THE CIVIL COURT PRACTICE 2019

VOLUME 2

THE CIVIL COURT PRACTICE 2019

Members of the LexisNexis Group worldwide

United Kingdom	RELX (UK) Limited, trading as LexisNexis, 1–3 Strand, London, WC2N 5JR
Australia	Reed International Books Australia Pty Ltd trading as LexisNexis, Chatswood, New South Wales
Austria	LexisNexis Verlag ARD Orac GmbH & Co KG, Vienna
Benelux	LexisNexis Benelux, Amsterdam
Canada	LexisNexis Canada, Markham, Ontario
China	LexisNexis China, Beijing and Shanghai
France	LexisNexis SA, Paris
Germany	LexisNexis GmbH, Dusseldorf
Hong Kong	LexisNexis Hong Kong, Hong Kong
India	LexisNexis India, New Delhi
Italy	Giuffrè Editore, Milan
Japan	LexisNexis Japan, Tokyo
Malaysia	Malayan Law Journal Sdn Bhd, Kuala Lumpur
New Zealand	LexisNexis NZ Ltd, Wellington
Singapore	LexisNexis Singapore, Singapore
South Africa	LexisNexis Butterworths, Durban
USA	LexisNexis, Dayton, Ohio

Published by RELX (UK) Limited

A CIP Catalogue record for this book is available from the British Library.

ISBN for Volume 2: ISBN 978-1-4743-1077-2

9 781474 310772

ISBN for the set: ISBN 978-1-4743-1075-8

9 781474 310758

Printed and bound by CPI Group (UK) Ltd, Croydon, CR0 4YY

Visit LexisNexis Butterworths at www.lexisnexis.co.uk

CONTENTS

PART II GENERAL JURISDICTION

PART III SPECIAL JURISDICTION

TABLE OF STATUTES

Paragraph references printed in **bold** type indicate where the Act is set out in part or in full.

TABLE OF STATUTORY INSTRUMENTS

Paragraph references printed in **bold** type indicate where the Statutory Instrument is set out in part or in full.

TABLE OF PRACTICE DIRECTIONS

Paragraph references printed in **bold** type indicate where the Practice Direction is set out in part or in full.

Civil Procedure Rules – Practice Directions

Other Practice Directions

Pre-Action Protocols

TABLE OF CASES

Adams v Bracknell Forest Borough Council [2003] EWCA Civ 706, [2003] ELR 409, [2003] 26 LS Gaz R 39, (2003) Times, 14 May, 147 Sol Jo LB 599, [2003] All ER (D) 50 (May); revsd [2004] UKHL 29, [2005] 1 AC 76, [2004] 3 All ER 897, [2004] 3 WLR 89, [2004] 26 LS Gaz R 28, (2004) Times, 24 June, 148 [2005] PIQR P2, Sol Jo LB 761, [2004] All ER (D) 163 (Jun) .... **III LIM [13.2], [17.2], [17.4], [17.4A], [36.1B]**

Adams v Rhymney Valley District Council (2000) 33 HLR 446, [2000] 3 EGLR 25, [2000] NLJR 1231, [2000] 39 EG 144, [2000] EGCS 94, [2001] PNLR 68, CA ..... **III L&T [164.6]**

Adams v Watkins (1989) 88 LGR 576, 60 P & CR 72, 22 HLR 107, [1990] 2 EGLR 185, [1990] 30 EG 89, CA .... **III MOB [4.1]**

Adan v Newham London Borough Council [2001] EWCA Civ 1916, [2002] 1 All ER 931, [2002] 1 WLR 2120, [2002] HLR 515, [2002] 09 LS Gaz R 29, 146 Sol Jo LB 28, (2002) Times, 16 January .... **II CCA [21.2A]; III L&T [304.2], [306.2]**

Adbury Park Estates Ltd [2003] BCC 696, sub nom Juer v Lomas [2001] All ER (D) 309 (Jun) .... **III COM [54K.2]**

Adcock v Co-operative Insurance Society Ltd [2000] Lloyd's Rep IR 657, Times, 26 April, CA .... **II CCA [48.1]; II SCA [36.4]**

Addiscombe Garden Estates Ltd v Crabbe [1958] 1 QB 513, [1957] 3 All ER 563, [1957] 3 WLR 980, 101 Sol Jo 959, 170 Estates Gazette 704, CA .... **III L&T [14.4]**

Addison v Denholm Ship Management (UK) Ltd [1997] ICR 770, [1997] IRLR 389, EAT .... **II SCA [18.5]**

Addison Lee v Lange [2018] 11 WLUK 193 .... **III EMP [1]**

Adeeko v Solicitors Regulation Authority [2012] EWHC 841 (Admin), [2012] NLJR 363, [2012] All ER (D) 21 (Mar) .... **III SOL [66.1A]**

Adelson (Sheldon) v Associated Newspapers Ltd [2007] EWCA Civ 701, [2007] 4 All ER 330, [2008] 1 WLR 585, (2007) Times, 18 July, [2008] EMLR 324, [2007] All ER (D) 117 (Jul) .... **III LIM [39.9A]**

Adelson v Associated Newspapers Ltd [2007] EWHC 3028 (QB), [2007] All ER (D) 305 (Dec) .... **III LIM [37.2]**

Adeneler v Ellinikos Organismos Galaktos: C-212/04 [2006] ECR I-6057, [2007] All ER (EC) 82, [2006] 3 CMLR 867, [2006] IRLR 716, [2006] All ER (D) 25 (Jul), ECJ ... **III EUR [11]**

Adidas AG, Re: C-223/98 [1999] ECR I-7081, [1999] 3 CMLR 895, ECJ .... **III EUR [388.4]**

Adidas-Salomon AG v Fitnessworld Trading Ltd: C-408/01 (2003) Times, 31 October, ECJ .... **III PAT [41.2]**

Adler v Blackman [1953] 1 QB 146, [1952] 2 All ER 945, 96 Sol Jo 802, [1952] 2 TLR 809, 160 Estates Gazette 436, CA .... **III L&T [93.2]**

Admiral Taverns (Cygnet) Ltd v Daniel [2008] EWHC 1688 (QB), [2008] 37 EG 153, [2008] All ER (D) 274 (Jul); affd [2008] EWCA Civ 1501, [2008] 48 EG 100 (CS), (2009) Times, 12 January, [2008] All ER (D) 251 (Nov) .... **III L&T 98.1**

Adriana Chimel v Damian Chibwana and Lloyd Williams (25 October 2016, unreported), CC (Brighton) .... **III PID [2D]**

Adris v Royal Bank of Scotland (Cartel Client Review Ltd, additional parties) [2010] EWHC 941 (QB), [2010] NLJR 767, [2010] 4 Costs LR 598, [2010] All ER (D) 156 (May) .... **II SCA [50.5F]**

Aegis Group plc v IRC [2005] EWHC 1468 (Ch), [2006] STC 23, sub nom Aegis, Re [2005] All ER (D) 209 (May) .... **III LIM [36.6]**

Aer Lingus plc v Gildacroft Ltd [2006] EWCA Civ 4, [2006] 2 All ER 290, [2006] 1 WLR 1173, [2006] 06 LS Gaz R 32, [2006] NLJR 147, (2006) Times, 23 January, 150 Sol Jo LB 129, [2006] All ER (D) 71 (Jan) .... **III LIM [12.1], [12.2A]**

Afala, The. See Interatlantic (Namibia) (Pty) Ltd v Okeanski Ribolov Ltd, The Afala

Afolabi v Solicitors Regulation Authority [2012] EWHC 3502 (Admin), [2012] NLJR 1562, [2012] All ER (D) 25 (Dec) .... **III SOL [66.1A]**

Afolabi v Southwark London Borough Council [2003] EWCA Civ 15, [2003] IRLR 220, [2003] ICR 800, [2003] 11 LS Gaz R 32, (2003) Times, 30 January, 147 Sol Jo LB 115, [2003] All ER (D) 217 (Jan) .... **III EQU [119.1]**

African Export-Import Bank v Shebah Exploration and Production Company Ltd (2017) Times, 1 September, CA .... **III CON [58.3]**

Agarwal v Cardiff University [2018] EWCA Civ 2084, [2018] All ER (D) 68 (Sep) ... **III EMP [3]**

Agassi v Robinson (Inspector of Taxes) (Bar Council intervening) [2005] EWCA Civ 1507, [2006] 1 All ER 900, [2006] 1 WLR 2126, [2006] STC 580, [2005] NLJR 1885, (2005) Times, 22 December, 150 Sol Jo LB 28, [2006] 2 Costs LR 283, [2005] SWTI 1994, [2005] All ER (D) 40 (Dec) .... **III SOL [5.2], [8.3]**

B

B (adult: refusal of medical treatment), Re [2002] EWHC 429 (Fam), [2002] 2 All ER 449, [2002] 2 FCR 1, 65 BMLR 149, [2002] 17 LS Gaz R 37, (2002) Times, 26 March, sub nom B (consent to treatment: capacity), Re [2002] 1 FLR 1090 .... **III MEN [404.1]**
B (a child) (disclosure), Re [2004] EWHC 411 (Fam), [2004] 3 FCR 1, [2004] 2 FLR 142, [2004] Fam Law 493, [2004] NLJR 498, [2004] Lloyd's Rep Med 303, [2004] All ER (D) 500 (Mar) .... **III COT [8.1A], [8.2]**
B (a child), Re [2017] EWCA Civ 1579, [2017] 4 WLR 202, [2017] Fam Law 1298, [2017] All ER (D) 100 (Oct) .... **III DAT [35.1]**
B v B (injunction: restraint on leaving jurisdiction) [1997] 3 All ER 258, [1998] 1 WLR 329, [1997] 2 FLR 148 .... **II CCA [21.5]**
B v B [2010] EWHC 543 (Fam) .... **III MEN [5]**
B v Birmingham City Council. See B (children) (adoption: removal from jurisdiction), Re [2004] EWCA Civ 515
B v IB [2013] EWHC 3755 (Fam), [2013] All ER (D) 36 (Dec) .... **III FMY [16C.1]**
B v M [1990] FCR 581. See Brown v Matthews
B v S (contempt: imprisonment of mother) [2009] EWCA Civ 548, [2009] 2 FLR 1005, [2009] Fam Law 1028 .... **III HUM [30.11]**
B v Secretary of State for the Home Department [2011] EWCA Civ 828, [2011] NLJR 1060, [2011] All ER (D) 188 (Jul) .... **III COT [21.2A]**
B v United Kingdom (1987) 10 EHRR 87 .... **III HUM [30.1]**
B v United Kingdom [2000] 1 FCR 289, [2000] 1 FLR 1, [2000] Fam Law 88, ECtHR .... **III HUM [35.2]**
B v United Kingdom (Application Nos 36337/97, 35974/97) (2001) 34 EHRR 529, [2001] 2 FCR 221, [2001] 2 FLR 261, [2001] Fam Law 506, 11 BHRC 667, [2001] ECHR 36337/97, [2001] All ER (D) 241 (Apr), ECtHR ...... **III COT [8.1]; III HUM [28.2], [32.5]**
B and L v United Kingdom (2006) 42 EHRR 11 .... **III HUM [16.1]**
BAT Industries plc v Windward Prospects Ltd [2013] EWHC 3612 (Comm), [2013] All ER (D) 265 (Nov) .... **II SCA [38.2]**
BD Shipsnavo GmbH & Co Reederei KG v African Fertilizers and Chemicals NIG Ltd (Nigeria) [2011] EWHC 2452 (Comm), [2011] 2 Lloyd's Rep 531, [2011] NLJR 1417, [2011] All ER (D) 03 (Oct) .... **III ARB [19.1]**
BDW Trading Ltd and Comet Square Phase 2 Block Management Co Ltd v South Anglia Housing Ltd [2013] EWHC 2169 (Ch), [2013] All ER (D) 183 (Jul) .... **III L&T [173.3C]**
BHP Petroleum Great Britain Ltd v Chesterfield Properties Ltd [2002] Ch 12, [2001] 2 All ER 914, [2001] 3 WLR 277, [2002] 1 P & CR 18, [2001] 2 EGLR 11, [2001] 22 EG 155, 145 Sol Jo LB 76, 82 P & CR D22; upheld sub nom BHP Petroleum Great Britain Ltd v Chesterfield Properties Ltd [2001] EWCA Civ 1797, [2002] Ch 194, [2002] 1 All ER 821, [2002] 2 WLR 672, [2002] 2 P & CR 117, [2002] 05 LS Gaz R 29, 146 Sol Jo LB 5, [2001] 50 EG 88 (CS), [2001] All ER (D) 451 (Nov), sub nom Chesterfield Properties Ltd v BHP Great Britain Petroleum Ltd [2002] 1 P & CR D33 ...... **III L&T [7.5]**
BICC Ltd v Cumbrian Industrials Ltd [2001] EWCA Civ 1621, [2002] Lloyd's Rep PN 526, [2001] All ER (D) 436 (Oct), sub nom Parkman Consulting Engineers (an unlimited company) v Cumbrian Industrials Ltd 79 Con LR 112 .... **III PID [16.4]**
BICC plc v Burndy Corpn [1985] Ch 232, [1985] 1 All ER 417, [1985] 2 WLR 132, [1985] RPC 273, 128 Sol Jo 750, [1984] LS Gaz R 3011, CA .... **III CON [34.2]**
BIM, DM and AM, Re [2014] EWCOP 39, [2014] All ER (D) 39 (Nov) ..... **III MEN [48.2]**
BJ (incapacitated adult), Re [2009] EWHC 3310 (Fam), [2010] 1 FLR 1373, [2010] Fam Law 242 .... **III MEN [35.1]**
BLCT (13096) Ltd v J Sainsbury plc [2003] EWCA Civ 884, [2004] 2 P & CR 32, 147 Sol Jo LB 815, [2003] All ER (D) 03 (Jul) .... **III ARB [22.6]**
BE Studios Ltd v Smith & Williamson Ltd [2005] EWHC 2730 (Ch), [2006] 2 All ER 811, (2005) Times, 16 December, [2005] All ER (D) 33 (Dec) .... **II SCA [50.5]**
BH (AP) v Lord Advocate [2012] UKSC 24, [2013] 1 AC 413, [2012] 4 All ER 600, [2012] 3 WLR 151, (2012) Times, 03 July, 2012 SC (UKSC) 308, 2012 SLT 799, 2012 SCCR 562, [2012] All ER (D) 126 (Jun), 2012 Scot (D) 14/6, SC .... **III WAL [4.1]**
BM, Re [2014] EWCOP B20 .... **III MEN [48.2], [52.1]**
BN, Re [2015] EWCOP 11, [2015] All ER (D) 50 (Mar) .... **III MEN [707.1], [707.5]**
BNM v MGN Ltd [2016] Lexis Citation 62, [2016] 3 Costs LO 441 .... **III FUND [41]**
BNM v MGN Ltd [2017] EWCA Civ 1767, (2018) Times, 12 January, [2017] All ER (D) 53 (Nov) .... **III PID [5D]**
BNP Paribas v Deloitte and Touche LLP [2003] EWHC 2874 (Comm), [2004] 1 Lloyd's Rep 233, [2003] NLJR 1841, [2004] BLR 90, [2003] All ER (D) 431 (Nov) . **III ARB [13,1]**

Barber v RJB Mining (UK) Ltd [1999] 2 CMLR 833, [1999] ICR 679, [1999] IRLR 308, 143 Sol Jo LB 141 .... III EMP [1]
Barber v Staffordshire County Council [1996] 2 All ER 748, [1996] IRLR 209, [1996] 06 LS Gaz R 26, sub nom Staffordshire County Council v Barber [1996] ICR 379, CA .... II CCA [7.5]; III EQU [A1]
Barbulescu v Romania (Application No 61496/08) [2017] ECHR 754 ...... III HUM [30.5D]
Barca v Mears [2004] EWHC 2170 (Ch), [2005] 2 FLR 1, [2004] All ER (D) 153 (Sep) .... III REA [36A.1]
Barcham, Re [2008] EWHC 1505 (Ch), [2009] 1 All ER 145, [2008] 2 P & CR D49, [2008] 2 FCR 643, [2008] 39 EG 126, (2008) Times, 24 July, [2008] All ER (D) 64 (Jul) .... III REA [57.1]
Barclays Bank Ltd v Ascott [1961] 1 All ER 782, [1961] 1 WLR 717, 105 Sol Jo 323, 178 Estates Gazette 189 .... III L&T [22.1]
Barclays Bank Ltd v Cole [1967] 2 QB 738, [1966] 3 All ER 948, [1967] 2 WLR 166, 110 Sol Jo 833, CA .... II SCA [56.1]
Barclays Bank plc v Alcorn [2002] 2 P & CR D19, [2002] All ER (D) 146 (Mar); on appeal [2002] EWCA Civ 817 .... III REA [23.3A], [23.4]
Barclays Bank plc v Bee [2001] EWCA Civ 1126, [2002] 1 WLR 332, [2002] 1 P & CR 321, [2001] 34 LS Gaz R 40, [2001] 37 EG 153, 145 Sol Jo LB 206, 82 P & CR D41, [2001] 29 EG 121 (CS) .... III L&T [17.1B]
Barclays Bank plc v Boulter [1999] 4 All ER 513, [1999] 1 WLR 1919, [1999] 3 FCR 529, [1999] 2 FLR 986, [2000] Fam Law 25, 32 HLR 170, [1999] 42 LS Gaz R 41, [1999] NLJR 1645, [1999] 49 EG 97, [1999] EGCS 121, 143 Sol Jo LB 250, 79 P & CR D1, HL .... II CCA [11.6B]
Barclays Bank plc v Brooks [1997] CCLR 60 .... II CCA [22.5]; III CON [52.1]
Barclays Bank plc v Coleman [2001] QB 20, [2000] 1 All ER 385, [2000] 3 WLR 405, [2000] 1 FCR 398, [2000] 1 FLR 343, [2000] Fam Law 245, 33 HLR 86, [2000] 03 LS Gaz R 37, [2000] EGCS 4, 144 Sol Jo LB 42, [2000] Lloyd's Rep Bank 67, 79 P & CR D28, CA; affd sub nom Barclays Bank plc v Coleman [2001] UKHL 44, [2001] 4 All ER 449, [2001] 3 WLR 1021, [2001] 3 FCR 481, [2001] 2 FLR 1364 .. II CCA [11.6C]
Barclays Bank plc v Fairclough Building Ltd [1995] QB 214, [1995] 1 All ER 289, [1994] 3 WLR 1057, 39 Con LR 86, [1995] PIQR P152, 68 BLR 1, [1994] BLM (June) 1, CA .... III PID [9.4]
Barclays Bank plc v Goff [2001] EWCA Civ 635, [2001] 2 All ER (Comm) 847, [2001] Lloyd's Rep Bank 189, [2001] NPC 48, [2001] 20 LS Gaz R 45, [2001] All ER (D) 42 (May) .... II CCA [11.6C]
Barclays Bank plc v Nylon Capital LLP [2011] EWCA Civ 826, [2011] 2 Lloyd's Rep 347, [2011] BLR 614, (2011) Times, 18 August, [2011] All ER (D) 214 (Jul) .... III ARB [5.4]
Barclays Bank plc v O'Brien [1994] 1 AC 180, [1993] 4 All ER 417, [1993] 3 WLR 786, [1994] 1 FCR 357, [1994] 1 FLR 1, [1994] Fam Law 78, 26 HLR 75, [1993] 46 LS Gaz R 37, [1993] NLJR 1511, 137 Sol Jo LB 240, HL .... II CCA [11.6]
Barclays Bank plc v Prudential Assurance Co Ltd [1998] BCC 928, [1998] 1 EGLR 44, [1998] 10 EG 159, [1997] EGCS 131 .... III L&T [2.2]
Barclays Bank plc v RBS Advanta [1996] RPC 307, [1997] ETMR 199 .... III PAT [41.2]
Barclays Bank plc v Walters (1988) Times, 20 October, CA .... III LIM [25.3]
Barclays Bank plc v Waterson [1989] CLY 2505 .... II CCA [11.5]
Barings plc, Re, Secretary of State for Trade and Industry v Baker (No 3) [1999] 1 All ER 1017, [2000] 1 WLR 634, [1999] 1 BCLC 262, [1998] NLJR 1474, [1998] All ER (D) 430 .... III COM [55.1]
Barings plc, Re, Secretary of State for Trade and Industry v Baker (No 5) [2000] 1 BCLC 523, CA .... III COM [54.2]
Barings plc (No 2), Re, Secretary of State for Trade and Industry v Baker [1999] 1 All ER 311, [1999] 1 BCLC 226, sub nom Secretary of State for Trade and Industry v Baker (No 2) [1999] 1 WLR 1985, CA .... III COM [50]
Barker v Corus UK Ltd [2006] UKHL 20, [2006] 2 AC 572, [2006] 3 All ER 785, [2006] 2 WLR 1027, [2006] ICR 809, 89 BMLR 1, [2006] NLJR 796, [2006] PIQR P390, (2006) Times, 4 May, [2006] 5 LRC 271, [2006] All ER (D) 23 (May) .... III PID [40C.2]
Barker v Johnson (1889) 60 LT 64, 5 TLR 278 .... II CCA [28.1]
Barking and Dagenham London Borough Council v Hyatt and Hyatt (1991) 24 HLR 406, CA .... III L&T [109.2]
Barlow Clowes International Ltd v Henwood. See Henwood v Barlow Clowes International Ltd (in liq)

C

Cherfi v G4S Security Services Ltd (UKEAT/0379/10/DM) (24 May 2011, unreported) .... III EQU [19.1]

Cherney v Deripaska [2007] EWHC 965 (Comm), [2007] 2 All ER (Comm) 785, [2007] All ER (D) 60 (May) .... III EUR [158.1], [273.1]

Cheryl Investments Ltd v Saldanha [1979] 1 All ER 5, [1978] 1 WLR 1329, 37 P & CR 349, 122 Sol Jo 777, CA .... III L&T [14.4]

Cheshire West and Chester Council v P [2011] EWCA Civ 1333 .... III MEN [93.1]. [620.2], [707.6]

Cheshire West and Chester Council v P [2011] EWHC 1330 (Fam), [2011] All ER (D) 155 (Jun); revsd [2011] EWCA Civ 1257, [2012] PTSR 1447, [2012] 1 FLR 693, [2012] Fam Law 137, [2011] NLJR 1670, [2011] All ER (D) 150 (Nov) . III HUM [27.1A]; III MEN [10], [35.1], [55.1], [93.1]

Cheshire West and Chester Council v P [2011] EWCA Civ 1257, [2012] PTSR 1447, [2012] 1 FLR 693, [2012] Fam Law 137, [2011] NLJR 1670, [2011] All ER (D) 150 (Nov); sub nom P (MIG) and Q (MEG) v Surrey County Council [2011] EWCA Civ 190, [2012] Fam 170, [2012] 2 WLR 1056, [2012] PTSR 727, [2011] 2 FLR 583, [2011] 1 FCR 559, [2011] Fam Law 475, 120 BMLR 44, [2011] All ER (D) 286 (Feb) .... III MEN [17A], [620.1]

Chesterfield Borough Council v Crossley (24 April 1998, unreported) .... III L&T [108.1]

Chesterfield Properties Ltd v BHP Great Britain Petroleum Ltd. See BHP Petroleum Great Britain Ltd v Chesterfield Properties Ltd

Chez Gerard Ltd v Greene Ltd [1983] 2 EGLR 79, 268 Estates Gazette 575, CA .... III L&T [14.7]

Chichester District Council v First Secretary of State [2004] EWCA Civ 1248, [2005] 1 WLR 279, [2005] LGR 427, [2005] 1 FCR 231, [2004] NLJR 1498, [2004] All ER (D) 181 (Sep), sub nom First Secretary of State v Chichester District Council (2004) Times, 14 October, 148 Sol Jo LB 1152 .... III HUM [30.5A]

Chief Adjudication Officer v Foster [1993] AC 754, [1993] 1 All ER 705, [1993] 2 WLR 292, [1993] 14 LS Gaz R 45, [1993] NLJR 296n, 136 Sol Jo LB 37, HL .... III L&T [306.4]

Chief Constable of the Bedfordshire Police v Golding [2015] EWHC 1875 (QB), 165 NLJ 7661, [2015] All ER (D) 23 (Jul) .... III ANSB [54.1]

Chief Constable of British Transport Police v Soods Solicitors Ltd [2012] EWHC 3780 (Admin), 156 Sol Jo (29) 31, [2012] All ER (D) 163 (Jul) .... III SOL [55]

Chief Constable of Greater Manchester v McNally [2002] EWCA Civ 14, [2002] 2 Cr App Rep 617, [2002] Crim LR 832, [2002] All ER (D) 221 (Jan), Times, 6 March .... III CRO [20.3A]

Chief Constable of Greater Manchester Police v Bailey [2017] EWCA Civ 425, (2017) Times, 28 June .... III EQU [27.1A]

Chief Constable of Hampshire Constabulary v Southampton City Council [2014] EWCA Civ 1541, [2014] All ER (D) 01 (Dec) .... III LIM [12.2B]

Chief Constable of Humberside Police v Information Comr (Secretary of State for the Home Dept intervening) [2009] EWCA Civ 1079, (2009) Times, 22 October, 153 Sol Jo (no 40) 35, [2009] All ER (D) 180 (Oct) .... III DAT [46.1]

Chief Constable of Kent v V [1983] QB 34, [1982] 3 All ER 36, [1982] 3 WLR 462, 126 Sol Jo 536, CA .... II CCA [21.3]

Chief Constable of Lancashire v Potter [2003] EWHC 2272 (Admin), [2003] 42 LS Gaz R 31, (2003) Times, 10 November, [2003] All ER (D) 199 (Oct) .... III ANSB [13.4]

Chief Constable of Leicestershire v M [1988] 3 All ER 1015, [1989] 1 WLR 20, 133 Sol Jo 47, [1989] 4 LS Gaz R 43, [1988] NLJR 295 .... II SCA [38.1D]; III ANSB [1], [26.1]

Chief Constable of Norfolk v Coffey [2017] UKEAT/0260/16 .... III EQU [6.3]

Chief Constable of West Midlands Police v Harrod. See Harrod v Chief Constable of West Midlands Police

Chief Constable of West Yorkshire Police v Khan [2001] UKHL 48, [2001] 1 WLR 1947, [2001] IRLR 830, [2001] ICR 1065, [2001] 42 LS Gaz R 37, (2001) Times, 16 October, 145 Sol Jo LB 230, [2001] All ER (D) 158 (Oct), sub nom Khan v Chief Constable of West Yorkshire Police [2001] 4 All ER 834, HL .... III EQU [27.1A]

Chiltern Railway Co Ltd v Patel [2008] EWCA Civ 178, [2008] Bus LR 1295, [2008] 2 P & CR 225, [2008] 2 EGLR 33, [2008] All ER (D) 129 (Feb) .... III L&T [31A.1]

Chilton v Saga Holidays plc [1986] 1 All ER 841, [1986] BTLC 11, CA ...... III ARB [10.3]

Chiodi's Personal Representatives v De Marney (1988) 21 HLR 6, [1988] 2 EGLR 64, [1988] 41 EG 80, CA .... III L&T [164.8]

Chios Property Investment Co Ltd v Lopez [1988] Fam Law 384, 20 HLR 120, [1988] 1 EGLR 98, [1988] 05 EG 57, CA .... III L&T [81.3]

Chipperfield v Shell UK Ltd (1980) 42 P & CR 136, 257 Estates Gazette 1042, CA .. III L&T [26.2], [26.4]
Chiron Corpn v Murex Diagnostics Ltd (No 7) [1994] FSR 458 .... III PAT [19.4]
Chiron Corpn v Organon Teknika Ltd (No 7) [1994] FSR 458 .... III PAT [19.4]
Chittenden, Re, Chittenden v Doe [1970] 3 All ER 562, [1970] 1 WLR 1618, 114 Sol Jo 954 .... III FMY [10.3]
Chittock, Re [2000] 1 WTLR 643, (2000) Times, 5 April .... III TRU [43B.3]
Choice Investments Ltd v Jeromnimon [1981] QB 149, [1981] 1 All ER 225, [1980] 2 WLR 80, 124 Sol Jo 883, CA .... II CCA [102]
Chorion plc v Lane (1999) Times, 7 April .... II CCA [7.5]; III EMP [5]
Choudhary v Bhatter [2009] EWCA Civ 1176, [2009] NLJR 1628, (2009) Times, 20 November, [2009] All ER (D) 131 (Nov) .... III EUR [294.3]
Choudhary v Martin (2008) Times, 2 January, CA .... III EQU [119.2]; III HAR [7.5]
Chr Knudsen, The [1932] P 153, 101 LJP 72, 18 Asp MLC 347, [1932] All ER Rep 326, 148 LT 60, 48 TLR 619, 43 Ll L Rep 423 .... II SCA [18.9]
Chrisdell Ltd v Johnson (1987) 54 P & CR 257, 19 HLR 406, [1987] 2 EGLR 123, 283 Estates Gazette 1553, CA .... III L&T [76.1]
Christie v Birmingham City Council [2016] EWCA Civ 1339 .... III COT [21.4]
Christie v MacFarlane 1930 SLT (Sh Ct) 5 .... III L&T [85.7]
Christofi v National Bank of Greece (Cyprus) Ltd [2015] EWHC 986 (QB), [2015] 2 All ER (Comm) 844, 165 NLJ 7650, [2015] All ER (D) 84 (Apr) .... III EUR [314.1]
Christopher Moran Holdings Ltd v Bairstow. See Re Park Air Services
Church Comrs v Ibrahim [1997] 1 EGLR 13, [1997] 03 EG 136, CA ...... III L&T [216.3]
Church Comrs for England v Al-Emarah [1997] Fam 34, [1996] 3 WLR 633, [1996] 2 FLR 544, 29 HLR 351, [1996] 22 LS Gaz R 27, 140 Sol Jo LB 129, sub nom Church Comrs v Alemarah [1996] 3 FCR 252, CA .... III L&T [82.1]
Church Comrs for England v Meya [2006] EWCA Civ 821, (2006) Times, 4 July, [2007] 1 P & CR D9, [2006] All ER (D) 234 (Jun) .... III L & T [214.2A]
Church Comrs for England v Royale Enterprises (22 September 2011, unreported), Central London County Court .... III L&T [276.1]
Church of Jesus Christ of Latter-Day Saints v Gallagher (Valuation Officer) [2006] EWCA Civ 1598, [2007] P & CR D14, [2007] RA 1, 150 Sol Jo LB 1572, [2006] All ER (D) 344 (Nov); affd sub nom Gallagher (Valuation Officer) v Church of Jesus Christ of Latter-Day Saints [2008] UKHL 56, [2008] 4 All ER 640, [2008] 1 WLR 1852, [2008] 2 P & CR D60, [2008] RA 317, [2008] NLJR 1179, (2008) Times, 7 August, [2008] All ER (D) 416 (Jul) .... III HUM [35.2I]
Churchill v Roach [2002] EWHC 3230 (Ch), [2004] 3 FCR 744, [2004] 2 FLR 989, [2003] All ER (D) 348 (Apr) .... III FMY [7.4B]
Churchill Insurance Co Ltd v Wilkinson [2012] EWCA Civ 1166, [2013] 1 All ER 1146, [2013] 1 WLR 1776, [2013] 1 All ER (Comm) 881, [2012] 3 CMLR 1165, [2013] Lloyd's Rep IR 137, [2012] 34 LS Gaz R 23, [2012] NLJR 1217, [2012] All ER (D) 157 (Aug) .... III PID [23H.1]
Cia de Seguros Imperio (a body corporate) v Heath (REBX) Ltd (formerly CE Heath & Co (North America) Ltd) [1999] 1 All ER (Comm) 750, [1999] Lloyd's Rep IR 571, [1999] CLC 997; affd [2000] 2 All ER (Comm) 787, [2001] 1 WLR 112, [2001] Lloyd's Rep IR 109, [2000] PNLR 795, CA .... III LIM [36.2], [39.8], [40.1]
Cil v Owners of the Turiddu (First National Bank of Maryland intervening). See Turiddu, The
Cinematic Finance Ltd v Ryder [2010] All ER (D) 283 (Oct) .... III COM [261.1]
Cinnamon Ltd v Morgan [2001] EWCA Civ 1616, [2002] 2 P & CR 139 ... III L&T [171.1]
Citadel Management Inc v Equal Ltd [1998] 36 LS Gaz R 32, 142 Sol Jo LB 253, CA .... III SOL [67.1]
Citadel Management Inc v Thompson [1999] 1 FLR 21, [1998] Fam Law 738, sub nom Citadel Management Inc v Equal Ltd [1998] 36 LS Gaz R 32, 142 Sol Jo LB 253, Times, 25 September, CA .... III SOL [67.1]
Citibank International plc v Kessler [1999] 2 CMLR 603, [1999] NPC 32, [1999] 15 LS Gaz R 29, [1999] EGCS 40, 78 P & CR D7, CA .... II CCA [11.7]
Citibank Trust Ltd v Ayivor [1987] 3 All ER 241, [1987] 1 WLR 1157, 19 HLR 463, 131 Sol Jo 1122, [1987] LS Gaz R 2766 .... II CCA [11.4]
Citro (a bankrupt), Re [1991] Ch 142, [1990] 3 All ER 952, [1990] 3 WLR 880, [1991] 1 FLR 71, [1990] Fam Law 428, 134 Sol Jo 806, [1990] 28 LS Gaz R 43, [1990] NLJR 1073, CA .... III REA [36A.1], [52A]

Credit Lyonnais SA v Russell Jones & Walker (a firm) [2002] EWHC 1310 (Ch), [2003] Lloyd's Rep PN 7, [2002] 33 EG 99, (2002) Times, 9 October, [2002] All ER (D) 19 (Jul) .... III SOL [61]
Crédit Suisse v Beegas Nominees Ltd [1994] 4 All ER 803, 69 P & CR 177, [1994] 1 EGLR 76, [1994] 11 EG 151, 12 EG 189 .... III L&T [164.1]
Crehan v Inntrepreneur Pub Co CPC [2004] EWCA Civ 637, (2004) Times, 28 May, 148 Sol Jo LB 662, [2004] All ER (D) 322 (May) .... III EUR [389.2]
Cressey v E Timm & Son Ltd [2005] EWCA Civ 763, [2005] 1 WLR 3926, [2005] 28 LS Gaz R 33, (2005) Times, 25 July, [2005] All ER (D) 295 (Jun) .... III LIM [17.4]
Cresswell v Duke of Westminster [1985] 2 EGLR 151, 25 RVR 144, 275 Estates Gazette 461, CA .... III L&T [50.5]
Crest Homes plc v Marks [1987] AC 829, [1987] 2 All ER 1074, [1987] 3 WLR 293, [1988] RPC 21, 131 Sol Jo 1003, [1987] LS Gaz R 2362, [1987] NLJ Rep 662, HL .. II CCA [21.7]
Crestford Ltd v Tesco Stores Ltd [2005] EWHC 805, [2005] 37 EG 148 ...... III L& T [7.3]
Cricket Ltd v Shaftesbury plc [1999] 3 All ER 283, [1999] 2 EGLR 57, [1999] 28 EG 127 .... III L&T [32.1], [41.3]
Crimble (Roy) Ltd v Edgecombe (1981) 131 NLJ 928, CA .... III MOB [2]
Cripps v Britpal Ltd [1951] EGD 308, CA .... III L&T [70.2]
Cristina v Seear [1985] 2 EGLR 128, 275 Estates Gazette 898, CA .... III L&T [14.6]
Crocker v Fothergill (1819) 2 B & Ald 652 .... II CCA [132.1]
Croke (a minor) v Wiseman [1981] 3 All ER 852, [1982] 1 WLR 71, 125 Sol Jo 726, CA .... III PID [13.4]
Crompton (Alfred) Amusement Machines Ltd v Customs and Excise Comrs (No 2) [1972] 2 QB 102, [1972] 2 All ER 353, [1972] 2 WLR 835, 116 Sol Jo 198, CA; affd [1974] AC 405, [1973] 2 All ER 1169, [1973] 3 WLR 268, 117 Sol Jo 602, HL .... III CRO [20.1]
Crosbie v Munroe [2003] 8 of 2003 Supreme Court Cost Office Reports, CA .. III SOL [75.1]
Cross v British Airways plc [2005] IRLR 423, [2005] All ER (D) 10 (Apr), EAT; affd [2006] EWCA Civ 549, [2006] ICR 1239, [2006] IRLR 804, [2006] 21 LS Gaz R 24, (2006) Times, 5 June, [2006] All ER (D) 148 (May) .... III EQU [19.1]
Crossley v Westminster City Council [2006] EWCA Civ 140, [2006] All ER (D) 321 (Feb) .... III L&T [306.2AB]
Crossmore Electrical and Civil Engineering Ltd, Re [1989] BCLC 137, 5 BCC 37 ... III COM [994.2]
Crowhurst v Maidment [1953] 1 QB 23, [1952] 2 All ER 808, 96 Sol Jo 783, [1952] 2 TLR 723, CA .... III L&T [69.7], [71.7]
Crowhurst Park, Re, Sims-Hilditch v Simmons [1974] 1 All ER 991, [1974] 1 WLR 583, 28 P & CR 14, 118 Sol Jo 331 .... III L&T [17.5], [30.6]
Crowley t/a Crowley Civil Engineers Claimant v Rushmoor Borough Council [2009] EWHC 2237 (TCC) .... III REA [60A]
Crown Estate Comrs v Dorset County Council [1990] Ch 297, [1990] 1 All ER 19, [1990] 2 WLR 89, 88 LGR 132, 60 P & CR 1 .... II CCA [49.2]
Crown Estate Commrs v Governors of Peabody Trust [2011] EWHC 1467 (Ch), [2011] NLJR 884, [2011] 24 EG 109 (CS), [2011] All ER (D) 63 (Jun) .... III L&T [235.1]
Crown Prosecution Service v T (2006) Times, 13 April, QBD .... III ANSB [13.4B]
Crown Suppliers (Property Services Agency) v Dawkins [1991] ICR 583, [1991] IRLR 327, [1991] 22 LS Gaz R 36, EAT; affd [1993] ICR 517, sub nom Dawkins v Department of the Environment [1993] IRLR 284, CA .... III EQU [9.1]
Croydon London Borough Council v Gladden (1994) 92 LGR 561, 159 LG Rev 241, 68 P & CR 300, [1994] 1 PLR 30, [1994] 16 LS Gaz R 37, [1994] JPL 723, CA ... III ENV [14.1]
Croydon (Unique) Ltd v Wright [2001] Ch 318, [1999] 4 All ER 257, [2000] 2 WLR 683, [1999] NPC 113, [1999] 3 EGLR 28, [1999] 33 LS Gaz R 31, [1999] NLJR 1473, [1999] 40 EG 189, 143 Sol Jo LB 241, 78 P & CR D40, CA .. II CCA [133.5], III L&T [2.3]
Crozat v Brogden [1894] 2 QB 30, 63 LJQB 325, 9 R 296, 42 WR 353, 70 LT 522, 10 TLR 361, CA .... III COM [46.5]
Crumpton v Unifox Properties Ltd and De Alnie Property Holdings Ltd (1992) 25 HLR 121, [1992] 2 EGLR 82, [1992] 46 EG 105, CA .... III L&T [187.7]
Cullen Investments Ltd v Brown [2017] EWHC 1586 (Ch), [2017] All ER (D) 50 (Jul) .... III COM [175.1]
Culnane v Morris [2005] EWHC 2438 (QB), [2006] 2 All ER 149, [2006] 1 WLR 2880, [2005] NLJR 1810, [2006] EMLR 139, [2005] All ER (D) 211 (Nov) .... III HUM [32.3]
Cumming v Danson [1942] 2 All ER 653, 112 LJKB 145, 87 Sol Jo 21, 59 TLR 70, sub nom Cumming v Dawson 168 LT 35, CA .... III L&T [71.8]

D

E

Ebert v Official Receiver [2001] EWCA Civ 340, [2001] 3 All ER 942, [2002] 1 WLR 320 .... II SCA [44.5]
Eburne (S W) Ltd v Toome Investments [1977] CLY 445 .... III L&T [21.1]
Eclairs Group Ltd v JKX Oil and Gas plc [2015] UKSC 71, [2015] All ER (D) 20 (Dec) .... III COM [794.2]
Eco Swiss China Time Ltd v Benetton International NV: C-126/97 [1999] 2 All ER (Comm) 44, [2000] 5 CMLR 816, ECJ .... III ARB [32]
Ecobank Transnational Incorporated v Tanoh [2015] EWCA Civ 1309, [2015] All ER (D) 216 (Dec) .... III SCA [38.1A]
Ecom Agroindustrial Corpn Ltd v Mosharaf Composite Textile Mill Ltd [2013] EWHC 1276 (Comm), [2013] 2 All ER (Comm) 983, [2013] 2 Lloyd's Rep 196, [2013] All ER (D) 294 (May) .... II SCA [38.1A]
Edgar (Ian) (Liverpool) Ltd v Edgar (25 January 2000, unreported), ECtHR .. III HUM [39.1]
Edicron Ltd v William Whiteley Ltd (1983) 46 P & CR 288, 127 Sol Jo 257, 266 Estates Gazette 908; revsd [1984] 1 All ER 219, [1984] 1 WLR 59, 47 P & CR 625, 127 Sol Jo 785, 268 Estates Gazette 1035, CA .... III L&T [30.4], [30.7]
Edinburgh Castle, The [1999] 2 Lloyd's Rep 362 .... II SCA [18.23]
Edlington Properties Ltd v JH Fenner & Co Ltd [2005] EWHC 2158 (QB), [2006] 1 All ER 98, [2006] 05 EG 274, (2005) Times, 4 November, [2005] All ER (D) 216 (Oct); affd [2006] EWCA Civ 403, [2006] 13 EG 141 (CS), 150 Sol Jo LB 474, [2006] All ER (D) 363 (Mar) .... III L&T [164.10]
Edmunds v Jones [1957] 3 All ER 23n, [1957] 1 WLR 1118n, 101 Sol Jo 848, CA .. III L&T [81.4]
Edmunds v Lawson QC [2000] QB 501, [2000] 2 WLR 1091, [2000] ICR 567, [2000] IRLR 391, 144 Sol Jo LB 151, CA .... III EMP [1]
Edmunds v Lloyd Italico e L'Ancora Cia di Assicurazioni e Riassicurazioni SpA [1986] 2 All ER 249, [1986] 1 WLR 492, [1986] 1 Lloyd's Rep 326, 130 Sol Jo 242, CA .... II SCA [36.2]
Edmunds v Robinson. See Edmonds v Robinson
Edwards v Chesterfield Royal Hospital NHS Foundation Trust [2010] EWCA Civ 571, [2011] QB 339, [2010] 3 WLR 1285, [2010] ICR 1181, [2010] IRLR 702, 154 Sol Jo (no 21) 28, [2010] 23 LS Gaz R 19, [2010] NLJR 806, [2010] All ER (D) 247 (May); revsd [2011] UKSC 58, [2012] 2 WLR 55, [2012] ICR 201, [2012] 02 LS Gaz R 17, [2011] NLJR 30, (2012) Times, 23 January, 155 Sol Jo (no 48) 31, [2011] All ER (D) 101 (Dec) .... III EMP [2]
Edwards v Flamingo Land Ltd [2013] EWCA Civ 801, [2013] All ER (D) 84 (Jul) ... III EQU [29.1]
Edwards v Kumarasamy [2016] UKSC 40, [2016] HLR 543, 166 NLJ 7708, (2016) Times, 18 July, [2016] All ER (D) 54 (Jul) .... III L&T [164.2]
Edwards v Lloyds TSB Bank plc [2004] EWHC 1745 (Ch), [2005] 1 FCR 139, [2004] All ER (D) 335 (Jul) .... III REA [52A]
Edwards v Surrey Police [1999] IRLR 456, EAT .... III EMP [6.7]
Edwards v Thompson (1990) 60 P & CR 222, [1990] 2 EGLR 71, [1990] 29 EG 41, CA .... III L&T [22.9]
Edwards v United Kingdom (Application No 46477/99) (2002) 12 BHRC 190, Times, 1 April, ECtHR .... III HUM [24.4], [24.4A]
Edwards and Lewis v United Kingdom (2003) Times, 29 July .... III HUM [28.2]
Eeles v Cobham Hire Services Ltd [2009] EWCA Civ 204, [2010] 1 WLR 409, [2009] PIQR P273, 153 Sol Jo (no 11) 30, [2009] All ER (D) 144 (Mar) .... III PID [25.2A]
Egan v Motor Services (Bath) Ltd [2007] EWCA Civ 1002, 151 Sol Jo LB 1364, [2007] All ER (D) 256 (Oct) .... III CON [75.4]
Eichner v Midland Bank Executor and Trustee Co Ltd [1970] 2 All ER 597, [1970] 1 WLR 1120, 21 P & CR 503, 114 Sol Jo 373, CA .... III L&T [22.3], [22.5]
Ekinci v Hackney London Borough Council [2001] EWCA Civ 776, [2002] HLR 12, sub nom Hackney London Borough Council v Ekinci [2001] 28 LS Gaz R 43 .. III L&T [306.4E]
Ekpe v Metropolitan Police Comr [2001] ICR 1084, [2001] IRLR 605, EAT . III EQU [219.2]
Ekwuru v Westminster City Council [2003] EWCA Civ 1293, [2004] HLR 198 .... III L & T [306.2AB]
EI Du Pont De Nemours & Co v ST Dupont [2003] EWCA Civ 1368, [2006] 1 WLR 2793, [2004] IP & T 559, 147 Sol Jo LB 1207, [2003] All ER (D) 185 (Oct), sub nom Du Pont Trademark, Re [2004] FSR 293 .... III REA [60K.4]
El Naschie v The Pitt Place (Epsom) Ltd (1998) Times, 27 May, CA .... III L&T [188.1]

F

Fullard, Re, Fullard v King [1982] Fam 42, [1981] 2 All ER 796, [1981] 3 WLR 743, 11 Fam Law 116, 125 Sol Jo 747, CA .... **III FMY [7.14]**
Fuller v Happy Shopper Markets Ltd [2001] All ER (D) 156, [2001] 1 WLR 1681, [2001] 2 Lloyd's Rep 49, [2001] 2 EGLR 32, [2001] 25 EG 159 .... **III L&T [164.10]**

G

G (adult patient: publicity), Re [1996] 1 FCR 413, [1995] 2 FLR 528, [1995] Fam Law 677 .... **III COT [20.1]**
G (minors) (celebrities: publicity), Re [1999] 3 FCR 181, [1999] 1 FLR 409, CA .... **III COT [8.2], [8.5]**
G (a minor) (chambers hearing: assistance), Re [1999] 1 WLR 1828, [1999] 2 FLR 59, [1999] Fam Law 454, CA .... **III SOL [8.4]**
G (a child) (contempt: committal order), Re [2003] EWCA Civ 489, [2003] 1 WLR 2051, [2003] 2 FCR 231, [2003] 2 FLR 58, [2003] 24 LS Gaz R 35, [2003] All ER (D) 165 (Apr) .... **III COT [8.2], [21.2A]**
G (a Child) (litigants in person), Re [2003] EWCA Civ 1055, [2003] 2 FLR 963, [2003] Fam Law 808, (2003) Times, 31 July, [2003] All ER (D) 459 (Jul) .... **III SOL [8.4]**
G (adoption: unmarried couple), Re [2009] 1 AC 173. See P (adoption: unmarried couple), Re
G (Adult), Re [2014] EWHC 1361 (COP), [2014] All ER (D) 27 (May) .... **III MEN [223.2], [596.2]**
G (Adult), Re [2014] EWCOP 5 .... **III MEN [707.7]**
G (TJ), Re [2010] EWHC 3005 (COP), [2010] All ER (D) 218 (Nov) .... **III MEN [34.1]**
G (TJ), Re [2011] WTLR 231 .... **III MEN [51.1]**
G v Director of Legal Aid Casework (British Red Cross Society intervening) [2014] EWCA Civ 1622, 165 NLJ 7636, [2014] All ER (D) 157 (Dec) .... **III HUM [28.2A], [30.3]**
G v E (by his litigation friend, the Official Solicitor) [2010] EWCA Civ 822, [2010] 4 All ER 579, [2011] 3 WLR 652, [2011] PTSR 1574, [2010] 2 FCR 601, [2011] 1 FLR 239, [2010] Fam Law 1066, 116 BMLR 162, [2010] All ER (D) 180 (Jul) .... **III MEN [55.1]**
G v E [2010] EWHC 621 (Fam), [2010] 2 FLR 294, [2010] Fam Law 703, [2010] All ER (D) 120 (Apr) .... **III MEN [36.1]**
G v E (by his Litigation Friend, the Official Solicitor), Manchester City Council v F [2010] EWHC 2512 (COP), [2011] 1 FLR 1652, [2011] Fam Law 141 .... **III MEN [403.2]**
G v E (Costs) [2010] EWHC 3385 (Fam), [2011] 1 FLR 1566, [2011] Fam Law 473; affd sub nom Manchester City Council v E (by his litigation friend the Official Solicitor) [2011] EWCA Civ 939, [2011] 2 FLR 1297, [2011] Fam Law 1196, [2014] WTLR 449, [2011] All ER (D) 38 (Aug) .... **III MEN [707.1]**
G (by his litigation friend) v Head Teacher and Governors of St Gregory's Catholic Science College [2011] EWHC 1452 (Admin), [2011] NLJR 884, [2011] All ER (D) 113 (Jun) .... **III EQU [85.2]**
GE Capital Bank Ltd v Rushton [2005] EWCA Civ 1556, [2006] 3 All ER 865, [2006] 1 WLR 899, [2006] RTR 207, (2005) Times, 21 December, 150 Sol Jo LB 96, [2005] All ER (D) 207 (Dec) .... **III CON [32.6]**
GH v Catholic Child Welfare Society (Diocese of Middlesbrough) [2016] EWHC 3337 (QB), [2017] ELR 136 .... **III LIM [38.5]**
GHB v United Kingdom (Application No 42455/98) (4 May 2000, unreported), ECtHR .... **III HUM [30.1]**
GJ (incapacitated adults), Re [2008] EWHC 1097 (Fam), [2008] 2 FLR 1295, [2008] Fam Law 997 .... **III MEN [35.1], [620]**
GJ v Foundation Trust PCT and the Secretary of State for Health [2009] EWHC 2972 (Fam), [2010] Fam 70, [2010] 3 WLR 840, [2010] Fam Law 139, [2010] 1 FLR 1251 .... **III MEN [15], [17], [25.1]**
GM, Re [2013] COPLR 290 .... **III MEN [10A], [48.2]**
GMP, Re[2015] EWCOP 67, [2015] All ER (D) 171 (Oct) .... **III MEN[52.1]**
GUS Consulting GmbH v Leboeuf Lamb Greene & Macrae (a firm) [2006] EWCA Civ 683, [2006] ArbLR 31, [2006] All ER (D) 399 (May) .... **III SOL [56]**
Gaidowski v Gonville and Caius College, Cambridge [1975] 2 All ER 952, [1975] 1 WLR 1066, 119 Sol Jo 491, CA .... **III L&T [50.1]**
Gain v Gain [1962] 1 All ER 63, [1961] 1 WLR 1469, 105 Sol Jo 970 .... **III CRO [20.1]**

Geden Operations Ltd v Dry Bulk Handy Holdings Inc, The M/V Bulk Uruguay [2014] EWHC 885 (Comm), [2014] 2 All ER (Comm) 196, [2014] 2 Lloyd's Rep 66, 164 NLJ 7601, [2014] All ER (D) 271 (Mar) .... III ARB [22.2]
Gedye, Re (1851) 14 Beav 56, 20 LJ Ch 410, 15 Jur 851, 17 LTOS 149 .... III SOL [85.6]
Gee Whiz, The [1951] 1 All ER 876n, 95 Sol Jo 239, [1951] 1 TLR 407 ...... II SCA [18.25]
General Dental Council's application (Savery), Re [2011] EWHC 3011 (Admin), (2011) Times, 10 December, [2012] Med LR 204 .... III DAT [47.2]; III HUM [30.4]
General Management Ltd v Locke [1980] 2 EGLR 83, 255 Estates Gazette 155, CA . III L&T [81.5]
General Medical Council v BBC [1998] 3 All ER 426, [1998] 1 WLR 1573, 43 BMLR 143, [1998] 25 LS Gaz R 32, [1998] NLJR 942, 142 Sol Jo LB 182, [1998] EMLR 833, CA .... III COT [10.2], [23.1]
General Motors Corpn v Yplon SA: C-375/97 [1999] ECR I-5421, [1999] All ER (EC) 865, [1999] 3 CMLR 427, [2000] RPC 572, ECJ .... III PAT [41.2]
General of Berne Insurance Co v Jardine Reinsurance Management Ltd [1998] 2 All ER 301, [1998] 1 WLR 1231, 142 Sol Jo LB 86, [1998] Lloyd's Rep IR 211, CA .. III SOL [76.2]
General Rolling Stock Co, Re, Joint Stock Discount Co's Claim (1872) 7 Ch App 646, 41 LJ Ch 732, 20 WR 762, [1861–73] All ER Rep 434, 27 LT 88, CA in Ch ... III LIM [1G]
Generics (UK) Ltd v H Lundbeck A/S [2009] UKHL 12, [2009] 2 All ER 955, [2009] IP & T 496, 107 BMLR 121, 153 Sol Jo (no 8) 30, [2009] All ER (D) 258 (Feb) .. III PAT [17.2A]
Gent v de la Mare (1987) 20 HLR 199, [1988] 1 EGLR 104, [1988] 18 EG 63, CA . III L&T [83.8]
Geoffrey Silver & Drake (a firm) v Baines (t/a Wetherfield Baines & Baines, a firm) [1971] 1 QB 396, [1971] 1 All ER 473, [1971] 2 WLR 187, 114 Sol Jo 865, CA .... II CCA [136.1]
George v Chambers (1843) 7 JP 79, 2 Dowl NS 783, 12 LJMC 94, 7 Jur 836, 11 M & W 149 .... II CCA [142.1]
Georgiou (t/a Marios Chippery) v United Kingdom [2001] STC 80, ECtHR . III HUM [28.10]
Gerald Metals SA v Timis [2016] EWHC 2327 (Ch), [2016] All ER (D) 31 (Oct) .... III ARB [14.2]
Germany v EC Commission: C-156/98 [2000] ECR I-6857, ECJ .... III EUR [388.4]
Germax Securities Ltd v Spiegal (1978) 37 P & CR 204, 123 Sol Jo 164, 250 Estates Gazette 449, CA .... III L&T [17.2]
Gertrud, The [1927] WN 265, 17 Asp MLC 343, 138 LT 239, 44 TLR 1, 29 Ll L Rep 5 .... III SOL [67.1]
Geveran Trading Co Ltd v Skjevesland [2002] EWCA Civ 1567, [2003] 1 All ER 1, sub nom Skjevesland v Geveran Trading Co Ltd [2002] NLJR 1686, 146 Sol Jo LB 248, (2002) Times, 13 November .... III HUM [28.3B]
Geys v Societe Generale, London Branch [2011] EWCA Civ 307, [2011] IRLR 482, [2011] All ER (D) 350 (Mar); revsd [2012] UKSC 63, [2012] All ER (D) 196 (Dec) .. III EMP [6.4]
Ghai v Newcastle City Council (Ramgharia Gurdwara, Hitchin intervening) [2009] EWHC 978 (Admin), [2009] NLJR 713, (2009) Times, 18 May, [2009] All ER (D) 68 (May) .... III HUM [31.5]
Ghaidan v Godin-Mendoza [2002] EWCA Civ 1533, [2003] Ch 380, [2002] 4 All ER 1162, [2003] 2 WLR 478, [2003] Fam Law 87, [2003] 01 LS Gaz R 24, sub nom Mendoza v Ghaidan [2002] 3 FCR 591, [2003] 1 FLR 468, [2003] HLR 505, [2002] NLJR 1718, 146 Sol Jo LB 253, [2003] 1 P & CR D25; affd [2004] UKHL 30, [2004] 2 AC 557, [2004] 3 WLR 113, [2004] 2 FCR 481, [2004] 2 FLR 600, [2004] Fam Law 641, [2004] HLR 827, [2004] 27 LS Gaz R 30, [2004] NLJR 1013, 148 Sol Jo LB 792, (2004) Times, 24 June, [2004] All ER (D) 210 (Jun), sub nom Ghaidan v Mendoza [2004] 3 All ER 411 .... III HUM [3], [9.2], [35.1]; III L&T [81.2], [112.2], [119.1], [119.3], [223.3]
Ghosh v General Medical Council [2001] UKPC 29, [2001] 1 WLR 1915, [2001] All ER (D) 189 (Jun) .... III SOL [66.2]
Gibbon v Manchester City Council [2010] EWCA Civ 726, [2011] 2 All ER 258, [2010] 1 WLR 2081, [2010] 3 EGLR 85, [2010] 36 EG 120, [2010] 27 EG 84 (CS), [2010] All ER (D) 218 (Jun) .... III PID [2C], [5B]
Gibbons v Registrar, Stroud County Court (1990) Independent, 8 October, CA .. II CCA [6.5]
Gibbs v Cruikshank (1873) LR 8 CP 454, 37 JP 744, 42 LJCP 273, 21 WR 734, 28 LT 735 .... II CCA [142.3]
Gibbs v Guild (1881) 8 QBD 296; affd 9 QBD 59, CA .... III LIM [7.1]
Gibbs v Leeds United Football Club Ltd [2016] EWHC 960 (QB), [2016] IRLR 493, 166 NLJ 7698, [2016] All ER (D) 206 (Apr) .... III EMP [1]

Gibson v Douglas [2016] EWCA Civ 1266 .... III L&T [91.6]
Gibson Davies Ltd, Re [1995] BCC 11 .... III COM [54.1]
Gil v Baygreen Properties Ltd. See Baygreen Properties Ltd v Gil
Gilbank v Miles [2006] ICR 12, (2005) Times, 16 November, [2005] All ER (D) 355 (Oct), EAT; affd [2006] EWCA Civ 543, [2006] ICR 1297, [2006] IRLR 538, [2006] All ER (D) 160 (May) .... III EQU [119.4]
Giles v Law Society [1995] 38 LS Gaz R 25, 139 Sol Jo LB 218, (1995) Times, 20 October, [1995] Admin LR 105, CA .... III SOL [65.2]
Giles v Rhind [2008] EWCA Civ 118, [2008] 3 All ER 697, [2008] 3 WLR 1233, [2008] 2 BCLC 1, [2008] BPIR 342, [2008] All ER (D) 410 (Feb) .... III LIM [36.5]
Gilham v Ministry of Justice (2016) UKEAT0087/16, [2017] IRLR 23, [2017] ICR 404, [2016] All ER (D) 27 (Nov), EAT .... III EMP [1]
Gilje v Charlegrove Securities Ltd [2003] EWHC 1284 (Ch), [2004] 1 All ER 91, [2004] HLR 1, [2003] 3 EGLR 9, [2003] 36 EG 110, [2003] All ER (D) 162 (May) . III L&T [174.1]
Gill v Birmingham City Council [2016] EWCA Civ 608, [2016] HLR 494 ... III COT [21.2A]
Gill (Stewart) Ltd v Horatio Myer & Co Ltd [1992] QB 600, [1992] 2 All ER 257, [1992] 2 WLR 721, CA .... III CON [68.1]
Gillan v United Kingdom (Application No 4158/05) [2010] ECHR 4158/05, [2010] NLJR 104, (2010) Times, 15 January, 28 BHRC 420, [2010] All ER (D) 40 (Jan) .. III HUM [27.2J]
Gillett v Holt [2001] Ch 210, [2000] 2 All ER 289, [2000] 3 WLR 815, [2000] 1 FCR 705, [2000] 2 FLR 266, [2000] Fam Law 714, [2000] 12 LS Gaz R 40, 144 Sol Jo LB 141, 80 P & CR D3, CA .... III FMY [6]
Gillick v West Norfolk and Wisbech Area Health Authority [1986] AC 112, [1985] 3 All ER 402, [1985] 3 WLR 830, [1986] 1 FLR 224, [1986] Crim LR 113, 129 Sol Jo 738, 2 BMLR 11, [1985] LS Gaz R 3551, [1985] NLJ Rep 1055, HL .... III MEN [407]
Gillies v Secretary of State for Work and Pensions (Scotland) [2006] UKHL 2, [2006] 1 All ER 731, [2006] 09 LS Gaz R 33, (2006) Times, 30 January, 2006 SLT 77, 150 Sol Jo LB 127, [2006] All ER (D) 181 (Jan) .... III HUM [28.3C]
Gillow v United Kingdom (1986) 11 EHRR 335 .... III HUM [30.5]
Gilmour Caterers Ltd v St Bartholomew's Hospital Governors [1956] 1 QB 387, [1956] 1 All ER 314, [1956] 2 WLR 419, 100 Sol Jo 110, 167 Estates Gazette 67, CA ..... III L&T [22.9]
Giorgione v Knight (1848) 12 JP 506, sub nom Knight, Re 17 LJ Ex 168, Cox M & H 47, 1 Exch 802, 12 Jur 101, 10 LTOS 377 .... II CCA [141.2]
Gissing v Gissing [1971] AC 886, [1970] 2 All ER 780, [1970] 3 WLR 255, 21 P & CR 702, 114 Sol Jo 550, 216 Estates Gazette 1257, HL .... III REA [58.2A]
Gladding v Channel 4 Television Corpn (1998) 142 Sol Jo LB 217, [1999] EMLR 475, CA .... II SCA [14.2]
Gladehurst Properties Ltd v Hashemi (on behalf of himself and Matthew Johnson) [2011] EWCA Civ 604, [2011] 4 All ER 556, [2011] 2 P & CR D41, [2011] All ER (D) 180 (May) .... III L&T [323.3]
Gladyric Ltd v Collinson (1983) 11 HLR 12, [1983] 2 EGLR 98, 267 Estates Gazette 761, CA .... III L&T [85.4]
Gladys Meek, Re [2014] EWCOP 1, [2014] WTLR 1155 .... III MEN [52.2]
Glaser v United Kingdom (2000) 33 EHRR 1, [2000] 3 FCR 193, [2001] 1 FLR 153, [2000] Fam Law 880, ECtHR .... III HUM [30.1]
Glass v United Kingdom (Application No 61827/00) [2004] 1 FCR 553, [2004] 1 FLR 1019, [2004] Fam Law 410, 77 BMLR 120, (2004) Times, 11 March, [2004] All ER (D) 166 (Mar), ECtHR .... III MEN [7]
Glaxo Group Ltd v Vectura Ltd [2018] EWCA Civ 1496, 168 NLJ 7807, [2018] All ER (D) 165 (Jun) .... III PAT [13.1]
Glencore International AG v Metro Trading Inc [2001] 1 All ER (Comm) 103, [2001] 1 Lloyd's Rep 284 .... II SCA [38.1A]
Gliddon v Lloyd Maunder Ltd [2003] NLJR 318 .... III FUND [27B.3]
Glider Standard Austria SH 1964, Re [1965] P 463, [1965] 2 All ER 1022, [1965] 3 WLR 568, [1965] 2 Lloyd's Rep 189, 109 Sol Jo 649 .... II SCA [18.19]
Global Financial Recoveries Ltd v Jones [2000] BPIR 1029 ..... III LIM [7.1], [10.1]; III PTY [19.3]
Global Marine Drillships Ltd v Landmark Solicitors LLP [2011] EWHC 2685 (Ch), [2011] 44 LS Gaz R 20, [2011] All ER (D) 01 (Nov) .... III SOL [67.1]
Globe Equities Ltd v Globe Legal Services Ltd [1999] BLR 232, CA .... II SCA [50.5]
Gloucestershire County Council v Evans [2008] EWCA Civ 21, [2008] 1 WLR 1883, [2008] NLJR 219, [2008] 2 Costs LR 308, [2008] All ER (D) 284 (Jan) ..... III FUND [27.4]

H

India (Republic) v India Steamship Co Ltd (No 2) [1998] AC 878, [1997] 3 WLR 818, [1997] 43 LS Gaz R 29, 141 Sol Jo LB 230, sub nom Indian Endurance (No 2), The, Republic of India v India Steamship Co Ltd [1997] 4 All ER 380, [1997] NLJR 1581, sub nom India (Republic) v India Steamship Co Ltd (Indian Endurance and Indian Grace) (No 2) [1998] 1 Lloyd's Rep 1, HL .... II SCA [19.2]
Infante v Rai-Radiotelevisione Italiana SpA [1999] 11 LS Gaz R 70, CA .... II SCA [14.1]
Ingleton v Dibble. See Dibble v Ingleton
Inglewood Investments Co Ltd v Baker [2002] EWCA Civ 1733, [2003] 2 P & CR 319, 146 Sol Jo LB 255, [2002] All ER (D) 378 (Nov) .... III LIM [20.4]
Ingrams v Sykes [1987] NLJ Rep 1135, CA .... III SOL [87.4]
IRC v National Federation of Self Employed and Small Businesses [1982] AC 617, [1981] 2 All ER 93, [1981] 2 WLR 722, [1981] STC 260, 55 TC 133, 125 Sol Jo 325, HL ... II SCA [30.3]
Inline Logistics Ltd v UCI Logistics Ltd [2002] EWHC 519 (Ch), [2002] RPC 611, [2002] 19 LS Gaz R 28, [2002] All ER (D) 435 (Mar) .... III FUND [28.3]
Inntrepreneur Pub Co (CPC) Ltd v Langton [2000] 1 EGLR 34, [1999] 44 LS Gaz R 39, [2000] 08 EG 169, 143 Sol Jo LB 268, 79 P & CR D7, [1999] EGCS 124 . II CCA [133.6], II SCA [39.1]; III L&T [2.3]
Instance (David J) Ltd v Denny Bros Printing Ltd [2001] EWCA Civ 939, [2002] RPC 321 .... III PAT [17.2]
Integral Memory plc v Haines Watts [2012] EWHC 342 (Ch), [2012] SWTI 1385, [2012] All ER (D) 110 (Mar) .... III SOL [44]
Intellimedia Systems Ltd v Doyle [2015] EWHC 1200 (Ch), [2015] All ER (D) 58 (Jun) .... III COM [125.1]
Intellimedia Technologies Ltd v Richards [2015] EWHC 1200 (Ch), [2015] All ER (D) 58 (Jun) .... III COM [125.1]
Inter Lotto (UK) Ltd v Camelot Group plc [2003] EWHC 1256 (Ch), [2003] 3 All ER 191; affd sub nom Inter Lotto (UK) Ltd v Camelot Group plc [2003] EWCA Civ 1132, [2003] 4 All ER 575, Times, 20 August .... III PAT [41.2A]
Interatlantic (Namibia) (Pty) Ltd v Okeanski Ribolov Ltd, The Afala [1995] 2 Lloyd's Rep 286, 1996 SLT 819, Ct of Sess .... II SCA [19.7]
Interbrew SA v Financial Times [2002] 1 Lloyd's Rep 542, [2001] All ER (D) 313 (Dec), (2002) Times, 4 January; affd sub nom Interbrew SA v Financial Times Ltd [2002] EWCA Civ 274, [2002] All ER (D) 106 (Mar), [2002] 16 LS Gaz R 37, [2002] EMLR 446, [2002] 2 Lloyd's Rep 229, Times, 21 March .... III HUM [32.6]
Interbulk Ltd v Aiden Shipping Co Ltd, The Vimeira [1983] 2 Lloyd's Rep 424, [1984] 2 Lloyd's Rep 66, [1983] Com LR 142, 133 NLJ 575, CA .... III ARB [21.4]
International Drilling Fluids Ltd v Louisville Investments (Uxbridge) Ltd [1986] Ch 513, [1986] 1 All ER 321, [1986] 2 WLR 581, 51 P & CR 187, 129 Sol Jo 854, [1986] 1 EGLR 39, 277 Estates Gazette 62, CA .... III L&T [7.3]
International Transport Roth GmbH v Secretary of State for the Home Department [2002] EWCA Civ 158, [2003] QB 728, [2002] 3 WLR 344, [2002] All ER (D) 325 (Feb) . III HUM [10.2], [28.10]
Interprods Ltd v De La Rue International Ltd [2014] EWHC 68 (Comm), [2014] 1 Lloyd's Rep 540, [2014] All ER (D) 193 (Jan) .... III ARB [20.3]
Interserve FM Ltd v Tuleikyte (2017) UKEAT/0267/16, [2017] IRLR 615, [2017] All ER (D) 226 (Mar), EAT .... III EQU [17.1]
Intpro Properties (UK) Ltd v Sauvel [1983] QB 1019, [1983] 2 All ER 495, [1983] 2 WLR 908, 127 Sol Jo 325, 267 Estates Gazette 515, CA .... II CCA [7.4]
Invercargill City Council v Hamlin [1996] AC 624, [1996] 1 All ER 140, [1996] 2 WLR 367, 78 BLR 78, 50 Con LR 105, [1996] NLJR 246, 140 Sol Jo LB 86, CA .... III LIM [3.5]
Iperion Investments Corpn v Broadwalk House Residents Ltd (1994) 71 P & CR 34, 27 HLR 196, [1995] 2 EGLR 47, [1995] 46 EG 188, CA .... III L&T [175.1]
Iqbal v Ahmed [2011] EWCA Civ 900, [2011] 3 FCR 1, [2012] 1 FLR 31, [2011] Fam Law 1199, [2011] All ER (D) 32 (Aug) .... III FMY [7.13]
Iqbal v Dean Manson Solicitors [2011] EWCA Civ 123, [2011] IRLR 428, [2011] NLJR 288, [2011] All ER (D) 163 (Feb) .... III HAR [6.1C], [6.4], [7.4], [8.1]
Iqbal v Thakrar [2004] EWCA Civ 592, [2004] 3 EGLR 21, [2004] All ER (D) 304 (Apr) .... III L&T [7.6], III L&T [7.7]
Iraqi Civilian Litigation, Re. See Mohammed v Secretary of State for Defence
Iraqi Civilians v Ministry of Defence [2017] UKSC 1, [2017] 2 WLR 287 .. III HUM [27.2F], [28.4]

J

James v Thomas [2007] EWCA Civ 1212, [2007] 3 FCR 696, [2008] 1 FLR 1598, [2008] Fam Law 99, [2008] Fam Law 519, [2007] All ER (D) 373 (Nov) .... **III REA [58.2]**

James v United Kingdom (1986) 8 EHRR 123, [1986] RVR 139, ECtHR .... **III HUM [39.1]**

James v Williams [2000] Ch 1, [1999] 3 All ER 309, [1999] 3 WLR 451, 79 P & CR 421, [1999] 2 FCR 498, [1999] 15 LS Gaz R 30, 78 P & CR D17, CA ..... **III LIM [20.3], [26.2]**

James W Elwell, The [1921] P 351, 90 LJP 132, 355, 15 Asp MLC 418, 125 LT 796, 37 TLR 178, 835, 8 Ll L Rep 115 .... **II CCA [87.4]**

James, Wells and Lee v United Kingdom (Application Nos 25119/09, 57715/09 and 57877/09) (2013) 56 EHRR 12, [2012] 37 LS Gaz R 20, 176 CL&J 577, (2012) Times, 03 December, [2012] Lexis Citation 77, 33 BHRC 617, [2012] All ER (D) 109 (Sep), ECtHR .... **III HUM [8.1], [27.21]**

Jameson v Central Electricity Generating Board (Babcock Energy, third party) [1998] QB 323, [1997] 4 All ER 38, [1997] 3 WLR 151, [1997] PIQR Q89, 141 Sol Jo LB 55, CA; revsd [2000] 1 AC 455, [1999] 1 All ER 193, [1999] 2 WLR 141, [1999] 1 Lloyd's Rep 573, 143 Sol Jo LB 29, HL .... **III PID [10.1], [16.1A]**

Jameson v Manley [1987] CLY 2963, CA .... **II CCA [21.7]**

Janes (Gowns) Ltd v Harlow Development Corpn [1980] 1 EGLR 52, 253 Estates Gazette 799 .... **III L&T [16C.1], [27.8]**

Jarvis v Swans Tours Ltd [1973] QB 233, [1973] 1 All ER 71, [1972] 3 WLR 954, 116 Sol Jo 822, CA .... **III CON [84.2], [273.3]**

Jaura v Ahmed [2002] EWCA Civ 210, (2002) Times, 18 March .... **II SCA [36.3]**

Javad v Aqil [1991] 1 All ER 243, [1991] 1 WLR 1007, 61 P & CR 164, [1990] 2 EGLR 82, [1990] NLJR 1232, [1990] 41 EG 61, CA .... **III L&T [41.3]**

Jay Bola, The. See Payabi v Armstel Shipping Corpn, The Jay Bola

Jefford v Gee [1970] 2 QB 130, [1970] 1 All ER 1202, [1970] 2 WLR 702, [1970] 1 Lloyd's Rep 107, 114 Sol Jo 206, CA .... **II SCA [36.6], [36.7], [36.10]**

Jeffrey v Secretary of State for Transport [2004] EWHC 2772, [2005] UKHRR 154 . **III HUM [13.4]**

Jelley v Iliffe [1981] Fam 128, [1981] 2 All ER 29, [1981] 2 WLR 801, 125 Sol Jo 355, CA .... **III FMY [7.7], [7.8]**

Jelly v All Type Roofing Co. See Debtor (No 50A-SD-1995), Re

Jelson Ltd v Derby City Council [1999] 3 EGLR 91, [1999] 19 EG 149, [1999] EGCS 88 .... **III REA [38.1]**

Jemma Trust Co Ltd v Liptrott [2003] EWCA Civ 1476, [2004] 1 All ER 510, [2003] 45 LS Gaz R 29, [2003] NLJR 1633, 147 Sol Jo LB 1275 .... **III SOL [74.4]**

Jenkins v Holt [1999] RTR 411, CA .... **III PID [9.3]**

Jenkins v Young Brothers Transport Ltd [2006] EWHC 151 (QB), [2006] 2 All ER 798, [2006] 1 WLR 3189, [2006] NLJR 421, [2006] 3 Costs LR 495, [2006] All ER (D) 270 (Feb) .... **III FUND [27.1]**

Jennings, Re [1994] Ch 286, [1994] 3 All ER 27, [1994] 3 WLR 67, [1995] 1 FCR 257, sub nom Re Jennings, Harlow v National Westminster Bank plc [1994] 1 FLR 536, [1994] Fam Law 439, CA .... **III FMY [7.12], [7.15], [9.4], [9.5]**

Jennings v Rice [2002] EWCA Civ 159, [2003] 1 P & CR 100, [2003] 1 FCR 501, [2002] NPC 28, [2002] All ER (D) 324 (Feb), [2002] WTLR 367 .... **III FMY [6]**

Jennings and Jennings v Epping Forest District Council (1992) 25 HLR 241, [1992] NPC 93, CA .... **III L&T [122.1]**

Jephson Homes Housing Association v Moisejevs [2001] 2 All ER 901, 33 HLR 594, [2001] 41 EG 186, [2000] EGCS 123, CA .... **III L&T [110.1C]**

Jervis v Harris [1996] Ch 195, [1996] 1 All ER 303, [1996] 2 WLR 220, [1995] NPC 171, [1996] 1 EGLR 78, [1995] 10 EG 159, 140 Sol Jo LB 13, CA .... **III L&T [9]**

Jessamine Investment Co v Schwartz [1978] QB 264, [1976] 3 All ER 521, [1977] 2 WLR 145, 33 P & CR 346, 120 Sol Jo 384, CA .... **III L&T [69.11]**

Jessemey v Rowstock Ltd [2014] EWCA Civ 185, [2014] 3 All ER 409, [2014] 1 WLR 3615, [2014] 3 CMLR 541, [2014] IRLR 368, [2014] ICR 550, (2014) Times, 15 April, [2014] EqLR 230, [2014] All ER (D) 237 (Feb) .... **III EQU [108.1]**

Jessop v Jessop [1992] 1 FLR 591, [1992] 1 FCR 253, [1992] Fam Law 328, CA .... **III FMY [15.1]**

Jet2.com Ltd v Huzar [2014] EWCA Civ 791, [2014] 4 All ER 581, [2014] 2 All ER (Comm) 914, [2014] Bus LR 1324, [2014] 2 Lloyd's Rep 368, [2014] All ER (D) 86 (Jun) .... **III CON [88.3]**

Jetivia SA v Bilta (UK). See Bilta (UK) Ltd (in liq) v Nazir Ltd

Jeune v Queens Cross Properties Ltd [1974] Ch 97, [1973] 3 All ER 97, [1973] 3 WLR 378, 26 P & CR 98, 117 Sol Jo 680 .... **III L&T [170.5]**

Jewelcraft Ltd v Pressland [2015] EWCA Civ 1111, [2015] All ER (D) 278 (Oct) .... III L&T [50.1], [50.1A]
Jewson Ltd v Kelly [2002] All ER (D) 339 (Oct), Times, 3 October .... III CON [75.4]
Jim Ennis Construction Ltd v Premier Asphalt Ltd [2009] EWHC 1906 (TCC), 125 Con LR 141, [2009] 41 EG 116, [2009] All ER (D) 29 (Aug) .... III LIM [7.2A]
Jivraj v Hashwani [2011] UKSC 40, [2011] 1 WLR 1872, [2011] Bus LR 1182, [2011] 2 Lloyd's Rep 513, [2011] ICR 1004, [2011] IRLR 827, [2011] NLJR 1100, (2011) Times, 04 August, [2011] All ER (D) 246 (Jul) .... III ARB [9.1]; III EQU [39]
Joanna Borchard, The. See Katzenstein Adler Industries (1975) Ltd v Borchard Lines Ltd
Jockey Club Racecourses Ltd v Wilmott Dixon Construction Ltd [2016] EWHC 167 (TCC), [2016] 4 WLR 43, [2016] 1 Costs LR 123, [2016] All ER (D) 90 (Feb) .. III PID [5B]
Joddrell v Peaktone Ltd [2012] EWCA Civ 1035, [2012] All ER (D) 287 (Jul) ...... III COM [1032.2]
Joel v Morison (1834) 6 C & P 501 .... III PID [3A]
Joel v Swaddle [1957] 3 All ER 325, [1957] 1 WLR 1094, 101 Sol Jo 850, 170 Estates Gazette 505, CA .... III L&T [22.10]
Johan (Jerry) Developments SA v Avon Tyres Ltd (1999) Times, 25 January ... III PTY [22.2]
Johann MK Blumenthal GMBH & Co KG v Itochu Corpn [2012] EWCA Civ 996, [2012] NLJR 1028, (2012) Times, 27 September, [2012] All ER (D) 240 (Jul), sub nom Johann MK Blumenthal GMBH [2012] 2 Lloyd's Rep 437 .... III ARB [9.8]
John v Associated Newspapers Ltd [2006] EWHC 1611 (QB), [2006] EMLR 772 ... III HUM [18.3]
John v Express Newspapers [2000] 3 All ER 257, [2000] 1 WLR 1931, [2000] NLJR 615, 144 Sol Jo LB 217, [2000] EMLR 606, CA .... III COT [19.1]
John Fox (a firm) v Bannister King & Rigbeys [1988] QB 925n, [1987] 1 All ER 737, [1987] 3 WLR 480n, 131 Sol Jo 1063, [1987] LS Gaz R 2692, [1987] NLJ Rep 122 .... II CCA [136.1]
John Mowlem Construction plc v Neil F Jones & Co (a firm) [2004] EWCA Civ 768, [2004] BLR 387, (2004) Times, 27 August, 148 Sol Jo LB 825, [2004] All ER (D) 21 (Oct) .... III SOL [61]
John Romans Park Homes Ltd v Hancock [2018] UKUT 249 (LC) .... III MOB [4.1]
Johnson, Re [1987] CLY 3882 .... III FMY [19A.1]
Johnson v Awe plc (UKEAT/0131/08/CEA), unreported .... III EMP [4]
Johnson v Chief Constable of Surrey (1992) Times, 23 November, CA .... III LIM [36.1A]
Johnson v Chief Constable of Surrey (23 November 1992, unreported), CA .... III LIM [36.2]
Johnson v County Bideford Ltd [2012] UKUT 457 (LC) .... III L&T [203.3]
Johnson v Felton (1994) 27 HLR 265, [1994] EGCS 135, CA .... III L&T [154.1]
Johnson v Lord Mayor and Citizens of Westminster [2013] EWCA Civ 773, [2013] NLJR 19, [2013] HLR 45, [2013] All ER (D) 259 (Jun) .... III L&T [306A.1]
Johnson v Medical Defence Union [2007] EWCA Civ 262, [2007] 3 CMLR 181, 96 BMLR 99, (2007) Times, 10 April , [2007] All ER (D) 464 (Mar) .... III DAT [11.4], [31.4]
Johnson v Medical Defence Union (No 2) (2006) Times, 4 April .... III DAT [11.4]
Johnson v Medical Defence Union Ltd [2004] EWHC 2509 (Ch), [2005] 1 All ER 87, [2004] All ER (D) 131 (Nov), Times, 25 November .... III DAT [17.4], [25.1]
Johnson v Miller Bros & R P Butler Ltd (2002) Times, 18 April, EAT .... III EMP [2]
Johnson v Ministry of Defence [2012] EWCA Civ 1505, [2012] All ER (D) 254 (Nov) .... III LIM [17.4A]
Johnson v Old [2013] EWCA Civ 415, [2013] 2 P & CR D15, [2013] HLR 344, [2013] All ER (D) 219 (Apr) .... III L&T [321.2]
Johnson v Secretary of State for the Home Department [2016] UKSC 56, [2016] 3 WLR 1267, 166 NLJ 7720, (2016) Times, 26 October, [2016] All ER (D) 116 (Oct) ...... III HUM [10.2]
Johnson v Solihull Metropolitan Borough Council [2015] UKSC 30, [2015] 3 All ER 1053, [2015] 2 WLR 1341, [2015] LGR 530, [2015] HLR 460, 165 NLJ 7653, (2015) Times, 25 May, [2015] All ER (D) 110 (May) .... III L&T [303AA.3]
Johnson v United Kingdom (1997) 27 EHRR 296, 40 BMLR 1, ECtHR ..... III HUM [27.2]
Johnson v Valks [2000] 1 All ER 450, [2000] 1 WLR 1502, [1999] 46 LS Gaz R 40, 144 Sol Jo LB 10, CA .... II SCA [44.1], [44.3]
Johnston (David) v Chief Constable of Merseyside Police [2009] EWHC 2969 (QB), [2009] All ER (D) 226 (Nov) .... III MEN [27.1]
Johnston v Chief Constable of the Royal Ulster Constabulary: 222/84 [1987] QB 129, [1986] 3 All ER 135, [1986] ECR 1651, [1986] 3 WLR 1038, [1986] 3 CMLR 240, [1987] ICR 83, [1986] IRLR 263, 130 Sol Jo 953, [1987] LS Gaz R 188, ECJ . III EQU [17.1]

K

Kennedy, Re, Kennedy v Official Solicitor to the Supreme Court [1980] CLY 2820 ... **III FMY [16]**

Kennedy v Charity Commission [2012] EWCA Civ 317, [2012] 1 WLR 3524, [2012] 14 LS Gaz R 22, [2012] All ER (D) 143 (Mar); [2014] UKSC 20, [2014] 2 All ER 847, [2014] IP & T 733, (2014) Times, 02 April, [2014] All ER (D) 240 (Mar) .... **III HUM [9.2], [32.8A]**

Kennett v Brown [1988] 2 All ER 600, [1988] 1 WLR 582, 132 Sol Jo 752, CA ..... **III LIM [39.6]**

Kenny v Preen [1963] 1 QB 499, [1962] 3 All ER 814, [1962] 3 WLR 1233, 106 Sol Jo 854, CA .... **II CCA [21.3]; III L&T [88]**

Kensington and Chelsea Royal London Borough Council v Hayden (1984) 17 HLR 114, [1985] CLY 1643, CA .... **III L&T [156.4]**

Kensington and Chelsea Royal London Borough Council v Hislop [2003] EWHC 2944 (Ch), [2004] 1 All ER 1036, [2003] All ER (D) 113 (Dec) .... **III L&T [122.1]**

Kensington and Chelsea Royal London Borough Council v O'Sullivan [2003] EWCA Civ 371, [2003] 1 FCR 687, [2003] HLR 877, 147 Sol Jo LB 387, (2003) Times, 27 March .... **III L&T [106.3]**

Kensington and Chelsea Royal London Borough Council v Simmonds [1996] 3 FCR 246, 29 HLR 507, CA .... **III L&T [157.4]**

Kensington Heights Commercial Co Ltd v Campden Hill Developments Ltd [2007] EWCA Civ 245, [2007] Ch 318, [2007] 2 All ER 751, [2007] 2 WLR 1040, 151 Sol Jo LB 436, (2007) Times, 20 April, [2007] All ER (D) 353 (Mar) .... **III L&T [186.2]**

Kent v Kavanagh [2006] EWCA Civ 162, [2006] 2 All ER 645, [2006] 10 EG 155 (CS), [2006] All ER (D) 33 (Mar) .... III L&T [55.3]

Kent Coast Property Investments Ltd v Ward [1990] 2 EGLR 86, [1990] 45 EG 107, CA .... **III L&T [14.4]**

Keohane v Metropolitan Police Comr (2014) UKEAT/0463/12, [2014] ICR 1073, [2014] EqLR 386, [2014] All ER (D) 307 (Mar), EAT .... **III EQU [17.2]**

Kanu v The London Borough of Southwark [2014] EWCA Civ 1085, [2014] LGR 785, [2014] PTSR 1197, [2014] HLR 595, (2014) Times, 01 August .... **III L&T [303AA.3]**

Kerly, Son and Verden, Re [1901] 1 Ch 467, 70 LJ Ch 189, 49 WR 199, 211, [1900–3] All ER Rep 858, 45 Sol Jo 120, 206, 83 LT 524, 699, 17 TLR 123, 189, CA .... **III SOL [67.1]**

Kerner v WX [2015] EWHC 128 (QB), [2015] All ER (D) 214 (Jan) .... **III HUM 18.2]**

Kernott v Jones [2010] EWCA Civ 578, [2010] 2 FCR 372, 154 Sol Jo (no 21) 30, [2010] All ER (D) 244 (May) .... **III REA [58.2]**

Kershaw v Micklethwaite [2010] EWHC 506 (Ch) .... **III SOL [45.1A]**

Kershaw Mechanical Services Ltd v Kendrick Construction Ltd [2006] EWHC 727 (TCC), [2006] 4 All ER 79, [2006] 2 All ER (Comm) 81, [2006] All ER (D) 21 (Mar) ...... **III ARB [22.4]**

Kesslar v Moore [2004] EWCA Civ 1551, sub nom Kesslar v Moore and Tibbits 148 Sol Jo LB 1316, sub nom Kesslar v Moore & Tibb (incorporating Kundert & Co) (a firm) [2005] PNLR 17, [2004] All ER (D) 53 (Nov) .... **III LIM [39.9A]**

Ketley v Gilbert [2001] 1 WLR 986, [2001] RTR 327, (2001) Times, 17 January, (2001) Independent, 19 January, [2000] All ER (D) 2429, CA .... **III CON [24B]**

Kew v Bettamix Ltd (formerly Tarmac Roadstone Southern Ltd) [2006] EWCA Civ 1535, 150 Sol Jo LB 1534, [2006] All ER (D) 173 (Nov) .... **III LIM [38.3]**

Kewal Investments Ltd v Arthur Maiden Ltd [1990] 1 EGLR 193, [1990] 15 EG 58 . **III L&T [14.2]**

Keypak Homecare Ltd (No 2), Re [1990] BCLC 440, [1990] BCC 117 .... **III COM [54.2]**

Keyu v Secretary of State for Foreign and Commonwealth Affairs [2014] EWCA Civ 312, [2014] 4 All ER 99, [2014] 3 WLR 948, [2014] All ER (D) 187 (Mar) .... **III HUM [24.4]**

Keyu v Secretary of State for Foreign and Commonwealth Affairs [2015] UKSC 69, [2015] All ER (D) 223 (Nov) .... **III HUM [6A], [9.3], [23.4], [23.5], [24.4]**

Khairule v North West Strategic Health Authority [2008] EWHC 1537 (QB), [2008] All ER (D) 85 (Jul) .... **III LIM [17.4A]**

Khan v Chief Constable of West Yorkshire Police. See Chief Constable of West Yorkshire Police v Khan

Khan v Evans [2001] CLY 888 .... **III CON [24B]**

Khan v RM Falvey & Co (a firm) [2002] EWCA Civ 400, [2002] Lloyd's Rep PN 369, [2002] 19 LS Gaz R 30, [2002] PNLR 28, [2002] All ER (D) 361 (Mar), Times, 12 April .... **III LIM [3.6], [13.4]; III SOL [61]**

L

Lonrho Ltd v Shell Petroleum Co Ltd [1980] QB 358, [1980] 2 WLR 367, 124 Sol Jo 205, 130 NLJ 393, CA; affd [1981] 2 All ER 456, [1980] 1 WLR 627, 124 Sol Jo 412, 130 NLJ 605, HL .... **III CRO [20.1]**
Lonrho plc, Re [1990] 2 AC 154, [1989] 2 All ER 1100, [1989] 3 WLR 535, [1989] NLJR 1073, HL .... **III COT [16.2]**
Lonrho plc v Tebbit [1992] 4 All ER 280, [1993] BCLC 96, [1992] BCC 779, CA .... **II CCA [7.8]**
Lonzim plc v Sprague [2009] EWHC 2838 (QB), [2009] All ER (D) 132 (Nov) .... **III LIM [37.2]**
Lopez Ribalda v Spain (Applications 1874/13 and 8567/13) (2018) .... **III HUM [30.5C]**
Lord Chancellor, Ministry of Justice v McCloud [2017] UKEAT/0071/17 .... **III EQU [5.2]**
L'Oreal (UK) Ltd v Johnson & Johnson [2000] ETMR 691, [2000] FSR 686 .. **III PAT [15.3], [45.1]**
Lotteryking Ltd v AMEC Properties Ltd [1995] NPC 55, [1995] 2 EGLR 13, [1995] 28 EG 104 .... **III L&T [164.10]**
Lougheed v On The Beach Ltd [2014] EWCA Civ 1538, [2014] All ER (D) 299 (Nov) .... **III CON [102.2], [273.3]**
Loutchansky v Times Newspapers Ltd [2001] EWCA Civ 536, [2002] QB 321, [2001] 4 All ER 115, [2001] 3 WLR 404, [2001] NLJR 643, [2001] EMLR 685 .... **III HUM [32.3]**
Loutchansky v Times Newspapers Ltd (No 2) [2001] EMLR 876; on appeal sub nom Loutchansky v Times Newspapers Ltd (No 2) [2001] EWCA Civ 1805, [2002] QB 783, [2002] 1 All ER 652, [2002] 2 WLR 640, [2002] 06 LS Gaz R 30, 145 Sol Jo LB 277, [2002] EMLR 241 .... **III HUM [28.5], [32.5A]; III LIM [6.3]**
Love and Lugg v Herrity (1990) 23 HLR 217, CA .... **III L&T [214.3]**
Lovely and Orchard Services Ltd v Daejan Investments (Grove Hall) Ltd (1977) 121 Sol Jo 711, [1978] 1 EGLR 44, 246 Estates Gazette 651 .... **III L&T [16C.1]**
Loveridge v Mayor and Burgesses of the London Borough of Lambeth [2014] UKSC 65, [2014] 1 WLR 4516, (2014) Times, 11 December, [2014] All ER (D) 28 (Dec) ...... **III L&T [233.1]**
Loveridge and Loveridge v Healey [2004] EWCA Civ 173, (2004) Times, 27 February, 148 Sol Jo LB 264, [2004] All ER (D) 359 (Feb) .... **III MOB [11.1]**
Lovibond (John) & Sons Ltd v Vincent [1929] 1 KB 687, 27 LGR 471, 93 JP 161, 98 LJKB 402, [1929] All ER Rep 59, 73 Sol Jo 252, 141 LT 116, 45 TLR 383, CA .... **III L&T [69.7]**
Lowe v Londrum (1950) 156 Estates Gazette 423, CA .... **III L&T [82.6]**
Lower Street Properties Ltd v Jones (1996) 28 HLR 877, [1996] NPC 29, [1996] 48 EG 154, CA .... **III L&T [227.3], [229.4]**
Lowery v Walker [1911] AC 10, 80 LJKB 138, [1908–10] All ER Rep 12, 55 Sol Jo 62, 103 LT 674, 27 TLR 83, HL .... **II CCA [78.2]**
Lawrence v Fen Tigers Ltd (Secretary of State for Justice intervening). See Coventry v Lawrence
Lowsley v Forbes (t/a LE Design Services) [1999] 1 AC 329, [1998] 3 All ER 897, [1998] 3 WLR 501, [1998] 2 Lloyd's Rep 577, [1998] NLJR 1268, 142 Sol Jo LB 247, [1998] All ER (D) 382, HL ..... **II CCA [71.1], III LIM [29.2], [29.3], [29.4], [36.1A], [36.2]**
Lowther v Chatwin [2003] EWCA Civ 729, [2003] All ER (D) 294 (May), Times, 4 August .... **III PID [40.1]**
Lubren v Lambeth London Borough Council (1987) 20 HLR 165, CA .... **III L&T [164.8]**
Lucas v Lineham [1950] 1 KB 548, [1950] 1 All ER 586, 66 (pt 1) TLR 641, CA ... **III L&T [82.22]**
Luganda v Service Hotels Ltd [1969] 2 Ch 209, [1969] 2 All ER 692, [1969] 2 WLR 1056, 20 P & CR 337, 113 Sol Jo 206, 210 Estates Gazette 113, CA .... **III L&T [68.3]**
Lumb v Hampsey [2011] EWHC 2808 (QB), [2012] All ER (D) 18 (Feb) .... **III PID [5D]**
Lunt v Khelifa [2002] EWCA Civ 801, [2002] All ER (D) 352 (May) .... **III PID [9.3]**
Lupkovics, Re, ex p Trustee v Freville [1954] 2 All ER 125, [1954] 1 WLR 1234, 98 Sol Jo 590 .... **III CRO [19.4]**
Lusitania, The. See Pierce v Bemis, The Lusitania
Lustig-Prean and Beckett v United Kingdom (1999) 29 EHRR 548, ECtHR ... **III HUM [7.2], [30.2]**
Lütticke (Alfons) GmbH v EC Commission: 48/65 [1966] ECR 19, [1966] CMLR 378, ECJ .... **III EUR [9]**
Lynch v Paul Davidson Taylor (a firm) [2004] EWHC 89 (QB), [2004] 1 WLR 1753, [2004] All ER (D) 28 (Feb) .... **III SOL [90.3]**
Lyon (John) Free Grammar School (Keepers and Governors) v James [1996] QB 163, [1995] 4 All ER 740, [1995] 3 WLR 908, 27 HLR 727, CA .... **III L&T [76.5]**

Lyon (John) Free Grammar School (Keepers and Governors etc) v Mayhew [1997] 1 EGLR 88, [1997] 17 EG 163, CA .... III L&T [17.1B]
Lyon (John) Free Grammar School (Keepers and Governors) v Secchi (1999) 32 HLR 820, [1999] NPC 121, [1999] 3 EGLR 49, [1999] 49 EG 100, [1999] EGCS 118, [1999] All ER (D) 1087, CA .... III L&T [257.7]
Lyon (John) Free Grammar School Governors v Vignaud [1993] 2 EGLR 122, [1993] 26 EG 128 .... III L&T [46.8]
Lyons v Central Commercial Properties Ltd [1958] 2 All ER 767, [1958] 1 WLR 869, 102 Sol Jo 600, 172 Estates Gazette 111, CA .... III L&T [22.3], [26.2]

M

M, Re [1994] 1 AC 377, [1993] 3 WLR 433, [1993] 37 LS Gaz R 50, [1993] NLJR 1099, 137 Sol Jo LB 199, sub nom M v Home Office [1993] 3 All ER 537, HL ..... III CRO [13.1]
M (a minor) (contempt of court: committal of court's own motion), Re [1999] Fam 263, [1999] 2 All ER 56, [1999] 2 WLR 810, [1999] 1 FCR 683, [1999] 1 FLR 810, [1999] Fam Law 208, 143 Sol Jo LB 36, CA .... III COT [2]
M (a child) (children and family reporter: disclosure), Re [2002] EWCA Civ 1199, [2003] Fam 26, [2002] 4 All ER 401, [2002] 3 FCR 208, [2002] 2 FLR 893, [2003] Fam Law 96, [2002] 39 LS Gaz R 37, [2002] All ER (D) 482 (Jul) .... III COT [8.1A]
M (children) (contempt: committal order), Re [2005] EWCA Civ 615, (2005) Times, 18 April, 149 Sol Jo LB 477, [2005] All ER (D) 73 (Apr), sub nom M (contact order), Re [2005] 2 FLR 1006 .... III COT [21.2A]
M (vulnerable adult) (testamentary capacity), Re [2009] EWHC 2525 (Fam), [2010] 3 All ER 682, [2011] 1 WLR 344, [2009] All ER (D) 314 (Oct) ...... III MEN [34.1], [51.1], [604.1]
M (adult patient) (minimally conscious state: withdrawal of treatment), Re [2011] EWHC 2443 (Fam), [2012] 1 WLR 1653, [2012] PTSR 1040, [2011] Fam Law 1330, 122 BMLR 67, [2011] 39 LS Gaz R 18, (2011) Times, 01 December, [2011] All ER (D) 142 (Sep), sub nom W (by her litigation friend, B) v M (by her litigation friend, the Official Solicitor) [2012] 1 All ER 1313, [2012] 1 FCR 1, [2012] 1 FLR 495 . III HUM [24.1]; III MEN [58.2]
M, Re [2011] EWHC 3590 (COP) .... III MEN [49.1], [133.1]
M (Children), Re [2017] EWCA Civ 2164, 168 NLJ 7777, [2018] All ER (D) 16 (Jan) .... III EQU [10.4]
M (a child) (oral evidence: vulnerable witness), Re [2012] EWCA Civ 1905, [2012] All ER (D) 272 (Nov) .... III HUM [28.2]
M (Best Interests: Deprivation of Liberty), Re [2013] EWHC 3456 (COP) .... III MEN [34.1]
M, Re, N v O and P [2013] COPLR 91 .... III MEN [10A]
M (by her litigation friend, B) v A Hospital [2017] EWCOP 19, [2018] 1 WLR 465, [2017] Fam Law 1296, [2017] All ER (D) 76 (Sep) .... III MEN [7]
M v B [2005] EWHC 1681 (Fam), [2005] Fam Law 860, (2005) Times, 10 August, [2005] All ER (D) 449 (Jul) .... III MEN [7]
M (by his litigation friend TM) v Hackney London Borough Council [2011] EWCA Civ 4, [2011] 3 All ER 529, [2011] 1 WLR 2873, [2011] PTSR 1419, (2011) Times, 17 February, [2011] All ER (D) 76 (Jan) .... III MEN [27.1], [27.2]
M v Home Office. See M, Re [1994] 1 AC 377
M v Islington London Borough Council and L [2002] 1 FLR 95, [2002] Fam Law 103, [2001] NLJR 1665 .... III HUM [28.3A]
M (a minor by his litigation friend LT) v Ministry of Justice [2009] EWCA Civ 419, [2009] NLJR 860, [2009] All ER (D) 44 (Jun) .... III HUM [13.4]
M v N (By her litigation friend, the Official Solicitor) [2015] EWCOP 76, 148 BMLR 116, 165 NLJ 7679, [2015] All ER (D) 198 (Nov) .... III MEN [34.1], [47.4]
M (a minor) v Newham London Borough Council [1995] 2 AC 633, HL .... III HUM [30.1]
M v Plymouth Health Authority [1993] 4 Med LR 108, [1993] PIQR P223 .... II CCA [31.3]
M v Press Association [2016] EWCOP 34, [2016] All ER (D) 08 (Jul) .... III MEN [6]
M v Secretary of State for Work and Pensions [2006] UKHL 11, [2006] 2 AC 91, [2006] 4 All ER 929, [2006] 2 WLR 637, [2006] Fam Law 524, (2006) Times, 14 March, 21 BHRC 254, [2006] All ER (D) 99 (Mar), sub nom Secretary of State for Work and Pensions v M [2006] 1 FCR 497, [2006] 2 FLR 56, 150 Sol Jo LB 363 .... III HUM [9.2]
M v United Kingdom (Application No 6638/03) (2005) Times, 15 September . III HUM [35.2]

Macmillan Inc v Bishopsgate Investment Trust plc (No 4) (1998) Times, 7 December, [1999] CLC 417, 478, CA .... **II CCA [41.2]**

McMullen v Great Southern Cemetery and Crematorium Co Ltd (1958) 172 Estates Gazette 855, CA .... **III L&T [18.4]**

McNerny v Lambeth London Borough Council (1988) 21 HLR 188, [1989] 1 EGLR 81, [1989] NLJR 114, [1989] 19 EG 77, CA .... **III L&T [164.6]**

McNulty v McNulty [2002] WTLR 737 .... **III FMY [10.1]**

McPhail v Persons, Names Unknown [1973] Ch 447, [1973] 3 All ER 393, [1973] 3 WLR 71, 117 Sol Jo 448, 227 Estates Gazette 985, CA .... **III HUM [30.5A]**

MacShannon v Rockware Glass Ltd. See Rockware Glass Ltd v MacShannon

McVicar v United Kingdom [2002] NLJR 759, ECtHR .... **III HUM [28.2A]**

Madurasinghe v Penguin Electronics (a firm) [1993] 3 All ER 20, [1993] 1 WLR 989, [1993] 2 LS Gaz R 43, 136 Sol Jo LB 328, CA .... **III SOL [80.1]**

Maga v Roman Catholic Archdiocese of Birmingham [2010] EWCA Civ 256, [2010] PTSR 1618, (2010) Times, 25 March, 154 Sol Jo (no 11) 28, [2010] All ER (D) 141 (Mar) .... **III LIM [31.2]; III PID [3A]**

Magnohard Ltd v Earl Cadogan [2012] EWCA Civ 594, [2013] 1 WLR 24, [2012] HLR 495, [2012] 28 Estates Gazette 82, [2012] 2 P & CR D35, [2012] All ER (D) 47 (May) .... **III L&T [50.1]**

Magyar Telecom BV, Re [2013] EWHC 3800 (Ch), [2013] All ER (D) 20 (Dec) ..... **III COM [899.3]**

Maharaj v Motor One Insurance Co Ltd (2018) Times, 8 May, PC .... **III LIM [11.1]**

Maher v Groupama Grand Est [2009] EWCA Civ 1191, [2009] All ER (D) 143 (Nov) .... **III PID [4A]**

Maher v Groupama Grand Est [2009] EWHC 38 (QB), [2009] 1 All ER 1116, [2009] 1 All ER (Comm) 793, [2009] 1 WLR 1752, [2009] RTR 248, [2009] Lloyd's Rep IR 659, [2009] NLJR 158, [2009] All ER (D) 183 (Jan) .... **III PID [4A]**

Mahmud v BCCI SA [1998] AC 20, [1997] 3 All ER 1, [1997] 3 WLR 95, [1997] ICR 606, [1997] IRLR 462, [1997] 94 LS Gaz R 33, [1997] NLJR 917, HL .... **III EMP [6.4B]**

Mahomed v Bank of Baroda [1998] 47 LS Gaz R 29, sub nom Bank of Baroda v Mahomed [1999] l Lloyd's Rep Bank 14, CA .... **III LIM [8.1]**

Mainwaring v Goldtech Investments Ltd (1991) Times, 19 February, CA ...... **III SOL [75.3]**

Mainwaring v Henry Smith's Charity Trustees [1998] QB 1, [1996] 2 All ER 220, [1996] 3 WLR 1033, 73 P & CR 395, 28 HLR 583, [1996] 29 EG 110, CA .... **III L&T [186.1]**

Mainwaring v Henry Smith's Charity Trustees (No 2) (1996) 29 HLR 572, [1997] 1 EGLR 93, [1997] 12 EG 152, CA .... **III L&T [186.8]**

Maistry v Solicitors Regulation Authority [2012] EWHC 3041 (Admin) ...... **III SOL [66.1A]**

Majorstake Ltd v Curtis [2006] EWCA Civ 1171, [2007] Ch 300, [2006] 4 All ER 1326, [2006] 3 WLR 1114, [2006] 33 LS Gaz R 25, [2006] BLR 461, [2007] 1 P & CR D24, [2006] All ER (D) 47 (Aug); revsd [2008] UKHL 10 , [2008] 1 AC 787, [2008] 2 All ER 303, [2008] 2 WLR 338, [2008] 1 P & CR D65, [2008] 2 P & CR 20, [2008] 14 EG 102, [2008] NLJR 262, [2008] 06 EG 131 (CS), (2008) Times, 12 February, [2008] All ER (D) 70 (Feb) .... **III L & T [259.1], [262A]**

Majrowski v Guy's and St Thomas's NHS Trust [2005] EWCA Civ 251, [2005] QB 848, [2005] 2 WLR 1503, [2005] ICR 977, [2005] IRLR 340, (2005) Times, March 21, 149 Sol Jo LB 358, [2005] All ER (D) 273 (Mar); affd [2006] UKHL 34, [2007] 1 AC 224, [2006] 4 All ER 395, [2006] 3 WLR 125, [2006] ICR 1199, [2006] IRLR 695, 91 BMLR 85, [2006] NLJR 1173, (2006) Times, 13 July, 150 Sol Jo LB 986, [2006] All ER (D) 146 (Jul) .... **III HAR [6.1B]**

Makhlouf (Appellant) v Secretary of State for the Home Department (Respondent) (Northern Ireland) Case ID: UKSC 2015/0092, [2014] NICA 86 .... **III HUM [30.10]**

Makhlouf v Secretary of State for the Home Department (Northern Ireland) [2016] UKSC 59, [2016] All ER (D) 93 (Nov) .... **III HUM [30.10]**

Makisi v Birmingham City Council [2011] EWCA Civ 355, [2011] PTSR 1545, [2011] HLR 444, [2011] 05 LS Gaz R 20, (2011) Times, 3 May, [2011] All ER (D) 12 (Apr) .... **III L&T [305.5]**

Malcolm v Ministry of Justice [2011] EWCA Civ 1538, [2011] All ER (D) 98 (Dec) . **III HUM [30.11]**

Malekshad v Howard de Walden Estates Ltd [2002] UKHL 49, [2003] 1 AC 1013, [2003] 1 All ER 193, [2002] 3 WLR 1881, [2003] 1 P & CR D35, [2003] HLR 418, [2003] 06 LS Gaz R 26, [2002] 50 EGCS 114, (2002) Times, 6 December, 146 Sol Jo LB 279, [2002] All ER (D) 68 (Dec) .... **III L&T [50.1], [50.4]**

Matthews (C & M) v Marsden Building Society [1951] Ch 758, [1951] 1 All ER 1053, [1951] 1 TLT 1114, 95 Sol Jo 366 .... **III LIM [3.3]**
Matthews v Ministry of Defence [2002] EWCA Civ 773, [2002] 3 All ER 513, [2002] 1 WLR 2621, [2002] ICR 1003, 12 BHRC 652, [2002] 27 LS Gaz R 33, [2002] NLJR 879, [2003] PIQR P49, (2002) Times, 31 May, 146 Sol Jo LB 144,, [2002] All ER (D) 448 (May); affd [2003] UKHL 4, [2003] 1 AC 1163, [2003] 1 All ER 689, [2003] 2 WLR 435, [2003] ICR 247, [2003] 13 LS Gaz R 26, [2003] NLJR 261, (2003) Times, 14 February, 147 Sol Jo LB 235, [2004] 1 LRC 318, [2003] All ER (D) 173 (Feb), 14 BHRC 585 .... **III CRO [1A]; III HUM [28.1]**
Matthews v Munster (1887) 20 QBD 141, 52 JP 260, 57 LJQB 49, 36 WR 178, [1886–90] All ER Rep 251, 57 LT 922, 4 TLR 102, CA .... **III SOL [59]**
Matuszowicz v Kingston-Upon-Hull City Council [2009] EWCA Civ 22, [2009] 3 All ER 685, [2009] IRLR 288, [2009] ICR 1170, [2009] All ER (D) 93 (Feb) .... **III EQU [118.1]**
Maud v Libyan Investment Authority. See Glenn Maud, Re
Maunder Taylor v Blaquire [2002] EWCA Civ 1633, [2003] 1 WLR 379, [2003] HLR 621, [2003] 03 LS Gaz R 33, [2003] 07 EG 138, [2002] All ER (D) 190, (Nov), Times, 21 November .... **III L&T [171.1]**
Maunsell v Olins [1975] AC 373, [1975] 1 All ER 16, [1974] 3 WLR 835, 30 P & CR 1, 118 Sol Jo 882, 233 Estates Gazette 591, HL .... **III L&T [76.6]**
Maurice v Hollow-Ware Products Ltd [2005] EWHC 815 (Ch), (2005) Times, 31 March, [2005] All ER (D) 254 (Mar) .... **III L & T [257.2]**
Mawan (now named) Mara, The [1988] 2 Lloyd's Rep 459 .... **II SCA [19.8]**
May and Baker Ltd v Boots Pure Drug Co Ltd (1950) 67 RPC 23, 94 Sol Jo 112, HL .... **III PAT [19.1]**
Mayhew v Free Grammar School of John Lyon (1991) 63 P & CR 53, 23 HLR 479, [1991] 2 EGLR 89, [1991] 45 EG 175, CA; affd sub nom Free Grammar School of John Lyon v Mayhew (1996) 29 HLR 719, CA .... **III L&T [46.10]**
Mayhew v Herrick (1849) 7 CB 229, 18 LJCP 179, 13 Jur 1078, 137 ER 92 .. **II CCA [87.4]**
Mayor and Burgesses of Newham London Borough Council v Hannan [2011] UKUT 406 (LC) .... **III L&T [173.3C]**
Mayor and Burgesses of the London Borough of Islington v Dyer [2017] EWCA Civ 150, [2017] 2 P & CR 268, [2017] HLR 331, 167 NLJ 7740, (2017) Times, 03 May , [2017] 2 P & CR D15, [2017] All ER (D) 164 (Mar) .... **III L&T [284.1]**
Mazur Media Ltd v Mazur Media GmbH [2004] EWHC 1566 (Ch), [2004] 1 WLR 2966, (2004) Times, 29 July, [2004] All ER (D) 110 (Jul) .... **III EUR [427.1]**
Mbutu v De la Rue Browne [2006] All ER (D) 170 (Mar) .... **III SOL [55]**
Meade-Hill and National Union of Civil and Public Servants v British Council [1996] 1 All ER 79, [1995] ICR 847, [1995] IRLR 478, CA .... **III EQU [144.1]**
Meadows v Clerical, Medical and General Life Assurance Society [1981] Ch 70, [1980] 1 All ER 454, [1980] 2 WLR 639, 40 P & CR 238, 124 Sol Jo 257, [1980] 2 EGLR 63, 255 Estates Gazette 883 .... **III L&T [15.5]**
Meah v Mouskos [1964] 2 QB 23, [1963] 3 All ER 908, [1964] 2 WLR 27, 107 Sol Jo 871, 188 Estates Gazette 593, CA .... **III L&T [40.1]**
Meah v Sector Properties Ltd [1974] 1 All ER 1074, [1974] 1 WLR 547, 27 P & CR 148, 118 Sol Jo 296, 231 Estates Gazette 367, CA .... **III L&T [37.1]**
Mecca, The. See Cory Bros & Co Ltd v Turkish SS Mecca (Owners), The Mecca
Medcalf v Mardell [2002] UKHL 27, [2003] 1 AC 120, [2002] 3 All ER 721, [2002] 3 WLR 172, [2002] 31 LS Gaz R 34, [2002] NLJR 1032 .... **II SCA [50.7]**
Medicaments and Related Classes of Goods (No 2), Re [2001] 1 WLR 700, [2001] ICR 564, [2001] 07 LS Gaz R 40, 145 Sol Jo LB 29, [2000] All ER (D) 2425, CA .... **II CCA [115.1A]; III HUM [28.3A]**
Medicaments and Related Clases of Goods (No 4), Re [2001] EWCA Civ 1217, [2002] 1 WLR 269, [2001] 34 LS Gaz R 37, 145 Sol Jo LB 209 ..... **III HUM [13.1A], [14.3], [28.3A]**
Medina Housing Association Ltd v Case [2002] EWCA Civ 2001, [2003] 1 All ER 1084, [2003] HLR 536 .... **III L&T [297.1]**
Medway Drydock and Engineering Co Ltd v MV Andrea Ursula, The Andrea Ursula [1973] QB 265, [1971] 1 All ER 821, [1971] 2 WLR 681, [1971] 1 Lloyd's Rep 145, 115 Sol Jo 32 .... **II SCA [19.10]**
Mehta v Royal Bank of Scotland plc (1999) 32 HLR 45, [1999] 3 EGLR 153, 78 P & CR D11 .... **III L&T [68.3], [232.5]**
Melville v Bruton (1996) 29 HLR 319, [1996] 13 LS Gaz R 26, 140 Sol Jo LB 117, CA .... **III L&T [233.3]**
Memco-Med Ltd's Patent [1992] RPC 403 .... **III PAT [10]-[11.1]**

Muir Group Housing Association Ltd v Thornley (1992) 91 LGR 1, 25 HLR 89, [1993] 1 EGLR 51, [1992] 43 LS Gaz R 31, [1993] 10 EG 144, CA .... **III L&T [122.1]**

Mukarkar v Secretary of State for the Home Department [2006] EWCA Civ 1045, (2006) Times, 16 August, [2006] All ER (D) 367 (Jul) .... **III HUM [30.10]**

Mularczyk v Azralnove Investments Ltd [1985] 2 EGLR 141, 276 Estates Gazette 1064, CA .... **III L&T [24.2]**

Mullaney v Maybourne Grange (Croydon) Management Co Ltd [1986] 1 EGLR 70, 277 Estates Gazette 1350 .... **III L&T [173.1]**

Mullen v Hackney London Borough Council [1997] 2 All ER 906, [1997] 1 WLR 1103, 29 HLR 592, CA .... **II CCA [21.7]; III L&T [164.12]**

Mullins v Howell (1879) 11 Ch D 763, 48 LJ Ch 679 .... **III SOL [67.1]**

Munjaz v United Kingdom (Application No 2913/06) [2012] ECHR 1704, (2012) Times, 09 October, ECtHR .... **III HUM [27.2], [30.2]; III MEN [9]**

Muñoz (Antonio) y Cia SA v Frumar Ltd: C-253/00 [2003] Ch 328, [2002] ECR I-7289, [2003] 3 WLR 58, [2003] All ER (EC) 56, [2002] 3 CMLR 734, (2002) Times, 20 November, [2002] All ER (D) 82 (Sep), ECJ .... **III EUR [9]**

Munro v Daw [1948] 1 KB 125, [1947] 2 All ER 360, [1948] LJR 96, 91 Sol Jo 504, 177 LT 481, 63 TLR 542, CA .... **III L&T [82.16]**

Munting v Hammersmith and Fulham London Borough Council [1998] CLY 3017 .. **III L&T [304.1]**

Murbarak v Murbarak [2001] 1 FCR 193, [2001] 1 FLR 698, [2001] Fam Law 178, [2001] All ER (D) 2302, CA .... **III HUM [28.9]**

Murfin v Campbell [2011] EWHC 1475 (Ch), [2011] NLJR 918, [2011] All ER (D) 190 (Jun) .... **III SOL [61]**

Murphy (dec'd), Re, Dalton V Latham [2003] EWCA Civ 796 (Ch), [2003] WTLR 687 .... **III TRU [43.1]**

Murphy v Brentwood District Council [1991] 1 AC 398, [1990] 2 All ER 908, [1990] 3 WLR 414, 89 LGR 24, [1990] 2 Lloyd's Rep 467, 22 HLR 502, 21 Con LR 1, 134 Sol Jo 1076, [1990] NLJR 1111, 50 BLR 1, HL .... **III LIM [3.5]**

Murphy v Gooch [2007] EWCA Civ 603, [2007] 3 FCR 96, [2007] 2 FLR 934, [2007] Fam Law 905, 151 Sol Jo LB 896, [2007] 2 P & CR D46, [2007] All ER (D) 350 (Jun) ... **III REA [57.1]**

Murphy v Wyatt [2011] EWCA Civ 408, [2011] 1 WLR 2129, [2011] 2 P & CR 81, [2011] HLR 488, [2011] All ER (D) 112 (Apr) .... **III MOB [6.5], [11.3]**

Murphy v Young & Co's Brewery plc and Sun Alliance and London Insurance plc [1997] 1 All ER 518, [1997] 1 WLR 1591, [1997] 1 Lloyd's Rep 236, CA .... **II SCA [50.4]**

Murphy's Settlements, Re, Murphy v Murphy [1998] 3 All ER 1, [1999] 1 WLR 282 .... **II CCA [21.9]**

Murray v Aslam (1994) 27 HLR 284, [1994] EGCS 160, CA .... **III L&T [232.1]**

Murray v Birmingham City Council (1987) 20 HLR 39, [1987] 2 EGLR 53, 283 Estates Gazette 962, CA .... **III L&T [164.1]**

Murray v Express Newspapers plc [2007] EWHC 1908 (Ch), [2007] 3 FCR 331, [2008] 1 FLR 704, [2007] Fam Law 1073, [2007] NLJR 1199, (2007) Times, 4 October, [2007] EMLR 583, [2007] All ER (D) 39 (Aug); revsd [2008] EWCA Civ 446, [2008] 3 WLR 1360, [2008] NLJR 706, (2008) Times, 12 May, [2008] EMLR 399, [2008] All ER (D) 70 (May), sub nom Murray v Big Pictures (UK) Ltd [2008] 3 FCR 661, [2008] 2 FLR 599, [2008] Fam Law 732 .... **III DAT [46.1]; III HUM [30.5D]**

Murray v Shuter [1972] 1 Lloyd's Rep 6, 115 Sol Jo 774, CA .... **III PID [10.1]**

Murray v VSP International Foundations (1993) Current Law Week, 8 October, 12 Litigation Letter (January 1994) p 79, CA .... **III COM [46.5]**

Muscat v Cable & Wireless plc. See Cable & Wireless plc v Muscat

Muscat v Smith [2003] EWCA Civ 962, [2003] 1 WLR 2853, (2003) Times, 12 August, sub nom Smith v Muscat [2003] 35 LS Gaz R 37, 147 Sol Jo LB 900, [2003] All ER (D) 192 (Jul) .... **III L&T [164.10]**

Muse v Brent London Borough Council [2008] EWCA Civ 1447, [2008] All ER (D) 233 (Dec) .... **III L&T [303E.6C]**

Muspratt v Johnston [1963] 2 QB 383, [1963] 2 All ER 339, [1963] 2 WLR 1153, 107 Sol Jo 252, CA .... **III L&T [76.1]**

Mustafa v Ruddock (1997) 30 HLR 495, [1997] EGCS 87, CA .... **III L&T [242.2]**

Muter v Newcastle upon Tyne Aero Club (17 December 2001, unreported) .... **III LIM [37.2]**

Mutua v Foreign and Commonwealth Office [2012] EWHC 2678 (QB), [2012] NLJR 1291, [2012] All ER (D) 48 (Oct) .... **III LIM [38.2], [38.3]**

N

O

Omnium de Traitement et de Valorisation SA v Hilmarton Ltd [1999] 2 All ER (Comm) 146, [1999] 2 Lloyd's Rep 222 .... III ARB [19.2]
On Demand Information plc (in administrative receivership) v Michael Gerson (Finance) plc [2000] 4 All ER 734, [2000] 2 All ER (Comm) 513, [2001] 1 WLR 155, [2000] NLJR 1300, CA .... III L&T [2.2]
One Step (Support) Ltd v Morris-Garner [2018] UKSC 20, [2018] 3 All ER 659, [2018] 2 WLR 1353, [2018] 2 All ER (Comm) 769, [2018] 1 Lloyd's Rep 495, [2018] IRLR 661, 168 NLJ 7790, (2018) Times, 24 April, [2018] All ER (D) 62 (Apr), SC .... III EMP [2]
Onigbanjo v Pearson [2008] BLR 5007, Mayor's and City of London's Ct ... III REA [60K.1], [60L.2]
Online Catering Ltd v Acton [2010] EWCA Civ 58, [2010] 3 All ER 869, [2010] 3 WLR 928, (2010) Times, 11 May, [2010] All ER (D) 112 (Feb) .... III CON [5.2], [7.5]
Onu v Akwiwu (UKEAT/0283/12/RN and UKEAT/0022/12/RN) [2014] EWCA Civ 279, [2014] 1 WLR 3636, [2013] ICR 1039, [2013] IRLR 523, EAT .... III EQU [108.1]
Opera Ltd, Re [1891] 3 Ch 260, 60 LJ Ch 839, 39 WR 705, 65 LT 371, 7 TLR 655, CA .... II CCA [87.4]
Orams v Apostolides: C-420/07 [2009] ECR I-3571, [2011] 2 WLR 324, [2010] 1 All ER (Comm) 950, (2009) Times, 1 May, [2009] All ER (D) 89 (May), ECJ ...... III EUR [305.3], [306.1]
Orams v Apostolides (British Residents' Association intervening) [2010] EWCA Civ 9, [2010] 1 All ER (Comm) 992, [2010] 05 LS Gaz R 18, [2010] 04 EG 112 (CS), (2010) Times, 24 February, [2010] All ER (D) 105 (Jan) .... III EUR [305.1]
O'Reilly v Mackman [1983] 2 AC 237, [1982] 3 All ER 680, [1982] 3 WLR 604, 126 Sol Jo 578, CA; affd [1983] 2 AC 237, [1982] 3 All ER 1124, [1982] 3 WLR 1096, 126 Sol Jo 820, HL .... II CCA [7.8]; III L&T [109.4]
Oren v Red Box Toy Factory Ltd [1999] FSR 785 .... III PAT [46]
Orlik (G) (Meat Products) Ltd v Hastings and Thanet Building Society (1974) 29 P & CR 126, 118 Sol Jo 811, 234 Estates Gazette 281, CA .... III L&T [28.2]
Orphanos v Queen Mary College [1985] AC 761, [1985] 2 All ER 233, [1985] 2 WLR 703, [1986] 2 CMLR 73, [1985] IRLR 349, 129 Sol Jo 284, [1985] LS Gaz R 1787, HL .... III EQU [9.2]
Orthet Ltd v Vince-Cain [2004] IRLR 857, [2005] ICR 374, [2004] All ER (D) 143 (May), EAT .... III EQU [119.5]
Orton v Collins [2007] EWHC 803 (Ch), [2007] 3 All ER 863, [2007] 1 WLR 2953, 151 Sol Jo LB 608, [2007] All ER (D) 175 (Apr) .... III REA [38.1]
Osada v Shepping [2000] 30 EG 125, 80 P & CR D13, CA .... III L&T [242.5A]
Osborn and Booth v Parole Board, Reilly, Re [2013] UKSC 61, [2014] 1 All ER 369, [2013] 3 WLR 1020, [2013] All ER (D) 88 (Oct) .... III HUM [27.2G]
Osborn (B) & Co Ltd v Dior [2003] EWCA Civ 281, [2003] HLR 649, [2003] 05 EG 144 (CS) .... III L&T [227.2A]
Oscroft v Benabo [1967] 2 All ER 548, [1967] 1 WLR 1087, 111 Sol Jo 520, CA ... III L&T [27.2]
Osei v Southwark London Borough Council [2007] EWCA Civ 787, [2007] All ER (D) 383 (Jul) .... III L&T [303C.1]
Osei-Antwi v South East London & Kent Bus Company Ltd [2010] EWCA Civ 132, [2010] All ER (D) 207 (Jan) .... III PID [9.3]
Osei-Bonsu v Wandsworth London Borough Council [1999] 1 All ER 265, [1999] 1 WLR 1011, sub nom Wandsworth London Borough Council v Osei-Bonsu [1999] 3 FCR 1, [1999] 1 FLR 276, 31 HLR 515, [1999] 1 EGLR 26, [1998] 42 LS Gaz R 34, [1998] NLJR 1641, [1999] 11 EG 167, [1998] EGCS 148, 143 Sol Jo LB 12, CA .. II CCA [21.2]; III L&T [106.3], [106.7], [168.2], [232.2], [232.9]
O'Shea v MGN Ltd [2001] EMLR 943 .... III HUM [32.5A]
Osman v United Kingdom (1998) 29 EHRR 245, [1999] 1 FLR 193, [1999] Fam Law 86, [1999] Crim LR 82, 5 BHRC 293, ECtHR .... III HUM [28.4]
Osmani v Camden London Borough Council [2004] EWCA Civ 1706, 149 Sol Jo LB 61, [2004] All ER (D) 268 (Dec) .... III L&T [303AA.3], [306.4A]
O'Sullivan v Herdmans Ltd [1987] 3 All ER 129, [1987] 1 WLR 1047, 131 Sol Jo 1003, [1987] LS Gaz R 2362, HL .... II SCA [34.3]
O'Sullivan v Metropolitan Police Comr (1995) 139 Sol Jo LB 164 .... III CRO [20.5]
Ottway v Jones [1955] 2 All ER 585, [1955] 1 WLR 706, 99 Sol Jo 432, CA . III L&T [71.9]
O_2 Holdings Ltd v Hutchison 3G UK Ltd: C-533/06 [2008] 3 CMLR 397, [2008] RPC 905, [2008] IP & T 1069, (2008) Times, 17 June, [2008] All ER (D) 155 (Jun), ECJ .... III PAT [41.2]

Overseas Medical Supplies Ltd v Orient Transport Services Ltd [1999] 1 All ER (Comm) 981, [1999] 2 Lloyd's Rep 273, [1999] CLC 1243, CA .... **III CON [66.2]**

Overstone Ltd v Shipway [1962] 1 All ER 52, [1962] 1 WLR 117, 106 Sol Jo 14, CA .... **II CCA [18.1]**

Owen v Martin [1992] PIQR Q151, CA .... **III PID [13.4]**

Owens Bank Ltd v Bracco (No 2): C-129/92 [1994] QB 509, [1994] 1 All ER 336, [1994] 2 WLR 759, [1994] ECR I-117, ECJ .... **III EUR [184.1]**

Oxford Gene Technology Ltd v Affymetric Inc [2001] FSR 136, [2001] IP & T 93, (2000) Times, 5 December, CA .... **III PAT [19.3]**

Oxley v Hiscock [2004] EWCA Civ 546, [2005] Fam 211, [2004] 3 All ER 703, [2004] 3 WLR 715, [2004] 2 P & CR D35, 6 ITELR 1091, [2004] 2 FCR 295, [2004] 2 FLR 295, [2004] Fam Law 569, [2004] 21 LS Gaz R 35, [2004] 20 EG 166 (CS), (2004) Times, 14 July, 148 Sol Jo LB 571, [2004] All ER (D) 48 (May) .... **III REA [58.2A]**

Oxley v Regional Properties Ltd [1944] KB 733n, [1944] 2 All ER 510, 88 Sol Jo 376, 171 LT 129, 60 TLR 519, CA; revsd sub nom Regional Properties Ltd v Oxley [1945] AC 347, [1945] 2 All ER 418, 114 LJKB 473, 173 LT 201, 61 TLR 563, HL ..... **III L&T [70.1]**

Ozbek v Ipswich Borough Council [2006] EWCA Civ 534, (2006) Times, 7 June, [2006] All ER (D) 51 (May) .... **III L & T [303G.2]**

P

P (minors) (diplomatic immunity), Re [1998] 2 FCR 480, [1998] 1 FLR 624, [1998] Fam Law 12 .... **II CCA [7.4]**

P, Re [2015] EWCOP 15, [2015] All ER (D) 196 (Mar) .... **III MEN [6]**

P, Re [2015] EWCOP 42, 145 BMLR 86, [2015] All ER (D) 292 (Jun) ...... **III MEN [34.1], [391.1]**

P, Re[2015] EWCOP 37, [2015] All ER (D) 117 (Jun) .... **III MEN [138.1]**

P, Re [2007] EWCA Civ 2, [2007] Fam Law 393, (2007) Times, 1 February, [2007] All ER (D) 05 (Jan), sub nom C (breach of human rights: damages), Re [2007] 3 FCR 288, [2007] 1 FLR 1957 .... **III HUM [14.2A]**

P (adoption: unmarried couple), Re [2008] UKHL 38, [2008] NI 310, [2008] 2 FCR 366, [2008] 2 FLR 1084, [2008] Fam Law 977, (2008) Times, 23 June, 24 BHRC 650, sub nom G (adoption: unmarried couple), Re [2009] 1 AC 173, [2008] 3 WLR 76 ...... **III HUM [30.1], [32.2F]**

P, Re [2009] EWHC 163 (Ch), [2010] Ch 33, [2009] 2 All ER 1198, [2009] All ER (D) 160 (Feb) .... **III MEN [34.1], [51.1], [400.1], [604.1]**

P (vulnerable adult) (capacity: appointment of deputies), Re [2010] EWHC 1592 (Fam), [2010] 2 FLR 1712, [2010] Fam Law 1073, [2010] All ER (D) 52 (Aug) ..... **III MEN [10A]**

P (Abortion), Re [2013] EWHC 50 (COP) .... **III MEN [32.1]**

P v F Ltd [2001] NLJR 1284, CA .... **III COM [28.2]**

P (by his litigation friend the Official Solicitor) v Independent Print Ltd [2011] EWCA Civ 756, [2012] 2 FCR 503, [2012] 1 FLR 212, [2011] Fam Law 1081, [2011] All ER (D) 36 (Jul) .... **III HUM [18.5], [32.5]; III MEN [13], [522.1]**

P v Liverpool Daily Post and Echo Newspapers plc. See Pickering v Liverpool Daily Post and Echo Newspapers plc

P v M [2011] COPLR Con Vol 947 .... **III MEN [9]**

P v Metropolitan Police Comr [2017] UKSC 65, [2018] IRLR 66, 167 NLJ 7768, [2017] All ER (D) 133 (Oct), SC .... **III EQU [39]**

P v United Kingdom [2001] 2 FCR 221, [2001] 2 FLR 261, [2001] Fam Law 506, ECtHR .... **III COT [8.1]; III HUM [28.2], [32.5]**

P (MIG) and Q (MEG) v Surrey County Council [2011] EWCA Civ 190, [2012] Fam 170, [2012] 2 WLR 1056, [2012] PTSR 727, [2011] 1 FCR 559, [2011] 2 FLR 583, [2011] Fam Law 475, 120 BMLR 44, [2011] All ER (D) 286 (Feb); sub nom Surrey County Council v P (Equality and Human Rights Commission intervening) [2014] UKSC 19, [2014] AC 896, [2014] 2 All ER 585, [2014] 2 WLR 642, [2014] PTSR 460, [2014] 2 FCR 71, 137 BMLR 16, (2014) Times, 01 April, [2014] 5 LRC 428, [2014] All ER (D) 185 (Mar) . **III HUM [27.1A]; III MEN [9], [10], [35.1], [49.2] [55.1], [620], [620.1]**

P, C and S v United Kingdom (Application No 56547/00), [2002] All ER (D) 239 (Jul), [2002] 3 FCR 1, [2002] 2 FLR 631, [2002] Fam Law 811, 35 EHRR 1075, Times, 16 August, ECtHR .... **III HUM [28.2A], [30.1]**

Q

R

R (on the application of Purdy) v DPP [2009] UKHL 45, [2009] 4 All ER 1147, [2009] 3 WLR 403, [2010] 1 Cr App Rep 1, 109 BMLR 153, [2009] NLJR 1175, (2009) Times, 31 July, 153 Sol Jo (no 31) 28, 27 BHRC 126, [2009] All ER (D) 335 (Jul) .. **III HUM [30.2]**

R v Disciplinary Committee of the Jockey Club, ex p Aga Khan [1993] 2 All ER 853, [1993] 1 WLR 909, CA .... **II SCA [30.5]**

R (on the application of W) v Doncaster Metropolitan Borough Council [2003] EWHC 192 (Admin), (2003) Times, 12 March, [2003] All ER (D) 177 (Feb); affd sub nom W v Doncaster Metropolitan Borough Council [2004] EWCA Civ 378, 148 Sol Jo LB 572, [2003] All ER (D) 177 (Feb), sub nom R (on the application of W) v Doncaster Metropolitan Borough Council [2004] 22 LS Gaz R 32, (2004) Times, 13 May ..... **III HUM [14.2A]**

R (on the application of Beeson) v Dorset County Council [2002] EWCA Civ 1812, [2003] HLR 550, [2003] 10 LS Gaz R 30 .... **III HUM [28.3]**

R v Dunn [2010] EWCA Crim 2395 .... **III MEN [82.1]**

R v Ealing District Health Authority, ex p Fox [1993] 3 All ER 170, [1993] 1 WLR 373, 11 BMLR 59, 136 Sol Jo LB 220 .... **III MEN [15]**

R (on the application of Bidar) v Ealing London Borough Council: C-209/03 [2005] QB 812, [2005] ECR I-2119, [2005] All ER (EC) 687, [2005] 2 WLR 1078, [2005] ELR 404, (2005) Times, 29 March, [2005] All ER (D) 235 (Mar), ECJ .... **III EQU [9.2]**

R (on the application of H) v Ealing London Borough Council (Equality and Human Rights Commission intervening) [2017] EWCA Civ 1127, [2017] All ER (D) 98 (Aug) .... **III EQU [19.2]**

R v Ealing London Borough Council, ex p Surdonja [2001] QB 97, sub nom Surdonja v Ealing London Borough Council [2000] 2 All ER 597, sub nom Ealing London Borough Council v Surdonja [2000] 3 WLR 481, CA .... **III L&T [304.2], [305.1]**

R (on the application of Von Brandenburg (also known as Hanley)) v East London and City Mental Health NHS Trust [2001] EWCA Civ 239, [2002] QB 235, [2001] 3 WLR 588; affd [2003] UKHL 58, [2004] 2 AC 280, [2004] 1 All ER 400, [2003] 3 WLR 1265, 76 BMLR 168, [2004] 05 LS Gaz R 28, (2003) Times, 14 November, 147 Sol Jo LB 1366, [2003] All ER (D) 174 (Nov) .... **III HUM [27.2]; III MEN [17]**

R (on the application of Bernard) v Enfield London Borough Council [2002] EWHC 2282 (Admin), [2003] HLR 354, [2002] 48 LS Gaz R 27, [2002] All ER (D) 383 (Oct); affd sub nom Bernard v Enfield London Borough Council [2001] EWCA Civ 1831, [2002] HLR 860 .... **III HUM [14.2]**

R (on the application of Mott) v Environment Agency [2018] UKSC 10, [2018] 2 All ER 663, [2018] 1 WLR 1022, 168 NLJ 7782, (2018) Times, 27 February, [2018] All ER (D) 77 (Feb), SC .... **III HUM [39.1]**

R v Epping and Harlow General Comrs, ex p Goldstraw [1983] 3 All ER 257, [1983] STC 693, 57 TC 536; affd [1983] 3 All ER 257, [1983] STC 693, 57 TC 536, CA . **II SCA [30.4]; III L&T [306.4]**

R v Ford [1989] QB 868, [1989] 3 All ER 445, [1989] 3 WLR 762, 89 Cr App Rep 278, [1989] Crim LR 828, [1989] NLJR 1193, CA .... **II SCA [56.3]**

R (on the application of Bonhoeffer) v General Medical Council [2011] EWHC 1585 (Admin), [2012] IRLR 37, [2011] All ER (D) 141 (Jun) ...... **III HUM [28.2]; III SOL [66.1]**

R (on the application of Burke) v General Medical Council [2004] EWHC 1879 (Admin), [2005] QB 424, [2005] 2 WLR 431, [2004] 3 FCR 579, [2004] 2 FLR 1121, 79 BMLR 126, (2004) Times, 6 August, [2004] All ER (D) 588 (Jul); revsd [2005] EWCA Civ 1003, [2006] QB 273, [2005] 3 WLR 1132, [2005] 3 FCR 169, [2005] 2 FLR 1223, [2005] Fam Law 776, 85 BMLR 1, [2005] NLJR 1457, (2005) Times, 2 August, [2005] All ER (D) 445 (Jul) .... **III HUM [25.2]**

R v George [2002] EWCA Crim 1923 [2003] Crim LR 282 .... **III COT [20.1]**

R (on the application of Green) v Gloucestershire County Council [2011] EWHC 2687 (Admin), [2011] 46 LS Gaz R 19, [2011] NLJR 1634, [2011] All ER (D) 111 (Nov) .... **III EQU [149.2]**

R v Goldstein [1983] 1 All ER 434, [1983] 1 WLR 151, [1983] 1 CMLR 252, [1983] Crim LR 249, 126 Sol Jo 84, HL .... **III EUR [389.1]**

R v Gough [1993] AC 646, [1993] 2 All ER 724, [1993] 2 WLR 883, 97 Cr App Rep 188, 157 JP 612, [1993] Crim LR 886, [1993] NLJR 775, 137 Sol Jo LB 168, HL . **III ARB [10.3]**

R (on the application of Watkins-Singh) v Governing Body of Aberdare Girls' High School [2008] EWHC 1865 (Admin), [2008] 3 FCR 203, [2008] ELR 561, [2008] All ER (D) 376 (Jul) .... **III EQU [85.2]**

R v Johnstone [2003] UKHL 28, [2003] 3 All ER 884, [2003] 1 WLR 1736, [2003] 2 Cr App Rep 493, 167 JP 281, [2003] 26 LS Gaz R 36, 147 Sol Jo LB 625 .... **III PAT [41.2]**

R v Jordan. See R v Staffordshire County Court Judge

R v Judge Sir Donald Hurst, ex p Smith [1960] 2 QB 133, [1960] 2 All ER 385, [1960] 2 WLR 961, 104 Sol Jo 468, DC .... **II CCA [82.3]**

R (on the application of Farrs Lane Developments Ltd) v Justices Of The Peace For Avon Somerset & Gloucestershire (2016) [2016] EWHC 982 (Admin) . **III REA [60K.3B], [60K.3C]**

R v Kansal (No 2) [2001] UKHL 62, [2002] 2 AC 69, [2002] 1 All ER 257, [2001] 3 WLR 1562, [2002] 1 Cr App Rep 478, [2002] 03 LS Gaz R 25, 145 Sol Jo LB 275, [2002] BPIR 370 .... **III HUM [6A], [23.3]**

R v Kenny (Charlie) [2011] EWCA Crim 1232 .... **III COT [9.3]**

R (on the application of McDonald) v Kensington and Chelsea Royal London Borough Council [2011] UKSC 33, [2011] 4 All ER 881, [2011] PTSR 1266, 121 BMLR 164, [2011] 29 LS Gaz R 17, [2011] NLJR 1026, (2011) Times, 7 July, [2011] All ER (D) 47 (Jul) .... **III HUM [30.6]**

R v Kensington and Chelsea Royal London Borough Council, ex p Byfield (1997) 31 HLR 913 .... **III L&T [304.2A], [306.4B]**

R (on the application of K) v Knowsley Metropolitan Borough Council [2004] EWHC 1933 (Admin) (2004) 168 JP 461, sub nom Keating v Knowsley Metropolitan Borough Council [2004] All ER (D) 383 (Jul) .... **III ANSB [5]**

R v Lambert [2001] UKHL 37, [2002] 2 AC 545, [2001] 3 All ER 577, [2001] 3 WLR 206, [2001] 2 Cr App Rep 511, [2001] 31 LS Gaz R 29, 145 Sol Jo LB 174 . **III HUM [6A], [9.2], [23.3]**

R v Lambeth County Court Judge and Jonas (1887) 36 WR 475, 4 TLR 158, DC .... **II CCA [115.3]**

R (on the application of Abdi) v Lambeth London Borough Council [2007] EWHC 1565 (Admin), (2007) Times, 11 July, [2007] All ER (D) 325 (Jun) ...... **III L&T [303A.3], [306.5]**

R (on the application of M) v Lambeth London Borough Council [2009] UKSC 8, [2009] 1 WLR 2557, [2009] 3 FCR 607, [2010] Fam Law 137, [2009] NLJR 1701, (2009) Times, 30 November, 153 Sol Jo (no 46) 34, [2009] All ER (D) 288 (Nov) ... **III HUM [28.1]**

R v Lambeth London Borough Council, ex p Alleyne (11 May 1999, unreported), CA .... **III L&T [306.2]**

R (on the application of Smith) v Land Registry (Cambridgeshire County Council, interested party) [2010] EWCA Civ 200, [2011] QB 413, [2010] 3 All ER 113, [2010] 3 WLR 1223, [2010] 2 P & CR 384, [2010] 2 EGLR 1, [2010] 21 EG 92, [2010] 11 EG 121 (CS), [2010] All ER (D) 82 (Mar) .... **III LIM [20.4], [42.11]**

R (on the application of Malik Law Chambers Solicitors) v Law Society [2010] EWHC 981 (Admin), [2010] All ER (D) 29 (May) .... **III SOL [85.11]**

R (on the application of Thompson) v Law Society [2004] EWCA Civ 167, [2004] 2 All ER 113, [2004] 1 WLR 2522, [2004] NLJR 307, (2004) Times, 1 April, 148 Sol Jo LB 265, [2004] All ER (D) 341 (Feb) .... **III HUM [28.1]**

R (on the application of A) v Leeds Magistrates' Court (2004) Times, 31 March .... **III ANSB [13.4A]**

R (on the application of Kenny) v Leeds Magistrates' Court [2003] EWHC 2963 (Admin), [2004] 1 All ER 1333, 168 JP 125, [2003] All ER (D) 104 (Dec); affd sub nom R (on the application of M) v Secretary of State for Constitutional Affairs and Lord Chancellor [2004] EWCA Civ 312, [2004] 2 All ER 531, [2004] 1 WLR 2298, [2004] LGR 417, 168 JP 529, (2004) Times, 31 March, 148 Sol Jo LB 385, [2004] All ER (D) 345 (Mar) .... **III ANSB [13.4A]**

R v Lefroy (1873) LR 8 QB 134, 37 JP 56, 42 LJQB 121, 21 WR 332, 28 LT 132 ... **II CCA [115.1], III COT [2]**

R v Legal Aid Board, ex p Kaim Todner (a firm) [1999] QB 966, [1998] 3 All ER 541, [1998] 3 WLR 925, [1998] 26 LS Gaz R 31, [1998] NLJR 941, 142 Sol Jo LB 189, CA .... **III COT [8.1], [20.1]**

R v Leicester City Justices, ex p Barrow [1991] 2 QB 260, [1991] 2 All ER 437, [1991] 2 WLR 974, [1991] RA 23, 155 JP 533, [1991] Crim LR 556; revsd [1991] 2 QB 260, [1991] 3 All ER 935, [1991] 3 WLR 368, [1991] RA 205, 155 JP 901, CA ..... **III SOL [8.4]**

R (on the application of Heather) v Leonard Cheshire Foundation [2002] EWCA Civ 366, [2002] 2 All ER 936, [2002] HLR 893 .... **III HUM [12.1B]**

R (on the application of Lonergan) v Lewes Crown Court (Secretary of State for the Home Department, interested party) [2005] EWHC 457 (Admin), [2005] 2 All ER 362, [2005] 1 WLR 2570, 169 JP 324, (2005) Times, 25 April, [2005] All ER (D) 382 (Mar) ... **III ANSB [13.4B]**

R (on the application of Manchester City Council) v Manchester Magistrates' Court [2005] EWHC 253 (Admin), (2005) Times, 8 March, [2005] All ER (D) 103 (Feb) .. **III ANSB [14.1]**

R (on the application of KB) v Mental Health Review Tribunal [2003] EWHC 193 (Admin), [2004] QB 936, [2003] 2 All ER 209, [2003] 3 WLR 185, [2003] 14 LS Gaz R 27, [2003] PIQR Q3, (2003) Times, 5 March, [2003] All ER (D) 168 (Feb) . **III HUM [14.2A]**

R (on the application of Munjaz) v Mersey Care NHS Trust [2003] EWCA Civ 1036, [2004] QB 395, [2003] 3 WLR 1505, 74 BMLR 178, (2003) Times, 25 July, 147 Sol Jo LB 903, [2003] All ER (D) 265 (Jul); revsd [2005] UKHL 58, [2006] 2 AC 148, [2006] 4 All ER 736, [2005] 3 WLR 793, 86 BMLR 84, (2005) Times, 18 October, [2005] All ER (D) 139 (Oct) .... **III HUM [25.5A], [27.2], [30.2]; III MEN [9], [403.2]**

R v Merton London Borough Council, ex p Sembi (1999) Times, 9 June .... **III L&T [304.2], [306.2], [306.4]**

R (on the application of C) v Metropolitan Police Comr [2011] UKSC 21, [2011] 3 All ER 859, [2011] 2 Cr App Rep 206, [2011] Crim LR 964, [2011] 22 LS Gaz R 18, [2011] NLJR 744, 175 CL&J 326, (2011) Times, 19 May, [2011] All ER (D) 167 (May) ... **III HUM [10.2], [30.4B]**

R (on the application of D) v Metropolitan Police Comr [2012] EWHC 309 (QB), [2012] All ER (D) 162 (Feb) .... **III HUM [13.1A]**

R (on the application of GC) v Metropolitan Police Comr [2011] UKSC 21, [2011] 3 All ER 859, [2011] 2 Cr App Rep 206, [2011] Crim LR 964, [2011] 22 LS Gaz R 18, [2011] NLJR 744, 175 CL&J 326, (2011) Times, 19 May, [2011] All ER (D) 167 (May) .... **III HUM [10.2], [30.4B]**

R (on the application of Hicks) v Metropolitan Police Comr [2012] EWHC 1947 (Admin), [2012] All ER (D) 232 (Jul) .... **III HUM [33.3]**

R (on the application of L) v Metropolitan Police Comr [2009] UKSC 3, [2010] 1 AC 410, [2010] 1 All ER 113, [2009] 3 WLR 1056, [2010] PTSR 245, [2010] 2 FCR 25, [2010] 1 FLR 643, [2010] Fam Law 21, [2009] NLJR 1549, 153 Sol Jo (no 42) 30, 28 BHRC 391, [2009] All ER (D) 296 (Oct) .... **III HUM [10.2], [20.6]**

R (on the application of Stanley) v Metropolitan Police Comr [2004] EWHC 2229 (Admin), 168 JP 623, [2004] 40 LS Gaz R 28, [2004] NLJR 1525, Times, 22 October, [2004] All ER (D) 67 (Oct) .... **III ANSB [5]**

R (on the application of T) v Metropolitan Police Comr [2013] EWCA Civ 192, [2013] 3 All ER 583, [2013] 1 WLR 3305, [2013] All ER (D) 126 (Mar) .... **III HUM [30.4D]**

R (on the application of TD) v Metropolitan Police Comr [2013] EWHC 2231 (Admin), [2013] All ER (D) 301 (Jul) .... **III HUM [30.4D]**

R (on the application of TD) v Metropolitan Police Comr [2014] EWCA Civ 585, 178 CL&J 364, 164 NLJ 7610, [2014] All ER (D) 37 (Jun) .... **III DAT [46.2]**

R (on the application of Catt) v Metropolitan Police Comr [2015] UKSC 9, [2015] AC 1065, [2015] 2 All ER 727, [2015] 2 WLR 664, [2015] IP & T 424, 165 NLJ 7644, (2015) Times, 11 March, [2015] All ER (D) 31 (Mar) .... **III DAT [46.2]; III HUM [30.6]**

R (on the application of T) v Metropolitan Police Comr [2015] UKSC 9, [2015] AC 1065, [2015] 2 All ER 727, [2015] 2 WLR 664, [2015] IP & T 424, 165 NLJ 7644, (2015) Times, 11 March, [2015] All ER (D) 31 (Mar) .... **III DAT [46.2]; III HUM [30.6]**

R (on the application of Wood) v Metropolitan Police Comr [2009] EWCA Civ 414, [2009] 4 All ER 951, (2009) Times, 1 June, 153 Sol Jo (no 21) 30, [2009] All ER (D) 208 (May) .... **III DAT [46.1], III HUM [30.5D]**

R v Mid Glamorgan Family Health Services Authority, ex p Martin [1995] 1 All ER 356, [1995] 1 WLR 110, [1995] 2 FCR 578, [1995] 1 FLR 283, [1994] 5 Med LR 383, 21 BMLR 1, [1994] 38 LS Gaz R 42, 138 Sol Jo LB 195, CA .... **II CCA [31.4]**

R v Ministry of Agriculture, Fisheries and Food, ex p Astonquest Ltd (21 December 1999, unreported), CA .... **III EUR [388.4]**

R (on the application of Purja) v Ministry of Defence [2003] EWCA Civ 1345, [2004] 1 WLR 289, [2003] 41 LS Gaz R 33, (2003) Times, 16 October .... **III HUM [35.1]**

R (on the application of the British Gurkha Welfare Society) v Ministry of Defence [2010] EWCA Civ 1098, [2010] All ER (D) 131 (Oct) .... **III HUM [35.1]**

R (on the application of Nicklinson) v Ministry of Justice [2012] EWHC 2381 (Admin), [2012] 3 FCR 233, 127 BMLR 197, [2012] 32 LS Gaz R 17, (2012) Times, 13 November, [2012] All ER (D) 105 (Aug); revsd in part sub nom R (on the application of Nicklinson) v Ministry of Justice (CNK Alliance Ltd and British Humanist Association intervening) [2013] EWCA Civ 961, 133 BMLR 46, (2013) Times, 08 October, [2013] HRLR 36, [2013] All ER (D) 392 (Jul) .. **III HUM [24.1A], [30.2], [31.1]**

R v Mirza [2004] UKHL 02, [2004] 1 AC 1118, [2004] 1 All ER 925, [2004] 2 WLR 201, [2004] 2 Cr App Rep 112, [2004] 07 LS Gaz R 34, [2004] NLJR 145, (2004) Times, 23 January, 16 BHRC 279, [2004] All ER (D) 189 (Jan) .... III COT [17.1]

R v Moore [2003] EWCA Crim 1574 [2003] 1 WLR 2170, [2003] 26 LS Gaz R 35, 147 Sol Jo LB 596 .... III COT [9.3]

R v Newcastle upon Tyne County Court, ex p Thompson (1988) 20 HLR 430, [1988] 2 EGLR 119, [1988] 26 EG 112 .... III L&T [71.5]

R (on the application of Khatun) v Newham London Borough Council [2003] EWHC 2326 (Admin), [2004] 08 EGCS 136, [2003] All ER (D) 188 (Oct); on appeal [2004] EWCA Civ 55, [2004] 3 WLR 417, [2004] LGR 696, (2004) Times, 27 February, 148 Sol Jo LB 268 .... III L&T [303E.5], [304.2A]

R (on the application of Laporte) v Newham London Borough Council [2004] EWHC 227 (Admin), [2004] All ER (D) 309 (Jan) .... III L&T [284.1], [285.4]

R (on the application of Morris) v Newham London Borough Council [2002] EWHC 1262 (Admin), [2002] All ER (D) 402 (May) .... III L&T [304.5]

R (on the application of Sacupima) v Newham London Borough Council [2000] All ER (D) 1947, [2001] 1 WLR 563, 33 HLR 18, (2000) Times, 1 December, CA .... III L&T [306.4D]

R v Newham London Borough Council, ex p Khan and Hussain (2000) 33 HLR 269, Times, 9 May .... III L&T [303E.6A], [304.4], [306.4D]

R v Newham London Borough Council, ex p Ojuri (No 2) (1998) Times, 29 August .... III L&T [306.3]

R v Newham London Borough Council, ex p Ojuri (No 5) (1998) 31 HLR 631 ..... III L&T [306.5]

R v Newington (1990) 91 Cr App R 247, CA .... III MEN [409]

R v Newtownabbey Magistrates' Court, ex p Belfast Telegraph Newspaper Ltd (1997) Times, 27 August .... III COT [13.2]

R (on the application of H) v North and East London Regional Mental Health Tribunal [2001] EWCA Civ 415, [2002] QB 1, [2001] 3 WLR 512, [2001] 21 LS Gaz R 40 . III HUM [10.2], [27.2B]

R (on the application of Hunt) v North Somerset Council [2013] EWCA Civ 1320, [2014] LGR 1, 177 CL&J 751, (2013) Times, 20 November, [2013] All ER (D) 51 (Nov); revsd in part sub nom Hunt v North Somerset Council [2015] UKSC 51, [2015] 1 WLR 3575, 165 NLJ 7663, (2015) Times, 27 July, [2015] All ER (D) 230 (Jul) .... III EQU [149.2]

R (on the application of Condliff) v North Staffordshire Primary Care Trust [2011] EWCA Civ 910, 121 BMLR 192, [2011] NLJR 1100, [2011] All ER (D) 254 (Jul) ... III HUM [30.6]

R (on the application of Douglas) v North Tyneside Metropolitan Borough Council [2003] EWCA Civ 1847, [2004] 1 All ER 709, [2004] 1 WLR 2363, [2004] NLJR 56, 148 Sol Jo LB 58, [2003] All ER (D) 375 (Dec) .... III HUM [35.2A], [40.2A]

R (on the application of Hurst) v Northern District of London Coroner [2007] UKHL 13, [2007] 2 AC 189, [2007] 2 All ER 1025, [2007] 2 WLR 726, [2007] NLJR 519, (2007) Times, 29 March, [2007] All ER (D) 470 (Mar) .... III HUM [9.3]

R (on the application of Veolia ES Nottinghamshire Ltd) v Nottinghamshire County Council [2010] EWCA Civ 1214, [2011] LGR 95, [2010] 44 LS Gaz R 18, (2010) Times, 9 November, [2010] All ER (D) 01 (Nov) .. III HUM [39.2A]

R (on the application of E) v Nottinghamshire Healthcare NHS Trust (Equality and Human Rights Commission intervening) [2009] EWCA Civ 795, 110 BMLR 87, [2009] All ER (D) 264 (Jul) .... III HUM [30.2]

R v OB. See OB v Director of the Serious Fraud Office

R (on the application of I-CD Publishing Ltd) v Office of the Deputy Prime Minister [2003] EWHC 1761 (Admin), [2003] All ER (D) 343 (Jul), Times, 11 August .... III DAT [21.4]

R v Panel on Take-overs and Mergers, ex p Datafin plc [1987] QB 815, [1987] 1 All ER 564, [1987] 2 WLR 699, [1987] BCLC 104, 3 BCC 10, 131 Sol Jo 23, [1987] LS Gaz R 264, [1986] NLJ Rep 1207, CA .... II SCA [30.5]

R (on the application of Brooke) v Parole Board [2007] EWHC 2036 (Admin), [2007] NLJR 463, (2007) Times, 18 October, [2007] All ER (D) 39 (Sep); affd [2008] EWCA Civ 29, [2008] 3 All ER 289, [2008] 1 WLR 1950, (2008) Times, 5 February, [2008] All ER (D) 21 (Feb) .... III HUM [27.2G]

R (on the application of Sturnham) v Parole Board [2013] UKSC 23, [2013] 2 AC 254, [2013] 2 All ER 1013, [2013] 2 WLR 1157, (2013) Times, 04 June, 157 Sol Jo (no 18) 31, 35 BHRC 378, [2013] All ER (D) 18 (May) .... III HUM [27.5A]

R (on the application of A) v Partnerships in Care Ltd [2002] EWHC 529 (Admin), [2002] 1 WLR 2611, (2002) Times, 23 April, [2002] All ER (D) 23 (Apr) .... III HUM [12.1B]

R (on the application of Hall (Roque)) v University College London Hospitals NHS Foundation Trust [2013] EWHC 198 (Admin), [2013] NLJR 208, [2013] ACD 55, [2013] All ER (D) 119 (Feb) .... III HUM [25.1]
R (on the application of Cart) v Upper Tribunal [2011] UKSC 28, [2011] 4 All ER 127, [2011] STC 1659, [2011] PTSR 1053, [2011] NLJR 916, (2011) Times, 23 June, [2011] All ER (D) 149 (Jun) .... III TCE [1]
R (on the application of Robertson) v Wakefield Metropolitan City Council [2001] EWHC Admin 915, [2002] QB 1052, [2002] 2 WLR 889, [2002] LGR 286, [2002] 02 LS Gaz R 28, (2001) Times, 27 November, 145 Sol Jo LB 267, [2001] All ER (D) 243 (Nov) .... III DAT [21.4]; III HUM [30.4A]
R (on the application of ZYN) v Walsall Metropolitan Borough Council [2014] EWHC 1918 (Admin), [2015] 1 All ER 165, [2014] PTSR 1356, [2014] WTLR 1649, [2014] All ER (D) 108 (Jun) .... III MEN [83.1]
R (on the application of Malik) v Waltham Forest NHS Primary Care Trust (Secretary of State for Health, interested party) [2007] EWCA Civ 265, [2007] 4 All ER 832, [2007] 1 WLR 2092, [2007] ICR 1101, [2007] IRLR 529, (2007) Times, 10 April , [2007] All ER (D) 462 (Mar) .... III HUM [14.2]
R v Wandsworth County Court, ex p London Borough of Wandsworth [1975] 3 All ER 390, [1975] 1 WLR 1314, 119 Sol Jo 529 .... III L&T [90.5]
R (on the application of Turley) v Wandsworth London Borough [2014] EWHC 4040 (Admin), [2014] All ER (D) 92 (Dec) .... III L&T [112.7]
R v Ward [2001] EWCA Crim 1648, (2001) Times, 10 August .... III COM [54.1]
R (on the application of PD) v West Midlands and North West Mental Health Review Tribunal (2003) Times, 31 October .... III HUM [28.3C]
R (on the application of Morris) v Westminster City Council [2004] EWHC 2191 (Admin), (2004) Times, 20 October .... III HUM [35.2B]; III L&T [303AA.4]
R (on the application of Gallastegui) v Westminster City Council and Comr of the Police for the Metropolis and Secretary of State for the Home Department [2012] EWHC 1123 (Admin), [2012] 4 All ER 401, [2012] LGR 789, [2012] NLJR 651, [2012] All ER (D) 144 (Apr); affd [2013] EWCA Civ 28, [2013] 2 All ER 579, [2013] 1 WLR 2377, [2013] LGR 337, (2013) Times, 05 March, [2013] All ER (D) 233 (Jan) ..... III HUM [19.1], [33.3]
R v Westminster City Council, ex p Residents' Association of Mayfair [1991] COD 182 .... III COM [46.2]
R v Williams [2001] 38 LS Gaz R 37, 145 Sol Jo LB 223, C-Mac .... III HUM [28.3C]
R v Wirral Metropolitan Borough Council [2009] EWCA Civ 827, [2009] Fam Law 1045, 153 Sol Jo (no 30) 28, [2009] All ER (D) 308 (Jul) .... III LIM [38.6A]
R v Wolverhampton Stipendiary Magistrate, ex p Mould (1992) Times, 16 November .... III SOL [8.4]
R (on the application of Snelgrove) v Woolwich Crown Court [2004] EWHC 2172 (Admin), [2005] 1 WLR 3223, [2005] 1 Cr App Rep 253, [2004] All ER (D) 177 (Sep) .... II SCA [28.1]
R v Worthing Borough Council, ex p Bruce (1991) 24 HLR 261, [1992] COD 42; on appeal [1994] 1 EGLR 116, [1994] 24 EG 149, CA .... III L&T [109.1]
R (on the application of Wilson) v Wychavon District Council [2007] EWCA Civ 52, [2007] QB 801, [2007] LGR 540, [2007] 2 P & CR 252, (2007) Times, 9 February, [2007] All ER (D) 79 (Feb) .... III HUM [30.9], [35.2C]
R v Young [1995] QB 324, [1995] 2 WLR 430, [1995] 2 Cr App Rep 379, [1995] 6 LS Gaz R 38, CA .... III COT [17.1]
R & B Customs Brokers Co Ltd v United Dominions Trust Ltd (Saunders Abbott (1980) Ltd, third party) [1988] 1 All ER 847, [1988] 1 WLR 321, [1988] RTR 134, [1988] BTLC 52, 132 Sol Jo 300, [1988] 11 LS Gaz R 42, CA .... III CON [75.2], [75.5]
RA (Sri Lanka) v Secretary of State for the Home Department [2008] EWCA Civ 1210, [2008] All ER (D) 51 (Nov) .... III HUM [30.10]
RB (Adult) (No 4), Re [2011] EWHC 3017 (Fam), [2012] 1 FLR 466 .... III COT [8.2A]; III MEN [13]
RB (by his litigation friend) v Brighton and Hove City Council [2014] EWCA Civ 561, (2014) Times, 12 June, [2014] All ER (D) 58 (May) .... III MEN [55.1], [55.2]
RB (Algeria) v Secretary of State for the Home Department [2009] UKHL 10, [2009] 4 All ER 1045, [2009] 2 WLR 512, [2009] NLJR 349, (2009) Times, 19 February, 153 Sol Jo (no 7) 32, 26 BHRC 90, [2009] All ER (D) 200 (Feb) .... III HUM [28.1]
RB Policies at Lloyd's v Butler [1950] 1 KB 76, [1949] 2 All ER 226, 82 Lloyd's Rep 841, [1949] WN 229, 93 Sol Jo 553, 65 TLR 436 .... III LIM [36.1C], [4.1]
RC (Dec'd), Re [2011] 1 FLR 1447, [2011] Fam Law 345 .... III MEN [93.1]

S

Saleem v The Mayor and Burgesses of the London Borough of Wandsworth [2015] EWCA Civ 780, [2015] LGR 695, [2015] HLR 762, (2015) Times, 27 August, [2015] All ER (D) 243 (Jul) .... III L&T [303C.1]
Salehabady v Trustees of the Eyre Estate [2017] UKUT 60 (LC) .... III L&T [260.2]
Salekipour v Parmar [2016] EWHC 1466 (QB), [2016] QB 987, [2016] 3 WLR 728, [2016] All ER (D) 186 (Jun); revsd sub nom Salekipour v Parmar (in her own right and as executrix of Parmar, deceased) [2017] EWCA Civ 2141, [2018] 2 WLR 1090, [2017] All ER (D) 108 (Dec) .... II CCA [21.1]
Salford City Council v Garner (2004) Times, 10 March, 148 Sol Jo LB 295, [2004] All ER (D) 465 (Feb), CA .... III L&T [286.1]
Salford Van Hire (Contracts) Ltd v Bocholt Developments Ltd [1996] RTR 103, [1995] 2 EGLR 50, [1995] 18 LS Gaz R 35, [1995] 47 EG 153, CA .... III PTY [2.3]
Salgueiro da Silva Mouta v Portugal (1999) 31 EHRR 47, [2001] 1 FCR 653, ECtHR .... III HUM [35.1]
Salmon, Re, Coard v National Westminster Bank Ltd [1981] Ch 167, [1980] 3 All ER 532, [1980] 3 WLR 748, 124 Sol Jo 813 .... III FMY [10.1]
Salomon v Akiens. See Akiens v Salomon
Salsbury v Law Society [2008] EWHC 889 (Admin), [2008] All ER (D) 251 (Mar); revsd [2008] EWCA Civ 1285, [2009] 2 All ER 487, [2009] 1 WLR 1286, (2009) Times, 15 January, 152 Sol Jo (no 46) 30, [2008] All ER (D) 240 (Nov) .... III SOL [66.1A], [66.1B]
Salter v Lask [1925] 1 KB 584, 23 LGR 327, 94 LJKB 522, 132 LT 830, 41 TLR 201, DC .... III L&T [81.3]
Samick Lines Co Ltd v Antonis P Lemos (Owners). See Antonis P Lemos, The
Samonini v London General Transport Services Ltd [2005] PIQR P20 ..... III FUND [27A.6]
Sampson v Wilson [1996] Ch 39, [1995] 3 WLR 455, 70 P & CR 359, 29 HLR 18, CA .... III L&T [232.5]
Samuel v Newbold. See Saunders v Newbold
Sancheti v City of London (2008) Times, 1 December, [2008] All ER (D) 204 (Nov), CA .... III ARB [6.2]
Sanctuary Housing Association v Campbell [1999] 3 All ER 460, [1999] 1 WLR 1279, [1999] 2 FCR 657, [1999] 2 FLR 383, [1999] Fam Law 449, 32 HLR 100, [1999] 2 EGLR 20, [1999] 18 EG 162, 78 P & CR D15, CA .... III L&T [106.7]
Sanderson v City of Bradford Metropolitan Borough Council [2016] EWHC 527 (QB), [2016] All ER (D) 16 (Apr) .... III LIM [38.5]
Sanders v Isaacs [1971] 1 All ER 755, [1971] 1 WLR 240, 114 Sol Jo 95 ..... III SOL [86.6], [87.3]
Sanders v United Kingdom (Application No 34129/96) (2000) Times, 12 May, ECtHR .... III HUM [28.3C]
Sandwell and West Birmingham Hospitals NHS Trust v CD [2014] EWCOP 23, 178 CL&J 530, [2014] All ER (D) 130 (Aug) .... III MEN [603.3]
Sandwell Metropolitan Borough Council v Hensley [2007] EWCA Civ 1425, 151 Sol Jo LB 1436, [2008] All ER (D) 34 (Jan) .... III L&T [157.2AA]
Sanghi Polyesters Ltd (India) v International Investor (KCFC) (Kuwait) [2000] 1 Lloyd's Rep 480 .... III ARB [22.3]
Sapir, Re EU:C:2013:228, C-645/11: .... III EUR [155.4]
Sardinia Sulcis and Al Tawwab, The [1991] 1 Lloyd's Rep 201, CA .. III L&T [21.1]; III LIM [39.9A]
Sargasso, The. See Neste Chemicals SA v DK Line SA and Tokumaru Kaiun KK, The Sargasso
Sargeant v Macepark (Whittlebury) Ltd [2004] EWHC 1333 (Ch), [2004] 4 All ER 662, [2004] 27 LS Gaz R 30, [2004] NLJR 925, (2004) Times, 6 July, [2004] All ER (D) 08 (Jun) .... III L&T [7.3], [7.6]
Sargeant v Sargeant [2018] EWHC 8 (Ch), [2018] WTLR 1451, [2018] All ER (D) 19 (Jan) .... III FMY [10.1]
Sarjantson v Humberside Police Chief Constable [2013] EWCA Civ 1252, [2013] 3 WLR 1540, [2013] All ER (D) 205 (Oct) .... III HUM [30.6], [33.3]
Sarum Trust v Duke of Westminster (1953) 161 Estates Gazette 104, [1953] CPL 86 .... III L&T [152.6]
Sarwar v Alam [2001] EWCA Civ 1401, [2001] 4 All ER 541, [2001] NLJR 1492, [2001] All ER (D) 44 (Sep) .... III FUND [28.1]
Sarwar v Ali [2007] LS Law Med 375 .... III PID [25.4]

Shell-Mex and BP Ltd v Manchester Garages Ltd [1971] 1 All ER 841, [1971] 1 WLR 612, 115 Sol Jo 111, 218 Estates Gazette 285, CA .... III L&T [14.2]
Shelley v United Artists Corpn Ltd (1990) 60 P & CR 241, [1990] 1 EGLR 103, [1990] 16 EG 73, CA .... III L&T [34.1], [34.3]
Shepherd v Post Office (1995) Times, 15 June, CA .... III PID [10.2]
Sheppard v Richmond-upon-Thames London Borough Council [2012] EWCA Civ 302 .... III L&T [303C.1]
Shepherd v Robinson [1919] 1 KB 474, 88 LJKB 873, 120 LT 492, 35 TLR 220, CA .... III SOL [59]
Shepherd Construction Ltd v Pinsent Masons LLP [2012] EWHC 43 (TCC), 141 Con LR 232, [2012] BLR 213 .... III SOL [44], [61]
Shepherd's Bush Housing Association v HATS Co-operative (1991) 24 HLR 176, [1991] EGCS 134, CA .... III L&T [103.4]
Shepping v Osada (2000) 33 HLR 146, sub nom Osada v Shepping [2000] 2 EGLR 38, [2000] 30 EG 125, 80 P & CR D13, CA .... III L&T [242.5A]
Sherdley v Nordea Life and Pension SA (Societe Anonyme) [2012] EWCA Civ 88, [2012] 2 All ER (Comm) 725, [2012] NLJR 293, [2012] All ER (D) 103 (Feb) ..... III EUR [165.1], [280.1]
Sheriff v Klyne Tugs (Lowestoft) Ltd [1999] ICR 1170, [1999] IRLR 481, 625 IRLB 6, CA .... III EMP [4]
Shiloh Spinners Ltd v Harding [1973] AC 691, [1973] 1 All ER 90, [1973] 2 WLR 28, 25 P & CR 48, 117 Sol Jo 34, HL .... III L&T [2.2]
Shilson, Coode & Co, Re [1904] 1 Ch 837, 73 LJ Ch 541, 52 WR 556, 90 LT 641, 20 TLR 418 .... II SOL [85.3]
Shine v English Churches Housing Group [2004] EWCA Civ 434, [2004] HLR 727, [2004] 20 LS Gaz R 35, (2004) Times, 2 June, 148 Sol Jo LB 476, [2004] All ER (D) 125 (Apr) .... III L&T [164.2B]
Shine v Freedman [1926] EGD 376 .... III L&T [82.3]
Shlosberg v Avonwick Holdings Ltd [2016] EWHC 1001 (Ch), [2016] 3 WLR 1330, [2016] BPIR 1012, [2016] All ER (D) 76 (May) .... III HUM [30.5]
Shogun Finance Ltd v Hudson [2001] EWCA Civ 1001, [2002] QB 834, [2002] 4 All ER 572, [2002] 2 WLR 867, [2002] RTR 288, (2001) Times, 4 July, (2001) Independent, 28 June, [2001] All ER (D) 306 (Jun); affd [2003] UKHL 62, [2004] 1 AC 919, [2004] 1 All ER 215, [2004] 1 All ER (Comm) 332, [2003] 3 WLR 1371, [2004] RTR 153, [2004] 1 Lloyd's Rep 532, [2003] 46 LS Gaz R 25, [2003] NLJR 1790, (2003) Times, 20 November, 147 Sol Jo LB 1368, [2004] 4 LRC 255, [2003] All ER (D) 258 (Nov) .... III CON [32.6]
Shore v Sedgwick Financial Services Ltd [2008] EWCA Civ 863, (2008) Times, 12 August, 152 Sol Jo (no 30) 31, [2008] All ER (D) 304 (Jul) .... III LIM [18.7]
Shoreditch County Court Bailiffs v De Madeiros (1988) Times, 24 February, CA ..... II CCA [115.2]
Short v Birmingham City Council [2004] EWHC 2112 (QB), [2004] All ER (D) 67 (Sep) .... III L&T [306.2B]
Shotley Point Marina (1986) Ltd v Spalding [1997] 1 EGLR 233, CA .... III L&T [37.3]
Shrewsbury and Atcham Borough Council v Evans (1997) 30 HLR 123, CA . III L&T [109.2], [157.5]
Shrewsbury and Atcham Borough Council v Tanriverdi [2005] EWCA Civ 1263, [2005] All ER (D) 158 (Sep) .... III COT [21.4], [21.5]
Shrimpton v Rabbits [1924] All ER Rep 694, 68 Sol Jo 685, 131 LT 478, 40 TLR 541, DC .... III L&T [71.8]
Sibohelle, The. See TTMI Sarl v Statoil ASA (The Sibohelle)
Sibthorpe v Southwark London Borough Council (Law Society intervening) [2011] EWCA Civ 25, [2011] 2 All ER 240, [2011] 1 WLR 2111, [2011] HLR 295, [2011] 06 LS Gaz R 18, [2011] NLJR 173, (2011) Times, 14 February, [2011] 3 Costs LR 427, [2011] All ER (D) 183 (Jan) .... III FUND [1], [27.6]
Siddiqui v Rashid [1980] 3 All ER 184, [1980] 1 WLR 1018, 40 P & CR 504, 124 Sol Jo 464, 256 Estates Gazette 169, CA .... III L&T [85.7]
Sidi Bishr, The [1987] 1 Lloyd's Rep 42 .... II SCA [18.35]
Siemens Hearing Instruments Ltd v Friends Life Ltd [2014] EWCA Civ 382, [2014] 2 P & CR 95, [2014] All ER (D) 94 (Aug) .... III L&T [15.1A]
Sienkiewicz v Greif (UK) Ltd [2011] UKSC 10, [2011] 2 AC 229, [2011] 2 All ER 857, [2011] 2 WLR 523, [2011] ICR 391, 119 BMLR 54, (2011) Times, 10 March, 155 Sol Jo (no 10) 30, [2011] All ER (D) 107 (Mar) .... III PID [40C.2]

Sierra Fishing Company v Farran [2015] EWHC 140 (Comm), [2015] 1 All ER (Comm) 560, 165 NLJ 7640, [2015] All ER (D) 04 (Feb) .... **III ARB [10.3]**

Sight and Sound Education Ltd v Books Etc Ltd [1999] 3 EGLR 45, [1999] 43 EG 161 .... **III L&T [30.5]**

Sigma Finance Corpn, Re [2009] UKSC 2, [2010] 1 All ER 571, [2009] NLJR 1550, 153 Sol Jo (no 42) 29, [2009] All ER (D) 297 (Oct) .... **III ARB [11.4]**

Signet Group plc v Hammerson UK Properties Ltd [1998] 03 LS Gaz R 25, 142 Sol Jo LB 70, 75 P & CR D33, CA .... **III LIM [39.9]**

Silih v Slovenia (Application No 71463/01) (2009) 49 EHRR 996, [2009] ECHR 71463/01, ECtHR .... **III HUM [24.4]**

Sills v Watkins [1956] 1 QB 250, [1955] 3 All ER 319, [1955] 3 WLR 520, 53 LGR 672, 99 Sol Jo 761, CA .... **III L&T [85.1]**

Silver v General Medical Council [2003] UKPC 33, (2003) Times, 9 May, [2003] All ER (D) 239 (Apr) .... **III SOL [66.2]**

Silver v United Kingdom (1983) 5 EHRR 347, ECtHR .... **III HUM [30.6]**

Silver Dry Bulk Co Ltd v Homer Hulbert Maritime Co Ltd [2017] EWHC 44 (Comm), [2017] 1 All ER (Comm) 791, [2017] 1 Lloyd's Rep 155, 167 NLJ 7734, [2017] All ER (D) 39 (Feb) .... **III ARB [9.9]**

Silvey v Pendragon plc [2001] EWCA Civ 784, [2001] IRLR 685 .... **III EMP [6.4A]**

Simaan General Contracting Co v Pilkington Glass Ltd [1987] 1 All ER 345, [1987] 1 WLR 516, 131 Sol Jo 297, [1987] LS Gaz R 819, [1986] NLJ Rep 824, 3 Const LJ 300, CA .... **III COM [46.5]**

Simmons v Castle [2012] EWCA Civ 1039, [2013] 1 All ER 334, [2013] 1 WLR 1239, [2012] 5 Costs LR 931, [2012] All ER (D) 335 (Jul) .... **III EQU [119.3], III PID [5D]**

Simmons v Castle (No 2) [2012] EWCA Civ 1288, [2013] 1 All ER 334, [2013] 1 WLR 1239, [2012] NLJR 1324, [2012] 6 Costs LR 1150, [2012] All ER (D) 90 (Oct) .. **III PID [4], [5D]**

Simmons and Politzer, Re [1954] 2 QB 296, [1954] 2 All ER 811, [1954] 3 WLR 423, 98 Sol Jo 573, CA .... **III SOL [77.2]**

Simms v London Borough of Islington [2008] EWCA Civ 1083, [2008] All ER (D) 146 (Oct) .... **III L&T [303AA.3], [306.4A]**

Simms v Simms [2002] EWHC 2734 (Fam), [2003] Fam 83, [2003] 1 All ER 669, [2003] 2 WLR 1465, [2003] 1 FCR 361, 71 BMLR 61, [2003] NLJR 21 .... **III MEN [7]**

Simon v Helmot [2012] UKPC 5, 126 BMLR 73, [2012] All ER (D) 215 (Mar) . **III PID [24.1]**

Simonite v Sheffield City Council [1992] NPC 9, [1992] 1 EGLR 105, [1992] 24 EG 134 .... **III L&T [16C.1], [27.6]**

Simpkin Marshall Ltd, Re [1959] Ch 229, [1958] 3 All ER 611, [1958] 3 WLR 693, 102 Sol Jo 878 .... **III SOL [75.1]**

Simpson v Norfolk & Norwich University Hospital NHS Trust [2011] EWCA Civ 1149, [2011] NLJR 1451, (2011) Times, 16 November, [2011] All ER (D) 102 (Oct) . **III PTY [19.4]**

Simpson v Norwest Holst Southern Ltd [1980] 2 All ER 471, [1980] 1 WLR 968, 124 Sol Jo 313, CA .... **III LIM [17.4]**

Sims v Dacorum Borough Council [2014] UKSC 63, [2014] 3 WLR 1600, [2014] LGR 898, 165 NLJ 7635, (2014) Times, 02 December, [2014] All ER (D) 126 (Nov) ..... **III HUM [30.5A]; III L&T [93.7]**

Sims v Wilson [1946] 2 All ER 261, 90 Sol Jo 570, 62 TLR 485, CA .... **III L&T [84.1]**

Sinclair Gardens Investments (Kensington) Ltd v Avon Estates (London) Ltd [2016] UKUT 317 (LC) .... **III L&T [175.1]**

Sinclair Gardens Investments (Kensington) Ltd v Poets Chase Freehold Co Ltd [2007] EWHC 1776 (Ch), [2007] 49 EG 104, [2007] NLJR 1427, [2007] 32 EG 89 (CS), [2007] All ER (D) 425 (Jul) .... **III L&T [249.4]**

Sinclair Investments (UK) Ltd v Versailles Trade Finance Ltd (in admin) [2011] EWCA Civ 347, [2012] Ch 453, [2011] 4 All ER 335, [2011] Bus LR 1126, [2011] 2 BCLC 501, [2011] 2 P & CR D14, [2011] All ER (D) 321 (Mar) .... **III LIM [26.2A]**

Singh v Libra Holidays Ltd [2003] EWHC 276 (QB), [2003] All ER (D) 319 (Feb) .. **III CON [102.1]**

Singh v Observer Ltd [1989] 2 All ER 751, 133 Sol Jo 485; revsd [1989] 3 All ER 777n, CA .... **II SCA [50.4]**

Singh v Yaqubi [2013] EWCA Civ 23, [2013] Lloyd's Rep IR 398, [2013] All ER (D) 225 (Jan) .... **III CON [30.3]**

Single Horse Properties Ltd v Surrey County Council. See Surrey County Council v Single Horse Properties Ltd

Southwark London Borough Council v Mills [2001] Ch 1, [1999] 2 WLR 409, 31 HLR 187, [1998] 2 EGLR 30, [1998] 34 LS Gaz R 31, [1998] 45 EG 151, [1998] EGCS 132, 142 Sol Jo LB 221, CA; affd sub nom Southwark London Borough Council v Tanner [2001] 1 AC 1, [1999] 3 WLR 939, sub nom Southwark London Borough Council v Mills [1999] 4 All ER 449, 32 HLR 148, [1999] 42 LS Gaz R 41, [1999] NLJR 1618, [1999] 45 EG 179, [1999] EGCS 122, 143 Sol Jo LB 249, [2000] Env LR 112, 79 P & CR D13, HL .... **III L&T [164.4], [164.6]**
Sovarex SA v Romero Alvarez SA [2011] EWHC 1661 (Comm), [2012] 1 All ER (Comm) 207, [2011] 2 Lloyd's Rep 320, [2011] NLJR 954, [2011] All ER (D) 225 (Jun) ..... **III ARB [19.1A]**
Sowden v Lodge [2004] EWCA Civ 1370, [2005] 1 All ER 581, [2005] 1 WLR 2129, 148 Sol Jo LB 1282, [2004] All ER (D) 304 (Oct) .... **III PID [25B.1]**
Sowerby v Charlton [2005] EWCA Civ 1610, [2006] 1 WLR 568, (2006) Times, 5 January, [2005] All ER (D) 343 (Dec) .... **III PID [2D]**
Span Terza, The [1982] 1 Lloyd's Rep 225, CA .... **II SCA [19.8]**
Spargo v North Essex District Health Authority [1997] 8 Med LR 125, [1997] 15 LS Gaz R 26, [1997] PIQR P235, 141 Sol Jo LB 90, CA .... **III LIM [17.3], [17.5]**
Sparks v Department for Transport [2016] EWCA Civ 360, [2016] IRLR 519, [2016] ICR 695, 166 NLJ 7697, [2016] All ER (D) 94 (Apr) .... **III EMP [1]**
Special Effects Ltd v L'Oreal SA [2007] EWCA Civ 1, 171 JP 381, [2007] IP & T 617, [2007] Bus LR 759, [2007] ETMR 815, [2007] RPC 381, (2007) 151 Sol Jo LB 126, (2007) Times, 24 January, [2007] All ER (D) 29 (Jan) .... **III PAT [41.1], [48.1]**
Spectravest Inc v Aperknit Ltd [1988] FSR 161 .... **III PAT [13.2]**
Speedwell Estates Ltd v Dalziel [2001] EWCA Civ 1277, [2001] All ER (D) 454 (Jul), [2002] HLR 813, [2001] 32 LS Gaz R 38, [2002] 02 EG 104, [2001] 35 EG 104 (CS), [2002] 1 P & CR D17 .... **III L&T [64.4]**
Spelman (by his litigation friends) v Express Newspapers [2012] EWHC 239 (QB), [2012] 09 LS Gaz R 18, [2012] All ER (D) 91 (Feb) .... **III HUM [18.5], [18.5A]**
Spence v Wilson (No 2) 1998 SLT 959, OH .... **III PID [37.2]**
Spencer v Gordon Wood (t/a Gordons Tyres (a firm)) [2004] EWCA Civ 352, 148 Sol Jo LB 356, [2004] All ER (D) 275 (Mar), sub nom Spencer v Wood (2004) Times, 30 March .... **III FUND [27A.6]**
Spencer v Secretary of Work and Pensions; Moore v Secretary of State for Transport [2008] EWCA Civ 750, [2009] 1 All ER 314, [2008] 3 CMLR 429, [2009] RTR 39, [2008] ICR 1359, [2008] IRLR 911, (2008) Times, 24 July, 152 Sol Jo (no 27) 31, [2008] All ER (D) 20 (Jul) .... **III LIM [3.5]**
Spencer v Taylor [2013] EWCA Civ 1600, [2014] HLR 113, [2013] All ER (D) 230 (Dec) .... **III L&T [229.3B], [229.4]**
Spielplatz Ltd v Pearson [2015] EWCA Civ 804, [2015] 2 P & CR 365, [2015] HLR 791, [2015] All ER (D) 40 (Aug) .... **III L&T [213.3A]**
Spier v Bernard. See Spyer v Bernard
Spiliada Maritime Corpn v Cansulex Ltd, The Spiliada [1987] AC 460, [1986] 3 All ER 843, [1986] 3 WLR 972, [1987] 1 Lloyd's Rep 1, 130 Sol Jo 925, [1987] LS Gaz R 113, [1986] NLJ Rep 1137, HL .... **II SCA [18.35], [48.2]**
Spirit of Independence, The (formerly known as Caribia Viva) [1999] 1 Lloyd's Rep 43 .... **II SCA [18.14]**
Spiro v Glencrown Properties Ltd [1991] Ch 537, [1991] 1 All ER 600, [1991] 2 WLR 931, 62 P & CR 402, [1990] NPC 90, 134 Sol Jo 1479, [1991] 1 EGLR 185, [1990] NLJR 1754, [1991] 02 EG 167 .... **III REA [38.1]**
Spittle v Bunney [1988] 3 All ER 1031, [1988] 1 WLR 847, [1988] Fam Law 433, 132 Sol Jo 754, [1988] NLJR 56, CA .... **II SCA [36.8]; III PID [13.2]**
Spook Erection Ltd v British Railways Board [1988] 1 EGLR 76, [1988] 21 EG 73, CA .... **III L&T [22.7], [22.9]**
Spraggs v Prentice (1950) 156 Estates Gazette 346, 100 L Jo 541 .... **III L&T [68.5]**
Spring Form Inc v Toy Brokers Ltd [2002] FSR 276 .... **III PAT [13.1A]**
Springfield Investments Ltd v Bell (1990) 22 HLR 440, [1991] 1 EGLR 115, [1991] 02 EG 157, CA .... **III L&T [83.2], [83.6]**
Spyer v Bernard (1863) 2 New Rep 172, sub nom Spier v Bernard 8 LT 396 ... **III SOL [85.7]**
Sritharan v Law Society [2005] EWCA Civ 476, [2005] 4 All ER 1105, [2005] 1 WLR 2708, [2005] NLJR 744, (2005) Times, 11 May, [2005] All ER (D) 395 (Apr) . **III SOL [66.3], [94.3A]**
Stack v Church Comrs for England [1952] 1 All ER 1352, 116 JP 334, 159 Estates Gazette 442, CA .... **III L&T [152.3]**

Stack v Dowden [2007] UKHL 17, [2007] 2 AC 432, [2007] 2 All ER 929, [2008] 2 P & CR 56, 9 ITELR 815, [2007] 2 FCR 280, [2007] 1 FLR 1858, [2007] Fam Law 593, [2007] NLJR 634, (2007) Times, 26 April, 151 Sol Jo LB 575, [2007] 2 P & CR D28, [2007] All ER (D) 208 (Apr) .... **III REA [57.1], [58.2A], [58.2C]**
Stafford v Camden London Borough Council [2012] EWCA Civ 839, [2012] 4 All ER 180, [2012] HLR 616, (2012) Times, 06 September, [2012] 2 P & CR D37, [2012] All ER (D) 129 (Jun) .... **III L&T [285.5]**
Stafford Borough Council v Haynes [2003] EWCA Civ 159, [2003] HLR 669 .... **III L&T [297.3]**
Staffordshire County Council v Barber. See Barber v Staffordshire County Council
Staffordshire County Council v SRK [2016] EWCOP 27, [2016] 3 WLR 867, [2016] All ER (D) 169 (May) .... **III MEN [50.1]**
Stainer v Lee [2010] EWHC 1539 (Ch), [2011] 1 BCLC 537, [2010] All ER (D) 56 (Jul) .... **III COM [262.2]**
Stakefield (Midlands) Ltd, Re [2010] EWHC 3175 (Ch), [2011] 2 BCLC 541, [2010] NLJR 1756, [2010] All ER (D) 89 (Dec) .... **III COM [306.2]**
Stakefield Ltd, Re, Secretary of State for Business, Enterprise & Regulatory Reform v Doffman [2010] EWHC 2518 (Ch), [2010] All ER (D) 94 (Oct) .... **III COM [50]**
Standingford v Bruce [1926] 1 KB 466, 24 LGR 141, 95 LJKB 223, 70 Sol Jo 346, 134 LT 282, 42 TLR 122, DC .... **III L&T [76.3], [82.8]**
Standingford v Probert [1950] 1 KB 377, [1949] 2 All ER 861, 93 Sol Jo 726, 65 TLR 704, CA .... **III L&T [85.2], [85.5]**
Stanley v Compton [1951] 1 All ER 859, CA .... **III L&T [76.5]**
Stanley v Saddique [1992] QB 1, [1991] 1 All ER 529, [1991] 2 WLR 459, CA . **III PID [14.1]**
Stanton v Collinson [2010] EWCA Civ 81, [2010] RTR 284, [2010] All ER (D) 276 (Feb) .... **III PID [9.3]**
Stapel v Bellshore Property Investments Ltd [2000] CLY 3948 ...... **III L&T [195.1], [206.1]**
Starrs v Procurator Fiscal, Linlithgow (1999) Times, 17 November .... **III HUM [28.3]**
Starsin, The. See Homburg Houtimport BV v Agrosin Private Ltd, The Starsin
Staszewski v Maribella Ltd (1997) 30 HLR 213, [1997] NPC 34, [1998] 1 EGLR 34, [1998] 04 EG 149, [1997] EGCS 35, 141 Sol Jo LB 74, CA .... **III L&T [187.4]**
State Bank of New South Wales (t/a Colonial State Bank) v Carey Harrison III [2002] EWCA Civ 363, [2002] All ER (D) 113 (Mar) .... **III REA [23.6A]**
Statoil v Sonatrach [2014] EWHC 875 (Comm), [2014] 2 All ER (Comm) 857, [2014] 2 Lloyd's Rep 252, 164 NLJ 7602, [2014] All ER (D) 31 (Apr) .... **III ARB [19.1]**
Staves and Staves v Leeds City Council (1990) 23 HLR 107, [1992] 2 EGLR 37, [1992] 29 EG 119, CA .... **III L&T [164.1]**
Stead v Stead [1985] FLR 16, [1985] Fam Law 154, CA .... **III FMY [8.1]**
Steamship Mutual Underwriting Association Ltd v Trollope & Colls (City) Ltd (1986) 6 Con LR 11, 33 BLR 77, 2 Const LJ 224, CA .... **III LIM [39.8]**
Stec v United Kingdom (2006) 43 EHRR 1017 .... **III HUM [35.4]**
Steedman v BBC [2001] EWCA Civ 1534, 145 Sol Jo LB 259, [2001] 47 LS Gaz R 27, (2001) Times, 13 December, [2002] EMLR 318, [2001] All ER (D) 316 (Oct) ...... **III HUM [28.5]; III LIM [37.2]**
Steedman v Scofield [1992] 2 Lloyd's Rep 163, sub nom Steadman v Scholfield [1992] 17 LS Gaz R 51, 136 Sol Jo LB 129 .... **II SCA [18.5]**
Steeds v Peverel Management Services Ltd (2001) Times, 16 May .... **III LIM [38.5]**
Steel v United Kingdom (1998) 28 EHRR 603, [1998] Crim LR 893, ECtHR . **III HUM [32.2]**
Steel v United Kingdom (Application No 68416/01) (2005) Times, 16 February ..... **III HUM [32.5A]**
Steel Linings Ltd and Harvey v Bibby & Co [1993] RA 27, [1993] NLJR 511, CA ... **II CCA [21.1], [142.2]; III PTY [2.7]**
Steel Wing Co Ltd, Re [1921] 1 Ch 349, 90 LJ Ch 116, [1920] B & CR 160, [1920] All ER Rep 292, 65 Sol Jo 240, 124 LT 664 .... **III PTY [19.2]**
Steen v A-G. See A-G v Punch Ltd
Steinfeld v Secretary of State for Education [2017] EWCA Civ 81, [2017] 4 All ER 47, [2017] 3 WLR 1237, [2017] 2 FLR 692, [2017] Fam Law 389, 167 NLJ 7736, [2017] All ER (D) 158 (Feb) .... **III HUM [10.2]**
Steinfeld and Anor v Secretary of State for Education [2016] EWHC 128 (Admin) .. **III HUM [34.1], [35.2K]**
Stenau Properties Ltd v Leek [2010] UKUT 478 (LC) .... **III L&T [173.3C]**
Stent v Monmouth District Council (1987) 54 P & CR 193, 19 HLR 269, [1987] 1 EGLR 59, 282 Estates Gazette 705, CA .... **III L&T [164.1]**

Syred v Powszecnny Zaklad Ubezpieczen (PZU) SA [2016] EWHC 254 (QB), [2016] 1 WLR 3211, [2016] All ER (D) 157 (Feb) .... **III PID [4A]**
Systech International Ltd v PC Harrington Contractors Ltd [2011] EWHC 2722 (TCC), [2012] 1 All ER (Comm) 381, [2012] Bus LR 1013, 139 Con LR 102, [2011] NLJR 1557, [2012] BLR 47, [2011] All ER (D) 240 (Oct); revsd [2012] EWCA Civ 1371, [2013] 2 All ER 69, [2013] 1 All ER (Comm) 1074, [2013] Bus LR 970, 145 Con LR 1, [2013] 1 EGLR 9, [2013] BLR 1, [2013] 03 Estates Gazette 88, (2013) Times, 01 January, [2012] All ER (D) 283 (Oct) .... **III ARB [10.4]; III L&T [308A]**
Szekeres v Alan Smeath & Co [2005] EWHC 1733 (Ch), [2005] 32 LS Gaz R 31, [2005] All ER (D) 08 (Aug) .... **III SOL [86.2]**
Szuluk v United Kingdom (Application No 36936/05) (2009) 108 BMLR 190, (2009) Times, 17 June, 27 BHRC 406, [2009] All ER (D) 02 (Jun), ECtHR .... **III HUM [30.11A]**

T

T (children) (costs), Re [2012] UKSC 36, [2012] 4 All ER 1137, [2012] 1 WLR 2281, [2012] PTSR 1379, [2012] 3 FCR 137, [2013] 1 FLR 133, [2012] Fam Law 1325, [2012] NLJR 1028, (2012) Times, 14 August, [2012] 5 Costs LR 914, [2012] All ER (D) 254 (Jul) .... **II SCA [50.5G]**
T v BBC [2007] EWHC 1683 (QB), [2008] 2 FCR 497, [2008] 1 FLR 281, [2007] Fam Law 904, [2007] All ER (D) 154 (Jul) .... **III HUM [18.4]**
T v P [2018] EWHC 685 (Ch), [2018] 3 All ER 469, 168 NLJ 7789, [2018] WTLR 109, [2018] 2 P & CR D21, [2018] All ER (D) 26 (Apr) .... **III TRU [38.1B]**
TA v AA (by his Litigation friend, the Official Solicitor) [2013] EWCA Civ 1661, [2014] 1 WLR 3773, [2014] All ER (D) 11 (Jan) .... **III MEN [91.1]**
TP and KM v United Kingdom [2001] 2 FCR 289, [2001] 2 FLR 549, [2001] Fam Law 590, ECtHR .... **III HUM [30.1]**
TSB Private Bank International SA v Chabra [1992] 2 All ER 245, [1992] 1 WLR 231 .... **II CCA [21.3]**
TTMI Sarl v Statoil ASA (The Sibohelle) [2011] EWHC 1150 (Comm), [2011] 2 All ER (Comm) 647, [2011] 2 Lloyd's Rep 220, [2011] All ER (D) 82 (May) .... **III ARB [20.2B]**
TW v Enfield London Borough Council (Secretary of State for Health intervening) [2013] EWHC 1180 (QB), 132 BMLR 227 .... **III MEN [27.1]**
Taberna Europe CDO II Plc v Selskabet AF 1.September 2008 [2016] EWCA Civ 1262, [2017] 2 WLR 803, [2017] 1 BCLC 319 , (2017) Times, 01 February, [2017] QB 633, [2017] All ER (D) 47 (Jan) .... **III CON [57.1]**
Tabernacle v Secretary of State for Defence [2009] EWCA Civ 23, (2009) Times, 25 February, [2009] All ER (D) 46 (Feb) .... **III HUM [33.3]**
Tacoma City, The [1991] 1 Lloyd's Rep 330, CA .... **II SCA [18.25]**
Tadema Holdings Ltd v Ferguson (1999) 32 HLR 866, [1999] 47 LS Gaz R 30, [1999] EGCS 138, CA .... **III L&T [217.5]**
Tagro v Cafane [1991] 2 All ER 235, [1991] 1 WLR 378, 23 HLR 250, [1991] 1 EGLR 279, CA .... **III L&T [232.2], [233.1]**
Taiwo v Olaigbe; Onu v Akwiwu [2016] UKSC 31, [2016] 1 WLR 2653, [2016] IRLR 719, [2016] ICR 756, 166 NLJ 7705, [2016] All ER (D) 134 (Jun) .... **III EQU [9.4]**
Taj v Ali [2000] 17 LS Gaz R 36, [2000] 43 EG 183, CA .... **III L&T [73.2]**
Talbot v Berkshire County Council [1994] QB 290, [1993] 4 All ER 9, [1993] 3 WLR 708, [1993] RTR 406, [1993] NLJR 402, [1993] PIQR P319, CA .... **III PID [16.5]**
Talbot v Talbot [1962] 3 All ER 174, 106 Sol Jo 613, sub nom Re Talbot [1962] 1 WLR 1113 .... **III FMY [7.14]**
Talling v Lawrence [1999] CLY 363, [1999] BPIR 414 .... **II CCA [28.3]**
Tame Shipping Ltd v Easy Navigation Ltd (2004) Times, 8 November .... **III ARB [21.2B]**
Tan v Sitkowski [2007] EWCA Civ 30, [2007] 1 WLR 1628, (2007) Times, 15 February, [2007] All ER (D) 16 (Feb) .... **III L&T [68.6]**
Tandon v Trustees of Spurgeons Homes [1982] AC 755, [1982] 1 All ER 1086, [1982] 2 WLR 735, 44 P & CR 307, 126 Sol Jo 260, [1982] RVR 228, 263 Estates Gazette 349, HL .... **III L&T [50.1]**
Tanfern Ltd v Cameron-MacDonald [2000] 2 All ER 801, [2000] 1 WLR 1311, CA .. **II SCA [13.3]**
Tankard v John Fredricks Plastics Ltd [2008] EWCA Civ 1375, [2009] 4 All ER 526, [2009] 1 WLR 1731, (2009) Times, 16 January, [2009] 1 Costs LR 101, [2008] All ER (D) 126 (Dec) .... **III FUND [5]**

Tillery Valley Foods v Channel Four Television [2004] EWHC 1075 (Ch), [2004] 22 LS Gaz R 31, (2004) Times, 21 May, [2004] All ER (D) 133 (May) ...... III HUM [18.4], [32.6]
Tilling v Whiteman [1980] AC 1, [1979] 1 All ER 737, [1979] 2 WLR 401, 38 P & CR 341, 123 Sol Jo 202, 250 Estates Gazette 51, HL .... III L&T [83.3]
Times Furnishing Co Ltd v Hutchings [1938] 1 KB 775, [1938] 1 All ER 422, 107 LJKB 432, 82 Sol Jo 315, 158 LT 335, 54 TLR 390 .... III PTY [2.3]
Times Newspapers Ltd, Re [2007] EWCA Crim 1925, [2008] 1 All ER 343, [2007] NLJR 1319, (2007) Times, 31 July , [2007] All ER (D) 473 (Jul) .... III COT [13.2], [20.1]
Times Newspapers Limited v Flood; Miller v Associated Newspapers Ltd; Frost and others v MGN Ltd [2017] UKSC 33, [2017] All ER (D) 46 (Apr), [2017] 1 WLR 1415, 167 NLJ 7743, (2017) Times, 17 April, [2017] 2 Costs LR 345 .... III HUM [32.3], [32.5A]
Times Newspapers Ltd, Re [2008] EWCA Crim 2559, [2009] 1 WLR 1015, [2009] Crim LR 114, (2008) Times, 31 October, [2008] All ER (D) 245 (Oct) .... III COT [20.1]
Times Newspapers Ltd v Chohan [2001] EWCA Civ 964, [2001] 1 WLR 1859, [2001] 30 LS Gaz R 38, 145 Sol Jo LB 165 .... III LIM [29.5]
Tingey v Sutton [1984] 3 All ER 561, [1984] 1 WLR 1154, 17 HLR 11, 128 Sol Jo 663, [1984] LS Gaz R 2294, 272 Estates Gazette 555, CA .... III L&T [78.2]
Tinseltime Ltd v Roberts [2012] EWHC 2628 (TCC), [2012] NLJR 1290, 156 Sol Jo (no 38) 31, [2012] 6 Costs LR 1094, [2012] All ER (D) 19 (Oct) .... II SCA [50.5F]; III SOL [47]
Tirkey v Chandhok (2014) UKEAT/0190/14, [2015] IRLR 195, [2015] ICR 527, [2015] All ER (D) 91 (Jan), EAT .... III EQU [9.2]
Titshall v Qwerty Travel Ltd [2011] EWCA Civ 1569, [2012] 2 All ER 627, [2012] 2 All ER (Comm) 347, [2012] 02 LS Gaz R 17, [2011] All ER (D) 107 (Dec) . III CON [90.2]
Tod-Heatly v Benham (1888) 40 Ch D 80, 58 LJ Ch 83, 37 WR 38, 60 LT 241, 5 TLR 9, [1886–90] All ER Rep Ext 1537, CA .... III L&T [82.3]
Tolputt (H) & Co Ltd v Mole [1911] 1 KB 87, 80 LJKB 232, 103 LT 607; on appeal [1911] 1 KB 836, 80 LJKB 686, 55 Sol Jo 293, 104 LT 148, CA .... II CCA [5F.2]
Tolstoy-Miloslavsky v Lord Aldington [1996] 2 All ER 556, [1996] 1 WLR 736, [1996] 01 LS Gaz R 22, 140 Sol Jo LB 26, [1996] PNLR 335, CA .... III SOL [75.3]
Tolten, The. See United Africa Co Ltd v Tolten (Owners), The Tolten
Tom Hoskins plc v EMW Law (a firm) [2010] EWHC 479 (Ch), [2010] NLJR 584, [2010] All ER (D) 54 (Apr) .... III SOL [61]
Tomkins v Jones (1889) 22 QBD 599, 58 LJQB 222, 37 WR 328, CA .... II CCA [141.2]
Tomlinson v Birmingham City Council [2010] UKSC 8, 154 Sol Jo (no 7) 37, [2010] All ER (D) 192 (Feb), sub nom Ali v Birmingham City Council [2010] 2 AC 39, [2010] 2 All ER 175, [2010] LGR 401, [2010] HLR 371, (2010) Times, 19 February .... III HUM [28.1], [28.2B]; L&T [303E.11]
Tomlinssons (R H) (Trowbridge) Ltd v Secretary of State for the Environment [1999] All ER (D) 870, [1999] 2 BCLC 760, [1999] NPC 110, CA .... III COM [5]
Toms v Ruberry [2017] EWHC 2970 (QB), [2017] All ER (D) 192 (Nov) .... III L&T [2.1B]
Tonicstar Ltd (on its own behalf and on behalf of the other corporate members of Lloyd's Syndicates 62, 1861 and 2255) v Allianz Insurance plc (Formerly Cornhill Insurance plc) [2017] EWHC 2753 (Comm), 167 NLJ 7769, [2017] All ER (D) 46 (Nov) .... III ARB [10.3A]
Toole v Bolton Metropolitan Borough Council [2002] EWCA Civ 588, [2002] All ER (D) 133 (Apr) .... III PID [9.2A]
Topplan Estates Ltd v Townley [2004] EWCA Civ 1369, (2004) 148 Sol Jo LB 1284, (2004)Times,15 November, [2004] All ER (D) 388 (Oct) .... III LIM [20.4]
Torridge District Council v Jones (1985) 18 HLR 107, [1985] 2 EGLR 54, 276 Estates Gazette 1253, CA .... III L&T [108.4]
Total Spares & Supplies Ltd v Antares SRL [2006] EWHC 1537 (Ch), [2006] All ER (D) 314 (Jun) .... II SCA [50.5C]
Totalise plc v Motley Fool Ltd [2001] 19 LS Gaz R 37, [2001] NLJR 644, 145 Sol Jo LB 71, [2001] EMLR 750; revsd [2001] EWCA Civ 1897, [2003] 2 All ER 872, [2002] 1 WLR 1233, [2002] 09 LS Gaz R 28, 146 Sol Jo LB 35, [2002] EMLR 358, [2001] All ER (D) 290 (Dec), Times, 10 January .... III COT [19.3]; III DAT [34.2]
Tower Hamlets London Borough Council v Azad (1997) 30 HLR 241, CA .. III L&T [110.1]
Tower Hamlets London Borough Council v BB, AM, SB and EL Trust [2011] EWHC 2853 (Fam), [2012] 1 FLR 1080, [2012] Fam Law 143 .... III MEN [51.5]
Tower Hamlets London Borough Council v Miah [1992] QB 622, [1992] 2 All ER 667, [1992] 2 WLR 761, 90 LGR 151, 24 HLR 199, [1992] 1 EGLR 39, [1992] 4 LS Gaz R 33, [1992] 18 EG 147, 136 Sol Jo LB 11, CA .... III L&T [156.5]

U

W

Westminster (Duke) v Birrane [1995] QB 262, [1995] 3 All ER 416, [1995] 2 WLR 270, 27 HLR 321, [1995] 1 EGLR 89, [1995] 03 LS Gaz R 37, [1995] 11 EG 141, CA ...... **III L&T [50.1], [50.4]**
Westminster (Duke) v Oddy (1984) 15 HLR 80, 128 Sol Jo 316, [1984] 1 EGLR 83, [1984] LS Gaz R 1443, [1984] RVR 112, 270 Estates Gazette 945, CA ...... **III L&T [46.4], [46.8], [64.6]**
Westminster City Council v Basson (1990) 62 P & CR 57, 23 HLR 225, [1991] 1 EGLR 277, [1990] EGCS 141, CA ...... **III L&T [68.2], [103.4]**
Westminster City Council v Boraliu [2007] EWCA Civ 1339, [2008] 1 WLR 2408, [2007] All ER (D) 34 (Nov) ...... **III L&T [156.4]**
Westminster City Council v British Waterways Board [1985] AC 676, [1984] 3 All ER 737, [1984] 3 WLR 1047, 83 LGR 113, 49 P & CR 117, 128 Sol Jo 783, [1984] LS Gaz R 3501, 272 Estates Gazette 1279, [1985] JPL 102, HL ...... **III L&T [22.12]**
Westminster City Council v Clarke [1992] 2 AC 288, [1992] 1 All ER 695, [1992] 2 WLR 229, 90 LGR 211, 24 HLR 260, [1992] 16 LS Gaz R 32, [1992] NLJR 196, 136 Sol Jo LB 82, HL ...... **III L&T [103.4]**
Westminster City Council v Horseferry Road Justices [2003] EWCA Civ 1007, [2003] 34 LS Gaz R 31, 147 Sol Jo LB 817, (2003) Times, 21 August, [2003] All ER (D) 26 (Jul) ...... **II SCA [27.1]**
Westminster City Council v Morris [2005] EWCA Civ 1184, [2006] 1 WLR 505 ... **III HUM [35.2B]**
Westminster City Council v O'Reilly [2003] EWCA Civ 1007, [2004] 1 WLR 195, [2003] 34 LS Gaz R 31, (2003) Times, 21 August, 147 Sol Jo LB 817, [2003] All ER (D) 26 (Jul) ...... **II SCA [27.1]**
Westminster City Council v Peart (1991) 24 HLR 389, CA ...... **III L&T [112.4], [223.3]**
Westminster Property Management Ltd, Re, Official Receiver v Stern [2000] 2 BCLC 396, [2000] 05 LS Gaz R 33, [2000] NLJR 21, 144 Sol Jo LB 80; affd [2000] 2 BCLC 396, CA ...... **III COM [51]**
Weston v Gribben [2006] EWCA Civ 1425, 150 Sol Jo LB 1463, [2006] All ER (D) 29 (Nov) ...... **III LIM [39.9A]**
Weston v Law Society [1998] 31 LS Gaz R 35, 142 Sol Jo LB 250 ...... **III SOL [66.4]**
Westport, The (No 3) [1966] 1 Lloyd's Rep 342 ...... **II SCA [18.26]**
Westport, The (No 4) [1968] 2 Lloyd's Rep 559 ...... **II SCA [18.25]**
Whalley v M'Connell. See Walley v M'Connell
Wharfland Ltd v South London Co-operative Building Co Ltd [1995] 2 EGLR 21, [1995] 30 EG 95 ...... **III PTY [2.4]**
Wheeler v Evans [1948] 1 KB 459, [1947] 2 All ER 740, CA ...... **III L&T [84.2]**
Wheeler v Mercer [1957] AC 416, [1956] 3 All ER 631, [1956] 3 WLR 841, 100 Sol Jo 836, 168 Estates Gazette 520, HL ...... **III L&T [41.3]**
Whelton Sinclair (a firm) v Hyland [1992] 2 EGLR 158, [1992] 41 EG 112, CA ...... **III L&T [17.5]**
Whiston v London Strategic Health Authority [2010] EWCA Civ 195, [2010] 3 All ER 452, [2010] 1 WLR 1582, 113 BMLR 110, (2010) Times, 4 May, [2010] All ER (D) 56 (Mar) ...... **III LIM [17.4A]**
Whitbread (Hotels) Ltd, Petitioners 2002 SLT 178, sub nom Whitbread (Hotels) Ltd v Walkmore (95) Ltd Times, 18 January, OH ...... **III LIM [38.2A]**
Whitbread West Pennines Ltd v Reedy [1988] ICR 807, 20 HLR 642, CA ... **III L&T [244.3]**
White, Re 102 LJP 71. See White v Hyde
White v Glass (1989) Times, 18 February, CA ...... **III LIM [38.8]**
White v Hyde [1933] P 105, [1933] All ER Rep 226, 77 Sol Jo 251, 149 LT 96, sub nom Re White 102 LJP 71, 49 TLR 325 ...... **III SOL [89.2]**
White v Wareing [1992] 1 EGLR 271, CA ...... **III L&T [69.7]**
White v White [2001] UKHL 9, [2001] 2 All ER 43, [2001] 1 All ER (Comm) 1105 [2001] 1 WLR 481, [2001] RTR 379, [2001] 1 Lloyd's Rep 679, [2001] NLJR 350, 145 Sol Jo LB 67 ...... **III EUR [388.1], [388.4]**
White v White [2003] EWCA Civ 924, [2004] 2 FLR 321, [2003] All ER (D) 252 (May) ...... **III REG [58.2D], [59.1], [59.1A]**
Whitefield v General Medical Council [2002] UKPC 62, [2003] IRLR 39, (2002) Times, 29 November ...... **III HUM [30.2]**
Whitfield v North Durham Health Authority [1995] 6 Med LR 32, 24 BMLR 39, [1995] PIQR P 361, CA ...... **III LIM [38.8]**
Whitehouse v Loi Lee [2009] EWCA Civ 375, [2009] 31 EG 74, [2009] 20 EG 103 (CS), (2009) Times, 13 July, [2009] 2 P & CR D28, [2009] All ER (D) 130 (May) .. **III L&T [71.8]**

Z

ZH (by his litigation friend) v Metropolitan Police Comr [2013] EWCA Civ 69, [2013] 3 All ER 113, [2013] 1 WLR 3021, (2013) Times, 12 April, [2013] All ER (D) 157 (Feb) .... **III EQU [29.1]; III HUM [25.3A], [27.1A]; III MEN [31.1], [38.4]**
ZH (Tanzania) v Secretary of State for the Home Department [2011] UKSC 4, [2011] 2 AC 166, [2011] 2 All ER 783, [2011] 2 WLR 148, [2011] 1 FCR 221, [2011] 1 FLR 2170, [2011] Fam Law 468, [2011] NLJR 212, (2011) Times, 08 February, 155 Sol Jo (no 5) 30, [2011] All ER (D) 02 (Feb) .... **III HUM [30.10]**
ZS (Jamaica) v Secretary of State for the Home Department [2012] EWCA Civ 1639, [2012] All ER (D) 144 (Dec) .... **III HUM [30.10]**
Zafiro, The, John Carlbom & Co Ltd v Owners of Zafiro [1960] P 1, [1959] 2 All ER 537, [1959] 3 WLR 123, [1959] 1 Lloyd's Rep 359, 103 Sol Jo 509 .... **II SCA [19.12]**
Zarb v Parry [2011] EWCA Civ 1306, [2012] 2 All ER 320, [2012] 1 WLR 1240, [2012] 1 P & CR 227, [2012] 1 EGLR 1, [2011] 46 LS Gaz R 21, [2011] NLJR 1633, [2012] 03 Estates Gazette 88, [2011] 47 EG 105 (CS), (2011) Times, 10 December, [2011] All ER (D) 100 (Nov) .... **III LIM [52.5]**
Zarvos v Pradhan [2003] EWCA Civ 208, [2003] 2 P & CR 122, [2003] 18 LS Gaz R 35, [2003] NLJR 404, [2003] 26 EG 180, 147 Sol Jo LB 301, [2003] 2 P & CR D11, [2003] 13 EG 114 (CS) .... **III L&T [22.12]**
Zealander v Lainghomes Ltd (2000) 2 TCLR 724 .... **III ARB [29]**
Zenith Investments (Torquay) Ltd v Kammins Ballrooms Co Ltd (No 2) [1971] 3 All ER 1281, [1971] 1 WLR 1751, 22 P & CR 1090, 115 Sol Jo 929, 221 Estates Gazette 147, CA .... **III L&T [37.1]**
Zeta, The. See Mersey Docks and Harbour Board v Turner, The Zeta
Zeus, The (1889) 13 PD 188, 6 Asp MLC 312, 37 WR 127, 59 LT 344 ...... **II SCA [18.14]**
Zirje, The [1989] 1 Lloyd's Rep 493 .... **II SCA [18.4]**
Zissis v Lukomski [2006] EWCA Civ 341, [2006] 1 WLR 2778, [2006] 15 EG 135 (CS), (2006) Times, 24 April, [2006] All ER (D) 63 (Apr) .... **III RE [60K.4]**
Zoan v Rouamba [2000] 2 All ER 620, [2000] 1 WLR 1509, [2000] NLJR 99, CA . **III CON [24B]**
Zohrab v Smith (1847) 5 Dow & L 635, 17 LJQB 174, Cox M & H 106, 12 Jur 603, 2 Saund & C 231, 11 LTOS 133 .... **II CCA [129.1]**
Zoumbas v Secretary of State for the Home Department [2013] UKSC 74, [2013] 1 WLR 3690, (2014) Times, 13 January, [2013] All ER (D) 310 (Nov) .... **III HUM [30.10]**
Zuliani v Veira [1994] 1 WLR 1149, PC .... **III SOL [85.6], [85.7]**
Zurich Professional Ltd v Karim [2006] EWHC 3355 (QB), [2006] All ER (D) 238 (Dec) .... **III SOL [62]**

Decisions of the European Court of Justice are listed below numerically. These decisions are also included in the preceding alphabetical list.

C-26/62: Algemene Transport-en Expeditie Onderneming van Gend en Loos NV v Nederlandse Belastingadministratie [1963] ECR 1, [1963] CMLR 105, ECJ . **III EUR [9], [11], [388.2], [388.4]**
C-6/64: Costa (Flaminio) v ENEL [1964] ECR 585, ECJ .... **III EUR [1], [4]**
48/65: Lütticke (Alfons) GmbH v EC Commission [1966] ECR 19, [1966] CMLR 378, ECJ .... **III EUR [9]**
9/70: Grad v Finanzamt Traunstein [1970] ECR 825, [1971] CMLR 1, ECJ ...... **III EUR [9]**
43/71: Politi SAS v Ministry for Finance of the Italian Republic [1971] ECR 1039, sub nom Politi SAS v Ministero delle Finanze: 43/71 [1973] CMLR 60, ECJ .... **III EUR [9]**
93/71: Leonesio v Italian Ministry for Agriculture and Forestry [1972] ECR 287, [1973] CMLR 343, ECJ .... **III EUR [9]**
C-41/74: Van Duyn v Home Office [1975] Ch 358, [1975] 3 All ER 190, [1974] ECR 1337, [1975] 2 WLR 760, [1975] 1 CMLR 1, 119 Sol Jo 302, ECJ .... **III EUR [9]**
43/75: Defrenne v Sabena [1981] 1 All ER 122, [1976] ECR 455, [1976] 2 CMLR 98, [1976] ICR 547, ECJ .... **III EUR [9]**
111/75: Impresa Costruzioni Comm Quirino Mazzalai v Ferrovia del Renon [1976] ECR 657, [1977] 1 CMLR 105, ECJ .... **III EUR [389.2]**
135/77: Bosch (Robert) GmbH v Hauptzollamt Hildesheim [1978] ECR 855, ECJ ... **III EUR [389.1]**

C-392/93: R v HM Treasury, ex p British Telecommunications plc [1996] QB 615, [1996] ECR I-1631, [1996] 3 WLR 203, [1996] All ER (EC) 411, [1996] 2 CMLR 217, [1996] IRLR 300, (1996) Times, 16 April, ECJ .... **III EUR [11]**
C-5/94: R v Ministry of Agriculture, Fisheries and Food, ex parte Hedley Lomas (Ireland) Ltd [1996] ALL ER (EC) 493 .... **III EUR [11]**
C-178/94, C-179/94, C-188/94, C-189/94 and C-190/94: Dillenkofer v Germany [1997] QB 259, [1996] ECR I-4845, [1997] 2 WLR 253, [1996] All ER (EC) 917, [1996] 3 CMLR 469, [1997] IRLR 60, ECJ .... **III EUR [11]**
C-194/94: CIA Security International SA v Signalson [1996] ECR I-2201, [1996] All ER (EC) 557, [1996] 2 CMLR 781, ECJ .... **III EUR [9]**
C-283/94, C-291/94 and C-292/94: Denkavit Internationaal BV, VITIC Amsterdam BV and Voormeer BV v Bundesamt für Finanzen [1996] ECR I-5063, [1996] STC 1445, ECJ .... **III EUR [11]**
C-168/95: Arcaro (criminal proceedings against) [1996] ECR I-4705, [1997] All ER (EC) 82, [1997] 1 CMLR 179, ECJ .... **III EUR [10], [388.4]**
C-373/95: Maso and Gazzetta v Instituto Nazionale della Prevedenza Sociale (INPS) and Italy [1997] ECR I-4051, [1997] 3 CMLR 1244, ECJ .... **III EUR [389.2]**
C-408/95: Eurotunnel SA v SeaFrance (formerly Societe Nouvelle d'Armement Transmanche SA) (International Duty Free Confederation and others, interveners) [1997] All ER (D) 65, ECJ .... **III EUR [389.2]**
C-319/96: Brinkmann Tabakfabriken GmbH v Skatteministeriet [1998] ECR I-5255, [1998] 3 CMLR 673, ECJ .... **III EUR [11]**
C-326/96: Levez v TH Jennings (Harlow Pools) Ltd [1999] All ER (EC) 1, [1998] ECR I-7835, [1999] 2 CMLR 363, [1999] ICR 521, [1999] IRLR 36, 608 IRLB 3, ECJ ..... **II CCA [7.5]**
C-126/97: Eco Swiss China Time Ltd v Benetton International NV [1999] 2 All ER (Comm) 44, [2000] 5 CMLR 816, ECJ .... **III ARB [32]**
C-237/97: Administrative Proceedings Concerning AFS Intercultural Programs Finland ry [1999] ECR I-825, [2000] 1 CMLR 845, ECJ .... **III CON [88]**
C-375/97: General Motors Corpn v Yplon SA [1999] ECR I-5421, [1999] All ER (EC) 865, [1999] 3 CMLR 427, [2000] RPC 572, ECJ .... **III PAT [41.2]**
C-156/98: Germany v EC Commission [2000] ECR I-6857, ECJ .... **III EUR [388.4]**
C-223/98: Re Adidas AG [1999] ECR I-7081, [1999] 3 CMLR 895, ECJ .... **III EUR [388.4]**
C-301/98: KVS International BV v Minister van Landbouw, Natuurbeheer en Visserij [2000] ECR I-3583, ECJ .... **III EUR [388.4]**
C-397/98: Metallgesellschaft Ltd v IRC and A-G [2001] Ch 620, [2001] 2 WLR 1497, [2001] All ER (EC) 496, [2001] STC 452, ECJ .... **III LIM [36.6]**
C-397, 410/98: Hoechst AG v IRC and A-G [2001] Ch 620, [2001] 2 WLR 1497, [2001] ECR I-1727, [2001] All ER (EC) 496, [2001] STC 452, sub nom Metallgesellschaft, Hoechst AG and Hoechst Ltd v IRC and AG [2001] 2 CMLR 700, ECJ .... **III LIM [36.3]**
C-411/98: Ferlini v Centre hospitalier de Luxembourg [2000] ECR I-8081, [2000] All ER (D) 1239, ECJ .... **III EUR [9]**
C-443/98: Unilever Italia SpA v Central Food SpA [2000] ECR I-7535, [2001] 1 CMLR 566, ECJ .... **III EUR [9]**
C-184/99: Grzelczyk v Centre Public d'Aide Sociale d'Ottignies-Louvain-la-Neuve [2001] ECR I-6193, [2003] All ER (EC) 385, [2002] 1 CMLR 543, [2002] ICR 566, (2001) Times, 16 November, [2001] All ER (D) 57 (Sep), ECJ .... **III EQU [9.2]**
C-191/99: Kvaerner plc v Staatssecretaris van Financiën [2002] QB 385, [2001] 3 WLR 1663, [2001] ECR I-4447, [2001] 3 CMLR 14, [2001] STC 1007, ECJ ...... **III EUR [388.4]**
C-118/00: Larsy v Institut National d'Assusurances Sociales pour Travailleurs Indépendants (INASTI) [2001] ECR I-5063, [2001] All ER (D) 317 (Jun), ECJ .. **III EUR [11]**
C-253/00: Muñoz (Antonio) y Cia SA v Frumar Ltd [2003] Ch 328, [2002] ECR I-7289, [2003] 3 WLR 58, [2003] All ER (EC) 56, [2002] 3 CMLR 734, (2002) Times, 20 November, [2002] All ER (D) 82 (Sep), ECJ .... **III EUR [9]**
C-400/00: Club-Tour, Viagens e Turismo SA v Garrido [2002] ECR I-4051, ECJ ..... **III CON [90.1]**
C-101/01: Lindqvist (Criminal proceedings against) [2004] QB 1014, [2004] All ER (EC) 561, [2004] 2 WLR 1385, (2003) Times, 13 November, [2004] IP & T 469, [2003] All ER (D) 77 (Nov), ECJ .... **III DAT [12.2]**
C-206/01: Arsenal Football Club plc v Reed [2003] Ch 454, [2003] 3 WLR 450, [2003] All ER (EC) 1, [2003] 1 CMLR 345, [2003] RPC 144, [2002] NLJR 1808, ECJ .... **III PAT [41.2]**

C-224/01: Köbler v Austria [2004] QB 848, [2004] All ER (EC) 23, [2004] 2 WLR 976, [2003] 3 CMLR 1003, (2003) Times, 3 October, [2003] All ER (D) 73 (Oct), ECJ ... **III EUR [11], [388.5]**
C-408/01: Adidas-Salomon AG v Fitnessworld Trading Ltd (2003) Times, 31 October, ECJ .... **III PAT [41.2]**
C-491/01: R v Secretary of State for Health, ex p British American Tobacco (Investments) Ltd: [2002] All ER (D) 126 (Dec), Times, 13 December, ECJ .. **III EUR [388.4], [389.2]**
C-159/02: Turner v Grovit [2004] All ER (EC) 485, [2004] 2 All ER (Comm) 381, [2004] 3 WLR 1193, [2004] 2 Lloyd's Rep 169, [2004] IRLR 899, (2004) Times, 29 April, [2004] All ER (D) 259 (Apr), ECJ .... **II SCA [38.1A]**
C-201/02: The Queen, on the application of Delena Wells v Secretary of State for Transport, Local Government and the Regions ECLI:EU:C:2004:12 .... **III EUR [9]**
C-105/03: Pupino (criminal proceedings against) [2006] QB 83, [2005] ECR I-5285, [2005] 3 WLR 1102, [2006] All ER (EC) 142, (2005) Times, 14 July, [2005] All ER (D) 147 (Jun), ECJ .... **III EUR [10], [388.3]**
C-173/03: Traghetti del Mediterraneo SpA v Italy [2006] ECR I-5177, [2006] All ER (EC) 983, [2006] 3 CMLR 586, [2006] All ER (D) 101 (Jun), ECJ .... **III EUR [11]**
C-209/03: R (on the application of Bidar) v Ealing London Borough Council [2005] QB 812, [2005] ECR I-2119, [2005] All ER (EC) 687, [2005] 2 WLR 1078, [2005] ELR 404, (2005) Times, 29 March, [2005] All ER (D) 235 (Mar), ECJ .... **III EQU [9.2]**
C-212/04: Adeneler v Ellinikos Organismos Galaktos [2006] ECR I-6057, [2007] All ER (EC) 82, [2006] 3 CMLR 867, [2006] IRLR 716, [2006] All ER (D) 25 (Jul), ECJ ... **III EUR [11]**
C-13/05: Chacon v Navas v Eurest Colectividadades , [2006] IRLR 706 .... **III EQU [6.2]**
C-303/06: Coleman v Attridge Law (2008) C-303/06, ECLI:EU:C:2008:415, [2008] ECR I-5603, [2008] All ER (EC) 1105, [2008] 3 CMLR 777, [2008] IRLR 722, [2008] ICR 1128, (2008) Times, 29 July, [2008] All ER (D) 245 (Jul), CSRC vol 32 iss 9/1, ECJ .... **III EQU [6.3]**
C-463/06: Odenbreit v FBTO Schadeverzekeringen NV [2007] ECR I-11321, [2008] 2 All ER (Comm) 733, [2008] Lloyd's Rep IR 354, [2007] All ER (D) 206 (Dec), ECJ .... **III EUR [165.1], [280.1]**
C-533/06: O_2 Holdings Ltd v Hutchison 3G UK Ltd [2008] 3 CMLR 397, [2008] RPC 905, [2008] IP & T 1069, (2008) Times, 17 June, [2008] All ER (D) 155 (Jun), ECJ .... **III PAT [41.2]**
C-185/07: Allianz SpA v West Tankers Inc C-185/07, [2009] AC 1138, [2009] ECR I-663, [2009] 3 WLR 696, [2009] 1 Lloyd's Rep 413, (2009) Times, 13 February, [2009] All ER (D) 82 (Feb), sub nom West Tankers Inc v Riunione Adriatica di Sicurta SpA, The Front Comor: C-185/07 [2009] 1 All ER (Comm) 435, [2009] All ER (EC) 491, [2008] 2 Lloyd's Rep 661 .... **II SCA [38.1A]; III EUR [155.1], [182.1], [272.1], [304.1]**
C-420/07: Orams v Apostolides [2009] ECR I-3571, [2011] 2 WLR 324, [2010] 1 All ER (Comm) 950, (2009) Times, 1 May, [2009] All ER (D) 89 (May), ECJ ...... **III EUR [305.3], [306.1]**
C-358/08: Aventis Pasteur SA v OB; sub nom O'Byrne v Aventis Pasteur SA (2009) Times, 9 December, [2009] All ER (D) 228 (Dec), ECJ .... **III LIM [14.3], [39.9A]**
C-282/10: Dominguez v Centre Informatique Du Centre Ouest Atlantique [2012] 2 CMLR 437, [2012] IRLR 321, [2012] ICR D23, ECJ .... **III EUR [10]**
C-412/10: Homawoo v GMF Assurances SA (2010/C 301/12), unreported, ECJ .. **III PID [4A]**
C-619/10: Trade Agency Ltd v Seramico Investments Ltd C-619/10, [2012] NLJR 1218, [2012] All ER (D) 66 (Sep) .... **III EUR [305.2], [305.3]**
C-335/11: HK Danmark v Dansk almennyttigt Boligselskab (2013) ECLI:EU:C:2013:222, [2014] All ER (EC) 1161, [2013] 3 CMLR 527, [2013] IRLR 571, [2013] ICR 851, 132 BMLR 58, [2013] EqLR 528, ECJ .... **III EQU [6.2]**
C-337/11: HK Danmark v Dansk Arbejdsgiverforening (2013) ECLI:EU:C:2013:222, [2014] All ER (EC) 1161, [2013] 3 CMLR 527, [2013] IRLR 571, [2013] ICR 851, 132 BMLR 58, [2013] EqLR 528, ECJ .... **III EQU [6.2]**
C-645/11:Sapir, Re EU:C:2013:228 .... **III EUR [155.4]**
C-49/12: Sunico, Re EU:C:2013:545 .... **III EUR [155.4]**
C-131/12: Google Spain SL v Agencia Espanola de proteccion de Datos (AEPD) [2014] QB 1022, [2014] 3 WLR 659, [2014] 2 All ER (Comm) 301, [2014] All ER (EC) 717, [2014] 3 CMLR 1247, [2014] IP & T 675, 164 NLJ 7607, 36 BHRC 589, [2014] All ER (D) 124 (May), ECJ .... **III DAT [11.4]**

Part II

General Jurisdiction

GENERAL NOTES ON JURISDICTION OF THE CIVIL COURTS

II GEN [1]

Jurisdiction of the Court of Appeal and the High Court The purpose of this Part is to set out the legislative base of the general jurisdiction of the civil courts that is, the Court of Appeal, the High Court and the County Court. The Senior Courts Act 1981 consolidated previous legislation and is now the main statutory authority under which justice is administered in the High Court and the Court of Appeal. The decision-making powers of judges derive from their appointment under the Act to carry out the judicial functions assigned to them under its provisions. The jurisdiction which litigants invoke is partly inherent in the Senior Courts, partly conferred in general terms by the Senior Courts 1981 and partly conferred by other statutes. Whereas Part 3 covers the jurisdiction conferred on the High Court by individual statutes, Part 2 sets out the jurisdiction conferred or, as the case may be, restated by the Senior Courts Act 1981.

II GEN [2]

Jurisdiction of the County Court In the same way, the jurisdiction of the County Court is made up of general jurlsdiction conferred by the County Courts Act 1984 (consolidating previous Acts going back to 1846) and specialist jurisdiction conferred by other Acts and instruments. Part 2 covers the general jurisdiction only.

II GEN [2A]

A new Supreme Court The new Supreme Court was created in October 2009. The Supreme Court replaces the judicial function of the House of Lords. The body of courts previously known as the Supreme Court (High Court, Crown Court, Court of Appeal) are known instead as the Senior Courts and the title of the Supreme Court Act 1981 has been changed to the Senior Courts Act 1981. It should also be noted that section 45 of the Mental Capacity Act 2005 establishes a superior court of record called the Court of Protection in place of the office of that name in the pre-existing Supreme Court.

II GEN [3]

High Court and County Courts Jurisdiction Order 1991 Straddling the High Court and the county court system is the High Court and County Courts Jurisdiction Order 1991, SI 1991/724, the text of which is set out later in this Part. Its effect is to regulate the flow of civil litigation so that it is started, managed, tried and enforced at a level which is appropriate to the value and weight of the case.

II GEN [4]

The Civil Procedure Act 1997: the Courts Act 2003 Two further pieces of legislation have sought to unify the administration of civil justice in the Senior Courts and the County Court. The Civil Procedure Act 1997 brought the rules and the rule-making functions together, leading to the introduction of a single set of rules, the Civil Procedure Rules 1998, which apply to all civil courts. The Courts Act 2003 has brought together other functions, such as court fees and the registration of judgments, and created a Head and Deputy Head of Civil Justice. The text of s 7 of the Civil Procedure Act 1997 which puts freezing orders and search orders on a statutory footing is set out at **II SCA [38.4]** as part of the commentary on the jurisdiction to grant injunctions provided by s 37 of the Senior Courts Act 1981. Material provisions of the Courts Act 2003 are set out later in this title at **II CA [1]–[6]**.

II GEN [5]

Practice and procedure The statutory text set out in this Part is directed at jurisdiction and the general powers of the courts in relation to civil matters. The section by section commentary draws attention to case-law development of the jurisdiction. It also cross-refers to the relevant rules of procedure, practice directions and forms.

II GEN [6]

Enforcement The enforcement of judgments has been the subject of 21st Century reforms, starting with s 98 of the Courts Act 2003 (Register of judgments and orders) and s 99 (High Court Writs of Execution). The relevant statutory text is at **II CA [5]–II CA [6]** with supporting commentary. More recently further changes have been made by the Tribunals, Courts and Enforcement Act 2007. See the text and commentary at **II TCE [1]** onwards.

Table of contents

SENIOR COURTS ACT 1981

(c 54)

PART I
CONSTITUTION OF THE SENIOR COURTS

THE SENIOR COURTS

II SCA [6]

1. The Senior Courts

(1) The Senior Courts of England and Wales shall consist of the Court of Appeal, the High Court of Justice and the Crown Court, each having such jurisdiction as is conferred on it by or under this or any other Act.

(2) . . .

II SCA [6.1]

A new Supreme Court The creation of a new Supreme Court was one of many important changes made by the Constitutional Reform Act 2005, with effect from 1 October 2009. The new Supreme Court is an appellate body whose jurisdiction includes hearing appeals which formerly were heard by the House of Lords. At the same time, by the same legislative process, the old Supreme Court (comprising the Court of Appeal, the High Court and the Crown Court) was renamed as the Senior Courts. Consequential amendments run right through the Act but mostly in Part I, the revised text of which is set out below.

THE COURT OF APPEAL

II SCA [7]

2. The Court of Appeal

(1) The Court of Appeal shall consist of:

- (a) ex-officio judges, and
- (b) ordinary judges, of whom the maximum full-time equivalent number is 39.

(2) The following shall be ex-officio judges of the Court of Appeal—

- (a) . . .
- (b) any person who was Lord Chancellor before 12 June 2003;
- (c) any judge of the Supreme Court who at the date of his appointment was, or was qualified for appointment as, an ordinary judge of the Court of Appeal or held an office within paragraphs (d) to (g);
- (d) the Lord Chief Justice;
- (e) the Master of the Rolls;
- (f) the President of the Queen's Bench Division;
- (g) the President of the Family Division; and
- (h) the Chancellor of the High Court;

but a person within paragraph (b) or (c) shall not be required to sit and act as a judge of the Court of Appeal unless at the request of the Lord Chief Justice he consents to do so.

(2A) The Lord Chief Justice may nominate a judicial office holder (as defined in section 109(4) of the Constitutional Reform Act 2005) to exercise his function under subsection (2) of making requests to persons within paragraphs (b) and (c) of that subsection.

(3) An ordinary judge of the Court of Appeal (including the vice-president, if any, of either division) shall be styled "Lords Justice of Appeal" or "Lady Justice of Appeal".

(4) Her Majesty may by Order in Council from time to time amend subsection (1) so as to increase or further increase the maximum full-time equivalent number of ordinary judges of the Court of Appeal.

(4A) It is for the Lord Chancellor to recommend to Her Majesty the making of an Order under subsection (4).

(5) No recommendation shall be made to Her Majesty in Council to make an Order under subsection (4) unless a draft of the Order has been laid before Parliament and approved by resolution of each House of Parliament.

(6) The Court of Appeal shall be taken to be duly constituted notwithstanding any vacancy in the office of . . . Lord Chief Justice, Master of the Rolls, President of the Queen's Bench Division, President of the Family Division or Chancellor of the High Court.

(7) For the purposes of this section the full-time equivalent number of ordinary judges is to be calculated by taking the number of full-time ordinary judges and adding, for each ordinary judge who is not a full-time ordinary judge, such fraction as is reasonable.

II SCA [7.1]

Judicial titles Section 62 of the Courts Act 2003, at **II CA [1]**, provides for the appointment of certain members of the Court of Appeal to be Head of Civil Justice and Deputy Head of Civil Justice. Section 63 of that Act substitutes a new sub-s (3), above. Section 64 empowers the Lord Chancellor, by order, to change the judicial title of certain members of the Court of Appeal and other judicial office holders.

II SCA [7A]

3. Divisions of Court of Appeal

(1) There shall be two divisions of the Court of Appeal, namely the criminal division and the civil division.

(2) The Lord Chief Justice shall be president of the criminal division of the Court of Appeal, and the Master of the Rolls shall be president of the civil division of that court.

(3) The Lord Chief Justice may, after consulting the Lord Chancellor appoint one of the ordinary judges of the Court of Appeal as vice-president of both divisions of that court, or one of those judges as vice-president of the criminal division and another of them as vice-president of the civil division.

(4) When sitting in a court of either division of the Court of Appeal in which no ex-officio judge of the Court of Appeal is sitting, the vice-president (if any) of that division shall preside.

(5) Any number of courts of either division of the Court of Appeal may sit at the same time.

(6) The Lord Chief Justice may nominate a judicial office holder (as defined in section 109(4) of the Constitutional Reform Act 2005) to exercise his functions under subsection (3).

THE HIGH COURT

II SCA [8]

4. The High Court

(1) The High Court shall consist of—

- (a) . . .
- (b) the Lord Chief Justice;
- (ba) the President of the Queen's Bench Division;
- (c) the President of the Family Division;
- (d) the Chancellor of the High Court;

(dd) the Senior Presiding Judge;
(ddd) the vice-president of the Queen's Bench Division; and
(e) the puisne judges of that court, of whom the maximum full-time equivalent number is 108.

(2) The puisne judges of the High Court shall be styled "Justices of the High Court".

(3) All the judges of the High Court shall, except where this Act expressly provides otherwise, have in all respects equal power, authority and jurisdiction.

(4) Her Majesty may by Order in Council from time to time amend subsection (1) so as to increase or further increase the maximum full-time equivalent number of puisne judges of the High Court.

(4A) It is for the Lord Chancellor to recommend to Her Majesty the making of an Order under subsection (4).

(5) No recommendation shall be made to Her Majesty in Council to make an Order under subsection (4) unless a draft of the Order has been laid before Parliament and approved by resolution of each House of Parliament.

(6) The High Court shall be taken to be duly constituted notwithstanding any vacancy in the office of . . . Lord Chief Justice, President of the Queen's Bench Division, President of the Family Division, Chancellor of the High Court or Senior Presiding Judge and whether or not an appointment has been made to the office of vice-president of the Queen's Bench Division.

(7) For the purposes of this section the full-time equivalent number of puisne judges is to be calculated by taking the number of full-time puisne judges and adding, for each puisne judge who is not a full-time puisne judge, such fraction as is reasonable.

II SCA [8.1]

The jurisdiction of Masters Masters are not part of the High Court but it has been held that they are judicial officers who are attached to the Queen's Bench and Chancery Divisions of the High Court and that their judgments are judgments of the High Court; they therefore have jurisdiction to hear proceedings under s 6 of the Justice and Security Act 2013 as 'proceedings before the High Court': *Abdule v Foreign and Commonwealth Office* [2018] EWHC 692 (QB), 28 March 2018.

II SCA [8A]

5. Divisions of High Court

(1) There shall be three divisions of the High Court namely—
(a) the Chancery Division, consisting of the Chancellor of the High Court, who shall be president thereof, and such of the puisne judges as are for the time being attached thereto in accordance with this section;
(b) the Queen's Bench Division, consisting of the Lord Chief Justice, the President of the Queen's Bench Division, the vice-president of the Queen's Bench Division and such of the puisne judges as are for the time being so attached thereto; and
(c) the Family Division, consisting of the President of the Family Division and such of the puisne judges as are for the time being so attached thereto.

(2) The puisne judges of the High Court shall be attached to the various Divisions by direction given by the Lord Chief Justice after consulting the Lord Chancellor; and any such judge may with his consent be transferred from one Division to another by direction given by the Lord Chief Justice after consulting the Lord Chancellor, but shall be so transferred only with the concurrence of the senior judge of the Division from which it is proposed to transfer him.

(3) Any judge attached to any Division may act as an additional judge of any other Division at the request of the Lord Chief Justice made with the concurrence of both of the following—

(a) the senior judge of the Division to which the judge is attached;

(b) the senior judge of the Division of which the judge is to act as an additional judge.

(4) Nothing in this section shall be taken to prevent a judge of any Division (whether nominated under section 6(2) or not) from sitting, whenever required, in a divisional court of another Division or for any judge of another Division.

(5) Without prejudice to the provisions of this Act relating to the distribution of business in the High Court, all jurisdiction vested in the High Court under this Act shall belong to all the Divisions alike.

(6) The Lord Chief Justice may nominate a judicial office holder (as defined in section 109(4) of the Constitutional Reform Act 2005) to exercise his functions under subsection (2).

II SCA [8B]

6. The Patents, Admiralty and Commercial Courts

(1) There shall be—

(a) as part of the Chancery Division, a Patents Court; and

(b) as parts of the Queen's Bench Division, an Admiralty Court and a Commercial Court.

(2) The judges of the Patents Court, of the Admiralty Court and of the Commercial Court shall be such of the puisne judges of the High Court as the Lord Chief Justice may, after consulting the Lord Chancellor, from time to time nominate to be judges of the Patents Court, Admiralty Judges and Commercial Judges respectively.

(3) The Lord Chief Justice may nominate a judicial office holder (as defined in section 109(4) of the Constitutional Reform Act 2005) to exercise his functions under subsection (2).

II SCA [8B.1]

Patents Court Proceedings in the Patents Court are subject to **CPR 63** and the supporting Practice Direction. See also chapter 23 of the Chancery Guide in Part 1 at **CHG 23.1**. For the jurisdiction conferred by other Acts see the Part III title PATENTS and OTHER INTELLECTUAL PROPERTY at **III PAT**.

II SCA [8B.2]

Admiralty Court and Commercial Court For further procedural guidance see **CPR 58 [1]** and **CPR PD 58** (Commercial Court), **CPR 61 [1]** and **CPR PD 61** (Admiralty Court) and the Admiralty and Commercial Courts Guide at **ACG App 6**.

II SCA [8B.3]

The Business and Property Courts of England and Wales Since 1 October 2017 the specialist jurisdictions (including the Admiralty Court, the Commercial Court, the Patents Court and the Chancery Division generally) were brought together as a specialist group, known as the Business and Property Courts of England and Wales (B&PCs). They operate out of the Rolls Building in Fetter Lane, London EC4A 1NL and this is the address for the issue of proceedings in these courts. Outside London, courts within B&PC are established in Birmingham, Bristol, Cardiff, Leeds and Manchester, each with their own District Registry for the issue of claims. The claim form should be marked in the top right hand corner 'Business and Property Courts'. The courts incorporate within this arrangement are:

(a) the Chancery Division of the High Court, which is sub-divided into Business List, Competition List, Financial List, Insolvency and Companies List, Intellectual Property List, Property, Trusts and Probate List and Revenue List;

(b) the Commercial Court (QBD);

(c) the Technology and Construction Court (QBD);

(d) the Circuit Commercial Court (QBD); and

(e) the Admiralty Court (QBD).

See CPR Part 57A and Practice Direction 57AA – Business and Property Courts for detailed provisions on the breakdown into courts and lists, the business assigned to each, the titles of claims, and the transfer of proceedings.

II SCA [8C]

7. Power to alter Divisions or transfer certain courts to different Divisions

(1) Her Majesty may from time to time, on a recommendation of the Lord Chancellor and the judges mentioned in subsection (2), by Order in Council direct that—

(a) any increase or reduction in the number of Divisions of the High Court; or

(b) the transfer of any of the courts mentioned in section 6(1) to a different Division,

be carried into effect in pursuance of the recommendation.

(2) Those judges are . . . the Lord Chancellor, the Lord Chief Justice, the Master of the Rolls, the President of the Queen's Bench Division, the President of the Family Division and the Chancellor of the High Court.

(3) An Order in Council under this section may include such incidental, supplementary or consequential provisions as appear to Her Majesty necessary or expedient, including amendments of provisions referring to particular Divisions contained in this Act or any other statutory provision.

(4) Any Order in Council under this section shall be subject to annulment in pursuance of a resolution of either House of Parliament.

OTHER PROVISIONS

II SCA [9]

9. Assistance for transaction of judicial business...

(1) A person within any entry in column 1 of the following Table may, subject to the proviso at the end of that Table, at any time, at the request of the appropriate authority, act—

(a) as a judge of a relevant court specified in the request; or

(b) if the request relates to a particular division of a relevant court so specified, as a judge of that court in that division.

Table

1 Judge or ex-judge	**2 Where competent to act on request**
1. A judge of the Court of Appeal.	The High Court and the Crown Court.
2. A person who has been a judge of the Court of Appeal.	The Court of Appeal, the High Court, the family court, the county court and the Crown Court.
3. A puisne judge of the High Court.	The Court of Appeal.
4. A person who has been a puisne judge of the High Court.	The Court of Appeal, the High Court, the family court, the county court and the Crown Court.
4A. The Senior President of Tribunals.	The Court of Appeal and the High Court.
5. A Circuit judge.	The High Court and the Court of Appeal.
6. A Recorder or a person within subsection (1ZB).	The High Court.

The entry in column 2 specifying the Court of Appeal in relation to a Circuit judge only authorises such a judge to act as a judge of a court in the criminal division of the Court of Appeal.

(1ZA) The Senior President of Tribunals is to be treated as not being within any entry in column 1 of the Table other than entry 4A.

(1ZB) A person is within this subsection if the person—

(a) is a Chamber President, or a Deputy Chamber President, of a chamber of the Upper Tribunal or of a chamber of the First-tier Tribunal,

(b) is a judge of the Upper Tribunal by virtue of appointment under paragraph 1(1) of Schedule 3 to the Tribunals, Courts and Enforcement Act 2007,

(c) is a transferred-in judge of the Upper Tribunal (see section 31(2) of that Act),

(d) is a deputy judge of the Upper Tribunal (whether under paragraph 7 of Schedule 3 to, or section 31(2) of, that Act), or

(e) is the President of Employment Tribunals (England and Wales) or the President of Employment Tribunals (Scotland).

(1A) A person shall not act as a judge by virtue of subsection (1) after the day on which he attains the age of 75.

(2) In subsection (1)—

the appropriate authority" means—

(a) the Lord Chief Justice or a judicial office holder (as defined in section 109(4) of the Constitutional Reform Act 2005) nominated by him to exercise his functions under this section, or

(b) at any time when the Lord Chief Justice or the nominated judicial office holder is unable to make such a request himself, or there is a vacancy in the office of Lord Chief Justice, the Master of the Rolls;

"relevant court", in the case of a person within any entry in column 1 of the Table, means a court specified in relation to that entry in column 2 of the Table,

. . .

(2A) The power of the appropriate authority to make a request under subsection (1) is subject to subsections (2B) to (2D).

(2B) In the case of a request to a person within entry 1, 3, 4A, 5 or 6 in column 1 of the Table, the appropriate authority may make the request only after consulting the Lord Chancellor.

(2C) In any other case the appropriate authority may make a request only with the concurrence of the Lord Chancellor.

(2CA) In the case of a request to a person within entry 5 or 6 in column 1 of the Table to act as a judge of the High Court, the appropriate authority may make the request only if the person is a member of the pool for requests under subsection (1) to persons within that entry.

(2D) In the case of a request to a Circuit judge... to act as a judge of the Court of Appeal, the appropriate authority may make the request only with the concurrence of the Judicial Appointments Commission.

(3) The person to whom a request is made under subsection (1) must comply with the request, but this does not apply to—

(a) a request made to a person who has been a judge of the Court of Appeal,

(b) a request made to a person who has been a puisne judge of the High Court and is not a judge of the Court of Appeal, or

(c) a request made to the Senior President of Tribunals if the holder of that office is a judge of the Court of Session or of the High Court, or Court of Appeal, in Northern Ireland.

it shall be the duty of the person to whom the request is made to comply with it.

(4) Without prejudice to section 24 of the Courts Act 1971 (temporary appointment of deputy Circuit judges...), if it appears to the Lord Chief Justice, after consulting the Lord Chancellor, that it is expedient as a temporary measure to

make an appointment under this subsection in order to facilitate the disposal of business in the High Court or the Crown Court or any other court or tribunal to which persons appointed under this subsection may be deployed, he may appoint a person qualified for appointment as a puisne judge of the High Court to be a deputy judge of the High Court during such period or on such occasions as the Lord Chief Justice may, after consulting the Lord Chancellor, think fit; and during the period or on the occasions for which a person is appointed as a deputy judge under this subsection, he may act as a puisne judge of the High Court.

(4A) No appointment of a person as a deputy judge of the High Court shall be such as to extend beyond the day on which he attains the age of 70, but this subsection is subject to section 26(4) to (6) of the Judicial Pensions and Retirement Act 1993 (Lord Chancellor's power to authorise continuance in office up to the age of 75).

(5) Every person while acting under this section shall, subject to subsections (6) and (6A), be treated for all purposes as, and accordingly may perform any of the functions of, a judge of the court in which he is acting.

(6) A person shall not by virtue of subsection (5)—

- (a) be treated as a judge of the court in which he is acting for the purposes of section 98(2) or of any statutory provision relating to—
  - (i) the appointment, retirement, removal or disqualification of judges of that court;
  - (ii) the tenure of office and oaths to be taken by such judges; or
  - (iii) the remuneration, allowances or pensions of such judges; or
- (b) subject to section 27 of the Judicial Pensions and Retirement Act 1993 be treated as having been a judge of a court in which he has acted only under this section.

(6A) A Circuit judge, Recorder or person within subsection (1ZB) shall not by virtue of subsection (5) exercise any of the powers conferred on a single judge by sections 31, 31B, 31C and 44 of the Criminal Appeal Act 1968 (powers of single judge in connection with appeals to the Court of Appeal and appeals from the Court of Appeal to the Supreme Court).

(7) [. . .]

(8) Such remuneration and allowances as the Lord Chancellor may, with the concurrence of the Minister for the Civil Service, determine may be paid out of money provided by Parliament—

- (a) to any person who has been—
  - (i) a judge of the Supreme Court; or
  - (ii) a judge of the Court of Appeal; or
  - (iii) a judge of the High Court,

  and is by virtue of subsection (1) acting as mentioned in that subsection;
- (b) to any deputy judge of the High Court appointed under subsection (4).

(8A) A person may be removed from office as a deputy judge of the High Court—

- (a) only by the Lord Chancellor with the agreement of the Lord Chief Justice, and
- (b) only on—
  - (i) the ground of inability or misbehaviour, or
  - (ii) a ground specified in the person's terms of appointment.

(8B) Subject to the preceding provisions of this section, a person appointed under subsection (4) is to hold and vacate office as a deputy judge of the High Court in accordance with the terms of the person's appointment, which are to be such as the Lord Chancellor may determine.

(9) The Lord Chief Justice may nominate a senior judge (as defined in section 109(5) of the Constitutional Reform Act 2005) to exercise functions of the Lord Chief Justice under this section.

II SCA [9.1]

Judge who lacks authority The fact that a person sitting as a High Court Judge lacks the necessary authority does not invalidate the exercise of jurisdiction where the judge-in-fact and all those involved honestly believe that he or she has that authority: *Coppard v Customs and Excise Comrs* [2003] EWCA Civ 511, [2003] QB 1428, [2003] 3 All ER 351.

The decision in a High Court matter of a district judge who has not been appointed under s 9 to sit as a High Court judge is not necessarily void. Where the district judge has reasonably assumed that the case was validly listed before him it may be saved by the common law doctrine of *de facto* jurisdiction: *Baldock v Webster* [2004] EWCA Civ 1869, [2006] QB 315, [2005] All ER 655.

II SCA [10]

10. Appointment of judges of Senior Courts

(1) Whenever the office of Lord Chief Justice, Master of the Rolls, President of the Queen's Bench Division, President of the Family Division or Chancellor of the High Court is vacant, Her Majesty may, on the recommendation of the Lord Chancellor, by letters patent appoint a qualified person to that office.

(2) Subject to the limits on full-time equivalent numbers for the time being imposed by sections 2(1) and 4(1), Her Majesty may, on the recommendation of the Lord Chancellor, from time to time by letters patent appoint qualified persons as Lords Justices of Appeal or as puisne judges of the High Court.

(3) No person shall be qualified for appointment—

- (a) as Lord Chief Justice, Master of the Rolls, President of the Queen's Bench Division, President of the Family Division or Chancellor of the High Court, unless he is qualified for appointment as a Lord Justice of Appeal or is a judge of the Court of Appeal;
- (b) as a Lord Justice of Appeal, unless—
  - (i) he satisfies the judicial-appointment eligibility condition on a 7-year basis; or
  - (ii) he is a judge of the High Court; or
- (c) as a puisne judge of the High Court, unless—
  - (i) he satisfies the judicial-appointment eligibility condition on a 7-year basis; or
  - (ii) he is a Circuit judge who has held that office for at least 2 years.

(4) A person appointed—

- (a) to any of the offices mentioned in subsection (1),
- (b) as a Lord Justice of Appeal, or
- (c) as a puisne judge of the High Court,

shall take the required oaths as soon as may be after accepting office.

(5) In the case of a person appointed to the office of Lord Chief Justice, the required oaths are to be taken in the presence of all of the following—

- (a) the Master of the Rolls;
- (b) the President of the Queen's Bench Division;
- (c) the President of the Family Division;
- (d) the Chancellor of the High Court.

(6) Where subsection (5) applies but there is a vacancy in one or more (but not all) of the offices mentioned in that subsection, the required oaths are to be taken in the presence of the holders of such of the offices as are not vacant.

(6A) Where the holder of an office mentioned in subsection (5) is incapable of exercising the functions of the office, the office is to be treated as vacant for the purposes of subsection (6).

(7) In the case of a person appointed other than to the office of Lord Chief Justice, the required oaths are to be taken in the presence of—

- (a) the Lord Chief Justice, or
- (b) a judicial office holder (as defined in section 109(4) of the Constitutional Reform Act 2005) nominated by him for this purpose.

(8) In this section "required oaths" means—

- (a) the oath of allegiance, and
- (b) the judicial oath,

as set out in the Promissory Oaths Act 1868.

II SCA [10A]

11. Tenure of office of judges of Senior Courts

(1) This section applies to the office of any judge of the Senior Courts.

(2) A person appointed to an office to which this section applies shall vacate it on the day on which he attains the age of seventy years unless by virtue of this section he has ceased to hold it before then.

(3) A person appointed to an office to which this section applies shall hold that office during good behaviour, subject to a power of removal by Her Majesty on an address presented to Her by both Houses of Parliament.

(3A) It is for the Lord Chancellor to recommend to Her Majesty the exercise of the power of removal under subsection (3).

(4) A person holding an office within section 2(2)(d) to (g) shall vacate that office on becoming a judge of the Supreme Court.

(5) A Lord Justice of Appeal shall vacate that office on becoming an ex-officio judge of the Court of Appeal.

(6) A puisne judge of the High Court shall vacate that office on becoming a judge of the Court of Appeal.

(7) A person who holds an office to which this section applies may at any time resign it by giving the Lord Chancellor notice in writing to that effect.

(8) The Lord Chancellor, if satisfied by means of a medical certificate that a person holding an office to which this section applies—

- (a) is disabled by permanent infirmity from the performance of the duties of his office; and
- (b) is for the time being incapacitated from resigning his office,

may, subject to subsection (9), by instrument under his hand declare that person's office to have been vacated; and the instrument shall have the like effect for all purposes as if that person had on the date of the instrument resigned his office.

(9) A declaration under subsection (8) with respect to a person shall be of no effect unless it is made—

- (a) in the case of any of the Lord Chief Justice, the Master of the Rolls, President of the Queen's Bench Division, President of the Family Division or Chancellor of the High Court, with the concurrence of two others of them;
- (b) in the case of a Lord Justice of Appeal, with the concurrence of the Master of the Rolls;
- (c) in the case of a puisne judge of any Division of the High Court, with the concurrence of the senior judge of that Division.

(10) . . .

II SCA [10B]

12. Salaries etc of judges of Senior Courts

(1) Subject to subsections (2) and (3), there shall be paid to judges of the Senior Courts . . . such salaries as may be determined by the Lord Chancellor with the concurrence of the Minister for the Civil Service.

(2) Until otherwise determined under this section, there shall be paid to the judges mentioned in subsection (1) the same salaries as at the commencement of this Act.

(3) Any salary payable under this section may be increased, but not reduced, by a determination or further determination under this section.

(4) [. . .]

(5) Salaries payable under this section shall be charged on and paid out of the Consolidated Fund.

(6) There shall be paid out of money provided by Parliament to any judge of the Court of Appeal or of the High Court, in addition to his salary, such allowances as may be determined by the Lord Chancellor with the concurrence of the Minister for the Civil Service.

(7) Pensions shall be payable to or in respect of the judges mentioned in subsection (1) in accordance with section 2 of the Judicial Pensions Act 1981 or, in the case of a judge who is a person to whom Part I of the Judicial Pensions and Retirement Act 1993 applies, in accordance with that Act.

II SCA [11]

13. Precedence of judges of Senior Courts

(1) When sitting in the Court of Appeal—

(a) the Lord Chief Justice and the Master of the Rolls shall rank in that order; and

(b) judges of the Supreme Court and persons who have been Lord Chancellor shall rank next after the Master of the Rolls and, among themselves, according to the priority of the dates on which they respectively became judges of the Supreme Court or Lord Chancellor, as the case may be.

(2) Subject to subsection (1)(b), the President of the Queen's Bench Division shall rank next after the Master of the Rolls.

(2A) The President of the Family Division shall rank next after the President of the Queen's Bench Division.

(3) The Chancellor of the High Court shall rank next after the President of the Family Division.

(4) The vice-president or vice-presidents of the divisions of the Court of Appeal shall rank next after the Chancellor of the High Court; and if there are two vice-presidents of those divisions, they shall rank, among themselves, according to the priority of the dates on which they respectively became vice-presidents.

(5) The Lords Justices of Appeal (other than the vice-president or vice-presidents of the divisions of the Court of Appeal) shall rank after the ex-officio judges of the Court of Appeal and, among themselves, according to the priority of the dates on which they respectively became judges of that court.

(6) The puisne judges of the High Court shall rank next after the judges of the Court of Appeal and, among themselves, according to the priority of the dates on which they respectively became judges of the High Court.

II SCA [12]

14. Power of judge of Senior Courts or Crown Court to act in cases relating to rates and taxes

(1) A judge of the Senior Courts or of the Crown Court shall not be incapable of acting as such in any proceedings by reason of being, as one of a class of ratepayers, taxpayers or persons of any other description, liable in common with others to pay, or contribute to, or benefit from, any rate or tax which may be increased, reduced or in any way affected by those proceedings.

(2) In this section "rate or tax" means any rate, tax, duty or liability, whether public, general or local, and includes—

(a) any fund formed from the proceeds of any such rate, tax, duty or liability; and

(b) any fund applicable for purposes the same as, or similar to, those for which the proceeds of any such rate, tax, duty or liability are or might be applied.

II SCA [12.1]

Judicial bias For a recent statement and application of the principles relating to actual and perceived judicial bias, and for citation of the relevant authority, see *R v Bow Street Metropolitan Stipendiary Magistrate, ex p Pinochet Ugarte (No 2)* [2000] 1 AC 119, [1999] 1 All ER 577, HL. For a comprehensive and authoritative analysis of these principles both in general and as applied to a number of specific situations, see *Locabail (UK) Ltd v Bayfield Properties Ltd* [2000] QB 451, [2000] 1 All ER 65, CA. An allegation of bias is not sustainable if based solely on the religion, ethnic or national origin, gender, age, class, means or sexual orientation of the judge hearing the case: *Seer Technologies Ltd v Abbas* [2000] 07 LS Gaz R 40, (2000) Times, 16 March.

Since the coming into force of the Human Rights Act 1998, matters of bias tend to be raised as depriving the litigant of his or her fundamental right, under Article 6, to an independent and impartial tribunal: see **III HUM [28]**.

PART II
JURISDICTION

(I) THE COURT OF APPEAL

II SCA [13]

15. General jurisdiction of Court of Appeal

(1) The Court of Appeal shall be a superior court of record.

(2) Subject to the provisions of this Act, there shall be exercisable by the Court of Appeal—

(a) all such jurisdiction (whether civil or criminal) as is conferred on it by this or any other Act; and

(b) all such other jurisdiction (whether civil or criminal) as was exercisable by it immediately before the commencement of this Act.

(3) For all purposes of or incidental to—

(a) the hearing and determination of any appeal to the civil division of the Court of Appeal; and

(b) the amendment, execution and enforcement of any judgment or order made on such an appeal,

the Court of Appeal shall have all the authority and jurisdiction of the court or tribunal from which the appeal was brought.

(4) It is hereby declared that any provision in this or any other Act which authorises or requires the taking of any steps for the execution or enforcement of a judgment or order of the High Court applies in relation to a judgment or order of the civil division of the Court of Appeal as it applies in relation to a judgment or order of the High Court.

II SCA [13.1]

Jurisdiction conferred by any other Act Appeals lie direct to the Court of Appeal from County Court (County Courts Act 1984 s 77 see para **II CCA [75]**) and from the Lands Tribunal (Lands Tribunal Act 1949 s 3(4)), among others.

II SCA [13.2]

Inherent powers of the Court of Appeal The Court of Appeal's inherent powers, preserved by this section, may be declared in practice directions as well as in judgments of the court; they include the power to propound a more stringent test for permission to appeal to the Court of Appeal in cases which have already been through one level of appeal without success: *Nascimento v Kerrigan* (1999) Times, 23 June, CA. See also the powers recited in **CPR 52.10**.

II SCA [13.2A]

Bail in proceedings for judicial review: Supreme Court Act 1981 s 15(3) It was decided in *Sezek v Secretary of State for the Home Department* [2001] Imm AR 657, CA, that the Court of Appeal could exercise the same original jurisdiction as the Administrative Court to grant bail to an applicant for judicial review, such jurisdiction having been established in *R v Secretary of State for the Home Department, ex p Turkoglu* [1988] QB 398, [1987] 2 All ER 823, CA.

II SCA [13.3]

Practice and procedure For the current practice and procedure of the Court of Appeal see **CPR 52** and the supporting Practice Direction at **CPR PD 52**. Recent changes are explained in *Tanfern Ltd v Cameron-Macdonald* [2000] 2 All ER 801, [2000] 1 WLR 1311, CA. Appeal notices should be presented on Form N161.

II SCA [13.4]

Assignment of appeals to Court of Appeal In addition to appeals which come to the Court of Appeal directly by appellant's notice to that Court there are also appeals which come there on assignment, as provided by s 57 of the Access to Justice Act 1999 at **CPR 52 [14]**.

II SCA [13.5]

Power of Court of Appeal to reopen its own decision The Court of Appeal may reopen its own decisions where it is effectively the final court of appeal (there being no prospect of permission for leave to appeal to the Lords) and fresh evidence shows something which would undermine public confidence in the administration of justice, such as judicial bias: *Taylor v Lawrence* [2002] EWCA Civ 90, [2003] QB 528, [2002] 2 All ER 353. For the procedure see **CPR 52.17**.

II SCA [13.6]

Jurisdiction of the court below Section 15(3) provides that the Court of Appeal has all the powers of the court below. It was held, in *Dar International FEF Co v Aon Ltd* [2003] EWCA Civ 1833, [2004] 3 All ER 986, [2004] 1 WLR 1395 that this includes the power to reinstate an order for security for costs which had lapsed and which the trial judge had refused to reinstate or extend.

II SCA [14]

16. Appeals from High Court

(1) Subject as otherwise provided by this or any other Act (and in particular to the provision in section 13(2)(a) of the Administration of Justice Act 1969 excluding appeals to the Court of Appeal in cases where leave to appeal from the High Court directly to the Supreme Court is granted under Part II of that Act), or as provided by any order made by the Lord Chancellor under section 56(1) of the Access to Justice Act 1999, the Court of Appeal shall have jurisdiction to hear and determine appeals from any judgment or order of the High Court.

(2) An appeal from a judgment or order of the High Court when acting as a prize court shall not be to the Court of Appeal, but shall be to Her Majesty in Council in accordance with the Prize Acts 1864 to 1944.

II SCA [14.1]

Appeals only available against orders of the court An appeal to the Court of Appeal lies only against an order of the court, and not against a finding in a reasoned judgment;

accordingly an order which omits the material decision should be made the subject of a request for amendment before it can become the subject of an appeal: *Infante v Rai – Radiotelevisione Italiana SpA* [1999] 11 LS Gaz R 70, CA.

II SCA [14.2]

Orders concerning juries The powers conferred by s 16(1) include the power to hear an appeal against a decision to discharge a civil jury: *Gladding v Channel 4 Television Corpn* [1999] EMLR 475, CA.

II SCA [14.3]

Second appeals Second appeals require the permission of the Court of Appeal which will be granted only where there is an important point of principle or some other compelling reason. See s 55 of the Access to Justice Act 1999 at **CPR 52 [12]**, which is restated as a rule of court in **CPR 52.13**.

II SCA [15]

17. Applications for new trial

(1) Where any cause or matter, or any issue in any cause or matter, has been tried in the High Court, any application for a new trial thereof, or to set aside a verdict, finding or judgment therein, shall be heard and determined by the Court of Appeal except where rules of court made in pursuance of subsection (2) provide otherwise.

(2) As regards cases where the trial was by a judge alone and no error of the court at the trial is alleged, or any prescribed class of such cases, rules of court may provide that any such application as is mentioned in subsection (1) shall be heard and determined by the High Court.

(3) Nothing in this section shall alter the practice in bankruptcy.

II SCA [16]

18. Restrictions on appeals to Court of Appeal

(1) No appeal shall lie to the Court of Appeal—

(a) except as provided by the Administration of Justice Act 1960 from any judgment of the High Court in any criminal cause or matter;

(b) from any order of the High Court or any other court or tribunal allowing an extension of time for appealing from a judgment or order;

(c) from any order, judgment or decision of the High Court or any other court or tribunal which, by virtue of any provision (however expressed) of this or any other Act, is final;

(d) from a decree absolute of *divorce or* nullity of marriage by a party who, having had time and opportunity to appeal from the decree nisi on which that decree was founded, has not appealed from the decree nisi;

(dd) from a divorce order;

(e) [. . .]

(f) [. . .]

(fa) from a dissolution order, nullity order or presumption of death order under Chapter 2 of Part 2 of the Civil Partnership Act 2004 that has been made final, by a party who, having had time and opportunity to appeal from the conditional order on which that final order was founded, has not appealed from the conditional order;

(g) except as provided by Part I of the Arbitration Act 1996, from any decision of the High Court under that Part;

(h) [. . .]

(1A) [. . .]

(1B) [. . .]

(2) [. . .]

II SCA [16.1]

Amendments to section 18 This section is printed as amended by the Access to Justice Act 1999.

II SCA [16.2]

Criminal cause As regards civil contempt, this is not a criminal cause or matter. An order made for criminal contempt may be appealed to the Court of Appeal under the Administration of Justice Act 1960 s 13. The appellate jurisdiction is exercised by the Criminal Division of the Court of Appeal under s 53: see para **II SCA [51]**.

The jurisdiction conferred on the High Court by Pt VI of the Criminal Justice Act 1988 (enforcement of confiscation by restraint orders) is civil; proceedings under it are outside the exception for any criminal cause or matter: *United States Government v Montgomery* [1999] 1 All ER 84, CA; affd [2001] UKHL 3, [2001] 1 All ER 815, [2001] 1 WLR 196.

II SCA [16.2A]

Decision which is final See for example s 28A which provides that any decision of the High Court on a case stated by magistrates in a non-criminal matter is final.

II SCA [16.3]–II SCA [16.4]

Arbitration Rights of appeal, subject to obtaining leave of the court, are provided by Arbitration Act 1996 ss 12(6), 17(4), 18(5), 21(6), 24(6), 25(5), 32(5), (6), 42(5), 44(7), 45(5), (6), 50(5), 56(7), 67(4), 68(4), 69(8), 77(4) and 79(6) in particular. The possibility of appealing against decisions under other sections, such as s 9 is not affected: *Inco Europe Ltd v First Choice Distribution (a Firm)* [2000] 2 All ER 109, [2000] 1 WLR 586, CA.

II SCA [16.5]

Requirement of permission Section 54 of the Access to Justice Act 1999 at **CPR 52 [11]** provides for the requirement of permission to appeal to be set by rules of court. See, in particular, **CPR 52.3**. The fact that permission to appeal is granted does not preclude the making of an order for security for costs: *Federal Bank of the Middle East Ltd v Hadkinson* [2000] 2 All ER 395, (1999) Times, 7 December, CA.

II SCA [16.6]

Routes of appeal The routes of appeal are determined in some cases by the Access to Justice Act 1999 (Destination of Appeals) Order 2000 (SI 2000/1071), made under s 56 of the Access to Justice Act 1999 at **CPR 52 [13]**. The terms of the order are set out at **CPR 52 [15]**.

(II) THE HIGH COURT

GENERAL JURISDICTION

II SCA [17]

19. General jurisdiction of High Court

(1) The High Court shall be a superior court of record.

(2) Subject to the provisions of this Act, there shall be exercisable by the High Court—

(a) all such jurisdiction (whether civil or criminal) as is conferred on it by this or any other Act; and

(b) all such other jurisdiction (whether civil or criminal) as was exercisable by it immediately before the commencement of this Act (including jurisdiction conferred on a judge of the High Court by any statutory provision).

(3) Any jurisdiction of the High Court shall be exercised only by a single judge of that court, except in so far as it is—

(a) by or by virtue of rules of court or any other statutory provision required to be exercised by a divisional court; or

(b) by rules of court made exercisable by a master, registrar or other officer of the court, or by any other person.

(4) The specific mention elsewhere in this Act of any jurisdiction covered by subsection (2) shall not derogate from the generality of that subsection.

II SCA [17.1]

Other jurisdiction exercisable by the High Court The reference, in s 19(2)(b), to all the other jurisdiction not expressly conferred by statute, is to the "inherent" jurisdiction exercised, or exercisable, by the Court in its long history of development. Powers are "inherent" if they are needed to enable a court to fulfil itself properly and effectively: per Lord Morris in *Connelly v DPP* [1964] AC 1254 at 1301, [1964] 2 All ER 401 at 409, HL and Lord Diplock in *Bremer Vulkan Schiffbau und Maschinenfabrik v South India Shipping Corpn Ltd* [1981] AC 909, [1981] 1 All ER 289 at 295, HL. For example, the High Court has the same inherent power as the Court of Appeal (considered at para **II SCA [13.5]**) to re-open its own decisions where this is necessary to maintain its character as a court of justice: *Seray-Wurle v Hackney London Borough Council* [2002] EWCA Civ 909, [2002] 3 All ER 448, (2002) Times, 4 July.

II SCA [17.2]

Declarations In *Greenwich Healthcare National Health Service Trust v London Quadrant Housing Trust* [1998] 3 All ER 437, [1998] 1 WLR 1749, Lightman J held that the court's power to grant declarations included the power to declare that a person was not entitled to apply for an injunction to prevent proposed development. The court has power to grant a declaration of non-liability, although it is an unusual remedy: *Messier-Dowty Ltd v Sabena SA* [2001] 1 All ER 275, [2000] 1 WLR 2040, CA. As to declarations of non-criminality of past acts, see *Imperial Tobacco Ltd v A-G* [1981] AC 718, [1980] 1 All ER 866, and as to lawfulness of future acts, see the cases on medical treatment noted at **III MEN [3]**. There is nothing, in Art 6 of the Human Rights Convention or elsewhere, to prevent a court from declaring that, on the balance of probabilities, a defendant has contravened the Banking Act 1987: *Financial Services Authority v Rourke* [2001] 46 LS Gaz R 36.

In a case in which two rival administrations claimed to be the legitimate government of Libya the court decided that it could and should grant a declaration that the applicant bank was entitled to act on the instructions of one, but not the other: *British Arab Commercial Bank plc v National Transitional Council of the State of Libya* [2011] EWHC 2274 (Comm), [2011] NLJR 1215, 155 Sol Jo (no 33) 31.

II SCA [18]

20. Admiralty jurisdiction of High Court

(1) The Admiralty jurisdiction of the High Court shall be as follows, that is to say—

- (a) jurisdiction to hear and determine any of the questions and claims mentioned in subsection (2);
- (b) jurisdiction in relation to any of the proceedings mentioned in subsection (3);
- (c) any other Admiralty jurisdiction which it had immediately before the commencement of this Act; and
- (d) any jurisdiction connected with ships or aircraft which is vested in the High Court apart from this section and is for the time being by rules of court made or coming into force after the commencement of this Act assigned to the Queen's Bench Division and directed by the rules to be exercised by the Admiralty Court.

(2) The questions and claims referred to in subsection (1)(a) are—

- (a) any claim to the possession or ownership of a ship or to the ownership of any share therein;
- (b) any question arising between the co-owners of a ship as to possession, employment or earnings of that ship;
- (c) any claim in respect of a mortgage of or charge on a ship or any share therein;
- (d) any claim for damage received by a ship;
- (e) any claim for damage done by a ship;

(f) any claim for loss of life or personal injury sustained in consequence of any defect in a ship or in her apparel or equipment, or in consequence of the wrongful act, neglect or default of—
    (i) the owners, charterers or persons in possession or control of a ship; or
    (ii) the master or crew of a ship, or any other person for whose wrongful acts, neglects or defaults the owners, charterers or persons in possession or control of a ship are responsible,

being an act, neglect or default in the navigation or management of the ship, in the loading, carriage or discharge of goods on, in or from the ship, or in the embarkation, carriage or disembarkation of persons on, in or from the ship;

(g) any claim for loss of or damage to goods carried in a ship;
(h) any claim arising out of any agreement relating to the carriage of goods in a ship or to the use or hire of a ship;
(j) any claim—
    (i) under the Salvage Convention 1989;
    (ii) under any contract for or in relation to salvage services; or
    (iii) in the nature of salvage not falling within (i) or (ii) above;

or any corresponding claim in connection with an aircraft;

(k) any claim in the nature of towage in respect of a ship or an aircraft;
(l) any claim in the nature of pilotage in respect of a ship or an aircraft;
(m) any claim in respect of goods or materials supplied to a ship for her operation or maintenance;
(n) any claim in respect of the construction, repair or equipment of a ship or in respect of dock charges or dues;
(o) any claim by a master or member of the crew of a ship for wages (including any sum allotted out of wages or adjudged by a superintendent to be due by way of wages);
(p) any claim by a master, shipper, charterer or agent in respect of disbursements made on account of a ship;
(q) any claim arising out of an act which is or is claimed to be a general average act;
(r) any claim arising out of bottomry;
(s) any claim for the forfeiture or condemnation of ship or of goods which are being or have been carried, or have been attempted to be carried, in a ship, or for the restoration of a ship or any such goods after seizure, or for droits of Admiralty.

(3) The proceedings referred to in subsection (1)(b) are—
(a) any application to the High Court under [the Merchant Shipping Act 1995];
(b) any action to enforce a claim for damage, loss of life or personal injury arising out of—
    (i) a collision between ships; or
    (ii) the carrying out of or omission to carry out a manoeuvre in the case of one or more of two or more ships; or
    (iii) non-compliance, on the part of one or more of two or more ships, with the collision regulations;
(c) any action by shipowners or other persons under the [Merchant Shipping Act 1995] for the limitation of the amount of their liability in connection with a ship or other property.

(4) The jurisdiction of the High Court under subsection (2)(b) includes power to settle any account outstanding and unsettled between the parties in relation to the ship, and to direct that the ship, or any share thereof, shall be sold, and to make such other order as the court thinks fit.

(5) Subsection (2)(e) extends to—

(a) any claim in respect of a liability incurred under Chapter III of Part VI of the Merchant Shipping Act 1995; and

(b) any claim in respect of a liability falling on the International Oil Pollution Compensation Fund, or on the International Oil Pollution Compensation Fund 1992, or on the International Oil Pollution Compensation Fund 2003, under Chapter IV of Part VI of the Merchant Shipping Act 1995.

(6) In subsection (2)(j)—

(a) the "Salvage Convention 1989" means the International Convention on Salvage, 1989 as it has effect under section 224 of the Merchant Shipping Act 1995;

(b) the reference to salvage services includes services rendered in saving life from a ship and the reference to any claim under any contract for or in relation to salvage services includes any claim arising out of such a contract whether or not arising during the provision of the services;

(c) the reference to a corresponding claim in connection with an aircraft is a reference to any claim corresponding to any claim mentioned in sub-paragraph (i) or (ii) of paragraph (j) which is available under section 87 of the Civil Aviation Act 1982.

(7) The preceding provisions of this section apply—

(a) in relation to all ships or aircraft, whether British or not and whether registered or not and wherever the residence or domicile of their owners may be;

(b) in relation to all claims, wherever arising (including, in the case of cargo or wreck salvage, claims in respect of cargo or wreck found on land); and

(c) so far as they relate to mortgages and charges, to all mortgages or charges, whether registered or not and whether legal or equitable, including mortgages and charges created under foreign law:

Provided that nothing in this subsection shall be construed as extending the cases in which money or property is recoverable under any of the provisions of the Merchant Shipping Act 1995.

II SCA [18.1]

Admiralty jurisdiction of the High Court Since 1 October 2017 the Admiralty Court has been grouped with other specialist jurisdictions within the Queen's Bench and Chancery Divisions as one of the Business and Property Courts of England and Wales. Admiralty proceedings may be issued out of the High Court of Justice at the Rolls Building, Fetter Lane, London EC4A 1NL or out of the District Registries in Birmingham, Bristol, Cardiff, Leeds or Manchester. See Part 57A and Practice Direction 57AA – Business and Property Courts.

II SCA [18.2]

Procedure Proceedings are regulated by CPR 61 (see para **CPR 61**).

There are provisions on offers to settle collision claims. Where an offer is made within the terms of Part 61 and the other side fails to do better, the offeree is liable for the offeror's costs after the expiry of the 21 days for acceptance. But the costs will not necessarily be awarded on an indemnity basis since provisions to this effect in Part 36 are not replicated in Part 61: *MIOM 1 Ltd v Sea Echo ENE (No 2)* [2011] EWHC 2715 (Admlty), [2011] All ER (D) 51 (Nov).

II SCA [18.3]

Precedents Any such application must be made in accordance with CPR 61 and the Practice Direction which supplements it.

II SCA [18.4]

Time limits Actions to enforce a claim against a ship or her owners, for loss or damage caused by that ship to another ship, her cargo, freight or property aboard, or for damages for loss of life or personal injury caused by that ship to any person on board another ship must be commenced within two years of the date of the damage or loss, or injury or death (s 190 Merchant Shipping Act 1995). It has been held, in the case of a claim for psychiatric injury as a result of a collision, that time starts to run under s 190(3) from the date of the development of the injury rather than from the date of the collision: *Sweet v Owners of Blyth Lifeboat* (2002) Times, 22 February. Actions to recover contribution payable under ss 187–189 of the Merchant Shipping Act 1995 must be commenced within one year of payment (Merchant Shipping Act 1995 s 190(4)). The court may extend these time limits: see *Waddon v Whitecroft-Scovell Ltd* [1988] 1 All ER 996, [1988] 1 WLR 309 HL; *The Zirje* [1989] 1 Lloyd's Rep 493; *The Gaz Fountain* [1987] 2 Lloyd's Rep 151, *The Seaspeed America* [1990] 1 Lloyd's Rep 150; *The Al Tabith and Alanfushi* [1993] 2 Lloyd's Rep 214; affd [1995] 2 Lloyd's Rep 336, CA. The court must consider whether a good reason for an extension has been demonstrated, and only then proceed to exercise its discretion taking into account the balance of hardship. A claimant guilty of unreasonable delay in bringing his action may be penalised in costs; see, eg *The Humbergate* [1952] 1 Lloyd's Rep 168. An action to enforce a claim in salvage is time-barred unless judicial or arbitral proceedings have been commenced within two years of the termination of the services: Merchant Shipping Act 1995 s 224, Sch 11, art 23. In time charter-parties, "detention" has its normal meaning, which involves physical or geographical constraint: *The Jalagouri* [2000] 1 All ER (Comm) 700, CA. See also *The Bumbesti* [2000] QB 559, [2000] All ER 692, [1999] 2 Lloyd's Rep 481, CA.

II SCA [18.5]

Ship The Supreme Court Act 1981 s 24(1) defines a ship as a "vessel used in navigation". This excludes a gas float: *Wells v Gas Float Whitton No 2* [1897] AC 337, HL; or a flying boat: *Polpen Shipping Co Ltd v Commercial Union Assurance Co Ltd* [1943] KB 161, [1943] 1 All ER 162. "Navigation" is used in the sense of proceeding from an originating place A to a terminus B for the purpose of discharging people or cargo at the destination point: *Curtis v Wild* [1991] 4 All ER 172. A "jet ski" is not "a vessel used in navigation" because navigation is planned or ordered movement from one place to another on water, and a jet-ski is not so, see *Steedman v Schofield* [1992] 2 Lloyd's Rep 163. Vessels held to be ships include a fishing coble (*ex p Ferguson and Hutchinson* (1871) MLC 8); dumb barges (*The Mac* (1882) 7 PD 126, CA; *St John Pilot Commrs v Cumberland Railway and Coal Co* [1910] AC 208, PC); a floating hotel used in the offshore industry *Addison v Denholm Management* [1997] ICR 770, EAT (Sc); and a jack-up oil rig *Lavery v MacLeod (Inspector of Taxes)* [2000] STC (SCD) 118.

II SCA [18.6]

(a) Any claim to the possession or ownership of a ship or to the ownership of any share of a ship The court may grant a declaration under this paragraph that a party is entitled to be registered as the owner of a British ship: *The Bineta* [1966] 2 Lloyd's Rep 419. The court may entertain an action whether or not the parties are resident within the jurisdiction provided the ship is within the jurisdiction of the court, see sub-s (7)(a): *The Jupiter (No 2)* [1925] P 69, CA.

II SCA [18.7]

(b) Any question arising between the co-owners of a ship as to possession, employment or earnings of that ship For the law regarding the co-ownership of partnership property see the Partnership Act 1980 s 20 at **III PAR [40]**.

II SCA [18.8]

(d) Any claim for damage received by a ship Proceedings may be brought where the damage is caused by a collision between a ship and some other object not a ship, see *Mersey Docks and Harbour Board v Turner, The Zeta* [1893] AC 468, HL. Proceedings *in rem* cannot be commenced for this claim: Supreme Court Act 1981 s 21(2) (see para **II SCA [19]**).

II SCA [18.9]

(e) Any claim for damage done by a ship The damage must be the direct result or natural consequence of something done by those engaged in the navigation of the ship and caused by the ship herself: *The Vera Cruz (No 2)* (1884) 9 PD 96; *The Minerva* [1933] P 224, 46 Ll L Rep 212. See also *The Chr Knudsen* [1932] P 153, 43 Ll L Rep 423. Damage need not be physical in nature, eg a claim arising from the deliberate action by a vessel to prevent another from fishing resulting in loss: *The Dagmara and Ama Antxine* [1988] 1 Lloyd's Rep 431.

II SCA [18.10]

Apportionment of liability The Merchant Shipping Act 1995 s 187 provides for the apportionment of liability where damage is caused by the fault of two or more vessels. The Court of Appeal will not readily interfere with the trial judge's apportionment; see eg *The Maloja II* [1994] 1 Lloyd's Rep 374, CA.

In a case where there is no counterclaim, the claimant whose award is reduced because of being partly to blame should not normally be deprived of full costs. The contention that the award of costs should be reduced by the same proportion as the award of damages was rejected in *Krysia Maritime Ltd v Intership Ltd* [2008] EWHC 1880 (Admlty), [2008] All ER (D) 12 (Aug).

II SCA [18.11]

Interest The court has a jurisdiction to award simple interest under (a) its inherent jurisdiction and (b) pursuant to s 35A of the Supreme Court Act 1981. Where both ships are to blame for a collision the judgment is for half the difference between the claims assessed. But where either ship delays the assessment her owners should not be allowed to increase the amount of interest due by their delay: *The St Charles* (1927) 29 Ll L Rep 312. The proper approach in circumstances where two vessels are each held to be partly to blame for a collision is to add interest to each claim before striking the balance between each such claim and setting one off against the other: *The Botany Triad and The Lu Shan* [1993] 2 Lloyd's Rep 259.

II SCA [18.12]

Collisions abroad An action *in rem* can be instituted in England in respect of a collision between a ship and a wharf abroad: *United Africa Co Ltd v Tolten (Owners), The Tolten* [1946] 1 All ER 79, see s 21(3), (4) of the Supreme Court Act 1981(see para **II SCA [19]**). Even though a ship is arrested abroad by a foreign court the claimants may be able to bring an action *in rem* within the jurisdiction here provided there is no breach of faith: *The Mansoor* [1968] 2 Lloyd's Rep 218. See, however, the provisions of the Civil Jurisdiction and Judgments Act 1982.

II SCA [18.13]

(g) Loss of or damage to goods Proceedings may be taken by the owner of cargo against the vessel on which it was laden for damage done to the cargo, but no action *in rem* lies if the ship has changed hands since the damage was sustained: *The Igor* [1956] 2 Lloyd's Rep 271. A provision in the bill of lading that all disputes under it shall be judged in a foreign country does not oust the court's jurisdiction, although the court will normally stay proceedings instituted in this country in breach of such an agreement, it will not do so where, for example, the owners of the ship against whom the claim is brought have no real connection with the foreign country and merely wish to avoid giving security: *The Fehmarn* [1958] 1 All ER 333, [1958] 1 WLR 159, CA.

II SCA [18.14]

(h) Carriage of goods and use or hire of ship Para (h) of sub-s (2) of the Supreme Court Act 1981 covers claims whether in contract or in tort arising out of any agreement relating to the carriage of goods in a ship: *The St Elefterio* [1957] P 179, [1957] 2 All ER 374, and a claim arising from a sub-charter, including claims for contribution or indemnity under the Civil Liability (Contribution) Act 1978, see *The Hamburg Star* [1994] 1 Lloyd's Rep 399. The agreement need not be made by the parties to the action: *The Antonis P Lemos* [1985] AC 711, [1985] 1 All ER 695, HL. The claim must arise out of an agreement relating to the use of a ship or to the carriage of goods in a ship, and if an action *in rem* is to be commenced under s 21(4) of the Supreme Court Act 1981 must also arise in connection with the same ship. "Arising out of" means "connected with" and not "arising under": *The Antonis P Lemos* [1985] AC 711, [1985] 1 All ER 695, HL. Examples of claims within para (h) are claims: for freight, demurrage and expenses: *Cargo ex Argos* (1873) LR 5 PC 134; for damages for breach of a charter-party: *The Montrosa* [1917] P 1; *The Alina* (1880) 5 Ex D 227, CA, and *Gunnestad v Price* (1875) LR 10 Exch 65; by the holder of a bill of lading for breach of the contract of carriage in the bill of lading: *The Rona* (1882) 7 PD 247; for damage for breach of contract of towage: *The Isca* (1886) 12 PD 34; on a bill of lading for demurrage: *Pugsley & Co v Ropkins & Co Ltd* [1892] 2 QB 184; for damage to a barge through the negligent loading of the defendants causing a carboy of acid to crack: *Thames Steam Tug and Lighterage Co Ltd v Universal Purifiers Ltd* [1951] 1 Lloyd's Rep 187; by watermen for mooring, unmooring and carriage of crew: *Corps v Paddle Steamer Queen of the South* [1968] P 449, [1968] 1 All ER 1163. Cases where it has been held that there was no Admiralty jurisdiction are claims: by brokers for commission for effecting a charter-party: *The Nuova Raffaelina* (1871) LR 3 A & E 483; for demurrage under a contract to load a ship with coal in a specified time: *The Zeus* (1889) 13 PD 188; upon an award made under the arbitration clause in a charter-party – not a claim "arising out of an agreement": *The Beldis* [1936] P 51; *The Bumbesti* [1999] 2

Lloyd's Rep 481; cf *The Saint Anna* [1983] 1 Lloyd's Rep 637, [1983] 1 WLR 895. "Goods" includes "baggage" and applies to the belongings of a passenger or traveller, but not those on board a ship as employees of the shipowners in order to man and operate her. Claims relating to passengers' luggage and the carriage of passengers by sea are now governed by the Athens Convention contained in the Merchant Shipping Act 1995, Sch 6. The words of sub-s 2(h) should be given their ordinary wide meaning and may include use of a ship under a salvage agreement: *The Eschersheim* [1976] 1 All ER 920, [1976] 1 WLR 430, HL.

Under French law, the right to arrest a vessel in respect of a charterer's debt does not necessarily give rise to a right of action against the vessel itself or to security from the owner which responds to the charterer's liability: *The Spirit of Independence* [1999] 1 Lloyd's Rep 43.

In time charter-parties "detention" has its normal meaning, which involves physical or geographical constraint: *The Jalgouri* [2000] 1 All ER (Comm) 700, CA. See also *The Bumbesti* [2000] QB 559, [1999] 2 Lloyd's Rep 481, CA.

Where there exists a contract for services in the form of a time charter, specific performance may not be ordered: *The Scaptrade* [1983] 2 AC 694. But injunctive relief may be granted in appropriate cases even where the effect may be to compel performance: *Lauritzencool AB v Lady Navigation Inc* [2005] EWCA Civ 579, (2005) Times, 26 May.

II SCA [18.15]

(j) Salvage Salvage is a complex subject – reference should be made to specialist works. The Merchant Shipping Act 1995 gave effect to the International Convention on Salvage 1989 as set out in Schedule 11 to the Merchant Shipping Act 1995. The Convention is a comprehensive, but not exhaustive, code of the law relating to salvage. Reference to the old established authorities (from which in large part the Convention is derived) is still necessary. Article 1 of the 1989 Convention defines "salvage operation" as "any act or activity undertaken to assist a vessel or other property in danger in navigable waters or in any other waters whatsoever". The Convention does not apply to a salvage operation in UK inland waters in which all of the vessels are of inland navigation (Pt II, para 2(1)), there is no right in English law to recover a salvage award for services to vessels in non-tidal waters: *The Goring* [1988] AC 831, [1988] 1 All ER 641, HL. The Convention does not apply to drilling platforms on location when engaged in exploration, exploitation or production: Article 3 of the Convention. The word "salvage" is also frequently used to denote the reward payable for such services. A claim for damages for breach of a salvage agreement under a standard form of salvage contract is not a claim in the nature of salvage: *The Tesaba* [1982] 1 Lloyd's Rep 397. Effectual assistance of any kind voluntarily rendered to a vessel or her cargo in danger of loss or damage may entitle those who render it to salvage reward. Success is a pre-condition to a reward: see Article 12 of the Convention. Salvage will not be payable where the services are rendered against the expressed wishes of the owner of the salved property: see Article 19 of the Convention; *The Pretoria* (1920) 5 Ll L Rep 112.

A full treatment of the law of salvage is beyond the scope of this text – reference should be made to specialist texts eg Geoffrey Brice *Maritime Law of Salvage* (3rd edn, 1999).

II SCA [18.16]

Special compensation Article 14 of the 1989 Convention provides for "special compensation" in relation to salvage operations where the ship or cargo threatened damage to the environment. See *The Nagasaki Spirit* [1997] AC 455, HL.

II SCA [18.17]

Life salvage No remuneration is due from persons whose lives are saved, but the salvor of human life may be entitled to a share of the payment awarded in respect of the salvage of the vessel or other property or preventing or minimising damage to the environment: see art 16 of the 1989 Convention.

II SCA [18.18]

HM ships Section 230 of the Merchant Shipping Act 1995 provides that the law relating to civil salvage shall, with certain exceptions, apply in relation to salvage services rendered by or to any of HM ships in the same manner as if the ship belonged to a private person. No claim for salvage services by one of HM ships may be finally adjudicated upon without the consent of the Secretary of State for Defence.

II SCA [18.19]

Aircraft The court has jurisdiction under s 20(1)(a) in respect of claims for salvage of aircraft, apparel and cargo, and towage and pilotage arising whilst the aircraft was waterborne: s 24(1) of the Supreme Court Act 1981 (see para **II SCA [22]**). See *Re Glider Standard Austria SH 1964* [1965] P 463, [1965] 2 All ER 1022.

II SCA [18.20]

Interest Interest may be awarded on salvage awards: *The Aldora* [1975] QB 748, and will generally be awarded from the date of termination of the services: *The Yoliane* [1995] 2 Lloyd's Rep 7.

II SCA [18.21]

(k) Towage Ordinary towage is "the employment of means, outside her own powers of propulsion, to expedite the voyage of a vessel, when the use of such means is unattended by any danger and when nothing more is required than to expedite her progress: *The Princess Alice* (1849) 3 Wm Rob 138, and is of two kinds: ordinary and extraordinary. Ordinary towage is rendered by contract to expedite the outward or homeward voyage of a ship. Extraordinary towage is the service rendered by towing and thus rescuing from peril a ship disabled and in distress: *The Kingalock* (1854) 1 Ecc & Ad 263. "Any claim in the nature of towage" includes a claim for damages for breach of a contract of towage, or for negligence in carrying out such a contract: *The Isca* (1886) 12 PD 34. The jurisdiction in respect of towage also extends to towage of an aircraft while waterborne: see s 24(1) of the Supreme Court Act 1981 (see para **II SCA [22]**). For the distinction between towage and salvage, see *The Troilus* [1951] AC 820, [1951] 2 All ER 40, HL.

II SCA [18.22]

(l) Pilotage The jurisdiction in respect of pilotage extends to both ships and aircraft, provided in the latter case that the services were rendered while the aircraft was waterborne; see Supreme Court Act 1981 s 24(1) (see para **II SCA [22]**).

II SCA [18.23]

(m) Goods or materials supplied to a ship Containers hired to shipowners under a general leasing agreement without specification as to any particular use or ship are not goods supplied to a ship: *The River Rima* [1988] 2 All ER 641, [1988] 1 WLR 758, HL. Sums paid to reimburse sub-agents who have supplied goods for the operation of a ship fall within s 20(2)(m) of the Supreme Court Act 1981: *The Kommunar* [1997] 1 Lloyd's Rep 1. The following claims also fall within this head: food, drink, stationary and consumables supplied for the officers and crew or for passengers; and the provision of services in the form of officers and crew for the operation and manning of the vessel: *The Edinburgh Castle* [1999] 2 Lloyd's Rep 362; *Lavington International Ltd v Bareboat Charterers of Nore Challenger and Nore Commander* [2001] 2 Lloyd's Rep 103.

II SCA [18.24]

(n) Construction, repair or equipment of a ship A claim in respect of repairs does not give rise to a maritime lien or other "charge" within the meaning of s 21(3) of the Supreme Court Act 1981, and cannot be the subject of an action *in rem* under that section: *The St Merriel, Smith's Dock Co Ltd v Owners of St Merriel* [1963] P 247, [1963] 1 All ER 537. However, such a claim may be brought in rem under s 21(4) of the Supreme Court Act 1981.

II SCA [18.25]

(o) Wages "Wages" include a claim for damages for wrongful dismissal: *The Blessing* (1878) 3 PD 35; *The Ferret* (1883) 8 App Cas 329, PC; but not for severance pay: *The Tacoma City* [1991] 1 Lloyd's Rep 330. The following may be included: national insurance contributions of the claimant, which the owner has agreed to pay, *The Gee Whiz* [1951] 1 All ER 876n; contributions to a seaman's union and insurance fund (as part of seamen's wages), *The Fairport (No 3)* [1966] 2 Lloyd's Rep 253; a master's claim for compensation after termination of his contract and costs of repatriation together with deductions for income tax and union dues, *The Westport (No 4)* [1968] 2 Lloyd's Rep 559. There is a maritime lien for all wages claims within s 20(2)(o): *The Ever Success* [1999] 1 Lloyd's Rep 824. On maritime liens see further note **II SCA [19.5]**.

II SCA [18.26]

(p) Disbursements A ship's agent's fees have been held to be properly included in a claim for disbursements: *The Westport (No 3)* [1966] 1 Lloyd's Rep 342. Where the only remedy for wages is the lien over the proceeds of sale of the ship such a claim takes priority over the claim for damage to the ship: *The Ruta* [2000] 1 WLR 2068.

II SCA [18.27]

(q) General average act Section 66(2) of the Marine Insurance Act 1906 defines a general average act as one "where any extraordinary sacrifice or expenditure is voluntarily and reasonably made or incurred in time of peril for the purpose of preserving the property imperilled in the common adventure." All parties to the venture are liable to contribute rateably. Reference should be made to specialist works on the subject. There is no maritime lien for a claim for general average contribution.

II SCA [18.28]

(r) Bottomry Bottomry bonds are contracts (now apparently obsolete) which are effectively mortgages of ships in which the owner borrows money to fit out a ship or finance her voyage, and pledges the keel or bottom of the ship as security; see *The Atlas* (1827) 2 Hag Adm 48. Bottomry bonds give rise to a maritime lien.

II SCA [18.29]

(s) Any claim for the forfeiture or condemnation of a ship or of goods The following provisions give rise to a right of forfeiture in the Crown: ss 3, 15 and 87 of the Merchant Shipping Act 1995, Customs and Excise Management Act 1979 and the Foreign Enlistment Act 1870.

II SCA [18.30]

Droits of Admiralty These include goods and property belonging to pirates, *flotsam* (goods from a lost ship found floating on the water), *jetsam* (goods thrown from a lost ship in an attempt to lighten her found floating on the water), *lagan* (goods cast from the ship which are too heavy to float found on the seabed), and property found at sea *derelict*. These goods are all included within the definition of wreck in s 255 of the Merchant Shipping Act 1995, although a shipwreck (goods cast or left on the land by the sea) is not strictly a droit of Admiralty but a prerogative of the Crown. See *Sir Henry Constable's Case* (1601) 5 Co Rep 106a and *R v Property Derelict* (1825) 1 Hag Adm 383. The Crown has no right to wreck outside territorial waters, see *The Lusitania* [1986] QB 384.

II SCA [18.31]

(a) Any application to the High Court under the Merchant Shipping Act 1995 See CPR Sch 1 RSC Ord 74 for the procedure.

II SCA [18.32]

Collision Regulations The Collision Regulations are contained in the Merchant Shipping (Distress Signals and Prevention of Collisions) Regulations 1989, SI 1989/1798. The Regulations apply to UK ships (including hovercraft) and seaplanes anywhere in the world, and all ships or seaplanes in the UK or UK waters. The Collision Regulations incorporate The International Regulations for Preventing of Collisions at Sea. Such regulations or any unwritten rules of seamanship, can only be applicable so far as the law of the place of collision makes them applicable: *The Esso Brussels* [1973] 2 Lloyd's Rep 73, CA.

II SCA [18.33]

Action *in personam* The court may not exercise jurisdiction in person save in the cases set out in s 22 of the Supreme Court Act 1981.

II SCA [18.34]

Action *in rem* See para **II SCA [19.2]**.

II SCA [18.35]

Staying proceedings on the grounds of *forum non conveniens* The principles governing an application for a stay are dealt with in *The Spiliada* [1987] AC 460. If the applicant shows that there is some other available forum having competent jurisdiction which is clearly more appropriate for trial the court will ordinarily grant a stay unless the interests of justice dictate that there should not be a stay. In collision actions there is often no "natural forum": *The Coral Isis* [1986] 1 Lloyd's Rep 413. The court will stay proceedings in collision actions where a collision occurred in foreign waters, provided there is no juridical disadvantage, when the most real and substantial connection of the action is with that place: *Aldington Shipping Ltd v Bradstock Shipping Corpn and Mabanaft GmbH* [1988] 1 Lloyd's Rep 475, CA; *The Sidi Bishr* [1987] 1 Lloyd's Rep 42; *The Vishva Ajay* [1989] 2 Lloyd's Rep 558.

II SCA [18.36]

(c) Any action under the Merchant Shipping Act 1995 for the limitation of their liability Limitation of liability is governed by the provisions of the Convention on Limitation of Liability for Maritime Claims 1976 (ss 185, 186 of the Merchant Shipping Act 1995).

A limitation action may be brought, under the Act, by a charterer. However, a charterer's right to limit liability to an owner does not extend to damage to the vessel or amounts paid to salvors: *CMA CGM SA v Classica Shipping Co Ltd* [2004] EWCA Civ 114, [2004] 1 All ER (Comm) 865.

II SCA [18.37]

Exclusion of liability Section 186 of the Merchant Shipping Act 1995 provides that the owner, charterer, manager or operator of a British ship and the master, crew member or servant of such persons when acting in the course of their employment are not liable for loss or damage (a) by fire on board the ship, (b) of gold, silver, watches, jewels or precious stones lost or damaged by reason of theft, robbery or other dishonest conduct if their nature or value were not at the time of shipment declared by the owner or shipper in the bill of lading or otherwise in writing. The right to exclude is lost if the damage results from the personal act or omission of the owner committed recklessly or with intent to cause loss.

II SCA [18.38]

Who may limit The following persons may limit liability: (1) Dock owners, canal owners, harbour authorities, a conservancy authority; (2) Ship owners and salvors; (3) Insurers of liability for claims subject to limitation.

II SCA [18.39]

What claims may be limited See s 187, Sch 7, art 2 of the Merchant Shipping Act 1995. (1) Claims for loss of life or personal injury or loss or damage to property on board or in connection with the operation of the ship or salvage operations; (2) claims in relation to loss from delay in carriage by sea of cargo, passengers or luggage; (3) claims in respect of other loss resulting from the infringement of rights other than contractual claims; (4) claims for removal, destruction and making cargo harmless; (5) claims of a person (other than a person liable in respect of measures taken in order to avert or minimise loss for which the person liable may limit his liability in accordance with this convention).

It has been held that the High Court has jurisdiction to entertain a limitation claim despite the absence of any *underlying court (or arbitration) proceedings within the jurisdiction: Seismic Shipping Inc v Total E and P UK plc* [2005] EWHC 460 (Admlty), [2005] 2 Lloyd's Rep 54.

II SCA [18.40]

What claims may not be limited Salvage or general average contribution; claims for oil pollution damage within the International Convention on Civil Liability for Oil Pollution Damage; claims under ss 7–11 of the Nuclear Installations Act 1965; claims against ship owners of a nuclear ship for nuclear damage; claims by servants of the shipowner or salvors involved in the salvage if the shipowner or salvor is not entitled to limit his liability for such claims.

II SCA [18.41]

Circumstances in which limitation will not apply A person is not entitled to limit liability if it is proved that the loss resulted from his personal act or omission, committed with the intent to cause such loss, or recklessly, with the knowledge that such loss would probably result: Merchant Shipping Act, Sch 7, art 4.

A carrier may still be entitled to limit liability although in breach of contract: *Daewoo Heavy Industries Ltd v Klipriver Shipping Ltd* [2003] EWCA Civ 451, [2002] 1 All ER (Comm) 801, (2003) Times, 17 April, a case in which the limitation provided by article IV, rule 5 of the Hague Rules 1924 was held to apply although the carrier had failed to see that the cargo was carried under deck.

II SCA [18.42]

Amount of limitation fund Limits are provided by reference to the gross tonnage of the ship and Special Drawing Rights (SDR), and the nature of the claim. The calculation of the conversion of Special Drawing Rights to sterling is governed by Merchant Shipping Act 1995, Sch 7, Part II, para 7.

Loss of life and Personal injury

500 tons	333,000 SDR

and for each additional ton from:

501–3000 tons	500 SDR per ton
3001–30,000 tons	333 SDR per ton
30,001–70,000 tons	250 SDR per ton

70,001 or more	167 SDR per ton
salvor under article 6(4)	833,000 SDR
Other claims	
Up to 500 tons	167,000 SDR
And for each additional ton from:	
501–30,000 tons	167 SDR per ton
30,001–70,000	125 SDR per ton
70,001 or more	83 SDR per ton
salvor under article 6(4)	833,000 SDR

The limitation on liability for passenger claims is 46,666 SDR multiplied by the number of passengers that the ship is authorised to carry up to a maximum of 25,000,000 SDR.

II SCA [18.43]

(c) Any other Admiralty jurisdiction The Admiralty Court has inherent jurisdiction (1) to award simple interest on sums outstanding at the date of judgment: *The Aldora* [1975] QB 748, *The La Pintada* [1985] AC 104; and (2) over acts done on the high seas: *The Turbantia* [1924] P 78. Prior to 1981 the court had statutory jurisdiction over claims for " necessaries": Admiralty Court Act 1840 s 6, Admiralty Court Act 1861 s 5. "Necessaries" include anchors, cables, rigging, etc, and all things actually needed for the service of the ship, eg fuel (*The West Friesland* (1859) Sw 454; *The D'Vora* [1952] 2 All ER 1127), provisions (*The N R Gosfabrick* (1858) Sw 344), clothing for the crew (*The William F Safford* (1860) Lush 69), and brokerage (*The Riga* (1872) LR 3 A & E 516). Sums paid to reimburse sub- sub-agents who have supplied goods for the operation of a ship fall within s 20(2)(m) of the Senior Courts Act 1981: *The Kommunar* [1997] 1 Lloyd's Rep 1.

II SCA [18.44]

(d) Any jurisdiction connected with ships or aircraft... apart from this section and... by rules of court... assigned to the Queen's Bench Division and directed by... rules to be exercised by the Admiralty Court There is no jurisdiction apart from this section and no rules have been made.

II SCA [19]

21. Mode of exercise of Admiralty jurisdiction

(1) Subject to section 22, an action in personam may be brought in the High Court in all cases within the Admiralty jurisdiction of that court.

(2) In the case of any such claim as is mentioned in section 20(2)(a), (c) or (s) or any such question as is mentioned in section 20(2)(b), an action in rem may be brought in the High Court against the ship or property in connection with which the claim or question arises.

(3) In any case in which there is a maritime lien or other charge on any ship, aircraft or other property for the amount claimed, an action in rem may be brought in the High Court against that ship, aircraft or property.

(4) In the case of any such claim as is mentioned in section 20(2)(e)–(r), where—

(a) the claim arises in connection with a ship; and

(b) the person who would be liable on the claim in an action in personam ("the relevant person") was, when the cause of action arose, the owner or charterer of, or in possession or in control of, the ship,

an action in rem may (whether or not the claim gives rise to a maritime lien on that ship) be brought in the High Court against—

(i) that ship, if at the time when the action is brought the relevant person is either the beneficial owner of that ship as respects all the shares in it or the charterer of it under a charter by demise; or

(ii) any other ship of which, at the time when the action is brought, the relevant person is the beneficial owner as respects all the shares in it.

(5) In the case of a claim in the nature of towage or pilotage in respect of an aircraft, an action in rem may be brought in the High Court against that aircraft if, at the time when the action is brought, it is beneficially owned by the person who would be liable on the claim in an action in personam.

(6) Where, in the exercise of its Admiralty jurisdiction, the High Court orders any ship, aircraft or other property to be sold, the court shall have jurisdiction to hear and determine any question arising as to the title to the proceeds of sale.

(7) In determining for the purposes of subsections (4) and (5) whether a person would be liable on a claim in an action in personam it shall be assumed that he has his habitual residence or a place of business within England or Wales.

(8) Where, as regards any such claim as is mentioned in section 20(2)(e) to (r), a ship has been served with a writ or arrested in an action in rem brought to enforce that claim, no other ship may be served with a writ or arrested in that or any other action in rem brought to enforce that claim; but this subsection does not prevent the issue, in respect of any one such claim, of a writ naming more than one ship or of two or more writs each naming a different ship.

II SCA [19.1]

Subsection (1) An action in personam An action *in personam* is a claim which is brought in the Admiralty Court in accordance with CPR 58 (para **CPR 58**) or, to the extent applicable, CPR 61 (para **CPR 61**).

II SCA [19.2]

Subsection (2) An action in rem Section 21 gives the right to proceed against a *res* – the thing (either the ship, her cargo, bunkers, or freight where subject to a maritime lien, or the aircraft): s 21(3), and the action is for many purposes treated as an action against the res. For procedure, see CPR 61 (para **CPR 61**). However, for the limits of this "fiction" and the extent to which the owners will be treated as parties to an in rem action, see *The Indian Grace* [1998] AC 878, HL. The merit of such an action is that the claimant can secure the arrest of the *res*, and upon proof of the claim ask the court to order the sale of the *res* and order the payment of the proceeds into court (net of the expenses of the Admiralty Marshall and of sale). It is even possible to commence an Admiralty action *in rem* against the proceeds of sale held in court. Although rarely done, because a claimant is anxious to obtain security for his claim, an action *in rem* may be brought by service of the proceedings without arrest. If after service the ship leaves the jurisdiction, the court will nevertheless give judgment against the ship. The court becomes seised of the action from the moment of service of the process or arrest of the ship: *The Nord Sea and Freccia Del Nord* [1989] 1 Lloyd's Rep 388. A claim for specific performance may be made in an Admiralty action *in rem*, equitable relief being available in every High Court action notwithstanding that it is purely personal in character: *The Conoco Britannia* [1972] 2 QB 543, [1972] 2 All ER 238.

II SCA [19.3]

Jurisdiction By arrest the claimant can obtain security for his claim and the court has jurisdiction provided that the *res* is within the jurisdiction of the court even if the owners are not. An arrest confers jurisdiction on English courts pursuant to s 2 of the Civil Jurisdiction and Judgments Act 1982, see Sch 1, art 57, The International Convention Relating to the Arrest of Sea Going Ships 1952 and *The Deichland* [1990] 1 QB 361, [1989] 2 All ER 1066, CA, as a court of the country in which an arrest is made. The court may, however, decline jurisdiction in such a case notwithstanding art 57, if related proceedings within the meaning of Articles 21 and 22 of the Brussels Convention have already been commenced before the court of another contracting state: *The Maciej Rataj* [1995] 1 Lloyd's Rep 302, ECJ. For these purposes it is required merely that the legal consequences of an arrest are that the ship becomes security for a maritime claim and a claimant's commercial motives are immaterial: *The Anna H* [1995] 1 Lloyd's Rep 11, CA. In order to ensure that the court has jurisdiction a claimant should either arrest and maintain the arrest or insist upon an undertaking to give security, accept service and submit to the jurisdiction of the court: *The Deichland* [1990] 1 QB 361, [1989] 2 All ER 1066, CA. For jurisdiction under the Collision Convention, however, the vessel need only be capable of being arrested, provided security is given: *The Po* [1991] 2 Lloyd's Rep 206, CA.

II SCA [19.4]

Ownership In an action *in rem* a change of ownership of the *res* after the jurisdiction has been properly invoked should not affect the right of the claimant to prosecute the action through all its stages: *The Monica S* [1968] P 741, [1967] 3 All ER 740. The transfer of ownership of a vessel after the issue of proceedings, but before service, does not affect the claimant's right to proceed *in rem* and the purchaser should arrange to be indemnified by the vendor against claims: *The Helene Roth* [1980] QB 273, [1980] 1 All ER 1078.

II SCA [19.5]

Subsection (3) Maritime lien In English law there is a maritime lien for (1) damage or loss caused by the negligent navigation of a ship, (2) salvage, (3) wages of a master or seaman, (4) wages of and disbursements made by a master, and (5) bottomry. A foreign law maritime lien will not found an action *in rem* unless it relates to the kind of claim recognised by the English courts as giving a maritime lien: *The Acrux* [1965] P 391, [1965] 2 All ER 323. The question whether a claim for pilotage carries a maritime lien was left open in *The Ambatielos* [1923] P 68. Social insurance contributions payable by a seaman's employer to a government body under foreign law are not part of the seaman's wages for which an action *in rem* will lie: *The Acrux* [1965] P 391, [1965] 2 All ER 323, but, if deducted by the master, may be included in any claim by him for wages and ordered to be paid over to the appropriate authority: *The Fairport* [1965] 2 Lloyd's Rep 183. The lien for wages arises out of service to the ship and does not depend on the consent of the shipowner, but the quantum of his claim is determined by reference to his contract of service during the relevant time: *The Ever Success* [1999] 1 Lloyd's Rep 824. The seaman does not lose his maritime lien by directing that part of his wages are to be paid to a national seaman's agency: *The Turiddu* [1999] 2 Lloyd's Rep 401. Where a lien exists, it attaches to the hull, tackle, apparel and furniture of the ship: *The Alexander* (1812) 1 Dods 278; *The Dundee* (1823) 1 Hag Adm 109. Cargo cannot be the subject of a lien in a collision case as it is not responsible for the damage, but it may be arrested to compel payment into court of the freight which would otherwise be received by the shipowner: *The Flora* (1866) LR 1 A & E 45. A person who pays off a debt for which there is a maritime lien does not thereby acquire the lien: *The Petone* [1917] P 198; *The Leoborg (No 2)* [1964] 1 Lloyd's Rep 380. Where the only remedy for wages is the lien over the proceeds of sale of the ship such a claim takes priority over the claim for damage to the ship: *The Ruta* [2001] 1 All ER 450.

II SCA [19.6]

Other charge The reference to other charge does not encompass contractual charges or mortgages, but is limited to statutory charges of the type arising under the Merchant Shipping Acts: *The St Merriel, Smith's Dock Co Ltd v Owners of St Merriel* [1963] P 247, [1963] 1 All ER 537.

II SCA [19.7]

Subsection (4) claims against sister ships An action *in rem* lies against the offending ship or one other sister ship only, for the claims in s 20(2)(e)–(r). Only one ship may be arrested under the provisions of sub-s (4)(ii): *The Banco, Owners of Monte Ulia v Owners of Banco* [1971] P 137, [1971] 1 All ER 524, CA; *The Afala* [1995] 2 Lloyd's Rep 286, Ct of Sess. A claimant may institute proceedings against more than one ship provided the claimant only serves and arrests one ship, (s 22(8)), but after service the proceedings should be amended by deleting all but one name: *The Nord Sea and Freccia Del Nord* [1989] 1 Lloyd's Rep 388.

II SCA [19.8]

Companies A ship cannot be arrested as a sister ship if the ownership of the alleged sister ship is vested in a different company even though the shares are held by the same person in both companies. The corporate veil can only be lifted if there is evidence to suggest fraud: *The Maritime Trader* [1981] 2 Lloyd's Rep 153. The right to proceed against a sister ship does not extend to a ship owned by a sister company where the registered owners are different companies: *The Evpo Agnic* [1988] 3 All ER 810, [1988] 1 WLR 1090, CA; *The Nazym Khikmet* [1996] 2 Lloyd's Rep 362, CA. Where at the time an action *in rem* is commenced the registered owner of that ship in connection with which the claim arose was not the owner of any share in an alleged sister ship that was sought to be arrested, the claimant had no right to proceed against the sister ship: *The Mawan* [1988] 2 Lloyd's Rep 459. A sister ship may be arrested in a claim based on a time charter as the word "charterer" includes a time charterer: *The Span Terza* [1982] 1 Lloyd's Rep 225, CA. See further para **II SCA [19.11]**.

II SCA [19.9]

"Person who would be liable" In sub-s (4) the purpose of the words "the person who would be liable on the claim in an action *in personam*" is simply to identify the person whose ship may be arrested; they mean "the person who would be liable on the assumption that the action succeeds": *The St Elefterio* [1957] P 179, [1957] 2 All ER 374. A reasonable belief that an owner would be liable in an action *in personam* is sufficient to justify an action *in rem*: *The Gulf Venture* [1984] 2 Lloyd's Rep 445.

II SCA [19.10]

Beneficial ownership A ship is "beneficially owned as respects all the shares therein" only by the person with a right to sell all the shares. Under s 3(4) of the Administration of Justice Act 1956 (now repealed) it was held that a ship under demise charter is "beneficially owned as respect of all the shares therein" and these words can be extended to cover cases where although the ship was not legally or equitably owned by a person it was in his full possession and control: *The Andrea Ursula* [1973] QB 265, [1971] 1 All ER 821. In *The Playa Larga (Owners of Cargo lately laden on board) v I Congreso del Partitdo* [1983] 1 AC 244, [1981] 2 All ER 1064, HL, *The Andrea Ursula* was not followed and in the case of a demise charter it has been held that the words "beneficially owned as respects all shares therein" did not apply to the charterer, although if there were a maritime lien an action *in rem* could still be brought: *The Father Thames* [1979] 2 Lloyd's Rep 364. The Court can look behind the registered owner to establish the beneficial ownership but it is for the claimant to prove on the balance of probabilities that at the time the action was brought the ship was beneficially owned by the same person who was the owner when the cause of action arose: *The Aventicum* [1978] 1 Lloyd's Rep 184 but see also *The Evpo Agnic* [1988] 3 All ER 810, [1988] 1 WLR 1090, CA.

II SCA [19.11]

Charterer Even if there is no formal demise charterer a "relevant person" who has the rights of a demise charterer against the owner of the ship will fall within s 21(4)(b) see *Bridge Oil Ltd v Owners and/or Demise Charterers of the ship Guissepe di Vittorio* [1998] 1 Lloyd's Rep 136, CA. The phrase "charterer of the ship" includes a demise charterer, a time charterer, a voyage charterer and a slot charterer: *The Tychy* [1999] 2 Lloyd's Rep 11, CA.

II SCA [19.12]

Winding up of owner company A ship which has been arrested is a security in the hands of the court, and the subsequent liquidation of the company owning the ship does not affect this: *The Cella* (1888) 13 PD 82. The arrest of a ship is a sequestration within the meaning of s 523 of the Companies Act 1985 (now repealed and replaced by s 128 of the Insolvency Act 1986): *Re Australian Direct Steam Navigation Co* (1875) LR 20 Eq 325; but it is not an execution within the meaning of that section or of Companies Act 1985 s 621 (now repealed and replaced by s 183 of the Insolvency Act 1986): *The Zafiro* [1960] P 1, [1959] 2 All ER 537. See also *The Constellation* [1965] 3 All ER 873, [1966] 1 WLR 272.

II SCA [20]

22. Restrictions on entertainment of actions in personam in collision and similar cases

(1) This section applies to any claim for damage, loss of life or personal injury arising out of—

- (a) a collision between ships; or
- (b) the carrying out of, or omission to carry out, a manoeuvre in the case of one or more of two or more ships; or
- (c) non-compliance, on the part of one or more of two or more ships, with the collision regulations.

(2) The High Court shall not entertain any action in personam to enforce a claim to which this section applies unless—

- (a) the defendant has his habitual residence or a place of business within England or Wales; or
- (b) the cause of action arose within inland waters of England or Wales or within the limits of a port of England or Wales; or
- (c) an action arising out of the same incident or series of incidents is proceeding in the court or has been heard and determined in the court.

In this subsection—

"inland waters" includes any part of the sea adjacent to the coast of the United Kingdom certified by the Secretary of State to be waters falling by international law to be treated as within the territorial sovereignty of Her Majesty apart from the operation of that law in relation to territorial waters;

"port" means any port, harbour, river, estuary, haven, dock, canal or other place so long as a person or body of persons is empowered by or under an Act to make charges in respect of ships entering it or using the facilities therein, and "limits of a port" means the limits thereof as fixed by or under the Act in question or, as the case may be, by the relevant charter or custom;

"charges" means any charges with the exception of light dues, local light dues and any other charges in respect of lighthouses, buoys or beacons and of charges in respect of pilotage.

(3) The High Court shall not entertain any action in personam to enforce a claim to which this section applies until any proceedings previously brought by the plaintiff in any court outside England and Wales against the same defendant in respect of the same incident or series of incidents have been discontinued or otherwise come to an end.

(4) Subsections (2) and (3) shall apply to counterclaims (except counterclaims in proceedings arising out of the same incident or series of incidents) as they apply to actions, the references to the plaintiff and the defendant being for this purpose read as references to the plaintiff on the counterclaim and the defendant to the counterclaim respectively.

(5) Subsections (2) and (3) shall not apply to any action or counterclaim if the defendant thereto submits or has agreed to submit to the jurisdiction of the court.

(6) Subject to the provisions of subsection (3), the High Court shall have jurisdiction to entertain an action in personam to enforce a claim to which this section applies whenever any of the conditions specified in subsection (2)(a) to (c) is satisfied, and the rules of court relating to the service of process outside the jurisdiction shall make such provision as may appear to the rule-making authority to be appropriate having regard to the provisions of this subsection.

(7) Nothing in this section shall prevent an action which is brought in accordance with the provisions of this section in the High Court being transferred, in accordance with the enactments in that behalf, to some other court.

(8) For the avoidance of doubt it is hereby declared that this section applies in relation to the jurisdiction of the High Court not being Admiralty jurisdiction, as well as in relation to its Admiralty jurisdiction.

II SCA [21]

23. High Court not to have jurisdiction in cases within Rhine Convention

The High Court shall not have jurisdiction to determine any claim or question certified by the Secretary of State to be a claim or question which, under the Rhine Navigation Convention, falls to be determined in accordance with the provisions of that Convention; and any proceedings to enforce such a claim which are commenced in the High Court shall be set aside.

II SCA [22]

24. Supplementary provisions as to Admiralty jurisdiction

(1) In sections 20 to 23 and this section, unless the context otherwise requires—

"collision regulations" means safety regulations under section 85 of the Merchant Shipping Act 1995;

"goods" includes baggage;

"master" has the same meaning as in the Merchant Shipping Act 1995, and accordingly includes every person (except a pilot) having command or charge of a ship;

"the Rhine Navigation Convention" means the Convention of the 7th October 1868 as revised by any subsequent Convention;

"ship" includes any description of vessel used in navigation and (except in the definition of "port" in section 22(2) and in subsection (2)(c) of this section) includes, subject to section 2(3) of the Hovercraft Act 1968, a hovercraft;

"towage" and "pilotage", in relation to an aircraft, mean towage and pilotage while the aircraft is waterborne.

(2) Nothing in sections 20 to 23 shall—

(a) be construed as limiting the jurisdiction of the High Court to refuse to entertain an action for wages by the master or a member of the crew of a ship, not being a British ship;

(b) affect the provisions of section 226 of the Merchant Shipping Act 1995 (power of a receiver of wreck to detain a ship in respect of a salvage claim); or

(c) authorise proceedings in rem in respect of any claim against the Crown, or the arrest, detention or sale of any of Her Majesty's ships or Her Majesty's aircraft, or, subject to section 2(3) of the Hovercraft Act 1968, Her Majesty's hovercraft, or of any cargo or other property belonging to the Crown.

(3) In this section—

"Her Majesty's ships" and "Her Majesty's aircraft" have the meanings given by section 38(2) of the Crown Proceedings Act 1947;

"Her Majesty's hovercraft" means hovercraft belonging to the Crown in right of Her Majesty's Government in the United Kingdom or Her Majesty's Government in Northern Ireland.

II SCA [22.1]

Ship See para **II SCA [18.5]**. As regards HM ships, admiralty jurisdiction may be exercised *in personam* against the Crown. A vessel chartered, but not demised to the Crown was held not to be a ship of the Crown: *The Nile* (1875) LR 4 A & E 449. Neither ships nor cargo of a foreign state in commercial use at the time of the cause of the action have sovereign immunity: State Immunity Act 1978 s 10.

OTHER PARTICULAR FIELDS OF JURISDICTION

II SCA [23]

25. Probate jurisdiction of High Court

(1) Subject to the provisions of Part V, the High Court shall, in accordance with section 19(2), have the following probate jurisdiction, that is to say all such jurisdiction in relation to probates and letters of administration as it had immediately before the commencement of this Act, and in particular all such contentious and non-contentious jurisdiction as it then had in relation to—

(a) testamentary causes or matters;

(b) the grant, amendment or revocation of probates and letters of administration; and

(c) the real and personal estate of deceased persons.

(2) Subject to the provisions of Part V, the High Court shall, in the exercise of its probate jurisdiction, perform all such duties with respect to the estates of deceased persons as fell to be performed by it immediately before the commencement of this Act.

II SCA [23.1]

Probate business Probate business generally is dealt with in Part V of the Act (ss 105–128).

Note also that the probate jurisdiction of the High Court is now assigned to the Property, Trusts and Probate List (ChD) within the structure of Business and Property Courts created by CPR Part 57A.

II SCA [23.2]

Contentious probate proceedings Proceedings started on or after 15 October 2001 must comply with section 1 of CPR Part 57, starting with **CPR 57.2** and the Practice Direction at **CPR PD 57**.

II SCA [23.3]

Rectification Section 20 of the Administration of Justice Act 1982 (set out at para **III TRU [43B]**) empowers the High Court to rectify a will in the circumstances set out in that section. In relation to estates whose value does not exceed £30,000 this power is exercisable by a county court by virtue of s 32 of the County Courts Act 1984, (see para **II CCA [16]**). For guidance on the scope and utility of this power see *Walker v Geo H Medlicott & Son (a firm)* [1999] 1 All ER 685, [1999] 1 WLR 727, CA, (considered in *Horsfall v Haywards (a Firm)* [1999] 1 FLR 1182, CA. For procedure see CPR Pt 57, particularly **CPR 57.11** and the Practice Direction at **CPR PD 57**.

II SCA [23.4]

Undue Influence Where undue influence is in issue the court has an inquisitorial function and a duty to ascertain the truth. Undue influence should not be inferred merely from the defendant's failure to defend: *Killick v Pountney* (1999) Times, 30 April, CA.

II SCA [24]

26. Matrimonial jurisdiction of High Court

The High Court shall, in accordance with section 19(2), have all such jurisdiction in relation to matrimonial causes and matters as was immediately before the commencement of the Matrimonial Causes Act 1857 vested in or exercisable by any ecclesiastical court or person in England or Wales in respect of—

(a) divorce a mensa et thoro (renamed judicial separation by that Act);

(b) nullity of marriage [. . .]; and

(c) any matrimonial cause or matter except marriage licences.

II SCA [24.1]

Acts conferring jurisdiction The main legislation conferring jurisdiction on the High Court in a matrimonial context is the Matrimonial Causes Act 1973 and the Matrimonial and Family Proceedings Act 1984. However, the latter Act also set up a system of Family courts in which proceedings under these Acts and, among others, the Children Act 1989 are heard. The procedure is regulated by the Family Procedure Rules 2010, which are outside the scope of this work.

II SCA [24.2]

The Family Court Note that from 22 April 2014 the matrimonial jurisdiction was conferred on the Family Court by section 17 of the Crime and Courts Act 1913, in the following terms:

17. Civil and family proceedings in England and Wales

(1) ...

(2) ...

(3) In the Matrimonial and Family Proceedings Act 1984 before Part 5 insert—

PART 4A THE FAMILY COURT

31A. Establishment of the family court

(1) There is to be a court in England and Wales, called the family court, for the purpose of exercising the jurisdiction and powers conferred on it—

(a) by or under this or any other Act, or

(b) by or under any Act, or Measure, of the National Assembly for Wales.

(2) The family court is to be a court of record and have a seal.

II SCA [25]

27. Prize jurisdiction of High Court

The High Court shall, in accordance with section 19(2), have as a prize court—

(a) all such jurisdiction as is conferred on it by the Prize Acts 1864 to 1944 (in which references to the High Court of Admiralty are by virtue of paragraph 1 of Schedule 4 to this Act to be construed as references to the High Court); and

(b) all such other jurisdiction on the high seas and elsewhere as it had as a prize court immediately before the commencement of this Act.

II SCA [25.1]

Procedure Proceedings in the High Court when acting as a Prize Court are not subject to the Civil Procedure Rules except to the extent that they are applied by rules made under the Prize Courts Act 1894 s 3: see **CPR 2.1**.

II SCA [26]

28. Appeals from Crown Court and inferior courts

(1) Subject to subsection (2), any order, judgment or other decision of the Crown Court may be questioned by any party to the proceedings, on the ground that it is wrong in law or is in excess of jurisdiction, by applying to the Crown Court to have a case stated by that court for the opinion of the High Court.

(2) Subsection (1) shall not apply to—

(a) a judgment or other decision of the Crown Court relating to trial on indictment; or

(b) any decision of that court under < . . . > the Local Government (Miscellaneous Provisions) Act 1982 which, by any provision of any of those Acts, is to be final.

(3) Subject to the provisions of this Act and to rules of court, the High Court shall, in accordance with section 19(2), have jurisdiction to hear and determine—

(a) any application, or any appeal (whether by way of case stated or otherwise), which it has power to hear and determine under or by virtue of this or any other Act; and

(b) all such other appeals as it had jurisdiction to hear and determine immediately before the commencement of this Act.

(4) In subsection (2)(a) the reference to a decision of the Crown Court relating to trial on indictment does not include a decision relating to a requirement to make a payment under regulations under section 23 or 24 of the Legal Aid, Sentencing and Punishment of Offenders Act 2012.

II SCA [27]

28A. Proceedings on case stated by magistrates' court

(1) The following provisions apply where a case is stated for the opinion of the High Court under section 111 of the Magistrates' Courts Act 1980 (case stated on question of law or jurisdiction).

(2) The High Court may, if it thinks fit, cause the case to be sent back for amendment, whereupon it shall be amended accordingly.

(3) The High Court shall hear and determine the question arising on the case (or the case as amended) and shall—

(a) reverse, affirm or amend the determination in respect of which the case has been stated, or

(b) remit the matter to the justice or justices with the opinion of the court,

and may make such other order in relation to the matter (including as to costs) as it thinks fit.

(4) Except as provided by the Administration of Justice Act 1960 (right of appeal to Supreme Court in criminal cases), a decision of the High Court under this section is final and conclusive on all parties.

II SCA [27.1]

No right of appeal to the Court of Appeal The effect of this section, in combination with s 18(1)(c), is that any decision of the High Court on a case stated by magistrates in a non-criminal matter is final and may not be appealed to the Court of Appeal. The argument that an alternative route to the Court of Appeal was provided by ss 54 and 55 of the Access to Justice Act 1999 and the Access to Justice (Destination of Appeals) Order 2000, SI 2000/1071, was rejected in *Westminster City Council v O'Reilly* [2003] EWCA Civ 1007, [2004] 1 WLR 195, (2003) Times, 21 August.

II SCA [28]

29. Mandatory, prohibiting and quashing orders

(1) The orders of mandamus, prohibition and certiorari shall be known instead as mandatory, prohibiting and quashing orders respectively.

(1A) The High Court shall have jurisdiction to make mandatory, prohibiting and quashing orders in those classes of case in which, immediately before 1st May 2004, it had jurisdiction to make orders of mandamus, prohibition and certiorari respectively.

(2) Every such order shall be final, subject to any right of appeal therefrom.

(3) In relation to the jurisdiction of the Crown Court, other than its jurisdiction in matters relating to trial on indictment, the High Court shall have all such jurisdiction to make mandatory, prohibiting or quashing orders as the High Court possesses in relation to the jurisdiction of an inferior court.

(3A) The High Court shall have no jurisdiction to make mandatory, prohibiting or quashing orders in relation to the jurisdiction of a court-martial in matters relating to—

(a) trial by court-martial for an offence, or

(b) appeals from a Standing Civilian Court;

and in this subsection "court-martial" means a court-martial under the Army Act 1955, the Air Force Act 1955 or the Naval Discipline Act 1957.

(4) The power of the High Court under any enactment to require justices of the peace or a judge or officer of the county court to do any act relating to the duties of their respective offices, or to require a magistrates' court to state a case for the opinion of the High Court, in any case where the High Court formerly had by virtue of any enactment jurisdiction to make a rule absolute, or an order, for any of those purposes, shall be exercisable by mandatory order.

(5) In any statutory provision—

(a) references to mandamus or to a writ or order of mandamus shall be read as references to a mandatory order;

(b) references to prohibition or to a writ or order of prohibition shall be read as references to a prohibiting order;

(c) references to certiorari or to a writ or order of certiorari shall be read as references to a quashing order; and

(d) references to the issue or award of a writ of mandamus, prohibition or certiorari shall be read as references to the making of the corresponding mandatory, prohibiting or quashing order.

(6) In subsection (3) the reference to the Crown Court's jurisdiction in matters relating to trial on indictment does not include its jurisdiction relating to requirements to make payments under regulations under section 23 or 24 of the Legal Aid, Sentencing and Punishment of Offenders Act 2012.

II SCA [28.1]

Jurisdiction in matters relating to trial on indictment Once a case has been sent to the Crown Court by magistrates all decisions concerning issues between the accused and Crown, for example as to whether to dismiss for abuse of process, are "matters relating to trial on indictment" within s 29(3) and are therefore not susceptible to judicial review: *R (on the application of Snelgrove) v Woolwich Crown Court* [2004] EWHC 2172 (Admin), [2005] 1 Cr App Rep 253. For example, s 29(3) has been held to exclude jurisdiction to entertain judicial review of a failure of the Crown Court to make a compensation order: *R (on the application of Faithfull) v Ipswich Crown Court* [2007] EWHC 2763 (Admin), [2008] 3 All ER 749.

It has also been held that the exclusion in s 29(3) applies even where the ground for applying for judicial review is that the sentence passed exceeded the jurisdiction of the sentencing court: *R (Crown Prosecution Service) v Guildford Crown Court* (2007) Times, 16 July, QBD.

II SCA [28.2]

Issues within the supervisory jurisdiction In a case of a remediation order made by the Crown Court it was held that, although the order arose from an earlier sentencing decision, it was not excluded from the supervisory jurisdiction: *R (Environment Agency) v Tapecrown Ltd* [2018] EWCA Crim 1345.

II SCA [29]

30. Applications to restrain persons from acting in offices in which they are not entitled to act

(1) Where a person not entitled to do so acts in an office to which this section applies, the High Court may—

(a) grant an injunction restraining him from so acting; and

(b) if the case so requires, declare the office to be vacant.

(2) This section applies to any substantive office of a public nature and permanent character which is held under the Crown or which has been created by any statutory provision or royal charter

II SCA [30]

31. Application for judicial review

(1) An application to the High Court for one or more of the following forms of relief, namely—

(a) a mandatory, prohibiting or quashing order;

(b) a declaration or injunction under subsection (2); or

(c) an injunction under section 30 restraining a person not entitled to do so from acting in an office to which that section applies,

shall be made in accordance with rules of court by a procedure to be known as an application for judicial review.

(2) A declaration may be made or an injunction granted under this subsection in any case where an application for judicial review, seeking that relief, has been made and the High Court considers that, having regard to—

(a) the nature of the matters in respect of which relief may be granted by mandatory, prohibiting or quashing orders;

(b) the nature of the persons and bodies against whom relief may be granted by such orders; and

(c) all the circumstances of the case,

it would be just and convenient for the declaration to be made or of the injunction to be granted, as the case may be.

(2A) The High Court—

(a) must refuse to grant relief on an application for judicial review, and

(b) may not make an award under subsection (4) on such an application,

if it appears to the court to be highly likely that the outcome for the applicant would not have been substantially different if the conduct complained of had not occurred.

(2B) The court may disregard the requirements in subsection (2A)(a) and (b) if it considers that it is appropriate to do so for reasons of exceptional public interest.

(2C) If the court grants relief or makes an award in reliance on subsection (2B), the court must certify that the condition in subsection (2B) is satisfied.

(3) No application for judicial review shall be made unless the leave of the High Court has been obtained in accordance with rules of court; and the court shall not grant leave to make such an application unless[—

(a)] it considers that the applicant has a sufficient interest in the matter to which the application relates[, and

(b) the applicant has provided the court with any information about the financing of the application that is specified in rules of court for the purposes of this paragraph.]

[(3A) The information that may be specified for the purposes of subsection (3)(b) includes—

(a) information about the source, nature and extent of financial resources available, or likely to be available, to the applicant to meet liabilities arising in connection with the application, and

(b) if the applicant is a body corporate that is unable to demonstrate that it is likely to have financial resources available to meet such liabilities, information about its members and about their ability to provide financial support for the purposes of the application.

(3B) Rules of court under subsection (3)(b) that specify information identifying those who are, or are likely to be, sources of financial support must provide that only a person whose financial support (whether direct or indirect) exceeds, or is likely to exceed, a level set out in the rules has to be identified.

This subsection does not apply to rules that specify information described in subsection (3A)(b).]

(3C) When considering whether to grant leave to make an application for judicial review, the High Court—

(a) may of its own motion consider whether the outcome for the applicant would have been substantially different if the conduct complained of had not occurred, and

(b) must consider that question if the defendant asks it to do so.

(3D) If, on considering that question, it appears to the High Court to be highly likely that the outcome for the applicant would not have been substantially different, the court must refuse to grant leave.

(3E) The court may disregard the requirement in subsection (3D) if it considers that it is appropriate to do so for reasons of exceptional public interest.

(3F) If the court grants leave in reliance on subsection (3E), the court must certify that the condition in subsection (3E) is satisfied.

(4) On an application for judicial review the High Court may award to the applicant damages, restitution or the recovery of a sum due if—

(a) the application includes a claim for such an award arising from any matter to which the application relates; and

(b) the court is satisfied that such an award would have been made if the claim had been made in an action begun by the applicant at the time of making the application.

(5) If, on an application for judicial review, the High Court quashes the decision to which the application relates, it may in addition—

(a) remit the matter to the court, tribunal or authority which made the decision, with a direction to reconsider the matter and reach a decision in accordance with the findings of the High Court, or

(b) substitute its own decision for the decision in question.

(5A) But the power conferred by subsection (5)(b) is exercisable only if—

(a) the decision in question was made by a court or tribunal,

(b) the decision is quashed on the ground that there has been an error of law, and

(c) without the error, there would have been only one decision which the court or tribunal could have reached.

(5B) Unless the High Court otherwise directs, a decision substituted by it under subsection (5)(b) has effect as if it were a decision of the relevant court or tribunal.

(6) Where the High Court considers that there has been undue delay in making an application for judicial review, the court may refuse to grant—

(a) leave for the making of the application; or
(b) any relief sought on the application,

if it considers that the granting of the relief sought would be likely to cause substantial hardship to, or substantially prejudice the rights of, any person or would be detrimental to good administration.

(7) Subsection (6) is without prejudice to any enactment or rule of court which has the effect of limiting the time within which an application for judicial review may be made.

(8) In this section "the conduct complained of", in relation to an application for judicial review, means the conduct (or alleged conduct) of the defendant that the applicant claims justifies the High Court in granting relief.

Amendment *Text in square brackets is inserted by the Criminal Justice and Courts Act 2015 with effect from a date to be appointed.*

II SCA [30.1]

Application for judicial review The provisions of s 31, as amended by the Civil Procedure (Modification of Supreme Court Act 1981) Order 2004, SI 2004/1033, bring together the jurisdictional provisions of ss 29, 30 and 31(2) and put them all under the new procedure for challenging the legality of decisions, acts and omissions by public bodies. The procedure is known as judicial review and s 31(3) establishes two essential requirements, the obtaining of leave and "sufficient interest" (sometimes referred to as *locus standi*). County courts may not make orders for mandamus, certiorari or prohibition: County Courts Act 1984 s 38(3).

With the coming into force of the Human Rights Act 1998, an Administrative Court was established, within the Queen's Bench Division, to hear applications for judicial review; and an Administration Court Office was set up to replace the old Crown Office: *Practice Note (Administrative Court: establishment)* [2000] 4 All ER 1071. The same note provided that parties to an application for judicial review should be described as "The Queen on the application of (name of applicant) – Claimant, versus, the public body against whom the proceedings are brought – Defendant".

A new subs-s (5) was substituted by the Tribunals, Courts and Enforcement Act 2007, s 141, with effect from 6 April 2008.

II SCA [30.2]

Procedure The procedure for applying for judicial review is now determined by **CPR 54**. Permission is required, as previously, but the application for it is to be included in the claim form (Form N461). The requirements which apply when Human Rights Act issues are raised, or remedies sought, are contained in para 5 of the Practice Direction at **CPR PD 54** and para 15 of the Practice Direction at **CPR PD 16**.

II SCA [30.3]

Sufficient interest An applicant with a direct personal interest in the relief sought will necessarily have a "sufficient interest". More difficult are the applications brought by individuals or organisations with a concern for the public good. The line needs to be drawn between the mere busybody and the person or organisation with an interest which is real but which may be affected only indirectly by the grant of the relief sought. The leading case on where to draw the line is the *Fleet Street Casuals* case: *IRC v National Federation of Self Employed and Small Businesses Ltd* [1982] AC 617, [1981] 2 All ER 93, HL. In *R (on the application of Bulger) v Secretary of State for the Home Department* [2001] EWHC Admin 119, [2001] 3 All ER 449, it was held that the victim's family did not have sufficient interest to challenge a sentencing tariff. See also cases noted in Volume 1 at **CPR 54.4[3]**.

II SCA [30.3A]

Promptness and undue delay Where the issue of promptness has been properly argued between the parties and the court has decided it in the applicant's favour, it may not usually be re-canvassed as part of a respondent's argument that relief should be refused because of undue delay, within s 31(6) of the Supreme Court Act 1981. However, it was decided in *R (on the application of Lichfield Securities Ltd) v Lichfield District Council* [2001] EWCA Civ 304, (2001) 81 P & CR 213, (2001) Times, 30 March that a re-canvassing of the issue was permissible in four situations:

- where the court hearing the initial application had so indicated;
- where new and relevant material was introduced;
- where, exceptionally, the issues as they had developed at the full hearing put a different aspect on the question of promptness;

- where the first judge had plainly overlooked some matter or reached a decision per incuriam.

II SCA [30.4]

Other available remedies to be used first It was stated, in *R v Epping and Harlow General Comrs, ex p Goldstraw* [1983] 3 All ER 257, to be a cardinal principle that, save in the most exceptional circumstances, judicial review should not be invoked where other remedies are available which have not been used. See also *R v Chief Constable of Merseyside Police, ex p Calveley* [1986] QB 424, [1986] 1 All ER 257, CA.

II SCA [30.5]

Extent of jurisdiction over public bodies Judicial review is a public law remedy by which the citizen may challenge the decisions of governmental and other public bodies. But it is not available against private bodies or to challenge private law arrangements: *R v Civil Service Appeal Board, ex p Bruce* [1989] 2 All ER 907, CA and *R v Disciplinary Committee of the Jockey Club, ex p Aga Khan* [1993] 2 All ER 853, [1993] 1 WLR 909, CA. Compare the successful application in *R v Panel of Take-Overs and Mergers, ex p Datafin plc* [1987] QB 815, [1987] 1 All ER 564, CA. As to whether judicial review or a private law action is the more appropriate course for an aggrieved person see the guidance of the Court of Appeal in *Dennis Rye Pension Fund Trustees v Sheffield City Council* [1997] 4 All ER 747, [1988] 1 WLR 840, CA.

In *R (Tucker) v Director General of the National Crime Squad* [2003] EWCA Civ 57, [2003] ICR 599 it was held that judicial review was not available in respect of a decision to terminate the applicant's secondment to the National Crime Squad.

II SCA [30.5A]

Extent of jurisdiction over courts The jurisdiction of the High Court to entertain challenges to decisions of inferior courts does not extend to decisions of the High Court itself, even when the decision is one given by a judge of an inferior court which is deemed by statute to be a decision of the High Court: *R (no the application of Okandeji) v Bow Street Magistrates Court* [2005] EWHC 2925 (Admin), [2006] 1 WLR 674, [2005] AlL ER (D) 166 (Nov), a decision on s 104(7) of the Extradition Act 2003.

II SCA [30.5B]

Power to substitute its own decision The power of the Divisional Court to substitute its own decision under sub-s (5)(b) is limited to circumstances where, without the error, there could have been only one decision. If this is not the case the decision must be remitted under sub-s (5)(a) for reconsideration by the court or tribunal: *R (on the application of Bar Standards Board) v Disciplinary Tribunal of the Council of the Inns of Court* [2016] EWCA Civ 478, [2016] All ER (D) 188 (May).

II SCA [30.6]

Precedents For precedents see **BCCP J[102]** onwards.

II SCA [30A]

31A. Transfer of judicial review applications to Upper Tribunal

(1) This section applies where an application is made to the High Court—

(a) for judicial review, or

(b) for permission to apply for judicial review.

(2) If Conditions 1, 2 and 3 are met, the High Court must by order transfer the application to the Upper Tribunal.

(2A) ...

(3) If Conditions 1 and 2 are met, but Condition 3 is not, the High Court may by order transfer the application to the Upper Tribunal if it appears to the High Court to be just and convenient to do so.

(4) Condition 1 is that the application does not seek anything other than—

(a) relief under section 31(1)(a) and (b);

(b) permission to apply for relief under section 31(1)(a) and (b);

(c) an award under section 31(4);

(d) interest;

(e) costs.

(5) Condition 2 is that the application does not call into question anything done by the Crown Court.

(6) Condition 3 is that the application falls within a class specified under section 18(6) of the Tribunals, Courts and Enforcement Act 2007.

(7) ...

(8) ...

II SCA [30A.1]

Specified classes of application The Lord Chief Justice has given directions under section 18(6) of the Tribunals, Courts and Enforcement Act 2007 specifying classes of application that must be transferred to the Upper Tribunal, as follows:

- Applications made on or after 3 November 2008 challenging any decision of the First-Tier tribunal on an appeal made in exercise of a right conferred by the Criminal Injuries Compensation Scheme in compliance with s 5(1) of the Criminal Injuries Compensation Act 1995 (appeals against decisions on review); and applications made on or after 3 November 2008 challenging any decision of the First-Tier tribunal made under Tribunal Procedure Rules or s 9 of the 2007 Act where there is no right of appeal to the Upper Tribunal and that decision is not an excluded decision within paragraph (b), (c) or (f) of s 11(5) of the 2007 Act.
- Applications made on or after 17 October 2011 calling into question a decision of the Secretary of State for the Home Department not to treat submissions as an asylum claim or a human rights claim within the meaning of Part 5 of the Nationality, Immigration and Asylum Act 2002 wholly or partly on the basis that they are not significantly different from material which has previously been considered, and such applications which also challenge a decision or decisions to remove or direct the removal of the applicant from the United Kingdom, or a failure or failures by the Secretary of State to make a decision on submissions said to support an asylum or human rights claim, but not those which also challenge any other decision.

Powers

II SCA [31]

32. Orders for interim payment

(1) As regards proceedings pending in the High Court, provision may be made by rules of court for enabling the court, in such circumstances as may be prescribed, to make an order requiring a party to the proceedings to make an interim payment of such amount as may be specified in the order, with provision for the payment to be made to such other party to the proceedings as may be so specified or, if the order so provides, by paying it into court.

(2) Any rules of court which make provision in accordance with subsection (1) may include provision for enabling a party to any proceedings who, in pursuance of such an order, has made an interim payment to recover the whole or part of the amount of the payment in such circumstances, and from such other party to the proceedings, as may be determined in accordance with the rules.

(3) Any rules made by virtue of this section may include such incidental, supplementary and consequential provisions as the rule-making authority may consider necessary or expedient.

(4) Nothing in this section shall be construed as affecting the exercise of any power relating to costs, including any power to make rules of court relating to costs.

(5) In this section "interim payment", in relation to a party to any proceedings, means a payment on account of any damages, debt or other sum (excluding any costs) which that party may be held liable to pay to or for the benefit of another party to the proceedings if a final judgment or order of the court in the proceedings is given or made in favour of that other party.

II SCA [31.1]

Procedure See **CPR 25.1** and Practice Direction 25B on interim payments at **CPR PD 25B**. For precedents see **BCCP C[39]–BCCP C[44]**.

II SCA [31.2]

"or other sum" The inclusion of the words "or other sum" in the definition of "interim payments" in sub-s (5) covers the ordering of interim payments in respect money that would have to be returned if a defence based on rescission of the contract were to succeed: *Deutsche Bank AG v United Global Ltd* [2016] EWCA Civ 119.

II SCA [32]

32A. Orders for provisional damages for personal injuries

(1) This section applies to an action for damages for personal injuries in which there is proved or admitted to be a chance that at some definite or indefinite time in the future the injured person will, as a result of the act or omission which gave rise to the cause of action, develop some serious disease or suffer some serious deterioration in his physical or mental condition.

(2) Subject to subsection (4) below, as regards any action for damages to which this section applies in which a judgment is given in the High Court, provision may be made by rules of court for enabling the court, in such circumstances as may be prescribed, to award the injured person—

(a) damages assessed on the assumption that the injured person will not develop the disease or suffer the deterioration in his condition; and

(b) further damages at a future date if he develops the disease or suffers the deterioration.

(3) Any rules made by virtue of this section may include such incidental, supplementary and consequential provisions as the rule-making authority may consider necessary or expedient.

(4) Nothing in this section shall be construed—

(a) as affecting the exercise of any power relating to costs, including any power to make rules of court relating to costs; or

(b) as prejudicing any duty of the court under any enactment or rule of law to reduce or limit the total damages which would have been recoverable apart from any such duty.

II SCA [32.1]

Serious deterioration "Serious deterioration" denotes a clear and severable deterioration going beyond ordinary or continuing deterioration: *Wilson v Ministry of Defence* [1991] 1 All ER 638. In the event of death, following an award of provisional damages, dependants are enabled, by the Damages Act 1996 s 3 to make claims under the Fatal Accidents Act 1976, which take the earlier award into account. See para **III PID [26]**.

II SCA [32.2]

Rules of court The relevant rules of court are at **CPR 36.7** and **CPR 41.1** onwards.

II SCA [32.3]

Practice See *Practice Note (Provisional Damages, Procedure)* [1985] 2 All ER 895, sub nom *Practice Direction* [1985] 1 WLR 961.

II SCA [32.4]

Precedents See **BCCP M[1254]** for a claim for provisional damages.

II SCA [33]

33. Powers of High Court exercisable before commencement of action

(1) On the application of any person in accordance with rules of court, the High Court shall, in such circumstances as may be specified in the rules, have power to make an order providing for any one or more of the following matters, that is to say—

(a) the inspection, photographing, preservation, custody and detention of property which appears to the court to be property which may become the subject-matter of subsequent proceedings in the High Court, or as to which any question may arise in any such proceedings; and

(b) the taking of samples of any such property as is mentioned in paragraph (a), and the carrying out of any experiment on or with any such property.

(2) On the application, in accordance with rules of court, of a person who appears to the High Court to be likely to be a party to subsequent proceedings in that court [. . .] the High Court shall, in such circumstances as may be specified in the rules, have power to order a person who appears to the court to be likely to be a party to the proceedings and to be likely to have or to have had in his possession, custody or power any documents which are relevant to an issue arising or likely to arise out of that claim—

(a) to disclose whether those documents are in his possession, custody or power; and

(b) to produce such of those documents as are in his possession, custody or power to the applicant or, on such conditions as may be specified in the order—

(i) to the applicant's legal advisers; or

(ii) to the applicant's legal advisers and any medical or other professional adviser of the applicant; or

(iii) if the applicant has no legal adviser, to any medical or other professional adviser of the applicant.

(3) This section applies in relation to the family court as it applies in relation to the High Court.

II SCA [33.1]

Rules of court See **CPR 31.16**.

II SCA [33.2]

Service of application abroad An application for pre-action disclosure is a free-standing set of proceedings which may be served abroad if the court so orders: *ED & F Capita Markets LLP v Obex Securities LLC* [2017] EWHC 265 (Ch).

II SCA [33.3]

A person likely to be a party In deciding whether an applicant or proposed respondent is "likely to be a party" to substantive proceedings, for the purposes of sub-s (2), the court should not have regard to limitation periods unless a defence of limitation is plainly bound to succeed: *Harris v Newcastle Health Authority* [1989] 2 All ER 273, [1989] 1 WLR 96, CA.

II SCA [33.4]

Precedents See **BCCP D[21]–BCCP D[22]**.

II SCA [34]

34. Power of High Court to order disclosure of documents, inspection of property etc in proceedings for personal injuries or death

(1) [. . .]

(2) On the application, in accordance with rules of court, of a party to any proceedings [. . .], the High Court shall, in such circumstances as may be specified in the rules, have power to order a person who is not a party to the proceedings and who appears to the court to be likely to have in his possession, custody or power any documents which are relevant to an issue arising out of the said claim—

(a) to disclose whether those documents are in his possession, custody or power; and

(b) to produce such of those documents, as are in his possession, custody or power to the applicant or, on such conditions as may be specified in the order—

(i) to the applicant's legal advisers; or

(ii) to the applicant's legal advisers and any medical or other professional adviser of the applicant; or

(iii) if the applicant has no legal adviser, to any medical or other professional adviser of the applicant.

(3) On the application, in accordance with rules of court, of a party to any proceedings [. . .], the High Court shall, in such circumstances as may be specified in the rules, have power to make an order providing for any one or more of the following matters, that is to say—

(a) the inspection, photographing, preservation, custody and detention of property which is not the property of, or in the possession of, any party to the proceedings but which is the subject-matter of the proceedings or as to which any question arises in the proceedings;

(b) the taking of samples of any such property as is mentioned in paragraph (a) and the carrying out of any experiment on or with any such property.

(4) The preceding provisions of this section are without prejudice to the exercise by the High Court of any power to make orders which is exercisable apart from those provisions.

(5) Subsections (2) and (3) apply in relation to the family court as they apply in relation to the High Court.

II SCA [34.1]

Extended scope of the section This section is no longer confined to proceedings for personal injury or death but relates to all proceedings in the High Court. The restriction was removed by the Civil Procedure (Modification of Enactments) Order 1998, SI 1998/2940, art 5(b) and the section is printed above in its present form.

II SCA [34.2]

Rules of court See **CPR 31.17**.

II SCA [34.3]

Hospital and medical notes The section provides a means of obtaining the disclosure of hospital and medical notes for the purposes of a claim against someone else: *Walker v Eli Lilly & Co* [1986] NLJ Rep 608. It may also be invoked by defendants eg to obtain documents held by DHSS in relation to the claimant's claim for disability benefit: *O'sullivan v Herdmans Ltd* [1987] 3 All ER 129, [1987] 1 WLR 1047, HL.

II SCA [34.4]

Precedents See **BCCP D[23]–BCCP D[24]**.

II SCA [35]

35. Provisions supplementary to ss 33 and 34

(1) A court shall not make an order under section 33 or 34 if it considers that compliance with the order, if made, would be likely to be injurious to the public interest.

(2) Rules of court may make provision as to the circumstances in which an order under section 33 or 34 can be made; and any rules making such provision may include such incidental, supplementary and consequential provisions as the rulemaking authority may consider necessary or expedient.

(3) Without prejudice to the generality of subsection (2), rules of court shall be made for the purpose of ensuring that the costs of and incidental to proceedings for an order under section 33(2) or 34 incurred by the person against whom the order is sought shall be awarded to that person unless the court otherwise directs.

(4) Sections 33(2) and 34 and this section bind the Crown; and section 33(1) binds the Crown so far as it relates to property as to which it appears to the court that it may become the subject-matter of subsequent proceedings involving a claim in respect of personal injuries to a person or in respect of a person's death.

In this subsection references to the Crown do not include references to Her Majesty in Her private capacity or to Her Majesty in right of Her Duchy of Lancaster or to the Duke of Cornwall.

(5) In sections 32A, 33 and 34 and this section—

"property" includes any land, chattel or other corporeal property of any description;

"personal injuries" includes any disease and any impairment of a person's physical or mental condition.

II SCA [36]

35A. Power of High Court to award interest on debts and damages

(1) Subject to rules of court, in proceedings (whenever instituted) before the High Court for the recovery of a debt or damages there may be included in any sum for which judgment is given simple interest, at such rate as the court thinks fit or as rules of court may provide, on all or any part of the debt or damages in respect of which judgment is given, or payment is made before judgment, for all or any part of the period between the date when the cause of action arose and—

- (a) in the case of any sum paid before judgment, the date of the payment; and
- (b) in the case of the sum for which judgment is given, the date of the judgment.

(2) In relation to a judgment given for damages for personal injuries or death which exceed £200 subsection (1) shall have effect—

- (a) with the substitution of "shall be included" for "may be included"; and
- (b) with the addition of "unless the court is satisfied that there are special reasons to the contrary" after "given", where first occurring.

(3) Subject to rules of court, where—

- (a) there are proceedings (whenever instituted) before the High Court for the recovery of a debt; and
- (b) the defendant pays the whole debt to the plaintiff (otherwise than in pursuance of a judgment in the proceedings),

the defendant shall be liable to pay the plaintiff simple interest at such rate as the court thinks fit or as rules of court may provide on all or any part of the debt for all or any part of the period between the date when the cause of action arose and the date of the payment.

(4) Interest in respect of a debt shall not be awarded under this section for a period during which, for whatever reason, interest on the debt already runs.

(5) Without prejudice to the generality of section 84, rules of court may provide for a rate of interest by reference to the rate specified in section 17 of the Judgments Act 1838 as that section has effect from time to time or by reference to a rate for which any other enactment provides.

(6) Interest under this section may be calculated at different rates in respect of different periods.

(7) In this section "plaintiff" means the person seeking the debt or damages and "defendant" means the person from whom the plaintiff seeks the debt or damages and "personal injuries" includes any disease and any impairment of a person's physical or mental condition.

(8) Nothing in this section affects the damages recoverable for the dishonour of a bill of exchange.

II SCA [36.1]

Subject to rules of court Interest may not be awarded unless a claim for it is made in accordance with rules of court: CPR 16.4 (1)(b), (2) (see para **CPR 16.4**). See *Ward v Chief Constable of Avon and Somerset* (1985) 129 Sol Jo 606, CA; *Edward Butler Vintners Ltd v Grange Seymour International Ltd* (1987) 131 Sol Jo 1188, CA.

II SCA [36.2]

Proceedings for the recovery of a debt or damages The power to award interest is not exercisable if payment of the debt or damages is made before the start of proceedings. But it may be awarded if the debt is paid after the start of proceedings: *Edmunds v Lloyd Italico e L'Ancora Cia di Assicurazioni e Riassicurazioni SpA* [1986] 2 All ER 249, [1986] 1 WLR 492, CA. Interest may be awarded on damages for loss of a non-profit-making chattel (*Metal Box Ltd v Currys Ltd* [1988] 1 All ER 341, [1988] 1 WLR 175) and on contractual damages which compensate in part for loss of interest which would have been earned: *Fansa v American Express International Banking Corpn* (1985) Times, 26 June. Conversely, interest may properly be withheld in respect of damages which include bank interest (*Wentworth v Wiltshire County Council* [1993] 2 All ER 256 at 269, CA) and in respect of damages for wrongful arrest and false imprisonment: *Holtham v Metropolitan Police Comr* (1987) Times, 28 November, CA. It may also be withheld in respect of other non-pecuniary losses eg damages for inconvenience: *Saunders v Edwards* [1987] 2 All ER 651, [1987] 1 WLR 1116, CA.

II SCA [36.3]

At such rate as the court thinks fit or as rules of court may provide If interest is claimed without specifying the rate, it may be awarded at whatever rate the court thinks fit. There are, however, advantages in specifying the rate payable on judgments (currently 8%) where the substantive claim is for the recovery of a liquidated debt. Provided the claim for interest is limited in this way, rules of court permit a default judgment to be entered for liquidated interest on top of the liquidated debt: CPR 12.6. For precedents where interest is claimed at the judgment rate on a liquidated debt, see **BCCP K[111]** and **BCCP K[221]**.

As to the rate to award on an assessment in a commercial case, the court should choose a rate one or two per cent over the base lending rate, but may discount for any tax advantage which non-payment has given the creditor: *Tate & Lyle Food and Distribution Ltd v Greater London Council* [1981] 3 All ER 716, [1982] 1 WLR 149. Interest may be awarded in commercial cases at 3 % over base rate in the case of small business claimants, because of the relatively higher cost of borrowing: *Jaura v Ahmed* [2002] EWCA Civ 210, (2002) Times, 18 March. Where the creditor has been indemnified by insurers who have rights of subrogation the mitigation of loss due to insurance should be left out of account: *H Cousins & Co Ltd v D & C Carriers Ltd* [1971] 2 QB 230, [1971] 1 All ER 55, CA. The judgment rate is appropriate for interest on damages for negligence by a solicitor in the conduct of proceedings on behalf of a claimant: *Pinnock v Wilkins & Sons* (1990) Times, 29 January, CA. For a precedent where interest is claimed on damages without specifying a rate, see **BCCP K[111]** and **BCCP K[224]**.

Interest in commercial cases may be awarded, under s 35A, at 3 % over base rate in the case of small business claimants, because of the relatively higher cost of borrowing: *Jaura v Ahmed* [2002] EWCA Civ 210, (2002) Times, 18 March.

II SCA [36.4]

For all or part of the period down to judgment Interest may be awarded for less than the full period where there has been unjustifiable delay by the claimant: *McDermid v Nash Dredging and Reclamation Co Ltd* [1986] QB 965, [1986] 2 All ER 676, CA. Where judgment is obtained for damages to be assessed interest should be given down to the date of assessment and not simply to the date of judgment: *Fablaine Ltd v Leygill Ltd* (*No 2*) [1982] Com LR 162. Interest under the Judgments Act 1838 runs from the latter date: *Thomas v Bunn* [1991] 1 AC 362, [1991] 1 All ER 193, HL. The Court of Appeal commented, in *Adcock v Co-operative Insurance Society Ltd* [2000] Lloyd's Rep IR 657, (2000) Times, 26 April, that penalising a dilatory claimant by disallowing part of a claim for interest could result in a defendant obtaining an unjustified windfall.

II SCA [36.5]

Debt paid before judgment Interest may not be awarded on sums paid before judgment, and therefore not included in it, unless paid by the defendant after the start of proceedings, as contemplated in sub-s (3). The section does not allow interest to be awarded on debts paid before the start of proceedings or on debts paid by third parties: *I M Properties plc v Cape and Dalgleish (a firm)* [1999] QB 297, [1998] 3 All ER 203, 457, CA.

On the other hand, the debt does not have to be a contract debt and the proceedings may be proceedings for judicial review: *R (on the application of Kemp) v Denbighshire Local Health Board* [2006] EWHC 181 (Admin), [2006] 3 All ER 141.

II SCA [36.6]

In relation to personal injuries or death The provisions of sub-s (2) derive from the Administration of Justice Act 1982 s 15(1) and narrow the court's discretion to withhold an award of interest in relation to damages for personal injuries or death, provided the substantive claim is above the insignificant threshold of £200. "Personal injuries" includes any disease and any impairment of a person's physical or mental condition: see sub-s (7). A separate body of case law has built up regarding the award of interest in relation to personal injuries or death, starting with the guidelines laid down in *Jefford v Gee* [1970] 2 QB 130, [1970] 1 All ER 1202, CA.

II SCA [36.7]

***Jefford v Gee* guidelines** Guidelines on award of interest in personal injury cases were laid down in *Jefford v Gee* [1970] 2 QB 130, [1970] 1 All ER 1202, CA and have been modified, and extended, by subsequent decisions of the courts. The main features of the guidelines, as applied today, are as follows:

(a) *Special damages*. Interest should be awarded on major items of special damage from the date of the loss at "the appropriate rate", which should be taken as the rate payable on the Special Account (formerly Short Term Investment Account) over the relevant period. Details of the rates payable since 1 October 1965 are set out below. However, in the normal case where special damages consist of, or include, loss of earnings which accrue over a long period, the better approach is to allow interest on the whole sum over the whole period but at half the Special Account rate. No interest should be awarded on damages in respect of future loss of earnings.

(b) *Pain, suffering, loss of amenity*. Interest on general damages for pain, suffering and loss of amenity should be awarded at the "conventional" rate of 2% pa from the date of service of proceedings: *Wright v British Railways Board* [1983] 2 AC 773, [1983] 2 All ER 698, HL. In *Lawrence v Chief Constable of Staffordshire* [2000] All ER (D) 894, (2000) Times, 25 July, CA the Court of Appeal rejected submissions that the rate should be raised to 3%.

(c) *Bereavement*. In *Sharman v Sheppard* [1989] CLY 1190 a county court judge awarded interest on bereavement damages, under s 1A of the Fatal Accidents Act 1976, at the Special Account rate as if it were special damages. An argument might perhaps be made for awarding interest at 2% pa instead, since the damages are intended as compensation for pain and suffering.

(d) *Loss of dependency under Fatal Accidents Act 1976*. In *Cookson v Knowles* [1979] AC 556, [1978] 2 All ER 604, HL, it was decided that interest should not be awarded on the whole of the dependency award (as originally recommended in *Jefford v Gee*) but only on the sum which represented the loss down to the date of the award; and that interest should be awarded at half the Special Account rate for the period from the service of proceedings. The Court of Appeal confirmed the correctness of this approach in *Fletcher (Executrix of the estate of Carl Fletcher (deceased)) v A Train & Sons Ltd* [2008] EWCA Civ 413, [2008] 4 All ER 698.

II SCA [36.8]

Departure from the guidelines Where there has been culpable delay by the claimant it may be appropriate to make a reduction in the interest period: *Birkett v Hayes* [1982] 2 All ER 710, [1982] 1 WLR 816, CA; *Spittle v Bunney* [1988] 3 All ER 1031, [1988] 1 WLR 847, CA; *Corbett v Barking, Havering and Brentwood Health Authority* [1991] 2 QB 408, [1991] 1 All ER 498, CA. Conversely, it may sometimes be appropriate to award interest for a period before service of proceedings: *Chadwick v Parsons* [1971] 2 Lloyd's Rep 49. Any special circumstances justifying an award in excess of the norm, as described above, should be pleaded, so that the defendant may take them into account when paying into court: *Dexter v Courtaulds Ltd* [1984] 1 All ER 70, [1984] 1 WLR 372, CA.

In a case of professional negligence in the handling of a personal injury claim the Court of Appeal chose the judgment rate of 8%, from the date of breach, as the appropriate rate for an award of interest in respect of special damages and chose it in preference to the special rate since the latter was too low: *Perry v Raleys Solicitors* [2017] EWCA Civ 314, [2017] All ER (D) 162 (Apr).

II SCA [36.9]

Social security benefits When calculating interest on damages for past losses, the court should ignore benefits received: *Wadey v Surrey County Council* [1999] 2 All ER 334, [1999] 1 WLR 1614, CA; *Wisely v John Fulton (Plumbers) Ltd, Wadey v Surrey County Council* [2000] 2 All ER 545, [2000] 1 WLR 820, HL.

II SCA [36.10]

Insured losses The fact that the claimant's loss is met by first party insurers on whose behalf the claim is made would not seem to be a sufficient reason for refusing an award of interest: *H Cousins & Co Ltd v D and C Carriers Ltd* [1971] 2 QB 230, [1971] 1 All ER 55, CA; but there are dicta to a contrary effect in *Jefford v Gee* [1970] 2 QB 130 at 146.

II SCA [36.11]

Rates payable on the Special Account The Special Rates recommended in the *Jefford v Gee* guidelines, above, have fluctuated from time to time, as set out in the following table:

Special Rate of Interest (formerly the Short Term Investment rate)	
From 1 February 2002	6%
From 1 February 2009	3%
From 1 June 2009	1½%
From 1 July 2009	½%

II SCA [36.12]

Period during which interest on a debt already runs Interest may run on a debt by reason of a contractual provision to this effect or by statute. For examples of the latter see the Land Compensation Act 1961 s 32(1); Housing Act 1985 Sch 10, para 4; Late Payments of Commercial Debts (Interest) Act 1998. The effect of sub-s (4) is to prevent the award of interest on interest.

II SCA [36.13]

Damages for dishonour of a bill of exchange The Bills of Exchange Act 1882 s 57 (measure of damages against parties to dishonoured bill) provides as follows

57. Measurement of damages against parties to dishonoured bills

Where a bill is dishonoured, the measure of damages, which shall be deemed to be liquidated damages, shall be as follows:

(1) The holder may recover from any party liable on the bill, and the drawer who has been compelled to pay the bill may recover from the acceptor, and an indorser who has been compelled to pay the bill may recover from the acceptor or from the drawer, or from a prior indorser—

- (a) The amount of the bill:
- (b) Interest thereon from the time of presentment for payment if the bill is payable on demand, and from the maturity of the bill in any other case:
- (c) The expenses of noting, or, when protest is necessary, and the protest has been extended, the expenses of protest.

(2) [. . .]

(3) Where by this Act interest may be recovered as damages, such interest may, if justice require it, be withheld wholly or in part, and where a bill is expressed to be payable with interest at a given rate, interest as damages may or may not be given at the same rate as interest proper.

As to the rate at which interest should be claimed for dishonour of a bill, the rate payable on judgments, or on the short term investment account, is a safe guide; but a higher rate at, or above, base rate may be justifiable in a commercial setting: *Practice Direction* [1983] 1 All ER 934 sub nom *Practice Note* [1983] 1 WLR 377. A precedent for a claim for damages for dishonour of a cheque, including a claim for interest, is provided at **BCCP K[843]**.

II SCA [36.14]

Late payment of commercial debts The Late Payment of Commercial Debts (Interest) Act 1998 confers a statutory right to claim interest on late payment of commercial debts and thus, in relation to any debt to which that Act applies, the operation of s 35A is excluded by sub-s (4). The text of the Act is set out at **CPR 16.4 [5.17]**.

II SCA [36.15]

Deduction of tax Statutory interest is "yearly interest" for the purposes of s 874 of the Income Tax Act 2007 and anyone liable to pay statutory interest must deduct tax at the basic rate and remit it to the tax authorities: *Re Lehman Bros International (Europe) (In administration) (No 7) v Revenue and Customs Comrs* [2017] EWCA Civ 2124, (2018) Times, 24 January.

II SCA [37]

36. Subpoena issued by High Court to run throughout United Kingdom

(1) If in any cause or matter in the High Court it appears to the court that it is proper to compel the personal attendance at any trial of a witness who may not be within the jurisdiction of the court, it shall be lawful for the court, if in the discretion of the court it seems fit so to do, to order that a writ of subpoena ad testificandum or writ of subpoena duces tecum shall issue in special form commanding the witness to attend the trial wherever he shall be within the United Kingdom; and the service of any such writ in any part of the United Kingdom shall be as valid and effectual for all purposes as if it had been served within the jurisdiction of the High Court.

(2) Every such writ shall have at its foot a statement to the effect that it is issued by the special order of the High Court, and no such writ shall issue without such a special order.

(3) If any person served with a writ issued under this section does not appear as required by the writ, the High Court, on proof to the satisfaction of the court of the service of the writ and of the default, may transmit a certificate of the default under the seal of the court or under the hand of a judge of the court—

- (a) if the service was in Scotland, to the Court of Session at Edinburgh; or
- (b) if the service was in Northern Ireland, to the High Court of Justice in Northern Ireland at Belfast;

and the court to which the certificate is sent shall thereupon proceed against and punish the person in default in like manner as if that person had neglected or refused to appear in obedience to process issued out of that court.

(4) No court shall in any case proceed against or punish any person for having made such default as aforesaid unless it is shown to the court that a reasonable and sufficient sum of money to defray —

- (a) the expenses of coming and attending to give evidence and of returning from giving evidence; and
- (b) any other reasonable expenses which he has asked to be defrayed in connection with his evidence,

was tendered to him at the time when the writ was served upon him.

(5) Nothing in this section shall affect—

- (a) the power of the High Court to issue a commission for the examination of witnesses out of the jurisdiction of the court in any case in which, notwithstanding this section, the court thinks fit to issue such a commission; or
- (b) the admissibility at any trial of any evidence which, if this section had not been enacted, would have been admissible on the ground of a witness being outside the jurisdiction of the court.

(6) In this section references to attendance at a trial include references to attendance before an examiner or commissioner appointed by the High Court in any cause or matter in that court, including an examiner or commissioner appointed to take evidence outside the jurisdiction of the court.

II SCA [37.1]

Witness who may not be within the jurisdiction of the court The purpose of this section is to extend the High Court's inherent jurisdiction over witnesses within the jurisdiction to situations where the witness is outside the jurisdiction but within the United Kingdom. The extension includes witnesses in Scotland and Northern Ireland but not witnesses in the Channel Islands or the Isle of Man: Interpretation Act 1978 s 5 and Sch 1.

II SCA [37.2]

Practice and procedure in respect of writs of subpoena The practice and procedure in respect of writs of subpoena is set out in CPR 34.2–34.5, see para **CPR 34.2** for the issue, service and setting aside of witness summonses.

II SCA [38]

37. Powers of High Court with respect to injunctions and receivers

(1) The High Court may by order (whether interlocutory or final) grant an injunction or appoint a receiver in all cases in which it appears to the court to be just and convenient to do so.

(2) Any such order may be made either unconditionally or on such terms and conditions as the court thinks just.

(3) The power of the High Court under subsection (1) to grant an interlocutory injunction restraining a party to any proceedings from removing from the jurisdiction of the High Court, or otherwise dealing with, assets located within that jurisdiction shall be exercisable in cases where that party is, as well as in cases where he is not, domiciled, resident or present within that jurisdiction.

(4) The power of the High Court to appoint a receiver by way of equitable execution shall operate in relation to all legal estates and interests in land; and that power—

- (a) may be exercised in relation to an estate or interest in land whether or not a charge has been imposed on that land under section 1 of the Charging Orders Act 1979 for the purpose of enforcing the judgment, order or award in question; and
- (b) shall be in addition to, and not in derogation of, any power of any court to appoint a receiver in proceedings for enforcing such a charge.

(5) Where an order under the said section 1 imposing a charge for the purpose of enforcing a judgment, order or award has been, or has effect as if, registered under section 6 of the Land Charges Act 1972, subsection (4) of the said section 6 (effect of non-registration of writs and orders registrable under that section) shall not apply to an order appointing a receiver made either—

- (a) in proceedings for enforcing the charge; or
- (b) by way of equitable execution of the judgment, order or award or, as the case may be, of so much of it as requires payment of moneys secured by the charge.

(6) This section applies in relation to the family court as it applies in relation to the High Court.

II SCA [38.1]

Applications for injunctions Section 37 restates the High Court's jurisdiction to grant injunctions. The jurisdiction may be invoked by applications made in the course of proceedings, or before the main proceedings have been started or after judgment, in aid of execution (eg a Mareva injunction to prevent dissipation of assets by judgment debtor: *Stewart Chartering Ltd v C and O Management SA* [1980] 1 All ER 718, [1982] 1 WLR 480).

The High Court has inherent jurisdiction, shared by the County Court, to prohibit the continuation, without leave, of proceedings which are likely to be an abuse of process: *Grepe v Loam* (1887) 37 Ch D 168, CA; similarly there is jurisdiction to prohibit the commencement of such proceedings: *Ebert v Birch* [2000] Ch 484, [1999] 3 WLR 670, CA. Neither the exercise of these powers in appropriate circumstances, nor of the powers under s 42 in relation to vexatious litigants, constitute a breach of Article 6 of the European Convention for the Protection of Human Rights and Fundamental Freedoms 1953, as to which see **III HUM [28]**. In *Cavannah v Blackburn with Darwen Borough Council* (23 November 2000, unreported), CA (Appeal ref A1/2000/2787) the Court of Appeal made an order that the appellant was not to be allowed to make further applications in the Employment Tribunal, the Employment Appeal Tribunal or the Court of Appeal in respect of her dismissal by the respondent, without leave of a judge of the Employment Appeal Tribunal being first obtained on notice to the respondent.

The High Court also has a long established jurisdiction to grant injunctions restricting the publication of reports affecting the interests of children and vulnerable adults. But it should balance the competing rights under Arts 8 (respect for family and private life) and 10 (freedom of expression) before doing so. *Local Authority v Health Authority (Inquiry: Restraint on publication)* [2003] EWHC 2745 (Fam), [2004] Fam 96, [2004] 1 All ER 480.

II SCA [38.1A]

Anti-suit Injunctions The courts of one member State may not restrain proceedings in another, except as provided by the Convention: *Turner v Grovit Case C-159/02* [2004] 2 All ER (Comm) 381. Outside the Convention, however, the English High Court has inherent jurisdiction to restrain by injunction proceedings in a foreign court which constitute an abuse of process in that their only purpose is to harass and oppress: *Turner v Grovit* [2000] QB 345, [1999] 3 All ER 616, CA. Similarly, an injunction may in appropriate circumstances, be granted to restrain foreign proceedings brought in breach of an arbitration clause: *Shell International Petroleum Co Ltd v Coral Oil Co Ltd* [1999] 1 Lloyd's Rep 72; *Bankers Trust Co v PT Jakarta International Hotels and Development* [1999] 1 All ER (Comm) 785; *Midgulf International Ltd v Groupe Chimique Tunisien* [2010] EWCA Civ 66, [2010] Lloyd's Rep 543, (2010) Times 3 March; or in breach of a contractual term conferring exclusive jurisdiction on the English court: *Continental Bank NA v Aeokos Cia Naviera SA* [1994] 2 All ER 540, [1994] 1 WLR 588, CA. However, a non-exclusive jurisdiction clause is usually to be construed as contemplating the possibility of parallel proceedings in another jurisdiction, in which case it would be inappropriate to grant an anti-suit injunction: *Highland Crusader Offshore Partners LP v Deutsche Bank AG* [2009] EWCA Civ 725, [2009] 2 All ER (Comm) 987, [2009] 2 Lloyd's Rep 617. An anti-suit injunction may be granted on a permanent basis where a party has been found, in a judgment on the merits, to be in breach of contract in bringing such proceedings: *National Westminster Bank v Utrecht-American Finance Co* [2001] EWCA Civ 658, [2001] 3 All ER 733. The English court has an ancillary power to protect the integrity of its judgments by restraining a foreign defendant from re-litigating the same issues abroad: *Masri v Consolidated Contractors International Co SAL (No 3)* [2008] EWCA Civ 625, [2008] 2 All ER (Comm) 1146.

In *Donohue v Armco Inc* [2001] UKHL 64, [2002] 1 All ER 749, the court refused an anti-suit injunction because there were strong reasons for doing so. An injunction was also refused in a case where the applicants had delayed and the respondents had already obtained judgments in the home courts: *Ecobank Transnational Incorporated v Tanoh* [2015] EWCA Civ 1309 (Comm), [2015] All ER (D) 51 (Jul). On the other hand, an anti-suit injunction was granted in *Navigation Maritime Bulgare v Rustal Trading Ltd (The Zagubanski)* [2002] 1 Lloyd's Rep 106 to restrain foreign proceedings in a Brussels Convention State. The court was satisfied that the respondent was acting in breach of a London arbitration clause and that the proceedings were within the "arbitration exception" in Art 2 of the Convention. Where the parties are bound by an arbitration clause, an anti-suit injunction may be granted under s 37 to restrain proceedings in breach of the arbitration clause even where the injunctive powers under s 44 of the Arbitration Act 1996 may be more limited: *Starlight Shipping Co v Tai Ping Insurance Co Ltd* [2007] EWHC 1893 (Comm), [2007] 2 CLC 440, Cooke J, QBD (Comm). An anti-suit injunction may be granted under this section, but not under s 44 of the 1996 Act, where no arbitration is pending or intended: *AES Ust-Kamenogorsk Hydropower Plant LLP v Ust-Kamenogorsk Hydropower Plant JSC* [2010] EWHC 722 (Comm). However, within the European Community, the grant of an anti-suit injunction may be in breach of the Convention, or the Council Regulation (EC) 44/2001, as was the opinion of the Advocate General in *Allianz SpA v West Tankers* Case C-185/07.

An application for an anti-suit injunction does not have to be made by claim – it may be made by application in proceedings which are already on foot: *Glencore International AG v Metro Trading Inc* [2001] 1 All ER (Comm) 103, [2002] All ER (D) 124 (Apr), CA.

The court's discretion to grant an anti-arbitration injunction should generally be exercised only in exceptional circumstances; and particular caution is required in respect of arbitrations outside the jurisdiction. As a minimum the applicant must establish either infringement of legal or equitable rights or that continuation of the arbitration would be vexatious, oppressive or unconscionable: *Claxton Engineering Services Ltd v TXM Olaj-Es Gazkutato KTF* [2011] EWHC 345 (Comm), [2011] 1 Lloyd's Rep 510, [2011] NLJR 437.

The Supreme Court reached the same conclusion: *AES Ust-Kamenogorsk Hydropower Plant LLP v Ust-Kamenogorsk Hydropower Plant JSC* [2013] UKSC 35, [2013] 1 WLR 1889, [2014] 1 All ER (Comm) 1. Conversely, where proceedings are started in a foreign court for an injunction to prevent submission to arbitration in the United Kingdom, our courts may grant an anti-suit injunction: *Ecom Agroindustrial Corpn Ltd v Mosharaf Composite Textile Mill Ltd* [2013] EWHC 1276 (Comm), [2013] 2 All ER (Comm) 983, [2013] 2 Lloyd's Rep 196.

II SCA [38.1B]

Covenant to obtain a Get However the court has no jurisdiction to enforce by mandatory injunction a covenant by a husband to obtain a Get, or a pre-nuptial agreement by him to comply with the instructions of the Beth Din in this regard. However, in such a case, the court may exercise its discretion to refuse to hear an application by the husband in family proceedings: *N v N (Divorce: Ante-Nuptial Agreement)* [1999] 2 FCR 583, [1999] 2 FLR 745.

II SCA [38.1C]

Injunction practice and precedents Practical guidance on injunction applications, particularly freezing orders and search orders, is provided in **CPR PD 25A**. Precedents for obtaining other kinds of interim (and perpetual) injunctions are set out in **BCCP C[31]**, **BCCP C[32]** and **BCCP C[551]**.

II SCA [38.1D]

Injunction to compel performance of public duty Where a local authority is empowered by statute to enforce a statute by prosecution the High Court has inherent power to grant a prohibitive injunction to prevent the commission of further offences: *Kirklees Metropolitan Borough Council v Wickes Building Supplies Ltd* [1993] AC 227. But such an inherent power does not extend to authorising an authority to interfere with property rights: *Worcestershire County Council v Tongue* [2003] 39 LS Gaz R 39, (2003) Times, 1 October, Neuberger J, [2004] EWCA Civ 140, [2004] Ch 236, (2004) Times, 26 February.

A deliberate and flagrant flouting of the law is an important factor, but not a necessary condition for the grant of an injunction and the broad questions to be asked are whether criminal proceedings are likely to prove ineffective to achieve the public interest purposes of the legislation or if there are good grounds for thinking that compliance will not be secured by prosecution: *Guildford Borough Council v Hein* [2005] EWCA Civ 979, (2005) Times, 21 September. In that case the Court concluded, by a majority, that an injunction was justified by the exceptional circumstances. However a declaration that the authority was entitled to dispose of animals removed from the defendant's control was set aside on the ground that such a disposal would be an illegal interference with property rights.

However, councils should not seek civil injunctions to restrain anti-social behaviour in reliance on s 27 of the Police and Justice Act 2006, since this would avoid the specific requirements applicable to ASBOs. The courts should not indulge in parallel activity by the extension of general common law principles: *Birmingham City Council v Shafi and Ellis* [2008] EWCA Civ 1186, applying principles laid down by Hoffmann J in *Chief Constable of Leicestershire v M* [1989] 1 WLR 20, ChD.

A defendant who persistently caused the sending of unsolicited emails in breach of the Privacy and Electronic Communications (EC Directive) Regulations 2003, SI 2003/2426 and thereby damaged the business of Microsoft Corporation, was enjoined on their application from committing further breaches, although the Regulations provided only damages by way of civil remedy: *Microsoft Corp v McDonald* [2006] EWHC 3410, (2007) Times, 26 January, Lewison J.

II SCA [38.1E]

Injunctions with effect in foreign jurisdictions Injunctive relief may be granted in respect of overseas assets of a company in administration. The comity owed by the courts of different jurisdictions to each other would normally make it inappropriate to grant injunctive relief affecting procedures in a foreign court but in certain circumstances such relief may be granted: *Harms Offshore AHT "Taurus" GmbH & Co KG v Bloom* [2009] EWCA Civ 632, [2009] 2 BCLC 473, (2009) Times, 10 July, CA.

Where a company is being wound up in the jurisdiction in which it had been incorporated an anti-suit injunction may be granted to stop creditors pursuing remedies in another jurisdiction, if it would give them unjustified priority. In so holding, the Supreme Court rejected the argument that foreign litigants should never be prevented from suing in their own courts: *Krys v Stichting Shell Pensioenfonds* (2015) 1 January, Sup Ct.

II SCA [38.2]

Appointment of receivers For the practice and procedure regarding the appointment of receivers, see **CPR 69.1** onwards and **CPR PD 69**. The court has power to appoint a receiver in relation to foreign assets where it is just and convenient to do so: *Masri v Consolidated Contractors* [2008] EWCA Civ 303, [2008] All ER (D) 359 (Jul). In an appropriate case a receiver may be appointed by way of equitable execution in support of a third party debt order: *Taurus Petroleum Ltd v State Oil Marketing Company of the Ministry of Oil, Republic of Iraq* [2017] UKSC 64. Precedents are provided in **BCCP H[40]** for the appointment of a receiver by way of equitable execution. See also *Atkin's Court Forms* Vol 33 (1997 Issue) title RECEIVERS.

In a case where one of several defendants was a foreign company and there were ongoing disputes between the company's shareholders and directors, who were also defendants, it was held to be appropriate to appoint a receiver for the purpose of defending the claim against the company: *JSC BTA Bank v Abylyazov* [2012] EWHC 2698 (Comm).

Appointment of receivers The court has power to appoint a receiver in relation to an estate where there is no current representative. Typical cases might be where the estate was entitled to an income but there was no one to receive it or where there were liabilities to meet, non-payment of which might lead to the loss of a valuable asset: *Joint Stock Company 'Aeroflot Russian Airlines' v Berezovsky* [2013] EWHC 1210 (Ch), [2013] NLJR 21.

A receiver may be appointed in respect of another party's very valuable civil claims in order to have them issued before being limitation-barred: *BAT Industries plc v Windward Prospects Ltd* [2013] EWHC 3612 (Comm), [2013] All ER (D) 265 (Nov).

II SCA [38.3]

Order for the preservation of evidence The power to grant an injunction may be exercised in order to preserve evidence. There are also statutory powers which may be exercised to allow a prospective claimant to inspect, photograph, preserve or sample property which may be the subject-matter of proceedings. Identical powers are conferred, in this regard, on the High Court and on the County Court by the Supreme Court Act 1981 s 33 and the County Courts Act 1984 s 52. Additional powers are conferred on the High Court alone by the Civil Procedure Act 1997 s 7, set out below.

II SCA [38.4]

7. Power of courts to make orders for preserving evidence etc.

(1) The court may make an order under this section for the purpose of securing, in the case of any existing or proposed proceedings in the court—

- (a) the preservation of evidence which is or may be relevant; or
- (b) the preservation of property which is or may be the subject-matter of the proceedings or as to which any question arises or may arise in the proceedings.

(2) A person who is, or appears to the court likely to be, a party to proceedings in the court may make an application for such an order.

(3) Such an order may direct any person to permit any person described in the order, or secure that any person so described is permitted—

- (a) to enter premises in England and Wales; and
- (b) while on the premises, to take in accordance with the terms of the order any of the following steps.

(4) Those steps are—

- (a) to carry out a search for or inspection of anything described in the order; and
- (b) to make or obtain a copy, photograph, sample or other record of anything so described.

(5) The order may also direct the person concerned—

- (a) to provide any person described in the order, or secure that any person so described is provided, with any information or article described in the order; and
- (b) to allow any person described in the order, or secure that any person so described is allowed, to retain for safe keeping anything described in the order.

(6) An order under this section is to have effect subject to such conditions as are specified in the order.

(7) This section does not affect any right of a person to refuse to do anything on the ground that to do so might tend to expose him or his spouse to proceedings for an offence or for the recovery of a penalty.

(8) In this section—

"court" means the High Court, and

"premises" includes any vehicle;

and an order under this section may describe anything generally, whether by reference to a class or otherwise.

II SCA [38.5]

Orders under CPA 1997 and Anton Piller orders Anton Piller orders (now known as "search orders") are broader in that they may include the administration of interrogatories and that the privilege against self-incrimination may be disapplied by the Supreme Court Act 1981 s 72. The county court could make Anton Piller orders in the circumstances set out in the County Courts Remedies Regulations 1991 (see para **II CCA [21.10]**), but there was no disapplication in the county court of the privilege against self-incrimination. See now the Practice Direction to CPR Part 25 (interim injunctions).

II SCA [38.6]

Injunctions against non-parties The general rule is that you cannot have an injunction except against a party to the suit: *Iveson v Harris* (1802) 32 ER 102, per LORD ELDON. But in *Venables v News Group Newspapers* [2001] Fam 430, [2001] 1 All ER 908, the President of the Family Division granted injunctions, based on the right to life of two 18-year-olds who were being released from prison, to prevent publication by *anyone* of confidential information about them. Injunctions were granted against unnamed would-be trespassers in *Hampshire Waste Service Ltd v Persons Unknown* [2003] EWHC 1738 (Ch), [2003] All ER (D) 124 (Jul). An injunction to stop harassment may be granted against un-named protesters where "just and convenient to do so": *Huntingdon Life Science Group plc v Cass* [2005] EWHC 2233 (QB), [2005] 4 All ER 899, Mackay J.

II SCA [39]

38. Relief against forfeiture for non-payment of rent

(1) In any action in the High Court for the forfeiture of a lease for non-payment of rent, the court shall have power to grant relief against forfeiture in a summary manner, and may do so subject to the same terms and conditions as to the payment of rent, costs or otherwise as could have been imposed by it in such an action immediately before the commencement of this Act.

(2) Where the lessee or a person deriving title under him is granted relief under this section, he shall hold the demised premises in accordance with the terms of the lease without the necessity for a new lease.

II SCA [39.1]

Forfeiture for non-payment of rent Where a lessee is proceeding by action in a county court to forfeit a lease for non-payment of rent, the county court has statutory powers to grant relief under County Courts Act 1984 ss 138 and 139: see paras **II CCA [133]** and **II CCA [134]**. Where the lessee fails to comply with the terms on which relief is granted under that section so that all further opportunity of obtaining relief is barred, the effect is to exclude also the possibility of relief being granted by the High Court under s 38: *Di Palma v Victoria Square Property Co Ltd* [1986] Ch 150, [1985] 2 All ER 676, CA. On the other hand, so long as the chance of further relief has not been lost, a mortgagee of a lease subject to forfeiture in the county court may apply to the High Court for relief under s 38: *United Dominions Trust Ltd v Shellpoint Trustees Ltd* [1993] 4 All ER 310, CA. As to the circumstances in which relief may be granted, the court needs to be satisfied, on the evidence, that arrears will be paid within a reasonable time: *Inntrepreneur Pub Co (CPC) Ltd v Langton* [1999] 44 LS Gaz R 39.

II SCA [39.2]

Relief to chargees It was held, in *Bland v Ingrams Estates Ltd* [2001] Ch 767, [2002] 1 All ER 221, CA, that a chargee of the leasehold did not have an interest sufficient to be granted relief directly. But relief could be granted indirectly, in the exercise of the court's inherent discretion, where the chargee joined the tenant as defendant and claimed relief in his shoes. See also the powers under s 146 of the Law of Property Act 1925 at **III L&T [2]**.

II SCA [40]

39. Execution of instrument by person nominated

(1) Where the High Court or family court has given or made a judgment or order directing a person to execute any conveyance, contract or other document, or to indorse any negotiable instrument, then, if that person—

(a) neglects or refuses to comply with the judgment or order; or

(b) cannot after reasonable inquiry be found, that court may, on such terms and conditions, if any, as may be just, order that the conveyance, contract or other document shall be executed, or that the negotiable instrument shall be indorsed, by such person as the court may nominate for that purpose.

(2) A conveyance, contract, document or instrument executed or indorsed in pursuance of an order under this section shall operate, and be for all purposes available, as if it had been executed or indorsed by the person originally directed to execute or indorse it.

II SCA [40.1]

Alternative to committal The powers under s 39 are appropriate for use where the only alternative is to commit the would-be signatory to prison for contempt. See *Danchevsky v Danchevsky* [1975] Fam 17, [1974] 3 All ER 934, CA; *Mir v Mir* [1992] Fam 79, [1992] 1 All ER 765.

II SCA [40.2]

On such terms and conditions as may be just In a case where the obstructive party was not only refusing to execute the conveyance, as ordered, but also intimidating any other party to the transaction, it was held that the court could order the redaction of the name and address of the other party from the document proffered to the obstructive one: *Welch v Welch* [2017] All ER (D) 27 (Jul).

II SCA [41]

40. Attachment of debts

(1) Subject to any order for the time being in force under subsection (4), this section applies to any deposit account, any withdrawable share account with a deposit-taker.

(2) In determining whether, for the purposes of the jurisdiction of the High Court to attach debts for the purpose of satisfying judgments or orders for the payment of money, a sum standing to the credit of a person in an account to which this section applies is a sum due or accruing to that person and, as such, attachable in accordance with rules of court, any condition mentioned in subsection (3) which applies to the account shall be disregarded.

(3) Those conditions are—

(a) any condition that notice is required before any money or share is withdrawn;

(b) any condition that a personal application must be made before any money or share is withdrawn;

(c) any condition that a deposit book or share-account book must be produced before any money or share is withdrawn; or

(d) any other prescribed condition.

(4) The Lord Chancellor may by order make such provision as he thinks fit, by way of amendment of this section or otherwise, for all or any of the following purposes, namely—

(a) including in, or excluding from, the accounts to which this section applies accounts of any description specified in the order;

(b) excluding from the accounts to which this section applies all accounts with any particular deposit-taker so specified or with any deposit-taker of a description so specified.

(5) Any order under subsection (4) shall be made by statutory instrument subject to annulment in pursuance of a resolution of either House of Parliament.

(6) "Deposit-taker" means a person who may, in the course of his business, lawfully accept deposits in the United Kingdom.

(7) Subsection (6) must be read with—

(a) section 22 of the Financial Services and Markets Act 2000;

(b) any relevant order under that section; and

(c) Schedule 2 to that Act.

II SCA [41.1]

Third party debt orders (garnishee proceedings) The High Court has inherent jurisdiction to attach any debt owed by a third person (the garnishee) to the judgment debtor and to order that the debt owed by the third person should be paid to the judgment creditor instead. Enforcement proceedings started on or after 25 March 2002 are regulated by **CPR 72.1** onwards in place of **RSC 49** and **CCR 30**, which applied down to that date. The purpose of s 40 is to extend the jurisdiction to include debts owed by banks, building societies and other deposit-taking institutions even where the debts are not immediately payable by the rules of the institution.

II SCA [42]

40A Administrative and clerical expenses of garnishees

(1) Where an interim third party debt order made in the exercise of the jurisdiction mentioned in subsection (2) of the preceding section is served on a deposit-taker, it may, subject to the provisions of this section, deduct from the relevant debt or debts an amount not exceeding the prescribed sum towards its administrative and clerical expenses in complying with the order; and the right [. . .] to make a deduction under this subsection shall be exercisable as from the time the interim third party debt order is served on it.

(1A) In subsection (1) "the relevant debt or debts", in relation to an interim third party debt order served on a deposit-taker, means the amount, as at the time the order is served on it, of the debt or debts of which the whole or a part is expressed to be attached by the order.

(1B) A deduction may be made under subsection (1) in a case where the amount referred to in subsection (1A) is insufficient to cover both the amount of the deduction and the amount of the judgment debt and costs in respect of which the attachment was made, notwithstanding that the benefit of the attachment to the creditor is reduced as a result of the deduction.

(2) An amount may not in pursuance of subsection (1) be deducted or, as the case may be, retained in a case where, by virtue of section 346 of the Insolvency Act 1986 or section 183 of the Insolvency Act 1986 or otherwise, the creditor is not entitled to retain the benefit of the attachment.

(3) In this section—

"deposit-taker" has the meaning given by section 40(6); and

"prescribed" means prescribed by an order made by the Lord Chancellor.

(4) An order under this section—

(a) may make different provision for different cases; [. . .]

(b) without prejudice to the generality of paragraph (a) of this subsection, may prescribe sums differing according to the amount due under the judgment or order to be satisfied

(c) may provide for this section not to apply to deposit-takers of any prescribed description.

(5) Any such order shall be made by statutory instrument subject to annulment in pursuance of a resolution of either House of Parliament.

II SCA [42.1]

Expenses of the garnishee Where the garnishee is a deposit-taking institution s 40A creates an entitlement to expenses which may be deducted from the money owed by the institution to the judgment debtor. In the event that there is insufficient money to pay the expenses as well as the judgment debt the expenses take priority. The sum of £55 has been prescribed as the sum which may be deducted: Attachment of Debts (Expenses) Order 1996, SI 1996/3098.

II SCA [43]

41. Wards of court

(1) Subject to the provisions of this section, no minor shall be made a ward of court except by virtue of an order to that effect made by the High Court.

(2) Where an application is made for such an order in respect of a minor, the minor shall become a ward of court on the making of the application, but shall cease to be a ward of court at the end of such period as may be prescribed unless within that period an order has been made in accordance with the application.

(2A) Subsection (2) does not apply with respect to a child who is the subject of a care order (as defined by section 105 of the Children Act 1989).

(3) The High Court may, either upon an application in that behalf or without such an application, order that any minor who is for the time being a ward of court shall cease to be a ward of court.

II SCA [44]

42. Restriction of vexatious legal proceedings

(1) If, on an application made by the Attorney General under this section, the High Court is satisfied that any person has habitually and persistently and without any reasonable ground—

(a) instituted vexatious civil proceedings, whether in the High Court or the family court or any inferior court, and whether against the same person or against different persons; or

(b) made vexatious applications in any civil proceedings, whether in the High Court or the family court or any inferior court, and whether instituted by him or another, or

(c) instituted vexatious prosecutions (whether against the same person or different persons),

the court may, after hearing that person or giving him an opportunity of being heard, make a civil proceedings order, a criminal proceedings order or an all proceedings order.

(1A) In this section—

"civil proceedings order" means an order that—

(a) no civil proceedings shall without the leave of the High Court be instituted in any court by the person against whom the order is made;

(b) any civil proceedings instituted by him in any court before the making of the order shall not be continued by him without the leave of the High Court; and

(c) no application (other than one for leave under this section) shall be made by him, in any civil proceedings instituted in any court by any person, without the leave of the High Court;

"criminal proceedings order" means an order that—

(a) no information shall be laid before a justice of the peace by the person against whom the order is made without the leave of the High Court; and

(b) no application for leave to prefer a bill of indictment shall be made by him without the leave of the High Court; and

"all proceedings order" means an order which has the combined effect of the two other orders.

(2) An order under subsection (1) may provide that it is to cease to have effect at the end of a specified period, but shall otherwise remain in force indefinitely.

(3) Leave for the institution or continuance of, or for the making of an application in, any civil proceedings by a person who is the subject of an order for the time being in force under subsection (1) shall not be given unless the High Court is satisfied that the proceedings or application are not an abuse of the process of the court in question and that there are reasonable grounds for the proceedings or application.

(3A) Leave for the laying of an information or for an application for leave to prefer a bill of indictment by a person who is the subject of an order for the time being in force under subsection (1) shall not be given unless the High Court is satisfied that the institution of the prosecution is not an abuse of the criminal process and that there are reasonable grounds for the institution of the prosecution by the applicant.

(4) No appeal shall lie from a decision of the High Court refusing leave required by virtue of this section.

(5) A copy of any order made under subsection (1) shall be published in the London Gazette.

II SCA [44.1]

Institution of proceedings by appeal For guidance on proceedings under this section see no paragraph 16 of the Practice Direction supplementing Part 8 of the CPR, in volume 1 at para **CPR PD 8**. Where a vexatious litigant is given permission to bring specified proceedings, the permission does not cover the institution of an appeal against the judgment. The Court of Appeal so held in *Johnson v Valks* [2000] 1 All ER 450, [2000] 1 WLR 1502, CA, following *A-G v Jones* [1990] 2 All ER 636, [1990] 1 WLR 859, CA and *Henry J Garratt & Co v Ewing* [1991] 4 All ER 891, [1991] 1 WLR 1356, CA.

II SCA [44.2]

Civil restraint orders In *Bhamjee v Forsdick (Practice Note)* [2003] EWCA Civ 1113, [2004] 1 WLR 88 the Court of Appeal identified three kinds of civil restraint order: (1) a civil restraint order, (2) an extended civil restraint order and (3) a general restraint order: see now Practice Direction 3C - Civil Restraint Orders at **CPR PD 3C**. But the courts are unlikely to proceed even to the first category of restraining order without cogent evidence of the respondent litigant's persistently bringing proceedings or making applications which are struck out as being totally devoid of merit. Where, therefore, an application or proceeding is struck out on this basis the successful respondent should see that it is reflected in the terms of the order made eg "struck out under CPR 3.4 as being totally devoid of merit". The procedure is governed by **CPR 3.11** and the supporting Practice Direction. Note that forms are now provided for the three kinds of restraint order, N19, N19A and N19B, the text of which is reproduced at **BCCP C[701]**, **BCCP C[702]** and **BCCP C[703]**.

II SCA [44.3]

Practice For guidance on proceedings to restrain vexatious litigants see now paragraph 16 of the Practice Direction supplementing Part 8 in volume 1 at **CPR PD 8**.

It is not necessary for evidence to be led to prove authorisation of the application by the Attorney-General: *A-G v Foley* [2000] 2 All ER 609, CA. It was also held in the same case that the element of repetition is an essential ingredient of vexatious litigation, although not necessarily over a long period: *A-G v Foley* [2000] 2 All ER 609, CA. These requirements may be satisfied even where the litigant chooses a variety of different targets: *A-G v Covey; A-G v Matthews* [2001] All ER (D) 222, (2001) Times, 2 March, CA.

See **CPR 5.4A** for the rules relating to the Attorney-General's search for, and use of, documents within a court file for the purposes of an application under this section. Note that it is no part of the Divisional Court's role to consider the rightness or otherwise of a decision already made against the respondent in other proceedings, except where the law, or the understanding of the law, has changed subsequently: *A-G v Vaidya* [2017] EWHC 2152 (Admin).

It may in some circumstances be appropriate to include an order restraining a vexatious litigant from acting as a litigation friend, a McKenzie friend or otherwise assisting any third party in the conduct of civil proceedings, except with the permission of the court: *A-G v Chitolie* [2004] EWHC 1943 (Admin). The inclusion of such a provision is now recommended as standard practice: *A-G v Vaidya* [2017] EWHC 2152 (Admin).

II SCA [44.4]

Permission to appeal The grant of permission under s 42 to bring proceedings does not include permission to bring a substantive appeal: *Johnson v Valks* [2000] 1 All ER 450, [2000] 1 WLR 1502, CA.

II SCA [44.5]

Convention rights and vexatious litigants The fact that the Attorney General may exercise an advisory role in the selection and appointment of judges does not compromise the impartiality of the judges once appointed: *A-G v Covey; A-G v Matthews* [2001] All ER (D) 222, (2001) Times, 2 March, CA. It was held in the same case that it was not a breach of Article 6.1, at **III HUM [28]**, to restrict a person's access t the courts where the order pursued a legitimate aim and allowed the litigant to seek permission or to seek a variation of the order. It was also held that there was no breach in failing to disclose a bench memorandum provided that the litigant was not prejudiced by it.

In *Ebert v Official Receiver* [2001] EWCA Civ 340, [2001] 3 All ER 942, it was held that the restriction on appeal in s 42(4) does not infringe Convention rights and that a High Court judge is not prevented by the Human Rights Act 1998 from refusing to grant permission to appeal.

It was held, in *Senior-Milne v Secretary of State for Justice* [2012] EWHC 3062 (Admin), [2012] NLJR 1465 that restrictions on vexatious litigants had to pursue a legitimate aim and have a reasonable relationship of proportionality to the aim. In the instant case the limitations did not restrict the access left to the individual in such a way or to such an extent that the very essence of the right was impaired.

II SCA [44.6]

Injunction to restrain access to courts The court has power in an appropriate case to restrain a vexatious litigant from entering the Royal Courts of Justice: *A-G v Ebert* [2002] EWHC Admin 695, [2002] 2 All ER 789.

Following the decision in *A-G v Ebert*, above, the defendant made 37 unsuccessful challenges, in writing, to the bankruptcy order, in the light of which the court ordered that he should be restrained from making any application at all under s 42 relating to the bankruptcy order, or relating to a cause of action over 6 years old, and that, as regards other matters, he should be restrained from making more than one application in the first half of each year and one in the second: *A-G v Ebert* [2005] EWHC 1254 (Admin), [2005] BPIR 1056.

II SCA [45]

43. Power of High Court to vary sentence on application for quashing order

(1) Where a person who has been sentenced for an offence—

(a) by a magistrates' court; or

(b) by the Crown Court after being convicted of the offence by a magistrates' court and committed to the Crown Court for sentence; or

(c) by the Crown Court on appeal against conviction or sentence,

applies to the High Court in accordance with section 31 for a quashing order to remove the proceedings of the magistrates' court or the Crown Court into the High Court, then, if the High Court determines that the magistrates' court or the Crown Court had no power to pass the sentence, the High Court may, instead of quashing the conviction, amend it by substituting for the sentence passed any sentence which the magistrates' court or, in a case within paragraph (b), the Crown Court had power to impose.

(2) Any sentence passed by the High Court by virtue of this section in substitution for the sentence passed in the proceedings of the magistrates' court or the Crown Court shall, unless the High Court otherwise directs, begin to run from the time when it would have begun to run if passed in those proceedings; but in computing the term of the sentence, any time during which the offender was released on bail in pursuance of section 37(1)(d) of the Criminal Justice Act 1948 shall be disregarded.

(3) Subsections (1) and (2) shall, with the necessary modifications, apply in relation to any order of a magistrates' court or the Crown Court which is made on, but does not form part of, the conviction of an offender as they apply in relation to a conviction and sentence.

II SCA [45.1]

Quashing order "Quashing order" was substituted for the former order of *certiorari* by the Civil Procedure (Modification of Supreme Court Act 1981) Order 2004, SI 2004/1033.

II SCA [46]

43ZA. Power of High Court to vary committal in default

(1) Where the High Court quashes the committal of a person to prison or detention by a magistrates' court or the Crown Court for—

(a) a default in paying a sum adjudged to be paid by a conviction; or

(b) want of sufficient goods to satisfy such a sum,

the High Court may deal with the person for the default or want of sufficient goods in any way in which the magistrates' court or Crown Court would have power to deal with him if it were dealing with him at the time when the committal is quashed.

(2) If the High Court commits him to prison or detention, the period of imprisonment or detention shall, unless the High Court otherwise directs, be treated as having begun when the person was committed by the magistrates' court or the Crown Court (except that any time during which he was released on bail shall not be counted as part of the period).

(3) In subsection (1) references to want of sufficient goods to satisfy a sum are references to circumstances where—

(a) there is power to use the procedure in Schedule 12 to the Tribunals, Courts and Enforcement Act 2007 to recover the sum from a person, but

(b) it appears, after an attempt has been made to exercise the power, that the person's goods are insufficient to pay the amount outstanding (as defined by paragraph 50(3) of that Schedule).

II SCA [46.1]

Access to justice This section was inserted by the Access to Justice Act 1999 s 62.

II SCA [46A]

43A. Specific powers of arbitrator exercisable by High Court

In any cause or matter proceeding in the High Court in connection with any contract incorporating an arbitration agreement which confers specific powers upon the arbitrator, the High Court may, if all parties to the agreement agree, exercise any such powers.

OTHER PROVISIONS

II SCA [47]

44. Extraordinary functions of judges of High Court

(1) Subject to the provisions of this Act, every judge of the High Court shall be—

(a) liable to perform any duty not incident to the administration of justice in any court of law which a judge of the High Court was, as the successor of any judge formerly subject to that duty, liable to perform immediately before the commencement of this Act by virtue of any statute, law or custom; and

(b) empowered to exercise any authority or power not so incident which a judge of the High Court was, as the successor of any judge formerly possessing that authority or power, empowered to exercise immediately before that commencement by virtue of any statute, law or custom.

(2) Any such duty, authority or power which immediately before the commencement of this Act was imposed or conferred by any statute, law or custom on . . . the Lord Chief Justice or the Master of the Rolls shall continue to be performed and exercised by them respectively.

II SCA [47.1]

Appeals relating to regulations of the Bar From an appointed day, High Court judges will no longer have jurisdiction as visitors to the Inns of Court, but other arrangements for appeals to the High Court may be made in accordance with s 24 of the Crime and Courts Act 2013.

GENERAL PROVISIONS

Law and equity

II SCA [48]

49. Concurrent administration of law and equity

(1) Subject to the provisions of this or any other Act, every court exercising jurisdiction in England or Wales in any civil cause or matter shall continue to administer law and equity on the basis that, wherever there is any conflict or variance between the rules of equity and the rules of the common law with reference to the same matter, the rules of equity shall prevail.

(2) Every such court shall give the same effect as hitherto—

(a) to all equitable estates, titles, rights, reliefs, defences and counterclaims, and to all equitable duties and liabilities; and

(b) subject thereto, to all legal claims and demands and all estates, titles, rights, duties, obligations and liabilities existing by the common law or by any custom or created by any statute,

and, subject to the provisions of this or any other Act, shall so exercise its jurisdiction in every cause or matter before it as to secure that, as far as possible, all matters in dispute between the parties are completely and finally determined, and all multiplicity of legal proceedings with respect to any of those matters is avoided.

(3) Nothing in this Act shall affect the power of the Court of Appeal or the High Court to stay any proceedings before it, where it thinks fit to do so, either of its own motion or on the application of any person, whether or not a party to the proceedings.

II SCA [48.1]

The rules of equity shall prevail Section 49 restates the position established by the Judicature Acts 1873–75 that law and equity must be administered concurrently in all courts and that the rules of equity must prevail. Practical examples of the effect given to equitable remedies in legal actions are to be found in the context of mortgage actions, claims and counterclaims and the doctrine of estoppel. In these and many other situations equitable remedies, the equitable right to set off damages against debts and the doctrine of promissory estoppel may be invoked to prevent or postpone the enforcement of legal rights.

II SCA [48.2]

Stay of proceedings The court has the power to stay proceedings as part of its inherent jurisdiction. There are various grounds on which it may do so eg to prevent an abuse of court process, to give effect to an arbitration agreement and to allow the parties to reach a compromise out of court. It is comparatively rare to stay proceedings in one United Kingdom court in order that the same issues may be litigated in another; but increasingly the High Court is being asked to stay proceedings in this country in order that equivalent proceedings in another country may take precedence. In cases where there is concurrent jurisdiction a ruling has to be made as to which is the more appropriate forum. See, for example, Civil Jurisdiction and Judgments Act 1982 s 49 at para **III EUR [31]** and, for a review of the authorities, *Spiliada Maritime Corpn v Consulex Ltd, The Spiliada* [1987] AC 460, [1986] 3 All ER 843, HL.

Where a claim has been issued against a defendant and the defendant's insurers are involved, it is not generally appropriate to stay parallel proceedings for a declaration of non-liability to the defendant's insurers. Reinsurance is not a general exception to the normal rule that a stay of proceedings properly brought should only be granted in rare and compelling circumstances: *Amlin Corporate Member Ltd v Oriental Assurance Corpn* [2012] EWCA Civ 1341, [2012] NLJR 1376.

II SCA [49]

50. Power to award damages as well as, or in substitution for, injunction or specific performance

Where the Court of Appeal or the High Court has jurisdiction to entertain an application for an injunction or specific performance, it may award damages in addition to, or in substitution for, an injunction or specific performance.

II SCA [49.1]

Damages for future losses Normally damages will be awarded in substitution for an injunction only where the loss can be adequately compensated by a small money payment and the grant of an injunction would be oppressive: *Shelfer v City of London Electric Lighting Co* [1895] 1 Ch 287 as interpreted in *Jaggard v Sawyer* [1995] 2 All ER 189, CA. However, in the case of a nuisance which infringes Convention rights a substantial award of damages may be made to cover losses in the future, whether or not an injunction would have been granted: *Marcic v Thames Water Utilities Ltd* [2001] 3 All ER 698.

See also the award of damages made in respect of past and future nuisance by noise in *Dennis v Ministry of Defence* [2003] EWHC 793 (QB), [2003] All ER (D) 300 (Apr), (2003) Times, 6 May.

II SCA [49.2]

Damages without proof of financial loss Where an injunction has been granted to restrain breach in the future and the defendant has obtained a benefit by a breach in the past, the court may award damages or order an account for the past breach although the claimant has not proved financial loss: *Experience Hendrix LLC v PPX Enterprises Inc* [2003] EWCA Civ 323, [2003] 1 All ER (Comm) 830, following *A-G v Blake* [2001] 1 AC 268, [2000] 4 All ER 385, HL.

In addition to an injunction to stop a private nuisance the court may award as damages a sum to represent the diminution in the value of the property: *Raymond v Young* [2015] EWCA Civ 456, [2015] All ER (D) 160 (May).

Where a former employee had for several years broken restrictive covenants designed to protect the former employer's business, damages were awarded although actual financial loss could not be proved. The court took as the measure of damage the reasonable price for a release from the covenants: *One Step (Support) Ltd v Morris-Garner* [2016] EWCA Civ 180. This was consistent with the approach to damages taken in *Wrotham Park Estate Co Ltd v Parkside Homes Ltd* [1974] 2 All ER 321.

II SCA [49.3]

Damages in substitution for injunction Where a claimant seeks an injunction to stop a continuing nuisance that invades his, or her, legal right (for, example right to light), the discretion to award damages in substitution for an injunction should be exercised only in very exceptional circumstances: *Regan v Paul Properties DPE No.1 Ltd* [2006] EWCA Civ 1391, [2007] 4 All ER 48, [2006] All ER (D) 327 (Oct), following the principles laid down in *Shelfer v City of London Electric Lighting Co (No 1)* [1895] 1 Ch 287.

See also *Watson v Croft Promo-Sport Ltd* [2009] EWCA Civ 15, [2009] 3 All ER 249, [2009] 18 EG 86, in which the trial judge's award of damages was set aside in favour of an injunction. The case concerned nuisance caused by car racing for which planning permission had been granted. Also the Supreme Court set aside an award of damages and granted an injunction in another case about noise in a residential area: *Coventry v Lawrence* [2014] UKSC 13, [2014] P & CR 11, [2014] PTSR 384, in which guidance was also given on the grant of *Shelfer* damages in cases about the right to light or breaches of restrictive covenants. Although the need for a flexible approach has been adopted in recent cases, there is a burden on the defendant to show why an injunction should not be granted and this has proved hard to discharge. See *Prophet plc v Huggett* [2014] EWHC 615 (Ch), [2014] IRLR 618, [2014] All ER (D) 136 (Mar) (a restriction on competitive employment) and *Higson v Guenault* [2014] EWCA Civ 703, [2014] 2 P&CR D33 (a right of way case).

II SCA [50]

51. Costs in civil division of Court of Appeal, High Court and county courts

(1) Subject to the provisions of this or any other enactment and to rules of court, the costs of and incidental to all proceedings in—

(a) the civil division of the Court of Appeal;

(b) the High Court;

(ba) the family court; and

(c) the county court,

shall be in the discretion of the court.

(2) Without prejudice to any general power to make rules of court, such rules may make provision for regulating matters relating to the costs of those proceedings including, in particular, prescribing scales of costs to be paid to legal or other representatives or for securing that the amount awarded to a party in respect of costs to be paid by him to such representatives is not limited to what would have been payable by him to them if he had not been awarded costs.

(3) The court shall have full power to determine by whom and to what extent the costs are to be paid.

(4) In subsections (1) and (2) "proceedings" includes the administration of estates and trusts.

(5) Nothing in subsection (1) shall alter the practice in any criminal cause, or in bankruptcy.

(6) In any proceedings mentioned in subsection (1), the court may disallow, or (as the case may be) order the legal or other representative concerned to meet, the whole of any wasted costs or such part of them as may be determined in accordance with rules of court.

(7) In subsection (6), "wasted costs" means any costs incurred by a party—

(a) as a result of any improper, unreasonable or negligent act or omission on the part of any legal or other representative or any employee of such a representative; or

(b) which, in the light of any such act or omission occurring after they were incurred, the court considers it is unreasonable to expect that party to pay.

(7A) Where the court exercises a power under subsection (6) in relation to costs incurred by a party, it must inform such of the following as it considers appropriate—

(a) an approved regulator;

(b) the Director of Legal Aid Casework.

(8) Where—

(a) a person has commenced proceedings in the High Court; but

(b) those proceedings should, in the opinion of the court, have been commenced in the county court or family court in accordance with any provision made under section 1 of the Courts and Legal Services Act 1990 or by or under any other enactment,

the person responsible for determining the amount which is to be awarded to that person by way of costs shall have regard to those circumstances.

(9) Where, in complying with subsection (8), the responsible person reduces the amount which would otherwise be awarded to the person in question—

(a) the amount of that reduction shall not exceed 25 per cent; and

(b) on any taxation of the costs payable by that person to his legal representative, regard shall be had to the amount of the reduction.

(10) The Lord Chancellor may by order amend subsection (9)(a) by substituting, for the percentage for the time being mentioned there, a different percentage.

(11) Any such order shall be made by statutory instrument and may make such transitional or incidental provision as the Lord Chancellor considers expedient.

(12) No such statutory instrument shall be made unless a draft of the instrument has been approved by both Houses of Parliament.

(12A) In subsection (7A)—

"approved regulator" has the meaning given by section 20 of the Legal Services Act 2007;

"the Director of Legal Aid Casework" means the civil servant designated under section 4 of the Legal Aid, Sentencing and Punishment of Offenders Act 2012.

(13) In this section "legal or other representative", in relation to a party to proceedings, means any person exercising a right of audience or right to conduct litigation on his behalf.

II SCA [50.1]

Rules of court under sub-section (2) **CPR 43.2** now provides, in paragraphs (3) and (4), for the limited application of the indemnity principle to the costs recoverable by a client who has made a conditional fee agreement on or after 2 June 2003.

II SCA [50.2]

Costs of and incidental to all proceedings The jurisdiction to order the payment of costs is confined by s 51(1) to costs of and incidental to proceedings. There is no power to order the payment of costs where there are no proceedings. As a general rule costs incurred in complying with a pre-action protocol may be recoverable as "incidental to" the proceedings, but not where they are incurred in persuading a claimant to drop a claim, wholly or in part: *McGlinn v Waltham Contractors Ltd* [2005] EWHC 1419 (TCC), [2005] 3 All ER 1126. It has been held that 'costs of and incidental to the proceedings' does not cover the costs of a separate pre-action mediation: *Lobster Group Ltd v Heidelberg Graphic Equipment Ltd* [2008] EWHC 413 (TCC), [2008] 2 All ER 1173, Coulson J.

On the other hand, the costs of attendance at a coroner's inquest may be recoverable in subsequent proceedings against a tortfeasor liable for the death in question: *Roach v Home Office* [2009] EWHC 312 (QB), [2009] 3 All ER 510, [2009] NLJR 474.

II SCA [50.3]

The discretion of the court, subject to rules Rules which limit the court's discretion as to costs are contained in CPR Part 44.

See also **CPR 48.7** regarding the personal liability of legal representatives for costs. Where proceedings have been settled and stayed by the making of a *Tomlin* order it is not necessary to lift the stay before an application can be made for a wasted costs order against the solicitors acting for one of the parties: *Wagstaff v Colls* [2003] EWCA Civ 469, (2003) Times, 17 April.

II SCA [50.4]

Full power to determine by whom the costs are to be paid Normally it is the unsuccessful party in the case who is ordered to pay the successful party's costs. Exceptionally, however, the Court may exercise its power to order a non-party to pay costs eg where the non-party has funded the bringing, or defence, of the case. See *Singh v Observer Ltd* [1989] 2 All ER 751: *Condliffe v Hislop* [1996] 1 All ER 431, [1996] 1 WLR 753, CA; *Murphy v Young & Co's Brewery plc* [1997] 1 All ER 518, [1997] 1 WLR 1591, CA.

For a case where costs were ordered to be paid *to* a non-party, see *J v Oyston* [2002] EWHC 819 (QB), [2002] Lloyd's Rep PN 427, in which the Defendant was ordered to pay the Solicitors Indemnity Fund the costs incurred on J's behalf.

II SCA [50.5]

Power to order costs against a non-party The discretion afforded by this section includes a power to order costs against a non-party. Where a non-party has an interest in the outcome of litigation by virtue of a champertous agreement, this constitutes a firm basis for the exercise of the statutory discretion to award costs against him. But, even if the agreement is not strictly champertous, a non-party's financial interest remains an important factor in the exercise of this discretion: *Nordstern Allgemeine Versicherungs AG v Internav Ltd* [1999] 2 Lloyd's Rep 139, CA. There has to be more than just a close relationship between a litigant and a non-party for a costs order to be made against the latter: *Symphony Group plc v Hodgson* [1994] QB 179, [1993] 4 All ER 143, CA (sixth guideline of BALCOMBE LJ, followed in *Wiggins v Richard Read (Transport) Ltd* (1999) Times 14 January, CA).

Unlike the "wasted costs" jurisdiction whose primary function is disciplinary, controlling the conduct of lawyers, the jurisdiction under s 51(3) is truly compensatory, designed to ensure that the costs burden of the winning party is borne by the person responsible for it, whether a party or not. Accordingly applications under s 51(3) are not subject to the procedural restrictions which apply to applications for wasted costs orders: *Robertson Research International Ltd v ABG Exploration BV* (1999) Times, 3 November.

The power to order a non-party to pay costs extends to a non-party domiciled outside the jurisdiction: *National Justice Compania Naviera SA v Prudential Assurance Co Ltd (No 2)* [1999] 2 Lloyd's Rep 621; affd [2000] 1 All ER 37, [2000] 1 Lloyd's Rep 129, CA. Solicitors acting for an unsuccessful party will not usually be at risk of an order that they pay the successful party's costs, but it may be appropriate so to order where the litigation is being continued for the benefit of the solicitors. It is not necessary to establish some exceptional circumstances before such an order is made: *Globe Equities Ltd v Globe Legal Services Ltd* [1999] BLR 232, CA. However, liability should not be imposed on a party's insurers unless their conduct has been so self-motivated that such an order is justified: *TGA Chapman Ltd v Christopher* [1998] 2 All ER 873, [1998] 1 WLR 12, CA; *Cormack v Westbourne* [1999] Lloyd's Rep PN 389. There is no justification for ordering the costs of an unsuccessful claim to be paid by the receiver of an insolvent company, since the defendant's usual and proper remedy is to apply for security for costs: *Mills v Birchall and Gilbertson* [2008] EWCA Civ 385, [2008] All ER (D) 257 (Apr).

Pure funders, who have no financial stake in the outcome, will not be liable if they have reasonable grounds for believing that the litigant has a reasonable case, but may be liable if, with quixotic philanthropy, they support cases willy-nilly against targeted institutions: *Hamilton v Al Fayed (Costs)* (2001) Times, 25 July. An appeal against this decision was dismissed: *Hamilton v Al Fayed (No 2)* [2002] EWCA Civ 665, [2003] QB 1175, [2002] 3 All ER 641. A similar view, that pure funders should not normally be vulnerable, was expressed in *Dymocks Franchise Systems (NSW) Pty Ltd v Todd* [2004] 1 WLR 2807, [2004] UKPC 39.But in that case it was held that exceptional circumstances were not required to justify an order in the case of a non-party who funded litigation and either controlled or was, at any rate to benefit from them. The most difficult cases are where non-parties fund receivers or liquidators in litigation designed to advance the funder's own financial interests. A costs order against receivers will be made more readily where the company is in liquidation and the receiver's agency has been terminated, or where the successful party has not been able to obtain security for costs, or there has been impropriety or unreasonableness: *Dolphin Quays Development Ltd v Mills* [2008] EWCA Civ 385, [2008] 4 All ER 58.

The Court of Appeal made an order against a commercial funder in *Arkin v Borchard Lines Ltd* [2005] EWCA Civ 655, [2005] 3 All ER 613, (2005) Times, 3 June. The Court's starting point was that a commercial funder who financed part, or indeed all, of the costs of litigation in a manner which facilitated access to justice and which was not otherwise objectionable should nevertheless be potentially liable for the costs of the opposing party to the extent of the funding provided. The judge at first instance had given insufficient weight to the rule that costs should normally follow the event and that the funder in the instant case had purchased a stake in the action for a commercial motive. The principles applicable to the exercise of the court's discretion under s 51(1) and (3) are helpfully summarised by Lord Brown in *Dymocks Franchise Systems (NSW) Pty Ltd v Todd* [2004] UKPC 39, [2004] 1 WLR 2807, at paragraph 25. In *Ewing v Office of the Deputy Prime Minister* [2005] EWCA Civ 1583, [2006] 1 WLR 1260 a vexatious litigant who was not himself a party but who funded and controlled unsuccessful litigation brought by someone else was ordered to pay the other side's costs. Similarly a director who controls unsuccessful litigation through his control of a company may be held liable for costs although not funding the case personally: *Petromec Inc v Petroleo Brasilieiro SA Petrobras (No 4)* [2006] EWCA Civ 1038, [2007] 2 Costs LR 212.

A director of a company who funds its litigation because he has a real interest in its outcome is nevertheless not normally to be ordered to meet the company's liability in costs to the other side since this would be contrary to the doctrine of separate liability: *Floods of Queensferry Ltd v Shand Construction Ltd* [2002] EWCA Civ 918, [2003] Lloyd's Rep IR 181, [2002] All ER (D) 467 (May); *Adris v Royal Bank of Scotland* [2010] EWHC 941 (QB), [2010] NLJR 767. But it is not necessary to prove impropriety, on the part of the director, in the prosecution of the claim: *B E Studios Ltd v Smith and Williamson Ltd* [2005] EWHC 2730 (Ch), [2006] 2 All ER 811, Evans-Lombe J; and a director may be ordered to pay the costs of unsuccessful litigation brought by him in the company's name even though bad faith is not proved against him: *Goodwood Recoveries Ltd v Breen* [2005] EWCA Civ 414, [2006] 2 All ER 533. Where the interests of a company and the director who set it up to run his business are very similar, a defendant who defeats a claim by the company may in some circumstances be awarded a third party costs order against the director: *Alan Phillips Associates Ltd v Dowling* [2007] EWCA Civ 64, (2007) 151 Sol Jo LB 122. But an order may not be made where the funder's intervention has not caused an increase in the other side's costs: *Jackson v Thakrar* [2007] EWHC 626 (TCC)[2007] BLR 241, Judge Peter Coulson QC, QBD (TCC), [2008] 1 All ER 601. On the other hand, a shareholder who is not a director but who funds, controls and directs litigation by a company in order to protect his own financial interests is as vulnerable to an order to pay the successful party's costs as any other funder: *CIBC Mellon Trust Co v Wolfgang Otto Stoltzenberg (No 3)* (2005) Times, 8 June, CA.

Where a claimant is ordered to pay a successful defendant's costs on the indemnity basis, professional funders of the claimant may be held similarly liable although not contributing directly to the factors which justified the basis: *Excalibur Ventures LLC v Texas Keystone Inc*

[2014] EWHC 3436 (Comm), 23 October 2014, in which 'the Arkin cap' was applied to limit the individual funders' liability to the amount of their financial contribution to the litigation, but leaving out of account their contribution to providing security for the other side's costs.

II SCA [50.5A]

Power to order a witness to pay costs The court has power to order a witness to pay costs occasioned by the witness's breach of duty to the court. An expert witness who gives evidence in breach of his, or her, duties under Part 35 may be joined for the purposes of making a costs order for the payment of the costs incurred and wasted by one or other of the parties as a result of the breach of duty. Although a warning might need to be given in the case of some witnesses this was not necessary in the case of an expert who had had made a declaration or statement of truth as required by the Practice Direction: *Phillips v Symes* [2004] EWHC 2329 (Ch), [2004] All ER (D) 269 (Oct), 2004) Times, 5 November, Smith J.

II SCA [50.5B]

Costs order against unincorporated association Where an order for costs is made against an unincorporated association and that association has a credit balance in a bank account, the order may be enforced against the balance by means of a third party debt order, although the individual members of the association may not have been identified: *Huntingdon Life Sciences Group Ltd v Stop Huntingdon Animal Cruelty* (2005) Times 2 November, QBD, Mackay J.

II SCA [50.5C]

Costs order against a non-party who did not cause costs to be incurred Circumstances may exist which make it just to order costs to be paid by a non-party who cannot be said to have caused the costs in question: *Total Spares & Supplies Ltd v Antares SRL* [2006] EWHC 1537 (Ch), [2006] All ER (D) 314 (Jun). In that case the defendant company transferred a substantial part of its business to a newly incorporated enterprise (the non-party) two weeks before the start of the trial and was struck off three months after judgment. The court ordered the newly incorporated enterprise to pay the successful claimant's costs.

II SCA [50.5D]

Costs order against a non-party who could have been sued Where an applicant has a cause of action against a non-party the court is most unlikely to order the non-party to pay costs unless (1) there are good reasons for not joining that person as a party and (2) he, or she, was warned at the earliest opportunity that such an order might be sought: *Oriakhel v Vickers* [2008] EWCA Civ 748, [2008] All ER (D) 69 (Jul).

Conversely, considerations in favour of ordering a non-party to pay costs should not be left out of account where the person concerned happens to be a party: *Threlfall v ECD Insight Ltd* [2013] EWCA Civ 1444, [2013] All ER (D) 195 (Nov).

II SCA [50.5E]

Costs order again a trustee in bankruptcy Where a trustee in bankruptcy assigns the right to sue on a claim to the bankrupt there is no general principal that the trustee cannot be held liable for the costs if the proceedings were to fail: *Hunt (as trustee in bankruptcy of Janan George Harb) v Harb* [2011] EWCA Civ 1239, [2011] 44 LS Gaz R 20, [2011] NLJR 1556.

II SCA [50.5F]

Costs order against solicitors It has been held that a successful party may obtain an order for costs against the solicitors for the unsuccessful party where the solicitors had the major interest in the outcome: *Myatt v National Coal Board (No 2)* [2007] EWCA Civ 307, [2007] 4 All ER 1094, [2007] 1 WLR 1559. Solicitors were also ordered to pay costs where they failed to obtain ATE insurance at the start of the litigation as instructed by their unsuccessful clients: *Adris v Royal Bank of Scotland (Cartel Client Review Ltd, additional parties)* [2010] EWHC 941 (QB), [2010] NLJR 767, [2010] 4 Costs LR 598. Similarly costs may be ordered against the unsuccessful defendant's professional indemnity insurers: *Plymouth & South West Co-operative Society Ltd v Architecture, Structure & Management Ltd* [2006] EWHC 3252 (TCC), 111 Con LR 189. A non-party costs order was refused in the case of a solicitor acting under a CFA, although it was considered that such an order might, in some circumstances, be justified: *Tinseltime Ltd v Roberts* [2012] EWHC 2628 (TCC), [2012] NLJR 1290, 156 Sol Jo (no 38) 31.

Since the legislation for conditional fee agreements visualises the possibility of the solicitor funding disbursements, it would not be right to conclude, on this fact alone, that a solicitor who did so was 'the real party' and potentially liable to an adverse costs order: *Flatman v Germany; Weddall v Barchester Healthcare Ltd* [2013] EWCA Civ 278, [2013] 4 All ER 349, [2013] 1 WLR 2676. The court has to see whether the solicitor has acted outside his, or her, role as a solicitor for the client or for a purpose outside that role: *Harcus Sinclair (a firm) v*

Buttonwood Legal Capital Ltd [2013] EWHC 2974 (Ch), [2013] All ER (D) 134 (Oct). A solicitor's failure to obtain ATE insurance has also been held insufficient to make the solicitor liable for the other side's costs: *Heron v TNT (UK) Ltd* [2013] EWCA Civ 469, [2013] 3 All ER 479, [2013] NLJR 21.

Sub-s (3) does not empower the court to order a solicitor who has failed to issue a claim in time to pay the defendant's costs of defending the claim when subsequently issued by another firm. This is because the original solicitor did not actively promote the litigation or cause the costs to be incurred: *Byrne v South Sefton (Merseyside) Health Authority* [2001] EWCA Civ 1904, [2002] 1 WLR 775, [2002] 01 LS Gaz R 19.

In a case where the solicitors who prepared the will allowed it to be executed by the wrong person it was held that they should be ordered to pay the costs of the resulting litigation: *Marley v Rawlings* [2014] UKSC 51, [2014] 4 All ER 619, [2014] 3 WLR 1015.

II SCA [50.5G]

Costs order against local authority In care proceedings a local authority should not normally be ordered to pay the other parties' costs of care proceedings which are held not to be justified, in the absence of reprehensible behaviour or an unreasonable stance: *Re T (children) (costs)* [2012] UKSC 36, [2012] 4 All ER 1137, [2012] 1 WLR 2281. On the other hand an order was made in a case where the evidence provided by a local authority under s 37 of the Children Act 1989 failed fundamentally to investigate, address or analyse the serious allegations (that illnesses were being fabricated): *HB v PB, OP and Croydon London Borough Council* [2013] EWHC 1956 (Fam), [2013] 3 FCR 318, [2013] Fam Law 1258.

II SCA [50.5H]

Costs order against a non-party who was not warned Where a non-party has participated in and funded the defence of proceedings it is not unfair to order him, or her, to pay the costs, if the defence is unsuccessful and it is not necessary that a warning of such a possibility should have been given at an earlier stage: *Deutsche Bank AG v Sebastian Holdings Incorporated* [2016] EWCA Civ 23.

An order for the defendant's insurers to pay the claimant's costs was upheld in *Travelers Insurance Co Ltd v XYZ* [2018] EWCA Civ 1099.

II SCA [50.5I]

Order for a third party funder to be identified Where there is good reason to believe that a claimant has funding falling within CPR 25.14(2)(b), the court has power to order the funder to provide security for costs and, if the identity of the funder is not known to the applicant, to order the funded party to identify the funder: *Wall v The Royal Bank of Scotland plc* [2016] EWHC 2460 (Comm), [2016] All ER (D) 84 (Oct).

II SCA [50.6]

Insolvency Act 1986 section 382 Since an award of costs is a matter for the court's discretion, the person ultimately ordered to pay costs does not, prior to the making of such an order, have a "contingent liability" within the meaning of s 382 of the Insolvency Act 1986: *Glenister v Rowe* [2000] Ch 76, [1999] 3 All ER 452, CA.

II SCA [50.7]

Wasted costs to be disallowed or ordered to be paid The principles governing the making of "wasted costs" orders are set out in *Ridehalgh v Horsefield* [1994] Ch 205, [1994] 3 All ER 848, CA. The practice and procedure is governed by CPR 48.7, see para **CPR 48.7**. See also *Re a Barrister (Wasted Costs Order No 1 of 1991)* [1993] QB 293, [1992] 3 All ER 429, CA. A "wasted costs" order may be made in the client's favour against his own legal representatives or against those of his opponent: *Brown v Bennett* [2002] 2 All ER 273, [2002] 1 WLR 713. Also the "wasted costs" of engaging counsel are not limited to court work (exercising a right of audience) but may include advisory and drafting work too: *Medcalf v Mardell* [2002] UKHL 27, [2003] 1 AC 120, [2002] 3 All ER 721. It was further decided in *Brown v Bennett* that the main question was whether, on the balance of probabilities, the applicant would have incurred the costs claimed to be wasted if the opponent had not acted improperly as he or she did. Where, as in that case, the opponent had to exercise judgment as to whether the evidence available was sufficient to justify the steps taken, a "wasted costs" order would not be appropriate unless the opponent's opinion was one at which no reasonable lawyer could in the circumstances have arrived.

An order may not be made against a solicitor who did not conduct the litigation in which the costs were incurred because he is not a "legal representative" for the purposes of s 51(6) having regard to the definition in s 119: *Byrne v Sefton Health Authority* [2001] EWCA Civ 1904, [2002] 1 WLR 775.

Where a wasted costs order is made on or after 13 April 2015, the court is required, by sub-ss (7A) and (12A), to inform an approved regulator or the Director of Legal Aid Casework, or both, as appropriate.

II SCA [50.8]

Wasted costs and non-parties Sub-section (3) does not empower the court to order a solicitor who has failed to issue a claim in time to pay the defendant's costs of defending the claim when issued by another firm. This is because the original solicitor did not actively promoted the litigation and his conduct was not causative of the incurring of the costs. Also the former solicitor is not a "legal representative" for the purposes of s 51(6), having regard to the definition in sub-s (13): *Byrne v Sefton Health Authority* [2001] EWCA Civ 1904, [2002] 1 WLR 775

II SCA [50.9]

Costs-capping The court's powers include capping the amount of costs for which a defendant may be liable at the trial: *King v Telegraph Group Ltd* [2004] EWCA Civ 613, [2004] 25 LS Gaz R 27. See the note at **CPR 44 [8A]**.

PART III
PRACTICE AND PROCEDURE
THE COURT OF APPEAL

Distribution of Business

II SCA [51]

53. Distribution of business between civil and criminal divisions

(1) Rule of court may provide for the distribution of business in the Court of Appeal between the civil and criminal divisions, but subject to any such rules business shall be distributed in accordance with the following provisions of this section.

(2) The criminal division of the Court of Appeal shall exercise—

(a) all jurisdiction of the Court of Appeal under Parts I and II of the Criminal Appeal Act 1968;

(b) the jurisdiction of the Court of Appeal under section 13 of the Administration of Justice Act 1960 (appeals in cases of contempt of court) in relation to appeals from orders and decisions of the Crown Court;

(c) all other jurisdiction expressly conferred on that division by this or any other Act; and

(d) the jurisdiction to order the issue of writs of venire de novo.

(3) The civil division of the Court of Appeal shall exercise the whole of the jurisdiction of that court not exercisable by the criminal division.

(4) Where any class of proceedings in the Court of Appeal is by any statutory provision assigned to the criminal division of that court, rules of court may provide for any enactment relating to—

(a) appeals to the Court of Appeal under Part I of the Criminal Appeal Act 1968; or

(b) any matter connected with or arising out of such appeals,

to apply in relation to proceedings of that class or, as the case may be, to any corresponding matter connected with or arising out of such proceedings, as it applies in relation to such appeals or, as the case may be, to the relevant matter within paragraph (b), with or without prescribed modifications in either case.

Composition of Court

II SCA [51A]

54. Court of civil division

(1) This section relates to the civil division of the Court of Appeal; and in this section "court", except where the context otherwise requires, means a court of that division.

(2) Subject as follows, a court shall be duly constituted for the purpose of exercising any of its jurisdiction if it consists of one or more judges.

(3) The Master of the Rolls may, with the concurrence of the Lord Chancellor, give (or vary or revoke) directions about the minimum number of judges of which a court must consist if it is to be duly constituted for the purpose of any description of proceedings.

(4) The Master of the Rolls, or any Lord Justice of Appeal designated by him, may (subject to any directions under subsection (3)) determine the number of judges of which a court is to consist for the purpose of any particular proceedings.

(4A) The Master of the Rolls may give directions as to what is to happen in any particular case where one or more members of a court which has partly heard proceedings are unable to continue.

(5) Where—

(a) an appeal has been heard by a court consisting of an even number of judges; and

(b) the members of the court are equally divided, the case shall, on the application of any party to the appeal, be re-argued before and determined by an uneven number of judges not less than three, before any appeal to the Supreme Court.

(6) [. . .]

(7) [. . .]

(8) Subsections (1) and (2) of section 70 (assessors in the High Court) shall apply in relation to causes and matters before the civil division of the Court of Appeal as they apply in relation to causes and matters before the High Court.

(9) Subsections (3) and (4) of section 70 (scientific advisers to assist the Patents Court in proceedings under the Patents Act 1949 and the Patents Act 1977) shall apply in relation to the civil division of the Court of Appeal and proceedings on appeal from any decision of the Patents Court in proceedings under those Acts as they apply in relation to the Patents Court and proceedings under those Acts.

(10) [. . .]

II SCA [51A.1]

Amendments This section is printed as amended by the Access to Justice Act 1999 s 59.

II SCA [51A.2]

Decision of single Lord Justice An application to a single Lord Justice for permission to appeal is an application to the Court of Appeal, so that court has no power to hear an appeal from or to review that decision: *Paragon Finance v Noueiri* [2001] EWCA Civ 1402, [2001] 1 WLR 2357.

II SCA [51B]

56. Judges not to sit on appeal from their own judgments, etc

(1) No judge shall sit as a member of the civil division of the Court of Appeal on the hearing of, or shall determine any application in proceedings incidental or preliminary to, an appeal from a judgment or order made in any case by himself or by any court of which he was a member.

(2) No judge shall sit as a member of the criminal division of the Court of Appeal on the hearing of, or shall determine any application in proceedings incidental or preliminary to, an appeal against—

(a) a conviction before himself or a court of which he was a member; or

(b) a sentence passed by himself or such a court.

Sittings and Vacations

II SCA [51C]

57. Sittings and vacations

(1) Sittings of the Court of Appeal may be held, and any other business of the Court of Appeal may be conducted, at any place in England or Wales.

(2) Subject to rules of court—

(a) the places at which the Court of Appeal sits outside the Royal Courts of Justice; and

(b) the days and times at which the Court of Appeal sits at any place outside the Royal Courts of Justice, shall be determined in accordance with directions given by the Lord Chancellor after consulting the Lord Chief Justice.

(3) Rules of court may make provision for regulating the vacations to be observed by the Court of Appeal and in the offices of that court.

(4) Rules of court—

(a) may provide for securing such sittings of the civil division of the Court of Appeal during vacation as the Master of the Rolls may with the concurrence of the Lord Chancellor determine;

(b) without prejudice to paragraph (a), shall provide for the transaction during vacation by judges of the Court of Appeal of all such business in the civil division of that court as may require to be immediately or promptly transacted; and

(c) shall provide for securing sittings of the criminal division of that court during vacation if necessary.

(5) The Lord Chief Justice may nominate a judicial office holder (as defined in section 109(4) of the Constitutional Reform Act 2005) to exercise his functions under this section.

Other Provisions

II SCA [51D]

58. Calling into question of incidental decisions in civil division

(1) Rules of court may provide that decisions of the Court of Appeal which—

(a) are taken by a single judge or any officer or member of staff of that court in proceedings incidental to any cause or matter pending before the civil division of that court; and

(b) do not involve the determination of an appeal or of an application for permission to appeal,

may be called into question in such manner as may be prescribed.

(2) No appeal shall lie to the Supreme Court from a decision which may be called into question pursuant to rules under subsection (1).

II SCA [51D.1]

New section This section was introduced, in substitution for the original, by the Access to Justice Act 1999 s 60.

II SCA [51E]

60. Rules of court, and decisions of Court of Appeal, as to whether judgment or order is final or interlocutory

(1) Rules of court may provide for orders or judgments of any prescribed description to be treated for any prescribed purpose connected with appeals to the Court of Appeal as final or as interlocutory.

(2) No appeal shall lie from a decision of the Court of Appeal as to whether a judgment or order is, for any purpose connected with an appeal to that court, final or interlocutory.

THE HIGH COURT

Distribution of business

II SCA [52]

61. Distribution of business among Divisions

(1) Subject to any provision made by or under this or any other Act (and in particular to any rules of court made in pursuance of subsection (2) and any order under subsection (3)), business in the High Court of any description mentioned in Schedule 1, as for the time being in force, shall be distributed among the Divisions in accordance with that Schedule.

(2) Rules of court may provide for the distribution of business in the High Court among the Divisions; but any rules made in pursuance of this subsection shall have effect subject to any orders for the time being in force under subsection (3).

(3) Subject to subsection (5), the Lord Chief Justice may, with the concurrence of the Lord Chancellor by order—

- (a) direct that any business in the High Court which is not for the time being assigned by or under this or any other Act to any Division be assigned to such Division as may be specified in the order;
- (b) if at any time it appears to the Lord Chief Justice and the Lord Chancellor desirable to do so with a view to the more convenient administration of justice, direct that any business for the time being assigned by or under this or any other Act to any Division be assigned to such other Division as may be specified in the order; and
- (c) amend Schedule 1 so far as may be necessary in consequence of provision made by order under paragraph (a) or (b).

(4) The powers conferred by subsection (2) and subsection (3) include power to assign business of any description to two or more Divisions concurrently.

(5) No order under subsection (3)(b) relating to any business shall be made without the concurrence of the senior judge of—

- (a) the Division or each of the Divisions to which the business is for the time being assigned; and
- (b) the Division or each of the Divisions to which the business is to be assigned by the order.

(6) Subject to rules of court, the fact that a cause or matter commenced in the High Court falls within a class of business assigned by or under this Act to a particular Division does not make it obligatory for it to be allocated or transferred to that Division.

(7) Without prejudice to subsections (1) to (5) and section 63, rules of court may provide for the distribution of the business (other than business required to be heard by a divisional court) in any Division of the High Court among the judges of that Division.

(8) Any order under subsection (3) shall be made by statutory instrument, which shall be laid before Parliament after being made.

(9) The Lord Chief Justice may nominate a judicial office holder (as defined in section 109(4) of the Constitutional Reform Act 2005) to exercise his functions under subsection (3).

II SCA [52.1]

The Business and Property Courts of England and Wales From 1 October 2017 most of the business identified in Schedule 1 as business of the Queen's Bench Division or the Chancery Division has been grouped as business of a new organisation, The Business and Property Courts of England and Wales. See CPR Part 57A.

II SCA [52A]

62. Business of Patents, Admiralty and Commercial Courts

(1) The Patents Court shall take such proceedings relating to patents as are within the jurisdiction conferred on it by the Patents Act 1977, and such other proceedings relating to patents or other matters as may be prescribed.

(2) The Admiralty Court shall take Admiralty business, that is to say causes and matters assigned to the Queen's Bench Division and involving the exercise of the High Court's Admiralty jurisdiction or its jurisdiction as a prize court.

(3) The Commercial Court shall take such causes and matters as may in accordance with rules of court be entered in the commercial list.

II SCA [52A.1]

Procedure See the notes on procedure and jurisdiction at **II SCA [8B.1]**, and **II SCA [8B.2]**.

II SCA [52A.2]

The Business and Property Courts of England and Wales From 1 October 2017 the Patents Court, the Admiralty Court and the Commercial Court are listed within the Business and Property Courts of England and Wales and managed as such.

See CPR Part 57A and Practice Direction 57AA – Business and Property Courts for detailed provisions on the breakdown into courts and lists, the business assigned to each, the titles of claims, and the transfer of proceedings.

II SCA [52B]

63. Business assigned to specially nominated judges

(1) Any business assigned, in accordance with this or any other Act or rules of court, to one or more specially nominated judges of the High Court may—

- (a) during vacation; or
- (b) during the illness or absence of that judge or any of those judges; or
- (c) for any other reasonable cause,

be dealt with by any judge of the High Court named for that purpose by the Lord Chief Justice after consulting the Lord Chancellor.

(2) If at any time it appears to the Lord Chief Justice, after consulting the Lord Chancellor, to be desirable to do so with a view to the more convenient administration of justice, he may by order direct that business of any description which is for the time being assigned, in accordance with this or any other Act or rules of court, to one or more specially nominated judges of the High Court shall cease to be so assigned and may be dealt with by any one or more judges of the High Court.

(3) An order under subsection (2) shall not be made in respect of any business without the concurrence of the senior judge of the Division to which the business is for the time being assigned.

(4) The Lord Chief Justice may nominate a judicial office holder (as defined in section 109(4) of the Constitutional Reform Act 2005) to exercise his functions under subsection (1) or (2).

II SCA [52C]

64. Choice of Division by plaintiff

(1) Without prejudice to the power of transfer under section 65, the person by whom any cause or matter is commenced in the High Court shall in the prescribed manner allocate it to whichever Division he thinks fit.

(2) Where a cause or matter is commenced in the High Court, all subsequent interlocutory or other steps or proceedings in the High Court in that cause or matter shall be taken in the Division to which the cause or matter is for the time being allocated (whether under subsection (1) or in consequence of its transfer under section 65).

II SCA [52D]

65. Power of transfer

(1) Any cause or matter may at any time and at any stage thereof, and either with or without application from any of the parties, be transferred, by such authority and in such manner as rules of court may direct, from one Division or judge of the High Court to another Division or judge thereof.

(2) The transfer of a cause or matter under subsection (1) to a different Division or judge of the High Court shall not affect the validity of any steps or proceedings taken or order made in that cause or matter before the transfer.

Divisional Courts

II SCA [53]

66. Divisional courts of the High Court

(1) Divisional courts may be held for the transaction of any business in the High Court which is, by or by virtue of rules of court or any other statutory provision, required to be heard by a divisional court.

(2) Any number of divisional courts may sit at the same time.

(3) A divisional court shall be constituted of not less than two judges.

(4) Every judge of the High Court shall be qualified to sit in any divisional court.

(5) The judge who is, according to the order of precedence under this Act, the senior of the judges constituting a divisional court shall be the president of the court.

Mode of Conducting Business

II SCA [54]

67. Proceedings in court and in chambers

Business in the High Court shall be heard and disposed of in court except in so far as it may, under this or any other Act, under rules of court or in accordance with the practice of the court, be dealt with in chambers.

II SCA [54.1]

The practice of the court The courts have acknowledged the public interest in seeing justice done and that the exclusion of the public from a hearing needs to be justified: *R v Chief Registrar of Building Societies, ex p New Cross Building Society* [1984] QB 227, [1984] 2 All ER 27, CA; *Polly Peck International plc v Nadir (No 2)* [1992] 4 All ER 769, CA. Classes of proceedings which are frequently heard in private are identified in the Administration of Justice Act 1960 s 12, where the purpose of the section is to ease the restriction on reporting in these and other cases. In addition many court decisions are taken in chambers in proceedings which are outside these categories: see CPR 39.2, see para **CPR 39.2** and the Part 39 Practice Direction, paras 1.5–1.14. The Human Rights Act 1998 may lead to a reassessment of established practice with regard to the requirements of Article 6 of the European Convention on Human Rights, that hearings should be in public and that decisions should be published.

II SCA [55]

68. Exercise of High Court jurisdiction otherwise than by judges of that court

(1) Provision may be made by rules of court as to the cases in which jurisdiction of the High Court may be exercised by—

(a) such Circuit judges, deputy Circuit judges or Recorders as the Lord Chief Justice may, after consulting the Lord Chancellor, from time to time nominate to deal with official referees' business; or

(b) special referees;

(c) . . .

(2) Without prejudice to the generality of subsection (1), rules of court may in particular—

(a) . . .

(b) authorise any question arising in any cause or matter to be referred to a special referee for inquiry and report.

(3) Rules of court shall not authorise the exercise of powers of attachment and committal by a special referee or any officer or other staff of the court.

(4) Subject to subsection (5), the decision of:

(a) any such person as is mentioned in subsection (1); or

(b) any officer or other staff of the court

may be called in question in such manner as may be prescribed by rules of court, whether by appeal to the Court of Appeal, or by an appeal or application to a divisional court or a judge in court or a judge in chambers, or by an adjournment to a judge in court or a judge in chambers.

(5) Rules of court may provide either generally or to a limited extent for decisions of persons nominated under subsection (1)(a) being called in question only by appeal on a question of law.

(6) The cases in which jurisdiction of the High Court may be exercised by persons nominated under subsection (1)(a) shall be known as "official referees' business"; and, subject to rules of court, the distribution of official referees' business among persons so nominated shall be determined in accordance with directions given by the Lord Chief Justice after consulting the Lord Chancellor.

(7) Any reference to an official referee in any enactment, whenever passed, or in rules of court or any other instrument or document, whenever made, shall, unless the context otherwise requires, be construed as, or (where the context requires) as including, a reference to a person nominated under subsection (1)(a).

(8) The Lord Chief Justice may nominate a judicial office holder (as defined in section 109(4) of the Constitutional Reform Act 2005) to exercise his functions under subsections (1)(a) and (6).

II SCA [56]

69. Trial by jury

(1) Where, on the application of any party to an action to be tried in the Queen's Bench Division, the court is satisfied that there is in issue—

(a) a charge of fraud against that party; or

(b) a claim in respect of malicious prosecution or false imprisonment; or

(c) any question or issue of a kind prescribed for the purposes of this paragraph,

the action shall be tried with a jury, unless the court is of opinion that the trial requires any prolonged examination of documents or accounts or any scientific or local investigation which cannot conveniently be made with a jury or unless the court is of opinion that the trial will involve section 6 proceedings.

(2) An application under subsection (1) must be made not later than such time before the trial as may be prescribed.

(3) An action to be tried in the Queen's Bench Division which does not by virtue of subsection (1) fall to be tried with a jury shall be tried without a jury unless the court in its discretion orders it to be tried with a jury.

(3A) An action in the Queen's Bench Division which by virtue of subsection (1) or (3) is being, or is to be, tried with a jury may, at any stage in the proceedings, be tried without a jury if the court concerned—

(a) is of opinion that the action involves, or will involve, section 6 proceedings, and

(b) in its discretion orders the action to be tried without a jury.

(3B) Where the court makes an order under subsection (3A)(b), it may make such other orders as it considers appropriate (including an order dismissing the jury).

(4) Nothing in subsections (1) to (3B) shall affect the power of the court to order, in accordance with rules of court, that different questions of fact arising in any action be tried by different modes of trial; and where any such order is made, subsection (1) shall have effect only as respects questions relating to any such charge, claim, question or issue as is mentioned in that subsection.

(5) Where for the purpose of disposing of any action or other matter which is being tried in the High Court by a judge with a jury it is necessary to ascertain the law of any other country which is applicable to the facts of the case, any question as to the effect of the evidence given with respect to that law shall, instead of being submitted to the jury, be decided by the judge alone.

(6) In this section "section 6 proceedings" has the meaning given by section 14(1) of the Justice and Security Act 2013 (certain civil proceedings in which closed material applications may be made).

II SCA [56.0]

Note that claims in respect of libel or slander were removed from section 69(1) by section 11 of the Defamation Act 2013, as from 1 January 2014, but that claims based on causes of action before that date are unaffected.

II SCA [56.1]

Discretion as to jury Where the case falls outside sub-s (1) the usual rule is for cases to be tried by judge alone: *Williams v Beesley* [1973] 3 All ER 144, [1973] 1 WLR 1295, HL. This rule applies to personal injury litigation unless the circumstances are wholly exceptional: *Ward v James* [1966] 1 QB 273, [1965] 1 All ER 563, CA; *H v Ministry of Defence* [1991] 2 QB 103, [1991] 2 All ER 834, CA. It also applies to claims for assault, or for malicious falsehood, but without a claim in respect of any cause of action within sub-s (1)(b): *Hendry v Chief Constable of Leicestershire* (1993) unreported, 93/1521, CA; *Joyce v Sengupta* [1993] 1 All ER 897, [1993] 1 WLR 337, CA. To come within sub-s (1)(a) a relevant issue of fraud must be raised which will have to be decided to determine the rights of the parties: *Everett v Islington Guardians* [1923] 1 KB 44. Compare *Newton Chemicals Ltd v Arsenis* [1989] 1 WLR 1297, CA. A "charge of fraud" means an actionable deceit including detriment: *Barclays Bank Ltd v Cole* [1967] 2 QB 738, [1966] 3 All ER 948, CA. The words "scientific investigation" are capable of including a medical investigation relevant to the quantum of damage: *Darragh v Chief Constable of Thames Valley Police* [1998] 43 LS Gaz R 32, CA.

II SCA [56.1A]

Split trial The court has a discretion, under s 69(4), to order the trial of some issues by a jury and others by judge alone. But if it is clear that jury trial is not convenient for the case as a whole (for example because of the need for prolonged examination of documents or scientific investigation) trial of all the issues by judge alone is normally appropriate: *Phillips v Metropolitan Police Comr* [2003] EWCA Civ 382, (2003) Times, 2 April. In that case the Court stated that the question of convenience should be determined by a series of questions. First, would there be a prolonged examination of documents or any scientific investigation? Second, if so, could that examination be conveniently made with a jury? Third, if not, should the court nevertheless exercise its discretion to order trial with a jury?

Where the main trial is to be by judge alone the court should take account of the disadvantages consequent on having a jury decide the meaning of the words complained of, as a preliminary issue. In *Armstrong v Times Newspapers Ltd* [2005] EWHC 2816 (QB), [2006] EMLR 9, Eady J rejected an application for jury trial of a preliminary issue, adopting the same approach as in *Philips v Metropolitan Police Comr*, above. An appeal was unsuccessful. The Court of Appeal concluded that the first part of sub-section (4) gave the judge an open discretion which was not moderated by the second part. The judge was therefore correct not to start with any predisposition in favour of jury trial and to take account of the general advantage of having all the issues tried by the same tribunal: *Armstrong v Times Newspapers Ltd* (2006) Times 7, July, CA.

II SCA [56.1B]

Application for jury made after the prescribed period Where an application for trial by jury is made outside the 28 day period following service of the defence, as provided in **CPR 26.11**, the right to a jury is lost and although a jury may be ordered as a matter of discretion, there is a presumption in favour of trial by judge alone: *Bento v Chief Constable of Bedfordshire* [2012] EWCA Civ 956, [2012] All ER (D) 189 (Jul).

II SCA [56.2]

Convenience The application of the proviso to sub-s (1) has more to do with the efficient administration of justice than with the complexity or difficulty of the issues involved: *Viscount De L'Isle v Times Newspapers Ltd* [1987] 3 All ER 499, [1988] 1 WLR 49, CA. As regards the examination of documents see *Goldsmith v Pressdram Ltd* [1987] 3 All ER 485, [1988] 1 WLR 64n, CA. In *Beta Construction Ltd v Channel Four Television Co Ltd* [1990] 2 All ER 1012, [1990] 1 WLR 1042, CA four instances are given of considerations justifying the refusal of jury trial within the proviso of convenience. See also *Taylor v Anderton* (*Police Complaints Authority Intervening*) [1995] 2 All ER 420, [1995] 1 WLR 447, CA. It was held in *Darragh v Chief Constable of Thames Valley Police* [1998] 43 LS Gaz R 32, CA, that trial by judge alone may be appropriate where the medical reports are complicated so as to raise issues of "scientific investigation". Note that the right to trial by jury is not affected by rules of court made under the Civil Procedure Act 1997, such as CPR 24.2 and CPR 24.3 which provide for summary judgment to be available in "any proceedings": *Safeway plc v Tate* [2001] QB 1120, [2001] 4 All ER 193, CA.

II SCA [56.3]

Composition of the jury There is no general principle that a jury must be racially balanced: *R v Ford* (*Royston*) [1989] QB 868, [1989] 3 All ER 445, CA. Indeed, juror selection must be carried out by the court administration as a random process, in accordance with the Juries Act 1974, ss 2, 5 and 6; *R v Tarrant* [1998] Crim LR 342, CA.

II SCA [57]

70. Assessors and scientific advisers

(1) In any cause or matter before the High Court the court may, if it thinks it expedient to do so, call in the aid of one or more assessors specially qualified, and hear and dispose of the cause or matter wholly or partially with their assistance.

(2) The remuneration, if any, to be paid to an assessor for his services under subsection (1) in connection with any proceedings shall be determined by the court, and shall form part of the costs of the proceedings.

(3) Rules of court shall make provision for the appointment of scientific advisers to assist the Patents Court in proceedings under the Patents Act 1949 and the Patents Act 1977 and for regulating the functions of such advisers.

(4) The remuneration of any such adviser shall be determined by the Lord Chancellor with the concurrence of the Minister for the Civil Service and shall be defrayed out of money provided by Parliament.

(5) Subsections (1) and (2) apply in relation to the family court as they apply in relation to the High Court.

II SCA [57.1]

Procedure For rules of court and practice see **CPR 35.15** and **CPR PD 35**.

II SCA [57.2]

Admiralty Assessors' remuneration A *Practice Note – Admiralty Assessors' Remuneration* was issued by Mr Justice Teare on 1 April 2018 and is expected to be replaced every twelve months.

Sittings and Vacations

II SCA [58]

71. Sittings and vacations

(1) Sittings of the High Court may be held, and any other business of the High Court may be conducted, at any place in England or Wales.

(2) Subject to rules of court—

- (a) the places at which the High Court sits outside the Royal Courts of Justice; and
- (b) the days and times when the High Court sits at any place outside the Royal Courts of Justice,

shall be determined in accordance with directions given by the Lord Chancellor after consulting the Lord Chief Justice.

(3) Rules of court may make provision for regulating the vacations to be observed by the High Court and in the offices of that court.

(4) Rules of court—

- (a) may provide for securing such sittings of any Division of the High Court during vacation as the senior judge of that Division may with the concurrence of the Lord Chancellor determine; and
- (b) without prejudice to paragraph (a), shall provide for the transaction during vacation by judges of the High Court of all such business in the High Court as may require to be immediately or promptly transacted.

(5) Different provision may be made in pursuance of subsection (3) for different parts of the country.

(6) The Lord Chief Justice may nominate a judicial office holder (as defined in section 109(4) of the Constitutional Reform Act 2005) to exercise his functions under this section.

II SCA [58.1]

Rules of court CPR 2.7 (see para **CPR 2.7**) regarding the places where cases are tried and the relevant Practice Direction regarding sittings, vacations and office hours.

There is nothing in this section or in **CPR 34.13** to prevent the court from appointing the trial judge to take the evidence of witnesses as a special examiner, outside England and Wales: *Peer International Corpn v Termidor Music Publishers Ltd* [2005] EWHC 1048 (Ch), (2005) Times, 2 June.

II SCA [59]

72. Withdrawal of privilege against incrimination of self or spouse in certain proceedings

(1) In any proceedings to which this subsection applies a person shall not be excused, by reason that to do so would tend to expose that person, or his or her spouse or civil partner, to proceedings for a related offence or for the recovery of a related penalty—

- (a) from answering any question put to that person in the first-mentioned proceedings; or
- (b) from complying with any order made in those proceedings.

(2) Subsection (1) applies to the following civil proceedings in the High Court, namely—

- (a) proceedings for infringement of rights pertaining to any intellectual property or for passing off;

(b) proceedings brought to obtain disclosure of information relating to any infringement of such rights or to any passing off; and

(c) proceedings brought to prevent any apprehended infringement of such rights or any apprehended passing off.

(3) Subject to subsection (4), no statement or admission made by a person—

(a) in answering a question put to him in any proceedings to which subsection (1) applies; or

(b) in complying with any order made in any such proceedings,

shall, in proceedings for any related offence or for the recovery of any related penalty, be admissible in evidence against that person or (unless they married or became civil partners after the making of the statement or admission) against the spouse or civil partner of that person.

(4) Nothing in subsection (3) shall render any statement or admission made by a person as there mentioned inadmissible in evidence against that person in proceedings for perjury or contempt of court.

(5) In this section—

"intellectual property" means any patent, trade mark, copyright, design right, registered design, technical or commercial information or other intellectual property;

"related offence", in relation to any proceedings to which subsection (1) applies, means—

(a) in the case of proceedings within subsection (2)(a) or (b)—

(i) any offence committed by or in the course of the infringement or passing off to which those proceedings relate; or

(ii) any offence not within sub-paragraph (i) committed in connection with that infringement or passing off, being an offence involving fraud or dishonesty;

(b) in the case of proceedings within subsection (2)(c), any offence revealed by the facts on which the plaintiff relies in those proceedings;

"related penalty", in relation to any proceedings to which subsection (1) applies means—

(a) in the case of proceedings within subsection (2)(a) or (b), any penalty incurred in respect of anything done or omitted in connection with the infringement or passing off to which those proceedings relate;

(b) in the case of proceedings within subsection (2)(c), any penalty incurred in respect of any act or omission revealed by the facts on which the plaintiff relies in those proceedings.

(6) Any reference in this section to civil proceedings in the High Court of any description includes a reference to proceedings on appeal arising out of civil proceedings in the High Court of that description.

II SCA [59.1]

Technical or commercial information or other intellectual property The definition of "intellectual property" in sub-section (5) has been held wide enough to include commercial and non-commercial information imparted in confidence over the telephone. An interceptor of such telephoned information would be unable claim privilege against self-incrimination as a ground for resisting an order to identify the person directing him. This is because directing the contravention of s 1(1) of the Regulation of Investigatory Powers Act 2000 (offence of telephone tapping) would be part and parcel of the interception and within the meaning of "related offence": *Coogan v News Group Newspapers Ltd* [2012] EWCA Civ 48, [2012] 2 All ER 74, [2012] 2 WLR 848.

Note, however, that the Supreme Court construed 'other intellectual property' as limited to other intellectual property which came within the general description 'technical and commercial information' and did not include personal information: *Phillips v News Group Newspapers Ltd* (2012) Times, 20 July, Supreme Court.

II SCA [59.2]

Related offence The words "any offence" in para (b) of the definition of "related offence" in sub-s (5) are not to be read as limited to offences of the kind mentioned in para (a): *Universal City Studios Inc v Hubbard* [1983] Ch 241, [1983] 2 All ER 596; on appeal [1984] Ch 225, [1984] 1 All ER 661, CA.

In a case where there were infringements of intellectual property rights in commercial information, by phone-hacking, it was held that a conspiracy to commit such offences was a related offence and continued from the time when the unlawful agreement was brought into existence until it was terminated. Every interception pursuant to the unlawful agreement would be a related offence committed in the course of the infringement: *Phillips v News Group Newspapers Ltd* [2012] UKSC 28, [2012] 4 All ER 207, [2012] 3 WLR 312.

GENERAL NOTES ON SECTIONS 73 TO 83

II SCA [60]

Sections 73 to 83 have been omitted because they concern the jurisdiction of the Crown Court.

GENERAL NOTES ON SECTIONS 84, 86 AND 87 (RULES OF COURT)

II SCA [61]

The rule-making powers under the Senior Courts Act 1981 are now confined to regulating the procedure of the Crown Court and the criminal division of the Court of Appeal and are contained in ss 84, 86 and 87 of the Act. This is the result of radical amendments made by the Civil Procedure Act 1997, which also set up an entirely new Civil Procedure Rule Committee to make rules of court governing the practice and procedure of the civil division of the Court of Appeal, the High Court and the County Court. See ss 1–6 of the Civil Procedure Act 1997, as amended by ss 82 to 85 of the Courts Act 2003. Since 7 October 2005 Family Procedure Rules are made by the Family Procedure Rule Committee in accordance with ss 75 to 81 of the Courts Act 2003.

PART IV
OFFICERS AND OFFICES

APPOINTMENT OF CERTAIN OFFICERS OF THE SENIOR COURTS

II SCA [62]

88. Qualifications for office

A person shall not be qualified for appointment to any office in the Senior Courts listed in column 1 of any Part of Schedule 2 unless he is a person of any description specified in relation to that office in column 2 of that Part.

II SCA [62.1]

Judicial titles Note that s 64 of the Courts Act 2003 empowers the Lord Chancellor, by order, to alter the name and style of many of these offices.

II SCA [62A]

89. Masters and registrars

(1) The power to make appointments to the offices in the Senior Courts listed in column 1 of Parts II and III of Schedule 2 shall be exercisable by Her Majesty.

(1A) The maximum number of appointments under subsection (1) is such as may be determined from time to time by the Lord Chancellor with the concurrence of the Treasury.

(2) The person appointed to the office of Queen's coroner and attorney and master of the Crown Office and Registrar of criminal appeals shall, by virtue of his appointment, be a master of the Queen's Bench Division.

(3) Her Majesty shall, on the recommendation of the Lord Chancellor, appoint a person to each office listed in the first column of the table in subsection (3C) ("a senior office").

(3A) A person may be appointed to a senior office only if—

(a) he holds the office in the corresponding entry in the second column of that table ("the qualifying office"), or

(b) he does not hold the qualifying office but could be appointed to it in compliance with section 88.

(3B) Where a person who is to be appointed to a senior office meets the condition in subsection (3A)(b) he shall, when appointed to the senior office, also be appointed to the qualifying office.

(3C) This is the table referred to in subsections (3) and (3A)—

Senior office	**Qualifying office**
Senior Master of the Queen's Bench Division	Master of the Queen's Bench Division
Chief Chancery Master	Master of the Chancery Division
Chief Taxing Master	Taxing master of the Senior Courts
Chief Bankruptcy Registrar	Insolvency and Companies Court Judge
Senior District Judge of the Family Division	Registrar of the Principal Registry of the Family Division.

(4) The person appointed Senior Master of the Queen's Bench Division under subsection (3)(a) shall hold and perform the duties of the offices of the Queen's Remembrancer and registrar of judgments.

(5)–(7) . . .

(7A) A person appointed under subsection (1) is to be paid such salary, and a person appointed to a senior office is to be paid such additional salary, as may be determined by the Lord Chancellor with the concurrence of the Treasury.

(7B) A salary payable under or by virtue of this section—

(a) may in any case be increased, but

(b) may not, in the case of a salary payable in respect of an office listed in column 1 of Part 2 of Schedule 2 or of a senior office, be reduced,

by a determination or further determination under this section.

(8) Salaries payable under or by virtue of this section shall be paid out of money provided by Parliament.

II SCA [62A.1]

ICC Judges A person appointed under s 89(1) to the office of Insolvency and Companies Court Judge (previously Registrar in Bankruptcy) is referred to in relevant Rules and Practice Directions as an ICC judge.

II SCA [62B]

90. Official Solicitor

(1) There shall continue to be an Official Solicitor to the Senior Courts, who shall be appointed by the Lord Chancellor.

(2) There shall be paid to the Official Solicitor out of money provided by Parliament such salary as the Lord Chancellor may, with the concurrence of the Minister for the Civil Service, determine.

(3) The Official Solicitor shall have such powers and perform such duties as may for the time being be conferred or imposed on the holder of that office—

(a) by or under this or any other Act; or

(b) by or in accordance with any direction given (before or after the commencement of this Act) by the Lord Chancellor.

(3A) The holder for the time being of the office of Official Solicitor shall have the right to conduct litigation in relation to any proceedings.

(3B) When acting as Official Solicitor a person who would otherwise have the right to conduct litigation by virtue of section 28(2)(a) of the Courts and Legal Services Act 1990 shall be treated as having acquired that right solely by virtue of subsection (3A).

(4) If—

(a) the Official Solicitor is not available because of his absence or for some other reason; or

(b) his office is vacant,

then, during such unavailability or vacancy, any powers or duties of the Official Solicitor shall be exercisable or fall to be performed by any person for the time being appointed by the Lord Chancellor as deputy to the Official Solicitor (and any property vested in the Official Solicitor may accordingly be dealt with by any such person in all respects as if it were vested in him instead).

II SCA [62C]

91. Deputies and temporary appointments

(1) If it appears to the Lord Chief Justice that it is expedient to do so in order to facilitate the disposal of business in the Senior Courts or any other court or tribunal to which a person appointed under this subsection may be deployed, he may appoint a person—

(a) to act as a deputy for any person holding an office listed in column 1 of Part II . . . of Schedule 2; or

(b) to act as a temporary additional officer in any such office,

during such period or on such occasions as the Lord Chancellor may think fit.

(1ZA) The Lord Chief Justice may not appoint a holder of relevant office under subsection (1) without the concurrence of the Lord Chancellor.

(1ZB) Section 85 of the Constitutional Reform Act 2005 (selection of certain office holders) does not apply to an appointment to which subsection (1ZA) applies.

(1ZC) In this section a "holder of relevant office" means a person who holds, or has held within two years ending with the date when his appointment under this section takes effect—

(a) any office listed in column 1 of Part 2 or 3 of Schedule 2, or

(b) the office of district judge.

(1A) If it appears to the Lord Chancellor that it is expedient to do so in order to facilitate the disposal of business in the Senior Courts, he may appoint a person—

(a) to act as a deputy for any person holding an office listed in column 1 of Part 3 of Schedule 2; or

(b) to act as a temporary additional officer in any such office,

during such period or on such occasions as the Lord Chancellor may think fit.

(2) Subject to subsection (3), a person shall not be qualified for appointment under this section if the office in which he would act by virtue of the appointment is one to which he is not qualified for permanent appointment.

(3) An appointment under this section may extend until the day on which a person attains the age of seventy-five years if it is an appointment of a holder of relevant office.

(4) Every person, while acting under this section, shall have all the jurisdiction of a person permanently appointed to the office in which he is acting.

(5) < . . . >

(6) The Lord Chancellor may, out of money provided by Parliament, pay to any person appointed under this section such remuneration and allowances as he may, with the concurrence of the Minister for the Civil Service, determine.

(6A) A person appointed under subsection (1) may be removed from office—

(a) only by the Lord Chancellor with the agreement of the Lord Chief Justice, and

(b) only on—

(i) the ground of inability or misbehaviour, or

(ii) a ground specified in the person's terms of appointment.

(6B) Subject to subsection (6C), the period of a person's appointment under subsection (1) (including a period already extended under this subsection) must be extended by the Lord Chancellor before its expiry; and for this purpose a person appointed under subsection (1) to act under this section on certain occasions is to be treated as having been appointed for a period that expires when the occasions end.

(6C) Extension under subsection (6B)—

(a) requires the person's agreement,

(b) is to be for such period as the Lord Chancellor thinks fit, and

(c) may be refused on—

(i) the ground of inability or misbehaviour, or

(ii) a ground specified in the person's terms of appointment,

but only with any agreement of the Lord Chief Justice, or a nominee of the Lord Chief Justice, that may be required by those terms.

(6D) Subject to the preceding provisions of this section (but subject in the first place to the Judicial Pensions and Retirement Act 1993), a person appointed under subsection (1) is to hold and vacate office in accordance with the terms of the person's appointment, which are to be such as the Lord Chancellor may determine.

(7) The Lord Chief Justice may nominate a judicial office holder (as defined in section 109(4) of the Constitutional Reform Act 2005) to exercise his functions under subsection (1) or (6A)(a).

OTHER PROVISIONS RELATING TO OFFICERS OF SENIOR COURTS

II SCA [63]

92. Tenure of office

(1) Subject to the following provisions of this section, to section 91(3) and to subsections (4) to (6) of section 26 of the Judicial Pensions and Retirement Act 1993 (Lord Chancellor's power to authorise continuance in office up to the age of 75), a person who holds an office to which this subsection applies shall vacate it on the day on which he attains the age of seventy years.

(2) Subsection (1) applies to the offices listed in column 1 of Part II of Schedule 2 . . . .

(2A) Subject to the following provisions of this section, a person who holds an office to which this subsection applies shall vacate it at the end of the completed year of service in the course of which he attains the age of sixty-two years.

(2B) Subsection (2A) applies to the offices listed in column 1 of Part I of Schedule 2 . . .

(2C) . . .

(2D) . . .

(2E) . . .

(3) . . .

(3A) Where the Lord Chancellor considers it desirable in the public interest to retain in office a person who holds an office to which subsection (2A) applies after the time when he would otherwise retire in accordance with that subsection, the Lord Chancellor may from time to time authorise the continuance in office of that person until such date, not being later than the date on which he attains the age of sixty-five years, as he thinks fit.

(4) A person appointed to an office listed in column 1 of Part 1 or 2 of Schedule 2 shall hold that office during good behaviour.

(5) The power to remove such a person from his office on account of misbehaviour shall be exercisable by the Lord Chancellor with the concurrence of the Lord Chief Justice.

(6) The Lord Chancellor may also, with the concurrence of the Lord Chief Justice, remove such a person from his office on account of inability to perform the duties of his office.

(7) A person appointed to an office listed in column 1 of Part III of Schedule 2 shall hold that office during Her Majesty's pleasure.

(8) It is for the Lord Chancellor to recommend to Her Majesty the exercise of any power under subsection (7).

II SCA [63A]

93. Status of officers for purposes of salary and pension

(1) Subject to subsection (2), any person who holds an office listed in column 1 of any Part of Schedule 2 or the office of Accountant General of the Senior Courts and is not employed in the civil service of the State shall be deemed to be so employed for the purposes of salary and pension.

(2) Subsection (1), so far as it relates to pension, shall not apply to a person holding qualifying judicial office, within the meaning of the Judicial Pensions and Retirement Act 1993.

II SCA [63B]

94. . . .

CENTRAL OFFICE AND ACCOUNTANT GENERAL

II SCA [64]

96. Central Office

(1) The Central Office of the Senior Courts shall perform such business as the Lord Chief Justice may, with the concurrence of the Lord Chancellor, direct.

(2) Subject to any direction under subsection (1), the Central Office shall perform such business as it performed immediately before the commencement of this Act.

(3) The Lord Chief Justice may nominate a judicial office holder (as defined in section 109(4) of the Constitutional Reform Act 2005) to exercise his functions under this section.

II SCA [64A]

97. Accountant General

(1) There shall continue to be an Accountant General of, and an accounting department for, the Senior Courts.

(2) The Lord Chancellor shall appoint such person as he thinks fit to the office in the Senior Courts of Accountant General of the Senior Courts and the person so appointed shall hold and vacate office in accordance with the terms of his appointment.

(3) The Accountant General shall be paid such salary or fees as the Lord Chancellor determines with the consent of the Treasury.

(4) If one person holds office both as the Accountant General and as the Public Trustee then, if he ceases to be the Public Trustee, he shall also cease to be the Accountant General unless the Lord Chancellor otherwise directs.

(5) If a vacancy occurs in the office of Accountant General or the person appointed to hold the office is for any reason unable to act for any period such person as the Lord Chancellor appoints as deputy in that office shall, during the vacancy or that period, perform the functions of that office (and any property vested in the Accountant General may accordingly be dealt with by the deputy in all respects as if it were vested in him instead).

JUDGES' CLERKS AND SECRETARIES

II SCA [65]

98. Judges' clerks and secretaries

(1) A clerk and a secretary shall be attached to each of the following judges of the Senior Courts, namely the Lord Chief Justice, the Master of the Rolls, the President of the Queen's Bench Division, the President of the Family Division and the Chancellor of the High Court.

(2) A clerk shall be attached to each of the following judges of the Senior Courts, namely the Lords Justices of Appeal and the puisne judges of the High Court.

(3) Any clerk or secretary attached as mentioned in subsection (1) or (2)—

- (a) shall be appointed by the Lord Chancellor; and
- (b) if not already employed in the civil service of the State shall be deemed for all purposes to be so employed.

(4) If at any time it appears to any of the judges mentioned in subsection (1) desirable that there should be attached to him a legal secretary (that is to say a secretary with legal qualifications) in addition to the secretary provided for by that subsection, he may, with the concurrence of the Lord Chancellor, appoint a person who has a general qualification (within the meaning of section 71 of the Courts and Legal Services Act 1990) as his legal secretary.

(5) An appointment under subsection (4) may be on either a full-time or a part-time basis; and a person appointed by a judge as his legal secretary shall, except as regards remuneration, hold and vacate that office in accordance with such terms as the judge may, with the concurrence of the Lord Chancellor, determine when making the appointment.

(6) A person appointed under subsection (4)—

- (a) shall not be treated as employed in the civil service of the State by reason only of that appointment; and
- (b) if the Lord Chancellor so determines in his case, shall be paid out of money provided by Parliament such remuneration as the Lord Chancellor may, with the concurrence of the Minister for the Civil Service, determine.

DISTRICT REGISTRIES AND DISTRICT JUDGES

II SCA [66]

99. District registries

(1) The Lord Chancellor may, after consulting the Lord Chief Justice, by order direct that there shall be district registries of the High Court at such places and for such districts as are specified in the order.

(2) Any order under this section shall be made by statutory instrument, which shall be laid before Parliament after being made.

(3) The Lord Chief Justice may nominate a judicial office holder (as defined in section 109(4) of the Constitutional Reform Act 2005) to exercise his functions under this section.

II SCA [66.1]

The Civil Courts Order 2014 By the Civil Courts Order 2014, SI 2014/819 the Lord Chancellor specified the various district registries of the High Court and identified the 10 Chancery district registries. The geographical boundaries of each district are substantially the same as before and, under the terms of the Order, are set by reference to areas served by the County Court hearing centres, formerly county court districts.

II SCA [66A]

100. District judges

(1) The Lord Chief Justice, after consulting the Lord Chancellor—

- (a) may assign a district judge to one or more district registries;
- (b) may change an assignment so as to assign the district judge to a different district registry or registries (or to no district registry).

(2) A reference in any enactment or other instrument to the district judge of a district registry is a reference to any district judge assigned to the registry concerned.

(3) Every district judge is, by virtue of his office, capable of acting in any district registry whether or not assigned to it, but may do so only in accordance with arrangements made by or on behalf of the Lord Chief Justice.

(4) Whilst a district judge is assigned to one or more district registries in accordance with subsection (1) he is a district judge of the High Court.

(5) The Lord Chief Justice may nominate a judicial office holder (as defined in section 109(4) of the Constitutional Reform Act 2005) to exercise his functions under subsection (1).

II SCA [66B]

101. . . .

Repealed by the Constitutional Reform Act 2005, s 14, Sch 3, para 2(1) with effect from 3 April 2006.

II SCA [66C]

102. Deputy district judges

(1) If it appears to the Lord Chief Justice that it is expedient to do so in order to facilitate the disposal of business in the High Court or any other court or tribunal to which a person appointed under this subsection may be deployed, he may appoint a person to be a deputy district judge.

(1A) A person is qualified for appointment under subsection (1) only if the person—

- (a) is qualified for appointment as a district judge, or
- (b) holds, or has held, the office of district judge.

(1B) The Lord Chief Justice may not appoint a person under subsection (1) without the concurrence of the Lord Chancellor if the person—

- (a) holds the office of district judge, or
- (b) ceased to hold the office of district judge within two years ending with the date when the appointment takes effect.

(1C) Section 85 of the Constitutional Reform Act 2005 (c 4) (selection of certain office holders) does not apply to an appointment to which subsection (1B) applies.

(3) No appointment to which subsection (1B) applies shall be such as to extend beyond the day on which the person in question attains the age of seventy-five years.

(4A) The Lord Chief Justice, after consulting the Lord Chancellor—

- (a) may assign a deputy district judge appointed under this section to one or more district registries;

(b) may change an assignment so as to assign the deputy district judge to a different district registry or registries (or to no district registry).

(4B) A deputy district judge appointed under this section and assigned to a district registry has, while acting under his assignment, the same jurisdiction as a district judge assigned to that registry.

(4C) Every deputy district judge appointed under this section is, by virtue of his office, capable of acting as a district judge in any district registry to which he is not assigned, but may act in a district registry to which he is not assigned only in accordance with arrangements made by or on behalf of the Lord Chief Justice.

(5) Subsection (6) of section 91 applies in relation to a deputy district judge appointed under this section as it applies in relation to a person appointed under that section.

(5ZA) A person appointed under this section may be removed from office as a deputy district judge—

(a) only by the Lord Chancellor with the agreement of the Lord Chief Justice, and

(b) only on—

(i) the ground of inability or misbehaviour, or

(ii) a ground specified in the person's terms of appointment.

(5ZB) Subject to subsection (5ZC), the term of a person's appointment under this section (including a term already extended under this subsection) must be extended by the Lord Chancellor before its expiry.

(5ZC) Extension under subsection (5ZB)—

(a) requires the person's agreement,

(b) is to be for such term as the Lord Chancellor thinks fit, and

(c) may be refused on—

(i) the ground of inability or misbehaviour, or

(ii) a ground specified in the person's terms of appointment,

but only with any agreement of the Lord Chief Justice, or a nominee of the Lord Chief Justice, that may be required by those terms.

(5ZD) Subject to the preceding provisions of this section (but subject in the first place to the Judicial Pensions and Retirement Act 1993), a person appointed under this section is to hold and vacate office as a deputy district judge in accordance with the terms of the person's appointment, which are to be such as the Lord Chancellor may determine.

(5ZE) The Lord Chief Justice may nominate a senior judge (as defined in section 109(5) of the Constitutional Reform Act 2005) to exercise the Lord Chief Justice's functions under subsection (1) or (5ZA)(a).

(5A) The Lord Chief Justice may nominate a judicial office holder (as defined in section 109(4) of the Constitutional Reform Act 2005) to exercise his functions under subsection... (4A).

(6) < . . . >

II SCA [66D]

103. Assistant district judges
Repealed by the Judicial Pensions and Retirement Act 1993 s 31(4), Sch 9.

DISTRICT PROBATE REGISTRIES

II SCA [66E]

104. District probate registries

(1) The Lord Chancellor may, after consulting the Lord Chief Justice, by order direct that there shall be district probate registries of the High Court at such places and for such districts as are specified in the order.

(2) Any order under this section shall be made by statutory instrument, which shall be laid before Parliament after being made.

(3) The Lord Chief Justice may nominate a judicial office holder (as defined in section 109(4) of the Constitutional Reform Act 2005) to exercise his functions under this section.

PART V
PROBATE CAUSES AND MATTERS

PROCEDURE IN PROBATE REGISTRIES IN RELATION TO GRANTS OF REPRESENTATION

II SCA [67]

105. Applications

Applications for grants of probate or administration and for the revocation of grants may be made to—

(a) the Principal Registry of the Family Division (in this Part referred to as "the Principal Registry"); or

(b) a district probate registry.

II SCA [67A]

106. Grants by district probate registrars

(1) Any grant made by a district probate registrar shall be made in the name of the High Court under the seal used in the registry.

(2)–(4) [. . .]

II SCA [67B]

107. No grant where conflicting applications

Subject to probate rules, no grant in respect of the estate, or part of the estate, of a deceased person shall be made out of the Principal Registry or any district probate registry on any application if, at any time before the making of a grant, it appears to the registrar concerned that some other application has been made in respect of that estate or, as the case may be, that part of it and has not been either refused or withdrawn.

II SCA [67C]

108. Caveats

(1) A caveat against a grant of probate or administration may be entered in the Principal Registry or in any district probate registry.

(2) On a caveat being entered in a district probate registry, the district probate registrar shall immediately send a copy of it to the Principal Registry to be entered among the caveats in that Registry.

II SCA [67D]

109. Refusal of grant where inheritance tax unpaid

(1) Subject to subsections (2) and (3), no grant shall be made, and no grant made outside the United Kingdom shall be resealed, except on the production of an account prepared in pursuance of [the Inheritance Tax Act 1984] showing by means of such receipt or certification as may be prescribed by the Commissioners of Inland Revenue (in this and the following section referred to as "the Commissioners") either—

(a) that the inheritance tax payable on the delivery of the account has been paid; or

(b) that no such tax is so payable.

(2) Arrangements may be made between the President of the Family Division and the Commissioners providing for the purposes of this section in such cases as may be specified in the arrangements that the receipt or certification of an account may be dispensed with or that some other document may be substituted for the account required by the Inheritance Tax Act 1984.

(3) Nothing in subsection (1) applies in relation to a case where the delivery of the account required by that Part of that Act has for the time being been dispensed with by any regulations under section 256(1)(a) of the Inheritance Tax Act 1984.

II SCA [67E]

110. Documents to be delivered to Commissioners of Inland Revenue

Subject to any arrangements which may from time to time be made between the President of the Family Division and the Commissioners, the Principal Registry and every district probate registry shall, within such period after a grant as the President may direct, deliver to the Commissioners or their proper officer the following documents—

(a) in the case of a grant of probate or of administration with the will annexed, a copy of the will;

(b) in every case, such certificate or note of the grant as the Commissioners may require.

II SCA [67F]

111. Records of grants

(1) There shall continue to be kept records of all grants which are made in the Principal Registry or in any district probate registry.

(2) Those records shall be in such form, and shall contain such particulars, as the President of the Family Division may direct.

POWER OF COURT IN RELATION TO PERSONAL REPRESENTATIVES

II SCA [67G]

112. Summons to executor to prove or renounce

The High Court may summon any person named as executor in a will to prove, or renounce probate of, the will, and to do such other things concerning the will as the court had power to order such a person to do immediately before the commencement of this Act.

II SCA [67H]

113. Power of court to sever grant

(1) Subject to subsection (2), the High Court may grant probate or administration in respect of any part of the estate of a deceased person, limited in any way the court thinks fit.

(2) Where the estate of a deceased person is known to be insolvent, the grant of representation to it shall not be severed under subsection (1) except as regards a trust estate in which he had no beneficial interest.

II SCA [67I]

114. Number of personal representatives

(1) Probate or administration shall not be granted by the High Court to more than four persons in respect of the same part of the estate of a deceased person.

(2) Where under a will or intestacy any beneficiary is a minor or a life interest arises, any grant of administration by the High Court shall be made either to a trust corporation (with or without an individual) or to not less than two individuals, unless it appears to the court to be expedient in all the circumstances to appoint an individual as sole administrator.

(3) For the purpose of determining whether a minority or life interest arises in any particular case, the court may act on such evidence as may be prescribed.

(4) If at any time during the minority of a beneficiary or the subsistence of a life interest under a will or intestacy there is only one personal representative (not being a trust corporation), the High Court may, on the application of any person interested or the guardian or receiver of any such person, and in accordance with probate rules, appoint one or more additional personal representatives to act while the minority or life interest subsists and until the estate is fully administered.

(5) An appointment of an additional personal representative under subsection (4) to act with an executor shall not have the effect of including him in any chain of representation.

II SCA [67J]

115. Grants to trust corporations

(1) The High Court may—

(a) where a trust corporation is named in a will as executor, grant probate to the corporation either solely or jointly with any other person named in the will as executor, as the case may require; or

(b) grant administration to a trust corporation, either solely or jointly with another person;

and the corporation may act accordingly as executor or administrator, as the case may be.

(2) Probate or administration shall not be granted to any person as nominee of a trust corporation.

(3) Any officer authorised for the purpose by a trust corporation or its directors or governing body may, on behalf of the corporation, swear affidavits, give security and do any other act which the court may require with a view to the grant to the corporation of probate or administration; and the acts of an officer so authorised shall be binding on the corporation.

[(4) Subsections (1) to (3) shall also apply in relation to any body which is exempt from the provisions of section 23(1) of the Solicitors Act 1974 (unqualified persons not to prepare papers for probate etc) by virtue of any of paragraphs (e) to (h) of subsection (2) of that section.]

Amendment *Sub-section (4) is inserted by the Courts and Legal Services Act 1990, as from a day to be appointed.*

II SCA [67K]

116. Power of court to pass over prior claims to grant

(1) If by reason of any special circumstances it appears to the High Court to be necessary or expedient to appoint as administrator some person other than the person who, but for this section, would in accordance with probate rules have been entitled to the grant, the court may in its discretion appoint as administrator such person as it thinks expedient.

(2) Any grant of administration under this section may be limited in any way the court thinks fit.

II SCA [67K.1]

Special circumstances for passing over prior claims to grant The court is empowered by s 116 to pass over prior claims to grant where this is justified by special circumstances. In a case where the deceased was an Australian of Aboriginal origin who was adopted in England, the court held special circumstances (concerning burial rites) existed. But the court further held that they did not justify passing over the prior claim to a grant of the deceased's daughter: *Buchanan v Milton* [1999] 2 FLR 844, Hale J.

II SCA [67L]

117. Administration pending suit

(1) Where any legal proceedings concerning the validity of the will of a deceased person, or for obtaining, recalling or revoking any grant, are pending, the High Court may grant administration of the estate of the deceased person in question to an administrator pending suit, who shall, subject to subsection (2), have all the rights, duties and powers of a general administrator.

(2) An administrator pending suit shall be subject to the immediate control of the court and act under its direction; and, except in such circumstances as may be prescribed, no distribution of the estate, or any part of the estate, of the deceased person in question shall be made by such an administrator without the leave of the court.

(3) The court may, out of the estate of the deceased, assign an administrator pending suit such reasonable remuneration as it thinks fit.

II SCA [67L.1]

Practice For practical guidance see para 8 of **CPR PD 57**.

II SCA [67M]

118. Effect of appointment of minor as executor

Where a testator by his will appoints a minor to be an executor, the appointment shall not operate to vest in the minor the estate, or any part of the estate, of the testator, or to constitute him a personal representative for any purpose, unless and until probate is granted to him in accordance with probate rules.

II SCA [67N]

119. Administration with will annexed

(1) Administration with the will annexed shall be granted, subject to and in accordance with probate rules, in every class of case in which the High Court had power to make such a grant immediately before the commencement of this Act.

(2) Where administration with the will annexed is granted, the will of the deceased shall be performed and observed in the same manner as if probate of it had been granted to an executor.

II SCA [67O]

120. Power to require administrators to produce sureties

(1) As a condition of granting administration to any person the High Court may, subject to the following provisions of this section and subject to and in accordance with probate rules, require one or more sureties to guarantee that they will make good, within any limit imposed by the court on the total liability of the surety or sureties, any loss which any person interested in the administration of the estate of the deceased may suffer in consequence of a breach by the administrator of his duties as such.

(2) A guarantee given in pursuance of any such requirement shall enure for the benefit of every person interested in the administration of the estate of the deceased as if contained in a contract under seal made by the surety or sureties with every such person and, where there are two or more sureties, as if they had bound themselves jointly and severally.

(3) No action shall be brought on any such guarantee without the leave of the High Court.

(4) Stamp duty shall not be chargeable on any such guarantee.

(5) This section does not apply where administration is granted to the Treasury Solicitor, the Official Solicitor, the Public Trustee, the Solicitor for the affairs of the Duchy of Lancaster or the Duchy of Cornwall or the Crown Solicitor for Northern Ireland, or to the consular officer of a foreign state to which section 1 of the Consular Conventions Act 1949 applies, or in such other cases as may be prescribed.

REVOCATION OF GRANTS AND CANCELLATION OF RESEALING AT INSTANCE OF COURT

II SCA [68]

121. Revocation of grants and cancellation of resealing at instance of court

(1) Where it appears to the High Court that a grant either ought not to have been made or contains an error, the court may call in the grant and, if satisfied that it would be revoked at the instance of a party interested, may revoke it.

(2) A grant may be revoked under subsection (1) without being called in, if it cannot be called in.

(3) Where it appears to the High Court that a grant resealed under the Colonial Probates Acts 1892 and 1927 ought not to have been resealed, the court may call in the relevant document and, if satisfied that the resealing would be cancelled at the instance of a party interested, may cancel the resealing.

In this and the following subsection "the relevant document" means the original grant or, where some other document was sealed by the court under those Acts, that document.

(4) A resealing may be cancelled under subsection (3) without the relevant document being called in, if it cannot be called in.

ANCILLARY POWERS OF COURT

II SCA [68A]

122. Examination of person with knowledge of testamentary document

(1) Where it appears that there are reasonable grounds for believing that any person has knowledge of any document which is or purports to be a testamentary document, the High Court may, whether or not any legal proceedings are pending, order him to attend for the purpose of being examined in open court.

(2) The court may—

(a) require any person who is before it in compliance with an order under subsection (1) to answer any question relating to the document concerned; and

(b) if appropriate, order him to bring in the document in such manner as the court may direct.

(3) Any person who, having been required by the court to do so under this section, fails to attend for examination, answer any question or bring in any document shall be guilty of contempt of court.

II SCA [68A.1]

Practice For practical guidance see para 7 of **CPR PD 57**.

II SCA [68B]

123. Subpoena to bring in testamentary document

Where it appears that any person has in his possession, custody or power any document which is or purports to be a testamentary document, the High Court may, whether or not any legal proceedings are pending, issue a subpoena requiring him to bring in the document in such manner as the court may in the subpoena direct.

PROVISIONS AS TO DOCUMENTS

II SCA [68C]

124. Place for deposit of original wills and other documents

All original wills and other documents which are under the control of the High Court in the Principal Registry or in any district probate registry shall be deposited and preserved in such places as may be provided for in directions given in accordance with Part 1 of Schedule 2 to the Constitutional Reform Act 2005; and any wills or other documents so deposited shall, subject to the control of the High Court and to probate rules, be open to inspection.

II SCA [68D]

125. Copies of wills and grants

An office copy, or a sealed and certified copy, of any will or part of a will open to inspection under section 124 or of any grant may, on payment of the fee prescribed by an order under section 92 of the Courts Act 2003 (fees), be obtained—

(a) from the registry in which in accordance with section 124 the will or documents relating to the grant are preserved; or

(b) where in accordance with that section the will or such documents are preserved in some place other than a registry, from the Principal Registry; or

(c) subject to the approval of the Senior Registrar of the Family Division, from the Principal Registry in any case where the will was proved in or the grant was issued from a district probate registry.

II SCA [68E]

126. *Depositories for wills of living persons*

(1) There shall be provided, under the control and direction of the High Court, safe and convenient depositories for the custody of the wills of living persons; and any person may deposit his will in such a depository on payment of the fee

prescribed by an order under section 92 of the Courts Act 2003 (fees) and subject to such conditions as may be prescribed by regulations made by the President of the Family Division with the concurrence of the Lord Chancellor.

(2) Any regulations made under this section shall be made by statutory instrument which shall be laid before Parliament after being made; and the Statutory Instruments Act 1946 shall apply to a statutory instrument containing regulations under this section in like manner as if they had been made by a Minister of the Crown.

II SCA [68E.1]

Prospective repeal This section was prospectively repealed by the Administration of Justice Act 1982 s 75, Sch 9 Part 1 from a day to be appointed.

PROBATE RULES

II SCA [68F]

127. Probate rules

(1) Rules of court (in this Part referred to as "probate rules") may be made in accordance with Part 1 of Schedule 1 to the Constitutional Reform Act 2005 for regulating and prescribing the practice and procedure of the High Court with respect to non-contentious or common form probate business.

(2) Without prejudice to the generality of subsection (1), probate rules may make provision for regulating the classes of persons entitled to grants of probate or administration in particular circumstances and the relative priorities of their claims thereto.

(3) . . .

II SCA [68F.1]

Non-contentious Probate Rules See the Non-Contentious Probate Rules 1987, SI 1987/2024, as amended.

INTERPRETATION OF PART V AND OTHER PROBATE PROVISIONS

II SCA [68G]

128. Interpretation of Part V and other probate provisions

In this Part, and in the other provisions of this Act relating to probate causes and matters, unless the context otherwise requires—

"administration" includes all letters of administration of the effects of deceased persons, whether with or without a will annexed, and whether granted for general, special or limited purposes;

"estate" means real and personal estate, and "real estate" includes—

(a) chattels real and land in possession, remainder or reversion and every interest in or over land to which the deceased person was entitled at the time of his death, and

(b) real estate held on trust or by way of mortgage or security, but not [. . .] money secured or charged on land;

"grant" means a grant of probate or administration;

"non-contentious or common form probate business" means the business of obtaining probate and administration where there is no contention as to the right thereto, including—

(a) the passing of probates and administrations through the High Court in contentious cases where the contest has been terminated,

(b) all business of a non-contentious nature in matters of testacy and intestacy not being proceedings in any action, and

(c) the business of lodging caveats against the grant of probate or administration;

"Principal Registry" means the Principal Registry of the Family Division;

"probate rules" means rules of court made under section 127;

"trust corporation" means the Public Trustee or a corporation either appointed by the court in any particular case to be a trustee or authorised by rules made under section 4(3) of the Public Trustee Act 1906 to act as a custodian trustee;

"will" includes a nuncupative will and any testamentary document of which probate may be granted.

PART VI
MISCELLANEOUS AND SUPPLEMENTARY

MISCELLANEOUS PROVISIONS

II SCA [69]–II SCA [69A]

129. Lords Commissioners to represent Lord Chancellor when Great Seal in commission

When the Great Seal is in commission, the Lords Commissioners shall represent the Lord Chancellor for the purposes of this Act; but the powers vested in him by this Act in relation to—

(a) the appointment of officers, and

(b) any act for which the concurrence or presence of the Lord Chancellor is required by this Act,

may be exercised by the senior Lord Commissioner for the time being.

II SCA [69B]

131. Conveyancing counsel of Senior Courts

(1) The conveyancing counsel of the Senior Courts shall be persons who have a 10 year High Court qualification, within the meaning of section 71 of the Courts and Legal Services Act 1990 who have practised as such for not less than ten years.

(2) The conveyancing counsel of the court shall be not more than six, nor less than three, in number, and shall be appointed by the Lord Chancellor with the concurrence of the Lord Chief Justice.

(3) The Lord Chief Justice may nominate a judicial office holder (as defined in section 109(4) of the Constitutional Reform Act 2005) to exercise his functions under this section.

II SCA [69C]

132. Proof of documents bearing seal or stamp of the Senior Courts or any office thereof

Every document purporting to be sealed or stamped with the seal or stamp of the Senior Courts or of any office of the Senior Courts shall be received in evidence in all parts of the United Kingdom without further proof.

II SCA [69D]

133. Enrolment and engrossment of instruments

(1) The Master of the Rolls may make regulations for authorising and regulating the enrolment or filing of instruments in the Senior Courts, and for prescribing the form in which certificates of enrolment or filing are to be issued.

(2) Regulations under subsection (1) shall not affect the operation of any enactment requiring or authorising the enrolment of any instrument in the Senior Courts or prescribing the manner in which any instrument is to be enrolled there.

(3) Any instrument which is required or authorised by or under this or any other Act to be enrolled or engrossed in the Senior Courts shall be deemed to have been duly enrolled or engrossed if it is written on material authorised or required by regulations under subsection (1) and has been filed or otherwise preserved in accordance with regulations under that subsection.

(4) The Lord Chancellor may, with the concurrence of the Master of the Rolls and of the Treasury, make regulations prescribing the fees to be paid on the enrolment or filing of any instrument in the Senior Courts, including any additional fees payable on the enrolment or filing of any instrument out of time.

(5) Any regulations under this section shall be made by statutory instrument, which shall be laid before Parliament after being made; and the Statutory Instruments Act 1946 shall apply to a statutory instrument containing regulations under subsection (1) in like manner as if the regulations had been made by a Minister of the Crown.

II SCA [69D.1]

Change of name See the Enrolment of Deeds (Change of Name) Regulations 1994, SI 1994/604, as amended by SI 2005/2056. The practice regarding the enrolment of deeds is set out in **CPR PD 5** at paragraph 6; and the text of the regulations is included as an Appendix to the Practice Direction.

II SCA [69E]

134. Powers of attorney deposited before October 1971

(1) This section applies to any instrument creating, or verifying the execution of, a power of attorney which was deposited in the Central Office of the Senior Courts before 1st October 1971.

(2) A separate file of such instruments shall continue to be kept and, subject to payment of the fee prescribed by an order under section 92 of the Courts Act 2003 (fees)—

- (a) any person may search that file, and may inspect any such instrument; and
- (b) an office copy of any such instrument shall be issued to any person on request.

(3) A document purporting to be an office copy of any such instrument shall, in any part of the United Kingdom, without further proof be sufficient evidence of the contents of the instrument and of its having been deposited as mentioned in subsection (1).

II SCA [69F]

135. Bonds given under order of court

(1) A bond to be given by any person under or for the purposes of any order of the High Court or the civil division of the Court of Appeal shall be given in such form and to such officer of the court as may be prescribed and, if the court so requires, with one or more sureties.

(2) An officer of the court to whom a bond is given in accordance with subsection (1) shall as such have power to enforce it or to assign it, pursuant to an order of the court under subsection (4), to some other person.

(3) Where by rules of court made for the purposes of this section another officer is at any time substituted for the officer previously prescribed as the officer to whom bonds of any class are to be given, the rules may provide that bonds of that

class given before the rules come into operation shall have effect as if references in the bonds to the officer previously prescribed were references to the substituted officer.

(4) Where it appears to the court that the condition of a bond given in accordance with subsection (1) has been broken, the court may, on an application in that behalf, order the bond to be assigned to such person as may be specified in the order.

(5) A person to whom a bond is ordered to be assigned under subsection (4) shall be entitled by virtue of the order to sue on the bond in his own name as if it had been originally given to him, and to recover on it as trustee for all persons interested the full amount recoverable in respect of the breach of condition.

II SCA [69G]

136. Production of documents filed in, or in custody of, Senior Courts

(1) Rules may be made in accordance with Part 1 of Schedule 1 to the Constitutional Reform Act 2005 for providing that, in any case where a document filed in, or in the custody of, any office of the Senior Courts is required to be produced to any court or tribunal (including an umpire or arbitrator) sitting elsewhere than at the Royal Courts of Justice—

- (a) it shall not be necessary for any officer, whether served with a subpoena in that behalf or not, to attend for the purpose of producing the document; but
- (b) the document may be produced to the court or tribunal by sending it to the court or tribunal, in the manner prescribed in the rules, together with a certificate, in the form so prescribed, to the effect that the document has been filed in, or is in the custody of, the office;

and any such certificate shall be prima facie evidence of the facts stated in it.

(2) Rules under this section may contain—

- (a) provisions for securing the safe custody and return to the proper office of the Senior Courts of any document sent to a court or tribunal in pursuance of the rules; and
- (b) such incidental and supplementary provisions as appear to the person making the rules to be necessary or expedient.

(3) . . .

II SCA [69G.1]

Court documents The procedure for obtaining documents that are in court custody is now regulated by CPR 5 and Practice Direction 5A – Court Documents.

II SCA [69H]

137. Money paid into court under enactment subsequently repealed

Where in pursuance of any enactment, whenever passed, any money has (before or after the commencement of this Act) been paid—

- (a) into the Bank of England in the name of the Accountant General of the Senior Courts; or
- (b) into the Senior Courts,

then, if that enactment has been or is subsequently repealed—

- (i) the Accountant General may continue to deal with the money; and
- (ii) any powers of the High Court with respect to the money shall continue to be exercisable,

in all respects as if that enactment had not been repealed.

II SCA [69I]–II SCA [69K]

Amendment *Sections 138, 138A and 138B of the Supreme Court Act 1981, which relate to the taking and sale by sheriffs of goods under execution, were repealed by the Courts Act 2003 and replaced by the provisions of Schedule 7 to that Act with effect from 15 March 2004 (see* **II CA [6]** *below).*

II SCA [69L]

139. Attachment of National Savings Bank deposits

(1) [. . .]

(2) The Lord Chancellor may by order direct that section 27(1) and (2) of the Crown Proceedings Act 1947 (attachment of moneys payable by the Crown) shall not apply in relation to any money payable by the Crown to any person on account of—

(a) any deposit in the National Savings Bank; or

(b) a deposit in that Bank of any description specified in the order.

(3) Any order under subsection (2) shall be made by statutory instrument subject to annulment in pursuance of a resolution of either House of Parliament.

(4) Without prejudice to section 153(4), this section extends to England and Wales only.

II SCA [69M]

140. Enforcement of fines and forfeited recognizances

(1) Payment of a fine imposed, or sum due under a recognizance forfeited, by the High Court or the civil division of the Court of Appeal may be enforced upon the order of the court—

(a) in like manner as a judgment of the High Court for the payment of money; or

(b) in like manner as a fine imposed by the Crown Court.

(2) Where payment of a fine or other sum falls to be enforced as mentioned in paragraph (a) of subsection (1) upon an order of the High Court or the civil division of the Court of Appeal under that subsection—

(a) the court shall, if the fine or other sum is not paid in full forthwith or within such time as the court may allow, certify to Her Majesty's Remembrancer the sum payable; and

(b) Her Majesty's Remembrancer shall thereupon proceed to enforce payment of that sum as if it were due to him as a judgment debt.

(3) Where payment of a fine or other sum falls to be enforced as mentioned in paragraph (b) of subsection (1) upon an order of the High Court or the civil division of the Court of Appeal under that subsection, the provisions of sections 139 and 140 of the Powers of Criminal Courts (Sentencing) Act 2000 shall apply to that fine or other sum as they apply to a fine imposed by the Crown Court.

(4) Where payment of a fine or other sum has become enforceable by Her Majesty's Remembrancer by virtue of this section or section 16 of the Contempt of Court Act 1981, any payment received by him in respect of that fine or other sum shall be dealt with by him in such manner as the Lord Chancellor may direct.

(5) In this section, and in sections 139 and 140 of the Powers of Criminal Courts (Sentencing) Act 2000 as extended by this section, "fine" includes a penalty imposed in civil proceedings.

II SCA [69N]

141. [. . .]

Repealed by the Statute Law (Repeals) Act 2004.

II SCA [69O]

142. Selection of judges for trial of election petitions

(1) The judges to be placed on the rota for the trial of parliamentary election petitions in England and Wales under Part III of the Representation of the People Act 1983 in each year shall be selected, in such manner as may be provided by rules of court, from the judges of the Queen's Bench Division of the High Court exclusive of any who are members of the House of Lords.

(2) Notwithstanding the expiry of the year for which a judge has been placed on the rota he may act as if that year had not expired for the purpose of continuing to deal with, giving judgment in, or dealing with any ancillary matter relating to, any case with which he may have been concerned during that year.

(3) Any judge placed on the rota shall be eligible to be placed on the rota again in the succeeding or any subsequent year.

II SCA [690.1]

Election petitions Jurisdiction, to hear petitions, applications and appeals, is conferred on the High Court by the Representation of the People Act 1983 and also, in a more limited way, on the County Court. The provisions of the 1983 Act are applied by regulations to local government elections and also European Assembly elections: see the Local Elections (Principal Areas) Rules 1986, SI 1986/2214 (as amended by SI 1998/578 and modified by SI 1998/746), the Local Elections (Parishes and Communities) Rules 1986, SI 1986/2215 (as amended by SI 1998/585) and the European Parliament Election Regulations 1986, SI 1986/2209. See CPR Sch 1 RSC Ord 94 r 5 at para **RSC 94r5** and CPR Sch 2 CCR Ord 45 at para **CCR 45**.

II SCA [70]

151. Interpretation of this Act, and rules of construction for other Acts and documents

(1) In this Act, unless the context otherwise requires—

"action" means any civil proceedings commenced by writ or in any other manner prescribed by rules of court;

"appeal", in the context of appeals to the civil division of the Court of Appeal, includes—

(a) an application for a new trial; and

(b) an application to set aside a verdict, finding or judgment in any cause or matter in the High Court which has been tried, or in which any issue has been tried, by a jury;

"arbitration agreement" has the same meaning as it has in Part I of the Arbitration Act 1996;

"cause" means any action or any criminal proceedings;

"Division", where it appears with a capital letter, means a division of the High Court;

"judgment" includes a decree;

"jurisdiction" includes powers;

"matter" means any proceedings in court not in a cause;

"party", in relation to any proceedings, includes any person who pursuant to or by virtue of rules of court or any other statutory provision has been served with notice of, or has intervened in, those proceedings;

"prescribed" means—

(a) except in relation to fees, prescribed by rules of court; and

(b) in relation to fees, prescribed by an order under section 130;

"qualifying judge advocate" means—

(a) the Judge Advocate General; or

(b) a person appointed under section 30(1)(a) or (b) of the Courts-Martial (Appeals) Act 1951 (assistants to the Judge Advocate General);

senior judge", where the reference is to the senior judge of a Division, means the president of that Division;

"solicitor" means a solicitor of the Senior Courts;

"statutory provision" means any enactment, whenever passed, or any provision contained in subordinate legislation (as defined in section 21(1) of the Interpretation Act 1978), whenever made;

"this or any other Act" includes an Act passed after this Act.

(2) Section 128 contains definitions of expressions used in Part V and in the other provisions of this Act relating to probate causes and matters.

(3) Any reference in this Act to rules of court under section 84 includes a reference to rules of court in relation to the Senior Courts under any provision of this or any other Act which confers on the Civil Procedure Rule Committee power to make rules of court.

(4) Except where the context otherwise requires, in this or any other Act—

[. . .]

[. . .]

"divisional court" (with or without capital letters) means a divisional court constituted under section 66;

"judge of the Senior Courts" means—

(a) a judge of the Court of Appeal other than an ex-officio judge within paragraph (b) or (c) of section 2(2); or

(b) a judge of the High Court,

and accordingly does not include, as such, a judge of the Crown Court;

"official referees' business" has the meaning given by section 68(6);

[. . .]

(5) The provisions of Schedule 4 (construction of references to superseded courts and officers) shall have effect.

SCHEDULE 1

DISTRIBUTION OF BUSINESS IN HIGH COURT

Chancery Division

II SCA [71]

1 To the Chancery Division are assigned all causes and matters relating to—

(a) the sale, exchange or partition of land, or the raising of charges on land;

(b) the redemption or foreclosure of mortgages;

(c) the execution of trusts;

(d) the administration of the estates of deceased persons;

(e) bankruptcy;

(f) the dissolution of partnerships or the taking of partnership or other accounts;

(g) the rectification, setting aside or cancellation of deeds or other instruments in writing;

(h) probate business, other than non-contentious or common form business;

(i) patents, trade marks, registered designs, copyright or design right;

(j) the appointment of a guardian of a minor's estate,

and all causes and matters involving the exercise of the High Court's jurisdiction under the enactments relating to companies.

QUEEN'S BENCH DIVISION

2 To the Queen's Bench Division are assigned—
(a) applications for writs of habeas corpus, except applications made by a parent or guardian of a minor for such a writ concerning the custody of the minor;
(b) applications for judicial review;
(ba) [. . .];
(bb) all financial restrictions proceedings within the meaning of Chapter 2 of Part 6 of the Counter-Terrorism Act 2008 (see section 65 of that Act);
(bc) *all proceedings—*
(i) *on an appeal under section 26, or an application under section 27, of the Terrorist Asset-Freezing etc Act 2010 (appeals and reviews by the court), or*
(ii) *on a claim arising from any matter to which such an appeal or application relates;*
(bd) all TPIM proceedings (within the meaning of the Terrorism Prevention and Investigation Measures Act 2011);
(be) all TEO proceedings (within the meaning given by paragraph 1 of Schedule 3 to the Counter-Terrorism and Security Act 2015 (proceedings relating to temporary exclusion orders));
[(bf) all proceedings—
(i) on an application under section 38 of the Sanctions and Anti-Money Laundering Act 2018 (court review of decisions), or
(ii) on a claim arising from any matter to which such an application relates;]
(c) all causes and matters involving the exercise of the High Court's Admiralty jurisdiction or its jurisdiction as a prize court; and
(d) all causes and matters entered in the commercial list.

FAMILY DIVISION

3 To the Family Division are assigned—
(a) all matrimonial causes and matters (whether at first instance or on appeal);
(aa) applications for a writ of habeas corpus for release relating to a minor;
(b) all causes and matters (whether at first instance or on appeal) relating to—
(i) legitimacy;
(ii) the exercise of the inherent jurisdiction of the High Court with respect to minors, the maintenance of minors and any proceedings under the Children Act 1989, except proceedings solely for the appointment of a guardian of a minor's estate;
(iii) [. . .] adoption;
(iv) non-contentious or common form probate business;
(c) applications for consent to the marriage of a minor or for a declaration under section 27B(5) of the Marriage Act 1949;
(d) ...
(e) applications under Part III of the Family Law Act 1986;
(e) proceedings under the Children Act 1989;
(ea) proceedings under section 79 of the Childcare Act 2006;
(eb) proceedings under section 43 of the Children and Families (Wales) Measure 2010;

(ec) proceedings under Part 6 of the Social Services and Well-being (Wales) Act 2014;

(f) all proceedings under—

(i) the Part IV or 4A of the Family Law Act 1996;

(ii) the Child Abduction and Custody Act 1985;

(iii) the Family Law Act 1986;

(iv) section 30 of the Human Fertilisation and Embryology Act 1990;

(v) Council Regulation (EC) No 2201/2003 of 27th November 2003 concerning jurisdiction and the recognition and enforcement of judgments in matrimonial matters and matters of parental responsibility, so far as that Regulation relates to jurisdiction, recognition and enforcement in parental responsibility matters;

(vi) the Convention on Jurisdiction, Applicable Law, Recognition, Enforcement and Co-Operation in respect of Parental Responsibility and Measures for the Protection of Children that was signed at The Hague on 19 October 1996;

(fa) all proceedings relating to a debit or credit under section 29(1) or 49(1) of the Welfare Reform and Pensions Act 1999;

(g) all proceedings for the purpose of enforcing an order made in any proceedings of a type described in this paragraph;

(h) all proceedings under the Child Support Act 1991;

(ha) all proceedings under Part 1 of Schedule 2 to the Female Genital Mutilation Act 2003;

(i) all proceedings under sections 6 and 8 of the Gender Recognition Act 2004;

(i) all civil partnership causes and matters (whether at first instance or on appeal);

(j) applications for consent to the formation of a civil partnership by a minor or for a declaration under paragraph 7 of Schedule 1 to the Civil Partnership Act 2004;

(k) applications under section 58 of that Act (declarations relating to civil partnerships);

(l) proceedings under Regulation (EU) No 606/2013 of the European Parliament and of the Council of 12 June 2013 on mutual recognition of protection measures in civil matters, so far as relating to the recognition and enforcement in England and Wales of a protection measure (within the meaning of that Regulation) ordered in a Member State other than the United Kingdom.

SCHEDULE 2

LIST OF OFFICES IN SENIOR COURTS FOR PURPOSES OF PART 4

PART 1

II SCA [72]

References in this Schedule to a person having a general qualification shall be construed in accordance with section 71 of the Courts and Legal Services Act 1990.

Office	*Persons qualified*
Official Solicitor	A person who has a 10 year general qualification (within the meaning of

section 71 of the Courts and Legal Services Act 1990).

Part 2

Office	*Persons qualified*
Master, Queen's Bench Division	A person who satisfies the judicial-appointment eligibility condition on a 5-year basis.
Queen's Coroner and Attorney and Master of the Crown Office and Registrar of Criminal Appeals	A person who satisfies the judicial-appointment eligibility condition on a 7-year basis.
Admiralty Registrar	A person who satisfies the judicial-appointment eligibility condition on a 5-year basis.
Master, Chancery Division	A person who satisfies the judicial-appointment eligibility condition on a 5-year basis.
Registrar in Bankruptcy of the High Court	A person who satisfies the judicial-appointment eligibility condition on a 5-year basis.
Taxing Master of the Senior Courts	A person who satisfies the judicial-appointment eligibility condition on a 5-year basis.
District judge of the principal registry of the Family Division	1 A person who satisfies the judicial-appointment eligibility condition on a 5-year basis. 2 A district probate registrar who either— (a) is of at least 5 years' standing, or (b) has, during so much of the 5 years immediately preceding his appointment as he has not been a district probate registrar, served as a civil servant in the principal registry or a district probate registry. 3 A civil servant who has served at least 7 years in the principal registry or a district probate registry.

Part 3

Office	*Persons qualified*
District probate registrar.	1 A person who has a 5 year general qualification. 2 A civil servant who has served at least 5 years in the principal

registry of the Family Division or a district probate registry.

In para 2, sub-para (bc) is deleted and sub-para (bf) is inserted by the Sanctions and Anti-Money Laundering Act 2018 with effect from a date to be appointed.

II SCA [72.1]

Amendments Note that s 64 of the Courts Act 2003 empowers the Lord Chancellor, by order, to alter the name and style of many of these offices.

COUNTY COURTS ACT 1984

(c 28)

TABLE OF CONTENTS

COUNTY COURT

Amendment *Italics and square brackets in the table above indicate amendments made by the Tribunals, Courts and Enforcement Act 2007, with effect from a date to be appointed.*

GENERAL NOTES ON COUNTY COURTS ACT 1984

II CCA [1]

The county courts derive their jurisdiction and powers from statute, principally the County Courts Act 1984. In 1990 county courts were given the same competence as the High Court in the general run of litigation regardless of the sums involved. The new regime removed most of the former "county court limits" (the Courts and Legal Services Act 1990 and the High Court and County Courts Jurisdiction Order 1991, SI 1991/724, see para **II HCJ [1]** post). Extensive changes have been made by the Tribunals, Courts and Enforcement Act 2007, and also by the Crime and Courts Act 2013, which replaced the district-based jurisdiction with a single county court with effect from 22 April 2014.

PART I
CONSTITUTION AND ADMINISTRATION

II CCA [2]

A1. Establishment of a single county court

(1) There is to be a court in England and Wales, called the county court, for the purpose of exercising the jurisdiction and powers conferred on it—

(a) by or under this or any other Act, or

(b) by or under any Act, or Measure, of the National Assembly for Wales.

(2) The county court is to be a court of record and have a seal.

II CCA [2.1]

The single County Court Article 2 of the Crime and Courts Act 2013 (Commencement No 10 and Transitional Provision) Order 2014, SI 2014/954 specified 22 April 2014 as the date when the new (single) County Court replaced all the district-based county courts in England and Wales.

PLACES AND TIMES OF SITTINGS OF COURTS

II CCA [3]

3. Places and times of sittings

(1) Sittings of the county court may be held, and any other business of the county court may be conducted, anywhere in England and Wales.

(1A) Sittings of the county court at any place may be continuous or intermittent or occasional.

(2) Sittings of the county court may be held simultaneously to take any number of different cases in the same place or different places, and the court may adjourn cases from place to place at any time.

(2A) The places at which the county court sits, and the days and times at which it sits in any place, are to be determined in accordance with directions given by the Lord Chancellor after consulting the Lord Chief Justice.

(3) [. . .]

(4) [. . .]

(5) The Lord Chief Justice may nominate a judicial office holder (as defined in section 109(4) of the Constitutional Reform Act 2005) to exercise his functions under this section.

II CCA [4]

4. Use of public buildings for courts

(1) Where, in any place in which a sitting of the county court is to be held or a sitting of the family court is held, there is a building, being a town hall, court-

COUNTY COURT

house or other public building belonging to any local or other public authority, that building shall, with all necessary rooms, furniture and fittings in it, be used for the purpose of holding the sitting of the court, without any charge for rent or other payment, except the reasonable and necessary charges for lighting, heating and cleaning the building when used for that purpose.

(2) Where any such building is used for the purpose of holding sittings of the county court, the sittings of the court shall be so arranged as not to interfere with the business of the local or other public authority usually transacted in the building or with any purpose for which the building may be used by virtue of any local Act.

(3) This section shall not apply to any place in which a building was erected before 1st January 1889 for the purpose of holding and carrying on the business of a county court.

II CCA [4.1]

As to the provision of courts, offices, judges' lodgings and accommodation generally see s 28 of the Courts Act 1971. As to payment of the cost of the supply of books, etc, see s 132(b) at para **II CCA [128]**.

JUDGES

II CCA [5]

5. Judges of the county court

(1) A person is a judge of the county court if the person—

(a) is a Circuit judge,

(b) is a district judge (which, by virtue of section 8(1C), here includes a deputy district judge appointed under section 8), or

(c) is within subsection (2),

but see also section 9 of the Senior Courts Act 1981 (certain ex-judges may act as judges of the county court).

(2) A person is within this subsection (and so, by virtue of subsection (1)(c), is a judge of the county court) if the person—

(a) is the Lord Chief Justice,

(b) is the Master of the Rolls,

(c) is the President of the Queen's Bench Division,

(d) is the President of the Family Division,

(e) is the Chancellor of the High Court,

(f) is an ordinary judge of the Court of Appeal (including the vice-president, if any, of either division of that court),

(g) is the Senior President of Tribunals,

(h) is a puisne judge of the High Court,

(i) is a deputy judge of the High Court,

(j) is the Judge Advocate General,

(k) is a Recorder,

(l) is a person who holds an office listed—

(i) in the first column of the table in section 89(3C) of the Senior Courts Act 1981 (senior High Court masters etc), or

(ii) in column 1 of Part 2 of Schedule 2 to that Act (High Court masters etc),

(m) is a deputy district judge appointed under section 102 of that Act,

(n) is a Chamber President, or a Deputy Chamber President, of a chamber of the Upper Tribunal or of a chamber of the First-tier Tribunal,

(o) is a judge of the Upper Tribunal by virtue of appointment under paragraph 1(1) of Schedule 3 to the Tribunals, Courts and Enforcement Act 2007,

(p) is a transferred-in judge of the Upper Tribunal (see section 31(2) of that Act),

(q) is a deputy judge of the Upper Tribunal (whether under paragraph 7 of Schedule 3 to, or section 31(2) of, that Act),

(r) is a District Judge (Magistrates' Courts),

(s) is a person appointed under section 30(1)(a) or (b) of the Courts-Martial (Appeals) Act 1951 (assistants to the Judge Advocate General),

(t) is a judge of the First-tier Tribunal by virtue of appointment under paragraph 1(1) of Schedule 2 to the Tribunals, Courts and Enforcement Act 2007,

(u) is a transferred-in judge of the First-tier Tribunal (see section 31(2) of that Act), or

(v) is a member of a panel of Employment Judges established for England and Wales or for Scotland.

II CCA [5.1]

Circuit judges Circuit judges being appointed by Her Majesty consequently become Her Majesty's Circuit Judges. The following declaration is made by Royal Warrant dated 29 March 1972 (published in the *London Gazette* dated 12 April 1972): "We do hereby declare Our Royal Will and Pleasure that at all times hereafter Our Circuit Judges in England and Wales shall be called known and addressed by the style and title of 'His Honour' prefixed to the word 'Judge' before their respective names and shall have rank and precedence next after Knights Bachelor and as between themselves have rank and precedence in manner following [as set out therein] And that Our Circuit Judges upon retirement may retain the style and title of 'His Honour' before their respective names."

II CCA [5.2]

Appointment of Circuit judges See s 16 of the Courts Act 1971. Appointment is limited to persons who have a 7-year Crown Court or a 7-year county court qualification within the meaning of s 71 of the 1990 Act, or who are recorders, or who have held for not less than three years one of a number of full-time offices including those of district judge and of stipendiary magistrate.

II CCA [5.3]

Appointment of deputy Circuit judges and assistant Recorders See s 24 of the Courts Act 1971 and s 71(2), Sch 10 para 32 of the Courts and Legal Services Act 1990 provide as follows:

"**24(1)** If it appears to the Lord Chancellor that it is expedient as a temporary measure to make an appointment under this section in order to facilitate the disposal of business in the Crown Court or a county court or official referees business in the High Court, he may –

(a) appoint to be a deputy Circuit judge, during such period or on such occasions as he thinks fit, any person who has held office as a judge of the Court of Appeal or of the High Court or as a Circuit judge; or

(b) appoint to be an assistant Recorder, during such period or on such occasions as he thinks fit, any person who has a 10 year Crown Court or 10 year county court qualification, within the meaning of section 71 of the Courts and Legal Services Act 1990.

(1A) No appointment of a person under subsection (I) above shall be such as to extend-

(a) in the case of appointment as a deputy Circuit Judge, beyond the day on which he attains the age of seventy-five; or

(b) in the case of appointment as an assistant Recorder, beyond the day on which he attains the age of seventy;

but paragraph (b) above is subject to section 26(4) to (6) of the Judicial Pensions and Retirement Act 1993 (Lord Chancellor's power to authorise continuance in office up to the age of 75).

(2) Except as provided by subsection (3) below, during the period or on the occasions for which a deputy Circuit judge or assistant Recorder is appointed under this section, he shall be treated for all purposes as, and accordingly may perform any of the functions of, a Circuit judge or a Recorder, as the case may be.

(3) A deputy Circuit judge appointed under this section shall not be treated as a Circuit judge for the purpose of any provision made by or under any enactment and relating to the appointment, retirement, removal or disqualification of Circuit judges, the tenure of office and oaths to be taken by such judges, or the remuneration, allowances or pensions of such judges; and section 21 of this Act shall not apply to an assistant Recorder appointed under this section.

[*Repealed*]

(4) There shall be paid out of money provided by Parliament to deputy Circuit judges and assistant Recorders appointed under this section such remuneration and allowances as the Lord Chancellor may, with the approval of the Minister for the Civil Service, determine."

II CCA [5.4]

Death or incapacity during trial The Lord Chancellor may, if he thinks fit, reimburse a party who incurs additional costs consequent upon the trial judge suffering incapacity or death in the course of the proceedings: s 53 of the Administration of Justice Act 1985. Provision for the costs to be taxed on an indemnity basis, if not agreed, is made by CPR Sch 2. This section came into force on 1 October 1988 (The Administration of Justice Act (Commencement No 5) Order 1988, SI 1988/1341). The maximum payable is at present £8,000 (The Reimbursement of Costs (Monetary Limit) Order 1988, SI 1988/1342).

II CCA [5.5]

Judicial titles Note that s 64 of the Courts Act 2003 empowers the Lord Chancellor, by order, to alter the name and style of certain judicial offices, including circuit judge, deputy circuit judge, recorder, assistant recorder, district judge and deputy district judge.

DISTRICT JUDGES AND DEPUTY DISTRICT JUDGES

II CCA [5A]

6. District judges

(1) Her Majesty may, on the recommendation of the Lord Chancellor, appoint district judges.

(2) [. . .]

(3) A reference in any enactment or other instrument to the district judge for a district or of a county court is—

- (a) if the context permits, a reference to the county court, and
- (b) otherwise is a reference to a judge of the county court.

(4) [. . .]

(5) A district judge is to be paid such salary as may be determined by the Lord Chancellor with the concurrence of the Treasury.

(6) A salary payable under this section may be increased but not reduced by a determination or further determination under this section.

(7) [. . .]

II CCA [5A.1]

Powers of district judge As to the powers of a district judge to try actions, see **CPR PD 2B**.

II CCA [5B]

8. Deputy district judges

(1) If it appears to the Lord Chief Justice that it is expedient to do so in order to facilitate the disposal of business in the county court or any other court or tribunal to which a person appointed under this subsection may be deployed, he may appoint a person to be a deputy district judge.

(1ZA) A person is qualified for appointment under subsection (1) only if the person—

(a) is qualified for appointment as a district judge, or

(b) holds, or has held, the office of district judge.

(1ZB) The Lord Chief Justice may not appoint a person under subsection (1) without the concurrence of the Lord Chancellor if the person—

(a) holds the office of district judge, or

(b) ceased to hold the office of district judge within two years ending with the date when the appointment takes effect.

(1ZC) Section 85 of the Constitutional Reform Act 2005 (c 4) (selection of certain office holders) does not apply to an appointment to which subsection (1ZB) applies.

(1A) Any appointment of a person as a deputy district judge—

(a) if subsection (1ZB) applies to the appointment, shall not be such as to, or be extended under subsection (3B) so as to, extend beyond the day on which he attains the age of 75 years; and

(b) in any other case, shall not be such as to, or be extended under subsection (3B) so as to, extend beyond the day on which he attains the age of 70 years, but subject to section 26(4) to (6) of the Judicial Pensions and Retirement Act 1993 (power to authorise continuance in office up to the age of 75).

(1B) [. . .]

(1C) A deputy district judge appointed under this section has the same powers as if he were a district judge other than a district judge's power to act in a district registry of the High Court.

(1D) [. . .]

(2) [. . .]

(3) The Lord Chancellor may pay to any person appointed under this section as deputy district judge such remuneration and allowances as he may, with the approval of the Treasury, determine.

(3A) A person appointed under this section may be removed from office as a deputy district judge—

(a) only by the Lord Chancellor with the agreement of the Lord Chief Justice, and

(b) only on—

(i) the ground of inability or misbehaviour, or

(ii) a ground specified in the person's terms of appointment.

(3B) Subject to subsections (1A) and (3C), the term of a person's appointment under this section (including a term already extended under this subsection) must be extended by the Lord Chancellor before its expiry.

(3C) Extension under subsection (3B)—

(a) requires the person's agreement,

(b) is to be for such term as the Lord Chancellor thinks fit, and

(c) may be refused on—

(i) the ground of inability or misbehaviour, or

(ii) a ground specified in the person's terms of appointment.

but only with any agreement of the Lord Chief Justice, or a nominee of the Lord Chief Justice, that may be required by those terms.

(3D) Subject to the preceding provisions of this section, a person appointed under this section is to hold and vacate office as a deputy district judge in accordance with the terms of the person's appointment, which are to be such as the Lord Chancellor may determine.

(3E) The Lord Chief Justice may nominate a senior judge (as defined in section 109(5) of the Constitutional Reform Act 2005) to exercise the Lord Chief Justice's functions under subsection (1) or (3A)(a).

(4) The Lord Chief Justice may nominate a judicial office holder (as defined in section 109(4) of the Constitutional Reform Act 2005) to exercise his functions under subsection (1B).

II CCA [5C]

9. Qualifications for appointment as district judge

No person shall be appointed a district judge, unless he satisfies the judicial-appointment condition on a 5-year basis.

II CCA [5D]

11. Tenure of office

(1) This subsection applies to the office of district judge.

(2) Subject to the following provisions of this section and to subsections (4) to (6) of section 26 of the Judicial Pensions and Retirement Act 1993 (Lord Chancellor's power to authorise continuance in office up to the age of 75), a person who holds an office to which subsection (1) applies shall vacate his office on the day on which he attains the age of 70 years.

(3) [. . .]

(4) A person appointed to an office to which subsection (1) applies shall hold that office during good behaviour.

(5) The power to remove such a person from his office on account of misbehaviour shall be exercisable by the Lord Chancellor, but only with the concurrence of the Lord Chief Justice.

(6) The Lord Chancellor, with the concurrence of the Lord Chief Justice, may also remove such a person from his office on account of inability to perform the duties of his office.

II CCA [5E]

12. Records of proceedings to be kept

(1) The Lord Chancellor may by regulations made by statutory instrument provide for the keeping of records of and in relation to proceedings of the county court.

(2) Any entry in a book or other document required by the said regulations to be kept for the purposes of this section, or a copy of any such entry or document purporting to be signed and certified as a true copy by a judge of the county court, shall at all times without further proof be admitted in any court or place whatsoever as evidence of the entry and of the proceeding referred to by it and of the regularity of that proceeding.

(3) The Lord Chancellor must consult the Lord Chief Justice before making regulations under this section.

(4) The Lord Chief Justice may nominate a judicial office holder (as defined in section 109(4) of the Constitutional Reform Act 2005) to exercise his functions under this section.

II CCA [5E.1]

Regulations The County Court (Records of Proceedings) Regulations 1967, SI 1967/1194, made by the Lord Chancellor under this section are printed below, as amended in 1988:

"1. These Regulations may be cited as the County Court (Records of Proceedings) Regulations 1967 and shall come into operation on 1 September 1967;

2. The [district judge] of every county court shall keep or cause to be kept the records of proceedings in that court specified in column 1 of the Schedule to these Regulations and those records shall constitute the books of the court;

3. Without prejudice to any requirement imposed by or under any enactment every record kept pursuant to the last foregoing Regulations shall contain in relation to each proceeding appearing in the record the details specified opposite thereto in column 2 of the said Schedule;

4. So much of the General Regulations for Registrars and High Bailiffs of County Courts as relates to the records to be kept of and in relation to proceedings in county courts is hereby revoked;

5. The Interpretation Act 1889 shall apply to the interpretation of these Regulations as it applies to the interpretation of an Act of Parliament.

Column 1 *Records to be kept*	*Column 2* *Details to be contained therein*
1. A record of ordinary [now claims] actions and matters begun in, and actions, counterclaims and matters transferred to, the court, other than actions and matters hereinafter mentioned. 2. A record of default actions [now claims] begun in or transferred to the court. 3. A record of actions and matters begun in the court under [section 23 or 24 of the County Courts Act 1984]. 4. A record of Admiralty actions begun in the court.	(a) The names addresses and descriptions (if any) of the parties. (b) The nature and amount of the claim or the nature of the relief sought. (c) Concise minutes of the proceedings, including a note of any judgement given, order made or decree granted.
5. A record of judgement summonses and interpleader proceedings issued by the court.	(a) In the case of a judgement summons (i) the name of the judgement creditor and the name, address and description (if any) of the judgement debtor; (ii) the amount in respect of which the judgement summons was issued. (b) In the case of interpleading proceedings (i) the names, addresses and descriptions (if any) of the parties other than the [district judge]; (ii) the nature of the relief sought. (c) Concise minutes of the proceedings, including the note of any order made.
6. A record of warrants and orders of commitment issued by the court and orders made by the court for the recovery of money by distress under the title Acts 1836 to 1951. 7. A record of warrants and orders of commitment received from other courts for execution.	(a) The name of the judgement creditor and the name, address and description (if any) of the judgement debtor (b) The amount in respect of which the warrant or order was issued. (c) In the case of a warrant or order received from another court for execution the name of that court. (d) In the case of a warrant of execution, a note of any claim made to or in respect of any goods seized in execution under the warrant and of any subsequent proceedings thereon. (e) A note of any return made to the warrant or order. (f) A note of any suspension or re-issue of the warrant or order.
8. A record of proceedings under Part I of the Family Law 1986. [1988]	(a) A note of the transmission of documents to the Court of Session and to the High Court in Northern Ireland. (b) A note of the particulars of the application to register a custody order, including the name and address of the applicant and of the child. (c) A note of any order varying or revoking a registered custody order [1988]

II CCA [5E.2]

Interpretation Act 1889 See now the Interpretation Act 1978.

II CCA [5E.3]

Inspection Under **CPR 5.4** a party to the proceedings may apply in writing for a copy of a document to be supplied from the records of the court. Any other person can apply for a copy of the claim form and any judgment or order or any document if the court gives permission in respect of such document.

II CCA [5E.4]

"Shall be... evidence of... the regularity" The entry of an order by the district judge in the minute book is conclusive evidence of the order, and cannot be contradicted by a memorandum made by the judge as to what were his intentions: *Dews v Riley* (1851) 11 CB 434, but see, *Saunders v Swansea Finance Co Ltd and Home* (1905) 21 TLR 317, CA, where such an entry was described as "only a step towards the formal order which was afterwards to be drawn up". See, too, *Pears v Wilson* (1851) 20 LJ Ex 381. In *R v Brompton County Court Judge* (1886) 18 QBD 213 (reversed in HL sub nom *Stonor v Fowle* (1887) 13 App Cas 20), the CA appear to have looked at a separate paper given by the judge to the district judge as to the case. A judgment may also be proved by oral admission, see *R v Stokes* [1988] Crim LR 110, CA.

A certified copy of minutes, expressed to be those of proceedings before the deputy of a county court judge, is sufficient evidence of the regularity of his appointment in an indictment for perjury: *R v Roberts* (1878) 38 LT 690. See also *R v Davies* (1861) 30 LJMC 159. So, too, the defendant on a counterclaim is estopped by the adverse record, even though the county court had no jurisdiction to enforce the counterclaim: *Webster v Armstrong* (1885) 54 LJQB 236.

COUNTY COURT

II CCA [5F]

13. Officers of court not to act as solicitors in that court

(1) A fee-paid part-time judge of the county court may not act as a judge of the court in relation to any proceedings in the court in which—

(a) the judge,

(b) a partner or employer of the judge,

(c) a body of which the judge is a member or officer, or

(d) a body of whose governing body the judge is a member,

is directly or indirectly engaged as legal representative or agent for any party.

(2) Every person who contravenes this section shall for each offence be liable on summary conviction to a fine of an amount not exceeding level 3 on the standard scale.

II CCA [5F.1]

Legal representative For definition see s 147(1).

II CCA [5F.2]

"Officer of a court" By s 147, "officer" in relation to a court means "any [district judge] or [deputy district judge] of that court, and any clerk, bailiff, usher or messenger in the service of that court".

This section does not prevent a district judge from acting as a solicitor on his own behalf in an action brought against him in his own court alleging negligence by him in his capacity as district judge and high bailiff: *H Tolputt & Co Ltd v Mole* [1911] 1 KB 87, DC and 836, CA.

No action lies against a district judge for non-compliance by him with the rules of practice: see *Robinson v Gell* (1852) 12 CB 191.

II CCA [5F.3]

"Standard scale" See s 14(1) at para **II CCA [6]** and the notes at para **II CCA [6.3]**.

II CCA [5F.4]

Section 6(5) This subsection provides for a district judge of any district acting for the district judge of another district.

II CCA [6]

14. Penalty for assaulting officers

(1) If any person assaults an officer of the county court while in the execution of his duty, he shall be liable—

(a) on summary conviction, to imprisonment for a term not exceeding *3 months* [51 weeks] or to a fine of an amount not exceeding level 5 on the standard scale, or both; or

(b) on an order made by the court in that behalf, to be committed for a specified period not exceeding 3 months to [. . .] prison [. . .] to such a fine as aforesaid, or to be so committed and to such a fine,

and an officer of the court may take the offender into custody, with or without warrant, and bring him before the court.

(2) The judge may at any time revoke an order committing a person to prison under this section and, if he is already in custody, order his discharge.

(3) [. . .]

Amendment *Text in italic is deleted and text in square brackets is inserted by the Criminal Justice Act 2003, with effect from a date to be appointed.*

II CCA [6.1]

Assaulting an officer of a court An honest factual mistake as to whether the victim of an assault was an officer of a court or was acting in the execution of official duty is a defence to liability under this section: *Blackburn v Bowering* [1994] 3 All ER 380, [1994] 1 WLR 1324, CA.

II CCA [6.2]

In the execution of duty In certain circumstances a bailiff may enter premises by opening doors and breaking locks in execution of a warrant to seize goods. But there are limits: see paras **II CCA [87.1]–[87.3]**.

II CCA [6.3]

Standard scale The standard scale is laid down in the Criminal Justice Act 1982 s 37 (as amended). Currently it provides as follows:

Level on the scale	*Amount of fine*
1	£200
2	£500
3	£1,000
4	£2,500
5	£5,000

The standard scale can be altered by order under the Magistrates' Court Act 1980 s 143.

II CCA [6.4]

Take the offender into custody Note that the arrest is only for the purpose of taking the offender before the judge, not for the purpose of taking him to a police station. Where the offender is not taken into custody and brought before the court a summons should be issued and served personally: see **CPR 81.34**.

II CCA [6.5]

Order of committal The judge should not normally order committal without giving an opportunity to explain conduct and to say why committal should not take place: *Stilwell v Williamson* (1986) Times, 1 September, CA; *Gibbons v Registrar Stroud County Court* (1990) Independent, 8 October, CA. An alleged contemnor has a common law right to adequate notice of what is being alleged. It is a matter of good practice to put the charge in writing to the alleged contemnor and unless it is clear that he has already read and understood it, it should be read out to him at the outset of the hearing. Where a court is considering possible imprisonment the court should ask an unrepresented defendant whether he wished publicly-funded representation: *Newman (t/a Mantella Publishing) v Modern Bookbinders Ltd* [2000] 2 All ER 814, [2000] 1 WLR 2559, CA.

The alleged contemnor must be given an effective opportunity to apply for legal assistance and this requirement outweighs all other considerations: *Berry Trade Ltd v Moussavi* [2002] EWCA Civ 477, [2002] 1 WLR 1910, (2002) Times, 10 April.

II CCA [6.6]

Appeal Proceedings under this section in relation to an assault on a bailiff are in the nature of proceedings for contempt of court: *Southam v Smout* [1964] 1 QB 308, [1963] 3 All ER 104, CA. An appeal lies to the Court of Appeal under the Administration of Justice Act 1960 s 13: see para **III COT [9]**. However, an appeal from a decision of a district judge lies to a Circuit judge: *Read v King* [1997] CLY 1262, CA. Notice of appeal to the Court of Appeal need not be given to the bailiff or other officer concerned: *Brown v Crowley* [1963] 3 All ER 655, [1963] 1 WLR 1102, CA.

II CCA [6.7]

Resisting or obstructing a bailiff A person who resists or obstructs a bailiff may be arrested without warrant under the Criminal Law Act 1977 s 10.

II CCA [6.8]

Representation As from 2 April 2001 legal advice and representation in proceedings under s 14, s 92 or s 118 is available as part of the Criminal Defence Service under the Access to Justice Act 1999. Sections 12 to 18 and Sch 3 of that Act came into operation on that date concurrently with the repeal of s 29 of the Legal Aid Act 1988. See Legal Services Commission Manual ID-041.

PART II
JURISDICTION AND TRANSFER OF PROCEEDINGS
ACTIONS OF CONTRACT AND TORT

II CCA [7]

15. General jurisdiction in actions of contract and tort

(1) Subject to subsection (2), the county court shall have jurisdiction to hear and determine any action founded on contract or tort [. . .]

(2) The county court shall not, except as in this Act provided, have jurisdiction to hear and determine—

- (a) [. . .]
- (b) any action in which the title to [. . .] any toll, fair, market or franchise is in question; or
- (c) any action for libel or slander.

(3) [. . .]

II CCA [7.1]

Amendment The financial limits on the ordinary jurisdiction of the county courts were removed by the Courts and Legal Services Act 1990 but proceedings may be transferred to and from the High Court for hearing or enforcement; see the High Court and County Courts Jurisdiction Order 1991, SI 1991/724, see para **II HCJ [1]** and CPR Pt 30 (see para **CPR 30**).

II CCA [7.2]

Arbitration agreement Although the court has unlimited jurisdiction to entertain claims in contract, proceedings will be stayed if the parties have already agreed on arbitration instead: see the Arbitration Act 1996 s 9 (see para **III ARB [6]**).

II CCA [7.3]

Devastavit County courts are enabled by this section to hear actions against executors for devastavit: *Winch v Winch* (1853) 13 CB 128: for a precedent see **BCCP Q[411]**.

II CCA [7.4]

Diplomatic privilege Diplomatic immunity is a procedural bar which may be waived. Process against a diplomat is not a nullity: it may continue after diplomatic immunity is removed by

COUNTY COURT

legislation although started before: *Empson v Smith* [1966] 1 QB 426, [1965] 2 All ER 881, CA. On the other hand it may not be waived by the individual without the authority of the sending state: *Re P (minors) (diplomatic immunity)* [1998] 2 FCR 480, [1998] 1 FLR 624. Facts relating to the question of entitlement to immunity may be proved conclusively, under the Diplomatic Privileges Act 1964 s 4, by the certificate of the Secretary of State for Foreign and Commonwealth Affairs. Requests for certificates should be addressed to the Head of Appointments Section, Protocol Department, Foreign and Commonwealth Office. See also the Consular Relations Act 1968, the International Organisations Act 1968 and the State Immunity Act 1978 for other aspects of immunity. Limits to the scope of immunity are illustrated by *Intpro Properties (UK) Ltd v Sauvel* [1983] QB 1019, [1983] 2 All ER 495, CA; *Amalgamated Metal Trading Ltd v Department of Trade and Industry (No 2)* (1989) Times, 16 May.

II CCA [7.5]

Employment rights An employee may not bring a claim in the county court for deduction of wages, in breach of s 13 of the Employment Rights Act 1996 or for other statutory employment rights over which the Tribunal has been given exclusive jurisdiction by s 205 of that Act, for example, claims for unfair dismissal. However, it seems that, if the claimant simply claims at common law for unpaid wages due under a contract of employment or for wrongful dismissal in breach of contract, the county court may entertain the claim. Moreover, the employee may have recourse to the ordinary courts in reliance on most other contractual rights at common law eg for unpaid commission: *Rickard v P B Glass Supplies Ltd* [1990] ICR 150, CA. An employee whose statutory remedy has been barred by the employers' deceit may be able to recover equivalent redress by a county court claim in tort: *Levez v T H Jennings (Harlow Pools) Ltd*: C-326/96 [1999] All ER (EC) 1, ECJ. Where the subject matter of an action in a county court is the same as that of a claim which has already been the subject of a decision in an industrial tribunal, the defence of res judicata is available in the county court: *Barber v Staffordshire County Council* [1996] 2 All ER 748, sub nom *Staffordshire County Council v Barber* [1996] ICR 379, CA. However this defence will not be available if the issues were different or if the tribunal cannot be regarded as having reached a decision (as opposed, for example, to having noted the fact of a compromise): *Dattani v Trio Supermarkets Ltd* [1998] ICR 872, CA. Where essentially the same issues arise in proceedings pending before a tribunal and the High Court it is the former which should normally be stayed: *Chorion plc v Lane* (1999) Times, 7 April. As to staying such proceedings see further **III EMP [5]**.

II CCA [7.6]

Libel, slander A county court has no jurisdiction to hear a claim founded on libel or slander unless

(a) the pleaded cause of action is confined to malicious falsehood: *Joyce v Sengupta* [1993] 1 All ER 897, [1993] 1 WLR 337, CA; or
(b) by agreement under s 18; or
(c) on transfer from the High Court under s 40.

II CCA [7.7]

Pension entitlement The court may decide pension entitlement as a matter of contract even though the scheme may provide for an appeal system with the Secretary of State as final adjudicator: *Hutchings v Islington London Borough Council* [1998] 3 All ER 445, [1998] 1 WLR 1629, CA.

II CCA [7.8]

Public bodies The normal route for challenging the acts and decisions of public bodies is by judicial review: *O'Reilly v Mackman* [1983] 2 AC 237, [1982] 3 All ER 680, CA; *Cocks v Thanet District Council* [1983] 2 AC 286, [1982] 3 All ER 1135, HL. The limitations on such rights of challenge are considered in the commentary on Supreme Court Act 1981 (now the Senior Courts Act 1981), s 31(3) at **II SCA [30.1]–II SCA [30.5]**. The fact that a public law remedy (judicial review) may be available is not a bar to the pursuit of a private law claim, if there is one, by ordinary action: *Roy v Kensington and Chelsea and Westminster Family Practitioner Committee* [1992] 1 AC 624, [1992] 1 All ER 705, HL; *Lonrho plc v Tebbit* [1992] 4 All ER 280, CA. Questions of *vires* may be raised by way of defence to a claim by a housing authority for arrears of rent: *Wandsworth London Borough Council v Winder* [1985] AC 461, [1984] 3 All ER 976, HL. But a challenge to the decision by an authority to bring proceedings for possession was held to be sustainable only by judicial review in *Avon County Council v Buscott* [1988] QB 656, [1988] 1 All ER 841, CA, although the decision in this case should be compared with those in *Waverley Borough Council v Hilden* [1988] 1 All ER 807, [1988] 1 WLR 246 and *Thrasyvoulou v Secretary of State for the Environment* [1988] QB 809, [1988] 2 All ER 781, CA.

II CCA [7.9]

In *Doyle v Northumbria Probation Committee* [1991] 4 All ER 294, [1991] 1 WLR 1340, the defendant raised a public law issue by way of defence to a private law claim at a time when the claimant was out of time for proceeding by judicial review. The court rejected an application to have the claim struck out as an abuse of process.

In considering whether a litigant should have brought judicial review proceedings or an action against a public body, the court should look at the practical consequences of the choice made rather than just at technical questions concerning the distinction between public and private rights. If the choice made has no significant disadvantages for the parties, the public or the court, it should not be regarded as an abuse of process: *Dennis Rye Pension Fund Trustees v Sheffield City Council* [1997] 4 All ER 747, [1998] 1 WLR 840, CA. Guidance was given in this case as to the appropriate way of proceeding when it is not clear whether judicial review or ordinary action is the correct procedure.

II CCA [8]

16. Money recoverable by statute

The county court shall have jurisdiction to hear and determine an action for the recovery of a sum recoverable by virtue of any enactment for the time being in force, if—

(a) it is not provided by that or any other enactment that such sums shall only be recoverable in the High Court or shall only be recoverable summarily; [. . .]

(b) [. . .]

II CCA [9]

17. Abandonment of part of claim to give court jurisdiction

(1) Where a claimant has a cause of action for more than the county court limit in which, if it were not for more than the county court limit the county court would have jurisdiction, the plaintiff may abandon the excess, and thereupon the county court shall have jurisdiction to hear and determine the action, but the claimant shall not recover in the action an amount exceeding the county court limit.

(2) Where the court has jurisdiction to hear and determine an action by virtue of this section, the judgment of the court in the action shall be in full discharge of all demands in respect of the cause of action, and entry of the judgment shall be made accordingly

II CCA [10]

18. Jurisdiction by agreement in certain actions

If the parties to any action, other than an action which, if commenced in the High Court, would have been assigned to the Chancery Division or to the Family Division or have involved the exercise of the High Court's Admiralty jurisdiction, agree, by a memorandum signed by them or by their respective legal representatives, that the county court shall have jurisdiction in the action, that court shall have jurisdiction to hear and determine the action accordingly

RECOVERY OF LAND AND ACTIONS WHERE TITLE IN QUESTION

II CCA [11]

21. Actions for recovery of land and actions where title in question

(1) The county court shall have jurisdiction to hear and determine any action for the recovery of land [. . .]

(2) The county court shall have jurisdiction to hear and determine any action in which the title to any hereditament comes in question [. . .]

(3) Where a mortgage of land consists of or includes a dwelling-house and no part of the land is situated in Greater London then, subject to subsection (4), if the county court] has jurisdiction by virtue of this section to hear and determine an action in which the mortgagee under that mortgage claims possession of the mortgaged property, no court other than the county court shall have jurisdiction to hear and determine that action.

(4) Subsection (3) shall not apply to an action for foreclosure or sale in which a claim for possession of the mortgaged property is also made.

(5) [. . .]

(6) [. . .]

(7) In this section—

"dwelling-house" includes any building or part of a building which is used as a dwelling;

"mortgage" includes a charge and "mortgagor" and "mortgagee" shall be construed accordingly;

"mortgagor" and "mortgagee" includes any person deriving title under the original mortgagor or mortgagee.

(8) The fact that part of the premises comprised in a dwelling-house is used as a shop or office or for business, trade or professional purposes shall not prevent the dwelling-house from being a dwelling-house for the purposes of this section.

(9) This section does not apply to a mortgage securing an agreement which is a regulated agreement within the meaning of the Consumer Credit Act 1974.

II CCA [11.1]

Recovery of land The county courts have unlimited jurisdiction, under s 21, to make possession orders, for the recovery of land. Eviction is, and always has been, a major head of county court business and protective legislation extends over a wide range of transactions and circumstances. In a landlord and tenant context the protection takes the form of relief against forfeiture (see s 138), security of tenure and the right, in some situations, to be granted a further lease. For the relevant statutes (which supplement the Supreme Court Act 1981 and the County Courts Act 1984 in this regard) see para **III L&T [2]**. In the context of a mortgage of residential property, the protection derives in part from equity and in part from the discretion, conferred on the court by legislation, to order or defer possession on terms which disadvantage the mortgagor as little as possible.

II CCA [11.1A]

Consumer Credit Act 1974: Financial Services and Markets Act 2000 The protection of the Consumer Credit Act 1974 in relation to mortgages securing regulated agreements is examined in the title CONSUMER CONTRACTS in Part III, see, in particular, the power to make time orders under s 129, see para **III CON [40]**. As regards the protection conferred by the Financial Services and Markets Act 2000, loans secured on land are regulated activities: see s 22 and para 23 of Sch 2. A person who carries on a regulated activity without authorisation (or exemption) commits an offence: see ss 19 and 23. The consequence for the mortgagor of an unauthorised mortgage is that the agreement is unenforceable unless the court allows it to be enforced. But if the mortgagor succeeds in having the mortgage lifted it will be on the terms that the mortgage is repaid: see s 28(7).

II CCA [11.2]

Mortgagee's right to possession The mortgagee has a legal right to possession; but the courts will not allow the legal right to be exercised oppressively. "A mortgagee will be restrained from getting possession except where it is sought bona fide and reasonably for the purpose of enforcing the security and then only subject to such conditions as the court thinks fit to impose": *Quennell v Maltby* [1979] 1 All ER 568, [1979] 1 WLR 318, CA, per Lord Denning MR. Note, however, that a mortgagee is entitled to exercise his common law right to take possession of a mortgaged dwelling house by peaceable entry without a court order: see s 36 of the Administration of Justice Act 1970 (as to which see para **III REA [22]**). This section only applies where the lender has brought an action for possession: *Ropaigealach v Barclays Bank plc* [2000] 1 QB 263, [1999] 4 All ER 235, CA. This section does not apply so as to impose upon any purchaser from a mortgagee exercising its power of sale an obligation to seek a court order for possession against the mortgagor if still in possession and to confer upon the court in such circumstances the same discretion as it would have on an application for possession by the mortgagee itself: *Horsham Properties Group Ltd v Paul Clark* [2008] EWHC 2327 (Ch).

The mere existence of a sub-mortgage does not divest the principal lender of the right to possession in the event of default by the borrower in paying the mortgage loan: *Credit and Mercantile plc v Marks* [2004] EWCA Civ 568, [2004] All ER (D) 174 (May).

For similar reasons, the registered proprietor of the charge may enforce it, even where there have been subsequent securitisation arrangements that involved a transfer of a portfolio of mortgages to a special purposes vehicle but without the legal title having been vested by registration to the transferee. The original proprietor may enforce it without the need to add others as parties: *Paragon Finance plc v Pender* [2005] EWCA Civ 760, (2005) Times, 19 July.

A suspended possession order remains operative even after the mortgage arrears have been cleared: *Bank of Scotland plc v Zinda* [2011] EWCA Civ 706, [2012] 1 WLR 728, [2011] 2 All ER (Comm) 839.

II CCA [11.3]

Dwelling-houses Subsection (3) gives the county court exclusive jurisdiction in actions by mortgagees for possession of dwelling-houses. Accordingly such actions may not be transferred to the High Court, even after consolidation of cases within the jurisdiction of the High Court: *Yorkshire Bank plc v Hall* [1999] 1 All ER 879, [1999] 1 WLR 1713, CA.

II CCA [11.4]

Mortgagor's counterclaim for damages Although a mortgagor may have a counterclaim for damages which may be set off against the mortgage debt, this is not a defence to a claim for possession: *National Westminster Bank plc v Skelton* [1993] 1 All ER 242, [1993] 1 WLR 72n, CA; *Ashley Guarantee plc v Zacaria* [1993] 1 All ER 254, [1993] 1 WLR 62, CA. Nor does it provide a ground for postponing or suspending an order for possession: *Western Bank Ltd v Schindler* [1977] Ch 1, [1976] 2 All ER 393, CA; *Citibank Trust Ltd v Ayivor* [1987] 3 All ER 241, [1987] 1 WLR 1157.

II CCA [11.5]

Mortgagor's counterclaim for rescission Misrepresentation on the part of the mortgagee may be ground for resisting the claim for possession and counterclaiming for rescission: *Barclays Bank plc v Waterson* [1989] CLY 2505. But a mortgagee's failure to disclose financial information about one mortgagor to another does not amount to misrepresentation: *Lloyds Bank plc v Egremont* [1990] FCR 770, [1990] 2 FLR 351, CA. It may, however, be an element in a claim by the other that the mortgagee had notice of undue influence by a joint mortgagor (see separate note, below). It was held in *UCB Corporate Services Ltd v Williams* [2002] EWCA Civ 555, [2002] 3 FCR 448 that where a wife was induced by her husband's misrepresentation to execute the charge it was not a sufficient reason for withholding rescission that she might have executed it without the misrepresentation.

II CCA [11.6]

Undue influence by a joint mortgagor There have been various cases, starting with *Barclays Bank plc v O'Brien* [1994] 1 AC 180, [1993] 4 All ER 417, HL, in which one joint mortgagor has contended that the other one used undue influence to obtain her (or his) signature and that the mortgagee, although aware of the trusting relationship and the financial disadvantage to the signatory, nevertheless failed to see that the joint mortgagor obtained independent legal advice before signing. The court concluded that the mortgagee had constructive notice of the fact that the joint mortgagor was vulnerable to undue influence and was barred on this ground from enforcing the claim for possession against the second mortgagor. More recently this situation has been reviewed in *Royal Bank of Scotland v Etridge (No 2)* [2001] UKHL 44, [2002] 2 AC 773, [2001] 4 All ER 449.

In *First National Bank plc v Achampong* [2003] EWCA Civ 487, [2004] 1 FCR 18, the question was raised as to what happens when the legal charge is vacated because of undue influence by one mortgagor over the other. The Court ruled that the legal charge is set aside and the charges register is rectified, but the mortgagee retains an equitable charge over the beneficial interest of the unduly influential mortgagor by operation of section 63(1) of the Law of Property Act 1925.

If a mortgage is voidable for undue influence, a replacement mortgage, taken out with the same lender as a condition of discharging the earlier mortgage, is similarly voidable although there was no undue influence in relation to the replacement mortgage: *Yorkshire Bank plc v Tinsley* [2004] EWCA Civ 816, [2004] 3 All ER 463, (2004) Times, 12 August.

II CCA [11.6A]

Manifest disadvantage It has been held that undue influence will not be implied from a trusting relationship unless there is a manifest disadvantage. In *Dunbar Bank plc v Nadeem* [1998] 3 All ER 876, CA, the Court held that there was no such disadvantage where an element in the transaction was that the wife acquired a joint interest in equity of the home,

COUNTY COURT

and in *Leggatt v National Westminster Bank plc* [2001] 1 FLR 523, CA it was considered that there was no manifest disadvantage in the case of a wife who signed a charge as surety to secure business liabilities, since the change replaced an open ended guarantee which she had signed years ago and was necessary to save the business.

II CCA [11.6B]

Constructive notice The defence of undue influence cannot succeed if the mortgagee is not put on notice of the relevant facts: *CIBC Mortgage plc v Pitt* [1994] 1 AC 200, [1993] 4 All ER 433, HL; *Britannia Building Society v Pugh* (1997) 29 HLR 423, CA. Where a bank sought to enforce a guarantee and legal charge against a wife and had written to the husband's solicitors asking them to confirm that they had ensured that the wife had received legal advice before execution of the guarantee and the legal charge but had not received such confirmation, it was held to be arguable that the bank had constructive notice of possible undue influence: *Cooke v National Westminster Bank plc* [1998] 3 FCR 643, [1998] 2 FLR 783, CA. The burden of proving that the mortgagee had actual or constructive notice of these facts is upon the party so alleging: *Barclays Bank plc v Boulter* [1999] 4 All ER 513, [1999] 1 WLR 1919, HL. However, the mortgagee is put on enquiry wherever a spouse or partner in a relationship offers to stand surety for the other spouse or partner's debt, and the mortgagee is aware of the relationship: *Royal Bank of Scotland v Etridge (No 2)* [2001] UKHL 44, [2002] 2 AC 773, [2001] 4 All ER 449.

In the case of a gift of property the presumption of undue influence is not rebutted by proof that the donee put no pressure on the donor but only by evidence that the donor's decision was made after full, free and informed thought: *Hammond v Osborn* [2002] EWCA Civ 885, [2002] All ER (D) 232 (Jun), (2002) Times, 18 July.

II CCA [11.6C]

Steps to be taken by a mortgagee Following *O'Brien*, a defence to a claim for possession by a joint mortgagor based on undue influence could not succeed if the risks had been made clear and he or she had been advised to take independent legal advice: *National Bank of Abu Dhabi v Mohamed* [1997] NPC 62, CA. It was sufficient for the mortgagees to have relied on a certificate of independent legal advice given not by a solicitor but by a legal executive acting with the authority of the principal: *Barclays Bank plc v Coleman* [2000] 1 All ER 385, [2000] 3 WLR 405, CA. The need for a wife to have independent legal advice was not satisfied by advice from the solicitor who was secretary of the husband's company which was the main beneficiary of the mortgage loan, and in which she held no shares: *National Westminster Bank plc v Breeds* [2001] Lloyd's Rep Bank 98, [2001] NPC 12. In *Barclay's Bank plc v Goff* [2001] EWCA Civ 635, [2001] 2 All ER (Comm) 847 it was held that in an ordinary case a bank would release itself of constructive notice by instructing a solicitor to give independent legal advice and then relying on confirmation that this had been done. An exception would be in respect of a transaction into which no competent solicitor could properly advise his client to enter.

The steps to be taken by a mortgagee when put on enquiry of possible undue influence were reviewed in *Etridge* and the court produced guidelines to apply to future transactions. The mortgagee was to insist that the wife attend a private meeting with its representative at which she was told of the extent of her liability and of the risk she was running and urged to take independent legal advice and exceptionally, to be safe, the mortgagee had to insist on the wife being separately advised. When independent legal advice is sought, the mortgagee should provide the solicitors with all necessary financial information and any suspicions they might have.

In *Wright v Cherry Tree Finance Ltd* [2001] EWCA Civ 449, [2001] 2 All ER (Comm) 877 a recently widowed mother mortgaged her home at an extravagant rate of interest to oblige her daughter and son-in-law. It was held that the presumption of the constructive notice of undue influence was not dispelled by the fact that she signed various explanatory documents provided by the lenders without having read them or having them explained at a meeting with the lenders.

In *National Westminster Bank plc v Amin* [2002] UKHL 9, [2002] 1 FLR 735 it was held that a wife had an arguable case for relief where the mortgagees were aware that neither she nor her husband could speak English but omitted this fact from their letter of instruction to the solicitors and the solicitors had failed to confirm that the mortgagors had understood what had been explained to them.

II CCA [11.6D]

Nature of legal advice The obligation of mortgagees as laid down in *Etridge* to satisfy themselves that a spouse or partner had been advised of the practical implications of the proposed transaction could be met by steps taken by the mortgagees themselves but alternatively it was reasonable for the mortgagees to rely on that task being performed by an independent legal advisor. Where the mortgagees were seeking to rely on independent legal advice, written confirmation should be obtained from the solicitors that the nature and practical implications of the documents had been explained to the spouse or partner. The nature of the legal advice given should be comprehensive following the guidelines in *Etridge* to include consideration of the terms of the documents, the risks involved and an assessment of the parties current and before financial position.

However, a solicitor's certificate may not be enough if the only advice given was bald advice not to go ahead with the transaction when a solicitor giving proper advice would explore why the home was being put seriously at risk and, where the main beneficiary would be someone who had acted fraudulently, the extent of the fraud: *Padden v Bevan Ashford Solicitors* [2011] EWCA Civ 1616, [2012] 2 All ER 718, [2012] 1 WLR 1759.

II CCA [11.6E]

Order for possession Where one of two joint mortgagors has an arguable defence of undue influence, the court should not in the meantime order possession against the other: *Albany Home Ltd v Massey and Massey* [1997] 2 All ER 609, CA.

II CCA [11.7]

Tenants of the mortgagor A mortgagee normally has the right to possession vis-à-vis tenants let into possession after the creation and registration of the mortgage: *Dudley and District Benefit Building Society v Emerson* [1949] Ch 707, [1949] 2 All ER 252, CA; *Britannia Building Society v Earl* [1990] 2 All ER 469, [1990] 1 WLR 422, CA. But a mortgagee cannot succeed against tenants who already have an overriding interest in the form of security of tenure vis-à-vis the mortgagor: *Woolwich Building Society v Dickman* [1996] 3 All ER 204, CA. A standard clause in a domestic mortgage by which the borrower agrees not to let the mortgaged property without the prior written consent of the lender does not contravene Article 48 of the Treaty of Rome, which guarantees freedom of movement for workers within the EC: *Citibank International plc v Kessler* [1999] 2 CMLR 603, CA. For further commentary refer to the notes to CPR Sch 2 CCR Ord 6 r 5 (see para **CCR 6r5 [1]**). Section 1 of the Mortgage Repossessions (Protection of Tenants etc) Act 2010 gives the courts power in some circumstances to give unlawful tenants up to 2 months before they can be evicted. The Act is set out at **III REA [88]**.

II CCA [11.8]

Duties owed by a mortgagor to joint guarantors Where a joint mortgage was entered into to secure a guarantee given by one of the mortgagors in respect of a company debt, the mortgagees were not entitled to vary the liability of the other joint mortgagor by increasing the limit of the guarantee without giving notice to the other joint mortgagor. This was despite the terms contained in the mortgage: *Lloyds TSB Bank plc v Shorney* [2001] EWCA Civ 1161, [2002] 1 FCR 673.

II CCA [11.9]

Administration of Justice Act provisions For the relevant provisions of the Administration of Justice Act 1970 see para **III REA [22]**, together with case law and commentary.

EQUITY PROCEEDINGS

II CCA [12]

23. Equity jurisdiction

The county court shall have all the jurisdiction of the High Court to hear and determine—

(a) proceedings for the administration of the estate of a deceased person, where the estate does not exceed in amount or value the county court limit;

(b) proceedings—

(i) for the execution of any trust, or

(ii) for a declaration that a trust subsists, or

(iii) under section 1 of the Variation of Trusts Act 1958,

where the estate or fund subject, or alleged to be subject, to the trust does not exceed in amount or value the county court limit;

(c) proceedings for foreclosure or redemption of any mortgage or for enforcing any charge or lien, where the amount owing in respect of the mortgage, charge or lien does not exceed the county court limit;

COUNTY COURT

(d) proceedings for the specific performance, or for the rectification, delivery up or cancellation, of any agreement for the sale, purchase or lease of any property, where, in the case of a sale or purchase, the purchase money, or in the case of a lease, the value of the property, does not exceed the county court limit;

(e) proceedings relating to the maintenance or advancement of a minor, where the property of the minor does not exceed in amount or value the county court limit;

(f) proceedings for the dissolution or winding-up of any partnership (whether or not the existence of the partnership is in dispute), where the whole assets of the partnership do not exceed in amount or value the county court limit;

(g) proceedings for relief against fraud or mistake, where the damage sustained or the estate or fund in respect of which relief is sought does not exceed in amount or value the county court limit

II CCA [12.1]

County court limit The Jurisdiction Order 1991 was amended by the County Court jurisdiction Order 2014, SI 2014/503, which increased the equity jurisdiction of the county from £30,000 to £350,000. The text of the revised order is at **II HCJ [1]**. Note, however, that the jurisdiction to hear proceedings under s 1 of the Variation of Trusts Act (s 1(b)(iii)) was deleted by the amendment order SI 2014/821.

II CCA [12.2]

Proceedings for the administration of the estate Proceedings started before 26 April 1999 should follow RSC Ord 44 (see **RSC 44**) or CCR Ord 23. Proceedings after that date should follow CPR Sch 1 RSC Ord 44 (see para **RSC 44**).

II CCA [12.3]

Foreclosure An action for possession under a mortgage is an action for the recovery of land within s 21, where the jurisdiction is unlimited: *West Penwith RDC v Gunnell* [1968] 2 All ER 1005, [1968] 1 WLR 1153, CA.

II CCA [12.4]

Specific performance The jurisdiction is not limited to land transactions but does not cover the enforcement of an undertaking to re-erect a boundary fence, which rests on s 38 powers instead: *Bourne v McDonald* [1950] 2 KB 422, [1950] 2 All ER 183, CA. A precedent for a claim for specific performance is provided at **BCCP P[1105]**.

II CCA [12.5]

Advancement "Advancement" is for placing the minor out in life, or otherwise for some special benefit to him, as distinct from ordinary maintenance and education. The court has no power to charge the real estate of a minor for the purpose of his advancement: *Re De Tessier's Settled Estate, De Tessier v De Tessier* [1893] 1 Ch 153.

II CCA [12.6]

Partnership See Partnership Act 1890 at para **III PAR [21]**. A Precedent for the dissolution or winding-up of solvent and insolvent partnerships is provided in **BCCP R[1251]**.

II CCA [12.7]

Relief against fraud and mistake The equitable jurisdiction extends to setting aside a deed of release of a judgment debt obtained by fraud: *Stephenson v Garnett* [1898] 1 QB 677, CA.

II CCA [13]

24. Jurisdiction by agreement in certain equity proceedings

(1) If, as respects any proceedings to which this section applies, the parties agree, by a memorandum signed by them or by their respective legal representatives or agents, that the county court shall have jurisdiction in the proceedings, that court shall, notwithstanding anything in any enactment, have jurisdiction to hear and determine the proceedings accordingly.

(2) Subject to subsection (3), this section applies to any proceedings in which the county court would have jurisdiction by virtue of—

(a) section 113(3) of the Settled Land Act 1925,

(b) section 63A of the Trustee Act 1925,

(c) sections 3(7), [. . .], 49(4), 66(4), 89(7), 90(3), 91(8), 92(2), 136(3), [. . .], 181(2), 188(2) of, and paragraph 3A of Part III and paragraph 1(3A) and (4A) of Part IV of Schedule 1 to, the Law of Property Act 1925,

(d) sections 17(2), 38(4), 41(1A), and 43(4) of the Administration of Estates Act 1925,

(e) section 6(1) of the Leasehold Property (Repairs) Act 1938,

(f) sections 1(6A) and 5(11) of the Land Charges Act 1972, and

(g) sections 23 [. . .] of this Act,

but for the limits of the jurisdiction of the court provided in those enactments.

(3) This section does not apply to proceedings under section 1 of the Variation of Trusts Act 1958

II CCA [13.1]

Jurisdiction by agreement This section is the counterpart of s 18. For transfer down from the High Court by consent see s 40(1).

II CCA [13.2]

Variation of Trusts Act 1958 See para **III TRU [37]**.

II CCA [13.3]

Legal representatives For definition see para **II CCA [141]**.

FAMILY PROVISION PROCEEDINGS

II CCA [14]

25. Jurisdiction under Inheritance (Provision for Family and Dependants) Act 1975

The county court shall have jurisdiction to hear and determine any application for an order under section 2 of the Inheritance (Provision for Family and Dependants) Act 1975 (including any application for permission to apply for such an order and any application made, in the proceedings on an application for such an order, for an order under any other provision of that Act) [. . .]

II CCA [14.1]

Jurisdiction and procedure The county courts have concurrent jurisdiction with the High Court. See para **III FMY [3]**. Note the extensive changes made by the Inheritance and Trustees' Powers Act 2014 with effect from 1 October 2014.

ADMIRALTY PROCEEDINGS

II CCA [15]

26. ***Districts for Admiralty purposes***

Repealed.

II CCA [15.1]

Admiralty county courts The Lord Chancellor may appoint county courts to exercise the Admiralty jurisdiction conferred by s 27. See the Civil Courts Order 1983, SI 1983/713. However, the admiralty jurisdiction was removed from all county courts by the Civil Courts (Amendment)(No 2) Order 1999, SI 1999/1011.

COUNTY COURT

PROBATE PROCEEDINGS

II CCA [16]

32. ***Contentious probate jurisdiction***
Repealed.

II CCA [16.1]

County court limit Jurisdiction depends on whether the net value of the deceased's estate as a whole (after making allowances for funeral expenses and for debts and liabilities) exceeds the county court limit which is £30,000 (County Courts Jurisdiction Order 1981, SI 1981/1123, art 2. Also see paras **II CCA [12.1]–[12.4]**); the limited jurisdiction conferred by s 32 of the County Courts Act 1984 was not affected by the High Court and County Courts Jurisdiction Order 1991, SI 1991/724 which does not refer to s 32, although it does refer to ss 15, 16, 21, 25 and 139.

II CCA [16.2]

Costs An executor unless he has acted unreasonably or for his own benefit is always allowed his costs either against the parties or out of the estate: See para **CPR 48.4**.

II CCA [16.3]

Procedure See **CPR 57**.

II CCA [17]

33. ***Effect of order of judge in probate proceedings***
Repealed.

MISCELLANEOUS PROVISIONS AS TO JURISDICTION

II CCA [18]

35. Division of causes of action
It shall not be lawful for any plaintiff to divide any cause of action for the purpose of bringing two or more actions in the county court.

II CCA [18.1]

Dividing a cause of action This provision is of less significance now that county courts have unlimited jurisdiction in actions of contract and tort. A claimant must prove and receive damages arising from the same cause of action once and for all: *Clark v Urguhart* [1930] AC 28, HL and see *Buckland v Palmer* [1984] 3 All ER 554, [1984] 1 WLR 1109, CA. Where goods are seized for arrears of hire under a hire-purchase agreement, this is an action for debt and a later action for damages for breach of contract is not barred by this provision: *Overstone Ltd v Shipway* [1962] 1 All ER 52, [1962] 1 WLR 117, CA.

II CCA [19]

36. No action on judgment of High Court
No action shall be brought in the county court on any judgment of the High Court.

II CCA [19.1]

Judgment of High Court "Judgment" is defined in Supreme Court Act 1981 s 151(1) (see para **II SCA [70]**). This section has been applied to protect an executor from being sued in the county court upon a debt founded on a judgment of the High Court previously obtained against his testator: *Cheetham v Hollingworth* [1914] WN 25.

EXERCISE OF JURISDICTION AND ANCILLARY JURISDICTION

II CCA [20]

37. Persons who may exercise jurisdiction of court

(1) Any jurisdiction and powers conferred by this or any other Act on the county court may be exercised by any judge of the county court.

II CCA [20.1]

The judge of a county court This section refers specifically to the Circuit judge (see para **II CCA [5]**) not the district judge; however, see **CPR 2.4** and the associated practice direction (at para **CPR PD 2B**) which deals with the allocation of functions between Circuit judges and district judges.

II CCA [21]

38. Remedies available in county courts

(1) Subject to what follows, in any proceedings in the county court the court may make any order which could be made by the High Court if the proceedings were in the High Court.

(2) Any order made by the county court may be—

(a) absolute or conditional;

(b) final or interlocutory.

(3) Neither the county court nor the family court has power—

(a) to order mandamus, certiorari or prohibition; or

(b) to make any order of a prescribed kind.

(4) Regulations under subsection (3)—

(a) may provide for any of their provisions not to apply in such circumstances or descriptions of case as may be specified in the regulations;

(b) may provide for the transfer of the proceedings to the High Court for the purpose of enabling an order of a kind prescribed under subsection (3) to be made;

(c) . . . and

(d) may make provision amending or repealing any provision made by or under any enactment, so far as may be necessary or expedient in consequence of the regulations; and

(e) may make different provision for different purposes.

(4A) If regulations are made under subsection (3), rules may be made in accordance with Part 1 of Schedule 1 to the Constitutional Reform Act 2005 about procedure relevant to the matters prescribed in the regulations.

(5) In this section "prescribed" means prescribed by regulations made under this section by the Lord Chancellor after consulting the Lord Chief Justice.

(6) The power to make regulations under this section shall be exercised by statutory instrument.

(7) No such statutory instrument shall be made unless a draft of the instrument has been approved by both Houses of Parliament.

II CCA [21.1]

Any order which could be made by the High Court Except as regards judicial review, Freezing injunctions and Search orders (as to which see the County Courts Remedies Regulations 1991, SI 1991/1222, below), the county court's general powers to award remedies and relief are the same as in the High Court. This is illustrated by *Kingswood Estate Co Ltd v Anderson* [1963] 2 QB 169, [1962] 3 All ER 593, CA (equitable defences); *Goker v NWS Bank plc* [1990] CCLR 34, Times, 23 May, CA (relief against forfeiture of a chattel); and *Steel Linings Ltd and Harvey v Bibby & Co* [1993] RA 27, [1993] NLJR 511, CA

COUNTY COURT

(injunction to restrain excessive distress). It has been held that the county court , like the High Court, has power to rescind its own judgments, for example on the ground of perjurious evidence given at the trial: *Salekipour v Parmar* [2017] EWCA Civ 2141, (2018) Times 22 January.

II CCA [21.2]

Declarations The county courts' jurisdiction to grant declaratory relief does not depend on the existence of a claim for money, see for example *Osei-Bonsu v Wandsworth London Borough Council* [1999] 1 All ER 265, [1999] 1 WLR 1011, CA. However, this jurisdiction exists only if the proceedings in which it is sought are of a kind which a county court has jurisdiction to entertain. Nevertheless, however the proceedings may be framed, if the true nature of the relief sought is such as to bring the matter within the court's jurisdiction, jurisdiction to grant a declaration will also exist: *Agodzo v Bristol City Council* [1999] 1 WLR 1971, CA. A court which has granted a declaration is *functus officio* and has no jurisdiction to vary it thereafter at a subsequent hearing: *R v British Coal Corpn, ex p Price (No 2)* (1993) Times, 23 February. The court has power to grant a declaration that a person is not entitled to apply for an injunction to prevent proposed development: *Greenwich Healthcare National Health Service Trust v London Quadrant Housing Trust* [1998] 3 All ER 437, [1998] 1 WLR 1749.

There is now jurisdiction to grant an interim declaration (see CPR 25.1(1)(b) at para **CPR 25.1**).

II CCA [21.2A]

Mandamus The judge of a county court has no power to give directions to a housing authority on an appeal under s 204 of the Housing Act 1996 because this is prevented by s 38(3)(a): *Adan v Newham London Borough Council* [2001] EWCA Civ 1916, [2002] 1 All ER 931, (2002) Times, 16 January.

II CCA [21.3]

Injunctions The county courts' jurisdiction to grant injunctions is no longer, as formerly, only available in relation to land or under specific statutory authority or where there is a claim for money or other relief (but see the County Courts Remedies Regulations 1991, SI 1991/1222 and the Practice Direction to CPR Part 25). Note, however, that the county courts' jurisdiction, including the jurisdiction to grant injunctions, derives only from statute (including, of course, the County Courts Act 1984) and that it has no inherent jurisdiction other than that of the High Court exercised under this section: *D v D (child case: powers of court)* [1994] 3 FCR 28, sub nom *D v D (County court jurisdiction: injunction)* [1993] 2 FLR 802, CA; and see *Devon County Council v B* [1997] 3 FCR 333, [1997] 1 FLR 591, CA. Note also that an injunction will only be granted to a defendant or respondent if it is ancillary to or comes within the scope of the substantive relief sought in the proceedings: *Des Salles d'Epinoix v Des Salles d'Epinoix* [1967] 2 All ER 539, [1967] 1 WLR 553, CA; compare *Chief Constable of Kent v V* [1983] QB 34, [1982] 3 All ER 36, CA. It was held, in *Ali v Westminster City Council* [1999] 1 All ER 450, [1991] 1 WLR 384, CA that a county court to which an individual was appealing against an authority's decision not to provide accommodation had no power to grant an interim injunction that accommodation be provided. The reasoning was that the individual had no cause of action, only a right of appeal and the county court had no inherent powers; the better course might be to apply for judicial review. "Ancillary" means "subservient to" see per Donovan LJ in *Kenny v Preen* [1962] 3 All ER 814 at 822 and *Watts v Wallter* [1972] 3 All ER 257 at 266, CA. Furthermore the right to an interlocutory injunction is dependent upon there being a cause of action subsisting at the time of the grant of the injunction: *The Siskina (Cargo Owners) v Distos Compania Naviera SA* [1979] AC 210; *Veracruz Transportation Inc v V C Shipping Co Inc* [1992] 1 Lloyd's Rep 353, CA; and jurisdiction to grant an injunction or other ancillary relief depends on the existence, in the court to which application for such relief is made, of jurisdiction to entertain the substantive proceedings: *Department of Social Security v Butler* [1995] 4 All ER 193, [1995] 1 WLR 1528, CA. But, provided that there is a cause of action against one defendant, the lack of such a cause of action against another does not necessarily prevent the grant of an injunction against that other defendant if the circumstances make this appropriate: *TSB Private Bank International SA v Chabra* [1992] 2 All ER 245, [1992] 1 WLR 231.

II CCA [21.4]

Injunctions in divorce proceedings In divorce proceedings the court has no jurisdiction to grant an injunction to exclude a spouse from the matrimonial home after decree absolute: *O'Malley v O'Malley* [1982] 2 All ER 112, [1982] 1 WLR 244, save where it is in the interests of the children to do so: *Quinn v Quinn* (1983) 4 FLR 394; *Wilde v Wilde* [1988] FCR 551, [1988] 2 FLR 83, CA. However, the Family Law Act 1996 Part IV gives the court power to grant occupation orders after decree absolute. The draconian nature of ouster orders has frequently been stressed in the Court of Appeal: *Tuck v Nicholls* [1989] FCR 300, [1989] 1

FLR 283, CA. An ouster order, if appropriate, must be expressed to take effect within not more than two or three weeks: *Dunsire v Dunsire* [1991] FCR 292, [19991] 2 FLR 314, CA. Where a court is faced with conflicting affidavits, oral evidence must be heard to resolve the dispute before an injunction can be granted: *Whitlock v Whitlock* [1990] FCR 129, [1989] 1 FLR 208, CA. As to the principles to be applied where the respondent is under disability see *Wookey v Wookey* [1991] Fam 121, [1991] 3 All ER 365, CA.

II CCA [21.5]

Injunctions in other proceedings The power to order surrender of his passport by a foreign debtor under an English judgment is only available as an aid to the court's established procedures. There is no power to grant a free-standing injunction for this purpose: *B v B* [1997] 3 All ER 258, [1998] 1 WLR 329. Where a claimant accepts a payment into court in an action in which he claims both damages and an injunction he cannot accept it simply in satisfaction of the money claim and leave the claim for an injunction alive: *Hargreaves Construction (Lineside) Ltd v Williams* (1982) Times, 3 July. In *Amey Roadstone Corpn v Purdey* [1986] CLY 2654 an injunction was granted in a representative action to prevent squatters on the claimant's land from moving to other land owned by the claimant. An injunction against molestation may not be founded on nuisance alone at the instance of a licensee (*Hunter v Canary Wharf Ltd* [1997] AC 655, [1997] 2 All ER 426, HL, overruling *Khorasandjian v Bush* [1993] QB 727, [1993] 3 All ER 669, CA on this point). But where it is appropriate eg because the claimant is a tenant, the injunction may specify an exclusion zone if necessary for the claimant's protection: *Burris v Azadani* [1995] 4 All ER 802, [1995] 1 WLR 1372, CA. Where an application for an injunction is made under different statutes any order made should include specific reference to the statute or statutes concerned: *Power v Power* [1986] CA Transcript 923.

II CCA [21.5A]

Civil Restraint Orders The court has powers to restrict abuse of court process by the issue of civil restraint orders. The circumstances under which these orders can be issued and the types of order are set out in **CPR PD 3C**. Where a statement of case or application is struck out or dismissed and is totally without merit, the court must consider whether to make a civil restraint order. The relevant forms for such orders are N19, N19A and N19B.

II CCA [21.6]

Injunctions: third parties and the public interest The court is entitled to take into consideration the rights of third parties who have not been joined in the proceedings: *Merrill Lynch Pierce Fenner & Smith Inc v Besman* [1985] CA Transcript 814. However, the court may grant an injunction to prevent a defendant from fulfilling a contract with an innocent third party, though it should do so only in clearly appropriate cases: *PSM International plc v Whitehouse* [1992] IRLR 279, CA. An injunction will not be granted to restrain publication of confidential information by a public servant unless it can be shown that publication is contrary to the public interest and will not be granted to prevent wrongdoing in general but only a specific wrong: *A-G v Guardian Newspapers Ltd (No 2)* [1990] 1 AC 109, [1988] 3 All ER 545, HL. It is well settled that an injunction to restrain breach of a contract for personal services will not be granted if its effect is to order performance of the contract: *Warren v Mendy* [1989] 3 All ER 103, [1989] 1 WLR 853, CA; *Provident Financial Group plc v Hayward* [1989] 3 All ER 298, [1989] ICR 160, CA. Only in exceptional circumstances will a mandatory injunction be granted to compel the carrying on of a business: *Co-operative Insurance Society Ltd v Argyll Stores (Holdings) Ltd* [1998] AC 1, [1997] 3 All ER 297, HL.

II CCA [21.7]

Undertakings A formal undertaking given by one of the parties in an action and recorded in court is equivalent to an injunction and the breach of it can be punished in the same way as for breach of an injunction: *Neath Canal Co v Ynisarwed Resolven Colliery Co* (1875) 10 Ch App 450; *Milburn v Newton Colliery Ltd* (1908) 52 Sol Jo 317; *Gandolfo v Gandolfo* [1981] QB 359, [1980] 1 All ER 833, CA; *Camden London Borough Council v Alpenoak Ltd* [1985] NLJ Rep 1209. An undertaking can be accepted from a minor provided that he or she understands its meaning and the consequences of a breach: *Leach v Taylor* [1996] CLY 928. Where such an undertaking is accepted the person giving it should be required to sign **FORM N117**.

A person not himself included in an undertaking, nor a party to the action, who knowing of the undertaking aids and abets a defendant in committing breach of it may be committed for contempt: *Thorne RDC v Bunting (No 2)* [1972] 3 All ER 657. An undertaking by a party or his solicitors not to use documents obtained under a Search order for any collateral or ulterior purpose may be modified by the court: *Crest Homes plc v Marks* [1987] AC 829, [1987] 2 All ER 1074, HL. Where a person has proved entitlement to an injunction it is not open to the court to impose a compromise by accepting an undertaking from the defendant without the claimant's agreement: *Jameson v Manley* [1987] CLY 2963, CA. In fixing a penalty for breach of an undertaking given by a local authority, the court may take judicial notice of previous breaches of undertakings given to that court by that local authority in previous cases: *Mullen v Hackney London Borough Council* [1997] 2 All ER 906, [1996] 1 WLR 1103, CA.

II CCA [21.8]

Receiver For the rule and practice as to receivers generally see CPR Sch 1 RSC Ord 30 (see para **RSC 30**) which applies to county courts. County courts have the same wide powers as the High Court has under Supreme Court Act 1981 s 37(1) (see para **II SCA [38]**) and specific powers under County Courts Act 1984 s 107 (see para **II CCA [101]**). Application may be made before or after judgment and by way of equitable execution (*R v Selfe* [1908] 2 KB 121). A receiver may be appointed to manage property and collect rent: *Hart v Emelkirk Ltd, Howroyd v Emelkirk Ltd* [1983] 3 All ER 15, [1983] 1 WLR 1289; *Daiches v Bluelake Investments Ltd* (1985) 51 P & CR 51.

II CCA [21.9]

Trusts The equitable jurisdiction to assist beneficiaries included the power to order the disclosure of the identity of the trustee of a discretionary trust to a potential beneficiary: *Re Murphy's Settlement* [1998] 3 All ER 1, [1999] 1 WLR 282.

II CCA [21.10]

Remedies Regulations The text of the County Court Remedies Regulations 2014, SI 2014/982, which took effect on 9 April 2014, is as follows:

1. Citation, commencement and interpretation

(1) These Regulations may be cited as the County Court Remedies Regulations 2014 and come into force on 22nd April 2014 or, if made on or after that date, on the day after the day on which they are made.

(2) In these Regulations—

"judge of the County Court" is to be construed in accordance with section 5 of the County Courts Act 1984 Act; and

"search order" means an order under section 7 of the Civil Procedure Act 1997 (order requiring a party to admit another party to premises for the purpose of preserving evidence, etc).

2. Revocation of the 1991 Regulations

The County Court Remedies Regulations 1991 ("the 1991 Regulations") are revoked.

3. The County Court's jurisdiction to make search orders

(1) Subject to the following provisions of this regulation, a county court shall not grant prescribed relief or vary or revoke an order made by the High Court granting such relief.

(2) Paragraph (1) shall not apply to a judge of the Court of Appeal or a High Court Judge sitting as a judge of the County Court.

(3) Paragraph (1) shall not—

(a) affect or modify powers expressly conferred on the County Court by or under any enactment other than section 38 of the County Courts Act 1984; or

(b) prevent the County Court from varying a search order where all the parties are agreed on the terms of the variation.

4. Applications for search orders in County Court proceedings

An application to the High Court for a search order in County Court proceedings shall be deemed to include an application for transfer of the proceedings to the High Court.

5. Transfer of proceedings to the County Court

(1) After an application for a search order has been disposed of by the High Court, the proceedings shall, unless the High Court orders otherwise, be transferred to the County Court if—

(a) they were transferred to the High Court; or

(b) apart from these Regulations, they should have been commenced in the County Court.

(2) Where a search order is made on an application made without notice, the application shall not be treated as disposed of for the purposes of paragraph (1) until any application to set aside or vary the order has been heard, or until the expiry of 28 days (or such other period as the Court may specify) during which no such application has been made.

II CCA [21.11]

Freezing injunctions and Search orders The Regulations restrict the grant of search injunctions by the County Court but note that there are now no restrictions on the power of the County Court to grant freezing injunctions. A useful precedent can be found at **CPR PD 25A**.

TRANSFER OF PROCEEDINGS

II CCA [22]

40. Transfer of proceedings to county court

(1) Where the High Court is satisfied that any proceedings before it are required by any provision of a kind mentioned in subsection (8) to be in the county court it shall—

(a) order the transfer of the proceedings to the county court; or

(b) if the court is satisfied that the person bringing the proceedings knew, or ought to have known, of that requirement, order that they be struck out.

(2) Subject to any such provision, the High Court may order the transfer of any proceedings before it to the county court.

(3) An order under this section may be made either on the motion of the High Court itself or on the application of any party to the proceedings.

(4) ...

(5) The transfer of any proceedings under this section shall not affect any right of appeal from the order directing the transfer.

(6) Where proceedings for the enforcement of any judgment or order of the High Court are transferred under this section—

(a) the judgment or order may be enforced as if it were a judgment or order of the county court; and

(b) subject to subsection (7), it shall be treated as a judgment or order of that court for all purposes.

(7) Where proceedings for the enforcement of any judgment or order of the High Court are transferred under this section—

(a) the powers of any court to set aside, correct, vary or quash a judgment or order of the High Court, and the enactments relating to appeals from such a judgment or order, shall continue to apply; and

(b) the powers of any court to set aside, correct, vary or quash a judgment or order of the county court, and the enactments relating to appeals from such a judgment or order, shall not apply.

(8) The provisions referred to in subsection (1) are any made—

(a) under section 1 of the Courts and Legal Services Act 1990; or

(b) by or under any other enactment.

(9) ...

COUNTY COURT

II CCA [22.1]

Background This section is printed as substituted by the Courts and Legal Services Act 1990 s 2(1). Sections 40, 41 and 42, provide the statutory framework for implementing the jurisdiction provisions contained in the High Court and County Courts Jurisdiction Order 1991, SI 1991/724, (see para **II HCJ [1]**).

II CCA [22.2]

Procedure and criteria for transfer for trial As to the procedure for the transfer of pending actions, see **CPR 30**; as to transfer of High Court judgments for enforcement see CPR Sch 2 CCR Ord 25 r 11 (see para **CCR 25r11**). See also *Practice Direction* [1991] 3 All ER 349, [1991] 1 WLR 643]. Note that a case may be transferred to the county court although the court is satisfied that the conditions for striking out under s 40(1)(b) are met: *Restick v Crickmore* [1994] 2 All ER 112, [1994] 1 WLR 420, CA.

II CCA [22.3]

Position after transfer Transfer to the County Court does not affect the right of appeal from the order directing the transfer or the right to apply to set aside a judgment transferred for enforcement: s 40(5), (7). But appeals against earlier orders of a High Court district judge or master lie to the county court judge after transfer: *Kings Quality Homes Ltd v A J Paints Ltd* [1997] 3 All ER 267, [1998] 1 WLR 124, CA.

II CCA [22.4]

Transfer for enforcement A High Court order for transfer is necessary for enforcement in the county court except in the case of enforcement by attachment of earnings, charging order or judgment summons.

II CCA [22.5]

Regulated credit agreements Proceedings to enforce regulated agreements should be brought in the county court. They are not invalid if brought in the High Court (Consumer Credit Act 1974 s 141(2)) but are likely to be struck out under s 40(1)(b) unless High Court issue can be justified: *Barclays Bank plc v Brooks* [1997] CCLR 60.

II CCA [22.6]

The transfer of any proceedings before it The power to transfer to the county court under sub-s (2) may be exercised even where the county court would not otherwise have jurisdiction to entertain the proceedings: *National Westminster Bank plc v King* [2008] EWHC 280 (Ch), [2008] All ER (D) 292 (Feb), (2008) Times, 14 April, Ch D (a claim to enforce a charging order where the value of the property exceeded the county court limit).

II CCA [23]

41. Transfer to High Court by order of High Court

(1) If at any stage in proceedings commenced in the county court or transferred to the county court under section 40, the High Court thinks it desirable that the proceedings, or any part of them, should be heard and determined in the High Court, it may order the transfer to the High Court of the proceedings or, as the case may be, of that part of them.

(2) The power conferred by subsection (1) is without prejudice to section 29 of the Senior Courts Act 1981 (power of High Court to issue prerogative orders).

(3) The power conferred by subsection (1) shall be exercised subject to any provision made—

- (a) under section 1 of the Courts and Legal Services Act 1990; or
- (b) by or under any other enactment.

II CCA [24]

42. Transfer of proceedings to High Court by order of the county court

(1) Where the county court is satisfied that any proceedings before it are required by any provision of a kind mentioned in subsection (7) to be in the High Court, it shall—

- (a) order the transfer of the proceedings to the High Court; or
- (b) if the court is satisfied that the person bringing the proceedings knew, or ought to have known, of that requirement, order that they be struck out.

(2) Subject to any such provision, the county court may order the transfer of any proceedings before it to the High Court.

(3) An order under this section may be made either on the motion of the court itself or on the application of any party to the proceedings.

(4) The transfer of any proceedings under this section shall not affect any right of appeal from the order directing the transfer.

(5) Where proceedings for the enforcement of any judgment or order of the county court are transferred under this section—

- (a) the judgment or order may be enforced as if it were a judgment or order of the High Court; and

(b) subject to subsection (6), it shall be treated as a judgment or order of that court for all purposes.

(6) Where proceedings for the enforcement of any judgment or order of the county court are transferred under this section—

(a) the powers of any court to set aside, correct, vary or quash a judgment or order of the county court, and the enactments relating to appeals from such a judgment or order, shall continue to apply; and

(b) the powers of any court to set aside, correct, vary or quash a judgment or order of the High Court, and the enactments relating to appeals from such a judgment or order, shall not apply.

(7) The provisions referred to in subsection (1) are any made—

(a) under section 1 of the Courts and Legal Services Act 1990; or

(b) by or under any other enactment.

(8) *Repealed.*

II CCA [24.1]

Criteria for transfer Section 42 gives to the county courts duties and powers relating to transfer to the High Court broadly corresponding to the duties and powers given by s 40 to the High Court relating to transfer to a county court. In deciding whether to order transfer under s 42(2) the judge must take into account the matters set out in CPR 30.3 (see para **CPR 30.3**) but, provided he does so, the decision whether to transfer or not is a matter for his discretion. He should not concern himself with the division of the High Court to which any transfer should be made: *McLaughlin v British Coal Corpn* (1992) Times, 16 December, CA.

II CCA [24.2]

Any other enactment The words "any other enactment" in s 42(7)(b) includes the 1984 Act itself, with the result that a mortgage claim which is, by s 21, within the exclusive jurisdiction of the county court cannot be transferred under s 42(2): *Yorkshire Bank plc v Hall* [1999] 1 All ER 879, [1999] 1 WLR 1713, CA.

II CCA [24.3]

Transfer of possession order for enforcement by a High Court writ of possession The transfer to the High Court of an order for possession enables the owner to apply for permission, on notice to the occupants, to issue a writ of possession, in accordance with **CPR 83.13**.

II CCA [25]

45. Costs in transferred cases

(1) Where an action, counterclaim or matter is ordered to be transferred—

(a) from the High Court to the county court; or

(b) from the county court to the High Court,

(c) ...

the costs of the whole proceedings both before and after the transfer shall, subject to any order of the court which ordered the transfer, be in the discretion of the court to which the proceedings are transferred; and that court shall have power to make orders with respect to the costs . . . , and the costs of the whole proceedings shall be taxed in that court.

(2) [. . .]

II CCA [25.1]

Taxed costs CPR Parts 44 and 47 (see para **CPR 44** and see para **CPR 47**) provide for assessment of costs in place of taxation.

PART III
PROCEDURE

PARTIES

II CCA [26]

46. Proceedings by the Crown

(1) Subject to the provisions of any enactment limiting the jurisdiction of the county court, whether by reference to the subject matter of the proceedings to be brought or the amount sought to be recovered in the proceedings or otherwise, proceedings by the Crown may be instituted in the county court.

(2) Subject to section 40(5), all rules of law and enactments regulating the removal or transfer of proceedings from the county court to the High Court and the transfer of proceedings in the High Court to the county court shall apply respectively to the removal or transfer of proceedings by the Crown in the county court and to the transfer of proceedings by the Crown in the High Court.

(3) Nothing in this section shall apply to proceedings affecting Her Majesty in Her private capacity.

II CCA [26.1]

Crown proceedings Proceedings by and against the Crown are subject to the provisions of the Crown Proceedings Act 1947 ss 15–18, 20 and 21, set out in notes to CPR Sch 2 CCR Ord 42, see para **CCR 42**. Note also that income tax collectors may sue for the recovery of income tax under the Taxes Management Act 1970 s 66.

II CCA [27]

48. Persons jointly liable

(1) Where a plaintiff has a demand recoverable under this Act against two or more persons jointly liable, it shall be sufficient to serve any of those persons with process, and judgment may be obtained and execution issued against any person so served, notwithstanding that others jointly liable may not have been served or sued or may not be within the jurisdiction of the court.

(2) Where judgment is so obtained against any person by virtue of subsection (1) and is satisfied by that person, he shall be entitled to recover in the court contribution from any other person jointly liable with him.

II CCA [27.1]

Rule against double recovery Judgment against one of two or more joint defendants does not bar proceedings against the others: Civil Liability (Contribution) Act 1978 s 3. On the other hand a judgment creditor may not recover more than his loss and must give credit in proceedings against one defendant for sums recovered from another, after applying those proceeds to sums and interest: *Banque Keyser Ullman SA v Skandia (UK) Insurance Ltd (No 2)* [1988] 2 All ER 880, [1988] NLJR 31.

II CCA [28]

49. Bankruptcy of plaintiff

(1) The bankruptcy of the plaintiff in any action in the county court which the trustee might maintain for the benefit of the creditors shall not cause the action to abate if, within such reasonable time as the court orders, the trustee elects to continue the action and to give security for the costs of the action.

(2) The hearing of the action may be adjourned until such an election is made.

(3) Where the trustee does not elect to continue the action and to give such security as is mentioned in subsection (1) within the time limited by the order, the defendant may avail himself of the bankruptcy as a defence to the action.

II CCA [28.1]

High Court practice In the High Court, where a claimant is adjudicated bankrupt after action brought, and his trustee declines to proceed with it, the action may be stayed by an order in chambers, and the defendant need not plead the bankruptcy in bar: *Warder v Saunders* (1882) 10 QBD 114. The stay will be binding on any assignee: *Selig v Lion* [1891] 1 QB 513. But if no steps towards a stay have been taken by the defendant, and after discharge the trustee assigns the right of action to the bankrupt, he may proceed: *Barker v Johnson* (1889) 60 LT 64.

II CCA [28.2]

Election by a trustee The election by a trustee not to continue a pending action commenced by the bankrupt is no bar to a subsequent action by him in his representative capacity, founded on the same cause of action: *Bennett v Gamgee* (1877) 36 LT 48, CA. If a trustee elects to go on with a pending action he must adopt the whole of it. Where a trustee adopted a defence he was ordered to pay the costs of an interlocutory appeal presented by the bankrupt which the trustee abandoned: *Borneman v Wilson* (1884) 28 Ch D 53, CA.

II CCA [28.3]

Security for costs The section expressly provides that the trustee shall give security for costs if he elects to continue a pending action. But a trustee who brings an action for the benefit of the estate will not be required to give security for costs, even though he is in insolvent circumstances: *Cowell v Taylor* (1885) 31 Ch D 34, CA. A bankrupt claimant will not be required to give security where the cause of action has arisen since his bankruptcy, and he is not suing merely as agent for the trustee: *Cook v Whellock* (1890) 24 QBD 658, CA. Where an action in contract is remitted under s 40 and, before the claimant has lodged the original writ and order with the district judge (now the proper officer) of the county court, he becomes bankrupt, and a trustee is appointed who obtains an order in the High Court joining himself as claimant in the action, the county court judge has no jurisdiction under this section, after the writ and order have been lodged, to order the trustee to give security for costs: *Hemming v Davies* [1898] 1 QB 660. Where an existing claimant has a bankruptcy order made against him, and the trustee subsequently assigns the cause of action back to the claimant, no security for costs order can be made against the trustee as the action is not maintained by the trustee: *Talling v Lawrence* [1999] BPIR 414, [1999] CLY 363.

II CCA [28.4]

Cause of action accruing after bankruptcy Where the cause of action has accrued after bankruptcy, an undischarged bankrupt may sue personally until the trustee intervenes: *Bailey v Thurston & Co Ltd* [1903] 1 KB 137, CA. However, a bankrupt has no locus standi to appeal against the judgment on which the bankruptcy petition was founded: *Heath v Tang* [1993] 4 All ER 694, [1993] 1 WLR 1421, CA.

II CCA [29]

50. Orders for interim payments

(1) Provision may be made by rules of court for enabling the court, in such circumstances as may be prescribed, to make an order requiring a party to the proceedings to make an interim payment of such amount as may be specified in the order, with provision for the payment to be made to such other party to the proceedings as may be so specified or, if the order so provides, by paying it into court.

(2) Any rules of court which make provision in accordance with subsection (1) may include provision for enabling a party to any proceedings who, in pursuance of such an order, has made an interim payment to recover the whole or part of the amount of the payment in such circumstances, and from such other party to the proceedings, as may be determined in accordance with the rules.

(3) Any rules made by virtue of this section may include such incidental, supplementary and consequential provisions as the Civil Procedure Rule Committee may consider necessary or expedient.

(4) Nothing in this section shall be construed as affecting the exercise of any power relating to costs, including any power to make rules of court relating to costs.

(5) In this section "interim payment", in relation to a party to any proceedings, means a payment on account of any damages, debt or other sum (excluding any costs) which that party may be held liable to pay to or for the benefit of another party to the proceedings if a final judgment or order of the court in the proceedings is given or made in favour of that other party; and any reference to a party to any proceedings includes a reference to any person who for the purposes of the proceedings acts as next friend or guardian of a party to the proceedings.

II CCA [29.1]

Provision is made for interim payments at **CPR 25.6**.

PROVISIONAL DAMAGES FOR PERSONAL INJURIES

II CCA [30]

51. Orders for provisional damages for personal injuries

(1) This section applies to an action for damages for personal injuries in which there is proved or admitted to be a chance that at some definite or indefinite time in the future the injured person will, as a result of the act or omission which gave rise to the cause of action, develop some serious disease or suffer some serious deterioration in his physical or mental condition.

(2) Subject to subsection (4), as regards any action for damages to which this section applies in which a judgment is given in the county court, provision may be made by rules of court for enabling the court, in such circumstances as may be prescribed, to award the injured person—

(a) damages assessed on the assumption that the injured person will not develop the disease or suffer the deterioration in his condition; and

(b) further damages at a future date if he develops the disease or suffers the deterioration.

(3) Any rules made by virtue of this section may include such incidental, supplementary and consequential provisions as the Civil Procedure Rule Committee may consider necessary or expedient.

(4) Nothing in this section shall be construed—

(a) as affecting the exercise of any power relating to costs, including any power to make rules of court relating to costs; or

(b) as prejudicing any duty of the court under any enactment or rule of law to reduce or limit the total damages which would have been recoverable apart from any such duty.

(5) In this section "personal injuries" includes any disease and any impairment of a person's physical or mental condition.

II CCA [30.1]

For the rules relating to the application for provisional damages see **CPR 41**.

Serious deterioration

II CCA [30.2]

"Serious deterioration" denotes a clear and severable deterioration going beyond ordinary or continuing deterioration: *Willson v Ministry of Defence* [1991] 1 All ER 638.

DISCLOSURE AND RELATED PROCEDURES

II CCA [31]

52. Powers of court exercisable before commencement of action

(1) On the application of any person in accordance with rules of court, the county court shall, in such circumstances as may be prescribed, have power to make an order providing for any one or more of the following matters, that is to say—

(a) the inspection, photographing, preservation, custody and detention of property which appears to the court to be property which may become the subject-matter of subsequent proceedings in the court, or as to which any question may arise in any such proceedings; and

(b) the taking of samples of any such property as is mentioned in paragraph (a), and the carrying out of any experiment on or with any such property.

(2) On the application, in accordance with rules of court, of a person who appears to the county court to be likely to be a party to subsequent proceedings in that court [. . .] the county court shall, in such circumstances as may be prescribed, have power to order a person who appears to the court to be likely to be a party to the proceedings and to be likely to have or to have had in his possession, custody or power any documents which are relevant to an issue arising or likely to arise out of that claim—

(a) to disclose whether those documents are in his possession, custody or power; and

(b) to produce such of those documents as are in his possession, custody or power to the applicant or on such conditions as may be specified in the order,—

(i) to the applicant's legal advisers; or

(ii) to the applicant's legal advisers and any medical or other professional adviser of the applicant; or

(iii) if the applicant has no legal adviser, to any medical or other professional adviser of the applicant.

(3) This section is subject to any provision made under section 38.

COUNTY COURT

II CCA [31.1]

Extension of section 52 The Civil Procedure (Modification of Enactments) Order 1998, SI 1998/2940 amended the application of this section so it applies to all proceedings and is not limited to personal injury or death. For the procedure see **CPR 31.16**.

II CCA [31.2]

Provision made under section 38 Each of ss 52, 53 and 54 has been amended by the Courts and Legal Services Act 1990, Sch 18, so as to make their application subject to limitations on remedies laid down in regulations under s 38 (see para **II CCA [21]**). For the County Court Remedies Regulations 1991, SI 1991/1222, made under that section see the notes at paras **II CCA [21.1]–[21.11]**. These regulations do not limit the court's powers under any of these three sections.

II CCA [31.3]

"Likely to be a party" A would-be claimant should be treated as "likely to be a party" and, in general, limitation issues should not be taken into account on an application for pre-commencement disclosure unless it is plain beyond doubt that a limitation defence must succeed: *Harris v Newcastle Health Authority* [1989] 2 All ER 273, [1989] 1 WLR 96, CA. A Health Authority's obligation to make pre-action disclosure does not include a requirement that it provide an itemised list of every document that it has disclosed: *M v Plymouth Health Authority* [1993] 4 Med LR 108.

II CCA [31.4]

Medical records The claimant is now in any event entitled, subject to the limitations set out in the Act, to see his own medical records under the Access to Health Records Act 1990, though this right applies only to records made on or after 1 November 1991. It is subject to an exception in respect of records, disclosure of which would be likely to cause serious harm to the physical or mental health of a patient or of any other individual; a similar principle applies to records made before 1 November 1991: *R v Mid Glamorgan Family Health Services, ex p Martin* [1995] 1 All ER 356, [1995] 1 WLR 110, CA.

II CCA [32]

53. Power of court to order disclosure of documents, inspection of property etc in proceedings for personal injuries or death

(1) [. . .]

(2) On the application, in accordance with rules of court, of a party to any proceedings [. . .], the county court shall, in such circumstances as may be prescribed, have power to order a person who is not a party to the proceedings and who appears to the court to be likely to have in his possession, custody or power any documents which are relevant to any issue arising out of the said claim—

- (a) to disclose whether those documents are in his possession, custody or power; and
- (b) to produce such of those documents as are in his possession, custody or power to the applicant or, on such conditions as may be specified in the order,—
  - (i) to the applicant's legal advisers; or
  - (ii) to the applicant's legal advisers and any medical or other professional adviser of the applicant; or
  - (iii) if the applicant has no legal adviser, to any medical or other professional adviser of the applicant.

(3) On the application, in accordance with rules of court, of a party to any proceedings [. . .], the county court shall, in such circumstances as may be prescribed, have power to make an order providing for any one or more of the following matters, that is to say—

- (a) the inspection, photographing, preservation, custody and detention of property which is not the property of, or in the possession of, any party to the proceedings but which is the subject-matter of the proceedings or as to which any question arises in the proceedings;
- (b) the taking of samples of any such property as is mentioned in paragraph (a) and the carrying out of any experiment on or with any such property.

(4) The preceding provisions of this section are without prejudice to the exercise by the county court of any power to make orders which is exercisable apart from those provisions.

(5) This section is subject to any provision made under section 38.

II CCA [32.1]

Extension of s 53 The Civil Procedure (Modification of Enactments) Order 1998, SI 1998/2940 amended the application of this section so it applies to all proceedings and is not limited to personal injury or death. For the procedure see **CPR 31.17**.

II CCA [32.2]

Video recording Under this section the court may order the defendants to allow the claimants to make video recording of the process in which an injured claimant was engaged: *Ash v Buxted Poultry Ltd* (1989) Times, 29 November.

II CCA [33]

54. Provisions supplementary to sections 52 and 53

(1) The county court shall not make an order under section 52 or 53 if it considers that compliance with the order, if made, would be likely to be injurious to the public interest.

(2) Rules of court may make provision as to the circumstances in which an order under section 52 or 53 can be made; and any rules making such provision may include such incidental, supplementary and consequential provisions as the Civil Procedure Rule Committee may consider necessary or expedient.

(3) Without prejudice to the generality of subsection (2), rules of court shall be made for the purpose of ensuring that the costs of and incidental to proceedings for an order under section 52(2) or 53 incurred by the person against whom the order is sought shall be awarded to that person unless the court otherwise directs.

(4) Sections 52(2) and 53 and this section bind the Crown; and section 52(1) binds the Crown so far as it relates to property as to which it appears to the court that it may become the subject-matter of subsequent proceedings involving a claim in respect of personal injuries to a person or in respect of a person's death.

In this subsection references to the Crown do not include references to Her Majesty in Her private capacity or to Her Majesty in right of Her Duchy of Lancaster or to the Duke of Cornwall.

(5) In sections 52 and 53 and this section—

"property" includes any land, chattel or other corporal property of any description;

"personal injuries" includes any disease and any impairment of a person's physical or mental condition.

(6) This section is subject to any provision made under section 38.

COUNTY COURT

WITNESSES AND EVIDENCE

II CCA [34]

55. Penalty for neglecting or refusing to give evidence

(1) Subject to subsections (2) and (3), any person who—

(a) having been summoned in pursuance of rules of court as a witness in the county court refuses or neglects, without sufficient cause, to appear or to produce any documents required by the summons to be produced; or

(b) having been so summoned or being present in court and being required to give evidence, refuses to be sworn or give evidence,

shall forfeit such fine as the court may direct.

(2) The court shall not have power under subsection (1) to direct that a person shall forfeit a fine of an amount exceeding £1,000.

(3) No person summoned in pursuance of rules of court as a witness in the county court shall forfeit a fine under this section unless there has been paid or tendered to him at the time of the service of the summons such sum in respect of his expenses (including, in such cases as may be prescribed, compensation for loss of time) as may be prescribed for the purposes of this section.

(4) The court may at its discretion direct that the whole or any part of any such fine, after deducting the costs, shall be applicable towards indemnifying the party injured by the refusal or neglect.

(4A) *Repealed.*

(5) This section does not apply to a debtor summoned to attend by a judgment summons.

II CCA [34.1]

Failure by party to appear Section 12 of the Courts and Legal Services Act 1990 (when brought into force) will enable the High Court or a county court to fine a party who fails to attend a hearing or who fails to give notice of his inability to attend; such a fine is not to exceed level 3 on the standard scale (s 12(4)).

II CCA [35]

56. Examination of witnesses abroad

The High Court shall have the same power to issue a commission, request or order to examine witnesses abroad for the purpose of proceedings in the county court as it has for the purpose of an action or matter in the High Court.

II CCA [35.1]

Procedure For the relevant procedure, see para **CPR 34.13** and in relation to the taking of depositions from witnesses in other Regulation States, the procedure is governed by Council Regulation (EC) No 1206/2001: see para **CPR 34.23**.

II CCA [36]

57. Evidence of prisoners

(1) Subject to subsection (2), in any proceedings pending before the county court, the court may, if it thinks fit, upon application on affidavit by any party, issue an order for bringing up before the court any person (in this section referred to as a "prisoner") confined in any place under any sentence or under committal for trial or otherwise, to be examined as a witness in the proceedings.

(2) No such order shall be made with respect to a person confined under process in any civil action or matter.

(3) Subject to subsection (4) the prisoner mentioned in any such order shall be brought before the court under the same custody, and shall be dealt with in the same manner in all respects, as a prisoner required by a writ of habeas corpus to be brought before the High Court and examined there as a witness.

(4) The person having the custody of the prisoner shall not be bound to obey the order unless there is tendered to him a reasonable sum for the conveyance and maintenance of a proper officer or officers and of the prisoner in going to, remaining at, and returning from, the court.

(5) This section applies in relation to the family court as it applies in relation to the county court.

II CCA [36.1]

Practice In cases where a prisoner is party to the proceedings and a production order is necessary to secure his or her attendance at court, a court will generally be prepared to issue an order based on an informal application and it would appear that the practice of the prison service is not to require payment for any expenses incurred in the process.

II CCA [37]

58. Persons who may take affidavits for use in county courts

(1) An affidavit to be used in the county court may be sworn before—

(a) a judge of the county court; or

(b) any justice of the peace; or

(c) an officer of the county court appointed by a judge of the county court for the purpose,

as well as before a commissioner for oaths or any other person authorised to take affidavits under the Commissioners for Oaths Acts 1889 and 1891 [. . .]

(2) An affidavit sworn before any such judge or officer may be sworn without the payment of any fee

II CCA [37.1]

Commissioner for oaths Section 113 of the Courts and Legal Services Act 1990 gives to "authorised persons" (defined by s 119 to include barristers) the powers enjoyed by commissioners for oaths; public notaries have the same powers as commissioners: Administration of Justice Act 1985 s 65.

II CCA [37.2]

Legal executives Legal executives may take affidavits: Commissioners for Oaths (Prescribed Bodies) Regulations 1995, SI 1995/1676.

II CCA [37.3]

Licensed conveyancers Licensed conveyancers may take affidavits: Commissioners for Oaths (Prescribed Bodies) Regulations 1994, SI 1994/1380.

II CCA [37.4]

Family proceedings Section 58 is extended for family proceedings, see Family Proceedings Rules 1991 r 10. 13.

II CCA [38]

59. ***Evidence in Admiralty proceedings***

Repealed.

RIGHT OF AUDIENCE

II CCA [39]

60. Rights of audience

(1) [. . .]

(2) Where an action is brought in the county court by a local authority for either or both of the following—

(a) the recovery of possession of a house belonging to the authority;

(b) the recovery of any rent, mesne profits, damages or other sum claimed by the authority in respect of the occupation by any person of such a house,

then, except where rules of court provide otherwise, any officer of the authority authorised by the authority for the purpose may address the court.

(3) In this section—

"local authority" means a county council, [...] a district council, the Broads Authority, any National Park authority, a London borough council, a police and crime commissioner, the Mayor's Office for Policing and Crime [...], a joint authority established by Part IV of the Local Government Act 1985, an economic prosperity board established under section 88 of the Local Democracy, Economic Development and Construction Act 2009, a combined authority established under section 103 of that Act, a fire and rescue authority created by an order under section 4A of the Fire and Rescue Services Act 2004, the London Fire Commissioner or the Common Council of the City of London; and

"house" includes a part of a house, a flat or any other dwelling and also includes any yard, garden, outhouse or appurtenance occupied with a house or part of a house or with a flat or other dwelling,

and any reference to the occupation of a house by a person includes a reference to anything done by that person, or caused or permitted by him to be done, in relation to the house as occupier of the house, whether under a tenancy or licence or otherwise.

II CCA [39.1]

Rights of audience See paras **III SOL [38]–III SOL [39]**, for the rights arising under the Courts and Legal Services Act 1990, ss 27 and 28 including the right of audience in chambers of persons employed to assist in the conduct of litigation *Re HS (minors) (chambers proceedings: rights of audience)* [1998] 3 FCR 245, [1998] 1 FLR 868, CA. See CPR 39.6 (see para **CPR 39.6**) for the discretion to allow a corporation to be represented by an employee or director and see para **III SOL [48.5]** for the further discretion to allow a friend of a litigant in person to give assistance at the hearing.

II CCA [40]

61. Right of audience by direction of Lord Chancellor

(1) The Lord Chancellor may, with the concurrence of the Lord Chief Justice, at any time direct that such categories of persons in relevant legal employment as may be specified in the direction may address the court in any proceedings in the county court, or in proceedings in the county court of such description as may be so specified.

(2) In subsection (1), "relevant legal employment" means employment which consists of or includes giving assistance in the conduct of litigation to a [legal representative] whether in private practice or not.

(3) A direction under this section may be given subject to such conditions and restrictions as appear to the Lord Chancellor to be necessary or expedient, and may be expressed to have effect as respects every place where the county court sits or or as respects one or more specified places where the county court sits.

(3A) Subsections (1) to (3) apply in relation to the family court as they apply in relation to the county court.

(4) The power to give directions conferred by this section includes a power to vary or rescind any direction given under this section.

(5) The Lord Chief Justice may nominate a judicial office holder (as defined in section 109(4) of the Constitutional Reform Act 2005) to exercise his functions under this section.

II CCA [40.1]

Directions On 1 April the Lord Chancellor gave the County Courts (Right of Audience) Direction 1978 in the following terms–

Right of audience in county courts direction by the Lord Chancellor under section 89A of the County Courts Act 1959

In exercise of the power conferred on him by section 89A of the County Courts Act 1959 (as inserted by section 16 of the Administration of Justice Act 1977) the Lord Chancellor hereby directs that—

1. A Fellow of the Institute of Legal Executives whose employment consists of or includes giving assistance in the conduct of litigation to a solicitor, whether in private practice or not, may address the court in any of the following proceedings in a county court in which that solicitor is acting, namely—
   (a) an unopposed application for an adjournment; or
   (b) an application for judgment by consent (except where, notwithstanding the consent, a question arises as to the applicant's entitlement to the judgment or its terms).
2. This Direction may be cited as the County Courts (Right of Audience) Direction 1978 and shall come into force on 1st April 1978.

See now the Institute of Legal Executives Order 1998, SI 1998/1077, art 2 whereby the Institute of Legal Executives is designated as an authorised body for the purposes of s 27 of the Courts and Legal Services Act 1990 (rights of audience). The Institute is enabled to grant limited extended rights of audience to suitably qualified Fellows.

MODE OF TRIAL

II CCA [41]

62. General power of judge to determine questions of fact and law

Subject to the provisions of this Act and of rules of court, a judge of the county court shall be the sole judge in all proceedings brought in the court, and shall determine all questions of fact as well as of law.

II CCA [41.1]

"Shall Determine" It is the duty of the judge to set out a coherent narrative of events based on factual findings and clearly to identify and list the issues: *Heffer v Tiffin Green (a firm)* (1998) Times, 28 December, CA.

II CCA [41.2]

Determining issues of foreign law On matters of statutory interpretation where there is no evidence that foreign rules of construction are different, the English Court may properly interpret according to English rules: *Macmillan Inc v Bishopsgate Investment Trust plc (No 4)* (1998) Times, 7 December, CA.

II CCA [41.3]

Questions of Community law The meaning of a provision of Community law is a matter for legal argument, not factual proof: European Communities Act 1972 s 3(1) (see para **III EUR [4]**). In interpreting domestic legislation the courts should endeavour to construe ambiguities in a way which is compatible with Treaty obligations: *R v Secretary of State for the Home Department, ex p Brind* [1991] 1 AC 696, sub nom *Brind v Secretary of State for the Home Department* [1991] 1 All ER 720, HL. But if such a provision is not possible the statutory provision which is incompatible must be declared inapplicable: *Customs and Excise Comrs v Apple and Pear Development Council* [1987] 2 CMLR 634, HL.

II CCA [41.4]

Treaty of Amsterdam The Treaty of Amsterdam, replacing the Treaty of Rome contains 314 Articles which provides for the setting up of a common market in which the suppliers of goods and services may operate across member state boundaries and compete on an equal footing with other suppliers within the Community. Some articles create rights and obligations with direct effect, eg art 141 (equal pay) and the decision in *Barber v Guardian Royal Exchange Assurance Group:* C-262/88 [1991] 1 QB 344, [1990] 2 All ER 660, ECJ. Others, although not of direct effect, may nevertheless be relied on in proceedings against the state or emanations of the state: *Marshall v Southampton and South West Hampshire Area Health Authority (Teaching):* 152/84 [1986] QB 401, [1986] 2 All ER 584, ECJ; *Foster v British Gas plc*: C-188/89 [1991] 1 QB 405, [1990] 3 All ER 897, ECJ. However, a directive which requires member states to adopt rules specifically intended to govern relations between private individuals may not be relied on in proceedings between such persons in the absence of measures to transpose the directive into national law, although, when applying provisions of national law, the national court should consider these provisions as far as possible in the light of the wording and purpose of the directive: *Faccini Dori v Recreb Srl*: C-91/92 [1995] All ER (EC) 1, [1994] ECR 1-3325, ECJ.

II CCA [41.5]

Reference to European Court When a question of Community law is raised in county court proceedings the judge has a discretion to refer it to the European Court of Justice for a preliminary ruling under Art 234; otherwise he or she must decide it. But Community legislation, such as a regulation or directive, may not be declared invalid by a court in a member state; only the European Court of Justice is competent to give such a ruling: *Foto-Frost v Hauptzollamt Lübeck-Ost*: 314/85 [1987] ECR 4199, ECJ. Reference procedure is set out in **CPR 68.1** onwards.

II CCA [41.6]

Convention rights In determining a question which has arisen in connection with a Convention right, a court must take into account a judgment or opinion of the European Court of Human Rights: Human Rights Act 1998 s 2. See **III HUM [8]**.

COUNTY COURT

II CCA [42]

63. Assessors

(1) In any proceedings [in the county court a judge of the court] may, if he thinks fit . . ., summon to his assistance, in such manner as may be prescribed, one or more persons of skill and experience in the matter to which the proceedings relate who may be willing to sit with the judge and act as assessors.

(2) ...

[(1) In any proceedings in the county court a judge of the court may, on the application of a party to the proceedings, summon to his assistance one or more persons—

(a) of skill and experience in the matter to which the proceedings relate; and

(b) who may be willing to sit with him and act as assessors.

(2) In any proceedings prescribed for the purposes of this subsection a judge of the county court may summon to his assistance one or more such persons even though no application has been made for him to do so.

(2A) *Repealed.*

(2B) *Repealed*

(2C) The summons shall be made in such manner as may be prescribed.]

(3) Subject to subsection (4), the remuneration of assessors for sitting under this section shall be determined by the court and shall be costs in the proceedings unless otherwise ordered by the court.

(4) Where one or more assessors are summoned for the purposes of assisting a judge in reviewing the taxation of the costs of any proceedings the remuneration of any such assessor—

(a) shall be at such rate as may be determined by the Lord Chancellor with the approval of the Treasury; and

(b) shall be payable out of moneys provided by Parliament.

[(4) In such cases as may be specified by order made by the Lord Chancellor with the consent of the Treasury, the remuneration of any assessor summoned under this section shall be paid, at such rate as may be so specified, out of money provided by Parliament.

(4A) Any power to make an order under subsection (4) shall be exercisable by statutory instrument subject to annulment by resolution of either House of Parliament.]

(5) Where any person is proposed to be summoned as an assessor, objection to him, either personally or in respect of his qualification, may be taken by any party in the prescribed manner.

Amendment *Sub-sections (1) and (2) substituted by new sub-ss (1) to (2C) and new sub-ss (4) and (4A) substituted by the Courts and Legal Services Act 1990, from a date to be appointed.*

II CCA [42.1]

Assessors Assessors are merely advisers of the judge and the judge ought to decide in accordance with his own opinions as to the law and merits of the case: *The Aid* (1881) 6 PD 84. **CPR 35.15** (see para **CPR 35.15**).

III CCA [42.2]

Practice and procedure The practice regarding the appointment of assessors is set out in **CPR PD 35.10**. In specified proceedings for contravention of the Equality Act 2010, s 114 provides that the power to appoint assessors must be exercised "unless the judge is satisfied that there are good reasons for not doing so". For the recommended practice in regard to the appointment of assessors in discrimination cases see the extensive guidance in *Cary v Comr of Police of the Metropolis (Equality and Human Rights Commission intervening)* [2014] EWCA Civ 987, [2015] ICR 71, [2014] EqLR 707. Provision is made by CPR 35.15 for the role of an assessor on appointment.

II CCA [43]

64. Reference to arbitration

(1) Rules of court—

(a) may prescribe cases in which proceedings in the county court are (without any order of the court) to be referred to arbitration; and

(b) may prescribe the manner in which and the terms on which cases are to be so referred; and

(c) may, where cases are so referred, require other matters within the jurisdiction of the court in dispute between the parties also to be referred to arbitration.

(2) Rules of court—

(a) may prescribe cases in which proceedings in the county court may be referred to arbitration by order of the court; and

(b) may authorise the court also to order other matters in dispute between the parties and within the jurisdiction of the court to be so referred.

(2A) Rules of court may prescribe the procedures and rules of evidence to be followed on any reference under subsection (1) or (2).

(2B) Rules made under subsection (2A) may, in particular, make provision with respect to the manner of taking and questioning evidence.

(3) On a reference under subsection (1) or (2) the award of the arbitrator, arbitrators or umpire shall be entered as the judgment in the proceedings and shall be as binding and effectual to all intents, subject to subsection (4), as if it had been given by the court.

(4) The court may, if it thinks fit, on application made to it within such time as may be prescribed, set aside the award, or may, with the consent of the parties, revoke the reference or order another reference to be made in the manner specified in this section.

(5) In this section "award" includes an interim award.

II CCA [43.1]

Arbitration Act 1996 Section 92 of the Arbitration Act 1996 disapplies that Act in relation to references to arbitration under s 64.

II CCA [43.2]

Small claims Provision is made by **CPR 26.6** (see para **CPR 26.6**) for the allocation to the small claims track of disputed claims involving £10,000 or less (or in the case of housing repairs or personal injury £1,000).

II CCA [44]

65. Power of judge to refer to district judge or referee

(1) Subject to rules of court, a judge of the county court may refer to another judge of the county court or a referee for inquiry and report—

(a) any proceedings which require any prolonged examination of documents or any scientific or local investigation which cannot, in the opinion of the judge, conveniently be made before him;

(b) any proceedings where the question in dispute consists wholly or in part of matters of account;

(c) with the consent of the parties, any other proceedings;

(d) subject to any right to have particular cases tried with a jury, any question arising in any proceedings.

(2) *Repealed.*

(3) Where any proceedings or question are referred under subsection (1), a judge of the county court may direct how the reference shall be conducted, and may remit any report for further inquiry and report, and on consideration of any report or further report may give such judgment or make such order in the proceedings as may be just.

(4) A judge of the county court may, after deciding or reserving any question of liability, refer to another judge of the county court any mere matter of account which is in dispute between the parties and, after deciding the question of liability, may give judgment on the other judge's report.

II CCA [44.1]

Procedure It is a nullity to refer the whole case for inquiry and report including proceedings outside s 65(1)(a) and (b): *Morgan v Cullen* [1936] 2 KB 324, [1936] 2 All ER 147, CA, in which the reference was held to be a nullity. The same applies to a reference to determine whether a person is a statutory tenant or whether rent book entries are forgeries: *Butler v Hudson* [1953] 2 QB 407, [1953] 2 All ER 418, CA.

JURIES

II CCA [45]

66. Trial by jury

(1) In the following proceedings in the county court the trial shall be without a jury—

(a) Admiralty proceedings;

(b) proceedings arising—

(i) under Part I, II or III of the Rent (Agriculture) Act 1976, or

(ii) under any provision of the Rent Act 1977 other than a provision contained in Part V, sections 103 to 106 or Part IX, or

(iii) under Part I of the Protection from Eviction Act 1977 or

(iv) under Part I of the Housing Act 1988;

(c) any appeal to the county court under the Housing Act 1985.

(2) In all other proceedings in the county court the trial shall be without a jury unless the court otherwise orders on an application made in that behalf by any party to the proceedings in such manner and within such time before the trial as may be prescribed.

(3) Where, on any such application, the court is satisfied that there is in issue—

(a) a charge of fraud against the party making the application; or

(b) a claim in respect of malicious prosecution or false imprisonment; or

(c) any question or issue of a kind prescribed for the purposes of this paragraph,

the action shall be tried with a jury, unless the court is of opinion that the trial requires any prolonged examination of documents or accounts or any scientific or local investigation which cannot conveniently be made with a jury.

(4) There shall be payable, in respect of the trial with a jury of proceedings in the county court, such fees as may be prescribed by the fees orders.

II CCA [45.1]

Discretion as to jury See para **II SCA [56.1]**. For notes on the court's discretion as to ordinary trial by jury and related topics see notes to s 69 of the Supreme Court Act 1981 at paras **II SCA [56.1]–II SCA [56.3]**.

II CCA [45.2]

Convenience See para **II SCA [56.2]**.

II CCA [45.3]

Transfer from High Court As for transfer of High Court jury actions to the county court see *Practice Note* [1989] 2 All ER 128, sub nom *Practice Statement* [1989] 1 WLR 1179.

II CCA [46]

67. Impanelling and swearing of jury

Where any proceedings in the county court are to be tried with a jury, eight jurymen shall be impanelled and sworn as occasion requires to give their verdicts in the proceedings brought before them, and being once sworn need not be re-sworn in each trial.

II CCA [46.1]

Majority verdicts The verdict need not be unanimous if seven jurymen agree on a verdict. The court may not accept a majority verdict unless the jury has had a reasonable period of time for deliberation. This, however, is without prejudice to any practice by which the parties may agree to proceed with an incomplete jury. See the Juries Act 1974 s 17.

II CCA [46.2]

Challenge Peremptory challenge was abolished by Criminal Justice Act 1988 s 118. Any party to county court proceedings has the same right of challenge to the jurors as in the High Court: Juries Act 1974 s 12.

II CCA [47]

68. Duty of judge to determine foreign law in jury trials

Where, for the purpose of disposing of any proceedings which are being tried in the county court by a judge of the court with a jury, it is necessary to ascertain the law of any other country which is applicable to the facts of the case, any question as to the effect of the evidence given with respect to that law shall, instead of being submitted to the jury, be decided by the judge alone.

II CCA [47.1]

Proof of foreign law The proof of foreign law is regulated by the Civil Evidence Act 1979 s 4. For procedure see **CPR 33.7**. Note, however, that Community law does not have to be proved as a fact: European Communities Act 1972 s 3(1).

INTEREST ON DEBTS AND DAMAGES

II CCA [48]

69. Power to award interest on debts and damages

(1) Subject to rules of court, in proceedings (whenever instituted) before the county court for the recovery of a debt or damages there may be included in any sum for which judgment is given simple interest, at such rate as the court thinks fit or as may be prescribed, on all or any part of the debt or damages in respect of which judgment is given, or payment is made before judgment, for all or any part of the period between the date when the cause of action arose and—

(a) in the case of any sum paid before judgment, the date of the payment; and

(b) in the case of the sum for which judgment is given, the date of the judgment.

(2) In relation to a judgment given for damages for personal injuries or death which exceed £200 subsection (1) shall have effect—

(a) with the substitution of "shall be included" for "may be included"; and

(b) with the addition of "unless the court is satisfied that there are special reasons to the contrary" after "given", where first occurring.

(3) Subject to rules of court, where—

(a) there are proceedings (whenever instituted) before the county court for the recovery of a debt; and

(b) the defendant pays the whole debt to the plaintiff (otherwise than in pursuance of a judgment in the proceedings),

the defendant shall be liable to pay the plaintiff simple interest, at such rate as the court thinks fit or as may be prescribed, on all or any part of the debt for all or any part of the period between the date when the cause of action arose and the date of the payment.

(4) Interest in respect of a debt shall not be awarded under this section for a period during which, for whatever reason, interest on the debt already runs.

(5) Interest under this section may be calculated at different rates in respect of different periods.

(6) In this section "plaintiff" means the person seeking the debt or damages and "defendant" means the person from whom the plaintiff seeks the debt or damages and "personal injuries" includes any disease and any impairment of a person's physical or mental condition.

COUNTY COURT

(7) Nothing in this section affects the damages recoverable for the dishonour of a bill of exchange.

(8) In determining whether the amount of any debt or damages exceeds that prescribed by or under any enactment, no account shall be taken of any interest payable by virtue of this section except where express provision to the contrary is made by or under that or any other enactment.

II CCA [48.1]

Jurisdiction to award interest The terms of s 69 are the same as those of Senior Courts Act 1981, s 35A and the county courts have the same powers as the High Court. For a commentary on their scope and exercise see para **II SCA [36.1]–II SCA [36.6]**. The Court of Appeal commented, in *Adcock v Co-operative Insurance Society Ltd* (2000) Times, 26 April, that penalising a dilatory claimant by disallowing part of a claim for interest could result in a defendant obtaining an unjustified windfall.

II CCA [48.2]

Deduction of tax Statutory interest is 'yearly interest' for the purposes of section 874 of the Income Tax Act 2007 and anyone liable to pay statutory interest must deduct tax at the basic rate and remit it to the tax authorities: *Re Lehman Bros International (Europe) (In administration) (No 7) v Revenue and Customs Comrs* [2017] EWCA Civ 2124, (2018) Times 24 January.

JUDGMENTS AND ORDERS

II CCA [49]

70. Finality of judgments and orders

Every judgment and order of the county court shall, except as provided by this or any other Act or as may be prescribed, be final and conclusive between the parties.

II CCA [49.1]

Final and conclusive Once a judgment is made and entered, the judge cannot, except by consent, alter it: *Irving v Askew* (1870) LR 5 QB 208; *The Recepta* [1893] P 255, CA. But a judge has power under CPR 40.12 to correct accidental slips and errors: *Moore v Buchanan* [1967] 3 All ER 273, [1967] 1 WLR 1341, CA. Moreover, until the order is drawn up the judge may recall it and alter it, without permitting counsel to make further submissions: *Hyde and South Bank Housing Association v Kain* (1989) 133 Sol Jo 1578, Times, 30 August (1989), CA. Conversely, a judge who has reserved judgment is entitled to refuse to consider a point drawn to his attention only after judgment has been reserved: *Sella House Ltd v Mears* (1988) 21 HLR 147, CA.

Where a judgment omits to deal with a particular issue, raised by the defendant, and the judge gives a second judgment, after hearing submissions, and states reasons for deciding the issue in the claimant's favour, the Court of Appeal may take account of the reasons in the second judgment as grounds for upholding the first: *Roche v Chief Constable of Greater Manchester Police* [2005] EWCA Civ 1454, (2005) Times, 10 November.

II CCA [49.2]

Issue estoppel Issue estoppel can be established by an inferior court: *Crown Estate Comrs v Dorset County Council* [1990] Ch 297, [1990] 1 All ER 19. As to the scope of issue estoppel see *Arnold v National Westminster Bank plc* [1990] Ch 573, [1990] 1 All ER 529, CA and, for a case where the estoppel was upheld in separate proceedings between different parties, see *North West Water Ltd v Binnie & Partners* [1990] 3 All ER 547. A bank which obtains a money judgment on a mortgage securing "all monies and liabilities" is estopped from bringing a separate action in respect of monies due from the same debtor upon a personal guarantee: *Lloyds Bank plc v Hawkins* [1998] 47 EG 137, CA.

II CCA [49.3]

Ex parte order The court may set aside an order made ex parte, but only where the applicant is a party or a person who is entitled to be a party: *Jones v Vans Colina* [1997] 1 All ER 768, CA.

II CCA [49.4]

Death of judge before delivering judgment Where a judge dies after preparing but before delivering a reserved judgment it would seem that (unless the parties consent to judgment according to the terms of the written judgment) a new trial is necessary. A decision cannot be said to be effective until it has been communicated to the parties in some way: *R v Greater Manchester Valuation Panel, ex p Shell Chemicals (UK) Ltd* [1982] QB 255, [1981] 3 WLR 752. Where one judge dies and a second takes over the hearing it may be proper to read over the notes of evidence taken, provided that there is no conflict of evidence: *Coleshill v Manchester Corpn* [1928] 1 KB 776, CA; *Bolton v Bolton* [1949] 2 All ER 908; *The Forest Lake* [1968] P 270, [1966] 3 All ER 833. As to the reimbursement of additional costs resulting from the death or incapacity of the judge, see the Administration of Justice Act 1985 s 53.

II CCA [49.5]

Staying proceedings on judgment The power to stay proceedings on a judgment, exercisable by the district judge under CPR Sch 2 CCR Ord 25 r 8 (see para **CCR 25r8**), arises under ss 71 and 88.

II CCA [50]

71. Satisfaction of judgments and orders for payment of money

(1) Where a judgment is given or an order is made by the county court under which a sum of money of any amount is payable, whether by way of satisfaction of the claim or counterclaim in the proceedings or by way of costs or otherwise, the court may, as it thinks fit, order the money to be paid either—

(a) in one sum, whether forthwith or within such period as the court may fix; or

(b) by such instalments payable at such times as the court may fix.

(2) If at any time it appears to the satisfaction of the county court that any party to any proceedings in the court is unable from any cause to pay any sum recovered against him (whether by way of satisfaction of the claim or counterclaim in the proceedings or by way of costs or otherwise) or any instalment of such a sum, the court may, in its discretion, suspend or stay any judgment or order given or made in the proceedings for such time and on such terms as the court thinks fit, and so from time to time until it appears that the cause of inability has ceased

(3) Subsections (1) and (2), so far as relating to costs, apply in relation to the family court as they apply in relation to the county court.

II CCA [50.1]

Execution in default of payment of instalments Section 86 (see para **II CCA [84]**).

II CCA [50.2]

Suspension of possession There is no inconsistency in making a suspended possession order coupled with a money judgment for the whole mortgage debt, suspended for so long as the order for possession is suspended: *Cheltenham and Gloucester Building Society v Grattidge and Grattidge* (1993) 25 HLR 454, CA.

II CCA [50.3]

Execution A stay of execution only prevents the claimant from putting into operation the machinery of the law, it does not prevent him exercising any right or remedy he may have apart from the process of the court: *Clifton Securities Ltd v Huntley* [1948] 2 All ER 283.

II CCA [50.4]

Reserve and Auxiliary Forces (Protection of Civil Interests) Act 1951 Persons in the armed forces are protected against the enforcement of certain judgments without leave.

II CCA [51]

72. Set-off in cases of cross judgments in county courts and High Court

(1) Where one person has obtained a judgment or order in the county court against another person, and that other person has obtained a judgment or order against the first-mentioned person in the county court or in the High Court,

either such person may, in accordance with rules of court, give notice in writing to the court or the several courts as the case may be, and may apply to the court or any of the said courts in accordance with rules of court for leave to set off any sums, including costs, payable under the several judgments or orders.

(2) Upon any such application, the set-off may be allowed in accordance with the practice for the time being in force in the High Court as to the allowance of set-off and in particular in relation to any solicitor's lien for costs.

(3) Where the cross judgments or orders have not been obtained in the same court, a copy of the order made on any such application shall be sent by the proper officer of the court to which the application is made to the proper officer of the other court.

GENERAL NOTES ON SECTIONS 73–73A

II CCA [52]

Register of judgments, orders and fines Sections 73 and 73A of the County Courts Act 1984 relating to the registration of county court judgments were repealed by the Courts Act 2003. The registration of county court judgments is now determined by regulations made under s 98 of the Courts Act 2003. The relevant regulations are set out in the Register of Judgments, Orders and Fines Regulations 2005, SI 2005/3595 consolidating the Register of County Court Judgments Regulations 1985 (SI 1985/1807 as amended by SI 1990/491, SI 1990/768, SI 1991/1815, SI 1993/710 and SI 1993/2173) and the Register of Fines Regulations 2003 (SI 2003/3184). The new Regulations provide for:

(a) judgments, administration orders and fines to be registered (regs 8 and 9);
(b) cancellation of entries in the register and endorsement of notices against entries (regs 11 to 17)
(c) certification of to the payment in full of a debt owed under a judgment or administration otrder and as to payment in full of a fine (regs 18 to 20);
(d) amendment of entries in the register (regs 21 to 26);
(e) removalof an entry in the register (reg 27);
(f) searches of the register and provision of certified copies (regs 28 and 29); and
(g) refusal of access to the register and appeals against that refusal (reg 30).

II CCA [52.1]

Set-off of Costs awarded by a Tribunal The High Court has jurisdiction to permit a set-off under this section of costs ordered by the VAT and Duties Tribunal (and assessed by the Supreme Court Costs Office) to be paid by Revenue and Customs Commissioners so as to set-off that amount against a judgment for unpaid tax, but will not necessarily exercise its discretion to allow the set-off: *Revenue and Customs Commissioners v Xicom Systems Ltd* [2008] EWHC 1945 (Ch), [2008] All ER (D) 39 (Aug).

II CCA [53]

Register of Judgments, Orders and Fines Regulations 2005, SI 2005/3595 The register is now by agreement of the Lord Chancellor kept by Registry Trust Ltd at 173/175 Cleveland Street, London W1P 5PE (telephone: 020 7380 0133; e-mail: info@registry-trust.org.uk).

Under the Civil Proceedings Fees Order 2004, a fee of £15 is payable on a request to cancel the registration of a judgment which has been satisfied. The fee is payable at the court at which satisfaction is made. Fees for searches of the Register are payable to Registry Trust Ltd and currently stand at £8.00 per name and address to be searched.

For the purposes of the regulations "judgment" does not include a "Tomlin" Order staying an action on agreed terms, even if one of the terms is that the defendant do pay the plaintiff a specified sum of money.

The main text of the Register of Judgments, Orders and Fines Regulations 2005, SI 2005/3595, as amended by SI 2009/474, is as follows:

II CCA [54]

1. Citation, commencement and duration

These Regulations may be cited as the Register of Judgments, Orders and Fines Regulations 2005.

II CCA [55]

2.

These Regulations shall come into force—

(a) for the purposes of this regulation and regulations 1 and 4, on the day after the day on which these Regulations are made; and

(b) for all other purposes, on 6th April 2006.

II CCA [56]

3. Interpretation

In these Regulations—

"the 1998 Rules" means the Civil Procedure Rules 1998;

"the Act" means the Courts Act 2003;

"Administrative Court" has the same meaning as in Part 54 of the 1998 Rules;

"amendment notice" means the notice given to the Registrar in accordance with regulation 21;

"applicable charge" means the charge fixed by the Lord Chancellor in accordance with section 98(4) of the Act, or in accordance with section 98(4) as applied by section 98(7)(b) of the Act;

"appropriate officer" means—

(a) in the case of the High Court or a county court, an officer of the court in which the judgment is entered;

(b) in the case of a registration under paragraph 38(1)(b) of Schedule 5 to the Act—

(i) where a fines officer exercises the power to register following service of a notice under paragraph 37(6)(b) of that Schedule, that officer; or

(ii) where a court exercises the power to register by virtue of paragraph 39(3) or (4) of that Schedule, an officer of that court;

(c) in respect of a liability order designated for the purposes of section 33(5) of the Child Support Act 1991, the Secretary of State;

"appropriate fee" means the fee prescribed under section 92(1) of the Act;

"certificate of satisfaction" means the certificate applied for under regulation 17;

"data protection principles" means the principles set out in Part 1 of Schedule 1 to the Data Protection Act 1998, as read subject to Part 2 of that Schedule and section 27(1) of that Act;

"debt" means the sum of money owed by virtue of a judgment, administration order or fine, and "debtor" means the individual, incorporated or unincorporated body liable to pay that sum;

"family proceedings" has the same meaning as in section 63 (interpretation) of the Family Law Act 1996;

"judgment" means any judgment or order of the court for a sum of money and, in respect of a county court, includes a liability order designated by the Secretary of State for the purposes of section 33(5) of the Child Support Act 1991;

"Local Justice Area" means the area specified in an order made under section 8(2) of the Act;

"Registrar" means—

(a) where the Register is kept by a body corporate in accordance with section 98(6) of the Act, that body corporate; or

(b) otherwise, the Lord Chancellor;

"the Register" means the register kept in accordance with section 98(1) of the Act;

"satisfied", in relation to a debt, means that the debt has been paid in full, and "satisfaction" is to be construed accordingly;

"Technology and Construction Court" has the same meaning as in Part 60 of the 1998 Rules.

II CCA [57]

4. Amendment to the Register of Fines Regulations 2003

In regulation 1(2) of the Register of Fines Regulations 2003, for "31st March 2006" substitute "6th April 2006".

II CCA [58]

5. Performance of steps under these Regulations

Any step to be taken under these Regulations by the appropriate officer or the Registrar shall be taken—

(a) in respect of—

(i) the registration of judgments to which regulation 8(1)(a) applies; and

(ii) the registration of administration orders to which regulation 8(1)(b) applies,

within one working day;

(b) in respect of the registration of sums to which regulation 8(1)(c) applies, as soon as may be reasonably practicable.

II CCA [59]

Return For the form of return of a judgment for registration, cancellation or satisfaction, see Form N442. Where a judgment is transferred to another court before it is due to be registered, it remains the responsibility of the court of judgment to effect the registration but before doing so it will inquire of the court of transfer whether the judgment has been satisfied.

II CCA [60]

6. Manner, etc, in which the Register is to be kept

(1) Where the Registrar is a body corporate, the Register shall be kept in accordance with the terms of the agreement between the Lord Chancellor and that body.

(2) The terms of the agreement between the Lord Chancellor and the body corporate shall specify—

(a) the manner in which the Register is to be kept;

(b) the form of the Register; and

(c) the place at which the Register is to be kept.

II CCA [61]

7

Where the Registrar is not a body corporate, the Register shall be kept by the Lord Chancellor in such a manner and at such a place as he shall determine.

II CCA [62]

8. Registration of judgments, administration orders and fines

(1) The appropriate officer shall send to the Registrar a return of—

(a) subject to regulation 9, every judgment entered in—

(i) the High Court; and

(ii) a county court;

(b) every administration order made under section 112 of the County Courts Act 1984 (power of county courts to make administration orders);

(c) every sum to be registered by virtue of paragraph 38(1)(b) of Schedule 5 to the Act (further steps available against defaulters).

(2) Following receipt of a return sent in accordance with paragraph (1), the Registrar shall record the details of the return as an entry in the Register.

II CCA [63]

9. Exempt judgments—High Court and county courts

Regulation 8(1)(a) does not apply to—

(a) any judgment made—

(i) in family proceedings;

(ii) by the Administrative Court; or

(iii) by the Technology and Construction Court;

(b) any judgment made in proceedings which are the subject of an appeal under Part 52 of the 1998 Rules, until that appeal has been determined;

(c) any judgment, other than a liability order designated under section 33(5) of the Child Support Act 1991, where the hearing was contested, until—

(i) an order is made for payment by instalments following an application by the judgment creditor;

(ii) an application is made for payment by instalments by the judgment debtor;

(iii) the judgment creditor takes any step to enforce the judgment under Part 70 of the 1998 Rules (general rules about enforcement of judgments and orders);

(iv) the judgment creditor applies for an order under Part 71 of the 1998 Rules (orders to obtain information from judgment debtors);

(v) the judgment creditor applies for a certificate of judgment under rule 8 of CCR Order 22 in Schedule 2 to the 1998 Rules;

(d) an order for the payment of money arising from an action for the recovery of land (whether for costs, payments due under a mortgage, arrears of rent, or otherwise), until the creditor takes any step to enforce the order under Part 70 of the 1998 Rules;

(e) an order of a county court under—

(i) section 73(15) of the Road Traffic Act 1991 (order for the recovery of an amount which is payable under an adjudication of a parking adjudicator); or

(ii) paragraph 7 of Schedule 6 to that Act (order for the recovery of an increased penalty charge).

II CCA [64]

10. Information contained in the appropriate officer's return

The return sent by virtue of regulation 8(1) shall contain details of—

(a) the full name and address of the debtor in respect of whom the entry in the Register is to be made;

(b) if the entry is to be in respect of an individual, that individual's date of birth (where known);

(c) the amount of the debt;

(d) the case number;

(e) in respect of a return sent by virtue of regulation 8(1)(a) regarding a liability order designated under section 33(5) of the Child Support Act 1991, the date of the judgment;

(f) in respect of all other returns sent by virtue of regulation 8(1)(a)—

(i) the name of the court which made the judgment; and

(ii) the date of the judgment;

(g) in respect of a return sent by virtue of regulation 8(1)(b)—

(i) the name of the court which made the administration order; and

(ii) the date of the order;

(h) in respect of a return sent by virtue of regulation 8(1)(c)—

(i) the Local Justice Area which imposed the fine; and

(ii) the date of conviction.

II CCA [65]

11. Cancellation or endorsement of entries relating to judgments of the High Court or a county court

(1) This regulation applies where an entry in the Register is one to which regulation 8(1)(a) applies (judgments entered in the High Court or a county court).

(2) Where it comes to the attention of the appropriate officer that—

(a) the debt to which the entry relates has been satisfied one month or less from the date of the judgment; or

(b) the judgment to which the entry relates has been set aside or reversed,

that officer shall send a request to the Registrar to cancel the entry.

(3) Where it comes to the attention of the appropriate officer that the debt has been satisfied more than one month from the date of the judgment, that officer shall send a request to the Registrar to endorse the entry as to the satisfaction of the debt.

II CCA [66]

12. Endorsement of entries relating to county court administration orders

(1) This regulation applies where an entry in the Register is one to which regulation 8(1)(b) applies (administration orders of a county court).

(2) Where it comes to the attention of the appropriate officer that—

(a) an administration order has been varied;

(b) an administration order has been revoked; or

(c) the debt has been satisfied,

that officer shall send a request to the Registrar to endorse the entry accordingly.

II CCA [67]

13. Cancellation or endorsement of entries relating to fines

(1) This regulation applies where an entry in the Register is one to which regulation 8(1)(c) applies (fines subject to registration under Schedule 5 to the Act).

(2) Where it comes to the attention of the appropriate officer that—

(a) the debt to which the entry relates has been satisfied one month or less from the date on which the fine was registered;

(b) the conviction for which the fine was imposed has been set aside or reversed; or

(c) the fine has been remitted in full,

that officer shall send a request to the Registrar to cancel the entry.

(3) Where it comes to the attention of the appropriate officer that the debt has been satisfied more than one month from the date on which the fine was registered, that officer shall send a request to the Registrar to endorse the entry as to the satisfaction of the debt.

II CCA [68]

14. Cancellation of entries in the Register—additional provisions

Where an entry in the Register is endorsed in accordance with regulations 11(3) or 13(3) and the appropriate officer is later of the opinion that the debt was satisfied one month or less from—

(a) the date of the judgment or administration order; or

(b) the date on which the fine was registered,

that officer shall send a request to the Registrar to cancel the relevant entry.

II CCA [69]

15.

Where—

(a) it comes to the attention of the appropriate officer that an administrative error has been made; and

(b) he is of the opinion that the error is such to require the cancellation of an entry in the Register,

that officer shall send a request to the Registrar to cancel the relevant entry.

II CCA [70]

16. Cancellation and endorsement of entries in the Register by the Registrar

Following receipt of a request under—

(a) regulation 11(2), 13(2), 14 or 15 (debt due satisfied in one month or less, etc), the Registrar shall cancel the relevant entry;

(b) regulation 11(3) or 13(3) (debt due satisfied in more than one month), the Registrar shall endorse the relevant entry as to the satisfaction of the debt;

(c) regulation 12(2) (administration order has been varied, revoked or debt has been satisfied), the Registrar shall endorse the relevant entry accordingly.

II CCA [70A]

17. Application for, and issue of, a certificate of satisfaction

(1) A registered debtor may apply to the appropriate officer for a certificate ("certificate of satisfaction") as to the satisfaction of the debt.

(2) An application under paragraph (1) shall be—

(a) made in writing; and

(b) accompanied by the appropriate fee.

II CCA [70B]

18

(1) In the case of an application for a certificate of satisfaction in respect of an entry in the Register to which regulation 8(1)(a) applies (judgments entered in the High Court or a county court), the application under regulation 17(1) shall be accompanied by—

(a) sufficient evidence that the debt has been satisfied;

(b) a statement that the registered debtor has taken reasonable steps to obtain such evidence, but has been unable to do so; or

(c) a statement that the registered debtor believes such evidence is already in the possession of the appropriate officer.

(2) For the purposes of paragraph (1)(a), sufficient evidence that the debt has been satisfied includes a signed statement by the creditor to that effect.

(3) Where paragraph (1)(b) applies, the appropriate officer shall send notice of the registered debtor's application under regulation 17(1) to the creditor together with a request that the creditor confirms within one month of the date of the notice whether the debt has been satisfied.

(4) For the purposes of paragraph (1)(c), evidence which is already in the possession of the appropriate officer includes where—

(a) the debt has been paid as the result of court enforcement proceedings taken under Part 70 of the 1998 Rules;

(b) payment of the debt has otherwise been made to the court.

II CCA [70C]

19

Where an application has been made under regulation 17(1) and—

(a) the appropriate officer is of the opinion that the debt has been satisfied; or

(b) a notice has been sent in accordance with regulation 18(3) and the creditor has not responded within the time limit provided,

the appropriate officer shall issue a certificate of satisfaction to the registered debtor.

II CCA [70D]

20. Amendment of the Register in respect of the amount registered

(1) Where it comes to the attention of the appropriate officer that the amount liable to be paid differs from the amount entered in the Register, due to—

(a) the issue of a final costs certificate; or

(b) an increase in the amount of the debt,

the appropriate officer shall send a return to the Registrar to amend the Register to reflect the revised amount.

(2) The return sent in accordance with paragraph (1) shall contain the same information as prescribed by regulation 10 in respect of the return sent in accordance with regulation 8(1).

(3) Following receipt of a return sent in accordance with this regulation, the Registrar shall amend the Register accordingly.

II CCA [70E]

21. Correction of registered details of the judgment, administration order or fine

(1) Where it comes to the attention of a registered debtor that the entry in the Register relating to his debt is inaccurate with respect to the details of the judgment, administration order or fine, that debtor may give notice to the Registrar requiring an amendment to be made ("amendment notice").

(2) The amendment notice shall—

(a) identify the entry which is alleged to be inaccurate; and

(b) state the amendment which is required.

II CCA [70F]

22.

Following receipt of an amendment notice in respect of an entry in the Register, the Registrar shall request that the appropriate officer verify the details of that entry.

II CCA [70G]

23.

Following receipt of a request for verification under regulation 22, the appropriate officer shall—

(a) check the information contained in the entry against the official records; and

(b) reply to the request, where applicable stating any necessary amendment.

II CCA [70H]

24.

(1) Where the appropriate officer informs the Registrar that the entry is inaccurate and requests an amendment, the Registrar shall amend the Register to rectify the inaccuracy.

(2) Following an amendment to the Register in accordance with paragraph (1), the Registrar shall inform the registered debtor of the action taken and the reasons for having taken that action.

II CCA [70I]

25.

Where the appropriate officer informs the Registrar that the entry is accurate, the Registrar shall inform the registered debtor that no action is to be taken and the reasons for not taking any action.

II CCA [70J]

26. Removal of entries in the Register

The Registrar shall remove any entry in the Register registered—

(a) by virtue of regulation 8(1)(a) or (b), six years from the date of the judgment;

(b) by virtue of regulation 8(1)(c), five years from the date of conviction.

II CCA [70K]

27. Searches of the Register

(1) Subject to regulation 29, searches of a section of the Register may be carried out on payment of the applicable charge relevant to the type and method of search.

(2) The types of search which may be carried out are—

(a) at a stated address, against a named individual or unincorporated body;

(b) against a named incorporated body;

(c) a periodical search—

(i) relating to a named court;

(ii) within a named county; or

(iii) with the agreement of the Registrar, against such other criteria as may be requested.

II CCA [70L]

28. Certified copies

On receipt of—

(a) a written request for a certified copy of an entry in the Register; and

(b) the applicable charge for such a request,

the Registrar shall provide a copy of that entry, certified by him as a true and complete copy of the entry in the Register.

II CCA [70M]

29. Refusal of access to the Register and appeals

(1) The Registrar may—

(a) refuse a person access to the Register, or to a part of the Register; and

(b) refuse to carry out a search of the Register,

if he believes that the purpose for which access has been requested or for which the results of the search will be used contravenes—

(i) any of the data protection principles; or

(ii) the provisions of any other enactment.

(2) Where a refusal is made under paragraph (1), the person who has been denied access to, or has been denied a search of, the Register may appeal to a county court against the decision of the Registrar.

II CCA [71]

74. Interest on judgment debts etc.

(1) The Lord Chancellor may by order made with the concurrence of the Treasury provide that any sums to which this subsection applies shall carry interest at such rate and between such times as may be prescribed by the order.

(2) The sums to which subsection (1) applies are—

(a) sums payable under judgments or orders given or made in the county court, including sums payable by instalments; and

(b) sums which by virtue of any enactment are, if the county court so orders, recoverable as if payable under an order of that court, and in respect of which the county court has so ordered.

(3) The payment of interest due under subsection (1) shall be enforceable as a sum payable under the judgment or order.

(4) The power conferred by subsection (1) includes power—

(a) to specify the descriptions of judgment or order in respect of which interest shall be payable;

(b) to provide that interest shall be payable only on sums exceeding a specified amount;

(c) to make provision for the manner in which and the periods by reference to which the interest is to be calculated and paid;

(d) to provide that any enactment shall or shall not apply in relation to interest payable under subsection (1) or shall apply to it with such modifications as may be specified in the order; and

(e) to make such incidental or supplementary provisions as the Lord Chancellor considers appropriate.

(5) Without prejudice to the generality of subsection (4), an order under subsection (1) may provide that the rate of interest shall be the rate specified in section 17 of the Judgments Act 1838 as that enactment has effect from time to time.

(5A) The power conferred by subsection (1) includes power to make provision enabling the county court to order that the rate of interest applicable to a sum expressed in a currency other than sterling shall be such rate as the court thinks fit (instead of the rate otherwise applicable).

(6) The power to make an order under subsection (1) shall be exercisable by statutory instrument subject to annulment in pursuance of a resolution of either House of Parliament.

II CCA [71.1]

The County Courts (Interest on Judgment Debts) Order 1991, SI 1991/1184 The 1991 Order, made under this section, provides for interest on some judgment debts of £5,000 or more. It appears that the whole amount of the liability under the judgment is taken into account, including costs. However interest awarded under s 69 was excluded in the unreported case of *Evans v Gwent County Council*, decided in the Newport County Court on

COUNTY COURT

8 April 1994, on the wording of s 69(8). The statutory rate of interest since 1 April 1993 has been 8% in line within the Judgment Debts (Rate of Interest) Order 1993, SI 1993/564. Judgment interest is barred by lapse of time under the Limitation Act 1980 s 24(2): *Lowsley v Forbes (t/a LE Design Services)* [1999] 1 AC 329, [1998] 3 All ER 897, HL. See CPR 40.8 (see para **CPR 40.8**) for time from which interest begins to run.

II CCA [71.1A]

Contractual interest after judgment Contractual interest due under an agreement continues to accrue after judgment and does not merge with the judgment: *Re Sneyd, ex p Fewings* (1883) 25 Ch D 338; *Ealing London Borough v El Isaac* [1980] 2 All ER 548, CA. However, in an agreement covered by the Unfair Terms in Consumer Contracts Regulations 1994, SI 1994/3159, the term "in respect of interest" had to satisfy the requirement of fairness provided by reg 4: *Director General of Fair Trading v First National Bank plc* [2001] UKHL 52, [2002] 1 AC 481, [2001] 2 All ER (Comm) 1000.

II CCA [71.2]

Small Commercial Debts The County Courts (Interest on Judgment Debts) (Amendment) Order 1998, SI 1998/2400 extended the awards on interest to judgments and orders under £5,000 in respect of qualifying debts for the purposes of the Late Payment of Commercial Debts (Interest) Act 1998. Qualifying debts are those owed to small suppliers by large businesses or public authorities: see Late Payment of Commercial Debts (Interest) Act 1998 (Commencement No 1) Order 1998, SI 1998/2479.

II CCA [71.3]

The text of the Order, as amended The County Courts (Interest on Judgment Debts) Order 1991, SI 1991/1184 (as amended by SI 1996/2516 and SI 1998/2400) is set out below.

II CCA [71.4]

1. Citation, commencement, interpretation and savings

(1) This Order may be cited as the County Courts (Interest on Judgment Debts) Order 1991 and shall come into force on 1 July 1991.

(2) In this Order, unless the context otherwise requires,—

"administration order" means an order under section 112 of the 1984 Act;

"given", in relation to a relevant judgment, means "given or made";

"judgment creditor" means the person who has obtained or is entitled to enforce the relevant judgment and "debtor" means the person against whom it was given;

"judgment debt" means a debt under a relevant judgment;

"relevant judgment" means a judgment or order of a county court for the payment of a sum of money—

(a) of not less than £5,000, or

(b) in respect of a debt which is a qualifying debt for the purposes of the Late Payment of Commercial Debts (Interest) Act 1998 and, in relation to a judgment debt, means the judgment or order which gives rise to the judgment debt."

"the 1984 Act" means the County Courts Act 1984.

(3) Where in accordance with the provisions of this Order interest ceases to accrue on a specified day, interest shall cease to accrue at the end of that day.

(4) Nothing in this Order shall apply where the relevant judgment is given before 1 July 1991.

II CCA [71.5]

2. The general rule

(1) Subject to the following provisions of this Order, every judgment debt under a relevant judgment shall, to the extent that it remains unsatisfied, carry interest under this Order from the date on which the relevant judgment was given.

(2) In the case of a judgment or order for the payment of a judgment debt, other than costs, the amount of which has to be determined at a later date, the judgment debt shall carry interest from that later date.

(3) Interest shall not be payable under this Order where the relevant judgment—

(a) is given in proceedings to recover money due under an agreement regulated by the Consumer Credit Act 1974;

(b) grants—
(i) the landlord of a dwelling house, or
(ii) the mortgagee under a mortgage of land which consists of or includes a dwelling house,

a suspended order for possession.

(4) Where the relevant judgment makes financial provision for a spouse or a child, interest shall only be payable on an order for the payment of not less than £5,000 as a lump sum (whether or not the sum is payable by instalments).

For the purpose of this paragraph, no regard shall be had to any interest payable under section 23(6) of the Matrimonial Causes Act 1973.

II CCA [71.6]

3. Interest where payment deferred

Where under the terms of the relevant judgment payment of a judgment debt—
(a) is not required to be made until a specified date, or
(b) is to be made by instalments,

interest shall not accrue under this Order—
(i) until that date, or
(ii) on the amount of any instalment, until it falls due,

as the case may be.

II CCA [71.7]

4. Interest and enforcement or other proceedings

(1) Where a judgment creditor takes proceedings in a county court to enforce payment under a relevant judgment, the judgment debt shall cease to carry interest thereafter, except where those proceedings fail to produce any payment from the debtor in which case interest shall accrue as if those proceedings had never been taken.

(2) For the purposes of this article "proceedings to enforce payment under a relevant judgment" include any proceeding for examining or summoning a judgment debtor or attaching a debt owed to him, but do not include proceedings under the Charging Orders Act 1979.

(3) Where an administration order or an attachment of earnings order is made, interest shall not accrue during the time the order is in force.

II CCA [71.8]

5. Rate of interest

(1) Subject to paragraph (2), where a judgment debt carries interest the rate of interest shall be the rate for the time being specified in section 17 of the Judgments Act 1838.

(2) Where a judgment debt carries interest and has been given for a sum expressed in a currency other than sterling, a county court may order that the rate of interest shall be such rate as the court thinks fit (instead of the rate otherwise applicable under paragraph (1)) and, where the court makes such an order, section 17 of the Judgments Act 1838 shall have effect in relation to the judgment debt as if the rate specified in the order were substituted for the rate specified in that section.

II CCA [71.9]

Article 5 Only applies in relation to judgments and orders given after 1 November 1996.

II CCA [71.10]

6. Appropriation of interest

(1) Where the debtor is indebted to the same judgment creditor under two or more judgments or orders, money paid by him shall be applied to satisfy such of the judgments as the debtor may stipulate or, where no such stipulation is made, according to their priority in time.

(2) Money paid by the debtor in respect of any judgment debt shall be appropriated first to discharge or reduce the principal debt and then towards the interest.

COUNTY COURT

II CCA [72]

74A. *Practice Directions*
Repealed.

GENERAL RULES OF PROCEDURE
GENERAL NOTES ON SECTION 75

II CCA [73]

County Court Rules Section 75 enabled the County Court Rule Committee to make rules of court regulating the practice of the county courts. Section 75 is repealed by the Civil Procedure Act 1997 and the power to make rules of court for proceedings in county courts is now exercised by the Civil Procedure Rule Committee.

II CCA [74]

76. Application of practice of High Court
In any case not expressly provided for by or in pursuance of this Act, the general principles of practice in the High Court may be adopted and applied to proceedings in the county court.

II CCA [74.1]

General principles A "general principle" means a general guiding rule and does not include specific directions which vary according to the subject-matter: *McCreagh v Frearson* (1921) 91 LJKB 365; *Williamson v Rider* [1963] 1 QB 89, [1962] 2 All ER 268 at 271. A county court judge possesses powers to stay frivolous and improper action similar to those enjoyed by the High Court: *R v Bayley* (1882) 8 QBD 411. This power is inherent as well as statutory: *Norman v Mathews* (1916) 85 LJKB 857, DC; see also *Gore v Van der Lann (Liverpool Corpn Intervening)* [1967] 2 QB 31, [1967] 1 All ER 360, CA. For form of order as to stay see *Grepe v Loam* (1887) 37 Ch D 168, CA, in which it was held that the court can hear an application for such a stay or dismissal in camera. In *Fitzpatrick v Batger & Co Ltd* [1967] 2 All ER 657, [1967] 1 WLR 706, CA, an action was dismissed for want of prosecution following inordinate and inexcusable delay. But the section cannot be read as supplementing the rules as to cases for which provision is made eg to authorise the entry of judgment on a motion for a new trial: *Robinson v Fawcett and Firth* [1901] 2 KB 325. See also *Rolph v Zolan* [1993] 4 All ER 202, [1993] 1 WLR 1305, CA.

II CCA [74.2]

The lacuna rule "It is only when there is a lacuna in the County Court Rules, some general principle not dealt with at all, that one is justified in applying (s 76) and seeking inspiration from the High Court Rules instead" per Lord Widgery in *R v Bloomsbury and Marylebone County Court, ex p Villerwest Ltd* [1975] 2 All ER 562, [1975] 1 WLR 1175, DC. But see the reversal of the decision in [1976] 1 All ER 897, [1976] 1 WLR 362, CA on the ground that county courts have a wide inherent jurisdiction to control their own procedure. Also in *Ager v Ager* [1998] 1 All ER 703, [1998] 1 WLR 1074, CA the Court held that the High Court practice of enforcing orders of the Court of Appeal could be followed in the county court in reliance on s 76.

PART IV
APPEALS ETC

APPEALS

II CCA [75]

77. Appeals: general provisions
(1) Subject to the provisions of this section and the following provisions of this Part of this Act and to any order made by the Lord Chancellor under section 56(1) of the Access to Justice Act 1999, if any party to any proceedings in the county court is dissatisfied with the determination of a judge or jury, he may appeal from it to the Court of Appeal in such manner and subject to such conditions as may be provided by the rules of the Supreme Court.

(1A) Without prejudice to the generality of the power to make rules of court, such rules may make provision for any appeal from the exercise by a judge of the county court of any power given to him by virtue of any enactment to be to another judge of the county court.

(2)–(4) . . .

(5) Subject to the provisions of this section and the following provisions of this Part of this Act, where an appeal is brought under subsection (1) in any action, an appeal may be brought under that subsection in respect of any claim or counterclaim in the action notwithstanding that there could have been no such appeal if that claim had been the subject of a separate action.

(6) In proceedings in which either the plaintiff or the defendant is claiming possession of any premises this section shall not confer any right of appeal on any question of fact if by virtue of—

- (a) section 13(4) of the Landlord and Tenant Act 1954; or
- (b) Cases III to IX in Schedule 4 to the Rent (Agriculture) Act 1976; or
- (c) section 98 of the Rent Act 1977, as it applies to Cases 1 to 6 and 8 and 9 in Schedule 15 to that Act, or that section as extended or applied by any other enactment; or
- (d) section 99 of the Rent Act 1977, as it applies to Cases 1 to 6 and 9 in Schedule 15 to that Act; or
- (e) section 84(2)(a) of the Housing Act 1985; or
- (ee) section 7 of the Housing Act 1988, as it applies to the grounds in Part II of Schedule 2 to that Act; or
- [(ef) paragraph 13(4) of Schedule 10 to the Local Government and Housing Act 1989; or]
- (f) any other enactment,

the court can only grant possession on being satisfied that it is reasonable to do so.

(7) This section shall not—

- (a) confer any right of appeal from any judgment or order where a right of appeal is conferred by some other enactment; or
- (b) take away any right of appeal from any judgment or order where a right of appeal is so conferred,

and shall have effect subject to any enactment other than this Act.

(8) In this section—

"enactment" means an enactment whenever passed.

Amendment *Text in square brackets is inserted by the Local Government and Housing Act 1989, with effect from a date to be appointed.*

COUNTY COURT

II CCA [75.1]

General restrictions on appeal to Court of Appeal Section 56(1) of the Access to Justice Act 1999 enables the Lord Chancellor by order to prescribe destination for appeals. The Access to Justice Act 1999 (Destination of Appeals) Order 2000, SI 2000/1071, describes the route for appeals. See **CPR 52 [15]**.

II CCA [75.2]

Leave requirement and conditions prescribed by rules See **CPR 52.3** by which permission to appeal is required for every appeal except an appeal against a committal order, refusal to grant habeas corpus or a secure accommodation order under s 25 of the Children Act 1989.

II CCA [75.3]

Appeal against findings of fact on preliminary issues The Court of Appeal has jurisdiction under s 77 to entertain an appeal against a finding of fact on preliminary issues made at a split hearing and will do so in care proceedings where the findings are crucial to the final care decision: *Re B (a Minor) (split hearings: jurisdiction)* [2000] 1 WLR 790, [2000] 1 FCR 297, CA.

II CCA [75.4]

Application to the court below for leave Where leave is required from the same court or tribunal that heard the proceedings such leave may be granted by another judge of the same court or tribunal: *Warren v T Kilroe & Sons Ltd* [1988] 1 All ER 638, [1988] 1 WLR 516, CA. If an application for leave is made ex parte and the judge to whom it is made does not dismiss the application he should follow the practice of the Court of Appeal and adjourn the application to give the other party an opportunity to make representations: *Aveyard v Aveyard* [1984] 1 All ER 159, [1984] 1 WLR 467n, CA.

II CCA [75.5]

Findings of fact Findings of fact on preliminary issues made at a split hearing in care proceedings which were crucial to the final decision as to whether to make a care order could be treated as determinative for the purposes of s 77 of the County Courts Act 1984. Although no order or declaration had been made, the Court of Appeal had power to hear an appeal against the findings: *Re B (A Minor) (split hearings: jurisdiction)* [2000] 1 WLR 790, [2000] 1 FCR 297.

II CCA [76]

78. Assistance of Trinity masters for Court of Appeal in Admiralty proceedings
Where, on an appeal by a party to any Admiralty proceedings which have been heard in the county court with the assistance of assessors, any party makes application to the Court of Appeal in that behalf, the court shall summon Trinity masters to assist on the hearing of the appeal if the court is of opinion that such assistance is necessary or desirable

II CCA [77]

79. Agreement not to appeal
(1) No appeal shall lie from any judgment, direction, decision or order of a judge of the county court if, before the judgment, direction, decision or order is given or made, the parties agree, in writing signed by themselves or their legal representatives or agents, that it shall be final.
(2) [. . .]

II CCA [78]

80. Judge's note on appeal
(1) At the hearing of any proceedings in the county court in which there is a right of appeal or from which an appeal may be brought with leave, the judge shall, at the request of any party, make a note—
- (a) of any question of law raised at the hearing; and
- (b) of the facts in evidence in relation to any such question; and
- (c) of his decision on any such question and of his determination of the proceedings.

(2) Where such a note has been taken, the judge shall (whether notice of appeal has been served or not), on the application of any party to the proceedings, and on payment by that party of such fee as may be prescribed by an order under section 92 of the Courts Act 2003 (fees), furnish him with a copy of the note, and shall sign the copy, and the copy so signed shall be used at the hearing of the appeal.

II CCA [78.1]

Request to take a note of the particular point This section has been predominately overtaken by **CPR PD 39A** requiring the judgment to be recorded unless the judge directs otherwise. However, it may still be pertinent particularly in interlocutory hearings although it is the duty of the legal representative who raises a question of law which may be the subject of an appeal to request the making of a note. Although the making of a request is not a condition precedent to an appeal on the point (*Wohlegemuthe v Coste* [1899] 1 QB 501; *Abrahams v Dimmock* [1915] 1 KB 662, CA), failure to do so often means that there is no proper note; and the Court of Appeal has stressed the need for one on many occasions. The legal representative should make a specific request, identifying each and every point of law:

Wohlegemuthe v Coste [1899] 1 QB 501. If one party is not represented the legal representative of the other should request the taking of a note of perceived irregularities in the conduct of the hearing: *Sebastian Coltman & Co v Caute* (1991) Times, 25 March, CA.

II CCA [78.2]

Contents of the note The note must comply with the three requirements of the section and the judge may add his own observations (*Clifford v Thames Ironworks and Shipbuilding Co* [1898] 1 QB 314) and subsequent corrections to resolve ambiguities (*Lowery v Walker* [1911] AC 10, HL).

Wherever a party applies for permission to appeal against a judgment or order at the hearing at which the judgment or order was made, the judge is required, by **CPR 40.2** to note the following (a) whether or not the judgment or order is final (b) whether an appeal lies from the judgment or order and, if so, to which appeal court (c) whether the court gives permission to appeal and (d) if not, the appropriate appeal court to which any further application for permission may be made. The judge is required by this rule to include all such information in the judgment or order. The judge is also required to complete form N460 — Reasons for allowing or refusing permission to appeal. This form can be found in the FORMS section on your CD-Rom.

II CCA [78.3]

Judge's reasons If the judge gives a written judgment, copies should be provided for the parties: *Collier v Wischnia* (1975) 119 Sol Jo 592, CA. It should contain reasons for the judgment and reasons should be given to explain every judicial decision, for example, to set aside a judgment by default: *Eagil Trust Co Ltd v Pigott Brown* [1985] 3 All ER 119, CA; *Banaskiewicz v Mulholland* (1985) Times, 19 April, CA; *Lennard v International Institute for Medical Science* (1985) Times, 29 April, CA. A judgment has to enable the parties and the appellate court to understand why the judge reached his decision and to enable ready analysis of his reasoning: *English v Emery Reimbold & Strick Ltd* [2002] EWCA Civ 605, [2002] 3 All ER 385. Although short judgments and short reasons are to be encouraged the reasons must be sufficient to support the decision; otherwise the case may have to be remitted for a fresh hearing before a different judge: *Baird v Thurrock Borough Council* [2005] EWCA Civ 1499, (2005) Times, 15 November. On appeal the core bundle, lodged under **CPR PD 52**, para 5.6, must contain a record of the judge's reasons in the form of a written judgment, a transcript or a note agreed between the legal representatives and approved by the judge. But references to the amount paid into court should be excluded: *Beaumont v British Uralite Ltd* (1973) 117 Sol Jo 914, CA; CPR 52.12 (see para **CPR 52.12**).

II CCA [78.4]

Disclosure of judge's note in subsequent actions In *R v Brighton County Court, ex p Westminster Press Ltd* [1990] 1 QB 628, [1990] 2 All ER 732, the Divisional Court stated that a judge is under no duty to disclose his trial notes except for the purpose of an appeal and that, while he has power to do so, this power should only be exercised in exceptional circumstances and where the parties to a subsequent action make an agreed request. If a judge refuses and receives a subpoena the Lord Chancellor's Department should be told with a view to instructing the Treasury Solicitor.

II CCA [78.5]

Shorthand note Where the judge has delivered a written judgment, copies of that judgment (one copy signed by the judge) and not a shorthand note of it must be lodged for the use of the Court of Appeal: *Practice Direction* [1943] WN 221. When it is desired to use a shorthand note of evidence on appeal the transcript should be sent to the judge for approval and a copy to the other side: Bucknill LJ in *Neil v Harland and Wolff Ltd* (1949) 82 Ll L Rep 515, CA. The cost of a transcript will not be allowed as of course on appeal. Tape recording of proceedings is mandatory unless the judge otherwise directs: **CPR PD 39A**. If a judgment is so recorded the judge has no discretion to refuse to supply a transcript to an appellant: *Ewing v Hartley* (1988) Times, 7 April, CA.

II CCA [78.6]

Counsel's or solicitor's note It is the duty of counsel always to take a note of a judgment in a county court: *Letts v Letts* (1987) Times, 8 April, CA. The brief fee includes having the note transcribed, submitted to the judge, revised and copied: *Practice Note (barrister fees)* [1994] 1 All ER 96, [1994] 1 WLR 74, CA. Solicitor representatives are under similar duties and the notes of solicitors or of counsel must be submitted to the judge for approval or comment, otherwise the Court of Appeal may feel unable to reverse the decision: *Bruen v Bruce* [1959] 2 All ER 375, [1959] 1 WLR 684, CA; *Belsham v William Dawson & Sons Ltd* (1986) Times, 27 November, CA. The above cases should be read in the light of the Practice Direction set out at **CPR PD 52B** and in particular paragraph 6.2 thereof. Where there is an official transcript it will normally be required by the Court of Appeal.

II CCA [79]

81. Powers of Court of Appeal on appeal from county court

(1) On the hearing of an appeal, the Court of Appeal may draw any inference of fact and either—

(a) order a new trial on such terms as the court thinks just; or

(b) order judgment to be entered for any party; or

(c) make a final or other order on such terms as the court thinks proper to ensure the determination on the merits of the real question in controversy between the parties.

(2) Subject to Civil Procedure Rules, on any appeal from the county court the Court of Appeal may reverse or vary, in favour of a party seeking to support the judgment or order of the county court in whole or in part, any determinations made in the county court on questions of fact, notwithstanding that the appeal is an appeal on a point of law only, or any such determinations on points of law, notwithstanding that the appeal is an appeal on a question of fact only.

(3) Subsection (2) shall not enable the Court of Appeal to reverse or vary any determination, unless the party dissatisfied with the determination would have been entitled to appeal in respect of it is aggrieved by the judgment or order.

II CCA [79.1]

Powers on appeal **CPR 52.10** provides that in relation to an appeal, the appeal court has all the powers of the lower court.

II CCA [80]

82. Decision of Court of Appeal on probate appeals to be final

No appeal shall lie from the decision of the Court of Appeal on any appeal from the county court in any proceedings in respect of any contentious matter arising with any grant, or revocation, of probate or administration that under section 105 of the Senior Courts Act 1981 has been applied for through the principal registry of the Family Division or a district probate registry.

II CCA [80.1]

Application for a new trial An application for a new trial should normally be made to the County Court and not the Court of Appeal: *O'Connor v Din* [1997] 1 FLR 226, [1997] Fam Law 244, CA.

II CCA [81]

83. Stay of proceedings in case of certiorari or prohibition

(1) The grant by the High Court of leave to make an application for an order of certiorari or prohibition to the county court shall, if the High Court so directs, operate as a stay of the proceedings in question until the determination of the application, or until the High Court otherwise orders.

(2) Where any proceedings are so stayed, the county court shall from time to time adjourn the hearing of the proceedings to such day as the court thinks fit.

II CCA [82]

84. Prohibition

(1) Where an application is made to the High Court for an order of prohibition addressed to the county court, the matter shall be finally disposed of by order.

(2) Upon any such application, no judge of the county court is to be served with notice of it or, except by the order of a judge of the High Court—

(a) be required to appear or be heard; or

(b) be liable to any order for the payment of the costs of the application;

but the application shall be proceeded with and heard in the same manner in all respects as an appeal duly brought from a decision of a judge of the county court, and notice of the application shall be given to or served upon the same parties as in the case of an order made or refused by a judge of the county court in a matter within his jurisdiction.

II CCA [82.1]

Origins of the section Sections 115 and 118 of the County Courts Act 1959, which dealt respectively with orders or certiorari and mandamus were repealed by the Supreme Court Act 1981 and replaced by s 29 of that Act (see **II SCA [28]**). Section 116 of the County Courts Act 1959 was not then repealed but was reproduced in the 1984 Act as s 84.

II CCA [82.2]

Precedents Precedents for remedies by way of judicial review are in **BCCP Division J**. For procedure see CPR Sch 1.

II CCA [82.3]

Mandamus, prohibition, certiorari Mandamus is appropriate where there has been an improper refusal to perform a duty, prohibition to prevent a court from acting in excess of its jurisdiction and certiorari to quash a decision. Although challenges are much more frequently launched by appeal under s 77, the remedies under CPR Sch 1 will lie against a county court judge, as in *R v Judge Sir Donald Hurst, ex p Smith* [1960] 2 QB 133, [1960] 2 All ER 385.

PART V
ENFORCEMENT OF JUDGMENTS AND ORDERS

Note Part V of the County Court Act 1984 has been substantially repealed by s 62 of the Tribunals, Courts and Enforcement Act 2007 giving effect on a date to be announced to Schedule 12 and 13 of the Act. This provides a revised framework for enforcement by the taking of control of goods (see **III PTY [2.8]**). The terminology in various pieces of primary legislation relating to current powers to seize and sell goods has been amended so that warrants of execution are renamed warrants of control. Section 67 of the Act transfers the district judges' responsibility for the execution of control to any person authorised for or on behalf of the Chancellor.

EXECUTION AGAINST GOODS

II CCA [83]

85. Execution of judgments or orders for payment of money

(1) Subject to article 8 of the High Court and County Courts Jurisdiction Order 1991, any sum of money payable under a judgment or order of the county cour may be recovered, in case of default or failure of payment, forthwith or at the time or times and in the manner thereby directed, under a warrant under subsection (2).

(2) A judge of the county court, on the application of the party prosecuting any such judgment or order, shall issue a warrant of control whereby any person authorised by or on behalf of the Lord Chancellor is empowered to use the procedure in Schedule 12 to the Tribunals, Courts and Enforcement Act 2007 (taking control of goods) to recover the money payable under the judgment or order.

(2A) The person to whom a warrant under subsection (2) must be directed is to be determined in accordance with arrangements made by a person authorised by or on behalf of the Lord Chancellor.]

(3) Repealed.

(4) It shall be the duty of every constable within his jurisdiction to assist in the execution of every such warrant

COUNTY COURT

II CCA [83.1]

Subject to article 8 Article 8(1) of the High Court and County Courts Jurisdiction Order 1991, SI 1991/724, (see para **II HCJ [7]**) requires execution of judgments for £5,000 or more to be effected in the High Court, unless the debt arises out of an agreement regulated by the Consumer Credit Act 1974, in which case it must be effected in the county court.

II CCA [83.2]

Judgments and orders of the Court of Appeal Judgments or orders of the Court of Appeal may be enforced by the High Court under Senior Courts Act 1981, s 54(1). Where the county court is the court of first instance it has been held (*Ager v Ager* [1998] 1 All ER 703, [1998] 1 WLR 1074, CA) that the combined effect of s 54(1) and County Courts Act 1984, s 76 empowers the county court to enforce orders of the Court of Appeal eg as to costs. Also s 81(1): see para **II CCA [79]**.

II CCA [83.3]

The Crown as creditor The Crown has a prerogative right to priority over other unsatisfied warrants of execution provided that the goods have not been sold: *New South Wales Taxation Comrs v Palmer* [1907] AC 179, PC; *A-G v Leonard* (1888) 38 Ch D 622; *Re Bonham, ex p Postmaster-General* (1879) 10 Ch D 595; *Bainbridge v Postmaster-General* [1906] 1 KB 178, CA. It would seem that the Crown Proceedings Act 1947 s 26(1) was concerned only with procedure and that the Crown right to priority is still effective.

II CCA [83.4]

The Crown as debtor See Crown Proceedings Act 1947 s 27.

II CCA [83.5]

Persons serving in armed forces Execution against serving members of the armed force requires leave in certain circumstances under the Reserve and Auxiliary Forces (Protection of Civil Interests) Act 1951.

II CCA [83.6]

Corporation Subject to the Debtors Acts 1869 and 1878, any judgment or order against a corporation wilfully disobeyed may, by leave of the judge, be enforced by the committal of directors or other officers under CPR Sch 2 CCR Ord 29 (see para **CCR 29**).

II CCA [83.7]

Warrant of control In the County Court the old warrant of execution has been replaced by the warrant of control: Tribunals Courts and Enforcement Act 2007, s 62. There is a standard form of request. This should be presented, together with a fee, to the County Court hearing centre, or posted to the County Court Money Claims Centre, where the judgment was obtained or to the County Court hearing centre to which the case has been transferred. In addition, the judgment creditor may file a request for a warrant to enforce a High Court judgment in the County Court hearing centre that serves the address where execution is to be levied: the warrant of control will then be issued to an enforcement officer not, as formerly, to the county court bailiff.

II CCA [83.8]

Schedule 12, Rules and Regulations The framework of the new regime for taking control of goods is set out in Schedule 12 to the Tribunals, Courts and Enforcement Act 2007, the text of which is at **II TCE 30**. The rules of court that apply are in Volume 1 at **CPR 83.1** onwards, followed by the Practice Direction at **CPR PD 83**, and in Part 84, starting at **CPR 84.1**. The provisions of Schedule 12 are supplement by Taking Control of Goods Regulations 2013, SI 2013/1894, which cover such matters as categories of exempt goods and giving notice of the intention to take control, also controlled goods agreements. The text of these regulations is set out in Volume 1 at **CPR 83.30**.

II CCA [83.9]

Consequential, Transitional and Saving Provisions There are transitional provisions in the Tribunals, Courts and Enforcement Act 2007 (Consequential, Transitional and Saving Provision) Order 2014, SI 2014/606 in respect of writs and warrants issued under the old law.

II CCA [84]

86. Execution of orders for payment by instalments

(1) Where the court has made an order for payment of any sum of money by instalments, a warrant of control to recover any of that sum shall not be issued until after default in payment of some instalment according to the order.

(2) Rules of court may prescribe the cases in which a warrant of control is to be issued if there is any such default and limit the amounts for which and the times at which a warrant of control may be issued.

(3) Except so far as may be otherwise provided by rules of court made for those purposes, a warrant or successive warrants of control may be issued if there is any such default for the whole of the said sum of money and costs then remaining unpaid or for such part as the court may order either at the time of the original order or at any subsequent time; but except so far as may be otherwise provided by such rules, no warrant of control may be issued unless when it is issued the whole or some part of an instalment which has already become due remains unpaid.

II CCA [84.1]

Power to make instalment order By s 71(1)(b) a county court has power to make an instalment order where judgment is given or an order is made under which a sum of money of any amount is payable whether by way of costs or otherwise.

II CCA [84.2]

Charging order The court has jurisdiction to make a final charging order despite the making of an instalment order under s 71(1)(b) of the County Courts Act 1984 where such instalment order was made after the date of the interim charging order. There is no reason why an instalment order and a charging order should not co-exist: *Ropaigealach v Allied Irish Bank plc* [2001] EWCA Civ 1790, [2002] 03 EG 130. Section 93 of the Tribunals, Courts and Enforcement Act 2007, which was brought into force on 1 October 2012, provides for charging orders to be made in respect of judgment debts which are the subject of instalment orders even where there has been no default in payment.

II CCA [85]

87. Indorsement of amount on warrant

(1) In or upon every warrant of control issued from the county court against the goods of any person, the court shall cause to be inserted or indorsed the total amount to be recovered, inclusive of the fee for issuing the warrant but exclusive of the fees for its execution.

(2) Repealed.

II CCA [86]

88. Power to stay execution

If at any time it appears to the satisfaction of the court that any party to any proceedings is unable from any cause to pay any sum recovered against him (whether by way of satisfaction of the claim or counterclaim in the proceedings or by way of costs or otherwise), or any instalment of such a sum, the court may, in its discretion, stay any execution issued in the proceedings for such time and on such terms as the court thinks fit, and so from time to time until it appears that the cause of inability has ceased

II CCA [86.1]

Stay For notes see para **II CCA [49.5]**.

COUNTY COURT

SECURITY AND CUSTODY OF GOODS ETC.

II CCA [87]

89. *Goods which may be seized*
Repealed.

II CCA [87.1]

Execution of the warrant by seizure Seizure in execution of the warrant may take the form of "close possession" (that is, actual physical possession) or "walking possession", whereby the debtor remains in physical possession on terms which allow the bailiff to walk in and take the goods at any time. However, the bailiff's right to seize the goods does not include the right to enter the debtor's premises by force, except in the circumstances considered below.

II CCA [87.2]

Walking possession A signed agreement to the effect that, in consideration of the bailiff not remaining in close possession of the goods seized, he should be allowed to re-enter at any time with force if necessary amounts in law to a seizure of the goods: *Watson v Murray & Co* [1955] 2 QB 1, [1955] 1 All ER 350. A walking possession agreement need not be signed by the judgment debtor personally but can be signed by any responsible person in the house such as the debtor's wife even though the debtor himself objects: *National Commercial Bank of Scotland Ltd v Arcam Demolition and Construction Ltd* [1966] 2 QB 593, [1966] 3 All ER 113, CA. For form of request to hold walking possession, see Form N 46, post. Goods are only impounded or otherwise secured when there is a distinct act making it manifest that they are not to be taken away. A "walking possession" agreement is not binding against an owner of goods who knows nothing of such agreement, is unaware of any distraint and removes his goods. In such circumstances an owner is not guilty of pound breach: *Abingdon RDC v O'Gorman* [1968] 2 QB 811, [1968] 3 All ER 79, CA. A valid distress for the purpose of the community charge legislation is not constituted, without entry, by the mere posting through the letter box of a document forbidding disposal of goods within a house: *Evans v South Ribble Borough Council* [1992] QB 757[1992] 2 All ER 695.

II CCA [87.3]

Forcible entry The bailiff may open doors in order to gain access, but may not normally force or break a lock: *Southam v Smout* [1964] 1 QB 308, [1963] 3 All ER 104, CA; *Vaughan v McKenzie* [1969] 1 QB 557, [1968] 1 All ER 1154. Forcible re-entry is not justified by a walking possession agreement, but only by the debtor's showing an intention deliberately to exclude the bailiff from coming in lawfully: *Khazanch v Faircharm Investments Ltd, McLeod v Butterwick* [1998] 2 All ER 901, [1998] 1 WLR 1603, CA.

II CCA [87.4]

Any of that person's goods The goods of the debtor include goods owned jointly by the debtor and another person: *Farrar v Beswick* (1836) 1 M & W 682; *Mayhew v Herrick* (1849) 7 CB 229; *The James W Ewell* [1921] P 351. But goods which are owned by a third party or are subject to a third party lien may not be seized even though in the apparent ownership of the debtor: *Jones Bros (Holloway) Ltd v Woodhouse* [1923] 2 KB 117, a hire-purchase case. On the other hand, the existence of a floating charge in favour of another creditor is not a bar to execution if the charge has not crystallised: *Re Opera Ltd* [1891] 3 Ch 260, CA; *Taunton v Sheriff of Warwickshire* [1895] 2 Ch 319, CA; *Heaton and Dugard Ltd v Cutting Bros Ltd* [1925] 1 KB 655, DC.

II CCA [87.5]

Exceptions Exempt goods are taken at the bailiff's peril: it is not for the debtor to make a case for having them returned: *Newman (t/a Mantella Publishing) Modern Bookbinders Ltd* [2000] 2 All ER 814, CA.

In addition to the exceptions made by s 89(1)(a) for the goods needed for work or for domestic life, there are other statutory exceptions which protect the military needs of members of the armed forces: Army Act 1955 s 185, Air Force Act 1955 s 185 and Naval Discipline Act 1957 s 102.

II CCA [87.6]

Anything else that may lawfully be seized Tenant's fixtures which the debtor has the right to remove may be seized as goods of the debtor: *Poole's Case* (1703) 1 Salk 368.

II CCA [88]

90. ***Custody of goods seized***
Repealed.

II CCA [88.1]

Inventory and notice If the goods are removed an inventory and notice of the time and place of sale must be served on the defendant in accordance with CPR Sch 2 CCR Ord 26 r 12 (see para **CCR 26r12**).

II CCA [89]

91. ***Disposal of bills of exchange seized***
Repealed.

II CCA [89.1]

Proceeds of sale If a District Judge holds a balance of money, the proceeds of the sale of goods which have been seized, such money is not liable to be seized in further execution unless the district judge has appropriated and set apart specific money to meet the first execution debt: *Wood v Wood* (1843) 4 QB 397; *Harrison v Paynter* (1840) 6 M & W 387.

II CCA [89.2]

Bank notes Bank notes seized in execution are not to be treated as the property of the execution creditor, so as to be available in the district judge's hands to satisfy a writ of execution lodged against the execution creditor: *Collingridge v Paxton* (1851) 11 CB 683; *France v Campbell* (1841) 9 Dowl 914.

II CCA [89.3]

Bills of exchange A "bill of exchange" includes a cheque: Bills of Exchange Act 1882 s 73.

II CCA [90]

92. Penalty for rescuing goods seized

(1) If any person rescues or attempts to rescue any goods seized in execution under process of the county court, he shall be liable—

(a) on summary conviction, to imprisonment for a term not exceeding *one month* [51 weeks] or to a fine of an amount not exceeding level 4 on the standard scale, or both; or

(b) on an order made by the county court in that behalf, to be committed for a specified period not exceeding one month to [. . .] prison [. . .] or to a fine of an amount not exceeding level 4 on the standard scale or to be so committed and to such a fine,

and an officer of the court may take the offender into custody, with or without warrant, and bring him before the county court.

(2) A judge of the county court may at any time revoke an order committing a person to prison under this section and, if he is already in custody, order his discharge.

(3) This section does not apply in the case of goods seized under Schedule 12 to the Tribunals, Courts and Enforcement Act 2007.

Amendment *Text in italic is repealed and text in square brackets substituted by the Criminal Justice Act 2003, from a date to be appointed.*

II CCA [90.1]

Procedure A charge of rescue of goods under this section amounts to a criminal charge for the purposes of Art 6(3) of the European Convention on Human Rights. As such it carries a number of basic procedural rights including the right to be told why one is arrested and to have adequate notice of what is being alleged. It is a matter of good practice to put the charge in writing to the alleged contemnor and unless it is clear that he has already read and understood it, it should be read over to him at the outset of the hearing. Where a court is

COUNTY COURT

considering possible imprisonment the court should ask an unrepresented defendant whether he wished representation: *Newman (t/a Mandella Publishing) v Modern Bookbinders Ltd* [2000] 2 All ER 814, CA.

As from 2 April 2001 legal advice and representation in proceedings under s 14, s 92 or s 118 is available as part of the Criminal Defence Service under the Access to Justice Act 1999. Sections 12 to 18 and Sch 3 of that Act came into operation on that date concurrently with the repeal of s 29 of the Legal Aid Act 1988. See Legal Services Commission Manual ID-041.

Where the offender is not taken into custody and brought before the court, a summons should be issued and served personally: see **CPR 81.34**.

SALE OF GOODS SEIZED

II CCA [91]–II CCA [94]

Taking control of goods The Tribunals, Courts and Enforcement Act 2007 has made substantial changes to the law on such matters as sale of seized goods and the new law is contained in Schedule 12 to the Act supplemented by regulations in SI 2013/1984. The text of Schedule 12 is at **II TCE [30]** and the regulations are in Volume 1 at **CPR 83.30**.

CLAIMS IN RESPECT OF GOODS SEIZED

II CCA [95]

99. Endorsement of warrants of control etc

(1) This section applies to—

(a) a warrant of control issued under section 85(2);

(b) a warrant of delivery or of possession, but only if it includes a power to take control of and sell goods to recover a sum of money and only for the purposes of exercising that power.

(2) The person to whom the warrant is directed must, as soon as possible after receiving it, endorse it by inserting on the back the date and time when he received it.

(3) No fee may be charged for endorsing a warrant under this section.

II CCA [95.1]

Claims in respect of goods seized under warrants of control The Tribunals, Courts and Enforcement Act 2007 made substantial changes to ss 99 to 104 with effect from 6 April 2014 and these sections are printed as amended. Provision is made in Schedule 12 to the Tribunals, Courts and Enforcement Act 2007 for claims in respect of goods wrongfully taken: see **II TCE 30**. The cases cited in the commentary on these sections were decided under the old law and should be interpreted accordingly.

II CCA [96]

100. ***Sale of goods to which claim is made***

Repealed.

II CCA [96.1]

"The claimant may... deposit" Where a claimant deposits with the bailiff an amount which is not the value of the goods, the bailiff must not withdraw from possession; even if he does so, the judge has power to order him to retake possession, and, further, in the case of a claimant under a bill of sale, can order a sale in accordance with CPR Sch 1 RSC Ord 17 r 6: *Miller & Co v Solomon* [1906] 2 KB 91: "I must point out that the dispute referred to . . . is a dispute between the parties interested, the claimant and the execution creditor": per Kennedy J, *Miller & Co v Solomon* [1906] 2 KB 91. "In order that the execution creditor may be in a position to determine whether he will take an issue, it is most important for him that the real amount of the value of the goods shall be paid into court, for if the amount is sufficient to satisfy both the claimant's security and the judgment debt and costs, it becomes unnecessary for the execution creditor to dispute the title of the claimant": per A. T. Lawrence J, *Miller & Co v Solomon* [1906] 2 KB 91 and CPR Sch 1 RSC Ord 17 r 6 see para **RSC 17r6**.

II CCA [96.2]

Where, however, the claimant makes a deposit which, although considerably less than the value of the goods seized, is more than sufficient to cover the costs of the judgment debt and execution, the bailiff must not remain in possession after the date of the deposit and he is not entitled to possession fees after that date: *Newsum, Sons & Co Ltd v James* [1909] 2 KB 384.

II CCA [96.3]

Where the bailiff retires from possession of goods on an equivalent sum of money being paid into court, he leaves them free goods which any other execution creditor putting in a *fi fa* can seize. In such a case the remedy of the original execution creditor is no longer against the goods but against the sum of money in court: *Wells v Hughes* [1907] 2 KB 845, CA.

II CCA [96.4]

"In default of the claimant complying" If no deposit is made or security given the bailiff is entitled under the above section to sell the goods without first applying for an interpleader summons under the next following section: *Cramer v Matthews* (1881) 7 QBD 425.

II CCA [96.5]

Payment out of deposit In *Haddow v Morton* [1894] 1 QB 565, CA, goods which had been taken in execution under a county court judgment were claimed by a person who deposited their value with the bailiff under the above section. On the trial of the interpleader issue the claim was not established and the money deposited was paid out to the judgment creditor. The money being insufficient to satisfy the judgment, the judgment creditor seized the goods again and the claimant again claimed them and deposited their value. On a second interpleader issue it was held that by taking out of court the money deposited by the claimant on the first occasion the judgment creditor accepted the money in lieu of the goods, and that the claimant was entitled to judgment on the issue. See also *Kotchie v Golden Sovereigns Ltd* [1898] 2 QB 164, CA.

II CCA [96.6]

Where the claimant deposited the full amount of the warrant, and subsequently failed to make title to some of the goods, it was held that the claimant was entitled to be paid out of the sum deposited the value of the goods to which title had been made, in spite of the failure to make title to the other goods, and that the judgment creditor was not entitled to be paid out of the deposit the value of the goods to which title had not been made: *Tellus Super Vacuum Cleaners v Ireland* [1938] LJNCCR 54.

II CCA [96.7]

Withdrawal of execution As to withdrawal and reissue refer to CPR Sch 2 CCR Ord 26 r 10 see para **CCR 26r10**.

II CCA [97]

101. Interpleader by district judge

(1) If a claim is made to or in respect of any goods seized in execution under process of the county court, or in respect of the proceeds or value of any such goods, the court may, as well before as after any action brought in respect of the claim, issue a summons calling before the court the party at whose instance the process issued and the party making the claim.

(2) Upon the issue of the summons, any action brought in the county court or any other court in respect of the claim or of any damage arising out of the execution of the warrant shall be stayed.

(3) On the hearing of the summons, the court shall adjudicate upon the claim, and shall also adjudicate between the parties or either of them and the person executing the warrant upon any claim to damages arising or capable of arising out of the execution of the warrant , and shall make such order in respect of any such claim and the costs of the proceedings as he thinks fit.

(4) This section does not apply in the case of goods seized under Schedule 12 to the Tribunals, Courts and Enforcement Act 2007.

II CCA [97.1]

"Any goods... or... the proceeds... thereof" Sections 100 and 101 relate to a claim to the goods of the debtor or "the proceeds" thereof; therefore where a creditor, who has by deed assigned all debts then and thereafter to become owing to him, subsequently recovers judgment against a debtor and the goods of this debtor are sold under an execution, the assignee under the deed cannot claim the proceeds of the sale under either of these sections: *Plant v Collins (Deeley, Claimant)* [1913] 1 KB 242, CA. "The case is clearly not within that section [that is s 157 of the Act of 1888; now s 101], which deals with goods taken in execution, or the proceeds of a sale of them as representing the goods, in a case where a question arises as to whether the goods seized belonged to the execution debtor or to a claimant of them. In this case no question arises or could have been raised by the claimant as to the title to the goods taken in execution": per KENNEDY LJ at 247.

II CCA [97.2]

Jurisdiction Under this section, the county courts have jurisdiction in interpleader, in the case of rival claimants to goods taken in execution. They have also jurisdiction by s 38, and, in the case of interpleader proceedings transferred from the High Court to the county court, by s 40.

II CCA [97.3]

The Crown See Crown Proceedings Act 1947 s 16.

II CCA [97.4]

Procedure See CPR Sch 2 CCR Ord 33 see also **CCR 33** for procedure. Any claim for damages should be made at the time of the interpleader as the right to damages merges in the decision and cannot provide the basis for a subsequent claim: *Kershaw v Automatic Salesman Ltd* (1937) 4 LJCCR 60; *West v Automatic Salesman Ltd* [1937] 2 KB 398, [1937] 2 All ER 706, CA. A claim for damages against the district judge requires notice to be given in accordance with CPR Sch 2 CCR Ord 33 r 5 see also **CCR 33r5**. As to liability see s 98 of the County Courts Act 1984 see also **II CCA [94]**.

II CCA [98]

102. ***Claims for rent where goods seized in execution***
Repealed.

EXECUTION OUT OF JURISDICTION OF COURT

II CCA [99]

103. ***Execution out of jurisdiction of court***
Repealed.

II CCA [100]

104. Information as to writs and warrants of execution

(1) Where a writ against the goods of any person issued from the High Court is delivered to an enforcement officer who is under a duty to execute the writ or to a sheriff, then on demand from a judge of the county court that person shall—

- (a) in the case of an enforcement officer, by writing signed by that officer or a person acting under his authority, and
- (b) in the case of a sheriff, by writing signed by any clerk in the office of the under-sheriff,

inform the judge of the precise time the writ was delivered to him.

(2) A person to whom a warrant issued by the county court is directed shall on demand show his warrant to any enforcement officer, any person acting under the authority of an enforcement officer and any sheriff's officer.

(3) Any writing purporting to be signed as mentioned in subsection (1) and the endorsement on any warrant issued from the county court shall respectively be sufficient justification to any judge, or enforcement officer or sheriff, acting on it.

(4) In this section "enforcement officer" means an individual who is authorised to act as an enforcement officer under the Courts Act 2003.

RECEIVERS AND ATTACHMENT OF DEBTS

II CCA [101]

107. Receivers

(1) The power of the county court to appoint a receiver by way of equitable execution shall operate in relation to all legal estates and interests in land.

(2) The said power may be exercised in relation to an estate or interest in land whether or not a charge has been imposed on that land under section 1 of the Charging Orders Act 1979 for the purpose of enforcing the judgment, decree, order or award in question, and the said power shall be in addition to and not in derogation of any power of any court to appoint a receiver in proceedings for enforcing such a charge.

(3) Where an order under section 1 of the Charging Orders Act 1979 imposing a charge for the purpose of enforcing a judgment, decree, order or award has been registered under section 6 of the Land Charges Act 1972, subsection (4) of that section (which provides that, amongst other things, an order appointing a receiver and any proceedings pursuant to the order or in obedience to it, shall be void against a purchaser unless the order is for the time being registered under that section) shall not apply to an order appointing a receiver made either in proceedings for enforcing the charge or by way of equitable execution of the judgment, decree, order or award or, as the case may be, of so much of it as requires payment of moneys secured by the charge.

II CCA [102]–II CCA [103]

108. Attachment of debts

(1) Subject to any order for the time being in force under subsection (4), this section applies to any deposit account, and any withdrawable share account, with a deposit-taker.

(2) In determining whether, for the purposes of the jurisdiction of the county court to attach debts for the purpose of satisfying judgments or orders for the payment of money, a sum standing to the credit of a person in an account to which this section applies is a sum due or accruing to that person and, as such, attachable in accordance with rules of court, any condition mentioned in subsection (3) which applies to the account shall be disregarded.

(3) Those conditions are—

- (a) any condition that notice is required before any money or share is withdrawn;
- (b) any condition that a personal application must be made before any money or share is withdrawn;
- (c) any condition that a deposit book or share-account book must be produced before any money or share is withdrawn; or
- (d) any other prescribed condition.

(4) The Lord Chancellor may by order make such provision as he thinks fit, by way of amendment of this section or otherwise, for all or any of the following purposes, namely—

- (a) including in, or excluding from, the accounts to which this section applies accounts of any description specified in the order;
- (b) excluding from the accounts to which this section applies all accounts with any particular deposit-taker so specified or with any deposit-taker of a description so specified.

COUNTY COURT

(5) An order under subsection (4) shall be made by statutory instrument subject to annulment in pursuance of a resolution of either House of Parliament.

II CCA [102]–II CCA [103.1]

Attachment of debts The effect of this section is to bring within the ambit of the provisions building societies, trustee savings banks, the National Savings Bank and, to the extent that they carry on a deposit-taking business, credit unions. For procedure regarding the attachment of third party debts (formerly known as garnishee proceedings), see para **CPR 72**, Third Party Debt Orders.

II CCA [102]–II CCA [103.2]

Foreign currency Foreign currency held in a judgment debtor's account is attachable under a third party debt order to satisfy a judgment given in sterling and the orders nisi and absolute should be appropriately worded: *Choice Investments Ltd v Jeromnimon (Midland Bank Ltd, garnishee)* [1981] QB 149, [1981] 1 All ER 225, CA.

II CCA [104]

109. Administrative and clerical expenses of garnishees

(1) Where an interim third party debt order made in the exercise of the jurisdiction mentioned in subsection (2) of the preceding section is served on a deposit-taker, it may, subject to the provisions of this section, deduct from the relevant debt or debts an amount not exceeding the prescribed sum towards its administrative and clerical expenses in complying with the order; and the right [. . .] to make a deduction under this subsection shall be exercisable as from the time the interim third party debt order is served on it.

(1A) In subsection (1) "the relevant debt or debts", in relation to an interim third party debt order served on a deposit-taker, means the amount, as at the time the order is served on it, of the debt or debts of which the whole or a part is expressed to be attached by the order.

(1B) A deduction may be made under subsection (1) in a case where the amount referred to in subsection (1A) is insufficient to cover both the amount of the deduction and the amount of the judgment debt and costs in respect of which the attachment was made, notwithstanding that the benefit of the attachment to the creditor is reduced as a result of the deduction.]

(2) An amount may not in pursuance of subsection (1)] be deducted or, as the case may be, retained in a case where by virtue of section 346 of the Insolvency Act 1986 or section 325 of the Companies Act 1948 or otherwise, the creditor is not entitled to retain the benefit of the attachment.

(3) In this section "prescribed" means prescribed by an order made by the Lord Chancellor.

(4) An order under this section—

- (a) may make different provision for different cases; [. . .]
- (b) without prejudice to the generality of paragraph (a) may prescribe sums differing according to the amount due under the judgment or order to be satisfied.
- (c) may provide for this section not to apply to [deposit-takers] of any prescribed description.

(5) Any such order shall be made by statutory instrument subject to annulment in pursuance of a resolution of either House of Parliament.

II CCA [104.1]

Administrative expenses of garnishees A deposit-taking institution may deduct from the debt being attached a sum not exceeding £55 (under the Attachment of Debts (Expenses) Order 1996, SI 1996/3098) towards its administrative and clerical expenses in complying with the third party debt order. The deduction can be made when the interim order is served and notwithstanding that the debt is insufficient to cover the attachment debt and the expenses. For further commentary see para **II SCA [41]** and see para **II SCA [42]** on the parallel provisions in the Senior Courts Act 1981 ss 40 (as amended), 40A (as inserted).

MISCELLANEOUS PROVISIONS AS TO ENFORCEMENT OF JUDGMENTS AND ORDERS

II CCA [105]

110. Penalty for non-attendance on judgment summons

(1) If a debtor summoned to attend the county court by a judgment summons fails to attend on the day and at the time fixed for any hearing of the summons, the court may adjourn or further adjourn the summons to a specified time on a specified day and order the debtor to attend at that time on that day.

(2) If—

(a) a debtor, having been ordered under subsection (1) to attend at a specified time on a specified day, fails to do so; [. . .]

(b) [. . .]

the court may make an order committing him to prison for a period not exceeding 14 days in respect of the failure or refusal.

(3) In any case where the court has power to make an order of committal under subsection (2) for failure to attend, he may in lieu of or in addition to making that order, order the debtor to be arrested and brought before the court either forthwith or at such time as the court may direct.

(4) A debtor shall not be committed to prison under subsection (2) for having failed to attend as required by an order under subsection (1) unless there was paid to him at the time of the service of the judgment summons, or paid or tendered to him at the time of the service of the order, such sum in respect of his expenses as may be prescribed for the purposes of this section.

(5) The court may at any time revoke an order committing a person to prison under this section and, if he is already in custody, order his discharge

II CCA [105.1]

Enforcing a debtor's attendance The procedure Is in CPR Sch 2 CCR Ord 28 r 4, see para **CCR 28r4**.

II CCA [106]

111. Provisions as to warrants of possession

(1) For the purpose of executing a warrant to give possession of any premises, it shall not be necessary to remove any goods from those premises.

(2) The duration of any warrant of possession issued by the county court to enforce a judgment or order for the recovery of land or for the delivery of possession of land shall be such as may be fixed by or in accordance with rules of court.

PART VI
ADMINISTRATION ORDERS

Amendment *Part VI has been substituted by the Tribunals, Courts and Enforcement Act 2007, with effect from a date to be appointed. The new Part 6A is set out below at para* **II CCA [114]**.

II CCA [106A]

112. ***Power to make administration order***

(1) Where a debtor—

(a) is unable to pay forthwith the amount of a judgment obtained against him; and

(b) alleges that his whole indebtedness amounts to a sum not exceeding the county court limit, inclusive of the debt for which the judgment was obtained;

COUNTY COURT

the county court may make an order providing for the administration of his estate.

[(1) Where a debtor is unable to pay forthwith the amount of any debt owed by him, the county court may make an order providing for the administration of his estate.

(1A) The order may be made—

- *(a) on the application of the debtor (whether or not a judgment debt has been obtained against the debtor in respect of his debt, or any of his debts);*
- *(b) on the application of any creditor under a judgment obtained against the debtor; or*
- *(c) of the court's own motion during the course of, or on the determination of, any enforcement or other proceedings.]*

(2) In this Part of this Act—

"administration order" means an order under this section; and

"the appropriate court", in relation to an administration order, means the court which has the power to make the order.

(3) Before an administration order is made, the county court shall, in accordance with rules of court, send to every person whose name the debtor has notified to the county court as being a creditor of him, a notice that that person's name has been so notified.

(4) So long as an administration order is in force, a creditor whose name is included in the schedule to the order shall not, without the leave of the county court, be entitled to present, or join in, a bankruptcy petition against the debtor unless—

- *(a) his name was so notified; and*
- *(b) the debt by virtue of which he presents, or joins in, the petition, exceeds £1,500; and*
- *(c) the notice given under subsection (3) was received by the creditor within 28 days immediately preceding the day on which the petition is presented.*

(4A) Subsection (4) is subject to section 112A.

(5) An administration order shall not be invalid by reason only that the total amount of the debts is found at any time to exceed the county court limit, but in that case the court may, if it thinks fit, set aside the order.

(6) An administration order may provide for the payment of the debts of the debtor by instalments or otherwise, and either in full or to such extent as appears practicable to the court under the circumstances of the case, and subject to any conditions as to his future earnings or income which the court may think just.

(7) The Secretary of State may by regulations increase or reduce the sum for the time being specified in subsection (4)(b); but no such increase in the sum so specified shall affect any case in which the bankruptcy petition was presented before the coming into force of the increase.

(8) The power to make regulations under subsection (7) shall be exercisable by statutory instrument; and no such regulations shall be made unless a draft of them has been approved by resolution of each House of Parliament.

(9) An administration order shall cease to have effect—

- *(a) at the end of the period of three years beginning with the date on which it is made; or*
- *(b) on such earlier date as may be specified in the order.*

Amendment *A new Part 6 has been substituted for Part VI by the Tribunals, Courts and Enforcement Act 2007, with effect from a date to be appointed. See para* **II CCA [113A]** *below.*

II CCA [106A.1]

Amendments This section has been substantially amended by s 13 of the Courts and Legal Services Act 1990, but no date has yet been fixed for the implementation of the amendments. The section is printed in its amended form except as regards the provisions which are due to be repealed: these are still shown, but in italics. The major reforms introduced by these amendments will be to remove the £5,000 limit of indebtedness; to allow a debtor to apply for an order without waiting for a judgment against him; to allow judgment creditors to apply; to permit the court to make an order of its own motion; and to provide for the order to cease to have effect not longer than three years after it is made. Sections 112A and 112B were similarly introduced by s 13 of the Courts and Legal Services Act 1990 but have not yet come into force. They will do so at the same time as the implementation of the amendments to this section for which no date is in immediate prospect.

For the procedure see CPR Sch 2, CCR Ord 39 (see para **CCR 39**).

As to the power to order summary administration upon the making of a bankruptcy order, see now s 275 of the Insolvency Act 1986.

II CCA [106A.2]

Attachment of earnings Any creditor scheduled to an administration order may apply for the making of an attachment of earnings order (see Attachment of Earnings Act 1971 s 3 and CPR Sch 2, CCR Ord 27r 1 (at para **CCR 27r1**). Where, on an application for an attachment of earnings order to secure payment of a judgment debt it appears that the debtor has other debts the court is required to consider whether the case be one for the making of an administration order (see Attachment of Earnings Act 1971 s 4). Pay or allowances payable to a member of HM Forces are not earnings within the Attachment of Earnings Act 1971: s 24(2). But deductions from pay in respect of an order or judgment may be made pursuant to s 151A of the Army Act 1955, as inserted by the Armed Forces Act 1971.

II CCA [106A.3]

Community charge A liability for unpaid community charge ranks as a debt for the purpose of sub-s (6) of this section: *Preston Borough Council v Riley* [1995] RA 227, [1995] BCC 700, CA.

II CCA [106A.4]

Procedure See CPR Sch 2, CCR Ord 39 (at para **CCR 39**). The judge, district judge, or, in the circumstances set out in CPR Sch 2, CCR Ord 39 r 5 (at para **CCR 39r5**), the proper officer, can make an administration order (see CPR Sch 2, CCR Ord 39 r 1, at para **CCR 39r1**). When an administration order is made in lieu of committal, it always is necessarily made by a judge, since the judge alone has jurisdiction over judgment summonses.

As long as the order is in force a creditor named in the order must not, without leave of the court making the order, present or join in a bankruptcy petition against the debtor except where the debt exceeds £1,500 and the petition is presented within 28 days after the creditor received notice from the district judge (s 20(3) of Administration of Justice Act 1965 which was brought into force on 29 December 1986 by the Insolvency Act 1985 (Commencement No 5) Order 1986, SI 1986/1924.

II CCA [106A.5]

Transfer of proceedings See CPR Sch 2.

II CCA [106A.6]

Revocation of order Cases in which the order may be revoked are given in CPR Sch 2, CCR 39 r 14 (at para **CCR 39r14**).

II CCA [106A.7]

Review of order See CPR Sch 2.

II CCA [106A.8]

Rules The power to make rules for the purposes of administration orders is contained in s 12 of the Insolvency Act 1976.

II CCA [106A.9]

Reserve and Auxiliary Forces (Protection of Civil Interests) Act 1951 Persons serving in the armed forces and in some other forms of national service are protected against the enforcement of certain judgments or orders without leave of the court if their inability to pay is due to circumstances arising from the period of service either by themselves or others.

II CCA [107]

112A. ***Further powers of the court***

(1) Where the court is satisfied—

- *(a) that it has power to make an administration order with respect to the debtor concerned; but*
- *(b) that an order restricting enforcement would be a more satisfactory way of dealing with the case,*

it may make such an order instead of making an administration order.

(2) Where an order restricting enforcement is made, no creditor specified in the order shall have any remedy against the person or property of the debtor in respect of any debt so specified, without the leave of the court.

(3) Subsection (4) applies to any creditor—

- *(a) who is named in the schedule to an administration order or in an order restricting enforcement; and*
- *(b) who provides the debtor with mains gas, electricity or water for the debtor's own domestic purposes.*

(4) While the order has effect, the creditor may not stop providing the debtor with—

- *(a) mains gas, electricity or (as the case may be) water for the debtor's own domestic purposes; or*
- *(b) any associated service which it provides for its customers,*

without leave of the court unless the reason for doing so relates to the non-payment of charges incurred by the debtor after the making of the order or is unconnected with non-payment by him of any charges.

(5) In this section "mains gas" means a supply of gas by a public gas supplier within the meaning of Part I of the Gas Act 1986.

(6) Rules of court may make provision with respect to the period for which any order restricting enforcement is to have effect and for the circumstances in which any such order may be revoked.

Amendment *A new Part 6 has been substituted for Part VI by the Tribunals, Courts and Enforcement Act 2007, with effect from a date to be appointed. See para* **II CCA [113A]** *below.*

II CCA [107.1]

This section, introduced, with effect from a day not yet appointed, by s 13(5) of the Courts and Legal Services Act 1990, will enable the court, instead of making and administration order under s 112, to make an order restricting creditors from pursing remedies against the debtor without leave. See further notes to s 112 at paras **II CCA [106A.1]–[106A.9]**.

II CCA [108]

112B. Administration orders with composition provisions

(1) Where the court is satisfied—

- *(a) that it has power to make an administration order with respect to the debtor concerned; and*
- *(b) that the addition of a composition provision would be a more satisfactory way of dealing with the case,*

it may make an administration order subject to such a provision.

(2) Where, at any time while an administration order is in force—

- *(a) the debtor has not discharged the debts to which that order relates; and*
- *(b) the court considers that he is unlikely to be able to discharge them,*

the court may add a composition provision to that order.

(3) A composition provision shall specify an amount to which the debtor's total indebtedness in respect of debts owed to creditors scheduled to the administration order is to be reduced.

(4) The amount of the debt owed to each of the creditors so scheduled shall be reduced in proportion to the reduction in his total indebtedness specified by the composition provision.

(5) Where a composition provision is added to an administration order after the order is made, section 113(a) shall apply as if the addition of the composition provision amounted to the making of a new administration order.

Amendment *A new Part 6 has been substituted for Part VI by the Tribunals, Courts and Enforcement Act 2007, with effect from a date to be appointed. See para* **II CCA [113A]** *below.*

II CCA [108.1]

This section introduced, with effect from a day not yet appointed, by s 13 of the Courts and Legal Services Act 1990 will enable the court to add to an administration order under s 112A composition provision stating the amount to which a debtor's total indebtedness to scheduled creditors is to be reduced, and proportionately reducing the debt owed to each scheduled debtor. See, further, notes to s 112 at paras **II CCA [106A.1]–[106A.9]**.

II CCA [109]

113. *Notice of order and proof of debts*

Where an administration order has been made—

(a) notice of the order—

(i) [. . .]

(ii) shall be posted on an appropriate website, and

(iii) shall be sent to every person whose name the debtor has notified to the county court as being a creditor of his or who has proved;

(b) any creditor of the debtor, on proof of his debt before the county court, shall be entitled to be scheduled as a creditor of the debtor for the amount of his proof;

(c) any creditor may object in the prescribed manner to any debt scheduled, or to the manner in which payment is directed to be made by instalments;

(d) any person who, after the date of the order, becomes a creditor of the debtor shall, on proof of his debt before the county court, be scheduled as a creditor of the debtor for the amount of his proof, but shall not be entitled to any dividend under the order until the creditors who are scheduled as having been creditors before the date of the order have been paid to the extent provided by the order.

Amendment *A new Part 6 has been substituted for Part VI by the Tribunals, Courts and Enforcement Act 2007, with effect from a date to be appointed. See para* **II CCA [113A]** *below.*

II CCA [109.1]

"Creditor notified by the debtor" This is to be construed as a requirement that notice shall be sent to every person whose name a debtor has notified to the appropriate county court as being a creditor of his.

II CCA [109.2]

"Any creditor may... object" Objections by creditors who have not received notice of scheduled debts, or to the manner in which payment by instalments is directed, should be made as soon as possible. See CPR Sch 2, CCR Ord 39 r 6 (at para **CCR 39r6**), for the procedure in the case of objection before the order is made and CPR Sch 2, CCR Ord 39 r 10 (at para **CCR 39r10**) in the case of objection after the order is made.

II CCA [109.3]

Creditor after the date of the order Creditors scheduled under s 113 (d) rank equally in proportion to their debts subject to the priority given to creditors scheduled before the date of the order: see CPR Sch 2, CCR Ord 39 r 18 (at para **CCR 39r18**).

II CCA [110]

114. ***Effect of administration order***

(1) Subject to sections 115 and 116, when an administration order is made, no creditor shall have any remedy against the person or property of the debtor in respect of any debt—

(a) of which the debtor notified the county court before the administration order was made; or

(b) which has been scheduled to the order,

except with the leave of the county court, and on such terms as that court may impose.

(2) Subject to subsection (3), when an administration order is made, the county court is to stay any proceedings in the county court which are pending against the debtor in respect of any debt so notified or scheduled shall, on receiving notice of the administration order, stay the proceedings, but may allow costs already incurred by the creditor, and such costs may, on application, be added to the debt.

(3) The requirement to stay proceedings shall not operate as a requirement to stay any proceedings in bankruptcy which are pending against the debtor.

Amendment *A new Part 6 has been substituted for Part VI by the Tribunals, Courts and Enforcement Act 2007, with effect from a date to be appointed. See para* **II CCA [113A]** *below.*

II CCA [110.1]

Where an administration order is made, and until it is revoked on one of the grounds specified in CPR Sch 2, CCR Ord 39 r 14 (at para **CCR 39r14**), a creditor cannot get leave to issue execution, for the object of the rule is to secure equal division of the debtor's property among all his creditors: *Re Frank* [1894] 1 QB 9.

The requirement to stay proceedings in this section does not apply to pending bankruptcy proceedings.

An attachment of earnings order may be made in order to secure payments required by an administration order. (See CPR Sch 2, CCR Ord 27 at para **CCR 27**).

II CCA [111]

115. ***Execution by district judge***

(1) Where it appears to the county court at any time while an administration order is in force that property of the debtor exceeds in value the minimum amount, the court shall, at the request of any creditor, and without fee, issue execution against the debtor's goods.

(1A) In subsection (1) above "the minimum amount" means £50 or such other amount as the Lord Chancellor may by order specify instead of that amount or the amount for the time being specified in such an order; and an order under this subsection shall be made by statutory instrument subject to annulment in pursuance of a resolution of either House of Parliament.

(2) Section 89 applies on an execution under this section as it applies on an execution under Part V.

Amendment *A new Part 6 has been substituted for Part VI by the Tribunals, Courts and Enforcement Act 2007, with effect from a date to be appointed. See para* **II CCA [113A]** *below.*

II CCA [111.1]

Section 89 This section specifies the nature of the goods that may be seized.

II CCA [112]

116. ***Right of landlord to distrain notwithstanding order***

Repealed.

II CCA [113]

117. Appropriation of money paid under order and discharge of order

(1) Money paid into court under an administration order shall be appropriated—

(a) first in satisfaction of the costs of administration (which shall not exceed 10 pence in the pound on the total amount of the debts); and

(b) then in liquidation of debts in accordance with the order.

(2) Where the amount received is sufficient to pay—

(a) each creditor scheduled to the order to the extent provided by the order;

(b) the costs of the plaintiff in the action in respect of which the order was made; and

(c) the costs of the administration,

the order shall be superseded, and the debtor shall be discharged from his debts to the scheduled creditors.

Amendment *A new Part 6 has been substituted for Part VI by the Tribunals, Courts and Enforcement Act 2007, with effect from a date to be appointed. See para* **II CCA [113A]** *below.*

[PART 6
ADMINISTRATION ORDERS]

[ADMINISTRATION ORDERS]

Note Section 106(1) of the Tribunals, Courts and Enforcement Act 2007 replaces the existing Part VI of the County Court Act 1984 with s 112 of the Act, to come into effect on a date to be announced. Section 112 of the Act provides that an administration order is an order to which certain debts are scheduled, which imposes a requirement on the debtor and which imposes requirements on certain creditors. Debts are to be scheduled to the order in accordance with the provisions in ss 112C, 112D, 112Y(3) and 112Y(4). The requirement that must be imposed on the debtor is set out in s 112E and this is a requirement to make repayments towards scheduled debts whilst the administration order is in force. The requirements which must be imposed on certain creditors are set out in ss 112F to 112I and these are all requirements that restrict the ability of those creditors to take enforcement action whilst an administration order is in force.

II CCA [113A]

[112A. Administration orders]

[An administration order is an order—

(a) to which certain debts are scheduled in accordance with section 112C, 112D or 112Y(3) or (4),

(b) which imposes the requirement specified in section 112E on the debtor, and

(c) which imposes the requirements specified in sections 112F to 112I on certain creditors.]

Amendment *Section 112A is inserted by the Tribunals, Courts and Enforcement Act 2007, with effect from a date to be appointed.*

II CCA [113B]

[112B. Power to make order]

[(1) The county court may make an administration order if the conditions in subsections (2) to (7) are met.

(2) The order must be made in respect of an individual who is a debtor under two or more qualifying debts.

(3) That individual ("the debtor") must not be a debtor under any business debts.

(4) The debtor must not be excluded under any of the following—

(a) the AO exclusion;

(b) the voluntary arrangement exclusion;

(c) the bankruptcy exclusion.

(5) The debtor must be unable to pay one or more of his qualifying debts.

(6) The total amount of the debtor's qualifying debts must be less than, or the same as, the prescribed maximum.

(7) The debtor's surplus income must be more than the prescribed minimum.

(8) Before making an administration order, the county court must have regard to any representations made—

(a) by any person about why the order should not be made, or

(b) by a creditor under a debt about why the debt should not be taken into account in calculating the total amount of the debtor's qualifying debts.]

Amendment *Section 112B is inserted by the Tribunals, Courts and Enforcement Act 2007, with effect from a date to be appointed.*

[SCHEDULING DEBTS]

II CCA [113C]

[112C. Scheduling declared debts]

[(1) This section applies to a qualifying debt ("the declared debt") if—

(a) an administration order is made, and

(b) when the order is made, the debt is taken into account in calculating the total amount of the debtor's qualifying debts for the purposes of section 112B(6).

(2) If the declared debt is already due at the time the administration order is made, the county court must schedule the debt to the order when the order is made.

(3) If the declared debt becomes due after the administration order is made, the county court must schedule the debt to the order if the debtor, or the creditor under the debt, applies to the court for the debt to be scheduled.

(4) This section is subject to section 112AG(5).]

Amendment *Section 112C is inserted by the Tribunals, Courts and Enforcement Act 2007, with effect from a date to be appointed.*

II CCA [113D]

[112D. Scheduling new debts]

[(1) This section applies to a qualifying debt ("the new debt") if the debt—

(a) arises after an administration order is made, and

(b) becomes due during the currency of the order.

(2) The county court may schedule the new debt to the administration order if these conditions are met—

(a) the debtor, or the creditor under the new debt, applies to the court for the debt to be scheduled;

(b) the total amount of the debtor's qualifying debts (including the new debt) is less than, or the same as, the prescribed maximum.]

Amendment *Section 112D is inserted by the Tribunals, Courts and Enforcement Act 2007, with effect from a date to be appointed.*

[Requirements imposed by order]

II CCA [113E]

[112E. Repayment requirement]

[(1) An administration order must, during the currency of the order, impose a repayment requirement on the debtor.

(2) A repayment requirement is a requirement for the debtor to repay the scheduled debts.

(3) The repayment requirement may provide for the debtor to repay a particular scheduled debt in full or to some other extent.

(4) The repayment requirement may provide for the debtor to repay different scheduled debts to different extents.

(5) In the case of a new debt scheduled to the order in accordance with section 112D, the repayment requirement may provide that no due repayment in respect of the new debt is to be made until the debtor has made all due repayments in respect of declared debts.

(6) The repayment requirement must provide that the due repayments are to be made by instalments.

(7) It is for the county court to decide when the instalments are to be made.

(8) But the county court is to determine the amount of the instalments in accordance with repayment regulations.

(9) Repayment regulations are regulations which make provision for instalments to be determined by reference to the debtor's surplus income.

(10) The repayment requirement may provide that the due repayments are to be made by other means (including by one or more lump sums) in addition to the instalments required in accordance with subsection (6).

(11) The repayment requirement may include provision in addition to any that is required or permitted by this section.

(12) In this section—

"declared debt" has the same meaning as in section 112C (and for this purpose it does not matter whether a declared debt is scheduled to the administration order when it is made, or afterwards);

"due repayments" means repayments which the repayment requirement requires the debtor to make;

"new debt" has the same meaning as in section 112D.]

Amendment *Section 112E is inserted by the Tribunals, Courts and Enforcement Act 2007, with effect from a date to be appointed.*

II CCA [113F]

[112F. Presentation of bankruptcy petition]

[(1) An administration order must, during the currency of the order, impose the following requirement.

(2) The requirement is that no qualifying creditor of the debtor is to present a bankruptcy petition against the debtor in respect of a qualifying debt, unless the creditor has the permission of the county court.

(3) The county court may give permission for the purposes of subsection (2) subject to such conditions as it thinks fit.]

Amendment *Section 112F is inserted by the Tribunals, Courts and Enforcement Act 2007, with effect from a date to be appointed.*

II CCA [113G]

[112G. Remedies other than bankruptcy]

[(1) An administration order must, during the currency of the order, impose the following requirement.

(2) The requirement is that no qualifying creditor of the debtor is to pursue any remedy for the recovery of a qualifying debt unless—

(a) regulations under subsection (3) provide otherwise, or

(b) the creditor has the permission of the proper county court.

(3) Regulations may specify classes of debt which are exempted (or exempted for specified purposes) from the restriction imposed by subsection (2).

(4) The county court may give permission for the purposes of subsection (2)(b) subject to such conditions as it thinks fit.

(5) This section does not have any effect in relation to bankruptcy proceedings.]

Amendment *Section 112G is inserted by the Tribunals, Courts and Enforcement Act 2007, with effect from a date to be appointed.*

II CCA [113H]

[112H. Charging of interest etc]

[(1) An administration order must, during the currency of the order, impose the following requirement.

(2) The requirement is that no creditor under a scheduled debt is to charge any sum by way of interest, fee or other charge in respect of that debt.]

Amendment *Section 112H is inserted by the Tribunals, Courts and Enforcement Act 2007, with effect from a date to be appointed.*

II CCA [113I]

[112I. Stopping supplies of gas or electricity]

[(1) An administration order must, during the currency of the order, impose the requirement in subsection (3).

(2) In relation to that requirement, a domestic utility creditor is any person who—

(a) provides the debtor with a supply of mains gas or mains electricity for the debtor's own domestic purposes, and

(b) is a creditor under a qualifying debt that relates to the provision of that supply.

(3) The requirement is that no domestic utility creditor is to stop the supply of gas or electricity, or the supply of any associated services, except in the cases in subsections (4) to (6).

(4) The first case is where the reason for stopping a supply relates to the non-payment by the debtor of charges incurred in connection with that supply after the making of the administration order.

(5) The second case is where the reason for stopping a supply is unconnected with the non-payment by the debtor of any charges incurred in connection with—

(a) that supply, or

(b) any other supply of mains gas or mains electricity, or of associated services, that is provided by the domestic utility creditor.

(6) The third case is where the county court gives permission to stop a supply.

(7) The county court may give permission for the purposes of subsection (6) subject to such conditions as it thinks fit.

(8) A supply of mains gas is a supply of the kind mentioned in section 5(1)(b) of the Gas Act 1986.

(9) A supply of mains electricity is a supply of the kind mentioned in section 4(1)(c) of the Electricity Act 1989.]

Amendment *Section 112I is inserted by the Tribunals, Courts and Enforcement Act 2007, with effect from a date to be appointed.*

II CCA [113J]

[112J. Application for an order]

[(1) The county court may make an administration order only on the application of the debtor.

(2) The debtor may make an application for an administration order whether or not a judgment has been obtained against him in respect of any of his debts.]

Amendment *Section 112J is inserted by the Tribunals, Courts and Enforcement Act 2007, with effect from a date to be appointed.*

II CCA [113K]

[112K. Duration]

[(1) The county court may, at the time it makes an administration order, specify a day on which the order will cease to have effect.

(2) The court may not specify a day which falls after the last day of the maximum permitted period.

(3) If the court specifies a day under this section, the order ceases to have effect on that day.

(4) If the court does not specify a day under this section, the order ceases to have effect at the end of the maximum permitted period.

(5) The maximum permitted period is the period of five years beginning with the day on which the order is made.

(6) This section is subject to—

(a) section 112S (variation of duration);

(b) section 112W (effect of revocation).

(7) This section is also subject to the following (effect of enforcement restriction order or debt relief order on administration order)—

(a) section 117I of this Act;

(b) section 251F of the Insolvency Act 1986.]

Amendment *Section 112K is inserted by the Tribunals, Courts and Enforcement Act 2007, with effect from a date to be appointed.*

II CCA [113L]

[112L. Effect on other debt management arrangements]

[(1) This section applies if—

(a) an administration order is made, and

(b) immediately before the order is made, other debt management arrangements are in force in respect of the debtor.

(2) The other debt management arrangements cease to be in force when the administration order is made.

(3) If the county court is aware of the other debt management arrangements, the court must give the relevant authority notice that the order has been made.

(4) In a case where the county court is aware of other debt management arrangements at the time it makes the order, it must give the notice as soon as practicable after making the order.

(5) In a case where the county court becomes aware of those arrangements after it makes the order, it must give the notice as soon as practicable after becoming aware of them.

(6) "Other debt management arrangements" means any of the following—

(a) an enforcement restriction order under Part 6A of this Act;

(b) a debt relief order under Part 7A of the Insolvency Act 1986;

(c) a debt repayment plan arranged in accordance with a debt management scheme that is approved under Chapter 4 of Part 5 of the Tribunals, Courts and Enforcement Act 2007.

(7) "The relevant authority" means—

(a) in relation to an enforcement restriction order: the *proper* county court;

(b) in relation to a debt relief order: the official receiver;

(c) in relation to a debt repayment plan: the operator of the debt management scheme in accordance with which the plan is arranged.

(8) For the purposes of this section a debt relief order is "in force" if the moratorium applicable to the order under section 251H of the Insolvency Act 1986 has not yet ended.]

Amendment *Section 112L is inserted by the Tribunals, Courts and Enforcement Act 2007, with effect from a date to be appointed.*

II CCA [113M]

[112M. Duty to provide information]

[(1) This section applies if, and for as long as, an administration order has effect in respect of a debtor.

(2) The debtor must, at the prescribed times, provide the county court with particulars of his—

(a) earnings,

(b) income,

(c) assets, and

(d) outgoings.

(3) The debtor must provide particulars of those matters—

(a) as the matters are at the time the particulars are provided, and

(b) as the debtor expects the matters to be at such times in the future as are prescribed.

(4) If the debtor intends to dispose of any of his property he must, within the prescribed period, provide the county court with particulars of the following matters—

(a) the property he intends to dispose of;

(b) the consideration (if any) he expects will be given for the disposal;

(c) such other matters as may be prescribed;

(d) such other matters as the court may specify.

(5) But subsection (4) does not apply if the disposal is of—

(a) goods that are exempt goods for the purposes of Schedule 12 to the Tribunals, Courts and Enforcement Act 2007,

(b) goods that are protected under any other enactment from being taken control of under that Schedule, or

(c) prescribed property.

(6) The duty under subsection (4) to provide the county court with particulars of a proposed disposal of property applies whether the debtor is the sole owner, or one of several owners, of the property.

(7) In any provision of this section "prescribed" means prescribed in regulations for the purposes of that provision.]

Amendment *Section 112M is inserted by the Tribunals, Courts and Enforcement Act 2007, with effect from a date to be appointed.*

II CCA [113N]

[112N. Offence if information not provided]

[(1) A person commits an offence if he fails to comply with—

(a) section 112M(2) and (3), or

(b) section 112M(4).

(2) A person who commits an offence under subsection (1) may be ordered by a judge of the *proper* county court to pay a fine of not more than £250 or to be imprisoned for not more than 14 days.

(3) Where under subsection (2) a person is ordered to be imprisoned by a judge of the county court, a judge of the county court may at any time—

(a) revoke the order, and

(b) if the person is already in custody, order his discharge.

(4) Section 129 of this Act (enforcement of fines) applies to payment of a fine imposed under subsection (2).

(5) For the purposes of section 13 of the Administration of Justice Act 1960 (appeal in cases of contempt of court), subsection (2) is to be treated as an enactment enabling the county court to deal with an offence under subsection (1) as if it were a contempt of court.

(6) A district judge or deputy district judge shall have the same powers under this section as a judge of a county court.]

Amendment *Section 112N is inserted by the Tribunals, Courts and Enforcement Act 2007, with effect from a date to be appointed.*

II CCA [113O]

[112O. Existing county court proceedings to be stayed]

[(1) This section applies if these conditions are met—

(a) an administration order is made;

(b) proceedings in the county court (other than bankruptcy proceedings) are pending against the debtor in respect of a qualifying debt;

(c) by virtue of a requirement included in the order by virtue of section 112G, the creditor under the qualifying debt is not entitled to continue the proceedings in respect of the debt;

(d) the county court receives notice of the administration order.

(2) The county court must stay the proceedings.

(3) The court may allow costs already incurred by the creditor.

(4) If the court allows such costs, it may on application or of its motion add them—

(a) to the debt, or

(b) if the debt is a scheduled debt, to the amount scheduled to the order in respect of the debt.

(5) But the court may not add the costs under subsection (4)(b) if the court is under a duty under section 112U(6)(b) to revoke the order because the total amount of the debtor's qualifying debts (including the costs) is more than the prescribed maximum.]

Amendment *Section 112O is inserted by the Tribunals, Courts and Enforcement Act 2007, with effect from a date to be appointed.*

II CCA [113P]

[112P. Appropriation of money paid]

[(1) Money paid into court under an administration order is to be appropriated—

(a) first in satisfaction of any relevant court fees, and

(b) then in liquidation of debts.

(2) Relevant court fees are any fees under an order made under section 92 of the Courts Act 2003 which are payable by the debtor in respect of the administration order.]

Amendment *Section 112P is inserted by the Tribunals, Courts and Enforcement Act 2007, with effect from a date to be appointed.*

II CCA [113Q]

[112Q. Discharge from debts]

[(1) If the debtor repays a scheduled debt to the extent provided for by the administration order, the county court must—

(a) order that the debtor is discharged from the debt, and

(b) de-schedule the debt.

(2) If the debtor repays all of the scheduled debts to the extent provided for by the administration order, the county court must revoke the order.

(3) Subsections (1) and (2) apply to all scheduled debts, including any which, under the administration order, are to be repaid other than to their full extent.]

Amendment *Section 112Q is inserted by the Tribunals, Courts and Enforcement Act 2007, with effect from a date to be appointed.*

II CCA [113R]

[112R. Variation]

[(1) The county court may vary an administration order.

(2) The power under this section is exercisable—

(a) on the application of the debtor;

(b) on the application of a qualifying creditor;

(c) of the court's own motion.]

Amendment *Section 112R is inserted by the Tribunals, Courts and Enforcement Act 2007, with effect from a date to be appointed.*

II CCA [113S]

[112S. Variation of duration]

[(1) The power under section 112R includes power to vary an administration order so as to specify a day, or (if a day has already been specified under section 112K or this subsection) a different day, on which the order will cease to have effect.

(2) But the new termination day must fall on or before the last day of the maximum permitted period.

(3) If the county court varies an administration under subsection (1), the order ceases to have effect on the new termination day.

(4) In this section—

(a) "new termination day" means the day on which the order will cease to have effect in accordance with the variation under subsection (1);

(b) "maximum permitted period" means the period of five years beginning with the day on which the order was originally made.

(5) This section is subject to section 112W (effect of revocation).]

Amendment *Section 112S is inserted by the Tribunals, Courts and Enforcement Act 2007, with effect from a date to be appointed.*

II CCA [113T]

[112T. De-scheduling debts]

[(1) The power under section 112R includes power to vary an administration order by de-scheduling a debt.

(2) But the debt may be de-scheduled only if it appears to the county court that it is just and equitable to do so.]

Amendment *Section 112T is inserted by the Tribunals, Courts and Enforcement Act 2007, with effect from a date to be appointed.*

II CCA [113U]

[112U. Duty to revoke order]

[(1) The county court must revoke an administration order in either of these cases—

(a) where it becomes apparent that, at the time the order was made, the condition in subsection 112B(2) was not met (debtor in fact did not have two or more qualifying debts);

(b) where the debtor is no longer a debtor under any qualifying debts.

(2) The county court must revoke an administration order in either of these cases—

(a) where it becomes apparent that, at the time the order was made, the condition in subsection 112B(3) was not met (debtor in fact had business debt), and he is still a debtor under the business debt, or any of the business debts, in question;

(b) where the debtor subsequently becomes a debtor under a business debt, and he is still a debtor under that debt.

(3) The county court must revoke an administration order where it becomes apparent that, at the time the order was made, the condition in section 112B(4) was not met (debtor in fact excluded under AO, voluntary arrangement or bankruptcy exclusion).

(4) The county court must revoke an administration order where, after the order is made—

(a) the debtor becomes excluded under the voluntary arrangement exclusion, or

(b) a bankruptcy order is made against the debtor, and is still in force.

(5) The county court must revoke an administration order in either of these cases—

(a) where it becomes apparent that, at the time the order was made, the condition in section 112B(5) was not met (debtor in fact able to pay qualifying debts);

(b) where the debtor is now able to pay all of his qualifying debts.

(6) The county court must revoke an administration order in either of these cases—

(a) where it becomes apparent that, at the time the order was made, the condition in section 112B(6) was not met (debtor's qualifying debts in fact more than prescribed maximum);

(b) where the total amount of the debtor's qualifying debts is now more than the prescribed maximum.

(7) The county court must revoke an administration order in either of these cases—

(a) where it becomes apparent that, at the time the order was made, the condition in section 112B(7) was not met (debtor's surplus income in fact less than, or the same as, the prescribed minimum);

(b) where the debtor's surplus income is now less than, or the same as, the prescribed minimum.]

Amendment *Section 112U is inserted by the Tribunals, Courts and Enforcement Act 2007, with effect from a date to be appointed.*

II CCA [113V]

[112V. Power to revoke order]

[(1) The county court may revoke an administration order in any case where there is no duty under this Part to revoke it.

(2) The power of revocation under this section may, in particular, be exercised in any of the following cases—

(a) where the debtor has failed to make two payments (whether consecutive or not) required by the order;

(b) where the debtor has failed to provide the county court with the particulars required by—

(i) section 112M(2) and (3), or

(ii) section 112M(4).

(3) The power of revocation under this section is exercisable—

(a) on the application of the debtor;

(b) on the application of a qualifying creditor;

(c) of the court's own motion.]

Amendment *Section 112V is inserted by the Tribunals, Courts and Enforcement Act 2007, with effect from a date to be appointed.*

II CCA [113W]

[112W. Effect of revocation]

[(1) This section applies if, under any duty or power in this Part, the county court revokes an administration order.

(2) The order ceases to have effect in accordance with the terms of the revocation.]

Amendment *Section 112W is inserted by the Tribunals, Courts and Enforcement Act 2007, with effect from a date to be appointed.*

II CCA [113X]

[112X. Notice when order made, varied, revoked etc]

[(1) If a notifiable event occurs in relation to an administration order, the *proper* county court must send notice of the event to the creditor under every scheduled debt.

(2) There is a notifiable event in any of the following cases—

(a) when the administration order is made;

(b) when a debt is scheduled to the administration order at any time after the making of the order;

(c) when the administration order is varied;

(d) when the administration order is revoked;

(e) when the county court is given notice under any of the provisions listed in section 112K(7) (effect of enforcement restriction order or debt relief order on administration order).]

Amendment *Section 112X is inserted by the Tribunals, Courts and Enforcement Act 2007, with effect from a date to be appointed.*

II CCA [113Y]

[112Y. Failure to take account of all qualifying debts]

[(1) This section applies if—

(a) an administration order has been made, but

(b) it becomes apparent that the total amount of the debtor's qualifying debts was not properly calculated for the purposes of section 112B(6), because of an undeclared debt.

(2) A debt is undeclared if it ought to have been, but was not, taken into account in the calculation for the purposes of section 112B(6).

(3) If these conditions are met—

(a) the undeclared debt is due (whether it became due before or after the making of the order);

(b) the total debt is less than, or the same as, the prescribed maximum;
the county court must schedule the undeclared debt to the order.
(4) If these conditions are met—
(a) the undeclared debt is not due;
(b) the total debt is less than, or the same as, the prescribed maximum;
the county court must schedule the undeclared debt to the order when the debt becomes due.
(5) If the total debt is more than the prescribed maximum, the county court must revoke the administration order (whether or not the undeclared debt is due).
(6) In this section "total debt" means the total amount of the debtor's qualifying debts (including the undeclared debt).
(7) Subsections (3) and (4) are subject to section 112AG(5).]

Amendment *Section 112Y is inserted by the Tribunals, Courts and Enforcement Act 2007, with effect from a date to be appointed.*

II CCA [113Z]

[112Z. Introduction]
[Sections 112AA to 112AH apply for the purposes of this Part.]

Amendment *Section 112Z is inserted by the Tribunals, Courts and Enforcement Act 2007, with effect from a date to be appointed.*

II CCA [113AA]

[112AA. Main definitions]
[(1) In this Part—
"administration order" has the meaning given by section 112A;
"debtor" has the meaning given by section 112B;
"prescribed maximum" means the amount prescribed in regulations for the purposes of section 112B(6);
"prescribed minimum" means the amount prescribed in regulations for the purposes of section 112B(7);
"qualifying creditor" means a creditor under a qualifying debt.
(2) References to the currency of an administration order are references to the period which—
(a) begins when the order first has effect, and
(b) ends when the order ceases to have effect.
(3) *Repealed.*
(4) *Repealed.*]

Amendment *Section 112AA is inserted by the Tribunals, Courts and Enforcement Act 2007, with effect from a date to be appointed.*

II CCA [113AB]

[112AB. Expressions relating to debts]
[(1) All debts are qualifying debts, except for the following—
(a) any debt secured against an asset;
(b) any debt of a description specified in regulations.
(2) A business debt is any debt (whether or not a qualifying debt) which is incurred by a person in the course of a business.
(3) Only debts that have already arisen are included in references to debts; and accordingly such references do not include any debt that will arise only on the happening of some future contingency.]

Amendment *Section 112AB is inserted by the Tribunals, Courts and Enforcement Act 2007, with effect from a date to be appointed.*

II CCA [113AC]

[112AC. Inability to pay debts]

[(1) In a case where an individual is the debtor under a debt that is repayable by a single payment, the debtor is to be regarded as unable to pay the debt only if—

(a) the debt has become due,

(b) the debtor has failed to make the single payment, and

(c) the debtor is unable to make that payment.

(2) In a case where an individual is the debtor under a debt that is repayable by a number of payments, the debtor is to be regarded as unable to pay the debt only if—

(a) the debt has become due,

(b) the debtor has failed to make one or more of the payments, and

(c) the debtor is unable to make all of the missed payments.]

***Amendment** Section 112AC is inserted by the Tribunals, Courts and Enforcement Act 2007, with effect from a date to be appointed.*

II CCA [113AD]

[112AD. Calculating the debtor's qualifying debts]

[(1) The total amount of a debtor's qualifying debts is to be calculated in accordance with subsections (2) and (3).

(2) All of the debtor's qualifying debts which have arisen before the calculation must be taken into account (whether or not the debts are already due at the time of the calculation).

(3) Regulations must make further provision about how the total amount of a debtor's qualifying debts is to be calculated.

(4) Regulations may make provision about how the amount of any particular qualifying debt is to be calculated.

(5) That includes the calculation of the amount of a debt for these purposes—

(a) calculating the total amount of the debtor's qualifying debts;

(b) scheduling the debt to an administration order.]

***Amendment** Section 112AD is inserted by the Tribunals, Courts and Enforcement Act 2007, with effect from a date to be appointed.*

II CCA [113AE]

[112AE. Calculating the debtor's surplus income]

[(1) The debtor's surplus income is to be calculated in accordance with regulations.

(2) Regulations under this section must, in particular, make the following provision—

(a) provision about what is surplus income;

(b) provision about the period by reference to which the debtor's surplus income is to be calculated.

(3) Regulations under this section may, in particular, provide for the debtor's assets to be taken account of when calculating his surplus income.]

***Amendment** Section 112AE is inserted by the Tribunals, Courts and Enforcement Act 2007, with effect from a date to be appointed.*

II CCA [113AF]

[112AF. Debts becoming due]

[(1) A debt that is repayable by a single payment becomes due when the time for making that payment is reached.

(2) A debt that is repayable by a number of payments becomes due when the time for making the first of the payments is reached.]

Amendment *Section 112AF is inserted by the Tribunals, Courts and Enforcement Act 2007, with effect from a date to be appointed.*

II CCA [113AG]

[112AG. Scheduling and de-scheduling debts]

[(1) A debt is scheduled to an administration order if the relevant information is included in a schedule to the order.

(2) A debt is de-scheduled if the relevant information is removed from a schedule in which it was included as mentioned in subsection (1).

(3) In relation to a debt, the relevant information is—

- (a) the amount of the debt, and
- (b) the name of the creditor under the debt.

(4) A scheduled debt is a debt that is scheduled to an administration order.

(5) The county court must not schedule a debt to an administration order unless the court has had regard to any representations made by any person about why the debt should not be scheduled.

(6) But subsection (5) does not apply to any representations which are made by the debtor in relation to the scheduling of a debt under section 112Y.

(7) The county court must not de-schedule a debt unless the court has had regard to any representations made by any person about why the debt should not be de-scheduled.

(8) But subsection (7) does not apply in relation to the de-scheduling of a debt under section 112Q.

(9) A court must not schedule a debt to an administration order, or de-schedule a debt, except in accordance with the provisions of this Part.]

Amendment *Section 112AG is inserted by the Tribunals, Courts and Enforcement Act 2007, with effect from a date to be appointed.*

II CCA [113AH]

[112AH. The AO, voluntary arrangement and bankruptcy exclusions]

[(1) The debtor is excluded under the AO exclusion if—

- (a) an administration order currently has effect in respect of him, or
- (b) an administration order has previously had effect in respect of him, and the period of 12 months—beginning with the day when that order ceased to have effect—has yet to finish.

(2) But in a case that falls within subsection (1)(b), the debtor is not excluded under the AO exclusion if the previous administration order—

- (a) ceased to have effect in accordance with any of the provisions listed in section 112K(7) (effect of enforcement restriction order or debt relief order on administration order), or
- (b) was revoked in accordance with section 112U(1)(b) (debtor no longer has any qualifying debts).

(3) The debtor is excluded under the voluntary arrangement exclusion if—

- (a) an interim order under section 252 of the Insolvency Act 1986 has effect in respect of him (interim order where debtor intends to make proposal for voluntary arrangement), or
- (b) he is bound by a voluntary arrangement approved under Part 8 of the Insolvency Act 1986.

(4) The debtor is excluded under the bankruptcy exclusion if—

- (a) a petition for a bankruptcy order to be made against him has been presented but not decided, or

COUNTY COURT

(b) he is an undischarged bankrupt.]

Amendment *Section 112AH is inserted by the Tribunals, Courts and Enforcement Act 2007, with effect from a date to be appointed.*

II CCA [113AI]

[112AI. Regulations under this Part]

[(1) It is for the Lord Chancellor to make regulations under this Part.

(2) Any power to make regulations under this Part is exercisable by statutory instrument.

(3) A statutory instrument containing regulations under this Part is subject to annulment in pursuance of a resolution of either House of Parliament.]

Amendment *Section 112AI is inserted by the Tribunals, Courts and Enforcement Act 2007, with effect from a date to be appointed.*

[PART 6A
ENFORCEMENT RESTRICTION ORDERS]

Amendment *Part 6A is inserted by the Tribunals, Courts and Enforcement Act 2007, with effect from a date to be appointed.*

II CCA [114]

[117A. Enforcement restriction orders]

[(1) An enforcement restriction order is an order that imposes the requirements specified in sections 117C to 117E on certain creditors.

(2) An enforcement restriction order may also impose a requirement in accordance with section 117F on the debtor.]

Amendment *Section 117A is inserted by the Tribunals, Courts and Enforcement Act 2007, with effect from a date to be appointed.*

II CCA [114A]

[117B. Power to make order]

[(1) The county court may make an enforcement restriction order if the conditions in subsections (2) to (8) are met.

(2) The order must be made in respect of an individual who is a debtor under two or more qualifying debts.

(3) That individual ("the debtor") must not be a debtor under any business debts.

(4) The debtor must not be excluded under any of the following—

(a) the ERO exclusion;

(b) the voluntary arrangement exclusion;

(c) the bankruptcy exclusion.

(5) The debtor must be unable to pay one or more of his qualifying debts.

(6) The debtor must be suffering from a sudden and unforeseen deterioration in his financial circumstances.

(7) There must be a realistic prospect that the debtor's financial circumstances will improve within the period of six months beginning when the order is made.

(8) It must be fair and equitable to make the order.

(9) Before making an enforcement restriction order, the county court must have regard to any representations made by any person about why the order should not be made.

(10) Subsection (9) is subject to Civil Procedure Rules.]

Amendment *Section 117B is inserted by the Tribunals, Courts and Enforcement Act 2007, with effect from a date to be appointed.*

II CCA [114B]

[117C. Presentation of bankruptcy petition]

[(1) An enforcement restriction order must, during the currency of the order, impose the following requirement.

(2) The requirement is that no qualifying creditor of the debtor is to present a bankruptcy petition against the debtor in respect of a qualifying debt, unless the creditor has the permission of the proper county court.

(3) The county court may give permission for the purposes of subsection (2) subject to such conditions as it thinks fit.]

Amendment *Section 117C is inserted by the Tribunals, Courts and Enforcement Act 2007, with effect from a date to be appointed.*

II CCA [114C]

[117D. Remedies other than bankruptcy]

[(1) An enforcement restriction order must, during the currency of the order, impose the following requirement.

(2) The requirement is that no qualifying creditor of the debtor is to pursue any remedy for the recovery of a qualifying debt unless—

(a) regulations under subsection (3) provide otherwise, or

(b) the creditor has the permission of the county court.

(3) Regulations may specify classes of debt which are exempted (or exempted for specified purposes) from any requirement imposed by subsection (2).

(4) The county court may give permission for the purposes of subsection (2)(b) subject to such conditions as it thinks fit.

(5) This section does not have any effect in relation to bankruptcy proceedings.]

Amendment *Section 117D is inserted by the Tribunals, Courts and Enforcement Act 2007, with effect from a date to be appointed.*

II CCA [114D]

[117E. Stopping supplies of gas or electricity]

[(1) An enforcement restriction order must, during the currency of the order, impose the requirement in subsection (3).

(2) In relation to that requirement, a domestic utility creditor is any person who—

(a) provides the debtor with a supply of mains gas or mains electricity for the debtor's own domestic purposes, and

(b) is a creditor under a qualifying debt that relates to the provision of that supply.

(3) The requirement is that no domestic utility creditor is to stop the supply of gas or electricity, or the supply of any associated services, except in the cases in subsections (4) to (6).

(4) The first case is where the reason for stopping a supply relates to the non-payment by the debtor of charges incurred in connection with that supply after the making of the enforcement restriction order.

(5) The second case is where the reason for stopping a supply is unconnected with the non-payment by the debtor of any charges incurred in connection with—

(a) that supply, or

(b) any other supply of mains gas or mains electricity, or of associated services, that is provided by the domestic utility creditor.

(6) The third case is where the county court gives permission to stop a supply.

(7) The county court may give permission for the purposes of subsection (6) subject to such conditions as it thinks fit.

(8) A supply of mains gas is a supply of the kind mentioned in section 5(1)(b) of the Gas Act 1986.

(9) A supply of mains electricity is a supply of the kind mentioned in section 4(1)(c) of the Electricity Act 1989.]

Amendment *Section 117E is inserted by the Tribunals, Courts and Enforcement Act 2007, with effect from a date to be appointed.*

II CCA [114E]

[117F. Repayment requirement]

[(1) An enforcement restriction order may impose a repayment requirement on the debtor.

(2) The county court may include the requirement in the order at the time it makes the order.

(3) The county court may, at any time after an enforcement restriction order has been made, vary the order so as to include a repayment requirement.

(4) The county court may, at any time when an enforcement restriction order includes a repayment requirement, vary the order so as to—

- (a) remove the repayment requirement, or
- (b) include a different repayment requirement.

(5) A repayment requirement is a requirement that the debtor make payments, in respect of one or more of his qualifying debts, to the person or persons to whom he owes the debt or debts.

(6) The county court may include a repayment requirement in an order only if—

- (a) the debtor has surplus income at the time of the inclusion of the requirement, and
- (b) the inclusion of the requirement would be fair and equitable.

(7) The debtor's surplus income is to be calculated in accordance with regulations.

(8) Regulations under subsection (7) must make the following provision—

- (a) provision about what is surplus income;
- (b) provision about the period by reference to which the debtor's surplus income is to be calculated.

(9) Regulations under subsection (7) may, in particular, provide for the debtor's assets to be taken account of for the purpose of calculating his surplus income.

(10) The county court may vary an enforcement restriction order under this section—

- (a) of its own motion;
- (b) on the application of the debtor;
- (c) on the application of a qualifying creditor.]

Amendment *Section 117F is inserted by the Tribunals, Courts and Enforcement Act 2007, with effect from a date to be appointed.*

II CCA [114F]

[117G. Application for order]

[(1) The county court may make an enforcement restriction order only on the application of the debtor.

(2) The debtor may make an application for an enforcement restriction order whether or not a judgment has been obtained against him in respect of any of his debts.]

Amendment *Section 117G is inserted by the Tribunals, Courts and Enforcement Act 2007, with effect from a date to be appointed.*

II CCA [114G]

[117H. Duration]

[(1) The county court may, at the time it makes an enforcement restriction order, specify a day on which the order will cease to have effect.

(2) The court may not specify a day which falls after the last day of the maximum permitted period.

(3) If the court specifies a day under this section, the order ceases to have effect on that day.

(4) If the court does not specify a day under this section, the order ceases to have effect at the end of the maximum permitted period.

(5) The maximum permitted period is the period of 12 months beginning with the day on which the order is made.

(6) This section is subject to—

- (a) section 117N (variation of duration);
- (b) section 117Q (effect of revocation);

(7) This section is also subject to the following (effect of administration order or debt relief order on enforcement restriction order)—

- (a) section 112L of this Act;
- (b) section 251F of the Insolvency Act 1986.]

Amendment *Section 117H is inserted by the Tribunals, Courts and Enforcement Act 2007, with effect from a date to be appointed.*

II CCA [114H]

[117I. Effect on other debt management arrangements]

[(1) This section applies if—

- (a) an enforcement restriction order is made, and
- (b) immediately before the order is made, other debt management arrangements are in force in respect of the debtor.

(2) The other debt management arrangements cease to be in force when the enforcement restriction order is made.

(3) If the county court is aware of the other debt management arrangements, the court must give the relevant authority notice that the order has been made.

(4) In a case where the county court is aware of those arrangements at the time it makes the order, it must give the notice as soon as practicable after making the order.

(5) In a case where the county court only becomes aware of those arrangements after it makes the order, it must give the notice as soon as practicable after becoming aware of them.

(6) "Other debt management arrangements" means any of the following—

- (a) an administration order under Part 6 of this Act;
- (b) a debt relief order under Part 7A of the Insolvency Act 1986;
- (c) a debt repayment plan arranged in accordance with a debt management scheme that is approved under Chapter 4 of Part 5 of the Tribunals, Courts and Enforcement Act 2007.

(7) "The relevant authority" means—

- (a) in relation to an administration order: the county court;
- (b) in relation to a debt relief order: the official receiver;
- (c) in relation to a debt repayment plan: the operator of the debt management scheme in accordance with which the plan is arranged.

(8) For the purposes of this section a debt relief order is "in force" if the moratorium applicable to the order under section 251H of the Insolvency Act 1986 has not yet ended.]

COUNTY COURT

Amendment *Section 117I is inserted by the Tribunals, Courts and Enforcement Act 2007, with effect from a date to be appointed.*

II CCA [114I]

[117J. Duty to provide information]

[(1) This section applies if, and for as long as, an enforcement restriction order has effect in respect of a debtor.

(2) The debtor must, at the prescribed times, provide the county court with particulars of his—

- (a) earnings,
- (b) income,
- (c) assets, and
- (d) outgoings.

(3) The debtor must provide particulars of those matters—

- (a) as the matters are at the time the particulars are provided, and
- (b) as the debtor expects the matters to be at such times in the future as may be prescribed.

(4) If the debtor intends to dispose of any of his property he must, within the prescribed period, provide the county court with particulars of the following matters—

- (a) the property he intends to dispose of;
- (b) the consideration (if any) he expects will be given for the disposal;
- (c) such other matters as may be prescribed;
- (d) such other matters as the court may specify.

(5) But subsection (4) does not apply if the disposal is of—

- (a) goods that are exempt goods for the purposes of Schedule 12 to the Tribunals, Courts and Enforcement Act 2007,
- (b) goods that are protected under any other enactment from being taken control of under that Schedule, or
- (c) prescribed property.

(6) The duty under subsection (4) to provide the county court with particulars of a proposed disposal of property applies whether the debtor is the sole owner, or one of several owners, of the property.

(7) In any provision of this section "prescribed" means prescribed in regulations for the purposes of that provision.]

Amendment *Section 117J is inserted by the Tribunals, Courts and Enforcement Act 2007, with effect from a date to be appointed.*

II CCA [114J]

[117K. Offence if information not provided]

[(1) A person commits an offence if he fails to comply with—

- (a) section 117J(2) and (3), or
- (b) section 117J(4).

(2) A person who commits an offence under subsection (1) may be ordered by a judge of the *proper* county court to pay a fine of not more than £250 or to be imprisoned for not more than 14 days.

(3) Where under subsection (2) a person is ordered to be imprisoned by a judge of the county court, a judge of the county court may at any time—

- (a) revoke the order, and
- (b) if the person is already in custody, order his discharge.

(4) Section 129 of this Act (enforcement of fines) applies to payment of a fine imposed under subsection (2).

(5) For the purposes of section 13 of the Administration of Justice Act 1960 (appeal in cases of contempt of court), subsection (2) is to be treated as an enactment enabling the county court to deal with an offence under subsection (1) as if it were a contempt of court.

(6) A district judge or deputy district judge shall have the same powers under this section as a judge of a county court.]

Amendment *Section 117K is inserted by the Tribunals, Courts and Enforcement Act 2007, with effect from a date to be appointed.*

II CCA [114K]

[117L. Existing county court proceedings to be stayed]

[(1) This section applies if these conditions are met—

(a) an enforcement restriction order is made;

(b) proceedings in the county court (other than bankruptcy proceedings) are pending against the debtor in respect of a qualifying debt;

(c) by virtue of a requirement included in the order by virtue of section 117D, the creditor under the qualifying debt is not entitled to continue the proceedings in respect of the debt;

(d) the county court receives notice of the enforcement restriction order.

(2) The county court must stay the proceedings.

(3) The county court—

(a) may allow costs already incurred by the creditor, and

(b) if the court allows such costs, may on application or of its own motion add them to the debt owed to the creditor.]

Amendment *Section 117L is inserted by the Tribunals, Courts and Enforcement Act 2007, with effect from a date to be appointed.*

II CCA [114L]

[117M. Charges]

[(1) This section applies during, and after, the currency of an enforcement restriction order.

(2) A qualifying creditor may not make any charge in respect of a protected qualifying debt, unless the charge—

(a) is interest, or

(b) is not interest but relates to a time before or after the currency of the order.

(3) A charge made in breach of subsection (2) is not recoverable.

(4) In subsection (2) "protected qualifying debt" means any qualifying debt under which the debtor was a debtor at some time during the currency of the enforcement restriction order.]

Amendment *Section 117M is inserted by the Tribunals, Courts and Enforcement Act 2007, with effect from a date to be appointed.*

II CCA [114M]

[117N. Variation of duration]

[(1) The county court may vary an enforcement restriction order so as to specify a day, or (if a day has already been specified under section 117H or this section) a different day, on which the order will cease to have effect.

(2) But the new termination day must fall on or before the last day of the maximum permitted period.

(3) If the county court varies an enforcement restriction order under subsection (1), the order ceases to have effect on the new termination day.

(4) The power under this section is exercisable—

(a) on the application of the debtor;
(b) on the application of a qualifying creditor;
(c) of the court's own motion.

(5) In this section—
(a) "new termination day" means the day on which the order will cease to have effect in accordance with the variation under subsection (1);
(b) "maximum permitted period" means the period of 12 months beginning with the day on which the order was originally made.

(6) This section is subject to section 117Q (effect of revocation).]

Amendment *Section 117N is inserted by the Tribunals, Courts and Enforcement Act 2007, with effect from a date to be appointed.*

II CCA [114N]

[117O. Duty to revoke order]

[(1) The county court must revoke an enforcement restriction order in either of these cases—
(a) where it becomes apparent that, at the time the order was made, the condition in subsection 117B(2) was not met (debtor in fact did not have two or more qualifying debts);
(b) where the debtor is no longer a debtor under any qualifying debts.

(2) The county court must revoke an enforcement restriction order in either of these cases—
(a) where it becomes apparent that, at the time the order was made, the condition in subsection 117B(3) was not met (debtor in fact had business debt), and he is still a debtor under the business debt, or any of the business debts, in question;
(b) where the debtor subsequently becomes a debtor under a business debt, and he is still a debtor under that debt.

(3) The county court must revoke an enforcement restriction order where it becomes apparent that, at the time the order was made, the condition in section 117B(4) was not met (debtor in fact excluded under ERO, voluntary arrangement or bankruptcy exclusion).

(4) The county court must revoke an enforcement restriction order where, after the order is made—
(a) the debtor becomes excluded under the voluntary arrangement exclusion, or
(b) a bankruptcy order is made against the debtor, and is still in force.

(5) The county court must revoke an enforcement restriction order in either of these cases—
(a) where it becomes apparent that, at the time the order was made, the condition in section 117B(5) was not met (debtor in fact able to pay qualifying debts);
(b) where the debtor is now able to pay all of his qualifying debts.

(6) The county court must revoke an enforcement restriction order in either of these cases—
(a) where it becomes apparent that, at the time the order was made, the condition in section 117B(6) was not met (debtor in fact not suffering from sudden and unforeseen deterioration in financial circumstances);
(b) where the debtor is no longer suffering from the deterioration in financial circumstances which was taken into account for the purposes of section 117B(6) (even if he is suffering from some other sudden and unforeseen deterioration in his financial circumstances).

(7) The county court must revoke an enforcement restriction order in either of these cases—

(a) where it becomes apparent that, at the time the order was made, the condition in section 117B(7) was not met (in fact no realistic prospect of improvement in debtor's financial circumstances);

(b) where there is no longer a realistic prospect that the debtor's financial circumstances will improve during the period within which the order would continue to have effect (if not revoked).

(8) The county court must revoke an enforcement restriction order in either of these cases—

(a) where it becomes apparent that, at the time the order was made, the condition in section 117B(8) was not met (not in fact fair and equitable to make order);

(b) where it is not fair and equitable for the order to continue to have effect.]

Amendment *Section 117O is inserted by the Tribunals, Courts and Enforcement Act 2007, with effect from a date to be appointed.*

II CCA [114O]

[117P. Power to revoke order]

[(1) The county court may revoke an enforcement restriction order in any case where there is no duty under this Part to revoke it.

(2) The power of revocation under this section may, in particular, be exercised in any of the following cases—

(a) where the order includes, or has previously included, a repayment requirement, and the debtor has failed to comply with that requirement;

(b) where the debtor has failed to provide the county court with the particulars required by—

(i) section 117J(2) and (3), or

(ii) section 117J(4).

(3) The power of revocation under this section is exercisable—

(a) on the application of the debtor;

(b) on the application of a qualifying creditor;

(c) of the court's own motion.]

Amendment *Section 117P is inserted by the Tribunals, Courts and Enforcement Act 2007, with effect from a date to be appointed.*

II CCA [114P]

[117Q. Effect of revocation]

[(1) This section applies if, under any duty or power in this Part, the county court revokes an enforcement restriction order.

(2) The order ceases to have effect in accordance with the terms of the revocation.]

Amendment *Section 117Q is inserted by the Tribunals, Courts and Enforcement Act 2007, with effect from a date to be appointed.*

II CCA [114Q]

[117R. Notice when order made, varied, revoked etc]

[(1) If a notifiable event occurs in relation to an enforcement restriction order, the county court must give notice of the event to every identified qualifying creditor of the debtor.

(2) There is a notifiable event in any of the following cases—

(a) when the enforcement restriction order is made;

(b) when the enforcement restriction order is varied;

(c) when the enforcement restriction order is revoked;
(d) when the county court is given notice under any of the provisions listed in section 117H(7) (effect of administration order or debt relief order on enforcement restriction order).

(3) A person is an identified qualifying creditor of the debtor if—
(a) the debtor has notified the county court that the person is a qualifying creditor, or
(b) the county court is satisfied that the person is a qualifying creditor.]

Amendment *Section 117R is inserted by the Tribunals, Courts and Enforcement Act 2007, with effect from a date to be appointed.*

II CCA [114R]

[117S. Introduction]

[Sections 117T to 117W apply for the purposes of this Part.]

Amendment *Section 117S is inserted by the Tribunals, Courts and Enforcement Act 2007, with effect from a date to be appointed.*

II CCA [114S]

[117T. Main definitions]

[(1) In this Part—
"enforcement restriction order" has the meaning given by section 117A;
"debtor" has the meaning given by section 117B;
"qualifying creditor" means a creditor under a qualifying debt.

(2) References to the currency of an enforcement restriction order are references to the period which—
(a) begins when the order first has effect, and
(b) ends when the order ceases to have effect.

(3) *Repealed.*

(4) *Repealed.*]

Amendment *Section 117T is inserted by the Tribunals, Courts and Enforcement Act 2007, with effect from a date to be appointed.*

II CCA [114T]

[117U. Expressions relating to debts]

[(1) All debts are qualifying debts, except for the following—
(a) any debt secured against an asset;
(b) any debt of a description specified in regulations.

(2) A business debt is any debt (whether or not a qualifying debt) which is incurred by a person in the course of a business.

(3) Only debts that have already arisen are included in references to debts; and accordingly such references do not include any debt that will arise only on the happening of some future contingency.]

Amendment *Section 117U is inserted by the Tribunals, Courts and Enforcement Act 2007, with effect from a date to be appointed.*

II CCA [114U]

[117V. Inability to pay debts]

[(1) In a case where an individual is the debtor under a debt that is repayable by a single payment, the debtor is to be regarded as unable to pay the debt only if—
(a) the time for making the payment has been reached,
(b) the debtor has failed to make the single payment, and
(c) the debtor is unable to make that payment.

(2) In a case where an individual is the debtor under a debt that is repayable by a number of payments, the debtor is to be regarded as unable to pay the debt only if—

(a) the time for making the first of the payments has been reached,

(b) the debtor has failed to make one or more of the payments, and

(c) the debtor is unable to make all of the missed payments.]

Amendment *Section 117V is inserted by the Tribunals, Courts and Enforcement Act 2007, with effect from a date to be appointed.*

II CCA [114V]

[117W. The ERO, voluntary arrangement and bankruptcy exclusions]

[(1) The debtor is excluded under the ERO exclusion if—

(a) an enforcement restriction order currently has effect in respect of him, or

(b) an enforcement restriction order has previously had effect in respect of him, and the period of 12 months—beginning with the day when that order ceased to have effect—has yet to finish.

(2) But in a case that falls within subsection (1)(b), the debtor is not excluded under the ERO exclusion if the previous enforcement restriction order—

(a) ceased to have effect in accordance with any of the provisions listed in section 117H(7) (effect of administration order or debt relief order on enforcement restriction order), or

(b) was revoked in accordance with section 117O(1)(b) (debtor no longer has any qualifying debts).

(3) The debtor is excluded under the voluntary arrangement exclusion if—

(a) an interim order under section 252 of the Insolvency Act 1986 has effect in respect of him (interim order where debtor intends to make proposal for voluntary arrangement), or

(b) he is bound by a voluntary arrangement approved under Part 8 of the Insolvency Act 1986.

(4) The debtor is excluded under the bankruptcy exclusion if—

(a) a petition for a bankruptcy order to be made against him has been presented but not decided, or

(b) he is an undischarged bankrupt.]

Amendment *Section 117W is inserted by the Tribunals, Courts and Enforcement Act 2007, with effect from a date to be appointed.*

II CCA [114W]

[117X. Power to make regulations]

[(1) It is for the Lord Chancellor to make regulations under this Part.

(2) Any power to make regulations under this Part is exercisable by statutory instrument.

(3) A statutory instrument containing regulations under this Part is subject to annulment in pursuance of a resolution of either House of Parliament.]

Amendment *Section 117X is inserted by the Tribunals, Courts and Enforcement Act 2007, with effect from a date to be appointed.*

PART VII
COMMITTALS

II CCA [115]

118. Power to commit for contempt

(1) If any person—

COUNTY COURT

(a) wilfully insults a judge of the county court, or any juror or witness, or any officer of the court during his sitting or attendance in court, or in going to or returning from the court; or

(b) wilfully interrupts the proceedings of the county court or otherwise misbehaves in court;

any officer of the court, with or without the assistance of any other person, may, by order of the judge, take the offender into custody and detain him until the rising of the court, and the judge may, if he thinks fit,—

(i) make an order committing the offender for a specified period not exceeding one month to [. . .] prison [. . .]; or

(ii) impose upon the offender, for every offence, a fine of an amount not exceeding £2,500, or may both make such an order and impose such a fine.

(2) A judge of the county court may at any time revoke an order committing a person to prison under this section and, if he is already in custody, order his discharge.

(3) *Repealed.*

II CCA [115.1]

Wilfully insults, wilfully interrupts The jurisdiction under this section, in respect of insults during the sitting or attendance in court, is confined to contempts committed in court: *R v Lefroy* (1873) LR 8 QB 134. However acts outside the courtroom may amount to a wilful interruption: *Bodden v Metropolitan Police Comr* [1990] 2 QB 397, [1989] 3 All ER 833, CA. Further, a threat to a witness on his way home from court was held to be a wilful insult which was within the scope of s 118(1)(a) and punishable accordingly: *Manchester City Council v McCann* [1999] QB 1214, [1999] 2 WLR 590, CA. A county court judge has no power to commit someone for acting as a solicitor in court when unqualified: *R v Brompton County Court Judge and Vague* [1893] 2 QB 195. When there is an undignified display of contempt of court it is often tactically wise for the judge to rise for a short adjournment: *R v Lewis* (1999) Times, 4 November, CA, Cr Div.

The offence of wilfully insulting the judge may be committed by a party maintaining, in open court, rudely and unambiguously that he or she intends to thwart any attempt to execute an order of the court. It was held in *Bell v Tuohy* [2002] EWCA Civ 423, [2002] 3 All ER 975 that the judge should, in such a case, where this was the only contempt, adjourn for a proper application to commit to be prepared and served.

II CCA [115.1A]

Punishment of misbehaviour The High Court has inherent power to detain a person beyond the rising of the court if this is necessary in order to make arrangements for a summary trial. The county court's powers are more limited. In either court the original judge may deal with the substantive committal issue provided that the circumstances would not give a reasonable bystander concerns as to impartiality: *Wilkinson v S* [2003] EWCA Civ 95, [2003] 2 All ER 184, [2003] 1 WLR 1254. The Court applied the impartiality test in *Re Medicaments and Related Classes of Goods (No 2)* [2001] 1 WLR 700, 726-727, CA.

II CCA [115.1B]

Issue of a summons Where the offender is not taken into custody and brought before the court, a summons should be issued and served personally: see **CPR 81.34**.

II CCA [115.2]

May make an order The Contempt of Court Act 1981 provides that a contemnor may be fined and committed on the same occasion. An unrepresented contemnor should be given the opportunity to apologise and to address the court as to penalty: *Shoreditch County Court Bailiffs v de Madeiros* (1988) Times, 24 February, CA. An order under this section would effectively be a penal order similar to an order under s 92 of the Act. For the procedure see **II CCA [90.1]**.

II CCA [115.3]

Committal to prison A warrant of committal for contempt is not good unless it specifies in what particulars the person committed has been guilty of contempt, in such a way as to enable him to purge his contempt: *R v Lambeth County Court Judge and Jonas* (1887) 36 WR 475; *McIlraith v Grady* [1968] 1 QB 468, [1967] 3 All ER 625, CA. But when the contempt consists in insulting the court the nature of the insult need not be set out in the warrant: *Levy* *v Moylan* (1850) 10 CB 189. A warrant of commitment regularly made out at the rising of the court is not rendered void by a previous irregular oral sentence having been pronounced by the judge, and entered in the district judge's book: *R v Staffordshire County Court Judge* (1888) 57 LJQB 483, sub nom *R v Jordan* 36 WR 797. For observations on the circumstances in which summary jurisdiction to commit for contempt should be exercised, see *Balogh v Crown Court at St Albans* [1975] QB 73, [1974] 3 All ER 283, CA.

II CCA [115.4]

Standard scale For notes to s 14 see para **II CCA [6.3]**.

II CCA [115.5]

Appeal Under s 13 of the Administration of Justice Act 1960, an appeal lies to the Court of Appeal from an order under this section and the Court of Appeal may reverse or vary the order or make such other order including the release of the appellant on bail as may be just. When appealing against a decision of a district judge, the appropriate course is to appeal to the circuit judge not the Court of Appeal: *Read v King* [1997] CLY 1262, CA.

II CCA [115.6]

Privilege The privilege from arrest claimed by suitors, witnesses and advocates while they are in the precincts of the court is the privilege of the court and not that of the litigant. The court, therefore, in a proper case may have a man arrested under a committal order even though he is a litigant before that court: *Re Hunt* [1959] 2 QB 69, [1959] 2 All ER 252, CA.

II CCA [115.7]

Representation As from 2 April 2001 legal advice and representation in proceedings under s 14, s 92 or s 118 is available as part of the Criminal Defence Service under the Access to Justice Act 1999. Sections 12 to 18 and Sch 3 of that Act came into operation on that date concurrently with the repeal of s 29 of the Legal Aid Act 1988. See Legal Services Commission Manual ID-041.

II CCA [116]

119. Issue and execution of orders of committal

(1) Whenever any order or warrant for the committal of any person to prison is made or issued by the county court (whether in pursuance of this or any other Act or of rules of court), the order or warrant shall be directed to the officers of the court, who shall thereby be empowered to take the body of the person against whom the order is made or warrant issued.

(2) It shall be the duty of every constable within his jurisdiction to assist in the execution of every such order or warrant.

(3) The governor of the prison mentioned in any such order or warrant shall be bound to receive and keep the person mentioned in it until he is lawfully discharged.

II CCA [117]

120. Prisons to which committals may be made

Any person committed to prison by the county court, in pursuance of this or any other Act or of rules of court, shall be committed to such prison as may from time to time be directed in the case of that court by order of the Secretary of State.

II CCA [118]

121. Power of judge to order discharge

(1) If at any time it appears to the satisfaction of the county court that any debtor arrested or confined in prison by order of the court is unable from any cause to pay any sum recovered against him (whether by way of satisfaction of a claim or counterclaim or by way of costs or otherwise), or any instalment thereof, and ought to be discharged, the court may order his discharge upon such terms (including liability to re-arrest if the terms are not complied with) as the court thinks fit.

II CCA [118.1]

Release of contemnor Where any punitive purpose of the committal has been achieved and further incarceration has no coercive effect, the contemnor should be released: *Enfield London Borough Council v Mahoney* [1983] 2 All ER 901, [1983] 1 WLR 749, CA.

II CCA [119]

122. ***Execution of committal orders out of jurisdiction of court***
Repealed.

PART VIII
RESPONSIBILITIES AND PROTECTION OF OFFICERS

II CCA [120]

123. ***District judge to have the same responsibilities as sheriff***
Repealed.

II CCA [121]

124. Liability of bailiff for neglect to levy execution

(1) Where the county court issues a warrant of execution, control, possession or delivery and the person to whom it is directed loses the opportunity of executing it by reason of neglect, connivance or omission, any party aggrieved thereby may complain to the court.

(2) On any such complaint the court, if the neglect, connivance or omission is proved to his satisfaction, shall order that person to pay such damages as it appears that the complainant has sustained by reason of it, not exceeding in any case the sum for which the warrant was issued.

II CCA [121.1]

Procedure For the procedure under this section see CPR Sch 2, CCR Order 34 r 1 (at para **CCR 34r1**). As to the liabilities of a district judge in executing a warrant see paras **II CCA [120]**, **II CCA [120.1]** and **II CCA [120.2]**.

This section does not prevent a district judge, in the case of his neglecting to levy execution, from being liable to an action for damages: *Watson v White* [1896] 2 QB 9. In an action for damages for wrongful execution on goods the owner need only show that the warrant did not authorise the officer to levy execution to the value of the goods which were in fact seized: *Moore v Lambeth County Court Registrar (No 2)* [1970] 1 QB 560, [1970] 1 All ER 980, CA.

As to irregularity in procedure in levying execution see *Domine v M Cohen & Co* [1936] 1 All ER 55, CA and as to the recovery of damage suffered in such a case and remoteness, see *Domine v Grimsdall* [1937] 2 All ER 119.

II CCA [122]

125. Irregularity in executing warrants

(1) No officer of the county court in executing any warrant of the court, and no person at whose instance any such warrant is executed, shall be deemed a trespasser by reason of any irregularity or informality—

(a) in any proceeding on the validity of which the warrant depends; or

(b) in the form of the warrant or in the mode of executing it;

But, except in the case of a warrant of control (to which Schedule 12 to the Tribunals, Courts and Enforcement Act 2007 applies), any person aggrieved may bring an action for any special damage sustained by him by reason of the irregularity or informality against the person guilty of it.

(2) No costs shall be recovered in such an action unless the damages awarded exceed £2.

II CCA [122.1]

Protection As to the protection of a sheriff's officer executing a writ of possession, see *Williams v Williams and Nathan* [1937] 2 All ER 559, CA.

As to penalties for assaulting officers of the court in the execution of their duty, see s 14 at para **II CCA [6]**.

II CCA [123]

126. Actions against bailiffs acting under warrants

(1) No action shall be commenced against any bailiff for anything done in obedience to a warrant issued by the county court, unless—

(a) a demand for inspection of the warrant and for a copy of it is made or left at the office of the bailiff by the party intending to bring the action, or his legal representative or agent; and

(b) the bailiff refuses or neglects to comply with the demand within six days after it is made.

(2) The demand must be in writing and signed by the person making it.

(3) If an action is commenced against a bailiff in a case where such a demand has been made and not complied with, judgment shall be given for the bailiff if the warrant is produced or proved at the trial, notwithstanding any defect of jurisdiction or other irregularity in the warrant; .

(4) In this section "bailiff" in relation to a warrant means the person to whom the warrant is directed, and (except in paragraph (a) of subsection (1)) includes any person acting by the order and in aid of a that person.

(5) This section does not apply to an action for anything done under a power to use the procedure in Schedule 12 to the Tribunals, Courts and Enforcement Act 2007.

COUNTY COURT

II CCA [123.1]

Protection As to the protection afforded by this section, see *Aspey v Jones* (1884) 54 LJQB 98, CA.

District judges are within the protection of the above enactment; *Dews v Riley* (1851) 11 CB 434; contra, *Andrews v Marris* (1841) 1 QB 3 and see notes to ss 123 and 124 ante.

A motion by a trustee in bankruptcy against a high bailiff (ie district judge) for an order on him to deliver up property is not an "action" within the meaning of this section: see *Re Lock, ex p Poppleton* (1890) 39 WR 15.

As to a bailiff's right to enter a house see paras **II CCA [87.1]–[87.4]**.

II CCA [123.2]

Legal representative For the definition see s 147 at para **II CCA [141]**.

II CCA [123A]

127. Warrants evidence of authority

In any action commenced against a person for anything done in pursuance of this Act, the production of the warrant of the county court shall be deemed sufficient proof of the authority of the court previous to the issue of the warrant.

II CCA [124]

128. ***Fees***

Repealed.

II CCA [125]

129. Enforcement of fines

Payment of any fine imposed by the county court under this Act may be enforced upon the order of the court in like manner—

(a) as payment of a debt adjudged by the court to be paid may be enforced under this Act; or

(b) as payment of a sum adjudged to be paid by a conviction of a magistrates' court may be enforced under the Magistrates' Courts Act 1980 (disregarding section 81(1) of that Act).

II CCA [125.1]

Magistrates' Courts Act 1980 See particularly s 75 (power to dispense with immediate payment), s.76 (enforcement of sums adjudged to be paid), s 77 (postponement of issue of warrant), s 79 (release from custody and reduction of detention on payment), s 80 (application of money found on defaulter to satisfy sum adjudged), s 82 (restriction on power to impose imprisonment for default), s 83 (process for securing attendance of offender for purposes of s 82), s 84 (power to require statement of means), s 85 (power to remit fine), s 86 (power to fix day for appearance of offender at means inquiry, etc) and s 88 (supervision pending payment).

II CCA [126]

130. Payment and application of fees, fines etc

(1) Subject to subsection (2), all fees, forfeitures and fines payable under this Act and any penalty to an officer of the county court under any other Act shall be paid to officers designated by the Lord Chancellor and dealt with by them in such manner as the Lord Chancellor, after consultation with the Treasury, may direct.

(2) Subsection (1) does not apply to fines imposed on summary conviction or to so much of a fine as is applicable under section 55(4) to indemnify a party injured.

(3) The Lord Chancellor, with the concurrence of the Treasury, shall from time to time make such rules as he thinks fit for securing the balances and other sums of money in the hands of any officers of the county court, and for the due accounting for and application of those balances and sums.

II CCA [126.1]

Officers designated These are the chief clerks of all county courts.

II CCA [127]

131. Appointment of auditors and other officers

The Lord Chancellor may, subject to the consent of the Treasury as to numbers and salaries, appoint as officers in his department such auditors and other officers as he may consider necessary for the purpose of controlling the accounts of the family court or the county court.

II CCA [128]

132. Payment of salaries and expenses

There shall be paid out of money provided by Parliament—

(a) all salaries, remuneration and other sums payable under Part I of this Act or under section 131;

(b) the expenses of supplying the county court and its offices, and the family court and its offices, with law and office books and stationery and postage stamps;

(c) expenses incurred in conveying to prison persons committed by the family court or the county court; and

(d) all other expenses arising out of any jurisdiction for the time being conferred on the family court or any officer of the family court or on the county court or any officer of the county court.

II CCA [128.1]

By s 18 of the Courts Act 1971 the salaries of judges are payable out of the Consolidated Fund and by ss 5(6) and 31 of the Judicial Pensions Act 1981 their pensions are also so payable. Part I of the 1984 Act provides for the appointment and remuneration of district judges, and officers in court service; s 131 at para **II CCA [127]** provides for the appointment of certain officers in the Lord Chancellor's Department.

II CCA [129]

133. Proof of service of summonses etc.

(1) Where any summons or other process issued from the county court is served by an officer of the court, the service may be proved by a certificate in a prescribed form [. . .] showing the fact and mode of the service.

(2) Any officer of the court wilfully and corruptly giving a false certificate under subsection (1) in respect of the service of a summons or other process shall be guilty of an offence and, on conviction thereof, shall be removed from office and shall be liable—

- (a) on conviction on indictment, to imprisonment for any term not exceeding 2 years; or
- (b) on summary conviction, to imprisonment for any term not exceeding 6 months or to a fine not exceeding the statutory maximum or to both such imprisonment and fine.

As amended by SI 1998/2940 art 6(e).

II CCA [129.1]

Service The question of service is one of fact for the judge: *Robinson v Lenaghan* (1848) 2 Exch 333; *Zohrab v Smith* (1847) 5 Dow & L 635; *Waters v Handley* (1848) 6 Dow & L 88.

II CCA [130]

135. Penalty for falsely pretending to act under authority of court

Any person who—

- (a) delivers or causes to be delivered to any other person any paper falsely purporting to be a copy of any summons or other process of the county court, knowing it to be false; or
- (b) acts or professes to act under any false colour or pretence of the process or authority of the county court;

shall be guilty of an offence and shall for each offence be liable on conviction on indictment to imprisonment for a term not exceeding 7 years.

II CCA [131]

136. Penalty for falsely representing document to have been issued from county court

(1) It shall not be lawful to deliver or cause to be delivered to any person any document which was not issued under the authority of the county court but which, by reason of its form or contents or both, has the appearance of having been issued under such authority.

(2) If any person contravenes this section, he shall for each offence be liable on summary conviction to a fine of an amount not exceeding level 3 on the standard scale.

(3) Nothing in this section shall be taken to prejudice section 135.

II CCA [131.1]

Standard scale See para **II CCA [6.3]**.

II CCA [132]

137. Lessee to give notice of summons for recovery of land

(1) Every lessee to whom there is delivered any summons issued from the county court for the recovery of land demised to or held by him, or to whose knowledge any such summons comes, shall forthwith give notice of the summons to his lessor or his bailiff or receiver.

(2) If a lessee fails to give notice as required by subsection (1), he shall be liable to forfeit to the person of whom he holds the land an amount equal to the value of 3 years' improved or rack rent of the land to be recovered by action in the county court or any other court having jurisdiction in respect of claims for such an amount

II CCA [132.1]

"Improved or rack rent" This does not mean the rent reserved by the contract of tenancy, but such rent as the premises would fetch at the time of service of the writ: *Crocker v Fothergill* (1819) 2 B & Ald 652.

FORFEITURE FOR NON-PAYMENT OF RENT

II CCA [133]

138. Provisions as to forfeiture for non-payment of rent

(1) This section has effect where a lessor is proceeding by action in the county court (being an action in which the county court has jurisdiction) to enforce against a lessee a right of re-entry or forfeiture in respect of any land for non-payment of rent.

(2) If the lessee pays into court or to the lessor not less than 5 clear days before the return day all the rent in arrear and the costs of the action, the action shall cease, and the lessee shall hold the land according to the lease without any new lease.

(3) If—

(a) the action does not cease under subsection (2); and

(b) the court at the trial is satisfied that the lessor is entitled to enforce the right of re-entry or forfeiture,

the court shall order possession of the land to be given to the lessor at the expiration of such period, not being less than 4 weeks from the date of the order, as the court thinks fit, unless within that period the lessee pays into court or to the lessor all the rent in arrear and the costs of the action.

(4) The court may extend the period specified under subsection (3) at any time before possession of the land is recovered in pursuance of the order under that subsection.

(5) [. . .] if—

(a) within the period specified in the order; or

(b) within that period as extended under subsection (4),

the lessee pays into court or to the lessor—

(i) all the rent in arrear; and

(ii) the costs of the action,

he shall hold the land according to the lease without any new lease.

(6) Subsection (2) shall not apply where the lessor is proceeding in the same action to enforce a right of re-entry or forfeiture on any other ground as well as for non-payment of rent, or to enforce any other claim as well as the right of re-entry or forfeiture and the claim for arrears of rent.

(7) If the lessee does not—

(a) within the period specified in the order; or

(b) within that period as extended under subsection (4),

pay into court or to the lessor—

(i) all the rent in arrear; and

(ii) the costs of the action,

the order shall be enforceable in the prescribed manner and so long as the order remains unreversed the lessee shall, subject to subsections (8) and (9A), be barred from all relief.

(8) The extension under subsection (4) of a period fixed by a court shall not be treated as relief from which the lessee is barred by subsection (7) if he fails to pay into court or to the lessor all the rent in arrear and the costs of the action within that period.

(9) Where the court extends a period under subsection (4) at a time when—

(a) that period has expired; and

(b) a warrant has been issued for the possession of the land, the court shall suspend the warrant for the extended period; and, if, before the expiration period, the lessee pays into court or to the lessor all the rent in arrear and all the costs of the action, the court shall cancel the warrant.

(9A) Where the lessor recovers possession of the land at any time after the making of the order under subsection (3) (whether as a result of the enforcement of the order or otherwise) the lessee may, at any time within six months from the date on which the lessor recovers possession, apply to the court for relief; and on any such application the court may, if it thinks fit, grant to the lessee such relief, subject to such terms and conditions, as it thinks fit.

(9B) Where the lessee is granted relief on an application under subsection (9A) he shall hold the land according to the lease without any new lease.

(9C) An application under subsection (9A) may be made by a person with an interest under a lease of the land derived (whether immediately or otherwise) from the lessee's interest therein in like manner as if he were the lessee; and on any such application the court may make an order which (subject to such terms and conditions as the court thinks fit) vests the land in such a person, as lessee of the lessor, for the remainder of the term of the lease under which he has any such interest as aforesaid, or for any lesser term.

In this subsection any reference to the land includes a reference to a part of the land.

(10) Nothing in this section or section 139 shall be taken to affect—

(a) the power of the court to make any order which it would otherwise have power to make as respects a right of re-entry or forfeiture on any ground other than non-payment of rent; or

(b) section 146(4) of the Law of Property Act 1925 (relief against forfeiture)

COUNTY COURT

II CCA [133.1]

Forfeiture for non-payment of rent Relief under s 138 is confined to cases where forfeiture is for non-payment of rent. The section does not apply if the landlord is proceeding on other grounds as well, as is made clear by sub-s (6), but the opportunity to seek relief under Law of Property Act 1925 s 146(4) is preserved by sub-s (10). In the case of premises let as a dwelling, s 81 of the Housing Act 1996 provides that as a pre-condition to the exercise of the rights to forfeiture based on outstanding service or administration charges, there must be a final determination by the leasehold valuation tribunal or by the court or admission by the tenant that these charges are payable: see **III L&T [276]**. A landlord may retain, and exercise, a right of re-entry for non-payment of rent, whilst making a legal assignment of the right to the arrears: *Kataria v Safeland plc* [1998] 1 EGLR 39, [1998] 05 EG 155, CA.

Where a tenant owes rent but has not admitted or agreed to owing service charges as well the landlord's right of re-entry is exercisable only in respect of the rent; and the jurisdiction, under s 146 of the Law of Property Act 1925, to impose the payment of such unpaid services as a condition of relief, is not available. However, for the purposes of s 138 of the County Courts Act 1984, the court's discretion to grant relief provides for the payment of "all the rent in arrear" and this might be interpreted as including service charges, if treated as rent by the terms of the lease: *Mohammadi v Anston Investments Ltd* [2003] EWCA Civ 981, [2004] HLR 88.

A landlord's claim for arrears of rent is not subject to a duty to take steps to mitigate, for example by negotiating a surrender or agreeing to an assignment: *Reichman v Beveridge* [2006] EWCA Civ 1659.

II CCA [133.2]

If the lessee pays all the rent in arrears The entitlement to rent does not end with service of proceedings: for the purpose of obtaining relief the lessee must pay all rent due at the time of the court order, or payment, if earlier: *Maryland Estates Ltd v Bar-Joseph* [1998] 3 All ER 193, [1999] 1 WLR 83 CA. If the forfeiture proceeds, money is recoverable for use and occupation from the date of the service of proceedings: *Canas Property Co Ltd v KL Television Services Ltd* [1970] 2 QB 433, [1970] 2 All ER 795, CA; *Capital and City Holdings Ltd v Dean Warburg Ltd* (1988) 58 P & CR 346, [1989] 1 EGLR 90, CA. Payment by someone other than the lessee is not usually effective (*Matthews v Dobbins* [1963] 1 All ER 417, [1963] 1 WLR 227, CA), but a mortgagee of the leasehold is entitled to relief under the section by paying off the arrears: *Escalus Properties Ltd v Robinson* [1996] QB 231, [1995] 4 All ER 852, CA. Comparable relief may be granted, as a matter of equity, to an equitable chargee: *Ladup Ltd v Williams & Glyn's Bank plc* [1985] 2 All ER 577, [1985] 1 WLR 851.

II CCA [133.3]

Five clear days before the return day "Five clear days" means five days excluding both the day when the payment is made into court and also the return day. As to "return day" this is defined in s 147 (see para **II CCA [141]**) and has been held to mean the hearing date specified in the summons: *Swordheath Properties Ltd v Bolt* [1992] 2 EGLR 68, [1992] 38 EG 152, CA.

II CCA [133.4]

Relief after recovery of possession The barring of all relief, pursuant to sub-s (7), was held in *Di Palma v Victoria Square Property Co Ltd* [1986] Ch 150, [1985] 2 All ER 676, CA to prevent an application to the High Court for relief. The insertion of sub-s (9A) remedies the situation by conferring jurisdiction on the county court, equivalent to the High Court jurisdiction, to entertain late applications for relief, within six months of recovery of possession.

II CCA [133.5]

Not less than four weeks An order giving less than four weeks until possession must be given is made without jurisdiction and may be set aside on this ground even after the lapse of a substantial period of time: *Croydon (Unique) Ltd v Wright* [2001] Ch 318, [1999] 4 All ER 257, CA.

II CCA [133.6]

Extension of period The barring of relief does not prevent the extension of the period. In *Varndeon Estates Ltd v Buckland and Buckland* (1967) 111 Sol Jo 684, CA, it was held that in the special circumstances a period of 18 months for the payment of the arrears of rent was reasonable and that arrears of rent under an earlier judgment should be included in the sum to be paid. However, evidence of ability to pay in the event of success in a collateral warranty claim is not sufficient for relief against forfeiture in the absence of evidence of an actual ability to pay within a reasonable time: *Inntrepreneur Pub Co (CPC) Ltd v Langton* [2000] 1 EGLR 34, [2000] 08 EG 169.

II CCA [133.7]

Position of mortgagee A mortgagee's application for relief may, like that of the lessee, be made at any time within six months of the date on which the lessor recovers possession and is not barred by sub-s (7) although such relief is discretionary: *United Dominions Trust Ltd v Shellpoint Trustees Ltd* [1993] 4 All ER 310, CA. The court may grant relief, notwithstanding that the tenant has been a bad payer: *Re Brompton Securities Ltd (No 2)* [1988] 3 All ER 677.

II CCA [133.8]

Law of Property Act 1925 s 146. For text and commentary see para **III L&T [2]**.

II CCA [133.9]

Security of tenure Where the lessee has security of tenure under the Rent Act 1977 the court should, nevertheless, exercise its jurisdiction under s 138. The lessee of a forfeited lease may be protected from eviction by other legislation but that does not absolve the court from its responsibilities under s 138: *Wolmer Securities Ltd v Corne* [1966] 2 QB 243, [1966] 2 All ER 691, CA. The position in the case of an assured tenancy for a fixed term is not the same as for a regulated tenancy. If the court decides to bring such a tenancy to an end, eg for arrears of rent, there is no scope for additional relief under s 138: *Artesian Residential Investments Ltd v Beck* [2000] QB 541, [1999] 3 All ER 113, CA.

II CCA [133.10]

Subsection (9C) A creditor of a lessee who has a charging order against the leasehold estate is not entitled to claim relief in his own name as a person with an interest in the lease under s 138(9C) but may claim indirectly, relying on the inherent jurisdiction of the High Court. The creditor can join the lessee as a defendant to the application for relief on the basis that the creditor is effectively a beneficiary of a trust by which the lessee held the estate: *Bland v Ingram's Estates Ltd* [2001] Ch 767, [2002] 1 All ER 221.

Where a lessee/mortgagee obtains relief on the usual terms as to payment of arrears and costs, any subsequent lessee who takes a lease with knowledge of the forfeiture has his, or her, leasehold term postponed to that of the original lessee once restored. The arrears of rent and interest payable by the applicant should be paid to the subsequent lessee for the period of the subsequent lease: s 141 of the Law of Property Act 1925 and *Re King, Robinson v Gray* [1963] Ch 459, [1963] 1 All ER 781, CA. As for the period when the lessor was in occupation, he should be charged (and should bring into account) a full occupation rent in determining the amount the applicant should pay as the price of relief: *Bland v Ingram's Estates Ltd (No 2)* [2001] EWCA Civ 1088, [2002] Ch 177, [2002] 1 All ER 244.

COUNTY COURT

II CCA [134]

139. Service of summons and re-entry

(1) In a case where section 138 has effect, if—

(a) one-half-year's rent is in arrear at the time of the commencement of the action; and

(b) the lessor has a right to re-enter for non-payment of that rent; and

(c) the power under section 72(1) of the Tribunals, Courts and Enforcement Act 2007 (commercial rent arrears recovery) is exercisable to recover the arrears; and

(d) there are not sufficient goods on the premises to recover the arrears by that power,

the service of the summons in the action in the prescribed manner shall stand in lieu of a demand and re-entry.

(2) Where a lessor has enforced against a lessee, by re-entry without action, a right of re-entry or forfeiture as respects any land for non-payment of rent, the lessee may [. . .] at any time within six months from the date on which the lessor re-entered apply to the county court for relief, and on any such application the court may, if it thinks fit, grant to the lessee such relief as the High Court could have granted.

(3) Subsections (9B) and (9C) of section 138 shall have effect in relation to an application under subsection (2) of this section as they have effect in relation to an application under subsection (9A) of that section.

II CCA [134.1]

No sufficient distress It is not a condition precedent to an action under s 138 that a landlord should prove no sufficient distress by an actual levy before action; the fact that there was no sufficient distress may be proved by other evidence: *Rickett v Green* [1910] 1 KB 253.

II CCA [135]

140. Interpretation of sections 138 and 139

For the purposes of sections 138 and 139—

"lessee" includes—

(a) an original or derivative under-lessee;
(b) the persons deriving title under a lessee;
(c) a grantee under a grant at a fee farm rent, or under a grant securing a rent by condition; and
(d) the persons deriving title under such a grantee;

"lessor" includes—

(a) an original or derivative under-lessor;
(b) the persons deriving title under a lessor;
(c) a person making a grant at a fee farm rent, or a grant securing a rent by condition; and
(d) the persons deriving title under such a grantor;

"under-lease" includes an agreement for an under-lease where the under-lessee has become entitled to have his underlease granted; and

"under-lessee" includes any person deriving title under an under-lessee

SOLICITORS

II CCA [136]

142. Power to enforce undertakings by solicitors

The county court shall have the same power to enforce an undertaking given by a solicitor in relation to any proceedings in that court as the High Court has to enforce an undertaking so given in relation to any proceedings in the High Court.

II CCA [136.1]

Power to enforce undertaking See *John Fox (a firm) v Bannister King & Rigbeys (a firm)* [1988] QB 925n[1987] 1 All ER 737, CA. If an order were made by way of punishment for contempt an appeal would lie to the Court of Appeal under Administration of Justice Act 1960 s 13. The procedure for enforcement is at CPR Sch 2 CCR Ord 29 r 2 (see para **CCR 29r2**). Summary procedure for enforcement is appropriate only in a clear case: *Geoffrey Silver and Drake v Baines* [1971] 1 QB 396, [1971] 1 All ER 473, CA; *Udall v Capri Lightning Ltd (in liquidation)* [1988] QB 907, [1987] 3 All ER 262, CA; *United Bank of Kuwait v Hammoud* [1988] 3 All ER 418, [1988] 1 WLR 1051, CA and *City Trust Ltd v Levy* [1988] 3 All ER 418, [1988] 1 WLR 1051, CA. See now **CPR 81.11**.

II CCA [136.2]

Implementation of an undertaking A breach of an undertaking to issue proceedings "forthwith" is punishable as contempt and "forthwith" means "as soon as practicable": *P S Refson & Co Ltd v Saggers* [1984] 3 All ER 111, [1984] 1 WLR 1025. Where the purpose of an undertaking is the protection of a third party, the solicitor may be liable in damages to the third party for breach of the undertaking: *Al-Kandari v J R Brown & Co* [1988] QB 665, [1988] 1 All ER 833, CA. An undertaking given within the normal ambit of the solicitor's function will bind the partners even where given fraudulently: *United Bank of Kuwait v Hammoud* [1988] 3 All ER 418, [1988] 1 WLR 1051; *City Trust Ltd v Levy* [1988] 3 All ER 418, [1988] 1 WLR 1051, CA.

II CCA [137]

143. Prohibition on persons other than solicitors receiving remuneration for business done in county courts

(1) No person other than—

(a) a legal representative; or
(b) a person exercising a right of audience or a right to conduct litigation by virtue of an order made under section 11 of the Courts and Legal Services Act 1990 (representation in county courts),

shall be entitled to have or recover any fee or reward for acting on behalf of a party in proceedings in the county court.

(2) < . . . >

REPLEVIN

II CCA [138]

144. Replevin

Schedule 1 to this Act shall have effect

II CCA [138.1]

Replevin Replevin is a judicial redelivery to their owner of chattels alleged to have been wrongfully seized. See Sch 1 and the notes, see paras **II CCA [142.1]–II CCA [142.4]**.

POWER TO RAISE MONETARY LIMITS

II CCA [139]

145. Power to raise monetary limits

(1) If it appears to Her Majesty in Council—

(a) that the county court limit for the purposes of any enactment referring to that limit, or

(b) that the higher limit or the lower limit referred to in section 20 of this Act,

should be increased, Her Majesty may by Order in Council direct that the limit in question shall be such amount as may be specified in the Order.

(2) An Order under subsection (1) may contain such incidental or transitional provisions as Her Majesty considers appropriate.

(2A) It is for the Lord Chancellor to recommend to Her Majesty the making of an Order under subsection (1).

(3) No recommendation shall be made to Her Majesty in Council to make an Order under this section unless a draft of the Order has been laid before Parliament and approved by resolution of each House of Parliament.

II CCA [139.1]

County court limits The county court limit has been abolished for those proceedings set out in art 2(1) of the High Court and County Courts Jurisdiction Order 1991, SI 1991/724, see paras **II HCJ [3.1]–II HCJ [3.4]**.

GENERAL

II CCA [140]

146. Lord Commissioners to represent Lord Chancellor when Great Seal in commission

When the Great Seal is in commission, the Lords Commissioners shall represent the Lord Chancellor for the purposes of this Act; but the powers vested in him by this Act in relation to the appointment of officers may be exercised by the senior Lord Commissioners for the time being.

II CCA [141]

147. Interpretation

(1) In this Act, unless the context otherwise requires—

"action" means any proceedings in the county court which may be commenced as prescribed by plaint;

[. . .]

"Admiralty proceedings" means proceedings which, if commenced in the High Court, would involve the exercise of the High Court's Admiralty jurisdiction;

COUNTY COURT

"the county court limit" means—

(a) in relation to any enactment contained in this Act for which a limit is for the time being specified by an Order under section 145, that limit,

(b) [. . .]

(c) in relation to any enactment contained in this Act and not within paragraph (a) [. . .], the county court limit for the time being specified by any other Order in Council or order defining the limit of county court jurisdiction for the purposes of that enactment;

[. . .]

"court" means the county court;

"deposit-taking institution" means a person who may, in the course of his business, lawfully accept deposits in the United Kingdom;

[...]

"hearing" includes trial, and "hear" and "heard" shall be construed accordingly;

"hereditament" includes both a corporeal and an incorporeal hereditament;

[. . .]

"judgment summons" means a summons issued on the application of a person entitled to enforce a judgment or order under section 5 of the Debtors Act 1869 requiring a person, or, where two or more persons are liable under the judgment or order, requiring any one or more of them to attend court;

"landlord", in relation to any land, means the person entitled to the immediate reversion or, if the property therein is held in joint tenancy, any of the persons entitled to the immediate reversion;

"legal representative" means a person who, for the purposes of the Legal Services Act 2007, is an authorised person in relation to an activity which constitutes the exercise of a right of audience or the conduct of litigation (within the meaning of that Act);

[. . .]

"matter" means every proceeding in the county court which may be commenced as prescribed otherwise than by plaint;

"officer", in relation to the county court, means any clerk, bailiff, usher or messenger in the service of that court;

[. . .]

"party" includes every person served with notice of, or attending, any proceeding, whether named as a party to that proceeding or not;

"prescribed" means prescribed by rules of court;

[. . .]

"proceedings" includes both actions and matters;

[. . .]

"return day" means the day appointed in any summons or proceeding for the appearance of the defendant or any other day fixed for the hearing of any proceedings;

[. . .]

"ship" includes any description of vessel used in navigation;

"solicitor" means solicitor of the Senior Courts;

[. . .]

(1A) The definition of "deposit-taking institution" in subsection (1) must be read with—

(a) section 22 of the Financial Services and Markets Act 2000;

(b) any relevant order under that section; and

(c) Schedule 2 to that Act.

(2), (3) [. . .]

II CCA [141.1]

Repeals The definitions of "county court rules" and "the rule committee" are repealed by the Civil Procedure Act 1997 Sch 2, para 2.

II CCA [141.2]

Hereditament The words "incorporeal hereditament" have been held to include leaseholds (*Tomkins v Jones* (1889) 22 QBD 599) and the office of parish clerk (*Stephenson v Raine* (1853) 2 E & B 744) but not a local rate: *Stuart v Jones* (1852) 1 E & B 22; *Re Baddeley* (1849) 4 Exch 508; *Re Knight* (1848) 1 Exch 802.

II CCA [141.3]

Legal representative This definition was inserted by the Courts and Legal Services Act 1990 Sch 18, para 60.

Schedules

SCHEDULE 1

Section 144

II CCA [142]

Replevin

1. (1) The sheriff shall have no power or responsibility with respect to replevin bonds or replevins.

(2) Where any goods subject to replevin are taken, the county court shall have power, subject to the provisions of this Schedule, to approve of replevin bonds and to grant replevins and to issue all necessary process in relation to them, and any such process shall be executed by an officer of the court.

(3) The court shall, at the instance of the party whose goods have been seized, cause the goods to be replevied to that party on his giving such security as is provided in this Schedule.

2. (1) It shall be a condition of any security given under paragraph 1 that the replevisor will—

- (a) commence an action of replevin against the seizor in the High Court within one week from the date when the security is given; or
- (b) commence such an action in the county court within one month from that date.

(2) In either case—

- (a) the replevisor shall give security, to be approved by the county court, for such an amount as the court thinks sufficient to cover both the probable costs of the action and either—
  - (i) the alleged rent or damage in respect of which the distress has been made; or
  - (ii) in a case where the goods replevied have been seized otherwise than under colour of distress, the value of the goods; and
- (b) it shall be a further condition of the security that the replevisor will—
  - (i) prosecute the action with effect and without delay; and
  - (ii) make a return of the goods, if a return of them is ordered in the action.

(3) [. . .]

[. . .]

II CCA [142.1]

The nature of replevin Replevin is a judicial redelivery to their owner of chattels alleged to have been wrongfully seized and is a remedy available to a bailee: *Swaffer v Mulcahy* [1934]

1 KB 608. It lies for goods taken under a court order if the court had no power to make the order: *George v Chambers* (1843) 11 M & W 149; but this does not apply to orders of the High Court. The process has two stages, the grant of replevin and the trial.

II CCA [142.2]

The power to grant replevin is given exclusively to the district judge of the county court. Replevin in respect of distress for unpaid domestic rates is available only where there was no right to vary the rate: *Steel Linings Ltd and Harvey v Bibby & Co* [1993] RA 27, [1993] NLJR 511, CA.

II CCA [142.3]

In an action of replevin the damages may be assessed as in an action of trespass and they may include an item for illegal distress and for annoyance and loss of replevin: *Smith v Enright* (1893) 63 LJQB 220; *Gibbs v Cruikshank* (1873) LR 8 CP 454.

II CCA [142.4]

With effect and without delay The first two words mean prosecuted to a successful conclusion: *Tummons v Ogle* (1856) 6 E & B 571. As to the requirement to act "without delay", a lapse of two years in bringing proceedings has been held to break the condition and to amount to an abandonment of the suit: *Axford v Perrett* (1828) 4 Bing 586; *Morris v Matthews* (1841) 2 QB 293; *Evans v Bowen* (1850) 19 LJQB 8.

HIGH COURT AND COUNTY COURTS JURISDICTION ORDER 1991

(SI 1991/724)

TABLE OF CONTENTS

II HCJ [1]

Amendments The Order was amended, as from 22 April 2014, by SI 2014/821, following the establishment of the single County Court. Note however, that the articles 6D and 6E introduced by SI 2014/821 do not apply to proceedings issued before that date.

II HCJ [2]

1. Title and commencement

This Order may be cited as the High Court and County Courts Jurisdiction Order 1991 and shall come into force on 1st July 1991.

II HCJ [2A]

1A. Interpretation

In this Order—

(a) *"the EOP Regulation" means Regulation (EC) No 1896/2006 of the European Parliament and of the Council of 12 December 2006 creating a European order for payment procedure;*

(b) *"the ESCP Regulation" means Regulation (EC) No 861/2007 of the European Parliament and of the Council of 11 July 2007 establishing a European small claims procedure; and*

(c) "the London insolvency district" means the insolvency district designated by the London Insolvency District (County Court at Central London) Order 2014.

Amendment *Text in italic is omitted by the European Enforcement Order, European Order for Payment and European Small Claims Procedure (Amendment etc) (EU Exit) Regulations 2018 with effect from exit day (as defined in the European Union (Withdrawal) Act 2018).*

II HCJ [3]

2. Jurisdiction

(1) The County Court shall have jurisdiction under—

(a) sections [. . .] 146 and 147 of the Law of Property Act 1925,
(b) [. . .],
(c) section 26 of the Arbitration Act 1950,
(d) section 63(2) of the Landlord and Tenant Act 1954,
(e) section 28(3) of the Mines and Quarries (Tips) Act 1969,
(f) section 66 of the Taxes Management Act 1970,
(g) section 41 of the Administration of Justice Act 1970,
(h) [. . .],
(i) section 13 of the Torts (Interference with Goods) Act 1977,
(j) section 87 of the Magistrates' Courts Act 1980,
(k) sections 17 and 18 of the Audit Commission Act 1998,
(l) sections 15, 16, 21, 25 and 139 of the County Courts Act 1984,
(m) section 39(4) of, and paragraph 3(1) of Schedule 3 to, the Legal Aid Act 1988,
(n) sections 99, 102(5), 114, 195, 204, 230, 231 and 235(5) of the Copyright, Designs and Patents Act 1988, [. . .]
(o) section 40 of the Housing Act 1988, and
(p) sections 13 and 14 of the Trusts of Land and Appointment of Trustees Act 1996,
(q) *the EOP Regulation,*
(r) *the ESCP Regulation,*

whatever the amount involved in the proceedings and whatever the value of any fund or asset connected with the proceedings.

(2) The County Court shall have jurisdiction under—

(a) section 10 of the Local Land Charges Act 1975, and
(b) section 10(4) of the Rentcharges Act 1977,

where the sum concerned or amount claimed does not exceed £5,000.

(3) The County Court shall have jurisdiction under the following provisions of the Law of Property Act 1925 where the capital value of the land or interest in land which is to be dealt with does not exceed £30,000:

(a) sections 3, 49, 66, 181 and 188;
(b) proviso (iii) to paragraph 3 of Part III of Schedule 1;
(c) proviso (v) to paragraph 1(3) of Part IV of Schedule 1;
(d) proviso (iii) and (iv) to paragraph 1(4) of Part IV of Schedule 1.

(4) The County Court shall have jurisdiction under sections 89, 90, 91 and 92 of the Law of Property Act 1925 where the amount owing in respect of the mortgage or charge at the commencement of the proceedings does not exceed £30,000.

(5) The County Court shall have jurisdiction under the proviso to section 136(1) of the Law of Property Act 1925 where the amount or value of the debt or thing in action does not exceed £30,000.

(6) The County Court shall have jurisdiction under section 1(6) of the Land Charges Act 1972—

(a) in the case of a land charge of Class C (i), C (ii) or D (i), if the amount does not exceed £30,000;
(b) in the case of a land charge of Class C (iii), if it is for a specified capital sum of money not exceeding £30,000 or, where it is not for a specified capital sum, if the capital value of the land affected does not exceed £30,000;
(c) in the case of a land charge of Class A, Class B, Class C (iv), Class D (ii), Class D (iii) or Class E, if the capital value of the land affected does not exceed £30,000;
(d) in the case of a land charge of Class F, if the land affected by it is the subject of an order made by the court under section 1 of the

Matrimonial Homes Act 1983 or an application for an order under that section relating to that land has been made to the court;

(e) [...]

(7) The County Court shall have jurisdiction under sections 69, 70 and 71 of the Solicitors Act 1974 where a bill of costs relates wholly or partly to contentious business done in the County Court and the amount of the bill does not exceed £5,000.

(7A) The County Court shall have jurisdiction under the following provisions of the Trade Marks Act 1994—

(a) sections 15, 16, 19, 23(5), 25(4)(b), 30, 31, 46, 47, 64, 73 and 74;

(b) paragraph 12 of Schedule 1; and

(c) paragraph 14 of Schedule 2,

to include jurisdiction to hear and determine any claims or matters ancillary to, or arising from proceedings brought under such provisions.

(7B) The County Court has jurisdiction in respect of any contentious probate matter arising in connection with an application for the grant or revocation of probate or administration where—

(a) the grant or application is made through the principal registry of the Family Division or a district probate registry under section 105 of the Senior Courts Act 1981; and

(b) it is shown to the satisfaction of the County Court that the value of the deceased's net estate at the date of death does not exceed £30,000.

(7C) In paragraph (7B), "net estate", in relation to a deceased person, means the estate of that person exclusive of any property the deceased was possessed of or entitled to as a trustee and not beneficially, and after making allowances for funeral expenses and for debts and liabilities.

(8) *Omitted.*

Amendment *Text in italic is omitted by the European Enforcement Order, European Order for Payment and European Small Claims Procedure (Amendment etc) (EU Exit) Regulations 2018 with effect from exit day (as defined in the European Union (Withdrawal) Act 2018).*

II HCJ [3.1]

Unlimited jurisdiction Article 2 has removed the financial limits on large areas of jurisdiction conferred on county courts by the County Courts Act 1984 (see para **II CCA [1]**): s 15 (contract and tort, except libel and slander), s 16 (money recoverable by statute), s 21 (recovery of land: see also Landlord and Tenant Act 1954, s 63(2) and Housing Act 1988 s 40), s 25 (inheritance family provision: and s 139 (relief against forfeiture after re-entry). See para **II HCJ [3.5]** for the other areas of more specialised jurisdiction.

II HCJ [3.2]

The £5,000 limit The £5,000 limit applies to Local Land Charges Act 1975 s 10 (compensation recoverable from registering authority for defective search certificate), Rentcharges Act 1977 s 10(4) (payment into court) and Solicitors Act 1974 ss 69, 70 and 71 (liability for costs).

II HCJ [3.3]

The £30,000 limit The £30,000 limit applies to any proceedings in the county court under the Law of Property Act 1925 and under the Land Charges Act 1972 s 1(6) (vacating registered land charges) except those arising under Law of Property Act 1925 ss 146 and 147 (relief from forfeiture) where the jurisdiction is unlimited.

II HCJ [3.4]

Savings for other limits There are savings for admiralty proceedings to which County Courts Act 1984 s 27(1), (2) applies: see art 12. The old financial limits under s 27(2) are still in force: £15,000 for salvage claims and £5,000 for everything else. Also the equity jurisdiction, set out in County Courts Act 1984 s 23, is still subject to "the county court limit" which was set at £30,000 in 1981 by the County Courts Jurisdiction Order 1981, SI 1981/1123.

HIGH COURT

II HCJ [3.5]

Administration of Justice Act 1970 s 41 This provision enables orders for costs and compensation, made in criminal courts to be recovered through the county courts.

Arbitration Act 1950 s 26 See now Arbitration Act 1996 s 66, (for enforcement of the award see para **III ARB [19]**).

Consumer Credit Act 1974 s 139(5)(b) This provision enables the court to reopen extortionate credit agreements (see para **III CON [50]**).

Copyright, Designs and Patents These areas of jurisdiction are explained more fully in Part III: see para **III PAT [35]**.

Legal Aid Act 1988 s 39(4) and Schedule 3 These provisions concern the recovery of money of legal aid contributions and losses caused by misrepresentations or non-compliance. Section 39(4) has now been repealed and replaced by the Access to Justice Act 1999. Section 21(5) of that Act gives the county court jurisdiction to hear claims for losses arising from misrepresentation.

Local Government Finance Act 1982 ss 19 and 20 Although the county court is given unlimited jurisdiction to determine applications and appeals under these sections the proceedings are required, by art 6, to be started in the High Court.

Magistrates Court Act 1980 s 87 This provision enables the payment of fines and other money due on conviction to be enforced through the county court.

Mines and Quarries (Tips) Act 1969 Local authorities are empowered by this Act to take steps to prevent disused tips from becoming dangerous. The county court has limited jurisdiction to resolve disputes about liability and compensation.

Taxes Management Act 1970 s 66 By this provision, proceedings for the recovery of tax may be brought in the county court in the name of the collector; and any barrister who is an officer of the Board may appear in such proceedings as an advocate. The effect of art 2 is to remove any financial limit on the sums recoverable.

Torts (Interference with Goods) Act 1977 s 13 This section provides for the sale, by order of the court, of uncollected goods (see para **III PTY [22]**).

Trusts of Land and Appointment of Trustees Act 1996 ss 13 and 14 These provisions replace Law of Property Act 1925 s 30 and empower the court to make orders regarding trusts of land: see para **III REA [50]**.

II HCJ [3.6]

Trade Marks Extensive jurisdiction under the Trade Marks Act 1994 was conferred on the patents county court and the county courts listed in para (7B) by the High Court and County Courts Jurisdiction (Amendment) Order 2005, SI 2005/587, with effect from 1 April 2005. Although s 75(a) of the Trade Marks Act 1994, as enacted, conferred jurisdiction on the High Court alone, the section was amended by s 1 of the Courts and Legal Services Act 1990 to enable the Lord Chancellor to designate business to county courts.

II HCJ [3.7]

Community trade marks The Community Trade Mark Regulations 1996, SI 1996/1908, made provision for the operation of the Community Trade Marks Regulation (Council Regulation (EC) No 40/95 of 20 December 1993 (OJ No L11, 14.1.94 p1) by applying certain provisions of the 1994 Act and the Trade Marks Rules to Community trade marks. Regulation 9 appointed the High Court as the Community Trade Marks Court. But the original regulation 9 was replaced by the Community Trade Mark (Designation of Community Trade Mark Courts) Regulations 2005, SI 2005/440; and the new regulation 9 designates the patents county court and the county courts listed in article 2(7B), above, as Community trade mark courts, in addition to the High Court, with effect from 1 April 2005.

II HCJ [3.8]

Artist's Resale Right Regulations 2006 The Artist's Resale Right Regulations 2006, SI 2006/346, give artists and their successors certain royalty rights on resale of their creations. They do not confer any special jurisdiction on the civil courts but reg 15 gives the artist, or successor, the right to obtain information about the terms of the resale within 3 years of the sale to which it relates and may apply to the county court for an order for that information to be supplied.

II HCJ [4]

3. Injunctions

The High Court shall have jurisdiction to hear an application for an injunction made in the course of or in anticipation of proceedings in the County Court where the County Court may not, by virtue of regulations under section 38(3)(b) of the County Courts Act 1984 or otherwise, grant such an injunction.

II HCJ [4.1]

Regulations under County Courts Act 1984 section 38(3) The broad effect of the County Court Remedies Regulations 1991, SI 1991/1222 is to limit the circumstances in which the County Court may grant an Anton Piller order but to allow the county court applicant to apply to the High Court instead on a notional transfer up of the proceedings: see para **II CCA [21.10]**. See also the Practice Direction to CPR Part 25 (interim injunctions).

An application to the High Court for a search order in the course of, or in anticipation of, county court proceedings should be made in accordance with Part 23 and should explain, in the body of the application, that it is made pursuant to paragraph 3 of the High Court and County Courts Jurisdiction Order 1991 because the county court has no jurisdiction to grant the relief sought by reason of reg 3(1) of the County Court Remedies Regulations 2014, SI 2014/982: *Schmidt v Wong* (2005) Times 13 December, CA.

II HCJ [5]

4. Allocation

Subject to articles 4A, 5, 6, 6A to 6E, proceedings in which both the County Court and the High Court have jurisdiction may be commenced either in the County Court or in the High Court.

II HCJ [6]

4A

Except for proceedings to which article 5 applies a claim for money in which the County Court has jurisdiction may only be commenced in the High Court if the financial value of the claim is more than £100,000.

5

(1) Proceedings which include a claim for damages in respect of personal injuries may only be commenced in the High Court if the value of the claim is £50,000 or more.

(2) In this article "personal injuries" means personal injuries to the claimant or any other person, and includes disease, impairment of physical or mental condition, and death.

(3) This article does not apply to proceedings which include a claim for damages in respect of an alleged breach of duty of care committed in the course of the provision of clinical or medical services (including dental or nursing services).

6

Applications and appeals under section 17 of the Audit Commission Act 1998 and appeals under section 18 of that Act shall be commenced in the High Court.

6A

Applications under section 1 of the Access to Neighbouring Land Act 1992 shall be commenced in the County Court.

6B

Applications under article 4 of the ESCP Regulation must be commenced in the County Court.

6C
Proceedings for the exercise of the jurisdiction to wind up a company registered in England and Wales may be commenced only in the High Court if the place which has longest been the company's registered office during the 6 months immediately preceding the presentation of the petition for winding up is in the district that is the London insolvency district for the purposes of the second Group of Parts of the Insolvency Act 1986.

6D
Proceedings under section 1 of the Variation of Trusts Act 1958 may be commenced and taken only in the High Court.

6E
Proceedings under sections 98, 641(1)(b) and 645 to 651 of the Companies Act 2006 may be commenced and taken only in the High Court.

6F
The enactments listed in Part 1 of the Schedule to this Order are amended as specified therein, being amendments which are consequential on the amendments in articles 6C to 6E.

6G
(1) In this article—
(a) "the Judgments Regulation" means Regulation (EU) No 1215/2012 of the European Parliament and of the Council of 12 December 2012 on jurisdiction and the recognition and enforcement of judgments in civil and commercial matters (recast), as amended from time to time and as applied by virtue of the Agreement made on 19 October 2005 between the European Community and the Kingdom of Denmark on jurisdiction and the recognition and enforcement of judgments in civil and commercial matters (OJ No L 299, 16.11.2005, p 62; OJ No L79, 21.3.2013, p 4);
(b) "adaptation order" means an order for the adaptation of a legal remedy which is contained in a foreign judgment but is unknown under the law of England and Wales pursuant to article 54 of the Judgments Regulation.
(2) An application for an adaptation order or a challenge under article 54(2) of the Judgments Regulation to the adaptation of any measure without an adaptation order must be made to the High Court.

Amendment *Text in italic is omitted by the European Enforcement Order, European Order for Payment and European Small Claims Procedure (Amendment etc) (EU Exit) Regulations 2018 with effect from exit day (as defined in the European Union (Withdrawal) Act 2018).*

II HCJ [6.1]

Proceedings which include a claim for personal injuries The wording of art 5 covers all claims for damages for personal injury whatever the cause of action. On the other hand, a claim against a solicitor for negligence in allowing a personal injury claim to be struck out is probably not within the wording of art 5, applying the reasoning in *Hopkins v MacKenzie* [1995] 6 Med LR 26, 23 BMLR 132, CA.

II HCJ [6.2]

Value of action for personal injuries The order does not deal expressly with the effect of recoverable social security benefits. The Social Security (Recovery of Benefits) Act 1997 provides for the amount payable to the claimant to be reduced by offsetting certain recoverable benefits against certain heads of pecuniary loss. The court is required to leave the benefit position out of account when assessing the damages (s 17). On the other hand, the compensation which the claimant is entitled to be paid is required, by s 8, to be reduced by offsetting certain recoverable benefits against certain financial losses. It is the net sum which the claimant "reasonably expects to receive" and it is only if the net sum is £50,000 or more that it is appropriate to start proceedings in the High Court.

II HCJ [6.3]

Civil Procedure Rules See now CPR Part 26 and the Practice Direction to Part 26.

II HCJ [7]

8. Enforcement

(1) Subject to paragraph (1A), a judgment or order of the County Court for the payment of a sum of money which it is sought to enforce wholly or partially by execution against goods—

(a) [. . .] shall be enforced only in the High Court where the sum which it is sought to enforce is £5,000 or more; and

(b) shall be enforced only in the County Court where the sum which it is sought to enforce is less than £600;

(c) in any other case may be enforced in either the High Court or the County Court.

(1A) A judgment or order of the County Court for the payment of a sum of money in proceedings arising out of an agreement regulated by the Consumer Credit Act 1974 shall be enforced only in the County Court.

(2) Subject to paragraph (3), where—

(a) an enactment provides that a sum of money shall be or may be recoverable as if it were payable under the County Court order; and

(b) the recovery of that sum is sought wholly or partially by execution against goods,

payment of that sum shall be enforced in accordance with paragraphs (1)(a) to (c).

(3) Paragraph (1)(b) does not apply to the enforcement of—

(a) a sum of money recoverable under section 15(1) of the Employment Tribunals Act 1996; or

(b) a compromise sum which is recoverable under section 19A(3) of that Act.

II HCJ [7.1]

Enforcement of county court judgment in High Court The procedure for enforcing the County Court judgment in the High Court is set out in the Senior Master's *Practice Direction of 31 August 1998* [1998] 4 All ER 63, [1998] 1 WLR 1557 (see para **CCR 25r13 [2]**). It requires the judgment creditor to go to the Action department in the Royal Courts of Justice with a signed certificate of the judgment of the county court and a copy. The signed certificate must be sealed with the seal of the issuing court and must comply with the formal requirements eg it must state that it is granted "for the purpose of enforcing the judgment in the High Court". The certificate will then be given a reference number, a letter and so on and will be treated, for enforcement purposes, as if it were a High Court judgment.

II HCJ [7.2]

Enforcement of High Court judgment in county court See CPR 70 (para **CPR 70**).

II HCJ [7.3]

Agreement regulated by Consumer Credit Act A consumer credit agreement is regulated by the Consumer Credit Act if the amount involved is less than the consumer credit limit of £25,000 for agreements on or after 1 May 1998 (Consumer Credit (Increase of Monetary Limits) (Amendment) Order 1998, SI 1998/996). See the changes made by the Consumer Credit Act 2006.

II HCJ [7.4]

County Courts Act 1984 section 85 The general rule in s 85(1) of the Act is that the county court judgment creditor may always issue execution in the county court. Article 8 provides an exception by prohibiting county court execution for £5,000 or more.

II HCJ [8]

8A. Enforcement of traffic penalties

(1) Proceedings for the recovery of—

(a) increased penalty charges provided for in charge certificates issued under—
  (i) paragraph 6 of Schedule 6 to the 1991 Act;
  (ii) paragraph 8 of Schedule 1 to the London Local Authorities Act 1996;
  (iii) regulation 17 of the Road User Charging (Enforcement and Adjudication) (London) Regulations 2001;
  (iv) regulation 21 of the Civil Enforcement of Parking Contraventions (England) General Regulations 2007; and
  (v) regulation 13 of the Civil Enforcement of Parking Contraventions (Penalty Charge Notices, Enforcement and Adjudication) (Wales) Regulations 2008;

(b) amounts payable by a person other than a local authority under an adjudication of a parking adjudicator pursuant to section 73 of the 1991 Act;

(c) amounts payable by a person other than a local authority under an adjudication pursuant to—
  (i) the Road User Charging (Enforcement and Adjudication) (London) Regulations 2001;
  (ii) the Civil Enforcement of Parking Contraventions (England) Representations and Appeals Regulations 2007; and
  (iii) the Civil Enforcement of Parking Contraventions (Representations and Appeals) (Wales) Regulations 2008; and

(d) increased fixed penalties referred to in—
  (i) regulation 17(6) of the Road Traffic (Vehicle Emissions) (Fixed Penalty) (England) Regulations 2002; and
  (ii) regulation 17(6) of the Road Traffic (Vehicle Emissions) (Fixed Penalty) (Wales) Regulations 2003,

shall be taken in the County Court.

(2) In this article, "the 1991 Act" means the Road Traffic Act 1991.

(3) In this article, "a local authority" means:—

(a) in England, a London borough council, the Common Council of the City of London, Transport for London, a county or district council or the Council of the Isles of Scilly; and

(b) in Wales, a county or county borough council.

II HCJ [8.1]

Recovery of fixed penalties and charges: High Court and County Courts Jurisdiction Order 1991, art 8A The current version of art 8A was inserted by the High Court and County Courts Jurisdiction (Amendment) Order 2001, SI 2001/1387. The new article provides that proceedings to recover certain parking charges and charges in connection with bus lanes must be started in the Northampton County Court.

II HCJ [8A]

8B. Enforcement of possession orders against trespassers

(1) A judgment or order of the County Court for possession of land made in a possession claim against trespassers may be enforced in the High Court or the County Court.

(2) In this article "a possession claim against trespassers" has the same meaning as in Part 55 of the Civil Procedure Rules 1998.

II HCJ [8A.1]

Certificate of judgment Before applying to the High Court for the issue of the writ it is necessary to obtain a certificate of judgment in Form N 293A.

II HCJ [8A.2]

Possession claim against trespassers **CPR 55.1** defines a possession claim against trespassers as a claim for the recovery of land which the claimant alleges is occupied only by a person or persons who entered or remained on the land without the consent of a person entitled to possession of that land but does not include a claim against a tenant or sub-tenant whether his tenancy has been terminated or not.

II HCJ [9]

9. Value of claim

For the purposes of articles 4A and 5, the value of the claim shall be calculated in accordance with rule 16.3(6) of the Civil Procedure Rules 1998.

II HCJ [10]

11. Crown proceedings – Transitional provisions

For a period of two years from the date upon which this Order comes into force no order shall be made transferring proceedings in the High Court to which the Crown is a party to the County Court, except—

(a) when the proceedings are set down to be tried or heard; or

(b) with the consent of the Crown.

II HCJ [10.1]

Crown proceedings The two-year period of restriction on transfer expired long ago.

II HCJ [11]

12. Savings

This Order shall not apply to:

(a) family proceedings within the meaning of Part V of the Matrimonial and Family Proceedings Act 1984.

(b) [. . .]

COURTS ACT 2003

(c 39)

TABLE OF CONTENTS

PART 6: JUDGES

OFFICES, TITLES, STYLES ETC

II CA [1]

62. Head and Deputy Head of Civil Justice

(1) There is to be a Head of Civil Justice.

(2) The Head of Civil Justice is—

(a) the Master of the Rolls, or

(b) if the Lord Chief Justice appoints another person, that person.

(3) The Lord Chief Justice may appoint a person to be Deputy Head of Civil Justice.

(4) The Lord Chief Justice must not appoint a person under subsection (2)(b) or (3) unless these conditions are met—

(a) the Lord Chief Justice has consulted the Lord Chancellor;

(b) the person to be appointed is one of the following—

(i) the Chancellor of the High Court;

(ii) an ordinary judge of the Court of Appeal.

(5) A person appointed under subsection (2)(b) or (3) holds the office to which he is appointed in accordance with the terms of his appointment.

(6) The Lord Chief Justice may nominate a judicial office holder (as defined in section 109(4) of the Constitutional Reform Act 2005) to exercise his functions under this section.

II CA [2]

66. Judges having powers of District Judges (Magistrates' Courts)

(1) Every holder of a judicial office specified in subsection (2) has the powers of a justice of the peace who is a District Judge (Magistrates' Courts) in relation to—

(a) criminal causes and matters,

(b) . . .

(2) The offices are—

(a) judge of the High Court;

(aa) Master of the Rolls;

(ab) ordinary judge of the Court of Appeal;

(ac) Senior President of Tribunals;

(b) deputy judge of the High Court;

(c) Circuit judge;

(d) deputy Circuit judge;

(e) recorder;

(f) Chamber President, or Deputy Chamber President, of a chamber of the Upper Tribunal or of a chamber of the First-tier Tribunal;

(g) judge of the Upper Tribunal by virtue of appointment under paragraph 1(1) of Schedule 3 to the Tribunals, Courts and Enforcement Act 2007;

(h) transferred-in judge of the Upper Tribunal (see section 31(2) of that Act);

(i) deputy judge of the Upper Tribunal (whether under paragraph 7 of Schedule 3 to, or section 31(2) of, that Act);

(j) office listed—

(i) in the first column of the table in section 89(3C) of the Senior Courts Act 1981 (senior High Court Masters etc), or

(ii) in column 1 of Part 2 of Schedule 2 to that Act (High Court Masters etc);

(k) district judge (which, by virtue of section 8(1C) of the County Courts Act 1984, here includes deputy district judge appointed under section 8 of that Act);

(l) deputy district judge appointed under section 102 of the Senior Courts Act 1981;

(m) judge of the First-tier Tribunal by virtue of appointment under paragraph 1(1) of Schedule 2 to the Tribunals, Courts and Enforcement Act 2007;

(n) transferred-in judge of the First-tier Tribunal (see section 31(2) of that Act);

(o) member of a panel of Employment Judges established for England and Wales or for Scotland.

(2A) A qualifying judge advocate has the powers of a justice of the peace who is a District Judge (Magistrates' Courts) in relation to criminal causes and matters.

(3) For the purposes of section 45 of the 1933 Act, every holder of a judicial office specified in subsection (2) is qualified to sit as a member of a youth court.

(4) . . .

(5) In this section "qualifying judge advocate" means—

(a) the Judge Advocate General; or

(b) a person appointed under section 30(1)(a) or (b) of the Courts-Martial (Appeals) Act 1951 (assistants to the Judge Advocate General).

(6) Subsection (2A) is without prejudice to the powers conferred by this section on a person within subsection (2) where that person is also a qualifying judge advocate.

(7) This section does not give a person any powers that a District Judge (Magistrates' Courts) may have to act in a court or tribunal that is not a magistrates' court.

II CA [2.1]

Commencement This provision was brought into force on 26 January 2004 by the Courts Act 2003 (Commencement No 1) Order 2003, SI 2003/3345, except as regards paragraph (b) of subsection (1) and subsection (4).

PART 8
MISCELLANEOUS

FEES AND COSTS

II CA [3]

92. Fees

(1) The Lord Chancellor may with the consent of the Treasury by order prescribe fees payable in respect of anything dealt with by—

(a) the Senior Courts,
(aa) the family court,
(b) the county court, and
(c) magistrates' courts.

(2) An order under this section may, in particular, contain provision as to—

(a) scales or rates of fees;
(b) exemptions from or reductions in fees;
(c) remission of fees in whole or in part.

(3) When including any provision in an order under this section, the Lord Chancellor must have regard to the principle that access to the courts must not be denied.

(4) The Lord Chancellor may not under this section prescribe fees which he or another authority has power to prescribe apart from this section.

(5) Before making an order under this section, the Lord Chancellor must consult—

(a) the Lord Chief Justice;
(b) the Master of the Rolls;
(ba) the President of the Queen's Bench Division;
(c) the President of the Family Division;
(d) the Chancellor of the High Court;
(e) the Head of Civil Justice;
(f) the Deputy Head of Civil Justice (if there is one).

(6) Before making an order under this section in relation to civil proceedings, the Lord Chancellor must consult the Civil Justice Council.

(7) The Lord Chancellor must take such steps as are reasonably practicable to bring information about fees to the attention of persons likely to have to pay them.

(8) Fees payable under this section are recoverable summarily as a civil debt.

(9) Subsection (10) applies in relation to an authority which has power to prescribe fees payable in any of the courts referred to in subsection (1).

(10) Nothing in this section prevents the authority from applying to any extent provisions contained in an order made under this section; and an instrument made in exercise of the power is to be read (unless the contrary intention appears) as applying those provisions as amended from time to time.

II CA [3.1]

Commencement This section was brought into force on 4 January 2005.

REGISTER OF JUDGMENTS ETC AND EXECUTION OF WRITS

II CA [4]

98. Register of judgments and orders etc

(1) A register is to be kept, in accordance with regulations, of—

(a) judgments entered in the High Court;
(b) judgments entered in the county court;

COURTS ACT 2003

(c) administration orders made under *section 112* [Part 6] of the County Courts Act 1984 (c 28) (power of county court to make administration orders);

(d) orders restricting enforcement made under section 112A of that Act (power of county courts to restrict enforcement of debts in lieu of administration order);

[(d) enforcement restriction orders under Part 6A of that Act (power of county court to make enforcement restriction orders);]

(e) sums which are, for the purposes of the 1980 Act, sums adjudged to be paid by a conviction or order of a magistrates' court.

(f) a decision or award of—

(i) the First-tier Tribunal,

(ii) the Upper Tribunal,

(iii) an employment tribunal, or

(iv) the Employment Appeal Tribunal,

in pursuance of which any sum is payable.

(2) "Regulations" means regulations made by the Lord Chancellor for the purposes of this section.

(3) The regulations may—

(a) provide for prescribed classes of judgments, orders, decisions, awards or adjudged sums to be exempt from registration;

(b) prescribe circumstances in which judgments, orders, decisions, awards or adjudged sums (or classes of them) are to be exempt from registration;

(c) prescribe circumstances in which an entry in the register is to be cancelled;

(d) in the case of sums adjudged to be paid by conviction of a magistrates' court or in the case of sums payable in pursuance of decisions or awards of a tribunal mentioned in subsection (1)(f), provide for sums to be registered only in prescribed circumstances or subject to prescribed conditions.

(4) The Lord Chancellor may fix charges to be made for—

(a) making information in an entry in the register available for inspection;

(b) carrying out an official search of the register;

(c) supplying a certified copy of information in an entry in the register.

(5) The proceeds of those charges are to be applied in paying the expenses incurred in maintaining the register; and any surplus is to be paid into the Consolidated Fund.

(6) If there is in force an agreement between the Lord Chancellor and a body corporate relating to the keeping by that body corporate of the register the register is to be kept by that body corporate.

(7) If, under subsection (6), the register is kept by a body corporate—

(a) the Lord Chancellor may recover from the body corporate any expenses incurred by the Lord Chancellor in connection with the supply of information to that body for the purposes of the register,

(b) subsection (4) applies as if it enabled the Lord Chancellor to fix the maximum charges to be made (instead of the charges to be made), and

(c) subsection (5) does not apply.

(8) If subsection (6) ceases to apply to a body corporate as a result of the termination (for any reason) of the agreement, the Lord Chancellor may require the information contained in the entries in the register to be transferred to such person as he may direct.

Amendment *Text in italic is deleted and text in square brackets is inserted by the Tribunals, Courts and Enforcement Act 2007, from a date to be appointed.*

II CA [4.1]

The new regime for registering judgments orders and fines Section 98 was brought fully into force on 6 April 2006 by the Courts Act 2003 (Commencement No 12 and Transitional Provision) Order 2005, SI 2005/3518 which also repealed ss 73 and 73A of the County Courts Act 1984 (register of county court judgments) from the same date, subject to the saving provision in paragraph 16 of Sch 9 to the Courts Act 2003. The effect of the saving provision is that the register of county court judgments (noted in detail at **II CCA [52]—II CCA [70]**) is to be treated as part of the register required by s 98. As for the keeping of the new register, reg 6 of the Register of Judgments, Orders and Fines Regulations 2005, SI 2005/3595, below, anticipates that the new Registrar may be a body corporate, such as Registry Trust Ltd which has hitherto kept the register of county court judgments under an agreement with the Lord Chancellor. Any such agreement which is in operation on 6 April 2006 is carried over into the new regime by s 98(6), above.

II CA [4.2]

The Register of Judgments, Orders and Fines Regulations 2005 The main text of the Register of Judgments, Orders and Fines Regulations 2005, SI 2005/3595, as amended by SI 2009/474, is as follows:

REGISTER OF JUDGMENTS, ORDERS AND FINES REGULATIONS 2005, SI 2005/3595

1. Citation, commencement and duration

These Regulations may be cited as the Register of Judgments, Orders and Fines Regulations 2005.

2

These Regulations shall come into force—

(a) for the purposes of this regulation and regulations 1 and 4, on the day after the day on which these Regulations are made; and

(b) for all other purposes, on 6th April 2006.

3. Interpretation

In these Regulations—

"the 1998 Rules" means the Civil Procedure Rules 1998;

"the Act" means the Courts Act 2003;

"Administrative Court" has the same meaning as in Part 54 of the 1998 Rules;

"amendment notice" means the notice given to the Registrar in accordance with regulation 21;

"applicable charge" means the charge fixed by the Lord Chancellor in accordance with section 98(4) of the Act, or in accordance with section 98(4) as applied by section 98(7)(b) of the Act;

"appropriate officer" means—

(a) in the case of the High Court or a county court, an officer of the court in which the judgment is entered or with which a tribunal decision is filed;

(b) in the case of a registration under paragraph 38(1)(b) of Schedule 5 to the Act—

(i) where a fines officer exercises the power to register following service of a notice under paragraph 37(6)(b) of that Schedule, that officer; or

(ii) where a court exercises the power to register by virtue of paragraph 39(3) or (4) of that Schedule, an officer of that court;

(c) in respect of a liability order designated for the purposes of section 33(5) of the Child Support Act 1991, the Secretary of State;

"appropriate fee" means the fee prescribed under section 92(1) of the Act;

"certificate of satisfaction" means the certificate applied for under regulation 17;

"data protection principles" means the principles set out in Article 5(1) of the GDPR;

"debt" means the sum of money owed by virtue of a judgment, administration order, fine or tribunal decision, and "debtor" means the individual, incorporated or unincorporated body liable to pay that sum;

"family proceedings" has the same meaning as in section 63 (interpretation) of the Family Law Act 1996;

COURTS ACT 2003

"judgment" means any judgment or order of the court for a sum of money and, in respect of a county court, includes a liability order designated by the Secretary of State for the purposes of section 33(5) of the Child Support Act 1991;

"Local Justice Area" means the area specified in an order made under section 8(2) of the Act;

"Registrar" means—

(a) where the Register is kept by a body corporate in accordance with section 98(6) of the Act, that body corporate; or

(b) otherwise, the Lord Chancellor;

"the Register" means the register kept in accordance with section 98(1) of the Act;

"satisfied", in relation to a debt, means that the debt has been paid in full, and "satisfaction" is to be construed accordingly;

"Technology and Construction Court" has the same meaning as in Part 60 of the 1998 Rules;

"tribunal decision" includes an award.

4. Amendment to the Register of Fines Regulations 2003

In regulation 1(2) of the Register of Fines Regulations 2003, for "31st March 2006" substitute "6th April 2006".

5. Performance of steps under these Regulations

Any step to be taken under these Regulations by the appropriate officer or the Registrar shall be taken—

(a) in respect of—

(i) the registration of judgments to which regulation 8(1)(a) applies; . . .

(ii) the registration of administration orders to which regulation 8(1)(b) applies; and

(iii) the registration of tribunal decisions to which regulation 8(1)(d) applies,

within one working day;

(b) in respect of the registration of sums to which regulation 8(1)(c) applies, as soon as may be reasonably practicable.

6. Manner, etc, in which the Register is to be kept

(1) Where the Registrar is a body corporate, the Register shall be kept in accordance with the terms of the agreement between the Lord Chancellor and that body.

(2) The terms of the agreement between the Lord Chancellor and the body corporate shall specify—

(a) the manner in which the Register is to be kept;

(b) the form of the Register; and

(c) the place at which the Register is to be kept.

7

Where the Registrar is not a body corporate, the Register shall be kept by the Lord Chancellor in such a manner and at such a place as he shall determine.

8. Registration of judgments, administration orders, fines and tribunal decisions

(1) The appropriate officer shall send to the Registrar a return of—

(a) subject to regulation 9, every judgment entered in—

(i) the High Court; and

(ii) a county court;

(b) every administration order made under section 112 of the County Courts Act 1984 (power of county courts to make administration orders);

(c) every sum to be registered by virtue of paragraph 38(1)(b) of Schedule 5 to the Act (further steps available against defaulters);

(d) subject to regulation 9A, every tribunal decision made by—

(i) the First-tier Tribunal;

(ii) the Upper Tribunal;

(iii) an employment tribunal; or

(iv) the Employment Appeal Tribunal,

in pursuance of which a sum of money is payable.

(2) Following receipt of a return sent in accordance with paragraph (1), the Registrar shall record the details of the return as an entry in the Register.

9. Exempt judgments—High Court and county courts

Regulation 8(1)(a) does not apply to—

(a) any judgment made—

(i) in family proceedings;

(ii) by the Administrative Court; or

(iii) by the Technology and Construction Court;

(b) any judgment made in proceedings which are the subject of an appeal under Part 52 of the 1998 Rules, until that appeal has been determined;

(c) any judgment, other than a liability order designated under section 33(5) of the Child Support Act 1991, where the hearing was contested, until—

(i) an order is made for payment by instalments following an application by the judgment creditor;

(ii) an application is made for payment by instalments by the judgment debtor;

(iii) the judgment creditor takes any step to enforce the judgment under Part 70 of the 1998 Rules (general rules about enforcement of judgments and orders);

(iv) the judgment creditor applies for an order under Part 71 of the 1998 Rules (orders to obtain information from judgment debtors);

(v) the judgment creditor applies for a certificate of judgment under rule 8 of CCR Order 22 in Schedule 2 to the 1998 Rules;

(d) an order for the payment of money arising from an action for the recovery of land (whether for costs, payments due under a mortgage, arrears of rent, or otherwise), until the creditor takes any step to enforce the order under Part 70 of the 1998 Rules;

(e) an order of a county court under—

(i) section 73(15) of the Road Traffic Act 1991 (order for the recovery of an amount which is payable under an adjudication of a parking adjudicator); or

(ii) paragraph 7 of Schedule 6 to that Act (order for the recovery of an increased penalty charge).

9A. Exempt tribunal decisions

Regulation 8(1)(d) does not apply until, pursuant to rule 70.5(2A)(a) of the 1998 Rules—

(a) in the case of a tribunal decision made by the First-tier Tribunal or the Upper Tribunal, a copy of the tribunal decision is filed with the High Court or a county court; or

(b) in the case of a tribunal decision made by an employment tribunal or the Employment Appeal Tribunal, a copy of the tribunal decision is filed with a county court.

10. Information contained in the appropriate officer's return

The return sent by virtue of regulation 8(1) shall contain details of—

(a) the full name and address of the debtor in respect of whom the entry in the Register is to be made;

(b) if the entry is to be in respect of an individual, that individual's date of birth (where known);

(c) the amount of the debt;

(d) the case number;

(e) in respect of a return sent by virtue of regulation 8(1)(a) regarding a liability order designated under section 33(5) of the Child Support Act 1991, the date of the judgment;

(f) in respect of all other returns sent by virtue of regulation 8(1)(a)—

(i) the name of the court which made the judgment; and

(ii) the date of the judgment;

(g) in respect of a return sent by virtue of regulation 8(1)(b)—

(i) the name of the court which made the administration order; and

(ii) the date of the order;

(h) in respect of a return sent by virtue of regulation 8(1)(c)—
  (i) the Local Justice Area which imposed the fine; and
  (ii) the date of conviction;

(i) in respect of a return sent by virtue of regulation 8(1)(d)—
  (i) the name of the court with which the tribunal decision was filed in accordance with regulation 9A; and
  (ii) the date on which the tribunal decision was filed with the court.

11. Cancellation or endorsement of entries relating to judgments of the High Court or a county court or tribunal decisions

(1) This regulation applies where an entry in the Register is one to which regulation 8(1)(a) applies (judgments entered in the High Court or a county court) or to which regulation 8(1)(d) applies (tribunal decisions).

(2) Where it comes to the attention of the appropriate officer that—

(a) the debt to which the entry relates has been satisfied one month or less from the date of the judgment or the date on which the tribunal decision was filed with the court in accordance with regulation 9A;

(b) the judgment to which the entry relates has been set aside or reversed; or

(c) the tribunal decision to which the entry relates has been set aside,

that officer shall send a request to the Registrar to cancel the entry.

(3) Where it comes to the attention of the appropriate officer that the debt has been satisfied more than one month from the date of the judgment or the date on which the tribunal decision was filed with the court in accordance with regulation 9A, that officer shall send a request to the Registrar to endorse the entry as to the satisfaction of the debt.

12. Endorsement of entries relating to county court administration orders

(1) This regulation applies where an entry in the Register is one to which regulation 8(1)(b) applies (administration orders of a county court).

(2) Where it comes to the attention of the appropriate officer that—

(a) an administration order has been varied;

(b) an administration order has been revoked; or

(c) the debt has been satisfied,

that officer shall send a request to the Registrar to endorse the entry accordingly.

13. Cancellation or endorsement of entries relating to fines

(1) This regulation applies where an entry in the Register is one to which regulation 8(1)(c) applies (fines subject to registration under Schedule 5 to the Act).

(2) Where it comes to the attention of the appropriate officer that—

(a) the debt to which the entry relates has been satisfied one month or less from the date on which the fine was registered;

(b) the conviction for which the fine was imposed has been set aside or reversed; or

(c) the fine has been remitted in full,

that officer shall send a request to the Registrar to cancel the entry.

(3) Where it comes to the attention of the appropriate officer that the debt has been satisfied more than one month from the date on which the fine was registered, that officer shall send a request to the Registrar to endorse the entry as to the satisfaction of the debt.

14. Cancellation of entries in the Register—additional provisions

Where an entry in the Register is endorsed in accordance with regulations 11(3) or 13(3) and the appropriate officer is later of the opinion that the debt was satisfied one month or less from—

(a) the date of the judgment or administration order; . . .

(b) the date on which the fine was registered; or

(c) the date on which the tribunal decision was filed with the court in accordance with regulation 9A,

that officer shall send a request to the Registrar to cancel the relevant entry.

15

Where—

(a) it comes to the attention of the appropriate officer that an administrative error has been made; and

(b) he is of the opinion that the error is such to require the cancellation of an entry in the Register,

that officer shall send a request to the Registrar to cancel the relevant entry.

16. Cancellation and endorsement of entries in the Register by the Registrar

Following receipt of a request under—

(a) regulation 11(2), 13(2), 14 or 15 (debt due satisfied in one month or less, etc), the Registrar shall cancel the relevant entry;

(b) regulation 11(3) or 13(3) (debt due satisfied in more than one month), the Registrar shall endorse the relevant entry as to the satisfaction of the debt;

(c) regulation 12(2) (administration order has been varied, revoked or debt has been satisfied), the Registrar shall endorse the relevant entry accordingly.

17. Application for, and issue of, a certificate of satisfaction

(1) A registered debtor may apply to the appropriate officer for a certificate ("certificate of satisfaction") as to the satisfaction of the debt.

(2) An application under paragraph (1) shall be—

(a) made in writing; and

(b) accompanied by the appropriate fee.

18

(1) In the case of an application for a certificate of satisfaction in respect of an entry in the Register to which regulation 8(1)(a) applies (judgments entered in the High Court or a county court) or to which regulation 8(1)(d) applies (tribunal decisions), the application under regulation 17(1) shall be accompanied by—

(a) sufficient evidence that the debt has been satisfied;

(b) a statement that the registered debtor has taken reasonable steps to obtain such evidence, but has been unable to do so; or

(c) a statement that the registered debtor believes such evidence is already in the possession of the appropriate officer.

(2) For the purposes of paragraph (1)(a), sufficient evidence that the debt has been satisfied includes a signed statement by the creditor to that effect.

(3) Where paragraph (1)(b) applies, the appropriate officer shall send notice of the registered debtor's application under regulation 17(1) to the creditor together with a request that the creditor confirms within one month of the date of the notice whether the debt has been satisfied.

(4) For the purposes of paragraph (1)(c), evidence which is already in the possession of the appropriate officer includes where—

(a) the debt has been paid as the result of court enforcement proceedings taken under Part 70 of the 1998 Rules;

(b) payment of the debt has otherwise been made to the court.

19

Where an application has been made under regulation 17(1) and—

(a) the appropriate officer is of the opinion that the debt has been satisfied; or

(b) a notice has been sent in accordance with regulation 18(3) and the creditor has not responded within the time limit provided,

the appropriate officer shall issue a certificate of satisfaction to the registered debtor.

20. Amendment of the Register in respect of the amount registered

(1) Where it comes to the attention of the appropriate officer that the amount liable to be paid differs from the amount entered in the Register, due to—

(a) the issue of a final costs certificate; . . .

(b) an increase in the amount of the debt[; or

(c) in the case of an entry to which regulation 8(1)(d) applies, a tribunal decision on appeal],

the appropriate officer shall send a return to the Registrar to amend the Register to reflect the revised amount.

(2) The return sent in accordance with paragraph (1) shall contain the same information as prescribed by regulation 10 in respect of the return sent in accordance with regulation 8(1).

(3) Following receipt of a return sent in accordance with this regulation, the Registrar shall amend the Register accordingly.

21. Correction of registered details of the judgment, administration order, fine or tribunal decision

(1) Where it comes to the attention of a registered debtor that the entry in the Register relating to his debt is inaccurate with respect to the details of the judgment, administration order, fine or tribunal decision, that debtor may give notice to the Registrar requiring an amendment to be made ("amendment notice").

(2) The amendment notice shall—

(a) identify the entry which is alleged to be inaccurate; and

(b) state the amendment which is required.

22

Following receipt of an amendment notice in respect of an entry in the Register, the Registrar shall request that the appropriate officer verify the details of that entry.

23

Following receipt of a request for verification under regulation 22, the appropriate officer shall—

(a) check the information contained in the entry against the official records; and

(b) reply to the request, where applicable stating any necessary amendment.

24

(1) Where the appropriate officer informs the Registrar that the entry is inaccurate and requests an amendment, the Registrar shall amend the Register to rectify the inaccuracy.

(2) Following an amendment to the Register in accordance with paragraph (1), the Registrar shall inform the registered debtor of the action taken and the reasons for having taken that action.

25

Where the appropriate officer informs the Registrar that the entry is accurate, the Registrar shall inform the registered debtor that no action is to be taken and the reasons for not taking any action.

26. Removal of entries in the Register

The Registrar shall remove any entry in the Register registered—

(a) by virtue of regulation 8(1)(a) or (b), six years from the date of the judgment;

(b) by virtue of regulation 8(1)(c), five years from the date of conviction;

(c) by virtue of regulation 8(1)(d), six years from the date on which the tribunal decision was filed with the court in accordance with regulation 9A.

27. Searches of the Register

(1) Subject to regulation 29, searches of a section of the Register may be carried out on payment of the applicable charge relevant to the type and method of search.

(2) The types of search which may be carried out are—

(a) at a stated address, against a named individual or unincorporated body;

(b) against a named incorporated body;

(c) a periodical search—

(i) relating to a named court;

(ii) within a named county; or

(iii) with the agreement of the Registrar, against such other criteria as may be requested.

28. Certified copies

On receipt of—

(a) a written request for a certified copy of an entry in the Register; and

(b) the applicable charge for such a request,

the Registrar shall provide a copy of that entry, certified by him as a true and complete copy of the entry in the Register.

29. Refusal of access to the Register and appeals

(1) The Registrar may—

(a) refuse a person access to the Register, or to a part of the Register; and

(b) refuse to carry out a search of the Register,

if he believes that the purpose for which access has been requested or for which the results of the search will be used contravenes—

(i) any of the data protection principles; or

(ii) the provisions of any other enactment.

(2) Where a refusal is made under paragraph (1), the person who has been denied access to, or has been denied a search of, the Register may appeal to a county court against the decision of the Registrar.

II CA [5]

99. High Court writs of execution

(1) Schedule 7 contains provisions about High Court writs of execution and about warrants issued in connection with the compulsory acquisition of land.

(2) Any rule of law requiring a writ of execution issued from the High Court to be directed to a sheriff is abolished.

II CA [5.1]

This section was brought into force on 15 March 2004.

SCHEDULE 7

ENFORCEMENT OF CERTAIN WRITS AND WARRANTS

Section 99

ENFORCEMENT OFFICERS: GENERAL

II CA [6]

1 Districts for writs and warrants enforced by enforcement officers

(1) England and Wales is to be divided into districts for the purposes of this Schedule.

(2) The districts are to bc those specified in regulations made under paragraph 12.

2 Enforcement officers: authorisation and assignment to districts

(1) An enforcement officer is an individual who is authorised to act as such by the Lord Chancellor or a person acting on his behalf.

(2) The Lord Chancellor or a person acting on his behalf must assign at least one enforcement officer to each district.

(3) The Lord Chancellor or a person acting on his behalf may—

(a) assign an enforcement officer to more than one district, and

(b) change any assignment of an enforcement officer so that he is assigned to a different district or to different districts.

3 Direction of writs of execution to enforcement officers

(1) A writ of execution issued from the High Court may be directed—

(a) if only one enforcement officer is assigned to the district in which the writ is to be executed, to that officer,

(b) if two or more enforcement officers are assigned to that district, to those officers collectively, or

(c) to a named enforcement officer who, whether or not assigned to that district, has undertaken to execute the writ.

(2) In this paragraph "writ of execution" does not include—

(a) a writ of sequestration, or

(b) a writ relating to ecclesiastical property.

3A Issue of certain warrants to enforcement officers

(1) Sub-paragraph (2) applies for the purpose of identifying the enforcement officer to whom a warrant may be issued under—

(a) section 91(1) of the Lands Clauses Consolidation Act 1845 (proceedings in case of refusal to deliver possession of lands), or

(b) section 13(1) of the Compulsory Purchase Act 1965 (refusal to give possession to acquiring authority).

(2) The enforcement officer, in relation to such a warrant, is—

(a) the enforcement officer assigned to a relevant district or, if two or more enforcement officers are assigned to that district, those officers collectively, or

(b) a named enforcement officer who, whether or not assigned to a relevant district, has undertaken to execute the warrant.

(3) In sub-paragraph (2), "a relevant district", in relation to a warrant, means—

(a) the district where the land in respect of which the warrant was issued is situated, or

(b) if that land (being land in one ownership) is not situated wholly in one district, a district where any part of that land is situated.

4 Enforcement officers to have traditional powers etc of sheriff

(1) This paragraph applies in relation to writs directed to one or more enforcement officers under paragraph 3 and warrants issued to one or more enforcement officers under an enactment mentioned in paragraph 3A(1)(a) or (b).

(1A) But it is subject to Schedule 12 to the Tribunals, Courts and Enforcement Act 2007 in the case of a writ conferring power to use the procedure in that Schedule.

(2) The relevant officer has, in relation to the writ, the duties, powers, rights, privileges and liabilities that a sheriff of a county would have had at common law if—

(a) the writ had been directed to him, and

(b) the district in which it is to be executed had been within his county.

(2A) The relevant officer has, in relation to the warrant, the duties, powers, rights, privileges and liabilities that a sheriff of a county would have had at common law if—

(a) the warrant had been issued to him, and

(b) the district in which it is to be executed had been within his county.

(3) "The relevant officer" means—

(a) in relation to a writ—

(i) if the writ is directed to a single enforcement officer under paragraph 3(1)(a) or (c), that officer;

(ii) if the writ is directed to two or more enforcement officers collectively under paragraph 3(1)(b), the officer to whom, in accordance with approved arrangements, the execution of the writ is allocated,

(b) in relation to a warrant—

(i) if the warrant is issued to a single enforcement officer in accordance with paragraph 3A(2)(a) or (b), that officer;

(ii) if the warrant is issued to two or more enforcement officers collectively in accordance with paragraph 3A(2)(a), the officer to whom, in accordance with approved arrangements, the execution of the warrant is allocated.

(4) Sub-paragraphs (2) and (2A) apply to a person acting under the authority of the relevant officer as they apply to the relevant officer.

(5) In this Schedule "approved arrangements" means arrangements approved by the Lord Chancellor or a person acting on his behalf.

5 Constable's duty to assist enforcement officers

It is the duty of every constable, at the request of—

(a) an enforcement officer, or

(b) a person acting under the officer's authority,

to assist the officer or that person in the execution of a writ or warrant.

WRITS OF EXECUTION AGAINST GOODS

6 Application of paragraphs 7 to 11

(1) Paragraph 7 applies to any writ of execution against goods which is issued from the High Court.

(2) Paragraphs 8 to 11—

- (a) do not apply to any writ that confers power to use the procedure in Schedule 12 to the Tribunals, Courts and Enforcement Act 2007, but
- (b) apply to any other writ of execution against goods which is issued from the High Court.

7 Endorsement of writ with date and time of receipt

(1) If the writ is directed to a single enforcement officer under paragraph 3(1)(a) or (c), that officer must endorse it as soon as possible after receiving it.

(2) If the writ is directed to two or more enforcement officers collectively under paragraph 3(1)(b), the individual who, in accordance with approved arrangements, is responsible for allocating its execution to one of those officers, must endorse it as soon as possible after receiving it.

(3) If the writ is directed to a person who is not an enforcement officer but is under a duty to execute it, that person must endorse it as soon as possible after receiving it.

(4) For the purposes of this paragraph, a person endorses a writ by endorsing on the back of it the date and time when he received it.

(5) No fee may be charged for endorsing a writ under this paragraph.

8 Effect of writ

(1) Subject to sub-paragraph (2), the writ binds the property in the goods of the execution debtor from the time when the writ is received by the person who is under a duty to endorse it.

(2) The writ does not prejudice the title to any goods of the execution debtor acquired by a person in good faith and for valuable consideration.

(3) Sub-paragraph (2) does not apply if the person acquiring goods of the execution debtor had notice, at the time of the acquisition, that—

- (a) the writ, or
- (b) any other writ by virtue of which the goods of the execution debtor might be seized or attached,

had been received by the person who was under a duty to endorse it but had not been executed.

(4) Sub-paragraph (2) does not apply if the person acquiring goods of the execution debtor had notice, at the time of the acquisition, that—

- (a) an application for the issue of a warrant of execution against the goods of the execution debtor had been made to the court, and
- (b) the warrant issued on the application remained unexecuted in the hands of a person charged with its execution.

Repealed.

(6) For the purposes of sub-paragraph (2) a thing shall be treated as done in good faith if it is in fact done honestly (whether it is done negligently or not).

(7) Any reference in this paragraph to the goods of the execution debtor includes anything else of his that may lawfully be seized in execution.

9 Seizure of goods

(1) This paragraph applies where an enforcement officer or other person who is under a duty to execute the writ is executing it.

(2) The officer may, by virtue of the writ, seize—

- (a) any goods of the execution debtor that are not exempt goods, and

COURTS ACT 2003

(b) any money, banknotes, bills of exchange, promissory notes, bonds, specialties or securities for money belonging to the execution debtor.

(3) "Exempt goods" means—

(a) such tools, books, vehicles and other items of equipment as are necessary to the execution debtor for use personally by him in his employment, business or vocation;

(b) such clothing, bedding, furniture, household equipment and provisions as are necessary for satisfying the basic domestic needs of the execution debtor and his family.

10 Sale of goods seized

(1) This paragraph applies if—

(a) a writ of execution has been issued from the High Court,

(b) goods are seized under the writ by an enforcement officer or other person under a duty to execute it, and

(c) the goods are to be sold for a sum which, including legal incidental expenses, exceeds £20.

(2) The sale must be—

(a) made by public auction, and not by bill of sale or private contract, unless the court otherwise orders, and

(b) publicly advertised on, and during the three days preceding, the day of sale.

(3) If the person who seized the goods has notice of another execution or other executions, the court must not consider an application for leave to sell privately until the notice prescribed by Civil Procedure Rules has been given to the other execution creditor or creditors.

(4) An execution creditor given notice under sub-paragraph (3) is entitled—

(a) to appear before the court, and

(b) to be heard on the application for the order.

11 Protection of officers selling seized goods

(1) This paragraph applies if—

(a) a writ of execution has been issued from the High Court,

(b) goods in the possession of an execution debtor are seized by an enforcement officer or other person under a duty to execute the writ, and

(c) the goods are sold by that officer without any claims having been made to them.

(2) If this paragraph applies—

(a) the purchaser of the goods acquires a good title to them, and

(b) no person is entitled to recover against the officer or anyone acting under his authority—

(i) for any sale of the goods, or

(ii) for paying over the proceeds prior to the receipt of a claim to the goods,

unless it is proved that the person from whom recovery is sought had notice, or might by making reasonable enquiry have ascertained, that the goods were not the property of the execution debtor.

(3) Nothing in this paragraph affects the right of a lawful claimant to any remedy to which he is entitled against any person other than the enforcement officer or other officer charged with the execution of the writ.

(4) "Lawful claimant" means a person who proves that at the time of sale he had a title to any goods seized and sold.

(5) This paragraph is subject to sections 183, 184 and 346 of the Insolvency Act 1986.

SUPPLEMENTARY

12 Regulations

(1) The Lord Chancellor may make regulations for the purpose of giving effect to the provisions of this Schedule that relate to enforcement officers.

(2) The regulations may, in particular, make provision as to—

(a) conditions to be met by individuals seeking to be authorised to act as enforcement officers;

(b) the circumstances in which authorisations may be terminated;

(c) the procedures to be followed in relation to the assignment of enforcement officers or changes in their assignments;

(d) the publication of—

(i) lists of enforcement officers assigned to each district, and

(ii) addresses to which writs of execution issued from the High Court to enforcement officers, or warrants issued to enforcement officers under an enactment mentioned in paragraph 3A(1)(a) or (b), may be sent.

(3) Subject to paragraph 7(5) the regulations may make provision for the determination of fees that may be charged by enforcement officers.

(4) Before making any regulations under this paragraph, the Lord Chancellor must consult—

(a) the Lord Chief Justice,

(b) the Master of the Rolls,

(ba) the President of the Queen's Bench Division,

(c) the President of the Family Division,

(d) the Chancellor of the High Court, and

(d) the Head of Civil Justice.

II CA [6.1]

Commencement This Schedule was brought into force on 15 March 2004, at the same time as the High Court Enforcement Officers Regulations 2004, SI 2004/400 came into effect. The latter instrument has been amended by SI 2004/673.

II CA [6.2]

Powers and duties of enforcement officers The powers and duties of the enforcement officer to whom the writ is directed are the same as those traditionally exercisable by the sheriff and include the power to require assistance from police constables: see paras 4 and 5. The enforcement officer's first task on receiving the writ is to endorse the time and date on the back of it, in accordance with para 7. Except in the case of an Admiralty writ *in rem*, the execution must not take place on a Sunday, Good Friday or Christmas Day, unless the court so orders. A breach of duty is actionable on proof of financial loss: *Watson v White* [1896] 2QB 9; *Six Arlington Street Investments v Persons Unknown* [1987] 1 All ER 474. Where a certificated bailiff commits torts in the course of enforcing a warrant of control, the applicant for the warrant is not liable vicariously: *Kafagi v JBW Group Ltd* [2018] EWCA Civ 1157.

II CA [6.3]

Entry and seizure As a general rule, the enforcement officer may not use force on any outer door of domestic premises to effect an entry but may use force on inner doors and to re-enter if expelled by force or deliberately prevented from re-entering: *Khazanchi v Faircharm Investments Ltd* [1998] 2 All ER 901; *McLeod v Butterwick* [1996] 3 All ER 236. For exceptions see paragraph 17 onwards of Schedule 12 to the Tribunals, Courts and Enforcement Act 2007 at **II TCE [31]**.

II CA [6.4]

Third party rights Third party rights are not defeated by seizure but unless these rights are brought to the enforcement officer's attention, so as to allow him to withdraw or interplead, a purchaser in good faith without notice will acquire good title: paragraphs 10 and 11 of Sch 7, above. In the case of goods which are rightly claimed to be owned by the debtor jointly with someone else, the sale may proceed but half the proceeds must be paid to the joint owner: *John Fox & Co v Ward* (1952) 102 LJ 725. On the other hand, partnership property is protected from seizure and sale by s 23 of the Partnership Act 1890: see **III PAR [43]**.

II CA [6.5]

Seizure, walking possession and sale Execution requires there to be seizure of the goods and it is not enough to post a notice of distress and a walking possession agreement, signed by the enforcement officer, through the letter box: *Evans v South Ribble Borough Council* [1992] 2 All ER 695. Certain household necessaries and equipment for work are exempt from seizure by para 9. As regards the goods which may be seized it is usual for them to be left on the premises subject to a walking possession agreement. A standard form of agreement is provided in Sch 4 to the High Court Enforcement Officers Regulations 2004, SI 2004/400. Goods which are seized may be sold and this must be by public auction unless the court orders otherwise: see para 7 of Sch 7, above, and also **RSC 47r6** in Volume 1.

II CA [6.6]

Fees The fees which may be charged by the enforcement officer are to be found in Sch 3 to the High Court Enforcement Officers Regulations 2004, SI 2004/400: see **FEE 6** in the Procedure and Guidance Supplement. Where the execution of the writ is completed by sale the fees may be deducted from the proceeds, but where the writ is withdrawn or satisfied, or its execution is stopped, they must be paid by the person on whose application the writ was issued, or, as the case may be, the person at whose insistence the execution was stopped: see reg 13 of the High Court Enforcement Officers Regulations 2004.

II CA [6.7]

Forms The standard forms of writ of execution, including writs of possession are to be found in the Civil Court Practice Book of Forms, starting at Form No 53.

II CA [6.8]

Precedents Precedents for claims by and against enforcement officers and for defences to such claims are set out in **BCCP H[46]–H[47.1]**.

TRIBUNALS, COURTS AND ENFORCEMENT ACT 2007

(c 15)

TABLE OF CONTENTS

GENERAL NOTES ON TRIBUNALS, COURTS AND ENFORCEMENT ACT 2007

II TCE [1]

Tribunals Part 1 (ss 1–49) set up a new integrated structure of First-tier Tribunals with appeals to the Upper Tribunal and enforcement through the county court (s 27).

Section 13 provides a right of appeal from the Upper Tribunal to the Court of Appeal subject to the grant of permission by either the Tribunal or the Court. But there is no right of appeal under this section against a refusal of permission: *Sarfraz v Disclosure and Barring Service* [2015] EWCA Civ 544.

II TCE [2]

Courts Part 2 (sections 50-61) is concerned with judicial appointments and the introduction of a "judicial-appointment eligibility condition"; the Supreme Court Act 1981 is amended accordingly. Part 2 is now fully in force and s 141, which amends s 31 of the Supreme Court Act 1981 (application for judicial review: see **II SCA [30]**) was brought into force on 6 April 2008.

II TCE [3]

Enforcement by taking control of goods Part 3 has a chapter on procedure (sections 62 to 70) and a second chapter on rent arrears recovery (sections 71 to 87).

The first chapter rewrites the old law of writs of *fieri facias* and warrants of execution and distress and seizure in terms of enforcement agents "taking control of goods". The County Courts Act 1984 is heavily amended. The free-standing provisions on the enforcement process are included in the sections set out below. The second chapter (rent arrears recovery) is dealt with in the LANDLORD AND TENANT AND HOUSING title. A third chapter (sections 88 to 90) applies Part 3 to the Crown and abolishes Crown preference. But it should be noted that provision is made in Part 6 (sections 134 to 138) for protecting works of art from seizure while on loan to a museum.

II TCE [4]

Enforcement of judgments and orders Part 4 (sections 91 to 105) amends the Charging Orders Act 1979 and the Attachment of Earnings Act 1971 and introduces a new procedure for eliciting information about the judgment debtor by court orders for disclosure by Departments and prescribed third parties.

II TCE [5]

Debt management and relief Part 5 (sections 106 to 133) provides in various ways for debt management and relief. Sections 106 and 107 amend the County Courts Act 1984 by substituting a new regime for administration orders and introducing a facility for making enforcement restriction orders. The text is set out, in square brackets, in the County Courts Act section, although not yet in force. Section 108 amends the Insolvency Act 1986 to include provision for debt relief orders and debt relief restrictions orders in the context of bankruptcy, for which see the INSOLVENCY title. The rest of Part 5 (sections 109 to 133) gives statutory support to the creation of debt management schemes subject to a supervising authority and with rights of appeal to the county court. The provisions on debt relief orders and debt relief restrictions were brought into force as part of bankruptcy law on 6 April 2009 by the Tribunals, Courts and Enforcement Act 2007 (Commencement No 7) Order 2009, SI 2009/382. The debt management and other provisions of Part 5 are not yet in force and the only one which is reproduced below is s 122, at **II TCE [29]**, which gives creditors affected by a debt repayment plan a right of appeal to the county court.

II TCE [6]–II TCE [10]

Commencement The provisions of Part 3: Enforcement by Taking Control of Goods were brought into force by commencement order on 6 April 2014: SI 2014/1768.

PART 3: ENFORCEMENT BY TAKING CONTROL OF GOODS

PROCEDURE

II TCE [11]

62. Enforcement by taking control of goods

(1) Schedule 12 applies where an enactment, writ or warrant confers power to use the procedure in that Schedule (taking control of goods and selling them to recover a sum of money).

(2) The power conferred by a writ or warrant of control to recover a sum of money, and any power conferred by a writ or warrant of possession or delivery to take control of goods and sell them to recover a sum of money, is exercisable only by using that procedure.

(3) Schedule 13—

(a) amends some powers previously called powers to distrain, so that they become powers to use that procedure;

(b) makes other amendments relating to Schedule 12 and to distress or execution.

(4) The following are renamed—

(a) writs of fieri facias, except writs of fieri facias de bonis ecclesiasticis, are renamed writs of control;

(b) warrants of execution are renamed warrants of control;

(c) warrants of distress, unless the power they confer is exercisable only against specific goods, are renamed warrants of control.

II TCE [12]

63. Enforcement agents

(1) This section and section 64 apply for the purposes of Schedule 12.

(2) An individual may act as an enforcement agent only if one of these applies—

(a) he acts under a certificate under section 64;

(b) he is exempt;

(c) he acts in the presence and under the direction of a person to whom paragraph (a) or (b) applies.

(3) An individual is exempt if he acts in the course of his duty as one of these—

(a) a constable;

(b) an officer of Revenue and Customs;

(ba) a person authorised to use the procedure in Schedule 12 by the Welsh Revenue Authority (or by a person to whom the Welsh Revenue Authority has delegated the function of authorising the use of the procedure);

(c) a person appointed under section 2(1) of the Courts Act 2003 (c 39) (court officers and staff).

(4) An individual is exempt if he acts in the course of his duty as an officer of a government department.

(5) For the purposes of an enforcement power conferred by a warrant, an individual is exempt if in relation to the warrant he is a civilian enforcement officer, as defined in section 125A of the Magistrates' Courts Act 1980 (c 43).

(6) A person is guilty of an offence if, knowingly or recklessly, he purports to act as an enforcement agent without being authorised to do so by subsection (2).

(7) A person guilty of an offence under this section is liable on summary conviction to a fine not exceeding level 5 on the standard scale.

II TCE [12.1]

Liability for bailiff's torts Where a certificated bailiff commits torts in the course of enforcing a warrant of control, the applicant for the warrant is not liable vicariously: *Kafagi v JBW Group Ltd* [2018] EWCA Civ 1157.

II TCE [13]

64. Certificates to act as an enforcement agent

(1) A certificate may be issued under this section by a judge of the county court.

(2) The Lord Chancellor must make regulations about certificates under this section.

(3) The regulations may in particular include provision—

(a) for fees to be charged for applications;

(b) for certificates to be issued subject to conditions, including the giving of security;

(c) for certificates to be limited to purposes specified by or under the regulations;

(d) about complaints against holders of certificates;

(e) about suspension and cancellation of certificates;

(f) to modify or supplement Schedule 12 for cases where a certificate is suspended or cancelled or expires;

(g) requiring courts to make information available relating to certificates.

(4) A certificate under section 7 of the Law of Distress Amendment Act 1888 (c 21) which is in force on the coming into force of this section has effect as a certificate under this section, subject to any provision made by regulations.

II TCE [14]

65. Common law rules replaced

(1) This Chapter replaces the common law rules about the exercise of the powers which under it become powers to use the procedure in Schedule 12.

(2) The rules replaced include—

(a) rules distinguishing between an illegal, an irregular and an excessive exercise of a power;

(b) rules that would entitle a person to bring proceedings of a kind for which paragraph 66 of Schedule 12 provides (remedies available to the debtor);

(c) rules of replevin;

(d) rules about rescuing goods.

II TCE [15]

66. Pre-commencement enforcement not affected

Where—

(a) by any provision of this Part a power becomes a power to use the procedure in Schedule 12, and

(b) before the commencement of that provision, goods have been distrained or executed against, or made subject to a walking possession agreement, under the power,

this Part does not affect the continuing exercise of the power in relation to those goods.

II TCE [16]

67. Transfer of county court enforcement

In section 85(2) of the County Courts Act 1984 (c 28) (under which writs of control give the district judge, formerly called the registrar, power to execute judgments or orders for payment of money) for "the registrar shall be" substitute "any person authorised by or on behalf of the Lord Chancellor is".

II TCE [17]

69. County court warrants of control etc

For section 99 of the County Courts Act 1984 substitute—

"99 Endorsement of warrants of control etc

(1) This section applies to—

(a) a warrant of control issued under section 85(2);

(b) a warrant of delivery or of possession, but only if it includes a power to take control of and sell goods to recover a sum of money and only for the purposes of exercising that power.

(2) The person to whom the warrant is directed must, as soon as possible after receiving it, endorse it by inserting on the back the date and time when he received it.

(3) No fee may be charged for endorsing a warrant under this section."

II TCE [18]

70. Power of High Court to stay execution

(1) If, at any time, the High Court is satisfied that a party to proceedings is unable to pay—

(a) a sum recovered against him (by way of satisfaction of the claim or counterclaim in the proceedings or by way of costs or otherwise), or

(b) any instalment of such a sum,

the court may stay the execution of any writ of control issued in the proceedings, for whatever period and on whatever terms it thinks fit.

(2) The court may act under subsection (1) from time to time until it appears that the cause of the inability to pay has ceased.

(3) In this section a party to proceedings includes every person, whether or not named as a party, who is served with notice of the proceedings or attends them.

PART 4
ENFORCEMENT OF JUDGMENTS AND ORDERS

INFORMATION REQUESTS AND ORDERS

II TCE [19]

95. Application for information about action to recover judgment debt

(1) A person who is the creditor in relation to a judgment debt may apply to the High Court, the family court or the county court for information about what kind of action it would be appropriate to take in court to recover that particular debt.

(2) An application under subsection (1) must comply with any provision made in regulations about the making of such applications.

II TCE [20]

96. Action by the court

(1) This section applies if the creditor in relation to a judgment debt makes an application for information under section 95.

(2) The relevant court may make one or more of the following in relation to the debtor—

- (a) a departmental information request;
- (b) an information order.

(3) The relevant court may exercise its powers under subsection (2) only if it is satisfied that to do so will help it to deal with the creditor's application.

(4) Before exercising its powers under subsection (2), the relevant court must give notice to the debtor that the court intends to make a request or order.

(5) The relevant court may not make a departmental information request to the Commissioners unless regulations are in force that have been made under section 102(4) and (7) and relate to the use or disclosure of debtor information disclosed by the Commissioners.

(6) The relevant court may disclose such information (including information identifying the debtor) as it considers necessary to assist the recipient of a request or order to comply with the request or order.

(7) A disclosure under subsection (6) is not to be taken to breach any restriction on the disclosure of information (however imposed).

(8) Nothing in this section is to be taken to prejudice any power that exists apart from this section to request or order the disclosure of information.

II TCE [21]

97. Departmental information requests

(1) A departmental information request is a request for the disclosure of information held by, or on behalf of, a government department.

(2) The request is to be made to the Minister of the Crown, or other person, who is in charge of the department.

(3) In the case of a request made to the designated Secretary of State, the disclosure of some or all of the following information may be requested—

- (a) the full name of the debtor;
- (b) the address of the debtor;
- (c) the date of birth of the debtor;
- (d) the national insurance number of the debtor;
- (e) prescribed information.

(4) In the case of a request made to the Commissioners, the disclosure of some or all of the following information may be requested—

- (a) whether or not the debtor is employed;

(b) the name and address of the employer (if the debtor is employed);
(c) the national insurance number of the debtor;
(d) prescribed information.

(5) In the case of any other request, the disclosure of prescribed information may be requested.

(6) In this section—

"designated Secretary of State" means the Secretary of State designated for the purpose of this section by regulations;

"government department" does not include the following—

(a) any part of the Scottish Administration;
(b) a Northern Ireland department;
(c) the Welsh Assembly Government or any member of staff appointed under section 52 of the Government of Wales Act 2006 (c 32);

"prescribed information", in relation to a departmental information request, means information that falls within the category or categories of information (if any) prescribed by regulations in relation to the department to which the request relates.

II TCE [22]

98. Information orders

(1) An information order is an order of the relevant court which—

(a) specifies a prescribed person ("the information discloser"),
(b) specifies prescribed information relating to the debtor ("the required information"), and
(c) orders the information discloser to disclose the required information to the relevant court.

(2) In subsection (1) "prescribed" means prescribed in regulations.

(3) Regulations under this section may be made by reference to—

(a) particular persons or particular descriptions of person (or both);
(b) particular information or particular descriptions of information (or both).

(4) Regulations may, in particular, be made under this section so as to ensure that—

(a) an information order made against a particular person, or a person of a particular description, may order that person to disclose only particular information, or information of a particular description;
(b) an information order that orders the disclosure of particular information, or information of a particular description, may only be made against a particular person, or a person of a particular description.

(5) Regulations under this section must not make provision that would allow the relevant court to order—

(a) the disclosure of information by the debtor, or
(b) the disclosure of information held by, or on behalf of, a government department.

II TCE [23]

99. Responding to a departmental information request

(1) This section applies if the relevant court makes a departmental information request.

(2) The recipient of the request may disclose to the relevant court any information (whether held by the department or on its behalf) that the recipient considers is necessary to comply with the request.

(3) A disclosure under subsection (2) is not to be taken to breach any restriction on the disclosure of information (however imposed).

(4) Nothing in this section is to be taken to prejudice any power that exists apart from this section to disclose information.

II TCE [24]

100. Information order: required information not held etc

(1) An information discloser is not to be regarded as having breached an information order because of a failure to disclose some or all of the required information, if that failure is for one of the permitted reasons.

(2) These are the permitted reasons—

- (a) the information provider does not hold the information;
- (b) the information provider is unable to ascertain whether the information is held, because of the way in which the information order identifies the debtor;
- (c) the disclosure of the information would involve the information discloser in unreasonable effort or expense.

(3) It is to be presumed that a failure to disclose required information is for a permitted reason if—

- (a) the information discloser gives the relevant court a certificate that complies with subsection (4), and
- (b) there is no evidence that the failure is not for a permitted reason.

(4) The certificate must state—

- (a) which of the required information is not being disclosed;
- (b) what the permitted reason is, or permitted reasons are, for the failure to disclose that information.

(5) Any reference in this section to the information discloser holding, or not holding, information includes a reference to the information being held, or not being held, on the information discloser's behalf.

II TCE [25]

101. Using the information about the debtor

(1) This section applies if—

- (a) the creditor in relation to a judgment debt makes an application for information under section 95, and
- (b) information ("debtor information") is disclosed to the relevant court in compliance with a request or order made under section 96.

(2) The relevant court may use the debtor information for the purpose of making another request or order under section 96 in relation to the debtor.

(3) The relevant court may use the debtor information for the purpose of providing the creditor with information about what kind of action (if any) it would be appropriate to take in court (whether the relevant court or another court) to recover the judgment debt.

(4) If the creditor takes any action in the relevant court to recover the judgment debt, the relevant court may use the debtor information in carrying out functions in relation to that action.

(5) If the creditor takes any action in another court to recover the judgment debt—

- (a) the relevant court may disclose the debtor information to the other court, and

(b) the other court may use that information in carrying out functions in relation to that action.

(6) Debtor information may be used or disclosed under any of subsections (3) to (5) only if—

(a) regulations about such use or disclosure of information are in force, and

(b) the use or disclosure complies with those regulations.

(7) In addition, if the debtor information was disclosed by the Commissioners, the information may be used or disclosed under any of subsections (3) to (5) only with the consent of the Commissioners.

(8) Consent for the purposes of subsection (7) may be given—

(a) in relation to particular use or a particular disclosure, or

(b) in relation to use, or a disclosure made, in such circumstances as may be specified or described in the consent.

(9) The use or disclosure of information in accordance with this section is not to be taken to breach any restriction on the use or disclosure of information (however imposed).

(10) Nothing in this section is to be taken to prejudice any power that exists apart from this section to use or disclose information.

II TCE [26]

102. Offence of unauthorised use or disclosure

(1) This section applies if—

(a) an application is made under section 95 in relation to recovery of a judgment debt ("the relevant judgment debt"),

(b) a departmental information request or an information order is made in consequence of that application, and

(c) information ("debtor information") is disclosed in accordance with the request or order.

(2) A person to whom the debtor information is disclosed commits an offence if he—

(a) uses or discloses the debtor information, and

(b) the use or disclosure is not authorised by any of subsections (3) to (6).

(3) The use or disclosure of the debtor information is authorised if it is in accordance with section 101.

(4) The use or disclosure of the debtor information is authorised if it is—

(a) in accordance with an enactment or order of court, or

(b) for the purposes of any proceedings before a court,

and it is in accordance with regulations.

(5) The use or disclosure of the debtor information is authorised if the information has previously been lawfully disclosed to the public.

(6) The use or disclosure of the debtor information is authorised if it is in accordance with rules of court that comply with regulations under subsection (7).

(7) Regulations may make provision about the circumstances, if any, in which rules of court may allow access to, or the supply of, information disclosed in accordance with a department information request or an information order.

(8) It is a defence for a person charged with an offence under subsection (2) to prove that he reasonably believed that the use or disclosure was lawful.

(9) A person guilty of an offence under subsection (2) is liable—

(a) on conviction on indictment, to imprisonment for a term not exceeding two years, to a fine or to both;

(b) on summary conviction, to imprisonment for a term not exceeding twelve months, to a fine not exceeding the statutory maximum, or to both.

II TCE [27]

104. Interpretation

(1) This section applies for the purposes of sections 95 to 103.

(2) In those provisions—

"Commissioners" means the Commissioners for Her Majesty's Revenue and Customs;

"creditor", in relation to a judgment debt, means—

(a) the person to whom the debt is payable (whether directly or through any court, an officer of any court or another person);

(b) where the debt is payable under an administration order (within the meaning of Part 6 of the County Courts Act 1984 (c 28)), any one of the creditors scheduled to the order;

"debtor", in relation to a judgment debt, means the person by whom the debt is payable;

"departmental information request" has the meaning given by section 97;

"information" means information held in any form;

"information discloser", in relation to an information order, has the meaning given by section 98(1)(a);

"information order" has the meaning given by section 98;

"judgment debt" means either of the following—

(a) a sum which is payable under a judgment or order enforceable by the High Court, the family court or the county court;

(b) a sum which, by virtue of an enactment, is recoverable as if it were payable under a judgment or order of the High Court, the family court or of the county court (including a sum which is so recoverable because a court so orders);

"required information", in relation to an information order, has the meaning given by section 98(1)(b);

"relevant court", in relation to an application under section 95, means the court to which the application is made.

(3) Any reference to information held on behalf of a government department, or on behalf of an information discloser, includes a reference to any information which—

(a) is held by a person who provides services to the department or to the information discloser, and

(b) is held by that person in connection with the provision of those services.

II TCE [28]

105. Application and transitional provision

(1) Sections 95 to 104 apply in relation to any judgment debt, whether it became payable, or recoverable, before or after the commencement of those sections.

(2) In relation to an offence committed before the commencement of section 154(1) of the Criminal Justice Act 2003 (c 44), the reference in section 102(9)(b) to 12 months is to be read as a reference to 6 months.

PART5
DEBT MANAGEMENT AND RELIEF

APPEALS

II TCE [29]

122. Right of appeal

(1) This section applies if a debt repayment plan is arranged for a debtor in accordance with an approved scheme.

(2) An affected creditor may appeal to the county court against any of the following—

- (a) the fact that the plan has been arranged;
- (b) the fact that a debt owed to the affected creditor has been specified in the plan;
- (c) the terms of the plan (including any provision included in the plan in accordance with section 110(3)).

(3) Subsection (2)(c) does not allow an affected creditor to appeal against the fact that a debt owed to any other creditor has been specified in the plan.

(4) In this section "affected creditor" means the creditor under any debt which is specified in the plan.

SCHEDULE 12
TAKING CONTROL OF GOODS

Section 62(1)

PART 1
INTRODUCTORY

II TCE [30]

1 The procedure

(1) Using the procedure in this Schedule to recover a sum means taking control of goods and selling them to recover that sum in accordance with this Schedule and regulations under it.

(2) In this Schedule a power to use the procedure to recover a particular sum is called an "enforcement power".

(3) The following apply in relation to an enforcement power.

(4) "Debt" means the sum recoverable.

(5) "Debtor" means the person liable to pay the debt or, if two or more persons are jointly or jointly and severally liable, any one or more of them.

(6) "Creditor" means the person for whom the debt is recoverable.

2 Enforcement agents

(1) In this Schedule "enforcement agent" means an individual authorised by section 63(2) to act as an enforcement agent.

(2) Only an enforcement agent may take control of goods and sell them under an enforcement power.

(3) An enforcement agent, if he is not the person on whom an enforcement power is conferred, may act under the power only if authorised by that person.

(4) In relation to goods taken control of by an enforcement agent under an enforcement power, references to the enforcement agent are references to any person for the time being acting as an enforcement agent under the power.

3 General interpretation

(1) In this Schedule—

"amount outstanding" is defined in paragraph 50(3);

"control" (except in paragraph 5(4)(a)) means control under an enforcement power;

"controlled goods" means goods taken control of that—

(a) have not been sold or abandoned,

(b) if they have been removed, have not been returned to the debtor (unless subject to a controlled goods agreement), and

(c) if they are goods of another person, have not been returned to that person;

"controlled goods agreement" has the meaning given by paragraph 13(4);

"co-owner" in relation to goods of the debtor means a person other than the debtor who has an interest in the goods, but only if the enforcement agent—

(a) knows that the person has an interest in the particular goods, or

(b) would know, if he made reasonable enquiries;

"the court", unless otherwise stated, and subject to rules of court, means—

(a) the High Court, in relation to an enforcement power under a writ of the High Court;

(b) the county court, in relation to an enforcement power under a warrant issued by the county court;

(c) in any other case, a magistrates' court;

"disposal" and related expressions, in relation to securities, are to be read in accordance with paragraph 48(2);

"exempt goods" means goods that regulations exempt by description or circumstances or both;

"goods" means property of any description, other than land;

"interest" means a beneficial interest;

"money" means money in sterling or another currency;

"premises" means any place, and in particular includes—

(a) a vehicle, vessel, aircraft or hovercraft;

(b) a tent or movable structure;

"securities" includes bills of exchange, promissory notes, bonds, specialties and securities for money.

(2) In this Schedule—

(a) references to goods of the debtor or another person are references to goods in which the debtor or that person has an interest, but

(b) references to goods of the debtor do not include references to trust property in which either the debtor or a co-owner has an interest not vested in possession.

PART 2
THE PROCEDURE

II TCE [31]

4 Binding property in the debtor's goods

(1) For the purposes of any enforcement power, the property in all goods of the debtor, except goods that are exempt goods for the purposes of this Schedule or are protected under any other enactment, becomes bound in accordance with this paragraph.

(2) Where the power is conferred by a writ issued from the High Court the writ binds the property in the goods from the time when it is received by the person who is under a duty to endorse it.

(3) Where the power is conferred by a warrant to which section 99 of the County Courts Act 1984 (c 28) or section 125ZA of the Magistrates' Courts Act

1980 (c 43) applies, the warrant binds the property in the goods from the time when it is received by the person who is under a duty to endorse it under that section.

(4) Where sub-paragraphs (2) and (3) do not apply but notice is given to the debtor under paragraph 7(1), the notice binds the property in the goods from the time when the notice is given.

5 Effect of property in goods being bound

(1) An assignment or transfer of any interest of the debtor's in goods while the property in them is bound for the purposes of an enforcement power—

(a) is subject to that power, and

(b) does not affect the operation of this Schedule in relation to the goods, except as provided by paragraph 61 (application to assignee or transferee).

(2) Sub-paragraph (1) does not prejudice the title to any of the debtor's goods that a person acquires—

(a) in good faith,

(b) for valuable consideration, and

(c) without notice.

(3) For the purposes of sub-paragraph (2)(a), a thing is to be treated as done in good faith if it is in fact done honestly (whether it is done negligently or not).

(4) In sub-paragraph (2)(c) "notice" means—

(a) where the property in the goods is bound by a writ or warrant, notice that the writ or warrant, or any other writ or warrant by virtue of which the goods of the debtor might be seized or otherwise taken control of, had been received by the person who was under a duty to endorse it and that goods remained bound under it;

(b) where the property in the goods is bound by notice under paragraph 7(1), notice that that notice had been given and that goods remained bound under it.

(5) In sub-paragraph (4)(a) "endorse" in relation to a warrant to which section 99 of the County Courts Act 1984 (c 28) or section 125ZA of the Magistrates' Courts Act 1980 (c 43) applies, means endorse under that section.

6 Time when property ceases to be bound

(1) For the purposes of any enforcement power the property in goods of the debtor ceases to be bound in accordance with this paragraph.

(2) The property in any goods ceases to be bound—

(a) when the goods are sold;

(b) in the case of money used to pay any of the amount outstanding, when it is used.

(3) The property in all goods ceases to be bound when any of these happens—

(a) the amount outstanding is paid, out of the proceeds of sale or otherwise;

(b) the instrument under which the power is exercisable ceases to have effect;

(c) the power ceases to be exercisable for any other reason.

7 Notice of enforcement

(1) An enforcement agent may not take control of goods unless the debtor has been given notice.

(2) Regulations must state—

(a) the minimum period of notice;

(b) the form of the notice;

(c) what it must contain;

(d) how it must be given;

(e) who must give it.

(3) The enforcement agent must keep a record of the time when the notice is given.

(4) If regulations authorise it, the court may order in prescribed circumstances that the notice given may be less than the minimum period.

(5) The order may be subject to conditions.

8 Time limit for taking control

(1) An enforcement agent may not take control of goods after the prescribed period.

(2) The period may be prescribed by reference to the date of notice of enforcement or of any writ or warrant conferring the enforcement power or any other date.

(3) Regulations may provide for the period to be extended or further extended by the court in accordance with the regulations.

9 Goods which may be taken

An enforcement agent may take control of goods only if they are—

- (a) on premises that he has power to enter under this Schedule, or
- (b) on a highway.

10 An enforcement agent may take control of goods only if they are goods of the debtor.

11 (1) Subject to paragraphs 9 and 10 and to any other enactment under which goods are protected, an enforcement agent—

- (a) may take control of goods anywhere in England and Wales;
- (b) may take control of any goods that are not exempt.

(2) Regulations may authorise him to take control of exempt goods in prescribed circumstances, if he provides the debtor with replacements in accordance with the regulations.

12 Value of goods taken

(1) Unless sub-paragraph (2) applies, an enforcement agent may not take control of goods whose aggregate value is more than—

- (a) the amount outstanding, and
- (b) an amount in respect of future costs, calculated in accordance with regulations.

(2) An enforcement agent may take control of goods of higher value on premises or on a highway, only to the extent necessary, if there are not enough goods of a lower value within a reasonable distance—

- (a) on a highway, or
- (b) on premises that he has power to enter under this Schedule, either under paragraph 14 or under an existing warrant.

(3) For the purposes of this paragraph goods are above a given value only if it is or ought to be clear to the enforcement agent that they are.

(4) Sub-paragraph (1) does not affect the power to keep control of goods if they rise in value once they have been taken.

13 Ways of taking control

(1) To take control of goods an enforcement agent must do one of the following—

- (a) secure the goods on the premises on which he finds them;
- (b) if he finds them on a highway, secure them on a highway, where he finds them or within a reasonable distance;
- (c) remove them and secure them elsewhere;
- (d) enter into a controlled goods agreement with the debtor.

(2) Any liability of an enforcement agent (including criminal liability) arising out of his securing goods on a highway under this paragraph is excluded to the extent that he acted with reasonable care.

(3) Regulations may make further provision about taking control in any of the ways listed in sub-paragraph (1), including provision—

- (a) determining the time when control is taken;
- (b) prohibiting use of any of those ways for goods by description or circumstances or both.

(4) A controlled goods agreement is an agreement under which the debtor—

- (a) is permitted to retain custody of the goods,
- (b) acknowledges that the enforcement agent is taking control of them, and
- (c) agrees not to remove or dispose of them, nor to permit anyone else to, before the debt is paid.

14 Entry without warrant

(1) An enforcement agent may enter relevant premises to search for and take control of goods.

(2) Where there are different relevant premises this paragraph authorises entry to each of them.

(3) This paragraph authorises repeated entry to the same premises, subject to any restriction in regulations.

(4) If the enforcement agent is acting under section 72(1) (CRAR), the only relevant premises are the demised premises.

(5) [...]

(6) Otherwise premises are relevant if the enforcement agent reasonably believes that they are the place, or one of the places, where the debtor—

- (a) usually lives, or
- (b) carries on a trade or business.

15 Entry under warrant

(1) If an enforcement agent applies to the court it may issue a warrant authorising him to enter specified premises to search for and take control of goods.

(2) Before issuing the warrant the court must be satisfied that all these conditions are met—

- (a) an enforcement power has become exercisable;
- (b) there is reason to believe that there are goods on the premises that the enforcement power will be exercisable to take control of if the warrant is issued;
- (c) it is reasonable in all the circumstances to issue the warrant.

(3) The warrant authorises repeated entry to the same premises, subject to any restriction in regulations.

16 Re-entry

(1) This paragraph applies where goods on any premises have been taken control of and have not been removed by the enforcement agent.

(2) The enforcement agent may enter the premises to inspect the goods or to remove them for storage or sale.

(3) This paragraph authorises repeated entry to the same premises.

17 General powers to use reasonable force

Where paragraph 18, 18A, 19 or 19A applies, an enforcement agent may if necessary use reasonable force to enter premises or to do anything for which the entry is authorised.

18 This paragraph applies if these conditions are met—

- (a) the enforcement agent has power to enter the premises under paragraph 14 or 16 or under a warrant under paragraph 15;
- (b) he is acting under an enforcement power conferred by a warrant of control under section 76(1) of the Magistrates' Courts Act 1980 (c 43) for the recovery of a sum adjudged to be paid by a conviction;

(c) he is entitled to execute the warrant by virtue of section 125A (civilian enforcement officers) or 125B (approved enforcement agencies) of that Act.

18A (1) This paragraph applies if these conditions are met—

(a) the enforcement agent has power to enter the premises under paragraph 14;

(b) the enforcement agent reasonably believes that the debtor carries on a trade or business on the premises;

(c) the enforcement agent is acting under a writ or warrant of control issued for the purpose of recovering a sum payable under a High Court or county court judgment;

(d) the sum so payable is not a traffic contravention debt.

(2) "Traffic contravention debt" has the meaning given by section 82(2) of the Traffic Management Act 2004.

19 (1) This paragraph applies if these conditions are met—

(a) the enforcement agent has power to enter the premises under paragraph 16;

(b) he reasonably believes that the debtor carries on a trade or business on the premises;

(c) he is acting under an enforcement power within sub-paragraph (2).

(2) The enforcement powers are those under any of the following—

(a) a writ or warrant of control issued for the purpose of recovering a sum payable under a High Court or county court judgment;

(b) section 127 of the Finance Act 2008.

19A (1) This paragraph applies if these conditions are met—

(a) the enforcement agent has power to enter the premises under paragraph 16;

(b) the enforcement agent has taken control of the goods by entering into a controlled goods agreement with the debtor;

(c) the debtor has failed to comply with any provision of the controlled goods agreement relating to the payment by the debtor of the debt;

(d) the debtor has been given notice of the intention of the enforcement agent to enter the premises to inspect the goods or to remove them for storage or sale;

(e) neither paragraph 18 nor paragraph 19 applies.

(2) For the purposes of a notice under sub-paragraph (1)(d), regulations must state—

(a) the minimum period of notice;

(b) the form of the notice;

(c) what it must contain;

(d) how it must be given;

(e) who must give it.

(3) The enforcement agent must keep a record of the time when a notice under sub-paragraph (1)(d) is given.

(4) If regulations authorise it, the court may order in prescribed circumstances that the notice given may be less than the minimum period.

(5) The order may be subject to conditions.

20 Application for power to use reasonable force

(1) This paragraph applies if an enforcement agent has power to enter premises under paragraph 14 or 16 or under a warrant under paragraph 15.

(2) If the enforcement agent applies to the court it may issue a warrant which authorises him to use, if necessary, reasonable force to enter the premises or to do anything for which entry is authorised.

21 (1) This paragraph applies if an enforcement agent is applying for power to enter premises under a warrant under paragraph 15.

(2) If the enforcement agent applies to the court it may include in the warrant provision authorising him to use, if necessary, reasonable force to enter the premises or to do anything for which entry is authorised.

22 (1) The court may not issue a warrant under paragraph 20 or include provision under paragraph 21 unless it is satisfied that prescribed conditions are met.

(2) A warrant under paragraph 20 or provision included under paragraph 21 may require any constable to assist the enforcement agent to execute the warrant.

23 Other provisions about powers of entry

Paragraphs 24 to 30 apply where an enforcement agent has power to enter premises under paragraph 14 or 16 or under a warrant under paragraph 15.

24 (1) The power to enter and any power to use force are subject to any restriction imposed by or under regulations.

(2) A power to use force does not include power to use force against persons <...>.

25 (1) The enforcement agent may enter and remain on the premises only within prescribed times of day.

(2) Regulations may give the court power in prescribed circumstances to authorise him to enter or remain on the premises at other times.

(3) The authorisation—

- (a) may be by order or in a warrant under paragraph 15;
- (b) may be subject to conditions.

26 (1) The enforcement agent must on request show the debtor and any person who appears to him to be in charge of the premises evidence of—

- (a) his identity, and
- (b) his authority to enter the premises.

(2) The request may be made before the enforcement agent enters the premises or while he is there.

27 (1) The enforcement agent may take other people onto the premises.

(2) They may assist him in exercising any power, including a power to use force.

(3) They must not remain on the premises without the enforcement agent.

(4) The enforcement agent may take any equipment onto the premises.

(5) He may leave equipment on the premises if he leaves controlled goods there.

28 (1) After entering the premises the enforcement agent must provide a notice for the debtor giving information about what the enforcement agent is doing.

(2) Regulations must state—

- (a) the form of the notice;
- (b) what information it must give.

(3) Regulations may prescribe circumstances in which a notice need not be provided after re-entry to premises.

(4) If the debtor is on the premises when the enforcement agent is there, the enforcement agent must give him the notice then.

(5) If the debtor is not there, the enforcement agent must leave the notice in a conspicuous place on the premises.

(6) If the enforcement agent knows that there is someone else there or that there are other occupiers, a notice he leaves under sub-paragraph (5) must be in a sealed envelope addressed to the debtor.

29 If the premises are occupied by any person apart from the debtor, the enforcement agent must leave at the premises a list of any goods he takes away.

30 The enforcement agent must leave the premises as effectively secured as he finds them.

31 Goods on a highway

(1) If the enforcement agent applies to the court it may issue a warrant which authorises him to use, if necessary, reasonable force to take control of goods on a highway.

(2) The court may not issue a warrant unless it is satisfied that prescribed conditions are met.

(3) The warrant may require any constable to assist the enforcement agent to execute it.

(4) The power to use force is subject to any restriction imposed by or under regulations.

(5) The power to use force does not include power to use force against persons [...]

32 (1) The enforcement agent may not exercise any power under this Schedule on a highway except within prescribed times of day.

(2) Regulations may give the court power in prescribed circumstances to authorise him to exercise a power at other times.

(3) The authorisation may be subject to conditions.

33 (1) If the enforcement agent takes control of goods on a highway or enters a vehicle on a highway with the intention of taking control of goods, he must provide a notice for the debtor giving information about what he is doing.

(2) Regulations must state—

(a) the form of the notice;

(b) what information it must give.

(3) If the debtor is present when the enforcement agent is there, the enforcement agent must give him the notice then.

(4) Otherwise the enforcement agent must deliver the notice to any relevant premises (as defined by paragraph 14) in a sealed envelope addressed to the debtor.

34 Inventory

(1) If an enforcement agent takes control of goods he must provide the debtor with an inventory of them as soon as reasonably practicable.

(2) But if there are co-owners of any of the goods, the enforcement agent must instead provide the debtor as soon as reasonably practicable with separate inventories of goods owned by the debtor and each co-owner and an inventory of the goods without a co-owner.

(3) The enforcement agent must as soon as reasonably practicable provide the co-owner of any of the goods with—

(a) the inventory of those goods, and

(b) a copy of the notice under paragraph 28.

(4) Regulations must state—

(a) the form of an inventory, and

(b) what it must contain.

35 Care of goods removed

(1) An enforcement agent must take reasonable care of controlled goods that he removes from the premises or highway where he finds them.

(2) He must comply with any provision of regulations about their care while they remain controlled goods.

36 Valuation

(1) Before the end of the minimum period, the enforcement agent must—

(a) make or obtain a valuation of the controlled goods in accordance with regulations;

(b) give the debtor, and separately any co-owner, an opportunity to obtain an independent valuation of the goods.

(2) In this paragraph "minimum period" means the period specified by regulations under—

(a) paragraph 49, in the case of securities;

(b) paragraph 39, in any other case.

37 Best price

(1) An enforcement agent must sell or dispose of controlled goods for the best price that can reasonably be obtained in accordance with this Schedule.

(2) That does not apply to money that can be used for paying any of the outstanding amount, unless the best price is more than its value if used in that way.

38 Sale

Paragraphs 39 to 42 apply to the sale of controlled goods, except where—

(a) the controlled goods are securities, or

(b) the sale is by exchange of one currency for another.

39 (1) The sale must not be before the end of the minimum period except with the agreement of the debtor and any co-owner.

(2) Regulations must specify the minimum period.

40 (1) Before the sale, the enforcement agent must give notice of the date, time and place of the sale to the debtor and any co-owner.

(2) Regulations must state—

(a) the minimum period of notice;

(b) the form of the notice;

(c) what it must contain (besides the date, time and place of sale);

(d) how it must be given.

(3) The enforcement agent may replace a notice with a new notice, subject to any restriction in regulations.

(4) Any notice must be given within the permitted period.

(5) Unless extended the permitted period is 12 months beginning with the day on which the enforcement agent takes control of the goods.

(6) Any extension must be by agreement in writing between the creditor and debtor before the end of the period.

(7) They may extend the period more than once.

41 (1) The sale must be by public auction unless the court orders otherwise.

(2) The court may make an order only on an application by the enforcement agent.

(3) Regulations may make provision about the types of sale the court may order.

(4) In an application for an order under sub-paragraph (2) the enforcement agent must state whether he has reason to believe that an enforcement power has become exercisable by another creditor against the debtor or a co-owner.

(5) If the enforcement agent states that he does, the court may not consider the application until notice of it has been given to the other creditor in accordance with regulations (or until the court is satisfied that an enforcement power is not exercisable by the other creditor against the debtor or a co-owner).

42 Regulations may make further provision about the sale of controlled goods, including in particular—

(a) requirements for advertising;

(b) provision about the conduct of a sale.

43 Place of sale

(1) Regulations may make provision about the place of sale of controlled goods.

(2) They may prescribe circumstances in which the sale may be held on premises where goods were found by the enforcement agent.

(3) Except where the regulations provide otherwise, the sale may not be held on those premises without the consent of the occupier.

(4) Paragraphs 44 to 46 apply if the sale may be held on those premises.

44 (1) The enforcement agent and any person permitted by him—

(a) may enter the premises to conduct or attend the sale;

(b) may bring equipment onto the premises for the purposes of the sale.

(2) This paragraph authorises repeated entry to the premises.

(3) If necessary the enforcement agent may use reasonable force to enable the sale to be conducted and any person to enter under this paragraph.

45 (1) The enforcement agent must on request show the debtor and any person who appears to him to be in charge of the premises evidence of—

(a) his identity, and

(b) his authority to enter and hold the sale on the premises.

(2) The request may be made before the enforcement agent enters the premises or while he is there.

46 The enforcement agent must leave the premises as effectively secured as he finds them.

47 Holding and disposal of securities

Paragraphs 48 and 49 apply to securities as controlled goods.

48 (1) Regulations may make provision about how securities are to be held and disposed of.

(2) In this Schedule, references to disposal include, in relation to securities, realising the sums secured or made payable by them, suing for the recovery of those sums or assigning the right to sue for their recovery.

(3) Regulations may in particular make provision for purposes corresponding to those for which provision is made in this Schedule in relation to the disposal of other controlled goods.

(4) The power to make regulations under this paragraph is subject to paragraph 49.

49 (1) The creditor may sue in the name of the debtor, or in the name of any person in whose name the debtor might have sued, for the recovery of any sum secured or made payable by securities, when the time of payment arrives.

(2) Before any proceedings under sub-paragraph (1) are commenced or the securities are otherwise disposed of, the enforcement agent must give notice of the disposal to the debtor and any co-owner.

(3) Regulations must state—

(a) the minimum period of notice;

(b) the form of the notice;

(c) what it must contain;

(d) how it must be given.

(4) The enforcement agent may replace a notice with a new notice, subject to any restriction in regulations.

(5) Any notice must be given within the permitted period.

(6) Unless extended the permitted period is 12 months beginning with the time of payment.

(7) Any extension must be by agreement in writing between the creditor and debtor before the end of the period.

(8) They may extend the period more than once.

50 Application of proceeds

(1) Proceeds from the exercise of an enforcement power must be used to pay the amount outstanding.

(2) Proceeds are any of these—

(a) proceeds of sale or disposal of controlled goods;

(b) money taken in exercise of the power, if paragraph 37(1) does not apply to it.

(3) The amount outstanding is the sum of these—

(a) the amount of the debt which remains unpaid (or an amount that the creditor agrees to accept in full satisfaction of the debt);

(b) any amounts recoverable out of proceeds in accordance with regulations under paragraph 62 (costs).

(4) If the proceeds are less than the amount outstanding, which amounts in sub-paragraph (3)(a) and (b) must be paid, and how much of any amount, is to be determined in accordance with regulations.

(5) If the proceeds are more than the amount outstanding, the surplus must be paid to the debtor.

(6) If there is a co-owner of any of the goods, the enforcement agent must—

(a) first pay the co-owner a share of the proceeds of those goods proportionate to his interest;

(b) then deal with the rest of the proceeds under sub-paragraphs (1) to (5).

(7) Regulations may make provision for resolving disputes about what share is due under sub-paragraph (6)(a).

51 Passing of title

(1) A purchaser of controlled goods acquires good title, with two exceptions.

(2) The exceptions apply only if the goods are not the debtor's at the time of sale.

(3) The first exception is where the purchaser, the creditor, the enforcement agent or a related party has notice that the goods are not the debtor's.

(4) The second exception is where a lawful claimant has already made an application to the court claiming an interest in the goods.

(5) A lawful claimant in relation to goods is a person who has an interest in them at the time of sale, other than an interest that was assigned or transferred to him while the property in the goods was bound for the purposes of the enforcement power.

(6) A related party is any person who acts in exercise of an enforcement power, other than the creditor or enforcement agent.

(7) "The court" has the same meaning as in paragraph 60.

52 Abandonment of goods other than securities

Paragraphs 53 and 54 apply to controlled goods other than—

(a) securities;

(b) money to which paragraph 37(1) does not apply.

53 (1) Controlled goods are abandoned if the enforcement agent does not give the debtor or any co-owner notice under paragraph 40 (notice of sale) within the permitted period.

(2) [...]

(3) Regulations may prescribe other circumstances in which controlled goods are abandoned.

54 (1) If controlled goods are abandoned then, in relation to the enforcement power concerned, the following apply—

(a) the enforcement power ceases to be exercisable;

(b) as soon as reasonably practicable the enforcement agent must make the goods available for collection by the debtor, if he removed them from where he found them.

(2) Regulations may make further provision about arrangements under sub-paragraph (1)(b), including in particular provision about the disposal of goods uncollected after a prescribed period.

(3) Where the enforcement power was under a writ or warrant, sub-paragraph (1) does not affect any power to issue another writ or warrant.

55 Abandonment of securities

Paragraphs 56 and 57 apply to securities as controlled goods.

56 (1) Securities are abandoned if the enforcement agent does not give the debtor or any co-owner notice under paragraph 49 (notice of disposal) within the permitted period.

(2) [...]

(3) Regulations may prescribe other circumstances in which securities are abandoned.

57 (1) If securities are abandoned then, in relation to the enforcement power concerned, the following apply—

(a) the enforcement power ceases to be exercisable;

(b) as soon as reasonably practicable the enforcement agent must make the securities available for collection by the debtor, if he removed them from where he found them.

(2) Where the enforcement power was under a writ or warrant, sub-paragraph (1) does not affect any power to issue another writ or warrant.

58 Payment of amount outstanding

(1) This paragraph applies where the debtor pays the amount outstanding in full—

(a) after the enforcement agent has taken control of goods, and

(b) before they are sold or abandoned.

(2) If the enforcement agent has removed the goods he must as soon as reasonably practicable make them available for collection by the debtor.

(3) No further step may be taken under the enforcement power concerned.

(4) For the purposes of this paragraph the amount outstanding is reduced by the value of any controlled goods consisting of money required to be used to pay that amount, and sub-paragraph (2) does not apply to that money.

59 (1) This paragraph applies if a further step is taken despite paragraph 58(3).

(2) The enforcement agent is not liable unless he had notice, when the step was taken, that the amount outstanding had been paid in full.

(3) Sub-paragraph (2) applies to a related party as to the enforcement agent.

(4) If the step taken is sale of any of the goods the purchaser acquires good title unless, at the time of sale, he or the enforcement agent had notice that the amount outstanding had been paid in full.

(5) A person has notice that the amount outstanding has been paid in full if he would have found it out if he had made reasonable enquiries.

(6) Sub-paragraphs (2) to (4) do not affect any right of the debtor or a co-owner to a remedy against any person other than the enforcement agent or a related party.

(7) In this paragraph, "related party" has the meaning given by paragraph 65(4).

60 Third party claiming goods

(1) This paragraph applies where a person makes an application to the court claiming that goods taken control of are his and not the debtor's.

(2) After receiving notice of the application the enforcement agent must not sell the goods, or dispose of them (in the case of securities), unless directed by the court under this paragraph.

(3) The court may direct the enforcement agent to sell or dispose of the goods if the applicant fails to make, or to continue to make, the required payments into court.

(4) The required payments are—
(a) payment on making the application (subject to sub-paragraph (5)) of an amount equal to the value of the goods, or to a proportion of it directed by the court;
(b) payment, at prescribed times (on making the application or later), of any amounts prescribed in respect of the enforcement agent's costs of retaining the goods.

(5) If the applicant makes a payment under sub-paragraph (4)(a) but the enforcement agent disputes the value of the goods, any underpayment is to be—
(a) determined by reference to an independent valuation carried out in accordance with regulations, and
(b) paid at the prescribed time.

(6) If sub-paragraph (3) does not apply the court may still direct the enforcement agent to sell or dispose of the goods before the court determines the applicant's claim, if it considers it appropriate.

(7) If the court makes a direction under sub-paragraph (3) or (6)—
(a) paragraphs 38 to 49, and regulations under them, apply subject to any modification directed by the court;
(b) the enforcement agent must pay the proceeds of sale or disposal into court.

(8) In this paragraph "the court", subject to rules of court, means—
(a) the High Court, in relation to an enforcement power under a writ of the High Court;
(b) the county court, in relation to an enforcement power under a warrant issued by the county court;
(c) in any other case, the High Court or the county court.

61 Application to assignee or transferee

(1) This Schedule applies as follows where an interest of the debtor's in goods is assigned or transferred while the property in the goods is bound for the purposes of an enforcement power, and the enforcement agent—
(a) knows that the assignee or transferee has an interest in the particular goods, or
(b) would know, if he made reasonable enquiries.

(2) These apply as if the assignee or transferee were a co-owner of the goods with the debtor—
(a) paragraph 34 (inventory);
(b) paragraph 36 (valuation);
(c) paragraphs 39 to 41 (sale);
(d) paragraph 59(6) (remedies after payment of amount outstanding).

(3) If the interest of the assignee or transferee was acquired in good faith, for valuable consideration and without notice, paragraph 50(6) applies as if "co-owner" included the assignee or transferee.

(4) If the interest of the assignee or transferee was not acquired in good faith, for valuable consideration and without notice, the enforcement agent must pay any surplus under paragraph 50(5) to the assignee or transferee and to the debtor (if he retains an interest).

(5) If the surplus is payable to two or more persons it must be paid in shares proportionate to their interests.

(6) Paragraph 5(3) and (4) ("good faith" and "notice") apply for the purposes of this paragraph.

62 Costs

(1) Regulations may make provision for the recovery by any person from the debtor of amounts in respect of costs of enforcement-related services.

(2) The regulations may provide for recovery to be out of proceeds or otherwise.

(3) The amount recoverable under the regulations in any case is to be determined by or under the regulations.

(4) The regulations may in particular provide for the amount, if disputed, to be assessed in accordance with rules of court.

(5) "Enforcement-related services" means anything done under or in connection with an enforcement power, or in connection with obtaining an enforcement power, or any services used for the purposes of a provision of this Schedule or regulations under it.

63 Limitation of liability for sale or payment of proceeds

(1) Any liability of an enforcement agent or related party to a lawful claimant for the sale of controlled goods is excluded except in two cases.

(2) The first exception is where at the time of the sale the enforcement agent had notice that the goods were not the debtor's, or not his alone.

(3) The second exception is where before sale the lawful claimant had made an application to the court claiming an interest in the goods.

(4) A lawful claimant in relation to goods is a person who has an interest in them at the time of sale, other than an interest that was assigned or transferred to him while the property in the goods was bound for the purposes of the enforcement power.

64 (1) Any liability of an enforcement agent or related party to a lawful claimant for paying over proceeds is excluded except in two cases.

(2) The first exception is where at the time of the payment he had notice that the goods were not the debtor's, or not his alone.

(3) The second exception is where before that time the lawful claimant had made an application to the court claiming an interest in the goods.

(4) A lawful claimant in relation to goods is a person who has an interest in them at the time of sale.

65 (1) Paragraphs 63 and 64—

- (a) do not affect the liability of a person other than the enforcement agent or a related party;
- (b) do not apply to the creditor if he is the enforcement agent.

(2) The following apply for the purposes of those paragraphs.

(3) The enforcement agent or a related party has notice of something if he would have found it out if he had made reasonable enquiries.

(4) A related party is any person who acts in exercise of an enforcement power, other than the creditor or enforcement agent.

(5) "The court" has the same meaning as in paragraph 60.

66 Remedies available to the debtor

(1) This paragraph applies where an enforcement agent—

- (a) breaches a provision of this Schedule, or
- (b) acts under an enforcement power under a writ, warrant, liability order or other instrument that is defective.

(2) The breach or defect does not make the enforcement agent, or a person he is acting for, a trespasser.

(3) But the debtor may bring proceedings under this paragraph.

(4) Subject to rules of court, the proceedings may be brought—

- (a) in the High Court, in relation to an enforcement power under a writ of the High Court;
- (b) in the county court, in relation to an enforcement power under a warrant issued by the county court;
- (c) in any other case, in the High Court or the county court.

(5) In the proceedings the court may—

- (a) order goods to be returned to the debtor;

(b) order the enforcement agent or a related party to pay damages in respect of loss suffered by the debtor as a result of the breach or of anything done under the defective instrument.

(6) A related party is either of the following (if different from the enforcement agent)—

(a) the person on whom the enforcement power is conferred,

(b) the creditor.

(7) Sub-paragraph (5) is without prejudice to any other powers of the court.

(8) Sub-paragraph (5)(b) does not apply where the enforcement agent acted in the reasonable belief—

(a) that he was not breaching a provision of this Schedule, or

(b) (as the case may be) that the instrument was not defective.

(9) This paragraph is subject to paragraph 59 in the case of a breach of paragraph 58(3).

67 Remedies available to the creditor

If a debtor wrongfully interferes with controlled goods and the creditor suffers loss as a result, the creditor may bring a claim against the debtor in respect of the loss.

68 Offences

(1) A person is guilty of an offence if he intentionally obstructs a person lawfully acting as an enforcement agent.

(2) A person is guilty of an offence if he intentionally interferes with controlled goods without lawful excuse.

(3) A person guilty of an offence under this paragraph is liable on summary conviction to—

(a) imprisonment for a term not exceeding 51 weeks, or

(b) a fine not exceeding level 4 on the standard scale, or

(c) both.

(4) In relation to an offence committed before the commencement of section 281(5) of the Criminal Justice Act 2003 (c 44), the reference in sub-paragraph (3)(a) to 51 weeks is to be read as a reference to 6 months.

69 Relation to insolvency provisions

This Schedule is subject to sections 183, 184 and 346 of the Insolvency Act 1986 (c 45).

II TCE [31.1]

Rights of entry Note the additional powers of entry conferred by amendments to paragraphs 17 onwards of Schedule 12 made by section 25 of the Crime and Courts Act 2013, with effect from 6 April 2014. The broad effect is to enable enforcement officers to enter residential premises where there is reason to believe that a trade or business is being carried on, in order to seize goods by way of enforcement, but not in respect of traffic penalties.

II TCE [31.2]

Regulations Regulation-making powers in section 90 provide for the Secretary of State to supplement or place conditions on the powers expressed in the Schedule. Regulations made in the context of commercial rent arrears recovery are contained in the Taking Control of Goods Regulations 2013, SI 2013/1894, the text of which is set out in Volume 1 at **CPR 83.30 [1]** .

Part III

Special Jurisdiction of the Civil Courts

ANTI-SOCIAL BEHAVIOUR

TABLE OF CONTENTS

GENERAL NOTES ON ANTI-SOCIAL BEHAVIOUR

III ANSB [1]

Jurisdiction For the power to attach powers of arrest in local authority cases see s 27 of the Police and Justice Act 2006 at **III ANSB [26]**.

However, councils should not seek civil injunctions to restrain anti-social behaviour in reliance on section 27 of the Police and Justice Act 2006, since this would avoid the specific requirements applicable to ASBOs. The courts should not indulge in parallel activity by the extension of general common law principles: *Birmingham City Council v Shafi* [2008] EWCA Civ 1186, [2009] 3 All ER 127, [2009] 1 WLR 1961, applying principles laid down by Hoffmann J in *Chief Constable of Leicestershire v M* [1989] 1 WLR 20, Ch D.

There are overlapping remedies to curb anti-social behaviour.

III ANSB [2]

Relevant authority It will be noted that the applicants for anti-social orders under this legislation have to be within the definition of 'relevant authority' which is limited to councils, police, housing action trusts and social landlords; but others may be added by order of the Secretary of State under section 1A, as amended.

Local authorities also have the right to apply for anti-social behaviour injunctions under s 152 of the Housing Act 1996: see **III L&T [297]**.

III ANSB [3]

Procedure The procedure for applying in county court proceedings for anti-social behaviour orders and interim orders and for applications to join or be joined is set out in **CPR 65.21** to **CPR 65.26** and is supported by Part IV of the Practice Direction at **CPR PD 65**. Breach of an anti-social behaviour order is made an offence, by s 1(10). It may also be enforced by committal.

III ANSB [4]

Guidance on anti-social behaviour orders Guidance on anti-social behaviour orders has been published by the Home Office in *A guide to anti-social behaviour orders and acceptable behaviour contracts*.

See also the guidance given by the Housing Corporation to registered social landlords in *Statutory housing management guidance on policies and procedures on tackling anti-social behaviour*.

III ANSB [5]

Publicity It is has been held that publicity, including photographs and names and partial addresses of those against whom the order is made may be justified as necessary and proportionate for the purposes of effective enforcement: *R (Stanley) v Commissioner of Police of the Metropolis* [2004] EWHC 2229 (Admin), (2004) Times, 22 October, QBD. In the case of a child or young person the court may direct, under s 39 of the Children and Young Persons Act 1933, that no newspaper report of the proceedings shall reveal the name, address or school or include identifying details and that publication of any photograph requires the court's permission. Publicity is unlikely to be appropriate in the case of an interim order, where the allegations are still unproved: *R (Keating) v Knowsley Metropolitan Borough Council* [2004] EWHC 1933 (Admin). But in the case of a final order the public interest considerations in favour of publicity (so that the defendants and their activities are known and can be reported on) have weight in the case of children and young persons as they do in the case of adults. See the decision of Elias J in *R (T) v St Albans Crown Court* [2002] EWHC 1129 (Admin) and the Home Office *Guidance on Publicising Anti-Social Behaviour Orders*.

Note that, in relation to proceedings brought against a child or young person for an offence under section 1(1), the powers to restrict reporting are those conferred by section 45 of the Youth Justice and Criminal Evidence Act 1999, as provided in section 1(10D).

III ANSB [6]–III ANSB [7]

Parenting orders County courts were empowered to make parenting orders by s 26A of the Anti-social Behaviour Act 2003, with effect from 29 June 2007. The relevant sections are set out at **III ANSB [16]–III ANSB [18]** and define the circumstances in which such orders may be made by, or on behalf of, local authorities and registered social landlords. The procedure for parenting order applications is laid down in **CPR 65.37** onwards.

III ANSB [8]–III ANSB [15]

Remedies for individuals Individuals have no remedies under the Crime and Disorder Act 1998. However they have remedies under the Protection from Harassment Act 1997: see **III HAR [1]**. Remedies are also available in domestic situations covered by Part IV of the Family Law Act 1996. They include the making of occupation orders and non-molestation orders: see **III FAM [96]** and **III FAM [107]**. In addition, of course, injunctions may be sought to restrain nuisance, trespass and infringement of property rights.

ANTI-SOCIAL BEHAVIOUR ACT 2003

(c 38)

III ANSB [16]

26A. Parenting orders in respect of anti-social behaviour: local authorities

(1) A local authority may apply for a parenting order in respect of a parent of a child or young person if—

(a) the local authority has reason to believe that the child or young person has engaged in anti-social behaviour, and

(b) the child or young person resides, or appears to reside, in the local authority's area.

An application for such an order may be made to a magistrates' court or, where section 26C so allows, to the county court.

(2) If such an application is made, the court may make a parenting order in respect of a parent of the child or young person if it is satisfied—

(a) that the child or young person has engaged in anti-social behaviour, and

(b) that making the order would be desirable in the interests of preventing the child or young person from engaging in further anti-social behaviour.

(3) A parenting order is an order which requires the parent—

(a) to comply, for a period not exceeding twelve months, with such requirements as are specified in the order, and

(b) subject to subsection (4), to attend, for a concurrent period not exceeding three months, such counselling or guidance programme as may be specified in directions given by the responsible officer.

(4) A parenting order under this section may, but need not, include a requirement mentioned in subsection (3)(b) in any case where a parenting order under this section or any other enactment has been made in respect of the parent on a previous occasion.

(5) A counselling or guidance programme which a parent is required to attend by virtue of subsection (3)(b) may be or include a residential course but only if the court is satisfied that the following two conditions are fulfilled.

(6) The first condition is that the attendance of the parent at a residential course is likely to be more effective than his attendance at a non-residential course in preventing the child or young person from engaging in further anti-social behaviour.

(7) The second condition is that any interference with family life which is likely to result from the attendance of the parent at a residential course is proportionate in all the circumstances.

(8) A person is eligible to be the responsible officer in relation to a parenting order under this section only if he is—

- (a) an officer of the local authority which applied for the order, or
- (b) a person nominated by that authority or by a person or body requested by the authority to make a nomination.

A person may not be nominated under paragraph (b) without his consent.

III ANSB [16.1]

Parenting orders The provisions on parenting orders in this and the following two sections were inserted by s 24 of the Police and Justice Act 2006, with effect from 29 June 2007.

III ANSB [16.2]

Contracting out functions The Secretary of State is empowered, by the new s 28A inserted by s 25 of the Police and Justice Act 2006, to make an order authorising a local authority to contract out its functions under s 26A.

III ANSB [17]

26B. Parenting orders in respect of anti-social behaviour: relevant housing providers

(1) A relevant housing provider may apply for a parenting order in respect of a parent of a child or young person if—

- (a) the relevant housing provider has reason to believe that the child or young person has engaged in anti-social behaviour, and
- (b) the behaviour in question directly or indirectly relates to or affects the housing management functions of the relevant housing provider.

An application for such an order may be made to a magistrates' court or, where section 26C so allows, to the county court.

(2) If such an application is made, the court may make a parenting order in respect of a parent of the child or young person if it is satisfied—

- (a) that the child or young person has engaged in anti-social behaviour, and
- (b) that making the order would be desirable in the interests of preventing the child or young person from engaging in further anti-social behaviour.

(3) A parenting order is an order which requires the parent—

- (a) to comply, for a period not exceeding twelve months, with such requirements as are specified in the order, and
- (b) subject to subsection (4), to attend, for a concurrent period not exceeding three months, such counselling or guidance programme as may be specified in directions given by the responsible officer.

ANTI-SOCIAL BEHAVIOUR

(4) A parenting order under this section may, but need not, include a requirement mentioned in subsection (3)(b) in any case where a parenting order under this section or any other enactment has been made in respect of the parent on a previous occasion.

(5) A counselling or guidance programme which a parent is required to attend by virtue of subsection (3)(b) may be or include a residential course but only if the court is satisfied that the following two conditions are fulfilled.

(6) The first condition is that the attendance of the parent at a residential course is likely to be more effective than his attendance at a non-residential course in preventing the child or young person from engaging in further anti-social behaviour.

(7) The second condition is that any interference with family life which is likely to result from the attendance of the parent at a residential course is proportionate in all the circumstances.

(8) A relevant housing provider must not make an application under this section without first consulting the local authority [(or, if subsection (8A) applies, each local authority)] in whose area the child or young person in question resides or appears to reside.

(8A) This subsection applies if the place where the child or young person resides or appears to reside is within the area of a county council and within the area of a district council.

(9) A person is eligible to be the responsible officer in relation to a parenting order under this section only if he is—

- (a) an officer of the relevant housing provider which applied for the order, or
- (b) a person nominated by that relevant housing provider.

A person may not be nominated under paragraph (b) without his consent.

(10) In deciding whom to nominate under subsection (9)(b) a relevant housing provider must take into account the views of—

- (a) the local authority (or authorities) mentioned in subsection (8), and
- (b) such other persons or bodies as the relevant housing provider thinks appropriate.

III ANSB [18]–III ANSB [25]

26C. Applications under s 26A or s 26B in county court proceedings

(1) Where a local authority or relevant housing provider (a "relevant authority")—

- (a) is a party to proceedings in the county court, and
- (b) considers that a party to those proceedings is a person in relation to whom it would be reasonable for it to make an application for a parenting order under section 26A or 26B (a "parenting order application"),

it may make such an application to that court in relation to that person.

(2) Where—

- (a) a relevant authority considers that a party to proceedings in the county court is a person in relation to whom it would be reasonable for it to make a parenting order application, but
- (b) the relevant authority is not a party to those proceedings,

it may apply to be joined to those proceedings to enable it to make a parenting order application.

(3) Where—

- (a) there are proceedings in the county court to which a relevant authority is a party, and

(b) the relevant authority considers that a child or young person has engaged in anti-social behaviour that is material in relation to the proceedings,

the relevant authority may apply for a person who is a parent of the child or young person to be joined to the proceedings to enable it to make a parenting order application in relation to him.

(4) A person must not be joined to proceedings in pursuance of subsection (3) unless the anti-social behaviour in question is material in relation to those proceedings.

III ANSB [25.1]

Applications for parenting orders in the county court This section confers jurisdiction on county courts with effect from 29 June 2007. Applications to county courts for parenting orders must follow the procedure set out in **CPR 65.37–CPR 65.41**. Note also the points made in paragraph 16 of the Practice Direction supplementing Part 65, at **CPR PD 65**, that (1) where the applicant is a registered social landlord there must be evidence of consultation of the relevant local authority (2) an order under s 26A or 26B must be served personally and (3) an application by a local authority to join a person under s 26C(3) may only be made against a person aged 18 or over.

POLICE AND JUSTICE ACT 2006

(c 48)

III ANSB [26]

27. Injunctions in local authority proceedings: power of arrest and demand

(1) This section applies to proceedings in which a local authority is a party by virtue of section 222 of the Local Government Act 1972 (c 70) (power of local authority to bring, defend or appear in proceedings for the promotion or protection of the interests of inhabitants of their area).

(2) If the court grants an injunction which prohibits conduct which is capable of causing nuisance or annoyance to a person it may, if subsection (3) applies, attach a power of arrest to any provision of the injunction.

(3) This subsection applies if the local authority applies to the court to attach the power of arrest and the court thinks that either—

(a) the conduct mentioned in subsection (2) consists of or includes the use or threatened use of violence, or

(b) there is a significant risk of harm to the person mentioned in that subsection.

(4) Where a power of arrest is attached to any provision of an injunction under subsection (2), a constable may arrest without warrant a person whom he has reasonable cause for suspecting to be in breach of that provision.

(5) After making an arrest under subsection (4) the constable must as soon as is reasonably practicable inform the local authority.

(6) Where a person is arrested under subsection (4)—

(a) he shall be brought before the court within the period of 24 hours beginning at the time of his arrest, and

(b) if the matter is not then disposed of forthwith, the court may remand him.

(7) For the purposes of subsection (6), when calculating the period of 24 hours referred to in paragraph (a) of that subsection, no account shall be taken of Christmas Day, Good Friday or any Sunday.

(8) Schedule 10 applies in relation to the power to remand under subsection (6).

(9) If the court has reason to consider that a medical report will be required, the power to remand a person under subsection (6) may be exercised for the purpose of enabling a medical examination and report to be made.

(10) If such a power is so exercised the adjournment shall not be in force—

(a) for more than three weeks at a time in a case where the court remands the accused person in custody, or

(b) for more than four weeks at a time in any other case.

(11) If there is reason to suspect that a person who has been arrested under subsection (4) is suffering from mental disorder within the meaning of the Mental Health Act 1983 the court shall have the same power to make an order under section 35 of that Act (remand for report on accused's mental condition) as the Crown Court has under that section in the case of an accused person within the meaning of that section.

(12) For the purposes of this section—

(a) "harm" includes serious ill-treatment or abuse (whether physical or not);

(b) "local authority" has the same meaning as in section 222 of the Local Government Act 1972 (c 70);

(c) "the court" means the High Court or the county court and includes—

(i) in relation to the High Court, a judge of that court, and

(ii) in relation to the county court, a judge of that court.

III ANSB [26.1]

New provisions This section and Schedule 10, below, set out powers and obligations regarding the arrest and remand of person alleged to have broken injunctions in local authority proceedings. The provisions replace those in s 91 of the Anti-Social Behaviour Act 2003 which were repealed by s 52 and Sch 15, Part 3 of this Act, with effect from 6 April 2007.

However, councils should not seek civil injunctions to restrain anti-social behaviour in reliance on s 27 of the Police and Justice Act 2006, since this would avoid the specific requirements applicable to ASBOs. The courts should not indulge in parallel activity by the extension of general common law principles: *Birmingham City Council v Shafi* [2008] EWCA Civ 1186, [2009] 3 All ER 127, [2009] 1 WLR 1961, applying principles laid down by Hoffmann J in *Chief Constable of Leicestershire v M* [1989] 1 WLR 20, Ch D.

SCHEDULE 10 INJUNCTIONS IN LOCAL AUTHORITY PROCEEDINGS: POWERS TO REMAND

INTRODUCTORY

III ANSB [27]

1

(1) The provisions of this Schedule apply where the court has power to remand a person under section 27(6) (injunctions in local authority proceedings: power of arrest and remand).

(2) In this Schedule "the court" has the same meaning as in section 27.

REMAND IN CUSTODY OR ON BAIL

2

(1) The court may—

(a) remand the person in custody, that is, commit him to custody to be brought before the court at the end of the period of remand or at such earlier time as the court may require, or

(b) remand him on bail, in accordance with the following provisions.

(2) The court may remand the person on bail—

(a) by taking from him a recognizance, with or without sureties, conditioned as provided in paragraph 3, or

(b) by fixing the amount of the recognizances with a view to their being taken subsequently, and in the meantime committing him to custody as mentioned in sub-paragraph (1)(a).

(3) Where a person is brought before the court after remand, the court may further remand him.

3

(1) Where a person is remanded on bail, the court may direct that his recognizance be conditioned for his appearance—

(a) before that court at the end of the period of remand, or

(b) at every time and place to which during the course of the proceedings the hearing may from time to time be adjourned.

(2) Where a recognizance is conditioned for a person's appearance as mentioned in sub-paragraph (1)(b), the fixing of any time for him next to appear shall be deemed to be a remand.

(3) Nothing in this paragraph affects the power of the court at any subsequent hearing to remand him afresh.

4

(1) The court shall not remand a person for a period exceeding eight clear days except that—

(a) if the court remands him on bail, it may remand him for a longer period if he and the other party consent, and

(b) if the court adjourns a case under section 27(9) (remand for medical examination and report) the court may remand him for the period of adjournment.

(2) Where the court has the power to remand a person in custody it may, if the remand is for a period not exceeding three clear days, commit him to the custody of a constable.

FURTHER REMAND

5

(1) If the court is satisfied that a person who has been remanded is unable by reason of illness or accident to appear or be brought before the court at the expiration of the period for which he was remanded, the court may, in his absence, remand him for a further time.

(2) The power mentioned in sub-paragraph (1) may, in the case of a person who was remanded on bail, be exercised by enlarging his recognizance and those of any sureties for him to a later time.

(3) Where a person remanded on bail is bound to appear before the court at any time and the court has no power to remand him under sub-paragraph (1), the court may in his absence enlarge his recognizance and those of any sureties for him to a later time.

(4) The enlargement of his recognizance shall be deemed to be a further remand.

(5) Paragraph 4(1) (limit of remand) does not apply to the exercise of the powers conferred by this paragraph.

Postponement of taking recognizance

6

Where under paragraph 2(2)(b) the court fixes the amount in which the principal and his sureties, if any, are to be bound, the recognizance may afterwards be taken by such person as may be prescribed by rules of court, with the same consequences as if it had been entered into before the court.

Requirements imposed on remand on bail

7

The court may when remanding a person on bail under this Schedule require him to comply, before release on bail or later, with such requirements as appear to the court to be necessary to secure that he does not interfere with witnesses or otherwise obstruct the course of justice.

POLICING AND CRIME ACT 2009

(c 26)

III ANSB [28]–III ANSB [33]

General Notes on Part 4 of the Policing and Crime Act 2009 Part 4 of the Policing and Crime Act 2009 is made up of ss 34 to 50 and Schedule 5, all of which are set out below. Section 34 confers power on the High Court and the county court (see s 49) to grant injunctions, on application, to protect individuals from gang violence. It should be noted that the magistrates' courts have no power to grant injunctions under this Part and that to be amenable to a Part 4 injunction the gang violence must include three elements: there must be at least three members, they must be associated with a particular area and they must be identifiable by sharing a group name, emblem or colour 'or any other characteristic'. The only persons who may apply for injunctions are the police and the local authority (s 37) and they must carry out limited consultations before applying (s 38). There are provisions for injunctions to be made with or without notice (s 39) and for the grant of interim injunctions (s 40) and for injunctions to be varied or discharged (s 41). The grant of an injunction may include a power of arrest (s 36) which may be exercised without obtaining a warrant (s 43). An arrested person must be brought before the appropriate court and may be remanded for reports in accordance with s 45 and Sch 5. The powers and procedures closely resemble those arising under ss 153A to 155 of the Housing Act 1996 for the control of anti-social behaviour on council estates: see **III L&T [298]** to **III L&T [158]**.

All the relevant provisions were brought into force on 31 January 2011 by the Policing and Crime Act 2009 (Commencement No 7) Order 2010, SI 2010/2988.

A new section 34 (Injunctions to Prevent Gang-related Violence and Drug-Dealing Activity) was substituted, as from 1 June 2015, by section 51 of the Serious Crime Act 2015.

PART 4
INJUNCTIONS: GANG-RELATED VIOLENCE AND DRUG-DEALING ACTIVITY

POWER TO GRANT INJUNCTIONS

III ANSB [34]

34. Injunctions to prevent gang-related violence and drug-dealing activity

(1) A court may grant an injunction under this section against a respondent aged 14 or over if the first and second conditions are met.

(2) The first condition is that the court is satisfied on the balance of probabilities that the respondent has engaged in or has encouraged or assisted—

(a) gang-related violence, or

(b) gang-related drug-dealing activity.

(3) The second condition is that the court thinks it is necessary to grant the injunction for either or both of the following purposes—

(a) to prevent the respondent from engaging in, or encouraging or assisting, gang-related violence or gang-related drug-dealing activity;

(b) to protect the respondent from gang-related violence or gang-related drug-dealing activity.

(4) An injunction under this section may (for either or both of those purposes)—

(a) prohibit the respondent from doing anything described in the injunction;

(b) require the respondent to do anything described in the injunction.

(5) For the purposes of this section, something is "gang-related" if it occurs in the course of, or is otherwise related to, the activities of a group that—

(a) consists of at least three people, and

(b) has one or more characteristics that enable its members to be identified by others as a group.

(6) In this section "violence" includes a threat of violence.

(7) In this Part "drug-dealing activity" means—

(a) the unlawful production, supply, importation or exportation of a controlled drug, or

(b) the unlawful production, supply, importation or exportation of a psychoactive substance.

(8) In subsection (7)—

(a) in paragraph (a), "production", "supply" and "controlled drug" have the meaning given by section 37(1) of the Misuse of Drugs Act 1971;

(b) in paragraph (b), "production", "supply" and "psychoactive substance" have the meaning given by section 59 of the Psychoactive Substances Act 2016.

III ANSB [34.1]

Standard burden of proof It has been held that proceedings under this Part are essentially civil proceedings to which the standard burden of proof, on the balance of probabilities, applies; and that they do not involve the bringing of a criminal charge, for the purposes of Article 6 of the Convention: *Jones v Birmingham City Council* [2018] EWCA Civ 1189, [2018] All ER (D) 129 (May).

CONTENTS OF INJUNCTIONS

III ANSB [35]

35. Contents of injunctions

(1) This section applies in relation to an injunction under section 34.

(2) The prohibitions included in the injunction may, in particular, have the effect of prohibiting the respondent from—

- (a) being in a particular place;
- (b) being with particular persons in a particular place;
- (c) being in charge of a particular species of animal in a particular place;
- (d) wearing particular descriptions of articles of clothing in a particular place;
- (e) using the internet to facilitate or encourage violence or drug-dealing activity.

(3) The requirements included in the injunction may, in particular, have the effect of requiring the respondent to—

- (a) notify the person who applied for the injunction of the respondent's address and of any change to that address;
- (b) be at a particular place between particular times on particular days;
- (c) present himself or herself to a particular person at a place where he or she is required to be between particular times on particular days;
- (d) participate in particular activities between particular times on particular days.

(4) A requirement of the kind mentioned in subsection (3)(b) may not be such as to require the respondent to be at a particular place for more than 8 hours in any day.

(5) The prohibitions and requirements included in the injunction must, so far as practicable, be such as to avoid—

- (a) any conflict with the respondent's religious beliefs, and
- (b) any interference with the times, if any, at which the respondent normally works or attends any educational establishment.

(6) Nothing in subsection (2) or (3) affects the generality of section 34(4).

(7) In subsection (2) "place" includes an area.

III ANSB [36]

36. Contents of injunctions: supplemental

(1) This section applies in relation to an injunction under section 34.

(2) The injunction may not include a prohibition or requirement that has effect after the end of the period of 2 years beginning with the day on which the injunction is granted ("the injunction date").

(3) The court may order the applicant and the respondent to attend one or more review hearings on a specified date or dates.

(4) If any prohibition or requirement in the injunction is to have effect after the end of the period of 1 year beginning with the injunction date, the court must order the applicant and the respondent to attend a review hearing on a specified date within the last 4 weeks of the 1 year period (whether or not the court orders them to attend any other review hearings).

(4A) Where—

(a) the respondent is under the age of 18 on the injunction date, and

(b) any prohibition or requirement in the injunction is to have effect after the respondent reaches that age and for at least the period of four weeks beginning with the respondent's 18th birthday,

the court must order the applicant and the respondent to attend a review hearing on a specified date within that period.

(5) A review hearing is a hearing held for the purpose of considering whether the injunction should be varied or discharged.

(6) The court may attach a power of arrest in relation to—

(a) any prohibition in the injunction, or

(b) any requirement in the injunction, other than one which has the effect of requiring the respondent to participate in particular activities.

(7) If the court attaches a power of arrest, it may specify that the power is to have effect for a shorter period than the prohibition or requirement to which it relates.

III ANSB [36.1]

Provisions to which a power of arrest is attached For the form of the injunction with a power of arrest and the requirement to deliver a copy to any police station for the area see **CPR 65.44**.

Applications

III ANSB [37]

37. Applications for injunctions under section 34

(1) An application for an injunction under section 34 may be made by—

(a) the chief officer of police for a police area,

(b) the chief constable of the British Transport Police Force, or

(c) a local authority.

(2) In this Part "local authority" means—

(a) in relation to England, a district council, a county council, a London borough council, the Common Council of the City of London or the Council of the Isles of Scilly;

(b) in relation to Wales, a county council or a county borough council.

III ANSB [37.1]

Procedure for applications An application for an injunction should be made in accordance with the Part 8 procedure and the other provisions of **CPR 65.43**. As regards applications for a power of arrest to be attached see **CPR 65.49**.

III ANSB [38]

38. Consultation by applicants for injunctions

(1) Before applying for an injunction under section 37, the applicant must comply with the consultation requirement.

(2) The consultation requirement is that the applicant must consult—

(a) any local authority, and any chief police officer, that the applicant thinks it appropriate to consult, and

(aa) where the respondent is under the age of 18 (and will be under that age when the application is made), the youth offending team established under section 39 of the Crime and Disorder Act 1998 in whose area it appears to the applicant that the respondent resides, and

(b) any other body or individual that the applicant thinks it appropriate to consult.

(3) If it appears to the applicant that the respondent resides in the area of two or more youth offending teams, the obligation in subsection (2)(aa) is to consult such of those teams as the applicant thinks appropriate.

III ANSB [39]

39. Applications without notice

(1) An application under section 37 may be made without the respondent being given notice.

(2) In this Part, such an application is referred to as an application without notice.

(3) Section 38(1) does not apply in relation to an application without notice.

(4) If an application without notice is made the court must either—

(a) dismiss the application, or

(b) adjourn the proceedings.

(5) If the court acts under subsection (4)(b), the applicant must comply with the consultation requirement before the date of the first full hearing.

(6) In this section "full hearing" means a hearing of which notice has been given to the applicant and respondent in accordance with rules of court.

Interim injunctions

III ANSB [40]

40. Interim injunctions: adjournment of on notice hearing

(1) This section applies if—

(a) the court adjourns the hearing of an application for an injunction under section 34, and

(b) the respondent was notified of the hearing in accordance with rules of court.

(2) The court may grant an interim injunction if it thinks that it is just and convenient to do so.

(3) An interim injunction under this section may include any provision which the court has power to include in an injunction granted under section 34 (including a power of arrest).

III ANSB [41]

41. Interim injunctions: adjournment of without notice hearing

(1) This section applies if—

(a) an application without notice is made by virtue of section 39, and

(b) the proceedings are adjourned (otherwise than at a full hearing within the meaning of that section).

(2) The court may grant an interim injunction if it thinks that it is necessary to do so.

(3) An interim injunction under this section may not have the effect of requiring the respondent to participate in particular activities.

(4) Except as provided by subsection (3), an interim injunction under this section may include any provision which the court has power to include in an injunction granted under section 34 (including a power of arrest).

Variation and discharge

III ANSB [42]

42. Variation or discharge of injunctions

(1) The court may vary or discharge an injunction under this Part if—

(a) a review hearing is held, or

(b) an application to vary or discharge the injunction is made.

(2) An application to vary or discharge the injunction may be made by—

(a) the person who applied for the injunction;

(b) the respondent.

(3) The power to vary an injunction includes power to—

(a) include an additional prohibition or requirement in the injunction;

(b) extend the period for which a prohibition or requirement in the injunction has effect (subject to section 36(2));

(c) attach a power of arrest or extend the period for which a power of arrest attached to the injunction has effect.

(4) Section 36(4) does not apply where an injunction is varied to include a prohibition or requirement which is to have effect as mentioned in that provision but the variation is made within (or at any time after) the period of 4 weeks mentioned in it.

(4A) Section 36(4A) does not apply where an injunction is varied to include a prohibition or requirement which is to have effect as mentioned in that provision but the variation is made within (or at any time after) the period of four weeks ending with the respondent's 18th birthday.

(5) Before applying for the variation or discharge of an injunction, a person mentioned in subsection (2)(a) must notify the persons consulted under section 38(1) or 39(5).

(6) If an application to vary or discharge an injunction under this Part is dismissed, no further application to vary or discharge it may be made by any person without the consent of the court.

III ANSB [42.1]

Application to vary or discharge An application to vary or discharge an injunction must be made in accordance with Part 23 and if made without notice must state the reasons: **CPR 65.45**.

Arrest and remand

III ANSB [43]

43. Arrest without warrant

(1) This section applies if a power of arrest is attached to a provision of an injunction under this Part.

(2) A constable may arrest without warrant a person whom the constable has reasonable cause to suspect to be in breach of the provision.

(3) If a constable arrests a person under subsection (2), the constable must inform the person who applied for the injunction.

(4) A person arrested under subsection (2) must be brought before a relevant judge within the period of 24 hours beginning with the time of the arrest.

(5) If the matter is not disposed of when the person is brought before the judge, the judge may remand the person.

(6) In calculating when the period of 24 hours mentioned in subsection (4) ends, Christmas Day, Good Friday and any Sunday are to be disregarded.

(7) In this Part "relevant judge", in relation to an injunction, means a judge of the court that granted the injunction, except that where—

(a) the respondent is aged 18 or over, but

(b) the injunction was granted by a youth court,

it means a judge of the county court.

III ANSB [44]

44. Issue of warrant of arrest

(1) This section applies in relation to an injunction under this Part.

(2) If the person who applied for the injunction considers that the respondent is in breach of any of its provisions, the person may apply to a relevant judge for the issue of a warrant for the arrest of the respondent.

(3) A relevant judge may not issue a warrant on an application under subsection (2) unless the judge has reasonable grounds for believing that the respondent is in breach of any provision of the injunction.

(4) If a person is brought before a court by virtue of a warrant under subsection (3), but the matter is not disposed of, the court may remand the person.

III ANSB [44.1]

Application for issue of a warrant of arrest An application for the issue of a warrant of arrest under s 44(2) must be made in accordance with Part 23 and **CPR 65.46**. For proceedings following arrest see **CPR 65.47**.

III ANSB [45]

45. Remand for medical examination and report

(1) This section applies in relation to a person who is brought before the relevant judge or the court under section 43 or 44.

(2) If the relevant judge or the court has reason to consider that a medical report will be required, the judge or the court may remand the person under section 43(5) or (as the case may be) 44(4) for the purpose of enabling a medical examination to take place and a report to be made.

(3) If the person is remanded in custody for that purpose, the adjournment may not be for more than 3 weeks at a time.

(4) If the person is remanded on bail for that purpose, the adjournment may not be for more than 4 weeks at a time.

(5) If the relevant judge or the court has reason to suspect that the person is suffering from a mental disorder within the meaning of the Mental Health Act 1983, the judge or the court has the same power to make an order under section 35 of that Act (remand for report on accused's medical condition) as the Crown Court has under that section in the case of an accused person (within the meaning of that section).

III ANSB [46]

46. Further provision about remands

Schedule 5 (which makes further provision about the remand of a person under sections 43(5) and 44(4)) has effect.

III ANSB [46A]

46A. Breach of injunction: supplementary powers in respect of under-18s

Schedule 5A (which makes provision about the powers of the court in relation to breach of an injunction by a respondent aged under 18) has effect.

III ANSB [46A.1]

Committal to prison for breach of injunction *Practice Guidance: Committal for Contempt of Court – Open Court*, issued by the Lord Chief Justice on 24 June 2015, explains that the Practice Direction (Committal for Contempt: Open Court, issued on 26 March 2015, at **CPR PD 81** and **III COT [000]**, applies to committal hearings under the Act in respect of adults but not to individuals under the age of 18.

MISCELLANEOUS

III ANSB [47]

47. Guidance

(1) The Secretary of State must issue guidance relating to injunctions under this Part.

(2) The Secretary of State may revise any guidance issued under subsection (1).

(3) Before issuing or revising any guidance under this section the Secretary of State must consult the Lord Chief Justice of England and Wales and such other persons as the Secretary of State thinks appropriate.

(4) The Secretary of State must lay any guidance issued or revised under this section before Parliament.

(5) The Secretary of State must publish any guidance issued or revised under this section.

(6) Each of the following must have regard to any guidance published under subsection (5)—

(a) a chief officer of police for a police area;

(b) the chief constable of the British Transport Police Force;

(c) a local authority.

III ANSB [48]

48. Supplemental

(1) *Repealed.*

(2) Rules of court may provide that an appeal from a decision ... to which this subsection applies may be made without notice being given to the respondent.

(3) Subsection (2) applies—

(a) to a decision under section 39(4)(a) that an application without notice be dismissed, and

(b) to a decisio to refuse to grant an interim injunction under section 41.

(4) In relation to a respondent attaining the age of 18 after the commencement of proceedings under this Part, rules of court may—

(a) provide for the transfer of the proceedings from a youth court to the High Court or the county court;

(b) prescribe circumstances in which the proceedings may or must remain in a youth court.

III ANSB [49]

49. Interpretation

(1) In this Part—

"application without notice" has the meaning given by section 39(2);

"consultation requirement" has the meaning given by section 38(2);

"court" (except in Schedule 5A)—

(a) in the case of a respondent aged under 18, means a youth court, and

(b) in any other case, means the High Court or the county court, but this is subject to any provision in rules of court that is or could be made under section 48(4);

"drug-dealing activity" has the meaning given by section 34(7);

"judge", in relation to a youth court, means a person qualified to sit as a member of that court;

"local authority" has the meaning given by section 37(2);

"relevant judge" has the meaning given by section 43(7);

"respondent" means the person in respect of whom an application for an injunction is made or (as the context requires) the person against whom such an injunction is granted;

"review hearing" has the meaning given by section 36(5);

"specify", in relation to an injunction, means specify in the injunction;

"violence" includes violence against property.

(2) Any reference in this Part to an injunction under this Part includes a reference to an interim injunction.

III ANSB [50]

50. Review of operation of this Part

(1) The Secretary of State must—

(a) review the operation of this Part, and

(b) prepare and publish a report on the outcome of the review.

(2) The report must be published before the end of the period of 3 years beginning with the day on which this Part comes into force.

(3) The Secretary of State must lay the report before Parliament.

SCHEDULE 5 INJUNCTIONS: POWERS TO REMAND

Introductory

III ANSB [51]

1

(1) The provisions of this Schedule apply where the court has power to remand a person under section 43(5) or 44(4).

(2) In this Schedule, "the court" means the High Court, the county court or a youth court and includes—

(a) in relation to the High Court, a judge of that court,

(b) in relation to the county court, a judge of that court, and

(c) in relation to a youth court, a judge of that court.

Remand in custody or on bail

2

(1) The court may—

(a) in the case of a person aged 18 or over remand the person in custody, that is, commit the person to custody to be brought before the court at the end of the period of remand or at such earlier time as the court may require, or

(b) remand the person on bail.

(2) The court may remand the person on bail—

(a) by taking from the person a recognizance, with or without sureties, conditioned as provided in paragraph 3, or

(b) by fixing the amount of the recognizances with a view to their being taken subsequently and, in the meantime, committing the person to custody as mentioned in sub-paragraph (1)(a).

(3) Where a person is brought before the court after remand, the court may further remand the person.

3

(1) Where a person is remanded on bail, the court may direct that the person's recognizance be conditioned for the person's appearance—

(a) before that court at the end of the period of remand, or

(b) at every time and place to which during the course of the proceedings the hearing may from time to time be adjourned.

(2) Where a recognizance is conditioned for a person's appearance as mentioned in sub-paragraph (1)(b), the fixing of any time for the person next to appear is to be treated as a remand.

(3) Nothing in this paragraph affects the power of the court at any subsequent hearing to remand the person afresh.

4

(1) The court may not remand a person for a period exceeding 8 clear days unless—

(a) the person is remanded on bail, and

(b) both that person and the person who applied for the injunction consent to a longer period.

(2) Where the court has power to remand a person in custody it may, if the remand is for a period not exceeding 3 clear days, commit the person to the custody of a constable.

Further remand

5

(1) If the court is satisfied that a person who has been remanded is unable by reason of illness or accident to appear or be brought before the court at the expiration of the period of remand, the court may, in the absence of the person, further remand the person.

(2) The power mentioned in sub-paragraph (1) may, in the case of a person who was remanded on bail, be exercised by enlarging the person's recognizance and those of any sureties for the person to a later time.

(3) Where a person remanded on bail is bound to appear before the court at any time and the court has no power to remand the person under sub-paragraph (1), the court may (in the person's absence) enlarge the person's recognizance and those of any sureties for the person to a later time.

(4) The enlargement of the person's recognizance is to be treated as a further remand.

(5) Paragraph 4(1) (limit of remand) does not apply to the exercise of the powers conferred by this paragraph.

Postponement of taking recognizance

6

Where under paragraph 2(2)(b) the court fixes the amount in which the principal and the sureties, if any, are to be bound, the recognizance may afterwards be taken by such person as may be prescribed by rules of court, with the same consequences as if it had been entered into before the court.

REQUIREMENTS IMPOSED ON REMAND ON BAIL

7

The court may when remanding a person on bail under this Schedule require the person to comply, before release on bail or later, with such requirements as appear to the court to be necessary to secure that the person does not interfere with witnesses or otherwise obstruct the course of justice.

III ANSB [51.1]

Recognizance For the procedure for taking a recognizance see **CPR 65.48**.

ANTI-SOCIAL BEHAVIOUR, CRIME AND POLICING ACT 2014

(c 12)

III ANSB [52]

Injunctions to stop anti-social behaviour Part 1 of the Anti-social Behaviour, Crime and Policing Act 2014 is made up of 21 sections on the theme of injunctions to stop anti-social behaviour, including a forward reference to Schedule 1 about remands under ss 9 and 10. Fresh powers are conferred on the High Court and the County Court and, as regards defendants under the age of 18, the youth courts.

Amendments to existing legislation are made by Schedule 11 and much of the existing legislation on the injunctive powers of the High Court and County Court is repealed, including ss 1 to 1F of the Crime and Disorder Act 1998 and ss 1 to 4, 9 and 14 of the Violent Crime Reduction Act 2006 (drinking banning orders). Part 1 of the Act of 2014 stands in their place but the changes require the making of a commencement order under s 185.

III ANSB [52A]

Housing Act amendments Amendments to the housing legislation are made by Part 5 of the Act, ss 94 to 100. They take the form of new provisions inserted in the Housing Act 1985 and the Housing Act 1988 and are set out in the Landlord and Tenant and Housing title at **III L&T [107]** onwards. They include new grounds for ordering possession where they has been anti-social behaviour connected with a secure tenancy or an assured tenancy: see, in particular, the new mandatory grounds for possession under s 84A of the Housing Act 1985 and the insertion of additional grounds for possession in Schedule 2 to the Housing Act 1988.

PART 1
INJUNCTIONS

INJUNCTIONS

III ANSB [53]

1. Power to grant injunctions

(1) A court may grant an injunction under this section against a person aged 10 or over ("the respondent") if two conditions are met.

(2) The first condition is that the court is satisfied, on the balance of probabilities, that the respondent has engaged or threatens to engage in anti-social behaviour.

(3) The second condition is that the court considers it just and convenient to grant the injunction for the purpose of preventing the respondent from engaging in anti-social behaviour.

(4) An injunction under this section may for the purpose of preventing the respondent from engaging in anti-social behaviour—

- (a) prohibit the respondent from doing anything described in the injunction;
- (b) require the respondent to do anything described in the injunction.

(5) Prohibitions and requirements in an injunction under this section must, so far as practicable, be such as to avoid—

- (a) any interference with the times, if any, at which the respondent normally works or attends school or any other educational establishment;
- (b) any conflict with the requirements of any other court order or injunction to which the respondent may be subject.

(6) An injunction under this section must—

- (a) specify the period for which it has effect, or
- (b) state that it has effect until further order.

In the case of an injunction granted before the respondent has reached the age of 18, a period must be specified and it must be no more than 12 months.

(7) An injunction under this section may specify periods for which particular prohibitions or requirements have effect.

(8) An application for an injunction under this section must be made to—

- (a) a youth court, in the case of a respondent aged under 18;
- (b) the High Court or the county court, in any other case.

Paragraph (b) is subject to any rules of court made under section 18(2).

III ANSB [53.1]

Standard burden of proof It has been held that proceedings under this Part are essentially civil proceedings to which the standard burden of proof, on the balance of probabilities, applies; and that they do not involve the bringing of a criminal charge, for the purposes of Article 6 of the Convention: *Jones v Birmingham City Council* [2018] EWCA Civ 1189, [2018] All ER (D) 129 (May).

III ANSB [53.2]

Injunction against travellers with power of arrest The court has powers, under s 1 of this Act also s 187B of the Town and Country Planning Act 1990 and s 222 of the Local Government Act 1972 to grant a local authority an injunction, with powers of arrest, to stop unauthorised encampments by travellers where there is a history of damage and nuisance over a significant period: *London Borough of Barking and Dagenham v Stokes* (2017) High Court decision of Turner J in the Queen's Bench Division on 30 October 2017.

III ANSB [54]

2. Meaning of "anti-social behaviour"

(1) In this Part "anti-social behaviour" means—

(a) conduct that has caused, or is likely to cause, harassment, alarm or distress to any person,

(b) conduct capable of causing nuisance or annoyance to a person in relation to that person's occupation of residential premises, or

(c) conduct capable of causing housing-related nuisance or annoyance to any person

(2) Subsection (1)(b) applies only where the injunction under section 1 is applied for by—

(a) a housing provider,

(b) a local authority, or

(c) a chief officer of police.

(3) In subsection (1)(c) "housing-related" means directly or indirectly relating to the housing management functions of—

(a) a housing provider, or

(b) a local authority.

(4) For the purposes of subsection (3) the housing management functions of a housing provider or a local authority include—

(a) functions conferred by or under an enactment;

(b) the powers and duties of the housing provider or local authority as the holder of an estate or interest in housing accommodation.

III ANSB [54.1]

Practice Interim injunctions (see section 7) have been granted to prohibit individuals with anti-Muslim views from entering any mosque or Islamic Cultural Centre, or its private grounds, within England and Wales without prior invitation and also from publishing words or images that were likely to stir up religious or racial hatred: *Chief Constable of Bedfordshire Police v Golding* [2015] EWHC 1875 (QB), 165 NLJ 7661, [2015] All ER (D) 23 (Jul).

Contents of injunctions

III ANSB [55]

3. Requirements included in injunctions

(1) An injunction under section 1 that includes a requirement must specify the person who is to be responsible for supervising compliance with the requirement. The person may be an individual or an organisation.

(2) Before including a requirement, the court must receive evidence about its suitability and enforceability from—

(a) the individual to be specified under subsection (1), if an individual is to be specified;

(b) an individual representing the organisation to be specified under subsection (1), if an organisation is to be specified.

(3) Before including two or more requirements, the court must consider their compatibility with each other.

(4) It is the duty of a person specified under subsection (1)—

(a) to make any necessary arrangements in connection with the requirements for which the person has responsibility (the "relevant requirements");

(b) to promote the respondent's compliance with the relevant requirements;

(c) if the person considers that the respondent—

(i) has complied with all the relevant requirements, or

(ii) has failed to comply with a relevant requirement,

to inform the person who applied for the injunction and the appropriate chief officer of police.

(5) In subsection (4)(c) "the appropriate chief officer of police" means—

(a) the chief officer of police for the police area in which it appears to the person specified under subsection (1) that the respondent lives, or

(b) if it appears to that person that the respondent lives in more than one police area, whichever of the relevant chief officers of police that person thinks it most appropriate to inform.

(6) A respondent subject to a requirement included in an injunction under section 1 must—

(a) keep in touch with the person specified under subsection (1) in relation to that requirement, in accordance with any instructions given by that person from time to time;

(b) notify the person of any change of address.

These obligations have effect as requirements of the injunction.

III ANSB [56]

4. Power of arrest

(1) A court granting an injunction under section 1 may attach a power of arrest to a prohibition or requirement of the injunction if the court thinks that—

(a) the anti-social behaviour in which the respondent has engaged or threatens to engage consists of or includes the use or threatened use of violence against other persons, or

(b) there is a significant risk of harm to other persons from the respondent.

"Requirement" here does not include one that has the effect of requiring the respondent to participate in particular activities.

(2) If the court attaches a power of arrest, the injunction may specify a period for which the power is to have effect which is shorter than that of the prohibition or requirement to which it relates.

Applications for injunctions

III ANSB [57]

5. Applications for injunctions

(1)

(a) a local authority,

(b) a housing provider,

(c) the chief officer of police for a police area,
(d) the chief constable of the British Transport Police Force,
(e) Transport for London,
(f) the Environment Agency,
(g) the Natural Resources Body for Wales,
(h) the Secretary of State exercising security management functions, or a Special Health Authority exercising security management functions on the direction of the Secretary of State, or
(i) the Welsh Ministers exercising security management functions, or a person or body exercising security management functions on the direction of the Welsh Ministers or under arrangements made between the Welsh Ministers and that person or body.

(2) In subsection (1) "security management functions" means—
(a) the Secretary of State's security management functions within the meaning given by section 195(3) of the National Health Service Act 2006;
(b) the functions of the Welsh Ministers corresponding to those functions.

(3) A housing provider may make an application only if the application concerns anti-social behaviour that directly or indirectly relates to or affects its housing management functions.

(4) For the purposes of subsection (3) the housing management functions of a housing provider include—
(a) functions conferred by or under an enactment;
(b) the powers and duties of the housing provider as the holder of an estate or interest in housing accommodation.

(5) The Secretary of State may by order—
(a) amend this section;
(b) amend section 20 in relation to expressions used in this section.

III ANSB [58]

6. Applications without notice

(1) An application for an injunction under section 1 may be made without notice being given to the respondent.

(2) If an application is made without notice the court must either—
(a) adjourn the proceedings and grant an interim injunction (see section 7), or
(b) adjourn the proceedings without granting an interim injunction, or
(c) dismiss the application.

Interim injunctions

III ANSB [59]

7. Interim injunctions

(1) This section applies where the court adjourns the hearing of an application (whether made with notice or without) for an injunction under section 1.

(2) The court may grant an injunction under that section lasting until the final hearing of the application or until further order (an "interim injunction") if the court thinks it just to do so.

(3) An interim injunction made at a hearing of which the respondent was not given notice may not have the effect of requiring the respondent to participate in particular activities.

(4) Subject to that, the court has the same powers (including powers under section 4) whether or not the injunction is an interim injunction.

VARIATION AND DISCHARGE

III ANSB [60]

8. Variation or discharge of injunctions

(1) The court may vary or discharge an injunction under section 1 on the application of—

(a) the person who applied for the injunction, or

(b) the respondent.

(2) In subsection (1) "the court" means—

(a) the court that granted the injunction, except where paragraph (b) applies;

(b) the county court, where the injunction was granted by a youth court but the respondent is aged 18 or over.

(3) The power to vary an injunction includes power—

(a) to include an additional prohibition or requirement in the injunction, or to extend the period for which a prohibition or requirement has effect;

(b) to attach a power of arrest, or to extend the period for which a power of arrest has effect.

(4) If an application under this section is dismissed, the party by which the dismissed application was made may make no further application under this section without—

(a) the consent of the court, or

(b) the agreement of the other party.

(5) Section 3 applies to additional requirements included under subsection (3)(a) above as it applies to requirements included in a new injunction.

ARREST AND REMAND

III ANSB [61]

9. Arrest without warrant

(1) Where a power of arrest is attached to a provision of an injunction under section 1, a constable may arrest the respondent without warrant if he or she has reasonable cause to suspect that the respondent is in breach of the provision.

(2) A constable who arrests a person under subsection (1) must inform the person who applied for the injunction.

(3) A person arrested under subsection (1) must, within the period of 24 hours beginning with the time of the arrest, be brought before—

(a) a judge of the High Court or a judge of the county court, if the injunction was granted by the High Court;

(b) a judge of the county court, if—

(i) the injunction was granted by the county court, or

(ii) the injunction was granted by a youth court but the respondent is aged 18 or over;

(c) a justice of the peace, if neither paragraph (a) nor paragraph (b) applies.

(4) In calculating when the period of 24 hours ends, Christmas Day, Good Friday and any Sunday are to be disregarded.

(5) The judge before whom a person is brought under subsection (3)(a) or (b) may remand the person if the matter is not disposed of straight away.

(6) The justice of the peace before whom a person is brought under subsection (3)(c) must remand the person to appear before the youth court that granted the injunction.

III ANSB [62]

10. Issue of arrest warrant

(1) If the person who applied for an injunction under section 1 thinks that the respondent is in breach of any of its provisions, the person may apply for the issue of a warrant for the respondent's arrest.

(2) The application must be made to—

(a) a judge of the High Court, if the injunction was granted by the High Court;

(b) a judge of the county court, if—

(i) the injunction was granted by the county court, or

(ii) the injunction was granted by a youth court but the respondent is aged 18 or over;

(c) a justice of the peace, if neither paragraph (a) nor paragraph (b) applies.

(3) A judge or justice may issue a warrant under this section only if the judge or justice has reasonable grounds for believing that the respondent is in breach of a provision of the injunction.

(4) A warrant issued by a judge of the High Court must require the respondent to be brought before that court.

(5) A warrant issued by a judge of the county court must require the respondent to be brought before that court.

(6) A warrant issued by a justice of the peace must require the respondent to be brought before—

(a) the youth court that granted the injunction, if the person is aged under 18;

(b) the county court, if the person is aged 18 or over.

(7) A constable who arrests a person under a warrant issued under this section must inform the person who applied for the injunction.

(8) If the respondent is brought before a court by virtue of a warrant under this section but the matter is not disposed of straight away, the court may remand the respondent.

III ANSB [63]

11. Arrest without warrant

Schedule 1 (remands under sections 9 and 10) has effect.

III ANSB [64]

12. Powers in respect of under-18s

Schedule 2 (breach of injunctions: powers of court in respect of under-18s) has effect.

III ANSB [64.1]

Committal to prison for breach of injunction *Practice Guidance: Committal for Contempt of Court – Open Court*, issued by the Lord Chief Justice on 24 June 2015, explains that the Practice Direction (Committal for Contempt: Open Court, issued on 26 March 2015, at **CPR PD 81** and **III COT [004]**, applies to committal hearings under the Act in respect of adults but not to individuals under the age of 18.

EXCLUSION FROM HOME

III ANSB [65]

13. Power to exclude person from home in cases of violence or risk of harm

(1) An injunction under section 1 may have the effect of excluding the respondent from the place where he or she normally lives ("the premises") only if—

(a) the respondent is aged 18 or over,

(b) the injunction is granted on the application of—

(i) a local authority,

(ii) the chief officer of police for the police area that the premises are in, or

(iii) if the premises are owned or managed by a housing provider, that housing provider, and

(c) the court thinks that—

(i) the anti-social behaviour in which the respondent has engaged or threatens to engage consists of or includes the use or threatened use of violence against other persons, or

(ii) there is a significant risk of harm to other persons from the respondent.

(2) For the purposes of this section a housing provider owns a place if—

(a) the housing provider is a person (other than a mortgagee not in possession) entitled to dispose of the fee simple of the place, whether in possession or in reversion, or

(b) the housing provider is a person who holds or is entitled to the rents and profits of the place under a lease that (when granted) was for a term of not less then 3 years.

SUPPLEMENTAL

III ANSB [66]

14. Requirements to consult etc

(1) A person applying for an injunction under section 1 must before doing so—

(a) consult the local youth offending team about the application, if the respondent will be aged under 18 when the application is made;

(b) inform any other body or individual the applicant thinks appropriate of the application.

This subsection does not apply to a without-notice application.

(2) Where the court adjourns a without-notice application, before the date of the first on-notice hearing the applicant must—

(a) consult the local youth offending team about the application, if the respondent will be aged under 18 on that date;

(b) inform any other body or individual the applicant thinks appropriate of the application.

(3) A person applying for variation or discharge of an injunction under section 1 granted on that person's application must before doing so—

(a) consult the local youth offending team about the application for variation or discharge, if the respondent will be aged under 18 when that application is made;

(b) inform any other body or individual the applicant thinks appropriate of that application.

(4) In this section—

"local youth offending team" means—

(a) the youth offending team in whose area it appears to the applicant that the respondent lives, or

(b) if it appears to the applicant that the respondent lives in more than one such area, whichever one or more of the relevant youth offending teams the applicant thinks it appropriate to consult;

"on-notice hearing" means a hearing of which notice has been given to the applicant and the respondent in accordance with rules of court;

"without-notice application" means an application made without notice under section 6.

III ANSB [67]

15. Appeals against decisions of youth court

(1) An appeal lies to the Crown Court against a decision of a youth court made under this Part.

(2) On an appeal under this section the Crown Court may make—

(a) whatever orders are necessary to give effect to its determination of the appeal;

(b) whatever incidental or consequential orders appear to it to be just.

(3) An order of the Crown Court made on an appeal under this section (other than one directing that an application be re-heard by the youth court) is to be treated for the purposes of section 8 as an order of the youth court.

III ANSB [68]

16. Special measures for witnesses

(1) Chapter 1 of Part 2 of the Youth Justice and Criminal Evidence Act 1999 (special measures directions in the case of vulnerable and intimidated witnesses) applies to proceedings under this Part as it applies to criminal proceedings, but with—

(a) the omission of the provisions of that Act mentioned in subsection (2) (which make provision appropriate only in the context of criminal proceedings), and

(b) any other necessary modifications.

(2) The provisions are—

(a) section 17(4) to (7);

(b) section 21(4C)(e);

(c) section 22A;

(d) section 27(10);

(e) section 32.

(3) Rules of court made under or for the purposes of Chapter 1 of Part 2 of that Act apply to proceedings under this Part—

(a) to the extent provided by rules of court, and

(b) subject to any modifications provided by rules of court.

(4) Section 47 of that Act (restrictions on reporting special measures directions etc) applies with any necessary modifications—

(a) to a direction under section 19 of that Act as applied by this section;

(b) to a direction discharging or varying such a direction.

Sections 49 and 51 of that Act (offences) apply accordingly.

III ANSB [69]

17. Children and young persons: disapplication of reporting restrictions

Section 49 of the Children and Young Persons Act 1933 (restrictions on reports of proceedings in which children and young persons are concerned) does not apply to proceedings under this Part.

III ANSB [70]

18. Rules of court

(1) Rules of court may provide that an appeal from a decision of the High Court, the county court or a youth court—

(a) to dismiss an application for an injunction under section 1 made without notice being given to the respondent, or

(b) to refuse to grant an interim injunction when adjourning proceedings following such an application,

may be made without notice being given to the respondent.

(2) Rules of court may provide for a youth court to give permission for an application for an injunction under section 1 against a person aged 18 or over to be made to the youth court if—

(a) an application to the youth court has been made, or is to be made, for an injunction under that section against a person aged under 18, and

(b) the youth court thinks that it would be in the interests of justice for the applications to be heard together.

(3) In relation to a respondent attaining the age of 18 after proceedings under this Part have begun, rules of court may—

(a) provide for the transfer of the proceedings from the youth court to the High Court or the county court;

(b) prescribe circumstances in which the proceedings may or must remain in the youth court.

III ANSB [71]

19. Guidance

(1) The Secretary of State may issue guidance to persons entitled to apply for injunctions under section 1 (see section 5) about the exercise of their functions under this Part.

(2) The Secretary of State may revise any guidance issued under this section.

(3) The Secretary of State must arrange for any guidance issued or revised under this section to be published.

III ANSB [72]

20. Interpretation etc

(1) In this Part—

"anti-social behaviour" has the meaning given by section 2;

"harm" includes serious ill-treatment or abuse, whether physical or not;

"housing accommodation" includes—

(a) flats, lodging-houses and hostels;

(b) any yard, garden, outhouses and appurtenances belonging to the accommodation or usually enjoyed with it;

(c) any common areas used in connection with the accommodation;

"housing provider" means—

(a) a housing trust, within the meaning given by section 2 of the Housing Associations Act 1985, that is a charity;

(b) a housing action trust established under section 62 of the Housing Act 1988;

(c) in relation to England, a non-profit private registered provider of social housing;

(d) in relation to Wales, a Welsh body registered as a social landlord under section 3 of the Housing Act 1996;

(e) any body (other than a local authority or a body within paragraphs (a) to (d)) that is a landlord under a secure tenancy within the meaning given by section 79 of the Housing Act 1985;

"local authority" means—

(a) in relation to England, a district council, a county council, a London borough council, the Common Council of the City of London or the Council of the Isles of Scilly;

(b) in relation to Wales, a county council or a county borough council;

"respondent" has the meaning given by section 1(1).

(2) A person's age is treated for the purposes of this Part as being that which it appears to the court to be after considering any available evidence.

III ANSB [73]

21. Saving and transitional provision

(1) In this section "existing order" means any of the following injunctions and orders—

(a) an anti-social behaviour injunction under section 153A of the Housing Act 1996;

(b) an injunction under section 153B of that Act (injunction against unlawful use of premises);

(c) an injunction in which anything is included by virtue of section 153D(3) or (4) of that Act (power to include provision banning person from premises or area, or to include power of arrest, in injunction against breach of tenancy agreement);

(d) an order under section 1 or 1B of the Crime and Disorder Act 1998 (anti-social behaviour orders etc);

(e) an individual support order under section 1AA of that Act made in connection with an order under section 1 or 1B of that Act;

(f) an intervention order under section 1G of that Act;

(g) a drinking banning order under section 3 or 4 of the Violent Crime Reduction Act 2006.

(2) The repeal or amendment by this Act of provisions about any of the existing orders specified in subsection (1)(a) to (d), (f) and (g) does not apply in relation to—

(a) an application made before the commencement day for an existing order;

(b) an existing order (whether made before or after that day) applied for before that day;

(c) anything done in connection with such an application or order.

(3) The repeal or amendment by this Act of provisions about an order specified in subsection (1)(e) does not apply in relation to—

(a) an individual support order made before the commencement day;

(b) anything done in connection with such an order.

(4) As from the commencement day there may be no variation of an existing order that extends the period of the order or of any of its provisions.

(5) At the end of the period of 5 years beginning with the commencement day—

(a) in relation to any of the existing orders specified in subsection (1)(a), (b) and (d) to (g) that is still in force, this Part has effect, with any necessary modifications (and with any modifications specified in an order under section 185(7)), as if the provisions of the order were provisions of an injunction under section 1;

(b) the provisions of this Part set out in subsection (6) apply to any injunction specified in subsection (1)(c) that is still in force as they apply to an injunction under section 1;

(c) subsections (2) to (4) cease to have effect.

(6) The provisions referred to in subsection (5)(b) are—

(a) section 1(7);

(b) sections 4(2) and 9 (if a power of arrest is attached);

(c) sections 6 to 8;

(d) section 10;

(e) section 11 and Schedule 1;

(f) section 12 and Schedule 2;

(g) section 18(1).

(7) In deciding whether to grant an injunction under section 1 a court may take account of conduct occurring up to 6 months before the commencement day.

(8) In this section "commencement day" means the day on which this Part comes into force.

III ANSB [73.1

Conduct before 23 September 2014 The purpose of sub-s (7) is to enable the court to grant an injunction on the basis of pre-commencement conduct, but not to prevent the court from considering conduct prior to 23 September 2014 when deciding whether the grant of an injunction is, in all the circumstances, an appropriate remedy: *Birmingham City Council v Pardoe* [2016] EWHC 3119 (QB), 5 December 2016. However, the court cannot grant an injunction unless at least one incident of anti-social behaviour is proved to have occurred after 23 September 2014.

SCHEDULE 1 REMANDS UNDER SECTIONS 9 AND 10

INTRODUCTORY

III ANSB [74]

1

(1) This Schedule applies where—

(a) a judge has power to remand a person under section 9(5),

(b) a justice of the peace is required to remand a person under section 9(6), or

(c) a court has power to remand a person under section 10(8).

(2) A reference in the following paragraphs of this Schedule to a judge is to be read as including a justice of the peace.

REMAND IN CUSTODY OR ON BAIL

2

(1) The judge or the court may remand the person—

(a) in custody, or

(b) on bail.

But a person aged under 18 may not be remanded in custody unless paragraph 6 applies.

(2) A reference in this Schedule to remanding a person in custody is a reference to committing the person to custody to be brought before the court at the end of the period of remand or at whatever earlier time the court may require.

(3) The judge or the court may remand the person on bail—

(a) by taking from the person a recognizance, with or without sureties, conditioned as provided in paragraph 3, or

(b) by fixing the amount of the recognizances with a view to their being taken subsequently and, in the meantime, committing the person to custody as mentioned in sub-paragraph (2).

(4) Where a person is brought before the court after remand, the court may further remand the person.

3

(1) Where a person is remanded on bail, the judge or the court may direct that the person's recognizance be conditioned for his or her appearance—

(a) before that court at the end of the period of remand, or

(b) at every time and place to which during the course of the proceedings the hearing may from time to time be adjourned.

(2) Where a recognizance is conditioned for a person's appearance as mentioned in sub-paragraph (1)(b), the fixing of a time for the person next to appear is to be treated as a remand.

(3) Nothing in this paragraph affects the power of the court at any subsequent hearing to remand the person afresh.

4

(1) The judge or the court may not remand a person for a period exceeding 8 clear days unless—

(a) paragraph 5 or 6 applies, or

(b) the person is remanded on bail and both that person and the person who applied for the injunction consent to a longer period.

(2) Where the judge or the court has power to remand a person in custody, the person may be committed to the custody of a constable if the remand is for a period not exceeding 3 clear days.

Remand for medical examination and report

5

(1) This paragraph applies where—

(a) the judge or the court has reason to think that a medical report will be needed, and

(b) the judge or the court remands the person in order to enable a medical examination to take place and a report to be made.

(2) If (in the case of a person aged 18 or over) the person is remanded in custody, the adjournment may not be for more than 3 weeks at a time.

(3) If the person is remanded on bail, the adjournment may not be for more than 4 weeks at a time.

6

(1) If the judge or the court—

(a) is satisfied, on the written or oral evidence of a registered medical practitioner, that there is reason to suspect that the person is suffering from mental disorder, and

(b) is of the opinion that it would be impracticable for a report on the person's mental condition to be made if he or she were remanded on bail,

the judge or the court may remand the person to a hospital or registered establishment specified by the judge or the court for such a report to be made.

(2) In sub-paragraph (1)—

"hospital" has the meaning given by section 145(1) of the Mental Health Act 1983;

"mental disorder" has the meaning given by section 1 of that Act (reading subsection (2B) of that section as if it included a reference to sub-paragraph (1) above);

"registered establishment" has the meaning given by 34(1) of that Act.

(3) Subsections (4) to (10) of section 35 of the Mental Health Act 1983 apply for the purposes of sub-paragraph (1) with any necessary modifications (in particular, with references to the accused person being read as references to the person mentioned in that sub-paragraph, and references to the court being read as references to the judge or the court).

Further remand

7

(1) If the court is satisfied that a person who has been remanded is unable by reason of illness or accident to appear or be brought before the court at the end of the period of remand, the court may further remand the person in his or her absence.

(2) The power in sub-paragraph (1) may, in the case of a person who was remanded on bail, be exercised by enlarging the person's recognizance and those of any sureties for the person to a later time.

(3) Where a person remanded on bail is bound to appear before the court at any time and the court has no power to remand the person under sub-paragraph (1), the court may (in the person's absence) enlarge the person's recognizance and those of any sureties for the person to a later time.

(4) The enlargement of the person's recognizance is to be treated as a further remand.

(5) Paragraph 4(1) (limit of remand) does not apply to the exercise of the powers conferred by this paragraph.

Postponement of taking recognizance

8

Where under paragraph 2(3)(b) the court fixes the amount in which the principal and the sureties, if any, are to be bound, the recognizance may afterwards be taken by a person prescribed by rules of court, with the same consequences as if it had been entered into before the court.

Requirements imposed on remand on bail

9

The court may when remanding a person on bail under this Schedule require the person to comply, before release on bail or later, with any requirements that appear to the court to be necessary to secure that the person does not interfere with witnesses or otherwise obstruct the course of justice.

Co-option arrangements

10

(1) The responsible authorities in a local government area must make arrangements ("co-option arrangements") for the inclusion of local providers of social housing among the relevant bodies in that area.

(2) In this paragraph "responsible authorities" means—

- (a) in relation to a local government area in England—
  - (i) the relevant district council or the unitary authority,
  - (ii) the chief officer of police for the police area which that local government area is within, and
  - (iii) each clinical commissioning group established under section 14V of the National Health Service Act 2006 whose area is wholly or partly within that local government area;

(b) in relation to a local government area in Wales—
   (i) the council for the area,
   (ii) the chief officer of police for the police area which that local government area is within, and
   (iii) each Local Health Board whose area is wholly or partly within that local government area.

ARBITRATION

TABLE OF CONTENTS

GENERAL NOTES ON ARBITRATION

III ARB [1]

The provisions of the Arbitration Act 1996 replace the Arbitration Act (Northern Ireland) 1937, Arbitration Act 1950, Part I, Arbitration Act 1975, Arbitration Act 1979 and the Consumer Arbitration Agreements Act 1988.

Proceedings under the Arbitration Act 1996 may be heard in the High Court or the County Court at Central London but not other county courts, except as regards s 9 (stay) and ss 66 and 101(2) (enforcement): High Court and County Courts (Allocation of Arbitration Proceedings) Order 1996, SI 1996/3215, as amended by SI 1999/1010.

Except as regards an application for a stay, every proceeding under the Arbitration Act 1996 must be by arbitration claim form which may be issued in one of the courts identified below which are within the group known collectively as The Business and Property Courts of England and Wales:

- either the Admiralty Court or the Commercial Court in the Rolls Building, Fetter Lane, London EC4 1NL;
- the Technology and Construction Court in the Rolls Building;
- the Circuit Commercial Court in the District Registry in Manchester, Birmingham, Leeds, Bristol and Cardiff.

Specialist County Court cases that fall within the Business and Property Courts ambit will be heard in a re-designated 'Business and Property Courts List', in the Central London County Court or a County Court hearing centre in Manchester, Birmingham, Leeds, Bristol or Cardiff.

III ARB [2]

Form and content of arbitration claim form The claimant should use the arbitration claim form (Form N8) (except when applying for a stay under s 9) and must complete the claim form in accordance with the requirements of **CPR 62.4**.

III ARB [3]

Procedure for applications under the Arbitration Act 1996 The procedure for arbitration applications, covering service and all subsequent steps, is set out in **CPR 62** and the accompanying Practice Direction.

The court's power to extend time under **CPR 3.1** may be exercised in relation to the statutory time limits, in accordance with s 80(5) of the Act. But the exercise of discretion should have regard to the principles underlying arbitration, including party autonomy, finality of awards, comparative freedom from intervention by the courts and avoiding unnecessary delay and expense: *Kalmneft JSC v Glencore International AG* [2002] 1 All ER 76.

Service abroad is dealt with in **CPR 62.5** and the general rule is that permission for service abroad will be allowed if, and only if, the seat of the arbitration is in England and Wales: see s 53 of the Arbitration Act 1996 and *Vale Do Rio Navegaçao SA v Shanghai Bao Steel Ocean Shipping Co Ltd* [2000] 2 All ER (Comm) 70. The location of the seat is to be determined at the start of the arbitration and cannot be changed afterwards except by common agreement of the parties: *Dubai Islamic Bank PJSC v Paymentech Merchant Services Inc* [2001] 1 Lloyd's Rep 65.

III ARB [4]

Proceedings under other Acts or for enforcement The procedure for arbitration claims under other Acts is set out at **CPR 62.11** onwards and the procedure for enforcement and registration of awards is at **CPR 62.17** onwards.

For the substantive law see 2 *Halsbury's Laws* (4th edn reissue) title ARBITRATION, para 601.

III ARB [5]

Precedents For precedents, see **BCCP K[321]–BCCP K[325]**.

ARBITRATION ACT 1996

(c 23)

III ARB [5]

1. General principles

The provisions of this Part are founded on the following principles, and shall be construed accordingly—

(a) the object of arbitration is to obtain the fair resolution of disputes by an impartial tribunal without unnecessary delay or expense;

(b) the parties should be free to agree how their disputes are resolved, subject only to such safeguards as are necessary in the public interest.

III ARB [5.1]

Confidentiality A term of confidentiality is implicit in an arbitration agreement, covering pleadings, submissions and proofs of evidence as well as awards: *Ali Shipping Corpn v Shipyard Trogir* [1998] 2 All ER 136, [1999] 1 WLR 136, CA.

However, the courts when called upon to exercise the supervisory role assigned by statute are acting as a branch of the state, not as a mere extension of the consensual arbitration process. Nevertheless they are acting in the public interest to facilitate the fairness and well-being of a consensual method of dispute resolution, and both the rule committee and the courts can still take into account the parties' expectations regarding privacy and confidentiality when agreeing to arbitrate: *Department of Economic Policy and Development of the City of Moscow v Bankers Trust* [2004] EWCA Civ 314, [2004] 4 All ER 746 per

Mance LJ who suggested that the starting point where permission to appeal was required should be to treat the public interest in a public hearing as having the greater weight: otherwise the presumption should be the other way round.

III ARB [5.2]

Parties free to agree on powers It was held in *Kastner v Jason* [2004] EWHC 592 (Ch), (2004) Times, 21 December that the parties to an arbitration agreement had empowered the Beth Din to make freezing directions pending satisfaction of a final award as this fell within the scope of s 48(1) and that similar powers in relation to a provisional award fell within s 39. However, the court held that the directions and award given by the Beth Din did not in the particular circumstances confer a proprietary interest in the nature of a charge.

III ARB [5.3]

Subject-matter of arbitration There is nothing in the Act or in the Companies Act 2006 to exclude arbitration as a possible means of determining disputes between the company and its members regarding, for example, allegations of unfair prejudice: *Fulham Football Club Ltd v Richards* [2011] EWCA Civ 855, [2011] All ER (D) 197 (Jul).

III ARB [5.4]

Expert determination A clause that provides for the expert determination of some but not all issues in dispute, is different from an arbitration clause that provides for disputes to be decided by a single forum. In a case where an expert determination clause provided for the expert to determine the extent of his jurisdiction it was held that the issue should be determined by the court without first having it determined by the expert: *Barclay's Bank plc v Nylon Capital LLP* [2011] EWCA Civ 826, [2011] 2 Lloyd's Rep 347, [2011] BLR 61.

A dispute resolution clause that provides for expert determination will not be construed as an arbitration agreement unless the provisions of the agreement support such an interpretation: *Wilky Property Holdings plc v London and Surrey Investments Ltd* [2011] EWHC 2226 (Ch), [2011] All ER (D) 86 (Aug).

III ARB [5.5]

Resolution by friendly discussion In a case where the arbitration agreement provided for the deferment of arbitration, to allow four weeks in which to seek a resolution by friendly discussion, the court held the provision for four weeks' deferment to be valid and enforceable: *Emirates Trading Agency LLC v Prime Mineral Exports Private Ltd* [2014] EWHC 2104 (Comm), [2014] 2 Lloyd's Rep 457, 164 NLJ 7615.

III ARB [6]

9. Stay of legal proceedings

(1) A party to an arbitration agreement against whom legal proceedings are brought (whether by way of claim or counterclaim) in respect of a matter which under the agreement is to be referred to arbitration may (upon notice to the other parties to the proceedings) apply to the court in which the proceedings have been brought to stay the proceedings so far as they concern that matter.

(2) An application may be made notwithstanding that the matter is to be referred to arbitration only after the exhaustion of other dispute resolution procedures.

(3) An application may not be made by a person before taking the appropriate procedural step (if any) to acknowledge the legal proceedings against him or after he has taken any step in those proceedings to answer the substantive claim.

(4) On an application under this section the court shall grant a stay unless satisfied that the arbitration agreement is null and void, inoperative, or incapable of being performed.

(5) If the court refuses to stay the legal proceedings, any provision that an award is a condition precedent to the bringing of legal proceedings in respect of any matter is of no effect in relation to those proceedings.

III ARB [6.1]

A party to an arbitration agreement An "arbitration agreement" means an agreement in writing to submit to arbitration any present or future disputes (whether they are contractual or not): ss 5 and 6. Most of the provisions in Part I of the Arbitration Act 1996 apply only where the seat of the arbitration (at the start of the arbitration: see s 3 and *Dubai Islamic Bank IJSC v Paymentech Merchant Services* [2001] 1 Lloyd's Rep 65, is in England and Wales or

ARBITRATION

Northern Ireland); but ss 9 to 11 are not limited in this way: s 2. Also the right to apply to the court under ss 9 to 11 is made mandatory by s 4 and Sch 1; and unless otherwise agreed an arbitration agreement remains valid and enforceable despite the death of a party: s 8. The provisions of Part I bind the Crown where the Crown is a party: s 106. A "dispute resolution" clause has been held to be different from an arbitration agreement and to provide no basis for the grant of a stay: *Halifax Financial Services Ltd v Intuitive Systems Ltd* [1999] 1 All ER (Comm) 303. However, it was held in *Cable & Wireless plc v IBM (United Kingdom) Ltd* [2003] EWHC 2059 (Comm), [2002] 2 All ER (Comm) 1041 that a dispute resolution clause which included a sufficiently defined mutual obligation upon the parties could, and should, be enforced. But a stay should be refused where the provision for dispute resolution is in terms of mediation rather than arbitration: *Flight Training International Inc v International Fire Training Equipment Ltd* [2004] EWHC 721, [2004] 2 All ER (Comm) 568, Cresswell, J, QBD.

Where the arbitration agreement provides for disputes or differences to be referred, the "difference" should be construed as including a failure to agree, falling short of a dispute: *Amec Civil Engineering Ltd v Secretary of State for Transport* (2005) Times, 22 March, CA.

Where a third party is treated as a party to the arbitration agreement, by virtue of s 8(1) of the Contracts (Rights of Third Parties) Act 1999, but only as regards issues between the third party and the promisor, the stay may not be granted on the third party's application in respect of other issues: *Fortress Value Recovery Fund I LLC v Blue Skye Special Opportunities Fund LP* [2013] EWCA Civ 367, [2013] 1 WLR 3466, [2013] 2 All ER (Comm) 315.

III ARB [6.2]

The court shall grant a stay unless The discretion which the court had under the Arbitration Act 1950 s 4, as regards domestic arbitrations, has gone. Instead the court has a general duty, formerly confined by the Arbitration Act 1975 s 1 to non-domestic arbitrations, to grant the stay unless satisfied that the agreement is null and void etc. The fact that the claimant would be entitled to summary judgment if the case proceeded is not a ground for refusing a stay: *Halki Shipping Corpn v Sopex Oils Ltd* [1998] 2 All ER 23, [1998] 1 WLR 726, CA. The fact that the defendant's withholding of payment contravenes s 111(1) of the Housing Grants, Construction and Regeneration Act 1996 is not a sufficient reason for refusing a stay provided that there is a dispute: *Collins (Contractors) Ltd v Baltic Quay Management (1994) Ltd* (2005) Times, 3 January, CA. Where there is an issue as to whether there is an arbitration agreement the court may decide it even where the arbitrator would be competent to do so: *Birse Construction Ltd v St David Ltd* [1999] BLR 194.

Similarly where there is an issue as to whether the matters in dispute fall within the arbitration agreement: *Al-Naimi (t/a Buildmaster Construction Services) v Islamic Press Agency Inc* [2000] 1 Lloyd's Rep 522, CA.

Similarly, the fact that the defendant's withholding of payment contravenes section III(1) of the Housing Grants, Construction and Regeneration Act 1996 is not a sufficient reason for refusing a stay provided that there is a dispute: *Collins (Contractors) Ltd v Baltic Quay Management (1994) Ltd* [2004] EWCA Civ 1757, (2005) Times, 3 January.

Where parties have voluntarily entered into an arbitration agreement they are to be treated as waiving their rights under Article 6, but the agreement must be made without constraint and must not run counter to any important public interest: *Stretford v Football Association* [2007] EWCA Civ 238, [2007] All ER (D) 346 (Mar), (2007) Times, 13 April.

III ARB [6.2A]

Arbitration agreement inoperative A stay may be refused under sub-s(4) where the arbitration agreement has been repudiated and has become inoperative at the date when proceedings were issued: *Traube v Perelman* [2001] All ER (D) 346, Jacob J. It was held in *Downing v Al Tameer Establishment* [2002] EWCA Civ 721, [2002] 2 All ER (Comm) 545 that where the claimant accepted the defendant's repudiation by issuing and serving a claim, the arbitration agreement became inoperative. On the other hand the referral of a dispute to adjudication under the Housing Grants, Construction and Regeneration Act 1996 does not necessarily preclude a subsequent reference to arbitration under a clause in the contract: *Peterhead Harbour Trustees v Lilley Construction Ltd* 2003 SLT 731, Ct of Sess, OH.

The right to apply to the Companies Court for relief under s 459 of the Companies Act 1985 (s 994 of the Companies Act 2006) has been held to be inalienable. Accordingly, such proceedings may not be stayed under s 9 of the Arbitration Act 1996, or under the inherent jurisdiction of the court, even where the petition is in respect of a matter which, under agreement between the parties, should be referred to arbitration: *Exeter City AFC Ltd v Football Conference Ltd* [2004] EWHC 2304 (Ch), [2004] 4 All ER 1179, (2004) Times, 12 February.

The person whose claim is sought to be stayed must be a party to the arbitration agreement or to be claiming through such a party; a legal or commercial connection with the party is not enough: *Sancheti v City of London* (2008) Times, 1 December, CA.

Where a person who is alleged to be a party to the arbitration contends that the agreement was obtained by bribery and subsequently rescinded on this ground, the arbitrator has jurisdiction to determine whether the agreement is valid as one of the issues arising out of an application for a stay and this is a more appropriate course than challenging the validity by court proceedings under s 72(1): *Fiona Trust and Holding Corporation v Privalov* [2007] EWCA Civ 20, [2007] All ER (D) 169 (Jan) (2007) Times, 29 January, upheld on further appeal to the House of Lords (2007) Times, 25 October, HL.

Where an arbitration agreement is alleged to be a forgery this issue should be decided before the statutory power to grant a stay may be exercised. Normally it is appropriate for the court to make the decision but exceptionally the court may exercise its inherent power to grant a stay pending a decision by the arbitrator: *Albon (trading as N A Carriage Company) v Naza Motor Trading Sdn Bhd (No 3)* [2007] EWHC 665 (Ch), [2007] 2 All ER 1075.

III ARB [6.3]

Any step in those proceedings It has been held that the phrase "any step in those proceedings" does not include applying to set aside a default judgment and applying for leave to defend and counterclaim: *Patel v Patel* [2000] QB 551, [1999] 3 WLR 322, CA. A defendant who is appealing against a decision that the court has jurisdiction may protect himself against the claimant's applying for judgment by applying for (a) an extension of time to acknowledge service or (b) a stay pending appeal. Neither step amounts to a submission to the jurisdiction: *Sithole v Thor Chemical Holdings Ltd* [1999] 09 LS Gaz R 32.

A defendant's application for summary judgment, if made conditionally on the court's refusing to grant a stay, is not a step in the proceedings, within para (3), and the court is not barred from granting the stay: *Capital Trusts Investments Ltd v Radio Design TJ AB* [2001] 3 All ER 756.

III ARB [6.4]

Application to statutory arbitrations For the purposes of s 9 and all the other provisions set out below except ss 12 and 71(4), a statutory arbitration is to be treated as if the arbitration were pursuant to an agreement on the terms contained in the enactment but with the provisions of the enactment, and rules made under it, prevailing over inconsistent provisions in the Arbitration Act 1996: ss 94 and 95. The seat of a statutory arbitration is required, by s 95(2), to be treated as being in England and Wales or, as the case may be, Northern Ireland.

III ARB [6.5]

Legal proceedings by way of interpleader The court's duty to stay proceedings under s 9 is extended by s 10 to legal proceedings in which relief by way of interpleader is granted. Third party proceedings were ordered to be stayed in *Wealand v CLC Contractors Ltd* [1998] CLC 808; *Wealands v CLC Contractors Ltd and Key Scaffolding Ltd* [2000] 1 All ER (Comm) 30, CA.

III ARB [6.6]

Admiralty proceedings where security has been given Where a stay is granted, in Admiralty proceedings in which property has been arrested or bail or other security has been given to obtain release from arrest, the court granting the stay may make orders under s 11 to preserve the property or the security.

III ARB [6.7]

Application under this section The application for a stay must be made by an application notice in accordance with CPR Pt 23, using **FORM N244**. It must also comply with **CPR 62.8**. For a precedent see **BCCP C[21]**. For a form of order staying proceedings see **FORM PF 167**.

III ARB [6.7A]

Inherent jurisdiction to stay proceedings Even where the statutory requirements for a stay under s 9 are not satisfied the court may exercise its inherent jurisdiction to grant a stay if the sensible course is for an arbitrator to consider the issues first: *Al-Naimi (t/a Buildmaster Construction Services) v Islamic Press Agency Inc* [2000] 1 Lloyd's Rep 522, CA.

III ARB [6.8]

Injunction to restrain foreign court proceedings Where a party to an agreement with an arbitration clause starts foreign court proceedings in breach of the clause, the English court may, in appropriate circumstances, grant an injunction to restrain that party from proceeding further with the action: *Bankers Trust Co v P T Jakarta International Hotels and Development* [1999] 1 All ER (Comm) 785, Cresswell J. See **II SCA [48.2]** for the court's inherent power to grant a stay.

Note, however, that it has been doubted whether an anti-suit injunction may be granted to stay proceedings in a member State in such circumstances; see the opinion of the Advocate General in *Allianz SpA v West Tankers Case C-185/07*. The European Court of Justice went on to hold that the jurisdiction point, that the effect of the arbitration was to exclude jurisdiction, was one which the court in which the case was proceeding had jurisdiction under the Regulation to decide and that the anti-suit injunction was contrary to the Regulation: *Allianz SpA v West Tankers Inc Case C-185/07* (2009) Times, 13 February, ECJ.

See para **II SCA [38.1A]** for further case law and comment on anti-suit injunctions.

III ARB [6.9]

Appeal A refusal of a stay may be appealed, with leave: *Inco Europe Ltd v First Choice Distribution (a firm)* [1999] 1 All ER 820, [1999] 1 WLR 270, CA. The exclusion, by Supreme Court Act 1981 s 18(1)(g), of rights of appeal against decisions under Part 1 of the Arbitration Act 1996 is confined to appeals under those sections which confer rights of appeal. The possibility of appealing against decisions under other sections, such as s 9, is not affected: *Inco Europe Ltd v First Choice Distribution (a firm)* [2000] 2 All ER 109[2000] 1 WLR 586, HL.

On the other hand, the Court of Appeal has no power to grant permission which has been refused below, nor to review the correctness of that refusal: *Henry Boot Construction (UK) Ltd v Malmaison Hotel (Manchester) Ltd* [2000] 1 All ER 257, [2000] 3 WLR 1824, CA.

III ARB [6.10]

Indemnity costs Where an applicant for a stay is successful an award of costs should normally be on an indemnity basis: *Re Boodhoo* [2007] EWCA Crim 14, (2007) Times, 5 February.

III ARB [7]

12. Power of court to extend time for beginning arbitral proceedings etc

(1) Where an arbitration agreement to refer future disputes to arbitration provides that a claim shall be barred, or the claimant's right extinguished, unless the claimant takes within a time fixed by the agreement some step—

(a) to begin arbitral proceedings, or

(b) to begin other dispute resolution procedures which must be exhausted before arbitral proceedings can be begun,

the court may by order extend the time for taking that step.

(2) Any party to the arbitration agreement may apply for such an order (upon notice to the other parties), but only after a claim has arisen and after exhausting any available arbitral process for obtaining an extension of time.

(3) The court shall make an order only if satisfied—

(a) that the circumstances are such as were outside the reasonable contemplation of the parties when they agreed the provision in question, and that it would be just to extend the time, or

(b) that the conduct of one party makes it unjust to hold the other party to the strict terms of the provision in question.

(4) The court may extend the time for such period and on such terms as it thinks fit, and may do so whether or not the time previously fixed (by agreement or by a previous order) has expired.

(5) An order under this section does not affect the operation of the Limitation Acts (see section 13).

(6) The leave of the court is required for any appeal from a decision of the court under this section.

III ARB [7.1]

Where an arbitration agreement provides Sections 12 and 13 apply only where the seat of the arbitration is in England and Wales or Northern Ireland (ss 2 and 3). Section 12 does not apply to statutory arbitrations but s 13 does: s 97.

III ARB [7.2]

The court may by order extend The parties may not, by agreement, exclude the right to apply to the court for an extension of time or for a period of limitation to be excluded (s 4 and

Sch 1), but the parties are free to agree when arbitral proceedings are to be regarded as commencing. In the absence of agreement, commencement takes place in accordance with the provisions of s 14. The purpose of s 12(3) is to allow an extension only where, if the circumstances had been drawn to the parties' attention at the time of making the agreement, they would have contemplated that the time bar might not apply: *Harbour and General Works Ltd v Environmental Agency* [2000] 1 All ER 50, [2000] 1 WLR 950, CA. Note that the requirements of sub-s (2) that application may not be made to the court until a claim has arisen and any available arbitral process for extending time has been exhausted.

III ARB [7.3]

Procedure for applying to the court See the notes at **III ARB [1]** for details of the courts with power to entertain applications under the Arbitration Act 1996 and the notes at **III ARB [2], [3]** for a summary of the procedure for applying.

III ARB [7.4]

Restrictive conditions An extension of time was reversed in *Cathiship SA v Allonasons Ltd, The Catherine Helen* [1998] 3 All ER 714 because of a failure to satisfy the requirement in s 12(3)(a) that the circumstances were outside the reasonable contemplation of the parties.

III ARB [8]

13. Application of Limitation Acts

(1) The Limitation Acts apply to arbitral proceedings as they apply to legal proceedings.

(2) The court may order that in computing the time prescribed by the Limitation Acts for the commencement of proceedings (including arbitral proceedings) in respect of a dispute which was the subject matter—

- (a) of an award which the court orders to be set aside or declares to be of no effect, or
- (b) of the affected part of an award which the court orders to be set aside in part, or declares to be in part of no effect,

the period between the commencement of the arbitration and the date of the order referred to in paragraph (a) or (b) shall be excluded.

(3) In determining for the purposes of the Limitation Acts when a cause of action accrued, any provision that an award is a condition precedent to the bringing of legal proceedings in respect of a matter to which an arbitration agreement applies shall be disregarded.

(4) In this Part "the Limitation Acts" means—

- (a) in England and Wales, the Limitation Act 1980, the Foreign Limitation Periods Act 1984 and any other enactment (whenever passed) relating to the limitation of actions;
- (b) in Northern Ireland, the Limitation (Northern Ireland) Order 1989, the Foreign Limitation Periods (Northern Ireland) Order 1985 and any other enactment (whenever passed) relating to the limitation of actions.

III ARB [9]

18. Failure of appointment procedure

(1) The parties are free to agree what is to happen in the event of a failure of the procedure for the appointment of the arbitral tribunal.

There is no failure if an appointment is duly made under section 17 (power in case of default to appoint sole arbitrator), unless that appointment is set aside.

(2) If or to the extent that there is no such agreement any party to the arbitration agreement may (upon notice to the other parties) apply to the court to exercise its powers under this section.

(3) Those powers are—

- (a) to give directions as to the making of any necessary appointments;
- (b) to direct that the tribunal shall be constituted by such appointments (or any one or more of them) as have been made;

> (c) to revoke any appointments already made;
> (d) to make any necessary appointments itself.
>
> (4) An appointment made by the court under this section has effect as if made with the agreement of the parties.
>
> (5) The leave of the court is required for any appeal from a decision of the court under this section.

III ARB [9.1]

The parties are free to agree The parties are free to agree on the constitution of the arbitral tribunal and on the procedure for making appointment (ss 15 and 16) and on a procedure in case of default to appoint (s 17) and on a failure of the procedure for the appointment of the tribunal (s 18). They are also free to agree on the functions of any chairman or umpire (ss 20 and 21) and when the umpire is to replace the other arbitrators (s 20). In cases where the parties had agreed 30 days for the appointment of an arbitrator but had not specified a time for appointment of a substitute arbitrator, the court held that 30 days should be allowed rather than 14 as provided by ss 16(5)(a) and 27: *Federal Insurance Co v Transamerica Occidental Life Insurance Co* [1999] 2 All ER (Comm) 138.

An arbitration clause which provides for the appointment of an arbitrator in accordance with discriminatory provisions is not invalidated by Part V of the Equality Act 2010. This is because an arbitrator has a judicial role and the contract that underpins the appointment is not one of employment: *Jivraj v Haswani* [2011] UKSC 40, [2011] 1 WLR 1872, [2011] Bus LR 1182, in which it was held that the Employment Equality (Religion or Belief) Regulations 2003, SI 2003/1660, which have since been revoked, did not apply to the selection or appointment of arbitrators.

III ARB [9.2]

Appointment of the arbitral tribunal: appointment of judges Subject to the conditions laid down in s 93, a judge of the Commercial Court or a judge of the Technology and Construction Court may accept appointment as a sole arbitrator or as umpire by or by virtue of an arbitration agreement.

III ARB [9.3]

Appointment under section 17 is set aside Where a sole arbitrator is appointed under s 17(2), the party in default may (upon notice to the appointing party) apply to the court which may set aside the appointment: s 17(3).

III ARB [9.4]

A party to an arbitration agreement See para **III ARB [6.1]**.

III ARB [9.4A]

Exercise, by court, of discretion to appoint or direct In *Durtnell (R) & Sons Ltd v Secretary of State for Trade and Industry* [2001] 1 All ER (Comm) 41, the court held that, where the application was made after a long period of delay the court should exercise its discretion according to whether, in the circumstances, there could be a fair resolution of the dispute, not whether there had been undue delay.

III ARB [9.5]

Agreement of the parties as to qualifications required of the arbitrators In the exercise of its powers under s 18, which are also exercisable where there is no agreed or other procedure under s 16 for the appointment of arbitrators, the court is required by s 19 to have due regard to any agreement of the parties as to the qualifications required of the arbitrators.

III ARB [9.6]

Additional powers regarding umpires In addition to the powers under s 18 the court has the power, in circumstances set out in s 21(5), to order that the umpire should replace the other arbitrators and make decisions, orders and awards as if he were sole arbitrator.

III ARB [9.7]

Procedure for applying to the court See the notes at **III ARB [1]** for details of the courts with power to entertain applications under Arbitration Act 1996 and the notes at **III ARB [2]–[3]** for a for a summary of the procedure for applying.

III ARB [9.8]

Leave to appeal Only the court of first instance may grant leave to appeal and there is no right of appeal against a refusal: *Johann MK Blumenthal GMBH & Co KG v Itochu Corpn* [2012] EWCA Civ 996, [2012] 2 Lloyd's Rep 437, [2012] NLJR 1028.

III ARB [9.9]

Dissolution of a party An arbitrator may not give orders or directions once one of the parties has been dissolved, since the consequence of the dissolution is the failure of the arbitrator's appointment: *Silver Dry Bulk Co Ltd v Homer Hulbert Maritime Company Ltd* [2017] EWHC 44 (Comm).

III ARB [10]

24. Power of court to remove arbitrator

(1) A party to arbitral proceedings may (upon notice to the other parties, to the arbitrator concerned and to any other arbitrator) apply to the court to remove an arbitrator on any of the following grounds—

(a) that circumstances exist that give rise to justifiable doubts as to his impartiality;

(b) that he does not possess the qualifications required by the arbitration agreement;

(c) that he is physically or mentally incapable of conducting the proceedings or there are justifiable doubts as to his capacity to do so;

(d) that he has refused or failed—

(i) properly to conduct the proceedings, or

(ii) to use all reasonable despatch in conducting the proceedings or making an award,

and that substantial injustice has been or will be caused to the applicant.

(2) If there is an arbitral or other institution or person vested by the parties with power to remove an arbitrator, the court shall not exercise its power of removal unless satisfied that the applicant has first exhausted any available recourse to that institution or person.

(3) The arbitral tribunal may continue the arbitral proceedings and make an award while an application to the court under this section is pending.

(4) Where the court removes an arbitrator, it may make such order as it thinks fit with respect to his entitlement (if any) to fees or expenses, or the repayment of any fees or expenses already paid.

(5) The arbitrator concerned is entitled to appear and be heard by the court before it makes any order under this section.

(6) The leave of the court is required for any appeal from a decision of the court under this section.

III ARB [10.1]

Procedure for applying to the court See the notes at **III ARB [1]** for details of the courts with power to entertain applications under the Arbitration Act 1996 and the notes at **III ARB [2]** and **III ARB [3]** for a summary of the procedure for applying. Each arbitrator must be a defendant and must be given notice in accordance with **CPR 62.6**.

III ARB [10.2]

Inquiry into impartiality In *AT & T Corpn v Saudi Cable Co* [2000] 2 All ER (Comm) 625, CA the court decided that the English court had power under s 23 of the Arbitration Act 1950 to consider the question of impartiality even where a decision on the issue had been made in accordance with the International Chamber of Commerce Rules of Conciliation and Arbitration 1988. The court further held that the test was the same as in relation to any judicial authority, namely whether there was any real danger that he or she was biased.

In *A v B* [2011] EWHC 2345 (Comm), [2011] 2 Lloyd's Rep 591, [2011] NLJJR 1291 Flaux J took the test for s 24(1)(a) to be whether a fair minded and informed observer would conclude that there was a real possibility of apparent or unconscious bias. The arbitrator was

ARBITRATION

a senior barrister who had in the past been instructed by solicitors on both sides and it was held, on the particular facts, that this was not sufficient to raise a real possibility of apparent or unconscious bias.

The impartiality of an arbitrator was questioned when it emerged that he had acted as arbitrator in 137 disputes in 25 of which one of the parties was the same company and 25% of his income was derived from those arbitrations. Mr Justice Hamblen ordered his removal in *Cofely Ltd v Bingham* [2016] EWHC 240 (Comm), [2016] 2 All ER (Comm) 129, [2016] BLR 187.

Inside information and knowledge may be a legitimate concern for the parties in overlapping arbitrations involving a common arbitrator and only one common party. But that by itself would not justify an inference of apparent bias and the concerns would be adequately met by disclosure: *Halliburton Company v Chubb Bermuda Insurance Ltd* [2018] EWCA Civ 817.

III ARB [10.3]

Proper conduct of proceedings As for "justifiable doubts as to impartiality", it is not necessary to prove actual bias: *R v Gough* [1993] AC 646, [1993] 2 All ER 724, HL, as long as circumstances exist that give rise to justifiable doubts. The existence of such circumstances must be proved and it is not enough to show that the arbitrator is a barrister practising in the same chambers as the barrister for one of the parties: *Laker Airways Inc v FLS Aerospace Ltd* [2000] 1 WLR 113, R IX J. Also, an arbitrator is not removable on the grounds only of irritability and lack of patience: *Andrews (t/a BA Contractors) v Bradshaw* [2000] BLR 6, CA. The arbitrator must not break the rules of natural justice, eg by refusing to allow cross-examination: *Chilton v Saga Holidays plc* [1986] 1 All ER 841, CA. It is also a breach to receive evidence from outside without allowing the parties to comment: *McMichael v United Kingdom* (1995) 20 EHRR 205, ECtHR. For other examples of serious irregularities in an arbitration context see s 68 (challenging the award: serious irregularity). For a case where a sole arbitrator was removed for misconduct and apparent bias see *Sierra Fishing Co v Hasan Said Farran* [2015] EWHC 140 (Comm), [2015] 1 All ER (Comm) 560, 165 NLJ 7640. Note however, that s 73 provides that a party may lose the right to complain later of improper conduct if he, or she, does not object at the time.

III ARB [10.3A]

Qualifications Where the qualifications necessary for appointment as an arbitrator are set out in the arbitration agreement, an arbitrator who does not have them may be removed: *Tonicstar Ltd v Allianz Insurance* [2017] EWHC 2753 (Comm), [2017] All ER (D) 46 (Nov), a case where a Queen's Counsel with experience in insurance litigation was held not to be a 'person from the trade or business of insurance'.

The *Allianz* case was reversed on appeal, however, on the ground that the condition as to qualifications was satisfied: *Allianz Insurance plc v Tonicstar Ltd* [2018] EWCA Civ 434, [2018] All ER (D) 125 (Mar).

III ARB [10.4]

Arbitrator's entitlement to fees The court is given a wide discretion, under s 24(4) to order the payment or repayment of all or some of the arbitrator's fees, on removal, but must first give the arbitrator the opportunity to be heard, under s 24(5). Where the arbitrator has resigned and the position as to fees is unresolved s 25(3) provides for the arbitrator, upon notice to the parties, to apply to the court: (a) for relief from liability; and (b) for an order regarding the payment or repayment of fees. In addition, any party may apply to the court (upon notice to the other parties and to the arbitrators) for the amount of his, or her, liability for the arbitrator's fees and expenses to be considered and adjusted. This right is given by s 28(2); and ss 56, 63(4) and 64 provide further opportunities to seek a court ruling on the reasonableness of arbitrators' fees and expenses, where they cannot be agreed.

Systech International Ltd v PC Harrington Contractors Ltd [2011] EWHC 2722 (TCC), [2011] NLJR 1557, [2011] All ER (D) 240 (Oct) was a case where an arbitrator made an award which the court declared to be unenforceable because of the arbitrator's breaches of the rules of natural justice. But this did not excuse the party against whom the award had been made from having to pay the arbitrator's fees, as ordered. The Court of Appeal found that the consideration for the payment of the fees had not failed totally and that there was no implied term that the arbitrator would act in accordance with the rules of natural justice.

III ARB [11]

32. Determination of preliminary point of jurisdiction

(1) The court may, on the application of a party to arbitral proceedings (upon notice to the other parties), determine any question as to the substantive jurisdiction of the tribunal.

A party may lose the right to object (see section 73).

(2) An application under this section shall not be considered unless—

(a) it is made with the agreement in writing of all the other parties to the proceedings, or

(b) it is made with the permission of the tribunal and the court is satisfied—

(i) that the determination of the question is likely to produce substantial savings in costs,

(ii) that the application was made without delay, and

(iii) that there is good reason why the matter should be decided by the court.

(3) An application under this section, unless made with the agreement of all the other parties to the proceedings, shall state the grounds on which it is said that the matter should be decided by the court.

(4) Unless otherwise agreed by the parties, the arbitral tribunal may continue the arbitral proceedings and make an award while an application to the court under this section is pending.

(5) Unless the court gives leave, no appeal lies from a decision of the court whether the conditions specified in subsection (2) are met.

(6) The decision of the court on the question of jurisdiction shall be treated as a judgment of the court for the purposes of an appeal.

But no appeal lies without the leave of the court which shall not be given unless the court considers that the question involves a point of law which is one of general importance or is one which for some other special reason should be considered by the Court of Appeal.

III ARB [11.1]

Procedure for applying to the court See the notes at **III ARB [1]** for details of the courts with power to entertain applications under Arbitration Act 1996 and the notes at **III ARB [2]** and **III ARB [3]**.

III ARB [11.2]

Any question as to the substantive jurisdiction Note the provision in s 73 that an objection must be raised as soon as grounds for objection are known, or could be known with reasonable diligence; otherwise the right to object is lost. As to "substantive jurisdiction", this is confined by s 82(1), to the matters specified in s 30(1)(a)–(c):

(a) whether there is a valid arbitration agreement,
(b) whether the tribunal is properly constituted, and
(c) what matters have been submitted to arbitration in accordance with the arbitration agreement.

III ARB [11.3]

Agreement in writing of all the parties The High Court has no jurisdiction to decide a question as to the substantive jurisdiction without the written agreement of all the parties: *Vale Do Rio Navegaçao SA v Shanghai Bao Steel Ocean Shipping Co Ltd* [2000] 2 All ER (Comm) 70.

III ARB [11.4]

Construing a jurisdiction clause When looking at a complex series of agreements it is necessary to construe an arbitration agreement which is part of the series by taking into account the overall scheme: *Re Sigma Finance Corpn* [2009] UKSC 2, [2010] 1 All ER 571, [2009] NLJR 1550. The task of determining whether a dispute falls within the jurisdiction clauses of one or more related agreements depends on the intention of the parties, as revealed by the agreements: *Satyam Computer Services Ltd v Upaid Systems Ltd* [2008] EWCA Civ 487, 2 All ER (Comm) 465, [2008] Bus LR D131; *Deutsche Bank AG v Sebastian Holdings Inc* [2010] EWCA Civ 998, [2010] NLJR 1190, [2010] NLJR 1230.

An agreement about the seat of an arbitration is analogous to an exclusive jurisdiction clause. The seat is in most cases sufficiently indicated by the country chosen as the place of the arbitration. Any claim for a remedy going to the existence or scope of the arbitrator's jurisdiction or as to the validity of an existing interim or final award should be made only to the courts of the place designated as the seat of the arbitration: *U&M Mining Zambia Ltd v Konkola Copper Mines plc* [2013] EWHC 260 (Comm), [2013] Bus LR D54, [2013] 2 Lloyd's Rep 218.

III ARB [11.5]

Establishing the proper law of the arbitration agreement The arbitration clause may provide for a London arbitration in a contract which is agreed to be governed by the law of a country other than the United Kingdom. In such a situation is the proper law of the arbitration agreement the law governing the contract generally or the law of England? In favour of applying English law is the argument that it is the logical consequence of the parties choosing a London arbitration to which the Arbitration Act 1996 would apply: *Sulamerica Cia Nacional De Seguros SA v Enesa Engenharia SA* [2012] EWCA Civ 638, [2012] 2 All ER (Comm) 795, [2012] 1 Lloyd's Rep 671.

III ARB [12]

42. Enforcement of peremptory orders of tribunal

(1) Unless otherwise agreed by the parties, the court may make an order requiring a party to comply with a peremptory order made by the tribunal.

(2) An application for an order under this section may be made—

- (a) by the tribunal (upon notice to the parties),
- (b) by a party to the arbitral proceedings with the permission of the tribunal (and upon notice to the other parties), or
- (c) where the parties have agreed that the powers of the court under this section shall be available.

(3) The court shall not act unless it is satisfied that the applicant has exhausted any available arbitral process in respect of failure to comply with the tribunal's order.

(4) No order shall be made under this section unless the court is satisfied that the person to whom the tribunal's order was directed has failed to comply with it within the time prescribed in the order or, if no time was prescribed, within a reasonable time.

(5) The leave of the court is required for any appeal from a decision of the court under this section.

III ARB [12.1]

Scheme for construction contracts Section 108–114 of the Housing, Grants, Construction and Regeneration Act 1996 provide for disputes in certain construction contracts to be referred for adjudication in accordance with the Scheme for Construction Contracts (England and Wales) Regulations 1998, SI 1998/694. The recovery of money due under the decision is governed by s 42 of the Arbitration Act 1996 (**III ARB [12]**), and may be the subject of a court decision. In one such case the Court of Appeal held that the arbitrator was not entitled to fees for arriving at a decision in breach of the rules of natural justice: *Systech International Ltd v PC Harrington Contractors Ltd* (2013) Times, 1 January, CA.

III ARB [12.2]

Exercise of discretion The court has a discretion whether to enforce and is not merely to rubber-stamp the order. On the other hand the court is not required to revisit the making of the order since this would lead to lengthy hearings, disproportionate to their objective: *Patley Wood Farm LLP v Brake* [2013] EWHC 4035 (Ch), 164 NLJ 7591, 164 NLJ 7625.

III ARB [13]

43. Securing the attendance of witnesses

(1) A party to arbitral proceedings may use the same court procedures as are available in relation to legal proceedings to secure the attendance before the tribunal of a witness in order to give oral testimony or to produce documents or other material evidence.

(2) This may only be done with the permission of the tribunal or the agreement of the other parties.

(3) The court procedures may only be used if—

(a) the witness is in the United Kingdom, and

(b) the arbitral proceedings are being conducted in England and Wales or, as the case may be, Northern Ireland.

(4) A person shall not be compelled by virtue of this section to produce any document or other material evidence which he could not be compelled to produce in legal proceedings.

III ARB [13.1]

Practice The applicant to the appropriate registry for the issue of a witness summons must file an affidavit or witness summons which shows that the application is made with the permission of the tribunal or the agreement of the other parties. This section does not give the court power to order disclosure from a third party: *BNP Paribas v Deloitte and Touche LLP* [2003] EWHC 2874 (Comm), [2003] NLJR 1841, Morison J.

A witness summons to produce documents must identify the documents, either individually or by class, with sufficient certainty to leave no doubt about what is required: *Tajik Aluminium Plant v Hydro Aluminium Plant AS* [2005] EWCA Civ 1218, [2005] 4 All ER 1232, in which it was also held that doubts about the adequacy of the description of the documents should be resolved in favour of the witness.

III ARB [14]

44. Court powers exercisable in support of arbitral proceedings

(1) Unless otherwise agreed by the parties, the court has for the purposes of and in relation to arbitral proceedings the same power of making orders about the matters listed below as it has for the purposes of and in relation to legal proceedings.

(2) Those matters are—

(a) the taking of the evidence of witnesses;

(b) the preservation of evidence;

(c) making orders relating to property which is the subject of the proceedings or as to which any question arises in the proceedings—

(i) for the inspection, photographing, preservation, custody or detention of the property, or

(ii) ordering that samples be taken from, or any observation be made of or experiment conducted upon, the property;

and for that purpose authorising any person to enter any premises in the possession or control of a party to the arbitration;

(d) the sale of any goods the subject of the proceedings;

(e) the granting of an interim injunction or the appointment of a receiver.

(3) If the case is one of urgency, the court may, on the application of a party or proposed party to the arbitral proceedings, make such orders as it thinks necessary for the purpose of preserving evidence or assets.

(4) If the case is not one of urgency, the court shall act only on the application of a party to the arbitral proceedings (upon notice to the other parties and to the tribunal) made with the permission of the tribunal or the agreement in writing of the other parties.

(5) In any case the court shall act only if or to the extent that the arbitral tribunal, and any arbitral or other institution or person vested by the parties with power in that regard, has no power or is unable for the time being to act effectively.

(6) If the court so orders, an order made by it under this section shall cease to have effect in whole or in part on the order of the tribunal or of any such arbitral or other institution or person having power to act in relation to the subject-matter of the order.

(7) The leave of the court is required for any appeal from a decision of the court under this section.

III ARB [14.1]

Charging order Where the Beth Din included in a provisional award a direction that one party was not to sell a certain house, it was held that the Beth Din had power to give the direction, because the parties had agreed to confer such powers, under s 39 (4), but that it did not create a charge over the property and that a caution to this effect was invalid: *Kastner v Jason* [2004] EWHC 592 (Ch), [2004] 2 Lloyd's Rep 233, Lightman J.

On the other hand, where a party is ordered to make a payment pursuant to an adjudicator's decision, it may be appropriate to enforce payment by a charging order and sale even where other claims and cross-claims by the parties may be the subject of ongoing arbitration proceedings: *Harlow & Milner Ltd v Teasdale* [2006] EWHC 1708, [2006] BLR 359.

III ARB [14.2]

If the case is one of urgency The effect of sub-s (3) is to limit the powers of the court, in cases of urgency, to making orders only where necessary for the purpose of preserving evidence or assets: *Cetelem SA v Roust Holdings Ltd* [2005] EWCA Civ 618, [2005] 4 All ER 52, (2005) Times, 13 June. In that case the Court held that the grant of an interim mandatory injunction to produce certain documents was, in the circumstances of the case, necessary and within the powers. It has been held, on an application for an urgent freezing injunction, that it is only in cases where the powers of an arbitral tribunal are inadequate or where the practical ability is lacking to exercise those powers that the court may act under s 44: *Gerald Metals SA v Timis* [2016] EWHC 2327 (Ch), [2016] All ER (D) 31 (Oct).

III ARB [14.3]

Power to make orders about the matters listed The court has no power under this section to order disclosure by a non-party of documents relevant to the arbitration unless such an order would come within one of the matters listed such as s 44(2)(b) or (c): *Assimina Maritime Ltd v Pakistan National Shipping Corpn, The Tasman Spirit* [2004] EWHC 3005 (Comm), [2005] 1 All ER (Comm) 460.

The section does not confer jurisdiction to stop legal proceedings started in breach of an arbitration agreement. However, power to grant such an injunction is available under s 37 of the Senior Courts Act 1981: *AES Ust-Kamenogorsk Hydropower Plant LLP v Ust-Kamenogorsk Hydropower Plant JSC* [2013] UKSC 35, [2013] 1 WLR 1889, [2014] 1 All ER (Comm) 1.

III ARB [14.4]

Relief available where there is no pending or intended arbitration Where there is no pending or intended arbitration there is no power to grant an injunction prohibiting court proceedings: *Cetelem SA v Roust Holdings Ltd* [2005] EWCA Civ 618, [2005] 4 All ER 52, [2005] All ER (Comm) 203. But a declaration may be granted as to the validity of the arbitration agreement: *AES Ust-Kamenogorsk Hydropower Plant LLP v Ust-Kamenogorsk Hydropower Plant JSC* [2010] EWHC 722 (Comm), [2010] 2 All ER (Comm) 1033, [2010] 2 Lloyd's Rep 493, in which it was held that injunctive relief, although not available under s 44, might nevertheless be granted under the Senior Courts Act 1981, s 37.

The Supreme Court reached the same conclusion: *AES Ust-Kamenogorsk Hydropower Plant LLP v Ust-Kamenogorsk Hydropower Plant JSC* (2013) Times 5 August, Sup Ct.

III ARB [15]

45. Determination of preliminary point of law

(1) Unless otherwise agreed by the parties, the court may on the application of a party to arbitral proceedings (upon notice to the other parties) determine any question of law arising in the course of the proceedings which the court is satisfied substantially affects the rights of one or more of the parties.

An agreement to dispense with reasons for the tribunal's award shall be considered an agreement to exclude the court's jurisdiction under this section.

(2) An application under this section shall not be considered unless—

- (a) it is made with the agreement of all the other parties to the proceedings, or
- (b) it is made with the permission of the tribunal and the court is satisfied—
  - (i) that the determination of the question is likely to produce substantial savings in costs, and
  - (ii) that the application was made without delay.

(3) The application shall identify the question of law to be determined and, unless made with the agreement of all the other parties to the proceedings, shall state the grounds on which it is said that the question should be decided by the court.

(4) Unless otherwise agreed by the parties, the arbitral tribunal may continue the arbitral proceedings and make an award while an application to the court under this section is pending.

(5) Unless the court gives leave, no appeal lies from a decision of the court whether the conditions specified in subsection (2) are met.

(6) The decision of the court on the question of law shall be treated as a judgment of the court for the purposes of an appeal.

But no appeal lies without the leave of the court which shall not be given unless the court considers that the question is one of general importance, or is one which for some other special reason should be considered by the Court of Appeal.

III ARB [15.1]

Unless otherwise agreed It will be noted that the right of a party to use court procedures to secure the attendance of witnesses (s 43) is unqualified, whereas the rights of access to the court under ss 42, 44 and 45 may be removed or restricted by agreement.

III ARB [15.2]

Procedure for applying to the court See the notes at **III ARB [1]** for details of the courts with power to entertain applications under the Arbitration Act 1996 and the notes at **III ARB [2]** and **III ARB [3]** or a summary of the procedure for applying.

III ARB [15.3]

An order requiring a party to comply The court has power to compel compliance by punishing non-compliance as contempt or, in some circumstances, by requiring the necessary acts to be performed by others eg under the Supreme Court Act 1981 s 39; see para **II SCA [40]**.

III ARB [15.4]

Peremptory order This is defined by s 82(1) as meaning an order under s 41(5), or in exercise of corresponding powers conferred on the tribunal by the parties. Section 41(5) is in the following terms: if without showing sufficient cause a party fails to comply with any order or directions of the tribunal, the tribunal may make a peremptory order to the same effect, prescribing such time for compliance with it as the tribunal considers appropriate.

III ARB [15.5]

Securing attendance of witnesses Where a witness has failed to attend as required by a witness summons, the court may issue a warrant for arrest and committal for contempt.

III ARB [15.6]

Court powers in relation to legal proceedings For example see para **CPR 25** (Interim Remedies). The court granted a Mareva injunction in *Re Q's Estate* [1999] 1 Lloyd's Rep 931.

III ARB [15.7]

Determination of preliminary point of law These provisions have their origins in the Arbitration Act 1979.

III ARB [15.8]

Any question of law Section 82(1) defines "question of law" as meaning:

(a) for a court in England and Wales, a question of the law of England and Wales, and
(b) for a court in Northern Ireland, a question of the law of Northern Ireland.

III ARB [16]

50. Extension of time for making award

(1) Where the time for making an award is limited by or in pursuance of the arbitration agreement, then, unless otherwise agreed by the parties, the court may in accordance with the following provisions by order extend that time.

ARBITRATION

(2) An application for an order under this section may be made—

(a) by the tribunal (upon notice to the parties), or

(b) by any party to the proceedings (upon notice to the tribunal and the other parties),

but only after exhausting any available arbitral process for obtaining an extension of time.

(3) The court shall only make an order if satisfied that a substantial injustice would otherwise be done.

(4) The court may extend the time for such period and on such terms as it thinks fit, and may do so whether or not the time previously fixed (by or under the agreement or by a previous order) has expired.

(5) The leave of the court is required for any appeal from a decision of the court under this section.

III ARB [16.1]

Procedure for applying to the court See the notes at **III ARB [1]** for details of the courts with power to entertain applications under the Arbitration Act 1996 and the notes at **III ARB [2]** and **III ARB [3]** for a summary of the procedure for applying. Note that sub-s (4) precludes an application to the court where there is any available arbitral process for appeal or review of the amount of the fees or expenses demanded.

III ARB [17]

56. Power to withhold award in case of non-payment

(1) The tribunal may refuse to deliver an award to the parties except upon full payment of the fees and expenses of the arbitrators.

(2) If the tribunal refuses on that ground to deliver an award, a party to the arbitral proceedings may (upon notice to the other parties and the tribunal) apply to the court, which may order that—

(a) the tribunal shall deliver the award on the payment into court by the applicant of the fees and expenses demanded, or such lesser amount as the court may specify,

(b) the amount of the fees and expenses properly payable shall be determined by such means and upon such terms as the court may direct, and

(c) out of the money paid into court there shall be paid out such fees and expenses as may be found to be properly payable and the balance of the money (if any) shall be paid out to the applicant.

(3) For this purpose the amount of fees and expenses properly payable is the amount the applicant is liable to pay under section 28 or any agreement relating to the payment of the arbitrators.

(4) No application to the court may be made where there is any available arbitral process for appeal or review of the amount of the fees or expenses demanded.

(5) References in this section to arbitrators include an arbitrator who has ceased to act and an umpire who has not replaced the other arbitrators.

(6) The above provisions of this section also apply in relation to any arbitral or other institution or person vested by the parties with powers in relation to the delivery of the tribunal's award.

As they so apply, the references to the fees and expenses of the arbitrators shall be construed as including the fees and expenses of that institution or person.

(7) The leave of the court is required for any appeal from a decision of the court under this section.

(8) Nothing in this section shall be construed as excluding an application under section 28 where payment has been made to the arbitrators in order to obtain the award.

III ARB [17.1]

The court As to the allocation of jurisdiction between High Court and county court, see para **III ARB [10.1]**. For the procedure for applying, see **CPR 62.3**, **CPR 62.4** and **CPR 62.6**.

III ARB [17.2]

Arbitrator's entitlement to fees The Arbitration Act 1996 provides other opportunities for obtaining court ruling on the arbitrator's entitlement to fees, see para **III ARB [10.4]**.

III ARB [18]

63. The recoverable costs of the arbitration

(1) The parties are free to agree what costs of the arbitration are recoverable.

(2) If or to the extent there is no such agreement, the following provisions apply.

(3) The tribunal may determine by award the recoverable costs of the arbitration on such basis as it thinks fit.

If it does so, it shall specify—

(a) the basis on which it has acted, and

(b) the items of recoverable costs and the amount referable to each.

(4) If the tribunal does not determine the recoverable costs of the arbitration, any party to the arbitral proceedings may apply to the court (upon notice to the other parties) which may—

(a) determine the recoverable costs of the arbitration on such basis as it thinks fit, or

(b) order that they shall be determined by such means and upon such terms as it may specify.

(5) Unless the tribunal or the court determines otherwise—

(a) the recoverable costs of the arbitration shall be determined on the basis that there shall be allowed a reasonable amount in respect of all costs reasonably incurred, and

(b) any doubt as to whether costs were reasonably incurred or were reasonable in amount shall be resolved in favour of the paying party.

(6) The above provisions have effect subject to section 64 (recoverable fees and expenses of arbitrators).

(7) Nothing in this section affects any right of the arbitrators, any expert, legal adviser or assessor appointed by the tribunal, or any arbitral institution, to payment of their fees and expenses.

III ARB [18.1]

Procedure for applying to the court See the notes at **III ARB [1]** for details of the courts with power to entertain applications under the Arbitration Act 1996 and the notes at **III ARB [2]** and **III ARB [3]** for a summary of the procedure for applying.

III ARB [18.2]

Subject to section 64 Section 64(1)–(2) provides that, unless otherwise agreed, the recoverable costs of the arbitration include the reasonable fees and expenses of the arbitrators which are appropriate in the circumstances; and the court is empowered, on application, to determine any question arising in this connection or to order its determination by others on such terms as the court may specify.

III ARB [19]

66. Enforcement of the award

(1) An award made by the tribunal pursuant to an arbitration agreement may, by leave of the court, be enforced in the same manner as a judgment or order of the court to the same effect.

(2) Where leave is so given, judgment may be entered in terms of the award.

(3) Leave to enforce an award shall not be given where, or to the extent that, the person against whom it is sought to be enforced shows that the tribunal lacked substantive jurisdiction to make the award.

The right to raise such an objection may have been lost (see section 73).

(4) Nothing in this section affects the recognition or enforcement of an award under any other enactment or rule of law, in particular under Part II of the Arbitration Act 1950 (enforcement of awards under Geneva Convention) or the provisions of Part III of this Act relating to the recognition and enforcement of awards under the New York Convention or by an action on the award.

III ARB [19.1]

Award enforced in the same manner as a judgment or order of the court The procedure for enforcing an arbitration award is set out in **CPR 62.18** and, as regards interest on awards, **CPR 62.19**.

Note that the sums awarded will not carry interest unless the arbitrator exercises the powers in s 69(4) to award prospective interest. The court does not have jurisdiction to add interest post-award under s 35A of the Supreme Court Act 1981: *Walker v Rose* [2000] 1 Lloyd's Rep 116. The same point was made in In re Arbitration Claim: *Statoil v Sonatrach* [2014] EWHC 875 (Comm), [2014] 2 All ER (Comm) 857, [2014] 2 Lloyd's Rep 252. However, in that case it was held that the award carried interest at the Judgment Act rate from the moment that it became enforceable as a judgment.

The grant of leave, under sub-s (1), to enforce an award is not the same as entering a judgment under sub-s (2); and a failure to comply by making payment is not contempt: *ASM Shipping Ltd of India v TTMI Ltd of England* [2007] EWHC 927 (Comm), [2007] 1 CLC 555.

An application for a court award, under sub-section (1), would be justified where it could be shown that such an order would confer a material benefit, for example to establish primacy of the award over an inconsistent award in another jurisdiction: *West Tankers Inc v Allianz Spa* [2011] EWHC 829 (Comm), [2011] 2 All ER (Comm) 1, [2011] NLJR 551.

The limitation period for enforcement is six years from the date on which the cause of action accrued. See s 7 of the Limitation Act 1980, as applied in *ED & F Man Sugar Ltd v Lendoudis* [2007] EWHC 2268 (Comm), [2008] 1 All ER 952; *National Ability SA v Tinna Oils and Chemicals Ltd* (2009) Times, 24 December, CA. The text of s 7 is at **III LIM [9]**.

The arbitrator has power to decide questions of jurisdiction. Where a party denies the existence of an arbitration the proper course is to apply to the arbitrator for a ruling, not to the court: *Noble Denton Middle East v Noble Denton International Ltd* [2010] EWHC 2574 (Comm), [2010] NLJR 1650.

A declaratory award may be enforced under s 66 and where the court has granted a declaration as to the validity of an award the declaratory judgment may be enforced by the issue of a writ of sequestration: *BD SHIPSNAVO GmbH & Co Reederel KG v African Fertilizers and Chemical NIG Ltd (Nigeria)* [2011] EWHC 2452 (Comm), [2011] All ER (D) 03 (Oct).

III ARB [19.1A]

Showing a lack of jurisdiction In a case where the respondent contended that there was no binding arbitration agreement and that the award was therefore invalid, it was held that such issues could be determined on the application to enforce. It was further held that it was for the respondent to prove the facts on which resistance to the application was based: *Sovarex SA v Romero Alvarez SA* [2011] EWHC 1661 (Comm), [2012] 1 All ER (Comm) 207, [2011] 2 Lloyd's Rep 320.

III ARB [19.2]

Illegality There is no general principle that questions of illegality may be raised as grounds for not enforcing an arbitrator's award where they were raised before the arbitrator as grounds for not making the award but were rejected: *Westacre Investments Ltd v Jugoimport-SPDR Holding Co Ltd* [2000] 1 QB 288, [1999] 3 All ER 864, CA. It was also decided in that case that enforcement may not be refused on public policy grounds if enforcement would not offend the public policy of the place of performance. See also *Omnium de Traitement et de Valorisation SA v Hilmarton Ltd* [1999] 2 All ER (Comm) 146. On the other hand enforcement was refused in *Soleimany v Soleimany* [1999] QB 785, [1999] 3 All ER 847, CA having regard to the illegality of the underlying contract and transaction.

III ARB [19.3]

New York Convention and other international awards The enforcement of New York Convention awards is dealt with in ss 99–104. In *Irvani v Irvani* [2000] 1 Lloyd's Rep, CA a New York Convention award was held unenforceable under s 103(2)(c) because the arbitrator had prevented one of the parties from presenting his case.

It has been held that a court when reviewing an international award, on an application under s 101, to permit enforcement, should pay careful attention to the type of hearing and the standard of proof required. Further, the court should not treat a finding by the tribunal that the respondent was a party to the arbitration as creating an estoppel, merely because the respondent had not challenged the award at the time: the respondent was entitled to challenge the finding on the subsequent application for permission to enforce: *Dallah Estate and Tourism Holding Co v Ministry of Religious Affairs, Government of Pakistan* [2009] EWCA Civ 755, 125 Con LR 37, [2009] 30 EG 67 (CS). It was also held in that case that the discretion conferred by s 103 (and by extension s 66) should not be exercised in favour of enforcement of an award which the court was satisfied was fundamentally flawed.

An appeal to the Supreme Court was dismissed: *Dallah Real Estates and Tourism Holding Co v Ministry of Religious Affairs, Government of Pakistan* [2010] UKSC 46, [2010] 3 All ER 1472, [2010] Lloyd's Rep 691.

It has been held that the grounds set out in s 103, for not recognising or enforcing an award, should be construed restrictively and should not be accepted unless there is a real prospect of success on one of the grounds or there is some other compelling reason why the issue should be disposed of at a trial: *Honeywell International Middle East Ltd v Meydan Group LLC* [2014] EWHC 1344 (TCC), 154 Con L R 113, [2014] BLR 401.

III ARB [19.4]

Security for costs The court has jurisdiction to order security for costs against a judgment-and-award creditor under a New York Convention award. **CPR 25.12** applies to claims under s 66 of the Arbitration Act 1996, to enforce domestic awards, and also to claims made under s 101 to enforce a Convention award: *Gater Assets Ltd v Nak Naftogaz Ukrainiy* [2007] EWHC 697 (Comm), [2007] 1 Lloyd's Rep 522, Field J, QBD. In that case the defendant was defending the clam to enforce the award by applying to have it set aside.

III ARB [19.5]

Freezing orders A freezing order granted in aid of enforcement of an arbitration award ought ordinarily to contain an ordinary course of business exception: *Mobile Telesystems Finance SA v Nomihold Securities Inc* [2011] EWCA Civ 1040, [2012] 1 Lloyd's Rep 6, [2011] NLJR 121.

III ARB [20]

67. Challenging the award: substantive jurisdiction

(1) A party to arbitral proceedings may (upon notice to the other parties and to the tribunal) apply to the court—

- (a) challenging any award of the arbitral tribunal as to its substantive jurisdiction; or
- (b) for an order declaring an award made by the tribunal on the merits to be of no effect, in whole or in part, because the tribunal did not have substantive jurisdiction.

A party may lose the right to object (see section 73) and the right to apply is subject to the restrictions in section 70 (2) and (3).

(2) The arbitral tribunal may continue the arbitral proceedings and make a further award while an application to the court under this section is pending in relation to an award as to jurisdiction.

(3) On an application under this section challenging an award of the arbitral tribunal as to its substantive jurisdiction, the court may by order—

- (a) confirm the award,
- (b) vary the award, or
- (c) set aside the award in whole or in part.

(4) The leave of the court is required for any appeal from a decision of the court under this section.

ARBITRATION

III ARB [20.1]

Procedure for applying to the court See the notes at **III ARB [1]** for details of the courts with power to entertain applications under the Arbitration Act 1996 and the notes at **III ARB [2]** and **III ARB [3]** for a summary of the procedure for applying. Oral evidence and cross-examination may be appropriate on an issue of fact such as whether a party joined in the arbitration was a party to the arbitration agreement and the challenger may be ordered to provide security for costs: *Azov Shipping Co v Baltic Shipping Co* [1999] 1 All ER 476.

A challenge may be presented on the basis of evidence that was not before the arbitrator; but the court has a discretion whether to admit it: *Central Trading & Exports Ltd v Fioralba Shipping Company, The Kalisti* [2014] EWHC 2397 (Comm), [2014] Bus LR D19, [2014] 2 Lloyd's Rep 449.

An arbitrator with jurisdiction to hear a dispute does not have jurisdiction to hear a counterclaim, unless it is itself a dispute within the arbitration clause: *Metal Distributors (UK) Ltd v ZCCM Investment Holdings plc* [2005] EWHC 156 (Comm), (2005) Times, 9 March, Cresswell J QBD (Comm).

Where one of the arbitrators is not validly appointed within the applicable rules, the non-compliance renders that arbitrator's participation unlawful and the award may be set aside as a nullity: *Sumukan Ltd v Commonwealth Secretariat (No 2)* [2007] EWCA Civ 1148, [2007] All ER (D) 253 (Nov), (2007) Times, 18 December.

III ARB [20.2]

Service abroad Service abroad will be permitted if the award was made in England and Wales; and this condition is treated as satisfied where the seat of the arbitration was in England and Wales: see ss 3 and 53 and **CPR 62.5**.

III ARB [20.2A]

Challenging a late award of interest on the award Where no order is made at the time for the award to carry interest, an additional award of interest may not be made subsequently except in the limited circumstances covered by s 57(3)(b). A subsequent award which is made in excess of jurisdiction may be set aside under this section: *Pirtek (UK) Ltd v Deanswood Ltd* [2005] EWHC 2301 (Comm), [2005] 2 Lloyd's Rep 728, QBD, Aikens J.

III ARB [20.2B]

Absence of a contract If there is no concluded contract between the parties, there can be no jurisdiction for an arbitrator: *Pacific Inter-Link SDN BHD v EFKO Food Ingredients Ltd* [2011] EWHC 923 (Comm), [2011] All ER (D) 191 (May) in which Steel J held that there were no effective contracts because the requirements for stamping, signing and returning had not been met. On the other hand a contract may be held to have been brought into existence by performance: *TTMI SARL v Statoil ASA (The Sibohelle)* [2011] EWHC 1150 (Comm), [2011] 2 All ER (Comm) 647, [2011] 2 Lloyd's Rep 220.

III ARB [20.3]

Challenging a ruling that the arbitrator had no substantive jurisdiction A ruling by an arbitrator that the respondents were not parties to the agreement, with the result that the arbitrator had no jurisdiction to make an award on the merits, has been held to be an award as to substantive jurisdiction within s 67(1)(a): *LG Caltex Gas Co Ltd v China National Petroleum Corpn* [2001] EWCA Civ 788, [2001] 4 All ER 875, [2001] 1 WLR 1892. The decision of the court below that the right to object was barred by s 73 depended on a finding, rejected by the Court of Appeal, that jurisdiction to make an award on the merits had been conferred by an ad hoc agreement.

Once the arbitrator has given his ruling, an application may be made to set aside as wrong but not on the ground that the ruling should have been deferred: *Kalmneft JSC v Glencore International AG* [2002] 1 All ER 76.

Although the courts will not entertain a challenge based on the interpretation of an international treaty, this doctrine of judicial restraint does not necessarily apply where the State parties have made a domestic contract which incorporates a treaty but also provides for dispute resolution by consensual arbitration: *Republic of Ecuador v Occidental Exploration and Production Co* [2005] EWCA Civ 1116, (2005) Times, 23 September.

It has been held, in a case where the award included findings of illegality, that the arbitration should be construed widely as covering all disputes arising out of the particular relationship, including issues of legality, unless excluded by express wording in the agreement: *Interprods Ltd v De La rue International Ltd* [2014] EWHC 68 (Comm), [2014] 1 Lloyd's Rep 540, in which the challenge to the award was rejected.

III ARB [20.4]

Permission to appeal against a decision under s 67 Only the trial judge may grant permission under sub-s (4) to appeal against a decision under this section. If permission is refused at this level the Court of Appeal has no power to grant it: *Athletic Union of Constantinople v National Basketball Association (No 2)* [2002] EWCA Civ 830, [2002] 3 All ER 897, [2002] 1 WLR 2863. See also the note at para **III ARB [22.4]**.

III ARB [20.5]

Effect of a successful challenge An arbitrator is not *functus officio* (no longer having jurisdiction) by reason only of an award being set aside. When this happens the arbitration reverts to the position before the publication of the award; and the same applies where the award has been declared to be 'of no effect': *Hussmann (Europe) Ltd v Pharaoh* [2003] EWCA Civ 266, [2003] 1 All ER (Comm) 879.

III ARB [20.6]

Duty to raise a point which counsel appears to have missed If an arbitrator appreciates that a party has missed a point, fairness requires that the arbitrator should raise it: *The Vimeira* [1984] 2 Lloyd's Rep 66. But the duty does not arise unless the arbitrator appreciates that the point has been missed: *Bandwidth Shipping Corporation v Intaari* [2007] EWCA Civ 998, (2007) Times, 31 October, [2007] All ER (D) 229 (Oct).

III ARB [21]

68. Challenging the award: serious irregularity

(1) A party to arbitral proceedings may (upon notice to the other parties and to the tribunal) apply to the court challenging an award in the proceedings on the ground of serious irregularity affecting the tribunal, the proceedings or the award. A party may lose the right to object (see section 73) and the right to apply is subject to the restrictions in section 70 (2) and (3).

(2) Serious irregularity means an irregularity of one or more of the following kinds which the court considers has caused or will cause substantial injustice to the applicant—

- (a) failure by the tribunal to comply with section 33 (general duty of tribunal);
- (b) the tribunal exceeding its powers (otherwise than by exceeding its substantive jurisdiction: see section 67);
- (c) failure by the tribunal to conduct the proceedings in accordance with the procedure agreed by the parties;
- (d) failure by the tribunal to deal with all the issues that were put to it;
- (e) any arbitral or other institution or person vested by the parties with powers in relation to the proceedings or the award exceeding its powers;
- (f) uncertainty or ambiguity as to the effect of the award;
- (g) the award being obtained by fraud or the award or the way in which it was procured being contrary to public policy;
- (h) failure to comply with the requirements as to the form of the award; or
- (i) any irregularity in the conduct of the proceedings or in the award which is admitted by the tribunal or by any arbitral or other institution or person vested by the parties with powers in relation to the proceedings or the award.

(3) If there is shown to be serious irregularity affecting the tribunal, the proceedings or the award, the court may—

- (a) remit the award to the tribunal, in whole or in part, for reconsideration,
- (b) set the award aside in whole or in part, or
- (c) declare the award to be of no effect, in whole or in part.

The court shall not exercise its power to set aside or to declare an award to be of no effect, in whole or in part, unless it is satisfied that it would be inappropriate to remit the matters in question to the tribunal for reconsideration.

(4) The leave of the court is required for any appeal from a decision of the court under this section.

III ARB [21.1]

A party to arbitral proceedings Section 72(2) confirms that a party to arbitral proceedings has rights of challenge under ss 67 and 68, although taking no part in the proceedings, and s 70(2) does not apply to such a party.

III ARB [21.2]

Apply to the court See the notes at **III ARB [1]** for details of the courts with power to entertain applications under the Arbitration Act 1996 and the notes at **III ARB [2]** and **III ARB [3]** for a summary of the procedure for applying. Note the restrictions imposed by the Arbitration Act 1996 s 70(2) and (3). As to service abroad see **III ARB [20.2]**.

III ARB [21.2A]

Tribunal exceeding its powers A tribunal does not exceed its powers, for the purposes of sub s(2)(b), by reason only of an erroneous exercise of the power under s 48(4) to make an award in a currency other than the proper currency of the contract: *Lesotho Highlands Development Authority v Impreglio SpA* [2005] UKHL 43, [2005] 3 All ER 749, (2005) Times, 6 July, reversing the Court of Appeal decision at [2003] EWCA Civ 1159, [2003] BLR 347.

A decision by an arbitrator as to jurisdiction may not be set aside on the sole ground of a failure to allow parties to make representations: *Amec Capital Projects Ltd v Whitefriars City Estates Ltd* [2004] EWCA Civ 1418, [2005] 1 All ER 723, (2004) Times, 8 November.

A party may not use s 68 to argue that the arbitration was in breach of Article 6 of the Human Rights Convention on the ground that arbitration was not agreed to willingly. A challenge under s 68 assumes the existence of an arbitration agreement: *Shuttari v Solicitors' Indemnity Fund* [2007] EWCA Civ 244, [2007] 1 CLC 303.

III ARB [21.2B]

Agreement by the parties not to use separately published reasons on appeal Where the parties agree as terms of the arbitration that separately published reasons should not be used in appellate proceedings, the court should uphold that agreement and not take the published reasons into account on appeal: *Tame Shipping Ltd v Easy Navigation Ltd* [2004] 2 All ER (Comm) 521, (2004) Times, 8 November, Moore-Blick J.

III ARB [21.2C]

Irregularity causing substantial injustice The opening words of sub-s (2) make the establishment of "substantial injustice" a precondition to a successful challenge on the ground of serious irregularity. An irregular exercise of the power under s 49(3) to award interest has been held not to satisfy the pre-condition: *Lesotho Highlands Development Authority v Impreglio SpA* (2005) Times, 6 July, HL, reversing the Court of Appeal decision at [2003] EWCA Civ 1159, [2003] BLR 347. It was observed in that case that an applicant alleging an irregularity on the part of the arbitrator in the discharge of his duties under s 33 faced "a high hurdle". The Court of Appeal has since confirmed the importance of maintaining the high hurdle in order to exclude challenges on issues of fact and confining this ground of appeal to cases were the arbitrator has acted unfairly in not allowing a party a reasonable opportunity of putting its case or answering that of its opponent: *Bandwith Shipping Corp v Antaari (a Firm)* [2007] EWCA Civ 998, (2007) Times 31 October. On the other hand there was held to be substantial injustice as to interest rates and double counting of works in a case where the arbitrator gave a very brief award without stating reasons for going against the evidence: *Van der Giessen De-Noord v Imtech* [2008] All ER (D) 284 (Nov).

In specialist arbitrations prior contact between parties and their lawyers and arbitrators is to be expected and not necessarily objectionable. But if a properly informed independent observer would conclude that there was a real possibility of bias, this would qualify as a serious irregularity causing substantial injustice, without it being necessary to show that bias had caused prejudice: *ASM Shipping Ltd of India v TTMI Ltd of England* [2005] EWHC 2338 (Comm), [2006] 1 Lloyd's Rep 375, QBD, M ORISON J.

In a case where an arbitrator's firm regularly advised an affiliate of the defendant, in apparent breach of 'non-waivable' guideline 1.4 in the 2014 IBA Guidelines on Conflict of Interest in international Arbitration, the challenge under section 68 was nevertheless dismissed: *W Ltd v M Sdn Bhd* [2016] EWHC 422 (Comm), [2016] 1 Lloyd's Rep 552, 164 ConLR 66.

III ARB [21.2D]

Award obtained by fraud Paragraph (g) of s 68(2) provides for challenging an award obtained by fraud, but this is not satisfied by an innocent failure to provide proper disclosure or the innocent production of false evidence. Where an application alleges fraud in the production of evidence it must be supported by evidence not available at the time of the arbitration which would have had an important influence on the result: *Double K Oil & Products 1996 Ltd v Neste Oil OYJ* [2009] EWHC 3380 (Comm), [2010] 1 Lloyd's Rep 141, [2010] NLJR 68.

III ARB [21.3]

Substantive jurisdiction Section 82(1) provides that, in relation to an arbitral tribunal, "substantive jurisdiction" refers to the matters specified in s 30(1)(a)–(c):

(a) whether there is a valid arbitration agreement,
(b) whether the tribunal is properly constituted, and
(c) what matters have been submitted to arbitration in accordance with the arbitration agreement.

III ARB [21.4]

Findings on facts not in issue It has been held under the old law, to be "misconduct" for an arbitrator to make contrary findings on facts not put in issue by the parties: *Strachan and Henshaw Ltd v Stein Industrie (UK) Ltd* (1997) 13 Const LJ 418, following *Interbulk Ltd v Aiden Shipping Co Ltd* [1984] 2 Lloyd's Rep 66, CA. Although the position is not free from doubt, such misconduct would seem to be a serious irregularity within s 68(2)(a) or (c). It was held in *Gbangbola v Smith & Sheriff Ltd* [1998] 3 All ER 730 to be serious misconduct, contrary to s 68(2)(a), for an arbitrator to base an award of costs on matters of concern to him which he had not brought to the attention of the parties.

Likewise in *Pacol Ltd v Joint Stock Co Rossakhar* [2000] 1 Lloyd's Rep 109 a finding of non-liability was set aside where liability had been admitted. On the other hand, it is not necessarily an error of procedure for an arbitrator to be appointed who has a trade connection with one of the parties: *Rustal Trading Ltd v Gill & Duffus SA* [2000] 1 Lloyd's Rep 14. Nor should an arbitrator be criticised for failing to address each and every argument and item of evidence when making an award. It would be wrong to allow s 68 to be used to challenge a finding of fact. Procedural irregularity is not a ground for appeal unless it is serious and has given rise to substantial injustice: *Schwebel v Schwebel* [2010] EWHC 3280 (TCC), [2010] All ER (D) 226 (Dec).

III ARB [21.5]

Procedural irregularity In *Hussman (Europe) Ltd v Al Ameen Development & Trade Co* [2000] 2 Lloyd's Rep 83 the tribunal had instructed an expert under s 37(1) to assist them on Saudi Arabian law and had acted irregularly by discussing the case with the expert without the prior consent of the parties. But the court held that the irregularity was not a serious one within s 68(2). For a further example of an error which was not, in the circumstances, a serious irregularity, see *Weldon Plant Ltd v Commission for the New Towns* [2000] BLR 496.

It was held in *Warborough Investments Ltd v S Robinson & Sons (Holdings) Ltd* [2003] EWCA Civ 751, [2003] 2 P & CR 68, (2003) Times, 9 July that although the arbitrator had acted irregularly in a rent review arbitration the error was within the margin of appreciation allowed to enable arbitrators to arrive at a fair resolution of a dispute without unnecessary delay or expense. In *A v B* [2011] EWHC 2345 (Comm), [2011] All ER (D) 71 (Sep) Flaux J held that a failure by the arbitrator to disclose involvement in another case until late on in the arbitration was not a serious irregularity and that, in any case, it had not caused substantial injustice.

It is not necessarily a procedural irregularity for an arbitrator who has heard a case in private to give the decision in public. The arbitrator has a discretion to do so where confidentiality is not prejudiced by publicity, in the interests of putting a decision on an important point into the public domain and demonstrating the fairness of the process: *Department of Economic Policy and Development of the City of Moscow v Bankers Trust Co* [2004] EWCA Civ 34, [2004] 4 All ER 746, CA.

On the other hand it has been held to be a serious irregularity for an arbitrator to contact witnesses directly without informing the parties that he had done so: *Norbrook Laboratories Ltd v Tank* [2006] EWHC 1055, [2006] 2 Lloyd's Rep 485.

The focus of a judge's enquiry under section 68 should be into whether there had been "due process" rather than analysing the correctness of the actual decision. Sometimes a more appropriate application would be for a correction under section 57: *Primera Maritime (Hellas) Ltd v Jiangsu Eastern Heavy Industry Co Ltd* [2013] EWHC 3066 (Comm), [2014] 1 All ER (Comm) 813, [2014] 1 Lloyd's Rep 255.

ARBITRATION

III ARB [21.5A]

Accidental slip An arbitrator has power, under s 57(3)(a), to correct an accidental slip or omission or to clarify. If there has been a mathematical mistake which has an impact on the award of costs the arbitrator may reconsider the award of costs too: *Gannet Shipping Ltd v Eastrade Commodities Inc* [2002] 1 All ER (Comm) 297.

III ARB [21.5B]

Arbitrator's use of personal knowledge An arbitrator may rely on his general expert knowledge but should disclose his knowledge of any special facts relevant to the case. Otherwise he would be discarding the role of an impartial arbitrator: *Fox v PG Wellfair Ltd* [1981] 2 Lloyd's Rep 514, CA. In *Checkpoint Ltd v Strathclyde Pension Fund* [2003] EWCA Civ 84, [2003] 14 EG 124, (2003) Times, 12 February the Court of Appeal gave practical guidance on the application of these principles in a rent review arbitration.

III ARB [21.5C]

Failure to deal with all the issues It is not a failure to deal with an issue, for the purposes of s 68(2)(d), if an arbitrator fails, when dealing with an issue, to take certain evidence into account: *World Trade Corpn Ltd v C Czarnikow Sugar Ltd* [2004] EWHC 2332 (Comm), [2004] 2 All ER (Comm) 813. Similarly, the issue utself must be sufficiently important for the failure to be capable of causing substantial injustice, a requirement which was not met in *Fidelity Management CA v Myriad International Holdings BV* [2005] EWHC 1193, [2005] 2 All ER (Comm), Morrison J, QBD.

III ARB [21.6]

Loss of the right to object For cases where the right to object was held to have been lost under s 73 see *Rustal Trading Ltd v Gill & Duffus SA* [2000] 1 Lloyd's Rep 14, [2000] CLY 224; and *Thyssen Canada Ltd v Mariana Maritime SA* [2005] EWHC 219, [2005] 1 Lloyd's Rep 640.

III ARB [21.7]

Service abroad Service abroad of an application notice challenging an award will be permitted if the award was made in England and Wales. This condition is treated as satisfied where the seat of the arbitration was in England and Wales: see **CPR 62.5**.

III ARB [22]

69. Appeal on point of law

(1) Unless otherwise agreed by the parties, a party to arbitral proceedings may (upon notice to the other parties and to the tribunal) appeal to the court on a question of law arising out of an award made in the proceedings.

An agreement to dispense with reasons for the tribunal's award shall be considered an agreement to exclude the court's jurisdiction under this section.

(2) An appeal shall not be brought under this section except—

(a) with the agreement of all the other parties to the proceedings, or

(b) with the leave of the court.

The right to appeal is also subject to the restrictions in section 70 (2) and (3).

(3) Leave to appeal shall be given only if the court is satisfied—

(a) that the determination of the question will substantially affect the rights of one or more of the parties,

(b) that the question is one which the tribunal was asked to determine,

(c) that, on the basis of the findings of fact in the award—

(i) the decision of the tribunal on the question is obviously wrong, or

(ii) the question is one of general public importance and the decision of the tribunal is at least open to serious doubt, and

(d) that, despite the agreement of the parties to resolve the matter by arbitration, it is just and proper in all the circumstances for the court to determine the question.

(4) An application for leave to appeal under this section shall identify the question of law to be determined and state the grounds on which it is alleged that leave to appeal should be granted.

(5) The court shall determine an application for leave to appeal under this section without a hearing unless it appears to the court that a hearing is required.

(6) The leave of the court is required for any appeal from a decision of the court under this section to grant or refuse leave to appeal.

(7) On an appeal under this section the court may by order—

(a) confirm the award,

(b) vary the award,

(c) remit the award to the tribunal, in whole or in part, for reconsideration in the light of the court's determination, or

(d) set aside the award in whole or in part.

The court shall not exercise its power to set aside an award, in whole or in part, unless it is satisfied that it would be inappropriate to remit the matters in question to the tribunal for reconsideration.

(8) The decision of the court on an appeal under this section shall be treated as a judgment of the court for the purposes of a further appeal.

But no such appeal lies without the leave of the court which shall not be given unless the court considers that the question is one of general importance or is one which for some other special reason should be considered by the Court of Appeal.

III ARB [22.1]

Procedure for appealing to the court The procedure for appealing to the court is laid down in CPR Part 52, at para **CPR 52**. The appellant's notice should follow Form 161 and should be accompanied by the documents required by paragraph 5.6 of the Practice Direction, at para **CPR PD 52**. As to service abroad, see **CPR 62.5**.

III ARB [22.2]

Question of law Section 82(1) of the Arbitration Act 1996 defines "question of law" as meaning—

(a) for a court in England and Wales, a question of the law of England and Wales, and
(b) for a court in Northern Ireland, a question of the law of Northern Ireland.

Where the law is applied by the arbitrator is not English law but some other law, there is no jurisdiction to entertain an appeal under this section: *Schwebel v Schwebel* [2010] EWHC 3280 (TCC), [2010] All ER (D) 226 (Dec), concerning an arbitration where Jewish law was applied.

The court has no jurisdiction to grant leave on a question of law where the issue in dispute is really one of fact: *Geden Operations Ltd v Dry Bulk Handy Holdings Inc, "M/V Bulk Uruguay"* [2014] EWHC 885 (Comm), [2014] 2 All ER (Comm) 196, [2014] 2 Lloyd's Rep 66; *Sun United Maritime Ltd v Kasteli Marine Inc, "The Imme"* [2014] EWHC 1476, [2015] 1 WLR 1527, [2014] 2 Lloyd's Rep 386. Similarly there is no question of law to found an application for leave to appeal where the decision of the arbitral panel was made in the exercise of an absolute discretion: *Kaneria v England and Wales Cricket Board Limited (ECB)* [2014] EWHC 1348 (Comm), 164 NLJ 7606, [2014] All ER (D) 45 (May).

III ARB [22.2A]

Question the arbitrator was asked to determine; acceptance of findings of fact Subsection (3) sets various restrictions on the grant of leave to appeal. There are particular requirements that the question is one which the tribunal was asked to determine and that the findings of fact should be accepted, neither of which was met in *Surefire Systems Ltd v Guardian ECL Ltd* [2005] EWHC 1860, [2005] BLR 534, QBD (T&CC), Jackson J.

III ARB [22.2B]

'Obviously wrong' To be 'obviously wrong' the error should be such that it can be grasped simply by studying the award itself: it must be easily and demonstrably wrong. If the error does not satisfy this test leave may be granted if the correctness of the decision is open to serious doubt but only if the question is one of public importance: *HMV UK Ltd v Propinvest Friar Ltd Partnership* [2011] EWCA Civ 1708, [2011] 1 Lloyd's Rep 416 per Arden LJ as regards the interpretation of s 29(3)(c)(i) and per Longmore LJ as regards the interpretation of s 69(3)(c)(ii).

The 'major intellectual aberration' test has judicial support: *AMEC Group Ltd v Secretary of State for Defence* [2013] EWHC 110 (TCC), 146 Con LR 152, [2013] All ER (D) 93 (Feb).

ARBITRATION

III ARB [22.3]

Unless otherwise agreed In *Sanghi Polyesters Ltd (India) v International Investor (KCFC) (Kuwait)* [2000] 1 Lloyd's Rep 480, the rights under s 69 were held to be unavailable because of the agreement of the parties. They were bound by the 1988 International Chamber of Commerce Rules of Conciliation and Arbitration, art 24 which provided for rights of appeal to be waived.

The Court of Appeal has jurisdiction to consider an appeal from the High Court about the existence of an agreement excluding the right of appeal: *Sumukan Ltd v Commonwealth Secretariat* [2007] EWCA Civ 243, [2007] All ER (D) 341 (Mar), (2007) Times, 13 April. The conclusion of such an agreement is not contrary to Article 6 of the Convention.

A provision in the arbitration agreement that the decision of the arbitrator should be 'final, conclusive and binding on the parties' does not amount to a waiver of the right to appeal on a point of law: *Shell Egypt West Manzala GmbH v Dana Gas Egypt Ltd* [2009] EWHC 2097 (Comm), [2009] All ER (D) 82 (Aug).

III ARB [22.4]

Refusal of permission to appeal The Court of Appeal has no jurisdiction to grant permission for an appeal. The effect of sub-s (6) is to preclude the possibility of further appeal from the court without the court's granting leave in the circumstances covered by the sub-section: *Henry Boot Construction (UK) Ltd v Malmaison Hotel (Manchester) Ltd* [2000] 1 All ER 257, [2000] 3 WLR 1824, CA.

However, the Court of Appeal has a residual discretion to review a judge's grant or refusal of permission in the rare case where there was such a substantial defect in the fairness of the process as to invalidate the judge's decision: *AstraZeneca Insurance Co Ltd v CGU International Insurance plc* [2006] EWCA Civ 1340, [2006] All ER (D) 176 (Oct), (2006) Times, 3 November, a case on sub-s (8), in which the Court approved the reasoning in *North Range Shipping Ltd v Seatrans Shipping Corpn* [2002] EWCA Civ 405, [2002] 4 All ER 390, a case on sub-s (6). The residual jurisdiction to set aside may be exercised (a) where the High Court judge had never reached a decision at all; and (b) where the decision was reached through a process incompatible with the European Convention on Human Rights: *Philip Hanby Ltd v Clarke* [2013] EWCA Civ 647, [2013] NLJR 29. For a case where the Court held there to be no basis for exercising the residual discretion see *Bunge SA v Kyla Shipping Co Ltd, The Kyla* [2013] EWCA Civ 734, [2013] 3 All ER 1006, [2013] 2 Lloyd's Rep 463.

III ARB [22.4A]

Reasons for refusal of permission A failure to provide reasons for refusing to grant permission to appeal does not infringe Convention rights under Art 6: *Mousaka Inc v Golden Seagull Maritime Inc* [2001] 2 Lloyd's Rep 657, Steel J. The Court of Appeal has since decided, in *North Range Shipping Ltd v Seatrans Shipping Corpn* [2002] EWCA Civ 405, [2002] 4 All ER 390, that a judge should, at the very least, tell an unsuccessful applicant which of the threshold tests under s 69(3) it had failed.

The High Court should not grant permission to appeal to the Court of Appeal unless the grant or refusal of leave to appeal against the award calls for elucidation as to the manner of the application of the statutory criteria: *CMA CGM SA v Beteiligungs-KG* [2002] EWCA Civ 1878, [2003] 3 All ER 330.

III ARB [22.4B]

Court's approach where parties agree to a right of appeal In a case within sub-s (2)(a), where the parties have agreed that there should be a right of appeal, the court should read the award in a fair and reasonable way and should defer to the arbitrator's experience where he or she has drawn on it and, as regards the question of law, the court should examine the way that the arbitrator has stated the law and consider whether the correct application of the law would have led to a different conclusion: *Kershaw Mechanical Services Ltd v Kendrick Construction Ltd* [2006] EWHC 727 (TCC), [2006] 4 All ER 79.

Since the appeal has to be on a point of law, it may not be used to re-open issues of fact: the appeal is confined to the findings of fact made by the arbitrator and it is irrelevant whether the court considers those findings to be wrong: *Dolphin Tanker Srl v Westport Petroleum Inc* [2010] EWHC 2617 (Comm), [2010] NLJR 1532; *Guangzhou Dockyards Company v E N E Aegiali I* [2010] EWHC 2826 (Comm), [2010] NLJR 1568.

III ARB [22.5]

Service abroad Service of the appellant's notice abroad will be permitted if the award was made in England and Wales. This condition is treated as satisfied where the seat of the arbitration was in England and Wales: see ss 3 and 53 and **CPR 62.5**.

III ARB [22.6]

Convention rights The provisions of sub-s (6) do not offend Art 6 of the Convention: where the requirements of that article have been satisfied at first instance, the Convention does not require a right of appeal: *BLCT (13096) Ltd v J Sainsbury plc* [2003] EWCA Civ 884, [2004] 2 P & CR 3.

III ARB [23]

70. Challenge or appeal: supplementary provisions

(1) The following provisions apply to an application or appeal under sections 67, 68 or 69.

(2) An application or appeal may not be brought if the applicant or appellant has not first exhausted—

- (a) any available arbitral process of appeal or review, and
- (b) any available recourse under section 57 (correction of award or additional award).

(3) Any application or appeal must be brought within 28 days of the date of the award or, if there has been any arbitral process of appeal or review, of the date when the applicant or appellant was notified of the result of that process.

(4) If on an application or appeal it appears to the court that the award—

- (a) does not contain the tribunal's reasons, or
- (b) does not set out the tribunal's reasons in sufficient detail to enable the court properly to consider the application or appeal,

the court may order the tribunal to state the reasons for its award in sufficient detail for that purpose.

(5) Where the court makes an order under subsection (4), it may make such further order as it thinks fit with respect to any additional costs of the arbitration resulting from its order.

(6) The court may order the applicant or appellant to provide security for the costs of the application or appeal, and may direct that the application or appeal be dismissed if the order is not complied with.

The power to order security for costs shall not be exercised on the ground that the applicant or appellant is—

- (a) an individual ordinarily resident outside the United Kingdom, or
- (b) a corporation or association incorporated or formed under the law of a country outside the United Kingdom, or whose central management and control is exercised outside the United Kingdom.

(7) The court may order that any money payable under the award shall be brought into court or otherwise secured pending the determination of the application or appeal, and may direct that the application or appeal be dismissed if the order is not complied with.

(8) The court may grant leave to appeal subject to conditions to the same or similar effect as an order under subsection (6) or (7).

This does not affect the general discretion of the court to grant leave subject to conditions.

III ARB [23.1]

Recourse under section 57 Section 57(a) may be used by an arbitrator to clarify an ambiguity in an award or to provide reasons: *Al Hadha Trading Co v Tradigrain SA* [2002] 2 Lloyds Rep 512; and a failure to apply to the arbitrator for clarification will usually bring s 70(2) into play: *Torch Offshore LLC v Cable Shipping Inc* [2004] EWHC 787, [2004] 2 All ER (Comm) 365, Cooke J, QBD (Comm Ct). On the other hand, the failure to apply under sub-s (3) for the arbitrator to clarify or remove an ambiguity does not necessarily prevent a party from challenging an ambiguous part of an award of costs on the grounds of serious irregularity (s 68): *Gbangbola v Smith & Sheriff Ltd* [1998] 3 All ER 730.

III ARB [23.2]

Within 28 days The rules of court on reckoning, extending and abridging the time for appealing are applied by s 80(5). See **CPR 62.9** regarding applications for the 28-day period to be varied and the decision in *Kalmneft JSC v Glencore International AG* [2002] 1 All ER 76 regarding the factors to be taken into account.

III ARB [23.3]

Security for costs Subject to s 70(6), the court may order any applicant (including an applicant who has been granted permission to appeal) to provide security for costs of any arbitration agreement.

The conditions for granting an order for security for costs are set out at CPR 25.13, **CPR 25.13**. Where the court has ordered security for costs it has a residual discretion to vary the order where there has been a material change of circumstances: *Kristjansson v R Verney & Co Ltd* (CA Civ Div Transcript No 1154/1998). The fact that the parties have agreed on the giving of security in a certain sum does not by itself exclude the court's power to vary on a material change of circumstances: *Republic of Kazakhstan v Istil Group Inc* (2005) Times, 17 November, CA. The Court went further, in the latter case. and held that even where the parties had agreed that the amount of security should not be variable the court might still exercise its discretion to vary, but only in wholly exceptional circumstances. The jurisdiction conferred by s 726 of the Companies Act 1985 is considered at **III COM [46]**.

III ARB [24]

71. Challenge or appeal: effect of order of Court

(1) The following provisions have effect where the court makes an order under sections 67, 68 or 69 with respect to an award.

(2) Where the award is varied, the variation has effect as part of the tribunal's award.

(3) Where the award is remitted to the tribunal, in whole or in part, for reconsideration, the tribunal shall make a fresh award in respect of the matters remitted within three months of the date of the order for remission or such longer or shorter period as the court may direct.

(4) Where the award is set aside or declared to be of no effect, in whole or in part, the court may also order that any provision that an award is a condition precedent to the bringing of legal proceedings in respect of a matter to which the arbitration agreement applies, is of no effect as regards the subject matter of the award or, as the case may be, the relevant part of the award.

III ARB [24.1]

Arbitrator's powers where award remitted in part In a case where an award was remitted to the arbitrator for him to put it in a form in which it would be capable of enforcement it was held that this did not allow the arbitrator to reconsider the merits. The part not remitted continued valid: *Carter (t/a Michael Carter Partnership) v Harold Simpson Associates (Architects) Ltd* [2004] UKPC 29, [2004] 2 Lloyd's Rep 512, (2004) Times, 25 June.

III ARB [25]

72. Saving for rights of person who takes no part in proceedings

(1) A person alleged to be a party to arbitral proceedings but who takes no part in the proceedings may question—

(a) whether there is a valid arbitration agreement,

(b) whether the tribunal is properly constituted, or

(c) what matters have been submitted to arbitration in accordance with the arbitration agreement,

by proceedings in the court for a declaration or injunction or other appropriate relief.

(2) He also has the same right as a party to the arbitral proceedings to challenge an award—

(a) by an application under section 67 on the ground of lack of substantive jurisdiction in relation to him, or

(b) by an application under section 68 on the ground of serious irregularity (within the meaning of that section) affecting him;

and section 70 (2) (duty to exhaust arbitral procedures) does not apply in his case.

III ARB [25.1]

A person alleged to be a party For the purposes of s 72(1), a question may be raised for the court's decision by someone who has been joined as a party but whose status as a party has not been determined: *Law Debenture Trust Corpn plc v Elektrim Finance BV* [2005] EWHC 1412 (Ch), [2005] 2 All ER 476, (2005) Times, 4 August, Mann J.

III ARB [25.2]

Challenging the validity of the agreement Where a person who is alleged to be a party to the arbitration contends that the agreement was obtained by bribery and subsequently rescinded on this ground, the arbitrator has jurisdiction to determine whether the agreement is valid as one of the issues arising out of an application for a stay and this is a more appropriate course than challenging the validity by court proceedings under s 72(1): *Fiona Trust and Holding Corporation v Privalov* [2007] EWCA Civ 20, [2007] All ER (D) 169 (Jan), (2007) Times, 29 January, upheld on further appeal to the House of Lords (2007) Times, 25 October, HL.

III ARB [25.3]

Person who takes no part in proceedings The words 'takes no part in the proceedings' are not limited to proceedings relating to the jurisdiction of the arbitrator but include participation in the substantive proceedings: *Alfred C Toepfer International GmbH v Broda Agro Trade (Cyprus) Ltd* [2010] EWCA Civ 1100, 132 ConLR 1, [2010] NLJR 1458.

III ARB [26]

73. Loss of right to object

(1) If a party to arbitral proceedings takes part, or continues to take part, in the proceedings without making, either forthwith or within such time as is allowed by the arbitration agreement or the tribunal or by any provision of this Part, any objection—

(a) that the tribunal lacks substantive jurisdiction,

(b) that the proceedings have been improperly conducted,

(c) that there has been a failure to comply with the arbitration agreement or with any provision of this Part, or

(d) that there has been any other irregularity affecting the tribunal or the proceedings,

he may not raise that objection later, before the tribunal or the court, unless he shows that, at the time he took part or continued to take part in the proceedings, he did not know and could not with reasonable diligence have discovered the grounds for the objection.

(2) Where the arbitral tribunal rules that it has substantive jurisdiction and a party to arbitral proceedings who could have questioned that ruling—

(a) by any available arbitral process of appeal or review, or

(b) by challenging the award,

does not do so, or does not do so within the time allowed by the arbitration agreement or any provision of this Part, he may not object later to the tribunal's substantive jurisdiction on any ground which was the subject of that ruling.

III ARB [26.1]

Refusal of extension of time to appeal Where the right to object has been lost an application to challenge on the ground of serious irregularity will be rejected. See the cases noted at **III ARB [21.6]**.

III ARB [26.2]

Forthwith Objections which are required to be raised 'forthwith' must be raised as soon as reasonably possible which may mean raising an objection immediately after a procedural ruling: *O'Donoghue v Enterprise Inns plc* [2008] EWHC 2273 (Ch), [2008] All ER (D) 43 (Oct).

III ARB [26.3]

Continuing to take part Objections to jurisdiction must be taken as soon as possible; continuing to take part may mean the opportunity is lost, as happened in *Exportadora de Las LA de CV v Corretaje Maritimo Sud-Americano Inc* [2018] EWHC 224 (Comm), [2018] All ER (D) 93 (Feb).

III ARB [27]

77. Powers of court in relation to service of documents

(1) This section applies where service of a document on a person in the manner agreed by the parties, or in accordance with provisions of section 76 having effect in default of agreement, is not reasonably practicable.

(2) Unless otherwise agreed by the parties, the court may make such order as it thinks fit—

(a) for service in such manner as the court may direct, or

(b) dispensing with service of the document.

(3) Any party to the arbitration agreement may apply for an order, but only after exhausting any available arbitral process for resolving the matter.

(4) The leave of the court is required for any appeal from a decision of the court under this section.

III ARB [27.1]

Service in accordance with provision of section 76 Section 76 enables the parties to an arbitration agreement to provide, by agreement, for the manner of service of documents in arbitration proceedings. However, it is made clear in s 76(5) that service for the purposes of legal proceedings (defined in s 82(1) as "civil proceedings in the High Court or a county court") is outside the scope of s 76.

Section 76(3) provides that 'A notice or other document may be served by any effective means' and email has held to be an effective means, at least where an appropriate email address has been published by the person to be served: *Bernuth Lines Ltd v High Seas Shipping Ltd* [2005] EWHC 3020 (Comm), [2006] 1 All ER (Comm) 359. Service on a company by email sent to a generic company address would be within section 76 but an email is not effective unless the individual has actual, or ostensible, authority to accept it: *Glencore Agriculture BV v Conqueror Holdings Ltd* [2017] EWHC 2893 (Comm), Popplewell J.

III ARB [27.2]

The court As to the allocation of jurisdiction between High Court and county court, see para **III ARB [1]**.

III ARB [27.3]

Discretion to make orders In addition to the power under s 77(2) to order substituted service or to dispense with service, the court has power under s 79(1) to extend time for taking steps in the arbitral proceedings, once started.

III ARB [28]

79. Power of court to extend time limits relating to arbitral proceedings

(1) Unless the parties otherwise agree, the court may by order extend any time limit agreed by them in relation to any matter relating to the arbitral proceedings or specified in any provision of this Part having effect in default of such agreement.

This section does not apply to a time limit to which section 12 applies (power of court to extend time for beginning arbitral proceedings, &c).

(2) An application for an order may be made—

(a) by any party to the arbitral proceedings (upon notice to the other parties and to the tribunal), or

(b) by the arbitral tribunal (upon notice to the parties).

(3) The court shall not exercise its power to extend a time limit unless it is satisfied—

(a) that any available recourse to the tribunal, or to any arbitral or other institution or person vested by the parties with power in that regard, has first been exhausted, and

(b) that a substantial injustice would otherwise be done.

(4) The court's power under this section may be exercised whether or not the time has already expired.

(5) An order under this section may be made on such terms as the court thinks fit.

(6) The leave of the court is required for any appeal from a decision of the court under this section.

III ARB [28.1]

Procedure for applying to the court See the notes at **III ARB [1]** for details of the courts with power to entertain applications under the Arbitration Act 1996 and the notes at **III ARB [2]** and **III ARB [3]** for a summary of the procedure for applying.

III ARB [28.2]

Power to extend time There is no power under this section to extend time where a timetable has already been agreed between the parties: *Minermet SpA Milan v Luckyfield Shipping Corpn SA* [2004] EWHC 729 (Comm), [2004] 2 Lloyd's Rep 348, Cooke J, QBD (Comm Ct).

Also the power to extend time may not be exercised unless a substantial injustice would otherwise be done, as provided in sub-s (3)(b); and it may be refused even so, having regard to other considerations such as the length and nature of any delay and prejudice to the respondent. But where all these considerations support an extension of time it may be allowed with retrospective effect: *Gold Coast Ltd v Naval Gijon SA* [2006] EWHC 1044 (Comm), [2006] 2 Lloyd's Rep 400, [2006] All ER (D) 209 (May) in which the court extended time for an application under s 57 to correct an error which the arbitrator admitted had been made.

III ARB [28.3]

Extension of time for appeal The court may extend the 28–day time limit for appealing which is set by s 70(3): see **CPR 62.9**, as applied by s 80(5): *S v A* [2016] EWHC 846 (Comm), [2016] 1 Lloyd's Rep 604, [2016] All ER (D) 180 (Apr).

GENERAL NOTES ON SECTIONS 89–92 (CONSUMER AND SMALL CLAIMS ARBITRATIONS)

III ARB [29]

Consumer arbitration agreements Sections 89 to 92 replace the protection from unfair arbitration clauses provided by the Consumer Arbitration Agreements Act 1988. New protection is given by extending the application of the Unfair Terms in Consumer Contracts Regulations 1994, SI 1994/3159 to cover agreements to submit to arbitration (s 89) and by making it clear that the protection applies where the consumer is a legal person as they apply where the consumer is a natural person: s 90. Such agreements are classified by s 91 as unfair for the purposes of the regulations so far as they relate to claims for pecuniary remedies which do not exceed the amount specified by order. The Unfair Arbitration Agreements (Specified Amount) Order 1999, SI 1999/2167, has the specified amount of £5,000.

In the case of an arbitration clause in an agreement with a consumer whose claim exceeds the specified sum, the clause may be struck down by application of the Unfair Terms in Consumer Contracts Regulations 1999, at para **III CON [106]**. This was the outcome in *Zealander v Laing Homes Ltd* (2000) 2 TCLR 724. The same conclusion was reached in *Mylcrist Builders v Mrs Buck* [2008] EWHC 2172 (TCC), applying the principles in *Director General of Fair Trading v First National Bank plc* [2002] 1 AC 481 and *Bryan & Langley v Martin Boston* [2005] BLR 508.

III ARB [30]

Small claims arbitrations Small claims arbitrations have their own statutory base in the County Courts Act 1984 s 64: see para **II CCA [43]**. They are outside the scope of the 1996 Act and are excluded by s 92 from the provisions relating to statutory arbitrations.

GENERAL NOTES ON SECTIONS 99–104 (NEW YORK CONVENTION AWARDS)

III ARB [31]

New York Convention award This means an award made in the territory of a state, other than the United Kingdom, which is a party to the New York Convention on the Recognition and Enforcement of Foreign Arbitral Awards adopted by the United Nations Conference on International Commercial Arbitration on 10 June 1958: s 100. Foreign awards which are not also New York Convention awards continue to be enforceable according to Part II of the Arbitration Act 1950.

A judge enforcing an award made in a New York Convention arbitration is entitled to order part enforcement, provided that the part to be enforced can be ascertained from the face of the award and judgment can be given in the same terms as those of the award: *IPCO (Nigeria) Ltd v Nigerian National Petroleum Corporation* [2008] EWCA Civ 1157, (2008) Times, 11 November, [2008] All ER (D) 197 (Oct), [2009] 1 Lloyd's Rep 89.

In subsequent proceedings the Court of Appeal adjourned the claimant's application to enforce the Nigerian award, pending a determination under s 103(3) as to whether there were public policy reasons for not enforcing it: *IPCO (Nigeria) Ltd v Nigerian National Petroleum Co* [2015] EWCA Civ 1144, [2015] All ER (D) 103 (Nov), [2009] 1 Lloyd's Rep 89.

III ARB [32]

The court For the purposes of enforcement, application for leave may be made to the High Court or to any county court: High Court and County Courts (Allocation of Arbitration Proceedings) Order 1996, SI 1996/3215, art 4. See **CPR 62.20** and **CPR 62.21** for the registration of foreign awards in the High Court. Grounds for refusing enforcement are set out in s 103(2), including (a) that a party was under an incapacity (b) that the arbitration agreement was not valid and (c) that the person against whom the award was made was unable to present his, or her, case. Grounds (a) and (c) were considered, and ground (c) was applied, in *Kanoria v Guinness* [2006] EWCA Civ 222, (2006) Times, 28 February. Note also the ruling in *Eco Swiss China Time Ltd v Benetton International NV* [1999] 2 All ER (Comm) 44, ECJ that the enforcement of an award which is contrary to art 81 (art 85) of the EC Treaty is contrary to public policy for the purposes of the New York Convention and should be annulled on this ground. Where a State agrees to submit a dispute to arbitration it renders itself amenable to such enforcement processes as may be necessary to render the arbitration effective: s 9 of the State Immunity Act 1978, as applied in *Svenska Petroleum Exploration AB v Government of the Republic of Lithuania (No 2)* (2006) Times, 17 November, CA.

See **III ARB [19.3]** for further notes on the enforcement of New York Convention awards.

COMPANIES

TABLE OF CONTENTS

COMPANY DIRECTORS DISQUALIFICATION ACT 1986

(c 46)

COMPANIES

GENERAL NOTES ON COMPANY DIRECTORS DISQUALIFICATION ACT 1986

III COM [1]–III COM [48]

Jurisdction As regards the Company Directors Disqualification Act 1986, the jurisdiction of the county courts with bankruptcy jurisdiction is concurrent with that of the High Court, but subject to the same restrictions as in the case of applications and orders under the Companies Act 2006.

For the purposes of s 6, however, the disqualification of a director of a company which is being, or has been, wound up by the court is provided by s 6(3)(a) to be the exclusive jurisdiction of that court. Further, the variation under s 8A of an undertaking given under s 9B can be heard only by the High Court. Proceedings in one county court may not be transferred to another: *Secretary of State for Trade and Industry v Shakespeare* [2005] 2 BCLC 471, [2005] BCC 891, District Judge Mithani. The jurisdiction conferred by s 6(3)(c) exists even where automatic dissolution has occurred by operation of the Insolvency Act 1986, Sch B1, para 84(6): *Secretary of State for Trade and Industry v Arnold* [2007] EWHC 1933 (Ch), [2008] 1 BCLC 581, [2008] BCC 119.

The jurisdiction of the courts has been enlarged (a) by the Insolvency Act 2000 which has put disqualification undertakings on a statutory footing and provided for their variation and (b) by the Enterprise Act 2002, s 204 which has introduced competition disqualifications, undertakings and investigations. Also the application of the Act to companies and their directors and officers has been extended by ss 22A, 22B and 22C to building societies, incorporated friendly societies and NHS foundation trusts.

Multiple amendments were made by the Small Business, Enterprise and Employment Act 2015 and they are incorporated in the text below. They were all brought into effect on 1 October 2015 by the Commencement No 2 Order, SI 2015/1689.

III COM [48A]

Statutory notice of intent A statutory notice of intent to seek disqualification is required by s 16. It should name the lead company but need not name others: *Re Surrey Leisure Ltd* [1999] 1 BCLC 731. The applicant for a disqualification order is required, by s 16(1), to give the intended recipient not less than 10 days' notice and a failure to do so may, when taken with other factors, render the proceedings a nullity: *Secretary of State for Trade and Industry v Swan* [2003] EWHC 1780 (Ch), [2003] All ER (D) 372 (Jul), (2003) Times, 18 August.

III COM [48B]

Other remedies for wrongdoing by directors Where a company has been the victim of wrongdoing by its directors, or of which its directors had notice, then the wrongdoing or knowledge cannot be attributed to the company as a defence to a claim brought against the directors by the liquidator of the company and its creditors: *Bilta (UK) Ltd (in liquidation) v Nazir (No 2)* [2015] UKSC 23, [2015] 2 All ER 1083, [2015] 2 WLR 1168. It was also held in that case that the liquidator's powers under section 213 of the Insolvency Act 1986 had worldwide effect and could be exercised against company defendants registered abroad.

III COM [49]

Procedure Proceedings for a disqualification order must be commenced by the issue of a claim form, using the CPR Pt 8 procedure but subject to the modifications provided in the Practice Direction: Directors Disqualification Proceedings at **III COM [56]** and certain provisions of the Insolvent Companies (Disqualification of Unfit Directors) Proceedings Rules 1987, SI 1987/2023. Two model claim forms, numbered N500 (for obtaining a disqualification order) and N501 (for obtaining a variation of an undertaking) are annexed to the Practice Direction and can be found at **III COM [69]** and **III COM [72]**. Every claim form and all affidavits, notices and other documents in proceedings under the Act must be entitled in the matter of the company in question and in the matter of the Act. All disqualification proceedings are allocated to the multi-track. Proceedings for permission to act as director although disqualified should be started by using Form N208 under CPR Pt 8 or by application notice (Pt 23, Form N244) in the disqualification proceedings. These and other requirements are set out in the Practice Direction at **III COM [56]**. Note that disqualification proceedings have their own versions of the Part 8 Claim Form, the Acknowledgment of Service and the Listing Questionnaire.

III COM [50]

Practice The Practice Direction on Directors Disqualification Proceedings is to be found at **III COM [56]**. It has been revised to take account of the expansion of the courts' jurisdiction by the Insolvency Act 2000 and the Enterprise Act 2002: it covers the various kinds of proceedings and applications in some detail, including a form of summary procedure.

It is in the public interest that proceedings should be shortened by agreement: see *Re Carecraft Construction Co Ltd* [1993] 4 All ER 499, [1994] 1 WLR 172 and the Vice-Chancellor's Practice Note [1996] 1 All ER 445, sub nom Practice Direction [1996] 1 WLR 170. But that is not to say that the Secretary of State is bound to agree to directors' undertakings instead of seeking orders for disqualification: *Re Blackspur Group plc* [1998] 1 WLR 422, CA. Also the Secretary of State may properly make his acceptance of an undertaking conditional on the director's delivering a statement as to the factual basis for admitting unfitness: *Re Blackspur Group plc (No 3)* [2002] 2 BCLC 263, upheld on appeal: [2001] EWCA Civ 1595, [2002] 2 BCLC 263.

As to double jeopardy, the Court of Appeal rejected the argument, in *Re Barings plc (No 2) Secretary of State for Trade and Industry v Baker (No 2)* [1999] 1 All ER 311, CA, that the disqualification proceedings put the director in double jeopardy because he had already been taken through disciplinary proceedings before the Securities and Futures Authority. The Court adopted the test that double jeopardy should be accepted as a ground for a stay only where allowing the second proceedings to continue would risk bringing the administration of justice into disrepute among right thinking people, having a proper understanding of the characteristics of the two sets of proceedings. See also *Re Barings plc (No 2)* [1999] 1 All ER 311, Ch D and, on appeal at p 333, CA. Note also *Re Dennis Hilton Ltd* [2001] 2 BCLC 302, (2001) Times, 4 July, where it was decided that the Secretary of State may start disqualification proceedings after a conviction by a criminal court in which disqualification could have been ordered but was not. Indeed, the ordering of a disqualification under s 2 is not a bar to proceedings under s 6 which are not an abuse of process: *Re Cedarwood Productions Ltd* (2001) Times, 12 July, CA. On the other hand, where the Secretary of State has agreed the statement of facts and the evidence the court should not take account of other evidence in fixing the disqualification period: *Re SIG Security Services Ltd* under the name of *Official Receiver v Bond* [1998] BCC 978. For the same reason the court should not make findings of misconduct where sufficient justification for the conduct in question has been advanced by the director in an affidavit which has not been contradicted: *Re Hopes (Heathrow) Ltd* [2001] 1 BCLC 575. Where the affirmation of the chief examiner includes an overstatement and unfair assessment of the evidence this may provide ground for striking out the whole proceedings or the offending parts of the affirmation. But if the proceedings are not struck out and much of the affirmation is not open to criticism it should not be struck out in its entirety: *Secretary of State for Trade and Industry v Swan* [2003] EWHC 1780 (Ch), [2003] All ER (D) 372 (Jul), (2003) Times, 18 August.

On the other hand, if proceedings are delayed for an unreasonable length of time they may be struck out for breach of the director's Convention right to a fair trial, under Article 6: *Eastaway v United Kingdom (74976/01)* (2005) 40 EHRR 17, ECtHR. The Secretary of State has to disclose materials in his possession but not those that could be in his possession. He has no absolute obligation to obtain documents or interview 3rd parties: *Re Stakefield Ltd, Secretary of State for Business Enterprise & Regulatory Reform v Doffman* [2010] EWHC 2518 (Ch).

III COM [50A]

Undertaking out of court Sections 5 to 8 of the Insolvency Act 2000 provide that disqualification for a period of between 2 and 15 years may be achieved by the Secretary of State's acceptance of an undertaking in appropriate terms, whether or not there have been disqualification proceedings in court. The amendments are included in the statutory text printed below as ss 1A, 7, 8, 8A, 9 and 17.

III COM [51]

Self-incrimination The court may receive evidence of self-incriminating answers given when interviewed under s 235 of the Insolvency Act 1986: See *Re Westminster Property Management Ltd* [2000] 2 BCLC 396, Sir Richard Scott V-C. The use of compulsorily obtained statements has been held not to be unfair, for the purposes of Art 6 of the Convention on Human Rights, given the civil nature of the proceedings: *DC, HC and AD v United Kingdom* [2000] BCC 710, ECHR, *WGS and MSLS v United Kingdom* [2000] BCC 719, ECHR.

The fact that civil proceedings will require the defendant director to provide evidence which may be useful in a prosecution of him is not by itself sufficient ground for a stay. Countervailing considerations are (a) that the director's civil evidence is excluded by s 20(2) from admission in the criminal proceedings and (b) that the trial judge has further power to exclude evidence under s 78 of the Police and Criminal Evidence Act 1984: *Secretary of State for Trade and Industry v Crane* [2001] 2 BCLC 222.

III COM [51A]

Findings of fact in earlier proceedings A respondent is not necessarily bound by findings made against him in proceedings between him and someone other than the Secretary of State: *Secretary of State for Trade and Industry v Bairstow* [2003] EWCA Civ 321, [2004] Ch 1, [2004] 4 All ER 325.

Although the strict rules on hearsay evidence, opinion evidence and the rule in *Hollington v F Hewthorn & Co Ltd* [1943] KB 587, [1943] 2 All ER 35, CA do not apply, findings of fact made by other institutions, such as the Financial Ombudsman Services, which are included in documents not produced under the statutory scheme are inadmissible and should be ignored by the trial judge: *Secretary of State for Business Enterprise and Regulatory Reform v Aaron* [2008] EWCA Civ 1146, [2009] 1 BCLC 55, (2008) Times, 11 November.

III COM [52]

Precedents Precedents are provided in **BCCP R[601]** and **BCCP R[602]** for a director's case opposing disqualification and for a disqualified director's application for permission to act as a director.

III COM [53]

1. Disqualification orders: general

(1) In the circumstances specified below in this Act a court may, and under sections 6 and 9A shall, make against a person a disqualification order, that is to say an order that for a period specified in the order—

(a) he shall not be a director of a company, act as receiver of a company's property or in any way, whether directly or indirectly, be concerned or take part in the promotion, formation or management of a company unless (in each case) he has the leave of the court, and

(b) he shall not act as an insolvency practitioner.

(2) In each section of this Act which gives to a court power or, as the case may be, imposes on it the duty to make a disqualification order there is specified the maximum (and, in sections 6 and 8ZA, the minimum) period of disqualification which may or (as the case may be) must be imposed by means of the order and, unless the court otherwise orders, the period of disqualification so imposed shall begin at the end of the period of 21 days beginning with the date of the order.

(3) Where a disqualification order is made against a person who is already subject to such an order or to a disqualification undertaking, the periods specified in those orders or, as the case may be, in the order and the undertaking shall run concurrently.

(4) A disqualification order may be made on grounds which are or include matters other than criminal convictions, notwithstanding that the person in respect of whom it is to be made may be criminally liable in respect of those matters.

III COM [53.1]

The making of disqualification orders Disqualification orders are mandatory in two situations (1) where the director of an insolvent company is unfit to be a director (s 6) and (2) where a company, or other organisation, has committed a breach of competition law for which the director is responsible (s 9A). The two relevant sections are set out at **III COM [54]** and **III COM [54E]**, respectively. Orders may also be made, as a matter of discretion, under s 2 (conviction of indictable offences), s 3 (persistent breaches of companies legislation), s 4 (fraud in winding up), s 5 (summary conviction) and under s 17, at **III COM [54A]** or s 8 at **III COM [54B]**. Applications for disqualification orders must comply with the Practice Direction at **III COM [56]** including the procedural provisions at **III COM [58]**. Note that the procedural directions are modified, by Part 6 of the Practice Direction at **III COM [64]**, in their application to claim forms issued other than in the Royal Courts of Justice.

In *Secretary of State for Business Innovation and Skills v Weston* [2014] EWHC 2933 (Ch), [2014] All ER (D) 43 Sept, ChD the Court held that there was an abuse of process and refused an application to disqualify a director under s 2 when a similar application on identical issues had previously been unsuccessful in criminal proceedings.

III COM [53.2]

Setting aside disqualification orders Any disqualification order made in the absence of the defendant may be set aside or varied: see para 14 of the Practice Direction at **III COM [60]**. As regards procedure see Part 5 of the Practice Direction at **III COM [63]**.

III COM [53.3]

Appeals Provisions regarding appeals are set out at para 35 of the Practice Direction at **III COM [67]**.

III COM [53.4]

The court's discretion, under s 1(1)(a) to give permission to act as a director A director may apply under s 1(1) for permission to continue as a director, as an alternative to applying under s 17. In such a case the application should be made early enough to be considered by the judge dealing with disqualification under s 6 and should be supported by clear evidence of the precise role which the director seeks permission to exercise: *Secretary of State for Trade and Industry v Collins* [2000] 2 BCLC 223, CA. Where the application is part and parcel of winding-up proceedings in a county court the application should be made in that court: *Re Britannia Homes Centres Ltd* [2001] 2 BCLC 63.

The general discretion requires the balancing of factors that include (i) the protection of the public (ii) deterrence and (iii) the need and legitimate interest of the claimant; and there is no rule against exercising the discretion in favour of a director who has acted dishonestly: *Re a Company 8097 of 2011* [2012] NLJR 912.

III COM [53.5]

Particulars of orders to be furnished to the Secretary of State Where a disqualification or grant of leave is made by the High Court or a county court, the Court Manager is required to furnish particulars of it to the Secretary of State in the form specified by regulations 6 and 7 of the Companies (Disqualification Orders) Regulations 2009, SI 2009/2471.

III COM [53A]

1A. Disqualification undertakings: general

(1) In the circumstances specified in sections 5A, 7, 8, 8ZC and 8ZE the Secretary of State may accept a disqualification undertaking, that is to say an undertaking by any person that, for a period specified in the undertaking, the person—

(a) will not be a director of a company, act as receiver of a company's property or in any way, whether directly or indirectly, be concerned or take part in the promotion, formation or management of a company unless (in each case) he has the leave of a court, and

(b) will not act as an insolvency practitioner.

(2) The maximum period which may be specified in a disqualification undertaking is 15 years; and the minimum period which may be specified in a disqualification undertaking under section 7 or 8ZC is two years.

(3) Where a disqualification undertaking by a person who is already subject to such an undertaking or to a disqualification order is accepted, the periods specified in those undertakings or (as the case may be) the undertaking and the order shall run concurrently.

(4) In determining whether to accept a disqualification undertaking by any person, the Secretary of State may take account of matters other than criminal convictions, notwithstanding that the person may be criminally liable in respect of those matters.

III COM [53A.1]

Secretary of State may accept undertakings This section was inserted by the Insolvency Act 2000 and is to be read with s 8A and the linked provisions in ss 7, 8, 9 and 17. They provide a statutory base for the pre-existing practice noted at **III COM [50]**. For the general rule on costs see Part 7 of the Practice Direction at **III COM [65]**. A director whose undertaking has been accepted may apply for permission to act as director in accordance with Part 4 of the Practice Direction at **III COM [62]**.

III COM [53B]

5A. Disqualification for certain convictions abroad

(1) If it appears to the Secretary of State that it is expedient in the public interest that a disqualification order under this section should be made against a person, the Secretary of State may apply to the court for such an order.

(2) The court may, on an application under subsection (1), make a disqualification order against a person who has been convicted of a relevant foreign offence.

(3) A "relevant foreign offence" is an offence committed outside Great Britain—

- (a) in connection with—
  - (i) the promotion, formation, management, liquidation or striking off of a company (or any similar procedure),
  - (ii) the receivership of a company's property (or any similar procedure), or
  - (iii) a person being an administrative receiver of a company (or holding a similar position), and
- (b) which corresponds to an indictable offence under the law of England and Wales or (as the case may be) an indictable offence under the law of Scotland.

(4) Where it appears to the Secretary of State that, in the case of a person who has offered to give a disqualification undertaking—

- (a) the person has been convicted of a relevant foreign offence, and
- (b) it is expedient in the public interest that the Secretary of State should accept the undertaking (instead of applying, or proceeding with an application, for a disqualification order),

the Secretary of State may accept the undertaking.

(5) In this section—

"company" includes an overseas company;

"the court" means the High Court or, in Scotland, the Court of Session.

(6) The maximum period of disqualification under an order under this section is 15 years.

III COM [54]

6. Duty of court to disqualify unfit directors of insolvent companies

(1) The court shall make a disqualification order against a person in any case where, on an application under this section, it is satisfied—

- (a) that he is or has been a director of a company which has at any time become insolvent (whether while he was a director or subsequently), and
- (b) that his conduct as a director of that company (either taken alone or taken together with his conduct as a director of one or more other companies or overseas companies) makes him unfit to be concerned in the management of a company.

(1A) In this section references to a person's conduct as a director of any company or overseas company include, where that company or overseas company has become insolvent, references to that person's conduct in relation to any matter connected with or arising out of the insolvency.

(2) For the purposes of this section, a company becomes insolvent if—

- (a) the company goes into liquidation at a time when its assets are insufficient for the payment of its debts and other liabilities and the expenses of the winding up,
- (b) the company enters administration, or
- (c) an administrative receiver of the company is appointed;

(2A) For the purposes of this section, an overseas company becomes insolvent if the company enters into insolvency proceedings of any description (including interim proceedings) in any jurisdiction.

(3) In this section and section 7(2), "the court" means—

(a) where the company in question is being or has been wound up by the court, that court,

(b) where the company in question is being or has been wound up voluntarily, any court which has or (as the case may be) had jurisdiction to wind it up,

(c) where neither paragraph (a) nor (b) applies but an administrator or administrative receiver has at any time been appointed in respect of the company in question, any court which has jurisdiction to wind it up.

(3A) Sections 117 and 120 of the Insolvency Act 1986 (jurisdiction) shall apply for the purposes of subsection (3) as if the references in the definitions of "registered office" to the presentation of the petition for winding up were references—

(a) in a case within paragraph (b) of that subsection, to the passing of the resolution for voluntary winding up,

(b) in a case within paragraph (c) of that subsection, to the appointment of the administrator or (as the case may be) administrative receiver.

(3B) Nothing in subsection (3) invalidates any proceedings by reason of their being taken in the wrong court; and proceedings—

(a) for or in connection with a disqualification order under this section, or

(b) in connection with a disqualification undertaking accepted under section 7,

may be retained in the court in which the proceedings were commenced, although it may not be the court in which they ought to have been commenced.

(3C) In this section and section 7, "director" includes a shadow director.

(4) Under this section the minimum period of disqualification is 2 years, and the maximum period is 15 years.

III COM [54.1]

Jurisdiction, scope and duration of disqualification Section 6(3)(c) confers jurisdiction to commence disqualification proceedings even where automatic dissolution had occurred by operation of the Insolvency Act 1986 Sch.B1 para.84(6): *Secretary of State for Trade & Industry v Arnold* [2007] EWHC 1933 (Ch), [2008] BCLC 581. Wherever disqualification is ordered it should normally be expressed as precluding the individual from being a director, liquidator, administrator, receiver or manager of a company's property or, in any way, taking part in the promotion, formation or management of a company. It should be expressed as applying to all companies and may not be limited to public companies: *R v Ward (Michael Granger)* [2001] EWCA Crim 1648, (2001) Times, 10 August. However, the court may grant leave, under the Company Directors Disqualification Act 1996 s 17, for the individual to be a director (liquidator or manager) of a particular company during the disqualification period or to be a receiver or manager of its property or to do other acts for which he would otherwise be disqualified. The court may make the grant of leave conditional on the director's giving specific undertakings which safeguard the public interest: *Re Gibson Davies Ltd* [1995] BCC 11. As to the period of disqualification, the court's practice is to consider the cases within three brackets, 2-5 years, 5-10 years and 10-15 years, according to the seriousness of the misconduct: *Re Grayan Building Services Ltd* [1995] Ch 241, [1995] 1 BCLC 276.

III COM [54.2]

Unfitness A director is not necessarily unfit because he has been imprudent: *Re Bath Glass Ltd* [1988] BCLC 329. Whilst proof of dishonesty is not essential and a finding of breach of duty, contractual, tortious, statutory or equitable, is not necessary, the court needs to be very careful before finding a director to be unfit without either: *Re Dawson Print Group Ltd* [1987] BCLC 601, 3 BCC 322; *Re Barings plc (No 5)* [2000] 1 BCLC 523; *Secretary of State for Trade and Industry v Goldberg* (2003) Times, 2 December. A clear breach of commercial morality, on the other hand, points strongly to unfitness: *Re Keypak Homecare Ltd (No 2)* [1990] BCLC 440.

A director's knowledge that the company has become insolvent does not by itself make a director unfit. He, or she, must also know that there is no reasonable prospect of meeting creditors' claims: *Secretary of State for Trade and Industry v Creegan* [2001] EWCA Civ 1742, [2002] 1 BCLC 99.

In determining the issue of unfitness the court is required by s 9 to have regard in particular to the matters mentioned in Part I of Sch 1 to the Act, at **III COM [55A]**, and also, where the company has become insolvent, to the matters mentioned in Part II of that Schedule.

III COM [54.2A]

Company registered in Scotland or Northern Ireland Proceedings to disqualify a director of a company registered in Scotland should be brought in Scotland. However, where proceedings are brought to disqualify a director of a company registered in England and Wales, the court may, in accordance with s 6(1)(b) take into account also the director's conduct as a director of a Scottish company: *Secretary of State for Trade and Industry v Forsythe* [2000] 2 BCLC 249.

As regards persons subject to a disqualification order or undertaking under Northern Ireland legislation, sections 12A and 12B now prevent that person from acting as a director or receiver of a company, or as an insolvency practitioner, without the leave of the High Court of Northern Ireland.

III COM [54.3]

Disqualification of companies Companies may be disqualified from acting as directors under this section and the *Carecraft* procedure (see **III COM [50]**) may be applied: *Official Receiver v Brady* [1999] BCC 258, Jacob J.

III COM [54.4]

Singular includes the plural Section 6 does not limit the number of companies which may be nominated in a single set of proceedings: *Re Surrey Leisure Ltd* [1999] 2 BCLC 457, CA.

III COM [54.5]

Breaches of the Act to be taken into account Paragraph 10 of Sch 1 specifies sections of the Act, breach of which should be taken into account on a disqualification application. But the list is not exhaustive. The breach of other sections, such as s 216, may also be taken into account: see *Re Migration Services International Ltd* [2000] 1 BCLC 666.

The conduct of a director in the witness box may be "conduct as a director . . . in relation to any matter connected with or arising out of the insolvency" for the purposes of s 6(2); it may therefore provide an additional ground of unfitness, so long as the charge is dealt with in a procedurally fair manner: *Secretary of State for Trade and Industry v Reynard* [2002] EWCA Civ 497, [2002] 2 BCLC 625, (2002) Times, 8 May.

III COM [54.6]

Shadow directors Shadow directors are brought within the section by sub-section (3). A shadow director is defined, by s 22(5) as "a person in accordance with whose directions or instructions the directors of the company are accustomed to act (but so that a person is not deemed a shadow director by reason only that the directors act on advice given by him in a professional capacity)". The purpose of the definition has been held to be to identify those, other than professional advisers, with real influence over the corporate affairs of the company, but not necessarily the whole field: *Secretary of State for Trade and Industry v Deverell* [2001] Ch 340, [2000] 2 All ER 365, CA. It was also held in that case that "directions or instructions" might take the form of non-professional advice and that the giving of "directions" might be proved by evidence of communications and their consequences, without necessarily establishing that the appointed directors assumed a subservient role.

III COM [54.7]

De facto directors An individual who has not been appointed a director may come within the scope of the legislation by reason of control and influence exerted over the duly appointed directors and this applies where the individual is a director of a corporate director of the company. But the individual does not become a de facto director unless he has assumed the status and functions of the appointed director: *Secretary of State for Trade and Industry v Hall* [2006] EWHC 1995 (Ch), (2006) Times, 28 July, Ch D, Evans-Lombe J.

For a case where a company secretary was held not to have acted as a de facto director see *Gemma Ltd (in liquidation) v Davies* [2008] EWHC 546 (Ch), [2008] All ER (D) 216 (Mar), (2008) Times, 4 April.

A human director of a company which in turn is a corporate director of a second company will not necessarily be regarded as a de facto director of the second company: *Revenue and Customs Comrs v Holland, Re Paycheck Services 3 Ltd* [2010] UKSC 51, [2010] 1 WLR 2793, [2010] NLJR 1686, a decision on the liability of company directors under s 212 of the Insolvency Act 1986.

III COM [54A]

7. Disqualification orders under section 6: applications and acceptance of undertakings

(1) If it appears to the Secretary of State that it is expedient in the public interest that a disqualification order under section 6 should be made against any person, an application for the making of such an order against that person may be made—

(a) by the Secretary of State, or

(b) if the Secretary of State so directs in the case of a person who is or has been a director of a company which is being or has been wound up by the court in England and Wales, by the official receiver.

(2) Except with the leave of the court, an application for the making under that section of a disqualification order against any person shall not be made after the end of the period of 3 years beginning with the day on which the company of which that person is or has been a director became insolvent.

(2A) If it appears to the Secretary of State that the conditions mentioned in section 6(1) are satisfied as respects any person who has offered to give him a disqualification undertaking, he may accept the undertaking if it appears to him that it is expedient in the public interest that he should do so (instead of applying, or proceeding with an application, for a disqualification order).

(3) ...

(4) The Secretary of State or the official receiver may require any person—

(a) to furnish him with such information with respect to [that person's or another person's conduct as a director of a company which has at any time become insolvent (whether while the person was a director or subsequently), and

(b) to produce and permit inspection of such books, papers and other records [as are considered by the Secretary of State or (as the case may be) the official receiver to be relevant to that person's or another person's conduct as such a director

as the Secretary of State or the official receiver may reasonably require for the purpose of determining whether to exercise, or of exercising, any function of his under this section.

(5) Subsections (1A) and (2) of section 6 apply for the purposes of this section as they apply for the purposes of that section.

III COM [54A.1]

Applications and undertakings The responsibility for applying to the court for a disqualification order under s 6 lies with the Secretary of State or, as the case may be, the official receiver; and sub-section (2) imposes a time limit of 2 years from the date when the relevant company became insolvent. Sub-sections (3) and (4) require certain office-holders to provide reports and information to the Secretary of State regarding the director's conduct. Sub-section (2A) confirms that the Secretary of State has power, in appropriate cases, to accept a disqualification undertaking, as provided in s 1A, as an alternative to seeking a disqualification order. Other sections relevant to applications for disqualification orders are s.9 (matters for determining unfitness of directors) and s 16 (application for disqualification order)

III COM [54A.2]

Information obtained by the Official Receiver and hearsay evidence The Secretary of State has power under s 7(4) to require the liquidator to provide information which may be used in disqualification proceedings, including information obtained by the exercise of powers under ss 235 and 236 of the Insolvency Act 1986. The House of Lords has held, reversing the decision of the Court of Appeal, that the Official Receiver may lawfully exercise the powers under these sections for the sole purpose of obtaining information for use in disqualification proceedings: *Re Pantmaenog Timber Co Ltd* [2003] UKHL 49, [2003] 4 All ER 18, (2003) Times, 7 August. Whether proceedings are brought under s 7 or under s 8 for a disqualification order under s 6, there is an implied exception to the strict rules of evidence relating to hearsay and opinion evidence: *Secretary of State for Business Enterprise & Regulatory Reform v Aaron* [2008] EWCA Civ 1146, [2008] All ER (D) 144 (Oct).

III COM [54A.3]

Applications under section 7(2) and (4) An application for permission to make a disqualification application after 2 years from the date of the insolvency should usually be made by claim form N208, as should an application under s 7(4) for extra information. Further guidance is provided in paras 17 to 19 of the Practice Direction at **III COM [61]**.

III COM [54AA]

7A. Office-holder's report on conduct of directors

(1) The office-holder in respect of a company which is insolvent must prepare a report (a "conduct report") about the conduct of each person who was a director of the company—

(a) on the insolvency date, or

(b) at any time during the period of 3 years ending with that date.

(2) For the purposes of this section a company is insolvent if—

(a) the company is in liquidation and at the time it went into liquidation its assets were insufficient for the payment of its debts and other liabilities and the expenses of the winding up,

(b) the company has entered administration, or

(c) an administrative receiver of the company has been appointed;

and subsection (1A) of section 6 applies for the purposes of this section as it applies for the purpose of that section.

(3) A conduct report must, in relation to each person, describe any conduct of the person which may assist the Secretary of State in deciding whether to exercise the power under section 7(1) or (2A) in relation to the person.

(4) The office-holder must send the conduct report to the Secretary of State before the end of—

(a) the period of 3 months beginning with the insolvency date, or

(b) such other longer period as the Secretary of State considers appropriate in the particular circumstances.

(5) If new information comes to the attention of an office-holder, the office-holder must send that information to the Secretary of State as soon as reasonably practicable.

(6) "New information" is information which an office-holder considers should have been included in a conduct report prepared in relation to the company, or would have been so included had it been available before the report was sent.

(7) If there is more than one office-holder in respect of a company at any particular time (because the company is insolvent by virtue of falling within more than one paragraph of subsection (2) at that time), subsection (1) applies only to the first of the office-holders to be appointed.

(8) In the case of a company which is at different times insolvent by virtue of falling within one or more different paragraphs of subsection (2)—

(a) the references in subsection (1) to the insolvency date are to be read as references to the first such date during the period in which the company is insolvent, and

(b) subsection (1) does not apply to an office-holder if at any time during the period in which the company is insolvent a conduct report has already been prepared and sent to the Secretary of State.

(9) The "office-holder" in respect of a company which is insolvent is—

(a) in the case of a company being wound up by the court in England and Wales, the official receiver;
(b) in the case of a company being wound up otherwise, the liquidator;
(c) in the case of a company in administration, the administrator;
(d) in the case of a company of which there is an administrative receiver, the receiver.

(10) The "insolvency date"—
(a) in the case of a company being wound up by the court, means the date on which the court makes the winding-up order (see section 125 of the Insolvency Act 1986);
(b) in the case of a company being wound up by way of a members' voluntary winding up, means the date on which the liquidator forms the opinion that the company will be unable to pay its debts in full (together with interest at the official rate) within the period stated in the directors' declaration of solvency under section 89 of the Insolvency Act 1986;
(c) in the case of a company being wound up by way of a creditors' voluntary winding up where no such declaration under section 89 of that Act has been made, means the date of the passing of the resolution for voluntary winding up;
(d) in the case of a company which has entered administration, means the date the company did so;
(e) in the case of a company in respect of which an administrative receiver has been appointed, means the date of that appointment.

(11) For the purposes of subsection (10)(e), any appointment of an administrative receiver to replace an administrative receiver who has died or vacated office pursuant to section 45 of the Insolvency Act 1986 is to be ignored.

(12) In this section—
"court" has the same meaning as in section 6;
"director" includes a shadow director.

III COM [54B]

8. Disqualification of director on finding of unfitness

(1) If it appears to the Secretary of State that it is expedient in the public interest that a disqualification order should be made against a person who is, or has been, a director or shadow director of a company, he may apply to the court for such an order.

(1A) ...

(2) The court may make a disqualification order against a person where, on an application under this section, it is satisfied that his conduct in relation to the company (either taken alone or taken together with his conduct as a director or shadow director of one or more other companies or overseas companies) makes him unfit to be concerned in the management of a company.

(2A) Where it appears to the Secretary of State that, in the case of a person who has offered to give him a disqualification undertaking—
(a) the conduct of the person in relation to a company of which the person is or has been a director or shadow director (either taken alone or taken together with his conduct as a director or shadow director of one or more other companies or overseas companies) makes him unfit to be concerned in the management of a company, and
(b) it is expedient in the public interest that he should accept the undertaking (instead of applying, or proceeding with an application, for a disqualification order),

he may accept the undertaking.

(2B) Subsection (1A) of section 6 applies for the purposes of this section as it applies for the purposes of that section.

(3) In this section "the court" means the High Court or, in Scotland, the Court of Session.

(4) The maximum period of disqualification under this section is 15 years.

III COM [54B.1]

Disqualification undertaking Note that the section now provides expressly for the Secretary of State to accept a disqualification undertaking, in an appropriate case, as an alternative to applying for a disqualification order under this section.

III COM [54B.2]

Procedure for applying to the court Proceedings under this section should be started by claim form, using the model form numbered N500 which is annexed to the Practice Direction (see para **III COM [69]**) and following the Part 8 procedure. Note the requirement in s 16(1), at **III COM [54J]**, to give 10 days' notice of the intention to apply for the making of a disqualification order by the court having jurisdiction to wind up a company. Further directions, regarding commencement, headings, claim form, service, acknowledgment of service, evidence, case managements and trial, are set out in Part 2 of the Practice Direction at **III COM [58]**.

III COM [54B.3]

Principles to be applied when determining unfitness and fixing the period of disqualification The same approach and principles should apply to cases under s 8 as under s 6 when determining unfitness and fixing the period of disqualification: *Secretary of State for Trade and Industry v Hollier* [2006] EWHC 1804, [2007] BCC 11, Etherton J, Ch D.

III COM [54BA]

8ZA. Order disqualifying person instructing unfit director of insolvent company

(1) The court may make a disqualification order against a person ("P") if, on an application under section 8ZB, it is satisfied—

(a) either—

(i)that a disqualification order under section 6 has been made against a person who is or has been a director (but not a shadow director) of a company, or

(ii)that the Secretary of State has accepted a disqualification undertaking from such a person under section 7(2A), and

(b) that P exercised the requisite amount of influence over the person.

That person is referred to in this section as "the main transgressor".

(2) For the purposes of this section, P exercised the requisite amount of influence over the main transgressor if any of the conduct—

(a) for which the main transgressor is subject to the order made under section 6, or

(b) in relation to which the undertaking was accepted from the main transgressor under section 7(2A),

was the result of the main transgressor acting in accordance with P's directions or instructions.

(3) But P does not exercise the requisite amount of influence over the main transgressor by reason only that the main transgressor acts on advice given by P in a professional capacity.

(4) Under this section the minimum period of disqualification is 2 years and the maximum period is 15 years.

(5) In this section and section 8ZB "the court" has the same meaning as in section 6; and subsection (3B) of section 6 applies in relation to proceedings mentioned in subsection (6) below as it applies in relation to proceedings mentioned in section 6(3B)(a) and (b).

(6) The proceedings are proceedings—
- (a) for or in connection with a disqualification order under this section, or
- (b) in connection with a disqualification undertaking accepted under section 8ZC.

III COM [54BB]

8ZB. Application for order under section 8ZA

(1) If it appears to the Secretary of State that it is expedient in the public interest that a disqualification order should be made against a person under section 8ZA, the Secretary of State may—
- (a) make an application to the court for such an order, or
- (b) in a case where an application for an order under section 6 against the main transgressor has been made by the official receiver, direct the official receiver to make such an application.

(2) Except with the leave of the court, an application for a disqualification order under section 8ZA must not be made after the end of the period of 3 years beginning with the day on which the company in question became insolvent (within the meaning given by section 6(2)).

(3) Subsection (4) of section 7 applies for the purposes of this section as it applies for the purposes of that section.

III COM [54BC]

8ZC. Disqualification undertaking instead of an order under section 8ZA

(1) If it appears to the Secretary of State that it is expedient in the public interest to do so, the Secretary of State may accept a disqualification undertaking from a person ("P") if—
- (a) any of the following is the case—
  - (i) a disqualification order under section 6 has been made against a person who is or has been a director (but not a shadow director) of a company,
  - (ii) the Secretary of State has accepted a disqualification undertaking from such a person under section 7(2A), or
  - (iii) it appears to the Secretary of State that such an undertaking could be accepted from such a person (if one were offered), and
- (b) it appears to the Secretary of State that P exercised the requisite amount of influence over the person.

That person is referred to in this section as "the main transgressor".

(2) For the purposes of this section, P exercised the requisite amount of influence over the main transgressor if any of the conduct—
- (a) for which the main transgressor is subject to the disqualification order made under section 6,
- (b) in relation to which the disqualification undertaking was accepted from the main transgressor under section 7(2A), or
- (c) which led the Secretary of State to the conclusion set out in subsection (1)(a)(iii),

was the result of the main transgressor acting in accordance with P's directions or instructions.

(3) But P does not exercise the requisite amount of influence over the main transgressor by reason only that the main transgressor acts on advice given by P in a professional capacity.

(4) Subsection (4) of section 7 applies for the purposes of this section as it applies for the purposes of that section.]

III COM [54BD]

8ZD. Order disqualifying person instructing unfit director: other cases

(1) The court may make a disqualification order against a person ("P") if, on an application under this section, it is satisfied—

(a) either—

(i) that a disqualification order under section 8 has been made against a person who is or has been a director (but not a shadow director) of a company, or

(ii) that the Secretary of State has accepted a disqualification undertaking from such a person under section 8(2A), and

(b) that P exercised the requisite amount of influence over the person.

That person is referred to in this section as "the main transgressor".

(2) The Secretary of State may make an application to the court for a disqualification order against P under this section if it appears to the Secretary of State that it is expedient in the public interest for such an order to be made.

(3) For the purposes of this section, P exercised the requisite amount of influence over the main transgressor if any of the conduct—

(a) for which the main transgressor is subject to the order made under section 8, or

(b) in relation to which the undertaking was accepted from the main transgressor under section 8(2A),

was the result of the main transgressor acting in accordance with P's directions or instructions.

(4) But P does not exercise the requisite amount of influence over the main transgressor by reason only that the main transgressor acts on advice given by P in a professional capacity.

(5) Under this section the maximum period of disqualification is 15 years.

(6) In this section "the court" means the High Court or, in Scotland, the Court of Session.

III COM [54BE]

8ZE. Disqualification undertaking instead of an order under section 8ZD

(1) If it appears to the Secretary of State that it is expedient in the public interest to do so, the Secretary of State may accept a disqualification undertaking from a person ("P") if—

(a) any of the following is the case—

(i) a disqualification order under section 8 has been made against a person who is or has been a director (but not a shadow director) of a company,

(ii) the Secretary of State has accepted a disqualification undertaking from such a person under section 8(2A), or

(iii) it appears to the Secretary of State that such an undertaking could be accepted from such a person (if one were offered), and

(b) it appears to the Secretary of State that P exercised the requisite amount of influence over the person.

That person is referred to in this section as "the main transgressor".

(2) For the purposes of this section, P exercised the requisite amount of influence over the main transgressor if any of the conduct—

(a) for which the main transgressor is subject to the disqualification order made under section 8,

(b) in relation to which the disqualification undertaking was accepted from the main transgressor under section 8(2A), or

(c) which led the Secretary of State to the conclusion set out in subsection (1)(a)(iii),

was the result of the main transgressor acting in accordance with P's directions or instructions.

(3) But P does not exercise the requisite amount of influence over the main transgressor by reason only that the main transgressor acts on advice given by P in a professional capacity.

III COM [54C]

8A. Variation etc of disqualification undertaking

(1) The court may, on the application of a person who is subject to a disqualification undertaking—

(a) reduce the period for which the undertaking is to be in force, or

(b) provide for it to cease to be in force.

(2) On the hearing of an application under subsection (1), the Secretary of State shall appear and call the attention of the court to any matters which seem to him to be relevant, and may himself give evidence or call witnesses.

(2A) Subsection (2) does not apply to an application in the case of an undertaking given under section 9B, and in such a case on the hearing of the application whichever of the Competition and Markets Authority or a specified regulator (within the meaning of section 9E) accepted the undertaking—

(a) must appear and call the attention of the court to any matters which appear to it or him (as the case may be) to be relevant;

(b) may give evidence or call witnesses.

(3) In this section "the court"—

(za) in the case of an undertaking given under section 8ZC has the same meaning as in section 8ZA;

(zb) in the case of an undertaking given under section 8ZE means the High Court or, in Scotland, the Court of Session;

(a) in the case of an undertaking given under section 9B means the High Court or (in Scotland) the Court of Session;

(b) in any other case has the same meaning as in section 5A(5), 7(2) or 8 (as the case may be).

III COM [54C.1]

Procedure for applying for a variation Proceedings to obtain a variation should be started by claim form, using the model Form N501, which is annexed to the Practice Direction (see para **III COM [72]**), and following the Part 8 procedure. Further directions, regarding commencement, claim form, acknowledgment of service, evidence, hearings, case management, trial and appeals are set out in paras 29 to 35 of the Practice Direction **III COM [66]**. A precedent is provided at **BCCP R[603]**.

III COM [54C.2]

Discretion to provide for undertaking to cease to be in force Although the discretion is unfettered, it requires the existence of special circumstances to justify an order that the undertaking should cease to have effect, as happened in *Secretary of State for Trade and Industry v Jonkler* [2006] EWHC 135 (Ch), [2006] 2 All ER 902, (2006) Times, 3 March, Ch D, Hart J (Companies Ct).

III COM [54D]

9. Matters for determining unfitness of directors

Repealed by the Small Business, Enterprise and Employment Act 2015.

III COM [54D.1]

Orders and undertakings Note that the insertion by the Insolvency Act 2000 of subsection (1A) obliges the Secretary of State to have regard to the Schedule 1 matters, at **III COM [55A]**, before accepting a disqualification undertaking.

III COM [54E]

9A. Competition disqualification order

(1) The court must make a disqualification order against a person if the following two conditions are satisfied in relation to him.

(2) The first condition is that an undertaking which is a company of which he is a director commits a breach of competition law.

(3) The second condition is that the court considers that his conduct as a director makes him unfit to be concerned in the management of a company.

(4) An undertaking commits a breach of competition law if it engages in conduct which infringes any of the following—

- (a) the Chapter 1 prohibition (within the meaning of the Competition Act 1998) (prohibition on agreements, etc preventing, restricting or distorting competition);
- (b) the Chapter 2 prohibition (within the meaning of that Act) (prohibition on abuse of a dominant position);
- (c) Article 101 of the Treaty on the Functioning of the European Union (prohibition on agreements, etc preventing, restricting or distorting competition);
- (d) Article 102 of that Treaty (prohibition on abuse of a dominant position).

(5) For the purpose of deciding under subsection (3) whether a person is unfit to be concerned in the management of a company the court—

- (a) must have regard to whether subsection (6) applies to him;
- (b) may have regard to his conduct as a director of a company in connection with any other breach of competition law;
- (c) must not have regard to the matters mentioned in Schedule 1.

(6) This subsection applies to a person if as a director of the company—

- (a) his conduct contributed to the breach of competition law mentioned in subsection (2);
- (b) his conduct did not contribute to the breach but he had reasonable grounds to suspect that the conduct of the undertaking constituted the breach and he took no steps to prevent it;
- (c) he did not know but ought to have known that the conduct of the undertaking constituted the breach.

(7) For the purposes of subsection (6)(a) it is immaterial whether the person knew that the conduct of the undertaking constituted the breach.

(8) For the purposes of subsection (4)(a) or (c) references to the conduct of an undertaking are references to its conduct taken with the conduct of one or more other undertakings.

(9) The maximum period of disqualification under this section is 15 years.

(10) An application under this section for a disqualification order may be made by the Competition and Markets Authority or by a specified regulator.

(11) Section 60 of the Competition Act 1998 (c 41) (consistent treatment of questions arising under United Kingdom and EU law) applies in relation to any question arising by virtue of subsection (4)(a) or (b) above as it applies in relation to any question arising under Part 1 of that Act.

III COM [54E.1]

Disqualification for competition infringements This section and the next four were inserted by s 204 of the Competition Act 2002. Their broad purpose is to provide for the disqualification of directors of companies (or other undertakings) which commit a breach of competition law where the breach is one for which the director in question has a responsibility within subsection (6). The applicant for an order is the Competition and Markets Authority or a specified regulator ie one of the regulators listed in s 9E(2). The only court with jurisdiction to hear the application is the High Court. The claim should be made using the model Form N501, annexed to the Practice Direction at **III COM [72]**: a precedent is provided in **BCCP R[605]**.

III COM [54F]

9B Competition undertakings

(1) This section applies if—

(a) the Competition and Markets Authority or a specified regulator thinks that in relation to any person an undertaking which is a company of which he is a director has committed or is committing a breach of competition law,

(b) the Competition and Markets Authority or the specified regulator thinks that the conduct of the person as a director makes him unfit to be concerned in the management of a company, and

(c) the person offers to give the Competition and Markets Authority or the specified regulator (as the case may be) a disqualification undertaking.

(2) The Competition and Markets Authority or the specified regulator (as the case may be) may accept a disqualification undertaking from the person instead of applying for or proceeding with an application for a disqualification order.

(3) A disqualification undertaking is an undertaking by a person that for the period specified in the undertaking he will not—

(a) be a director of a company;

(b) act as receiver of a company's property;

(c) in any way, whether directly or indirectly, be concerned or take part in the promotion, formation or management of a company;

(d) act as an insolvency practitioner.

(4) But a disqualification undertaking may provide that a prohibition falling within subsection (3)(a) to (c) does not apply if the person obtains the leave of the court.

(5) The maximum period which may be specified in a disqualification undertaking is 15 years.

(6) If a disqualification undertaking is accepted from a person who is already subject to a disqualification undertaking under this Act or to a disqualification order the periods specified in those undertakings or the undertaking and the order (as the case may be) run concurrently.

(7) Subsections (4) to (8) of section 9A apply for the purposes of this section as they apply for the purposes of that section but in the application of subsection (5) of that section the reference to the court must be construed as a reference to the Competition and Markets Authority or a specified regulator (as the case may be).

III COM [54F.1]

Variation order Proceedings to obtain a variation should be started by claim form, using the model Form N501, which is annexed to the Practice Direction at **III COM [72]**, and following the Part 8 procedure. Further directions, regarding commencement, claim form, acknowledgment of service, evidence, hearings, case management, trial and appeals are set out in paras 29 to 35 of the Practice Direction at **III COM [66]**. A precedent is provided at **BCCP R[604]**.

III COM [54G]

9C. Competition investigations

(1) If the Competition and Markets Authority or a specified regulator has reasonable grounds for suspecting that a breach of competition law has occurred it or he (as the case may be) may carry out an investigation for the purpose of deciding whether to make an application under section 9A for a disqualification order.

(2) For the purposes of such an investigation sections 26 to 30 of the Competition Act 1998 (c 41) apply to the Competition and Markets Authority and the specified regulators as they apply to the Competition and Markets Authority for the purposes of an investigation under section 25 of that Act.

(3) Subsection (4) applies if as a result of an investigation under this section the Competition and Markets Authority or a specified regulator proposes to apply under section 9A for a disqualification order.

(4) Before making the application the Competition and Markets Authority or regulator (as the case may be) must—

- (a) give notice to the person likely to be affected by the application, and
- (b) give that person an opportunity to make representations.

III COM [54H]

9D. Co-ordination

(1) The Secretary of State may make regulations for the purpose of co-ordinating the performance of functions under sections 9A to 9C (relevant functions) which are exercisable concurrently by two or more persons.

(2) Section 54(5) to (7) of the Competition Act 1998 (c 41) applies to regulations made under this section as it applies to regulations made under that section and for that purpose in that section—

- (a) references to Part 1 functions must be read as references to relevant functions;
- (b) references to a regulator must be read as references to a specified regulator;
- (ba) the reference in subsection (6A)(b) to notice under section 31(1) of the Competition Act 1998 that the regulator proposes to make a decision within the meaning given by section 31(2) of that Act is to be read as notice under section 9C(4) that the specified regulator proposes to apply under section 9A for a disqualification order;
- (c) a competent person also includes any of the specified regulators.

(3) The power to make regulations under this section must be exercised by statutory instrument subject to annulment in pursuance of a resolution of either House of Parliament.

(4) Such a statutory instrument may—

- (a) contain such incidental, supplemental, consequential and transitional provision as the Secretary of State thinks appropriate;
- (b) make different provision for different cases.

III COM [54J]

9E. Interpretation

(1) This section applies for the purposes of sections 9A to 9D.

(2) Each of the following is a specified regulator for the purposes of a breach of competition law in relation to a matter in respect of which he or it has a function—

- (a) the Office of Communications;
- (b) the Gas and Electricity Markets Authority;

(c) the Water Services Regulation Authority;
(d) the Office of Rail and Road;
(e) the Civil Aviation Authority;
(f) Monitor.
(g) the Payment Systems Regulator established under section 40 of the Financial Services (Banking Reform) Act 2013;
(h) the Financial Conduct Authority.

(3) The court is the High Court or (in Scotland) the Court of Session.

(4) Conduct includes omission.

(5) Director includes shadow director.

III COM [54JA]

12C. Determining unfitness etc: matters to be taken into account

(1) This section applies where a court must determine—
(a) whether a person's conduct as a director of one or more companies or overseas companies makes the person unfit to be concerned in the management of a company;
(b) whether to exercise any discretion it has to make a disqualification order under any of sections 2 to 4, 5A, 8 or 10;
(c) where the court has decided to make a disqualification order under any of those sections or is required to make an order under section 6, what the period of disqualification should be.

(2) But this section does not apply where the court in question is one mentioned in section 2(2)(b) or (c).

(3) This section also applies where the Secretary of State must determine—
(a) whether a person's conduct as a director of one or more companies or overseas companies makes the person unfit to be concerned in the management of a company;
(b) whether to exercise any discretion the Secretary of State has to accept a disqualification undertaking under section 5A, 7 or 8.

(4) In making any such determination in relation to a person, the court or the Secretary of State must—
(a) in every case, have regard in particular to the matters set out in paragraphs 1 to 4 of Schedule 1;
(b) in a case where the person concerned is or has been a director of a company or overseas company, also have regard in particular to the matters set out in paragraphs 5 to 7 of that Schedule.

(5) In this section "director" includes a shadow director.

(6) Subsection (1A) of section 6 applies for the purposes of this section as it applies for the purposes of that section.

(7) The Secretary of State may by order modify Schedule 1; and such an order may contain such transitional provision as may appear to the Secretary of State to be necessary or expedient.

(8) The power to make an order under this section is exercisable by statutory instrument.

(9) An order under this section may not be made unless a draft of the instrument containing it has been laid before, and approved by a resolution of, each House of Parliament.

III COM [54JB]

15A. Compensation orders and undertakings

(1) The court may make a compensation order against a person on the application of the Secretary of State if it is satisfied that the conditions mentioned in subsection (3) are met.

(2) If it appears to the Secretary of State that the conditions mentioned in subsection (3) are met in respect of a person who has offered to give the Secretary of State a compensation undertaking, the Secretary of State may accept the undertaking instead of applying, or proceeding with an application, for a compensation order.

(3) The conditions are that—

(a) the person is subject to a disqualification order or disqualification undertaking under this Act, and

(b) conduct for which the person is subject to the order or undertaking has caused loss to one or more creditors of an insolvent company of which the person has at any time been a director.

(4) An "insolvent company" is a company that is or has been insolvent and a company becomes insolvent if—

(a) the company goes into liquidation at a time when its assets are insufficient for the payment of its debts and other liabilities and the expenses of the winding up,

(b) the company enters administration, or

(c) an administrative receiver of the company is appointed.

(5) The Secretary of State may apply for a compensation order at any time before the end of the period of two years beginning with the date on which the disqualification order referred to in paragraph (a) of subsection (3) was made, or the disqualification undertaking referred to in that paragraph was accepted.

(6) In the case of a person subject to a disqualification order under section 8ZA or 8ZD, or a disqualification undertaking under section 8ZC or 8ZE, the reference in subsection (3)(b) to conduct is a reference to the conduct of the main transgressor in relation to which the person has exercised the requisite amount of influence.

(7) In this section and sections 15B and 15C "the court" means—

(a) in a case where a disqualification order has been made, the court that made the order,

(b) in any other case, the High Court or, in Scotland, the Court of Session.

III COM [54JC]

15B. Amounts payable under compensation orders and undertakings

(1) A compensation order is an order requiring the person against whom it is made to pay an amount specified in the order—

(a) to the Secretary of State for the benefit of—

(i) a creditor or creditors specified in the order;

(ii) a class or classes of creditor so specified;

(b) as a contribution to the assets of a company so specified.

(2) A compensation undertaking is an undertaking to pay an amount specified in the undertaking—

(a) to the Secretary of State for the benefit of—

(i) a creditor or creditors specified in the undertaking;

(ii) a class or classes of creditor so specified;

(b) as a contribution to the assets of a company so specified.

(3) When specifying an amount the court (in the case of an order) and the Secretary of State (in the case of an undertaking) must in particular have regard to—

(a) the amount of the loss caused;

(b) the nature of the conduct mentioned in section 15A(3)(b);

(c) whether the person has made any other financial contribution in recompense for the conduct (whether under a statutory provision or otherwise).

(4) An amount payable by virtue of subsection (2) under a compensation undertaking is recoverable as if payable under a court order.

(5) An amount payable under a compensation order or compensation undertaking is provable as a bankruptcy debt.

III COM [54JD]

15C. Variation and revocation of compensation undertakings

(1) The court may, on the application of a person who is subject to a compensation undertaking—

(a) reduce the amount payable under the undertaking, or

(b) provide for the undertaking not to have effect.

(2) On the hearing of an application under subsection (1), the Secretary of State must appear and call the attention of the court to any matters which the Secretary of State considers relevant, and may give evidence or call witnesses.

III COM [54K]

16. Application for disqualification order

(1) A person intending to apply for the making of a disqualification order shall give not less than 10 days' notice of his intention to the person against whom the order is sought; and on the hearing of the application the last-mentioned person may appear and himself give evidence or call witnesses.

(2) An application to a court, other than a court mentioned in section 2(2)(b) or (c), for the making against any person of a disqualification order under any of sections 2 to 4 may be made by the Secretary of State or the official receiver, or by the liquidator or any past or present member or creditor of any company or overseas company in relation to which that person has committed or is alleged to have committed an offence or other default.

(3) On the hearing of any application under this Act made by a person falling within subsection (4), the applicant shall appear and call the attention of the court to any matters which seem to him to be relevant, and may himself give evidence or call witnesses.

(4) The following fall within this subsection—

(a) the Secretary of State;

(b) the official receiver;

(c) the Competition and Markets Authority;

(d) the liquidator;

(e) a specified regulator (within the meaning of section 9E).

III COM [54K.1]

Procedure Whereas an application for a disqualification order may be made by the Secretary of State or the official receiver in a variety of courts, an application for a competition disqualification may be made only by the Competition and Markets Authority or a specified regulator and must be made to the High Court. In either case the proceedings should be started by claim form, using the model form N500 which is annexed to the Practice Direction: Directors Disqualification Proceedings at **III COM [69]**. A precedent is provided at **BCCP R[605]**. The case should then follow the Part 8 procedure, as modified by the Practice Direction.

Where fraud is alleged and there is more than one defendant the application should particularise the case against each: *Secretary of State for Trade and Industry v Gee* [2006] BCC 384, Ch D (Comp Ct), in which Chief Registrar Baister observed that the Secretary of State had been wrong to serve expert evidence at the outset and without permission.

III COM [54K.2]

Application by a liquidator In a case where a liquidator applied for the disqualification of a previous liquidator on grounds of serious misconduct it was held that the application should not be refused because of the applicant liquidator's lack of financial interest: *Wood v Mistry* [2012] EWHC 1899 (Ch), [2012] Bus LR 1607, (2012) Times, 04 October, in which Newey J declined to follow observations by Jacob J in *Re Adbury Park Estates Ltd* [2003] BCC 696 to the effect that a lack of financial interest meant that the liquidator had no standing.

III COM [55]

17. Application for leave under an order or undertaking

(1) Where a person is subject to a disqualification order made by a court having jurisdiction to wind up companies, any application for leave for the purposes of section 1(1)(a) shall be made to that court.

(2) Where—

(a) a person is subject to a disqualification order made under section 2 by a court other than a court having jurisdiction to wind up companies, or

(b) a person is subject to a disqualification order made under section 5,

any application for leave for the purposes of section 1(1)(a) shall be made to any court which, when the order was made, had jurisdiction to wind up the company (or, if there is more than one such company, any of the companies) to which the offence (or any of the offences) in question related.

(3) Where a person is subject to a disqualification undertaking accepted at any time under section 5A, 7 or 8, any application for leave for the purposes of section 1A(1)(a) shall be made to any court to which, if the Secretary of State had applied for a disqualification order under the section in question at that time, his application could have been made.

(3ZA) Where a person is subject to a disqualification undertaking accepted at any time under section 8ZC, any application for leave for the purposes of section 1A(1)(a) must be made to any court to which, if the Secretary of State had applied for a disqualification order under section 8ZA at that time, that application could have been made.

(3ZB) Where a person is subject to a disqualification undertaking accepted at any time under section 8ZE, any application for leave for the purposes of section 1A(1)(a) must be made to the High Court or, in Scotland, the Court of Session.

(3A) Where a person is subject to a disqualification undertaking accepted at any time under section 9B any application for leave for the purposes of section 9B(4) must be made to the High Court or (in Scotland) the Court of Session.

(4) But where a person is subject to two or more disqualification orders or undertakings (or to one or more disqualification orders and to one or more disqualification undertakings), any application for leave for the purposes of section 1(1)(a), 1A(1)(a) or 9B(4) shall be made to any court to which any such application relating to the latest order to be made, or undertaking to be accepted, could be made.

(5) On the hearing of an application for leave for the purposes of section 1(1)(a) or 1A(1)(a), the Secretary of State shall appear and call the attention of the court to any matters which seem to him to be relevant, and may himself give evidence or call witnesses.

(6) Subsection (5) does not apply to an application for leave for the purposes of section 1(1)(a) if the application for the disqualification order was made under section 9A.

(7) In such a case and in the case of an application for leave for the purposes of section 9B(4) on the hearing of the application whichever of the Competition and Markets Authority or a specified regulator (within the meaning of section 9E) applied for the order or accepted the undertaking (as the case may be)—

(a) must appear and draw the attention of the court to any matters which appear to it or him (as the case may be) to be relevant;

(b) may give evidence or call witnesses.

III COM [55.1]

Allowing disqualified director to work A director may be allowed to continue although the company has not demonstrated a need for his services. The need of the applicant must be balanced against the importance of protecting the public: *Re Barings plc (No 3)* [1999] 1 All ER 1017, [2000] 1 WLR 634. An application may be granted even where a need for the applicant to continue as director has not been established: *Re Barings plc (No 3)* [1999] 1 All ER 1017, [2000] 1 WLR 634. Also, the court is not bound to exclude consideration of the applicant's personal non-business purpose: *Secretary of State for Trade and Industry v Rosenfield* [1999] BCC 413.

In *Secretary of State for Business Enterprise and Reform v Meade* [2011] All ER (D) 35 (Aug) the court granted the applicant permission to act as a director for a limited time so that he could organise the company's affairs and ensure its viability during the period of his disqualification.

III COM [55.1A]

Procedure The application may be made either by claim form N208 under CPR Pt 8 or by application notice (N244) in existing disqualification proceedings. Special procedural requirements are set out in Part Four of the Practice Direction – Directors Disqualification Proceedings at **III COM [56]**.

III COM [55.2]

Application for leave under section 1(1) A director may apply under s 1(1) for permission to continue as a director, as an alternative to applying under s 17. In such a case the application should be made early enough to be considered by the judge dealing with disqualification under s 6 and should be supported by clear evidence of the precise role which the director seeks permission to exercise: *Secretary of State for Trade and Industry v Collins* [2000] 2 BCLC 223, CA. Where the application is part and parcel of winding-up proceedings in a county court the application should be made in that court: *Re Britannia Homes Centres Ltd* [2001] 2 BCLC 63.

III COM [55.2A]

Appeals Under r 2(4) of the Insolvent Companies (Disqualification of Unfit Directors) Rules 1987, SI 1987/2023, an appeal against the rejection of a leave application should be made, in accordance with r 7.47(2) of the Insolvency Rules 1986, SI 1986/1925, to a single High Court judge: *Re Britannia Homes Centres Ltd* [2001] 2 BCLC 63.

In considering an appeal the judge is not entitled to tinker with the sentence but has to identify some error of legal reasoning before interfering with the application of the familiar principles, by the trial judge, to the facts of the instant case: *Kotonou v Secretary of State for Business, Enterprise and Regulatory Reform* [2010] EWHC 19 (Ch), [2010] NLJR 905.

III COM [55.3]

Costs of the Secretary of State In the ordinary way the successful applicant should be ordered to pay the costs of the Secretary of State: *Secretary of State for Trade and Industry v Collins* [2000] 2 BCLC 223, CA.

SCHEDULE 1
DETERMINING UNFITNESS ETC: MATTERS TO BE TAKEN INTO ACCOUNT

Section 9

PART I

...

MATTERS TO BE TAKEN INTO ACCOUNT IN ALL CASES

III COM [55A]

1 The extent to which the person was responsible for the causes of any material contravention by a company or overseas company of any applicable legislative or other requirement.

2 Where applicable, the extent to which the person was responsible for the causes of a company or overseas company becoming insolvent.

3 The frequency of conduct of the person which falls within paragraph 1 or 2.

4 The nature and extent of any loss or harm caused, or any potential loss or harm which could have been caused, by the person's conduct in relation to a company or overseas company.

ADDITIONAL MATTERS TO BE TAKEN INTO ACCOUNT WHERE PERSON IS OR HAS BEEN A DIRECTOR

5 Any misfeasance or breach of any fiduciary duty by the director in relation to a company or overseas company.

6 Any material breach of any legislative or other obligation of the director which applies as a result of being a director of a company or overseas company.

7 The frequency of conduct of the director which falls within paragraph 5 or 6.

INTERPRETATION

8 Subsections (1A) to (2A) of section 6 apply for the purposes of this Schedule as they apply for the purposes of that section.

9 In this Schedule "director" includes a shadow director.

PRACTICE DIRECTION—DIRECTORS DISQUALIFICATION PROCEEDINGS

PART ONE
GENERAL

1. Application and interpretation

III COM [56]–III COM [57]

1.1. In this Practice Direction:

(1) "the Act" means the Company Directors Disqualification Act 1986 (as amended);

(2) "the Disqualification Rules" means the rules for the time being in force made under section 411 of the Insolvency Act 1986 in relation to disqualification proceedings[1];

(3) "the Insolvency Rules" means the rules for the time being in force made under sections 411 and 412 of the Insolvency Act 1986 in relation to insolvency proceedings;

(4) "CPR" means the Civil Procedure Rules 1998 and "CPR" followed by "Part" or "Rule" and a number means the part or Rule with that number in those Rules;

(5) "disqualification proceedings" has the meaning set out in paragraph 1.3 below;

(6) "a disqualification application" is an application under the Act for the making of a disqualification order;

(7) References to a "Registrar" are to a Registrar in Bankruptcy of the High Court and (save in cases where it is clear from the context that a particular provision applies only to the High Court in London) include a District Judge in a District Registry of the High Court and in County Court having insolvency jurisdiction;

(8) except where the context otherwise requires references to:

(a) "company" or "companies" shall include references to "partnership" or "partnerships" and to "limited liability partnership" and "limited liability partnerships";

(b) "director" shall include references to an "officer" of a partnership and to a "member" of a limited liability partnership;

(c) "shadow director" shall include references to a "shadow member" of a limited liability partnership

and, in appropriate cases, the forms annexed to this practice direction shall be varied accordingly;

(9) Where the Act applies to other entities as it applies to companies, references in this practice direction to director or officer of a company and to other terms in the Act as provided for by legislation shall also apply for the purposes of this practice direction.

1.2. This practice direction shall come into effect on 9 December 2014, and shall replace the practice direction which came into effect on 26 April 1999 (as subsequently amended). Steps taken prior to 9 December 2014, and steps taken on or after that date in accordance with an obligation which arose before that date or a court direction made before that date, shall not thereby be invalidated.

1.3. This practice direction applies to all proceedings brought under the Act and/or the Disqualification Rules ("disqualification proceedings").[2]

2. Multi-track

2.1. All disqualification proceedings are allocated to the multi-track. The CPR relating to direction questionnaires and track allocation shall not apply.

3. Rights of audience

3.1. Official receivers and deputy official receivers have right of audience in any proceedings to which this Practice Direction applies, including cases where a disqualification application is made by the Secretary of State or by the official receiver at his direction[3].

COMPANIES

PART TWO
DISQUALIFICATION APPLICATIONS
4. Commencement

III COM [58]–III COM [59]

4.1. A disqualification application must be commenced by a claim form in the form annexed hereto.

4.2. The procedure set out in CPR Part 8[4], as modified by this practice direction and (where the application is made under sections 7, 8 or 9A of the Act) the Disqualification Rules shall apply to all disqualification applications. CPR rule 8.2 (contents of the claim form) shall not apply. CPR rule 8.1(3) (power of the Court to order the application to continue as if the claimant had not used the Part 8 Procedure) shall not apply.

4.3. When the claim form is issued, the claimant will be given a date for the first hearing of the disqualification application. This date is to be not less than eight weeks from the date of issue of the claim form . The first hearing will be before a registrar.[5]

5. Headings

5.1. Every court document in disqualification applications shall be headed:

IN THE HIGH COURT OF JUSTICE

CHANCERY DIVISION

[DISTRICT REGISTRY] or [COMPANIES COURT] if in the Royal Courts of Justice

or

IN THE COUNTY COURT SITTING AT [ ]

followed by

IN THE MATTER OF [name of company]

AND IN THE MATTER OF THE COMPANY DIRECTORS DISQUALIFICATION ACT 1986.

6. Service of the claim form

6.1. Service of claim forms in disqualification applications will be the responsibility of the Claimant and will not be undertaken by the court.

6.2. If serving by first class post on the defendant's last known address, the day of service shall, unless the contrary is shown, be deemed to be the 7th day next following that on which the claim form was posted[6]. Otherwise, Sections I and II of CPR Part 6 apply. Attention is drawn to CPR 16.17 regarding a certificate of service of the claim form.

6.3 The claim form served on the defendant shall be accompanied by an acknowledgment of service.

6.4 Section IV of CPR Part 6 shall not apply. In any disqualification proceedings where a claim form or order of the court or other document is required to be served on any person who is not in England and Wales, the court may order service on him to be effected within such time and in such manner as it thinks fit[7], may require such proof of service as it thinks fit, and may give such directions as to acknowledgment of service as it thinks fit.

7. Acknowledgment of service

7.1. The form of acknowledgment of service annexed to this Practice Direction shall be used in disqualification proceedings. CPR rule 8.3(2) and 8.3(3)(a) shall not apply.

7.2. The defendant shall:

(1) (subject to any directions to the contrary given under paragraph 6.4 above) file an acknowledgment of service in the prescribed form not more than 14 days after service of the claim form; and

(2) serve a copy of the acknowledgment of service on the claimant and any other party.

7.3. Where the defendant has failed to file an acknowledgment of service and the time period for doing so has expired, the defendant may attend the hearing of the application but (unless the court orders otherwise) may not take part in the hearing unless the court gives permission and the defendant undertakes to file and serve an acknowledgment of service.

8. Evidence

8.1. Evidence in disqualification applications shall be by affidavit, except where the official receiver is a party, in which case his evidence may be in the form of a written report (with or without affidavits by other persons) which shall be treated as if it had been verified by affidavit by him and shall be prima facie evidence of any matter contained in it.[8]

8.2. The affidavits or the official receiver's report in support of the application shall include a statement of the matters by reference to which it is alleged that a disqualification order should be made against the defendant.[9]

8.3. When the claim form is issued:

(1) the affidavit or report in support of the disqualification application must be filed in court; and

(2) except where the court requires otherwise, exhibits must be lodged with the court where they shall be retained until the conclusion of the proceedings; and

(3) copies of the affidavit/report and exhibits shall be served with the claim form on the defendant.[10].

(4) If, as a result of the court's requirement, exhibits are not lodged in accordance with 8.3(2), the exhibits should be available at the trial and any other hearing at which reference to them may be made.

8.4. The defendant shall, within 28 days from the date of service of the claim form [11]:

(1) file in court any affidavit evidence in opposition to the disqualification application that he or she wishes the court to take into consideration; and

(2) except where the court requires otherwise, lodge the exhibits with the court where they shall be retained until the conclusion of the proceedings; and

(3) at the same time, serve upon the claimant a copy of the affidavits and exhibits.

If, as a result of the court's requirement, exhibits are not lodged in accordance with 8.4(2), the exhibits should be available at the trial and any other hearing at which reference to them may be made.

8.5. In cases where there is more than one defendant, each defendant is required to serve his evidence on the other defendants at the same time as service on the claimant unless the court otherwise orders.

8.6. The claimant shall, within 14 days from receiving the copy of the defendant's evidence[12]:

COMPANIES

(1) file in court any further affidavit or report in reply he wishes the court to take into consideration; and

(2) except where the court requires otherwise, lodge the exhibits with the court where they shall be retained until the conclusion of the proceedings; and

(3) at the same time serve a copy of the affidavits/reports and exhibits upon the defendant.

If, as a result of the court's requirement, exhibits are not lodged in accordance with 8.6(2), the exhibits should be available at the trial and any other hearing at which reference to them may be made.

8.7. Prior to the first hearing of the disqualification application, the time for serving evidence may be extended by written agreement between the parties. After the first hearing, any extension of time for serving evidence is governed by CPR rules 2.11 and 29.5.

8.8. So far as is possible all evidence should be filed before the first hearing of the disqualification application.

9. The first hearing of the disqualification application

9.1. The registrar shall either determine the case at the first hearing or give directions and adjourn it.[13].

9.2. All directions should insofar as possible be sought at the first hearing of the disqualification application so that the disqualification application can be determined at the earliest possible date. The parties should take all possible steps to avoid successive directions hearings.

10. The trial

10.1. Trial bundles containing copies of:

(1) the claim form;

(2) the acknowledgment of service;

(3) all evidence filed by or on behalf of each of the parties to the proceedings, together with the exhibits thereto;

(4) all relevant correspondence; and

(5) such other documents as the parties consider necessary;

shall be lodged with the court, in accordance with the time limits and guidelines specified in the Chancery Guide.

10.2. Skeleton arguments should be prepared by all parties, whether the case is to be heard by a registrar or a judge. They should comply with all relevant guidelines, in particular the Chancery Guide.

10.3. Where appropriate the advocate for the claimant should also provide: (a) a chronology; and (b) a list of persons involved in the facts of the case.

10.4. The documents mentioned in paragraph 10.1–10.3 above must be delivered to the appropriate court office.

10.5. Copies of documents delivered to the court must, so far as possible, be provided to each of the other parties to the disqualification application.

10.6. The provisions in paragraphs 10.1 to 10.5 above are subject to any order of the court making different provision.

11. Uncontested disposals

11.1. If the defendant fails to file evidence within the time set out in paragraph 9.4 above and/or within any extension of time granted by the court, the court may make an order that unless the defendant files evidence by a specified date he shall be debarred from filing evidence without the permission of the court. If the defendant then fails to file evidence within the time specified by the debarring order and subject to any further court order, the disqualification application will be determined by way of an uncontested disposal hearing.

11.2 Not less than 3 days prior to an uncontested disposal hearing, bundles containing copies of:

(1) the claim form;

(2) the acknowledgment of service;

(3) all evidence filed by the claimant together with the exhibits thereto;

(4) any relevant correspondence;

shall be lodged with the court.

11.3. The claimant should in all cases prepare a skeleton argument, which shall be lodged no later than 2 days before the hearing.

11.4. The provisions in paragraphs 11.1 to 11.3 above are subject to any order of the court making different provision.

11.6 In all cases, the parties must inform the court immediately of any material change to the information provided in a pre-trial check list.

12. *Carecraft* procedure

12.1. The parties may invite the court to deal with the disqualification application under the procedure adopted in *Re Carecraft Construction Co Ltd* [1994] 1 WLR 172, as clarified by the decision of the Court of Appeal in *Secretary of State for Trade and Industry v Rogers* [1996] 4 All ER 854 . The claimant must submit a written statement of agreed or undisputed facts, and an agreed period of disqualification or an agreed range of years (e.g. 2 to 5 years; 6 to 10 years; 11 to 15 years).

12.2. Unless the Court otherwise orders, a hearing under the *Carecraft* procedure will be held in private.

12.3. If the Court is minded to make a disqualification order having heard the parties' representations, it will usually give judgment and make the disqualification order in public. Unless the Court otherwise orders, the written statement referred to in paragraph 12.1 shall be annexed to the disqualification order.

13. Making and setting aside of disqualification order

13.1. The court may make a disqualification order against the defendant, whether or not the defendant appears, and whether or not he has completed and returned the acknowledgment of service of the claim form, or filed evidence.[14]

13.2. Any disqualification order made in the absence of the defendant may be set aside or varied by the court on such terms as it thinks just.[15]

14. Service of orders

14.1. Service of orders (including any disqualification order) will be the responsibility of the claimant.

PART THREE
APPLICATIONS UNDER SECTIONS 7(2) AND 7(4) OF THE ACT

15. Provisions applicable to applications under section 7(2) of the Act to make a disqualification application after the end of the 2 year period specified

III COM [60]

15.1. Applications under section 7(2) of the Act shall be made by Practice Form N208 under CPR Part 8 save where it is sought to join a director or former director to existing proceedings, in which case such application shall be made by application notice under CPR Part 23, and Practice Direction 23A shall apply save as modified below.

15.2 Service of claim forms and application notices seeking orders under section 7(2) of the Act will be the responsibility of the applicant and will not be undertaken by the court.

15.3 Every claim form and application notice by which such an application is begun and all witness statements, affidavits, notices and other documents in relation thereto must be entitled in the matter of the company or companies in question and in the matter of the Act.

16. Applications for extra information made under section 7(4) of the Act

16.1. Such applications may be made:

(1) by Practice Form N208 under CPR Part 8;

(2) by Application Notice in existing disqualification proceedings; or

(3) by application under the Insolvency Rules in the relevant insolvency, if the insolvency practitioner against whom the application is made remains the officeholder.

16.2 Service of claim forms and application notices seeking orders under section 7(4) of the Act will be the responsibility of the applicant and will not be undertaken by the court.

16.3 Every claim form and application notice by which such an application is begun and all witness statements, affidavits, notices and other documents in relation thereto must be entitled in the matter of the company or companies in question and in the matter of the Act.

PART FOUR
APPLICATIONS FOR PERMISSION TO ACT

17. Commencing an application for permission to act

III COM [61]

17.1. This Practice Direction governs applications for permission to act made under:

(1) section 17 of the Act for the purposes of any of sections 1(1)(a), 1A(1)(a) or 9B(4); and

(2) section 12(2) of the Act.

17.2. Sections 12 and 17 of the Act identify the courts which have jurisdiction to deal with applications for permission to act. Subject to these sections, such applications may be made:

(1) by Practice Form N208 under CPR Part 8; or

(3) by application notice in an existing disqualification application.

17.3 In the case of a person subject to disqualification under section 12A or 12B of the Act (by reason of being disqualified in Northern Ireland), permission to act notwithstanding disqualification can only be granted by the High Court of Northern Ireland.

18. Headings

18.1. Every claim form by which an application for permission to act is begun, and all affidavits, notices and other documents in the application must be entitled in the matter of the company or companies in question and in the matter of the Act.

18.2 Every application notice by which an application for permission to act is made and all affidavits, notices and other documents in the application shall be entitled in the same manner as the heading of the claim form in the existing disqualification application.

19. Evidence

19.1. Evidence in support of an application for permission to act shall be by affidavit.

20. Service

20.1 Where a disqualification application has been made under section 9A of the Act or a disqualification undertaking has been accepted under section 9B of the Act, the claim form or application notice for permission to act (as appropriate), together with the evidence in support thereof, must be served on the Office of Fair Trading or specified regulator which made the relevant disqualification application or accepted the disqualification undertaking (as the case may be).

20.2. In all other cases, the claim form or application notice (as appropriate), together with the evidence in support thereof, must be served on the Secretary of State.

20.3 Addresses for service on government departments are set out in the List of Authorised Government Departments issued by the Cabinet Office under section 17 of the Crown Proceedings Act 1947, which is annexed to the Practice Direction supplementing Part 66.

PART FIVE
APPLICATIONS IN THE COURSE OF PROCEEDINGS

21. Form of application

III COM [62]

21.1. CPR Part 23 and Practice Direction 23A shall apply in relation to applications governed by this Practice Direction save as modified below.

22. Headings

22.1. Every notice and all witness statements and affidavits in relation thereto must be entitled in the same manner as the Claim Form in the proceedings in which the application is made.

23. Service

23.1. Service of an application notice in disqualification proceedings will be the responsibility of the party making such application and will not be undertaken by the court.

23.2. Where any application notice or order of the court or other document is required in any application to be served on any person who is not in England and Wales, the court may order service on him to be effected within such time and in such manner as it thinks fit, and may also require such proof of service as it thinks fit. Section IV of CPR Part 6 does not apply.

PART SIX
DISQUALIFICATION PROCEEDINGS OTHER THAN IN THE ROYAL COURTS OF JUSTICE

24. Modifications

III COM [63]

24.1 Where a disqualification application or a section 8A application is made by a claim form issued other than in the Royal Courts of Justice this Practice Direction shall apply with the following modifications.

(1) Upon the issue of the claim form the court shall endorse it with the date and time for the first hearing before a district judge. The powers exercisable by a registrar under this Practice Direction shall be exercised by a district judge.

(2) If the district judge (either at the first hearing or at any adjourned hearing before him) directs that the disqualification claim or section 8A application is to be heard by a High Court judge or by an authorised circuit judge he will direct that the case be entered forthwith in the list for hearing by that judge and the court will allocate (i) a date for the hearing of the trial by that judge and (ii) unless the district judge directs otherwise a date for the hearing of a Pre Trial Review by the trial judge.

PART SEVEN
DISQUALIFICATION UNDERTAKINGS

25. Costs

III COM [64]

25.1 The general rule is that where an undertaking is given after a disqualification application has been commenced the court will order the defendant to pay the costs where the claimant has accepted a disqualification undertaking.

25.2. The general rule will not apply where the court considers that the circumstances are such that it should make another order.

PART EIGHT
APPLICATIONS UNDER SECTION 8A OF THE ACT TO REDUCE THE PERIOD FOR WHICH A DISQUALIFICATION UNDERTAKING IS IN FORCE OR TO PROVIDE FOR IT TO CEASE TO BE IN FORCE

26. Headings

III COM [65]

26.1. Every claim form by which a section 8A application is begun and all affidavits, notices and other documents in the proceedings must be entitled in the matter of a disqualification undertaking and its date and in the matter of the Act.

27. Commencement: the claim form

27.1 Section 8A(3) of the Act identifies the courts which have jurisdiction to deal with section 8A applications.

27.2 A section 8A application shall be commenced by a claim form in the form annexed hereto issued:

(1) in the case of a disqualification undertaking given under section 9B of the Act, in the High Court out of the office of the companies court at the Royal Courts of Justice;

(2) in any other case,

(a) in the High Court out of the office of the companies court or a chancery district registry which has jurisdiction under the Act; and

(b) in the County Court which has jurisdiction under the Act, out of the appropriate county court office.

27.3 In section 8A applications the procedure set out in CPR Part 8, as modified by the Disqualification Rules and this Practice Direction shall apply. CPR rule 8.2 (contents of the claim form) shall not apply. CPR rule 8.1 (3) (power of the Court to order the application to continue as if the claimant had not used the Part 8 procedure) shall not apply.

27.4 In the case of a disqualification undertaking given under section 9B of the Act, the defendant to the section 8A application shall be the Office of Fair Trading or specified regulator which accepted the undertaking. In all other cases, the Secretary of State shall be made the defendant to the section 8A application.

27.5 Service of claim forms in section 8A applications will be the responsibility of the claimant and will not be undertaken by the court. If serving by first class post on the defendant's last known address the day of service shall, unless the contrary is shown, be deemed to be the 7th day next following that on which the claim form was posted. Otherwise, Sections I and II of CPR Part 6 apply. Attention is drawn to CPR r 6.14(2) regarding a certificate of service of the claim form.

27.6 Section IV of CPR Part 6 shall not apply. In any disqualification proceedings where a claim form or other document is required to be served on any person who is not in England and Wales, the court may order service on him to be effected within such time and in such manner as it thinks fit, may require such proof of service as it thinks fit, and may give such directions as to acknowledgment of service as it thinks fit.

27.7 The claim form served on the defendant shall be accompanied by an acknowledgment of service in the form annexed hereto.

28. Acknowledgement of service

28.1. The defendant shall:

(1) file an acknowledgment of service in the relevant practice form not more than 14 days after service of the claim form; and

(2) serve a copy of the acknowledgment of service on the claimant and any other party.

28.2. Where the defendant has failed to file an acknowledgment of service and the time period for doing so has expired, the defendant may nevertheless attend the hearing of the application and take part in the hearing as provided for by section 8A(2) or (2A) of the Act. However, this is without prejudice to the Court's case management powers and its powers to make costs orders.

29. Evidence

29.1. Evidence in section 8A applications shall be by affidavit. The undertaking (or a copy) shall be exhibited to the affidavit.

29.2. When the claim form is issued:

(1) the affidavit in support of the section 8A application must be filed in court;

(2) except where the court requires otherwise, exhibits must be lodged with the court where they shall be retained until the conclusion of the proceedings; and

COMPANIES

(3) copies of the affidavit and exhibits shall be served with the claim form on the defendant.

(4) If, as a result of the court's requirement, exhibits are not lodged in accordance with 28.2(2), the exhibits should be available at the trial and any other hearing at which reference to them may be made.

29.3 The defendant shall, within 28 days from the date of service of the claim form:

(1) file in court any affidavit evidence that he wishes the court to take into consideration on the application; and

(2) except where the court requires otherwise, lodge the exhibits with the court where they shall be retained until the conclusion of the proceedings; and

(3) at the same time, serve upon the claimant a copy of the affidavits and exhibits.

If, as a result of the court's requirement, exhibits are not lodged in accordance with 28.3(2), the exhibits should be available at the trial and any other hearing at which reference to them may be made.

29.4. The claimant shall, within 14 days from receiving the copy of the defendant's evidence:

(1) file in court any further affidavit evidence in reply he wishes the court to take into consideration; and

(2) except where the court requires otherwise, lodge the exhibits with the court where they shall be retained until the conclusion of the proceedings; and

(3) at the same time serve a copy of the affidavits and exhibits upon the defendant.

If, as a result of the court's requirement, exhibits are not lodged in accordance with 28.4(2), the exhibits should be available at the trial and any other hearing at which reference to them may be made.

29.5 Prior to the first hearing of the section 8A application, the time for serving evidence may be extended by written agreement between the parties. After the first hearing, the extension of time for serving evidence is governed by CPR rules 2.11 and 29.5.

29.6 So far as is possible all evidence should be filed before the first hearing of the section 8A application.

30. Hearings

30.1 Insofar as is relevant the provisions of paragraph 9 in Part Two above concerning hearings shall apply in respect of section 8A applications as they do in respect of disqualification applications.

31. The trial

31.1 Insofar as is relevant the provisions of paragraph 10 in Part Two above concerning trials shall apply in respect of section 8A applications as they do in respect of disqualification applications.

PART NINE
APPEALS

32. Appeals

III COM [66]

32.1 Rules 7.47 and 7.49A of the Insolvency Rules, as supplemented by Part Four of the Insolvency Proceedings Practice Direction, apply to an appeal from, or review of, a decision made by the court in the course of:

(1) disqualification proceedings under any of sections 6 to 8A or 9A of the Act;

(2) an application made under section 17 of the Act for the purposes of any of sections 1(1)(a), 1A(1)(a) or 9B(4), for permission to act notwithstanding a disqualification order made, or a disqualification undertaking accepted, under any of sections 6 to 10.

Any such decision, and any appeal from it, constitutes 'insolvency proceedings' for the purposes of the Insolvency Proceedings Practice Direction.

32.2 An appeal from a decision made by the court in the course of disqualification proceedings under any of sections 2(2)(a), 3 or 4 of the Act or on an application for permission to act notwithstanding a disqualification order made under any of those sections is governed by CPR Part 52 and Practice Direction 52.

NOTE TO ACCOMPANY DRAFT UPDATED CDDA 1986 PRACTICE DIRECTION

Background

III COM [67]–III COM [68]

1. This draft came about because it had been noted that the 1999 CDDA 1986 Practice Direction (as updated) was in a number of respects out of date. In particular:

1.1 It contained references to the 2000 edition of the Chancery Guide.

1.2 It made cross-references to CPR provisions on service which were no longer correct because of amendments to the CPR.

1.3 It had ceased to reflect current practice in the Companies Court (e.g. as to the way uncontested hearings were dealt with, and the fact that PTRs were no longer ordered as a matter of routine).

2. It was decided that the opportunity should be taken to do a general review of the contents of the Practice Direction.

The drafting committee

3. A committee was formed consisting of Chief Registrar Baister, Michael Gibbon QC of Maitland Chambers (who was heavily involved with disqualification as a junior barrister, and regularly appeared in the general Monday lists and PTR lists), Morris Peacock of Howes Percival (who has more than a decade of very close involvement with numerous disqualification cases at one of the government agents) and Catherine Doran of Radcliffe Chambers (who has over recent years spent a substantial amount of her practice as one of the disqualification list counsel). As drafting progressed, Malcolm Davis-White QC (whose expertise in this field is well-known, and who was involved in the drafting of the original 1999 Practice Direction) became involved.

4. Once the initial committee had reached consensus on a provisional draft, then other individuals with particular relevant experience were given the opportunity to consider the draft. DJ Andrew Saffmann of the Insolvency Court Users Committee, who has great experience of insolvency matters in the County Court context, agreed to take part at this stage, as did Colin Evans, Head of the Technical Team at the Insolvency Service. HH Judge Mithani (whose expertise in this field is also well-known) was also provided with a copy to consider.

5. Various modifications were made to the draft in the light of the observations received.

What the draft Practice Direction does not do

6. The 1999 Practice Direction had a difficult job: the intentions behind it included creating a procedural regime for civil disqualification proceedings to which the 1987 DQ Rules did not apply (e.g., proceedings under ss3 and 4 of CDDA 1986), and

COMPANIES

identifying how the DQ Rules should mesh effectively with the CPR and Insolvency Rules. The Practice Direction would be relatively straightforward to write if it had its source in a single set of rules: but it does not.

7. Practical examples of the complexity encountered and considered during the committee's work are numerous. Here are a variety:

7.1 In disqualification proceedings "application" may mean one of two different things: sometimes it is a reference to the substantive "claim" for the making of a disqualification order, sometimes it is a reference to a CPR Part 23 application. In this Note the two are distinguished by referring to the application for the making of a disqualification order as an "application/claim".

7.2 The 1987 Rules prescribe the use of affidavits in the relevant application/claims. That is now out of step with both the CPR and the IR 1986 (as amended). However, we do not consider that a change can be made to this by practice direction. The compulsory use of affidavits in the 1987 Rules seems intrinsically hard to justify in current circumstances.

7.3 Moreover, the Practice Direction shows how this creates practical complications for the unwary. Evidence in a disqualification application/claim must be by affidavit (leaving to one side the official receiver's report); but if an application is made within the proceedings, it is made under CPR Part 23, and is therefore to be supported by a witness statement.

7.4 The 1987 Rules apply to the vast majority (in number) of civil application/claims. However, it does not apply to all such application/claims. Given the same application/claim may seek an order under different sections (and this has occurred) and to ensure that in such cases one procedure applies to the application/claim and also to avoid the confusion that might arise where different procedures govern different application/claims the current PD seeks to apply a uniform regime to all civil disqualification applications/claims. We consider this approach should continue. We also consider that the written evidence rules for applications for permission to act notwithstanding disqualification should be governed by the same rule as applies to disqualification application/claims as the evidence on the two will often be inextricably bound together, the Courts having indicated that in the normal way any leave application should follow straight on from disqualification.

7.5 The 1987 Rules are now also out of step with IR 1986 on service out of the jurisdiction. Old IR 1986 r 12.12 was in similar terms to r 5(2) of the 1987 Rules, but under new r 12A.20, CPR Part 6 applies "with such modifications as the court may direct". Disqualification law and practice in this respect therefore is an island in a sea of otherwise superseded insolvency law. Again the PD cannot change the provision laid down by the 1987 Rules.

7.6 In terms of the organisation of the DQ Practice Direction, it is difficult to cut back on the apparent repetitiveness, because so many quirks of the different underlying regimes/types of applications need to be catered for. A related problem is that where attempts were made (e.g.) to combine provisions covering the same subject matter in different sections (e.g. service) the drafting got very dense trying to deal with exceptions: one virtue of the slightly lengthier approach is that is clearer.

8. We question whether now might be the time to consider the interaction between the 1987 Rules and the PD and, in particular, whether the time has come (a) to let the matter be governed solely by PD and (b) to bring the written evidence position more in line with modern practice. We recognise that these are policy issues, especially for the government.

Changes made by the draft

9. Notwithstanding the above, it has been possible to take the opportunity to use some cross-referencing and make some pruning of the text. Some elements of the 1999 Practice Direction were considered no longer necessary: for example, the old

para 6.1 set out in detail the required contents of the claim form (which was already annexed), whereas the new draft simply states that the claim form should be in the form annexed to the Practice Direction. By way of further example, it was felt that setting out matters which were essentially legal matters for the claimant to get right should be avoided (see for example old para 4.1A, which dealt with which courts had jurisdiction).

10. This Note is not intended to cover the specific changes in detail, but we highlight certain matters below.

10.1 Para 7.3 highlights current practice on participation in proceedings by defendants who have not filed acknowledgments of services. The court will normally require an undertaking that an acknowledgment will be filed: the reason for this is that the court has in the past found that defendants would attend for (say) directions hearings, but would afterwards prove untraceable if there was no acknowledgment on file.

10.2 The provisions for lodging exhibits (para 8.3 etc) reflect the Companies Court reality that exhibits have for a number of years often not been accepted by the court office because of lack of space.

10.3 In para 8.5, we make specific reference to the time when defendants should serve evidence on each other (which was left open by old para 9.5). We recognise that when there are cut-throat defences the court may consider it appropriate to order that defendants are only to exchange when they are all ready with their evidence, but we consider that the default position should simply be that they should serve on other defendants when they serve on the claimant.

10.4 Para 10.2 reflects current practice in requiring skeleton arguments in all cases (rather than "in all but the simplest cases"). See also para 11.3.

10.5 By contrast (and again reflecting current practice), para 10.3 leaves the issue of whether there should be a chronology and dramatis personae to the advocate, rather than requiring them in all but the simplest cases. Further, the requirement of a list of references to the defendant has been taken out: it was virtually entirely ignored in practice.

10.6 Section 11 has been introduced to deal with practice in relation to uncontested disposals, which form a significant part of the work in the general lists.

Chief Registrar Baister

Malcolm Davis-White QC

Michael Gibbon QC

Morris Peacock

Catherine Doran

---

1 The current rules are the Insolvent Companies (Disqualification of Unfit Directors) Proceedings Rules 1987, as amended ("the 1987 Rules"). For convenience, relevant references to the 1987 Rules, which apply to disqualification applications under sections 7, 8 and 9A of the Act (see rule 1(3)), are set out in footnotes to this Practice Direction. This Practice Direction applies certain provisions contained in the 1987 Rules to disqualification proceedings other than applications under sections 7, 8 and 9A of the Act.

2 This includes any applications under the Act to the extent provided for by subordinate legislation.

3 Rule 10 of the 1987 Rules.

4 Rule 2(2) of the 1987 Rules.

5 Rule 7(1) of the 1987 Rules.

6 Rule 5(1) of the 1987 Rules.

7 Rule 5(2) of the 1987 Rules.

8 Rule 3(2) of the 1987 Rules. Section 441 of the Companies Act 1985 makes provision for

the admissibility in legal proceedings of a certified copy of a report of inspectors appointed under Part XIV of the Companies Act 1985.

[9] Rule 3(3) of the 1987 Rules.

[10] Rule 3(1) of 1987 Rules.

[11] Rule 6(1) of the 1987 Rules.

[12] Rule 6(2) of the 1987 Rules.

[13] Rule 7(3) of the 1987 Rules.

[14] Rule 8(1) of the 1987 Rules.

[15] Rule 8(2) of the 1987 Rules.

III COM [69]

Notes n500a Notes n500b

Claim form

Directors disqualification application

In the	
Claim No.	
Fee Account no.	

In the matter of

SEAL

And in the matter of The Company Directors Disqualification Act 1986.

Name of Claimant	Name(s) of Defendant(s)

The hearing

(This section will be completed by the court)

The defendant(s) must attend before the (Registrar/District Judge) on

Date Time

Place

on the hearing of an application by , the claimant, for a disqualification order under section of the Company Directors Disqualification Act 1986 that:

The grounds upon which the claimant seeks a disqualification order are set out (in the details of claim overleaf and) in the (affidavit/report) of (sworn/dated) a true copy of which is served herewith.

Note: If you do not attend, the court may make such order as it thinks fit

Does your claim include any issues under the Human Rights Act 1998? ☐ Yes ☐ No

The court office at

Please address forms or letters to the Operational Delivery Manager and quote the claim number.

N500 Claim form - Directors disqualification proceedings (05.14)

COMPANIES

Claim No.	

Details of your claim

Defendant's(s) name(s) and address(es)

	£
Court fee	
Legal Representative Costs	
Issue date	

Claim No.	

Endorsement

1,CPR Part 8 as modified by the Directors Disqualification Proceedings Pratice Direction applies to this claim.

2. Any evidence which the defendant wishes to be taken into consideration by the court must be filed in court within 28 days from the date of service of the claim form and copies must then be served forthwith on the claimant. The evidence must be in the form of one or more affidavits.

[3. This claim is made in accordance with the Insolvent Companies (Disqualification of Unfit Directors) Proceedings Rules 1987 (S.I. 1987/2023, as amended).]

4. The court has the power to impose a disqualification period as follows:
where the application is under section 2 or section 4 of the Company Directors Disqualification Act, for a period of up to 15 years;
where the application is under section 3 of the Company Directors Disqualification Act, for a period of up to 5 years;
where the application is under section 7 of the Company Directors Disqualification Act, for a period of not less than 2 years and up to 15 years;
where the application is under section 8 or section 9A of the Company Directors Disqualification Act, for a period of up to 15 years.

[5. On the first hearing of the claim, the court may hear and determine the claim summarily, without further or other notice to you and if it is so determined, the court may impose disqualification for a period of up to 5 years.]

[6. If at the hearing of the application the court, on the evidence then before it, is minded to impose, in the case of any defendant, disqualification for any period longer than 5 years, it will not make a disqualification order on the first hearing but will adjourn the application to be heard (with further evidence, if any) at a later date that will be notified to the defendant. At the second hearing, the court may impose disqualification period of more than 5 years without any further reference to you.]

7. Your attention is drawn to the possibility of resolving the claim by offering an undertaking pursuant to section 1A or 9B of the Company Directors Disqualification Act (as applicable) or pursuant to the summary procedure adopted in Re Carecraft Construction Co. Ltd [1994] 1 WLR 172 (as clarified by the decision of the Court of Appeal in Secretary of State v Rogers [1996] 1 WLR 1569).

Statement of Truth

*(I believe)(The claimant believes) that the facts stated in this claim form are true.
* I am duly authorised by the claimant to sign this statement.

Full name of claimant

Name of claimant's legal representative's firm

position or office held

Signed

*(Claimant)(Claimant's legal representative) (if signing on behalf of firm or company)

delete as appropriate

Claimant's or claimant's legal representative's address to which documents should be sent if different from overleaf. If you are prepared to accept service by DX, fax or e-mail, please add details

Sign and Lock >

COMPANIES

III COM [70]

Notes for claimant on completing claim form N500

Directors disqualification application

Please read all of these guidance notes before you begin completing the claim form. The notes follow the order in which information is required on the form.

- Court staff can help you fill in the claim form and give information about procedure once it has been issued. But they cannot give legal advice. If you need legal advice, for example, about the likely success of your claim or the evidence you need to prove it, you should contact a solicitor or a Citizens Advice Bureau.
- If you are filing in the claim form by hand, please use black ink and write in block capitals.
- You must file evidence to support your claim with the claim form in the form of an affidavit or affirmation or where permitted by rule 3(2) of the Insolvent Companies (Disqualification of Unfit Directors) Proceedings Rules 1986, a report by the Official Receiver.
- Copy the completed claim form, the defendant's notes for guidance and your written evidence so that you have one copy for yourself, one copy for the court and one copy for each defendant. Send or take the forms and evidence to the court office with the appropriate fee. The court will tell you how much this is.

Notes on completing the claim form

Heading
You must fill in the heading of the form to indicate whether you want the claim to be issued in a county court or in the High Court (The High Court means either a District Registry (attached to a county court) or the Companies Court at the Royal Courts of Justice in London).

Use whichever of the following is appropriate:

'In the .... county court'
(inserting the name of the court)

or

'In the High Court of Justice Chancery Division
.... District Registry'
(inserting the name of the District Registry)

or

'In the High Court of Justice Chancery Division, Companies Court'

A disqualification application under section 9A of the Company Directors Disqualification Act must be issued in the High Court, out of the office of the Companies Court Registrar at the Royal Courts of Justice.

The section of text beginning 'In the matter of...' is included to comply with paragraph 5.1 of the Directors Disqualification Proceedings Practice Direction. You should insert the name of the relevant company(ies) after this text.

Claimant and defendant details
As the person issuing the claim, you are called the 'claimant'; the person you are suing is called the 'defendant'. You must provide the following information about yourself **and** the defendant according to the capacity on which you are suing and in which the defendant is being sued. When suing or being sued as:-

an individual:
All known forenames and surname (whether Mr, Mrs, Miss, Ms or Other e.g. Dr) and residential address (**including** postcode and telephone and any fax or e-mail number) in England and Wales. Where the defendant is a proprietor of a business, a partner in a firm or an individual sued in the name of a club or other unincorporated association, the address for service should be the usual or last known place of residence or principal place of business of the company, firm or club or other unincorporated association.

Where the individual is:

a firm
Enter the name of the firm followed by the words 'a firm' e.g. 'Bandbow - a firm' and an address for service which is either a partner's residential address or the principal or last known place of business.

a corporation (other than a company):
Enter the full name of the corporation and the address which is either its principal office or any other place where the corporation carries on activities and which has a real connection with the claim.

N500A Notes for claimant on completing a Part 8 claim form (06.05) HMCS

a company registered in England and Wales:
Enter the name of the company and an address which is either the company's registered office or any place of business that has a real, or the most, connection with the claim e.g. the shop where the goods were bought.

an oversea company (defined by s744 of the Companies Act 1985):
Enter the name of the company and either the address registered under s691 of the Act or the address of the place of business having a real, or the most, connection with the claim.

Hearing
Paragraph 4.3 of the Practice Direction states that 'When the claim form is issued, the claimant will be given a date for the first hearing of the disqualification application'. Court staff will complete these details when a date for a hearing is fixed, before the claim form is served. You should fill in the blanks in the sentence below the dates with the claimant's name and the section of the Company Directors Disqualification Act 1986 under which you are seeking the defendant's disqualification. You should then complete the empty section with the details of the order you wish the court to make, and delete the sections in the following sentence as appropriate.

Details of your claim
You should set out the details of your claim here, unless you have chosen to set them out only in an attached affidavit or report

Evidence
The evidence in support of the claim must be set out in an attached affidavit or report, which must include a statement of the matters by reference to which it is alleged that a disqualification order should be made against the defendant.

Defendant's name and address
Enter in this box the full name and address of the defendant to be served with the claim form (i.e. one claim form for each defendant). If the defendant is to be served outside England and Wales, you may need to obtain the court's permission.

Endorsement
If the claim is not brought under section 7, 8 or 9A of the Company Directors Disqualification Act 1986, paragraphs 3, 5 and 6 of the endorsement should be deleted.

Statement of truth
This must be signed by you, by your solicitor or your litigation friend, as appropriate.

Where the claimant is a registered company or a corporation the claim must be signed by either the director, treasurer, secretary, chief executive, manager or other officer of the company or (in the case of a corporation) the mayor, chairman, president or town clerk.

Address for documents
Insert in this box the address at which you wish to receive documents, if different from the address you have already given under the heading 'Claimant'. The address you give must be either that of your solicitors or your residential or business address and must be in England or Wales. If you live or carry on business outside of England and Wales, you can give some other address within England and Wales.

COMPANIES

III COM [71]

Notes for defendant
Directors disqualification application

Please read these notes carefully - they will help you to decide what to do about this claim.

- You have 14 days from the date on which you were served with the claim form (see below) in which to respond to the claim by completing and returning the acknowledgment of service enclosed with this claim form. The acknowledgement of service should be completed and returned to the court offce and a copy sent to the claimant named on the claim form.
- If you **do not return** the acknowledgment of service (Form N502), you will be allowed to attend any hearing of this claim but you will not be allowed to take part in the hearing unless the court gives you permission to do so.

Court staff can tell you about procedures but they cannot give legal advice. If you need legal advice, you should contact a solicitor or Citizens Advice Bureau immediately

Responding to this claim

Time for responding
The completed acknowledgment of service must be returned to the court office and a copy sent to the claimant named on the claim form within 14 days of the date on which the claim form was served on you. If the claim form was

- sent by post, the 14 days begins 7 days from the date of the postmark on the envelope.
- delivered or left at your address, the 14 days begins the day after it was delivered or left.
- handed to you personally, the 14 days begins on the day it was given to you.

Completing the acknowledgment of service (N502)
You should complete section A, B, or C as appropriate and all of section D.

Section A - contesting the claim
If you wish to contest the remedy sought by the claimant in the claim form, you should complete section A.

Section B - mitigation
If you do not wish to resist the claim for a disqualifcation order, but would like to offer evidence of mitigating circumstances with a view to justifying a shorter period of disqualifcation, you should complete section B.

Section C - disputing the court's jurisdiction
You should indicate your intention by completing section C and fling an application disputing the court's jurisdiction within 14 days of fling your acknowledgment of service at the court. The court will arrange a hearing date for the application and tell you and the claimant when and where to attend.

Section D - Statement of truth
This must be signed by you, by your solicitor or your litigation friend, as appropriate.

Where the defendant is a registered company or a corporation the claim must be signed by either the director, treasurer, secretary, chief executive, manager or other offcer of the company or (in the case of a corporation) the mayor, chairman, president or town clerk.

Written evidence
Any evidence which you wish to be taken into consideration by the court must be fled in court within 28 days from the date of service of the claim form upon you. The evidence must be in the form of an affidavit

Serving other parties
At the same time as you file your affidavit evidence with the court, you must also send copies of both the form and any written evidence to the claimant named on the claim form.

What happens next
The date of the first hearing of the claim is set out under 'Hearing'.

N500B Notes for defendant - Directors disqualifcation application (06.05) HMCS

III COM [72]

Claim form

Directors disqualification section 8A application

In the

Claim No.

In the matter of a disqualification undertaking date

and in the matter of the Company Directors Disqualifcation Act 1986.

SEAL

Name of Claimant

Name of Defendant(s)

The hearing

(This section will be completed by the court)

The defendant(s) must attend before the (Registrar/District Judge) on

Date Time

Place

on the hearing of an application by , the claimant, for an order under Section 8A of the Company Directors Disqualifcation Act 1986 that:

The grounds upon which the claimant seeks the order are set out (in the details of claim overleaf and) in the affidavit of) sworn on a true copy of which is served herewith.

Note: If you do not attend, the court may make such order as it thinks fit

The court office at

is open between 10 am and 4 pm Monday to Friday. When corresponding with the court, please address forms or letters to the Court Manager and quote the claim number.

N501 Claim form - Directors disqualifcation section 8A application (06.05)

COMPANIES

Claim No.	

Does your claim include any issues under the Human Rights Act 1998? ☐ Yes ☐ No

Details of your claim

Defendant's(s) name(s) and address(es)

	£
Court fee	
Solicitor's costs	
Issue date	

Endorsement

1. CPR Part 8 as modified by the Directors Disqualication Proceedings Pratice Direction applies to this claim.
2. Any evidence which the defendant wishes to be taken into consideration by the court must be filed in court within 28 days from the date of service of the claim form and copies must then be served forthwith on the claimant. The evidence must be in the form of one or more affdavits.

Statement of Truth

*(I believe)(The claimant believes) that the facts stated in this claim form are true.
* I am duly authorised by the claimant to sign this statement.

Full name of claimant ______________________________

Name of claimant's solicitor's firm ______________________________

signed ______________ position or offce held ______________

*(Claimant)(Litigation friend)(Claimant's solicitor) (if signing on behalf of firm or company)

**delete as appropriate*

Claimant's or claimant's solicitor's address to which documents should be sent if different from overleaf. If you are prepared to accept service by DX, fax or e-mail, please add details.

COMPANIES

III COM [73]

Notes for claimant on completing claim form N501

Directors disqualification section 8A application

Please read all of these guidance notes before you begin completing the claim form. The notes follow the order in which information is required on the form.

- Court staff can help you fill in the claim form and give information about procedure once it has been issued But they cannot give legal advice. If you need legal advice for example, about the likely success of your claim or the evidence you need to prove it, you should contact a solicitor or a Citizens Advice Bureau.
- If you are filling in the claim form by hand, please use black ink and write in block capitals.
- You must file evidence to support your claim with the claim form in the form of an affidavit or affirmation.
- Copy the completed claim form, the defendant's notes for guidance and your written evidence so that you have one copy for yourself, one copy for the court and one copy for each defendant. Send or take the forms and evidence to the court office with the appropriate fee. The court will tell you how much this is.

Notes on completing the claim form

Heading
You must fill in the heading of the form to indicate whether you want the claim to be issued in a county court or in the High Court (The High Court means either a District Registry (attached to a county court) or the Royal Courts of Justice in London). Section 8A(3) of the Company Directors Disqualification Act 1986 identifies the courts which have jurisdiction to deal with Section 8A applications.

An application under section 8A of the Company Directors Disqualification Act which relates to a disqualification undertaking given under section 9B of the Act must be issued in the High Court, out of the office of the Companies Court Registrar at the Royal Courts of Justice.

Use whichever of the following is appropriate:

'In the ....county court'
(inserting the court name)

or

'In the High Court of Justice Chancery Division
....District Registry'
(inserting the name of the District Registry)

or

'In the High Court of Justice Chancery Division, Companies Court'

Claimant and defendant details
As the person issuing the claim, you are called the 'claimant'; the person you are suing is called the 'defendant'. You must provide the following information about yourself **and** the defendant according to the capacity on which you are suing and in which the defendant is being sued. When suing or being sued as:-

an individual:
All known forenames and surname (whether Mr, Mrs, Miss, Ms or Other e.g. Dr) and residential address (**including** postcode and telephone and any fax or e-mail number) in England and Wales. Where the defendant is a proprietor of a business, a partner in a firm or an individual sued in the name of a club or other unincorporated association, the address for service should be the usual or last known place of residence or principal place of business of the company, firm or club or other unincorporated association.

Where the individual is:

a firm
Enter the name of the firm followed by the words 'a firm' e.g. 'Bandbow - a firm' and an address for service which is either a partner's residential address or the principal or last known place of business.

a corporation (other than a company):
Enter the full name of the corporation and the address which is either its principal office or any other place where the corporation carries on activities and which has a real connection with the claim.

N501A Notes for claimant on completing claim form N501 (06.05)

a company registered in England and Wales:
Enter the name of the company and an address which is either the company's registered office or any place of business that has a real, or the most, connection with the claim e.g. the shop where the goods were bought.

an oversea company (defined by s744 of the Companies Act 1985):
Enter the name of the company and either the address registered under s691 of the Act or the address of the place of business having a real, or the most, connection with the claim.

Hearing
Paragraph 30.3 of the Directors Disqualif cation Proceedings Practice Direction states that 'When the claim form is issued, the claimant will be given a date for the first hearing of the section 8 application'. Court staff will complete these details when a date for a hearing is fixed, before the claim form is served. However, you must complete the section below this with the details of the order you wish the court to make and fill in the details of your affidavit if you are attaching one to the form.

Details of your claim
You should set out the details of your claim here, unless you have chosen to set them out only in an attached affidavit.

Evidence
Evidence in section 8A applications must be by affidavit. The affidavit in support of the section 8A application must be filed in court at the same time as the claim form. Any exhibits to the affidavit must be lodged with the court at the same time. Copies of the affidavit and exhibits must be served with the claim form on the defendant.

Defendant's name and address
Enter in this box the full name and address of the defendant to be served with the claim form (i.e. one claim form for each defendant).

In the case of a disqualification undertaking given under section 9B of the Act, the defendant to the section 8A application shall be the Office of Fair Trading or specif ed regulator which accepted the undertaking. In all other cases, the defendant shall be the Secretary of State for Trade and Industry.

Addresses for service on government departments are set out in the List of Authorised government Departments issued by the Cabinet Office under section 17 of the Crown Proceedings Act 1947, which is annexed to the Practice Direction supplementing Part 66 of the Civil Procedure Rules.

Statement of truth
This must be signed by you, by your solicitor or your litigation friend, as appropriate.

Where the claimant is a registered company or a corporation the claim must be signed by either the director, treasurer, secretary, chief executive, manager or other officer of the company or (in the case of a corporation) the mayor, chairman, president or town clerk.

Address for documents
Insert in this box the address at which you wish to receive documents, if different from the address you have already given under the heading 'Claimant'. The address you give must be either that of your solicitors or your residential or business address and must be in England or Wales. If you live or carry on business outside of England and Wales, you can give some other address within England and Wales.

COMPANIES

III COM [74]

Notes for defendant

Directors disqualification section 8A application

Please read these notes carefully - they will help you to decide what to do about this claim.

- You have 14 days from the date on which you were served with the claim form (see below) in which to respond to the claim by completing and returning the acknowledgment of service enclosed with this claim form. The acknowledgement of service should be completed and returned to the court office and a copy sent to the claimant named on the claim form.
- If you **do not return** the acknowledgment of service (Form N503), you will be allowed to attend any hearing of this claim but you will not be allowed to take part in the hearing unless the court gives you permission to do so.

Court staff can tell you about procedures but they cannot give legal advice. If you need legal advice, you should contact a solicitor or Citizens Advice Bureau immediately

Responding to this claim

Time for responding
The completed acknowledgment of service must be returned to the court office (and a copy sent to the claimant named on the claim form) within 14 days of the date on which the claim form was served on you. If the claim form was:

sent by post, the 14 days begins 7 days from the date of the postmark on the envelope.

delivered or left at your address, the 14 days begins the day after it was delivered.

handed to you personally, the 14 days begins on the day it was given to you.

If the claim form was issued in the High Court in London, the acknowledgment of service should be returned to the Companies Court, General Off ce, Room TM 2.09, Royal Courts of Justice, The Strand, London, WC2A 2LL

Completing the acknowledgment of service (N503)
You should complete section A or B as appropriate and all of section C.

Statement of truth
This must be signed by you, your solicitor or your litigation friend, as appropriate.

Written evidence
Any evidence which you wish to be taken into consideration by the court must be filed in court withir 28 days from the date of service of the claim form upon you. The evidence must be in the form of an affidavit

Serving other parties
At the same time as you file your affidavit evidence with the court, you must also send copies of both the form and any written evidence to the claimant named on the claim form.

What happens next
The date of the first hearing of the claim is set out under 'hearing'.

N501B Notes for defendant - Directors disqualif cation section 8A application (06.05)

III COM [75]

Acknowledgment of service

Directors disqualification application

In the	
Claim No.	
Claimant (including ref)	
Defendant	

You should read the 'notes for defendant' (Form N500B) attached to the claim form which will tell you how to complete this form, and when and where to send it.

State the full name of the defendant

Section A

☐ I intend to contest the claim on the grounds that:

☐ I was not a director or shadow director of

at the time when my conduct, or the conduct of other persons, is in question.
(Please insert the name of each of the companies concerned in the box above)

☐ My conduct as a director or shadow director was not as alleged in support of the application for a disqualification order.

☐ I dispute the allegation that my conduct makes me unfit to be involved in the management of a company.

☐ I intend to contest the claim on the grounds that:
(Only complete this if the case has been brought under section 7 of the Company Directors Disqualification Act 1986. In the box below insert the name of any company listed on the claim form after the words 'In the matter of' to which this statement applies)

has at no time become insolvent within the meaning of section 6(2) of the Company Directors Disqualification Act 1986.

☐ I intend to contest the claim on the grounds that:
(Only complete this if the case has been brought under section 9A of the Company Directors Disqualification Act 1986. Please insert the name of any relevant company in the box below.)

has not committed a breach of competition law within the meaning of section 9A(4) of the Company Directors Disqualification Act 1986.

The court office at

is open between 10 am and 4 pm Monday to Friday. When corresponding with the court, please address forms or letters to the Court Manager and quote the claim number.

N502 Acknowledgment of service - Directors disqualification applications (06.05) HMCS

Section B

☐ I do not wish to dispute the claim for a disqualification order.

☐ I would like to offer evidence with a view to reducing the period of disqualification.

Section C

☐ The claim form was served outside England or Wales and I intend to dispute jurisdiction.

(You should file your application within 14 days of the date on which you file this acknowledgment of service with the court)

Section D

Statement of Truth

*(I believe)(The defendant believes) that the facts stated in this form are true.

*I am duly authorised by the defendant to sign this statement.

Full name ______________________________

Name of defendant's solicitor's firm ______________________________

Signed ____________________ position or office held ____________________

*(Defendant)(Litigation friend)(Defendant's solicitor) (if signing on behalf of firm or company)

Dated ____________________

**delete as appropriate*

Give an address (including post code) to which notices about this case can be sent to you.

Telephone no.	

If applicable	
Ref no.	
Fax no.	
DX no.	
E-mail	

III COM [76]

Acknowledgment of service

Directors disqualification section 8A application

You should read the 'notes for defendant' (Form N501B) attached to the claim form which will tell you how to complete this form, and when and where to send it.

In the	
Claim No.	
Claimant (including ref)	
Defendant	

Section A

☐ The defendant currently intends to appear at the hearing of the section 8A application.

☐ The defendant currently intends to file evidence on the section 8A application.

Section B

☐ The defendant intends to dispute jurisdiction

(You should file your application within 14 days of the date on which you file this acknowledgment of service with the court.)

Section C

Statement of Truth

*(I believe)(The defendant believes) that the facts stated in this form are true.

*I am duly authorised by the defendant to sign this statement.

Full name ______________________________

Name of defendant's solicitor's firm ______________________________

Signed ____________________ position or office held ____________________

*(Defendant)(Defendant's solicitor) (if signing on behalf of firm or company)

Dated ____________________

*delete as appropriate

Give an address (including post code) to which notices about this case can be sent to you.

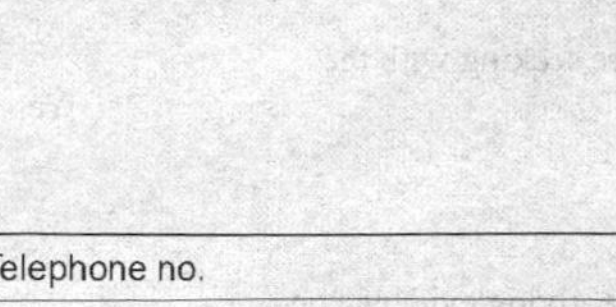

Telephone no.

If applicable	
Ref no.	
Fax no.	
DX no.	
E-mail	

The court office at

is open between 10 am and 4 pm Monday to Friday. When corresponding with the court, please address forms or letters to the Court Manager and quote the claim number.

N503 Acknowledgment of service - Directors disqualification section 8A application (06.05) HMCS

III COM [77]

Pre-trial checklist
Directors disqualification

To be completed by, or on behalf of,

who is [1st][2nd][3rd][ ][Claimant][Defendant] in this claim

Name of company to which claim relates

In the	
Claim no.	
Last date for filing with court office	
Date(s) fixed for trial or trial period	
Claimant	
Defendant	

This form must be **completed** and **returned** to the court no later than the date given above. If not, your evidence may be struck out or some other sanction imposed.

If the claim has settled, or settles before the trial date, you must let the court know immediately.

Legal representatives only: You must **attach** estimates of costs incurred to date, and of your likely overall costs. In substantial cases, these should be provided in compliance with CPR Part 43.

You must also **attach** a proposed timetable for the trial itself.

A Confirmation of compliance with directions

1. I confirm that I have complied with those directions already given which require action by me. ☐Yes ☐No

If you are unable to give confirmation, state which directions you have still to comply with and the date by which this will be done.

Directions	Date

2. I believe that additional directions are necessary before the trial takes place. ☐Yes ☐No

If Yes, you should attach an application and a draft order.

Include in your application all directions needed to enable the claim ***to be tried on the date, or within the trial period, already fixed.*** *These should include any issues relating to experts and their evidence, and any orders needed in respect of directions still requiring action by any other party.*

3. Have you agreed the additional directions you are seeking with the other party(ies)? ☐Yes ☐No

B Witnesses

1. How many witnesses (including yourself) will be giving evidence on your behalf at the trial? *(Do not include experts - see Section C)* ☐

Continued over

Witnesses continued

2. If the trial date is not yet fixed, are there any days within the trial period you or your witnesses would wish to avoid if possible? *(Do not include experts - see Section C)*

Please give details

Name of witness	Dates to be avoided, if possible	Reason

Please specify any special facilities or arrangements needed at court for the party or any witness (e.g. witness with a disability).

3. Will you be providing an interpreter for any of your witnesses? ☐ Yes ☐ No

C Experts

You are reminded that you may not use an expert's report or have your expert give oral evidence unless the court has given permission. If you do not have permission, you must make an application (see section A2 above)

1. Please give the information requested for your expert(s)

Name	Field of expertise	Joint expert?	Is report agreed?	Has permission been given for oral evidence?
		☐ Yes ☐ No	☐ Yes ☐ No	☐ Yes ☐ No
		☐ Yes ☐ No	☐ Yes ☐ No	☐ Yes ☐ No
		☐ Yes ☐ No	☐ Yes ☐ No	☐ Yes ☐ No

2. Has there been discussion between experts? ☐ Yes ☐ No

3. Have the experts signed a joint statement? ☐ Yes ☐ No

4. If your expert is giving oral evidence and the trial date is not yet fixed, is there any day within the trial period which the expert would wish to avoid, if possible? ☐ Yes ☐ No

If Yes, please give details

Name	Dates to be avoided, if possible	Reason

2 of 4

COMPANIES

D Legal representation

1. Who will be presenting your case at the trial? ☐ You ☐ Solicitor ☐ Counsel

2. If the trial date is not yet fixed, is there any day within the trial period that the person presenting your case would wish to avoid, if possible? ☐ Yes ☐ No

   If Yes, please give details

Name	Dates to be avoided, if possible	Reason

E Summary disposal under the Carecraft procedure or by disqualification undertaking

1. Have you considered the possibility of resolving this case by a disqualification undertaking or under the procedure adopted in *Re Carecraft Construction Co. Ltd* [1994] 1 WLR 172 ('a Carecraft application'). If not this should be considered as soon as possible. ☐ Yes ☐ No

2. Please state whether the case should be listed for a Carecraft disposal or full trial at a time and date to be fixed. ☐ Carecraft ☐ Full trial

3. If such a Carecraft application is to be made, the agreed written statement of facts must be submitted by the claimant as set out in the Practice Direction relating to disqualification proceedings and delivered to the court not later than 2 working days before the date upon which it is intended to make the application and in any event as soon as possible.

F The trial

1. Has the estimate of the time needed for trial changed? ☐ Yes ☐ No

   If Yes, say how long you estimate the whole trial will take, including both parties' cross-examination and closing arguments ☐ days ☐ hours ☐ minutes

2. If different from original estimate have you agreed with the other party(ies) that this is now the **total** time needed? ☐ Yes ☐ No

3. Is the timetable for trial you have attached agreed with the other party(ies)? ☐ Yes ☐ No

G Document and fee checklist

Tick as appropriate

I attach to this questionnaire -

- ☐ An application and fee for additional directions
- ☐ A proposed timetable for trial
- ☐ A draft order
- ☐ An estimate of costs
- ☐ Listing fee

Signed

[Counsel][Solicitor][for the][1st][2nd][3rd][ ]
[Claimant][Defendant]

Date

Please enter your [firm's] name, reference number and full postal address including (if appropriate) details of DX, fax or e-mail

Postcode

Tel. no.		DX no.		E-mail	
Fax no.		Ref. no.			

4 of 4

COMPANIES

COMPANIES ACT 2006

(c 46)

GENERAL NOTES ON COMPANIES ACT 2006

III COM [78]

General purpose and effect This legislation derives from the recommendations of the Company Law Review the object of which was "to bring forward proposals for a modern law for the modern world". The legislation replaced the existing law on companies and incidentally implements certain European Directives: the latter were brought into effect by the first two Commencement Orders.

III COM [79]–III COM [85]

Jurisdiction conferred on the High Court and certain county courts The jurisdiction to entertain claims and applications under the Act is conferred on the High Court and the county courts by s 1156, at **III COM [1133]**.

III COM [86]

Business and Property Courts On 4 July 2017 specialist jurisdictions across England and Wales, including the Companies Court and the Commercial Court were brought together under a single umbrella: The Business and Property Courts of England and Wales (B&PCs). In London the courts exercising the specialist jurisdictions continue to function in the Rolls Building in Fetter Lane. Outside London there are courts exercising the specialist jurisdictions in Birmingham, Bristol, Cardiff, Leeds and Manchester. In the five regional centres the cases are heard in what is now known as the Business and Property Courts List. In London all claims and applications under the Company Directors Disqualification Act 1986 or under the Companies Act 2006 should be assigned to the Insolvency and Companies list (Ch D). All High Court claims in London should be titled as follows:

IN THE HIGH COURT OF JUSTICE

BUSINESS AND PROPERTY COURTS OF ENGLAND AND WALES

INSOLVENCY AND COMPANIES LIST

If issued in a Regional Centre the second line of the title should be BUSINESS AND PROPERTY COURTS IN BIRMINGHAM, BRISTOL, CARDIFF, LEEDS or MANCHESTER, as the case may be.

III COM [87]

County courts with specialist jurisdiction Specialist jurisdiction cases that are within the competence of the county court may be issued for hearing in the County Court at Central London, Birmingham, Bristol, Cardiff or Manchester, also Newcastle, Leeds, Liverpool or Preston. Such cases will be marked 'Business and Property work' on allocation if not before.

They will be managed and heard only by judges specialising in this work, known as ICC judges. All claims and applications under the Company Directors Disqualification Act 1986 or under the Companies Act 2006 must be entitled 'IN THE MATTER OF [the name of the Company] and IN THE MATTER OF [the Company Directors Disqualification Act 1986, or as the case may be]. Proceedings must be started by Part 8 claim form except under ss 370, 955 or 968, where Part 7 is specified.

III COM [88]

European Companies The civil courts also have certain new powers in relation to the Societas Europaea, a public limited-liability company which is regulated by Council Regulation (EC) No 2157/2001 of 8 October 2001 on the Statute for a European Company. The courts of England and Wales may be involved with the affairs of such companies in relation to mergers (see paras 16 and 17 of the Practice Direction at **III COM [1501]**).

III COM [89]

Commencement The Companies Act 2006 (Commencement No 3, Consequential Amendments, Transitional Provisions and Savings) Order 2007, SI 2007/2194 and the Companies Act 2006 (Commencement No 4 and Commencement No 3 (Amendment)) Order 2007 brought into force many of its substantive provisions on 1 October 2007. They include ss 117 and 118 (inspection of register), s 169 (removal of directors), s 229 (directors' service contracts), s 238 (directors' indemnity provisions), ss 260-264 (derivative claims), s 295 (members' statements) s 306 (meeting by court order), s 317 (members' statements), s 358 (inspection of records), ss 369-373 (control of political donations except for independent election candidates) ss 994-996 (protection of members against unfair prejudice) and s 1132 (production and inspection of documents where offence suspected). The text of these provisions is set out below.

The Companies Act 2006 (Commencement No 5, Transitional Provisions and Savings) Order 2007, SI 2007/3495 appointed further days for commencement. As regards the sections set out below, the No 5 Order appointed 6 April 2008 for the commencement of ss 452, 456, 527, 745, 746, 749, 757-759, 782, 812, 896, 899, 900, 934 and 938. It appointed 1 October 2008 for the commencement of ss 74, 175-177 and 1157.

The 6th, 7th and 8th commencement orders (SI 2008/674, SI 2008/1886 and SI 2008/2860) provided for the remaining sections to be in force by 1 October 2009 save that following the final commencement on 1 October 2009, four provisions of the 2006 Act have not been commenced. These are s 327(2)(c), 330(6)(c), s 1175 as it applies in Northern Ireland and Part 2 of Schedule 9.

III COM [90]

Rules of court Proceedings under the Companies Acts are within the scope of the Civil Proceedings Rules 1998, as amended. Most of the claims are required by the Practice Direction to be brought by Case 8 procedure. However derivative claims are governed by **CPR 19.9** onwards and it will be noted that new rules were introduced by the Civil Procedure (Amendment) Rules 2007, SI 2007/2204, for derivative claims under the Companies Act 2006, ss 260-264. Exceptional provision is also made for proceedings under ss 994-996 for the protection of members against unfair prejudice. These are required by statute to be brought by petition.

III COM [91]

Practice and procedure See Practice Direction – Applications under the Companies Acts and Related Legislation, which is reproduced at the end of this title. Note in particular that the claim form in proceedings under the Companies Act 2006 should be entitled "In the matter of *[the name of the company in question]* and in the matter of the Companies Act 2006" and will, where issued in the High Court, be issued out of the Companies Court or a Chancery district registry. In a county court it will be issued out of a county court office. The company, if not the claimant, should be made a defendant.

III COM [92]

Enforcement of court orders against companies In addition to the enforcement remedies available against individuals, companies against which judgment debts have been obtained can be subject to winding-up petitions. See **III INS [11]**.

III COM [93]–III COM [94]

Service Paragraph 20 of the Practice Direction provides that the parties are responsible for service of documents in proceedings to which it applies.

PART 3
A COMPANY'S CONSTITUTION

III COM [95]

41. Constitutional limitations: transactions involving directors or their associates

(1) This section applies to a transaction if or to the extent that its validity depends on section 40 (power of directors deemed to be free of limitations under company's constitution in favour of person dealing with company in good faith).

Nothing in this section shall be read as excluding the operation of any other enactment or rule of law by virtue of which the transaction may be called in question or any liability to the company may arise.

(2) Where—

- (a) a company enters into such a transaction, and
- (b) the parties to the transaction include—
  - (i) a director of the company or of its holding company, or
  - (ii) a person connected with any such director,

the transaction is voidable at the instance of the company.

(3) Whether or not it is avoided, any such party to the transaction as is mentioned in subsection (2)(b)(i) or (ii), and any director of the company who authorised the transaction, is liable—

- (a) to account to the company for any gain he has made directly or indirectly by the transaction, and
- (b) to indemnify the company for any loss or damage resulting from the transaction.

(4) The transaction ceases to be voidable if—

- (a) restitution of any money or other asset which was the subject matter of the transaction is no longer possible, or
- (b) the company is indemnified for any loss or damage resulting from the transaction, or
- (c) rights acquired bona fide for value and without actual notice of the directors' exceeding their powers by a person who is not party to the transaction would be affected by the avoidance, or
- (d) the transaction is affirmed by the company.

(5) A person other than a director of the company is not liable under subsection (3) if he shows that at the time the transaction was entered into he did not know that the directors were exceeding their powers.

(6) Nothing in the preceding provisions of this section affects the rights of any party to the transaction not within subsection (2)(b)(i) or (ii).

But the court may, on the application of the company or any such party, make an order affirming, severing or setting aside the transaction on such terms as appear to the court to be just.

(7) In this section—

- (a) "transaction" includes any act; and
- (b) the reference to a person connected with a director has the same meaning as in Part 10 (company directors).

III COM [95.1]

Derivation and commencement This section derives from Companies Act 1985, 322A which it replaced on 1 October 2009.

III COM [95.2]

Procedure A claim for an order under this section is required by para 5 of the Practice Direction to be made by Part 8 claim form. A person connected with a director is defined in ss 252-254 to include family members (such as spouse, civil partner, live in partner, children, step children, children or step children of a partner) companies in which a director has at least a 20% stake, trustees of a family trust, business partners and firms in which a director or family member is a partner.

PART 5
A COMPANY'S NAME

III COM [96]

74. Appeal from adjudicator's decision

(1) An appeal lies to the court from any decision of a company names adjudicator to uphold or dismiss an application under section 69.

(2) Notice of appeal against a decision upholding an application must be given before the date specified in the adjudicator's order by which the respondent company's name is to be changed.

(3) If notice of appeal is given against a decision upholding an application, the effect of the adjudicator's order is suspended.

(4) If on appeal the court—

(a) affirms the decision of the adjudicator to uphold the application, or

(b) reverses the decision of the adjudicator to dismiss the application,

the court may (as the case may require) specify the date by which the adjudicator's order is to be complied with, remit the matter to the adjudicator or make any order or determination that the adjudicator might have made.

(5) If the court determines a new name for the company it must give notice of the determination—

(a) to the parties to the appeal, and

(b) to the registrar.

III COM [96.1]

Procedure Applicants who object to a company's name may apply under s 69 to the company names adjudicator from whom any appeal is a statutory appeal to which **CPR 52** applies and which should be started by appellant's notice in Form 161. The section, together with the Company Names Adjudicator Rules 2008 (SI 2008/ 1738) came into force on 1 October 2008.

PART 7
RE-REGISTRATION AS A MEANS OF ALTERING A COMPANY'S STATUS

III COM [97]

97. Re-registration of public company as private limited company

(1) A public company may be re-registered as a private limited company if—

(a) a special resolution that it should be so re-registered is passed,

(b) the conditions specified below are met, and

(c) an application for re-registration is delivered to the registrar in accordance with section 100, together with—

(i) the other documents required by that section, and

(ii) a statement of compliance.

(2) The conditions are that—

(a) where no application under section 98 for cancellation of the resolution has been made—

(i) having regard to the number of members who consented to or voted in favour of the resolution, no such application may be made, or

COMPANIES

(ii) the period within which such an application could be made has expired, or

(b) where such an application has been made—

(i) the application has been withdrawn, or

(ii) an order has been made confirming the resolution and a copy of that order has been delivered to the registrar.

(3) The company must make such changes—

(a) in its name, and

(b) in its articles,

as are necessary in connection with its becoming a private company limited by shares or, as the case may be, by guarantee.

III COM [97.1]

Derivation and commencement This section and the two which follow it derive from the Companies Act 1985, ss 53 and 54 which they replaced on 1 October 2009.

III COM [98]

98. Application to court to cancel resolution

(1) Where a special resolution by a public company to be re-registered as a private limited company has been passed, an application to the court for the cancellation of the resolution may be made—

(a) by the holders of not less in the aggregate than 5% in nominal value of the company's issued share capital or any class of the company's issued share capital (disregarding any shares held by the company as treasury shares);

(b) if the company is not limited by shares, by not less than 5% of its members; or

(c) by not less than 50 of the company's members;

but not by a person who has consented to or voted in favour of the resolution.

(2) The application must be made within 28 days after the passing of the resolution and may be made on behalf of the persons entitled to make it by such one or more of their number as they may appoint for the purpose.

(3) On the hearing of the application the court shall make an order either cancelling or confirming the resolution.

(4) The court may—

(a) make that order on such terms and conditions as it thinks fit,

(b) if it thinks fit adjourn the proceedings in order that an arrangement may be made to the satisfaction of the court for the purchase of the interests of dissentient members, and

(c) give such directions, and make such orders, as it thinks expedient for facilitating or carrying into effect any such arrangement.

(5) The court's order may, if the court thinks fit—

(a) provide for the purchase by the company of the shares of any of its members and for the reduction accordingly of the company's capital; and

(b) make such alteration in the company's articles as may be required in consequence of that provision.

(6) The court's order may, if the court thinks fit, require the company not to make any, or any specified, amendments to its articles without the leave of the court.

(7) In this section and section 99(3) "the court", in England and Wales, means the High Court".

III COM [98.1]

Procedure An application for an order under this section is required by para 5 of the Practice Direction to be made by Part 8 claim form. See also s 99 for the requirement to notify the registrar.

III COM [99]

99. Notice to registrar of court application or order

(1) On making an application under section 98 (application to court to cancel resolution) the applicants, or the person making the application on their behalf, must immediately give notice to the registrar.

This is without prejudice to any provision of rules of court as to service of notice of the application.

(2) On being served with notice of any such application, the company must immediately give notice to the registrar.

(3) Within 15 days of the making of the court's order on the application, or such longer period as the court may at any time direct, the company must deliver to the registrar a copy of the order.

(4) If a company fails to comply with subsection (2) or (3) an offence is committed by—

- (a) the company, and
- (b) every officer of the company who is in default.

(5) A person guilty of an offence under this section is liable on summary conviction to a fine not exceeding level 3 on the standard scale and, for continued contravention, a daily default fine not exceeding one-tenth of level 3 on the standard scale.

PART 8
REGISTER OF MEMBERS

III COM [100]–III COM [117]

117. Register of members: response to request for inspection or copy

(1) Where a company receives a request under section 116 (register of members: right to inspect and require copy), it must within five working days either—

- (a) comply with the request, or
- (b) apply to the court.

(2) If it applies to the court it must notify the person making the request.

(3) If on an application under this section the court is satisfied that the inspection or copy is not sought for a proper purpose—

- (a) it shall direct the company not to comply with the request, and
- (b) it may further order that the company's costs (in Scotland, expenses) on the application be paid in whole or in part by the person who made the request, even if he is not a party to the application.

(4) If the court makes such a direction and it appears to the court that the company is or may be subject to other requests made for a similar purpose (whether made by the same person or different persons), it may direct that the company is not to comply with any such request.

The order must contain such provision as appears to the court appropriate to identify the requests to which it applies.

(5) If on an application under this section the court does not direct the company not to comply with the request, the company must comply with the request immediately upon the court giving its decision or, as the case may be, the proceedings being discontinued.

III COM [117.1]

Challenging the member's request This provision is entirely new and it came into force on 1 October 2007. An application to the court for an order under this section is required by para 5 of the Practice direction to be made by Part 8 claim form. The 2006 Act does not provide any guidance as to what would not be a proper purpose for the inspection or copy. Courts may be influenced by the views of the Company Law Review Steering Group (CLRSG) whose work formed the basis for the 2006 Act. The CLRSG recommended that use of information in a company's register of members be restricted to purposes relevant to either the holding of interests recorded in the register, or the exercise of rights attached to them, and to other purposes approved by the company (CLRSG *The Final Report* URN 01/943 (July 2001) para 11.44.

A proper purpose test applies to requests to inspect a company's register of shareholders, see *Burry & Knight Ltd v Knight* [2014] EWCA Civ 604, [2015] 1 All ER 37, [2014] 1 WLR 4046 where a combination of proper and improper purposes meant that a company did not need to comply with such a request. In *Fox Davies v Burberry Plc* [2017] EWCA Civ 1129, [2017] BCC 387 the Court of Appeal held that a company was entitled to refuse to allow the claimant to inspect its register of members because the claimant's requests did not comply with s 116(4)(d) in that they did not identify the names and addresses of the persons to whom the information would be disclosed and because the requests were not for a proper purpose, the onus being on the company to prove the lack of proper purpose.

III COM [118]

118. Register of members: refusal of inspection or default in providing copy

(1) If an inspection required under section 116 (register of members: right to inspect and require copy) is refused or default is made in providing a copy required under that section, otherwise than in accordance with an order of the court, an offence is committed by—

(a) the company, and

(b) every officer of the company who is in default.

(2) A person guilty of an offence under this section is liable on summary conviction to a fine not exceeding level 3 on the standard scale and, for continued contravention, a daily default fine not exceeding one-tenth of level 3 on the standard scale.

(3) In the case of any such refusal or default the court may by order compel an immediate inspection or, as the case may be, direct that the copy required be sent to the person requesting it.

III COM [118.1]

Derivation, commencement and procedure This section derives in part from the Companies Act 1985, s 356 which it replaced on 1 October 2007. Proceedings should be started by Part 8 claim form.

III COM [119]–III COM [125]

125. Power of court to rectify register

(1) If—

(a) the name of any person is, without sufficient cause, entered in or omitted from a company's register of members, or

(b) default is made or unnecessary delay takes place in entering on the register the fact of any person having ceased to be a member,

the person aggrieved, or any member of the company, or the company, may apply to the court for rectification of the register.

(2) The court may either refuse the application or may order rectification of the register and payment by the company of any damages sustained by any party aggrieved.

(3) On such an application the court may decide any question relating to the title of a person who is a party to the application to have his name entered in or omitted from the register, whether the question arises between members or alleged

members, or between members or alleged members on the one hand and the company on the other hand, and generally may decide any question necessary or expedient to be decided for rectification of the register.

(4) In the case of a company required by this Act to send a list of its members to the registrar of companies, the court, when making an order for rectification of the register, shall by its order direct notice of the rectification to be given to the registrar.

III COM [125.1]

Derivation, commencement and procedure This section derives from the Companies Act 1985, s 359, which it replaced on 1 October 2009. Proceedings should be started by Part 8 claim form. The company, as well as any relevant members should be joined as defendants, see para 9 of the Practice Direction. Where a purported transfer of a member's shares has been held to be invalid it is appropriate for the court to order the rectification of the register and to restore the member's name as the owner, but such an order is not necessarily an indication as to the beneficial ownership of the company: *Smith v Charles Building Services Ltd* [2006] EWCA Civ 14, [2006] BCC 334. The rectification can be ordered with retrospective effect even though a company may be in the process of being wound up: *Re New Millenium Experience Co Ltd* [2003] EWHC 1823 (Ch), [2004] 1 All ER 687.

See *Avenue Road Developments Ltd v Reggiesco Ltd* [2012] EWHC 1625 (Ch), [2012] All ER (D) 135 (Jun), ChD and *Blindley Heath Investments Ltd v Bass* [2015] EWCA Civ 1023, for examples of cases involving claims for rectification of the company's register under s 125.

In *Nilon Ltd v Royal Westminster Investments SA* [2015] UKPC 2, [2015] 3 All ER 372, [2015] 2 BCLC 1 the Privy Council held that the right to rectify the share register under s 125 only arises where there has been a valid transfer of legal title and (contrary to the Court of Appeal's decision in *Re Hoicrest Ltd, Keene v Martin* [2000] 1 WLR 414, [2000] 1 BCLC 194, [1999] 44 LS Gaz R 39, CA) it is insufficient to merely have a prospective right against the company dependent upon the conversion of an equitable right to a legal title by an order for specific performance of the contract by which the shares were to be transferred. This principle was considered in *Intellimedia Technologies Ltd v Richards; Intellimedia Systems Ltd v Doyle* [2015] EWHC 1200 (Ch), [2015] All ER (D) 58 (Jun) where it was said that, although *Hoicrest* remains binding, rectification applications were essentially concerned with an applicant's rights vis à vis the company rather than with the resolution of inter shareholder contractual disputes.

PART 10
A COMPANY'S DIRECTORS

III COM [126]–III COM [169]

169. Director's right to protest against removal

(1) On receipt of notice of an intended resolution to remove a director under section 168, the company must forthwith send a copy of the notice to the director concerned.

(2) The director (whether or not a member of the company) is entitled to be heard on the resolution at the meeting.

(3) Where notice is given of an intended resolution to remove a director under that section, and the director concerned makes with respect to it representations in writing to the company (not exceeding a reasonable length) and requests their notification to members of the company, the company shall, unless the representations are received by it too late for it to do so—

(a) in any notice of the resolution given to members of the company state the fact of the representations having been made; and

(b) send a copy of the representations to every member of the company to whom notice of the meeting is sent (whether before or after receipt of the representations by the company).

(4) If a copy of the representations is not sent as required by subsection (3) because received too late or because of the company's default, the director may (without prejudice to his right to be heard orally) require that the representations shall be read out at the meeting.

(5) Copies of the representations need not be sent out and the representations need not be read out at the meeting if, on the application either of the company or of any other person who claims to be aggrieved, the court is satisfied that the rights conferred by this section are being abused.

(6) The court may order the company's costs (in Scotland, expenses) on an application under subsection (5) to be paid in whole or in part by the director, notwithstanding that he is not a party to the application.

III COM [169.1]

Derivation, commencement and procedure This section derives from the Companies Act 1985, s 304, which it replaced on 1 October 2007. Proceedings by a director, to challenge an intended removal of resolution under s 168, should be started by Part 8 claim form. Paragraph 10 of the Practice Direction provides that a copy of the claim form must be served on the company (if it is not the claimant) and on the director concerned unless this is not reasonably practicable in which case the claimant must provide evidence that it has otherwise notified the company and the director of the application.

III COM [170]

170. Scope and nature of general duties

(1) The general duties specified in sections 171 to 177 are owed by a director of a company to the company.

(2) A person who ceases to be a director continues to be subject—

- (a) to the duty in section 175 (duty to avoid conflicts of interest) as regards the exploitation of any property, information or opportunity of which he became aware at a time when he was a director, and
- (b) to the duty in section 176 (duty not to accept benefits from third parties) as regards things done or omitted by him before he ceased to be a director.

To that extent those duties apply to a former director as to a director, subject to any necessary adaptations.

(3) The general duties are based on certain common law rules and equitable principles as they apply in relation to directors and have effect in place of those rules and principles as regards the duties owed to a company by a director.

(4) The general duties shall be interpreted and applied in the same way as common law rules or equitable principles, and regard shall be had to the corresponding common law rules and equitable principles in interpreting and applying the general duties.

(5) The general duties apply to a shadow director of a company where and to the extent that they are capable of so applying.

III COM [170.1]

Commencement Sections 170 to 174 came into force on 1 October 2007.

THE GENERAL DUTIES

III COM [171]

171. Duty to act within powers

A director of a company must—

- (a) act in accordance with the company's constitution, and
- (b) only exercise powers for the purposes for which they are conferred.

III COM [172]

172. Duty to promote the success of the company

(1) A director of a company must act in the way he considers, in good faith, would be most likely to promote the success of the company for the benefit of its members as a whole, and in doing so have regard (amongst other matters) to—

- (a) the likely consequences of any decision in the long term,
- (b) the interests of the company's employees,
- (c) the need to foster the company's business relationships with suppliers, customers and others,
- (d) the impact of the company's operations on the community and the environment,
- (e) the desirability of the company maintaining a reputation for high standards of business conduct, and
- (f) the need to act fairly as between members of the company.

(2) Where or to the extent that the purposes of the company consist of or include purposes other than the benefit of its members, subsection (1) has effect as if the reference to promoting the success of the company for the benefit of its members were to achieving those purposes.

(3) The duty imposed by this section has effect subject to any enactment or rule of law requiring directors, in certain circumstances, to consider or act in the interests of creditors of the company.

III COM [173]

173. Duty to exercise independent judgment

(1) A director of a company must exercise independent judgment.

(2) This duty is not infringed by his acting—

- (a) in accordance with an agreement duly entered into by the company that restricts the future exercise of discretion by its directors, or
- (b) in a way authorised by the company's constitution.

III COM [174]

174. Duty to exercise reasonable care, skill and diligence

(1) A director of a company must exercise reasonable care, skill and diligence.

(2) This means the care, skill and diligence that would be exercised by a reasonably diligent person with—

- (a) the general knowledge, skill and experience that may reasonably be expected of a person carrying out the functions carried out by the director in relation to the company, and
- (b) the general knowledge, skill and experience that the director has.

III COM [175]

175. Duty to avoid conflicts of interest

(1) A director of a company must avoid a situation in which he has, or can have, a direct or indirect interest that conflicts, or possibly may conflict, with the interests of the company.

(2) This applies in particular to the exploitation of any property, information or opportunity (and it is immaterial whether the company could take advantage of the property, information or opportunity).

(3) This duty does not apply to a conflict of interest arising in relation to a transaction or arrangement with the company.

(4) This duty is not infringed—

(a) if the situation cannot reasonably be regarded as likely to give rise to a conflict of interest; or

(b) if the matter has been authorised by the directors.

(5) Authorisation may be given by the directors—

(a) where the company is a private company and nothing in the company's constitution invalidates such authorisation, by the matter being proposed to and authorised by the directors; or

(b) where the company is a public company and its constitution includes provision enabling the directors to authorise the matter, by the matter being proposed to and authorised by them in accordance with the constitution.

(6) The authorisation is effective only if—

(a) any requirement as to the quorum at the meeting at which the matter is considered is met without counting the director in question or any other interested director, and

(b) the matter was agreed to without their voting or would have been agreed to if their votes had not been counted.

(7) Any reference in this section to a conflict of interest includes a conflict of interest and duty and a conflict of duties.

III COM [175.1]

Commencement Sections 175 to 177 came into force on 1 October 2008.

In *Premier Waste Management v Towers* [2011] EWCA Civ 923, [2011] IRLR 73, [2012] 1 BCLC 67, the strict nature of the 'no conflict' duty was noted together with the irrelevance to its application of factors such as absence of good faith on the part of the director or absence of loss by the company. The test for directors' breach of duty under s 175 is objective; see *Richmond Pharmacology Ltd v Chester Overseas Ltd* [2014] EWHC 2692 (Ch), [2014] Bus LR 1110. See also *Killen v Horseworld Ltd* [2012] EWHC 363 (QB), [2012] All ER (D) 03 (Mar) and *Harbro Supplies Ltd v Hampton* [2014] EWHC 1781 (Ch) where the courts applied the s 175 duty to former directors. See also *Cullen Investments Ltd v Brown* [2017] EWHC 1586 (Ch) where a director of a joint venture who had an interest in a competitor was in breach of his duties under ss 172 and 175–177 and *Bhullar v Bhullar* [2017] EWHC 407 (Ch) where a director breached his fiduciary duty by procuring payments to be made to a company he controlled without the authority of his fellow directors and, having not acted reasonably, was not relieved of liability under s 1157.

In a case where the defendants assisted the sole director in conduct in breach of s 175, they too were held liable for the breach: *Goldtrail Travel Ltd (in liquidation) v Aydin* [2016] EWCA Civ 371, [2016] All ER (D) 91 (Apr).

III COM [176]

176. Duty not to accept benefits from third parties

(1) A director of a company must not accept a benefit from a third party conferred by reason of—

(a) his being a director, or

(b) his doing (or not doing) anything as director.

(2) A "third party" means a person other than the company, an associated body corporate or a person acting on behalf of the company or an associated body corporate.

(3) Benefits received by a director from a person by whom his services (as a director or otherwise) are provided to the company are not regarded as conferred by a third party.

(4) This duty is not infringed if the acceptance of the benefit cannot reasonably be regarded as likely to give rise to a conflict of interest.

(5) Any reference in this section to a conflict of interest includes a conflict of interest and duty and a conflict of duties.

III COM [177]

177. Duty to declare interest in proposed transaction or arrangement

(1) If a director of a company is in any way, directly or indirectly, interested in a proposed transaction or arrangement with the company, he must declare the nature and extent of that interest to the other directors.

(2) The declaration may (but need not) be made—

- (a) at a meeting of the directors, or
- (b) by notice to the directors in accordance with—
  - (i) section 184 (notice in writing), or
  - (ii) section 185 (general notice).

(3) If a declaration of interest under this section proves to be, or becomes, inaccurate or incomplete, a further declaration must be made.

(4) Any declaration required by this section must be made before the company enters into the transaction or arrangement.

(5) This section does not require a declaration of an interest of which the director is not aware or where the director is not aware of the transaction or arrangement in question. For this purpose a director is treated as being aware of matters of which he ought reasonably to be aware.

(6) A director need not declare an interest—

- (a) if it cannot reasonably be regarded as likely to give rise to a conflict of interest;
- (b) if, or to the extent that, the other directors are already aware of it (and for this purpose the other directors are treated as aware of anything of which they ought reasonably to be aware); or
- (c) if, or to the extent that, it concerns terms of his service contract that have been or are to be considered—
  - (i) by a meeting of the directors, or
  - (ii) by a committee of the directors appointed for the purpose under the company's constitution.

SUPPLEMENTARY PROVISIONS

III COM [178]

178. Civil consequences of breach of general duties

(1) The consequences of breach (or threatened breach) of sections 171 to 177 are the same as would apply if the corresponding common law rule or equitable principle applied.

(2) The duties in those sections (with the exception of section 174 (duty to exercise reasonable care, skill and diligence)) are, accordingly, enforceable in the same way as any other fiduciary duty owed to a company by its directors.

III COM [178.1]

Commencement Sections 178 and 179 came into force on 1 October 2007.

III COM [179]

179. Cases within more than one of the general duties

Except as otherwise provided, more than one of the general duties may apply in any given case.

III COM [180]

180. Consent, approval or authorisation by members

(1) In a case where—

COMPANIES

(a) section 175 (duty to avoid conflicts of interest) is complied with by authorisation by the directors, or
(b) section 177 (duty to declare interest in proposed transaction or arrangement) is complied with, the transaction or arrangement is not liable to be set aside by virtue of any common law rule or equitable principle requiring the consent or approval of the members of the company.

This is without prejudice to any enactment, or provision of the company's constitution, requiring such consent or approval.

(2) The application of the general duties is not affected by the fact that the case also falls within Chapter 4 or 4A (transactions requiring approval of members), except that where either of those Chapters applies and—
(a) approval is given under the Chapter concerned, or
(b) the matter is one as to which it is provided that approval is not needed,
it is not necessary also to comply with section 175 (duty to avoid conflicts of interest) or section 176 (duty not to accept benefits from third parties).

(3) Compliance with the general duties does not remove the need for approval under any applicable provision of Chapter 4 or 4A (transactions requiring approval of members).

(4) The general duties—
(a) have effect subject to any rule of law enabling the company to give authority, specifically or generally, for anything to be done (or omitted) by the directors, or any of them, that would otherwise be a breach of duty, and
(b) where the company's articles contain provisions for dealing with conflicts of interest, are not infringed by anything done (or omitted) by the directors, or any of them, in accordance with those provisions.

(5) Otherwise, the general duties have effect (except as otherwise provided or the context otherwise requires) notwithstanding any enactment or rule of law.

III COM [180.1]

Derivation, commencement and procedure These provisions provide a statutory statement of directors' duties and are an innovation introduced by the Companies Act 2006. The statement of duties is not intended to be an exhaustive list of all the duties owed by a director to his company. No attempt has been made to codify the principle that directors are regarded as trustees of the company's property, but in the light of s 170(3) such principle survives. According to ministerial statements, the statutory statement of general duties is based on and intended to replace the common law rules and equitable principles but the courts should continue to have regard to the continuing development of those rules and principles: *Lord Goldsmith, Lords Grand Committee, 6 February 2006, column 243-4*. The case law which has established the duties in equity and at Common Law will therefore continue to be relevant. This section came into force on 1 October 2007 save that sub-ss (1), (2) (in part) and 4(b) came into force on 1 October 2008. A director's duties under these sections are owed to his company and in case of breach, the company is the proper plaintiff and the claim should be brought by CPR Part 8 claim form.

III COM [181]–III COM [229]

229. Right of member to inspect and request copy

(1) Every copy or memorandum required to be kept under section 228 must be open to inspection by any member of the company without charge.

(2) Any member of the company is entitled, on request and on payment of such fee as may be prescribed, to be provided with a copy of any such copy or memorandum.

The copy must be provided within seven days after the request is received by the company.

(3) If an inspection required under subsection (1) is refused, or default is made in complying with subsection (2), an offence is committed by every officer of the company who is in default.

(4) A person guilty of an offence under this section is liable on summary conviction to a fine not exceeding level 3 on the standard scale and, for continued contravention, a daily default fine not exceeding one-tenth of level 3 on the standard scale.

(5) In the case of any such refusal or default the court may by order compel an immediate inspection or, as the case may be, direct that the copy required be sent to the person requiring it.

III COM [229.1]

Derivation, commencement and procedure This section derives from the Companies Act 1985, s 318, which it replaced on 1 October 2007. Proceedings for an order for the inspection or copying of the director's service contract should be started by Part 8 claim form.

III COM [230]–III COM [238]

238. Right of member to inspect and request copy

(1) Every copy or memorandum required to be kept by a company under section 237 must be open to inspection by any member of the company without charge.

(2) Any member of the company is entitled, on request and on payment of such fee as may be prescribed, to be provided with a copy of any such copy or memorandum.

The copy must be provided within seven days after the request is received by the company.

(3) If an inspection required under subsection (1) is refused, or default is made in complying with subsection (2), an offence is committed by every officer of the company who is in default.

(4) A person guilty of an offence under this section is liable on summary conviction to a fine not exceeding level 3 on the standard scale and, for continued contravention, a daily default fine not exceeding one-tenth of level 3 on the standard scale.

(5) In the case of any such refusal or default the court may by order compel an immediate inspection or, as the case may be, direct that the copy required be sent to the person requiring it.

III COM [238.1]

Derivation, commencement and procedure This section derives from the Companies Act 1985, s 309C, which it replaced on 1 October 2007. Proceedings for an order for the inspection or copying of the director's indemnity provision should be started by Part 8 claim form.

PART 11
DERIVATIVE CLAIMS AND PROCEEDINGS BY MEMBERS

III COM [239]–III COM [260]

260. Derivative claims

(1) This Chapter applies to proceedings in England and Wales or Northern Ireland by a member of a company—

(a) in respect of a cause of action vested in the company, and

(b) seeking relief on behalf of the company.

This is referred to in this Chapter as a "derivative claim".

(2) A derivative claim may only be brought—

(a) under this Chapter, or
(b) in pursuance of an order of the court in proceedings under section 994 (proceedings for protection of members against unfair prejudice).

(3) A derivative claim under this Chapter may be brought only in respect of a cause of action arising from an actual or proposed act or omission involving negligence, default, breach of duty or breach of trust by a director of the company.

The cause of action may be against the director or another person (or both).

(4) It is immaterial whether the cause of action arose before or after the person seeking to bring or continue the derivative claim became a member of the company.

(5) For the purposes of this Chapter—
(a) "director" includes a former director;
(b) a shadow director is treated as a director; and
(c) references to a member of a company include a person who is not a member but to whom shares in the company have been transferred or transmitted by operation of law.

III COM [260.1]

Derivation and commencement The provisions in Part 11 derive from the common law jurisdiction to entertain claims by members in the name of the company, arising out of wrongs done to the company by the directors, in circumstances identified in *Foss v Harbottle* (1843) 2 Hare 461. This section and the ones which follow consolidate and clarify the existing law, with minor changes. They came into force on 1 October 2007. Derivative claims can also be brought in pursuance to an order of the court in proceedings under s 994 (Unfair Prejudice).

It has been held that the statutory provisions abolished and replaced the common law derivative action in relation to proceedings by members of the wronged company. However, the statute did not abolish the common law multiple derivative action, which it has been held may still be used where members of a holding company are seeking to protect a company owned by the holding company: *Re Fort Gilkicker Ltd, Universal Project Management Services Ltd v Fort Gilkicker Ltd* [2013] EWHC 348 (Ch), [2013] Ch 551, [2013] 3 All ER 546. A multiple derivative action is not within ss 260 to 264 of the Companies Act 2006, see *Bhullar v Bhullar* [2015] EWHC 1943 (Ch), 165 NLJ 7662, [2015] All ER (D) 130 (Jul).

In *Harris v Microfusion 2013 LLP* [2016] EWCA Civ 1212 the Court of Appeal considered the fraud on a minority exception to the rule in *Foss v Harbottle* in the context of limited liability partnerships.

III COM [260.2]

Directors' conduct The scope of s 260(3) includes a broader range of conduct on the part of directors. It goes further than the common law, as decided in *Pavlides v Jensen* [1956] 2 All ER 518 by covering negligence in circumstances where the directors have not benefited from their negligence. The cause of action may be against a director or against another person or both. Scenarios in which a third party would be a proper defendant include where a third party dishonestly assisted a director to act in breach of his fiduciary obligations, or where a tracing claim is made against a third party arising out of a primary wrongdoing committed by the director.

III COM [261]

261. Application for permission to continue derivative claim

(1) A member of a company who brings a derivative claim under this Chapter must apply to the court for permission (in Northern Ireland, leave) to continue it.

(2) If it appears to the court that the application and the evidence filed by the applicant in support of it do not disclose a prima facie case for giving permission (or leave), the court—
(a) must dismiss the application, and
(b) may make any consequential order it considers appropriate.

(3) If the application is not dismissed under subsection (2), the court—
(a) may give directions as to the evidence to be provided by the company, and
(b) may adjourn the proceedings to enable the evidence to be obtained.

(4) On hearing the application, the court may—

(a) give permission (or leave) to continue the claim on such terms as it thinks fit,

(b) refuse permission (or leave) and dismiss the claim, or

(c) adjourn the proceedings on the application and give such directions as it thinks fit.

III COM [261.1]

Procedure The procedure for derivative claims is set out in **CPR 19.9**, **19.9A-19.9F**. It is excluded from the ambit of the Companies Acts Practice Direction by para 2 of Section I and has a Practice Direction of its own: Practice Direction 1 – Derivative Claims at **CPR PD 19C**. As set out in **CPR 19.9**, the proceedings must be started by a claim form (Part 7) and headed 'derivative claim' and the company must be made a defendant. The next step is to make a Part 23 application, supported by written evidence, for permission to proceed and to serve them on the company, together with a notice in the form set out in Practice Direction 19C and copies of the claim form and particulars of claim. The procedure set out in **CPR 19.9C** applies in the case of a trade union or a body corporate to which Chapter 1 of Part 11 does not apply. The application procedure is also applicable in cases where derivative claims arise in the course of other proceedings: **CPR 19.9D**. Where, in any such proceedings, notifying the company of the permission application would be likely to frustrate some part of the remedy sought, an application may be made, without notice to the company to delay the serving of the notice but reasons must be stated together with any written evidence in support: **CPR 19.9A(7)** and para 3 of the Practice Direction at **CPR 19C**. The decision whether the claimant's evidence discloses a prima facie case will normally be made at an ex parte hearing without submissions from or (in the case of an oral hearing to reconsider such a decision reached pursuant to **CPR 19.9A(9)**) attendance by the company. If without invitation from the court the company volunteers a submission or attendance, the company will not normally be allowed any costs of that submission or attendance: **CPR PD 19C** para 5. If at the ex parte hearing the court is satisfied that there is a prima facie case for giving permission to bring a derivative claim, the court is likely to order that an inter partes hearing take place to consider the merits of the application in more detail. However, that inter partes hearing should not amount to 'anything like a mini trial of the action'. See *Fanmailuk.com v Cooper* [2008 EWHC 3131 (Ch), [2008] All ER (D) 183 (Dec) and *Iesini v Westrip Holdings Ltd* [2009] EWHC 2526 (Ch). It would require very exceptional circumstances for a derivative claim to be brought by a majority shareholder in control of the company. See *Cinematic Finance v Ryder* [2010] All ER (D) 283 (Oct). If the applicants serve the defendants with notice of the application the court may proceed to the second stage of the application (the hearing) without making a decision on the papers as contemplated by **CPR 19.9A**: *Mission Capital plc v Sinclair* [2010] 1 BCLC 304; *Stimpson v Southern Landlords Association* [2010] BCC 387.

In *Wilton UK Ltd v Shuttleworth* [2017] EWHC 2195 (Ch) the Court considered the consequences of the claimant serving a derivative claim and particulars of claim without first obtaining the Court's permission under s 261. It was held that the failure invalidated the steps taken but that the court had jurisdiction to grant retrospective permission.

In *Langley Ward Ltd v Trevor* [2011] EWHC 1893 (Ch), [2011] All ER (D) 78 (Jul), ChD the court refused permission to commence a derivative action where there were two equal shareholders and the company was deadlocked and some of the allegations were more relevant to an application to wind up the company on just and equitable grounds. In *Phillips v Fryer* [2012] EWHC 1611 (Ch), [2012] All ER (D) 74 (Jun) ChD the court allowed a claimant to proceed with a derivative claim despite the fact that an unfair prejudice petition under s 994 had been issued.

For a case where an essentially intra-shareholder dispute was allowed to proceed by way of a derivative claim but the claimant was refused an indemnity against costs see *Hook v Sumner* [2015] EWHC 3820 (Ch), [2016] BCC 220.

III COM [262]

262. Application for permission to continue claim as a derivative claim

(1) This section applies where—

(a) a company has brought a claim, and

(b) the cause of action on which the claim is based could be pursued as a derivative claim under this Chapter.

(2) A member of the company may apply to the court for permission (in Northern Ireland, leave) to continue the claim as a derivative claim on the ground that—

(a) the manner in which the company commenced or continued the claim amounts to an abuse of the process of the court,

(b) the company has failed to prosecute the claim diligently, and

(c) it is appropriate for the member to continue the claim as a derivative claim.

(3) If it appears to the court that the application and the evidence filed by the applicant in support of it do not disclose a prima facie case for giving permission (or leave), the court—

(a) must dismiss the application, and

(b) may make any consequential order it considers appropriate.

(4) If the application is not dismissed under subsection (3), the court—

(a) may give directions as to the evidence to be provided by the company, and

(b) may adjourn the proceedings to enable the evidence to be obtained.

(5) On hearing the application, the court may—

(a) give permission (or leave) to continue the claim as a derivative claim on such terms as it thinks fit,

(b) refuse permission (or leave) and dismiss the application, or

(c) adjourn the proceedings on the application and give such directions as it thinks fit.

III COM [262.1]

Procedure In the case of proceedings under s 262(1), the procedure in **CPR 19.9B** should be followed.

III COM [262.2]

Costs of derivative claim The court may order the company body corporate or trade union for the benefit of which a derivative claim is brought to indemnify the claimant against liability for costs incurred in the permission application or in the derivative claim or both: **CPR 19.9E**. This reflects the Common Law position and has been held to be analogous to the indemnity which a trustee is entitled to in respect of trust proceedings: *Wallersteiner v Moir (No2)* [1975] QB 373. Where it is intended to seek such an order this should be stated in the application notice or, as the case may be, the claim form. An equal shareholder who brings a derivative action against his co-shareholder is unlikely to be entitled to an order for the company to indemnify his costs: *Halle v Trax BW Ltd* [2000] BCC 1020.

As regards awarding costs on an indemnity basis, see *Carlisle & Cumbria United Independent Supporters' Society Ltd v CUFC Holdings Ltd* [2010] EWCA Civ 463, [2010] All ER (D) 25 (May); *Kiani v Cooper* [2010] EWHC 577 (Ch), [2010] 2 BCLC 427, [2010] BCC 463 and *Stainer v Lee* [2010] EWHC 1539 (Ch), [2011] 1 BCLC 537.

III COM [263]

263. Whether permission to be given

(1) The following provisions have effect where a member of a company applies for permission (in Northern Ireland, leave) under section 261 or 262.

(2) Permission (or leave) must be refused if the court is satisfied—

(a) that a person acting in accordance with section 172 (duty to promote the success of the company) would not seek to continue the claim, or

(b) where the cause of action arises from an act or omission that is yet to occur, that the act or omission has been authorised by the company, or

(c) where the cause of action arises from an act or omission that has already occurred, that the act or omission—

(i) was authorised by the company before it occurred, or

(ii) has been ratified by the company since it occurred.

(3) In considering whether to give permission (or leave) the court must take into account, in particular—

(a) whether the member is acting in good faith in seeking to continue the claim;

(b) the importance that a person acting in accordance with section 172 (duty to promote the success of the company) would attach to continuing it;

(c) where the cause of action results from an act or omission that is yet to occur, whether the act or omission could be, and in the circumstances would be likely to be—

(i) authorised by the company before it occurs, or

(ii) ratified by the company after it occurs;

(d) where the cause of action arises from an act or omission that has already occurred, whether the act or omission could be, and in the circumstances would be likely to be, ratified by the company;

(e) whether the company has decided not to pursue the claim;

(f) whether the act or omission in respect of which the claim is brought gives rise to a cause of action that the member could pursue in his own right rather than on behalf of the company.

(4) In considering whether to give permission (or leave) the court shall have particular regard to any evidence before it as to the views of members of the company who have no personal interest, direct or indirect, in the matter.

(5) The Secretary of State may by regulations—

(a) amend subsection (2) so as to alter or add to the circumstances in which permission (or leave) is to be refused;

(b) amend subsection (3) so as to alter or add to the matters that the court is required to take into account in considering whether to give permission (or leave).

(6) Before making any such regulations the Secretary of State shall consult such persons as he considers appropriate.

(7) Regulations under this section are subject to affirmative resolution procedure.

III COM [263.1]

Exercise of discretion Where permission is given to continue a derivative claim the court may order that the claim may not be discontinued or settled without the permission of the court: **CPR 19.9F**.

III COM [263.2]

The appropriate test for permission The factors listed in s 263(3) are consistent with the approach which would be taken by a hypothetical and independent board of directors, as recommended in *Airey v Cordell* [2006] EWHC 2728 (Ch), [2006] All ER (D) 111 (Aug). Courts are less likely to allow a derivative action if the member has any alternative remedies, (for example a claim for breach of a shareholders' agreement as in *Franbar Holdings v Patel* [2008] EWHC 1534 (Ch), [2008] All ER (D) 14 (Jul) or member's unfair prejudice petition under s 994 - **III COM [994]**) or has an ulterior motive: *Barrett v Duckett* [1995] 1 BCLC 243, [1995] BCC 362. However, where a claimant intends to bring a derivative claim for the benefit of a company he will not be disqualified from doing so just because there are other benefits that he will derive from the claim. See *Iesini v Westrip Holdings Ltd* [2009] EWHC 2526. The new statutory procedure was considered in *Mission Capital PLC v Sinclair* [2008] EWHC 1339 (Ch), [2008] All ER (D) 225 (Mar) where it was held that permission to continue with the derivative action should be refused where a notional director was unlikely to attach much importance to the claim and the alleged damage was speculative. In *Kleanthous v Paphitis* [2011] EWHC 2287 (Ch), [2011] All ER (D) 33 (Sep) and *Langley Ward Ltd v Trevor* [2011] EWHC 1893 (Ch) the court refused permission to pursue actions as derivative claims on the basis that a person acting in accordance with their duties under s 172 would not seek to continue the claim. If a company is incorporated overseas it is not normally appropriate to commence a derivative action in this jurisdiction: *Reeves v Sprecher* [2007] EWHC 117 (Ch), [2007] 2 BCLC 614.

III COM [263.3]

The views of independent members The importance of the views of independent members is highlighted by the fact that under s 263(4) the courts shall have *particular regard* to those views rather than merely taking them into account. This reflects the approach adopted by the courts: *Smith v Croft (No 2)* [1988] Ch 114, [1987] 3 All ER 909, CA.

III COM [263.4]

Mandatory refusal of permission A mandatory refusal, under s 263(2)(a) would be justified only where the court was satisfied that no director acting in accordance with s 172 would seek to continue the claim. If some directors would, and others would not, the case would not fall within subsection (2)(a) but rather within subsection (3)(b): *Iesini v Westrip Holdings Ltd* [2009] EWHC 2526 (Ch), [2011] 1 BCLC 498, [2010] NLJR 1045.

III COM [264]

264. Application for permission to continue derivative claim brought by another member

(1) This section applies where a member of a company ("the claimant")—

(a) has brought a derivative claim,

(b) has continued as a derivative claim a claim brought by the company, or

(c) has continued a derivative claim under this section.

(2) Another member of the company ("the applicant") may apply to the court for permission (in Northern Ireland, leave) to continue the claim on the ground that—

(a) the manner in which the proceedings have been commenced or continued by the claimant amounts to an abuse of the process of the court,

(b) the claimant has failed to prosecute the claim diligently, and

(c) it is appropriate for the applicant to continue the claim as a derivative claim.

(3) If it appears to the court that the application and the evidence filed by the applicant in support of it do not disclose a prima facie case for giving permission (or leave), the court—

(a) must dismiss the application, and

(b) may make any consequential order it considers appropriate.

(4) If the application is not dismissed under subsection (3), the court—

(a) may give directions as to the evidence to be provided by the company, and

(b) may adjourn the proceedings to enable the evidence to be obtained.

(5) On hearing the application, the court may—

(a) give permission (or leave) to continue the claim on such terms as it thinks fit,

(b) refuse permission (or leave) and dismiss the application, or

(c) adjourn the proceedings on the application and give such directions as it thinks fit.

III COM [264.1]

Procedure In the case of proceedings under s. 264(1) the procedure in **CPR 19.9B** should be followed.

PART 13
RESOLUTIONS AND MEETINGS

III COM [265]–III COM [295]

295. Application not to circulate members' statement

(1) A company is not required to circulate a members' statement under section 293 if, on an application by the company or another person who claims to be aggrieved, the court is satisfied that the rights conferred by section 292 and that section are being abused.

(2) The court may order the members who requested the circulation of the statement to pay the whole or part of the company's costs (in Scotland, expenses) on such an application, even if they are not parties to the application.

III COM [295.1]

Derivation, commencement and procedure This section is entirely new and it came into force on 1 October 2007. It mirrors the provisions concerning members' statements in s 317. Proceedings for an order that a members' statement should not be circulated should be started by Part 8 claim form. Paragraph 11 of the Practice Direction provides that the claimant must serve a copy of the claim form on the company (if it is not the claimant) and on each member who requested the circulation of the statement, unless that is not reasonably practicable, in which case the claimant must provide evidence that it has notified the company and the members concerned in some other way. There is no definition in the Act of what amounts to abuse. However, it is presumed that guidance as to what amounts to abuse may be obtained from s 292(2) which states that a resolution which if passed would be ineffective, is defamatory, or is frivolous or vexatious cannot be properly moved as a written resolution.

III COM [265]–III COM [306]

306. Power of court to order meeting

(1) This section applies if for any reason it is impracticable—

(a) to call a meeting of a company in any manner in which meetings of that company may be called, or

(b) to conduct the meeting in the manner prescribed by the company's articles or this Act.

(2) The court may, either of its own motion or on the application—

(a) of a director of the company, or

(b) of a member of the company who would be entitled to vote at the meeting,

order a meeting to be called, held and conducted in any manner the court thinks fit.

(3) Where such an order is made, the court may give such ancillary or consequential directions as it thinks expedient.

(4) Such directions may include a direction that one member of the company present at the meeting be deemed to constitute a quorum.

(5) A meeting called, held and conducted in accordance with an order under this section is deemed for all purposes to be a meeting of the company duly called, held and conducted.

III COM [306.1]

Derivation, commencement and procedure This section derives from the Companies Act 1985, s 371, which it replaced on 1 October 2007. Proceedings for an order for a meeting to be held should be started by Part 8 claim form.

III COM [306.2]

In *Smith v Butler* [2011] EWHC 2301 (Ch), [2011] All ER (D) 21 (Sep), the court exercised its powers to authorise the holding of a company meeting under CA 2006 s 306 to remove a director where the company articles required a quorum of two members at a meeting but one of the two members refused to attend. In *Schofield v Schofield* [2011] EWCA Civ 154, [2011] All ER (D) 274 (Feb) the Court of Appeal considered the application of the principle in *Re Duomatic Ltd* [1969] 2 Ch 365, [1969] 1 All ER 161 that a company can be bound by the informal unanimous agreement of the shareholders. The claimant had relied on this principle when arguing that a shareholder had waived the requirements as to notice of a meeting which are set out in s 303. However, the Court of Appeal held that this principle could not be applied in a situation where the shareholder had not treated the meeting as valid. The principle required some outward and objective manifestation of unqualified agreement or acquiescence. See also Secretary of State for Business Innovation and *Skills v Doffman, Re Stakefield (Midlands) Ltd* [2010] EWHC 3175 (Ch), [2010] All ER (D) 89 (Dec) where the court considered various limitations of the *Re Duomatic* principle, particularly where the interests of the company included that of its creditors.

III COM [307]–III COM [317]

317. Application not to circulate members' statement

(1) A company is not required to circulate a members' statement under section 315 if, on an application by the company or another person who claims to be aggrieved, the court is satisfied that the rights conferred by section 314 and that section are being abused.

(2) The court may order the members who requested the circulation of the statement to pay the whole or part of the company's costs (in Scotland, expenses) on such an application, even if they are not parties to the application.

III COM [317.1]

Derivation, commencement and procedure This section derives from s 377(3) and it came into force on 1 October 2007. Proceedings for an order that a members' statement should not be circulated should be started by Part 8 claim form. Paragraph 11 of the Practice Direction provides that the claimant must serve a copy of the claim form on the company (if it is not the claimant) and on each member who requested the circulation of the statement, unless that is not reasonably practicable, in which case the claimant must provide evidence that it has notified the company and the members concerned in some other way.

III COM [318]–III COM [358]

358. Inspection of resolutions and meetings of class members

(1) The records referred to in section 355 (records of resolutions etc) relating to the previous ten years must be kept available for inspection—

- (a) at the company's registered office, or
- (b) at a place specified in regulations under section 1136.

(2) The company must give notice to the registrar—

- (a) of the place at which the records are kept available for inspection, and
- (b) of any change in that place,

unless they have at all times been kept at the company's registered office.

(3) The records must be open to the inspection of any member of the company without charge.

(4) Any member may require a copy of any of the records on payment of such fee as may be prescribed.

(5) If default is made for 14 days in complying with subsection (2) or an inspection required under subsection (3) is refused, or a copy requested under subsection (4) is not sent, an offence is committed by every officer of the company who is in default.

(6) A person guilty of an offence under this section is liable on summary conviction to a fine not exceeding level 3 on the standard scale and, for continued contravention, a daily default fine not exceeding one-tenth of level 3 on the standard scale.

(7) In a case in which an inspection required under subsection (3) is refused or a copy requested under subsection (4) is not sent, the court may by order compel an immediate inspection of the records or direct that the copies required be sent to the persons who requested them.

III COM [358.1]

Derivation, commencement and procedure This section derives from the Companies Act 1985, s 383, which it replaced on 1 October 2007. Proceedings for an order for inspection should be started by Part 8 claim form.

PART 14
CONTROL OF POLITICAL DONATIONS AND EXPENDITURE

III COM [359]–III COM [369]

369. Liability of directors in case of unauthorised donation or expenditure

(1) This section applies where a company has made a political donation or incurred political expenditure without the authorisation required by this Part.

(2) The directors in default are jointly and severally liable—

(a) to make good to the company the amount of the unauthorised donation or expenditure, with interest, and

(b) to compensate the company for any loss or damage sustained by it as a result of the unauthorised donation or expenditure having been made.

(3) The directors in default are—

(a) those who, at the time the unauthorised donation was made or the unauthorised expenditure was incurred, were directors of the company by which the donation was made or the expenditure was incurred, and

(b) where—

(i) that company was a subsidiary of a relevant holding company, and

(ii) the directors of the relevant holding company failed to take all reasonable steps to prevent the donation being made or the expenditure being incurred,

the directors of the relevant holding company.

(4) For the purposes of subsection (3)(b) a "relevant holding company" means a company that, at the time the donation was made or the expenditure was incurred—

(a) was a holding company of the company by which the donation was made or the expenditure was incurred,

(b) was a UK-registered company, and

(c) was not a subsidiary of another UK-registered company.

(5) The interest referred to in subsection (2)(a) is interest on the amount of the unauthorised donation or expenditure, so far as not made good to the company—

(a) in respect of the period beginning with the date when the donation was made or the expenditure was incurred, and

(b) at such rate as the Secretary of State may prescribe by regulations.

Section 379(2) (construction of references to date when donation made or expenditure incurred) does not apply for the purposes of this subsection.

(6) Where only part of a donation or expenditure was unauthorised, this section applies only to so much of it as was unauthorised.

III COM [369.1]

Derivation and Commencement The provisions in this Part derive from the Companies Act 1985, s 347F onwards. Sections 362 to 379 of the Act, which relate to the control of political donations and expenditure, were brought into force on 1 October 2007 by article 3 of the Companies Act 2006 (Commencement No 3, Consequential Amendments, Transitional Provisions and Savings) Order 2007, SI 2007/2194 except in relation to independent election candidates. They have effect in relation to independent election candidates from 1 October 2008.

III COM [369.2]

Political expenditure exemption The Companies (Political Expenditure Exemption) Order 2007, SI 2007/2081, exempts political expenditure from the need for authorisation if it is expenditure to which article 3 applies and is incurred by a company to which article 4 applies. Very broadly, the exemption covers political expenditure by the news media in relation to news material which could reasonably be regarded as intended to influence voters or encourage support for a political party.

III COM [369.3]

Rate of interest payable on unauthorised political donation or expenditure The interest rate, for the purposes of s 369(5)(b) has been set at 8% per annum by the Companies (Interest Rate for Unauthorised Political Donation or Expenditure) Regulations 2007, SI 2007/2242.

III COM [369.4]

Directors Pursuant to s 379(1), in this part of the Act, references to directors includes shadow directors.

III COM [370]

370. Enforcement of directors' liabilities by shareholder action

(1) Any liability of a director under section 369 is enforceable—

(a) in the case of a liability of a director of a company to that company, by proceedings brought under this section in the name of the company by an authorised group of its members;

(b) in the case of a liability of a director of a holding company to a subsidiary, by proceedings brought under this section in the name of the subsidiary by—

(i) an authorised group of members of the subsidiary, or

(ii) an authorised group of members of the holding company.

(2) This is in addition to the right of the company to which the liability is owed to bring proceedings itself to enforce the liability.

(3) An "authorised group" of members of a company means—

(a) the holders of not less than 5% in nominal value of the company's issued share capital,

(b) if the company is not limited by shares, not less than 5% of its members, or

(c) not less than 50 of the company's members.

(4) The right to bring proceedings under this section is subject to the provisions of section 371.

(5) Nothing in this section affects any right of a member of a company to bring or continue proceedings under Part 11 (derivative claims or proceedings).

III COM [370.1]

Commencement and Procedure Sections 370 to 373 were brought into force, with exceptions, on 1 October 2007. Paragraph 12 of the Practice Direction provides for proceedings under this section to be brought by Part 7 claim form. Further procedural requirements are set out in ss 371-373.

III COM [371]

371. Enforcement of directors' liabilities by shareholder action: supplementary

(1) A group of members may not bring proceedings under section 370 in the name of a company unless—

(a) the group has given written notice to the company stating—

(i) the cause of action and a summary of the facts on which the proceedings are to be based,

(ii) the names and addresses of the members comprising the group, and

(iii) the grounds on which it is alleged that those members constitute an authorised group; and

(b) not less than 28 days have elapsed between the date of the giving of the notice to the company and the bringing of the proceedings.

(2) Where such a notice is given to a company, any director of the company may apply to the court within the period of 28 days beginning with the date of the giving of the notice for an order directing that the proposed proceedings shall not be brought, on one or more of the following grounds—

(a) that the unauthorised amount has been made good to the company;

(b) that proceedings to enforce the liability have been brought, and are being pursued with due diligence, by the company;

(c) that the members proposing to bring proceedings under this section do not constitute an authorised group.

(3) Where an application is made on the ground mentioned in subsection (2)(b), the court may as an alternative to directing that the proposed proceedings under section 370 are not to be brought, direct—

(a) that such proceedings may be brought on such terms and conditions as the court thinks fit, and

(b) that the proceedings brought by the company—

(i) shall be discontinued, or

(ii) may be continued on such terms and conditions as the court thinks fit.

(4) The members by whom proceedings are brought under section 370 owe to the company in whose name they are brought the same duties in relation to the proceedings as would be owed by the company's directors if the proceedings were being brought by the company.

But proceedings to enforce any such duty may be brought by the company only with the permission of the court.

(5) Proceedings brought under section 370 may not be discontinued or settled by the group except with the permission of the court, which may be given on such terms as the court thinks fit.

III COM [372]

372. Costs of shareholder action

(1) This section applies in relation to proceedings brought under section 370 in the name of a company ("the company") by an authorised group ("the group").

(2) The group may apply to the court for an order directing the company to indemnify the group in respect of costs incurred or to be incurred by the group in connection with the proceedings.

The court may make such an order on such terms as it thinks fit.

(3) The group is not entitled to be paid any such costs out of the assets of the company except by virtue of such an order.

(4) If no such order has been made with respect to the proceedings, then—

(a) if the company is awarded costs in connection with the proceedings, or it is agreed that costs incurred by the company in connection with the proceedings should be paid by any defendant, the costs shall be paid to the group; and

(b) if any defendant is awarded costs in connection with the proceedings, or it is agreed that any defendant should be paid costs incurred by him in connection with the proceedings, the costs shall be paid by the group.

(5) In the application of this section to Scotland for "costs" read "expenses" and for "defendant" read "defender".

III COM [373]

373. Information for purposes of shareholder action

(1) Where proceedings have been brought under section 370 in the name of a company by an authorised group, the group is entitled to require the company to provide it with all information relating to the subject matter of the proceedings that is in the company's possession or under its control or which is reasonably obtainable by it.

(2) If the company, having been required by the group to do so, refuses to provide the group with all or any of that information, the court may, on an application made by the group, make an order directing—

(a) the company, and

(b) any of its officers or employees specified in the application,

to provide the group with the information in question in such form and by such means as the court may direct.

PART 15
ACCOUNTS AND REPORTS

III COM [374]–III COM [452]

452. Default in filing accounts and reports: court order

(1) If—

(a) the requirements of section 441 (duty to file accounts and reports) are not complied with in relation to a company's accounts and reports for a financial year before the end of the period for filing those accounts and reports, and

(b) the directors of the company fail to make good the default within 14 days after the service of a notice on them requiring compliance,

the court may, on the application of any member or creditor of the company or of the registrar, make an order directing the directors (or any of them) to make good the default within such time as may be specified in the order.

(2) The court's order may provide that all costs (in Scotland, expenses) of and incidental to the application are to be borne by the directors.

III COM [452.1]

Derivation and commencement This section derives from the Companies Act 1985, s 242. This section and s 456 came into force on 6 April 2008.

III COM [452.2]

Revision of accounts See the Companies (Revision of Defective Accounts and Reports) Regulations 2008, SI 2008/373.

The law relating to the preparation and filing of annual accounts was amended by the Companies, Partnerships and Groups (Accounts and Reports) Regulations 2015, SI 2015/980, which implement Directive 2013/34/EU with effect from 6 April 2015. They apply to financial years beginning on or after 1 January 2016 or, if the directors so decide, a financial year beginning on or after 1 January 2015.

III COM [453]–III COM [456]

456. Application to court in respect of defective accounts or reports

(1) An application may be made to the court—

(a) by the Secretary of State, after having complied with section 455, or

(b) by a person authorised by the Secretary of State for the purposes of this section,

for a declaration (in Scotland, a declarator) that the annual accounts of a company do not comply, or a strategic report or a directors' report does not comply, with the requirements of this Act (or, where applicable, of Article 4 of the IAS Regulation) and for an order requiring the directors of the company to prepare revised accounts or a revised report.

(2) Notice of the application, together with a general statement of the matters at issue in the proceedings, shall be given by the applicant to the registrar for registration.

(3) If the court orders the preparation of revised accounts, it may give directions as to—

- (a) the auditing of the accounts,
- (b) the revision of any directors' remuneration report, strategic report and supplementary material or, directors' report, and
- (c) the taking of steps by the directors to bring the making of the order to the notice of persons likely to rely on the previous accounts,

and such other matters as the court thinks fit.

(4) If the court orders the preparation of a revised strategic report or directors' report it may give directions as to—

- (a) the review of the report by the auditors,
- (b) ...
- (c) the taking of steps by the directors to bring the making of the order to the notice of persons likely to rely on the previous report, and
- (d) such other matters as the court thinks fit.

(5) If the court finds that the accounts or report did not comply with the requirements of this Act (or, where applicable, of Article 4 of the IAS Regulation) it may order that all or part of—

- (a) the costs (in Scotland, expenses) of and incidental to the application, and
- (b) any reasonable expenses incurred by the company in connection with or in consequence of the preparation of revised accounts or a revised report,

are to be borne by such of the directors as were party to the approval of the defective accounts or report.

For this purpose every director of the company at the time of the approval of the accounts or report shall be taken to have been a party to the approval unless he shows that he took all reasonable steps to prevent that approval.

(6) Where the court makes an order under subsection (5) it shall have regard to whether the directors party to the approval of the defective accounts or report knew or ought to have known that the accounts or report did not comply with the requirements of this Act (or, where applicable, of Article 4 of the IAS Regulation), and it may exclude one or more directors from the order or order the payment of different amounts by different directors.

(7) On the conclusion of proceedings on an application under this section, the applicant must send to the registrar for registration a copy of the court order or, as the case may be, give notice to the registrar that the application has failed or been withdrawn.

(8) The provisions of this section apply equally to revised annual accounts, revised strategic reports and revised directors' reports, in which case they have effect as if the references to revised accounts or reports were references to further revised accounts or reports.

III COM [456.1]

Procedure Proceedings under this section, which came into force on 6 April 2008, should be by Part 8 claim form, as was the practice in relation to proceedings under the Companies Act 1985, s 245B. The application may be made by the Secretary of State or by any persons authorised by the Secretary of State in accordance with s 457. Persons so authorised may obtain information under s 458 on which to base their claim.

PART 16
AUDIT

III COM [457]–III COM [527]

527. Members' power to require website publication of audit concerns

(1) The members of a quoted company may require the company to publish on a website a statement setting out any matter relating to—

(a) the audit of the company's accounts (including the auditor's report and the conduct of the audit) that are to be laid before the next accounts meeting, or

(b) any circumstances connected with an auditor of the company ceasing to hold office since the previous accounts meeting,

that the members propose to raise at the next accounts meeting of the company.

(2) A company is required to do so once it has received requests to that effect from—

(a) members representing at least 5% of the total voting rights of all the members who have a relevant right to vote (excluding any voting rights attached to any shares in the company held as treasury shares), or

(b) at least 100 members who have a relevant right to vote and hold shares in the company on which there has been paid up an average sum, per member, of at least £100.

See also section 153 (exercise of rights where shares held on behalf of others).

(3) In subsection (2) a "relevant right to vote" means a right to vote at the accounts meeting.

(4) A request—

(a) may be sent to the company in hard copy or electronic form,

(b) must identify the statement to which it relates,

(c) must be authenticated by the person or persons making it, and

(d) must be received by the company at least one week before the meeting to which it relates.

(5) A quoted company is not required to place on a website a statement under this section if, on an application by the company or another person who claims to be aggrieved, the court is satisfied that the rights conferred by this section are being abused.

(6) The court may order the members requesting website publication to pay the whole or part of the company's costs (in Scotland, expenses) on such an application, even if they are not parties to the application.

III COM [527.1]

Commencement This provision is entirely new and came into force on 6 April 2008.

III COM [528]–III COM [557]

557. Offence of failure to make return

(1) If a company makes default in complying with—

section 555 (return of allotment of shares by limited company), or

section 556 (return of allotment of new class of shares by unlimited company),

an offence is committed by every officer of the company who is in default.

(2) A person guilty of an offence under this section is liable—

(a) on conviction on indictment, to a fine;

(b) on summary conviction, to a fine not exceeding the statutory maximum and, for continued contravention, a daily default fine not exceeding one-tenth of the greater of £5,000 or the amount corresponding to level 4 on the standard scale for summary offences.

(3) In the case of default in delivering to the registrar within one month after the allotment the return required by section 555 or 556—

(a) any person liable for the default may apply to the court for relief, and

(b) the court, if satisfied—

(i) that the omission to deliver the document was accidental or due to inadvertence, or

(ii) that it is just and equitable to grant relief,

may make an order extending the time for delivery of the document for such period as the court thinks proper.

III COM [557.1]

Derivation and commencement This section derives from the Companies Act 1985, ss 88 and 128 and came into force on 1 October 2009.

III COM [558]–III COM [589]

589. Power of court to grant relief

(1) This section applies in relation to liability under—

section 585(2) (liability of allottee in case of breach by public company of prohibition on accepting undertaking to do work or perform services),

section 587(2) or (4) (liability of allottee in case of breach by public company of prohibition on payment by long-term undertaking), or

section 588 (liability of subsequent holders of shares),

as it applies in relation to a contravention of those sections.

(2) A person who—

(a) is subject to any such liability to a company in relation to payment in respect of shares in the company, or

(b) is subject to any such liability to a company by virtue of an undertaking given to it in, or in connection with, payment for shares in the company,

may apply to the court to be exempted in whole or in part from the liability.

(3) In the case of a liability within subsection (2)(a), the court may exempt the applicant from the liability only if and to the extent that it appears to the court just and equitable to do so having regard to—

(a) whether the applicant has paid, or is liable to pay, any amount in respect of—

(i) any other liability arising in relation to those shares under any provision of this Chapter or Chapter 6, or

(ii) any liability arising by virtue of any undertaking given in or in connection with payment for those shares;

(b) whether any person other than the applicant has paid or is likely to pay, whether in pursuance of any order of the court or otherwise, any such amount;

(c) whether the applicant or any other person—

(i) has performed in whole or in part, or is likely so to perform any such undertaking, or

(ii) has done or is likely to do any other thing in payment or part payment for the shares.

(4) In the case of a liability within subsection (2)(b), the court may exempt the applicant from the liability only if and to the extent that it appears to the court just and equitable to do so having regard to—

(a) whether the applicant has paid or is liable to pay any amount in respect of liability arising in relation to the shares under any provision of this Chapter or Chapter 6;

(b) whether any person other than the applicant has paid or is likely to pay, whether in pursuance of any order of the court or otherwise, any such amount.

(5) In determining whether it should exempt the applicant in whole or in part from any liability, the court must have regard to the following overriding principles—

(a) a company that has allotted shares should receive money or money's worth at least equal in value to the aggregate of the nominal value of those shares and the whole of any premium or, if the case so requires, so much of that aggregate as is treated as paid up;

(b) subject to that, where a company would, if the court did not grant the exemption, have more than one remedy against a particular person, it should be for the company to decide which remedy it should remain entitled to pursue.

(6) If a person brings proceedings against another ("the contributor") for a contribution in respect of liability to a company arising under any provision of this Chapter or Chapter 6 and it appears to the court that the contributor is liable to make such a contribution, the court may, if and to the extent that it appears to it just and equitable to do so having regard to the respective culpability (in respect of the liability to the company) of the contributor and the person bringing the proceedings—

(a) exempt the contributor in whole or in part from his liability to make such a contribution, or

(b) order the contributor to make a larger contribution than, but for this subsection, he would be liable to make.

III COM [589.1]

Derivation and commencement This section derives from the Companies Act 1985, s 113 and came into force on 1 October 2009.

III COM [590]–III COM [606]

606. Power of court to grant relief

(1) A person who—

(a) is liable to a company under any provision of this Chapter in relation to payment in respect of any shares in the company, or

(b) is liable to a company by virtue of an undertaking given to it in, or in connection with, payment for any shares in the company,

may apply to the court to be exempted in whole or in part from the liability.

(2) In the case of a liability within subsection (1)(a), the court may exempt the applicant from the liability only if and to the extent that it appears to the court just and equitable to do so having regard to—

(a) whether the applicant has paid, or is liable to pay, any amount in respect of—

(i) any other liability arising in relation to those shares under any provision of this Chapter or Chapter 5, or

(ii) any liability arising by virtue of any undertaking given in or in connection with payment for those shares;

(b) whether any person other than the applicant has paid or is likely to pay, whether in pursuance of any order of the court or otherwise, any such amount;

(c) whether the applicant or any other person—

(i) has performed in whole or in part, or is likely so to perform any such undertaking, or

(ii) has done or is likely to do any other thing in payment or part payment for the shares.

(3) In the case of a liability within subsection (1)(b), the court may exempt the applicant from the liability only if and to the extent that it appears to the court just and equitable to do so having regard to—

(a) whether the applicant has paid or is liable to pay any amount in respect of liability arising in relation to the shares under any provision of this Chapter or Chapter 5;

(b) whether any person other than the applicant has paid or is likely to pay, whether in pursuance of any order of the court or otherwise, any such amount.

(4) In determining whether it should exempt the applicant in whole or in part from any liability, the court must have regard to the following overriding principles—

(a) that a company that has allotted shares should receive money or money's worth at least equal in value to the aggregate of the nominal value of those shares and the whole of any premium or, if the case so requires, so much of that aggregate as is treated as paid up;

(b) subject to this, that where such a company would, if the court did not grant the exemption, have more than one remedy against a particular person, it should be for the company to decide which remedy it should remain entitled to pursue.

(5) If a person brings proceedings against another ("the contributor") for a contribution in respect of liability to a company arising under any provision of this Chapter or Chapter 5 and it appears to the court that the contributor is liable to make such a contribution, the court may, if and to the extent that it appears to it, just and equitable to do so having regard to the respective culpability (in respect of the liability to the company) of the contributor and the person bringing the proceedings—

(a) exempt the contributor in whole or in part from his liability to make such a contribution, or

(b) order the contributor to make a larger contribution than, but for this subsection, he would be liable to make.

(6) Where a person is liable to a company under section 604(2) (agreement for transfer of non-cash asset: effect of contravention), the court may, on application, exempt him in whole or in part from that liability if and to the extent that it appears to the court to be just and equitable to do so having regard to any benefit accruing to the company by virtue of anything done by him towards the carrying out of the agreement mentioned in that subsection.

III COM [606.1]

Derivation and commencement This section derives from the Companies Act 1985, s 113 and came into force on 1 October 2009.

III COM [607]–III COM [633]

633. Right to object to variation: companies having a share capital

(1) This section applies where the rights attached to any class of shares in a company are varied under section 630 (variation of class rights: companies having a share capital).

(2) The holders of not less in the aggregate than 15% of the issued shares of the class in question (being persons who did not consent to or vote in favour of the resolution for the variation) may apply to the court to have the variation cancelled.

For this purpose any of the company's share capital held as treasury shares is disregarded.

(3) If such an application is made, the variation has no effect unless and until it is confirmed by the court.

(4) Application to the court—

COMPANIES

(a) must be made within 21 days after the date on which the consent was given or the resolution was passed (as the case may be), and

(b) may be made on behalf of the shareholders entitled to make the application by such one or more of their number as they may appoint in writing for the purpose.

(5) The court, after hearing the applicant and any other persons who apply to the court to be heard and appear to the court to be interested in the application, may, if satisfied having regard to all the circumstances of the case that the variation would unfairly prejudice the shareholders of the class represented by the applicant, disallow the variation, and shall if not so satisfied confirm it. The decision of the court on any such application is final.

(6) References in this section to the variation of the rights of holders of a class of shares include references to their abrogation.

III COM [633.1]

Derivation and commencement This section derives from the Companies Act 1985, s 127 and came into force on 1 October 2009.

III COM [634]–III COM [645]

645. Application to court for order of confirmation

(1) Where a company has passed a resolution for reducing share capital, it may apply to the court for an order confirming the reduction.

(2) If the proposed reduction of capital involves either—

(a) diminution of liability in respect of unpaid share capital, or

(b) the payment to a shareholder of any paid-up share capital,

section 646 (creditors entitled to object to reduction) applies unless the court directs otherwise.

(3) The court may, if having regard to any special circumstances of the case it thinks proper to do so, direct that section 646 is not to apply as regards any class or classes of creditors.

(4) The court may direct that section 646 is to apply in any other case.

III COM [645.1]

Derivation and commencement This section derives from the Companies Act 1985, s 136 and came into force on 1 October 2009. Note that while proceedings under the old law were by petition, an application under the new section must be made by Part 8 claim form. Note that under s 641(1)(a) a private company may reduce its share capital by special resolution without a court order if the resolution is supported by a solvency statement. The prescribed form of solvency statement is set out in the Companies (Reduction of Share Capital) Order 2008, SI 2008/1915.

III COM [645.2]

Evidence As regards evidence in support of an application to confirm a reduction of capital, see the guidance in paragraph 19 of the Practice Direction.

III COM [646]

646. Creditors entitled to object to reduction

(1) Where this section applies (see section 645(2) and (4)), every creditor of the company who—

(a) at the date fixed by the court is entitled to any debt or claim that, if that date were the commencement of the winding up of the company would be admissible in proof against the company, and

(b) can show that there is a real likelihood that the reduction would result in the company being unable to discharge his debt or claim when it fell due,

is entitled to object to the reduction of capital.

(2) The court shall settle a list of creditors entitled to object.

(3) For that purpose the court—

(a) shall ascertain, as far as possible without requiring an application from any creditor, the names of those creditors and the nature and amount of their debts or claims, and

(b) may publish notices fixing a day or days within which creditors not entered on the list are to claim to be so entered or are to be excluded from the right of objecting to the reduction of capital.

(4) If a creditor entered on the list whose debt or claim is not discharged or has not determined does not consent to the reduction, the court may, if it thinks fit, dispense with the consent of that creditor on the company securing payment of his debt or claim.

(5) For this purpose the debt or claim must be secured by appropriating (as the court may direct) the following amount—

(a) if the company admits the full amount of the debt or claim or, though not admitting it, is willing to provide for it, the full amount of the debt or claim;

(b) if the company does not admit, and is not willing to provide for, the full amount of the debt or claim, or if the amount is contingent or not ascertained, an amount fixed by the court after the like enquiry and adjudication as if the company were being wound up by the court.

III COM [646.1]

Derivation and commencement This section derives from the Companies Act 1985, s 136 and came into force on 1 October 2009.

III COM [647]–III COM [648]

648. Court order confirming reduction

(1) The court may make an order confirming the reduction of capital on such terms and conditions as it thinks fit.

(2) The court must not confirm the reduction unless it is satisfied, with respect to every creditor of the company who is entitled to object to the reduction of capital that either—

(a) his consent to the reduction has been obtained, or

(b) his debt or claim has been discharged, or has determined or has been secured.

(3) Where the court confirms the reduction, it may order the company to publish (as the court directs) the reasons for reduction of capital, or such other information in regard to it as the court thinks expedient with a view to giving proper information to the public, and (if the court thinks fit) the causes that led to the reduction.

(4) The court may, if for any special reason it thinks proper to do so, make an order directing that the company must, during such period (commencing on or at any time after the date of the order) as is specified in the order, add to its name as its last words the words "and reduced".

If such an order is made, those words are, until the end of the period specified in the order, deemed to be part of the company's name.

III COM [648.1]

Derivation and commencement This section derives from the Companies Act 1985, s 137 and came into force on 1 October 2009.

PART 18
ACQUISITION BY COMPANY OF ITS OWN SHARES

III COM [649]–III COM [703]

703. Enforcement of right to inspect copy or memorandum

(1) If default is made in complying with section 702(2), (3) or (4) or default is made for 14 days in complying with section 702(5), or an inspection required under section 702(6) is refused, an offence is committed by—

(a) the company, and

(b) every officer of the company who is in default.

(2) A person guilty of an offence under this section is liable on summary conviction to a fine not exceeding level 3 on the standard scale and, for continued contravention, a daily default fine not exceeding one-tenth of level 3 on the standard scale.

(3) In the case of refusal of an inspection required under section 702(6) the court may by order compel an immediate inspection.

III COM [703.1]

Derivation and commencement This section derives from the Companies Act 1985, s 169 and came into force on 1 October 2009.

III COM [703.2]

Amendment of Part 18 The provisions of Part 18 have been substantially amended by the Companies Act 2006 (Amendment of Part 18) Regulations 2013, SI 2013/999.

III COM [704]–III COM [720]

720. Directors' statement and auditor's report to be available for inspection

(1) The directors' statement and auditor's report must be kept available for inspection throughout the period—

(a) beginning with the day on which the company—

(i) first publishes the notice required by section 719(1), or

(ii) if earlier, first publishes or gives the notice required by section 719(2), and

(b) ending five weeks after the date of the resolution for payment out of capital.

(2) They must be kept available for inspection—

(a) at the company's registered office, or

(b) at a place specified in regulations under section 1136.

(3) The company must give notice to the registrar—

(a) of the place at which the statement and report are kept available for inspection, and

(b) of any change in that place,

unless they have at all times been kept at the company's registered office.

(4) They must be open to the inspection of any member or creditor of the company without charge.

(5) If default is made for 14 days in complying with subsection (3), or an inspection under subsection (4) is refused, an offence is committed by—

(a) the company, and

(b) every officer of the company who is in default.

(6) A person guilty of an offence under this section is liable on summary conviction to a fine not exceeding level 3 on the standard scale and, for continued contravention, a daily default fine not exceeding one-tenth of level 3 on the standard scale.

(7) In the case of a refusal of an inspection required by subsection (4), the court may by order compel an immediate inspection.

III COM [720.1]

Derivation and commencement This section derives from the Companies Act 1985, s 175 and came into force on 1 October 2009.

III COM [721]

721. Application to court to cancel resolution

(1) Where a private company passes a special resolution approving a payment out of capital for the redemption or purchase of any of its shares—

- (a) any member of the company (other than one who consented to or voted in favour of the resolution), and
- (b) any creditor of the company,

may apply to the court for the cancellation of the resolution.

(2) The application—

- (a) must be made within five weeks after the passing of the resolution, and
- (b) may be made on behalf of the persons entitled to make it by such one or more of their number as they may appoint in writing for the purpose.

(3) On an application under this section the court may if it thinks fit—

- (a) adjourn the proceedings in order that an arrangement may be made to the satisfaction of the court—
  - (i) for the purchase of the interests of dissentient members, or
  - (ii) for the protection of dissentient creditors, and
- (b) give such directions and make such orders as it thinks expedient for facilitating or carrying into effect any such arrangement.

(4) Subject to that, the court must make an order either cancelling or confirming the resolution, and may do so on such terms and conditions as it thinks fit.

(5) If the court confirms the resolution, it may by order alter or extend any date or period of time specified—

- (a) in the resolution, or
- (b) in any provision of this Chapter applying to the redemption or purchase to which the resolution relates.

(6) The court's order may, if the court thinks fit—

- (a) provide for the purchase by the company of the shares of any of its members and for the reduction accordingly of the company's capital, and
- (b) make any alteration in the company's articles that may be required in consequence of that provision.

(7) The court's order may, if the court thinks fit, require the company not to make any, or any specified, amendments of its articles without the leave of the court.

III COM [721.1]

Derivation and commencement This section derives from the Companies Act 1985, s 176 and came into force on 1 October 2009.

III COM [722]

722. Notice to registrar of court application or order

(1) On making an application under section 721 (application to court to cancel resolution) the applicants, or the person making the application on their behalf, must immediately give notice to the registrar.

COMPANIES

This is without prejudice to any provision of rules of court as to service of notice of the application.

(2) On being served with notice of any such application, the company must immediately give notice to the registrar.

(3) Within 15 days of the making of the court's order on the application, or such longer period as the court may at any time direct, the company must deliver to the registrar a copy of the order.

(4) If a company fails to comply with subsection (2) or (3) an offence is committed by—

(a) the company, and

(b) every officer of the company who is in default.

(5) A person guilty of an offence under this section is liable on summary conviction to a fine not exceeding level 3 on the standard scale and, for continued contravention, a daily default fine not exceeding one-tenth of level 3 on the standard scale.

III COM [722.1]

Derivation and commencement This section derives from the Companies Act 1985, s 176 and came into force on 1 October 2009.

PART 19
DEBENTURES

III COM [723]–III COM [745]

745. Register of debenture holders: response to request for inspection or copy

(1) Where a company receives a request under section 744 (register of debenture holders: right to inspect and require copy), it must within five working days either—

(a) comply with the request, or

(b) apply to the court.

(2) If it applies to the court it must notify the person making the request.

(3) If on an application under this section the court is satisfied that the inspection or copy is not sought for a proper purpose—

(a) it shall direct the company not to comply with the request, and

(b) it may further order that the company's costs (in Scotland, expenses) on the application be paid in whole or in part by the person who made the request, even if he is not a party to the application.

(4) If the court makes such a direction and it appears to the court that the company is or may be subject to other requests made for a similar purpose (whether made by the same person or different persons), it may direct that the company is not to comply with any such request.

The order must contain such provision as appears to the court appropriate to identify the requests to which it applies.

(5) If on an application under this section the court does not direct the company not to comply with the request, the company must comply with the request immediately upon the court giving its decision or, as the case may be, the proceedings being discontinued.

III COM [745.1]

Commencement This provision is entirely new and came into force on 6 April 2008.

III COM [746]

746. Register of debenture holders: refusal of inspection or default in providing copy

(1) If an inspection required under section 744 (register of debenture holders: right to inspect and require copy) is refused or default is made in providing a copy required under that section, otherwise than in accordance with an order of the court, an offence is committed by—

(a) the company, and

(b) every officer of the company who is in default.

(2) A person guilty of an offence under this section is liable on summary conviction to a fine not exceeding level 3 on the standard scale and, for continued contravention, a daily default fine not exceeding one-tenth of level 3 on the standard scale.

(3) In the case of any such refusal or default the court may by order compel an immediate inspection or, as the case may be, direct that the copy required be sent to the person requesting it.

III COM [746.1]

Derivation and commencement This section derives from the Companies Act 1985, s 191 and came into force on 6 April 2008.

III COM [747]–III COM [749]

749. Right of debenture holder to copy of deed

(1) Any holder of debentures of a company is entitled, on request and on payment of such fee as may be prescribed, to be provided with a copy of any trust deed for securing the debentures.

(2) If default is made in complying with this section, an offence is committed by every officer of the company who is in default.

(3) A person guilty of an offence under this section is liable on summary conviction to a fine not exceeding level 3 on the standard scale and, for continued contravention, a daily default fine not exceeding one-tenth of level 3 on the standard scale.

(4) In the case of any such default the court may direct that the copy required be sent to the person requiring it.

III COM [749.1]

Derivation and commencement This section derives from the Companies Act 1985, s 191 and came into force on 6 April 2008.

PART 20
PRIVATE AND PUBLIC COMPANIES

III COM [750]–III COM [757]

757. Enforcement of prohibition: order restraining proposed contravention

(1) If it appears to the court—

(a) on an application under this section, or

(b) in proceedings under Part 30 (protection of members against unfair prejudice),

that a company is proposing to act in contravention of section 755 (prohibition of public offers by private companies), the court shall make an order under this section.

(2) An order under this section is an order restraining the company from contravening that section.

(3) An application for an order under this section may be made by—

(a) a member or creditor of the company, or

(b) the Secretary of State.

III COM [757.1]

Derivation and commencement This provision is entirely new and came into force on 6 April 2008.

III COM [758]

758. Enforcement of prohibition: orders available to the court after contravention

(1) This section applies if it appears to the court—

(a) on an application under this section, or

(b) in proceedings under Part 30 (protection of members against unfair prejudice),

that a company has acted in contravention of section 755 (prohibition of public offers by private companies).

(2) The court must make an order requiring the company to re-register as a public company unless it appears to the court—

(a) that the company does not meet the requirements for re-registration as a public company, and

(b) that it is impractical or undesirable to require it to take steps to do so.

(3) If it does not make an order for re-registration, the court may make either or both of the following—

(a) a remedial order (see section 759), or

(b) an order for the compulsory winding up of the company.

(4) An application under this section may be made by—

(a) a member of the company who—

(i) was a member at the time the offer was made (or, if the offer was made over a period, at any time during that period), or

(ii) became a member as a result of the offer,

(b) a creditor of the company who was a creditor at the time the offer was made (or, if the offer was made over a period, at any time during that period), or

(c) the Secretary of State.

III COM [758.1]

Derivation and commencement This provision is entirely new and came into force on 6 April 2008.

III COM [759]

759. Enforcement of prohibition: remedial orders

(1) A "remedial order" is an order for the purpose of putting a person affected by anything done in contravention of section 755 (prohibition of public offers by private company) in the position he would have been in if it had not been done.

(2) The following provisions are without prejudice to the generality of the power to make such an order.

(3) Where a private company has—

(a) allotted securities pursuant to an offer to the public, or

(b) allotted or agreed to allot securities with a view to their being offered to the public,

a remedial order may require any person knowingly concerned in the contravention of section 755 to offer to purchase any of those securities at such price and on such other terms as the court thinks fit.

(4) A remedial order may be made—

(a) against any person knowingly concerned in the contravention, whether or not an officer of the company;

(b) notwithstanding anything in the company's constitution (which includes, for this purpose, the terms on which any securities of the company are allotted or held);

(c) whether or not the holder of the securities subject to the order is the person to whom the company allotted or agreed to allot them.

(5) Where a remedial order is made against the company itself, the court may provide for the reduction of the company's capital accordingly.

III COM [759.1]

Derivation and commencement This provision is entirely new and came into force on 6 April 2008.

PART 21
CERTIFICATION AND TRANSFER OF CERTIFICATES

III COM [760]–III COM [782]

782. Issue of certificates etc: court order to make good default

(1) If a company on which a notice has been served requiring it to make good any default in complying with—

(a) section 769(1) (duty of company as to issue of certificates etc on allotment),

(b) section 776(1) (duty of company as to issue of certificates etc on transfer), or

(c) section 780(1) (duty of company as to issue of certificates etc on surrender of share warrant),

fails to make good the default within ten days after service of the notice, the person entitled to have the certificates or the debentures delivered to him may apply to the court.

(2) The court may on such an application make an order directing the company and any officer of it to make good the default within such time as may be specified in the order.

(3) The order may provide that all costs (in Scotland, expenses) of and incidental to the application are to be borne by the company or by an officer of it responsible for the default.

III COM [782.1]

Derivation and commencement This section derives from the Companies Act 1985, s 185 and came into force on 6 April 2008.

III COM [783]–III COM [794]

794. Notice requiring information: order imposing restrictions on shares

(1) Where—

(a) a notice under section 793 (notice requiring information about interests in company's shares) is served by a company on a person who is or was interested in shares in the company, and

(b) that person fails to give the company the information required by the notice within the time specified in it,

the company may apply to the court for an order directing that the shares in question be subject to restrictions.

For the effect of such an order see section 797.

(2) If the court is satisfied that such an order may unfairly affect the rights of third parties in respect of the shares, the court may, for the purpose of protecting those rights and subject to such terms as it thinks fit, direct that such acts by such persons or descriptions of persons and for such purposes as may be set out in the order shall not constitute a breach of the restrictions.

(3) On an application under this section the court may make an interim order. Any such order may be made unconditionally or on such terms as the court thinks fit.

(4) Sections 798 to 802 make further provision about orders under this section.

III COM [794.1]

Derivation and commencement This section derives in part from the Companies Act 1985, s 216 and came into force on 20 January 2007.

III COM [794.2]

The imposition of voting and transfer restrictions on shareholders who had failed to provide accurate information in answer to disclosure notices under s 793 was held to be subject to the proper purpose rule so was invalid where the directors had primarily imposed the restrictions for the improper purpose of preventing shareholders voting at an annual general meeting rather than to enforce the demand for information, see *Eclairs Group Ltd v JKX Oil & Gas Plc* [2015] UKSC 71.

III COM [795]–III COM [799]

799. Relaxation of restrictions

(1) An application may be made to the court on the ground that an order directing that shares shall be subject to restrictions unfairly affects the rights of third parties in respect of the shares.

(2) An application for an order under this section may be made by the company or by any person aggrieved.

(3) If the court is satisfied that the application is well-founded, it may, for the purpose of protecting the rights of third parties in respect of the shares, and subject to such terms as it thinks fit, direct that such acts by such persons or descriptions of persons and for such purposes as may be set out in the order do not constitute a breach of the restrictions.

III COM [799.1]

Derivation and commencement This section derives from the Companies Act 1985, s 456 and came into force on 20 January 2007.

III COM [800]

800. Removal of restrictions

(1) An application may be made to the court for an order directing that the shares shall cease to be subject to restrictions.

(2) An application for an order under this section may be made by the company or by any person aggrieved.

(3) The court must not make an order under this section unless—

(a) it is satisfied that the relevant facts about the shares have been disclosed to the company and no unfair advantage has accrued to any person as a result of the earlier failure to make that disclosure, or

(b) the shares are to be transferred for valuable consideration and the court approves the transfer.

(4) An order under this section made by virtue of subsection (3)(b) may continue, in whole or in part, the restrictions mentioned in section 797(1)(c) and (d) (restrictions on issue of further shares or making of payments) so far as they relate to a right acquired or offer made before the transfer.

(5) Where any restrictions continue in force under subsection (4)—

(a) an application may be made under this section for an order directing that the shares shall cease to be subject to those restrictions, and

(b) subsection (3) does not apply in relation to the making of such an order.

III COM [800.1]

Derivation and commencement This section derives from the Companies Act 1985, s 456 and came into force on 20 January 2007.

III COM [801]

801. Order for sale of shares

(1) The court may order that the shares subject to restrictions be sold, subject to the court's approval as to the sale.

(2) An application for an order under subsection (1) may only be made by the company.

(3) Where the court has made an order under this section, it may make such further order relating to the sale or transfer of the shares as it thinks fit.

(4) An application for an order under subsection (3) may be made—

(a) by the company,

(b) by the person appointed by or in pursuance of the order to effect the sale, or

(c) by any person interested in the shares.

(5) On making an order under subsection (1) or (3) the court may order that the applicant's costs (in Scotland, expenses) be paid out of the proceeds of sale.

III COM [801.1]

Derivation and commencement This section derives from the Companies Act 1985, s 456 and came into force on 20 January 2007.

III COM [802]

802. Application of proceeds of sale under court order

(1) Where shares are sold in pursuance of an order of the court under section 801, the proceeds of the sale, less the costs of the sale, must be paid into court for the benefit of the persons who are beneficially interested in the shares.

(2) A person who is beneficially interested in the shares may apply to the court for the whole or part of those proceeds to be paid to him.

(3) On such an application the court shall order the payment to the applicant of—

(a) the whole of the proceeds of sale together with any interest on them, or

(b) if another person had a beneficial interest in the shares at the time of their sale, such proportion of the proceeds and interest as the value of the applicant's interest in the shares bears to the total value of the shares.

This is subject to the following qualification.

(4) If the court has ordered under section 801(5) that the costs (in Scotland, expenses) of an applicant under that section are to be paid out of the proceeds of sale, the applicant is entitled to payment of his costs (or expenses) out of those proceeds before any person interested in the shares receives any part of those proceeds.

III COM [802.1]

Derivation and commencement This section derives from the Companies Act 1985, s 457 and came into force on 20 January 2007.

III COM [803]–III COM [807]

807. Right to inspect and request copies of reports

(1) Any report prepared under section 805 must be open to inspection by any person without charge.

(2) Any person is entitled, on request and on payment of such fee as may be prescribed, to be provided with a copy of any such report or any part of it. The copy must be provided within ten days after the request is received by the company.

(3) If an inspection required under subsection (1) is refused, or default is made in complying with subsection (2), an offence is committed by—

(a) the company, and

(b) every officer of the company who is in default.

(4) A person guilty of an offence under this section is liable on summary conviction to a fine not exceeding level 3 on the standard scale and, for continued contravention, a daily default fine not exceeding one-tenth of level 3 on the standard scale.

(5) In the case of any such refusal or default the court may by order compel an immediate inspection or, as the case may be, direct that the copy required be sent to the person requiring it.

III COM [807.1]

Derivation and commencement This section derives from the Companies Act 1985, ss 215 and 219 and came into force on 20 January 2007.

III COM [808]–III COM [812]

812. Court supervision of purpose for which rights may be exercised

(1) Where a company receives a request under section 811 (register of interests disclosed: right to inspect and require copy), it must—

(a) comply with the request if it is satisfied that it is made for a proper purpose, and

(b) refuse the request if it is not so satisfied.

(2) If the company refuses the request, it must inform the person making the request, stating the reason why it is not satisfied.

(3) A person whose request is refused may apply to the court.

(4) If an application is made to the court—

(a) the person who made the request must notify the company, and

(b) the company must use its best endeavours to notify any persons whose details would be disclosed if the company were required to comply with the request.

(5) If the court is not satisfied that the inspection or copy is sought for a proper purpose, it shall direct the company not to comply with the request.

(6) If the court makes such a direction and it appears to the court that the company is or may be subject to other requests made for a similar purpose (whether made by the same person or different persons), it may direct that the company is not to comply with any such request.

The order must contain such provision as appears to the court appropriate to identify the requests to which it applies.

(7) If the court does not direct the company not to comply with the request, the company must comply with the request immediately upon the court giving its decision or, as the case may be, the proceedings being discontinued.

III COM [812.1]

Derivation and commencement This provision is entirely new and came into force on 6 April 2008.

III COM [813]

813 Register of interests disclosed: refusal of inspection or default in providing copy

(1) If an inspection required under section 811 (register of interests disclosed: right to inspect and require copy) is refused or default is made in providing a copy required under that section, otherwise than in accordance with section 812, an offence is committed by—

(a) the company, and

(b) every officer of the company who is in default.

(2) A person guilty of an offence under this section is liable on summary conviction to a fine not exceeding level 3 on the standard scale and, for continued contravention, a daily default fine not exceeding one-tenth of level 3 on the standard scale.

(3) In the case of any such refusal or default the court may by order compel an immediate inspection or, as the case may be, direct that the copy required be sent to the person requesting it.

III COM [813.1]

Derivation and commencement This section derives from the Companies Act 1985, ss 211, 213 and 219 and came into force on 20 January 2007.

III COM [814]–III COM [817]

817. Removal of entries from register: incorrect entry relating to third party

(1) This section applies where in pursuance of an obligation imposed by a notice under section 793 (notice requiring information about interests in company's shares) a person gives to a company the name and address of another person as being interested in shares in the company.

(2) That other person may apply to the company for the removal of the entry from the register.

(3) If the company is satisfied that the information in pursuance of which the entry was made is incorrect, it shall remove the entry.

(4) If an application under subsection (3) is refused, the applicant may apply to the court for an order directing the company to remove the entry in question from the register.

The court may make such an order if it thinks fit.

III COM [817.1]

Derivation and commencement This section derives from the Companies Act 1985, s 217 and came into force on 20 January 2007.

III COM [818]

818. Adjustment of entry relating to share acquisition agreement

(1) If a person who is identified in the register kept by a company under section 808 (register of interests disclosed) as being a party to an agreement to which section 824 applies (certain share acquisition agreements) ceases to be a party to the agreement, he may apply to the company for the inclusion of that information in the register.

(2) If the company is satisfied that he has ceased to be a party to the agreement, it shall record that information (if not already recorded) in every place where his name appears in the register as a party to the agreement.

(3) If an application under this section is refused (otherwise than on the ground that the information has already been recorded), the applicant may apply to the court for an order directing the company to include the information in question in the register.

The court may make such an order if it thinks fit.

III COM [818.1]

Derivation and commencement This section derives from the Companies Act 1985, s 217 and came into force on 20 January 2007.

PART 25
COMPANY CHARGES

III COM [819]–III COM [859F]

859F. Extension of period allowed for delivery

(1) Subsection (3) applies if the court is satisfied that—

(a) neither the company nor any other person interested in the charge has delivered to the registrar the documents required under section 859A or (as the case may be) 859B before the end of the period allowed for delivery under the section concerned, and

(b) the requirement in subsection (2) is met.

(2) The requirement is—

(a) that the failure to deliver those documents—

(i) was accidental or due to inadvertence or to some other sufficient cause, or

(ii) is not of a nature to prejudice the position of creditors or shareholders of the company, or

(b) that on other grounds it is just and equitable to grant relief.

(3) The court may, on the application of the company or a person interested, and on such terms and conditions as seem to the court just and expedient, order that the period allowed for delivery be extended.

III COM [859F.1]

Derivation and procedure Sections 860 to 877 of Part 25, as enacted, were repealed by the Companies Act 2006 (Amendment of Part 25) Regulations 2013, SI 2013/600, an amending instrument made under section 894. Instead of the repealed sections 860 to 877 the Regulations inserted Chapter A1, comprising new sections 859A to 859Q. The repealed section 873 empowered the court to extend time to register a charge and also to rectify any omission or mist-statement. The power to extend time is now conferred by the new section 859F, above, and the power to rectify is conferred by the new section 859M, below. Proceedings under section 859F are required to be started by claim form using the Part 8 procedure; and no other party than the Claimant need be involved. The claim form should identify the charge and state whether reliance is place of s 859F(2)(a)(i) or on (ii). A copy of the charge should be exhibited and the original brought to the hearing. Evidence of solvency from a company officer needs to be filed. The evidence needs to confirm that no winding up order has been made, no resolution for winding up has been passed, that no winding up petition is pending, that no notice of a resolution to wind up has been given by an officer of the company, that the company is carrying on business, and that no unsatisfied judgment has been given against the company. If there is a significant delay between the filing of such evidence and the hearing of the application then an up to date statement should be provided at the hearing.

III COM [859F.2]

Transitional provisions Regulation 6 provides for the original Part 25 to continue to apply for charges created before 26 April 2013. Note that one of the effects of the change was to remove the statutory register of charges from that date. A rectification order under the new s 859M will result in an alteration to information on a statement or notice not on the statutory register.

III COM [859M]–III COM [877]

859M. Rectification of register

(1) Subsection (3) applies if the court is satisfied that—

(a) there has been an omission or mis-statement in any statement or notice delivered to the registrar in accordance with this Chapter, and

(b) the requirement in subsection (2) is met.

(2) The requirement is that the court is satisfied—

(a) that the omission or mis-statement—

(i) was accidental or due to inadvertence or to some other sufficient cause, or

(ii) is not of a nature to prejudice the position of creditors or shareholders of the company, or

(b) that on other grounds it is just and equitable to grant relief.

(3) The court may, on the application of the company or a person interested, and on such terms and conditions as seem to the court just and expedient, order that the omission or mis-statement be rectified.

(4) A copy of the court's order must be sent by the applicant to the registrar for registration.

III COM [877.1]

Procedure The Part 8 procedure must be used and the charge must be exhibited and the omission or mis-statement fully explained and the terms of rectification proposed. It is very important that the registrar is joined as a party and indeed that his lawyers are consulted beforehand to advise and assist in the drafting of the terms of rectification.

PART 26
ARRANGEMENTS AND RECONSTRUCTIONS

III COM [878]–III COM [896]

896. Court order for holding of meeting

(1) The court may, on an application under this section, order a meeting of the creditors or class of creditors, or of the members of the company or class of members (as the case may be), to be summoned in such manner as the court directs.

(2) An application under this section may be made by—

(a) the company,

(b) any creditor or member of the company,

(c) if the company is being wound up, the liquidator, or

(d) if the company is in administration, the administrator.

(3) Section 323 (representation of corporations at meetings) applies to a meeting of creditors under this section as to a meeting of the company (references to a member of the company being read as references to a creditor).

III COM [896.1]

Derivation and commencement This section derives from the Companies Act 1985, s 425 and came into force on 6 April 2008.

III COM [896.2]

Arrangement with creditors A scheme of arrangement under Part 26 requires the arrangement to be made between the company and its creditors, not with former clients with proprietary interests held in trust, since the latter are not 'creditors' and their rights cannot be affected: *Re Lehman Brothers International (Europe) (in Administration) (No 2)* [2009] EWCA Civ 1161, [2010] 1 BCLC 496, (2009) Times, 12 November, CA.

III COM [897]–III COM [899]

899. Court sanction for compromise or arrangement

(1) If a majority in number representing 75% in value of the creditors or class of creditors or members or class of members (as the case may be), present and voting either in person or by proxy at the meeting summoned under section 896, agree a compromise or arrangement, the court may, on an application under this section, sanction the compromise or arrangement.

(2) An application under this section may be made by—

- (a) the company,
- (b) any creditor or member of the company, or
- (c) if the company is being wound up, the liquidator, or
- (d) if the company is in administration, the administrator.

(3) A compromise or arrangement sanctioned by the court is binding on—

- (a) all creditors or the class of creditors or on the members or class of members (as the case may be), and
- (b) the company or, in the case of a company in the course of being wound up, the liquidator and contributories of the company.

(4) The court's order has no effect until a copy of it has been delivered to the registrar.

(5) Section 323 (representation of corporations at meetings) applies to a meeting of creditors under this section as to a meeting of the company (references to a member of the company being read as references to a creditor).

III COM [899.1]

Derivation and commencement This section derives from the Companies Act 1985, s 425 and came into force on 6 April 2008.

III COM [899.2]

Arrangement with a class of creditors In entering into an arrangement it is not necessary for a company to consult any class of creditors who are not affected. But where this is issue the court is entitled to ascertain whether a purported class actually has an economic interest in a real sense and to take action accordingly: *Re Bluebrook Ltd* [2009] EWHC 2114 (Ch), [2010] 1 BCLC 338.

In section (3) the word 'arrangement' was substituted for 'agreement' by article 8 of the Companies Act 2006 (Consequential Amendments and Transitional Provisions) Order 2011, SI 2011/1265.

III COM [899.3]

Jurisdiction in the case of a foreign company The fact that a foreign company would not be wound up by the English court in the circumstances prevailing at the time of a scheme is not a bar to the court sanctioning the scheme, provided that there is a sufficient connection with the English jurisdiction: *Re Magyar Telecom BV* [2013] EWHC 3800 (Ch), [2013] All ER (D) 20 (Dec), Richards J.

III COM [899.4]

A majority in number of the class of members present The votes of members of the class who acquired shares by share-splitting in order to oppose the scheme were held to be invalid in *Re Dee Valley Group Ltd* (2017) Times, 21 March, Ch D, Sir Geoffrey Vos.

III COM [900]

900. Powers of court to facilitate reconstruction or amalgamation

(1) This section applies where application is made to the court under section 899 to sanction a compromise or arrangement and it is shown that—

- (a) the compromise or arrangement is proposed for the purposes of, or in connection with, a scheme for the reconstruction of any company or companies, or the amalgamation of any two or more companies, and

(b) under the scheme the whole or any part of the undertaking or the property of any company concerned in the scheme ("a transferor company") is to be transferred to another company ("the transferee company").

(2) The court may, either by the order sanctioning the compromise or arrangement or by a subsequent order, make provision for all or any of the following matters—

(a) the transfer to the transferee company of the whole or any part of the undertaking and of the property or liabilities of any transferor company;

(b) the allotting or appropriation by the transferee company of any shares, debentures, policies or other like interests in that company which under the compromise or arrangement are to be allotted or appropriated by that company to or for any person;

(c) the continuation by or against the transferee company of any legal proceedings pending by or against any transferor company;

(d) the dissolution, without winding up, of any transferor company;

(e) the provision to be made for any persons who, within such time and in such manner as the court directs, dissent from the compromise or arrangement;

(f) such incidental, consequential and supplemental matters as are necessary to secure that the reconstruction or amalgamation is fully and effectively carried out.

(3) If an order under this section provides for the transfer of property or liabilities—

(a) the property is by virtue of the order transferred to, and vests in, the transferee company, and

(b) the liabilities are, by virtue of the order, transferred to and become liabilities of that company.

(4) The property (if the order so directs) vests freed from any charge that is by virtue of the compromise or arrangement to cease to have effect.

(5) In this section—

"property" includes property, rights and powers of every description; and

"liabilities" includes duties.

(6) Every company in relation to which an order is made under this section must cause a copy of the order to be delivered to the registrar within seven days after its making.

(7) If default is made in complying with subsection (6) an offence is committed by—

(a) the company, and

(b) every officer of the company who is in default.

(8) A person guilty of an offence under subsection (7) is liable on summary conviction to a fine not exceeding level 3 on the standard scale and, for continued contravention, a daily default fine not exceeding one-tenth of level 3 on the standard scale.

III COM [900.1]

Derivation and commencement This section derives from the Companies Act 1985, s 427 and came into force on 6 April 2008.

PART 27
MERGERS AND DIVISIONS OF PUBLIC COMPANIES

III COM [901]–III COM [934]

934. Power of court to exclude certain requirements (division)

(1) In the case of a division, the court may by order direct that—

(a) in relation to any company involved in the division, the requirements of—

(i) section 921 (publication of draft terms), and

(ii) section 926 (inspection of documents),

do not apply, and

(b) in relation to an existing transferee company, section 932 (circumstances in which meeting of members of transferee company not required) has effect with the omission of the first and second conditions specified in that section,

if the court is satisfied that the following conditions will be fulfilled in relation to that company.

(2) The first condition is that the members of that company will have received, or will have been able to obtain free of charge, copies of the documents listed in section 926—

(a) in time to examine them before the date of the first meeting of the members, or any class of members, of that company summoned for the purposes of agreeing to the scheme, or

(b) in the case of an existing transferee company where in the circumstances described in section 932 no meeting is held, in time to require a meeting as mentioned in subsection (4) of that section.

(3) The second condition is that the creditors of that company will have received or will have been able to obtain free of charge copies of the draft terms in time to examine them—

(a) before the date of the first meeting of the members, or any class of members, of the company summoned for the purposes of agreeing to the scheme, or

(b) in the circumstances mentioned in subsection (2)(b) above, at the same time as the members of the company.

(4) The third condition is that no prejudice would be caused to the members or creditors of the transferor company or any transferee company by making the order in question.

III COM [934.1]

Derivation and commencement This section derives from the Companies Act 1985, Sch 15B, para 11 and came into force on 6 April 2008.

III COM [934.2]

Merger and Societas Europaea As explained in Section IV of the Practice Direction, Societas Europaea is a European public limited-liability company which is regulated by the Council Regulation (EC) No 2157/2001 of 8 October 2001 on the Statute for a European Company (SE). Before a Societas Europaea formed by merger can be registered in Great Britain, an application must be made to the court for the issue of a certificate which confirms the completion of the pre-merger acts and formalities. This is required by Article 25 of the Regulation and the procedure is set out in paragraph 16 of the Practice Direction. Also, proceedings must be taken, by claim form, to obtain a court order which confirms compliance with Article 26 of the Regulation. Here again the procedure is set out in paragraph 17 of the Practice Direction.

III COM [935]–III COM [938]

938. Power of court to summon meeting of members or creditors of existing transferee company

(1) The court may order a meeting of—

(a) the members of an existing transferee company, or any class of them, or

(b) the creditors of an existing transferee company, or any class of them, to be summoned in such manner as the court directs.

(2) An application for such an order may be made by—

(a) the company concerned,

(b) a member or creditor of the company, or

(c) if the company is being wound up, the liquidator, or

(d) if the company is in administration, the administrator.

(3) Section 323 (representation of corporations at meetings) applies to a meeting of creditors under this section as to a meeting of the company (references to a member being read as references to a creditor).

III COM [938.1]

Derivation and commencement This section derives from the Companies Act 1985, s 427A and came into force on 6 April 2008.

PART 28
TAKEOVERS ETC

III COM [939]–III COM [955]

955. Enforcement by the court

(1) If, on the application of the Panel, the court is satisfied—

(a) that there is a reasonable likelihood that a person will contravene a rule-based requirement, or

(b) that a person has contravened a rule-based requirement or a disclosure requirement,

the court may make any order it thinks fit to secure compliance with the requirement.

(2) In subsection (1) "the court" means the High Court or, in Scotland, the Court of Session.

(3) Except as provided by subsection (1), no person—

(a) has a right to seek an injunction, or

(b) in Scotland, has title or interest to seek an interdict or an order for specific performance,

to prevent a person from contravening (or continuing to contravene) a rule-based requirement or a disclosure requirement.

(4) In this section—

"contravene" includes fail to comply;

"disclosure requirement" means a requirement imposed under section 947;

"rule-based requirement" means a requirement imposed by or under rules.

III COM [955.1]

Derivation and commencement This provision is entirely new and came into force on 6 April 2007.

III COM [955.2]

Procedure Paragraph 13 of the Practice Direction provides for proceedings for an order under s 955 to be begun by a Part 7 claim form.

III COM [956]–III COM [968]

968. Takeovers – effect on contractual restrictions

(1) The following provisions have effect where a takeover bid is made for an opted-in company.

(2) An agreement to which this section applies is invalid in so far as it places any restriction—

- (a) on the transfer to the offeror, or at his direction to another person, of shares in the company during the offer period;
- (b) on the transfer to any person of shares in the company at a time during the offer period when the offeror holds shares amounting to not less than 75% in value of all the voting shares in the company;
- (c) on rights to vote at a general meeting of the company that decides whether to take any action which might result in the frustration of the bid;
- (d) on rights to vote at a general meeting of the company that—
  - (i) is the first such meeting to be held after the end of the offer period, and
  - (ii) is held at a time when the offeror holds shares amounting to not less than 75% in value of all the voting shares in the company.

(3) This section applies to an agreement—

- (a) entered into between a person holding shares in the company and another such person on or after 21st April 2004, or
- (b) entered into at any time between such a person and the company,

and it applies to such an agreement even if the law applicable to the agreement (apart from this section) is not the law of a part of the United Kingdom.

(4) The reference in subsection (2)(c) to rights to vote at a general meeting of the company that decides whether to take any action which might result in the frustration of the bid includes a reference to rights to vote on a written resolution concerned with that question.

(5) For the purposes of subsection (2)(c), action which might result in the frustration of a bid is any action of that kind specified in rules under section 943(1) giving effect to Article 9 of the Takeovers Directive.

(6) If a person suffers loss as a result of any act or omission that would (but for this section) be a breach of an agreement to which this section applies, he is entitled to compensation, of such amount as the court considers just and equitable, from any person who would (but for this section) be liable to him for committing or inducing the breach.

(7) In subsection (6) "the court" means the High Court or, in Scotland, the Court of Session.

(8) A reference in this section to voting shares in the company does not include—

- (a) debentures, or
- (b) shares that, under the company's articles of association, do not normally carry rights to vote at its general meetings (for example, shares carrying rights to vote that, under those articles, arise only where specified pecuniary advantages are not provided).

III COM [968.1]

Derivation and commencement This provision is new and came into force on 6 April 2007.

III COM [968.2]

Procedure Paragraph 24 of the Practice Direction provides for proceedings for an order under s 968(6) to be brought by a Part 7 claim form.

III COM [969]–III COM [986]

986. Applications to the court

(1) Where a notice is given under section 979 to a shareholder the court may, on an application made by him, order—

- (a) that the offeror is not entitled and bound to acquire the shares to which the notice relates, or
- (b) that the terms on which the offeror is entitled and bound to acquire the shares shall be such as the court thinks fit.

(2) An application under subsection (1) must be made within six weeks from the date on which the notice referred to in that subsection was given.

If an application to the court under subsection (1) is pending at the end of that period, section 981(6) does not have effect until the application has been disposed of.

(3) Where a shareholder exercises his rights under section 983 in respect of any shares held by him, the court may, on an application made by him or the offeror, order that the terms on which the offeror is entitled and bound to acquire the shares shall be such as the court thinks fit.

(4) On an application under subsection (1) or (3)—

- (a) the court may not require consideration of a higher value than that specified in the terms of the offer ("the offer value") to be given for the shares to which the application relates unless the holder of the shares shows that the offer value would be unfair;
- (b) the court may not require consideration of a lower value than the offer value to be given for the shares.

(5) No order for costs or expenses may be made against a shareholder making an application under subsection (1) or (3) unless the court considers that—

- (a) the application was unnecessary, improper or vexatious,
- (b) there has been unreasonable delay in making the application, or
- (c) there has been unreasonable conduct on the shareholder's part in conducting the proceedings on the application.

(6) A shareholder who has made an application under subsection (1) or (3) must give notice of the application to the offeror.

(7) An offeror who is given notice of an application under subsection (1) or (3) must give a copy of the notice to—

- (a) any person (other than the applicant) to whom a notice has been given under section 979;
- (b) any person who has exercised his rights under section 983.

(8) An offeror who makes an application under subsection (3) must give notice of the application to—

- (a) any person to whom a notice has been given under section 979;
- (b) any person who has exercised his rights under section 983.

(9) Where a takeover offer has not been accepted to the extent necessary for entitling the offeror to give notices under subsection (2) or (4) of section 979 the court may, on an application made by him, make an order authorising him to give notices under that subsection if it is satisfied that—

- (a) the offeror has after reasonable enquiry been unable to trace one or more of the persons holding shares to which the offer relates,
- (b) the requirements of that subsection would have been met if the person, or all the persons, mentioned in paragraph (a) above had accepted the offer, and
- (c) the consideration offered is fair and reasonable.

This is subject to subsection (10).

(10) The court may not make an order under subsection (9) unless it considers that it is just and equitable to do so having regard, in particular, to the number of shareholders who have been traced but who have not accepted the offer.

III COM [986.1]

Derivation and commencement This section derives from the Companies Act 1985, s 430C and came into force on 6 April 2007.

PART 30
PROTECTION OF MEMBERS AGAINST UNFAIR PREJUDICE

III COM [987]–III COM [994]

994. Petition by company member

(1) A member of a company may apply to the court by petition for an order under this Part on the ground—

(a) that the company's affairs are being or have been conducted in a manner that is unfairly prejudicial to the interests of members generally or of some part of its members (including at least himself), or

(b) that an actual or proposed act or omission of the company (including an act or omission on its behalf) is or would be so prejudicial.

(1A) For the purposes of subsection (1)(a), a removal of the company's auditor from office—

(a) on grounds of divergence of opinions on accounting treatments or audit procedures, or

(b) on any other improper grounds,

shall be treated as being unfairly prejudicial to the interests of some part of the company's members.

(2) The provisions of this Part apply to a person who is not a member of a company but to whom shares in the company have been transferred or transmitted by operation of law as they apply to a member of a company.

(3) In this section, and so far as applicable for the purposes of this section in the other provisions of this Part, "company" means—

(a) a company within the meaning of this Act, or

(b) ...

III COM [994.1]

Derivation and commencement This section derives from the Companies Act 1985, s 459 and came into force on 1 October 2007.

Procedure

III COM [994.2]

Proceedings are commenced by petition. A person who is not a member of the company because he has transferred his share to another member to hold on trust for him can petition under s 994: see *Harris v Jones* [2011] EWHC 1518 (Ch), [2011] All ER (D) 94 (Jun). A member whose shares have been sold but remains a registered shareholder has standing to petition under s 994: see *Re ASA Resource Group Plc* [2018] EWHC 1102 (Ch). See *Re AMT Coffee Ltd* [2018] EWHC 1562 (Ch) for the steps that personal representatives need to take in order to acquire standing to petition. The company is a purely nominal party since the substantial dispute is usually between the shareholders. Accordingly, it is inappropriate for directors to use the company's funds to pay legal expenses of the shareholders who are the true respondents to the petition: *Re Crossmore Electrical & Civil Engineering Ltd* [1989] BCLC 137. It is not always necessary for the other culpable shareholders to be in the majority or that they be joined as respondents: *Re Ravenhart Service (Hastings) Ltd* [2004] EWHC 76 (Ch), [2004] 2 BCLC 377. The petition can be struck out if the court is satisfied that the case is unarguable or the likelihood of the trial judge exercising his discretion to grant the claimed relief is so remote that the case can be described as perfectly hopeless: *Legal Costs Negotiators Ltd* [1999] 2 BCLC 171, CA. The nature of a claim under s 994 is one of relief from unfairly prejudicial conduct of the company's affairs. This does not necessarily provide a remedy for misconduct and a derivative claim in accordance with Part 11 of the Act will often be more appropriate. Accordingly, a freezing order against directors who allegedly misappropriated assets will not be granted in s 994 proceedings where only the company not the petitioner has a relevant cause of action: *Re Premier Electronics (GB) Ltd* [2002] 2 BCLC 634. Proceedings under s 994 should not normally be combined with a winding-up petition on just and equitable grounds under s 122(1)(g) of the Insolvency Act 1986: *see Practice Direction – Order Under section 127 Insolvency Act 1986* at **III INS PD [37A]**. A shareholder's right to petition under s 994 is not inalienable so can be subject to an arbitration agreement and award provided that third parties are not bound by the award. See *Fulham Football Club (1987) Ltd v Sir David Richards* [2011] EWCA Civ 855, [2011] All ER (D) 197 (Jul). For an example of a case involving a limited liability partnership which the unfair prejudice under s 994 also involved a complete breakdown of the relationship between members and an entitlement to seek to have the partnership wound up on a just and equitable basis see *Eaton v Caulfield* [2011] EWHC 173 (Ch).

In *Graham v Every* [2014] EWCA Civ 191, [2014] All ER (D) 260 (Feb) the reasonableness of an offer to buy the claimant's shares was considered in the context of a s 994 petition and the guidelines set out in *Re a Company (No 00709 of 1992) O'Neill v Phillips* [1999] 1 WLR 1092, [1999] 2 All ER 961, HL. *Thomas v Dawson* [2015] EWCA Civ 706, [2015] All ER (D) 106 (Jul) highlights the extent of trial judges' discretion as to the remedy for unfair prejudice. In *Arbuthnott v Bonyman* [2015] EWCA Civ 536, [2015] All ER (D) 218 (May) the Court of Appeal considered a s 994 petition in the context of amendment of articles of association and said that a power to amend articles will be validly exercised, even though the amendment is not for the benefit of the company if it relates to a matter in which the company as an entity has no interest but rather is only for the benefit of shareholders or some of them, provided that the amendment does not amount to oppression of the minority or is otherwise unjust or is outside the scope of the power.

A company, even one with only a few shareholders, is not to be treated as a quasi-partnership company if the formal documents indicate that it was set up on an arms-length basis and there is no evidence of informal arrangements qualifying the formal position. In such circumstances, the exclusion of a director from a company in which he held a minority shareholding, and the compulsory acquisition of his shares by the majority shareholder does not amount to unfair conduct. See *Re Migration Solutions Holdings Ltd, Brett v Migration Solutions Holdings Ltd* [2016] EWHC 523 (Ch), [2016] All ER (D) 126 (Mar). For a case where a quasi partnership was found, see *Re Foundries Miniatures Ltd* [2017] EWHC 889 (Ch).

Where a company is worthless at the relevant time, petitioning shareholders, who had succeeded in establishing unfairly prejudicial conduct on the part of a fellow shareholder, were not entitled to financial relief, see *Ashdown v Griffin* [2017] EWHC 2601 (Ch), [2017] All ER (D) 147 (Oct).

In respect of any unfair prejudice petition issued in the High Court (Rolls Building) for initial hearing before a registrar, the court will give automatic directions. The parties should presume that the court will engage in costs budgeting unless one of the exceptions provided for by the CPR applies. They should notify the court as soon as possible if the 1 hour time estimate is too long or too short. The automatic directions provide as follows:

> 'UPON THE PETITION of the above named Petitioner(s) presented to the court on [insert date of presentation]
>
> OF ITS OWN MOTION THE COURT ORDERS:
>
> 1. The Petitioner(s) serve the petition by 4.00 pm [*insert date 14 days after date of issue*];
>
> 2. the petition stand as points of claim;
>
> 3. the Respondent(s) (save for the company) file and serve points of defence by 4.00 pm [*insert date 28 days after date in 1. above*];
>
> 4. the Petitioner(s) file and serve points of reply (if so advised) by 4.00 pm [*insert date 14 days after date in 3. above*];
>
> 5. the petition be adjourned to [*insert date 28 days after date in 4. above – 1 hour appointment*] for case management and (where appropriate) costs management
>
> 6. where there is to be costs management:
>
> (a) the parties file and exchange costs budgets by 4.00 pm [*21 days before hearing fixed by para 5 above*];
>
> (b) the parties consider each other's costs budget(s) and by 4.00 pm [*insert date 14 days before date in 5 above*] identify to each other which phases in the other party's/parties' budget(s) are agreed and which are not agreed, in the latter case giving brief reasons and suggested alternative figures;
>
> (c) by 4.00 pm [*7 days before hearing fixed by para 5 above*] the Petitioner's solicitors file and serve:

COMPANIES

(i) confirmation that all phases in the budgets are agreed; or

(ii) a one page summary in tabular form setting out the figures for the phases in the budgets indicating which phases have been agreed and which have not been agreed together with a summary of the reasons for disagreement and suggested alternative figures;

(d) the parties file and serve in the form below a non-binding indication of what they believe to be the approximate value of the shares in issue in the petition by 4.00 pm [*insert date 7 days before the date in 5*];

7. the parties be permitted to vary the above orders by consent so as to extend any period provided for by no more than 28 days (the court to be notified so that the hearing fixed by paragraph 5 can be vacated and re-fixed) or to apply to the court to vary the foregoing;

8. costs be in the petition.

Estimate of value

For the purpose of the hearing mentioned in paragraph 6 of the order dated [. . . . .] I/ we put the following non-binding estimate on the value of the shares in issue in this petition on [*insert date(s)*]: £. . . . .

Petitioner/petitioner's solicitors/Respondent/respondent's solicitors

III COM [994.3]

Directors' fiduciary duties When a business opportunity for the company arises it is not for the director who learns of it to decide whether or not the company would be interested. The director should not decide that the company would not be interested and then take advantage of the opportunity without reference to the company. The director's fiduciary duty is to inform the company. Failure to do so is a good ground for a petition although the claimant must also establish unfair prejudice to the claimant as a result: *O'Donnell v Shanahan* [2009] EWCA Civ 751, [2009] 2 BCLC 666, (2009) Times 21 August. A no dividend policy combined with excessive remuneration may be unfairly prejudicial and a breach of directors' duties: *Booth v Booth* [2017] EWHC 457 (Ch).

III COM [994.4]

Costs Unfair prejudice claims frequently give rise to "sprawling litigation" which is very expensive for the parties. The costs regime must therefore give clear and predictable signals about the costs consequences of rejecting a reasonable offer of settlement made at an early stage: *F&C Alternative Investments (Holdings) Ltd v Barthelemy* [2011] EWHC 2807 (Ch), [2012] Bus LR 891, [2011] NLJR 1596.

III COM [995]

995. Petition by Secretary of State

(1) This section applies to a company in respect of which—

(a) the Secretary of State has received a report under section 437 of the Companies Act 1985 (c 6) (inspector's report);

(b) the Secretary of State has exercised his powers under section 447 or 448 of that Act (powers to require documents and information or to enter and search premises);

(c) the Secretary of State, the Financial Conduct Authority, the Prudential Regulation Authority or the Bank of England has exercised his or its powers under Part 11 of the Financial Services and Markets Act 2000 (c 8) (information gathering and investigations); or

(d) the Secretary of State has received a report from an investigator appointed by him, the Financial Conduct Authority, the Prudential Regulation Authority or the Bank of England under that Part.

(2) If it appears to the Secretary of State that in the case of such a company—

(a) the company's affairs are being or have been conducted in a manner that is unfairly prejudicial to the interests of members generally or of some part of its members, or

(b) an actual or proposed act or omission of the company (including an act or omission on its behalf) is or would be so prejudicial,

he may apply to the court by petition for an order under this Part.

(3) The Secretary of State may do this in addition to, or instead of, presenting a petition for the winding up of the company.

(4) In this section, and so far as applicable for the purposes of this section in the other provisions of this Part, "company" means any body corporate that is liable to be wound up under the Insolvency Act 1986 (c 45) or the Insolvency (Northern Ireland) Order 1989 (SI 1989/2405 (NI 19)).

III COM [995.1]

Derivation and commencement This section derives from the Companies Act 1985, s 460 and came into force on 1 October 2007.

III COM [996]

996. Powers of the Court under this Part

(1) If the court is satisfied that a petition under this Part is well founded, it may make such order as it thinks fit for giving relief in respect of the matters complained of.

(2) Without prejudice to the generality of subsection (1), the court's order may—

- (a) regulate the conduct of the company's affairs in the future;
- (b) require the company—
  - (i) to refrain from doing or continuing an act complained of, or
  - (ii) to do an act that the petitioner has complained it has omitted to do;
- (c) authorise civil proceedings to be brought in the name and on behalf of the company by such person or persons and on such terms as the court may direct;
- (d) require the company not to make any, or any specified, alterations in its articles without the leave of the court;
- (e) provide for the purchase of the shares of any members of the company by other members or by the company itself and, in the case of a purchase by the company itself, the reduction of the company's capital accordingly.

III COM [996.1]

Derivation and commencement This section derives from the Companies Act 1985, s 461 and came into force on 1 October 2007.

PART 31
DISSOLUTION AND RESTORATION TO THE REGISTER

III COM [997]–III COM [1021]

1021. Power of court to make vesting order

(1) The court may—

- (a) on application by a person who either claims an interest in disclaimed property or is under a liability not discharged by this Act in respect of disclaimed property, and
- (b) on hearing such persons as it thinks fit,

make an order for the vesting of the property in or its delivery to any persons entitled to it, or to whom it may seem just that the property should be delivered by way of compensation for such liability, or a trustee for him.

(2) The order may be made on such terms as the court thinks fit.

(3) On a vesting order being made under this section, the property comprised in it vests accordingly in the person named in that behalf in the order, without conveyance or assignation for that purpose.

III COM [1021.1]

Derivation and commencement This section derives from the Companies Act 1985, s 657 and came into force on 1 October 2009.

III COM [1022]–III COM [1029]

1029. Application to court for restoration to the register

(1) An application may be made to the court to restore to the register a company—

(a) that has been dissolved under Chapter 9 of Part 4 of the Insolvency Act 1986 (c 45) or Chapter 9 of Part 5 of the Insolvency (Northern Ireland) Order 1989 (SI 1989/2405 (NI 19)) (dissolution of company after winding up),

(b) that is deemed to have been dissolved under paragraph 84(6) of Schedule B1 to that Act or paragraph 85(6) of Schedule B1 to that Order (dissolution of company following administration), or

(c) that has been struck off the register—

(i) under section 1000 or 1001 (power of registrar to strike off defunct company), or

(ii) under section 1003 (voluntary striking off),

whether or not the company has in consequence been dissolved.

(2) An application under this section may be made by—

(a) the Secretary of State,

(b) any former director of the company,

(c) any person having an interest in land in which the company had a superior or derivative interest,

(d) any person having an interest in land or other property—

(i) that was subject to rights vested in the company, or

(ii) that was benefited by obligations owed by the company,

(e) any person who but for the company's dissolution would have been in a contractual relationship with it,

(f) any person with a potential legal claim against the company,

(g) any manager or trustee of a pension fund established for the benefit of employees of the company,

(h) any former member of the company (or the personal representatives of such a person),

(i) any person who was a creditor of the company at the time of its striking off or dissolution,

(j) any former liquidator of the company,

(k) where the company was struck off the register under section 1003 (voluntary striking off), any person of a description specified by regulations under section 1006(1)(f) or 1007(2)(f) (persons entitled to notice of application for voluntary striking off),

or by any other person appearing to the court to have an interest in the matter.

III COM [1029.1]

Derivation and commencement This provision is entirely new and came into force on 1 October 2009. It replaces ss 651 and 653 of the Companies Act 1985 and provides for a new procedure

III COM [1029.1A]

Procedure The Court has the power under CPR 19.2(2) to join a third party to restoration proceedings in an appropriate case, see *Welsh Ministers v Price* [2017] EWCA Civ 1768 (Civ), [2018] 1 WLR 738, [2018] 1 BCLC 1.

III COM [1029.2]

Alternative procedure It should be noted that there are alternative provisions under ss 1024 to 1028 for applications to be made by former members or directors of the company to the registrar to restore to the register companies which the registrar has struck off less than 6 years before.

III COM [1030]

1030. When application to the court may be made

(1) An application to the court for restoration of a company to the register may be made at any time for the purpose of bringing proceedings against the company for damages for personal injury.

(2) No order shall be made on such an application if it appears to the court that the proceedings would fail by virtue of any enactment as to the time within which proceedings must be brought.

(3) In making that decision the court must have regard to its power under section 1032(3) (power to give consequential directions etc) to direct that the period between the dissolution (or striking off) of the company and the making of the order is not to count for the purposes of any such enactment.

(4) In any other case an application to the court for restoration of a company to the register may not be made after the end of the period of six years from the date of the dissolution of the company, subject as follows.

(5) In a case where—

- (a) the company has been struck off the register under section 1000 or 1001 (power of registrar to strike off defunct company),
- (b) an application to the registrar has been made under section 1024 (application for administrative restoration to the register) within the time allowed for making such an application, and
- (c) the registrar has refused the application,

an application to the court under this section may be made within 28 days of notice of the registrar's decision being issued by the registrar, even if the period of six years mentioned in subsection (4) above has expired.

(6) For the purposes of this section—

- (a) "personal injury" includes any disease and any impairment of a person's physical or mental condition; and
- (b) references to damages for personal injury include—
  - (i) any sum claimed by virtue of section 1(2)(c) of the Law Reform (Miscellaneous Provisions) Act 1934 (c 41) or section 14(2)(c) of the Law Reform (Miscellaneous Provisions) Act (Northern Ireland) 1937 (1937 c 9 (NI)) (funeral expenses)), and
  - (ii) damages under the Fatal Accidents Act 1976 (c 30), the Damages (Scotland) Act 1976 (c 13) or the Fatal Accidents (Northern Ireland) Order 1977 (SI 1977/1251 (NI 18)).

III COM [1030.1]

Derivation and commencement This provision is entirely new and came into force on 1 October 2009. It replaced s 651(4) but is different in content.

III COM [1030.2]

Amendments The section was amended on 23 November 2018 by the Third Parties (Rights Against Insurers) Act 2010 (Consequential Amendment of Companies Act 2006) Regulations 2018, SI 2018/1162.

III COM [1031]

1031. Decision on application for restoration by the court

(1) On an application under section 1029 the court may order the restoration of the company to the register—

(a) if the company was struck off the register under section 1000 or 1001 (power of registrar to strike off defunct companies) and the company was, at the time of the striking off, carrying on business or in operation;

(b) if the company was struck off the register under section 1003 (voluntary striking off) and any of the requirements of sections 1004 to 1009 was not complied with;

(c) if in any other case the court considers it just to do so.

(2) If the court orders restoration of the company to the register, the restoration takes effect on a copy of the court's order being delivered to the registrar.

(3) The registrar must cause to be published in the Gazette notice of the restoration of the company to the register.

(4) The notice must state—

(a) the name of the company or, if the company is restored to the register under a different name (see section 1033), that name and its former name,

(b) the company's registered number, and

(c) the date on which the restoration took effect.

III COM [1031.1]

Derivation and commencement This provision is entirely new and came into force on 1 October 2009.

III COM [1032]

1032. Effect of court order for restoration to the register

(1) The general effect of an order by the court for restoration to the register is that the company is deemed to have continued in existence as if it had not been dissolved or struck off the register.

(2) The company is not liable to a penalty under section 453 or any corresponding earlier provision (civil penalty for failure to deliver accounts) for a financial year in relation to which the period for filing accounts and reports ended—

(a) after the date of dissolution or striking off, and

(b) before the restoration of the company to the register.

(3) The court may give such directions and make such provision as seems just for placing the company and all other persons in the same position (as nearly as may be) as if the company had not been dissolved or struck off the register.

(4) The court may also give directions as to—

(a) the delivery to the registrar of such documents relating to the company as are necessary to bring up to date the records kept by the registrar,

(b) the payment of the costs (in Scotland, expenses) of the registrar in connection with the proceedings for the restoration of the company to the register,

(c) where any property or right previously vested in or held on trust for the company has vested as *bona vacantia*, the payment of the costs (in Scotland, expenses) of the Crown representative—

(i) in dealing with the property during the period of dissolution, or

(ii) in connection with the proceedings on the application.

(5) In this section the "Crown representative" means—

(a) in relation to property vested in the Duchy of Lancaster, the Solicitor to that Duchy;

(b) in relation to property vested in the Duke of Cornwall, the Solicitor to the Duchy of Cornwall;

(c) in relation to property in Scotland, the Queen's and Lord Treasurer's Remembrancer;

(d) in relation to other property, the Treasury Solicitor.

III COM [1032.1]

Derivation and commencement This provision is entirely new and came into force on 1 October 2009.

III COM [1032.2]

Effect of restoration in relation to pending claims In a case where a personal injury claim was issued and served at the registered office after a company had been struck off it was held that the effect of the restoration was to validate, retrospectively both the issue of the claim and the service: *Joddrell v Peakstone Ltd* [2012] EWCA Civ 1035, [2012] All ER (D) 287 (Jul). In *Hawkes v County Leasing Asset Management Ltd* [2015] EWCA Civ 1251, [2015] All ER (D) 73 (Dec) the Court of Appeal gave guidance on the exercise of the courts' discretion to provide a limitation direction under s 1032(3) so that the period of dissolution should not count for limitation purposes. A company seeking a limitation direction has the burden of demonstrating the existence of exceptional circumstances and normally has to show that had it not been dissolved then the claim would have been brought on time. The burden on a creditor who seeks such a direction is less onerous.

On the other hand, a third party applying for an extension of the limitation period to cover the time between the company's being struck off and subsequently restored has to show a clear causal link between the dissolution and the failure to bring proceedings in time. The third party must show that the claim would probably have been brought in time but for the strike-off: *Davy v Pickering* [2017] EWCA Civ 30, (2017) Times, 08 March, [2017] All ER (D) 104 (Jan). See also *Housemaker Services Ltd v Cole* [2017] EWHC 753 (Ch).

III COM [1032.3]

Effect of Crown's termination of lease Between dissolution and restoration the assets, including business leases, vest in the Crown. If the Crown's response is to disclaim a company lease, the disclaimer operates to terminate it, in accordance with s 1015(1) of the Act, with the consequence, as decided by the Inner House of the Court of Session, that it is not included in the assets which re-vest, contrary to the 'general effect' of restoration: *ELB Securities Ltd v Alan Love and Prestwick Hotels Ltd* [2015] CSIH 67.

PART 35
THE REGISTRAR OF COMPANIES

III COM [1032A]

1096. Rectification of the register under court order

(1) The registrar shall remove from the register any material—

(a) that derives from anything that the court has declared to be invalid or ineffective, or to have been done without the authority of the company, or

(b) that a court declares to be factually inaccurate, or to be derived from something that is factually inaccurate, or forged,

and that the court directs should be removed from the register.

(2) The court order must specify what is to be removed from the register and indicate where on the register it is.

(3) The court must not make an order for the removal from the register of anything the registration of which had legal consequences as mentioned in section 1094(3) unless satisfied—

(a) that the presence of the material on the register has caused, or may cause, damage to the company, and

(b) that the company's interest in removing the material outweighs any interest of other persons in the material continuing to appear on the register.

(4) Where in such a case the court does make an order for removal, it may make such consequential orders as appear just with respect to the legal effect (if any) to be accorded to the material by virtue of its having appeared on the register.

(5) A copy of the court's order must be sent to the registrar for registration.

(6) This section does not apply where the court has other, specific, powers to deal with the matter, for example under—

(a) the provisions of Part 15 relating to the revision of defective accounts and reports, or

(b) section 859M (rectification of register).

III COM [1032A.1]

Derivation and commencement This section is entirely new and came into force on 1 October 2009.

III COM [1032A.2]

Procedure It is recommended that the registrar of companies be joined as a party to any application under s 1096 and, where this has not occurred, it is the informal practice at some courts to require that step to be taken. This enables those acting for the registrar to identify relevant issues in advance of any hearing and to confirm in writing if they have been resolved, thereby reducing the risk of an inappropriate form of order. There is usually no need for the registrar to be represented at the hearing.

III COM [1033]–III COM [1113]

1113. Enforcement of company's filing obligations

(1) This section applies where a company has made default in complying with any obligation under the Companies Acts—

(a) to deliver a document to the registrar, or

(b) to give notice to the registrar of any matter.

(2) The registrar, or any member or creditor of the company, may give notice to the company requiring it to comply with the obligation.

(3) If the company fails to make good the default within 14 days after service of the notice, the registrar, or any member or creditor of the company, may apply to the court for an order directing the company, and any specified officer of it, to make good the default within a specified time.

(4) The court's order may provide that all costs (in Scotland, expenses) of or incidental to the application are to be borne by the company or by any officers of it responsible for the default.

(5) This section does not affect the operation of any enactment making it an offence, or imposing a civil penalty, for the default.

III COM [1113.1]

Derivation and commencement This section derives from the Companies Act 1985, s 713 and came into force on 1 October 2009.

PART 36
OFFENCES UNDER THE COMPANIES ACTS

III COM [1114]–III COM [1132]

1132. Production and inspection of documents where offence suspected

(1) An application under this section may be made—

(a) in England and Wales, to a judge of the High Court by the Director of Public Prosecutions, the Secretary of State or a chief officer of police;

(b) in Scotland, to one of the Lords Commissioners of Justiciary by the Lord Advocate;

(c) in Northern Ireland, to the High Court by the Director of Public Prosecutions for Northern Ireland, the Department of Enterprise, Trade and Investment or a chief superintendent of the Police Service of Northern Ireland.

(2) If on an application under this section there is shown to be reasonable cause to believe—

(a) that any person has, while an officer of a company, committed an offence in connection with the management of the company's affairs, and

(b) that evidence of the commission of the offence is to be found in any documents in the possession or control of the company,

an order under this section may be made.

(3) The order may—

(a) authorise any person named in it to inspect the documents in question, or any of them, for the purpose of investigating and obtaining evidence of the offence, or

(b) require the secretary of the company, or such other officer of it as may be named in the order, to produce the documents (or any of them) to a person named in the order at a place so named.

(4) This section applies also in relation to documents in the possession or control of a person carrying on the business of banking, so far as they relate to the company's affairs, as it applies to documents in the possession or control of the company, except that no such order as is referred to in subsection (3)(b) may be made by virtue of this subsection.

(5) The decision under this section of a judge of the High Court, any of the Lords Commissioners of Justiciary or the High Court is not appealable.

(6) In this section "document" includes information recorded in any form.

III COM [1132.1]

Derivation and commencement This section derives from the Companies Act 1985, s 721 and came into force on 1 October 2007.

III COM [1133]–III COM [1139]

1139. Service of documents on company

(1) A document may be served on a company registered under this Act by leaving it at, or sending it by post to, the company's registered office.

(2) A document may be served on an overseas company whose particulars are registered under section 1046—

(a) by leaving it at, or sending it by post to, the registered address of any person resident in the United Kingdom who is authorised to accept service of documents on the company's behalf, or

(b) if there is no such person, or if any such person refuses service or service cannot for any other reason be effected, by leaving it at or sending by post to any place of business of the company in the United Kingdom.

(3) For the purposes of this section a person's "registered address" means any address for the time being shown as a current address in relation to that person in the part of the register available for public inspection.

(4) Where a company registered in Scotland or Northern Ireland carries on business in England and Wales, the process of any court in England and Wales may be served on the company by leaving it at, or sending it by post to, the company's principal place of business in England and Wales, addressed to the manager or other head officer in England and Wales of the company.

Where process is served on a company under this subsection, the person issuing out the process must send a copy of it by post to the company's registered office.

(5) Further provision as to service and other matters is made in the company communications provisions (see section 1143).

III COM [1139.1]

Service on a company registered in Scotland A company registered in Scotland may be validly served by post at its registered office with a claim form issued in England and Wales even where there are business premises within the jurisdiction where it could have been served. Because service in Scotland is service outside the jurisdiction the rules allow six months under CPR 7.5(2) instead of four: *Ashley v Tesco Stores* [2015] EWCA Civ 414, [2015] All ER (D) 269 (Jan).

III COM [1140]

1140. Service of documents on directors, secretaries and others

(1) A document may be served on a person to whom this section applies by leaving it at, or sending it by post to, the person's registered address.

(2) This section applies to—

- (a) a director or secretary of a company;
- (b) in the case of an overseas company whose particulars are registered under section 1046, a person holding any such position as may be specified for the purposes of this section by regulations under that section;
- (c) a person appointed in relation to a company as—
  - (i) a judicial factor (in Scotland),
  - (ii) [an interim manager] appointed under section 76 of the Charities Act 2011 [or section 33 of Charities Act (Northern Ireland) 2008], or
  - (iii) a manager appointed under section 47 of the Companies (Audit, Investigations and Community Enterprise) Act 2004 (c 27).

(3) This section applies whatever the purpose of the document in question. It is not restricted to service for purposes arising out of or in connection with the appointment or position mentioned in subsection (2) or in connection with the company concerned.

(4) For the purposes of this section a person's "registered address" means any address for the time being shown as a current address in relation to that person in the part of the register available for public inspection.

(5) If notice of a change of that address is given to the registrar, a person may validly serve a document at the address previously registered until the end of the period of 14 days beginning with the date on which notice of the change is registered.

(6) Service may not be effected by virtue of this section at an address—

- (a) if notice has been registered of the termination of the appointment in relation to which the address was registered and the address is not a registered address of the person concerned in relation to any other appointment;
- (b) in the case of a person holding any such position as is mentioned in subsection (2)(b), if the overseas company has ceased to have any connection with the United Kingdom by virtue of which it is required to register particulars under section 1046.

(7) Further provision as to service and other matters is made in the company communications provisions (see section 1143).

(8) Nothing in this section shall be read as affecting any enactment or rule of law under which permission is required for service out of the jurisdiction.

Amendment *Text in square brackets is inserted by the Charities Act (Northern Ireland) 2008, with effect from a date to be appointed.*

III COM [1141]

1141. Service addresses

(1) In the Companies Acts a "service address", in relation to a person, means an address at which documents may be effectively served on that person.

(2) The Secretary of State may by regulations specify conditions with which a service address must comply.

(3) Regulations under this section are subject to negative resolution procedure.

III COM [1142]

1142. Requirement to give service address

Any obligation under the Companies Acts to give a person's address is, unless otherwise expressly provided, to give a service address for that person.

III COM [1143]–III COM [1156]

1156. Meaning of "the court"

(1) Except as otherwise provided, in the Companies Acts "the court" means—

- (a) in England and Wales, the High Court or the county court;
- (b) in Scotland, the Court of Session or the sheriff court;
- (c) in Northern Ireland, the High Court.

(2) The provisions of the Companies Acts conferring jurisdiction on "the court" as defined above have effect subject to any enactment or rule of law relating to the allocation of jurisdiction or distribution of business between courts in any part of the United Kingdom.

(3) ...

III COM [1156.1]

Distribution of county court business As a result of the Insolvency (England and Wales) Rules 2016, SI 2016/1024 and the Practice Directions, the county court hearing centres in which cases under the Insolvency legislation or under the Companies Act 2006 can be heard are limited to the Central London County Court Hearing Centre and those county court hearing centres located at a District Registry.

III COM [1156.2]

Jurisdiction based on English law governing creditor arrangements The fact that English law is the governing law for all creditor arrangements provides a sufficient ground to warrant the exercise of jurisdiction by the English court: *Re Icopal AS* [2013] EWHC 3469 (Ch), [2013] All ER (D) 295 (Jul).

III COM [1157]–III COM [1500]

1157. Power to grant relief in certain cases

(1) If in proceedings for negligence, default, breach of duty or breach of trust against—

- (a) an officer of a company, or
- (b) a person employed by a company as auditor (whether he is or is not an officer of the company),

it appears to the court hearing the case that the officer or person is or may be liable but that he acted honestly and reasonably, and that having regard to all the circumstances of the case (including those connected with his appointment) he ought fairly to be excused, the court may relieve him, either wholly or in part, from his liability on such terms as it thinks fit.

(2) If any such officer or person has reason to apprehend that a claim will or might be made against him in respect of negligence, default, breach of duty or breach of trust—

- (a) he may apply to the court for relief, and

(b) the court has the same power to relieve him as it would have had if it had been a court before which proceedings against him for negligence, default, breach of duty or breach of trust had been brought.

(3) Where a case to which subsection (1) applies is being tried by a judge with a jury, the judge, after hearing the evidence, may, if he is satisfied that the defendant (in Scotland, the defender) ought in pursuance of that subsection to be relieved either in whole or in part from the liability sought to be enforced against him, withdraw the case from the jury and forthwith direct judgment to be entered for the defendant (in Scotland, grant decree of absolvitor) on such terms as to costs (in Scotland, expenses) or otherwise as the judge may think proper.

III COM [1157.1]

Derivation and commencement This section derives from the Companies Act 1985, s 727 and came into force on 1 October 2008.

PRACTICE DIRECTION 49A—APPLICATIONS UNDER THE COMPANIES ACTS AND RELATED LEGISLATION

III COM [1501]

THIS PRACTICE DIRECTION SUPPLEMENTS CPR PART 49

SECTION I GENERAL

Definitions

1. In this practice direction—

'the 1985 Act' means the Companies Act 1985[1];

'the 2006 Act' means the Companies Act 2006[2];

'the CJPA' means the Criminal Justice and Police Act 2001[3];

'the EC Regulation' means Council Regulation (EC) No. 2157/2001 of 8 October 2001 on the Statute for a European Company (SE)[4];

'Part VII FSMA' means Part VII of the Financial Services and Markets Act 2000[5];

'the Cross-Border Mergers Regulations' means the Companies (Cross-Border Mergers) Regulations 2007[6].

Application of this practice direction

2. This practice direction applies to proceedings under—

(a) the 1985 Act;

(b) the 2006 Act (except proceedings under Chapter 1 of Part 11 or Part 30 of that Act);

(c) section 59 of the CJPA;

(d) Articles 22, 25 and 26 of the EC Regulation;

(e) Part VII FSMA; and

(f) the Cross-Border Mergers Regulations.

(Part 19 and Practice Direction 19C contain provisions about proceedings under Chapter 1 of Part 11 of the 2006 Act (derivative claims).)

Application of this practice direction to certain proceedings in relation to limited liability partnerships

3. This practice direction applies to proceedings under the 1985 Act and 2006 Act as applied to limited liability partnerships by regulations made under the Limited Liability Partnerships Act 2000.

Title of documents

4.

(1) The claim form in proceedings under the 1985 Act, the 2006 Act, Part VII FSMA, the EC Regulation or the Cross-Border Mergers Regulations, and any application, affidavit, witness statement, notice or other document in such proceedings, must be entitled 'In the matter of [*the name of the company in question*] and in the matter of [*the relevant law*]', where '[*the relevant law*]' means 'the Companies Act 1985', 'the Companies Act 2006', 'Part VII of the Financial Services and Markets Act 2000', 'Council Regulation (EC) No 2157/2001 of 8 October 2001 on the Statute for a European Company (SE)' or 'the Companies (Cross-Border Merger) Regulations 2007', as the case may be.

(2) Where a company changes its name in the course of proceedings, the title must be altered by—

  (a) substituting the new name for the old; and

  (b) inserting the old name in brackets at the end of the title.

Starting proceedings and notification of application made

5.

(1) Proceedings to which this practice direction applies must be started by a Part 8 claim form—

  (a) unless a provision of this or another practice direction provides otherwise, but

  (b) subject to any modification of that procedure by this or any other practice direction.

(2) The claim form—

  (a) will, where issued in the High Court, be issued out of the Companies Court or a Chancery district registry; or

  (b) will, where issued in a county court, be issued out of a County Court hearing centre office.

(3) Where this practice direction requires a party to proceedings to notify another person of an application, such notification must, unless the court orders otherwise, be given by sending to that other person a copy of the claim form as soon as reasonably practicable after the claim form has been issued.

SECTION II PARTICULAR APPLICATIONS UNDER THE 2006 ACT

References to provisions of the 2006 Act in this Section

6. In this Section, a reference to a section by number, not otherwise identified, is to the section so numbered in the 2006 Act.

Company generally to be made a party to a claim under the 2006 Act

7.

COMPANIES

(1) Where in a claim under the 2006 Act the company concerned is not the claimant, the company is to be made a defendant to the claim unless—

(a) any other enactment, the CPR or this or another practice direction makes a different provision; or

(b) the court orders otherwise.

(2) Where an application is made in the course of proceedings to which the company is or is required to be a defendant, the company must be made a respondent to the application unless—

(a) any other enactment, the CPR or this or another practice direction makes a different provision; or

(b) the court orders otherwise.

Applications under section 169 (Director's right to protest against removal)

8.

(1) This paragraph applies to an application for an order under section 169(5).

(2) The claimant must notify the director concerned of the application.

Applications under section 244 (Disclosure under court order of protected information)

9.

(1) This paragraph applies to an application for an order under section 244.

(2) The claimant must notify the director concerned of the application.

Applications under section 295 (Application not to circulate members' statement) or section 317 (Application not to circulate members' statement)

10.

(1) This paragraph applies to an application for an order under section 295 or 317.

(2) The claimant must notify each member who requested the circulation of the relevant statement of the application.

Proceedings under section 370 (Unauthorised donations – enforcement of directors' liabilities by shareholder action)

11. Proceedings to enforce a director's liability under section 370 must be started by a Part 7 claim form.

Proceedings under section 456 (Application in respect of defective accounts or directors' report)

12.

(1) This paragraph applies to an application for a declaration under section 456(1).

(2) The claimant must notify any former director who was a director at the time of the approval of the annual accounts or directors' report of the application.

Proceedings under section 511, 514, 515 or 518 (Representations or statements made by the auditor)

13.

(1) This paragraph applies to an application for an order under section 511(6), 514(7), 515(7) or 518(9).

(2) The claimant must notify the auditor of the application.

Proceedings under section 527 (Members' powers to require website publication of audit concerns)

14.

(1) This paragraph applies to an application for an order under section 527(5).

(2) The claimant must, unless the court orders otherwise, notify each member who requested a statement to be placed on the website of the application.

Proceedings under Parts 26 and 27 of the 2006 Act (Applications to sanction a compromise or arrangement)

15.

(1) This paragraph applies to an application for an order under Parts 26 and 27 of the 2006 Act to sanction a compromise or arrangement.

(2) Where the application is made by the company concerned, or by a liquidator or administrator of the company, there need be no defendant to the claim unless the court so orders.

(3) The claim form must be supported by written evidence, including—

(a) statutory information about the company; and

(b) the terms of the proposed compromise or arrangement.

(4) The claim form must seek—

(a) directions for convening a meeting of creditors or members or both, as the case requires;

(b) the sanction of the court to the compromise or arrangement, if it is approved at the meeting or meetings, and a direction for a further hearing for that purpose; and

(c) a direction that the claimant files a copy of a report to the court by the chairman of the meeting or of each meeting.

Proceedings under section 955 (Takeovers – enforcement by the court)

16. Proceedings for an order under section 955 must be started by a Part 7 claim form.

Proceedings under section 968 (Takeovers – effect on contractual restrictions)

17. Proceedings to recover compensation under section 968(6) must be started by a Part 7 claim form.

Applications under section 1132 (Production and inspection of documents where offence suspected)

18.

(1) This paragraph applies to an application for an order under section 1132.

(2) No notice need be given to any person against whom the order is sought.

SECTION III OTHER APPLICATIONS

Applications under the EC Regulation – Article 25

19.

(1) In this paragraph and paragraphs 20 and 21—

COMPANIES

(a) a reference to an Article by number is a reference to the Article so numbered in the EC Regulation; and

(b) 'SE' means a European public limited-liability company (Societas Europaea) within the meaning of the EC Regulation.

(1A) Any document that is filed with the court must, if not in English, be accompanied by a translation of that document into English—

(a) certified by a notary public or other qualified person; or

(b) accompanied by written evidence confirming that the translation is accurate.

(2) An application for a certificate under Article 25(2)—

(a) must set out the pre-merger acts and formalities applicable to the applicant company;

(b) must be accompanied by evidence that those acts and formalities have been completed; and

(c) must be accompanied by copies of—

(i) the draft terms of merger, as provided for in Article 20;

(ii) the entry in the London Gazette containing the particulars specified in Article 21;

(iii) a directors' report;

(iv) an expert's report; and

(v) the resolution of the applicant company approving the draft terms of merger in accordance with Article 23.

(3) In paragraph (2)(c)—

'directors' report' in relation to a company means a report by the directors of the company containing the information required by section 908 of the 2006 Act;

'expert's report' in relation to a company means a report to the members of the company drawn up in accordance with—

(a) section 909 of the 2006 Act; or

(b) Article 22.

(4) There need be no defendant to the application.

Applications under the EC Regulation – Article 22 (Appointment of an independent expert)

20.

(1) An application under Article 22 for the appointment of an independent expert must be made—

(a) where the application is made at the same time as or after the application under Article 25(2) for the approval of the pre-merger acts and formalities has been filed with the court, by application notice pursuant to Part 23; or

(b) where no application under Article 25(2) has been made, by a Part 8 claim form.

(2) The application (whether by a claim form or application notice, as the case may be) must be accompanied by evidence in support of the application.

Applications under the EC Regulation – Article 26

21.

(1) Where under Article 26(2) a merging company is required to submit a certificate to the High Court, that company must, if no other merging company has begun proceedings under Article 26, start such proceedings by way of a Part 8 claim form.

(2) There need be no defendant to the claim.

(3) The claim form—

(a) must name the SE and all of the merging companies;

(b) must be accompanied by the documents referred to in sub-paragraph (5); and

(c) must be served on each of the other merging companies.

(4) Where under Article 26(2) a merging company is required to submit a certificate to the High Court, and proceedings under Article 26 have already been begun, the company—

(a) must, not more than 14 days after service on it of the claim form, file an acknowledgment of service and serve it on each of the other merging companies; and

(b) must file the documents, in relation to each merging company, referred to in sub-paragraph (5) within the time limit specified in Article 26(2), and serve copies of them on each of the other merging companies.

(5) The documents in relation to each merging company are—

(a) the certificate issued under Article 25(2) in respect of the company;

(b) a copy of the draft terms of merger approved by the company;

(c) evidence that arrangements for employee involvement have been determined by the company pursuant to Council Directive 2001/86/EC of 8 October 2001 supplementing the Statute for a European company with regard to the involvement of employees; and

(d) evidence that the SE has been formed in accordance with Article 26(4).

Applications under the Cross-Border Mergers Regulations

22.

(1) In this paragraph and paragraphs 23 to 25 a reference to a regulation by number is a reference to the regulation so numbered in the Cross-Border Mergers Regulations.

(2) Any document that is filed with the court must, if not in English, be accompanied by a translation of that document into English—

(a) certified by a notary public or other qualified person; or

(b) accompanied by written evidence confirming that the translation is accurate.

Application for approval of pre-merger requirements

23.

(1) This paragraph applies to an application under regulation 6.

(2) There need be no defendant to the application.

(3) The application must—

(a) set out the pre-merger acts and formalities required by regulations 7 to 10 and 12 to 15 applicable to the applicant company; and

(b) be accompanied by evidence that those acts and formalities have been completed properly.

(4) Where an application under regulation 11 to summon a meeting of creditors has been made, the court will not determine the application under regulation 6 to approve the pre-merger requirements until the result of the meeting is known.

(5) Where the court makes an order certifying that all pre-merger acts and formalities have been completed properly, the applicant must draw up the

COMPANIES

order and file it no later than 7 days after the date on which the order was made so that it can be sealed[GL] by the court. The court will seal[GL] and return the order to the applicant within 15 days of receipt.

Application for appointment of independent expert or to summon a meeting of members or creditors

24.

(1) This paragraph applies to—

(a) an application for the appointment of an independent expert under regulation 9;

(b) an application under regulation 11 for an order to summon a meeting of members or creditors or both.

(2) The application must be made—

(a) where the application is made at the same time as or after the application for approval of the pre-merger acts and formalities under regulation 6 has been filed with the court, by application notice pursuant to Part 23; or

(b) where no application under regulation 6 has been made, by a Part 8 claim form.

(3) The application (whether by claim form or application notice, as the case may be) must be accompanied by evidence in support of the application.

Application for the approval of the completion of the merger

25.

(1) This paragraph applies to an application under regulation 16.

(2) The application must be made by a Part 8 claim form.

(3) There need be no defendant to the application.

(4) The claim form must be accompanied by –

(a) the documents referred to in regulation 16(1)(b), (c) and (e);

(b) where appropriate, evidence that regulation 16(1)(f) has been complied with; and

(c) such other evidence as may be required to enable the court to decide the application.

(5) Where the court makes an order under regulation 16 approving the merger, it will fix a date on which the consequences of the merger are to take effect.

Applications under section 59 of the CJPA

26.

(1) In sub-paragraphs (2) to (8)—

(a) a reference to a section by number, not otherwise identified, is a reference to the section so numbered in the CJPA; and

(b) references to a relevant interest in property have the same meaning as in section 59 of the CJPA.

(2) This paragraph applies to applications under section 59 in respect of property seized in exercise of the power conferred by section 448(3) of the 1985 Act (including any additional powers of seizure conferred by section 50 that are exercisable by reference to that power).

(3) The application must be supported by evidence—

(a) that the claimant has a relevant interest in the property to which the application relates; and

(b) in the case of an application under section 59(2), that one or more of the grounds set out in section 59(3) is satisfied in relation to the property.

(4) Where the claimant has a relevant interest in the property, the defendants to the claim are to be—

(a) the person in possession of the property; and

(b) any other person who appears to have a relevant interest in the property.

(5) Where the claimant is in possession of the property, the defendants are to be—

(a) the person from whom the property was seized; and

(b) any other person who appears to have a relevant interest in the property.

(6) In the case of an application for the return of seized property, the claimant must serve a copy of the claim form and the claimant's evidence in support of it on the person specified, by the notice given under section 52 when the property was seized, as the person to whom notice of such an application should be given.

(7) If the claimant knows the identity of the person who seized the property, the claimant must also notify that person of the application.

(8) When the court issues the claim form it will fix a date for the hearing.

SECTION IV CONDUCT OF PROCEEDINGS

Reduction of capital – evidence

27. In the case of an application to confirm a reduction in capital, if any shares were issued otherwise than for cash—

(a) for any shares so issued on or after 1st January 1901, it is sufficient to set out in the application the extent to which the shares are, or are treated as being, paid up; and

(b) for any shares so issued between 1st September 1867 and 31st December 1900, the application must also show that the requirement as to the filing of the relevant contract with the Registrar of Joint Stock Companies in section 25 of the Companies Act 1867 was complied with.

SECTION V MISCELLANEOUS

Service of documents

28. The parties are responsible for service of documents in proceedings to which this practice direction applies.

Transitional provisions

29. A claim started, or an application made, before 1st October 2007 may be continued in accordance with the practice direction in force on 30th September 2007 as if it had not been revoked.

---

[1] 1985 c. 6

[2] 2006 c. 46

[3] 2001 c. 16

[4] OJ No. L294, 10.11.2001, p.1

[5] 2000 c. 8

[6] S.I. 2007/2974

CONSUMER CONTRACTS

TABLE OF CONTENTS

GENERAL NOTES ON CONSUMER CONTRACTS

III CON [1]

Jurisdiction of the civil courts In addition to the equitable remedies, which are available to mitigate the rigours of the common law of contract, there are various statutory controls. These enable the courts, mostly the county courts, to prevent one party, usually a creditor, from holding the other, usually a consumer, to the strict letter of the contract. The courts' jurisdiction is in most cases discretionary and the main criterion for its exercise is reasonableness in all the circumstances. In some situations, however, the protection takes the form of a statutory ban on enforcement, subject, in some cases, to a discretion to allow it.

III CON [2]

Substantive law The substantive law of sale and supply of goods and services was codified in the 1970–80s and the main provisions are set out in this title. This is because the application of these provisions is at the heart of most of the millions of disputes which are decided every year by the small claims procedure, in which legal representation is comparatively rare. For a fuller exposition of the law see the publications collected at the end of these General Notes.

More recently, contracting consumers have been given additional protection by the implementation of Council Directives. Areas of particular relevance, which are covered in this title, are package holidays, distance selling, unfair terms in consumer contracts and additional terms in contracts for the sale and supply of goods.

From 1 October 2015 a new code of consumer rights and remedies has been brought into force by the enactment of the Consumer Rights Act 2015. It sets out the rights of consumers in respect of contracts made on or after that date for the sale or supply of goods, digital content or services. Alongside the primary legislation are the Alternative Dispute Resolution for Consumer Disputes (Competent Authorities and Information) Regulations 2015, SI 2015/542, which are intended to encourage the resolution of consumer/trader disputes by a simple, low cost out of court procedure.

III CON [2A]

Codes and Rules The paragraphs that follow set out the substantive rights and duties imputed into consumer contracts by various statutes, orders and regulations. In addition, providers of financial services are required to comply with rules and codes of conduct promulgated under the Financial Services Act 2000, as amended by section 24 of the

Financial Services Act 2012. Section 150 of the Act of 2000 created a statutory cause of action for the benefit of consumers where financial loss resulted from non-compliance with the rules or code of conduct. This cause of action has been upheld by the Court of Appeal in cases where the consumers would otherwise have failed: *Saville v Central Capital Ltd* [2014] EWCA Civ 337, [2014] All ER (D) 216 (Mar) also *Figurasin v Central Capital Ltd* [2014] EWCA Civ 504, [2014] 2 All ER (Comm) 257. These were both cases of insurance being arranged in breach of the Insurance Code of Business promulgated by the Financial Services Authority. The Financial Services Act 2012 replaced the Financial Services Authority with the Financial Conduct Authority and, by s 24 of that Act, conferred on the new authority comparable powers to regulate the provision of financial services by rules and codes of conduct. The cause of action created in the consumer's favour by s 150 of the Act of 2000 was replaced for the future by a comparable cause of action for financial loss caused by non-compliance with the rules and codes of conduct laid down by the new authority. The replacement cause of action was inserted in the Act of 2000 as a new s 138D.

It may be concluded that the protection of consumers buying financial services, including personal indemnity insurance, is not limited to the contractual and statutory rights set out in the paragraphs that follow. There is in addition a right to compensation for loss caused by non-compliance with the regulator's rules and code of conduct; and the party in breach has the burden of disproving causation, according to Sir Stanley Burnton's judgment in *Saville*. For precedents for claims based on the breach of such rules and codes see BCCP Div K, Section H and in particular paragraph **H[1530.1]**.

III CON [3]

Definition of "consumer" There is no universal definition of "consumer" but the highest common factor is that, in a contractual situation, it is a person who contracts for the supply of goods or services but does not do so in the course of a business. Community law leans towards a consumer being a "natural" person but UK law is willing to include corporations within the protective provisions on unreasonable exemption clauses. See **III CON [67.1]**.

III CON [4]

Precedents See **BCCP Division K** for claims and defences which are designed to meet the requirements of the Civil Procedure Rules 1998 and which cover the main areas of consumer contract law: agency; bills of exchange, consumer credit financial services; sale of goods and suretyship. See also for precedents **BCCP M[901]–BCCP M[909]**.

For the substantive law see 4 *Halsbury's Laws* (4th edn reissue) title BILLS OF SALE, para 601; 9(1) *Halsbury's Laws* (4th edn reissue) title CONSUMER CREDIT, para 1; 2 *Halsbury's Laws* (4th edn reissue) title BAILMENT, para 1801; 20 *Halsbury's Laws* (4th edn reissue) title GUARANTEE AND INDEMNITY, para 101; 41 *Halsbury's Laws* (4th edn reissue) title SALE OF GOODS, para 601.

BILLS OF SALE (1878) AMENDMENT ACT 1882

(c 43)

III CON [5]

7. Bills of sale with power to seize except in certain events to be void

Personal chattels assigned under a bill of sale shall not be liable to be seized or taken possession of by the grantee for any other than the following causes—

(1) If the grantor shall make default in payment of the sum or sums of money thereby secured at the time therein provided for payment, or in the performance of any covenant or agreement contained in the bill of sale and necessary for maintaining the security;

(2) If the grantor shall become a bankrupt, or suffer the said goods or any of them to be distrained, or taken control of using the power in Schedule 12 to the Tribunals, Courts and Enforcement Act 2007, for rent, rates, or taxes;

(3) If the grantor shall fraudulently either remove or suffer the said goods, or any of them, to be removed from the premises;

(4) If the grantor shall not, without reasonable excuse, upon demand in writing by the grantee, produce to him his last receipts for rent, rates, and taxes;

(5) If execution shall have been levied against the goods of the grantor under any judgment at law:

Provided that the grantor may within five days from the seizure or taking possession of any chattels on account of any of the above-mentioned causes, apply to the High Court, or to a judge thereof in chambers, and such court or judge, if satisfied that by payment of money or otherwise the said cause of seizure no longer exists, may restrain the grantee from removing or selling the said chattels, or may make such other order as may seem just.

III CON [5.1]

Procedure The application should be made in the Queen's Bench Division of the High Court by a Part 8 claim form, using form N208. See **QBG 13.4.9**.

III CON [5.2]

The grantor Having regard to the wording of the Bills of Sale Acts and s 17 of the Act of 1882 in particular, the protection applies only to individuals, not to corporations: *Slavenburg's Bank NV v Intercontinental Natural Resources Ltd* [1980] 1 All ER 955, [1980] 1 WLR 1076; *Online Catering Ltd v Acton* [2010] EWCA Civ 58, [2010] 3 All ER 869, [2010] 3 WLR 928.

III CON [6]

7A. Defaults under consumer credit agreements

(1) Paragraph (1) of section 7 of this Act does not apply to a default relating to a bill of sale given by way of security for the payment of money under a regulated agreement to which section 87 (1) of the Consumer Credit Act 1974 applies—

(a) unless the restriction imposed by section 88 (2) of that Act has ceased to apply to the bill of sale; or

(b) if, by virtue of section 89 of that Act, the default is to be treated as not having occurred.

(2) Where paragraph (1) of section 7 of this Act does apply in relation to a bill of sale such as is mentioned in subsection (1) of this section, the proviso to that section shall have effect with the substitution of "county court" for "High Court".

III CON [6.1]

Procedure to restrain grantee In the case of a consumer credit agreement the application should be made in the county court by claim form N208. The opportunity should be taken to apply at the same time for relief under the Consumer Credit Act 1974, for example a time order under s 129 or to vary the terms on the ground that they are extortionate (s 136) or that the agreement arose out of an unfair relationship (s 140A): *Southern and District Finance plc v Barnes* [1996] 1 FCR 679.

III CON [6.2]

Consumer Credit Act The effect of this section is to prevent the creditor from exercising powers under s 7 (1) after the service of a default notice in accordance with s 88 of the Consumer Credit Act 1974 if the period allowed by the notice has not expired or the debtor has, during that period, made good the default.

III CON [7]

11. Local registration of contents of bills of sale

Where the affidavit (which under section ten of the principal Act is required to accompany a bill of sale when presented for registration) describes the residence of the person making or giving the same or of the person against whom the process is issued to be in some place outside the London insolvency district, or where the bill of sale describes the chattels enumerated therein as being in some place outside the London insolvency district, the registrar under the principal Act shall forthwith and within three clear days after registration in the principal registry and in accordance with the prescribed directions, transmit an abstract in the prescribed form of the contents of such bill of sale to the county court.

Every abstract so transmitted shall be filed, kept, and indexed by the county court in the prescribed manner, and any person may search, inspect, make extracts from, and obtain copies of the abstract so registered in the like manner and upon the like terms as to payment or otherwise as near as may be as in the case of bills of sale registered by the registrar under the principal Act.

III CON [7.1]

Local registration Section 23 (1) of the Administration of Justice Act 1925 provides that a copy of the bill of sale instead of an abstract shall be sent for local registration.

III CON [7.2]

Registrar The "registrar under the principal Act" is the Chief Bankruptcy Registrar.

III CON [7.3]

Registered under the principal Act Section 16 of the Bills of Sale Act 1878 provides that any person shall be entitled to have an office copy or extract of any registered bill of sale and affidavit on payment at the same rate as for office copies of judgments of the High Court. An application for a search of the register must be made in accordance with paragraph 11A of the Practice Direction supplementing Part 8 in Volume1, at **CPR PD 8**.

III CON [7.4]

Rectification An application to the High Court, under Bill of Sale Act 1878, s 14, should be made by witness statement or Part 8 claim form, as provided in paragraph 10A of the Practice Direction supplementing Part 8 in Volume 1, at **CPR PD 8**. Applications under s 15 are governed by paragraph 11 of the same Practice Direction.

III CON [7.5]

Corporations The Bills of Sale Acts do not apply to corporations: *Slavenburg's Bank NV v Intercontinental Natural Resources Ltd* [1980] 1 All ER 955, [1980] 1 WLR 1076; *Online Catering Ltd v Acton* [2010] EWCA Civ 58, [2010] 3 All ER 869, [2010] 3 WLR 928.

III CON [8]

16. Inspection of registered bills of sale

Any person shall be entitled at all reasonable times to search the register, on payment of a fee of one shilling, or such other fee as may be prescribed, and subject to such regulations as may be prescribed, and shall be entitled at all reasonable times to inspect, examine, and make extracts from any and every registered bill of sale without being required to make a written application, or to specify any particulars in reference thereto, upon payment of one shilling for each bill of sale inspected, and such payment shall be made by a judicature stamp. Provided that the said extracts shall be limited to the dates of execution, registration, renewal of registration, and satisfaction, to the names, addresses, and occupations of the parties, to the amount of the consideration, and to any further prescribed particulars.

BILLS OF SALE (LOCAL REGISTRATION) RULES 1960

(SI 1960/2326)

III CON [9]

1. Commencement

These Rules may be cited as the Bills of Sale (Local Registration) Rules 1960, and shall come into operation on the second day of January 1961.

III CON [10]

2. Interpretation

(1) The Interpretation Act 1889 shall apply to the interpretation of these Rules as it applies to the interpretation of an Act of Parliament.

(2) In these Rules—

"affidavit of renewal" means an affidavit made for the purpose of renewing the registration of a bill of sale pursuant to section 11 of the Bills of Sale Act 1878;

"registrar of bills of sale" means the registrar for the purposes of the said Act of 1878;

"section 11 of the Act of 1882" means section 11 of the Bills of Sale Act (1878) Amendment Act 1882, as amended by section 23 of the Administration of Justice Act 1925.

III CON [10.1]

Interpretation Act 1889 See now the Interpretation Act 1978.

III CON [10.2]

Registrar References to the registrar should be interpreted as referring to the district judge: Courts and Legal Services Act 1990 s 74.

III CON [11]

3. Certificate of registration of bill of sale or affidavit

Every copy of a bill of sale or of an affidavit of renewal which is transmitted to a district judge under section 11 of the Act of 1882 shall bear a certificate by the registrar of bills of sale showing the date on which the registration or, as the case may be, the renewal of registration, of the bill of sale was effected and the date on which the copy of the bill of sale or affidavit is transmitted to the district judge.

III CON [12]

4. Notice of satisfaction of bill of sale

Where a memorandum of satisfaction has been written on a registered copy of a bill of sale, the registrar of bills of sale shall transmit a notice of satisfaction in the form set out in the Schedule to these Rules to every district judge to whom a copy of the bill of sale was transmitted under section 11 of the Act of 1882.

III CON [13]

5. Numbering and filing of copies of bills of sale and affidavits

Every district judge shall number consecutively the copies of bills of sale and of affidavits of renewal transmitted to him under section 11 of the Act of 1882 and shall file and keep them in the court office.

III CON [14]

6. Indexing of copies of bills of sale

Every district judge shall keep an alphabetical index of the copies of bills of sale and of affidavits of renewal transmitted to him under section 11 of the Act of 1882 and shall enter in the index under the first letter of the surname of the grantor of every bill the grantor's full name, address and description and the number of the copy of the bill of sale or affidavit.

III CON [15]

7. Annexing of notice of satisfaction to bill of sale

7. A district judge to whom a notice of satisfaction is transmitted shall annex the notice to the copy of the bill of sale to which it relates and shall add to the entry in the index relating to the bill of sale a note that it has been satisfied.

SUPPLY OF GOODS (IMPLIED TERMS) ACT 1973

(c 13)

GENERAL NOTES ON SUPPLY OF GOODS

III CON [16]

This Act is concerned, primarily, with contracts for the supply of goods on hire-purchase terms. It sets out the terms which are to be implied for the benefit of the customer. The rights of a customer who is a consumer are now to be found in the Consumer Rights Act 2015, ss 7 to 18, at **III CON [191]** to **III CON [202]**.

As regards contracts made on or after 1 October 2015, amendments to the Act made by Schedule 1 to the Consumer Rights Act 2015 have effect and are included in the text below.

III CON [17]

8. Implied terms as to title

(1) In every relevant hire-purchase agreement, other than one to which subsection (2) below applies, there is—

(a) an implied term on the part of the creditor that he will have a right to sell the goods at the time when the property is to pass; and

(b) an implied term that—

(i) the goods are free, and will remain free until the time when the property is to pass, from any charge or encumbrance not disclosed or known to the person to whom the goods are bailed or (in Scotland) hired before the agreement is made, and

(ii) that person will enjoy quiet possession of the goods except so far as it may be disturbed by any person entitled to the benefit of any charge or encumbrance so disclosed or known.

(2) In a relevant hire-purchase agreement, in the case of which there appears from the agreement or is to be inferred from the circumstances of the agreement an intention that the creditor should transfer only such title as he or a third person may have, there is—

(a) an implied term that all charges or encumbrances known to the creditor and not known to the person to whom the goods are bailed or hired have been disclosed to that person before the agreement is made; and

(b) an implied term that neither—

(i) the creditor; nor

(ii) in a case where the parties to the agreement intend that any title which may be transferred shall be only such title as a third person may have, that person; nor

(iii) anyone claiming through or under the creditor or that third person otherwise than under a charge or encumbrance disclosed or known to the person to whom the goods are bailed or hired, before the agreement is made;

will disturb the quiet possession of the person to whom the goods are bailed or hired.

(3) As regards England and Wales and Northern Ireland, the term implied by subsection (1)(a) above is a condition and the terms implied by subsections (1)(b), (2)(a) and (2)(b) above are warranties.

III CON [17.1]

Exclusion by contract Liability cannot be excluded: see the Unfair Contract Terms Act 1977 s 6 (1) (see para **III CON [61]**).

III CON [17.2]

Relevant hire purchase agreement Amendments made to this section and section 15 by Schedule 1 to the Consumer Rights Act 2015 make it clear that a hire purchase agreement that is covered by Chapter 2 of that Act is not 'relevant'. So an agreement is not within the protection of the Act of 1973 if made on or after 1 October 2015 but is covered instead by Chapter 2 of the Consumer Rights Act 2015.

III CON [18]

9. Bailing or hiring by description

(1) Where under a relevant hire-purchase agreement goods are bailed or (in Scotland) hired by description, there is an implied [term] that the goods will correspond with the description, and if under the agreement the goods are bailed

or hired by reference to a sample as well as a description, it is not sufficient that the bulk of the goods corresponds with the sample if the goods do not also correspond with the description.

(1A) As regards England and Wales and Northern Ireland, the term implied by subsection (1) above is a condition.

(2) Goods shall not be prevented from being bailed or hired by description by reason only that, being exposed for sale, bailment or hire, they are selected by the person to whom they are bailed or hired.

III CON [18.1]

Exclusion by contract Liability cannot be excluded where the hirer "deals as a consumer": see Unfair Contract Terms Act 1977 ss 6 (2) and 12 (see paras **III CON [61]** and **III CON [67]**). Also reg 8 of the Unfair Terms in Consumer Contracts Regulations 1999 (SI 1999/2083), at **III CON [116]**, deprives unfair terms of binding effect; and an exclusion of a consumer's statutory rights is an unfair term within regs 5 and 6 and Sch 2, para 1(b). In the case of hirers who do not so deal, an exclusion of liability may be relied on only in so far as it satisfies the requirement of reasonableness, set out in s 11. See para **III CON [66]** for the "reasonableness" test and see para **III CON [67]** for the meaning of "dealing as a consumer".

III CON [19]

10. Implied undertakings as to quality or fitness

(1) Except as provided by this section and section 11 below and subject to the provisions of any other enactment, including any enactment of the Parliament of Northern Ireland, or the Northern Ireland Assembly, there is no implied term as to the quality or fitness for any particular purpose of goods bailed or (in Scotland) hired under a relevant hire-purchase agreement.

(2) Where the creditor bails or hires goods under a hire-purchase agreement in the course of a business, there is an implied term that the goods supplied under the agreement are of satisfactory quality.

(2A) For the purposes of this Act, goods are of satisfactory quality if they meet the standard that a reasonable person would regard as satisfactory, taking account of any description of the goods, the price (if relevant) and all the other relevant circumstances.

(2B) For the purposes of this Act, the quality of goods includes their state and condition and the following (among others) are in appropriate cases aspects of the quality of goods—

- (a) fitness for all the purposes for which goods of the kind in question are commonly supplied,
- (b) appearance and finish,
- (c) freedom from minor defects,
- (d) safety, and
- (e) durability.

(2C) The term implied by subsection (2) above does not extend to any matter making the quality of goods unsatisfactory—

- (a) which is specifically drawn to the attention of the person to whom the goods are bailed or hired before the agreement is made,
- (b) where that person examines the goods before the agreement is made, which that examination ought to reveal, or
- (c) where the goods are bailed or hired by reference to a sample, which would have been apparent on a reasonable examination of the sample.

(2D) ...

(2E) ...

(2F) ...

(3) Where the creditor bails or hires goods under a relevant hire-purchase agreement in the course of a business and the person to whom the goods are bailed or hired, expressly or by implication, makes known—

(a) to the creditor in the course of negotiations conducted by the creditor in relation to the making of the relevant hire-purchase agreement, or

(b) to a credit-broker in the course of negotiations conducted by that broker in relation to goods sold by him to the creditor before forming the subject matter of the relevant hire-purchase agreement,

any particular purpose for which the goods are being bailed or hired, there is an implied term that the goods supplied under the agreement are reasonably fit for that purpose, whether or not that is a purpose for which such goods are commonly supplied, except where the circumstances show that the person to whom the goods are bailed or hired does not rely, or that it is unreasonable for him to rely, on the skill or judgment of the creditor or credit-broker.

(4) An implied term as to the quality or fitness for a particular purpose may be annexed to a hire-purchase agreement by usage.

(5) The preceding provisions of this section apply to a relevant hire-purchase agreement made by a person who in the course of a business is acting as agent for the creditor as they apply to an agreement made by the creditor in the course of a business, except where the creditor is not bailing or hiring in the course of a business and either the person to whom the goods are bailed or hired knows that fact or reasonable steps are taken to bring it to the notice of that person before the agreement is made.

(6) In subsection (3) above and this subsection—

(a) "credit-broker" means a person acting in the course of a business of credit brokerage,

(b) "credit brokerage" means the effecting of introductions of individuals desiring to obtain credit—

(i) to persons carrying on any business so far as it relates to the provision of credit, or

(ii) to other persons engaged in credit brokerage.

(7) As regards England and Wales and Northern Ireland, the terms implied by subsections (2) and (3) above are conditions.

(8) ...

III CON [19.1]

Satisfactory quality This section, as amended, provides for "satisfactory" rather than "merchantable" quality. Sub-sections (2D), (2E) and (2F) were inserted by reg 13 of the Sale and Supply of Goods to Consumers Regulations 2002, SI 2002/3045, with effect from 31 March 2003. Provisions to the same effect were inserted in contracts of sale by reg 3 and in contracts of hire and contracts for the supply of goods and services together by reg 7 of the same Regulations.

III CON [19.2]

Exclusion by contract Liability cannot be excluded where the hirer "deals as a consumer": see the Unfair Contract Terms Act 1977 ss 6 (2) and 12 (see paras **III CON [61]** and **III CON [67]**). Also reg 8 of the Unfair Terms in Consumer Contracts Regulations 1999 (SI 1999/2083), at **III CON [116]**, deprives unfair terms of binding effect; and an exclusion of a consumer's statutory rights is an unfair term within regs 5 and 6 and Sch 2, para 1(b). In the case of hirers who do not so deal, an exclusion of liability may be relied on only in so far as it satisfies the requirement of reasonableness, set out in s 11 of the Unfair Contract Terms Act 1977. See para **III CON [66]** for the "reasonableness" test and para **III CON [67]** for the meaning of "dealing as a consumer".

III CON [19.3]

Fitness for a particular purpose Where the customer has made known the particular purpose for which the goods are required and the goods are not fit for that purpose the customer is entitled to reject them. If the supplier then offers to modify the goods to make them fit, the offer may reasonably be rejected unless the offer is clear and cogent, which was not the case in *Albury Asset Rentals Ltd v Ash Manor Cheese Company Ltd (Pt 20 claimant) and Manton Hire and Sales Ltd (Pt 20 defendant)* [2013] EWCA Civ 548, [2013] All ER (D) 215 (May).

III CON [20]

11. Samples

(1) Where under a relevant hire-purchase agreement goods are bailed or (in Scotland) hired by reference to a sample, there is an implied term—

(a) that the bulk will correspond with the sample in quality; and

(b) that the person to whom the goods are bailed or hired will have a reasonable opportunity of comparing the bulk with the sample; and

(c) that the goods will be free from any defect, making their quality unsatisfactory, which would not be apparent on reasonable examination of the sample.

(2) As regards England and Wales and Northern Ireland, the term implied by subsection (1) above is a condition.

III CON [20.1]

Exclusion by contract Liability cannot be excluded where the hirer "deals as a consumer": see the Unfair Contract Terms Act 1977 ss 6 (2) and 12 (see paras **III CON [61]** and **III CON [67]**). Also reg 8 of the Unfair Terms in Consumer Contracts Regulations 1999 (SI 1999/2083), at **III CON [116]**, deprives unfair terms of binding effect; and an exclusion of a consumer's statutory rights is an unfair term within regs 5 and 6 and Sch 2, para 1(b). In the case of hirers who do not so deal, an exclusion of liability may be relied on only in so far as it satisfies the requirement of reasonableness, set out in s 11 of the Unfair Contract Terms Act 1977. See para **III CON [66]** for the "reasonableness" test and para **III CON [67]** for the meaning of "dealing as a consumer".

III CON [21]–III CON [22]

11A. Modification of remedies for breach of statutory condition in non-consumer cases

(1) Where in the case of a relevant hire-purchase agreement—

(a) the person to whom goods are bailed would, apart from this subsection, have the right to reject them by reason of a breach on the part of the creditor of a term implied by section 9, 10 or 11 (1)(a) or (c) above, but

(b) the breach is so slight that it would be unreasonable for him to reject them,

the breach is not to be treated as a breach of condition but may be treated as a breach of warranty.

(2) This section applies unless a contrary intention appears in, or is to be implied from, the agreement.

(3) It is for the creditor to show—

(a) that a breach fell within subsection (1)(b) above, and

(b) that the agreement was a relevant hire-purchase agreement.

(4) ...

(5) This section does not apply to Scotland.

III CON [23]

15. Supplementary

(1) In sections 8 to 14 above and this section—

"business" includes a profession and the activities of any government department (including a Northern Ireland department), or local or public authority;

"buyer" and "seller" includes a person to whom rights and duties under a conditional sale agreement have passed by assignment or operation of law;

"conditional sale agreement" means an agreement for the sale of goods under which the purchase price or part of it is payable by instalments, and the property in the goods is to remain in the seller (notwithstanding that the buyer is to be in possession of the goods) until such conditions as to the payment of instalments or otherwise as may be specified in the agreement are fulfilled;

"creditor" means the person by whom the goods are bailed or (in Scotland) hired under a hire-purchase agreement or the person to whom his rights and duties under the agreement have passed by assignment or operation of law; and

"hire-purchase agreement" means an agreement, other than a conditional sale agreement, under which—

(a) goods are bailed or (in Scotland) hired in return for periodical payments by the person to whom they are bailed or hired, and

(b) the property in the goods will pass to that person if the terms of the agreement are complied with and one or more of the following occurs—

(i) the exercise of an option to purchase by that person,

(ii) the doing of any other specified act by any party to the agreement,

(iii) the happening of any other specified event.

and a hire-purchase agreement is relevant if it is not a contract to which Chapter 2 of Part 1 of the Consumer Rights Act 2015 applies;

(2) ...

(3) ...

(4) Nothing in sections 8 to 13 above shall prejudice the operation of any other enactment including any enactment of the Parliament of Northern Ireland or the Northern Ireland Assembly or any rule of law whereby any term, other than one relating to quality or fitness, is to be implied in any relevant hire-purchase agreement.

CONSUMER CREDIT ACT 1974

(c 39)

GENERAL NOTES ON CONSUMER CREDIT ACT 1974

III CON [24]

Regulated agreements "Regulated agreement" is defined by s 189 (1) as "a consumer credit agreement, or consumer hire agreement, other than an exempt agreement". A "consumer credit agreement" is explained in s 8 as a personal credit agreement, whereby a creditor provides an individual with credit not exceeding the monetary limit. The limit was raised from £15,000 to £25,000 by the Consumer Credit (Increase of Monetary Limits) (Amendment) Order 1988, SI 1998/996 in respect of agreements made on or after 1 May 1998. Where credit facilities are agreed at an amount in excess of the monetary limit, the individual transactions for less than the limit may nevertheless be unregulated: *National Westminster Bank plc v Story* [1999] 20 LS Gaz R 41, CA. Conversely it has been held that where, due to an oversight, customers of a bank were invited to sign documents appropriate to a regulated agreement the statutory provisions on regulated agreements (eg section 77A) applied although the sums involved were over the monetary limit of £25,000: *NRAM plc v McAdam* [2014] EWHC 4174 (Comm), [2015] 2 All ER 340, [2015] 1 All ER (Comm) 1239. But this was reversed on appeal: the Court of Appeal decided that the statutory provisions were not incorporated but that the customers would be entitled to sue for misrepresentation, or breach of collateral warranty instead: *NRAM plc v McAdam* (2015) Times, 8 September, CA.

The regulatory scope of the Act is changed by the opening sections of the Consumer Credit Act 2006. They amend the Consumer Credit Act 1974 by removing monetary limits, redefining "individual" and introducing new exemptions for debtors who have a "high net worth" (new s 16A) and for agreements over £25,000 which are wholly or predominantly for the debtor's business purposes (new s 16B). A further exemption was added by the insertion of a new s 16C (exemption relating to investment properties): see SI 2008/2826. Section 1 of the Consumer Credit Act 2006 was brought into force on 6 April 2007 by SI 2007/123, subject to transitional provisions. Section 2 (removal of financial limits) was brought fully into force by SI 2008/831 on 6 April 2008 except as regards existing agreements for more than £25,000 and agreements secured by a land mortgage on land outside the United Kingdom or on land less than 40% of which is used as a dwelling-house. The same instrument appointed 1 October 2008 as the commencement date for all provisions not already in force, subsequently extended by SI 2008/2444 to 31 October 2008.

Note that residential renovation agreements made after 16 March 2016 are excepted by the Mortgage Credit Directive Order 2015, SI 2015/910, implementing EU Directive 2014/17/EU.

III CON [24A]

Changes made by EU Directive 2008/448/EC In order to implement EU Directive 2008/448/EC, it has been necessary to amend all the main provisions of the Consumer Credit Act 1974 and the secondary legislation too. This has been achieved by means of an instrument made by the Minister designated for the purpose of section 2(2) of the European Communities Act 1972: the Consumer Credit (EU Directive) Regulations 2010, SI 2010/1010, as amended by SI 2010/1969 and SI 2011/11 to correct drafting errors. The amendments to the primary legislation are in regulations 3 to 46 of this instrument and have been carried into the text set out below. Regulations 47 to 98 make amendments to the secondary legislation and these too have been incorporated. Most of the amendments affect the form rather than the substance but there are some significant changes of substance, such as the new s 66A which gives the consumer a right of unilateral withdrawal within 14 days and in the new Part VA on Current Account Overdrafts. The amendments apply in general to agreements entered into on or after 1 February 2011. Confusingly, however, some of the amendments apply to agreements made before that date, in which case the earlier date is stated in the commentary on the amended section. In addition there is an overriding transitional provision that applies all the amendments to any agreement made after 30 April 2010 and before 1 February 2011 to which any of six qualifying conditions applies. This is the effect of regulation 101 of the Consumer Credit (EU Directive) Regulations 2010, SI 2010/1010, regulation 101A (inserted by SI 2010/1969) and regulation 102, which provides for their interpretation. The text of these three regulations is as follows:

101. Early application of regulations to certain agreements before 1st February 2011

(1) Where one of the conditions A to E is satisfied in relation to a prospective regulated consumer credit agreement on a date on or after 30th April 2010 and before 1st February

2011, Parts 1 to 3 of these Regulations apply to that agreement (and to any subsequent regulated consumer credit agreement entered into before 1st February 2011), from the date and time that the condition is satisfied.

(2) Condition A is that information relating to the agreement is disclosed by a creditor or a credit intermediary before the agreement is made in compliance or in purported compliance with the Information Regulations 2010.

(3) Condition B is that—

(a) the agreement would, if made, be an agreement entered into at the debtor's request using a means of distance communication (other than voice telephony) which does not enable the provision before the agreement is made of the information referred to in regulation 3(4) of the Information Regulations 2010, and

(b) the debtor is informed by the creditor before the agreement is made that the information referred to in regulation 3(4) of the Information Regulations 2010 will be disclosed immediately after the agreement is made in accordance with regulation 5 of those Regulations.

(4) Condition C is that—

(a) the agreement would, if made, be a distance agreement entered into by the debtor wholly or predominantly for the purposes of a business carried on, or intended to be carried on, by him, and

(b) the debtor is informed by the creditor before the agreement is made that information referred to in regulation 3(4) of the Information Regulations 2010 will be disclosed immediately after the agreement is made in accordance with regulation 6 of those Regulations.

(5) Condition D is that—

(a) the agreement would, if made, be an authorised non-business overdraft agreement (other than a qualifying overdraft agreement referred to in paragraph (7)(b)),

(b) the agreement would, if made, be one made at the debtor's request using a means of distance communication which does not enable the provision before the agreement is made of the information referred to in regulation 10(2) of the Information Regulations 2010, and

(c) the creditor has informed the debtor before the agreement is made that a document containing the terms of the agreement will be provided immediately after the agreement is made as though the amendment made by regulation 9 of these Regulations (insertion of section 61B in the Consumer Credit Act 1974) applied.

(6) Condition E is that the agreement would, if made, be a qualifying overdraft agreement and—

(a) the creditor has provided a document containing the terms of the agreement before the agreement is made as though the amendment made by regulation 9 (insertion of section 61B in the Consumer Credit Act 1974) applied, or

(b) the creditor has informed the debtor before the agreement is made that a document containing the terms of the agreement will be provided at, or immediately after, the time the agreement is made as though the amendment made by regulation 9 applied.

(7) In paragraph (6) "qualifying overdraft agreement" means—

(a) an authorised business overdraft agreement, or

(b) an authorised non-business overdraft agreement under which the creditor provides the debtor with credit exceeding £60,260 or which is secured on land.

101A.

(1) Where condition F is satisfied on a date on or after 26th August 2010 and before 1st February 2011 in relation to a prospective regulated consumer credit agreement falling within paragraph (2), Parts 1 to 3 of these Regulations apply to that agreement (and to any subsequent regulated consumer credit agreement entered into before 1st February 2011), from the date and time that the condition is satisfied.

(2) An agreement falls within this paragraph if it is an agreement which would, if made, be—

(a) an agreement under which the creditor provides the debtor with credit exceeding £60,260 and is not an authorised non-business overdraft agreement, or

(b) an agreement entered into by the debtor wholly or predominantly for the purposes of a business carried on, or intended to be carried on, by him.

(3) Condition F is that the Consumer Credit (Disclosure of Information) Regulations 2004 apply to the agreement, but the creditor—

(a) does what would be required by regulations 3(1)(a) and (c) of those Regulations (pre-contractual information requirement to disclose information and statements required by the Consumer Credit (Agreements) Regulations 1983) if the amendments to the Consumer Credit (Agreements) Regulations 1983 made by regulations 52 to 56 were in force; and

(b) also provides the debtor with a statement before the agreement is made that, if the creditor decides not to proceed with the agreement on the basis of information obtained from a credit reference agency, the creditor will, when informing the debtor of the decision—

(i) inform the debtor that this decision has been reached on the basis of information from a credit reference agency, and

(ii) provide the debtor with the particulars of the agency including its name, address and telephone number.

102. Interpretation

In this Part—

(a) "authorised business overdraft agreement", "authorised non-business overdraft agreement", "consumer credit agreement", "creditor", "debtor", "open-end" and "regulated" have the meanings given by section 189(1) of the Consumer Credit Act 1974;

(b) "distance agreement" means any regulated consumer credit agreement made under an organised distance sales or service-provision scheme run by the creditor or on behalf of the creditor who, in any such case, for the purpose of that agreement makes exclusive use of one or more means of distance communication up to and including the time at which the agreement is made;

(c) "Information Regulations 2010" means the Consumer Credit (Disclosure of Information) Regulations 2010;

(d) "means of distance communication" means any means which, without the simultaneous physical presence of the creditor or a person acting on behalf of the creditor and of the debtor, may be used for the making of a regulated consumer credit agreement between the parties to that agreement.

III CON [24B]

Procedure and precedents Claims relating to money only should be started by claim form in accordance with CPR Pt 7 see para **CPR 7**; claims relating to land should also be started by claim form but should comply in addition with **CPR 55.3** and **CPR 55.10** whilst hire-purchase and other claims under the Act must comply with the Practice Directions at **CPR PD 7B** and **CPR PD 16**, para 6. For claims and defences under the Consumer Credit Act 1974 see **BCCP K[1466]** onwards.

PART II
CREDIT AGREEMENTS, HIRE AGREEMENTS AND LINKED TRANSACTION

III CON [24C]

8. Consumer credit agreements

(1) A consumer credit agreement is an agreement between an individual ("the debtor") and any other person ("the creditor") by which the creditor provides the debtor with credit of any amount.

(2) . . .

(3) A consumer credit agreement is a regulated credit agreement within the meaning of this Act if it—

(a) is a regulated credit agreement for the purposes of Chapter 14A of Part 2 of the Regulated Activities Order; and

(b) if entered into on or after 21st March 2016, is not an agreement of the type described in Article 3(1)(b) of Directive 2014/17/EU of the European Parliament and of the Council of 4th February 2014 on credit agreements for consumers relating to residential immovable property.

(4) Subsection (1) does not apply in relation to an agreement that is a green deal plan (see instead section 189B.

III CON [24C.1]

Raising and removal of financial ceiling As enacted, s 8 confined the application of the Act to agreements that provided for credit not exceeding £5,000. But, as explained at **III CON [24]**, the limits were raised at various times and eventually removed so as to bring more and more consumer credit agreements within the scope of the Act. However, the categories of exemption have been expanded as well: see sections 16 to 16C.

III CON [24C.2]

A green deal plan Subsection (4) is one of many insertions in the Act made by the Consumer Credit Act 1974 (Green Deal) ((Amendment) Order 2014, SI 2014/436 that came into force on 28 February 2014. Their general effect is that credit agreements relating to 'green deal' improvements of domestic premises are regulated by the Act, but differently from mainstream consumer credit agreements. For the detail see ss 189B and 189C at **III CON [55A]** and **III CON [55B]**.

III CON [24D]

9. Meaning of credit

(1) In this Act "credit" includes a cash loan, and any other form of financial accommodation.

(2) Where credit is provided otherwise than in sterling, it shall be treated for the purposes of this Act as provided in sterling of an equivalent amount.

(3) Without prejudice to the generality of subsection (1), the person by whom goods are bailed or (in Scotland) hired to an individual under a hire-purchase agreement shall be taken to provide him with fixed-sum credit to finance the transaction of an amount equal to the total price of the goods less the aggregate of the deposit (if any) and the total charge for credit.

(4) For the purposes of this Act, an item entering into the total charge for credit shall not be treated as credit even though time is allowed for its payment.

III CON [24E]

10. Running-account credit and fixed-sum credit

(1) For the purposes of this Act—

(a) running-account credit is a facility under a consumer credit agreement whereby the debtor is enabled to receive from time to time (whether in his own person, or by another person) from the creditor or a third party cash, goods and services (or any of them) to an amount or value such that, taking into account payments made by or to the credit of the debtor, the credit limit (if any) is not at any time exceeded; and

(b) fixed-sum credit is any other facility under a consumer credit agreement whereby the debtor is enabled to receive credit (whether in one amount or by instalments).

(2) In relation to running-account credit, "credit limit" means, as respects any period, the maximum debit balance which, under the credit agreement, is allowed to stand on the account during that period, disregarding any term of the agreement allowing that maximum to be exceeded merely temporarily.

(3) For the purposes of any provision of this Act that specifies an amount of credit (except section 17(1)(a)), running-account credit shall be taken not to exceed the amount specified in that provision ("the specified amount") if—

(a) the credit limit does not exceed the specified amount; or

(b) whether or not there is a credit limit, and if there is, notwithstanding that it exceeds the specified amount,—

(i) the debtor is not enabled to draw at any one time an amount which, so far as (having regard to section 9(4)) it represents credit, exceeds the specified amount, or

(ii) the agreement provides that, if the debit balance rises above a given amount (not exceeding the specified amount), the rate of the total charge for credit increases or any other condition favouring the creditor or his associate comes into operation, or

(iii) at the time the agreement is made it is probable, having regard to the terms of the agreement and any other relevant considerations, that the debit balance will not at any time rise above the specified amount.

III CON [24E.1]

EU Directive change In sub-section (3) the words "any provision of this Act that specifies an amount of credit (except section 17(1)(a))"have been inserted to give effect to EU Directive 2008/448/EC, and SI 2010/1010, in respect of agreements made on or after 1 February 2011.

III CON [24F]

11. Restricted-use credit and unrestricted-use credit

(1) A restricted-use credit agreement is a regulated consumer credit agreement—

(a) to finance a transaction between the debtor and the creditor, whether forming part of that agreement or not, or

(b) to finance a transaction between the debtor and a person (the "supplier") other than the creditor, or

(c) to refinance any existing indebtedness of the debtor's, whether to the creditor or another person,

and "restricted-use credit" shall be construed accordingly.

(2) An unrestricted-use credit agreement is a regulated consumer credit agreement not falling within subsection (1), and "unrestricted-use credit" shall be construed accordingly.

(3) An agreement does not fall within subsection (1) if the credit is in fact provided in such a way as to leave the debtor free to use it as he chooses, even though certain uses would contravene that or any other agreement.

(4) An agreement may fall within subsection (1)(b) although the identity of the supplier is unknown at the time the agreement is made.

III CON [24G]

12. Debtor-creditor supply agreements

A debtor-creditor-supplier agreement is a regulated consumer credit agreement being—

(a) a restricted-use credit agreement which falls within section 11(1)(a), or

(b) a restricted-use credit agreement which falls within section 11(1)(b) and is made by the creditor under pre-existing arrangements, or in contemplation of future arrangements, between himself and the supplier, or

(c) an unrestricted-use credit agreement which is made by the creditor under pre-existing arrangements between himself and a person (the "supplier") other than the debtor in the knowledge that the credit is to be used to finance a transaction between the debtor and the supplier.

III CON [24G.1]

Debtor-creditor-supplier agreements A very usual form of regulated agreement is one where the customer (debtor) needs credit in order to acquire goods supplied by the retailer (supplier) and finance is provided by a bank (creditor) either by means of a hire-purchase agreement made between the creditor (who buys the goods from the supplier) and the debtor or by means of a credit card account. Section 56 protects the customer by providing that antecedent negotiations with the supplier are deemed to be conducted by the supplier on behalf of the creditor as well as on his own behalf. Section 75 provides further protection by holding the creditor jointly liable with the supplier for the supplier's misrepresentations or breaches of contract. The protective provisions of s 75 have been held to apply to foreign as well as domestic transactions: *Office of Fair Trading v Lloyds TSB Bank plc* [2006] EWCA Civ 268, [2007] QB 1, [2006] 2 AIL ER 821; affd [2007] UKHL 48, [2008] 1 AC 316, [2008] 1 All ER 205.

III CON [24H]

13. Debtor-creditor agreements

A debtor-creditor agreement is a regulated consumer credit agreement being—

(a) a restricted-use credit agreement which falls within section 11(1)(b) but is not made by the creditor under pre-existing arrangements, or in contemplation of future arrangements, between himself and the supplier, or

(b) a restricted-use credit agreement which falls within section 11(1)(c), or

(c) an unrestricted-use credit agreement which is not made by the creditor under pre-existing arrangements between himself and a person (the "supplier") other than the debtor in the knowledge that the credit is to be used to finance a transaction between the debtor and the supplier.

III CON [24I]

14. Credit-token agreements

(1) A credit-token is a card, check, voucher, coupon, stamp, form, booklet or other document or thing given to an individual by a person carrying on a consumer credit business, who undertakes—

(a) that on the production of it (whether or not some other action is also required) he will supply cash, goods and services (or any of them) on credit, or

(b) that where, on the production of it to a third party (whether or not any other action is also required), the third party supplies cash, goods and services (or any of them), he will pay the third party for them (whether or not deducting any discount or commission), in return for payment to him by the individual.

(2) A credit-token agreement is a regulated agreement for the provision of credit in connection with the use of a credit-token.

(3) Without prejudice to the generality of section 9(1), the person who gives to an individual an undertaking falling within subsection (1)(b) shall be taken to provide him with credit drawn on whenever a third party supplies him with cash, goods or services.

(4) For the purposes of subsection (1), use of an object to operate a machine provided by the person giving the object or a third party shall be treated as the production of the object to him.

III CON [24I.1]

Credit cards A card which includes statements that satisfy sub-section (1) is a credit-token although none of the statements are true: *Eliott v Director General of Fair Trading* [1980] 1 WLR 977, [1980] ICR 629.

III CON [24J]–III CON [24N]

15. Consumer hire agreements

(1) A consumer hire agreement is an agreement made by a person with an individual (the "hirer") for the bailment or (in Scotland) the hiring of goods to the hirer, being an agreement which—

(a) is not a hire-purchase agreement, and

(b) is capable of subsisting for more than three months, . . .

(c) . . .

(2) A consumer hire agreement is a regulated agreement with the meaning of this Act if it is a regulated consumer hire agreement for the purposes of Chapter 14B of Part 2 of the Regulated Activities Order.

III CON [24O]

17. Small agreements

(1) A small agreement is—

(a) a regulated consumer credit agreement for credit not exceeding £50, other than a hire-purchase or conditional sale agreement; or

(b) a regulated consumer hire agreement which does not require the hirer to make payments exceeding £50,

being an agreement which is either unsecured or secured by a guarantee or indemnity only (whether or not the guarantee or indemnity is itself secured).

(2) For the purposes of paragraph (a) of subsection (1), running-account credit shall be taken not to exceed the amount specified in that paragraph if the credit limit does not exceed that amount.

(3) Where—

(a) two or more small agreements are made at or about the same time between the same parties, and

(b) it appears probable that they would instead have been made as a single agreement but for the desire to avoid the operation of provisions of this Act which would have applied to that single agreement but, apart from this subsection, are not applicable to the small agreements,

this Act applies to the small agreements as if they were regulated agreements other than small agreements.

(4) If, apart from this subsection, subsection (3) does not apply to any agreements but would apply if, for any party or parties to any of the agreements, there were substituted an associate of that party, or associates of each of those parties, as the case may be, then subsection (3) shall apply to the agreements.

III CON [24O.1]

EU Directive change A new sub-section (2) has been inserted to give effect to EU Directive 2008/448/EC, and SI 2010/1010, in respect of agreements made on or after 1 February 2011.

III CON [24P]

18. Multiple agreements

(1) This section applies to an agreement (a "multiple agreement") if its terms are such as—

(a) to place a part of it within one category of agreement mentioned in this Act, and another part of it within a different category of agreements so mentioned, or within a category of agreement not so mentioned, or

(b) to place it, or a part of it, within two or more categories of agreement so mentioned.

(2) Where a part of an agreement falls within subsection (1), that part shall be treated for the purposes of this Act as a separate agreement.

(3) Where an agreement falls within subsection (1)(b), it shall be treated as an agreement in each of the categories in question, and this Act shall apply to it accordingly.

(4) Where under subsection (2) a part of a multiple agreement is to be treated as a separate agreement, the multiple agreement shall (with any necessary modifications) be construed accordingly; and any sum payable under the multiple agreement, if not apportioned by the parties, shall for the purposes of proceedings in any court relating to the multiple agreement be apportioned by the court as may be requisite.

(5) In the case of an agreement for running-account credit, a term of the agreement allowing the credit limit to be exceeded merely temporarily shall not be treated as a separate agreement or as providing fixed-sum credit in respect of the excess.

(6) This Act does not apply to a multiple agreement so far as the agreement relates to goods if under the agreement payments are to be made in respect of the goods in the form of rent (other than a rent-charge) issuing out of land.

III CON [24Q]

19. Linked transactions

(1) A transaction entered into by the debtor or hirer, or a relative of his, with any other person ("the other party"), except one for the provision of security, is a linked transaction in relation to an actual or prospective regulated agreement (the "principal agreement") of which it does not form part if—

- (a) the transaction is entered into in compliance with a term of the principal agreement; or
- (b) the principal agreement is a debtor-creditor-supplier agreement and the transaction is financed, or to be financed, by the principal agreement; or
- (c) the other party is a person mentioned in subsection (2), and a person so mentioned initiated the transaction by suggesting it to the debtor or hirer, or his relative, who enters into it—
  - (i) to induce the creditor or owner to enter into the principal agreement, or
  - (ii) for another purpose related to the principal agreement, or
  - (iii) where the principal agreement is a restricted-use credit agreement, for a purpose related to a transaction financed, or to be financed, by the principal agreement.

(2) The persons referred to in subsection (1)(c) are—

- (a) the creditor or owner, or his associate;
- (b) a person who, in the negotiation of the transaction, is represented by a credit-broker who is also a negotiator in antecedent negotiations for the principal agreement;
- (c) a person who, at the time the transaction is initiated, knows that the principal agreement has been made or contemplates that it might be made.

(3) A linked transaction entered into before the making of the principal agreement has no effect until such time (if any) as that agreement is made.

(4) Regulations may exclude linked transactions of the prescribed description from the operation of subsection (3).

III CON [24Q.1]

Exclusions The Consumer Credit (Linked Transaction)(Exemptions) Regulations 1983, SI 1983/1560 exclude contracts of insurance, those that contain a guarantee of goods and those comprising or effected under agreements for the operation of deposit or current accounts.

III CON [24R]

20. Total charge for credit

In this Act, "the total charge for credit" has the meaning given by the Regulated Activities Order for the purposes of Chapter 14A of Part 2 of that Order.

Amendment *Section 20 was substituted by the Financial Services and Markets Act 2000 (Regulated Activities) (Amendment) (No 2) Order 2013, SI 2013/1881 with effect from 26 July 2013 (for certain purposes) and 1 April 2014 (for remaining purposes). For transitional provisions see Part 8 of SI 2013/1881.*

III CON [24R.1]

The 1980 Regulations The contractual terms as to credit and charges must comply with the requirements of the Consumer Credit (Total Charge for Credit) Regulations 1980, SI 1980/51, as most recently amended by SI 2010/1010. In *Watchtower Investments Ltd v Payne* [2001] EWCA Civ 1159, [2001] 35 LS Gaz R 32, (2001) Times, 22 August, it was held that the paying off of mortgage arrears as a term of the loan was correctly shown as part of the credit. The argument that it should have been specified as a charge was rejected. In *McGinn v Grangewood Securities Ltd* [2002] EWCA Civ 522, (2002) Times, 30 May, however, the Court concluded that payment to the first mortgagee was not part of the objective purpose of the loan but was part of its true cost. It was therefore one of the "other charges" in regulation 4(b) below, and was part of the total charge for credit. A similar conclusion, that an obligation to pay off arrears was a charge for credit, which should have been specified as such, was reached in *Ocwen Ltd v Coxall* (2004) Ipswich county court 5 May, reported in Legal Action (2005) April 25. The court held that the failure to specify the charge meant that the agreement was improperly executed for the purposes of s 65(1) and also that the failure to include a prescribed term was a failure within s 127(3) which made the agreement wholly unenforceable. See also *Southern Pacific Personal Loans Ltd v Walker* [2010] UKSC 32, [2010] 4 All ER 277, [2010] 1 WLR 1819. The Court held in that case that the broker's fee and interest on it were part of the "total charge for credit" but that the amount of credit was what was left after such charges had been stripped out. The agreement was therefore correct in stating as the amount of credit a figure that did not include elements in the total charge.

III CON [24R.2]

The 2010 Regulations The Consumer Credit (Total Charge for Credit) Regulations 2010, SI 2010/1011, implement the EU Directive 2008/448/EC by setting out the basis on which the annual percentage rate of charge (APR) and the total charge for credit must be calculated.

The 2010 Regulations were amended, with effect from 1 January 2013 by the Consumer Credit (Total Charge for Credit) (Amendment) Regulations 2012, SI 2012/1745. The changes add to the assumptions for calculating the APR and implement Directive 2011/90/EU.

PART V
ENTRY INTO CREDIT OR HIRE AGREEMENTS

PRELIMINARY MATTERS

III CON [25]

55. Disclosure of information

(1) Regulations may require specified information to be disclosed in the prescribed manner to the debtor or hirer before a regulated agreement is made.

(2) If regulations under subsection (1) are not complied with, the agreement is enforceable against the debtor or hirer on an order of the court only (and for these purposes a retaking of goods or land to which the agreement relates is an enforcement of the agreement).

III CON [25.1]

Disclosure of Information Regulations 2004 Pre-contract disclosure of extensive information was made a legal requirement by the Consumer Credit (Disclosure of Information) Regulations 2004, SI 2004/1481 with effect from 31 May 2005. Amendments were made by SI 2010/1010 with effect from 1 February 2011: but the amendments do not apply to agreements to which the. Consumer Credit (Disclosure of Information) Regulations 2010, SI 2010/1013 apply.

III CON [25.2]

EU Directive change A new sub-section (2) has been substituted to give effect to EU Directive 2008/448/EC, and SI 2010/1010, as amended by SI 2010/1969 and SI 2011/11, in respect of agreements made on or after 1 February 2011. New disclosure requirements are imposed in respect of such agreements by the Consumer Credit (Disclosure of Information) Regulations 2010, SI 2010/1013.

III CON [25A]

55A. *Pre-contractual explanations etc*

Repealed.

Amendment *Section 55A was repealed by the Financial Services and Markets Act 2000 (Regulated Activities) (Amendment) (No 2) Order 2013, SI 2013/1881 with effect from 26 July 2013 (for certain purposes). For transitional provisions see Part 8 of SI 2013/1881.*

III CON [25B]

55B. *Assessment of credit-worthiness*

Repealed.

Amendment *Section 55B was repealed by the Financial Services and Markets Act 2000 (Regulated Activities) (Amendment) (No 2) Order 2013, SI 2013/1881 with effect from 26 July 2013 (for certain purposes). For transitional provisions see Part 8 of SI 2013/1881.*

III CON [25C]

55C. Copy of draft consumer agreement

(1) Before a regulated consumer credit agreement, other than an excluded agreement, is made, the creditor must, if requested, give to the debtor without delay a copy of the prospective agreement (or such of its terms as have at that time been reduced to writing).

(2) Subsection (1) does not apply if at the time the request is made, the creditor is unwilling to proceed with the agreement.

(3) A breach of the duty imposed by subsection (1) is actionable as a breach of statutory duty.

(4) For the purposes of this section an agreement is an excluded agreement if it is—

- (a) an agreement secured on land,
- (b) an agreement under which a person takes an article in pawn,
- (c) an agreement under which the creditor provides the debtor with credit which exceeds £60,260 and which is not a residential renovation agreement, or
- (d) an agreement entered into by the debtor wholly or predominantly for the purposes of a business carried on, or intended to be carried on, by him.

(5) Article 60C(5) and (6) of the Regulated Activities Order applies for the purposes of subsection (4)(d).

Amendment *Sub-section (5) was substituted by the Financial Services and Markets Act 2000 (Regulated Activities) (Amendment) (No 2) Order 2013, SI 2013/1881 with effect from 26 July 2013 (for certain purposes) and 1 April 2014 (for remaining purposes). For transitional provisions see Part 8 of SI 2013/1881.*

III CON [25C.1]

EU Directive change This section has been inserted to give effect to EU Directive 2008/448/EC, and SI 2010/1010, in respect of agreements made on or after 1 February 2011.

III CON [26]

56. Antecedent negotiations

(1) In this Act "antecedent negotiations" means any negotiations with the debtor or hirer—

(a) conducted by the creditor or owner in relation to the making of any regulated agreement, or

(b) conducted by a credit-broker in relation to goods sold or proposed to be sold by the credit-broker to the creditor before forming the subject-matter of a debtor-creditor-supplier agreement within section 12(a), or

(c) conducted by the supplier in relation to a transaction financed or proposed to be financed by a debtor-creditor-supplier agreement within section 12(b) or (c),

and "negotiator" means the person by whom negotiations are so conducted with the debtor or hirer.

(2) Negotiations with the debtor in a case falling within subsection (1)(b) or (c) shall be deemed to be conducted by the negotiator in the capacity of agent of the creditor as well as in his actual capacity.

(3) An agreement is void if, and to the extent that, it purports in relation to an actual or prospective regulated agreement—

(a) to provide that a person acting as, or on behalf of, a negotiator is to be treated as the agent of the debtor or hirer, or

(b) to relieve a person from liability for acts or omissions of any person acting as, or on behalf of, a negotiator.

(4) For the purposes of this Act, antecedent negotiations shall be taken to begin when the negotiator and the debtor or hirer first enter into communication (including communication by advertisement), and to include any representations made by the negotiator to the debtor or hirer and any other dealings between them.

III CON [26.1]

Misrepresentation by negotiator In the ordinary hire-purchase case, where the goods are supplied by a dealer but the agreement is entered into with a finance company, the section deems the dealer as "credit broker" to be acting as the agent of the finance company in any antecedent negotiations and both will be liable for any misrepresentation.

Note, however, that the protection provided by s 56 (supplier, or credit-broker, deemed to be the creditor's agent) has been held to apply only where the creditor buys direct from the supplier, or credit-broker, and not when the creditor has purchased from an intermediary credit-broker who has made no representations: *Black Horse Ltd v Langford* [2007] EWHC 907 (QB), [2007] RTR 462. However, the deemed agency was found to exist in a case involving representations by a PPI salesman: *British Credit Trust Ltd v Scotland* [2014] EWCA Civ 790, [2015] 1 All ER 708, [2015] 1 All ER (Comm) 401.

See also s 75 at **III CON [30M]**.

III CON [27]

57. Withdrawal from prospective agreement

(1) The withdrawal of a party from a prospective regulated agreement shall operate to apply this Part to the agreement, any linked transaction and any other thing done in anticipation of the making of the agreement as it would apply if the agreement were made and then cancelled under section 69.

(2) The giving to a party of a written or oral notice which, however expressed, indicates the intention of the other party to withdraw from a prospective regulated agreement operates as a withdrawal from it.

(3) Each of the following shall be deemed to be the agent of the creditor or owner for the purpose of receiving a notice under subsection (2)—

(a) a credit-broker or supplier who is the negotiator in antecedent negotiations, and

(b) any person who, in the course of a business carried on by him, acts on behalf of the debtor or hirer in any negotiations for the agreement.

(4) Where the agreement, if made, would not be a cancellable agreement, subsection (1) shall nevertheless apply as if the contrary were the case.

III CON [28]

58. Opportunity for withdrawal from prospective land mortgage

(1) Before sending to the debtor or hirer, for his signature, an unexecuted agreement in a case where the prospective regulated agreement is to be secured on land (the "mortgaged land"), the creditor or owner shall give the debtor or hirer a copy of the unexecuted agreement which contains a notice in the prescribed form indicating the right of the debtor or hirer to withdraw from the prospective agreement, and how and when the right is exercisable, together with a copy of any other document referred to in the unexecuted agreement.

(2) Subsection (1) does not apply to—

(a) a restricted-use credit agreement to finance the purchase of the mortgaged land, or

(b) an agreement for a bridging loan in connection with the purchase of the mortgaged land or other land.

III CON [28.1]

Notice in the prescribed form A form of notice is prescribed by the Consumer Credit (Cancellation Notices and Copies of Documents) Regulations 1983, SI 1983/1557, as amended by SI 2010/1010.

III CON [29]

59. Agreement to enter future agreement void

(1) An agreement is void if, and to the extent that, it purports to bind a person to enter as debtor or hirer into a prospective regulated agreement.

(2) Regulations may exclude from the operation of subsection (1) agreements such as are described in the regulations.

III CON [29.1]

Certain agreements are excluded from the operation of this section by the Consumer Credit (Agreements to Enter Prospective Agreements) (Exemptions) Regulations 1983, SI 1983/1552.

Making the agreement

III CON [29A]

60. Form and content of agreements

(1) The Treasury shall make regulations as to the form and content of documents embodying regulated agreements, and the regulations shall contain such provisions as appear to them appropriate with a view to ensuring that the debtor or hirer is made aware of—

(a) the rights and duties conferred or imposed on him by the agreement,

(b) the amount and rate of the total charge for credit (in the case of a consumer credit agreement),

(c) the protection and remedies available to him under this Act, and

(d) any other matters which, in the opinion of the Treasury, it is desirable for him to know about in connection with the agreement.

(2) Regulations under subsection (1) may in particular—

(a) require specified information to be included in the prescribed manner in documents, and other specified material to be excluded;

(b) contain requirements to ensure that specified information is clearly brought to the attention of the debtor or hirer, and that one part of a document is not given insufficient or excessive prominence compared with another.

(3) If, on an application made to the FCA by a person carrying on a consumer credit business or a consumer hire business, it appears to the FCA impracticable for the applicant to comply with any requirement of regulations under subsection (1) in a particular case, it may, by notice to the applicant, direct that the requirement be waived or varied in relation to such agreements, and subject to such conditions (if any), as it may specify, and this Act and the regulations shall have effect accordingly.

(4) The FCA shall give a notice under subsection (3) only if it is satisfied that to do so would not prejudice the interests of debtors or hirers.

(5) An application may be made under subsection (3) only if it relates to—

(a) a consumer credit agreement secured on land,

(b) a consumer credit agreement under which a person takes an article in pawn,

(c) a consumer credit agreement under which the creditor provides the debtor with credit which exceeds £60,260 and which is not a residential renovation agreement,

(d) a consumer credit agreement entered into by the debtor wholly or predominantly for the purposes of a business carried on, or intended to be carried on, by him, or

(e) a consumer hire agreement.

(6) Article 60C(5) and (6) of the Regulated Activities Order applies for the purposes of subsection (5)(d).

Amendment *Section 60 is shown as amended by the Financial Services and Markets Act 2000 (Regulated Activities) (Amendment) (No 2) Order 2013, SI 2013/1881 with effect from 26 July 2013 (for certain purposes) and 1 April 2014 (for remaining purposes). For transitional provisions see Part 8 of SI 2013/1881.*

III CON [29A.1]

The Consumer Credit (Agreement) Regulations 1983/1553 provide for the form and content of regulated agreements. Major amendments were made by SI 2004/1482 and 2619, with effect from 31 May 2005. Further extensive amendments were made by SI 2010/1010, as amended by SI 2010/909 and SI 2011/11, to give effect to EU Directive 200/448/EC applying to agreements made on or after 1 February 2011.

III CON [29A.2]

EU Directive change This section has been inserted to give effect to EU Directive 2008/448/EC, and SI 2010/1010, in respect of agreements made on or after 1 February 2011.

III CON [29B]

61. Signing of agreement

(1) A regulated agreement is not properly executed unless—

(a) a document in the prescribed form itself containing all the prescribed terms and conforming to regulations under section 60(1) is signed in the prescribed manner both by the debtor or hirer and by or on behalf of the creditor or owner, and

(b) the document embodies all the terms of the agreement, other than implied terms, and

(c) the document is, when presented or sent to the debtor or hirer for signature, in such a state that all its terms are readily legible.

(2) In addition, where the agreement is one to which section 58(1) applies, it is not properly executed unless—

(a) the requirements of section 58(1) were complied with, and

(b) the unexecuted agreement was sent, for his signature, to the debtor or hirer by an appropriate method not less than seven days after a copy of it was given to him under section 58(1), and

(c) during the consideration period, the creditor or owner refrained from approaching the debtor or hirer (whether in person, by telephone or letter, or in any other way) except in response to a specific request made by the debtor or hirer after the beginning of the consideration period, and

(d) no notice of withdrawal by the debtor or hirer was received by the creditor or owner before the sending of the unexecuted agreement.

(3) In subsection (2)(c), "the consideration period" means the period beginning with the giving of the copy under section 58(1) and ending—

(a) at the expiry of seven days after the day on which the unexecuted agreement is sent, for his signature, to the debtor or hirer, or

(b) on its return by the debtor or hirer after signature by him,

whichever first occurs.

(4) Where the debtor or hirer is a partnership or an unincorporated body of persons, subsection (1)(a) shall apply with the substitution for "by the debtor or hirer" of "by or on behalf of the debtor or hirer".

III CON [29C]

61A. Duty to supply copy of executed consumer credit agreement

(1) Where a regulated consumer credit agreement, other than an excluded agreement, has been made, the creditor must give a copy of the executed agreement, and any other document referred to in it, to the debtor.

(2) Subsection (1) does not apply if—

(a) a copy of the unexecuted agreement (and of any other document referred to in it) has already been given to the debtor, and

(b) the unexecuted agreement is in identical terms to the executed agreement.

(3) In a case referred to in subsection (2), the creditor must inform the debtor in writing—

(a) that the agreement has been executed,

(b) that the executed agreement is in identical terms to the unexecuted agreement a copy of which has already been given to the debtor, and

(c) that the debtor has the right to receive a copy of the executed agreement if the debtor makes a request for it at any time before the end of the period referred to in section 66A(2).

(4) Where a request is made under subsection (3)(c) the creditor must give a copy of the executed agreement to the debtor without delay.

(5) If the requirements of this section are not observed, the agreement is not properly executed.

(6) For the purposes of this section, an agreement is an excluded agreement if it is—

(a) a cancellable agreement, or

(b) an agreement—

(i) secured on land,

(ii) under which the creditor provides the debtor with credit which exceeds £60,260, or

(iii) entered into by the debtor wholly or predominantly for the purposes of a business carried on, or intended to be carried on, by him,

unless the creditor or a credit intermediary has complied with or purported to comply with regulation 3(2) of the Consumer Credit (Disclosure of Information) Regulations 2010.

(6A) An agreement is not an excluded agreement by virtue of subsection (6)(b)(ii) if it is a residential renovation agreement.

(7) Article 60C(5) and (6) of the Regulated Activities Order applies for the purposes of subsection (6)(b)(iii).

(8) In this section, "credit intermediary" means a person who in the course of business—

(a) carries on any of the activities specified in article 36A(1)(d) to (f) of the Regulated Activities Order for a consideration that is or includes a financial consideration, and

(b) does not do so as a creditor.

Amendment *Section 61A is shown as amended by the Financial Services and Markets Act 2000 (Regulated Activities) (Amendment) (No 2) Order 2013, SI 2013/1881 with effect from 26 July 2013 (for certain purposes) and 1 April 2014 (for remaining purposes). For transitional provisions see Part 8 of SI 2013/1881.*

III CON [29C.1]

EU Directive change Sub-sections (5) and (6)have been inserted to give effect to EU Directive 2008/448/EC, and SI 2010/1010, in respect of agreements made on or after 1 February 2011.

III CON [29D]

61B. Duty to supply copy of overdraft agreement

(1) Where an authorised business overdraft agreement or an authorised non-business overdraft agreement has been made, a document containing the terms of the agreement must be given to the debtor.

(2) The creditor must provide the document referred to in subsection (1) to the debtor before or at the time the agreement is made unless—

(a) the creditor has provided the debtor with the information referred to in regulation 10(3) of the Consumer Credit (Disclosure of Information) Regulations 2010, in which case it may be provided after the agreement is made,

(b) the creditor has provided the debtor with the information referred to in regulation 10(3)(c), (e), (f), (h) and (k) of those Regulations, in which case it must be provided immediately after the agreement is made, or

(c) the agreement is an agreement of a description referred to in regulation 10(4)(b) of those Regulations, in which case it must be provided immediately after the agreement is made.

(3) If the requirements of this section are not observed, the agreement is enforceable against the debtor on an order of the court only (and for these purposes a retaking of goods or land to which the agreement relates is an enforcement of the agreement).

III CON [29D.1]

EU Directive change This section has been inserted to give effect to EU Directive 2008/448/EC, and SI 2010/1010, in respect of agreements made on or after 1 February 2011.

III CON [29E]

62. Duty to supply copy of unexecuted agreement

(1) If in the case of a regulated agreement which is an excluded agreement the unexecuted agreement is presented personally to the debtor or hirer for his signature, but on the occasion when he signs it the document does not become an executed agreement, a copy of it, and of any other document referred to in it, must be there and then delivered to him.

(2) If the unexecuted agreement is sent to the debtor or hirer for his signature, a copy of it, and of any other document referred to in it, must be sent to him at the same time.

(3) A regulated agreement which is an excluded agreement is not properly executed if the requirements of this section are not observed.

(4) In this section, "excluded agreement" has the same meaning as in section 61A.

III CON [29E.1]

EU Directive change This section has been amended to give effect to EU Directive 2008/448/EC, and SI 2010/1010, in respect of agreements made on or after 1 February 2011. As amended, the section imposes a duty only if the regulated agreement is an excluded agreement. The same applies to s 63, which has been amended in the same way.

III CON [29F]

63. Duty to supply copy of executed agreement

(1) If in the case of a regulated agreement which is an excluded agreement the unexecuted agreement is presented personally to the debtor or hirer for his signature, and on the occasion when he signs it the document becomes an executed agreement, a copy of the executed agreement, and of any other document referred to in it, must be there and then delivered to him.

(2) A copy of the executed agreement, and of any other document referred to in it, must be given to the debtor or hirer within the seven days following the making of the agreement unless—

- (a) subsection (1) applies, or
- (b) the unexecuted agreement was sent to the debtor or hirer for his signature and, on the occasion of his signing it, the document became an executed agreement.

(3) In the case of a cancellable agreement, a copy under subsection (2) must be sent by an appropriate method.

(4) In the case of a credit-token agreement, a copy under subsection (2) need not be given within the seven days following the making of the agreement if it is given before or at the time when the credit-token is given to the debtor.

(5) A regulated agreement which is an excluded agreement is not properly executed if the requirements of this section are not observed.

(6) In this section, "excluded agreement" has the same meaning as in section 61A.

III CON [29G]

64. Duty to give notice of cancellation rights

(1) In the case of a cancellable agreement, a notice in the prescribed form indicating the right of the debtor or hirer to cancel the agreement, how and when that right is exercisable, and the name and address of a person to whom notice of cancellation may be given,—

- (a) must be included in every copy given to the debtor or hirer under section 62 or 63, and
- (b) except where section 63(2) applied, must also be sent by an appropriate method to the debtor or hirer within the seven days following the making of the agreement.

(2) In the case of a credit-token agreement, a notice under subsection (1)(b) need not be sent by an appropriate method within the seven days following the making of the agreement if either—

- (a) it is sent by an appropriate method to the debtor or hirer before the credit-token is given to him, or

(b) it is sent by an appropriate method to him together with the credit-token.

(3) Regulations may provide that except where section 63(2) applied a notice sent under subsection (1)(b) shall be accompanied by a further copy of the executed agreement, and of any other document referred to in it.

(4) Regulations may provide that subsection (1)(b) is not to apply in the case of agreements such as are described in the regulations, being agreements made by a particular person, if—

(a) on an application by that person to the FCA, the FCA has determined that, having regard to—

(i) the manner in which antecedent negotiations for agreements with the applicant of that description are conducted, and

(ii) the information provided to debtors or hirers before such agreements are made,

the requirement imposed by subsection (1)(b) can be dispensed with without prejudicing the interests of debtors or hirers; and

(b) any conditions imposed by the FCA in making the determination are complied with.

(5) A cancellable agreement is not properly executed if the requirements of this section are not observed.

Amendment *Section 64 is shown as amended by the Financial Services and Markets Act 2000 (Regulated Activities) (Amendment) (No 2) Order 2013, SI 2013/1881 with effect from 26 July 2013 (for certain purposes) and 1 April 2014 (for remaining purposes). For transitional provisions see Part 8 of SI 2013/1881.*

III CON [29G.1]

Regulations Forms of notice and obligations to provide copies are governed by the Consumer Credit (Cancellation Notices and Copies of Documents) Regulations 1983, SI 1983/1557. Major amendments were made by SI 2004/2619 with effect from 31 May 2010/1010. A further amendment was made by SI 2010/1010, to apply the regulations to agreements within s 66A.

III CON [30]

65. Consequences of improper execution

(1) An improperly-executed regulated agreement is enforceable against the debtor or hirer on an order of the court only.

(2) A retaking of goods or land to which a regulated agreement relates is an enforcement of the agreement.

III CON [30.1]

Improper execution of the agreement Examples of improper execution are breach of the requirements of ss 60 and 61 and the Consumer Credit (Agreement) Regulations 1983, SI 1983/1553 (as amended) as to form, content, legibility and signatures noting in particular the more stringent requirements which apply to agreements made on or after 31 May 2005 as a result of the Consumer Credit (Agreements) (Amendment) Regulations 2004, SI 2004/1482, as amended by the Consumer Credit (Miscellaneous Amendments) Regulations 2004, SI 2004/2619. Further obligations arise under the Consumer Credit (EU Directive) Regulations 2010 SI 2010/1010, with effect from no later than 1 February 2011. Others concern failures to deliver copies of the agreement (ss 62 and 63) and to give notice of cancellation rights in compliance with the Consumer Credit (Cancellation Notices and Copies of Documents) Regulations 1983, SI 1983/1557 (as amended by the Consumer Credit (Miscellaneous Amendments) Regulations 2004, SI 2004/2619). The enforcement of an agreement, which fails to bring to the attention of the hirer the liability for accelerated payments in the event of breach, requires the leave of the court. The court's discretion is limited by the provisions of s 127 Consumer Credit Act 1974 (see para **III CON [38]**). The court's leave may be given on terms that the accelerated payments are reduced: *Rank Xerox v Hepple* [1994] CCLR 1, [1993] CLY 461. In order to comply with the regulations under s 60 (1) as to making the debtor or hirer aware of the rights and duties, the terms must be presented in a way which will convey those rights and duties to the average reader: *Lombard Tricity Finance Ltd v Paton* [1989] 1 All ER 918, CA. The term in that case related to the creditor's right to vary the rate of interest. Stating the rate of interest but not the amount to be repaid complies with para 5 of Sch 6 but not with para 13 of Sch 1: *Hurstanger Ltd v Wilson* [2007] EWCA Civ 299, (2007) Times, 11 May, [2007] All ER (D) 66 (Apr). Where there has been no loss or prejudice as a result of the breach, decided cases indicate that the court should readily exercise its discretion to allow enforcement: *Nissan Finance UK Ltd v Lockhart* [1993] CCLR 39, [1993] CLY 462, CA; *P B Leasing Ltd v Patel* [1995] CCLR 82. It has been held that a failure to execute an agreement properly by signing it does not necessarily make the transaction illegal or void: *Carlyle Finance Ltd v Pallas Industrial Finance Ltd* [1999] 1 All ER (Comm) 659, CA. On the other hand, it was held in *Wilson First County Trust Ltd* [2001] QB 407, [2001] 2 WLR 302, CA, that the court had no discretion to allow enforcement in cases which fell within s 127(3) or (4) (below at para **III CON [38]**).

The obligations introduced by EU Directive 2008/448/EC and SI 210/1010, with effect from 1 February 2011, provide fresh opportunities for improper execution.

III CON [30.1A]

Requirement to give information in advance The Consumer Credit (Disclosure of Information) Regulations 2004, SI 2004/1481 apply to any agreement made on or after 31 May 2005 and impose obligations on the creditors and owners to give prospective customers in advance virtually all the information made obligatory for the agreement itself and in a document separate from the agreement. Non-compliance renders any subsequent agreement improperly executed and thus potentially unenforceable.

III CON [30.1B]

Disclosure of broker's commission Where the lender has paid the broker a commission without ensuring that the borrower's informed consent has been obtained, the lender may be found to have procured a breach of fiduciary duty by the broker and may be liable, in equity, to account to the borrower for the amount of the commission and interest: *Hurstanger Ltd v Wilson* [2007] EWCA Civ 299, [2007] All ER (D) 66 (Apr), (2007) Times, 11 May.

III CON [30.2]

Procedure The creditor's application for an order to enforce an improperly executed agreement for the recovery of goods must be made in accordance with the Consumer Credit Act which supplements the CPR Part 7B Practice Direction (see para **CPR PD 7B**). The debtor may rely on the improper execution and other breaches of the Act as a defence. For a precedent see **BCCP K[1570]**.

III CON [30.3]

Traffic accident: hire charges for a replacement vehicle In a vehicle damage case the defendant may resist a claim for the cost of hiring a replacement vehicle on the ground that the claimant's hiring agreement was unenforceable for improper execution or other reasons. In *Dimond v Lovell* [2000] 1 QB 216, [1999] 3 All ER 1, CA, the Court of Appeal held that the hiring of the replacement car was a consumer credit agreement because payment was deferred. It held also that the agreement was improperly made in breach of the Act. Therefore the loan of the car had been of benefit to the claimant but the benefit had been conferred in breach of statute, so the claimant was not a trustee for the third party and she had suffered no loss. The result was that the defendant was not liable for the notional cost of the hire. In *Dimond v Lovell* [2002] 1 AC 384, [2000] 2 All ER 897, HL, the House of Lords upheld the decision of the Court of Appeal, reported at [1999] 3 All ER 1, that the cost of hiring a replacement vehicle could not be recovered if the hiring contravened the requirements for a regulated credit agreement. Even where those requirements were satisfied, the claimant was not necessarily entitled to full reimbursement of the hire charges. If they exceeded the hire charges under an ordinary hiring agreement because of additional benefits conferred, the claimant was not entitled, in their Lordships' opinion, to recover the excess. Lord Hoffman gave as examples the benefits conferred by relieving the claimant against:

(1) the necessity of laying out money to pay for the car;
(2) the trouble and anxiety of pursuing a claim;
(3) having to bear irrecoverable costs if successful; and
(4) the expense of unsuccessful litigation.

The value of such benefits should be deducted, thereby reducing the recoverable charges to those which would be made under an ordinary hiring agreement. However, the cost of credit hire may be recoverable in full where the claimant is unable to pay ordinary hire charges without making sacrifices that it would not be reasonable for him, or her, to make: *Lagden v O'Connor* [2003] UKHL 64, [2004] 1 AC 1067, [2004] 1 All ER 277.

The tortfeasor is protected by the requirement that the claimant can recover no more than the reasonable cost of hiring a comparable vehicle as a replacement, typically by reference to the spot hire charge: *Bee v Jensen (No 2)* [2007] EWCA Civ 923, (2007) Times, 17 October, [2007] All ER (D) 73 (Sept), [2007] 4 All ER 791.

Where the claimant is able to hire a replacement vehicle he, or she, should be entitled to the basic hire rate for a reasonable equivalent vehicle, having regard to hire rates available from the chosen hire company and local competitors. The phrase 'basic hire rate' is preferable to 'spot hire rate': *Pattni v First Leicester Buses Ltd* [2011] EWCA Civ 1384, [2011] All ER (D) 230 (Nov). In that case the Court rejected a claim for interest from the end of the period of hire down to judgment on the ground that no interest had in fact been paid.

Where a claimant who is not impecunious makes a credit-hire agreement for a vehicle to use during repairs, the recovery rate should be the 'basic hire rate' for the area, ascertained by identifying the lowest reasonable rate charged by a mainstream supplier or a local reputable supplier. In this way the collateral benefits of the credit-hire arrangement that are not recoverable are stripped out: *Stevens v Equity Syndicate Management Ltd* [2015] EWCA Civ 93, [2015] RTR 257, 165 NLJ 7644.

Hire charges for a replacement vehicle may be rejected if the claimant does not need a replacement as where he has a fleet of other vehicles at his disposal: *Singh v Yaqubi* [2013] EWCA Civ 23, [2013] Lloyd's Rep IR 398.

III CON [30.3A]

Traffic accident: the Helpline cases In *Clark v Ardington* [2002] Lloyd's Rep IR 138, Oxford Cty Ct, the recoverability of hire charges was challenged in a group of cases in some of which the charges had been incurred under Helpline agreements. The court ruled that the agreements which were made with the car owners concerned were exempt agreements and that the charges were recoverable, although subject to certain deductions. Interest was awarded on the money paid (for the hire or for the repairs) from the date of payment. Claims made under agreements which were made with Helpline on the initiative of certain insurance brokers (the A Plan cases) were held to fail for a lack of consideration moving from the car owner. In the cases which were successful deductions were made under various heads:

- the credit hire rates were reduced to the standard hire rates available locally except in the case of an impecunious owner who had no alternative but to use credit hire;
- delivery charges were disallowed;
- the period of hire was reduced to the period reasonably needed to do the repairs;
- the engineer's fee was disallowed where the damage was slight.

The full text of the judgment, which was given by His Honour Judge Charles Harris QC on 14 September 2001, is available on the Court Service web site (http://www.hmcourts-service.gov.uk).

Where the claimant has entered a No Win No Fee agreement which would protect him or her from liability for the hire charges if the case were lost that does not provide the defendant with a defence to the claim: *Irving v Morgan Sindall plc* [2018] EWHC 1147 (QB), [2018] All ER (D) 85 (May).

III CON [30.3B]

Traffic accident: insurers' subrogated right to recover hire charges In a case where the claimant sought to recover the hire charges incurred by his insurers the court held that the hire rates were reasonable when compared with other spot rates and therefore recoverable. No discount would be made in respect of the commission earned by the insurers or their ability to negotiate corporate rates, which would be lower: *Bee v Jenson* [2006] EWHC 3359 (Comm), (2007) Times, 16 January, [2006] All ER (D) 352 (Dec).

On the other hand a claimant who unreasonably rejects a defendant's offer of a replacement vehicle may nevertheless recover the cost which the defendant would have incurred in providing it: *Strutt v Whitnell* [1975] 2 All ER 510, [1975] 1 WLR 870, CA. Similarly, where a defendant offers a free replacement the offer should reveal the cost to the defendant of providing it since the claimant needs this information in order to decide whether to accept or reject: *Copley v Lawn* (2009) Times, 15 July, CA.

III CON [30.3C]

Credit hire without a right of cancellation An issue similar to that in *Dimond v Lovell* arises where the claimant hires a vehicle under a credit hire agreement that does not comply with the Cancellation of Contracts Made in a Consumer's Home Regulations: see **III CON [130]**. The Court of Appeal has held that the unenforceable hire charges are not recoverable from the tortfeasor: *Salat v Barutis* [2013] EWCA Civ 1499, [2013] All ER (D) 232.

III CON [30.4]

Traffic accident: repairs on credit It may be contended that the cost of repairs may be recovered by the car owner even where the contract with the repairer is in breach of the Consumer Credit Act 1974. The argument is that the cost of repair (whether payable or not) is an indicator of the diminution in value of the damaged car and it was adopted by the court, in the claimant's favour in *Taylor v Cook* [1999] CLY 2504, a county court decision following *The London Corpn* [1935] P 70, *Darbishire v Warran* [1963] 1 WLR 1067 and *Jones (Alfred John) v Stroud District Council* [1986] 1 WLR 1141. Car damage following a collision is an immediate loss representing the diminution in the car's value whereas a hire charge for a replacement vehicle is a potential future loss, only sustained where the charge is recoverable. For this reason the decision in *Dimond v Lovell* [2002] 1 AC 384, [2000] 2 All ER 897, HL (that the cost for hire in breach of the Act may not be recovered) does not prevent the recovery of the cost of repairs under an agreement in breach of the Act: *Burdis v Livsey* [2002] EWCA Civ 510, [2003] QB 36.

As to the reasonableness of the cost of repair this would depend on what a person in the position of the claimant could obtain on the open market rather than on what the claimant's insurer could obtain: *Coles v Hetherton* [2012] EWHC 1599 (Comm), [2012] RTR 457, [2012] NLJR 873.

III CON [30A]

66. Acceptance of credit-tokens

(1) The debtor shall not be liable under a credit-token agreement for use made of the credit-token by any person unless the debtor had previously accepted the credit-token, or the use constituted an acceptance of it by him.

(2) The debtor accepts a credit-token when—

- (a) it is signed, or
- (b) a receipt for it is signed, or
- (c) it is first used,

either by the debtor himself or by a person who, pursuant to the agreement, is authorised by him to use it.

WITHDRAWAL FROM CERTAIN AGREEMENTS

III CON [30B]

66A. Withdrawal from consumer credit agreement

(1) The debtor under a regulated consumer credit agreement, other than an excluded agreement, may withdraw from the agreement, without giving any reason, in accordance with this section.

(2) To withdraw from an agreement under this section the debtor must give oral or written notice of the withdrawal to the creditor before the end of the period of 14 days beginning with the day after the relevant day.

(3) For the purposes of subsection (2) the relevant day is whichever is the latest of the following—

- (a) the day on which the agreement is made;
- (b) where the creditor is required to inform the debtor of the credit limit under the agreement, the day on which the creditor first does so;
- (c) in the case of an agreement to which section 61A (duty to supply copy of executed consumer credit agreement) applies, the day on which the debtor receives a copy of the agreement under that section or on which the debtor is informed as specified in subsection (3) of that section;
- (d) in the case of an agreement to which section 63 (duty to supply copy of executed agreement: excluded agreements) applies, the day on which the debtor receives a copy of the agreement under that section.

(4) Where oral notice under this section is given to the creditor it must be given in a manner specified in the agreement.

(5) Where written notice under this section is given by facsimile transmission or electronically—

- (a) it must be sent to the number or electronic address specified for the purpose in the agreement, and
- (b) where it is so sent, it is to be regarded as having been received by the creditor at the time it is sent (and section 176A does not apply).

(6) Where written notice under this section is given in any other form—

(a) it must be sent by post to, or left at, the postal address specified for the purpose in the agreement, and

(b) where it is sent by post to that address, it is to be regarded as having been received by the creditor at the time of posting (and section 176 does not apply).

(7) Subject as follows, where the debtor withdraws from a regulated consumer credit agreement under this section—

(a) the agreement shall be treated as if it had never been entered into, and

(b) where an ancillary service relating to the agreement is or is to be provided by the creditor, or by a third party on the basis of an agreement between the third party and the creditor, the ancillary service contract shall be treated as if it had never been entered into.

(8) In the case referred to in subsection (7)(b) the creditor must without delay notify any third party of the fact that the debtor has withdrawn from the agreement.

(9) Where the debtor withdraws from an agreement under this section—

(a) the debtor must repay to the creditor any credit provided and the interest accrued on it (at the rate provided for under the agreement), but

(b) the debtor is not liable to pay to the creditor any compensation, fees or charges except any non-returnable charges paid by the creditor to a public administrative body.

(10) An amount payable under subsection (9) must be paid without undue delay and no later than the end of the period of 30 days beginning with the day after the day on which the notice of withdrawal was given (and if not paid by the end of that period may be recovered by the creditor as a debt).

(11) Where a regulated consumer credit agreement is a conditional sale, hire-purchase or credit-sale agreement and—

(a) the debtor withdraws from the agreement under this section after the credit has been provided, and

(b) the sum payable under subsection (9)(a) is paid in full by the debtor,

title to the goods purchased or supplied under the agreement is to pass to the debtor on the same terms as would have applied had the debtor not withdrawn from the agreement.

(12) In subsections (2), (4), (5), (6) and (9)(a) references to the creditor include a person specified by the creditor in the agreement.

(13) In subsection (7)(b) the reference to an ancillary service means a service that relates to the provision of credit under the agreement and includes in particular an insurance or payment protection policy.

(14) For the purposes of this section, an agreement is an excluded agreement if it is—

(a) an agreement for credit exceeding £60,260, other than a residential renovation agreement,

(b) an agreement secured on land,

(c) a restricted-use credit agreement to finance the purchase of land, or

(d) an agreement for a bridging loan in connection with the purchase of land.

III CON [30B.1]

EU Directive change This section has been inserted to give effect to EU Directive 2008/448/EC, and SI 2010/1010, in respect of agreements made on or after 1 February 2011.

Cancellation of certain agreements within cooling-off period

III CON [30C]

67. Cancellable agreements

(1) Subject to subsection (2) a regulated agreement may be cancelled by the debtor or hirer in accordance with this Part if the antecedent negotiations included oral representations made when in the presence of the debtor or hirer by an individual acting as, or on behalf of, the negotiator, unless—

(a) the agreement is secured on land, or is a restricted-use credit agreement to finance the purchase of land or is an agreement for a bridging loan in connection with the purchase of land, or

(b) the unexecuted agreement is signed by the debtor or hirer at premises at which any of the following is carrying on any business (whether on a permanent or temporary basis)—

(i) the creditor or owner;

(ii) any party to a linked transaction (other than the debtor or hirer or a relative of his);

(iii) the negotiator in any antecedent negotiations.

(2) This section does not apply where section 66A applies.

III CON [30C.1]

EU Directive change Sub-section (2) has been inserted to give effect to EU Directive 2008/448/EC, and SI 2010/1010, in respect of agreements made on or after 1 February 2011.

III CON [30C.2]

Contracts made in a Consumer's Home or Place of Work See also the cancellation rights under the Cancellation of Contracts made in a Consumer's Home or Place of Work etc Regulations 2008, SI 2008/1816, as amended by SI 2010/1010.

III CON [30D]

68. Cooling-off period

The debtor or hirer may serve notice of cancellation of a cancellable agreement between his signing of the unexecuted agreement and—

(a) the end of the fifth day following the day on which he received a copy under section 63(2) or a notice under section 64(1)(b), or

(b) if (by virtue of regulations made under section 64(4)) section 64(1)(b) does not apply, the end of the fourteenth day following the day on which he signed the unexecuted agreement.

III CON [30E]

69. Notice of cancellation

(1) If within the period specified in section 68 the debtor or hirer under a cancellable agreement serves on—

(a) the creditor or owner, or

(b) the person specified in the notice under section 64(1), or

(c) a person who (whether by virtue of subsection (6) or otherwise) is the agent of the creditor or owner,

a notice (a "notice of cancellation") which, however expressed and whether or not conforming to the notice given under section 64(1), indicates the intention of the debtor or hirer to withdraw from the agreement, the notice shall operate—

(i) to cancel the agreement, and any linked transaction, and

(ii) to withdraw any offer by the debtor or hirer, or his relative, to enter into a linked transaction.

(2) In the case of a debtor-creditor-supplier agreement for restricted-use credit financing—

(a) the doing of work or supply of goods to meet an emergency, or

(b) the supply of goods which, before service of the notice of cancellation, had by the act of the debtor or his relative become incorporated in any land or thing not comprised in the agreement or any linked transaction,

subsection (1) shall apply with the substitution of the following for paragraph (i)—

"(i) to cancel only such provisions of the agreement and any linked transaction as—

(aa) relate to the provision of credit, or

(bb) require the debtor to pay an item in the total charge for credit, or

(cc) subject the debtor to any obligation other than to pay for the doing of the said work, or the supply of the said goods".

(3) Except so far as is otherwise provided, references in this Act to the cancellation of an agreement or transaction do not include a case within subsection (2).

(4) Except as otherwise provided by or under this Act, an agreement or transaction cancelled under subsection (1) shall be treated as if it had never been entered into.

(5) Regulations may exclude linked transactions of the prescribed description from subsection (1)(i) or (ii).

(6) Each of the following shall be deemed to be the agent of the creditor or owner for the purpose of receiving a notice of cancellation—

(a) a credit-broker or supplier who is the negotiator in antecedent negotiations, and

(b) any person who, in the course of a business carried on by him, acts on behalf of the debtor or hirer in any negotiations for the agreement.

(7) Whether or not it is actually received by him, a notice of cancellation sent to a person shall be deemed to be served on him—

(a) in the case of a notice sent by post, at the time of posting, and

(b) in the case of a notice transmitted in the form of an electronic communication in accordance with section 176A(1), at the time of the transmission.

III CON [30F]

70. Cancellation: recovery of money paid by debtor or hirer

(1) On the cancellation of a regulated agreement, and of any linked transaction,—

(a) any sum paid by the debtor or hirer, or his relative, under or in contemplation of the agreement or transaction, including any item in the total charge for credit, shall become repayable, and

(b) any sum, including any item in the total charge for credit, which but for the cancellation is, or would or might become, payable by the debtor or hirer, or his relative, under the agreement or transaction shall cease to be, or shall not become, so payable, and

(c) in the case of a debtor-creditor-supplier agreement falling within section 12(b) any sum paid on the debtor's behalf by the creditor to the supplier shall become repayable to the creditor.

(2) If, under the terms of a cancelled agreement or transaction, the debtor or hirer, or his relative, is in possession of any goods, he shall have a lien on them for any sum repayable to him under subsection (1) in respect of that agreement or transaction, or any other linked transaction.

(3) A sum repayable under subsection (1) is repayable by the person to whom it was originally paid, but in the case of a debtor-creditor-supplier agreement falling within section 12(b) the creditor and the supplier shall be under a joint and several liability to repay sums paid by the debtor, or his relative, under the agreement or under a linked transaction falling within section 19(1)(b) and accordingly, in such a case, the creditor shall be entitled, in accordance with rules of court, to have the supplier made a party to any proceedings brought against the creditor to recover any such sums.

(4) Subject to any agreement between them, the creditor shall be entitled to be indemnified by the supplier for loss suffered by the creditor in satisfying his liability under subsection (3), including costs reasonably incurred by him in defending proceedings instituted by the debtor.

(5) Subsection (1) does not apply to any sum which, if not paid by a debtor, would be payable by virtue of section 71, and applies to a sum paid or payable by a debtor for the issue of a credit-token only where the credit-token has been returned to the creditor or surrendered to a supplier.

(6) If the total charge for credit includes an item in respect of a fee or commission charged by a credit-broker, the amount repayable under subsection (1) in respect of that item shall be the excess over £5 of the fee or commission.

(7) If the total charge for credit includes any sum payable or paid by the debtor to a credit-broker otherwise than in respect of a fee or commission charged by him, that sum shall for the purposes of subsection (6) be treated as if it were such a fee or commission.

(8) So far only as is necessary to give effect to section 69(2), this section applies to an agreement or transaction within that subsection as it applies to a cancelled agreement or transaction.

III CON [30G]

71. Cancellation: repayment of credit

(1) Notwithstanding the cancellation of a regulated consumer credit agreement, other than a debtor-creditor-supplier agreement for restricted-use credit, the agreement shall continue in force so far as it relates to repayment of credit and payment of interest.

(2) If, following the cancellation of a regulated consumer credit agreement, the debtor repays the whole or a portion of a credit—

- (a) before the expiry of one month following service of the notice of cancellation, or
- (b) in the case of a credit repayable by instalments, before the date on which the first instalment is due,

no interest shall be payable on the amount repaid.

(3) If the whole of a credit repayable by instalments is not repaid on or before the date specified in subsection (2) (b), the debtor shall not be liable to repay any of the credit except on receipt of a request in writing in the prescribed form, signed by or on behalf of the creditor, stating the amounts of the remaining instalments (recalculated by the creditor as nearly as may be in accordance with the agreement and without extending the repayment period), but excluding any sum other than principal and interest.

(4) Repayment of a credit, or payment of interest, under a cancelled agreement shall be treated as duly made if it is made to any person on whom, under section 69, a notice of cancellation could have been served, other than a person referred to in section 69(6)(b).

III CON [30G.1]

Form of request The Consumer Credit (Repayment of Credit on Cancellation) Regulations 1983, SI 1983/1559, prescribe the form of a request for repayment under this section.

III CON [30H]

72. Cancellation: return of goods

(1) This section applies where any agreement or transaction relating to goods, being—

(a) a restricted-use debtor-creditor-supplier agreement, a consumer hire agreement, or a linked transaction to which the debtor or hirer under any regulated agreement is a party, or

(b) a linked transaction to which a relative of the debtor or hirer under any regulated agreement is a party,

is cancelled after the debtor or hirer (in a case within paragraph (a)) or the relative (in a case within paragraph (b)) has acquired possession of the goods by virtue of the agreement or transaction.

(2) In this section—

(a) "the possessor" means the person who has acquired possession of the goods as mentioned in subsection (1),

(b) "the other party" means the person from whom the possessor acquired possession, and

(c) "the pre-cancellation period" means the period beginning when the possessor acquired possession and ending with the cancellation.

(3) The possessor shall be treated as having been under a duty throughout the pre-cancellation period—

(a) to retain possession of the goods, and

(b) to take reasonable care of them.

(4) On the cancellation, the possessor shall be under a duty, subject to any lien, to restore the goods to the other party in accordance with this section, and meanwhile to retain possession of the goods and take reasonable care of them.

(5) The possessor shall not be under any duty to deliver the goods except at his own premises and in pursuance of a request in writing signed by or on behalf of the other party and served on the possessor either before, or at the time when, the goods are collected from those premises.

(6) If the possessor—

(a) delivers the goods (whether at his own premises or elsewhere) to any person on whom, under section 69, a notice of cancellation could have been served (other than a person referred to in section 69(6)(b)), or

(b) sends the goods at his own expense to such a person,

he shall be discharged from any duty to retain the goods or deliver them to any person.

(7) Where the possessor delivers the goods as mentioned in subsection (6)(a) his obligation to take care of the goods shall cease; and if he sends the goods as mentioned in subsection (6)(b), he shall be under a duty to take reasonable care to see that they are received by the other party and not damaged in transit, but in other respects his duty to take care of the goods shall cease.

(8) Where, at any time during the period of 21 days following the cancellation, the possessor receives such a request as is mentioned in subsection (5), and unreasonably refuses or unreasonably fails to comply with it, his duty to take reasonable care of the goods shall continue until he delivers or sends the goods as mentioned in subsection (6), but if within that period he does not receive such a request his duty to take reasonable care of the goods shall cease at the end of that period.

(9) The preceding provisions of this section do not apply to—

(a) perishable goods, or

(b) goods which by their nature are consumed by use and which, before the cancellation, were so consumed, or

(c) goods supplied to meet an emergency, or

(d) goods which, before the cancellation, had become incorporated in any land or thing not comprised in the cancelled agreement or a linked transaction.

(10) Where the address of the possessor is specified in the executed agreement, references in this section to his own premises are to that address and no other.

(11) Breach of a duty imposed by this section is actionable as a breach of statutory duty.

III CON [30I]

73. Cancellation: goods given in part-exchange

(1) This section applies on the cancellation of a regulated agreement where, in antecedent negotiations, the negotiator agreed to take goods in part-exchange (the "part-exchange goods") and those goods have been delivered to him.

(2) Unless, before the end of the period of ten days beginning with the date of cancellation, the part-exchange goods are returned to the debtor or hirer in a condition substantially as good as when they were delivered to the negotiator, the debtor or hirer shall be entitled to recover from the negotiator a sum equal to the part-exchange allowance (as defined in subsection (7)(b)).

(3) In the case of a debtor-creditor-supplier agreement within section 12(b), the negotiator and the creditor shall be under a joint and several liability to pay to the debtor a sum recoverable under subsection (2).

(4) Subject to any agreement between them, the creditor shall be entitled to be indemnified by the negotiator for loss suffered by the creditor in satisfying his liability under subsection (3), including costs reasonably incurred by him in defending proceedings instituted by the debtor.

(5) During the period of ten days beginning with the date of cancellation, the debtor or hirer, if he is in possession of goods to which the cancelled agreement relates, shall have a lien on them for—

(a) delivery of the part-exchange goods, in a condition substantially as good as when they were delivered to the negotiator, or

(b) a sum equal to the part-exchange allowance;

and if the lien continues to the end of that period it shall thereafter subsist only as a lien for a sum equal to the part-exchange allowance.

(6) Where the debtor or hirer recovers from the negotiator or creditor, or both of them jointly, a sum equal to the part-exchange allowance, then, if the title of the debtor or hirer to the part-exchange goods has not vested in the negotiator, it shall so vest on the recovery of that sum.

(7) For the purposes of this section—

(a) the negotiator shall be treated as having agreed to take goods in part-exchange if, in pursuance of the antecedent negotiations, he either purchased or agreed to purchase those goods or accepted or agreed to accept them as part of the consideration for the cancelled agreement, and

(b) the part-exchange allowance shall be the sum agreed as such in the antecedent negotiations or, if no such agreement was arrived at, such sum as it would have been reasonable to allow in respect of the part-exchange goods if no notice of cancellation had been served.

(8) In an action brought against the creditor for a sum recoverable under subsection (2), he shall be entitled, in accordance with rules of court, to have the negotiator made a party to the proceedings.

EXCLUSION OF CERTAIN AGREEMENTS FROM PART V

III CON [30J]

74. Exclusion of certain agreements from Part V

(1) Except as provided in subsections (1A) to (2), this Part does not apply to—

(a) a non-commercial agreement,

(b) a debtor-creditor agreement enabling the debtor to overdraw on a current account,

(c) a debtor-creditor agreement to finance the making of such payments arising on, or connected with, the death of a person as may be prescribed, or

(d) a small debtor-creditor-supplier agreement for restricted-use credit.

(1A) Section 56 (antecedent negotiations) applies to a non-commercial agreement.

(1B) Where an agreement that falls within subsection (1)(b) is an authorised business overdraft agreement the following provisions apply—

(a) . . .

(b) section 56 (antecedent negotiations);

(c) section 60 (regulations on form and content of agreements);

(d) section 61B (duty to supply copy of overdraft agreement).

(1C) Where an agreement that falls within subsection (1)(b) is an authorised non-business overdraft agreement the following provisions apply—

(a) section 55 (regulations on disclosure of information);

(b) . . .

(c) section 55C (copy of draft consumer credit agreement);

(d) section 56 (antecedent negotiations);

(e) section 60 (regulations on form and content of agreements);

(f) section 61B (duty to supply copy of overdraft agreement).

(1D) Where an agreement that falls within subsection (1)(b) would be an authorised non-business overdraft agreement but for the fact that the credit is not repayable on demand or within three months the following provisions apply—

(a) section 55 (regulations on disclosure of information);

(b) . . .

(c) . . .

(d) section 55C (copy of draft consumer credit agreement);

(e) section 56 (antecedent negotiations);

(f) section 60 (regulations on form and content of agreements);

(g) section 61 (signing of agreement);

(h) section 61A (duty to supply copy of executed agreement);

(i) section 66A (withdrawal from consumer credit agreement).

(1E) In the case of an agreement that falls within subsection (1)(b) but does not fall within subsection (1B), (1C) or (1D), section 56 (antecedent negotiations) applies.

(1F) The following provisions apply to a debtor-creditor agreement to finance the making of such payments arising on, or connected with, the death of a person as may be prescribed—

(a) section 55 (regulations on disclosure of information);

(b) . . .

(c) . . .

(d) section 55C (copy of draft consumer credit agreement);

(e) section 56 (antecedent negotiations);

(f) section 60 (regulations on form and content of agreements);

(g) section 61 (signing of agreement);

(h) section 61A (duty to supply copy of executed agreement);

(i) section 66A (withdrawal from consumer credit agreement).

(2) The following provisions apply to a small debtor-creditor-supplier agreement for restricted-use credit—

(a) section 55 (regulations on disclosure of information);

(b) section 56 (antecedent negotiations);

(c) section 66A (withdrawal from consumer credit agreement).

(2A) In the case of an agreement to which the Cancellation of Contracts made in a Consumer's Home or Place of Work etc Regulations 2008 apply the reference in subsection (2) to a small agreement shall be construed as if in section 17(1)(a) and (b) "£35" were substituted for "£50".

(3) Subsection (1)(c) applies only where the FCA so determines, and such a determination—

(a) may be made subject to such conditions as the FCA thinks fit, and

(b) shall be made only if the FCA is of opinion that it is not against the interests of debtors.

(3A) . . .

(4) If any term of an agreement falling within subsection (1)(d) is expressed in writing, regulations under section 60(1) shall apply to that term (subject to section 60(3)) as if the agreement was a regulated agreement not falling within subsection (1)(d).

Amendment *Section 74 is shown as amended by the Financial Services and Markets Act 2000 (Regulated Activities) (Amendment) (No 2) Order 2013, SI 2013/1881 with effect from 26 July 2013 (for certain purposes) and 1 April 2014 (for remaining purposes). For transitional provisions see Part 8 of SI 2013/1881.*

III CON [30J.1]

Payments arising on death The Consumer Credit (Payments Arising on Death) Regulations 1983, SI 1983. 1554, as amended by SI 2010/1010, prescribe under s 74(1)(c), payments that arise in connection with death to which Part V of the Act does not apply.

III CON [30J.2]

EU Directive change This section has been amended to give effect to EU Directive 2008/448/EC, and SI 2010/1010, in respect of agreements made on or after 1 February 2011. The main change is the introduction of new sub-sections (1) to (1F) and (2)

PART VA
CURRENT ACCOUNT OVERDRAFTS

III CON [30K]

74A. *Information to be provided on a current account agreement*

Repealed.

Amendment *Section 74A was repealed by the Financial Services and Markets Act 2000 (Regulated Activities) (Amendment) (No 2) Order 2013, SI 2013/1881 with effect from 26 July 2013 (for certain purposes) and 1 April 2014 (for remaining purposes). For transitional provisions see Part 8 of SI 2013/1881.*

III CON [30K.1]

EU Directive change This section has been inserted to give effect to EU Directive 2008/448/EC, and SI 2010/1010, in respect of agreements made on or after 1 February 2011.

III CON [30L]

74B. *Information to be provided on significant overdrawing without prior arrangement*

Repealed.

Amendment *Section 74B was repealed by the Financial Services and Markets Act 2000 (Regulated Activities) (Amendment) (No 2) Order 2013, SI 2013/1881 with effect from 26 July 2013 (for certain purposes) and 1 April 2014 (for remaining purposes). For transitional provisions see Part 8 of SI 2013/1881.*

III CON [30L.1]

EU Directive change This section has been inserted to give effect to EU Directive 2008/448/EC, and SI 2010/1010, in respect of agreements made on or after 1 February 2011.

PART VI
MATTERS ARISING DURING THE CURRENCY OF CREDIT OR HIRE AGREEMENTS

III CON [30M]

75. Liability of creditor for breaches by supplier

(1) If the debtor under a debtor-creditor-supplier agreement falling within section 12(b) or (c) has, in relation to a transaction financed by the agreement, any claim against the supplier in respect of a misrepresentation or breach of contract, he shall have a like claim against the creditor, who, with the supplier, shall accordingly be jointly and severally liable to the debtor.

(2) Subject to any agreement between them, the creditor shall be entitled to be indemnified by the supplier for loss suffered by the creditor in satisfying his liability under subsection (1), including costs reasonably incurred by him in defending proceedings instituted by the debtor.

(3) Subsection (1) does not apply to a claim—

- (a) under a non-commercial agreement, . . .
- (b) so far as the claim relates to any single item to which the supplier has attached a cash price not exceeding £100 or more than £30,000, or.
- (c) under a debtor-creditor-supplier agreement for running-account credit—
  - (i) which provides for the making of payments by the debtor in relation to specified periods which, in the case of an agreement which is not secured on land, do not exceed three months, and
  - (ii) which requires that the number of payments to be made by the debtor in repayments of the whole amount of the credit provided in each such period shall not exceed one.

(4) This section applies notwithstanding that the debtor, in entering into the transaction, exceeded the credit limit or otherwise contravened any term of the agreement.

(5) In an action brought against the creditor under subsection (1) he shall be entitled, in accordance with rules of court, to have the supplier made a party to the proceedings.

III CON [30M.1]

Foreign transactions The protective provisions of this section apply to overseas transactions as well as domestic: *Office of Fair Trading v Lloyds TSB Bank plc* [2007] UKHL 48, [2008] 1 AC 316, [2008] 1 All ER 205.

III CON [30M.2]

EU Directive change Sub-section (3)(c) has been inserted to give effect to EU Directive 2008/448/EC, and SI 2010/1010, in respect of agreements made on or after 1 February 2011.

III CON [30M.3]

Rescission of the credit agreement Where the supplier has repudiated the contract and the consumer has accepted the repudiation and returned the goods he or she will remain liable to the creditor until the credit contract has been rescinded, by notice to the creditor of the repudiation by the supplier. Where the creditor continues after rescission to treat the customer as a defaulter, the creditor may be liable for damages resulting from the damage to the credit rating: *Durkin v DSG Retail Ltd* [2014] UKSC 21, [2014] 2 All ER 715, [2014] 1 WLR 1148.

III CON [30N]

75A. Further provision for liability of creditor for breaches by supplier

(1) If the debtor under a linked credit agreement has a claim against the supplier in respect of a breach of contract the debtor may pursue that claim against the creditor where any of the conditions in subsection (2) are met.

(2) The conditions in subsection (1) are—

- (a) that the supplier cannot be traced,
- (b) that the debtor has contacted the supplier but the supplier has not responded,
- (c) that the supplier is insolvent, or
- (d) that the debtor has taken reasonable steps to pursue his claim against the supplier but has not obtained satisfaction for his claim.

(3) The steps referred to in subsection (2)(d) need not include litigation.

(4) For the purposes of subsection (2)(d) a debtor is to be deemed to have obtained satisfaction where he has accepted a replacement product or service or other compensation from the supplier in settlement of his claim.

(5) In this section "linked credit agreement" means a regulated consumer credit agreement which serves exclusively to finance an agreement for the supply of specific goods or the provision of a specific service and where—

- (a) the creditor uses the services of the supplier in connection with the preparation or making of the credit agreement, or
- (b) the specific goods or provision of a specific service are explicitly specified in the credit agreement.

(6) This section does not apply where—

- (a) the cash value of the goods or service is £30, 000 or less,
- (b) the linked credit agreement is for credit which exceeds £60,260 and is not a residential renovation agreement, or
- (c) the linked credit agreement is entered into by the debtor wholly or predominantly for the purposes of a business carried on, or intended to be carried on, by him.

(7) Article 60C(5) and (6) of the Regulated Activities Order applies for the purposes of subsection (6)(c).

(8) This section does not apply to an agreement secured on land.

Amendment *Section 75A is shown as amended by the Financial Services and Markets Act 2000 (Regulated Activities) (Amendment) (No 2) Order 2013, SI 2013/1881 with effect from 26 July 2013 (for certain purposes) and 1 April 2014 (for remaining purposes). For transitional provisions see Part 8 of SI 2013/1881.*

III CON [30N.1]

EU Directive change This section has been inserted to give effect to EU Directive 2008/448/EC, and SI 2010/1010, in respect of any regulated consumer credit agreement made on or after 11 June 2010.

III CON [30O]

76. Duty to give notice before taking certain action

(1) The creditor or owner is not entitled to enforce a term of a regulated agreement by—

(a) demanding earlier payment of any sum, or

(b) recovering possession of any goods or land, or

(c) treating any right conferred on the debtor or hirer by the agreement as terminated, restricted or deferred,

except by or after giving the debtor or hirer not less than seven days' notice of intention to do so.

(2) Subsection (1) applies only where—

(a) a period for the duration of the agreement is specified in the agreement, and

(b) that period has not ended when the creditor or owner does an act mentioned in subsection (1),

but so applies notwithstanding that, under the agreement, any party is entitled to terminate it before the end of the period so specified.

(3) A notice under subsection (1) is ineffective if not in the prescribed form.

(4) Subsection (1) does not prevent a creditor from treating the right to draw on any credit as restricted or deferred and taking such steps as may be necessary to make the restriction or deferment effective.

(5) Regulations may provide that subsection (1) is not to apply to agreements described by the regulations.

(6) Subsection (1) does not apply to a right of enforcement arising by reason of any breach by the debtor or hirer of the regulated agreement.

III CON [300.1]

Form of notice The form of the notice is prescribed by the Consumer Credit (Enforcement, Default and Termination Notices) Regulations 1983, SI 1983/1561, as amended by SI 1984/1109, 2004/3237 and 2007/1167.

III CON [30P]

77. Duty to give information to debtor under fixed-sum term agreement

(1) The creditor under a regulated agreement for fixed-sum credit, within the prescribed period after receiving a request in writing to that effect from the debtor and payment of a fee of £1, shall give the debtor a copy of the executed agreement (if any) and of any other document referred to in it, together with a statement signed by or on behalf of the creditor showing, according to the information to which it is practicable for him to refer,—

(a) the total sum paid under the agreement by the debtor;

(b) the total sum which has become payable under the agreement by the debtor but remains unpaid, and the various amounts comprised in that total sum, with the date when each became due; and

(c) the total sum which is to become payable under the agreement by the debtor, and the various amounts comprised in that total sum, with the date, or mode of determining the date, when each becomes due.

(1A) Where a request under subsection (1) also amounts to a request under regulation 49 of the Payment Services Regulations 2017 (information during period of contract), subsection (1) applies as if the words "and payment of a fee of £1" were omitted.

(2) If the creditor possesses insufficient information to enable him to ascertain the amounts and dates mentioned in subsection (1)(c), he shall be taken to comply with that paragraph if his statement under subsection (1) gives the basis on which, under the regulated agreement, they would fall to be ascertained.

(2A) Subsection (2B) applies if the regulated agreement is a green deal plan . . .

(2B) The duty imposed on the creditor by subsection (1) may be discharged by another person acting on the creditor's behalf.

(3) Subsection (1) does not apply to—

(a) an agreement under which no sum is, or will or may become, payable by the debtor, or

(b) a request made less than one month after a previous request under that subsection relating to the same agreement was complied with.

(4) If the creditor under an agreement fails to comply with subsection (1)—

(a) he is not entitled, while the default continues, to enforce the agreement; . . .

(b) . . .

(5) This section does not apply to a non-commercial agreement.

III CON [30P.1]

It has been held that the information may be provided in several documents, not necessarily bearing signatures and that a breach of the section does not, by itself, give rise to an unfair relationship for the purposes of s 140A: *Carey v HSBC Bank plc* [2009] EWHC 3417 (QB), (2010) Times, 25 January. A creditor who is prevented by sub-section (4) from enforcing the agreement while a request for documents is outstanding may nevertheless report the default in payment to credit reference agencies: *McGuffick v Royal Bank of Scotland plc* [2009] EWHC 2386 (Comm), [2010] 1 All ER 634, [2010] 1 All ER (Comm) 48. In *Rankine v American Express Services Europe Ltd* [2009] CCLR 3, the view was expressed that the issue of a claim form was not 'enforcement', but only a step in this direction. This view was approved in *McGuffick*.

III CON [30Q]

77A. Statements to be provided in relation to fixed-sum agreements

(1) The creditor under a regulated agreement for fixed-sum credit must give the debtor statements under this section.

(1A) The statements must relate to consecutive periods.

(1B) The first such period must begin with either—

(a) the day on which the agreement is made, or

(b) the day the first movement occurs on the debtor's account with the creditor relating to the agreement.

(1C) No such period may exceed a year.

(1D) For the purposes of subsection (1C), a period of a year which expires on a non-working day may be regarded as expiring on the next working day.

(1E) Each statement under this section must be given to the debtor before the end of the period of thirty days beginning with the day after the end of the period to which the statement relates.

(2) Regulations may make provision about the form and content of statements under this section.

(2A) Subsection (2B) applies if the regulated agreement is a green deal plan . . .

(2B) Any duty imposed on the creditor by this section may be discharged by another person acting on the creditor's behalf.

(3) The debtor shall have no liability to pay any sum in connection with the preparation or the giving to him of a statement under this section.

(4) The creditor is not required to give the debtor any statement under this section once the following conditions are satisfied—

(a) that there is no sum payable under the agreement by the debtor; and

(b) that there is no sum which will or may become so payable.

(5) Subsection (6) applies if at a time before the conditions mentioned in subsection (4) are satisfied the creditor fails to give the debtor—

(a) a statement under this section within the period mentioned in subsection (1E); . . .

(b) . . .

(6) Where this subsection applies in relation to a failure to give a statement under this section to the debtor—

(a) the creditor shall not be entitled to enforce the agreement during the period of non-compliance;

(b) the debtor shall have no liability to pay any sum of interest to the extent calculated by reference to the period of non-compliance or to any part of it; and

(c) the debtor shall have no liability to pay any default sum which (apart from this paragraph)—

(i) would have become payable during the period of non-compliance; or

(ii) would have become payable after the end of that period in connection with a breach of the agreement which occurs during that period (whether or not the breach continues after the end of that period).

(7) In this section "the period of non-compliance" means, in relation to a failure to give a statement under this section to the debtor, the period which—

(a) begins immediately after the end of the period mentioned in . . . subsection (5); and

(b) ends at the end of the day on which the statement is given to the debtor or on which the conditions mentioned in subsection (4) are satisfied, whichever is earlier.

(8) This section does not apply in relation to a non-commercial agreement or to a small agreement.

(9) This section does not apply where the holder of a current account overdraws on the account without a pre-arranged overdraft or exceeds a pre-arranged overdraft limit.

III CON [30Q.1]

Consumer Credit Act 2006 This section was introduced by the Consumer Credit Act 2006, s 6 with effect from 1 October 2008. The statement must comply with the Consumer Credit (Information Requirements and Duration of Licences and Charges) Regulations 2007, SI 27/1167 and the relevant transitional provisions.

III CON [30R]

77B. Fixed-sum credit agreement: statement of account to be provided on request

(1) This section applies to a regulated consumer credit agreement—

(a) which is for fixed-sum credit,

(b) which is of fixed duration,

(c) where the credit is repayable in instalments by the debtor, and

(d) which is not an excluded agreement.

(2) Upon a request from the debtor, the creditor must as soon as reasonably practicable give to the debtor a statement in writing which complies with subsections (3) to (5).

(3) The statement must include a table showing the details of each instalment owing under the agreement as at the date of the request.

(4) Details to be provided under subsection (3) must include—

(a) the date on which the instalment is due,

(b) the amount of the instalment,

(c) any conditions relating to payment of the instalment, and

(d) a breakdown of the instalment showing how much of it is made up of capital repayment, interest payment and other charges.

(5) Where the rate of interest is variable or the charges under the agreement may be varied, the statement must also indicate clearly and concisely that the information in the table is valid only until the rate of interest or charges are varied.

(6) The debtor may make a request under subsection (2) at any time that the agreement is in force unless a previous request has been made less than a month before and has been complied with.

(7) The debtor shall have no liability to pay any sum in connection with the preparation or the giving of a statement under this section.

(7A) Subsection (7B) applies if the regulated agreement is a green deal plan . . .

(7B) Any duty imposed on the creditor by this section may be discharged by another person acting on the creditor's behalf.

(8) A breach of the duty imposed by this section is actionable as a breach of statutory duty.

(9) For the purposes of this section, an agreement is an excluded agreement if it is—

- (a) an agreement secured on land,
- (b) an agreement under which a person takes an article in pawn,
- (c) an agreement under which the creditor provides the debtor with credit which exceeds £60,260 and which is not a residential renovation agreement, or
- (d) an agreement entered into by the debtor wholly or predominantly for the purpose of a business carried on, or intended to be carried on, by him.

(10) Article 60C(5) and (6) of the Regulated Activities Order applies for the purposes of subsection (9)(d).

Amendment *Section 77B is shown as amended by the Financial Services and Markets Act 2000 (Regulated Activities) (Amendment) (No 2) Order 2013, SI 2013/1881 with effect from 26 July 2013 (for certain purposes) and 1 April 2014 (for remaining purposes). For transitional provisions see Part 8 of SI 2013/1881.*

III CON [30R.1]

EU Directive change This section has been inserted to give effect to EU Directive 2008/448/EC, and SI 2010/1010, in respect of any agreement other than an open-end agreement made on or after 11 June 2010 and open-end agreements made on or after 1 February 2011.

III CON [30S]

78. Duty to give information to debtor under running-account credit agreement

(1) The creditor under a regulated agreement for running-account credit, within the prescribed period after receiving a request in writing to that effect from the debtor and payment of a fee of £1, shall give the debtor a copy of the executed agreement (if any) and of any other document referred to in it, together with a statement signed by or on behalf of the creditor showing, according to the information to which it is practicable for him to refer,—

- (a) the state of the account, and
- (b) the amount, if any, currently payable under the agreement by the debtor to the creditor, and
- (c) the amounts and due dates of any payments which, if the debtor does not draw further on the account, will later become payable under the agreement by the debtor to the creditor.

(1A) Where a request under subsection (1) also amounts to a request under regulation 49 of the Payment Services Regulations 2017 (information during period of contract), subsection (1) applies as if the words "and payment of a fee of £1" were omitted.

(2) If the creditor possesses insufficient information to enable him to ascertain the amounts and dates mentioned in subsection (1)(c), he shall be taken to comply

with that paragraph if his statement under subsection (1) gives the basis on which, under the regulated agreement, they would fall to be ascertained.

(3) Subsection (1) does not apply to—

(a) an agreement under which no sum is, or will or may become, payable by the debtor, or

(b) a request made less than one month after a previous request under that subsection relating to the same agreement was complied with.

(4) Where running-account credit is provided under a regulated agreement, the creditor shall give the debtor statements in the prescribed form, and with the prescribed contents—

(a) showing according to the information to which it is practicable for him to refer, the state of the account at regular intervals of not more than twelve months, and

(b) where the agreement provides, in relation to specified periods, for the making of payments by the debtor, or the charging against him of interest or any other sum, showing according to the information to which it is practicable for him to refer the state of the account at the end of each of those periods during which there is any movement in the account.

(4A) Regulations may require a statement under subsection (4) to contain also information in the prescribed terms about the consequences of the debtor—

(a) failing to make payments as required by the agreement; or

(b) only making payments of a prescribed description in prescribed circumstances.

(5) A statement under subsection (4) shall be given within the prescribed period after the end of the period to which the statement relates.

(6) If the creditor under an agreement fails to comply with subsection (1)—

(a) he is not entitled, while the default continues, to enforce the agreement; . . .

(b) . . .

(7) This section does not apply to a non-commercial agreement, and subsections (4) to (5) do not apply to a small agreement.

III CON [30S.1]

Regulations See the Consumer Credit (Running-Account Credit Information) Regulations 1983, SI 1983/1570, as amended by SI 2010/1010. The statement must also, in some cases, comply with regulations 13 to 18 of the Consumer Credit (Information Requirements and Duration of Licences and Charges) Regulations 2007, SI 2007/1167.

III CON [30S.2]

Non-commercial agreement The provision in subsection (6) that prevents a creditor from enforcing an agreement for which he has failed to provide a copy does not apply to a non-commercial agreement. This is defined in section 189 as a consumer credit agreement or a consumer hire agreement not made by the creditor or owner in the course of a business carried on by him.

III CON [30T]

78A. Duty to give information to debtor on change of rate of interest

(1) Where the rate of interest charged under a regulated consumer credit agreement, other than an excluded agreement, is to be varied, the creditor must inform the debtor in writing of the matters mentioned in subsection (3) before the variation can take effect.

(2) But subsection (1) does not apply where—

(a) the agreement provides that the creditor is to inform the debtor in writing periodically of the matters mentioned in subsection (3) in relation to any variation, at such times as may be provided for in the agreement,

(b) the agreement provides that the rate of interest is to vary according to a reference rate,

(c) the reference rate is publicly available,

(d) information about the reference rate is available on the premises of the creditor, and

(e) the variation of the rate of interest results from a change to the reference rate.

(3) The matters referred to in subsections (1) and (2)(a) are—

(a) the variation in the rate of interest,

(b) the amount of any payments that are to be made after the variation has effect, if different, expressed as a sum of money where practicable, and

(c) if the number or frequency of payments changes as a result of the variation, the new number or frequency.

(4) In the case of an agreement mentioned in subsection (5) this section applies as follows—

(a) the obligation in subsection (1) only applies if the rate of interest increases, and

(b) subsection (3) is to be read as if paragraphs (b) and (c) were omitted.

(5) The agreements referred to in subsection (4) are—

(a) an authorised business overdraft agreement,

(b) an authorised non-business overdraft agreement, or

(c) an agreement which would be an authorised non-business overdraft agreement but for the fact that the credit is not repayable on demand or within three months.

(6) For the purposes of this section an agreement is an excluded agreement if it is—

(a) a debtor-creditor agreement arising where the holder of a current account overdraws on the account without a pre-arranged overdraft or exceeds a pre-arranged overdraft limit, or

(b) an agreement secured on land.

III CON [30T.1]

EU Directive change This section has been inserted to give effect to EU Directive 2008/448/EC, and SI 2010/1010, in respect of any open-end agreement, whenever made, and all agreements made on or after 1 February 2011.

III CON [30U]

79. Duty to give hirer information

(1) The owner under a regulated consumer hire agreement, within the prescribed period after receiving a request in writing to that effect from the hirer and payment of a fee of £1, shall give to the hirer a copy of the executed agreement and of any other document referred to in it, together with a statement signed by or on behalf of the owner showing, according to the information to which it is practicable for him to refer, the total sum which has become payable under the agreement by the hirer but remains unpaid and the various amounts comprised in that total sum, with the date when each became due.

(2) Subsection (1) does not apply to—

(a) an agreement under which no sum is, or will or may become, payable by the hirer, or

(b) a request made less than one month after a previous request under that subsection relating to the same agreement was complied with.

(3) If the owner under an agreement fails to comply with subsection (1)—

(a) he is not entitled, while the default continues, to enforce the agreement; . . .

(b) . . .

(4) This section does not apply to a non-commercial agreement.

III CON [30V]

80. Debtor or hirer to give information about goods

(1) Where a regulated agreement, other than a non-commercial agreement, requires the debtor or hirer to keep goods to which the agreement relates in his possession or control, he shall, within seven working days after he has received a request in writing to that effect from the creditor or owner, tell the creditor or owner where the goods are.

(2) If the debtor or hirer fails to comply with subsection (1), and the default continues for 14 days, he commits an offence.

III CON [30W]

81. ***Appropriation of payments***

Repealed.

Amendment *Section 81 was repealed by the Financial Services and Markets Act 2000 (Regulated Activities) (Amendment) (No 2) Order 2013, SI 2013/1881 with effect from 26 July 2013 (for certain purposes) and 1 April 2014 (for remaining purposes). For transitional provisions see Part 8 of SI 2013/1881.*

III CON [30X]

82. Variation of agreements

(1) Where, under a power contained in a regulated agreement, the creditor or owner varies the agreement, the variation shall not take effect before notice of it is given to the debtor or hirer in the prescribed manner.

(1A) Subsection (1) does not apply to a variation in the rate of interest charged under an agreement not secured on land (see section 78A).

(1B) Subsection (1) does not apply to a variation in the rate of interest charged under an agreement secured on land if—

(a) the agreement falls within subsection (1D), and

(b) the variation is a reduction in the rate.

(1C) Subsection (1) does not apply to a variation in any other charge under an agreement if—

(a) the agreement falls within subsection (1D), and

(b) the variation is a reduction in the charge.

(1D) The agreements referred to in subsections (1B) and (1C) are—

(a) an authorised business overdraft agreement,

(b) an authorised non-business overdraft agreement, or

(c) an agreement which would be an authorised non-business overdraft agreement but for the fact that the credit is not repayable on demand or within three months.

(1E) Subsection (1) does not apply to a debtor-creditor agreement arising where the holder of a current account overdraws on the account without a pre-arranged overdraft or exceeds a pre-arranged overdraft limit.

(2) Where an agreement (a "modifying agreement") varies or supplements an earlier agreement, the modifying agreement shall for the purposes of this Act be treated as—

(a) revoking the earlier agreement, and

(b) containing provisions reproducing the combined effect of the two agreements, and obligations outstanding in relation to the earlier agreement shall accordingly be treated as outstanding instead in relation to the modifying agreement.

(2A) Subsection (2) does not apply if the earlier agreement or the modifying agreement is an exempt agreement.

(2B) Subsection (2) does not apply if the modifying agreement varies—

- (a) the amount of the repayment to be made under the earlier agreement, or
- (b) the duration of the agreement,

as a result of the discharge of part of the debtor's indebtedness under the earlier agreement by virtue of section 94(3).

(3) If the earlier agreement is a regulated agreement but (apart from this subsection) the modifying agreement is not then, unless the modifying agreement is—

- (a) for running account credit; or
- (b) an exempt agreement,

it shall be treated as a regulated agreement.

(4) If the earlier agreement is a regulated agreement for running-account credit, and by the modifying agreement the creditor allows the credit limit to be exceeded but intends the excess to be merely temporary, Part V (except section 56) shall not apply to the modifying agreement.

(5) If—

- (a) the earlier agreement is a cancellable agreement, and
- (b) the modifying agreement is made within the period applicable under section 68 to the earlier agreement,

then, whether or not the modifying agreement would, apart from this subsection, be a cancellable agreement, it shall be treated as a cancellable agreement in respect of which a notice may be served under section 68 not later than the end of the period applicable under that section to the earlier agreement.

(5A) Subsection (5) does not apply where the modifying agreement is an exempt agreement.

(6) Except under subsection (5), a modifying agreement shall not be treated as a cancellable agreement.

(6A) If—

- (a) the earlier agreement is an agreement to which section 66A (right of withdrawal) applies, and
- (b) the modifying agreement is made within the period during which the debtor may give notice of withdrawal from the earlier agreement (see section 66A(2)),

then, whether or not the modifying agreement would, apart from this subsection, be an agreement to which section 66A applies, it shall be treated as such an agreement in respect of which notice may be given under subsection (2) of that section within the period referred to in paragraph (b) above.

(6B) Except as provided for under subsection (6A) section 66A does not apply to a modifying agreement.

(7) This section does not apply to a non-commercial agreement.

Amendment *Section 82 is shown as amended by the Financial Services and Markets Act 2000 (Regulated Activities) (Amendment) (No 2) Order 2013, SI 2013/1881 with effect from 26 July 2013 (for certain purposes) and 1 April 2014 (for remaining purposes). For transitional provisions see Part 8 of SI 2013/1881.*

III CON [30X.1]

EU Directive change Sub-sections (1A), (1B), (1C), (1D), (1E), (2B), (6A) and (6B) have been inserted to give effect to EU Directive 2008/448/EC, and SI 2010/1010, in respect of any open-end agreement, whenever made, and all agreements made on or after 11 June 2010.

III CON [30X.2]

The prescribed manner As to the manner of giving notice see the Consumer Credit (Notice of Variation of Agreements) Regulations 1977, SI 1977/328, as amended by SI 1979/661 and 2010/101.

III CON [30Y]

82A. *Assignment of rights*
Repealed.

Amendment *Section 82A was repealed by the Financial Services and Markets Act 2000 (Regulated Activities) (Amendment) (No 2) Order 2013, SI 2013/1881 with effect from 26 July 2013 (for certain purposes) and 1 April 2014 (for remaining purposes). For transitional provisions see Part 8 of SI 2013/1881.*

III CON [30Y.1]

EU Directive change This section has been inserted to give effect to EU Directive 2008/448/EC, and SI 2010/1010, in respect of any open-end agreement, whenever made, and all agreements made on or after 1 February 2011.

III CON [30Z]

83. Liability for misuse of credit facilities

(1) The debtor under a regulated consumer credit agreement shall not be liable to the creditor for any loss arising from use of the credit facility by another person not acting, or to be treated as acting, as the debtor's agent.

(2) This section does not apply to a non-commercial agreement, or to any loss in so far as it arises from misuse of an instrument to which section 4 of the Cheques Act 1957 applies.

III CON [30AA]

84. Misuse of credit-tokens

(1) Section 83 does not prevent the debtor under a credit-token agreement from being made liable to the extent of £35 (or the credit limit if lower) for loss to the creditor arising from use of the credit-token by other persons during a period beginning when the credit-token ceases to be in the possession of any authorised person and ending when the credit-token is once more in the possession of an authorised person.

(2) Section 83 does not prevent the debtor under a credit-token agreement from being made liable to any extent for loss to the creditor from use of the credit-token by a person who acquired possession of it with the debtor's consent.

(3) Subsections (1) and (2) shall not apply to any use of the credit-token after the creditor has been given oral or written notice that it is lost or stolen, or is for any other reason liable to misuse.

(3A) . . .

(3B) . . .

(3C) . . .

(4) Subsections (1) and (2) shall not apply unless there are contained in the credit-token agreement in the prescribed manner particulars of the name, address and telephone number of a person stated to be the person to whom notice is to be given under subsection (3).

(5) Notice under subsection (3) takes effect when received, but where it is given orally, and the agreement so requires, it shall be treated as not taking effect if not confirmed in writing within seven days.

(6) Any sum paid by the debtor for the issue of the credit-token, to the extent (if any) that it has not been previously offset by use made of the credit token, shall be treated as paid towards satisfaction of any liability under subsection (1) or (2).

(7) The debtor, the creditor, and any person authorised by the debtor to use the credit-token, shall be authorised persons for the purposes of subsection (1).

(8) Where two or more credit-tokens are given under one credit-token agreement, the preceding provisions of this section apply to each credit-token separately.

III CON [30AB]

85. Duty on owner of new credit-tokens

(1) Whenever, in connection with a credit-token agreement, a credit-token (other than the first) is given by the creditor to the debtor, the creditor shall give the debtor a copy of the executed agreement (if any) and of any other document referred to in it.

(2) If the creditor fails to comply with this section—

(a) he is not entitled, while the default continues, to enforce the agreement; . . .

(b) . . .

(3) This section does not apply to a small agreement.

III CON [31]

86. Death of debtor or hirer

(1) The creditor or owner under a regulated agreement is not entitled, by reason of the death of the debtor or hirer, to do an act specified in paragraphs (a) to (e) of section 87(1) if at the death the agreement is fully secured.

(2) If at the death of the debtor or hirer a regulated agreement is only partly secured or is unsecured, the creditor or owner is entitled, by reason of the death of the debtor or hirer, to do an act specified in paragraphs (a) to (e) of section 87(1) on an order of the court only.

(3) This section applies in relation to the termination of an agreement only where—

(a) a period for its duration is specified in the agreement, and

(b) that period has not ended when the creditor or owner purports to terminate the agreement,

but so applies notwithstanding that, under the agreement, any party is entitled to terminate it before the end of the period so specified.

(4) This section does not prevent the creditor from treating the right to draw on any credit as restricted or deferred, and taking such steps as may be necessary to make the restriction or deferment effective.

(5) This section does not affect the operation of any agreement providing for payment of sums—

(a) due under the regulated agreement, or

(b) becoming due under it on the death of the debtor or hirer,

out of the proceeds of a policy of assurance on his life.

(6) For the purposes of this section an act is done by reason of the death of the debtor or hirer if it is done under a power conferred by the agreement which is—

(a) exercisable on his death, or

(b) exercisable at will and exercised at any time after his death.

III CON [31.1]

Procedure Proceedings under s 86(2) for an order for the recovery of goods must comply with the Consumer Credit Act Procedure set out in Practice Direction 7B at **CPR PD 7B**. The procedure for obtaining an order for the recovery of mortgaged residential property is set out at para **CPR 55.10**.

PART VII
DEFAULT AND TERMINATION

Information sheets

III CON [31A]

86A. FCA to prepare information sheets on arrears and defaults

(1) The FCA shall prepare and issue an arrears information sheet and a default information sheet.

(2) The arrears information sheet shall include information to help debtors and hirers who receive notices under section 86B or 86C

(3) The default information sheet shall include information to help debtors and hirers who receive default notices.

(4) Regulations may make provision about the information to be included in an information sheet.

(5) An information sheet takes effect for the purposes of this Part at the end of the period of three months beginning with the day on which it is issued.

(6) If the FCA revises an information sheet after it has been issued, it shall issue the revised information sheet.

(7) A revised information sheet takes effect for the purposes of this Part at the end of the period of three months beginning with the day on which it is issued.

Amendment *Section 86A is shown as amended by the Financial Services and Markets Act 2000 (Regulated Activities) (Amendment) (No 2) Order 2013, SI 2013/1881 with effect from 26 July 2013 (for certain purposes) and 1 April 2014 (for remaining purposes). For transitional provisions see Part 8 of SI 2013/1881.*

Sums in arrears and default sums

III CON [31B]

86B. Notice of sums in arrears under fixed-sum credit agreements etc

(1) This section applies where at any time the following conditions are satisfied—

- (a) that the debtor or hirer under an applicable agreement is required to have made at least two payments under the agreement before that time;
- (b) that the total sum paid under the agreement by him is less than the total sum which he is required to have paid before that time;
- (c) that the amount of the shortfall is no less than the sum of the last two payments which he is required to have made before that time;
- (d) that the creditor or owner is not already under a duty to give him notices under this section in relation to the agreement; and
- (e) if a judgment has been given in relation to the agreement before that time, that there is no sum still to be paid under the judgment by the debtor or hirer.

(2) The creditor or owner—

- (a) shall, within the period of 14 days beginning with the day on which the conditions mentioned in subsection (1) are satisfied, give the debtor or hirer a notice under this section; and
- (b) after the giving of that notice, shall give him further notices under this section at intervals of not more than six months.

(3) The duty of the creditor or owner to give the debtor or hirer notices under this section shall cease when either of the conditions mentioned in subsection (4) is satisfied; but if either of those conditions is satisfied before the notice required by subsection (2)(a) is given, the duty shall not cease until that notice is given.

(4) The conditions referred to in subsection (3) are—

- (a) that the debtor or hirer ceases to be in arrears;

(b) that a judgment is given in relation to the agreement under which a sum is required to be paid by the debtor or hirer.

(5) For the purposes of subsection (4)(a) the debtor or hirer ceases to be in arrears when—

(a) no payments, which he has ever failed to make under the agreement when required, are still owing;

(b) no default sum, which has ever become payable under the agreement in connection with his failure to pay any sum under the agreement when required, is still owing;

(c) no sum of interest, which has ever become payable under the agreement in connection with such a default sum, is still owing; and

(d) no other sum of interest, which has ever become payable under the agreement in connection with his failure to pay any sum under the agreement when required, is still owing.

(6) A notice under this section shall include a copy of the current arrears information sheet under section 86A.

(7) The debtor or hirer shall have no liability to pay any sum in connection with the preparation or the giving to him of a notice under this section.

(8) Regulations may make provision about the form and content of notices under this section.

(9) In the case of an applicable agreement under which the debtor or hirer must make all payments he is required to make at intervals of one week or less, this section shall have effect as if in subsection (1)(a) and (c) for "two" there were substituted "four".

(10) If an agreement mentioned in subsection (9) was made before the beginning of the relevant period, only amounts resulting from failures by the debtor or hirer to make payments he is required to have made during that period shall be taken into account in determining any shortfall for the purposes of subsection (1)(c).

(11) In subsection (10) "relevant period" means the period of 20 weeks ending with the day on which the debtor or hirer is required to have made the most recent payment under the agreement.

(12) In this section "applicable agreement" means an agreement which falls within subsection (12A) or (12B).

(12A) An agreement falls within this subsection if—

(a) it is a regulated agreement for fixed-sum credit; and

(b) it is not—

(i) a non-commercial agreement;

(ii) a small agreement; or

(iii) a green deal plan.

(12B) An agreement falls within this subsection if—

(a) it is a regulated consumer hire agreement; and

(b) it is neither a non-commercial agreement nor a small agreement.

(13) In this section—

(a) "payments" in relation to an applicable agreement which is a regulated agreement for fixed-sum credit means payments to be made at predetermined intervals provided for under the terms of the agreement; and

(b) "payments" in relation to an applicable agreement which is a regulated consumer hire agreement means any payments to be made by the hirer in relation to any period in consideration of the bailment or hiring to him of goods under the agreement.

III CON [31B.1]

Information and notices The notice must comply with the Consumer Credit (Information Requirements and Duration of Licences and Charges) Regulations 2007, SI 2007/1167.

III CON [31C]

86C. Notice of sums in arrears under running account credit agreements

(1) This section applies where at any time the following conditions are satisfied—

- (a) that the debtor under an applicable agreement is required to have made at least two payments under the agreement before that time;
- (b) that the last two payments which he is required to have made before that time have not been made;
- (c) that the creditor has not already been required to give a notice under this section in relation to either of those payments; and
- (d) if a judgment has been given in relation to the agreement before that time, that there is no sum still to be paid under the judgment by the debtor.

(2) The creditor shall, no later than the end of the period within which he is next required to give a statement under section 78(4) in relation to the agreement, give the debtor a notice under this section.

(3) The notice shall include a copy of the current arrears information sheet under section 86A.

(4) The notice may be incorporated in a statement or other notice which the creditor gives the debtor in relation to the agreement by virtue of another provision of this Act.

(5) The debtor shall have no liability to pay any sum in connection with the preparation or the giving to him of the notice.

(6) Regulations may make provision about the form and content of notices under this section.

(7) In this section "applicable agreement" means an agreement which—

- (a) is a regulated agreement for running-account credit; and
- (b) is neither a non-commercial agreement nor a small agreement.

(8) In this section "payments" means payments to be made at predetermined intervals provided for under the terms of the agreement.

III CON [31C.1]

Sums in arrears The statement must comply with the Consumer Credit (Information Requirements and Duration of Licences and Charges) Regulations 2007, SI 2007/1167.

III CON [31D]

86D. Failure to give notice of sums in arrears

(1) This section applies where the creditor or owner under an agreement is under a duty to give the debtor or hirer notices under section 86B but fails to give him such a notice—

- (a) within the period mentioned in subsection (2)(a) of that section; or
- (b) within the period of six months beginning with the day after the day on which such a notice was last given to him.

(2) This section also applies where the creditor under an agreement is under a duty to give the debtor a notice under section 86C but fails to do so before the end of the period mentioned in subsection (2) of that section.

(3) The creditor or owner shall not be entitled to enforce the agreement during the period of non-compliance.

(4) The debtor or hirer shall have no liability to pay—

- (a) any sum of interest to the extent calculated by reference to the period of non-compliance or to any part of it; or
- (b) any default sum which (apart from this paragraph)—
  - (i) would have become payable during the period of non-compliance; or

(ii) would have become payable after the end of that period in connection with a breach of the agreement which occurs during that period (whether or not the breach continues after the end of that period).

(5) In this section "the period of non-compliance" means, in relation to a failure to give a notice under section 86B or 86C to the debtor or hirer, the period which—

(a) begins immediately after the end of the period mentioned in (as the case may be) subsection (1)(a) or (b) or (2); and

(b) ends at the end of the day mentioned in subsection (6).

(6) That day is—

(a) in the case of a failure to give a notice under section 86B as mentioned in subsection (1)(a) of this section, the day on which the notice is given to the debtor or hirer;

(b) in the case of a failure to give a notice under that section as mentioned in subsection (1)(b) of this section, the earlier of the following—

(i) the day on which the notice is given to the debtor or hirer;

(ii) the day on which the condition mentioned in subsection (4)(a) of that section is satisfied;

(c) in the case of a failure to give a notice under section 86C, the day on which the notice is given to the debtor.

III CON [31E]

86E. Notice of default sums

(1) This section applies where a default sum becomes payable under a regulated agreement by the debtor or hirer.

(2) The creditor or owner shall, within the prescribed period after the default sum becomes payable, give the debtor or hirer a notice under this section.

(3) The notice under this section may be incorporated in a statement or other notice which the creditor or owner gives the debtor or hirer in relation to the agreement by virtue of another provision of this Act.

(4) The debtor or hirer shall have no liability to pay interest in connection with the default sum to the extent that the interest is calculated by reference to a period occurring before the 29th day after the day on which the debtor or hirer is given the notice under this section.

(5) If the creditor or owner fails to give the debtor or hirer the notice under this section within the period mentioned in subsection (2), he shall not be entitled to enforce the agreement until the notice is given to the debtor or hirer.

(6) The debtor or hirer shall have no liability to pay any sum in connection with the preparation or the giving to him of the notice under this section.

(7) Regulations may—

(a) provide that this section does not apply in relation to a default sum which is less than a prescribed amount;

(b) make provision about the form and content of notices under this section.

(8) This section does not apply in relation to a non-commercial agreement or to a small agreement.

III CON [31E.1]

Notice of default sums The statement must comply with the Consumer Credit (Information Requirements and Duration of Licences and Charges) Regulations 2007, SI 2007/1167.

III CON [31F]

86F. Interest on default sums

(1) This section applies where a default sum becomes payable under a regulated agreement by the debtor or hirer.

(2) The debtor or hirer shall only be liable to pay interest in connection with the default sum if the interest is simple interest.

Default notices

III CON [31G]

87. Need for default notice

(1) Service of a notice on the debtor or hirer in accordance with section 88 (a "default notice") is necessary before the creditor or owner can become entitled, by reason of any breach by the debtor or hirer of a regulated agreement,—

- (a) to terminate the agreement, or
- (b) to demand earlier payment of any sum, or
- (c) to recover possession of any goods or land, or
- (d) to treat any right conferred on the debtor or hirer by the agreement as terminated, restricted or deferred, or
- (e) to enforce any security.

(2) Subsection (1) does not prevent the creditor from treating the right to draw upon any credit as restricted or deferred, and taking such steps as may be necessary to make the restriction or deferment effective.

(3) The doing of an act by which a floating charge becomes fixed is not enforcement of a security.

(4) Regulations may provide that subsection (1) is not to apply to agreements described by the regulations.

(5) Subsection (1)(d) does not apply in a case referred to in section 98A(4) (termination or suspension of debtor's right to draw on credit under open-end agreement).

III CON [31G.1]

Notice of default sums Sub-section (5) has been inserted to give effect to EU Directive 2008/448/EC, and SI 2010/1010, in respect of any open-end agreement, whenever made, and all agreements made on or after 1 February 2011.

III CON [31H]

88. Contents and effect of default notice

(1) The default notice must be in the prescribed form and specify—

- (a) the nature of the alleged breach;
- (b) if the breach is capable of remedy, what action is required to remedy it and the date before which that action is to be taken;
- (c) if the breach is not capable of remedy, the sum (if any) required to be paid as compensation for the breach, and the date before which it is to be paid.

(2) A date specified under subsection (1) must not be less than 14 days after the date of service of the default notice, and the creditor or owner shall not take action such as is mentioned in section 87(1) before the date so specified or (if no requirement is made under subsection (1)) before those 14 days have elapsed.

(3) The default notice must not treat as a breach failure to comply with a provision of the agreement which becomes operative only on breach of some other provision, but if the breach of that other provision is not duly remedied or

compensation demanded under subsection (1) is not duly paid, or (where no requirement is made under subsection (1)) if the 14 days mentioned in subsection (2) have elapsed, the creditor or owner may treat the failure as a breach and section 87(1) shall not apply to it.

(4) The default notice must contain information in the prescribed terms about the consequences of failure to comply with it and any other prescribed matters relating to the agreement.

(4A) The default notice must also include a copy of the current default information sheet under section 86A.

(5) A default notice making a requirement under subsection (1) may include a provision for the taking of action such as is mentioned in section 87(1) at any time after the restriction imposed by subsection (2) will cease, together with a statement that the provision will be ineffective if the breach is duly remedied or the compensation duly paid.

III CON [31H.1]

Form of notice The form of the notice is prescribed by the Consumer Credit (Enforcement, Default and Termination Notices) Regulations 1983, SI 1983/1561, as amended by SI 1984/1109, 2004/3237 and 2007/1167.

A default notice which allows 14 days from the date of the notice (rather than the date of service) is defective and must be treated as such: *American Express Services Europe Ltd v Brandon* [2011] EWCA Civ 1187, [2011] All ER (D) 206 (Oct).

III CON [31I]

89. Compliance with default notice

If before the date specified for that purpose in the default notice the debtor or hirer takes the action specified under section 88(1)(b) or (c) the breach shall be treated as not having occurred.

FURTHER RESTRICTION OF REMEDIES FOR DEFAULT

III CON [32]

90. Retaking of protected hire-purchase etc goods

(1) At any time when—

(a) the debtor is in breach of a regulated hire-purchase or a regulated conditional sale agreement relating to goods, and

(b) the debtor has paid to the creditor one-third or more of the total price of the goods, and

(c) the property in the goods remains in the creditor,

the creditor is not entitled to recover possession of the goods from the debtor except on an order of the court.

(2) Where under a hire-purchase or conditional sale agreement the creditor is required to carry out any installation and the agreement specifies, as part of the total price, the amount to be paid in respect of the installation (the "installation charge") the reference in subsection (1)(b) to one-third of the total price shall be construed as a reference to the aggregate of the installation charge and one-third of the remainder of the total price.

(3) In a case where—

(a) subsection (1)(a) is satisfied, but not subsection (1)(b), and

(b) subsection (1)(b) was satisfied on a previous occasion in relation to an earlier agreement, being a regulated hire-purchase or regulated conditional sale agreement, between the same parties, and relating to any of the goods comprised in the later agreement (whether or not other goods were also included),

subsection (1) shall apply to the later agreement with the omission of paragraph (b).
(4) If the later agreement is a modifying agreement, subsection (3) shall apply with the substitution, for the second reference to the later agreement, of a reference to the modifying agreement.
(5) Subsection (1) shall not apply, or shall cease to apply, to an agreement if the debtor has terminated, or terminates, the agreement.
(6) Where subsection (1) applies to an agreement at the death of the debtor, it shall continue to apply (in relation to the possessor of the goods) until the grant of probate or administration, or (in Scotland) confirmation (on which the personal representative would fall to be treated as the debtor).
(7) Goods falling within this section are in this Act referred to as "protected goods".

III CON [32.1]

Procedure and precedent Proceedings for the retaking of protected hire-purchase goods must comply with the Consumer Credit Act Procedure, set out in Practice Direction 7B at **CPR PD 7B**, as applied in *Hunter v Lex Vehicle Finance Ltd* [2005] EWHC 223 (Ch), [2005] BPIR 586. A precedent for a claim by a creditor, under s 90 is at **BCCP K[1468]**.

III CON [32.2]

Recovery of possession An order for recovery of possession is not needed for recovery with the hirer's consent: s 173 (3). But the consent must be informed by knowledge of the hirer's rights to be effective: *Chartered Trust plc v Pitcher* [1988] RTR 72, CA. When an owner seeks to recover from a non-party the onus of proving the acquisition of a good title is on that person: *Thomas v Heelas* [1986] CA Transcript 1065.

III CON [32.3]

Need for a default notice The creditor's right to recover possession (among other rights) depends on the service on the debtor of a valid default notice in compliance with ss 87 and 88. But the notice will not be valid if it asserts an excessive amount to be due under the agreement: *Woodchester Lease Management Services Ltd v Swain & Co (a Firm)* [1999] 1 WLR 263, CA. Note that any default notice served after 1 October 2006 must allow 14 days, not 7: the longer period is required by an amending provision in s 14(1) of the Consumer Credit Act 2006.

III CON [32.4]

Defence based on failure to serve default notice The creditor has no right to the return of goods unless a valid default notice has been served in accordance with s 88 Consumer Credit Act 1974. For a precedent for a defence based on a failure to serve a valid default notice see **BCCP K[1576]**.

III CON [32.5]

The total price For the purpose of s 90 the total price does not include money due as contractual interest in respect of late payments: *Julian Hodge Bank Ltd v Hall* [1998] CCLR 14, CA.

III CON [32.6]

Where goods on hire-purchase have been sold to a third party Section 27 of the Hire-Purchase Act 1964, as substituted by para 22 of Sch 4 to the Consumer Credit Act 1974, protects a bona fide purchaser of an article from someone in possession of it on hire-purchase terms: the buyer acquires a good title vis-à-vis the finance company. But this does not apply where a dishonest seller has acquired possession by means of a false identity so that the hire-purchase agreement is void: *Shogun Finance Ltd v Hudson* [2001] EWCA Civ 1001, [2002] QB 834, [2002] 4 All ER 572; affd [2003] UKHL 62, [2004] 1 AC 919, [2004] 1 All ER 215.

The bona fide purchaser must be a "private purchaser" and not a "trade or finance purchaser": see the interpretation in *GE Capital Bank Ltd v Rushton* [2005] EWCA Civ 1556, [2006] 3 All ER 865, [2006] 1 WLR 899 of the definitions in s 29(2) of the Hire Purchase Act 1964, as substituted by the Consumer Credit Act 1974.

III CON [33]

91. Consequences of breach of section 90

If goods are recovered by the creditor in contravention of section 90—

(a) the regulated agreement, if not previously terminated, shall terminate, and

(b) the debtor shall be released from all liability under the agreement, and shall be entitled to recover from the creditor all sums paid by the debtor under the agreement.

III CON [34]

92. Recovery of possession of goods or land

(1) Except under an order of the court, the creditor or owner shall not be entitled to enter any premises to take possession of goods subject to a regulated hire-purchase agreement, regulated conditional sale agreement or regulated consumer hire agreement.

(2) At any time when the debtor is in breach of a regulated conditional sale agreement relating to land, the creditor is entitled to recover possession of the land from the debtor, or any person claiming under him, on an order of the court only.

(3) An entry in contravention of subsection (1) or (2) is actionable as a breach of statutory duty.

III CON [34.1]

Procedure and precedents Proceedings under s 92 (1) must comply with the Consumer Credit Act procedure, set out in Practice Direction 7B at **CPR PD 7B**). A precedent for such a claim is provided at **BCCP K[1468]** and a precedent for a defence based on failure to serve a default notice is at **BCCP K[1576]**. Proceedings for the recovery of land must comply with Part I of **CPR 55**. A defendant may apply for a time order under s 129(1)(c) (see para **III CON [40]**).

III CON [34.2]

Relief from forfeiture The county court's powers under County Courts Act 1984 s 38 (see para **II CCA [21]**) include a general equitable jurisdiction to grant relief from forfeiture of proprietary or possessory rights: *BICC plc v Burndy Corpn* [1985] Ch 232, [1985] 1 All ER 417, CA; *Transag Haulage Ltd v Leyland DAF Finance plc* [1994] 2 BCLC 88, [1994] CCLR 111.

III CON [34A]

93. Interest not to be increased on default

The debtor under a regulated consumer credit agreement shall not be obliged to pay interest on sums which, in breach of the agreement, are unpaid by him at a rate—

(a) where the total charge for credit includes an item in respect of interest, exceeding the rate of that interest, or

(b) in any other case, exceeding what would be the rate of the total charge for credit if any items included in the total charge for credit by virtue of rules made by the FCA under paragraph (2)(d) of article 60M of the Regulated Activities Order were disregarded.

Amendment *Section 93 is shown as amended by the Financial Services and Markets Act 2000 (Regulated Activities) (Amendment) (No 2) Order 2013, SI 2013/1881 with effect from 26 July 2013 (for certain purposes) and 1 April 2014 (for remaining purposes). For transitional provisions see Part 8 of SI 2013/1881.*

Early payment by debtor

III CON [34B]

94. Right to complete payments ahead of time

(1) The debtor under a regulated consumer credit agreement is entitled at any time, by notice to the creditor and the payment to the creditor of all amounts payable by the debtor to him under the agreement and any amount which the creditor claims under section 95A(2) (less any rebate allowable under section 95), to discharge the debtor's indebtedness under the agreement.

(2) A notice under subsection (1) may embody the exercise by the debtor of any option to purchase goods conferred on him by the agreement, and deal with any other matter arising on, or in relation to, the termination of the agreement.

(3) The debtor under a regulated consumer credit agreement, other than an agreement secured on land, is entitled at any time to discharge part of his indebtedness by taking the steps in subsection (4).

(4) The steps referred to in subsection (3) are as follows—

- (a) he provides notice to the creditor,
- (b) he pays to the creditor some of the amount payable by him to the creditor under the agreement before the time fixed by the agreement, and
- (c) he makes the payment—
  - (i) before the end of the period of 28 days beginning with the day following that on which notice under paragraph (a) was received by the creditor, or
  - (ii) on or before any later date specified in the notice.

(5) Where a debtor takes the steps in subsection (4) his indebtedness shall be discharged by an amount equal to the sum of the amount paid and any rebate allowable under section 95 less any amount which the creditor claims under section 95A(2) or section 95B(2).

(6) A notice—

- (a) under subsection (1), other than a notice relating to a regulated consumer credit agreement secured on land, or
- (b) under subsection (4)(a),

need not be in writing.

III CON [34B.1]

EU Directive change Sub-sections (3) to (6) have been inserted to give effect to EU Directive 2008/448/EC, and SI 2010/1010, in respect of any agreement made on or after 11 June 2010.

III CON [34C]

95. Rebate on early settlement

(1) Regulations may provide for the allowance of a rebate of charges for credit to the debtor under a regulated consumer credit agreement where, under section 94, on refinancing, on breach of the agreement, or for any other reason, his indebtedness is discharged or is discharged in part or becomes payable before the time fixed by the agreement, or any sum becomes payable by him before the time so fixed.

(2) Regulations under subsection (1) may provide for calculation of the rebate by reference to any sums paid or payable by the debtor or his relative under or in connection with the agreement (whether to the creditor or some other person), including sums under linked transactions and other items in the total charge for credit.

III CON [34C.1]

Calculating the rebate Formulae for calculating the rebate are provided by the Consumer Credit (Early Settlement) Regulations 2004 SI 2004/1483,as amended by SI 2004/2619 and 2010/1010.

III CON [34C.2]

EU Directive change The words "or is discharged in part" have been inserted in subsection (1) to give effect to EU Directive 2008/448/EC, and SI 2010/1010, in respect of any agreement made on or after 11 June 2010.

III CON [34D]

95A. Compensatory amount

(1) This section applies where—

(a) a regulated consumer credit agreement, other than an agreement secured on land, provides for the rate of interest on the credit to be fixed for a period of time, and

(b) under section 94 the debtor discharges all or part of his indebtedness during that period.

(2) The creditor may claim an amount equal to the cost which the creditor has incurred as a result only of the debtor's indebtedness being discharged during that period if—

(a) the amount of the payment under section 94 exceeds £8,000 or, where more than one such payment is made in any 12 month period, the total of those payments exceeds £8,000,

(b) the agreement is not a debtor-creditor agreement enabling the debtor to overdraw on a current account, and

(c) the amount of the payment under section 94 is not paid from the proceeds of a contract of payment protection insurance.

(3) The amount in subsection (2)—

(a) must be fair,

(b) must be objectively justified, and

(c) must not exceed whichever is the lower of—

(i) the relevant percentage of the amount of the payment under section 94, and

(ii) the total amount of interest that would have been paid by the debtor under the agreement in the period from the date on which the debtor makes the payment under section 94 to the date fixed by the agreement for the discharge of the indebtedness of the debtor.

(4) In subsection (3)(c)(i) "relevant percentage" means—

(a) 1%, where the period from the date on which the debtor makes the payment under section 94 to the date fixed by the agreement for the discharge of the indebtedness of the debtor is more than one year, or

(b) 0.5%, where that period is equal to or less than one year.

III CON [34D.1]

EU Directive change This section has been inserted to give effect to EU Directive 2008/448/EC, and SI 2010/1010, in respect of any agreement made on or after 11 June 2010.

III CON [34E]

96. Effect on linked transactions

(1) Where for any reason the indebtedness of the debtor under a regulated consumer credit agreement is discharged before the time fixed by the agreement, he, and any relative of his, shall at the same time be discharged from any liability under a linked transaction, other than a debt which has already become payable.

(2) Subsection (1) does not apply to a linked transaction which is itself an agreement providing the debtor or his relative with credit.
(3) Regulations may exclude linked transactions of the prescribed description from the operation of subsection (1).

III CON [34E1]

Exclusions The Consumer Credit (Linked Transaction)(Exemptions) Regulations 1983, SI 1983/1560 exclude contracts of insurance, those that contain a guarantee of goods and those comprising or effected under agreements for the operation of deposit or current accounts.

III CON [34F]

97. Duty to give information

(1) The creditor under a regulated consumer credit agreement, within the prescribed period after he has received a request . . . to that effect from the debtor, shall give the debtor a statement in the prescribed form indicating, according to the information to which it is practicable for him to refer, the amount of the payment required to discharge the debtor's indebtedness under the agreement, together with the prescribed particulars showing how the amount is arrived at.
(2) Subsection (1) does not apply to a request made less than one month after a previous request under that subsection relating to the same agreement was complied with.
(2A) A request under subsection (1) need not be in writing unless the agreement is secured on land.
(3) If the creditor fails to comply with subsection (1)—
(a) he is not entitled, while the default continues, to enforce the agreement; . . .
(b) . . .

III CON [34F.1]

Statement in the prescribed form The form and procedure are set out in the Consumer Credit (Settlement Information) Regulations 1983 SI 1983/1564, as amended by SI 2004/14883, 2004/3236 and 2010/1010.

III CON [34F.2]

EU Directive change Sub-section (2A) has been inserted to give effect to EU Directive 2008/448/EC, and SI 2010/1010, in respect of any agreement made on or after 11 June 2010.

III CON [34G]

97A. Duty to give information on partial repayment

(1) Where a debtor under a regulated consumer credit agreement—
(a) makes a payment by virtue of which part of his indebtedness is discharged under section 94, and
(b) at the same time or subsequently requests the creditor to give him a statement concerning the effect of the payment on the debtor's indebtedness,

the creditor must give the statement to the debtor before the end of the period of seven working days beginning with the day following that on which the creditor receives the request.
(2) The statement shall be in writing and shall contain the following particulars—
(a) a description of the agreement sufficient to identify it,
(b) the name, postal address and, where appropriate, any other address of the creditor and the debtor,

(c) where the creditor is claiming an amount under section 95A(2) or section 95B(2), that amount and the method used to determine it,

(d) the amount of any rebate to which the debtor is entitled—

(i) under the agreement, or

(ii) by virtue of section 95 where that is higher,

(e) where the amount of the rebate mentioned in paragraph (d)(ii) is given, a statement indicating that this amount has been calculated having regard to the Consumer Credit (Early Settlement) Regulations 2004,

(f) where the debtor is not entitled to any rebate, a statement to this effect,

(g) any change to—

(i) the number, timing or amount of repayments to be made under the agreement, or

(ii) the duration of the agreement,

which results from the partial discharge of the indebtedness of the debtor, and

(h) the amount of the debtor's indebtedness remaining under the agreement at the date the creditor gives the statement.

III CON [34G.1]

EU Directive change This section has been inserted to give effect to EU Directive 2008/448/EC, and SI 2010/1010, in respect of any agreement made on or after 11 June 2010.

III CON [34H]

98. Duty to give notice of termination (non-default cases)

(1) The creditor or owner is not entitled to terminate a regulated agreement except by or after giving the debtor or hirer not less than seven days' notice of the termination.

(2) Subsection (1) applies only where—

(a) a period for the duration of the agreement is specified in the agreement, and

(b) that period has not ended when the creditor or owner does an act mentioned in subsection (1),

but so applies notwithstanding that, under the agreement, any party is entitled to terminate it before the end of the period so specified.

(3) A notice under subsection (1) is ineffective if not in the prescribed form.

(4) Subsection (1) does not prevent a creditor from treating the right to draw on any credit as restricted or deferred and taking such steps as may be necessary to make the restriction or deferment effective.

(5) Regulations may provide that subsection (1) is not to apply to agreements described by the regulations.

(6) Subsection (1) does not apply to the termination of a regulated agreement by reason of any breach by the debtor or hirer of the agreement.

III CON [34H.1]

Form of notice The form of the notice is prescribed by the Consumer Credit (Enforcement, Default and Termination Notices) Regulations 1983, SI 1983/1561, as amended by SI 1984/1109, 2004/3237 and 2007/1167.

III CON [34I]

98A. Termination etc of open-end consumer credit agreements

(1) The debtor under a regulated open-end consumer credit agreement, other than an excluded agreement, may by notice terminate the agreement, free of charge, at any time, subject to any period of notice not exceeding one month provided for by the agreement.

(2) Notice under subsection (1) need not be in writing unless the creditor so requires.

(3) Where a regulated open-end consumer credit agreement, other than an excluded agreement, provides for termination of the agreement by the creditor—

(a) the termination must be by notice served on the debtor, and

(b) the termination may not take effect until after the end of the period of two months, or such longer period as the agreement may provide, beginning with the day after the day on which notice is served.

(4) Where a regulated open-end consumer credit agreement, other than an excluded agreement, provides for termination or suspension by the creditor of the debtor's right to draw on credit—

(a) to terminate or suspend the right to draw on credit the creditor must serve a notice on the debtor before the termination or suspension or, if that is not practicable, immediately afterwards,

(b) the notice must give reasons for the termination or suspension, and

(c) the reasons must be objectively justified.

(5) Subsection (4)(a) and (b) does not apply where giving the notice—

(a) is prohibited by *an* [a retained] EU obligation, or

(b) would, or would be likely to, prejudice—

(i) the prevention or detection of crime,

(ii) the apprehension or prosecution of offenders, or

(iii) the administration of justice.

(6) An objectively justified reason under subsection (4)(c) may, for example, relate to—

(a) the unauthorised or fraudulent use of credit, or

(b) a significantly increased risk of the debtor being unable to fulfil his obligation to repay the credit.

(7) Subsections (1) and (3) do not affect any right to terminate an agreement for breach of contract.

(8) For the purposes of this section an agreement is an excluded agreement if it is—

(a) an authorised non-business overdraft agreement,

(b) an authorised business overdraft agreement,

(c) a debtor-creditor agreement arising where the holder of a current account overdraws on the account without a pre-arranged overdraft or exceeds a pre-arranged overdraft limit, or

(d) an agreement secured on land.

Amendment *Text in italic is deleted and text in square brackets is inserted by the Consumer Credit (Amendment) (EU Exit) Regulations 2018, SI 2018/1038, with effect from exit day (as defined in the European Union (Withdrawal) Act 2018.*

III CON [34I.1]

EU Directive change This section has been inserted to give effect to EU Directive 2008/448/EC, and SI 2010/1010, in respect of any open-end agreement, whenever made, and all agreements made on or after 1 February 2011.

III CON [34J]

99. Right to terminate hire-purchase etc. agreements

(1) At any time before the final payment by the debtor under a regulated hire-purchase or regulated conditional sale agreement falls due, the debtor shall be entitled to terminate the agreement by giving notice to any person entitled or authorised to receive the sums payable under the agreement.

(2) Termination of an agreement under subsection (1) does not affect any liability under the agreement which has accrued before the termination.

(3) Subsection (1) does not apply to a conditional sale agreement relating to land after the title to the land has passed to the debtor.

(4) In the case of a conditional sale agreement relating to goods, where the property in the goods, having become vested in the debtor, is transferred to a person who does not become the debtor under the agreement, the debtor shall not thereafter be entitled to terminate the agreement under subsection (1).

(5) Subject to subsection (4), where a debtor under a conditional sale agreement relating to goods, terminates the agreement under this section after the property in the goods has become vested in him, the property in the goods shall thereupon vest in the person (the "previous owner") in whom it was vested immediately before it became vested in the debtor:

Provided that if the previous owner has died, or any other event has occurred whereby that property, if vested in him immediately before that event, would thereupon have vested in some other person, the property shall be treated as having devolved as if it had been vested in the previous owner immediately before his death or immediately before that event, as the case may be.

III CON [34J.1]

Prescribed form See the Consumer Credit (Enforcement, Default and Termination Notices) Regulations 1983, SI 1983/1561, as amended by SI 1984/1109, 2004/3237 and 2007/1167.

III CON [34K]

100. Liability of debtor on termination of hire-purchase etc agreement

(1) Where a regulated hire-purchase or regulated conditional sale agreement is terminated under section 99 the debtor shall be liable, unless the agreement provides for a smaller payment, or does not provide for any payment, to pay to the creditor the amount (if any) by which one-half of the total price exceeds the aggregate of the sums paid and the sums due in respect of the total price immediately before the termination.

(2) Where under a hire-purchase or conditional sale agreement the creditor is required to carry out any installation and the agreement specifies, as part of the total price, the amount to be paid in respect of the installation (the "installation charge") the reference in subsection (1) to one-half of the total price shall be construed as a reference to the aggregate of the installation charge and one-half of the remainder of the total price.

(3) If in any action the court is satisfied that a sum less than the amount specified in subsection (1) would be equal to the loss sustained by the creditor in consequence of the termination of the agreement by the debtor, the court may make an order for the payment of that sum in lieu of the amount specified in subsection (1).

(4) If the debtor has contravened an obligation to take reasonable care of the goods or land, the amount arrived at under subsection (1) shall be increased by the sum required to recompense the creditor for that contravention, and subsection (2) shall have effect accordingly.

(5) Where the debtor, on the termination of the agreement, wrongfully retains possession of goods to which the agreement relates, then, in any action brought by the creditor to recover possession of the goods from the debtor, the court, unless it is satisfied that having regard to the circumstances it would not be just to do so, shall order the goods to be delivered to the creditor without giving the debtor an option to pay the value of the goods.

III CON [34L]

101. Right to terminate hire agreement

(1) The hirer under a regulated consumer hire agreement is entitled to terminate the agreement by giving notice to any person entitled or authorised to receive the sums payable under the agreement.

(2) Termination of an agreement under subsection (1) does not affect any liability under the agreement which has accrued before the termination.

(3) A notice under subsection (1) shall not expire earlier than eighteen months after the making of the agreement, but apart from that the minimum period of notice to be given under subsection (1), unless the agreement provides for a shorter period, is as follows.

(4) If the agreement provides for the making of payments by the hirer to the owner at equal intervals, the minimum period of notice is the length of one interval or three months, whichever is less.

(5) If the agreement provides for the making of such payments at differing intervals, the minimum period of notice is the length of the shortest interval or three months, whichever is less.

(6) In any other case, the minimum period of notice is three months.

(7) This section does not apply to—

(a) any agreement which provides for the making by the hirer of payments which in total (and without breach of the agreement) exceed £1,500 in any year, or

(b) any agreement where—

(i) goods are bailed or (in Scotland) hired to the hirer for the purposes of a business carried on by him, or the hirer holds himself out as requiring the goods for those purposes, and

(ii) the goods are selected by the hirer, and acquired by the owner for the purposes of the agreement at the request of the hirer from any person other than the owner's associate, or

(c) any agreement where the hirer requires, or holds himself out as requiring, the goods for the purpose of bailing or hiring them to other persons in the course of a business carried on by him.

(8) If, on an application made to the FCA by a person carrying on a consumer hire business, it appears to the FCA that it would be in the interest of hirers to do so, it may direct that, subject to such conditions (if any) as it may specify, this section shall not apply to consumer hire agreements made by the applicant; and this Act shall have effect accordingly.

(8A) If it appears to the FCA that it would be in the interests of hirers to do so, it may direct that, subject to such conditions (if any) as it may specify, this section shall not apply to a consumer hire agreement if the agreement falls within a specified description; and this Act shall have effect accordingly.

(9) In the case of a modifying agreement subsection (3) shall apply with the substitution, for "the making of the agreement" of "the making of the original agreement".

Amendment *Section 101 is shown as amended by the Financial Services and Markets Act 2000 (Regulated Activities) (Amendment) (No 2) Order 2013, SI 2013/1881 with effect from 26 July 2013 (for certain purposes) and 1 April 2014 (for remaining purposes). For transitional provisions see Part 8 of SI 2013/1881.*

III CON [34M]

102. Agency for receiving notice of rescission

(1) Where the debtor or hirer under a regulated agreement claims to have a right to rescind the agreement, each of the following shall be deemed to be the agent of the creditor or owner for the purpose of receiving any notice rescinding the agreement which is served by the debtor or hirer—

(a) a credit-broker or supplier who was the negotiator in antecedent negotiations, and

(b) any person who, in the course of a business carried on by him, acted on behalf of the debtor or hirer in any negotiations for the agreement.

(2) In subsection (1) "rescind" does not include—

(a) service of a notice of cancellation, or

(b) termination of an agreement under section 99 or 101, or by the exercise of a right or power in that behalf expressly conferred by the agreement.

III CON [34N]

103. Termination statements

(1) If an individual (the "customer") serves on any person (the "trader") a notice—

(a) stating that—

(i) the customer was the debtor or hirer under a regulated agreement described in the notice, and the trader was the creditor or owner under the agreement, and

(ii) the customer has discharged his indebtedness to the trader under the agreement, and

(iii) the agreement has ceased to have any operation; and

(b) requiring the trader to give the customer a notice, signed by or on behalf of the trader, confirming that those statements are correct,

the trader shall, within the prescribed period after receiving the notice, either comply with it or serve on the customer a counter-notice stating that, as the case may be, he disputes the correctness of the notice or asserts that the customer is not indebted to him under the agreement.

(2) Where the trader disputes the correctness of the notice he shall give particulars of the way in which he alleges it to be wrong.

(3) Subsection (1) does not apply in relation to any agreement if the trader has previously complied with that subsection on the service of a notice under it with respect to that agreement.

(4) Subsection (1) does not apply to a non-commercial agreement.

(5) . . .

(6) A breach of the duty imposed by subsection (1) is actionable as a breach of statutory duty.

III CON [34N.1]

Prescribed period The Consumer Credit (Prescribed Periods for Giving Information) Regulations 1983, SI 1983/1569, prescribe a period of 12 days after receipt of the notice within which to comply or serve a counter-notice.

PART VIII
SECURITY

NEGOTIABLE INSTRUMENTS

III CON [35]

123. Restrictions on taking and negotiating instruments

(1) A creditor or owner shall not take a negotiable instrument, other than a bank note or cheque, in discharge of any sum payable—

(a) by the debtor or hirer under a regulated agreement, or

(b) by any person as surety in relation to the agreement.

(2) The creditor or owner shall not negotiate a cheque taken by him in discharge of a sum payable as mentioned in subsection (1) except to a banker (within the meaning of the Bills of Exchange Act 1882).

(3) The creditor or owner shall not take a negotiable instrument as security for the discharge of any sum payable as mentioned in subsection (1).

(4) A person takes a negotiable instrument as security for the discharge of a sum if the sum is intended to be paid in some other way, and the negotiable instrument is to be presented for payment only if the sum is not paid in that way.

(5) This section does not apply where the regulated agreement is a non-commercial agreement.

(6) The Treasury may by order provide that this section shall not apply where the regulated agreement has a connection with a country outside the United Kingdom.

Amendment *Section 123 is shown as amended by the Financial Services and Markets Act 2000 (Regulated Activities) (Amendment) (No 2) Order 2013, SI 2013/1881 with effect from 26 July 2013 (for certain purposes) and 1 April 2014 (for remaining purposes). For transitional provisions see Part 8 of SI 2013/1881.*

III CON [36]

124. Consequences of breach of section 123

(1) After any contravention of section 123 has occurred in relation to a sum payable as mentioned in section 123 (1)(a), the agreement under which the sum is payable is enforceable against the debtor or hirer on an order of the court only.

(2) After any contravention of section 123 has occurred in relation to a sum payable by any surety, the security is enforceable on an order of the court only.

(3) Where an application for an order under subsection (2) is dismissed (except on technical grounds only) section 106 shall apply to the security.

III CON [36.1]

Procedure and precedents Proceedings for an enforcement order under s 124 (2) in order to recover goods, must comply with the Consumer Credit Act Procedure, set out in Practice Direction 7B at **CPR PD 7B**.

III CON [36.2]

The court's discretion The exercise of the court's discretion is limited by s 127 (1) and (2) Consumer Credit Act 1974 (see para **III CON [38]**).

LAND MORTGAGES

III CON [37]

126. Enforcement of land mortgages

(1) A land mortgage securing an agreement of one the following types is enforceable (so far as is provided in relation to the agreement) on an order of the court only—

(a) a regulated agreement;

(b) a regulated mortgage contract;

(c) a consumer credit agreement which would, but for article 60D of the Regulated Activities Order (exempt agreements: exemption relating to the purchase of land for non-residential purposes), be a regulated agreement.

(2) Subject to section 140A(5) (unfair relationships between creditors and debtors), a regulated mortgage contract which would, but for article 60C(2) of the Regulated Activities Order (exempt agreements: exemption relating to the nature of the agreement), be a regulated agreement is to be treated for the purposes of Part 9 (judicial control) as if it were a regulated agreement.

(3) In this section, "regulated mortgage contract" has the meaning given by article 61(3) of the Regulated Activities Order (regulated mortgage contracts)).

III CON [37.1]

Order of the court "The court" means the county court (s 189) and its orders may provide for an extension of time (s 129), suspension (s 135) and variation of terms (s 136). Proceedings must comply with **CPR 55.10**.

PART IX
JUDICIAL CONTROL

ENFORCEMENT OF CERTAIN REGULATED AGREEMENTS AND SECURITIES

III CON [38]

127. Enforcement orders in case of infringement

(1) In the case of an application for an enforcement order under—

(za) section 55(2) (disclosure of information), or

(zb) section 61B(3) (duty to supply copy of overdraft agreement), or

(a) section 65 (1) (improperly executed agreements), or

(b) section 105 (7)(a) or (b) (improperly executed security instruments), or

(c) section 111 (2) (failure to serve copy of notice on surety), or

(d) section 124 (1) or (2) (taking of negotiable instrument in contravention of section 123),

the court shall dismiss the application if, but only if, it considers it just to do so having regard to—

(i) prejudice caused to any person by the contravention in question, and the degree of culpability for it; and

(ii) the powers conferred on the court by subsection (2) and sections 135 and 136.

(2) If it appears to the court just to do so, it may in an enforcement order reduce or discharge any sum payable by the debtor or hirer, or any surety, so as to compensate him for prejudice suffered as a result of the contravention in question.

(3) . . .

(4) . . .

(5) . . .

III CON [38.1]

Procedure A claim for an order to enforce an agreement under this section must use the Consumer Credit Act procedure unless the agreement relates only to money, in which case it should be started by the issue of a Part 7 claim form: **CPR PD 7B**.

III CON [38.2]

Compensation for prejudice In *National Guardian Mortgage Corpn v Wilkes* [1993] CCLR 1, the court held that the failure to supply a copy of the agreement deprived the debtor of the opportunity to borrow at a lower rate of interest and reduced the amount of accrued interest by 40%. In *Rank Xerox v Hepple* [1994] CCLR 1, the court reduced the sum due as accelerated payment from £5,000 to £500.

III CON [38.3]

Repeal of sub-sections (3), (4) and (5) The repeal of sub-sections (3), (4) and (5) by s 15 of the Consumer Credit Act 2006 reverses the effect of *Wilson v First County Trust Ltd (No 2)* [2003] UKHL 40, [2004] 1 AC 816, [2003] 4 All ER 97 and allows the courts a discretion regarding enforcement in all cases of infringement where the contract was made on or after 6 April 2007.

III CON [38.4]

EU Directive change Sub-section (1) has been inserted to give effect to EU Directive 2008/448/EC, and SI 2010/1010, in respect of agreements made on or after 1 February 2011.

III CON [39]

128. Enforcement orders on death of debtor or hirer

The court shall make an order under section 86 (2) if, but only if, the creditor or owner proves that he has been unable to satisfy himself that the present and future obligations of the debtor or hirer under the agreement are likely to be discharged.

EXTENSION OF TIME

III CON [40]

129. Time orders

(1) If it appears to the court just to do so—

- (a) on an application for an enforcement order; or
- (b) on an application made by a debtor or hirer under this paragraph after service on him of—
  - (i) a default notice, or
  - (ii) a notice under section 76 (1) or 98 (1); or
- (ba) on an application made by a debtor or hirer under this paragraph after he has been given a notice under section 86B or 86C; or
- (c) in an action brought by a creditor or owner to enforce a regulated agreement or any security, or recover possession of any goods or land to which a regulated agreement relates,

the court may make an order under this section (a "time order").

(2) A time order shall provide for one or both of the following, as the court considers just—

- (a) the payment by the debtor or hirer or any surety of any sum owed under a regulated agreement or a security by such instalments, payable at such times, as the court, having regard to the means of the debtor or hirer and any surety, considers reasonable;
- (b) the remedying by the debtor or hirer of any breach of a regulated agreement (other than non-payment of money) within such period as the court may specify.

III CON [40.1]

Procedure An application for a time order by a debtor, if made under s 129 (1)(b), must comply with the Consumer Credit Act Procedure set out in Practice Direction 7B (at **CPR PD 7B**) and the claim must include the particulars required by para 7.3 of that Practice Direction.

III CON [40.2]

Time orders In *First National Bank plc v Syed* [1991] 2 All ER 250, CA, it was held that, in considering whether to make a time order, the court should consider the creditor's position as well as the debtor's and should not make a time order where there has been a history of default and an order which the debtor could afford would not meet the accruing interest and there is no realistic prospect of the debtor's financial position improving. In *Southern and District Finance plc v Barnes* [1996] 1 FCR 679, [1995] CCLR 62, CA, the Court of Appeal examined the jurisdiction under s 129 and made the following observations:

(1) Where a time order is sought the court should consider first whether it is just to make such an order at all.
(2) On the first issue the court should have regard to all the circumstances of the case, including the particular positions of the debtor and of the creditor.
(3) In a case of temporary financial difficulties the time allowed should be a specified period.
(4) No order should be made unless the debtor is likely to resume payments at no less than the contractual rate.
(5) The expression "the sum owed" means every sum owing.
(6) The court must consider what instalments would be reasonable as to amount and timing, having regard to the debtor's means.
(7) The time order may include amendments to the agreement, provided that they are just to the parties and consequential on the order.
(8) Where the whole balance is owing a time order must necessarily alter the term of the loan and the rate of interest.
(9) If a time order is made any possession order must be suspended during compliance with the order.
(10) Where a creditor brings a possession action that is a calling in of the whole loan which is "the sum owed".
(11) The court may make a time order in respect of future instalments.

In *London North Securities Ltd v Meadows* [2004] Legal Action Group, December p 32, decision of HHJ Howarth in Liverpool County Court 28 October 2004, the court held under s 136 that the default rate of interest (34.9 % APR, compounding monthly) was extortionate, and that s 129 empowered the court to make a time order for the payment of default interest at rates reduced retrospectively to the special account simple rate.

III CON [40A]

129A. Debtor or hirer to give notice of intent etc to creditor or owner

(1) A debtor or hirer may make an application under section 129(1)(ba) in relation to a regulated agreement only if—

(a) following his being given the notice under section 86B or 86C, he gave a notice within subsection (2) to the creditor or owner; and
(b) a period of at least 14 days has elapsed after the day on which he gave that notice to the creditor or owner.

(2) A notice is within this subsection if it—

(a) indicates that the debtor or hirer intends to make the application;
(b) indicates that he wants to make a proposal to the creditor or owner in relation to his making of payments under the agreement; and
(c) gives details of that proposal.

III CON [41]

130. Supplemental provisions about time orders

(1) Where in accordance with rules of court an offer to pay any sum by instalments is made by the debtor or hirer and accepted by the creditor or owner, the court may in accordance with rules of court make a time order under section 129 (2)(a) giving effect to the offer without hearing evidence of means.

(2) In the case of a hire-purchase or conditional sale agreement only, a time order under section 129 (2)(a) may deal with sums which, although not payable by the debtor at the time the order is made, would if the agreement continued in force become payable under it subsequently.

(3) A time order under section 129 (2)(a) shall not be made where the regulated agreement is secured by a pledge if, by virtue of regulations made under section 76 (5), 87 (4) or 98 (5), service of a notice is not necessary for enforcement of the pledge.

(4) Where, following the making of a time order in relation to a regulated hire-purchase or conditional sale agreement or a regulated consumer hire agreement, the debtor or hirer is in possession of the goods, he shall be treated (except in the case of a debtor to whom the creditor's title has passed) as a bailee or (in Scotland) a custodier of the goods under the terms of the agreement, notwithstanding that the agreement has been terminated.

(5) Without prejudice to anything done by the creditor or owner before the commencement of the period specified in a time order made under section 129 (2)(b) ("the relevant period"),—

- (a) he shall not while the relevant period subsists take in relation to the agreement any action such as is mentioned in section 87 (1);
- (b) where—
  - (i) a provision of the agreement ("the secondary provision") becomes operative only on breach of another provision of the agreement ("the primary provision"), and
  - (ii) the time order provides for the remedying of such a breach of the primary provision within the relevant period,

  he shall not treat the secondary provision as operative before the end of that period;
- (c) if while the relevant period subsists the breach to which the order relates is remedied it shall be treated as not having occurred.

(6) On the application of any person affected by a time order, the court may vary or revoke the order.

INTEREST

III CON [41A]

130A. Interest payable on judgment debts etc

(1) If the creditor or owner under a regulated agreement wants to be able to recover from the debtor or hirer post-judgment interest in connection with a sum that is required to be paid under a judgment given in relation to the agreement (the "judgment sum"), he—

- (a) after the giving of that judgment, shall give the debtor or hirer a notice under this section (the "first required notice"); and
- (b) after the giving of the first required notice, shall give the debtor or hirer further notices under this section at intervals of not more than six months.

(2) The debtor or hirer shall have no liability to pay post-judgment interest in connection with the judgment sum to the extent that the interest is calculated by reference to a period occurring before the day on which he is given the first required notice.

(3) If the creditor or owner fails to give the debtor or hirer a notice under this section within the period of six months beginning with the day after the day on which such a notice was last given to the debtor or hirer, the debtor or hirer shall have no liability to pay post-judgment interest in connection with the judgment sum to the extent that the interest is calculated by reference to the whole or to a part of the period which—

- (a) begins immediately after the end of that period of six months; and
- (b) ends at the end of the day on which the notice is given to the debtor or hirer.

(4) The debtor or hirer shall have no liability to pay any sum in connection with the preparation or the giving to him of a notice under this section.

(5) A notice under this section may be incorporated in a statement or other notice which the creditor or owner gives the debtor or hirer in relation to the agreement by virtue of another provision of this Act.

(6) Regulations may make provision about the form and content of notices under this section.

(7) This section does not apply in relation to post-judgment interest which is required to be paid by virtue of any of the following—

- (a) section 4 of the Administration of Justice (Scotland) Act 1972;
- (b) Article 127 of the Judgments Enforcement (Northern Ireland) Order 1981;
- (c) section 74 of the County Courts Act 1984.

(8) This section does not apply in relation to a non-commercial agreement or to a small agreement.

(9) In this section "post-judgment interest" means interest to the extent calculated by reference to a period occurring after the giving of the judgment under which the judgment sum is required to be paid.

III CON [41A.1]

Interest after judgment From 1 October 2008 a creditor under an agreement which provides for post-judgment interest may give notice under s 130A(1) of the Consumer Credit Act 1974, as amended by the Act of 2006, of an intention to recover such interest. Note, however, that the Consumer Credit (Enforcement, Default and Termination Notices) Regulations 1983, SI 1983/1561 were amended by reg 33 of the Consumer Credit (Information Requirements and Duration of Licences and Charges) Regulations 2007, SI 2007/1167 to require the giving of a statement about the inclusion of a right to post-judgment interest in the agreement; and that regs 34 and 35 of SI 2007/1167 prescribe the content of the notice of intention to enforce it.

PROTECTION OF PROPERTY PENDING PROCEEDINGS

III CON [42]

131. Protection orders

The court, on the application of the creditor or owner under a regulated agreement, may make such orders as it thinks just for protecting any property of the creditor or owner, or property subject to any security, from damage or depreciation pending the determination of any proceedings under this Act, including orders restricting or prohibiting use of the property or giving directions as to its custody.

III CON [43]

132. Financial relief for hirer

(1) Where the owner under a regulated consumer hire agreement recovers possession of goods to which the agreement relates otherwise than by action, the hirer may apply to the court for an order that—

- (a) the whole or part of any sum paid by the hirer to the owner in respect of the goods shall be repaid, and
- (b) the obligation to pay the whole or part of any sum owed by the hirer to the owner in respect of the goods shall cease,

and if it appears to the court just to do so, having regard to the extent of the enjoyment of the goods by the hirer, the court shall grant the application in full or in part.

(2) Where in proceedings relating to a regulated consumer hire agreement the court makes an order for the delivery to the owner of goods to which the agreement relates the court may include in the order the like provision as may be made in an order under subsection (1).

III CON [44]

133. Hire-purchase etc agreements: special powers of court

(1) If, in relation to a regulated hire-purchase or conditional sale agreement, it appears to the court just to do so—

(a) on an application for an enforcement order or time order; or

(b) in an action brought by the creditor to recover possession of goods to which the agreement relates,

the court may—

(i) make an order (a "return order") for the return to the creditor of goods to which the agreement relates,

(ii) make an order (a "transfer order") for the transfer to the debtor of the creditor's title to certain goods to which the agreement relates ("the transferred goods"), and the return to the creditor of the remainder of the goods.

(2) In determining for the purposes of this section how much of the total price has been paid ("the paid-up sum"), the court may—

(a) treat any sum paid by the debtor, or owed by the creditor, in relation to the goods as part of the paid-up sum;

(b) deduct any sum owed by the debtor in relation to the goods (otherwise than as part of the total price) from the paid-up sum,

and make corresponding reductions in amounts so owed.

(3) Where a transfer order is made, the transferred goods shall be such of the goods to which the agreement relates as the court thinks just; but a transfer order shall be made only where the paid-up sum exceeds the part of the total price referable to the transferred goods by an amount equal to at least one-third of the unpaid balance of the total price.

(4) Notwithstanding the making of a return order or transfer order, the debtor may at any time before the goods enter the possession of the creditor, on payment of the balance of the total price and the fulfilment of any other necessary conditions, claim the goods ordered to be returned to the creditor.

(5) When, in pursuance of a time order or under this section, the total price of goods under a regulated hire-purchase agreement or regulated conditional sale agreement is paid and any other necessary conditions are fulfilled, the creditor's title to the goods vests in the debtor.

(6) If, in contravention of a return order or transfer order, any goods to which the order relates are not returned to the creditor, the court, on the application of the creditor, may—

(a) revoke so much of the order as relates to those goods, and

(b) order the debtor to pay the creditor the unpaid portion of so much of the total price as is referable to those goods.

(7) For the purposes of this section, the part of the total price referable to any goods is the part assigned to those goods by the agreement or (if no such assignment is made) the part determined by the court to be reasonable.

III CON [45]

134. Evidence of adverse detention in hire-purchase etc cases

(1) Where goods are comprised in a regulated hire-purchase agreement, regulated conditional sale agreement or regulated consumer hire agreement, and the creditor or owner—

(a) brings an action or makes an application to enforce a right to recover possession of the goods from the debtor or hirer, and

(b) proves that a demand for the delivery of the goods was included in the default notice under section 88 (5), or that, after the right to recover possession of the goods accrued but before the action was begun or the application was made, he made a request in writing to the debtor or hirer to surrender the goods,

then, for the purposes of the claim of the creditor or owner to recover possession of the goods, the possession of them by the debtor or hirer shall be deemed to be adverse to the creditor or owner.

(2) In subsection (1) "the debtor or hirer" includes a person in possession of the goods at any time between the debtor's or hirer's death and the grant of probate or administration, or (in Scotland) confirmation.

(3) Nothing in this section affects a claim for damages for conversion or (in Scotland) for delict.

SUPPLEMENTAL PROVISIONS AS TO ORDERS

III CON [46]

135. Power to impose conditions or suspend operation of order

(1) If it considers it just to do so, the court may in an order made by it in relation to a regulated agreement include provisions—

(a) making the operation of any term of the order conditional on the doing of specified acts by any party to the proceedings;

(b) suspending the operation of any term of the order either—

(i) until such time as the court subsequently directs, or

(ii) until the occurrence of a specified act or omission.

(2) The court shall not suspend the operation of a term requiring the delivery up of goods by any person unless satisfied that the goods are in his possession or control.

(3) In the case of a consumer hire agreement, the court shall not so use its powers under subsection (1)(b) as to extend the period for which, under the terms of the agreement, the hirer is entitled to possession of the goods to which the agreement relates.

(4) On the application of any person affected by a provision included under subsection (1), the court may vary the provision.

III CON [47]–III CON [51]

136. Power to vary agreements and securities

The court may in an order made by it under this Act include such provision as it considers just for amending any agreement or security in consequence of a term of the order.

III CON [47.1]

Use in conjunction with time orders For the use of the powers under this section in conjunction with the power to make time orders under s 129 see the notes to the latter section (see para **III CON [40.2]**).

UNFAIR RELATIONSHIPS

III CON [51A]

140A. Unfair relationships between creditors and debtors

(1) The court may make an order under section 140B in connection with a credit agreement if it determines that the relationship between the creditor and the debtor arising out of the agreement (or the agreement taken with any related agreement) is unfair to the debtor because of one or more of the following—

(a) any of the terms of the agreement or of any related agreement;

(b) the way in which the creditor has exercised or enforced any of his rights under the agreement or any related agreement;

(c) any other thing done (or not done) by, or on behalf of, the creditor (either before or after the making of the agreement or any related agreement).

(2) In deciding whether to make a determination under this section the court shall have regard to all matters it thinks relevant (including matters relating to the creditor and matters relating to the debtor).

(3) For the purposes of this section the court shall (except to the extent that it is not appropriate to do so) treat anything done (or not done) by, or on behalf of, or in relation to, an associate or a former associate of the creditor as if done (or not done) by, or on behalf of, or in relation to, the creditor.

(4) A determination may be made under this section in relation to a relationship notwithstanding that the relationship may have ended.

(5) An order under section 140B shall not be made in connection with a credit agreement which is an exempt agreement for the purposes of Chapter 14A of Part 2 of the Regulated Activities Order by virtue of article 60C(2) of that Order (regulated mortgage contracts and regulated home purchase plans).

III CON [51A.1]

Unfair relationship It has been held that a failure to provide information in accordance with s 77, when requested, does not, by itself, give rise to an unfair relationship for the purposes of s 140A: *Carey v HSBC Bank plc* [2009] EWHC 3417 (QB), (2010) Times, 25 January.

In a case where the lenders earned a commission from an insurance agency through which the borrower acquired a payment protection policy for £10,200, the court decided that the lenders and the borrower were not in an unfair relationship although the lenders had failed to disclose that the PPI contract earned them a commission of £8,887: *Harrison v Black Horse Ltd* [2011] EWCA Civ 1128, [2011] All ER (D) 112 (Oct). However, the Supreme Court reached the opposite conclusion in a later case: *Plevin v Paragon Personal Finance Ltd* [2014] UKSC 61, [2015] 1 All ER 625, [2014] 1 WLR 4222. It was there held that non-disclosure of commissions payable out of the claimant's PPI premium made her relationship with the defendants unfair and that *Harrison v Black Horse Ltd* was wrongly decided. Note, however, that the Supreme Court disagreed with the view of Briggs LJ that, in determining the fairness of the relationship, the court should take account of the acts and omissions of the PPI salesman although not an agent of the creditor. This is to be contrasted with case law on section 56 in favour of a deemed agency. See *British Credit Trust Ltd v Scotland* [2014] EWCA Civ 790, [2015] 1 All ER 708, [2015] 1 All ER (Comm) 401.

III CON [51A.2]

Penalty clauses Outside the statute the court's powers at common law and in equity include the grant of relief against unfair or oppressive bargains for example rescission of the contract. There is also power to disallow the enforcement of penalty clauses that require the payment of a penal sum on breach, which is in excess of the real loss suffered. The enforceability of a penalty clause depends on whether it is extortionate or extravagant, these being the main tests for striking it down: *Cavendish Square Holdings BV v El Makdessi and Beavis v ParkingEye Ltd* [2015] UKSC 67, 162 ConLR 1, [2015] All ER (D) 47 (Nov).

III CON [51B]

140B. Powers of court in relation to unfair relationships

(1) An order under this section in connection with a credit agreement may do one or more of the following—

(a) require the creditor, or any associate or former associate of his, to repay (in whole or in part) any sum paid by the debtor or by a surety by virtue of the agreement or any related agreement (whether paid to the creditor, the associate or the former associate or to any other person);

(b) require the creditor, or any associate or former associate of his, to do or not to do (or to cease doing) anything specified in the order in connection with the agreement or any related agreement;

(c) reduce or discharge any sum payable by the debtor or by a surety by virtue of the agreement or any related agreement;

(d) direct the return to a surety of any property provided by him for the purposes of a security;

(e) otherwise set aside (in whole or in part) any duty imposed on the debtor or on a surety by virtue of the agreement or any related agreement;

(f) alter the terms of the agreement or of any related agreement;

(g) direct accounts to be taken, or (in Scotland) an accounting to be made, between any persons.

(2) An order under this section may be made in connection with a credit agreement only—

(a) on an application made by the debtor or by a surety;

(b) at the instance of the debtor or a surety in any proceedings in any court to which the debtor and the creditor are parties, being proceedings to enforce the agreement or any related agreement; or

(c) at the instance of the debtor or a surety in any other proceedings in any court where the amount paid or payable under the agreement or any related agreement is relevant.

(3) An order under this section may be made notwithstanding that its effect is to place on the creditor, or any associate or former associate of his, a burden in respect of an advantage enjoyed by another person.

(4) An application under subsection (2)(a) may only be made—

(a) in England and Wales, to the county court;

(b) in Scotland, to the sheriff court;

(c) in Northern Ireland, to the High Court (subject to subsection (6)).

(5) In Scotland such an application may be made in the sheriff court for the district in which the debtor or surety resides or carries on business.

(6) In Northern Ireland such an application may be made to the county court if the credit agreement is an agreement under which the creditor provides the debtor with—

(a) fixed-sum credit not exceeding £15,000; or

(b) running-account credit on which the credit limit does not exceed £15,000.

(7) Without prejudice to any provision which may be made by rules of court made in relation to county courts in Northern Ireland, such rules may provide that an application made by virtue of subsection (6) may be made in the county court for the division in which the debtor or surety resides or carries on business.

(8) A party to any proceedings mentioned in subsection (2) shall be entitled, in accordance with rules of court, to have any person who might be the subject of an order under this section made a party to the proceedings.

(9) If, in any such proceedings, the debtor or a surety alleges that the relationship between the creditor and the debtor is unfair to the debtor, it is for the creditor to prove to the contrary.

III CON [51C]

140C. Interpretation of ss 140A and 140B

(1) In this section and in sections 140A and 140B "credit agreement" means any agreement between an individual (the "debtor") and any other person (the "creditor") by which the creditor provides the debtor with credit of any amount.

(2) References in this section and in sections 140A and 140B to the creditor or to the debtor under a credit agreement include—

(a) references to the person to whom his rights and duties under the agreement have passed by assignment or operation of law;

(b) where two or more persons are the creditor or the debtor, references to any one or more of those persons.

(3) The definition of "court" in section 189(1) does not apply for the purposes of sections 140A and 140B.

(4) References in sections 140A and 140B to an agreement related to a credit agreement (the "main agreement") are references to—

(a) a credit agreement consolidated by the main agreement;

(b) a linked transaction in relation to the main agreement or to a credit agreement within paragraph (a);

(c) a security provided in relation to the main agreement, to a credit agreement within paragraph (a) or to a linked transaction within paragraph (b).

(5) In the case of a credit agreement which is not a regulated consumer credit agreement, for the purposes of subsection (4) a transaction shall be treated as being a linked transaction in relation to that agreement if it would have been such a transaction had that agreement been a regulated consumer credit agreement.

(6) For the purposes of this section and section 140B the definitions of "security" and "surety" in section 189(1) apply (with any appropriate changes) in relation to—

(a) a credit agreement which is not a consumer credit agreement as if it were a consumer credit agreement; and

(b) a transaction which is a linked transaction by virtue of subsection (5).

(7) For the purposes of this section a credit agreement (the "earlier agreement") is consolidated by another credit agreement (the "later agreement") if—

(a) the later agreement is entered into by the debtor (in whole or in part) for purposes connected with debts owed by virtue of the earlier agreement; and

(b) at any time prior to the later agreement being entered into the parties to the earlier agreement included—

(i) the debtor under the later agreement; and

(ii) the creditor under the later agreement or an associate or a former associate of his.

(8) Further, if the later agreement is itself consolidated by another credit agreement (whether by virtue of this subsection or subsection (7)), then the earlier agreement is consolidated by that other agreement as well.

MISCELLANEOUS

III CON [52]

141. Jurisdiction and parties

(1) In England and Wales, the county court shall have jurisdiction to hear and determine—

(a) any action by the creditor or owner to enforce a regulated agreement or any security relating to it;

(b) any action to enforce any linked transaction against the debtor or hirer or his relative;

and such an action shall not be brought in any other court.

(2) Where an action or application is brought in the High Court which, by virtue of this Act, ought to have been brought in the county court it shall not be treated as improperly brought, but shall be transferred to the county court.

(5) Except as may be provided by rules of court, all the parties to a regulated agreement, and any surety, shall be made parties to any proceedings relating to the agreement.

III CON [52.1]

Transfer to county court Under the old rules the Senior Master of the Queen's Bench Division issued a practice direction which drew attention to the requirement to commence in, or transfer to, a county court any action to enforce a regulated agreement or linked transaction: Practice Direction: Consumer Credit Act 1974 (1988) 132 Sol Jo 186. It was later held that the exercise of the power to strike out depended on whether the conditions in County Courts Act 1984 s 40 (1)(b) (see para **II CCA [22]**) are satisfied: *Barclays Bank plc v Brooks* [1997] CCLR 60; *Restick v Crickmore* [1994] 2 All ER 112, [1994] 1 WLR 420, CA.

III CON [52.2]

Jurisdiction to enforce a judgment or order As to the exclusive jurisdiction of the county court to enforce judgments or orders by execution against goods, see the High Court and County Courts Jurisdiction Order 1991, SI 1991/724, art 8 (1)(b) (as amended) at para **II HCJ [7]**. Section 141 does not prevent service of a statutory demand: *Mills v Grove Securities Ltd* [1996] CCLR 74, CA.

III CON [53]

142. Power to declare rights of parties

(1) Where under any provision of this Act a thing can be done by a creditor or owner on an enforcement order only, and either—

(a) the court dismisses (except on technical grounds only) an application for an enforcement order, or

(b) where no such application has been made or such an application has been dismissed on technical grounds only, an interested party applies to the court for a declaration under this subsection,

the court may if it thinks just make a declaration that the creditor or owner is not entitled to do that thing, and thereafter no application for an enforcement order in respect of it shall be entertained.

(2) Where—

(a) a regulated agreement or linked transaction is cancelled under section 69 (1), or becomes subject to section 69 (2), or

(b) a regulated agreement is terminated under section 91,

and an interested party applies to the court for a declaration under this subsection, the court may make a declaration to that effect.

PART XI
ENFORCEMENT OF ACT

III CON [54]

172. Statements by creditor or owner to be binding

(1) A statement by a creditor or owner is binding on him if given under—

section 77 (1),
section 78 (1),
section 79 (1),
section 97 (1),
section 107 (1)(c),
section 108 (1)(c), or
section 109 (1)(c).

(2) Where a trader—

(a) gives a customer a notice in compliance with section 103 (1)(b), or

(b) gives a customer a notice under section 103 (1) asserting that the customer is not indebted to him under an agreement,

the notice is binding on the trader.

(3) Where in proceedings before any court—

(a) it is sought to rely on a statement or notice given as mentioned in subsection (1) or (2), and
(b) the statement or notice is shown to be incorrect,

the court may direct such relief (if any) to be given to the creditor or owner from the operation of subsection (1) or (2) as appears to the court to be just.

PART XII
SUPPLEMENTAL

III CON [55]

189. Definitions

(1) In this Act, unless the context otherwise requires—

"advertisement" includes every form of advertising, whether in a publication, by television or radio, by display of notices, signs, labels, showcards or goods, by distribution of samples, circulars, catalogues, price lists or other material, by exhibition of pictures, models or films, or in any other way, and references to the publishing of advertisements shall be construed accordingly;

"ancillary credit business" has the meaning given by section 145(1);

"antecedent negotiations" has the meaning given by section 56;

"appropriate method" means—

(a) post, or
(b) transmission in the form of an electronic communication in accordance with section 176A(1);

"associate" shall be construed in accordance with section 184;

"authorised business overdraft agreement" means a debtor-creditor agreement which provides authorisation in advance for the debtor to overdraw on a current account, where the agreement is entered into by the debtor wholly or predominantly for the purposes of the debtor's business (see subsection (2A));

"authorised non-business overdraft agreement" means a debtor-creditor agreement which provides authorisation in advance for the debtor to overdraw on a current account where—

(a) the credit must be repaid on demand or within three months, and
(b) the agreement is not entered into by the debtor wholly or predominantly for the purposes of the debtor's business (see subsection (2A));

"bill of sale" has the meaning given by section 4 of the Bills of Sale Act 1878 or, for Northern Ireland, by section 4 of the Bills of Sale (Ireland) Act 1879;

"building society" means a building society within the meaning of the Building Societies Act 1986;

"business" includes profession or trade, and references to a business apply subject to subsection (2);

"cancellable agreement" means a regulated agreement which, by virtue of section 67, may be cancelled by the debtor or hirer;

"canvass" shall be construed in accordance with sections 48 and 153;

"cash" includes money in any form;

"charity" means as respects England and Wales a charity registered under the Charities Act 1993 or an exempt charity (within the meaning of that Act), as respects Northern Ireland an institution or other organisation established for charitable purposes only ("organisation" including any persons administering a trust and "charitable" being construed in the same way as if it were contained in the Income Tax Acts) and as respects Scotland a body entered in the Scottish Charity Register;

"conditional sale agreement" means an agreement for the sale of goods or land under which the purchase price or part of it is payable by instalments, and the property in the goods or land is to remain in the seller (notwithstanding that the buyer is to be in possession of the goods or land) until such conditions as to the payment of instalments or otherwise as may be specified in the agreement are fulfilled;

"consumer credit agreement" has the meaning given by section 8, and includes a consumer credit agreement which is cancelled under section 69(1), or becomes subject to section 69(2), so far as the agreement remains in force;

"consumer credit business" means any business being carried on by a person so far as it comprises or relates to—

(a) the provision of credit by him, or

(b) otherwise his being a creditor,

under regulated consumer credit agreements;

"consumer hire agreement" has the meaning given by section 15;

"consumer hire business" means any business being carried on by a person so far as it comprises or relates to—

(a) the bailment or (in Scotland) the hiring of goods by him, or

(b) otherwise his being an owner,

under regulated consumer hire agreements;

"controller", in relation to a body corporate, means a person—

(a) in accordance with whose directions or instructions the directors of the body corporate or of another body corporate which is its controller (or any of them) are accustomed to act, or

(b) who, either alone or with any associate or associates, is entitled to exercise or control the exercise of, one third or more of the voting power at any general meeting of the body corporate or of another body corporate which is its controller;

"copy" shall be construed in accordance with section 180;

"court" means in relation to England and Wales the county court, in relation to Scotland the sheriff court and in relation to Northern Ireland the High Court or the county court;

"credit" shall be construed in accordance with section 9;

"credit-broker" means a person carrying on a business of credit brokerage;

"credit brokerage" has the meaning given by section 145(2);

"credit information services" is to be read in accordance with section 145(7B);

"credit intermediary" has the meaning given by section 160A;

"credit limit" has the meaning given by section 10(2);

"creditor" means "(except in relation to green deal plans: see instead section 189B(2)) the person providing credit under a consumer credit agreement or the person to whom his rights and duties under the agreement have passed by assignment or operation of law, and in relation to a prospective consumer credit agreement, includes the prospective creditor;

"credit reference agency" is to be read in accordance with section 145(8);

"credit-sale agreement" means an agreement for the sale of goods, under which the purchase price or part of it is payable by instalments, but which is not a conditional sale agreement;

"credit-token" has the meaning given by section 14(1);

"credit-token agreement" means a regulated agreement for the provision of credit in connection with the use of a credit-token;

"debt-adjusting" has the meaning given by section 145(5);

"debt administration" has the meaning given by section 145(7A);

"debt-collecting" has the meaning given by section 145(7);

"debt-counselling" has the meaning given by section 145(6);

"debtor" means "(except in relation to green deal plans: see instead section 189B(3)) the individual receiving credit under a consumer credit agreement or the person to whom his rights and duties under the agreement have passed by assignment or operation of law, and in relation to a prospective consumer credit agreement includes the prospective debtor;

"debtor-creditor agreement" has the meaning given by section 13;

"debtor-creditor-supplier agreement" has the meaning given by section 12;

"default notice" has the meaning given by section 87(1);

"default sum" has the meaning given by section 187A;

"deposit" means any sum payable by a debtor or hirer by way of deposit or down-payment, or credited or to be credited to him on account of any deposit or down-payment, whether the sum is to be or has been paid to the creditor or owner or any other person, or is to be or has been discharged by a payment of money or a transfer or delivery of goods or by any other means;

"documents" includes information recorded in any form;

"electric line" has the meaning given by the Electricity Act 1989 or, for Northern Ireland, the Electricity (Northern Ireland) Order 1992;

"electronic communication" means an electronic communication within the meaning of the Electronic Communications Act 2000 (c 7);

"embodies" and related words shall be construed in accordance with subsection (4);

"enforcement authority" has the meaning given by section 161(1);

"enforcement order" means an order under section 65(1), 105(7)(a) or (b), 111(2) or 124(1) or (2);

"executed agreement" means a document, signed by or on behalf of the parties, embodying the terms of a regulated agreement, or such of them as have been reduced to writing;

"FCA" means the Financial Conduct Authority;

"finance" means to finance wholly or partly and "financed" and "refinanced" shall be construed accordingly;

"file" and "copy of the file" have the meanings given by section 158(5);

"fixed-sum credit" has the meaning given by section 10(1)(b);

"friendly society" means a society registered under the Friendly Societies Acts 1896 to 1971 [. . .];

"future arrangements" shall be construed in accordance with section 187;

"the GDPR" has the same meaning as in Parts 5 to 7 of the Data Protection Act 2018 (see section 3(10), (11) and (14) of that Act);

"give", means, deliver or send by an appropriate method to;

"goods" has the meaning given by section 61(1) of the Sale of Goods Act 1979;

"green deal plan" has the meaning given by section 1 of the Energy Act 2011;

"High Court" means Her Majesty's High Court of Justice, or the Court of Session in Scotland or the High Court of Justice in Northern Ireland;

"hire-purchase agreement" means an agreement, other than a conditional sale agreement, under which—

(a) goods are bailed or (in Scotland) hired in return for periodical payments by the person to whom they are bailed or hired, and

(b) the property in the goods will pass to that person if the terms of the agreement are complied with and one or more of the following occurs—

(i) the exercise of an option to purchase by that person,

(ii) the doing of any other specified act by any party to the agreement,

(iii) the happening of any other specified event;

"hirer" means the individual to whom goods are bailed or (in Scotland) hired under a consumer hire agreement, or the person to whom his rights and duties under the agreement have passed by assignment or operation of law, and in relation to a prospective consumer hire agreement includes the prospective hirer;

"individual" includes—

(a) a partnership consisting of two or three persons not all of whom are bodies corporate; and

(b) an unincorporated body of persons which does not consist entirely of bodies corporate and is not a partnership;

"installation" means—

(a) the installing of any electric line or any gas or water pipe,

(b) the fixing of goods to the premises where they are to be used, and the alteration of premises to enable goods to be used on them,

(c) where it is reasonably necessary that goods should be constructed or erected on the premises where they are to be used, any work carried out for the purpose of constructing or erecting them on those premises;

"judgment" includes an order or decree made by any court;

"land", includes an interest in land, and in relation to Scotland includes heritable subjects of whatever description;

"land improvement company" means an improvement company as defined by section 7 of the Improvement of Land Act 1899;

"land mortgage" includes any security charged on land;

"linked transaction" has the meaning given by section 19(1);

"local authority", in relation to England [. . .], means [. . .] a county council, a London borough council, a district council, the Common Council of the City of London, or the Council of Isles of Scilly, in relation to Wales means a county council or a county borough council, and in relation to Scotland, means a council constituted under section 2 of the Local Government etc (Scotland) Act 1994, and, in relation to Northern Ireland, means a district council;

"modifying agreement" has the meaning given by section 82(2);

"multiple agreement" has the meaning given by section 18(1);

"negotiator" has the meaning given by section 56(1);

"non-commercial agreement" means a consumer credit agreement or a consumer hire agreement not made by the creditor or owner in the course of a business carried on by him;

"notice" means notice in writing;

"notice of cancellation" has the meaning given by section 69(1);

"open-end" in relation to a consumer credit agreement, means of no fixed duration;

"owner" means a person who bails or (in Scotland) hires out goods under a consumer hire agreement or the person to whom his rights and duties under the agreement have passed by assignment or operation of law, and in relation to a prospective consumer hire agreement, includes the prospective bailor or persons from whom the goods are to be hired;

"pawn" means any article subject to a pledge;

"pawn-receipt" has the meaning given by section 114;

"pawnee" and "pawnor" include any person to whom the rights and duties of the original pawnee or the original pawnor, as the case may be, have passed by assignment or operation of law;

"payment" includes tender;

"pledge" means the pawnee's rights over an article taken in pawn;

"prescribed" means prescribed by regulations made by the Secretary of State;

"pre-existing arrangements" shall be construed in accordance with section 187;

"principal agreement" has the meaning given by section 19(1);

"protected goods" has the meaning given by section 90(7);

"redemption period" has the meaning given by section 116(3);

"Regulated Activities Order" means the Financial Services and Markets Act 2000 (Regulated Activities) Order 2001;

"regulated agreement" means a consumer credit agreement which is a regulated agreement (within the meaning of section 8(3)) or a consumer hire agreement which is a regulated agreement (within the meaning of section 15(2));

"regulations" means regulations made by the Treasury;

"relative", except in section 184, means a person who is an associate by virtue of section 184(1);

"representation" includes any condition or warranty, and any other statement or undertaking, whether oral or in writing;

"residential renovation agreement" means a consumer credit agreement entered into on or after 21st March 2016—

(a) which is unsecured; and

(b) the purpose of which is the renovation of residential property, as described in Article 2(2a) of Directive 2008/48/EC of the European Parliament and of the Council of 23rd April 2008 on credit agreements for consumers.

"restricted-use credit agreement" and "restricted-use credit" have the meanings given by section 11(1);

"rules of court", in relation to Northern Ireland means, in relation to the High Court, rules made under section 7 of the Northern Ireland Act 1962, and, in relation to any other court, rules made by the authority having for the time being power to make rules regulating the practice and procedure in that court;

"running-account credit" shall be construed in accordance with section 10;

"security", in relation to an actual or prospective consumer credit agreement or consumer hire agreement, or any linked transaction, means a mortgage, charge, pledge, bond, debenture, indemnity, guarantee, bill, note or other right provided by the debtor or hirer, or at his request (express or implied), to secure the carrying out of the obligations of the debtor or hirer under the agreement;

"security instrument" has the meaning given by section 105(2);

"serve on" means deliver or send by post to;

"signed" shall be construed in accordance with subsection (3);

"small agreement" has the meaning given by section 17(1), and "small" in relation to an agreement within any category shall be construed accordingly;

"supplier" has the meaning given by section 11(1)(b) or 12(c) or 13(c) or, in relation to an agreement falling within section 11(1)(a), means the creditor, and includes a person to whom the rights and duties of a supplier (as so defined) have passed by assignment or operation of law, or (in relation to a prospective agreement) the prospective supplier;

"surety" means the person by whom any security is provided, or the person to whom his rights and duties in relation to the security have passed by assignment or operation of law;

"technical grounds" shall be construed in accordance with subsection (5);

"time order" has the meaning given by section 129(1);

"total charge for credit" has the meaning given by section 20;

"total price" means the total sum payable by the debtor under a hire-purchase agreement or a conditional sale agreement, including any sum payable on the exercise of an option to purchase, but excluding any sum payable as a penalty or as compensation or damages for a breach of the agreement;

"unexecuted agreement" means a document embodying the terms of a prospective regulated agreement, or such of them as it is intended to reduce to writing;

"unrestricted-use credit agreement" and "unrestricted-use credit" have the meanings given by section 11(2);

"working day" means any day other than—

(a) Saturday or Sunday,

(b) Christmas Day or Good Friday,

(c) a bank holiday within the meaning given by section 1 of the Banking and Financial Dealings Act 1971.

(1A) In sections 70(4), 73(4) and 75(2) . . . "costs", in relation to proceedings in Scotland, means expenses.

(2) A person is not to be treated as carrying on a particular type of business merely because occasionally he enters into transactions belonging to a business of that type.

(2A) For the purpose of the definitions of "authorised business overdraft agreement" and "authorised non-business overdraft agreement" article 60C(5) and (6) of the Regulated Activities Order applies.

(3) Any provision of this Act requiring a document to be signed is complied with by a body corporate if the document is sealed by that body.

This subsection does not apply to Scotland.

(4) A document embodies a provision if the provision is set out either in the document itself or in another document referred to in it.

(5) An application dismissed by the court or the FCA shall, if the court or the FCA so certifies, be taken to be dismissed on technical grounds only.

(6) Except in so far as the context otherwise requires, any reference in this Act to an enactment shall be construed as a reference to that enactment as amended by or under any other enactment, including this Act.

(7) In this Act, except where otherwise indicated—

(a) a reference to a numbered Part, section or Schedule is a reference to the Part or section of, or the Schedule to, this Act so numbered, and

(b) a reference in a section to a numbered subsection is a reference to the subsection of that section so numbered, and

(c) a reference in a section, subsection or Schedule to a numbered paragraph is a reference to the paragraph of that section, subsection or Schedule so numbered.

Amendment *Section 189 is shown as amended by the Financial Services and Markets Act 2000 (Regulated Activities) (Amendment) (No 2) Order 2013, SI 2013/1881 with effect from 26 July 2013 (for certain purposes) and 1 April 2014 (for remaining purposes). For transitional provisions see Part 8 of SI 2013/1881.*

III CON [55.1]

EU Directive change This section has been expanded to give effect to EU Directive 2008/448/EC, and SI 2010/1010, in respect of agreements made on or after 1 February 2011.

III CON [55.2]

The Court Extensive civil jurisdiction is conferred by this Act on the county court; and references to "the court" are to be interpreted accordingly. As regards the enforcement of money judgments, the High Court and County Courts Jurisdiction Order 1991, SI 1991/724, article 8, as amended, provides that a money judgment, arising out of proceedings on a regulated agreement may be enforced only in the county court: see **II HCJ [7]**.

III CON [55A]

189B. Green deal plans

(1) A green deal plan is to be treated as a consumer credit agreement for the purposes of this Act if (and only if)—

(a) the property in relation to the plan is a domestic property at the time when the plan is commenced, or

(b) if paragraph (a) does not apply, the occupier or owner of the property who makes the arrangement for the plan is an individual.

(2) In the application of this Act to a green deal consumer credit agreement—

(a) the creditor is to be treated as being—

(i) the green deal provider (within the meaning of Chapter 1 of Part 1 of the Energy Act 2011) for the plan, or

(ii) the person to whom the provider's rights and duties under the plan have passed by assignment or operation of law,

(b) credit is to be treated as advanced under the agreement of an amount equal to the amount of the improvement costs, and

(c) the advance of credit is to be treated as made on the completion of the installation of the energy efficiency improvements to the property (but this paragraph is subject to any term of the green deal plan providing that part of the advance is to be treated as made on completion of any part of the installation).

(3) A reference in a provision of this Act listed in the first column of the table in Schedule 2A to the debtor is, in the application of the provision in relation to a green deal consumer credit agreement, to be read as a reference to—

(a) a person who at the relevant time falls (or fell) within the description or descriptions specified in the corresponding entry in the second column of the table, or

(b) if more than one description is specified and at the relevant time different persons fall (or fell) within the descriptions, each of those persons,

and except as provided by this subsection, a person is not and is not to be treated as the debtor in relation to the agreement.

(4) Where by virtue of subsection (3) a reference to the debtor in a listed provision is to be read as a reference to the improver, it is to be assumed in applying the provision in relation to the green deal consumer credit agreement that the improver is provided with credit on the terms of the green deal plan.

(5) Where by virtue of subsection (3) a reference to the debtor in a listed provision is to be read as a reference to a person who is not the improver, it is to be assumed in applying the provision in relation to the green deal consumer credit agreement—

(a) if the provision in question is any of sections 94 to 97A (which together make provision about early payment by the debtor), that the person is provided with credit on terms that the person is liable to pay all the instalments under the green deal plan;

(b) in any other case, that the person is provided with credit on those terms of the green deal plan that bind or benefit the person for any period by virtue of regulations under section 6(2)(b) of the Energy Act 2011.

(6) References in this section and in Schedule 2A to the "improver", "first bill payer", "current bill payer" and "previous bill payer" are to be read as follows—

(a) a person is the "improver" if the person—

(i) is the owner or occupier of the property, and

(ii) is the person who makes (or has made or proposes to make) the arrangement for the green deal plan,

but this is subject to section 189C(4) in cases where the person is not an individual;

(b) a person is the "first bill payer" if the person is liable to pay the energy bills for the property at the time when the green deal plan is commenced;

(c) a person is the "current bill payer" if the person is liable by virtue of section 1(6)(a) of the Energy Act 2011 to pay instalments under the plan as a result of being for the time being liable to pay the energy bills for the property;

(d) a person is a "previous bill payer" if, as a result of previously falling within paragraph (c) for an earlier period, the person has an outstanding payment liability under the plan in respect of that period.

(7) References in this Act to a prospective consumer credit agreement, and references to the creditor and debtor in relation to such an agreement, are to be read in accordance with this section in the case of prospective green deal consumer credit agreements.

(8) In this section and in section 189C—

"domestic property" means a building or part of a building that is occupied as a dwelling or (if not occupied) is intended to be occupied as a dwelling;

"energy bill" has the same meaning as in section 1 of the Energy Act 2011;

"energy efficiency improvements" has the meaning given by section 2(4) of the Energy Act 2011;

"green deal consumer credit agreement" means a green deal plan that is to be treated as a consumer credit agreement for the purposes of this Act by virtue of subsection (1);

"improvement costs", in relation to a green deal plan, are the costs of the energy efficiency improvements to the property which are to be paid by instalments under the plan after the time when credit is to be treated as being advanced by virtue of subsection (2) (but ignoring any interest or other charges for credit in determining those costs);

"listed provision" means a provision of this Act listed in the first column of Schedule 2A;

"occupier" and "owner" have the same meanings as in Chapter 1 of Part 1 of the Energy Act 2011;

"property", in relation to a green deal plan, means the property to which the energy efficiency improvements under the plan are or are intended to be made.

III CON [55A.1]

Green Deal The new ss 189B and 189C and Schedule 2A were inserted, with effect from 28 February 2014, by the Consumer Credit Act 1974 (Green Deal) (Amendment) Order 2014, SI 2014/436. They provide for the circumstances in which a green deal plan is to be treated as a consumer credit agreement and the persons who are to be treated as the creditor and the debtor in relation to a green deal plan. The interpretation provisions in the new Schedule 2A provide for references to "debtor" to be construed as references to the improver or, sometimes, the current bill payer.

III CON [55A.2]

Temporary provisions For the period between 27 February and 1 April 2014, the new s 189B and Schedule 2A are to be read as if references to "debtor" were to the improver or to various categories of bill payer. For the detailed glossing of the text see article 6 of the Consumer Credit 1974 (Green Deal (Amendment) Order 2014, SI 2014/436.

III CON [55B]

189C. Section 189B: supplementary provision

(1) A green deal consumer credit agreement is to be treated—

(a) as an agreement for fixed-sum credit within the meaning of section 10(1)(b);

(b) as a credit agreement for the purposes of sections 140A and 140B (and section 140C(1) is to be read accordingly).

(2) Where a green deal consumer credit agreement is a regulated agreement within the meaning of this Act (see section 8(3)), it is to be treated as a restricted-use agreement that falls within section 11(1)(a).

(3) Sections 81, 140C(2) and 176(5) do not apply in the case of a green deal consumer credit agreement.

(4) A person who is not an individual is to be treated as the improver in relation to any listed provision in the first column of the table in Schedule 2A only if the corresponding entry in the second column of the table so specifies.

(5) For the purposes of section 189B—

(a) a green deal plan is commenced when—

(i) the occupier or owner of the property signs in the prescribed manner a document in relation to the plan in accordance with section 61(1) (requirements as to form and content of regulated agreements), or

(ii) if the occupier or owner of the property does not sign such a document, the green deal plan is made;

(b) a person is liable to pay the energy bills for a property at any time if the person would be treated as the bill payer for the property at that time for the purposes of Chapter 1 of Part 1 of the Energy Act 2011 (see section 2(3) and (10)).

SCHEDULE 2A
MEANING OF "DEBTOR" IN RELATION TO GREEN DEAL AGREEMENTS

III CON [55C]

Section of this Act	*References to "debtor" are to be read as references to the . . .*
Section 19	—improver
Section 55	—improver
Section 55C	—improver —first bill payer
Section 56	—improver —first bill payer
Section 57	—improver
Section 59	—improver
Sections 60 and 61	—improver (including an improver who is not an individual)
Section 61A	—improver
Sections 62, 63, 64	—improver
Section 65	—improver

	—current bill payer —previous bill payer
Section 66A	—improver
Sections 67, 68, 69, 70, 71, 72, 73	—improver
Section 75A	—improver
Sections 76 and 77	—current bill payer —previous bill payer
Section 77A	—current bill payer
Section 77B	—improver —current bill payer
Section 78A	—improver —current bill payer
Section 80	—improver
Section 82	—improver —current bill payer —previous bill payer
Section 86	—current bill payer —previous bill payer
Section 86E	—current bill payer —previous bill payer
Section 86F	—current bill payer —previous bill payer
Section 87	—current bill payer —previous bill payer
Section 89	—current bill payer —previous bill payer
Section 93	—current bill payer —previous bill payer
Sections 94, 95, 95A, 95B, 96, 97, 97A	—improver —current bill payer
Section 98	—current bill payer —previous bill payer
Sections 102, 103, 105, 107, 110, 113	—improver
Sections 123, 124	—current bill payer —previous bill payer
Section 127	—improver —current bill payer —previous bill payer
Sections 128, 129, 130, 130A	—current bill payer —previous bill payer
Sections 140A, 140B, 140C	—improver —current bill payer

	—previous bill payer
Section 141(1), (2), (3A), (3B)	—improver —current bill payer —previous bill payer
Section 157	—improver —first bill payer
Section 173	—improver —current bill payer —previous bill payer
Section 179	—improver —first bill payer —current bill payer —previous bill payer
Section 185(1), (2), (2A), (2B), (2C), (2D), (4)	—current bill payer
Section 187A	—current bill payer —previous bill payer
Section 189(1), so far as relating to definition of "security"	—improver

UNFAIR CONTRACT TERMS ACT 1977

(c 50)

Amendments Editorial Note: As regards contracts made on or after 1 October 2015, amendments to the Act made by Schedule 4 to the Consumer Rights Act 2015 have effect and are included in the text below.

III CON [56]

1. Scope of Part 1

(1) For the purposes of this Part of this Act, "negligence" means the breach—

(a) of any obligation, arising from the express or implied terms of a contract, to take reasonable care or exercise reasonable skill in the performance of the contract;

(b) of any common law duty to take reasonable care or exercise reasonable skill (but not any stricter duty);

(c) of the common duty of care imposed by the Occupiers' Liability Act 1957 or the Occupiers' Liability Act (Northern Ireland) 1957.

(2) This Part of this Act is subject to Part III; and in relation to contracts, the operation of sections 2, 3 and 7 is subject to the exceptions made by Schedule 1.

(3) In the case of both contract and tort, sections 2 to 7 apply (except where the contrary is stated in section 6 (4)) only to business liability, that is liability for breach of obligations or duties arising—

(a) from things done or to be done by a person in the course of a business (whether his own business or another's); or

(b) from the occupation of premises used for business purposes of the occupier;

and references to liability are to be read accordingly but liability of an occupier of premises for breach of an obligation or duty towards a person obtaining access to the premises for recreational or educational purposes, being liability for loss or damage suffered by reason of the dangerous state of the premises, is not a business liability of the occupier unless granting that person such access for the purposes concerned falls within the business purposes of the occupier.

(4) In relation to any breach of duty or obligation, it is immaterial for any purpose of this Part of this Act whether the breach was inadvertent or intentional, or whether liability for it arises directly or vicariously.

III CON [56.1]

Contracts outside the scope The effect of sub-s (2) is to exclude international supply contracts (s 26), foreign contracts where English law has been chosen to apply (s 27), contract terms authorised or approved by statute, treaty or competent authority (ss 28 and 29) and contracts in Sch 1, in particular those concerning insurance, land transactions, company formation, securities, charterparties and carriage by sea. An anti set-off provision in a lease was held to be outside the scope of the Act in *Electricity Supply Nominees Ltd v IAF Group plc* [1993] 3 All ER 372, [1993] 1 WLR 1059; and the Court of Appeal reached the same conclusion in proceedings between tenant and management company: *Unchained Growth III plc v Granby Village (Manchester) Management Co Ltd* [2000] 1 WLR 739, CA. A provision in a contract of employment relating to share options was similarly held to be excluded in *Micklefield v SAC Technology Ltd* [1991] 1 All ER 275, [1990] 1 WLR 1002.

A contract for the hire of goods where it was contemplated that the goods would be carried from one territory to another has been held to be an international supply contract for the purposes of s 26: *Trident Turboprop (Dublin) Ltd v First Flight Couriers Ltd* [2009] EWCA Civ 290, [2009] 2 All ER (Comm) 1050, [2009] 3 WLR 861, with the result that clauses excluding liability for contractual breach or misrepresentation were found to be outside the scope of the 1977 Act.

III CON [56.2]

Unfair Terms in Consumer Contracts Regulations The Unfair Terms in Consumer Contracts Regulations 1999, SI 1999/2083 replace those of 1994 (SI 1994/3159). They protect individuals who contract as consumers against having their rights removed or restricted by unfair terms. Land transactions are not excluded. The Regulations overlap the area covered by the Act, being narrower in some respects but wider in others. Although revoked by the Consumer Rights Act 2015 they continue to apply to contracts made before 1 October 2015: see General Notes on the Regulations at **III CON [106]**.

The Regulations have now been replaced by the Consumer Rights Act 2015 at **III CON [183]** as regards contracts made with consumers after 1 October 2015.

III CON [56.3]

Precedent Reliance on the Unfair Contract Terms Act 1977 but not the Unfair Terms in Consumer Contracts Regulations 1999 is pleaded in a precedent at **BCCP K[2514]**.

III CON [57]

2. Negligence liability

(1) A person cannot by reference to any contract term or to a notice given to persons generally or to particular persons exclude or restrict his liability for death or personal injury resulting from negligence.

(2) In the case of other loss or damage, a person cannot so exclude or restrict his liability for negligence except in so far as the term or notice satisfies the requirement of reasonableness.

(3) Where a contract term or notice purports to exclude or restrict liability for negligence a person's agreement to or awareness of it is not of itself to be taken as indicating his voluntary acceptance of any risk.

(4) This section does not apply to—

(a) a term in a consumer contract, or

(b) a notice to the extent that it is a consumer notice,

(but see the provision made about such contracts and notices in sections 62 and 65 of the Consumer Rights Act 2015).

III CON [57.1]

Situations within the section The effect of s 2 is to bring under scrutiny all clauses which exclude or restrict liability for negligence in the performance of services. This could include a surveyor making a report to a local authority but owing a duty of care to a house-buyer: *Smith v Eric S Bush (a firm)*; *Harris v Wyre Forest District Council* [1990] 1 AC 831, [1989] 2 All ER 514, HL. Also, in *Phillips Products Ltd v Hyland* [1987] 2 All ER 620, [1987] 1 WLR 659n, CA the Court applied s 2 (2) as striking down a clause whereby the suppliers of plant and a driver under a contract of hire excluded their liability for negligence on the part of the driver. A contract of employment which required a junior doctor to work excessive overtime to the prejudice of his health but at his own risk would be within the scope of s 2: *Johnstone v Bloomsbury Health Authority* [1992] QB 333, [1991] 2 All ER 293, CA.

Subject to reasonableness, a disclaimer notice may be effective in excluding or restricting liability under the Misrepresentation Act 1967 for pre-contractual misrepresentations: *Taberna Europe CDO II plc v Selskabet af 1 September 2008 A/S (in bankruptcy)* (2017) Times, 1 February, CA.

III CON [57.2]

Situations outside the section The only duty situations which are unaffected are those put outside the scope of Part 1 by s 1(2): (see para **III CON [56.1]**).

III CON [57.3]

The requirement of reasonableness See para **III CON [66]**.

III CON [57.4]

Company schemes of arrangement It has been held that a scheme of arrangement approved by the court under s 425 of the Companies Act 1985, at **III COM [35]**, is not rendered ineffective by s 2(1), as regards provisions in respect of liability for personal injury claims, since such a scheme is not a contract or notice for the purposes of that subsection: *Re Cape plc* [2006] EWHC 1316 (Ch), [2006] 3 All ER 1222.

III CON [58]

3. Liability arising in contract

(1) This section applies as between contracting parties where one of them deals on the other's written standard terms of business.

(2) As against that party, the other cannot by reference to any contract term—

(a) when himself in breach of contract, exclude or restrict any liability of his in respect of the breach; or

(b) claim to be entitled—

(i) to render a contractual performance substantially different from that which was reasonably expected of him, or

(ii) in respect of the whole or any part of his contractual obligation, to render no performance at all,

except in so far as (in any of the cases mentioned above in this subsection) the contract term satisfies the requirement of reasonableness.

(3) This section does not apply to a term in a consumer contract (but see the provision made about such contracts in section 62 of the Consumer Rights Act 2015).

III CON [58.1]

Requirement of reasonableness See para **III CON [66]**.

III CON [58.2]

Dealing as consumer See para **III CON [67]**.

An employee who receives a bonus or commission as a form of wages under a personal contract for services has been held not to be dealing as a consumer; and a condition of payment that he or she should be employed on the pay date has been held to be outside the scope of s 3: *Keen v Commerzbank AG* [2006] EWCA Civ 1536, [2006] All ER (D) 239 (Nov).

III CON [58.3]

Written standard terms In the case of a written contract made between companies in the course of business the claimant company cannot rely on s 3 unless it is established that the contract is on standard terms habitually used: *British Fermentation Products Ltd v Compair Reavell Ltd* [1999] 2 All ER (Comm) 389. It is not enough that a standard terms contract is sometimes used or was used for the transaction in question; and a substantial variation in the terms may mean that the terms cannot be relied on as 'standard': *African Export-Import Bank v Shebah Exploration and Production Company Ltd* (2017) Times, 1 September, CA.

A guarantee signed by a company director in respect of a loan to the company has been held to be within s 3 because the guarantee was in the bank's standard terms: *Governor and Company of the Bank of Scotland v Reuben Singh* (2005) QBD 17 June, in which it was also held that the terms were not unreasonable and were therefore binding. See also the decision in *Barclays Bank plc v Alfons Kufner* [2008] EWHC 2319, [2008] All ER (D) 102 (Oct) to the same effect.

III CON [59]

4. ***Unreasonable indemnity clauses***

Repealed.

III CON [60]

5. ***"Guarantee" of consumer goods***

Repealed.

III CON [61]

6. Sale and hire-purchase

(1) Liability for breach of the obligations arising from—

(a) section 12 of the Sale of Goods Act 1979 (seller's implied undertakings as to title, etc);

(b) section 8 of the Supply of Goods (Implied Terms) Act 1973 (the corresponding thing in relation to hire-purchase),

cannot be excluded or restricted by reference to any contract term.

(1A) Liability for breach of the obligations arising from—

(a) section 13, 14 or 15 of the 1979 Act (seller's implied undertakings as to conformity of goods with description or sample, or as to their quality or fitness for a particular purpose);

(b) section 9, 10 or 11 of the 1973 Act (the corresponding things in relation to hire purchase), cannot be excluded or restricted by reference to a contract term except in so far as the term satisfies the requirement of reasonableness.

(2) ...

(3) ...

(4) The liabilities referred to in this section are not only the business liabilities defined by section 1 (3), but include those arising under any contract of sale of goods or hire-purchase agreement.

(5) This section does not apply to a consumer contract (but see the provision made about such contracts in section 31 of the Consumer Rights Act 2015).

III CON [61.1]

Sale of Goods Act 1979 See paras **III CON [70]–III CON [81]**.

III CON [61.2]

Supply of Goods (Implied Terms) Act 1973 See paras **III CON [16]–III CON [23]**.

III CON [62]

7. Miscellaneous contracts under which goods pass

(1) Where the possession or ownership of goods passes under or in pursuance of a contract not governed by the law of sale of goods or hire-purchase, subsections (2) to (4) below apply as regards the effect (if any) to be given to contract terms excluding or restricting liability for breach of obligation arising by implication of law from the nature of the contract.

(1A) Liability in respect of the goods' correspondence with description or sample, or their quality or fitness for any particular purpose, cannot be excluded or restricted by reference to such a term except in so far as the term satisfies the requirement of reasonableness.

(2) ...

(3) ...

(3A) Liability for breach of the obligations arising under section 2 of the Supply of Goods and Services Act 1982 (implied terms about title etc in certain contracts for the transfer of the property in goods) cannot be excluded or restricted by references to any such term.

(4) Liability in respect of—

(a) the right to transfer ownership of the goods, or give possession; or

(b) the assurance of quiet possession to a person taking goods in pursuance of the contract,

cannot (in a case to which subsection (3A) above does not apply) be excluded or restricted by reference to any such term except in so far as the term satisfies the requirement of reasonableness.

(4A) This section does not apply to a consumer contract (but see the provision made about such contracts in section 31 of the Consumer Rights Act 2015).

(5) ...

III CON [63]

8. Misrepresentation

If a contract contains a term which would exclude or restrict—

(a) any liability to which a party to a contract may be subject by reason of any misrepresentation made by him before the contract was made; or

(b) any remedy available to another party to the contract by reason of such a misrepresentation,

that term shall be of no effect except in so far as it satisfies the requirement of reasonableness as stated in section 11 (1) of the Unfair Contract Terms Act 1977; and it is for those claiming that the term satisfies that requirement to show that it does.

III CON [64]

9. *Effect of breach*

Repealed.

III CON [65]

10. Evasion by means of secondary contract

A person is not bound by any contract term prejudicing or taking away rights of his which arise under, or in connection with the performance of, another contract, so far as those rights extend to the enforcement of another's liability which this Part of this Act prevents that other from excluding or restricting.

III CON [65.1]

Enforcement of another's liability The reference to "another" is to someone other than the contracting parties and s 10 has no effect on contracts which settle or compromise disputes about their liabilities to each other. The policy of the Act is to prohibit or restrict exemption from prospective liability, not past: *Tudor Grange Holdings Ltd v Citibank NA* [1992] Ch 53, [1991] 4 All ER 1.

III CON [66]

11. The "reasonableness" test

(1) In relation to a contract term, the requirement of reasonableness for the purposes of this Part of this Act, section 3 of the Misrepresentation Act 1967 and section 3 of the Misrepresentation Act (Northern Ireland) 1967 is that the term shall have been a fair and reasonable one to be included having regard to the circumstances which were, or ought reasonably to have been, known to or in the contemplation of the parties when the contract was made.

(2) In determining for the purposes of section 6 or 7 above whether a contract term satisfies the requirement of reasonableness, regard shall be had in particular to the matters specified in Schedule 2 to this Act; but this subsection does not prevent the court or arbitrator from holding, in accordance with any rule of law, that a term which purports to exclude or restrict any relevant liability is not a term of the contract.

(3) In relation to a notice (not being a notice having contractual effect), the requirement of reasonableness under this Act is that it should be fair and reasonable to allow reliance on it, having regard to all the circumstances obtaining when the liability arose or (but for the notice) would have arisen.

(4) Where by reference to a contract term or notice a person seeks to restrict liability to a specified sum of money, and the question arises (under this or any other Act) whether the term or notice satisfies the requirement of reasonableness, regard shall be had in particular (but without prejudice to subsection (2) above in the case of contract terms) to—

- (a) the resources which he could expect to be available to him for the purpose of meeting the liability should it arise; and
- (b) how far it was open to him to cover himself by insurance.

(5) It is for those claiming that a contract term or notice satisfies the requirement of reasonableness to show that it does.

III CON [66.1]

Matters specified in Schedule 2 Sch 2 sets out guidelines as follows:

The matters to which regard is to be had in particular for the purposes of ss 6 (3), 7 (3) and (4), 20 and 21 are any of the following which appear to be relevant:

- (a) the strength of the bargaining positions of the parties relative to each other, taking into account (among other things) alternative means by which the customer's requirements could have been met;

(b) whether the customer received an inducement to agree to the term, or in accepting it had an opportunity of entering into a similar contract with other persons, but without having to accept a similar term;
(c) whether the customer knew or ought reasonably to have known of the existence and extent of the term (having regard, among other things, to any custom of the trade and any previous course of dealing between the parties);
(d) where the term excludes or restricts any relevant liability if some condition is not complied with, whether it was reasonable at the time of the contract to expect that compliance with that condition would be practicable;
(e) whether the goods were manufactured, processed or adapted to the special order of the customer.

III CON [66.2]

Businesses dealing at arms' length In *WRM Group Ltd v Wood* [1998] CLC 189, CA it was held that an agreed limit of £300,000 on rights of set-off for breach or misrepresentation was fairly negotiated at arms' length and should be upheld. The court reached the same result in respect of a "no set-off" clause in a company director's guarantee of the company's borrowing from a bank where he had taken legal advice before signing: *Governor and Company of the Bank of Scotland v Reuben Singh* (2005) QBD 17 June. The opposite conclusion was reached in the case of a limitation on liability which suppliers of a computer system insisted on in all its contracts with local authority customers: *St Albans City and District Council v International Computers Ltd* [1996] 4 All ER 481, CA. See also *Overseas Medical Supplies Ltd v Orient Transport Services Ltd* [1999] 1 All ER (Comm) 981, CA where exemptive provisions were not upheld. On the other hand, in *South West Water Services Ltd v International Computers Ltd* [1999] BLR 420 the court held that an "entire contract clause" which excluded liability for fraudulent misrepresentation inducing the contract was unreasonable and could not be enforced.

In *Watford Electronics Ltd v Sanderson CFL Ltd* [2001] EWCA Civ 317, [2001] 1 All ER (Comm) 696 the Court of Appeal overturned a finding of unreasonableness in the case of an entire agreement clause, coupled with an acknowledgment that the making of the agreement had not been induced by representations. The court held that, since the acknowledgment was capable of raising an estoppel if relied on, the clause might well pass the reasonableness test, particularly where the parties were of equal bargaining power and had the benefit of professional advice. For other cases where the provisions of the contract were held to be reasonable in a commercial context see *JP Morgan Chase v Springwell Navigation* [2008] EWHC 1186 Comm, [2008] All ER (D) 167 and *Barclays Bank plc v Alfons Kufner* [2008] EWHC 2319, [2008] All ER (D) 102 (Oct).

In *Britvic Soft Drinks Ltd v Messer UK Ltd* [2002] EWCA Civ 548, [2002] 2 All ER (Comm) 321, (2002) Times, 22 May, the Court of Appeal upheld a claim under s 14 of the Sale of Goods Act 1979 in respect of contaminated supplies of carbon dioxide and rejected an unreasonable exemption clause.

III CON [66.3]

Surveyor reporting for a building society In *Smith v Eric S Bush (a firm)* [1990] 1 AC 831, [1987] 3 All ER 179, CA, the court held that an exclusion clause could not be relied upon by a negligent surveyor as a defence to a claim by a purchaser who had relied on his report to a building society.

III CON [67]

12. *"Dealing as consumer"*
Repealed.

III CON [68]

13. Varieties of exemption clause

(1) To the extent that this Part of this Act prevents the exclusion or restriction of any liability it also prevents—
(a) making the liability or its enforcement subject to restrictive or onerous conditions;
(b) excluding or restricting any right or remedy in respect of the liability, or subjecting a person to any prejudice in consequence of his pursuing any such right or remedy;
(c) excluding or restricting rules of evidence or procedure;

and (to that extent) sections 2, 6 and 7 also prevent excluding or restricting liability by reference to terms and notices which exclude or restrict the relevant obligation or duty.

(2) But an agreement in writing to submit present or future differences to arbitration is not to be treated under this Part of this Act as excluding or restricting any liability.

III CON [68.1]

Exclusion of the right of set-off An exclusion, or restriction, of the right of set-off is within the scope of s 13. Where the exclusion operates to exclude payments or credits from being set-off it is on the face of it unreasonable, unless those relying on it show otherwise: *Stewart Gill Ltd v Horatio Myer & Co Ltd* [1992] QB 600, [1992] 2 All ER 257, CA.

III CON [69]

14. Interpretation of Part I

In this Part of this Act—

"business" includes a profession and the activities of any government department or local or public authority;

"consumer contract" has the same meaning as in the Consumer Rights Act 2015 (see section 61);

"consumer notice" has the same meaning as in the Consumer Rights Act 2015 (see section 61);

"goods" has the same meaning as in [the Sale of Goods Act 1979]:

"hire-purchase agreement" has the same meaning as in the Consumer Credit Act 1974;

"negligence" has the meaning given by section 1 (1);

"notice" includes an announcement, whether or not in writing, and any other communication or pretended communication; and

"personal injury" includes any disease and any impairment of physical or mental condition.

SALE OF GOODS ACT 1979

(c 54)

Amendments **Editorial Note:** As regards contracts made on or after 1 October 2015, amendments to the Act made by Schedule 1 to the Consumer Rights Act 2015 have effect and are included in the text below.

III CON [70]

1. Contracts to which Act applies

(1) This Act applies to contracts of sale of goods made on or after (but not to those made before) 1 January 1894.

(2) In relation to contracts made on certain dates, this Act applies subject to the modification of certain of its sections as mentioned in Schedule 1 below.

(3) Any such modification is indicated in the section concerned by a reference to Schedule 1 below.

(4) Accordingly, where a section does not contain such a reference, this Act applies in relation to the contract concerned without such modification of the section.

(5) Certain sections or subsections of this Act do not apply to a contract to which Chapter 2 of Part 1 of the Consumer Rights Act 2015 applies.

(6) Where that is the case it is indicated in the section concerned.

III CON [70.1]

Contracts to which Chapter 2 of Part 1 of the Consumer Rights Act 2015 applies The Consumer Rights Act 2015, Part 1, chapter 2, applies to contracts for the sale of goods made on or after 1 October 2015. These contracts do not have the benefit of subss 11(4), 12, 13, 14, 15, 15B(1), 20, 29(3), 30, 31, 32, 33, 35, 35A, 36, Part 5A, 51, 52, 53, 53A, 54, 55(1) or 58. Similar protection is provided instead by the Consumer Rights Act 2015.

III CON [71]

2. Contract of sale

(1) A contract of sale of goods is a contract by which the seller transfers or agrees to transfer the property in goods to the buyer for a money consideration, called the price.

(2) There may be a contract of sale between one part owner and another.

(3) A contract of sale may be absolute or conditional.

(4) Where under a contract of sale the property in the goods is transferred from the seller to the buyer the contract is called a sale.

(5) Where under a contract of sale the transfer of the property in the goods is to take place at a future time or subject to some condition later to be fulfilled the contract is called an agreement to sell.

(6) An agreement to sell becomes a sale when the time elapses or the conditions are fulfilled subject to which the property in the goods is to be transferred.

III CON [71.1]

Hire-purchase A contract of hire-purchase falls outside the definition because there is no legal obligation to buy. The hirer in possession is therefore unable to pass title under s 25(2): *Close Asset Finance Ltd v Care Graphics Machinery Ltd* [2000] 12 LS Gaz R 42. The court followed *Helby v Matthews* [1895] AC 471, HL and distinguished the case where the hirer deemed to have agreed to buy subject to an option not to do so, *Forthright Finance Ltd v Carlyle Finance Ltd* [1997] 4 All ER 90, CA. But a purchaser in good faith from a person in possession on hire-purchase terms may acquire a good title under s 27 of the Hire-Purchase Act 1964. See **III CON [25A]**.

III CON [72]

11. When condition to be treated as warranty

(1) This section does not apply to Scotland.

(2) Where a contract of sale is subject to a condition to be fulfilled by the seller, the buyer may waive the condition, or may elect to treat the breach of the condition as a breach of warranty and not as a ground for treating the contract as repudiated.

(3) Whether a stipulation in a contract of sale is a condition, the breach of which may give rise to a right to treat the contract as repudiated, or a warranty, the breach of which may give rise to a claim for damages but not to a right to reject the goods and treat the contract as repudiated, depends in each case on the construction of the contract; and a stipulation may be a condition, though called a warranty in the contract.

(4) Subject to section 35A below where a contract of sale is not severable and the buyer has accepted the goods or part of them, the breach of a condition to be fulfilled by the seller can only be treated as a breach of warranty, and not as a ground for rejecting the goods and treating the contract as repudiated, unless there is an express or implied term of the contract to that effect.

(4A) Subsection (4) does not apply to a contract to which Chapter 2 of Part 1 of the Consumer Rights Act 2015 applies (but see the provision made about such contracts in sections 19 to 22 of that Act).

(5) [. . .]

(6) Nothing in this section affects a condition or warranty whose fulfilment is excused by law by reason of impossibility or otherwise.

(7) Paragraph 2 of Schedule 1 below applies in relation to a contract made before 22 April 1967 or (in the application of this Act to Northern Ireland) 28 July 1967.

III CON [73]

12. Implied terms about title, etc

(1) In a contract of sale, other than one to which subsection (3) below applies, there is an implied term on the part of the seller that in the case of a sale he has a right to sell the goods, and in the case of an agreement to sell he will have such a right at the time when the property is to pass.

(2) In a contract of sale, other than one to which subsection (3) below applies, there is also an implied term that—

- (a) the goods are free, and will remain free until the time when the property is to pass, from any charge or encumbrance not disclosed or known to the buyer before the contract is made, and
- (b) the buyer will enjoy quiet possession of the goods except so far as it may be disturbed by the owner or other person entitled to the benefit of any charge or encumbrance so disclosed or known.

(3) This subsection applies to a contract of sale in the case of which there appears from the contract or is to be inferred from its circumstances an intention that the seller should transfer only such title as he or a third person may have.

(4) In a contract to which subsection (3) above applies there is an implied [term] that all charges or encumbrances known to the seller and not known to the buyer have been disclosed to the buyer before the contract is made.

(5) In a contract to which subsection (3) above applies there is also an implied [term] that none of the following will disturb the buyer's quiet possession of the goods, namely—

- (a) the seller;
- (b) in a case where the parties to the contract intend that the seller should transfer only such title as a third person may have, that person;
- (c) anyone claiming through or under the seller or that third person otherwise than under a charge or encumbrance disclosed or known to the buyer before the contract is made.

(5A) As regards England and Wales and Northern Ireland, the term implied by subsection (1) above is a condition and the terms implied by subsections (2), (4) and (5) above are warranties.

(6) Paragraph 3 of Schedule 1 below applies in relation to a contract made before 18 May 1973.

(7) This section does not apply to a contract to which Chapter 2 of Part 1 of the Consumer Rights Act 2015 applies (but see the provision made about such contracts in section 17 of that Act).

III CON [73.1]

Precedents A precedent for a claim for breach of the terms as to title is set out at **BCCP K[2455]**. See **BCCP K[2461]** for a claim based on the right to quiet possession and **BCCP K[2533]** and **BCCP K[2534]** for defence relying on s 12.

III CON [73.2]

Exclusion by contract Liability cannot be excluded: see the Unfair Contract Terms Act 1977 s 6(1) (see **III CON [61]**).

III CON [73.3]

Quiet possession In *Rubicon Computer Systems Ltd v United Paints Ltd* (2000) 2 TCLR 453, CA the seller of a computer system who installed a time-lock by which he rendered the system unusable was held to have broken the term implied by s 12(2)(b) and to have repudiated the contract.

III CON [74]

13. Sale by description

(1) Where there is a contract for the sale of goods by description, there is an implied term that the goods will correspond with the description.

(1A) As regards England and Wales and Northern Ireland, the term implied by subsection (l) above is a condition.

(2) If the sale is by sample as well as by description it is not sufficient that the bulk of the goods corresponds with the sample if the goods do not also correspond with the description.

(3) A sale of goods is not prevented from being a sale by description by reason only that, being exposed for sale or hire, they are selected by the buyer.

(4) Paragraph 4 of Schedule 1 below applies in relation to a contract made before 18 May 1973.

(5) This section does not apply to a contract to which Chapter 2 of Part 1 of the Consumer Rights Act 2015 applies (but see the provision made about such contracts in section 11 of that Act).

III CON [74.1]

Attribution of an artist The attribution of an artist to a painting does not necessarily make a sale of the painting a sale by description, with the attribution being part of the description: *Harlingdon & Leinster Enterprises Ltd v Christopher Hull Fine Art Ltd* [1991] 1 QB 564, [1990] 1 All ER 737, CA.

III CON [74.2]

Exclusion by contract See the limits placed on exemption clauses by the Unfair Contract Terms Act 1977 s 6(2) and (3) and also by the Unfair Terms in Consumer Contracts Regulations 1999, SI 1999/2083 regs 5–8 and Sch 2, para 1(b) at **III CON [106]** and following.

III CON [74.3]

Precedents A precedent for a claim for goods not complying with the description is set out at **BCCP K[2471]** and see **BCCP K[2544]** and **BCCP K[2545]** for defences based on ss 13 and 15.

III CON [75]

14. Implied terms about quality or fitness

(1) Except as provided by this section and section 15 below and subject to any other enactment, there is no implied [term] about the quality or fitness for any particular purpose of goods supplied under a contract of sale.

(2) Where the seller sells goods in the course of a business, there is an implied term that the goods supplied under the contract are of satisfactory quality.

(2A) For the purposes of this Act, goods are of satisfactory quality if they meet the standard that a reasonable person would regard as satisfactory, taking account of any description of the goods, the price (if relevant) and all the other relevant circumstances.

(2B) For the purposes of this Act, the quality of goods includes their state and condition and the following (among others) are in appropriate cases aspects of the quality of goods—

- (a) fitness for all the purposes for which goods of the kind in question are commonly supplied,
- (b) appearance and finish,
- (c) freedom from minor defects,
- (d) safety, and
- (e) durability.

(2C) The term implied by subsection (2) above does not extend to any matter making the quality of goods unsatisfactory—

- (a) which is specifically drawn to the buyer's attention before the contract is made,
- (b) where the buyer examines the goods before the contract is made, which that examination ought to reveal, or
- (c) in the case of a contract for sale by sample, which would have been apparent on a reasonable examination of the sample.

(2D) ...

(2E) ...

(2F) ...

(3) Where the seller sells goods in the course of a business and the buyer, expressly or by implication, makes known—

- (a) to the seller, or
- (b) where the purchase price or part of it is payable by instalments and the goods were previously sold by a credit-broker to the seller, to that credit-broker,

any particular purpose for which the goods are being bought, there is an implied term that the goods supplied under the contract are reasonably fit for that purpose, whether or not that is a purpose for which such goods are commonly supplied, except where the circumstances show that the buyer does not rely, or that it is unreasonable for him to rely, on the skill or judgment of the seller or credit-broker.

(4) An implied term about quality or fitness for a particular purpose may be annexed to a contract of sale by usage.

(5) The preceding provisions of this section apply to a sale by a person who in the course of a business is acting as agent for another as they apply to a sale by a principal in the course of a business, except where that other is not selling in the course of a business and either the buyer knows that fact or reasonable steps are taken to bring it to the notice of the buyer before the contract is made.

(6) As regards England and Wales and Northern Ireland, the terms implied by subsections (2) and (3) above are conditions.

(7) Paragraph 5 of Schedule 1 below applies in relation to a contract made on or after 18 May 1973 and before the appointed day, and paragraph 6 in relation to one made before 18 May 1973.

(8) In subsection (7) above and paragraph 5 of Schedule 1 below references to the appointed day are to the day appointed for the purposes of those provisions by an order of the Secretary of State made by statutory instrument.

(9) This section does not apply to a contract to which Chapter 2 of Part 1 of the Consumer Rights Act 2015 applies (but see the provision made about such contracts in sections 9, 10 and 18 of that Act).

III CON [75.1]

Precedents For statements of case based on breach of the terms implied by s 14, see **BCCP K[2462]– BCCP K[2465]** and **BCCP K[2535]– BCCP K[2543]**. For a claim against a seller for injuries caused in an accident due to defects in a car, see **BCCP M[901]**.

III CON [75.2]

Visible defects The fact that goods have a defect which the buyer sees before taking delivery does not mean that the goods are merchantable if the seller agreed to put the defect right: *R & B Customs Brokers Co Ltd v United Dominions Trust Ltd* [1988] 1 All ER 847, [1988] 1 WLR 321, CA.

III CON [75.3]

Fitness for purpose The seller's obligation is to supply goods fit for the purpose for which they would ordinarily be used. If the intended purpose arises from an abnormal feature, the term as to fitness is not implied unless the feature is made known: *Slater v Finning Ltd* [1997] AC 473, [1996] 3 All ER 398, HL.

For the application of the section to a defective car which was driven 5,000 miles before it was rejected see *Rogers v Parrish (Scarborough) Ltd* [1987] QB 933, [1987] 2 All ER 232, CA: the car had persistent serious faults which the seller tried unsuccessfully to put right.

III CON [75.4]

Merchantable quality, satisfactory quality It has been held that a painting may be of merchantable quality although not in fact painted by the attributed artist: *Harlingdon & Leinster Enterprises Ltd v Christopher Hull Fine Art Ltd* [1991] 1 QB 564, [1990] 1 All ER 737, CA. The effect of sub-ss (2A) and (2B) is to require the court to apply the standards of a reasonable person who takes account of the description of the goods, their price and such relevant circumstances as the claims made as to their effectiveness: *Jewson Ltd v Kelly* [2002] All ER (D) 339 (Oct), (2002) Times, 3 October. Sub-sections (2D), (2E) and (2F) were inserted by reg 3 of the Sale and Supply of Goods to Consumers Regulations 2002, SI 2002/3045, with effect from 31 March 2003. Provisions to the same effect were inserted in contracts of hire and hire-purchase and contracts for the supply of goods and services together by regs 7 and 13 of the same Regulations.

The test for whether goods are of satisfactory quality is objective: *Egan v Motor Services (Bath) Ltd* [2007] EWCA Civ 1002, [2007] All ER (D) 256 (Oct) (in which the court rejected a claim by the purchaser of a new car which was "camber sensitive").

III CON [75.5]

Sale in the course of a business The words "in the course of a business" should be construed broadly without regard for the narrow construction placed on the same words in a different part of the Act: *Stevenson v Rogers* [1999] QB 1028, [1999] 1 All ER 613, CA, distinguishing *R & B Customs Brokers Co Ltd v United Dominions Trust Ltd* [1988] 1 All ER 847, [1988] 1 WLR 321, CA.

III CON [75.6]

Sale by agent The buyer from an agent for an undisclosed principal is not precluded by s 14 (5) from suing the principal if the goods are not of satisfactory quality: *Boyter v Thomson* [1995] 2 AC 628, [1995] 3 All ER 135, HL.

III CON [75.7]

Exclusion by contract See the limits placed on exemption clauses by the Unfair Contract Terms Act 1977 s 6(2) and (3) and also by the Unfair Terms in Consumer Contracts Regulations 1999, SI 1999/2083 regs 5–8 and Sch 2, para 1(b) at **III CON [106]** and following.

III CON [75.8]

Replacement parts provided under warranty In *VAI Industries (UK) Ltd v Bostock & Bramley Transmissions Ltd* [2003] EWCA Civ 1069, [2003] BLR 359, CA, goods were sold subject to a two-year warranty that the equipment would be free of design faults and would be replaced if they proved to be defective within three years. The equipment turned out to be defective and was replaced but the replacement equipment was defective too. The Court held that for the limitation period for any claim for breach of the warranty started with the date of the sale, not the end of the two year warranty period. On the other hand it was implied in the replacement transaction that the replacement equipment would meet the original contractual requirements. Accordingly, the limitation period for a claim in respect of defects in the replacement equipment started when they were delivered.

III CON [76]

15. Sale by sample

(1) A contract of sale is a contract for sale by sample where there is an express or implied term to that effect in the contract.

(2) In the case of a contract for sale by sample there is an implied term—

- (a) that the bulk will correspond with the sample in quality;
- (b) [. . .]
- (c) that the goods will be free from any defect, making their quality unsatisfactory, which would not be apparent on reasonable examination of the sample.

(3) As regards England and Wales and Northern Ireland, the term implied by subsection (2) above is a condition.

(4) Paragraph 7 of Schedule 1 below applies in relation to a contract made before 18 May 1973.

(5) This section does not apply to a contract to which Chapter 2 of Part 1 of the Consumer Rights Act 2015 applies (but see the provision made about such contracts in sections 13 and 18 of that Act).

III CON [76.1]

Exclusion by contract See the limits placed on exemption clauses by the Unfair Contract Terms Act 1977 s 6(2) and (3) and also by the Unfair Terms in Consumer Contracts Regulations 1999 (SI 1999/2083) regs 5–8 and Sch 2, para 1(b) at **III CON [106]** and following.

III CON [76.2]

Precedents For claims and defences based on breach of the terms implied by s 15, see **BCCP K[2472]**, **BCCP K[2544]** and **BCCP K[2545]**.

III CON [77]

15A. Modifications of remedies for breach of condition in non-consumer cases

(1) Where in the case of a contract of sale—

- (a) the buyer would, apart from this subsection, have the right to reject goods by reason of a breach on the part of the seller of a term implied by section 13, 14 or 15 above, but
- (b) the breach is so slight that it would be unreasonable for him to reject them,

... the breach is not to be treated as a breach of condition but may be treated as a breach of warranty.

(2) This section applies unless a contrary intention appears in, or is to be implied from, the contract.

(3) It is for the seller to show that a breach fell within subsection (1)(b) above.

(4) This section does not apply to Scotland.

III CON [78]

35. Acceptance

(1) The buyer is deemed to have accepted the goods subject to subsection (2) below—

- (a) when he intimates to the seller that he has accepted them, or
- (b) when the goods have been delivered to him and he does any act in relation to them which is inconsistent with the ownership of the seller.

(2) Where goods are delivered to the buyer, and he has not previously examined them, he is not deemed to have accepted them under subsection (1) above until he has had a reasonable opportunity of examining them for the purpose—

(a) of ascertaining whether they are in conformity with the contract, and

(b) in the case of a contract for sale by sample, of comparing the bulk with the sample.

(3) ...

(4) The buyer is also deemed to have accepted the goods when after the lapse of a reasonable time he retains the goods without intimating to the seller that he has rejected them.

(5) The questions that are material in determining for the purposes of subsection (4) above whether a reasonable time has elapsed include whether the buyer has had a reasonable opportunity of examining the goods for the purpose mentioned in subsection (2) above.

(6) The buyer is not by virtue of this section deemed to have accepted the goods merely because—

(a) he asks for, or agrees to, their repair by or under an arrangement with the seller, or

(b) the goods are delivered to another under a sub-sale or other disposition.

(7) Where the contract is for the sale of goods making one or more commercial units, a buyer accepting any goods included in a unit is deemed to have accepted all the goods making the unit; and in this subsection "commercial unit" means a unit division of which would materially impair the value of the goods or the character of the unit.

(8) Paragraph 10 of Schedule 1 below applies in relation to a contract made before 22 April 1967 or (in the application of this Act to Northern Ireland) 28 July 1967.

(9) This section does not apply to a contract to which Chapter 2 of Part 1 of the Consumer Rights Act 2015 applies (but see the provision made about such contracts in section 21 of that Act).

III CON [78.1]

Retention after a reasonable time Time taken in requesting or agreeing to repairs, and in carrying them out is to be left out of account in deciding whether the buyer has retained the goods for a reasonable time without intimating their rejection: *Clegg v Olle Andersson* [2003] EWCA Civ 320, [2003] 1 All ER (Comm) 721, (2003) Times, 14 April.

On the other hand, the Court of Appeal upheld a ruling at first instance that although the suppliers of kitchen units had broken the contract by providing and installing units of the wrong colour the purchaser was rightly held to have accepted them by allowing a reasonable time to elapse without rejecting them: *Jones v Callagher (t/a Gallery Kitchens and Bathrooms)* [2004] EWCA Civ 10, [2005] 1 Lloyd's Rep 377.

III CON [78.2]

Rejection after repair The buyer is not deemed to have accepted the goods merely because he has agreed to repair work: sub-s (6) so provides. If, however, the agreement was that the repairs would be at the seller's expense and if they were carried out satisfactorily the right to reject would, in the ordinary way, be lost. However, the circumstances might give rise to an implied obligation on the seller to say what the defect was and the corrective effect of the repairs. In such a case a refusal by the seller to give the buyer this information could be a basis for rejecting the goods even if the repairs had cured the defect: *JH Ritchie Ltd v Lloyd Ltd* [2007] UKHL 9, [2007] All ER (D) 109 (Mar), (2007) Times, 8 March (a decision on the Act as applied in Scotland).

III CON [79]

35A. Right of partial rejection

(1) If the buyer—

(a) has the right to reject the goods by reason of a breach on the part of the seller that affects some or all of them, but

(b) accepts some of the goods, including, where there are any goods unaffected by the breach, all such goods,

he does not by accepting them lose his right to reject the rest.

(2) In the case of a buyer having the right to reject an instalment of goods, subsection (1) above applies as if references to the goods were references to the goods comprised in the instalment.

(3) For the purposes of subsection (1) above, goods are affected by a breach if by reason of the breach they are not in conformity with the contract.

(4) This section applies unless a contrary intention appears in, or is to be implied from, the contract.

(5) This section does not apply to a contract to which Chapter 2 of Part 1 of the Consumer Rights Act 2015 applies (but see the provision made about such contracts in section 21 of that Act).

III CON [80]

36. Buyer not bound to return rejected goods

(1) Unless otherwise agreed, where goods are delivered to the buyer, and he refuses to accept them, having the right to do so, he is not bound to return them to the seller, but it is sufficient if he intimates to the seller that he refuses to accept them.

(2) This section does not apply to a contract to which Chapter 2 of Part 1 of the Consumer Rights Act 2015 applies (but see the provision made about such contracts in section 20 of that Act).

PART 5A
ADDITIONAL RIGHTS OF BUYER IN CONSUMER CASES

III CON [81]

53. Remedy for breach of warranty

(1) Where there is a breach of warranty by the seller, or where the buyer elects (or is compelled) to treat any breach of a condition on the part of the seller as a breach of warranty, the buyer is not by reason only of such breach of warranty entitled to reject the goods; but he may—

(a) set up against the seller the breach of warranty in diminution or extinction of the price, or

(b) maintain an action against the seller for damages for the breach of warranty.

(2) The measure of damages for breach of warranty is the estimated loss directly and naturally resulting, in the ordinary course of events, from the breach of warranty.

(3) In the case of breach of warranty of quality such loss is prima facie the difference between the value of the goods at the time of delivery to the buyer and the value they would have had if they had fulfilled the warranty.

(4) The fact that the buyer has set up the breach of warranty in diminution or extinction of the price does not prevent him from maintaining an action for the same breach of warranty if he has suffered further damage.

(4A) This section does not apply to a contract to which Chapter 2 of Part 1 of the Consumer Rights Act 2015 applies (but see the provision made about such contracts in section 19 of that Act).

(5) This section does not apply to Scotland.

III CON [81A]

61. Interpretation

(1) In this Act, unless the context or subject matter otherwise requires—

"action" includes counterclaim and set-off, and in Scotland condescendence and claim and compensation;

"bulk" means a mass or collection of goods of the same kind which—

(a) is contained in a defined space or area; and

(b) is such that any goods in the bulk are interchangeable with any other goods therein of the same number or quantity;

"business" includes a profession and the activities of any government department (including a Northern Ireland department) or local or public authority;

"buyer" means a person who buys or agrees to buy goods;

...

"contract of sale" includes an agreement to sell as well as a sale;

"credit-broker" means a person acting in the course of a business of credit brokerage carried on by him, that is a business of effecting introductions of individuals desiring to obtain credit—

(a) to persons carrying on any business so far as it relates to the provision of credit, or

(b) to other persons engaged in credit brokerage;

"defendant" includes in Scotland defender, respondent, and claimant in a multiple poinding;

"delivery" means voluntary transfer of possession from one person to another [except that in relation to sections 20A and 20B above it includes such appropriation of goods to the contract as results in property in the goods being transferred to the buyer;]

"document of title to goods" has the same meaning as it has in the Factors Acts;

"Factors Acts" means the Factors Act 1889, the Factors (Scotland) Act 1890, and any enactment amending or substituted for the same;

"fault" means wrongful act or default;

"future goods" means goods to be manufactured or acquired by the seller after the making of the contract of sale;

"goods" includes all personal chattels other than things in action and money, and in Scotland all corporeal moveables except money; and in particular "goods" includes emblements, industrial growing crops, and things attached to or forming part of the land which are agreed to be severed before sale or under the contract of sale and includes an undivided share in goods;

"plaintiff" includes pursuer, complainer, claimant in a multiplepoinding and defendant or defender counter-claiming;

...

"property" means the general property in goods, and not merely a special property;

. . .

...

"sale" includes a bargain and sale as well as a sale and delivery;

"seller" means a person who sells or agrees to sell goods;

"specific goods" means goods identified and agreed on at the time a contract of sale is made and includes an undivided share, specified as a fraction or percentage, of goods identified and agreed on as aforesaid;

"warranty" (as regards England and Wales and Northern Ireland) means an agreement with reference to goods which are the subject of a contract of sale, but collateral to the main purpose of such contract, the breach of which gives rise to a claim for damages, but not to a right to reject the goods and treat the contract as repudiated.

(2) < . . . >

(3) A thing is deemed to be done in good faith within the meaning of this Act when it is in fact done honestly, whether it is done negligently or not.

(4) A person is deemed to be insolvent within the meaning of this Act if he has either ceased to pay his debts in the ordinary course of business or he cannot pay his debts as they become due, < . . . >

(5) Goods are in a deliverable state within the meaning of this Act when they are in such a state that the buyer would under the contract be bound to take delivery of them.

(5A) ...

(6) As regards the definition of "business" in subsection (1) above, paragraph 14 of Schedule 1 below applies in relation to a contract made on or after 18th May 1973 and before 1st February 1978, and paragraph 15 in relation to one made before 18th May 1973.

III CON [81A.1]

Definition of 'goods' A computer disk is within the definition of 'goods' whereas a computer program is not. Nevertheless, if a disk is sold, encoded with a program to instruct or enable a computer, the buyer will have the benefit of the implied terms as to the quality and fitness of the encoded disk: *St Albans City and District Council v International Computers Ltd* [1996] 4 All ER 481, CA.

SUPPLY OF GOODS AND SERVICES ACT 1982

(c 29)

GENERAL NOTES ON SUPPLY OF GOODS AND SERVICES

III CON [82]

The Supply of Goods and Services Act 1982 sets out the terms to be implied in contracts for the supply of goods where the contracts are not covered by either the Supply of Goods (Implied Terms) Act 1973 or the Sale of Goods Act 1979. The main targets in Part I are contracts under which goods and services are provided together and contracts of hire. Part I of the Act confirms that contracts for the supply of goods and services together are subject to the same implied terms as to title in the goods (s 2), description (s 3), quality or fitness (s 4) and sample (s 5) as if they were sales governed by ss 12, 13, 14 and 15 of the Sale of Goods Act 1979. It does broadly the same for contracts of hire as regards title (s 7), description (s 8), quality or fitness (s 9) and sample (s 10). The terms may be varied by agreement, subject to Unfair Contract Terms Act 1977 s 7 see para **III CON [62]** and the Unfair Terms in Consumer Contracts Regulations 1999 (SI 1999/2083) at **III CON [106]**.

The provisions of Part I were held to cover the supply of meals to the purchaser from a tour company of a package holiday at a Dominican Republic hotel, although the claim under the Package Travel etc Regulations 1992 failed because the hotelier was not at fault: *Wood v TUI Travel plc t/a First Choice* [2017] EWCA Civ 11.

The rights of a customer who is a consumer are set out in the Consumer Rights Act 2015, ss 9 to 18 in the case of hire, at **III CON [193]** onwards, and ss 48 to 57 for services, at **III CON [232]** onwards.

PART II
SUPPLY OF SERVICES

III CON [83]

12. The contracts concerned

(1) In this Act a "relevant contract for the supply of a service" means, subject to subsection (2) below, a contract under which a person ("the supplier") agrees to carry out a service, other than a contract to which Chapter 4 of Part 1 of the Consumer Rights Act 2015 applies.

(2) For the purposes of this Act, a contract of service or apprenticeship is not a relevant contract for the supply of a service.

(3) Subject to subsection (2) above, a contract is a relevant contract for the supply of a service for the purposes of this Act whether or not goods are also—

(a) transferred or to be transferred, or

(b) bailed or to be bailed by way of hire,

under the contract, and whatever is the nature of the consideration for which the service is to be carried out.

(4) The Secretary of State may by order provide that one or more of sections 13 to 15 below shall not apply to services of a description specified in the order, and such an order may make different provision for different circumstances.

(5) The power to make an order under subsection (4) above shall be exercisable by statutory instrument subject to annulment in pursuance of a resolution of either House of Parliament.

III CON [83.1]

Orders Of particular significance are the Supply of Services (Exclusion of Implied Terms) Order 1982 (SI 1982/1771) which excludes the terms in the case of the supply of services by advocates, and the Supply of Services (Exclusion of Implied Terms) Order 1985 (SI 1985/1) which excludes the terms in the case of services supplied by an arbitrator.

III CON [83.2]

Relevant contract for the supply of a service The effect of sub-s (1) is to disapply the provisions of ss 12–16 of the Act in relation to services supplied on or after 1 October 2015, since these are services to which Chapter 4 of Part 1 of the Consumer Rights Act 2015 applies instead. They are therefore not 'relevant' contracts for the purposes of the 1982 Act.

III CON [84]

13. Implied term about care and skill

In a relevant contract for the supply of a service where the supplier is acting in the course of a business, there is an implied term that the supplier will carry out the service with reasonable care and skill.

III CON [84.1]

Duty of tour operators In *Wilson v Best Travel Ltd* [1993] 1 All ER 353 it was held that the duty owed by a tour operator under s 13 was to exercise reasonable care to exclude accommodation which was not reasonably safe. If a hotel complied with local safety standards, the tour operator was not in breach by reason only of a higher standard being required in the United Kingdom. Where a contract is made for the benefit of a party of people, the one who made the contract may sue for damages on behalf of all: *Jackson v Horizon Holidays Ltd* [1975] 3 All ER 92, [1975] 1 WLR 1468, CA.

III CON [84.2]

Damages for frustration and distress A contract breaker is not in general liable for distress, frustration, etc unless the contract is to provide pleasure, relaxation and peace of mind, as in *Jarvis v Swans Tours Ltd* [1973] QB 233, [1973] 1 All ER 71, CA and *Heywood v Wellers* [1976] QB 446. [1976] 1 All ER 300, CA. The general rule, as stated in *Watts v Morrow* [1991] 1 WLR 1421, CA, does, however, allow damages to be recovered for physical inconvenience and discomfort. In *Hobbs v London and South Western Rly Co* (1875) LR 10 QB 111, damages were awarded to Mr Hobbs for the inconvenience and discomfort of having to walk eight miles home in the rain after being taken to the wrong destination. In *Farley v Skinner* [2001] UKHL 49, [2002] 2 AC 732, [2001] 4 All ER 801, a surveyor who, in breach of his duty of reasonable skill and care, advised the prospective purchaser of a cottage that he was not likely to be affected by aircraft noise, was held liable for its interference with the purchaser's pleasure, relaxation and peace of mind (£10,000). A decision in the other direction in *Knott v Bolton* (1995) 11 Const LJ 375 was held to have been wrongly decided.

III CON [84.3]

Precedents Precedents for claims for breach of the terms implied in contracts for the supply of professional services are set out at **BCCP N[201]** onwards.

III CON [85]

14. Implied term about time for performance

(1) Where, under a relevant contract for the supply of a service by a supplier acting in the course of a business, the time for the service to be carried out is not fixed by the contract, left to be fixed in a manner agreed by the contract or determined by the course of dealing between the parties, there is an implied term that the supplier will carry out the service within a reasonable time.

(2) What is a reasonable time is a question of fact.

III CON [86]

15. Implied term about consideration

(1) Where, under a relevant contract for the supply of a service, the consideration for the service is not determined by the contract, left to be determined in a manner agreed by the contract or determined by the course of dealing between the parties, there is an implied term that the party contracting with the supplier will pay a reasonable charge.

(2) What is a reasonable charge is a question of fact.

III CON [87]–III CON [105]

16. Exclusion of implied terms, etc

(1) Where a right, duty or liability would arise under a relevant contract for the supply of a service by virtue of this Part of this Act, it may (subject to subsection (2) below and the 1977 Act) be negatived or varied by express agreement, or by the course of dealing between the parties, or by such usage as binds both parties to the contract.

(2) An express term does not negative a term implied by this Part of this Act unless inconsistent with it.

(3) Nothing in this Part of this Act prejudices—

- (a) any rule of law which imposes on the supplier a duty stricter than that imposed by section 13 or 14 above; or
- (b) subject to paragraph (a) above, any rule of law whereby any term not inconsistent with this Part of this Act is to be implied in a relevant contract for the supply of a service.

(4) This Part of this Act has effect subject to any other enactment which defines or restricts the rights, duties or liabilities arising in connection with a service of any description.

III CON [87.1]

The 1977 Act The duty of care and skill, arising under s 13, falls within the definition of "negligence" in the Unfair Contract Terms Act 1977 s 1(1) see para **III CON [56]** and the exclusion or restriction of liability for negligence is controlled by s 2 see para **III CON [57]**, whereas exclusion or restriction of liability in respect of the other duties is controlled by s 3 see para **III CON [58]**.

III CON [87.2]

Unfair Terms in Consumer Contracts Regulations 1999 The Unfair Terms in Consumer Contracts Regulations 1999, SI 1999/2083 at **III CON [106]** place further limitations on the power to exclude or restrict consumer rights.

UNFAIR TERMS IN CONSUMER CONTRACTS REGULATIONS 1999

(SI 1999/2083)

GENERAL NOTES ON THE REGULATIONS

III CON [106]–III CON [125]

Revocation These Regulations are revoked by Schedule 4 to the Consumer Rights Act 2015, except that they continue to apply to contracts made before 1 October 2015. For the text of the Regulations and commentary relating to them, see Volume 2 of the 2016, and earlier, editions of the *Civil Court Practice*.

CONSUMER PROTECTION (DISTANCE SELLING) REGULATIONS 2000

(SI 2000/2334, as amended by SI 2004/2095, SI 2005/689)

GENERAL NOTES ON THE REGULATIONS

III CON [125A]

These regulations apply to consumer contracts made on or after 31 October 2000 and before 13 June 2014, when they were superseded by the Consumer Contracts (Information, Cancellation and Additional Charges) Regulations 2013, SI 2013/3134, the text of which is set out at **III CON [132]**, onwards. The text of the superseded Distance Selling Regulations 2000 is to be found in Volume 2 of the Civil Court Practice for 2014 and preceding editions, starting at **III CON [125A]**.

STOP NOW ORDERS (EC DIRECTIVE) REGULATIONS 2001

(SI 2001/1422)

GENERAL NOTES ON THE STOP NOW ORDERS REGULATIONS 2001

III CON [126]

Background The Stop Now Orders (EC Directive) Regulations 2001, SI 2001/1422 confer jurisdiction on the High Court to grant orders in the nature of injunctions to stop Community infringements, that is to say, infringements of certain Community directives which have been incorporated into domestic law. The domestic law which has, as a result, become enforceable by Stop Now orders includes provisions of the Consumer Credit Act 1974 at **III CON [24]**, the Package, Travel, Package Holidays and Package Tours Regulations 1992 at **III CON [88]** and the Unfair Contract Terms in Consumer Contracts Regulations 1994 at **III CON [106]**. Other subject areas listed in reg 2 include cancellation rights, various kinds of advertising, timeshares and regulation of the supply of goods and services to consumers. Before the bringing into force of the new Regulations, the Director General had the right to seek injunctions to compel compliance under Part III of the Fair Trading Act 1973 and also under the various sets of regulations whereby EC directives for consumer protection were given effect. See, for example, *Director General of Fair Trading v Tobyward* [1989] 2 All ER 266, CA and *Director General of Fair Trading v First National Bank plc* [2000] QB 672, [2000] 2 All ER 759, CA. The broad effect of the new Regulations is to amend and enlarge the jurisdictional provisions in Part III of the Fair Trading Act 1973 so as to enable the court to make Stop Now orders under that Act in the case of Community infringements. Section 41A of that Act makes it clear that, in England and Wales, the jurisdiction is not exercisable by the county court but only by the High Court.

III CON [127]

Qualified entities The Stop Now Regulations break new ground in two respects. First, they provide for persons and bodies other than the Director General of Fair Trading to make the application. Prominent in the Schedule 3 list of Public UK Qualified Entities is "every weights and measures authority in Great Britain". It is anticipated that the Consumers Association and similar organisations may apply to be added to the list.

III CON [127A]

Transfer of the functions of the Director General The functions of the Director General of Fair Trading under these, and other, Regulations, were transferred by s 2 of the Enterprise Act 2002 to the Office of Fair Trading, with effect from 1 April 2003.

III CON [128]

Undertakings The other respect in which the Stop New Regulations break new ground is by providing for undertakings given to the OFT or other qualified entities to be enforceable as if they were undertakings given to the court. This is the effect of paragraphs 14 and 15 of Schedule 2 (Provisions having effect in place of Part III of the Act). The usual methods of enforcement would be committal proceedings or by sequestration.

SALE AND SUPPLY OF GOODS TO CONSUMERS REGULATIONS 2002

(SI 2002/3045)

III CON [129]

15. *Consumer guarantees*
Revoked.

III CON [129.1]

Revocation These regulations were revoked, as from 1 October 2015 by the Consumer Rights Act 2015.

CANCELLATION OF CONTRACTS MADE IN A CONSUMER'S HOME OR PLACE OF WORK ETC REGULATIONS 2008

(SI 2008/1816)

A GENERAL NOTE

III CON [130]

These Regulations give the consumer the right to cancel certain contracts provided that a cancellation notice is served within seven days. The contracts concerned are contracts for goods or services made during a visit by a trader to a consumer's home or place of work or on an excursion organised by the trader. The trader is required to give the consumer notice in writing of the right to cancel. The Regulations replace earlier, slightly narrower, regulations and re-implement Council Directive 85/577/EEC.

The Regulations do not apply to contracts made on or after 13 June 2014. They are superseded by the Consumer Contracts (Information, Cancellation and Additional Charges) Regulations 2013, SI 2013/3134, which cover the same ground but in a different way.

III CON [131]

Consequences of breach of the regulations In a transaction to which the Regulations apply the consumer must be given written notice, in a prescribed form, of his, or her, right to cancel the contract and a failure to provide such a notice invalidates the agreement. In those circumstances the creditor is unable to recover the debt. This was the result in an unreported case in the Cambridge County Court; *Chen Wei v Cambridge Power and Light Ltd* (2010) 10th September, before His Honour Judge Moloney QC. In this case the court considered but rejected an argument that the effect of the Regulations was to deprive the creditor of his possessions in breach of article 1 of the First Protocol to the Convention on Human Rights. A different point was taken in *W v Veolia Environmental Services (UK) plc* [2011] EWHC 2020 (QB), [2011] All ER (D) 280 (Jul). In that case the claimant paid the hire charges due under an unenforceable agreement and it was held that the claimant was therefore entitled to recover the charges from the defendant since he would have to account to the insurers for the amount recovered and therefore there would be no double recovery which would otherwise bar the claim.

In a case where the would-be customer cancelled a contract, although not given notice of his right to do so as required by reg 7, the Supreme Court held, reversing the Court of Appeal that, since the contract was non-compliant and invalid he was entitled not only to cancel but also to have his deposit returned: *Robertson v Swift* [2014] UKSC 50, (2014) Times, 10 October.

CONSUMER CONTRACTS (INFORMATION, CANCELLATION AND ADDITIONAL CHARGES) REGULATIONS 2013

(SI 2013/3134)

GENERAL NOTES ON THE REGULATIONS

III CON [132]

These Regulations apply to contracts made on or after 13 June 2014 and cover the same ground as the Consumer Protection (Distance Selling) Regulations 2000, SI 2000/2334 and the Cancellation of Contracts made in a Consumer's Home or Place of Work etc Regulations 2008, SI 2008/1816, which they replace.

They provide certain rights to consumers in their dealings with traders (both defined in reg 4). The trader is required, by regs 7 to 18, to make certain information available to the consumer before making the contract and in this respect different provision is made for on-premises contracts, off-premises contracts and distance contracts. Regulations 27 to 38 confer rights of cancellation or withdrawal. Minor amendments were made to the Regulations by the Consumer Protection (Amendment) Regulations 2014, SI 2014/870.

PART 1
GENERAL

III CON [133]

1. Citation and commencement

(1) These Regulations may be cited as the Consumer Contracts (Information, Cancellation and Additional Charges) Regulations 2013 and come into force on 13th June 2014.

(2) These Regulations apply in relation to contracts entered into on or after that date.

III CON [134]

2. Regulations superseded

The following do not apply in relation to contracts entered into on or after 13th June 2014—

(a) the Consumer Protection (Distance Selling) Regulations 2000;

(b) the Cancellation of Contracts made in a Consumer's Home or Place of Work etc Regulations 2008.

III CON [134.1]

The Distance Selling Regulations 2000 These Consumer Protection (Distance Selling) Regulations 2000 apply to consumer contracts made on or after 31 October 2000 and before 13 June 2014. The text is to be found in Volume 2 of the Civil Court Practice for 2014 and preceding editions, starting at **III CON [125A]**.

III CON [134.2]

Cancellation of Contracts made in a Consumer's Home or Place of Work etc Regulations 2008 The Cancellation of Contracts made in a Consumer's Home or Place of Work etc Regulations 2008 apply to contracts made before 13 June 2014 and a General Note on them is provided at **III CON [130]**. The commentary at **III CON [131]** on Consequences of breach of the regulations is relevant to the construction and application of the current regulations that follow.

III CON [135]

3. Review

(1) The Secretary of State must before the end of each review period—

(a) carry out a review of these Regulations,

(b) set out the conclusions of the review in a report, and

(c) publish the report.

(2) In carrying out the review, the Secretary of State must, so far as is reasonable, have regard to what is done in other member States to implement Directive 2011/83/EU of the European Parliament and of the Council of 25 October 2011 on consumer rights, amending Council Directive 93/13/EEC and Directive 1999/44/EC of the European Parliament and of the Council and repealing Council Directive 85/577/EC and Directive 97/7/EC of the European Parliament and of the Council.

(3) The report must in particular—

(a) set out the objectives intended to be achieved by these Regulations,

(b) assess the extent to which those objectives have been achieved, and

(c) assess whether those objectives remain appropriate and, if so, the extent to which they could be achieved in a way that imposes less regulation.

(4) A review period is—

(a) the period of 5 years beginning with the day on which these Regulations come into force, and

(b) each successive period of 5 years.

III CON [136]

4. "Consumer" and "trader"

In these Regulations—

"consumer" means an individual acting for purposes which are wholly or mainly outside that individual's trade, business, craft or profession;

"trader" means a person acting for purposes relating to that person's trade, business, craft or profession, whether acting personally or through another person acting in the trader's name or on the trader's behalf.

III CON [137]

5. Other definitions

In these Regulations—

"business" includes the activities of any government department or local or public authority;

"business premises" in relation to a trader means—

(a) any immovable retail premises where the activity of the trader is carried out on a permanent basis, or

(b) any movable retail premises where the activity of the trader is carried out on a usual basis;

"CMA" means the Competition and Markets Authority;

"commercial guarantee", in relation to a contract, means any undertaking by the trader or producer to the consumer (in addition to the trader's duty to supply goods that are in conformity with the contract) to reimburse the price paid or to replace, repair or service goods in any way if they do not meet the specifications or any other requirements not related to conformity set out in the guarantee statement or in the relevant advertising available at the time of the contract or before it is entered into;

"court"—

(a) in relation to England and Wales, means the county court or the High Court,

(b) in relation to Northern Ireland, means a county court or the High Court, and

(c) in relation to Scotland means the sheriff court or the Court of Session;

"delivery" means voluntary transfer of possession from one person to another;

"digital content" means data which are produced and supplied in digital form;

"distance contract" means a contract concluded between a trader and a consumer under an organised distance sales or service-provision scheme without the simultaneous physical presence of the trader and the consumer, with the exclusive use of one or more means of distance communication up to and including the time at which the contract is concluded;

"district heating" means the supply of heat (in the form of steam or hot water or otherwise) from a central source of production through a transmission and distribution system to heat more than one building;

"durable medium" means paper or email, or any other medium that—

(a) allows information to be addressed personally to the recipient,

(b) enables the recipient to store the information in a way accessible for future reference for a period that is long enough for the purposes of the information, and

(c) allows the unchanged reproduction of the information stored;

"functionality" in relation to digital content includes region coding, restrictions incorporated for the purposes of digital rights management, and other technical restrictions;

"goods" means any tangible moveable items, but that includes water, gas and electricity if and only if they are put up for sale in a limited volume or a set quantity;

"off-premises contract" means a contract between a trader and a consumer which is any of these—

(a) a contract concluded in the simultaneous physical presence of the trader and the consumer, in a place which is not the business premises of the trader;

(b) a contract for which an offer was made by the consumer in the simultaneous physical presence of the trader and the consumer, in a place which is not the business premises of the trader;

(c) a contract concluded on the business premises of the trader or through any means of distance communication immediately after the consumer was personally and individually addressed in a place which is not the business premises of the trader in the simultaneous physical presence of the trader and the consumer;

(d) a contract concluded during an excursion organised by the trader with the aim or effect of promoting and selling goods or services to the consumer;

"on-premises contract" means a contract between a trader and a consumer which is neither a distance contract nor an off-premises contract;

"public auction" means a method of sale where—

(a) goods or services are offered by a trader to consumers through a transparent, competitive bidding procedure run by an auctioneer,

(b) the consumers attend or are given the possibility to attend in person, and

(c) the successful bidder is bound to purchase the goods or services;

"sales contract" means a contract under which a trader transfers or agrees to transfer the ownership of goods to a consumer and the consumer pays or agrees to pay the price, including any contract that has both goods and services as its object;

"service" includes—

(a) the supply of water, gas or electricity if they are not put up for sale in a limited volume or a set quantity, and

(b) the supply of district heating;

"service contract" means a contract, other than a sales contract, under which a trader supplies or agrees to supply a service to a consumer and the consumer pays or agrees to pay the price.

III CON [138]

6. Limits of application: general

(1) These Regulations do not apply to a contract, to the extent that it is—

(a) for—

(i) gambling within the meaning of the Gambling Act 2005 (which includes gaming, betting and participating in a lottery);

(ii) in relation to Northern Ireland, for betting, gaming or participating lawfully in a lottery within the meaning of the Betting, Gaming, Lotteries and Amusements (Northern Ireland) Order 1985; or

(iii) participating in a lottery which forms part of the National Lottery within the meaning of the National Lottery etc Act 1993;

(b) for services of a banking, credit, insurance, personal pension, investment or payment nature;

(c) for the creation of immovable property or of rights in immovable property;

(d) for rental of accommodation for residential purposes;

(e) for the construction of new buildings, or the construction of substantially new buildings by the conversion of existing buildings;

(f) for the supply of foodstuffs, beverages or other goods intended for current consumption in the household and which are supplied by a trader on frequent and regular rounds to the consumer's home, residence or workplace;

(g) a package travel contract, within the scope of Directive (EU) 2015/2302 of the European Parliament and of the Council on package travel and linked travel arrangements, amending Regulation (EC) No 2006/2004 and Directive 2011/83/EU of the European Parliament and of the Council and repealing Council Directive 90/314/EEC;

(h) within the scope of Directive 2008/122/EC of the European Parliament and of the Council on the protection of consumers in respect of certain aspects of timeshare, long-term holiday product, resale and exchange contracts.

(2) These Regulations do not apply to contracts—

(a) concluded by means of automatic vending machines or automated commercial premises;

(b) concluded with a telecommunications operator through a public telephone for the use of the telephone;

(c) concluded for the use of one single connection, by telephone, internet or fax, established by a consumer;

(d) under which goods are sold by way of execution or otherwise by authority of law.

(3) Paragraph (1)(b) is subject to regulations 38(4) (ancillary contracts) and 40(3) (additional payments).

PART 2
INFORMATION REQUIREMENTS

CHAPTER 1
PROVISION OF INFORMATION

III CON [139]

7. Application of Part 2

(1) This Part applies to on-premises, off-premises and distance contracts, subject to paragraphs (2), (3) and (4) and regulation 6.

(2) This Part does not apply to contracts to the extent that they are—

(a) for the supply of a medicinal product by administration by a prescriber, or under a prescription or directions given by a prescriber;

(b) for the supply of a product by a health care professional or a person included in a relevant list, under arrangements for the supply of services as part of the health service, where the product is one that, at least in some circumstances is available under such arrangements free or on prescription.

(3) This Part, except for regulation 14(1) to (5), does not apply to contracts to the extent that they are for passenger transport services.

(4) This Part does not apply to off-premises contracts under which the payment to be made by the consumer is not more than £42.

(5) In paragraph (2)—

"health care professional" and "prescriber" have the meaning given by regulation 2(1) of the National Health Service (Pharmaceutical and Local Pharmaceutical Services) Regulations 2013;

"health service" means—

(a) the health service as defined by section 275(1) of the National Health Service Act 2006 or section 206(1) of the National Health Service (Wales) Act 2006,

(b) the health service as defined by section 108(1) of the National Health Service (Scotland) Act 1978, or

(c) any of the health services under section 2(1)(a) of the Health and Social Care (Reform) Act (Northern Ireland) 2009;

"medicinal product" has the meaning given by regulation 2(1) of the Human Medicines Regulations 2012;

"relevant list" means—

(a) a relevant list for the purposes of the National Health Service (Pharmaceutical and Local Pharmaceutical Services) Regulations 2013, or

(b) a list maintained under those Regulations.

III CON [140]

8. Making information etc available to a consumer

For the purposes of this Part, something is made available to a consumer only if the consumer can reasonably be expected to know how to access it.

III CON [141]

9. Information to be provided before making an on-premises contract

(1) Before the consumer is bound by an on-premises contract, the trader must give or make available to the consumer the information described in Schedule 1 in a clear and comprehensible manner, if that information is not already apparent from the context.

(2) Paragraph (1) does not apply to a contract which involves a day-to-day transaction and is performed immediately at the time when the contract is entered into.

(3) If the contract is for the supply of digital content other than for a price paid by the consumer—

(a) any information that the trader gives the consumer as required by this regulation is to be treated as included as a term of the contract, and

(b) a change to any of that information, made before entering into the contract or later, is not effective unless expressly agreed between the consumer and the trader.

(4) ...

III CON [142]

10. Information to be provided before making an off-premises contract

(1) Before the consumer is bound by an off-premises contract, the trader—

(a) must give the consumer the information listed in Schedule 2 in a clear and comprehensible manner, and

(b) if a right to cancel exists, must give the consumer a cancellation form as set out in part B of Schedule 3.

(2) The information and any cancellation form must be given on paper or, if the consumer agrees, on another durable medium and must be legible.

(3) The information referred to in paragraphs (l), (m) and (n) of Schedule 2 may be provided by means of the model instructions on cancellation set out in part A of Schedule 3; and a trader who has supplied those instructions to the consumer, correctly filled in, is to be treated as having complied with paragraph (1) in respect of those paragraphs.

(4) If the trader has not complied with paragraph (1) in respect of paragraph (g), (h) or (m) of Schedule 2, the consumer is not to bear the charges or costs referred to in those paragraphs.

(5) If the contract is for the supply of digital content other than for a price paid by the consumer—

(a) any information that the trader gives the consumer as required by this regulation is to be treated as included as a term of the contract, and

(b) a change to any of that information, made before entering into the contract or later, is not effective unless expressly agreed between the consumer and the trader.

(6) ...

(7) This regulation is subject to regulation 11.

III CON [143]

11. Provision of information in connection with repair or maintenance contracts

(1) If the conditions in paragraphs (2), (3) and (4) are met, regulation 10(1) does not apply to an off-premises contract where—

(a) the contract is a service contract,

(b) the consumer has explicitly requested the trader to supply the service for the purpose of carrying out repairs or maintenance,

(c) the obligations of the trader and the consumer under the contract are to be performed immediately, and

(d) the payment to be made by the consumer is not more than £170.

(2) The first condition is that, before the consumer is bound by the contract, the trader gives or makes available to the consumer on paper or, if the consumer expressly agrees, on another durable medium—

(a) the information referred to in paragraphs (b) to (d), (f) and (g) of Schedule 2,

(b) an estimate of the total price, where it cannot reasonably be calculated in advance, and

(c) where a right to cancel exists, a cancellation form as set out in part B of Schedule 3.

(3) The second condition is that, before the consumer is bound by the contract, the trader gives or makes available to the consumer the information referred to in paragraphs (a), (l) and (o) of Schedule 2, either on paper or another durable medium or otherwise if the consumer expressly agrees.

(4) The third condition is that the confirmation of the contract provided in accordance with regulation 12 contains the information required by regulation 10(1).

(5) For the right to cancel where this regulation applies, see in particular—

(a) regulation 28(1)(e) and (2) (cases where cancellation excluded: visit requested for urgent work);

(b) regulation 36 (form of consumer's request, and consequences).

III CON [144]

12. Provision of copy or confirmation of off-premises contracts

(1) In the case of an off-premises contract, the trader must give the consumer—

(a) a copy of the signed contract, or

(b) confirmation of the contract.

(2) The confirmation must include all the information referred to in Schedule 2 unless the trader has already provided that information to the consumer on a durable medium prior to the conclusion of the off-premises contract.

(3) The copy or confirmation must be provided on paper or, if the consumer agrees, on another durable medium.

(4) The copy or confirmation must be provided within a reasonable time after the conclusion of the contract, but in any event—

(a) not later than the time of the delivery of any goods supplied under the contract, and

(b) before performance begins of any service supplied under the contract.

(5) If the contract is for the supply of digital content not on a tangible medium and the consumer has given the consent and acknowledgement referred to in regulation 37(1)(a) and (b), the copy or confirmation must include confirmation of the consent and acknowledgement.

III CON [145]

13. Information to be provided before making a distance contract

(1) Before the consumer is bound by a distance contract, the trader—

(a) must give or make available to the consumer the information listed in Schedule 2 in a clear and comprehensible manner, and in a way appropriate to the means of distance communication used, and

(b) if a right to cancel exists, must give or make available to the consumer a cancellation form as set out in part B of Schedule 3.

(2) In so far as the information is provided on a durable medium, it must be legible.

(3) The information referred to in paragraphs (l), (m) and (n) of Schedule 2 may be provided by means of the model instructions on cancellation set out in part A of Schedule 3; and a trader who has supplied those instructions to the consumer, correctly filled in, is to be treated as having complied with paragraph (1) in respect of those paragraphs.

(4) Where a distance contract is concluded through a means of distance communication which allows limited space or time to display the information—

(a) the information listed in paragraphs (a), (b), (f), (g), (h), (l) and (s) of Schedule 2 must be provided on that means of communication in accordance with paragraphs (1) and (2), but

(b) the other information required by paragraph (1) may be provided in another appropriate way.

(5) If the trader has not complied with paragraph (1) in respect of paragraph (g), (h) or (m) of Schedule 2, the consumer is not to bear the charges or costs referred to in those paragraphs.

(6) If the contract is for the supply of digital content other than for a price paid by the consumer—

(a) any information that the trader gives the consumer as required by this regulation is to be treated as included as a term of the contract, and

(b) a change to any of that information, made before entering into the contract or later, is not effective unless expressly agreed between the consumer and the trader.

(7) ...

III CON [146]

14. Requirements for distance contracts concluded by electronic means

(1) This regulation applies where a distance contract is concluded by electronic means.

(2) If the contract places the consumer under an obligation to pay, the trader must make the consumer aware in a clear and prominent manner, and directly before the consumer places the order, of the information listed in paragraphs (a), (f), (g), (h), (s) and (t) of Schedule 2.

(3) The trader must ensure that the consumer, when placing the order, explicitly acknowledges that the order implies an obligation to pay.

(4) If placing an order entails activating a button or a similar function, the trader must ensure that the button or similar function is labelled in an easily legible manner only with the words 'order with obligation to pay' or a corresponding unambiguous formulation indicating that placing the order entails an obligation to pay the trader.

(5) If the trader has not complied with paragraphs (3) and (4), the consumer is not bound by the contract or order.

(6) The trader must ensure that any trading website through which the contract is concluded indicates clearly and legibly, at the latest at the beginning of the ordering process, whether any delivery restrictions apply and which means of payment are accepted.

III CON [147]

15. Telephone calls to conclude a distance contract

If the trader makes a telephone call to the consumer with a view to concluding a distance contract, the trader must, at the beginning of the conversation with the consumer, disclose—

(a) the trader's identity,

(b) where applicable, the identity of the person on whose behalf the trader makes the call, and

(c) the commercial purpose of the call.

III CON [148]

16. Confirmation of distance contracts

(1) In the case of a distance contract the trader must give the consumer confirmation of the contract on a durable medium.

(2) The confirmation must include all the information referred to in Schedule 2 unless the trader has already provided that information to the consumer on a durable medium prior to the conclusion of the distance contract.

(3) If the contract is for the supply of digital content not on a tangible medium and the consumer has given the consent and acknowledgment referred to in regulation 37(1)(a) and (b), the confirmation must include confirmation of the consent and acknowledgement.

(4) The confirmation must be provided within a reasonable time after the conclusion of the contract, but in any event—

(a) not later than the time of delivery of any goods supplied under the contract, and

(b) before performance begins of any service supplied under the contract.

(5) For the purposes of paragraph (4), the confirmation is treated as provided as soon as the trader has sent it or done what is necessary to make it available to the consumer.

III CON [149]

17. Burden of proof in relation to off-premises and distance contracts

(1) In case of dispute about the trader's compliance with any provision of regulations 10 to 16, it is for the trader to show that the provision was complied with.

(2) That does not apply to proceedings—

(a) for an offence under regulation 19, or

(b) relating to compliance with an injunction, interdict or order under regulation 45.

III CON [150]

18. Effect on contract of failure to provide information

Every contract to which this Part applies is to be treated as including a term that the trader has complied with the provisions of—

(a) regulations 9 to 14, and

(b) regulation 16.

CHAPTER 2
OFFENCES

III CON [151]

19. Offence relating to the failure to give notice of the right to cancel

(1) A trader is guilty of an offence if the trader enters into an off-premises contract to which regulation 10 applies but fails to give the consumer the information listed in paragraph (l), (m) or (n) of Schedule 2 in accordance with that regulation.

(2) A person who is guilty of an offence under paragraph (1) is liable on summary conviction to a fine not exceeding level 5 on the standard scale.

III CON [152]

20. Defence of due diligence

(1) In any proceedings against a person (A) for an offence under regulation 19 it is a defence for A to prove—

- (a) that the commission of the offence was due to—
  - (i) the act or default of another, or
  - (ii) reliance on information given by another, and
- (b) that A took all reasonable precautions and exercised all due diligence to avoid the commission of such an offence by A or any person under A's control.

(2) A person is not entitled to rely on the defence provided by paragraph (1) without leave of the court unless—

- (a) that person has served on the prosecutor a notice in writing giving such information as was in that person's possession identifying or assisting in the identification of the other person; and
- (b) the notice is served on the prosecutor not less than 7 days before the hearing of the proceedings or, in Scotland, 7 days before the intermediate diet or 14 days before the trial diet, whichever is earlier.

III CON [153]

21. Liability of persons other than the principal offender

Where the commission by a person of an offence under regulation 19 is due to the act or default of another person, that other person is guilty of the offence and may be proceeded against and punished whether or not proceedings are taken against the first person.

III CON [154]

22. Offences committed by bodies of persons

(1) Where an offence under regulation 19 committed by a body corporate is proved—

- (a) to have been committed with the consent or connivance of an officer of the body corporate or
- (b) to be attributable to any neglect on the part of an officer of the body corporate,

the officer, as well as the body corporate, is guilty of the offence and liable to be proceeded against and punished accordingly.

(2) In paragraph (1) a reference to an officer of a body corporate includes a reference to—

- (a) a director, manager, secretary or other similar officer; and

(b) a person purporting to act as a director, manager, secretary or other similar officer.

(3) Where an offence under regulation 19 committed in Scotland by a Scottish partnership is proved—

(a) to have been committed with the consent or connivance of a partner, or

(b) to be attributable to any neglect on the part of a partner,

that partner, as well as the partnership shall be guilty of the offence and liable to be proceeded against and punished accordingly.

(4) In paragraph (3) a reference to a partner includes a person purporting to act as a partner.

III CON [155]

23. Duty to enforce

(1) Subject to paragraphs (2) and (3)—

(a) it is the duty of every weights and measures authority in Great Britain to enforce regulation 19 within its area; and

(b) it is the duty of the Department of Enterprise, Trade and Investment in Northern Ireland to enforce regulation 19 within Northern Ireland.

(2) No proceedings for an offence under regulation 19 may be instituted in England and Wales except by or on behalf of an enforcement authority.

(3) Nothing in paragraph (1) authorises any weights and measures authority to bring proceedings in Scotland for an offence.

III CON [156]

24. ***Powers of investigation***

Revoked.

III CON [157]

25. ***Obstruction of authorised officers***

Revoked.

III CON [158]

26. ***Freedom from self-incrimination***

Revoked.

PART 3
RIGHT TO CANCEL

III CON [159]

27. Application of Part 3

(1) This Part applies to distance and off-premises contracts between a trader and a consumer, subject to paragraphs (2) and (3) and regulations 6 and 28.

(2) This Part does not apply to contracts to the extent that they are—

(a) for the supply of a medicinal product by administration by a prescriber, or under a prescription or directions given by a prescriber;

(b) for the supply of a product by a health care professional or a person included in a relevant list, under arrangements for the supply of services as part of the health service, where the product is one that, at least in some circumstances is available under such arrangements free or on prescription;

(c) for passenger transport services.

(3) This Part does not apply to off-premises contracts under which the payment to be made by the consumer is not more than £42.

(4) In paragraph (2)(a) and (b), expressions defined in regulation 7(5) have the meaning given there.

III CON [160]

28. Limits of application: circumstances excluding cancellation

(1) This Part does not apply as regards the following—

(a) the supply of—

(i) goods, or

(ii) services, other than supply of water, gas, electricity or district heating,

for which the price is dependent on fluctuations in the financial market which cannot be controlled by the trader and which may occur within the cancellation period;

(b) the supply of goods that are made to the consumer's specifications or are clearly personalised;

(c) the supply of goods which are liable to deteriorate or expire rapidly;

(d) the supply of alcoholic beverages, where—

(i) their price has been agreed at the time of the conclusion of the sales contract,

(ii) delivery of them can only take place after 30 days, and

(iii) their value is dependent on fluctuations in the market which cannot be controlled by the trader;

(e) contracts where the consumer has specifically requested a visit from the trader for the purpose of carrying out urgent repairs or maintenance;

(f) the supply of a newspaper, periodical or magazine with the exception of subscription contracts for the supply of such publications;

(g) contracts concluded at a public auction;

(h) the supply of accommodation, transport of goods, vehicle rental services, catering or services related to leisure activities, if the contract provides for a specific date or period of performance.

(2) Sub-paragraph (e) of paragraph (1) does not prevent this Part applying to a contract for—

(a) services in addition to the urgent repairs or maintenance requested, or

(b) goods other than replacement parts necessarily used in making the repairs or carrying out the maintenance,

if the trader supplies them on the occasion of a visit such as is mentioned in that sub-paragraph.

(3) The rights conferred by this Part cease to be available in the following circumstances—

(a) in the case of a contract for the supply of sealed goods which are not suitable for return due to health protection or hygiene reasons, if they become unsealed after delivery;

(b) in the case of a contract for the supply of sealed audio or sealed video recordings or sealed computer software, if the goods become unsealed after delivery;

(c) in the case of any sales contract, if the goods become mixed inseparably (according to their nature) with other items after delivery.

III CON [161]

29. Right to cancel

(1) The consumer may cancel a distance or off-premises contract at any time in the cancellation period without giving any reason, and without incurring any liability except under these provisions—

(a) regulation 34(3) (where enhanced delivery chosen by consumer);

(b) regulation 34(9) (where value of goods diminished by consumer handling);

(c) regulation 35(5) (where goods returned by consumer);

(d) regulation 36(4) (where consumer requests early supply of service).

(2) The cancellation period begins when the contract is entered into and ends in accordance with regulation 30 or 31.

(3) Paragraph (1) does not affect the consumer's right to withdraw an offer made by the consumer to enter into a distance or off-premises contract, at any time before the contract is entered into, without giving any reason and without incurring any liability.

III CON [162]

30. Normal cancellation period

(1) The cancellation period ends as follows, unless regulation 31 applies.

(2) If the contract is—

(a) a service contract, or

(b) a contract for the supply of digital content which is not supplied on a tangible medium,

the cancellation period ends at the end of 14 days after the day on which the contract is entered into.

(3) If the contract is a sales contract and none of paragraphs (4) to (6) applies, the cancellation period ends at the end of 14 days after the day on which the goods come into the physical possession of—

(a) the consumer, or

(b) a person, other than the carrier, identified by the consumer to take possession of them.

(4) If the contract is a sales contract under which multiple goods are ordered by the consumer in one order but some are delivered on different days, the cancellation period ends at the end of 14 days after the day on which the last of the goods come into the physical possession of—

(a) the consumer, or

(b) a person, other than the carrier, identified by the consumer to take possession of them.

(5) If the contract is a sales contract under which goods consisting of multiple lots or pieces of something are delivered on different days, the cancellation period ends at the end of 14 days after the day on which the last of the lots or pieces come into the physical possession of—

(a) the consumer, or

(b) a person, other than the carrier, identified by the consumer to take possession of them.

(6) If the contract is a sales contract for regular delivery of goods during a defined period of more than one day, the cancellation period ends at the end of 14 days after the day on which the first of the goods come into the physical possession of—

(a) the consumer, or

(b) a person, other than the carrier, identified by the consumer to take possession of them.

III CON [163]

31. Cancellation period extended for breach of information requirement

(1) This regulation applies if the trader does not provide the consumer with the information on the right to cancel required by paragraph (l) of Schedule 2, in accordance with Part 2.

(2) If the trader provides the consumer with that information in the period of 12 months beginning with the first day of the 14 days mentioned in regulation 30(2) to (6), but otherwise in accordance with Part 2, the cancellation period ends at the end of 14 days after the consumer receives the information.

(3) Otherwise the cancellation period ends at the end of 12 months after the day on which it would have ended under regulation 30.

III CON [164]

32. Exercise of the right to withdraw or cancel

(1) To withdraw an offer to enter into a distance or off-premises contract, the consumer must inform the trader of the decision to withdraw it.

(2) To cancel a contract under regulation 29(1), the consumer must inform the trader of the decision to cancel it.

(3) To inform the trader under paragraph (2) the consumer may either—

(a) use a form following the model cancellation form in part B of Schedule 3, or

(b) make any other clear statement setting out the decision to cancel the contract.

(4) If the trader gives the consumer the option of filling in and submitting such a form or other statement on the trader's website—

(a) the consumer need not use it, but

(b) if the consumer does, the trader must communicate to the consumer an acknowledgement of receipt of the cancellation on a durable medium without delay.

(5) Where the consumer informs the trader under paragraph (2) by sending a communication, the consumer is to be treated as having cancelled the contract in the cancellation period if the communication is sent before the end of the period.

(6) In case of dispute it is for the consumer to show that the contract was cancelled in the cancellation period in accordance with this regulation.

III CON [165]

33. Effect of withdrawal or cancellation

(1) If a contract is cancelled under regulation 29(1)—

(a) the cancellation ends the obligations of the parties to perform the contract, and

(b) regulations 34 to 38 apply.

(2) Regulations 34 and 38 also apply if the consumer withdraws an offer to enter into a distance or off-premises contract.

III CON [166]

34. Reimbursement by trader in the event of withdrawal or cancellation

(1) The trader must reimburse all payments, other than payments for delivery, received from the consumer, subject to paragraph (10).

(2) The trader must reimburse any payment for delivery received from the consumer, unless the consumer expressly chose a kind of delivery costing more than the least expensive common and generally acceptable kind of delivery offered by the trader.

(3) In that case, the trader must reimburse any payment for delivery received from the consumer up to the amount the consumer would have paid if the consumer had chosen the least expensive common and generally acceptable kind of delivery offered by the trader.

(4) Reimbursement must be without undue delay, and in any event not later than the time specified in paragraph (5) or (6).

(5) If the contract is a sales contract and the trader has not offered to collect the goods, the time is the end of 14 days after—

- (a) the day on which the trader receives the goods back, or
- (b) if earlier, the day on which the consumer supplies evidence of having sent the goods back.

(6) Otherwise, the time is the end of 14 days after the day on which the trader is informed of the consumer's decision to withdraw the offer or cancel the contract, in accordance with regulation 32.

(7) The trader must make the reimbursement using the same means of payment as the consumer used for the initial transaction, unless the consumer has expressly agreed otherwise.

(8) The trader must not impose any fee on the consumer in respect of the reimbursement.

(9) If (in the case of a sales contract) the value of the goods is diminished by any amount as a result of handling of the goods by the consumer beyond what is necessary to establish the nature, characteristics and functioning of the goods, the trader may recover that amount from the consumer, up to the contract price.

(10) An amount that may be recovered under paragraph (9)—

- (a) may be deducted from the amount to be reimbursed under paragraph (1);
- (b) otherwise, must be paid by the consumer to the trader.

(11) Paragraph (9) does not apply if the trader has failed to provide the consumer with the information on the right to cancel required by paragraph (l) of Schedule 2, in accordance with Part 2.

(12) For the purposes of paragraph (9) handling is beyond what is necessary to establish the nature, characteristics and functioning of the goods if, in particular, it goes beyond the sort of handling that might reasonably be allowed in a shop.

(13) Where the provisions of this regulation apply to cancellation of a contract, the contract is to be treated as including those provisions as terms.

III CON [167]

35. Return of goods in the event of cancellation

(1) Where a sales contract is cancelled under regulation 29(1), it is the trader's responsibility to collect the goods if—

- (a) the trader has offered to collect them, or
- (b) in the case of an off-premises contract, the goods were delivered to the consumer's home when the contract was entered into and could not, by their nature, normally be returned by post.

(2) If it is not the trader's responsibility under paragraph (1) to collect the goods, the consumer must—

- (a) send them back, or
- (b) hand them over to the trader or to a person authorised by the trader to receive them.

(3) The address to which goods must be sent under paragraph (2)(a) is—

- (a) any address specified by the trader for sending the goods back;
- (b) if no address is specified for that purpose, any address specified by the trader for the consumer to contact the trader;

(c) if no address is specified for either of those purposes, any place of business of the trader.

(4) The consumer must send off the goods under paragraph (2)(a), or hand them over under paragraph (2)(b), without undue delay and in any event not later than 14 days after the day on which the consumer informs the trader as required by regulation 32(2).

(5) The consumer must bear the direct cost of returning goods under paragraph (2), unless—

(a) the trader has agreed to bear those costs, or

(b) the trader failed to provide the consumer with the information about the consumer bearing those costs, required by paragraph (m) of Schedule 2, in accordance with Part 2.

(6) The contract is to be treated as including a term that the trader must bear the direct cost of the consumer returning goods under paragraph (2) where paragraph (5)(b) applies.

(7) The consumer is not required to bear any other cost of returning goods under paragraph (2).

(8) The consumer is not required to bear any cost of collecting goods under paragraph (1) unless the trader has offered to collect the goods and the consumer has agreed to bear the costs of the trader doing so.

III CON [168]

36. Supply of service in cancellation period

(1) The trader must not begin the supply of a service before the end of the cancellation period provided for in regulation 30(1) unless the consumer—

(a) has made an express request, and

(b) in the case of an off-premises contract, has made the request on a durable medium.

(2) In the case of a service other than supply of water, gas, electricity or district heating, the consumer ceases to have the right to cancel a service contract under regulation 29(1) if the service has been fully performed, and performance of the service began—

(a) after a request by the consumer in accordance with paragraph (1), and

(b) with the acknowledgement that the consumer would lose that right once the contract had been fully performed by the trader.

(3) Paragraphs (4) to (6) apply where a contract is cancelled under regulation 29(1) and a service has been supplied in the cancellation period.

(4) Where the service is supplied in response to a request in accordance with paragraph (1), the consumer must (subject to paragraph (6)) pay to the trader an amount—

(a) for the supply of the service for the period for which it is supplied, ending with the time when the trader is informed of the consumer's decision to cancel the contract, in accordance with regulation 32(2), and

(b) which is in proportion to what has been supplied, in comparison with the full coverage of the contract.

(5) The amount is to be calculated—

(a) on the basis of the total price agreed in the contract, or

(b) if the total price is excessive, on the basis of the market value of the service that has been supplied, calculated by comparing prices for equivalent services supplied by other traders.

(6) The consumer bears no cost for supply of the service, in full or in part, in the cancellation period, if—

(a) the trader has failed to provide the consumer with the information on the right to cancel required by paragraph (l) of Schedule 2, or the information on payment of that cost required by paragraph (n) of that Schedule, in accordance with Part 2, or

(b) the service is not supplied in response to a request in accordance with paragraph (1).

III CON [169]

37. Supply of digital content in cancellation period

(1) Under a contract for the supply of digital content not on a tangible medium, the trader must not begin supply of the digital content before the end of the cancellation period provided for in regulation 30(1), unless—

(a) the consumer has given express consent, and

(b) the consumer has acknowledged that the right to cancel the contract under regulation 29(1) will be lost.

(2) The consumer ceases to have the right to cancel such a contract under regulation 29(1) if, before the end of the cancellation period, supply of the digital content has begun after the consumer has given the consent and acknowledgement required by paragraph (1).

(3) Paragraph (4) applies where a contract is cancelled under regulation 29(1) and digital content has been supplied, not on a tangible medium, in the cancellation period.

(4) The consumer bears no cost for supply of the digital content, in full or in part, in the cancellation period, if—

(a) the consumer has not given prior express consent to the beginning of the performance of the digital content before the end of the 14-day period referred to in regulation 30,

(b) the consumer gave that consent but did not acknowledge when giving it that the right to cancel would be lost, or

(c) the trader failed to provide confirmation required by regulation 12(5) or 16(3).

III CON [170]

38. Effects of withdrawal or cancellation on ancillary contracts

(1) If a consumer withdraws an offer to enter into a distance or off-premises contract, or cancels such a contract under regulation 29(1), any ancillary contracts are automatically terminated, without any costs for the consumer, other than any costs under these provisions—

(a) regulation 34(3) (where enhanced delivery chosen by consumer);

(b) regulation 34(9) (where value of goods diminished by consumer handling);

(c) regulation 35(5) (where goods returned by consumer);

(d) regulation 36(4) (where consumer requests early supply of service).

(2) When a trader is informed by a consumer under regulation 32(1) or (2) of a decision to withdraw an offer or cancel a contract, the trader must inform any other trader with whom the consumer has an ancillary contract that is terminated by paragraph (1).

(3) An "ancillary contract", in relation to a distance or off-premises contract (the "main contract"), means a contract by which the consumer acquires goods or services related to the main contract, where those goods or services are provided—

(a) by the trader, or

(b) by a third party on the basis of an arrangement between the third party and the trader.

(4) Regulation 6(1)(b) (exclusion of financial services contracts) does not limit the contracts that are ancillary contracts for the purposes of this regulation.

PART 4
PROTECTION FROM INERTIA SELLING AND ADDITIONAL CHARGES

III CON [171]

39. Inertia selling

(1) Before regulation 28 of the Consumer Protection from Unfair Trading Regulations 2008. (and in Part 5 of those Regulations) insert—

"27A Inertia selling

(1) This regulation applies where a trader engages in the unfair commercial practice described in paragraph 29 of Schedule 1 (inertia selling).

(2) The consumer is exempted from any obligation to provide consideration for the products supplied by the trader.

(3) The absence of a response from the consumer following the supply does not constitute consent to the provision of consideration for, or the return or safekeeping of, the products.

(4) In the case of an unsolicited supply of goods, the consumer may, as between the consumer and the trader, use, deal with or dispose of the goods as if they were an unconditional gift to the consumer."

III CON [172]

40. Additional payments under a contract

(1) Under a contract between a trader and a consumer, no payment is payable in addition to the remuneration agreed for the trader's main obligation unless, before the consumer became bound by the contract, the trader obtained the consumer's express consent.

(2) There is no express consent (if there would otherwise be) for the purposes of this paragraph if consent is inferred from the consumer not changing a default option (such as a pre-ticked box on a website).

(3) This regulation does not apply if the trader's main obligation is to supply services within regulation 6(1)(b), but in any other case it applies even if an additional payment is for such services.

(4) Where a trader receives an additional payment which, under this regulation, is not payable under a contract, the contract is to be treated as providing for the trader to reimburse the payment to the consumer.

III CON [173]

41. Help-line charges over basic rate

(1) Where a trader operates a telephone line for the purpose of consumers contacting the trader by telephone in relation to contracts entered into with the trader, a consumer contacting the trader must not be bound to pay more than the basic rate.

(2) If in those circumstances a consumer who contacts a trader in relation to a contract is bound to pay more than the basic rate, the contract is to be treated as providing for the trader to pay to the consumer any amount by which the charge paid by the consumer for the call is more than the basic rate.

PART 5
DELIVERY AND RISK

III CON [174]

42. ***Time for delivery of goods***
Revoked.

III CON [175]

43. Passing of risk
Revoked.

PART 6
ENFORCEMENT

III CON [176]

44. Complaints

(1) It is the duty of an enforcement authority to consider any complaint made to it about a contravention of these Regulations, unless—

- (a) the complaint appears to the authority to be frivolous or vexatious, or
- (b) another enforcement authority has notified the CMA that it agrees to consider the complaint.

(2) If an enforcement authority has notified the CMA as mentioned in paragraph (1)(b), that authority is under a duty to consider the complaint.

(3) The following are enforcement authorities for the purposes of these Regulations—

- (a) every local weights and measures authority in Great Britain;
- (b) the Department of Enterprise, Trade and Investment in Northern Ireland.

III CON [177]

45. Orders to secure compliance

(1) An enforcement authority may apply for an injunction, or in Scotland an interdict or order of specific implement, against any person who appears to the authority to be responsible for a contravention of these Regulations.

(2) The court on an application under this regulation may grant an injunction, interdict or order on such terms as it thinks fit to secure compliance with these Regulations.

III CON [178]

46. Notification of undertakings and orders to the CMA

An enforcement authority must notify the CMA—

- (a) of any undertaking given to it by or on behalf of any person who appears to it to be responsible for a contravention of these Regulations;
- (b) of the outcome of any application made by it under regulation 45, and of the terms of any undertaking given to the court or of any order made by the court;

PART 7
CONSEQUENTIAL AMENDMENTS

III CON [179]

47. Consequential amendments
Schedule 4 makes amendments that are consequential on these Regulations.

SCHEDULE 1
INFORMATION RELATING TO ON-PREMISES CONTRACTS

III CON [180]

The information referred to in regulation 9(1) is—

(a) the main characteristics of the goods, services or digital content, to the extent appropriate to the medium of communication and to the goods, services or digital content;
(b) the identity of the trader (such as the trader's trading name), the geographical address at which the trader is established and the trader's telephone number;
(c) the total price of the goods, services or digital content inclusive of taxes, or where the nature of the goods, services or digital content is such that the price cannot reasonably be calculated in advance, the manner in which the price is to be calculated;
(d) where applicable, all additional delivery charges or, where those charges cannot reasonably be calculated in advance, the fact that such additional charges may be payable;
(e) where applicable, the arrangements for payment, delivery, performance, and the time by which the trader undertakes to deliver the goods, to perform the service or to supply the digital content;
(f) where applicable, the trader's complaint handling policy;
(g) in the case of a sales contract, a reminder that the trader is under a legal duty to supply goods that are in conformity with the contract;
(h) where applicable, the existence and the conditions of after-sales services and commercial guarantees;
(i) the duration of the contract, where applicable, or, if the contract is of indeterminate duration or is to be extended automatically, the conditions for terminating the contract;
(j) where applicable, the functionality, including applicable technical protection measures, of digital content;
(k) where applicable, any relevant compatibility of digital content with hardware and software that the trader is aware of or can reasonably be expected to have been aware of.

SCHEDULE 2
INFORMATION RELATING TO DISTANCE AND OFF-PREMISES CONTRACTS

III CON [181]

The information referred to in regulations 10(1) and 13(1) is (subject to the note at the end of this Schedule)—

(a) the main characteristics of the goods, services or digital content, to the extent appropriate to the medium of communication and to the goods, services or digital content;

(b) the identity of the trader (such as the trader's trading name), the geographical address at which the trader is established and the trader's telephone number;

(c) the geographical address at which the trader is established and, where available, the trader's telephone number, fax number and e-mail address, to enable the consumer to contact the trader quickly and communicate efficiently;

(d) where the trader is acting on behalf of another trader, the geographical address and identity of that other trader;

(e) if different from the address provided in accordance with paragraph (c), the geographical address of the place of business of the trader, and, where the trader acts on behalf of another trader, the geographical address of the place of business of that other trader, where the consumer can address any complaints;

(f) the total price of the goods, services or digital content inclusive of taxes, or where the nature of the goods, services or digital content is such that the price cannot reasonably be calculated in advance, the manner in which the price is to be calculated,

(g) where applicable, all additional delivery charges and any other costs or, where those charges cannot reasonably be calculated in advance, the fact that such additional charges may be payable;

(h) in the case of a contract of indeterminate duration or a contract containing a subscription, the total costs per billing period or (where such contracts are charged at a fixed rate) the total monthly costs;

(i) the cost of using the means of distance communication for the conclusion of the contract where that cost is calculated other than at the basic rate;

(j) the arrangements for payment, delivery, performance, and the time by which the trader undertakes to deliver the goods, to perform the services or to supply the digital content;

(k) where applicable, the trader's complaint handling policy;

(l) where a right to cancel exists, the conditions, time limit and procedures for exercising that right in accordance with regulations 27 to 38;

(m) where applicable, that the consumer will have to bear the cost of returning the goods in case of cancellation and, for distance contracts, if the goods, by their nature, cannot normally be returned by post, the cost of returning the goods;

(n) that, if the consumer exercises the right to cancel after having made a request in accordance with regulation 36(1), the consumer is to be liable to pay the trader reasonable costs in accordance with regulation 36(4);

(o) where under regulation 28, 36 or 37 there is no right to cancel or the right to cancel may be lost, the information that the consumer will not benefit from a right to cancel, or the circumstances under which the consumer loses the right to cancel;

(p) in the case of a sales contract, a reminder that the trader is under a legal duty to supply goods that are in conformity with the contract;

(q) where applicable, the existence and the conditions of after-sale customer assistance, after-sales services and commercial guarantees;

(r) the existence of relevant codes of conduct, as defined in regulation 5(3)(b) of the Consumer Protection from Unfair Trading Regulations 2008, and how copies of them can be obtained, where applicable;

(s) the duration of the contract, where applicable, or, if the contract is of indeterminate duration or is to be extended automatically, the conditions for terminating the contract;

(t) where applicable, the minimum duration of the consumer's obligations under the contract;

(u) where applicable, the existence and the conditions of deposits or other financial guarantees to be paid or provided by the consumer at the request of the trader;

(v) where applicable, the functionality, including applicable technical protection measures, of digital content;

(w) where applicable, any relevant compatibility of digital content with hardware and software that the trader is aware of or can reasonably be expected to have been aware of;

(x) where applicable, the possibility of having recourse to an out-of-court complaint and redress mechanism, to which the trader is subject, and the methods for having access to it.

Note: In the case of a public auction, the information listed in paragraphs (b) to (e) may be replaced with the equivalent details for the auctioneer.

SCHEDULE 3
INFORMATION ABOUT THE EXERCISE OF THE RIGHT TO CANCEL

A MODEL INSTRUCTIONS FOR CANCELLATION

III CON [182]

Right to Cancel

You have the right to cancel this contract within 14 days without giving any reason.

The cancellation period will expire after 14 days from the day [See Note 1].

To exercise the right to cancel, you must inform us [See Note 2] of your decision to cancel this contract by a clear statement (eg a letter sent by post, fax or e-mail). You may use the attached model cancellation form, but it is not obligatory. [See Note 3]

To meet the cancellation deadline, it is sufficient for you to send your communication concerning your exercise of the right to cancel before the cancellation period has expired.

Effects of cancellation

If you cancel this contract, we will reimburse to you all payments received from you, including the costs of delivery (except for the supplementary costs arising if you chose a type of delivery other than the least expensive type of standard delivery offered by us).

We may make a deduction from the reimbursement for loss in value of any goods supplied, if the loss is the result of unnecessary handling by you.

We will make the reimbursement without undue delay, and not later than—

(a) 14 days after the day we receive back from you any goods supplied, or

(b) (if earlier) 14 days after the day you provide evidence that you have returned the goods, or

(c) if there were no goods supplied, 14 days after the day on which we are informed about your decision to cancel this contract.

We will make the reimbursement using the same means of payment as you used for the initial transaction, unless you have expressly agreed otherwise; in any event, you will not incur any fees as a result of the reimbursement. [See Note 4]

[See Note 5]

[See Note 6]

Notes on instructions for completion:

1 Insert one of the following texts between the inverted commas:

(a) in the case of a service contract or a contract for the supply of digital content which is not supplied on a tangible medium: "of the conclusion of the contract.";

(b) in the case of a sales contract: "on which you acquire, or a third party other than the carrier and indicated by you acquires, physical possession of the goods.";

(c) in the case of a contract relating to multiple goods ordered by the consumer in one order and delivered separately: "on which you acquire, or a third party other than the carrier and indicated by you acquires, physical possession of the last good.";

(d) in the case of a contract relating to delivery of a good consisting of multiple lots or pieces: "on which you acquire, or a third party other than the carrier and indicated by you acquires, physical possession of the last lot or piece.";

(e) in the case of a contract for the regular delivery of goods during a defined period of time: "on which you acquire, or a third party other than the carrier and indicated by you acquires, physical possession of the first good.".

2 Insert your name, geographical address and, where available, your telephone number, fax number and e-mail address.

3 If you give the option to the consumer to electronically fill in and submit information about the consumer's cancellation from the contract on your website, insert the following: "You can also electronically fill in and submit the model cancellation form or any other clear statement on our website [insert Internet address]. If you use this option, we will communicate to you an acknowledgement of receipt of such a cancellation on a durable medium (eg by e-mail) without delay.".

4 In the case of sales contracts in which you have not offered to collect the goods in the event of cancellation insert the following: "We may withhold reimbursement until we have received the goods back or you have supplied evidence of having sent back the goods, whichever is the earliest.".

5 If the consumer has received goods in connection with the contract

(a) insert:

— "We will collect the goods."; or,

— "You shall send back the goods or hand them over to us or . . . [insert the name and geographical address, where applicable, of the person authorised by you to receive the goods], without undue delay and in any event not later than 14 days from the day on which you communicate your cancellation from this contract to us. The deadline is met if you send back the goods before the period of 14 days has expired."

(b) insert:

— "We will bear the cost of returning the goods.";

— "You will have to bear the direct cost of returning the goods";

— If, in a distance contract, you do not offer to bear the cost of returning the goods and the goods, by their nature, cannot normally be returned by post: "You will have to bear the direct cost of returning the goods, . . . EUR [insert the amount]."; or if the cost of returning the goods cannot reasonably be calculated in advance: "You will have to bear the direct cost of returning the goods. The cost is estimated at a maximum of approximately . . . EUR [insert the amount]."; or

— If, in an off-premises contract, the goods, by their nature, cannot normally be returned by post and have been delivered to the consumer's home at the time of the conclusion of the contract: "We will collect the goods at our own expense."; and,

(c) insert:

"You are only liable for any diminished value of the goods resulting from the handling other than what is necessary to establish the nature, characteristics and functioning of the goods."

6 In the case of a service contract insert the following: "If you requested to begin the performance of services during the cancellation period, you shall pay us an amount which is in proportion to what has been performed until you have communicated us your cancellation from this contract, in comparison with the full coverage of the contract.".

B MODEL CANCELLATION FORM

To [here the trader's name, geographical address and, where available, fax number and e-mail address are to be inserted by the trader]:
I/We [*] hereby give notice that I/We [*] cancel my/our [*] contract for the sale of the following goods [*]/for the supply of the following service [*],
Ordered on [*]/received on [*],
Name of consumer(s),
Address of consumer(s),
Signature of consumer(s) (only if this form is notified on paper),
Date
[*] Delete as appropriate.

CONSUMER PROTECTION (AMENDMENT) REGULATIONS 2014

(SI 2014/870)

III CON [183]

New Remedies Provided by the Consumer Protection (Amendment) Regulations 2014 The Consumer Protection (Amendment) Regulations 2014, SI 2014/870 amend the Consumer Protection from Unfair Trading Regulations 2008, SI 2008/1277 by providing new rights of redress in respect of misleading or aggressive commercial practices. The changes implement the EU Unfair Commercial Practices Directive (2005/29) and apply to contracts entered into on or after 14 October 2014.

CONSUMER RIGHTS ACT 2015

(c 15)

III CON [184]

General Notes on the Consumer Rights Act 2015 The Consumer Rights Act 2015 applies to all consumer contracts made on or after 1 October 2015, which is the commencement date. It has a broader sweep than the sale or supply of goods or services. These are covered in Chapter 2 (sections 3 to 32) and Chapter 4 (sections 48 to 57). In between the two, Chapter 3 confers rights and remedies on consumers in relation to a newly identified category of consumer contract: the digital content contract. The control and invalidation of unfair terms in any of the three categories of consumer contract is dealt with in sections 61 to 70. The existing law on consumer rights is pulled together and restated in a single statute but includes small changes to the pre-existing law and these are listed in Schedules 1 and 4. The law governing contracts made with someone who is not a consumer is untouched by the legislation.

The Consumer Rights Act 2015 (Commencement No 3) sets two main dates for the coming into force of ss 1 to 76. In the main everything comes into force on 1 October 2015 as regards new contracts, whereas contracts made and notices given before that date continue to be governed by the pre-existing law: see arts 3, 5 and 6. But in their application to a contract to supply a consumer transport service, the commencement of s 48(1) to (4), 49 to 59 and related consequential amendments the date for commencement is 6 April 2016 as regards consumer contracts made on or after that date: see arts 4, 5 and 6.

Part 1 (ss 1 to 60) contains 5 chapters which set out the rights which are built into consumer contracts and the remedies available on breach. Part 2 (ss 61 to 76) sets out the powers and duties of the civil courts in to relation terms imported into such contracts that are unfair. The rest of the Act, down to s 101, protects consumers in other ways, which are outside the remit of the civil courts and involve other enforcement agencies. Sections 77 to 101 are therefore not reproduced here; nor are the Schedules except Schedules 1, 2 and 4 which are tied in with Parts 1 and 2.

PART 1
CONSUMER CONTRACTS FOR GOODS, DIGITAL CONTENT AND SERVICES

CHAPTER 1
INTRODUCTION

III CON [185]

1. Where Part 1 applies

(1) This Part applies where there is an agreement between a trader and a consumer for the trader to supply goods, digital content or services, if the agreement is a contract.

(2) It applies whether the contract is written or oral or implied from the parties' conduct, or more than one of these combined.

(3) Any of Chapters 2, 3 and 4 may apply to a contract—
(a) if it is a contract for the trader to supply goods, see Chapter 2;
(b) if it is a contract for the trader to supply digital content, see Chapter 3 (also, subsection (6));
(c) if it is a contract for the trader to supply a service, see Chapter 4 (also, subsection (6)).

(4) In each case the Chapter applies even if the contract also covers something covered by another Chapter (a mixed contract).

(5) Two or all three of those Chapters may apply to a mixed contract.

(6) For provisions about particular mixed contracts, see—
(a) section 15 (goods and installation);
(b) section 16 (goods and digital content).

(7) For other provisions applying to contracts to which this Part applies, see Part 2 (unfair terms).

III CON [186]

2. Key definitions

(1) These definitions apply in this Part (as well as the definitions in section 59).

(2) "Trader" means a person acting for purposes relating to that person's trade, business, craft or profession, whether acting personally or through another person acting in the trader's name or on the trader's behalf.

(3) "Consumer" means an individual acting for purposes that are wholly or mainly outside that individual's trade, business, craft or profession.

(4) A trader claiming that an individual was not acting for purposes wholly or mainly outside the individual's trade, business, craft or profession must prove it.

(5) For the purposes of Chapter 2, except to the extent mentioned in subsection (6), a person is not a consumer in relation to a sales contract if—
(a) the goods are second hand goods sold at public auction, and
(b) individuals have the opportunity of attending the sale in person.

(6) A person is a consumer in relation to such a contract for the purposes of—
(a) sections 11(4) and (5), 12, 28 and 29, and
(b) the other provisions of Chapter 2 as they apply in relation to those sections.

(7) "Business" includes the activities of any government department or local or public authority.

(8) "Goods" means any tangible moveable items, but that includes water, gas and electricity if and only if they are put up for supply in a limited volume or set quantity.

(9) "Digital content" means data which are produced and supplied in digital form.

CHAPTER 2
GOODS

WHAT GOODS CONTRACTS ARE COVERED?

III CON [187]

3. Contracts covered by this Chapter

(1) This Chapter applies to a contract for a trader to supply goods to a consumer.

(2) It applies only if the contract is one of these (defined for the purposes of this Part in sections 5 to 8)—
(a) a sales contract;

(b) a contract for the hire of goods;
(c) a hire-purchase agreement;
(d) a contract for transfer of goods.

(3) It does not apply—
(a) to a contract for a trader to supply coins or notes to a consumer for use as currency;
(b) to a contract for goods to be sold by way of execution or otherwise by authority of law;
(c) to a contract intended to operate as a mortgage, pledge, charge or other security;
(d) in relation to England and Wales or Northern Ireland, to a contract made by deed and for which the only consideration is the presumed consideration imported by the deed;
(e) in relation to Scotland, to a gratuitous contract.

(4) A contract to which this Chapter applies is referred to in this Part as a "contract to supply goods".

(5) Contracts to supply goods include—
(a) contracts entered into between one part owner and another;
(b) contracts for the transfer of an undivided share in goods;
(c) contracts that are absolute and contracts that are conditional.

(6) Subsection (1) is subject to any provision of this Chapter that applies a section or part of a section to only some of the kinds of contracts listed in subsection (2).

(7) A mixed contract (see section 1(4)) may be a contract of any of those kinds.

III CON [188]

4. Ownership of goods

(1) In this Chapter ownership of goods means the general property in goods, not merely a special property.

(2) For the time when ownership of goods is transferred, see in particular the following provisions of the Sale of Goods Act 1979 (which relate to contracts of sale)—

section 16:	goods must be ascertained
section 17:	property passes when intended to pass
section 18:	rules for ascertaining intention
section 19:	reservation of right of disposal
section 20A:	undivided shares in goods forming part of a bulk
section 20B:	deemed consent by co-owner to dealings in bulk goods

III CON [189]

5. Sales contracts

(1) A contract is a sales contract if under it—
(a) the trader transfers or agrees to transfer ownership of goods to the consumer, and
(b) the consumer pays or agrees to pay the price.

(2) A contract is a sales contract (whether or not it would be one under subsection (1)) if under the contract—
(a) goods are to be manufactured or produced and the trader agrees to supply them to the consumer,
(b) on being supplied, the goods will be owned by the consumer, and

(c) the consumer pays or agrees to pay the price.

(3) A sales contract may be conditional (see section 3(5)), but in this Part "conditional sales contract" means a sales contract under which—

(a) the price for the goods or part of it is payable by instalments, and

(b) the trader retains ownership of the goods until the conditions specified in the contract (for the payment of instalments or otherwise) are met;

and it makes no difference whether or not the consumer possesses the goods.

III CON [190]

6. Contracts for the hire of goods

(1) A contract is for the hire of goods if under it the trader gives or agrees to give the consumer possession of the goods with the right to use them, subject to the terms of the contract, for a period determined in accordance with the contract.

(2) But a contract is not for the hire of goods if it is a hire-purchase agreement.

III CON [191]

7. Hire-purchase agreements

(1) A contract is a hire-purchase agreement if it meets the two conditions set out below.

(2) The first condition is that under the contract goods are hired by the trader in return for periodical payments by the consumer (and "hired" is to be read in accordance with section 6(1)).

(3) The second condition is that under the contract ownership of the goods will transfer to the consumer if the terms of the contract are complied with and—

(a) the consumer exercises an option to buy the goods,

(b) any party to the contract does an act specified in it, or

(c) an event specified in the contract occurs.

(4) But a contract is not a hire-purchase agreement if it is a conditional sales contract.

III CON [192]

8. Contracts for transfer of goods

A contract to supply goods is a contract for transfer of goods if under it the trader transfers or agrees to transfer ownership of the goods to the consumer and—

(a) the consumer provides or agrees to provide consideration otherwise than by paying a price, or

(b) the contract is, for any other reason, not a sales contract or a hire-purchase agreement.

What Statutory Rights are There under a Goods Contract?

III CON [193]

9. Goods to be of satisfactory quality

(1) Every contract to supply goods is to be treated as including a term that the quality of the goods is satisfactory.

(2) The quality of goods is satisfactory if they meet the standard that a reasonable person would consider satisfactory, taking account of—

(a) any description of the goods,

(b) the price or other consideration for the goods (if relevant), and

(c) all the other relevant circumstances (see subsection (5)).

(3) The quality of goods includes their state and condition; and the following aspects (among others) are in appropriate cases aspects of the quality of goods—

(a) fitness for all the purposes for which goods of that kind are usually supplied;
(b) appearance and finish;
(c) freedom from minor defects;
(d) safety;
(e) durability.

(4) The term mentioned in subsection (1) does not cover anything which makes the quality of the goods unsatisfactory—
(a) which is specifically drawn to the consumer's attention before the contract is made,
(b) where the consumer examines the goods before the contract is made, which that examination ought to reveal, or
(c) in the case of a contract to supply goods by sample, which would have been apparent on a reasonable examination of the sample.

(5) The relevant circumstances mentioned in subsection (2)(c) include any public statement about the specific characteristics of the goods made by the trader, the producer or any representative of the trader or the producer.

(6) That includes, in particular, any public statement made in advertising or labelling.

(7) But a public statement is not a relevant circumstance for the purposes of subsection (2)(c) if the trader shows that—
(a) when the contract was made, the trader was not, and could not reasonably have been, aware of the statement,
(b) before the contract was made, the statement had been publicly withdrawn or, to the extent that it contained anything which was incorrect or misleading, it had been publicly corrected, or
(c) the consumer's decision to contract for the goods could not have been influenced by the statement.

(8) In a contract to supply goods a term about the quality of the goods may be treated as included as a matter of custom.

(9) See section 19 for a consumer's rights if the trader is in breach of a term that this section requires to be treated as included in a contract.

III CON [194]

10. Goods to be fit for particular purpose

(1) Subsection (3) applies to a contract to supply goods if before the contract is made the consumer makes known to the trader (expressly or by implication) any particular purpose for which the consumer is contracting for the goods.

(2) Subsection (3) also applies to a contract to supply goods if—
(a) the goods were previously sold by a credit-broker to the trader,
(b) in the case of a sales contract or contract for transfer of goods, the consideration or part of it is a sum payable by instalments, and
(c) before the contract is made, the consumer makes known to the credit-broker (expressly or by implication) any particular purpose for which the consumer is contracting for the goods.

(3) The contract is to be treated as including a term that the goods are reasonably fit for that purpose, whether or not that is a purpose for which goods of that kind are usually supplied.

(4) Subsection (3) does not apply if the circumstances show that the consumer does not rely, or it is unreasonable for the consumer to rely, on the skill or judgment of the trader or credit-broker.

(5) In a contract to supply goods a term about the fitness of the goods for a particular purpose may be treated as included as a matter of custom.

(6) See section 19 for a consumer's rights if the trader is in breach of a term that this section requires to be treated as included in a contract.

III CON [195]

11. Goods to be as described

(1) Every contract to supply goods by description is to be treated as including a term that the goods will match the description.

(2) If the supply is by sample as well as by description, it is not sufficient that the bulk of the goods matches the sample if the goods do not also match the description.

(3) A supply of goods is not prevented from being a supply by description just because—

(a) the goods are exposed for supply, and

(b) they are selected by the consumer.

(4) Any information that is provided by the trader about the goods and is information mentioned in paragraph (a) of Schedule 1 or 2 to the Consumer Contracts (Information, Cancellation and Additional Charges) Regulations 2013 (SI 2013/3134) (main characteristics of goods) is to be treated as included as a term of the contract.

(5) A change to any of that information, made before entering into the contract or later, is not effective unless expressly agreed between the consumer and the trader.

(6) See section 2(5) and (6) for the application of subsections (4) and (5) where goods are sold at public auction.

(7) See section 19 for a consumer's rights if the trader is in breach of a term that this section requires to be treated as included in a contract.

III CON [196]

12. Other pre-contract information included in contract

(1) This section applies to any contract to supply goods.

(2) Where regulation 9, 10 or 13 of the Consumer Contracts (Information, Cancellation and Additional Charges) Regulations 2013 (SI 2013/3134) required the trader to provide information to the consumer before the contract became binding, any of that information that was provided by the trader other than information about the goods and mentioned in paragraph (a) of Schedule 1 or 2 to the Regulations (main characteristics of goods) is to be treated as included as a term of the contract.

(3) A change to any of that information, made before entering into the contract or later, is not effective unless expressly agreed between the consumer and the trader.

(4) See section 2(5) and (6) for the application of this section where goods are sold at public auction.

(5) See section 19 for a consumer's rights if the trader is in breach of a term that this section requires to be treated as included in the contract.

III CON [197]

13. Goods to match a sample

(1) This section applies to a contract to supply goods by reference to a sample of the goods that is seen or examined by the consumer before the contract is made.

(2) Every contract to which this section applies is to be treated as including a term that—

(a) the goods will match the sample except to the extent that any differences between the sample and the goods are brought to the consumer's attention before the contract is made, and

(b) the goods will be free from any defect that makes their quality unsatisfactory and that would not be apparent on a reasonable examination of the sample.

(3) See section 19 for a consumer's rights if the trader is in breach of a term that this section requires to be treated as included in a contract.

III CON [198]

14. Goods to match a model seen or examined

(1) This section applies to a contract to supply goods by reference to a model of the goods that is seen or examined by the consumer before entering into the contract.

(2) Every contract to which this section applies is to be treated as including a term that the goods will match the model except to the extent that any differences between the model and the goods are brought to the consumer's attention before the consumer enters into the contract.

(3) See section 19 for a consumer's rights if the trader is in breach of a term that this section requires to be treated as included in a contract.

III CON [199]

15. Installation as part of conformity of the goods with the contract

(1) Goods do not conform to a contract to supply goods if—

(a) installation of the goods forms part of the contract,

(b) the goods are installed by the trader or under the trader's responsibility, and

(c) the goods are installed incorrectly.

(2) See section 19 for the effect of goods not conforming to the contract.

III CON [200]

16. Goods not conforming to contract if digital content does not conform

(1) Goods (whether or not they conform otherwise to a contract to supply goods) do not conform to it if—

(a) the goods are an item that includes digital content, and

(b) the digital content does not conform to the contract to supply that content (for which see section 42(1)).

(2) See section 19 for the effect of goods not conforming to the contract.

III CON [201]

17. Trader to have right to supply the goods etc

(1) Every contract to supply goods, except one within subsection (4), is to be treated as including a term—

(a) in the case of a contract for the hire of goods, that at the beginning of the period of hire the trader must have the right to transfer possession of the goods by way of hire for that period,

(b) in any other case, that the trader must have the right to sell or transfer the goods at the time when ownership of the goods is to be transferred.

(2) Every contract to supply goods, except a contract for the hire of goods or a contract within subsection (4), is to be treated as including a term that—

(a) the goods are free from any charge or encumbrance not disclosed or known to the consumer before entering into the contract,

(b) the goods will remain free from any such charge or encumbrance until ownership of them is to be transferred, and

(c) the consumer will enjoy quiet possession of the goods except so far as it may be disturbed by the owner or other person entitled to the benefit of any charge or encumbrance so disclosed or known.

(3) Every contract for the hire of goods is to be treated as including a term that the consumer will enjoy quiet possession of the goods for the period of the hire except so far as the possession may be disturbed by the owner or other person entitled to the benefit of any charge or encumbrance disclosed or known to the consumer before entering into the contract.

(4) This subsection applies to a contract if the contract shows, or the circumstances when they enter into the contract imply, that the trader and the consumer intend the trader to transfer only—

(a) whatever title the trader has, even if it is limited, or

(b) whatever title a third person has, even if it is limited.

(5) Every contract within subsection (4) is to be treated as including a term that all charges or encumbrances known to the trader and not known to the consumer were disclosed to the consumer before entering into the contract.

(6) Every contract within subsection (4) is to be treated as including a term that the consumer's quiet possession of the goods—

(a) will not be disturbed by the trader, and

(b) will not be disturbed by a person claiming through or under the trader, unless that person is claiming under a charge or encumbrance that was disclosed or known to the consumer before entering into the contract.

(7) If subsection (4)(b) applies (transfer of title that a third person has), the contract is also to be treated as including a term that the consumer's quiet possession of the goods—

(a) will not be disturbed by the third person, and

(b) will not be disturbed by a person claiming through or under the third person, unless the claim is under a charge or encumbrance that was disclosed or known to the consumer before entering into the contract.

(8) In the case of a contract for the hire of goods, this section does not affect the right of the trader to repossess the goods where the contract provides or is to be treated as providing for this.

(9) See section 19 for a consumer's rights if the trader is in breach of a term that this section requires to be treated as included in a contract.

III CON [202]

18. No other requirement to treat term about quality or fitness as included

(1) Except as provided by sections 9, 10, 13 and 16, a contract to supply goods is not to be treated as including any term about the quality of the goods or their fitness for any particular purpose, unless the term is expressly included in the contract.

(2) Subsection (1) is subject to provision made by any other enactment (whenever passed or made).

What Remedies are There if Statutory Rights under a Goods Contract are not Met?

III CON [203]

19. Consumer's rights to enforce terms about goods

(1) In this section and sections 22 to 24 references to goods conforming to a contract are references to—

(a) the goods conforming to the terms described in sections 9, 10, 11, 13 and 14,

(b) the goods not failing to conform to the contract under section 15 or 16, and

(c) the goods conforming to requirements that are stated in the contract.

(2) But, for the purposes of this section and sections 22 to 24, a failure to conform as mentioned in subsection (1)(a) to (c) is not a failure to conform to the contract if it has its origin in materials supplied by the consumer.

(3) If the goods do not conform to the contract because of a breach of any of the terms described in sections 9, 10, 11, 13 and 14, or if they do not conform to the contract under section 16, the consumer's rights (and the provisions about them and when they are available) are—

(a) the short-term right to reject (sections 20 and 22);

(b) the right to repair or replacement (section 23); and

(c) the right to a price reduction or the final right to reject (sections 20 and 24).

(4) If the goods do not conform to the contract under section 15 or because of a breach of requirements that are stated in the contract, the consumer's rights (and the provisions about them and when they are available) are—

(a) the right to repair or replacement (section 23); and

(b) the right to a price reduction or the final right to reject (sections 20 and 24).

(5) If the trader is in breach of a term that section 12 requires to be treated as included in the contract, the consumer has the right to recover from the trader the amount of any costs incurred by the consumer as a result of the breach, up to the amount of the price paid or the value of other consideration given for the goods.

(6) If the trader is in breach of the term that section 17(1) (right to supply etc) requires to be treated as included in the contract, the consumer has a right to reject (see section 20 for provisions about that right and when it is available).

(7) Subsections (3) to (6) are subject to section 25 and subsections (3)(a) and (6) are subject to section 26.

(8) Section 28 makes provision about remedies for breach of a term about the time for delivery of goods.

(9) This Chapter does not prevent the consumer seeking other remedies—

(a) for a breach of a term that this Chapter requires to be treated as included in the contract,

(b) on the grounds that, under section 15 or 16, goods do not conform to the contract, or

(c) for a breach of a requirement stated in the contract.

(10) Those other remedies may be ones—

(a) in addition to a remedy referred to in subsections (3) to (6) (but not so as to recover twice for the same loss), or

(b) instead of such a remedy, or

(c) where no such remedy is provided for.

(11) Those other remedies include any of the following that is open to the consumer in the circumstances—

(a) claiming damages;

(b) seeking specific performance;

(c) seeking an order for specific implement;

(d) relying on the breach against a claim by the trader for the price;

(e) for breach of an express term, exercising a right to treat the contract as at an end.

(12) It is not open to the consumer to treat the contract as at an end for breach of a term that this Chapter requires to be treated as included in the contract, or on the grounds that, under section 15 or 16, goods do not conform to the contract, except as provided by subsections (3), (4) and (6).

(13) In this Part, treating a contract as at an end means treating it as repudiated.

(14) For the purposes of subsections (3)(b) and (c) and (4), goods which do not conform to the contract at any time within the period of six months beginning with the day on which the goods were delivered to the consumer must be taken not to have conformed to it on that day.

(15) Subsection (14) does not apply if—

(a) it is established that the goods did conform to the contract on that day, or

(b) its application is incompatible with the nature of the goods or with how they fail to conform to the contract.

III CON [204]

20. Right to reject

(1) The short-term right to reject is subject to section 22.

(2) The final right to reject is subject to section 24.

(3) The right to reject under section 19(6) is not limited by those sections.

(4) Each of these rights entitles the consumer to reject the goods and treat the contract as at an end, subject to subsections (20) and (21).

(5) The right is exercised if the consumer indicates to the trader that the consumer is rejecting the goods and treating the contract as at an end.

(6) The indication may be something the consumer says or does, but it must be clear enough to be understood by the trader.

(7) From the time when the right is exercised—

(a) the trader has a duty to give the consumer a refund, subject to subsection (18), and

(b) the consumer has a duty to make the goods available for collection by the trader or (if there is an agreement for the consumer to return rejected goods) to return them as agreed.

(8) Whether or not the consumer has a duty to return the rejected goods, the trader must bear any reasonable costs of returning them, other than any costs incurred by the consumer in returning the goods in person to the place where the consumer took physical possession of them.

(9) The consumer's entitlement to receive a refund works as follows.

(10) To the extent that the consumer paid money under the contract, the consumer is entitled to receive back the same amount of money.

(11) To the extent that the consumer transferred anything else under the contract, the consumer is entitled to receive back the same amount of what the consumer transferred, unless subsection (12) applies.

(12) To the extent that the consumer transferred under the contract something for which the same amount of the same thing cannot be substituted, the consumer is entitled to receive back in its original state whatever the consumer transferred.

(13) If the contract is for the hire of goods, the entitlement to a refund extends only to anything paid or otherwise transferred for a period of hire that the consumer does not get because the contract is treated as at an end.

(14) If the contract is a hire-purchase agreement or a conditional sales contract and the contract is treated as at an end before the whole of the price has been paid, the entitlement to a refund extends only to the part of the price paid.

(15) A refund under this section must be given without undue delay, and in any event within 14 days beginning with the day on which the trader agrees that the consumer is entitled to a refund.

(16) If the consumer paid money under the contract, the trader must give the refund using the same means of payment as the consumer used, unless the consumer expressly agrees otherwise.

(17) The trader must not impose any fee on the consumer in respect of the refund.

(18) There is no entitlement to receive a refund—

- (a) if none of subsections (10) to (12) applies,
- (b) to the extent that anything to which subsection (12) applies cannot be given back in its original state, or
- (c) where subsection (13) applies, to the extent that anything the consumer transferred under the contract cannot be divided so as to give back only the amount, or part of the amount, to which the consumer is entitled.

(19) It may be open to a consumer to claim damages where there is no entitlement to receive a refund, or because of the limits of the entitlement, or instead of a refund.

(20) Subsection (21) qualifies the application in relation to England and Wales and Northern Ireland of the rights mentioned in subsections (1) to (3) where—

- (a) the contract is a severable contract,
- (b) in relation to the final right to reject, the contract is a contract for the hire of goods, a hire-purchase agreement or a contract for transfer of goods, and
- (c) section 26(3) does not apply.

(21) The consumer is entitled, depending on the terms of the contract and the circumstances of the case—

- (a) to reject the goods to which a severable obligation relates and treat that obligation as at an end (so that the entitlement to a refund relates only to what the consumer paid or transferred in relation to that obligation), or
- (b) to exercise any of the rights mentioned in subsections (1) to (3) in respect of the whole contract.

III CON [205]

21. Partial rejection of goods

(1) If the consumer has any of the rights mentioned in section 20(1) to (3), but does not reject all of the goods and treat the contract as at an end, the consumer—

- (a) may reject some or all of the goods that do not conform to the contract, but
- (b) may not reject any goods that do conform to the contract.

(2) If the consumer is entitled to reject the goods in an instalment, but does not reject all of those goods, the consumer—

- (a) may reject some or all of the goods in the instalment that do not conform to the contract, but
- (b) may not reject any goods in the instalment that do conform to the contract.

(3) If any of the goods form a commercial unit, the consumer cannot reject some of those goods without also rejecting the rest of them.

(4) A unit is a "commercial unit" if division of the unit would materially impair the value of the goods or the character of the unit.

(5) The consumer rejects goods under this section by indicating to the trader that the consumer is rejecting the goods.

(6) The indication may be something the consumer says or does, but it must be clear enough to be understood by the trader.

(7) From the time when a consumer rejects goods under this section—

(a) the trader has a duty to give the consumer a refund in respect of those goods (subject to subsection (10)), and

(b) the consumer has a duty to make those goods available for collection by the trader or (if there is an agreement for the consumer to return rejected goods) to return them as agreed.

(8) Whether or not the consumer has a duty to return the rejected goods, the trader must bear any reasonable costs of returning them, other than any costs incurred by the consumer in returning those goods in person to the place where the consumer took physical possession of them.

(9) Section 20(10) to (17) apply to a consumer's right to receive a refund under this section (and in section 20(13) and (14) references to the contract being treated as at an end are to be read as references to goods being rejected).

(10) That right does not apply—

(a) if none of section 20(10) to (12) applies,

(b) to the extent that anything to which section 20(12) applies cannot be given back in its original state, or

(c) to the extent that anything the consumer transferred under the contract cannot be divided so as to give back only the amount, or part of the amount, to which the consumer is entitled.

(11) It may be open to a consumer to claim damages where there is no right to receive a refund, or because of the limits of the right, or instead of a refund.

(12) References in this section to goods conforming to a contract are to be read in accordance with section 19(1) and (2), but they also include the goods conforming to the terms described in section 17.

(13) Where section 20(21)(a) applies the reference in subsection (1) to the consumer treating the contract as at an end is to be read as a reference to the consumer treating the severable obligation as at an end.

III CON [206]

22. Time limit for short-term right to reject

(1) A consumer who has the short-term right to reject loses it if the time limit for exercising it passes without the consumer exercising it, unless the trader and the consumer agree that it may be exercised later.

(2) An agreement under which the short-term right to reject would be lost before the time limit passes is not binding on the consumer.

(3) The time limit for exercising the short-term right to reject (unless subsection (4) applies) is the end of 30 days beginning with the first day after these have all happened—

(a) ownership or (in the case of a contract for the hire of goods, a hire-purchase agreement or a conditional sales contract) possession of the goods has been transferred to the consumer,

(b) the goods have been delivered, and

(c) where the contract requires the trader to install the goods or take other action to enable the consumer to use them, the trader has notified the consumer that the action has been taken.

(4) If any of the goods are of a kind that can reasonably be expected to perish after a shorter period, the time limit for exercising the short-term right to reject in relation to those goods is the end of that shorter period (but without affecting the time limit in relation to goods that are not of that kind).

(5) Subsections (3) and (4) do not prevent the consumer exercising the short-term right to reject before something mentioned in subsection (3)(a), (b) or (c) has happened.

(6) If the consumer requests or agrees to the repair or replacement of goods, the period mentioned in subsection (3) or (4) stops running for the length of the waiting period.

(7) If goods supplied by the trader in response to that request or agreement do not conform to the contract, the time limit for exercising the short-term right to reject is then either—

(a) 7 days after the waiting period ends, or

(b) if later, the original time limit for exercising that right, extended by the waiting period.

(8) The waiting period—

(a) begins with the day the consumer requests or agrees to the repair or replacement of the goods, and

(b) ends with the day on which the consumer receives goods supplied by the trader in response to the request or agreement.

III CON [207]

23. Right to repair or replacement

(1) This section applies if the consumer has the right to repair or replacement (see section 19(3) and (4)).

(2) If the consumer requires the trader to repair or replace the goods, the trader must—

(a) do so within a reasonable time and without significant inconvenience to the consumer, and

(b) bear any necessary costs incurred in doing so (including in particular the cost of any labour, materials or postage).

(3) The consumer cannot require the trader to repair or replace the goods if that remedy (the repair or the replacement)—

(a) is impossible, or

(b) is disproportionate compared to the other of those remedies.

(4) Either of those remedies is disproportionate compared to the other if it imposes costs on the trader which, compared to those imposed by the other, are unreasonable, taking into account—

(a) the value which the goods would have if they conformed to the contract,

(b) the significance of the lack of conformity, and

(c) whether the other remedy could be effected without significant inconvenience to the consumer.

(5) Any question as to what is a reasonable time or significant inconvenience is to be determined taking account of—

(a) the nature of the goods, and

(b) the purpose for which the goods were acquired.

(6) A consumer who requires or agrees to the repair of goods cannot require the trader to replace them, or exercise the short-term right to reject, without giving the trader a reasonable time to repair them (unless giving the trader that time would cause significant inconvenience to the consumer).

(7) A consumer who requires or agrees to the replacement of goods cannot require the trader to repair them, or exercise the short-term right to reject, without giving the trader a reasonable time to replace them (unless giving the trader that time would cause significant inconvenience to the consumer).

(8) In this Chapter, "repair" in relation to goods that do not conform to a contract, means making them conform.

III CON [208]

24. Right to price reduction or final right to reject

(1) The right to a price reduction is the right—

(a) to require the trader to reduce by an appropriate amount the price the consumer is required to pay under the contract, or anything else the consumer is required to transfer under the contract, and

(b) to receive a refund from the trader for anything already paid or otherwise transferred by the consumer above the reduced amount.

(2) The amount of the reduction may, where appropriate, be the full amount of the price or whatever the consumer is required to transfer.

(3) Section 20(10) to (17) applies to a consumer's right to receive a refund under subsection (1)(b).

(4) The right to a price reduction does not apply—

(a) if what the consumer is (before the reduction) required to transfer under the contract, whether or not already transferred, cannot be divided up so as to enable the trader to receive or retain only the reduced amount, or

(b) if anything to which section 20(12) applies cannot be given back in its original state.

(5) A consumer who has the right to a price reduction and the final right to reject may only exercise one (not both), and may only do so in one of these situations—

(a) after one repair or one replacement, the goods do not conform to the contract;

(b) because of section 23(3) the consumer can require neither repair nor replacement of the goods; or

(c) the consumer has required the trader to repair or replace the goods, but the trader is in breach of the requirement of section 23(2)(a) to do so within a reasonable time and without significant inconvenience to the consumer.

(6) There has been a repair or replacement for the purposes of subsection (5)(a) if—

(a) the consumer has requested or agreed to repair or replacement of the goods (whether in relation to one fault or more than one), and

(b) the trader has delivered goods to the consumer, or made goods available to the consumer, in response to the request or agreement.

(7) For the purposes of subsection (6) goods that the trader arranges to repair at the consumer's premises are made available when the trader indicates that the repairs are finished.

(8) If the consumer exercises the final right to reject, any refund to the consumer may be reduced by a deduction for use, to take account of the use the consumer has had of the goods in the period since they were delivered, but this is subject to subsections (9) and (10).

(9) No deduction may be made to take account of use in any period when the consumer had the goods only because the trader failed to collect them at an agreed time.

(10) No deduction may be made if the final right to reject is exercised in the first 6 months (see subsection (11)), unless—

(a) the goods consist of a motor vehicle, or

(b) the goods are of a description specified by order made by the Secretary of State by statutory instrument.

(11) In subsection (10) the first 6 months means 6 months beginning with the first day after these have all happened—

(a) ownership or (in the case of a contract for the hire of goods, a hire-purchase agreement or a conditional sales contract) possession of the goods has been transferred to the consumer,

(b) the goods have been delivered, and

(c) where the contract requires the trader to install the goods or take other action to enable the consumer to use them, the trader has notified the consumer that the action has been taken.

(12) In subsection (10)(a) "motor vehicle"—

(a) in relation to Great Britain, has the same meaning as in the Road Traffic Act 1988 (see sections 185 to 194 of that Act);

(b) in relation to Northern Ireland, has the same meaning as in the Road Traffic (Northern Ireland) Order 1995 (SI 1995/2994 (NI 18)) (see Parts I and V of that Order).

(13) But a vehicle is not a motor vehicle for the purposes of subsection (10)(a) if it is constructed or adapted—

(a) for the use of a person suffering from some physical defect or disability, and

(b) so that it may only be used by one such person at any one time.

(14) An order under subsection (10)(b)—

(a) may be made only if the Secretary of State is satisfied that it is appropriate to do so because of significant detriment caused to traders as a result of the application of subsection (10) in relation to goods of the description specified by the order;

(b) may contain transitional or transitory provision or savings.

(15) No order may be made under subsection (10)(b) unless a draft of the statutory instrument containing it has been laid before, and approved by a resolution of, each House of Parliament.

Other Rules about Remedies under Goods Contracts

III CON [209]

25. Delivery of wrong quantity

(1) Where the trader delivers to the consumer a quantity of goods less than the trader contracted to supply, the consumer may reject them, but if the consumer accepts them the consumer must pay for them at the contract rate.

(2) Where the trader delivers to the consumer a quantity of goods larger than the trader contracted to supply, the consumer may accept the goods included in the contract and reject the rest, or may reject all of the goods.

(3) Where the trader delivers to the consumer a quantity of goods larger than the trader contracted to supply and the consumer accepts all of the goods delivered, the consumer must pay for them at the contract rate.

(4) Where the consumer is entitled to reject goods under this section, any entitlement for the consumer to treat the contract as at an end depends on the terms of the contract and the circumstances of the case.

(5) The consumer rejects goods under this section by indicating to the trader that the consumer is rejecting the goods.

(6) The indication may be something the consumer says or does, but it must be clear enough to be understood by the trader.

(7) Subsections (1) to (3) do not prevent the consumer claiming damages, where it is open to the consumer to do so.

(8) This section is subject to any usage of trade, special agreement, or course of dealing between the parties.

III CON [210]

26. Instalment deliveries

(1) Under a contract to supply goods, the consumer is not bound to accept delivery of the goods by instalments, unless that has been agreed between the consumer and the trader.

(2) The following provisions apply if the contract provides for the goods to be delivered by stated instalments, which are to be separately paid for.

(3) If the trader makes defective deliveries in respect of one or more instalments, the consumer, apart from any entitlement to claim damages, may be (but is not necessarily) entitled—

- (a) to exercise the short-term right to reject or the right to reject under section 19(6) (as applicable) in respect of the whole contract, or
- (b) to reject the goods in an instalment.

(4) Whether paragraph (a) or (b) of subsection (3) (or neither) applies to a consumer depends on the terms of the contract and the circumstances of the case.

(5) In subsection (3), making defective deliveries does not include failing to make a delivery in accordance with section 28.

(6) If the consumer neglects or refuses to take delivery of or pay for one or more instalments, the trader may—

- (a) be entitled to treat the whole contract as at an end, or
- (b) if it is a severable breach, have a claim for damages but not a right to treat the whole contract as at an end.

(7) Whether paragraph (a) or (b) of subsection (6) (or neither) applies to a trader depends on the terms of the contract and the circumstances of the case.

III CON [211]

27. Consignation, or payment into court, in Scotland

(1) Subsection (2) applies where—

- (a) a consumer has not rejected goods which the consumer could have rejected for breach of a term mentioned in section 19(3) or (6),
- (b) the consumer has chosen to treat the breach as giving rise only to a claim for damages or to a right to rely on the breach against a claim by the trader for the price of the goods, and
- (c) the trader has begun proceedings in court to recover the price or has brought a counter-claim for the price.

(2) The court may require the consumer—

- (a) to consign, or pay into court, the price of the goods, or part of the price, or
- (b) to provide some other reasonable security for payment of the price.

Other Rules about Goods Contracts

III CON [212]

28. Delivery of goods

(1) This section applies to any sales contract.

(2) Unless the trader and the consumer have agreed otherwise, the contract is to be treated as including a term that the trader must deliver the goods to the consumer.

(3) Unless there is an agreed time or period, the contract is to be treated as including a term that the trader must deliver the goods—

- (a) without undue delay, and

(b) in any event, not more than 30 days after the day on which the contract is entered into.

(4) In this section—

(a) an "agreed" time or period means a time or period agreed by the trader and the consumer for delivery of the goods;

(b) if there is an obligation to deliver the goods at the time the contract is entered into, that time counts as the "agreed" time.

(5) Subsections (6) and (7) apply if the trader does not deliver the goods in accordance with subsection (3) or at the agreed time or within the agreed period.

(6) If the circumstances are that—

(a) the trader has refused to deliver the goods,

(b) delivery of the goods at the agreed time or within the agreed period is essential taking into account all the relevant circumstances at the time the contract was entered into, or

(c) the consumer told the trader before the contract was entered into that delivery in accordance with subsection (3), or at the agreed time or within the agreed period, was essential,

then the consumer may treat the contract as at an end.

(7) In any other circumstances, the consumer may specify a period that is appropriate in the circumstances and require the trader to deliver the goods before the end of that period.

(8) If the consumer specifies a period under subsection (7) but the goods are not delivered within that period, then the consumer may treat the contract as at an end.

(9) If the consumer treats the contract as at an end under subsection (6) or (8), the trader must without undue delay reimburse all payments made under the contract.

(10) If subsection (6) or (8) applies but the consumer does not treat the contract as at an end—

(a) that does not prevent the consumer from cancelling the order for any of the goods or rejecting goods that have been delivered, and

(b) the trader must without undue delay reimburse all payments made under the contract in respect of any goods for which the consumer cancels the order or which the consumer rejects.

(11) If any of the goods form a commercial unit, the consumer cannot reject or cancel the order for some of those goods without also rejecting or cancelling the order for the rest of them.

(12) A unit is a "commercial unit" if division of the unit would materially impair the value of the goods or the character of the unit.

(13) This section does not prevent the consumer seeking other remedies where it is open to the consumer to do so.

(14) See section 2(5) and (6) for the application of this section where goods are sold at public auction.

III CON [213]

29. Passing of risk

(1) A sales contract is to be treated as including the following provisions as terms.

(2) The goods remain at the trader's risk until they come into the physical possession of—

(a) the consumer, or

(b) a person identified by the consumer to take possession of the goods.

(3) Subsection (2) does not apply if the goods are delivered to a carrier who—

(a) is commissioned by the consumer to deliver the goods, and

(b) is not a carrier the trader named as an option for the consumer.

(4) In that case the goods are at the consumer's risk on and after delivery to the carrier.

(5) Subsection (4) does not affect any liability of the carrier to the consumer in respect of the goods.

(6) See section 2(5) and (6) for the application of this section where goods are sold at public auction.

III CON [214]

30. Goods under guarantee

(1) This section applies where—

(a) there is a contract to supply goods, and

(b) there is a guarantee in relation to the goods.

(2) "Guarantee" here means an undertaking to the consumer given without extra charge by a person acting in the course of the person's business (the "guarantor") that, if the goods do not meet the specifications set out in the guarantee statement or in any associated advertising—

(a) the consumer will be reimbursed for the price paid for the goods, or

(b) the goods will be repaired, replaced or handled in any way.

(3) The guarantee takes effect, at the time the goods are delivered, as a contractual obligation owed by the guarantor under the conditions set out in the guarantee statement and in any associated advertising.

(4) The guarantor must ensure that—

(a) the guarantee sets out in plain and intelligible language the contents of the guarantee and the essential particulars for making claims under the guarantee,

(b) the guarantee states that the consumer has statutory rights in relation to the goods and that those rights are not affected by the guarantee, and

(c) where the goods are offered within the territory of the United Kingdom, the guarantee is written in English.

(5) The contents of the guarantee to be set out in it include, in particular—

(a) the name and address of the guarantor, and

(b) the duration and territorial scope of the guarantee.

(6) The guarantor and any other person who offers to supply to consumers the goods which are the subject of the guarantee must, on request by the consumer, make the guarantee available to the consumer within a reasonable time, in writing and in a form accessible to the consumer.

(7) What is a reasonable time is a question of fact.

(8) If a person fails to comply with a requirement of this section, the enforcement authority may apply to the court for an injunction or (in Scotland) an order of specific implement against that person requiring that person to comply.

(9) On an application the court may grant an injunction or (in Scotland) an order of specific implement on such terms as it thinks appropriate.

(10) In this section—

"court" means—

(a) in relation to England and Wales, the High Court or the county court,

(b) in relation to Northern Ireland, the High Court or a county court, and

(c) in relation to Scotland, the Court of Session or the sheriff;

"enforcement authority" means—

(a) the Competition and Markets Authority,

(b) a local weights and measures authority in Great Britain, and
(c) the Department of Enterprise, Trade and Investment in Northern Ireland.

Can a Trader Contract out of Statutory Rights and Remedies under a Goods Contract?

III CON [215]

31. Liability that cannot be excluded or restricted

(1) A term of a contract to supply goods is not binding on the consumer to the extent that it would exclude or restrict the trader's liability arising under any of these provisions—

- (a) section 9 (goods to be of satisfactory quality);
- (b) section 10 (goods to be fit for particular purpose);
- (c) section 11 (goods to be as described);
- (d) section 12 (other pre-contract information included in contract);
- (e) section 13 (goods to match a sample);
- (f) section 14 (goods to match a model seen or examined);
- (g) section 15 (installation as part of conformity of the goods with the contract);
- (h) section 16 (goods not conforming to contract if digital content does not conform);
- (i) section 17 (trader to have right to supply the goods etc);
- (j) section 28 (delivery of goods);
- (k) section 29 (passing of risk).

(2) That also means that a term of a contract to supply goods is not binding on the consumer to the extent that it would—

- (a) exclude or restrict a right or remedy in respect of a liability under a provision listed in subsection (1),
- (b) make such a right or remedy or its enforcement subject to a restrictive or onerous condition,
- (c) allow a trader to put a person at a disadvantage as a result of pursuing such a right or remedy, or
- (d) exclude or restrict rules of evidence or procedure.

(3) The reference in subsection (1) to excluding or restricting a liability also includes preventing an obligation or duty arising or limiting its extent.

(4) An agreement in writing to submit present or future differences to arbitration is not to be regarded as excluding or restricting any liability for the purposes of this section.

(5) Subsection (1)(i), and subsection (2) so far as it relates to liability under section 17, do not apply to a term of a contract for the hire of goods.

(6) But an express term of a contract for the hire of goods is not binding on the consumer to the extent that it would exclude or restrict a term that section 17 requires to be treated as included in the contract, unless it is inconsistent with that term (and see also section 62 (requirement for terms to be fair)).

(7) See Schedule 3 for provision about the enforcement of this section.

III CON [216]

32. Contracts applying law of non-EEA State

(1) If—

- (a) the law of a country or territory other than an EEA State is chosen by the parties to be applicable to a sales contract, but

(b) the sales contract has a close connection with the United Kingdom,

this Chapter, except the provisions in subsection (2), applies despite that choice.

(2) The exceptions are—

(a) sections 11(4) and (5) and 12;

(b) sections 28 and 29;

(c) section 31(1)(d), (j) and (k).

(3) For cases where those provisions apply, or where the law applicable has not been chosen or the law of an EEA State is chosen, see Regulation (EC) No 593/2008 of the European Parliament and of the Council of 17 June 2008 on the law applicable to contractual obligations.

CHAPTER 3
DIGITAL CONTENT

What Digital Content Contracts are Covered?

III CON [217]

33. Contracts covered by this Chapter

(1) This Chapter applies to a contract for a trader to supply digital content to a consumer, if it is supplied or to be supplied for a price paid by the consumer.

(2) This Chapter also applies to a contract for a trader to supply digital content to a consumer, if—

(a) it is supplied free with goods or services or other digital content for which the consumer pays a price, and

(b) it is not generally available to consumers unless they have paid a price for it or for goods or services or other digital content.

(3) The references in subsections (1) and (2) to the consumer paying a price include references to the consumer using, by way of payment, any facility for which money has been paid.

(4) A trader does not supply digital content to a consumer for the purposes of this Part merely because the trader supplies a service by which digital content reaches the consumer.

(5) The Secretary of State may by order provide for this Chapter to apply to other contracts for a trader to supply digital content to a consumer, if the Secretary of State is satisfied that it is appropriate to do so because of significant detriment caused to consumers under contracts of the kind to which the order relates.

(6) An order under subsection (5)—

(a) may, in particular, amend this Act;

(b) may contain transitional or transitory provision or savings.

(7) A contract to which this Chapter applies is referred to in this Part as a "contract to supply digital content".

(8) This section, other than subsection (4), does not limit the application of section 46.

(9) The power to make an order under subsection (5) is exercisable by statutory instrument.

(10) No order may be made under subsection (5) unless a draft of the statutory instrument containing it has been laid before, and approved by a resolution of, each House of Parliament.

What Statutory Rights are There under a Digital Content Contract?

III CON [218]

34. Digital content to be of satisfactory quality

(1) Every contract to supply digital content is to be treated as including a term that the quality of the digital content is satisfactory.

(2) The quality of digital content is satisfactory if it meets the standard that a reasonable person would consider satisfactory, taking account of—

- (a) any description of the digital content,
- (b) the price mentioned in section 33(1) or (2)(b) (if relevant), and
- (c) all the other relevant circumstances (see subsection (5)).

(3) The quality of digital content includes its state and condition; and the following aspects (among others) are in appropriate cases aspects of the quality of digital content—

- (a) fitness for all the purposes for which digital content of that kind is usually supplied;
- (b) freedom from minor defects;
- (c) safety;
- (d) durability.

(4) The term mentioned in subsection (1) does not cover anything which makes the quality of the digital content unsatisfactory—

- (a) which is specifically drawn to the consumer's attention before the contract is made,
- (b) where the consumer examines the digital content before the contract is made, which that examination ought to reveal, or
- (c) where the consumer examines a trial version before the contract is made, which would have been apparent on a reasonable examination of the trial version.

(5) The relevant circumstances mentioned in subsection (2)(c) include any public statement about the specific characteristics of the digital content made by the trader, the producer or any representative of the trader or the producer.

(6) That includes, in particular, any public statement made in advertising or labelling.

(7) But a public statement is not a relevant circumstance for the purposes of subsection (2)(c) if the trader shows that—

- (a) when the contract was made, the trader was not, and could not reasonably have been, aware of the statement,
- (b) before the contract was made, the statement had been publicly withdrawn or, to the extent that it contained anything which was incorrect or misleading, it had been publicly corrected, or
- (c) the consumer's decision to contract for the digital content could not have been influenced by the statement.

(8) In a contract to supply digital content a term about the quality of the digital content may be treated as included as a matter of custom.

(9) See section 42 for a consumer's rights if the trader is in breach of a term that this section requires to be treated as included in a contract.

III CON [219]

35. Digital content to be fit for particular purpose

(1) Subsection (3) applies to a contract to supply digital content if before the contract is made the consumer makes known to the trader (expressly or by implication) any particular purpose for which the consumer is contracting for the digital content.

(2) Subsection (3) also applies to a contract to supply digital content if—

(a) the digital content was previously sold by a credit-broker to the trader,

(b) the consideration or part of it is a sum payable by instalments, and

(c) before the contract is made, the consumer makes known to the credit-broker (expressly or by implication) any particular purpose for which the consumer is contracting for the digital content.

(3) The contract is to be treated as including a term that the digital content is reasonably fit for that purpose, whether or not that is a purpose for which digital content of that kind is usually supplied.

(4) Subsection (3) does not apply if the circumstances show that the consumer does not rely, or it is unreasonable for the consumer to rely, on the skill or judgment of the trader or credit-broker.

(5) A contract to supply digital content may be treated as making provision about the fitness of the digital content for a particular purpose as a matter of custom.

(6) See section 42 for a consumer's rights if the trader is in breach of a term that this section requires to be treated as included in a contract.

III CON [220]

36. Digital content to be as described

(1) Every contract to supply digital content is to be treated as including a term that the digital content will match any description of it given by the trader to the consumer.

(2) Where the consumer examines a trial version before the contract is made, it is not sufficient that the digital content matches (or is better than) the trial version if the digital content does not also match any description of it given by the trader to the consumer.

(3) Any information that is provided by the trader about the digital content that is information mentioned in paragraph (a), (j) or (k) of Schedule 1 or paragraph (a), (v) or (w) of Schedule 2 (main characteristics, functionality and compatibility) to the Consumer Contracts (Information, Cancellation and Additional Charges) Regulations 2013 (SI 2013/3134) is to be treated as included as a term of the contract.

(4) A change to any of that information, made before entering into the contract or later, is not effective unless expressly agreed between the consumer and the trader.

(5) See section 42 for a consumer's rights if the trader is in breach of a term that this section requires to be treated as included in a contract.

III CON [221]

37. Other pre-contract information included in contract

(1) This section applies to any contract to supply digital content.

(2) Where regulation 9, 10 or 13 of the Consumer Contracts (Information, Cancellation and Additional Charges) Regulations 2013 (SI 2013/3134) required the trader to provide information to the consumer before the contract became binding, any of that information that was provided by the trader other than information about the digital content and mentioned in paragraph (a), (j) or (k) of Schedule 1 or paragraph (a), (v) or (w) of Schedule 2 to the Regulations (main characteristics, functionality and compatibility) is to be treated as included as a term of the contract.

(3) A change to any of that information, made before entering into the contract or later, is not effective unless expressly agreed between the consumer and the trader.

(4) See section 42 for a consumer's rights if the trader is in breach of a term that this section requires to be treated as included in a contract.

III CON [222]

38. No other requirement to treat term about quality or fitness as included

(1) Except as provided by sections 34 and 35, a contract to supply digital content is not to be treated as including any term about the quality of the digital content or its fitness for any particular purpose, unless the term is expressly included in the contract.

(2) Subsection (1) is subject to provision made by any other enactment, whenever passed or made.

III CON [223]

39. Supply by transmission and facilities for continued transmission

(1) Subsection (2) applies where there is a contract to supply digital content and the consumer's access to the content on a device requires its transmission to the device under arrangements initiated by the trader.

(2) For the purposes of this Chapter, the digital content is supplied—

- (a) when the content reaches the device, or
- (b) if earlier, when the content reaches another trader chosen by the consumer to supply, under a contract with the consumer, a service by which digital content reaches the device.

(3) Subsections (5) to (7) apply where—

- (a) there is a contract to supply digital content, and
- (b) after the trader (T) has supplied the digital content, the consumer is to have access under the contract to a processing facility under arrangements made by T.

(4) A processing facility is a facility by which T or another trader will receive digital content from the consumer and transmit digital content to the consumer (whether or not other features are to be included under the contract).

(5) The contract is to be treated as including a term that the processing facility (with any feature that the facility is to include under the contract) must be available to the consumer for a reasonable time, unless a time is specified in the contract.

(6) The following provisions apply to all digital content transmitted to the consumer on each occasion under the facility, while it is provided under the contract, as they apply to the digital content first supplied—

- (a) section 34 (quality);
- (b) section 35 (fitness for a particular purpose);
- (c) section 36 (description).

(7) Breach of a term treated as included under subsection (5) has the same effect as breach of a term treated as included under those sections (see section 42).

III CON [224]

40. Quality, fitness and description of content supplied subject to modifications

(1) Where under a contract a trader supplies digital content to a consumer subject to the right of the trader or a third party to modify the digital content, the following provisions apply in relation to the digital content as modified as they apply in relation to the digital content as supplied under the contract—

- (a) section 34 (quality);
- (b) section 35 (fitness for a particular purpose);
- (c) section 36 (description).

(2) Subsection (1)(c) does not prevent the trader from improving the features of, or adding new features to, the digital content, as long as—

- (a) the digital content continues to match the description of it given by the trader to the consumer, and
- (b) the digital content continues to conform to the information provided by the trader as mentioned in subsection (3) of section 36, subject to any change to that information that has been agreed in accordance with subsection (4) of that section.

(3) A claim on the grounds that digital content does not conform to a term described in any of the sections listed in subsection (1) as applied by that subsection is to be treated as arising at the time when the digital content was supplied under the contract and not the time when it is modified.

III CON [225]

41. Trader's right to supply digital content

(1) Every contract to supply digital content is to be treated as including a term—

- (a) in relation to any digital content which is supplied under the contract and which the consumer has paid for, that the trader has the right to supply that content to the consumer;
- (b) in relation to any digital content which the trader agrees to supply under the contract and which the consumer has paid for, that the trader will have the right to supply it to the consumer at the time when it is to be supplied.

(2) See section 42 for a consumer's rights if the trader is in breach of a term that this section requires to be treated as included in a contract.

What Remedies are There if Statutory Rights under a Digital Content Contract are not Met?

III CON [226]

42. Consumer's rights to enforce terms about digital content

(1) In this section and section 43 references to digital content conforming to a contract are references to the digital content conforming to the terms described in sections 34, 35 and 36.

(2) If the digital content does not conform to the contract, the consumer's rights (and the provisions about them and when they are available) are—

- (a) the right to repair or replacement (see section 43);
- (b) the right to a price reduction (see section 44).

(3) Section 16 also applies if an item including the digital content is supplied.

(4) If the trader is in breach of a term that section 37 requires to be treated as included in the contract, the consumer has the right to recover from the trader the amount of any costs incurred by the consumer as a result of the breach, up to the amount of the price paid for the digital content or for any facility within section 33(3) used by the consumer.

(5) If the trader is in breach of the term that section 41(1) (right to supply the content) requires to be treated as included in the contract, the consumer has the right to a refund (see section 45 for provisions about that right and when it is available).

(6) This Chapter does not prevent the consumer seeking other remedies for a breach of a term to which any of subsections (2), (4) or (5) applies, instead of or in addition to a remedy referred to there (but not so as to recover twice for the same loss).

(7) Those other remedies include any of the following that is open to the consumer in the circumstances—

- (a) claiming damages;
- (b) seeking to recover money paid where the consideration for payment of the money has failed;
- (c) seeking specific performance;
- (d) seeking an order for specific implement;
- (e) relying on the breach against a claim by the trader for the price.

(8) It is not open to the consumer to treat the contract as at an end for breach of a term to which any of subsections (2), (4) or (5) applies.

(9) For the purposes of subsection (2), digital content which does not conform to the contract at any time within the period of six months beginning with the day on which it was supplied must be taken not to have conformed to the contract when it was supplied.

(10) Subsection (9) does not apply if—

- (a) it is established that the digital content did conform to the contract when it was supplied, or
- (b) its application is incompatible with the nature of the digital content or with how it fails to conform to the contract.

III CON [227]

43. Right to repair or replacement

(1) This section applies if the consumer has the right to repair or replacement.

(2) If the consumer requires the trader to repair or replace the digital content, the trader must—

- (a) do so within a reasonable time and without significant inconvenience to the consumer; and
- (b) bear any necessary costs incurred in doing so (including in particular the cost of any labour, materials or postage).

(3) The consumer cannot require the trader to repair or replace the digital content if that remedy (the repair or the replacement)—

- (a) is impossible, or
- (b) is disproportionate compared to the other of those remedies.

(4) Either of those remedies is disproportionate compared to the other if it imposes costs on the trader which, compared to those imposed by the other, are unreasonable, taking into account—

- (a) the value which the digital content would have if it conformed to the contract,
- (b) the significance of the lack of conformity, and
- (c) whether the other remedy could be effected without significant inconvenience to the consumer.

(5) Any question as to what is a reasonable time or significant inconvenience is to be determined taking account of—

- (a) the nature of the digital content, and
- (b) the purpose for which the digital content was obtained or accessed.

(6) A consumer who requires or agrees to the repair of digital content cannot require the trader to replace it without giving the trader a reasonable time to repair it (unless giving the trader that time would cause significant inconvenience to the consumer).

(7) A consumer who requires or agrees to the replacement of digital content cannot require the trader to repair it without giving the trader a reasonable time to replace it (unless giving the trader that time would cause significant inconvenience to the consumer).

(8) In this Chapter, "repair" in relation to digital content that does not conform to a contract, means making it conform.

III CON [228]

44. Right to price reduction

(1) The right to a price reduction is the right to require the trader to reduce the price to the consumer by an appropriate amount (including the right to receive a refund for anything already paid above the reduced amount).

(2) The amount of the reduction may, where appropriate, be the full amount of the price.

(3) A consumer who has that right may only exercise it in one of these situations—

- (a) because of section 43(3)(a) the consumer can require neither repair nor replacement of the digital content, or
- (b) the consumer has required the trader to repair or replace the digital content, but the trader is in breach of the requirement of section 43(2)(a) to do so within a reasonable time and without significant inconvenience to the consumer.

(4) A refund under this section must be given without undue delay, and in any event within 14 days beginning with the day on which the trader agrees that the consumer is entitled to a refund.

(5) The trader must give the refund using the same means of payment as the consumer used to pay for the digital content, unless the consumer expressly agrees otherwise.

(6) The trader must not impose any fee on the consumer in respect of the refund.

III CON [229]

45. Right to a refund

(1) The right to a refund gives the consumer the right to receive a refund from the trader of all money paid by the consumer for the digital content (subject to subsection (2)).

(2) If the breach giving the consumer the right to a refund affects only some of the digital content supplied under the contract, the right to a refund does not extend to any part of the price attributable to digital content that is not affected by the breach.

(3) A refund must be given without undue delay, and in any event within 14 days beginning with the day on which the trader agrees that the consumer is entitled to a refund.

(4) The trader must give the refund using the same means of payment as the consumer used to pay for the digital content, unless the consumer expressly agrees otherwise.

(5) The trader must not impose any fee on the consumer in respect of the refund.

Compensation for Damage to Device or to other Digital Content

III CON [230]

46. Remedy for damage to device or to other digital content

(1) This section applies if—

- (a) a trader supplies digital content to a consumer under a contract,
- (b) the digital content causes damage to a device or to other digital content,
- (c) the device or digital content that is damaged belongs to the consumer, and

(d) the damage is of a kind that would not have occurred if the trader had exercised reasonable care and skill.

(2) If the consumer requires the trader to provide a remedy under this section, the trader must either—

(a) repair the damage in accordance with subsection (3), or

(b) compensate the consumer for the damage with an appropriate payment.

(3) To repair the damage in accordance with this subsection, the trader must—

(a) repair the damage within a reasonable time and without significant inconvenience to the consumer, and

(b) bear any necessary costs incurred in repairing the damage (including in particular the cost of any labour, materials or postage).

(4) Any question as to what is a reasonable time or significant inconvenience is to be determined taking account of—

(a) the nature of the device or digital content that is damaged, and

(b) the purpose for which it is used by the consumer.

(5) A compensation payment under this section must be made without undue delay, and in any event within 14 days beginning with the day on which the trader agrees that the consumer is entitled to the payment.

(6) The trader must not impose any fee on the consumer in respect of the payment.

(7) A consumer with a right to a remedy under this section may bring a claim in civil proceedings to enforce that right.

(8) The Limitation Act 1980 and the Limitation (Northern Ireland) Order 1989 (SI 1989/1339 (NI 11)) apply to a claim under this section as if it were an action founded on simple contract.

(9) The Prescription and Limitation (Scotland) Act 1973 applies to a right to a remedy under this section as if it were an obligation to which section 6 of that Act applies.

Can a Trader Contract out of Statutory Rights and Remedies under a Digital Content Contract?

III CON [231]

47. Liability that cannot be excluded or restricted

(1) A term of a contract to supply digital content is not binding on the consumer to the extent that it would exclude or restrict the trader's liability arising under any of these provisions—

(a) section 34 (digital content to be of satisfactory quality),

(b) section 35 (digital content to be fit for particular purpose),

(c) section 36 (digital content to be as described),

(d) section 37 (other pre-contract information included in contract), or

(e) section 41 (trader's right to supply digital content).

(2) That also means that a term of a contract to supply digital content is not binding on the consumer to the extent that it would—

(a) exclude or restrict a right or remedy in respect of a liability under a provision listed in subsection (1),

(b) make such a right or remedy or its enforcement subject to a restrictive or onerous condition,

(c) allow a trader to put a person at a disadvantage as a result of pursuing such a right or remedy, or

(d) exclude or restrict rules of evidence or procedure.

(3) The reference in subsection (1) to excluding or restricting a liability also includes preventing an obligation or duty arising or limiting its extent.

(4) An agreement in writing to submit present or future differences to arbitration is not to be regarded as excluding or restricting any liability for the purposes of this section.

(5) See Schedule 3 for provision about the enforcement of this section.

(6) For provision limiting the ability of a trader under a contract within section 46 to exclude or restrict the trader's liability under that section, see section 62.

CHAPTER 4
SERVICES

What Services Contracts are Covered?

III CON [232]

48. Contracts covered by this Chapter

(1) This Chapter applies to a contract for a trader to supply a service to a consumer.

(2) That does not include a contract of employment or apprenticeship.

(3) In relation to Scotland, this Chapter does not apply to a gratuitous contract.

(3A) This Chapter does not apply to anything that is governed by Regulation (EU) No 181/2011 of the European Parliament and of the Council of 16 February 2011 concerning the rights of passengers in bus and coach transport and amending Regulation (EC) No 2006/2004.

(4) A contract to which this Chapter applies is referred to in this Part as a "contract to supply a service".

(5) The Secretary of State may by order made by statutory instrument provide that a provision of this Chapter does not apply in relation to a service of a description specified in the order.

(6) The power in subsection (5) includes power to provide that a provision of this Chapter does not apply in relation to a service of a description specified in the order in the circumstances so specified.

(7) An order under subsection (5) may contain transitional or transitory provision or savings.

(8) No order may be made under subsection (5) unless a draft of the statutory instrument containing it has been laid before, and approved by a resolution of, each House of Parliament.

What Statutory Rights are There under a Services Contract?

III CON [233]

49. Service to be performed with reasonable care and skill

(1) Every contract to supply a service is to be treated as including a term that the trader must perform the service with reasonable care and skill.

(2) See section 54 for a consumer's rights if the trader is in breach of a term that this section requires to be treated as included in a contract.

III CON [234]

50. Information about the trader or service to be binding

(1) Every contract to supply a service is to be treated as including as a term of the contract anything that is said or written to the consumer, by or on behalf of the trader, about the trader or the service, if—

(a) it is taken into account by the consumer when deciding to enter into the contract, or

(b) it is taken into account by the consumer when making any decision about the service after entering into the contract.

(2) Anything taken into account by the consumer as mentioned in subsection (1)(a) or (b) is subject to—

(a) anything that qualified it and was said or written to the consumer by the trader on the same occasion, and

(b) any change to it that has been expressly agreed between the consumer and the trader (before entering into the contract or later).

(3) Without prejudice to subsection (1), any information provided by the trader in accordance with regulation 9, 10 or 13 of the Consumer Contracts (Information, Cancellation and Additional Charges) Regulations 2013 (SI 2013/3134) is to be treated as included as a term of the contract.

(4) A change to any of the information mentioned in subsection (3), made before entering into the contract or later, is not effective unless expressly agreed between the consumer and the trader.

(5) See section 54 for a consumer's rights if the trader is in breach of a term that this section requires to be treated as included in a contract.

III CON [235]

51. Reasonable price to be paid for a service

(1) This section applies to a contract to supply a service if—

(a) the consumer has not paid a price or other consideration for the service,

(b) the contract does not expressly fix a price or other consideration, and does not say how it is to be fixed, and

(c) anything that is to be treated under section 50 as included in the contract does not fix a price or other consideration either.

(2) In that case the contract is to be treated as including a term that the consumer must pay a reasonable price for the service, and no more.

(3) What is a reasonable price is a question of fact.

III CON [236]

52. Service to be performed within a reasonable time

(1) This section applies to a contract to supply a service, if—

(a) the contract does not expressly fix the time for the service to be performed, and does not say how it is to be fixed, and

(b) information that is to be treated under section 50 as included in the contract does not fix the time either.

(2) In that case the contract is to be treated as including a term that the trader must perform the service within a reasonable time.

(3) What is a reasonable time is a question of fact.

(4) See section 54 for a consumer's rights if the trader is in breach of a term that this section requires to be treated as included in a contract.

III CON [237]

53. Relation to other law on contract terms

(1) Nothing in this Chapter affects any enactment or rule of law that imposes a stricter duty on the trader.

(2) This Chapter is subject to any other enactment which defines or restricts the rights, duties or liabilities arising in connection with a service of any description.

III CON [237.1]

Penalty clauses Outside the statute the court's powers at common law and in equity include the grant of relief against unfair or oppressive bargains for example rescission of the contract. There is also power to disallow the enforcement of penalty clauses that require the payment of a penal sum on breach, which is in excess of the real loss suffered. The enforceability of a penalty clause depends on whether it is extortionate or extravagant, these being the main tests for striking it down: *Cavendish Square Holdings BV v El Makdessi and Beavis v ParkingEye Ltd* [2015] UKSC 67, [2015] All ER (D) 47 (Nov).

What Remedies are There if Statutory Rights under a Services Contract are not Met?

III CON [238]

54. Consumer's rights to enforce terms about services

(1) The consumer's rights under this section and sections 55 and 56 do not affect any rights that the contract provides for, if those are not inconsistent.

(2) In this section and section 55 a reference to a service conforming to a contract is a reference to—

- (a) the service being performed in accordance with section 49, or
- (b) the service conforming to a term that section 50 requires to be treated as included in the contract and that relates to the performance of the service.

(3) If the service does not conform to the contract, the consumer's rights (and the provisions about them and when they are available) are—

- (a) the right to require repeat performance (see section 55);
- (b) the right to a price reduction (see section 56).

(4) If the trader is in breach of a term that section 50 requires to be treated as included in the contract but that does not relate to the service, the consumer has the right to a price reduction (see section 56 for provisions about that right and when it is available).

(5) If the trader is in breach of what the contract requires under section 52 (performance within a reasonable time), the consumer has the right to a price reduction (see section 56 for provisions about that right and when it is available).

(6) This section and sections 55 and 56 do not prevent the consumer seeking other remedies for a breach of a term to which any of subsections (3) to (5) applies, instead of or in addition to a remedy referred to there (but not so as to recover twice for the same loss).

(7) Those other remedies include any of the following that is open to the consumer in the circumstances—

- (a) claiming damages;
- (b) seeking to recover money paid where the consideration for payment of the money has failed;
- (c) seeking specific performance;
- (d) seeking an order for specific implement;
- (e) relying on the breach against a claim by the trader under the contract;
- (f) exercising a right to treat the contract as at an end.

III CON [239]

55. Right to repeat performance

(1) The right to require repeat performance is a right to require the trader to perform the service again, to the extent necessary to complete its performance in conformity with the contract.

(2) If the consumer requires such repeat performance, the trader—

- (a) must provide it within a reasonable time and without significant inconvenience to the consumer; and
- (b) must bear any necessary costs incurred in doing so (including in particular the cost of any labour or materials).

(3) The consumer cannot require repeat performance if completing performance of the service in conformity with the contract is impossible.

(4) Any question as to what is a reasonable time or significant inconvenience is to be determined taking account of—

- (a) the nature of the service, and
- (b) the purpose for which the service was to be performed.

III CON [240]

56. Right to price reduction

(1) The right to a price reduction is the right to require the trader to reduce the price to the consumer by an appropriate amount (including the right to receive a refund for anything already paid above the reduced amount).

(2) The amount of the reduction may, where appropriate, be the full amount of the price.

(3) A consumer who has that right and the right to require repeat performance is only entitled to a price reduction in one of these situations—

- (a) because of section 55(3) the consumer cannot require repeat performance; or
- (b) the consumer has required repeat performance, but the trader is in breach of the requirement of section 55(2)(a) to do it within a reasonable time and without significant inconvenience to the consumer.

(4) A refund under this section must be given without undue delay, and in any event within 14 days beginning with the day on which the trader agrees that the consumer is entitled to a refund.

(5) The trader must give the refund using the same means of payment as the consumer used to pay for the service, unless the consumer expressly agrees otherwise.

(6) The trader must not impose any fee on the consumer in respect of the refund.

Can a Trader Contract out of Statutory Rights and Remedies under a Services Contract?

III CON [241]

57. Liability that cannot be excluded or restricted

(1) A term of a contract to supply services is not binding on the consumer to the extent that it would exclude the trader's liability arising under section 49 (service to be performed with reasonable care and skill).

(2) Subject to section 50(2), a term of a contract to supply services is not binding on the consumer to the extent that it would exclude the trader's liability arising under section 50 (information about trader or service to be binding).

(3) A term of a contract to supply services is not binding on the consumer to the extent that it would restrict the trader's liability arising under any of sections 49 and 50 and, where they apply, sections 51 and 52 (reasonable price and reasonable time), if it would prevent the consumer in an appropriate case from recovering the price paid or the value of any other consideration. (If it would not prevent the consumer from doing so, Part 2 (unfair terms) may apply.)

(4) That also means that a term of a contract to supply services is not binding on the consumer to the extent that it would —

(a) exclude or restrict a right or remedy in respect of a liability under any of sections 49 to 52,

(b) make such a right or remedy or its enforcement subject to a restrictive or onerous condition,

(c) allow a trader to put a person at a disadvantage as a result of pursuing such a right or remedy, or

(d) exclude or restrict rules of evidence or procedure.

(5) The references in subsections (1) to (3) to excluding or restricting a liability also include preventing an obligation or duty arising or limiting its extent.

(6) An agreement in writing to submit present or future differences to arbitration is not to be regarded as excluding or restricting any liability for the purposes of this section.

(7) See Schedule 3 for provision about the enforcement of this section.

CHAPTER 5
GENERAL AND SUPPLEMENTARY PROVISIONS

III CON [242]

58. Powers of the court

(1) In any proceedings in which a remedy is sought by virtue of section 19(3) or (4), 42(2) or 54(3), the court, in addition to any other power it has, may act under this section.

(2) On the application of the consumer the court may make an order requiring specific performance or, in Scotland, specific implement by the trader of any obligation imposed on the trader by virtue of section 23, 43 or 55.

(3) Subsection (4) applies if—

(a) the consumer claims to exercise a right under the relevant remedies provisions, but

(b) the court decides that those provisions have the effect that exercise of another right is appropriate.

(4) The court may proceed as if the consumer had exercised that other right.

(5) If the consumer has claimed to exercise the final right to reject, the court may order that any reimbursement to the consumer is reduced by a deduction for use, to take account of the use the consumer has had of the goods in the period since they were delivered.

(6) Any deduction for use is limited as set out in section 24(9) and (10).

(7) The court may make an order under this section unconditionally or on such terms and conditions as to damages, payment of the price and otherwise as it thinks just.

(8) The "relevant remedies provisions" are—

(a) where Chapter 2 applies, sections 23 and 24;

(b) where Chapter 3 applies, sections 43 and 44;

(c) where Chapter 4 applies, sections 55 and 56.

III CON [243]

59. Interpretation

(1) These definitions apply in this Part (as well as the key definitions in section 2)—

"conditional sales contract" has the meaning given in section 5(3);

"Consumer Rights Directive" means Directive 2011/83/EU of the European Parliament and of the Council of 25 October 2011 on consumer rights, amending Council Directive 93/13/EEC and Directive 1999/44/EC of the European Parliament and of the Council and repealing Council Directive 85/577/EEC and Directive 97/7/EC of the European Parliament and of the Council;

"credit-broker" means a person acting in the course of a business of credit brokerage carried on by that person;

"credit brokerage" means—

(a) introducing individuals who want to obtain credit to persons carrying on any business so far as it relates to the provision of credit,

(b) introducing individuals who want to obtain goods on hire to persons carrying on a business which comprises or relates to supplying goods under a contract for the hire of goods, or

(c) introducing individuals who want to obtain credit, or to obtain goods on hire, to other persons engaged in credit brokerage;

"delivery" means voluntary transfer of possession from one person to another;

"enactment" includes—

(a) an enactment contained in subordinate legislation within the meaning of the Interpretation Act 1978,

(b) an enactment contained in, or in an instrument made under, a Measure or Act of the National Assembly for Wales,

(c) an enactment contained in, or in an instrument made under, an Act of the Scottish Parliament, and

(d) an enactment contained in, or in an instrument made under, Northern Ireland legislation;

"producer", in relation to goods or digital content, means—

(a) the manufacturer,

(b) the importer into the European Economic Area, or

(c) any person who purports to be a producer by placing the person's name, trade mark or other distinctive sign on the goods or using it in connection with the digital content.

(2) References in this Part to treating a contract as at an end are to be read in accordance with section 19(13).

III CON [244]

60. Changes to other legislation

Schedule 1 (amendments consequential on this Part) has effect.

PART 2
UNFAIR TERMS

What Contracts and Notices are Covered by this Part?

III CON [245]

61. Contracts and notices covered by this Part

(1) This Part applies to a contract between a trader and a consumer.

(2) This does not include a contract of employment or apprenticeship.

(3) A contract to which this Part applies is referred to in this Part as a "consumer contract".

(4) This Part applies to a notice to the extent that it—

(a) relates to rights or obligations as between a trader and a consumer, or

(b) purports to exclude or restrict a trader's liability to a consumer.

(5) This does not include a notice relating to rights, obligations or liabilities as between an employer and an employee.

(6) It does not matter for the purposes of subsection (4) whether the notice is expressed to apply to a consumer, as long as it is reasonable to assume it is intended to be seen or heard by a consumer.

(7) A notice to which this Part applies is referred to in this Part as a "consumer notice".

(8) In this section "notice" includes an announcement, whether or not in writing, and any other communication or purported communication.

What are the General Rules about Fairness of Contract Terms and Notices?

III CON [246]

62. Requirement for contract terms and notices to be fair

(1) An unfair term of a consumer contract is not binding on the consumer.

(2) An unfair consumer notice is not binding on the consumer.

(3) This does not prevent the consumer from relying on the term or notice if the consumer chooses to do so.

(4) A term is unfair if, contrary to the requirement of good faith, it causes a significant imbalance in the parties' rights and obligations under the contract to the detriment of the consumer.

(5) Whether a term is fair is to be determined—

(a) taking into account the nature of the subject matter of the contract, and

(b) by reference to all the circumstances existing when the term was agreed and to all of the other terms of the contract or of any other contract on which it depends.

(6) A notice is unfair if, contrary to the requirement of good faith, it causes a significant imbalance in the parties' rights and obligations to the detriment of the consumer.

(7) Whether a notice is fair is to be determined—

(a) taking into account the nature of the subject matter of the notice, and

(b) by reference to all the circumstances existing when the rights or obligations to which it relates arose and to the terms of any contract on which it depends.

(8) This section does not affect the operation of—

(a) section 31 (exclusion of liability: goods contracts),

(b) section 47 (exclusion of liability: digital content contracts),

(c) section 57 (exclusion of liability: services contracts), or

(d) section 65 (exclusion of negligence liability).

III CON [246.1]

Guidance on the unfair terms provisions On 31 July 2015 the Competition & Markets Authority (CMA) published Unfair Contract Terms Guidance [CMA 37].

III CON [246.2]

Penalty clauses Outside the statute the court's powers at common law and in equity include the grant of relief against unfair or oppressive bargains for example rescission of the contract. There is also power to disallow the enforcement of penalty clauses that require the payment of a penal sum on breach, which is in excess of the real loss suffered. The enforceability of a penalty clause depends on whether it is extortionate or extravagant, these being the main tests for striking it down: *Cavendish Square Holdings BV v El Makdessi and Beavis v ParkingEye Ltd* [2015] UKSC 67, [2015] All ER (D) 47 (Nov).

III CON [247]

63. Contract terms which may or must be regarded as unfair

(1) Part 1 of Schedule 2 contains an indicative and non-exhaustive list of terms of consumer contracts that may be regarded as unfair for the purposes of this Part.

(2) Part 1 of Schedule 2 is subject to Part 2 of that Schedule; but a term listed in Part 2 of that Schedule may nevertheless be assessed for fairness under section 62 unless section 64 or 73 applies to it.

(3) The Secretary of State may by order made by statutory instrument amend Schedule 2 so as to add, modify or remove an entry in Part 1 or Part 2 of that Schedule.

(4) An order under subsection (3) may contain transitional or transitory provision or savings.

(5) No order may be made under subsection (3) unless a draft of the statutory instrument containing it has been laid before, and approved by a resolution of, each House of Parliament.

(6) A term of a consumer contract must be regarded as unfair if it has the effect that the consumer bears the burden of proof with respect to compliance by a distance supplier or an intermediary with an obligation under any enactment or rule implementing the Distance Marketing Directive.

(7) In subsection (6)—

"the Distance Marketing Directive" means Directive 2002/65/EC of the European Parliament and of the Council of 23 September 2002 concerning the distance marketing of consumer financial services and amending Council Directive 90/619/EEC and Directives 97/7/EC and 98/27/EC;

"distance supplier" means—

(a) a supplier under a distance contract within the meaning of the Financial Services (Distance Marketing) Regulations 2004 (SI 2004/2095), or

(b) a supplier of unsolicited financial services within the meaning of regulation 15 of those regulations;

"enactment" includes an enactment contained in subordinate legislation within the meaning of the Interpretation Act 1978;

"intermediary" has the same meaning as in the Financial Services (Distance Marketing) Regulations 2004;

"rule" means a rule made by the Financial Conduct Authority or the Prudential Regulation Authority under the Financial Services and Markets Act 2000 or by a designated professional body within the meaning of section 326(2) of that Act.

III CON [248]

64. Exclusion from assessment of fairness

(1) A term of a consumer contract may not be assessed for fairness under section 62 to the extent that—

- (a) it specifies the main subject matter of the contract, or
- (b) the assessment is of the appropriateness of the price payable under the contract by comparison with the goods, digital content or services supplied under it.

(2) Subsection (1) excludes a term from an assessment under section 62 only if it is transparent and prominent.

(3) A term is transparent for the purposes of this Part if it is expressed in plain and intelligible language and (in the case of a written term) is legible.

(4) A term is prominent for the purposes of this section if it is brought to the consumer's attention in such a way that an average consumer would be aware of the term.

(5) In subsection (4) "average consumer" means a consumer who is reasonably well-informed, observant and circumspect.

(6) This section does not apply to a term of a contract listed in Part 1 of Schedule 2.

III CON [249]

65. Bar on exclusion or restriction of negligence liability

(1) A trader cannot by a term of a consumer contract or by a consumer notice exclude or restrict liability for death or personal injury resulting from negligence.

(2) Where a term of a consumer contract, or a consumer notice, purports to exclude or restrict a trader's liability for negligence, a person is not to be taken to have voluntarily accepted any risk merely because the person agreed to or knew about the term or notice.

(3) In this section "personal injury" includes any disease and any impairment of physical or mental condition.

(4) In this section "negligence" means the breach of—

- (a) any obligation to take reasonable care or exercise reasonable skill in the performance of a contract where the obligation arises from an express or implied term of the contract,
- (b) a common law duty to take reasonable care or exercise reasonable skill,
- (c) the common duty of care imposed by the Occupiers' Liability Act 1957 or the Occupiers' Liability Act (Northern Ireland) 1957, or
- (d) the duty of reasonable care imposed by section 2(1) of the Occupiers' Liability (Scotland) Act 1960.

(5) It is immaterial for the purposes of subsection (4)—

- (a) whether a breach of duty or obligation was inadvertent or intentional, or
- (b) whether liability for it arises directly or vicariously.

(6) This section is subject to section 66 (which makes provision about the scope of this section).

III CON [250]

66. Scope of section 65

(1) Section 65 does not apply to—

- (a) any contract so far as it is a contract of insurance, including a contract to pay an annuity on human life, or
- (b) any contract so far as it relates to the creation or transfer of an interest in land.

(2) Section 65 does not affect the validity of any discharge or indemnity given by a person in consideration of the receipt by that person of compensation in settlement of any claim the person has.

(3) Section 65 does not—

- (a) apply to liability which is excluded or discharged as mentioned in section 4(2)(a) (exception to liability to pay damages to relatives) of the Damages (Scotland) Act 2011, or
- (b) affect the operation of section 5 (discharge of liability to pay damages: exception for mesothelioma) of that Act.

(4) Section 65 does not apply to the liability of an occupier of premises to a person who obtains access to the premises for recreational purposes if—

- (a) the person suffers loss or damage because of the dangerous state of the premises, and
- (b) allowing the person access for those purposes is not within the purposes of the occupier's trade, business, craft or profession.

III CON [251]

67. Effect of an unfair term on the rest of a contract

Where a term of a consumer contract is not binding on the consumer as a result of this Part, the contract continues, so far as practicable, to have effect in every other respect.

III CON [252]

68. Requirement for transparency

(1) A trader must ensure that a written term of a consumer contract, or a consumer notice in writing, is transparent.

(2) A consumer notice is transparent for the purposes of subsection (1) if it is expressed in plain and intelligible language and it is legible.

III CON [253]

69. Contract terms that may have different meanings

(1) If a term in a consumer contract, or a consumer notice, could have different meanings, the meaning that is most favourable to the consumer is to prevail.

(2) Subsection (1) does not apply to the construction of a term or a notice in proceedings on an application for an injunction or interdict under paragraph 3 of Schedule 3.

How are the General Rules Enforced?

III CON [254]

70. Enforcement of the law on unfair contract terms

(1) Schedule 3 confers functions on the Competition and Markets Authority and other regulators in relation to the enforcement of this Part.

(2) For provision about the investigatory powers that are available to those regulators for the purposes of that Schedule, see Schedule 5.

Supplementary Provisions

III CON [255]

71. Duty of court to consider fairness of term

(1) Subsection (2) applies to proceedings before a court which relate to a term of a consumer contract.

(2) The court must consider whether the term is fair even if none of the parties to the proceedings has raised that issue or indicated that it intends to raise it.
(3) But subsection (2) does not apply unless the court considers that it has before it sufficient legal and factual material to enable it to consider the fairness of the term.

III CON [256]

72. Application of rules to secondary contracts

(1) This section applies if a term of a contract ("the secondary contract") reduces the rights or remedies or increases the obligations of a person under another contract ("the main contract").
(2) The term is subject to the provisions of this Part that would apply to the term if it were in the main contract.
(3) It does not matter for the purposes of this section—
- (a) whether the parties to the secondary contract are the same as the parties to the main contract, or
- (b) whether the secondary contract is a consumer contract.

(4) This section does not apply if the secondary contract is a settlement of a claim arising under the main contract.

III CON [257]

73. Disapplication of rules to mandatory terms and notices

(1) This Part does not apply to a term of a contract, or to a notice, to the extent that it reflects—
- (a) mandatory statutory or regulatory provisions, or
- (b) the provisions or principles of an international convention to which the United Kingdom or the EU is a party.

(2) In subsection (1) "mandatory statutory or regulatory provisions" includes rules which, according to law, apply between the parties on the basis that no other arrangements have been established.

III CON [258]

74. Contracts applying law of non-EEA State

(1) If—
- (a) the law of a country or territory other than an EEA State is chosen by the parties to be applicable to a consumer contract, but
- (b) the consumer contract has a close connection with the United Kingdom,

this Part applies despite that choice.
(2) For cases where the law applicable has not been chosen or the law of an EEA State is chosen, see Regulation (EC) No 593/2008 of the European Parliament and of the Council of 17 June 2008 on the law applicable to contractual obligations.

III CON [259]

75. Changes to other legislation

Schedule 4 (amendments consequential on this Part) has effect.

III CON [260]

76. Interpretation of Part 2

(1) In this Part—
"consumer contract" has the meaning given by section 61(3);

"consumer notice" has the meaning given by section 61(7);

"transparent" is to be construed in accordance with sections 64(3) and 68(2).

(2) The following have the same meanings in this Part as they have in Part 1—

"trader" (see section 2(2));

"consumer" (see section 2(3));

"goods" (see section 2(8));

"digital content" (see section 2(9)).

(3) Section 2(4) (trader who claims an individual is not a consumer must prove it) applies in relation to this Part as it applies in relation to Part 1.

Schedules

SCHEDULE 2
CONSUMER CONTRACT TERMS WHICH MAY BE REGARDED AS UNFAIR

Section 63

PART 1
LIST OF TERMS

III CON [261]

1. A term which has the object or effect of excluding or limiting the trader's liability in the event of the death of or personal injury to the consumer resulting from an act or omission of the trader.

2. A term which has the object or effect of inappropriately excluding or limiting the legal rights of the consumer in relation to the trader or another party in the event of total or partial non-performance or inadequate performance by the trader of any of the contractual obligations, including the option of offsetting a debt owed to the trader against any claim which the consumer may have against the trader.

3. A term which has the object or effect of making an agreement binding on the consumer in a case where the provision of services by the trader is subject to a condition whose realisation depends on the trader's will alone.

4. A term which has the object or effect of permitting the trader to retain sums paid by the consumer where the consumer decides not to conclude or perform the contract, without providing for the consumer to receive compensation of an equivalent amount from the trader where the trader is the party cancelling the contract.

5. A term which has the object or effect of requiring that, where the consumer decides not to conclude or perform the contract, the consumer must pay the trader a disproportionately high sum in compensation or for services which have not been supplied.

6. A term which has the object or effect of requiring a consumer who fails to fulfil his obligations under the contract to pay a disproportionately high sum in compensation.

7. A term which has the object or effect of authorising the trader to dissolve the contract on a discretionary basis where the same facility is not granted to the consumer, or permitting the trader to retain the sums paid for services not yet supplied by the trader where it is the trader who dissolves the contract.

8. A term which has the object or effect of enabling the trader to terminate a contract of indeterminate duration without reasonable notice except where there are serious grounds for doing so.

9. A term which has the object or effect of automatically extending a contract of fixed duration where the consumer does not indicate otherwise, when the deadline fixed for the consumer to express a desire not to extend the contract is unreasonably early.

10. A term which has the object or effect of irrevocably binding the consumer to terms with which the consumer has had no real opportunity of becoming acquainted before the conclusion of the contract.

11. A term which has the object or effect of enabling the trader to alter the terms of the contract unilaterally without a valid reason which is specified in the contract.

12. A term which has the object or effect of permitting the trader to determine the characteristics of the subject matter of the contract after the consumer has become bound by it.

13. A term which has the object or effect of enabling the trader to alter unilaterally without a valid reason any characteristics of the goods, digital content or services to be provided.

14. A term which has the object or effect of giving the trader the discretion to decide the price payable under the contract after the consumer has become bound by it, where no price or method of determining the price is agreed when the consumer becomes bound.

15. A term which has the object or effect of permitting a trader to increase the price of goods, digital content or services without giving the consumer the right to cancel the contract if the final price is too high in relation to the price agreed when the contract was concluded.

16. A term which has the object or effect of giving the trader the right to determine whether the goods, digital content or services supplied are in conformity with the contract, or giving the trader the exclusive right to interpret any term of the contract.

17. A term which has the object or effect of limiting the trader's obligation to respect commitments undertaken by the trader's agents or making the trader's commitments subject to compliance with a particular formality.

18. A term which has the object or effect of obliging the consumer to fulfil all of the consumer's obligations where the trader does not perform the trader's obligations.

19. A term which has the object or effect of allowing the trader to transfer the trader's rights and obligations under the contract, where this may reduce the guarantees for the consumer, without the consumer's agreement.

20. A term which has the object or effect of excluding or hindering the consumer's right to take legal action or exercise any other legal remedy, in particular by—

(a) requiring the consumer to take disputes exclusively to arbitration not covered by legal provisions,

(b) unduly restricting the evidence available to the consumer, or

(c) imposing on the consumer a burden of proof which, according to the applicable law, should lie with another party to the contract.

PART 2
SCOPE OF PART 1

Financial services

21. Paragraph 8 (cancellation without reasonable notice) does not include a term by which a supplier of financial services reserves the right to terminate unilaterally a contract of indeterminate duration without notice where there is a valid reason, if the supplier is required to inform the consumer of the cancellation immediately.

22. Paragraph 11 (variation of contract without valid reason) does not include a term by which a supplier of financial services reserves the right to alter the rate of interest payable by or due to the consumer, or the amount of other charges for financial services without notice where there is a valid reason, if—

(a) the supplier is required to inform the consumer of the alteration at the earliest opportunity, and

(b) the consumer is free to dissolve the contract immediately.

CONTRACTS WHICH LAST INDEFINITELY

23. Paragraphs 11 (variation of contract without valid reason), 12 (determination of characteristics of goods etc after consumer bound) and 14 (determination of price after consumer bound) do not include a term under which a trader reserves the right to alter unilaterally the conditions of a contract of indeterminate duration if—

(a) the trader is required to inform the consumer with reasonable notice, and

(b) the consumer is free to dissolve the contract.

SALE OF SECURITIES, FOREIGN CURRENCY ETC

24. Paragraphs 8 (cancellation without reasonable notice), 11 (variation of contract without valid reason), 14 (determination of price after consumer bound) and 15 (increase in price) do not apply to—

(a) transactions in transferable securities, financial instruments and other products or services where the price is linked to fluctuations in a stock exchange quotation or index or a financial market rate that the trader does not control, and

(b) contracts for the purchase or sale of foreign currency, traveller's cheques or international money orders denominated in foreign currency.

PRICE INDEX CLAUSES

25. Paragraphs 14 (determination of price after consumer bound) and 15 (increase in price) do not include a term which is a price-indexation clause (where otherwise lawful), if the method by which prices vary is explicitly described.

PACKAGE TRAVEL AND LINKED TRAVEL ARRANGEMENTS REGULATIONS 2018

(SI 2018/634)

GENERAL NOTES ON THE REGULATIONS

III CON [262]

These Regulations give effect, within the United Kingdom, to the Package Travel Directive (EU) 2015/2302, as from 1 July 2018, from which date the previous Regulations, SI 1992/3288 are revoked by Part 8 (reg 37), except as regards contracts concluded before that date. Part 2 (regs 4 to 8 together with Schs 1 to 5) imposes information duties on the retailer or organiser, whichever is the 'relevant person', with penal sanctions for non-compliance; and reg 8 puts the burden of proving compliance on the relevant person, rather than on the traveller to prove non-compliance. Part 3 and 4 (regs 9 to 18) impose contractual duties on the provider of package travel by introducing implied terms into the contract. Part 5 (regs 10 to 26 together with Schs 6 to 10)) requires the organiser (as defined in reg 2(1) to provide insolvency protection in a variety of ways, with penal sanctions for non-compliance. Part 7 (regs 31 to 36) provides for enforcement by prosecution subject to a defence of due diligence (reg 32) and time limits (reg 34). The text below sets out those provisions that create private law obligations and civil remedies for breach, described in the regulations as 'non-conformity'. The provisions that impose public law duties and sanctions (Parts 2, 5 and 7 onwards) have been omitted.

III CON [263]

1. Citation and commencement

(1) These Regulations may be cited as the Package Travel and Linked Travel Arrangements Regulations 2018.

(2) Except as set out in paragraph (3), these Regulations come into force on 1st July 2018.

(3) Regulation 38(4) comes into force on the later of the following—

(a) 1st July 2018;

(b) the day on which Schedule 1 to the Wales Act 2017 (which inserts Schedule 7A into the Government of Wales Act 2006, which regulation 38(4) amends) comes into force.

III CON [264]

2. Interpretation

(1) In these Regulations—

"the Directive" means Directive (EU) 2015/2302 of the European Parliament and of the Council on package travel and linked travel arrangements, amending Regulation (EC) No 2006/2004 and Directive 2011/83/EU of the European Parliament and of the Council and repealing Council Directive 90/314/EEC;

"commencement date" means the date on which these Regulations come into force;

"durable medium" means any instrument which—

(a) enables the traveller or the trader to store information addressed personally to them in a way accessible for future reference for a period of time adequate for the purposes of the information; and

(b) allows the unchanged reproduction of the information stored;

"lack of conformity" means a failure to perform, or the improper performance of, the travel services included in a package;

"minor" means a person below the age of 18;

"organiser" means—

(a) a trader who combines and sells, or offers for sale, packages, either directly or through another trader or together with another trader; or

(b) the trader who transmits the traveller's data to another trader in accordance with paragraph (5)(b)(v);

"package travel contract" means a contract on a package as a whole or, if the package is provided under separate contracts, all contracts covering the travel services included in the package;

"point of sale" means—

(a) any retail premises, whether movable or immovable;

(b) a retail website or similar online sales facility, including where retail websites or online sales facilities are presented to travellers as a single facility; or

(c) a telephone service;

"repatriation" means the traveller's return to the place of departure or to another place the contracting parties agree upon;

"retailer" means a trader other than the organiser who sells or offers for sale packages combined by an organiser;

"start of the package" means the beginning of the performance of travel services included in the package;

"trader" means any person who is acting, including through any other person acting in their name or on their behalf, for purposes relating to their trade, business, craft or profession in relation to contracts covered by these Regulations, whether acting in the capacity of organiser, retailer, trader facilitating a linked travel arrangement or as a travel service provider;

"travel service" means—

(a) the carriage of passengers;

(b) the provision of accommodation which is not intrinsically part of the carriage of passengers and is not for residential purposes;

(c) the rental of—

(i) cars;

(ii) other motor vehicles within the meaning of Article 3(11) of Directive 2007/46/EC of the European Parliament and of the Council establishing a framework for the approval of motor vehicles and their trailers, and of systems, components and separate technical units intended for such vehicles; or

(iii) motorcycles requiring a Category A driving licence in accordance with point (c) of Article 4(3) of Directive 2006/126/EC of the European Parliament and of the Council on driving licences;

(d) any other tourist service not intrinsically part of a travel service within the meaning of paragraph (a), (b) or (c);

"traveller" means any individual who is seeking to conclude a contract, or is entitled to travel on the basis of a contract concluded, within the scope of these Regulations;

"unavoidable and extraordinary circumstances" means a situation—

(a) beyond the control of the party who seeks to rely on such a situation for the purpose of regulation 12(7), 13(2)(b), 15(14) or (16), 16(4)(c) or 28(3)(b); and

(b) the consequences of which could not have been avoided even if all reasonable measures had been taken;

"Union passenger rights legislation" means—

(a) Regulation (EC) No 261/2004 of the European Parliament and of the Council establishing common rules on compensation and assistance to passengers in the event of denied boarding and of cancellation or long delay of flights, and repealing Regulation (EEC) No 295/91;

(b) Regulation (EC) No 1371/2007 of the European Parliament and of the Council on rail passengers' rights and obligations;

(c) Regulation (EC) No 392/2009 of the European Parliament and of the Council on the liability of carriers of passengers by sea in the event of accidents;

(d) Regulation (EU) No 1177/2010 of the European Parliament and of the Council concerning the rights of passengers when travelling by sea and inland waterway and amending Regulation (EC) No 2006/2004; and

(e) Regulation (EU) No 181/2011 of the European Parliament and of the Council concerning the rights of passengers in bus and coach transport and amending Regulation (EC) No 2006/2004.

(2) In these Regulations, a reference to an organiser or a retailer being "established" is to be construed according to the meaning of "establishment" given by point 5 of Article 4 of Directive 2006/123/EC of the European Parliament and of the Council on services in the international market.

(3) In these Regulations, subject to paragraph (4), a "linked travel arrangement" means at least two different types of travel service purchased for the purpose of the same trip or holiday, not constituting a package, resulting in the conclusion of separate contracts with the individual service providers, if a trader facilitates—

(a) on the occasion of a single visit to, or contact with, a trader's point of sale, the separate selection and separate payment of each travel service by travellers; or

(b) in a targeted manner, the procurement of at least one additional travel service from another trader where a contract with such other trader is concluded at the latest 24 hours after the confirmation of the booking of the first travel service.

(4) Where—

(a) not more than one travel service of the kind listed in paragraph (a), (b) or (c) of the definition of "travel service", and

(b) one or more tourist services of the kind listed in paragraph (d) of that definition,

are purchased, those services do not constitute a linked travel arrangement if the tourist services referred to in sub-paragraph (b) do not account for a significant proportion of the combined value of the services and are not advertised as, and do not otherwise represent, an essential feature of the trip or holiday.

(5) In these Regulations, subject to paragraph (6), a "package" means a combination of at least two different types of travel services for the purpose of the same trip or holiday, if—

(a) those services are combined by one trader, including at the request of, or in accordance with, the selection of the traveller, before a single contract on all services is concluded; or

(b) those services are—

(i) purchased from a single point of sale and selected before the traveller agrees to pay,

(ii) offered, sold or charged at an inclusive or total price,

(iii) advertised or sold under the term "package" or under a similar term,

(iv) combined after the conclusion of a contract by which a trader entitles the traveller to choose among a selection of different types of travel services, or

(v) purchased from separate traders through linked online booking processes where—

(aa) the traveller's name, payment details and e-mail address are transmitted from the trader with whom the first contract is concluded to another trader or traders, and

(bb) a contract with the latter trader or traders is concluded at the latest 24 hours after the confirmation of the booking of the first travel service,

irrespective of whether the traveller concludes separate contracts with one or more travel service providers in respect of the services.

(6) A combination of travel services where not more than one type of travel service of the kind listed in paragraph (a), (b) or (c) of the definition of "travel service" is combined with one or more tourist services of the kind listed in paragraph (d) of that definition is not a package if the latter services—

(a) do not account for a significant proportion of the value of the combination and are not advertised as, and do not otherwise represent, an essential feature of the combination; or

(b) are selected and purchased after the performance of a travel service of the kind listed in paragraph (a), (b) or (c) of the definition of "travel service" has started.

III CON [265]

3. Application

(1) These Regulations apply to—

(a) packages offered for sale or sold by traders to travellers, and

(b) linked travel arrangements,

which are concluded on or after the commencement date.

(2) These Regulations do not apply to—

(a) packages and linked travel arrangements covering a period of less than 24 hours, unless overnight accommodation is included;

(b) packages offered, and linked travel arrangements facilitated, occasionally on a not-for-profit basis for a limited group of travellers;

(c) packages and linked travel arrangements purchased on the basis of a general agreement.

(3) In paragraph (2)(c), a "general agreement" means an agreement which is concluded between a trader and another person acting for a trade, business, craft or profession, for the purpose of booking travel arrangements in connection with that trade, business, craft or profession.

III CON [265.1]

Packages, traders, travellers and linked travel arrangements For the definition of "packages", "traders" and "travellers" see reg 2(1) and for "linked travel arrangement" see reg 2(3).

III CON [266]

9. Transfer of the package travel contract to another traveller

(1) A traveller ("the transferor") may transfer the package travel contract once it is concluded to a person ("the transferee") who satisfies all the conditions applicable to that contract.

(2) The transferor must give the organiser, on a durable medium, reasonable notice of the transfer and, for those purposes, notice which is given 7 days or more before the day on which the package starts is always deemed to be reasonable.

(3) The organiser must inform the transferor about the additional fees, charges or other costs arising from the transfer of the package travel contract ("the transfer costs") and must provide proof of those costs.

(4) The transfer costs—

(a) must not be unreasonable; and

(b) must not exceed the cost incurred by the organiser as a result of the transfer.

(5) The transferor and the transferee are jointly and severally liable for the transfer costs.

(6) The provisions of paragraphs (3) and (4) are implied as a term in every package travel contract.

III CON [267]

10. Alteration of the price

(1) The provisions of this regulation are implied as a term in every package travel contract.

(2) The prices specified in a package travel contract must not be increased once the contract is concluded unless the contract—

(a) states expressly that such an increase may be made;

(b) states that price increases are to be made solely to allow for increases which are a direct consequence of changes in—

(i) the price of the carriage of passengers resulting from the cost of fuel or other power sources;

(ii) the level of taxes or fees on the travel services included in the contract imposed by third parties not directly involved in the performance of the package, including tourist taxes, landing taxes or embarkation or disembarkation fees at ports and airports; and

(iii) the exchange rates relevant to the package;

(c) provides that the traveller has the right to a price reduction corresponding to any decrease in the costs referred to in sub-paragraph (b) that occurs before the start of the package once the contract is concluded; and

(d) provides how the revisions referred to in sub-paragraphs (a) and (b) are to be calculated.

(3) Irrespective of its extent, a price increase may only be made if the organiser notifies the traveller clearly and comprehensibly of it with a justification for that increase and a calculation, on a durable medium, at the latest 20 days before the start of the package.

(4) Where a price increase exceeds 8% of the total price of the package, paragraphs (4) to (11) of regulation 11 apply.

(5) Where, under the terms of the package travel contract, the traveller has the right to a price reduction which corresponds to a decrease in the costs referred to in paragraph (2)(b), the organiser—

(a) may deduct administrative expenses from any refund owed to the traveller as a result of the reduction in price; and

(b) must, at the traveller's request, provide proof of any expenses so deducted.

III CON [268]

11. Alteration of other package travel contract terms

(1) The provisions of this regulation are implied as a term in every package travel contract.

(2) The organiser must not unilaterally change the terms of a package travel contract before the start of the package, other than the price in accordance with regulation 10, unless—

(a) the contract allows the organiser to make such changes;

(b) the change is insignificant; and

(c) the organiser informs the traveller of the change in a clear, comprehensible and prominent manner on a durable medium.

(3) Paragraphs (4) to (11) apply where, before the start of the package, the organiser—

(a) is constrained by circumstances beyond the control of the organiser to alter significantly any of the main characteristics of the travel services specified in paragraphs 1 to 10 of Schedule 1;

(b) cannot fulfil the special requirements specified in paragraph 1 of Schedule 5; or

(c) proposes to increase the price of the package by more than 8% in accordance with regulation 10(4).

(4) The organiser must, without undue delay, inform the traveller in a clear, comprehensible and prominent manner on a durable medium, of—

(a) the proposed changes referred to in paragraph (3) and, where appropriate, in accordance with paragraph (7), their impact on the price of the package;

(b) a reasonable period within which the traveller must inform the organiser of the decision pursuant to paragraph (5);

(c) the consequences of the traveller's failure to respond within the period referred to in sub-paragraph (b); and

(d) any substitute package, of an equivalent or higher quality, if possible, offered to the traveller and its price.

(5) The traveller may, within a reasonable period specified by the organiser—

(a) accept the proposed changes; or

(b) terminate the contract without paying a termination fee.

(6) Where the traveller terminates the contract pursuant to paragraph (5)(b), the traveller may accept a substitute package, where this is offered by the organiser.

(7) Where—

(a) the changes to the package travel contract referred to in paragraph (3), or

(b) the substitute package referred to in paragraph (6),

result in a package of lower quality or cost, the traveller is entitled to an appropriate price reduction.

(8) Where—

(a) the traveller terminates the contract pursuant to paragraph (5)(b), and

(b) the traveller does not accept a substitute package,

the organiser must refund all payments made by or on behalf of the traveller without undue delay and in any event not later than 14 days after the contract is terminated.

(9) Where paragraph (8) applies, regulation 16(2) to (10) applies.

(10) Where the traveller does not confirm, within the period specified in paragraph (5), whether the traveller wishes to—

(a) accept the proposed change, or

(b) terminate the contract,

in accordance with that paragraph, the organiser must notify the traveller, a second time, of the matters in sub-paragraphs (a) to (d) of paragraph (4).

(11) If, having been notified under paragraph (10), the traveller fails to respond, the organiser may terminate the contract and refund all payments made by or on behalf of the traveller without undue delay and in any event not later than 14 days after the contract is terminated.

III CON [269]

12. Termination of the package travel contract by the traveller

(1) The provisions of this regulation are implied as a term in every package travel contract.

(2) A traveller may terminate the package travel contract at any time before the start of the package.

(3) Where the traveller terminates the package travel contract under paragraph (2), the traveller may be required to pay an appropriate and justifiable termination fee to the organiser.

(4) The package travel contract may specify reasonable standard termination fees based on—

(a) the time of the termination of the contract before the start of the package; and

(b) the expected cost savings and income from alternative deployment of the travel services.

(5) In the absence of standardised termination fees, the amount of the termination fee must correspond to the price of the package minus the cost savings and income from alternative deployment of the travel services.

(6) The organiser must provide a justification for the amount of the termination fee if the traveller so requests.

(7) Notwithstanding paragraphs (2) to (6), in the event of unavoidable and extraordinary circumstances occurring at the place of destination or its immediate vicinity and which significantly affect—

(a) the performance of the package, or

(b) the carriage of passengers to the destination,

the traveller may terminate the package travel contract before the start of the package without paying any termination fee.

(8) Where the package travel contract is terminated under paragraph (7), the traveller is entitled to a full refund of any payments made for the package but is not entitled to additional compensation.

III CON [270]

13. Termination of the package travel contract by the organiser

(1) The provisions of this regulation are implied as a term in every package travel contract.

(2) Paragraph (3) applies where—

(a) the number of persons enrolled for the package is smaller than the minimum number stated in the contract and the organiser notifies the traveller of the termination of the contract within the period fixed in the contract but not later than—

(i) in the case of trips lasting more than 6 days, 20 days before the start of the package;

(ii) in the case of trips lasting between 2 and 6 days, 7 days before the start of the package;

(iii) in the case of trips lasting less than 2 days, 48 hours before the start of the package; or

(b) the organiser is prevented from performing the contract because of unavoidable and extraordinary circumstances and notifies the traveller of the termination of the contract without undue delay before the start of the package.

(3) The organiser—

(a) may terminate the package travel contract and provide the traveller with a full refund of any payments made for the package;

(b) is not liable for additional compensation.

III CON [271]

14. Refunds in the event of termination

(1) The provisions of this regulation are implied as a term in every package travel contract.

(2) Following a termination under regulation 12(2), the organiser must reimburse any payments made by or on behalf of the traveller, having deducted any termination fee.

(3) Any—

(a) reimbursement required under paragraph (2), or

(b) refund required pursuant to—

(i) regulation 12(8), or

(ii) a termination under regulation 13(3),

must be made to the traveller without undue delay and in any event not later than 14 days after the package travel contract is terminated.

III CON [272]

15. Responsibility for the performance of the package

(1) The provisions of this regulation are implied as a term in every package travel contract.

(2) The organiser is liable to the traveller for the performance of the travel services included in the package travel contract, irrespective of whether those services are to be performed by the organiser or by other travel service providers.

(3) The traveller must inform the organiser without undue delay, taking into account the circumstances of the case, of any lack of conformity which the traveller perceives during the performance of a travel service included in the package travel contract.

(4) If any of the travel services are not performed in accordance with the package travel contract, the organiser must remedy the lack of conformity within a reasonable period set by the traveller unless that—

(a) is impossible; or

(b) entails disproportionate costs, taking into account the extent of the lack of conformity and the value of the travel services affected.

(5) Where the organiser does not remedy the lack of conformity within a reasonable period set by the traveller for a reason mentioned in sub-paragraph (a) or (b) of paragraph (4), regulation 16 applies.

(6) Where the organiser refuses to remedy the lack of conformity or where immediate remedy is required, the traveller—

(a) may remedy the lack of conformity; and

(b) is entitled to reimbursement of the necessary expenses.

(7) A traveller to whom paragraph (6)(a) applies is not required to—

(a) set a reasonable period pursuant to paragraph (4), and
(b) if such a period has been set, wait until the end of the period,

before the traveller remedies the lack of conformity.

(8) Where the organiser is unable to provide a significant proportion of the travel services as agreed in the package travel contract, the organiser must offer, at no extra cost to the traveller, suitable alternative arrangements of, where possible, equivalent or higher quality than those specified in the contract, for the continuation of the package, including where the traveller's return to the place of departure is agreed.

(9) Where the organiser offers proposed alternative arrangements which result in a package of lower quality than that specified in the package travel contract, the organiser must grant the traveller an appropriate price reduction.

(10) The traveller may reject the proposed alternative arrangements offered under paragraph (8) only if—

(a) they are not comparable to the arrangements which were agreed in the package travel contract; or
(b) the price reduction granted is inadequate.

(11) Where—

(a) a lack of conformity substantially affects the performance of the package; and
(b) the organiser fails to remedy the lack of conformity within the reasonable period,

the traveller may terminate the package travel contract without paying a termination fee and, where appropriate, is entitled to a price reduction, or compensation for damages, or both, in accordance with regulation 16.

(12) If—

(a) the organiser is unable to make alternative arrangements, or
(b) the traveller rejects the proposed alternative arrangements in accordance with paragraph (10),

the traveller is, where appropriate, entitled to a price reduction, or compensation for damages, or both, in accordance with regulation 16 without terminating the package travel contract.

(13) If the package includes the carriage of passengers, the organiser must, in the cases referred to in paragraphs (11) and (12), also provide repatriation of the traveller with equivalent transport without undue delay and at no extra cost to the traveller.

(14) Where the organiser is unable to ensure the traveller's return as agreed in the package travel contract because of unavoidable and extraordinary circumstances, the organiser must bear the cost of necessary accommodation, if possible of equivalent category—

(a) for a period not exceeding 3 nights per traveller; or
(b) where a different period is specified in the Union passenger rights legislation applicable to the relevant means of transport for the traveller's return, for the period specified in that legislation.

(15) The limitation of costs referred to in paragraph (14) does not apply to persons with reduced mobility as defined in point (a) of Article 2 of Regulation (EC) No 1107/2006 of the European Parliament and of the Council, concerning the rights of disabled persons and persons with reduced mobility when travelling by air and any person accompanying them, pregnant women and unaccompanied minors, as well as persons in need of specific medical assistance, provided that the organiser has been notified of their particular needs at least 48 hours before the start of the package.

(16) The organiser's liability under paragraph (14) may not be limited by reason of unavoidable and extraordinary circumstances if the relevant transport provider may not rely on such circumstances under the applicable Union passenger rights legislation.

III CON [272.1]

Organiser's liability for performance of travel services by others Regulation 15(2) imposes liability on the organiser for non-conformity by other travel service providers in the provision of travel services included in the package travel contract. In a case where the travellers paid for a package holiday which included hotel accommodation in the Dominican Republic, the travel company was held liable for food poisoning caused by breach of the Supply of Goods and Services Act 1982 but not under the previous regulations: *Wood v TUI Travel plc t/a First Choice* [2017] EWCA Civ 11. The new regulations would probably impose liability for the food-poisoning on the organiser, because of reg 15(2).

III CON [273]

16. Price reduction and compensation for damages

(1) The provisions of this regulation are implied as a term in every package travel contract.

(2) The organiser must offer the traveller an appropriate price reduction for any period during which there is a lack of conformity, unless the organiser proves that the lack of conformity is attributable to the traveller.

(3) The organiser must offer the traveller, without undue delay, appropriate compensation for any damage which the traveller sustains as a result of any lack of conformity.

(4) The traveller is not entitled to compensation for damages under paragraph (3) if the organiser proves that the lack of conformity is—

(a) attributable to the traveller;

(b) attributable to a third party unconnected with the provision of the travel services included in the package travel contract and is unforeseeable or unavoidable; or

(c) due to unavoidable and extraordinary circumstances.

(5) In so far as the international conventions limit the extent of, or the conditions under which, compensation is to be paid by a provider carrying out a travel service which is part of a package, the same limitations are to apply to the organiser.

(6) In other cases, the package travel contract may limit compensation to be paid by the organiser as long as that limitation—

(a) does not apply to personal injury or damage caused intentionally or with negligence or does not limit any liability that cannot be limited by law; and

(b) does not amount to less than 3 times the total price of the package.

(7) Any right to compensation or price reduction under these Regulations does not affect the rights of travellers under—

(a) the Union passenger rights legislation; and

(b) the international conventions.

(8) Travellers may present claims under—

(a) these Regulations;

(b) the Union passenger rights legislation; and

(c) the international conventions.

(9) Where a traveller is granted compensation or a price reduction under—

(a) these Regulations, and

(b) the Union passenger rights legislation or the international conventions,

the organiser must deduct the compensation or price reductions referred to in sub-paragraph (b) from the compensation or price reduction referred to in sub-paragraph (a) to avoid overcompensation.

(10) In this regulation, the "international conventions" means—

(a) the Carriage by Air Conventions, within the meaning given in section 1(5) of the Carriage by Air Act 1961;

(b) the Athens Convention of 1974 on the Carriage of Passengers and their Luggage by Sea;

(c) the Convention of 1980 concerning International Carriage by Rail (COTIF).

III CON [273.1]

Union passenger rights legislation "Union passenger rights legislation" is defined in reg 2(1) and includes regulation (EC) No 261/2004 about compensation and assistance in the event of denied board and cancellations or long delay of flights.

III CON [273.2]

Right to price reduction The right to a price reduction reflects the provisions of ss 54 and 56 of the Consumer Rights Act 2015, at **III CON [238]**, **III CON [240]**, as a right arising when the service provided does not conform.

III CON [273.3]

Compensation for damage due to non-conformity Where the con-conformity (ie breach of contract) causes physical inconvenience, general damages may be awarded: *Hobbs v London and South Eestern Rly Co* (1875) LR 10 QB 111. Also where the contract is to provide pleasure, relaxation and peace of mind, damages for frustration and disappointment may be awarded: *Jarvis v Swans Tours Ltd* [1973] QB 233, [1973] 1 All ER 71.

Claims may be made for personal injury where caused by non-conformity or breach of a duty of care. But note that local standards have to be taken into account in establishing the standard of care: *Lougheed v On the Beach* [2014] EWCA Civ 1538, [2014] All ER (D) 299 (Nov).

III CON [273.4]

Unavoidable and extraordinary circumstances It has been held that owners of a swimming pool cannot be expected to protect users against obvious dangers such as diving head first into the shallow end: *Evans v Kosmar Villa Holidays plc* [2007] EWCA Civ 1003, [2008] 1 All ER 530. Also the liability for non-conformity is unlikely to extend to actions totally outside the contract. In a case under the previous regulations, a holiday maker was raped by an electrician employee of the hotel where she was staying, having offered to show her a short cut to the reception area. It was held that the actions of the employee were not part of the services agreed to be provided by the travel agents. They were therefore not liable: *X v Kuoni Travel Ltd* [2018] EWCA Civ 938, [2018] All ER (D) 121 (Apr).

III CON [273.5]

Protocols In addition to the Pre-action Protocol for Personal Injury Claims, at **III PID [42]**, and the Pre-action Protocol for Disease and Illness Claims, at **III [PID [44]**, there is also a Pre-action Protocol for Resolution of Package Travel Claims. The Text is set out at **PRO 14**, in Volume 1.

III CON [274]

17. Possibility of contacting the organiser via the retailer

(1) The provisions of this regulation are implied as a term in every package travel contract.

(2) The traveller may address messages, requests or complaints in relation to the performance of the package directly to the retailer through which it was purchased.

(3) The retailer must forward those messages, requests or complaints to the organiser without undue delay.

(4) For the purpose of compliance with time-limits or limitation periods, receipt of the messages, requests or complaints referred to in this regulation by the retailer are to be considered as receipt by the organiser.

III CON [275]

18. Obligation to provide assistance

(1) The provisions of this regulation are implied as a term in every package travel contract.

(2) Where a traveller is in difficulty, the organiser must give appropriate assistance without undue delay, including in the circumstances referred to in regulation 15(14), in particular by—

- (a) providing appropriate information on health services, local authorities and consular assistance; and
- (b) assisting the traveller to make distance communications and helping the traveller to find alternative travel arrangements.

(3) The organiser may charge a fee for such assistance if the difficulty is caused intentionally by the traveller or through the traveller's negligence but that fee—

- (a) must be reasonable; and
- (b) must not exceed the actual costs incurred by the organiser.

III CON [276]

27. Specific obligations of the retailer where the organiser is established outside the European Economic Area

Where—

- (a) an organiser is established outside the European Economic Area, and
- (b) a retailer established in the United Kingdom sells or offers for sale packages combined by that organiser,

the retailer is subject to the obligations for organisers set out in Parts 4 and 5, unless the retailer provides evidence that the organiser complies with those Parts.

III CON [277]

28. Liability for booking errors

(1) The provisions of this regulation are implied as a term in every package travel contract.

(2) A trader is liable—

- (a) for any errors due to technical defects in the booking system which are attributable to that trader; and
- (b) where the trader agrees to arrange the booking of a package or of travel services which are part of linked travel arrangements, for the errors made during the booking process.

(3) A trader is not liable for booking errors which—

- (a) are attributable to the traveller; or
- (b) are caused by unavoidable and extraordinary circumstances.

III CON [278]

29. Right of redress

Where an organiser or, in a case under regulation 27, a retailer—

- (a) pays compensation,
- (b) grants a price reduction, or
- (c) meets the other obligations incumbent on the organiser or the retailer under these Regulations,

the organiser or retailer may seek redress from any third parties which contributed to the event triggering compensation, a price reduction or other obligations.

III CON [278.1]

Redress from third party This right of redress already exists under the Civil Liability (Contribution) Act 1978, at **III PID [16]**.

III CON [279]

30. Rights and obligations under these Regulations

(1) A declaration by an organiser of a package or a trader facilitating a linked travel arrangement that—

(a) the organiser or trader is acting exclusively as a travel service provider, as an intermediary or in any other capacity, or

(b) a package or a linked travel arrangement does not constitute a package or a linked travel arrangement,

does not absolve that organiser or trader from the obligations imposed upon them under these Regulations.

(2) A traveller may not waive any right granted to the traveller by these Regulations.

(3) Any contractual arrangement or any statement by the traveller which—

(a) directly or indirectly waives or restricts the rights conferred on travellers pursuant to these Regulations, or

(b) aims to circumvent the application of these Regulations,

is not binding on the traveller.

CONTEMPT OF COURT

TABLE OF CONTENTS

GENERAL NOTES ON CONTEMPT OF COURT

III COT [1]

Civil and criminal contempt Contempts have traditionally been classified as civil or criminal, although the importance of the distinction has lessened as the procedures for dealing with the two classes have converged: see eg *Daltel Europe Ltd v Makki* [2006] EWCA Civ 94, [2006] 1 WLR 2704.

In general terms:

(a) civil contempts consist in disobedience to judgments and court orders; and
(b) criminal contempts consist in conduct impeding or interfering with the administration of justice, or creating a risk of such impediment or interference.

Contempt in connection with civil proceedings is punishable by committal, sequestration or a fine. The procedure in relation to any application for committal or sequestration is, in the civil courts, regulated by CPR Part 81. Part 81 embraces acts or omissions of the following descriptions:

(a) disobedience to a court order;
(b) breach of an undertaking to the court;
(c) making a false statement of truth (**CPR 32.14**);
(d) making a false disclosure statement (**CPR 31.23**);
(e) conduct which either obstructs or is calculated to obstruct or prejudice the administration of justice (for example, exerting pressure on a witness not to give evidence or even exerting pressure upon the judge); or
(f) contempt in the face of the court (for example, disrupting proceedings) (both at common law and under the Contempt of Court Act 1981).

See **CPR 81 [1]** onwards.

The common law jurisdiction to punish the publication of court proceedings as contempt has been redefined by the sections of the Administration of Justice 1960 and the Contempt of Court Act 1981, reproduced below. See also the application of articles 6, 8 and 10 pursuant to the Human Rights Act 1998 at **III HUM [18]**: it is clear that committal proceedings are to be categorised as criminal proceedings for the purposes of art 6, whether the contempt involved is classified as civil or as criminal: *Daltel Europe Ltd v Makki* [2006] EWCA Civ 94, [2006] 1 WLR 2704, (2006) Times, 8 March; *Barnes (t/a Pool Motors) v Seabrook* [2010] EWHC 1849 (Admin) at para 42.

Both criminal and civil contempts must be proved beyond reasonable doubt (see, eg, *A-G v Leveller Magazine Ltd* [1979] AC 440, [1979] 1 All ER 745, HL (criminal contempt); *A-G v Express Newspapers* [2004] EWHC 2859 (Admin), (2005) EMLR 13, DC (criminal contempt - breach of strict liability rule); *Dean v Dean* [1987] FCR 96, [1987] 1 FLR 517, CA (civil contempt).

Taking photographs in court could merit a prison sentence: *HM Solicitor General v Cox* [2016] EWHC 1241 (QB), [2016] All ER (D) 03 (Jun).

III COT [2]

High Court The High Court, as a court of record, has an inherent power to punish for contempt, whether criminal or civil. It has jurisdiction to make an order of committal of its own motion.

By CPR 81.18(1) a committal application in relation to a false statement of truth (**CPR 32.14**) or disclosure statement (**CPR 31.23**) in connection with proceedings in the High Court, a Divisional Court or the Court of Appeal, may be made only:

(a) with the permission of the court dealing with the proceedings in which the false statement or disclosure statement was made; or
(b) by the Attorney General.

Swearing a false affidavit is properly categorised as a criminal contempt rather than a civil contempt, and the High Court retains an inherent jurisdiction to punish criminal contempt by the summary process of committal in civil proceedings: *Hydropool Hot Tubs Ltd v Roberjot* [2011] EWHC 121 (Ch), para 62, [2011] All ER (D) 106 (Feb).

County courts County courts, on the other hand, have purely statutory powers derived from the County Courts Act 1984.

The county court does not have power to punish for contempt in relation to a false statement of truth (CPR 32.14) or a false disclosure statement (CPR 31.23): in simple terms: the Act does not give it such a power.

A committal application in relation to a false statement of truth or disclosure statement in connection with proceedings in a county court may be made only:

(a) with the permission of a single judge of the Queen's Bench Division; or
(b) by the Attorney General: CPR 81.18(3) (see para **CPR 81.18**).

A county court has power under s 38 of the County Courts Act 1984 to punish for civil contempt but has no statutory power to deal with criminal contempts (*R v Lefroy* (1893) LR 8 QB 134; *Bush v Green* [1985] 3 All ER 721, [1985] 1 WLR 1143, CA; *Manchester City Council v McCann* [1999] QB 1214, CA), except those covered specifically by the Act of 1984.

A county court has jurisdiction to make an order of committal of its own motion by virtue of s 38 of the County Courts Act 1984: *Re M (a minor) (contempt of court: committal of court's own motion)* [1999] Fam 263, [1999] 2 All ER 56, CA.

The jurisdiction of the county court to punish criminal contempts is limited to the circumstances specified in the County Courts Act 1984. These are:

(a) assaulting an officer of the court while in the execution of his duty (s 14; see para **II CCA [6]** and *King v Read and Slack* [1999] 1 FLR 425, CA);
(b) rescuing goods seized in execution under process of a county court (s 92; see **II CCA [90]**);
(c) non attendance on judgment summons (s 110; see para **II CCA [105]**);
(d) wilfully insulting a judge, juror or witness going to, attending or returning from a sitting, or wilfully interrupting the proceedings or otherwise misbehaving in court (s 118; see para **II CCA [115]**).

III COT [3]

Appeals Rights of appeal are governed by s 13 of the Administration of Justice Act 1960 (see para **III COT [9]**) and CPR 52.

There are particular and complex provisions relating to appeals in respect of the grant or refusal of an order for committal: **CPR 52.3 [5]**.

III COT [4]

Practice Directions CPR 81 is accompanied and supplemented by both a Practice Direction (**CPR PD 81**) and by a Practice Guidance Note: Practice Guidance: Committal for Contempt of Court – Open Court, issued by the Lord Chief Justice on 24 June 2015. The Note explains that the Practice Direction (Committal for Contempt: Open Court), issued on 26 March 2015, at **CPR PG 81**, applies to committal hearings under the Act in respect of adults but not to individuals under the age of 18.

III COT [5]

Precedents For a precedent for an application for an order of committal see **BCCP H[602]**. For the substantive law see 9(1) Halsbury's Laws (4th edn reissue) title CONTEMPT OF COURT, para 401.

ADMINISTRATION OF JUSTICE ACT 1960

(c 65)

III COT [8]

12. Publication of information relating to proceedings in private

(1) The publication of information relating to proceedings before any court sitting in private shall not of itself be contempt of court except in the following cases, that is to say—

(a) where the proceedings—

(i) relate to the exercise of the inherent jurisdiction of the High Court with respect to minors;

(ii) are brought under the Children Act 1989 or the Adoption and Children Act 2002; or

(iii) otherwise relate wholly or mainly to the maintenance or upbringing of a minor;

(b) where the proceedings are brought under the Mental Capacity Act 2005, or under any provision of the Mental Health Act 1983 authorising an application or reference to be made to the First-tier Tribunal, the Mental Health Review Tribunal for Wales or the county court;

(c) where the court sits in private for reasons of national security during that part of the proceedings about which the information in question is published;

(d) where the information relates to a secret process, discovery or invention which is in issue in the proceedings;

(e) where the court (having power to do so) expressly prohibits the publication of all information relating to the proceedings or of information of the description which is published.

(2) Without prejudice to the foregoing subsection, the publication of the text or a summary of the whole or part of an order made by a court sitting in private shall not of itself be contempt of court except where the court (having power to do so) expressly prohibits the publication.

(3) In this section references to a court include references to a judge and to a tribunal and to any person exercising the functions of a court, a judge or a tribunal; and references to a court sitting in private include references to a court sitting in camera or in chambers.

(4) Nothing in this section shall be construed as implying that any publication is punishable as contempt of court which would not be so punishable apart from this section (and in particular where the publication is not so punishable by reason of being authorised by rules of court).

[(5) Subsection (1) is subject to Part 2 of the Children, Schools and Families Act 2010 (family proceedings), and nothing in subsection (2) applies in relation to a contempt of court under section 11 of that Act (restriction on publication of information relating to family proceedings).]

Amendment *Sub-section (5) is inserted by the Children, Schools and Families Act 2010, s 25 from a date to be appointed.*

III COT [8.1]

Restrictions on publication Section 12 sets out four statutory exceptions (at s 12(1)(a) to (d)) to the general principle that, save in exceptional circumstances, court proceedings should be conducted in public, and regulates the breach of orders made by way of exception to the general principle (s 12(1)(e) and s 12(2)). Outside the specific situations covered by s 12(1)(a) to (d), a court may sit in camera or impose restrictions on the publication of information relating to court proceedings but this is an exceptional course, which will be adopted only where the court is persuaded that justice could not otherwise be done in the proceedings, either because the case could not be effectively tried or because the parties entitled to justice would be reasonably deterred from seeking it at the hands of the court: *Scott v Scott* [1913] AC 417, HL (Viscount Haldane LC at 437–439) and Earl Loreburn at 446); *A-G v Leveller Magazine Ltd* [1979] AC 440, HL. The general rule and its qualifications now appear in **CPR 39.2** and CPR PD 39, paras 1.1–1.15. Reporting restrictions may, in an appropriate case, be extended beyond the death of the patient and include, for example, the reporting of the inquest: *V v Associated Newspapers Ltd* [2016] EWCOP 21, [2016] All ER (D) 195 (Apr).

A presumption that, in cases under the Children Act 1989, the court will sit in private and will not give judgment publicly, while retaining a discretion to sit in public in appropriate cases, does not breach Arts 6 or 10 of the European Convention on Human Rights: *B v United Kingdom, P v United Kingdom (Application Nos 36337/97, 35974/97)* [2001] 2 FLR 261, [2001] Fam Law 506, ECtHR; *Clibbery v Allan* [2002] EWCA Civ 45, [2002] Fam 261, [2002] 1 All ER 865. The balancing exercise required in relation to Arts 8 and 10 of the European Convention on Human Rights may lead a court hearing a case under the Children Act 1989 to relax the usual restrictions and to sit in open court or give judgment in public: *Re Webster (a Child)* [2006] EWHC 2733, [2007] EMLR 7, or to discharge an injunction preventing publication of information relating to court proceedings: *Clayton v Clayton* [2006] EWCA Civ 878, [2006] Fam 83. The court will be particularly vigilant where the parties have agreed between themselves that there should be a prohibition on publication of information relating to the proceedings: see, eg *R v Legal Aid Board, ex p Kaim Todner* [1999] QB 966 at 977, [1998] 3 All ER 541 at 549, CA.

For rules of court in relation to hearings in private, see **CPR 39.2** and **CPR 81.28**(5).

For the position in relation to the publication of judgments in family courts and the Court of Protection see **III COT [8.2A]**.

III COT [8.1A]

Effect of s 12 The effect of s 12 is to make it, at least prima facie, a contempt of court to publish information relating to proceedings before a court sitting in private in the specific cases set out at sub-ss (1)(a) to (d) (see *Pickering v Liverpool Daily Post and Echo Newspapers plc* [1991] 2 AC 370 at 416H, HL), or where the court has expressly prohibited the publication of information relating to the proceedings or of a specified description (sub-s (1)(e)).

The communication by a children and family reporter appointed in proceedings brought under the Children Act 1989 to the relevant statutory authority of concerns about inappropriate sexual behaviour by a parent does not constitute "publication" within the meaning of s 12: *Re M (a child) (disclosure: children and family reporter)* [2002] EWCA Civ 1199, [2003] Fam 26, [2002] 4 All ER 401.

For publication to constitute a contempt of court under s 12(1)(a), the publisher must know that the information published related to court proceedings, and that those proceedings were in private: *Re F (a minor) (publication of information)* [1977] Fam 58 at 74, [1977] 1 All ER 114, CA. Where the publisher has the requisite knowledge, the advice of experienced counsel that publication will not amount to a contempt is not a defence: *X v Dempster* [1999] 3 FCR 757, [1999] 1 FLR 894. Further, the court may give permission for publication of information relating even to proceedings which fall within s 12(1)(a) to (d): *Re R (MJ) (a minor)* [1975] Fam 89, [1975] 2 All ER 749.

The publication of a text or summary of the whole or part of an order made by a court sitting in private is not a contempt unless the proceedings fall within s 12(1)(a) to (d) or the court has expressly prohibited such publication: s 12(2); *AF Noonan (Architectural Practice) Ltd v Bournemouth & Boscombe Athletic Community Football Club Ltd* [2007] EWCA Civ 848, [2007] 1 WLR 2614. For the power to postpone the reporting of proceedings, see s 4(2) of the Contempt of Court Act 1981 at para **III COT [13]**. For a summary of the effect of s 12, see *Re B* [2004] EWHC 411 (Fam), [2004] 2 FLR 142, [2004] Lloyd's Rep Med 303, para 82, per Munby J.

For the position in relation to the publication of judgments in family courts and the Court of Protection see **III COT [8.2A]**.

For discussion and explanation of the application of s 12, the exercise of the judge's discretion and, more particularly, the concept of good reason please refer to *Independent News and Media Ltd v A (by his litigation friend, the Official Solicitor)* [2010] EWCA Civ 343 (Lord Judge CJ, Lord Neuberger MR and Sir Mark Potter P).

III COT [8.1B]

Status of judgments given in chambers Except in the specific cases identified in s 12(1)(a) to (d), a judgment, even when given in chambers, is normally to be regarded as a public document: *Hodgson v Imperial Tobacco Ltd* [1998] 1 WLR 1056, at 1070, CA; *Forbes v Smith* [1998] 1 All ER 973, at 975j (Jacob J). However, where secrecy is sought and granted, a judgment will normally be regarded as given in camera: see, eg, *Forbes v Smith* [1998] 1 All ER 973 at 976a–b, Ch D. Even where there is no restriction as to publication, lawyers are expected to exercise self restraint as to what is said in relation to any order, judgment or account of proceedings in chambers: *Hodgson v Imperial Tobacco Ltd* [1998] 1 WLR 1056, at 1071, CA.

For additional notes on hearings in private please refer to the notes at **CPR 39.2 [1]** onwards.

For the position in relation to the publication of judgments in family courts and the Court of Protection see **III COT [8.2A]**.

III COT [8.2]

Matters which may nevertheless be published Section 12(1) prohibits publication of information regarding the substance of matters which the court has closed its doors to consider, and accordingly does not prohibit the publication of the fact that the court will sit, is sitting or sat at a certain date, time or place behind closed doors to consider those matters, or indeed the fact that a named patient in hospital has applied to a mental health review tribunal or that the tribunal has decided to release the patient from detention: *Pickering v Liverpool Daily Post and Echo Newspapers plc* [1991] 2 AC 370 at 423A and G–H, HL.

Similarly, an account of events unfolding outside the room in which the hearing is conducted, including the comings and goings of the parties and of witnesses, is not "information relating to proceedings before any court", and its publication is not prohibited by s 12(1)(a) to (d): *Re G (minors) (celebrities: publicity)* [1999] 3 FCR 181, [1999] 1 FLR 409, CA.

What is protected from publication are details of the actual proceedings of the court; these include statements of evidence, and reports and accounts of interviews prepared for use in court: *Re F (a minor) (publication of information)* [1977] Fam 58, 99 and 105; and the submissions of the advocates: *Re G (a child) (contempt: committal)* [2003] EWCA Civ 489, [2003] 1 WLR 2051, para 27. Section 12(1)(a) prohibits only the publication of information relating to the proceedings there referred to: *Re F (a minor) (publication of information)* [1977] Fam 58 at 74, [1977] 1 All ER 114, CA; *R v Central Television plc* [1994] Fam 192, [1994] 3 All ER 641, CA.

The common law may restrict publication of information of a much wider scope in relation to a child: see, eg, *R v Central Television plc* [1994] Fam 192, [1994] 3 All ER 641, CA; *Re Z (a minor) (identification: restrictions on publication)* [1997] Fam 1, [1995] 4 All ER 961, CA. If the court wishes to prohibit the publication of such information, it must make an appropriate order, in respect of which the criteria governing situations which fall outside s 12(1)(a) to (d) are applicable (see para **III COT [8.1]**). For an example of such an order, see *Re G (minors) (celebrities: publicity)* [1999] 3 FCR 181, [1999] 1 FLR 409, CA. However, neither s 12(1)(a), nor s 97(2) of the Children Act 1989, as amended, prevents the media from interviewing a ward of court about matters not within the scope of s 12(1)(a), or from publishing or broadcasting such an interview: *Kelly v BBC* [2001] Fam 59, [2001] 1 All ER 323. Similarly, s 12 does not prohibit publication of documents held by social workers which have neither been filed with the court nor used in court proceedings: *Re W (minors) (social worker: disclosure)* [1998] 2 All ER 801, [1999] 1 WLR 205, CA; and in the absence of an order, such as under s 39(1) of the Children and Young Persons Act 1933, it is not a breach of s 12(1)(a) to publish the name and address of, or to indicate the identity of, a child, nor to publish the fact that proceedings are taking place: *Cleveland County Council v W* [1989] FCR 625, sub nom *Re W (wards) (publication of information)* [1989] 1 FLR 246; *Re G (a child) (contempt: committal)* [2003] EWCA Civ 489, [2003] 1 WLR 2051, para 27 (discussion of whether publication of details of case and circumstances surrounding it on "Families Need Fathers" website constituted contempt of court); nor is it a breach of s 12(1)(a) to publish the names of parties or witnesses: see *Re B* [2004] EWHC 411 (Fam), [2004] 2 FLR 142, [2004] Lloyd's Rep Med 303, para 82, per Munby J.

Every court, when making what it believes to be a final order in proceedings under the Children Act 1989, should consider whether or not there is an outstanding welfare issue which needs to be addressed by a continuing order for anonymity; if no outstanding welfare issue arises, it is likely that the penal consequences of s 97 of the 1989 Act will cease to have effect, and the parties will be able to put into the public domain any matter relating to themselves and their children which they wish to publish, provided that the publication does not offend against s 12: *Clayton v Clayton* [2006] EWCA Civ 878, [2006] Fam 83, para 77.

A judge might authorise the publication of the terms of a final order in a financial remedy case on the grounds that the issues in the case were already a matter of public comment, it was in the public interest that the outcome should be published and that the public should be aware that a settlement had been negotiated: *Wyatt v Vince* [2015] UKSC 14, [2015] 2 All ER 75 (on the other hand, the amount of Mrs Wyatt's costs bill was still a matter of speculation and the court refused permission for it to be published).

III COT [8.2A]

Communication of information concerning children and publication of information relating to family proceedings For the position in proceedings concerning children and incapacitated or vulnerable adults see the guidance at www.judiciary.gov.uk/wp-content/uploads/JCO/Documents/Guidance/transparency-in-the-family-courts-jan2014.pdf and the amendments to rules of court etc which will follow.

This Guidance (together with similar Guidance issued at the same time for the Court of Protection) is intended to bring about an immediate and significant change in practice in relation to the publication of judgments in family courts and the Court of Protection.

Transparency in the Family Courts Publication of Judgments
Practice Guidance issued on 16 January 2014 by Sir James Munby, President of the Family Division

The purpose of this Guidance

1. This Guidance (together with similar Guidance issued at the same time for the Court of Protection) is intended to bring about an immediate and significant change in practice in relation to the publication of judgments in family courts and the Court of Protection.

2. In both courts there is a need for greater transparency in order to improve public understanding of the court process and confidence in the court system. At present too few judgments are made available to the public, which has a legitimate interest in being able to read what is being done by the judges in its name. The Guidance will have the effect of increasing the number of judgments available for publication (even if they will often need to be published in appropriately anonymised form).

3. In July 2011 Sir Nicholas Wall P issued, jointly with Bob Satchwell, Executive Director of the Society of Editors, a paper, *The Family Courts: Media Access & Reporting (Media Access & Reporting)*, setting out a statement of the current state of the law. In their preface they recognised that the debate on increased transparency and public confidence in the family courts would move forward and that future consideration of this difficult and sensitive area would need to include the questions of access to and reporting of proceedings by the media, whilst maintaining the privacy of the families involved. The paper is to be found at: http://www.judiciary.gov.uk/Resources/JCO/Documents/Guidance/family-courts-media-july2011.pdf.

4. In April 2013 I issued a statement, *View from the President's Chambers: the Process of Reform*, [2013] Fam Law 548, in which I identified transparency as one of the three strands in the reforms which the family justice system is currently undergoing. I said:

> 'I am determined to take steps to improve access to and reporting of family proceedings. I am determined that the new Family Court should not be saddled, as the family courts are at present, with the charge that we are a system of secret and unaccountable justice. Work, commenced by my predecessor, is well underway. I hope to be in a position to make important announcements in the near future.'

5. That applies just as much to the issue of transparency in the Court of Protection.

6. Very similar issues arise in both the Family Court (as it will be from April 2014) and the Court of Protection in relation to the need to protect the personal privacy of children and vulnerable adults. The applicable rules differ, however, and this is something that needs attention. My starting point is that so far as possible the same rules and principles should apply in both the family courts (in due course the Family Court) and the Court of Protection.

7. I propose to adopt an incremental approach. Initially I am issuing this Guidance. This will be followed by further Guidance and in due course more formal Practice Directions and changes to the Rules (the Court of Protection Rules 2007 and the Family Procedure Rules 2010). Changes to primary legislation are unlikely in the near future.

8. As provided in paragraph 14 below, this Guidance applies only to judgments delivered by certain judges. In due course, following the introduction of the Family Court, consideration will be given to extending it to judgments delivered by other judges (including lay justices).

The legal framework

9. The effect of section 12 of the Administration of Justice Act 1960 is that it is a contempt of court to publish a judgment in a family court case involving children unless either the judgment has been delivered in public or, where delivered in private, the judge has authorised publication. In the latter case, the judge normally gives permission for the judgment to be published on condition that the published version protects the anonymity of the children and members of their family.

10. In every case the terms on which publication is permitted are a matter for the judge and will be set out by the judge in a rubric at the start of the judgment.

11. The normal terms as described in paragraph 9 may be appropriate in a case where no-one wishes to discuss the proceedings otherwise than anonymously. But they may be inappropriate, for example, where parents who have been exonerated in care proceedings wish to discuss their experiences in public, identifying themselves and making use of the judgment. Equally, they may be inappropriate in cases where findings have been made against a person and someone else contends and/or the judge concludes that it is in the public interest for that person to be identified in any published version of the judgment.

12. If any party wishes to identify himself or herself, or any other party or person, as being a person referred to in any published version of the judgment, their remedy is to seek an order of the court and a suitable modification of the rubric: Media Access & Reporting, para 82; *Re RB (Adult) (No 4)* [2011] EWHC 3017 (Fam), [2012] 1 FLR 466, paras [17], [19].

13. Nothing in this Guidance affects the exercise by the judge in any particular case of whatever powers would otherwise be available to regulate the publication of material relating to the proceedings. For example, where a judgment is likely to be used in a way that would defeat the purpose of any anonymisation, it is open to the judge to refuse to publish the judgment or to make an order restricting its use.

Guidance

14. This Guidance takes effect from 3 February 2014. It applies:

(i) in the family courts (and in due course in the Family Court), to judgments delivered by Circuit Judges, High Court Judges and persons sitting as judges of the High Court; and

(ii) to all judgments delivered by High Court Judges (and persons sitting as judges of the High Court) exercising the inherent jurisdiction to make orders in respect of children and incapacitated or vulnerable adults.

15. The following paragraphs of this Guidance distinguish between two classes of judgment:

(i) those that the judge *must* ordinarily allow to be published (paragraphs 16 and 17); and

(ii) those that *may* be published (paragraph 18).

16. Permission to publish a judgment should always be given whenever the judge concludes that publication would be in the public interest and whether or not a request has been made by a party or the media.

17. Where a judgment relates to matters set out in Schedule 1 or 2 below and a written judgment already exists in a publishable form or the judge has already ordered that the judgment be transcribed, the starting point is that permission should be given for the judgment to be published unless there are compelling reasons why the judgment should not be published.

SCHEDULE 1

In the family courts (and in due course in the Family Court), including in proceedings under the inherent jurisdiction of the High Court relating to children, judgments arising from:

(i) a substantial contested fact-finding hearing at which serious allegations, for example allegations of significant physical, emotional or sexual harm, have been determined;

(ii) the making or refusal of a final care order or supervision order under Part 4 of the Children Act 1989, or any order for the discharge of any such order, except where the order is made with the consent of all participating parties;

(iii) the making or refusal of a placement order or adoption order under the Adoption and Children Act 2002, or any order for the discharge of any such order, except where the order is made with the consent of all participating parties;

(iv) the making or refusal of any declaration or order authorising a deprivation of liberty, including an order for a secure accommodation order under section 25 of the Children Act 1989;

(v) any application for an order involving the giving or withholding of serious medical treatment;

(vi) any application for an order involving a restraint on publication of information relating to the proceedings.

SCHEDULE 2

CONTEMPT OF COURT

In proceedings under the inherent jurisdiction of the High Court relating to incapacitated or vulnerable adults, judgments arising from:

(i) any application for a declaration or order involving a deprivation or possible deprivation of liberty;
(ii) any application for an order involving the giving or withholding of serious medical treatment;
(iii) any application for an order that an incapacitated or vulnerable adult be moved into or out of a residential establishment or other institution;
(iv) any application for a declaration as to capacity to marry or to consent to sexual relations;
(v) any application for an order involving a restraint on publication of information relating to the proceedings.

18. In all other cases, the starting point is that permission may be given for the judgment to be published whenever a party or an accredited member of the media applies for an order permitting publication, and the judge concludes that permission for the judgment to be published should be given.

19. In deciding whether and if so when to publish a judgment, the judge shall have regard to all the circumstances, the rights arising under any relevant provision of the European Convention on Human Rights, including Articles 6 (right to a fair hearing), 8 (respect for private and family life) and 10 (freedom of expression), and the effect of publication upon any current or potential criminal proceedings.

20. In all cases where a judge gives permission for a judgment to be published:

(i) public authorities and expert witnesses should be named in the judgment approved for publication, unless there are compelling reasons why they should not be so named;
(ii) the children who are the subject of the proceedings in the family courts, and other members of their family, and the person who is the subject of proceedings under the inherent jurisdiction of the High Court relating to incapacitated or vulnerable adults, and other members of their family, should not normally be named in the judgment approved for publication unless the judge otherwise orders;
(iii) anonymity in the judgment as published should not normally extend beyond protecting the privacy of the children and adults who are the subject of the proceedings and other members of their families, unless there are compelling reasons to do so.

21. Unless the judgment is already in anonymised form or the judge otherwise orders, any necessary anonymisation of the judgment shall be carried out, in the case of judgments being published pursuant to paragraphs 16 and 17 above, by the solicitor for the applicant in the proceedings and, in the case of a judgment being published pursuant to paragraph 18 above, by the solicitor for the party or person applying for publication of the judgment. The anonymised version of the judgment must be submitted to the judge within a period specified by the judge for approval. The version approved for publication will contain such rubric as the judge specifies. Unless the rubric specified by the judge provides expressly to the contrary every published judgment shall be deemed to contain the following rubric:

> 'This judgment was delivered in private. The judge has given leave for this version of the judgment to be published on condition that (irrespective of what is contained in the judgment) in any published version of the judgment the anonymity of the children and members of their family must be strictly preserved. All persons, including representatives of the media, must ensure that this condition is strictly complied with. Failure to do so will be a contempt of court.'

22. The judge will need to consider who should be ordered to bear the cost of transcribing the judgment. Unless the judge otherwise orders:

(i) in cases falling under paragraph 16 the cost of transcribing the judgment is to be at public expense;
(ii) subject to (i), in cases falling under paragraph 17 the cost of transcribing the judgment shall be borne equally by the parties to the proceedings;
(iii) in cases falling under paragraph 18, the cost of transcribing the judgment shall be borne by the party or person applying for publication of the judgment.

23. In all cases where permission is given for a judgment to be published, the version of the judgment approved for publication shall be made available, upon payment of any appropriate charge that may be required, to any person who requests a copy. Where a

judgment to which paragraph 16 or 17 applies is approved for publication, it shall as soon as reasonably practicable be placed by the court on the BAILII website. Where a judgment to which paragraph 18 applies is approved for publication, the judge shall consider whether it should be placed on the BAILII website and, if so, it shall as soon as reasonably practicable be placed by the court on the BAILII website.

III COT [8.3]

Mental Health Acts The reference to the Mental Health Act 1959 in s 12(1)(b) should be read as a reference to the Mental Health Act 1983: Interpretation Act 1978 s 17(2); *Pickering v Liverpool Daily Post and Echo Newspapers plc* [1991] 2 AC 370 at 417D, HL.

III COT [8.4]

Standard of proof of contempt Proof of an allegation in civil proceedings that a person is in contempt of court, including in relation to the cases covered by s 12, has to be to the criminal standard, ie, beyond reasonable doubt: *X v Dempster* [1999] 3 FCR 757, [1999] 1 FLR 894.

III COT [8.5]

Section 12(2) The power under s 12(2) to prohibit publication either of the text of an order or of a summary thereof is likely to be exercised only in the rarest of cases. In *Re G (minors) (celebrities: publicity)* [1999] 3 FCR 181, [1999] 1 FLR 409, CA, the Court of Appeal varied an order of this nature to allow publication of a brief summary by the Official Solicitor.

III COT [8.6]

Section 12(4) Section 12(4), which on its face is ambiguous, prevents a finding of contempt of court in circumstances which would not have amounted to a contempt under the pre-existing law: *Re F (a minor) (publication of information)* [1977] Fam 58 at 74, [1977] 1 All ER 114, CA.

III COT [8.7]

Application for normal restrictions on publicity to be lifted: timing and costs An application by the press for the lifting of restrictions on publicity should normally be made ahead of the hearing. If an arguable, but unsuccessful, case is presented at this stage an adverse order for costs is unlikely to be made; but a late, unsuccessful application which unnecessarily disrupts the hearing may result in an order that the applicant pay the resulting costs: *A v Times Newspapers Ltd* [2003] EWHC 2444 (Fam), [2003] 1 All ER 587.

III COT [9]

13. Appeal in cases of contempt of court

(1) Subject to the provisions of this section, an appeal shall lie under this section from any order or decision of a court in the exercise of jurisdiction to punish for contempt of court (including criminal contempt); and in relation to any such order or decision the provisions of this section shall have effect in substitution for any other enactment relating to appeals in civil or criminal proceedings.

(2) An appeal under this section shall lie in any case at the instance of the defendant and, in the case of an application for committal or attachment, at the instance of the applicant; and the appeal shall lie—

(a) from an order or decision of any inferior court not referred to in the next following paragraph, to [. . .] the High Court;

(b) from an order or decision of the county court or any other inferior court from which appeals generally lie to the Court of Appeal, and from an order or decision (other than a decision on an appeal under this section) of a single judge of the High Court, or of any court having the powers of the High Court or of a judge of that court, to the Court of Appeal;

(bb) from an order or decision of the Crown Court to the Court of Appeal;

(c) from a decision of a single judge of the High Court on an appeal under this section, from an order or decision of a Divisional Court or the Court of Appeal (including a decision of either of those courts on an appeal under this section), and from an order or decision (except

CONTEMPT OF COURT

one made in Scotland or Northern Ireland) of the Court Martial Appeal Court, to the Supreme Court.

(2A) Paragraphs (a) to (c) of subsection (2) of this section do not apply in relation to appeals under this section from an order or decision of the family court, but (subject to any provision made under section 56 of the Access of Justice Act 1999 or by or under any other enactment) such an appeal shall lie to the Court of Appeal.

(3) The court to which an appeal is brought under this section may reverse or vary the order or decision of the court below, and make such other order as may be just; and without prejudice to the inherent powers of any court referred to in subsection (2) of this section, provision may be made by rules of court for authorising the release on bail of an appellant under this section.

(4) Subsections (2) to (4) of section one and section two of this Act shall apply to an appeal to the Supreme Court under this section as they apply to an appeal to the Supreme Court under the said section one, except that so much of the said subsection (2) as restricts the grant of leave to appeal shall apply only where the decision of the court below is a decision on appeal to that court under this section.

(5) In this section "court" includes any tribunal or person having power to punish for contempt; and references in this section to an order or decision of a court in the exercise of jurisdiction to punish for contempt of court include references—

- *(a) to an order or decision of the High Court, the family court, the Crown Court or the county court under any enactment enabling that court to deal with an offence as if it were contempt of court;*
- *(b) to an order or decision of the county court, or of any court having the powers of the county court, under section 14, 92 or 118 of the County Courts Act 1984;*
- *(c) to an order or decision of a magistrates' court under subsection (3) of section 63 of the Magistrates' Courts Act 1980,*
- *(d) to an order or decision (except one made in Scotland or Northern Ireland) of the Court Martial, the Summary Appeal Court or the Service Civilian Court under section 309 of the Armed Forced Act 2006,*

but do not include references to orders under section five of the Debtors Act 1869, or under any provision of the Magistrates' Courts Act 1980, or the County Courts Act 1984, except those referred to in paragraphs (b) and (c) of this subsection and except sections 38 and 142 of the last mentioned Act so far as those sections confer jurisdiction in respect of contempt of court.

(6) This section does not apply to a conviction or sentence in respect of which an appeal lies under Part I of the Criminal Appeal Act 1968, or to a decision of the criminal division of the Court of Appeal under that Part of that Act; [. . .]

Repeal *Section 13 is repealed in part by the Legal Aid (Scotland) Act 1986, in part by the Legal Aid Act 1988 and in part by the Access to Justice (Northern Ireland) Order 2003, with effect from a date to be appointed.*

III COT [9.1]

Right of appeal Section 13 provides a general right of appeal in any case involving the jurisdiction to punish for contempt of court, which must now be read in conjunction with the Access to Justice Act 1999, the Access to Justice Act 1999 (Destination of Appeals) Order 2000 (SI 2000/1071) and CPR 52: *Barnet London Borough Council v Hurst* [2002] EWCA Civ 1009, [2002] 4 All ER 457, [2003] 1 WLR 722.

The language of s 13 is sufficiently wide to relate to orders or decisions made in the course of proceedings which may result in a conviction of and sentence for contempt, including a refusal to grant bail: *R v Serumaga* [2005] EWCA Crim 370, [2005] 1 WLR 3366, [2005] 2 All ER 160.

The appropriate procedure for a challenge to a refusal by the Crown Court to grant bail is an appeal to the Court of Appeal (Criminal Division) under s 13(1) rather than an application for judicial review: *R v Serumaga* [2005] EWCA Crim 370, [2005] 1 WLR 3366.

Although the Court of Appeal has jurisdiction under s 13 to hear an appeal from a decision of a district judge, the appropriate course is to appeal to the circuit judge, unless the criteria set out in CPR 52.14 are satisfied: *Barnet London Borough Council v Hurst* [2002] EWCA Civ 1009, [2002] 4 All ER 457, [2003] 1 WLR 722. Any appeal against committal should be heard as quickly as possible: *Mesham v Clarke* [1989] FCR 782, [1989] 1 FLR 370, CA.

The reference to the Court of Appeal in s 13(2)(c) encompasses both divisions of the Court of Appeal: *OB v Director of the Serious Fraud Office* [2012] EWCA Crim 901, [2012] 3 All ER 1017, [2012] 1 WLR 3188.

There are particular and complex provisions relating to appeals in respect of the grant or refusal of an order for committal: **CPR 52.3 [5]**.

III COT [9.2]

Permission to appeal A person who has been committed to prison does not require permission to appeal (even where the committal order was suspended: *Wilkinson v S* [2003] EWCA Civ 95, [2003] 2 All ER 184, [2003] 1 WLR 1254, and even where the appeal is not strictly against a 'committal order' within the meaning of CPR 52.3(1)(a)(i) but is an appeal against a refusal of a judge to order the applicant's early discharge from prison: *CJ v Flintshire Borough Council* [2010] EWCA Civ 393, [2010] 2 FLR 1224, [2010] 3 FCR 40, [2010] Fam Law 697, para 4), except in the case of a second appeal from a committal order originally made by a district judge; permission is required in all other cases including appeals by an applicant for a committal order: CPR 52.3(1)(a)(i); *Barnet London Borough Council v Hurst* [2002] EWCA Civ 1009, [2002] 4 All ER 457, [2003] 1 WLR 722; *Kynaston v Carroll* [2004] EWCA Civ 1434; *Poole Borough Council v Hambridge* [2007] EWCA Civ 990 (*Wood v Collins* [2006] EWCA Civ 743, [2006] All ER (D) 165 (May) not followed).

A company cannot be committed to prison and requires permission to appeal against an order finding it to be in contempt: such a finding is is not a 'committal order' within the meaning of CPR 52.3(1)(a): *Masri v Consolidated Contractors International Company SAL* [2011] EWCA Civ 898, (2011) Times, 30 November.

Permission is required for all second appeals, and may only be granted by the Court of Appeal: CPR 52.13: *Barnet London Borough Council v Hurst* [2002] EWCA Civ 1009, [2002] 4 All ER 457, [2003] 1 WLR 722.

There are particular and complex provisions relating to appeals in respect of the grant or refusal of an order for committal: **CPR 52.3 [5]**.

For appeals to the Supreme Court please refer to para **II SCR [A1.1]**.

III COT [9.2A]

Bail pending appeal The Court of Appeal may release an appellant on bail pending an appeal to the Court of Appeal or Supreme Court under s 13: CPR Sch 1 RSC Ord 109, r 4. There does not appear to be any provision for the grant of bail pending an appeal to the High Court, although CPR Sch 1 RSC Ord 79 applies in relation to the grant of bail in 'criminal proceedings', which arguably includes criminal contempt of court.

The appropriate procedure for a challenge to a refusal by the Crown Court to grant bail is an appeal to the Court of Appeal under s 13(1) rather than an application for judicial review: *R v Serumaga* [2005] EWCA Crim 370, [2005] 1 WLR 3366.

III COT [9.3]

Court's powers on appeal The appeal court has power to reverse or vary the order or decision of the court below, and make such other order as may be just: s 13(3).

Section 13(3) probably includes within it a power to award costs against one of the parties to the proceedings: *R v Moore* [2003] EWCA Crim 1574, [2003] 1 WLR 2170, para 17. Section 13(3) does not, however, confer a power to order payment of costs out of central funds: *R v Moore* [2003] EWCA Crim 1574, [2003] 1 WLR 2170, para 24 (successful appeal against conviction for contempt of court in the Crown Court).

The appeal court may remit a matter to the court below for a rehearing: *R v Kenny (Charlie)* [2011] EWCA Crim 1232; for an example, see *Manchester City Council v McCann* [1999] QB 1214, CA.

Section 13(2) does not prevent a court to which an appeal has been made from increasing the sentence imposed by the court below: *Wilson v Webster* [1998] 2 FCR 575, [1998] 1 FLR 1097, CA, applied in *Neil v Ryan* [1999] 1 FCR 241, [1998] 2 FLR 1068, CA.

For guidance on the approach to be adopted by the appeal court in committal cases, see *Nicholls v Nicholls* [1997] 1 WLR 314, CA, at 326-327.

CONTEMPT OF COURT ACT 1981

(c 49)

III COT [10]

1. The strict liability rule

In this Act "the strict liability rule" means the rule of law whereby conduct may be treated as a contempt of court as tending to interfere with the course of justice in particular legal proceedings regardless of intent to do so.

III COT [10.1]

Intention Mens rea, in the sense of an intention to interfere with or impede the administration of justice, is required for criminal contempt of court: *A-G v Times Newspapers Ltd* [1992] 1 AC 191, [1992] 2 All ER 398, HL. The "strict liability rule" is a rule by virtue of which conduct may be treated as a contempt of court as tending to interfere with the course of justice in particular legal proceedings regardless of intent to do so. For the conduct to which the strict liability rule applies, and the statutory defences, see ss 2–6 (see paras **III COT [11]–III COT [15]**).

A person who deliberately took an illegal photograph in court and a person who deliberately disseminated it thereby showed the intention to impede the due administration of justice: the question of whether he had intended to create a real risk of prejudice was not distinguishable from the question of whether he had intended to take the illegal photograph: *HM Solicitor General v Cox* [2016] EWHC 1241 (QB), QBD, Div Ct, Lord Thomas CJ and Ouseley J where it was held that:

(1) Illegal photography would, in general, interfere with the proper administration of justice through the very fact that it defied the criminal law relating to the administration of justice. Further, the statutory prohibition on photography in court was also a reflection of the serious risk to the administration of justice necessarily inherent in photography in court without the permission of the court, which could be given under the relevant statutory provisions in very limited circumstances. Such photograph inevitably posed serious risks to proceedings or participants in them. Those serious risks might be continued or enhanced by the use made of illegal photographs, whether by publication or some other use. The real and specific risk of serious interference with the proper administration of justice was evident. Those involved in upholding the proper administration of the criminal justice system, including witnesses, would be aware of the publicity which could be given to them through the use of illegal photographs. That obviously created a serious risk to the due administration of justice. The sentencing of a criminal and its immediate aftermath, and the respect to which victims were entitled, were an essential part of the due administration of justice. The due administration of justice plainly also included the protection of victims and their families from the use of illegally taken photographs for

whatever purpose, including to undermine or belittle the outcome of the criminal process or the court's authority. The fact that taking photographs in court and publishing them were criminal offences did not prevent those acts being punishable as contempts of court, as those actions posed serious risks to, and interfered with, the due administration of justice. The court obviously had power, as it needed, to deal immediately with anyone seen taking photographs, in order to maintain control over its proceedings and to avoid it standing powerless while the law designed to protect the administration of justice was broken before it. Whilst the later publication of such photographs might not be a contempt in the face of the court, it was still a contempt, quite apart from the fact that it was a criminal offence, since publication for a variety of reasons might be the very purpose behind the taking of the photograph illegally (see [23], [24], [27], [28], [30], [31] of the judgment).

(2) The circumstances in which contempt of court arose were too varied for one mens rea to be applicable to all forms of contempt. Nor was that the law. In the overwhelming majority of cases, it would be readily inferred that the person deliberately taking photographs had intended to interfere with the due administration of justice. However, there might be rare cases where that was not the inference. Accordingly, specific intent was not required. It was sufficient mens rea that the acts had to be deliberate and in breach of the criminal law or a court order of which the person knew. No specific intent was required beyond that. The intent required could not depend on the foresight, knowledge or understanding which the ignorant or foolish might have of the ways in which his acts risked or actually did interfere with the administration of justice. The questions whether the breach had been knowing and deliberate, and whether it had been intended to interfere with the course of justice amounted to the same question, even if the person might not have realised or understood quite how the administration of justice could be interfered with. Alternatively, it was sufficient mens rea, for the specific intent to impede the course of justice, if the contemnor intended to risk impeding the course of justice by his acts, even if he had not intended the precise manner in which his acts would have that effect (see [60], [66], [68]–[70], [73] of the judgment).

CONTEMPT OF COURT

III COT [10.2]

Legal proceedings "Court" includes any tribunal or body exercising the judicial power of the state, and "legal proceedings" are to be construed accordingly: s 19 (see para **III COT [23]**).

The following are "courts" within the meaning of s 19, and the strict liability rule applies: a mental health review tribunal (*Pickering v Liverpool Daily Post and Echo Newspapers plc* [1991] 2 AC 370, HL, at 417E–G); and an employment tribunal (*Peach Grey & Co v Sommers* [1995] 2 All ER 513, [1995] ICR 549).

In *A-G v Associated Newspapers Group plc* [1989] 1 All ER 604, [1989] 1 WLR 322, DC (Mann LJ and Henry J) it was held that a mental health review tribunal is not a 'court' for the purposes of the 1981 Act and, therefore, an article published in a newspaper prior to or during the hearing by such a tribunal of an application by a restricted patient for release from a secure hospital was not contempt of court under s 1 of that Act.

The Disciplinary Committee of the GMC is a judicial body but not a 'court' for these purposes because it does not exercise the power of the state as required by the definition in s 19; its proceedings are therefore not 'legal proceedings' and the strict liability rule does not apply: *General Medical Council v BBC* [1998] 3 All ER 426, [1998] 1 WLR 1573, CA.

III COT [11]

2. Limitation of scope of strict liability

(1) The strict liability rule applies only in relation to publications, and for this purpose "publication" includes any speech, writing, programme included in a programme service or other communication in whatever form, which is addressed to the public at large or any section of the public.

(2) The strict liability rule applies only to a publication which creates a substantial risk that the course of justice in the proceedings in question will be seriously impeded or prejudiced.

(3) The strict liability rule applies to a publication only if the proceedings in question are active within the meaning of this section at the time of the publication.

(4) Schedule 1 applies for determining the times at which proceedings are to be treated as active within the meaning of this section.

(5) In this section "programme service" has the same meaning as in the Broadcasting Act 1990.

III COT [11.1]

"Substantial risk" and "serious prejudice" The test of substantial risk and serious prejudice means that neither a slight risk of serious prejudice, nor a substantial risk of slight prejudice, is sufficient to fulfil the requirements of the test: *A-G v Times Newspapers Ltd* (1983) Times, 12 February.

Whereas "seriously" should be construed in its ordinary meaning: *A-G v English* [1983] 1 AC 116, [1982] 2 All ER 903, HL, "substantial" has been taken as intending to exclude a risk that is only remote, or "not substantial" or "not minimal": *A-G v English; A-G v News Group Newspapers Ltd* [1987] QB 1, [1986] 2 All ER 833, CA.

The risk is to be assessed as at the time of publication: *A-G v English* [1983] 1 AC 116, [1982] 2 All ER 903, HL per Lord Diplock at 141F, 917, and must be practical and not theoretical: *A-G v Guardian Newspapers Ltd* [1992] 1 WLR 874, DC (per Mann LJ at 881C).

Unless a publication materially affects the course of a trial by causing it to be moved or delayed to minimise the prejudice occasioned, or requires directions from the court well beyond those ordinarily required and routinely given to juries to focus their attention on evidence called before them rather than whatever they may have heard or read outside court, or creates at the very least a seriously arguable ground for an appeal on the basis of prejudice, it is unlikely to be vulnerable to contempt proceedings under the strict liability rule: *A-G v Unger* [1998] 1 Cr App Rep 308 at 318G–319A, DC (in which newspaper reports of an alleged confession to an offence were held not to amount to a contempt). Nevertheless, a publication may constitute a contempt and yet, even though not substantially mitigated in its effect by a temporary stay and/or change of venue, not so prejudice the trial as to undermine the safety of any subsequent conviction: *A-G v Birmingham Post and Mail Ltd* [1998] 4 All ER 49, [1999] 1 WLR 361, DC.

In assessing the risk that a juror might see a photograph (of the accused in a murder trial holding a gun), the court should consider whether its appearance online was only fleeing or remained available for a substantial period: the longer it was available, the greater the chance that a juror might see it: *A-G v Associated Newspapers Ltd* [2011] EWHC 418 (Admin), [2011] 1 WLR 2097, para 27. In *A-G v Express Newspapers* [2004] EWHC 2859 (Admin), (2005) EMLR 13, DC, publication of the identity of two men charged with rape was held to have created a substantial risk that the course of justice in the criminal proceedings would be seriously impeded or prejudiced because it rendered the complainant highly vulnerable to cross-examination on the basis that her evidence as to identification was tainted by what she had read or by what she had heard from others.

A publication may fall within the protective ambit of s 2(2) as a potential impediment to the course of justice because it may deter or discourage witnesses from coming forward and providing information helpful to a suspect, which may (depending on the circumstances) help immediately to clear him of suspicion or enable his defence to be fully developed at trial: *A-G v MGN Ltd* [2011] EWHC 2074 (Admin), para 31, [2012] 1 Cr App Rep 1, [2011] All ER (D) 06 (Aug). In this context, any interference with the art 10 rights of the alleged contemnors depends on proof to the criminal standard that the publications in question have created a substantial risk of serious impediment or prejudice to the course of justice, and this falls comfortably within the limitations acknowledged in the Convention itself, including the art 6 right to a fair hearing: *A-G v MGN Ltd* [2011] EWHC 2074 (Admin), para 32, [2012] 1 Cr App Rep 1, [2011] All ER (D) 06 (Aug).

An article published during and concerning the phone-hacking trial was held to have been in contempt of court, since it was established that (a) it was likely to come to the attention of jurors, (b) there was a risk of serious prejudice, and (c) it was unrealistic to suppose that any juror who read it would not be influenced: *A-G v Conde Nast Publications Ltd* [2015] EWHC 3322 (Admin), [2015] All ER (D) 147 (Nov).

For Practice Guidance as to the use which may be made in court of live text-based communications, see the commentary to s 4 below.

III COT [12]

3. Defence of innocent publication or distribution

(1) A person is not guilty of contempt of court under the strict liability rule as the publisher of any matter to which that rule applies if at the time of publication (having taken all reasonable care) he does not know and has no reason to suspect that relevant proceedings are active.

(2) A person is not guilty of contempt of court under the strict liability rule as the distributor of a publication containing any such matter if at the time of distribution (having taken all reasonable care) he does not know that it contains such matter and has no reason to suspect that it is likely to do so.

(3) The burden of proof of any fact tending to establish a defence afforded by this section to any person lies upon that person.

(4) [. . .]

III COT [12.1]

Availability of defence The defence under this section is available only where the strict liability rule applies, so that it is not available where the contempt is alleged to have been intended to prejudice proceedings, or where there is a breach of s 12 of the Administration of Justice Act 1960 (see para **III COT [8]**).

III COT [13]

4. Contemporary reports of proceedings

(1) Subject to this section a person is not guilty of contempt of court under the strict liability rule in respect of a fair and accurate report of legal proceedings held in public, published contemporaneously and in good faith.

(2) In any such proceedings the court may, where it appears to be necessary for avoiding a substantial risk of prejudice to the administration of justice in those proceedings, or in any other proceedings pending or imminent, order that the publication of any report of the proceedings, or any part of the proceedings, be postponed for such period as the court thinks necessary for that purpose.

(2A) Where in proceedings for any offence which is an administration of justice offence for the purposes of section 54 of the Criminal Procedure and Investigations Act 1996 (acquittal tainted by an administration of justice offence) it appears to the court that there is a possibility that (by virtue of that section) proceedings may be taken against a person for an offence of which he has been acquitted, subsection (2) of this section shall apply as if those proceedings were pending or imminent.

(3) For the purposes of subsection (1) of this section [. . .] a report of proceedings shall be treated as published contemporaneously—

(a) in the case of a report of which publication is postponed pursuant to an order under subsection (2) of this section, if published as soon as practicable after that order expires;

(b) in the case of a report of allocation or sending proceedings of which publication is permitted by virtue only of subsection (6) of section 52A of the Crime and Disorder Act 1998 ("the 1998 Act"), if published as soon as practicable after publication is so permitted;

(c) in the case of a report of an application of which publication is permitted by virtue only of sub-paragraph (5) or (7) of paragraph 3 of Schedule 3 to the 1998 Act, if published as soon as practicable after publication is so permitted.

(4) [. . .]

III COT [13.1]

General Subject to the provisions of s 4, a person is not guilty of contempt of court under the strict liability rule in respect of a fair and accurate report of legal proceedings held in public, published contemporaneously and in good faith. For the principles governing reports of proceedings held in private, see **III COT [8.1]**.

Practice Guidance: The use of live text-based forms of communication (including Twitter) from court for the purposes of fair and accurate reporting (see **CPR PD 39A.6 [2]**) issued on 14 December 2011 (and replacing the Interim Practice Guidance of 20 December 2010) permits the use by a representative of the media or 'a legal commentator' of live text-based communications, such as mobile email, social media (including Twitter) and internet-enabled laptops in and from courts throughout England and Wales, without making an application to the court; a member of the public who wishes to use such communications during court proceedings must make an application, formally or informally (eg by communicating a request to the judge through court staff). In both cases, compliance with the strict prohibition rules created by ss 1, 2 and 4 of the Contempt of Court Act 1981 in relation to the reporting of court proceedings is required; and permission to use live, text-based communications from court may be withdrawn by the court at any time.

III COT [13.2]

Postponement order A court considering whether to make an order under s 4(2) must balance the competing interests under Arts 6 and 10 of the European Convention on Human Rights, and should apply the three-part test laid down by the Court of Appeal in *Ex p Telegraph Group plc* [2001] EWCA Crim 1075, [2001] 1 WLR 1983, CA.

The statutory power is exhaustive, and there is no inherent power to order postponement in cases falling outside the scope of s 4(2): *R v Newtownabbey Magistrates' Court, ex p Belfast Telegraph Newspapers Ltd* (1997) Times, 27 August; *Independent Publishing Co Ltd v A-G of Trinidad and Tobago* [2004] UKPC 26, [2005] 1 AC 190; *Re Times Newspapers Ltd* [2007] EWCA Crim 1925, [2008] 1 All ER 343.

The court may hear representations from the press before making an order under s 4(2): *R v Clerkenwell Metropolitan Stipendiary Magistrates, ex p Telegraph plc* [1993] QB 462, [1993] 2 All ER 183, DC. In deciding whether to make an order under s 4(2) the court will take into account the fact that juries follow directions given to them by the trial judge to focus exclusively on the evidence and ignore anything they may have heard or read out of court: see eg *Re B* [2006] EWCA Crim 2692, [2006] All ER (D) 348 (Oct).

Even where there is a not insubstantial risk of prejudice which a postponement order would eliminate, the court should consider other less restrictive ways of eliminating the risk of prejudice and should not use the provisions of sub-s (2) for the purposes of alleviating the difficulties of witnesses giving evidence: *Re MGN Ltd* [2011] EWCA Crim 100, [2011] 1 Cr App Rep 387, [2011] NLJR 552.

III COT [13.3]

Form of order An order made under s 4(2) must be formulated in precise terms, must be committed to writing either by the judge personally or by the clerk of the court under the judge's directions, and must state (a) its precise scope, (b) the time at which it shall cease to have effect, if appropriate, and (c) the specific purpose of making the order: *Practice Direction (Contempt: Reporting Restrictions)* [1983] 1 All ER 64, [1982] 1 WLR 1475, CA.

III COT [13.4]

Breach of order Publication in breach of an order made under s 4(2) is a contempt: *R v Horsham Justices, ex p Farquharson* [1982] QB 762, [1982] 2 All ER 269, CA; *A-G v Guardian Newspapers Ltd (No 3)* [1992] 3 All ER 38, [1992] 1 WLR 874, DC.

III COT [14]

5. Discussion of public affairs

A publication made as or as part of a discussion in good faith of public affairs or other matters of general public interest is not to be treated as a contempt of court under the strict liability rule if the risk of impediment or prejudice to particular legal proceedings is merely incidental to the discussion.

III COT [14.1]

General Once the court has determined that a publication falls within s 2(2), it must consider whether s 5 applies, the burden of proof on both issues being on the prosecution: *A-G v English* [1983] 1 AC 116, [1982] 2 All ER 903, HL.

III COT [14.2]

Incidental risk A risk is incidental to the discussion if it is "no more than an incidental consequence of expounding its main theme": *A-G v English* [1983] 1 AC 116, [1982] 2 All ER 903, HL.

III COT [15]

6. Savings

Nothing in the foregoing provisions of this Act—

(a) prejudices any defence available at common law to a charge of contempt of court under the strict liability rule;

(b) implies that any publication is punishable as contempt of court under that rule which would not be so punishable apart from those provisions;

(c) restricts liability for contempt of court in respect of conduct intended to impede or prejudice the administration of justice.

III COT [15.1]

Conduct intended to impede The "strict liability rule" in s 1 (para **III COT [10]**) does not apply where conduct (whether the conduct consists of publication or otherwise) is intended to impede or prejudice the administration of justice, in relation to which the common law continues to apply (see para **III COT [4A]**).

III COT [16]

7. Consent required for institution of proceedings

Proceedings for a contempt of court under the strict liability rule (other than Scottish proceedings) shall not be instituted except by or with the consent of the Attorney General or on the motion of a court having jurisdiction to deal with it.

III COT [16.1]

Attorney-General's consent There is no formal procedure for seeking the Attorney-General's consent to proceedings; an application is simply made by writing to him. A refusal of consent cannot be challenged: *R v Solicitor-General, ex p Taylor* [1996] 1 FCR 206.

III COT [16.2]

Proceedings by trial on indictment The proper approach to allegations of contempt of court by the media is by way of committal proceedings in the High Court, not by trial on indictment: *Re Lonrho Plc* [1990] 2 AC 154, [1989] 2 All ER 1100, HL per Lord Keith; *A-G v Dallas* [2012] EWHC 156 (Admin), [2012] 1 WLR 991, [2012] Cr App Rep 436.

III COT [17]

8. *Confidentiality of jury's deliberations*

(1) Subject to subsection (2) below, it is a contempt of court to obtain, disclose or solicit any particulars of statements made, opinions expressed, arguments advanced or votes cast by members of a jury in the course of their deliberations in any legal proceedings.

(2) This section does not apply to any disclosure of any particulars—

(a) in the proceedings in question for the purpose of enabling the jury to arrive at their verdict, or in connection with the delivery of that verdict, or

(b) in evidence in any subsequent proceedings for an offence alleged to have been committed in relation to the jury in the first mentioned proceedings,

or to the publication of any particulars so disclosed.

(3) Proceedings for a contempt of court under this section (other than Scottish proceedings) shall not be instituted except by or with the consent of the Attorney General or on the motion of a court having jurisdiction to deal with it.

Repeal *Section 8 is repealed in relation to England and Wales by the Criminal Justice and Courts Act 2015 with effect from 13 April 2015.*

III COT [17.1]

Section 8(1) "Disclose" is apt to describe both the revelation of jury deliberations by an individual juror and the further disclosure of those same deliberations by publication in a newspaper: *A-G v Associated Newspapers Ltd* [1994] 2 AC 238, HL. The requisite *mens rea* is an intention to disclose: *A-G v Scotcher* [2005] UKHL 36, [2005] 1 WLR 1867, [2005] 3 All ER 1.

A jury's stay in a hotel is a hiatus between sessions in the jury room and discussions between jurors at the hotel are not "deliberations" for the purposes of s 8(1) of the Contempt of Court Act 1981: *R v Young (Stephen)* [1995] QB 324, CA.

Section 8(1) does not apply to the court, which may enquire into a jury's deliberations in exceptional cases in order to determine whether a miscarriage of justice has occurred, or to complaints by a juror to the court about misconduct during the jury's deliberations: *R v Mirza* [2004] UKHL 02, [2004] 1 AC 1118, [2004] 1 All ER 925 (*R v Young (Stephen)* [1995] QB 324, CA, not followed on this issue); *A-G v Scotcher* [2005] UKHL 36, [2005] 1 WLR 1867.

It is the duty of jurors to bring such conduct to the judge's attention while the case is continuing: *Practice Direction (Crown Court: Guidance to Jurors)* [2004] 1 WLR 665: *A-G v Pardon* [2012] EWHC 3401 (Admin).

The Court of Appeal has repeatedly emphasised the seriousness with which it will view any incident which serves to undermine the system of trial by jury, and *A-G v Scotcher* [2003] EWHC 1380 (Admin), [2003] All ER (D) 221 (May) does not represent current sentencing practice: *A-G v Pardon* [2012] EWHC 3401 (Admin), para 19.

III COT [18]

9. Use of tape recorders

(1) Subject to subsection (4) below, it is a contempt of court—

(a) to use in court, or bring into court for use, any tape recorder or other instrument for recording sound, except with the leave of the court;

(b) to publish a recording of legal proceedings made by means of any such instrument, or any recording derived directly or indirectly from it, by playing it in the hearing of the public or any section of the public, or to dispose of it or any recording so derived, with a view to such publication;

(c) to use any such recording in contravention of any conditions of leave granted under paragraph (a).

(d) to publish or dispose of any recording in contravention of any conditions of leave granted under subsection (1A).

(1A) In the case of a recording of Supreme Court proceedings, subsection (1)(b) does not apply to its publication or disposal with the leave of the Court.

(2) Leave under paragraph (a) of subsection (1), or under subsection (1A), may be granted or refused at the discretion of the court, and if granted—

(a) may, in the case of leave under subsection (1)(a), be granted subject to such conditions as the court thinks proper with respect to the use of any recording made pursuant to the leave; and

(b) may, in the case of leave under subsection (1A), be granted subject to such conditions as the Supreme Court thinks proper with respect to publication or disposal of any recording to which the leave relates;

and where leave has been granted the court may at the like discretion withdraw or amend it either generally or in relation to any particular part of the proceedings.

(3) Without prejudice to any other power to deal with an act of contempt under paragraph (a) of subsection (1), the court may order the instrument, or any recording made with it, or both, to be forfeited; and any object so forfeited shall (unless the court otherwise determines on application by a person appearing to be the owner) be sold or otherwise disposed of in such manner as the court may direct.

(4) This section does not apply to the making or use of sound recordings for purposes of official transcripts of proceedings.

(5) See section 32 of the Crime and Courts Act 2013 for power to provide for further exceptions.

III COT [18.1]

Practice Direction See para **CPR PD 39A.6 [2]**: *Practice Direction (Tape Recorders)* [1981] 3 All ER 848, [1981] 1 WLR 1526. *Practice Guidance: The use of live text-based forms of communication (including Twitter) from court for the purposes of fair and accurate reporting* issued on dated 14 December 2011 (and replacing the Interim Practice Guidance of 20 December 2010) is intended to be consistent with s 9: see para 2.

This section is printed as amended by s 31 of the Crime and Courts Act 2013, with effect from 25 June 2013.

The Lord Chancellor has power, under s 32 of the Crime and Courts Act 2013, by order to disapply s 9 as regards tape-recording and filming subject to conditions and circumstances prescribed in the order. This power came into force on 15 July 2013.

III COT [18.2]

It is not clear whether mens rea is required for there to be a contempt under s 9(1): *Re Hooker (Patricia) and the Contempt of Court Act 1981* [1993] COD 190, DC.

III COT [19]

10. Sources of information

No court may require a person to disclose, nor is any person guilty of contempt of court for refusing to disclose, the source of information contained in a publication for which he is responsible, unless it be established to the satisfaction of the court that disclosure is necessary in the interests of justice or national security or for the prevention of disorder or crime.

III COT [19.1]

Disclosure Where an injunction has been granted preventing further publication on the grounds of a breach of legal professional confidence and the applicant seeks an order for disclosure under s 10 in order to find who has been responsible for the past breach, the court will not order disclosure on the grounds that it is necessary in the interests of justice in the absence of evidence that further breaches are likely and that the disclosure sought would help to avert them: *Saunders v Punch Ltd* [1998] 1 All ER 234, [1998] 1 WLR 986; nor will the court order disclosure on this basis where other means of identifying the source of a leak of confidential information have not been explored: *John v Express Newspapers* [2000] 3 All ER 257, [2000] 1 WLR 1931, CA.

For guidance as to the balance to be struck in deciding whether to compel a journalist to disclose the source of his or her information, see *X Ltd v Morgan-Grampion (Publishers) Ltd* [1991] 1 AC 1, [1990] 2 All ER 1, HL; *Camelot Group plc v Centaur Communications Ltd* [1999] QB 124, [1998] 1 All ER 251, CA; and *Ashworth Hospital Authority v MGN Ltd* [2002] UKHL 29, [2002] 4 All ER 193, [2002] 1 WLR 2033 (see also *Mersey Care NHS Trust v Ackroyd* (2006) Times, 9 February).

The court may order disclosure to be given on oath: see, for example, *Michael O'Mara Books Ltd v Express Newspapers plc* [1998] EMLR 383.

Summary judgment will be appropriate only in exceptional cases: *Ackroyd v Mersey Care NHS Trust* [2003] EWCA Civ 663, (2003) 73 BMLR 88, (2003) Times, 21 May.

III COT [19.2]

Relationship between s 10 and Art 10 of the European Convention on Human Rights The application of s 10 of the Contempt of Court Act 1981 involves an application of the principles developed by the European Court of Human Rights in relation to Art 10 of the European Convention on Human Rights: *Ashworth Hospital Authority v MGN Ltd* [2002] UKHL 29, [2002] 4 All ER 193, [2002] 1 WLR 2033. The art 10 right to freedom of expression is a right that is given to all people; similarly, s 10 of the Contempt of Court Act 1981 makes no distinction between journalists and others; the Strasbourg jurisprudence distinguishes between types of speech rather than types of speaker, and the type of speech to which it gives most protection is that which is directed to informing public debate (or, as it sometimes put, imparting information and ideas on political questions and on other matters of public interest); art 10 and s 10 are amongst the best known examples of the special status given by the law to journalism, and are designed to enhance the freedom of the press by protecting journalistic sources, and that includes sources who may have acted unlawfully in leaking information: *Metropolitan Police Comr v Times Newspapers Ltd* [2011] EWHC 2705 (QB), paras 127, 132 and 134. For an extensive discussion of the relationship between s 10 and Art 10 of the European Convention on Human Rights see: *Richard v British Broadcasting Corporation* [2017] EWHC 1291 (Ch), [2017] All ER (D) 33 (Jun) (Mann J).

III COT [19.3]

Publication for which he is responsible In *Totalise plc v Motley Fool Ltd* [2001] EWCA Civ 1897, [2002] 1 WLR 1233 (in which statements defamatory of the claimants were posted by an unidentified data-user on the discussion boards operated by the defendants), the defendants were held not to be entitled to the protection provided by s 10 because they took no responsibility for what was posted on their websites and exercised no editorial control.

CONTEMPT OF COURT

III COT [19.3]

Where a company suffers economic loss by reason of the leaking of confidential information the company has a remedy against the perpetrator and may seek information leading to identification from third parties. Where, however, the third party is a journalist or newspaper the information may be withheld in reliance on s 10. This section protects the source of the information except where disclosure is necessary in the interests of justice or national security or the prevention of disorder or crime. In *Financial Times Ltd v United Kingdom (Application No 821/03)* (2009) Times, 16 December, ECtHR, the European Court found that public interest in protecting the journalist's sources outweighed the interest in protecting the company from further breach of confidentiality and enabling them to recover damages. This effectively overturned the decision of the High Court and Court of Appeal in favour of ordering disclosure.

III COT [20]

11. Publication of matters exempted from disclosure in court

In any case where a court (having power to do so) allows a name or other matter to be withheld from the public in proceedings before the court, the court may give such directions prohibiting the publication of that name or matter in connection with the proceedings as appear to the court to be necessary for the purpose for which it was so withheld.

III COT [20.1]

Necessary for the purpose Section 11 does not give the court power to withhold information from the public, but makes provision for reporting restrictions in those cases where the court, having power to withhold information, does so: *A-G's Reference (No 3 of 1999), Re British Broadcasting Corpn* [2009] UKHL 34, [2010] 1 All ER 235, [2009] 3 WLR 142; *Re Times Newspapers Ltd* [2009] EWCA Crim 2396, [2009] 1 WLR 1015.

The court has such a power at common law (and see s 12 of the Administration of Justice Act 1960, as amended, at para **III COT [8]**), but exercises it only exceptionally, where it is persuaded that justice could not otherwise be done in the proceedings, either because the case could not be effectively tried or because the parties entitled to justice would be reasonably deterred from seeking it at the hands of the court: *Scott v Scott* [1913] AC 417, HL (Viscount Haldane LC at 437–439 and Earl Loreburn at 446); *A-G v Leveller Magazine Ltd* [1979] AC 440, [1979] 1 All ER 745, HL.

The court is also bound by s 6 of the Human Rights Act 1998 to act compatibly with any rights arising under the European Convention of Human Rights, which involves striking the appropriate balance between an individual's article 8 rights to respect for his private life and a broadcaster's article 10 rights to freedom of expression and communication: *A-G's Reference (No 3 of 1999), Re British Broadcasting Corpn* [2009] UKHL 34, [2010] 1 All ER 235, [2009] 3 WLR 142. An anonymity order may also be justified where there would otherwise be a real and immediate risk to life engaging article 2: *Re Times Newspapers Ltd* [2008] EWCA Crim 2559, [2009] 1 WLR 1015, [2009] Crim LR 114.

Any interference with the public nature of court proceedings is to be avoided unless justice requires it, and it is appropriate to take into account the restriction on disclosure sought, the nature of the proceedings, the identity of the party seeking the order and the reasonableness of the claim as well as the fact that any person who initiates proceedings may reasonably be taken to have accepted the consequences of the public nature of court proceedings: *R v Legal Aid Board, ex p Kaim Todner* [1999] QB 966, [1998] 3 All ER 541, CA.

In circumstances where the parties have agreed between themselves that there should be a prohibition on publication of information relating to the proceedings, the court will be particularly vigilant: see, eg, *R v Legal Aid Board, ex p Kaim Todner* [1999] QB 966, at 977, [1998] 3 All ER 541, at 549, CA.

Where it is necessary to protect witnesses or the ability of medical and nursing staff to carry out their duties effectively to care for a patient who is the subject of litigation, the court may prohibit the publication of the identity of the patient and the NHS Trust who are parties to the litigation: *Re G (adult patient: publicity)* [1996] 1 FCR 413, [1995] 2 FLR 538.

There is no justification for lawyers to be treated differently from other litigants: *R v Legal Aid Board, ex p Kaim Todner* [1999] QB 966, [1998] 3 All ER 541, CA.

The need for proceedings to be held in public means that an order under s 11 should only remain in force for the time necessary to fulfil its purpose: *R v George* [2002] EWCA Crim 1923, para 28, (2002) Times, 30 August, [2003] Crim LR 282. Publication of inaccurate speculation about matters which are the subject of a restriction under s 11 does not breach that restriction but may constitute an attempt to flout the order made by the court under s 11 and thereby constitute a contempt at common law: *Re Times Newspapers Ltd* [2007] EWCA Crim 1925, [2008] 1 All ER 343.

There is no respondent to be notified or heard in opposition to an application for an order under s 11 but, if an order is made without notice, the media may challenge it as a violation of their Article 10 rights: *A v British Broadcasting Corporation* [2014] UKSC 25.

On 1 August 2011, the Master of the Rolls issued *Practice Guidance: Interim Non-Disclosure Orders* setting out the recommended practice regarding any application for interim injunctive relief in civil proceedings to restrain the publication of information.

III COT [20.2]

Proceedings in the Crown Court The section does not apply to proceedings in the Crown Court and there is no other power, by statute or at common law, for a Crown Court judge to impose restrictions on the publication of evidence given in public: *Re Trinity Mirror plc* [2008] EWCA Crim 50, [2008] 2 All ER 1159.

III COT [21]

14. Proceedings in England and Wales

(1) In any case where a court has power to commit a person to prison for contempt of court and (apart from this provision) no limitation applies to the period of committal, the committal shall (without prejudice to the power of the court to order his earlier discharge) be for a fixed term, and that term shall not on any occasion exceed two years in the case of committal by a superior court, or one month in the case of committal by an inferior court.

(2) In any case where an inferior court has power to fine a person for contempt of court and (apart from this provision) no limit applies to the amount of the fine, the fine shall not on any occasion exceed £2,500.

(2A) In the exercise of jurisdiction to commit for contempt of court or any kindred offence the court shall not deal with the offender by making an order under section 60 of the Powers of Criminal Courts (Sentencing) Act 2000 (an attendance centre order) if it appears to the court, after considering any available evidence, that he is under 17 years of age.

(2A) A fine imposed under subsection (2) above shall be deemed, for the purposes of any enactment, to be a sum adjudged to be paid by a conviction.

(3) [. . .]

(4) Each of the superior courts shall have the like power to make a hospital order or guardianship order under section 37 of the Mental Health Act 1983 or an interim hospital order under section 38 of that Act in the case of a person suffering from mental disorder within the meaning of that Act who could otherwise be committed to prison for contempt of court as the Crown Court has under that section in the case of a person convicted of an offence.

(4A) Each of the superior courts shall have the like power to make an order under section 35 of the said Act of 1983 (remand for report on accused's mental condition) where there is reason to suspect that a person who could be committed to prison for contempt of court is suffering from mental disorder within the meaning of that Act as the Crown Court has under that section in the case of an accused person within the meaning of that section.

(4A) For the purposes of the preceding provisions of this section the county court shall be treated as a superior court and not an inferior court.

(4B) The preceding provisions of this section do not apply to the family court, but—

- (a) this is without prejudice to the operation of section 31E(1)(a) of the Matrimonial and Family Proceedings Act 1984 (family court has High Court's powers) in relation to the powers of the High Court that are limited or conferred by those provisions of this section, and
- (b) section 31E(1)(b) of that Act (family court has county court's powers) does not apply in relation to the powers of the county court that are limited or conferred by those provisions of this section.

CONTEMPT OF COURT

(5) The enactments specified in Part III of Schedule 2 shall have effect subject to the amendments set out in that Part, being amendments relating to the penalties and procedure in respect of certain offences of contempt in coroners' courts, county courts and magistrates' courts.

Amendment *First sub-s (2A) is repealed by the Criminal Justice and Immigration Act 2008 with effect from a date to be appointed.*

III COT [21.1]

Superior court 'Superior court' is defined in s 19 (see para **III COT [23]**). A county court is an inferior court, but is treated as a superior court for the purposes of s 14 (1)–(4A): see the second sub-s (4A).

III COT [21.1A]

Consideration of all contempts on one occasion While it is desirable so far as possible to consider on a single occasion all extant allegations of contempt of court, there is no fixed rule to such effect. The aim is desirable because the Contempt of Court Act 1981 limits the sentence for contempt of court which could be imposed on any occasion to a maximum term of two years' imprisonment. That timetable should not be manipulated by multiple applications in an attempt to procure a term of imprisonment in excess of two years; efforts to do so were overwhelmingly likely to fail. However there is not and could not be an invariable rule. A decision whether or not to leave over for future consideration extant allegations of contempt was a case management decision for the judge with which the court would be slow to interfere save on well-recognised grounds. Where alleged contempts arose in the context of a worldwide freezing order, coupled with a variety of ancillary and related provisions, there is likely to be a strong public interest in ensuring that the freezing order was appropriately policed, enforced and thus made effective; in that regard, the bringing of contempt proceedings could encourage improved compliance with its terms (see paras [29], [32], [33], [35], [36] of the judgment): *JSC BTA Bank v Ablyazov* [2011] EWCA Civ 1386, [2012] 2 All ER 575, [2012] 1 WLR 1988 (Sir Andrew Morritt C, Moses and Gross LJJ) (a case involving 32 allegations of contempt).

III COT [21.2]

Sentencing powers In the High Court and in the county courts (by virtue of the second sub-s (4A)), the jurisdiction to punish for contempt of court is the same.

Section 14 provides that punishment of the contemnor by imprisonment may not exceed two years, although the power to fine is unlimited.

Committal for civil contempt plainly comes within art 5(1)(b) of the European Convention on Human Rights, and when a court is considering whether to commit for contempt or to make an order for early release, it must consider the extent to which an order imprisoning the person for contempt is necessary and proportionate in the interests of the prevention of disorder or crime and to uphold the rule of law and the lawful orders of the court: *CJ v Flintshire Borough Council* [2010] EWCA Civ 393, [2010] 2 FLR 1224, [2010] 3 FCR 40, [2010] Fam Law 697, paras 30 and 37.

Committal must be for a fixed and not an indefinite term: *Linnett v Coles* [1987] QB 555, [1986] 3 All ER 652, CA. The court may impose consecutive sentences for different contempts: *Lee v Walker* [1985] QB 1191, [1985] 1 All ER 781, CA; but consecutive sentences imposed on the same occasion, even where one of them was a suspended sentence which is being activated, may not exceed two years in total: *Villiers v Villiers* [1994] 2 All ER 149, [1994] 1 WLR 493, CA. Where a substantial sentence of imprisonment is imposed it will normally (but not always: *Ablyazov v JSC BTA Bank* [2011] EWCA Civ 1386) be inappropriate to leave over other matters for future consideration, and a previous suspended sentence should be activated or discharged: *Phillips v Symes (No 3)* [2005] EWCA Civ 533 and [2005] EWCA Civ 663, [2005] 1 WLR 2986 (per Pill LJ at paras 50-55).

Where a judge promises a reduction in sentence to take account of mitigating factors, he may not impose individually reduced sentences consecutively so as to result in a total sentence which amounts to the maximum of two years: *Re R (a minor) (contempt: sentence)* [1994] 2 All ER 144, [1994] 1 WLR 487, CA.

A contemnor sentenced for failure to comply with an order requiring compliance within a specified time cannot be punished again for a continuing failure to comply since this is not a fresh breach of the order: *Kumari v Jalal* [1996] 4 All ER 65, [1997] 1 WLR 97, CA. As in the case of prohibitive injunctions, however, the court may make successive mandatory injunctions requiring positive action, such as the disclosure of information, notwithstanding a past failure to comply with an identical request; and a failure to comply with any fresh order would properly expose the defaulter to fresh contempt proceedings and the possibility of a further term of imprisonment: *Re W (a Child) (Abduction: Contempt)* [2011] EWCA Civ 1196, (2011) Times, 15 September, para 37.

It is neither an abuse of process nor a breach of the European Convention on Human Rights to bring contempt proceedings and criminal charges arising out of the same facts: *DPP v Tweddell* [2001] EWHC Admin 188, [2002] 1 FCR 438, approved in *Barnet London Borough Council v Hurst* [2002] EWCA Civ 1009, [2002] 4 All ER 457, [2003] 1 WLR 722 (see also **III COT [21.2A]**).

The Crown Court has the power when passing a sentence of imprisonment in respect of a criminal conviction to order that it should run consecutively to a sentence imposed in the county court for contempt in respect of the same act: *R v Anomo* [1998] 2 Cr App Rep (S) 269, CA.

A confiscation order under the Drug Trafficking Act 1994 is not part of the sentence of imprisonment for a drug trafficking offence but is a conditional order intended to persuade the defendant to pay over the proceeds he or she has unlawfully made from dealing in drugs; accordingly, an order committing the defendant to prison for contempt of court does not amount to a second sentence for the same "offence": *DPP v Scarlett* [2000] 1 WLR 515, CA.

A fine may be imposed which increases automatically at intervals until the contemnor complies with the order: see, for example, *Raja v Van Hoogstraten* [2002] EWHC 2233 (Ch), [2002] All ER (D) 155 (Oct).

The court may make a transcript of its judgment available at public expense where it is in the interests of justice to do so: see, eg *Cambridgeshire County Council v D* [1999] 3 FCR 613, [1999] 2 FLR 42, CA.

A minor cannot be committed to prison (and an injunction should not be granted against a minor unless the court is satisfied that he has sufficient means to allow for enforcement by way of a fine or sequestration of assets): *Harrow London Borough Council v G* [2004] EWHC 17 (QB), [2004] NPC 4, [2004] 1 P & CR D43.

III COT [21.2A]

Sentencing principles The appropriate sentence for contempt in the face of the court in the nature of outbursts from the public gallery is a strong judicial rebuke, coupled if necessary with a fine, rather than a custodial sentence: *R v Lewis* (1999) Times, 4 November, CA.

A short custodial sentence may be justified where abusive remarks are directed at a judge: *R v McDaniel* (1990) 12 Cr App R (S) 44, CA (appellant called judge who had just sentenced his brother 'a dog' and 14 days' imprisonment was upheld); *R v Hill* [1986] Crim LR 457, CA (member of public who shouted that judge was biased and racist was imprisoned for 7 days), or a warning has been ignored and remarks are directed at a jury trying to do their duty: *R v Barrington White* [2011] EWCA Crim 2804 (sentence of 7 days' imprisonment substituted for 14 days).

Where contempt proceedings and a criminal prosecution are brought in respect of the same events, the first court to sentence must not anticipate or allow for a likely future sentence; it is for the second court to sentence to reflect the prior sentence in its judgment to ensure that the defendant is not punished twice for the same act; and there is an obligation on the first court to ensure that the basis of its sentence is fully expressed, and that a transcript of its judgment is made available to the second court: *Lomas v Parle (Practice Note)* [2003] EWCA Civ 1804, [2004] 1 WLR 1642, paras 46–49, applied in *Slade v Slade* [2009] EWCA Civ 748, [2010] 1 WLR 1262, [2010] 1 All ER 1231, [2009] Fam Law 925.

Where the respondent has already pleaded guilty and been sentenced for substantially the same offences this should be taken into account when imposing a sentence on the hearing, subsequently, of an application to commit in civil proceedings for breach of an injunction: *Gill v Birmingham City Council* [2016] EWCA Civ 608.

In cases where there is a coercive element in a sentence for disobeying an order of the court, consideration may be given to imposing the maximum sentence of two years' imprisonment, leaving it to the contemnor to purge his contempt and secure his release by complying with the order: *Lightfoot v Lightfoot* [1989] FCR 305, [1989] 1 FLR 414, CA.

The terminology of 'purging' a contempt is not particularly helpful in the context of a contempt which amounts to a breach of a prohibitory order and which, once done, cannot be undone: *CJ v Flintshire Borough Council* [2010] EWCA Civ 393, [2010] 2 FLR 1224, [2010] 3 FCR 40, [2010] Fam Law 697, para 6.

Breach of an order or undertaking does not automatically, or even normally, lead to committal: *Smith v Smith* [1988] FCR 225, [1988] 1 FLR 179, CA. A committal order, even if suspended, is a last resort normally reserved for serious, intentional and, in most cases, repeated contempt of court: *Re G (a child) (contempt: committal)* [2003] EWCA Civ 489, [2003] 1 WLR 2051, para 21. There is not, however, a principle to the effect that imprisonment cannot be imposed for a first breach of an order or undertaking in a family case: *Thorpe v Thorpe* [1998] 2 FCR 384, [1998] 2 FLR 127, CA.

The factors to be considered when sentencing for contempt in family cases are summarised in *Hale v Tanner (Practice Note)* [2000] 1 WLR 2377, [2000] 3 FCR 62, CA, confirmed in *Robinson v Murray* [2005] EWCA Civ 935, [2005] 3 FCR 504 (per Woolf LCJ, paras 18-20)

CONTEMPT OF COURT

and applied in *Slade v Slade* [2009] EWCA Civ 748, (2009) Times, 20 August; and they have also been applied by the Court of Appeal in relation to a breach of an order excluding the appellant from a particular area of a town: *Turnbull v Middlesbrough Borough Council* (2003) Times, 15 September, CA, and their application by analogy, at least to some extent, has been recognised in cases other than family cases: see eg *Prosser v Prosser* [2011] EWHC 2172 (Ch), para 121.

In cases of actual or threatened violence, so far as is consistent with avoiding duplicated punishment, sentences for contempt of court for breach of non-molestation orders made under s 42 of the Family Law Act 1996 should not be manifestly discrepant with sentences passed in the Crown Court for comparable offences, such as under the Offences against the Person Act 1861: *Head v Orrow* [2004] EWCA Civ 1691, (2005) 2 FLR 329. Where proceedings might be brought under s 42 Family Law Act 1996 or the Protection from Harassment Act 1997 and a sentence near the top of the range for contempt of court (two years) might be warranted, the appropriate course is probably to bring proceedings under the 1997 Act so that greater powers of punishment are available to the Court: *Robinson v Murray* [2005] EWCA Civ 935, [2005] 3 FCR 504 (per Woolf LCJ, paras 11-13).

Where the alleged contemnor is a single parent, the right of the children to respect for their family life under Art 8 of the European Convention on Human Rights should be considered before an order for committal is made: *R (on the application of Stokes) v Gwent Magistrates' Court* [2001] EWHC Admin 569, 165 JP 766.

While the court will be mindful of the background which made an injunction necessary, a sentence is imposed for its breach rather than for the background history: *Cambridgeshire County Council v D* [1999] 3 FCR 613, [1999] 2 FLR 42, CA. The court will be reluctant to order the committal of a party for breach of an order when the applicant is in breach of a related order: *Waite v Waite* [2001] EWCA Civ 1186, [2001] All ER (D) 203 (Jul). The court will be reluctant to impose a custodial sentence merely because the contemnor would be unable to pay a fine: *Re M (a Child) (Contact Order)* [2005] EWCA Civ 615, [2005] 2 FLR 1006.

The usual starting point in determining the appropriate sanction to be applied for a contempt is an order for indemnity costs: *Elvington Park Ltd v Mellor* (19 March 2001, unreported), Neuberger J. In commercial litigation, an application to commit for contempt of court should be made only as a last resort, where there has been a flagrant breach of a court order (*Belgolaise SA v Purchandani* (1998) 152 Sol Jo LB 252, Comm Ct) and committal for contempt is only appropriate where there has been a serious contumacious flouting of court orders: *Gulf Azov Shipping Co Ltd v Idisi* [2001] EWCA Civ 491, [2001] 1 Lloyd's Rep 727.

The following propositions apply in relation to sentencing for civil contempt consisting of non-compliance with the disclosure provisions of a freezing order:

JSC BTA Bank v Solodchenko [2011] EWCA Civ 1241, para 55:

(i) Freezing orders are made for good reason and in order to prevent the dissipation or spiriting away of assets. Any substantial breach of such an order is a serious matter, which merits condign punishment.
(ii) Condign punishment for such contempt normally means a prison sentence. However, there may be circumstances in which a substantial fine is sufficient: for example, if the contempt has been purged and the relevant assets recovered.
(iii) Where there is a continuing failure to disclose relevant information, the court should consider imposing a long sentence, possibly even the maximum of two years, in order to encourage future co-operation by the contemnor.

Further, in the case of continuing breach, out of fairness to the contemnor, the court may see fit to indicate (a) what portion of the sentence should be served in any event as punishment for past breaches and (b) what portion of the sentence the court might consider remitting in the event of prompt and full compliance thereafter; any such indication would be persuasive, but not binding upon a future court (para 56).

Where there has been a technical breach of an order, in circumstances where the contemnor believed that his actions complied with the order, the court will impose no penalty and will consider the appropriateness of the application for committal; if it concludes that the application was a wholly disproportionate response to a trivial or blameless breach, it will dismiss the application with costs: *Adam Phones Ltd v Goldschmidt* [1999] 4 All ER 486; see also *Bhimji v Chatwani* [1991] 1 All ER 705, [1991] 1 WLR 989 (no penalty imposed for non-contumacious breach of Anton Piller (search and seizure) order).

A sentence of immediate imprisonment was appropriate where the contemnor had dissipated money held on trust for her brother, in flagrant and deliberate breach of a court order and with the object of frustrating a financial order which the court had indicated it might make following the brother's imprisonment for a number of offences: *R v Spokes* [2010] EWCA Crim 3211.

Those who make false claims in court in relation to liability or in relation to compensation as a result of liability should expect to go to prison: *South Wales Fire and Rescue Service v Smith* [2011] EWHC 1749 (Admin), [2011] All ER (D) 39 (Oct), cited with approval: *Fairclough Homes Ltd v Summers* [2012] UKSC 26, [2012] 34 All ER 317, [2012] 1 WLR 2004; *R (London Borough of Havering) v Bowyer* [2012] EWHC 2237 (Admin).

The guidelines for breaches of antisocial behaviour orders issued by the Sentencing Guidelines Council in December 2008 are directed at criminal proceedings but are equally relevant in relation to committal for breach of an antisocial behaviour order made by a civil court: *Amicus Horizon Ltd v Brand* [2012] EWCA Civ 817, [2012] All ER (D) 252 (May).

In cases under the Family Law Act 1996, where there is a power to remand in custody pending the committal hearing, any time spent in custody before sentence does not go to reduce the sentence of a contemnor (contemnors being excluded from the ambit of the relevant provisions of the Criminal Justice Act 1967 by s 104(1) thereof; see *Delaney v Delaney* [1996] QB 387, per Bingham MR at 398–399). The judge should therefore bear in mind, when considering what is the appropriate period of imprisonment to impose in respect of a contempt of court, that any time spent on remand will not be deducted: *Sevketoglu v Sevketoglu* [2003] EWCA Civ 1570, (2003) Times, 27 November.

The immediate committal of a seriously disabled contemnor should not be ordered without inquiry as to the conditions in which he or she will be detained: *Price v United Kingdom (Application 33394/96)* [2001] Crim LR 916, (2001) Times, 13 August (in which the prison conditions were such as to constitute degrading treatment contrary to Art 3 of the European Convention on Human Rights).

It is only in circumstances where the very fact of imprisonment itself might expose the contemnor to a real risk of an art 3 breach that the court will be called upon to enquire into whether sentencing a person to custody will mean a breach of art 3: *R v Qazi* [2010] EWCA Crim 2579, para 35, [2011] 2 Cr App Rep (S) 32, [2011] Crim LR 159; applied: *B v Secretary of State for the Home Department* [2011] EWCA Civ 828, para 15, [2011] NLJR 1060, [2011] All ER (D) 188 (Jul).

III COT [21.2B]

Mitigation Whether represented or not, a person who is liable to be committed to prison should be given a proper opportunity to mitigate: *Taylor v Persico* (1992) Times, 12 February, CA; *Goldsmith v Goldsmith* (2006) Times, 22 November, CA.

A claim that a defendant acted in accordance with legal advice will not be taken into account in mitigation for breach of an injunction where the advice was not recorded and was based on instructions which had no factual basis, and where it was not the case that the defendant had a genuine belief in the correctness of legal advice which later turned out to be untrue: *Parker v Rasalingham* (2000) Times, 25 July.

In *Pan Petroleum Aje Ltd v Yinka Folawiyo Petroleum Co Ltd* [2017] EWCA Civ 1525 (Court of Appeal, Civil Division; Gross, Lewison and Flaux LJJ) Court orders were to be construed objectively and in the context in which they had been made, including the reasons given by the court for the making of the order at the time that it had been made. When a court concluded that the party in contempt had acted on the basis of an interpretation of the order which had not been reasonably arguable, it was not necessary for the applicant to also show that the breach of the order had been committed with actual knowledge. There was no defence for a party in breach to show that it had acted on the basis of legal advice. That would only go to issues of mitigation not to whether there had been contempt (see paras [42], [43], [44], [64], [65] of the judgment). The relevant wording of the order had the clear an unambiguous meaning for which the claimant contended and which the judge had found. Further the context and the object of the order supported that construction. Given the firm conclusion about the wording of the order and the clear and unequivocal meaning, the defendants contrary construction of the order was not reasonably arguable. Accordingly, the judge had been justified in concluding that the defendants had been in contempt and that the claimant was entitled to the declaratory relief sought (see paras [55], [57], [61], [63], [64], [65] of the judgment).

Although duress is not a defence in civil contempt proceedings, it may be a mitigating factor; the legal burden of proving duress is on the defendant: *Coca-Cola Co v Aytacli* [2003] EWHC 91 (Ch), (2003) Times, 11 February.

III COT [21.2C]

Power to remand in custody In cases of criminal contempt (which include contempt in the face of the court; see, further, **III COT [1]**), the superior courts have an inherent power of detention until the rising of the court on the day of the alleged contempt (see *Delaney v Delaney* [1996] QB 387, CA, per Bingham MR at 401), and the county court and magistrates' courts have similar powers by virtue of s 118(1) of the County Courts Act 1984 and s 12(1) of the Contempt of Court Act 1981 (see, further, **III COT [3]**).

In cases of civil contempt, with the exception of cases under the Family Law Act 1996, there is no power to remand in custody before sentence, whether before or after a finding of contempt has been made: see *Delaney v Delaney* [1996] QB 387, CA.

In cases under the Family Law Act 1996, there is a power to remand in custody pending the committal hearing, but any time spent in custody before sentence does not go to reduce the sentence of a contemnor (contemnors being excluded from the ambit of the relevant provisions of the Criminal Justice Act 1967 by s 104(1) thereof; see *Delaney v Delaney* [1996] QB 387, CA, per Bingham MR at 398–399). The judge should therefore bear in mind, when considering what is the appropriate period of imprisonment to impose in respect of a contempt of court, that any time spent on remand will not be deducted: *Sevketoglu v Sevketoglu* [2003] EWCA Civ 1570, (2003) Times, 27 November.

III COT [21.3]

Contemnors under 21 Where a contemnor is aged at least 18 but under 21 the court should have regard to s 108 of the Powers of Criminal Courts (Sentencing) Act 2000 (detention of persons aged at least 18 but under 21 for default or contempt) (s 108 is prospectively repealed by the Criminal Justice and Court Services Act 2000, ss 74, 75, Sch 7, Pt II, paras 160, 188, Sch 8, as from a day to be appointed under s 80 of that Act). Section 61 of the Criminal Justice and Court Services Act 2000 (not yet in force) provides that no court may pass a sentence of detention in a young offender institution or make a custodial order except in relation to a person who is aged at least 17 but under 18 (s 61(1)); and that no court is to commit a person to be detained under s 108 of the Powers of Criminal Courts (Sentencing) Act 2000 or make an order fixing a term of detention under that section (s 61(2)).

III COT [21.4]

Suspension If a term of imprisonment for breach of an injunction is to be suspended it should be for a finite period: *Pidduck v Molloy* [1992] 1 FCR 418, [1992] 2 FLR 202, CA; see also *Griffin v Griffin* [2000] 2 FCR 302, [2000] 2 FLR 44, CA. However, there is power to suspend for an indefinite period. The restrictions imposed by section 14(1) do not apply to periods of suspension. Nevertheless, orders suspending a period of imprisonment should be drafted carefully so as to ensure that the contemnor has a degree of certainty over its effect and duration: *Christie v Birmingham City Council* [2016] EWCA Civ 1339.

An order for suspended committal should state the terms and conditions upon, and the period for which, it is suspended: *Bluffield v Curtis* [1988] 1 FLR 170, CA; see also *Griffin v Griffin* [2000] 2 FCR 302, [2000] 2 FLR 44, CA.

In the county court, failure to serve a suspended committal order in Form N79 on the contemnor is a fundamental defect not capable of cure: *Couzens v Couzens* [2001] EWCA Civ 992, [2001] 3 FCR 289, [2001] 2 FLR 701.

A contemnor who has been committed to prison may not be discharged on terms that the remaining part of his sentence be suspended: *Harris v Harris (No 2)* [2001] EWCA Civ 1645, [2002] Fam 253, [2002] 1 All ER 185 (although this was ordered by the Court of Appeal, apparently *per incuriam*, in *Shrewsbury and Atcham Borough Council v Tanriverdi* [2005] EWCA Civ 1263), [2005] All ER (D) 158 (Sep)).

III COT [21.5]

Release and discharge From 4 April 2005, the Secretary of State is required by s 258 of the Criminal Justice Act 2003 to release anyone in prison for contempt of court once half the sentence has been served; the same section also confers a discretion to order early release in exceptional circumstances on compassionate grounds (for transitional and saving provisions see Criminal Justice Act 2003 (Commencement No 8 and Transitional and Saving Provisions) Order 2005 (SI 2005/950), Sch 2, paras 14 and 24).

The court has the power to discharge a contemnor on an application made in accordance with **CPR 81.31** and **CPR 81.32**.

In *CJ v Flintshire Borough Council* [2010] EWCA Civ 393, [2010] 2 FLR 1224, [2010] 3 FCR 40, [2010] Fam Law 697, para 21, the Court of Appeal set out eight overlapping questions which a judge considering an application for early discharge might usefully consider (the questions are not a tick-list but windows on a problem which will always be case specific: para 36):

(i) Can the court conclude, in all the circumstances as they now are, that the contemnor has suffered punishment proportionate to his contempt;

(ii) Would the interest of the State in upholding the rule of law be significantly prejudiced by early discharge?

(iii) How genuine is the contemnor's expression of contrition?

(iv) Has he done all that he reasonably can to demonstrate a resolve and an ability not to commit a further breach if discharged early?

(v) In particular has he done all that he reasonably can (bearing in mind the difficulties of his so doing while in prison) in order to construct for himself proposed living and other practical arrangements in the event of early discharge in such a way as to minimise the risk of his committing a further breach?

(vi) Does he make any specific proposal to augment the protection against any further breach of those whom the order which he breached was designed to protect?

(vii) What is the length of time which he has served in prison, including its relation to (a) the full term imposed upon him and (b) the term which he will otherwise be required to serve prior to release pursuant to s 258(2) of the Criminal Justice Act 2003?

(viii) Are there any special factors which impinge upon the exercise of the discretion in one way or the other?

An order for early discharge does not depend on favourable answers to all eight questions, but (i) probably needs an affirmative answer before early discharge should be ordered; (ii) requires a negative answer; an affirmative answer to (iii) will usually (but not always: see eg *Enfield London Borough Council v Mahoney* [1983] 2 All ER 901, [1983] 1 WLR 749, CA) be necessary but may not be sufficient; subject to this, the answers to the questions go into the melting pot, out of which comes the conclusion: *CJ v Flintshire Borough Council* (see above), para 23.

Early discharge may not be ordered on the terms that the remaining part of the sentence be suspended: *Harris v Harris* [2001] EWCA Civ 1645, [2002] Fam 253, [2002] 1 All ER 185; *CJ v Flintshire Borough Council* (see above), paras 33-34 (although such an order was made by the Court of Appeal, apparently *per incuriam*, in *Shrewsbury and Atcham Borough Council v Tanriverdi* [2005] EWCA Civ 1263).

III COT [22]

16. Enforcement of fines imposed by certain superior courts

(1) Payment of a fine for contempt of court imposed by a superior court, other than the Crown Court or one of the courts specified in subsection (4) below, may be enforced upon the order of the court—

(a) in like manner as a judgment of the High Court for the payment of money; or

(b) in like manner as a fine imposed by the Crown Court.

(2) Where payment of a fine imposed by any court falls to be enforced as mentioned in paragraph (a) of subsection (1)—

(a) the court shall, if the fine is not paid in full forthwith or within such time as the court may allow, certify to Her Majesty's Remembrancer the sum payable;

(b) Her Majesty's Remembrancer shall thereupon proceed to enforce payment of that sum as if it were due to him as a judgment debt; [. . .]

(c) [. . .]

(3) Where payment of a fine imposed by any court falls to be enforced as mentioned in paragraph (b) of subsection (1), the provisions of sections 139 and 140 of the Powers of Criminal Courts (Sentencing) Act 2000 shall apply as they apply to a fine imposed by the Crown Court.

(4) Subsection (1) of this section does not apply to fines imposed by the criminal division of the Court of Appeal or by the Supreme Court on appeal from that division.

(5) The Fines Act 1833 shall not apply to a fine to which subsection (1) of this section applies.

(6) [. . .]

III COT [22.1]

Superior court See definition in s 19 (see para **III COT [23]**).

III COT [22.2]

Minors An injunction should not be granted against a minor unless the court is satisfied that he has sufficient means to allow for enforcement by way of a fine or sequestration of assets, as a minor cannot be committed to prison: *Harrow London Borough Council v G* [2004] EWHC 17 (QB), [2004] NPC 4, [2004] 1 P & CR D43.

III COT [23]

19. Interpretation

In this Act—

[. . .]

"court" includes any tribunal or body exercising the judicial power of the State, and "legal proceedings" shall be construed accordingly;

"publication" has the meaning assigned by subsection (1) of section 2, and "publish" (except in section 9) shall be construed accordingly;

"Scottish proceedings" means proceedings before any court, including the Court Martial Appeal Court... and the Employment Appeal Tribunal, sitting in Scotland, and includes proceedings before the Supreme Court in the exercise of any appellate jurisdiction over proceedings in such a court;

"the strict liability rule" has the meaning assigned by section 1;

"superior court" means the Supreme Court, Court of Appeal, the High Court, the Crown Court, the Court Martial Appeal Court,... the Employment Appeal Tribunal and any other court exercising in relation to its proceedings powers equivalent to those of the High Court.

III COT [23.1]

Court The following are "courts" within the meaning of s 19: a mental health review tribunal (*Pickering v Liverpool Daily Post and Echo Newspapers plc* [1991] 2 AC 370, HL, at 417E–G); an employment tribunal (*Peach Grey & Co v Sommers* [1995] 2 All ER 513, [1995] ICR 549). The Disciplinary Committee of the GMC is not a "court" for these purposes because, although it is a judicial body, it does not exercise the power of the state as required by the definition in s 19: *General Medical Council v BBC* [1998] 3 All ER 426, [1998] 1 WLR 1573, CA.

Schedule

SCHEDULE 1
TIMES WHEN PROCEEDINGS ARE ACTIVE FOR PURPOSES OF SECTION 2

Section 2

PRELIMINARY

III COT [24]

1 In this Schedule "criminal proceedings" means proceedings against a person in respect of an offence, not being appellate proceedings or proceedings commenced by motion for committal or attachment in England and Wales or Northern Ireland; and "appellate proceedings" means proceedings on appeal from or for the review of the decision of a court in any proceedings.

1ZA Proceedings under the Double Jeopardy (Scotland) Act 2011 (asp 16) are criminal proceedings for the purposes of this Schedule.

1A In paragraph 1 the reference to offence includes a service offence within the meaning of the Armed Forces Act 2006.

2 Criminal, appellate and other proceedings are active within the meaning of section 2 at the times respectively prescribed by the following paragraphs of this Schedule; and in relation to proceedings in which more than one of the steps described in any of those paragraphs is taken, the reference in that paragraph is a reference to the first of those steps.

CRIMINAL PROCEEDINGS

3 Subject to the following provisions of this Schedule, criminal proceedings are active from the relevant initial step specified in paragraph 4 or 4A until concluded as described in paragraph 5.

4 The initial steps of criminal proceedings are:—

(a) arrest without warrant;

(b) the issue, or in Scotland the grant, of a warrant for arrest;

(c) the issue of a summons to appear, or in Scotland the grant of a warrant to cite;

(d) the service of an indictment or other document specifying the charge;

(e) except in Scotland, oral charge.

(f) the making of an application under section 2(2) (tainted acquittals), 3(3)(b) (admission made or becoming known after acquittal), 4(3)(b) (new evidence), 11(3) (eventual death of injured person) or 12(3) (nullity of previous proceedings) of the Double Jeopardy (Scotland) Act 2011 (asp 16).

4A Where as a result of an order under section 54 of the Criminal Procedure and Investigations Act 1996 (acquittal tainted by an administration of justice offence) proceedings are brought against a person for an offence of which he has previously been acquitted, the initial step of the proceedings is a certification under subsection (2) of that section; and paragraph 4 has effect subject to this.

5 Criminal proceedings are concluded—

(a) by acquittal or, as the case may be, by sentence;

(b) by any other verdict, finding, order or decision which puts an end to the proceedings;

(c) by discontinuance or by operation of law.

(d) where the initial steps of the proceedings are as mentioned in paragraph 4(f)—

(i) by refusal of the application;

(ii) if the application is granted and within the period of 2 months mentioned in section 6(3) of the Double Jeopardy (Scotland) Act 2011 (asp 16) a new prosecution is brought, by acquittal or, as the case may be, by sentence in the new prosecution.

6 The reference in paragraph 5(a) to sentence includes any order or decision consequent on conviction or finding of guilt which disposes of the case, either absolutely or subject to future events, and a deferment of sentence under section 1 of the Powers of Criminal Courts (Sentencing) Act 2000, section 219 or 432 of the Criminal Procedure (Scotland) Act 1975 or Article 14 of the Treatment of Offenders (Northern Ireland) Order 1976.

7 Proceedings are discontinued within the meaning of paragraph 5(c)—

(a) in England and Wales or Northern Ireland, if the charge or summons is withdrawn or a *nolle prosequi* entered;

(aa) in England and Wales if they are discontinued by virtue of section 23 of the Prosecution of Offences Act 1985;

(ab) in England and Wales, if they are discontinued by virtue of paragraph 11 of Schedule 17 to the Crime and Courts Act 2013 (deferred prosecution agreements);

(b) in Scotland, if the proceedings are expressly abandoned by the prosecutor or are deserted *simpliciter;*

(c) in the case of proceedings in Northern Ireland commenced by arrest without warrant, if the person arrested is released, otherwise than on bail, without having been charged.

(ca) in the case of proceedings in England and Wales commenced by arrest without warrant, if the person arrested is notified that the person is not to be prosecuted (whether under section 34(5C), 37(6B), 37B(5), 37CA(6), 41(11), 42(13), 43(21) or 44(10) of the Police and Criminal Evidence Act 1984 or otherwise);

(d) where the initial steps of the proceedings are as mentioned in paragraph 4(f) and the application is granted, if no new prosecution is brought within the period of 2 months mentioned in section 6(3) of the Double Jeopardy (Scotland) Act 2011 (asp 16).

8 . . .

9 Criminal proceedings in England and Wales or Northern Ireland cease to be active if an order is made for the charge to lie on the file, but become active again if leave is later given for the proceedings to continue.

9A Where proceedings in England and Wales have been discontinued by virtue of section 23 of the Prosecution of Offences Act 1985, but notice is given by the accused under subsection (7) of that section to the effect that he wants the proceedings to continue, they become active again with the giving of that notice.

10 Without prejudice to paragraph 5(b) above, criminal proceedings against a person cease to be active—

(a) if the accused is found to be under a disability such as to render him unfit to be tried or unfit to plead or, in Scotland, is found to be insane in bar of trial; or

(b) if a hospital order is made in his case under section 51(5) of the Mental Health Act 1983 or Article 57(5) of the Mental Health (Northern Ireland) Order 1986 or, in Scotland, where an assessment order or a treatment order ceases to have effect by virtues of sections 52H or 52R respectively of the Criminal Procedure (Scotland) Act 1995,

but become active again if they are later resumed.

11 Criminal proceedings against a person which become active on the issue or the grant of a warrant for his arrest cease to be active at the end of the period of twelve months beginning with the date of the warrant unless he has been arrested within that period, but become active again if he is subsequently arrested.

OTHER PROCEEDINGS AT FIRST INSTANCE

12 Proceedings other than criminal proceedings and appellate proceedings are active from the time when arrangements for the hearing are made or, if no such arrangements are previously made, from the time the hearing begins, until the proceedings are disposed of or discontinued or withdrawn; and for the purposes of this paragraph any motion or application made in or for the purposes of any proceedings, and any pre-trial review in the county court, is to be treated as a distinct proceeding.

13 In England and Wales or Northern Ireland arrangements for the hearing of proceedings to which paragraph 12 applies are made within the meaning of that paragraph—

(a) in the case of proceedings in the High Court for which provision is made by rules of court for setting down for trial, when the case is set down;

(b) in the case of any proceedings, when a date for the trial or hearing is fixed.

14 In Scotland arrangements for the hearing of proceedings to which paragraph 12 applies are made within the meaning of that paragraph—

(a) in the case of an ordinary action in the Court of Session or in the sheriff court, when the Record is closed;
(b) in the case of a motion or application, when it is enrolled or made;
(c) in any other case, when the date for a hearing is fixed or a hearing is allowed.

APPELLATE PROCEEDINGS

15 Appellate proceedings are active from the time when they are commenced—
(a) by application for leave to appeal or apply for review, or by notice of such an application;
(b) by notice of appeal or of application for review;
(c) by other originating process,
until disposed of or abandoned, discontinued or withdrawn.

16 Where, in appellate proceedings relating to criminal proceedings, the court—
(a) remits the case to the court below; or
(b) orders a new trial or a *venire de novo*, or in Scotland grants authority to bring a new prosecution,
any further or new proceedings which result shall be treated as active from the conclusion of the appellate proceedings.

CROWN PROCEEDINGS

CROWN PROCEEDINGS ACT 1947

(c 44)

TABLE OF CONTENTS

GENERAL NOTES ON CROWN PROCEEDINGS ACT 1947

III CRO [1]

Provisions Part I of the Act (ss 1–12) changed the substantive law in 1947 by creating a *right* to sue to the Crown in contract and tort (and for infringement of intellectual property rights) and by applying to the Crown the existing law as to indemnity, contribution, joint and several tortfeasors and contributory negligence. Part II of the Act (ss 13–23) conferred jurisdiction on the High Court, the Court of Appeal and the county courts to entertain civil proceedings by or against the Crown and to grant remedies and relief, including interpleader, and to hear summary applications in relation to certain revenue matters. It also made provision for the institution of proceedings by and against authorised Government departments (s 17) and service of such proceedings (s 18), venue (s 19) and removal and transfer (s 20). Part III (ss 24–27) established a new regime for judgments and enforcement and Part IV provided for miscellaneous matters, including discovery, as the process was then known.

III CRO [1A]

The repeal of s 10 The effect of s 10 of the Act was to replace the right of members of the Armed Forces to sue the Ministry of Defence for injuries with a right to participate in a compensation scheme. The right to sue was effectively barred by a claim to public interest immunity. Although the section was repealed by s 1 of the Crown Proceedings (Armed Forces) Act 1987, the repeal did not apply to acts or omissions before 15 May 1987. In *Matthews v Ministry of Defence* [2002] EWCA Civ 773, [2002] 3 All ER 513, (2002) Times, 30 January, it was contended that the continuing effect of s 10 in relation to old cases contravened the claimant's Convention right under Art 6(1) to a fair hearing. But the Court of Appeal concluded that the bar to proceedings against the Crown for damages and the right to a pension instead were matters of substantive law not procedure and that Art 6(1) of the Convention on Human Rights was not engaged.

The Court of Appeal decision was upheld in *Matthews v Ministry of Defence* [2003] UKHL 4, [2003] 1 AC 1163, [2003] 1 All ER 689.

III CRO [1B]

Acts of parliament that bind the Crown The Crown is not bound by an Act of Parliament unless the statute so provides. For a case where the Crown was held exempt from the smoking ban imposed by Chapter 1 of Part 1 of the Health Act 2006 see *R (on the application of Black) v Secretary of State for Justice* (2016) Times, 6 May, CA.

The decision of the Court of Appeal was affirmed, reluctantly, by the Supreme Court in *R (on the application of Black) v Secretary of State for Justice* [2017] UKSC 81, where it was held that the smoking ban imposed by the Health Act 2006 on enclosed public spaces and workplaces did not apply to prisons or the myriad other premises occupied by central government departments.

III CRO [2]

Procedure The rules of court applicable to civil proceedings by or against the Crown are contained in **CPR 66** which has replaced the old RSC Order 77 and CCR Order 42. Most of the old litigation privileges of the Crown have been swept away; but there are still some restrictions on the processes by which orders may be enforced against the Crown: see **CPR 66.6** and **CPR 66.7**. See also the Practice Direction at **CPR PD 66** and the accompanying note by the Attorney-General on factors to be taken into consideration in the determination of disputes over venue.

Concurrently with the introduction of the new **CPR 66**, various amendments to the Crown Proceedings Act were made by the Civil Procedure (Modification of Crown Proceedings Act 1947) Order 2005, SI 2005/2712, to enable the procedural privileges of the Crown to be removed.

III CRO [3]

Costs Costs generally are in the discretion of the court to be exercised on the same principles as in cases between subjects; see s 7 of the Administration of Justice (Miscellaneous Provisions) Act 1933. Discretionary items in the bill of costs of a salaried solicitor representing the Crown should be taxed as if it were an independent solicitor's: *Re Eastwood, Lloyds Bank Ltd v Eastwood* [1975] Ch 112, [1974] 3 All ER 603, CA; *Leopold Lazarus Ltd v Secretary of State for Trade and Industry* (1976) 120 Sol Jo 268.

III CRO [4]

Future questions Nothing in the Act or Rules enables a future and hypothetical question to be raised in proceedings against the Crown: *Re Barnato, Joel v Sanges* [1949] Ch 258, [1949] 1 All ER 515, CA, and see *Blackburn v A-G* [1971] 2 All ER 1380, [1971] 1 WLR 1037, CA and *R v Halton Borough Council, ex p Poynton* (1989) Times, 10 March.

For the substantive law see 11(2) *Halsbury's Laws* (4th edn reissue) title CROWN PROCEEDINGS AND CROWN PRACTICE, para 101.

PART II
JURISDICTION AND PROCEDURE

III CRO [5]

13. Civil Proceedings in the High Court

Subject to the provisions of this Act, all such civil proceedings by or against the Crown as are mentioned in the First Schedule to this Act are hereby abolished, and all civil proceedings by or against the Crown in the High Court shall be instituted and proceeded with in accordance with rules of court and not otherwise.

In this section the expression "rules of court" means, in relation to any claim against the Crown in the High Court which falls within the jurisdiction of that court as a prize court, rules of court made under section three of the Prize Courts Act 1894.

III CRO [5.1]

Rules of court The relevant rules of court are those contained in CPR Part 66 at **CPR 66**. Rules for prize courts are, however, excluded from the scope of the Civil Procedure Rules 1998 by Part 2, at **CPR 2.1**. On the other hand, notice must be given to the Crown, in accordance with **CPR 19.4A**, in the case of proceedings under s 4 of the Human Rights Act 1998 for a declaration of incompatibility or under s 9 for damages in respect of a judicial act.

III CRO [5.2]

Liability in tort Section 2 (1) of the Crown Proceedings Act 1947 made the Crown liable in tort as if it were a private person and expressly conferred vicarious liability for torts committed by servants and agents. It was held in *Racz v Home Office* [1994] 2 AC 45, [1994] 1 All ER 97, HL that the Home Office might be liable for misfeasance in public office on the part of prison officers.

Act of State may still be available as a defence to private law claims founded on foreign law, principally in cases where the claim is non-justiciable. However, in a private law claim for unlawful detention by HM armed forces, contrary to Afghan law, it was held that Act of State was not available as a defence since there were no compelling reasons of public policy why it should be: *Mohammad v Secretary of State for Defence* [2015] EWCA Civ 843.

III CRO [5.3]

Liability of the Crown to make restitution of money paid under a mistake It has been held that tax wrongly paid under a mistake of law may in some circumstances be recovered on a restitutionary basis, provided that the claim is brought within six years of discovering the mistake: *Deutsche Morgan Grenfell Group Plc v Inland Revenue Comrs* [2006] UKHL 49, [2006] All ER (D) 298 (Oct).

III CRO [6]

14. Summary applications to High Court in certain revenue matters

(1) Subject to and in accordance with rules of court, the Crown may apply in a summary manner to the High Court:—

- (a) for the furnishing of information required to be furnished by any person under the enactments relating to inheritance tax;
- (b) for the delivery of accounts and payment of inheritance tax under the Inheritance Tax Act 1984;
- (c) for the delivery of an account under section two of the Stamp Duties Management Act 1891, or under that section as amended or applied by any subsequent enactment;
- (d) for the payment of sums improperly withheld or retained within the meaning of the said section two.

(2) Subject to and in accordance with rules of court, the Crown may apply in a summary manner to the High Court:—

- (a) for the payment of duty under the enactments relating to excise duties;
- (b) for the delivery of any accounts required to be delivered, or the furnishing of any information required to be furnished, by the enactments relating to excise duties or by any regulations relating to such duties;
- (c) for the payment of tax under the enactments relating to value added tax;
- (d) for the delivery of any accounts, the production of any books, or the furnishing of any information, required to be delivered, produced or furnished under the enactments relating to value added tax.

III CRO [6.1]

Procedure The procedure is set out in CPR 66.5 (para **CPR 66.5**).

III CRO [7]

15. Civil proceedings in the county court

(1) Subject to the provisions of this Act, and to any enactment limiting the jurisdiction of the county court (whether by reference to the subject matter of the proceedings to be brought or the amount sought to be recovered in the proceedings or otherwise) any civil proceedings against the Crown may be instituted in the county court.

(2) Any proceedings by or against the Crown in the county court shall be instituted and proceeded with in accordance with rules of court and not otherwise.

III CRO [7.1]

Proceedings by the Crown Arrears of contributions payable under the Social Security Acts may be recovered in the county court as a debt to the Crown: *Ministry of National Insurance v Barrs* [1951] 1 All ER 532. Income tax (and interest thereon) which is due and payable under any assessment may be recovered as a debt due to the Crown by proceedings in a county court commenced in the name of a collector of taxes: s 66 of the Taxes Management Act 1970; see also CPR Sch 2 CCR Ord 42 r 10 (see para **CCR 42r10**).

III CRO [7.2]

Procedure See **CPR 66**.

General

III CRO [8]

16. Interpleader

The Crown may obtain relief by way of interpleader proceedings, and may be made a party to such proceedings, in the same manner in which a subject may obtain relief by way of such proceedings or be made a party thereto, and may be made a party to such proceedings notwithstanding that the application for relief is made by a sheriff or other like officer; and all rules of court relating to interpleader proceedings shall, subject to the provisions of this Act, have effect accordingly.

III CRO [9]

17. Parties to proceedings

(1) The Minister for the Civil Service shall publish a list specifying the several Government departments which are authorised departments for the purposes of this Act, and the name and address for service of the person who is, or is acting for the purposes of this Act as, the solicitor for each such department, and may from time to time amend or vary the said list.

Any document purporting to be a copy of a list published under this section and purporting to be printed under the superintendence or the authority of His Majesty's Stationery Office shall in any legal proceedings be received as evidence for the purpose of establishing what departments are authorised departments for the purposes of this Act, and what person is, or is acting for the purposes of this Act as, the solicitor for any such department.

(2) Civil proceedings by the Crown may be instituted either by an authorised Government department in its own name, whether that department was or was not at the commencement of this Act authorised to sue, or by the Attorney General.

(3) Civil proceedings against the Crown shall be instituted against the appropriate authorised Government department, or, if none of the authorised Government departments is appropriate or the person instituting the proceedings has any reasonable doubt whether any and if so which of those departments is appropriate, against the Attorney General.

(4) Where any civil proceedings against the Crown are instituted against the Attorney General, an application may at any stage of the proceedings be made to the court by or on behalf of the Attorney General to have such of the authorised Government departments as may be specified in the application substituted for him as defendant to the proceedings; and where any such proceedings are brought against an authorised Government department, an application may at any stage of the proceedings be made to the court on behalf of that department to have the Attorney General or such of the authorised Government departments as may be specified in the application substituted for the applicant as the defendant to the proceedings.

Upon any such application the court may if it thinks fit make an order granting the application on such terms as the court thinks fit; and on such an order being made the proceedings shall continue as if they had been commenced against the department specified in that behalf in the order, or, as the case may require, against the Attorney General.

(5) No proceedings instituted in accordance with this Part of this Act by or against the Attorney General or an authorised government department shall abate or be affected by any change in the person holding the office of Attorney General or in the person or body of persons constituting the department.

III CRO [9.1]

Service For service on the crown, see Crown Proceedings Act 1947 s 18 (see para **III CRO [10]**), and CPR 6.5(8) at **CPR 6.5**.

III CRO [9.2]

Scotland Sections 17 (3) and 18 do not apply to Scotland, where (in accordance with the Crown Suits (Scotland) Act 1857) civil proceedings against the Crown or any Government department may be directed against the Lord Advocate. The Lord Advocate's address for service is the Crown Office, 5–7 Regents Road, Edinburgh EH 7 5 BL. In the event that proceedings are directed against the Secretary of State for Scotland as such, the Reorganisation of Offices (Scotland) Act 1939 provides that it is sufficient to describe him by the title "the Secretary of State for Scotland" without naming him. His address for service is St Andrew's House, Edinburgh EH 1 3 TE.

III CRO [9.3]

Claim outside Act Where a certificate under s 40(3) (see **III CRO [23]**) precludes the bringing of proceedings under or in accordance with the Act, the Crown cannot be sued in tort outside the Act by joining the Attorney-General as defendant, even if only declaratory relief is sought: *Trawnik v Lennox* [1985] 2 All ER 368[1985] 1 WLR 532, CA.

III CRO [9.4]

Service of proceedings against Government Departments On 4 April 2018 the Chancellor of the Duchy of Lancaster and Minister for the Cabinet Office published a list of Authorised Government Departments, in accordance with s 17(1), and the names and addresses of the solicitors on whom proceedings against such Departments should be served. The text of the List of Authorised Government Departments is available at www.gov.uk/government/publications and is reproduced below.

As will be seen, proceedings against most Authorised Government Departments should be served on the Treasury Solicitor at the Government Legal Department, One Kemble Street, London WC2B 4TS.

Service at this address may be by post or by DX delivery to DX 123242 Kingsway 6. Service by email is generally not accepted, except with prior agreement. The Litigation Enquiries line is 0207 210 4700 – option 2.

CROWN PROCEEDINGS

AUTHORISED GOVERNMENT DEPARTMENTS	SOLICITOR AND ADDRESSES FOR SERVICE
Advisory, Conciliation and Arbitration Service (see Note (3))	
Cabinet Office	
Commissioners for the Reduction of National Debt (see Note (4))	
Crown Prosecution Service	
Department for Business, Energy and Industrial Strategy	
Department for Communities and Local Government	
Department for Digital, Culture, Media and Sport	
Department for Education	
Department for Environment, Food and Rural Affairs	
Department for Exiting the European Union	
Department for International Development	
Department for International Trade	
Department for Transport	
The Treasury Solicitor	
Department of Health	Government Legal Department
Foreign and Commonwealth Office	One Kemble Street
Forestry Commission	London
Government Actuary's Department	WC2B 4TS
Health and Safety Executive (see Note (5))	
Her Majesty's Treasury	(see Notes (1) and (2))
Home Office	
Department of Communities and Local Government	
Ministry of Defence	
Ministry of Justice	
National Savings and Investments (NS&I)	
Northern Ireland Office	
Office for Budget Responsibility (see Note (6))	
Privy Council Office (see Note (7))	
Public Works Loan Board (see Note (4))	
Serious Fraud Office	
Statistics Board (UK Statistics Authority)	
The National Archives	
Wales Office (Office of the Secretary of State for Wales)	

Competition and Markets Authority	Director of Litigation Competition and Markets Authority Victoria House Southampton Row London WC1B 4AD
Department for Work and Pensions	Legal Director's Office Department for Work and Pensions Caxton House Tothill Street London SW1H 9NA
Food Standards Agency	Director of Legal Services Food Standards Agency Aviation House 125 Kingsway London WC2B 6NH
Her Majesty's Revenue and Customs	General Counsel and Solicitor to Her Majesty's Revenue and Customs HM Revenue and Customs South West Wing Bush House, Strand London WC2B 4RD
National Crime Agency	The Legal Adviser National Crime Agency Units 1-6 Citadel Place Tinworth Street London SE11 5EF
Office for Standards in Education, Children's Services and Skills (Ofsted)	Deputy Director, Legal Services Ofsted Clive House 70 Petty France Westminster London SW1H 9EX

Office of Gas and Electricity Markets Authority (Ofgem)	Senior Legal Director Office of Gas and Electricity Markets 9 Millbank London SW1P 3GE
Office of Qualifications and Examinations Regulation (Ofqual)	Legal Director Ofqual 1410 Spring Place Herald Avenue Coventry Business Park Coventry West Midlands CV5 6UB
Office of Rail and Road	Director of Legal Services ORR One Kemble Street London WC2B 4AN
Water Services Regulation Authority (Ofwat)	General Counsel Water Services Regulation Authority (Ofwat) Centre City Tower 7 Hill Street Birmingham B5 4UA
Welsh Government	The Director of Legal Services to the Welsh Government Cathays Park Cardiff CF10 3NG
UK Export Finance	The General Counsel, UK Export Finance, 1 Horse Guards Road, London SW1A 2HQ

NOTES

(1) Section 17(3) and section 18 of the Crown Proceedings Act 1947 provide as follows:

17(3) Civil proceedings against the Crown shall be instituted against the appropriate authorised Government department, or, if none of the authorised Government departments is appropriate or the person instituting the proceedings has any reasonable doubt whether any and if so which of those departments is appropriate, against the Attorney General.

18 All documents required to be served on the Crown for the purpose of or in connection with any civil proceedings by or against the Crown shall, if those proceedings are by or against an authorised Government department, be served on the solicitor, if any, for that department, or the person, if any, acting for the purposes of this Act as solicitor for that department, or if there is no such solicitor and no person so acting, or if the proceedings are brought by or against the Attorney General, on the Solicitor for the affairs of His Majesty's Treasury.

Proceedings brought against the Attorney General should be served on the Treasury Solicitor.

(2) The above-mentioned provisions do not apply to Scotland, where in accordance with the Crown Suits (Scotland) Act 1857, as amended by the Scotland Act 1998, civil proceedings against the Scottish Government may be directed against the Scottish Ministers or against the Lord Advocate for and on behalf of the Scottish Government and the address for service is the Office of the Solicitor to the Scottish Government, Victoria Quay, Edinburgh EH6 6QQ.
Civil proceedings against any other office holder in the Scottish Administration or body which is part of the Scottish Administration may be directed against the Lord Advocate or the relevant body or office holder in the Scottish Administration. Civil proceedings against the Crown (other than the Scottish Administration) or any Government Department (other than the Scottish Government) may be directed against the Advocate General for Scotland. The Advocate General's address for service is the Office of the Advocate General for Scotland, Victoria Quay, Edinburgh EH6 6QQ.

(3) Under section 247 of the Trade Union and Labour Relations (Consolidation) Act 1992, the Crown Proceedings Act 1947 applies to the Advisory, Conciliation and Arbitration Service as if it were a Government department for the purposes of civil proceedings arising out of its statutory functions.

(4) The functions of the Commissioners for the Reduction of National Debt and the Public Works Loan Board are carried out within the UK Debt Management Office.

(5) Under section 10 of Health and Safety at Work etc. Act 1974, the Crown Proceedings Act 1947 applies to the Health and Safety Executive as if it were a Government department for the purposes of civil proceedings arising out of its functions in England and Wales and Northern Ireland. Section 10 also provides that in Scotland the Crown Suits (Scotland) Act 1857 shall apply to the Executive as it if were a public department within the meaning of that Act, with the effect that civil proceedings against it may be directed against the Advocate General for Scotland as explained above.

(6) Under paragraph 7 of Schedule 1 to the Budget Responsibility and National Audit Act 2011, the Crown Proceedings Act 1947 applies to the Office for Budget Responsibility as if it were a Government department for the purposes of civil proceedings arising out of its functions.

(7) The Privy Council Office supports the Privy Council and the Lord President of the Council in exercising their functions as an advisory council of state, independent of government, which can be the subject of civil proceedings.

III CRO [9.5]

Executive Agencies Most of the authorised Government departments have set up Executive Agencies through which much of the Department's business is carried on, particularly, the provision of services to the public. Executive Agencies which have been set up in this way are not separate legal entities but remain part of their Department. Civil Proceedings which arise out of an Executive Agency's activities should therefore be treated as proceedings by or against the Department; and the address for service for authorised Departments should be read as applying equally to their Executive Agencies.

III CRO [10]

18. Service of documents

All documents required to be served on the Crown for the purpose of or in connection with any civil proceedings by or against the Crown shall, if those proceedings are by or against an authorised Government department, be served on the solicitor, if any, for that department, or the person, if any, acting for the purposes of this Act as solicitor for that department, or if there is no such solicitor and no person so acting, or if the proceedings are brought by or against the Attorney General on the Solicitor for the affairs of His Majesty's Treasury.

III CRO [11]

19. Venue and related matters

[Repealed by the Civil Procedure (Modification of Crown Proceedings Act 1947) Order 2005, SI 2005/2712.]

III CRO [12]

20. Removal and transfer of proceedings

(1) *[Repealed by the Civil Procedure (Modification of Crown Proceedings Act 1947) Order 2005, SI 2005/2712.]*

(2) All rules of law and enactments relating to the removal or transfer of proceedings from the county court to the High Court, or the transfer of proceedings from the High Court to the county court, shall apply in relation to proceedings against the Crown.

III CRO [13]

21. Nature of relief

(1) In any civil proceedings by or against the Crown the court shall, subject to the provisions of this Act, have power to make all such orders as it has power to make in proceedings between subjects, and otherwise to give such appropriate relief as the case may require:

- (a) Where any proceedings against the Crown any such relief is sought as might in proceedings between subjects be granted by way of injunction or specific performance, the court shall not grant an injunction or make an order for specific performance, but may in lieu thereof make an order declaratory of the rights of the parties; and
- (b) In any proceedings against the Crown for the recovery of land or other property the court shall not make an order for the recovery of the land or the delivery of the property, but may in lieu thereof make an order declaring that the claimant is entitled as against the Crown to the land or property or to the possession thereof.

(2) The court shall not in any civil proceedings grant any injunction or make any order against an officer of the Crown if the effect of granting the injunction or making the order would be to give any relief against the Crown which could not have been obtained in the proceedings against the Crown.

III CRO [13.1]

Injunction against Crown As to the jurisdiction of a county court to grant an injunction, see s 38 of the County Courts Act 1984 (see para **II CCA [21]**). Subsection (1) is concerned with proceedings in contract or tort against a Government department; it does not prevent the grant of an injunction against health authorities even though they may be carrying out functions on behalf of the Crown: *British Medical Association v Greater Glasgow Health Board*

[1989] AC 1211, [1989] 1 All ER 984, HL. Nor does it prevent the grant of injunctive relief against a Minister or Department in proceedings for judicial review: *Re M* [1994] 1 AC 377, sub nom *M v Home Office* [1993] 3 All ER 537, HL. Nor, finally, does it prevent the grant of injunctive relief against the Crown to protect rights under EEC Treaty: *R v Secretary of State for Transport, ex p Factortame Ltd (No 2)* [1991] 1 AC 603, sub nom *Factortame Ltd v Secretary of State for Transport (No 2)* [1991] 1 All ER 70, HL.

III CRO [13.2]

Injunction in favour of Crown Although the Crown may now be required to give an undertaking in damages on the grant of an interlocutory injunction to protect its proprietary or contractual right, an undertaking will not be insisted upon where the Crown is seeking to enforce a statutory order which is good on its face: *F Hoffmann-La Roche & Co AG v Secretary of State for Trade and Industry* [1975] AC 295, [1974] 2 All ER 1128, HL.

III CRO [13.3]

Civil proceedings "Civil proceedings" are defined in s 38(2) at **III CRO [22]**. The definition does not include "proceedings on the Crown side of the King's Bench Division", that is to say proceedings in England and Wales for judicial review. In Scotland the equivalent public law remedy is achieved by invoking the supervisory jurisdiction of the Court of Session. It has been held that proceedings invoking the supervisory jurisdiction in Scotland are within the definition of "civil proceedings" for the purposes of the opening words of s 21(1) and that the restrictions imposed by sub-paragraph (a) do not apply since they are confined to private law claims: *Davidson v Scottish Ministers* (2005) Times, 19 December, HL. The result in that case was that the Scottish courts were held to have jurisdiction to grant injunctive relief against ministers of the Scottish Executive in proceedings under the supervisory jurisdiction. No penal notice is necessary in the case of injunctive relief ordered by the Administrative Court against any government department, or officer of the Crown or against a local authority: *MSA v Croydon London Borough Council* [2009] EWHC 2474 (Admin), [2009] All ER (D) 106 (Oct).

III CRO [14]

22. Appeals and stay of execution

Subject to the provisions of this Act, all enactments and rules of court relating to appeals and stay of execution shall, with any necessary modifications, apply to civil proceedings by or against the Crown as they apply to proceedings between subjects.

III CRO [15]

23. Scope of Part II

(1) Subject to the provisions of this section, any reference in this Part of this Act to civil proceedings by the Crown shall be construed as a reference to the following proceedings only:—

(a) proceedings for the enforcement or vindication of any right or the obtaining of any relief which, if this Act had not been passed, might have been enforced or vindicated or obtained by any such proceedings as are mentioned in paragraph 1 of the First Schedule to this Act;

(b) proceedings for the enforcement or vindication of any right or the obtaining of any relief which, if this Act had not been passed, might have been enforced or vindicated or obtained by an action at the suit of any Government department or any officer of the Crown as such;

(c) all such proceedings as the Crown is entitled to bring by virtue of this Act;

and the expression "civil proceedings by or against the Crown" shall be construed accordingly.

(2) Subject to the provisions of this section, any reference in this Part of this Act to civil proceedings against the Crown shall be construed as a reference to the following proceedings only:—

(a) proceedings for the enforcement or vindication of any right or the obtaining of any relief which, if this Act had not been passed, might have been enforced or vindicated or obtained by any such proceedings as are mentioned in paragraph 2 of the First Schedule to this Act;

(b) proceedings for the enforcement or vindication of any right or the obtaining of any relief which, if this Act had not been passed, might have been enforced or vindicated or obtained by an action against the Attorney General, any Government department, or any officer of the Crown as such; and

(c) all such proceedings as any person is entitled to bring against the Crown by virtue of this Act;

and the expression "civil proceedings by or against the Crown" shall be construed accordingly.

(3) Notwithstanding anything in the preceding provisions of this section, the provisions of this Part of this Act shall not have effect with respect to any of the following proceedings, that is to say:—

(a) proceedings brought by the Attorney General on the relation of some other person;

(b) proceedings by or against the Public Trustee;

(c) proceedings by or against the Charity Commission;

(d), (e) [. . .]

(f) proceedings by or against the Registrar of the Land Registry or any officers of that registry.

(4) Subject to the provisions of any Order in Council made under the provisions hereinafter contained, this part of this Act shall not affect proceedings initiated in any court other than the High Court or the county court.

PART III
JUDGMENTS AND EXECUTION

III CRO [16]

24. Interest on debts, damages and costs

(1) Section seventeen of the Judgments Act 1938 (which provides that a judgment debt shall carry interest) shall apply to judgment debts due from or to the Crown.

(3) Section 35A of the Senior Courts Act 1981 and section 69 of the County Courts Act 1984 (which respectively empower the High Court and the county court to award interest on debts and damages) and section 3 of the Law Reform (Miscellaneous Provisions) Act 1934 (which empowers other courts of record to do so) shall apply to judgments given in proceedings by and against the Crown.

III CRO [17]

25. Satisfaction of orders against the Crown

(1) Where in any civil proceedings by or against the Crown, or in any proceedings on the Crown side of the King's Bench Division, or in connection with any arbitration to which the Crown is a party, any order (including an order for costs) is made by any court in favour of any person against the Crown or against a Government department or against an officer of the Crown as such, the court officer of the court shall, on an application in that behalf made by or on behalf of that person at any time after the expiration of twenty-one days from the date of the order or, in case the order provides for the payment of costs and the costs require to be taxed, at any time after the costs have been taxed, whichever is the later, issue to that person a certificate in the prescribed form containing particulars of the order:

Provided that, if the court so directs, a separate certificate shall be used with respect to the costs (if any) ordered to be paid to the applicant.

(2) A copy of any certificate issued under this section may be served by the person in whose favour the order is made upon the person for the time being named in the record as the solicitor, or as the person acting as solicitor, for the Crown or for the Government department or officer concerned.

(3) If the order provides for the payment of any money by way of damages or otherwise, or of any costs, the certificate shall state the amount so payable, and the appropriate Government department shall, subject as hereinafter provided, pay to the person entitled or to his solicitor the amount appearing by the certificate to be due to him together with the interest, if any, lawfully due thereon:

Provided that the court by which any such order as aforesaid is made or any court to which an appeal against the order lies may direct that, pending an appeal or otherwise, payment of the whole of any amount so payable, or any part thereof, shall be suspended, and if the certificate has not been issued may order any such directions to be inserted therein.

(4) Save as aforesaid no execution or attachment or process in the nature thereof shall be issue out of any court for enforcing payment by the Crown of any such money or costs as aforesaid, and no person shall be individually liable under any order for the payment by the Crown, or any government department, or any officer of the Crown as such, of any such money or costs.

III CRO [17.1]

Certificate An application under section 25(1) of the Act for a separate certificate of costs payable to the applicant may be made without notice: CPR 66.6(3).

III CRO [17.2]

Visiting forces By s 9 of the Visiting Forces Act 1952 the Minister of Defence is empowered to make arrangements for the satisfaction by him of judgments given against members of visiting forces. The arrangements made by the Minister of Defence will be found in the Law Journal, 4 June 1954.

III CRO [17.3]

Arrears of social security benefit The Crown Proceedings Act 1947 s 25(4) does not prevent an order being made for arrears of social security to be paid into a bank account the subject of a *Mareva* injunction: *Bank Mellat v Kazmi* [1989] QB 541, [1989] 1 All ER 925, CA.

III CRO [18]

26. Execution by the Crown

(1) Subject to the provisions of this Act, any order made in favour of the Crown against any person in any civil proceedings to which the Crown is a party may be enforced in the same manner as an order made in an action between subjects, and not otherwise.

(2) Sections four and five of the Debtors Act 1869 (which provide respectively for the abolition of imprisonment for debt, and for saving the power of committal in case of small debts), shall apply to sums of money payable and debts due to the Crown:

Provided that for the purpose of the application of the said section four to any sum of money payable or debt due to the Crown, the section shall have effect as if there were included among the exceptions therein mentioned default in payment of any sum payable in respect of death duties.

(3) Nothing in this section shall affect any procedure which immediately before the commencement of this Act was available for enforcing an order made in favour of the Crown in proceedings brought by the Crown for the recovery of any fine or penalty, or the forfeiture or condemnation of any goods, or the forfeiture of any ship or any share in a ship.

III CRO [18.1]

Debtors Act 1869 Debtors Act 1869 s 4 provides that, with certain exceptions, no person shall be arrested or imprisoned for making default in payment of a sum of money. Debtors Act 1869 s 5, see notes to CPR Sch 2 CCR Ord 28 r 1 (see para **CCR 28r1[3]**).

III CRO [19]

27. Attachment of moneys payable by the Crown

(1) Where any money is payable by the Crown to some person who, under any order of any court, is liable to pay any money to any person, and that other person would, if the money so payable by the Crown were money payable by a subject, be entitled under rules of court to obtain an order for the attachment thereof as a debt due or accruing due, or an order for the appointment of an sequestrator or receiver to receive the money on his behalf, the High Court may, subject to the provisions of this Act and in accordance with rules of court, make an order restraining the first-mentioned person from receiving that money and directing payment thereof to that other person, or to the sequestrator or receiver: Provided that no such order shall be made in respect of:

(a) any wages or salary payable to any officer of the Crown as such;

(b) any money which is subject to the provisions of any enactment prohibiting or restricting assignment or charging or taking in execution;

(c) [. . .]

(2) The provisions of the preceding subsection shall, so far as they relate to forms of relief falling within the jurisdiction of the county court, have effect in relation to the county court as they have effect in relation to the High Court.

(3) In their application to England and Wales the preceding provisions of this section shall have effect subject to any order for the time being in force under section 139 (2) of the Senior Courts Act 1981.

III CRO [19.1]

Attachment of debts For attachment of debts by third party debt orders, see CPR Pt 72 (at para **CPR 72.1** onwards). The county court has no jurisdiction to appoint a sequestrator. Under s 22 of the Attachment of Earnings Act 1971 an attachment of earnings order may be made in respect of a debtor who is in the employment of the Crown.

III CRO [19.2]

Order under section For the procedure on applying for an order restraining the Crown's creditor from receiving the money and directing it to be paid to the judgment creditor, see CPR 66.7 at **CPR 66.7**. But a Mareva injunction may inhibit the enjoined party's free disposition of sums received in the form of social security: *Bank Mellat v Kazmi* [1989] QB 541, [1989] 1 All ER 925, CA.

III CRO [19.3]

"Any enactment" See, eg s 203 of the Army Act 1955, which generally precludes the assignment or charging of military pay, pensions etc.

III CRO [19.4]

Bankruptcy Proceedings under this section are proceedings by way of attachment for the purposes of s 346(1) of the Insolvency Act 1986 (see para **II CCA [94.1]**, notes to s 98 of the County Courts Act 1984). Hence, if the order directs payment to the judgment creditor's solicitors on terms that they retain the money for six months and during that time the judgment debtor is adjudged bankrupt, the judgment creditor cannot retain the benefit of the order against the trustee in bankruptcy: *Re Lupkovics, ex p Trustee v Freville* [1954] 2 All ER 125, [1954] 1 WLR 1234.

III CRO [19.5]

National Savings Bank Crown Proceedings Act 1947 s 27(1)(c), which precluded the making of an order under s 27 (1) in respect of any money payable by the Crown to any person on account of a deposit in the National Savings Bank, was repealed by the Supreme Court Act 1981 s 152(4) schedule 7, but the new s 27 (3) (as inserted by s 139(1)(b) of the Supreme Court Act 1981) makes s 27(1) and (2) subject to any order made by the Lord Chancellor under the Supreme Court Act 1981 s 139(2), which enables him to direct that those subsections shall not apply in relation to any money payable by the Crown to any person on account of any deposit in the National Savings Bank or a deposit in that Bank of any description specified in the order. At the time of going to press no such order had been made. Accordingly, the court can make an order under Crown Proceedings Act 1947 s 27, in respect of money in an ordinary or investment account with the National Savings Bank even though the principal office of the Bank, being in Glasgow, is outside England and Wales: *Brooks Associates Inc v Basu* [1983] QB 220, [1983] 1 All ER 508.

III CRO [19.6]

Striking out in the public interest Where the claimant's case turns on the reception of evidence which the public interest requires to be excluded (for example, evidence relating to the role of informers in police investigations) the court may strike it out on the ground that a fair trial is not possible: *Carnduff v Rock* [2001] EWCA Civ 680, [2001] 1 WLR 1786.

PART IV
MISCELLANEOUS AND SUPPLEMENTAL

III CRO [20]

28. Discovery

(1) Subject to and in accordance with rules of court:

(a) in any civil proceedings in the High Court or the county court to which the Crown is a party, the Crown may be required by the court to make discovery of documents and produce documents for inspection; and

(b) in any such proceedings as aforesaid, the Crown may be required by the court to answer interrogatories;

Provided that this section shall be without prejudice to any rule of law which authorises or requires the withholding of any document or the refusal to answer any question on the ground that the disclosure of the document or the answering of the question would be injurious to the public interest.

Any order of the court made upon the powers conferred by paragraph (b) of this subsection shall direct by what officer of the Crown the interrogatories are to be answered.

(2) Without prejudice to the proviso to the preceding subsection, any rules made for the purposes of this section shall be such as to secure that the existence of a document will not be disclosed if, in the opinion of a Minister of the Crown, it would be injurious to the public interest to disclose the existence thereof.

CROWN PROCEEDINGS

III CRO [20.1]

Discovery Now termed disclosure, at CPR Pt 31 (see para **CPR 31**). The notes which follow were decided on discovery. Where a Government department claims what used to be called Crown privilege the claim is usually made by a written certificate, signed (but not necessarily sworn) by an appropriate Minister or official, or by the Attorney-General: *Auten v Rayner (No 2)* [1960] 1 All ER 692; *Alfred Crompton Amusement Machines Ltd v Customs and Excise Comrs (No 2)* [1972] 2 QB 102, [1972] 2 All ER 353, CA; affd [1974] AC 405, [1973] 2 All ER 1169, HL. In *Lonrho Ltd v Shell Petroleum Co Ltd* [1980] 1 WLR 627 at 637, a certificate of the appropriate Minister was lodged by the Attorney-General, who was given leave to intervene to assert, on behalf of the Crown, public interest immunity from disclosure of documents which had come into existence under an assurance of confidentiality in connection with a private inquiry set up by the Foreign Secretary. Where a claim to immunity is established, not only must the document be withheld from production but oral evidence relating to it will also be excluded: *Gain v Gain* [1962] 1 All ER 63, [1961] 1 WLR 1469; *Re Grosvenor Hotel, London* [1964] Ch 464, [1963] 3 All ER 426. A party's agreement not to challenge the Minister's certificate does not, however, prevent him from denying matters stated in it: *Sethia v Stern* (1987) Times, 4 November, CA. Where a Minister finds that the public interest is finely balanced, both for and against disclosure, he or she may give a written decision not to disclose but at the same time leave the ultimate decision to the court: *R v Chief Constable of the West Midlands Police, ex p Wiley* [1995] 1 AC 274, [1994] 3 All ER 420, HL.

III CRO [20.2]

Ending of class claims for Government documents On 18 December 1996 the Attorney-General made a statement in Parliament (Hansard, HC, 949) that, as regards Government documents and information, claims to public interest immunity would not be based on either class or contents but simply on the ground that disclosure would cause real damage or harm to the public interest ("the new test based on serious damage").

III CRO [20.3]

Balancing the public interests When considering whether Crown documents ought to be disclosed the Minister, or, as the case may be, the court should balance the alleged public interest in non-disclosure against the public interest that the administration of justice should not be frustrated. See now CPR 31.19 (Claim to withhold inspection or disclosure of document) and the note on **Saving for the public interest** at **CPR 31.19[1]** in volume 1, where the modern case law is reviewed.

III CRO [20.3A]

Convention rights The judge is entitled, having regard to Art 6 of the Human Rights Convention, to balance the conflicting interests in the instant case rather than to start with a rule that the identity of an informer should be protected unless the case falls within one of the exceptions noted in *D v NSPCC* [1978] AC 171 at 218. See *Chief Constable of Greater Manchester v McNally* [2002] EWCA Civ 14, [2002] All ER (D) 221, (2002) Times, 6 March. But it has also been held that a person who made a complaint to the Police Complaints Authority was not entitled to disclosure of documents containing eye-witness accounts before the conclusion of the police investigation, if at all: *R (on the application of Green) v Police Complaints Authority* [2002] EWCA Civ 389, [2002] All ER (D) 397 (May), (2002) Times, 6 May.

III CRO [20.4]

Ministerial decision not to disclose There is no equivalent duty to disclose documents outside litigation. Accordingly a ministerial decision not to disclose a report on the inquiry into the death of a soldier could not be judicially reviewed on the application of his parents: *R v Secretary of State for Defence, ex p Sancto* [1993] COD 144. Nor does a Minister owe a duty of care, as a matter of private law, when deciding whether to claim public interest immunity: *Bennett v Metropolitan Police Comr* [1995] 2 All ER 1, [1995] 1 WLR 488.

III CRO [20.5]

Police complaints documents In *R v Chief Constable of West Midlands Police, ex p Wiley* [1995] 1 AC 274, [1994] 3 All ER 420, it was doubted whether documents created for the purposes of police investigations came within a recognised class of public interest immunity: but immunity was claimed successfully in relation to investigating officers' reports and working papers in *Taylor v Anderton* [1995] 2 All ER 420, [1995] 1 WLR 447, CA: likewise in *O'Sullivan v Metropolitan Police Comr* (1995) 139 Sol Jo LB 164, concerning a police report to the Crown Prosecution Service. Contrast *Wallace Smith Trust Co Ltd v Deloitte Haskins & Sells* [1996] 4 All ER 403, [1997] 1 WLR 257, CA, regarding records of interviews with Serious Fraud Office.

III CRO [21]

29. Exclusion of proceedings in rem against the Crown

(1) Nothing in this Act shall authorise proceedings in rem in respect of any claim against the Crown, or the arrest, detention or sale of any of His Majesty's ships or aircraft, or of any cargo or other property belonging to the Crown, or give to any person any lien on any such ship, aircraft, cargo or other property.

(2) Where proceedings in rem have been instituted in the High Court or in the county court against any such ship, aircraft, cargo or other property, the court may, if satisfied, either on an application by the plaintiff for an order under this subsection or an application by the Crown to set aside the proceedings, that the proceedings were so instituted by the plaintiff in the reasonable belief that the ship, aircraft, cargo or other property did not belong to the Crown, order that the proceedings shall be treated as if they were in personam duly instituted against the Crown in accordance with the provisions of this Act, or duly instituted against any other person whom the court regards as the proper person to be sued in the circumstances, and that the proceedings shall continue accordingly.

Any such order may be made upon such terms, if any, as the court thinks just; and where the court makes any such order it may make such consequential orders as the court thinks expedient.

III CRO [22]

38. Interpretation

(1) Any reference in this Act to the provisions of this Act shall, unless the context otherwise requires, include a reference to rules of court made for the purposes of this Act.

(2) In this Act, except in so far as the context otherwise requires or it is otherwise expressly provided, the following expressions have the meanings hereby respectively assigned to them, that is to say—

"Agent", when used in relation to the Crown, includes an independent contractor employed by the Crown:

"Civil proceedings" includes proceedings in the High Court or the county court for the recovery of fines or penalties, but does not include proceedings on the Crown side of the King's Bench Division;

"Officer" in relation to the Crown, includes any servant of Her Majesty, and accordingly (but without prejudice to the generality of the foregoing provision) includes a Minister of the Crown and a member of the Scottish Executive;

"Order" includes a judgment, decree rule, award or declaration;

"Prescribed" means prescribed by rules of court;

"Proceedings against the Crown" includes a claim by way of set-off or counterclaim raised in proceedings by the Crown;

(3) Any reference in this Act to Her Majesty in Her private capacity shall be construed as including a reference to Her Majesty in right of Her Duchy of Lancaster and to the Duke of Cornwall.

(4) Any reference in Parts III or IV of this Act to civil proceedings by or against the Crown or to civil proceedings to which the Crown is a party, shall be construed as including a reference to civil proceedings to which the Attorney General, or any Government department, or any officer of the Crown as such is a party:

Provided that the Crown shall not for the purposes of Parts III and IV of this Act be deemed to be a party to any proceedings by reason only that they are brought by the Attorney General upon the relation of some other person.

(5) [. . .]

(6) References in this Act to any enactment shall be construed as references to that enactment as amended by or under any other enactment, including this Act.

III CRO [22.1]

"Officer" This expression does not include independent contractors such as the BOAC: *Moukataff v British Overseas Airways Corpn* [1967] 1 Lloyd's Rep 396.

III CRO [23]

40. Savings

(1) Nothing in this Act shall apply to proceedings by or against, or authorise proceedings in tort to be brought against, His Majesty in His private capacity.

(2) Except as therein otherwise expressly provided, nothing in this Act shall:—

(a) affect the law relating to prize salvage, or apply to proceedings in causes or matters within the jurisdiction of the High Court as a prize court or to any criminal proceedings; or

(b) authorise proceedings to be taken against the Crown under or in accordance with this Act in respect of any alleged liability of the Crown arising otherwise than in respect of His Majesty's Government in the

CROWN PROCEEDINGS

United Kingdom or the Scottish Administration, or affect proceedings against the Crown in respect of any such alleged liability as aforesaid; or

(c) affect any proceedings by the Crown otherwise than in right of His Majesty's Government in the United Kingdom or the Scottish Administration; or

(d) subject the Crown to any greater liabilities in respect of the acts or omissions of any independent contractor employed by the Crown than those to which the Crown would be subject in respect of such acts or omissions if it were a private person; or

(e) < . . . >

(f) affect any rules of evidence or any presumption relating to the extent to which the Crown is bound by any Act of Parliament; or

(g) affect any right of the Crown to demand a trial at bar or to control or otherwise intervene in proceedings affecting its rights, property or profits; or

(h) affect any liability imposed on the public trustee < . . . > or the Scottish Administration by the Public Trustee Act 1906;

and, without prejudice to the general effect of the foregoing provisions, Part III of this Act shall not apply to the Crown except in right of His Majesty's Government in the United Kingdom or the Scottish Administration.

(3) A certificate of a Secretary of State:—

(a) to the effect that any alleged liability of the Crown arises otherwise than in respect of His Majesty's Government in the United Kingdom;

(b) to the effect that any proceedings by the Crown are proceedings otherwise than in right of His Majesty's Government in the United Kingdom;

shall, for the purposes of this Act, be conclusive as to the matter so certified.

(3A) A certificate of the Scottish Ministers to the effect that—

(a) any alleged liability of the Crown arises otherwise than in respect of the Scottish Administration,

(b) any proceedings by the Crown are proceedings otherwise than in right of the Scottish Administration,

shall, for the purposes of this Act, be conclusive as to that matter.

(4) Where any property vests in the Crown by virtue of any rule of law which operates independently of the acts or the intentions of the Crown, the Crown shall not by virtue of this Act be subject to any liabilities in tort by reason only of the property being so vested; but the provisions of this subsection shall be without prejudice to the liabilities of the Crown under this Act in respect of any period after the Crown or any person acting for the Crown has in fact taken possession or control of any such property, or entered into occupation thereof.

(5) This Act shall not operate to limit the discretion of the court to grant relief by way of mandamus in cases in which such relief might have been granted before the commencement of this Act, notwithstanding that by reason of the provisions of this Act some other and further remedy is available.

III CRO [23.1]

"Under or in accordance with this Act" For the purposes of s 40(2)(b) of the Crown Proceedings Act 1947 proceedings brought against an authorised government department in reliance on s 17 of the Crown Proceedings Act 1947 (see para **III CRO [9]**) are proceedings "under or in accordance with this Act" and will therefore be barred by a certificate under s 40(3) of the Crown Proceedings Act 1947: *Trawnik v Ministry of Defence* [1984] 2 All ER 791 (reversed on another point [1985] 2 All ER 368, [1985] 1 WLR 532, CA).

DATA PROTECTION

TABLE OF CONTENTS

GENERAL NOTES ON DATA PROTECTION

III DAT [A1]

The text of the Data Protection Act 2018 is set out below, except where summarised as General Notes. The provisions of Part 5 are summarised in General Notes because they provide for the role and functions of the Information Commissioner as the supervisory authority but do not create rights that are enforceable by direct access to the courts. The main source of civil rights and remedies in protection of personal data is the General Data Protection Regulation (GDPR). Its provisions are applied and interpreted and added to by the Data Protection Act 2018 but the text of GDPR is not reproduced as part of the Act. The GDPR and the Act have therefore to be read together. The text of the GDPR is available on the internet at gdpr-info.eu. It provides a new regime for the processing and protection of personal data in place of that provided by the Data Protection Directive 95/46/EC but it leaves some matters to be decided by individual member states. The Data Protection Act 2018 operates in the areas delegated to member States and also in new areas outside the GDPR.

The Regulation is of direct effect throughout the European Union from 25 May 2018. The Data Protection Act 2018, which is also fully in force, takes the GDPR as its starting point and extends its application to areas outside, such as the manual unstructured processing of personal data held by an FOPI public authority (ss 21–28) and it makes provision for the textual implementation of the Law Enforcement Directive (Part 3, ss 29–54). As regards Intelligence services processing, Part 4 provides a free-standing exposition of the data subject's rights and duties which reflects the principles and provisions of GDPR. Elsewhere in Parts 1,2, 3, 6 and 7 the Act fills in the blanks left to Member States, by, for example, specifying the courts with jurisdiction to entertain claims for breach of duty (s 180) and by clarifying the meaning to be given to the provisions of GDPR as applied in the United Kingdom.

DATA PROTECTION ACT 2018

(c 12)

PART 1
PRELIMINARY

III DAT [1]

1 Overview

(1) This Act makes provision about the processing of personal data.

(2) Most processing of personal data is subject to the GDPR.

(3) Part 2 supplements the GDPR (see Chapter 2) and applies a broadly equivalent regime to certain types of processing to which the GDPR does not apply (see Chapter 3).

(4) Part 3 makes provision about the processing of personal data by competent authorities for law enforcement purposes and implements the Law Enforcement Directive.

(5) Part 4 makes provision about the processing of personal data by the intelligence services.

(6) Part 5 makes provision about the Information Commissioner.

(7) Part 6 makes provision about the enforcement of the data protection legislation.

(8) Part 7 makes supplementary provision, including provision about the application of this Act to the Crown and to Parliament.

III DAT [2]

2 Protection of personal data

(1) The GDPR, the applied GDPR and this Act protect individuals with regard to the processing of personal data, in particular by—

- (a) requiring personal data to be processed lawfully and fairly, on the basis of the data subject's consent or another specified basis,
- (b) conferring rights on the data subject to obtain information about the processing of personal data and to require inaccurate personal data to be rectified, and
- (c) conferring functions on the Commissioner, giving the holder of that office responsibility for monitoring and enforcing their provisions.

(2) When carrying out functions under the GDPR, the applied GDPR and this Act, the Commissioner must have regard to the importance of securing an appropriate level of protection for personal data, taking account of the interests of data subjects, controllers and others and matters of general public interest.

III DAT [2.1]

Liability of controllers and processors Underpinning the protection of personal data is the right of the data subject to be compensated for damage (including distress: s 168) caused by the contravention of GDPR by controllers or processors. The right is conferred by GDPR, Articles 79 and 82 and contraventions are actionable as torts. Proceedings may be taken in the High Court or the county court: s 180. The same remedies are available for contravention of similar regimes of data protection made enforceable by provisions in Part 2 of the Act (manual unstructured data held by Freedom of Information Public Authorities), Part 3 (law enforcement) and Part 4 (Intelligence Services).

III DAT [2.2]

Liability of employers An employer may be vicariously liable for the unauthorised publication of personal data by an employee, as was held in a case under the Data Protection Act 1998: *Various Claimants v Wm Morrison Supermarkets plc* [2018] EWCA Civ 2339, (2018) Times 10 December. Note, however, that an exemption from liability is provided by Article 82(3) of GDPR for events for which the controller was not in any way responsible.

III DAT [3]

3 Terms relating to the processing of personal data

(1) This section defines some terms used in this Act.

(2) "Personal data" means any information relating to an identified or identifiable living individual (subject to subsection (14)(c)).

(3) "Identifiable living individual" means a living individual who can be identified, directly or indirectly, in particular by reference to—

- (a) an identifier such as a name, an identification number, location data or an online identifier, or
- (b) one or more factors specific to the physical, physiological, genetic, mental, economic, cultural or social identity of the individual.

(4) "Processing", in relation to information, means an operation or set of operations which is performed on information, or on sets of information, such as—

- (a) collection, recording, organisation, structuring or storage,
- (b) adaptation or alteration,
- (c) retrieval, consultation or use,
- (d) disclosure by transmission, dissemination or otherwise making available,
- (e) alignment or combination, or
- (f) restriction, erasure or destruction,

(subject to subsection (14)(c) and sections 5(7), 29(2) and 82(3), which make provision about references to processing in the different Parts of this Act).

(5) "Data subject" means the identified or identifiable living individual to whom personal data relates.

(6) "Controller" and "processor", in relation to the processing of personal data to which Chapter 2 or 3 of Part 2, Part 3 or Part 4 applies, have the same meaning as in that Chapter or Part (see sections 5, 6, 32 and 83 and see also subsection (14)(d)).

(7) "Filing system" means any structured set of personal data which is accessible according to specific criteria, whether held by automated means or manually and whether centralised, decentralised or dispersed on a functional or geographical basis.

(8) "The Commissioner" means the Information Commissioner (see section 114).

(9) "The data protection legislation" means—

- (a) the GDPR,
- (b) the applied GDPR,
- (c) this Act,
- (d) regulations made under this Act, and
- (e) regulations made under section 2(2) of the European Communities Act 1972 which relate to the GDPR or the Law Enforcement Directive.

(10) "The GDPR" means Regulation (EU) 2016/679 of the European Parliament and of the Council of 27 April 2016 on the protection of natural persons with regard to the processing of personal data and on the free movement of such data (General Data Protection Regulation).

(11) "The applied GDPR" means the GDPR as applied by Chapter 3 of Part 2.

(12) "The Law Enforcement Directive" means Directive (EU) 2016/680 of the European Parliament and of the Council of 27 April 2016 on the protection of natural persons with regard to the processing of personal data by competent authorities for the purposes of the prevention, investigation, detection or

prosecution of criminal offences or the execution of criminal penalties, and on the free movement of such data, and repealing Council Framework Decision 2008/977/JHA.

(13) "The Data Protection Convention" means the Convention for the Protection of Individuals with regard to Automatic Processing of Personal Data which was opened for signature on 28 January 1981, as amended up to the day on which this Act is passed.

(14) In Parts 5 to 7, except where otherwise provided—

(a) references to the GDPR are to the GDPR read with Chapter 2 of Part 2 and include the applied GDPR read with Chapter 3 of Part 2 ;

(b) references to Chapter 2 of Part 2, or to a provision of that Chapter, include that Chapter or that provision as applied by Chapter 3 of Part 2;

(c) references to personal data, and the processing of personal data, are to personal data and processing to which Chapter 2 or 3 of Part 2, Part 3 or Part 4 applies;

(d) references to a controller or processor are to a controller or processor in relation to the processing of personal data to which Chapter 2 or 3 of Part 2, Part 3 or Part 4 applies.

(15) There is an index of defined expressions in section 206.

III DAT [3.1]

Definitions The definitions of "personal data", "processing" and "controller" reflect those in Article 4 of the GDPR.

PART 2
GENERAL PROCESSING

CHAPTER 1 SCOPE AND DEFINITIONS

III DAT [4]

4 Processing to which this Part applies

(1) This Part is relevant to most processing of personal data.

(2) Chapter 2 of this Part—

(a) applies to the types of processing of personal data to which the GDPR applies by virtue of Article 2 of the GDPR, and

(b) supplements, and must be read with, the GDPR.

(3) Chapter 3 of this Part—

(a) applies to certain types of processing of personal data to which the GDPR does not apply (see section 21), and

(b) makes provision for a regime broadly equivalent to the GDPR to apply to such processing.

III DAT [4.1]

Article 2 of the GDPR Key provisions in Article 2 of GDPR are:

'1. This Regulation applies to the processing of personal data wholly or partly by automated means and to the processing other than by automated means of personal data which form part of a filing system or are intended to form part of a filing system.

2. This Regulation does not apply to the processing of personal data:

(a)–(b)...

(c) by a natural person in the course of a purely personal or household activity;

(d) by competent authorities for the purposes of the prevention, investigation, detection or prosecution of criminal offences or the execution of criminal penalties, including the safeguarding against and the prevention of threats to public security.'

III DAT [4.2]

A purely personal or household activity It has been held that Jehovah's Witnesses who collected personal information about people to whom they were preaching could not rely on the exclusion of 'processing of personal data by a natural person in the course of a purely personal or household activity': *Tietosuojavaituutettu v Jehovan todistajat – uskonnellinen yhdyskunta Case C-25/17* (2018) Times, 24 September, Court of Justice of the European Union

III DAT [5]

5 Definitions

(1) Terms used in Chapter 2 of this Part and in the GDPR have the same meaning in Chapter 2 as they have in the GDPR.

(2) In subsection (1), the reference to a term's meaning in the GDPR is to its meaning in the GDPR read with any provision of Chapter 2 which modifies the term's meaning for the purposes of the GDPR.

(3) Subsection (1) is subject to any provision in Chapter 2 which provides expressly for the term to have a different meaning and to section 204.

(4) Terms used in Chapter 3 of this Part and in the applied GDPR have the same meaning in Chapter 3 as they have in the applied GDPR.

(5) In subsection (4), the reference to a term's meaning in the applied GDPR is to its meaning in the GDPR read with any provision of Chapter 2 (as applied by Chapter 3) or Chapter 3 which modifies the term's meaning for the purposes of the applied GDPR.

(6) Subsection (4) is subject to any provision in Chapter 2 (as applied by Chapter 3) or Chapter 3 which provides expressly for the term to have a different meaning.

(7) A reference in Chapter 2 or Chapter 3 of this Part to the processing of personal data is to processing to which the Chapter applies.

(8) Sections 3 and 205 include definitions of other expressions used in this Part.

CHAPTER 2 THE GDPR

MEANING OF CERTAIN TERMS USED IN THE GDPR

III DAT [6]

6 Meaning of "controller"

(1) The definition of "controller" in Article 4(7) of the GDPR has effect subject to—

(a) subsection (2),

(b) section 209, and

(c) section 210.

(2) For the purposes of the GDPR, where personal data is processed only—

(a) for purposes for which it is required by an enactment to be processed, and

(b) by means by which it is required by an enactment to be processed,

the person on whom the obligation to process the data is imposed by the enactment (or, if different, one of the enactments) is the controller.

III DAT [7]

7 Meaning of "public authority" and "public body"

(1) For the purposes of the GDPR, the following (and only the following) are "public authorities" and "public bodies" under the law of the United Kingdom—

- (a) a public authority as defined by the Freedom of Information Act 2000,
- (b) a Scottish public authority as defined by the Freedom of Information (Scotland) Act 2002 (asp 13), and
- (c) an authority or body specified or described by the Secretary of State in regulations,

subject to subsections (2), (3) and (4).

(2) An authority or body that falls within subsection (1) is only a "public authority" or "public body" for the purposes of the GDPR when performing a task carried out in the public interest or in the exercise of official authority vested in it.

(3) The references in subsection (1)(a) and (b) to public authorities and Scottish public authorities as defined by the Freedom of Information Act 2000 and the Freedom of Information (Scotland) Act 2002 (asp 13) do not include any of the following that fall within those definitions—

- (a) a parish council in England;
- (b) a community council in Wales;
- (c) a community council in Scotland;
- (d) a parish meeting constituted under section 13 of the Local Government Act 1972;
- (e) a community meeting constituted under section 27 of that Act;
- (f) charter trustees constituted—
  - (i) under section 246 of that Act,
  - (ii) under Part 1 of the Local Government and Public Involvement in Health Act 2007, or
  - (iii) by the Charter Trustees Regulations 1996 (SI 1996/263).

(4) The Secretary of State may by regulations provide that a person specified or described in the regulations that is a public authority described in subsection (1)(a) or (b) is not a "public authority" or "public body" for the purposes of the GDPR.

(5) Regulations under this section are subject to the affirmative resolution procedure.

LAWFULNESS OF PROCESSING

III DAT [8]

8 Lawfulness of processing: public interest etc

In Article 6(1) of the GDPR (lawfulness of processing), the reference in point (e) to processing of personal data that is necessary for the performance of a task carried out in the public interest or in the exercise of the controller's official authority includes processing of personal data that is necessary for—

- (a) the administration of justice,
- (b) the exercise of a function of either House of Parliament,
- (c) the exercise of a function conferred on a person by an enactment or rule of law,
- (d) the exercise of a function of the Crown, a Minister of the Crown or a government department, or
- (e) an activity that supports or promotes democratic engagement.

III DAT [8.1]

Principles relating to processing of personal data The requirement that personal data should be processed lawfully is one of the Principles set out in Article 5 of GDPR. These reflect the Data Protection Principles specified in Schedule 1 to the Data Protection Act 1998, by which the European Data Protection Directive (95/46/EC) was implemented. The same six data protection principles are restated in Part 3 (Law Enforcement Processing) at ss 35 to 40 and Part 4 (Intelligence Services Processing) at ss 86 to 91, but subject to qualifications appropriate to the processing of personal data for the purposes of those Parts.

III DAT [8.2]

Tasks carried out in the public interest As regards the areas of processing specified in s 8, Article 6(2) of GDPR allows Member States to add to the tasks carried out in the public interest or in the exercise of official authority for which processing is necessary.

III DAT [9]

9 Child's consent in relation to information society services

In Article 8(1) of the GDPR (conditions applicable to child's consent in relation to information society services)—

(a) references to "16 years" are to be read as references to "13 years", and

(b) the reference to "information society services" does not include preventive or counselling services.

III DAT [9.1]

Consent Article 6(1)(a) specifies the giving of consent by the data subject as a basis for lawful processing of personal data. The conditions for consent are set out in Article 7 and one of them is that the controller should be able to demonstrate that the data subject has consented. Article 8 is concerned with the processing of personal data of a child in the context of 'information society services'. It deals with the giving of consent on behalf of a child of under 13, by the holder of parental responsibility. Above that age a child can give valid consent. Note that 'information society services' do not include preventive or counselling services.

Special categories of personal data

III DAT [10]

10 Special categories of personal data and criminal convictions etc data

(1) Subsections (2) and (3) make provision about the processing of personal data described in Article 9(1) of the GDPR (prohibition on processing of special categories of personal data) in reliance on an exception in one of the following points of Article 9(2)—

(a) point (b) (employment, social security and social protection);

(b) point (g) (substantial public interest);

(c) point (h) (health and social care);

(d) point (i) (public health);

(e) point (j) (archiving, research and statistics).

(2) The processing meets the requirement in point (b), (h), (i) or (j) of Article 9(2) of the GDPR for authorisation by, or a basis in, the law of the United Kingdom or a part of the United Kingdom only if it meets a condition in Part 1 of Schedule 1.

(3) The processing meets the requirement in point (g) of Article 9(2) of the GDPR for a basis in the law of the United Kingdom or a part of the United Kingdom only if it meets a condition in Part 2 of Schedule 1.

(4) Subsection (5) makes provision about the processing of personal data relating to criminal convictions and offences or related security measures that is not carried out under the control of official authority.

(5) The processing meets the requirement in Article 10 of the GDPR for authorisation by the law of the United Kingdom or a part of the United Kingdom only if it meets a condition in Part 1, 2 or 3 of Schedule 1.

(6) The Secretary of State may by regulations—

(a) amend Schedule 1—

(i) by adding or varying conditions or safeguards, and

(ii) by omitting conditions or safeguards added by regulations under this section, and

(b) consequentially amend this section.

(7) Regulations under this section are subject to the affirmative resolution procedure.

III DAT [10.1]

Special categories of personal data Section 2 of the Data Protection Act 1998 identified certain categories of personal data as "sensitive" and Schedule 3 set out special conditions, such as where the data subject has given explicit consent for the processing of personal data in these categories. The list of special categories in Article 9 is broadly the same as in s 2 of the 1998 Act but instead of laying down special conditions for processing, the Article prohibits processing subject to exceptions, such as where the data subject has given explicit consent. Note that the scope of some of the exceptions is qualified by the provisions in Schedule 1, which include a great variety of conditions, for example that an appropriate policy is in place.

III DAT [11]

11 Special categories of personal data etc: supplementary

(1) For the purposes of Article 9(2)(h) of the GDPR (processing for health or social care purposes etc), the circumstances in which the processing of personal data is carried out subject to the conditions and safeguards referred to in Article 9(3) of the GDPR (obligation of secrecy) include circumstances in which it is carried out—

(a) by or under the responsibility of a health professional or a social work professional, or

(b) by another person who in the circumstances owes a duty of confidentiality under an enactment or rule of law.

(2) In Article 10 of the GDPR and section 10, references to personal data relating to criminal convictions and offences or related security measures include personal data relating to—

(a) the alleged commission of offences by the data subject, or

(b) proceedings for an offence committed or alleged to have been committed by the data subject or the disposal of such proceedings, including sentencing.

III DAT [11.1]

Special provision for special categories The processing of personal data relating to criminal convictions and offences is not a special category within Article 9 of GDPR but is dealt with in Article 10, as clarified by sub-s (2) of s 10.

Rights of the data subject

III DAT [12]

12 Limits on fees that may be charged by controllers

(1) The Secretary of State may by regulations specify limits on the fees that a controller may charge in reliance on—

(a) Article 12(5) of the GDPR (reasonable fees when responding to manifestly unfounded or excessive requests), or

(b) Article 15(3) of the GDPR (reasonable fees for provision of further copies).

(2) The Secretary of State may by regulations—

DATA PROTECTION

(a) require controllers of a description specified in the regulations to produce and publish guidance about the fees that they charge in reliance on those provisions, and

(b) specify what the guidance must include.

(3) Regulations under this section are subject to the negative resolution procedure.

III DAT [12.1]

Rights of the data subject The data subject's right of access under Article 15 carries with it the right, under Article 12, to have the information provided in intelligible form and in clear language.

III DAT [12.2]

Charges for responding to subject access requests The general rule is that the controller must respond to a subject access request within a month and without charge. Regulations under s 12 may provide for reasonable charges for extra copies and for responding to manifestly unfounded or excessive requests. Note the provision in Article 11 that the controller may ask for information which identifies the subject and in paragraph (6) of Article 12 information which identifies the person making the request in Articles 15 to 21.

III DAT [12.3]

Information to be provided to the data subject The GDPR requires the controller to give the data subject information at the point when the data is collected, including, for example the contact details of the controller's data protection officer and the purpose of the processing. See Article 13 for where the data subject provides the data and Article 14 for where the obtaining of the data has been achieved in some other way.

III DAT [13]

13 Obligations of credit reference agencies

(1) This section applies where a controller is a credit reference agency (within the meaning of section 145(8) of the Consumer Credit Act 1974).

(2) The controller's obligations under Article 15(1) to (3) of the GDPR (confirmation of processing, access to data and safeguards for third country transfers) are taken to apply only to personal data relating to the data subject's financial standing, unless the data subject has indicated a contrary intention.

(3) Where the controller discloses personal data in pursuance of Article 15(1) to (3) of the GDPR, the disclosure must be accompanied by a statement informing the data subject of the data subject's rights under section 159 of the Consumer Credit Act 1974 (correction of wrong information).

III DAT [13.1]

The Consumer Credit Act 1974 This section makes special provision for subject access requests made to a credit reference agency and covers the same ground as s 9 of the Data Protection Act 1998.

III DAT [14]

14 Automated decision-making authorised by law: safeguards

(1) This section makes provision for the purposes of Article 22(2)(b) of the GDPR (exception from Article 22(1) of the GDPR for significant decisions based solely on automated processing that are authorised by law and subject to safeguards for the data subject's rights, freedoms and legitimate interests).

(2) A decision is a "significant decision" for the purposes of this section if, in relation to a data subject, it—

(a) produces legal effects concerning the data subject, or

(b) similarly significantly affects the data subject.

(3) A decision is a "qualifying significant decision" for the purposes of this section if—

(a) it is a significant decision in relation to a data subject,
(b) it is required or authorised by law, and
(c) it does not fall within Article 22(2)(a) or (c) of the GDPR (decisions necessary to a contract or made with the data subject's consent).

(4) Where a controller takes a qualifying significant decision in relation to a data subject based solely on automated processing—
(a) the controller must, as soon as reasonably practicable, notify the data subject in writing that a decision has been taken based solely on automated processing, and
(b) the data subject may, before the end of the period of 1 month beginning with receipt of the notification, request the controller to—
(i) reconsider the decision, or
(ii) take a new decision that is not based solely on automated processing.

(5) If a request is made to a controller under subsection (4), the controller must, within the period described in Article 12(3) of the GDPR—
(a) consider the request, including any information provided by the data subject that is relevant to it,
(b) comply with the request, and
(c) by notice in writing inform the data subject of—
(i) the steps taken to comply with the request, and
(ii) the outcome of complying with the request.

(6) In connection with this section, a controller has the powers and obligations under Article 12 of the GDPR (transparency, procedure for extending time for acting on request, fees, manifestly unfounded or excessive requests etc) that apply in connection with Article 22 of the GDPR.

(7) The Secretary of State may by regulations make such further provision as the Secretary of State considers appropriate to provide suitable measures to safeguard a data subject's rights, freedoms and legitimate interests in connection with the taking of qualifying significant decisions based solely on automated processing.

(8) Regulations under subsection (7)—
(a) may amend this section, and
(b) are subject to the affirmative resolution procedure.

III DAT [14.1]

Data subject's rights in relation to automated decision-making Article 22 of the GDPR, as expanded by s 14, carries forward in a different form the data subject's rights under s 12 of the Data Protection Act 1998.

RESTRICTIONS ON DATA SUBJECT'S RIGHTS

III DAT [15]

15 Exemptions etc

(1) Schedules 2, 3 and 4 make provision for exemptions from, and restrictions and adaptations of the application of, rules of the GDPR.

(2) In Schedule 2—
(a) Part 1 makes provision adapting or restricting the application of rules contained in Articles 13 to 21 and 34 of the GDPR in specified circumstances, as allowed for by Article 6(3) and Article 23(1) of the GDPR;
(b) Part 2 makes provision restricting the application of rules contained in Articles 13 to 21 and 34 of the GDPR in specified circumstances, as allowed for by Article 23(1) of the GDPR;

(c) Part 3 makes provision restricting the application of Article 15 of the GDPR where this is necessary to protect the rights of others, as allowed for by Article 23(1) of the GDPR;

(d) Part 4 makes provision restricting the application of rules contained in Articles 13 to 15 of the GDPR in specified circumstances, as allowed for by Article 23(1) of the GDPR;

(e) Part 5 makes provision containing exemptions or derogations from Chapters II, III, IV, V and VII of the GDPR for reasons relating to freedom of expression, as allowed for by Article 85(2) of the GDPR;

(f) Part 6 makes provision containing derogations from rights contained in Articles 15, 16, 18, 19, 20 and 21 of the GDPR for scientific or historical research purposes, statistical purposes and archiving purposes, as allowed for by Article 89(2) and (3) of the GDPR.

(3) Schedule 3 makes provision restricting the application of rules contained in Articles 13 to 21 of the GDPR to health, social work, education and child abuse data, as allowed for by Article 23(1) of the GDPR.

(4) Schedule 4 makes provision restricting the application of rules contained in Articles 13 to 21 of the GDPR to information the disclosure of which is prohibited or restricted by an enactment, as allowed for by Article 23(1) of the GDPR.

(5) In connection with the safeguarding of national security and with defence, see Chapter 3 of this Part and the exemption in section 26.

III DAT [15.1]

Exemptions, restrictions and adaptations Articles 13 to 21 of GDPR confer substantive rights on the data subject in respect of his or her personal data and corresponding duties on the controller. They include rights to information, data access, rectification, erasure, restriction of processing, notification, portability and the right to object. Article 34 obliges the controller to inform the data subject of breaches of personal data duties, in certain circumstances. But the rights and duties are qualified by exemptions, restrictions and adaptations in Schedules 2, 3 and 4. Those in Schedule 2 are permitted to be made by national law in relation to the maintenance of law and order, national security and defence and the protection of the rights of others. Also special provision is made for reasons relating to freedom of expression in Part 5 of the Schedule and, in Part 6, for scientific or historical research purposes, statistical purposes and archiving persons.

The substantive rights of the data subject, in the context of Law Enforcement Processing (Part 3) and Intelligence Services Processing (Part 4) are set out at ss 43 to 50 in Part 3 and ss 92 to 100 in Part 4.

III DAT [15.2]

Rectification or erasure without compensation In a case under the 1998 Act where inaccurate data had been processed and published but the controller has taken reasonable care, within s 13(3), the court, whilst denying compensation, made an order under s 4 for the rectification or erasure of the data shown to be inaccurate: *NT1 and NT2 v Google LLC (Information Commissioner Intervening)* [2018] EWHC 799 (QB).

III DAT [15.3]

Schedule 3 The provisions of Schedule 3 reflect those in s 30 of the Data Protection Act 1998.

III DAT [16]

16 Power to make further exemptions etc by regulations

(1) The following powers to make provision altering the application of the GDPR may be exercised by way of regulations made by the Secretary of State under this section—

(a) the power in Article 6(3) for Member State law to lay down a legal basis containing specific provisions to adapt the application of rules of the GDPR where processing is necessary for compliance with a legal obligation, for the performance of a task in the public interest or in the exercise of official authority;

(b) the power in Article 23(1) to make a legislative measure restricting the scope of the obligations and rights mentioned in that Article where necessary and proportionate to safeguard certain objectives of general public interest;

(c) the power in Article 85(2) to provide for exemptions or derogations from certain Chapters of the GDPR where necessary to reconcile the protection of personal data with the freedom of expression and information.

(2) Regulations under this section may—

(a) amend Schedules 2 to 4—

(i) by adding or varying provisions, and

(ii) by omitting provisions added by regulations under this section, and

(b) consequentially amend section 15.

(3) Regulations under this section are subject to the affirmative resolution procedure.

Accreditation of certification providers

III DAT [17]

17 Accreditation of certification providers

(1) Accreditation of a person as a certification provider is only valid when carried out by—

(a) the Commissioner, or

(b) the national accreditation body.

(2) The Commissioner may only accredit a person as a certification provider where the Commissioner—

(a) has published a statement that the Commissioner will carry out such accreditation, and

(b) has not published a notice withdrawing that statement.

(3) The national accreditation body may only accredit a person as a certification provider where the Commissioner—

(a) has published a statement that the body may carry out such accreditation, and

(b) has not published a notice withdrawing that statement.

(4) The publication of a notice under subsection (2)(b) or (3)(b) does not affect the validity of any accreditation carried out before its publication.

(5) Schedule 5 makes provision about reviews of, and appeals from, a decision relating to accreditation of a person as a certification provider.

(6) The national accreditation body may charge a reasonable fee in connection with, or incidental to, the carrying out of the body's functions under this section, Schedule 5 and Article 43 of the GDPR.

(7) The national accreditation body must provide the Secretary of State with such information relating to its functions under this section, Schedule 5 and Article 43 of the GDPR as the Secretary of State may reasonably require.

(8) In this section—

"certification provider" means a person who issues certification for the purposes of Article 42 of the GDPR;

"the national accreditation body" means the national accreditation body for the purposes of Article 4(1) of Regulation (EC) No 765/2008 of the European Parliament and of the Council of 9 July 2008 setting out the requirements for accreditation and market surveillance relating to the marketing of products and repealing Regulation (EEC) No 339/93.

III DAT [17.1]

Codes of conduct Articles 40 to 43 providing for the drawing up, by the Information Commissioner and others, of codes of conduct. Once the codes have been approved, independent persons and bodies are needed to monitor compliance and their accreditation is the responsibility of the Information Commissioner. Data protection certificates may be issued to demonstrate the existence of appropriate data protection safeguards and Article 43 provides for the setting up of accredited certification bodies. Section 17 and Schedule 5 explain how these provisions will be made to work within the United Kingdom.

TRANSFERS OF PERSONAL DATA TO THIRD COUNTRIES ETC

III DAT [18]

18 Transfers of personal data to third countries etc

(1) The Secretary of State may by regulations specify, for the purposes of Article 49(1)(d) of the GDPR—

- (a) circumstances in which a transfer of personal data to a third country or international organisation is to be taken to be necessary for important reasons of public interest, and
- (b) circumstances in which a transfer of personal data to a third country or international organisation which is not required by an enactment is not to be taken to be necessary for important reasons of public interest.

(2) The Secretary of State may by regulations restrict the transfer of a category of personal data to a third country or international organisation where—

- (a) the transfer is not authorised by an adequacy decision under Article 45(3) of the GDPR, and
- (b) the Secretary of State considers the restriction to be necessary for important reasons of public interest.

(3) Regulations under this section—

- (a) are subject to the made affirmative resolution procedure where the Secretary of State has made an urgency statement in respect of them;
- (b) are otherwise subject to the affirmative resolution procedure.

(4) For the purposes of this section, an urgency statement is a reasoned statement that the Secretary of State considers it desirable for the regulations to come into force without delay.

III DAT [18.1]

Regulations No regulations have yet been made under this section.

SPECIFIC PROCESSING SITUATIONS

III DAT [19]

19 Processing for archiving, research and statistical purposes: safeguards

(1) This section makes provision about—

- (a) processing of personal data that is necessary for archiving purposes in the public interest,
- (b) processing of personal data that is necessary for scientific or historical research purposes, and
- (c) processing of personal data that is necessary for statistical purposes.

(2) Such processing does not satisfy the requirement in Article 89(1) of the GDPR for the processing to be subject to appropriate safeguards for the rights and freedoms of the data subject if it is likely to cause substantial damage or substantial distress to a data subject.

(3) Such processing does not satisfy that requirement if the processing is carried out for the purposes of measures or decisions with respect to a particular data subject, unless the purposes for which the processing is necessary include the purposes of approved medical research.

(4) In this section—

"approved medical research" means medical research carried out by a person who has approval to carry out that research from—

- (a) a research ethics committee recognised or established by the Health Research Authority under Chapter 2 of Part 3 of the Care Act 2014, or
- (b) a body appointed by any of the following for the purpose of assessing the ethics of research involving individuals—
    - (i) the Secretary of State, the Scottish Ministers, the Welsh Ministers, or a Northern Ireland department;
    - (ii) a relevant NHS body;
    - (iii) United Kingdom Research and Innovation or a body that is a Research Council for the purposes of the Science and Technology Act 1965;
    - (iv) an institution that is a research institution for the purposes of Chapter 4A of Part 7 of the Income Tax (Earnings and Pensions) Act 2003 (see section 457 of that Act);

"relevant NHS body" means—

- (a) an NHS trust or NHS foundation trust in England,
- (b) an NHS trust or Local Health Board in Wales,
- (c) a Health Board or Special Health Board constituted under section 2 of the National Health Service (Scotland) Act 1978,
- (d) the Common Services Agency for the Scottish Health Service, or
- (e) any of the health and social care bodies in Northern Ireland falling within paragraphs (a) to (e) of section 1(5) of the Health and Social Care (Reform) Act (Northern Ireland) 2009 (c 1 (NI)).

(5) The Secretary of State may by regulations change the meaning of "approved medical research" for the purposes of this section, including by amending subsection (4).

(6) Regulations under subsection (5) are subject to the affirmative resolution procedure.

III DAT [19.1]

Archiving, research and statistics This section qualifies the rights and freedoms of the data subject where the processing identified in sub-s (1) is necessary for medical research but safeguards the data subject from such processing if it is likely to cause substantial damage or distress.

Minor definition

III DAT [20]

20 Meaning of "court"

Section 5(1) (terms used in this Chapter to have the same meaning as in the GDPR) does not apply to references in this Chapter to a court and, accordingly, such references do not include a tribunal.

CHAPTER 3 OTHER GENERAL PROCESSING

GENERAL NOTES ON CHAPTER 3 (OTHER GENERAL PROCESSING)

III DAT [21]–III DAT [28]

Chapter 3 comprises ss 21 to 28. Their purpose is broadly to apply the GDPR to manual unstructured data held by freedom of Information public authorities and thus to carry forward the Freedom of Information Act amendments made to the Data Protection Act 1998. The provisions include qualifications and exemptions for, in particular, historical research, national security and defence.

PART 3
LAW ENFORCEMENT PROCESSING

CHAPTER 1 SCOPE AND DEFINITIONS

Scope

III DAT [29]

29 Processing to which this Part applies

(1) This Part applies to—

(a) the processing by a competent authority of personal data wholly or partly by automated means, and

(b) the processing by a competent authority otherwise than by automated means of personal data which forms part of a filing system or is intended to form part of a filing system.

(2) Any reference in this Part to the processing of personal data is to processing to which this Part applies.

(3) For the meaning of "competent authority", see section 30.

III DAT [29.1]

Scope and purpose of Part 3 Part 3 gives legal effect in the United Kingdom to the EU Data protection Directive 2016/680. It provides a bespoke regime for the processing of personal data by the police, prosecutors and other criminal justice agencies (listed in Schedule 7) for law enforcement purposes (defined in s 31). It also allows the unhindered flow of data internationally whilst providing safeguards to protect personal data (ss 72 to 78).

Definitions

III DAT [30]

30 Meaning of "competent authority"

(1) In this Part, "competent authority" means—

(a) a person specified or described in Schedule 7, and

(b) any other person if and to the extent that the person has statutory functions for any of the law enforcement purposes.

(2) But an intelligence service is not a competent authority within the meaning of this Part.

(3) The Secretary of State may by regulations amend Schedule 7—

(a) so as to add or remove a person or description of person;

(b) so as to reflect any change in the name of a person specified in the Schedule.

(4) Regulations under subsection (3) which make provision of the kind described in subsection (3)(a) may also make consequential amendments of section 73(4)(b).

(5) Regulations under subsection (3) which make provision of the kind described in subsection (3)(a), or which make provision of that kind and of the kind described in subsection (3)(b), are subject to the affirmative resolution procedure.

(6) Regulations under subsection (3) which make provision only of the kind described in subsection (3)(b) are subject to the negative resolution procedure.

(7) In this section—

"intelligence service" means—

(a) the Security Service;

(b) the Secret Intelligence Service;

(c) the Government Communications Headquarters;

"statutory function" means a function under or by virtue of an enactment.

III DAT [31]

31 "The law enforcement purposes"

For the purposes of this Part, "the law enforcement purposes" are the purposes of the prevention, investigation, detection or prosecution of criminal offences or the execution of criminal penalties, including the safeguarding against and the prevention of threats to public security.

III DAT [32]

32 Meaning of "controller" and "processor"

(1) In this Part, "controller" means the competent authority which, alone or jointly with others—

(a) determines the purposes and means of the processing of personal data, or

(b) is the controller by virtue of subsection (2).

(2) Where personal data is processed only—

(a) for purposes for which it is required by an enactment to be processed, and

(b) by means by which it is required by an enactment to be processed,

the competent authority on which the obligation to process the data is imposed by the enactment (or, if different, one of the enactments) is the controller.

(3) In this Part, "processor" means any person who processes personal data on behalf of the controller (other than a person who is an employee of the controller).

III DAT [33]

33 Other definitions

(1) This section defines certain other expressions used in this Part.

(2) "Employee", in relation to any person, includes an individual who holds a position (whether paid or unpaid) under the direction and control of that person.

(3) "Personal data breach" means a breach of security leading to the accidental or unlawful destruction, loss, alteration, unauthorised disclosure of, or access to, personal data transmitted, stored or otherwise processed.

(4) "Profiling" means any form of automated processing of personal data consisting of the use of personal data to evaluate certain personal aspects relating to an individual, in particular to analyse or predict aspects concerning that individual's performance at work, economic situation, health, personal preferences, interests, reliability, behaviour, location or movements.

(5) "Recipient", in relation to any personal data, means any person to whom the data is disclosed, whether a third party or not, but it does not include a public authority to whom disclosure is or may be made in the framework of a particular inquiry in accordance with the law.

(6) "Restriction of processing" means the marking of stored personal data with the aim of limiting its processing for the future.

(7) "Third country" means a country or territory other than a member State.

(8) Sections 3 and 205 include definitions of other expressions used in this Part.

CHAPTER 2 PRINCIPLES

III DAT [34]

34 Overview and general duty of controller

(1) This Chapter sets out the six data protection principles as follows—

- (a) section 35(1) sets out the first data protection principle (requirement that processing be lawful and fair);
- (b) section 36(1) sets out the second data protection principle (requirement that purposes of processing be specified, explicit and legitimate);
- (c) section 37 sets out the third data protection principle (requirement that personal data be adequate, relevant and not excessive);
- (d) section 38(1) sets out the fourth data protection principle (requirement that personal data be accurate and kept up to date);
- (e) section 39(1) sets out the fifth data protection principle (requirement that personal data be kept for no longer than is necessary);
- (f) section 40 sets out the sixth data protection principle (requirement that personal data be processed in a secure manner).

(2) In addition—

- (a) each of sections 35, 36, 38 and 39 makes provision to supplement the principle to which it relates, and
- (b) sections 41 and 42 make provision about the safeguards that apply in relation to certain types of processing.

(3) The controller in relation to personal data is responsible for, and must be able to demonstrate, compliance with this Chapter.

III DAT [35]

35 The first data protection principle

(1) The first data protection principle is that the processing of personal data for any of the law enforcement purposes must be lawful and fair.

(2) The processing of personal data for any of the law enforcement purposes is lawful only if and to the extent that it is based on law and either—

- (a) the data subject has given consent to the processing for that purpose, or
- (b) the processing is necessary for the performance of a task carried out for that purpose by a competent authority.

(3) In addition, where the processing for any of the law enforcement purposes is sensitive processing, the processing is permitted only in the two cases set out in subsections (4) and (5).

(4) The first case is where—

- (a) the data subject has given consent to the processing for the law enforcement purpose as mentioned in subsection (2)(a), and
- (b) at the time when the processing is carried out, the controller has an appropriate policy document in place (see section 42).

(5) The second case is where—

- (a) the processing is strictly necessary for the law enforcement purpose,
- (b) the processing meets at least one of the conditions in Schedule 8, and
- (c) at the time when the processing is carried out, the controller has an appropriate policy document in place (see section 42).

(6) The Secretary of State may by regulations amend Schedule 8—

(a) by adding conditions;

(b) by omitting conditions added by regulations under paragraph (a).

(7) Regulations under subsection (6) are subject to the affirmative resolution procedure.

(8) In this section, "sensitive processing" means—

(a) the processing of personal data revealing racial or ethnic origin, political opinions, religious or philosophical beliefs or trade union membership;

(b) the processing of genetic data, or of biometric data, for the purpose of uniquely identifying an individual;

(c) the processing of data concerning health;

(d) the processing of data concerning an individual's sex life or sexual orientation.

III DAT [36]

36 The second data protection principle

(1) The second data protection principle is that—

(a) the law enforcement purpose for which personal data is collected on any occasion must be specified, explicit and legitimate, and

(b) personal data so collected must not be processed in a manner that is incompatible with the purpose for which it was collected.

(2) Paragraph (b) of the second data protection principle is subject to subsections (3) and (4).

(3) Personal data collected for a law enforcement purpose may be processed for any other law enforcement purpose (whether by the controller that collected the data or by another controller) provided that—

(a) the controller is authorised by law to process the data for the other purpose, and

(b) the processing is necessary and proportionate to that other purpose.

(4) Personal data collected for any of the law enforcement purposes may not be processed for a purpose that is not a law enforcement purpose unless the processing is authorised by law.

III DAT [37]

37 The third data protection principle

The third data protection principle is that personal data processed for any of the law enforcement purposes must be adequate, relevant and not excessive in relation to the purpose for which it is processed.

III DAT [38]

38 The fourth data protection principle

(1) The fourth data protection principle is that—

(a) personal data processed for any of the law enforcement purposes must be accurate and, where necessary, kept up to date, and

(b) every reasonable step must be taken to ensure that personal data that is inaccurate, having regard to the law enforcement purpose for which it is processed, is erased or rectified without delay.

(2) In processing personal data for any of the law enforcement purposes, personal data based on facts must, so far as possible, be distinguished from personal data based on personal assessments.

(3) In processing personal data for any of the law enforcement purposes, a clear distinction must, where relevant and as far as possible, be made between personal data relating to different categories of data subject, such as—

- (a) persons suspected of having committed or being about to commit a criminal offence;
- (b) persons convicted of a criminal offence;
- (c) persons who are or may be victims of a criminal offence;
- (d) witnesses or other persons with information about offences.

(4) All reasonable steps must be taken to ensure that personal data which is inaccurate, incomplete or no longer up to date is not transmitted or made available for any of the law enforcement purposes.

(5) For that purpose—

- (a) the quality of personal data must be verified before it is transmitted or made available,
- (b) in all transmissions of personal data, the necessary information enabling the recipient to assess the degree of accuracy, completeness and reliability of the data and the extent to which it is up to date must be included, and
- (c) if, after personal data has been transmitted, it emerges that the data was incorrect or that the transmission was unlawful, the recipient must be notified without delay.

III DAT [39]

39 The fifth data protection principle

(1) The fifth data protection principle is that personal data processed for any of the law enforcement purposes must be kept for no longer than is necessary for the purpose for which it is processed.

(2) Appropriate time limits must be established for the periodic review of the need for the continued storage of personal data for any of the law enforcement purposes.

III DAT [40]

40 The sixth data protection principle

The sixth data protection principle is that personal data processed for any of the law enforcement purposes must be so processed in a manner that ensures appropriate security of the personal data, using appropriate technical or organisational measures (and, in this principle, "appropriate security" includes protection against unauthorised or unlawful processing and against accidental loss, destruction or damage).

III DAT [41]

41 Safeguards: archiving

(1) This section applies in relation to the processing of personal data for a law enforcement purpose where the processing is necessary—

- (a) for archiving purposes in the public interest,
- (b) for scientific or historical research purposes, or
- (c) for statistical purposes.

(2) The processing is not permitted if—

- (a) it is carried out for the purposes of, or in connection with, measures or decisions with respect to a particular data subject, or
- (b) it is likely to cause substantial damage or substantial distress to a data subject.

III DAT [42]

42 Safeguards: sensitive processing

(1) This section applies for the purposes of section 35(4) and (5) (which require a controller to have an appropriate policy document in place when carrying out sensitive processing in reliance on the consent of the data subject or, as the case may be, in reliance on a condition specified in Schedule 8).

(2) The controller has an appropriate policy document in place in relation to the sensitive processing if the controller has produced a document which—

(a) explains the controller's procedures for securing compliance with the data protection principles (see section 34(1)) in connection with sensitive processing in reliance on the consent of the data subject or (as the case may be) in reliance on the condition in question, and

(b) explains the controller's policies as regards the retention and erasure of personal data processed in reliance on the consent of the data subject or (as the case may be) in reliance on the condition in question, giving an indication of how long such personal data is likely to be retained.

(3) Where personal data is processed on the basis that an appropriate policy document is in place, the controller must during the relevant period—

(a) retain the appropriate policy document,

(b) review and (if appropriate) update it from time to time, and

(c) make it available to the Commissioner, on request, without charge.

(4) The record maintained by the controller under section 61(1) and, where the sensitive processing is carried out by a processor on behalf of the controller, the record maintained by the processor under section 61(3) must include the following information—

(a) whether the sensitive processing is carried out in reliance on the consent of the data subject or, if not, which condition in Schedule 8 is relied on,

(b) how the processing satisfies section 35 (lawfulness of processing), and

(c) whether the personal data is retained and erased in accordance with the policies described in subsection (2)(b) and, if it is not, the reasons for not following those policies.

(5) In this section, "relevant period", in relation to sensitive processing in reliance on the consent of the data subject or in reliance on a condition specified in Schedule 8, means a period which—

(a) begins when the controller starts to carry out the sensitive processing in reliance on the data subject's consent or (as the case may be) in reliance on that condition, and

(b) ends at the end of the period of 6 months beginning when the controller ceases to carry out the processing.

CHAPTER 3 RIGHTS OF THE DATA SUBJECT

Overview and scope

III DAT [43]

43 Overview and scope

(1) This Chapter—

(a) imposes general duties on the controller to make information available (see section 44);

(b) confers a right of access by the data subject (see section 45);

(c) confers rights on the data subject with respect to the rectification of personal data and the erasure of personal data or the restriction of its processing (see sections 46 to 48);

(d) regulates automated decision-making (see sections 49 and 50);

(e) makes supplementary provision (see sections 51 to 54).

(2) This Chapter applies only in relation to the processing of personal data for a law enforcement purpose.

(3) But sections 44 to 48 do not apply in relation to the processing of relevant personal data in the course of a criminal investigation or criminal proceedings, including proceedings for the purpose of executing a criminal penalty.

(4) In subsection (3), "relevant personal data" means personal data contained in a judicial decision or in other documents relating to the investigation or proceedings which are created by or on behalf of a court or other judicial authority.

(5) In this Chapter, "the controller", in relation to a data subject, means the controller in relation to personal data relating to the data subject.

Information: controller's general duties

III DAT [44]

44 Information: controller's general duties

(1) The controller must make available to data subjects the following information (whether by making the information generally available to the public or in any other way)—

(a) the identity and the contact details of the controller;

(b) where applicable, the contact details of the data protection officer (see sections 69 to 71);

(c) the purposes for which the controller processes personal data;

(d) the existence of the rights of data subjects to request from the controller—

(i) access to personal data (see section 45),

(ii) rectification of personal data (see section 46), and

(iii) erasure of personal data or the restriction of its processing (see section 47);

(e) the existence of the right to lodge a complaint with the Commissioner and the contact details of the Commissioner.

(2) The controller must also, in specific cases for the purpose of enabling the exercise of a data subject's rights under this Part, give the data subject the following—

(a) information about the legal basis for the processing;

(b) information about the period for which the personal data will be stored or, where that is not possible, about the criteria used to determine that period;

(c) where applicable, information about the categories of recipients of the personal data (including recipients in third countries or international organisations);

(d) such further information as is necessary to enable the exercise of the data subject's rights under this Part.

(3) An example of where further information may be necessary as mentioned in subsection (2)(d) is where the personal data being processed was collected without the knowledge of the data subject.

(4) The controller may restrict, wholly or partly, the provision of information to the data subject under subsection (2) to the extent that and for so long as the restriction is, having regard to the fundamental rights and legitimate interests of the data subject, a necessary and proportionate measure to—

(a) avoid obstructing an official or legal inquiry, investigation or procedure;

(b) avoid prejudicing the prevention, detection, investigation or prosecution of criminal offences or the execution of criminal penalties;

(c) protect public security;

(d) protect national security;

(e) protect the rights and freedoms of others.

(5) Where the provision of information to a data subject under subsection (2) is restricted, wholly or partly, the controller must inform the data subject in writing without undue delay—

(a) that the provision of information has been restricted,

(b) of the reasons for the restriction,

(c) of the data subject's right to make a request to the Commissioner under section 51,

(d) of the data subject's right to lodge a complaint with the Commissioner, and

(e) of the data subject's right to apply to a court under section 167.

(6) Subsection (5)(a) and (b) do not apply to the extent that complying with them would undermine the purpose of the restriction.

(7) The controller must—

(a) record the reasons for a decision to restrict (whether wholly or partly) the provision of information to a data subject under subsection (2), and

(b) if requested to do so by the Commissioner, make the record available to the Commissioner.

Data subject's right of access

III DAT [45]

45 Right of access by the data subject

(1) A data subject is entitled to obtain from the controller—

(a) confirmation as to whether or not personal data concerning him or her is being processed, and

(b) where that is the case, access to the personal data and the information set out in subsection (2).

(2) That information is—

(a) the purposes of and legal basis for the processing;

(b) the categories of personal data concerned;

(c) the recipients or categories of recipients to whom the personal data has been disclosed (including recipients or categories of recipients in third countries or international organisations);

(d) the period for which it is envisaged that the personal data will be stored or, where that is not possible, the criteria used to determine that period;

(e) the existence of the data subject's rights to request from the controller—

(i) rectification of personal data (see section 46), and

(ii) erasure of personal data or the restriction of its processing (see section 47);

(f) the existence of the data subject's right to lodge a complaint with the Commissioner and the contact details of the Commissioner;

(g) communication of the personal data undergoing processing and of any available information as to its origin.

(3) Where a data subject makes a request under subsection (1), the information to which the data subject is entitled must be provided in writing—

(a) without undue delay, and

(b) in any event, before the end of the applicable time period (as to which see section 54).

(4) The controller may restrict, wholly or partly, the rights conferred by subsection (1) to the extent that and for so long as the restriction is, having regard to the fundamental rights and legitimate interests of the data subject, a necessary and proportionate measure to—

(a) avoid obstructing an official or legal inquiry, investigation or procedure;

(b) avoid prejudicing the prevention, detection, investigation or prosecution of criminal offences or the execution of criminal penalties;

(c) protect public security;

(d) protect national security;

(e) protect the rights and freedoms of others.

(5) Where the rights of a data subject under subsection (1) are restricted, wholly or partly, the controller must inform the data subject in writing without undue delay—

(a) that the rights of the data subject have been restricted,

(b) of the reasons for the restriction,

(c) of the data subject's right to make a request to the Commissioner under section 51,

(d) of the data subject's right to lodge a complaint with the Commissioner, and

(e) of the data subject's right to apply to a court under section 167.

(6) Subsection (5)(a) and (b) do not apply to the extent that the provision of the information would undermine the purpose of the restriction.

(7) The controller must—

(a) record the reasons for a decision to restrict (whether wholly or partly) the rights of a data subject under subsection (1), and

(b) if requested to do so by the Commissioner, make the record available to the Commissioner.

DATA SUBJECT'S RIGHTS TO RECTIFICATION OR ERASURE ETC

III DAT [46]

46 Right to rectification

(1) The controller must, if so requested by a data subject, rectify without undue delay inaccurate personal data relating to the data subject.

(2) Where personal data is inaccurate because it is incomplete, the controller must, if so requested by a data subject, complete it.

(3) The duty under subsection (2) may, in appropriate cases, be fulfilled by the provision of a supplementary statement.

(4) Where the controller would be required to rectify personal data under this section but the personal data must be maintained for the purposes of evidence, the controller must (instead of rectifying the personal data) restrict its processing.

III DAT [47]

47 Right to erasure or restriction of processing

(1) The controller must erase personal data without undue delay where—

(a) the processing of the personal data would infringe section 35, 36(1) to (3), 37, 38(1), 39(1), 40, 41 or 42, or

(b) the controller has a legal obligation to erase the data.

(2) Where the controller would be required to erase personal data under subsection (1) but the personal data must be maintained for the purposes of evidence, the controller must (instead of erasing the personal data) restrict its processing.

(3) Where a data subject contests the accuracy of personal data (whether in making a request under this section or section 46 or in any other way), but it is not possible to ascertain whether it is accurate or not, the controller must restrict its processing.

(4) A data subject may request the controller to erase personal data or to restrict its processing (but the duties of the controller under this section apply whether or not such a request is made).

III DAT [48]

48 Rights under section 46 or 47: supplementary

(1) Where a data subject requests the rectification or erasure of personal data or the restriction of its processing, the controller must inform the data subject in writing—

(a) whether the request has been granted, and

(b) if it has been refused—

(i) of the reasons for the refusal,

(ii) of the data subject's right to make a request to the Commissioner under section 51,

(iii) of the data subject's right to lodge a complaint with the Commissioner, and

(iv) of the data subject's right to apply to a court under section 167.

(2) The controller must comply with the duty under subsection (1)—

(a) without undue delay, and

(b) in any event, before the end of the applicable time period (see section 54).

(3) The controller may restrict, wholly or partly, the provision of information to the data subject under subsection (1)(b)(i) to the extent that and for so long as the restriction is, having regard to the fundamental rights and legitimate interests of the data subject, a necessary and proportionate measure to—

(a) avoid obstructing an official or legal inquiry, investigation or procedure;

(b) avoid prejudicing the prevention, detection, investigation or prosecution of criminal offences or the execution of criminal penalties;

(c) protect public security;

(d) protect national security;

(e) protect the rights and freedoms of others.

(4) Where the rights of a data subject under subsection (1) are restricted, wholly or partly, the controller must inform the data subject in writing without undue delay—

(a) that the rights of the data subject have been restricted,

(b) of the reasons for the restriction,

(c) of the data subject's right to lodge a complaint with the Commissioner, and

(d) of the data subject's right to apply to a court under section 167.

(5) Subsection (4)(a) and (b) do not apply to the extent that the provision of the information would undermine the purpose of the restriction.

(6) The controller must—

- (a) record the reasons for a decision to restrict (whether wholly or partly) the provision of information to a data subject under subsection (1)(b)(i), and
- (b) if requested to do so by the Commissioner, make the record available to the Commissioner.

(7) Where the controller rectifies personal data, it must notify the competent authority (if any) from which the inaccurate personal data originated.

(8) In subsection (7), the reference to a competent authority includes (in addition to a competent authority within the meaning of this Part) any person that is a competent authority for the purposes of the Law Enforcement Directive in a member State other than the United Kingdom.

(9) Where the controller rectifies, erases or restricts the processing of personal data which has been disclosed by the controller—

- (a) the controller must notify the recipients, and
- (b) the recipients must similarly rectify, erase or restrict the processing of the personal data (so far as they retain responsibility for it).

(10) Where processing is restricted in accordance with section 47(3), the controller must inform the data subject before lifting the restriction.

AUTOMATED INDIVIDUAL DECISION-MAKING

III DAT [49]

49 Right not to be subject to automated decision-making

(1) A controller may not take a significant decision based solely on automated processing unless that decision is required or authorised by law.

(2) A decision is a "significant decision" for the purpose of this section if, in relation to a data subject, it—

- (a) produces an adverse legal effect concerning the data subject, or
- (b) significantly affects the data subject.

III DAT [50]

50 Automated decision-making authorised by law: safeguards

(1) A decision is a "qualifying significant decision" for the purposes of this section if—

- (a) it is a significant decision in relation to a data subject, and
- (b) it is required or authorised by law.

(2) Where a controller takes a qualifying significant decision in relation to a data subject based solely on automated processing—

- (a) the controller must, as soon as reasonably practicable, notify the data subject in writing that a decision has been taken based solely on automated processing, and
- (b) the data subject may, before the end of the period of 1 month beginning with receipt of the notification, request the controller to—
  - (i) reconsider the decision, or
  - (ii) take a new decision that is not based solely on automated processing.

(3) If a request is made to a controller under subsection (2), the controller must, before the end of the period of 1 month beginning with receipt of the request—

- (a) consider the request, including any information provided by the data subject that is relevant to it,
- (b) comply with the request, and
- (c) by notice in writing inform the data subject of—

(i) the steps taken to comply with the request, and
(ii) the outcome of complying with the request.

(4) The Secretary of State may by regulations make such further provision as the Secretary of State considers appropriate to provide suitable measures to safeguard a data subject's rights, freedoms and legitimate interests in connection with the taking of qualifying significant decisions based solely on automated processing.

(5) Regulations under subsection (4)—
(a) may amend this section, and
(b) are subject to the affirmative resolution procedure.

(6) In this section "significant decision" has the meaning given by section 49(2).

Supplementary

III DAT [51]

51 Exercise of rights through the Commissioner

(1) This section applies where a controller—
(a) restricts under section 44(4) the information provided to the data subject under section 44(2) (duty of the controller to give the data subject additional information),
(b) restricts under section 45(4) the data subject's rights under section 45(1) (right of access), or
(c) refuses a request by the data subject for rectification under section 46 or for erasure or restriction of processing under section 47.

(2) The data subject may—
(a) where subsection (1)(a) or (b) applies, request the Commissioner to check that the restriction imposed by the controller was lawful;
(b) where subsection (1)(c) applies, request the Commissioner to check that the refusal of the data subject's request was lawful.

(3) The Commissioner must take such steps as appear to the Commissioner to be appropriate to respond to a request under subsection (2) (which may include the exercise of any of the powers conferred by sections 142 and 146).

(4) After taking those steps, the Commissioner must inform the data subject—
(a) where subsection (1)(a) or (b) applies, whether the Commissioner is satisfied that the restriction imposed by the controller was lawful;
(b) where subsection (1)(c) applies, whether the Commissioner is satisfied that the controller's refusal of the data subject's request was lawful.

(5) The Commissioner must also inform the data subject of the data subject's right to apply to a court under section 167.

(6) Where the Commissioner is not satisfied as mentioned in subsection (4)(a) or (b), the Commissioner may also inform the data subject of any further steps that the Commissioner is considering taking under Part 6 .

III DAT [52]

52 Form of provision of information etc

(1) The controller must take reasonable steps to ensure that any information that is required by this Chapter to be provided to the data subject is provided in a concise, intelligible and easily accessible form, using clear and plain language.

(2) Subject to subsection (3), the information may be provided in any form, including electronic form.

(3) Where information is provided in response to a request by the data subject under section 45, 46, 47 or 50, the controller must provide the information in the same form as the request where it is practicable to do so.

(4) Where the controller has reasonable doubts about the identity of an individual making a request under section 45, 46 or 47, the controller may—

(a) request the provision of additional information to enable the controller to confirm the identity, and

(b) delay dealing with the request until the identity is confirmed.

(5) Subject to section 53, any information that is required by this Chapter to be provided to the data subject must be provided free of charge.

(6) The controller must facilitate the exercise of the rights of the data subject under sections 45 to 50.

III DAT [53]

53 Manifestly unfounded or excessive requests by the data subject

(1) Where a request from a data subject under section 45, 46, 47 or 50 is manifestly unfounded or excessive, the controller may—

(a) charge a reasonable fee for dealing with the request, or

(b) refuse to act on the request.

(2) An example of a request that may be excessive is one that merely repeats the substance of previous requests.

(3) In any proceedings where there is an issue as to whether a request under section 45, 46, 47 or 50 is manifestly unfounded or excessive, it is for the controller to show that it is.

(4) The Secretary of State may by regulations specify limits on the fees that a controller may charge in accordance with subsection (1)(a).

(5) Regulations under subsection (4) are subject to the negative resolution procedure.

III DAT [54]

54 Meaning of "applicable time period"

(1) This section defines "the applicable time period" for the purposes of sections 45(3)(b) and 48(2)(b).

(2) "The applicable time period" means the period of 1 month, or such longer period as may be specified in regulations, beginning with the relevant time.

(3) "The relevant time" means the latest of the following—

(a) when the controller receives the request in question;

(b) when the controller receives the information (if any) requested in connection with a request under section 52(4);

(c) when the fee (if any) charged in connection with the request under section 53 is paid.

(4) The power to make regulations under subsection (2) is exercisable by the Secretary of State.

(5) Regulations under subsection (2) may not specify a period which is longer than 3 months.

(6) Regulations under subsection (2) are subject to the negative resolution procedure.

CHAPTER 4 CONTROLLER AND PROCESSOR

Overview and scope

III DAT [55]

55 Overview and scope

(1) This Chapter—

(a) sets out the general obligations of controllers and processors (see sections 56 to 65);
(b) sets out specific obligations of controllers and processors with respect to security (see section 66);
(c) sets out specific obligations of controllers and processors with respect to personal data breaches (see sections 67 and 68);
(d) makes provision for the designation, position and tasks of data protection officers (see sections 69 to 71).

(2) This Chapter applies only in relation to the processing of personal data for a law enforcement purpose.

(3) Where a controller is required by any provision of this Chapter to implement appropriate technical and organisational measures, the controller must (in deciding what measures are appropriate) take into account—
(a) the latest developments in technology,
(b) the cost of implementation,
(c) the nature, scope, context and purposes of processing, and
(d) the risks for the rights and freedoms of individuals arising from the processing.

General obligations

III DAT [56]

56 General obligations of the controller

(1) Each controller must implement appropriate technical and organisational measures to ensure, and to be able to demonstrate, that the processing of personal data complies with the requirements of this Part.

(2) Where proportionate in relation to the processing, the measures implemented to comply with the duty under subsection (1) must include appropriate data protection policies.

(3) The technical and organisational measures implemented under subsection (1) must be reviewed and updated where necessary.

III DAT [57]

57 Data protection by design and default

(1) Each controller must implement appropriate technical and organisational measures which are designed—
(a) to implement the data protection principles in an effective manner, and
(b) to integrate into the processing itself the safeguards necessary for that purpose.

(2) The duty under subsection (1) applies both at the time of the determination of the means of processing the data and at the time of the processing itself.

(3) Each controller must implement appropriate technical and organisational measures for ensuring that, by default, only personal data which is necessary for each specific purpose of the processing is processed.

(4) The duty under subsection (3) applies to—
(a) the amount of personal data collected,
(b) the extent of its processing,
(c) the period of its storage, and
(d) its accessibility.

(5) In particular, the measures implemented to comply with the duty under subsection (3) must ensure that, by default, personal data is not made accessible to an indefinite number of people without an individual's intervention.

III DAT [58]

58 Joint controllers

(1) Where two or more competent authorities jointly determine the purposes and means of processing personal data, they are joint controllers for the purposes of this Part.

(2) Joint controllers must, in a transparent manner, determine their respective responsibilities for compliance with this Part by means of an arrangement between them, except to the extent that those responsibilities are determined under or by virtue of an enactment.

(3) The arrangement must designate the controller which is to be the contact point for data subjects.

III DAT [59]

59 Processors

(1) This section applies to the use by a controller of a processor to carry out processing of personal data on behalf of the controller.

(2) The controller may use only a processor who provides guarantees to implement appropriate technical and organisational measures that are sufficient to secure that the processing will—

- (a) meet the requirements of this Part, and
- (b) ensure the protection of the rights of the data subject.

(3) The processor used by the controller may not engage another processor ("a sub-processor") without the prior written authorisation of the controller, which may be specific or general.

(4) Where the controller gives a general written authorisation to a processor, the processor must inform the controller if the processor proposes to add to the number of sub-processors engaged by it or to replace any of them (so that the controller has the opportunity to object to the proposal).

(5) The processing by the processor must be governed by a contract in writing between the controller and the processor setting out the following—

- (a) the subject-matter and duration of the processing;
- (b) the nature and purpose of the processing;
- (c) the type of personal data and categories of data subjects involved;
- (d) the obligations and rights of the controller and processor.

(6) The contract must, in particular, provide that the processor must—

- (a) act only on instructions from the controller,
- (b) ensure that the persons authorised to process personal data are subject to an appropriate duty of confidentiality,
- (c) assist the controller by any appropriate means to ensure compliance with the rights of the data subject under this Part,
- (d) at the end of the provision of services by the processor to the controller—
  - (i) either delete or return to the controller (at the choice of the controller) the personal data to which the services relate, and
  - (ii) delete copies of the personal data unless subject to a legal obligation to store the copies,
- (e) make available to the controller all information necessary to demonstrate compliance with this section, and
- (f) comply with the requirements of this section for engaging sub-processors.

(7) The terms included in the contract in accordance with subsection (6)(a) must provide that the processor may transfer personal data to a third country or international organisation only if instructed by the controller to make the particular transfer.

(8) If a processor determines, in breach of this Part, the purposes and means of processing, the processor is to be treated for the purposes of this Part as a controller in respect of that processing.

III DAT [60]

60 Processing under the authority of the controller or processor

A processor, and any person acting under the authority of a controller or processor, who has access to personal data may not process the data except—

- (a) on instructions from the controller, or
- (b) to comply with a legal obligation.

III DAT [61]

61 Records of processing activities

(1) Each controller must maintain a record of all categories of processing activities for which the controller is responsible.

(2) The controller's record must contain the following information—

- (a) the name and contact details of the controller;
- (b) where applicable, the name and contact details of the joint controller;
- (c) where applicable, the name and contact details of the data protection officer;
- (d) the purposes of the processing;
- (e) the categories of recipients to whom personal data has been or will be disclosed (including recipients in third countries or international organisations);
- (f) a description of the categories of—
  - (i) data subject, and
  - (ii) personal data;
- (g) where applicable, details of the use of profiling;
- (h) where applicable, the categories of transfers of personal data to a third country or an international organisation;
- (i) an indication of the legal basis for the processing operations, including transfers, for which the personal data is intended;
- (j) where possible, the envisaged time limits for erasure of the different categories of personal data;
- (k) where possible, a general description of the technical and organisational security measures referred to in section 66.

(3) Each processor must maintain a record of all categories of processing activities carried out on behalf of a controller.

(4) The processor's record must contain the following information—

- (a) the name and contact details of the processor and of any other processors engaged by the processor in accordance with section 59(3);
- (b) the name and contact details of the controller on behalf of which the processor is acting;
- (c) where applicable, the name and contact details of the data protection officer;
- (d) the categories of processing carried out on behalf of the controller;
- (e) where applicable, details of transfers of personal data to a third country or an international organisation where explicitly instructed to

do so by the controller, including the identification of that third country or international organisation;

(f) where possible, a general description of the technical and organisational security measures referred to in section 66.

(5) The controller and the processor must make the records kept under this section available to the Commissioner on request.

III DAT [62]

62 Logging

(1) A controller (or, where personal data is processed on behalf of the controller by a processor, the processor) must keep logs for at least the following processing operations in automated processing systems—

(a) collection;
(b) alteration;
(c) consultation;
(d) disclosure (including transfers);
(e) combination;
(f) erasure.

(2) The logs of consultation must make it possible to establish—

(a) the justification for, and date and time of, the consultation, and
(b) so far as possible, the identity of the person who consulted the data.

(3) The logs of disclosure must make it possible to establish—

(a) the justification for, and date and time of, the disclosure, and
(b) so far as possible—
  (i) the identity of the person who disclosed the data, and
  (ii) the identity of the recipients of the data.

(4) The logs kept under subsection (1) may be used only for one or more of the following purposes—

(a) to verify the lawfulness of processing;
(b) to assist with self-monitoring by the controller or (as the case may be) the processor, including the conduct of internal disciplinary proceedings;
(c) to ensure the integrity and security of personal data;
(d) the purposes of criminal proceedings.

(5) The controller or (as the case may be) the processor must make the logs available to the Commissioner on request.

III DAT [63]

63 Co-operation with the Commissioner

Each controller and each processor must co-operate, on request, with the Commissioner in the performance of the Commissioner's tasks.

III DAT [64]

64 Data protection impact assessment

(1) Where a type of processing is likely to result in a high risk to the rights and freedoms of individuals, the controller must, prior to the processing, carry out a data protection impact assessment.

(2) A data protection impact assessment is an assessment of the impact of the envisaged processing operations on the protection of personal data.

(3) A data protection impact assessment must include the following—

(a) a general description of the envisaged processing operations;
(b) an assessment of the risks to the rights and freedoms of data subjects;

(c) the measures envisaged to address those risks;

(d) safeguards, security measures and mechanisms to ensure the protection of personal data and to demonstrate compliance with this Part, taking into account the rights and legitimate interests of the data subjects and other persons concerned.

(4) In deciding whether a type of processing is likely to result in a high risk to the rights and freedoms of individuals, the controller must take into account the nature, scope, context and purposes of the processing.

III DAT [65]

65 Prior consultation with the Commissioner

(1) This section applies where a controller intends to create a filing system and process personal data forming part of it.

(2) The controller must consult the Commissioner prior to the processing if a data protection impact assessment prepared under section 64 indicates that the processing of the data would result in a high risk to the rights and freedoms of individuals (in the absence of measures to mitigate the risk).

(3) Where the controller is required to consult the Commissioner under subsection (2), the controller must give the Commissioner—

(a) the data protection impact assessment prepared under section 64, and

(b) any other information requested by the Commissioner to enable the Commissioner to make an assessment of the compliance of the processing with the requirements of this Part.

(4) Where the Commissioner is of the opinion that the intended processing referred to in subsection (1) would infringe any provision of this Part, the Commissioner must provide written advice to the controller and, where the controller is using a processor, to the processor.

(5) The written advice must be provided before the end of the period of 6 weeks beginning with receipt of the request for consultation by the controller or the processor.

(6) The Commissioner may extend the period of 6 weeks by a further period of 1 month, taking into account the complexity of the intended processing.

(7) If the Commissioner extends the period of 6 weeks, the Commissioner must—

(a) inform the controller and, where applicable, the processor of any such extension before the end of the period of 1 month beginning with receipt of the request for consultation, and

(b) provide reasons for the delay.

Obligations relating to security

III DAT [66]

66 Security of processing

(1) Each controller and each processor must implement appropriate technical and organisational measures to ensure a level of security appropriate to the risks arising from the processing of personal data.

(2) In the case of automated processing, each controller and each processor must, following an evaluation of the risks, implement measures designed to—

(a) prevent unauthorised processing or unauthorised interference with the systems used in connection with it,

(b) ensure that it is possible to establish the precise details of any processing that takes place,

(c) ensure that any systems used in connection with the processing function properly and may, in the case of interruption, be restored, and
(d) ensure that stored personal data cannot be corrupted if a system used in connection with the processing malfunctions.

Obligations relating to personal data breaches

III DAT [67]

67 Notification of a personal data breach to the Commissioner

(1) If a controller becomes aware of a personal data breach in relation to personal data for which the controller is responsible, the controller must notify the breach to the Commissioner—
(a) without undue delay, and
(b) where feasible, not later than 72 hours after becoming aware of it.

(2) Subsection (1) does not apply if the personal data breach is unlikely to result in a risk to the rights and freedoms of individuals.

(3) Where the notification to the Commissioner is not made within 72 hours, the notification must be accompanied by reasons for the delay.

(4) Subject to subsection (5), the notification must include—
(a) a description of the nature of the personal data breach including, where possible, the categories and approximate number of data subjects concerned and the categories and approximate number of personal data records concerned;
(b) the name and contact details of the data protection officer or other contact point from whom more information can be obtained;
(c) a description of the likely consequences of the personal data breach;
(d) a description of the measures taken or proposed to be taken by the controller to address the personal data breach, including, where appropriate, measures to mitigate its possible adverse effects.

(5) Where and to the extent that it is not possible to provide all the information mentioned in subsection (4) at the same time, the information may be provided in phases without undue further delay.

(6) The controller must record the following information in relation to a personal data breach—
(a) the facts relating to the breach,
(b) its effects, and
(c) the remedial action taken.

(7) The information mentioned in subsection (6) must be recorded in such a way as to enable the Commissioner to verify compliance with this section.

(8) Where a personal data breach involves personal data that has been transmitted by or to a person who is a controller under the law of another member State, the information mentioned in subsection (6) must be communicated to that person without undue delay.

(9) If a processor becomes aware of a personal data breach (in relation to personal data processed by the processor), the processor must notify the controller without undue delay.

III DAT [68]

68 Communication of a personal data breach to the data subject

(1) Where a personal data breach is likely to result in a high risk to the rights and freedoms of individuals, the controller must inform the data subject of the breach without undue delay.

(2) The information given to the data subject must include the following—

(a) a description of the nature of the breach;
(b) the name and contact details of the data protection officer or other contact point from whom more information can be obtained;
(c) a description of the likely consequences of the personal data breach;
(d) a description of the measures taken or proposed to be taken by the controller to address the personal data breach, including, where appropriate, measures to mitigate its possible adverse effects.

(3) The duty under subsection (1) does not apply where—
(a) the controller has implemented appropriate technological and organisational protection measures which were applied to the personal data affected by the breach,
(b) the controller has taken subsequent measures which ensure that the high risk to the rights and freedoms of data subjects referred to in subsection (1) is no longer likely to materialise, or
(c) it would involve a disproportionate effort.

(4) An example of a case which may fall within subsection (3)(a) is where measures that render personal data unintelligible to any person not authorised to access the data have been applied, such as encryption.

(5) In a case falling within subsection (3)(c) (but not within subsection (3)(a) or (b)), the information mentioned in subsection (2) must be made available to the data subject in another equally effective way, for example, by means of a public communication.

(6) Where the controller has not informed the data subject of the breach the Commissioner, on being notified under section 67 and after considering the likelihood of the breach resulting in a high risk, may—
(a) require the controller to notify the data subject of the breach, or
(b) decide that the controller is not required to do so because any of paragraphs (a) to (c) of subsection (3) applies.

(7) The controller may restrict, wholly or partly, the provision of information to the data subject under subsection (1) to the extent that and for so long as the restriction is, having regard to the fundamental rights and legitimate interests of the data subject, a necessary and proportionate measure to—
(a) avoid obstructing an official or legal inquiry, investigation or procedure;
(b) avoid prejudicing the prevention, detection, investigation or prosecution of criminal offences or the execution of criminal penalties;
(c) protect public security;
(d) protect national security;
(e) protect the rights and freedoms of others.

(8) Subsection (6) does not apply where the controller's decision not to inform the data subject of the breach was made in reliance on subsection (7).

(9) The duties in section 52(1) and (2) apply in relation to information that the controller is required to provide to the data subject under this section as they apply in relation to information that the controller is required to provide to the data subject under Chapter 3 .

Data protection officers

III DAT [69]

69 Designation of a data protection officer

(1) The controller must designate a data protection officer, unless the controller is a court, or other judicial authority, acting in its judicial capacity.

(2) When designating a data protection officer, the controller must have regard to the professional qualities of the proposed officer, in particular—

(a) the proposed officer's expert knowledge of data protection law and practice, and

(b) the ability of the proposed officer to perform the tasks mentioned in section 71.

(3) The same person may be designated as a data protection officer by several controllers, taking account of their organisational structure and size.

(4) The controller must publish the contact details of the data protection officer and communicate these to the Commissioner.

III DAT [70]

70 Position of data protection officer

(1) The controller must ensure that the data protection officer is involved, properly and in a timely manner, in all issues which relate to the protection of personal data.

(2) The controller must provide the data protection officer with the necessary resources and access to personal data and processing operations to enable the data protection officer to—

(a) perform the tasks mentioned in section 71, and

(b) maintain his or her expert knowledge of data protection law and practice.

(3) The controller—

(a) must ensure that the data protection officer does not receive any instructions regarding the performance of the tasks mentioned in section 71;

(b) must ensure that the data protection officer does not perform a task or fulfil a duty other than those mentioned in this Part where such task or duty would result in a conflict of interests;

(c) must not dismiss or penalise the data protection officer for performing the tasks mentioned in section 71.

(4) A data subject may contact the data protection officer with regard to all issues relating to—

(a) the processing of that data subject's personal data, or

(b) the exercise of that data subject's rights under this Part.

(5) The data protection officer, in the performance of this role, must report to the highest management level of the controller.

III DAT [71]

71 Tasks of data protection officer

(1) The controller must entrust the data protection officer with at least the following tasks—

(a) informing and advising the controller, any processor engaged by the controller, and any employee of the controller who carries out processing of personal data, of that person's obligations under this Part,

(b) providing advice on the carrying out of a data protection impact assessment under section 64 and monitoring compliance with that section,

(c) co-operating with the Commissioner,

(d) acting as the contact point for the Commissioner on issues relating to processing, including in relation to the consultation mentioned in section 65, and consulting with the Commissioner, where appropriate, in relation to any other matter,

(e) monitoring compliance with policies of the controller in relation to the protection of personal data, and

(f) monitoring compliance by the controller with this Part.

(2) In relation to the policies mentioned in subsection (1)(e), the data protection officer's tasks include—

(a) assigning responsibilities under those policies,

(b) raising awareness of those policies,

(c) training staff involved in processing operations, and

(d) conducting audits required under those policies.

(3) In performing the tasks set out in subsections (1) and (2), the data protection officer must have regard to the risks associated with processing operations, taking into account the nature, scope, context and purposes of processing.

CHAPTER 5 TRANSFERS OF PERSONAL DATA TO THIRD COUNTRIES ETC

Overview and interpretation

III DAT [72]

72 Overview and interpretation

(1) This Chapter deals with the transfer of personal data to third countries or international organisations, as follows—

(a) sections 73 to 76 set out the general conditions that apply;

(b) section 77 sets out the special conditions that apply where the intended recipient of personal data is not a relevant authority in a third country or an international organisation;

(c) section 78 makes special provision about subsequent transfers of personal data.

(2) In this Chapter, "relevant authority", in relation to a third country, means any person based in a third country that has (in that country) functions comparable to those of a competent authority.

General principles for transfers

III DAT [73]

73 General principles for transfers of personal data

(1) A controller may not transfer personal data to a third country or to an international organisation unless—

(a) the three conditions set out in subsections (2) to (4) are met, and

(b) in a case where the personal data was originally transmitted or otherwise made available to the controller or another competent authority by a member State other than the United Kingdom, that member State, or any person based in that member State which is a competent authority for the purposes of the Law Enforcement Directive, has authorised the transfer in accordance with the law of the member State.

(2) Condition 1 is that the transfer is necessary for any of the law enforcement purposes.

(3) Condition 2 is that the transfer—

(a) is based on an adequacy decision (see section 74),

(b) if not based on an adequacy decision, is based on there being appropriate safeguards (see section 75), or

(c) if not based on an adequacy decision or on there being appropriate safeguards, is based on special circumstances (see section 76).

(4) Condition 3 is that—

(a) the intended recipient is a relevant authority in a third country or an international organisation that is a relevant international organisation, or

(b) in a case where the controller is a competent authority specified in any of paragraphs 5 to 17, 21, 24 to 28, 34 to 51, 54 and 56 of Schedule 7—

(i) the intended recipient is a person in a third country other than a relevant authority, and

(ii) the additional conditions in section 77 are met.

(5) Authorisation is not required as mentioned in subsection (1)(b) if—

(a) the transfer is necessary for the prevention of an immediate and serious threat either to the public security of a member State or a third country or to the essential interests of a member State, and

(b) the authorisation cannot be obtained in good time.

(6) Where a transfer is made without the authorisation mentioned in subsection (1)(b), the authority in the member State which would have been responsible for deciding whether to authorise the transfer must be informed without delay.

(7) In this section, "relevant international organisation" means an international organisation that carries out functions for any of the law enforcement purposes.

III DAT [74]

74 Transfers on the basis of an adequacy decision

A transfer of personal data to a third country or an international organisation is based on an adequacy decision where—

(a) the European Commission has decided, in accordance with Article 36 of the Law Enforcement Directive, that—

(i) the third country or a territory or one or more specified sectors within that third country, or

(ii) (as the case may be) the international organisation,

ensures an adequate level of protection of personal data, and

(b) that decision has not been repealed or suspended, or amended in a way that demonstrates that the Commission no longer considers there to be an adequate level of protection of personal data.

III DAT [75]

75 Transfers on the basis of appropriate safeguards

(1) A transfer of personal data to a third country or an international organisation is based on there being appropriate safeguards where—

(a) a legal instrument containing appropriate safeguards for the protection of personal data binds the intended recipient of the data, or

(b) the controller, having assessed all the circumstances surrounding transfers of that type of personal data to the third country or international organisation, concludes that appropriate safeguards exist to protect the data.

(2) The controller must inform the Commissioner about the categories of data transfers that take place in reliance on subsection (1)(b).

(3) Where a transfer of data takes place in reliance on subsection (1)—

(a) the transfer must be documented,

(b) the documentation must be provided to the Commissioner on request, and

(c) the documentation must include, in particular—
 (i) the date and time of the transfer,
 (ii) the name of and any other pertinent information about the recipient,
 (iii) the justification for the transfer, and
 (iv) a description of the personal data transferred.

III DAT [76]

76 Transfers on the basis of special circumstances

(1) A transfer of personal data to a third country or international organisation is based on special circumstances where the transfer is necessary—

(a) to protect the vital interests of the data subject or another person,
(b) to safeguard the legitimate interests of the data subject,
(c) for the prevention of an immediate and serious threat to the public security of a member State or a third country,
(d) in individual cases for any of the law enforcement purposes, or
(e) in individual cases for a legal purpose.

(2) But subsection (1)(d) and (e) do not apply if the controller determines that fundamental rights and freedoms of the data subject override the public interest in the transfer.

(3) Where a transfer of data takes place in reliance on subsection (1)—

(a) the transfer must be documented,
(b) the documentation must be provided to the Commissioner on request, and
(c) the documentation must include, in particular—
 (i) the date and time of the transfer,
 (ii) the name of and any other pertinent information about the recipient,
 (iii) the justification for the transfer, and
 (iv) a description of the personal data transferred.

(4) For the purposes of this section, a transfer is necessary for a legal purpose if—

(a) it is necessary for the purpose of, or in connection with, any legal proceedings (including prospective legal proceedings) relating to any of the law enforcement purposes,
(b) it is necessary for the purpose of obtaining legal advice in relation to any of the law enforcement purposes, or
(c) it is otherwise necessary for the purposes of establishing, exercising or defending legal rights in relation to any of the law enforcement purposes.

Transfers to particular recipients

III DAT [77]

77 Transfers of personal data to persons other than relevant authorities

(1) The additional conditions referred to in section 73(4)(b)(ii) are the following four conditions.

(2) Condition 1 is that the transfer is strictly necessary in a specific case for the performance of a task of the transferring controller as provided by law for any of the law enforcement purposes.

(3) Condition 2 is that the transferring controller has determined that there are no fundamental rights and freedoms of the data subject concerned that override the public interest necessitating the transfer.

DATA PROTECTION

(4) Condition 3 is that the transferring controller considers that the transfer of the personal data to a relevant authority in the third country would be ineffective or inappropriate (for example, where the transfer could not be made in sufficient time to enable its purpose to be fulfilled).

(5) Condition 4 is that the transferring controller informs the intended recipient of the specific purpose or purposes for which the personal data may, so far as necessary, be processed.

(6) Where personal data is transferred to a person in a third country other than a relevant authority, the transferring controller must inform a relevant authority in that third country without undue delay of the transfer, unless this would be ineffective or inappropriate.

(7) The transferring controller must—

(a) document any transfer to a recipient in a third country other than a relevant authority, and

(b) inform the Commissioner about the transfer.

(8) This section does not affect the operation of any international agreement in force between member States and third countries in the field of judicial co-operation in criminal matters and police co-operation.

Subsequent transfers

III DAT [78]

78 Subsequent transfers

(1) Where personal data is transferred in accordance with section 73, the transferring controller must make it a condition of the transfer that the data is not to be further transferred to a third country or international organisation without the authorisation of the transferring controller or another competent authority.

(2) A competent authority may give an authorisation under subsection (1) only where the further transfer is necessary for a law enforcement purpose.

(3) In deciding whether to give the authorisation, the competent authority must take into account (among any other relevant factors)—

(a) the seriousness of the circumstances leading to the request for authorisation,

(b) the purpose for which the personal data was originally transferred, and

(c) the standards for the protection of personal data that apply in the third country or international organisation to which the personal data would be transferred.

(4) In a case where the personal data was originally transmitted or otherwise made available to the transferring controller or another competent authority by a member State other than the United Kingdom, an authorisation may not be given under subsection (1) unless that member State, or any person based in that member State which is a competent authority for the purposes of the Law Enforcement Directive, has authorised the transfer in accordance with the law of the member State.

(5) Authorisation is not required as mentioned in subsection (4) if—

(a) the transfer is necessary for the prevention of an immediate and serious threat either to the public security of a member State or a third country or to the essential interests of a member State, and

(b) the authorisation cannot be obtained in good time.

(6) Where a transfer is made without the authorisation mentioned in subsection (4), the authority in the member State which would have been responsible for deciding whether to authorise the transfer must be informed without delay.

CHAPTER 6 SUPPLEMENTARY

III DAT [79]

79 National security: certificate

(1) A Minister of the Crown may issue a certificate certifying, for the purposes of section 44(4), 45(4), 48(3) or 68(7), that a restriction is a necessary and proportionate measure to protect national security.

(2) The certificate may—

(a) relate to a specific restriction (described in the certificate) which a controller has imposed or is proposing to impose under section 44(4), 45(4), 48(3) or 68(7), or

(b) identify any restriction to which it relates by means of a general description.

(3) Subject to subsection (6), a certificate issued under subsection (1) is conclusive evidence that the specific restriction or (as the case may be) any restriction falling within the general description is, or at any time was, a necessary and proportionate measure to protect national security.

(4) A certificate issued under subsection (1) may be expressed to have prospective effect.

(5) Any person directly affected by the issuing of a certificate under subsection (1) may appeal to the Tribunal against the certificate.

(6) If, on an appeal under subsection (5), the Tribunal finds that, applying the principles applied by a court on an application for judicial review, the Minister did not have reasonable grounds for issuing the certificate, the Tribunal may—

(a) allow the appeal, and

(b) quash the certificate.

(7) Where in any proceedings under or by virtue of this Act, it is claimed by a controller that a restriction falls within a general description in a certificate issued under subsection (1), any other party to the proceedings may appeal to the Tribunal on the ground that the restriction does not fall within that description.

(8) But, subject to any determination under subsection (9), the restriction is to be conclusively presumed to fall within the general description.

(9) On an appeal under subsection (7), the Tribunal may determine that the certificate does not so apply.

(10) A document purporting to be a certificate under subsection (1) is to be—

(a) received in evidence, and

(b) deemed to be such a certificate unless the contrary is proved.

(11) A document which purports to be certified by or on behalf of a Minister of the Crown as a true copy of a certificate issued by that Minister under subsection (1) is—

(a) in any legal proceedings, evidence of that certificate, and

(b) in any legal proceedings in Scotland, sufficient evidence of that certificate.

(12) The power conferred by subsection (1) on a Minister of the Crown is exercisable only by—

(a) a Minister who is a member of the Cabinet, or

(b) the Attorney General or the Advocate General for Scotland.

(13) No power conferred by any provision of Part 6 may be exercised in relation to the imposition of—

(a) a specific restriction in a certificate under subsection (1), or

(b) a restriction falling within a general description in such a certificate.

III DAT [80]

80 Special processing restrictions

(1) Subsections (3) and (4) apply where, for a law enforcement purpose, a controller transmits or otherwise makes available personal data to an EU recipient or a non-EU recipient.

(2) In this section—

"EU recipient" means—

(a) a recipient in a member State other than the United Kingdom, or

(b) an agency, office or body established pursuant to Chapters 4 and 5 of Title V of the Treaty on the Functioning of the European Union;

"non-EU recipient" means—

(a) a recipient in a third country, or

(b) an international organisation.

(3) The controller must consider whether, if the personal data had instead been transmitted or otherwise made available within the United Kingdom to another competent authority, processing of the data by the other competent authority would have been subject to any restrictions by virtue of any enactment or rule of law.

(4) Where that would be the case, the controller must inform the EU recipient or non-EU recipient that the data is transmitted or otherwise made available subject to compliance by that person with the same restrictions (which must be set out in the information given to that person).

(5) Except as provided by subsection (4), the controller may not impose restrictions on the processing of personal data transmitted or otherwise made available by the controller to an EU recipient.

(6) Subsection (7) applies where—

(a) a competent authority for the purposes of the Law Enforcement Directive in a member State other than the United Kingdom transmits or otherwise makes available personal data to a controller for a law enforcement purpose, and

(b) the competent authority in the other member State informs the controller, in accordance with any law of that member State which implements Article 9(3) and (4) of the Law Enforcement Directive, that the data is transmitted or otherwise made available subject to compliance by the controller with restrictions set out by the competent authority.

(7) The controller must comply with the restrictions.

III DAT [81]

81 Reporting of infringements

(1) Each controller must implement effective mechanisms to encourage the reporting of an infringement of this Part.

(2) The mechanisms implemented under subsection (1) must provide that an infringement may be reported to any of the following persons—

(a) the controller;

(b) the Commissioner.

(3) The mechanisms implemented under subsection (1) must include—

(a) raising awareness of the protections provided by Part 4A of the Employment Rights Act 1996 and Part 5A of the Employment Rights (Northern Ireland) Order 1996 (SI 1996/1919 (NI 16)), and

(b) such other protections for a person who reports an infringement of this Part as the controller considers appropriate.

(4) A person who reports an infringement of this Part does not breach—

(a) an obligation of confidence owed by the person, or

(b) any other restriction on the disclosure of information (however imposed).

(5) Subsection (4) does not apply if or to the extent that the report includes a disclosure which is prohibited by any of Parts 1 to 7 or Chapter 1 of Part 9 of the Investigatory Powers Act 2016.

(6) Until the repeal of Part 1 of the Regulation of Investigatory Powers Act 2000 by paragraphs 45 and 54 of Schedule 10 to the Investigatory Powers Act 2016 is fully in force, subsection (5) has effect as if it included a reference to that Part.

PART 4
INTELLIGENCE SERVICES PROCESSING

CHAPTER 1 SCOPE AND DEFINITIONS

SCOPE

III DAT [82]

82 Processing to which this Part applies

(1) This Part applies to—

(a) the processing by an intelligence service of personal data wholly or partly by automated means, and

(b) the processing by an intelligence service otherwise than by automated means of personal data which forms part of a filing system or is intended to form part of a filing system.

(2) In this Part, "intelligence service" means—

(a) the Security Service;

(b) the Secret Intelligence Service;

(c) the Government Communications Headquarters.

(3) A reference in this Part to the processing of personal data is to processing to which this Part applies.

III DAT [82.1]

The intelligence services As this section makes clear, Part 4 provides a special set of rules for the processing of personal data by the Security Service, the Secret intelligence Service and GCHQ. It is to be read with Schedules 9, 10 and 11.

DEFINITIONS

III DAT [83]

83 Meaning of "controller" and "processor"

(1) In this Part, "controller" means the intelligence service which, alone or jointly with others—

(a) determines the purposes and means of the processing of personal data, or

(b) is the controller by virtue of subsection (2).

(2) Where personal data is processed only—

(a) for purposes for which it is required by an enactment to be processed, and

(b) by means by which it is required by an enactment to be processed,

the intelligence service on which the obligation to process the data is imposed by the enactment (or, if different, one of the enactments) is the controller.

(3) In this Part, "processor" means any person who processes personal data on behalf of the controller (other than a person who is an employee of the controller).

III DAT [84]

84 Other definitions

(1) This section defines other expressions used in this Part.

(2) "Consent", in relation to the processing of personal data relating to an individual, means a freely given, specific, informed and unambiguous indication of the individual's wishes by which the individual, by a statement or by a clear affirmative action, signifies agreement to the processing of the personal data.

(3) "Employee", in relation to any person, includes an individual who holds a position (whether paid or unpaid) under the direction and control of that person.

(4) "Personal data breach" means a breach of security leading to the accidental or unlawful destruction, loss, alteration, unauthorised disclosure of, or access to, personal data transmitted, stored or otherwise processed.

(5) "Recipient", in relation to any personal data, means any person to whom the data is disclosed, whether a third party or not, but it does not include a person to whom disclosure is or may be made in the framework of a particular inquiry in accordance with the law.

(6) "Restriction of processing" means the marking of stored personal data with the aim of limiting its processing for the future.

(7) Sections 3 and 205 include definitions of other expressions used in this Part.

CHAPTER 2 PRINCIPLES

OVERVIEW

III DAT [85]

85 Overview

(1) This Chapter sets out the six data protection principles as follows—

- (a) section 86 sets out the first data protection principle (requirement that processing be lawful, fair and transparent);
- (b) section 87 sets out the second data protection principle (requirement that the purposes of processing be specified, explicit and legitimate);
- (c) section 88 sets out the third data protection principle (requirement that personal data be adequate, relevant and not excessive);
- (d) section 89 sets out the fourth data protection principle (requirement that personal data be accurate and kept up to date);
- (e) section 90 sets out the fifth data protection principle (requirement that personal data be kept for no longer than is necessary);
- (f) section 91 sets out the sixth data protection principle (requirement that personal data be processed in a secure manner).

(2) Each of sections 86, 87 and 91 makes provision to supplement the principle to which it relates.

THE DATA PROTECTION PRINCIPLES

III DAT [86]

86 The first data protection principle

(1) The first data protection principle is that the processing of personal data must be—

- (a) lawful, and

(b) fair and transparent.

(2) The processing of personal data is lawful only if and to the extent that—

(a) at least one of the conditions in Schedule 9 is met, and

(b) in the case of sensitive processing, at least one of the conditions in Schedule 10 is also met.

(3) The Secretary of State may by regulations amend Schedule 10—

(a) by adding conditions;

(b) by omitting conditions added by regulations under paragraph (a).

(4) Regulations under subsection (3) are subject to the affirmative resolution procedure.

(5) In determining whether the processing of personal data is fair and transparent, regard is to be had to the method by which it is obtained.

(6) For the purposes of subsection (5), data is to be treated as obtained fairly and transparently if it consists of information obtained from a person who—

(a) is authorised by an enactment to supply it, or

(b) is required to supply it by an enactment or by an international obligation of the United Kingdom.

(7) In this section, "sensitive processing" means—

(a) the processing of personal data revealing racial or ethnic origin, political opinions, religious or philosophical beliefs or trade union membership;

(b) the processing of genetic data for the purpose of uniquely identifying an individual;

(c) the processing of biometric data for the purpose of uniquely identifying an individual;

(d) the processing of data concerning health;

(e) the processing of data concerning an individual's sex life or sexual orientation;

(f) the processing of personal data as to—

(i) the commission or alleged commission of an offence by an individual, or

(ii) proceedings for an offence committed or alleged to have been committed by an individual, the disposal of such proceedings or the sentence of a court in such proceedings.

III DAT [87]

87 The second data protection principle

(1) The second data protection principle is that—

(a) the purpose for which personal data is collected on any occasion must be specified, explicit and legitimate, and

(b) personal data so collected must not be processed in a manner that is incompatible with the purpose for which it is collected.

(2) Paragraph (b) of the second data protection principle is subject to subsections (3) and (4).

(3) Personal data collected by a controller for one purpose may be processed for any other purpose of the controller that collected the data or any purpose of another controller provided that—

(a) the controller is authorised by law to process the data for that purpose, and

(b) the processing is necessary and proportionate to that other purpose.

(4) Processing of personal data is to be regarded as compatible with the purpose for which it is collected if the processing—

(a) consists of—

(i) processing for archiving purposes in the public interest,
(ii) processing for the purposes of scientific or historical research, or
(iii) processing for statistical purposes, and

(b) is subject to appropriate safeguards for the rights and freedoms of the data subject.

III DAT [88]

88 The third data protection principle

The third data protection principle is that personal data must be adequate, relevant and not excessive in relation to the purpose for which it is processed.

III DAT [89]

89 The fourth data protection principle

The fourth data protection principle is that personal data undergoing processing must be accurate and, where necessary, kept up to date.

III DAT [90]

90 The fifth data protection principle

The fifth data protection principle is that personal data must be kept for no longer than is necessary for the purpose for which it is processed.

III DAT [91]

91 The sixth data protection principle

(1) The sixth data protection principle is that personal data must be processed in a manner that includes taking appropriate security measures as regards risks that arise from processing personal data.

(2) The risks referred to in subsection (1) include (but are not limited to) accidental or unauthorised access to, or destruction, loss, use, modification or disclosure of, personal data.

CHAPTER 3 RIGHTS OF THE DATA SUBJECT

Overview

III DAT [92]

92 Overview

(1) This Chapter sets out the rights of the data subject as follows—

(a) section 93 deals with the information to be made available to the data subject;
(b) sections 94 and 95 deal with the right of access by the data subject;
(c) sections 96 and 97 deal with rights in relation to automated processing;
(d) section 98 deals with the right to information about decision-making;
(e) section 99 deals with the right to object to processing;
(f) section 100 deals with rights to rectification and erasure of personal data.

(2) In this Chapter, "the controller", in relation to a data subject, means the controller in relation to personal data relating to the data subject.

Rights

III DAT [93]

93 Right to information

(1) The controller must give a data subject the following information—

(a) the identity and the contact details of the controller;

(b) the legal basis on which, and the purposes for which, the controller processes personal data;

(c) the categories of personal data relating to the data subject that are being processed;

(d) the recipients or the categories of recipients of the personal data (if applicable);

(e) the right to lodge a complaint with the Commissioner and the contact details of the Commissioner;

(f) how to exercise rights under this Chapter;

(g) any other information needed to secure that the personal data is processed fairly and transparently.

(2) The controller may comply with subsection (1) by making information generally available, where the controller considers it appropriate to do so.

(3) The controller is not required under subsection (1) to give a data subject information that the data subject already has.

(4) Where personal data relating to a data subject is collected by or on behalf of the controller from a person other than the data subject, the requirement in subsection (1) has effect, in relation to the personal data so collected, with the following exceptions—

(a) the requirement does not apply in relation to processing that is authorised by an enactment;

(b) the requirement does not apply in relation to the data subject if giving the information to the data subject would be impossible or involve disproportionate effort.

III DAT [94]

94 Right of access

(1) An individual is entitled to obtain from a controller—

(a) confirmation as to whether or not personal data concerning the individual is being processed, and

(b) where that is the case—

(i) communication, in intelligible form, of the personal data of which that individual is the data subject, and

(ii) the information set out in subsection (2).

(2) That information is—

(a) the purposes of and legal basis for the processing;

(b) the categories of personal data concerned;

(c) the recipients or categories of recipients to whom the personal data has been disclosed;

(d) the period for which the personal data is to be preserved;

(e) the existence of a data subject's rights to rectification and erasure of personal data (see section 100);

(f) the right to lodge a complaint with the Commissioner and the contact details of the Commissioner;

(g) any information about the origin of the personal data concerned.

(3) A controller is not obliged to provide information under this section unless the controller has received such reasonable fee as the controller may require, subject to subsection (4).

(4) The Secretary of State may by regulations—

(a) specify cases in which a controller may not charge a fee;

(b) specify the maximum amount of a fee.

(5) Where a controller—

(a) reasonably requires further information—

(i) in order that the controller be satisfied as to the identity of the individual making a request under subsection (1), or

(ii) to locate the information which that individual seeks, and

(b) has informed that individual of that requirement,

the controller is not obliged to comply with the request unless the controller is supplied with that further information.

(6) Where a controller cannot comply with the request without disclosing information relating to another individual who can be identified from that information, the controller is not obliged to comply with the request unless—

(a) the other individual has consented to the disclosure of the information to the individual making the request, or

(b) it is reasonable in all the circumstances to comply with the request without the consent of the other individual.

(7) In subsection (6), the reference to information relating to another individual includes a reference to information identifying that individual as the source of the information sought by the request.

(8) Subsection (6) is not to be construed as excusing a controller from communicating so much of the information sought by the request as can be communicated without disclosing the identity of the other individual concerned, whether by the omission of names or other identifying particulars or otherwise.

(9) In determining for the purposes of subsection (6)(b) whether it is reasonable in all the circumstances to comply with the request without the consent of the other individual concerned, regard must be had, in particular, to—

(a) any duty of confidentiality owed to the other individual,

(b) any steps taken by the controller with a view to seeking the consent of the other individual,

(c) whether the other individual is capable of giving consent, and

(d) any express refusal of consent by the other individual.

(10) Subject to subsection (6), a controller must comply with a request under subsection (1)—

(a) promptly, and

(b) in any event before the end of the applicable time period.

(11) If a court is satisfied on the application of an individual who has made a request under subsection (1) that the controller in question has failed to comply with the request in contravention of this section, the court may order the controller to comply with the request.

(12) A court may make an order under subsection (11) in relation to a joint controller whose responsibilities are determined in an arrangement under section 104 only if the controller is responsible for compliance with the obligation to which the order relates.

(13) The jurisdiction conferred on a court by this section is exercisable by the High Court or, in Scotland, by the Court of Session.

(14) In this section—

"the applicable time period" means—

(a) the period of 1 month, or

(b) such longer period, not exceeding 3 months, as may be specified in regulations made by the Secretary of State,

beginning with the relevant time;

"the relevant time", in relation to a request under subsection (1), means the latest of the following—

(a) when the controller receives the request,

(b) when the fee (if any) is paid, and

(c) when the controller receives the information (if any) required under subsection (5) in connection with the request.

(15) Regulations under this section are subject to the negative resolution procedure.

III DAT [95]

95 Right of access: supplementary

(1) The controller must comply with the obligation imposed by section 94(1)(b)(i) by supplying the data subject with a copy of the information in writing unless—

(a) the supply of such a copy is not possible or would involve disproportionate effort, or

(b) the data subject agrees otherwise;

and where any of the information referred to in section 94(1)(b)(i) is expressed in terms which are not intelligible without explanation the copy must be accompanied by an explanation of those terms.

(2) Where a controller has previously complied with a request made under section 94 by an individual, the controller is not obliged to comply with a subsequent identical or similar request under that section by that individual unless a reasonable interval has elapsed between compliance with the previous request and the making of the current request.

(3) In determining for the purposes of subsection (2) whether requests under section 94 are made at reasonable intervals, regard must be had to—

(a) the nature of the data,

(b) the purpose for which the data is processed, and

(c) the frequency with which the data is altered.

(4) The information to be supplied pursuant to a request under section 94 must be supplied by reference to the data in question at the time when the request is received, except that it may take account of any amendment or deletion made between that time and the time when the information is supplied, being an amendment or deletion that would have been made regardless of the receipt of the request.

(5) For the purposes of section 94(6) to (8), an individual can be identified from information to be disclosed to a data subject by a controller if the individual can be identified from—

(a) that information, or

(b) that and any other information that the controller reasonably believes the data subject making the request is likely to possess or obtain.

III DAT [96]

96 Right not to be subject to automated decision-making

(1) The controller may not take a decision significantly affecting a data subject that is based solely on automated processing of personal data relating to the data subject.

(2) Subsection (1) does not prevent such a decision being made on that basis if—

(a) the decision is required or authorised by law,

(b) the data subject has given consent to the decision being made on that basis, or

(c) the decision is a decision taken in the course of steps taken—

(i) for the purpose of considering whether to enter into a contract with the data subject,

(ii) with a view to entering into such a contract, or

(iii) in the course of performing such a contract.

(3) For the purposes of this section, a decision that has legal effects as regards an individual is to be regarded as significantly affecting the individual.

III DAT [97]

97 Right to intervene in automated decision-making

(1) This section applies where—

(a) the controller takes a decision significantly affecting a data subject that is based solely on automated processing of personal data relating to the data subject, and

(b) the decision is required or authorised by law.

(2) This section does not apply to such a decision if—

(a) the data subject has given consent to the decision being made on that basis, or

(b) the decision is a decision taken in the course of steps taken—

(i) for the purpose of considering whether to enter into a contract with the data subject,

(ii) with a view to entering into such a contract, or

(iii) in the course of performing such a contract.

(3) The controller must as soon as reasonably practicable notify the data subject that such a decision has been made.

(4) The data subject may, before the end of the period of 1 month beginning with receipt of the notification, request the controller—

(a) to reconsider the decision, or

(b) to take a new decision that is not based solely on automated processing.

(5) If a request is made to the controller under subsection (4), the controller must, before the end of the period of 1 month beginning with receipt of the request—

(a) consider the request, including any information provided by the data subject that is relevant to it, and

(b) by notice in writing inform the data subject of the outcome of that consideration.

(6) For the purposes of this section, a decision that has legal effects as regards an individual is to be regarded as significantly affecting the individual.

III DAT [98]

98 Right to information about decision-making

(1) Where—

(a) the controller processes personal data relating to a data subject, and

(b) results produced by the processing are applied to the data subject,

the data subject is entitled to obtain from the controller, on request, knowledge of the reasoning underlying the processing.

(2) Where the data subject makes a request under subsection (1), the controller must comply with the request without undue delay.

III DAT [99]

99 Right to object to processing

(1) A data subject is entitled at any time, by notice given to the controller, to require the controller—

- (a) not to process personal data relating to the data subject, or
- (b) not to process such data for a specified purpose or in a specified manner,

on the ground that, for specified reasons relating to the situation of the data subject, the processing in question is an unwarranted interference with the interests or rights of the data subject.

(2) Where the controller—

- (a) reasonably requires further information—
  - (i) in order that the controller be satisfied as to the identity of the individual giving notice under subsection (1), or
  - (ii) to locate the data to which the notice relates, and
- (b) has informed that individual of that requirement,

the controller is not obliged to comply with the notice unless the controller is supplied with that further information.

(3) The controller must, before the end of 21 days beginning with the relevant time, give a notice to the data subject—

- (a) stating that the controller has complied or intends to comply with the notice under subsection (1), or
- (b) stating the controller's reasons for not complying with the notice to any extent and the extent (if any) to which the controller has complied or intends to comply with the notice under subsection (1).

(4) If the controller does not comply with a notice under subsection (1) to any extent, the data subject may apply to a court for an order that the controller take steps for complying with the notice.

(5) If the court is satisfied that the controller should comply with the notice (or should comply to any extent), the court may order the controller to take such steps for complying with the notice (or for complying with it to that extent) as the court thinks fit.

(6) A court may make an order under subsection (5) in relation to a joint controller whose responsibilities are determined in an arrangement under section 104 only if the controller is responsible for compliance with the obligation to which the order relates.

(7) The jurisdiction conferred on a court by this section is exercisable by the High Court or, in Scotland, by the Court of Session.

(8) In this section, "the relevant time", in relation to a notice under subsection (1), means—

- (a) when the controller receives the notice, or
- (b) if later, when the controller receives the information (if any) required under subsection (2) in connection with the notice.

III DAT [100]

100 Rights to rectification and erasure

(1) If a court is satisfied on the application of a data subject that personal data relating to the data subject is inaccurate, the court may order the controller to rectify that data without undue delay.

(2) If a court is satisfied on the application of a data subject that the processing of personal data relating to the data subject would infringe any of sections 86 to 91, the court may order the controller to erase that data without undue delay.

(3) If personal data relating to the data subject must be maintained for the purposes of evidence, the court may (instead of ordering the controller to rectify or erase the personal data) order the controller to restrict its processing without undue delay.

(4) If—

(a) the data subject contests the accuracy of personal data, and

(b) the court is satisfied that the controller is not able to ascertain whether the data is accurate or not,

the court may (instead of ordering the controller to rectify or erase the personal data) order the controller to restrict its processing without undue delay.

(5) A court may make an order under this section in relation to a joint controller whose responsibilities are determined in an arrangement under section 104 only if the controller is responsible for carrying out the rectification, erasure or restriction of processing that the court proposes to order.

(6) The jurisdiction conferred on a court by this section is exercisable by the High Court or, in Scotland, by the Court of Session.

CHAPTER 4 CONTROLLER AND PROCESSOR

OVERVIEW

III DAT [101]

101 Overview

This Chapter sets out—

(a) the general obligations of controllers and processors (see sections 102 to 106);

(b) specific obligations of controllers and processors with respect to security (see section 107);

(c) specific obligations of controllers and processors with respect to personal data breaches (see section 108).

GENERAL OBLIGATIONS

III DAT [102]

102 General obligations of the controller

Each controller must implement appropriate measures—

(a) to ensure, and

(b) to be able to demonstrate, in particular to the Commissioner,

that the processing of personal data complies with the requirements of this Part.

III DAT [103]

103 Data protection by design

(1) Where a controller proposes that a particular type of processing of personal data be carried out by or on behalf of the controller, the controller must, prior to the processing, consider the impact of the proposed processing on the rights and freedoms of data subjects.

(2) A controller must implement appropriate technical and organisational measures which are designed to ensure that—

(a) the data protection principles are implemented, and

(b) risks to the rights and freedoms of data subjects are minimised.

III DAT [104]

104 Joint controllers

(1) Where two or more intelligence services jointly determine the purposes and means of processing personal data, they are joint controllers for the purposes of this Part.

(2) Joint controllers must, in a transparent manner, determine their respective responsibilities for compliance with this Part by means of an arrangement between them, except to the extent that those responsibilities are determined under or by virtue of an enactment.

(3) The arrangement must designate the controller which is to be the contact point for data subjects.

III DAT [105]

105 Processors

(1) This section applies to the use by a controller of a processor to carry out processing of personal data on behalf of the controller.

(2) The controller may use only a processor who undertakes—

(a) to implement appropriate measures that are sufficient to secure that the processing complies with this Part;

(b) to provide to the controller such information as is necessary for demonstrating that the processing complies with this Part.

(3) If a processor determines, in breach of this Part, the purposes and means of processing, the processor is to be treated for the purposes of this Part as a controller in respect of that processing.

III DAT [106]

106 Processing under the authority of the controller or processor

A processor, and any person acting under the authority of a controller or processor, who has access to personal data may not process the data except—

(a) on instructions from the controller, or

(b) to comply with a legal obligation.

Obligations relating to security

III DAT [107]

107 Security of processing

(1) Each controller and each processor must implement security measures appropriate to the risks arising from the processing of personal data.

(2) In the case of automated processing, each controller and each processor must, following an evaluation of the risks, implement measures designed to—

(a) prevent unauthorised processing or unauthorised interference with the systems used in connection with it,

(b) ensure that it is possible to establish the precise details of any processing that takes place,

(c) ensure that any systems used in connection with the processing function properly and may, in the case of interruption, be restored, and

(d) ensure that stored personal data cannot be corrupted if a system used in connection with the processing malfunctions.

OBLIGATIONS RELATING TO PERSONAL DATA BREACHES

III DAT [108]

108 Communication of a personal data breach

(1) If a controller becomes aware of a serious personal data breach in relation to personal data for which the controller is responsible, the controller must notify the Commissioner of the breach without undue delay.

(2) Where the notification to the Commissioner is not made within 72 hours, the notification must be accompanied by reasons for the delay.

(3) Subject to subsection (4), the notification must include—

- (a) a description of the nature of the personal data breach including, where possible, the categories and approximate number of data subjects concerned and the categories and approximate number of personal data records concerned;
- (b) the name and contact details of the contact point from whom more information can be obtained;
- (c) a description of the likely consequences of the personal data breach;
- (d) a description of the measures taken or proposed to be taken by the controller to address the personal data breach, including, where appropriate, measures to mitigate its possible adverse effects.

(4) Where and to the extent that it is not possible to provide all the information mentioned in subsection (3) at the same time, the information may be provided in phases without undue further delay.

(5) If a processor becomes aware of a personal data breach (in relation to data processed by the processor), the processor must notify the controller without undue delay.

(6) Subsection (1) does not apply in relation to a personal data breach if the breach also constitutes a relevant error within the meaning given by section 231(9) of the Investigatory Powers Act 2016.

(7) For the purposes of this section, a personal data breach is serious if the breach seriously interferes with the rights and freedoms of a data subject.

CHAPTER 5 TRANSFERS OF PERSONAL DATA OUTSIDE THE UNITED KINGDOM

III DAT [109]

109 Transfers of personal data outside the United Kingdom

(1) A controller may not transfer personal data to—

- (a) a country or territory outside the United Kingdom, or
- (b) an international organisation,

unless the transfer falls within subsection (2).

(2) A transfer of personal data falls within this subsection if the transfer is a necessary and proportionate measure carried out—

- (a) for the purposes of the controller's statutory functions, or
- (b) for other purposes provided for, in relation to the controller, in section 2(2)(a) of the Security Service Act 1989 or section 2(2)(a) or 4(2)(a) of the Intelligence Services Act 1994.

CHAPTER 6 EXEMPTIONS

III DAT [110]

110 National security

(1) A provision mentioned in subsection (2) does not apply to personal data to which this Part applies if exemption from the provision is required for the purpose of safeguarding national security.

(2) The provisions are—

- (a) Chapter 2 (the data protection principles), except section 86(1)(a) and (2) and Schedules 9 and 10;
- (b) Chapter 3 (rights of data subjects);
- (c) in Chapter 4 , section 108 (communication of a personal data breach to the Commissioner);
- (d) in Part 5—
  - (i) section 119 (inspection in accordance with international obligations);
  - (ii) in Schedule 13 (other general functions of the Commissioner), paragraphs 1(a) and (g) and 2;
- (e) in Part 6—
  - (i) sections 142 to 154 and Schedule 15 (Commissioner's notices and powers of entry and inspection);
  - (ii) sections 170 to 173 (offences relating to personal data);
  - (iii) sections 174 to 176 (provision relating to the special purposes).

III DAT [111]

111 National security: certificate

(1) Subject to subsection (3), a certificate signed by a Minister of the Crown certifying that exemption from all or any of the provisions mentioned in section 110(2) is, or at any time was, required for the purpose of safeguarding national security in respect of any personal data is conclusive evidence of that fact.

(2) A certificate under subsection (1)—

- (a) may identify the personal data to which it applies by means of a general description, and
- (b) may be expressed to have prospective effect.

(3) Any person directly affected by the issuing of a certificate under subsection (1) may appeal to the Tribunal against the certificate.

(4) If on an appeal under subsection (3), the Tribunal finds that, applying the principles applied by a court on an application for judicial review, the Minister did not have reasonable grounds for issuing the certificate, the Tribunal may—

- (a) allow the appeal, and
- (b) quash the certificate.

(5) Where, in any proceedings under or by virtue of this Act, it is claimed by a controller that a certificate under subsection (1) which identifies the personal data to which it applies by means of a general description applies to any personal data, another party to the proceedings may appeal to the Tribunal on the ground that the certificate does not apply to the personal data in question.

(6) But, subject to any determination under subsection (7), the certificate is to be conclusively presumed so to apply.

(7) On an appeal under subsection (5), the Tribunal may determine that the certificate does not so apply.

(8) A document purporting to be a certificate under subsection (1) is to be—

- (a) received in evidence, and
- (b) deemed to be such a certificate unless the contrary is proved.

(9) A document which purports to be certified by or on behalf of a Minister of the Crown as a true copy of a certificate issued by that Minister under subsection (1) is—

(a) in any legal proceedings, evidence of that certificate, and

(b) in any legal proceedings in Scotland, sufficient evidence of that certificate.

(10) The power conferred by subsection (1) on a Minister of the Crown is exercisable only by—

(a) a Minister who is a member of the Cabinet, or

(b) the Attorney General or the Advocate General for Scotland.

III DAT [112]

112 Other exemptions

Schedule 11 provides for further exemptions.

III DAT [113]

113 Power to make further exemptions

(1) The Secretary of State may by regulations amend Schedule 11—

(a) by adding exemptions from any provision of this Part;

(b) by omitting exemptions added by regulations under paragraph (a).

(2) Regulations under this section are subject to the affirmative resolution procedure.

PART 5
THE INFORMATION COMMISSIONER

III DAT [114]–III DAT [141]

The intelligence services The Information Commissioner is identified, by s 115 as the Supervisory Authority for Data Protection within the United Kingdom. The need for such an office is stated in Article 51 of the GDPR and the role and functions of the Information Commissioner are conferred by Articles 57 and 58. They are the subject of detailed provisions in this Part and in Schedules 12 and 13, which carry forward the provisions of Articles 51 to 59. The functions include the preparation and approval of codes of practice, co-operation and exchange of information under the Law Enforcement Directive and the Data Protection Convention (Schedule 14) and reporting to Parliament. However, s 117 provides that the Commissioner may not exercise functions in relation to the processing of personal data by a court, tribunal or individual acting in a judicial capacity. The Commissioner is given extensive power to charge fees for services provided; and data controllers are required by Data Protection (Charges and Information) Regulations 2018, SI 2018/480 to provide information and to pay annual charges to the Information Commissioner. This instrument includes a Schedule of Exemptions. Provision for the Information Commissioner's power to issue and enforce notices and orders is made in Part 6.

PART 6
ENFORCEMENT

III DAT [142]–III DAT [166]

General Notes on the Enforcement Powers of the Information Commissioner Sections 142 to 166 empower the Information Commissioner to supervise and influence the activities of controllers and processors by the issue of information notices, assessment notices, enforcement notices, penalty notices and penalty variation notices, Anyone given such a notice has a right of appeal to the Tribunal. Sections 165 and 165 allow complaints about contraventions of GDPR to be made by data subjects to the Information Commissioner and to the Tribunal if the Information Commissioner does not take appropriate action on the complaint. Provision is also made by ss 201 to 203 for other powers to be conferred on the Tribunal and regarding its rules of procedure. Section 164 provides a limited role for the courts: where an information notice, an assessment notice or an enforcement notice contains an urgency statement the recipient may apply to the court for the urgency statement to be disapplied or varied. The application to the court should be made in accordance with Part 23.

Remedies in the court

III DAT [167]

167 Compliance orders

(1) This section applies if, on an application by a data subject, a court is satisfied that there has been an infringement of the data subject's rights under the data protection legislation in contravention of that legislation.

(2) A court may make an order for the purposes of securing compliance with the data protection legislation which requires the controller in respect of the processing, or a processor acting on behalf of that controller—

- (a) to take steps specified in the order, or
- (b) to refrain from taking steps specified in the order.

(3) The order may, in relation to each step, specify the time at which, or the period within which, it must be taken.

(4) In subsection (1)—

- (a) the reference to an application by a data subject includes an application made in exercise of the right under Article 79(1) of the GDPR (right to an effective remedy against a controller or processor);
- (b) the reference to the data protection legislation does not include Part 4 of this Act or regulations made under that Part.

(5) In relation to a joint controller in respect of the processing of personal data to which Part 3 applies whose responsibilities are determined in an arrangement under section 58, a court may only make an order under this section if the controller is responsible for compliance with the provision of the data protection legislation that is contravened.

III DAT [167.1]

Application to the Court The claimant may proceed by the issue of a claim form or, where the facts are undisputed, using the procedure under Part 8. Remedies that may be sought include orders for rectification, erasure, restriction or injunction. Note that the section may not be used to enforce rights under Part 4 (intelligence services processing) but it may be used to enforce all other rights under the GDPR, the applied GDPR, the Act and regulations under it and regulations made under s 2(2) of the European Communities Act 1972 which relate to the GDPR or the Law Enforcement Direction (see the definition in s 3 of the "data protection legislation").

III DAT [168]

168 Compensation for contravention of the GDPR

(1) In Article 82 of the GDPR (right to compensation for material or non-material damage), "non-material damage" includes distress.

(2) Subsection (3) applies where—

- (a) in accordance with rules of court, proceedings under Article 82 of the GDPR are brought by a representative body on behalf of a person, and
- (b) a court orders the payment of compensation.

(3) The court may make an order providing for the compensation to be paid on behalf of the person to—

- (a) the representative body, or
- (b) such other person as the court thinks fit.

III DAT [168.1]

Damages for distress Case law on awards for distress made under s 13 of the Data Protection Act 1998 may be relevant, in particular *Vidal-Hall v Google Inc* [2015] EWCA Civ 311.

III DAT [168.2]

Proceedings by a representative Where several people have the same interest in a claim **CPR 19.6** provides for one or more of them to represent the rest. Article 80(1) of the GDPR and s 187 of the Act go further and enable data subjects to authorise organisations to represent them and to exercise certain rights on their behalf, including the right to claim compensation under Article 82.

III DAT [169]

169 Compensation for contravention of other data protection legislation

(1) A person who suffers damage by reason of a contravention of a requirement of the data protection legislation, other than the GDPR, is entitled to compensation for that damage from the controller or the processor, subject to subsections (2) and (3).

(2) Under subsection (1)—

- (a) a controller involved in processing of personal data is liable for any damage caused by the processing, and
- (b) a processor involved in processing of personal data is liable for damage caused by the processing only if the processor—
  - (i) has not complied with an obligation under the data protection legislation specifically directed at processors, or
  - (ii) has acted outside, or contrary to, the controller's lawful instructions.

(3) A controller or processor is not liable as described in subsection (2) if the controller or processor proves that the controller or processor is not in any way responsible for the event giving rise to the damage.

(4) A joint controller in respect of the processing of personal data to which Part 3 or 4 applies whose responsibilities are determined in an arrangement under section 58 or 104 is only liable as described in subsection (2) if the controller is responsible for compliance with the provision of the data protection legislation that is contravened.

(5) In this section, "damage" includes financial loss and damage not involving financial loss, such as distress.

III DAT [169.1]

Requirement of the data protection legislation other than the GDPR Given the broad definition in s 3 of "data protection legislation" it would seem that compensation in the form of damages is available for, among other things, breach of rights under Part 4 (intelligence services processing) as well as breach of rights under Part 3.

Offences relating to personal data

III DAT [170]–III DAT [173]

General Notes on Offences relating to Personal Data Various offences are created in relation to personal data: unlawful obtaining etc of personal data (s 170), re-identification of de-identified personal data (ss 171 and 172) and alteration etc of personal data to prevent disclosure to data subject (s 173). Provision is made in ss 196 to 200 for the prosecution of offences and penalties.

THE SPECIAL PURPOSES

III DAT [174]

174 The special purposes

(1) In this Part, "the special purposes" means one or more of the following—

(a) the purposes of journalism;

(b) academic purposes;

(c) artistic purposes;

(d) literary purposes.

(2) In this Part, "special purposes proceedings" means legal proceedings against a controller or processor which relate, wholly or partly, to personal data processed for the special purposes and which are—

(a) proceedings under section 167 (including proceedings on an application under Article 79 of the GDPR), or

(b) proceedings under Article 82 of the GDPR or section 169.

(3) The Commissioner may make a written determination, in relation to the processing of personal data, that—

(a) the personal data is not being processed only for the special purposes;

(b) the personal data is not being processed with a view to the publication by a person of journalistic, academic, artistic or literary material which has not previously been published by the controller.

(4) The Commissioner must give written notice of the determination to the controller and the processor.

(5) The notice must provide information about the rights of appeal under section 162.

(6) The determination does not take effect until one of the following conditions is satisfied—

(a) the period for the controller or the processor to appeal against the determination has ended without an appeal having been brought, or

(b) an appeal has been brought against the determination and—

(i) the appeal and any further appeal in relation to the determination has been decided or has otherwise ended, and

(ii) the time for appealing against the result of the appeal or further appeal has ended without another appeal having been brought.

III DAT [175]

175 Provision of assistance in special purposes proceedings

(1) An individual who is a party, or prospective party, to special purposes proceedings may apply to the Commissioner for assistance in those proceedings.

(2) As soon as reasonably practicable after receiving an application under subsection (1), the Commissioner must decide whether, and to what extent, to grant it.

(3) The Commissioner must not grant the application unless, in the Commissioner's opinion, the case involves a matter of substantial public importance.

(4) If the Commissioner decides not to provide assistance, the Commissioner must, as soon as reasonably practicable, notify the applicant of the decision, giving reasons for the decision.

(5) If the Commissioner decides to provide assistance, the Commissioner must—

(a) as soon as reasonably practicable, notify the applicant of the decision, stating the extent of the assistance to be provided, and

(b) secure that the person against whom the proceedings are, or are to be, brought is informed that the Commissioner is providing assistance.

(6) The assistance that may be provided by the Commissioner includes—

(a) paying costs in connection with the proceedings, and

(b) indemnifying the applicant in respect of liability to pay costs, expenses or damages in connection with the proceedings.

(7) In England and Wales or Northern Ireland, the recovery of expenses incurred by the Commissioner in providing an applicant with assistance under this section (as taxed or assessed in accordance with rules of court) is to constitute a first charge for the benefit of the Commissioner—

(a) on any costs which, by virtue of any judgment or order of the court, are payable to the applicant by any other person in respect of the matter in connection with which the assistance is provided, and

(b) on any sum payable to the applicant under a compromise or settlement arrived at in connection with that matter to avoid, or bring to an end, any proceedings.

(8) In Scotland, the recovery of such expenses (as taxed or assessed in accordance with rules of court) is to be paid to the Commissioner, in priority to other debts—

(a) out of any expenses which, by virtue of any judgment or order of the court, are payable to the applicant by any other person in respect of the matter in connection with which the assistance is provided, and

(b) out of any sum payable to the applicant under a compromise or settlement arrived at in connection with that matter to avoid, or bring to an end, any proceedings.

III DAT [176]

176 Staying special purposes proceedings

(1) In any special purposes proceedings before a court, if the controller or processor claims, or it appears to the court, that any personal data to which the proceedings relate—

(a) is being processed only for the special purposes,

(b) is being processed with a view to the publication by any person of journalistic, academic, artistic or literary material, and

(c) has not previously been published by the controller,

the court must stay or, in Scotland, sist the proceedings.

(2) In considering, for the purposes of subsection (1)(c), whether material has previously been published, publication in the immediately preceding 24 hours is to be ignored.

(3) Under subsection (1), the court must stay or sist the proceedings until either of the following conditions is met—

(a) a determination of the Commissioner under section 174 with respect to the personal data or the processing takes effect;

(b) where the proceedings were stayed or sisted on the making of a claim, the claim is withdrawn.

III DAT [177]

177 Guidance about how to seek redress against media organisations

(1) The Commissioner must produce and publish guidance about the steps that may be taken where an individual considers that a media organisation is failing or has failed to comply with the data protection legislation.

(2) In this section, "media organisation" means a body or other organisation whose activities consist of or include journalism.

(3) The guidance must include provision about relevant complaints procedures, including—

(a) who runs them,

(b) what can be complained about, and

(c) how to make a complaint.

(4) For the purposes of subsection (3), relevant complaints procedures include procedures for making complaints to the Commissioner, the Office of Communications, the British Broadcasting Corporation and other persons who produce or enforce codes of practice for media organisations.

(5) The guidance must also include provision about—

(a) the powers available to the Commissioner in relation to a failure to comply with the data protection legislation,

(b) when a claim in respect of such a failure may be made before a court and how to make such a claim,

(c) alternative dispute resolution procedures,

(d) the rights of bodies and other organisations to make complaints and claims on behalf of data subjects, and

(e) the Commissioner's power to provide assistance in special purpose proceedings.

(6) The Commissioner—

(a) may alter or replace the guidance, and

(b) must publish any altered or replacement guidance.

(7) The Commissioner must produce and publish the first guidance under this section before the end of the period of 1 year beginning when this Act is passed.

III DAT [178]

178 Review of processing of personal data for the purposes of journalism

(1) The Commissioner must—

(a) review the extent to which, during each review period, the processing of personal data for the purposes of journalism complied with—

(i) the data protection legislation, and

(ii) good practice in the processing of personal data for the purposes of journalism,

(b) prepare a report of the review, and

(c) submit the report to the Secretary of State.

(2) In this section—

"good practice in the processing of personal data for the purposes of journalism" has the same meaning as in section 124;

"review period" means—

(a) the period of 4 years beginning with the day on which Chapter 2 of Part 2 of this Act comes into force, and

(b) each subsequent period of 5 years beginning with the day after the day on which the previous review period ended.

(3) The Commissioner must start a review under this section, in respect of a review period, within the period of 6 months beginning when the review period ends.

(4) The Commissioner must submit the report of a review under this section to the Secretary of State—

(a) in the case of the first review, before the end of the period of 18 months beginning when the Commissioner started the review, and

(b) in the case of each subsequent review, before the end of the period of 12 months beginning when the Commissioner started the review.

(5) The report must include consideration of the extent of compliance (as described in subsection (1)(a)) in each part of the United Kingdom.

(6) The Secretary of State must—

(a) lay the report before Parliament, and

(b) send a copy of the report to—
  (i) the Scottish Ministers,
  (ii) the Welsh Ministers, and
  (iii) the Executive Office in Northern Ireland.

(7) Schedule 17 makes further provision for the purposes of a review under this section.

III DAT [179]

179 Effectiveness of the media's dispute resolution procedures

(1) The Secretary of State must, before the end of each review period, lay before Parliament a report produced by the Secretary of State or an appropriate person on—

(a) the use of relevant alternative dispute resolution procedures, during that period, in cases involving a failure, or alleged failure, by a relevant media organisation to comply with the data protection legislation, and

(b) the effectiveness of those procedures in such cases.

(2) In this section—

"appropriate person" means a person who the Secretary of State considers has appropriate experience and skills to produce a report described in subsection (1);

"relevant alternative dispute resolution procedures" means alternative dispute resolution procedures provided by persons who produce or enforce codes of practice for relevant media organisations;

"relevant media organisation" means a body or other organisation whose activities consist of or include journalism, other than a broadcaster;

"review period" means—
  (a) the period of 3 years beginning when this Act is passed, and
  (b) each subsequent period of 3 years.

(3) The Secretary of State must send a copy of the report to—

(a) the Scottish Ministers,

(b) the Welsh Ministers, and

(c) the Executive Office in Northern Ireland.

Jurisdiction of courts

III DAT [180]

180 Jurisdiction

(1) The jurisdiction conferred on a court by the provisions listed in subsection (2) is exercisable—

(a) in England and Wales, by the High Court or the county court,

(b) in Northern Ireland, by the High Court or a county court, and

(c) in Scotland, by the Court of Session or the sheriff,

subject to subsections (3) and (4).

(2) Those provisions are—

(a) section 145 (information orders);

(b) section 152 (enforcement notices and processing for the special purposes);

(c) section 156 (penalty notices and processing for the special purposes);

(d) section 167 and Article 79 of the GDPR (compliance orders);

(e) sections 168 and 169 and Article 82 of the GDPR (compensation).

(3) In relation to the processing of personal data to which Part 4 applies, the jurisdiction conferred by the provisions listed in subsection (2) is exercisable only by the High Court or, in Scotland, the Court of Session.

(4) In relation to an information notice which contains a statement under section 142(7), the jurisdiction conferred on a court by section 145 is exercisable only by the High Court or, in Scotland, the Court of Session.

(5) The jurisdiction conferred on a court by section 164 (applications in respect of urgent notices) is exercisable only by the High Court or, in Scotland, the Court of Session.

Definitions

III DAT [181]

181 Interpretation of Part 6

In this Part—

"assessment notice" has the meaning given in section 146;

"certification provider" has the meaning given in section 17;

"enforcement notice" has the meaning given in section 149;

"information notice" has the meaning given in section 142;

"penalty notice" has the meaning given in section 155;

"penalty variation notice" has the meaning given in Schedule 16;

"representative", in relation to a controller or processor, means a person designated by the controller or processor under Article 27 of the GDPR to represent the controller or processor with regard to the controller's or processor's obligations under the GDPR.

PART 7
SUPPLEMENTARY AND FINAL PROVISION

Regulations under this Act

III DAT [182]

182 Regulations and consultation

(1) Regulations under this Act are to be made by statutory instrument.

(2) Before making regulations under this Act, the Secretary of State must consult—

(a) the Commissioner, and

(b) such other persons as the Secretary of State considers appropriate.

(3) Subsection (2) does not apply to regulations made under—

(a) section 23;

(b) section 30;

(c) section 211;

(d) section 212;

(e) section 213;

(f) paragraph 15 of Schedule 2.

(4) Subsection (2) does not apply to regulations made under section 18 where the Secretary of State has made an urgency statement in respect of them.

(5) Regulations under this Act may—

(a) make different provision for different purposes;

(b) include consequential, supplementary, incidental, transitional, transitory or saving provision.

(6) Where regulations under this Act are subject to "the negative resolution procedure" the statutory instrument containing the regulations is subject to annulment in pursuance of a resolution of either House of Parliament.

(7) Where regulations under this Act are subject to "the affirmative resolution procedure" the regulations may not be made unless a draft of the statutory instrument containing them has been laid before Parliament and approved by a resolution of each House of Parliament.

(8) Where regulations under this Act are subject to "the made affirmative resolution procedure"—

- (a) the statutory instrument containing the regulations must be laid before Parliament after being made, together with the urgency statement in respect of them, and
- (b) the regulations cease to have effect at the end of the period of 120 days beginning with the day on which the instrument is made, unless within that period the instrument is approved by a resolution of each House of Parliament.

(9) In calculating the period of 120 days, no account is to be taken of any time during which—

- (a) Parliament is dissolved or prorogued, or
- (b) both Houses of Parliament are adjourned for more than 4 days.

(10) Where regulations cease to have effect as a result of subsection (8), that does not—

- (a) affect anything previously done under the regulations, or
- (b) prevent the making of new regulations.

(11) Any provision that may be included in regulations under this Act subject to the negative resolution procedure may be made by regulations subject to the affirmative resolution procedure or the made affirmative resolution procedure.

(12) If a draft of a statutory instrument containing regulations under section 7 would, apart from this subsection, be treated for the purposes of the standing orders of either House of Parliament as a hybrid instrument, it is to proceed in that House as if it were not such an instrument.

(13) A requirement under a provision of this Act to consult may be satisfied by consultation before, as well as by consultation after, the provision comes into force.

(14) In this section, "urgency statement" has the meaning given in section 18(4).

CHANGES TO THE DATA PROTECTION CONVENTION

III DAT [183]

183 Power to reflect changes to the Data Protection Convention

(1) The Secretary of State may by regulations make such provision as the Secretary of State considers necessary or appropriate in connection with an amendment of, or an instrument replacing, the Data Protection Convention which has effect, or is expected to have effect, in the United Kingdom.

(2) The power under subsection (1) includes power—

- (a) to amend or replace the definition of "the Data Protection Convention" in section 3;
- (b) to amend Chapter 3 of Part 2 of this Act;
- (c) to amend Part 4 of this Act;
- (d) to make provision about the functions of the Commissioner, courts or tribunals in connection with processing of personal data to which Chapter 3 of Part 2 or Part 4 of this Act applies, including provision amending Parts 5 to 7 of this Act;

(e) to make provision about the functions of the Commissioner in connection with the Data Protection Convention or an instrument replacing that Convention, including provision amending Parts 5 to 7 of this Act;

(f) to consequentially amend this Act.

(3) Regulations under this section are subject to the affirmative resolution procedure.

(4) Regulations under this section may not be made after the end of the period of 3 years beginning with the day on which this Act is passed.

RIGHTS OF THE DATA SUBJECT

III DAT [184]

184 Prohibition of requirement to produce relevant records

(1) It is an offence for a person ("P1") to require another person to provide P1 with, or give P1 access to, a relevant record in connection with—

(a) the recruitment of an employee by P1,

(b) the continued employment of a person by P1, or

(c) a contract for the provision of services to P1.

(2) It is an offence for a person ("P2") to require another person to provide P2 with, or give P2 access to, a relevant record if—

(a) P2 is involved in the provision of goods, facilities or services to the public or a section of the public, and

(b) the requirement is a condition of providing or offering to provide goods, facilities or services to the other person or to a third party.

(3) It is a defence for a person charged with an offence under subsection (1) or (2) to prove that imposing the requirement—

(a) was required or authorised by an enactment, by a rule of law or by the order of a court or tribunal, or

(b) in the particular circumstances, was justified as being in the public interest.

(4) The imposition of the requirement referred to in subsection (1) or (2) is not to be regarded as justified as being in the public interest on the ground that it would assist in the prevention or detection of crime, given Part 5 of the Police Act 1997 (certificates of criminal records etc).

(5) In subsections (1) and (2), the references to a person who requires another person to provide or give access to a relevant record include a person who asks another person to do so—

(a) knowing that, in the circumstances, it would be reasonable for the other person to feel obliged to comply with the request, or

(b) being reckless as to whether, in the circumstances, it would be reasonable for the other person to feel obliged to comply with the request,

and the references to a "requirement" in subsections (3) and (4) are to be interpreted accordingly.

(6) In this section—

"employment" means any employment, including—

(a) work under a contract for services or as an office-holder,

(b) work under an apprenticeship,

(c) work experience as part of a training course or in the course of training for employment, and

(d) voluntary work,

and "employee" is to be interpreted accordingly;

DATA PROTECTION

"relevant record" has the meaning given in Schedule 18 and references to a relevant record include—

(a) a part of such a record, and

(b) a copy of, or of part of, such a record.

III DAT [185]

185 Avoidance of certain contractual terms relating to health records

(1) A term or condition of a contract is void in so far as it purports to require an individual to supply another person with a record which—

(a) consists of the information contained in a health record, and

(b) has been or is to be obtained by a data subject in the exercise of a data subject access right.

(2) A term or condition of a contract is also void in so far as it purports to require an individual to produce such a record to another person.

(3) The references in subsections (1) and (2) to a record include a part of a record and a copy of all or part of a record.

(4) In this section, "data subject access right" means a right under—

(a) Article 15 of the GDPR (right of access by the data subject);

(b) Article 20 of the GDPR (right to data portability);

(c) section 45 of this Act (law enforcement processing: right of access by the data subject);

(d) section 94 of this Act (intelligence services processing: right of access by the data subject).

III DAT [186]

186 Data subject's rights and other prohibitions and restrictions

(1) An enactment or rule of law prohibiting or restricting the disclosure of information, or authorising the withholding of information, does not remove or restrict the obligations and rights provided for in the provisions listed in subsection (2), except as provided by or under the provisions listed in subsection (3).

(2) The provisions providing obligations and rights are—

(a) Chapter III of the GDPR (rights of the data subject),

(b) Chapter 3 of Part 3 of this Act (law enforcement processing: rights of the data subject), and

(c) Chapter 3 of Part 4 of this Act (intelligence services processing: rights of the data subject).

(3) The provisions providing exceptions are—

(a) in Chapter 2 of Part 2 of this Act, sections 15 and 16 and Schedules 2, 3 and 4,

(b) in Chapter 3 of Part 2 of this Act, sections 23, 24, 25 and 26,

(c) in Part 3 of this Act, sections 44(4), 45(4) and 48(3), and

(d) in Part 4 of this Act, Chapter 6 .

Representation of data subjects

III DAT [187]

187 Representation of data subjects with their authority

(1) In relation to the processing of personal data to which the GDPR applies—

(a) Article 80(1) of the GDPR (representation of data subjects) enables a data subject to authorise a body or other organisation which meets the conditions set out in that Article to exercise the data subject's rights under Articles 77, 78 and 79 of the GDPR (rights to lodge complaints and to an effective judicial remedy) on the data subject's behalf, and

(b) a data subject may also authorise such a body or organisation to exercise the data subject's rights under Article 82 of the GDPR (right to compensation).

(2) In relation to the processing of personal data to which the GDPR does not apply, a body or other organisation which meets the conditions in subsections (3) and (4), if authorised to do so by a data subject, may exercise some or all of the following rights of a data subject on the data subject's behalf—

(a) rights under section 165(2), (4)(d) and (6)(c) (complaints to the Commissioner);

(b) rights under section 166(2) (orders for the Commissioner to progress complaints);

(c) rights under section 167(1) (compliance orders);

(d) the right to bring judicial review proceedings against the Commissioner.

(3) The first condition is that the body or organisation, by virtue of its constitution or an enactment—

(a) is required (after payment of outgoings) to apply the whole of its income and any capital it expends for charitable or public purposes,

(b) is prohibited from directly or indirectly distributing amongst its members any part of its assets (otherwise than for charitable or public purposes), and

(c) has objectives which are in the public interest.

(4) The second condition is that the body or organisation is active in the field of protection of data subjects' rights and freedoms with regard to the protection of their personal data.

(5) In this Act, references to a "representative body", in relation to a right of a data subject, are to a body or other organisation authorised to exercise the right on the data subject's behalf under Article 80 of the GDPR or this section.

III DAT [188]

188 Representation of data subjects with their authority: collective proceedings

(1) The Secretary of State may by regulations make provision for representative bodies to bring proceedings before a court or tribunal in England and Wales or Northern Ireland combining two or more relevant claims.

(2) In this section, "relevant claim", in relation to a representative body, means a claim in respect of a right of a data subject which the representative body is authorised to exercise on the data subject's behalf under Article 80(1) of the GDPR or section 187.

(3) The power under subsection (1) includes power—

(a) to make provision about the proceedings;

(b) to confer functions on a person, including functions involving the exercise of a discretion;

(c) to make different provision in relation to England and Wales and in relation to Northern Ireland.

(4) The provision mentioned in subsection (3)(a) includes provision about—

(a) the effect of judgments and orders;

(b) agreements to settle claims;

(c) the assessment of the amount of compensation;

(d) the persons to whom compensation may or must be paid, including compensation not claimed by the data subject;

(e) costs.

DATA PROTECTION

(5) Regulations under this section are subject to the negative resolution procedure.

III DAT [189]

189 Duty to review provision for representation of data subjects

(1) Before the end of the review period, the Secretary of State must—

- (a) review the matters listed in subsection (2) in relation to England and Wales and Northern Ireland,
- (b) prepare a report of the review, and
- (c) lay a copy of the report before Parliament.

(2) Those matters are—

- (a) the operation of Article 80(1) of the GDPR,
- (b) the operation of section 187,
- (c) the merits of exercising the power under Article 80(2) of the GDPR (power to enable a body or other organisation which meets the conditions in Article 80(1) of the GDPR to exercise some or all of a data subject's rights under Articles 77, 78 and 79 of the GDPR without being authorised to do so by the data subject),
- (d) the merits of making equivalent provision in relation to data subjects' rights under Article 82 of the GDPR (right to compensation), and
- (e) the merits of making provision for a children's rights organisation to exercise some or all of a data subject's rights under Articles 77, 78, 79 and 82 of the GDPR on behalf of a data subject who is a child, with or without being authorised to do so by the data subject.

(3) "The review period" is the period of 30 months beginning when section 187 comes into force.

(4) In carrying out the review, the Secretary of State must—

- (a) consider the particular needs of children separately from the needs of adults,
- (b) have regard to the fact that children have different needs at different stages of development,
- (c) carry out an analysis of the particular challenges that children face in authorising, and deciding whether to authorise, other persons to act on their behalf under Article 80(1) of the GDPR or section 187,
- (d) consider the support and advice available to children in connection with the exercise of their rights under Articles 77, 78, 79 and 82 of the GDPR by another person on their behalf and the merits of making available other support or advice, and
- (e) have regard to the United Kingdom's obligations under the United Nations Convention on the Rights of the Child.

(5) Before preparing the report under subsection (1), the Secretary of State must consult the Commissioner and such other persons as the Secretary of State considers appropriate, including—

- (a) persons active in the field of protection of data subjects' rights and freedoms with regard to the protection of their personal data,
- (b) children and parents,
- (c) children's rights organisations and other persons who appear to the Secretary of State to represent the interests of children,
- (d) child development experts, and
- (e) trade associations.

(6) In this section—

"children's rights organisation" means a body or other organisation which—

- (a) is active in representing the interests of children, and

(b) has objectives which are in the public interest;

"trade association" includes a body representing controllers or processors;

"the United Nations Convention on the Rights of the Child" means the Convention on the Rights of the Child adopted by the General Assembly of the United Nations on 20 November 1989 (including any Protocols to that Convention which are in force in relation to the United Kingdom), subject to any reservations, objections or interpretative declarations by the United Kingdom for the time being in force.

III DAT [190]

190 Post-review powers to make provision about representation of data subjects

(1) After the report under section 189(1) is laid before Parliament, the Secretary of State may by regulations—

(a) exercise the powers under Article 80(2) of the GDPR in relation to England and Wales and Northern Ireland,

(b) make provision enabling a body or other organisation which meets the conditions in Article 80(1) of the GDPR to exercise a data subject's rights under Article 82 of the GDPR in England and Wales and Northern Ireland without being authorised to do so by the data subject, and

(c) make provision described in section 189(2)(e) in relation to the exercise in England and Wales and Northern Ireland of the rights of a data subject who is a child.

(2) The powers under subsection (1) include power—

(a) to make provision enabling a data subject to prevent a body or other organisation from exercising, or continuing to exercise, the data subject's rights;

(b) to make provision about proceedings before a court or tribunal where a body or organisation exercises a data subject's rights;

(c) to make provision for bodies or other organisations to bring proceedings before a court or tribunal combining two or more claims in respect of a right of a data subject;

(d) to confer functions on a person, including functions involving the exercise of a discretion;

(e) to amend sections 166 to 168, 180, 187, 203, 205 and 206;

(f) to insert new sections and Schedules into Part 6 or 7 ;

(g) to make different provision in relation to England and Wales and in relation to Northern Ireland.

(3) The powers under subsection (1)(a) and (b) include power to make provision in relation to data subjects who are children or data subjects who are not children or both.

(4) The provision mentioned in subsection (2)(b) and (c) includes provision about—

(a) the effect of judgments and orders;

(b) agreements to settle claims;

(c) the assessment of the amount of compensation;

(d) the persons to whom compensation may or must be paid, including compensation not claimed by the data subject;

(e) costs.

(5) Regulations under this section are subject to the affirmative resolution procedure.

Framework for Data Processing by Government

III DAT [191]

191 Framework for Data Processing by Government

(1) The Secretary of State may prepare a document, called the Framework for Data Processing by Government, which contains guidance about the processing of personal data in connection with the exercise of functions of—

(a) the Crown, a Minister of the Crown or a United Kingdom government department, and

(b) a person with functions of a public nature who is specified or described in regulations made by the Secretary of State.

(2) The document may make provision relating to all of those functions or only to particular functions or persons.

(3) The document may not make provision relating to, or to the functions of, a part of the Scottish Administration, the Welsh Government, a Northern Ireland Minister or a Northern Ireland department.

(4) The Secretary of State may from time to time prepare amendments of the document or a replacement document.

(5) Before preparing a document or amendments under this section, the Secretary of State must consult—

(a) the Commissioner, and

(b) any other person the Secretary of State considers it appropriate to consult.

(6) Regulations under subsection (1)(b) are subject to the negative resolution procedure.

(7) In this section, "Northern Ireland Minister" includes the First Minister and deputy First Minister in Northern Ireland.

III DAT [192]

192 Approval of the Framework

(1) Before issuing a document prepared under section 191, the Secretary of State must lay it before Parliament.

(2) If, within the 40-day period, either House of Parliament resolves not to approve the document, the Secretary of State must not issue it.

(3) If no such resolution is made within that period—

(a) the Secretary of State must issue the document, and

(b) the document comes into force at the end of the period of 21 days beginning with the day on which it is issued.

(4) Nothing in subsection (2) prevents another version of the document being laid before Parliament.

(5) In this section, "the 40-day period" means—

(a) if the document is laid before both Houses of Parliament on the same day, the period of 40 days beginning with that day, or

(b) if the document is laid before the Houses of Parliament on different days, the period of 40 days beginning with the later of those days.

(6) In calculating the 40-day period, no account is to be taken of any period during which Parliament is dissolved or prorogued or during which both Houses of Parliament are adjourned for more than 4 days.

(7) This section applies in relation to amendments prepared under section 191 as it applies in relation to a document prepared under that section.

III DAT [193]

193 Publication and review of the Framework

(1) The Secretary of State must publish a document issued under section 192(3).

(2) Where an amendment of a document is issued under section 192(3), the Secretary of State must publish—

(a) the amendment, or

(b) the document as amended by it.

(3) The Secretary of State must keep under review the document issued under section 192(3) for the time being in force.

(4) Where the Secretary of State becomes aware that the terms of such a document could result in a breach of an international obligation of the United Kingdom, the Secretary of State must exercise the power under section 191(4) with a view to remedying the situation.

III DAT [194]

194 Effect of the Framework

(1) When carrying out processing of personal data which is the subject of a document issued under section 192(3) which is for the time being in force, a person must have regard to the document.

(2) A failure to act in accordance with a provision of such a document does not of itself make a person liable to legal proceedings in a court or tribunal.

(3) A document issued under section 192(3), including an amendment or replacement document, is admissible in evidence in legal proceedings.

(4) In any legal proceedings before a court or tribunal, the court or tribunal must take into account a provision of any document issued under section 192(3) in determining a question arising in the proceedings if—

(a) the question relates to a time when the provision was in force, and

(b) the provision appears to the court or tribunal to be relevant to the question.

(5) In determining a question arising in connection with the carrying out of any of the Commissioner's functions, the Commissioner must take into account a provision of a document issued under section 192(3) if—

(a) the question relates to a time when the provision was in force, and

(b) the provision appears to the Commissioner to be relevant to the question.

DATA-SHARING: HMRC AND RESERVE FORCES

III DAT [195]–III DAT [203]

195 Reserve forces: data-sharing by HMRC

(1) The Reserve Forces Act 1996 is amended as follows.

(2) After section 125 insert—

"125A Supply of contact details by HMRC

(1) This subsection applies to contact details for—

(a) a member of an ex-regular reserve force, or

(b) a person to whom section 66 (officers and former servicemen liable to recall) applies,

which are held by HMRC in connection with a function of HMRC.

(2) HMRC may supply contact details to which subsection (1) applies to the Secretary of State for the purpose of enabling the Secretary of State—

DATA PROTECTION

(a) to contact a member of an ex-regular reserve force in connection with the person's liability, or potential liability, to be called out for service under Part 6;

(b) to contact a person to whom section 66 applies in connection with the person's liability, or potential liability, to be recalled for service under Part 7.

(3) Where a person's contact details are supplied under subsection (2) for a purpose described in that subsection, they may also be used for defence purposes connected with the person's service (whether past, present or future) in the reserve forces or regular services.

(4) In this section, "HMRC" means Her Majesty's Revenue and Customs.

125B Prohibition on disclosure of contact details supplied under section 125A

(1) A person who receives information supplied under section 125A may not disclose it except with the consent of the Commissioners for Her Majesty's Revenue and Customs (which may be general or specific).

(2) A person who contravenes subsection (1) is guilty of an offence.

(3) It is a defence for a person charged with an offence under this section to prove that the person reasonably believed—

(a) that the disclosure was lawful, or

(b) that the information had already lawfully been made available to the public.

(4) Subsections (4) to (7) of section 19 of the Commissioners for Revenue and Customs Act 2005 apply to an offence under this section as they apply to an offence under that section.

(5) Nothing in section 107 or 108 (institution of proceedings and evidence) applies in relation to an offence under this section.

125C Data protection

(1) Nothing in section 125A or 125B authorises the making of a disclosure which contravenes the data protection legislation.

(2) In this section, "the data protection legislation" has the same meaning as in the Data Protection Act 2018 (see section 3 of that Act)."

INTERPRETATION

III DAT [204]

204 Meaning of "health professional" and "social work professional"

(1) In this Act, "health professional" means any of the following—

(a) a registered medical practitioner;

(b) a registered nurse or midwife;

(c) a registered dentist within the meaning of the Dentists Act 1984 (see section 53 of that Act);

(d) a registered dispensing optician or a registered optometrist within the meaning of the Opticians Act 1989 (see section 36 of that Act);

(e) a registered osteopath with the meaning of the Osteopaths Act 1993 (see section 41 of that Act);

(f) a registered chiropractor within the meaning of the Chiropractors Act 1994 (see section 43 of that Act);

(g) a person registered as a member of a profession to which the Health *and Social Work* Professions Order 2001 (SI 2002/254) for the time being extends, *other than the social work profession in England*;

(h) a registered pharmacist or a registered pharmacy technician within the meaning of the Pharmacy Order 2010 (SI 2010/231) (see article 3 of that Order);

(i) a registered person within the meaning of the Pharmacy (Northern Ireland) Order 1976 (SI 1976/1213 (NI 22)) (see Article 2 of that Order);

(j) a child psychotherapist;

(k) a scientist employed by a health service body as head of a department.

(2) In this Act, "social work professional" means any of the following—

(a) a person registered as a social worker in England in the register maintained under the Health and Social Work Professions Order 2001 (SI 2002/254);

[(a) a person registered as a social worker in the register maintained by Social Work England under section 39(1) of the Children and Social Work Act 2017;]

(b) a person registered as a social worker in the register maintained by Social Care Wales under section 80 of the Regulation and Inspection of Social Care (Wales) Act 2016 (anaw 2);

(c) a person registered as a social worker in the register maintained by the Scottish Social Services Council under section 44 of the Regulation of Care (Scotland) Act 2001 (asp 8);

(d) a person registered as a social worker in the register maintained by the Northern Ireland Social Care Council under section 3 of the Health and Personal Social Services Act (Northern Ireland) 2001 (c 3 (NI)).

(3) In subsection (1)(a) "registered medical practitioner" includes a person who is provisionally registered under section 15 or 21 of the Medical Act 1983 and is engaged in such employment as is mentioned in subsection (3) of that section.

(4) In subsection (1)(k) "health service body" means any of the following—

(a) the Secretary of State in relation to the exercise of functions under section 2A or 2B of, or paragraph 7C, 8 or 12 of Schedule 1 to, the National Health Service Act 2006;

(b) a local authority in relation to the exercise of functions under section 2B or 111 of, or any of paragraphs 1 to 7B or 13 of Schedule 1 to, the National Health Service Act 2006;

(c) a National Health Service trust first established under section 25 of the National Health Service Act 2006;

(d) a Special Health Authority established under section 28 of the National Health Service Act 2006;

(e) an NHS foundation trust;

(f) the National Institute for Health and Care Excellence;

(g) the Health and Social Care Information Centre;

(h) a National Health Service trust first established under section 5 of the National Health Service and Community Care Act 1990;

(i) a Local Health Board established under section 11 of the National Health Service (Wales) Act 2006;

(j) a National Health Service trust first established under section 18 of the National Health Service (Wales) Act 2006;

(k) a Special Health Authority established under section 22 of the National Health Service (Wales) Act 2006;

(l) a Health Board within the meaning of the National Health Service (Scotland) Act 1978;

(m) a Special Health Board within the meaning of the National Health Service (Scotland) Act 1978;

(n) a National Health Service trust first established under section 12A of the National Health Service (Scotland) Act 1978;

(o) the managers of a State Hospital provided under section 102 of the National Health Service (Scotland) Act 1978;

(p) the Regional Health and Social Care Board established under section 7 of the Health and Social Care (Reform) Act (Northern Ireland) 2009 (c 1 (NI));

(q) a special health and social care agency established under the Health and Personal Social Services (Special Agencies) (Northern Ireland) Order 1990 (SI 1990/247 (NI 3));

(r) a Health and Social Care trust established under Article 10 of the Health and Personal Social Services (Northern Ireland) Order 1991 (SI 1991/194 (NI 1)).

Amendment *Text in italic is deleted and text in square brackets is inserted with effect from a date to be appointed.*

III DAT [205]

205 General interpretation

(1) In this Act—

"biometric data" means personal data resulting from specific technical processing relating to the physical, physiological or behavioural characteristics of an individual, which allows or confirms the unique identification of that individual, such as facial images or dactyloscopic data;

"data concerning health" means personal data relating to the physical or mental health of an individual, including the provision of health care services, which reveals information about his or her health status;

"enactment" includes—

(a) an enactment passed or made after this Act,

(b) an enactment comprised in subordinate legislation,

(c) an enactment comprised in, or in an instrument made under, a Measure or Act of the National Assembly for Wales,

(d) an enactment comprised in, or in an instrument made under, an Act of the Scottish Parliament, and

(e) an enactment comprised in, or in an instrument made under, Northern Ireland legislation;

"genetic data" means personal data relating to the inherited or acquired genetic characteristics of an individual which gives unique information about the physiology or the health of that individual and which results, in particular, from an analysis of a biological sample from the individual in question;

"government department" includes the following (except in the expression "United Kingdom government department")—

(a) a part of the Scottish Administration;

(b) a Northern Ireland department;

(c) the Welsh Government;

(d) a body or authority exercising statutory functions on behalf of the Crown;

"health record" means a record which—

(a) consists of data concerning health, and

(b) has been made by or on behalf of a health professional in connection with the diagnosis, care or treatment of the individual to whom the data relates;

"inaccurate", in relation to personal data, means incorrect or misleading as to any matter of fact;

"international obligation of the United Kingdom" includes—

(a) an EU obligation, and

(b) an obligation that arises under an international agreement or arrangement to which the United Kingdom is a party;

"international organisation" means an organisation and its subordinate bodies governed by international law, or any other body which is set up by, or on the basis of, an agreement between two or more countries;

"Minister of the Crown" has the same meaning as in the Ministers of the Crown Act 1975;

"publish" means make available to the public or a section of the public (and related expressions are to be read accordingly);

"subordinate legislation" has the meaning given in the Interpretation Act 1978;

"tribunal" means any tribunal in which legal proceedings may be brought;

"the Tribunal", in relation to an application or appeal under this Act, means—

(a) the Upper Tribunal, in any case where it is determined by or under Tribunal Procedure Rules that the Upper Tribunal is to hear the application or appeal, or

(b) the First-tier Tribunal, in any other case.

(2) References in this Act to a period expressed in hours, days, weeks, months or years are to be interpreted in accordance with Article 3 of Regulation (EEC, Euratom) No 1182/71 of the Council of 3 June 1971 determining the rules applicable to periods, dates and time limits, except in—

(a) section 125(4), (7) and (8);
(b) section 161(3), (5) and (6);
(c) section 176(2);
(d) section 178(2);
(e) section 182(8) and (9);
(f) section 183(4);
(g) section 192(3), (5) and (6);
(h) section 197(3) and (4);
(i) paragraph 23(4) and (5) of Schedule 1;
(j) paragraphs 5(4) and 6(4) of Schedule 3;
(k) Schedule 5;
(l) paragraph 11(5) of Schedule 12;
(m) Schedule 15;

(and the references in section 5 to terms used in Chapter 2 or 3 of Part 2 do not include references to a period expressed in hours, days, weeks, months or years).

(3) Section 3(14)(b) (interpretation of references to Chapter 2 of Part 2 in Parts 5 to 7) and the amendments in Schedule 19 which make equivalent provision are not to be treated as implying a contrary intention for the purposes of section 20(2) of the Interpretation Act 1978, or any similar provision in another enactment, as it applies to other references to, or to a provision of, Chapter 2 of Part 2 of this Act.

III DAT [206]

206 Index of defined expressions

The Table below lists provisions which define or otherwise explain terms defined for this Act, for a Part of this Act or for Chapter 2 or 3 of Part 2 of this Act.

the affirmative resolution procedure	section 182
the applied Chapter 2 (in Chapter 3 of Part 2)	section 22
the applied GDPR	section 3
assessment notice (in Part 6)	section 181
biometric data	section 205
certification provider (in Part 6)	section 181

DATA PROTECTION

the Commissioner	section 3
competent authority (in Part 3)	section 30
consent (in Part 4)	section 84
controller	section 3
data concerning health	section 205
the Data Protection Convention	section 3
the data protection legislation	section 3
data subject	section 3
employee (in Parts 3 and 4)	sections 33 and 84
enactment	section 205
enforcement notice (in Part 6)	section 181
filing system	section 3
FOI public authority (in Chapter 3 of Part 2)	section 21
the GDPR	section 3
genetic data	section 205
government department	section 205
health professional	section 204
health record	section 205
identifiable living individual	section 3
inaccurate	section 205
information notice (in Part 6)	section 181
intelligence service (in Part 4)	section 82
international obligation of the United Kingdom	section 205
international organisation	section 205
the Law Enforcement Directive	section 3
the law enforcement purposes (in Part 3)	section 31
the made affirmative resolution procedure	section 182
Minister of the Crown	section 205
the negative resolution procedure	section 182
penalty notice (in Part 6)	section 181
penalty variation notice (in Part 6)	section 181
personal data	section 3
personal data breach (in Parts 3 and 4)	sections 33 and 84
processing	section 3
processor	section 3
profiling (in Part 3)	section 33
public authority (in the GDPR and Part 2)	section 7
public body (in the GDPR and Part 2)	section 7
publish	section 205
recipient (in Parts 3 and 4)	sections 33 and 84
representative (in Part 6)	section 181
representative body (in relation to a right of a data subject)	section 187
restriction of processing (in Parts 3 and 4)	sections 33 and 84
social work professional	section 204
the special purposes (in Part 6)	section 174
special purposes proceedings (in Part 6)	section 174
subordinate legislation	section 205

third country (in Part 3)	section 33
tribunal	section 205
the Tribunal	section 205

TERRITORIAL APPLICATION

III DAT [207]

207 Territorial application of this Act

(1) This Act applies only to processing of personal data described in subsections (2) and (3).

(2) It applies to the processing of personal data in the context of the activities of an establishment of a controller or processor in the United Kingdom, whether or not the processing takes place in the United Kingdom.

(3) It also applies to the processing of personal data to which Chapter 2 of Part 2 (the GDPR) applies where—

- (a) the processing is carried out in the context of the activities of an establishment of a controller or processor in a country or territory that is not a member State, whether or not the processing takes place in such a country or territory,
- (b) the personal data relates to a data subject who is in the United Kingdom when the processing takes place, and
- (c) the processing activities are related to—
  - (i) the offering of goods or services to data subjects in the United Kingdom, whether or not for payment, or
  - (ii) the monitoring of data subjects' behaviour in the United Kingdom.

(4) Subsections (1) to (3) have effect subject to any provision in or made under section 120 providing for the Commissioner to carry out functions in relation to other processing of personal data.

(5) Section 3(14)(c) does not apply to the reference to the processing of personal data in subsection (2).

(6) The reference in subsection (3) to Chapter 2 of Part 2 (the GDPR) does not include that Chapter as applied by Chapter 3 of Part 2 (the applied GDPR).

(7) In this section, references to a person who has an establishment in the United Kingdom include the following—

- (a) an individual who is ordinarily resident in the United Kingdom,
- (b) a body incorporated under the law of the United Kingdom or a part of the United Kingdom,
- (c) a partnership or other unincorporated association formed under the law of the United Kingdom or a part of the United Kingdom, and
- (d) a person not within paragraph (a), (b) or (c) who maintains, and carries on activities through, an office, branch or agency or other stable arrangements in the United Kingdom,

and references to a person who has an establishment in another country or territory have a corresponding meaning.

GENERAL

III DAT [208]

208 Children in Scotland

(1) Subsections (2) and (3) apply where a question falls to be determined in Scotland as to the legal capacity of a person aged under 16 to—

(a) exercise a right conferred by the data protection legislation, or

(b) give consent for the purposes of the data protection legislation.

(2) The person is to be taken to have that capacity where the person has a general understanding of what it means to exercise the right or give such consent.

(3) A person aged 12 or over is to be presumed to be of sufficient age and maturity to have such understanding, unless the contrary is shown.

III DAT [209]

209 Application to the Crown

(1) This Act binds the Crown.

(2) For the purposes of the GDPR and this Act, each government department is to be treated as a person separate from the other government departments (to the extent that is not already the case).

(3) Where government departments are not able to enter into contracts with each other, a provision of the GDPR or this Act that would require relations between them to be governed by a contract (or other binding legal act) in writing is to be treated as satisfied if the relations are the subject of a memorandum of understanding between them.

(4) Where the purposes for which and the manner in which personal data is, or is to be, processed are determined by a person acting on behalf of the Royal Household, the Duchy of Lancaster or the Duchy of Cornwall, the controller in respect of that data for the purposes of the GDPR and this Act is—

(a) in relation to the Royal Household, the Keeper of the Privy Purse,

(b) in relation to the Duchy of Lancaster, such person as the Chancellor of the Duchy appoints, and

(c) in relation to the Duchy of Cornwall, such person as the Duke of Cornwall, or the possessor for the time being of the Duchy of Cornwall, appoints.

(5) Different persons may be appointed under subsection (4)(b) or (c) for different purposes.

(6) As regards criminal liability—

(a) a government department is not liable to prosecution under this Act;

(b) nothing in subsection (4) makes a person who is a controller by virtue of that subsection liable to prosecution under this Act;

(c) a person in the service of the Crown is liable to prosecution under the provisions of this Act listed in subsection (7).

(7) Those provisions are—

(a) section 119;

(b) section 170;

(c) section 171;

(d) section 173;

(e) paragraph 15 of Schedule 15.

III DAT [210]

210 Application to Parliament

(1) Parts 1, 2 and 5 to 7 of this Act apply to the processing of personal data by or on behalf of either House of Parliament.

(2) Where the purposes for which and the manner in which personal data is, or is to be, processed are determined by or on behalf of the House of Commons, the controller in respect of that data for the purposes of the GDPR and this Act is the Corporate Officer of that House.

(3) Where the purposes for which and the manner in which personal data is, or is to be, processed are determined by or on behalf of the House of Lords, the controller in respect of that data for the purposes of the GDPR and this Act is the Corporate Officer of that House.

(4) Subsections (2) and (3) do not apply where the purposes for which and the manner in which the personal data is, or is to be, processed are determined by or on behalf of the Intelligence and Security Committee of Parliament.

(5) As regards criminal liability—

(a) nothing in subsection (2) or (3) makes the Corporate Officer of the House of Commons or the Corporate Officer of the House of Lords liable to prosecution under this Act;

(b) a person acting on behalf of either House of Parliament is liable to prosecution under the provisions of this Act listed in subsection (6).

(6) Those provisions are—

(a) section 170;

(b) section 171;

(c) section 173;

(d) paragraph 15 of Schedule 15.

III DAT [211]

211 Minor and consequential provision

(1) In Schedule 19—

(a) Part 1 contains minor and consequential amendments of primary legislation;

(b) Part 2 contains minor and consequential amendments of other legislation;

(c) Part 3 contains consequential modifications of legislation;

(d) Part 4 contains supplementary provision.

(2) The Secretary of State may by regulations make provision that is consequential on any provision made by this Act.

(3) Regulations under subsection (2)—

(a) may include transitional, transitory or saving provision;

(b) may amend, repeal or revoke an enactment.

(4) The reference to an enactment in subsection (3)(b) does not include an enactment passed or made after the end of the Session in which this Act is passed.

(5) Regulations under this section that amend, repeal or revoke primary legislation are subject to the affirmative resolution procedure.

(6) Any other regulations under this section are subject to the negative resolution procedure.

(7) In this section, "primary legislation" means—

(a) an Act;

(b) an Act of the Scottish Parliament;

(c) a Measure or Act of the National Assembly for Wales;

(d) Northern Ireland legislation.

FINAL

III DAT [212]

212 Commencement

(1) Except as provided by subsections (2) and (3), this Act comes into force on such day as the Secretary of State may by regulations appoint.

(2) This section and the following provisions come into force on the day on which this Act is passed—

- (a) sections 1 and 3;
- (b) section 182;
- (c) sections 204, 205 and 206;
- (d) sections 209 and 210;
- (e) sections 213(2), 214 and 215;
- (f) any other provision of this Act so far as it confers power to make regulations or Tribunal Procedure Rules or is otherwise necessary for enabling the exercise of such a power on or after the day on which this Act is passed.

(3) The following provisions come into force at the end of the period of 2 months beginning when this Act is passed—

- (a) section 124;
- (b) sections 125, 126 and 127, so far as they relate to a code prepared under section 124;
- (c) section 177;
- (d) section 178 and Schedule 17;
- (e) section 179.

(4) Regulations under this section may make different provision for different areas.

III DAT [212.1]

Commencement order See the Data Protection Act 2018 (Commencement No 1 and Transitional and Saving Provisions) Regulations 2018, SI 2018/625.

III DAT [213]

213 Transitional provision

(1) Schedule 20 contains transitional, transitory and saving provision.

(2) The Secretary of State may by regulations make transitional, transitory or saving provision in connection with the coming into force of any provision of this Act or with the GDPR beginning to apply, including provision amending or repealing a provision of Schedule 20.

(3) Regulations under this section that amend or repeal a provision of Schedule 20 are subject to the negative resolution procedure.

III DAT [214]

214 Extent

(1) This Act extends to England and Wales, Scotland and Northern Ireland, subject to—

- (a) subsections (2) to (5), and
- (b) paragraph 12 of Schedule 12.

(2) Section 199 extends to England and Wales only.

(3) Sections 188, 189 and 190 extend to England and Wales and Northern Ireland only.

(4) An amendment, repeal or revocation made by this Act has the same extent in the United Kingdom as the enactment amended, repealed or revoked.

(5) This subsection and the following provisions also extend to the Isle of Man—

(a) paragraphs 332 and 434 of Schedule 19;

(b) sections 211(1), 212(1) and 213(2), so far as relating to those paragraphs.

(6) Where there is a power to extend a part of an Act by Order in Council to any of the Channel Islands, the Isle of Man or any of the British overseas territories, the power may be exercised in relation to an amendment or repeal of that part which is made by or under this Act.

III DAT [215]

215 Short title

This Act may be cited as the Data Protection Act 2018.

SCHEDULE 1

SPECIAL CATEGORIES OF PERSONAL DATA AND CRIMINAL CONVICTIONS ETC DATA

Section 10

PART 1

CONDITIONS RELATING TO EMPLOYMENT, HEALTH AND RESEARCH ETC

Employment, social security and social protection

III DAT [216]

1 (1) This condition is met if—

(a) the processing is necessary for the purposes of performing or exercising obligations or rights which are imposed or conferred by law on the controller or the data subject in connection with employment, social security or social protection, and

(b) when the processing is carried out, the controller has an appropriate policy document in place (see paragraph 39 in Part 4 of this Schedule).

(2) See also the additional safeguards in Part 4 of this Schedule.

(3) In this paragraph—

"social security" includes any of the branches of social security listed in Article 3(1) of Regulation (EC) No 883/2004 of the European Parliament and of the Council on the co-ordination of social security systems (as amended from time to time);

"social protection" includes an intervention described in Article 2(b) of Regulation (EC) 458/2007 of the European Parliament and of the Council of 25 April 2007 on the European system of integrated social protection statistics (ESSPROS) (as amended from time to time).

Health or social care purposes

2 (1) This condition is met if the processing is necessary for health or social care purposes.

(2) In this paragraph "health or social care purposes" means the purposes of—

(a) preventive or occupational medicine,

(b) the assessment of the working capacity of an employee,

(c) medical diagnosis,

(d) the provision of health care or treatment,

(e) the provision of social care, or

(f) the management of health care systems or services or social care systems or services.

(3) See also the conditions and safeguards in Article 9(3) of the GDPR (obligations of secrecy) and section 11(1).

PUBLIC HEALTH

3 This condition is met if the processing—
 (a) is necessary for reasons of public interest in the area of public health, and
 (b) is carried out—
  (i) by or under the responsibility of a health professional, or
  (ii) by another person who in the circumstances owes a duty of confidentiality under an enactment or rule of law.

RESEARCH ETC

4 This condition is met if the processing—
 (a) is necessary for archiving purposes, scientific or historical research purposes or statistical purposes,
 (b) is carried out in accordance with Article 89(1) of the GDPR (as supplemented by section 19), and
 (c) is in the public interest.

PART 2
SUBSTANTIAL PUBLIC INTEREST CONDITIONS

REQUIREMENT FOR AN APPROPRIATE POLICY DOCUMENT WHEN RELYING ON CONDITIONS IN THIS PART

5 (1) Except as otherwise provided, a condition in this Part of this Schedule is met only if, when the processing is carried out, the controller has an appropriate policy document in place (see paragraph 39 in Part 4 of this Schedule).
 (2) See also the additional safeguards in Part 4 of this Schedule.

STATUTORY ETC AND GOVERNMENT PURPOSES

6 (1) This condition is met if the processing—
 (a) is necessary for a purpose listed in sub-paragraph (2), and
 (b) is necessary for reasons of substantial public interest.
 (2) Those purposes are—
 (a) the exercise of a function conferred on a person by an enactment or rule of law;
 (b) the exercise of a function of the Crown, a Minister of the Crown or a government department.

ADMINISTRATION OF JUSTICE AND PARLIAMENTARY PURPOSES

7 This condition is met if the processing is necessary—
 (a) for the administration of justice, or
 (b) for the exercise of a function of either House of Parliament.

EQUALITY OF OPPORTUNITY OR TREATMENT

8 (1) This condition is met if the processing—
 (a) is of a specified category of personal data, and
 (b) is necessary for the purposes of identifying or keeping under review the existence or absence of equality of opportunity or treatment between

groups of people specified in relation to that category with a view to enabling such equality to be promoted or maintained,

subject to the exceptions in sub-paragraphs (3) to (5).

(2) In sub-paragraph (1), "specified" means specified in the following table—

Category of personal data	*Groups of people (in relation to a category of personal data)*
Personal data revealing racial or ethnic origin	People of different racial or ethnic origins
Personal data revealing religious or philosophical beliefs	People holding different religious or philosophical beliefs
Data concerning health	People with different states of physical or mental health
Personal data concerning an individual's sexual orientation	People of different sexual orientation

(3) Processing does not meet the condition in sub-paragraph (1) if it is carried out for the purposes of measures or decisions with respect to a particular data subject.

(4) Processing does not meet the condition in sub-paragraph (1) if it is likely to cause substantial damage or substantial distress to an individual.

(5) Processing does not meet the condition in sub-paragraph (1) if—

(a) an individual who is the data subject (or one of the data subjects) has given notice in writing to the controller requiring the controller not to process personal data in respect of which the individual is the data subject (and has not given notice in writing withdrawing that requirement),

(b) the notice gave the controller a reasonable period in which to stop processing such data, and

(c) that period has ended.

RACIAL AND ETHNIC DIVERSITY AT SENIOR LEVELS OF ORGANISATIONS

9 (1) This condition is met if the processing—

(a) is of personal data revealing racial or ethnic origin,

(b) is carried out as part of a process of identifying suitable individuals to hold senior positions in a particular organisation, a type of organisation or organisations generally,

(c) is necessary for the purposes of promoting or maintaining diversity in the racial and ethnic origins of individuals who hold senior positions in the organisation or organisations, and

(d) can reasonably be carried out without the consent of the data subject,

subject to the exception in sub-paragraph (3).

(2) For the purposes of sub-paragraph (1)(d), processing can reasonably be carried out without the consent of the data subject only where—

(a) the controller cannot reasonably be expected to obtain the consent of the data subject, and

(b) the controller is not aware of the data subject withholding consent.

(3) Processing does not meet the condition in sub-paragraph (1) if it is likely to cause substantial damage or substantial distress to an individual.

(4) For the purposes of this paragraph, an individual holds a senior position in an organisation if the individual—

(a) holds a position listed in sub-paragraph (5), or

(b) does not hold such a position but is a senior manager of the organisation.

(5) Those positions are—

(a) a director, secretary or other similar officer of a body corporate;

(b) a member of a limited liability partnership;

(c) a partner in a partnership within the Partnership Act 1890, a limited partnership registered under the Limited Partnerships Act 1907 or an entity of a similar character formed under the law of a country or territory outside the United Kingdom.

(6) In this paragraph, "senior manager", in relation to an organisation, means a person who plays a significant role in—

(a) the making of decisions about how the whole or a substantial part of the organisation's activities are to be managed or organised, or

(b) the actual managing or organising of the whole or a substantial part of those activities.

(7) The reference in sub-paragraph (2)(b) to a data subject withholding consent does not include a data subject merely failing to respond to a request for consent.

Preventing or detecting unlawful acts

10 (1) This condition is met if the processing—

(a) is necessary for the purposes of the prevention or detection of an unlawful act,

(b) must be carried out without the consent of the data subject so as not to prejudice those purposes, and

(c) is necessary for reasons of substantial public interest.

(2) If the processing consists of the disclosure of personal data to a competent authority, or is carried out in preparation for such disclosure, the condition in sub-paragraph (1) is met even if, when the processing is carried out, the controller does not have an appropriate policy document in place (see paragraph 5 of this Schedule).

(3) In this paragraph—

"act" includes a failure to act;

"competent authority" has the same meaning as in Part 3 of this Act (see section 30).

Protecting the public against dishonesty etc

11 (1) This condition is met if the processing—

(a) is necessary for the exercise of a protective function,

(b) must be carried out without the consent of the data subject so as not to prejudice the exercise of that function, and

(c) is necessary for reasons of substantial public interest.

(2) In this paragraph, "protective function" means a function which is intended to protect members of the public against—

(a) dishonesty, malpractice or other seriously improper conduct,

(b) unfitness or incompetence,

(c) mismanagement in the administration of a body or association, or

(d) failures in services provided by a body or association.

Regulatory requirements relating to unlawful acts and dishonesty etc

12 (1) This condition is met if—

(a) the processing is necessary for the purposes of complying with, or assisting other persons to comply with, a regulatory requirement which involves a person taking steps to establish whether another person has—

(i) committed an unlawful act, or

(ii) been involved in dishonesty, malpractice or other seriously improper conduct,

(b) in the circumstances, the controller cannot reasonably be expected to obtain the consent of the data subject to the processing, and

(c) the processing is necessary for reasons of substantial public interest.

(2) In this paragraph—

"act" includes a failure to act;

"regulatory requirement" means—

(a) a requirement imposed by legislation or by a person in exercise of a function conferred by legislation, or

(b) a requirement forming part of generally accepted principles of good practice relating to a type of body or an activity.

Journalism etc in connection with unlawful acts and dishonesty etc

13 (1) This condition is met if—

(a) the processing consists of the disclosure of personal data for the special purposes,

(b) it is carried out in connection with a matter described in sub-paragraph (2),

(c) it is necessary for reasons of substantial public interest,

(d) it is carried out with a view to the publication of the personal data by any person, and

(e) the controller reasonably believes that publication of the personal data would be in the public interest.

(2) The matters mentioned in sub-paragraph (1)(b) are any of the following (whether alleged or established)—

(a) the commission of an unlawful act by a person;

(b) dishonesty, malpractice or other seriously improper conduct of a person;

(c) unfitness or incompetence of a person;

(d) mismanagement in the administration of a body or association;

(e) a failure in services provided by a body or association.

(3) The condition in sub-paragraph (1) is met even if, when the processing is carried out, the controller does not have an appropriate policy document in place (see paragraph 5 of this Schedule).

(4) In this paragraph—

"act" includes a failure to act;

"the special purposes" means—

(a) the purposes of journalism;

(b) academic purposes;

(c) artistic purposes;

(d) literary purposes.

Preventing fraud

14 (1) This condition is met if the processing—

(a) is necessary for the purposes of preventing fraud or a particular kind of fraud, and

(b) consists of—

(i) the disclosure of personal data by a person as a member of an anti-fraud organisation,

(ii) the disclosure of personal data in accordance with arrangements made by an anti-fraud organisation, or

(iii) the processing of personal data disclosed as described in sub-paragraph (i) or (ii).

(2) In this paragraph, "anti-fraud organisation" has the same meaning as in section 68 of the Serious Crime Act 2007.

SUSPICION OF TERRORIST FINANCING OR MONEY LAUNDERING

15 This condition is met if the processing is necessary for the purposes of making a disclosure in good faith under either of the following—

(a) section 21CA of the Terrorism Act 2000 (disclosures between certain entities within regulated sector in relation to suspicion of commission of terrorist financing offence or for purposes of identifying terrorist property);

(b) section 339ZB of the Proceeds of Crime Act 2002 (disclosures within regulated sector in relation to suspicion of money laundering).

SUPPORT FOR INDIVIDUALS WITH A PARTICULAR DISABILITY OR MEDICAL CONDITION

16 (1) This condition is met if the processing—

(a) is carried out by a not-for-profit body which provides support to individuals with a particular disability or medical condition,

(b) is of a type of personal data falling within sub-paragraph (2) which relates to an individual falling within sub-paragraph (3),

(c) is necessary for the purposes of—

(i) raising awareness of the disability or medical condition, or

(ii) providing support to individuals falling within sub-paragraph (3) or enabling such individuals to provide support to each other,

(d) can reasonably be carried out without the consent of the data subject, and

(e) is necessary for reasons of substantial public interest.

(2) The following types of personal data fall within this sub-paragraph—

(a) personal data revealing racial or ethnic origin;

(b) genetic data or biometric data;

(c) data concerning health;

(d) personal data concerning an individual's sex life or sexual orientation.

(3) An individual falls within this sub-paragraph if the individual is or has been a member of the body mentioned in sub-paragraph (1)(a) and—

(a) has the disability or condition mentioned there, has had that disability or condition or has a significant risk of developing that disability or condition, or

(b) is a relative or carer of an individual who satisfies paragraph (a) of this sub-paragraph.

(4) For the purposes of sub-paragraph (1)(d), processing can reasonably be carried out without the consent of the data subject only where—

(a) the controller cannot reasonably be expected to obtain the consent of the data subject, and

(b) the controller is not aware of the data subject withholding consent.

(5) In this paragraph—

"carer" means an individual who provides or intends to provide care for another individual other than—

(a) under or by virtue of a contract, or

(b) as voluntary work;

"disability" has the same meaning as in the Equality Act 2010 (see section 6 of, and Schedule 1 to, that Act).

(6) The reference in sub-paragraph (4)(b) to a data subject withholding consent does not include a data subject merely failing to respond to a request for consent.

Counselling etc

17 (1) This condition is met if the processing—

(a) is necessary for the provision of confidential counselling, advice or support or of another similar service provided confidentially,

(b) is carried out without the consent of the data subject for one of the reasons listed in sub-paragraph (2), and

(c) is necessary for reasons of substantial public interest.

(2) The reasons mentioned in sub-paragraph (1)(b) are—

(a) in the circumstances, consent to the processing cannot be given by the data subject;

(b) in the circumstances, the controller cannot reasonably be expected to obtain the consent of the data subject to the processing;

(c) the processing must be carried out without the consent of the data subject because obtaining the consent of the data subject would prejudice the provision of the service mentioned in sub-paragraph (1)(a).

Safeguarding of children and of individuals at risk

18 (1) This condition is met if—

(a) the processing is necessary for the purposes of—

(i) protecting an individual from neglect or physical, mental or emotional harm, or

(ii) protecting the physical, mental or emotional well-being of an individual,

(b) the individual is—

(i) aged under 18, or

(ii) aged 18 or over and at risk,

(c) the processing is carried out without the consent of the data subject for one of the reasons listed in sub-paragraph (2), and

(d) the processing is necessary for reasons of substantial public interest.

(2) The reasons mentioned in sub-paragraph (1)(c) are—

(a) in the circumstances, consent to the processing cannot be given by the data subject;

(b) in the circumstances, the controller cannot reasonably be expected to obtain the consent of the data subject to the processing;

(c) the processing must be carried out without the consent of the data subject because obtaining the consent of the data subject would prejudice the provision of the protection mentioned in sub-paragraph (1)(a).

(3) For the purposes of this paragraph, an individual aged 18 or over is "at risk" if the controller has reasonable cause to suspect that the individual—

(a) has needs for care and support,

(b) is experiencing, or at risk of, neglect or physical, mental or emotional harm, and

(c) as a result of those needs is unable to protect himself or herself against the neglect or harm or the risk of it.

(4) In sub-paragraph (1)(a), the reference to the protection of an individual or of the well-being of an individual includes both protection relating to a particular individual and protection relating to a type of individual.

Safeguarding of economic well-being of certain individuals

19 (1) This condition is met if the processing—

(a) is necessary for the purposes of protecting the economic well-being of an individual at economic risk who is aged 18 or over,

(b) is of data concerning health,
(c) is carried out without the consent of the data subject for one of the reasons listed in sub-paragraph (2), and
(d) is necessary for reasons of substantial public interest.

(2) The reasons mentioned in sub-paragraph (1)(c) are—
(a) in the circumstances, consent to the processing cannot be given by the data subject;
(b) in the circumstances, the controller cannot reasonably be expected to obtain the consent of the data subject to the processing;
(c) the processing must be carried out without the consent of the data subject because obtaining the consent of the data subject would prejudice the provision of the protection mentioned in sub-paragraph (1)(a).

(3) In this paragraph, "individual at economic risk" means an individual who is less able to protect his or her economic well-being by reason of physical or mental injury, illness or disability.

INSURANCE

20 (1) This condition is met if the processing—
(a) is necessary for an insurance purpose,
(b) is of personal data revealing racial or ethnic origin, religious or philosophical beliefs or trade union membership, genetic data or data concerning health, and
(c) is necessary for reasons of substantial public interest,

subject to sub-paragraphs (2) and (3).

(2) Sub-paragraph (3) applies where—
(a) the processing is not carried out for the purposes of measures or decisions with respect to the data subject, and
(b) the data subject does not have and is not expected to acquire—
(i) rights against, or obligations in relation to, a person who is an insured person under an insurance contract to which the insurance purpose mentioned in sub-paragraph (1)(a) relates, or
(ii) other rights or obligations in connection with such a contract.

(3) Where this sub-paragraph applies, the processing does not meet the condition in sub-paragraph (1) unless, in addition to meeting the requirements in that sub-paragraph, it can reasonably be carried out without the consent of the data subject.

(4) For the purposes of sub-paragraph (3), processing can reasonably be carried out without the consent of the data subject only where—
(a) the controller cannot reasonably be expected to obtain the consent of the data subject, and
(b) the controller is not aware of the data subject withholding consent.

(5) In this paragraph—

"insurance contract" means a contract of general insurance or long-term insurance;

"insurance purpose" means—
(a) advising on, arranging, underwriting or administering an insurance contract,
(b) administering a claim under an insurance contract, or
(c) exercising a right, or complying with an obligation, arising in connection with an insurance contract, including a right or obligation arising under an enactment or rule of law.

(6) The reference in sub-paragraph (4)(b) to a data subject withholding consent does not include a data subject merely failing to respond to a request for consent.

(7) Terms used in the definition of "insurance contract" in sub-paragraph (5) and also in an order made under section 22 of the Financial Services and Markets Act 2000 (regulated activities) have the same meaning in that definition as they have in that order.

OCCUPATIONAL PENSIONS

21 (1) This condition is met if the processing—

(a) is necessary for the purpose of making a determination in connection with eligibility for, or benefits payable under, an occupational pension scheme,

(b) is of data concerning health which relates to a data subject who is the parent, grandparent, great-grandparent or sibling of a member of the scheme,

(c) is not carried out for the purposes of measures or decisions with respect to the data subject, and

(d) can reasonably be carried out without the consent of the data subject.

(2) For the purposes of sub-paragraph (1)(d), processing can reasonably be carried out without the consent of the data subject only where—

(a) the controller cannot reasonably be expected to obtain the consent of the data subject, and

(b) the controller is not aware of the data subject withholding consent.

(3) In this paragraph—

"occupational pension scheme" has the meaning given in section 1 of the Pension Schemes Act 1993;

"member", in relation to a scheme, includes an individual who is seeking to become a member of the scheme.

(4) The reference in sub-paragraph (2)(b) to a data subject withholding consent does not include a data subject merely failing to respond to a request for consent.

POLITICAL PARTIES

22 (1) This condition is met if the processing—

(a) is of personal data revealing political opinions,

(b) is carried out by a person or organisation included in the register maintained under section 23 of the Political Parties, Elections and Referendums Act 2000, and

(c) is necessary for the purposes of the person's or organisation's political activities,

subject to the exceptions in sub-paragraphs (2) and (3).

(2) Processing does not meet the condition in sub-paragraph (1) if it is likely to cause substantial damage or substantial distress to a person.

(3) Processing does not meet the condition in sub-paragraph (1) if—

(a) an individual who is the data subject (or one of the data subjects) has given notice in writing to the controller requiring the controller not to process personal data in respect of which the individual is the data subject (and has not given notice in writing withdrawing that requirement),

(b) the notice gave the controller a reasonable period in which to stop processing such data, and

(c) that period has ended.

(4) In this paragraph, "political activities" include campaigning, fund-raising, political surveys and case-work.

ELECTED REPRESENTATIVES RESPONDING TO REQUESTS

23 (1) This condition is met if—

(a) the processing is carried out—
(i) by an elected representative or a person acting with the authority of such a representative,
(ii) in connection with the discharge of the elected representative's functions, and
(iii) in response to a request by an individual that the elected representative take action on behalf of the individual, and
(b) the processing is necessary for the purposes of, or in connection with, the action reasonably taken by the elected representative in response to that request,

subject to sub-paragraph (2).

(2) Where the request is made by an individual other than the data subject, the condition in sub-paragraph (1) is met only if the processing must be carried out without the consent of the data subject for one of the following reasons—
(a) in the circumstances, consent to the processing cannot be given by the data subject;
(b) in the circumstances, the elected representative cannot reasonably be expected to obtain the consent of the data subject to the processing;
(c) obtaining the consent of the data subject would prejudice the action taken by the elected representative;
(d) the processing is necessary in the interests of another individual and the data subject has withheld consent unreasonably.

(3) In this paragraph, "elected representative" means—
(a) a member of the House of Commons;
(b) a member of the National Assembly for Wales;
(c) a member of the Scottish Parliament;
(d) a member of the Northern Ireland Assembly;
(e) a member of the European Parliament elected in the United Kingdom;
(f) an elected member of a local authority within the meaning of section 270(1) of the Local Government Act 1972, namely—
(i) in England, a county council, a district council, a London borough council or a parish council;
(ii) in Wales, a county council, a county borough council or a community council;
(g) an elected mayor of a local authority within the meaning of Part 1A or 2 of the Local Government Act 2000;
(h) a mayor for the area of a combined authority established under section 103 of the Local Democracy, Economic Development and Construction Act 2009;
(i) the Mayor of London or an elected member of the London Assembly;
(j) an elected member of—
(i) the Common Council of the City of London, or
(ii) the Council of the Isles of Scilly;
(k) an elected member of a council constituted under section 2 of the Local Government etc (Scotland) Act 1994;
(l) an elected member of a district council within the meaning of the Local Government Act (Northern Ireland) 1972 (c 9 (NI));
(m) a police and crime commissioner.

(4) For the purposes of sub-paragraph (3), a person who is—
(a) a member of the House of Commons immediately before Parliament is dissolved,
(b) a member of the National Assembly for Wales immediately before that Assembly is dissolved,
(c) a member of the Scottish Parliament immediately before that Parliament is dissolved, or

(d) a member of the Northern Ireland Assembly immediately before that Assembly is dissolved,

is to be treated as if the person were such a member until the end of the fourth day after the day on which the subsequent general election in relation to that Parliament or Assembly is held.

(5) For the purposes of sub-paragraph (3), a person who is an elected member of the Common Council of the City of London and whose term of office comes to an end at the end of the day preceding the annual Wardmotes is to be treated as if he or she were such a member until the end of the fourth day after the day on which those Wardmotes are held.

Disclosure to elected representatives

24 (1) This condition is met if—

(a) the processing consists of the disclosure of personal data—

(i) to an elected representative or a person acting with the authority of such a representative, and

(ii) in response to a communication to the controller from that representative or person which was made in response to a request from an individual,

(b) the personal data is relevant to the subject matter of that communication, and

(c) the disclosure is necessary for the purpose of responding to that communication,

subject to sub-paragraph (2).

(2) Where the request to the elected representative came from an individual other than the data subject, the condition in sub-paragraph (1) is met only if the disclosure must be made without the consent of the data subject for one of the following reasons—

(a) in the circumstances, consent to the processing cannot be given by the data subject;

(b) in the circumstances, the elected representative cannot reasonably be expected to obtain the consent of the data subject to the processing;

(c) obtaining the consent of the data subject would prejudice the action taken by the elected representative;

(d) the processing is necessary in the interests of another individual and the data subject has withheld consent unreasonably.

(3) In this paragraph, "elected representative" has the same meaning as in paragraph 23.

Informing elected representatives about prisoners

25 (1) This condition is met if—

(a) the processing consists of the processing of personal data about a prisoner for the purpose of informing a member of the House of Commons, a member of the National Assembly for Wales or a member of the Scottish Parliament about the prisoner, and

(b) the member is under an obligation not to further disclose the personal data.

(2) The references in sub-paragraph (1) to personal data about, and to informing someone about, a prisoner include personal data about, and informing someone about, arrangements for the prisoner's release.

(3) In this paragraph—

"prison" includes a young offender institution, a remand centre, a secure training centre or a secure college;

"prisoner" means a person detained in a prison.

PUBLICATION OF LEGAL JUDGMENTS

26 This condition is met if the processing—

(a) consists of the publication of a judgment or other decision of a court or tribunal, or

(b) is necessary for the purposes of publishing such a judgment or decision.

ANTI-DOPING IN SPORT

27 (1) This condition is met if the processing is necessary—

(a) for the purposes of measures designed to eliminate doping which are undertaken by or under the responsibility of a body or association that is responsible for eliminating doping in a sport, at a sporting event or in sport generally, or

(b) for the purposes of providing information about doping, or suspected doping, to such a body or association.

(2) The reference in sub-paragraph (1)(a) to measures designed to eliminate doping includes measures designed to identify or prevent doping.

(3) If the processing consists of the disclosure of personal data to a body or association described in sub-paragraph (1)(a), or is carried out in preparation for such disclosure, the condition in sub-paragraph (1) is met even if, when the processing is carried out, the controller does not have an appropriate policy document in place (see paragraph 5 of this Schedule).

STANDARDS OF BEHAVIOUR IN SPORT

28 (1) This condition is met if the processing—

(a) is necessary for the purposes of measures designed to protect the integrity of a sport or a sporting event,

(b) must be carried out without the consent of the data subject so as not to prejudice those purposes, and

(c) is necessary for reasons of substantial public interest.

(2) In sub-paragraph (1)(a), the reference to measures designed to protect the integrity of a sport or a sporting event is a reference to measures designed to protect a sport or a sporting event against—

(a) dishonesty, malpractice or other seriously improper conduct, or

(b) failure by a person participating in the sport or event in any capacity to comply with standards of behaviour set by a body or association with responsibility for the sport or event.

PART 3
ADDITIONAL CONDITIONS RELATING TO CRIMINAL CONVICTIONS ETC

CONSENT

29 This condition is met if the data subject has given consent to the processing.

PROTECTING INDIVIDUAL'S VITAL INTERESTS

30 This condition is met if—

(a) the processing is necessary to protect the vital interests of an individual, and

(b) the data subject is physically or legally incapable of giving consent.

PROCESSING BY NOT-FOR-PROFIT BODIES

31 This condition is met if the processing is carried out—
(a) in the course of its legitimate activities with appropriate safeguards by a foundation, association or other not-for-profit body with a political, philosophical, religious or trade union aim, and
(b) on condition that—
(i) the processing relates solely to the members or to former members of the body or to persons who have regular contact with it in connection with its purposes, and
(ii) the personal data is not disclosed outside that body without the consent of the data subjects.

PERSONAL DATA IN THE PUBLIC DOMAIN

32 This condition is met if the processing relates to personal data which is manifestly made public by the data subject.

LEGAL CLAIMS

33 This condition is met if the processing—
(a) is necessary for the purpose of, or in connection with, any legal proceedings (including prospective legal proceedings),
(b) is necessary for the purpose of obtaining legal advice, or
(c) is otherwise necessary for the purposes of establishing, exercising or defending legal rights.

JUDICIAL ACTS

34 This condition is met if the processing is necessary when a court or tribunal is acting in its judicial capacity.

ADMINISTRATION OF ACCOUNTS USED IN COMMISSION OF INDECENCY OFFENCES INVOLVING CHILDREN

35 (1) This condition is met if—
(a) the processing is of personal data about a conviction or caution for an offence listed in sub-paragraph (2),
(b) the processing is necessary for the purpose of administering an account relating to the payment card used in the commission of the offence or cancelling that payment card, and
(c) when the processing is carried out, the controller has an appropriate policy document in place (see paragraph 39 in Part 4 of this Schedule).
(2) Those offences are an offence under—
(a) section 1 of the Protection of Children Act 1978 (indecent photographs of children),
(b) Article 3 of the Protection of Children (Northern Ireland) Order 1978 (SI 1978/1047 (NI 17)) (indecent photographs of children),
(c) section 52 of the Civic Government (Scotland) Act 1982 (indecent photographs etc of children),
(d) section 160 of the Criminal Justice Act 1988 (possession of indecent photograph of child),
(e) Article 15 of the Criminal Justice (Evidence etc) (Northern Ireland) Order 1988 (SI 1988/1847 (NI 17)) (possession of indecent photograph of child), or

(f) section 62 of the Coroners and Justice Act 2009 (possession of prohibited images of children),

or incitement to commit an offence under any of those provisions.

(3) See also the additional safeguards in Part 4 of this Schedule.

(4) In this paragraph—

"caution" means a caution given to a person in England and Wales or Northern Ireland in respect of an offence which, at the time when the caution is given, is admitted;

"conviction" has the same meaning as in the Rehabilitation of Offenders Act 1974 or the Rehabilitation of Offenders (Northern Ireland) Order 1978 (SI 1978/1908 (NI 27));

"payment card" includes a credit card, a charge card and a debit card.

EXTENSION OF CONDITIONS IN PART 2 OF THIS SCHEDULE REFERRING TO SUBSTANTIAL PUBLIC INTEREST

36 This condition is met if the processing would meet a condition in Part 2 of this Schedule but for an express requirement for the processing to be necessary for reasons of substantial public interest.

EXTENSION OF INSURANCE CONDITIONS

37 This condition is met if the processing—

(a) would meet the condition in paragraph 20 in Part 2 of this Schedule (the "insurance condition"), or

(b) would meet the condition in paragraph 36 by virtue of the insurance condition,

but for the requirement for the processing to be processing of a category of personal data specified in paragraph 20(1)(b).

PART 4
APPROPRIATE POLICY DOCUMENT AND ADDITIONAL SAFEGUARDS

APPLICATION OF THIS PART OF THIS SCHEDULE

38 This Part of this Schedule makes provision about the processing of personal data carried out in reliance on a condition in Part 1, 2 or 3 of this Schedule which requires the controller to have an appropriate policy document in place when the processing is carried out.

REQUIREMENT TO HAVE AN APPROPRIATE POLICY DOCUMENT IN PLACE

39 The controller has an appropriate policy document in place in relation to the processing of personal data in reliance on a condition described in paragraph 38 if the controller has produced a document which—

(a) explains the controller's procedures for securing compliance with the principles in Article 5 of the GDPR (principles relating to processing of personal data) in connection with the processing of personal data in reliance on the condition in question, and

(b) explains the controller's policies as regards the retention and erasure of personal data processed in reliance on the condition, giving an indication of how long such personal data is likely to be retained.

ADDITIONAL SAFEGUARD: RETENTION OF APPROPRIATE POLICY DOCUMENT

40 (1) Where personal data is processed in reliance on a condition described in paragraph 38, the controller must during the relevant period—

(a) retain the appropriate policy document,

(b) review and (if appropriate) update it from time to time, and

(c) make it available to the Commissioner, on request, without charge.

(2) "Relevant period", in relation to the processing of personal data in reliance on a condition described in paragraph 38, means a period which—

(a) begins when the controller starts to carry out processing of personal data in reliance on that condition, and

(b) ends at the end of the period of 6 months beginning when the controller ceases to carry out such processing.

Additional safeguard: record of processing

41 A record maintained by the controller, or the controller's representative, under Article 30 of the GDPR in respect of the processing of personal data in reliance on a condition described in paragraph 38 must include the following information—

(a) which condition is relied on,

(b) how the processing satisfies Article 6 of the GDPR (lawfulness of processing), and

(c) whether the personal data is retained and erased in accordance with the policies described in paragraph 39(b) and, if it is not, the reasons for not following those policies.

SCHEDULE 2

EXEMPTIONS ETC FROM THE GDPR

Section 15

PART 1

ADAPTATIONS AND RESTRICTIONS BASED ON ARTICLES 6(3) AND 23(1)

III DAT [217]

GDPR provisions to be adapted or restricted: "the listed GDPR provisions"

1 In this Part of this Schedule, "the listed GDPR provisions" means—

(a) the following provisions of the GDPR (the rights and obligations in which may be restricted by virtue of Article 23(1) of the GDPR)—

(i) Article 13(1) to (3) (personal data collected from data subject: information to be provided);

(ii) Article 14(1) to (4) (personal data collected other than from data subject: information to be provided);

(iii) Article 15(1) to (3) (confirmation of processing, access to data and safeguards for third country transfers);

(iv) Article 16 (right to rectification);

(v) Article 17(1) and (2) (right to erasure);

(vi) Article 18(1) (restriction of processing);

(vii) Article 19 (notification obligation regarding rectification or erasure of personal data or restriction of processing);

(viii) Article 20(1) and (2) (right to data portability);

(ix) Article 21(1) (objections to processing);

(x) Article 5 (general principles) so far as its provisions correspond to the rights and obligations provided for in the provisions mentioned in sub-paragraphs (i) to (ix); and

(b) the following provisions of the GDPR (the application of which may be adapted by virtue of Article 6(3) of the GDPR)—

(i) Article 5(1)(a) (lawful, fair and transparent processing), other than the lawfulness requirements set out in Article 6;
(ii) Article 5(1)(b) (purpose limitation).

CRIME AND TAXATION: GENERAL

2 (1) The listed GDPR provisions and Article 34(1) and (4) of the GDPR (communication of personal data breach to the data subject) do not apply to personal data processed for any of the following purposes—
(a) the prevention or detection of crime,
(b) the apprehension or prosecution of offenders, or
(c) the assessment or collection of a tax or duty or an imposition of a similar nature,

to the extent that the application of those provisions would be likely to prejudice any of the matters mentioned in paragraphs (a) to (c).

(2) Sub-paragraph (3) applies where—
(a) personal data is processed by a person ("Controller 1") for any of the purposes mentioned in sub-paragraph (1)(a) to (c), and
(b) another person ("Controller 2") obtains the data from Controller 1 for the purpose of discharging statutory functions and processes it for the purpose of discharging statutory functions.

(3) Controller 2 is exempt from the obligations in the following provisions of the GDPR—
(a) Article 13(1) to (3) (personal data collected from data subject: information to be provided),
(b) Article 14(1) to (4) (personal data collected other than from data subject: information to be provided),
(c) Article 15(1) to (3) (confirmation of processing, access to data and safeguards for third country transfers), and
(d) Article 5 (general principles) so far as its provisions correspond to the rights and obligations provided for in the provisions mentioned in paragraphs (a) to (c),

to the same extent that Controller 1 is exempt from those obligations by virtue of sub-paragraph (1).

CRIME AND TAXATION: RISK ASSESSMENT SYSTEMS

3 (1) The GDPR provisions listed in sub-paragraph (3) do not apply to personal data which consists of a classification applied to the data subject as part of a risk assessment system falling within sub-paragraph (2) to the extent that the application of those provisions would prevent the system from operating effectively.

(2) A risk assessment system falls within this sub-paragraph if—
(a) it is operated by a government department, a local authority or another authority administering housing benefit, and
(b) it is operated for the purposes of—
(i) the assessment or collection of a tax or duty or an imposition of a similar nature, or
(ii) the prevention or detection of crime or apprehension or prosecution of offenders, where the offence concerned involves the unlawful use of public money or an unlawful claim for payment out of public money.

(3) The GDPR provisions referred to in sub-paragraph (1) are the following provisions of the GDPR (the rights and obligations in which may be restricted by virtue of Article 23(1) of the GDPR)—

(a) Article 13(1) to (3) (personal data collected from data subject: information to be provided);
(b) Article 14(1) to (4) (personal data collected other than from data subject: information to be provided);
(c) Article 15(1) to (3) (confirmation of processing, access to data and safeguards for third country transfers);
(d) Article 5 (general principles) so far as its provisions correspond to the rights and obligations provided for in the provisions mentioned in paragraphs (a) to (c).

Immigration

4 (1) The GDPR provisions listed in sub-paragraph (2) do not apply to personal data processed for any of the following purposes—
(a) the maintenance of effective immigration control, or
(b) the investigation or detection of activities that would undermine the maintenance of effective immigration control,

to the extent that the application of those provisions would be likely to prejudice any of the matters mentioned in paragraphs (a) and (b).

(2) The GDPR provisions referred to in sub-paragraph (1) are the following provisions of the GDPR (the rights and obligations in which may be restricted by virtue of Article 23(1) of the GDPR)—
(a) Article 13(1) to (3) (personal data collected from data subject: information to be provided);
(b) Article 14(1) to (4) (personal data collected other than from data subject: information to be provided);
(c) Article 15(1) to (3) (confirmation of processing, access to data and safeguards for third country transfers);
(d) Article 17(1) and (2) (right to erasure);
(e) Article 18(1) (restriction of processing);
(f) Article 21(1) (objections to processing);
(g) Article 5 (general principles) so far as its provisions correspond to the rights and obligations provided for in the provisions mentioned in sub-paragraphs (a) to (f).

(That is, the listed GDPR provisions other than Article 16 (right to rectification), Article 19 (notification obligation regarding rectification or erasure of personal data or restriction of processing) and Article 20(1) and (2) (right to data portability) and, subject to sub-paragraph (2)(g) of this paragraph, the provisions of Article 5 listed in paragraph 1(b).)

(3) Sub-paragraph (4) applies where—
(a) personal data is processed by a person ("Controller 1"), and
(b) another person ("Controller 2") obtains the data from Controller 1 for any of the purposes mentioned in sub-paragraph (1)(a) and (b) and processes it for any of those purposes.

(4) Controller 1 is exempt from the obligations in the following provisions of the GDPR—
(a) Article 13(1) to (3) (personal data collected from data subject: information to be provided),
(b) Article 14(1) to (4) (personal data collected other than from data subject: information to be provided),
(c) Article 15(1) to (3) (confirmation of processing, access to data and safeguards for third country transfers), and
(d) Article 5 (general principles) so far as its provisions correspond to the rights and obligations provided for in the provisions mentioned in paragraphs (a) to (c),

to the same extent that Controller 2 is exempt from those obligations by virtue of sub-paragraph (1).

INFORMATION REQUIRED TO BE DISCLOSED BY LAW ETC OR IN CONNECTION WITH LEGAL PROCEEDINGS

5 (1) The listed GDPR provisions do not apply to personal data consisting of information that the controller is obliged by an enactment to make available to the public, to the extent that the application of those provisions would prevent the controller from complying with that obligation.

(2) The listed GDPR provisions do not apply to personal data where disclosure of the data is required by an enactment, a rule of law or an order of a court or tribunal, to the extent that the application of those provisions would prevent the controller from making the disclosure.

(3) The listed GDPR provisions do not apply to personal data where disclosure of the data—

(a) is necessary for the purpose of, or in connection with, legal proceedings (including prospective legal proceedings),

(b) is necessary for the purpose of obtaining legal advice, or

(c) is otherwise necessary for the purposes of establishing, exercising or defending legal rights,

to the extent that the application of those provisions would prevent the controller from making the disclosure.

PART 2
RESTRICTIONS BASED ON ARTICLE 23(1): RESTRICTIONS OF RULES IN ARTICLES 13 TO 21 AND 34

GDPR PROVISIONS TO BE RESTRICTED: "THE LISTED GDPR PROVISIONS"

6 In this Part of this Schedule, "the listed GDPR provisions" means the following provisions of the GDPR (the rights and obligations in which may be restricted by virtue of Article 23(1) of the GDPR)—

(a) Article 13(1) to (3) (personal data collected from data subject: information to be provided);

(b) Article 14(1) to (4) (personal data collected other than from data subject: information to be provided);

(c) Article 15(1) to (3) (confirmation of processing, access to data and safeguards for third country transfers);

(d) Article 16 (right to rectification);

(e) Article 17(1) and (2) (right to erasure);

(f) Article 18(1) (restriction of processing);

(g) Article 19 (notification obligation regarding rectification or erasure of personal data or restriction of processing);

(h) Article 20(1) and (2) (right to data portability);

(i) Article 21(1) (objections to processing);

(j) Article 5 (general principles) so far as its provisions correspond to the rights and obligations provided for in the provisions mentioned in sub-paragraphs (a) to (i).

FUNCTIONS DESIGNED TO PROTECT THE PUBLIC ETC

7 The listed GDPR provisions do not apply to personal data processed for the purposes of discharging a function that—

(a) is designed as described in column 1 of the Table, and

(b) meets the condition relating to the function specified in column 2 of the Table,

to the extent that the application of those provisions would be likely to prejudice the proper discharge of the function.

TABLE

Description of function design	*Condition*
1 The function is designed to protect members of the public against— (a) financial loss due to dishonesty, malpractice or other seriously improper conduct by, or the unfitness or incompetence of, persons concerned in the provision of banking, insurance, investment or other financial services or in the management of bodies corporate, or (b) financial loss due to the conduct of discharged or undischarged bankrupts.	The function is— (a) conferred on a person by an enactment, (b) a function of the Crown, a Minister of the Crown or a government department, or (c) of a public nature, and is exercised in the public interest.
2 The function is designed to protect members of the public against— (a) dishonesty, malpractice or other seriously improper conduct, or (b) unfitness or incompetence.	The function is— (a) conferred on a person by an enactment, (b) a function of the Crown, a Minister of the Crown or a government department, or (c) of a public nature, and is exercised in the public interest.
3 The function is designed— (a) to protect charities or community interest companies against misconduct or mismanagement (whether by trustees, directors or other persons) in their administration, (b) to protect the property of charities or community interest companies from loss or misapplication, or (c) to recover the property of charities or community interest companies.	The function is— (a) conferred on a person by an enactment, (b) a function of the Crown, a Minister of the Crown or a government department, or (c) of a public nature, and is exercised in the public interest.
4 The function is designed— (a) to secure the health, safety and welfare of persons at work, or (b) to protect persons other than those at work against risk to health or safety arising out of or in connection with the action of persons at work.	The function is— (a) conferred on a person by an enactment, (b) a function of the Crown, a Minister of the Crown or a government department, or (c) of a public nature, and is exercised in the public interest.
5 The function is designed to protect members of the public against— (a) maladministration by public bodies, (b) failures in services provided by public bodies, or (c) a failure of a public body to provide a service which it is a function of the body to provide.	The function is conferred by any enactment on— (a) the Parliamentary Commissioner for Administration, (b) the Commissioner for Local Administration in England, (c) the Health Service Commissioner for England, (d) the Public Services Ombudsman for Wales, (e) the Northern Ireland Public Services Ombudsman,

DATA PROTECTION

	(f) the Prison Ombudsman for Northern Ireland, or (g) the Scottish Public Services Ombudsman.
6 The function is designed— (a) to protect members of the public against conduct which may adversely affect their interests by persons carrying on a business, (b) to regulate agreements or conduct which have as their object or effect the prevention, restriction or distortion of competition in connection with any commercial activity, or (c) to regulate conduct on the part of one or more undertakings which amounts to the abuse of a dominant position in a market.	The function is conferred on the Competition and Markets Authority by an enactment.

Audit functions

8 (1) The listed GDPR provisions do not apply to personal data processed for the purposes of discharging a function listed in sub-paragraph (2) to the extent that the application of those provisions would be likely to prejudice the proper discharge of the function.

(2) The functions are any function that is conferred by an enactment on—

(a) the Comptroller and Auditor General;

(b) the Auditor General for Scotland;

(c) the Auditor General for Wales;

(d) the Comptroller and Auditor General for Northern Ireland.

Functions of the Bank of England

9 (1) The listed GDPR provisions do not apply to personal data processed for the purposes of discharging a relevant function of the Bank of England to the extent that the application of those provisions would be likely to prejudice the proper discharge of the function.

(2) "Relevant function of the Bank of England" means—

(a) a function discharged by the Bank acting in its capacity as a monetary authority (as defined in section 244(2)(c) and (2A) of the Banking Act 2009);

(b) a public function of the Bank within the meaning of section 349 of the Financial Services and Markets Act 2000;

(c) a function conferred on the Prudential Regulation Authority by or under the Financial Services and Markets Act 2000 or by another enactment.

Regulatory functions relating to legal services, the health service and children's services

10 (1) The listed GDPR provisions do not apply to personal data processed for the purposes of discharging a function listed in sub-paragraph (2) to the extent that the application of those provisions would be likely to prejudice the proper discharge of the function.

(2) The functions are—

(a) a function of the Legal Services Board;

(b) the function of considering a complaint under the scheme established under Part 6 of the Legal Services Act 2007 (legal complaints);

(c) the function of considering a complaint under—

(i) section 14 of the NHS Redress Act 2006,

(ii) section 113(1) or (2) or section 114(1) or (3) of the Health and Social Care (Community Health and Standards) Act 2003,

(iii) section 24D or 26 of the Children Act 1989, or

(iv) Part 2A of the Public Services Ombudsman (Wales) Act 2005;

(d) the function of considering a complaint or representations under Chapter 1 of Part 10 of the Social Services and Well-being (Wales) Act 2014 (anaw 4).

Regulatory functions of certain other persons

11 The listed GDPR provisions do not apply to personal data processed for the purposes of discharging a function that—

(a) is a function of a person described in column 1 of the Table, and

(b) is conferred on that person as described in column 2 of the Table,

to the extent that the application of those provisions would be likely to prejudice the proper discharge of the function.

TABLE

Person on whom function is conferred	*How function is conferred*
1 The Commissioner.	By or under— (a) the data protection legislation; (b) the Freedom of Information Act 2000; (c) section 244 of the Investigatory Powers Act 2016; (d) the Privacy and Electronic Communications (EC Directive) Regulations 2003 (SI 2003/2426); (e) the Environmental Information Regulations 2004 (SI 2004/3391); (f) the INSPIRE Regulations 2009 (SI 2009/3157); (g) Regulation (EU) No 910/2014 of the European Parliament and of the Council of 23 July 2014 on electronic identification and trust services for electronic transactions in the internal market and repealing Directive 1999/93/EC; (h) the Re-use of Public Sector Information Regulations 2015 (SI 2015/1415); (i) the Electronic Identification and Trust Services for Electronic Transactions Regulations 2016 (SI 2016/696).
2 The Scottish Information Commissioner.	By or under— (a) the Freedom of Information (Scotland) Act 2002 (asp 13); (b) the Environmental Information (Scotland) Regulations 2004 (SSI 2004/520); (c) the INSPIRE (Scotland) Regulations 2009 (SSI 2009/440).
3 The Pensions Ombudsman.	By or under Part 10 of the Pension Schemes Act 1993 or any corresponding legislation having equivalent effect in Northern Ireland.

4 The Board of the Pension Protection Fund.	By or under sections 206 to 208 of the Pensions Act 2004 or any corresponding legislation having equivalent effect in Northern Ireland.
5 The Ombudsman for the Board of the Pension Protection Fund.	By or under any of sections 209 to 218 or 286(1) of the Pensions Act 2004 or any corresponding legislation having equivalent effect in Northern Ireland.
6 The Pensions Regulator.	By an enactment.
7 The Financial Conduct Authority.	By or under the Financial Services and Markets Act 2000 or by another enactment.
8 The Financial Ombudsman.	By or under Part 16 of the Financial Services and Markets Act 2000.
9 The investigator of complaints against the financial regulators.	By or under Part 6 of the Financial Services Act 2012.
10 A consumer protection enforcer, other than the Competition and Markets Authority.	By or under the CPC Regulation.
11 The monitoring officer of a relevant authority.	By or under the Local Government and Housing Act 1989.
12 The monitoring officer of a relevant Welsh authority.	By or under the Local Government Act 2000.
13 The Public Services Ombudsman for Wales.	By or under the Local Government Act 2000.
14 The Charity Commission.	By or under— (a) the Charities Act 1992; (b) the Charities Act 2006; (c) the Charities Act 2011.

12 In the Table in paragraph 11—

"consumer protection enforcer" has the same meaning as "CPC enforcer" in section 213(5A) of the Enterprise Act 2002;

the "CPC Regulation" has the meaning given in section 235A of the Enterprise Act 2002;

the "Financial Ombudsman" means the scheme operator within the meaning of Part 16 of the Financial Services and Markets Act 2000 (see section 225 of that Act);

the "investigator of complaints against the financial regulators" means the person appointed under section 84(1)(b) of the Financial Services Act 2012;

"relevant authority" has the same meaning as in section 5 of the Local Government and Housing Act 1989, and "monitoring officer", in relation to such an authority, means a person designated as such under that section;

"relevant Welsh authority" has the same meaning as "relevant authority" in section 49(6) of the Local Government Act 2000, and "monitoring officer", in relation to such an authority, has the same meaning as in Part 3 of that Act.

PARLIAMENTARY PRIVILEGE

13 The listed GDPR provisions and Article 34(1) and (4) of the GDPR (communication of personal data breach to the data subject) do not apply to personal data where this is required for the purpose of avoiding an infringement of the privileges of either House of Parliament.

Judicial appointments, judicial independence and judicial proceedings

14 (1) The listed GDPR provisions do not apply to personal data processed for the purposes of assessing a person's suitability for judicial office or the office of Queen's Counsel.

(2) The listed GDPR provisions do not apply to personal data processed by—

(a) an individual acting in a judicial capacity, or

(b) a court or tribunal acting in its judicial capacity.

(3) As regards personal data not falling within sub-paragraph (1) or (2), the listed GDPR provisions do not apply to the extent that the application of those provisions would be likely to prejudice judicial independence or judicial proceedings.

Crown honours, dignities and appointments

15 (1) The listed GDPR provisions do not apply to personal data processed for the purposes of the conferring by the Crown of any honour or dignity.

(2) The listed GDPR provisions do not apply to personal data processed for the purposes of assessing a person's suitability for any of the following offices—

(a) archbishops and diocesan and suffragan bishops in the Church of England;

(b) deans of cathedrals of the Church of England;

(c) deans and canons of the two Royal Peculiars;

(d) the First and Second Church Estates Commissioners;

(e) lord-lieutenants;

(f) Masters of Trinity College and Churchill College, Cambridge;

(g) the Provost of Eton;

(h) the Poet Laureate;

(i) the Astronomer Royal.

(3) The Secretary of State may by regulations amend the list in sub-paragraph (2) to—

(a) remove an office, or

(b) add an office to which appointments are made by Her Majesty.

(4) Regulations under sub-paragraph (3) are subject to the affirmative resolution procedure.

PART 3
RESTRICTION BASED ON ARTICLE 23(1): PROTECTION OF RIGHTS OF OTHERS

Protection of the rights of others: general

16 (1) Article 15(1) to (3) of the GDPR (confirmation of processing, access to data and safeguards for third country transfers), and Article 5 of the GDPR so far as its provisions correspond to the rights and obligations provided for in Article 15(1) to (3), do not oblige a controller to disclose information to the data subject to the extent that doing so would involve disclosing information relating to another individual who can be identified from the information.

(2) Sub-paragraph (1) does not remove the controller's obligation where—

(a) the other individual has consented to the disclosure of the information to the data subject, or

(b) it is reasonable to disclose the information to the data subject without the consent of the other individual.

(3) In determining whether it is reasonable to disclose the information without consent, the controller must have regard to all the relevant circumstances, including—

(a) the type of information that would be disclosed,

(b) any duty of confidentiality owed to the other individual,

(c) any steps taken by the controller with a view to seeking the consent of the other individual,

(d) whether the other individual is capable of giving consent, and

(e) any express refusal of consent by the other individual.

(4) For the purposes of this paragraph—

(a) "information relating to another individual" includes information identifying the other individual as the source of information;

(b) an individual can be identified from information to be provided to a data subject by a controller if the individual can be identified from—

(i) that information, or

(ii) that information and any other information that the controller reasonably believes the data subject is likely to possess or obtain.

ASSUMPTION OF REASONABLENESS FOR HEALTH WORKERS, SOCIAL WORKERS AND EDUCATION WORKERS

17 (1) For the purposes of paragraph 16(2)(b), it is to be considered reasonable for a controller to disclose information to a data subject without the consent of the other individual where—

(a) the health data test is met,

(b) the social work data test is met, or

(c) the education data test is met.

(2) The health data test is met if—

(a) the information in question is contained in a health record, and

(b) the other individual is a health professional who has compiled or contributed to the health record or who, in his or her capacity as a health professional, has been involved in the diagnosis, care or treatment of the data subject.

(3) The social work data test is met if—

(a) the other individual is—

(i) a children's court officer,

(ii) a person who is or has been employed by a person or body referred to in paragraph 8 of Schedule 3 in connection with functions exercised in relation to the information, or

(iii) a person who has provided for reward a service that is similar to a service provided in the exercise of any relevant social services functions, and

(b) the information relates to the other individual in an official capacity or the other individual supplied the information—

(i) in an official capacity, or

(ii) in a case within paragraph (a)(iii), in connection with providing the service mentioned in paragraph (a)(iii).

(4) The education data test is met if—

(a) the other individual is an education-related worker, or

(b) the other individual is employed by an education authority (within the meaning of the Education (Scotland) Act 1980) in pursuance of its functions relating to education and—

(i) the information relates to the other individual in his or her capacity as such an employee, or

(ii) the other individual supplied the information in his or her capacity as such an employee.

(5) In this paragraph—

"children's court officer" means a person referred to in paragraph 8(1)(q), (r), (s), (t) or (u) of Schedule 3;

"education-related worker" means a person referred to in paragraph 14(4)(a) or (b) or 16(4)(a), (b) or (c) of Schedule 3 (educational records);

"relevant social services functions" means functions specified in paragraph 8(1)(a), (b), (c) or (d) of Schedule 3.

PART 4
RESTRICTIONS BASED ON ARTICLE 23(1): RESTRICTIONS OF RULES IN ARTICLES 13 TO 15

GDPR provisions to be restricted: "the listed GDPR provisions"

18 In this Part of this Schedule, "the listed GDPR provisions" means the following provisions of the GDPR (the rights and obligations in which may be restricted by virtue of Article 23(1) of the GDPR)—

(a) Article 13(1) to (3) (personal data collected from data subject: information to be provided);
(b) Article 14(1) to (4) (personal data collected other than from data subject: information to be provided);
(c) Article 15(1) to (3) (confirmation of processing, access to data and safeguards for third country transfers);
(d) Article 5 (general principles) so far as its provisions correspond to the rights and obligations provided for in the provisions mentioned in sub-paragraphs (a) to (c).

Legal professional privilege

19 The listed GDPR provisions do not apply to personal data that consists of—

(a) information in respect of which a claim to legal professional privilege or, in Scotland, confidentiality of communications, could be maintained in legal proceedings, or
(b) information in respect of which a duty of confidentiality is owed by a professional legal adviser to a client of the adviser.

Self incrimination

20 (1) A person need not comply with the listed GDPR provisions to the extent that compliance would, by revealing evidence of the commission of an offence, expose the person to proceedings for that offence.

(2) The reference to an offence in sub-paragraph (1) does not include an offence under—

(a) this Act,
(b) section 5 of the Perjury Act 1911 (false statements made otherwise than on oath),
(c) section 44(2) of the Criminal Law (Consolidation) (Scotland) Act 1995 (false statements made otherwise than on oath), or
(d) Article 10 of the Perjury (Northern Ireland) Order 1979 (SI 1979/1714 (NI 19)) (false statutory declarations and other false unsworn statements).

(3) Information disclosed by any person in compliance with Article 15 of the GDPR is not admissible against the person in proceedings for an offence under this Act.

Corporate finance

21 (1) The listed GDPR provisions do not apply to personal data processed for the purposes of or in connection with a corporate finance service provided by a relevant person to the extent that either Condition A or Condition B is met.

(2) Condition A is that the application of the listed GDPR provisions would be likely to affect the price of an instrument.

DATA PROTECTION

(3) Condition B is that—

(a) the relevant person reasonably believes that the application of the listed GDPR provisions to the personal data in question could affect a decision of a person—

(i) whether to deal in, subscribe for or issue an instrument, or

(ii) whether to act in a way likely to have an effect on a business activity (such as an effect on the industrial strategy of a person, the capital structure of an undertaking or the legal or beneficial ownership of a business or asset), and

(b) the application of the listed GDPR provisions to that personal data would have a prejudicial effect on the orderly functioning of financial markets or the efficient allocation of capital within the economy.

(4) In this paragraph—

"corporate finance service" means a service consisting in—

(a) underwriting in respect of issues of, or the placing of issues of, any instrument,

(b) services relating to such underwriting, or

(c) advice to undertakings on capital structure, industrial strategy and related matters and advice and service relating to mergers and the purchase of undertakings;

"instrument" means an instrument listed in section C of Annex 1 to Directive 2004/39/EC of the European Parliament and of the Council of 21 April 2004 on markets in financial instruments, and references to an instrument include an instrument not yet in existence but which is to be or may be created;

"price" includes value;

"relevant person" means—

(a) a person who, by reason of a permission under Part 4A of the Financial Services and Markets Act 2000, is able to carry on a corporate finance service without contravening the general prohibition;

(b) an EEA firm of the kind mentioned in paragraph 5(a) or (b) of Schedule 3 to that Act which has qualified for authorisation under paragraph 12 of that Schedule, and may lawfully carry on a corporate finance service;

(c) a person who is exempt from the general prohibition in respect of any corporate finance service—

(i) as a result of an exemption order made under section 38(1) of that Act, or

(ii) by reason of section 39(1) of that Act (appointed representatives);

(d) a person, not falling within paragraph (a), (b) or (c), who may lawfully carry on a corporate finance service without contravening the general prohibition;

(e) a person who, in the course of employment, provides to their employer a service falling within paragraph (b) or (c) of the definition of "corporate finance service";

(f) a partner who provides to other partners in the partnership a service falling within either of those paragraphs.

(5) In the definition of "relevant person" in sub-paragraph (4), references to "the general prohibition" are to the general prohibition within the meaning of section 19 of the Financial Services and Markets Act 2000.

Management forecasts

22 The listed GDPR provisions do not apply to personal data processed for the purposes of management forecasting or management planning in relation to a

business or other activity to the extent that the application of those provisions would be likely to prejudice the conduct of the business or activity concerned.

NEGOTIATIONS

23 The listed GDPR provisions do not apply to personal data that consists of records of the intentions of the controller in relation to any negotiations with the data subject to the extent that the application of those provisions would be likely to prejudice those negotiations.

CONFIDENTIAL REFERENCES

24 The listed GDPR provisions do not apply to personal data consisting of a reference given (or to be given) in confidence for the purposes of—

(a) the education, training or employment (or prospective education, training or employment) of the data subject,

(b) the placement (or prospective placement) of the data subject as a volunteer,

(c) the appointment (or prospective appointment) of the data subject to any office, or

(d) the provision (or prospective provision) by the data subject of any service.

EXAM SCRIPTS AND EXAM MARKS

25 (1) The listed GDPR provisions do not apply to personal data consisting of information recorded by candidates during an exam.

(2) Where personal data consists of marks or other information processed by a controller—

(a) for the purposes of determining the results of an exam, or

(b) in consequence of the determination of the results of an exam,

the duty in Article 12(3) or (4) of the GDPR for the controller to provide information requested by the data subject within a certain time period, as it applies to Article 15 of the GDPR (confirmation of processing, access to data and safeguards for third country transfers), is modified as set out in sub-paragraph (3).

(3) Where a question arises as to whether the controller is obliged by Article 15 of the GDPR to disclose personal data, and the question arises before the day on which the exam results are announced, the controller must provide the information mentioned in Article 12(3) or (4)—

(a) before the end of the period of 5 months beginning when the question arises, or

(b) if earlier, before the end of the period of 40 days beginning with the announcement of the results.

(4) In this paragraph, "exam" means an academic, professional or other examination used for determining the knowledge, intelligence, skill or ability of a candidate and may include an exam consisting of an assessment of the candidate's performance while undertaking work or any other activity.

(5) For the purposes of this paragraph, the results of an exam are treated as announced when they are first published or, if not published, first communicated to the candidate.

PART 5
EXEMPTIONS ETC BASED ON ARTICLE 85(2) FOR REASONS OF FREEDOM OF EXPRESSION AND INFORMATION

Journalistic, academic, artistic and literary purposes

26 (1) In this paragraph, "the special purposes" means one or more of the following—
(a) the purposes of journalism;
(b) academic purposes;
(c) artistic purposes;
(d) literary purposes.

(2) Sub-paragraph (3) applies to the processing of personal data carried out for the special purposes if—
(a) the processing is being carried out with a view to the publication by a person of journalistic, academic, artistic or literary material, and
(b) the controller reasonably believes that the publication of the material would be in the public interest.

(3) The listed GDPR provisions do not apply to the extent that the controller reasonably believes that the application of those provisions would be incompatible with the special purposes.

(4) In determining whether publication would be in the public interest the controller must take into account the special importance of the public interest in the freedom of expression and information.

(5) In determining whether it is reasonable to believe that publication would be in the public interest, the controller must have regard to any of the codes of practice or guidelines listed in sub-paragraph (6) that is relevant to the publication in question.

(6) The codes of practice and guidelines are—
(a) BBC Editorial Guidelines;
(b) Ofcom Broadcasting Code;
(c) Editors' Code of Practice.

(7) The Secretary of State may by regulations amend the list in sub-paragraph (6).

(8) Regulations under sub-paragraph (7) are subject to the affirmative resolution procedure.

(9) For the purposes of this paragraph, the listed GDPR provisions are the following provisions of the GDPR (which may be exempted or derogated from by virtue of Article 85(2) of the GDPR)—
(a) in Chapter II of the GDPR (principles)—
(i) Article 5(1)(a) to (e) (principles relating to processing);
(ii) Article 6 (lawfulness);
(iii) Article 7 (conditions for consent);
(iv) Article 8(1) and (2) (child's consent);
(v) Article 9 (processing of special categories of data);
(vi) Article 10 (data relating to criminal convictions etc);
(vii) Article 11(2) (processing not requiring identification);
(b) in Chapter III of the GDPR (rights of the data subject)—
(i) Article 13(1) to (3) (personal data collected from data subject: information to be provided);
(ii) Article 14(1) to (4) (personal data collected other than from data subject: information to be provided);
(iii) Article 15(1) to (3) (confirmation of processing, access to data and safeguards for third country transfers);
(iv) Article 16 (right to rectification);
(v) Article 17(1) and (2) (right to erasure);
(vi) Article 18(1)(a), (b) and (d) (restriction of processing);

(vii) Article 19 (notification obligation regarding rectification or erasure of personal data or restriction of processing);

(viii) Article 20(1) and (2) (right to data portability);

(ix) Article 21(1) (objections to processing);

(c) in Chapter IV of the GDPR (controller and processor)—

(i) Article 34(1) and (4) (communication of personal data breach to the data subject);

(ii) Article 36 (requirement for controller to consult Commissioner prior to high risk processing);

(d) in Chapter V of the GDPR (transfers of data to third countries etc), Article 44 (general principles for transfers);

(e) in Chapter VII of the GDPR (co-operation and consistency)—

(i) Articles 60 to 62 (co-operation);

(ii) Articles 63 to 67 (consistency).

PART 6
DEROGATIONS ETC BASED ON ARTICLE 89 FOR RESEARCH, STATISTICS AND ARCHIVING

Research and statistics

27 (1) The listed GDPR provisions do not apply to personal data processed for—

(a) scientific or historical research purposes, or

(b) statistical purposes,

to the extent that the application of those provisions would prevent or seriously impair the achievement of the purposes in question.

(2) For the purposes of this paragraph, the listed GDPR provisions are the following provisions of the GDPR (the rights in which may be derogated from by virtue of Article 89(2) of the GDPR)—

(a) Article 15(1) to (3) (confirmation of processing, access to data and safeguards for third country transfers);

(b) Article 16 (right to rectification);

(c) Article 18(1) (restriction of processing);

(d) Article 21(1) (objections to processing).

(3) The exemption in sub-paragraph (1) is available only where—

(a) the personal data is processed in accordance with Article 89(1) of the GDPR (as supplemented by section 19), and

(b) as regards the disapplication of Article 15(1) to (3), the results of the research or any resulting statistics are not made available in a form which identifies a data subject.

Archiving in the public interest

28 (1) The listed GDPR provisions do not apply to personal data processed for archiving purposes in the public interest to the extent that the application of those provisions would prevent or seriously impair the achievement of those purposes.

(2) For the purposes of this paragraph, the listed GDPR provisions are the following provisions of the GDPR (the rights in which may be derogated from by virtue of Article 89(3) of the GDPR)—

(a) Article 15(1) to (3) (confirmation of processing, access to data and safeguards for third country transfers);

(b) Article 16 (right to rectification);

(c) Article 18(1) (restriction of processing);

(d) Article 19 (notification obligation regarding rectification or erasure of personal data or restriction of processing);

(e) Article 20(1) (right to data portability);

(f) Article 21(1) (objections to processing).

(3) The exemption in sub-paragraph (1) is available only where the personal data is processed in accordance with Article 89(1) of the GDPR (as supplemented by section 19).

SCHEDULE 3
EXEMPTIONS ETC FROM THE GDPR: HEALTH, SOCIAL WORK, EDUCATION AND CHILD ABUSE DATA

Section 15

PART 1
GDPR PROVISIONS TO BE RESTRICTED

III DAT [218]

1 In this Schedule "the listed GDPR provisions" means the following provisions of the GDPR (the rights and obligations in which may be restricted by virtue of Article 23(1) of the GDPR)—

(a) Article 13(1) to (3) (personal data collected from data subject: information to be provided);

(b) Article 14(1) to (4) (personal data collected other than from data subject: information to be provided);

(c) Article 15(1) to (3) (confirmation of processing, access to data and safeguards for third country transfers);

(d) Article 16 (right to rectification);

(e) Article 17(1) and (2) (right to erasure);

(f) Article 18(1) (restriction of processing);

(g) Article 20(1) and (2) (right to data portability);

(h) Article 21(1) (objections to processing);

(i) Article 5 (general principles) so far as its provisions correspond to the rights and obligations provided for in the provisions mentioned in sub-paragraphs (a) to (h).

PART 2
HEALTH DATA

Definitions

2 (1) In this Part of this Schedule—

"the appropriate health professional", in relation to a question as to whether the serious harm test is met with respect to data concerning health, means—

(a) the health professional who is currently or was most recently responsible for the diagnosis, care or treatment of the data subject in connection with the matters to which the data relates,

(b) where there is more than one such health professional, the health professional who is the most suitable to provide an opinion on the question, or

(c) a health professional who has the necessary experience and qualifications to provide an opinion on the question, where—

(i) there is no health professional available falling within paragraph (a) or (b), or

(ii) the controller is the Secretary of State and data is processed in connection with the exercise of the functions conferred on the Secretary of State by or under the Child Support Act 1991 and the Child Support Act 1995, or the Secretary of State's functions in relation to social security or war pensions, or

(iii) the controller is the Department for Communities in Northern Ireland and data is processed in connection with the exercise of the functions conferred on the Department by or under the Child Support (Northern Ireland) Order 1991 (SI 1991/2628 (NI 23)) and the Child Support (Northern Ireland) Order 1995 (SI 1995/2702 (NI 13));

"war pension" has the same meaning as in section 25 of the Social Security Act 1989 (establishment and functions of war pensions committees).

(2) For the purposes of this Part of this Schedule, the "serious harm test" is met with respect to data concerning health if the application of Article 15 of the GDPR to the data would be likely to cause serious harm to the physical or mental health of the data subject or another individual.

Exemption from the listed GDPR provisions: data processed by a court

3 (1) The listed GDPR provisions do not apply to data concerning health if—

(a) it is processed by a court,

(b) it consists of information supplied in a report or other evidence given to the court in the course of proceedings to which rules listed in subparagraph (2) apply, and

(c) in accordance with those rules, the data may be withheld by the court in whole or in part from the data subject.

(2) Those rules are—

(a) the Magistrates' Courts (Children and Young Persons) Rules (Northern Ireland) 1969 (SR (NI) 1969 No 221);

(b) the Magistrates' Courts (Children and Young Persons) Rules 1992 (SI 1992/2071 (L 17));

(c) the Family Proceedings Rules (Northern Ireland) 1996 (SR (NI) 1996 No 322);

(d) the Magistrates' Courts (Children (Northern Ireland) Order 1995) Rules (Northern Ireland) 1996 (SR (NI) 1996 No 323);

(e) the Act of Sederunt (Child Care and Maintenance Rules) 1997 (SI 1997/291 (S 19));

(f) the Sheriff Court Adoption Rules 2009;

(g) the Family Procedure Rules 2010 (SI 2010/2955 (L 17));

(h) the Children's Hearings (Scotland) Act 2011 (Rules of Procedure in Children's Hearings) Rules 2013 (SSI 2013/194).

Exemption from the listed GDPR provisions: data subject's expectations and wishes

4 (1) This paragraph applies where a request for data concerning health is made in exercise of a power conferred by an enactment or rule of law and—

(a) in relation to England and Wales or Northern Ireland, the data subject is an individual aged under 18 and the person making the request has parental responsibility for the data subject,

(b) in relation to Scotland, the data subject is an individual aged under 16 and the person making the request has parental responsibilities for the data subject, or

(c) the data subject is incapable of managing his or her own affairs and the person making the request has been appointed by a court to manage those affairs.

(2) The listed GDPR provisions do not apply to data concerning health to the extent that complying with the request would disclose information—

(a) which was provided by the data subject in the expectation that it would not be disclosed to the person making the request,

(b) which was obtained as a result of any examination or investigation to which the data subject consented in the expectation that the information would not be so disclosed, or

(c) which the data subject has expressly indicated should not be so disclosed.

(3) The exemptions under sub-paragraph (2)(a) and (b) do not apply if the data subject has expressly indicated that he or she no longer has the expectation mentioned there.

Exemption from Article 15 of the GDPR: serious harm

5 (1) Article 15(1) to (3) of the GDPR (confirmation of processing, access to data and safeguards for third country transfers) do not apply to data concerning health to the extent that the serious harm test is met with respect to the data.

(2) A controller who is not a health professional may not rely on sub-paragraph (1) to withhold data concerning health unless the controller has obtained an opinion from the person who appears to the controller to be the appropriate health professional to the effect that the serious harm test is met with respect to the data.

(3) An opinion does not count for the purposes of sub-paragraph (2) if—

(a) it was obtained before the beginning of the relevant period, or

(b) it was obtained during that period but it is reasonable in all the circumstances to re-consult the appropriate health professional.

(4) In this paragraph, "the relevant period" means the period of 6 months ending with the day on which the opinion would be relied on.

Restriction of Article 15 of the GDPR: prior opinion of appropriate health professional

6 (1) Article 15(1) to (3) of the GDPR (confirmation of processing, access to data and safeguards for third country transfers) do not permit the disclosure of data concerning health by a controller who is not a health professional unless the controller has obtained an opinion from the person who appears to the controller to be the appropriate health professional to the effect that the serious harm test is not met with respect to the data.

(2) Sub-paragraph (1) does not apply to the extent that the controller is satisfied that the data concerning health has already been seen by, or is within the knowledge of, the data subject.

(3) An opinion does not count for the purposes of sub-paragraph (1) if—

(a) it was obtained before the beginning of the relevant period, or

(b) it was obtained during that period but it is reasonable in all the circumstances to re-consult the appropriate health professional.

(4) In this paragraph, "the relevant period" means the period of 6 months ending with the day on which the opinion would be relied on.

PART 3
SOCIAL WORK DATA

Definitions

7 (1) In this Part of this Schedule—

"education data" has the meaning given by paragraph 17 of this Schedule;

"Health and Social Care trust" means a Health and Social Care trust established under the Health and Personal Social Services (Northern Ireland) Order 1991 (SI 1991/194 (NI 1));

"Principal Reporter" means the Principal Reporter appointed under the Children's Hearings (Scotland) Act 2011 (asp 1), or an officer of the Scottish Children's Reporter Administration to whom there is delegated under paragraph 10(1) of Schedule 3 to that Act any function of the Principal Reporter;

"social work data" means personal data which—

(a) is data to which paragraph 8 applies, but

(b) is not education data or data concerning health.

(2) For the purposes of this Part of this Schedule, the "serious harm test" is met with respect to social work data if the application of Article 15 of the GDPR to the data would be likely to prejudice carrying out social work, because it would be likely to cause serious harm to the physical or mental health of the data subject or another individual.

(3) In sub-paragraph (2), "carrying out social work" is to be taken to include doing any of the following—

(a) the exercise of any functions mentioned in paragraph 8(1)(a), (d), (f) to (j), (m), (p), (s), (t), (u), (v) or (w);

(b) the provision of any service mentioned in paragraph 8(1)(b), (c) or (k);

(c) the exercise of the functions of a body mentioned in paragraph 8(1)(e) or a person mentioned in paragraph 8(1)(q) or (r).

(4) In this Part of this Schedule, a reference to a local authority, in relation to data processed or formerly processed by it, includes a reference to the Council of the Isles of Scilly, in relation to data processed or formerly processed by the Council in connection with any functions mentioned in paragraph 8(1)(a)(ii) which are or have been conferred on the Council by an enactment.

8 (1) This paragraph applies to personal data falling within any of the following descriptions—

(a) data processed by a local authority—

(i) in connection with its social services functions (within the meaning of the Local Authority Social Services Act 1970 or the Social Services and Well-being (Wales) Act 2014 (anaw 4)) or any functions exercised by local authorities under the Social Work (Scotland) Act 1968 or referred to in section 5(1B) of that Act, or

(ii) in the exercise of other functions but obtained or consisting of information obtained in connection with any of the functions mentioned in sub-paragraph (i);

(b) data processed by the Regional Health and Social Care Board—

(i) in connection with the provision of social care within the meaning of section 2(5) of the Health and Social Care (Reform) Act (Northern Ireland) 2009 (c 1 (NI)), or

(ii) in the exercise of other functions but obtained or consisting of information obtained in connection with the provision of that care;

(c) data processed by a Health and Social Care trust—

(i) in connection with the provision of social care within the meaning of section 2(5) of the Health and Social Care (Reform) Act (Northern Ireland) 2009 (c 1 (NI)) on behalf of the Regional Health and Social Care Board by virtue of an authorisation made under Article 3(1) of the Health and Personal Social Services (Northern Ireland) Order 1994 (SI 1994/429 (NI 2)), or

(ii) in the exercise of other functions but obtained or consisting of information obtained in connection with the provision of that care;

(d) data processed by a council in the exercise of its functions under Part 2 of Schedule 9 to the Health and Social Services and Social Security Adjudications Act 1983;

(e) data processed by—

(i) a probation trust established under section 5 of the Offender Management Act 2007, or

DATA PROTECTION

(ii) the Probation Board for Northern Ireland established by the Probation Board (Northern Ireland) Order 1982 (SI 1982/713 (NI 10));

(f) data processed by a local authority in the exercise of its functions under section 36 of the Children Act 1989 or Chapter 2 of Part 6 of the Education Act 1996, so far as those functions relate to ensuring that children of compulsory school age (within the meaning of section 8 of the Education Act 1996) receive suitable education whether by attendance at school or otherwise;

(g) data processed by the Education Authority in the exercise of its functions under Article 55 of the Children (Northern Ireland) Order 1995 (SI 1995/755 (NI 2)) or Article 45 of, and Schedule 13 to, the Education and Libraries (Northern Ireland) Order 1986 (SI 1986/594 (NI 3)), so far as those functions relate to ensuring that children of compulsory school age (within the meaning of Article 46 of the Education and Libraries (Northern Ireland) Order 1986) receive efficient full-time education suitable to their age, ability and aptitude and to any special educational needs they may have, either by regular attendance at school or otherwise;

(h) data processed by an education authority in the exercise of its functions under sections 35 to 42 of the Education (Scotland) Act 1980 so far as those functions relate to ensuring that children of school age (within the meaning of section 31 of the Education (Scotland) Act 1980) receive efficient education suitable to their age, ability and aptitude, whether by attendance at school or otherwise;

(i) data relating to persons detained in a hospital at which high security psychiatric services are provided under section 4 of the National Health Service Act 2006 and processed by a Special Health Authority established under section 28 of that Act in the exercise of any functions similar to any social services functions of a local authority;

(j) data relating to persons detained in special accommodation provided under Article 110 of the Mental Health (Northern Ireland) Order 1986 (SI 1986/595 (NI 4)) and processed by a Health and Social Care trust in the exercise of any functions similar to any social services functions of a local authority;

(k) data which—

(i) is processed by the National Society for the Prevention of Cruelty to Children, or by any other voluntary organisation or other body designated under this paragraph by the Secretary of State or the Department of Health in Northern Ireland, and

(ii) appears to the Secretary of State or the Department, as the case may be, to be processed for the purposes of the provision of any service similar to a service provided in the exercise of any functions specified in paragraph (a), (b), (c) or (d);

(l) data processed by a body mentioned in sub-paragraph (2)—

(i) which was obtained, or consists of information which was obtained, from an authority or body mentioned in any of paragraphs (a) to (k) or from a government department, and

(ii) in the case of data obtained, or consisting of information obtained, from an authority or body mentioned in any of paragraphs (a) to (k), fell within any of those paragraphs while processed by the authority or body;

(m) data processed by a National Health Service trust first established under section 25 of the National Health Service Act 2006, section 18 of the National Health Service (Wales) Act 2006 or section 5 of the

National Health Service and Community Care Act 1990 in the exercise of any functions similar to any social services functions of a local authority;

(n) data processed by an NHS foundation trust in the exercise of any functions similar to any social services functions of a local authority;

(o) data processed by a government department—

(i) which was obtained, or consists of information which was obtained, from an authority or body mentioned in any of paragraphs (a) to (n), and

(ii) which fell within any of those paragraphs while processed by that authority or body;

(p) data processed for the purposes of the functions of the Secretary of State pursuant to section 82(5) of the Children Act 1989;

(q) data processed by—

(i) a children's guardian appointed under Part 16 of the Family Procedure Rules 2010 (SI 2010/2955 (L 17)),

(ii) a guardian ad litem appointed under Article 60 of the Children (Northern Ireland) Order 1995 (SI 1995/755 (NI 2)) or Article 66 of the Adoption (Northern Ireland) Order 1987 (SI 1987/2203 (NI 22)), or

(iii) a safeguarder appointed under section 30(2) or 31(3) of the Children's Hearings (Scotland) Act 2011 (asp 1);

(r) data processed by the Principal Reporter;

(s) data processed by an officer of the Children and Family Court Advisory and Support Service for the purpose of the officer's functions under section 7 of the Children Act 1989 or Part 16 of the Family Procedure Rules 2010 (SI 2010/2955 (L 17));

(t) data processed by the Welsh family proceedings officer for the purposes of the functions under section 7 of the Children Act 1989 or Part 16 of the Family Procedure Rules 2010;

(u) data processed by an officer of the service appointed as guardian ad litem under Part 16 of the Family Procedure Rules 2010;

(v) data processed by the Children and Family Court Advisory and Support Service for the purpose of its functions under section 12(1) and (2) and section 13(1), (2) and (4) of the Criminal Justice and Court Services Act 2000;

(w) data processed by the Welsh Ministers for the purposes of their functions under section 35(1) and (2) and section 36(1), (2), (4), (5) and (6) of the Children Act 2004;

(x) data processed for the purposes of the functions of the appropriate Minister pursuant to section 12 of the Adoption and Children Act 2002 (independent review of determinations).

(2) The bodies referred to in sub-paragraph (1)(l) are—

(a) a National Health Service trust first established under section 25 of the National Health Service Act 2006 or section 18 of the National Health Service (Wales) Act 2006;

(b) a National Health Service trust first established under section 5 of the National Health Service and Community Care Act 1990;

(c) an NHS foundation trust;

(d) a clinical commissioning group established under section 14D of the National Health Service Act 2006;

(e) the National Health Service Commissioning Board;

(f) a Local Health Board established under section 11 of the National Health Service (Wales) Act 2006;

(g) a Health Board established under section 2 of the National Health Service (Scotland) Act 1978.

Exemption from the listed GDPR provisions: data processed by a court

9 (1) The listed GDPR provisions do not apply to data that is not education data or data concerning health if—

(a) it is processed by a court,

(b) it consists of information supplied in a report or other evidence given to the court in the course of proceedings to which rules listed in subparagraph (2) apply, and

(c) in accordance with any of those rules, the data may be withheld by the court in whole or in part from the data subject.

(2) Those rules are—

(a) the Magistrates' Courts (Children and Young Persons) Rules (Northern Ireland) 1969 (SR (NI) 1969 No 221);

(b) the Magistrates' Courts (Children and Young Persons) Rules 1992 (SI 1992/2071 (L 17));

(c) the Family Proceedings Rules (Northern Ireland) 1996 (SR (NI) 1996 No 322);

(d) the Magistrates' Courts (Children (Northern Ireland) Order 1995) Rules (Northern Ireland) 1996 (SR (NI) 1996 No 323);

(e) the Act of Sederunt (Child Care and Maintenance Rules) 1997 (SI 1997/291 (S 19));

(f) the Sheriff Court Adoption Rules 2009;

(g) the Family Procedure Rules 2010 (SI 2010/2955 (L 17));

(h) the Children's Hearings (Scotland) Act 2011 (Rules of Procedure in Children's Hearings) Rules 2013 (SSI 2013/194).

Exemption from the listed GDPR provisions: data subject's expectations and wishes

10 (1) This paragraph applies where a request for social work data is made in exercise of a power conferred by an enactment or rule of law and—

(a) in relation to England and Wales or Northern Ireland, the data subject is an individual aged under 18 and the person making the request has parental responsibility for the data subject,

(b) in relation to Scotland, the data subject is an individual aged under 16 and the person making the request has parental responsibilities for the data subject, or

(c) the data subject is incapable of managing his or her own affairs and the person making the request has been appointed by a court to manage those affairs.

(2) The listed GDPR provisions do not apply to social work data to the extent that complying with the request would disclose information—

(a) which was provided by the data subject in the expectation that it would not be disclosed to the person making the request,

(b) which was obtained as a result of any examination or investigation to which the data subject consented in the expectation that the information would not be so disclosed, or

(c) which the data subject has expressly indicated should not be so disclosed.

(3) The exemptions under sub-paragraph (2)(a) and (b) do not apply if the data subject has expressly indicated that he or she no longer has the expectation mentioned there.

Exemption from Article 15 of the GDPR: serious harm

11 Article 15(1) to (3) of the GDPR (confirmation of processing, access to data and safeguards for third country transfers) do not apply to social work data to the extent that the serious harm test is met with respect to the data.

Restriction of Article 15 of the GDPR: prior opinion of Principal Reporter

12 (1) This paragraph applies where—

(a) a question arises as to whether a controller who is a social work authority is obliged by Article 15(1) to (3) of the GDPR (confirmation of processing, access to data and safeguards for third country transfers) to disclose social work data, and

(b) the data—

(i) originated from or was supplied by the Principal Reporter acting in pursuance of the Principal Reporter's statutory duties, and

(ii) is not data which the data subject is entitled to receive from the Principal Reporter.

(2) The controller must inform the Principal Reporter of the fact that the question has arisen before the end of the period of 14 days beginning when the question arises.

(3) Article 15(1) to (3) of the GDPR (confirmation of processing, access to data and safeguards for third country transfers) do not permit the controller to disclose the data to the data subject unless the Principal Reporter has informed the controller that, in the opinion of the Principal Reporter, the serious harm test is not met with respect to the data.

(4) In this paragraph "social work authority" means a local authority for the purposes of the Social Work (Scotland) Act 1968.

PART 4
EDUCATION DATA

Educational records

13 In this Part of this Schedule "educational record" means a record to which paragraph 14, 15 or 16 applies.

14 (1) This paragraph applies to a record of information which—

(a) is processed by or on behalf of the proprietor of, or a teacher at, a school in England and Wales specified in sub-paragraph (3),

(b) relates to an individual who is or has been a pupil at the school, and

(c) originated from, or was supplied by or on behalf of, any of the persons specified in sub-paragraph (4).

(2) But this paragraph does not apply to information which is processed by a teacher solely for the teacher's own use.

(3) The schools referred to in sub-paragraph (1)(a) are—

(a) a school maintained by a local authority;

(b) an Academy school;

(c) an alternative provision Academy;

(d) an independent school that is not an Academy school or an alternative provision Academy;

(e) a non-maintained special school.

(4) The persons referred to in sub-paragraph (1)(c) are—

(a) an employee of the local authority which maintains the school;

(b) in the case of—

(i) a voluntary aided, foundation or foundation special school (within the meaning of the School Standards and Framework Act 1998),

(ii) an Academy school,

(iii) an alternative provision Academy,

(iv) an independent school that is not an Academy school or an alternative provision Academy, or

(v) a non-maintained special school,

a teacher or other employee at the school (including an educational psychologist

DATA PROTECTION

engaged by the proprietor under a contract for services);

(c) the pupil to whom the record relates;

(d) a parent, as defined by section 576(1) of the Education Act 1996, of that pupil.

(5) In this paragraph—

"independent school" has the meaning given by section 463 of the Education Act 1996;

"local authority" has the same meaning as in that Act (see sections 579(1) and 581 of that Act);

"non-maintained special school" has the meaning given by section 337A of that Act;

"proprietor" has the meaning given by section 579(1) of that Act.

15 (1) This paragraph applies to a record of information which is processed—

(a) by an education authority in Scotland, and

(b) for the purpose of the relevant function of the authority.

(2) But this paragraph does not apply to information which is processed by a teacher solely for the teacher's own use.

(3) For the purposes of this paragraph, information processed by an education authority is processed for the purpose of the relevant function of the authority if the processing relates to the discharge of that function in respect of a person—

(a) who is or has been a pupil in a school provided by the authority, or

(b) who receives, or has received, further education provided by the authority.

(4) In this paragraph "the relevant function" means, in relation to each education authority, its function under section 1 of the Education (Scotland) Act 1980 and section 7(1) of the Self-Governing Schools etc (Scotland) Act 1989.

16 (1) This paragraph applies to a record of information which—

(a) is processed by or on behalf of the Board of Governors, proprietor or trustees of, or a teacher at, a school in Northern Ireland specified in sub-paragraph (3),

(b) relates to an individual who is or has been a pupil at the school, and

(c) originated from, or was supplied by or on behalf of, any of the persons specified in sub-paragraph (4).

(2) But this paragraph does not apply to information which is processed by a teacher solely for the teacher's own use.

(3) The schools referred to in sub-paragraph (1)(a) are—

(a) a grant-aided school;

(b) an independent school.

(4) The persons referred to in sub-paragraph (1)(c) are—

(a) a teacher at the school;

(b) an employee of the Education Authority, other than a teacher at the school;

(c) an employee of the Council for Catholic Maintained Schools, other than a teacher at the school;

(d) the pupil to whom the record relates;

(e) a parent, as defined by Article 2(2) of the Education and Libraries (Northern Ireland) Order 1986 (SI 1986/594 (NI 3)).

(5) In this paragraph, "grant-aided school", "independent school", "proprietor" and "trustees" have the same meaning as in the Education and Libraries (Northern Ireland) Order 1986 (SI 1986/594 (NI 3)).

OTHER DEFINITIONS

17 (1) In this Part of this Schedule—

"education authority" and "further education" have the same meaning as in the Education (Scotland) Act 1980;

"education data" means personal data consisting of information which—

(a) constitutes an educational record, but

(b) is not data concerning health;

"Principal Reporter" means the Principal Reporter appointed under the Children's Hearings (Scotland) Act 2011 (asp 1), or an officer of the Scottish Children's Reporter Administration to whom there is delegated under paragraph 10(1) of Schedule 3 to that Act any function of the Principal Reporter;

"pupil" means—

(a) in relation to a school in England and Wales, a registered pupil within the meaning of the Education Act 1996,

(b) in relation to a school in Scotland, a pupil within the meaning of the Education (Scotland) Act 1980, and

(c) in relation to a school in Northern Ireland, a registered pupil within the meaning of the Education and Libraries (Northern Ireland) Order 1986 (SI 1986/594 (NI 3));

"school"—

(a) in relation to England and Wales, has the same meaning as in the Education Act 1996,

(b) in relation to Scotland, has the same meaning as in the Education (Scotland) Act 1980, and

(c) in relation to Northern Ireland, has the same meaning as in the Education and Libraries (Northern Ireland) Order 1986;

"teacher" includes—

(a) in Great Britain, head teacher, and

(b) in Northern Ireland, the principal of a school.

(2) For the purposes of this Part of this Schedule, the "serious harm test" is met with respect to education data if the application of Article 15 of the GDPR to the data would be likely to cause serious harm to the physical or mental health of the data subject or another individual.

EXEMPTION FROM THE LISTED GDPR PROVISIONS: DATA PROCESSED BY A COURT

18 (1) The listed GDPR provisions do not apply to education data if—

(a) it is processed by a court,

(b) it consists of information supplied in a report or other evidence given to the court in the course of proceedings to which rules listed in subparagraph (2) apply, and

(c) in accordance with those rules, the data may be withheld by the court in whole or in part from the data subject.

(2) Those rules are—

(a) the Magistrates' Courts (Children and Young Persons) Rules (Northern Ireland) 1969 (SR (NI) 1969 No 221);

(b) the Magistrates' Courts (Children and Young Persons) Rules 1992 (SI 1992/2071 (L 17));

(c) the Family Proceedings Rules (Northern Ireland) 1996 (SR (NI) 1996 No 322);

(d) the Magistrates' Courts (Children (Northern Ireland) Order 1995) Rules (Northern Ireland) 1996 (SR (NI) 1996 No 323);

(e) the Act of Sederunt (Child Care and Maintenance Rules) 1997 (SI 1997/291 (S 19));

(f) the Sheriff Court Adoption Rules 2009;

(g) the Family Procedure Rules 2010 (SI 2010/2955 (L 17));

(h) the Children's Hearings (Scotland) Act 2011 (Rules of Procedure in Children's Hearings) Rules 2013 (SSI 2013/194).

Exemption from Article 15 of the GDPR: serious harm

19 Article 15(1) to (3) of the GDPR (confirmation of processing, access to data and safeguards for third country transfers) do not apply to education data to the extent that the serious harm test is met with respect to the data.

Restriction of Article 15 of the GDPR: prior opinion of Principal Reporter

20 (1) This paragraph applies where—

(a) a question arises as to whether a controller who is an education authority is obliged by Article 15(1) to (3) of the GDPR (confirmation of processing, access to data and safeguards for third country transfers) to disclose education data, and

(b) the controller believes that the data—

(i) originated from or was supplied by or on behalf of the Principal Reporter acting in pursuance of the Principal Reporter's statutory duties, and

(ii) is not data which the data subject is entitled to receive from the Principal Reporter.

(2) The controller must inform the Principal Reporter of the fact that the question has arisen before the end of the period of 14 days beginning when the question arises.

(3) Article 15(1) to (3) of the GDPR (confirmation of processing, access to data and safeguards for third country transfers) do not permit the controller to disclose the data to the data subject unless the Principal Reporter has informed the controller that, in the opinion of the Principal Reporter, the serious harm test is not met with respect to the data.

PART 5
CHILD ABUSE DATA

Exemption from Article 15 of the GDPR: child abuse data

21 (1) This paragraph applies where a request for child abuse data is made in exercise of a power conferred by an enactment or rule of law and—

(a) the data subject is an individual aged under 18 and the person making the request has parental responsibility for the data subject, or

(b) the data subject is incapable of managing his or her own affairs and the person making the request has been appointed by a court to manage those affairs.

(2) Article 15(1) to (3) of the GDPR (confirmation of processing, access to data and safeguards for third country transfers) do not apply to child abuse data to the extent that the application of that provision would not be in the best interests of the data subject.

(3) "Child abuse data" is personal data consisting of information as to whether the data subject is or has been the subject of, or may be at risk of, child abuse.

(4) For this purpose, "child abuse" includes physical injury (other than accidental injury) to, and physical and emotional neglect, ill-treatment and sexual abuse of, an individual aged under 18.

(5) This paragraph does not apply in relation to Scotland.

SCHEDULE 4

EXEMPTIONS ETC FROM THE GDPR: DISCLOSURE PROHIBITED OR RESTRICTED BY AN ENACTMENT

Section 15

GDPR PROVISIONS TO BE RESTRICTED: "THE LISTED GDPR PROVISIONS"

III DAT [219]

1 In this Schedule "the listed GDPR provisions" means the following provisions of the GDPR (the rights and obligations in which may be restricted by virtue of Article 23(1) of the GDPR)—

(a) Article 15(1) to (3) (confirmation of processing, access to data and safeguards for third country transfers);

(b) Article 5 (general principles) so far as its provisions correspond to the rights and obligations provided for in Article 15(1) to (3).

HUMAN FERTILISATION AND EMBRYOLOGY INFORMATION

2 The listed GDPR provisions do not apply to personal data consisting of information the disclosure of which is prohibited or restricted by any of sections 31, 31ZA to 31ZE and 33A to 33D of the Human Fertilisation and Embryology Act 1990.

ADOPTION RECORDS AND REPORTS

3 (1) The listed GDPR provisions do not apply to personal data consisting of information the disclosure of which is prohibited or restricted by an enactment listed in sub-paragraph (2), (3) or (4).

(2) The enactments extending to England and Wales are—

(a) regulation 14 of the Adoption Agencies Regulations 1983 (SI 1983/1964);

(b) regulation 41 of the Adoption Agencies Regulations 2005 (SI 2005/389);

(c) regulation 42 of the Adoption Agencies (Wales) Regulations 2005 (SI 2005/1313 (W 95));

(d) rules 5, 6, 9, 17, 18, 21, 22 and 53 of the Adoption Rules 1984 (SI 1984/265);

(e) rules 24, 29, 30, 65, 72, 73, 77, 78 and 83 of the Family Procedure (Adoption) Rules 2005 (SI 2005/2795 (L 22));

(f) in the Family Procedure Rules 2010 (SI 2010/2955 (L 17)), rules 14.6, 14.11, 14.12, 14.13, 14.14, 14.24, 16.20 (so far as it applies to a children's guardian appointed in proceedings to which Part 14 of those Rules applies), 16.32 and 16.33 (so far as it applies to a children and family reporter in proceedings to which Part 14 of those Rules applies).

(3) The enactments extending to Scotland are—

(a) regulation 23 of the Adoption Agencies (Scotland) Regulations 1996 (SI 1996/3266 (S 254));

(b) rule 67.3 of the Act of Sederunt (Rules of the Court of Session 1994) 1994 (SI 1994/1443 (S 69));

(c) rules 10.3, 17.2, 21, 25, 39, 43.3, 46.2 and 47 of the Act of Sederunt (Sheriff Court Rules Amendment) (Adoption and Children (Scotland) Act 2007) 2009 (SSI 2009/284);

(d) sections 53 and 55 of the Adoption and Children (Scotland) Act 2007 (asp 4);

(e) regulation 28 of the Adoption Agencies (Scotland) Regulations 2009 (SSI 2009/154);

(f) regulation 3 of the Adoption (Disclosure of Information and Medical Information about Natural Parents) (Scotland) Regulations 2009 (SSI 2009/268).

(4) The enactments extending to Northern Ireland are—

(a) Articles 50 and 54 of the Adoption (Northern Ireland) Order 1987 (SI 1987/2203 (NI 22));

(b) rule 53 of Order 84 of the Rules of the Court of Judicature (Northern Ireland) 1980 (SR (NI) 1980 No 346);

(c) rules 4A.4(5), 4A.5(1), 4A.6(6), 4A.22(5) and 4C 7 of Part IVA of the Family Proceedings Rules (Northern Ireland) 1996 (SR (NI) 1996 No 322).

Statements of special educational needs

4 (1) The listed GDPR provisions do not apply to personal data consisting of information the disclosure of which is prohibited or restricted by an enactment listed in sub-paragraph (2).

(2) The enactments are—

(a) regulation 17 of the Special Educational Needs and Disability Regulations 2014 (SI 2014/1530);

(b) regulation 10 of the Additional Support for Learning (Co-ordinated Support Plan) (Scotland) Amendment Regulations 2005 (SSI 2005/518);

(c) regulation 22 of the Education (Special Educational Needs) Regulations (Northern Ireland) 2005 (SR (NI) 2005 No 384).

Parental order records and reports

5 (1) The listed GDPR provisions do not apply to personal data consisting of information the disclosure of which is prohibited or restricted by an enactment listed in sub-paragraph (2), (3) or (4).

(2) The enactments extending to England and Wales are—

(a) sections 60, 77, 78 and 79 of the Adoption and Children Act 2002, as applied with modifications by regulation 2 of and Schedule 1 to the Human Fertilisation and Embryology (Parental Orders) Regulations 2010 (SI 2010/985) in relation to parental orders made under—

(i) section 30 of the Human Fertilisation and Embryology Act 1990, or

(ii) section 54 of the Human Fertilisation and Embryology Act 2008;

(b) rules made under section 144 of the Magistrates' Courts Act 1980 by virtue of section 141(1) of the Adoption and Children Act 2002, as applied with modifications by regulation 2 of and Schedule 1 to the Human Fertilisation and Embryology (Parental Orders) Regulations 2010, so far as the rules relate to—

(i) the appointment and duties of the parental order reporter, and

(ii) the keeping of registers and the custody, inspection and disclosure of documents and information relating to parental order proceedings or related proceedings;

(c) rules made under section 75 of the Courts Act 2003 by virtue of section 141(1) of the Adoption and Children Act 2002, as applied with modifications by regulation 2 of Schedule 1 to the Human Fertilisation and Embryology (Parental Orders) Regulations 2010 (SI 2010/985), so far as the rules relate to—

(i) the appointment and duties of the parental order reporter, and

(ii) the keeping of registers and the custody, inspection and disclosure of documents and information relating to parental order proceedings or related proceedings.

(3) The enactments extending to Scotland are—

(a) sections 53 and 55 of the Adoption and Children (Scotland) Act 2007 (asp 4), as applied with modifications by regulation 4 of and Schedule 3 to the Human Fertilisation and Embryology (Parental Orders) Regulations 2010 (SI 2010/985) in relation to parental orders made under—

(i) section 30 of the Human Fertilisation and Embryology Act 1990, or

(ii) section 54 of the Human Fertilisation and Embryology Act 2008;

(b) rules 2.47 and 2.59 of the Act of Sederunt (Child Care and Maintenance Rules) 1997 (SI 1997/291 (S 19));

(c) rules 21 and 25 of the Sheriff Court Adoption Rules 2009.

(4) The enactments extending to Northern Ireland are—

(a) Articles 50 and 54 of the Adoption (Northern Ireland) Order 1987 (SI 1987/2203 (NI 22)), as applied with modifications by regulation 3 of and Schedule 2 to the Human Fertilisation and Embryology (Parental Orders) Regulations 2010 in respect of parental orders made under—

(i) section 30 of the Human Fertilisation and Embryology Act 1990, or

(ii) section 54 of the Human Fertilisation and Embryology Act 2008;

(b) rules 4, 5 and 16 of Order 84A of the Rules of the Court of Judicature (Northern Ireland) 1980 (SR (NI) 1980 No 346);

(c) rules 3, 4 and 15 of Order 50A of the County Court Rules (Northern Ireland) 1981 (SR (NI) 1981 No 225).

Information provided by Principal Reporter for children's hearing

6 The listed GDPR provisions do not apply to personal data consisting of information the disclosure of which is prohibited or restricted by any of the following enactments—

(a) section 178 of the Children's Hearings (Scotland) Act 2011 (asp 1);

(b) the Children's Hearings (Scotland) Act 2011 (Rules of Procedure in Children's Hearings) Rules 2013 (SSI 2013/194).

EMPLOYMENT

TABLE OF CONTENTS

GENERAL NOTES ON EMPLOYMENT

III EMP [1]

Introduction At common law the relationship of employer and employee is governed by contract. In addition, legislative provisions have superimposed certain statutory rights such as: the right to a redundancy payment; the right not to be unfairly dismissed; the right not to be discriminated against on grounds of race, gender, disability, sexual orientation, age, religious or philosophical belief. The impact of employment protection legislation has been so far-reaching that it has distorted the contractual basis of the relationship of employment.

Each of these statutory rights may only be asserted in employment tribunals which have an exclusive jurisdiction to determine such matters in the field of employment. Since 6 May 2014 it has become compulsory for the vast majority of claimants to notify ACAS of their claim before a tribunal claim can be issued. However, the requirement to pay fees in order to bring claims in the Employment Tribunal (and appeals to the Employment Appeal Tribunal) which was introduced in July 2013 was found to be unlawful by the Supreme Court in July 2017 on the basis that it had the effect of preventing access to justice (*R on the application of Unison) v Lord Chancellor* [2017] UKSC 51). While exclusive jurisdiction for the vast majority of the employment legislation lies with the Employment Tribunal, the Tribunal itself cannot enforce an order for damages or costs. If a party does not comply with an order for payment made by the Employment Tribunal, it must be enforced in the County Court or in the High Court (see **III EMP [2]**).

Courts have often to determine whether a benefit given to an employee is merely an expectation which can be lawfully withdrawn by the employer or whether by custom and practice it has become a contractual term the breach of which is unlawful. This means that courts or tribunals have to examine the terms of the contract and the precise practices that pertained. There is a useful summary of the list of factors to be considered in determining whether or not a term has been incorporated into a contract in the Court of Appeal judgment in *Albion Automotive v Walker* [2002] EWCA Civ 946. In many jobs there is an expectation that an annual increase in salary will be paid. In *Earle v Equality and Human Rights Commission (UKEAT/0011/14)* [2014] IRLR 845, [2014] All ER (D) 33 (Sep), EAT it was held there was no right to pay progression (see also *Thorne v House of Commons Commission* [2014] EWHC 93 (QB), [2014] IRLR 260) whereas in *McAlinden v CSC Computer Sciences Ltd* [2013] EWCA Civ 1435 it was held there was such an implied term. Whether a provision in a company handbook has contractual force is considered in *Sparks v Department of Transport* [2016] EWCA Civ 360, [2016] IRLR 519, [2016] ICR 695, Lord Dyson.

Under reg 4(1) of the Working Time Regulations 1998 there is a free-standing right for workers to bring claims in the civil courts. Workers who had not opted out of that right were entitled to a declaration that they could refuse to work until their average working hours fell below the 48-hour maximum. See *Barber v RJB Mining (UK) Ltd* [1999] ICR 679, [1999] IRLR 308. As to whether regulations concerning the minimum wage apply, see *Edmunds v Lawson* [2000] QB 501, [2000] ICR 567.

A person will only have rights under the Working Time Regulations or minimum wage legislation if he or she is a 'worker' within the meaning of those Regulations. In ascertaining whether a person is a 'worker' within, for example, the Working Time Regulations 1998, SI 1998/1833, the court or tribunal should find what was the true agreement of the parties, having regard to all the circumstances of the case and should not be constrained from doing so by the terms of any documentation: *Autoclenz Ltd v Belcher* [2011] UKSC 41, [2011] 4 All ER 745, [2011] ICR 1157.

For the purpose of minimum wage legislation time that counts is when the employee is required to be at work not merely to be available for work, ie sleeping employee who could be roused to meet an emergency. See the judgment of Underhill LJ in *Royal Mencap Society v Tomlinson-Blake* [2018] EWCA Civ 1641, [2018] IRLR 932.

There is increasing jurisprudence as to what constitutes being a worker. Such cases are very fact specific and it is difficult to distil general principles, albeit there appears to be an increasing tendency for the courts and tribunals to look behind the wording of contracts to the working reality. This approach has been adopted in a number of claims in the Employment Tribunal relating to the employment status of people in the 'gig economy'. As a result cyclists working as couriers in London have been successful at first instance claiming that they are 'workers' (*Boxer v Excel Group Services* ET/3200365/16 and *Dewhurst v CitySprint UK Ltd* ET/2202512/2016) and Employment Tribunal decisions which found that Uber and Addison Lee drivers were also 'workers' were upheld by the EAT in *Uber BV v Aslam* [2018] IRLR 97 and *Addison Lee v Lange* [2018] 11 WLUK 193. Uber has appealed to the Court of Appeal and Addison Lee is also expected to seek permission to appeal the decision further. The issue of the boundary between true self-employment and being a worker has now been authoritatively considered by the Supreme Court in *Pimlico Plumbers Ltd and Mullins v Smith* [2018] UKSC 29 in which the Court upheld an Employment Tribunal's decision which found that plumbers who were required to wear a company uniform, drive company vans and provide their services on a full-time basis were not carrying out their own business undertaking (despite written terms suggesting otherwise) but rather were workers who were integrated into the company's business. It is likely there will be legislative intervention to clarify the issue.

Tribunals have a much more flexible procedure than courts and are not bound by rules of evidence. However, the time limits are strict: in most cases early conciliation via ACAS must be commenced within three months of the act or omission complained of, although those time limits can be extended in various situations. In *Abdulla v Birmingham City Council* [2012] UKSC 47, [2012] ICR 1419, [2012] NLJR 1377 it was held by a majority that equal pay claims which would have been out of time in an employment tribunal could proceed as a breach of contract in the High Court. Costs do not follow the event in tribunals and there is only a limited power to award costs against an unsuccessful partly. Because tribunals are the creatures of statute they have no inherent powers and issues as to jurisdiction frequently arise. Thus in unfair dismissal cases there are frequent arguments as to whether the applicant is an employee within the definition of s 230. Employees who had wrongly been characterised as self-employed were not precluded from claiming in later litigation that they were employees. The contract was not tainted by illegality if there had been no concealment of the true facts: see *Payne v Enfield Technical Services Ltd* [2008] ICR 1423. A volunteer working for a charity has been held not to be in employment: *X v Mid-Sussex Citizens Advice Bureau* [2012] UKSC 59, [2013] 1 All ER 1038, [2013] 2 CMLR 423.

In *Gilham v Ministry of Justice* UKEAT0087/16/LA, [2017] IRLR 23 it was held that a District Judge was not an employee. This decision followed a long line of cases concerning the status of ministers of religion (see *Sharp v Worcester Diocesan Board of Finance Ltd* UKEAT/0243/12/DM, [2013] All ER (D) 356 (Nov) for the latest of such decisions).

Findings made in unfair dismissal cases can be binding on actions for breach of contract in the courts. Courts have to have regard to statutory provisions which are normally litigated in employment tribunals. Thus in *Bernadone v Pall Mall Services Group Ltd* [1999] IRLR 617, Blofeld J held the benefit of a transferor's insurance policy transferred with the liability of the transferor.

In both unfair dismissal and wrongful dismissal it should be noted that there has to be a dismissal. A retirement on the ground of ill health is not a dismissal: *Healey v Bridgend County Borough Council* [2004] ICR 561n, (2002) Times, 2 December, CA. However, employees who volunteer for redundancy are dismissed as opposed to having their employment terminated by mutual consent: *Optare Group Ltd v Transport and General Workers Union* [2007] IRLR 931. The fact that an employee is prepared to discuss a consensual termination of his employment does not preclude the right to claim constructive dismissal: *Gibbs v Leeds United Football Club* [2016] IRLR 493, EAT.

III EMP [2]

Concurrent jurisdiction: breach of contract The Industrial Tribunals Extension of Jurisdiction (England and Wales) Order 1994, SI 1994/1623 confers jurisdiction on employment tribunals to determine claims for breach of contract. There are a number of significant limitations on this power. The claim must arise or be outstanding on the termination of the employee's employment (art 3(c)). Thus claims which arise whilst the employment still subsists must be brought in the county court. Termination of employment is a finite date rather than a process: *Johnson v Miller Bros and FP Butler Ltd* [2002] ICR 744, (2002) Times, 18 April, EAT. If commission is payable in arrears and therefore not payable at the termination of the contract, the Employment Tribunal does not have jurisdiction: *Peninsula Business Services Ltd v Sweeney* [2004] IRLR 49, EAT.

An action for wrongful dismissal and unfair dismissal may well arise out of the same factual context. However, the test to be applied to the two causes of action is different. In cases of wrongful dismissal the reasonableness of the employer's actions is irrelevant once the employer has established a repudiatory breach. The question is simply whether the employee was in fact in breach of contract on the balance of probabilities. This contrasts with unfair dismissal cases in which an Employment Tribunal must consider the reasonableness of the decision to dismiss as it appeared to the employer at the time: *Brito-Babapulle v Ealing Hospital NHS Trust (UKEAT/0358/12)* [2013] IRLR 854.

Certain types of claim are excluded; namely those relating to personal injuries (art 3); and living accommodation, confidentiality, intellectual property and covenants in restraint of trade (art 5). Article 4 allows counterclaims by the employer but subject to the same limitations as to the nature of the claims, and only in circumstances in which the claimant has brought a claim for breach of contract by virtue of the Extension of Jurisdiction Order 1994. There is a time limit of six weeks from the date of the receipt of the claim (art 8). Article 10 imposes a limit of £25,000 on the jurisdiction of a tribunal. An employment tribunal has no jurisdiction to give injunctive relief. If the original claim fails, for example, if it is time-barred, the counterclaim still stands as an independent claim: *Patel v RCMS Ltd* [1999] IRLR 161, EAT. An employer who sues an employee for failing to take up a job would be wiser to sue in a court because of the issue of jurisdiction: *Tullett Prebon Group Ltd v El-Hajjali* [2008] IRLR 760, QBD.

An employee who is dismissed in breach of a contractual disciplinary procedure cannot bring a claim for damages for breach of contract on the basis that they have suffered loss by reason of the manner of their dismissal: *Edwards v Chesterfield Royal Hospital and Botham (FC) v Ministry of Defence* [2011] UKSC 58.

Employment tribunal awards and compromises can now be enforced through application to the High Court in accordance with **CPR 70.5** and para 4 of **CPR PD 70**.

Wrotham Park damages are potentially available in employment cases in which the test for the award for such damages is met. Specifically, where: a defendant has deliberately breached its contractual obligations for its own benefit, the claimant cannot easily show a specific financial loss from that breach, and the claimant has a legitimate interest in preventing the defendant from making a profit from the breach, then it may be just for the claimant to receive *Wrotham Park* damages. These are damages to reflect the sum which they might reasonably have requested as compensation had there been a (hypothetical) negotiation in which the claimant had given permission for the breach in exchange for compensation. A case need not be exceptional for *Wrotham Park* damages to be awarded; the question is simply whether such an award would be a 'just response'. In exceptional cases it may be appropriate for damages to be awarded on the basis of an account of profits. For a discussion of *Wrotham Park* damages and the award of an account of profits in an employment context see the decision of the Supreme Court (*Morris-Garner v One Step (Support) Ltd* [2018] UKSC 20).

III EMP [3]

Concurrent jurisdiction: unauthorised deductions and equal pay Employees and workers are protected from unauthorised deductions being made to their wages. The general rule is that an employer is not entitled to make deductions unless authorised to do so either by statute or a contractual term or the employee has signified his agreement to the deduction. The relevant sections are ss 13 onward of the Employment Rights Act 1996. The effect of s 25(4) is that where an employer has a valid claim against the employee but asserts it by making an unauthorised deduction then the amount of the employer's claim is reduced (or extinguished) by the amount of the unlawful deduction. Such authority as there is (*Rickard v PB Glass Supplies Ltd* [1990] ICR 150, CA and *Delaney v Staples* [1992] ICR 483, HL, and see also judgment of Nicholls LJ in *Delaney v Staples* [1991] ICR 331 at 341, CA) makes it clear that an employee may still pursue his claim for unpaid wages in the courts. In the case of *Watts v Silwood Crane Hire Ltd*, a district judge's order that there was no jurisdiction was overruled by HHJ Colyer QC: see [1999] CLY 2017. Anomalies result. If an employee proceeds in the tribunal the fact that a deduction was unauthorised would mean that the employer loses his right to a set off by virtue of the operation of s 25(4) of the Employment Rights Act 1996. If the employee proceeds to claim unpaid wages in the courts the provision concerning unauthorised payment do not apply and the employer can set off his counter-claim. This seems to be the only conclusion which can be derived from the wording of s 205(2). The remedy of a worker in respect of any contravention of ss 13, 15, 18(1) or 21(1) is by way of a complaint under s 23 and not otherwise.

In an unauthorised deduction case an employment tribunal has jurisdiction not only to hear the claim but also to construe the terms of the employment contract in question, at least insofar as such a construction exercise is necessary to determine the sum of wages which should have been payable: *Weatherilt v Cathay Pacific Airways Ltd* (2017) UKEAT/0333/16 and *Agarwal v Cardiff University*, [2018] EWCA Civ 2084.

Claims under s 2 of the Equal Pay Act 1970 may be presented to the court rather than the tribunal but the court has power to strike out a claim in respect of an equality clause where it appears to the court that the claim could be more conveniently disposed of separately by an employment tribunal. In a case where the claimant acted reasonably in not claiming in the tribunal within the time limit this would be a factor in favour of the court claim not being struck out: *Ashby v Birmingham City Council* [2011] EWHC 424 (QB), [2011] IRLR 473, [2011] NLJR 405.

Concurrent jurisdiction: unauthorised deductions and equal pay The Supreme Court has now held, by a majority, that it can never be more convenient for a claim to be disposed of by an employment tribunal than by a court if the time limit for proceedings in the tribunal has already run out: *Abdulla v Birmingham City Council* [2012] UKSC 47, [2013] 1 All ER 649, [2012] ICR 1419, a case concerning breach of an equality clause. Abuse of process was not raised as a factor in this case.

III EMP [3A]

Claims under the Protection from Harassment Act 1997 An employee who has been harassed at work can bring a claim under the Protection from Harassment Act 1997 in the County Court, but the conduct complained of must be so serious that a criminal sanction would be appropriate. For a case in which the High Court found that the Claimant's allegations fell well short of that threshold see *Hammond v International Network Services UK Ltd* [2007] EWHC 2604 (QB). See also *Conn v Sunderland City Council* (2007) Times, 23 November, in which the Court of Appeal overturned a first instance decision for the claimant on the basis that the conduct complained of was not sufficiently serious. For a case in which the high hurdle of establishing harassment in the workplace was met see: *Veakins v Kier Islington Ltd* [2009] EWCA Civ 1288, (2010) Times, 13 January in which Lord Justice Maurice Kay noted that the facts of the instant case were 'extraordinary' and commented that he did not expect that many workplace cases would give rise to that liability. A wife who is the victim of harassment aimed at her husband may receive damages albeit that the campaign is not directed at her: *Levi v Bates* [2015] EWCA Civ 206, [2015] 3 WLR 769, [2015] All ER (D) 139 (Mar).

For further comment on the interpretation of harassment see **III DIS [8]**.

III EMP [4]

Res judicata and issue estoppel The need for finality in litigation has resulted in the doctrine that where a matter has been litigated and a decision reached the parties are not free to open up the matters yet again in subsequent proceedings. Res judicata (also known as cause of action estoppel) applies as a defence to the cause of action when the whole action has already been determined by a court of competent jurisdiction. Issue estoppel applies to a particular issue rather than the whole cause of action. Where an employment tribunal has reached a decision on a cause of action or an issue which was a necessary finding in order for the Court to determine the claim, this binds the parties in any subsequent action in the courts (see *O'Laoire v Jackel International Ltd* [1990] ICR 197, [1990] IRLR 70, CA and *Bon Groundwork Ltd v Foster* [2012] EWCA Civ 252, [2012] ICR 1027, [2012] IRLR 517). In *Sheriff v Klyne Tugs (Lowestoft) Ltd* [1999] ICR 1170, [1999] IRLR 481, CA, it was held that as psychiatric harm caused by discrimination was within the jurisdiction of an employment tribunal, a subsequent court action was barred by the terms of settlement of the employment tribunal case. See also *Eastwood v Magnox Electric plc* [2002] EWCA Civ 463, [2002] IRLR 447. It was held in *Bank of Credit and Commerce International SA v Ali* [2001] UKHL 8, [2001] 1 All ER 961, [2001] ICR 337 that a compromise did not preclude an action for a claim of damages which had not been contemplated.

A claimant may not sue in the county court on a claim which an Employment Tribunal has dismissed even where the dismissal was not on the merits but on the withdrawal of the claim by the claimant: *Lennon v Birmingham City Council* [2001] EWCA Civ 435, [2001] IRLR 826. See also *Sivanandan v Enfield London Borough Council* [2005] EWCA Civ 10, (2005) Times, 25 January: the attempt to litigate the matter was an abuse of process of the court. Where in a tribunal a case has been dismissed because the application was out of time, an action may be brought before the courts: see *Nayif v The High Commission of Brunei Darussalam* [2014] EWCA Civ 1521, [2014] 4 All ER 159, [2015] ICR 517.

Where the claimant's intention is to discontinue a claim before the tribunal, rather than to withdraw it (as in *Lennon v Birmingham City Council* [2001] EWCA Civ 435, [2001] IRLR 826), a second claim is not barred: *Ako v Rothschild Asset Management Ltd* [2002] EWCA Civ 236, [2002] 2 All ER 693.

Where the employee makes the position clear and reserves the right to pursue an action in the courts and withdraws a tribunal claim to avoid multiplicity of action, subsequent litigation in the court is not barred: *Sajid v Sussex Muslim Society* [2001] EWCA Civ 1684, [2002] IRLR 113. However, where an employee brings a successful claim for wrongful dismissal and is awarded the statutory maximum he, or she, may not sue in the courts to recover the excess, even though this was the declared intention from the outset. This is because the cause of action merges with the award: *Fraser v HLMAD Ltd* [2006] EWCA Civ 738, [2006] All ER (D) 152 (Jun). In *Vaughan v Lewisham Borough Council* [2013] EWHC 795 (QB), [2013] IRLR 720, [2013] NLJR 21 the High Court refused an application for an injunction restraining seven defendants from allegedly making defamatory statements in the course of responding to Employment Tribunal claims.

Where a claimant has brought proceedings in the ET for unfair dismissal he may subsequently sue in the courts for breach of the obligations of mutual trust and confidence if occurring before the dismissal (eg by ordering suspension). The employee may also sue for injury to health caused by events such as the employer's failure to investigate complaints and failure to conduct disciplinary proceedings fairly: *Eastwood v Magnox Electric plc; McCabe v Cornwall County Council* (2004) Times, 16 July, HL.

Where a personal injury claim in the County Court is the subject of a settlement agreement this does not necessarily mean that there will be an issue estoppel in relation to a subsequent claim of disability discrimination: *Johnson v Awe plc* UKEAT/0131/08/CEA.

III EMP [5]

Staying proceedings The binding nature of employment tribunal decisions means that there is often considerable tactical advantage in choosing the venue of the initial hearing. This is especially the position when evidence will be admissible before a tribunal but not before a court. The tribunal has power to adjourn proceedings pending a court action when this is appropriate. The employment tribunal has to balance the inevitable delay which will occur against the complexity of the issues, the nature of the evidence, the amount involved and the similarity of the issues between the two actions. For examples of the way in which this discretion has been exercised see *Carter v Credit Change Ltd* [1980] 1 All ER 252, [1979] ICR 908, CA and *JMCC Holdings Ltd v Conroy* [1990] ICR 179, EAT. For a case in which the High Court ordered a stay see *Chorion plc v Lane* (1999) Times, 7 April, Ch, Laddie J. However, there is no power in the Employment Tribunal to relinquish jurisdiction to the High Court against the wishes of the claimants merely because it considers that would be the most appropriate forum: *Asda Stores v Brierley* [2016] EWCA Civ 566, [2016] IRLR 709.

For the substantive law see 16 *Halsbury's Laws* (4th edn reissue) title EMPLOYMENT, para 1. A stay may be ordered even if no High Court proceedings have been issued: see *Paymentshield Group Holdings Ltd v Halstead* UKEAT/0479/11. However there is no need to order a stay of employment tribunal proceedings merely because a claim in the High Court had been indicated in correspondence: *Halstead v Paymentshield Group Holdings Ltd* [2012] EWCA Civ 524, [2012] IRLR 586.

III EMP [6]

Precedents For precedents see **BCCP K[1602]–BCCP K[1609]**.

EMPLOYMENT RIGHTS ACT 1996

(c 18)

Periods of Notice

III EMP [6]

86. Rights of employer and employee to minimum notice

(1) The notice required to be given by an employer to terminate the contract of employment of a person who has been continuously employed for one month or more—

(a) is not less than one week's notice if his period of continuous employment is less than two years,

(b) is not less than one week's notice for each year of continuous employment if his period of continuous employment is two years or more but less than twelve years, and

(c) is not less than twelve weeks' notice if his period of continuous employment is twelve years or more.

(2) The notice required to be given by an employee who has been continuously employed for one month or more to terminate his contract of employment is not less than one week.

(3) Any provision for shorter notice in any contract of employment with a person who has been continuously employed for one month or more has effect subject to subsections (1) and (2); but this section does not prevent either party from waiving his right to notice on any occasion or from accepting a payment in lieu of notice.

(4) Any contract of employment of a person who has been continuously employed for three months or more which is a contract for a term certain of one month or less shall have effect as if it were for an indefinite period; and, accordingly, subsections (1) and (2) apply to the contract.

(5) [. . .]

(6) This section does not affect any right of either party to a contract of employment to treat the contract as terminable without notice by reason of the conduct of the other party.

III EMP [6.1]

General The common law position is preserved in that contracts may contain express periods of notice or periods of notice may be implied. In a case in which the notice period has to be implied because there is no express agreement, the court or tribunal will determine what notice is reasonable having regard to the parties' intentions and factors such as the employee's seniority and normal practice in the particular industry (see *Reda v Flag Ltd* [2002] IRLR 747). It should be noted that the protection is only given to a person who is an employee as defined by s 230(1) of the Employment Rights Act 1996. There are certain occupations which are exempted from the provision. It does not apply to merchant seamen subject to a crew agreement approved by the Secretary of State for Trade (s 199(1)) but does apply to share fishermen (s 199(2)) and to other merchant seamen (s 199(4)). It applies to the police force (s 200) but not to civil servants (s 191(2)(d)) and not to the armed services (s 192(2)(d)). For the territorial scope of the Employment Rights Act and its jurisdiction in relation to those who work wholly or partly abroad, see *Lawson v Serco Ltd* [2006] UKHL 3, [2006] 1 All ER 823.

III EMP [6.1A]

A worker who is paid by an employment agency to provide services to an organisation may have an implied contract of employment with that organisation. The essentials of a contract of employment are the obligation to provide work for remuneration and the obligation to perform it coupled with control: it does not matter whether the arrangements for payment are made directly or indirectly. But the contract between the worker and the agency has to be examined in its entirety to see whether it excludes the possibility of a contract of employment between the worker and the end-user: *Cable and Wireless plc v Muscat* [2006] EWCA Civ 220, [2006] IRLR 354, (2006) Times, 10 April in which the Court of Appeal approved the guidance given in *Dacas v Brook Street Bureau* [2004] EWCA Civ 217, [2004] ICR 1437 and confirmed the decision below that there was an implied contract of employment with the end user.

On the other hand, the Employment Appeal Tribunal has shown a strong reluctance to imply a contract of employment where this would be inconsistent with the contract in writing between the agency and the agency worker: *Astbury v Gist* [2007] All ER (D) 480 (March); and *Heatherwood and Wexham Park Hospitals NHS Trust v Kulubowila* [2007] All ER (D) 496 (Mar), EAT. See also *James v Greenwich London Borough Council* [2007] ICR 577.

Disputes as to the correct identity of the employer of an agency worker have become less common since the coming into force of the Agency Workers Regulations 2010 which provide for certain basic rights for agency workers from the start of their assignment and for parity of some other conditions (including pay and annual leave) between agency and non-agency workers at a hirer after a period of twelve weeks' continuous work.

III EMP [6.2]

Continuous employment In the majority of cases the calculation of continuous periods of employment should cause no difficulty if the employer has served a statement in accordance with the statutory requirements setting out the date from which the period is to be calculated. Difficult issues can arise where there has been a transfer of a business or where there has been intermittent working. There are detailed provisions in the Employment Rights Act 1996 which deal with the definition of continuity and the Transfer of Undertakings (Protection of Employment) Regulations 2006, SI 2006/246 (as amended) apply where there has been a transfer of an undertaking. Continuous employment need not be pursuant to one contract but can be under successive contracts *Re Mack Trucks (Britain) Ltd* [1967] 1 All ER 977, [1967] 1 WLR 780.

III EMP [6.3]

Statutory notice to be given by an employee It is of course possible to increase this by agreement but it is to be noted that the statutory notice required of an employee does not increase with the length of service. For the right of an employer to exercise a contractual right to make a payment in lieu of notice when an employee has given notice see *Marshall (Cambridge) Ltd v Hamblin* [1994] ICR 362, [1994] IRLR 260, EAT. This prevented an employee from working out his notice where his income mainly consisted of commission.

III EMP [6.4]

Effect of contract provision for shorter notice If the contract provides for a shorter notice it is of no effect but the parties may waive notice, see *Trotter v Forth Ports Authority* [1991] IRLR 419, Ct of Sess, or the employee accept money in lieu of notice. A contractual term empowering an employer to dismiss an employee with immediate effect was insufficient to exclude a contractual right to payment in lieu of notice: *Skilton v T & K Home Improvements Ltd* [2000] ICR 1162, [2000] IRLR 595. However, if there is a contractual term that an employer may terminate a contract on payment of money in lieu of notice the contract is terminated with the employee's consent even though the employee was not aware of the payment at the time; see *Geys v Société Générale London Branch* [2011] EWCA Civ 307, [2011] IRLR 482. In *Abrahams v Performing Right Society* [1995] ICR 1028, [1995] IRLR 486, CA, it was held that a payment in lieu of notice was a contractual debt and there was no duty on the employee to mitigate. In *Cerberus Software Ltd v Rowley* [2001] EWCA Civ 78, [2001] ICR 376, it was held that where there was no contractual right to a payment in lieu (as in the *Abrahams* case), the claim was one in damages and was subject to mitigation in the normal way.

For the position of bonuses, see *Clark v Nomura International plc* [2000] IRLR 766 and *Manor House Healthcare v Hays* EAT (Transcript) 16 October 2000.

III EMP [6.4A]

Other claims If the wrongful dismissal precludes the employee from acquiring other rights damages may flow. In *Silvey v Pendragon plc* [2001] EWCA Civ 784, [2001] IRLR 685, it was decided that an employee could recover damages in respect of the enhanced pension rights which he lost when his employment was terminated without due notice 12 days before his 55th birthday. In *Fox v British Airways plc* (UKEAT/0033/12/RN), [2013] ICR 51, EAT the EAT ruled that the father of an employee who was unfairly dismissed thereby losing his £85,000 death in service award could recover that sum on behalf of the estate. As a general rule, an employee who is dismissed in breach of contract in circumstances in which they would have met the qualifying period for a claim of unfair dismissal had they been granted their contractual notice entitlement cannot recover damages for loss of that chance to claim unfair dismissal. See *Harper v Virgin Net Ltd* [2003] IRLR 831. The decision to the opposite effect in *Raspin v United News Shops Ltd* [1999] IRLR 9, EAT has not been followed. However, an employee who is given less than the statutory notice entitlement will have the relevant continuity of employment to claim unfair dismissal if they would have reached the two year qualifying period within the statutory notice period (Employment Rights Act 1996, s 97(2))

In circumstances in which the disciplinary procedure was part of the employee's contract (as often applies in respect of NHS staff) an injunction has been granted to prevent an employee from being dismissed without pursuing disciplinary procedures: see *Kircher v Hillingdon Primary Care Trust* [2006] Lloyd's Rep Med 215. This principle has been extended to granting an injunction restraining an employee from being suspended from work: *Mezey v South West London and St George's Mental Health NHS Trust* [2007] EWCA Civ 106, [2007]IRLR 244, CA. Courts are reluctant to intervene in minor irregularities in contractual disciplinary procedures but have residual power to do so when the irregularities are significant and make the breach of the contractual disciplinary procedure unlawful: *West London Mental Health NHS Trust v Chhabra* [2013] UKSC 80, [2014] 1 All ER 943, [2014] IRLR 227.

III EMP [6.4B]

Stigma damages An employee may be awarded stigma damages on the basis that an employer has breached an implied term not to conduct a corrupt and dishonest business and the employee has thereby suffered a disadvantage in the labour market: *Malik v BCCI SA (in liquidation); Mahmud v BCCI SA (in liquidation)* [1998] AC 20, [1997] 3 All ER 1, HL. Difficult issues of causation may arise: *BCCI SA v Ali (No 3)* [2002] EWCA Civ 82, [2002] IRLR 460, CA. A breach of the implied term of mutual trust and obligation resulting in a depressive illness made the employer liable for damages: *Gogay v Hertfordshire County Council* [2000] IRLR 703, CA. However, no damages will be awarded for a breach of contract as to the distress caused by the manner of the dismissal: *Dunnachie v Kingston Upon Hull Council* [2003] ICR 1294, [2003] IRLR 384. It would be an impermissible exercise of judicial discretion to give a parallel remedy for the unfair circumstances attending dismissal because it would be contrary to the evident intent of Parliament that there should be such a remedy, but it should be limited in its application and extent. See *Eastwood v Magnox Electric plc*

[2002] EWCA Civ 463, [2002] IRLR 447. There is no reason in principle why a claim should not be brought for harassment in the work place under the 1997 Act although an Employment Tribunal would in most cases be a more appropriate venue: *Veakins v Kier Islington Ltd* [2009] EWCA Civ 1288, (2010) Times, 13 January.

III EMP [6.5]

Short term contracts In a short term contract no notice is necessary, and a series of short fixed term contracts might, in the absence of this provision, defeat the object of the Act. This sub-section enables an employee who has in fact been employed for three months or more under a contract for a term certain of one month to receive the statutory notice and requires him to give not less than one week's notice.

III EMP [6.6]

Sub-section (5) This sub-section in effect takes the seasonal worker such as a hop picker out of the ambit of the section.

III EMP [6.7]

Sub-section (6) This sub-section makes it clear that the existing common law position is preserved; namely that an employer or employee may terminate the contract summarily. Many contracts of employment or staff handbooks give examples of gross misconduct. In *Ardron v Sussex Partnership NHS Trust* [2018] EWHC 1535 (QB) it was decided that, although contractual terms about what constitutes gross misconduct are the starting point, the employer was required to consider independently whether the breach was serious enough to come within the rubric of gross misconduct. In other words it is for the court or tribunal to determine whether there was gross misconduct and the employer's designation of what is misconduct is not determinative of the issue. It should be noticed that contracts of employment can come to an end other than by dismissal as in cases of frustration (in practice long term sickness and imprisonment are the most usual examples) or by mutual agreement or by performance. In the case of constructive dismissal it has been held that the resignation must be communicated before it becomes effective: *Edwards v Surrey Police* [1999] IRLR 456, EAT. This equates with the position when notice is given by an employer: See *McMaster v Manchester Airport plc* [1998] IRLR 112, EAT.

III EMP [6.8]

Money payable for the notice period Although in the normal way compensation for the loss of wages during the contractual, or statutory, notice period would be the employee's normal working wage for that period, the employee will only be entitled to his normal weekly wage if that is what he would have received had he been given notice. Where an employee would only have been in receipt of statutory sick pay during her notice period, as she would have been unable to work through sickness, in the absence of contractual provision to the contrary, the proper measure of her loss is the amount of statutory sick pay she would have received. *Burlo v Langley* [2006] EWCA Civ 1778, (2006) Times, 3 April, EAT.

ENVIRONMENT

TABLE OF CONTENTS

GENERAL NOTES ON ENVIRONMENT LAW

III ENV [1]

Judicial review of planning decisions Decisions by a local planning authority, the Environment Agency or Ministers may be challenged by applying for judicial review, following the procedure set out in **CPR 54**. Questions of human rights and, in particular, the Convention right to a fair hearing before an independent tribunal, at **III HUM [28]**, may be raised by judicial review. Although the decision-maker is not an independent and impartial tribunal, the decision may not be challenged on this ground if an appeal lies to an independent and impartial tribunal *with full jurisdiction*. The European Court of Human Rights concluded, in *Chapman v United Kingdom* (Application 27238/95) (2001) Times, 30 January, that the scope of review by the High Court which was available to the applicants after a public procedure before an inspector met the requirement under Art 6.1 of access to an independent tribunal. This is to be contrasted with the decision of the Divisional Court in *R (on application of Holding & Barnes plc) v Secretary of State for the Environment, Transport and the Regions* [2001] NLJR 135, Times, 24 January. The Court there held that the restrictions on the jurisdiction of the High Court to review Ministerial decisions under the Town and Country Planning Act 1990, ss 77–79 and Ministerial orders under the Transport and Works Act 1992, the Highways Act 1980 and the Acquisition of Land Act 1981 were incompatible with Art 6.1 of the European Convention on Human Rights, at **III HUM [28]**. The Ministerial decisions and orders were saved by s 6(2) of the Human Rights Act 1998, at **III HUM [12]**, from being unlawful; and declarations of incompatibility were made under s 4(2), at **III HUM [10]**. However, the decision to grant a declaration of incompatibility was set aside by the House of Lords in *R (on the application of Holding & Barnes plc) v Secretary of State for the Environment, Transport and the Regions* [2001] UKHL 23, [2003] 2 AC 295, [2001] 2 All ER 929.

III ENV [1A]

Planning court claims As regards the presentation of a claim in the newly formed Planning Court see the Practice Directions 8C, 54D and 54E, as from 5 October 2015.

LOCAL GOVERNMENT (MISCELLANEOUS PROVISIONS) ACT 1976

(c 57)

III ENV [2]

21. Appeal to county court against certain notices under s 20

(1) A person on whom a notice other than an occasional notice is served in pursuance of the preceding section may, within six weeks beginning with the date of service of the notice, appeal to the county court against the notice on one or both of the following grounds, namely—

(a) that a requirement of the notice is unreasonable; and

(b) that it would have been fairer to serve the notice on another person who is an owner or occupier of the relevant place in question.

(2) Where a ground of an appeal in pursuance of the preceding subsection is the ground mentioned in paragraph (b) of that subsection the other person in question shall be made a respondent to the appeal in accordance with rules of court except in a case where the rules provide that he shall not be made a respondent to the appeal.

(3) On an appeal in pursuance of subsection (1) of this section the court shall either—

(a) quash the notice to which the appeal relates; or

(b) modify the notice so that, instead of imposing its requirements on the appellant, it imposes them upon another person who is an owner or occupier of the relevant place in question; or

(c) order that the appellant be entitled to recover from such a person a specified part of the expenses incurred by the appellant in complying with the notice; or

(d) dismiss the appeal;

but the court shall not be entitled to exercise its powers under paragraph (b) or (c) of this subsection unless a ground of the appeal is that mentioned in paragraph (b) of subsection (1) of this section.

(4) Where the court modifies a notice in pursuance of paragraph (b) of the preceding subsection the notice shall be deemed to be served in pursuance of the preceding section on the other person in question on the date on which the modification is made; but that person shall not be entitled to appeal against the notice in pursuance of this section.

(5) It shall be the duty of the court, in determining whether to order that the appellant be entitled to recover from another person a part of the cost of complying with a notice, to have regard to the terms of any agreement relating to the relevant place in question to which either person is a party.

(6) Where a person appeals in pursuance of this section against a notice, the notice shall be of no effect pending the determination of the appeal; and where the court determines the appeal otherwise than by quashing the notice it may extend the period specified in the notice in pursuance of subsection (1)(a) of the preceding section.

III ENV [2.1]

Notices under section 20 Notices under s 20 are notices requiring the provision of sanitary appliances at places of entertainment. 'Relevant places' for the purposes of s 20 will include places where it is normal for customers to sit down and eat on the premises: *R (on the application of Kingston upon Hull City Council) v Secretary of State for Business, Innovation and Skills* [2016] EWHC 1064 (Admin), [2016] PTSR 967.

III ENV [2.2]

Procedure and precedent The appeal procedure is set out in CPR Part 52 and **CPR PD 52B** which allows a maximum period of 7 days for service (see para CPR 52.4(3)). A precedent for a statutory appeal to the county court is provided at **BCCP F[301]**.

III ENV [3]

23. Power of local authorities to deal with dangerous trees

(1) Where a district council, a London borough council or the Common Council, or a county or county borough council in Wales—

- (a) receives from a person appearing to the council to be an owner or occupier of any land in the area of the council on which a tree is situated a notice requesting the council to make the tree safe; and
- (b) considers that the tree is in such a condition that there is imminent danger of its causing damage to persons or property,

the council may take such steps on the land, whether by felling the tree or otherwise, as it thinks are appropriate for the purpose of making the tree safe and may recover the expenses reasonably incurred in doing so from the person who gave the notice.

(2) Where such a council—

- (a) receives from a person appearing to the council to be an owner or occupier of land a notice requesting the council to make safe a tree on other land which is in its area and which appears to the council not to be owned or occupied by that person; and
- (b) considers that the tree is in such a condition that it is likely to cause damage to persons or property on the first-mentioned land; and
- (c) knows the name and address of no person appearing to the council to be an owner or occupier of the land and either—
  - (i) has made reasonable but unsuccessful enquiries for the purpose of ascertaining the name and address of such a person, or
  - (ii) considers that in view of the imminence of the danger of such damage from the tree the delay involved in making enquiries or further enquiries about the name and address of such a person is unwarranted,

the council may take such steps on the other land as are mentioned in the preceding subsection and may recover the expenses reasonably incurred in doing so from any person who was an owner or occupier of the other land when the council took those steps.

(3) Where such a council—

- (a) receives from a person appearing to the council to be an owner or occupier of land a notice requesting the council to make safe a tree on other land which is in its area and which appears to the council not to be owned or occupied by that person; and
- (b) considers that the tree is in such condition that it is likely to cause damage to persons or property on the first-mentioned land; and
- (c) knows the name and address of a person appearing to the council to be an owner or occupier of the other land,

the council may serve on such a person as is mentioned in paragraph (c) of this subsection a notice requiring him to take on the other land, within a reasonable period specified in the notice (which must not expire before the expiration of 21 days beginning with the date of service of the notice), such steps for making the tree safe as are so specified.

(4) Where it appears to such a council that a tree on land in the area of the council which is not owned or occupied by the council is in such a condition that it is likely to cause damage to persons or property on other land in that area which is owned or occupied by the council, subsection (2) (except paragraph (b)) of this section, or as the case may require subsection (3) (except paragraph (b)) of this section, shall apply as if the other land were occupied by another person and he had duly given notice to the council in pursuance of that subsection in respect of the tree.

(5) A person on whom a notice is served by a council in pursuance of subsection (3) of this section may, within 21 days beginning with the date of service of the notice, appeal to the county court against the notice on one or more of the following grounds, namely—

- (a) that he is neither an owner nor an occupier of the land on which the tree is situated;
- (b) that the tree is not in such condition as is mentioned in paragraph (b) of that subsection;
- (c) that less expensive steps than those specified in the notice would suffice for the purpose of making the tree safe;
- (d) that it would have been fairer to serve the notice on another person who is an owner or occupier of the land aforesaid;

and any other person who is an owner or occupier of the land to which the notice relates may within the period aforesaid appeal to the county court against the notice on one or both of the grounds mentioned in paragraphs (b) and (c) of this subsection.

(6) Subsections (2) to (6) of section 21 of this Act shall apply to an appeal in pursuance of the preceding subsection as they apply to an appeal in pursuance of subsection (1) of that section as if for the references in subsections (2) and (3) of that section to paragraph (b) of subsection (1) of that section there were substituted references to paragraph (d) of the preceding subsection, for the references in subsections (3) and (5) of that section to the relevant place there were substituted references to the land on which the tree is situated and for the reference in subsection (4) of that section to section 20 of this Act and the reference in subsection (6) of that section to section 20(1)(a) of this Act there were substituted a reference to subsection (3) of this section.

(7) If a person on whom a notice is served by a council in pursuance of subsection (3) of this section fails to comply with the notice, the council may take the steps specified in the notice and recover from that person the expenses reasonably incurred in doing so.

III ENV [3.1]

Procedure The appeal procedure is set out in CPR Part 52 and **CPR PD 52B** which allows a maximum period of 7 days for service (see para CPR 52.4(3)). A precedent for a statutory appeal to the county court is provided at **BCCP F[301]**.

III ENV [4]

25. Power of certain councils with respect to dangerous excavations

(1) Where a district council, a London borough council or the Common Council, or a county or county borough council in Wales—

- (a) considers that an excavation made at any time by some person on land in the area of the council is accessible to the public from a highway or a place of public resort and, by reason of its being unenclosed or inadequately enclosed, is a danger to the public; and
- (b) knows the name and address of no person appearing to the council to be an owner or occupier of the land on which it appears to the council that works to remove the danger should be carried out and either—
  - (i) has made reasonable but unsuccessful enquiries for the purpose of ascertaining the name and address of such a person, or
  - (ii) considers that in view of the imminence of the danger the delay involved in making enquiries or further enquiries about the name and address of such a person is unwarranted,

the council may carry out on the land mentioned in paragraph (b) of this subsection such works as appear to the council to be necessary for the purpose of removing the danger.

(2) Where such a council—

(a) considers that an excavation made at any time by some person on land in the area of the council is as mentioned in paragraph (a) of the preceding subsection; and

(b) knows the name and address of a person appearing to the council to be an owner or occupier of the land on which it appears to the council that works to remove the danger in question should be carried out,

the council may serve on an owner or occupier of the land a notice specifying the excavation and stating that the council proposes to carry out, for the purpose of removing the danger in question, such works as are specified in the notice at such places on the land as are so specified.

(3) If any person having an interest in or a right over land in respect of which a notice is served in pursuance of the preceding subsection objects to the notice on one or more of the following grounds, namely—

(a) that the excavation is not a danger to the public; or

(b) that works other than some or all of those specified in the notice are appropriate for the purpose of removing the danger; or

(c) that places other than some or all of those so specified are appropriate as the site of works for removing the danger,

he may, during the period of 21 days beginning with the date on which the notice was served, appeal to the county court against the notice.

(4) On such an appeal the court shall either quash the notice or dismiss the appeal or, where a ground of the appeal is the ground specified in paragraph (b) or (c) of the preceding subsection, modify the notice so that it refers only to works or, as the case may be, places which the appellant agrees or the appellants agree are appropriate for the purpose of removing the danger; but the notice shall not be modified by the court so as to refer to a place on land of which no appellant is an owner or occupier.

(5) If no appeal in pursuance of subsection (3) of this section is made against a notice within the period mentioned in that subsection or if on such an appeal the appeal is dismissed or the notice is modified as mentioned in the preceding subsection, the council which served the notice may, at any time after the expiration of that period or, as the case may be, after the appeal is dismissed or the notice is modified, carry out the works specified in the notice at the places so specified.

(6) It shall be the duty of a council by which works have been carried out in pursuance of this section to maintain and repair the works except—

(a) so far as they consist of the filling in of the excavation in question;

(b) after the works have been removed in pursuance of the following subsection;

(c) in a case where the council has agreed with a person who is for the time being an owner or occupier of the land on which the works are situated that he shall maintain and repair the works and he has performed his obligations under the agreement.

(7) Where it appears to a council by which works have been carried out in pursuance of this section that if the works were removed the excavation in question would not be a danger to the public, then—

(a) the council may remove the works; and

(b) it shall be the duty of the council to remove the works, except so far as they consist of the filling in of the excavation in question, if it is requested to do so by a person having an interest in or a right over the land on which the works are situated.

(8) [. . .] A district council, a London borough council or the Common Council, or a county or county borough council in Wales, may pay to any person the whole or part of the expenses incurred by him in carrying out

ENVIRONMENT

works for preventing or removing danger to the public from an excavation made at any time by some person on land in the area of the authority, whether or not the person who incurred the expenses had a duty to carry out any such works.

III ENV [4.1]

Procedure The procedure for an appeal to the county court under this section is provided by Part 52 and **CPR PD 52B**, which allows a maximum period of 7 days for service (see para CPR 52.4(3)). A precedent for a statutory appeal to the county court is provided at **BCCP F[301]**.

III ENV [5]

35. Removal of obstructions from private sewers

(1) If a private sewer is obstructed at a point within the area of a local authority (other than a county council in England [. . .]) the authority may serve on each of the persons who is an owner or occupier of premises served by the sewer, or on each of such of those persons as the authority thinks fit, a notice requiring the recipients of notices in pursuance of this subsection in respect of the obstruction to remove it before a time specified in the notice; and that time shall not be earlier than forty-eight hours after the service of the notice or, if different notices in respect of the same obstruction are served in pursuance of this subsection at different times, shall not be earlier than forty-eight hours after the latest of those times.

(2) If an obstruction in respect of which notices have been served by an authority in pursuance of the preceding subsection is not removed within the period specified in the notices, the authority may remove it.

(3) Where an authority has reasonably incurred expenses in removing an obstruction in pursuance of the preceding subsection, the authority may serve on each of the persons on whom it served notice in pursuance of subsection (1) of this section in respect of the obstruction a further notice—

- (a) requiring him to pay to the authority a sum equal to so much of the expenses as is specified in the further notice; and
- (b) specifying the other persons on whom notices in pursuance of this subsection have been or are to be served in respect of the expenses and the amount specified or to be specified in each of those notices;

and it shall be the duty of the authority, in determining what amounts to specify in notices to be served by the authority in pursuance of this subsection in respect of any expenses, to have regard to any matters which appear to the authority to indicate the cause of the obstruction and, so far as the authority are aware of the obligations, to any obligations to remove the obstruction which arose under agreements between persons on whom the notices are to be served.

(4) A person on whom a notice is served in pursuance of the preceding subsection may, within the period of six weeks beginning with the date of service of the notice, appeal to the county court against the notice on the ground that it would be reasonable for the whole or part of the sum specified in the notice to be paid by some other person who is an owner or occupier of premises served by the sewer in question.

(5) On an appeal in pursuance of the preceding subsection against a notice the court shall either dismiss the appeal or order that the whole or part of the sum specified in the notice shall be paid to the authority which served the notice by—

- (a) a person, other than the appellant, who is an owner or occupier of premises served by the sewer in question; or
- (b) persons, other than the appellant, each of whom is such an owner or occupier, in such proportions as are specified in the order,

and that the sum specified in the notice shall be reduced accordingly; but the court shall not order any payment by a person other than the appellant unless that person has, not later than the beginning of the period of eight days ending with that on which the hearing of the appeal is begun, been made a respondent to the appeal in accordance with rules of court.

(6) Where a local authority has served a notice on a person in pursuance of subsection (3) of this section, then—

(a) if the person has not appealed against the notice in pursuance of subsection (4) of this section within the period specified in that subsection, the authority shall be entitled after the expiration of that period to recover from him the sum specified in the notice; and

(b) if he has so appealed within that period and the court has not reduced to nil the sum specified in the notice, the authority shall be entitled after the determination of the appeal to recover from him the sum specified in the notice or, if the court has reduced that sum to a smaller sum, the smaller sum.

(7) Expressions used in this section and in Part II of the Public Health Act 1936 have the same meanings in this section as in that Part; and sections 287 and 288 of that Act (which confer power to enter premises and penalise obstruction) shall have effect as if references to that Act included references to this section.

III ENV [5.1]

Procedure The procedure for an appeal to the county court under this section is provided by Part 52 and **CPR PD 52B**, which allows a maximum period of 7 days for service (see para CPR 52.4(3)). A precedent for a statutory appeal to the county court is provided at **BCCP F[301]**.

LOCAL GOVERNMENT (MISCELLANEOUS PROVISIONS) ACT 1982

(c 30)

GENERAL NOTES ON LOCAL GOVERNMENT (MISCELLANEOUS PROVISIONS) ACT 1982

III ENV [6]

Jurisdiction This Act confers no jurisdiction on the High Court, but ss 29 to 32 confer jurisdiction on the county courts. A local authority is enabled by these sections to undertake work on unoccupied buildings and to recover the expense from owners and occupiers who are served with notices. Any person so served has a right, under s 31, to appeal to a county court within 21 days. A person from whom recovery is sought although not so served may apply to a county court under s 32 for a declaration that the work was unnecessary or undertaken unreasonably.

III ENV [7]

Procedure The procedure for an appeal to the county court under this section is provided by Part 52 and **CPR PD 52B**, which allows a maximum period of 7 days for service (see para CPR 52.4(3)). A precedent for a statutory appeal to the county court is provided at **BCCP F[301]**.

HOUSING ACT 1985

(c 68)

GENERAL NOTES ON HOUSING ACT 1985

III ENV [8]–III ENV [13]

Sections 283 to 288 of the Housing Act 1985 made provision for obstructive building orders and rights of appeal to the county court. But they were all repealed by Schedule 16 to the Housing Act 2004 with effect, subject to transitional provisions, from 6 April 2006: see SI 2006/1060.

TOWN AND COUNTRY PLANNING ACT 1990

(c 8)

III ENV [14]

187B. Injunctions restraining breaches of planning control

(1) Where a local planning authority consider it necessary or expedient for any actual or apprehended breach of planning control to be restrained by injunction, they may apply to the court for an injunction, whether or not they have exercised or are proposing to exercise any of their other powers under this Part.

(2) On an application under subsection (1) the court may grant such an injunction as the court thinks appropriate for the purpose of restraining the breach.

(3) Rules of court may provide for such an injunction to be issued against a person whose identity is unknown.

(4) In this section "the court" means the High Court or the county court.

III ENV [14.1]

Jurisdiction These provisions confer jurisdiction on both the High Court and the county courts to restrain breaches of planning control by injunction. In the case of actual breach the court may compel compliance by a mandatory injunction: *Runnymede Borough Council v Harwood* (1994) 92 LGR 561, CA. In the case of an apprehended breach an injunction restraining development may need to be qualified by the words "in breach of the requirement for planning permission or otherwise than as permitted by Sch 2, Part 1, to the General Development Order 1988" (SI 1988/1813): *Croydon London Borough Council v Gladden* (1994) 92 LGR 561, CA. An interim injunction against persons unknown was granted by the Court of Appeal in *South Cambridgeshire District Council v Persons Unknown* [2004] EWCA Civ 1280, (2004) Times, 11 November to restrain unauthorised development on land adjacent to a gipsy caravan site. Where mobile homes are moved on to agricultural land in flagrant breach of a court order and an injunction is granted for their removal, the court is not justified in suspending the order pending the determination of the planning application: *Mid Bedfordshire District Council v Brown* (2005) Times, 3 January, CA (affd [2012] EWCA Civ 160, [2012] 2 All ER 1039). In *Harlow District Council v Stokes* [2015] EWHC 953 (QB) Patterson J granted a district-wide interim injunction against named defendants.

The breadth of the order was necessary and proportionate having regard to the geographic range of unauthorised encampments by the defendant travellers in the preceding 17 months and the lack of success which other methods of control had met with.

An injunction was granted under this section for the removal of the tents put up by protesters near St Paul's Cathedral, on the ground that no planning permission had been applied for in respect of this change of use: *Mayor, Commonalty and Citizens of the City of London v Samede* [2012] EWHC 34 (QB), [2012] 05 LS Gaz R 21, (2012) Times, 27 January.

An occupier who has withdrawn an appeal under s 285 against an enforcement notice is not barred for this reason from challenging its validity as a ground for resisting the grant of an injunction under s 187B: *North West Estates plc v Buckinghamshire County Council* [2003] EWCA Civ 719, (2003) 147 Sol Jo LB 661, Times, 11 June.

The power to grant injunctions under s 187B is distinct from the power to grant injunctions enforcing planning obligations contained within agreements under s 106 of the Town and Country Planning Act 1990. In *Ali v Newham* [2014] 1 WLR 2743 an injunction was granted under s 106(5) to enforce the terms of a planning obligation and require a land-owning trust to carry out removal works and the court refused to suspend it pending the determination of planning appeals. Lord Dyson MR held that factors to be taken into account on such an application were different to those on an application under s 187B and were not to be conflated, even if the breach of the planning obligation was also a breach of planning control. It followed that in the absence of circumstances that would on normal equitable principles lead to the denial of an injunction, where there has been a substantial breach of a planning obligation under s 106, the discretion conferred by s 106(5) should normally be exercised in favour of the grant of an injunction

III ENV [14.2]

Comparable powers under other Acts The powers under s 187B are similar to powers conferred by the Planning (Listed Buildings and Conservation Areas) Act 1990 s 44A and by the Planning (Hazardous Substances) Act 1990 s 26AA. All three sets of provisions were brought into existence by the Planning and Compensation Act 1991.

III ENV [14.2A]

Inherent power to enjoin unnamed persons There is inherent power in the courts to entertain proceedings for an injunction where the defendants are unnamed. Such proceedings are not invalidated by the failure to name: see **CPR 3.10 [4]**. Injunctions were granted against unnamed would-be trespassers in *Hampshire Waste Services Ltd v Persons Unknown* [2003] EWHC 1738 (Ch), [2003] All ER (D) 124 (Jul) Ch D.

III ENV [14.3]

Procedure The procedure for obtaining injunctions in these, and comparable, circumstances is set out in paragraph 20 of the Practice Direction supplementing Part 8, in volume 1 at **CPR PD 8**.

In *South Cambridgeshire District Council v Persons Unknown* [2004] EWCA Civ 1280, (2004) Times, 11 November the Court ordered service of the claim form and injunction to be effected by placing copies in clear plastic envelopes and nailing them to stakes or gateposts or other prominent locations on the site. Further, the claimants were required to check that the notice was still there once a week. The notice should inform the defendants that they could obtain copies of the application notice and the witness statements and exhibits by applying to the council's planning officer during working hours.

III ENV [14.4]

Injunctions to evict from home Where the land-owner places a mobile home on his land and lives in it as his home, in breach of planning controls, the court should not grant an injunction which would effectively remove him from his home except where such a step is appropriate and proportionate: *South Buckinghamshire District Council v Porter* [2001] EWCA Civ 1549, [2002] 1 All ER 425; affd [2003] UKHL 26, [2003] 2 AC 558, [2003] 3 All ER 1. On the other hand, appropriate enforcement measures do not infringe Convention rights: *Smith (Jane) v United Kingdom (Application 25154/94)* (2001) 33 EHRR 30, ECtHR; *Lee v United Kingdom (Application 25289/94)* (2001) 33 EHRR 29, ECtHR.

In *Davis v Tonbridge and Malling Borough Council* (2004) Times, 5 March, CA the Court of Appeal upheld the grant of an injunction to evict travelling showmen from a site where they had caused damage and deliberately acted unlawfully although the injunction would necessarily cause hardship to the families involved.

The principles in *South Bucks* (about balancing environmental interests against the Article 8 interests of the occupier) do not arise in the case of unnamed defendants, which made it important to grant such injunctions only where identification was impossible: *South Cambridgeshire District Council v Gammell* [2005] EWCA Civ 1429, (2005) Times, 3 November, in which it was also held that someone coming to the land with knowledge of the injunction would be in contempt and that the proper course was to apply to the court to set aside or vary the order, applying the *South Bucks* principles.

The possibility of owing a duty under s 193(2) of the Housing Act 1996 to families evicted from their own land, for breach of planning control, is not necessarily a sufficient ground for refusing an injunction to evict them, but the authority would need to receive and consider homelessness applications before implementing the eviction: *McCarthy v Basildon District Council, Equality and Human Rights Commission intervening* [2009] EWCA Civ 13, [2009] All ER (D) 160 (Jan).

III ENV [14.5]

Injunction against travellers with power of arrest The court has powers, under s 187B of the Town and Country Panning Act 1990 and s 222 of the Local Government Act 1972 to grant a local authority an injunction, with powers of arrest, to stop unauthorised encampments by travellers where there is a history of damage and nuisance over a significant period: decision of Turner J in *London Borough of Barking and Dagenham v Stokes* (2017) 30 October 2017, unreported.

III ENV [15]

214A. Injunctions

(1) Where a local planning authority consider it necessary or expedient for an actual or apprehended offence under section 210 or 211 to be restrained by injunction, they may apply to the court for an injunction, whether or not they have exercised or are proposing to exercise any of their other powers under this Chapter.

(2) Subsections (2) to (4) of section 187B apply to an application under this section as they apply to an application under that section.

III ENV [15.1]

Offences under section 210 or 211 These sections create offences in relation to cutting down trees and the like.

III ENV [15.2]

Procedure The procedure for obtaining an injunction under this section is set out in paragraph 20 of the Practice Direction supplementing Part 8, in volume 1 at **CPR PD 8**.

III ENV [16]

289. Appeals to High Court relating to enforcement notices and notices under sections 207 and 215

(1) Where the Secretary of State gives a decision in proceedings on an appeal under Part VII against an enforcement notice the appellant or the local planning authority or any other person having an interest in the land to which the notice relates may, according as rules of court may provide, either appeal to the High Court against the decision on a point of law or require the Secretary of State to state and sign a case for the opinion of the High Court.

(2) Where the Secretary of State gives a decision in proceedings on an appeal under Part VIII against a notice under section 207, the appellant or the local planning authority or any person (other than the appellant) on whom the notice was served may, according as rules of court may provide, either appeal to the High Court against the decision on a point of law or require the Secretary of State to state and sign a case for the opinion of the High Court.

(2A) Where the Welsh Ministers give a decision in proceedings on an appeal under Part 8 against a notice under section 215, the appellant or the local planning authority or any other person having an interest in the land to which the notice relates may, according as rules of court may provide, either appeal to the High Court against the decision on a point of law or require the Welsh Ministers to sign and state a case for the opinion of the High Court.

(3) At any stage of the proceedings on any such appeal as is mentioned in subsection (1), the Secretary of State may state any question of law arising in the course of the proceedings in the form of a special case for the decision of the High Court.

(4) A decision of the High Court on a case stated by virtue of subsection (3) shall be deemed to be a judgment of the court within the meaning of section 16 of the Senior Courts Act 1981 (jurisdiction of the Court of Appeal to hear and determine appeals from any judgment of the High Court).

(4A) In proceedings brought by virtue of this section in respect of an enforcement notice, the High Court or, as the case may be, the Court of Appeal may, on such terms if any as the Court thinks fit (which may include terms requiring the local planning authority to give an undertaking as to damages or any other matter), order that the notice shall have effect, or have effect to such extent as may be specified in the order, pending the final determination of those proceedings and any re-hearing and determination by the Secretary of State.

(4B) Where proceedings are brought by virtue of this section in respect of any notice under section 207 [or 215], the notice shall be of no effect pending the final determination of those proceedings and any re-hearing and determination by the Secretary of State.

(5) In relation to any proceedings in the High Court or the Court of Appeal brought by virtue of this section the power to make rules of court shall include power to make rules—

(a) prescribing the powers of the High Court or the Court of Appeal with respect to the remitting of the matter with the opinion or direction of the court for re-hearing and determination by the Secretary of State [or the Welsh Ministers]; and

(b) providing for the Secretary of State or the Welsh Ministers, either generally or in such circumstances as may be prescribed by the rules, to be treated as a party to any such proceedings and to be entitled to appear and to be heard accordingly.

(5A) Rules of court may also provide for the High Court or, as the case may be, the Court of Appeal to give directions as to the exercise, until such proceedings in respect of an enforcement notice are finally concluded and any re-hearing and determination by the Secretary of State has taken place, of any other powers in respect of the matters to which such a notice relates.

(6) No proceedings in the High Court shall be brought by virtue of this section except with the leave of that Court and no appeal to the Court of Appeal shall be so brought except with the leave of the Court of Appeal or of the High Court.

(7) In this section "decision" includes a direction or order, and references to the giving of a decision shall be construed accordingly.

ENVIRONMENT

III ENV [16.1]

Application for permission to appeal An application for permission to appeal to the High Court under s 289 must comply with paragraph 22.6.1 of the Practice Direction—Statutory Appeals and Appeals Subject to Special Provision at **CPR PD 52E**. So also must an application for permission to appeal to the High Court under Planning (Listed Buildings and Conservation Areas) Act 1990, s 65.

III ENV [16.2]

Appeals The procedure for appeals and applications is contained in Part 52 at **CPR 52** and paragraph 22.6.1 of the Practice Direction—Statutory Appeals and Appeals Subject to Special Provision at **CPR PD 52D**.

III ENV [16.3]

Cases stated The procedure for cases started under s 289(1), (3) or under Planning (Listed Buildings and Conservation Areas) Act 1990 s 65(2) is set out in CPR Part 52 at **CPR 52** and Practice Direction—Appeals by Way of Case Stated at **CPR PD 52E**. Although s 289(1) appears to give an interested party a choice as to how to proceed following an unsuccessful appeal, it is considered that the right to require a case to be stated post appeal is effectively redundant given the breadth of the right to appeal on a point of law.

III ENV [16.4]

Challenging Secretary of State's decision under s 177(1)(a) Where the Secretary of State has set aside a council's refusal of planning permission the decision may be challenged by the council, under s 288(1), by issuing proceedings in the High Court, using Form N208, within six weeks. In *Thurrock Borough Council v Secretary of State for the Environment, Transport and the Regions* [2000] All ER (D) 2258, (2000) Times, 20 December, CA the council had mistakenly applied instead for permission to appeal the decision under s 289. The Court of Appeal concluded that the applicant council should be allowed to amend the form of application for permission so as to turn it into a challenge under s 288.

III ENV [16.5]

Challenging a decision not to hold a further public inquiry Whilst a local plan may be challenged by an application to quash under s 287, the procedure may not be used to challenge an earlier decision not to hold a further inquiry. The better course would have been to apply, under CPR Pt 54 (Judicial Review), for a declaration or remission: *First Corporate Shipping Ltd (t/a Bristol Port Co) v North Somerset District Council* [2001] EWCA Civ 693, (2001) Times, 15 June, CA.

III ENV [16.6]

Challenging a decision for infringement of Convention rights One of the grounds for allowing an appeal could be infringement of Art 8 of the Convention, as in *Clarke v Secretary of State for the Environment, Transport and the Regions* (2001) Times, 9 November. In this case, which was an appeal under s 288, the inspector had wrongly taken account of a gypsy family's rejection of an offer of conventional accommodation as a reason for refusing planning permission for a caravan. On the other hand, Art 8 does not confer a right on every gypsy to the site of his or her choice: the legitimate needs of the community for the preservation of the local environment should also be taken into account and may prevail as in *Coster v United Kingdom (Application 24876/94)* (2001) 33 EHRR 20, ECtHR and *Beard v United Kingdom (Application 224882/94)* (2001) 33 EHRR 19, ECtHR.

WATER RESOURCES ACT 1991

(c 57)

GENERAL NOTES ON WATER RESOURCES ACT 1991

III ENV [17]

Jurisdiction to hear appeals This Act, which has subsequently been amended, re-enacts many of the provisions of the Water Resources Act 1963 although the right to appeal to the county court against curtailment of abstraction rights has now been removed by the Water Act 2003.

Under Schedule 15 of the Act owners of chargeable land are liable to pay a drainage charge. Aggrieved persons may appeal demands to the county court under para 11 of the Schedule.

There is also a right of appeal to a single judge of the Chancery Division under s 205(4) in relation to the disclosure of information relating to underground water.

III ENV [18]

Procedure The procedure for appeals and applications is contained in Part 52 at **CPR 52** and the Practice Direction—Statutory Appeals and Appeals Subject to Special Provision at **CPR PD 52D**.

ENERGY PERFORMANCE OF BUILDINGS (ENGLAND AND WALES) REGULATIONS 2012

(SI 2012/3118)

GENERAL NOTES ON ENERGY PERFORMANCE OF BUILDINGS (ENGLAND AND WALES) REGULATIONS 2012

III ENV [19]

These Regulations implement in England and Wales articles 7 (energy performance certificates), 9 (air-conditioning system inspections) and 10 (energy assessors) of the (recast) Energy Performance of Buildings Directive, OJ No L 153, 18.6.2010 which lays down requirements for the production of energy performance certificates when buildings are constructed, sold or rented out, display of certificates in large public buildings, and regular inspections of air-conditioning systems. There have been subsequent amendments and additions to that Directive.

Part 3 of these Regulations concerns display energy certificates and includes in reg 15 a new provision enacting requirements of articles 11(2), 12(1)(b) and 13(1) of the recast Directive. Excluded buildings are dealt with under reg 15A. A display energy certificate must give operational and other information relating to energy performance of buildings of specified sizes which are occupied by public authorities and frequently visited by the public.

Part 4, concerning inspection of air-conditioning systems, provides that the person who has control of the operation of an air-conditioning system over a specified output must ensure the system is inspected at regular intervals not exceeding 5 years (reg 18).

Part 5 requires that energy assessors who produce specified certificates or inspect air-conditioning systems must be members of an accreditation scheme approved by the Secretary of State (reg 22).

Part 6 requires certain documents produced by energy assessors to be entered onto a register maintained by the Secretary of State. Regulations 30 to 32 set out who may be given information from the register.

These Regulations revoke and replace the Energy Performance of Buildings (Certificates and Inspections) (England and Wales) Regulations 2007, SI 2007/991 and the various amending instruments, so as to achieve a consolidation of the secondary legislation in this area. However, there have been amendments since. See in particular, SI 2013/10, SI 2013/181, SI 2013/603, SI 2014/880, SI 2015/609, SI 2015/1681, SI 2016/284, SI 2016/888, SI 2017/368 and SI 2018/362.

A guide to energy performance certificates for the construction, sale and let of non-dwellings was produced by the Department for Communities and Local Government in December 2017.

III ENV [20]

Enforcement and appeals An authorised officer of an enforcement authority may serve a penalty charge notice for breach of the Regulations (reg 36) and the recipient has the right to request a review (reg 39) and, after the review, to appeal to the county court (reg 40).

The appellant should follow the appeal procedure in CPR 52.4 and para 5 of **CPR PD 52B** and use **Form N161**. Note that the right of appeal does not arise until there has been a review and notice of the outcome has been given.

The penalty is recoverable in the county court as a civil debt.

EQUALITY

TABLE OF CONTENTS

EQUALITY ACT 2010

(c 15)

GENERAL NOTE

III EQU [A1]

Most of the provisions in the Equality Act 2010 have been in force since 1 October 2010. They repeal and replace all the pre-existing legislation on unlawful discrimination, except as regards conduct before that date and subject to other savings and transitional provisions in the Equality Act 2010 (Commencement No 4, Savings, Consequential, Transitional, Transitory and Incidental Provisions and Revocation) Order 2010, SI 2010/2317 (the No 4 Order). The commencement dates for provisions brought into effect by subsequent orders are noted against the relevant sections. Amendments were made, before commencement, by the Equality Act 2010 (Consequential Amendments, Saving and Supplementary Provisions) Order 2010, SI 2010/2279. The affected provisions are ss 87, 94, 108, Sch 3 and Sch 9 and they are printed below as amended.

The provisions which apply to proceedings in the civil courts, and to which the Civil Procedure Rules 1998 apply, are set out below, with appropriate commentary. They all came into force on or before 1 October 2010 except as otherwise indicated in the notes. Provisions relating to the jurisdiction of Tribunals (Part 5), or to family property (Part 15), have been omitted as have provisions on the advancement of equality generally (Part 11) and the detailed provisions on transport of disabled persons (Part 12).

Note that in civil proceedings an assessor has normally to be appointed, as provided in s 114 and that practice and procedure are the subject-matter of a Practice Direction- Proceedings under Enactments relating to Equality, set out at the end of this title at **III EQU PD 1**.

Although s 114 of the Equality Act gives jurisdiction to hear claims to the County Court, there may be situations in which a discrimination claim can be brought as part of an application for judicial review: eg *R (on the application of Dowsett) v Secretary of State for Justice* [2011] EWHC 2877 (Admin).

Claims of discrimination which have been litigated in the employment tribunal (or would have been but for the unwillingness of the party in question to put them to the test) should not be reopened in the county court: see *Barber v Staffordshire County Council* [1996] 2 All ER 748, [1996] IRLR 209, [1996] ICR 379; *Lennon v Birmingham City Council* [2001] EWCA Civ 435, [2001] IRLR 826 and *Ako v Rothschild Asset Management Ltd* [2002] EWCA Civ 236, [2002] 2 All ER 693, [2002] ICR 899. However, not every order dismissing the case in the Tribunal will result in issue estoppel applying. In *Nayif v High Commission of Brunei Darussalam* [2014] EWCA Civ 1521, [2015] 4 All ER 159, [2015] IRLR 134, a race discrimination claim had been issued in the Employment Tribunal and found to be out of time. The subsequent claim for breach of statutory duty in the Court based on the same facts was not barred by res judicata.

Comprehensive Codes of Practice have been published by the Commission for Equality and Human Rights, in accordance with s 14 of the Equality Act 2006 and given legal force, from 6 April 2011, by the Equality Act 2010 Codes of Practice (Services, Public Functions and Associations, Employment, and Equal Pay) Order 2011, SI 211/857. For the text see http://www.equalityhumanrights.com/legal-and-policy/equality-act/equality-act-codes-of-practice/.

PART 1
SOCIO-ECONOMIC INEQUALITIES

III EQU [1]

1. Public sector duty regarding socio-economic inequalities

(1) An authority to which this section applies must, when making decisions of a strategic nature about how to exercise its functions, have due regard to the desirability of exercising them in a way that is designed to reduce the inequalities of outcome which result from socio-economic disadvantage.

(2) In deciding how to fulfil a duty to which it is subject under subsection (1), an authority must take into account any guidance issued in accordance with subsection (2A).

(2A) The guidance to be taken into account under subsection (2) is—

- (a) in the case of a duty imposed on an authority in relation to devolved Scottish functions, guidance issued by the Scottish Ministers;
- (aa) in the case of a duty imposed on an authority in relation to devolved Welsh functions, guidance issued by the Welsh Ministers;
- (b) in any other case, guidance issued by a Minister of the Crown.

(3) The authorities to which this section applies are—

- (a) a Minister of the Crown;
- (b) a government department other than the Security Service, the Secret Intelligence Service or the Government Communications Headquarters;
- (c) a county council or district council in England;
- (d) the Greater London Authority;
- (e) a London borough council;
- (f) the Common Council of the City of London in its capacity as a local authority;
- (g) the Council of the Isles of Scilly;
- (h) ...
- (i) ...
- (j) ...
- (k) a police and crime commissioner established for an area in England.

(4) ...

(5) ...

(6) The reference to inequalities in subsection (1) does not include any inequalities experienced by a person as a result of being a person subject to immigration control within the meaning given by section 115(9) of the Immigration and Asylum Act 1999.

III EQU [1.1]

Commencement of Part 1 This Part needs a commencement order to bring it into force in respect of England and Wales. Sections 1(1)–(3)(k), (6), 2 and 3 were brought into force with effect from 1 April 2018 in relation to Scotland by SSI 2017/403, art 2(1)(a), (b), (c).

III EQU [2]

2. Power to amend section 1

(1) A Minister of the Crown may by regulations amend section 1 so as to—

- (a) add a public authority to the authorities that are subject to the duty under subsection (1) of that section;
- (b) remove an authority from those that are subject to the duty;
- (c) make the duty apply, in the case of a particular authority, only in relation to certain functions that it has;

EQUALITY

(d) in the case of an authority to which the application of the duty is already restricted to certain functions, remove or alter the restriction.

(2) In subsection (1) "public authority" means an authority that has functions of a public nature.

(3) Provision made under subsection (1) may not impose a duty on an authority in relation to any devolved Scottish functions or devolved Welsh functions.

(4) The Scottish Ministers or the Welsh Ministers may by regulations amend section 1 so as to—

(a) add a relevant authority to the authorities that are subject to the duty under subsection (1) of that section;

(b) remove a relevant authority from those that are subject to the duty;

(c) make the duty apply, in the case of a particular relevant authority, only in relation to certain functions that it has;

(d) in the case of a relevant authority to which the application of the duty is already restricted to certain functions, remove or alter the restriction.

(5) For the purposes of the power conferred by subsection (4) on the Scottish Ministers, "relevant authority" means an authority whose functions—

(a) are exercisable only in or as regards Scotland,

(b) are wholly or mainly devolved Scottish functions, and

(c) correspond or are similar to those of an authority for the time being specified in section 1(3).

(6) For the purposes of the power conferred by subsection (4) on the Welsh Ministers, "relevant authority" means a devolved Welsh authority (within the meaning given by section 157A of the Government of Wales Act 2006) whose functions correspond or are similar to those of an authority for the time being specified in subsection (3) of section 1 or referred to in subsection (4) of that section.

(7) ...

(8) Regulations under this section may make any amendments of section 1 that appear to the Minister or Ministers to be necessary or expedient in consequence of provision made under subsection (1) or (as the case may be) subsection (4).

(9) ...

(10) ...

(11) ...

III EQU [3]

3. Enforcement

A failure in respect of a performance of a duty under section 1 does not confer a cause of action at private law.

PART 2
EQUALITY: KEY CONCEPTS

CHAPTER 1 PROTECTED CHARACTERISTICS

III EQU [4]

4. The protected characteristics

The following characteristics are protected characteristics—

age;
disability;
gender reassignment;
marriage and civil partnership;
pregnancy and maternity;

race;
religion or belief;
sex;
sexual orientation.

III EQU [4.1]

Commencement of Part 2 Part 2 was brought into force on 1 October 2010 by Order 4, SI 2010/2317, except s 14.

III EQU [5]

5. Age

(1) In relation to the protected characteristic of age—

(a) a reference to a person who has a particular protected characteristic is a reference to a person of a particular age group;

(b) a reference to persons who share a protected characteristic is a reference to persons of the same age group.

(2) A reference to an age group is a reference to a group of persons defined by reference to age, whether by reference to a particular age or to a range of ages.

III EQU [5.1]

Contractual retirement age A mandatory contractual retirement age, say 65, is not necessarily discriminatory on grounds of age. The Supreme Court decision in *Seldon v Clarkson Wright and Jakes* [2012] UKSC 16, [2012] 3 All ER 1301, [2012] 2 CMLR 50 restated the three legitimate aims of a fixed retirement age in the context of retirement from a partnership of solicitors:

(1) ensuring that associates were given the opportunity of partnership after a reasonable period, thus ensuring that they did not leave;

(2) facilitating the planning of the partnership by having a realistic long term expectation as to when vacancies would arise; and

(3) limiting the need to expel partners by way of performance management, thus contributing to a congenial and supportive culture in the firm.

See also *Harrod v Chief Constable of West Midlands* [2017] EWCA Civ 191, [2017] ICR 869 where a complaint of indirect age discrimination was rejected in relation to the use of the Police Pensions Regulations 1987 to impose compulsory retirement on officers with service of more than 30 years.

III EQU [5.2]

Judicial pensions In *Lord Chancellor, Ministry of Justice v McCloud* [2017] UKEAT/0071/17, transitional provisions of the Judicial Pension Regulations 2015 were found to be discriminatory because of age. The EAT upheld the Tribunal's finding that this could not be justified as a proportionate means of pursuing a legitimate aim.

III EQU [6]

6. Disability

(1) A person (P) has a disability if—

(a) P has a physical or mental impairment, and

(b) the impairment has a substantial and long-term adverse effect on P's ability to carry out normal day-to-day activities.

(2) A reference to a disabled person is a reference to a person who has a disability.

(3) In relation to the protected characteristic of disability—

(a) a reference to a person who has a particular protected characteristic is a reference to a person who has a particular disability;

(b) a reference to persons who share a protected characteristic is a reference to persons who have the same disability.

(4) This Act (except Part 12 and section 190) applies in relation to a person who has had a disability as it applies in relation to a person who has the disability; accordingly (except in that Part and that section)—

(a) a reference (however expressed) to a person who has a disability includes a reference to a person who has had the disability, and

(b) a reference (however expressed) to a person who does not have a disability includes a reference to a person who has not had the disability.

(5) A Minister of the Crown may issue guidance about matters to be taken into account in deciding any question for the purposes of subsection (1).

(6) Schedule 1 (disability: supplementary provision) has effect.

III EQU [6.1]

Parts to which this section does not apply Part 12 is about disabled person's transport and s 190 is about improvements to let dwelling houses.

III EQU [6.2]

A person who has a disability The Equality Act 2010 has brought some changes to the way in which disability is defined with the intention of making it easier for a person to show that they are disabled. In particular there is no longer a requirement to consider whether the person is restricted in respect of one of the eight capacities which were specified under the old Disability Discrimination Act 1995. The basic definition of a disabled person (in s 6, and see also Schedule 1) remains the same and hence decisions under the old law will still apply (save in respect of the eight capacities). Decisions under the old law as to what constitutes a disability include *Goodwin v Patent Office* [1999] ICR 302, [1999] IRLR 4, EAT and *Hewett v Motorola Ltd* [2004] IRLR 545. See also *J v DLA Piper UK LLP* [2010] ICR 1052, [2010] IRLR 936 for guidance relating to how to approach the issue of mental disability. While there is no free-standing prohibition of discrimination on the grounds of obesity under European law, a person may be disabled as a result of obesity – for example, because of reduced mobility – if the effect is sufficient to meet the test set out in section 6: see *Walker v Sita Information Networking Computing Ltd* [2013] UKEAT 0097/12/0802, [2013] EqLR 476, EAT; *Fag og Arbejde (FOA) v Kommunernes Landsforening (KL) (Case C-354/13)* [2015] All ER (EC) 265, [2015] 2 CMLR 500, [2015] ICR 322. See also guidance from the CJEU as to the meaning of disability under Directive 2000/78/EC: *Chacon Navas v Eurest Colectividades SA (C-13/05)* [2006] 3 CMLR 40. Since 2009, the UN Convention on the Rights of Persons with Disabilities binds the EU and the Directive must be interpreted in a manner consistent with the Convention: see *HK Danmark v Dansk almennyttigt Boligselskab (Case C-335/11)* [2013] 3 CMLR 21, [2013] ICR 851.

III EQU [6.3]

Beyond being disabled Having a disability is not the only way in which a person can be protected. In *Coleman v Attridge Law (Case C-303/06)* [2008] IRLR 722 the CJEU held that Directive 2000/78 must be interpreted in such a way so as to include claims where the impugned treatment was based upon the disability of a person with whom the claimant was associated. Thus, there, Ms Coleman could advance claims of direct discrimination and harassment on grounds of/related to the disability of her son. The perception that a person has a protected characteristic has been enough to found a cause of action in respect of some protected characteristics (see *English v Thomas Sanderson Blinds Ltd* [2009] ICR 206 (sexual orientation); see also para 7.10 of the EHRC Code of Practice). However in the case of disability additional complexities have been considered sufficient to require a reference to the CJEU before such a claim can be recognised: *J v DLA Piper UK LLP* [2010] IRLR 936; and see *Aitken v Metropolitan Police Comr* [2011] 1 CMLR 58. These concerns were, however, overcome in *Chief Constable of Norfolk v Coffey* [2017] UKEAT/0260/16 in which the EAT (considering *CHEZ Rapredelenie Bulgaria AD v Komisia za zashtita ot diskriminatsia (Case C-83/14)* [2015] IRLR 746) recognised the ability to claim where an employer did not perceive that the claimant was disabled, but that s/he might become disabled at a future date. The mere assertion of a disability is, however, insufficient to found a claim for discrimination or harassment: see *Peninsula Business Services Ltd v Baker* [2017] ICR 714, [2017] IRLR 394. The Court of Appeal has held that the duty to make reasonable adjustments does not extend to the making of adjustments where the person disabled is associated with the claimant: see *Hainsworth v Ministry of Defence* [2014] EWCA Civ 763, [2014] 3 CMLR 43.

III EQU [6.4]

General approach in disability cases The approach to issues such as justification in disability cases will not necessarily follow that for other protected characteristics. In *Buchanan v Metropolitan Police Comr* (2016) UKEAT/0112/16, [2016] IRLR 918, [2017] ICR 184 the EAT held that it would be rare in disability cases concerned with attendance management for the approach in *Seldon v Clarkson Wright & Jakes* [2012] UKSC 16, [2012]

3 All ER 1301 (see **III EQU [5.1]**) to be applicable. There can also be a relation with other causes of action, such as unfair dismissal: see *O'Brien v Bolton St Catherine's Academy* [2017] EWCA Civ 145, [2017] ICR 737 where it was held that unfair dismissal on medical grounds was in the circumstances an act of disability discrimination. However, In *York City Council v Grosset* [2018] ICR 1492, the Court of Appeal held that the test of justification was an objective one under which the court/tribunal had to make its own assessment, in contrast to the test in relation to unfair dismissal.

III EQU [6.5]

Guidance Article 13 of the No 4 Order 2010, SI 2010/2317 saved the published guidance 'Guidance on matters to be taken into account in determining questions relating to the definition of disability' ISBN 978-0-11-703686-4 until fresh guidance was issued. New guidance came into force on 1 May 2011 and is available from www.gov.uk/government/publications/equality-act-guidance.

III EQU [6.6]

Schedule 1 and the Regulations Detailed provision for the meaning of disability is made in Sch 1 and the regulations made under it: **III EQU [219]**. See also the notes to s 22 regarding impairment: **III EQU [22.1]**.

III EQU [7]

7. Gender reassignment

(1) A person has the protected characteristic of gender reassignment if the person is proposing to undergo, is undergoing or has undergone a process (or part of a process) for the purpose of reassigning the person's sex by changing physiological or other attributes of sex.

(2) A reference to a transsexual person is a reference to a person who has the protected characteristic of gender reassignment.

(3) In relation to the protected characteristic of gender reassignment—
- (a) a reference to a person who has a particular protected characteristic is a reference to a transsexual person;
- (b) a reference to persons who share a protected characteristic is a reference to transsexual persons.

III EQU [7.1]

State Pension The Court of Justice of the European Union has ruled as discriminatory a provision (Gender Recognition Act 2004, s 4) that the retirement age for a state pension in the case of a person who changed gender should not be age appropriate to the acquired gender if that person was married to someone of the same gender. Such a provision was held to be contrary to arts 3, 4 and 7 of the Council Directive (EEC) 79/7 on the Equality of Treatment of Men and Women: *MB v Secretary of State for Work and Pensions (C-451/16)* [2019] 1 CMLR 4.

III EQU [8]

8. Marriage and civil partnership

(1) A person has the protected characteristic of marriage and civil partnership if the person is married or is a civil partner.

(2) In relation to the protected characteristic of marriage and civil partnership—
- (a) a reference to a person who has a particular protected characteristic is a reference to a person who is married or is a civil partner;
- (b) a reference to persons who share a protected characteristic is a reference to persons who are married or are civil partners.

III EQU [8.1]

Marital status In an employment case it was held that a person had been discriminated against by reason of marital status when she was less favourably treated because she was married to a particular man: see *Dunn v Institute of Cemetery and Crematorium Management* [2012] ICR 941. However the reasoning in that case was disapproved in *Hawkins v Atex Group Ltd* [2012] ICR 1315 in which Underhill P emphasised the protected characteristic is being married (whether generally or to a particular person) and the appropriate comparator

EQUALITY

will usually be someone in a relationship akin to marriage but who is not actually married. The reason for the treatment must be because the close relationship in question takes the form of marriage. See the other case law considered in *Hawkins*. In *Gould v Trustees of St John's Downshire Hill* [2017] UKEAT/0115/17, Simler P held that the status of divorce did not inform the scope of the protection for the status of marriage.

III EQU [9]

9. Race

(1) Race includes—

(a) colour;

(b) nationality;

(c) ethnic or national origins.

(2) In relation to the protected characteristic of race—

(a) a reference to a person who has a particular protected characteristic is a reference to a person of a particular racial group;

(b) a reference to persons who share a protected characteristic is a reference to persons of the same racial group.

(3) A racial group is a group of persons defined by reference to race; and a reference to a person's racial group is a reference to a racial group into which the person falls.

(4) The fact that a racial group comprises two or more distinct racial groups does not prevent it from constituting a particular racial group.

(5) A Minister of the Crown—

(a) must by order amend this section so as to provide for caste to be an aspect of race;

(b) may by order amend this Act so as to provide for an exception to a provision of this Act to apply, or not to apply, to caste or to apply, or not to apply, to caste in specified circumstances.

(6) The power under section 207(4)(b), in its application to subsection (5), includes power to amend this Act.

III EQU [9.1]

Racial group The provisions on racial groups are in line with s 3 of the Race Relations Act 1976 and cases decided under the old law are therefore noted below.

Sikhs are a racial group within the definition in sub-s (1) and therefore it is discriminatory to require a Sikh boy to remove his turban and cut his hair before being admitted as a pupil at a school: *Mandla v Dowell Lee* [1983] 2 AC 548, [1983] 1 All ER 1062, HL. But Rastafarians have been held not to be a racial group: *Crown Suppliers (Property Services Agency) v Dawkins* [1991] ICR 583, [1991] IRLR 327, EAT, since confirmed by the Court of Appeal [1993] ICR 517, CA. Essential characteristics of a "racial group" defined by reference to its ethnic origins are (1) a long shared history, of which the group is conscious as distinguishing it from other groups, and the memory of which it has kept alive; and (2) a cultural tradition of its own, including family and social customs and manners, often but not necessarily associated with religious observance: *Mandla v Dowell Lee* [1983] 2 AC 548, [1983] 1 All ER 1062, HL. A publican's refusal to admit a Sikh wearing a turban cannot be justified on the ground that customers with hats on are not allowed on the premises: *Gurmit Singh Kambo v Vaulkhard* (1984) Times, 7 December, CA. Gypsies, in the primary sense, are a racial group and therefore a publican's refusal to serve "travellers" may be indirectly discriminatory against them: *Commission for Racial Equality v Dutton* [1989] QB 783, [1989] 1 All ER 306, CA. Romany Gypsies and Irish Travellers each form a distinct racial group, and by virtue of s 9(4) form a composite group: *Moore and Coates v Secretary of State for Communities and Local Government* [2015] EWHCC 44 (Admin), [2015] JPL 762. Ability to speak a particular language, however, is not of itself a significant factor in determining a racial group and so it is not discriminatory to refuse a Welsh woman a job because she cannot speak Welsh: *Gwynedd County Council v Jones* [1986] ICR 833, [1986] LS Gaz R 3836, EAT.

In *Tirkey v Chandhok* (2014) UKEAT/0190/14, [2015] IRLR 195, [2015] ICR 527, [2015] All ER (D) 91 (Jan), EAT the EAT considered that 'ethnic origins' was a wide and flexible phrase capable of covering questions of descent, and caste could fall within it. Thus even before the exercise of s 9(5) powers, caste discrimination could fall within the concept of race in s 9. Section 9(5) did not limit the scope of 'race' as currently defined: it contained a power to extend so as expressly to include caste within the definition, and not limit the meaning of existing elements of the definition.

III EQU [9.2]

Nationality Cases on 'nationality' and its significance under the old law are noted below.

The policy of a college in charging higher fees to students not ordinarily resident (in the sense of having no real home) in the EEC is so closely related to their nationality as to constitute discrimination against a Cypriot student: *Orphanos v Queen Mary College* [1985] AC 761, [1985] 2 All ER 233, HL. A marriage registrar's practice of requesting applicants from abroad to produce their passports for their residence and other particulars to be checked is not discriminatory as, being addressed to persons from anywhere abroad, it is not based on the applicants' racial or national origins: *Tejani v Superintendent Registrar for the District of Peterborough* [1986] IRLR 502, CA, but see the criticism of this decision in 137 NLJ at p 196. *Grzelczyk v Centre Public d'aide sociale d'Ottignie-Louvain-la-Nouve: C-184/99* [2001] ECR I-6193, [2003] All ER (EC) 385, ECJ has held the refusal of social assistance on the ground of nationality to be unlawful, at least in the case of an individual who is a citizen of the European Union. The decision is based on Arts 6 and 8a of the Treaty of Rome. However see *R (on the application of Mohammed) v Secretary of State for Defence* [2007] EWCA Civ 1023, (2007) Times, 9 May, 151 Sol Jo LB 610. It was held that making payments to surviving prisoners of war of specified nationalities was not racially discriminatory, since the determination was by nationality, not race or colour. See *Hounga v Allen* [2014] UKSC 47, [2014] 4 All ER 595, [2014] 1 WLR 2889 (see below) for the position of an illegal immigrant.

The requirement that a student should be ordinarily resident in the country for three years as a condition of entitlement to subsidised loans and grants has been held to be justifiable even in the case of EU nationals, but the further condition of "settlement" (effectively nationality) may be applied only against nationals of countries outside the European Union: *R (on the application of Bidar) v Ealing London Borough Council: C-209/03* [2005] QB 812, [2005] All ER (EC) 687, ECJ. The Court was considering the effect of the restrictions in Schedule 1 to the Education (Student Support) Regulations (SI 2001/951) in the light of articles 12 and 149(1) EC about freedom of movement and the development of quality education within the Community by encouraging cooperation between member states.

III EQU [9.3]

Illegal presence in the United Kingdom In *Allen v Hounga* [2014] UKSC 47 [2014] 4 All ER 595, [2014] 1 WLR 2889 the Supreme Court rejected a defence against a claim for race discrimination made on the basis that the claimant was in the United Kingdom illegally. A claim for discrimination will only be defeated by a defence of illegality in circumstances in which there is an inextricable link between the claim and the claimant's illegal conduct. Even then, the illegality defence is grounded in public policy, and can therefore be overridden by a competing, stronger public policy aim. See also *Vakante v Addey & Stanhope School* [2004] EWCA Civ 1065, [2004] 4 All ER 1056, [2015] All ER (D) 219 (Jun) and its consideration in *Hounga*.

III EQU [9.4]

Modern Slavery In *Taiwo v Olaigbe, Onu v Akwiwu* [2016] UKSC 31, [2016] 1 WLR 2653 the Supreme Court held that whilst it was wrong to mistreat migrant workers on the basis of their vulnerable immigration status, any such treatment did not automatically amount to direct or indirect discrimination on the ground of nationality contrary to the Equality Act 2010. The Supreme Court invited Parliament to consider whether the remedy provided by the Modern Slavery Act 2015, s 8 was too restrictive.

III EQU [10]

10. Religion or belief

(1) Religion means any religion and a reference to religion includes a reference to a lack of religion.

(2) Belief means any religious or philosophical belief and a reference to belief includes a reference to a lack of belief.

(3) In relation to the protected characteristic of religion or belief—

(a) a reference to a person who has a particular protected characteristic is a reference to a person of a particular religion or belief;

(b) a reference to persons who share a protected characteristic is a reference to persons who are of the same religion or belief.

III EQU [10.1]

General Cases on the application of the equivalent wording in s 44 of the Equality Act 2006, now repealed, are included in the notes below.

III EQU [10.2]

Philosophical and political belief There is a growing body of case law as to what constitutes religious or philosophical or religious belief. In *Nicholson v Grainger plc* [2010] 2 All ER 253, [2010] IRLR 4, [2009] NLJR 1582 an asserted philosophical belief that mankind was heading towards catastrophic climate change and the claimant had a moral duty to lead a life in a manner that mitigated that catastrophe for the benefit of future generations and to persuade others to do the same was capable of being a 'religious or philosophical belief' and a tribunal finding that the criteria were satisfied was upheld. See also *Harron v Chief Constable of Dorset* [2016] IRLR 481. Political beliefs can be a philosophical belief: *Olivier v Department for Work and Pensions*, Employment Tribunal decision noted in IDS, February 2014, at 17. In *Gray v Mulberry Co (Design) Ltd* [2018] IRLR 893, the EAT upheld a decision that the claimant's belief that there was a 'statutory human or moral right to own the copyright and moral rights of her own creative works and output' had not attained the level of cogency, seriousness, cohesion and importance required by *Grainger*.

III EQU [10.3]

Religious belief Usually establishing the possession of a religious belief will be relatively straightforward. A factual enquiry will be made: see *R (on the application of Williamson) v Secretary of State for Education and Employment* [2005] UKHL 15, [2005] 2 AC 246. More difficult is separating out what is a true component of the belief from other desires. An example is *Gareddu v London Underground* [2017] IRLR 404. When dealing with the case of an employee who had been denied 5 weeks' annual leave to attend religious festivals with his family, it was found that the true reason for the request was not the manifestation of belief, but a desire to spend time with his family. It is clear that protection extends to the absence of a religious belief. Thus in *Eweida v UK* (above) at para 79, the Court emphasised that rights under article 9 were 'a precious asset for atheists, agnostics, sceptics and the unconcerned'. Scientology has been held to be a 'religion' in the context of a decision relating to whether a chapel owned by a scientology college was 'a place of meeting for religious worship' within the meaning of the Places of Worship Registration Act 1855: see *R (on the application of Hodkin) v Registrar General of Births, Deaths and Marriages* [2013] UKSC 77, [2014] 1 All ER 737, [2014] 2 WLR 23.

III EQU [10.4]

Religious beliefs and other rights It was inevitable that cases would be brought where the assertion of religious belief by one employee could be construed as a denial of another employee's right not to be discriminated against on the grounds of his or her sexual orientation. Four such cases were litigated through the UK Courts and ended up before the ECtHR: *Eweida v United Kingdom (Application No 48420/10)* (2013) 57 EHRR 8. See the note at **III HUM [31.5]**. One of the Claimants was a registrar who objected to conducting civil partnership ceremonies. She was not permitted to set up her religious beliefs as a valid reason for a refusal when her beliefs involved discrimination against same sex partners: *Ladele v Islington London Borough Council* [2009] EWCA Civ 1357, [2010] 1 WLR 955, [2010] LGR 690. Similarly, in *McFarlane v Relate Avon Ltd* [2010] EWCA Civ 880, [2010] IRLR 872, 29 BHRC 249 a sex therapy and relationship counsellor could not refuse to provide services to homosexual couples because of his religious beliefs. In two cases about employees who wanted to wear visible crosses at work, the question was the extent to which the infringement of Article 9 rights can be justified. In *Eweida v British Airways Plc* [2010] EWCA Civ 80, [2010] ICR 890 the airline's dress code had sought to pursue a legitimate aim but had not struck a fair balance. However in *Chaplin*, the hospital's policy did because it was designed to minimise infection and injury risks when handling patients. In *Re A (Children) (Contact: Ultra-Orthodox Judaism: Transgender Parent)* [2018] 44 WLR 60, the Court of Appeal held a judge had been wrong to refuse contact between a children and their father, who was a transgender person who had been shunned by their ultra-orthodox Jewish community. The approach of promoting contact was no different merely because religious belief was in play. In *Proceedings brought by Tietosuojavaltuutettu (C-25/17)* [2019] 1 CMLR 5, the CJEU held that the processing of personal data carried out in the context of door-to-door preaching by the Jehovah's Witnesses religious community must respect the rules of the Data Protection Directive.

III EQU [10.5]

Belief and manner of manifestation distinguished There is a growing body of case law for the proposition that there is a crucial distinction between discriminating against a person because of his or her religious or philosophical belief and the way in which that belief is manifested. The right to the belief is protected; the manner of manifestation is not, particularly if it is offensive to others. As Laws LJ stated in *McFarlane v Relate Avon Ltd* [2010] EWCA Civ 880, [2010] IRLR 872, 29 BHRC 249 (para 22): 'In a free constitution such as ours there is an important distinction to be drawn between the law's protection of the right to hold and express a belief and the law's protection of that belief's substance or content. The common law and ECHR Article 9 offer vigorous protection of the Christian's right (and every other person's right) to hold and express his or her beliefs. And so they should. By contrast they do not, and should not, offer any protection whatever of the substance or content of those beliefs on the ground only that they are based on religious precepts. These are twin conditions of a free society.' See also *Grace v Places for Children* UKEAT/0217/13/GE, 5 November 2013 and IDS Brief, February 2014, at 7 for an analysis of a dividing line between the holding of a belief and its manifestation. A couple whose application to foster children was refused on the basis of their religious belief that homosexuality was wrong failed in their application for judicial review of the decision: *R (on the application of Johns) v Derby City Council (Equality and Human Rights Commission intervening)* [2011] EWHC 375 (Admin), [2011] 1 FCR 493, [2011] 1 FLR 2094. In *Heafield v Times Newspapers Ltd* (UKEATPA/1305/12/BA), [2013] NLJR 235 a sub-editor, who was a Roman Catholic, failed in his action for harassment on the grounds of religious belief when an editor chased him for an article by referring to 'the fucking Pope'. In context, this did not fall within the statutory definition. In *Wasteney v East London NHS Foundation Trust* [2016] ICR 643, a senior employee tried to impose her religious views on a junior colleague and had been found guilty of serious misconduct by the employer. The EAT rejected a claim of discrimination and harassment because of religion or belief: the employer had been entitled to find the conduct went beyond a religious discussion and placed improper pressure on the junior colleague. Another example is *Amachree v Wandsworth Borough Council* (2010, 2328606/2009), a decision of an Employment Tribunal, which shows that a religious belief cannot be used as a shield for inappropriate conduct. An employee, a homeless prevention officer, told a terminally ill service user that her problem was that she did not have God or faith in her life and was ill as a result. Following her complaint and the officer's suspension, the officer issued a press release from which the terminally ill patient could be identified. An employment tribunal found the employer had not unfairly dismissed him or discriminated against him on grounds of religious belief.

III EQU [10.6]

Constitutional right to freedom of conscience The Judicial Committee of the Privy Council, when construing the constitution of the Bahamas, advised that a rule requiring Muslim members of the Royal Bahamas Defence Force to attend Christian prayers as a ceremonial obligation was contrary to their constitutional right to freedom of conscience: *Laramore v Commodore of the Royal Bahamas Defence Force* [2017] UKPC 13, [2017] 1 WLR 2752.

III EQU [11]

11. Sex

In relation to the protected characteristic of sex—

(a) a reference to a person who has a particular protected characteristic is a reference to a man or to a woman;

(b) a reference to persons who share a protected characteristic is a reference to persons of the same sex.

III EQU [11.1]

Civil partnerships The government has been held by the Supreme Court to have discriminated against a heterosexual couple by delaying a decision whether to amend the Civil Partnership Act 2004 so as to extend civil partnership to people of the opposite sex: *R (on the application of Steinfeld and Keidan) v Secretary of State for International Development* [2018] UKSC 32, [2018] 3 WLR 415.

III EQU [11.2]

Wide reach of indirect gender discrimination Indirect discrimination (see s 19 of the Act) can have a widespread effect. For example an industrial tribunal in Northern Ireland held that a requirement that a job candidate had two years' paid work experience within a 5 year period had a disproportionate adverse effect on women. The tribunal drew an inference that the vast proportion of people who take periods out of work to look after the family are women. The condition was therefore indirect discrimination against women: *Nuala Crilly v Ballymagroarty Hazelbank Community Partnership* (31 October 2011), see IDS, November 2012, page 5. See further *Essop v Home Office; Naeem v Secretary of State for Justice* [2017] IRLR 558 and the discussion below s 19 at para **III EQU [19]**.

EQUALITY

III EQU [12]

12. Sexual orientation

(1) Sexual orientation means a person's sexual orientation towards—

(a) persons of the same sex,

(b) persons of the opposite sex, or

(c) persons of either sex.

(2) In relation to the protected characteristic of sexual orientation—

(a) a reference to a person who has a particular protected characteristic is a reference to a person who is of a particular sexual orientation;

(b) a reference to persons who share a protected characteristic is a reference to persons who are of the same sexual orientation.

III EQU [12.1]

Examples It was held to be discrimination, contrary to reg 3(1) of the Equality Act (Sexual Orientation) Regulations 2007 (SI 2007/1263), for a hotelier to refuse accommodation with a double bed to a homosexual couple on the ground that the hotelier's religious beliefs prevented him from offering such bedrooms to anyone but couples who were married to each other: *Hall v Bull (Liberty intervening)* [2013] UKSC 73, [2013] 1 WLR 3741, (2014) Times, 09 January. In a similar case relating to the refusal to allow a homosexual couple to occupy a double room, a bed & breakfast owner was also found to have unlawfully discriminated on the grounds of sexual orientation *Black v Wilkinson* [2013] EWCA Civ 820, [2013] 4 All ER 1053, [2013] 1 WLR 2490.

In a Northern Ireland case, the Court of Appeal held that a refusal by a bakery to decorate a cake with the words 'Support Gay Marriage' discriminated against the customer on grounds of sexual orientation: *Lee v McArthur* [2016] NICA 39, [2017] IRLR 69, however this was overturned by the Supreme Court. The Supreme Court held that on the facts there was no discrimination based on sexual orientation, but simply a refusal to include a message promoting gay marriage which was a concept which the bakers rejected on sincerely held religious grounds. The objection was to the message not to serving the messengers as customers: *Lee v Ashers Baking Co Ltd* [2018] UKSC 49, [2018] 3 WLR 1294, (2018) Times, 11 October. A similar factual scenario (albeit with different legal considerations arising) came before the US Supreme Court: *Masterpiece Cakeshop Ltd v Colorado Civil Rights Commission* 584 US (2018). The Court found a failure by the Colorado Civil Rights Commission to employ religious neutrality when it concluded that the bakery had discriminated against the couple. The Supreme Court did not rule on broader questions concerning the intersection of anti-discrimination laws, free exercise of religion, and freedom of speech.

CHAPTER 2 PROHIBITED CONDUCT

DISCRIMINATION

III EQU [13]

13. Direct discrimination

(1) A person (A) discriminates against another (B) if, because of a protected characteristic, A treats B less favourably than A treats or would treat others.

(2) If the protected characteristic is age, A does not discriminate against B if A can show A's treatment of B to be a proportionate means of achieving a legitimate aim.

(3) If the protected characteristic is disability, and B is not a disabled person, A does not discriminate against B only because A treats or would treat disabled persons more favourably than A treats B.

(4) If the protected characteristic is marriage and civil partnership, this section applies to a contravention of Part 5 (work) only if the treatment is because it is B who is married or a civil partner.

(5) If the protected characteristic is race, less favourable treatment includes segregating B from others.

(6) If the protected characteristic is sex—

(a) less favourable treatment of a woman includes less favourable treatment of her because she is breast-feeding;

(b) in a case where B is a man, no account is to be taken of special treatment afforded to a woman in connection with pregnancy or childbirth.

(7) Subsection (6)(a) does not apply for the purposes of Part 5 (work).

(8) This section is subject to sections 17(6) and 18(7).

III EQU [13.1]

Protected characteristics Protected characteristics are listed in s 4. Protection extends beyond the possession of a protected characteristic: see the discussion above in the context of disability at **III EQU [6.3]**.

III EQU [13.2]

What may be worn at work An employer who bans the wearing of Islamic headscarves at work is not discriminating directly if this is part of a general ban on the wearing of wearing political, philosophical or religious signs in the workplace: *Achbita v G4S secure Solutions NV (Case C-157/15)* [2017] 3 CMLR 21, (2017) Times, 27 March, ECJ. On the other hand a ban on the wearing of Islamic headscarves is not justified by reference to the wishes of customers: *Bougnaoulv Micropole SA (Case C-188/15)* [2017] 3 CMLR 22, (2017) 27 March 2017, ECJ.

III EQU [14]

14. Combined discrimination: dual characteristics

(1) A person (A) discriminates against another (B) if, because of a combination of two relevant protected characteristics, A treats B less favourably than A treats or would treat a person who does not share either of those characteristics.

(2) The relevant protected characteristics are—

(a) age;

(b) disability;

(c) gender reassignment;

(d) race

(e) religion or belief;

(f) sex;

(g) sexual orientation.

(3) For the purposes of establishing a contravention of this Act by virtue of subsection (1), B need not show that A's treatment of B is direct discrimination because of each of the characteristics in the combination (taken separately).

(4) But B cannot establish a contravention of this Act by virtue of subsection (1) if, in reliance on another provision of this Act or any other enactment, A shows that A's treatment of B is not direct discrimination because of either or both of the characteristics in the combination.

(5) Subsection (1) does not apply to a combination of characteristics that includes disability in circumstances where, if a claim of direct discrimination because of disability were to be brought, it would come within section 116 (special educational needs).

(6) A Minister of the Crown may by order amend this section so as to—

(a) make further provision about circumstances in which B can, or in which B cannot, establish a contravention of this Act by virtue of subsection (1);

(b) specify other circumstances in which subsection (1) does not apply.

(7) The references to direct discrimination are to a contravention of this Act by virtue of section 13.

III EQU [14.1]

Commencement This section is not yet in force and awaits a commencement order.

III EQU [15]

15. Discrimination arising from disability

(1) A person (A) discriminates against a disabled person (B) if—

(a) A treats B unfavourably because of something arising in consequence of B's disability, and

(b) A cannot show that the treatment is a proportionate means of achieving a legitimate aim.

(2) Subsection (1) does not apply if A shows that A did not know, and could not reasonably have been expected to know, that B had the disability.

III EQU [15.1]

A new concept The cause of action 'discrimination arising from disability' is intended to overcome the perceived deficiencies in the pre-existing law which were identified in *London Borough of Lewisham v Malcolm* [2008] UKHL 43, [2008] 1 AC 1399, [2008] 4 All ER 525 and to avoid the difficult issue of identifying an appropriate comparator in disability discrimination cases. It may be that the stair-lift case, *Williams v Richmond Court (Swansea) Ltd* [2006] EWCA Civ 1719, (2006) Times, 29 December, would now be decided differently. For the questions to be asked see *Hensman v Ministry of Defence* UKEAT/007/14/DM, [2014] EqLR 670. In *Williams v Swansea University Pension and Assurance Scheme Trustees* [2018] UKSC 65, , [2019] 1 WLR 93, there was no unfavourable treatment of a disabled employee who had reduced his hours before taking ill health retirement when pension benefits were calculated by reference to his final part-time salary. It is to be noted that any discrimination established under s 15(1)(a) can be justified applying the test in s 15(1)(b). See *Bolton St Catherine's Academy v O'Brien* [2017] ICR 737 for observations concerning the relationship between a finding of disproportionality of dismissal for a period of sickness absence with the test for unfair dismissal under s 98(4) of the Employment Rights Act 1996, but note the subsequent clarification of those observations in *City of York Council v Grosset* [2018] ICR 1492.

See also the controversial case of *First Group plc v Paulley* [2017] UKSC 4, [2017] 1 WLR 423, (2017) Times, 24 January raising the question how should a bus company provide for wheelchair users if the space on the bus is taken by a buggy-pusher?

III EQU [15.2]

Knowledge of disability The section requires actual or constructive knowledge of a disability that substantially impairs the claimant's ability to carry out normal activities. Occupational health advice that the claimant is not so disabled may mean that an employer cannot reasonably know of the disability for the purposes of this section and the duty under s 29 to make adjustments: *Donellan v Liberata UK Ltd* [2018] EWCA Civ 129. Where there is knowledge of the disability, there is no additional requirement that the alleged discriminator should be aware that the 'something' referred to in s 15 arose in consequence of the disability: *City of York Council v Grosset* [2018] EWCA Civ 1105, [2018] ICR 1492.

III EQU [15.3]

Proportionate means In proceedings for possession against a tenant with a disability, the issue may be raised as to whether making an order would be a proportionate means of meeting the landlord's legitimate aims. It may also be raised on an application to enforce a possession order, but not if it has been decided in the landlord's favour on making the order for possession, unless there has been a material change of circumstances: *Paragon Asra Housing Ltd v Neville* [2018] EWCA Civ 1712, [2018] All ER (D) 09 (Aug).

III EQU [15.4]

Homelessness of disabled person On an application to be accepted as homeless because of the inadequacy of the accommodation occupied, the housing authority's decision under s 184 of the Housing Act 1996 is required by s 149(3)(b) and (4) to focus on the particular needs of that person not the generalised needs of others on the housing list: *Lomax v Gosport Borough Council* [2018] EWCA Civ 1846.

III EQU [16]

16. Gender reassignment discrimination: cases of absence from work

(1) This section has effect for the purposes of the application of Part 5 (work) to the protected characteristic of gender reassignment.

(2) A person (A) discriminates against a transsexual person (B) if, in relation to an absence of B's that is because of gender reassignment, A treats B less favourably than A would treat B if—

(a) B's absence was because of sickness or injury, or

(b) B's absence was for some other reason and it is not reasonable for B to be treated less favourably.

(3) A person's absence is because of gender reassignment if it is because the person is proposing to undergo, is undergoing or has undergone the process (or part of the process) mentioned in section 7(1).

III EQU [17]

17. Pregnancy and maternity discrimination: non-work cases

(1) This section has effect for the purposes of the application to the protected characteristic of pregnancy and maternity of—

(a) Part 3 (services and public functions);

(b) Part 4 (premises);

(c) Part 6 (education);

(d) Part 7 (associations).

(2) A person (A) discriminates against a woman if A treats her unfavourably because of a pregnancy of hers.

(3) A person (A) discriminates against a woman if, in the period of 26 weeks beginning with the day on which she gives birth, A treats her unfavourably because she has given birth.

(4) The reference in subsection (3) to treating a woman unfavourably because she has given birth includes, in particular, a reference to treating her unfavourably because she is breast-feeding.

(5) For the purposes of this section, the day on which a woman gives birth is the day on which—

(a) she gives birth to a living child, or

(b) she gives birth to a dead child (more than 24 weeks of the pregnancy having passed).

(6) Section 13, so far as relating to sex discrimination, does not apply to anything done in relation to a woman in so far as—

(a) it is for the reason mentioned in subsection (2), or

(b) it is in the period, and for the reason, mentioned in subsection (3).

EQUALITY

III EQU [17.1]

Proportionality in the treatment of pregnant women Special treatment of pregnant women should be ignored where reasonably necessary for the protection of women. But the principle of proportionality should be applied against the derogation in favour of pregnant women where the protection goes beyond what is reasonably necessary: *De Belin v Eversheds Legal Services Ltd* (2011) UKEAT/0352/10/JOJ, [2011] IRLR 448, [2011] 16 LS Gaz R 18, EAT applying dicta about proportionality in *Johnston v Chief Constable of the Royal Ulster Constabulary: 222/84* [1987] QB 129, [1986] 3 All ER 135, ECJ. The mere fact that a woman is on maternity leave when unfavourable treatment occurred was not enough to establish unlawful direct discrimination under s 18 (or by extension s 17): *Interserve FM Ltd v Tuleikyte* [2017] IRLR 615.

III EQU [17.2]

'Because' The test of causation denoted by the word 'because' has been considered in the context of s 18 (see **III EQU [18]** below). In *Metropolitan Police Comr v Keohane* [2014] ICR

1073, the EAT rejected the contention that the phrase 'because of' should be construed narrowly and preferred submissions that the underlying directive which fell to be implemented used the wording 'related to' which imported a broader test of connection.

III EQU [18]

18. Pregnancy and maternity discrimination: work cases

(1) This section has effect for the purposes of the application of Part 5 (work) to the protected characteristic of pregnancy and maternity.

(2) A person (A) discriminates against a woman if, in the protected period in relation to a pregnancy of hers, A treats her unfavourably—

- (a) because of the pregnancy, or
- (b) because of illness suffered by her as a result of it.

(3) A person (A) discriminates against a woman if A treats her unfavourably because she is on compulsory maternity leave.

(4) A person (A) discriminates against a woman if A treats her unfavourably because she is exercising or seeking to exercise, or has exercised or sought to exercise, the right to ordinary or additional maternity leave.

(5) For the purposes of subsection (2), if the treatment of a woman is in implementation of a decision taken in the protected period, the treatment is to be regarded as occurring in that period (even if the implementation is not until after the end of that period).

(6) The protected period, in relation to a woman's pregnancy, begins when the pregnancy begins, and ends—

- (a) if she has the right to ordinary and additional maternity leave, at the end of the additional maternity leave period or (if earlier) when she returns to work after the pregnancy;
- (b) if she does not have that right, at the end of the period of 2 weeks beginning with the end of the pregnancy.

(7) Section 13, so far as relating to sex discrimination, does not apply to treatment of a woman in so far as—

- (a) it is in the protected period in relation to her and is for a reason mentioned in paragraph (a) or (b) of subsection (2), or
- (b) it is for a reason mentioned in subsection (3) or (4).

III EQU [18.1]

General See the comments under s 17 above.

III EQU [18.2]

Relationship with the Maternity and Parental Leave etc Regulations 1999 The protection under reg 10 of the Maternity and Parental Leave etc Regulations 1999 (right to be offered a suitable available vacancy upon redundancy) is different to that arising under s 18 (where a finding of unfavourable treatment because of pregnancy etc is required). The Regulations grant special protection at penalty of unfair dismissal: see *Sefton Borough Council v Wainwright* [2015] ICR 652.

III EQU [19]

19. Indirect discrimination

(1) A person (A) discriminates against another (B) if A applies to B a provision, criterion or practice which is discriminatory in relation to a relevant protected characteristic of B's.

(2) For the purposes of subsection (1), a provision, criterion or practice is discriminatory in relation to a relevant protected characteristic of B's if—

- (a) A applies, or would apply, it to persons with whom B does not share the characteristic,

(b) it puts, or would put, persons with whom B shares the characteristic at a particular disadvantage when compared with persons with whom B does not share it,

(c) it puts, or would put, B at that disadvantage, and

(d) A cannot show it to be a proportionate means of achieving a legitimate aim.

(3) The relevant protected characteristics are—

age;

disability;

gender reassignment;

marriage and civil partnership;

race;

religion or belief;

sex;

sexual orientation.

III EQU [19.0]

General A claimant who is a member of a group that can be shown, statistically, to be disadvantaged by a relevant practice, criterion or procedure does not also have to show the reason. Once the causal link is shown it is for the employer to show justification: *Essop v Home Office (UK Border Agency); Naseem v Secretary of State for Justice* [2017] UKSC 27, [2017] 1 WLR 1343, [2017] ICR 640, (2017) Times, 18 April. In respect of justification, the Supreme Court noted that '[t]he requirement to justify a PCP should not be seen as placing an unreasonable burden upon respondents. Nor should it be seen as casting some sort of shadow or stigma upon them.' See also *R (on the application of C) v Secretary of State for Work and Pensions* [2017] UKSC 72, [2017] 1 WLR 4127 where the Supreme Court held that a special customer records policy which retained details of a transgender person's previous gender was a proportionate means of achieving a legitimate aim.

III EQU [19.1]

Cost as justification There was conflicting authority on the question of whether cost alone can be sufficient grounds on which to justify indirect discrimination. In *Cherfi v G4S Security Services Ltd* (UKEAT/0379/10/DM), (24 May 2011, unreported) the EAT said that there was no reason in principle why a justification defence that said that the cost of preventing the discriminatory impact would be disproportionately high could not succeed. This conflicted with the earlier EAT decision in *Cross v British Airways* [2005] IRLR 423 in which it was held that an employer could not rely solely on cost. See now *Woodcock v Cumbria PCT* [2012] EWCA Civ 330, [2012] ICR 1126, [2012] IRLR 491 where Rimer LJ held the guidance of the CJEU was clear that discriminatory treatment could not be justified solely by reason of cost. There needed to be something more. Budgetary consequences were held to be incapable of justifying discrimination on the basis of being a part time worker – fundamental principles of equal treatment could not depend on how much money was available or how the state chose to allocate available funds: *Ministry of Justice (formerly Department for Constitutional Affairs) v O'Brien (Council of Immigration Judges intervening)* [2013] UKSC 6, [2013] 2 All ER 1, [2013] 1 WLR 522 (see also per the CJEU (C-393/10) [2012] 2 CMLR 25).

III EQU [19.2]

Proportionate means of achieving a legitimate aim A scheme requiring dangerous prisoners to be accommodated in approved premises before release (where a shortage of approved premises for women meant they were less likely than male prisoners to be accommodated near their homes) could not be said to be justified where the Ministry of Justice had not addressed the possible impacts on women of the scheme, assessed whether there was a disadvantage, its significance and whether there were steps which could mitigate it: *R (Coll) v Secretary of State for Justice* [2017] UKSC 40, [2017] 1 WLR 2093. The scope of section 19(2)(d) fell to be considered in *R (H) v Ealing London Borough Council* [2017] EWCA Civ 1127, (2017) Times, 11 September. The Council's housing allocation policy gave priority to working households and was thus indirectly discriminatory in respect of those who were unable to work due to a protected characteristic. However, since the priority was to be applied to only 15% of the housing within the allocation scheme the Court held it to be a proportionate means of achieving a legitimate aim.

ADJUSTMENTS FOR DISABLED PERSONS

III EQU [20]

20. Duty to make adjustments

(1) Where this Act imposes a duty to make reasonable adjustments on a person, this section, sections 21 and 22 and the applicable Schedule apply; and for those purposes, a person on whom the duty is imposed is referred to as A.

(2) The duty comprises the following three requirements.

(3) The first requirement is a requirement, where a provision, criterion or practice of A's puts a disabled person at a substantial disadvantage in relation to a relevant matter in comparison with persons who are not disabled, to take such steps as it is reasonable to have to take to avoid the disadvantage.

(4) The second requirement is a requirement, where a physical feature puts a disabled person at a substantial disadvantage in relation to a relevant matter in comparison with persons who are not disabled, to take such steps as it is reasonable to have to take to avoid the disadvantage.

(5) The third requirement is a requirement, where a disabled person would, but for the provision of an auxiliary aid, be put at a substantial disadvantage in relation to a relevant matter in comparison with persons who are not disabled, to take such steps as it is reasonable to have to take to provide the auxiliary aid.

(6) Where the first or third requirement relates to the provision of information, the steps which it is reasonable for A to have to take include steps for ensuring that in the circumstances concerned the information is provided in an accessible format.

(7) A person (A) who is subject to a duty to make reasonable adjustments is not (subject to express provision to the contrary) entitled to require a disabled person, in relation to whom A is required to comply with the duty, to pay to any extent A's costs of complying with the duty.

(8) A reference in section 21 or 22 or an applicable Schedule to the first, second or third requirement is to be construed in accordance with this section.

(9) In relation to the second requirement, a reference in this section or an applicable Schedule to avoiding a substantial disadvantage includes a reference to—

- (a) removing the physical feature in question,
- (b) altering it, or
- (c) providing a reasonable means of avoiding it.

(10) A reference in this section, section 21 or 22 or an applicable Schedule (apart from paragraphs 2 to 4 of Schedule 4) to a physical feature is a reference to—

- (a) a feature arising from the design or construction of a building,
- (b) a feature of an approach to, exit from or access to a building,
- (c) a fixture or fitting, or furniture, furnishings, materials, equipment or other chattels, in or on premises, or
- (d) any other physical element or quality.

(11) A reference in this section, section 21 or 22 or an applicable Schedule to an auxiliary aid includes a reference to an auxiliary service.

(12) A reference in this section or an applicable Schedule to chattels is to be read, in relation to Scotland, as a reference to moveable property.

(13) The applicable Schedule is, in relation to the Part of this Act specified in the first column of the Table, the Schedule specified in the second column.

Part of this Act	*Applicable Schedule*
Part 3 (services and public functions)	Schedule 2
Part 4 (premises)	Schedule 4

Part of this Act	*Applicable Schedule*
Part 5 (work)	Schedule 8
Part 6 (education)	Schedule 13
Part 7 (associations)	Schedule 15
Each of the Parts mentioned above	Schedule 21

III EQU [20.1]

Further provisions on the duty to make adjustments There are further provisions on the duty to make adjustments at ss 189 and 190 and in regs 9 to 14 of the Equality Act 2010 (Disability) Regulations 2010, SI 2010/2128.

III EQU [20.1A]

Key cases As to the duty itself, the key cases are *Archibald v Fife Council* [2004] UKHL 32, [2004] 4 All ER 303, [2004] IRLR 651; *Lewisham London Borough Council v Malcolm* [2008] UKHL 43, [2008] 1 AC 1399, [2008] 4 All ER 525 and *Griffiths v Secretary of State for Work and Pensions* [2015] EWCA Civ 1265, [2016] IRLR 216.

III EQU [20.2]

Duty to make adjustments for mental incapacity It has been held, in a decision under the Disability Discrimination Act 1995, as amended, that a creditor discriminates against an incapacitated debtor if he, or she, obtains a bankruptcy order with knowledge of the incapacity and without making reasonable adjustments: *Haworth v Cartmel* [2011] EWHC 36 (Ch), [2011] All ER (D) 23 (Mar).

III EQU [20.3]

Duty of transport operators to make adjustments for wheelchair users A bus company which had a policy of asking customers to move from the wheelchair space of a bus to allow a wheelchair user to board, but if they refused not then compelling them to do so or take any further action, was found to breach the requirement to make reasonable adjustments under s 20(3) of the Equality Act 2010: *Paulley v Firstgroup plc* [2017] UKSC 4, [2017] 1 WLR 423. The Supreme Court accepted that there could be circumstances in which it would be unreasonable for a non-wheelchair user to vacate the space allocated for wheelchairs. As there could be a variety of circumstances in which a non-wheelchair user refused to vacate a space, the appropriate response of the driver would vary depending on the reason for refusal and the other circumstances. Where the driver concluded the refusal to move was unreasonable, it was unjustifiable for the company to have a policy which did not require some further step by the driver in any circumstances. It was not unreasonable for the company to train the driver to do a bit more when a request was not complied with.

III EQU [20.4]

No duty in association cases The duty does not extend to making adjustments where the disability in question is that of a person associated with the claimant: see *Hainsworth v Ministry of Justice* [2014] EWCA Civ 763, [2014] 3 CMLR 43.

III EQU [21]

21. Failure to comply with duty

(1) A failure to comply with the first, second or third requirement is a failure to comply with a duty to make reasonable adjustments.

(2) A discriminates against a disabled person if A fails to comply with that duty in relation to that person.

(3) A provision of an applicable Schedule which imposes a duty to comply with the first, second or third requirement applies only for the purpose of establishing whether A has contravened this Act by virtue of subsection (2); a failure to comply is, accordingly, not actionable by virtue of another provision of this Act or otherwise.

III EQU [22]

22. Regulations

(1) Regulations may prescribe—

EQUALITY

(a) matters to be taken into account in deciding whether it is reasonable for A to take a step for the purposes of a prescribed provision of an applicable Schedule;

(b) descriptions of persons to whom the first, second or third requirement does not apply.

(2) Regulations may make provision as to—

(a) circumstances in which it is, or in which it is not, reasonable for a person of a prescribed description to have to take steps of a prescribed description;

(b) what is, or what is not, a provision, criterion or practice;

(c) things which are, or which are not, to be treated as physical features;

(d) things which are, or which are not, to be treated as alterations of physical features;

(e) things which are, or which are not, to be treated as auxiliary aids.

(3) Provision made by virtue of this section may amend an applicable Schedule.

III EQU [22.1]

Regulations The Equality Act 2010 (Disability) Regulations 2010, SI 2010/2128, regs 3 and 4 exclude addictions from the concept of "impairment" and also certain criminal tendencies. Special provision is also made for babies and young children (reg 6) and blind people (reg 7).

DISCRIMINATION: SUPPLEMENTARY

III EQU [23]

23. Comparison by reference to circumstances

(1) On a comparison of cases for the purposes of section 13, 14, or 19 there must be no material difference between the circumstances relating to each case.

(2) The circumstances relating to a case include a person's abilities if—

(a) on a comparison for the purposes of section 13, the protected characteristic is disability;

(b) on a comparison for the purposes of section 14, one of the protected characteristics in the combination is disability.

(3) If the protected characteristic is sexual orientation, the fact that one person (whether or not the person referred to as B) is a civil partner while another is married to a person of the opposite sex is not a material difference between the circumstances relating to each case.

(4) If the protected characteristic is sexual orientation, the fact that one person (whether or not the person referred to as B) is married to a person of the same sex while another is married to a person of the opposite sex is not a material difference between the circumstances relating to each case.

III EQU [24]

24. Irrelevance of alleged discriminator's characteristics

(1) For the purpose of establishing a contravention of this Act by virtue of section 13(1), it does not matter whether A has the protected characteristic.

(2) For the purpose of establishing a contravention of this Act by virtue of section 14(1), it does not matter—

(a) whether A has one of the protected characteristics in the combination;

(b) whether A has both.

III EQU [25]

25. References to particular strands of discrimination

(1) Age discrimination is—

(a) discrimination within section 13 because of age;
(b) discrimination within section 19 where the relevant protected characteristic is age.

(2) Disability discrimination is—
(a) discrimination within section 13 because of disability;
(b) discrimination within section 15;
(c) discrimination within section 19 where the relevant protected characteristic is disability;
(d) discrimination within section 21.

(3) Gender reassignment discrimination is—
(a) discrimination within section 13 because of gender reassignment;
(b) discrimination within section 16;
(c) discrimination within section 19 where the relevant protected characteristic is gender reassignment.

(4) Marriage and civil partnership discrimination is—
(a) discrimination within section 13 because of marriage and civil partnership;
(b) discrimination within section 19 where the relevant protected characteristic is marriage and civil partnership.

(5) Pregnancy and maternity discrimination is discrimination within section 17 or 18.

(6) Race discrimination is—
(a) discrimination within section 13 because of race;
(b) discrimination within section 19 where the relevant protected characteristic is race.

(7) Religious or belief-related discrimination is—
(a) discrimination within section 13 because of religion or belief;
(b) discrimination within section 19 where the relevant protected characteristic is religion or belief.

(8) Sex discrimination is—
(a) discrimination within section 13 because of sex;
(b) discrimination within section 19 where the relevant protected characteristic is sex.

(9) Sexual orientation discrimination is—
(a) discrimination within section 13 because of sexual orientation;
(b) discrimination within section 19 where the relevant protected characteristic is sexual orientation.

Other prohibited conduct

III EQU [26]

26. Harassment

(1) A person (A) harasses another (B) if—
(a) A engages in unwanted conduct related to a relevant protected characteristic, and
(b) the conduct has the purpose or effect of—
(i) violating B's dignity, or
(ii) creating an intimidating, hostile, degrading, humiliating or offensive environment for B.

(2) A also harasses B if—
(a) A engages in unwanted conduct of a sexual nature, and
(b) the conduct has the purpose or effect referred to in subsection (1)(b).

(3) A also harasses B if—

(a) A or another person engages in unwanted conduct of a sexual nature or that is related to gender reassignment or sex,

(b) the conduct has the purpose or effect referred to in subsection (1)(b), and

(c) because of B's rejection of or submission to the conduct, A treats B less favourably than A would treat B if B had not rejected or submitted to the conduct.

(4) In deciding whether conduct has the effect referred to in subsection (1)(b), each of the following must be taken into account—

(a) the perception of B;

(b) the other circumstances of the case;

(c) whether it is reasonable for the conduct to have that effect.

(5) The relevant protected characteristics are—

age;
disability;
gender reassignment;
race;
religion or belief;
sex;
sexual orientation.

III EQU [26.1]

Definition It has been held, under the earlier legislation, that the term 'harassment' should not be construed by reference to the Protection from Harassment Act 1997, that 'purpose' and 'effect' are different and alternative elements and that the effect (of violating dignity etc) does not constitute harassment unless the response is reasonable: *Dhaliwali v Richmond Pharmacology* [2009] ICR 724, [2009] IRLR 336. As regards sexual orientation it was held, in a case decided under the Regulations, now revoked, that homophobic banter may amount to harassment even where the person concerned is known to be heterosexual: *English v Thomas Sanderson Blinds Ltd* [2008] EWCA Civ 1421, [2009] 2 All ER 468, [2009] 2 CMLR 437. The Court of Appeal upheld this principle. However, on remittal to the Employment Tribunal the action failed on its own facts. The person concerned had engaged in similar offensive conduct elsewhere: see *Thomas Sanderson Blinds Ltd v English* [2011] EqLR 688 and IDS 940, January 2012, page 24. However, revealing a person's sexuality to their colleagues at a new office is not harassment if that person had been open about the fact that they were gay while working in their previous office: *Grant v HM Land Registry* [2011] IRLR 748. While the protection extends beyond those possessing a protected characteristic (to cases of association, perception or attribution), it is not sufficient to assert the possession of a protected characteristic for the purposes of a claim: *Peninsula Business Services Ltd v Baker* [2017] ICR 714, [2017] IRLR 394.

III EQU [26.2]

Protected characteristics See ss 4 to 12 for an exposition of the protected characteristics.

III EQU [27]

27. Victimisation

(1) A person (A) victimises another person (B) if A subjects B to a detriment because—

(a) B does a protected act, or

(b) A believes that B has done, or may do, a protected act.

(2) Each of the following is a protected act—

(a) bringing proceedings under this Act;

(b) giving evidence or information in connection with proceedings under this Act;

(c) doing any other thing for the purposes of or in connection with this Act;

(d) making an allegation (whether or not express) that A or another person has contravened this Act.

(3) Giving false evidence or information, or making a false allegation, is not a protected act if the evidence or information is given, or the allegation is made, in bad faith.

(4) This section applies only where the person subjected to a detriment is an individual.

(5) The reference to contravening this Act includes a reference to committing a breach of an equality clause or rule.

III EQU [27.1]

Other protection Broader protection against victimisation is provided by s 47B of the Employment Rights Act 1996, as amended by the Public Interest Disclosure Act 1998.

III EQU [27.1A]

Key principles The detriment complained of must be shown to be 'because of' undertaking a protected act: see *Chief Constable of West Yorkshire Police v Khan* [2001] IRLR 830; *Derbyshire v St Helens Metropolitan Borough Council* [2007] ICR 841. This requires the alleged victimiser to have known of the protected act: see *Peninsula Business Services Ltd v Baker* [2017] ICR 714, [2017] IRLR 394 and (by analogy) *Royal Mail Ltd v Jhuti* [2017] EWCA Civ 1632. There is no 'doctrine of transferred malice': *Chief Constable of Greater Manchester v Bailey* [2017] EWCA Civ 425. The meaning of 'bad faith' for the purposes of s 27(3) was considered by the EAT in *Saad v Southampton University Hospitals NHS Trust* [2018] IRLR 1007. While motivation could be part of the context, the core meaning of bad faith was dishonesty.

III EQU [27.2]

Victimisation and legal proceedings Judicial proceedings immunity applies to witness statements in cases brought under discrimination legislation just as it does to common law claims. So it is not possible to bring a claim for victimisation on the basis of the content of witness statements produced in respect of an earlier claim for discrimination: *Parmar v East Leicester Medical Practice* [2011] IRLR 641, applying *Darker (as personal representative of Docker, deceased) v Chief Constable of the West Midlands Police* [2001] 1 AC 435, [2000] 4 All ER 193, [2000] 3 WLR 747, HL and *Heath v Metropolitan Police Comr* [2004] EWCA Civ 943, [2005] IRLR 270, [2005] ICR 329.

PART 3
SERVICES AND PUBLIC FUNCTIONS

Preliminary

III EQU [28]

28. Application of this Part

(1) This Part does not apply to the protected characteristic of—

(a) age, so far as relating to persons who have not attained the age of 18;

(b) marriage and civil partnership.

(2) This Part does not apply to discrimination, harassment or victimisation—

(a) that is prohibited by Part 4 (premises), 5 (work) or 6 (education), or

(b) that would be so prohibited but for an express exception.

(3) This Part does not apply to—

(a) a breach of an equality clause or rule;

(b) anything that would be a breach of an equality clause or rule but for section 69 or Part 2 of Schedule 7;

(c) a breach of a non-discrimination rule.

III EQU [28.1]

Commencement of Part 3 Part 3 was brought into force on 1 October 2010 by the No 4 Order SI 2010/2317, except so far as its provisions apply to the protected characteristic of age. Part 3 (Services and Public Functions) has effect in respect of age from 1 October 2012.

III EQU [28.2]

County court jurisdiction County courts have jurisdiction to entertain proceedings for contravention of Part 3 except s 115: see s 114(2).

PROVISION OF SERVICES, ETC

III EQU [29]

29. Provision of services, etc

(1) A person (a "service-provider") concerned with the provision of a service to the public or a section of the public (for payment or not) must not discriminate against a person requiring the service by not providing the person with the service.

(2) A service-provider (A) must not, in providing the service, discriminate against a person (B)—

(a) as to the terms on which A provides the service to B;
(b) by terminating the provision of the service to B;
(c) by subjecting B to any other detriment.

(3) A service-provider must not, in relation to the provision of the service, harass—

(a) a person requiring the service, or
(b) a person to whom the service-provider provides the service.

(4) A service-provider must not victimise a person requiring the service by not providing the person with the service.

(5) A service-provider (A) must not, in providing the service, victimise a person (B)—

(a) as to the terms on which A provides the service to B;
(b) by terminating the provision of the service to B;
(c) by subjecting B to any other detriment.

(6) A person must not, in the exercise of a public function that is not the provision of a service to the public or a section of the public, do anything that constitutes discrimination, harassment or victimisation.

(7) A duty to make reasonable adjustments applies to—

(a) a service-provider (and see also section 55(7));
(b) a person who exercises a public function that is not the provision of a service to the public or a section of the public.

(8) In the application of section 26 for the purposes of subsection (3), and subsection (6) as it relates to harassment, neither of the following is a relevant protected characteristic—

(a) religion or belief;
(b) sexual orientation.

(9) In the application of this section, so far as relating to race or religion or belief, to the granting of entry clearance (within the meaning of the Immigration Act 1971), it does not matter whether an act is done within or outside the United Kingdom.

(10) Subsection (9) does not affect the application of any other provision of this Act to conduct outside England and Wales or Scotland.

III EQU [29.1]

Discrimination in services to the public: some examples A local authority that discriminates against disabled people in its business plan for services to the public may be challenged by judicial review: *R (on the application of W) v Birmingham City Council* [2011] EWHC 1147 (Admin), [2011] All ER (D) 53 (Jun), a case brought in reliance on the now repealed s 49A of the Disability Discrimination Act 1995.

In *ZH (by his litigation friend) v Metropolitan Police Comr* [2013] EWCA Civ 69, [2013] 3 All ER 113, [2013] 1 WLR 3021 the Court of Appeal upheld a finding that the police had failed to make reasonable adjustments to its usual policy on control and restraint in the case of a severely autistic 16 year old boy. ZH was restrained with handcuffs and leg restraints and subsequently taken into custody in a situation in which the court found that the boy could not understand the officers' attempts to communicate and was therefore vulnerable to an escalation of the police's response.

In *Edwards v Flamingo Land Ltd* [2013] EWCA Civ 801, [2013] All ER (D) 84 (Jul) the Court of Appeal dismissed a claim brought on behalf of a disabled child against a restaurant which had refused to serve her food outside the restaurant's official seating area. It held that the duty to make reasonable adjustments did not extend to requiring a service provider to fundamentally alter the nature of its service, trade or business. In this case the restaurant was not a takeaway which provided food and drink to be consumed away from the premises, and hence an adjustment to provide what was in effect a takeaway service was a requirement to fundamentally alter the nature of the business.

The Court of Appeal has held that where a person wishes to challenge a road traffic order on the basis it breaches the Equality Act 2010, s 29, the claim must be made to the County Court under the procedure in the Equality Act. The provisions in the Road Traffic Regulation Act 1984, Sch 9 (providing for High Court jurisdiction by way of statutory review) were to be regarded as impliedly repealed: *Hamnett v Essex County Council* [2017] EWCA Civ 6.

In *R (on the application of VC) v Secretary of State for the Home Dept* [2018] EWCA Civ 57, the Court of Appeal held that the Secretary of State had failed to comply with a the duty to make adjustments for mentally ill detainees in respect of their ability to make representations before decisions concerning their detention and segregation. See also the note above at **III EQU [12.1]** in relation to the provision of hotel accommodation to homosexual couples.

It has been held that a coroner's declared policy of not prioritising a death because of the religion of the deceased or family discriminated indirectly, contrary to ss 19 and 29: *R (on the application of Adath Yisroel Burial Society) v Inner North London Coroner* [2018] EWHC 969 (Admin), (2018) Times, 15 May.

III EQU [29.2]

Reasonable adjustments It has been held that a wheelchair user who boards a bus is entitled to have reasonable adjustments made to accommodate the wheelchair, including by the driver taking further steps in the face of an unreasonable refusal to move by another passenger occupying the wheelchair space: *Paulley v Firstgroup plc* [2017] UKSC 4, [2017] 1 WLR 423.

III EQU [29.3]

Justification within Schedule 3 Discrimination in the provision of separate services to men and to women may be justified in the exceptional circumstances identified in Schedule 3, as in the provision of approved premises for the accommodation of dangerous prisoners released from custody: *Coll v Secretary of State for Justice* [2015] EWCA Civ 328, (2015) Times, 27 April, CA, [2015] All ER (D) 61 (Apr).

Supplementary

III EQU [30]

30. Ships and hovercraft

(1) This Part (subject to subsection (2)) applies only in such circumstances as are prescribed in relation to—

(a) transporting people by ship or hovercraft;

(b) a service provided on a ship or hovercraft.

(2) Section 29(6) applies in relation to the matters referred to in paragraphs (a) and (b) of subsection (1); but in so far as it relates to disability discrimination, section 29(6) applies to those matters only in such circumstances as are prescribed.

(3) It does not matter whether the ship or hovercraft is within or outside the United Kingdom.

(4) "Ship" has the same meaning as in the Merchant Shipping Act 1995.

(5) "Hovercraft" has the same meaning as in the Hovercraft Act 1968.

(6) Nothing in this section affects the application of any other provision of this Act to conduct outside England and Wales or Scotland.

III EQU [30.1]

Transitory provisions The commencement of this section is subject to detailed transitory provisions in arts 10 and 11 of the No 4 Order 2010, SI 2010/2317.

III EQU [31]

31. Interpretation and exceptions

(1) This section applies for the purposes of this Part.

(2) A reference to the provision of a service includes a reference to the provision of goods or facilities.

(3) A reference to the provision of a service includes a reference to the provision of a service in the exercise of a public function.

(4) A public function is a function that is a function of a public nature for the purposes of the Human Rights Act 1998.

(5) Where an employer arranges for another person to provide a service only to the employer's employees—

- (a) the employer is not to be regarded as the service-provider, but
- (b) the employees are to be regarded as a section of the public.

(6) A reference to a person requiring a service includes a reference to a person who is seeking to obtain or use the service.

(7) A reference to a service-provider not providing a person with a service includes a reference to—

- (a) the service-provider not providing the person with a service of the quality that the service-provider usually provides to the public (or the section of it which includes the person), or
- (b) the service-provider not providing the person with the service in the manner in which, or on the terms on which, the service-provider usually provides the service to the public (or the section of it which includes the person).

(8) In relation to the provision of a service by either House of Parliament, the service-provider is the Corporate Officer of the House concerned; and if the service involves access to, or use of, a place in the Palace of Westminster which members of the public are allowed to enter, both Corporate Officers are jointly the service-provider.

(9) Schedule 2 (reasonable adjustments) has effect.

(10) Schedule 3 (exceptions) has effect.

PART 4
PREMISES

PRELIMINARY

III EQU [32]

32. Application of this Part

(1) This Part does not apply to the following protected characteristics—

- (a) age;
- (b) marriage and civil partnership.

(2) This Part does not apply to discrimination, harassment or victimisation—

- (a) that is prohibited by Part 5 (work) or Part 6 (education), or
- (b) that would be so prohibited but for an express exception.

(3) This Part does not apply to the provision of accommodation if the provision—

- (a) is generally for the purpose of short stays by individuals who live elsewhere, or

(b) is for the purpose only of exercising a public function or providing a service to the public or a section of the public.

(4) The reference to the exercise of a public function, and the reference to the provision of a service, are to be construed in accordance with Part 3.

(5) This Part does not apply to—

(a) a breach of an equality clause or rule;

(b) anything that would be a breach of an equality clause or rule but for section 69 or Part 2 of Schedule 7;

(c) a breach of a non-discrimination rule.

III EQU [32.1]

Commencement of Part 4 Part 4 was brought into force on 1 October 2010 by the No 4 Order SI 2010/2317 but with exceptional provision for ss 36-38.

III EQU [32.2]

Jurisdiction of county courts County courts may entertain proceedings for contravention of Part 4: see s 114.

Disposal and management

III EQU [33]

33. Disposals, etc

(1) A person (A) who has the right to dispose of premises must not discriminate against another (B)—

(a) as to the terms on which A offers to dispose of the premises to B;

(b) by not disposing of the premises to B;

(c) in A's treatment of B with respect to things done in relation to persons seeking premises.

(2) Where an interest in a commonhold unit cannot be disposed of unless a particular person is a party to the disposal, that person must not discriminate against a person by not being a party to the disposal.

(3) A person who has the right to dispose of premises must not, in connection with anything done in relation to their occupation or disposal, harass—

(a) a person who occupies them;

(b) a person who applies for them.

(4) A person (A) who has the right to dispose of premises must not victimise another (B)—

(a) as to the terms on which A offers to dispose of the premises to B;

(b) by not disposing of the premises to B;

(c) in A's treatment of B with respect to things done in relation to persons seeking premises.

(5) Where an interest in a commonhold unit cannot be disposed of unless a particular person is a party to the disposal, that person must not victimise a person by not being a party to the disposal.

(6) In the application of section 26 for the purposes of subsection (3), neither of the following is a relevant protected characteristic—

(a) religion or belief;

(b) sexual orientation.

III EQU [34]

34. Permission for disposal

(1) A person whose permission is required for the disposal of premises must not discriminate against another by not giving permission for the disposal of the premises to the other.

(2) A person whose permission is required for the disposal of premises must not, in relation to an application for permission to dispose of the premises, harass a person—

(a) who applies for permission to dispose of the premises, or

(b) to whom the disposal would be made if permission were given.

(3) A person whose permission is required for the disposal of premises must not victimise another by not giving permission for the disposal of the premises to the other.

(4) In the application of section 26 for the purposes of subsection (2), neither of the following is a relevant protected characteristic—

(a) religion or belief;

(b) sexual orientation.

(5) This section does not apply to anything done in the exercise of a judicial function.

III EQU [35]

35. Management

(1) A person (A) who manages premises must not discriminate against a person (B) who occupies the premises—

(a) in the way in which A allows B, or by not allowing B, to make use of a benefit or facility;

(b) by evicting B (or taking steps for the purpose of securing B's eviction);

(c) by subjecting B to any other detriment.

(2) A person who manages premises must not, in relation to their management, harass—

(a) a person who occupies them;

(b) a person who applies for them.

(3) A person (A) who manages premises must not victimise a person (B) who occupies the premises—

(a) in the way in which A allows B, or by not allowing B, to make use of a benefit or facility;

(b) by evicting B (or taking steps for the purpose of securing B's eviction);

(c) by subjecting B to any other detriment.

(4) In the application of section 26 for the purposes of subsection (2), neither of the following is a relevant protected characteristic—

(a) religion or belief;

(b) sexual orientation.

III EQU [35.1]

Disability discrimination as a defence to a claim for possession Where disability discrimination is raised as a defence, under section 35(1)(b), to a landlord's claim for possession, and the possibility of discrimination is made out, the burden is on the landlord to show either that there was no discrimination contrary to section 15(1)(a) or that it was proportionate under section 15(1)(b): *Akerman-Livingstone v Aster Communities Ltd* [2015] UKSC 15, [2015] 2 WLR 721, [2015] HLR 346. Lord Neuberger observed, in that case, that summary judgment would not normally be a sensible or adequate procedure for dealing with disputed cases and that, although issues of proportionality arose in both, the protection afforded by section 35(1)(b) was stronger than that afforded by Article 8 of the Convention on Human Rights. In *Paragon Asra Housing Ltd (formerly Paragon Community Housing Ltd) v Neville* [2018] EWCA Civ 1712, the Court of Appeal held that where the court had held that making a suspended possession order would be proportionate under s 15(1)(b), and thus not discriminatory, the same question did not need to be considered again when the order came to be enforced (at least in the absence of a material change in circumstances).

Reasonable adjustments

III EQU [36]

36. Leasehold and commonhold premises and common parts

(1) A duty to make reasonable adjustments applies to—

(a) a controller of let premises;

(b) a controller of premises to let;

(c) a commonhold association;

(d) a responsible person in relation to common parts.

(2) A controller of let premises is—

(a) a person by whom premises are let, or

(b) a person who manages them.

(3) A controller of premises to let is—

(a) a person who has premises to let, or

(b) a person who manages them.

(4) The reference in subsection (1)(c) to a commonhold association is a reference to the association in its capacity as the person who manages a commonhold unit.

(5) A responsible person in relation to common parts is—

(a) where the premises to which the common parts relate are let (and are not part of commonhold land or in Scotland), a person by whom the premises are let;

(b) where the premises to which the common parts relate are part of commonhold land, the commonhold association.

(6) Common parts are—

(a) in relation to let premises (which are not part of commonhold land or in Scotland), the structure and exterior of, and any common facilities within or used in connection with, the building or part of a building which includes the premises;

(b) in relation to commonhold land, every part of the commonhold which is not for the time being a commonhold unit in accordance with the commonhold community statement.

(7) A reference to letting includes a reference to sub-letting; and for the purposes of subsection (1)(a) and (b), a reference to let premises includes premises subject to a right to occupy.

(8) This section does not apply to premises of such description as may be prescribed.

III EQU [36.1]

Commencement Sub-sections 36(1)(d), (5) and (6) still require a commencement order.

III EQU [37]

37. Adjustments to common parts in Scotland

(1) The Scottish Ministers may by regulations provide that a disabled person is entitled to make relevant adjustments to common parts in relation to premises in Scotland.

(2) The reference in subsection (1) to a disabled person is a reference to a disabled person who—

(a) is a tenant of the premises,

(b) is an owner of the premises, or

(c) is otherwise entitled to occupy the premises,

and uses or intends to use the premises as the person's only or main home.

(3) Before making regulations under subsection (1), the Scottish Ministers must consult a Minister of the Crown.

(4) Regulations under subsection (1) may, in particular—

(a) prescribe things which are, or which are not, to be treated as relevant adjustments;

(b) prescribe circumstances in which the consent of an owner of the common parts is required before a disabled person may make an adjustment;

(c) provide that the consent to adjustments is not to be withheld unreasonably;

(d) prescribe matters to be taken into account, or to be disregarded, in deciding whether it is reasonable to consent to adjustments;

(e) prescribe circumstances in which consent to adjustments is to be taken to be withheld;

(f) make provision about the imposition of conditions on consent to adjustments;

(g) make provision as to circumstances in which the sheriff may make an order authorising a disabled person to carry out adjustments;

(h) make provision about the responsibility for costs arising (directly or indirectly) from an adjustment;

(i) make provision about the reinstatement of the common parts to the condition they were in before an adjustment was made;

(j) make provision about the giving of notice to the owners of the common parts and other persons;

(k) make provision about agreements between a disabled person and an owner of the common parts;

(l) make provision about the registration of information in the Land Register of Scotland or the recording of documents in the Register of Sasines relating to an entitlement of a disabled person or an obligation on an owner of the common parts;

(m) make provision about the effect of such registration or recording;

(n) make provision about who is to be treated as being, or as not being, a person entitled to occupy premises otherwise than as tenant or owner.

(5) In this section—

"common parts" means, in relation to premises, the structure and exterior of, and any common facilities within or used in connection with, the building or part of a building which includes the premises but only in so far as the structure, exterior and common facilities are not solely owned by the owner of the premises;

"relevant adjustments" means, in relation to a disabled person, alterations or additions which are likely to avoid a substantial disadvantage to which the disabled person is put in using the common parts in comparison with persons who are not disabled.

III EQU [37.1]

This section, which relates only to Scotland, was brought into force on 11 July 2011.

SUPPLEMENTARY

III EQU [38]

38. Interpretation and exceptions

(1) This section applies for the purposes of this Part.

(2) A reference to premises is a reference to the whole or part of the premises.

(3) A reference to disposing of premises includes, in the case of premises subject to a tenancy, a reference to—

(a) assigning the premises,

(b) sub-letting them, or

(c) parting with possession of them.

(4) A reference to disposing of premises also includes a reference to granting a right to occupy them.

(5) A reference to disposing of an interest in a commonhold unit includes a reference to creating an interest in a commonhold unit.

(6) A reference to a tenancy is to a tenancy created (whether before or after the passing of this Act)—

(a) by a lease or sub-lease,

(b) by an agreement for a lease or sub-lease,

(c) by a tenancy agreement, or

(d) in pursuance of an enactment,

and a reference to a tenant is to be construed accordingly.

(7) A reference to commonhold land, a commonhold association, a commonhold community statement, a commonhold unit or a unit-holder is to be construed in accordance with the Commonhold and Leasehold Reform Act 2002.

(8) Schedule 4 (reasonable adjustments) has effect.

(9) Schedule 5 (exceptions) has effect.

III EQU [38.1]

Commencement Sub-section (8) (Schedule 4 and reasonable adjustments) has been brought into force by the No 4 Order only in relation to the provisions set out in sub-sections (1) to (7) and (9). A further commencement order is required to give it further effect.

PART 5
WORK

III EQU [39]–III EQU [83]

GENERAL NOTES ON PART 5: WORK Part 5 is about equality rights in the context of employment, although it is not confined strictly to the rights of employees: the definition of employment in s 83(2) is wider than work pursuant to a contract of employment (see eg *Pimlico Plumbers Ltd v Smith* [2018] UKSC 29, [2018] ICR 1511 and *Bates van Winkelhof v Clyde and Co LLP* [2014] UKSC 32, [2014] ICR 730). It also covers the rights of applicants for employment, contract workers (s 41), police officers (ss 42 and 43), partners (ss 44 to 46), barristers and advocates (ss 47 and 48), office-holders and others (ss 49 to 60). It has been held that arbitrators are not employees for the purposes of this Part of the Act: *Jivraj v Hashwani* [2011] UKSC 40 and hence it is lawful for an arbitration agreement to specify (or restrict) the nationality or religion of the arbitrator who may be appointed. Further, the Supreme Court has held that a police officer was not barred by judicial immunity from bringing a discrimination claim in relation to a decision of a misconduct panel: *P v Metropolitan Police Comr* [2017] UKSC 65, [2018] IRLR 66.

There are particular provisions about occupational pensions (ss 61 to 63), sex equality, pregnancy and maternity equality (ss 64 to 76) disclosure of information about pay (ss 77 and 78), comparators (ss 79 and 80) and ships, hovercraft and offshore work (ss 81 to 83).

No jurisdiction is conferred on the civil courts to entertain proceedings under Part 5: the jurisdiction is conferred on Employment Tribunals instead (s 120) and the text of Part V has therefore been omitted from this work.

PART 6
EDUCATION
CHAPTER 1 SCHOOLS

III EQU [84]

84. Application of this Chapter

This Chapter does not apply to the following protected characteristics—

(a) age;

(b) marriage and civil partnership.

III EQU [84.1]

Commencement of Part 6 Part 6 was brought into force on 1 October 2010 by the No 4 Order, SI 2010/2317.

III EQU [84.2]

Jurisdiction of county courts County courts may entertain proceedings for contravention of Part 4 except in relation to a claim within s 116: see s 114.

III EQU [85]

85. Pupils: admission and treatment, etc

(1) The responsible body of a school to which this section applies must not discriminate against a person—

(a) in the arrangements it makes for deciding who is offered admission as a pupil;

(b) as to the terms on which it offers to admit the person as a pupil;

(c) by not admitting the person as a pupil.

(2) The responsible body of such a school must not discriminate against a pupil—

(a) in the way it provides education for the pupil;

(b) in the way it affords the pupil access to a benefit, facility or service;

(c) by not providing education for the pupil;

(d) by not affording the pupil access to a benefit, facility or service;

(e) by excluding the pupil from the school;

(f) by subjecting the pupil to any other detriment.

(3) The responsible body of such a school must not harass—

(a) a pupil;

(b) a person who has applied for admission as a pupil.

(4) The responsible body of such a school must not victimise a person—

(a) in the arrangements it makes for deciding who is offered admission as a pupil;

(b) as to the terms on which it offers to admit the person as a pupil;

(c) by not admitting the person as a pupil.

(5) The responsible body of such a school must not victimise a pupil—

(a) in the way it provides education for the pupil;

(b) in the way it affords the pupil access to a benefit, facility or service;

(c) by not providing education for the pupil;

(d) by not affording the pupil access to a benefit, facility or service;

(e) by excluding the pupil from the school;

(f) by subjecting the pupil to any other detriment.

(6) A duty to make reasonable adjustments applies to the responsible body of such a school.

(7) In relation to England and Wales, this section applies to—

(a) a school maintained by a local authority;

(b) an independent educational institution (other than a special school);

(ba) an alternative provision Academy that is not an independent educational institution;

(c) a special school (not maintained by a local authority).

(8) In relation to Scotland, this section applies to—

(a) a school managed by an education authority;

(b) an independent school;

(c) a school in respect of which the managers are for the time being receiving grants under section 73(c) or (d) of the Education (Scotland) Act 1980.

(9) The responsible body of a school to which this section applies is—

(a) if the school is within subsection (7)(a), the local authority or governing body;

(b) if it is within subsection (7)(b), (ba) or (c), the proprietor;

(c) if it is within subsection (8)(a), the education authority;

(d) if it is within subsection (8)(b), the proprietor;

(e) if it is within subsection (8)(c), the managers.

(10) In the application of section 26 for the purposes of subsection (3), none of the following is a relevant protected characteristic—

(a) gender reassignment;

(b) religion or belief;

(c) sexual orientation.

III EQU [85.1]

School admissions A Jewish school which refused to admit a pupil on the basis that his mother was not recognised as Jewish by the Office of the Chief Rabbi (she having converted to Judaism but not in a manner recognised by orthodox standards) was found to have discriminated against that pupil on the grounds of race. See *R (on the application of E) v Governing Body of Jewish Free School (The United Synagogue intervening)* [2009] UKSC 15, [2010] 1 All ER 319, [2010] 2 WLR 153.

III EQU [85.2]

School uniform and hair styles The school uniform decisions under the old law have relevance to the new and include *R (on the application of Begum) v Headteacher and Governors of Denbigh High School* [2006] UKHL 15, [2007] 1 AC 100, [2006] 2 All ER 487 and *R (Sarika Angel Watkins-Singh) v Governing Body of Aberdare Girls High School* [2008] EWHC 1865 (Admin).

In a case where school policy was to allow girls, but not boys, to wear their hair in corn rows it was held that the different treatment of boys and girls was not discriminatory but that there was racial discrimination against a boy of African-Caribbean ethnicity who, for reasons based on his culture and ethnicity, attended wearing his hair in corn-rows: *G (by his litigation friend) v Head Teacher and Governors of St Gregory's Catholic Science College* [2011] EWHC 1452 (Admin), [2011] All ER (D) 113 (Jun).

III EQU [85.3]

Segregation of male and female pupils The complete segregation of male and female pupils over a certain age for all lessons, breaks, school clubs and trips was held to be direct discrimination, contrary to ss 13 and 85, in *HM Inspector of Education, Children's Services and Skills v Interim Executive Board of Al-Hijrah School (Secretary of State for Education intervening)* [2017] EWCA Civ 1426, [2017] All ER (D) 79 (Oct).

III EQU [86]

86. Victimisation of pupils, etc for conduct of parents, etc

(1) This section applies for the purposes of section 27 in its application to section 85(4) or (5).

(2) The references to B in paragraphs (a) and (b) of subsection (1) of section 27 include a reference to a parent or sibling of the child in question.

(3) Giving false evidence or information, or making a false allegation, in good faith is not a protected act in a case where—

(a) the evidence or information is given, or the allegation is made, by a parent or sibling of the child, and

(b) the child has acted in bad faith.

(4) Giving false evidence or information, or making a false allegation, in bad faith, is a protected act in a case where—

(a) the evidence or information is given, or the allegation is made, by a parent or sibling of the child, and

(b) the child has acted in good faith.

(5) In this section—

"child" means a person who has not attained the age of 18;

"sibling" means a brother or sister, a half-brother or half-sister, or a stepbrother or stepsister.

III EQU [87]

87. Application of certain powers under Education Act 1996

(A1) Subsections (1) and (2) do not apply in the case of a school in Wales.

(1) Sections 496 and 497 of the Education Act 1996 and section 70 of the Education (Scotland) Act 1980 (powers to give directions where responsible body of school in default of obligations, etc) apply to the performance of a duty under section 85.

(2) But neither of sections 496 and 497 of the Education Act 1996 applies to the performance of a duty under that section by the proprietor of an independent educational institution (other than a special school) or an alternative provision Academy that is not an independent educational institution; and section 70 of the Education (Scotland) Act 1980 does not apply to the performance of a duty under that section by the proprietor of an independent school.

(3) In the case of a school in Wales—

(a) Chapter 1 of Part 2 of the School Standards and Organisation (Wales) Act 2013 ("the 2013 Act") (intervention in conduct of maintained schools) applies to the performance of a duty under section 85, but as if—

(i) the only relevant grounds for intervention were grounds 5 and 6 in section 2 of that Act, and

(ii) sections 3 to 9 and 12 to 16 of that Act did not apply;

(b) Chapter 2 of Part 2 of the 2013 Act (intervention in local authorities) applies to the performance of a duty under section 85, but as if—

(i) the only relevant grounds for intervention were grounds 1 and 2 in section 21 of that Act, and

(ii) sections 24 to 27 of that Act did not apply.

(4) But neither of Chapters 1 and 2 of Part 2 of the 2013 Act applies to the performance of a duty under section 85 by the proprietor of an independent educational institution (other than a special school).

III EQU [88]

88. Disabled pupils: accessibility

Schedule 10 (accessibility) has effect.

III EQU [89]

89. Interpretation and exceptions

(1) This section applies for the purposes of this Chapter.

(2) Nothing in this Chapter applies to anything done in connection with the content of the curriculum.

(3) "Pupil"—

(a) in relation to England and Wales, has the meaning given in section 3(1) of the Education Act 1996;

(b) in relation to Scotland, has the meaning given in section 135(1) of the Education (Scotland) Act 1980.

(4) "Proprietor"—

(a) in relation to a school in England and Wales, has the meaning given in section 579(1) of the Education Act 1996;

(b) in relation to a school in Scotland, has the meaning given in section 135(1) of the Education (Scotland) Act 1980.

(5) "School"—

(a) in relation to England and Wales, has the meaning given in section 4 of the Education Act 1996;

(b) in relation to Scotland, has the meaning given in section 135(1) of the Education (Scotland) Act 1980.

(6) A reference to a school includes a reference to an independent educational institution in England; and a reference to an independent educational institution in England is to be construed in accordance with Chapter 1 of Part 4 of the Education and Skills Act 2008.

(7) A reference to an independent educational institution is a reference to—

(a) an independent educational institution in England, or

(b) an independent school in Wales.

(8) "Independent school"—

(a) in relation to Wales, has the meaning given in section 463 of the Education Act 1996;

(b) in relation to Scotland, has the meaning given in section 135(1) of the Education (Scotland) Act 1980.

(9) "Special school" has the meaning given in section 337 of the Education Act 1996.

(10) "Local authority" means—

(a) in relation to England, an English local authority within the meaning of section 162 of the Education and Inspections Act 2006;

(b) in relation to Wales, a Welsh local authority within the meaning of that section.

(11) "Education authority", in relation to Scotland, has the meaning given in section 135(1) of the Education (Scotland) Act 1980.

(12) Schedule 11 (exceptions) has effect.

CHAPTER 2 FURTHER AND HIGHER EDUCATION

III EQU [90]

90. Application of this Chapter

This Chapter does not apply to the protected characteristic of marriage and civil partnership.

III EQU [91]

91. Students: admission and treatment, etc

(1) The responsible body of an institution to which this section applies must not discriminate against a person—

(a) in the arrangements it makes for deciding who is offered admission as a student;

(b) as to the terms on which it offers to admit the person as a student;

(c) by not admitting the person as a student.

(2) The responsible body of such an institution must not discriminate against a student—

(a) in the way it provides education for the student;

(b) in the way it affords the student access to a benefit, facility or service;

(c) by not providing education for the student;

(d) by not affording the student access to a benefit, facility or service;

(e) by excluding the student;

EQUALITY

(f) by subjecting the student to any other detriment.

(3) The responsible body of such an institution must not discriminate against a disabled person—

(a) in the arrangements it makes for deciding upon whom to confer a qualification;

(b) as to the terms on which it is prepared to confer a qualification on the person;

(c) by not conferring a qualification on the person;

(d) by withdrawing a qualification from the person or varying the terms on which the person holds it.

(4) Subsection (3) applies only to disability discrimination.

(5) The responsible body of such an institution must not harass—

(a) a student;

(b) a person who has applied for admission as a student;

(c) a disabled person who holds or has applied for a qualification conferred by the institution.

(6) The responsible body of such an institution must not victimise a person—

(a) in the arrangements it makes for deciding who is offered admission as a student;

(b) as to the terms on which it offers to admit the person as a student;

(c) by not admitting the person as a student.

(7) The responsible body of such an institution must not victimise a student—

(a) in the way it provides education for the student;

(b) in the way it affords the student access to a benefit, facility or service;

(c) by not providing education for the student;

(d) by not affording the student access to a benefit, facility or service;

(e) by excluding the student;

(f) by subjecting the student to any other detriment.

(8) The responsible body of such an institution must not victimise a disabled person—

(a) in the arrangements it makes for deciding upon whom to confer a qualification;

(b) as to the terms on which it is prepared to confer a qualification on the person;

(c) by not conferring a qualification on the person;

(d) by withdrawing a qualification from the person or varying the terms on which the person holds it.

(9) A duty to make reasonable adjustments applies to the responsible body of such an institution.

(10) In relation to England and Wales, this section applies to—

(a) a university;

(b) any other institution within the higher education sector;

(c) an institution within the further education sector;

(d) a 16 to 19 Academy.

(11) In relation to Scotland, this section applies to—

(a) a university;

(b) a designated institution;

(c) a college of further education.

(12) A responsible body is—

(a) in the case of an institution within subsection (10)(a), (b) or (c), the governing body;

(aa) in the case of an institution within subsection (10)(d), the proprietor (within the meaning of the Education Act 1996);

(b) in the case of an institution within subsection (11)(a) or (b), the governing body;
(c) in the case of a college of further education under the management of a board of management, the board of management;
(d) in the case of any other college of further education, any board of governors of the college or any person responsible for the management of the college, whether or not formally constituted as a governing body or board of governors.

III EQU [92]

92. Further and higher education courses

(1) The responsible body in relation to a course to which this section applies must not discriminate against a person—

(a) in the arrangements it makes for deciding who is enrolled on the course;
(b) as to the terms on which it offers to enrol the person on the course;
(c) by not accepting the person's application for enrolment.

(2) The responsible body in relation to such a course must not discriminate against a person who is enrolled on the course in the services it provides or offers to provide.

(3) The responsible body in relation to such a course must not harass a person who—

(a) seeks enrolment on the course;
(b) is enrolled on the course;
(c) is a user of services provided by the body in relation to the course.

(4) The responsible body in relation to such a course must not victimise a person—

(a) in the arrangements it makes for deciding who is enrolled on the course;
(b) as to the terms on which it offers to enrol the person on the course;
(c) by not accepting the person's application for enrolment.

(5) The responsible body in relation to such a course must not victimise a person who is enrolled on the course in the services it provides or offers to provide.

(6) A duty to make reasonable adjustments applies to the responsible body.

(7) This section applies to—

(a) a course of further or higher education secured by a responsible body in England or Wales;
(b) a course of education provided by the governing body of a maintained school under section 80 of the School Standards and Framework Act 1998;
(c) a course of further education secured by an education authority in Scotland.

(8) A responsible body is—

(a) a local authority in England or Wales, for the purposes of subsection (7)(a);
(b) the governing body of a maintained school, for the purposes of subsection (7)(b);
(c) an education authority in Scotland, for the purposes of subsection (7)(c).

(9) In this section—

EQUALITY

"course", in relation to further education, includes each component part of a course if there is no requirement imposed on persons registered for a component part of the course to register for another component part of the course;

"enrolment" includes registration for a component part of a course;

"maintained school" has the meaning given in section 20(7) of the School Standards and Framework Act 1998;

"services" means services of any description which are provided wholly or mainly for persons enrolled on a course to which this section applies.

III EQU [93]

93. Recreational or training facilities

(1) The responsible body in relation to facilities to which this section applies must not discriminate against a person—

(a) in the arrangements it makes for deciding who is provided with the facilities;

(b) as to the terms on which it offers to provide the facilities to the person;

(c) by not accepting the person's application for provision of the facilities.

(2) The responsible body in relation to such facilities must not discriminate against a person who is provided with the facilities in the services it provides or offers to provide.

(3) The responsible body in relation to such facilities must not harass a person who—

(a) seeks to have the facilities provided;

(b) is provided with the facilities;

(c) is a user of services provided by the body in relation to the facilities.

(4) The responsible body in relation to such facilities must not victimise a person—

(a) in the arrangements it makes for deciding who is provided with the facilities;

(b) as to the terms on which it offers to provide the facilities to the person;

(c) by not accepting the person's application for provision of the facilities.

(5) The responsible body in relation to such facilities must not victimise a person who is provided with the facilities in the services it provides or offers to provide.

(6) A duty to make reasonable adjustments applies to the responsible body.

(7) This section applies to—

(a) facilities secured by a local authority in England under section 507A or 507B of the Education Act 1996;

(b) facilities secured by a local authority in Wales under section 508 of that Act;

(c) recreational or training facilities provided by an education authority in Scotland.

(8) A responsible body is—

(a) a local authority in England, for the purposes of subsection (7)(a);

(b) a local authority in Wales, for the purposes of subsection (7)(b);

(c) an education authority in Scotland, for the purposes of subsection (7)(c).

(9) This section does not apply to the protected characteristic of age, so far as relating to persons who have not attained the age of 18.

III EQU [94]

94. Interpretation and exceptions

(1) This section applies for the purposes of this Chapter.

(2) Nothing in this Chapter applies to anything done in connection with the content of the curriculum.

(3) A reference to a student, in relation to an institution, is a reference to a person for whom education is provided by the institution.

(4) A reference to a university includes a reference to a university college and a college, school or hall of a university.

(5) A reference to an institution within the further or higher education sector is to be construed in accordance with section 91 of the Further and Higher Education Act 1992.

(6) "Further education"—

(a) in relation to England and Wales, has the meaning given in section 2 of the Education Act 1996;

(b) in relation to Scotland, has the meaning given in section 1(3) of the Further and Higher Education (Scotland) Act 1992.

(7) "Higher education"—

(a) in relation to England and Wales, means education provided by means of a course of a description mentioned in Schedule 6 to the Education Reform Act 1988;

(b) in relation to Scotland, has the meaning given in section 38 of the Further and Higher Education (Scotland) Act 1992.

(8) "College of further education" has the meaning given in section 36 of the Further and Higher Education (Scotland) Act 1992.

(9) "Designated institution" has the meaning given in section 44 of that Act.

(10) "Local authority" means—

(a) in relation to England, an English local authority within the meaning of section 162 of the Education and Inspections Act 2006;

(b) in relation to Wales, a Welsh local authority within the meaning of that section.

(11) "Education authority" has the meaning given by section 135(1) of the Education (Scotland) Act 1980.

(11A) A reference to conferring a qualification includes a reference—

(a) to renewing or extending the conferment of a qualification;

(b) to authenticating a qualification conferred by another person.

(12) Schedule 12 (exceptions) has effect.

EQUALITY

CHAPTER 3 GENERAL QUALIFICATIONS BODIES

III EQU [95]

95. Application of this Chapter

This Chapter does not apply to the protected characteristic of marriage and civil partnership.

III EQU [96]

96. Qualifications bodies

(1) A qualifications body (A) must not discriminate against a person (B)—

(a) in the arrangements A makes for deciding upon whom to confer a relevant qualification;

(b) as to the terms on which it is prepared to confer a relevant qualification on B;

(c) by not conferring a relevant qualification on B.

(2) A qualifications body (A) must not discriminate against a person (B) upon whom A has conferred a relevant qualification—

(a) by withdrawing the qualification from B;
(b) by varying the terms on which B holds the qualification;
(c) by subjecting B to any other detriment.

(3) A qualifications body must not, in relation to conferment by it of a relevant qualification, harass—
(a) a person who holds the qualification, or
(b) a person who applies for it.

(4) A qualifications body (A) must not victimise a person (B)—
(a) in the arrangements A makes for deciding upon whom to confer a relevant qualification;
(b) as to the terms on which it is prepared to confer a relevant qualification on B;
(c) by not conferring a relevant qualification on B.

(5) A qualifications body (A) must not victimise a person (B) upon whom A has conferred a relevant qualification—
(a) by withdrawing the qualification from B;
(b) by varying the terms on which B holds the qualification;
(c) by subjecting B to any other detriment.

(6) A duty to make reasonable adjustments applies to a qualifications body.

(7) Subsection (6) does not apply to the body in so far as the appropriate regulator specifies provisions, criteria or practices in relation to which the body—
(a) is not subject to a duty to make reasonable adjustments;
(b) is subject to a duty to make reasonable adjustments, but in relation to which such adjustments as the regulator specifies should not be made.

(8) For the purposes of subsection (7) the appropriate regulator must have regard to—
(a) the need to minimise the extent to which disabled persons are disadvantaged in attaining the qualification because of their disabilities;
(b) the need to secure that the qualification gives a reliable indication of the knowledge, skills and understanding of a person upon whom it is conferred;
(c) the need to maintain public confidence in the qualification.

(9) The appropriate regulator—
(a) must not specify any matter for the purposes of subsection (7) unless it has consulted such persons as it thinks appropriate;
(b) must publish matters so specified (including the date from which they are to have effect) in such manner as is prescribed.

(10) The appropriate regulator is—
(a) in relation to a qualifications body that confers qualifications in England, a person prescribed by a Minister of the Crown;
(b) in relation to a qualifications body that confers qualifications in Wales, a person prescribed by the Welsh Ministers;
(c) in relation to a qualifications body that confers qualifications in Scotland, a person prescribed by the Scottish Ministers.

(11) For the purposes of subsection (10), a qualification is conferred in a part of Great Britain if there are, or may reasonably be expected to be, persons seeking to obtain the qualification who are or will be assessed for those purposes wholly or mainly in that part.

III EQU [97]

97. Interpretation

(1) This section applies for the purposes of section 96.

(2) A qualifications body is an authority or body which can confer a relevant qualification.

(3) A relevant qualification is an authorisation, qualification, approval or certification of such description as may be prescribed—

- (a) in relation to conferments in England, by a Minister of the Crown;
- (b) in relation to conferments in Wales, by the Welsh Ministers;
- (c) in relation to conferments in Scotland, by the Scottish Ministers.

(4) An authority or body is not a qualifications body in so far as—

- (a) it is the responsible body of a school to which section 85 applies,
- (b) it is the governing body of an institution to which section 91 applies,
- (c) it exercises functions under the Education Acts, or
- (d) it exercises functions under the Education (Scotland) Act 1980.

(5) A qualifications body does not include an authority or body of such description, or in such circumstances, as may be prescribed.

(6) A reference to conferring a relevant qualification includes a reference—

- (a) to renewing or extending the conferment of a relevant qualification;
- (b) to authenticating a relevant qualification conferred by another person.

(7) A reference in section 96(8), (10) or (11) to a qualification is a reference to a relevant qualification.

(8) Subsection (11) of section 96 applies for the purposes of subsection (3) of this section as it applies for the purposes of subsection (10) of that section.

CHAPTER 4 MISCELLANEOUS

III EQU [98]

98. Reasonable adjustments

Schedule 13 (reasonable adjustments) has effect.

III EQU [99]

99. Educational charities and endowments

Schedule 14 (educational charities and endowments) has effect.

PART 7
ASSOCIATIONS

PRELIMINARY

III EQU [100]

100. Application of this Part

(1) This Part does not apply to the protected characteristic of marriage and civil partnership.

(2) This Part does not apply to discrimination, harassment or victimisation—

- (a) that is prohibited by Part 3 (services and public functions), Part 4 (premises), Part 5 (work) or Part 6 (education), or
- (b) that would be so prohibited but for an express exception.

III EQU [100.1]

Commencement of Part 7 Part 7 was brought into force on 1 October 2010 by article 2(6) of the commencement provisions in SI 2010/2317, except so far as they apply to the protected characteristic of age. Part 7 (Associations) has effect in regards to age from 1 October 2012.

EQUALITY

III EQU [100.2]

Jurisdiction of county courts County courts may entertain proceedings for contravention of Part 7 except s 106: see s 114(4).

MEMBERSHIP, ETC

III EQU [101]

101. Members and associates

(1) An association (A) must not discriminate against a person (B)—
 (a) in the arrangements A makes for deciding who to admit to membership;
 (b) as to the terms on which A is prepared to admit B to membership;
 (c) by not accepting B's application for membership.

(2) An association (A) must not discriminate against a member (B)—
 (a) in the way A affords B access, or by not affording B access, to a benefit, facility or service;
 (b) by depriving B of membership;
 (c) by varying B's terms of membership;
 (d) by subjecting B to any other detriment.

(3) An association (A) must not discriminate against an associate (B)—
 (a) in the way A affords B access, or by not affording B access, to a benefit, facility or service;
 (b) by depriving B of B's rights as an associate;
 (c) by varying B's rights as an associate;
 (d) by subjecting B to any other detriment.

(4) An association must not harass—
 (a) a member;
 (b) a person seeking to become a member;
 (c) an associate.

(5) An association (A) must not victimise a person (B)—
 (a) in the arrangements A makes for deciding who to admit to membership;
 (b) as to the terms on which A is prepared to admit B to membership;
 (c) by not accepting B's application for membership.

(6) An association (A) must not victimise a member (B)—
 (a) in the way A affords B access, or by not affording B access, to a benefit, facility or service;
 (b) by depriving B of membership;
 (c) by varying B's terms of membership;
 (d) by subjecting B to any other detriment.

(7) An association (A) must not victimise an associate (B)—
 (a) in the way A affords B access, or by not affording B access, to a benefit, facility or service;
 (b) by depriving B of B's rights as an associate;
 (c) by varying B's rights as an associate;
 (d) by subjecting B to any other detriment.

III EQU [102]

102. Guests

(1) An association (A) must not discriminate against a person (B)—
 (a) in the arrangements A makes for deciding who to invite, or who to permit to be invited, as a guest;

(b) as to the terms on which A is prepared to invite B, or to permit B to be invited, as a guest;

(c) by not inviting B, or not permitting B to be invited, as a guest.

(2) An association (A) must not discriminate against a guest (B) invited by A or with A's permission (whether express or implied)—

(a) in the way A affords B access, or by not affording B access, to a benefit, facility or service;

(b) by subjecting B to any other detriment.

(3) An association must not harass—

(a) a guest;

(b) a person seeking to be a guest.

(4) An association (A) must not victimise a person (B)—

(a) in the arrangements A makes for deciding who to invite, or who to permit to be invited, as a guest;

(b) as to the terms on which A is prepared to invite B, or to permit B to be invited, as a guest;

(c) by not inviting B, or not permitting B to be invited, as a guest.

(5) An association (A) must not victimise a guest (B) invited by A or with A's permission (whether express or implied)—

(a) in the way A affords B access, or by not affording B access, to a benefit, facility or service;

(b) by subjecting B to any other detriment.

III EQU [103]

103. Sections 101 and 102: further provision

(1) A duty to make reasonable adjustments applies to an association.

(2) In the application of section 26 for the purposes of section 101(4) or 102(3), neither of the following is a relevant protected characteristic—

(a) religion or belief;

(b) sexual orientation.

SPECIAL PROVISION FOR POLITICAL PARTIES

III EQU [104]

104. Selection of candidates

(1) This section applies to an association which is a registered political party.

(2) A person does not contravene this Part only by acting in accordance with selection arrangements.

(3) Selection arrangements are arrangements—

(a) which the party makes for regulating the selection of its candidates in a relevant election,

(b) the purpose of which is to reduce inequality in the party's representation in the body concerned, and

(c) which, *subject to subsection (7)*, are a proportionate means of achieving that purpose.

(4) The reference in subsection (3)(b) to inequality in a party's representation in a body is a reference to inequality between—

(a) the number of the party's candidates elected to be members of the body who share a protected characteristic, and

(b) the number of the party's candidates so elected who do not share that characteristic.

EQUALITY

(5) For the purposes of subsection (4), persons share the protected characteristic of disability if they are disabled persons (and section 6(3)(b) is accordingly to be ignored).

(6) Selection arrangements do not include short-listing only such persons as have a particular protected characteristic.

(7) *But subsection (6) does not apply to the protected characteristic of sex; and subsection (3)(c) does not apply to short-listing in reliance on this subsection.*

(8) The following elections are relevant elections—

(a) Parliamentary Elections;

(b) elections to the European Parliament;

(c) elections to the Scottish Parliament;

(d) elections to the National Assembly for Wales;

(e) local government elections within the meaning of section 191, 203 or 204 of the Representation of the People Act 1983 (excluding elections for the Mayor of London).

Amendment *Text in italic is deleted by s 105(1) with effect from 31 December 2030, unless an order is made under subsection 105(2).*

III EQU [105]

105. Time-limited provision

(1) Section 104(7) and the words ", subject to subsection (7)," in section 104(3)(c) are repealed at the end of 2030 unless an order is made under subsection (2).

(2) At any time before the end of 2030, a Minister of the Crown may by order provide that subsection (1) is to have effect with the substitution of a later time for that for the time being specified there.

(3) In section 3 of the Sex Discrimination (Election Candidates) Act 2002 (expiry of that Act), in subsection (1) for "2015" substitute "2030".

(4) The substitution made by subsection (3) does not affect the power to substitute a later time by order under section 3 of that Act.

III EQU [106]

106. Information about diversity in range of candidates, etc

(1) This section applies to an association which is a registered political party.

(2) If the party had candidates at a relevant election, the party must, in accordance with regulations, publish information relating to protected characteristics of persons who come within a description prescribed in the regulations in accordance with subsection (3).

(3) One or more of the following descriptions may be prescribed for the purposes of subsection (2)—

(a) successful applicants for nomination as a candidate at the relevant election;

(b) unsuccessful applicants for nomination as a candidate at that election;

(c) candidates elected at that election;

(d) candidates who are not elected at that election.

(4) The duty imposed by subsection (2) applies only in so far as it is possible to publish information in a manner that ensures that no person to whom the information relates can be identified from that information.

(5) The following elections are relevant elections—

(a) Parliamentary Elections;

(b) elections to the European Parliament;

(c) elections to the Scottish Parliament;

(d) elections to the National Assembly for Wales.

(6) This section does not apply to the following protected characteristics—
  (a) marriage and civil partnership;
  (b) pregnancy and maternity.

(7) The regulations may provide that the information to be published—
  (a) must (subject to subsection (6)) relate to all protected characteristics or only to such as are prescribed;
  (b) must include a statement, in respect of each protected characteristic to which the information relates, of the proportion that the number of persons who provided the information to the party bears to the number of persons who were asked to provide it.

(8) Regulations under this section may prescribe—
  (a) descriptions of information;
  (b) descriptions of political party to which the duty is to apply;
  (c) the time at which information is to be published;
  (d) the form and manner in which information is to be published;
  (e) the period for which information is to be published.

(9) Provision by virtue of subsection (8)(b) may, in particular, provide that the duty imposed by subsection (2) does not apply to a party which had candidates in fewer constituencies in the election concerned than a prescribed number.

(10) Regulations under this section—
  (a) may provide that the duty imposed by subsection (2) applies only to such relevant elections as are prescribed;
  (b) may provide that a by-election or other election to fill a vacancy is not to be treated as a relevant election or is to be so treated only to a prescribed extent;
  (c) may amend this section so as to provide for the duty imposed by subsection (2) to apply in the case of additional descriptions of election.

(11) Nothing in this section authorises a political party to require a person to provide information to it.

III EQU [106.1]

Not yet in force This section awaits a commencement order.

SUPPLEMENTARY

III EQU [107]

107. Interpretation and exceptions

(1) This section applies for the purposes of this Part.

(2) An "association" is an association of persons—
  (a) which has at least 25 members, and
  (b) admission to membership of which is regulated by the association's rules and involves a process of selection.

(3) A Minister of the Crown may by order amend subsection (2)(a) so as to substitute a different number for that for the time being specified there.

(4) It does not matter—
  (a) whether an association is incorporated;
  (b) whether its activities are carried on for profit.

(5) Membership is membership of any description; and a reference to a member is to be construed accordingly.

(6) A person is an "associate", in relation to an association, if the person—
  (a) is not a member of the association, but
  (b) in accordance with the association's rules, has some or all of the rights as a member as a result of being a member of another association.

EQUALITY

(7) A reference to a registered political party is a reference to a party registered in the Great Britain register under Part 2 of the Political Parties, Elections and Referendums Act 2000.

(8) Schedule 15 (reasonable adjustments) has effect.

(9) Schedule 16 (exceptions) has effect.

PART 8
PROHIBITED CONDUCT: ANCILLARY

III EQU [108]

108. Relationships that have ended

(1) A person (A) must not discriminate against another (B) if—

  (a) the discrimination arises out of and is closely connected to a relationship which used to exist between them, and

  (b) conduct of a description constituting the discrimination would, if it occurred during the relationship, contravene this Act.

(2) A person (A) must not harass another (B) if—

  (a) the harassment arises out of and is closely connected to a relationship which used to exist between them, and

  (b) conduct of a description constituting the harassment would, if it occurred during the relationship, contravene this Act.

(3) It does not matter whether the relationship ends before or after the commencement of this section.

(4) A duty to make reasonable adjustments applies to A if B is placed at a substantial disadvantage as mentioned in section 20.

(5) For the purposes of subsection (4), sections 20, 21 and 22 and the applicable Schedules are to be construed as if the relationship had not ended.

(6) For the purposes of Part 9 (enforcement), a contravention of this section relates to the Part of this Act that would have been contravened if the relationship had not ended.

(7) But conduct is not a contravention of this section in so far as it also amounts to victimisation of B by A.

III EQU [108.1]

Victimisation after employment ends An argument that it is possible to construe sub-s (7) as precluding a claim for post-employment victimisation succeeded in the EAT: *Rowstock Ltd v Jessemey* (UKEAT/0112/12)[2013] ICR 807, [2013] IRLR 439, but was subsequently rejected by the Court of Appeal ([2014] EWCA Civ 185, [2014] 1 WLR 3615, [2014] 3 All ER 409, [2014] IRLR 368) on the basis that it was clear that the draftsman had not intended to remove the protection from victimisation that former employees had enjoyed prior to the passing of the Equality Act 2010. See also *Onu v Akwiwu* (UKEAT/0283/12/RN and UKEAT/0022/12/RN), [2013] ICR 1039, [2013] IRLR 523, based in part on the provisions of the EU Directive 2000/43/EC 29 June 2000 and the judgment of the Court of Appeal in *Onu v Akwiwu* [2014] EWCA Civ 279, [2014] 1 WLR 3636.

III EQU [109]

109. Liability of employers and principals

(1) Anything done by a person (A) in the course of A's employment must be treated as also done by the employer.

(2) Anything done by an agent for a principal, with the authority of the principal, must be treated as also done by the principal.

(3) It does not matter whether that thing is done with the employer's or principal's knowledge or approval.

(4) In proceedings against A's employer (B) in respect of anything alleged to have been done by A in the course of A's employment it is a defence for B to show that B took all reasonable steps to prevent A—

(a) from doing that thing, or

(b) from doing anything of that description.

(5) This section does not apply to offences under this Act (other than offences under Part 12 (disabled persons: transport)).

III EQU [110]

110. Liability of employees and agents

(1) A person (A) contravenes this section if—

(a) A is an employee or agent,

(b) A does something which, by virtue of section 109(1) or (2), is treated as having been done by A's employer or principal (as the case may be), and

(c) the doing of that thing by A amounts to a contravention of this Act by the employer or principal (as the case may be).

(2) It does not matter whether, in any proceedings, the employer is found not to have contravened this Act by virtue of section 109(4).

(3) A does not contravene this section if—

(a) A relies on a statement by the employer or principal that doing that thing is not a contravention of this Act, and

(b) it is reasonable for A to do so.

(4) A person (B) commits an offence if B knowingly or recklessly makes a statement mentioned in subsection (3)(a) which is false or misleading in a material respect.

(5) A person guilty of an offence under subsection (4) is liable on summary conviction to a fine not exceeding level 5 on the standard scale.

(5A) A does not contravene this section if A—

(a) does not conduct a relevant marriage,

(b) is not present at, does not carry out, or does not otherwise participate in, a relevant marriage, or

(c) does not consent to a relevant marriage being conducted,

for the reason that the marriage is the marriage of a same sex couple.

(5B) Subsection (5A) applies to A only if A is within the meaning of "person" for the purposes of section 2 of the Marriage (Same Sex Couples) Act 2013; and other expressions used in subsection (5A) and section 2 of that Act have the same meanings in that subsection as in that section.

(5C) A does not contravene this section by refusing to solemnise a relevant Scottish marriage for the reason that the marriage is the marriage of two persons of the same sex.

(5D) A does not contravene this section by refusing to register a relevant Scottish civil partnership for the reason that the civil partnership is between two persons of the same sex.

(5E) Subsections (5C) and (5D) apply only if A is an approved celebrant.

(5F) Expressions used in subsections (5C) to (5E) have the same meaning as in paragraph 25B of Schedule 3.

(5G) A chaplain does not contravene this section by refusing to solemnise a relevant Scottish forces marriage for the reason that the marriage is the marriage of two persons of the same sex.

(5H) Expressions used in subsection (5G) have the same meaning as in paragraph 25C of Schedule 3.

(6) Part 9 (enforcement) applies to a contravention of this section by A as if it were the contravention mentioned in subsection (1)(c).

(7) The reference in subsection (1)(c) to a contravention of this Act does not include a reference to disability discrimination in contravention of Chapter 1 of Part 6 (schools).

III EQU [111]

111. Instructing, causing or inducing contraventions

(1) A person (A) must not instruct another (B) to do in relation to a third person (C) anything which contravenes Part 3, 4, 5, 6 or 7 or section 108(1) or (2) or 112(1) (a basic contravention).

(2) A person (A) must not cause another (B) to do in relation to a third person (C) anything which is a basic contravention.

(3) A person (A) must not induce another (B) to do in relation to a third person (C) anything which is a basic contravention.

(4) For the purposes of subsection (3), inducement may be direct or indirect.

(5) Proceedings for a contravention of this section may be brought—

- (a) by B, if B is subjected to a detriment as a result of A's conduct;
- (b) by C, if C is subjected to a detriment as a result of A's conduct;
- (c) by the Commission.

(6) For the purposes of subsection (5), it does not matter whether—

- (a) the basic contravention occurs;
- (b) any other proceedings are, or may be, brought in relation to A's conduct.

(7) This section does not apply unless the relationship between A and B is such that A is in a position to commit a basic contravention in relation to B.

(8) A reference in this section to causing or inducing a person to do something includes a reference to attempting to cause or induce the person to do it.

(9) For the purposes of Part 9 (enforcement), a contravention of this section is to be treated as relating—

- (a) in a case within subsection (5)(a), to the Part of this Act which, because of the relationship between A and B, A is in a position to contravene in relation to B;
- (b) in a case within subsection (5)(b), to the Part of this Act which, because of the relationship between B and C, B is in a position to contravene in relation to C.

III EQU [112]

112. Aiding contraventions

(1) A person (A) must not knowingly help another (B) to do anything which contravenes Part 3, 4, 5, 6 or 7 or section 108(1) or (2) or 111 (a basic contravention).

(2) It is not a contravention of subsection (1) if—

- (a) A relies on a statement by B that the act for which the help is given does not contravene this Act, and
- (b) it is reasonable for A to do so.

(3) B commits an offence if B knowingly or recklessly makes a statement mentioned in subsection (2)(a) which is false or misleading in a material respect.

(4) A person guilty of an offence under subsection (3) is liable on summary conviction to a fine not exceeding level 5 on the standard scale.

(5) For the purposes of Part 9 (enforcement), a contravention of this section is to be treated as relating to the provision of this Act to which the basic contravention relates.

(6) The reference in subsection (1) to a basic contravention does not include a reference to disability discrimination in contravention of Chapter 1 of Part 6 (schools).

PART 9
ENFORCEMENT

CHAPTER 1 INTRODUCTORY

III EQU [113]

113. Proceedings

(1) Proceedings relating to a contravention of this Act must be brought in accordance with this Part.

(2) Subsection (1) does not apply to proceedings under Part 1 of the Equality Act 2006.

(3) Subsection (1) does not prevent—

(a) a claim for judicial review;

(b) proceedings under the Immigration Acts;

(c) proceedings under the Special Immigration Appeals Commission Act 1997;

(d) in Scotland, an application to the supervisory jurisdiction of the Court of Session.

(4) This section is subject to any express provision of this Act conferring jurisdiction on a court or tribunal.

(5) The reference to a contravention of this Act includes a reference to a breach of an equality clause or rule.

(6) Chapters 2 and 3 do not apply to proceedings relating to an equality clause or rule except in so far as Chapter 4 provides for that.

(7) This section does not apply to—

(a) proceedings for an offence under this Act;

(b) proceedings relating to a penalty under Part 12 (disabled persons: transport).

III EQU [113.1]

Exclusive jurisdiction In *Summers v Richmond upon Thames London Borough Council* [2018] EWHC 782 (Admin), the High Court held it did not have jurisdiction to determine whether exemptions in a Public Spaces Protection Order, were discriminatory towards disabled persons because s 113 and s 114 conferred exclusive jurisdiction on the County Court.

CHAPTER 2 CIVIL COURTS

III EQU [114]

114. Jurisdiction

(1) The county court or, in Scotland, the sheriff has jurisdiction to determine a claim relating to—

(a) a contravention of Part 3 (services and public functions);

(b) a contravention of Part 4 (premises);

(c) a contravention of Part 6 (education);

(d) a contravention of Part 7 (associations);

(e) a contravention of section 108, 111 or 112 that relates to Part 3, 4, 6 or 7.

(2) Subsection (1)(a) does not apply to a claim within section 115.

(3) Subsection (1)(c) does not apply to a claim within section 116.

(4) Subsection (1)(d) does not apply to a contravention of section 106.

(5) For the purposes of proceedings on a claim within subsection (1)(a)—

- (a) a decision in proceedings on a claim mentioned in section 115(1) that an act is a contravention of Part 3 is binding;
- (b) it does not matter whether the act occurs outside the United Kingdom.

(6) The county court or sheriff—

- (a) must not grant an interim injunction or interdict unless satisfied that no criminal matter would be prejudiced by doing so;
- (b) must grant an application to stay or sist proceedings under subsection (1) on grounds of prejudice to a criminal matter unless satisfied the matter will not be prejudiced.

(7) In proceedings in England and Wales on a claim within subsection (1), the power under section 63(1) of the County Courts Act 1984 (appointment of assessors) must be exercised unless the judge is satisfied that there are good reasons for not doing so.

(8) In proceedings in Scotland on a claim within subsection (1), the power under rule 44.3 of Schedule 1 to the Sheriff Court (Scotland) Act 1907 (appointment of assessors) must be exercised unless the sheriff is satisfied that there are good reasons for not doing so.

(9) The remuneration of an assessor appointed by virtue of subsection (8) is to be at a rate determined by the Lord President of the Court of Session.

III EQU [114.1]

Assessors For s 63 of the County Courts Act 1984 see **II CCA [42]**. The role of assessors is to assist the judge not merely by giving expert advice but also in evaluating the evidence. An assessor should have skill and experience in 'the matter to which the proceedings relate' (CPR 35.15). The Court of Appeal has held that whilst county court judges were trained in relation to certain discrimination issues, the assistance of someone who regularly dealt with discrimination issues was potentially very valuable. However, the requirement in CPR 35.15 does not mean that an assessor needs to have special skills relating to the particular protected characteristic or the particular kind of unlawful treatment that is the subject of the claim: *Cary v Metropolitan Police Comr (Equality and Human Rights Commission intervening)* [2014] EWCA Civ 987, [2015] ICR 71, [2014] EqLR 707 (see also the general guidance given by the Court about the selection and appointment of assessors). Expert evidence given by assessors should be disclosed so that the parties can respond to it. Any direction given them on the law by the judge should be given in open court but where a corporate judicial decision has to be made the discussion should remain confidential. If there is a serious disagreement between the judge and assessors the judge should spell it out in the judgment, giving reasons. All these points were made by the Court of Appeal in a case brought under the Race Relations Act 1976: *Ahmed v Governing Body of the University of Oxford* [2002] EWCA Civ 1907, [2003] 1 All ER 915, [2003] 1 WLR 995.

III EQU [114.2]

Death of claimant It was decided in *Harris (Andrews Personal representative) v Lewisham and Guys Mental Health NHS Trust* [2000] 3 All ER 769, [2000] IRLR 320, CA, that a discrimination claim is covered by the Law Reform (Miscellaneous Provisions) Act 1934, s 1(1) and that a cause of action therefore survives the death of the person making the complaint.

III EQU [115]

115. Immigration cases

(1) A claim is within this section if it relates to the act of an immigration authority in taking a relevant decision and—

- (a) the question whether the act is a contravention of Part 3 has been or could be raised on an appeal which is pending, or could be brought, under the immigration provisions, or
- (b) it has been decided on an appeal under those provisions that the act is not a contravention of Part 3.

(2) The relevant decision is not—

(a) subject to challenge in proceedings on a claim within section 114(1)(a), or

(b) affected by the decision of a court in such proceedings.

(3) For the purposes of subsection (1)(a) a power to grant permission to appeal out of time must be ignored.

(4) Each of the following is an immigration authority—

(a) the Secretary of State;

(b) an immigration officer;

(c) a person responsible for the grant or refusal of entry clearance (within the meaning of section 33(1) of the Immigration Act 1971).

(5) The immigration provisions are—

(a) the Special Immigration Appeals Commission Act 1997, or

(b) Part 5 of the Nationality, Immigration and Asylum Act 2002.

(6) A relevant decision is—

(a) a decision under the Immigration Acts relating to the entitlement of a person to enter or remain in the United Kingdom;

(b) a decision on an appeal under the immigration provisions relating to a decision within paragraph (a).

(7) An appeal is pending if it is pending for the purposes of section 104 of the Nationality, Immigration and Asylum Act 2002 or (as the case may be) for the purposes of that section as it is applied by section 2(2)(j) of the Special Immigration Appeals Commission Act 1997.

(8) This section applies in relation to reviews under section 2D and 2E of the Special Immigration Appeals Commission Act 1997 as it applies in relation to appeals under the immigration provisions.

III EQU [115.1]

No civil remedy in the county court The county court does not have jurisdiction to determine a claim relating to a contravention of this section: see s 114.

III EQU [116]

116. Education cases

(1) A claim is within this section if it may be made to—

(a) the First-tier Tribunal in accordance with Part 2 of Schedule 17,

(b) the *Special Educational Needs Tribunal for Wales* [Education Tribunal for Wales] in accordance with Part 2 of that Schedule, or

(c) the First-tier Tribunal for Scotland Health and Education Chamber in accordance with Part 3 of that Schedule.

(2) A claim is also within this section if it must be made in accordance with appeal arrangements within the meaning of Part 4 of that Schedule.

(3) Schedule 17 (disabled pupils: enforcement) has effect.

Amendment *Text in italic is deleted and text in square brackets is inserted by the Additional Learning Needs and Education Tribunal (Wales) Act 2018 with effect from a date to be appointed.*

III EQU [116.1]

No civil remedy in the county court The county court does not have jurisdiction to determine a claim relating to a contravention of this section: see s 114.

EQUALITY

III EQU [117]

117. National security

(1) Rules of court may, in relation to proceedings on a claim within section 114, confer power as mentioned in subsections (2) to (4); but a power so conferred is exercisable only if the court thinks it expedient to do so in the interests of national security.

(2) The rules may confer power to exclude from all or part of the proceedings—

(a) the claimant or pursuer;

(b) a representative of the claimant or pursuer;

(c) an assessor.

(3) The rules may confer power to permit a claimant, pursuer or representative who has been excluded to make a statement to the court before the commencement of the proceedings, or part of the proceedings, to which the exclusion relates.

(4) The rules may confer power to take steps to keep secret all or part of the reasons for the court's decision.

(5) The Attorney General or, in Scotland, the Advocate General for Scotland may appoint a person to represent the interests of a claimant or pursuer in, or in any part of, proceedings to which an exclusion by virtue of subsection (2)(a) or (b) relates.

(6) A person (P) may be appointed under subsection (5) only if—

(a) in relation to proceedings in England and Wales, P is a person who, for the purposes of the Legal Services Act 2007, is an authorised person in relation to an activity which constitutes the exercise of a right of audience or the conduct of litigation;

(b) in relation to proceedings in Scotland, P is an advocate or qualified to practice as a solicitor in Scotland.

(7) P is not responsible to the person whose interests P is appointed to represent.

III EQU [118]

118. Time limits

(1) Subject to sections 140A and 140AA proceedings on a claim within section 114 may not be brought after the end of—

(a) the period of 6 months starting with the date of the act to which the claim relates, or

(b) such other period as the county court or sheriff thinks just and equitable.

(2) If subsection (3) applies, subsection (1)(a) has effect as if for "6 months" there were substituted "9 months".

(3) This subsection applies if—

(a) the claim relates to the act of a qualifying institution, and

(b) a complaint relating to the act is referred under the student complaints scheme before the end of the period of 6 months starting with the date of the act.

(4) ...

(5) If it has been decided under the immigration provisions that the act of an immigration authority in taking a relevant decision is a contravention of Part 3 (services and public functions), subsection (1) has effect as if for paragraph (a) there were substituted—

"(a) the period of 6 months starting with the day after the expiry of the period during which, as a result of section 114(2), proceedings could not be brought in reliance on section 114(1)(a);".

(6) For the purposes of this section—

(a) conduct extending over a period is to be treated as done at the end of the period;

(b) failure to do something is to be treated as occurring when the person in question decided on it.

(7) In the absence of evidence to the contrary, a person (P) is to be taken to decide on failure to do something—

(a) when P does an act inconsistent with doing it, or

(b) if P does no inconsistent act, on the expiry of the period in which P might reasonably have been expected to do it.

(8) In this section—

"immigration authority", "immigration provisions" and "relevant decision" each have the meaning given in section 115;

"qualifying institution" has the meaning given in section 11 of the Higher Education Act 2004, and includes an institution which is treated as continuing to be a qualifying institution for the purposes of Part 2 of that Act (see section 20A(2) of that Act);

"the student complaints scheme" means a scheme for the review of qualifying complaints (within the meaning of section 12 of that Act) that is provided by the designated operator (within the meaning of section 13(5)(b) of that Act).

III EQU [118.1]

Just and equitable What is just and equitable for the purposes of subsection (1)(a) is a question of fact in each case: *Foster v South Glamorgan Health Authority* [1988] ICR 526, [1988] IRLR 277, EAT. For relevant factors to take into account see *British Coal Corp v Keeble* [1997] IRLR 336 and *Afolabi v Southwark London Borough Council* [2003] EWCA Civ 15, [2003] ICR 800, [2003] IRLR 220. See also *Robertson v Bexley Community Centre (t/a Leisure Link)* [2003] EWCA Civ 576, [2003] IRLR 434 and *Chief Constable of Lincolnshire v Caston* [2009] EWCA Civ 1298, [2010] IRLR 327.

III EQU [118.2]

Acts extending over a period Where an employer repeatedly refuses applications to move from full-time to part-time working, the time limit runs from the most recent refusal, provided it was a considered decision, not merely a reference back to the original decision. If it is a considered decision it does not matter whether fresh evidence is taken into account: *Cast v Croydon College* [1998] ICR 500, [1998] IRLR 318, CA.

In the employment field, the Court of Appeal has indicated that it is generally desirable for the question of whether an act extends over a period to be decided once all of the facts of the case have been found. Further, it may be that a Defendant being responsible for an ongoing discriminatory state of affairs or situation could be considered to be an act extending over a period. See the leading authority of *Hendricks v Metropolitan Police Comr* [2002] EWCA Civ 1686, [2003] 1 All ER 654, [2003] ICR 530. However, it is not sufficient for a claimant simply to assert that there was an ongoing discriminatory state of affairs. He or she must have a reasonably arguable basis for such a belief: *MA v Merck Sharp & Dohme Ltd* [2008] EWCA Civ 1426.

III EQU [118.3]

Reasonable adjustments For the operation of time limits to claims of failure to make reasonable adjustments, see *Matuszowicz v Kingston upon Hull City Council* [2009] EWCA Civ 22, [2009] 3 All ER 685, [2009] ICR 1170.

III EQU [119]

119. Remedies

(1) This section applies if the county court or the sheriff finds that there has been a contravention of a provision referred to in section 114(1).

(2) The county court has power to grant any remedy which could be granted by the High Court—

(a) in proceedings in tort;

(b) on a claim for judicial review.

(3) The sheriff has power to make any order which could be made by the Court of Session—

(a) in proceedings for reparation;

(b) on a petition for judicial review.

(4) An award of damages may include compensation for injured feelings (whether or not it includes compensation on any other basis).

(5) Subsection (6) applies if the county court or sheriff—

(a) finds that a contravention of a provision referred to in section 114(1) is established by virtue of section 19, but

(b) is satisfied that the provision, criterion or practice was not applied with the intention of discriminating against the claimant or pursuer.

(6) The county court or sheriff must not make an award of damages unless it first considers whether to make any other disposal.

(7) The county court or sheriff must not grant a remedy other than an award of damages or the making of a declaration unless satisfied that no criminal matter would be prejudiced by doing so.

III EQU [119.1]

No requirement of foreseeability Damages for discrimination are to be awarded in a like manner as for other torts, save that there is no requirement of foreseeability. See *Essa v Laing Ltd* [2004] EWCA Civ 02, [2004] ICR 746, [2004] IRLR 313 in which the complainant was found to have suffered race discrimination which caused a significant psychiatric injury and loss of earnings. The Employment Tribunal found that this was a an over-reaction to what had happened and declined to award his full loss on the grounds that it was not foreseeable. The Court of Appeal in *Essa* overturned that decision, holding that damages for discrimination, which is a statutory tort, are "strict liability" and do not require a finding of foreseeability.

III EQU [119.2]

Aggravated damages Exemplary damages are not available in discrimination claims. See *Ministry of Defence and Meredith* [1995] IRLR 539, EAT. Aggravated damages are recoverable in appropriate cases but are an aspect of injury to feelings rather than a separatehead of claim: *Metropolitan Police Comr v Shaw* [2011] UKEAT 0125/11. The tribunal should be careful to ensure that the factors which it considers to be aggravating are not merely the acts of discrimination themselves: See *Hardy & Hansons plc v Lax (No 2)* EAT/0700/04, unreported. For an analysis of cases in which claims are made for psychiatric harm, injury to feelings and aggravated damages see *Choudhury v Martin* (2008) Times, 2 January, CA.

III EQU [119.3]

Injury to feelings Damages will generally be awarded for injury to feelings. In *Vento v Chief Constable of the Yorkshire Police (No 2)* [2002] EWCA Civ 1871, [2003] ICR 318, [2003] IRLR 102, the Court of Appeal gave the following guidance to Employment Tribunals, but which also applies to claims in the civil courts:

(a) The top band should normally be between £15,000 and £25,000. Sums in this range should be awarded in the most serious cases, such as where there has been a lengthy campaign of discriminatory harassment on the ground of sex or race. This case falls within that band. Only in the most exceptional case should an award of compensation for injury to feelings exceed £25,000.

(b) The middle band of between £5,000 and £15,000 should be used for serious cases, which do not merit an award in the highest band.

(c) Awards of between £500 and £5,000 are appropriate for less serious cases, such as where the act of discrimination is an isolated or one-off occurrence. In general, awards of less than £500 are to be avoided altogether, as they risk being regarded as so low as not to be a proper recognition of injury to feelings.

In the employment case of *Da'Bell v National Society for the Prevention of Cruelty to Children* [2010] IRLR 19, EAT the Employment Appeal Tribunal held that the *Vento* guidelines should be increased to reflect inflation as follows:

(a) Top band increased to £30,000;
(b) Middle bank increased to £18,000;
(c) Lower band increased to £6,000.

Although note in *Bullimore v Pothecary Witham Weld Solicitors* (2010) UKEAT/0189/10, [2011] IRLR 18, [2010] EqLR 260, [2010] All ER (D) 269 (Dec), the EAT held that while employment tribunals should assess quantum for non-pecuniary loss in 'today's money', no explicit uprating exercise was required. *Da'Bell* represented a reminder to take inflation into account but did not mean that a decision without express uprating was wrong. The 10% uplift laid down in *Simmons v Castle* [2012] EWCA Civ 1039, [2013] 1 WLR 1239 apples to injury to feelings awards, whether in the Employment Tribunal or County Court: see *Pereira de Souza v Vinci Construction UK Ltd* [2017] EWCA Civ 879, [2017] IRLR 844.

Presidential guidance has been given regarding employment tribunal awards for injury to feelings and psychiatric injury, following the decision in *De Souza v Vinci Construction (UK) Ltd* [2017] EWCA Civ 879. The effect of the guidance is that the *Vento* guidelines have been further uprated as follows:

(a) Top band: £25,700 to £42,900
(b) Middle: £8,600 to 25,700
(c) Low: £900 to £8,600.

III EQU [119.4]

Flexibility There is, of course, within each band considerable flexibility: see *Gilbank v Miles* [2006] EWCA Civ 543, [2006] ICR 1297, [2006] IRLR 538 in which the Court of Appeal dismissed an appeal from the EAT albeit that the award was at the top end. The tribunal should first consider whether it is just and equitable to make an award for injury to feelings. If it decides that it is, then the level of the award made should then be arrived at on ordinary tortious principles, not on the basis of what the tribunal considers just and equitable: see *Hardy & Hansons plc v Lax (No 2)* EAT/0700/04, unreported.

Where allegations of two (or more) different forms of discrimination are claimed (including claims for discrimination and victimisation) it may be appropriate to make two separate awards for injury to feelings. See *Al Jumard v Clywd Leisure Ltd* [2008] IRLR 345 where the claimant in an employment case was found to be entitled to two separate awards for injury to feelings for his claims of race discrimination and disability discrimination.

III EQU [119.5]

Tax treatment of injury to feelings awards In *Moorthy v Revenue and Customs Commissioners* [2014] UKFTT 834 (TC), [2016] UKUT 13 (TCC), the Upper Tribunal (Tax and Chancery Chamber) held that a sum paid to an employee in respect of injury to feelings in a settlement agreement was not exempted from income tax on the basis it was 'on account of injury to . . . an employee' under s 406 of the Income Tax (Earnings and Pensions) Act 2003. Injury did not include injury to feelings and EAT decisions to the contrary (*Orthet Ltd v Vince-Cain* [2004] IRLR 857, [2005] ICR 374, [2004] All ER (D) 143 (May), EAT; *Wilton v Timothy James Consulting Ltd* (2015) UKEAT/82/14, [2015] IRLR 368, [2015] ICR 765, [2015] All ER (D) 70 (Apr), EAT) were wrongly decided.

See now the ruling of the Court of Appeal that injury to feelings are within the s 406 exemption for personal injury and that a part of a global settlement figure may be treated as for injury to feelings so as to obtain the exemption: *Moorthy v Revenue and Customs Comrs* [2018] EWCA Civ 847, [2018] ICR 1326, (2018) Times, 2 May.

CHAPTERS 3 AND 4 EMPLOYMENT TRIBUNALS

III EQU [120]–III EQU [135]

GENERAL NOTE ON JURISDICTION OF EMPLOYMENT TRIBUNALS AND EQUALITY OF TERMS These two chapters are omitted because they concern the jurisdiction of Employment Tribunals. Note, however, that powers are conferred on the county court to refer to an employment tribunal any question about a non-discrimination rule (s 122) or about an equality clause or rule (s 128) and to strike out any claim relating to such a rule or clause if it appears that it could be more conveniently determined by an employment tribunal.

A non-discrimination rule, a sex equality rule and a maternity equality rule are treated, by ss 61, 67 and 75, as included in every occupational pension scheme; and a sex equality clause and a maternity equality clause are treated, by ss 66 and 73, as included in terms of work.

As regards the meaning of non-discrimination and equality rules and equality clauses, their interpretation is provided for in s 212 as follows: 'a non-discrimination rule' is defined in s 61 and 'an equality clause' means a sex equality clause, as defined in s 66, or a maternity equality clause, as defined in s 73, whereas 'an equality rule' means a sex equality rule, as defined in s 67, or a maternity equality rule, as defined in s 75.

CHAPTER 5 MISCELLANEOUS

III EQU [136]

136. Burden of proof

(1) This section applies to any proceedings relating to a contravention of this Act.

(2) If there are facts from which the court could decide, in the absence of any other explanation, that a person (A) contravened the provision concerned, the court must hold that the contravention occurred.

(3) But subsection (2) does not apply if A shows that A did not contravene the provision.

(4) The reference to a contravention of this Act includes a reference to a breach of an equality clause or rule.

(5) This section does not apply to proceedings for an offence under this Act.

(6) A reference to the court includes a reference to—

(a) an employment tribunal;
(b) the Asylum and Immigration Tribunal;
(c) the Special Immigration Appeals Commission;
(d) the First-tier Tribunal;
(e) the *Special Educational Needs Tribunal for Wales* [Education Tribunal for Wales];
(f) the First-tier Tribunal for Scotland Health and Education Chamber.

Amendment *Text in italic is deleted and text in square brackets is inserted by the Additional Learning Needs and Education Tribunal (Wales) Act 2018 with effect from a date to be appointed.*

III EQU [136.1]

The two-stage process The burden of proof is initially on the claimant to prove facts from which it may be concluded, in the absence of an adequate explanation, that there has been discrimination; and the defendant then has the burden of proving the facts from which a non-discriminatory explanation may be established: *Transport for London and McGill v Aderemi* [2011] UKEAT/0006/11 following the guidance provided in *Wong v Igen Ltd (Equal Opportunities Commission intervening)* [2005] EWCA Civ 142, [2005] ICR 931, [2005] IRLR 258.

See now the guidance of the Supreme Court in *Hewage v Grampian Health Board* [2012] UKSC 37, [2012] 4 All ER 447, [2012] IRLR 870 and *Ayodele v Citylink Ltd* [2017] EWCA Civ 1913, [2018] IRLR 114.

III EQU [137]

137. Previous findings

(1) A finding in relevant proceedings in respect of an act which has become final is to be treated as conclusive in proceedings under this Act.

(2) Relevant proceedings are proceedings before a court or employment tribunal under any of the following—

(a) section 19 or 20 of the Race Relations Act 1968;
(b) the Equal Pay Act 1970;
(c) the Sex Discrimination Act 1975;
(d) the Race Relations Act 1976;
(e) section 6(4A) of the Sex Discrimination Act 1986;
(f) the Disability Discrimination Act 1995;
(g) Part 2 of the Equality Act 2006;
(h) the Employment Equality (Religion and Belief) Regulations 2003 (SI 2003/1660);
(i) the Employment Equality (Sexual Orientation) Regulations 2003 (SI 2003/1661);

(j) the Employment Equality (Age) Regulations 2006 (SI 2006/1031);
(k) the Equality Act (Sexual Orientation) Regulations 2007 (SI 2007/1263).

(3) A finding becomes final—
(a) when an appeal against the finding is dismissed, withdrawn or abandoned, or
(b) when the time for appealing expires without an appeal having been brought.

III EQU [138]

138. Obtaining information, etc

Repealed by the Enterprise and Regulatory Reform Act 2013 with effect from 6 April 2014 (except in relation to proceedings that relate to a contravention occurring before this date): see SI 2014/416, art 3(a) and the Enterprise and Regulatory Reform Act 2013, s 66(2).

III EQU [139]

139. Interest

(1) Regulations may make provision—
(a) for enabling an employment tribunal to include interest on an amount awarded by it in proceedings under this Act;
(b) specifying the manner in which, and the periods and rate by reference to which, the interest is to be determined.

(2) Regulations may modify the operation of an order made under section 14 of the Employment Tribunals Act 1996 (power to make provision as to interest on awards) in so far as it relates to an award in proceedings under this Act.

III EQU [139A]

139A. Equal pay audits

The text of this section has been omitted since it is concerned with the jurisdiction of employment tribunals, not the civil courts.

III EQU [140]

140. Conduct giving rise to separate proceedings

(1) This section applies in relation to conduct which has given rise to two or more separate proceedings under this Act, with at least one being for a contravention of section 111 (instructing, causing or inducing contraventions).

(2) A court may transfer proceedings to an employment tribunal.

(3) An employment tribunal may transfer proceedings to a court.

(4) A court or employment tribunal is to be taken for the purposes of this Part to have jurisdiction to determine a claim or complaint transferred to it under this section; accordingly—
(a) a reference to a claim within section 114(1) includes a reference to a claim transferred to a court under this section, and
(b) a reference to a complaint within section 120(1) includes a reference to a complaint transferred to an employment tribunal under this section.

(5) A court or employment tribunal may not make a decision that is inconsistent with an earlier decision in proceedings arising out of the conduct.

(6) "Court" means—
(a) in relation to proceedings in England and Wales, the county court;
(b) in relation to proceedings in Scotland, the sheriff.

EQUALITY

III EQU [140A]

140A. Extension of time limits because of mediation in certain cross-border disputes

(1) In this section—

(a) "Mediation Directive" means Directive 2008/52/EC of the European Parliament and of the Council of 21 May 2008 on certain aspects of mediation in civil and commercial matters,

(b) "mediation" has the meaning given by article 3(a) of the Mediation Directive,

(c) "mediator" has the meaning given by article 3(b) of the Mediation Directive, and

(d) "relevant dispute" means a dispute to which article 8(1) of the Mediation Directive applies (certain cross-border disputes).

(2) Subsection (3) applies where—

(a) a time limit is set by section 118(1)(a), 118(2) or 129(3) in relation to the whole or part of a relevant dispute,

(b) a mediation in relation to the relevant dispute starts before the time limit expires, and

(c) if not extended by this section, the time limit would expire before the mediation ends or less than eight weeks after it ends.

(3) The time limit expires instead at the end of eight weeks after the mediation ends (subject to subsection (4)).

(4) If a time limit mentioned in subsection (2)(a) has been extended by this section, subsections (2) and (3) apply to the extended time limit as they apply to a time limit mentioned in subsection (2)(a).

(5) Subsection (6) applies where—

(a) a time limit is set by section 123(1)(a) in relation to the whole or part of a relevant dispute,

(b) a mediation in relation to the relevant dispute starts before the time limit expires, and

(c) if not extended by this section the time limit would expire before the mediation ends or less than four weeks after it ends.

(6) The time limit expires instead at the end of four weeks after the mediation ends (subject to subsection (7)).

(7) If a time limit mentioned in subsection (5)(a) has been extended by this section, subsections (5) and (6) apply to the extended time limit as they apply to a time limit mentioned in subsection (5)(a).

(8) Where more than one time limit applies in relation to a relevant dispute, the extension by subsection (3) or (6) of one of those time limits does not affect the others.

(9) For the purposes of this section, a mediation starts on the date of the agreement to mediate that is entered into by the parties and the mediator.

(10) For the purposes of this section, a mediation ends on the date of the first of these to occur—

(a) the parties reach an agreement in resolution of the relevant dispute,

(b) a party completes the notification of the other parties that it has withdrawn from the mediation,

(c) a party to whom a qualifying request is made fails to give a response reaching the other parties within 14 days of the request,

(d) the parties, after being notified that the mediator's appointment has ended (by death, resignation or otherwise), fail to agree within 14 days to seek to appoint a replacement mediator,

(e) the mediation otherwise comes to an end pursuant to the terms of the agreement to mediate.

(11) For the purpose of subsection (10), a qualifying request is a request by a party that another (A) confirm to all parties that A is continuing with the mediation.

(12) In the case of any relevant dispute, references in this section to a mediation are references to the mediation so far as it relates to that dispute, and references to a party are to be read accordingly.

(13) Where a court or tribunal has power under section 118(1)(b) or 123(1)(b) to extend a period of limitation, the power is exercisable in relation to the period of limitation as extended by this section.

III EQU [140AA]

140AA. Extension of time limits because of alternative dispute resolution in certain cross border or domestic contractual disputes

(1) In this section—

- (a) "ADR Directive" means Directive 2013/11/EU of the European Parliament and of the Council of 21 May 2013 on alternative dispute resolution for consumer disputes and amending Regulation (EC) No 2006/2004 and Directive 2009/22/EC;
- (b) "ADR entity" has the meaning given by article 4(1)(h) of the ADR Directive;
- (c) . . .
- (d) "ADR procedure" has the meaning given by article 4(1)(g) of the ADR Directive;
- (e) "non-binding ADR procedure" means an ADR procedure the outcome of which is not binding on the parties;
- (f) "relevant dispute" means a dispute to which Article 12(1) of the ADR Directive applies (certain cross-border or domestic contractual disputes brought by a consumer against a trader).

(2) Subsection (3) applies where—

- (a) a time limit is set by section 118(1)(a) and (2) in relation to the whole or part of a relevant dispute;
- (b) a non-binding ADR procedure in relation to the relevant dispute starts before the time limit expires; and
- (c) if not extended by this section, the time limit would expire before the non-binding ADR procedure ends or less than eight weeks after it ends.

(3) For the purposes of initiating judicial proceedings, the time limit expires instead at the end of eight weeks after the non-binding ADR procedure ends (subject to subsection (4)).

(4) If a time limit has been extended by this section, subsections (2) and (3) apply to the extended time limit as they apply to a time limit mentioned in subsection (2)(a).

(5) Where more than one time limit applies in relation to a relevant dispute, the extension by subsection (3) of one of those time limits does not affect the others.

(6) For the purposes of this section, a non-binding ADR procedure starts in relation to a relevant dispute on the date when the dispute is first sent or otherwise communicated to the ADR entity in accordance with the entity's rules regarding the submission of complaints.

(7) For the purposes of this section, the non-binding ADR procedure ends on the date of the first of these to occur—

- (a) the parties reach an agreement in resolution of the relevant dispute;
- (b) a party completes the notification of the other parties that it has withdrawn from the non-binding ADR procedure;
- (c) a party to whom a qualifying request is made fails to give a response reaching the other parties within 14 days of the request;

EQUALITY

(d) that the ADR entity notifies the party that submitted the relevant dispute to the ADR entity that, in accordance with its policy, the ADR entity refuses to deal with the relevant dispute;

(e) after the parties are notified that the ADR entity can no longer act in relation to the relevant dispute (for whatever reason), the parties fail to agree within 14 days to submit the dispute to an alternative ADR entity;

(f) the non-binding ADR procedure otherwise comes to an end pursuant to the rules of the ADR entity.

(8) For the purpose of subsection (6), a qualifying request is a request by a party that another (A) confirm to all parties that A is continuing with the non-binding ADR procedure.

(9) In the case of any relevant dispute, references in this section to a non-binding ADR procedure are references to the non-binding ADR procedure so far as it relates to that dispute, and references to a party are to be read accordingly.

(10) Where a court or tribunal has power under section 118(1)(b) to extend a period of limitation, the power is exercisable in relation to the period of limitation as extended by this section.

III EQU [140B]

140B. Extension of time limits to facilitate conciliation before institution of proceedings

(1) This section applies where a time limit is set by section 123(1)(a) or 129(3) or (4).

But it does not apply to a dispute that is (or so much of a dispute as is) a relevant dispute for the purposes of section 140A.

(2) In this section—

(a) Day A is the day on which the complainant or applicant concerned complies with the requirement in subsection (1) of section 18A of the Employment Tribunals Act 1996 (requirement to contact ACAS before instituting proceedings) in relation to the matter in respect of which the proceedings are brought, and

(b) Day B is the day on which the complainant or applicant concerned receives or, if earlier, is treated as receiving (by virtue of regulations made under subsection (11) of that section) the certificate issued under subsection (4) of that section.

(3) In working out when the time limit set by section 123(1)(a) or 129(3) or (4) expires the period beginning with the day after Day A and ending with Day B is not to be counted.

(4) If the time limit set by section 123(1)(a) or 129(3) or (4) would (if not extended by this subsection) expire during the period beginning with Day A and ending one month after Day B, the time limit expires instead at the end of that period.

(5) The power conferred on the employment tribunal by subsection (1)(b) of section 123 to extend the time limit set by subsection (1)(a) of that section is exercisable in relation to that time limit as extended by this section.

III EQU [141]

141. Interpretation, etc

(1) This section applies for the purposes of this Part.

(2) A reference to the responsible person, in relation to an equality clause or rule, is to be construed in accordance with Chapter 3 of Part 5.

(3) A reference to a worker is a reference to the person to the terms of whose work the proceedings in question relate; and, for the purposes of proceedings relating to an equality rule or a non-discrimination rule, a reference to a worker includes a reference to a member of the occupational pension scheme in question.

(4) A reference to the terms of a person's work is to be construed in accordance with Chapter 3 of Part 5.

(5) A reference to a member of an occupational pension scheme includes a reference to a prospective member.

(6) In relation to proceedings in England and Wales, a person has an incapacity if the person—

(a) has not attained the age of 18, or

(b) lacks capacity (within the meaning of the Mental Capacity Act 2005).

(7) In relation to proceedings in Scotland, a person has an incapacity if the person—

(a) has not attained the age of 16, or

(b) is incapable (within the meaning of the Adults with Incapacity (Scotland) Act 2000 (asp 4)).

(8) "Service complaint" means a complaint made under section 340A(1) or (2) of the Armed Forces Act 2006.

(9) "Criminal matter" means—

(a) an investigation into the commission of an alleged offence;

(b) a decision whether to commence criminal proceedings;

(c) criminal proceedings.

PART 10
CONTRACTS, ETC

CONTRACTS AND OTHER AGREEMENTS

III EQU [142]

142. Unenforceable terms

(1) A term of a contract is unenforceable against a person in so far as it constitutes, promotes or provides for treatment of that or another person that is of a description prohibited by this Act.

(2) A relevant non-contractual term is unenforceable against a person in so far as it constitutes, promotes or provides for treatment of that or another person that is of a description prohibited by this Act, in so far as this Act relates to disability.

(3) A relevant non-contractual term is a term which—

(a) is a term of an agreement that is not a contract, and

(b) relates to the provision of an employment service within section 56(2)(a) to (e) or to the provision under a group insurance arrangement of facilities by way of insurance.

(4) A reference in subsection (1) or (2) to treatment of a description prohibited by this Act does not include—

(a) a reference to the inclusion of a term in a contract referred to in section 70(2)(a) or 76(2), or

(b) a reference to the failure to include a term in a contract as referred to in section 70(2)(b).

(5) Subsection (4) does not affect the application of section 148(2) to this section.

EQUALITY

III EQU [143]

143. Removal or modification of unenforceable terms

(1) The county court or the sheriff may, on an application by a person who has an interest in a contract or other agreement which includes a term that is unenforceable as a result of section 142, make an order for the term to be removed or modified.

(2) An order under this section must not be made unless every person who would be affected by it—

(a) has been given notice of the application (except where notice is dispensed with in accordance with rules of court), and

(b) has been afforded an opportunity to make representations to the county court or sheriff.

(3) An order under this section may include provision in respect of a period before the making of the order.

III EQU [144]

144. Contracting out

(1) A term of a contract is unenforceable by a person in whose favour it would operate in so far as it purports to exclude or limit a provision of or made under this Act.

(2) A relevant non-contractual term (as defined by section 142) is unenforceable by a person in whose favour it would operate in so far as it purports to exclude or limit a provision of or made under this Act, in so far as the provision relates to disability.

(3) This section does not apply to a contract which settles a claim within section 114.

(4) This section does not apply to a contract which settles a complaint within section 120 if the contract—

(a) is made with the assistance of a conciliation officer, or

(b) is a qualifying settlement agreement.

(5) A contract within subsection (4) includes a contract which settles a complaint relating to a breach of an equality clause or rule or of a non-discrimination rule.

(6) A contract within subsection (4) includes an agreement by the parties to a dispute to submit the dispute to arbitration if—

(a) the dispute is covered by a scheme having effect by virtue of an order under section 212A of the Trade Union and Labour Relations (Consolidation) Act 1992, and

(b) the agreement is to submit the dispute to arbitration in accordance with the scheme.

III EQU [144.1]

Jurisdiction of county court This Part was brought fully into force by Order No 4 on 1 October 2010 conferring jurisdiction on the county court in the matter of contract terms, including terms in contracts of employment: see *Meade-Hall v British Council* [1996] 1 All ER 79, [1995] ICR 847, CA. A term in a contract of employment that commits the parties to resolution of disputes by arbitration does not deprive the employee of the right to take a complaint of discrimination to the Tribunal: *Clyde & Co LLP v Van Winkelhof* [2011] EWHC 668 (QB), [2011] IRLR 467, [2011] NLJR 475. As regards terms in collective agreements and rules of undertakings, these may be challenged by complaint to an employment tribunal as provided in ss 145 to 148.

Collective agreements and rules of undertakings

III EQU [145]–III EQU [148]

The text of these provisions has been omitted since it is concerned with the jurisdiction of employment tribunals, not the civil courts.

PART 11
ADVANCEMENT OF EQUALITY

CHAPTER 1 PUBLIC SECTOR EQUALITY DUTY

III EQU [149]

149. Public sector equality duty

(1) A public authority must, in the exercise of its functions, have due regard to the need to—

- (a) eliminate discrimination, harassment, victimisation and any other conduct that is prohibited by or under this Act;
- (b) advance equality of opportunity between persons who share a relevant protected characteristic and persons who do not share it;
- (c) foster good relations between persons who share a relevant protected characteristic and persons who do not share it.

(2) A person who is not a public authority but who exercises public functions must, in the exercise of those functions, have due regard to the matters mentioned in subsection (1).

(3) Having due regard to the need to advance equality of opportunity between persons who share a relevant protected characteristic and persons who do not share it involves having due regard, in particular, to the need to—

- (a) remove or minimise disadvantages suffered by persons who share a relevant protected characteristic that are connected to that characteristic;
- (b) take steps to meet the needs of persons who share a relevant protected characteristic that are different from the needs of persons who do not share it;
- (c) encourage persons who share a relevant protected characteristic to participate in public life or in any other activity in which participation by such persons is disproportionately low.

(4) The steps involved in meeting the needs of disabled persons that are different from the needs of persons who are not disabled include, in particular, steps to take account of disabled persons' disabilities.

(5) Having due regard to the need to foster good relations between persons who share a relevant protected characteristic and persons who do not share it involves having due regard, in particular, to the need to—

- (a) tackle prejudice, and
- (b) promote understanding.

(6) Compliance with the duties in this section may involve treating some persons more favourably than others; but that is not to be taken as permitting conduct that would otherwise be prohibited by or under this Act.

(7) The relevant protected characteristics are—

age;
disability;
gender reassignment;
pregnancy and maternity;
race;
religion or belief;
sex;
sexual orientation.

(8) A reference to conduct that is prohibited by or under this Act includes a reference to—

- (a) a breach of an equality clause or rule;
- (b) a breach of a non-discrimination rule.

(9) Schedule 18 (exceptions) has effect.

III EQU [149.1]

Commencement This section came into force on 5 April 2011.

III EQU [149.2]

Nature of the duty The terms of s 149 are entirely general and apply to the carrying out of any functions of a public authority. It has been held to apply to a housing authority in connection with the taking of possession proceedings and also in the discharge of its duties to the disabled under Part 7 of the Housing Act 1996: *Barnsley Metropolitan Borough Council v Norton* [2011] EWCA Civ 834, (2011) Times, 8 September; *Powell v Dacorum Borough Council* [2019] EWCA Civ 23. See also the need to have regard to statutory equality needs: *R (on the application of Hajrula and Hamza) v London Councils* [2011] EWHC 448 (Admin), [2011] All ER (D) 119 (Apr). The duty applies to decisions to grant outline planning permission under the Town and Country Planning Act 1990: *R (on the application of Buckley) v Bath and North East Somerset Council* [2018] EWHC 1551 (Admin).

On the other hand, the question is whether the duties have been carried out in substance, rather than whether an Equality Impact Assessment ('EIA') has been produced: such an assessment is not conclusive proof that due regard has been given to the statutory equality needs: *R (on the application of Green) v Gloucestershire County Council* [2011] EWHC 268 (Admin), [2011] All ER (D) 111 (Nov). In *R (on the application of Hunt) v North Somerset Council* [2013] EWCA Civ 1320, [2014] LGR 1, [2013] All ER (D) 51 (Nov), the Court of Appeal held that the council had not complied with the s 149 duty where there was insufficient evidence that council members had read the relevant EIA (as opposed to the summary of the EIA). The Supreme Court in that case went on (when considering costs) to hold that this contained a lesson of general application for local authorities regarding the discharge by committee members of the duty: [2015] UKSC 51, [2015] 1 WLR 3575. An argument that s 149 precludes the contracting out of any function subject to that duty was not accepted in *Panayiotou v Waltham Forest London Borough Council* [2017] EWCA Civ 1624, [2017] HLR 48.

III EQU [149.3]

Having 'due regard' Having 'due regard' means the regard that is appropriate in the circumstances and the circumstances include the importance of the areas of life of the members of the disadvantaged group, the extent of the inequality and the need to gather relevant information. Performance of the 'due regard' duty has to be an integral part of the formation of the decision and not merely the justification for the making of the decision: *R (on the application of Coleman) v Barnet London Borough Council* [2012] EWHC 3725 (Admin), [2012] All ER (D) 256 (Dec). The s 149 duty may be discharged through carrying out assessments and consultations carried out pursuant to other duties or powers: *R (on the application of Robson) v Salford City Council* [2015] EWCA Civ 6, [2015] LGR 150, [2015] All ER (D) 150 (Jan). In *R (on the application of Unison) v Lord Chancellor* [2015] EWCA Civ 935, [2016] 1 CMLR 25, [2016] ICR 1, the Court of Appeal held that the Court should only go as far as identifying whether the essential questions had been conscientiously considered and that any conclusions were not irrational. Non-essential errors or misjudgements were not evidence of a breach of the duty. (This aspect of the Court of Appeal's duty was not the subject of appeal to the Supreme Court: [2017] UKSC 51, [2017] 3 WLR 409.)

In *Griffiths v Secretary of State for Justice* [2013] EWHC 4077 (Admin), [2014] All ER (D) 02 (Jan) the High Court found that the Secretary of State for Justice had failed to fulfil his equality duty in respect of the provision of approved premises to accommodate women released from prison on licence. Although the provision in question was not in fact found to be discriminatory the Secretary of State had provided no evidence that he had addressed the possible impacts on women, assessed whether there was a disadvantage, or considered what steps might be taken to mitigate any such disadvantage. The Court of Appeal, (the case now known as *R (on the application of Coll) v Secretary of State for Justice*) [2015] EWCA Civ 328, [2015] 1 WLR 3781), upheld the conclusion on the issue of sex discrimination, but there was no appeal against the finding of a breach of the s 149 duty. This meant when the issue of justification was considered in the Supreme Court, the Ministry was not in a position to show a proportionate means of fulfilling a legitimate aim: [2017] UKSC 40, [2017] 1 WLR 2093.

III EQU [149.4]

Weight and extent of the duty The duty does not require every consequence of a major government policy to be listed. In *R (on the application of Carmichael), R (on the application of Rutherford) v Secretary of State for Work and Pensions* [2016] UKSC 58, [2016] 1 WLR 4550, the fact that the Secretary of State had failed to identify a small specific group which was adversely affected by the scheme in question did not prevent the conclusion that he had complied with the s 149 duty where gender-based discrimination had been addressed (see also at first instance: *R (on the application of A) v Secretary of State for Work and Pensions* [2015] EWHC 159 (Admin), [2015] All ER (D) 255 (Jan) and in the Court of Appeal: *Rutherford v Secretary of State for Work and Pensions* [2016] EWCA Civ 29, [2016] All ER (D) 208 (Jan)).

In *Hotak v Southwark London Borough Council* [2015] UKSC 30, [2016] AC 811 the Supreme Court held that the weight and extent of the equality duty were highly fact sensitive and dependent on individual judgment (in a case concerning the assessment of whether a homeless person was 'vulnerable' for the purposes of the Housing Act 1996, s 189(1)(c)). This was followed in *Hackney London Borough Council v Haque* [2017] EWCA Civ 4, [2017] All ER (D) 68 (Jan) where the Court of Appeal held the aim of the duty was to bring equality duties into the mainstream so they became an essential part of decision making. It required the decision maker to focus sharply on the relevant aspects of the duty where engaged by the contextual facts in a particular case. See also in the same context *Birmingham City Council v Wilson* [2016] EWCA Civ 1137, [2017] HLR 4.

III EQU [149.5]

Homelessness of disabled person On an application to be accepted as homeless because of the inadequacy of the accommodation occupied, the housing authority's decision under s 184 of the Housing Act 1996 is required by s 149(3)(b) and (4) to focus on the particular needs of that person not the generalised needs of others on the housing list: *Lomax v Gosport Borough Council* [2018] EWCA Civ 1846.

III EQU [150]

150. Public authorities and public functions

(1) A public authority is a person who is specified in Schedule 19.

(2) In that Schedule—

Part 1 specifies public authorities generally;

Part 2 specifies relevant Welsh authorities;

Part 3 specifies relevant Scottish authorities.

(3) A public authority specified in Schedule 19 is subject to the duty imposed by section 149(1) in relation to the exercise of all of its functions unless subsection (4) applies.

(4) A public authority specified in that Schedule in respect of certain specified functions is subject to that duty only in respect of the exercise of those functions.

(5) A public function is a function that is a function of a public nature for the purposes of the Human Rights Act 1998.

III EQU [150.1]

Commencement This section was brought fully into force on 5 April 2011.

III EQU [151]

151. Power to specify public authorities

(1) A Minister of the Crown may by order amend Part 1, 2 or 3 of Schedule 19.

(2) The Welsh Ministers may by order amend Part 2 of Schedule 19.

(3) The Scottish Ministers may by order amend Part 3 of Schedule 19.

(4) The power under subsection (1), (2) or (3) may not be exercised so as to—

(a) add an entry to Part 1 relating to a relevant Welsh or Scottish authority or a cross-border Welsh or Scottish authority;

(b) add an entry to Part 2 relating to a person who is not a relevant Welsh authority;

(c) add an entry to Part 3 relating to a person who is not a relevant Scottish authority.

(5) A Minister of the Crown may by order amend Schedule 19 so as to make provision relating to a cross-border Welsh or Scottish authority.

(6) On the first exercise of the power under subsection (5) to add an entry relating to a cross-border Welsh or Scottish authority to Schedule 19, a Minister of the Crown must—

EQUALITY

(a) add a Part 4 to the Schedule for cross-border authorities, and
(b) add the cross-border Welsh or Scottish authority to that Part.

(7) Any subsequent exercise of the power under subsection (5) to add an entry relating to a cross-border Welsh or Scottish authority to Schedule 19 must add that entry to Part 4 of the Schedule.

(8) An order may not be made under this section so as to extend the application of section 149 unless the person making it considers that the extension relates to a person by whom a public function is exercisable.

(9) An order may not be made under this section so as to extend the application of section 149 to—

(a) the exercise of a function referred to in paragraph 3 of Schedule 18 (judicial functions, etc);
(b) a person listed in paragraph 4(2)(a) to (e) of that Schedule (Parliament, devolved legislatures and General Synod);
(c) the exercise of a function listed in paragraph 4(3) of that Schedule (proceedings in Parliament or devolved legislatures).

III EQU [151.1]

Commencement This section came into force on 18 January 2011.

III EQU [152]

152. Power to specify public authorities: consultation

(1) Before making an order under a provision specified in the first column of the Table, a Minister of the Crown must consult the person or persons specified in the second column.

Provision	*Consultees*
Section 151(1)	The Commission
Section 151(1), so far as relating to a relevant Welsh authority	The Welsh Ministers
Section 151(1), so far as relating to a relevant Scottish authority	The Scottish Ministers
Section 151(5)	The Commission
Section 151(5), so far as relating to a cross-border Welsh authority	The Welsh Ministers
Section 151(5), so far as relating to a cross-border Scottish authority	The Scottish Ministers

(2) Before making an order under section 151(2), the Welsh Ministers must consult the Commission, and after making such an order they must inform a Minister of the Crown

(3) Before making an order under section 151(3), the Scottish Ministers must consult the Commission, and after making such an order they must inform a Minister of the Crown

III EQU [152.1]

Commencement This section came into force on 18 January 2011.

III EQU [153]

153. Power to impose specific duties

(1) A Minister of the Crown may by regulations impose duties on a public authority specified in Part 1 of Schedule 19 for the purpose of enabling the better performance by the authority of the duty imposed by section 149(1).

(2) The Welsh Ministers may by regulations impose duties on a public authority specified in Part 2 of Schedule 19 for that purpose.

(3) The Scottish Ministers may by regulations impose duties on a public authority specified in Part 3 of Schedule 19 for that purpose.

(4) Before making regulations under this section, the person making them must consult the Commission.

III EQU [153.1]

Commencement This section came into force on 18 January 2011.

III EQU [153.2]

Specific Duties Regulations The Equality Act 2010 (Specific Duties and Public Authorities) Regulations 2017, SI 2017/353 impose duties on public authorities listed in the Schedules to publish information to demonstrate compliance with s 149(1) and to prepare and publish one or more objectives it thinks it should achieve to do any of the things mentioned in paragraphs (a) to (c) of s 149(1). This replicates the 2011 Regulations; and in addition the 2017 Regulations impose gender pay gap reporting requirements.

III EQU [154]

154. Power to impose specific duties: cross-border authorities

(1) If a Minister of the Crown exercises the power in section 151(5) to add an entry for a public authority to Part 4 of Schedule 19, the Minister must include after the entry a letter specified in the first column of the Table in subsection (3).

(2) Where a letter specified in the first column of the Table in subsection (3) is included after an entry for a public authority in Part 4 of Schedule 19, the person specified in the second column of the Table—

- (a) may by regulations impose duties on the authority for the purpose of enabling the better performance by the authority of the duty imposed by section 149(1), subject to such limitations as are specified in that column;
- (b) must in making the regulations comply with the procedural requirement specified in that column.

(3) This is the Table—

Letter	*Person by whom regulations may be made and procedural requirements*
A	Regulations may be made by a Minister of the Crown in relation to the authority's functions that are not devolved Welsh functions. The Minister of the Crown must consult the Welsh Ministers before making the regulations. Regulations may be made by the Welsh Ministers in relation to the authority's devolved Welsh functions. The Welsh Ministers must inform a Minister of the Crown after making the regulations.
B	Regulations may be made by a Minister of the Crown in relation to the authority's functions that are not devolved Scottish functions. The Minister of the Crown must consult the Scottish Ministers before making the regulations. Regulations may be made by the Scottish Ministers in relation to the authority's devolved Scottish functions. The Scottish Ministers must inform a Minister of the Crown after making the regulations.

EQUALITY

Letter	*Person by whom regulations may be made and procedural requirements*
C	Regulations may be made by a Minister of the Crown in relation to the authority's functions that are neither devolved Welsh functions nor devolved Scottish functions. The Minister of the Crown must consult the Welsh Ministers and the Scottish Ministers before making the regulations. Regulations may be made by the Welsh Ministers in relation to the authority's devolved Welsh functions. The Welsh Ministers must inform a Minister of the Crown after making the regulations. Regulations may be made by the Scottish Ministers in relation to the authority's devolved Scottish functions. The Scottish Ministers must inform a Minister of the Crown after making the regulations.
D	The regulations may be made by a Minister of the Crown. The Minister of the Crown must consult the Welsh Ministers before making the regulations.

(4) Before making regulations under subsection (2), the person making them must consult the Commission.

III EQU [154.1]

Commencement This section came into force on 18 January 2011.

III EQU [155]

155. Power to impose specific duties: supplementary

(1) Regulations under section 153 or 154 may require a public authority to consider such matters as may be specified from time to time by—

- (a) a Minister of the Crown, where the regulations are made by a Minister of the Crown;
- (b) the Welsh Ministers, where the regulations are made by the Welsh Ministers;
- (c) the Scottish Ministers, where the regulations are made by the Scottish Ministers.

(2) Regulations under section 153 or 154 may impose duties on a public authority that is a contracting authority within the meaning of the Public Sector Directive in connection with its public procurement functions.

(3) In subsection (2)—

"public procurement functions" means functions the exercise of which is regulated by the Public Sector Directive;

"the Public Sector Directive" means Directive 2014/24/EU of the European Parliament and of the Council of 26 February 2014 on public procurement and repealing Directive 2004/18/EC, as amended from time to time

(4) Subsections (1) and (2) do not affect the generality of section 153 or 154(2)(a).

(5) A duty imposed on a public authority under section 153 or 154 may be modified or removed by regulations made by—

- (a) a Minister of the Crown, where the original duty was imposed by regulations made by a Minister of the Crown;
- (b) the Welsh Ministers, where the original duty was imposed by regulations made by the Welsh Ministers;
- (c) the Scottish Ministers, where the original duty was imposed by regulations made by the Scottish Ministers.

III EQU [155.1]

Commencement This section came into force on 18 January 2011.

III EQU [156]

156. Enforcement

A failure in respect of a performance of a duty imposed by or under this Chapter does not confer a cause of action at private law.

III EQU [156.1]

Commencement This section came into force on 5 April 2011.

III EQU [157]

157. Interpretation

(1) This section applies for the purposes of this Chapter.

(2) A relevant Welsh authority is a devolved Welsh authority (within the meaning given by section 157A of the Government of Wales Act 2006) other than the Assembly Commission.

(3) A cross-border Welsh authority is a person other than a relevant Welsh authority (or the Assembly Commission) who has any function that—

- (a) is exercisable in or as regards Wales, and
- (b) is a devolved Welsh function.

(4) The Assembly Commission has the same meaning as in the Government of Wales Act 2006.

(5) A function is a devolved Welsh function if—

- (a) it relates to a matter in respect of which functions are exercisable by the Welsh Ministers, the First Minister for Wales or the Counsel General to the Welsh Government, or
- (b) provision conferring the function would be within the legislative competence of the National Assembly for Wales.

(6) A relevant Scottish authority is a public body, public office or holder of a public office—

- (a) which is not a cross-border Scottish authority or the Scottish Parliamentary Corporate Body,
- (b) whose functions are exercisable only in or as regards Scotland, and
- (c) at least some of whose functions do not relate to reserved matters.

(7) A cross-border Scottish authority is a cross-border public authority within the meaning given by section 88(5) of the Scotland Act 1998.

(8) A function is a devolved Scottish function if it—

- (a) is exercisable in or as regards Scotland, and
- (b) does not relate to reserved matters.

(9) Reserved matters has the same meaning as in the Scotland Act 1998.

III EQU [157.1]

Commencement This section came into force on 18 January 2011.

CHAPTER 2 POSITIVE ACTION

III EQU [158]

158. Positive action: general

(1) This section applies if a person (P) reasonably thinks that—

- (a) persons who share a protected characteristic suffer a disadvantage connected to the characteristic,

EQUALITY

(b) persons who share a protected characteristic have needs that are different from the needs of persons who do not share it, or

(c) participation in an activity by persons who share a protected characteristic is disproportionately low.

(2) This Act does not prohibit P from taking any action which is a proportionate means of achieving the aim of—

(a) enabling or encouraging persons who share the protected characteristic to overcome or minimise that disadvantage,

(b) meeting those needs, or

(c) enabling or encouraging persons who share the protected characteristic to participate in that activity.

(3) Regulations may specify action, or descriptions of action, to which subsection (2) does not apply.

(4) This section does not apply to—

(a) action within section 159(3), or

(b) anything that is permitted by virtue of section 104.

(5) If section 104(7) is repealed by virtue of section 105, this section will not apply to anything that would have been so permitted but for the repeal.

(6) This section does not enable P to do anything that is prohibited by or under an enactment other than this Act.

III EQU [158.1]

Commencement This section was brought fully into force on 18 April 2011.

III EQU [159]

159. Positive action: recruitment and promotion

(1) This section applies if a person (P) reasonably thinks that—

(a) persons who share a protected characteristic suffer a disadvantage connected to the characteristic, or

(b) participation in an activity by persons who share a protected characteristic is disproportionately low.

(2) Part 5 (work) does not prohibit P from taking action within subsection (3) with the aim of enabling or encouraging persons who share the protected characteristic to—

(a) overcome or minimise that disadvantage, or

(b) participate in that activity.

(3) That action is treating a person (A) more favourably in connection with recruitment or promotion than another person (B) because A has the protected characteristic but B does not.

(4) But subsection (2) applies only if—

(a) A is as qualified as B to be recruited or promoted,

(b) P does not have a policy of treating persons who share the protected characteristic more favourably in connection with recruitment or promotion than persons who do not share it, and

(c) taking the action in question is a proportionate means of achieving the aim referred to in subsection (2).

(5) "Recruitment" means a process for deciding whether to—

(a) offer employment to a person,

(b) make contract work available to a contract worker,

(c) offer a person a position as a partner in a firm or proposed firm,

(d) offer a person a position as a member of an LLP or proposed LLP,

(e) offer a person a pupillage or tenancy in barristers' chambers,

(f) take a person as an advocate's devil or offer a person membership of an advocate's stable,

(g) offer a person an appointment to a personal office,

(h) offer a person an appointment to a public office, recommend a person for such an appointment or approve a person's appointment to a public office, or

(i) offer a person a service for finding employment.

(6) This section does not enable P to do anything that is prohibited by or under an enactment other than this Act.

III EQU [159.1]

Commencement This section was brought fully into force on 6 April 2011.

PART 12
DISABLED PERSONS: TRANSPORT

III EQU [160]–III EQU [188]

GENERAL NOTE ON PART 12 Part 12 imposes certain public duties in the matter of transport which cannot be enforced in the civil courts except by the public law remedy of judicial review. On the other hand, a failure by a bus or train service or an airline to make reasonable provision for disabled passengers, for example by having wheelchairs available for use, may involve a contravention of Part 3 giving rise to a civil claim. See, for example *Roads v Central Trains Ltd* [2004] EWCA Civ 1541; *Ross v Ryanair Ltd* [2004] EWCA Civ 1751, [2005] 1 WLR 2447, (2005) Times, 11 January; and importantly *Paulley v Firstgroup plc* [2017] UKSC 4, [2017] 1 WLR 423.

PART 13
DISABILITY: MISCELLANEOUS

III EQU [189]

189. Reasonable adjustments

Schedule 21 (reasonable adjustments: supplementary) has effect.

III EQU [190]

190. Improvements to let dwelling houses

(1) This section applies in relation to a lease of a dwelling house if each of the following applies—

(a) the tenancy is not a protected tenancy, a statutory tenancy or a secure tenancy;

(b) the tenant or another person occupying or intending to occupy the premises is a disabled person;

(c) the disabled person occupies or intends to occupy the premises as that person's only or main home;

(d) the tenant is entitled, with the consent of the landlord, to make improvements to the premises;

(e) the tenant applies to the landlord for consent to make a relevant improvement.

(2) Where the tenant applies in writing for the consent—

(a) if the landlord refuses to give consent, the landlord must give the tenant a written statement of the reason why the consent was withheld;

(b) if the landlord neither gives nor refuses to give consent within a reasonable time, consent must be taken to have been unreasonably withheld.

EQUALITY

(3) If the landlord gives consent subject to a condition which is unreasonable, the consent must be taken to have been unreasonably withheld.
(4) If the landlord's consent is unreasonably withheld, it must be taken to have been given.
(5) On any question as to whether—

(a) consent was unreasonably withheld, or
(b) a condition imposed was unreasonable,

it is for the landlord to show that it was not.
(6) If the tenant fails to comply with a reasonable condition imposed by the landlord on the making of a relevant improvement, the failure is to be treated as a breach by the tenant of an obligation of the tenancy.
(7) An improvement to premises is a relevant improvement if, having regard to the disabled person's disability, it is likely to facilitate that person's enjoyment of the premises.
(8) Subsections (2) to (7) apply only in so far as provision of a like nature is not made by the lease.
(9) In this section—

"improvement" means an alteration in or addition to the premises and includes—

(a) an addition to or alteration in the landlord's fittings and fixtures;
(b) an addition or alteration connected with the provision of services to the premises;
(c) the erection of a wireless or television aerial;
(d) carrying out external decoration;

"lease" includes a sub-lease or other tenancy, and "landlord" and "tenant" are to be construed accordingly;
"protected tenancy" has the same meaning as in section 1 of the Rent Act 1977;
"statutory tenancy" is to be construed in accordance with section 2 of that Act;
"secure tenancy" has the same meaning as in section 79 of the Housing Act 1985.

PART 14
GENERAL EXCEPTIONS

III EQU [191]

191. Statutory provisions
Schedule 22 (statutory provisions) has effect.

III EQU [192]

192. National security
A person does not contravene this Act only by doing, for the purpose of safeguarding national security, anything it is proportionate to do for that purpose.

III EQU [193]

193. Charities
(1) A person does not contravene this Act only by restricting the provision of benefits to persons who share a protected characteristic if—

(a) the person acts in pursuance of a charitable instrument, and
(b) the provision of the benefits is within subsection (2).

(2) The provision of benefits is within this subsection if it is—

(a) a proportionate means of achieving a legitimate aim, or
(b) for the purpose of preventing or compensating for a disadvantage linked to the protected characteristic.

(3) It is not a contravention of this Act for—
(a) a person who provides supported employment to treat persons who have the same disability or a disability of a prescribed description more favourably than those who do not have that disability or a disability of such a description in providing such employment;
(b) a Minister of the Crown to agree to arrangements for the provision of supported employment which will, or may, have that effect.

(4) If a charitable instrument enables the provision of benefits to persons of a class defined by reference to colour, it has effect for all purposes as if it enabled the provision of such benefits—
(a) to persons of the class which results if the reference to colour is ignored, or
(b) if the original class is defined by reference only to colour, to persons generally.

(5) It is not a contravention of this Act for a charity to require members, or persons wishing to become members, to make a statement which asserts or implies membership or acceptance of a religion or belief; and for this purpose restricting the access by members to a benefit, facility or service to those who make such a statement is to be treated as imposing such a requirement.

(6) Subsection (5) applies only if—
(a) the charity, or an organisation of which it is part, first imposed such a requirement before 18 May 2005, and
(b) the charity or organisation has not ceased since that date to impose such a requirement.

(7) It is not a contravention of section 29 for a person, in relation to an activity which is carried on for the purpose of promoting or supporting a charity, to restrict participation in the activity to persons of one sex.

(8) A charity regulator does not contravene this Act only by exercising a function in relation to a charity in a manner which the regulator thinks is expedient in the interests of the charity, having regard to the charitable instrument.

(9) Subsection (1) does not apply to a contravention of—
(a) section 39;
(b) section 40;
(c) section 41;
(d) section 55, so far as relating to the provision of vocational training.

(10) Subsection (9) does not apply in relation to disability.

III EQU [193.1]

Charitable instrument In *Hugh-Jones v St John's College, Cambridge* [1979] ICR 848, 123 Sol Jo 603, EAT a university statute making research fellowships available only to men was held to be a charitable instrument and also a relevant statutory provision.

III EQU [194]

194. Charities: supplementary

(1) This section applies for the purposes of section 193.

(2) That section does not apply to race, so far as relating to colour.

(3) "Charity"—
(a) in relation to England and Wales, has the meaning given by section 1(1) of the Charities Act 2011;
(b) in relation to Scotland, means a body entered in the Scottish Charity Register.

(4) "Charitable instrument" means an instrument establishing or governing a charity (including an instrument made or having effect before the commencement of this section).

(5) The charity regulators are—

(a) the Charity Commission for England and Wales;

(b) the Scottish Charity Regulator.

(6) Section 107(5) applies to references in subsection (5) of section 193 to members, or persons wishing to become members, of a charity.

(7) "Supported employment" means facilities provided, or in respect of which payments are made, under section 15 of the Disabled Persons (Employment) Act 1944.

III EQU [195]

195. Sport

(1) A person does not contravene this Act, so far as relating to sex, only by doing anything in relation to the participation of another as a competitor in a gender-affected activity.

(2) A person does not contravene section 29, 33, 34 or 35, so far as relating to gender reassignment, only by doing anything in relation to the participation of a transsexual person as a competitor in a gender-affected activity if it is necessary to do so to secure in relation to the activity—

(a) fair competition, or

(b) the safety of competitors.

(3) A gender-affected activity is a sport, game or other activity of a competitive nature in circumstances in which the physical strength, stamina or physique of average persons of one sex would put them at a disadvantage compared to average persons of the other sex as competitors in events involving the activity.

(4) In considering whether a sport, game or other activity is gender-affected in relation to children, it is appropriate to take account of the age and stage of development of children who are likely to be competitors.

(5) A person who does anything to which subsection (6) applies does not contravene this Act only because of the nationality or place of birth of another or because of the length of time the other has been resident in a particular area or place.

(6) This subsection applies to—

(a) selecting one or more persons to represent a country, place or area or a related association, in a sport or game or other activity of a competitive nature;

(b) doing anything in pursuance of the rules of a competition so far as relating to eligibility to compete in a sport or game or other such activity.

(7) A person does not contravene this Act, so far as relating to age discrimination, only by doing anything in relation to the participation of another as a competitor in an age-banded activity if it is necessary to do so—

(a) to secure in relation to the activity fair competition or the safety of competitors,

(b) to comply with the rules of a national or international competition, or

(c) to increase participation in that activity.

(8) For the purposes of subsection (7), an age-banded activity is a sport, game or other activity of a competitive nature in circumstances in which the physical or mental strength, agility, stamina, physique, mobility, maturity or manual dexterity of average persons of a particular age group would put them at a disadvantage compared to average persons of another age group as competitors in events involving the activity.

III EQU [196]

196. General

Schedule 23 (general exceptions) has effect.

III EQU [197]

197. Age

(1) A Minister of the Crown may by order amend this Act to provide that any of the following does not contravene this Act so far as relating to age—

(a) specified conduct;
(b) anything done for a specified purpose;
(c) anything done in pursuance of arrangements of a specified description.

(2) Specified conduct is conduct—

(a) of a specified description,
(b) carried out in specified circumstances, or
(c) by or in relation to a person of a specified description.

(3) An order under this section may—

(a) confer on a Minister of the Crown or the Treasury a power to issue guidance about the operation of the order (including, in particular, guidance about the steps that may be taken by persons wishing to rely on an exception provided for by the order);
(b) require the Minister or the Treasury to carry out consultation before issuing guidance under a power conferred by virtue of paragraph (a);
(c) make provision (including provision to impose a requirement) that refers to guidance issued under a power conferred by virtue of paragraph (a).

(4) Guidance given by a Minister of the Crown or the Treasury in anticipation of the making of an order under this section is, on the making of the order, to be treated as if it has been issued in accordance with the order.

(5) For the purposes of satisfying a requirement imposed by virtue of subsection (3)(b), the Minister or the Treasury may rely on consultation carried out before the making of the order that imposes the requirement (including consultation carried out before the commencement of this section).

(6) Provision by virtue of subsection (3)(c) may, in particular, refer to provisions of the guidance that themselves refer to a document specified in the guidance.

(7) Guidance issued (or treated as issued) under a power conferred by virtue of subsection (3)(a) comes into force on such day as the person who issues the guidance may by order appoint; and an order under this subsection may include the text of the guidance or of extracts from it.

(8) This section is not affected by any provision of this Act which makes special provision in relation to age.

(9) The references to this Act in subsection (1) do not include references to—

(a) Part 5 (work);
(b) Chapter 2 of Part 6 (further and higher education).

III EQU [197.1]

Commencement This section was brought into force by the Equality Act 2010 (Commencement No 9) Order 2012/1569, art 2 with effect from 19 June 2012. Schedules 22 and 23 insofar as they apply to the protected characteristic of age were brought into force on 1 October 2012 (see art 3 of SI 2012/1569). Sections 191 to 196 were brought fully into force on 1 October 2010 by SI 2010/2317.

III EQU [198]–III EQU [201]

GENERAL NOTE ON PART 15: FAMILY PROPERTY The provisions of Part 15 amend or remove perceived inequalities in family law as it applies to family property such as the presumption of advancement and the common law duty of a husband to maintain his wife.

PART 16
GENERAL AND MISCELLANEOUS

CIVIL PARTNERSHIPS

III EQU [202]

202. Civil partnerships on religious premises

(1) The Civil Partnership Act 2004 is amended as follows.

(2) Omit section 6(1)(b) and (2) (prohibition on use of religious premises for registration of civil partnership).

(3) In section 6A (power to approve premises for registration of civil partnership), after subsection (2), insert—

"(2A) Regulations under this section may provide that premises approved for the registration of civil partnerships may differ from those premises approved for the registration of civil marriages.

(2B) Provision by virtue of subsection (2)(b) may, in particular, provide that applications for approval of premises may only be made with the consent (whether general or specific) of a person specified, or a person of a description specified, in the provision.

(2C) The power conferred by section 258(2), in its application to the power conferred by this section, includes in particular—

(a) power to make provision in relation to religious premises that differs from provision in relation to other premises;

(b) power to make different provision for different kinds of religious premises."

(4) In that section, after subsection (3), insert—

"(3A) For the avoidance of doubt, nothing in this Act places an obligation on religious organisations to host civil partnerships if they do not wish to do so.

(3B) "Civil marriage" means marriage solemnised otherwise than according to the rites of the Church of England or any other religious usages.

(3C) "Religious premises" means premises which—

(a) are used solely or mainly for religious purposes, or

(b) have been so used and have not subsequently been used solely or mainly for other purposes."

III EQU [202.1]

Commencement This section was brought into force by 5 December 2011.

EU OBLIGATIONS

III EQU [203]

203. Harmonisation

(1) This section applies if—

(a) there is an EU obligation of the United Kingdom which a Minister of the Crown thinks relates to the subject matter of the Equality Acts,

(b) the obligation is to be implemented by the exercise of the power under section 2(2) of the European Communities Act 1972 (the implementing power), and

(c) the Minister thinks that it is appropriate to make harmonising provision in the Equality Acts.

(2) The Minister may by order make the harmonising provision.

(3) If the Minister proposes to make an order under this section, the Minister must consult persons and organisations the Minister thinks are likely to be affected by the harmonising provision.

(4) If, as a result of the consultation under subsection (3), the Minister thinks it appropriate to change the whole or part of the proposal, the Minister must carry out such further consultation with respect to the changes as the Minister thinks appropriate.

(5) The Equality Acts are the Equality Act 2006 and this Act.

(6) Harmonising provision is provision made in relation to relevant subject matter of the Equality Acts—

- (a) which corresponds to the implementing provision, or
- (b) which the Minister thinks is necessary or expedient in consequence of or related to provision made in pursuance of paragraph (a) or the implementing provision.

(7) The implementing provision is provision made or to be made in exercise of the implementing power in relation to so much of the subject matter of the Equality Acts as implements an EU obligation.

(8) Relevant subject matter of the Equality Acts is so much of the subject matter of those Acts as does not implement an EU obligation.

(9) A harmonising provision may amend a provision of the Equality Acts.

(10) The reference to this Act does not include a reference to this section or Schedule 24 or to a provision specified in that Schedule.

(11) A Minister of the Crown must report to Parliament on the exercise of the power under subsection (2)—

- (a) at the end of the period of 2 years starting on the day this section comes into force;
- (b) at the end of each succeeding period of 2 years.

III EQU [204]

204. Harmonisation: procedure

(1) If, after the conclusion of the consultation required under section 203, the Minister thinks it appropriate to proceed with the making of an order under that section, the Minister must lay before Parliament—

- (a) a draft of a statutory instrument containing the order, together with
- (b) an explanatory document.

(2) The explanatory document must—

- (a) introduce and give reasons for the harmonising provision;
- (b) explain why the Minister thinks that the conditions in subsection (1) of section 203 are satisfied;
- (c) give details of the consultation carried out under that section;
- (d) give details of the representations received as a result of the consultation;
- (e) give details of such changes as were made as a result of the representations.

(3) Where a person making representations in response to the consultation has requested the Minister not to disclose them, the Minister must not disclose them under subsection (2)(d) if, or to the extent that, to do so would (disregarding any connection with proceedings in Parliament) constitute an actionable breach of confidence.

(4) If information in representations made by a person in response to consultation under section 203 relates to another person, the Minister need not disclose the information under subsection (2)(d) if or to the extent that—

- (a) the Minister thinks that the disclosure of information could adversely affect the interests of that other person, and
- (b) the Minister has been unable to obtain the consent of that other person to the disclosure.

(5) The Minister may not act under subsection (1) before the end of the period of 12 weeks beginning with the day on which the consultation under section 203(3) begins.

(6) Laying a draft of a statutory instrument in accordance with subsection (1) satisfies the condition as to laying imposed by subsection (8) of section 208, in so far as that subsection applies in relation to orders under section 203.

Application

III EQU [205]

205. Crown application

(1) The following provisions of this Act bind the Crown—

- (a) Part 1 (public sector duty regarding socio-economic inequalities);
- (b) Part 3 (services and public functions), so far as relating to the exercise of public functions;
- (c) Chapter 1 of Part 11 (public sector equality duty).

(2) Part 5 (work) binds the Crown as provided for by that Part.

(3) The remainder of this Act applies to Crown acts as it applies to acts done by a private person.

(4) For the purposes of subsection (3), an act is a Crown act if (and only if) it is done—

- (a) by or on behalf of a member of the executive,
- (b) by a statutory body acting on behalf of the Crown, or
- (c) by or on behalf of the holder of a statutory office acting on behalf of the Crown.

(5) A statutory body or office is a body or office established by an enactment.

(6) The provisions of Parts 2 to 4 of the Crown Proceedings Act 1947 apply to proceedings against the Crown under this Act as they apply to proceedings in England and Wales which, as a result of section 23 of that Act, are treated for the purposes of Part 2 of that Act as civil proceedings by or against the Crown.

(7) The provisions of Part 5 of that Act apply to proceedings against the Crown under this Act as they apply to proceedings in Scotland which, as a result of that Part, are treated as civil proceedings by or against the Crown.

(8) But the proviso to section 44 of that Act (removal of proceedings from the sheriff to the Court of Session) does not apply to proceedings under this Act.

III EQU [206]

206. Information society services

Schedule 25 (information society services) has effect.

III EQU [206.1]

Commencement This section came into force on 1 October 2010.

Subordinate legislation

III EQU [207]

207. Exercise of power

(1) A power to make an order or regulations under this Act is exercisable by a Minister of the Crown, unless there is express provision to the contrary.

(2) Orders, regulations or rules under this Act must be made by statutory instrument.

(3) Subsection (2) does not apply to—

(a) a transitional exemption order under Part 1 of Schedule 11,
(b) a transitional exemption order under Part 1 of Schedule 12, or
(c) an order under paragraph 1(3) of Schedule 14 that does not modify an enactment.

(4) Orders or regulations under this Act—
(a) may make different provision for different purposes;
(b) may include consequential, incidental, supplementary, transitional, transitory or saving provision.

(5) Nothing in section 163(4), 174(4), 181A(5), 181B(6) or 182(3) affects the generality of the power under subsection (4)(a).

(6) The power under subsection (4)(b), in its application to section 37, 139A, 153, 154(2), 155(5), 197 or 216 or to paragraph 7(1) of Schedule 11 or paragraph 1(3) or 2(3) of Schedule 14, includes power to amend an enactment (including, in the case of section 139A, 197 or 216, this Act).

(7) In the case of section 216 (commencement), provision by virtue of subsection (4)(b) may be included in a separate order from the order that provides for the commencement to which the provision relates; and, for that purpose, it does not matter—
(a) whether the order providing for the commencement includes provision by virtue of subsection (4)(b);
(b) whether the commencement has taken place.

(8) A statutory instrument containing an Order in Council under section 82 (offshore work) is subject to annulment in pursuance of a resolution of either House of Parliament.

III EQU [208]

208. Ministers of the Crown, etc

(1) This section applies where the power to make an order or regulations under this Act is exercisable by a Minister of the Crown or the Treasury.

(2) A statutory instrument containing (whether alone or with other provision) an order or regulations that amend this Act or another Act of Parliament, or an Act of the Scottish Parliament or an Act or Measure of the National Assembly for Wales, is subject to the affirmative procedure.

(3) But a statutory instrument is not subject to the affirmative procedure by virtue of subsection (2) merely because it contains—
(a) an order under section 59 (local authority functions);
(b) an order under section 151 (power to amend list of public authorities for the purposes of the public sector equality duty) that provides for the omission of an entry where the authority concerned has ceased to exist or the variation of an entry where the authority concerned has changed its name;
(c) an order under paragraph 1(3) of Schedule 14 (educational charities and endowments) that modifies an enactment.

(4) A statutory instrument containing (whether alone or with other provision) an order or regulations mentioned in subsection (5) is subject to the affirmative procedure.

(5) The orders and regulations referred to in subsection (4) are—
(a) regulations under section 30 (services: ships and hovercraft);
(b) regulations under section 78 (gender pay gap information);
(c) regulations under section 81 (work: ships and hovercraft);
(d) an order under section 105 (election candidates: expiry of provision);
(e) regulations under section 106 (election candidates: diversity information);
(ea) regulations under section 139A (equal pay audits);

(f) regulations under section 153 or 154(2) (public sector equality duty: powers to impose specific duties);
(fa) regulations under section 181A or 181B (information for bus passengers);
(g) . . .
(h) an order under section 203 (EU obligations: harmonisation);
(i) regulations under paragraph 9(3) of Schedule 20 (rail vehicle accessibility: determination of turnover for purposes of penalties).

(6) A statutory instrument that is not subject to the affirmative procedure by virtue of subsection (2) or (4) is subject to the negative procedure.

(7) But a statutory instrument is not subject to the negative procedure by virtue of subsection (6) merely because it contains—

(a) . . .
(b) an order under section 216 (commencement) that—
  (i) does not amend an Act of Parliament, an Act of the Scottish Parliament or an Act or Measure of the National Assembly for Wales, and
  (ii) is not made in reliance on section 207(7).

(8) If a statutory instrument is subject to the affirmative procedure, the order or regulations contained in it must not be made unless a draft of the instrument is laid before and approved by a resolution of each House of Parliament.

(9) If a statutory instrument is subject to the negative procedure, it is subject to annulment in pursuance of a resolution of either House of Parliament.

(10) If a draft of a statutory instrument containing an order or regulations under section 2, 151, 153, 154(2) or 155(5) would, apart from this subsection, be treated for the purposes of the Standing Orders of either House of Parliament as a hybrid instrument, it is to proceed in that House as if it were not a hybrid instrument.

III EQU [209]

209. The Welsh Ministers

(1) This section applies where the power to make an order or regulations under this Act is exercisable by the Welsh Ministers.

(2) A statutory instrument containing (whether alone or with other provision) an order or regulations mentioned in subsection (3) is subject to the affirmative procedure.

(3) The orders and regulations referred to in subsection (2) are—

(a) regulations under section 2 (socio-economic inequalities);
(b) an order under section 151 (power to amend list of public authorities for the purposes of the public sector equality duty);
(c) regulations under section 153 or 154(2) (public sector equality duty: powers to impose specific duties);
(d) regulations under section 155(5) that amend an Act of Parliament or an Act or Measure of the National Assembly for Wales (public sector equality duty: power to modify or remove specific duties);
[(e) regulations under paragraph 6, 6A or 6F of Schedule 17 (tribunal procedure, case friends and capacity of parents and persons over compulsory school age)].

(4) But a statutory instrument is not subject to the affirmative procedure by virtue of subsection (2) merely because it contains an order under section 151 that provides for—

(a) the omission of an entry where the authority concerned has ceased to exist, or
(b) the variation of an entry where the authority concerned has changed its name.

(5) A statutory instrument that is not subject to the affirmative procedure by virtue of subsection (2) is subject to the negative procedure.

(6) If a statutory instrument is subject to the affirmative procedure, the order or regulations contained in it must not be made unless a draft of the instrument is laid before and approved by a resolution of the National Assembly for Wales.

(7) If a statutory instrument is subject to the negative procedure, it is subject to annulment in pursuance of a resolution of the National Assembly for Wales.

Amendment *Sub-section (3)(e) is inserted by the Additional Learning Needs and Education Tribunal (Wales) Act 2018 with effect from a date to be appointed.*

III EQU [210]

210. The Scottish Ministers

(1) This section applies where the power to make an order, regulations or rules under this Act is exercisable by the Scottish Ministers.

(2) A statutory instrument containing (whether alone or with other provision) an order or regulations mentioned in subsection (3) is subject to the affirmative procedure.

(3) The orders and regulations referred to in subsection (2) are—

- (a) regulations under section 2 (socio-economic inequalities);
- (b) regulations under section 37 (power to make provision about adjustments to common parts in Scotland);
- (c) an order under section 151 (power to amend list of public authorities for the purposes of the public sector equality duty);
- (d) regulations under section 153 or 154(2) (public sector equality duty: powers to impose specific duties);
- (e) regulations under section 155(5) that amend an Act of Parliament or an Act of the Scottish Parliament (public sector equality duty: power to modify or remove specific duties).

(4) But a statutory instrument is not subject to the affirmative procedure by virtue of subsection (2) merely because it contains an order under section 151 that provides for—

- (a) the omission of an entry where the authority concerned has ceased to exist, or
- (b) the variation of an entry where the authority concerned has changed its name.

(5) A statutory instrument that is not subject to the affirmative procedure by virtue of subsection (2) is subject to the negative procedure.

(6) If a statutory instrument is subject to the affirmative procedure, the order or regulations contained in it must not be made unless a draft of the instrument is laid before and approved by a resolution of the Scottish Parliament.

(7) If a statutory instrument is subject to the negative procedure, it is subject to annulment in pursuance of a resolution of the Scottish Parliament.

AMENDMENTS, ETC

III EQU [211]

211. Amendments, repeals and revocations

(1) Schedule 26 (amendments) has effect.

(2) Schedule 27 (repeals and revocations) has effect.

III EQU [211.1]

Schedules 26 and 27 The text of these Schedules has not been included. The broad effect of Schedule 27 is to identify and repeal all the pre-existing law that this Act replaces.

EQUALITY

INTERPRETATION

III EQU [212]

212. General interpretation

(1) In this Act—

"armed forces" means any of the naval, military or air forces of the Crown;

"the Commission" means the Commission for Equality and Human Rights;

"detriment" does not, subject to subsection (5), include conduct which amounts to harassment;

"the Education Acts" has the meaning given in section 578 of the Education Act 1996;

"employment" and related expressions are (subject to subsection (11)) to be read with section 83;

"enactment" means an enactment contained in—

(a) an Act of Parliament,

(b) an Act of the Scottish Parliament,

(c) an Act or Measure of the National Assembly for Wales, or

(d) subordinate legislation;

"equality clause" means a sex equality clause or maternity equality clause;

"equality rule" means a sex equality rule or maternity equality rule;

"man" means a male of any age;

"maternity equality clause" has the meaning given in section 73;

"maternity equality rule" has the meaning given in section 75;

"non-discrimination rule" has the meaning given in section 61;

"occupational pension scheme" has the meaning given in section 1 of the Pension Schemes Act 1993;

"parent" has the same meaning as in—

(a) the Education Act 1996 (in relation to England and Wales);

(b) the Education (Scotland) Act 1980 (in relation to Scotland);

"prescribed" means prescribed by regulations;

"profession" includes a vocation or occupation;

"sex equality clause" has the meaning given in section 66;

"sex equality rule" has the meaning given in section 67;

"subordinate legislation" means—

(a) subordinate legislation within the meaning of the Interpretation Act 1978, or

(b) an instrument made under an Act of the Scottish Parliament or an Act or Measure of the National Assembly for Wales;

"substantial" means more than minor or trivial;

"trade" includes any business;

"woman" means a female of any age.

(2) A reference (however expressed) to an act includes a reference to an omission.

(3) A reference (however expressed) to an omission includes (unless there is express provision to the contrary) a reference to—

(a) a deliberate omission to do something;

(b) a refusal to do it;

(c) a failure to do it.

(4) A reference (however expressed) to providing or affording access to a benefit, facility or service includes a reference to facilitating access to the benefit, facility or service.

(5) Where this Act disapplies a prohibition on harassment in relation to a specified protected characteristic, the disapplication does not prevent conduct relating to that characteristic from amounting to a detriment for the purposes of discrimination within section 13 because of that characteristic.

(6) A reference to occupation, in relation to premises, is a reference to lawful occupation.

(7) The following are members of the executive—

(a) a Minister of the Crown;

(b) a government department;

(c) the Welsh Ministers, the First Minister for Wales or the Counsel General to the Welsh Government;

(d) any part of the Scottish Administration.

(8) A reference to a breach of an equality clause or rule is a reference to a breach of a term modified by, or included by virtue of, an equality clause or rule.

(9) A reference to a contravention of this Act does not include a reference to a breach of an equality clause or rule, unless there is express provision to the contrary.

(10) "Member", in relation to an occupational pension scheme, means an active member, a deferred member or a pensioner member (within the meaning, in each case, given by section 124 of the Pensions Act 1995).

(11) "Employer", "deferred member", "pension credit member", "pensionable service", "pensioner member" and "trustees or managers" each have, in relation to an occupational pension scheme, the meaning given by section 124 of the Pensions Act 1995.

(12) A reference to the accrual of rights under an occupational pension scheme is to be construed in accordance with that section.

(13) Nothing in section 28, 32, 84, 90, 95 or 100 is to be regarded as an express exception.

III EQU [213]

213. References to maternity leave, etc

(1) This section applies for the purposes of this Act.

(2) A reference to a woman on maternity leave is a reference to a woman on—

(a) compulsory maternity leave,

(b) ordinary maternity leave, or

(c) additional maternity leave.

(3) A reference to a woman on compulsory maternity leave is a reference to a woman absent from work because she satisfies the conditions prescribed for the purposes of section 72(1) of the Employment Rights Act 1996.

(4) A reference to a woman on ordinary maternity leave is a reference to a woman absent from work because she is exercising the right to ordinary maternity leave.

(5) A reference to the right to ordinary maternity leave is a reference to the right conferred by section 71(1) of the Employment Rights Act 1996.

(6) A reference to a woman on additional maternity leave is a reference to a woman absent from work because she is exercising the right to additional maternity leave.

(7) A reference to the right to additional maternity leave is a reference to the right conferred by section 73(1) of the Employment Rights Act 1996.

(8) "Additional maternity leave period" has the meaning given in section 73(2) of that Act.

III EQU [214]

214. Index of defined expressions

Schedule 28 lists the places where expressions used in this Act are defined or otherwise explained.

FINAL PROVISIONS

III EQU [215]

215. Money

There is to be paid out of money provided by Parliament any increase attributable to this Act in the expenses of a Minister of the Crown.

III EQU [216]

216. Commencement

(1) The following provisions come into force on the day on which this Act is passed—

(a) section 186(2) (rail vehicle accessibility: compliance);

(b) this Part (except sections 202 (civil partnerships on religious premises), 206 (information society services) and 211 (amendments, etc)).

(2) Part 15 (family property) comes into force on such day as the Lord Chancellor may by order appoint.

(3) Subject to subsections (4) and (6), the other provisions of this Act come into force on such day as a Minister of the Crown may by order appoint.

(4) The following provisions of Part 1 (socio-economic inequalities) come into force on such day as the Scottish Ministers may by order appoint—

(a) section 1, so far as it applies to a relevant authority as defined by section 2(5);

(b) section 2, so far as it confers a power on the Scottish Ministers;

(c) section 3, for the purposes of section 1 to the extent mentioned in paragraph (a).

(5) The following do not apply to an order under subsection (4)—

(a) section 207(2) (see instead section 27 of the Interpretation and Legislative Reform (Scotland) Act 2010: powers exercisable by Scottish statutory instrument), and

(b) section 210.

(6) The following provisions of Part 1 come into force on such day as the Welsh Ministers may by order appoint—

(a) section 1, so far as it applies to a relevant authority as defined by section 2(6);

(b) section 2, so far as it confers a power on the Welsh Ministers;

(c) section 3, for the purposes of section 1 to the extent mentioned in paragraph (a).

(7) Section 209 does not apply to an order under subsection (6).

III EQU [216.1]

Provisions commencing on the passing of the Act The whole of this Part came into force on 8 April 2010 except for s 202, which was brought into force by SI 2011/2646 by 5 December 2011, and s 206, which was brought into force on 1 October 2010 by the No 4 Commencement Order, SI 2010/2317.

III EQU [216.2]

Commencement orders The most important commencement order to date is the No 4 Order 2010, SI 2010/2317 which brings into force almost the whole of the Act and repeals the pre-existing law with effect from 1 October 2010, but with consequential transitional, transitory and incidental provisions in respect of the change over and pending cases.

III EQU [217]

217. Extent

(1) This Act forms part of the law of England and Wales.

(2) This Act, apart from section 190 (improvements to let dwelling houses) and Part 15 (family property), forms part of the law of Scotland.

(3) Each of the following also forms part of the law of Northern Ireland—

(a) section 82 (offshore work);

(b) section 105(3) and (4) (expiry of Sex Discrimination (Election Candidates) Act 2002);

(c) section 199 (abolition of presumption of advancement).

III EQU [218]

218. Short title

This Act may be cited as the Equality Act 2010.

SCHEDULE 1
DISABILITY: SUPPLEMENTARY PROVISION

Section 6

PART 1
DETERMINATION OF DISABILITY

IMPAIRMENT

III EQU [219]

1 Regulations may make provision for a condition of a prescribed description to be, or not to be, an impairment.

LONG-TERM EFFECTS

2 (1) The effect of an impairment is long-term if—

(a) it has lasted for at least 12 months,

(b) it is likely to last for at least 12 months, or

(c) it is likely to last for the rest of the life of the person affected.

(2) If an impairment ceases to have a substantial adverse effect on a person's ability to carry out normal day-to-day activities, it is to be treated as continuing to have that effect if that effect is likely to recur.

(3) For the purposes of sub-paragraph (2), the likelihood of an effect recurring is to be disregarded in such circumstances as may be prescribed.

(4) Regulations may prescribe circumstances in which, despite sub-paragraph (1), an effect is to be treated as being, or as not being, long-term.

SEVERE DISFIGUREMENT

3 (1) An impairment which consists of a severe disfigurement is to be treated as having a substantial adverse effect on the ability of the person concerned to carry out normal day-to-day activities.

(2) Regulations may provide that in prescribed circumstances a severe disfigurement is not to be treated as having that effect.
(3) The regulations may, in particular, make provision in relation to deliberately acquired disfigurement.

Substantial adverse effects

4 Regulations may make provision for an effect of a prescribed description on the ability of a person to carry out normal day-to-day activities to be treated as being, or as not being, a substantial adverse effect.

Effect of medical treatment

5 (1) An impairment is to be treated as having a substantial adverse effect on the ability of the person concerned to carry out normal day-to-day activities if—
(a) measures are being taken to treat or correct it, and
(b) but for that, it would be likely to have that effect.
(2) "Measures" includes, in particular, medical treatment and the use of a prosthesis or other aid.
(3) Sub-paragraph (1) does not apply—
(a) in relation to the impairment of a person's sight, to the extent that the impairment is, in the person's case, correctable by spectacles or contact lenses or in such other ways as may be prescribed;
(b) in relation to such other impairments as may be prescribed, in such circumstances as are prescribed.

Certain medical conditions

6 (1) Cancer, HIV infection and multiple sclerosis are each a disability.
(2) HIV infection is infection by a virus capable of causing the Acquired Immune Deficiency Syndrome.

Deemed disability

7 (1) Regulations may provide for persons of prescribed descriptions to be treated as having disabilities.
(2) The regulations may prescribe circumstances in which a person who has a disability is to be treated as no longer having the disability.
(3) This paragraph does not affect the other provisions of this Schedule.

Progressive conditions

8 (1) This paragraph applies to a person (P) if—
(a) P has a progressive condition,
(b) as a result of that condition P has an impairment which has (or had) an effect on P's ability to carry out normal day-to-day activities, but
(c) the effect is not (or was not) a substantial adverse effect.
(2) P is to be taken to have an impairment which has a substantial adverse effect if the condition is likely to result in P having such an impairment.
(3) Regulations may make provision for a condition of a prescribed description to be treated as being, or as not being, progressive.

Past disabilities

9 (1) A question as to whether a person had a disability at a particular time ("the relevant time") is to be determined, for the purposes of section 6, as if the

provisions of, or made under, this Act were in force when the act complained of was done had been in force at the relevant time.

(2) The relevant time may be a time before the coming into force of the provision of this Act to which the question relates.

PART 2
GUIDANCE

Preliminary

10 This Part of this Schedule applies in relation to guidance referred to in section 6(5).

Examples

11 The guidance may give examples of—

(a) effects which it would, or would not, be reasonable, in relation to particular activities, to regard as substantial adverse effects;

(b) substantial adverse effects which it would, or would not, be reasonable to regard as long-term.

Adjudicating bodies

12 (1) In determining whether a person is a disabled person, an adjudicating body must take account of such guidance as it thinks is relevant.

(2) An adjudicating body is—

(a) a court;

(b) a tribunal;

(c) a person (other than a court or tribunal) who may decide a claim relating to a contravention of Part 6 (education).

Representations

13 Before issuing the guidance, the Minister must—

(a) publish a draft of it;

(b) consider any representations made to the Minister about the draft;

(c) make such modifications as the Minister thinks appropriate in the light of the representations.

Parliamentary procedure

14 (1) If the Minister decides to proceed with proposed guidance, a draft of it must be laid before Parliament.

(2) If, before the end of the 40-day period, either House resolves not to approve the draft, the Minister must take no further steps in relation to the proposed guidance.

(3) If no such resolution is made before the end of that period, the Minister must issue the guidance in the form of the draft.

(4) Sub-paragraph (2) does not prevent a new draft of proposed guidance being laid before Parliament.

(5) The 40-day period—

(a) begins on the date on which the draft is laid before both Houses (or, if laid before each House on a different date, on the later date);

(b) does not include a period during which Parliament is prorogued or dissolved;

EQUALITY

(c) does not include a period during which both Houses are adjourned for more than 4 days.

Commencement

15 The guidance comes into force on the day appointed by order by the Minister.

Revision and revocation

16 (1) The Minister may—
(a) revise the whole or part of guidance and re-issue it;
(b) by order revoke guidance.
(2) A reference to guidance includes a reference to guidance which has been revised and re-issued.

III EQU [219.1]

Regulations For the purposes of paragraph 3, tattoos and piercings are excluded from the concept of "severe disfigurement" by the Equality Act 2010 (Disability) Regulations 2010, SI 2010/2128, reg 5.

III EQU [219.2]

Ability to carry out normal day to day activities The court or tribunal should focus on what the disabled person cannot do, not on what he or she can do: *Goodwin v Patent Office* [1999] ICR 302, [1999] IRLR 4, EAT. The role of guidance is to guide on marginal cases and the omission to refer to obvious day to day activities, like chopping vegetables and ironing did not mean that such activities were irrelevant: *Vicary v British Telecommunications plc* [1999] IRLR 680, EAT. The fact that the percentage of the population who engage in such activities as putting their hair in rollers and applying make-up is small does not preclude such activities being "day to day activities": *Ekpe v Metropolitan Police Comr* [2001] IRLR 605, EAT. The existence of a disability should be established on the basis of evidence available to the alleged discriminator at the time: *McDougall v Richmond Adult Community College* [2008] EWCA Civ 4, [2008] ICR 431, [2008] IRLR 227 (an employment case).

III EQU [219.3]

Effect of medical treatment A claimant whose contention turns on the effect of treatment should bring medical evidence in support: *Woodrup v Southwark London Borough Council* [2002] EWCA Civ 1716, [2003] IRLR 111.

SCHEDULE 2
SERVICES AND PUBLIC FUNCTIONS: REASONABLE ADJUSTMENTS

Section 31

Preliminary

III EQU [220]

1 This Schedule applies where a duty to make reasonable adjustments is imposed on A by this Part.

The duty

2 (1) A must comply with the first, second and third requirements.
(2) For the purposes of this paragraph, the reference in section 20(3), (4) or (5) to a disabled person is to disabled persons generally.
(3) Section 20 has effect as if, in subsection (4), for "to avoid the disadvantage" there were substituted—
"(a) to avoid the disadvantage, or

(b) to adopt a reasonable alternative method of providing the service or exercising the function."

(4) In relation to each requirement, the relevant matter is the provision of the service, or the exercise of the function, by A.

(5) Being placed at a substantial disadvantage in relation to the exercise of a function means—

(a) if a benefit is or may be conferred in the exercise of the function, being placed at a substantial disadvantage in relation to the conferment of the benefit, or

(b) if a person is or may be subjected to a detriment in the exercise of the function, suffering an unreasonably adverse experience when being subjected to the detriment.

(6) In relation to the second requirement, a physical feature includes a physical feature brought by or on behalf of A, in the course of providing the service or exercising the function, on to premises other than those that A occupies (as well as including a physical feature in or on premises that A occupies).

(7) If A is a service-provider, nothing in this paragraph requires A to take a step which would fundamentally alter—

(a) the nature of the service, or

(b) the nature of A's trade or profession.

(8) If A exercises a public function, nothing in this paragraph requires A to take a step which A has no power to take.

SPECIAL PROVISION ABOUT TRANSPORT

3 (1) This paragraph applies where A is concerned with the provision of a service which involves transporting people by land, air or water.

(2) It is never reasonable for A to have to take a step which would—

(a) involve the alteration or removal of a physical feature of a vehicle used in providing the service;

(b) affect whether vehicles are provided;

(c) affect what vehicles are provided;

(d) affect what happens in the vehicle while someone is travelling in it.

(3) But, for the purpose of complying with the first or third requirement, A may not rely on sub-paragraph (2)(b), (c) or (d) if the vehicle concerned is—

(a) a hire-vehicle designed and constructed for the carriage of passengers, comprising more than 8 seats in addition to the driver's seat and having a maximum mass not exceeding 5 tonnes,

(b) a hire-vehicle designed and constructed for the carriage of goods and having a maximum mass not exceeding 3.5 tonnes,

(c) a vehicle licensed under section 48 of the Local Government (Miscellaneous Provisions) Act 1976 or section 7 of the Private Hire Vehicles (London) Act 1998 (or under a provision of a local Act corresponding to either of those provisions),

(d) a private hire car (within the meaning of section 23 of the Civic Government (Scotland) Act 1982),

(e) a public service vehicle (within the meaning given by section 1 of the Public Passenger Vehicles Act 1981),

(f) a vehicle built or adapted to carry passengers on a railway or tramway (within the meaning, in each case, of the Transport and Works Act 1992),

(g) a taxi,

(h) a vehicle deployed to transport the driver and passengers of a vehicle that has broken down or is involved in an accident, or

(i) a vehicle deployed on a system using a mode of guided transport (within the meaning of the Transport and Works Act 1992).

(4) In so far as the second requirement requires A to adopt a reasonable alternative method of providing the service to disabled persons, A may not, for the purpose of complying with the requirement, rely on sub-paragraph (2)(b), (c) or (d) if the vehicle is within sub-paragraph (3)(h).

(5) A may not, for the purpose of complying with the first, second or third requirement rely on sub-paragraph (2) of this paragraph if A provides the service by way of a hire-vehicle built to carry no more than 8 passengers.

(6) For the purposes of sub-paragraph (5) in its application to the second requirement, a part of a vehicle is to be regarded as a physical feature if it requires alteration in order to facilitate the provision of—

- (a) hand controls to enable a disabled person to operate braking and accelerator systems in the vehicle, or
- (b) facilities for the stowage of a wheelchair.

(7) For the purposes of sub-paragraph (6)(a), fixed seating and in-built electrical systems are not physical features; and for the purposes of sub-paragraph (6)(b), fixed seating is not a physical feature.

(8) In the case of a vehicle within sub-paragraph (3), a relevant device is not an auxiliary aid for the purposes of the third requirement.

(9) A relevant device is a device or structure, or equipment, the installation, operation or maintenance of which would necessitate making a permanent alteration to, or which would have a permanent effect on, the internal or external fabric of the vehicle.

(10) Regulations may amend this paragraph so as to provide for sub-paragraph (2) not to apply, or to apply only so far as is prescribed, in relation to vehicles of a prescribed description.

INTERPRETATION

4 (1) This paragraph applies for the purposes of paragraph 3.

(2) A "hire-vehicle" is a vehicle hired (by way of a trade) under a hiring agreement to which section 66 of the Road Traffic Offenders Act 1988 applies.

(3) A "taxi", in England and Wales, is a vehicle—

- (a) licensed under section 37 of the Town Police Clauses Act 1847,
- (b) licensed under section 6 of the Metropolitan Public Carriage Act 1869, or
- (c) drawn by one or more persons or animals.

(4) A "taxi", in Scotland, is—

- (a) a hire car engaged, by arrangements made in a public place between the person to be transported (or a person acting on that person's behalf) and the driver, for a journey starting there and then, or
- (b) a vehicle drawn by one or more persons or animals.

III EQU [220.1]

Commencement Schedule 2 is fully in force except paragraph 2 for which special provision is made in article 2(3) of the commencement provisions in SI 2010/2317.

III EQU [220.2]

Reasonableness and design standards Circumstances are prescribed by para 9 of the Equality Act 2010 (Disability) Regulations 2010, SI 2010/2128 in which it is not reasonable to remove or alter a physical feature. The question whether a physical feature satisfies the relevant design is to be determined in accordance with the Schedule to the same Regulations.

SCHEDULE 3
SERVICES AND PUBLIC FUNCTIONS: EXCEPTIONS

Section 31

PART 1
CONSTITUTIONAL MATTERS

Parliament

III EQU [221]

1 (1) Section 29 does not apply to the exercise of—
(a) a function of Parliament;
(b) a function exercisable in connection with proceedings in Parliament.

(2) Sub-paragraph (1) does not permit anything to be done to or in relation to an individual unless it is done by or in pursuance of a resolution or other deliberation of either House or of a Committee of either House.

Legislation

2 (1) Section 29 does not apply to preparing, making or considering—
(a) an Act of Parliament;
(b) a Bill for an Act of Parliament;
(c) an Act of the Scottish Parliament;
(d) a Bill for an Act of the Scottish Parliament;
(e) an Act of the National Assembly for Wales;
(f) a Bill for an Act of the National Assembly for Wales.

(2) Section 29 does not apply to preparing, making, approving or considering—
(a) a Measure of the National Assembly for Wales;
(b) a proposed Measure of the National Assembly for Wales.

(3) Section 29 does not apply to preparing, making, confirming, approving or considering an instrument which is made under an enactment by—
(a) a Minister of the Crown;
(b) the Scottish Ministers or a member of the Scottish Executive;
(c) the Welsh Ministers, the First Minister for Wales or the Counsel General to the Welsh Government.

(4) Section 29 does not apply to preparing, making, confirming, approving or considering an instrument to which paragraph 6(a) of Schedule 2 to the Synodical Government Measure 1969 (1969 No 2) (Measures, Canons, Acts of Synod, orders, etc) applies.

(5) Section 29 does not apply to anything done in connection with the preparation, making, consideration, approval or confirmation of an instrument made by—
(a) Her Majesty in Council;
(b) the Privy Council.

(6) Section 29 does not apply to anything done in connection with the imposition of a requirement or condition which comes within Schedule 22 (statutory provisions).

Judicial functions

3 (1) Section 29 does not apply to—
(a) a judicial function;
(b) anything done on behalf of, or on the instructions of, a person exercising a judicial function;
(c) a decision not to commence or continue criminal proceedings;

EQUALITY

(d) anything done for the purpose of reaching, or in pursuance of, a decision not to commence or continue criminal proceedings.

(2) A reference in sub-paragraph (1) to a judicial function includes a reference to a judicial function conferred on a person other than a court or tribunal.

Armed forces

4 (1) Section 29(6), so far as relating to relevant discrimination, does not apply to anything done for the purpose of ensuring the combat effectiveness of the armed forces.

(2) "Relevant discrimination" is—

(a) age discrimination;
(b) disability discrimination;
(c) gender reassignment discrimination;
(d) sex discrimination.

Security services, etc

5 Section 29 does not apply to—

(a) the Security Service;
(b) the Secret Intelligence Service;
(c) the Government Communications Headquarters;
(d) a part of the armed forces which is, in accordance with a requirement of the Secretary of State, assisting the Government Communications Headquarters.

PART 2
EDUCATION

6 In its application to a local authority in England and Wales, section 29, so far as relating to age discrimination or religious or belief-related discrimination, does not apply to—

(a) the exercise of the authority's functions under section 14 of the Education Act 1996 (provision of schools);
(b) the exercise of its function under section 13 of that Act in so far as it relates to a function of its under section 14 of that Act.

7 In its application to an education authority, section 29, so far as relating to age discrimination or religious or belief-related discrimination, does not apply to—

(a) the exercise of the authority's functions under section 17 of the Education (Scotland) Act 1980 (provision of schools);
(b) the exercise of its functions under section 1 of that Act, section 2 of the Standards in Scotland's Schools etc Act 2000 (asp 6) or section 4 or 5 of the Education (Additional Support for Learning) (Scotland) Act 2004 (asp 4) (general responsibility for education) in so far as it relates to a matter specified in paragraph (a);
(c) the exercise of its functions under subsection (1) of section 50 of the Education (Scotland) Act 1980 (education of pupils in exceptional circumstances) in so far as it consists of making arrangements of the description referred to in subsection (2) of that section.

8 (1) In its application to a local authority in England and Wales or an education authority, section 29, so far as relating to sex discrimination, does not apply to the exercise of the authority's functions in relation to the establishment of a school.

(2) But nothing in sub-paragraph (1) is to be taken as disapplying section 29 in relation to the exercise of the authority's functions under section 14 of the Education Act 1996 or section 17 of the Education (Scotland) Act 1982.

9 Section 29, so far as relating to age discrimination, does not apply in relation to anything done in connection with—

(a) the curriculum of a school,
(b) admission to a school,
(c) transport to or from a school, or
(d) the establishment, alteration or closure of schools.

10 (1) Section 29, so far as relating to disability discrimination, does not require a local authority in England or Wales exercising functions under the Education Acts or an education authority exercising relevant functions to remove or alter a physical feature.

(2) Relevant functions are functions under—

(a) the Education (Scotland) Act 1980,
(b) the Education (Scotland) Act 1996,
(c) the Standards in Scotland's Schools etc Act 2000, or
(d) the Education (Additional Support for Learning) (Scotland) Act 2004.

11 Section 29, so far as relating to religious or belief-related discrimination, does not apply in relation to anything done in connection with—

(a) the curriculum of a school;
(b) admission to a school which has a religious ethos;
(c) acts of worship or other religious observance organised by or on behalf of a school (whether or not forming part of the curriculum);
(d) the responsible body of a school which has a religious ethos;
(e) transport to or from a school;
(f) the establishment, alteration or closure of schools.

12 This Part of this Schedule is to be construed in accordance with Chapter 1 of Part 6.

PART 3
HEALTH AND CARE

BLOOD SERVICES

13 (1) A person operating a blood service does not contravene section 29 only by refusing to accept a donation of an individual's blood if—

(a) the refusal is because of an assessment of the risk to the public, or to the individual, based on clinical, epidemiological or other data obtained from a source on which it is reasonable to rely, and
(b) the refusal is reasonable.

(2) A blood service is a service for the collection and distribution of human blood for the purposes of medical services.

(3) "Blood" includes blood components.

HEALTH AND SAFETY

14 (1) A service-provider (A) who refuses to provide the service to a pregnant woman does not discriminate against her in contravention of section 29 because she is pregnant if—

(a) A reasonably believes that providing her with the service would, because she is pregnant, create a risk to her health or safety,
(b) A refuses to provide the service to persons with other physical conditions, and
(c) the reason for that refusal is that A reasonably believes that providing the service to such persons would create a risk to their health or safety.

EQUALITY

(2) A service-provider (A) who provides, or offers to provide, the service to a pregnant woman on conditions does not discriminate against her in contravention of section 29 because she is pregnant if—

(a) the conditions are intended to remove or reduce a risk to her health or safety,

(b) A reasonably believes that the provision of the service without the conditions would create a risk to her health or safety,

(c) A imposes conditions on the provision of the service to persons with other physical conditions, and

(d) the reason for the imposition of those conditions is that A reasonably believes that the provision of the service to such persons without those conditions would create a risk to their health or safety.

Care within the family

15 A person (A) does not contravene section 29 only by participating in arrangements under which (whether or not for reward) A takes into A's home, and treats as members of A's family, persons requiring particular care and attention.

PART 4
IMMIGRATION

Age

15A (1) This paragraph applies in relation to age discrimination.

(2) Section 29 does not apply to anything done by a relevant person in the exercise of functions exercisable by virtue of a relevant enactment.

(3) A relevant person is—

(a) a Minister of the Crown acting personally, or

(b) a person acting in accordance with a relevant authorisation.

(4) A relevant authorisation is a requirement imposed or express authorisation given—

(a) with respect to a particular case or class of case, by a Minister of the Crown acting personally;

(b) with respect to a particular class of case, by a relevant enactment or by an instrument made under or by virtue of a relevant enactment.

(5) The relevant enactments are—

(a) the Immigration Acts,

(b) the Special Immigration Appeals Commission Act 1997,

(c) a provision made under section 2(2) of the European Communities Act 1972 which relates to immigration or asylum, and

(d) a provision of EU law which relates to immigration or asylum.

(6) The reference in sub-paragraph (5)(a) to the Immigration Acts does not include a reference to—

(a) sections 28A to 28K of the Immigration Act 1971 (powers of arrest, entry and search, etc), or

(b) section 14 of the Asylum and Immigration (Treatment of Claimants, etc) Act 2004 (power of arrest).

Disability

16 (1) This paragraph applies in relation to disability discrimination.

(2) Section 29 does not apply to—

(a) a decision within sub-paragraph (3);

(b) anything done for the purposes of or in pursuance of a decision within that sub-paragraph.

(3) A decision is within this sub-paragraph if it is a decision (whether or not taken in accordance with immigration rules) to do any of the following on the ground that doing so is necessary for the public good—

(a) to refuse entry clearance;

(b) to refuse leave to enter or remain in the United Kingdom;

(c) to cancel leave to enter or remain in the United Kingdom;

(d) to vary leave to enter or remain in the United Kingdom;

(e) to refuse an application to vary leave to enter or remain in the United Kingdom.

(4) Section 29 does not apply to—

(a) a decision taken, or guidance given, by the Secretary of State in connection with a decision within sub-paragraph (3);

(b) a decision taken in accordance with guidance given by the Secretary of State in connection with a decision within that sub-paragraph.

NATIONALITY AND ETHNIC OR NATIONAL ORIGINS

17 (1) This paragraph applies in relation to race discrimination so far as relating to—

(a) nationality, or

(b) ethnic or national origins.

(2) Section 29 does not apply to anything done by a relevant person in the exercise of functions exercisable by virtue of a relevant enactment.

(3) A relevant person is—

(a) a Minister of the Crown acting personally, or

(b) a person acting in accordance with a relevant authorisation.

(4) A relevant authorisation is a requirement imposed or express authorisation given—

(a) with respect to a particular case or class of case, by a Minister of the Crown acting personally;

(b) with respect to a particular class of case, by a relevant enactment or by an instrument made under or by virtue of a relevant enactment.

(5) The relevant enactments are—

(a) the Immigration Acts,

(b) the Special Immigration Appeals Commission Act 1997,

(c) a provision made under section 2(2) of the European Communities Act 1972 which relates to immigration or asylum, and

(d) a provision of EU law which relates to immigration or asylum.

(6) The reference in sub-paragraph (5)(a) to the Immigration Acts does not include a reference to—

(a) sections 28A to 28K of the Immigration Act 1971 (powers of arrest, entry and search, etc), or

(b) section 14 of the Asylum and Immigration (Treatment of Claimants, etc) Act 2004 (power of arrest).

RELIGION OR BELIEF

18 (1) This paragraph applies in relation to religious or belief-related discrimination.

(2) Section 29 does not apply to a decision within sub-paragraph (3) or anything done for the purposes of or in pursuance of a decision within that sub-paragraph.

(3) A decision is within this sub-paragraph if it is a decision taken in accordance with immigration rules—

(a) to refuse entry clearance or leave to enter the United Kingdom, or to cancel leave to enter or remain in the United Kingdom, on the grounds that the exclusion of the person from the United Kingdom is conducive to the public good, or

(b) to vary leave to enter or remain in the United Kingdom, or to refuse an application to vary leave to enter or remain in the United Kingdom, on the grounds that it is undesirable to permit the person to remain in the United Kingdom.

(4) Section 29 does not apply to a decision within sub-paragraph (5), or anything done for the purposes of or in pursuance of a decision within that sub-paragraph, if the decision is taken on grounds mentioned in sub-paragraph (6).

(5) A decision is within this sub-paragraph if it is a decision (whether or not taken in accordance with immigration rules) in connection with an application for entry clearance or for leave to enter or remain in the United Kingdom.

(6) The grounds referred to in sub-paragraph (4) are—

(a) the grounds that a person holds an office or post in connection with a religion or belief or provides a service in connection with a religion or belief,

(b) the grounds that a religion or belief is not to be treated in the same way as certain other religions or beliefs, or

(c) the grounds that the exclusion from the United Kingdom of a person to whom paragraph (a) applies is conducive to the public good.

(7) Section 29 does not apply to—

(a) a decision taken, or guidance given, by the Secretary of State in connection with a decision within sub-paragraph (3) or (5);

(b) a decision taken in accordance with guidance given by the Secretary of State in connection with a decision within either of those sub-paragraphs.

INTERPRETATION

19 A reference to entry clearance, leave to enter or remain or immigration rules is to be construed in accordance with the Immigration Act 1971.

PART 5
INSURANCE, ETC

SERVICES ARRANGED BY EMPLOYER

20 (1) Section 29 does not apply to the provision of a relevant financial service if the provision is in pursuance of arrangements made by an employer for the service-provider to provide the service to the employer's employees, and other persons, as a consequence of the employment.

(2) "Relevant financial service" means—

(a) insurance or a related financial service, or

(b) a service relating to membership of or benefits under a personal pension scheme (within the meaning given by section 1 of the Pension Schemes Act 1993).

AGE

20A (1) A person (A) does not contravene section 29, so far as relating to age discrimination, by doing anything in connection with the provision of a financial service.

(2) Where A conducts an assessment of risk for the purposes of providing the financial service to another person (B), A may rely on sub-paragraph (1) only if the assessment of risk, so far as it involves a consideration of B's age, is carried out by reference to information which is relevant to the assessment of risk and from a source on which it is reasonable to rely.

(3) In this paragraph, "financial service" includes a service of a banking, credit, insurance, personal pension, investment or payment nature.

Disability

21 (1) It is not a contravention of section 29, so far as relating to disability discrimination, to do anything in connection with insurance business if—

(a) that thing is done by reference to information that is both relevant to the assessment of the risk to be insured and from a source on which it is reasonable to rely, and

(b) it is reasonable to do that thing.

(2) "Insurance business" means business which consists of effecting or carrying out contracts of insurance; and that definition is to be read with—

(a) section 22 of the Financial Services and Markets Act 2000,

(b) any relevant order under that Act, and

(c) Schedule 2 to that Act.

Sex, gender reassignment, pregnancy and maternity

22 *Repealed by SI 2012/2992 with effect from 21 December 2012.*

Existing insurance policies

23 (1) It is not a contravention of section 29, so far as relating to relevant discrimination, to do anything in connection with insurance business in relation to an existing insurance policy.

(2) "Relevant discrimination" is—

(a) age discrimination;

(b) disability discrimination;

(c) gender reassignment discrimination;

(d) pregnancy and maternity discrimination;

(e) race discrimination;

(f) religious or belief-related discrimination;

(g) sex discrimination;

(h) sexual orientation discrimination.

(3) An existing insurance policy is a policy of insurance entered into before the date on which this paragraph comes into force.

(4) Sub-paragraph (1) does not apply where an existing insurance policy was renewed, or the terms of such a policy were reviewed, on or after the date on which this paragraph comes into force.

(5) A review of an existing insurance policy which was part of, or incidental to, a general reassessment by the service-provider of the pricing structure for a group of policies is not a review for the purposes of sub-paragraph (4).

(6) "Insurance business" has the meaning given in paragraph 21.

PART 6
MARRIAGE: GENDER REASSIGNMENT

Gender reassignment: England and Wales

24 (1) A person does not contravene section 29, so far as relating to gender reassignment discrimination, only because of anything done in reliance on section 5B of the Marriage Act 1949 (solemnisation of marriages involving person of acquired gender).

(2) A person (A) whose consent to the solemnisation of the marriage of a person (B) is required under section 44(1) of the Marriage Act 1949 (solemnisation in registered building) does not contravene section 29, so far as relating to gender reassignment discrimination, by refusing to consent if A reasonably believes that B's gender has become the acquired gender under the Gender Recognition Act 2004.

EQUALITY

(3) Sub-paragraph (4) applies to a person (A) who may, in a case that comes within the Marriage Act 1949 (other than the case mentioned in sub-paragraph (1)), solemnise marriages according to a form, rite or ceremony of a body of persons who meet for religious worship.

(4) A does not contravene section 29, so far as relating to gender reassignment discrimination, by refusing to solemnise, in accordance with a form, rite or ceremony as described in sub-paragraph (3), the marriage of a person (B) if A reasonably believes that B's gender has become the acquired gender under the Gender Recognition Act 2004.

PART 6ZA
MARRIAGE AND CIVIL PARTNERSHIP: SCOTLAND

Gender reassignment: Scotland

25 (1) An approved celebrant (A) does not contravene section 29, so far as relating to gender reassignment discrimination, only by refusing to solemnise the marriage of a person (B) if A reasonably believes that B's gender has become the acquired gender under the Gender Recognition Act 2004.

(2) In sub-paragraph (1) "approved celebrant" has the meaning given in section 8(2)(a) of the Marriage (Scotland) Act 1977 (persons who may solemnise marriage).

(3) An approved celebrant (A) does not contravene section 29, so far as relating to gender reassignment discrimination, only by refusing to register the civil partnership of a person (B) if A reasonably believes that B's gender has become the acquired gender under the Gender Recognition Act 2004.

(4) In sub-paragraph (3) "approved celebrant" has the meaning given in section 94A(4)(a) of the Civil Partnership Act 2004.

PART 6A
MARRIAGE OF SAME SEX COUPLES IN ENGLAND AND WALES

Marriage according to religious rites: no compulsion to solemnize etc

25A (1) A person does not contravene section 29 only because the person—

(a) does not conduct a relevant marriage,

(b) is not present at, does not carry out, or does not otherwise participate in, a relevant marriage, or

(c) does not consent to a relevant marriage being conducted,

for the reason that the marriage is the marriage of a same sex couple.

(2) Expressions used in this paragraph and in section 2 of the Marriage (Same Sex Couples) Act 2013 have the same meanings in this paragraph as in that section.

PART 6B
MARRIAGE OF SAME SEX COUPLES AND CIVIL PARTNERSHIP: SCOTLAND

Marriage of same sex couples and civil partnership: Scotland

25B (1) An approved celebrant does not contravene section 29 only by refusing to solemnise a relevant Scottish marriage for the reason that the marriage is the marriage of two persons of the same sex.

(2) An approved celebrant does not contravene section 29 only by refusing to register a relevant Scottish civil partnership for the reason that the civil partnership is between two persons of the same sex.

(3) A person does not contravene section 29 only by refusing to participate in a religious or belief ceremony forming part of, or connected with, the solemnising of

a relevant Scottish marriage for the reason that the marriage is the marriage of two persons of the same sex.

(4) A person does not contravene section 29 only by refusing to participate in a religious or belief ceremony forming part of, or connected with, the registration of a relevant Scottish civil partnership for the reason that the civil partnership is between two persons of the same sex.

(5) For the purposes of this paragraph, a person is an approved celebrant for the purposes of both marriage and civil partnership whether the person is an approved celebrant within the meaning of section 8(2)(a) of the Marriage (Scotland) Act 1977 2 or section 94A(4)(a) of the Civil Partnership Act 2004.

(6) In this paragraph—

"relevant Scottish civil partnership" means a religious or belief civil partnership within the meaning of section 94A(4)(b) of the Civil Partnership Act 2004;

"relevant Scottish marriage" means a religious or belief marriage of two persons of the same sex within the meaning of section 8(2)(a) of the Marriage (Scotland) Act 1977.

Marriage of same sex couples: Scottish forces marriages

25C (1) A chaplain does not contravene section 29 only by refusing to solemnise a relevant Scottish forces marriage according to religious rites or usages for the reason that the marriage is the marriage of two persons of the same sex.

(2) In this paragraph—

"chaplain" has the meaning given by paragraph (a) of the definition of "authorised person" in paragraph 12(2) of Schedule 6 to the Marriage (Same Sex Couples) Act 2013;

"forces marriage" has the meaning given by paragraph 12(2) of Schedule 6 to the Marriage (Same Sex Couples) Act 2013;

"relevant Scottish forces marriage" means a forces marriage of two persons of the same sex where Scotland is the relevant part of the United Kingdom within the meaning of paragraph 12 of Schedule 6 to the Marriage (Same Sex Couples) Act 2013.

PART 7
SEPARATE AND SINGLE SERVICES

Separate services for the sexes

26 (1) A person does not contravene section 29, so far as relating to sex discrimination, by providing separate services for persons of each sex if—

(a) a joint service for persons of both sexes would be less effective, and

(b) the limited provision is a proportionate means of achieving a legitimate aim.

(2) A person does not contravene section 29, so far as relating to sex discrimination, by providing separate services differently for persons of each sex if—

(a) a joint service for persons of both sexes would be less effective,

(b) the extent to which the service is required by one sex makes it not reasonably practicable to provide the service otherwise than as a separate service provided differently for each sex, and

(c) the limited provision is a proportionate means of achieving a legitimate aim.

(3) This paragraph applies to a person exercising a public function in relation to the provision of a service as it applies to the person providing the service.

Single-sex services

27 (1) A person does not contravene section 29, so far as relating to sex discrimination, by providing a service only to persons of one sex if—
(a) any of the conditions in sub-paragraphs (2) to (7) is satisfied, and
(b) the limited provision is a proportionate means of achieving a legitimate aim.
(2) The condition is that only persons of that sex have need of the service.
(3) The condition is that—
(a) the service is also provided jointly for persons of both sexes, and
(b) the service would be insufficiently effective were it only to be provided jointly.
(4) The condition is that—
(a) a joint service for persons of both sexes would be less effective, and
(b) the extent to which the service is required by persons of each sex makes it not reasonably practicable to provide separate services.
(5) The condition is that the service is provided at a place which is, or is part of—
(a) a hospital, or
(b) another establishment for persons requiring special care, supervision or attention.
(6) The condition is that—
(a) the service is provided for, or is likely to be used by, two or more persons at the same time, and
(b) the circumstances are such that a person of one sex might reasonably object to the presence of a person of the opposite sex.
(7) The condition is that—
(a) there is likely to be physical contact between a person (A) to whom the service is provided and another person (B), and
(b) B might reasonably object if A were not of the same sex as B.
(8) This paragraph applies to a person exercising a public function in relation to the provision of a service as it applies to the person providing the service.

Gender reassignment

28 (1) A person does not contravene section 29, so far as relating to gender reassignment discrimination, only because of anything done in relation to a matter within sub-paragraph (2) if the conduct in question is a proportionate means of achieving a legitimate aim.
(2) The matters are—
(a) the provision of separate services for persons of each sex;
(b) the provision of separate services differently for persons of each sex;
(c) the provision of a service only to persons of one sex.

Services relating to religion

29 (1) A minister does not contravene section 29, so far as relating to sex discrimination, by providing a service only to persons of one sex or separate services for persons of each sex, if—
(a) the service is provided for the purposes of an organised religion,
(b) it is provided at a place which is (permanently or for the time being) occupied or used for those purposes, and
(c) the limited provision of the service is necessary in order to comply with the doctrines of the religion or is for the purpose of avoiding conflict with the strongly held religious convictions of a significant number of the religion's followers.
(2) The reference to a minister is a reference to a minister of religion, or other person, who—

(a) performs functions in connection with the religion, and

(b) holds an office or appointment in, or is accredited, approved or recognised for purposes of, a relevant organisation in relation to the religion.

(3) An organisation is a relevant organisation in relation to a religion if its purpose is—

(a) to practise the religion,

(b) to advance the religion,

(c) to teach the practice or principles of the religion,

(d) to enable persons of the religion to receive benefits, or to engage in activities, within the framework of that religion, or

(e) to foster or maintain good relations between persons of different religions.

(4) But an organisation is not a relevant organisation in relation to a religion if its sole or main purpose is commercial.

SERVICES GENERALLY PROVIDED ONLY FOR PERSONS WHO SHARE A PROTECTED CHARACTERISTIC

30 If a service is generally provided only for persons who share a protected characteristic, a person (A) who normally provides the service for persons who share that characteristic does not contravene section 29(1) or (2)—

(a) by insisting on providing the service in the way A normally provides it, or

(b) if A reasonably thinks it is impracticable to provide the service to persons who do not share that characteristic, by refusing to provide the service.

CONCESSIONS

30A (1) A person does not contravene section 29, so far as relating to age discrimination, by giving a concession in respect of a service to persons of a particular age group.

(2) The reference to a concession in respect of a service is a reference to a benefit, right or privilege having the effect that the manner in which the service is provided is, or the terms on which it is provided are, more favourable than the manner in which, or the terms on which, it is usually provided to the public (or, where it is provided to a section of the public, that section).

AGE RELATED HOLIDAYS

30B (1) A person (P) does not contravene section 29, so far as relating to age discrimination, by providing a relevant holiday service to persons of a particular age group.

(2) In sub-paragraph (1) "relevant holiday service" means a service—

(a) which involves the provision of at least two of the following together for a single price—

(i) travel;

(ii) accommodation;

(iii) access to activities or services not ancillary to travel or accommodation which form a significant part of the service or its cost;

(b) the provision of which is for a period of more than 24 hours or includes the provision of overnight accommodation;

(c) which P provides only to persons of the age group in question; and

(d) an essential feature of which is the bringing together of persons of that age group with a view to facilitating their enjoyment of facilities or services designed with particular regard to persons of that age group.

(3) P may not rely on sub-paragraph (1) unless, before providing a person with a relevant holiday service, P provides the person with a written statement that the service is provided only to persons of the age group in question.

(4) For the purpose of sub-paragraph (2)(a)(i), "travel" includes an option for an individual to make alternative travel arrangements to those included in the relevant holiday service as offered by P.

Age restricted services

30C (1) This paragraph applies where a person (P)—

(a) provides a service the provision of which is prohibited by or under an enactment to persons under the age specified in or under the enactment ("the statutory age"), and

(b) displays on the premises on which the service is provided an age warning in relation to the provision of the service.

(2) An age warning in relation to the provision of a service is a statement to the effect that the service will not be provided to a person who—

(a) appears to P, or an employee or agent of P's, to be under the age specified in the statement, and

(b) on being required to do so by P or the employee or agent, fails to produce satisfactory identification.

(3) P does not contravene section 29, so far as relating to age discrimination, by not providing the service to a person, who—

(a) appears to P, or an employee or agent of P's, to be under the age specified in the age warning in relation to the provision of the service, and

(b) on being required to do so by P or the employee or agent, fails to produce satisfactory identification.

(4) In this paragraph—

(a) a reference to the provision of a service includes a reference to provision of access to the service, and

(b) "satisfactory identification", in relation to a person, means a valid document which—

(i) in the case of licensed premises where an age condition applies, meets that condition, and

(ii) in any other case includes a photograph of the person and establishes that the person has attained the statutory age in relation to the provision of a service;

"licensed premises" means premises in respect of which a relevant premises licence within the meaning of section 19A of the Licensing Act 2003 (mandatory conditions where alcohol sold) has effect; and

"age condition" means a condition specified in an order under subsection (1) of section 19A of that Act requiring the age of certain persons to be verified in the manner specified in the condition before they are served alcohol in premises where the condition applies.

Residential mobile homes

30D [*applicable in England and Scotland*]

(1) A person (A) who is the owner of a protected site does not contravene section 29, so far as relating to age discrimination, by—

(a) entering into a mobile home agreement with a person (B) that entitles only persons who have attained a particular age to station and occupy a mobile home on land forming part of the site, or

(b) refusing to permit assignment by B of a mobile home agreement to any person other than a person who has attained a particular age.

(2) A does not contravene section 29, so far as relating to age discrimination, by imposing a requirement in park rules that mobile homes stationed on land forming part of the site and occupied under mobile home agreements may be occupied only by persons who have attained a particular age.

(3) A does not contravene section 29, so far as relating to age discrimination, by—

- (a) imposing in or under a mobile home rental agreement with a person (C) a requirement that the mobile home to which the agreement relates may be occupied only by persons who have attained a particular age, or
- (b) refusing to permit assignment by C of a mobile home rental agreement to any person other than a person who has attained a particular age.

(4) But A may not rely on sub-paragraph (1) or (3) unless, before doing something mentioned in that sub-paragraph, A provides B or C, as the case may be, with a written statement to the effect that the mobile home in question may be occupied only by persons who have attained the age in question.

(5) In this paragraph,

"mobile home agreement" means an agreement to which the Mobile Homes Act 1983 applies; and "owner", "protected site" and "mobile home" have the same meaning as in that Act;

"park rules" means rules applying to residents of mobile homes on the protected site and required to be observed by a term in the mobile home agreement or the mobile home rental agreement as the case may be;

"mobile home rental agreement" means an agreement (other than an arrangement to occupy a mobile home for the purposes of a holiday) under which a person ("the occupier") is entitled to occupy a mobile home on the protected site as the occupier's residence whether for a specified period or for successive periods of a specified duration subject to payment of money and the performance of other obligations.

30D [*applicable in Wales*] (1) A person (A) who is the owner of a protected site does not contravene section 29, so far as relating to age discrimination, by—

- (a) entering into a mobile home agreement with a person (B) that entitles only persons who have attained a particular age to station and occupy a mobile home on land forming part of the site, or
- (b) refusing to permit assignment by B of a mobile home agreement to any person other than a person who has attained a particular age.

(2) A does not contravene section 29, so far as relating to age discrimination, by imposing a requirement in park rules that mobile homes stationed on land forming part of the site and occupied under mobile home agreements may be occupied only by persons who have attained a particular age.

(3) A does not contravene section 29, so far as relating to age discrimination, by—

- (a) imposing in or under a mobile home rental agreement with a person (C) a requirement that the mobile home to which the agreement relates may be occupied only by persons who have attained a particular age, or
- (b) refusing to permit assignment by C of a mobile home rental agreement to any person other than a person who has attained a particular age.

(4) But A may not rely on sub-paragraph (1) or (3) unless, before doing something mentioned in that sub-paragraph, A provides B or C, as the case may be, with a written statement to the effect that the mobile home in question may be occupied only by persons who have attained the age in question.

(5) In this paragraph,

"mobile home agreement" means an agreement to which the Mobile Homes Act 1983 or Part 4 of the Mobile Homes (Wales) Act 2013 applies; and "owner", "protected site" and "mobile home" have the same meaning as in that Act or that Part of that Act;

"park rules" means rules applying to residents of mobile homes on the protected site and required to be observed by a term in the mobile home agreement or the mobile home rental agreement as the case may be;

"mobile home rental agreement" means an agreement (other than an arrangement to occupy a mobile home for the purposes of a holiday) under which a person ("the occupier") is entitled to occupy a mobile home on the protected site as the occupier's residence whether for a specified period or for successive periods of a specified duration subject to payment of money and the performance of other obligations.

PART 8
TELEVISION, RADIO AND ON-LINE BROADCASTING AND DISTRIBUTION

31 (1) Section 29 does not apply to the provision of a content service (within the meaning given by section 32(7) of the Communications Act 2003).

(2) Sub-paragraph (1) does not apply to the provision of an electronic communications network, electronic communications service or associated facility (each of which has the same meaning as in that Act).

PART 9
TRANSPORT

Application to disability

32 This Part of this Schedule applies in relation to disability discrimination.

Transport by air

33 (1) Section 29 does not apply to—

(a) transporting people by air;

(b) a service provided on a vehicle for transporting people by air.

(2) Section 29 does not apply to anything governed by Regulation (EC) No 1107/2006 of the European Parliament and of the Council of 5 July 2006 concerning the rights of disabled persons and persons with reduced mobility when travelling by air.

Transport by land: road

34 (1) Section 29 does not apply to transporting people by land, unless the vehicle concerned is—

(a) a hire-vehicle designed and constructed for the carriage of passengers and comprising no more than 8 seats in addition to the driver's seat,

(b) a hire-vehicle designed and constructed for the carriage of passengers, comprising more than 8 seats in addition to the driver's seat and having a maximum mass not exceeding 5 tonnes,

(c) a hire-vehicle designed and constructed for the carriage of goods and having a maximum mass not exceeding 3.5 tonnes,

(d) a vehicle licensed under section 48 of the Local Government (Miscellaneous Provisions) Act 1976 or section 7 of the Private Hire Vehicles (London) Act 1998 (or under a provision of a local Act corresponding to either of those provisions),

(e) a private hire car (within the meaning of section 23 of the Civic Government (Scotland) Act 1982),

(f) a public service vehicle (within the meaning given by section 1 of the Public Passenger Vehicles Act 1981),

(g) a vehicle built or adapted to carry passengers on a railway or tramway (within the meaning, in each case, of the Transport and Works Act 1992),

(h) a taxi,

(i) a vehicle deployed to transport the driver and passengers of a vehicle that has broken down or is involved in an accident, or

(j) a vehicle deployed on a system using a mode of guided transport (within the meaning of the Transport and Works Act 1992).

(1A) Sections 20 to 22 and section 29 do not apply to anything that is governed by Regulation (EU) No 181/2011 of the European Parliament and of the Council of 16 February 2011 concerning the rights of passengers in bus and coach transport and amending Regulation (EC) No 2006/2004.

(2) Paragraph 4 of Schedule 2 applies for the purposes of this paragraph as it applies for the purposes of paragraph 3 of that Schedule.

Transport by land: rail

34A Section 29 does not apply to anything governed by Regulation (EC) No 1371/2007 of the European Parliament and of the Council of 23 October 2007 on rail passengers' rights and obligations.

PART 10
SUPPLEMENTARY

Power to amend

35 (1) A Minister of the Crown may by order amend this Schedule—

(a) so as to add, vary or omit an exception to section 29, so far as relating to disability, religion or belief or sexual orientation;

(b) so as to add, vary or omit an exception to section 29(6), so far as relating to gender reassignment, pregnancy and maternity, race or sex.

(2) But provision by virtue of sub-paragraph (1) may not amend this Schedule—

(a) so as to omit an exception in paragraph 1, 2 or 3;

(b) so as to reduce the extent to which an exception in paragraph 1, 2 or 3 applies.

(3) For the purposes of an order under sub-paragraph (1)(a), so far as relating to disability, which makes provision in relation to transport by air, it does not matter whether the transport is within or outside the United Kingdom.

(4) Before making an order under this paragraph the Minister must consult the Commission.

(5) Nothing in this paragraph affects the application of any other provision of this Act to conduct outside England and Wales or Scotland.

EQUALITY

SCHEDULE 4
PREMISES: REASONABLE ADJUSTMENTS

Section 38

Preliminary

III EQU [222]

1 This Schedule applies where a duty to make reasonable adjustments is imposed on A by this Part.

The duty in relation to let premises

2 (1) This paragraph applies where A is a controller of let premises.

(2) A must comply with the first and third requirements.

(3) For the purposes of this paragraph, the reference in section 20(3) to a provision, criterion or practice of A's includes a reference to a term of the letting.

(4) For those purposes, the reference in section 20(3) or (5) to a disabled person is a reference to a disabled person who—

(a) is a tenant of the premises, or

(b) is otherwise entitled to occupy them.

(5) In relation to each requirement, the relevant matters are—

(a) the enjoyment of the premises;

(b) the use of a benefit or facility, entitlement to which arises as a result of the letting.

(6) Sub-paragraph (2) applies only if A receives a request from or on behalf of the tenant or a person entitled to occupy the premises to take steps to avoid the disadvantage or provide the auxiliary aid.

(7) If a term of the letting that prohibits the tenant from making alterations puts the disabled person at the disadvantage referred to in the first requirement, A is required to change the term only so far as is necessary to enable the tenant to make alterations to the let premises so as to avoid the disadvantage.

(8) It is never reasonable for A to have to take a step which would involve the removal or alteration of a physical feature.

(9) For the purposes of this paragraph, physical features do not include furniture, furnishings, materials, equipment or other chattels in or on the premises; and none of the following is an alteration of a physical feature—

(a) the replacement or provision of a sign or notice;

(b) the replacement of a tap or door handle;

(c) the replacement, provision or adaptation of a door bell or door entry system;

(d) changes to the colour of a wall, door or any other surface.

(10) The terms of a letting include the terms of an agreement relating to it.

THE DUTY IN RELATION TO PREMISES TO LET

3 (1) This paragraph applies where A is a controller of premises to let.

(2) A must comply with the first and third requirements.

(3) For the purposes of this paragraph, the reference in section 20(3) or (5) to a disabled person is a reference to a disabled person who is considering taking a letting of the premises.

(4) In relation to each requirement, the relevant matter is becoming a tenant of the premises.

(5) Sub-paragraph (2) applies only if A receives a request by or on behalf of a disabled person within sub-paragraph (3) for A to take steps to avoid the disadvantage or provide the auxiliary aid.

(6) Nothing in this paragraph requires A to take a step which would involve the removal or alteration of a physical feature.

(7) Sub-paragraph (9) of paragraph 2 applies for the purposes of this paragraph as it applies for the purposes of that paragraph.

THE DUTY IN RELATION TO COMMONHOLD UNITS

4 (1) This paragraph applies where A is a commonhold association; and the reference to a commonhold association is a reference to the association in its capacity as the person who manages a commonhold unit.

(2) A must comply with the first and third requirements.

(3) For the purposes of this paragraph, the reference in section 20(3) to a provision, criterion or practice of A's includes a reference to—

(a) a term of the commonhold community statement, or

(b) any other term applicable by virtue of the transfer of the unit to the unit-holder.

(4) For those purposes, the reference in section 20(3) or (5) to a disabled person is a reference to a disabled person who—

(a) is the unit-holder, or

(b) is otherwise entitled to occupy the unit.

(5) In relation to each requirement, the relevant matters are—

(a) the enjoyment of the unit;

(b) the use of a benefit or facility, entitlement to which arises as a result of a term within sub-paragraph (3)(a) or (b).

(6) Sub-paragraph (2) applies only if A receives a request from or on behalf of the unit-holder or a person entitled to occupy the unit to take steps to avoid the disadvantage or provide the auxiliary aid.

(7) If a term within sub-paragraph (3)(a) or (b) that prohibits the unit-holder from making alterations puts the disabled person at the disadvantage referred to in the first requirement, A is required to change the term only so far as is necessary to enable the unit-holder to make alterations to the unit so as to avoid the disadvantage.

(8) It is never reasonable for A to have to take a step which would involve the removal or alteration of a physical feature; and sub-paragraph (9) of paragraph 2 applies in relation to a commonhold unit as it applies in relation to let premises.

THE DUTY IN RELATION TO COMMON PARTS

5 (1) This paragraph applies where A is a responsible person in relation to common parts.

(2) A must comply with the second requirement.

(3) For the purposes of this paragraph, the reference in section 20(4) to a physical feature is a reference to a physical feature of the common parts.

(4) For those purposes, the reference in section 20(4) to a disabled person is a reference to a disabled person who—

(a) is a tenant of the premises,

(b) is a unit-holder, or

(c) is otherwise entitled to occupy the premises,

and uses or intends to use the premises as the person's only or main home.

(5) In relation to the second requirement, the relevant matter is the use of the common parts.

(6) Sub-paragraph (2) applies only if—

(a) A receives a request by or on behalf of a disabled person within sub-paragraph (4) for A to take steps to avoid the disadvantage, and

(b) the steps requested are likely to avoid or reduce the disadvantage.

CONSULTATION ON ADJUSTMENTS RELATING TO COMMON PARTS

6 (1) In deciding whether it is reasonable to take a step for the purposes of paragraph 5, A must consult all persons A thinks would be affected by the step.

(2) The consultation must be carried out within a reasonable period of the request being made.

(3) A is not required to have regard to a view expressed against taking a step in so far as A reasonably believes that the view is expressed because of the disabled person's disability.

(4) Nothing in this paragraph affects anything a commonhold association is required to do pursuant to Part 1 of the Commonhold and Leasehold Reform Act 2002.

AGREEMENT ON ADJUSTMENTS RELATING TO COMMON PARTS

7 (1) If A decides that it is reasonable to take a step for the purposes of paragraph 5, A and the disabled person must agree in writing the rights and responsibilities of each of them in relation to the step.

(2) An agreement under this paragraph must, in particular, make provision as to the responsibilities of the parties in relation to—

(a) the costs of any work to be undertaken;
(b) other costs arising from the work;
(c) the restoration of the common parts to their former condition if the relevant disabled person stops living in the premises.

(3) It is always reasonable before the agreement is made for A to insist that the agreement should require the disabled person to pay—

(a) the costs referred to in paragraphs (a) and (b) of sub-paragraph (2), and
(b) the costs of the restoration referred to in paragraph (c) of that sub-paragraph.

(4) If an agreement under this paragraph is made, A's obligations under the agreement become part of A's interest in the common parts and pass on subsequent disposals accordingly.

(5) Regulations may require a party to an agreement under this paragraph to provide, in prescribed circumstances, prescribed information about the agreement to persons of a prescribed description.

(6) The regulations may require the information to be provided in a prescribed form.

(7) Regulations may make provision as to circumstances in which an agreement under this paragraph is to cease to have effect, in so far as the agreement does not itself make provision for termination.

VICTIMISATION

8 (1) This paragraph applies where the relevant disabled person comes within paragraph 2(4)(b), 4(4)(b) or 5(4)(c).

(2) A must not, because of costs incurred in connection with taking steps to comply with a requirement imposed for the purposes of paragraph 2, 4 or 5, subject to a detriment—

(a) a tenant of the premises, or
(b) the unit-holder.

REGULATIONS

9 (1) This paragraph applies for the purposes of section 36 and this Schedule.

(2) Regulations may make provision as to—

(a) circumstances in which premises are to be treated as let, or as not let, to a person;
(b) circumstances in which premises are to be treated as being, or as not being, to let;
(c) who is to be treated as being, or as not being, a person entitled to occupy premises otherwise than as tenant or unit-holder;
(d) who is to be treated as being, or as not being, a person by whom premises are let;
(e) who is to be treated as having, or as not having, premises to let;
(f) who is to be treated as being, or as not being, a manager of premises.

(3) Provision made by virtue of this paragraph may amend this Schedule.

III EQU [222.1]

Commencement This Schedule is not yet in force except as regards paras 1 to 4, 8 (except so far as it relates to paragraph 5(4)(c)) and para 9 (except so far as not already in force as a result of SI 2010/1736 art 2, Sch 1 para 1): see art 2(4)(e) of the commencement provisions in SI 2010/2317.

III EQU [222.2]

Auxiliary aids or services See the further provision made, for the purposes of paragraphs 2 to 4 by the Equality Act 2010 (Disability) Regulations 2010, SI 2010/2128, reg 8.

SCHEDULE 5

PREMISES: EXCEPTIONS

Section 38

Owner-occupier

III EQU [223]

1 (1) This paragraph applies to the private disposal of premises by an owner-occupier.

(2) A disposal is a private disposal only if the owner-occupier does not—

(a) use the services of an estate agent for the purpose of disposing of the premises, or

(b) publish (or cause to be published) an advertisement in connection with their disposal.

(3) Section 33(1) applies only in so far as it relates to race.

(4) Section 34(1) does not apply in so far as it relates to—

(a) religion or belief, or

(b) sexual orientation.

(5) In this paragraph—

"estate agent" means a person who, by way of profession or trade, provides services for the purpose of—

(a) finding premises for persons seeking them, or

(b) assisting in the disposal of premises;

"owner-occupier" means a person who—

(a) owns an estate or interest in premises, and

(b) occupies the whole of them.

2 (1) Section 36(1)(a) does not apply if—

(a) the premises are, or have been, the only or main home of a person by whom they are let, and

(b) since entering into the letting, neither that person nor any other by whom they are let has used a manager for managing the premises.

(2) A manager is a person who, by profession or trade, manages let premises.

(3) Section 36(1)(b) does not apply if—

(a) the premises are, or have been, the only or main home of a person who has them to let, and

(b) neither that person nor any other who has the premises to let uses the services of an estate agent for letting the premises.

(4) "Estate agent" has the meaning given in paragraph 1.

Small premises

3 (1) This paragraph applies to anything done by a person in relation to the disposal, occupation or management of part of small premises if—

(a) the person or a relative of that person resides, and intends to continue to reside, in another part of the premises, and

(b) the premises include parts (other than storage areas and means of access) shared with residents of the premises who are not members of the same household as the resident mentioned in paragraph (a).

(2) Sections 33(1), 34(1) and 35(1) apply only in so far as they relate to race.

(3) Premises are small if—

(a) the only other persons occupying the accommodation occupied by the resident mentioned in sub-paragraph (1)(a) are members of the same household,

(b) the premises also include accommodation for at least one other household,

(c) the accommodation for each of those other households is let, or available for letting, on a separate tenancy or similar agreement, and

(d) the premises are not normally sufficient to accommodate more than two other households.

(4) Premises are also small if they are not normally sufficient to provide residential accommodation for more than six persons (in addition to the resident mentioned in sub-paragraph (1)(a) and members of the same household).

(5) In this paragraph, "relative" means—

(a) spouse or civil partner,

(b) unmarried partner,

(c) parent or grandparent,

(d) child or grandchild (whether or not legitimate),

(e) the spouse, civil partner or unmarried partner of a child or grandchild,

(f) brother or sister (whether of full blood or half-blood), or

(g) a relative within paragraph (c), (d), (e) or (f) whose relationship arises as a result of marriage or civil partnership.

(6) In sub-paragraph (5), a reference to an unmarried partner is a reference to the other member of a couple consisting of—

(a) a man and a woman who are not married to each other but are living together as husband and wife, or

(b) two people of the same sex who are not civil partners of each other but are living together as if they were.

4 (1) Section 36(1) does not apply if—

(a) the premises in question are small premises,

(b) the relevant person or a relative of that person resides, and intends to continue to reside, in another part of the premises, and

(c) the premises include parts (other than storage areas and means of access) shared with residents of the premises who are not members of the same household as the resident mentioned in paragraph (b).

(2) The relevant person is the person who, for the purposes of section 36(1), is—

(a) the controller of the premises, or

(b) the responsible person in relation to the common parts to which the premises relate.

(3) "Small premises" and "relative" have the same meaning as in paragraph 3.

5 A Minister of the Crown may by order amend paragraph 3 or 4.

SCHEDULE 10
ACCESSIBILITY FOR DISABLED PUPILS

Section 88

Accessibility strategies

III EQU [224]

1 (1) A local authority in England and Wales must, in relation to schools for which it is the responsible body, prepare—
(a) an accessibility strategy;
(b) further such strategies at such times as may be prescribed.

(2) An accessibility strategy is a strategy for, over a prescribed period—
(a) increasing the extent to which disabled pupils can participate in the schools' curriculums;
(b) improving the physical environment of the schools for the purpose of increasing the extent to which disabled pupils are able to take advantage of education and benefits, facilities or services provided or offered by the schools;
(c) improving the delivery to disabled pupils of information which is readily accessible to pupils who are not disabled.

(3) The delivery in sub-paragraph (2)(c) must be—
(a) within a reasonable time;
(b) in ways which are determined after taking account of the pupils' disabilities and any preferences expressed by them or their parents.

(4) An accessibility strategy must be in writing.

(5) A local authority must keep its accessibility strategy under review during the period to which it relates and, if necessary, revise it.

(6) A local authority must implement its accessibility strategy.

2 (1) In preparing its accessibility strategy, a local authority must have regard to—
(a) the need to allocate adequate resources for implementing the strategy;
(b) guidance as to the matters mentioned in sub-paragraph (3).

(2) The authority must also have regard to guidance as to compliance with paragraph 1(5).

(3) The matters are—
(a) the content of an accessibility strategy;
(b) the form in which it is to be produced;
(c) persons to be consulted in its preparation.

(4) Guidance may be issued—
(a) for England, by a Minister of the Crown;
(b) for Wales, by the Welsh Ministers.

(5) A local authority must, if asked, make a copy of its accessibility strategy available for inspection at such reasonable times as it decides.

(6) A local authority in England must, if asked by a Minister of the Crown, give the Minister a copy of its accessibility strategy.

(7) A local authority in Wales must, if asked by the Welsh Ministers, give them a copy of its accessibility strategy.

Accessibility plans

3 (1) The responsible body of a school in England and Wales must prepare—
(a) an accessibility plan;
(b) further such plans at such times as may be prescribed.

(2) An accessibility plan is a plan for, over a prescribed period—

(a) increasing the extent to which disabled pupils can participate in the school's curriculum,

(b) improving the physical environment of the school for the purpose of increasing the extent to which disabled pupils are able to take advantage of education and benefits, facilities or services provided or offered by the school, and

(c) improving the delivery to disabled pupils of information which is readily accessible to pupils who are not disabled.

(3) The delivery in sub-paragraph (2)(c) must be—

(a) within a reasonable time;

(b) in ways which are determined after taking account of the pupils' disabilities and any preferences expressed by them or their parents.

(4) An accessibility plan must be in writing.

(5) The responsible body must keep its accessibility plan under review during the period to which it relates and, if necessary, revise it.

(6) The responsible body must implement its accessibility plan.

(7) A relevant inspection may extend to the performance by the responsible body of its functions in relation to the preparation, publication, review, revision and implementation of its accessibility plan.

(8) A relevant inspection is an inspection under—

(a) Part 1 of the Education Act 2005, or

(b) Chapter 1 of Part 4 of the Education and Skills Act 2008 (regulation and inspection of independent education provision in England).

4 (1) In preparing an accessibility plan, the responsible body must have regard to the need to allocate adequate resources for implementing the plan.

(2) The proprietor of an independent educational institution (other than an Academy) must, if asked, make a copy of the school's accessibility plan available for inspection at such reasonable times as the proprietor decides.

(3) The proprietor of an independent educational institution in England (other than an Academy) must, if asked by a Minister of the Crown, give the Minister a copy of the school's accessibility plan.

(4) The proprietor of an independent school in Wales (other than an Academy) must, if asked by the Welsh Ministers, give them a copy of the school's accessibility plan.

Power of direction

5 (1) This sub-paragraph applies if the appropriate authority is satisfied (whether or not on a complaint) that a responsible body—

(a) has acted or is proposing to act unreasonably in the discharge of a duty under this Schedule, or

(b) has failed to discharge such a duty.

(2) This sub-paragraph applies if the appropriate authority is satisfied (whether or not on a complaint) that a responsible body of a school specified in sub-paragraph (3)—

(a) has acted or is proposing to act unreasonably in the discharge of a duty the body has in relation to the provision to the authority of copies of the body's accessibility plan or the inspection of that plan, or

(b) has failed to discharge the duty.

(3) The schools are—

(a) schools approved under section 342 of the Education Act 1996 (non-maintained special schools);

(b) Academies.

[(b) Academy schools;

(c) alternative provision Academies.]

(4) This sub-paragraph applies if a Tribunal has made an order under paragraph 5 of Schedule 17 and the appropriate authority is satisfied (whether or not on a complaint) that the responsible body concerned—

(a) has acted or is proposing to act unreasonably in complying with the order, or

(b) has failed to comply with the order.

(5) If sub-paragraph (1), (2) or (4) applies, the appropriate authority may give a responsible body such directions as the authority thinks expedient as to—

(a) the discharge by the body of the duty, or

(b) compliance by the body with the order.

(6) A direction may be given in relation to sub-paragraph (1) or (2) even if the performance of the duty is contingent on the opinion of the responsible body.

(7) A direction may not, unless sub-paragraph (8) applies, be given to the responsible body of a school in England in respect of a matter—

(a) that has been complained about to a Local Commissioner in accordance with Chapter 2 of Part 10 of the Apprenticeships, Skills, Children and Learning Act 2009 (parental complaints against governing bodies etc), or

(b) that the appropriate authority thinks could have been so complained about.

(8) This sub-paragraph applies if—

(a) the Local Commissioner has made a recommendation to the responsible body under section 211(4) of the Apprenticeships, Skills, Children and Learning Act 2009 (statement following investigation) in respect of the matter, and

(b) the responsible body has not complied with the recommendation.

(9) A direction—

(a) may be varied or revoked by the appropriate authority;

(b) may be enforced, on the application of the appropriate authority, by a mandatory order obtained in accordance with section 31 of the Senior Courts Act 1981.

(10) The appropriate authority is—

(a) in relation to the responsible body of a school in England, the Secretary of State;

(b) in relation to the responsible body of a school in Wales, the Welsh Ministers.

SUPPLEMENTARY

6 (1) This paragraph applies for the purposes of this Schedule.

(2) Regulations may prescribe services which are, or are not, to be regarded as being—

(a) education;

(b) a benefit, facility or service.

(3) The power to make regulations is exercisable by—

(a) in relation to England, a Minister of the Crown;

(b) in relation to Wales, the Welsh Ministers.

(4) "Disabled pupil" includes a disabled person who may be admitted to the school as a pupil.

(5) "Responsible body" means—

(a) in relation to a maintained school or a maintained nursery school, the local authority or governing body;

(b) in relation to a pupil referral unit, the local authority;

(c) in relation to an independent educational institution or an alternative provision Academy that is not an independent educational institution, the proprietor;

(d) in relation to a special school not maintained by a local authority, the proprietor.

(6) "Governing body", in relation to a maintained school, means the body corporate (constituted in accordance with regulations under section 19 of the Education Act 2002) which the school has as a result of that section.

(7) "Maintained school" has the meaning given in section 20 of the School Standards and Framework Act 1998; and "maintained nursery school" has the meaning given in section 22 of that Act.

Amendment *In para 5(3)(b), the text in italic is deleted and the text in square brackets is inserted by the Education Act 2011, with effect from a date to be appointed.*

SCHEDULE 11
SCHOOLS: EXCEPTIONS

Section 89

PART 1
SEX DISCRIMINATION

Admission to single-sex schools

III EQU [225]

1 (1) Section 85(1), so far as relating to sex, does not apply in relation to a single-sex school.

(2) A single-sex school is a school which—

(a) admits pupils of one sex only, or

(b) on the basis of the assumption in sub-paragraph (3), would be taken to admit pupils of one sex only.

(3) That assumption is that pupils of the opposite sex are to be disregarded if—

(a) their admission to the school is exceptional, or

(b) their numbers are comparatively small and their admission is confined to particular courses or classes.

(4) In the case of a school which is a single-sex school by virtue of sub-paragraph (3)(b), section 85(2)(a) to (d), so far as relating to sex, does not prohibit confining pupils of the same sex to particular courses or classes.

Single-sex boarding at schools

2 (1) Section 85(1), so far as relating to sex, does not apply in relation to admission as a boarder to a school to which this paragraph applies.

(2) Section 85(2)(a) to (d), so far as relating to sex, does not apply in relation to boarding facilities at a school to which this paragraph applies.

(3) This paragraph applies to a school (other than a single-sex school) which has some pupils as boarders and others as non-boarders and which—

(a) admits as boarders pupils of one sex only, or

(b) on the basis of the assumption in sub-paragraph (4), would be taken to admit as boarders pupils of one sex only.

(4) That assumption is that pupils of the opposite sex admitted as boarders are to be disregarded if their numbers are small compared to the numbers of other pupils admitted as boarders.

Single-sex schools turning co-educational

3 (1) If the responsible body of a single-sex school decides to alter its admissions arrangements so that the school will cease to be a single-sex school, the body may apply for a transitional exemption order in relation to the school.

(2) If the responsible body of a school to which paragraph 2 applies decides to alter its admissions arrangements so that the school will cease to be one to which that paragraph applies, the body may apply for a transitional exemption order in relation to the school.

(3) A transitional exemption order in relation to a school is an order which, during the period specified in the order as the transitional period, authorises—

(a) sex discrimination by the responsible body of the school in the arrangements it makes for deciding who is offered admission as a pupil;

(b) the responsible body, in the circumstances specified in the order, not to admit a person as a pupil because of the person's sex.

(4) Paragraph 4 applies in relation to the making of transitional exemption orders.

(5) The responsible body of a school does not contravene this Act, so far as relating to sex discrimination, if—

(a) in accordance with a transitional exemption order, or

(b) pending the determination of an application for a transitional exemption order in relation to the school,

it does not admit a person as a pupil because of the person's sex.

4 (1) In the case of a maintained school within the meaning given by section 32 of the Education and Inspections Act 2006, a transitional exemption order may be made in accordance with such provision as is made in regulations under section 21 of that Act (orders made by local authority or adjudicator in relation to schools in England).

(2) In the case of a school in Wales maintained by a local authority, a transitional exemption order may be made in accordance section 82 of, or Part 3 of Schedule 3 to, the School Standards and Organisation (Wales) Act 2013 (orders made by Welsh Ministers).

(3) In the case of a school in Scotland managed by an education authority or in respect of which the managers are for the time being receiving grants under section 73(c) or (d) of the Education (Scotland) Act 1980—

(a) the responsible body may submit to the Scottish Ministers an application for the making of a transitional exemption order, and

(b) the Scottish Ministers may make the order.

(4) . . .

(5) . . .

(6) In the case of a school in England or Wales not coming within sub-paragraph (1), (2), (4) or (5) or an independent school in Scotland—

(a) the responsible body may submit to the Commission an application for the making of a transitional exemption order, and

(b) the Commission may make the order.

(7) An application under sub-paragraph (6) must specify—

(a) the period proposed by the responsible body as the transitional period to be specified in the order,

(b) the stages within that period by which the body proposes to move to the position where section 85(1)(a) and (c), so far as relating to sex, is complied with, and

(c) any other matters relevant to the terms and operation of the order applied for.

(8) The Commission must not make an order on an application under sub-paragraph (6) unless satisfied that the terms of the application are reasonable, having regard to—

(a) the nature of the school's premises,

(b) the accommodation, equipment and facilities available, and

(c) the responsible body's financial resources.

PART 2
RELIGIOUS OR BELIEF-RELATED DISCRIMINATION

School with religious character etc

5 Section 85(1) and (2)(a) to (d), so far as relating to religion or belief, does not apply in relation to—

- (a) a school designated under section 69(3) of the School Standards and Framework Act 1998 (foundation or voluntary school with religious character);
- (b) a school (other than an alternative provision Academy) listed in the register of independent schools for England or for Wales, if the school's entry in the register records that the school has a religious ethos;
- (c) a school transferred to an education authority under section 16 of the Education (Scotland) Act 1980 (transfer of certain schools to education authorities) which is conducted in the interest of a church or denominational body;
- (d) a school provided by an education authority under section 17(2) of that Act (denominational schools);
- (e) a grant-aided school (within the meaning of that Act) which is conducted in the interest of a church or denominational body;
- (f) a school registered in the register of independent schools for Scotland if the school admits only pupils who belong, or whose parents belong, to one or more particular denominations;
- (g) a school registered in that register if the school is conducted in the interest of a church or denominational body.

Curriculum, worship, etc

6 Section 85(2)(a) to (d), so far as relating to religion or belief, does not apply in relation to anything done in connection with acts of worship or other religious observance organised by or on behalf of a school (whether or not forming part of the curriculum).

Power to amend

7 (1) A Minister of the Crown may by order amend this Part of this Schedule—

- (a) so as to add, vary or omit an exception to section 85;
- (b) so as to make provision about the construction or application of section 19(2)(d) in relation to section 85.

(2) The power under sub-paragraph (1) is exercisable only in relation to religious or belief-related discrimination.

(3) Before making an order under this paragraph the Minister must consult—

- (a) the Welsh Ministers,
- (b) the Scottish Ministers, and
- (c) such other persons as the Minister thinks appropriate.

PART 3
DISABILITY DISCRIMINATION

Permitted form of selection

8 (1) A person does not contravene section 85(1), so far as relating to disability, only by applying a permitted form of selection.

(2) In relation to England and Wales, a permitted form of selection is—

(a) in the case of a maintained school which is not designated as a grammar school under section 104 of the School Standards and Framework Act 1998, a form of selection mentioned in section 99(2) or (4) of that Act;

(b) in the case of a maintained school which is so designated, its selective admission arrangements (within the meaning of section 104 of that Act);

(c) in the case of an independent educational institution, arrangements which provide for some or all of its pupils to be selected by reference to general or special ability or aptitude, with a view to admitting only pupils of high ability or aptitude.

(3) In relation to Scotland, a permitted form of selection is—

(a) in the case of a school managed by an education authority, arrangements approved by the Scottish Ministers for the selection of pupils for admission;

(b) in the case of an independent school, arrangements which provide for some or all of its pupils to be selected by reference to general or special ability or aptitude, with a view to admitting only pupils of high ability or aptitude.

(4) "Maintained school" has the meaning given in section 22 of the School Standards and Framework Act 1998.

SCHEDULE 12
FURTHER AND HIGHER EDUCATION EXCEPTIONS

Section 94

PART 1
SINGLE-SEX INSTITUTIONS, ETC

ADMISSION TO SINGLE-SEX INSTITUTIONS

III EQU [226]

1 (1) Section 91(1), so far as relating to sex, does not apply in relation to a single-sex institution.

(2) A single-sex institution is an institution to which section 91 applies, which—

(a) admits students of one sex only, or

(b) on the basis of the assumption in sub-paragraph (3), would be taken to admit students of one sex only.

(3) That assumption is that students of the opposite sex are to be disregarded if—

(a) their admission to the institution is exceptional, or

(b) their numbers are comparatively small and their admission is confined to particular courses or classes.

(4) In the case of an institution which is a single-sex institution by virtue of sub-paragraph (3)(b), section 91(2)(a) to (d), so far as relating to sex, does not prohibit confining students of the same sex to particular courses or classes.

SINGLE-SEX INSTITUTIONS TURNING CO-EDUCATIONAL

2 (1) If the responsible body of a single-sex institution decides to alter its admissions arrangements so that the institution will cease to be a single-sex institution, the body may apply for a transitional exemption order in relation to the institution.

(2) A transitional exemption order relating to an institution is an order which, during the period specified in the order as the transitional period, authorises—

(a) sex discrimination by the responsible body of the institution in the arrangements it makes for deciding who is offered admission as a student;

(b) the responsible body, in the circumstances specified in the order, not to admit a person as a student because of the person's sex.

(3) Paragraph 3 applies in relation to the making of a transitional exemption order.

(4) The responsible body of an institution does not contravene this Act, so far as relating to sex discrimination, if—

(a) in accordance with a transitional exemption order, or

(b) pending the determination of an application for a transitional exemption order in relation to the institution,

it does not admit a person as a student because of the person's sex.

(5) The responsible body of an institution does not contravene this Act, so far as relating to sex discrimination, if—

(a) in accordance with a transitional exemption order, or

(b) pending the determination of an application for a transitional exemption order in relation to the institution,

it discriminates in the arrangements it makes for deciding who is offered admission as a student.

3 (1) In the case of a single-sex institution—

(a) its responsible body may submit to the Commission an application for the making of a transitional exemption order, and

(b) the Commission may make the order.

(2) An application under sub-paragraph (1) must specify—

(a) the period proposed by the responsible body as the transitional period to be specified in the order,

(b) the stages, within that period, by which the body proposes to move to the position where section 91(1)(a) and (c), so far as relating to sex, is complied with, and

(c) any other matters relevant to the terms and operation of the order applied for.

(3) The Commission must not make an order on an application under sub-paragraph (1) unless satisfied that the terms of the application are reasonable, having regard to—

(a) the nature of the institution's premises,

(b) the accommodation, equipment and facilities available, and

(c) the responsible body's financial resources.

PART 2
OTHER EXCEPTIONS

Occupational requirements

4 A person (P) does not contravene section 91(1) or (2) if P shows that P's treatment of another person relates only to training that would help fit that other person for work the offer of which the other person could be refused in reliance on Part 1 of Schedule 9.

Institutions with a religious ethos

5 (1) The responsible body of an institution which is designated for the purposes of this paragraph does not contravene section 91(1), so far as relating to religion or belief, if, in the admission of students to a course at the institution—

(a) it gives preference to persons of a particular religion or belief,

(b) it does so to preserve the institution's religious ethos, and

(c) the course is not a course of vocational training.

(2) A Minister of the Crown may by order designate an institution if satisfied that the institution has a religious ethos.

BENEFITS DEPENDENT ON MARITAL STATUS, ETC

6 A person does not contravene section 91, so far as relating to sexual orientation, by providing married persons and civil partners (to the exclusion of all other persons) with access to a benefit, facility or service.

CHILD CARE

7 (1) A person does not contravene section 91(2)(b) or (d), so far as relating to age, only by providing, or making arrangements for or facilitating the provision of, care for children of a particular age group.

(2) Facilitating the provision of care for a child includes—

(a) paying for some or all of the cost of the provision;

(b) helping a parent of the child to find a suitable person to provide care for the child;

(c) enabling a parent of the child to spend more time providing care for the child or otherwise assisting the parent with respect to the care that the parent provides for the child.

(3) A child is a person who has not attained the age of 17.

(4) A reference to care includes a reference to supervision.

III EQU [226.1]

Designation of institutions The Equality Act 2010 (Designation of Institutions with Religious Ethos)(England and Wales) Order 2010, SI 2010/1915 designates 16 institutions as institutions with religious ethos.

SCHEDULE 13
EDUCATION: REASONABLE ADJUSTMENTS

Section 98

EQUALITY

PRELIMINARY

III EQU [227]

1 This Schedule applies where a duty to make reasonable adjustments is imposed on A by this Part.

THE DUTY FOR SCHOOLS

2 (1) This paragraph applies where A is the responsible body of a school to which section 85 applies.

(2) A must comply with the first and third requirements.

(3) For the purposes of this paragraph—

(a) the reference in section 20(3) to a provision, criterion or practice is a reference to a provision, criterion or practice applied by or on behalf of A;

(b) the reference in section 20(3) or (5) to a disabled person is—

(i) in relation to a relevant matter within sub-paragraph (4)(a), a reference to disabled persons generally;

(ii) in relation to a relevant matter within sub-paragraph (4)(b), a reference to disabled pupils generally.

(4) In relation to each requirement, the relevant matters are—

(a) deciding who is offered admission as a pupil;
(b) provision of education or access to a benefit, facility or service.

THE DUTY FOR FURTHER OR HIGHER EDUCATION INSTITUTIONS

3 (1) This paragraph applies where A is the responsible body of an institution to which section 91 applies.
(2) A must comply with the first, second and third requirements.
(3) For the purposes of this paragraph—
(a) the reference in section 20(3) to a provision, criterion or practice is a reference to a provision, criterion or practice applied by or on behalf of A;
(b) the reference in section 20(4) to a physical feature is a reference to a physical feature of premises occupied by A;
(c) the reference in section 20(3), (4) or (5) to a disabled person is—
(i) in relation to a relevant matter within sub-paragraph (4)(a), a reference to disabled persons generally;
(ii) in relation to a relevant matter within sub-paragraph (4)(b) or (c), a reference to disabled students generally;
(iii) in relation to a relevant matter within sub-paragraph (4)(d) or (e) below, a reference to an interested disabled person.
(4) In relation to each requirement, the relevant matters are—
(a) deciding who is offered admission as a student;
(b) provision of education;
(c) access to a benefit, facility or service;
(d) deciding on whom a qualification is conferred;
(e) a qualification that A confers.

4 (1) An interested disabled person is a disabled person who, in relation to a relevant matter specified in the first column of the table, is of a description specified in the second column.

Case	*Description of disabled person*
Deciding upon whom to confer a qualification.	A person who is, or has notified A that the person may be, an applicant for the conferment of the qualification.
A qualification that A confers.	An applicant for the conferment by A of the qualification.
	A person on whom A confers the qualification.

(2) A provision, criterion or practice does not include the application of a competence standard.
(3) A competence standard is an academic, medical or other standard applied for the purpose of determining whether or not a person has a particular level of competence or ability.

THE DUTY RELATING TO CERTAIN OTHER FURTHER OR HIGHER EDUCATION COURSES

5 (1) This paragraph applies where A is the responsible body in relation to a course to which section 92 applies.
(2) A must comply with the first, second and third requirements; but if A is the governing body of a maintained school (within the meaning given by that section), A is not required to comply with the second requirement.
(3) For the purposes of this paragraph—

(a) the reference in section 20(3) to a provision, criterion or practice is a reference to a provision, criterion or practice applied by or on behalf of A;

(b) the reference in section 20(4) to a physical feature is a reference to a physical feature of premises occupied by A;

(c) the reference in section 20(3), (4) or (5) to a disabled person is—

(i) in relation to a relevant matter within sub-paragraph (4)(a), a reference to disabled persons generally;

(ii) in relation to a relevant matter within sub-paragraph (4)(b), a reference to disabled persons generally who are enrolled on the course.

(4) In relation to each requirement, the relevant matters are—

(a) arrangements for enrolling persons on a course of further or higher education secured by A;

(b) services provided by A for persons enrolled on the course.

THE DUTY RELATING TO RECREATIONAL OR TRAINING FACILITIES

6 (1) This paragraph applies where A is the responsible body in relation to facilities to which section 93 applies.

(2) A must comply with the first, second and third requirements.

(3) For the purposes of this paragraph—

(a) the reference in section 20(3) to a provision, criterion or practice is a reference to a provision, criterion or practice applied by or on behalf of A;

(b) the reference in section 20(4) to a physical feature is a reference to a physical feature of premises occupied by A;

(c) the reference in section 20(3), (4) or (5) to a disabled person is a reference to disabled persons generally.

(4) In relation to each requirement, the relevant matter is A's arrangements for providing the recreational or training facilities.

CODE OF PRACTICE

7 In deciding whether it is reasonable for A to have to take a step for the purpose of complying with the first, second or third requirement, A must have regard to relevant provisions of a code of practice issued under section 14 of the Equality Act 2006.

CONFIDENTIALITY REQUESTS

8 (1) This paragraph applies if a person has made a confidentiality request of which A is aware.

(2) In deciding whether it is reasonable for A to have to take a step in relation to that person so as to comply with the first, second or third requirement, A must have regard to the extent to which taking the step is consistent with the request.

(3) In a case within paragraph 2, a "confidentiality request" is a request—

(a) that the nature or existence of a disabled person's disability be treated as confidential, and

(b) which satisfies either of the following conditions.

(4) The first condition is that the request is made by the person's parent.

(5) The second condition is that—

(a) it is made by the person, and

(b) A reasonably believes that the person has sufficient understanding of the nature and effect of the request.

(6) In a case within paragraph 3, a "confidentiality request" is a request by a disabled person that the nature or existence of the person's disability be treated as confidential.

THE DUTY FOR GENERAL QUALIFICATIONS BODIES

9 (1) This paragraph applies where A is a qualifications body for the purposes of section 96.

(2) Paragraphs 3 and 4(1), so far as relating to qualifications, apply to a qualifications body as they apply to a responsible body.

(3) This paragraph is subject to section 96(7).

III EQU [227.1]

Schedule 13 entered into force with effect from 1 October 2010 except as follows. Paragraph 2, so far as it relates to the third requirement, entered into force on 1 September 2012. Paragraph 5, so far as it relates to the third requirement in a case where A is the governing body of a maintained school (within the meaning of section 92), also entered into force on 1 September 2012. See Equality Act 2010 (Commencement No 4, Savings, Consequential, Transitional, Transitory and Incidental Provisions and Revocation) Order 2010, 2010/2317, art 2(6)(i) and Equality Act 2010 (Commencement No 10) Order 2012, 2012/2184, art 2(b).

SCHEDULE 14
EDUCATIONAL CHARITIES AND ENDOWMENTS

Section 99

EDUCATIONAL CHARITIES

III EQU [228]

1 (1) This paragraph applies to a trust deed or other instrument—

(a) which concerns property applicable for or in connection with the provision of education in an establishment in England and Wales to which section 85 or 91 applies, and

(b) which in any way restricts the benefits available under the instrument to persons of one sex.

(2) Sub-paragraph (3) applies if, on the application of the trustees or the responsible body (within the meaning of that section), a Minister of the Crown is satisfied that the removal or modification of the restriction would be conducive to the advancement of education without sex discrimination.

(3) The Minister may by order make such modifications of the instrument as appear to the Minister expedient for removing or modifying the restriction.

(4) If the trust was created by a gift or bequest, an order must not be made until the end of the period of 25 years after the date when the gift or bequest took effect.

(5) Sub-paragraph (4) does not apply if the donor or the personal representatives of the donor or testator consent in writing to making the application for the order.

(6) The Minister must require the applicant to publish a notice—

(a) containing particulars of the proposed order;

(b) stating that representations may be made to the Minister within a period specified in the notice.

(7) The period must be not less than one month beginning with the day after the date of the notice.

(8) The applicant must publish the notice in the manner specified by the Minister.

(9) The cost of publication may be paid out of the property of the trust.

(10) Before making the order, the Minister must take account of representations made in accordance with the notice.

EDUCATIONAL ENDOWMENTS

2 (1) This paragraph applies to an educational endowment—

(a) to which section 104 of the Education (Scotland) Act 1980 applies, and

(b) which in any way restricts the benefit of the endowment to persons of one sex.

(2) Sub-paragraph (3) applies if, on the application of the governing body of an educational endowment, the Scottish Ministers are satisfied that the removal or modification of the provision which restricts the benefit of the endowment to persons of one sex would be conducive to the advancement of education without sex discrimination.

(3) The Scottish Ministers may by order make such provision as they think expedient for removing or modifying the restriction.

(4) If the Scottish Ministers propose to make such an order they must publish a notice in such manner as they think sufficient for giving information to persons they think may be interested in the endowment—

(a) containing particulars of the proposed order;

(b) stating that representations may be made with respect to the proposal within such period as is specified in the notice.

(5) The period must be not less than one month beginning with the day after the date of publication of the notice.

(6) The cost of publication is to be paid out of the funds of the endowment to which the notice relates.

(7) Before making an order, the Scottish Ministers—

(a) must consider representations made in accordance with the notice;

(b) may cause a local inquiry to be held into the representations under section 67 of the Education (Scotland) Act 1980.

(8) A reference to an educational endowment includes a reference to—

(a) a scheme made or approved for the endowment under Part 6 of the Education (Scotland) Act 1980;

(b) in the case of an endowment the governing body of which is entered in the Scottish Charity Register, a scheme approved for the endowment under section 39 or 40 of the Charities and Trustee Investment (Scotland) Act 2005 (asp 10);

(c) an endowment which is, by virtue of section 108(1) of the Education (Scotland) Act 1980, treated as if it were an educational endowment (or which would, but for the disapplication of that section by section 122(4) of that Act, be so treated);

(d) a university endowment, the Carnegie Trust, a theological endowment and a new endowment.

(9) Expressions used in this paragraph and in Part 6 of the Education (Scotland) Act 1980 have the same meaning in this paragraph as in that Part.

SCHEDULE 15
ASSOCIATIONS: REASONABLE ADJUSTMENTS

Section 107

PRELIMINARY

III EQU [229]

1 This Schedule applies where a duty to make reasonable adjustments is imposed on an association (A) by this Part.

THE DUTY

2 (1) A must comply with the first, second and third requirements.

(2) For the purposes of this paragraph, the reference in section 20(3), (4) or (5) to a disabled person is a reference to disabled persons who—

(a) are, or are seeking to become or might wish to become, members,

(b) are associates, or

(c) are, or are likely to become, guests.

(3) Section 20 has effect as if, in subsection (4), for "to avoid the disadvantage" there were substituted—

"(a) to avoid the disadvantage, or

(b) to adopt a reasonable alternative method of affording access to the benefit, facility or service or of admitting persons to membership or inviting persons as guests."

(4) In relation to the first and third requirements, the relevant matters are—

(a) access to a benefit, facility or service;

(b) members' or associates' retaining their rights as such or avoiding having them varied;

(c) being admitted to membership or invited as a guest.

(5) In relation to the second requirement, the relevant matters are—

(a) access to a benefit, facility or service;

(b) being admitted to membership or invited as a guest.

(6) In relation to the second requirement, a physical feature includes a physical feature brought by or on behalf of A, in the course of or for the purpose of providing a benefit, facility or service, on to premises other than those that A occupies (as well as including a physical feature in or on premises that A occupies).

(7) Nothing in this paragraph requires A to take a step which would fundamentally alter—

(a) the nature of the benefit, facility or service concerned, or

(b) the nature of the association.

(8) Nor does anything in this paragraph require a member or associate in whose house meetings of the association take place to make adjustments to a physical feature of the house.

SCHEDULE 16
ASSOCIATIONS: EXCEPTIONS

Section 107

SINGLE CHARACTERISTIC ASSOCIATIONS

III EQU [230]

1 (1) An association does not contravene section 101(1) by restricting membership to persons who share a protected characteristic.

(2) An association that restricts membership to persons who share a protected characteristic does not breach section 101(3) by restricting the access by associates to a benefit, facility or service to such persons as share the characteristic.

(3) An association that restricts membership to persons who share a protected characteristic does not breach section 102(1) by inviting as guests, or by permitting to be invited as guests, only such persons as share the characteristic.

(4) Sub-paragraphs (1) to (3), so far as relating to race, do not apply in relation to colour.

(5) This paragraph does not apply to an association that is a registered political party.

Age

1A (1) An association does not contravene section 101(1) or (2), so far as relating to age discrimination, by giving a concession on admission to membership for—

(a) persons of a particular age group, or

(b) persons who have been members of the association for more than a number of years specified by the association for this purpose.

(2) An association does not contravene section 101(2) or (3), so far as relating to age discrimination, by giving a concession on access to a benefit, facility or service for—

(a) members of a particular age group, or

(b) persons who have been members of the association for more than a number of years specified by the association for this purpose.

(3) An association does not contravene section 102(1), so far as relating to age discrimination, by giving a concession on invitations of persons of a particular age group as guests.

(4) An association does not contravene section 102(2), so far as relating to age discrimination, by giving a concession on access to a benefit, facility or service for guests of a particular age group.

(5) For the purposes of this paragraph, affording only persons of a particular age group access to a benefit, facility or service for a limited time is to be regarded as a concession.

(6) The reference to a concession in respect of something done by an association is a reference to a benefit, right or privilege having the effect that the manner in which, or the terms on which, it does it are more favourable than the manner in which, or the terms on which, it usually does the thing.

Health and safety

2 (1) An association (A) does not discriminate against a pregnant woman in contravention of section 101(1)(b) because she is pregnant if—

(a) the terms on which A is prepared to admit her to membership include a term intended to remove or reduce a risk to her health or safety,

(b) A reasonably believes that admitting her to membership on terms which do not include that term would create a risk to her health or safety,

(c) the terms on which A is prepared to admit persons with other physical conditions to membership include a term intended to remove or reduce a risk to their health or safety, and

(d) A reasonably believes that admitting them to membership on terms which do not include that term would create a risk to their health or safety.

(2) Sub-paragraph (1) applies to section 102(1)(b) as it applies to section 101(1)(b); and for that purpose a reference to admitting a person to membership is to be read as a reference to inviting the person as a guest or permitting the person to be invited as a guest.

(3) An association (A) does not discriminate against a pregnant woman in contravention of section 101(2)(a) or (3)(a) or 102(2)(a) because she is pregnant if—

(a) the way in which A affords her access to a benefit, facility or service is intended to remove or reduce a risk to her health or safety,

(b) A reasonably believes that affording her access to the benefit, facility or service otherwise than in that way would create a risk to her health or safety,

(c) A affords persons with other physical conditions access to the benefit, facility or service in a way that is intended to remove or reduce a risk to their health or safety, and

(d) A reasonably believes that affording them access to the benefit, facility or service otherwise than in that way would create a risk to their health or safety.

(4) An association (A) which does not afford a pregnant woman access to a benefit, facility or service does not discriminate against her in contravention of section 101(2)(a) or (3)(a) or 102(2)(a) because she is pregnant if—

(a) A reasonably believes that affording her access to the benefit, facility or service would, because she is pregnant, create a risk to her health or safety,

(b) A does not afford persons with other physical conditions access to the benefit, facility or service, and

(c) the reason for not doing so is that A reasonably believes that affording them access to the benefit, facility or service would create a risk to their health or safety.

(5) An association (A) does not discriminate against a pregnant woman under section 101(2)(c) or (3)(c) because she is pregnant if—

(a) the variation of A's terms of membership, or rights as an associate, is intended to remove or reduce a risk to her health or safety,

(b) A reasonably believes that not making the variation to A's terms or rights would create a risk to her health or safety,

(c) A varies the terms of membership, or rights as an associate, of persons with other physical conditions,

(d) the variation of their terms or rights is intended to remove or reduce a risk to their health or safety, and

(e) A reasonably believes that not making the variation to their terms or rights would create a risk to their health or safety.

III EQU [230.1]

Schedule 16 is in force except so far as it applies to the protected characteristic of age. Its application to age has effect from 1 October 2012.

SCHEDULE 21

REASONABLE ADJUSTMENTS: SUPPLEMENTARY

Section 189

PRELIMINARY

III EQU [231]

1 This Schedule applies for the purposes of Schedules 2, 4, 8, 13 and 15.

BINDING OBLIGATIONS, ETC

2 (1) This paragraph applies if—

(a) a binding obligation requires A to obtain the consent of another person to an alteration of premises which A occupies,

(b) where A is a controller of let premises, a binding obligation requires A to obtain the consent of another person to a variation of a term of the tenancy, or

(c) where A is a responsible person in relation to common parts, a binding obligation requires A to obtain the consent of another person to an alteration of the common parts.

(2) For the purpose of discharging a duty to make reasonable adjustments—

(a) it is always reasonable for A to have to take steps to obtain the consent, but

(b) it is never reasonable for A to have to make the alteration before the consent is obtained.

(3) In this Schedule, a binding obligation is a legally binding obligation in relation to premises, however arising; but the reference to a binding obligation in sub-paragraph (1)(a) or (c) does not include a reference to an obligation imposed by a tenancy.

(4) The steps referred to in sub-paragraph (2)(a) do not include applying to a court or tribunal.

LANDLORD'S CONSENT

3 (1) This paragraph applies if—

(a) A occupies premises under a tenancy,

(b) A is proposing to make an alteration to the premises so as to comply with a duty to make reasonable adjustments, and

(c) but for this paragraph, A would not be entitled to make the alteration.

(2) This paragraph also applies if—

(a) A is a responsible person in relation to common parts,

(b) A is proposing to make an alteration to the common parts so as to comply with a duty to make reasonable adjustments,

(c) A is the tenant of property which includes the common parts, and

(d) but for this paragraph, A would not be entitled to make the alteration.

(3) The tenancy has effect as if it provided—

(a) for A to be entitled to make the alteration with the written consent of the landlord,

(b) for A to have to make a written application for that consent,

(c) for the landlord not to withhold the consent unreasonably, and

(d) for the landlord to be able to give the consent subject to reasonable conditions.

(4) If a question arises as to whether A has made the alteration (and, accordingly, complied with a duty to make reasonable adjustments), any constraint attributable to the tenancy must be ignored unless A has applied to the landlord in writing for consent to the alteration.

(5) For the purposes of sub-paragraph (1) or (2), A must be treated as not entitled to make the alteration if the tenancy—

(a) imposes conditions which are to apply if A makes an alteration, or

(b) entitles the landlord to attach conditions to a consent to the alteration.

PROCEEDINGS BEFORE COUNTY COURT OR SHERIFF

4 (1) This paragraph applies if, in a case within Part 3, 4, 6 or 7 of this Act—

(a) A has applied in writing to the landlord for consent to the alteration, and

(b) the landlord has refused to give consent or has given consent subject to a condition.

(2) A (or a disabled person with an interest in the alteration being made) may refer the matter to the county court or, in Scotland, the sheriff.

(3) The county court or sheriff must determine whether the refusal or condition is unreasonable.

(4) If the county court or sheriff finds that the refusal or condition is unreasonable, the county court or sheriff—

(a) may make such declaration as it thinks appropriate;

(b) may make an order authorising A to make the alteration specified in the order (and requiring A to comply with such conditions as are so specified).

EQUALITY

Joining landlord as party to proceedings

5 (1) This paragraph applies to proceedings relating to a contravention of this Act by virtue of section 20.

(2) A party to the proceedings may request the employment tribunal, county court or sheriff ("the judicial authority") to direct that the landlord is joined or sisted as a party to the proceedings.

(3) The judicial authority—

(a) must grant the request if it is made before the hearing of the complaint or claim begins;

(b) may refuse the request if it is made after the hearing begins;

(c) must refuse the request if it is made after the complaint or claim has been determined.

(4) If the landlord is joined or sisted as a party to the proceedings, the judicial authority may determine whether—

(a) the landlord has refused to consent to the alteration;

(b) the landlord has consented subject to a condition;

(c) the refusal or condition was unreasonable.

(5) If the judicial authority finds that the refusal or condition was unreasonable, it—

(a) may make such declaration as it thinks appropriate;

(b) may make an order authorising A to make the alteration specified in the order (and requiring A to comply with such conditions as are so specified);

(c) may order the landlord to pay compensation to the complainant or claimant.

(6) An employment tribunal may act in reliance on sub-paragraph (5)(c) instead of, or in addition to, acting in reliance on section 124(2); but if it orders the landlord to pay compensation it must not do so in reliance on section 124(2).

(7) If the county court or the sheriff orders the landlord to pay compensation, it may not order A to do so.

Regulations

6 (1) Regulations may make provision as to circumstances in which a landlord is taken for the purposes of this Schedule to have—

(a) withheld consent;

(b) withheld consent reasonably;

(c) withheld consent unreasonably.

(2) Regulations may make provision as to circumstances in which a condition subject to which a landlord gives consent is taken—

(a) to be reasonable;

(b) to be unreasonable.

(3) Regulations may make provision supplementing or modifying the preceding paragraphs of this Schedule, or provision made under this paragraph, in relation to a case where A's tenancy is a sub-tenancy.

(4) Provision made by virtue of this paragraph may amend the preceding paragraphs of this Schedule.

Interpretation

7 An expression used in this Schedule and in Schedule 2, 4, 8, 13 or 15 has the same meaning in this Schedule as in that Schedule.

III EQU [231.1]

Landlord withholding consent Particular circumstances are prescribed by the Equality Act 2010 (Disability) Regulations 2010, SI 2010/2128, reg 10 as circumstances in which a relevant landlord is to be taken, for the purposes of Sch 21, to have withheld consent for alterations to premises. Further provision is made by regs 10 to 13 for circumstances in which the withholding of consent is to be treated as unreasonable, or reasonable or subject to reasonable conditions.

III EQU [231.2]

Modifications in the case of a sub-tenancy The text of this Schedule must be read as modified by the provisions of the Equality Act 2010 (Disability) Regulations 2010, SI 2010/2128, reg 14 in its application to occupiers who are sub-tenants.

SCHEDULE 22
STATUTORY PROVISIONS

Section 191

STATUTORY AUTHORITY

III EQU [232]

1 (1) A person (P) does not contravene a provision specified in the first column of the table, so far as relating to the protected characteristic specified in the second column in respect of that provision, if P does anything P must do pursuant to a requirement specified in the third column.

Specified provision	*Protected characteristic*	*Requirement*
Parts 3 to 7	Age	A requirement of an enactment
Parts 3 to 7 and 12	Disability	A requirement of an enactment
		A relevant requirement or condition imposed by virtue of an enactment
Parts 3 to 7	Religion or belief	A requirement of an enactment
		A relevant requirement or condition imposed by virtue of an enactment
Section 29(6) and Parts 6 and 7	Sex	A requirement of an enactment
Parts 3, 4, 6 and 7	Sexual orientation	A requirement of an enactment
		A relevant requirement or condition imposed by virtue of an enactment

(2) A reference in the table to Part 6 does not include a reference to that Part so far as relating to vocational training.

(3) In this paragraph a reference to an enactment includes a reference to—

(a) a Measure of the General Synod of the Church of England;

(b) an enactment passed or made on or after the date on which this Act is passed.

(4) In the table, a relevant requirement or condition is a requirement or condition imposed (whether before or after the passing of this Act) by—

(a) a Minister of the Crown;

(b) a member of the Scottish Executive;

(c) the National Assembly for Wales (constituted by the Government of Wales Act 1998);

(d) the Welsh Ministers, the First Minister for Wales or the Counsel General to the Welsh Government.

EQUALITY

Protection of women

2 (1) A person (P) does not contravene a specified provision only by doing in relation to a woman (W) anything P is required to do to comply with—

(a) a pre-1975 Act enactment concerning the protection of women;
(b) a relevant statutory provision (within the meaning of Part 1 of the Health and Safety at Work etc Act 1974) if it is done for the purpose of the protection of W (or a description of women which includes W);
(c) a requirement of a provision specified in Schedule 1 to the Employment Act 1989 (provisions concerned with protection of women at work).

(2) The references to the protection of women are references to protecting women in relation to—

(a) pregnancy or maternity, or
(b) any other circumstances giving rise to risks specifically affecting women.

(3) It does not matter whether the protection is restricted to women.

(4) These are the specified provisions—

(a) Part 5 (work);
(b) Part 6 (education), so far as relating to vocational training.

(5) A pre-1975 Act enactment is an enactment contained in—

(a) an Act passed before the Sex Discrimination Act 1975;
(b) an instrument approved or made by or under such an Act (including one approved or made after the passing of the 1975 Act).

(6) If an Act repeals and re-enacts (with or without modification) a pre-1975 enactment then the provision re-enacted must be treated as being in a pre-1975 enactment.

(7) For the purposes of sub-paragraph (1)(c), a reference to a provision in Schedule 1 to the Employment Act 1989 includes a reference to a provision for the time being having effect in place of it.

(8) This paragraph applies only to the following protected characteristics—

(a) pregnancy and maternity;
(b) sex.

Educational appointments, etc: religious belief

3 (1) A person does not contravene Part 5 (work) only by doing a relevant act in connection with the employment of another in a relevant position.

(2) A relevant position is—

(a) the head teacher or principal of an educational establishment;
(b) the head, a fellow or other member of the academic staff of a college, or institution in the nature of a college, in a university;
(c) a professorship of a university which is a canon professorship or one to which a canonry is annexed.

(3) A relevant act is anything it is necessary to do to comply with—

(a) a requirement of an instrument relating to the establishment that the head teacher or principal must be a member of a particular religious order;
(b) a requirement of an instrument relating to the college or institution that the holder of the position must be a woman;
(c) an Act or instrument in accordance with which the professorship is a canon professorship or one to which a canonry is annexed.

(4) Sub-paragraph (3)(b) does not apply to an instrument taking effect on or after 16 January 1990 (the day on which section 5(3) of the Employment Act 1989 came into force).

(5) A Minister of the Crown may by order provide that anything in sub-paragraphs (1) to (3) does not have effect in relation to—

(a) a specified educational establishment or university;

(b) a specified description of educational establishments.

(6) An educational establishment is—

(a) a school within the meaning of the Education Act 1996 or the Education (Scotland) Act 1980;

(b) a college, or institution in the nature of a college, in a university;

(c) an institution designated by order made, or having effect as if made, under section 129 of the Education Reform Act 1988;

(d) a college of further education within the meaning of section 36 of the Further and Higher Education (Scotland) Act 1992;

(e) a university in Scotland;

(f) an institution designated by order under section 28 of the Further and Higher Education Act 1992 or section 44 of the Further and Higher Education (Scotland) Act 1992.

(7) This paragraph does not affect paragraph 2 of Schedule 9.

4 A person does not contravene this Act only by doing anything which is permitted for the purposes of—

(a) section 58(6) or (7) of the School Standards and Framework Act 1998 (dismissal of teachers because of failure to give religious education efficiently);

(b) section 60(4) and (5) of that Act (religious considerations relating to certain appointments);

(c) section 124A of that Act (preference for certain teachers at independent schools of a religious character);

(d) section 124AA(5) to (7) of that Act (religious considerations relating to certain teachers at Academies with religious character).

CROWN EMPLOYMENT, ETC

5 (1) A person does not contravene this Act—

(a) by making or continuing in force rules mentioned in sub-paragraph (2);

(b) by publishing, displaying or implementing such rules;

(c) by publishing the gist of such rules.

(2) The rules are rules restricting to persons of particular birth, nationality, descent or residence—

(a) employment in the service of the Crown;

(b) employment by a prescribed public body;

(c) holding a public office (within the meaning of section 50).

(3) The power to make regulations for the purpose of sub-paragraph (2)(b) is exercisable by the Minister for the Civil Service.

(4) In this paragraph "public body" means a body (whether corporate or unincorporated) exercising public functions (within the meaning given by section 31(4)).

EQUALITY

SCHEDULE 23
GENERAL EXCEPTIONS

Section 196

ACTS AUTHORISED BY STATUTE OR THE EXECUTIVE

III EQU [233]

1 (1) This paragraph applies to anything done—

(a) in pursuance of an enactment;

(b) in pursuance of an instrument made by a member of the executive under an enactment;

(c) to comply with a requirement imposed (whether before or after the passing of this Act) by a member of the executive by virtue of an enactment;

(d) in pursuance of arrangements made (whether before or after the passing of this Act) by or with the approval of, or for the time being approved by, a Minister of the Crown;

(e) to comply with a condition imposed (whether before or after the passing of this Act) by a Minister of the Crown.

(2) A person does not contravene Part 3, 4, 5 or 6 by doing anything to which this paragraph applies which discriminates against another because of the other's nationality.

(3) A person (A) does not contravene Part 3, 4, 5 or 6 if, by doing anything to which this paragraph applies, A discriminates against another (B) by applying to B a provision, criterion or practice which relates to—

(a) B's place of ordinary residence;

(b) the length of time B has been present or resident in or outside the United Kingdom or an area within it.

ORGANISATIONS RELATING TO RELIGION OR BELIEF

2 (1) This paragraph applies to an organisation the purpose of which is—

(a) to practise a religion or belief,

(b) to advance a religion or belief,

(c) to teach the practice or principles of a religion or belief,

(d) to enable persons of a religion or belief to receive any benefit, or to engage in any activity, within the framework of that religion or belief, or

(e) to foster or maintain good relations between persons of different religions or beliefs.

(2) This paragraph does not apply to an organisation whose sole or main purpose is commercial.

(3) The organisation does not contravene Part 3, 4 or 7, so far as relating to religion or belief or sexual orientation, only by restricting—

(a) membership of the organisation;

(b) participation in activities undertaken by the organisation or on its behalf or under its auspices;

(c) the provision of goods, facilities or services in the course of activities undertaken by the organisation or on its behalf or under its auspices;

(d) the use or disposal of premises owned or controlled by the organisation.

(4) A person does not contravene Part 3, 4 or 7, so far as relating to religion or belief or sexual orientation, only by doing anything mentioned in sub-paragraph (3) on behalf of or under the auspices of the organisation.

(5) A minister does not contravene Part 3, 4 or 7, so far as relating to religion or belief or sexual orientation, only by restricting—

(a) participation in activities carried on in the performance of the minister's functions in connection with or in respect of the organisation;

(b) the provision of goods, facilities or services in the course of activities carried on in the performance of the minister's functions in connection with or in respect of the organisation.

(6) Sub-paragraphs (3) to (5) permit a restriction relating to religion or belief only if it is imposed—

(a) because of the purpose of the organisation, or

(b) to avoid causing offence, on grounds of the religion or belief to which the organisation relates, to persons of that religion or belief.

(7) Sub-paragraphs (3) to (5) permit a restriction relating to sexual orientation only if it is imposed—

(a) because it is necessary to comply with the doctrine of the organisation, or

(b) to avoid conflict with strongly held convictions within sub-paragraph (9).

(8) In sub-paragraph (5), the reference to a minister is a reference to a minister of religion, or other person, who—

(a) performs functions in connection with a religion or belief to which the organisation relates, and

(b) holds an office or appointment in, or is accredited, approved or recognised for the purposes of the organisation.

(9) The strongly held convictions are—

(a) in the case of a religion, the strongly held religious convictions of a significant number of the religion's followers;

(b) in the case of a belief, the strongly held convictions relating to the belief of a significant number of the belief's followers.

(9A) An organisation does not contravene Part 3, 4 or 7 only by refusing to allow premises owned or controlled by the organisation to be used—

(a) to solemnise a relevant Scottish marriage for the reason that the marriage is the marriage of two persons of the same sex;

(b) to register a relevant Scottish civil partnership for the reason that the civil partnership is between two persons of the same sex.

(9B) A person (or a group of persons) does not contravene Part 3, 4 or 7 only by refusing to allow premises owned or controlled by the person (or the group) on behalf of an organisation to be used—

(a) to solemnise a relevant Scottish marriage for the reason that the marriage is the marriage of two persons of the same sex;

(b) to register a relevant Scottish civil partnership for the reason that the civil partnership is between two persons of the same sex.

(9C) An organisation does not contravene section 29 only by allowing an approved celebrant of the organisation to act as set out in sub-paragraph (1) or (2) of paragraph 25B of Schedule 3.

(9D) In sub-paragraphs (9A) to (9C), "approved celebrant", "relevant Scottish marriage" and "relevant Scottish civil partnership" have the same meaning as in paragraph 25B of Schedule 3.

(10) This paragraph does not permit anything which is prohibited by section 29, so far as relating to sexual orientation, if it is done—

(a) on behalf of a public authority, and

(b) under the terms of a contract between the organisation and the public authority.

(11) In the application of this paragraph in relation to sexual orientation, sub-paragraph (1)(e) must be ignored.

(12) In the application of this paragraph in relation to sexual orientation, in sub-paragraph (3)(d), "disposal" does not include disposal of an interest in premises by way of sale if the interest being disposed of is—

(a) the entirety of the organisation's interest in the premises, or

(b) the entirety of the interest in respect of which the organisation has power of disposal.

(13) In this paragraph—

(a) "disposal" is to be construed in accordance with section 38;

(b) "public authority" has the meaning given in section 150(1).

COMMUNAL ACCOMMODATION

3 (1) A person does not contravene this Act, so far as relating to sex discrimination or gender reassignment discrimination, only because of anything done in relation to—

(a) the admission of persons to communal accommodation;

(b) the provision of a benefit, facility or service linked to the accommodation.

(2) Sub-paragraph (1)(a) does not apply unless the accommodation is managed in a way which is as fair as possible to both men and women.

(3) In applying sub-paragraph (1)(a), account must be taken of—

(a) whether and how far it is reasonable to expect that the accommodation should be altered or extended or that further accommodation should be provided, and

(b) the frequency of the demand or need for use of the accommodation by persons of one sex as compared with those of the other.

(4) In applying sub-paragraph (1)(a) in relation to gender reassignment, account must also be taken of whether and how far the conduct in question is a proportionate means of achieving a legitimate aim.

(5) Communal accommodation is residential accommodation which includes dormitories or other shared sleeping accommodation which for reasons of privacy should be used only by persons of the same sex.

(6) Communal accommodation may include—

(a) shared sleeping accommodation for men and for women;

(b) ordinary sleeping accommodation;

(c) residential accommodation all or part of which should be used only by persons of the same sex because of the nature of the sanitary facilities serving the accommodation.

(7) A benefit, facility or service is linked to communal accommodation if—

(a) it cannot properly and effectively be provided except for those using the accommodation, and

(b) a person could be refused use of the accommodation in reliance on sub-paragraph (1)(a).

(8) This paragraph does not apply for the purposes of Part 5 (work) unless such arrangements as are reasonably practicable are made to compensate for—

(a) in a case where sub-paragraph (1)(a) applies, the refusal of use of the accommodation;

(b) in a case where sub-paragraph (1)(b) applies, the refusal of provision of the benefit, facility or service.

Training provided to non-EEA residents, etc

4 (1) A person (A) does not contravene this Act, so far as relating to nationality, only by providing a non-resident (B) with training, if A thinks that B does not intend to exercise in Great Britain skills B obtains as a result.

(2) A non-resident is a person who is not ordinarily resident in an EEA state.

(3) The reference to providing B with training is—

(a) if A employs B in relevant employment, a reference to doing anything in or in connection with the employment;

(b) if A as a principal allows B to do relevant contract work, a reference to doing anything in or in connection with allowing B to do the work;

(c) in a case within paragraph (a) or (b) or any other case, a reference to affording B access to facilities for education or training or ancillary benefits.

(4) Employment or contract work is relevant if its sole or main purpose is the provision of training in skills.

(5) In the case of training provided by the armed forces or Secretary of State for purposes relating to defence, sub-paragraph (1) has effect as if—

(a) the reference in sub-paragraph (2) to an EEA state were a reference to Great Britain, and

(b) in sub-paragraph (4), for "its sole or main purpose is" there were substituted "it is for purposes including".

(6) "Contract work" and "principal" each have the meaning given in section 41.

SCHEDULE 24
HARMONISATION: EXCEPTIONS

Section 203

III EQU [234]

Part 1 (public sector duty regarding socio-economic inequalities)
Chapter 2 of Part 5 (occupational pensions)
Section 78 (gender pay gap)
Section 106 (election candidates: diversity information)
Chapters 1 to 3 and 5 of Part 9 (enforcement), except section 136
Sections 142 and 146 (unenforceable terms, declaration in respect of void terms)
Chapter 1 of Part 11 (public sector equality duty)
Part 12 (disabled persons: transport)
Part 13 (disability: miscellaneous)
Section 197 (power to specify age exceptions)
Part 15 (family property)
Part 16 (general and miscellaneous)
Schedule 1 (disability: supplementary provision)
In Schedule 3 (services and public functions: exceptions)—

(a) in Part 3 (health and care), paragraphs 13 and 14;
(b) Part 4 (immigration);
(c) Part 5 (insurance);
(d) Part 6 (marriage);
(e) Part 7 (separate and single services), except paragraph 30;
(f) Part 8 (television, radio and on-line broadcasting and distribution);
(g) Part 9 (transport);
(h) Part 10 (supplementary)

Schedule 4 (premises: reasonable adjustments)
Schedule 5 (premises: exceptions), except paragraph 1
Schedule 6 (office-holders: excluded offices), except so far as relating to colour or nationality or marriage and civil partnership
Schedule 8 (work: reasonable adjustments)
In Schedule 9 (work: exceptions)—

(a) Part 1 (general), except so far as relating to colour or nationality;
(b) Part 2 (exceptions relating to age);
(c) Part 3 (other exceptions), except paragraph 19 so far as relating to colour or nationality

Schedule 10 (education: accessibility for disabled pupils)
Schedule 13 (education: reasonable adjustments), except paragraphs 2, 5, 6 and 9
Schedule 17 (education: disabled pupils: enforcement)
Schedule 18 (public sector equality duty: exceptions)
Schedule 19 (list of public authorities)
Schedule 20 (rail vehicle accessibility: compliance)
Schedule 21 (reasonable adjustments: supplementary)
In Schedule 22 (exceptions: statutory provisions), paragraphs 2 and 5
Schedule 23 (general exceptions), except paragraph 2
Schedule 25 (information society services)

III EQU [234.1]

Schedule 24 will come into force from a date to be appointed: s 216(3).

EQUALITY

SCHEDULE 25
INFORMATION SOCIETY SERVICES

Section 206

Service providers

III EQU [235]

1 (1) This paragraph applies where a person concerned with the provision of an information society service (an "information society service provider") is established in Great Britain.
(2) This Act applies to anything done by the person in an EEA state (other than the United Kingdom) in providing the service as this Act would apply if the act in question were done by the person in Great Britain.

2 (1) This paragraph applies where an information society service provider is established in an EEA state (other than the United Kingdom).
(2) This Act does not apply to anything done by the person in providing the service.

Exceptions for mere conduits

3 (1) An information society service provider does not contravene this Act only by providing so much of an information society service as consists in—
(a) the provision of access to a communication network, or
(b) the transmission in a communication network of information provided by the recipient of the service.
(2) But sub-paragraph (1) applies only if the service provider does not—
(a) initiate the transmission,
(b) select the recipient of the transmission, or
(c) select or modify the information contained in the transmission.
(3) For the purposes of sub-paragraph (1), the provision of access to a communication network, and the transmission of information in a communication network, includes the automatic, intermediate and transient storage of the information transmitted so far as the storage is solely for the purpose of carrying out the transmission in the network.
(4) Sub-paragraph (3) does not apply if the information is stored for longer than is reasonably necessary for the transmission.

Exception for caching

4 (1) This paragraph applies where an information society service consists in the transmission in a communication network of information provided by a recipient of the service.
(2) The information society service provider does not contravene this Act only by doing anything in connection with the automatic, intermediate and temporary storage of information so provided if—
(a) the storage of the information is solely for the purpose of making more efficient the onward transmission of the information to other recipients of the service at their request, and
(b) the condition in sub-paragraph (3) is satisfied.
(3) The condition is that the service-provider—
(a) does not modify the information,
(b) complies with such conditions as are attached to having access to the information, and

(c) (where sub-paragraph (4) applies) expeditiously removes the information or disables access to it.

(4) This sub-paragraph applies if the service-provider obtains actual knowledge that—

(a) the information at the initial source of the transmission has been removed from the network,

(b) access to it has been disabled, or

(c) a court or administrative authority has required the removal from the network of, or the disablement of access to, the information.

EXCEPTION FOR HOSTING

5 (1) An information society service provider does not contravene this Act only by doing anything in providing so much of an information society service as consists in the storage of information provided by a recipient of the service, if—

(a) the service provider had no actual knowledge when the information was provided that its provision amounted to a contravention of this Act, or

(b) on obtaining actual knowledge that the provision of the information amounted to a contravention of that section, the service provider expeditiously removed the information or disabled access to it.

(2) Sub-paragraph (1) does not apply if the recipient of the service is acting under the authority of the control of the service provider.

MONITORING OBLIGATIONS

6 An injunction or interdict under Part 1 of the Equality Act 2006 may not impose on a person concerned with the provision of a service of a description given in paragraph 3(1), 4(1) or 5(1)—

(a) a liability the imposition of which would contravene Article 12, 13 or 14 of the E-Commerce Directive;

(b) a general obligation of the description given in Article 15 of that Directive.

INTERPRETATION

7 (1) This paragraph applies for the purposes of this Schedule.

(2) "Information society service"—

(a) has the meaning given in Article 2(a) of the E-Commerce Directive (which refers to Article 1(2) of Directive 98/34/EC of the European Parliament and of the Council of 22 June 1998 laying down a procedure for the provision of information in the field of technical standards and regulations), and

(b) is summarised in recital 17 of the E-Commerce Directive as covering "any service normally provided for remuneration, at a distance, by means of electronic equipment for the processing (including digital compression) and storage of data, and at the individual request of a recipient of a service".

(3) "The E-Commerce Directive" means Directive 2000/31/EC of the European Parliament and of the Council of 8 June 2000 on certain legal aspects of information society services, in particular electronic commerce, in the Internal Market (Directive on electronic commerce).

(4) "Recipient" means a person who (whether for professional purposes or not) uses an information society service, in particular for seeking information or making it accessible.

(5) An information society service-provider is "established" in a country or territory if the service-provider—

(a) effectively pursues an economic activity using a fixed establishment in that country or territory for an indefinite period, and
(b) is a national of an EEA state or a body mentioned in Article 54 of the treaty on the Functioning of the European Union.

(6) The presence or use in a particular place of equipment or other technical means of providing an information society service is not itself sufficient to constitute the establishment of a service-provider.

(7) Where it cannot be decided from which of a number of establishments an information society service is provided, the service is to be regarded as provided from the establishment at the centre of the information society service provider's activities relating to that service.

(8) Section 212(4) does not apply to references to providing a service.

PRACTICE DIRECTION — PROCEEDINGS UNDER ENACTMENTS RELATING TO EQUALITY

SCOPE AND INTERPRETATION

III EQU PD 1

1.1 This Practice Direction applies to certain county court proceedings under the enactments defined in paragraph 1.2.

1.2 In this Practice Direction –

(1) 'the 2006 Act' means the Equality Act 2006;
(2) 'the 2010 Act' means the Equality Act 2010;
(3) 'the Commission' means the Commission for Equality and Human Rights;

1.3 For proceedings which relate to conduct before 1 October 2010, the Practice Direction on Proceedings Under Enactments Relating to Discrimination applies.

COMMISSION TO BE GIVEN NOTICE OF CLAIMS

2. When a claim under section 114 of the 2010 Act is commenced, the claimant must give notice of the commencement of the proceedings to the Commission and file a copy of that notice.

ASSESSORS

3. Rule 35.15 has effect in relation to an assessor who is to be appointed in proceedings under section 114 (7) of the 2010 Act.

EXCLUSION OF PERSONS FROM CERTAIN PROCEEDINGS

4.1 In a claim brought under section 114 of the 2010 Act the court may, where it considers it expedient in the interests of national security –

(a) exclude from all or part of the proceedings –
  (i) the claimant;
  (ii) a representative of the claimant;
  (iii) an assessor;
(b) permit a claimant or representative who has been excluded to make a statement to the court before the commencement of the proceedings, or the part of the proceedings, to which the exclusion relates:

(c) take steps to keep secret all or part of the reasons for its decision in the claim.

4.2 In this paragraph, a 'special advocate' means a person appointed under section 117(5) of the 2010 Act.

4.3 In proceedings to which this paragraph refers, where the claimant or a representative of the claimant has been excluded from all or part of the proceedings—

(a) the court will inform the Attorney General of the proceedings; and
(b) the Attorney General may appoint a special advocate to represent the interests of a claimant in, or in any part of, proceedings to which an exclusion under paragraph 4.1 relates.

4.4 In exercise of its powers under paragraph 4.1(c), the court may order the special advocate not to communicate (directly or indirectly) with any person (including the excluded claimant)—

(a) on any matter discussed or referred to; or
(b) with regard to any material disclosed,

during or with reference to any part of the proceedings to which an exclusion under paragraph 4.1 relates.

4.5 Where the court makes an order referred to in paragraph 4.4 (or any similar order), the special advocate may apply for permission to seek instructions from, or otherwise to communicate with an excluded person and the court may make directions for that purpose.

EXPENSES OF COMMISSION

5.1 This paragraph applies where the Commission has, in respect of a claim, provided a claimant with assistance under section 28 of the 2006 Act.

5.2 If the Commission claims a charge for expenses incurred by it in providing such assistance, it must give notice of the claim to –

(a) the court; and
(b) the claimant,

within 14 days of determination of the proceedings.

5.3 If notice is given to the court under paragraph 5.2—

(a) money paid into court for the benefit of the claimant that relates to costs and expenses must not be paid out unless this is permitted by an order of the court; and
(b) the court may order the expenses incurred by the Commission to be assessed and paid as if they were costs payable by claimant to own solicitor.

5.4 The court may either—

(a) make a summary assessment of the expenses; or
(b) order detailed assessment of the expenses by a costs officer.

EUROPE

TABLE OF CONTENTS

INTRODUCTION

III EUR [0]

At the time of submission of this Chapter the political landscape and potential outcome of the Brexit process is still unknown. Hence, it is virtually impossible to make an educated guess on whether the UK will leave the EU on 29 March 2019 with or without a deal; or if it will even leave the bloc altogether on that day, as an extension of article 50 of the Treaty on the European Union (TEU) could be requested. If the latter were the case, UK legislation, ie European Union (Withdrawal) Act 2018, would need to be adapted accordingly before that day.

The EU–UK Withdrawal Agreement, result of months of negotiations and approved by EU leaders on 25 November 2018, contains rules that would govern the transition, ie 30 March 2019 to 31 December 2020, in several areas including Jurisdiction in Civil and Commercial matters (see Title VI, articles 66–69). In order to do that it must enter into force and that seems unlikely as it was rejected by the House of Commons in mid-January 2019. The likelihood of the UK leaving the EU under the No Deal scenario on 29 March (even if that occurs by default) has increased unless 'the' or 'a' deal is agreed and ratified or an extension is requested by the UK (and granted by the EU) before that date.

In the context of Brexit it is important to mention the outcome of case *Wightman v Secretary of State for Exiting the European Union: C-621/18* ECLI:EU:C:2018:999. In this case the CJEU was asked to clarify the scope of article 50 TEU, in particular, whether the UK can unilaterally revoke article 50. The Court ruled that in the absence of an express provision governing revocation of the notification of the intention to withdraw, that revocation is subject

EUROPE

to the rules laid down in article 50(1) for the withdrawal itself, with the result that it may be decided upon unilaterally, in accordance with the constitutional requirements of the Member State concerned. In other words, where a Member State has notified the European Council of its intention to withdraw from the EU, that article allows that Member State – for as long as a withdrawal agreement concluded between them has not entered into force or, if no such agreement has been concluded, for as long as the two-year period laid down in article 50(3) TEU, possibly extended in accordance with that paragraph, has not expired – to revoke that notification unilaterally, in an unequivocal and unconditional manner, by a notice addressed to the European Council in writing, after the Member State concerned has taken the revocation decision in accordance with its constitutional requirements. The purpose of the revocation is to confirm the EU membership of the Member State concerned under terms that are unchanged as regards its status. That revocation brings the withdrawal procedure to an end. This is yet another option to conclude the Brexit process.

In light of the above, this Chapter will reflect the current status quo of the legislation and case law applicable pre-Brexit.

GENERAL NOTES ON THE EU AND ITS UNIQUE SYSTEM

III EUR [1]

The European Union (EU) is a unique supranational organization. It is not a country nor a federation or an intergovernmental organisation. Its structure and legal system do not fall into any traditional legal category and works in seemingly unusual ways, its own. Its Member States, remain independent sovereign nations, however, they have partially transferred sovereignty via the Treaties and internationally gained strength and influence they would have not achieved on their own.

From its inception the European Community (now EU) was intended to grow and become more than just an economic bloc. The founding Member States agreed to transfer parcels of sovereignty to the newly 'supranational' institutions where supranational means something placed over a national structure (different from 'intergovernmental' where decisions are taken by consensus and linked to national government interests). Member States are no longer able to adopt, independently, legislation in the areas delegated in the Treaties, ie the current Treaty on the European Union (TEU) and Treaty on the Functioning of the European Union (TFEU) and their predecessors. The original Member States created a new system that, according to established case law of the Court of Justice of the EU (CJEU), takes precedence over their national law (to that effect see *Costa (Flaminio) v ENEL: C-6/64* [1964] ECR 585, ECJ), which States joining the EU must accept without reservations.

III EUR [2]

The Member States The process of integration culminating in the EU began in 1951 between six countries (Belgium, Germany, France, Italy, Luxembourg and the Netherlands). After seven rounds of accessions or enlargements (1973: Denmark, Ireland and the UK; 1981: Greece; 1986: Spain and Portugal; 1995: Austria, Finland and Sweden; 2004: Cyprus, Czech Republic, Estonia, Hungary, Latvia, Lithuania, Malta, Poland, Slovakia and Slovenia; 2007: Bulgaria and Romania and 2013: Croatia), the EU has today 28 Member States and a handful of candidate states expected to join in the future.

In June 2016 the UK voted to leave the EU and as such the UK is the first Member State to use the exit clause set out in article 50 TEU. The exit process started on 29 March 2017, the date on which article 50 was activated and set the UK's departure date from the EU as 29 March 2019. Until that date the UK will be a full Member State and all its obligations under the Treaties will remain valid. Therefore, all existing EU legislation including any adopted during the exit negotiations are and will be applicable to the UK for as long as it remains a Member State in the strict sense of the word.

III EUR [3]

The EU institutions At present there are seven EU institutions:

The **European Council**, which was elevated to the rank of institution by the Treaty of Lisbon, is the political driving force of the EU and sets the goals that the Heads of State or Government of the Member States believe the EU needs to pursue.

The **Council of the EU** is co-legislator with the European Parliament. It represents the governments of the Member States (by Ministers or officials of equivalent rank) and has no permanent formation except for permanent committees. Its shape changes according to the matters debated during its meetings.

The **European Parliament** is co-legislator with the Council of the EU. It represents EU citizens (500+ million). Members of Parliament align according to political views not by nationality and aim to legislate protecting the interests of EU citizens.

The **European Commission** is the executive of the EU and 'Guardian of the Treaties'. It drafts legislation and ensures EU law is complied with. As such, it initiates infringement procedures against Member States when necessary. It is made up of a representative of each Member State (28 Commissioners). The Commissioners are said to have a "dual-hat" as they represent their Member State in the composition but as Commissioners they must have the interests of the EU at heart.

The **Court of Justice of the EU (CJEU)** is the judiciary and interprets EU law. Renamed by the Treaty of Lisbon, the CJEU (ex-ECJ) is 'one' institution that comprises two different Courts: the Court of Justice and the General Court.

Court of Justice: shares the name of the institution and comprises one judge per Member State. Its formations are: Chambers, Full Court and Grand Chamber. The Advocates General assist the Court by submitting conclusions on the merits of the case at hand facts and applicable law (known as Opinion of the Advocate General). The Court has no obligation to follow the Opinion but usually does.

General Court: formerly known as Court of First Instance (CFI) this court acts mainly as a first instance court. It comprises, as from 19 September 2016, 44 judges and has no Advocates General (AGs). Even though it does not have AGs if there is a need one of the judges may be called upon to perform that function. The court rules in Chambers or Grand Chamber.

The **Court of Auditors** is the auditor of the EU's finances. Its audit work starts with the EU's budget and policies meaning it checks how the EU institutions spend EU money including that contributed annually by the Member States. Auditors produce reports on the findings.

The **European Central Bank (ECB)** was elevated to the rank of institution by the Treaty of Lisbon. It is the central bank of the EU countries whose currency is the euro. Its main task is to maintain price stability in the Eurozone and preserve the purchasing power of the single currency. Its actions impact non-Euro zone Member States such as the UK.

III EUR [4]

The legal system (principles) The EU legal system is *sui generis* and cannot be compared to either the civil or common law systems. The key to understanding how it works is to avoid attempts to subsume it into (or compare it to) a national system and observe its rules and behaviour carefully.

Some of the most important principles that govern EU law are conferral, subsidiarity, proportionality and supremacy - though there are more. The first three are express in the Treaties and the latter has been developed by the CJEU via case law:

- *Conferral* (TUE, arts 4 and 5): Member States transferred some competences (or sovereignty if preferred) to the EU and agreed to refrain from adopting legislation in those areas (or, in other words, to act only in response to a specific instruction from the EU on the matter). Once the competence is transferred it cannot be recalled. A Member State will infringe the Treaty if it adopts legislation in the areas of EU exclusive competence (for catalogue of competences see TFEU, arts 3 to 6). Member States cannot recall powers nor redefine their relationship with the EU; they are 'in or out', however, there are a few exceptions in specific areas, eg the UK in Justice and Home Affairs.
- *Subsidiarity* (TUE, art 5 and Protocol on the application of the principles of subsidiarity and proportionality): it is paramount to the system. The EU will act only and in so far as its action has more chances of success than Member States' action in a particular area. Where Member States' action is more likely to be successful this principle is not complied with and the legislation should not be adopted as it could be later annulled or declared void by the CJEU.
- *Proportionality* (TUE, art 5 and Protocol on the application of the principles of subsidiarity and proportionality): closely linked to subsidiarity, it means that the EU action cannot go beyond what is necessary to achieve the objectives set out in the Treaties. Should the EU go over that limit the legislation could be annulled.
- *Supremacy*: logical and necessary to the system it was established by the CJEU in *Costa (Flaminio) v ENEL: C-6/64* [1964] ECR 585, ECJ. The provisions of EU law take precedence over national law. Where in conflict national legislation must be set aside (or applied in light of the conformity with EU law doctrine) and the EU norm applied. It covers primary, as well as secondary and tertiary sources of law.

In summary, conferral delimits the competences of the EU and those which remain with the Member States and the principles of subsidiarity and proportionality act as limits to the exercise of those conferred competences. As an umbrella, to ensure the correct functioning of the system, the supremacy or primacy of EU law over national law requires national judges to apply EU law when acting as EU judges. National judges act as two sides of the same coin: where the case has no EU element they rule solely on national law but where the case before them has an EU connection they need to act as EU judges and apply the principle of primacy.

III EUR [5]

EU law (typology) EU law comprises primary, secondary and tertiary sources of law and is wider than EU legislation as the latter refers to acts adopted by the EU institutions in application of the Treaties. The system as such takes precedence over national law, therefore, it is important to know its elements.

Primary: Treaties, their amendments, protocols and accession Treaties, ie the Founding Treaties (European Steel and Coal Community (ESCC), European Atomic Energy Community (EAEC), European Economic Community (EEC), Treaty on European Union (TEU)); their amendments (Single European Act, Maastricht, Amsterdam, Nice, Lisbon) and protocols attached to them as well as the Accession Treaties of Member States beyond the six founding States.

The commonly known as Treaty of Maastricht comprises two Treaties: the amendment to and rename of the EEC to European Community Treaty (ECT) and the creation of the EU via the TEU. From Maastricht onwards, until the Treaty of Lisbon, the amending Treaties cover modifications to both ECT and TEU. With the Treaty of Lisbon the system was simplified to the TEU and Treaty on the Functioning of the EU (TFEU), the EC ceased to exist. The European Community (EC) was transformed into the European Union with a major development; the latter has, unlike the former, legal personality and can enter into agreements and international treaties on its own name.

Secondary: legislation adopted by the EU institutions. According to TFEU, art 288 the different types are: Regulations, Directives, Decisions, Recommendations and Opinions (the last two, known as 'soft law', have no binding force but are usually taken into account in EU judgments – and are not covered in this section). The Treaty of Lisbon redefined the concept of secondary legislation which now comprises legislative and non-legislative acts, the latter are acts adopted by the European Commission as opposed to legislative acts which are adopted by the Council of the EU and Parliament, the co-legislators.

Non-legislative acts can be 'delegated' or 'implementing' acts (see TFEU, arts 290 and 291). In both the Commission will adopt new measures as stipulated in a legislative act (eg a Directive or Regulation) that delegates upon it the powers to issue those acts. When issued they will clearly indicate in the title whether they are delegated or implementing.

- **Regulation**: act of general application, binding in its entirety and directly applicable in the EU territory. No measures are required to incorporate it into national law. It can be of a legislative or non-legislative nature. Entry into force and application dates may differ but usually coincide.
- **Directive**: act used to harmonise areas, addressed to Member States, binding as to the result to be achieved which needs transposition into national law within the timeframe stipulated. It can be of a legislative or non-legislative nature. Entry into force and transposition deadline are usually up to 24 months apart. It can also have a different application date for the implementing legislation but usually it coincides with the transposition deadline. Unlike Regulations, which are used to uniform certain topics, Directives harmonise, ie gradually remove disparities.
- **Decision**: act that can be adopted by the Council of the EU (sometimes jointly with the Parliament) or by the Commission, hence, it can be legislative or non-legislative. It is fully binding upon its addressees (authorities, individuals, Member States) as it requires them to do something or stop doing something by a specific date and can also confer rights on them. It is a hybrid that has elements of both Regulations and Directives; hence, it needs careful consideration. No general rule on entry into force or application date (the Decision itself will stipulate that).

Tertiary: judgments (case law) of the CJEU and principles of EU law developed by it. The judgments interpret EU law and as such are to be complied with in the whole EU. If the judgments are not complied with the infringing Member State could, and most likely will, be fined. Sometimes those judgments formulate principles, eg direct and indirect effect, primacy of EU law, State liability, and become landmark cases.

III EUR [6]

Interpretation of EU law The rule is that Member States and the Commission, the latter via non-legislative acts of TFEU, arts 290 and 291, implement EU law but only the judiciaries (ie CJEU or national courts) can interpret it. The national judge has to act as an EU judge and set aside national legislation if it conflicts with EU law. If in doubt on the interpretation or validity of an EU provision, national courts can refer questions to the CJEU.

III EUR [7]

References to the CJEU: preliminary ruling procedure The relationship between national courts and the CJEU is reference-based with the CJEU interpreting EU law and national courts applying that interpretation. The procedure, called 'reference for a preliminary ruling', commences with a reference lodged at the CJEU by a court or tribunal of a Member State. A national judge may decide to make a reference to the CJEU because he finds interpretation of EU law ambiguous in relation to an ongoing court case. The national proceedings are stayed until the CJEU delivers its interpretation, then the national judge issues its ruling based on the CJEU interpretation.

All national courts 'can' refer questions to the CJEU but the highest courts or even administrative tribunals whose judgments or decisions cannot be appealed 'must' refer the case if there is a doubt on the interpretation of an EU provision or on its possible application to the national case (see TFEU, art 267):

'The Court of Justice of the European Union shall have jurisdiction to give preliminary rulings concerning:

(a) the interpretation of the Treaties;
(b) the validity and interpretation of acts of the institutions, bodies, offices or agencies of the Union;

Where such a question is raised before any court or tribunal of a Member State, that court or tribunal may, if it considers that a decision on the question is necessary to enable it to give judgment, request the Court to give a ruling thereon.

Where any such question is raised in a case pending before a court or tribunal of a Member State against whose decisions there is no judicial remedy under national law, that court or tribunal shall bring the matter before the Court.

If such a question is raised in a case pending before a court or tribunal of a Member State with regard to a person in custody, the Court of Justice of the European Union shall act with the minimum of delay.'

These rulings amount to well over half of cases reaching the CJEU. A recent example of this is case *Wightman v Secretary of State for Exiting the European Union: C-621/18* ECLI:EU:C:2018:999, referred by a UK court.

The CJEU's role is to provide the national court with an interpretation of EU law or to rule on its validity, not to apply that law to the factual situation of the main proceedings. That is the task of the national court or tribunal. The CJEU does not decide issues of fact nor resolves differences of opinion on the interpretation or application of national law. In references from national courts under TFEU, art 267, the CJEU is not exercising a normal appellate function and therefore cannot determine or reverse issues of fact: *Arsenal Football Club plc v Reed* [2002] EWHC 2695 (Ch), [2003] 1 All ER 137.

When ruling on the interpretation or validity of EU law, the CJEU will make every effort to give an answer which will be of assistance to the national court in resolving the dispute in the main proceedings. However, it is for that court or tribunal to draw specific conclusions from the ruling and, if necessary, disapply the rule of national law in question.

It is appropriate to refer a matter to the CJEU where it cannot be said with complete confidence that the Court would decide that implementation by a devolved government within the UK is to be treated, for the purposes of the principle of equality and non-discrimination, as if it were implementation by the Member State: *R (on the application of Horvath) v Secretary of State for the Environment, Food and Rural Affairs* [2007] EWCA Civ 620, (2007) Times, 30 July.

In the UK, the CPR Part 68 establishes the steps to follow to make a reference to the CJEU and Practice Direction 68 supplements them. In addition, the Supreme Court has issued some rules on the application of TFEU, art 267 via the Supreme Court Rules 2009, SI 2009/1603, as amended. The rules are found in Part 6, s 42 and are supplemented by Practice Direction 11 (European Communities Act 1972 (**III EUR [386]**) contains more UK-specific information and case law).

The EU has issued guidance on this procedure in *Recommendations to national courts and tribunals in relation to the initiation of preliminary ruling proceedings (2012/C 338/01).*

III EUR [8]

Remedies for non-compliance with EU law In addition to the means of enforcement of EU law available to the EU institutions, ie the infringement procedure (including the referral to the CJEU) there are some principles, developed by the CJEU, to enforce EU law at national level. These are remedies available to individuals when they face breaches of compliance with EU law. Those principles, known as judicial enforcement of EU law, are: direct effect, indirect effect and State liability. The infringement procedure comprises two phases: the administrative and the litigation phase or referral to the CJEU. Cases can be closed at the administrative phase so the litigation phase may not occur.

Their development took place in the context of the preliminary ruling procedure of TFEU, art 267 which is the way that national courts have to cooperate and collaborate with the CJEU in order to achieve a harmonised interpretation of EU law.

In other words, whenever individuals are affected by the non-compliance of EU law provisions they may resort to their national courts to seek enforcement of the rights conferred upon them by EU law, the interpretation of national law in light of EU law or claim damages where the State's action (or inaction) caused them damages or loss.

All three remedies stem from the principle of sincere cooperation (TEU, art 4(3) and its predecessors) which places upon national courts the duty to protect the rights conferred by EU law on individuals, including enforcement of these rights where the Member State is responsible for breaches of EU law.

III EUR [9]

Direct effect This is a fundamental principle of EU law developed by the CJEU in the early 1960s. It can be described as a mechanism for individuals to request national courts to enforce rights derived from EU provisions. It was established in *Van Gend en Loos (C-26/62)* which set the main criteria needed for direct effect which are, today, still applicable.

The CJEU held that:

'The Community constitutes a new legal order of international law for the benefit of which the states have limited their sovereign rights, albeit within limited fields, and the subjects of which comprise not only member states but also their nationals. Independently of the legislation of member states, Community law therefore not only imposes obligations on individuals but is also intended to confer upon them rights which become part of their legal heritage. These rights arise not only where they are expressly granted by the Treaty, but also by reason of obligations which the Treaty imposes in a clearly defined way upon individuals as well as upon the member states and upon the institutions of the Community.'

The provision in question was EEC, art 12 (now TFEU, art 30), ie primary law. The action raised the question of the conflict between national legislation and the EEC Treaty.

For it to have direct effect an EU provision must be:

- clear;
- precise;
- unconditional; and
- confer rights upon the individuals.

The CJEU decided the question referred by the Netherlands court by stating the doctrine of direct effect, thus conferring on the individual a direct guarantee of the rights conferred by EU law before the national court.

It is widely accepted that Treaty articles, Regulations, Decisions and Directives are capable of producing such effect whereas Recommendations and Opinions lack that capability due to their non-binding nature. It must be borne in mind that the direct effect of Directives is the most commonly known facet of the principle and that which causes more problems considering that, by definition, Directives are not addressed to individuals and require an act of the Member State in order for them to be fully operational.

Vertical and horizontal direct effect:

- vertical: individual seeks to enforce an EU provision against the State (or emanation of the State);
- horizontal: individual seeks to enforce an EU provision against another individual.

The vertical direct effect has been recognised for: Treaty articles (*Algemene Transport-en Expeditie Onderneming van Gend en Loos NV v Nederlandse Belastingadministratie: C-26/62* [1963] ECR 1, [1963] CMLR 105, ECJ; *Lütticke (Alfons) GmbH v EC Commission: C-48/65* [1966] ECR 19, [1966] CMLR 378, ECJ); Regulations (*Politi SAS v Ministry for Finance of the Italian Republic: C-43/71* [1971] ECR 1039, *sub nom Politi SAS v Ministero delle Finanze: C-43/71* [1973] CMLR 60, ECJ; *Leonesio v Italian Ministry for Agriculture and Forestry: C-93/71* [1972] ECR 287, [1973] CMLR 343, ECJ); Decisions (*Grad v Finanzamt Traunstein: C-9/70* [1970] ECR 825, [1971] CMLR 1, ECJ; *Hansa Fleisch Ernst Mundt GmbH & Co KG v Landrat des Kreises Schleswig-Flensburg: C-156/91* [1992] ECR I-5567, ECJ); Directives (*Van Duyn v Home Office: C-41/74* [1975] Ch 358, [1975] 3 All ER 190, ECJ; *Pubblico Ministero v Ratti: C-148/78* [1979] ECR 1629, [1980] 1 CMLR 96, ECJ; *Foster v British Gas plc: C-188/89* [1991] 1 QB 405, [1990] 3 All ER 897).

As regards horizontal direct effect: Treaty articles (*Defrenne v Sabena: C-43/75* [1981] 1 All ER 122, [1976] ECR 455; *Ferlini v Centre hospitalier de Luxembourg: C-411/98* [2000] ECR I-8081, [2000] All ER (D) 1239, ECJ) and Regulations (*Muñoz (Antonio) y Cia SA v Frumar Ltd: C-253/00* [2003] Ch 328, [2002] ECR I-7289) are capable of such effect whereas for Directives the principle is consistently denied by the CJEU (*Marshall v Southampton and South West Hampshire Area Health Authority (Teaching): C-152/84* [1986] QB 401, [1986] 2 All ER 584, ECJ; *Dori v Recreb Srl: C-91/92* [1995] All ER (EC) 1, [1994] ECR I-3325, ECJ).

It is worth mentioning that part of the doctrine recognises the existence of a so called 'incidental direct effect' which basically is the negative impact on third parties that the application of vertical direct effect can have (*CIA Security International SA v Signalson: C-194/94* [1996] ECR I-2201, [1996] All ER (EC) 557, ECJ; *Unilever Italia SpA v Central Food SpA: C-443/98* [2000] ECR I-7535, [2001] 1 CMLR 566; *R (on the application of Delena Wells) v Secretary of State for Transport, Local Government and the Regions: C-201/02* ECLI:EU:C:2004:12). In some cases it would be something close to a partial horizontal direct effect (*Wells*).

III EUR [10]

Indirect effect The principle of indirect effect, otherwise known as consistent interpretation, was developed by the CJEU in the *Von Colson and Kamann v Land Nordrhein-Westfalen: C-14/83* [1984] ECR 1891, [1986] 2 CMLR 430, ECJ and *Marleasing SA v La Comercial Internacional de Alimentación SA: C-106/89* [1990] ECR I-4135, [1992] 1 CMLR 305, ECJ cases and it is mainly an interpretative tool that national courts 'can use' when their legal orders permit so. It requires that national courts interpret as far as possible national law in light of the wording and purpose of an EU provision. Mostly applied for Directives, when they are not implemented or incorrectly implemented, it can be used for all types of EU legislation as established in *Grimaldi v Fonds Des Maladies Professionnelles: C-322/88* [1990] IRLR 400 and *Pupino (criminal proceedings against): C-105/03* [2006] QB 83, [2006] All ER (EC) 142.

In *Grimaldi* the CJEU stated '[t]he national courts are bound to take recommendations into consideration in order to decide disputes submitted to them, in particular where they cast light on the interpretation of national measures adopted in order to implement them or where they are designed to supplement binding Community provisions'. In *Pupino* it extended the consistent interpretation doctrine to framework decisions in the context of the (then) judicial cooperation in civil and criminal matters (inter-governmental pillar of the TEU now part of the TFEU, arts 81 and 82).

Indirect effect was also developed as a means to counteract the negative effects of the non-recognition of horizontal direct effect as it allows individuals to rely on Directives before a national court against another individual.

In *Von Colson* the CJEU held that:

'... [t]he member state's obligation arising from a Directive to achieve the result envisaged by the Directive [...], is binding on all the authorities of the member states, including for matters within their jurisdiction, the courts. It follows that, in applying the national law and in particular the provisions of a national law specifically introduced in order to implement a Directive, national courts are required to interpret their national law in the light of the wording and the purpose of the Directive.

The obligation was later widened in *Marleasing*: '[...] in applying national law, whether the provisions in question were adopted before or after the directive, the national court called upon to interpret it is required to do so, as far as possible, in the light of the wording and the purpose of the directive'.

In other words, before *Marleasing* national courts had to interpret national implementing legislation in light of the wording and purpose of the Directive. If there was no implementation of the Directive in the national legal order the obligation did not apply. The individual considered there was an incorrect or inadequate implementation and challenged that precisely.

After *Marleasing* the obligation arises whether there is implementing legislation or not (this includes legislation that predates the Directive which covers the same matter but cannot be considered implementing legislation as it was not adopted to give effect to the Directive or simply there is no legislation on the subject as the Member State did not implement it). Here the obligation seems absolute 'if the member state did not implement the Directive any piece of national law should be interpreted in light of the purpose of the Directive'. This created many problems which were later solved by setting the limits of the principle which are:

- if applying indirect effect would increase criminal liability or criminal charges (*Pretore di Salò v X: C-14/86* [1987] ECR 2545, [1989] 1 CMLR 71, ECJ; *Arcaro (criminal proceedings against): C-168/95* [1996] ECR I-4705, [1997] All ER (EC) 82, ECJ); or
- if it violates the principles of non-retroactivity, legitimate expectations or legal certainty (*Officier van Justitie v Kolpinghuis Nijmegen BV: C-80/86* [1987] ECR 3969, [1989] 2 CMLR 18, ECJ).

In *Harz v Deutsche Tradax GmbH: C-79/83* [1984] ECR 1921, [1986] 2 CMLR 430, ECJ the CJEU confirmed that Directives could have indirect effect in horizontal actions.

EUROPE

A few years later, the CJEU narrowed the principle by establishing that consistent interpretation must be applied when national law permits it. In other words, it cannot be the basis of a *contra legem* interpretation of national law. Where indirect effect cannot be used, in some cases, State liability is still a possibility: *Wagner Miret v Fondo de Garanatia Salarial: C-334/92* [1993] ECR I-6911, ECJ.

But it was in *Pupino* where the CJEU established more clearly the limits and scope of application of the principle. The case was about the possible direct or indirect effect of a Framework decision and the CJEU stated that:

'... the principle of conforming interpretation is binding in relation to framework decisions adopted in the context of Title VI of the TEU. When applying national law, the national court that is called upon to interpret it must do so as far as possible in the light of the wording and purpose of the framework decision in order to attain the result which it pursues. [T]he obligation on the national court to refer to the content of a framework decision when interpreting the relevant rules of its national law is limited by general principles of law, particularly those of legal certainty and non-retroactivity. In particular, those principles prevent that obligation from leading to the criminal liability of persons who contravene the provisions of a framework decision from being determined or aggravated on the basis of such a decision alone, independently of an implementing law.'

The result of the obligation to interpret national law in conformity with EU law depends on the flexibility of national law. When the provisions of national law that are inconsistent with EU law are very clear and precise, according to their interpreters, EU law will have little impact, because interpreting *contra legem* is not required (*Pupino*). Conversely, where national law is malleable, or considered so by its enforcers, the impact of EU law will be potentially much stronger. The CJEU does not leave entire discretion to national courts as it requires that they try as hard as possible to achieve consistent interpretation, which implies that they take 'the whole body of national law into consideration' and make use of the interpretative methods recognised by national law with a view to ensuring full effectiveness of EU law. But such interpretation is not always possible (see *Dominguez v Centre Informatique Du Centre Ouest Atlantique: C-282/10* [2012] 2 CMLR 437, [2012] IRLR 321).

III EUR [11]

State liability Arguably this is the last resort available to individuals who seek to enforce EU law in national courts, provided the non-compliance of EU provisions is found to be the direct result of the inaction or incorrect action of a Member State (ie where neither direct effect or indirect effect is possible). However, it can also be used where direct or indirect effect are available. The principle originated in the joined cases *Francovich and Bonifaci v Italy: C-6, 9/90* [1991] ECR I-5357, [1993] 2 CMLR 66, ECJ. Thus, since 1991, EU citizens have been able to bring an action for damages against a Member State which infringes EU law.

On the reference from the Italian court, the CJEU held that the Directive in question was designed to confer rights on individuals which they had been denied as a result of the failure to act of the Member State which had not implemented the Directive in question. In that way the Court opened up the possibility of an action for damages against the Member State itself: Francovich. The CJEU firstly denied the direct effect of key provisions of the Directive and then recalled *Van Gend en Loos* and *Costa* on the nature of the EU legal order to prepare the ground to say that '... [t]he full effectiveness of Community rules would be impaired and the protection of the rights which they grant would be weakened if individuals were unable to obtain redress when their rights are infringed by a breach of Community law for which a member state can be held responsible. It follows that the principle whereby a state must be liable for loss and damage caused to individuals as a result of breaches of Community law for which the state can be held responsible is inherent in the system of the Treaty.'

The requirements for State liability set in the landmark case were:

- EU provision (Directive in this case) must grant rights to the individual;
- the content of the right must be identifiable from the wording; and
- causal link between the breach of the State's obligation and the loss and damage suffered.

The conditions under which State liability gives rise to a right to reparation depend on the nature of the breach of EU law which causes the loss or damage. But the amount of reparation and the procedural steps to claim it in national courts is left to the national legal orders to establish always having in mind that the substantive and procedural conditions for reparation of loss and damage laid down by Member States' national law must not be less favourable than those relating to similar domestic claims and must not be so framed as to make it virtually impossible or excessively difficult to obtain reparation.

The *Francovich* test's requirements were later refined in *Brasserie du Pêcheur SA v Germany: C-46/93* [1996] QB 404, [1996] All ER (EC) 301, ECJ and *R v Secretary of State for Transport, ex p Factortame Ltd: C-48/93* [1996] QB 404, [1996] ECR I-1029, ECJ) which widened the notion of EU provision breached to all types of EU law (in *Brasserie* and

Factortame it was the Treaty, in *Francovich* it was a Directive). The former two cases put a number of questions to the Court concerning the principle of a Member State's liability in cases other than failure to transpose Directives and the right of individuals to obtain reparation. They dealt with the issue of whether or not the principle of State liability applies generally, particularly in cases where a national law infringes directly applicable provisions, and, if so, under which conditions.

The CJEU established that the principle of State liability for breaches of EU law was generally recognised, subject to precise conditions being met, irrespective of which organ of the Member State was responsible for the breach, including a national parliament, and whatever the nature of the EU legislation breached.

The conditions to be met are:

- the EU norm must confer rights;
- the breach must be sufficiently serious; and
- causal link breach-damages.

Further, *Francovich* seems to cover only total breaches whereas *Brasserie* deals also with partial or sufficiently serious breaches. As regards the factors to take into account when deciding whether a sufficiently serious breach has occurred Brasserie lists quite a few. Those include: the clarity and precision of the rule breached, the measure of discretion left by that rule to the national or EU authorities, whether the infringement and the damage caused was intentional or involuntary, whether any error of law was excusable or inexcusable, the fact that the position taken by an EU institution may have contributed towards the omission, and the adoption or retention of national measures or practices contrary to EU law. In any case, a breach of EU law will be sufficiently serious if it has persisted despite a judgment declaring the infringement, or a preliminary ruling or settled case law of the CJEU on the matter from which it is clear that the conduct in question constituted an infringement.

Dillenkofer dealt with non-implementation of a Directive which was held to equate to sufficiently serious breach: *Dillenkofer v Germany: C-178/94, C-179/94, C-188/94, C-189/94 and C-190/94* [1997] QB 259, [1996] All ER (EC) 917, ECJ.

In *British Telecommunications* the CJEU provided the solution to the national dispute on the incorrect implementation of the Directive and the possibility to originate State liability: *R v HM Treasury, ex p British Telecommunications plc: C-392/93* [1996] QB 615, [1996] ECR I-1631, ECJ. Since then, the CJEU has, on several occasions, chosen to adopt a position directly by making its own assessment of whether a particular situation constituted a serious breach of EU law and therefore rendered the Member State liable. The position in British Telecommunications was restated in *Denkavit Internationaal BV, VITIC Amsterdam BV and Voormeer BV v Bundesamt für Finanzen: C-283/94, C-291/94 and C-292/94* [1996] ECR I-5063, [1996] STC 1445, ECJ; *Brinkmann Tabakfabriken GmbH v Skatteministeriet: C-319/96* [1998] ECR I-5255, [1998] 3 CMLR 673, ECJ and *Larsy v Institut National d'Assusurances Sociales pour Travailleurs Indépendants (INASTI): C-118/00* [2001] ECR I-5063, [2001] All ER (D) 317 (Jun), ECJ.

In the application of a Treaty article the mere infringement equates to sufficiently serious breach: *R v Ministry of Agriculture, Fisheries and Food, ex p Hedley Lomas (Ireland) Ltd: C-5/94* [1996] All ER (EC) 493.

As regards whether State liability can arise from a breach of EU law attributable to the highest court of a Member State adjudicating at last instance the CJEU was clear: 'the principle applies to any case in which a member state breaches Community law, whichever is the authority of the member state whose act or omission was responsible for the breach'. It went on to say that 'in international law a state which incurs liability for breach of an international commitment is viewed as a single entity, irrespective of whether the breach which gave rise to the damage is attributable to the legislature, the judiciary or the executive. That principle must apply a fortiori in the Community legal order': *Köbler v Austria (C-224/01)* [2004] QB 848, [2004] All ER (EC) 23.

It also added a new criterion to recognise a manifest breach of EU law namely that non-compliance by the court in question with its obligation (mandatory for Courts adjudicating at last instance) to make a reference for a preliminary ruling under TFEU, art 267.

EU law precludes the application of national rules that exclude State liability in cases where the infringement results from the judicial function of interpreting the provisions of law or assessing facts or evidence. To exclude any possibility of holding the Member State liable when the infringement allegedly committed by the national court relates to its interpretation of provisions of law or its assessment of facts or evidence would render the principle of State liability meaningless and would mean that individuals have no legal protection if a national court adjudicating at last instance committed a manifest error in performing its functions of interpretation or assessment: *Traghetti del Mediterraneo SpA v Italy: C-173/03* [2006] ECR I-5177, [2006] All ER (EC) 983.

The Member State's obligation to refrain from making provisions that would seriously compromise achievement of the outcome sought by a Directive applies to national courts. From the date on which a Directive has entered into force, the courts of the Member State must refrain from interpreting national law in such a manner that, after the period for transposition has expired, might seriously compromise attainment of the Directive's objective: *Adeneler v Ellinikos Organismos Galaktos: C-212/04* [2006] ECR I-6057, [2007] All ER (EC) 82.

As regards adequate reparation the CJEU established in *Brasserie* that reparation had to be commensurate with the loss or damage sustained; it must ensure the effective protection of the rights of the individuals who have been caused loss or damage. Adequate reparation may take the form of retroactive and proper application in full of the Directive's implementing measures, provided that it was properly transposed, unless the beneficiaries establish the existence of additional loss sustained on account of the fact that they were unable to benefit, at the appropriate time, from the advantages guaranteed by the Directive with the result that such loss has to be made good.

The CJEU has tried to provide national courts and individuals with tools (ie principles and doctrines) to make good many breaches of (or non-compliance with) EU law provisions. So far these are the remedies available to individuals but we may have not yet seen the last act of the CJEU in this field. Practitioners must remain vigilant to developments in EU law to avoid unnecessary litigation.

III EUR [12]

The European Communities Act 1972 EU law meaning the EU Treaties and secondary legislation adopted by the EU institutions, sometimes requires per se to be incorporated in the legal orders of the Member States eg Directives, Decisions. But some instruments, notably those that created the new legal system ie the EU Treaties and all their amendments, are left to be dealt with in accordance with international law and the constitutional requirements of the Member States' legal systems.

In the UK, following the decision to accede to the European Communities (now EU) and signature of the Accession Treaty (EU instrument adopted when a State becomes a Member State by which it accepts the existing EU acquis and signed by the presidents of some EU institutions and the Heads of State or Government of the existing and new Member States) an Act of Parliament was required to internalise the EU Treaties. This was done via the European Communities Act 1972. The 1972 Act has been subsequently amended to incorporate each and every amendment to the EU Treaties – following signature by the UK Government – so as to give effect to those amendments in the UK legal order (detailed information on the Act in **III EUR [386]**)

The repeal of this Act is the subject matter of the European Union (Withdrawal) Act 2018 which is the direct result of the UK decision to leave the EU by activating the exit clause (art 50 TEU) in March 2017. The Act will – unless art 50 TEU is suspended and an amendment to the Act is passed in time – enter into force the date on which the UK leaves the EU which at the moment is set for 29 March 2019 at 23.00hs local time (see more on this in **III EUR [386]**).

The Act sets rules on the status of EU law post-Brexit mainly by listing some specific pieces of EU law that will be 'retained' ie converted into UK law, which EU-derived domestic legislation will be preserved and which pieces are expressly left behind, eg Charter of Fundamental Rights. The Act also tries to anticipate and solve potential conundrums as regards lacunae or deficiencies that may arise and sets rules on interpretation of retained EU law that Courts may follow.

III EUR [13]

Evolution of the system The term judicial cooperation in civil matters first appeared in the Maastricht Treaty, specifically in the Treaty establishing the EU (TEU), and established that judicial cooperation in civil matters was a subject of common interest to the Member States. With the Treaty of Amsterdam, this policy of cooperation, which had until then been solely under action taken by the Member States (ie intergovernmental) became a matter subject to legislative action by the EU institutions. The Treaty of Lisbon refers explicitly to the principle of mutual recognition of judgments in civil matters but leaves the legislative competence essentially untouched. TFEU, art 81 sets out a list of activities which may be the subject of legislation:

'1. The Union shall develop judicial cooperation in civil matters having cross-border implications, based on the principle of mutual recognition of judgments and of decisions in extrajudicial cases. Such cooperation may include the adoption of measures for the approximation of the laws and regulations of the Member States.

2. For the purposes of paragraph 1, the European Parliament and the Council, acting in accordance with the ordinary legislative procedure, shall adopt measures, particularly when necessary for the proper functioning of the internal market, aimed at ensuring:

(a) the mutual recognition and enforcement between Member States of judgments and of decisions in extrajudicial cases;

(b) the cross-border service of judicial and extrajudicial documents;

(c) the compatibility of the rules applicable in the Member States concerning conflict of laws and of jurisdiction;
(d) cooperation in the taking of evidence;
(e) effective access to justice;
(f) the elimination of obstacles to the proper functioning of civil proceedings, if necessary by promoting the compatibility of the rules on civil procedure applicable in the Member States;
(g) the development of alternative methods of dispute settlement;
(h) support for the training of the judiciary and judicial staff.

3. Notwithstanding paragraph 2, measures concerning family law with cross-border implications shall be established by the Council, acting in accordance with a special legislative procedure. The Council shall act unanimously after consulting the European Parliament.

The Council, on a proposal from the Commission, may adopt a decision determining those aspects of family law with cross-border implications which may be the subject of acts adopted by the ordinary legislative procedure. The Council shall act unanimously after consulting the European Parliament.

The proposal referred to in the second subparagraph shall be notified to the national Parliaments. If a national Parliament makes known its opposition within six months of the date of such notification, the decision shall not be adopted. In the absence of opposition, the Council may adopt the decision.'

Article 81 TFEU clarifies that judicial cooperation in civil matters may include the adoption of measures for the approximation of the laws of the Member States. With the exception of measures in family law, legislation in these matters is now adopted under the ordinary legislative procedure by which EU legislation is adopted jointly by the European Parliament and the Council, the co-legislators. Family law measures are adopted under the special procedure in which the Council acts unanimously after consulting the Parliament.

When applying legal instruments in this area, legal practitioners must bear in mind that not all pieces apply to 'all' Member States. Denmark, Ireland and the UK have special arrangements under the Treaty with respect to legislation adopted in the area of civil justice (see **III EUR [18]**). Denmark does not take part in the adoption of any legal acts in this area and is not bound by them. Nonetheless, a number of instruments have been extended to Denmark by means of a bilateral agreement with the EU. The UK and Ireland have the right to choose whether to take part in the adoption of legislative acts in this area and are only bound by them if they have 'opted in'. Until now the UK and Ireland have 'opted in' to many but not all the legislative acts in the area of civil and commercial matters eg the UK and Ireland did not opt in to the adoption of the Regulation on succession.

The amount of EU legislation in the area of judicial cooperation in civil and commercial matters has grown significantly over the past years. There are legal acts in place which govern jurisdiction, mutual recognition and enforcement of judgments and applicable law in a broad range of matters, extending from contract to successions and maintenance obligations. EU legislation also provides for direct cooperation between the courts and Member States' competent authorities eg when taking evidence abroad or in child abduction matters. Access to justice in cross-border cases has been improved through provisions on legal aid, mediation and simplified and low-cost procedures for small and uncontested claims.

In order to facilitate the application of the EU acquis in practice the European Judicial Network in civil and commercial matters was created in 2001. (More information on the network including detailed information for the UK, ie England and Wales, Scotland, Northern Ireland and Gibraltar in e-justice.europa.eu/content_about_the_network-431-en.do).

III EUR [14]

Mutual recognition The jurisdiction of the Member States' courts and rules on applicable law in civil and commercial matters are at the heart of judicial cooperation in civil matters in the EU. National rules of private international law and international civil procedures differ from State to State and this can hamper the functioning of the EU internal market. To avoid this potential harmful effect it is vital to have uniform provisions which determine the competent court as well as simplified procedural formalities to achieve rapid and simple recognition and enforcement of judicial decisions issued in another Member State.

The principle of mutual recognition is the cornerstone of the policy in this area. Mutual recognition of judicial decisions and judgments and the necessary approximation of legislation aim to facilitate cooperation between authorities and the judicial protection of individual rights. The final goal of mutual recognition is for judicial decisions of all kinds in the field of civil and commercial matters to circulate freely among all Member States, be recognised and enforced in other Member States without any intermediate steps. A key element in the development of EU law in this respect is the progressive removal of the barriers to recognition and enforcement of judgments between the judicial systems of the Member States.

III EUR [15]

From the Brussels Convention 1968 to the Brussels I Recast Regulation In order to simplify the formalities governing the mutual recognition and enforcement of judgments of courts or tribunals the six founding Member States decided to enter into a Convention (as the subject matter was not susceptible to be dealt with by Community legislation) and they signed the Brussels Convention in 1968.

The Brussels Convention 1968 and the 1971 Protocol to that Convention were the rules on jurisdiction applicable until 2002 in the EU. The Convention still applies to some territories not governed by EU law. See national legislation on the matter (Civil Jurisdiction and Judgments Act 1982, as amended). Those were almost entirely superseded by Regulation (EC) No 44/2001, commonly known as Brussels I, which was in force from 1 March 2002 until 10 January 2015. The Convention still applies in respect of a few dependent territories of the EU Member States. Brussels I was consequence of the Tampere Council of October 1999 which called for further reduction of the intermediate measures required to enable the recognition and enforcement of a decision or judgment in the requested State and the complete abolition of the procedure required to have a foreign judgment declared enforceable (*exequatur*). As a first step the intermediate procedures were abolished for small consumer or commercial claims as well as for uncontested claims.

In 2012, Regulation (EU) No 1215/2012, known as Brussels I Recast, replaced Brussels I and established new rules that the UK courts currently apply in civil and commercial matters as regards jurisdiction in claims against defendants domiciled in EU Member States and enforcement of judgments given in other EU Member States. Brussels I Recast goes further and abolishes the *exequatur* procedure for judicial decisions in civil and commercial matters as a general rule.

The UK courts follow Brussels I Recast because it is EU law and the European Communities Act 1972 obliges them to do so. Once the UK leaves the EU that obligation will cease (please note that the point in time on which the obligation will cease will depend on the terms on which the UK leaves the EU, ie with or without a deal. See also art 127 of the EU–UK Withdrawal Agreement). New rules will be enacted and applied post-Brexit (or post-implementation period, depending on the case). As a first step parts of the EU acquis will be internalised as UK law – as per the European Union (Withdrawal) Act 2018 – and then repealed piece by piece, as the case may be; some others, like Brussels I Recast (but also Brussels I, Lugano Conventions, etc), will cease or continue to apply depending on the terms of exit (see UK legislation section, para **III EUR [386B]**).

Adding to the above, careful consideration must be paid to the Lugano Convention on Jurisdiction and the Enforcement of Judgments in Civil and Commercial Matters of 1988 between the EC (now EU) and the members of the European Free Trade Association (EFTA), ie Norway, Switzerland and Iceland, which was intended as a parallel convention to the Brussels Convention 1968.

The Lugano Convention was revised in 2007. Its successor, known as the 'Revised Lugano Convention', was signed by Switzerland, the EC (the EU had no legal personality at the time so only the European Community could enter into this type of agreements; this changed with the entry into force of the Lisbon Treaty in December 2009), Denmark, Norway and Iceland and also serves as a parallel agreement to Brussels I, which was replaced by Brussels I Recast. The Revised Lugano Convention was incorporated into UK law by the Civil Jurisdiction and Judgments Regulations 2009. The Revised Lugano Convention entered into force for the EU, Denmark and Norway on 1 January 2010, for Switzerland on 1 January 2011 and for Iceland on 1 May 2011. For States that join the EU after the conclusion of the Lugano Convention, the Convention applies automatically from their EU accession date.

In summary, at present the pieces governing the matter are the Brussels I Recast (for EU Member States), the Revised Lugano Convention (for EU and EFTA States) and the Brussels Convention for EU territories not covered by Brussels I Recast. (Brussels I Recast Recital 9 states: 'The 1968 Brussels Convention continues to apply to the territories of the Member States which fall within the territorial scope of that Convention and which are excluded from this Regulation pursuant to article 355 of the TFEU'.)

Recital 34 of Brussels I Recast states that '[c]ontinuity between the 1968 Brussels Convention, Regulation (EC) 44/2001 and the Recast Regulation should be ensured, and transitional provisions should be laid down to that end'. The same need for continuity applies as regards the interpretation by the CJEU of the 1968 Brussels Convention and of the Regulations replacing it.

III EUR [16]

A word of caution Some Member States often decide to 'give effect' to EU Regulations by means of their own national instruments. This is a confusing practice as it misguides legal practitioners who assume that applying national law is correct and sufficient.

EU Regulations do not need transposition or internalisation into the national legal orders of the Member States (unlike Directives). This means that if legal practitioners only take into account national law and it is later proved that a mistake or omission between the Regulation and the national law 'giving effect' to it took place, the risks of relying on the wrong legal basis increase exponentially. In addition, infringement proceedings could be launched at EU level if a Member State applies incorrectly a Regulation – this could be the case if the national piece does not mirror the wording and spirit of the Regulation. Therefore, unless rigorous monitoring is carried out to be alerted of such cases, practitioners risk not being aware of those infringement procedures and could easily misinform their clients.

To eliminate risks, for cases falling under Brussels I or Brussels I Recast the texts of the Regulations (as amended) are to be looked at and assessed in the context of national cases not only the Civil Jurisdiction and Judgments Act 1982, as amended by, among other the Civil Jurisdiction and Judgments Order 2001. The 1982 Act is the first port of call for the Brussels and Revised Lugano Conventions (more on this in **III EUR [391]**).

III EUR [17]

Relationship between Brussels I Recast and application of Brussels I to cases lodged on or before 10 January 2015. Amendments to Brussels I and Brussels I Recast Even though Brussels I (Regulation (EC) 44/2001) was repealed and replaced by Brussels I Recast (Regulation (EU) 1215/2012) with effect from 10 January 2015 it continues to apply to cases not yet concluded on 10 January 2015 or, in other words, Brussels I Recast applies to legal proceedings instituted on or after 10 January 2015 (article 66(1)) and Brussels I to judgments handed down in proceedings instituted before 10 January 2015 (article 66(2)).

It is worth mentioning that Brussels I has been amended following its 'repeal' and that may seem confusing. However, if you consider it is still applicable to some proceedings the situation is clarified. Commission Regulation (EU) 2015/263 amending Annexes I to IV to Council Regulation (EC) No 44/2001 was adopted on 16 January 2015 and entered into force on 11 March 2015.

Since the annexes to Brussels I had been amended several times it was deemed necessary to consolidate the information by means of an amending regulation. Therefore, the rules of national jurisdiction referred to in articles 3(2) and 4(2) contained in Annex I; the courts or competent authorities that have jurisdiction in the Member States to deal with applications for a declaration of enforceability (Annex II); the courts with which appeals may be lodged against decisions on a declaration of enforceability (Annex III) and the final appeal procedures against such decisions (Annex IV) are now contained in Regulation (EU) 2015/263.

In addition, Brussels I Recast has also been amended namely by Regulation (EU) No 542/2014 of the European Parliament and of the Council of 15 May 2014 amending Regulation (EU) No 1215/2012 as regards the rules to be applied with respect to the Unified Patent Court and the Benelux Court of Justice and by Commission Delegated Regulation (EU) 2015/281 of 26 November 2014 replacing Annexes I and II of Regulation (EU) No 1215/2012 of the European Parliament and of the Council on jurisdiction and the recognition and enforcement of judgments in civil and commercial matters. The latter refers to the format of the certificate concerning a judgment in civil and commercial matters and that of the certificate concerning an authentic instrument/court settlement in civil and commercial matters. Please note it applies in Denmark. Denmark did not participate in the adoption of Brussels I Recast and is not bound by it. However, in accordance with article 3(2) of the Agreement between the EU and Denmark, Denmark notified the Commission, on 20 December 2012, of its decision to implement the contents of Regulation (EU) No 1215/2012. Thus, the references to Denmark and its currency are included in the forms.

Regulation (EU) 542/2014 applies from 10 January 2015 to align it with the general application date of Brussels I Recast. It inserted four new articles (71a to 71d) which deal with recognition of the Unified Patent Court and Benelux Court of Justice as common courts and set rules on jurisdiction, recognition and enforcement of judgments of those courts. The Unified Patent Court Agreement was signed on 19 February 2013 by Belgium, Bulgaria, Czech Republic, Denmark, Germany, Estonia, Ireland, Greece, France, Italy, Cyprus, Latvia, Lithuania, Luxembourg, Hungary, Malta, Netherlands, Austria, Portugal, Romania, Slovenia, Slovakia, Finland, Sweden and the UK. It provides for its entry into force not prior to the first day of the fourth month after the date of entry into force of the amendments to Regulation (EU) No 1215/2012 concerning the relationship of that Regulation with the UPC Agreement. On 15 October 2012, Belgium, Luxembourg and the Netherlands, parties to the Treaty of 31 March 1965 concerning the establishment and statute of a Benelux Court of Justice (Benelux Court of Justice Treaty), signed a Protocol amending that Treaty. That Protocol made it possible to transfer jurisdiction to the Benelux Court of Justice in specific matters falling within the scope of Regulation (EU) No 1215/2012.

In summary, at present there are two systems running in parallel:

- for proceedings instituted before 10 January 2015, Brussels I still applies (as amended for the last time by Regulation (EU) 2015/263);

- for proceedings commenced on 10 January 2015 onward the applicable legislation is Brussels I Recast, as amended.

Please note that as of late January 2019 the above mentioned is still the case as many judgments handed down by the CJEU in 2018 still refer to Brussels I.

III EUR [18]

Special status of the UK: 'opt ins' and applicable EU legislation in the UK The UK's participation in EU legislation in the field of Justice and Home Affairs (JHA) is mainly governed by Protocols 21 and 19 to the Treaty on the EU and the Treaty on the Functioning of the EU (TEU and TFEU, respectively), often referred to as the Lisbon Treaty.

Essentially, TFEU, Protocol 21 states that:

'[...none of the provisions of Title V of Part Three of the Treaty on the Functioning of the European Union [Area of freedom, security and justice], no measure adopted pursuant to that Title, no provision of any international agreement concluded by the Union pursuant to that Title, and no decision of the Court of Justice interpreting any such provision or measure shall be binding upon or applicable in the UK or Ireland; and no such provision, measure or decision shall in any way affect the competences, rights and obligations of those States; and no such provision, measure or decision shall in any way affect the Community or Union acquis nor form part of Union law as they apply to the UK or Ireland.'

However, according to article 3 '[t]he UK or Ireland may notify the President of the Council in writing, within three months after a proposal or initiative has been presented to the Council pursuant to Title V of Part Three of the Treaty on the Functioning of the European Union, that it wishes to take part in the adoption and application of any such proposed measure, whereupon that State shall be entitled to do so'. This has been the case with the Brussels I Recast Regulation.

Furthermore, according to article 4 '[t]he UK or Ireland may at any time after the adoption of a measure by the Council pursuant to Title V of Part Three of the Treaty on the Functioning of the European Union notify its intention to the Council and to the Commission that it wishes to accept that measure'.

Therefore, the UK may join in the adoption of a measure or communicate its intention to apply it after it has been passed as legislation. This is the so-called 'opt in'. Unlike the UK, Ireland may notify the Council in writing that it no longer wishes to be covered by the terms of Protocol N 21. In that case, the normal Treaty provisions, including legislation issued in line with the Treaties, will apply to Ireland.

In relation to Schengen, which governs border controls among Member States, article 4 of Protocol N 19 states that 'Ireland and the UK of Great Britain and Northern Ireland may at any time request to take part in some or all of the provisions of the Schengen acquis'. In other words, this is a permanent 'opt out' unless the UK changes its mind and decides to join Schengen (virtually impossible considering the undergoing Brexit process).

APPLICABLE LEGISLATION

III EUR [19]

EU legislation: Brussels I Recast: an approximation to the matter The novelties that Brussels I Recast incorporated into the EU acquis, and in UK law as a logical consequence, were a few but not minor in scope. Those affected:

- rules on jurisdiction;
- procedure to recognise and enforce EU judgments (elimination of the *exequatur*);
- scope of the arbitration exclusion;
- *lis pendens* and ability of EU courts to stay proceedings in favour of non-EU courts.

It is worth mentioning that Recital 34 of Brussels I Recast stresses the need for continuity in the interpretation of the Recast and its predecessors (Brussels I Regulation and Brussels Convention). This means that the CJEU case law interpreting a provision of its predecessors remains applicable where the relevant provision of the Brussels I Recast may be treated as equivalent.

Rules on jurisdiction: greater respect for jurisdiction clauses (choice of court agreements) and removal of the domicile requirement contained in Brussels I. Now, where parties to a contract, regardless of their domicile, agree that the courts of a particular EU Member State will have jurisdiction to settle any disputes which arise in connection with the contract, the jurisdiction clause must be recognised by all EU Member State courts. Brussels I Recast requires that effect be given to such clauses provided certain requirements are met. The chosen court will have jurisdiction unless the agreement is null and void as to its substantive validity under the law of the chosen Member State. Recital 20 adds that this includes the chosen State's conflict of laws rules.

Where parallel or related proceedings are commenced on either side of 10 January 2015, the two sets of proceedings will be subject to different Regulations. This is of particular importance when dealing with cases where the first set of proceedings are in breach of a jurisdiction clause as the new provisions apply from 10 January 2015.

New provisions require a first seised EU court to stay its proceedings as soon as the designated EU court under an exclusive jurisdiction clause has been seised. The non-chosen court will not be able to proceed unless (and until) the chosen court declines jurisdiction. Further, Recital 22 of Brussels I Recast makes it clear that, as a consequence, the chosen court will have priority to decide any issues concerning the validity or scope of the jurisdiction clause. Once seised, the chosen court is able to proceed irrespective of whether the non-chosen court has already decided on the stay of proceedings.

Under Brussels I, if a party, in breach of an exclusive jurisdiction clause, commenced proceedings in the courts of an EU Member State other than the chosen by the parties, and the other party brought parallel proceedings in respect of the same cause of action before the chosen court, the chosen court had to wait until the court first seised determined whether it had jurisdiction. This first in time rule seriously undermined the efficacy of exclusive jurisdiction clauses. Parties seeking to delay or frustrate proceedings which could properly be brought before the courts of the chosen Member State often brought proceedings in another Member State where it was likely to take a long time to determine the jurisdiction question. The court of the chosen Member State was required to stay the proceedings brought before it, while the court first seised decided the issue of jurisdiction, delaying the determination of the proceedings brought before the chosen court. This litigation tactic is known as an 'Italian torpedo'. Brussels I Recast eliminates the problem where there is an exclusive jurisdiction clause. But some commercial contracts contain unilateral or asymmetric jurisdiction clauses. Asymmetric clauses require one party to sue in a particular jurisdiction but give the other party freedom to sue in a number of jurisdictions. This means the risk of torpedo actions potentially remains where those type of clauses are used. It is yet to be seen whether asymmetric jurisdiction clauses will be assimilated to exclusive jurisdiction clauses by the EU courts and, more importantly, by the CJEU.

The chosen court is released from its obligation to stay proceedings irrespective of whether the non-chosen court has decided on the stay.

It is important to mention the Hague Convention 2005 on Choice of Court Agreements (see more on the Convention below). It applies only to wholly exclusive jurisdiction agreements in favour of the courts of one Contracting State (or one or more courts within one Contracting State). The Hague Convention does not apply to non-exclusive or asymmetric agreements in favour of an EU Member State court, those are governed by Brussels I Recast. There are provisions in the Hague Convention which will preserve Brussels I Recast's effect. When an EU court assesses an exclusive clause in its favour (or in favour of another EU Member State's court) the Hague Convention is capable of taking precedence over Brussels I Recast.

The Hague Convention does not have anything similar to the new mechanism of Brussels I Recast which requires a non-chosen EU court to stay its proceedings when a chosen EU court is seised. If the Hague Convention applies, one question that may arise, is whether a first seised non-chosen EU court must act in accordance with Brussels I Recast's provisions and stay its proceedings. Whatever the answer from the non-chosen court's perspective, under the Hague Convention, the chosen EU court is not obliged to stay its proceedings when another EU court is first seised. The CJEU may decide, should the question come before it, that the non-chosen EU court is obliged to apply Brussels I Recast on this point.

The Revised Lugano Convention is unaffected by Brussels I Recast. It will therefore continue to govern issues involving proceedings before an EU court and the courts of the Lugano States. As the Lugano Convention replicates Brussels I it appears that torpedo actions are still possible between EU courts and those of the Lugano States.

Recognition and enforcement of judgments: the procedure has been simplified with the elimination of the *exequatur*. The judgment creditor is only required to present a copy of the judgment and a standard form certificate from the court which issued the judgment. It can then begin whatever enforcement measures are available under the local law ie the State where enforcement is sought. The judgment debtor can still oppose enforcement but the grounds on which he can do so are very limited.

Arbitration: Brussels I Recast clarifies that all matters relating to arbitration fall outside its scope, including those relating to the establishment of an arbitral tribunal, the powers of arbitrators, the conduct of an arbitration procedure and the enforcement of an arbitral award. Where one party brings proceedings before an EU Member State court in breach of an arbitration agreement, the other party can ask the court of the seat of the arbitration to refer the matter to arbitration and the court of the seat cannot be prevented from doing so. The New York Convention is to take precedence over Brussels I Recast.

Non-EU Lis pendens: the new rules provide EU courts with discretion to stay proceedings in favour of non-EU proceedings if certain conditions are met namely the non-EU proceedings must be first in time, the stay must be necessary for the proper administration of justice and the judgment of the non-EU court must also be capable of recognition and enforcement in the EU Member State seized. The new rules are of fundamental importance to situations involving non-EU jurisdictional factors (ie anything jurisdictionally relevant, eg an exclusive jurisdiction clause in favour of a non-EU state).

III EUR [20]

EU law and the Hague Convention 2005 on choice of court agreements The Hague Convention is the first, potentially, world-wide instrument on choice of courts agreements even when some regional (such as within the EU) and bilateral arrangements exist. Depending on how many States ratify it in the future, it is possible that it may facilitate the creation of a recognition and enforcement regime for court judgments between the Contracting States with a similar effect to those the New York Convention has in the field of arbitration.

The Convention entered into force for Mexico and the EU Member States (excluding Denmark) on 1 October 2015. It only applies before the courts of those States and governs the jurisdictional effect of an exclusive choice of court agreement in favour of any of them, and the recognition and enforcement of judgments between them. To the extent that the Convention is relevant to any such matters, due to the transitional provisions, it will only apply to exclusive choice of court agreements in favour of an EU Member State or Mexico concluded on or after 1 October 2015. It is applicable to Singapore since 1 October 2016. The United States of America signed it in 2009 and Ukraine in 2016 but none of them has yet ratified it. China signed it in September 2017 but has not yet ratified it. Montenegro ratified it in April 2018 and it entered into force on 1 August 2018 and Denmark ratified it in May with entry into force set for 1 September 2018.

Insurance and reinsurance contracts fall within the scope of the Convention and provision is made for this to remain so even if the insurance contract relates to a matter to which the Convention does not apply. However, on 11 June 2015, the EU made a declaration pursuant to article 21 excluding insurance contracts from the scope of application of the Convention. The reason is that Brussels I Recast contains protective rules for insured parties and the Convention would conflict with/override such rules in the cases in which it applied. The declaration was thought necessary in order to maintain the effect of such rules. The declaration also specifies a number of defined situations in which the Convention will nonetheless apply which broadly correlate with the circumstances in which Brussels I Recast would otherwise permit effect to be given to a choice of court agreement in an insurance contract. Please note Denmark has tabled a Declaration on article 21 in very similar terms.

UK situation: the application of the Hague Convention post-Brexit is a matter that the UK government decided to tackle ahead of Brexit day. To that end, the UK ratified the Convention on 28 December 2018. It also tabled a 'Declaration' covering, among other matters, article 21 in similar terms to the EU's. Under Note Verbale, it states '[i]n accordance with Article 29 of the 2005 Hague Convention, the UK is bound by the Convention by virtue of its membership of the EU, which approved the Convention on behalf of its Member States. The UK intends to continue to participate in the 2005 Hague Convention after it withdraws from the EU'. It then focuses in two possible outcomes, ie that the EU–UK Withdrawal agreement governs the field post-Brexit (following approval and ratification) and the no deal scenario. In that event, 'the UK wishes to ensure continuity of application of the 2005 Hague Convention from the point at which it ceases to be a Member State of the EU'. The UK has therefore submitted the Instrument of Accession in accordance with Article 27(4) of the 2005 Hague Convention only in preparation for this situation. The Instrument of Accession declares that the UK accedes to the 2005 Hague Convention in its own right with effect from 1 April 2019. See the Declaration at https://www.hcch.net/en/instruments/conventions/status-table/notifications/?csid=1318&disp=resdn

More information on the status of the Hague Convention: www.hcch.net/en/instruments/conventions/status-table/?cid=98

III EUR [21]

Specific considerations In the international legal order there are a number of regional and bilateral arrangements which cover matters of jurisdiction and recognition and enforcement of judgments between States such as Regulation (EU) 1215/2012 (Brussels I Recast) and the Revised Lugano Convention 2007. Given the potentially global nature of the Hague Convention, any given Contracting State may therefore find itself in a position where it is party both to the Convention and an instrument of that nature. The question will then arise as to which instrument that Contracting State must apply where there is inconsistency. The Convention contains rules which clarify which instrument is to have priority, these are set out in article 26.

In the EU Brussels I Recast governs jurisdiction and recognition and enforcement of judgments and is already aligned with the Convention. As the Hague Convention was concluded by the EU it is to be regarded within the EU as an instrument of EU Law whose effect is preserved before the EU courts by article 67 of Brussels I Recast. As such, within the EU, the CJEU will be the supreme interpreter of the Convention since its jurisdiction extends to that instrument. This will, of course, change as regards the UK once it leaves the bloc. Please note a more in depth analysis of the Hague Convention exceeds the scope of this Chapter.

REGULATION (EU) NO 1215/2012 OF THE EUROPEAN PARLIAMENT AND OF THE COUNCIL OF 12 DECEMBER 2012 ON JURISDICTION AND THE RECOGNITION AND ENFORCEMENT OF JUDGMENTS IN CIVIL AND COMMERCIAL MATTERS

CHAPTER I
SCOPE AND DEFINITIONS

III EUR [22]–III EUR [154]

General Note This Regulation, known as Brussels I Recast, repealed and replaced Regulation (EC) No 44/2001, Brussels I, with effect from 10 January 2015. From that day on it applies to new proceedings, but not to those already started at that date. Article 66 provides for them to continue to be regulated by Brussels I. The new provisions on jurisdiction are, in some cases, similar to the old provisions. Case law on the interpretation and application of the provisions on jurisdiction under Brussels I are to be considered when dealing with equivalent provisions under Brussels I Recast and as such are included in this section. As regards enforcement of judgments to which Brussels I Recast applies, the procedure is now different: registration before enforcement is no longer required. The Civil Procedure (Amendment No 7) Rules 2014, SI 2014/2948 made amendments to the Civil Procedure Rules 1998, SI 1998/3132 which provide for the new procedure in rules 74.3A, 74.4A, 74.7A, 74.7B, 74.7C and 74.11A.

The Brussels I Recast Regulation was amended in two occasions before its provisions became applicable on 10 January 2015. To assist in its interpretation the text reproduced below includes the amendments made by Regulation (EU) 542/2014 and Commission Delegated Regulation (EU) 2015/281.

Article 1

III EUR [155]

This Regulation shall apply in civil and commercial matters whatever the nature of the court or tribunal. It shall not extend, in particular, to revenue, customs or administrative matters or to the liability of the State for acts and omissions in the exercise of State authority (*acta iure imperii*).

2. The Regulation shall not apply to:
   - (a) the status or legal capacity of natural persons, rights in property arising out of a matrimonial relationship or out of a relationship deemed by the law applicable to such relationship to have comparable effects to marriage;
   - (b) bankruptcy, proceedings relating to the winding-up of insolvent companies or other legal persons, judicial arrangements, compositions and analogous proceedings;
   - (c) social security;
   - (d) arbitration;
   - (e) maintenance obligations arising from a family relationship, parentage, marriage or affinity;
   - (f) wills and succession, including maintenance obligations arising by reason of death.

III EUR [155.1]

Arbitration In a case where a judgment was obtained in Greece for the enforcement of an arbitration award it was held that the Judgments Regulation could not be invoked to enforce the judgment: *ED & F Man Sugar Ltd v Lendoudis* [2007] EWHC 2268 (Comm), [2008] 1 All ER 952.

In *Allianz SpA v West Tankers Inc: C-185/07* [2009] AC 1138, [2009] ECR I-663, ECJ, the CJEU held that a preliminary issue concerning the application of an arbitration agreement, including its validity, fell within the scope of Brussels I if the main subject matter of the proceedings came within its scope. This narrow interpretation of the arbitration exception created various problems for EU-seated arbitrations. In particular, the other party could delay resolution of a dispute by means of a "torpedo action" in another Member State on the merits, claiming that the arbitration agreement was invalid. The court of the seat would be prevented from considering the validity of the arbitration agreement due to the rules on parallel proceedings which required any Member State court to stay its proceedings in favour of the court first seised. Recital 12 of Brussels I Recast clarifies the matter in favour of an absolute exclusion of arbitration from its scope. If an arbitral award and a Member State court judgment conflict, a Member State may enforce the arbitral award, if considered valid, under the New York Convention in preference to the court judgment as the Convention takes precedence. In *'Gazprom' OAO, Re: C-536/13* ECLI:EU:C:2015:316, [2015] 1 WLR 4937 the CJEU held that Brussels I does not preclude a court of a Member State from recognising and enforcing, or from refusing to recognise and enforce, an arbitral award prohibiting a party from bringing certain claims before a court of a Member State, since that Regulation does not govern the recognition and enforcement, in a Member State, of an arbitral award issued by an arbitral tribunal in another Member State.

In *Nori Holdings Ltd v Public Joint-Stock Company 'Bank Otkritie Financial Corporation'* [2018] EWHC 1343 (Comm), [2018] All ER (D) 30 (Jun), 6 June 2018, Male J concluded that there is nothing in the Recast Regulation to cast doubt on the continuing validity of the decision in *West Tankers* which remains an authoritative statement of EU law. The case was about granting anti-suit injunctions in Russia and Cyprus. As regards the latter it was decided that a court in one Member State cannot grant an injunction to restrain proceedings brought in another Member State in breach of an arbitration clause.

III EUR [155.2]

Winding up of insolvent company Where the principal claim in the winding up is for a declaration as to beneficial ownership, the litigation is not within the exception provided by article 1(2)(b) but is governed by article 2. The claim should therefore be brought in the courts of the state of the defendant's domicile: *Byers v Yacht Bull Corpn* [2010] EWHC 133 (Ch), [2010] 2 BCLC 169, (2010) Times, 15 February.

III EUR [155.3]

Insolvency proceedings As regards the delimitation of the scope of Brussels I Recast and Regulation No 1346/2000 the CJEU has held that the Regulations must be interpreted in such a way as to avoid any overlap between the rules of law that those instruments lay down and any legal vacuum. Accordingly, actions excluded under art 1(2)(b) of Brussels I Recast from the application of that regulation because they come under 'bankruptcy, proceedings relating to the winding-up of insolvent companies or other legal persons, judicial arrangements, compositions and analogous proceedings' fall within the scope of Regulation No 1346/2000 and, actions which fall outside the scope of art 3(1) of Regulation No 1346/2000 fall within the scope of Brussels I Recast: *Tünkers France and Tünkers Maschinenbau: C-641/16* (2017) EU:C:2017:847. As follows from Recital 10 of Brussels I Recast, the intention was to adopt a broad definition of 'civil and commercial matters' in art 1(1) and, consequently, to provide that the article should be broad in its scope. By contrast, the scope of Regulation No 1346/2000 should not be given a broad interpretation. It is settled case-law that it is the closeness of the link between a court action and the insolvency proceedings that is decisive for the purposes of deciding whether the exclusion in art 1(2)(b) of Brussels I Recast is applicable (citing *Tünkers France and Tünkers Maschinenbau*).

The obligations which form the basis of bringing an action for liability in tort against a committee of creditors originate in rules that are specific to insolvency proceedings. In order to ascertain whether the liability of the members of the committee of creditors may be engaged because of the rejection of the restructuring plan, it is necessary to analyse in particular the extent of that committee's obligations in the insolvency proceedings and the compatibility of the rejection with those obligations. Such an analysis clearly presents a direct and close link with the insolvency proceedings, and is closely connected with those proceedings. As such, the CJEU held that art 1(2)(b) of Brussels I Recast applies to an action

EUROPE

for liability in tort brought against the members of a committee of creditors because of their conduct in voting on a restructuring plan in insolvency proceedings and that such an action is therefore excluded from its scope ratione materiae: *Valach: C-649/16* (2017) ECLI:EU:C:2017:986.

III EUR [155.4]

Civil and commercial matters Brussels I Recast replaced Brussels I and the CJEU's interpretation of the provisions of the latter also applies to Brussels I Recast whenever the provisions of the two instruments are regarded as equivalent: *Schmidt: C-417/15* (2016) EU:C:2016:881. Article 1(1) of Brussels I Recast repeats the wording of article 1(1) of Brussels I and includes 'civil and commercial matters'. That concept should be regarded as an autonomous concept to be interpreted by reference, first, to the objectives and scheme of the regulation and, second, to the general principles which stem from the corpus of the national legal systems: *Aannemingsbedrijf Aertssen and Aertssen Terrassements: C-523/14* EU:C:2015:722. In order to determine whether a matter falls within the scope of Brussels I Recast it is necessary to identify the legal relationship between the parties and to examine the basis and rules governing the bringing of the action (citing *Sapir and Others: C-645/11* EU:C:2013:228 and *Sunico and Others: C-49/12* EU:C:2013:545). As such, the CJEU has held that enforcement proceedings brought by a company owned by a local authority against a natural person domiciled in another Member State, for the purposes of recovering an unpaid debt for parking in a public car park the operation of which has been delegated to that company by that authority, which merely constitute consideration for a service provided, fall within the scope of Brussels I Recast: *Pula Parking: C-551/16* (2017) ECLI:EU:C:2017:193.

In a case relating to an action brought by a natural person having acquired bonds issued by a Member State, against that State and seeking to contest the exchange of those bonds with bonds of a lower value, imposed on that natural person by the effect of a law adopted in exceptional circumstances by the national legislator, the CJEU decided that the matter does not fall within civil and commercial matters within the meaning of article 1(1) of Brussels I Recast: *Kuhn: C-307/18* ECLI:EU:C:2018:911.

Article 2

III EUR [156]

For the purposes of this Regulation:

(a) 'judgment' means any judgment given by a court or tribunal of a Member State, whatever the judgment may be called, including a decree, order, decision or writ of execution, as well as a decision on the determination of costs or expenses by an officer of the court.

For the purposes of Chapter III, 'judgment' includes provisional, including protective, measures ordered by a court or tribunal which by virtue of this Regulation has jurisdiction as to the substance of the matter. It does not include a provisional, including protective, measure which is ordered by such a court or tribunal without the defendant being summoned to appear, unless the judgment containing the measure is served on the defendant prior to enforcement;

(b) 'court settlement' means a settlement which has been approved by a court of a Member State or concluded before a court of a Member State in the course of proceedings;

(c) 'authentic instrument' means a document which has been formally drawn up or registered as an authentic instrument in the Member State of origin and the authenticity of which:

 (i) relates to the signature and the content of the instrument; and

 (ii) has been established by a public authority or other authority empowered for that purpose;

(d) 'Member State of origin' means the Member State in which, as the case may be, the judgment has been given, the court settlement has been approved or concluded, or the authentic instrument has been formally drawn up or registered;

(e) 'Member State addressed' means the Member State in which the recognition of the judgment is invoked or in which the enforcement of the judgment, the court settlement or the authentic instrument is sought;

(f) 'court of origin' means the court which has given the judgment the recognition of which is invoked or the enforcement of which is sought.

Article 3

III EUR [157]

For the purposes of this Regulation, 'court' includes the following authorities to the extent that they have jurisdiction in matters falling within the scope of this Regulation:

(a) in Hungary, in summary proceedings concerning orders to pay (fizetési meghagyásos eljárás), the notary (közjegyző);

(b) in Sweden, in summary proceedings concerning orders to pay (betalningsföreläggande) and assistance (handräckning), the Enforcement Authority (Kronofogdemyndigheten).

CHAPTER II
JURISDICTION

SECTION 1

GENERAL PROVISIONS

Article 4

III EUR [158]

1. Subject to this Regulation, persons domiciled in a Member State shall, whatever their nationality, be sued in the courts of that Member State.

2. Persons who are not nationals of the Member State in which they are domiciled shall be governed by the rules of jurisdiction applicable to nationals of that Member State.

III EUR [158.1]

Domicile Whether an individual is domiciled or not in a Member State is a matter of national law. As such, a defendant is not domiciled in a Member State merely because he has an address and establishment there if he is usually resident elsewhere and his business interests there are comparatively insignificant: *Cherney v Deripaska* [2007] EWHC 965 (Comm), [2007] 2 All ER (Comm) 785, Langley J, QBD; *High Tech International AG v Deripaska* [2006] EWHC 3276 (QB), [2007] EMLR 449, Easy J, QBD.

Article 5

III EUR [159]

1. Persons domiciled in a Member State may be sued in the courts of another Member State only by virtue of the rules set out in Sections 2 to 7 of this Chapter.

2. In particular, the rules of national jurisdiction of which the Member States are to notify the Commission pursuant to point (a) of Article 76(1) shall not be applicable as against the persons referred to in paragraph 1.

Article 6

III EUR [160]

1. If the defendant is not domiciled in a Member State, the jurisdiction of the courts of each Member State shall, subject to Article 18(1), Article 21(2) and Articles 24 and 25, be determined by the law of that Member State.
2. As against such a defendant, any person domiciled in a Member State may, whatever his nationality, avail himself in that Member State of the rules of jurisdiction there in force, and in particular those of which the Member States are to notify the Commission pursuant to point (a) of Article 76(1), in the same way as nationals of that Member State.

SECTION 2

SPECIAL JURISDICTION

Article 7

III EUR [161]

A person domiciled in a Member State may be sued in another Member State:

(1)

- (a) in matters relating to a contract, in the courts for the place of performance of the obligation in question;
- (b) for the purpose of this provision and unless otherwise agreed, the place of performance of the obligation in question shall be:
  - – in the case of the sale of goods, the place in a Member State where, under the contract, the goods were delivered or should have been delivered,
  - – in the case of the provision of services, the place in a Member State where, under the contract, the services were provided or should have been provided;
- (c) if point (b) does not apply then point (a) applies;

(2) in matters relating to tort, delict or quasi-delict, in the courts for the place where the harmful event occurred or may occur;

(3) as regards a civil claim for damages or restitution which is based on an act giving rise to criminal proceedings, in the court seised of those proceedings, to the extent that that court has jurisdiction under its own law to entertain civil proceedings;

(4) as regards a civil claim for the recovery, based on ownership, of a cultural object as defined in point 1 of Article 1 of Directive 93/7/EEC initiated by the person claiming the right to recover such an object, in the courts for the place where the cultural object is situated at the time when the court is seised;

(5) as regards a dispute arising out of the operations of a branch, agency or other establishment, in the courts for the place where the branch, agency or other establishment is situated;

(6) as regards a dispute brought against a settlor, trustee or beneficiary of a trust created by the operation of a statute, or by a written instrument, or created orally and evidenced in writing, in the courts of the Member State in which the trust is domiciled;

(7) as regards a dispute concerning the payment of remuneration claimed in respect of the salvage of a cargo or freight, in the court under the authority of which the cargo or freight in question:

- (a) has been arrested to secure such payment; or
- (b) could have been so arrested, but bail or other security has been given;

provided that this provision shall apply only if it is claimed that the defendant has an interest in the cargo or freight or had such an interest at the time of salvage.

III EUR [161.1]

Contract Article 7(1)(b) mentions the place of performance of contractual obligations as a connecting factor with a particular jurisdiction rather than the place of ultimate delivery: *Scottish and Newcastle International Ltd v Othon Ghalanos Ltd* [2006] EWCA Civ 1750, [2006] 2 CLC 1015.

In *Feniks sp. z o.o.: C-337/17* (2018) ECLI:EU:C:2018:805 the CJEU ruled that an actio pauliana, whereby the person entitled to a debt arising under a contract requests that an act by which his debtor has transferred an asset to a third party and which is allegedly detrimental to his rights be declared ineffective in relation to the creditor, is covered by article 7(1)(a) of Brussels I Recast.

Article 7(1) must be interpreted as meaning that the court with jurisdiction to hear a claim for compensation relating to the termination of a commercial concession agreement concluded between two companies established and operating in two different Member States for the distribution of goods on the domestic market of a third Member State in which neither of those companies has a branch or establishment, is that of the Member State in which the place of the main supply of services, if that is clear from the provisions of the contract and, in the absence of such provisions, the actual performance of that contract, and where it cannot be determined on that basis, the place where the agent is domiciled: *Saey Home & Garden NV/SA: C-64/17* (2018) ECLI:EU:C:2018:173.

In joined cases *C 274/16, C 447/16 and C 448/16 flightright GmbH* (2018) ECLI:EU:C:2018:160 the CJEU ruled that the second indent of article 7(1)(b) (and the second indent of article 5(1)(b) of Brussels I) must be interpreted as meaning that, in the case of a connecting flight, the 'place of performance' of that flight, for the purposes of those provisions, is the place of arrival of the second leg, where the carriage on both flights was operated by two different air carriers and the action for compensation for the long delay of that connecting flight under Regulation No 261/2004 is based on an irregularity which took place on the first of those flights, operated by the air carrier with which the passengers concerned do not have contractual relations.

III EUR [161.2]

Immovable property In the first ruling under Brussels I Recast the CJEU held that an action seeking the avoidance of a gift of immovable property on the ground of the donor's incapacity to contract does not fall within the exclusive jurisdiction of the courts of the Member State in which the property is situated, ie article 24(1), but within the special jurisdiction provided for under article 7(1)(a): *Schmidt (Wolfgang) v Schmidt (Christiane): C-417/15* ECLI:EU:C:2016:881.

III EUR [161.3]

Tort: the place where the harmful event occurred In a case on its predecessor, art 5(3) of Brussels I, it was held that the provision on jurisdiction in tort could not be read so broadly as to encompass any place where the adverse consequences of an event could be felt: *Universal Music International Holding BV v Schilling: C-12/15* ECLI:EU:C:2016:450, [2016] QB 967, [2016] 3 WLR 1139, distinguishing the earlier decision in *Kolassa v Barclays Bank plc: C-375/13* ECLI:EU:C:2015:37, [2016] 1 All ER (Comm) 733, [2015] All ER (D) 230 (Jan).

III EUR [161.4]

Online content The CJEU has held that injury caused by a defamatory publication to the reputation and good name of a legal person occurs in the places where the publication is distributed and in which the victim claims to have suffered injury to its reputation (citing *Shevill and Others: C-8/93* EU:C:1995:61). A person who considers his rights have been infringed by means of content placed online has the option of bringing an action for damages, in respect of all the harm caused, either before the courts of the Member State in which the publisher of that content is established or before the courts of the Member State in which the centre of his interests is based (citing *eDate Advertising and Others, C-509/09 and C-161/10* EU:C:2011:685). That principle was adopted specifically in the context of the infringement of the personality rights of a natural person, it has not been established that it also applies to legal persons.

As regards online content, the alleged infringement is usually felt most keenly at the centre of interests of the relevant person, given the reputation enjoyed by him in that place. For the purposes of art 7(2) the criterion of the 'victim's centre of interests' reflects the place where, in principle, the damage caused by online material occurs most significantly. The courts of the Member State in which the centre of interests of the person affected is located are, consequently, best placed to assess the impact of such content on the rights of that person. These considerations apply regardless of whether the damage allegedly suffered is material or non-material in nature as that has no bearing on the determination of the centre of

EUROPE

interests as the place in which a court can best assess the actual impact of the publication on the internet and its harmful nature. The centre of interests of a natural person generally corresponds to the Member State of his habitual residence. However, such a person may also have his centre of interests in a Member State in which he does not habitually reside, in so far as other factors, such as the pursuit of a professional activity, may establish the existence of a particularly close link with that State. A legal person claiming that its personality rights have been infringed by the publication of incorrect information concerning it on the internet and by a failure to remove comments relating to that person can bring an action for rectification of that information, removal of those comments and compensation in respect of all the damage sustained before the courts of the Member State in which its centre of interests is located. When the relevant legal person carries out the main part of its activities in a different Member State from the one in which its registered office is located, that person may sue the alleged perpetrator of the injury in that other Member State by virtue of it being where the damage occurred. However, a person who alleges that his personality rights have been infringed by the publication of incorrect information concerning him on the internet and by the failure to remove comments relating to him cannot bring an action for rectification of that information and removal of those comments before the courts of each Member State in which the information published on the internet is or was accessible: *Bolagsupplysningen OÜ: C-194/16* ECLI:EU:C:2017:766.

III EUR [161.5]

Credit agreements A credit agreement between a credit institution and a borrower is to be considered a contract for the supply of services within the meaning of the second indent of article 7(1)(b). The place where the services were provided is, in the case of a credit institution granting a loan, the place where that institution has its registered office except where it has been agreed otherwise: *Kareda: C-149/16* ECLI:EU:C:2017:472.

A recourse claim between jointly and severally liable debtors under a credit agreement constitutes a 'matter relating to a contract' as established in art 7(1). A recourse claim between jointly and severally liable debtors for a repayment obligation is founded on the credit agreement concluded between the jointly and severally liable debtors and the credit institution. It follows from Brussels I Recast objectives of predictability, unification and the proper administration of justice that the court that has territorial jurisdiction to hear and determine such claim is the court of the place in the Member State where that credit institution has its registered office as that is the place of performance of the obligation on which such a recourse action is based: *Kareda: C-149/16* ECLI:EU:C:2017:472.

Article 8

III EUR [162]

A person domiciled in a Member State may also be sued:

(1) where he is one of a number of defendants, in the courts for the place where any one of them is domiciled, provided the claims are so closely connected that it is expedient to hear and determine them together to avoid the risk of irreconcilable judgments resulting from separate proceedings;

(2) as a third party in an action on a warranty or guarantee or in any other third-party proceedings, in the court seised of the original proceedings, unless these were instituted solely with the object of removing him from the jurisdiction of the court which would be competent in his case;

(3) on a counter-claim arising from the same contract or facts on which the original claim was based, in the court in which the original claim is pending;

(4) in matters relating to a contract, if the action may be combined with an action against the same defendant in matters relating to rights in rem in immovable property, in the court of the Member State in which the property is situated.

III EUR [162.1]

One of a number of defendants where the claims are closely connected A sufficiently close connection was found to exist in *Cooper Tire & Rubber Co Europe Ltd v Dow Deutschland Inc* [2010] EWCA Civ 864, [2010] NLJR 1116.

III EUR [162.2]

Counterclaims Article 8(3) must be interpreted as applying, not exclusively, in a situation in which the court with jurisdiction to hear and determine a claim alleging infringement of the applicant's personality rights, on the ground that photographs were taken and videos recorded without his knowledge, is seised by the defendant bringing a counterclaim for compensation on the ground that the applicant is liable in tort, delict or quasi-delict for, inter alia, restrictions on his intellectual creations, which are the subject of the original application, where, when examining the counterclaim, that court is required to assess the lawfulness of the actions on which the applicant bases its own claims: *Nothartová: C-306/17* (2018) ECLI:EU:C:2018:360.

Article 9

III EUR [163]

Where by virtue of this Regulation a court of a Member State has jurisdiction in actions relating to liability from the use or operation of a ship, that court, or any other court substituted for this purpose by the internal law of that Member State, shall also have jurisdiction over claims for limitation of such liability.

SECTION 3

JURISDICTION IN MATTERS RELATING TO INSURANCE

Article 10

III EUR [164]

In matters relating to insurance, jurisdiction shall be determined by this Section, without prejudice to Article 6 and point 5 of Article 7.

III EUR [164.1]

Insurance The Declaration made by the EU pursuant to article 21 of the Hague Convention 2005 on choice of court agreements preserves the application of the rules of Brussels I Recast to insurance matters (see EU and the Hague Convention at **III EUR [20]**).

Article 11

III EUR [165]

1. An insurer domiciled in a Member State may be sued:
   - (a) in the courts of the Member State in which he is domiciled;
   - (b) in another Member State, in the case of actions brought by the policyholder, the insured or a beneficiary, in the courts for the place where the claimant is domiciled; or
   - (c) if he is a co-insurer, in the courts of a Member State in which proceedings are brought against the leading insurer.

2. An insurer who is not domiciled in a Member State but has a branch, agency or other establishment in one of the Member States shall, in disputes arising out of the operations of the branch, agency or establishment, be deemed to be domiciled in that Member State.

III EUR [165.1]

Forum in which insurer may be sued The discretion provided by article 11.1 depends on the circumstances applying at the time of suit, not at the time of contract: *Sherdley v Nordea Life and Pension SA (Société Anonyme)* [2012] EWCA Civ 88, [2012] 2 All ER (Comm) 725, [2012] NLJR 293. The CJEU has held that the reference in article 13(2) and article 11(1)(b) allows the injured party to bring an action directly against the insurer before the courts of the place where that injured party is domiciled, provided that such a direct action is permitted and the insurer is domiciled in a Member State, ie a German national injured in the Netherlands was entitled to sue the defendant's insurers (based in the Netherlands) in his local court in Germany: *Odenbreit v FBTO Schadeverzekeringen NV: C-463/06* [2007] ECR I-11321, [2008] 2 All ER (Comm) 733, ECJ.

Article 12

III EUR [166]

In respect of liability insurance or insurance of immovable property, the insurer may in addition be sued in the courts for the place where the harmful event occurred. The same applies if movable and immovable property are covered by the same insurance policy and both are adversely affected by the same contingency.

Article 13

III EUR [167]

1. In respect of liability insurance, the insurer may also, if the law of the court permits it, be joined in proceedings which the injured party has brought against the insured.
2. Articles 10, 11 and 12 shall apply to actions brought by the injured party directly against the insurer, where such direct actions are permitted.
3. If the law governing such direct actions provides that the policyholder or the insured may be joined as a party to the action, the same court shall have jurisdiction over them.

III EUR [167.1]

Insurance According to the CJEU, article 13(2), read in conjunction with article 11(1)(b), means that it may not be relied on by a natural person, whose professional activity consists in recovering claims for damages from insurers and who relies on a contract for the assignment of a claim concluded with the victim of a road accident, to bring a civil liability action against the insurer of the person responsible for that accident, which has its registered office in a Member State other than the Member State of the place of domicile of the injured party, before a court of the Member State in which the injured party is domiciled: *Paweł Hofsoe: C-106/17* (2018) ECLI:EU:C:2018:50.

Article 14

III EUR [168]

1. Without prejudice to Article 13(3), an insurer may bring proceedings only in the courts of the Member State in which the defendant is domiciled, irrespective of whether he is the policyholder, the insured or a beneficiary.
2. The provisions of this Section shall not affect the right to bring a counter-claim in the court in which, in accordance with this Section, the original claim is pending.

Article 15

III EUR [169]

The provisions of this Section may be departed from only by an agreement:

(1) which is entered into after the dispute has arisen;

(2) which allows the policyholder, the insured or a beneficiary to bring proceedings in courts other than those indicated in this Section;

(3) which is concluded between a policyholder and an insurer, both of whom are at the time of conclusion of the contract domiciled or habitually resident in the same Member State, and which has the effect of conferring jurisdiction on the courts of that Member State even if the harmful event were to occur abroad, provided that such an agreement is not contrary to the law of that Member State;

(4) which is concluded with a policyholder who is not domiciled in a Member State, except in so far as the insurance is compulsory or relates to immovable property in a Member State; or

(5) which relates to a contract of insurance in so far as it covers one or more of the risks set out in Article 16.

Article 16

III EUR [170]

The following are the risks referred to in point 5 of Article 15:

(1) any loss of or damage to:

(a) seagoing ships, installations situated offshore or on the high seas, or aircraft, arising from perils which relate to their use for commercial purposes;

(b) goods in transit other than passengers' baggage where the transit consists of or includes carriage by such ships or aircraft;

(2) any liability, other than for bodily injury to passengers or loss of or damage to their baggage:

(a) arising out of the use or operation of ships, installations or aircraft as referred to in point 1(a) in so far as, in respect of the latter, the law of the Member State in which such aircraft are registered does not prohibit agreements on jurisdiction regarding insurance of such risks;

(b) for loss or damage caused by goods in transit as described in point 1(b);

(3) any financial loss connected with the use or operation of ships, installations or aircraft as referred to in point 1(a), in particular loss of freight or charter-hire;

(4) any risk or interest connected with any of those referred to in points 1 to 3;

(5) notwithstanding points 1 to 4, all 'large risks' as defined in Directive 2009/138/EC of the European Parliament and of the Council of 25 November 2009 on the taking-up and pursuit of the business of Insurance and Reinsurance (Solvency II).

SECTION 4

JURISDICTION OVER CONSUMER CONTRACTS

Article 17

III EUR [171]

1. In matters relating to a contract concluded by a person, the consumer, for a purpose which can be regarded as being outside his trade or profession, jurisdiction shall be determined by this Section, without prejudice to Article 6 and point 5 of Article 7, if:

(a) it is a contract for the sale of goods on instalment credit terms;
(b) it is a contract for a loan repayable by instalments, or for any other form of credit, made to finance the sale of goods; or
(c) in all other cases, the contract has been concluded with a person who pursues commercial or professional activities in the Member State of the consumer's domicile or, by any means, directs such activities to that Member State or to several States including that Member State, and the contract falls within the scope of such activities.

2. Where a consumer enters into a contract with a party who is not domiciled in a Member State but has a branch, agency or other establishment in one of the Member States, that party shall, in disputes arising out of the operations of the branch, agency or establishment, be deemed to be domiciled in that Member State.
3. This Section shall not apply to a contract of transport other than a contract which, for an inclusive price, provides for a combination of travel and accommodation.

Article 18

III EUR [172]

1. A consumer may bring proceedings against the other party to a contract either in the courts of the Member State in which that party is domiciled or, regardless of the domicile of the other party, in the courts for the place where the consumer is domiciled.
2. Proceedings may be brought against a consumer by the other party to the contract only in the courts of the Member State in which the consumer is domiciled.
3. This Article shall not affect the right to bring a counter- claim in the court in which, in accordance with this Section, the original claim is pending.

III EUR [172.1]

The consumer may be sued only in the courts of the Member State in which he or she is domiciled (regardless of whether the trader is domiciled within or outside the EU). Conversely, the consumer has a choice of where to sue the trader. The extension of the rules to non-EU domiciled traders is new to Brussels I Recast.

Article 19

III EUR [173]

The provisions of this Section may be departed from only by an agreement:
(1) which is entered into after the dispute has arisen;
(2) which allows the consumer to bring proceedings in courts other than those indicated in this Section; or
(3) which is entered into by the consumer and the other party to the contract, both of whom are at the time of conclusion of the contract domiciled or habitually resident in the same Member State, and which confers jurisdiction on the courts of that Member State, provided that such an agreement is not contrary to the law of that Member State.

SECTION 5

JURISDICTION OVER INDIVIDUAL CONTRACTS OF EMPLOYMENT

Article 20

III EUR [174]

1. In matters relating to individual contracts of employment, jurisdiction shall be determined by this Section, without prejudice to Article 6, point 5 of Article 7 and, in the case of proceedings brought against an employer, point 1 of Article 8.
2. Where an employee enters into an individual contract of employment with an employer who is not domiciled in a Member State but has a branch, agency or other establishment in one of the Member States, the employer shall, in disputes arising out of the operations of the branch, agency or establishment, be deemed to be domiciled in that Member State.

Article 21

III EUR [175]

1. An employer domiciled in a Member State may be sued:
   (a) in the courts of the Member State in which he is domiciled; or
   (b) in another Member State:
      (i) in the courts for the place where or from where the employee habitually carries out his work or in the courts for the last place where he did so; or
      (ii) if the employee does not or did not habitually carry out his work in any one country, in the courts for the place where the business which engaged the employee is or was situated.
2. An employer not domiciled in a Member State may be sued in a court of a Member State in accordance with point (b) of paragraph 1.

III EUR [175.1]

The employee may be sued only in the courts of the Member State in which he or she is domiciled (article 22) but has a choice of where to sue the employer. The employer can be sued in the Member State where he is domiciled, where the employee habitually carried out his/her work or, if that was not in any one country, where the business which engaged the employee was situated (the last two options apply regardless of whether the employer is EU domiciled or not). The extension of the rules to non-EU domiciled employers is new to Brussels I Recast.

Article 22

III EUR [176]

1. An employer may bring proceedings only in the courts of the Member State in which the employee is domiciled.
2. The provisions of this Section shall not affect the right to bring a counter-claim in the court in which, in accordance with this Section, the original claim is pending.

EUROPE

Article 23

III EUR [177]

The provisions of this Section may be departed from only by an agreement:

(1) which is entered into after the dispute has arisen; or

(2) which allows the employee to bring proceedings in courts other than those indicated in this Section.

SECTION 6

EXCLUSIVE JURISDICTION

Article 24

III EUR [178]

The following courts of a Member State shall have exclusive jurisdiction, regardless of the domicile of the parties:

(1) in proceedings which have as their object rights in rem in immovable property or tenancies of immovable property, the courts of the Member State in which the property is situated.

However, in proceedings which have as their object tenancies of immovable property concluded for temporary private use for a maximum period of six consecutive months, the courts of the Member State in which the defendant is domiciled shall also have jurisdiction, provided that the tenant is a natural person and that the landlord and the tenant are domiciled in the same Member State;

(2) in proceedings which have as their object the validity of the constitution, the nullity or the dissolution of companies or other legal persons or associations of natural or legal persons, or the validity of the decisions of their organs, the courts of the Member State in which the company, legal person or association has its seat. In order to determine that seat, the court shall apply its rules of private international law;

(3) in proceedings which have as their object the validity of entries in public registers, the courts of the Member State in which the register is kept;

(4) in proceedings concerned with the registration or validity of patents, trade marks, designs, or other similar rights required to be deposited or registered, irrespective of whether the issue is raised by way of an action or as a defence, the courts of the Member State in which the deposit or registration has been applied for, has taken place or is under the terms of an instrument of the Union or an international convention deemed to have taken place.

Without prejudice to the jurisdiction of the European Patent Office under the Convention on the Grant of European Patents, signed at Munich on 5 October 1973, the courts of each Member State shall have exclusive jurisdiction in proceedings concerned with the registration or validity of any European patent granted for that Member State;

(5) in proceedings concerned with the enforcement of judgments, the courts of the Member State in which the judgment has been or is to be enforced.

III EUR [178.1]

The exclusive jurisdiction provisions now apply regardless of the domicile of the parties and do not deprive courts of non-Member States of jurisdiction since they are not bound by Brussels I Recast.

III EUR [178.2]

Rights *in rem* In the first ruling under Brussels I Recast the CJEU held that an application, seeking the enforcement of powers arising from a right in rem, falls under the exclusive jurisdiction of the courts of the Member State in which the property is situated. Thus, it held that an action seeking the removal from the land register of notices evidencing the donee's right of ownership falls within article 24(1): *Schmidt (Wolfgang) v Schmidt (Christiane): C-417/15* ECLI:EU:C:2016:881.

III EUR [178.3]

Not all actions on rights *in rem* The provisions of article 24(1) of Brussels I Recast (article 22(1) of Brussels I) must not be given an interpretation broader than is required by their objective. Those provisions have the effect of depriving the parties of the choice of forum which would otherwise be theirs and, in certain cases, of resulting in their being brought before a court which is not that of the domicile of any of them. The essential reason for the exclusive jurisdiction of the courts where the property is situated is that those courts are the best placed, for reasons of proximity, to ascertain the facts satisfactorily and to apply the rules and practices which are generally those of the State in which the property is situated. However, exclusive jurisdiction of the courts of that State does not encompass all actions concerning rights in rem in immovable property, but only those which both come within the scope of the Brussels Convention or Brussels I respectively and are actions which seek to determine the extent, content, ownership or possession of immovable property or the existence of other rights in rem therein and to provide the holders of those rights with protection for the powers which attach to their interest: *Schmidt (Wolfgang) v Schmidt (Christiane): C-417/15* ECLI:EU:C:2016:881 citing *Komu and Others: C-605/14).*

III EUR [178.4]

Trademarks Articles 22(4) and 71 of Brussels I have been reproduced in articles 24(4) and 71 of Brussels I Recast. In a case on Benelux trademarks and designs the CJEU held that the codified rule of article 4.6 of the BCIP (Benelux Convention on Intellectual Property of 2005) of the Benelux regime established by the three Member States, was consistent with Brussels I. The rule, which is founded on the defendant's domicile, ensures that the disputes relating to Benelux trademarks and designs may be dealt with by a Belgian, Luxembourg, or Dutch court, instead of being concentrated, pursuant to article 22(4), before the Dutch courts where the filing and registration of trademarks is centralised and the register is kept as it is indispensable for the proper functioning of the Benelux regime of trademarks and designs. Article 71 of Brussels I, read in light of TFEU, article 350, does not prevent Belgium, Luxembourg and the Netherlands from maintaining in force, in derogation from article 22(4) [now article 24(4)], the rule of jurisdiction for disputes on Benelux trademarks and designs of article 4.6 of the BCIP: *Brite Strike Technologies Inc. v Brite Strike Technologies SA: C-230/15* (2016), unreported.

More recently the CJEU has held that, as regards jurisdiction for Benelux trademarks, contrary to the facts of *Brite Strike Technologies: C-230/15* EU:C:2016:560), in which the Court clarified the relationship between the rule of jurisdiction set out in Paragraph 4.6 of the BCIP and that of art 22(4) of Brussels I, where the proceedings do not concern the registration or the validity of the Benelux trademark in question or any potential infringement of that trademark the specific features of the BCIP on jurisdiction are irrelevant eg the action is not founded on any substantive provision of the BCIP. Brussels I (and by analogy Brussels I Recast) does not apply to proceedings to determine whether a person was correctly registered as the proprietor of a trademark: *Hanssen: C-341/16* ECLI:EU:C:2017:738.

SECTION 7

PROROGATION OF JURISDICTION

Article 25

III EUR [179]

1. If the parties, regardless of their domicile, have agreed that a court or the courts of a Member State are to have jurisdiction to settle any disputes which have arisen or which may arise in connection with a particular legal relationship, that court or those courts shall have jurisdiction, unless the agreement is null and void as to its substantive validity under the law of that Member State. Such jurisdiction shall be exclusive unless the parties have agreed otherwise. The agreement conferring jurisdiction shall be either:

EUROPE

(a) in writing or evidenced in writing;
(b) in a form which accords with practices which the parties have established between themselves; or
(c) in international trade or commerce, in a form which accords with a usage of which the parties are or ought to have been aware and which in such trade or commerce is widely known to, and regularly observed by, parties to contracts of the type involved in the particular trade or commerce concerned.

2. Any communication by electronic means which provides a durable record of the agreement shall be equivalent to 'writing'.

3. The court or courts of a Member State on which a trust instrument has conferred jurisdiction shall have exclusive jurisdiction in any proceedings brought against a settlor, trustee or beneficiary, if relations between those persons or their rights or obligations under the trust are involved.

4. Agreements or provisions of a trust instrument conferring jurisdiction shall have no legal force if they are contrary to Articles 15, 19 or 23, or if the courts whose jurisdiction they purport to exclude have exclusive jurisdiction by virtue of Article 24.

5. An agreement conferring jurisdiction which forms part of a contract shall be treated as an agreement independent of the other terms of the contract.

The validity of the agreement conferring jurisdiction cannot be contested solely on the ground that the contract is not valid.

III EUR [179.1]

This provision is broader than its predecessor article 23 of Brussels I which only applied to jurisdiction agreements where one of the parties was domiciled in the EU. Brussels I Recast applies to jurisdiction clauses that confer jurisdiction on a Member State regardless of domicile.

In construing paras 1(a) and 1(c) the CJEU has held that, where the jurisdiction clause is in an unsigned prospectus, the requirements of 1(a) may be satisfied if there is an express reference to the prospectus in the signed contract and that the requirements of 1(c) could be satisfied if the usage, of including the jurisdiction clause in the prospectus, was generally recognised and an established practice: *Profit Investment Sim SpA v Ossi: C-366/13* (2016) ECLI:EU:C:2016:282, [2016] 1 WLR 3832, [2016] 2 All ER (Comm) 621.

The CJEU has held that a jurisdiction clause which is set out in the client's general terms and conditions, referred to in the instruments witnessing the contracts between those parties and forwarded upon their conclusion, and which designates as courts with jurisdiction those of a city of a Member State, meets the requirements of article 23(1) of Brussels I [now article 25(1)] relating to the consent of the parties and to the precision of the content of such a clause: *Hőszig (C-222/15)*.

In *Saey Home & Garden NV/SA: C-64/17* (2018) ECLI:EU:C:2018:173 the CJEU ruled that article 25(1) means that, subject to verifications being made by the referring court, a jurisdiction clause set out in the general conditions of sale mentioned in invoices issued by one of the contracting parties does not satisfy the requirements of that provision.

Article 26

III EUR [180]

1. Apart from jurisdiction derived from other provisions of this Regulation, a court of a Member State before which a defendant enters an appearance shall have jurisdiction. This rule shall not apply where appearance was entered to contest the jurisdiction, or where another court has exclusive jurisdiction by virtue of Article 24.

2. In matters referred to in Sections 3, 4 or 5 where the policyholder, the insured, a beneficiary of the insurance contract, the injured party, the consumer or the employee is the defendant, the court shall, before assuming jurisdiction under paragraph 1, ensure that the defendant is informed of his right to contest the jurisdiction of the court and of the consequences of entering or not entering an appearance.

SECTION 8

EXAMINATION AS TO JURISDICTION AND ADMISSIBILITY

Article 27

III EUR [181]

Where a court of a Member State is seised of a claim which is principally concerned with a matter over which the courts of another Member State have exclusive jurisdiction by virtue of Article 24, it shall declare of its own motion that it has no jurisdiction.

Article 28

III EUR [182]

1. Where a defendant domiciled in one Member State is sued in a court of another Member State and does not enter an appearance, the court shall declare of its own motion that it has no jurisdiction unless its jurisdiction is derived from the provisions of this Regulation.
2. The court shall stay the proceedings so long as it is not shown that the defendant has been able to receive the document instituting the proceedings or an equivalent document in sufficient time to enable him to arrange for his defence, or that all necessary steps have been taken to this end.
3. Article 19 of Regulation (EC) No 1393/2007 of the European Parliament and of the Council of 13 November 2007 on the service in the Member States of judicial and extrajudicial documents in civil or commercial matters (service of documents) (1) shall apply instead of paragraph 2 of this Article if the document instituting the proceedings or an equivalent document had to be transmitted from one Member State to another pursuant to that Regulation.
4. Where Regulation (EC) No 1393/2007 is not applicable, Article 15 of the Hague Convention of 15 November 1965 on the Service Abroad of Judicial and Extrajudicial Documents in Civil or Commercial Matters shall apply if the document instituting the proceedings or an equivalent document had to be transmitted abroad pursuant to that Convention.

SECTION 9

LIS PENDENS - RELATED ACTIONS

Article 29

III EUR [183]

1. Without prejudice to Article 31(2), where proceedings involving the same cause of action and between the same parties are brought in the courts of different Member States, any court other than the court first seised shall of its own motion stay its proceedings until such time as the jurisdiction of the court first seised is established.
2. In cases referred to in paragraph 1, upon request by a court seised of the dispute, any other court seised shall without delay inform the former court of the date when it was seised in accordance with Article 32.
3. Where the jurisdiction of the court first seised is established, any court other than the court first seised shall decline jurisdiction in favour of that court.

III EUR [183.1]

The same parties In a case where the UK court was the court first seised but a new claimant was substituted later, on an assignment after the foreign court had become seised, it was held that the UK court remained the court first seised for the purposes of Brussels I. The point of law on appeal was whether the parties to the UK proceedings and the parties to the Cyprus proceedings were the 'same parties' for the purposes of article 27 of Brussels I (now article 29) which gives priority to the courts of the Member State which is first seised. It was held that the question of 'the same parties' was to be determined by looking at the claims and not at the subsequent defences, thus the UK court remained the first seised: *Kolden Hollings Ltd v Rolette Commerce Ltd* [2007] EWHC 1597 (Com), [2007] 4 All ER 62, upheld on appeal; [2008] EWCA Civ 10, [2008] 2 All ER (Comm) 289.

Article 30

III EUR [184]

1. Where related actions are pending in the courts of different Member States, any court other than the court first seised may stay its proceedings.
2. Where the action in the court first seised is pending at first instance, any other court may also, on the application of one of the parties, decline jurisdiction if the court first seised has jurisdiction over the actions in question and its law permits the consolidation thereof.
3. For the purposes of this Article, actions are deemed to be related where they are so closely connected that it is expedient to hear and determine them together to avoid the risk of irreconcilable judgments resulting from separate proceedings.

III EUR [184.1]

Related actions If there is a related action pending in the court of another Member State, and that action was commenced before the UK proceedings, the UK court has a discretion to stay its proceedings. Actions are deemed to be related where they are so closely connected that it is expedient to hear and determine them together to avoid the risk of irreconcilable judgments resulting from separate proceedings. In determining whether discretion should be exercised in favour of a stay, a national court should consider three factors: (1) the extent of the relatedness of the proceedings and the risk of mutually irreconcilable decisions; (2) the stage reached in each set of proceedings and (3) the proximity of the courts to the subject matter of the case. This well-established approach was suggested by Advocate General Lenz in *Owens Bank Ltd v Bracco (C-129/92)* – see *Cooper Tire & Rubber Company v Dow Deutschland* [2010] EWCA Civ 864. However, it must be pointed out that these factors are not exhaustive. It is highly likely the UK court will however be slow to exercise the discretion to stay where its jurisdiction is based on an exclusive jurisdiction clause in its favour: *Nomura International Plc v Banca Monte Dei Paschi Di Siena SpA* [2013] EWHC 3187 (Comm).

Where the UK court is satisfied that there are in fact pending proceedings in the courts of another Member State, even though it may not consider that the proceedings in the other Member State involve the same cause of action as the proceedings in the UK, it may still find that the two proceedings are closely connected. If that connection is so close that it is expedient to hear and determine them together to avoid the risk of irreconcilable judgments resulting from separate proceedings it may grant a stay. There is a balance of factors to be weighed and, when that balance points strongly to resolving the issue which arises in the other Member State proceedings and equally strongly to staying the proceedings here in the meantime, it is likely to grant the stay: *Lehman Brothers Bankhaus AG I Ins v CMA CGM* [2013] EWHC 171 (Comm), [2013] 2 All ER (Comm) 557, [2013] NLJR 167.

III EUR [184.2]

Stay in favour of non-Member State court It is not clear whether a Member State court has discretion to stay its proceedings in favour of a non-Member State court where there are grounds for exclusive jurisdiction equivalent to article 24 in favour of that court. In *Ferrexpo AG v Gilson Investments Ltd* [2012] EWHC 721 (Comm) the English court exercised its discretion and stayed proceedings against an English domiciled defendant on the basis that the object of the proceedings was the validity of resolutions made by a Ukrainian company. Further, it was held that there was no significant argument in favour of the court assuming jurisdiction but there were powerful reasons for the dispute to be decided in Ukraine, in particular, a multiplicity of proceedings and a risk of inconsistent decisions and that other parties interested in the dispute had joined the Ukrainian proceedings.

Article 31

III EUR [185]

1. Where actions come within the exclusive jurisdiction of several courts, any court other than the court first seised shall decline jurisdiction in favour of that court.
2. Without prejudice to Article 26, where a court of a Member State on which an agreement as referred to in Article 25 confers exclusive jurisdiction is seised, any court of another Member State shall stay the proceedings until such time as the court seised on the basis of the agreement declares that it has no jurisdiction under the agreement.
3. Where the court designated in the agreement has established jurisdiction in accordance with the agreement, any court of another Member State shall decline jurisdiction in favour of that court.
4. Paragraphs 2 and 3 shall not apply to matters referred to in Sections 3, 4 or 5 where the policyholder, the insured, a beneficiary of the insurance contract, the injured party, the consumer or the employee is the claimant and the agreement is not valid under a provision contained within those Sections.

III EUR [185.1]

Exclusive jurisdiction Where proceedings come within an exclusive jurisdiction clause in favour of another Member State court and proceedings are commenced in that court, regardless of whether those proceedings commence before or after UK proceedings, the UK court must stay its proceedings in favour of the other Member State court. The UK court may only proceed if the chosen court has declined jurisdiction. Thus, if the chosen court establishes its jurisdiction, the UK court must decline jurisdiction.

Article 32

III EUR [186]

1. For the purposes of this Section, a court shall be deemed to be seised:
   (a) at the time when the document instituting the proceedings or an equivalent document is lodged with the court, provided that the claimant has not subsequently failed to take the steps he was required to take to have service effected on the defendant; or
   (b) if the document has to be served before being lodged with the court, at the time when it is received by the authority responsible for service, provided that the claimant has not subsequently failed to take the steps he was required to take to have the document lodged with the court.

The authority responsible for service referred to in point (b) shall be the first authority receiving the documents to be served.

2. The court, or the authority responsible for service, referred to in paragraph 1, shall note, respectively, the date of the lodging of the document instituting the proceedings or the equivalent document, or the date of receipt of the documents to be served.

III EUR [186.1]

The CA held that the court first seised is (1) the court where the proceedings were first lodged or, alternatively, (2) where the proceedings were first received by the authority responsible for service: *Benatti v WPP Holdings Italy Srl* [2007] EWCA Civ 263, (2007) Times, 16 April, CA.

It further held that, provided documents capable of being served and lodged have been received by the authority responsible for service, it does not matter whether or when service is actually effected.

Article 33

III EUR [187]

1. Where jurisdiction is based on Article 4 or on Articles 7, 8 or 9 and proceedings are pending before a court of a third State at the time when a court in a Member State is seised of an action involving the same cause of action and between the same parties as the proceedings in the court of the third State, the court of the Member State may stay the proceedings if:

(a) it is expected that the court of the third State will give a judgment capable of recognition and, where applicable, of enforcement in that Member State; and

(b) the court of the Member State is satisfied that a stay is necessary for the proper administration of justice.

2. The court of the Member State may continue the proceedings at any time if:

(a) the proceedings in the court of the third State are themselves stayed or discontinued;

(b) it appears to the court of the Member State that the proceedings in the court of the third State are unlikely to be concluded within a reasonable time; or

(c) the continuation of the proceedings is required for the proper administration of justice.

3. The court of the Member State shall dismiss the proceedings if the proceedings in the court of the third State are concluded and have resulted in a judgment capable of recognition and, where applicable, of enforcement in that Member State.

4. The court of the Member State shall apply this Article on the application of one of the parties or, where possible under national law, of its own motion.

III EUR [187.1]

Where prior proceedings involving the same cause of action and between the same parties have been brought in a non-Member State court first, the UK court has discretion to stay its proceedings under article 33. The rule does not apply where the UK court's jurisdiction is based on a jurisdiction clause under article 25 as under Brussels I Recast an exclusive jurisdiction clause prevails. Further, the discretion to stay only applies where the non-Member State proceedings were first in time. It does not allow the UK court to stay its proceedings in favour of a non-Member State court where the UK proceedings were commenced first.

Article 34

III EUR [188]

Where jurisdiction is based on Article 4 or on Articles 7, 8 or 9 and an action is pending before a court of a third State at the time when a court in a Member State is seised of an action which is related to the action in the court of the third State, the court of the Member State may stay the proceedings if:

(a) it is expedient to hear and determine the related actions together to avoid the risk of irreconcilable judgments resulting from separate proceedings;

(b) it is expected that the court of the third State will give a judgment capable of recognition and, where applicable, of enforcement in that Member State; and

(c) the court of the Member State is satisfied that a stay is necessary for the proper administration of justice.

2. The court of the Member State may continue the proceedings at any time if:

(a) it appears to the court of the Member State that there is no longer a risk of irreconcilable judgments;

(b) the proceedings in the court of the third State are themselves stayed or discontinued;

(c) it appears to the court of the Member State that the proceedings in the court of the third State are unlikely to be concluded within a reasonable time; or

(d) the continuation of the proceedings is required for the proper administration of justice.

3. The court of the Member State may dismiss the proceedings if the proceedings in the court of the third State are concluded and have resulted in a judgment capable of recognition and, where applicable, of enforcement in that Member State.

4. The court of the Member State shall apply this Article on the application of one of the parties or, where possible under national law, of its own motion.

III EUR [188.1]

Member State courts may stay their proceedings where related claims are brought in a non-Member State court, where the Member State court's jurisdiction is based on article 4 (domicile) or articles 7, 8 or 9 (special jurisdiction). However, that discretion may be exercised only if certain requirements are met including the need for the proceedings to have been commenced in the non-Member State first. Brussels I Recast is silent as regards what happens if the non-Member State court is second seised and, for instance, there is an exclusive jurisdiction agreement in favour of that court or other provisions confer upon it exclusive jurisdiction. It seems that a Member State court has discretion to stay proceedings in favour of a non-Member State court where there is an exclusive jurisdiction clause in favour of that court. It is expected that the UK court will stay its proceedings to give effect to the parties' choice of jurisdiction.

SECTION 10

PROVISIONAL, INCLUDING PROTECTIVE, MEASURES

Article 35

III EUR [189]

Application may be made to the courts of a Member State for such provisional, including protective, measures as may be available under the law of that Member State, even if the courts of another Member State have jurisdiction as to the substance of the matter.

CHAPTER III
RECOGNITION AND ENFORCEMENT

SECTION 1

RECOGNITION

Article 36

III EUR [190]

1. A judgment given in a Member State shall be recognised in the other Member States without any special procedure being required.

2. Any interested party may, in accordance with the procedure provided for in Subsection 2 of Section 3, apply for a decision that there are no grounds for refusal of recognition as referred to in Article 45.

3. If the outcome of proceedings in a court of a Member State depends on the determination of an incidental question of refusal of recognition, that court shall have jurisdiction over that question.

Article 37

III EUR [191]

1. A party who wishes to invoke in a Member State a judgment given in another Member State shall produce:

(a) a copy of the judgment which satisfies the conditions necessary to establish its authenticity; and

(b) the certificate issued pursuant to Article 53.

2. The court or authority before which a judgment given in another Member State is invoked may, where necessary, require the party invoking it to provide, in accordance with Article 57, a translation or a transliteration of the contents of the certificate referred to in point (b) of paragraph 1. The court or authority may require the party to provide a translation of the judgment instead of a translation of the contents of the certificate if it is unable to proceed without such a translation.

Article 38

III EUR [192]

The court or authority before which a judgment given in another Member State is invoked may suspend the proceedings, in whole or in part, if:

(a) the judgment is challenged in the Member State of origin; or

(b) an application has been submitted for a decision that there are no grounds for refusal of recognition as referred to in Article 45 or for a decision that the recognition is to be refused on the basis of one of those grounds.

SECTION 2

ENFORCEMENT

Article 39

III EUR [193]

A judgment given in a Member State which is enforceable in that Member State shall be enforceable in the other Member States without any declaration of enforceability being required.

III EUR [193.1]

This article eliminates the *exequatur* procedure.

Article 40

III EUR [194]

An enforceable judgment shall carry with it by operation of law the power to proceed to any protective measures which exist under the law of the Member State addressed.

Article 41

III EUR [195]

1. Subject to the provisions of this Section, the procedure for the enforcement of judgments given in another Member State shall be governed by the law of the Member State addressed. A judgment given in a Member State which is enforceable in the Member State addressed shall be enforced there under the same conditions as a judgment given in the Member State addressed.

2. Notwithstanding paragraph 1, the grounds for refusal or of suspension of enforcement under the law of the Member State addressed shall apply in so far as they are not incompatible with the grounds referred to in Article 45.

3. The party seeking the enforcement of a judgment given in another Member State shall not be required to have a postal address in the Member State addressed. Nor shall that party be required to have an authorised representative in the Member State addressed unless such a representative is mandatory irrespective of the nationality or the domicile of the parties.

Article 42

III EUR [196]

1. For the purposes of enforcement in a Member State of a judgment given in another Member State, the applicant shall provide the competent enforcement authority with:

(a) a copy of the judgment which satisfies the conditions necessary to establish its authenticity; and

(b) the certificate issued pursuant to Article 53, certifying that the judgment is enforceable and containing an extract of the judgment as well as, where appropriate, relevant information on the recoverable costs of the proceedings and the calculation of interest.

2. For the purposes of enforcement in a Member State of a judgment given in another Member State ordering a provisional, including a protective, measure, the applicant shall provide the competent enforcement authority with:

(a) a copy of the judgment which satisfies the conditions necessary to establish its authenticity;

(b) the certificate issued pursuant to Article 53, containing a description of the measure and certifying that:

(i) the court has jurisdiction as to the substance of the matter;

(ii) the judgment is enforceable in the Member State of origin; and

(c) where the measure was ordered without the defendant being summoned to appear, proof of service of the judgment.

3. The competent enforcement authority may, where necessary, require the applicant to provide, in accordance with Article 57, a translation or a transliteration of the contents of the certificate.

4. The competent enforcement authority may require the applicant to provide a translation of the judgment only if it is unable to proceed without such a translation.

III EUR [196.1]

See CPR Part 74 and Practice Direction 74A for detailed guidance on enforcement of judgments under Brussels I Recast and Brussels I (as different provisions apply depending on the proceedings under which the judgments were handed down).

EUROPE

Article 43

III EUR [197]

1. Where enforcement is sought of a judgment given in another Member State, the certificate issued pursuant to Article 53 shall be served on the person against whom the enforcement is sought prior to the first enforcement measure. The certificate shall be accompanied by the judgment, if not already served on that person.
2. Where the person against whom enforcement is sought is domiciled in a Member State other than the Member State of origin, he may request a translation of the judgment in order to contest the enforcement if the judgment is not written in or accompanied by a translation into either of the following languages:
   (a) a language which he understands; or
   (b) the official language of the Member State in which he is domiciled or, where there are several official languages in that Member State, the official language or one of the official languages of the place where he is domiciled.

Where a translation of the judgment is requested under the first subparagraph, no measures of enforcement may be taken other than protective measures until that translation has been provided to the person against whom enforcement is sought.
This paragraph shall not apply if the judgment has already been served on the person against whom enforcement is sought in one of the languages referred to in the first subparagraph or is accompanied by a translation into one of those languages.
3. This Article shall not apply to the enforcement of a protective measure in a judgment or where the person seeking enforcement proceeds to protective measures in accordance with Article 40.

Article 44

III EUR [198]

1. In the event of an application for refusal of enforcement of a judgment pursuant to Subsection 2 of Section 3, the court in the Member State addressed may, on the application of the person against whom enforcement is sought:
   (a) limit the enforcement proceedings to protective measures;
   (b) make enforcement conditional on the provision of such security as it shall determine; or
   (c) suspend, either wholly or in part, the enforcement proceedings.
2. The competent authority in the Member State addressed shall, on the application of the person against whom enforcement is sought, suspend the enforcement proceedings where the enforceability of the judgment is suspended in the Member State of origin.

SECTION 3

REFUSAL OF RECOGNITION AND ENFORCEMENT

SUBSECTION 1

Refusal of recognition

ARTICLE 45

III EUR [199]

1. On the application of any interested party, the recognition of a judgment shall be refused:

(a) if such recognition is manifestly contrary to public policy (ordre public) in the Member State addressed;

(b) where the judgment was given in default of appearance, if the defendant was not served with the document which instituted the proceedings or with an equivalent document in sufficient time and in such a way as to enable him to arrange for his defence, unless the defendant failed to commence proceedings to challenge the judgment when it was possible for him to do so;

(c) if the judgment is irreconcilable with a judgment given between the same parties in the Member State addressed;

(d) if the judgment is irreconcilable with an earlier judgment given in another Member State or in a third State involving the same cause of action and between the same parties, provided that the earlier judgment fulfils the conditions necessary for its recognition in the Member State addressed; or

(e) if the judgment conflicts with:

(i) Sections 3, 4 or 5 of Chapter II where the policyholder, the insured, a beneficiary of the insurance contract, the injured party, the consumer or the employee was the defendant; or

(ii) Section 6 of Chapter II.

2. In its examination of the grounds of jurisdiction referred to in point (e) of paragraph 1, the court to which the application was submitted shall be bound by the findings of fact on which the court of origin based its jurisdiction.

3. Without prejudice to point (e) of paragraph 1, the jurisdiction of the court of origin may not be reviewed. The test of public policy referred to in point (a) of paragraph 1 may not be applied to the rules relating to jurisdiction.

4. The application for refusal of recognition shall be made in accordance with the procedures provided for in Subsection 2 and, where appropriate, Section 4.

SUBSECTION 2

Refusal of enforcement

ARTICLE 46

III EUR [200]

On the application of the person against whom enforcement is sought, the enforcement of a judgment shall be refused where one of the grounds referred to in Article 45 is found to exist.

ARTICLE 47

III EUR [201]

1. The application for refusal of enforcement shall be submitted to the court which the Member State concerned has communicated to the Commission pursuant to point (a) of Article 75 as the court to which the application is to be submitted.

2. The procedure for refusal of enforcement shall, in so far as it is not covered by this Regulation, be governed by the law of the Member State addressed.

3. The applicant shall provide the court with a copy of the judgment and, where necessary, a translation or transliteration of it.

The court may dispense with the production of the documents referred to in the first subparagraph if it already possesses them or if it considers it unreasonable to require the applicant to provide them. In the latter case, the court may require the other party to provide those documents.

4. The party seeking the refusal of enforcement of a judgment given in another Member State shall not be required to have a postal address in the Member State addressed. Nor shall that party be required to have an authorised representative in the Member State addressed unless such a representative is mandatory irrespective of the nationality or the domicile of the parties.

III EUR [201.1]

Article 75(a) is equivalent to Annex II to Brussels I, which was amended in January 2015 by Regulation (EU) 2015/263 which entered into force on 11 March 2015. In what relates to the UK it states: '... in the United Kingdom: in England and Wales, the High Court of Justice, or in the case of a maintenance judgment, the Family Court on transmission by the Secretary of State; in Scotland, the Court of Session, or in the case of a maintenance judgment, the Sheriff Court on transmission by the Scottish Ministers; in Northern Ireland, the High Court of Justice, or in the case of a maintenance judgment, the Magistrates' Court on transmission by the Department of Justice; in Gibraltar, the Supreme Court of Gibraltar, or in the case of a maintenance judgment, the Magistrates' Court on transmission by the Attorney General of Gibraltar'.

The procedure to follow in so far as not covered by Brussels I Recast is left to national law and in the UK it is governed by CPR 74.7A. As regards enforcement of a judgment by a party not domiciled in the Member State where the enforcement is sought Brussels I Recast simplifies the situation as it now states that the party seeking enforcement cannot be asked to have a postal address in the Member State. However, it leaves the door open to require an authorised representative in such Member State if that requirement is a requisite under national law applicable irrespective of nationality or domicile.

ARTICLE 48

III EUR [202]

The court shall decide on the application for refusal of enforcement without delay.

ARTICLE 49

III EUR [203]

1. The decision on the application for refusal of enforcement may be appealed against by either party.
2. The appeal is to be lodged with the court which the Member State concerned has communicated to the Commission pursuant to point (b) of Article 75 as the court with which such an appeal is to be lodged.

ARTICLE 50

III EUR [204]

The decision given on the appeal may only be contested by an appeal where the courts with which any further appeal is to be lodged have been communicated by the Member State concerned to the Commission pursuant to point (c) of Article 75.

ARTICLE 51

III EUR [205]

1. The court to which an application for refusal of enforcement is submitted or the court which hears an appeal lodged under Article 49 or Article 50 may stay the proceedings if an ordinary appeal has been lodged against the judgment in the

Member State of origin or if the time for such an appeal has not yet expired. In the latter case, the court may specify the time within which such an appeal is to be lodged.

2. Where the judgment was given in Ireland, Cyprus or the United Kingdom, any form of appeal available in the Member State of origin shall be treated as an ordinary appeal for the purposes of paragraph 1.

SECTION 4

COMMON PROVISIONS

Article 52

III EUR [206]

Under no circumstances may a judgment given in a Member State be reviewed as to its substance in the Member State addressed.

Article 53

III EUR [207]

The court of origin shall, at the request of any interested party, issue the certificate using the form set out in Annex I.

III EUR [207.1]

Annex I was replaced by Commission Delegated Regulation (EU) 2015/281 which entered into force on 26 February 2015. When faced with the need to apply article 53 practitioners need to check the certificate complies with the requirements of the new Annex I. Thus, they need to look at the above-mentioned Regulation as well not only Brussels I Recast.

Article 54

III EUR [208]

1. If a judgment contains a measure or an order which is not known in the law of the Member State addressed, that measure or order shall, to the extent possible, be adapted to a measure or an order known in the law of that Member State which has equivalent effects attached to it and which pursues similar aims and interests.

Such adaptation shall not result in effects going beyond those provided for in the law of the Member State of origin.

2. Any party may challenge the adaptation of the measure or order before a court.

3. If necessary, the party invoking the judgment or seeking its enforcement may be required to provide a translation or a transliteration of the judgment.

Article 55

III EUR [209]

A judgment given in a Member State which orders a payment by way of a penalty shall be enforceable in the Member State addressed only if the amount of the payment has been finally determined by the court of origin.

EUROPE

Article 56

III EUR [210]

No security, bond or deposit, however described, shall be required of a party who in one Member State applies for the enforcement of a judgment given in another Member State on the ground that he is a foreign national or that he is not domiciled or resident in the Member State addressed.

III EUR [210.1]

Reinforcement of the lack of necessity for the party who seeks enforcement of a judgment to have an address, be domiciled in or be a national of the Member State addressed as no security, bond or deposit may be required.

Article 57

III EUR [211]

1. When a translation or a transliteration is required under this Regulation, such translation or transliteration shall be into the official language of the Member State concerned or, where there are several official languages in that Member State, into the official language or one of the official languages of court proceedings of the place where a judgment given in another Member State is invoked or an application is made, in accordance with the law of that Member State.
2. For the purposes of the forms referred to in Articles 53 and 60, translations or transliterations may also be into any other official language or languages of the institutions of the Union that the Member State concerned has indicated it can accept.
3. Any translation made under this Regulation shall be done by a person qualified to do translations in one of the Member States.

CHAPTER IV
AUTHENTIC INSTRUMENTS AND COURT SETTLEMENTS

Article 58

III EUR [212]

1. An authentic instrument which is enforceable in the Member State of origin shall be enforceable in the other Member States without any declaration of enforceability being required. Enforcement of the authentic instrument may be refused only if such enforcement is manifestly contrary to public policy (ordre public) in the Member State addressed.

The provisions of Section 2, Subsection 2 of Section 3, and Section 4 of Chapter III shall apply as appropriate to authentic instruments.

2. The authentic instrument produced must satisfy the conditions necessary to establish its authenticity in the Member State of origin.

Article 59

III EUR [213]

A court settlement which is enforceable in the Member State of origin shall be enforced in the other Member States under the same conditions as authentic instruments.

Article 60

III EUR [214]

The competent authority or court of the Member State of origin shall, at the request of any interested party, issue the certificate using the form set out in Annex II containing a summary of the enforceable obligation recorded in the authentic instrument or of the agreement between the parties recorded in the court settlement.

III EUR [214.1]

Annex II was replaced by Commission Delegated Regulation (EU) 2015/281 which entered into force on 26 February 2015. When faced with the need to apply article 60 practitioners need to check the certificate complies with the requirements of the new Annex II. Thus, they need to look at the above-mentioned Regulation as well not only Brussels I Recast.

CHAPTER V
GENERAL PROVISIONS

Article 61

III EUR [215]

No legalisation or other similar formality shall be required for documents issued in a Member State in the context of this Regulation.

Article 62

III EUR [216]

1. In order to determine whether a party is domiciled in the Member State whose courts are seised of a matter, the court shall apply its internal law.
2. If a party is not domiciled in the Member State whose courts are seised of the matter, then, in order to determine whether the party is domiciled in another Member State, the court shall apply the law of that Member State.

Article 63

III EUR [217]

1. For the purposes of this Regulation, a company or other legal person or association of natural or legal persons is domiciled at the place where it has its:
    (a) statutory seat;
    (b) central administration; or
    (c) principal place of business.
2. For the purposes of Ireland, Cyprus and the United Kingdom, 'statutory seat' means the registered office or, where there is no such office anywhere, the place of incorporation or, where there is no such place anywhere, the place under the law of which the formation took place.
3. In order to determine whether a trust is domiciled in the Member State whose courts are seised of the matter, the court shall apply its rules of private international law.

Article 64

III EUR [218]

Without prejudice to any more favourable provisions of national laws, persons domiciled in a Member State who are being prosecuted in the criminal courts of another Member State of which they are not nationals for an offence which was not intentionally committed may be defended by persons qualified to do so, even if they do not appear in person. However, the court seised of the matter may order appearance in person; in the case of failure to appear, a judgment given in the civil action without the person concerned having had the opportunity to arrange for his defence need not be recognised or enforced in the other Member States.

Article 65

III EUR [219]

1. The jurisdiction specified in point 2 of Article 8 and Article 13 in actions on a warranty or guarantee or in any other third-party proceedings may be resorted to in the Member States included in the list established by the Commission pursuant to point (b) of Article 76(1) and Article 76(2) only in so far as permitted under national law. A person domiciled in another Member State may be invited to join the proceedings before the courts of those Member States pursuant to the rules on third-party notice referred to in that list.
2. Judgments given in a Member State by virtue of point 2 of Article 8 or Article 13 shall be recognised and enforced in accordance with Chapter III in any other Member State. Any effects which judgments given in the Member States included in the list referred to in paragraph 1 may have, in accordance with the law of those Member States, on third parties by application of paragraph 1 shall be recognised in all Member States.
3. The Member States included in the list referred to in paragraph 1 shall, within the framework of the European Judicial Network in civil and commercial matters established by Council Decision 2001/470/EC (1) ('the European Judicial Network') provide information on how to determine, in accordance with their national law, the effects of the judgments referred to in the second sentence of paragraph 2.

CHAPTER VI
TRANSITIONAL PROVISIONS

Article 66

III EUR [220]

1. This Regulation shall apply only to legal proceedings instituted, to authentic instruments formally drawn up or registered and to court settlements approved or concluded on or after 10 January 2015.
2. Notwithstanding Article 80, Regulation (EC) No 44/2001 shall continue to apply to judgments given in legal proceedings instituted, to authentic instruments formally drawn up or registered and to court settlements approved or concluded before 10 January 2015 which fall within the scope of that Regulation.

III EUR [220.1]

Temporal scope In a case dealing with the recovery of an unpaid debt, payable under a contract entered into before Croatia acceded to the EU, the CJEU held that Brussels I Recast applies as the enforcement proceedings were brought on 27 February 2015, after Brussels I Recast entered into force and the dispute in the main proceedings was brought before the referring court, on 21 April 2015. According to art 66(1) the only necessary and sufficient condition for the regulation to be applicable to litigation relating to legal relationships created before its entry into force is that the judicial proceedings should have been instituted subsequently to that date: *Pula Parking: C-551/16* ECLI:EU:C:2017:193 citing *Sanicentral: C-25/79* EU:C:1979:255.

CHAPTER VII
RELATIONSHIP WITH OTHER INSTRUMENTS

Article 67

III EUR [221]

This Regulation shall not prejudice the application of provisions governing jurisdiction and the recognition and enforcement of judgments in specific matters which are contained in instruments of the Union or in national legislation harmonised pursuant to such instruments.

III EUR [221.1]

The Hague Convention of 2005 on choice of court agreements may apply in light of article 67 of Brussels I Recast (see article 26 of the Convention to assess applicability). Where there is an exclusive jurisdiction clause in favour of Mexico in an agreement concluded on or after 1 October 2015, or in favour of Singapore on or after 1 October 2016, the Hague Convention will apply. See the Declarations made by the EU in relation to the application of the Convention as those are applicable to the UK.

Article 68

III EUR [222]

1. This Regulation shall, as between the Member States, supersede the 1968 Brussels Convention, except as regards the territories of the Member States which fall within the territorial scope of that Convention and which are excluded from this Regulation pursuant to Article 355 of the TFEU.

2. In so far as this Regulation replaces the provisions of the 1968 Brussels Convention between the Member States, any reference to that Convention shall be understood as a reference to this Regulation.

Article 69

III EUR [223]

Subject to Articles 70 and 71, this Regulation shall, as between the Member States, supersede the conventions that cover the same matters as those to which this Regulation applies. In particular, the conventions included in the list established by the Commission pursuant to point (c) of Article 76(1) and Article 76(2) shall be superseded.

Article 70

III EUR [224]

1. The conventions referred to in Article 69 shall continue to have effect in relation to matters to which this Regulation does not apply.

2. They shall continue to have effect in respect of judgments given, authentic instruments formally drawn up or registered and court settlements approved or concluded before the date of entry into force of Regulation (EC) No 44/2001.

Article 71

III EUR [225]

1. This Regulation shall not affect any conventions to which the Member States are parties and which, in relation to particular matters, govern jurisdiction or the recognition or enforcement of judgments.
2. With a view to its uniform interpretation, paragraph 1 shall be applied in the following manner:
   (a) this Regulation shall not prevent a court of a Member State which is party to a convention on a particular matter from assuming jurisdiction in accordance with that convention, even where the defendant is domiciled in another Member State which is not party to that convention. The court hearing the action shall, in any event, apply Article 28 of this Regulation;
   (b) judgments given in a Member State by a court in the exercise of jurisdiction provided for in a convention on a particular matter shall be recognised and enforced in the other Member States in accordance with this Regulation.

Where a convention on a particular matter to which both the Member State of origin and the Member State addressed are parties lays down conditions for the recognition or enforcement of judgments, those conditions shall apply. In any event, the provisions of this Regulation on recognition and enforcement of judgments may be applied.

III EUR [225.1]

The CJEU has held that article 71, read in light of TFEU, art 350, does not preclude the application to trademarks disputes of the rule of jurisdiction for disputes relating to Benelux trademarks and designs, laid down in article 4.6 of the Benelux Convention on Intellectual Property (Trademarks and Designs) of 2005, signed by Belgium, Luxembourg and the Netherlands: *Brite Strike Technologies Inc. v Brite Strike Technologies SA: C-230/15* (2016), unreported.

The Convention on the Contract for the International Carriage of Goods by Road which creates jurisdiction over proceedings in respect of certain carriers in a series of carriage contracts but not others (see its article 36) may also apply: *British American Tobacco Denmark A/S v Kazemier Transport BV; British American Tobacco Switzerland SA v H Essers Security Logistics BV* [2015] UKSC 65, [2015] 3 WLR 1173.

Article 71A

III EUR [225A]

1. For the purposes of this Regulation, a court common to several Member States as specified in paragraph 2 (a 'common court') shall be deemed to be a court of a Member State when, pursuant to the instrument establishing it, such a common court exercises jurisdiction in matters falling within the scope of this Regulation.
2. For the purposes of this Regulation, each of the following courts shall be a common court:
   (a) the Unified Patent Court established by the Agreement on a Unified Patent Court signed on 19 February 2013 (the 'UPC Agreement'); and
   (b) the Benelux Court of Justice established by the Treaty of 31 March 1965 concerning the establishment and statute of a Benelux Court of Justice (the 'Benelux Court of Justice Treaty').

Article 71B

III EUR [225B]

The jurisdiction of a common court shall be determined as follows:

(1) a common court shall have jurisdiction where, under this Regulation, the courts of a Member State party to the instrument establishing the common court would have jurisdiction in a matter governed by that instrument;

(2) where the defendant is not domiciled in a Member State, and this Regulation does not otherwise confer jurisdiction over him, Chapter II shall apply as appropriate regardless of the defendant's domicile.

Application may be made to a common court for provisional, including protective, measures even if the courts of a third State have jurisdiction as to the substance of the matter;

(3) where a common court has jurisdiction over a defendant under point 2 in a dispute relating to an infringement of a European patent giving rise to damage within the Union, that court may also exercise jurisdiction in relation to damage arising outside the Union from such an infringement.

Such jurisdiction may only be established if property belonging to the defendant is located in any Member State party to the instrument establishing the common court and the dispute has a sufficient connection with any such Member State.

Article 71C

III EUR [225C]

1. Articles 29 to 32 shall apply where proceedings are brought in a common court and in a court of a Member State not party to the instrument establishing the common court.
2. Articles 29 to 32 shall apply where, during the transitional period referred to in Article 83 of the UPC Agreement, proceedings are brought in the Unified Patent Court and in a court of a Member State party to the UPC Agreement.

Article 71D

III EUR [225D]

This Regulation shall apply to the recognition and enforcement of:

(a) judgments given by a common court which are to be recognised and enforced in a Member State not party to the instrument establishing the common court; and

(b) judgments given by the courts of a Member State not party to the instrument establishing the common court which are to be recognised and enforced in a Member State party to that instrument.

However, where recognition and enforcement of a judgment given by a common court is sought in a Member State party to the instrument establishing the common court, any rules of that instrument on recognition and enforcement shall apply instead of the rules of this Regulation.

III EUR [225D.1]

This article deals with recognition and enforcement of judgments of common courts eg those of the Benelux Court of Justice and the Unitary Patent Court, among other. The last paragraph states that Brussels I Recast is to give way to the application of the agreements creating those courts when recognition and enforcement of judgments given by those Courts is sought in the territories covered by those agreements.

Article 72

III EUR [226]

This Regulation shall not affect agreements by which Member States, prior to the entry into force of Regulation (EC) No 44/2001, undertook pursuant to Article 59 of the 1968 Brussels Convention not to recognise judgments given, in particular in other Contracting States to that Convention, against defendants domiciled or habitually resident in a third State where, in cases provided for in Article 4 of that Convention, the judgment could only be founded on a ground of jurisdiction specified in the second paragraph of Article 3 of that Convention.

Article 73

III EUR [227]

1. This Regulation shall not affect the application of the 2007 Lugano Convention.
2. This Regulation shall not affect the application of the 1958 New York Convention.
3. This Regulation shall not affect the application of bilateral conventions and agreements between a third State and a Member State concluded before the date of entry into force of Regulation (EC) No 44/2001 which concern matters governed by this Regulation.

III EUR [227.1]

Questions of jurisdiction between EU Member States and European Free Trade Agreement States (Norway, Switzerland and Iceland) continue to be governed by the 2007 Revised Lugano Convention. For proceedings commenced before particular dates in 2010 and 2011, depending on which EFTA State it relates to, the original 1988 Lugano Convention applies (see **III EUR [15]**). The Lugano Convention applies when there is an exclusive jurisdiction clause in favour of an EFTA State, the defendant is domiciled in an EFTA State and/or there are parallel proceedings in an EFTA State (other factors need to be taken into consideration here, eg commencement of the proceedings, etc).

CHAPTER VIII
FINAL PROVISIONS

Article 74

III EUR [228]

The Member States shall provide, within the framework of the European Judicial Network and with a view to making the information available to the public, a description of national rules and procedures concerning enforcement, including authorities competent for enforcement, and information on any limitations on enforcement, in particular debtor protection rules and limitation or prescription periods. The Member States shall keep this information permanently updated.

III EUR [228.1]

There is a wealth of information on procedural issues under Brussels I Recast at e-justice.eu ropa.eu. For judges or practitioners alike the European Judicial Network has resources to profit from when dealing with cross-border cases including tools such as specialised guides, Memb er States case law in application of EU law (Member States' courts apply and interpret the law of the relevant Member States as well as EU law. Therefore, it is in the interest of citizens and legal practitioners to have access not only to case law of their own Member State, but also to that of other EU Member States), etc.

Article 75

III EUR [229]

By 10 January 2014, the Member States shall communicate to the Commission:

(a) the courts to which the application for refusal of enforcement is to be submitted pursuant to Article 47(1);

(b) the courts with which an appeal against the decision on the application for refusal of enforcement is to be lodged pursuant to Article 49(2);

(c) the courts with which any further appeal is to be lodged pursuant to Article 50; and

(d) the languages accepted for translations of the forms as referred to in Article 57(2).

The Commission shall make the information publicly available through any appropriate means, in particular through the European Judicial Network.

III EUR [229.1]

As regards article 75(1)(a) the UK communicated to the Commission that the court to which applications are to be submitted pursuant to articles 36(2), 45(4) and 47(1) is, in England and Wales, the High Court of Justice (Enforcement Section, Queen's Bench Division) which is also the court with which an appeal against the decision on the application for refusal of enforcement is to be lodged pursuant to article 49(2) as per article 75(1)(b). In what relates to article 75(1)(c) the courts to lodge, pursuant to article 50, any further appeal in England and Wales are the Court of Appeal (Civil Division, Royal Courts of Justice) or the Supreme Court (in accordance with national law providing for appeals to sometimes go directly from the High Court to the Supreme Court). The particular provisions for a 'leapfrog' appeal are set out in Part 2 of the Administration of Justice Act 1969. Sections 12 to 15 of Part 2 apply to England and Wales, and Section 16 provides for how Sections 12 to 15 apply to Northern Ireland.

Article 76

III EUR [230]

1. The Member States shall notify the Commission of:

(a) the rules of jurisdiction referred to in Articles 5(2) and 6(2);

(b) the rules on third-party notice referred to in Article 65; and

(c) the conventions referred to in Article 69.

2. The Commission shall, on the basis of the notifications by the Member States referred to in paragraph 1, establish the corresponding lists.

3. The Member States shall notify the Commission of any subsequent amendments required to be made to those lists. The Commission shall amend those lists accordingly.

4. The Commission shall publish the lists and any subsequent amendments made to them in the *Official Journal of the European Union*.

5. The Commission shall make all information notified pursuant to paragraphs 1 and 3 publicly available through any other appropriate means, in particular through the European Judicial Network.

III EUR [230.1]

The information notified to the Commission is as follows:

- Article 76(1)(a) Rules of jurisdiction referred to in articles 5(2) and 6(2):
  (a) the document instituting the proceedings having been served on the defendant during his temporary presence in the UK; or
  (b) the presence within the UK of property belonging to the defendant; or
  (c) the seizure by the plaintiff of property situated in the UK.
- Article 76(1)(c) Conventions referred to in article 69
  (a) the Convention between the UK and France providing for the Mutual Enforcement of Judgments in Civil and Commercial Matters, with Protocol, signed at Paris on 18 January 1934,

EUROPE

(b) the Convention between the UK and Belgium providing for the Mutual Enforcement of Judgments in Civil and Commercial Matters, with Protocol, signed at Brussels on 2 May 1934,

(c) the Convention between the UK and Germany for the Mutual Recognition and Enforcement of Judgments in Civil and Commercial Matters, signed at Bonn on 14 July 1960,

(d) the Convention between the UK and Austria providing for the Mutual Recognition and Enforcement of Judgments in Civil and Commercial Matters, signed at Vienna on 14 July 1961, with amending Protocol signed at London on 6 March 1970,

(e) the Convention between the UK and Italy for the Mutual Recognition and Enforcement of Judgments in Civil and Commercial Matters, signed at Rome on 7 February 1964, with amending Protocol signed at Rome on 14 July 1970,

(f) the Convention between the UK and the Netherlands providing for the Mutual Recognition and Enforcement of Judgments in Civil Matters, signed at The Hague on 17 November 1967.

Article 77

III EUR [231]

The Commission shall be empowered to adopt delegated acts in accordance with Article 78 concerning the amendment of Annexes I and II.

Article 78

III EUR [232]

1. The power to adopt delegated acts is conferred on the Commission subject to the conditions laid down in this Article.

2. The power to adopt delegated acts referred to in Article 77 shall be conferred on the Commission for an indeterminate period of time from 9 January 2013.

3. The delegation of power referred to in Article 77 may be revoked at any time by the European Parliament or by the Council. A decision to revoke shall put an end to the delegation of the power specified in that decision. It shall take effect the day following the publication of the decision in the *Official Journal of the European Union* or at a later date specified therein. It shall not affect the validity of any delegated acts already in force.

4. As soon as it adopts a delegated act, the Commission shall notify it simultaneously to the European Parliament and to the Council.

5. A delegated act adopted pursuant to Article 77 shall enter into force only if no objection has been expressed either by the European Parliament or the Council within a period of two months of notification of that act to the European Parliament and the Council or if, before the expiry of that period, the European Parliament and the Council have both informed the Commission that they will not object. That period shall be extended by two months at the initiative of the European Parliament or of the Council.

Article 79

III EUR [233]

By 11 January 2022 the Commission shall present a report to the European Parliament, to the Council and to the European Economic and Social Committee on the application of this Regulation. That report shall include an evaluation of the possible need for a further extension of the rules on jurisdiction to defendants not domiciled in a Member State, taking into account the operation of this Regulation and possible developments at international level. Where appropriate, the report shall be accompanied by a proposal for amendment of this Regulation.

Article 80

III EUR [234]

This Regulation shall repeal Regulation (EC) No 44/2001. References to the repealed Regulation shall be construed as references to this Regulation and shall be read in accordance with the correlation table set out in Annex III.

Article 81

III EUR [235]

This Regulation shall enter into force on the twentieth day following that of its publication in the *Official Journal of the European Union*.

It shall apply from 10 January 2015, with the exception of Articles 75 and 76, which shall apply from 10 January 2014.

This Regulation shall be binding in its entirety and directly applicable in the Member States in accordance with the Treaties.

Done at Strasbourg, 12 December 2012.
For the European Parliament
The President
M. Schulz
For the Council
The President
A. D. Mavroyiannis

ANNEXES

III EUR [236]–III EUR [261]

Editorial note. We are unable to reproduce the Annexes to Regulation (EU) 1215/2012 here, but they can be found online at: eur-lex.europa.eu/legal-content/EN/TXT/?uri=CELEX:02012R1215-20150226

Regulation (EU) 2015/281 replaced Annexes I and II to this Regulation (see **III EUR [268]** and **III EUR [269]** below). It entered into force on 26 February 2015. Annexes I and II to this Regulation remained in force until that date. Annex III, which contains a correlation table between Brussels I and Brussels I Recast, remains in force.

EUROPE

REGULATION (EU) NO 542/2014 OF THE EUROPEAN PARLIAMENT AND OF THE COUNCIL OF 15 MAY 2014 AMENDING REGULATION (EU) NO 1215/2012 AS REGARDS THE RULES TO BE APPLIED WITH RESPECT TO THE UNIFIED PATENT COURT AND THE BENELUX COURT OF JUSTICE

III EUR [262]

THE EUROPEAN PARLIAMENT AND THE COUNCIL OF THE EUROPEAN UNION,

Having regard to the Treaty on the Functioning of the European Union, and in particular points (a), (c) and (e) of Article 81(2) thereof,

Having regard to the proposal from the European Commission,

After transmission of the draft legislative act to the national parliaments,

Having regard to the opinion of the European Economic and Social Committee,

Having regard to the opinion of the Committee of the Regions[1],

Acting in accordance with the ordinary legislative procedure[2],

Whereas:

(1) On 19 February 2013, the Kingdom of Belgium, the Republic of Bulgaria, the Czech Republic, the Kingdom of Denmark, the Federal Republic of Germany, the Republic of Estonia, Ireland, the Hellenic Republic, the French Republic, the Italian Republic, the Republic of Cyprus, the Republic of Latvia, the Republic of Lithuania, the Grand-Duchy of Luxembourg, Hungary, the Republic of Malta, the Kingdom of the Netherlands, the Republic of Austria, the Portuguese Republic, Romania, the Republic of Slovenia, the Slovak Republic, the Republic of Finland, the Kingdom of Sweden and the United Kingdom of Great Britain and Northern Ireland signed the Agreement on a Unified Patent Court[3] (the 'UPC Agreement'). The UPC Agreement provides for its entry into force not prior to the first day of the fourth month after the date of entry into force of the amendments to Regulation (EU) No 1215/2012 of the European Parliament and of the Council[4] concerning the relationship of that Regulation with the UPC Agreement.

(2) On 15 October 2012, the Kingdom of Belgium, the Grand-Duchy of Luxembourg and the Kingdom of the Netherlands, parties to the Treaty of 31 March 1965 concerning the establishment and statute of a Benelux Court of Justice (the 'Benelux Court of Justice Treaty'), signed a Protocol amending that Treaty. That Protocol made it possible to transfer jurisdiction to the Benelux Court of Justice in specific matters falling within the scope of Regulation (EU) No 1215/2012.

(3) It is necessary to regulate the relationship of Regulation (EU) No 1215/2012 with the UPC Agreement and with the Benelux Court of Justice Treaty by way of amendments to that Regulation.

(4) The Unified Patent Court and the Benelux Court of Justice should be deemed to be courts within the meaning of Regulation (EU) No 1215/2012 in order to ensure legal certainty and predictability for defendants who could be sued in those two Courts at a location situated in a Member State other than the one designated by the rules of Regulation (EU) No 1215/2012.

(5) The amendments to Regulation (EU) No 1215/2012 provided for in this Regulation with regard to the Unified Patent Court are intended to establish the international jurisdiction of that Court and do not affect the internal allocation of proceedings among the divisions of that Court nor the arrangements laid down in the UPC Agreement concerning the exercise of jurisdiction, including exclusive jurisdiction, during the transitional period provided for in that Agreement.

(6) As courts common to several Member States, the Unified Patent Court and the Benelux Court of Justice cannot, unlike a court of one Member State, exercise jurisdiction on the basis of national law with respect to defendants not domiciled in a Member State. To allow those two Courts to exercise jurisdiction with respect to such defendants, the rules of Regulation (EU) No 1215/2012 should therefore, with regard to matters falling within the jurisdiction of, respectively, the Unified Patent Court and the Benelux Court of Justice, also apply to defendants domiciled in third States. The existing rules of jurisdiction of Regulation (EU) No 1215/2012 ensure a close connection between proceedings to which that Regulation applies and the territory of the Member States. It is therefore appropriate to extend those rules to proceedings against all defendants regardless of their domicile. When applying the rules of jurisdiction of Regulation (EU) No 1215/2012, the Unified Patent Court and the Benelux Court of Justice (hereinafter individually referred to as a 'common court') should apply only those rules which are appropriate for the subject-matter for which jurisdiction has been conferred on them.

(7) A common court should be able to hear disputes involving defendants from third States on the basis of a subsidiary rule of jurisdiction in proceedings relating to an infringement of a European patent giving rise to damage both inside and outside the Union. Such subsidiary jurisdiction should be exercised where property belonging to the defendant is located in any Member State party to the instrument establishing the common court and the dispute in question has a sufficient connection with any such Member State, for example because the claimant is domiciled there or the evidence relating to the dispute is available there. In establishing its jurisdiction, the common court should have regard to the value of the property in question, which should not be insignificant and which should be such as to make it possible to enforce the judgment, at least in part, in the Member States parties to the instrument establishing the common court.

(8) The rules of Regulation (EU) No 1215/2012 on lis pendens and related actions, aimed at preventing parallel proceedings and irreconcilable judgments, should apply when proceedings are brought in a common court and in a court of a Member State in which the UPC Agreement or, as the case may be, the Benelux Court of Justice Treaty does not apply.

(9) The rules of Regulation (EU) No 1215/2012 on lis pendens and related actions should likewise apply where, during the transitional period provided for in the UPC Agreement, proceedings concerning certain types of disputes are brought in, on the one hand, the Unified Patent Court and, on the other hand, a national court of a Member State party to the UPC Agreement.

(10) Judgments given by the Unified Patent Court or by the Benelux Court of Justice should be recognised and enforced in accordance with Regulation (EU) No 1215/2012 in a Member State not party to, as the case may be, the UPC Agreement or the Benelux Court of Justice Treaty.

(11) Judgments given by the courts of a Member State not party to, as the case may be, the UPC Agreement or the Benelux Court of Justice Treaty should be recognised and enforced in another Member State in accordance with Regulation (EU) No 1215/2012.

(12) Regulation (EU) No 1215/2012 should therefore be amended accordingly.

(13) Since the objective of this Regulation cannot be sufficiently achieved by the Member States but can rather, by reason of its scale and effects, be better achieved at Union level, the Union may adopt measures, in accordance with the principle of subsidiarity as set out in Article 5 of the Treaty on European Union (TEU). In accordance with the principle of proportionality, as set out in that Article, this Regulation does not go beyond what is necessary in order to achieve that objective.

(14) In accordance with Article 3 and Article 4a(1) of the Protocol (No 21) on the position of the United Kingdom and Ireland in respect of the area of freedom,

security and justice, annexed to the TEU and to the Treaty on the Functioning of the European Union (TFEU), those Member States have notified their wish to take part in the adoption and application of this Regulation.

(15) In accordance with Articles 1 and 2 of the Protocol (No 22) on the position of Denmark, annexed to the TEU and to the TFEU, Denmark is not taking part in the adoption of this Regulation and is not bound by it or subject to its application, without prejudice to the possibility for Denmark of applying the amendments to Regulation (EU) No 1215/2012 laid down in this Regulation pursuant to Article 3 of the Agreement of 19 October 2005 between the European Community and the Kingdom of Denmark on jurisdiction and the recognition and enforcement of judgments in civil and commercial matters[5],

---

1 Opinion of 26 February 2014 (not yet published in the Official Journal).

2 Position of the European Parliament of 15 April 2014 (not yet published in the Official Journal) and decision of the Council of 6 May 2014.

3 OJ C 175, 20.6.2013, p. 1.

4 Regulation (EU) No 1215/2012 of the European Parliament and of the Council of 12 December 2012 on jurisdiction and the recognition and enforcement of judgments in civil and commercial matters (OJ L 351, 20.12.2012, p. 1).

5 OJ L 299, 16.11.2005, p. 62.

HAVE ADOPTED THIS REGULATION:

Article 1

III EUR [263]

In Chapter VII of Regulation (EU) No 1215/2012, the following Articles are inserted:

Article 71a

1. For the purposes of this Regulation, a court common to several Member States as specified in paragraph 2 (a 'common court') shall be deemed to be a court of a Member State when, pursuant to the instrument establishing it, such a common court exercises jurisdiction in matters falling within the scope of this Regulation.
2. For the purposes of this Regulation, each of the following courts shall be a common court:
   (a) the Unified Patent Court established by the Agreement on a Unified Patent Court signed on 19 February 2013 (the 'UPC Agreement'); and
   (b) the Benelux Court of Justice established by the Treaty of 31 March 1965 concerning the establishment and statute of a Benelux Court of Justice (the 'Benelux Court of Justice Treaty').

Article 71b

The jurisdiction of a common court shall be determined as follows:

(1) a common court shall have jurisdiction where, under this Regulation, the courts of a Member State party to the instrument establishing the common court would have jurisdiction in a matter governed by that instrument;

(2) where the defendant is not domiciled in a Member State, and this Regulation does not otherwise confer jurisdiction over him, Chapter II shall apply as appropriate regardless of the defendant's domicile.

Application may be made to a common court for provisional, including protective, measures even if the courts of a third State have jurisdiction as to the substance of the matter;

(3) where a common court has jurisdiction over a defendant under point 2 in a dispute relating to an infringement of a European patent giving rise to damage within the Union, that court may also exercise jurisdiction in relation to damage arising outside the Union from such an infringement.

Such jurisdiction may only be established if property belonging to the defendant is located in any Member State party to the instrument establishing the common court and the dispute has a sufficient connection with any such Member State.

Article 71c

1. Articles 29 to 32 shall apply where proceedings are brought in a common court and in a court of a Member State not party to the instrument establishing the common court.

2. Articles 29 to 32 shall apply where, during the transitional period referred to in Article 83 of the UPC Agreement, proceedings are brought in the Unified Patent Court and in a court of a Member State party to the UPC Agreement.

Article 71d

This Regulation shall apply to the recognition and enforcement of:

(a) judgments given by a common court which are to be recognised and enforced in a Member State not party to the instrument establishing the common court; and

(b) judgments given by the courts of a Member State not party to the instrument establishing the common court which are to be recognised and enforced in a Member State party to that instrument.

However, where recognition and enforcement of a judgment given by a common court is sought in a Member State party to the instrument establishing the common court, any rules of that instrument on recognition and enforcement shall apply instead of the rules of this Regulation.

Article 2

III EUR [264]

This Regulation shall enter into force on the day following that of its publication in the *Official Journal of the European Union*.

It shall apply from 10 January 2015.

This Regulation shall be binding in its entirety and directly applicable in the Member States in accordance with the Treaties.

Done at Strasbourg, 12 June 2013.

For the European Parliament
The President
M. Schulz
For the Council
The President
D. Kourkoulas

EUROPE

COMMISSION DELEGATED REGULATION (EU) 2015/281 OF 26 NOVEMBER 2014 REPLACING ANNEXES I AND II OF REGULATION (EU) NO 1215/2012 OF THE EUROPEAN PARLIAMENT AND OF THE COUNCIL ON JURISDICTION AND THE RECOGNITION AND ENFORCEMENT OF JUDGMENTS IN CIVIL AND COMMERCIAL MATTERS

III EUR [265]

THE EUROPEAN COMMISSION,

Having regard to the Treaty on the Functioning of the European Union,

Having regard to Regulation (EU) No 1215/2012 of the European Parliament and of the Council of 12 December 2012 on jurisdiction and the recognition and enforcement of judgments in civil and commercial matters[1], and in particular Article 77 thereof,

Whereas:

(1) Regulation (EU) No 1215/2012 provides for the circulation of judgments, authentic instruments and court settlements in the Union. It will start to apply on 10 January 2015.

(2) Regulation (EU) No 1215/2012 established, in Annexes I and II, a form of the certificate concerning a judgment in civil and commercial matters and a form of the certificate concerning an authentic instrument/court settlement in civil and commercial matters.

(3) Latvia adopted the euro as from 1 January 2014. Therefore, all the references to the former currency of Latvia should be deleted from the forms. Lithuania will adopt the euro as from 1 January 2015. Therefore, all the references to the currency of Lithuania should be deleted from the forms.

(4) Croatia joined the Union as from 1 July 2013. Therefore, the references to Croatia and its currency should be included in the forms.

(5) In accordance with Articles 1 and 2 of Protocol (No 22) on the position of Denmark, annexed to the Treaty on European Union and to the Treaty on the Functioning of the European Union, Denmark did not take part in the adoption of Regulation (EU) No 1215/2012 and it is not bound by it or subject to its application.

(6) However, in accordance with Article 3(2) of the Agreement between the European Union and Denmark, Denmark has, by letter of 20 December 2012, notified[2] the Commission of its decision to implement the contents of Regulation (EU) No 1215/2012. Therefore the references to Denmark and its currency should be included in the forms.

(7) For reasons of clarity it is appropriate to replace Annexes I and II.

(8) Regulation (EU) No 1215/2012 should therefore be amended accordingly,

---

1 OJ L 351, 20.12.2012, p. 1.

2 OJ L 79, 21.3.2013, p. 4.

HAVE ADOPTED THIS REGULATION:

Article 1

III EUR [266]

Annexes I and II to Regulation (EU) No 1215/2012 are replaced by the text in the Annex to this Regulation.

Article 2

III EUR [267]

This Regulation shall enter into force on the day following that of its publication in the *Official Journal of the European Union*.

This Regulation shall be binding in its entirety and directly applicable in the Member States in accordance with the Treaties.

Done at Brussels, 26 November 2014.

For the Commission
The President
Jean-Claude Juncker

ANNEX I

III EUR [268]

ANNEX

'ANNEX I

CERTIFICATE CONCERNING A JUDGMENT IN CIVIL AND COMMERCIAL MATTERS

Article 53 of Regulation (EU) No 1215/2012 of the European Parliament and of the Council on jurisdiction and the recognition and enforcement of judgments in civil and commercial matters

1. COURT OF ORIGIN

1.1. Name:

1.2. Address:

1.2.1. Street and number/PO box:

1.2.2. Place and postal code:

1.2.3. Member State:

AT ☐ BE ☐ BG ☐ CY ☐ CZ ☐ DK ☐ DE ☐ EE ☐ EL ☐ ES ☐ FI ☐ FR ☐ HR ☐ HU ☐ IE ☐ IT ☐ LT ☐
LU ☐ LV ☐ MT ☐ NL ☐ PL ☐ PT ☐ RO ☐ SE ☐ SI ☐ SK ☐ UK ☐

1.3. Telephone:

1.4. Fax:

1.5. E-mail (if available):

2. CLAIMANT(S) ([1])

2.1. Surname and given name(s)/name of company or organisation:

2.2. Identification number (if applicable and if available):

2.3. Date (dd/mm/yyyy) and place of birth or, if legal person, of incorporation/formation/registration (if relevant and if available):

2.4. Address:

2.4.1. Street and number/PO box:

2.4.2. Place and postal code:

2.4.3. Country:

AT ☐ BE ☐ BG ☐ CY ☐ CZ ☐ DK ☐ DE ☐ EE ☐ EL ☐ ES ☐ FI ☐ FR ☐ HR ☐ HU ☐ IE ☐ IT ☐ LT ☐
LU ☐ LV ☐ MT ☐ NL ☐ PL ☐ PT ☐ RO ☐ SE ☐ SI ☐ SK ☐ UK ☐ Other (please specify (ISO-code)) ☐

2.5. E-mail (if available):

3. DEFENDANT(S) ([2])

3.1. Surname and given name(s)/name of company or organisation:

3.2. Identification number (if applicable and if available):

3.3. Date (dd/mm/yyyy) and place of birth or, if legal person, of incorporation/formation/registration (if relevant and if available):

3.4. Address:

3.4.1. Street and number/PO box:

3.4.2. Place and postal code:

3.4.3. Country:

AT ☐ BE ☐ BG ☐ CY ☐ CZ ☐ DK ☐ DE ☐ EE ☐ EL ☐ ES ☐ FI ☐ FR ☐ HR ☐ HU ☐ IE ☐ IT ☐ LT ☐
LU ☐ LV ☐ MT ☐ NL ☐ PL ☐ PT ☐ RO ☐ SE ☐ SI ☐ SK ☐ UK ☐ Other (please specify (ISO-code)) ☐

3.5. E-mail (if available):

4. THE JUDGMENT

4.1. Date (dd/mm/yyyy) of the judgment:

4.2. Reference number of the judgment:

4.3. The judgment was given in default of appearance:

4.3.1. ☐ No

4.3.2. ☐ Yes (please indicate the date (dd/mm/yyyy) on which the document instituting the proceedings or an equivalent document was served on the defendant):

4.4. The judgment is enforceable in the Member State of origin without any further conditions having to be met:

4.4.1. ☐ Yes (please indicate the date (dd/mm/yyyy) on which the judgment was declared enforceable, if applicable):

4.4.2. ☐ Yes, but only against the following person(s) (please specify):

4.4.3. ☐ Yes, but limited to part(s) of the judgment (please specify):

4.4.4. ☐ The judgment does not contain an enforceable obligation

4.5. As of the date of issue of the certificate, the judgment has been served on the defendant(s):

4.5.1. ☐ Yes (please indicate the date of service (dd/mm/yyyy) if known):

4.5.1.1. The judgment was served in the following language(s):

BG ☐ ES ☐ CS ☐ DK ☐ DE ☐ ET ☐ EL ☐ EN ☐ FR ☐ HR ☐ GA ☐ IT ☐ LV ☐ LT ☐ HU ☐ MT ☐ NL ☐ PL ☐ PT ☐ RO ☐ SK ☐ SL ☐ FI ☐ SV ☐ Other (please specify (ISO-code)) ☐

4.5.2. ☐ Not to the knowledge of the court

4.6. Terms of the judgment and interest:

4.6.1. Judgment on a monetary claim ([3])

4.6.1.1. Short description of the subject-matter of the case:

4.6.1.2. The court has ordered:

.... (surname and given name(s)/name of company or organisation) ([4])

to make a payment to:

.... (surname and given name(s)/name of company or organisation)

4.6.1.2.1. If more than one person has been held liable for one and the same claim, the whole amount may be collected from any one of them:

4.6.1.2.1.1. ☐ Yes

4.6.1.2.1.2. ☐ No

4.6.1.3. Currency:

☐ euro (EUR) ☐ Bulgarian lev (BGN) ☐ Czech koruna (CZK) ☐ Danish krone (DKK) ☐ kuna (HRK) ☐ Hungarian forint (HUF) ☐ Polish zloty (PLN) ☐ pound sterling (GBP) ☐ Romanian leu (RON) ☐ Swedish krona (SEK) ☐ other (please specify (ISO code)):

4.6.1.4. Principal amount:

4.6.1.4.1. ☐ Amount to be paid in one sum

EUROPE

4.6.1.4.2. ☐ Amount to be paid in instalments ([5])

Due date (dd/mm/yyyy)	Amount

4.6.1.4.3. ☐ Amount to be paid regularly

4.6.1.4.3.1. ☐ per day

4.6.1.4.3.2. ☐ per week

4.6.1.4.3.3. ☐ other (state frequency):

4.6.1.4.3.4. From date (dd/mm/yyyy) or event:

4.6.1.4.3.5. If applicable, until (date (dd/mm/yyyy) or event):

4.6.1.5. Interest, if applicable:

4.6.1.5.1. Interest:

4.6.1.5.1.1. ☐ Not specified in the judgment

4.6.1.5.1.2. ☐ Yes, specified in the judgment as follows:

4.6.1.5.1.2.1. Amount:

or:

4.6.1.5.1.2.2. Rate ... %

4.6.1.5.1.2.3. Interest due from .... (date (dd/mm/yyyy) or event) to .... (date (dd/mm/yyyy) or event) ([6])

4.6.1.5.2. ☐ Statutory interest (if applicable) to be calculated in accordance with (please specify relevant statute):

4.6.1.5.2.1. Interest due from .... (date (dd/mm/yyyy) or event) to .... (date (dd/mm/yyyy) or event) ([6])

4.6.1.5.3. ☐ Capitalisation of interest (if applicable, please specify):

4.6.2. Judgment ordering a provisional, including a protective, measure:

4.6.2.1. Short description of the subject matter of the case and the measure ordered:

4.6.2.2. The measure was ordered by a court having jurisdiction as to the substance of the matter:

4.6.2.2.1. ☐ Yes

4.6.3. Other type of judgment:

4.6.3.1. Short description of the subject-matter of the case and the ruling by the court:

4.7. Costs ([7]):

4.7.1. Currency:

☐ euro (EUR) ☐ Bulgarian lev (BGN) ☐ Czech koruna (CZK) ☐ Danish krone (DKK) ☐ kuna (HRK) ☐ Hungarian forint (HUF) ☐ Polish zloty (PLN) ☐ pound sterling (GBP) ☐ Romanian leu (RON) ☐ Swedish krona (SEK) ☐ other (please specify (ISO code)):

4.7.2. The following person(s) against whom enforcement is sought has/have been ordered to bear the costs:

4.7.2.1. Surname and given name(s)/name of company or organisation: ([8])

4.7.2.2. If more than one person has been ordered to bear the costs, the whole amount may be collected from any one of them:

4.7.2.2.1. ☐ Yes

4.7.2.2.2. ☐ No

4.7.3. The costs of which recovery is sought are as follows: ([9])

4.7.3.1. ☐ The costs have been fixed in the judgment by way of a total amount (please specify amount):

4.7.3.2. ☐ The costs have been fixed in the judgment by way of a percentage of total costs (please specify percentage of total):

4.7.3.3. ☐ Liability for the costs has been determined in the judgment and the exact amounts are as follows:

4.7.3.3.1. ☐ Court fees:

4.7.3.3.2. ☐ Lawyers' fees:

4.7.3.3.3. ☐ Cost of service of documents:

4.7.3.3.4. ☐ Other:

4.7.3.4. ☐ Other (please specify):

4.7.4. Interest on costs:

4.7.4.1. ☐ Not applicable

4.7.4.2. ☐ Interest specified in the judgment

4.7.4.2.1. ☐ Amount:

or

4.7.4.2.2. ☐ Rate … %

4.7.4.2.2.1. Interest due from .... (date (dd/mm/yyyy) or event) to .... (date (dd/mm/yyyy) or event) ([6])

4.7.4.3. ☐ Statutory interest (if applicable) to be calculated in accordance with (please specify relevant statute):

4.7.4.3.1. Interest due from .... (date (dd/mm/yyyy) or event) to .... (date (dd/mm/yyyy) or event): ([6])

4.7.4.4. ☐ Capitalisation of interest (if applicable, please specify):

Done at: …

Signature and/or stamp of the court of origin:

([1]) Insert information for all claimants if the judgment concerns more than one.
([2]) Insert information for all defendants if the judgment concerns more than one.
([3]) If the judgment only concerns costs relating to a claim which has been decided in an earlier judgment, leave point 4.6.1. blank and go to point 4.7.
([4]) If more than one person has been ordered to make a payment, insert information for all persons.
([5]) Insert information for each instalment.
([6]) Insert information for all periods if more than one.
([7]) This point also covers situations where the costs are awarded in a separate judgment.
([8]) Insert information for all persons if more than one.
([9]) In the event that the costs may be recovered from several persons, insert the breakdown for each person separately.

ANNEX II

III EUR [269]

ANNEX II

CERTIFICATE CONCERNING AN AUTHENTIC INSTRUMENT/COURT SETTLEMENT (1) IN CIVIL AND COMMERCIAL MATTERS

Article 60 of Regulation (EU) No 1215/2012 of the European Parliament and of the Council on jurisdiction and the recognition and enforcement of judgments in civil and commercial matters

1. COURT OR COMPETENT AUTHORITY ISSUING THE CERTIFICATE

1.1. Name:

1.2. Address:

1.2.1. Street and number/PO box:

1.2.2. Place and postal code:

1.2.3. Member State:

AT ☐ BE ☐ BG ☐ CY ☐ CZ ☐ DK ☐ DE ☐ EE ☐ EL ☐ ES ☐ FI ☐ FR ☐ HR ☐ HU ☐ IE ☐ IT ☐ LT ☐ LU ☐ LV ☐ MT ☐ NL ☐ PL ☐ PT ☐ RO ☐ SE ☐ SI ☐ SK ☐ UK ☐

1.3. Telephone:

1.4. Fax:

1.5. E-mail (if available):

2. AUTHENTIC INSTRUMENT

2.1. Authority which has drawn up the authentic instrument (if different from the authority issuing the certificate)

2.1.1. Name and designation of authority:

2.1.2. Address:

2.2. Date (dd/mm/yyyy) on which the authentic instrument was drawn up by the authority referred to in point 2.1:

2.3. Reference number of the authentic instrument (if applicable):

2.4. Date (dd/mm/yyyy) on which the authentic instrument was registered in the Member State of origin (to be filled in only if the date of registration determines the legal effect of the instrument and this date is different from the date indicated in point 2.2):

2.4.1. Reference number in the register (if applicable):

3. COURT SETTLEMENT

3.1. Court which approved the court settlement or before which the court settlement was concluded (if different from the court issuing the certificate)

3.1.1. Name of court:

3.1.2. Address:

3.2. Date (dd/mm/yyyy) of the court settlement:

3.3. Reference number of the court settlement:

4. PARTIES TO THE AUTHENTIC INSTRUMENT/COURT SETTLEMENT:

4.1. Name(s) of creditor(s) (surname and given name(s)/name of company or organisation) (2):

4.1.1. Identification number (if applicable and if available):

4.1.2. Date (dd/mm/yyyy) and place of birth or, if legal person, of incorporation/formation/registration (if relevant and if available):

4.2. Name(s) of debtor(s) (surname and given name(s)/name of company or organisation) (3):

4.2.1. Identification number (if applicable and if available):

4.2.2. Date (dd/mm/yyyy) and place of birth or, if legal person, of incorporation/formation/registration (if relevant and if available):

4.3. Name of other parties, if any (surname and given name(s)/name of company or organisation) (4):

4.3.1. Identification number (if applicable and if available):

4.3.2. Date (dd/mm/yyyy) and place of birth or, if legal person, of incorporation/formation/registration (if relevant and if available):

5. ENFORCEABILITY OF THE AUTHENTIC INSTRUMENT/COURT SETTLEMENT IN THE MEMBER STATE OF ORIGIN

5.1. The authentic instrument/court settlement is enforceable in the Member State of origin:

5.1.1. ☐ Yes

5.2. Terms of the authentic instrument/court settlement and interest

5.2.1. Authentic instrument/court settlement relating to a monetary claim

5.2.1.1. Short description of the subject matter:

5.2.1.2. Under the authentic instrument/court settlement:

.... (surname and given name(s)/name of company or organisation) (5)

has to make a payment to:

.... (surname and given name(s)/name of company or organisation)

5.2.1.2.1. If more than one person has been held liable for one and the same claim, the whole amount may be collected from any one of them:

5.2.1.2.1.1. ☐ Yes

5.2.1.2.1.2. ☐ No

5.2.1.3. Currency:

☐ euro (EUR) ☐ Bulgarian lev (BGN) ☐ Czech koruna (CZK) ☐ Danish krone (DKK) ☐ kuna (HRK) ☐ Hungarian forint (HUF) ☐ Polish zloty (PLN) ☐ pound sterling (GBP) ☐ Romanian leu (RON) ☐ Swedish krona (SEK) ☐ other (please specify (ISO code)):

5.2.1.4. Principal amount:

5.2.1.4.1. ☐ Amount to be paid in one sum

5.2.1.4.2. ☐ Amount to be paid in instalments (6)

Due date (dd/mm/yyyy)	Amount

5.2.1.4.3. ☐ Amount to be paid regularly

5.2.1.4.3.1. ☐ per day

5.2.1.4.3.2. ☐ per week

5.2.1.4.3.3. ☐ other (state frequency):

5.2.1.4.3.4. From date (dd/mm/yyyy) or event:

5.2.1.4.3.5. If applicable, until .... (date (dd/mm/yyyy) or event)

5.2.1.5. Interest, if applicable

5.2.1.5.1. Interest:

5.2.1.5.1.1. ☐ Not specified in the authentic instrument/court settlement

5.2.1.5.1.2. ☐ Yes, specified in the authentic instrument/court settlement as follows:

5.2.1.5.1.2.1. Amount:

or

5.2.1.5.1.2.2. Rate ... %

5.2.1.5.1.2.3. Interest due from .... (date (dd/mm/yyyy) or event) to .... (date (dd/mm/yyyy) or event) ([7])

5.2.1.5.2. ☐ Statutory interest (if applicable) to be calculated in accordance with (please specify relevant statute):

5.2.1.5.2.1. Interest due from .... (date (dd/mm/yyyy) or event) to .... (date (dd/mm/yyyy) or event) ([7])

5.2.1.5.3. ☐ Capitalisation of interest (if applicable, please specify):

5.2.2. Authentic instrument/court settlement relating to a non-monetary enforceable obligation:

5.2.2.1. Short description of the enforceable obligation

5.2.2.2. The obligation referred to in point 5.2.2.1. is enforceable against the following person(s) ([8]) (surname and given name(s)/name of company or organisation):

Done at: ...

Signature and/or stamp of the court or competent authority issuing the certificate:

([1]) Delete as appropriate throughout the certificate.
([2]) Insert information for all creditors if more than one.
([3]) Insert information for all debtors if more than one.
([4]) Insert information for other parties (if any).
([5]) If more than one person has been ordered to make a payment, insert information for all persons.
([6]) Insert information for each instalment.
([7]) Insert information for all periods if more than one.
([8]) Insert information for all persons if more than one.'

Note: this Regulation entered into force on 26 February 2015. The original Annexes to Regulation (EU) 1215/2012, Brussels I recast, remained valid until that date.

COUNCIL REGULATION (EC) NO 44/2001 OF 22 DECEMBER 2000 ON JURISDICTION AND THE RECOGNITION AND ENFORCEMENT OF JUDGMENTS IN CIVIL AND COMMERCIAL MATTERS

GENERAL NOTE ON COUNCIL REGULATION (EC) No 44/2001

III EUR [270]

Council Regulation (EC) No 44/2001, generally known as Brussels I but also as the Judgments Regulation in the UK, was repealed and replaced by Regulation (EU) No 1215/2012, known as Brussels I Recast or the new Judgments Regulation and so described in CPR Part 74. Brussels I Recast became applicable on 10 January 2015 date on which Brussels I ceased to apply except in relation to proceedings commenced before that date. For such proceedings the provisions of Brussels I continue to apply. For this reason the whole Regulation is reproduced below (information on interaction between the two EU Regulations in **III EUR [17]**).

III EUR [271]

THE COUNCIL OF THE EUROPEAN UNION,

Having regard to the Treaty establishing the European Community, and in particular Article 61(c) and Article 67(1) thereof,

Having regard to the proposal from the Commission[(1)],

Having regard to the opinion of the European Parliament[(2)],

Having regard to the opinion of the Economic and Social Committee[(3)],

Whereas:

(1) The Community has set itself the objective of maintaining and developing an area of freedom, security and justice, in which the free movement of persons is ensured. In order to establish progressively such an area, the Community should adopt, amongst other things, the measures relating to judicial cooperation in civil matters which are necessary for the sound operation of the internal market.

(2) Certain differences between national rules governing jurisdiction and recognition of judgments hamper the sound operation of the internal market. Provisions to unify the rules of conflict of jurisdiction in civil and commercial matters and to simplify the formalities with a view to rapid and simple recognition and enforcement of judgments from Member States bound by this Regulation are essential.

(3) This area is within the field of judicial cooperation in civil matters within the meaning of Article 65 of the Treaty.

(4) In accordance with the principles of subsidiarity and proportionality as set out in Article 5 of the Treaty, the objectives of this Regulation cannot be sufficiently achieved by the Member States and can therefore be better achieved by the Community. This Regulation confines itself to the minimum required in order to achieve those objectives and does not go beyond what is necessary for that purpose.

(5) On 27 September 1968 the Member States, acting under Article 293, fourth indent, of the Treaty, concluded the Brussels Convention on Jurisdiction and the Enforcement of Judgments in Civil and Commercial Matters, as amended by Conventions on the Accession of the New Member States to that Convention (hereinafter referred to as the 'Brussels Convention')[(4)]. On 16 September 1988 Member States and EFTA States concluded the Lugano Convention on Jurisdiction and the Enforcement of Judgments in Civil and Commercial Matters, which is a parallel Convention to the 1968 Brussels Convention. Work has been undertaken

for the revision of those Conventions, and the Council has approved the content of the revised texts. Continuity in the results achieved in that revision should be ensured.

(6) In order to attain the objective of free movement of judgments in civil and commercial matters, it is necessary and appropriate that the rules governing jurisdiction and the recognition and enforcement of judgments be governed by a Community legal instrument which is binding and directly applicable.

(7) The scope of this Regulation must cover all the main civil and commercial matters apart from certain well-defined matters.

(8) There must be a link between proceedings to which this Regulation applies and the territory of the Member States bound by this Regulation. Accordingly common rules on jurisdiction should, in principle, apply when the defendant is domiciled in one of those Member States.

(9) A defendant not domiciled in a Member State is in general subject to national rules of jurisdiction applicable in the territory of the Member State of the court seised, and a defendant domiciled in a Member State not bound by this Regulation must remain subject to the Brussels Convention.

(10) For the purposes of the free movement of judgments, judgments given in a Member State bound by this Regulation should be recognised and enforced in another Member State bound by this Regulation, even if the judgment debtor is domiciled in a third State.

(11) The rules of jurisdiction must be highly predictable and founded on the principle that jurisdiction is generally based on the defendant's domicile and jurisdiction must always be available on this ground save in a few well-defined situations in which the subject-matter of the litigation or the autonomy of the parties warrants a different linking factor. The domicile of a legal person must be defined autonomously so as to make the common rules more transparent and avoid conflicts of jurisdiction.

(12) In addition to the defendant's domicile, there should be alternative grounds of jurisdiction based on a close link between the court and the action or in order to facilitate the sound administration of justice.

(13) In relation to insurance, consumer contracts and employment, the weaker party should be protected by rules of jurisdiction more favourable to his interests than the general rules provide for.

(14) The autonomy of the parties to a contract, other than an insurance, consumer or employment contract, where only limited autonomy to determine the courts having jurisdiction is allowed, must be respected subject to the exclusive grounds of jurisdiction laid down in this Regulation.

(15) In the interests of the harmonious administration of justice it is necessary to minimise the possibility of concurrent proceedings and to ensure that irreconcilable judgments will not be given in two Member States. There must be a clear and effective mechanism for resolving cases of lis pendens and related actions and for obviating problems flowing from national differences as to the determination of the time when a case is regarded as pending. For the purposes of this Regulation that time should be defined autonomously.

(16) Mutual trust in the administration of justice in the Community justifies judgments given in a Member State being recognised automatically without the need for any procedure except in cases of dispute.

(17) By virtue of the same principle of mutual trust, the procedure for making enforceable in one Member State a judgment given in another must be efficient and rapid. To that end, the declaration that a judgment is enforceable should be issued virtually automatically after purely formal checks of the documents supplied, without there being any possibility for the court to raise of its own motion any of the grounds for non-enforcement provided for by this Regulation.

(18) However, respect for the rights of the defence means that the defendant should be able to appeal in an adversarial procedure, against the declaration of enforceability, if he considers one of the grounds for non-enforcement to be present. Redress procedures should also be available to the claimant where his application for a declaration of enforceability has been rejected.

(19) Continuity between the Brussels Convention and this Regulation should be ensured, and transitional provisions should be laid down to that end. The same need for continuity applies as regards the interpretation of the Brussels Convention by the Court of Justice of the European Communities and the 1971 Protocol[5] should remain applicable also to cases already pending when this Regulation enters into force.

(20) The United Kingdom and Ireland, in accordance with Article 3 of the Protocol on the position of the United Kingdom and Ireland annexed to the Treaty on European Union and to the Treaty establishing the European Community, have given notice of their wish to take part in the adoption and application of this Regulation.

(21) Denmark, in accordance with Articles 1 and 2 of the Protocol on the position of Denmark annexed to the Treaty on European Union and to the Treaty establishing the European Community, is not participating in the adoption of this Regulation, and is therefore not bound by it nor subject to its application.

(22) Since the Brussels Convention remains in force in relations between Denmark and the Member States that are bound by this Regulation, both the Convention and the 1971 Protocol continue to apply between Denmark and the Member States bound by this Regulation.

(23) The Brussels Convention also continues to apply to the territories of the Member States which fall within the territorial scope of that Convention and which are excluded from this Regulation pursuant to Article 299 of the Treaty.

(24) Likewise for the sake of consistency, this Regulation should not affect rules governing jurisdiction and the recognition of judgments contained in specific Community instruments.

(25) Respect for international commitments entered into by the Member States means that this Regulation should not affect conventions relating to specific matters to which the Member States are parties.

(26) The necessary flexibility should be provided for in the basic rules of this Regulation in order to take account of the specific procedural rules of certain Member States. Certain provisions of the Protocol annexed to the Brussels Convention should accordingly be incorporated in this Regulation.

(27) In order to allow a harmonious transition in certain areas which were the subject of special provisions in the Protocol annexed to the Brussels Convention, this Regulation lays down, for a transitional period, provisions taking into consideration the specific situation in certain Member States.

(28) No later than five years after entry into force of this Regulation the Commission will present a report on its application and, if need be, submit proposals for adaptations.

(29) The Commission will have to adjust Annexes I to IV on the rules of national jurisdiction, the courts or competent authorities and redress procedures available on the basis of the amendments forwarded by the Member State concerned; amendments made to Annexes V and VI should be adopted in accordance with Council Decision 1999/468/EC of 28 June 1999 laying down the procedures for the exercise of implementing powers conferred on the Commission[6],

1 OJ C 376, 28.12.1999, p. 1.

2 Opinion delivered on 21 September 2000 (not yet published in the Official Journal).

3 OJ C 117, 26.4.2000, p. 6.

4 OJ L 299, 31.12.1972, p. 32. OJ L 304, 30.10.1978, p. 1. OJ L 388, 31.12.1982, p. 1. OJ L 285, 3.10.1989, p. 1. OJ C 15, 15.1.1997, p. 1. For a consolidated text, see OJ C 27, 26.1.1998, p. 1.

5 OJ L 204, 2.8.1975, p. 28. OJ L 304, 30.10.1978, p. 1. OJ L 388, 31.12.1982, p. 1. OJ L 285, 3.10.1989, p. 1. OJ C 15, 15.1.1997, p. 1. For a consolidated text see OJ C 27, 26.1.1998, p. 28.

6 OJ L 184, 17.7.1999, p. 23.

HAVE ADOPTED THIS REGULATION:

CHAPTER I
SCOPE

Article 1

III EUR [272]

1. This Regulation shall apply in civil and commercial matters whatever the nature of the court or tribunal. It shall not extend, in particular, to revenue, customs or administrative matters.
2. The Regulation shall not apply to:
   (a) the status or legal capacity of natural persons, rights in property arising out of a matrimonial relationship, wills and succession;
   (b) bankruptcy, proceedings relating to the winding-up of insolvent companies or other legal persons, judicial arrangements, compositions and analogous proceedings;
   (c) social security;
   (d) arbitration.
3. In this Regulation, the term 'Member State' shall mean Member States with the exception of Denmark.

III EUR [272.1]

Arbitration In a case where a judgment was obtained in Greece for the enforcement of an arbitration award it was held that Brussels I could not be invoked to enforce the judgment: *ED & F Man Sugar Ltd v Lendoudis* [2007] EWHC 2268 (Comm), [2008] 1 All ER 952.

In *Allianz SpA v West Tankers Inc: C-185/07* [2009] AC 1138, [2009] ECR I-663, ECJ, the CJEU held that a preliminary issue concerning the application of an arbitration agreement, including in particular its validity, fell within the scope of Brussels I if the main subject matter of the proceedings came within its scope. This narrow interpretation of the arbitration exception created various problems for EU-seated arbitrations as, for instance, the other party could delay resolution of a dispute by means of a torpedo action in another Member State on the merits, claiming that the arbitration agreement was invalid. The court of the seat was prevented from considering the validity of the arbitration agreement due to the rules on parallel proceedings which require any Member State court to stay its proceedings in favour of the court first seised. In *'Gazprom' OAO, Re: C-536/13* ECLI:EU:C:2015:316, [2015] 1 WLR 4937 the CJEU held that Brussels I does not preclude a court of a Member State from recognising and enforcing, or from refusing to recognise and enforce, an arbitral award prohibiting a party from bringing certain claims before a court of that Member State, since that Regulation does not govern the recognition and enforcement, in a Member State, of an arbitral award issued by an arbitral tribunal in another Member State.

III EUR [272.2]

Winding up of insolvent company Where the principal claim in the winding up is for a declaration as to beneficial ownership, the litigation is not within the exception provided by article 1(2)(b) but is governed by article 2. The claim should therefore be brought in the courts of the State of the defendant's domicile: *Byers v Yacht Bull Corpn* [2010] EWHC 133 (Ch), [2010] 2 BCLC 169, (2010) Times, 15 February.

CHAPTER II
JURISDICTION

SECTION 1
GENERAL PROVISIONS

Article 2

III EUR [273]

1. Subject to this Regulation, persons domiciled in a Member State shall, whatever their nationality, be sued in the courts of that Member State.
2. Persons who are not nationals of the Member State in which they are domiciled shall be governed by the rules of jurisdiction applicable to nationals of that State.

III EUR [273.1]

Domicile Whether an individual is domiciled or not in a Member State is a matter of national law. As such, a defendant is not domiciled in a Member State merely because he has an address and establishment there if he is usually resident elsewhere and his business interests there are comparatively insignificant: *Cherney v Deripaska* [2007] EWHC 965 (Comm), [2007] 2 All ER (Comm) 785, QBD, Langley J; *High Tech International AG v Deripaska* [2006] EWHC 3276 (QB), [2007] EMLR 449, QBD, Easy J.

Article 3

III EUR [274]

1. Persons domiciled in a Member State may be sued in the courts of another Member State only by virtue of the rules set out in Sections 2 to 7 of this Chapter.
2. In particular the rules of national jurisdiction set out in Annex I shall not be applicable as against them.

Article 4

III EUR [275]

1. If the defendant is not domiciled in a Member State, the jurisdiction of the courts of each Member State shall, subject to Articles 22 and 23, be determined by the law of that Member State.
2. As against such a defendant, any person domiciled in a Member State may, whatever his nationality, avail himself in that State of the rules of jurisdiction there in force, and in particular those specified in Annex I, in the same way as the nationals of that State.

SECTION 2
SPECIAL JURISDICTION

Article 5

III EUR [276]

A person domiciled in a Member State may, in another Member State, be sued:
1.
- (a) in matters relating to a contract, in the courts for the place of performance of the obligation in question;
- (b) for the purpose of this provision and unless otherwise agreed, the place of performance of the obligation in question shall be:

— in the case of the sale of goods, the place in a Member State where, under the contract, the goods were delivered or should have been delivered,

— in the case of the provision of services, the place in a Member State where, under the contract, the services were provided or should have been provided,

(c) if subparagraph (b) does not apply then subparagraph (a) applies;

2. in matters relating to maintenance, in the courts for the place where the maintenance creditor is domiciled or habitually resident or, if the matter is ancillary to proceedings concerning the status of a person, in the court which, according to its own law, has jurisdiction to entertain those proceedings, unless that jurisdiction is based solely on the nationality of one of the parties;

3. in matters relating to tort, *delict* or *quasi-delict*, in the courts for the place where the harmful event occurred or may occur;

4. as regards a civil claim for damages or restitution which is based on an act giving rise to criminal proceedings, in the court seised of those proceedings, to the extent that that court has jurisdiction under its own law to entertain civil proceedings;

5. as regards a dispute arising out of the operations of a branch, agency or other establishment, in the courts for the place in which the branch, agency or other establishment is situated;

6. as settlor, trustee or beneficiary of a trust created by the operation of a statute, or by a written instrument, or created orally and evidenced in writing, in the courts of the Member State in which the trust is domiciled;

7. as regards a dispute concerning the payment of remuneration claimed in respect of the salvage of a cargo or freight, in the court under the authority of which the cargo or freight in question:

(a) has been arrested to secure such payment, or

(b) could have been so arrested, but bail or other security has been given;

provided that this provision shall apply only if it is claimed that the defendant has an interest in the cargo or freight or had such an interest at the time of salvage.

III EUR [276.1]

Matters relating to a contract The CJEU has held that actions seeking the annulment of a contract and the restitution of sums paid but not due on the basis of that contract constitute 'matters relating to a contract' within the meaning of article 5(1)(a): *Profit Investment Sim SpA (in liquidation) v Ossi (C-366/13)*.

The concept of 'matters relating to a contract' in article 5(1)(a) is to be interpreted, for the purposes of that provision, as covering a claim brought by air passengers for compensation for the long delay of a connecting flight, made under Regulation (EC) No 261/2004, against an operating air carrier with which the passenger concerned does not have contractual relations: *flightright GmbH: joined cases C 274/16, C 447/16 and C 448/16* (2018) ECLI:EU:C:2018:160.

III EUR [276.2]

Contract Article 5(1)(b) mentions the place of performance of contractual obligations as a connecting factor with a particular jurisdiction rather than the place of ultimate delivery: *Scottish and Newcastle International Ltd v Othon Ghalanos Ltd* [2006] EWCA Civ 1750, [2006] 2 CLC 1015.

In the context of a contract for the carriage of goods between Member States in several stages, with stops, and by a number of means of transport it was decided that both the place of dispatch and the place of delivery of the goods constitute places where transport services are provided for the purposes of the second indent of article 5(1)(b): *Zurich Insurance plc: C-88/17* (2018) ECLI:EU:C:2018:558.

As regards the second indent of article 5(1)(b) the Court has ruled that it does not apply to a defendant domiciled in a third State and that, the said provision must be interpreted as meaning that, in the case of a connecting flight, the place of performance of that flight, is the place of arrival of the second leg, where the carriage on both flights was operated by two different air carriers and the action for compensation for the long delay of that connecting flight under Regulation No 261/2004 is based on an irregularity which took place on the first of those flights, operated by the air carrier with which the passengers concerned do not have contractual relations: *flightright GmbH: joined cases C 274/16, C 447/16 and C 448/16* (2018) ECLI:EU:C:2018:160.

III EUR [276.3]

Tort: the place where the harmful event occurred The Court has held that the provision on jurisdiction in tort could not be read so broadly as to encompass any place where the adverse consequences of an event could be felt: *Universal Music International Holding BV v Schilling: C-12/15* ECLI:EU:C:2016:450, [2016] QB 967, [2016] 3 WLR 1139, distinguishing the earlier decision in *Kolassa v Barclays Bank plc: C-375/13* ECLI:EU:C:2015:37, [2016] 1 All ER (Comm) 733, [2015] All ER (D) 230 (Jan).

In *Löber C-304/17* (2018) ECLI:EU:C:2018:701 the CJEU ruled that article 5(3) must be interpreted to the effect that in a situation in which an investor brings, on the basis of the prospectus relating to a certificate in which he or she invested, a tort action against the bank which issued that certificate, the courts of that investor's domicile, as the courts for the place where the harmful event occurred within the meaning of that provision, have jurisdiction to hear and determine that action, where the damage the investor claims to have suffered consists in financial loss which occurred directly in that investor's bank account with a bank established within the jurisdiction of those courts.

III EUR [276.4]

Tort: online content In *Concurrence SARL v Samsung Electronics France SAS: C-618/15* (21 December 2016, unreported) the CJEU held that, in relation to an action to establish liability for infringement of the prohibition on resale outside a selective distribution network resulting from offers on websites operated in various Member States, of products covered by that network, the place where the 'damage occurred' is to be regarded as the territory of the Member State which protects the prohibition on resale, a territory on which the appellant alleges to have suffered a reduction in its sales. The fact that the websites on which the offer of the products covered by the selective distribution right appears operate in Member States other than that of the court seised is irrelevant, as long as the events which occurred in those Member States resulted in or may result in the alleged damage in the jurisdiction of the court seised (see *Coty Germany: C-360/12* EU:C:2014:1318).

Article 6

III EUR [277]

A person domiciled in a Member State may also be sued:

1. where he is one of a number of defendants, in the courts for the place where any one of them is domiciled, provided the claims are so closely connected that it is expedient to hear and determine them together to avoid the risk of irreconcilable judgments resulting from separate proceedings;
2. as a third party in an action on a warranty or guarantee or in any other third party proceedings, in the court seised of the original proceedings, unless these were instituted solely with the object of removing him from the jurisdiction of the court which would be competent in his case;
3. on a counter-claim arising from the same contract or facts on which the original claim was based, in the court in which the original claim is pending;
4. in matters relating to a contract, if the action may be combined with an action against the same defendant in matters relating to rights *in rem* in immovable property, in the court of the Member State in which the property is situated.

III EUR [277.1]

One of a number of defendants where the claims are closely connected Regarding article 6(1) a sufficiently close connection was found to exist in *Cooper Tire & Rubber Co Europe Ltd v Dow Deutschland Inc* [2010] EWCA Civ 864, [2010] NLJR 1116.

III EUR [277.2]

Irreconcilable judgments Where two actions, which have different subject-matters and bases and which are not connected by a link of subordination or incompatibility, are brought against several defendants, the fact that the upholding of one of those actions is potentially capable of affecting the extent of the right whose protection is sought by the other action

EUROPE

does not suffice to give rise to a risk of irreconcilable judgments within the meaning of article 6(1): *Profit Investment Sim SpA v Ossi: C-366/13* (2016) ECLI:EU:C:2016:282, [2016] 1 WLR 3832, [2016] 2 All ER (Comm) 621.

III EUR [277.3]

Any other third party proceedings Joinder of proceedings under article 6(2) depends on there being a close connection with the original proceedings. The court concluded that there was no such connection in *Barton v Golden Sun Holidays Ltd (in liquidation)* [2007] I L Pr 57, QBD, Wyn Williams J.

Article 7

III EUR [278]

Where by virtue of this Regulation a court of a Member State has jurisdiction in actions relating to liability from the use or operation of a ship, that court, or any other court substituted for this purpose by the internal law of that Member State, shall also have jurisdiction over claims for limitation of such liability.

SECTION 3

JURISDICTION IN MATTERS RELATING TO INSURANCE

Article 8

III EUR [279]

In matters relating to insurance, jurisdiction shall be determined by this Section, without prejudice to Article 4 and point 5 of Article 5.

Article 9

III EUR [280]

1. An insurer domiciled in a Member State may be sued:
   (a) in the courts of the Member State where he is domiciled, or
   (b) in another Member State, in the case of actions brought by the policyholder, the insured or a beneficiary, in the courts for the place where the plaintiff is domiciled,
   (c) if he is a co-insurer, in the courts of a Member State in which proceedings are brought against the leading insurer.
2. An insurer who is not domiciled in a Member State but has a branch, agency or other establishment in one of the Member States shall, in disputes arising out of the operations of the branch, agency or establishment, be deemed to be domiciled in that Member State.

III EUR [280.1]

Forum in which insurer may be sued The discretion provided by article 9(1) depends on the circumstances applying at the time of suit, not at the time of contract: *Sherdley v Nordea Life and Pension SA (Société Anonyme)* [2012] EWCA Civ 88, [2012] 2 All ER (Comm) 725, [2012] NLJR 293. The CJEU has held that the reference in article 11(2) to article 9(1)(b) allows the injured party to bring an action directly against the insurer before the courts of the place where that injured party is domiciled, provided that such a direct action is permitted and the insurer is domiciled in a Member State – a German national injured in the Netherlands was entitled to sue the defendant's insurers (based in the Netherlands) in his local court in Germany: *Odenbreit v FBTO Schadeverzekeringen NV: C-463/06* [2007] ECR I-11321, [2008] 2 All ER (Comm) 733, ECJ.

III EUR [280.2]

Subrogation The CJEU has held that, pursuant to article 11(2), employers to which the rights of their employees to compensation have passed may, as persons which have suffered damage and whatever their size and legal form, rely on the rules of special jurisdiction laid down in articles 8 to 10. Article 9(1)(b), read together with article 11(2), means that an employer, established in one Member State, which continued to pay the salary of its employee absent as the result of a road traffic accident and to which have passed the employee's rights with regard to the company insuring the civil liability resulting from the vehicle involved in that accident, which is established in a second Member State, may, in the capacity of 'injured party', within the meaning of article 11(2), sue the insurance company before the courts of the first Member State, where a direct action is permitted: *KABEG v MMA IARD SA: C-340/16* ECLI:EU:C:2017:576.

Article 10

III EUR [281]

In respect of liability insurance or insurance of immovable property, the insurer may in addition be sued in the courts for the place where the harmful event occurred. The same applies if movable and immovable property are covered by the same insurance policy and both are adversely affected by the same contingency.

Article 11

III EUR [282]

1. In respect of liability insurance, the insurer may also, if the law of the court permits it, be joined in proceedings which the injured party has brought against the insured.
2. Articles 8, 9 and 10 shall apply to actions brought by the injured party directly against the insurer, where such direct actions are permitted.
3. If the law governing such direct actions provides that the policyholder or the insured may be joined as a party to the action, the same court shall have jurisdiction over them.

Article 12

III EUR [283]

1. Without prejudice to Article 11(3), an insurer may bring proceedings only in the courts of the Member State in which the defendant is domiciled, irrespective of whether he is the policyholder, the insured or a beneficiary.
2. The provisions of this Section shall not affect the right to bring a counter-claim in the court in which, in accordance with this Section, the original claim is pending.

Article 13

III EUR [284]

The provisions of this Section may be departed from only by an agreement:
1. which is entered into after the dispute has arisen, or
2. which allows the policyholder, the insured or a beneficiary to bring proceedings in courts other than those indicated in this Section, or
3. which is concluded between a policyholder and an insurer, both of whom are at the time of conclusion of the contract domiciled or habitually resident in the same Member State, and which has the effect of conferring jurisdiction on the courts of that State even if the harmful event were to occur abroad, provided that such an agreement is not contrary to the law of that State, or

4. which is concluded with a policyholder who is not domiciled in a Member State, except in so far as the insurance is compulsory or relates to immovable property in a Member State, or

5. which relates to a contract of insurance in so far as it covers one or more of the risks set out in Article 14.

III EUR [284.1]

Insurance The CJEU has held that article 13(5), considered in conjunction with article 14(2)(a), means that a victim entitled [under national law] to bring a direct action against the insurer of the party which caused the harm which he has suffered is not bound by an agreement on jurisdiction concluded between the insurer and that party: *Assens Havn: C-368/16* ECLI:EU:C:2017:546.

Article 14

III EUR [285]

The following are the risks referred to in Article 13(5):

1. any loss of or damage to:
   - (a) seagoing ships, installations situated offshore or on the high seas, or aircraft, arising from perils which relate to their use for commercial purposes;
   - (b) goods in transit other than passengers' baggage where the transit consists of or includes carriage by such ships or aircraft;

2. any liability, other than for bodily injury to passengers or loss of or damage to their baggage:
   - (a) arising out of the use or operation of ships, installations or aircraft as referred to in point 1(a) in so far as, in respect of the latter, the law of the Member State in which such aircraft are registered does not prohibit agreements on jurisdiction regarding insurance of such risks;
   - (b) for loss or damage caused by goods in transit as described in point 1(b);

3. any financial loss connected with the use or operation of ships, installations or aircraft as referred to in point 1(a), in particular loss of freight or charter-hire;

4. any risk or interest connected with any of those referred to in points 1 to 3;

5. notwithstanding points 1 to 4, all 'large risks' as defined in Council Directive 73/239/EEC (1), as amended by Council Directives 88/357/EEC (2) and 90/618/EEC (3), as they may be amended.

SECTION 4
JURISDICTION OVER CONSUMER CONTRACTS

Article 15

III EUR [286]

1. In matters relating to a contract concluded by a person, the consumer, for a purpose which can be regarded as being outside his trade or profession, jurisdiction shall be determined by this Section, without prejudice to Article 4 and point 5 of Article 5, if:
   - (a) it is a contract for the sale of goods on instalment credit terms; or
   - (b) it is a contract for a loan repayable by instalments, or for any other form of credit, made to finance the sale of goods; or
   - (c) in all other cases, the contract has been concluded with a person who pursues commercial or professional activities in the Member State of the consumer's domicile or, by any means, directs such activities to that Member State or to several States including that Member State, and the contract falls within the scope of such activities.

2. Where a consumer enters into a contract with a party who is not domiciled in the Member State but has a branch, agency or other establishment in one of the Member States, that party shall, in disputes arising out of the operations of the branch, agency or establishment, be deemed to be domiciled in that State.
3. This Section shall not apply to a contract of transport other than a contract which, for an inclusive price, provides for a combination of travel and accommodation.

III EUR [286.1]

Concept of consumer In *Schrems v Facebook Ireland: C-498/16* (2018) ECLI:EU:C:2018:37 the Court ruled that article 15 is to be interpreted as meaning that the activities of publishing books, lecturing, operating websites, fundraising and being assigned the claims of numerous consumers for the purpose of their enforcement do not entail the loss of a private Facebook account user's status as a 'consumer' within the meaning of that article.

Article 16

III EUR [287]

1. A consumer may bring proceedings against the other party to a contract either in the courts of the Member State in which that party is domiciled or in the courts for the place where the consumer is domiciled.
2. Proceedings may be brought against a consumer by the other party to the contract only in the courts of the Member State in which the consumer is domiciled.
3. This Article shall not affect the right to bring a counter-claim in the court in which, in accordance with this Section, the original claim is pending.

III EUR [287.1]

Consumers claims Article 16(1) does not apply to the proceedings brought by a consumer for the purpose of asserting, in the courts of the place where he is domiciled, not only his own claims, but also claims assigned by other consumers domiciled in the same Member State, in other Member States or in non-member countries: *Schrems v Facebook Ireland: C-498/16* (2018) ECLI:EU:C:2018:37.

Article 17

III EUR [288]

The provisions of this Section may be departed from only by an agreement:
1. which is entered into after the dispute has arisen; or
2. which allows the consumer to bring proceedings in courts other than those indicated in this Section; or
3. which is entered into by the consumer and the other party to the contract, both of whom are at the time of conclusion of the contract domiciled or habitually resident in the same Member State, and which confers jurisdiction on the courts of that Member State, provided that such an agreement is not contrary to the law of that Member State.

SECTION 5

JURISDICTION OVER INDIVIDUAL CONTRACTS OF EMPLOYMENT

Article 18

III EUR [289]

1. In matters relating to individual contracts of employment, jurisdiction shall be determined by this Section, without prejudice to Article 4 and point 5 of Article 5.

2. Where an employee enters into an individual contract of employment with an employer who is not domiciled in a Member State but has a branch, agency or other establishment in one of the Member States, the employer shall, in disputes arising out of the operations of the branch, agency or establishment, be deemed to be domiciled in that Member State.

Article 19

III EUR [290]

An employer domiciled in a Member State may be sued:

1. in the courts of the Member State where he is domiciled; or
2. in another Member State:
   - (a) in the courts for the place where the employee habitually carries out his work or in the courts for the last place where he did so, or
   - (b) if the employee does not or did not habitually carry out his work in any one country, in the courts for the place where the business which engaged the employee is or was situated.

III EUR [290.1]

Employment: habitual place of work Where the work entrusted to the employee is carried out on the territory of more than one Member State the CJEU has held (see *Mulox IBC: C-125/92* EU:C:1993:306) that the habitual place of work can be defined as 'the place where or from which the employee principally discharges his obligations towards his employer'. To determine that place, national courts should adopt a circumstantial method ie take into account all the circumstances of the particular case in order to determine the State with which the professional activity has the greatest connection. Nevertheless, the determination of the court with jurisdiction over disputes brought before the courts of the Member States by the air crew of airlines raises a particular difficulty. The concept of 'place where the employee habitually carries out his work' of article 19(2)(a) refers to the place where, or from which, the employee in fact performs the essential part of his duties vis-à-vis his employer. As regards work relationships in the transport sector, the CJEU mentioned in *Koelzsch: C-29/10* EU:C:2011:151) and *Voogsgeerd: C-384/10* EU:C:2011:842) several indicia that might be taken into consideration by the national courts. In particular, in which Member State is situated (i) the place from which the employee carries out his transport-related tasks, (ii) the place where he returns after his tasks, receives instructions concerning his tasks and organises his work, and (iii) the place where his work tools are to be found. The CJEU has held that in the event of proceedings brought by a member of the air crew, assigned to or employed by an airline, in order to establish the jurisdiction of the court seised, the concept of 'place where the employee habitually carries out his work' of article 19(2)(a) cannot be equated with that of 'home base', within the meaning of Annex III to Regulation No 3922/91. The concept of 'home base' constitutes nevertheless a significant indicium for the purposes of determining the 'place where the employee habitually carries out his work': *Nogueira and Others: C-168/16 and C-169/16* ECLI:EU:C:2017:688.

Article 20

III EUR [291]

1. An employer may bring proceedings only in the courts of the Member State in which the employee is domiciled.
2. The provisions of this Section shall not affect the right to bring a counter-claim in the court in which, in accordance with this Section, the original claim is pending.

III EUR [291.1]

Counterclaims Article 20(2) gives an employer the right to bring, before the court properly seised of the original proceedings brought by an employee, a counterclaim based on a claim-assignment agreement concluded, after the introduction of the original proceedings, between the employer and the original holder of that claim: *Petronas Lubricants Italy SpA: C-1/17* (2018) ECLI:EU:C:2018:478.

Article 21

III EUR [292]

The provisions of this Section may be departed from only by an agreement on jurisdiction:

1. which is entered into after the dispute has arisen; or
2. which allows the employee to bring proceedings in courts other than those indicated in this Section.

III EUR [292.1]

Agreement on jurisdiction Article 21 restricts the conclusion by the parties to a contract of employment of an agreement on jurisdiction. Such an agreement must thus be concluded after the dispute has arisen or, if it was concluded beforehand, must allow the employee to bring proceedings before courts other than those on which those rules confer jurisdiction (see *Mahamdia: C-154/11* EU:C:2012:491). The provision cannot be interpreted as meaning that a jurisdiction clause could apply exclusively and thus prohibit the employee from bringing proceedings before the courts which have jurisdiction under articles 18 and 19: *Nogueira and Others: C-168/16 and C-169/16* ECLI:EU:C:2017:688.

SECTION 6

EXCLUSIVE JURISDICTION

Article 22

III EUR [293]

The following courts shall have exclusive jurisdiction, regardless of domicile:

1. in proceedings which have as their object rights *in rem* in immovable property or tenancies of immovable property, the courts of the Member State in which the property is situated.

   However, in proceedings which have as their object tenancies of immovable property concluded for temporary private use for a maximum period of six consecutive months, the courts of the Member State in which the defendant is domiciled shall also have jurisdiction, provided that the tenant is a natural person and that the landlord and the tenant are domiciled in the same Member State;
2. in proceedings which have as their object the validity of the constitution, the nullity or the dissolution of companies or other legal persons or associations of natural or legal persons, or of the validity of the decisions of their organs, the courts of the Member State in which the company, legal person or association has its seat. In order to determine that seat, the court shall apply its rules of private international law;
3. in proceedings which have as their object the validity of entries in public registers, the courts of the Member State in which the register is kept;
4. in proceedings concerned with the registration or validity of patents, trade marks, designs, or other similar rights required to be deposited or registered, the courts of the Member State in which the deposit or registration has been applied for, has taken place or is under the terms of a Community instrument or an international convention deemed to have taken place.

   Without prejudice to the jurisdiction of the European Patent Office under the Convention on the Grant of European Patents, signed at Munich on 5 October 1973, the courts of each Member State shall have exclusive jurisdiction, regardless of domicile, in proceedings concerned with the registration or validity of any European patent granted for that State;
5. in proceedings concerned with the enforcement of judgments, the courts of the Member State in which the judgment has been or is to be enforced.

III EUR [293.1]

Trademarks Articles 22(4) and 71 of Brussels I have been reproduced in articles 24(4) and 71 of Brussels I Recast. In a case on Benelux trademarks and designs the CJEU held that under the Benelux regime established by the three Member States, based on a decentralised system and a mechanism for referring questions for a preliminary ruling to the Benelux Court of Justice and the multilingual character of that regional union, the codified rule of article 4.6 of the BCIP (Benelux Convention on Intellectual Property of 2005), which is founded in particular on the defendant's domicile, must be treated as indispensable for the proper functioning of the Benelux regime of trademarks and designs. Disputes relating to Benelux trademarks and designs may be dealt with, as the case may be, by a Belgian, Luxembourg, or Dutch court, instead of being concentrated, pursuant to the Brussels I jurisdiction of article 22(4), before the Dutch courts where the filing and registration of trademarks is centralised and the register is kept. That is so because article 71 of Brussels I, read in light of TFEU, art 350, does not prevent Belgium, Luxembourg and the Netherlands from maintaining in force, in derogation from article 22(4), the rule of jurisdiction for disputes on Benelux trademarks and designs of BCIP, art 4.6: *Brite Strike Technologies Inc. v Brite Strike Technologies SA: C-230/15* (2016), unreported.

III EUR [293.2]

Establishment In *E.ON Czech Holding AG C-560/16* (2018) ECLI:EU:C:2018:167 it was decided that an action for review of the reasonableness of the consideration that the principal shareholder of a company is required to pay to the minority shareholders of that company in the event of the compulsory transfer of their shares to that principal shareholder comes within the exclusive jurisdiction of the courts of the Member State in which that company is established in accordance to article 22(2).

SECTION 7

PROROGATION OF JURISDICTION

Article 23

III EUR [294]

1. If the parties, one or more of whom is domiciled in a Member State, have agreed that a court or the courts of a Member State are to have jurisdiction to settle any disputes which have arisen or which may arise in connection with a particular legal relationship, that court or those courts shall have jurisdiction. Such jurisdiction shall be exclusive unless the parties have agreed otherwise. Such an agreement conferring jurisdiction shall be either:

(a) in writing or evidenced in writing; or

(b) in a form which accords with practices which the parties have established between themselves; or

(c) in international trade or commerce, in a form which accords with a usage of which the parties are or ought to have been aware and which in such trade or commerce is widely known to, and regularly observed by, parties to contracts of the type involved in the particular trade or commerce concerned.

2. Any communication by electronic means which provides a durable record of the agreement shall be equivalent to 'writing'.

3. Where such an agreement is concluded by parties, none of whom is domiciled in a Member State, the courts of other Member States shall have no jurisdiction over their disputes unless the court or courts chosen have declined jurisdiction.

4. The court or courts of a Member State on which a trust instrument has conferred jurisdiction shall have exclusive jurisdiction in any proceedings brought against a settlor, trustee or beneficiary, if relations between these persons or their rights or obligations under the trust are involved.

5. Agreements or provisions of a trust instrument conferring jurisdiction shall have no legal force if they are contrary to Articles 13, 17 or 21, or if the courts whose jurisdiction they purport to exclude have exclusive jurisdiction by virtue of Article 22.

III EUR [294.1]

In writing or in a form which accords with usage In construing paras 1(a) and 1(c) the CJEU has held that, where the jurisdiction clause is in an unsigned prospectus, the requirements of 1(a) may be satisfied if there is an express reference to the prospectus in the signed contract and that the requirements of 1(c) could be satisfied if the usage, of including the jurisdiction clause in the prospectus, was generally recognised and an established practice: *Profit Investment Sim SpA v Ossi: C-366/13* (2016) ECLI:EU:C:2016:282, [2016] 1 WLR 3832, [2016] 2 All ER (Comm) 621.

III EUR [294.2]

Jurisdiction clauses Jurisdiction clauses are severable from the substantive contract. Thus a court hearing a contractual claim, under an exclusive jurisdiction clause, may also consider alternative claims if the contract is held to be invalid: *Deutsche Bank v Asia Pacific* [2008] EWCA Civ 1091, [2008] All ER (D) 104 (Oct).

The CJEU has held that a jurisdiction clause which is set out in the client's general terms and conditions, referred to in the instruments witnessing the contracts between those parties and forwarded upon their conclusion, and which designates as courts with jurisdiction those of a city of a Member State, meets the requirements of article 23(1) relating to the consent of the parties and to the precision of the content of such a clause: *Hoszig Kft. v Alstom Power Thermal Services: C-222/15* (2016) ECLI:EU:C:2016:525.

III EUR [294.2A]

Jurisdiction clauses: insurance contracts Agreements on jurisdiction have no legal force if they are contrary to article 13. Brussels I establishes a system in which derogations from the jurisdictional rules in matters of insurance must be interpreted strictly (see by analogy *Société financière et industrielle du Peloux: C-112/03* EU:C:2005:280). The CJEU has held that an agreement on jurisdiction made between an insurer and an insured party cannot be invoked against a victim of insured damage who wishes to bring an action directly against the insurer before the courts of the place where the harmful event occurred or before the courts of the place where the victim is domiciled: *Assens Havn: C-368/16* ECLI:EU:C:2017:546.

III EUR [294.3]

Jurisdiction of courts of non-Member States The exclusive jurisdiction conferred by article 23 does not deprive courts of non-Member States of jurisdiction, since they are not bound by Brussels I; conversely, where one Member State would be bound by articles 6(1) and 22 to concede jurisdiction to another Member State, it may not claim jurisdiction over a person not domiciled in any Member State at all, since this is not the purpose of the words regardless of jurisdiction: *Choudhury v Bhatter* [2009] EWCA Civ 1176, [2009] NLJR 1628, (2009) Times, 20 November. The correctness of *Choudhury v Bhatter* was left open in *Dar Al Arkan Real Estate Development Co v Majid Al-Sayed Bader Hashim Al Refai* (2014) Times, 30 June, CA.

III EUR [294.4]

Damages: tortious acts A jurisdiction clause in a contract between two companies cannot be relied upon by the representatives of one of them to dispute the jurisdiction of a court over an action for damages which aims to render them jointly and severally liable for supposedly tortious acts carried out in the performance of their duties: *Leventis: C-436/16* ECLI:EU:C:2017:497.

III EUR [294.5]

Damages: competition law In *Apple Sales International: C-595/17* (2018) ECLI:EU:C:2018:854 the CJEU ruled that article 23 means that the application, in the context of an action for damages brought by a distributor against its supplier on the basis of article 102 TFEU, of a jurisdiction clause within the contract binding the parties is not excluded on the sole ground that that clause does not expressly refer to disputes relating to liability incurred as a result of an infringement of competition law. Further, it is not a prerequisite for the application of a jurisdiction clause, in the context of an action for damages brought by a distributor against its supplier on the basis of article 102 TFEU, that there be a finding of an infringement of competition law by a national or European authority.

Article 24

III EUR [295]

Apart from jurisdiction derived from other provisions of this Regulation, a court of a Member State before which a defendant enters an appearance shall have jurisdiction. This rule shall not apply where appearance was entered to contest the jurisdiction, or where another court has exclusive jurisdiction by virtue of Article 22.

SECTION 8

EXAMINATION AS TO JURISDICTION AND ADMISSIBILITY

Article 25

III EUR [296]

Where a court of a Member State is seised of a claim which is principally concerned with a matter over which the courts of another Member State have exclusive jurisdiction by virtue of Article 22, it shall declare of its own motion that it has no jurisdiction.

Article 26

III EUR [297]

1. Where a defendant domiciled in one Member State is sued in a court of another Member State and does not enter an appearance, the court shall declare of its own motion that it has no jurisdiction unless its jurisdiction is derived from the provisions of this Regulation.
2. The court shall stay the proceedings so long as it is not shown that the defendant has been able to receive the document instituting the proceedings or an equivalent document in sufficient time to enable him to arrange for his defence, or that all necessary steps have been taken to this end.
3. Article 19 of Council Regulation (EC) No 1348/2000 of 29 May 2000 on the service in the Member States of judicial and extrajudicial documents in civil or commercial matters (1) shall apply instead of the provisions of paragraph 2 if the document instituting the proceedings or an equivalent document had to be transmitted from one Member State to another pursuant to this Regulation.
4. Where the provisions of Regulation (EC) No 1348/2000 are not applicable, Article 15 of the Hague Convention of 15 November 1965 on the Service Abroad of Judicial and Extrajudicial Documents in Civil or Commercial Matters shall apply if the document instituting the proceedings or equivalent document had to be transmitted pursuant to that Convention.

SECTION 9

LIS PENDENS – RELATED ACTIONS

Article 27

III EUR [298]

1. Where proceedings involving the same cause of action and between the same parties are brought in the courts of different Member States, any court other than the court first seised shall of its own motion stay its proceedings until such time as the jurisdiction of the court first seised is established.

2. Where the jurisdiction of the court first seised is established, any court other than the court first seised shall decline jurisdiction in favour of that court.

III EUR [298.1]

The same parties In a case where the UK court was the court first seised but a new claimant was substituted later, on an assignment after the foreign court had become seised, it was held that the UK court remained the court first seised for the purposes of Brussels I. The point of law on the appeal was whether the parties to the UK proceedings and the parties to the Cyprus proceedings were the 'same parties' for the purposes of article 27 of Brussels I which gives priority to the courts of the Member State which is first seised. It was held that the question of 'the same parties' was to be determined by looking at the claims and not at the subsequent defences, thus the UK court remained the first seised: *Kolden Hollings Ltd v Rolette Commerce Ltd* [2007] EWHC 1597 (Comm), [2007] 4 All ER 62; upheld on appeal [2008] EWCA Civ 10, [2008] 2 All ER (Comm) 289.

III EUR [298.2]

Time when the Court is deemed to be seised Article 27(1) and point 1 of article 30 read together, in cases of lis pendens, mean that the date on which a procedure for a measure of inquiry prior to any legal proceedings was commenced cannot constitute the date on which a court called upon to rule on a substantive application, brought in the same Member State following the result of that measure, was 'deemed to be seised': *HanseYachts: C-29/16* ECLI:EU:C:2017:343.

Article 28

III EUR [299]

1. Where related actions are pending in the courts of different Member States, any court other than the court first seised may stay its proceedings.
2. Where these actions are pending at first instance, any court other than the court first seised may also, on the application of one of the parties, decline jurisdiction if the court first seised has jurisdiction over the actions in question and its law permits the consolidation thereof.
3. For the purposes of this Article, actions are deemed to be related where they are so closely connected that it is expedient to hear and determine them together to avoid the risk of irreconcilable judgments resulting from separate proceedings.

III EUR [299.1]

Related proceedings The application of article 28 requires an assessment of the degree of connection, and then a value judgment as to the expediency of hearing the two actions together in order to avoid the risk of inconsistent judgments: *Research in Motion UK Ltd v Visto Corp* [2008] FSR 20, CA in which the CA concluded that the area of potential conflict between the English claim regarding a certain patent and the Italian claim regarding a different product was not such as to require a single trial. If justified by the circumstances as at the date of hearing the application, the court may properly hold, taking a broad commonsense approach, that although the proceedings might, if tried separately, lead to inconsistent judgments, the risk is not sufficiently great to justify trying them together as related proceedings: *Lehman Brothers Bankhaus AG I Ins v CMA CGM* [2013] EWHC 171 (Comm), [2013] 2 All ER (Comm) 557, [2013] NLJR 167.

It has been held that there are three factors which may be relevant to the exercise of the discretion to stay proceedings: (1) the extent of the relatedness and the risk of mutually irreconcilable decisions (2) the stage reached in each set of proceedings and (3) the proximity of the courts to the subject matter of the case. The closer the connection between the proceedings in question, the more necessary it would appear for the court second seised to stay its proceedings: *Seven Licensing Co Sarl v FFG-Platinum SA* [2011] EWHC 2967 (Comm), [2011] 46 LS Gaz R 21, [2011] NLJR 1634.

Article 29

III EUR [300]

Where actions come within the exclusive jurisdiction of several courts, any court other than the court first seised shall decline jurisdiction in favour of that court.

Article 30

III EUR [301]

For the purposes of this Section, a court shall be deemed to be seised:

1. at the time when the document instituting the proceedings or an equivalent document is lodged with the court, provided that the plaintiff has not subsequently failed to take the steps he was required to take to have service effected on the defendant, or
2. if the document has to be served before being lodged with the court, at the time when it is received by the authority responsible for service, provided that the plaintiff has not subsequently failed to take the steps he was required to take to have the document lodged with the court.

III EUR [301.1]

The aim of article 30 is to determine which of two courts is first seised where the two parties have issued proceedings against each other in different EU jurisdictions. The CA has held that the court first seised is (1) the court where the proceedings were first lodged or, alternatively, (2) where the proceedings were first received by the authority responsible for service: *Benatti v WPP Holdings Italy Srl* [2007] EWCA Civ 263, (2007) Times, 16 April in which it was further held that, provided documents capable of being served and lodged have been received by the authority responsible for service, it does not matter whether or when service is actually effected.

III EUR [301.2]

Document instituting proceedings A court is deemed to be seised at the time of lodging of not only a 'document instituting the proceedings' but also an 'equivalent document'. The concept of an 'equivalent document' means that a document instituting proceedings for the taking of evidence cannot be regarded, for the purposes of assessing a situation of lis pendens and of determining which court is the court first seised within the meaning of article 27(1), as also being the document instituting the substantive proceedings. Such an interpretation would be incompatible with the objective pursued by point 1 of article 30 which seeks to permit the simple and uniform identification of the time at which a court is seised: *HanseYachts: C-29/16* ECLI:EU:C:2017:343.

SECTION 10

PROVISIONAL, INCLUDING PROTECTIVE, MEASURES

Article 31

III EUR [302]

Application may be made to the courts of a Member State for such provisional, including protective, measures as may be available under the law of that State, even if, under this Regulation, the courts of another Member State have jurisdiction as to the substance of the matter.

CHAPTER III
RECOGNITION AND ENFORCEMENT

Article 32

III EUR [303]

For the purposes of this Regulation, 'judgment' means any judgment given by a court or tribunal of a Member State, whatever the judgment may be called, including a decree, order, decision or writ of execution, as well as the determination of costs or expenses by an officer of the court.

SECTION 1
RECOGNITION

Article 33

III EUR [304]

1. A judgment given in a Member State shall be recognised in the other Member States without any special procedure being required.
2. Any interested party who raises the recognition of a judgment as the principal issue in a dispute may, in accordance with the procedures provided for in Sections 2 and 3 of this Chapter, apply for a decision that the judgment be recognised.
3. If the outcome of proceedings in a court of a Member State depends on the determination of an incidental question of recognition that court shall have jurisdiction over that question.

III EUR [304.1]

The CA has held, following *West Tankers* that a court decision in one Member State, judgment in relation to the incorporation of an arbitration clause covered by Brussels I, was a judgment to which article 33 applied: *National Navigation Co v Endesa Generacion SA, The Wadi Sudr* [2009] EWCA Civ 1397, [2010] 1 Lloyd's Rep 193. The CA held that, notwithstanding that the English court's proceedings were themselves non-Regulation proceedings, the English court was nevertheless bound to recognise a judgment of a Brussels I State given in Regulation proceedings.

Article 34

III EUR [305]

A judgment shall not be recognised:
1. if such recognition is manifestly contrary to public policy in the Member State in which recognition is sought;
2. where it was given in default of appearance, if the defendant was not served with the document which instituted the proceedings or with an equivalent document in sufficient time and in such a way as to enable him to arrange for his defence, unless the defendant failed to commence proceedings to challenge the judgment when it was possible for him to do so;
3. if it is irreconcilable with a judgment given in a dispute between the same parties in the Member State in which recognition is sought;
4. if it is irreconcilable with an earlier judgment given in another Member State or in a third State involving the same cause of action and between the same parties, provided that the earlier judgment fulfils the conditions necessary for its recognition in the Member State addressed.

III EUR [305.1]

Land in Cyprus Where a litigant in Nicosia succeeded in obtaining a judgment in his favour regarding his right to land in a part of North Cyprus controlled by the Turkish Cypriot administration, the CA (following the ruling of the CJEU in Case C-420/07) held that there was no principle of public policy to prevent the enforcement of the judgment by the English courts: *Orams v Apostolides* [2010] EWCA Civ 9, [2010] 1 All ER (Comm) 992, [2010] 05 LS Gaz R 18.

III EUR [305.2]

Manifestly contrary to public policy The Member State in which enforcement of a default judgment is sought is entitled to take the view that a judgment which contains no assessment of the subject-matter, basis and merits of the action is a restriction on a defendant's fundamental right and goes against its public policy. The CJEU has held that article 34(1), to which article 45(1) refers, allows the courts of the Member State in which enforcement is sought to refuse to enforce a judgment given in default of appearance which does not contain an assessment of the subject-matter or the basis of the action and which lacks any argument of its merits, only if it appears to the court, after an overall assessment of the proceedings, that that judgment is a manifest and disproportionate breach of the defendant's right to a fair trial on account of the impossibility of bringing an appropriate and effective appeal against it: *Trade Agency Ltd v Seramico Investments Ltd: C-619/10* [2012] NLJR 1218, [2012] All ER (D) 66 (Sep).

The CJEU has held that while the Member States in principle remain free to determine, according to their own national conceptions, what the requirements of their public policy are, the limits of that concept are a matter of interpretation of Brussels I. So, while it is not for the Court to define the content of the public policy of a Member State, it is none the less required to review the limits within which the courts of a Member State may have recourse to that concept for the purpose of refusing recognition of a judgment emanating from a court in another Member State: *flyLAL-Lithuanian Airlines AS, in liquidation v Starptautiska lidosta Riga VAS: C-302/13* ECLI:EU:C:2014:2319, [2014] 5 CMLR 1277, [2014] All ER (D) 324 (Oct). The fact that a judgment given in a Member State is contrary to EU law does not justify that judgment not being recognised in another Member State on the grounds that it infringes public policy in that State where the error of law relied on does not constitute a manifest breach of a rule of law regarded as essential in the EU legal order and therefore in the legal order of the Member State in which recognition is sought or of a right recognised as being fundamental in those legal orders: *Diageo Brands BV v Simiramida-04 EOOD: C-681/13* ECLI:EU:C:2015:471, [2016] Ch 147, [2015] 3 WLR 1632.

III EUR [305.3]

Judgment in default The CJEU is of the view that the court of the Member State in which enforcement is sought has jurisdiction to carry out an independent assessment of all the evidence and ascertain, where necessary, whether that evidence is consistent with the information in the certificate, for the purpose of establishing whether the defendant in default of appearance was served with the document instituting proceedings and, if service was effected in sufficient time and in such a way as to enable him to arrange for his defence: *Trade Agency Ltd v Seramico Investments Ltd: C-619/10* [2012] NLJR 1218, [2012] All ER (D) 66 (Sep). The recognition or enforcement of a default judgment cannot be refused under article 34(2) where the defendant was able to commence proceedings to challenge the default judgment and those proceedings enabled him to argue that he had not been served with the document which instituted the proceedings or with the equivalent document in sufficient time and in such a way as to enable him to arrange for his defence: *Orams v Apostolides: C-420/07* [2009] ECR I-3571, [2011] 2 WLR 324.

Article 35

III EUR [306]

1. Moreover, a judgment shall not be recognised if it conflicts with Sections 3, 4 or 6 of Chapter II, or in a case provided for in Article 72.
2. In its examination of the grounds of jurisdiction referred to in the foregoing paragraph, the court or authority applied to shall be bound by the findings of fact on which the court of the Member State of origin based its jurisdiction.
3. Subject to the paragraph 1, the jurisdiction of the court of the Member State of origin may not be reviewed. The test of public policy referred to in point 1 of Article 34 may not be applied to the rules relating to jurisdiction.

III EUR [306.1]

Recognition of grounds of jurisdiction The CJEU has held that the suspension of the application of the acquis communautaire in the northern area (of Cyprus, under Turkish control), provided for by article 1(1) of Protocol No 10 (to the Accession Acts and EU Treaties), does not preclude the application of Brussels I to a judgment which is given by a Cypriot court sitting in the government-controlled area, but concerns land situated in the northern area. Further, article 35(1) does not authorise the court of a Member State to refuse recognition or enforcement of a judgment given by the courts of another Member State concerning land situated in an area of the latter State over which its government does not exercise effective control: *Orams v Apostolides: C-420/07* [2009] ECR I-3571, [2011] 2 WLR 324.

Article 36

III EUR [307]

Under no circumstances may a foreign judgment be reviewed as to its substance.

III EUR [307.1]

Article 36 disallows any review of a judgment delivered in another Member State as to its substance and as such the CJEU has held that the court of the State in which recognition is sought may not review the accuracy of the findings of law or fact made by the court of the State of origin: *flyLAL-Lithuanian Airlines AS, in liquidation v Starptautiska lidosta Riga VAS: C-302/13* ECLI:EU:C:2014:2319, [2014] 5 CMLR 1277, [2014] All ER (D) 324 (Oct).

Article 37

III EUR [308]

1. A court of a Member State in which recognition is sought of a judgment given in another Member State may stay the proceedings if an ordinary appeal against the judgment has been lodged.
2. A court of a Member State in which recognition is sought of a judgment given in Ireland or the United Kingdom may stay the proceedings if enforcement is suspended in the State of origin, by reason of an appeal.

SECTION 2

ENFORCEMENT

Article 38

III EUR [309]

1. A judgment given in a Member State and enforceable in that State shall be enforced in another Member State when, on the application of any interested party, it has been declared enforceable there.
2. However, in the United Kingdom, such a judgment shall be enforced in England and Wales, in Scotland, or in Northern Ireland when, on the application of any interested party, it has been registered for enforcement in that part of the United Kingdom.

III EUR [309.1]

Time for enforcement The provision for enforcement of a registered judgment must be read subject to the provisions of article 47(3), to the effect that measures of enforcement may not be taken until the expiry of the time allowed for appeal: *Cyprus Popular Bank Public Co Ltd v Vgenopoulos* [2016] EWHC 1442 (QB).

Article 38 does not preclude legislation of a Member State which provides for the application of a time limit for the enforcement of a preventive attachment order from being applied in the case of an order which has been adopted in another Member State and is enforceable in the Member State in which enforcement is sought: *Società Immobiliare Al Bosco Srl: C-379/17* (2018) ECLI:EU:C:2018:806.

Article 39

III EUR [310]

1. The application shall be submitted to the court or competent authority indicated in the list in Annex II.
2. The local jurisdiction shall be determined by reference to the place of domicile of the party against whom enforcement is sought, or to the place of enforcement.

Article 40

III EUR [311]

1. The procedure for making the application shall be governed by the law of the Member State in which enforcement is sought.
2. The applicant must give an address for service of process within the area of jurisdiction of the court applied to. However, if the law of the Member State in which enforcement is sought does not provide for the furnishing of such an address, the applicant shall appoint a representative ad litem.
3. The documents referred to in Article 53 shall be attached to the application.

III EUR [311.1]

The procedure for enforcement in the UK of judgments obtained elsewhere in the EU is included in CPR Part 74. This part makes procedural provision for enforcing judgments to which Brussels I still applies, namely judgments in proceedings commenced before 10 January 2015. The procedure is saved for such judgments and is not affected by the Civil Procedure (Amendment No 7) Rules 2014, SI 2014/2948, which added a new procedure for judgments under Brussels I Recast or new Judgments Regulation. Thus, the provisions of CPR 74.4(1)(b) and (2)(c) and of CPR 74.5, 74.6, 74.7, 74.8, 74.9 74.10 and 74.11 continue to apply to the enforcement of judgments under Brussels I. Precedents are provided in BCCP Division H at **BCCP H[64]** for an application to register a judgment and at **BCCP H[64A]** for evidence in support. The certificate from the foreign court needs to follow the form and contents in Annex V.

Article 41

III EUR [312]

The judgment shall be declared enforceable immediately on completion of the formalities in Article 53 without any review under Articles 34 and 35. The party against whom enforcement is sought shall not at this stage of the proceedings be entitled to make any submissions on the application.

Article 42

III EUR [313]

1. The decision on the application for a declaration of enforceability shall forthwith be brought to the notice of the applicant in accordance with the procedure laid down by the law of the Member State in which enforcement is sought.
2. The declaration of enforceability shall be served on the party against whom enforcement is sought, accompanied by the judgment, if not already served on that party.

Article 43

III EUR [314]

1. The decision on the application for a declaration of enforceability may be appealed against by either party.
2. The appeal is to be lodged with the court indicated in the list in Annex III.
3. The appeal shall be dealt with in accordance with the rules governing procedure in contradictory matters.
4. If the party against whom enforcement is sought fails to appear before the appellate court in proceedings concerning an appeal brought by the applicant, Article 26(2) to (4) shall apply even where the party against whom enforcement is sought is not domiciled in any of the Member States.
5. An appeal against the declaration of enforceability is to be lodged within one month of service thereof. If the party against whom enforcement is sought is domiciled in a Member State other than that in which the declaration of enforceability was given, the time for appealing shall be two months and shall run from the date of service, either on him in person or at his residence. No extension of time may be granted on account of distance.

III EUR [314.1]

Time limit to appeal The High Court has held that there is no general power to extend the mandatory two month time limit for appealing. The Court is obliged to enforce that time limit strictly, subject only to the residual power to extend a mandatory time limit in the rare case where its application would impair the very essence of the right of appeal, and strict adherence to it would infringe article 6 of the ECHR: *Christofi v National Bank of Greece (Cyprus) Ltd* [2015] EWHC 986 (QB), 165 NLJ 7650, [2015] All ER (D) 84 (Apr).

Article 44

III EUR [315]

The judgment given on the appeal may be contested only by the appeal referred to in Annex IV.

Article 45

III EUR [316]

1. The court with which an appeal is lodged under Article 43 or Article 44 shall refuse or revoke a declaration of enforceability only on one of the grounds specified in Articles 34 and 35. It shall give its decision without delay.
2. Under no circumstances may the foreign judgment be reviewed as to its substance.

Article 46

III EUR [317]

1. The court with which an appeal is lodged under Article 43 or Article 44 may, on the application of the party against whom enforcement is sought, stay the proceedings if an ordinary appeal has been lodged against the judgment in the Member State of origin or if the time for such an appeal has not yet expired; in the latter case, the court may specify the time within which such an appeal is to be lodged.
2. Where the judgment was given in Ireland or the United Kingdom, any form of appeal available in the Member State of origin shall be treated as an ordinary appeal for the purposes of paragraph 1.

3. The court may also make enforcement conditional on the provision of such security as it shall determine.

III EUR [317.1]

Appellant lodges appeal in time but fails to lodge appeal bundle The High Court recalled *Denton* where the CA emphasised that the (*Denton*) test was not whether the breach was trivial but whether it was serious and significant. A failure to serve an appeal bundle in time is a significant breach essentially for the good administration reasons. The routine non-observance of procedural rules was one of the reasons why the CA in *Denton* urged the adoption of a more robust approach to case management. However, there are degrees of seriousness and a court is entitled to have regard to the context in which the default occurs. But adherence to procedural steps does, in practice, matter. Thus, the appeal may be struck out: *AB Snoras v Antonov* [2015] EWHC 2136 (QB).

Article 47

III EUR [318]

1. When a judgment must be recognised in accordance with this Regulation, nothing shall prevent the applicant from availing himself of provisional, including protective, measures in accordance with the law of the Member State requested without a declaration of enforceability under Article 41 being required.
2. The declaration of enforceability shall carry with it the power to proceed to any protective measures.
3. During the time specified for an appeal pursuant to Article 43(5) against the declaration of enforceability and until any such appeal has been determined, no measures of enforcement may be taken other than protective measures against the property of the party against whom enforcement is sought.

III EUR [318.1]

In *Banco Nacional de Commercio Exterior SNC v Empesa de Telecommunicationes de Cuba SA* [2007] EWHC 19 (Comm)[2007] 2 All ER (Comm) 46, David Steel J, QBD (Comm) it was held that article 47 provides an unrestricted and discrete code for granting provisional or protective measures in the context of enforcement. There are no basis for restricting the measures to the freezing of domestic assets and/or for limiting the disclosure to domestic assets. Thus, freezing or disclosure orders may be made worldwide. On appeal this decision was reversed. The CA held that all parts of article 47 are directed at enforcement. Article 47(1) is simply dealing with the position before a declaration of enforceability/registration has taken place. If the applicant is able to show that he has a judgment which must be recognised he is not prevented from availing himself of protective measures before the formalities which lead to registration have been completed. Each of the provisions of article 47 deals with the time at which things can or cannot be done. Thus, article 47 (1) deals with the time before registration; (2) with the time after registration; and (3) with the time after registration where there is an appeal pending: [2007] EWCA Civ 662.

III EUR [318.2]

Time for enforcement of judgment following registration Article 47(3) applies to the enforcement after registration of a judgment obtained in another Member State. The result is that measures of enforcement may not be taken until the expiry of the time allowed for appeal: *Cyprus Popular Bank Public Co Ltd v Vgenopoulos* [2016] EWHC 1442 (QB).

Article 48

III EUR [319]

1. Where a foreign judgment has been given in respect of several matters and the declaration of enforceability cannot be given for all of them, the court or competent authority shall give it for one or more of them.
2. An applicant may request a declaration of enforceability limited to parts of a judgment.

Article 49

III EUR [320]

A foreign judgment which orders a periodic payment by way of a penalty shall be enforceable in the Member State in which enforcement is sought only if the amount of the payment has been finally determined by the courts of the Member State of origin.

Article 50

III EUR [321]

An applicant who, in the Member State of origin has benefited from complete or partial legal aid or exemption from costs or expenses, shall be entitled, in the procedure provided for in this Section, to benefit from the most favourable legal aid or the most extensive exemption from costs or expenses provided for by the law of the Member State addressed.

Article 51

III EUR [322]

No security, bond or deposit, however described, shall be required of a party who in one Member State applies for enforcement of a judgment given in another Member State on the ground that he is a foreign national or that he is not domiciled or resident in the State in which enforcement is sought.

Article 52

III EUR [323]

In proceedings for the issue of a declaration of enforceability, no charge, duty or fee calculated by reference to the value of the matter at issue may be levied in the Member State in which enforcement is sought.

SECTION 3

COMMON PROVISIONS

Article 53

III EUR [324]

1. A party seeking recognition or applying for a declaration of enforceability shall produce a copy of the judgment which satisfies the conditions necessary to establish its authenticity.
2. A party applying for a declaration of enforceability shall also produce the certificate referred to in Article 54, without prejudice to Article 55.

Article 54

III EUR [325]

The court or competent authority of a Member State where a judgment was given shall issue, at the request of any interested party, a certificate using the standard form in Annex V to this Regulation.

III EUR [325.1]

No discretion to withhold certificate There is no discretion to refuse an application under article 54 for a certificate of judgment: *Re Snelling House Ltd; Alford v Barton* [2015] All ER (D) 22 (Dec).

Article 55

III EUR [326]

1. If the certificate referred to in Article 54 is not produced, the court or competent authority may specify a time for its production or accept an equivalent document or, if it considers that it has sufficient information before it, dispense with its production.
2. If the court or competent authority so requires, a translation of the documents shall be produced. The translation shall be certified by a person qualified to do so in one of the Member States.

Article 56

III EUR [327]

No legalisation or other similar formality shall be required in respect of the documents referred to in Article 53 or Article 55(2), or in respect of a document appointing a representative *ad litem*.

CHAPTER IV
AUTHENTIC INSTRUMENTS AND COURT SETTLEMENTS

Article 57

III EUR [328]

1. A document which has been formally drawn up or registered as an authentic instrument and is enforceable in one Member State shall, in another Member State, be declared enforceable there, on application made in accordance with the procedures provided for in Articles 38, et seq. The court with which an appeal is lodged under Article 43 or Article 44 shall refuse or revoke a declaration of enforceability only if enforcement of the instrument is manifestly contrary to public policy in the Member State addressed.
2. Arrangements relating to maintenance obligations concluded with administrative authorities or authenticated by them shall also be regarded as authentic instruments within the meaning of paragraph 1.
3. The instrument produced must satisfy the conditions necessary to establish its authenticity in the Member State of origin.
4. Section 3 of Chapter III shall apply as appropriate. The competent authority of a Member State where an authentic instrument was drawn up or registered shall issue, at the request of any interested party, a certificate using the standard form in Annex VI to this Regulation.

Article 58

III EUR [329]

A settlement which has been approved by a court in the course of proceedings and is enforceable in the Member State in which it was concluded shall be enforceable in the State addressed under the same conditions as authentic instruments. The court or competent authority of a Member State where a court settlement was approved shall issue, at the request of any interested party, a certificate using the standard form in Annex V to this Regulation.

CHAPTER V
GENERAL PROVISIONS

Article 59

III EUR [330]

1. In order to determine whether a party is domiciled in the Member State whose courts are seised of a matter, the court shall apply its internal law.

2. If a party is not domiciled in the Member State whose courts are seised of the matter, then, in order to determine whether the party is domiciled in another Member State, the court shall apply the law of that Member State.

Article 60

III EUR [331]

1. For the purposes of this Regulation, a company or other legal person or association of natural or legal persons is domiciled at the place where it has its:
   (a) statutory seat, or
   (b) central administration, or
   (c) principal place of business.

2. For the purposes of the United Kingdom and Ireland 'statutory seat' means the registered office or, where there is no such office anywhere, the place of incorporation or, where there is no such place anywhere, the place under the law of which the formation took place.

3. In order to determine whether a trust is domiciled in the Member State whose courts are seised of the matter, the court shall apply its rules of private international law.

Article 61

III EUR [332]

Without prejudice to any more favourable provisions of national laws, persons domiciled in a Member State who are being prosecuted in the criminal courts of another Member State of which they are not nationals for an offence which was not intentionally committed may be defended by persons qualified to do so, even if they do not appear in person. However, the court seised of the matter may order appearance in person; in the case of failure to appear, a judgment given in the civil action without the person concerned having had the opportunity to arrange for his defence need not be recognised or enforced in the other Member States.

Article 62

III EUR [333]

In Sweden, in summary proceedings concerning orders to pay (*betalningsföreläggande*) and assistance (*handräckning*), the expression 'court' includes the 'Swedish enforcement service' (*kronofogdemyndighet*).

Article 63

III EUR [334]

1. A person domiciled in the territory of the Grand Duchy of Luxembourg and sued in the court of another Member State pursuant to Article 5(1) may refuse to submit to the jurisdiction of that court if the final place of delivery of the goods or provision of the services is in Luxembourg.
2. Where, under paragraph 1, the final place of delivery of the goods or provision of the services is in Luxembourg, any agreement conferring jurisdiction must, in order to be valid, be accepted in writing or evidenced in writing within the meaning of Article 23(1)(a).
3. The provisions of this Article shall not apply to contracts for the provision of financial services.
4. The provisions of this Article shall apply for a period of six years from entry into force of this Regulation.

Article 64

III EUR [335]

1. In proceedings involving a dispute between the master and a member of the crew of a seagoing ship registered in Greece or in Portugal, concerning remuneration or other conditions of service, a court in a Member State shall establish whether the diplomatic or consular officer responsible for the ship has been notified of the dispute. It may act as soon as that officer has been notified.
2. The provisions of this Article shall apply for a period of six years from entry into force of this Regulation.

Article 65

III EUR [336]

1. The jurisdiction specified in Article 6(2) and Article 11 in actions on a warranty of guarantee or in any other third party proceedings may not be resorted to Germany, Austria and Hungary. Any person domiciled in another Member State may be sued in the courts:
   (a) of Germany, pursuant to Articles 68 and 72 to 74 of the Code of Civil Procedure (Zivilprozessordnung) concerning third-party notices;
   (b) of Austria, pursuant to Article 21 of the Code of Civil Procedure (Zivilprozessordnung) concerning third-party notices;
   (c) of Hungary, pursuant to Articles 58 to 60 of the Code of Civil Procedure (Polgári perrendtartás) concerning third-party notices.
2. Judgments given in other Member States by virtue of Article 6(2), or Article 11 shall be recognised and enforced in Germany, Austria and Hungary in accordance with Chapter III. Any effects which judgments given in these States may have on third parties

by application of the provisions in paragraph 1 shall also be recognised in the other Member States.

CHAPTER VI
TRANSITIONAL PROVISIONS

Article 66

III EUR [337]

1. This Regulation shall apply only to legal proceedings instituted and to documents formally drawn up or registered as authentic instruments after the entry into force thereof.

2. However, if the proceedings in the Member State of origin were instituted before the entry into force of this Regulation, judgments given after that date shall be recognised and enforced in accordance with Chapter III,

(a) if the proceedings in the Member State of origin were instituted after the entry into force of the Brussels or the Lugano Convention both in the Member State or origin and in the Member State addressed;

(b) in all other cases, if jurisdiction was founded upon rules which accorded with those provided for either in Chapter II or in a convention concluded between the Member State of origin and the Member State addressed which was in force when the proceedings were instituted.

CHAPTER VII
TRANSITIONAL PROVISIONS

Article 67

III EUR [338]

This Regulation shall not prejudice the application of provisions governing jurisdiction and the recognition and enforcement of judgments in specific matters which are contained in Community instruments or in national legislation harmonised pursuant to such instruments.

Article 68

III EUR [339]

1. This Regulation shall, as between the Member States, supersede the Brussels Convention, except as regards the territories of the Member States which fall within the territorial scope of that Convention and which are excluded from this Regulation pursuant to Article 299 of the Treaty.

2. In so far as this Regulation replaces the provisions of the Brussels Convention between Member States, any reference to the Convention shall be understood as a reference to this Regulation.

Article 69

III EUR [340]

Subject to Article 66(2) and Article 70, this Regulation shall, as between Member States, supersede the following conventions and treaty concluded between two or more of them:

— the Convention between Belgium and France on Jurisdiction and the Validity and Enforcement of Judgments, Arbitration Awards and Authentic Instruments, signed at Paris on 8 July 1899,

— the Convention between Belgium and the Netherlands on Jurisdiction, Bankruptcy, and the Validity and Enforcement of Judgments, Arbitration Awards and Authentic Instruments, signed at Brussels on 28 March 1925,

— the Convention between France and Italy on the Enforcement of Judgments in Civil and Commercial Matters, signed at Rome on 3 June 1930,

— the Convention between the United Kingdom and the French Republic providing for the reciprocal enforcement of judgments in civil and commercial matters, with Protocol, signed at Paris on 18 January 1934,

— the Convention between the United Kingdom and the Kingdom of Belgium providing for the reciprocal enforcement of judgments in civil and commercial matters, with Protocol, signed at Brussels on 2 May 1934,

— the Convention between Germany and Italy on the Recognition and Enforcement of Judgments in Civil and Commercial Matters, signed at Rome on 9 March 1936,

— the Convention between Belgium and Austria on the Reciprocal Recognition and Enforcement of Judgments and Authentic Instruments relating to Maintenance Obligations, signed at Vienna on 25 October 1957,

— the Convention between Germany and Belgium on the Mutual Recognition and Enforcement of Judgments, Arbitration Awards and Authentic Instruments in Civil and Commercial Matters, signed at Bonn on 30 June 1958,

— the Convention between the Netherlands and Italy on the Recognition and Enforcement of Judgments in Civil and Commercial Matters, signed at Rome on 17 April 1959,

— the Convention between Germany and Austria on the Reciprocal Recognition and Enforcement of Judgments, Settlements and Authentic Instruments in Civil and Commercial Matters, signed at Vienna on 6 June 1959,

— the Convention between Belgium and Austria on the Reciprocal Recognition and Enforcement of Judgments, Arbitral Awards and Authentic Instruments in Civil and Commercial Matters, signed at Vienna on 16 June 1959,

— the Convention between the United Kingdom and the Federal Republic of Germany for the reciprocal recognition and enforcement of judgments in civil and commercial matters, signed at Bonn on 14 July 1960,

— the Convention between the United Kingdom and Austria providing for the reciprocal recognition and enforcement of judgments in civil and commercial matters, signed at Vienna on 14 July 1961, with amending Protocol signed at London on 6 March 1970,

— the Convention between Greece and Germany for the Reciprocal Recognition and Enforcement of Judgments, Settlements and Authentic Instruments in Civil and Commercial Matters, signed in Athens on 4 November 1961,

— the Convention between Belgium and Italy on the Recognition and Enforcement of Judgments and other Enforceable Instruments in Civil and Commercial Matters, signed at Rome on 6 April 1962,

— the Convention between the Netherlands and Germany on the Mutual Recognition and Enforcement of Judgments and Other Enforceable Instruments in Civil and Commercial Matters, signed at The Hague on 30 August 1962,

— the Convention between the Netherlands and Austria on the Reciprocal Recognition and Enforcement of Judgments and Authentic Instruments in Civil and Commercial Matters, signed at The Hague on 6 February 1963,

— the Convention between the United Kingdom and the Republic of Italy for the reciprocal recognition and enforcement of judgments in civil and commercial matters, signed at Rome on 7 February 1964, with amending Protocol signed at Rome on 14 July 1970,

— the Convention between France and Austria on the Recognition and Enforcement of Judgments and Authentic Instruments in Civil and Commercial Matters, signed at Vienna on 15 July 1966,

— the Convention between the United Kingdom and the Kingdom of the Netherlands providing for the reciprocal recognition and enforcement of judgments in civil matters, signed at The Hague on 17 November 1967,

— the Convention between Spain and France on the Recognition and Enforcement of Judgment Arbitration Awards in Civil and Commercial Matters, signed at Paris on 28 May 1969,

— the Convention between Luxembourg and Austria on the Recognition and Enforcement of Judgments and Authentic Instruments in Civil and Commercial Matters, signed at Luxembourg on 29 July 1971,

— the Convention between Italy and Austria on the Recognition and Enforcement of Judgments in Civil and Commercial Matters, of Judicial Settlements and of Authentic Instruments, signed at Rome on 16 November 1971,

— the Convention between Spain and Italy regarding Legal Aid and the Recognition and Enforcement of Judgments in Civil and Commercial Matters, signed at Madrid on 22 May 1973,

— the Convention between Finland, Iceland, Norway, Sweden and Denmark on the Recognition and Enforcement of Judgments in Civil Matters, signed at Copenhagen on 11 October 1977,

— the Convention between Austria and Sweden on the Recognition and Enforcement of Judgments in Civil Matters, signed at Stockholm on 16 September 1982,

— the Convention between Spain and the Federal Republic of Germany on the Recognition and Enforcement of Judgments, Settlements and Enforceable Authentic Instruments in Civil and Commercial Matters, signed at Bonn on 14 November 1983,

— the Convention between Austria and Spain on the Recognition and Enforcement of Judgments, Settlements and Enforceable Authentic Instruments in Civil and Commercial Matters, signed at Vienna on 17 February 1984,

— the Convention between Finland and Austria on the Recognition and Enforcement of Judgments in Civil Matters, signed at Vienna on 17 November 1986,

— the Treaty between Belgium, the Netherlands and Luxembourg in Jurisdiction, Bankruptcy, and the Validity and Enforcement of Judgments, Arbitration Awards and Authentic Instruments, signed at Brussels on 24 November 1961, in so far as it is in force,

— the Convention between the Czechoslovak Republic and Portugal on the Recognition and Enforcement of Court Decisions, signed at Lisbon on 23 November 1927, still in force between the Czech Republic and Portugal,

— the Convention between the Federative People's Republic of Yugoslavia and the Republic of Austria on Mutual Judicial Cooperation, signed at Vienna on 16 December 1954,

— the Convention between the Polish People's Republic and the Hungarian People's Republic on the Legal Assistance in Civil, Family and Criminal Matters, signed at Budapest on 6 March 1959,

— the Convention between the Federative People's Republic of Yugoslavia and the Kingdom of Greece on the Mutual Recognition and Enforcement of Judgments, signed at Athens on 18 June 1959,

— the Convention between the Polish People's Republic and the Federative People's Republic of Yugoslavia on the Legal Assistance in Civil and Criminal Matters, signed at Warsaw on 6 February 1960, now in force between Poland and Slovenia, and between Poland and Croatia,

— the Agreement between the Federative People's Republic of Yugoslavia and the Republic of Austria on the Mutual Recognition and Enforcement of Arbitral Awards and Arbitral Settlements in Commercial Matters, signed at Belgrade on 18 March 1960,

— the Agreement between the Federative People's Republic of Yugoslavia and the Republic of Austria on the Mutual Recognition and Enforcement of Decisions in Alimony Matters, signed at Vienna on 10 October 1961,

— the Convention between Poland and Austria on Mutual Relations in Civil Matters and on Documents, signed at Vienna on 11 December 1963,

— the Treaty between the Czechoslovak Socialist Republic and the Socialist Federative Republic of Yugoslavia on Settlement of Legal Relations in Civil, Family and Criminal Matters, signed at Belgrade on 20 January 1964, still in force between the Czech Republic, Slovakia and Slovenia and between the Czech Republic, Slovakia and Croatia,

— the Convention between Poland and France on Applicable Law, Jurisdiction and the Enforcement of Judgments in the Field of Personal and Family Law, concluded in Warsaw on 5 April 1967,

— the Convention between the Governments of Yugoslavia and France on the Recognition and Enforcement of Judgments in Civil and Commercial Matters, signed at Paris on 18 May 1971,

— the Convention between the Federative Socialist Republic of Yugoslavia and the Kingdom of Belgium on the Recognition and Enforcement of Court Decisions in Alimony Matters, signed at Belgrade on 12 December 1973,

— the Convention between Hungary and Greece on Legal Assistance in Civil and Criminal Matters, signed at Budapest on 8 October 1979,

— the Convention between Poland and Greece on Legal Assistance in Civil and Criminal Matters, signed at Athens on 24 October 1979,

— the Convention between Hungary and France on Legal Assistance in Civil and Family Law, on the Recognition and Enforcement of Decisions and on Legal Assistance in Criminal Matters and on Extradition, signed at Budapest on 31 July 1980,

— the Treaty between the Czechoslovak Socialist Republic and the Hellenic Republic on Legal Aid in Civil and Criminal Matters, signed at Athens on 22 October 1980, still in force between the Czech Republic, Slovakia and Greece,

— the Convention between the Republic of Cyprus and the Hungarian People's Republic on Legal Assistance in Civil and Criminal Matters, signed at Nicosia on 30 November 1981,

— the Treaty between the Czechoslovak Socialistic Republic and the Republic of Cyprus on Legal Aid in Civil and Criminal Matters, signed at Nicosia on 23 April 1982, still in force between the Czech Republic, Slovakia and Cyprus,

— the Agreement between the Republic of Cyprus and the Republic of Greece on Legal Cooperation in Matters of Civil, Family, Commercial and Criminal Law, signed at Nicosia on 5 March 1984,

— the Treaty between the Government of the Czechoslovak Socialist Republic and the Government of the Republic of France on Legal Aid and the Recognition and Enforcement of Judgments in Civil, Family and Commercial Matters, signed at Paris on 10 May 1984, still in force between the Czech Republic, Slovakia and France,

— the Agreement between the Republic of Cyprus and the Socialist Federal Republic of Yugoslavia on Legal Assistance in Civil and Criminal Matters, signed at Nicosia on 19 September 1984, now in force between Cyprus and Slovenia,

— the Treaty between the Czechoslovak Socialist Republic and the Italian Republic on Legal Aid in Civil and Criminal Matters, signed at Prague on 6 December 1985, still in force between the Czech Republic, Slovakia and Italy,

— the Treaty between the Czechoslovak Socialist Republic and the Kingdom of Spain on Legal Aid, Recognition and Enforcement of Court Decisions in Civil Matters, signed at Madrid on 4 May 1987, still in force between the Czech Republic, Slovakia and Spain,

— the Treaty between the Czechoslovak Socialist Republic and the Polish People's Republic on Legal Aid and Settlement of Legal Relations in Civil, Family, Labour and Criminal Matters, signed at Warsaw on 21 December 1987, still in force between the Czech Republic, Slovakia and Poland,

— the Treaty between the Czechoslovak Socialist Republic and the Hungarian People's Republic on Legal Aid and Settlement of Legal Relations in Civil, Family and Criminal Matters, signed at Bratislava on 28 March 1989, still in force between the Czech Republic, Slovakia and Hungary,

— the Convention between Poland and Italy on Judicial Assistance and the Recognition and Enforcement of Judgments in Civil Matters, signed at Warsaw on 28 April 1989,

— the Treaty between the Czech Republic and the Slovak Republic on Legal Aid provided by Judicial Bodies and on Settlements of Certain Legal Relations in Civil and Criminal Matters, signed at Prague on 29 October 1992,

— the Agreement between the Republic of Latvia, the Republic of Estonia and the Republic of Lithuania on Legal Assistance and Legal Relationships, signed at Tallinn on 11 November 1992,

— the Agreement between the Republic of Poland and the Republic of Lithuania on Legal Assistance and Legal Relations in Civil, Family, Labour and Criminal Matters, signed in Warsaw on 26 January 1993,

— the Agreement between the Republic of Latvia and the Republic of Poland on Legal Assistance and Legal Relationships in Civil, Family, Labour and Criminal Matters, signed at Riga on 23 February 1994,

— the Agreement between the Republic of Cyprus and the Republic of Poland on Legal Cooperation in Civil and Criminal Matters, signed at Nicosia on 14 November 1996,

— the Agreement between Estonia and Poland on Granting Legal Assistance and Legal Relations on Civil, Labour and Criminal Matters, signed at Tallinn on 27 November 1998,

— the Convention between Bulgaria and Belgium on certain Judicial Matters, signed at Sofia on 2 July 1930,

— the Agreement between the People's Republic of Bulgaria and the Federative People's Republic of Yugoslavia on Mutual Legal Assistance, signed at Sofia on 23 March 1956, still in force between Bulgaria and Slovenia and between Bulgaria and Croatia,

— the Treaty between the People's Republic of Romania and the People's Republic of Hungary on Legal Assistance in Civil, Family and Criminal Matters, signed at Bucharest on 7 October 1958,

— the Treaty between the People's Republic of Romania and the Czechoslovak Republic on Legal Assistance in Civil, Family and Criminal Matters, signed at Prague on 25 October 1958, still in force between Romania and Slovakia,

— the Agreement between the People's Republic of Bulgaria and the Romanian People's Republic on Legal Assistance in Civil, Family and Criminal Matters, signed at Sofia on 3 December 1958,

— the Treaty between the People's Republic of Romania and the Federal People's Republic of Yugoslavia on Legal Assistance, signed at Belgrade on 18 October 1960 and its Protocol, still in force between Romania and Slovenia and between Romania and Croatia,

— the Agreement between the People's Republic of Bulgaria and the Polish People's Republic on Legal Assistance and Legal Relations in Civil, Family and Criminal Matters, signed at Warsaw on 4 December 1961,

— the Convention between the Socialist Republic of Romania and the Republic of Austria on Legal Assistance in Civil and Family law and the Validity and Service of Documents and its annexed Protocol, signed at Vienna on 17 November 1965,

— the Agreement between the People's Republic of Bulgaria and the Hungarian People's Republic on Legal Assistance in Civil, Family and Criminal Matters, signed at Sofia on 16 May 1966,

— the Convention between the Socialist Republic of Romania and the Hellenic Republic on Legal Assistance in Civil and Criminal Matters and its Protocol, signed at Bucharest on 19 October 1972,

— the Convention between the Socialist Republic of Romania and the Italian Republic on Judicial Assistance in Civil and Criminal Matters, signed at Bucharest on 11 November 1972,

— the Convention between the Socialist Republic of Romania and the French Republic on Legal Assistance in Civil and Commercial Matters, signed at Paris on 5 November 1974,

— the Convention between the Socialist Republic of Romania and the Kingdom of Belgium on Legal Assistance in Civil and Commercial Matters, signed at Bucharest on 30 October 1975,

— the Agreement between the People's Republic of Bulgaria and the Hellenic Republic on Legal Assistance in Civil and Criminal Matters, signed at Athens on 10 April 1976,

— the Agreement between the People's Republic of Bulgaria and the Czechoslovak Socialist Republic on Legal Assistance and Settlement of Relations in Civil, Family and Criminal Matters, signed at Sofia on 25 November 1976,

— the Convention between the Socialist Republic of Romania and the United Kingdom of Great Britain and Northern Ireland on Legal Assistance in Civil and Commercial Matters, signed at London on 15 June 1978,

— the Additional Protocol to the Convention between the Socialist Republic of Romania and the Kingdom of Belgium on Legal Assistance Civil and Commercial Matters, signed at Bucharest on 30 October 1979,

— the Convention between the Socialist Republic of Romania and the Kingdom of Belgium on Recognition and Enforcement of Decisions in Alimony Obligations, signed at Bucharest on 30 October 1979,

— the Convention between the Socialist Republic of Romania and the Kingdom of Belgium on Recognition and Enforcement of Divorce Decisions, signed at Bucharest on 6 November 1980,

— the Agreement between the People's Republic of Bulgaria and the Republic of Cyprus on Legal Assistance in Civil and Criminal Matters, signed at Nicosia on 29 April 1983,

— the Agreement between the Government of the People's Republic of Bulgaria and the Government of the French Republic on Mutual Legal Assistance in Civil Matters, signed at Sofia on 18 January 1989,

— the Agreement between the People's Republic of Bulgaria and the Italian Republic on Legal Assistance and Enforcement of Decisions in Civil Matters, signed at Rome on 18 May 1990,

— the Agreement between the Republic of Bulgaria and the Kingdom of Spain on Mutual Legal Assistance in Civil Matters, signed at Sofia on 23 May 1993,

— the Treaty between Romania and the Czech Republic on Judicial Assistance in Civil Matters, signed at Bucharest on 11 July 1994,

— the Convention between Romania and the Kingdom of Spain on Jurisdiction, Recognition and Enforcement of Decisions in Civil and Commercial Matters, signed at Bucharest on 17 November 1997,

— the Convention between Romania and the Kingdom of Spain — complementary to the Hague Convention relating to civil procedure law (Hague, 1 March 1954), signed at Bucharest on 17 November 1997,

— the Treaty between Romania and the Republic of Poland on Legal Assistance and Legal Relations in Civil Cases, signed at Bucharest on 15 May 1999,

— the Agreement between the Socialist Federative Republic of Yugoslavia and the People's Republic of Hungary on Mutual Legal Assistance, signed at Belgrade on 7 March 1968, still in force between Croatia and Hungary,

— the Agreement between the Republic of Croatia and the Republic of Slovenia on Legal Assistance in Civil and Criminal Matters, signed at Zagreb on 7 February 1994.

Article 70

III EUR [341]

1. The Treaty and the Conventions referred to in Article 69 shall continue to have effect in relation to matters to which this Regulation does not apply.
2. They shall continue to have effect in respect of judgments given and documents formally drawn up or registered as authentic instruments before the entry into force of this Regulation.

Article 71

III EUR [342]

1. This Regulation shall not affect any conventions to which the Member States are parties and which in relation to particular matters, govern jurisdiction or the recognition or enforcement of judgments.
2. With a view to its uniform interpretation, paragraph 1 shall be applied in the following manner:
   (a) this Regulation shall not prevent a court of a Member State, which is a party to a convention on a particular matter, from assuming jurisdiction in accordance with that convention, even where the defendant is domiciled in another Member State which is not a party to that convention. The court hearing the action shall, in any event, apply Article 26 of this Regulation;
   (b) judgments given in a Member State by a court in the exercise of jurisdiction provided for in a convention on a particular matter shall be recognised and enforced in the other Member States in accordance with this Regulation.

Where a convention on a particular matter to which both the Member State of origin and the Member State addressed are parties lays down conditions for the recognition or enforcement of judgments, those conditions shall apply. In any event, the provisions of this Regulation which concern the procedure for recognition and enforcement of judgments may be applied.

III EUR [342.1]

Trademarks The CJEU has held that article 71, read in light of TFEU, art 350, does not preclude the application to trademarks disputes of the rule of jurisdiction for disputes relating to Benelux trademarks and designs, laid down in article 4.6 of the Benelux Convention on Intellectual Property (Trademarks and Designs) of 2005, signed by Belgium, Luxembourg and the Netherlands: *Brite Strike Technologies Inc. v Brite Strike Technologies SA: C-230/15* (2016), unreported.

Article 72

III EUR [343]

This Regulation shall not affect agreements by which Member States undertook, prior to the entry into force of this Regulation pursuant to Article 59 of the Brussels Convention, not to recognise judgments given, in particular in other Contracting States to that Convention, against defendants domiciled or habitually resident in a third country where, in cases provided for in Article 4 of that Convention, the judgment could only be founded on a ground of jurisdiction specified in the second paragraph of Article 3 of that Convention.

CHAPTER VIII
FINAL PROVISIONS

Article 73

III EUR [344]

No later than five years after the entry into force of this Regulation, the Commission shall present to the European Parliament, the Council and the Economic and Social Committee a report on the application of this Regulation. The report shall be accompanied, if need be, by proposals for adaptations to this Regulation.

Article 74

III EUR [345]

1. The Member States shall notify the Commission of the texts amending the lists set out in Annexes I to IV. The Commission shall adapt the Annexes concerned accordingly.
2. The updating or technical adjustments of the forms, specimens of which appear in Annexes V and VI, shall be adopted by the Commission. Those measures, designed to amend non-essential elements of this Regulation, shall be adopted in accordance with the regulatory procedure with scrutiny referred to in Article 75(2).

Article 75

III EUR [346]

1. The Commission shall be assisted by a committee.
2. Where reference is made to this paragraph, Article 5a(1) to (4) and Article 7 of Decision 1999/468/EC shall apply, having regard to the provisions of Article 8 thereof.

Article 76

III EUR [347]

This Regulation shall enter into force on 1 March 2002.

This Regulation is binding in its entirety and directly applicable in the Member States in accordance with the Treaty establishing the European Community.

ANNEX I

III EUR [348]

Rules of jurisdiction referred to in Article 3 (2) and Article 4 (2)

— in Bulgaria: Article 4, paragraph 1, point 2, of the Private International Law Code,

— in the Czech Republic: Act No 91/2012 on private international law, in particular, its Article 6,

— in Denmark: Article 246(2) and (3) of the Administration of Justice Act (*lov om rettens pleje*),

— in Germany: Article 23 of the code of civil procedure (*Zivilprozeßordnung*),

— in Estonia: Article 86 (jurisdiction at the location of property) of the Code of Civil Procedure (*Tsiviilkohtumenetluse seadustik*), insofar as the claim is unrelated to that property of the person; Article 100 (claim for termination of application of standard terms) of the Code of Civil Procedure, insofar as the action is to be lodged with the court in whose territorial jurisdiction the standard term was applied,

— in Greece: Article 40 of the code of civil procedure (Κώδικας Πολιτικής Δικονομίας),

— in France: Articles 14 and 15 of the civil code (*Code civil*),

— in Croatia: Article 54 of the Act on the Resolution of Conflicts of Laws with the Regulations of Other Countries in Specific Relations,

— in Ireland: the rules which enable jurisdiction to be founded on the document instituting the proceedings having been served on the defendant during his temporary presence in Ireland,

— in Italy: Articles 3 and 4 of Law 218 of 31 May 1995,

— in Cyprus: section 21(2) of the Courts of Justice Law No 14 of 1960, as amended,

— in Latvia: section 27 and paragraphs 3, 5, 6 and 9 of section 28 of the Civil Procedure Law (*Civilprocesa likums*),

— in Lithuania: Articles 783(3), 787 and 789(3) of the Code of Civil Procedure (*Civilinio proceso kodeksas*),

— in Luxembourg: Articles 14 and 15 of the civil code (*Code civil*),

— in Hungary: Article 57 of Law Decree No 13 of 1979 on International Private Law (*a nemzetközi magánjogról szóló 1979. évi 13. törvényerejű rendelet*),

— in Malta: Articles 742, 743 and 744 of the Code of Organisation and Civil Procedure — Cap. 12 (*Kodiċi ta' Organizzazzjoni u Proċedura Ċivili — Kap. 12*) and Article 549 of the Commercial Code — Cap. 13 (*Kodiċi tal-kummerċ — Kap. 13*),

— in Austria: Article 99 of the Law on court Jurisdiction (*Jurisdiktionsnorm*),

— in Poland: Article 1103 point 4 and Article 1110 of the Code of Civil Procedure (*Kodeks postępowania cywilnego*) in so far as the latter establishes jurisdiction exclusively on the basis of one of the following circumstances: the applicant is a Polish citizen or has their habitual residence, domicile or registered office in Poland,

— in Portugal: Article 63(1) of the Code of Civil Procedure (*Código de Processo Civil*) in so far as it may encompass exorbitant grounds of jurisdiction, such as the courts for the place in which the branch, agency or other establishment is situated (if situated in Portugal) when the central administration (if situated in a foreign State) is the party sued and Article 10 of the Code of Labour Procedure (*Código de Processo do Trabalho*) in so far as it may encompass exorbitant grounds of jurisdiction, such as the courts for the place where the plaintiff is domiciled in proceedings relating to individual contracts of employment brought by the employee against the employer,

— in Romania: Articles 1065-1081 under Title I 'International jurisdiction of Romanian courts' in Book VII 'International civil procedure' of Act No 134/2010 on the Code of Civil Procedure,

— in Slovenia: Article 48(2) of the Private International Law and Procedure Act (*Zakon o medarodnem zasebnem pravu in postopku*) in relation to Article 47(2) of Civil Procedure Act (*Zakon o pravdnem postopku*) and Article 58 of the Private International Law and Procedure Act (*Zakon o medarodnem zasebnem pravu in postopku*) in relation to Article 59 of Civil Procedure Act (*Zakon o pravdnem postopku*),

— in Slovakia: Articles 37 to 37e of Act No 97/1963 on Private International Law and the Rules of Procedure relating thereto,

— in Finland: paragraphs 1 and 2 of Section 18(1) of Chapter 10 of the Code of Judicial Procedure (*oikeudenkäymiskaari/rättegångsbalken*),

— in Sweden: the first sentence of the first paragraph of Section 3 of Chapter 10 of the Code of Judicial Procedure (*rättegångsbalken*),

— in the United Kingdom: the rules which enable jurisdiction to be founded on:

(a) the document instituting the proceedings having been served on the defendant during his temporary presence in the United Kingdom; or
(b) the presence within the United Kingdom of property belonging to the defendant; or
(c) the seizure by the plaintiff of property situated in the United Kingdom.

ANNEX II

III EUR [349]

The courts or competent authorities to which the application referred to in Article 39 may be submitted are the following:

— in Belgium, the 'tribunal de première instance' or '*rechtbank van eerste aanleg*' or '*erstinstanzliches Gericht*'

— in Bulgaria, the '*окръжния съд*',

— in the Czech Republic, the '*okresní soudy*',

— in Denmark, the '*byret*',

— in Germany,

(a) the presiding judge of a chamber of the '*Landgericht*',
(b) a notary in a procedure of declaration of enforceability of an authentic instrument,

— in Estonia, the '*maakohus*' (county court),

— in Greece, the 'Μονομελές Πρωτοδικείο',

— in Spain, the '*Juzgado de Primera Instancia*',

— in France:

(a) the '*greffier en chef du tribunal de grande instance*',
(b) the '*président de la chambre départementale des notaires*' in the case of application for a declaration of enforceability of a notarial authentic instrument,

— in Croatia, the '*općinski sudovi*' in civil matters, the '*Općinski građanski sud u Zagrebu*' and the '*trgovački sudovi*' in commercial matters,

— in Ireland, the High Court,

— in Italy, the '*corte d'appello*',

— in Cyprus, the 'Επαρχιακό Δικαστήριο' or in the case of a maintenance judgment the 'Οικογενειακό Δικαστήριο',

— in Latvia, the '*rajona (pilsētas) tiesa*',

— in Lithuania, the '*Lietuvos apeliacinis teismas*',

— in Luxembourg, the presiding judge of the '*tribunal d'arrondissement*',

— in Hungary, the '*törvényszék székhelyén működő járásbíróság*', and in Budapest the '*Budai Központi Kerületi Bíróság*',

— in Malta, the '*Prim' Awla tal-Qorti Ċivili*' or '*Qorti tal-Maġistrati ta' Għawdex fil-ġurisdizzjoni superjuri tagħha*', or, in the case of a maintenance judgment, the '*Reġistratur tal-Qorti*' on transmission by the '*Ministru responsabbli għall-Ġustizzja*',

— in the Netherlands, the '*voorzieningenrechter van de rechtbank*',

— in Austria, the '*Bezirksgericht*',

— in Poland, the '*sąd okręgowy*',

— in Portugal, the '*Tribunal de Comarca*',

— in Romania, the '*Tribunal*',

— in Slovenia, the '*okrožno sodišče*',

— in Slovakia, '*okresný súd*',

— in Finland, the '*käräjäoikeus/tingsrätt*',

— in Sweden, the '*Svea hovrätt*',

— in the United Kingdom:

(a) in England and Wales, the High Court of Justice, or in the case of a maintenance judgment, the Family Court on transmission by the Secretary of State;
(b) in Scotland, the Court of Session, or in the case of a maintenance judgment, the Sheriff Court on transmission by the Scottish Ministers;
(c) in Northern Ireland, the High Court of Justice, or in the case of a maintenance judgment, the Magistrates' Court on transmission by the Department of Justice;
(d) in Gibraltar, the Supreme Court of Gibraltar, or in the case of a maintenance judgment, the Magistrates' Court on transmission by the Attorney General of Gibraltar.

ANNEX III

III EUR [350]

The courts with which appeals referred to in Article 43 (2) may be lodged are the following:

— in Belgium,
(a) as regards appeal by the defendant, the '*tribunal de première instance*' or '*rechtbank van eerste aanleg*' or '*erstinstanzliche Gericht*',
(b) as regards appeal by the applicant, the '*Cour d'appel*' or '*hof van beroep*',

— in Bulgaria, the '*Апелативен съд — София*',

— in the Czech Republic, the '*okresní soudy*',

— in Denmark, the '*landsret*',

— in Germany, the '*Oberlandesgericht*',

— in Estonia, the '*ringkonnakohus*',

— in Greece the 'Εφετείο',

— in Spain, the '*Juzgado de Primera Instancia*' which issued the contested decision, with the appeal to be solved by the '*Audiencia Provincial*',

— in France:
(a) the '*cour d'appel*' on decisions allowing the application,
(b) the presiding judge of the '*tribunal de grande instance*', on decisions rejecting the application,

— in Croatia, '*županijski sud*' through '*općinski sud*' in civil matters and '*Visoki trgovački sud Republike Hrvatske*' through '*trgovački sud*' in commercial matters,

— in Ireland, the High Court,

— in Italy, the '*corte d'appello*',

— in Cyprus, the 'Επαρχιακό Δικαστήριο' or in the case of a maintenance judgment the 'Οικογενειακό Δικαστήριο',

— in Latvia, the '*apgabaltiesa*' via the '*rajona (pilsētas) tiesa*',

— in Lithuania, the '*Lietuvos apeliacinis teismas*',

— in Luxembourg, the '*Cour supérieure de justice*' sitting as a court of civil appeal,

— in Hungary, the '*törvényszék székhelyén működő járásbíróság*' (in Budapest, the '*Budai Központi Kerületi Bíróság*'); the appeal is adjudicated by the '*törvényszék*' (in Budapest, the '*Fővárosi Törvényszék*'),

— in Malta, the '*Qorti tal-Appell*' in accordance with the procedure laid down for appeals in the *Kodiċi ta' Organizzazzjoni u Proċedura Ċivili — Kap.12* or in the case of a maintenance judgment by '*ċitazzjoni*' before the '*Prim' Awla tal-Qorti Ċivili jew il-Qorti tal-Maġistrati ta' Għawdex fil-ġurisdizzjoni superjuri tagħha*",

— in the Netherlands, the '*rechtbank*',

— in Austria, the '*Landesgericht*' via the '*Bezirksgericht*',

— in Poland, the '*sąd apelacyjny*' via the '*sąd okręgowy*',

EUROPE

— in Portugal, the '*Tribunal da Relação*' is the competent court. The appeals are launched, in accordance with the national law in force, by way of a request addressed to the court which issued the contested decision,

— in Romania, the '*Curte de Apel*',

— in Slovenia, the '*okrožno sodišče*',

— in Slovakia, the court of appeal through the district court whose decision is being appealed,

— in Finland, the '*hovioikeus/hovrätt*',

— in Sweden, the '*Svea hovrätt*',

— in the United Kingdom:

(a) in England and Wales, the High Court of Justice, or in the case of a maintenance judgment, the Family Court;

(b) in Scotland, the Court of Session, or in the case of a maintenance judgment, the Sheriff Court;

(c) in Northern Ireland, the High Court of Justice, or in the case of a maintenance judgment, the Magistrates' Court;

(d) in Gibraltar, the Supreme Court of Gibraltar, of in the case of a maintenance judgment, the Magistrates' Court.

ANNEX IV

III EUR [351]

The appeals which may be lodged pursuant to Article 44 are the following:

— in Belgium, Greece, Spain, France, Italy, Luxembourg and the Netherlands, an appeal in cassation,

— in Bulgaria, '*обжалване пред Върховния касационен съд*',

— in the Czech Republic, appellate review ('*dovolání*'), action to re-open proceedings ('*žaloba na obnovu řízení*') and action in annulment ('*žaloba pro zmatečnost*'),

— in Denmark, an appeal to the '*Højesteret*' with leave from the '*Procesbevillingsnævnet*',

— in Germany, a '*Rechtsbeschwerde*',

— in Estonia, a '*kassatsioonikaebus*',

— in Croatia, an appeal to the '*Vrhovni sud Republike Hrvatske*',

— in Ireland, an appeal on a point of law to the Supreme Court,

— in Cyprus, an appeal to the Supreme Court,

— in Latvia, an appeal in cassation to the '*Augstākās tiesas Senātā*' via the '*apgabaltiesā*',

— in Lithuania, an appeal in cassation to the '*Lietuvos Aukščiausiasis Teismas*',

— in Hungary, '*felülvizsgálati kérelem*',

— in Malta, no further appeal lies to any other court; in the case of a maintenance judgment the '*Qorti tal-Appell*' in accordance with the procedure laid down for appeal in the '*kodiċi ta' Organizzazzjoni u Procedura Ċivili — Kap. 12*',

— in Austria, a '*Revisionsrekurs*',

— in Poland, '*skarga kasacyjna*',

— in Portugal, an appeal on a point of law,

— in Romania, a '*recursul*',

— in Slovenia, an appeal to the '*Vrhovno sodišče Republike Slovenije*',

— in Slovakia, the '*dovolanie*',

— in Finland, an appeal to the '*korkein oikeus/högsta domstolen*',

— in Sweden, an appeal to the '*Högsta domstolen*',

— in the United Kingdom, a single further appeal on a point of law.

ANNEX V

III EUR [352]

Certificate referred to in Articles 54 and 58 of the Regulation on judgments and court settlements

(English, inglés, anglais, inglese, . . .)

1. Member State of origin
2. Court or competent authority issuing the certificate
   2.1. Name
   2.2. Address
   2.3. Tel./fax/e-mail
3. Court which delivered the judgment/approved the court settlement(*)
   3.1. Type of court
   3.2. Place of court
4. Judgment/court settlement(*)
   4.1. Date
   4.2. Reference number
   4.3. The parties to the judgment/court settlement(*)
   4.3.1. Name(s) of plaintiff(s)
   4.3.2. Name(s) of defendant(s)
   4.3.3. Name(s) of other party(ies), if any
   4.4. Date of service of the document instituting the proceedings where judgment was given in default of appearance
   4.5. Text of the judgment/court settlement(*) as annexed to this certificate
5. Names of parties to whom legal aid has been granted

The judgment/court settlement(*) is enforceable in the Member State of origin (Articles 38 and 58 of the Regulation) against:

Name:

Done at . . . ., date . . . .

Signature and/or stamp . . . .

(*) Delete as appropriate.

ANNEX VI

III EUR [353]

Certificate referred to in Article 57(4) of the Regulation on authentic instruments

(English, inglés, anglais, inglese . . . .)

1. Member State of origin
2. Competent authority issuing the certificate
   2.1. Name
   2.2. Address
   2.3. Tel./fax/e-mail
3. Authority which has given authenticity to the instrument
   3.1. Authority involved in the drawing up of the authentic instrument (if applicable)
   3.1.1. Name and designation of authority
   3.1.2. Place of authority
   3.2. Authority which has registered the authentic instrument (if applicable)
   3.2.1. Type of authority
   3.2.2. Place of authority

4. Authentic instrument
   4.1. Description of the instrument
   4.2. Date
   4.2.1. on which the instrument was drawn up
   4.2.2. if different: on which the instrument was registered
   4.3. Reference number
   4.4. Parties to the instrument
   4.4.1. Name of the creditor
   4.4.2. Name of the debtor
5. Text of the enforceable obligation as annexed to this certificate

The authentic instrument is enforceable against the debtor in the Member State of origin (Article 57(1) of the Regulation)

Done at . . . ., date . . . .

Signature and/or stamp . . . .

COMMISSION REGULATION (EU) 2015/263 OF 16 JANUARY 2015 AMENDING ANNEXES I TO IV TO COUNCIL REGULATION (EC) NO 44/2001 ON JURISDICTION AND THE RECOGNITION AND ENFORCEMENT OF JUDGMENTS IN CIVIL AND COMMERCIAL MATTERS

GENERAL NOTE ON COMMISSION REGULATION (EU) No 2015/263

III EUR [354]

Since the Annexes to Regulation (EC) No 44/2001 were amended on several occasions and taking into account that Member States notified the Commission of additional amendments to the lists set out in Annexes I to IV after their last amendment in 2013, it was considered appropriate to publish consolidated versions of the lists contained in those Annexes. As such this amending Regulation, which also applies to the relations between the EU and Denmark, was adopted. It entered into force on 11 March 2015.

III EUR [355]

THE EUROPEAN COMMISSION,

Having regard to the Treaty on the Functioning of the European Union,

Having regard to Council Regulation (EC) No 44/2001 of 22 December 2000 on jurisdiction and the recognition and enforcement of judgments in civil and commercial matters[(1)], and in particular Article 74(1) thereof,

Whereas:

(1) Annex I to Regulation (EC) No 44/2001 lists the rules of national jurisdiction referred to in Articles 3(2) and 4(2) of the Regulation. Annex II contains the lists of courts or competent authorities that have jurisdiction in the Member States to deal with applications for a declaration of enforceability. Annex III lists the courts with which appeals may be lodged against decisions on a declaration of enforce-

ability, and Annex IV enumerates the final appeal procedures against such decisions,

(2) The Annexes of Regulation (EC) No 44/2001 have been amended on several occasions, most recently by Commission Regulation (EC) No 566/2013[2],

(3) Member States have notified the Commission of additional amendments to the lists set out in Annexes I to IV. It is therefore appropriate to publish consolidated versions of the lists contained in those Annexes,

(4) Pursuant to Article 2 of the Agreement between the European Community and the Kingdom of Denmark on jurisdiction and the recognition and enforcement of judgments in civil and commercial matters[3], this Regulation should, under international law, apply to the relations between the European Union and Denmark,

(5) Regulation (EC) No 44/2001 should therefore be amended accordingly,

---

1 OJ L 12, 16.1.2001, p. 1.

2 OJ L 167, 19.6.2013, p. 29.

3 OJ L 299, 16.11.2005, p. 62.

HAVE ADOPTED THIS REGULATION:

Article 1

III EUR [356]

Annexes I to IV to Regulation (EC) No 44/2001 are replaced by the text in the Annex to this Regulation.

Article 2

III EUR [357]

This Regulation shall enter into force on the 20th day following that of its publication in the *Official Journal of the European Union*.

This Regulation shall be binding in its entirety and directly applicable in the Member States in accordance with the Treaties.

Done at Brussels, 16 January 2015.

For the Commission
The President
Jean-Claude Juncker

ANNEX I

III EUR [358]

Rules of jurisdiction referred to in Article 3(2) and Article 4(2)

— in Bulgaria: Article 4, paragraph 1, point 2, of the Private International Law Code,

— in the Czech Republic: Act No 91/2012 on private international law, in particular, its Article 6,

— in Denmark: Article 246(2) and (3) of the Administration of Justice Act (*lov om rettens pleje*),

— in Germany: Article 23 of the code of civil procedure (*Zivilprozeßordnung*),

— in Estonia: Article 86 (jurisdiction at the location of property) of the Code of Civil Procedure (*Tsiviilkohtumenetluse seadustik*), insofar as the claim is unrelated to that property of the person; Article 100 (claim for termination of application of standard terms) of the Code of Civil Procedure, insofar as the action is to be lodged with the court in whose territorial jurisdiction the standard term was applied,

— in Greece: Article 40 of the code of civil procedure (Κώδικας Πολιτικής Δικονομίας),

— in France: Articles 14 and 15 of the civil code (*Code civil*),

— in Croatia: Article 54 of the Act on the Resolution of Conflicts of Laws with the Regulations of Other Countries in Specific Relations,

— in Ireland: the rules which enable jurisdiction to be founded on the document instituting the proceedings having been served on the defendant during his temporary presence in Ireland,

— in Italy: Articles 3 and 4 of Law 218 of 31 May 1995,

— in Cyprus: section 21(2) of the Courts of Justice Law No 14 of 1960, as amended,

— in Latvia: section 27 and paragraphs 3, 5, 6 and 9 of section 28 of the Civil Procedure Law (*Civilprocesa likums*),

— in Lithuania: Articles 783(3), 787 and 789(3) of the Code of Civil Procedure (*Civilinio proceso kodeksas*),

— in Luxembourg: Articles 14 and 15 of the civil code (*Code civil*),

— in Hungary: Article 57 of Law Decree No 13 of 1979 on International Private Law (*a nemzetközi magánjogról szóló 1979. évi 13. törvényerejű rendelet*),

— in Malta: Articles 742, 743 and 744 of the Code of Organisation and Civil Procedure — Cap. 12 (*Kodiċi ta' Organizzazzjoni u Proċedura Ċivili — Kap. 12*) and Article 549 of the Commercial Code — Cap. 13 (*Kodiċi tal-kummerċ — Kap. 13*),

— in Austria: Article 99 of the Law on court Jurisdiction (*Jurisdiktionsnorm*),

— in Poland: Article 1103 point 4 and Article 1110 of the Code of Civil Procedure (*Kodeks postępowania cywilnego*) in so far as the latter establishes jurisdiction exclusively on the basis of one of the following circumstances: the applicant is a Polish citizen or has their habitual residence, domicile or registered office in Poland,

— in Portugal: Article 63(1) of the Code of Civil Procedure (*Código de Processo Civil*) in so far as it may encompass exorbitant grounds of jurisdiction, such as the courts for the place in which the branch, agency or other establishment is situated (if situated in Portugal) when the central administration (if situated in a foreign State) is the party sued and Article 10 of the Code of Labour Procedure (*Código de Processo do Trabalho*) in so far as it may encompass exorbitant grounds of jurisdiction, such as the courts for the place where the plaintiff is domiciled in proceedings relating to individual contracts of employment brought by the employee against the employer,

— in Romania: Articles 1065-1081 under Title I 'International jurisdiction of Romanian courts' in Book VII 'International civil procedure' of Act No 134/2010 on the Code of Civil Procedure,

— in Slovenia: Article 48(2) of the Private International Law and Procedure Act (*Zakon o medarodnem zasebnem pravu in postopku*) in relation to Article 47(2) of Civil Procedure Act (*Zakon o pravdnem postopku*) and Article 58 of the Private International Law and Procedure Act (*Zakon o medarodnem zasebnem pravu in postopku*) in relation to Article 59 of Civil Procedure Act (*Zakon o pravdnem postopku*),

— in Slovakia: Articles 37 to 37e of Act No 97/1963 on Private International Law and the Rules of Procedure relating thereto,

— in Finland: paragraphs 1 and 2 of Section 18(1) of Chapter 10 of the Code of Judicial Procedure (*oikeudenkäymiskaari/rättegångsbalken*),

— in Sweden: the first sentence of the first paragraph of Section 3 of Chapter 10 of the Code of Judicial Procedure (*rättegångsbalken*),

— in the United Kingdom: the rules which enable jurisdiction to be founded on:
(a) the document instituting the proceedings having been served on the defendant during his temporary presence in the United Kingdom; or
(b) the presence within the United Kingdom of property belonging to the defendant; or
(c) the seizure by the plaintiff of property situated in the United Kingdom.

ANNEX II

III EUR [359]

The courts or competent authorities to which the application referred to in Article 39 may be submitted are the following:

— in Belgium, the 'tribunal de première instance' or '*rechtbank van eerste aanleg*' or '*erstinstanzliches Gericht*'

— in Bulgaria, the '*окръжния съд*',

— in the Czech Republic, the '*okresní soudy*',

— in Denmark, the '*byret*',

— in Germany,
(a) the presiding judge of a chamber of the '*Landgericht*',
(b) a notary in a procedure of declaration of enforceability of an authentic instrument,

— in Estonia, the '*maakohus*' (county court),

— in Greece, the 'Μονομελές Πρωτοδικείο',

— in Spain, the '*Juzgado de Primera Instancia*',

— in France:
(a) the '*greffier en chef du tribunal de grande instance*',
(b) the '*président de la chambre départementale des notaires*' in the case of application for a declaration of enforceability of a notarial authentic instrument,

— in Croatia, the '*općinski sudovi*' in civil matters, the '*Općinski građanski sud u Zagrebu*' and the '*trgovački sudovi*' in commercial matters,

— in Ireland, the High Court,

— in Italy, the '*corte d'appello*',

— in Cyprus, the 'Επαρχιακό Δικαστήριο' or in the case of a maintenance judgment the 'Οικογενειακό Δικαστήριο',

— in Latvia, the '*rajona (pilsētas) tiesa*',

— in Lithuania, the '*Lietuvos apeliacinis teismas*',

— in Luxembourg, the presiding judge of the '*tribunal d'arrondissement*',

— in Hungary, the '*törvényszék székhelyén működő járásbíróság*', and in Budapest the '*Budai Központi Kerületi Bíróság*',

— in Malta, the '*Prim' Awla tal-Qorti Ċivili*' or '*Qorti tal-Maġistrati ta' Għawdex fil-ġurisdizzjoni superjuri tagħha*', or, in the case of a maintenance judgment, the '*Reġistratur tal-Qorti*' on transmission by the '*Ministru responsabbli għall-Ġustizzja*',

— in the Netherlands, the '*voorzieningenrechter van de rechtbank*',

— in Austria, the '*Bezirksgericht*',

— in Poland, the '*sąd okręgowy*',

— in Portugal, the '*Tribunal de Comarca*',

— in Romania, the '*Tribunal*',

— in Slovenia, the '*okrožno sodišče*',

— in Slovakia, '*okresný súd*',

— in Finland, the '*käräjäoikeus/tingsrätt*',

— in Sweden, the '*Svea hovrätt*',

— in the United Kingdom:

(a) in England and Wales, the High Court of Justice, or in the case of a maintenance judgment, the Family Court on transmission by the Secretary of State;

(b) in Scotland, the Court of Session, or in the case of a maintenance judgment, the Sheriff Court on transmission by the Scottish Ministers;

(c) in Northern Ireland, the High Court of Justice, or in the case of a maintenance judgment, the Magistrates' Court on transmission by the Department of Justice;

(d) in Gibraltar, the Supreme Court of Gibraltar, or in the case of a maintenance judgment, the Magistrates' Court on transmission by the Attorney General of Gibraltar.

ANNEX III

III EUR [360]

The courts with which appeals referred to in Article 43 (2) may be lodged are the following:

— in Belgium,

(a) as regards appeal by the defendant, the '*tribunal de première instance*' or '*rechtbank van eerste aanleg*' or '*erstinstanzliche Gericht*',

(b) as regards appeal by the applicant, the '*Cour d'appel*' or '*hof van beroep*',

— in Bulgaria, the '*Апелативен съд — София*',

— in the Czech Republic, the '*okresní soudy*',

— in Denmark, the '*landsret*',

— in Germany, the '*Oberlandesgericht*',

— in Estonia, the '*ringkonnakohus*',

— in Greece the 'Εφετείο',

— in Spain, the '*Juzgado de Primera Instancia*' which issued the contested decision, with the appeal to be solved by the '*Audiencia Provincial*',

— in France:

(a) the '*cour d'appel*' on decisions allowing the application,

(b) the presiding judge of the '*tribunal de grande instance*', on decisions rejecting the application,

— in Croatia, '*županijski sud*' through '*općinski sud*' in civil matters and '*Visoki trgovački sud Republike Hrvatske*' through '*trgovački sud*' in commercial matters,

— in Ireland, the High Court,

— in Italy, the '*corte d'appello*',

— in Cyprus, the 'Επαρχιακό Δικαστήριο' or in the case of a maintenance judgment the 'Οικογενειακό Δικαστήριο',

— in Latvia, the '*apgabaltiesa*' via the '*rajona (pilsētas) tiesa*',

— in Lithuania, the '*Lietuvos apeliacinis teismas*',

— in Luxembourg, the '*Cour supérieure de justice*' sitting as a court of civil appeal,

— in Hungary, the '*törvényszék székhelyén működő járásbíróság*' (in Budapest, the '*Budai Központi Kerületi Bíróság*'); the appeal is adjudicated by the '*törvényszék*' (in Budapest, the '*Fővárosi Törvényszék*'),

— in Malta, the '*Qorti tal-Appell*' in accordance with the procedure laid down for appeals in the *Kodiċi ta' Organizzazzjoni u Proċedura Ċivili — Kap.12* or in the case of a maintenance judgment by '*ċitazzjoni*' before the '*Prim' Awla tal-Qorti Ċivili jew il-Qorti tal-Maġistrati ta' Għawdex fil-ġurisdizzjoni superjuri tagħha*'',

— in the Netherlands, the '*rechtbank*',

— in Austria, the '*Landesgericht*' via the '*Bezirksgericht*',
— in Poland, the '*sąd apelacyjny*' via the '*sąd okręgowy*',
— in Portugal, the '*Tribunal da Relação*' is the competent court. The appeals are launched, in accordance with the national law in force, by way of a request addressed to the court which issued the contested decision,
— in Romania, the '*Curte de Apel*',
— in Slovenia, the '*okrožno sodišče*',
— in Slovakia, the court of appeal through the district court whose decision is being appealed,
— in Finland, the '*hovioikeus/hovrätt*',
— in Sweden, the '*Svea hovrätt*',
— in the United Kingdom:

(a) in England and Wales, the High Court of Justice, or in the case of a maintenance judgment, the Family Court;

(b) in Scotland, the Court of Session, or in the case of a maintenance judgment, the Sheriff Court;

(c) in Northern Ireland, the High Court of Justice, or in the case of a maintenance judgment, the Magistrates' Court;

(d) in Gibraltar, the Supreme Court of Gibraltar, of in the case of a maintenance judgment, the Magistrates' Court.

ANNEX IV

III EUR [361]

The appeals which may be lodged pursuant to Article 44 are the following:
— in Belgium, Greece, Spain, France, Italy, Luxembourg and the Netherlands, an appeal in cassation,
— in Bulgaria, '*обжалване пред Върховния касационен съд*',
— in the Czech Republic, appellate review ('*dovolání*'), action to re-open proceedings ('*žaloba na obnovu řízení*') and action in annulment ('*žaloba pro zmatečnost*'),
— in Denmark, an appeal to the '*Højesteret*' with leave from the '*Procesbevillingsnævnet*',
— in Germany, a '*Rechtsbeschwerde*',
— in Estonia, a '*kassatsioonikaebus*',
— in Croatia, an appeal to the '*Vrhovni sud Republike Hrvatske*',
— in Ireland, an appeal on a point of law to the Supreme Court,
— in Cyprus, an appeal to the Supreme Court,
— in Latvia, an appeal in cassation to the '*Augstākās tiesas Senātā*' via the '*apgabaltiesā*',
— in Lithuania, an appeal in cassation to the '*Lietuvos Aukščiausiasis Teismas*',
— in Hungary, '*felülvizsgálati kérelem*',
— in Malta, no further appeal lies to any other court; in the case of a maintenance judgment the '*Qorti tal-Appell*' in accordance with the procedure laid down for appeal in the '*kodiċi ta' Organizzazzjoni u Procedura Ċivili — Kap. 12*',
— in Austria, a '*Revisionsrekurs*',
— in Poland, '*skarga kasacyjna*',
— in Portugal, an appeal on a point of law,
— in Romania, a '*recursul*',
— in Slovenia, an appeal to the '*Vrhovno sodišče Republike Slovenije*',
— in Slovakia, the '*dovolanie*',
— in Finland, an appeal to the '*korkein oikeus/högsta domstolen*',
— in Sweden, an appeal to the '*Högsta domstolen*',

— in the United Kingdom, a single further appeal on a point of law.

REGULATION (EU) NO 606/2013 OF THE EUROPEAN PARLIAMENT AND OF THE COUNCIL OF 12 JUNE 2013 ON MUTUAL RECOGNITION OF PROTECTION MEASURES IN CIVIL MATTERS

GENERAL NOTE ON REGULATION (EU) No 606/2013

III EUR [362]

This Regulation aim is to provide for the enforcement in a Member State of a protection measure granted to an individual in civil litigation in another Member State. The Civil Jurisdiction and Judgments (Protection Measures) Regulations 2014, SI 2014/3298 made provision to facilitate its application in the UK from 11 January 2015. Regulation 3 specifies the family court, the county court and the High Court as the enforcing courts within England and Wales and for appeals from a decision of a court of summary jurisdiction to be made to the county court and from the county court to the High Court.

The procedure for certifying outgoing protection measures and for enforcing incoming protection measures is set out in CPR Part 74 as Section VI Recognition and enforcement of protection measures, starting at **CPR 74.34**. Note in particular the rules on applying for an article 5 certificate for an outgoing protection measure and requests for a translation, service requirements, rectification and withdrawal: **CPR 74.34** to **CPR 74.43**. Applications for an article 14 certificate are dealt with in **CPR 74.44** and **CPR 74.45**. The remaining rules provide for the enforcement of incoming protection measures, adjustments under article 11, applications for the refusal of recognition or enforcement under article 13 and, applications under article 14(2) for suspension or withdrawal.

III EUR [363]

THE EUROPEAN PARLIAMENT AND THE COUNCIL OF THE EUROPEAN UNION,

Having regard to the Treaty on the Functioning of the European Union, and in particular points (a), (c) and (e) of Article 81(2) thereof,

Having regard to the proposal from the European Commission,

After transmission of the draft legislative act to the national parliaments,

Having regard to the opinion of the European Economic and Social Committee,

Having regard to the opinion of the Committee of the Regions[(1)],

Acting in accordance with the ordinary legislative procedure[(2)],

Whereas:

(1) The Union has set itself the objective of maintaining and developing an area of freedom, security and justice in which the free movement of persons is ensured and access to justice is facilitated, in particular through the principle of mutual recognition of judicial and extrajudicial decisions in civil matters. For the gradual establishment of such an area, the Union is to adopt measures relating to judicial cooperation in civil matters having cross-border implications, particularly when necessary for the proper functioning of the internal market.

(2) Article 81(1) of the Treaty on the Functioning of the European Union (TFEU) provides that judicial cooperation in civil matters having cross-border implications is to be based on the principle of mutual recognition of judgments and of decisions in extrajudicial cases.

(3) In a common area of justice without internal borders, provisions to ensure rapid and simple recognition and, where applicable, enforcement in another Member State of protection measures ordered in a Member State are essential to

ensure that the protection afforded to a natural person in one Member State is maintained and continued in any other Member State to which that person travels or moves. It is necessary to ensure that the legitimate exercise by citizens of the Union of their right to move and reside freely within the territory of Member States, in accordance with Article 3(2) of the Treaty on European Union (TEU) and Article 21 TFEU, does not result in a loss of that protection.

(4) Mutual trust in the administration of justice in the Union and the aim of ensuring quicker and less costly circulation of protection measures within the Union justify the principle according to which protection measures ordered in one Member State are recognised in all other Member States without any special procedure being required. As a result, a protection measure ordered in one Member State ('Member State of origin') should be treated as if it had been ordered in the Member State where its recognition is sought ('Member State addressed').

(5) In order to attain the objective of free movement of protection measures, it is necessary and appropriate that the rules governing the recognition and, where applicable, enforcement of protection measures be governed by a legal instrument of the Union which is binding and directly applicable.

(6) This Regulation should apply to protection measures ordered with a view to protecting a person where there exist serious grounds for considering that that person's life, physical or psychological integrity, personal liberty, security or sexual integrity is at risk, for example so as to prevent any form of gender-based violence or violence in close relationships such as physical violence, harassment, sexual aggression, stalking, intimidation or other forms of indirect coercion. It is important to underline that this Regulation applies to all victims, regardless of whether they are victims of gender-based violence.

(7) Directive 2012/29/EU of the European Parliament and of the Council of 25 October 2012 establishing minimum standards on the rights, support and protection of victims of crime[3] ensures that victims of crime receive appropriate information and support.

(8) This Regulation complements Directive 2012/29/EU. The fact that a person is the object of a protection measure ordered in civil matters does not necessarily preclude that person from being defined as a 'victim' under that Directive.

(9) The scope of this Regulation is within the field of judicial cooperation in civil matters within the meaning of Article 81 TFEU. This Regulation applies only to protection measures ordered in civil matters. Protection measures adopted in criminal matters are covered by Directive 2011/99/EU of the European Parliament and of the Council of 13 December 2011 on the European Protection Order[4].

(10) The notion of civil matters should be interpreted autonomously, in accordance with the principles of Union law. The civil, administrative or criminal nature of the authority ordering a protection measure should not be determinative for the purpose of assessing the civil character of a protection measure.

(11) This Regulation should not interfere with the functioning of Council Regulation (EC) No 2201/2003 of 27 November 2003 concerning jurisdiction and the recognition and enforcement of judgments in matrimonial matters and the matters of parental responsibility[5] ('Brussels IIa Regulation'). Decisions taken under the Brussels IIa Regulation should continue to be recognised and enforced under that Regulation.

(12) This Regulation takes account of the different legal traditions of the Member States and does not interfere with the national systems for ordering protection measures. This Regulation does not oblige the Member States to modify their national systems so as to enable protection measures to be ordered in civil matters, or to introduce protection measures in civil matters for the application of this Regulation.

(13) In order to take account of the various types of authorities which order protection measures in civil matters in the Member States, and unlike in other areas of judicial cooperation, this Regulation should apply to decisions of both judicial authorities and administrative authorities provided that the latter offer guarantees with regard, in particular, to their impartiality and to the right of the parties to judicial review. In no event should police authorities be considered as issuing authorities within the meaning of this Regulation.

(14) Based on the principle of mutual recognition, protection measures ordered in civil matters in the Member State of origin should be recognised in the Member State addressed as protection measures in civil matters in accordance with this Regulation.

(15) According to the principle of mutual recognition, the recognition corresponds to the duration of the protection measure. However, taking into account the diversity of protection measures under the laws of the Member States, in particular in terms of their duration, and the fact that this Regulation will typically apply in urgent situations, the effects of recognition under this Regulation should, by way of exception, be limited to a period of 12 months from the issuing of the certificate provided for by this Regulation, irrespective of whether the protection measure itself (be it provisional, time- limited or indefinite in nature) has a longer duration.

(16) In cases where the duration of a protection measure is greater than 12 months, the limitation of the effects of recognition under this Regulation should be without prejudice to the right of the protected person to invoke that protection measure under any other available legal act of the Union providing for recognition or to apply for a national protection measure in the Member State addressed.

(17) The limitation of the effects of recognition is exceptional due to the special nature of the subject matter of this Regulation and should not serve as a precedent for other instruments in civil and commercial matters.

(18) This Regulation should deal only with the recognition of the obligation imposed by the protection measure. It should not regulate the procedures for implementation or enforcement of the protection measure, nor should it cover any potential sanctions that might be imposed if the obligation ordered by the protection measure is infringed in the Member State addressed. Those matters are left to the law of that Member State. However, in accordance with the general principles of Union law and particularly the principle of mutual recognition, Member States are to ensure that protection measures recognised under this Regulation can take effect in the Member State addressed.

(19) Protection measures covered by this Regulation should afford protection to the protected person at his or her place of residence or place of work, or at another place which that person visits on a regular basis, such as the residence of close relatives or the school or educational establishment attended by his or her child. Irrespective of whether the place in question or the extent of the area covered by the protection measure is described in the protection measure by one or more specific addresses or by reference to a circumscribed area which the person causing the risk may not approach or enter, respectively (or a combination of the two), the recognition of the obligation imposed by the protection measure relates to the purpose which the place serves for the protected person rather than to the specific address.

(20) In the light of the foregoing and provided that the nature and the essential elements of the protection measure are maintained, the competent authority of the Member State addressed should be allowed to adjust the factual elements of the protection measure where such adjustment is necessary in order for the recognition of the protection measure to be effective in practical terms in the Member State addressed. Factual elements include the address, the general location or the minimum distance the person causing the risk must keep from the protected person, the address or the general location. However, the type and the civil nature of the protection measure may not be affected by such adjustment.

(21) In order to facilitate any adjustment of a protection measure, the certificate should indicate whether the address specified in the protection measure constitutes the place of residence, the place of work or a place that the protected person visits on a regular basis. Furthermore, if relevant, the circumscribed area (approximate radius from the specific address) to which the obligation imposed by the protection measure on the person causing the risk applies should also be indicated in the certificate.

(22) In order to facilitate the free movement of protection measures within the Union, this Regulation should introduce a uniform model of certificate and provide for the establishment of a multilingual standard form for that purpose. The issuing authority should issue the certificate upon request by the protected person.

(23) Free text fields in the multilingual standard form for the certificate should be as limited as possible, so that translation or transliteration may be provided in most cases without imposing any costs on the protected person by making use of the standard form in the relevant language. Any costs for necessary translation that goes beyond the text of the multilingual standard form are to be allocated as provided under the law of the Member State of origin.

(24) Where a certificate contains free text, the competent authority of the Member State addressed should determine whether any translation or transliteration is required. This should not preclude the protected person or the issuing authority of the Member State of origin from providing a translation or transliteration on their own initiative.

(25) To ensure respect for the rights of defence of the person causing the risk, where the protection measure was ordered in default of appearance or under a procedure that does not provide for prior notice to that person ('*ex- parte* proceeding'), the issue of the certificate should only be possible if that person has had the opportunity to arrange for his or her defence against the protection measure. However, with a view to avoiding circumvention and taking into account the typical urgency of cases necessitating protection measures, it should not be required that the period for raising such defence has expired before a certificate may be issued. The certificate should be issued as soon as the protection measure is enforceable in the Member State of origin.

(26) Having regard to the objectives of simplicity and speed, this Regulation provides for simple and quick methods to be used for bringing procedural steps to the notice of the person causing the risk. Those specific methods of notification should apply only for the purposes of this Regulation due to the special nature of its subject matter, should not serve as a precedent for other instruments in civil and commercial matters and should not affect any obligations of a Member State concerning the service abroad of judicial and extrajudicial documents in civil matters arising from a bilateral or multilateral convention concluded between that Member State and a third country.

(27) When the certificate is brought to the notice of the person causing the risk and also when any adjustment is made to any factual elements of a protection measure in the Member State addressed, due regard should be paid to the interest of the protected person in not having his or her whereabouts or other contact details disclosed. Such details should not be disclosed to the person causing the risk unless such disclosure is necessary for compliance with, or the enforcement of, the protection measure.

(28) The issuing of the certificate should not be subject to appeal.

(29) The certificate should be rectified where, due to an obvious error or inaccuracy, such as a typing error or an error of transcription or copying, the certificate does not correctly reflect the protection measure, or should be withdrawn if it was clearly wrongly granted, for example where it was used for a measure that falls outside the scope of this Regulation or where it was issued in breach of the requirements for its issuing.

(30) The issuing authority of the Member State of origin should, upon request, assist the protected person in obtaining information on the authorities of the Member State addressed before which the protection measure is to be invoked or enforcement is to be sought.

(31) The harmonious functioning of justice requires that irreconcilable decisions should not be delivered in two Member States. To that end, this Regulation should provide for a ground for refusal of recognition or enforcement of the protection measure in cases of irreconcilability with a judgment given or recognised in the Member State addressed.

(32) Public interest considerations may, in exceptional circumstances, justify a refusal by the court of the Member State addressed to recognise or enforce a protection measure where its application would be manifestly incompatible with the public policy of that Member State. However, the court should not be able to apply the public-policy exception in order to refuse recognition or enforcement of

EUROPE

a protection measure when to do so would be contrary to the rights set out in the Charter of Fundamental Rights of the European Union, and in particular Article 21 thereof.

(33) In the event of suspension or withdrawal of the protection measure or withdrawal of the certificate in the Member State of origin, the competent authority of the Member State addressed should, upon submission of the relevant certificate, suspend or withdraw the effects of recognition and, where applicable, the enforcement of the protection measure.

(34) A protected person should have effective access to justice in other Member States. To ensure such effective access in procedures covered by this Regulation, legal aid is to be provided in accordance with Council Directive 2003/8/EC of 27 January 2003 to improve access to justice in cross-border disputes by establishing minimum common rules relating to legal aid for such disputes[(6)].

(35) In order to facilitate the application of this Regulation, Member States should be required to provide certain information regarding their national rules and procedures concerning protection measures in civil matters within the framework of the European Judicial Network in civil and commercial matters established by Council Decision 2001/470/EC[(7)]. Access to the information provided by the Member States should be made available through the European e-Justice Portal.

(36) In order to ensure uniform conditions for the implementation of this Regulation, implementing powers should be conferred on the Commission with regard to the establishment and subsequent amendment of the forms provided for in this Regulation. Those powers should be exercised in accordance with Regulation (EU) No 182/2011 of the European Parliament and of the Council of 16 February 2011 laying down the rules and general principles concerning mechanisms for control by Member States of the Commission's exercise of implementing powers[(8)].

(37) The examination procedure should be used for the adoption of implementing acts establishing and subsequently amending the forms provided for in this Regulation.

(38) This Regulation respects the fundamental rights and observes the principles recognised in the Charter of Fundamental Rights of the European Union. In particular, it seeks to ensure the rights of the defence and fair trial, as established in Articles 47 and 48 thereof. This Regulation should be applied according to those rights and principles.

(39) Since the objective of this Regulation, namely to establish rules for a simple and rapid mechanism for the recognition of protection measures ordered in a Member State in civil matters, cannot be sufficiently achieved by the Member States and can therefore be better achieved at Union level, the Union may adopt measures, in accordance with the principle of subsidiarity as set out in Article 5 TEU. In accordance with the principle of proportionality, as set out in that Article, this Regulation does not go beyond what is necessary in order to achieve that objective.

(40) In accordance with Article 3 of Protocol No 21 on the position of the United Kingdom and Ireland in respect of the Area of Freedom, Security and Justice, annexed to the TEU and to the TFEU, those Member States have notified their wish to take part in the adoption and application of this Regulation.

(41) In accordance with Articles 1 and 2 of Protocol No 22 on the position of Denmark, annexed to the TEU and to the TFEU, Denmark is not taking part in the adoption of this Regulation and is not bound by it or subject to its application.

(42) The European Data Protection Supervisor delivered an opinion on 17 October 2011[(9)], based on Article 41(2) of Regulation (EC) No 45/2001 of the European Parliament and of the Council of 18 December 2000 on the protection of individuals with regard to the processing of personal data by the Community institutions and bodies and on the free movement of such data[(10)],

1 OJ C 113, 18.4.2012, p. 56.

2 Position of the European Parliament of 22 May 2013 (not yet published in the Official Journal) and decision of the Council of 6 June 2013.

[3] OJ L 315, 14.11.2012, p. 57.
[4] OJ L 338, 21.12.2011, p. 2.
[5] OJ L 338, 23.12.2003, p. 1.
[6] OJ L 26, 31.1.2003, p. 41.
[7] OJ L 174, 27.6.2001, p. 25.
[8] OJ L 55, 28.2.2011, p. 13.
[9] OJ C 35, 9.2.2012, p. 10.
[10] OJ L 8, 12.1.2001, p. 1.

HAVE ADOPTED THIS REGULATION:

CHAPTER I
SUBJECT MATTER, SCOPE AND DEFINITIONS

Article 1 Subject matter

III EUR [364]

This Regulation establishes rules for a simple and rapid mechanism for the recognition of protection measures ordered in a Member State in civil matters.

Article 2 Scope

III EUR [365]

1. This Regulation shall apply to protection measures in civil matters ordered by an issuing authority within the meaning of point (4) of Article 3.
2. This Regulation shall apply to cross-border cases. For the purposes of this Regulation, a case shall be deemed to be a cross-border case where the recognition of a protection measure ordered in one Member State is sought in another Member State.
3. This Regulation shall not apply to protection measures falling within the scope of Regulation (EC) No 2201/2003.

Article 3 Definitions

III EUR [366]

For the purposes of this Regulation, the following definitions shall apply:

(1) 'protection measure' means any decision, whatever it may be called, ordered by the issuing authority of the Member State of origin in accordance with its national law and imposing one or more of the following obligations on the person causing the risk with a view to protecting another person, when the latter person's physical or psychological integrity may be at risk:

(a) a prohibition or regulation on entering the place where the protected person resides, works, or regularly visits or stays;
(b) a prohibition or regulation of contact, in any form, with the protected person, including by telephone, electronic or ordinary mail, fax or any other means;
(c) a prohibition or regulation on approaching the protected person closer than a prescribed distance;

(2) 'protected person' means a natural person who is the object of the protection afforded by a protection measure;

(3) 'person causing the risk' means a natural person on whom one or more of the obligations referred to in point (1) have been imposed;

(4) 'issuing authority' means any judicial authority, or any other authority designated by a Member State as having competence in the matters falling within the scope of this Regulation, provided that such other authority offers guarantees to the parties with regard to impartiality, and that its decisions in relation to the protection measure may, under the law of the Member State in which it operates, be made subject to review by a judicial authority and have similar force and effects to those of a decision of a judicial authority on the same matter;
(5) 'Member State of origin' means the Member State in which the protection measure is ordered;
(6) 'Member State addressed' means the Member State in which the recognition and, where applicable, the enforcement of the protection measure is sought.

CHAPTER II
RECOGNITION AND ENFORCEMENT OF PROTECTION MEASURES

Article 4 Recognition and enforcement

III EUR [367]

1. A protection measure ordered in a Member State shall be recognised in the other Member States without any special procedure being required and shall be enforceable without a declaration of enforceability being required.
2. A protected person who wishes to invoke in the Member State addressed a protection measure ordered in the Member State of origin shall provide the competent authority of the Member State addressed with:
   (a) a copy of the protection measure which satisfies the conditions necessary to establish its authenticity;
   (b) the certificate issued in the Member State of origin pursuant to Article 5; and
   (c) where necessary, a transliteration and/or a translation of the certificate in accordance with Article 16.
3. The certificate shall take effect only within the limits of the enforceability of the protection measure.
4. Irrespective of whether the protection measure has a longer duration, the effects of recognition pursuant to paragraph 1 shall be limited to a period of 12 months, starting from the date of the issuing of the certificate.
5. The procedure for the enforcement of protection measures shall be governed by the law of the Member State addressed.

Article 5 Certificate

III EUR [368]

1. The issuing authority of the Member State of origin shall, upon request by the protected person, issue the certificate using the multilingual standard form established in accordance with Article 19 and containing the information provided for in Article 7.
2. No appeal shall lie against the issuing of the certificate.
3. Upon request by the protected person, the issuing authority of the Member State of origin shall provide the protected person with a transliteration and/or a translation of the certificate by making use of the multilingual standard form established in accordance with Article 19.

Article 6 Requirements for the issuing of the certificate

III EUR [369]

1. The certificate may only be issued if the protection measure has been brought to the notice of the person causing the risk in accordance with the law of the Member State of origin.
2. Where the protection measure was ordered in default of appearance, the certificate may only be issued if the person causing the risk had been served with the document which instituted the proceeding or an equivalent document or, where relevant, had been otherwise informed of the initiation of the proceeding in accordance with the law of the Member State of origin in sufficient time and in such a way as to enable that person to arrange for his or her defence.
3. Where the protection measure was ordered under a procedure that does not provide for prior notice to be given to the person causing the risk ('ex-parte proceeding'), the certificate may only be issued if that person had the right to challenge the protection measure under the law of the Member State of origin.

Article 7 Contents of the certificate

III EUR [370]

The certificate shall contain the following information:

(a) the name and address/contact details of the issuing authority;
(b) the reference number of the file;
(c) the date of issue of the certificate;
(d) details concerning the protected person: name, date and place of birth, where available, and an address to be used for notification purposes, preceded by a conspicuous warning that that address may be disclosed to the person causing the risk;
(e) details concerning the person causing the risk: name, date and place of birth, where available, and address to be used for notification purposes;
(f) all information necessary for enforcement of the protection measure, including, where applicable, the type of the measure and the obligation imposed by it on the person causing the risk and specifying the function of the place and/or the circumscribed area which that person is prohibited from approaching or entering, respectively;
(g) the duration of the protection measure;
(h) the duration of the effects of recognition pursuant to Article 4(4);
(i) a declaration that the requirements laid down in Article 6 have been met;
(j) information on the rights granted under Articles 9 and 13;
(k) for ease of reference, the full title of this Regulation.

Article 8 Notification of the certificate to the person causing the risk

III EUR [371]

1. The issuing authority of the Member State of origin shall bring to the notice of the person causing the risk the certificate and the fact that the issuing of the certificate results in the recognition and, where applicable, in the enforceability of the protection measure in all Member States pursuant to Article 4.
2. Where the person causing the risk resides in the Member State of origin, the notification shall be effected in accordance with the law of that Member State. Where the person causing the risk resides in a Member State other than the Member State of origin

or in a third country, the notification shall be effected by registered letter with acknowledgment of receipt or equivalent.

Situations in which the address of the person causing the risk is not known or in which that person refuses to accept receipt of the notification shall be governed by the law of the Member State of origin.

3. The whereabouts or other contact details of the protected person shall not be disclosed to the person causing the risk unless their disclosure is necessary for compliance with, or the enforcement of, the protection measure.

Article 9 Rectification or withdrawal of the certificate

III EUR [372]

1. Without prejudice to Article 5(2) and upon request by the protected person or the person causing the risk to the issuing authority of the Member State of origin or on that authority's own initiative, the certificate shall be:

(a) rectified where, due to a clerical error, there is a discrepancy between the protection measure and the certificate; or

(b) withdrawn where it was clearly wrongly granted, having regard to the requirements laid down in Article 6 and the scope of this Regulation.

2. The procedure, including any appeal, with regard to the rectification or withdrawal of the certificate shall be governed by the law of the Member State of origin.

Article 10 Assistance to the protected person

III EUR [373]

Upon request by the protected person, the issuing authority of the Member State of origin shall assist that person in obtaining information, as made available in accordance with Articles 17 and 18, concerning the authorities of the Member State addressed before which the protection measure is to be invoked or enforcement is to be sought.

Article 11 Adjustment of the protection measure

III EUR [374]

1. The competent authority of the Member State addressed shall, where and to the extent necessary, adjust the factual elements of the protection measure in order to give effect to the protection measure in that Member State.

2. The procedure for the adjustment of the protection measure shall be governed by the law of the Member State addressed.

3. The adjustment of the protection measure shall be brought to the notice of the person causing the risk.

4. Where the person causing the risk resides in the Member State addressed, the notification shall be effected in accordance with the law of that Member State. Where the person causing the risk resides in a Member State other than the Member State addressed or in a third country, the notification shall be effected by registered letter with acknowledgment of receipt or equivalent.

Situations in which the address of the person causing the risk is not known or in which that person refuses to accept receipt of the notification shall be governed by the law of the Member State addressed.

5. An appeal against the adjustment of the protection measure may be lodged by the protected person or the person causing the risk. The appeal procedure shall be governed by the law of the Member State addressed. However, the lodging of an appeal shall not have suspensive effect.

Article 12 No review as to substance

III EUR [375]

Under no circumstances may a protection measure ordered in the Member State of origin be reviewed as to its substance in the Member State addressed.

Article 13 Refusal of recognition or enforcement

III EUR [376]

1. The recognition and, where applicable, the enforcement of the protection measure shall be refused, upon application by the person causing the risk, to the extent such recognition is:

(a) manifestly contrary to public policy in the Member State addressed; or

(b) irreconcilable with a judgment given or recognised in the Member State addressed.

2. The application for refusal of recognition or enforcement shall be submitted to the court of the Member State addressed as communicated by that Member State to the Commission in accordance with point (a)(iv) of Article 18(1).

3. The recognition of the protection measure may not be refused on the ground that the law of the Member State addressed does not allow for such a measure based on the same facts.

Article 14 Suspension or withdrawal of recognition or enforcement

III EUR [377]

1. In the event of suspension or withdrawal of the protection measure in the Member State of origin, suspension or limitation of its enforceability, or withdrawal of the certificate in accordance with point (b) of Article 9(1), the issuing authority of the Member State of origin shall, upon request by the protected person or the person causing the risk, issue a certificate indicating that suspension, limitation or withdrawal using the multilingual standard form established in accordance with Article 19.

2. Upon submission by the protected person or the person causing the risk of the certificate issued in accordance with paragraph 1, the competent authority of the Member State addressed shall suspend or withdraw the effects of the recognition and, where applicable, the enforcement of the protection measure.

CHAPTER III
GENERAL AND FINAL PROVISIONS

Article 15 Legalisation and other similar formalities

III EUR [378]

No legalisation or other similar formality shall be required for documents issued in a Member State in the context of this Regulation.

Article 16 Transliteration or translation

III EUR [379]

1. Any transliteration or translation required under this Regulation shall be into the official language or one of the official languages of the Member State addressed or into any other official language of the institutions of the Union which that Member State has indicated it can accept.
2. Subject to Article 5(3), any translation under this Regulation shall be done by a person qualified to do translations in one of the Member States.

Article 17 Information made available to the public

III EUR [380]

The Member States shall provide, within the framework of the European Judicial Network in civil and commercial matters established by Decision 2001/470/EC and with a view to making the information available to the public, a description of the national rules and procedures concerning protection measures in civil matters, including information on the type of authorities which are competent in the matters falling within the scope of this Regulation.
The Member States shall keep that information updated.

Article 18 Communication of information by the Member States

III EUR [381]

1. By 11 July 2014, Member States shall communicate to the Commission the following information:
   (a) the type of authorities which are competent in the matters falling within the scope of this Regulation, specifying, where applicable:
      (i) the authorities which are competent to order protection measures and issue certificates in accordance with Article 5;
      (ii) the authorities before which a protection measure ordered in another Member State is to be invoked and/or which are competent to enforce such a measure;
      (iii) the authorities which are competent to effect the adjustment of protection measures in accordance with Article 11(1);
      (iv) the courts to which the application for refusal of recognition and, where applicable, enforcement is to be submitted in accordance with Article 13;
   (b) the language or languages accepted for translations as referred to in Article 16(1).
2. The Commission shall make the information referred to in paragraph 1 available to the public through any appropriate means, in particular through the website of the European Judicial Network in civil and commercial matters.

Article 19 Establishment and subsequent amendment of the forms

III EUR [382]

The Commission shall adopt implementing acts establishing and subsequently amending the forms referred to in Articles 5 and 14. Those implementing acts shall be adopted in accordance with the examination procedure referred to in Article 20.

Article 20 Committee procedure

III EUR [383]

1. The Commission shall be assisted by a committee. That committee shall be a committee within the meaning of Regulation (EU) No 182/2011.
2. Where reference is made to this paragraph, Article 5 of Regulation (EU) No 182/2011 shall apply.

Article 21 Review

III EUR [384]

By 11 January 2020, the Commission shall submit to the European Parliament, the Council and the European Economic and Social Committee a report on the application of this Regulation. If necessary, the report shall be accompanied by proposals for amendments.

Article 22 Entry into force

III EUR [385]

This Regulation shall enter into force on the twentieth day following that of its publication in the *Official Journal of the European Union*.
It shall apply from 11 January 2015.
This Regulation shall apply to protection measures ordered on or after 11 January 2015, irrespective of when proceedings have been instituted.
This Regulation shall be binding in its entirety and directly applicable in the Member States in accordance with the Treaties.

Done at Strasbourg, 12 June 2013.
For the European Parliament
The President
M. Schulz
For the Council
The President
L Creighton

UK LEGISLATION

III EUR [386]

General Notes on UK legislation EU law, as in the EU Treaties and secondary legislation adopted by the EU institutions, sometimes requires *per se* to be incorporated in the legal orders of the Member States eg Directives. But some instruments, notably those that created the new legal system ie the EU Treaties and their amendments, are left to be dealt with in accordance with international law and the constitutional requirements of the Member States' legal systems. In the UK, following the decision to accede to the European Communities (now EU) and signature of the Accession Treaty (EU Treaty signed when a State becomes a Member State by which it accepts the existing EU acquis and signed by the presidents of some EU institutions and the Heads of State or Government of the existing and new Member States) an Act of Parliament was required to internalise the EU Treaties. This was done via the European Communities Act 1972. The Act has been subsequently amended to incorporate each amendment to the EU Treaties – following signature by the UK Government – so as to give effect to those amendments in the UK legal order. The Act has also been amended in other numerous occasions to reflect changes in UK law alone eg European Union Act 2011 (c 12) which covers steps to follow in case the EU Treaties are amended in the future, etc. This section covers the main UK legislation that you need to look at and apply when dealing with cases with an EU connection.

EUROPE

III EUR [386A]

Brexit: state of play (see also 'Introduction' at para III EUR [0]) Following the EU Referendum of June 2016 by which the UK voted to leave the EU and the activation of article 50 TEU on 29 March 2017 – which set as departure date of the UK from the EU 29 March 2019 – the standing of EU law post-Brexit was assessed. In particular, the survival of EU law in the UK and the necessary repeal of the ECA 1972. Those main subjects are the core of the European Union (Withdrawal) Act 2018.

Once in force the new Act will repeal the ECA 1972 and internalise most EU law necessary for the UK to continue to operate post-Brexit without a legal vacuum while it decides whether to maintain or replace certain provisions.

It is important to note that, at least until 29 March 2019, EU law will continue to apply in its normal fashion and the UK needs to comply with it including with any transposition deadlines, eg for Directives, required by EU instruments. However, should the EU–UK Withdrawal Agreement be approved and ratified, the UK will find itself in a sui generis position as it will no longer be a Member State but most pieces of EU law will continue to apply (see article 127) and the jurisdiction of the CJEU, for certain cases, will remain for some time.

At present it is difficult to ascertain whether the said agreement will ever enter into force. Having said that, a summary of what could happen if it does and also if a No Deal scenario materialises can be found below.

III EUR [386B]

UK–EU Withdrawal agreement enters into force Should the agreement enter into force on Brexit-day (whenever that may be), and provided nothing is altered in the coming weeks, the articles to look at are articles 67–68 part of Title VI: Ongoing Judicial Cooperation in Civil and Commercial matters.

That title in essence states that EU rules on jurisdiction (Brussels regime) will continue to apply to cases commenced before the end of the implementation/transition period (article 126: until 31 December 2020) and related proceedings ie proceedings concerning civil and commercial matters including Community intellectual property rights, data protection and posting of workers, family matters and maintenance. The rules on recognition and enforcement of judgments will apply to cross-border civil and commercial, family and maintenance cases that are commenced before the end of the implementation/transition period and court settlements and authentic instruments finalised before that point.

Further, EU rules on service of documents will apply to legal documents received for service before the end of the implementation/transition period, even if service actually takes place after that point. Similarly, EU rules on the taking of evidence will apply to requests received even if the evidence is not actually taken until afterwards. Rules governing the European Judicial Network will also continue to apply to requests for information received before the end of the implementation/transition period.

III EUR [386C]

No Deal scenario As things stand, on 29 March 2019, the UK will cease to be an EU Member State. The EU legislative instruments, the rights etc, deriving from the EU treaties and the domestic implementing legislation will become 'retained EU law' under sections 2, 3 and 4 of the European Union (Withdrawal) Act 2018. As retained, however, the instruments will cease to operate on a 'reciprocal basis' and the UK alone cannot legislate to restore that reciprocity. In addition, they will also contain numerous EU exit-related deficiencies that will render them largely unworkable (inapplicable). Hence, there is a need to legislate and prepare the statute books for the period post-Brexit. In that sense, the Civil Jurisdiction and Judgments (Amendment) (EU Exit) Regulations 2019 – Draft legislation – will:

- revoke Brussels I Recast (and its amending EU Regulations), Brussels I and the tertiary EU instruments related to them;
- revoke the Council Decision establishing the European Judicial Network in civil and commercial matters;
- extinguish the rights, powers, liabilities, obligations, restrictions, remedies and procedures derived from the Brussels Convention and Protocols (and subsequent accession Conventions), Revised Lugano Convention, Lugano Convention and the EU-Denmark Agreement;
- preserve the operation of Brussels I Recast and Brussels I, Brussels Convention, both Lugano Conventions and EU-Denmark Agreement, and the domestic legislation that implements these instruments and treaties, for transitional purposes so they continue to apply in England and Wales, Northern Ireland and Scotland to determine jurisdiction for proceedings commenced in the UK before exit day; in relation to the recognition or enforcement of a judgment or decision given by a court of an EU Member State or EFTA state where that court was seised before exit day; and in relation to recognition or enforcement of a court settlement concluded before a court of, or authentic instrument registered in, an EU or EFTA state before exit day;

- amend domestic primary and secondary legislation to reflect the fact that the Brussels regime will no longer apply in the UK after exit day;
- retain and restate rules contained in Brussels I Recast relating to jurisdiction in cases brought by and against UK domiciled consumers, by employees who work or have worked in the UK, and against employees domiciled in the UK, in the form of new provisions in the Civil Jurisdiction and Judgments Act 1982 (see reg 26); and
- retain and restate rules on the domicile of corporations or associations for the purposes of the retained and restated rules on jurisdiction in cases brought by and against UK domiciled employees and consumers, and of section 16 of the Civil Jurisdiction and Judgments Act 1982, ie allocation within the UK of jurisdiction in certain civil proceedings (see reg 42).

The effect of the above will be to remove the Brussels regime rules from domestic law, save for the retained provisions on jurisdiction in consumer and employee matters, and the rules on domicile of corporations and associations. In its place, jurisdiction and the recognition and enforcement of judgments will be determined by a combination of the existing common law and statute which currently applies to cases to which the Brussels regime does not apply, and (where it applies) the Hague 2005 Convention on Choice of Court Agreements to which the UK is acceding as an independent Contracting State post-Brexit (subject of a separate statutory instrument, the Civil Jurisdiction and Judgments (Hague Convention on Choice of Court Agreements 2005) (EU Exit) Regulations 2018, SI 2018/1124).

As regards transitional cases, it is intended that, where a case has commenced in the courts of England and Wales, Northern Ireland or Scotland before exit day, the Brussels regime rules should continue to apply until that case is concluded. Equally, where a case commenced in an EU Member State or a Lugano Convention State is concluded by a court settlement before exit day, or results in a judgment before or after exit day, courts of England and Wales, Northern Ireland or Scotland will recognise and enforce the outcome as if Brussels regime rules still applied. This is intended to make outcomes as predictable as possible for litigants in these categories of cases. There is one adjustment to the operation of the Brussels regime in relation to competing proceedings (lis pendens), contained in reg 93(2). Where a court of England and Wales, Northern Ireland or Scotland is seised before exit day, and a court of an EU Member State, or a state bound by the Revised Lugano Convention is seised at a point after the court in the UK in question has been seised, the UK court has a discretion, exceptionally, to decline jurisdiction despite being first seised. This is designed purely to enable that court to avoid an injustice, which could occur in particular if the second seised court refuses to stay the case and decline jurisdiction because the UK is no longer bound by the Brussels regime, notwithstanding that the UK court was seised first in time. This could result in litigants facing parallel proceedings in more than one court, both of which consider themselves bound, mandatorily, to hear the case. To avoid this result, some discretion is provided to an otherwise mandatory rule.

EUROPEAN COMMUNITIES ACT 1972

(c 68)

III EUR [387]

1. Short title and interpretation

(1) This Act may be cited as the European Communities Act 1972.

(2) In this Act [. . .]—

"the EU" means the European Union, being the Union established by the Treaty on European Union signed at Maastricht on 7th February 1992 (as amended by any later Treaty);

EUROPE

"the Communities" means the European Economic Community, the European Coal and Steel Community and the European Atomic Energy Community;

"the Treaties" or "the EU Treaties" means, subject to subsection (3) below, the pre-accession treaties, that is to say, those described in Part I of Schedule 1 to this Act, taken with—

(a) the treaty relating to the accession of the United Kingdom to the European Economic Community and to the European Atomic Energy Community, signed at Brussels on the 22nd January 1972; and

(b) the decision, of the same date, of the Council of the European Communities relating to the accession of the United Kingdom to the European Coal and Steel Community; and

(c) the treaty relating to the accession of the Hellenic Republic to the European Economic Community and to the European Atomic Energy Community, signed at Athens on 28th May 1979; and

(d) the decision, of 24th May 1979, of the Council relating to the accession of the Hellenic Republic to the European Coal and Steel Community; and

(e) the decisions of the Council of 7 May 1985, 24 June 1988, 31 October 1994, 29 September 2000 and 7 June 2007 on the Communities' system of own resources, and the decision of the Council of 26 May 2014 on the EU's system of own resources;

(g) the treaty relating to the accession of the Kingdom of Spain and the Portuguese Republic to the European Economic Community and to the European Atomic Energy Community, signed at Lisbon and Madrid on 12th June 1985; and

(h) the decision, of 11th June 1985, of the Council relating to the accession of the Kingdom of Spain and the Portuguese Republic to the European Coal and Steel Community; and

(j) the following provisions of the Single European Act signed at Luxembourg and The Hague on 17th and 28th February 1986, namely Title II (amendment of the treaties establishing the Communities) and, so far as they relate to any of the Communities or any Community institution, the preamble and Titles I (common provisions) and IV (general and final provisions); and

(k) Titles II, III and IV of the Treaty on European Union signed at Maastricht on 7th February 1992, together with the other provisions of the Treaty so far as they relate to those Titles, and the Protocols adopted at Maastricht on that date and annexed to the Treaty establishing the European Community with the exception of the Protocol on Social Policy on page 117 of Cm 1934 and

(l) the decision, of 1st February 1993, of the Council amending the Act concerning the election of the representatives of the European Parliament by direct universal suffrage annexed to Council Decision 76/787/ECSC, EEC, Euratom of 20th September 1976 and

(m) the Agreement on the European Economic Area signed at Oporto on 2nd May 1992 together with the Protocol adjusting that Agreement signed at Brussels on 17th March 1993 and

(n) the treaty concerning the accession of the Kingdom of Norway, the Republic of Austria, the Republic of Finland and the Kingdom of Sweden to the European Union, signed at Corfu on 24th June 1994; and

(o) the following provisions of the Treaty signed at Amsterdam on 2nd October 1997 amending the Treaty on European Union, the Treaties establishing the European Communities and certain related Acts—

(i) Articles 2 to 9,

(ii) Article 12, and

(iii) the other provisions of the Treaty so far as they relate to those Articles,

and the Protocols adopted on that occasion other than the Protocol on Article J.7 of the Treaty on European Union and

(p) the following provisions of the Treaty signed at Nice on 26th February 2001 amending the Treaty on European Union, the Treaties establishing the European Communities and certain related Acts—

(i) Articles 2 to 10, and

(ii) the other provisions of the Treaty so far as they relate to those Articles,

and the Protocols adopted on that occasion;

and any other treaty entered into by the EU (except in so far as it relates to, or could be applied in relation to, the Common Foreign and Security Policy), with or without any of the member States, or entered into, as a treaty ancillary to any of the Treaties, by the United Kingdom; and

(q) the treaty concerning the accession of the Czech Republic, the Republic of Estonia, the Republic of Cyprus, the Republic of Latvia, the Republic of Lithuania, the Republic of Hungary, the Republic of Poland, the Republic of Slovenia and the Slovak Republic to the European Union, signed at Athens on 16th April 2003; and

(r) the treaty concerning the accession of the Republic of Bulgaria and Romania to the European Union, signed at Luxembourg on 25th April 2005; and

(s) the Treaty of Lisbon Amending the Treaty on European Union and the Treaty Establishing the European Community signed at Lisbon on 13th December 2007 (together with its Annex and protocols), excluding any provision that relates to, or in so far as it relates to or could be applied in relation to, the Common Foreign and Security Policy; and

(t) the Protocol amending the Protocol (No 36) on transitional provisions annexed to the Treaty on European Union, to the Treaty on the Functioning of the European Union and to the Treaty establishing the European Atomic Energy Community, signed at Brussels on 23 June 2010; and

(u) the treaty concerning the accession of the Republic of Croatia to the European Union, signed at Brussels on 9 December 2011; and

(v) the Protocol on the concerns of the Irish people on the Treaty of Lisbon, adopted at Brussels on 16 May 2012;

and any expression defined in Schedule 1 to this Act has the meaning there given to it.

(3) If Her Majesty by Order in Council declares that a treaty specified in the Order is to be regarded as one of the EU Treaties as herein defined, the Order shall be conclusive that it is to be so regarded; but a treaty entered into by the United Kingdom after the 22nd January 1972, other than a pre-accession treaty to which

the United Kingdom accedes on terms settled on or before that date, shall not be so regarded unless it is so specified, nor be so specified unless a draft of the Order in Council has been approved by resolution of each House of Parliament.

(4) For purposes of subsections (2) and (3) above, "treaty" includes any international agreement, and any protocol or annex to a treaty or international agreement.

III EUR [388]

2. General interpretation of Treaties

(1) All such rights, powers, liabilities, obligations and restrictions from time to time created or arising by or under the Treaties, and all such remedies and procedures from time to time provided for by or under the Treaties, as in accordance with the Treaties are without further enactment to be given legal effect or used in the United Kingdom shall be recognised and available in law, and be enforced, allowed and followed accordingly; and the expression "enforceable Community right" and similar expressions shall be read as referring to one to which this subsection applies.

(2) Subject to Schedule 2 to this Act, at any time after its passing Her Majesty may by Order in Council, and any designated Minister or department may by regulations, make provision—

- (a) for the purpose of implementing any Community obligation of the United Kingdom, or enabling any such obligation to be implemented, or of enabling any rights enjoyed or to be enjoyed by the United Kingdom under or by virtue of the Treaties to be exercised; or
- (b) for the purpose of dealing with matters arising out of or related to any such obligation or rights or the coming into force, or the operation from time to time, of subsection (1) above;

and in the exercise of any statutory power or duty, including any power to give directions or to legislate by means of orders, rules, regulations or other subordinate instrument, the person entrusted with the power or duty may have regard to the objects of the Communities and to any such obligation or rights as aforesaid.

In this subsection "designated Minister or department" means such Minister of the Crown or government department as may from time to time be designated by Order in Council in relation to any matter or for any purpose, but subject to such restrictions or conditions (if any) as may be specified by the Order in Council.

(3) There shall be charged on and issued out of the Consolidated Fund or, if so determined by the Treasury, the National Loans Fund the amounts required to meet any Community obligation to make payments to any of the Communities or member States, or any Community obligation in respect of contributions to the capital or reserves of the European Investment Bank or in respect of loans to the Bank, or to redeem any notes or obligations issued or created in respect of any such Community obligation; and, except as otherwise provided by or under any enactment,—

- (a) any other expenses incurred under or by virtue of the Treaties or this Act by any Minister of the Crown or government department may be paid out of moneys provided by Parliament; and
- (b) any sums received under or by virtue of the Treaties or this Act by any Minister of the Crown or government department, save for such sums as may be required for disbursements permitted by any other enactment, shall be paid into the Consolidated Fund or, if so determined by the Treasury, the National Loans Fund.

(4) The provision that may be made under subsection (2) above includes, subject to Schedule 2 to this Act, any such provision (of any such extent) as might be made by Act of Parliament, and any enactment passed or to be passed, other than one

contained in this Part of this Act, shall be construed and have effect subject to the foregoing provisions of this section; but, except as may be provided by any Act passed after this Act, Schedule 2 shall have effect in connection with the powers conferred by this and the following sections of this Act to make Orders in Council and regulations.

(5) < . . . > and the references in that subsection to a Minister of the Crown or government department and to a statutory power or duty shall include a Minister or department of the Government of Northern Ireland and a power or duty arising under or by virtue of an Act of the Parliament of Northern Ireland.

(6) A law passed by the legislature of any of the Channel Islands or of the Isle of Man, or a colonial law (within the meaning of the Colonial Laws Validity Act 1865) passed or made for Gibraltar, if expressed to be passed or made in the implementation of the Treaties and of the obligations of the United Kingdom thereunder, shall not be void or inoperative by reason of any inconsistency with or repugnancy to an Act of Parliament, passed or to be passed, that extends to the Island or Gibraltar or any provision having the force and effect of an Act there (but not including this section), nor by reason of its having some operation outside the Island or Gibraltar; and any such Act or provision that extends to the Island or Gibraltar shall be construed and have effect subject to the provisions of any such law.

III EUR [388.1]

Interpreting in favour of compliance 'All such rights, [...] obligations and restrictions from time to time created or arising by or under the Treaties,[...], as in accordance with the Treaties are without further enactment to be given legal effect or used in the United Kingdom shall be recognised and available in law, and be enforced, allowed and followed accordingly [...]' (s 2(1)). This is key to understand how EU law operates and needs to be interpreted and applied in the UK. The caveat being that whenever EU law requires Member States to adopt legislation to internalise or give effect to some provisions Member States are not only allowed but obliged to do so (see **III EUR [5]**).

However, in *White v White* [2001] UKHL 9, [2001] 2 All ER 43, [2001] 1 Lloyd's Rep 679, the House of Lords held, citing *Francovich v Italy: C-6 and C-9/90* [1991] ECR I-5357 at 5408 and 5412, that the *Marleasing* principle cannot be stretched to the length of requiring contracts to be interpreted in a manner that would impose on one or other of the parties obligations which, the *Marleasing* case apart, the contract did not impose. This is so even in the case of a contract where one of the parties is an emanation of government, here the Secretary of State. The citizen's obligations are those to which he agreed, as construed in accordance with normal principles of interpretation.

Some confusion, if any, may arise when reading s 2(2)(a) as it would seem to contradict, to some extent, s 2(1) or at least give room to pass legislation that, in itself, may not be required as '[...] for the purpose of implementing any EU obligation of the United Kingdom, or enabling any such obligation to be implemented, or of enabling any rights enjoyed or to be enjoyed by the United Kingdom under or by virtue of the Treaties to be exercised' would seem to authorise. However, confusion will dispel if you read it in the context of EU law and its principles as 'implementing any EU obligation' means any EU obligation, provision or piece of EU legislation that by its nature requires implementation such as Directives but not Regulations or some Treaties provisions as those are directly applicable and/or have direct effect (see **III EUR [9]** on direct effect). Please note that s 2(2) is subject to what established in Schedule 2 which sets the limits of the powers conferred by it '[t]he powers conferred by section 2(2) of this Act to make provision for the purposes mentioned in section 2(2)(a) [...] shall not include power [...]'.

III EUR [388.2]

Direct effect fundamental principle of EU law developed by the CJEU in the early 1960s. It can be described as a mechanism for individuals to request national courts to enforce rights derived from EU provisions. It was established in the judgment in *Van Gend en Loos (C-26/62)* which set the main criteria needed for direct effect which are, today, still applicable.

For it to have direct effect the EU provision must be:

- clear;
- precise;
- unconditional; and
- confer rights upon the individuals.

In *Van Gend en Loos* the provision in question was EEC, art 12 (now TFEU, art 30), ie primary law. The action raised the question of the conflict between national legislation and the provisions of the EEC Treaty. The Court decided the question referred by a Netherlands court by stating the doctrine of direct effect, thus conferring on the individual, in this case a transport company, a direct guarantee of its rights under Community law before the national court.

It is widely accepted that Treaty articles, Regulations, Decisions and Directives are capable of producing such effect whereas Recommendations and Opinions lack that capability due to their non-binding nature. It must be borne in mind that the direct effect of Directives is the most commonly known facet of the principle and that which causes more problems considering that, by definition, Directives are not addressed to individuals and require an act of the Member State in order for them to be fully operational. There are two types of direct effect: vertical where an individual seeks to enforce an EU provision against the State (or emanation of the State) and horizontal where an individual seeks to enforce an EU provision against another individual (see **III EUR [9]** for case law).

In *Evans v Secretary of State and Motor Insurers Bureau (C-63/01)* the CJEU stated that if the compensation system set up in the UK were found to be 'subject to one or more defects of transposition', it was incumbent on the national court to determine 'whether or not those defects have adversely affected Mr Evans', and if so whether the non-fulfilment of the UK's obligation to transpose the Directive was 'sufficiently serious'. The CA, following Evans, said that that judgment could be seen as a template for consideration in the appeal and held that failure to transpose correctly a Directive gave rise not only to direct effect but also to damages under the State liability remedy: *Byrne v Motor Insurers' Bureau* [2008] EWCA Civ 574.

III EUR [388.3]

Interpreting in favour of compliance Read together s 2, sub-ss 1, 2 and 4, create an obligation of interpreting national law in compliance with EU law. Sub-section 4 states '[t]he provision that may be made under subsection (2) above includes, subject to Schedule 2 to this Act, any such provision (of any such extent) as might be made by Act of Parliament, and any enactment passed or to be passed, other than one contained in this part of this Act, shall be construed and have effect subject to the foregoing provisions of this section [...]'.

Indirect effect, or consistent interpretation, is mainly an interpretative tool that national courts can use when their legal orders so permit (see **III EUR [10]**). It requires that national courts interpret as far as possible national law in light of the wording and purpose of EU law. It achieves indirectly, via judicial interpretation of national law, the result obtainable through direct effect where that principle cannot be applied. The principle was developed by the CJEU in *Von Colson and Kamann v Land Nordrhein-Westfalen: C-14/83* [1984] ECR 1891, [1986] 2 CMLR 430, ECJ and its scope later widened in *Marleasing SA v La Comercial Internacional de Alimentación SA: C-106/89* [1990] ECR I-4135, [1992] 1 CMLR 305, ECJ. Mostly applied for Directives, when they are not implemented or incorrectly implemented, it can be used for all types of EU legislation as established in *Grimaldi v Fonds Des Maladies Professionnelles: C-322/88* [1990] IRLR 400 and *Pupino (criminal proceedings against): C-105/03* [2006] QB 83, [2006] All ER (EC) 142.

INDIRECT EFFECT IN UK COURTS

III EUR [388.4]

Section 2(4) of the European Communities Act 1972 does not enable or constrain a UK court to distort the meaning of a UK Statute in order to enforce against an individual a Community directive which has no direct effect between individuals, that it applies only where Community provisions are directly applicable. A UK court will always be willing and anxious to conclude that UK law is consistent with EU law. Where an Act is passed for the purpose of giving effect to an obligation imposed by a Directive or other instrument a UK court will seldom encounter difficulty in concluding that the language of the Act is effective for the intended purpose. But the construction of a UK Act of Parliament is a matter of judgment to be determined by UK courts and to be derived from the language of the legislation considered in the light of the circumstances prevailing at the date of enactment: *DUKE v GEC Reliance Ltd* [1988] 1 All ER 626, Lord Templeman.

A construction which permits the relevant UK legislation to operate as a proper fulfilment of the UK's obligation under the Treaty involves not so much doing violence to the language of the section as filling a gap by an implication which arises, not from the words used, but from the manifest purpose of the Act and the mischief it was intended to remedy. The question is whether that can be justified by the necessity – indeed the obligation – to apply a purposive construction which will implement the UK's obligations under the Treaty: *Pickstone v Freemans Plc* [1989] HL, Lord Aylmerton.

The courts of the UK are under a duty to follow the practice of the CJEU by giving a purposive construction to Directives and to regulations issued for the purpose of complying with Directives: *Litster v Forth Dry Dock* [1989] 1 All ER 1134, Lord Templeman.

It is the duty of the court to give to regulation 5 a construction which accords with the decisions of the EU Court upon the corresponding provisions of the Directive to which the regulation was intended by Parliament to give effect. The precedent established by *Pickstone v Freemans Plc*, indicates that this is to be done by implying the words necessary to achieve that result: *Litster v Forth Dry Dock*, Lord Keith of Kinkel. The approach to the construction of primary and subordinate legislation enacted to give effect to the UK's obligations under the EEC Treaty have been the subject matter of recent authority in this House (see *Pickstone v Freemans Plc*) and is not in doubt. If the legislation can reasonably be construed so as to conform with those obligations – obligations which are to be ascertained not only from the wording of the relevant Directive but from the interpretation placed upon it by the CJEU at Luxembourg – such a purposive construction will be applied even though, perhaps, it may involve some departure from the strict and literal application of the words which the legislature has elected to use: *Litster v Forth Dry Dock*, Lord Aylmerton.

In *Webb v EMO Air Cargo (No 2)* [1995] 4 All ER 577, Lord Keith of Kinkel adjusted his preliminary view, which did not include consideration of EU law, to accommodate the CJEU ruling. The original case *Webb v EMO* concerned the interpretation of the Sex Discrimination Act 1975 and was stayed until the CJEU gave its preliminary ruling following which the House of Lords complied with the EU judgment by interpreting the said Act in light of the Directive.

In summary, UK courts have gone from a strict approach to the indirect effect doctrine as seen in Duke (no distortion of UK legislation as no constrain to UK courts to do so under European Communities Act 1972), to supplying by implication words appropriate to comply with UK's obligations under the Treaty as it occurred in *Pickstone* (established flexibility in purposive construction of legislation that gives effect to EU law) and upholding that view in *Litster* to finally embracing indirect effect in Webb (interpreting pre-existing legislation in light of the objective of the Directive). The evolution has been consistent with that of the CJEU on this matter.

It is worth mentioning that indirect effect admits, contrary to *Van Gend en Loos*, that it is not possible for individuals to expect that EU law will have a pre-determined effect in national courts. As a result of consistent interpretation, individual claims will thrive in some national courts, and obligations will be imposed on individuals as a result, whereas, in others, they will be unsuccessful because of the limits in the courts' power to interpret national law.

Thus, in interpreting national legislation the courts should endeavour to construe ambiguities in a way which is compatible with EU law (or obligations): *Marleasing SA v La Comercial Internacional de Alimentación SA: C-106/89* [1990] ECR I-4135, [1992] 1 CMLR 305, ECJ; *Litster v Forth Dry Dock and Engineering Co Ltd* [1990] AC 546, [1989] 1 All ER 1134.

After *Marleasing* the obligation arises whether there is implementing legislation or not (this includes legislation that predates the Directive which covers the same matter but cannot be considered implementing legislation as it was not adopted to give effect to the Directive or simply there is no legislation on the subject as the Member State did not implement it). Here the obligation seems absolute 'if the member state did not implement the Directive any piece of national law should be interpreted in light of the purpose of the Directive'. This created many problems which the CJEU later solved by setting the limits of the principle which are: if applying indirect effect would increase criminal liability or criminal charges (*Pretore di Salò*, *Arcaro*) or if it violates the principles of non-retroactivity, legitimate expectations or legal certainty (*Kolpinghuis*).

The CJEU has held that when applying provisions of national law, the national court must interpret them as far as possible in the light of the wording and purpose of any relevant Directive, even if it does not have direct effect: *Faccini Dori: C-91/92* [1995] All ER (EC) 1, [1994] ECR I-3325. Further, the CJEU has consistently held that, in interpreting a provision of EU law, it is necessary to consider not only its wording but also the context in which it occurs and the objects of the rules of which it forms part, see *Adidas AG, Re: C-223/98* [1999] ECR I-7081, [1999] 3 CMLR 895, ECJ; *KVS International: C-301/98* [2000] ECR I-3583; *Germany v Commission: C-156/98* [2000] ECR I-6857; *Kvaerner: C-191/99* [2001] ECR I-4447: *R v Secretary of State for Health, ex p British American Tobacco (Investments) Ltd and Imperial Tobacco Ltd: C-491/01* [2002] All ER (D) 126 (Dec), (2002) Times, 13 December.

It is axiomatic as a result of s 2 that where a rule of national law conflicts with directly applicable Treaty rights it is the duty of the national court to override the offending rule of national law: *Alabaster v Woolwich plc* [2000] ICR 1037. The distinction between primary and secondary legislation either at EU or national level is of little assistance in determining the margin of appreciation available to a national decision maker. To give weight to such a distinction is inappropriate in view of the wide powers to amend primary legislation by Order in Council. The margin of appreciation depends on the nature of the decision including the extent to which it is circumscribed by EU law under which the decision maker is acting: *R v Ministry of Agriculture Fisheries and Food, ex p Astonquest Ltd* (21 December 1999, unreported), CA.

EUROPE

In *White v White* [2001] UKHL 9, [2001] 2 All ER 43, [2001] 1 Lloyd's Rep 679, the House of Lords held, that the provision in question was an agreement that, even though was meant to give effect to a Directive, it was not 'legislation' so the *Marleasing* principle was not applicable. Had the MIB agreement been embodied in legislation, whether primary or secondary, the English court would have been under an obligation to interpret its provisions, as far as possible, in a way which gives effect to the Directive [...]. *Litster v Forth Dry Dock* was cited as requiring a purposive construction to be applied to legislation even though, perhaps, it may involve some departure from the strict and literal application of the words which the legislature has elected to use. Further, it was held that the courts must apply national law accordingly, whenever the law was enacted or made. But it is one matter to apply this principle to national law. Whatever form it may take, law is made by authorities of the state. It is quite another matter to apply this principle to contracts made between citizens. The *Marleasing* principle cannot be stretched to the length of requiring contracts to be interpreted in a manner that would impose on one or other of the parties obligations which, *Marleasing* apart, the contract did not impose. This is so even in the case of a contract where one of the parties is an emanation of government, here, the Secretary of State. The citizen's obligations are those to which he agreed, as construed in accordance with normal principles of interpretation. This is an example of the reluctance of UK courts to apply the EU principle. Nothing in TFEU, art 289 says that a Directive needs to be implemented by 'legislation', in fact, it says 'a directive shall be binding, as to the result to be achieved, upon each Member State to which it is addressed, but shall leave to the national authorities the choice of form and methods'. It is widely accepted that Directives can be implemented by administrative rules provided those apply without discrimination of any kind. So the MIB agreement was, as recognised in the judgment, the implementing measure for the Directive in question and yet the Court chose to subsume the case in UK law only (contract law) when, if the reference to the CJEU had been permitted, the result most likely would have been different.

Although Parliament cannot bind its successors against repeal, the European Communities Act 1972 is a constitutional statute which by force of the common law cannot be impliedly repealed. The fundamental legal basis of the UK's relationship with the EU rests with domestic and not EU legal powers, a balance which gives full weight both to the supremacy of EU law and the supremacy of the UK Parliament. The amending power given by s 2(2) and the opening words of s 2(4) clearly envisage provision being made to give effect to a Directive. Parliament can and has delegated the power to amend primary legislation by s 2(2) read with s 2(4). As the 1972 Act is unambiguous on this issue it is improper to take account of ministerial statements made at the time of the passage of the 1972 Act, suggesting that consequential amendments would be minor: *Thoburn v Sunderland City Council; Hunt v Hackney London Borough Council; Harman v Cornwall County Council; Collins v Sutton London Borough Council* [2002] EWHC 195 (Admin), [2003] QB 151, [2002] 4 All ER 156.

Section 2(2)(a) is concerned primarily with bringing into force EU obligations arising from the Treaties. These obligations are primarily the Directives which should be implemented as a whole and not on a line by line basis. There should be no attempt to divide those things which a Member State has to do from those where it might not have to do if it chose to do something else. Accordingly it made no sense to hold that transitional provisions enabling the UK to retain existing law for a period needed primary legislation whereas the remaining provisions of a Directive did not: *Oakley Inc v Animal Ltd* [2005] EWCA Civ 1191, 20 October 2005.

III EUR [388.5]

State liability State liability is the last resort available to individuals who seek to enforce EU law in national courts, provided the non-compliance of EU provisions is found to be the direct result of the inaction or incorrect action of a Member State (ie where neither direct effect or indirect effect is possible). However, it must be stressed it can also be used where direct or indirect effect are available. The principle originated in the joined cases of *Francovich and others (C-6/90 and C-9/90)*. Thus, since 1991, EU citizens have been able to bring an action for damages against a Member State which infringes an EU provision (see **III EUR [11]**).

A State may be liable in damages for losses caused by a serious breach of EU law. Following the CJEU ruling in *Brasserie du Pêcheur SA v Germany, R v Secretary of State for Transport, ex p Factortame Ltd* [1996] QB 404, [1996] All ER (EC) 301, ECJ, the Divisional Court made a declaration. Its terms were that Her Majesty's Government's breaches of Community law in the *Factortame* case were sufficiently serious to give rise to liability for damage caused but not for exemplary damages: *R v Secretary of State for Transport, ex p Factortame: C-48/93* [1998] 1 All ER 736n. This decision was upheld on appeal: *R v Secretary of State for Transport, ex p Factortame Ltd* [1999] 2 All ER 640, CA and in the House of Lords [1999] 1 AC 524, [1999] 4 All ER 906. In order to justify a claim for compensation for breach of directly effective EU law it is necessary either a specific provision for reparation or an allegation that the breach of EU law is sufficiently serious: *Nabadda v Westminster City Council* [2000] ICR 951. A court can be liable for a breach of EU law although it has been held that the infringement did not meet the requirements for an award: *Köbler v Austria: C-224/01* [2003] 3 CMLR 1003, (2003) Times, 3 October, ECJ. A Köbler-based claim against the CA was dismissed because it did not establish 'manifest error': *Cooper v A-G* [2008] EWHC 2178 (Admin), [2008] 3 CMLR 1370, (2008) Times, 7 October, decision of Plender J.

On whether an incorrect implementation of a Directive gives rise to State liability and whether that amounts to sufficiently serious breach the CA agreed with the approach in *Evans: Byrne v Motor Insurers' Bureau* [2008] EWCA Civ 574.

A failure to issue a residence card within the time allowed by the Immigration (EEA) Regulations 2006, SI 2006/1003 entitles an applicant for a card to damages in respect of resulting financial loss: *R (on the application of Hana Zewdu) v Secretary of State for the Home Office* [2015] EWHC 2148 (Admin), [2015] All ER (D) 307 (Jun).

III EUR [388.6]

Nationality Whether a person is a national of the UK (and, as a consequence, a EU citizen) depends on the wording of the 1982 Declaration by the Government of the UK on the definition of 'nationals' which replaced the 1972 Declaration annexed to the Final Act of the Treaty of Accession: *R (on the application of Kaur) v Secretary of State for the Home Department (JUSTICE intervening): C-192/99* [2001] All ER (EC) 250, ECJ.

III EUR [388.7]

Wales Section 2(2) may be used to designate the National Assembly for Wales. See Government of Wales Act 1998, s 29(1).

III EUR [388.8]

Implied repeal by subsequent legislation A constitutional statute is one which (a) conditions the legal relationship between citizen and State in some general, overarching manner, or (b) enlarges or diminishes the scope of what we would now regard as fundamental constitutional rights. (a) and (b) are of necessity closely related: it is difficult to think of an instance of (a) that is not also an instance of (b). The special status of constitutional statutes follows the special status of constitutional rights. The European Communities Act 1972 clearly belongs in this family. It incorporated the whole corpus of substantive Community rights and obligations, and gave overriding domestic effect to the judicial and administrative machinery of Community law. It may be there has never been a statute having such profound effects on so many dimensions of our daily lives. The Act is, by force of the common law, a constitutional statute. Ordinary statutes may be impliedly repealed. Constitutional statutes may not. For the repeal of a constitutional Act or the abrogation of a fundamental right to be effected by statute, the court would apply this test: is it shown that the legislature's actual – not imputed, constructive or presumed – intention was to effect the repeal or abrogation? the test could only be met by express words in the later statute, or by words so specific that the inference of an actual determination to effect the result contended for was irresistible. The ordinary rule of implied repeal did not satisfy that test, and therefore has no application to constitutional statutes such as the European Communities Act 1972: *Thoburn v Sunderland City Council; Hunt v Hackney London Borough Council; Harman v Cornwall County Council; Collins v Sutton London Borough Council* [2002] EWHC 195 (Admin), [2003] QB 151, [2002] 4 All ER 156.

III EUR [389]

3. Decisions on, and proof of, Treaties and EU instruments etc

(1) For the purposes of all legal proceedings any question as to the meaning or effect of any of the Treaties, or as to the validity, meaning or effect of any EU instrument, shall be treated as a question of law (and, if not referred to the European Court, be for determination as such in accordance with the principles laid down by and any relevant decision of the European Court).

(2) Judicial notice shall be taken of the Treaties, of the Official Journal of the European Union and of any decision of, or expression of opinion by, the European Court on any such question as aforesaid; and the Official Journal shall be admissible as evidence of any instrument or other act thereby communicated of the EU or of any EU institution.

(3) Evidence of any instrument issued by a EU institution, including any judgment or order of the European Court, or of any document in the custody of a EU institution, or any entry in or extract from such a document, may be given in

any legal proceedings by production of a copy certified as a true copy by an official of that institution; and any document purporting to be such a copy shall be received in evidence without proof of the official position or handwriting of the person signing the certificate.

(4) Evidence of any EU instrument may also be given in any legal proceedings—

(a) by production of a copy purporting to be printed by the Queen's Printer;

(b) where the instrument is in the custody of a government department (including a department of the Government of Northern Ireland), by production of a copy certified on behalf of the department to be a true copy by an officer of the department generally or specially authorised so to do;

and any document purporting to be such a copy as is mentioned in paragraph (b) above of an instrument in the custody of a department shall be received in evidence without proof of the official position or handwriting of the person signing the certificate, or of his authority to do so, or of the document being in the custody of the department.

(5) *Omitted.*

III EUR [389.1]

Validity of EU law According to s 3(1) '[...] any question as to the meaning or effect of any of the Treaties, or as to the validity, meaning or effect of any EU instrument, shall be treated as a question of law (and, if not referred to the European Court, be for determination as such in accordance with the principles laid down by and any relevant decision of the European Court)'. This section is of great importance to understand the role EU law plays in UK proceedings and the extent of the obligation of the UK courts when it becomes apparent that they are dealing with a case with an EU connection. The effect or validity of any piece of EU law (ie Treaties or secondary legislation) are to be decided by applying principles of EU law created or developed by the CJEU's case law (called decision and European Court, respectively, by the Act). In other words, principles such as primacy of EU law, direct and indirect effect, State liability, etc need to be part of the domestic court reasoning when deciding proceedings before it. In applying EU law principles of interpretation a purposive approach must be taken: *Shanning International Ltd (in liquidation) v Lloyds TSB Bank plc* (2000) Times, 19 January, QBD, Commercial Court.

It is also important to note that EU legislation may not be declared invalid by a national court but only by the CJEU: *Foto-Frost: C-314/85* [1987] ECR 4199, ECJ and that the meaning of particular provisions of EU law is a matter for legal argument, not factual proof: *R v Goldstein* [1983] 1 All ER 434, [1983] 1 WLR 151. As regards challenges to national implementing legislation which go to the validity of EU legislation see *R v Secretary of State for Health, ex p Macrae Seafoods Ltd* [1995] COD 369; *R v Secretary of State for Health, ex p Imperial Tobacco Ltd* [2000] 1 All ER 572 and *R v Secretary of State for Health, ex p Imperial Tobacco Ltd* [2001] 1 All ER 850, [2001] 1 WLR 127, HL.

In *Arsenal Football Club plc v Reed* [2003] EWCA Civ 696, [2003] 3 All ER 865, the CA applied the ruling of the CJEU in allowing Arsenal's appeal. The CA held that (1) the CJEU was not competent to reverse findings of fact made by Laddie J, but that (2) the CJEU was entitled to base its ruling on findings of fact which had not been made but which were inevitable. The ruling of the CJEU is binding in so far as it is a ruling upon interpretation. Strictly speaking the judgment is the explanation of the ruling, but as explained in *Robert Bosch GmbH v Hamptzollant Hildestein* [1978] ECR 855: 'the operative part of the judgment of this Court should always be interpreted in the light of the reasoning that precedes it'. That is particularly apt in the present case as the ruling uses the words 'in the circumstances such as those in the present case'. This case illustrates the problems that may arise if the reference questions are not clear enough as the CJEU may end up assuming the facts upon which the reference is made as different from the reality.

III EUR [389.2]

Referrals to the CJEU under the preliminary ruling procedure (see particularly III EUR [7]) This procedure is available to all courts of the Member States, therefore, it is so for all UK courts. As explained in **III EUR [7]**, the UK court is to incorporate EU law and case law in its reasoning and the UK judge must act as an EU judge as well so if, at any point of that reasoning, doubt as to validity or interpretation of EU law or UK legislation implementing EU law arises it is possible and advisable to stay proceedings and refer questions to the CJEU.

This is applicable to any proceedings ie first instance or appeals. But, if doubt arises during proceedings before courts against whose decisions there are no other legal remedies ie last instance, the right to refer becomes an obligation under TFEU, art 267.

Like other final courts, the UK Supreme Court is, in the areas of EU law in which the UK is bound by the jurisdiction of the CJEU, under the duty imposed by article 267 of the TFEU to ask the CJEU to give preliminary rulings concerning the interpretation of the Treaties and the validity and interpretation of acts of the EU institutions, bodies, offices or agencies of the EU, where such a question is raised in proceedings before it and it considers that a decision on the question is necessary to enable it to give judgment.

Where an application for permission to appeal raises such a question, the UKSC does not, when considering whether in the light of that question to grant permission or to make a reference to the CJEU, apply a test of whether the question is of general public importance.

In reference cases from national courts under ECT, art 234 (now TFEU, art 267) the CJEU does not exercise a normal appellate function and therefore cannot determine or reverse issues of fact: *Arsenal Football Club plc v Reed* [2002] EWHC 2695 (Ch), [2003] 1 All ER 137.

It is not open to a national court to decide for itself that a decision of the European Commission in an anti-competition dispute had been wrongly decided and to determine the same question differently: *Crehan v Inntrepreneur Pub Co (CPC)* [2004] EWCA Civ 637, [2004] All ER (D) 322 (May).

It was appropriate to refer a matter to the CJEU where it could not be said with complete confidence that the CJEU would decide that implementation by a devolved government within the UK was to be treated, for the purposes of the principle of equality and non-discrimination, as if it were implementation by the Member State: *R (on the application of Horvath) v Secretary of State for the Environment, Food and Rural Affairs* [2007] EWCA Civ 620, (2007) Times, 30 July.

It must be borne in mind that since the CJEU case law is available and accessible by the general public at all times the CJEU may reject a reference if it is clear from the questions submitted that the same questions have been answered in earlier cases. Thus, it is advisable to monitor regularly the cases going through the CJEU system regardless of the Member State which refers them because the interpretation given by the CJEU may be applicable or have impact on cases you deal with.

The CJEU has held that under TFEU, art 267 it has jurisdiction to give preliminary rulings concerning the validity and interpretation of EU institutions acts, regardless of whether they are directly applicable (see, to that effect, *Impresa Costruzioni Comm Quirino Mazzalai v Ferrovia del Renon: C-111/75* [1976] ECR 657, [1977] 1 CMLR 105, ECJ and *Maso and Gazzetta v Instituto Nazionale della Prevedenza Sociale (INPS) and Italy: C-373/95* [1997] ECR I-4051, [1997] 3 CMLR 1244, ECJ). A Directive is an act covered by that article even though the period for its implementation has not yet expired, and a question concerning it may validly be referred to the Court provided that that reference also satisfies the conditions for admissibility laid down in the Court's case law. Thus, when a question on the validity of an EU instrument is raised before a national court, it is for that court to decide whether a decision on the matter is necessary to enable it to give judgment and consequently whether it should request the CJEU to rule on that question. Accordingly, where the national court's questions relate to the validity of a provision of EU law, the CJEU is obliged in principle to give a ruling (citing *Eurotunnel SA v SeaFrance (formerly Societe Nouvelle d'Armement Transmanche SA) (International Duty Free Confederation, interveners): C-408/95* [1997] All ER (D) 65, ECJ): *R v Secretary of State for Health, ex p British American Tobacco (Investments) Ltd: C-491/01* [2002] All ER (D) 126 (Dec), (2002) Times, 13 December, ECJ.

CPR Part 68 establishes the steps to follow to make a reference to the CJEU and Practice Direction 68 supplements them. In addition, the Supreme Court has issued some rules on the application TFEU, art 267 via the Supreme Court Rules 2009, SI 2009/1603, as amended. The rules are found in Part 6, s 42 and are supplemented by Practice Direction 11.

More information on this procedure has been issued by the EU in 'Recommendations to national courts and tribunals in relation to the initiation of preliminary ruling proceedings' (2012/C 338/01).

III EUR [390]

4. General provision for repeal and amendment

(1) The enactments mentioned in Schedule 3 to this Act (being enactments that are superseded or to be superseded by reason of EU obligations and of the provision made by this Act in relation thereto or are not compatible with EU obligations) are hereby repealed, to the extent specified in column 3 of the

Schedule, with effect from the entry date or other date mentioned in the Schedule; and in the enactments mentioned in Schedule 4 to this Act there shall, subject to any transitional provision there included, be made the amendments provided for by that Schedule.

(2) Where in any Part of Schedule 3 to this Act it is provided that repeals made by that Part are to take effect from a date appointed by order, the orders shall be made by statutory instrument, and an order may appoint different dates for the repeal of different provisions to take effect, or for the repeal of the same provision to take effect for different purposes; and an order appointing a date for a repeal to take effect may include transitional and other supplementary provisions arising out of that repeal, including provisions adapting the operation of other enactments included for repeal but not yet repealed by that Schedule, and may amend or revoke any such provisions included in a previous order.

(3) Where any of the following sections of this Act, or any paragraph of Schedule 4 to this Act, affects or is construed as one with an Act or Part of an Act similar in purpose to provisions having effect only in Northern Ireland, then—

(a) unless otherwise provided by Act of the Parliament of Northern Ireland, the Governor of Northern Ireland may by Order in Council make provision corresponding to any made by the section or paragraph, and amend or revoke any provision so made; and

(b) < . . . >

(4) Where Schedule 3 or 4 to this Act provides for the repeal or amendment of an enactment that extends or is capable of being extended to any of the Channel Islands or the Isle of Man, the repeal or amendment shall in like manner extend or be capable of being extended thereto.

CIVIL JURISDICTION AND JUDGMENTS ACT 1982

(c 27)

GENERAL NOTES ON THE CIVIL JURISDICTION AND JUDGMENTS ACT 1982 (SEE 'BREXIT: STATE OF PLAY' AT **III EUR [386A]** AND 'NO DEAL SCENARIO' AT **III EUR [386C]** FOR INFORMATION ON THIS ACT'S DRAFT AMENDMENT)

III EUR [391]

The main purpose of the Civil Jurisdiction and Judgments Act 1982 was to give effect in the UK (and in the three separate law districts: England and Wales, Scotland and Northern Ireland) to the 1968 Brussels Convention on Jurisdiction and Enforcement of Judgments in Civil and Commercial Matters and its 1971 Protocol on the Interpretation of the Convention. Please note that according to s 14(1), the Act (including its Schedules containing eg the text of the Convention) may be amended by Order in Council.

The Civil Jurisdiction and Judgments Act 1991 introduced amendments to give effect to the 1988 Lugano Convention on Jurisdiction and the Enforcement of Judgments in Civil and Commercial Matters and its Protocols, by means of inserting ss 3A and 3B and Schedule 3C to the 1982 Act. The objective of the Lugano Convention and the implementing legislation was, broadly, to set out similar arrangements on jurisdiction and enforcement of judgments to States parties to the European Free Trade Association (EFTA) namely Iceland, Norway and Switzerland to those existing under the Brussels Convention.

EUROPE

The Civil Jurisdiction and Judgments Order 2001, SI 2001/3929 made legislative changes needed in consequence of the coming into force of Council Regulation (EC) No 44/2001 of 22 December 2000 on Jurisdiction and the Recognition of Judgments in Civil and Commercial Matters, commonly known as Brussels I, from 1 March 2002. The Regulation is referred to in the Civil Procedure Rules 1998 and in the 1982 Act as "the Judgments Regulation" following the 2001 amendment. Schedule 1 and 2 of the Order, respectively, made amendments to the Act - mainly to Schedule 4 - to align it with the contents of Brussels I and the Conventions. the relationship between Brussels I, the Brussels Convention and the Lugano Convention (Schedule 2, paragraph 1(c)) was also clarified. The main aim of the Order was to create a regime on jurisdiction and the recognition and enforcement of judgments barely distinguishable from the earlier regimes established by the 1982 Act and its various Schedules applicable to Brussels I and the mentioned Conventions.

The Civil Jurisdiction and Judgments (Authentic Instruments and Court Settlements) Order 2001, SI 2001/3928. This Order in Council applies specified provisions of the Civil Jurisdiction and Judgments Order 2001 to authentic instruments and court settlements from other Member States bound by the Judgments Regulations (Brussels I), which by virtue of its Chapter IV, are enforceable in the same manner as judgments. Paragraphs 1 to 6 and 8 of the Civil Jurisdiction and Judgments Order 2001 are applied, with modifications, and section 48 of the Civil Jurisdiction and Judgments Act 1982 is applied, to such documents and settlements as if they were judgments to which the Judgments Regulation (Brussels I) applies.

The Civil Jurisdiction and Judgments Regulations 2009, SI 2009/3131 gave effect to the Revised Lugano Convention 2007 and repealed, among other amendments made to UK legislation, ss 3A and 3B of the 1982 Act. In October 2007 the European Community, Iceland, Norway, Denmark and Switzerland agreed on a convention to replace the 1988 Lugano Convention. The provisions of the new convention are generally parallel in nature to the equivalent provisions of Brussels I. The entry into force of the new convention re-established the parallelism which earlier existed between the 1988 Lugano and the 1968 Brussels Conventions, disrupted by the Judgments Regulation (Brussels I) from March 2002.

Of paramount importance is to keep in mind that the original Judgments Regulation (Brussels I) was repealed and replaced by Regulation (EU) No 1215/2012 of the European Parliament and of the Council of 12 December 2012 on Jurisdiction and the Recognition and Enforcement of Judgments in Civil and Commercial Matters (recast), with effect from 10 January 2015. However, for proceedings commenced before that date it continues to apply as does the implementing Order (see both Regulations in **III EUR [17]**).

The Civil Jurisdiction and Judgments (Amendment) Regulations 2014, SI 2014/2947 were made to facilitate the application of Regulation (EU) No 1215/2012 in the UK from 10 January 2015. The Brussels I Recast Regulation or Judgments Regulation recast replaces Brussels I and contains revised and new provisions both on jurisdiction, and on recognition and enforcement of judgments. The Regulations made amendments to various enactments, in particular the 1982 Act, the Civil Jurisdiction and Judgments Order 2001 and the Civil Jurisdiction and Judgments (Authentic Instruments and Court Settlements) Order 2001, which are consequential on the replacement of the original Judgments Regulation (Brussels I). It is worth mentioning that Regulation 6 made transitional and saving provision. The transitional provisions in article 66 of Brussels I Recast have the effect that the original version of Brussels I will continue to apply, in relation to judgments arising from existing proceedings, for a significant period. Rather than having two sets of provisions in the various enactments which were amended, the approach adopted was to make amendments which remove from those enactments the provisions relating to the original version of the Judgments Regulation, but to provide (as regulation 6 does) for the amendments not to apply where the original version of the Judgments Regulation continues to apply, so that the provisions relating to the original version of the Judgments Regulation also continue to apply.

The Civil Jurisdiction and Judgments (Hague Convention on Choice of Court Agreements 2005) Regulations 2015, SI 2015/1644 gave effect in the UK to the Hague Convention. The Regulations made amendments to UK legislation consequential on the entry into force of the Convention on 1 October 2015. Amendments to the 1982 Act provide, in particular, for foreign judgments required to be recognised and enforced under the Convention to be registered under that Act on the application of an interested party and for a decision on such an application to be appealable on the grounds set out in the Convention. Consequential amendments were made to the Civil Jurisdiction and Judgments Act (Interim Relief) Order 1997 (SI 1997/302) and the Civil Jurisdiction and Judgments Act 1982 (Provisional and Protective Measures) (Scotland) Order 1997 (SI 1997/2780 (S.174). The Civil Procedure Rules 1998, SI 1998/3132 were amended to provide for service of claims to which the Convention applies out of the jurisdiction and to make further provision as to the procedure for registration and enforcement of foreign judgments in England and Wales in accordance with the Convention. Provisions were also made in relation to the application the 1982 Act to judicial settlements.

With effect from 1 April 1997, the High Court in England and Wales has had the power to grant interim relief under s 25 of the Act for proceedings not in Brussels or Lugano Convention States and for proceedings whose subject matter is not within the scope of the Conventions.

The Civil Procedure Rules (CPR) and the relevant practice directions give effect to the Act, the Brussels and Lugano Conventions and both the original and recast Judgments Regulations (Brussels I and Brussels I Recast). CPR 6.18 states that a 'Regulation State' means a 'Member State' in the Judgments Regulation, that is all Member States including Denmark (see the Civil Jurisdiction and Judgments Regulations 2007, SI 2007/1655). Some of the most significant rules are **CPR 6.17–CPR 6.19** (service out of the jurisdiction), CPR 11 (disputing the court's jurisdiction), **CPR 12.10** at para (b) (entering default judgment in Convention cases), **CPR 25.13** (security for costs), **CPR 68** (references to the European Court) and **CPR 74** (enforcement of judgments in different jurisdictions).

III EUR [392]

Enforcement in different parts of the UK Schedule 4 to the 1982 Act established a regime for enforcement of UK judgments in other Member States and vice versa. Because there are three separate law districts within the UK it was necessary to make separate provision for jurisdiction within, and judgments going to and from, (a) England and Wales, (b) Scotland and (c) Northern Ireland. The CJEU has held that the interpretation of the regime for the allocation of jurisdiction is a matter within the sole jurisdiction of the national courts of the UK: *Kleinwort Benson Ltd v Glasgow City Council: C-346/93* [1996] QB 57, [1995] All ER (EC) 514, ECJ.

III EUR [393]

Special note on the Civil Jurisdiction and Judgments (Authentic Instruments and Court Settlements) Order 2001, SI 2001/3928 The Civil Jurisdiction and Judgments (Authentic Instruments and Court Settlements) Order 2001 was amended a couple of times, its latest amendment was made by the Civil and Judgments (Amendment) Regulations 2014. In particular, Regulation 4 and Schedule 3 made amendments to this Order to replace references to the Judgments Regulation (Brussels I) or to provisions of it, with references to the recast Judgments Regulation (Brussels I Recast), or to the corresponding provisions of it one of which was the replacement of the word "registration" for "enforcement" in its article 3.

III EUR [394]

Special note on the Civil Jurisdiction and Judgments Order 2001 The Civil Jurisdiction and Judgments Order 2001 has been amended a few times, usually to reflect changes to EU legislation but also to UK legislation, eg the Civil Jurisdiction and Judgments (Amendment) (Scotland) Regulations 2015 regarding adaptation measures of article 54 of the recast Judgments Regulation in Scotland.

Practitioners who need to serve proceedings outside the UK but inside the EU or who wish to have judgments recognised or enforced in a different Member State should rely on Brussels I or Brussels I Recast, as the case may be, but also on the above-mentioned Orders in their latest versions. The 1982 Act continues to have effect in cases involving the enforcement and recognition of judgments within the separate law districts within the UK and under the Brussels and Revised Lugano Conventions. Interactions between the Brussels and Lugano Conventions are governed by s 9 of the 1982 Act.

GENERAL NOTE

III EUR [395]

Comments and case law directly related to Brussels I and Brussels I Recast, ie old and new/ recast Judgments Regulation are located in the respective part of this Chapter and not reproduced here (see **III EUR [19]** et seq). Below some comments mainly applicable to the Brussels, 2005 Hague and Lugano Conventions.

EUROPE

III EUR [396]

1. Interpretation of references to the Conventions and Contracting States

(1) In this Act—

"the 1968 Convention" means the Convention on jurisdiction and and the enforcement of judgments in civil and commercial matters (including the Protocol annexed to that Convention), signed at Brussels on 27th September 1968;

"the 1971 Protocol" means the Protocol on the interpretation of the 1968 Convention by the European Court, signed at Luxembourg on 3rd June 1971;

"the Accession Convention" means the Convention on the accession to the 1968 Convention and the 1971 Protocol of Denmark, the Republic of Ireland and the United Kingdom, signed at Luxembourg on 9th October 1978;

"the 1982 Accession Convention" means the Convention on the accession of the Hellenic Republic to the 1968 Convention and the 1971 Protocol, with the adjustments made to them by the Accession Convention, signed at Luxembourg on 25th October 1982;

"the 1989 Accession Convention" means the Convention on the accession of the Kingdom of Spain and the Portuguese Republic to the 1968 Convention and the 1971 Protocol, with the adjustments made to them by the Accession Convention and the 1982 Accession Convention, signed at Donostia — San Sebastián on 26th May 1989;

"the 1996 Accession Convention" means the Convention on the accession of the Republic of Austria, the Republic of Finland and the Kingdom of Sweden to the 1968 Convention and the 1971 Protocol, with the adjustments made to them by the Accession Convention, the 1982 Accession Convention and the 1989 Accession Convention, signed at Brussels on 29th November 1996,

"the 2005 Hague Convention" means the Convention on Choice of Court Agreements concluded on 30th June 2005 at the Hague;

"the 2007 Hague Convention" means the Convention on the International Recovery of Child Support and other forms of Family Maintenance done at The Hague on 23 November 2007;

"the Brussels Conventions" means the 1968 Convention, the 1971 Protocol, the Accession Convention, the 1982 Accession Convention, the 1989 Accession Convention and the 1996 Accession Convention

"the Lugano Convention" means the Convention on jurisdiction and the recognition and enforcement of judgments in civil and commercial matters, between the European Community and the Republic of Iceland, the Kingdom of Norway, the Swiss Confederation and the Kingdom of Denmark signed on behalf of the European Community on 30th October 2007;

"the Regulation" means Regulation (EU) No 1215/2012 of the European Parliament and of the Council of 12 December 2012 on jurisdiction and the recognition and enforcement of judgments in civil and commercial matters (recast) as amended from time to time and as applied by virtue of the Agreement made on 19 October 2005 between the European Community and the Kingdom of Denmark on jurisdiction and the recognition and enforcement of judgments in civil and commercial matters (OJ No L 299, 16.11.2005, p 62; OJ No L79, 21.3.2013, p 4).

(2) In this Act, unless the context otherwise requires—

(a) references to, or to any provision of, the 1968 Convention or the 1971 Protocol are references to that Convention, Protocol or provision as amended by the Accession Convention, the 1982 Accession Convention, the 1989 Accession Convention and the 1996 Accession Convention; and

(aa) . . .

(b) any reference in any provision to a numbered Article without more is a reference—

(i) to the Article so numbered of the 1968 Convention, in so far as the provision applies in relation to that Convention, and

(ii) to the Article so numbered of the Lugano Convention, in so far as the provision applies in relation to that Convention, and any reference to a sub-division of a numbered Article shall be construed accordingly.

(3) In this Act—

"2005 Hague Convention State", in any provision, in the application of that provision in relation to the 2005 Hague Convention, means a State bound by that Convention;

"2007 Hague Convention State", in any provision, in the application of that provision in relation to the 2007 Hague Convention, means a State bound by that Convention;

"Contracting State", without more, in any provision means—

(a) in the application of the provision in relation to the Brussels Conventions, a Brussels Contracting State;

(b) in the application of the provision in relation to the Lugano Convention, a State bound by the Lugano Convention;

(c) in the application of the provision in relation to the 2005 Hague Convention, a 2005 Hague Convention State;

"Brussels Contracting State" means a state which is one of the original parties to the 1968 Convention or one of the parties acceding to that Convention under the Accession Convention, or under the 1982 Accession Convention, or under the 1989 Accession Convention, but only with respect to any territory—

(a) to which the Brussels Conventions apply; and

(b) which is excluded from the scope of the Regulation pursuant to Articles 349 and 355 of the Treaty on the Functioning of the European Union; and

"Maintenance Regulation State", in any provision, in the application of that provision in relation to the Maintenance Regulation means a Member State;

"State bound by the Lugano Convention" in any provision, in the application of that provision in relation to the Lugano Convention has the same meaning as in Article 1(3) of that Convention;

"Regulation State" in any provision, in the application of that provision in relation to the Regulation, means a Member State.

(4) Any question arising as to whether it is the Regulation, any of the Brussels Conventions, the Lugano Convention, or the 2005 Hague Convention which applies in the circumstances of a particular case shall be determined as follows—

(a) in accordance with Article 64 of the Lugano Convention (which determines the relationship between the Brussels Conventions and the Lugano Convention);

(b) in accordance with Article 68 of the Regulation (which determines the relationship between the Brussels Conventions and the Regulation).

(c) in accordance with Article 26 of the 2005 Hague Convention (which determines the relationship between the Brussels Conventions, the Lugano Convention, the Regulation and the 2005 Hague Convention).

III EUR [397]

2. The Brussels Conventions to have the force of law

(1) The Brussels Conventions shall have the force of law in the United Kingdom, and judicial notice shall be taken of them.

(2) For convenience of reference there are set out in Schedules 1, 2, 3, 3A, 3B and 3C respectively the English texts of—

(a) the 1968 Convention as amended by Titles II and III of the Accession Convention, by Titles II and III of the 1982

Accession Convention, by Titles II and III of, and Annex I(d) to, the 1989 Accession Convention and by Titles II and III of the 1996 Accession Convention;

(b) the 1971 Protocol as amended by Title IV of the Accession Convention, by Title IV of the 1982 Accession Convention, by Title IV of the 1989 Accession Convention and by Title IV of the 1996 Accession Convention;

(c) Titles V and VI of the Accession Convention (transitional and final provisions) as amended by Title V of the 1989 Accession Convention;

(d) Titles V and VI of the 1982 Accession Convention (transitional and final provisions); and

(e) Titles VI and VII of the 1989 Accession Convention (transitional and final provisions),

(f) Titles V and VI of the 1996 Accession Convention (transitional and final provisions),

being texts prepared from the authentic English texts referred to in Articles 37 and 41 of the Accession Convention, in Article 17 of the 1982 Accession Convention, in Article 34 of the 1989 Accession Convention and in Article 18 of the 1996 Accession Convention.

III EUR [398]

3. Interpretation of the Brussels Conventions

(1) Any question as to the meaning or effect of any provision of the Brussels Conventions shall, if not referred to the European Court in accordance with the 1971 Protocol, be determined in accordance with the principles laid down by and any relevant decision of the European Court.

(2) Judicial notice shall be taken of any decision of, or expression of opinion by, the European Court on any such question.

(3) Without prejudice to the generality of subsection (1), the following reports (which are reproduced in the Official Journal of the European Union), namely—

(a) the reports by Mr P Jenard on the 1968 Convention and the 1971 Protocol; and

(b) the report by Professor Peter Schlosser on the Accession Convention; and

(c) the report by Professor Demetrios I Evrigenis and Professor K D Kerameus on the 1982 Accession Convention; and

(d) the report by Mr Martinho de Almeida Cruz, Mr. Manuel Desantes Real and Mr P Jenard on the 1989 Accession Convention,

may be considered in ascertaining the meaning or effect of any provision of the Brussels Conventions and shall be given such weight as is appropriate in the circumstances.

III EUR [399]

4. Enforcement of judgments other than maintenance orders

(1) A judgment, other than a maintenance order, which is the subject of an application under Article 31 of the 1968 Convention for its enforcement in any part of the United Kingdom shall, to the extent that its enforcement is authorised by the appropriate court, be registered in the prescribed manner in that court.

In this subsection "the appropriate court" means the court to which the application is made in pursuance of Article 32 (that is to say, the High Court or the Court of Session).

(2) Where a judgment is registered under this section, the reasonable costs or expenses of and incidental to its registration shall be recoverable as if they were sums recoverable under the judgment.

(3) A judgment registered under this section shall, for the purposes of its enforcement, be of the same force and effect, the registering court shall have in relation to its enforcement the same powers, and proceedings for or with respect to its enforcement may be taken, as if the judgment had been originally given by the registering court and had (where relevant) been entered.

(4) Subsection (3) is subject to Article 39 (restriction on enforcement where appeal pending or time for appeal unexpired), to section 7 and to any provision made by rules of court as to the manner in which and conditions subject to which a judgment registered under this section may be enforced.

III EUR [399.1]

Application for registration An application for registration under s 4 must comply with the procedure laid down in CPR Part 74 and **CPR PD 74** and **CPR PD 74B** (see Volume I).

III EUR [400]

4A. Enforcement of judgments, other than maintenance orders, under the Lugano Convention

(1) Where a judgment, other than a maintenance order, is registered under the Lugano Convention, the reasonable costs or expenses of and incidental to its registration shall be recoverable as if they were sums recoverable under the judgment.

(2) A judgment other than a maintenance order registered under the Lugano Convention shall, for the purposes of its enforcement, be of the same force and effect, the registering court shall have in relation to its enforcement the same powers, and proceedings for or with respect to its enforcement may be taken, as if the judgment had been originally given by the registering court and had (where relevant) been entered.

(3) Subsection (2) is subject to Article 47(3) of the Lugano Convention (restriction on enforcement where appeal pending or time for appeal unexpired), to section 7 (interest on registered judgments) and to any provision made by rules of court as to the manner in which and conditions subject to which a judgment registered under the Lugano Convention may be enforced.

III EUR [400.1]

Application for registration An application for registration under s 4 must comply with the procedure laid down in CPR Part 74 and **CPR PD 74** and **CPR PD 74B** (see Volume I).

III EUR [401]

4B. Registration and enforcement of judgments under the 2005 Hague Convention

(1) A judgment which is required to be recognised and enforced under the 2005 Hague Convention in any part of the United Kingdom must be registered in the prescribed manner in the appropriate court, on the application of any interested party.

(2) In subsection (1) "the appropriate court" means—

(a) in England and Wales or Northern Ireland, the High Court;

(b) in Scotland, the Court of Session.

(3) A judgment which is required to be recognised and enforced under the 2005 Hague Convention must be registered without delay on completion of the formalities in Article 13 of the 2005 Hague Convention if the registering court considers that it meets the condition for recognition in Article 8(3) of the 2005 Hague Convention, without any review of whether a ground for refusal under Article 9 applies.

(4) The party against whom enforcement is sought shall not be entitled to make any submission on the application for registration.

(5) Where a judgment which is required to be recognised and enforced under the 2005 Hague Convention has been registered, the reasonable costs or expenses of and incidental to its registration shall be recoverable as if they were sums recoverable under the judgment.

(6) A judgment which is required to be recognised and enforced under the 2005 Hague Convention shall, for the purposes of its enforcement, be of the same force and effect, the registering court shall have in relation to its enforcement the same powers, and proceedings for or with respect to its enforcement may be taken, as if the judgment had been originally given by the registering court and had (where relevant) been entered.

(7) Subsection (6) is subject to section 7 (interest on registered judgments) and to any provision made by rules of court as to the manner in which and conditions subject to which a judgment registered under the 2005 Hague Convention may be enforced.

III EUR [401.1]

Application for registration An application for registration under s 4 must comply with the procedure laid down in CPR Part 74 and **CPR PD 74** and **CPR PD 74B** (see Volume I).

III EUR [402]

6. Appeals under Article 37, second paragraph and Article 41

(1) The single further appeal on a point of law referred to in the 1968 Convention in Article 37, second paragraph and Article 41 in relation to the recognition or enforcement of a judgment other than a maintenance order lies—

- (a) in England and Wales or Northern Ireland, to the Court of Appeal or to the Supreme Court in accordance with Part II of the Administration of Justice Act 1969 (appeals direct from the High Court to the Supreme Court);
- (b) in Scotland, to the Inner House of the Court of Session.

(2) Paragraph (a) of subsection (1) has effect notwithstanding section 15(2) of the Administration of Justice Act 1969 (exclusion of direct appeal to the Supreme Court in cases where no appeal to the Supreme Court lies from a decision of the Court of Appeal).

(3) The single further appeal on a point of law referred to in the 1968 Convention in Article 37, second paragraph and Article 41 in relation to the recognition or enforcement of a maintenance order lies—

- (a) ...
- (b) in Scotland, to the Inner House of the Court of Session;
- (c) in Northern Ireland, to the Court of Appeal.

III EUR [403]

6A. Appeals under Article 44 and Annex IV of the Lugano Convention

(1) The single further appeal on a point of law referred to in Article 44 and Annex IV of the Lugano Convention in relation to the recognition or enforcement of a judgment other than a maintenance order lies—

- (a) in England and Wales or Northern Ireland, to the Court of Appeal or to the Supreme Court in accordance with Part II of the Administration of Justice Act 1969 (appeals direct from the High Court to the Supreme Court);
- (b) in Scotland, to the Inner House of the Court of Session.

(2) Paragraph (a) of subsection (1) has effect notwithstanding section 15(2) of the Administration of Justice Act 1969 (exclusion of direct appeal to the Supreme Court in cases where no appeal to that House lies from a decision of the Court of Appeal).

(3) The single further appeal on a point of law referred to in Article 44 and Annex IV of the Lugano Convention in relation to the recognition or enforcement of a maintenance order lies—

(a) ...

(b) in Scotland, to the Inner House of the Court of Session;

(c) in Northern Ireland, to the Court of Appeal.

III EUR [404]

6B. Appeals in relation to registration of judgments under the 2005 Hague Convention

(1) A decision on the application for registration of a judgment required to be recognised and enforced under the 2005 Hague Convention may be appealed against by either party.

(2) The appeal referred to in subsection (1) lies—

(a) in England and Wales or Northern Ireland, to the High Court;

(b) in Scotland, to the Court of Session.

(3) The court to which an appeal referred to in subsection (1) is brought must refuse or revoke registration only if—

(a) the condition for recognition in Article 8(3) of the 2005 Hague Convention is not met;

(b) the ground for postponement or refusal of recognition in Article 8(4) of the 2005 Hague Convention applies; or

(c) one or more of the grounds specified in Article 9 of the 2005 Hague Convention apply.

(4) A single further appeal on a point of law against the judgment given on the appeal referred to in subsection (1) lies—

(a) in England and Wales or Northern Ireland, to the Court of Appeal or to the Supreme Court in accordance with Part II of the Administration of Justice Act 1969 (appeals direct from the High Court to the Supreme Court);

(b) in Scotland, to the Inner House of the Court of Session.

(5) Paragraph (a) of subsection (4) has effect notwithstanding section 15(2) of the Administration of Justice Act 1969 (exclusion of direct appeal to the Supreme Court in cases where no appeal to that Court lies from a decision of the Court of Appeal).

III EUR [405]

9. Provisions supplementary to Title VII of 1968 Convention

(1) The provisions of Title VII of the 1968 Convention and, apart from Article 64, of Title VII of the Lugano Convention and Article 26 of the 2005 Hague Convention (relationship between the Convention in question and other conventions to which Contracting States are or may become parties) shall have effect in relation to—

(a) any statutory provision, whenever passed or made, implementing any such other convention in the United Kingdom; and

(b) any rule of law so far as it has the effect of so implementing any such other convention,

as they have effect in relation to that other convention itself.

(1A) . . .

(2) . . .

III EUR [405.1]

This section governs the interaction among the main three Conventions, ie Brussels, Lugano and Hague 2005.

EUROPE

III EUR [406]

10. Allocation within UK of jurisdiction with respect to trusts and consumer contracts

(1) The provisions of this section have effect for the purpose of allocating within the United Kingdom jurisdiction in certain proceedings in respect of which the 1968 Convention or the Lugano Convention confers jurisdiction on the courts of the United Kingdom generally and to which section 16 does not apply.

(2) Any proceedings which by virtue of Article 5(6) (trusts) are brought in the United Kingdom shall be brought in the courts of the part of the United Kingdom in which the trust is domiciled.

(3) Any proceedings which by virtue of the first paragraph of Article 14 of the 1968 Convention or Article 16(1) of the Lugano Convention (consumer contracts) are brought in the United Kingdom by a consumer on the ground that he is himself domiciled there shall be brought in the courts of the part of the United Kingdom in which he is domiciled.

III EUR [406.1]

Proof and admissibility of judgments Sections 11, 11A and 11B provide for specific rules tailored to the specific Convention the judgments fall under. Essentially, a judgment of a court in a Contracting State, other than the UK, may be proved by production of a judgment document which bears the court seal or which is certified as a true copy by a judge or officer of that court. However, some specificities apply so see the relevant section. UK judgments may be certified for enforcement in other Contracting States in accordance with s 12. For more information on the certificate see CPR 74.

III EUR [407]

11. Proof and admissibility of certain judgments and related documents

(1) For the purposes of the 1968 Convention—

- (a) a document, duly authenticated, which purports to be a copy of a judgment given by a court of a Contracting State other than the United Kingdom shall without further proof be deemed to be a true copy, unless the contrary is shown; and
- (b) the original or a copy of any such document as is mentioned in Article 46(2) or 47 (supporting documents to be produced by a party seeking recognition or enforcement of a judgment) shall be evidence, and in Scotland sufficient evidence, of any matter to which it relates.

(2) A document purporting to be a copy of a judgment given by any such court as is mentioned in subsection (1)(a) is duly authenticated for the purposes of this section if it purports—

- (a) to bear the seal of that court; or
- (b) to be certified by any person in his capacity as a judge or officer of that court to be a true copy of a judgment given by that court.

(3) Nothing in this section shall prejudice the admission in evidence of any document which is admissible apart from this section.

III EUR [408]

11A. Proof and admissibility of certain judgments and related documents for the purposes of the Lugano Convention

(1) For the purposes of the Lugano Convention—

- (a) a document, duly authenticated, which purports to be a copy of a judgment given by a court of a State bound by the Lugano Convention other than the United Kingdom shall without further proof be deemed to be a true copy, unless the contrary is shown; and
- (b) a certificate obtained in accordance with Article 54 and Annex V shall be evidence, and in Scotland sufficient evidence, that the judgment is

enforceable in the State of origin which is bound by the Lugano Convention.

(2) A document purporting to be a copy of a judgment given by any such court as is mentioned in subsection (1)(a) is duly authenticated for the purposes of this section if it purports—

(a) to bear the seal of that court; or

(b) to be certified by any person in his capacity as a judge or officer of that court to be a true copy of a judgment given by that court.

(3) Nothing in this section shall prejudice the admission in evidence of any document which is admissible apart from this section.

III EUR [409]

11B. Proof and admissibility of certain judgments and related documents for the purposes of the 2005 Hague Convention

(1) For the purposes of the 2005 Hague Convention—

(a) a document, duly authenticated, which purports to be a copy of a judgment given by a court of a 2005 Hague Convention State other than the United Kingdom shall without further proof be deemed to be a true copy, unless the contrary is shown; and

(b) a certificate issued by the court of the 2005 Hague Convention State of origin, in the form recommended for use under the 2005 Hague Convention and published by the Hague Conference on Private International Law, as referred to in Article 13(3) of the 2005 Hague Convention, shall be evidence, and in Scotland sufficient evidence, as to whether the judgment has effect or is enforceable in the 2005 Hague Convention State of origin.

(2) A document purporting to be a copy of a judgment given by any such court as is mentioned in subsection (1)(a) is duly authenticated for the purposes of this section if it purports—

(a) to bear the seal of that court; or

(b) to be certified by any person in their capacity as judge or officer of that court to be a true copy of a judgment given by that court.

(3) Nothing in this section shall prejudice the admission in evidence of any document which is admissible apart from this section.

III EUR [410]

12. Provision for issue of copies of, and certificates in connection with, UK judgments

Rules of court may make provision for enabling any interested party wishing to secure under the 1968 Convention, the Lugano Convention or the 2005 Hague Convention the recognition or enforcement in another Contracting State of a judgment given by a court in the United Kingdom to obtain, subject to any conditions specified in the rules—

(a) a copy of the judgment; and

(b) a certificate giving particulars relating to the judgment and the proceedings in which it was given

III EUR [411]

13. Modifications to cover authentic instruments and court settlements

(1) Her Majesty may by Order in Council provide that—

(a) any provision of this Act relating to the recognition or enforcement in the United Kingdom or elsewhere of judgments to which the 1968 Convention applies; and

EUROPE

(b) any other statutory provision, whenever passed or made, so relating,
shall apply, with such modifications as may be specified in the Order, in relation to documents and settlements within Title IV of the 1968 Convention (authentic instruments and court settlements enforceable in the same manner as judgments) as if they were judgments to which [the Convention in question] applies.

(2) An Order in Council under this section may make different provision in relation to different descriptions of documents and settlements.

(3) Any Order in Council under this section shall be subject to annulment in pursuance of a resolution of either House of Parliament.

III EUR [412]

15. Interpretation of Part I and consequential amendments

(1) In this Part, unless the context otherwise requires—

"judgment" has the meaning given by Article 25 of the 1968 Convention or, as the case may be, Article 32 of the Lugano Convention or Article 4(1) of the 2005 Hague Convention;

"maintenance order" means a maintenance judgment within the meaning of the 1968 Convention or, as the case may be, the Lugano Convention;

"payer", in relation to a maintenance order, means the person liable to make the payments for which the order provides;

"prescribed" means prescribed by rules of court.

(2) References in this Part to a judgment registered under sections 4, 4A, 4B, 5 or 5A include, to the extent of its registration, references to a judgment so registered to a limited extent only.

(3) Anything authorised or required by the 1968 Convention, the Lugano Convention or this Part to be done by, to or before a particular magistrates' court in Northern Ireland may be done by, to or before any magistrates' court acting for the same petty sessions district as that court.

(4) The enactments specified in Part I of Schedule 12 shall have effect with the amendments specified there, being amendments consequential on this Part.

III EUR [413]

16. Allocation within UK of jurisdiction in certain civil proceedings

(1) The provisions set out in Schedule 4 (which contains a modified version of Chapter II of the Regulation) shall have effect for determining, for each part of the United Kingdom, whether the courts of law of that part, or any particular court of law in that part, have or has jurisdiction in proceedings where—

(a) the subject-matter of the proceedings is within the scope of the Regulation as determined by Article 1 of the Regulation (whether or not the Regulation has effect in relation to the proceedings); and

(b) the defendant or defender is domiciled in the United Kingdom or the proceedings are of a kind mentioned in Article 24 of the Regulation (exclusive jurisdiction regardless of domicile).

(2) [. . .]

(3) In determining any question as to the meaning or effect of any provision contained in Schedule 4—

(a) regard shall be had to any relevant principles laid down by the European Court in connection with Title II of the 1968 Convention or Chapter II of the Regulation and to any relevant decision of that court as to the meaning or effect of any provision of that Title or that Chapter; and

(b) without prejudice to the generality of paragraph (a), the reports mentioned in section 3(3) may be considered and shall, so far as relevant, be given such weight as is appropriate in the circumstances.

(4) The provisions of this section and Schedule 4 shall have effect subject to the Regulation, Schedule 6 to the Civil Jurisdiction and Judgments (Maintenance) Regulations 2011, the 1968 Convention, the Lugano Convention and the 2005 Hague Convention and to the provisions of section 17.

(5) [. . .]

III EUR [414]

17. Exclusion of certain proceedings from Schedule 4

(1) Schedule 4 shall not apply to proceedings of any description listed in Schedule 5 or to proceedings in Scotland under any enactment which confers jurisdiction on a Scottish court in respect of a specific subject-matter on specific grounds.

(2) Her Majesty may by Order in Council—

- (a) add to the list in Schedule 5 any description of proceedings in any part of the United Kingdom; and
- (b) remove from that list any description of proceedings in any part of the United Kingdom (whether included in the list as originally enacted or added by virtue of this subsection).

(3) An Order in Council under subsection (2)—

- (a) may make different provisions for different descriptions of proceedings, for the same description of proceedings in different courts or for different parts of the United Kingdom; and
- (b) may contain such transitional and other incidental provisions as appear to Her Majesty to be appropriate.

(4) An Order in Council under subsection (2) shall not be made unless a draft of the Order has been laid before Parliament and approved by a resolution of each House of Parliament.

III EUR [415]

18. Enforcement of UK judgments in other parts of UK

(1) In relation to any judgment to which this section applies—

- (a) Schedule 6 shall have effect for the purpose of enabling any money provisions contained in the judgment to be enforced in a part of the United Kingdom other than the part in which the judgment was given; and
- (b) Schedule 7 shall have effect for the purpose of enabling any non-money provisions so contained to be so enforced.

(2) In this section "judgment" means any of the following (references to the giving of a judgment being construed accordingly)—

- (a) any judgment or order (by whatever name called) given or made by a court of law in the United Kingdom;
- (b) any judgment or order not within paragraph (a) which has been entered in England and Wales in the High Court or the county court or in Northern Ireland in the High Court or a county court;
- (c) any document which in Scotland has been registered for execution in the Books of Council and Session or in the sheriff court books kept for any sheriffdom;
- (d) any award or order made by a tribunal in any part of the United Kingdom which is enforceable in that part without an order of a court of law;
- (e) an arbitration award which has become enforceable in the part of the United Kingdom in which it was given in the same manner as a judgment given by a court of law in that part;
- (f) an order made, or a warrant issued, under Part 8 of the Proceeds of Crime Act 2002 for the purposes of a civil recovery investigation

EUROPE

within the meaning given by section 341 of that Act or an unexplained wealth order made under that Part (see sections 362A and 396A of that Act;

(g) an order made, or a warrant issued, under Chapter 3 of Part 8 of the Proceeds of Crime Act 2002 for the purposes of a detained cash investigation, a detained property investigation or a frozen funds investigation within the meanings given by section 341 of that Act;

and, subject to the following provisions of this section, this section applies to all such judgments.

(3) Subject to subsection (4), (4ZA) and (4ZB), this section does not apply to—

(a) a judgment given in proceedings in a magistrates' court in England and Wales or Northern Ireland;

(b) a judgment given in proceedings other than civil proceedings;

(ba) a judgment given in the exercise of jurisdiction in relation to insolvency law, within the meaning of section 426 of the Insolvency Act 1986;

(c) a judgment given in proceedings relating to—

(i) [. . .]

(ii) [. . .]

(iii) the obtaining of title to administer the estate of a deceased person;

(d) an order made under Part 2, 3 or 4 of the Proceeds of Crime Act 2002 (confiscation).

(4) This section applies, whatever the nature of the proceedings in which it is made, to—

(a) a decree issued under section 13 of the Court of Exchequer (Scotland) Act 1856 (recovery of certain rent charges and penalties by process of the Court of Session);

(b) an order which is enforceable in the same manner as a judgment of the High Court in England and Wales by virtue of section 16 of the Contempt of Court Act 1981 or section 140 of the Senior Courts Act 1981 (which relate to fines for contempt of court and forfeiture of recognisances).

(4ZA) This section applies to a freezing order made under section 40D of the Immigration Act 2014 by a magistrates' court in England and Wales or a court of summary jurisdiction in Northern Ireland.

(4ZB) This section applies to the following orders made by a magistrates' court in England and Wales or Northern Ireland—

(a) an account freezing order made under section 303Z3 of the Proceeds of Crime Act 2002;

(b) an order for the forfeiture of money made under section 303Z14 of that Act;

(c) an account freezing order made under paragraph 10S of Schedule 1 to the Anti-terrorism, Crime and Security Act 2001;

(d) an order for the forfeiture of money made under paragraph 10Z2 of that Schedule.

(4A) This section does not apply as respects—

(a) the enforcement in Scotland of orders made by the High Court or the county court in England and Wales under or for the purposes of Part VI of the Criminal Justice Act 1988 or the Drug Trafficking Act 1994 (confiscation of the proceeds of certain offences or of drug trafficking); or

(b) the enforcement in England and Wales of orders made by the Court of Session or by the sheriff under or for the purposes of the Proceeds of Crime (Scotland) Act 1995.

(5) This section does not apply to so much of any judgment as—

(a) is an order to which section 16 of the Maintenance Orders Act 1950 applies (and is therefore an order for whose enforcement in another part of the United Kingdom provision is made by Part II of that Act);

(b) concerns the status or legal capacity of an individual;

(c) relates to the management of the affairs of a person not capable of managing his own affairs;

(d) is a provisional (including protective) measure other than an order of any of the following kinds—

(i) a freezing order of the kind mentioned in paragraph (a) or (c) of subsection (4ZB) made (in Scotland) by the sheriff (in addition to such orders made by a magistrates' court in England and Wales or Northern Ireland);

(ii) an order for the making of an interim payment;

(iii) an interim order made in connection with the civil recovery of proceeds of unlawful conduct;

(iv) an interim freezing order under section 362J of the Proceeds of Crime Act 2002;

(v) an interim freezing order under section 396J of that Act;

and except where otherwise stated references to a judgment to which this section applies are to such a judgment exclusive of any such provisions.

(6) The following are within subsection (5)(b), but without prejudice to the generality of that provision—

(a) an order or decree of judicial separation or of separation;

(b) any order which is a Part I order for the purposes of the Family Law Act 1986.

(6A) In subsection (5)(d), "an interim order made in connection with the civil recovery of proceeds of unlawful conduct" means any of the following made under Chapter 2 of Part 5 of the Proceeds of Crime Act 2002—

(a) a property freezing order or prohibitory property order;

(b) an order under section 245E or 245F of that Act (order relating to receivers in connection with property freezing order);

(c) an interim receiving order or interim administration order.

(7) This section does not apply to a judgment of a court outside the United Kingdom which falls to be treated for the purposes of its enforcement as a judgment of a court of law in the United Kingdom by virtue of registration under Part II of the Administration of Justice Act 1920, Part I of the Foreign Judgments (Reciprocal Enforcement) Act 1933, Part I of the Maintenance Orders (Reciprocal Enforcement) Act 1972, the International Recovery of Maintenance (Hague Convention 2007) Regulations 2012 or section 4 or 5 of this Act or by virtue of the Civil Jurisdiction and Judgments (Maintenance) Regulations 2011.

(8) A judgment to which this section applies, other than a judgment within paragraph (e) of subsection (2), shall not be enforced in another part of the United Kingdom except by way of registration under Schedule 6 or 7.

III EUR [416]

19. Recognition of UK judgments in other parts of UK

(1) A judgment to which this section applies given in one part of the United Kingdom shall not be refused recognition in another part of the United Kingdom solely on the ground that, in relation to that judgment, the court which gave it was not a court of competent jurisdiction according to the rules of private international law in force in that other part.

(2) Subject to subsection (3), this section applies to any judgment to which section 18 applies.

(3) This section does not apply to—

(a) the documents mentioned in paragraph (c) of the definition of "judgment" in section 18(2);
(b) the awards and orders mentioned in paragraphs (d) and (e) of that definition;
(c) the decrees and orders referred to in section 18(4).

III EUR [417]

24. Interim relief and protective measures in cases of doubtful jurisdiction

(1) Any power of a court in England and Wales or Northern Ireland to grant interim relief pending trial or pending the determination of an appeal shall extend to a case where—

(a) the issue to be tried, or which is the subject of the appeal, relates to the jurisdiction of the court to entertain the proceedings; or
(b) the proceedings involve the reference of any matter to the European Court under the 1971 Protocol; or
(c) the proceedings involve a reference of any matter relating to the Regulation or the Lugano Convention *or the 2005 Hague Convention* to the European Court under Article 267 of the Treaty on the Functioning of the European Union; or
(d) the proceedings involve a reference of any matter relating to the Maintenance Regulation to the European Court under Article 267 of the Treaty on the Functioning of the European Union.

(2) Any power of a court in Scotland to grant protective measures pending the decision of any hearing shall apply to a case where—

(a) the subject of the proceedings includes a question as to the jurisdiction of the court to entertain them; or
(b) the proceedings involve the reference of a matter to the European Court under the 1971 Protocol; or
(c) the proceedings involve a reference of any matter relating to the Regulation or the Lugano Convention *or the 2005 Hague Convention* to the European Court under Article 267 of the Treaty on the Functioning of the European Union; or
(d) the proceedings involve a reference of any matter relating to the Maintenance Regulation to the European Court under Article 267 of the Treaty on the Functioning of the European Union.

(3) Subsections (1) and (2) shall not be construed as restricting any power to grant interim relief or protective measures which a court may have apart from this section.

Amendment *Text in italic is deleted by the Civil Jurisdiction and Judgments (Hague Convention on Choice of Court Agreements 2005) (EU Exit) Regulations 2018, SI 2018/1124 with effect from exit day (as defined in the European Union (Withdrawal) Act 2018.*

III EUR [417.1]

In deciding whether to grant or refuse an interim declaration of invalidity the court should have regard, first, to the threshold condition that there is a serious case to be tried and then to the balance of convenience, namely the strength of the case in the CJEU and the loss to the parties if interim relief were granted or if it were refused: *R v Secretary of State for Transport, ex p Factortame (No 2)* [1991] 1 AC 603, 671-674 followed in *R v Secretary of State for Trade and Industry, ex p Trade Unions Congress* [2001] 1 CMLR 198, CA.

III EUR [418]

25. Interim relief in England and Wales and Northern Ireland in the absence of substantive proceedings

(1) The High Court in England and Wales or Northern Ireland shall have power to grant interim relief where—

(a) proceedings have been or are to be commenced in a Brussels Contracting State or a State bound by the Lugano Convention or a 2005 Hague Convention State or a Regulation State other than the United Kingdom or in a part of the United Kingdom other than that in which the High Court in question exercises jurisdiction; and

(b) they are or will be proceedings whose subject-matter is either within the scope of the Regulation, as determined by Article 1 of the Regulation, within the scope of the Maintenance Regulation as determined by Article 1 of that Regulation, within scope of the Lugano Convention as determined by Article 1 of the Lugano Convention or within scope of the 2005 Hague Convention as determined by Articles 1 and 2 of the 2005 Hague Convention (whether or not the Regulation, the Maintenance Regulation, the Lugano Convention or the 2005 Hague Convention has effect in relation to the proceedings).

(2) On an application for any interim relief under subsection (1) the court may refuse to grant that relief if, in the opinion of the court, the fact that the court has no jurisdiction apart from this section in relation to the subject-matter of the proceedings in question makes it inexpedient for the court to grant it.

(3) Her Majesty may by Order in Council extend the power to grant interim relief conferred by subsection (1) so as to make it exercisable in relation to proceedings of any of the following descriptions, namely—

(a) proceedings commenced or to be commenced otherwise than in a Brussels Contracting State or a State bound by the Lugano Convention or a 2005 Hague Convention State or Regulation State or a Maintenance Regulation State;

(b) proceedings whose subject-matter is not within the scope . . . of the Regulation as determined by Article 1 of the Regulation, the Maintenance Regulation as determined by Article 1 of that Regulation, the Lugano Convention as determined by Article 1 of the Lugano Convention or the 2005 Hague Convention as determined by Articles 1 and 2 of the 2005 Hague Convention;

(c) [. . .].

(4) An Order in Council under subsection (3)—

(a) may confer power to grant only specified descriptions of interim relief;

(b) may make different provision for different classes of proceedings, for proceedings pending in different countries or courts outside the United Kingdom or in different parts of the United Kingdom, and for other different circumstances; and

(c) may impose conditions or restrictions on the exercise of any power conferred by the Order.

(5) [. . .]

(6) Any Order in Council under subsection (3) shall be subject to annulment in pursuance of a resolution of either House of Parliament.

(7) In this section "interim relief", in relation to the High Court in England and Wales or Northern Ireland, means interim relief of any kind which that court has power to grant in proceedings relating to matters within its jurisdiction, other than—

(a) a warrant for the arrest of property; or

(b) provision for obtaining evidence.

III EUR [418.1]

The test of the UK courts' jurisdiction to grant injunctions under s 25 is one of expediency: *Republic of Haiti v Duvalier* [1990] 1 QB 202, [1989] 1 All ER 456, CA; *Refco Inc v Eastern Trading Co* [1999] 1 Lloyd's Rep 159.

III EUR [418.2]

The Civil Jurisdiction and Judgments Act 1982 (Interim Relief) Order 1997, SI 1997/302 The power to grant interim relief under this section was extended to proceedings in any part of the world.

The court has jurisdiction, in the strict sense, to grant an interlocutory or final injunction where it had in personam jurisdiction over the person against whom the injunction was sought and the court has the power to grant interim relief in relation to proceedings that had been or were about to be commenced in a foreign State. However, where those proceedings had not yet been issued, the court will require evidence that the claim for substantive relief has at least been formulated: *Fourie v Le Roux* [2007] UKHL 1, [2007] 1 All ER 1087.

III EUR [418.3]

Freezing orders A worldwide freezing order may be made under s 25 and served on a third party within the jurisdiction who also has assets outside the jurisdiction. But in *Bank of China v NBM LLC* [2001] 4 All ER 954, the court held, following the ruling in *Baltic Shipping Co v Translink Shipping Ltd* [1995] 1 Lloyd's Rep 673, that a proviso, for the protection of the third party, should normally be added to the standard form of order.

III EUR [418.4]

Insolvency Insolvency proceedings constituted by a compulsory winding-up order in a foreign court and the issue of letters of request to the English High Court are not 'proceedings' within s 25 in relation to which freezing orders may be made: *Fourie v Le Roux* [2005] EWCA Civ 204, (2005) Times, 25 April.

III EUR [419]

26. Security in Admiralty proceedings in England and Wales or Northern Ireland in case of stay, etc

(1) Where in England and Wales or Northern Ireland a court stays or dismisses Admiralty proceedings on the ground that the dispute in question should be submitted [. . .] to the determination of the courts of another part of the United Kingdom or of an overseas country, the court may, if in those proceedings property has been arrested or bail or other security has been given to prevent or obtain release from arrest—

- (a) order that the property arrested be retained as security for the satisfaction of any award or judgment which—
  - (i) is given in respect of the dispute in the [. . .] legal proceedings in favour of which those proceedings are stayed or dismissed; and
  - (ii) is enforceable in England and Wales or, as the case may be, in Northern Ireland; or
- (b) order that the stay or dismissal of those proceedings be conditional on the provision of equivalent security for the satisfaction of any such award or judgment.

(2) Where a court makes an order under subsection (1), it may attach such conditions to the order as it thinks fit, in particular conditions with respect to the institution or prosecution of the relevant [. . .] legal proceedings.

(3) Subject to any provision made by rules of court and to any necessary modifications, the same law and practice shall apply in relation to property retained in pursuance of an order made by a court under subsection (1) as would apply if it were held for the purposes of proceedings in that court.

III EUR [420]

39. Application of provisions corresponding to 1968 Convention in relation to certain territories

(1) Her Majesty may by Order in Council make provision corresponding to the provision made by the 1968 Convention as between the Contracting States to that Convention, with such modifications as appear to Her Majesty to be

appropriate, for regulating, as between the United Kingdom and any of the territories mentioned in subsection (2), the jurisdiction of courts and the recognition and enforcement of judgments.

(2) The territories referred to in subsection (1) are—

(a) the Isle of Man;

(b) any of the Channel Islands;

(c) any colony.

(3) An Order in Council under this section may contain such supplementary and incidental provisions as appear to Her Majesty to be necessary or expedient, including in particular provisions corresponding to or applying any of the provisions of Part I with such modifications as may be specified in the Order.

(4) Any Order in Council under this section shall be subject to annulment in pursuance of a resolution of either House of Parliament.

III EUR [421]

41. Domicile of individuals

(1) Subject to Article 52 (which contains provisions for determining whether a party is domiciled in a Contracting State), the following provisions of this section determine, for the purposes of the 1968 Convention and this Act, whether an individual is domiciled in the United Kingdom or in a particular part of, or place in, the United Kingdom or in a state other than a Contracting State.

(2) An individual is domiciled in the United Kingdom if and only if—

(a) he is resident in the United Kingdom; and

(b) the nature and circumstances of his residence indicate that he has a substantial connection with the United Kingdom.

(3) Subject to subsection (5), an individual is domiciled in a particular part of the United Kingdom if and only if—

(a) he is resident in that part; and

(b) the nature and circumstances of his residence indicate that he has a substantial connection with that part.

(4) An individual is domiciled in a particular place in the United Kingdom if and only if he—

(a) is domiciled in the part of the United Kingdom in which that place is situated; and

(b) is resident in that place.

(5) An individual who is domiciled in the United Kingdom but in whose case the requirements of subsection (3)(b) are not satisfied in relation to any particular part of the United Kingdom shall be treated as domiciled in the part of the United Kingdom in which he is resident.

(6) In the case of an individual who—

(a) is resident in the United Kingdom, or in a particular part of the United Kingdom; and

(b) has been so resident for the last three months or more,

the requirements of subsection (2)(b) or, as the case may be, subsection (3)(b) shall be presumed to be fulfilled unless the contrary is proved.

(7) An individual is domiciled in a state other than a Contracting State if and only if—

(a) he is resident in that state; and

(b) the nature and circumstances of his residence indicate that he has a substantial connection with that state.

III EUR [422]

42. Domicile and seat of corporation or association

(1) For the purposes of this Act the seat of a corporation or association (as determined by this section) shall be treated as its domicile.

(2) The following provisions of this section determine where a corporation or association has its seat—

(a) for the purpose of Article 53 (which for the purposes of the 1968 Convention equates the domicile of such a body with its seat); and

(b) for the purposes of this Act other than the provisions mentioned in section 43(1)(b) and (c).

(3) A corporation or association has its seat in the United Kingdom if and only if—

(a) it was incorporated or formed under the law of a part of the United Kingdom and has its registered office or some other official address in the United Kingdom; or

(b) its central management and control is exercised in the United Kingdom.

(4) A corporation or association has its seat in a particular part of the United Kingdom if and only if it has its seat in the United Kingdom and—

(a) it has its registered office or some other official address in that part; or

(b) its central management and control is exercised in that part; or

(c) it has a place of business in that part.

(5) A corporation or association has its seat in a particular place in the United Kingdom if and only if it has its seat in the part of the United Kingdom in which that place is situated and—

(a) it has its registered office or some other official address in that place; or

(b) its central management and control is exercised in that place; or

(c) it has a place of business in that place.

(6) Subject to subsection (7), a corporation or association has its seat in a state other than the United Kingdom if and only if—

(a) it was incorporated or formed under the law of that state and has its registered office or some other official address there; or

(b) its central management and control is exercised in that state.

(7) A corporation or association shall not be regarded as having its seat in a Contracting State other than the United Kingdom if it is shown that the courts of that state would not regard it as having its seat there.

(8) In this section—

"business" includes any activity carried on by a corporation or association, and "place of business" shall be construed accordingly;

"official address", in relation to a corporation or association, means an address which it is required by law to register, notify or maintain for the purpose of receiving notices or other communications.

III EUR [423]

43. Seat of Corporation or Association for purposes of Article 16 (2) and related provisions

(1) The following provisions of this section determine where a corporation or association has its seat for the purposes of—

(a) Article 16(2) of the 1968 Convention (which confers exclusive jurisdiction over proceedings relating to the formation or dissolution of such bodies, or to the decisions of their organs);

(b) Rules 4 and 11(b) in Schedule 4; and

(c) Rules 2(l) and 5(1)(b) in Schedule 8.

(2) A corporation or association has its seat in the United Kingdom if and only if—

- (a) it was incorporated or formed under the law of a part of the United Kingdom; or
- (b) its central management and control is exercised in the United Kingdom.

(3) A corporation or association has its seat in a particular part of the United Kingdom if and only if it has its seat in the United Kingdom and—

- (a) subject to subsection (5), it was incorporated or formed under the law of that part; or
- (b) being incorporated or formed under the law of a state other than the United Kingdom, its central management and control is exercised in that part.

(4) A corporation or association has its seat in a particular place in Scotland if and only if it has its seat in Scotland and—

- (a) it has its registered office or some other official address in that place; or
- (b) it has no registered office or other official address in Scotland, but its central management and control is exercised in that place.

(5) A corporation or association incorporated or formed under—

- (a) an enactment forming part of the law of more than one part of the United Kingdom; or
- (b) an instrument having effect in the domestic law of more than one part of the United Kingdom,

shall, if it has a registered office, be taken to have its seat in the part of the United Kingdom in which that office is situated, and not in any other part of the United Kingdom.

(6) Subject to subsection (7), a corporation or association has its seat in a Contracting State other than the United Kingdom if and only if—

- (a) it was incorporated or formed under the law of that state; or
- (b) its central management and control is exercised in that state.

(7) A corporation or association shall not be regarded as having its seat in a Contracting State other than the United Kingdom if—

- (a) it has its seat in the United Kingdom by virtue of subsection (2)(a); or
- (b) it is shown that the courts of that other state would not regard it for the purposes of Article 16(2) as having its seat there.

(8) In this section "official address" has the same meaning as in section 42.

III EUR [424]

44. Persons deemed to be domiciled in the United Kingdom for certain purposes

(1) This section applies to—

- (a) proceedings within Section 3 of Title II of the 1968 Convention (insurance contracts), and
- (b) proceedings within Section 4 of Title II of the 1968 Convention (consumer contracts).

(2) A person who, for the purposes of proceedings to which this section applies arising out of the operations of a branch, agency or other establishment in the United Kingdom, is deemed for the purposes of the 1968 Convention to be domiciled in the United Kingdom by virtue of—

- (a) Article 8, second paragraph (insurers); or
- (b) Article 13, second paragraph (suppliers of goods, services or credit to consumers),

shall, for the purposes of those proceedings, be treated for the purposes of this Act as so domiciled and as domiciled in the part of the United Kingdom in which the branch, agency or establishment in question is situated.

III EUR [425]

45. Domicile of trusts

(1) The following provisions of this section determine, for the purposes of the 1968 Convention the Lugano Convention and this Act, where a trust is domiciled.

(2) A trust is domiciled in the United Kingdom if and only if it is by virtue of subsection (3) domiciled in a part of the United Kingdom.

(3) A trust is domiciled in a part of the United Kingdom if and only if the system of law of that part is the system of law with which the trust has its closest and most real connection.

III EUR [426]

46. Domicile and the seat of the Crown

(1) For the purposes of this Act the seat of the Crown (as determined by this section) shall be treated as its domicile.

(2) The following provisions of this section determine where the Crown has its seat—

(a) for the purposes of the 1968 Convention (in which Article 53 equates the domicile of a legal person with its seat); and

(b) for the purposes of this Act.

(3) Subject to the provisions of any Order in Council for the time being in force under subsection (4)—

(a) the Crown in right of Her Majesty's government in the United Kingdom has its seat in every part of, and every place in, the United Kingdom; and

(aa) the Crown in right of the Scottish Administration has its seat in, and in every place in, Scotland,

(b) the Crown in right of Her Majesty's government in Northern Ireland has its seat in, and in every place in, Northern Ireland.

(4) Her Majesty may by Order in Council provide that, in the case of proceedings of any specified description against the Crown in right of Her Majesty's government in the United Kingdom, the Crown shall be treated for the purposes of the 1968 Convention as having its seat in, and in every place in, a specified part of the United Kingdom and not in any other part of the United Kingdom.

(5) An Order in Council under subsection (4) may frame a description of proceedings in any way, and in particular may do so by reference to the government department or officer of the Crown against which or against whom they fall to be instituted.

(6) Any Order in Council made under this section shall be subject to annulment in pursuance of a resolution of either House of Parliament.

(7) Nothing in this section applies to the Crown otherwise than in right of Her Majesty's government in the United Kingdom, the Scottish Administration or Her Majesty's government in Northern Ireland.

III EUR [427]

49. Saving for power to stay, sist, strike out or dismiss proceedings

Nothing in this Act shall prevent any court in the United Kingdom from staying, sisting, striking out or dismissing any proceedings before it, on the ground of forum non conveniens or otherwise, where to do so is not inconsistent with the 1968 Convention or, as the case may be, the Lugano Convention or the 2005 Hague Convention.

III EUR [427.1]

Power to stay The leading cases in this area are *Trendtex Trading Corpn v Crédit Suisse* [1980] QB 629, [1980] 3 All ER 721, CA and *Rockware Glass Ltd v MacShannon* [1978] AC 795, sub nom *MacShannon v Rockware Glass Ltd* [1978] 1 All ER 625, HL.

Where the court has jurisdiction under the Judgments Regulation (Brussels I), the power of the court to stay proceedings cannot be used simply because another Regulation State is the forum conveniens: *Mazur Media Ltd v Mazur Media GmbH* [2004] EWHC 1566 (Ch), [2004] 1 WLR 2966.

Section 49 has no application to jurisdictional disputes involving non-Contracting States: *Eli Lilly & Co v Novo Nordisk A/S* [2000] IL Pr 73, CA.

III EUR [428]

50. Interpretation: general

In this Act, unless the context otherwise requires—

"the Accession Convention", "the 1982 Accession Convention", "the 1989 Accession Convention" and "the 1996 Accession Convention" have the meaning given by section 1(1);

"Article" and references to sub-divisions of numbered Articles are to be construed in accordance with section 1(2)(b);

"association" means an unincorporated body of persons;

"Brussels Contracting State" has the meaning given by section 1(3);

"the Brussels Conventions" has the meaning given by section 1(1);

"Contracting State" has the meaning given by section 1(3);

"the 1968 Convention" has the meaning given by section 1(1), and references to that Convention and to provisions of it are to be construed in accordance with section 1(2)(a);

"the 2005 Hague Convention" has the meaning given by section 1(1);

"2005 Hague Convention State" has the meaning given by section 1(3);

"corporation" means a body corporate, and includes a partnership subsisting under the law of Scotland;

"court", without more, includes a tribunal;

"court of law", in relation to the United Kingdom, means any of the following courts, namely—

(a) the Supreme Court,

(aa) in England and Wales, the Court of Appeal, the High Court, the Crown Court, the family court, the county court and a magistrates' court,

(b) in . . . Northern Ireland, the Court of Appeal, the High Court, the Crown Court, a county court and a magistrates' court,

(c) in Scotland, the Court of Session, the Sheriff Appeal Court and a sheriff court;

"the Crown" is to be construed in accordance with section 51(2);

"enactment" includes an enactment comprised in Northern Ireland legislation;

"the 2007 Hague Convention" has the meaning given by section 1(1);

"2007 Hague Convention State" has the meaning given by section 1(3);

"judgment", subject to sections 15(1) and 18(2) and to paragraph 1 of Schedules 6 and 7, means any judgment or order (by whatever name called) given or made by a court in any civil proceedings;

"the Lugano Convention" has the meaning given by section 1(1);

"magistrates' court", in relation to Northern Ireland, means a court of summary jurisdiction;

"the Maintenance Regulation" has the meaning given by section 1(1);

"Maintenance Regulation State" has the meaning given by section 1(3);

"modifications" includes additions, omissions and alterations;

EUROPE

"overseas country" means any country or territory outside the United Kingdom;

"part of the United Kingdom" means England and Wales, Scotland or Northern Ireland;

"the 1971 Protocol" has the meaning given by section 1(1), and references to that Protocol and to provisions of it are to be construed in accordance with section 1(2)(a);

"the Regulation" has the meaning given by section 1(1);

"Regulation State" has the meaning given by section 1(3);

"rules of court", in relation to any court, means rules, orders or regulations made by the authority having power to make rules, orders or regulations regulating the procedure of that court, and includes—

(a) in Scotland, Acts of Sederunt;

(b) in Northern Ireland, Judgment Enforcement Rules;

"State bound by the Lugano Convention" has the meaning given by section 1(3);

"statutory provision" means any provision contained in an Act, or in any Northern Ireland legislation, or in—

(a) subordinate legislation (as defined in section 21(1) of the Interpretation Act 1978); or

(b) any instrument of a legislative character made under any Northern Ireland legislation;

"tribunal"—

(a) means a tribunal of any description other than a court of law;

(b) in relation to an overseas country, includes, as regards matters relating to maintenance within the meaning of the 1968 Convention, any authority having power to give, enforce, vary or revoke a maintenance order.

Schedules

SCHEDULE 4

CHAPTER II OF THE REGULATION AS MODIFIED: RULES FOR ALLOCATION OF JURISDICTION WITHIN UK

Section 16

GENERAL

III EUR [429]

1. Subject to the rules of this Schedule, persons domiciled in a part of the United Kingdom shall be sued in the courts of that part.

2. Persons domiciled in a part of the United Kingdom may be sued in the courts of another part of the United Kingdom only by virtue of rules 3 to 13 of this Schedule.

SPECIAL JURISDICTION

3. A person domiciled in a part of the United Kingdom may, in another part of the United Kingdom, be sued—

(a) in matters relating to a contract, in the courts for the place of performance of the obligation in question;

(b) in matters relating to maintenance, in the courts for the place where the maintenance creditor is domiciled or habitually resident or, if the matter is ancillary to proceedings concerning the status of a person, in the court which, according to its own law, has jurisdiction to entertain those proceedings, unless that jurisdiction is based solely on the nationality of one of the parties;

(c) in matters relating to tort, delict or quasi-delict, in the courts for the place where the harmful event occurred or may occur;

(d) as regards a civil claim for damages or restitution which is based on an act giving rise to criminal proceedings, in the court seised of those proceedings, to the extent that that court has jurisdiction under its own law to entertain civil proceedings;

(e) as regards a dispute arising out of the operations of a branch, agency or other establishment, in the courts for the place in which the branch, agency or other establishment is situated;

(f) as settlor, trustee or beneficiary of a trust created by the operation of a statute, or by a written instrument, or created orally and evidenced in writing, in the courts of the part of the United Kingdom in which the trust is domiciled;

(g) as regards a dispute concerning the payment of remuneration claimed in respect of the salvage of a cargo or freight, in the court under the authority of which the cargo or freight in question—

(i) has been arrested to secure such payment; or

(ii) could have been so arrested, but bail or other security has been given;

provided that this provision shall apply only if it is claimed that the defendant has an interest in the cargo or freight or had such an interest at the time of salvage;

(h) in proceedings—

(i) concerning a debt secured on immovable property; or

(ii) which are brought to assert, declare or determine proprietary or possessory rights, or rights of security, in or over movable property, or to obtain authority to dispose of movable property,

in the courts of the part of the United Kingdom in which the property is situated.

4. Proceedings which have as their object a decision of an organ of a company or other legal person or of an association of natural or legal persons may, without prejudice to the other provisions of this Schedule, be brought in the courts of the part of the United Kingdom in which that company, legal person or association has its seat.

5. A person domiciled in a part of the United Kingdom may, in another part of the United Kingdom, also be sued—

(a) where he is one of a number of defendants, in the courts for the place where any one of them is domiciled, provided the claims are so closely connected that it is expedient to hear and determine them together to avoid the risk of irreconcilable judgments resulting from separate proceedings;

(b) as a third party in an action on a warranty or guarantee or in any other third party proceedings, in the court seised of the original proceedings, unless these were instituted solely with the object of removing him from the jurisdiction of the court which would be competent in his case;

(c) on a counter-claim arising from the same contract or facts on which the original claim was based, in the court in which the original claim is pending;

(d) in matters relating to a contract, if the action may be combined with an action against the same defendant in matters relating to rights in rem in immovable property, in the court of the part of the United Kingdom in which the property is situated.

6. Where by virtue of this Schedule a court of a part of the United Kingdom has jurisdiction in actions relating to liability arising from the use or operation of a ship, that court, or any other court substituted for this purpose by the internal law of that part, shall also have jurisdiction over claims for limitation of such liability.

JURISDICTION OVER CONSUMER CONTRACTS

7. (1) In matters relating to a contract concluded by a person, the consumer, for a purpose which can be regarded as being outside his trade or profession, jurisdiction shall be determined by this rule and rules 8 and 9, without prejudice to rule 3(e) and (h)(ii), if—
   (a) it is a contract for the sale of goods on instalment credit terms; or
   (b) it is a contract for a loan repayable by instalments, or for any other form of credit, made to finance the sale of goods; or
   (c) in all other cases, the contract has been concluded with a person who pursues commercial or professional activities in the part of the United Kingdom in which the consumer is domiciled or, by any means, directs such activities to that part or to other parts of the United Kingdom including that part, and the contract falls within the scope of such activities.

(2) This rule shall not apply to a contract of transport other than a contract which, for an inclusive price, provides for a combination of travel and accommodation, or to a contract of insurance.

8. (1) A consumer may bring proceedings against the other party to a contract either in the courts of the part of the United Kingdom in which that party is domiciled or in the courts of the part of the United Kingdom in which the consumer is domiciled.
(2) Proceedings may be brought against a consumer by the other party to the contract only in the courts of the part of the United Kingdom in which the consumer is domiciled.
(3) The provisions of this rule shall not affect the right to bring a counter-claim in the court in which, in accordance with this rule and rules 7 and 9, the original claim is pending.

9. The provisions of rules 7 and 8 may be departed from only by an agreement—
   (a) which is entered into after the dispute has arisen; or
   (b) which allows the consumer to bring proceedings in courts other than those indicated in those rules; or
   (c) which is entered into by the consumer and the other party to the contract, both of whom are at the time of conclusion of the contract domiciled or habitually resident in the same part of the United Kingdom, and which confers jurisdiction on the courts of that part, provided that such an agreement is not contrary to the law of that part.

JURISDICTION OVER INDIVIDUAL CONTRACTS OF EMPLOYMENT

10. (1) In matters relating to individual contracts of employment, jurisdiction shall be determined by this rule, without prejudice to rule 3(e).
(2) An employer may be sued—
   (a) in the courts of the part of the United Kingdom in which he is domiciled; or
   (b) in the courts of the part of the United Kingdom where the employee habitually carries out his work or in the courts of that part where he last did so; or
   (c) if the employee does not or did not habitually carry out his work in any one place, in the courts of the part of the United Kingdom where the business which engaged the employee is or was situated.

(3) An employer may bring proceedings only in the courts of the part of the United Kingdom in which the employee is domiciled.

(4) The provisions of this rule shall not affect the right to bring a counter-claim in the court in which, in accordance with this rule, the original claim is pending.

(5) The provisions of this rule may be departed from only by an agreement on jurisdiction—

(a) which is entered into after the dispute has arisen; or

(b) which allows the employee to bring proceedings in courts other than those indicated in this rule.

Exclusive jurisdiction

11. The following courts shall have exclusive jurisdiction, regardless of domicile:—

(a)

(i) in proceedings which have as their object rights *in rem* in immovable property or tenancies of immovable property, the courts of the part of the United Kingdom in which the property is situated;

(ii) however, in proceedings which have as their object tenancies of immovable property concluded for temporary private use for a maximum period of six consecutive months, the courts of the part of the United Kingdom in which the defendant is domiciled shall also have jurisdiction, provided that the tenant is a natural person and that the landlord and the tenant are domiciled in the same part of the United Kingdom;

(b) in proceedings which have as their object the validity of the constitution, the nullity or the dissolution of companies or other legal persons or associations of natural or legal persons, the courts of the part of the United Kingdom in which the company, legal person or association has its seat;

(c) in proceedings which have as their object the validity of entries in public registers, the courts of the part of the United Kingdom in which the register is kept;

(d) in proceedings concerned with the enforcement of judgments, the courts of the part of the United Kingdom in which the judgment has been or is to be enforced.

Prorogation of jurisdiction

12. (1) If the parties have agreed that a court or the courts of a part of the United Kingdom are to have jurisdiction to settle any disputes which have arisen or which may arise in connection with a particular legal relationship, and, apart from this Schedule, the agreement would be effective to confer jurisdiction under the law of that part, that court or those courts shall have jurisdiction.

(2) The court or courts of a part of the United Kingdom on which a trust instrument has conferred jurisdiction shall have jurisdiction in any proceedings brought against a settlor, trustee or beneficiary, if relations between these persons or their rights or obligations under the trust are involved.

(3) Agreements or provisions of a trust instrument conferring jurisdiction shall have no legal force if they are contrary to the provisions of rule 9, or if the courts whose jurisdiction they purport to exclude have exclusive jurisdiction by virtue of rule 11.

13. (1) Apart from jurisdiction derived from other provisions of this Schedule, a court of a part of the United Kingdom before which a defendant enters an appearance shall have jurisdiction.

(2) This rule shall not apply where appearance was entered to contest the jurisdiction, or where another court has exclusive jurisdiction by virtue of rule 11.

EXAMINATION AS TO JURISDICTION AND ADMISSIBILITY

14. Where a court of a part of the United Kingdom is seised of a claim which is principally concerned with a matter over which the courts of another part of the United Kingdom have exclusive jurisdiction by virtue of rule 11, it shall declare of its own motion that it has no jurisdiction.

15. (1) Where a defendant domiciled in one part of the United Kingdom is sued in a court of another part of the United Kingdom and does not enter an appearance, the court shall declare of its own motion that it has no jurisdiction unless its jurisdiction is derived from the provisions of this Schedule.

(2) The court shall stay the proceedings so long as it is not shown that the defendant has been able to receive the document instituting the proceedings or an equivalent document in sufficient time to enable him to arrange for his defence, or that all necessary steps have been taken to this end.

PROVISIONAL, INCLUDING PROTECTIVE, MEASURES

16. Application may be made to the courts of a part of the United Kingdom for such provisional, including protective, measures as may be available under the law of that part, even if, under this Schedule, the courts of another part of the United Kingdom have jurisdiction as to the substance of the matter.

III EUR [429.1]

Schedule 4 was inserted by The Civil Jurisdiction and Judgments Implementing Order, SI 2001/3929 as amendments were needed in light of the Judgments Regulation (Brussels I) entry into force on 1 March 2002. It has been subsequently amended as a result of the repeal of Brussels I by Brussels I Recast (recast Judgments Regulation). Schedule 4 brought the jurisdictional arrangements between the separate law districts within the UK in line with the Brussels I Regulation, except as regards contract.

III EUR [429.2]

Contract The special jurisdiction in contract cases is still tied, by para 3(a), to the place of performance.

III EUR [429.3]

Tort In a case where insurers in England claimed that they had suffered damage by meeting a false claim put together in Scotland for the loss of a fishing vessel west of Shetland, it was held that the phrase "where the harmful event occurred" included the place of the event giving rise to the damage (in that case Scotland). The fact that the insurers were damaged in England was insufficient to establish jurisdiction: *Sunderland Marine Insurance Co Ltd v Wiseman (the Seaward Quest)* [2007] EWHC 1460 (Comm), [2007] 2 Lloyd's Rep 308, Langley J, QBD (Comm).

III EUR [429.4]

Jurisdiction by agreement The jurisdiction conferred by agreement need not be exclusive and the question of exclusivity is to be determined by the law governing the agreement: *McGowan v Summit* at Lloyds 2002 SLT 1258, (2002) Times, 21 July, Court of Session, Inner House.

III EUR [429.5]

District to grant a stay The discretion to stay proceedings in one law district in favour of proceedings in another law district within the same State should be exercised on grounds of lack of jurisdiction, not convenience of forum: *Cumming v Scottish Daily Record and Sunday Mail Ltd* [1995] EMLR 538, followed in *Ennstone Building Products Ltd v Stanger Ltd (Choice of Forum)* [2000] BLR 82.

SCHEDULE 5
PROCEEDINGS EXCLUDED FROM SCHEDULE 4

Section 17

III EUR [430]

1. Proceedings under the Companies Acts

Proceedings for the winding up of a company under the Insolvency Act 1986 or the Insolvency (Northern Ireland) Order 1989, or proceedings relating to a company as respects which jurisdiction is conferred on the court having winding up jurisdiction under either of those Acts.

2. Patents, trade marks, designs and similar rights

Proceedings concerned with the registration or validity of patents, trade marks, designs or other similar rights required to be deposited or registered.

3. Protection of Trading Interests Act 1980

Proceedings under section 6 of the Protection of Trading Interests Act 1980 (recovery of sums paid or obtained pursuant to a judgment for multiple damages).

4. Appeals etc from tribunals

Proceedings on appeal from, or for review of, decisions of tribunals.

5. Maintenance and similar payments to local and other public authorities

Proceedings for, or otherwise relating to, an order under any of the following provisions—

(a) paragraph 23 of Schedule 2 to the Children Act 1989, section 80 of the Social Work (Scotland) Act 1968 section 156 of the Children and Young Persons Act (Northern Ireland) 1968 or Article 41 of the Children (Northern Ireland) Order 1995 (contributions in respect of children in care, etc);

(b) section 49 or 50 of the Child Care Act 1980, section 81 of the Social Work (Scotland) Act 1968 or section 159 of the Children and Young Persons Act (Northern Ireland) 1968 (applications for, or for variation of, affiliation orders in respect of children in care, etc);

(c) *section 43 of the National Assistance Act 1948*, section 18 of the Supplementary Benefits Act 1976, section 24 of the Social Security Act 1986, section 106 of the Social Security Administration Act 1992 or any enactment applying in Northern Ireland and corresponding to either of them, Article 101 of the Health and Personal Social Services (Northern Ireland) Order 1972 or Article 23 of the Supplementary Benefits (Northern Ireland) Order 1977 (recovery of cost of assistance or benefit from person liable to maintain the assisted person);

(d) section 44 of the National Assistance Act 1948, section 19 of the Supplementary Benefits Act 1976, section 25 of the Social Security Act 1986 or any enactment applying in Northern Ireland and corresponding to it, Article 102 of the Health and Personal Social Services (Northern Ireland) Order 1972 or Article 24 of the Supplementary Benefits (Northern Ireland) Order 1977 (applications for, or for variation of, affiliation orders in respect of children for whom assistance or benefit provided).

6. Proceedings under certain conventions, etc

Proceedings brought in any court in pursuance of—

(a) any statutory provision which, in the case of any convention to which Article 57, or Article 71 of the Regulation, applies (conventions relating to specific matters which override the general rules [. . .]),

EUROPE

implements the convention or makes provision with respect to jurisdiction in any field to which the convention relates; and

(b) any rule of law so far as it has the effect of implementing any such convention.

7. Certain Admiralty proceedings in Scotland

Proceedings in Scotland in an admiralty action where the jurisdiction of the Court of Session or, as the case may be, of the sheriff is based on arrestment *in rem* or *ad fundandam jurisdictionem* of a ship, cargo or freight.

8. Register of aircraft mortgages

Proceedings for the rectification of the register of aircraft mortgages kept by the Civil Aviation Authority.

9. Continental Shelf Act 1964

Proceedings brought in any court in pursuance of an order under section 11 of the Petroleum Act 1998.

10. Financial Services Act 1986

Proceedings such as are mentioned in section 415 of the Financial Services and Marketing Act 2000.

11. Proceedings by third parties against insurers

Proceedings under the Third Parties (Rights against Insurers) Act 2010.

FINAL COMMENTS

III EUR [431]

Most of the authority of the case law under the old Judgments Regulation (Brussels I) is still applicable including in the context of the Brussels Convention, hence, practitioners should check the Brussels I section first (see **III EUR [19]** et seq). In addition, the website of the CJEU contains valuable information.

III EUR [432]

Brussels and Lugano Conventions on jurisdiction and the enforcement of judgments in civil and commercial matters – Exchange of information The Contracting States to the Lugano Convention set up a system for the exchange of information on judgments delivered under that convention and the Brussels Convention, which is largely identical to the Lugano Convention. The system, established pursuant to Protocol No 2 annexed to the Lugano Convention, includes, inter alia, the communication of information gathered by the Registrar of the CJEU, designated as the central body.

To that end, a selection of national decisions and certain judgments of the CJEU have been sent periodically since 1992 to the national authorities designated by the Contracting States. Since the entry into force of Council Regulation (EC) No 44/2001 – Brussels I – which replaced the Brussels Convention, the most important relevant decisions, likely to affect the interpretation of the Lugano Convention, have also been included.

At the request of the Contracting States, submitted in the context of the Standing Committee set up for the purposes of the mentioned Protocol, the documents sent are also published on curia.europa.eu/common/recdoc/convention/en/index.htm. The reports drawn up on the ba sis of the documents sent under the aegis of the Standing Committee are available on the w ebsite of the Federal Office of Justice (Switzerland).

FAMILY PROVISION

TABLE OF CONTENTS

INHERITANCE (PROVISION FOR FAMILY AND DEPENDANTS) ACT 1975

(c 63)

GENERAL NOTES ON INHERITANCE (PROVISION FOR FAMILY AND DEPENDANTS) ACT 1975

III FMY [1]

The Inheritance (Provision for Family and Dependants) Act 1975 gives the court jurisdiction to interfere with the exercise of a person's freedom of testamentary disposition. The Act enables the court to award financial provision for specified classes of applicants out of the estate of a deceased person. For the conceptual basis of the Act see generally *Ilott v Mitson (No 2)* [2017] UKSC 17, [2018] AC 545, [2017] 4 All ER 545, esp at [1]–[3], [49]–[66].

The Act only applies if the deceased died domiciled in England and Wales (sub-s 1(1)).

III FMY [2]

Amendments The Act was amended by the Family Law Act 1996. These amendments have not yet been brought into force and thus appear in the text as prospective amendments.

The Act was also amended by the Inheritance and Trustees' Powers Act 2014, which came into force on 1 October 2014, and it is printed here as so amended. The amendments apply only in relation to deaths occurring after 1 October 2014. For the text of the Act applicable to deaths before that date, see earlier editions of this work.

III FMY [3]

Jurisdiction Proceedings under the Act may be commenced in either the High Court or the County Court.

Claims under the Act in the High Court may be brought either in the Chancery Division or in the Family Division.

The Chancery Division is part of the Business and Property Courts. Claims under the Act in the Business and Property Courts should be issued in the Property, Trusts and Probate list: see Practice Direction 57AA – Business and Property Courts.

The Family Court, which is distinct from the Family Division of the High Court, does not have jurisdiction under the Act: *Practice Guidance (Family Court: Allocation and Transfer of Cases)* Family Division 28 February 2018 [2018] 1 WLR 2924.

The County Court has unlimited jurisdiction in claims under the Act: County Courts Act 1984, s 25 (para **II CCA [14]**). For the allocation of proceedings between the High Court and the County Court see the High Court and County Courts Jurisdiction Order 1991, SI 1991/724, Art 4 (para **II HCJ [5]**).

III FMY [4]

Procedure Procedure in both the High Court and the County Court is governed by CPR 57.14–57.16 and the Practice Direction to that part. Proceedings in the Family Division are subject to the CPR in all respects save for CPR 40 (drawing up and service of orders). For further notes on procedural matters, see CPR 57 (para **CPR 57**).

III FMY [4A]

Costs For the correct approach to costs where a claimant fails to beat a Part 36 offer but the defendants bear most of the responsibility for the case having been pursued in an inappropriate "no holds barred" manner, see *Lilleyman v Lilleyman* [2012] EWHC 1056 (Ch), [2013] 1 All ER 325, [2012] 1 WLR 2801.

III FMY [5]

Precedents For precedents for claims under the Act and further notes on procedure, see **BCCP Q[451]-BCCP Q[501]**.

III FMY [6]

Related remedies Where a will fails to carry out the deceased's intentions in consequence of a clerical error or a failure to understand his instructions, the court has jurisdiction to order that the will be rectified to carry out his intentions: see s 20 of the Administration of Justice Act 1982 (para **III TRU [43B]**). Where a person alters his position in reliance on representations made to him by another, a proprietary estoppel may arise which the court may order to be satisfied by an award of an interest in the estate of the representor: see *Thorner v Major* [2009] UKHL 18, [2009] 3 All ER 945, [2009] 1 WLR 776; *Gillett v Holt* [2001] Ch 210, [2000] 2 All ER 289. For examples of proprietary estoppel, see *Campbell v Griffin* [2001] EWCA Civ 990, [2001] WTLR 951 (lodger lived largely rent free in house but provided care to its owners in reliance on an unfulfilled assurance that he would have a home for life; an equity arose in his favour which the court ordered to be satisfied by an award of a lump sum charged on the house); *Jennings v Rice* [2002] EWCA Civ 1591, [2002] WTLR 367 (elderly widow and carer, claim by carer succeeded); *Grundy v Ottey* [2003] EWCA Civ 176, [2003] WTLR 1253 (quasi-matrimonial relationship, claim succeeded).

A resulting trust may arise where the purchase price of property is contributed in whole or part by a person other than the legal owner. A constructive trust may arise where it would be unconscionable for the legal owner of the property to deny the existence of another's beneficial interest in it: see further **III REA [58.2]–III REA [58.2B]**

A claim of these kinds may be more appropriate than, or may be combined with, a claim under the Inheritance (Provision for Family and Dependants Act) 1975.

III FMY [6A]

Forfeiture of gifts by claim under the Inheritance (Provision for Family and Dependants) Act 1975 A condition in a will depriving a beneficiary thereunder of a gift in the will if he, or another, brings a claim against the estate under the Inheritance (Provision for Family and Dependants) Act 1975 may be valid. However, the court has jurisdiction to relieve beneficiaries from the forfeiture of their gifts if the forfeiture occurs through no fault of theirs: *Nathan v Leonard* [2002] EWHC 1385 (Ch), [2003] 4 All ER 198, [2003] 1 WLR 827. Further, when assessing a claim under the Act by a beneficiary a gift to whom has been forfeited, the court can take account of the effect of the forfeiture.

III FMY [6B]

Standing of applicant to bring a probate claim A person who falls within the categories of persons able to bring a claim against an estate under the Inheritance (Provision for Family and Dependants) Act 1975 has a sufficient interest in the estate to bring a probate claim under **CPR 57.2**: *O'Brien v Seagrave* [2007] EWHC 788 (Ch); [2007] 3 All ER 633; [2007] 1 WLR 2002.

POWERS OF COURT TO ORDER FINANCIAL PROVISION FROM DECEASED'S ESTATE

III FMY [7]

1. Application for financial provision from deceased's estate

(1) Where after the commencement of this Act a person dies domiciled in England and Wales and is survived by any of the following persons—

- (a) the spouse or civil partner of the deceased;
- (b) a former spouse or former civil partner of the deceased, but not one who has formed a subsequent marriage or civil partnership;
- (ba) any person (not being a person included in paragraph (a) or (b) above) to whom subsection (1A) or (1B) below applies;
- (c) a child of the deceased;
- (d) any person (not being a child of the deceased) who in relation to any marriage or civil partnership to which the deceased was at any time a party, or otherwise in relation to any family in which the deceased at any time stood in the role of a parent, was treated by the deceased as a child of the family;

(e) any person (not being a person included in the foregoing paragraphs of this subsection) who immediately before the death of the deceased was being maintained, either wholly or partly, by the deceased;

that person may apply to the court for an order under section 2 of this Act on the ground that the disposition of the deceased's estate effected by his will or the law relating to intestacy, or the combination of his will and that law, is not such as to make reasonable financial provision for the applicant.

(1A) This subsection applies to a person if the deceased died on or after 1st January 1996 and, during the whole of the period of two years ending immediately before the date when the deceased died, the person was living—

(a) in the same household as the deceased, and

(b) as the husband or wife of the deceased.

(1B) This subsection applies to a person if for the whole of the period of two years ending immediately before the date when the deceased died the person was living—

(a) in the same household as the deceased, and

(b) as the civil partner of the deceased.

(2) In this Act "reasonable financial provision"—

(a) in the case of an application made by virtue of subsection (1)(a) above by the husband or wife of the deceased (except where *the marriage with the deceased was the subject of a decree of judicial separation and at the date of death the decree was in force* [, at the date of death, a separation order under the Family Law Act 1996 was in force in relation to the marriage] and the separation was continuing), means such financial provision as it would be reasonable in all the circumstances of the case for a husband or wife to receive, whether or not that provision is required for his or her maintenance;

(aa) in the case of an application made by virtue of subsection (1)(a) above by the civil partner of the deceased (except where, at the date of death, a separation order under Chapter 2 of Part 2 of the Civil Partnership Act 2004 was in force in relation to the civil partnership and the separation was continuing), means such financial provision as it would be reasonable in all the circumstances of the case for a civil partner to receive, whether or not that provision is required for his or her maintenance;

(b) in the case of any other application made by virtue of subsection (1) above, means such financial provision as it would be reasonable in all the circumstances of the case for the applicant to receive for his maintenance.

(2A) The reference in subsection (1)(d) above to a family in which the deceased stood in the role of a parent includes a family of which the deceased was the only member (apart from the applicant).

(3) For the purposes of subsection (1)(e) above, a person is to be treated as being maintained by the deceased (either wholly or partly, as the case may be) only if the deceased was making a substantial contribution in money or money's worth towards the reasonable needs of that person, other than a contribution made for full valuable consideration pursuant to an arrangement of a commercial nature.

Amendment *Text in italic is deleted and text in square brackets is inserted by the Family Law Act 1996 with effect from a date to be appointed.*

III FMY [7.1]

Claims under the Act A claim for financial provision under the Act involves the following three stages:

(1) Is the claimant within the categories (defined in sub-s 1(1) of the Act) of persons entitled to make a claim?

(2) If so, was the disposition of the deceased's estate effected by his will or the law relating to intestacy (or both) not such as to make reasonable financial provision for the claimant?

(3) If so, what (if any) financial provision should the court make for the claimant out of the deceased's estate?

The court is required to have regard to the matters specified in s 3 of the Act in relation to both questions (2) and (3). There is in most cases a substantial overlap between questions (2) and (3). There may be cases in which it will be convenient to separate questions (2) and (3), but in many cases the same conclusions will both answer the question whether reasonable financial provision has been made for the claimant and identify what that financial provision should be: *Ilott v Mitson (No 2)* [2017] UKSC 17, [2018] AC 545, [2017] 4 All ER 545 at [23]–[24].

III FMY [7.1A]

Civil partnership The Act was amended by the Civil Partnership Act 2004 to give civil partnership the same status as marriage for the purposes of the Act. Thus, claims can now be brought against the estate of a deceased person by the following additional classes of applicant: (i) a civil partner of the deceased, (ii) a former civil partner of the deceased who has not formed a subsequent civil partnership or marriage, (iii) a person treated by the deceased as a child of a civil partnership to which the deceased was a party and (iv) a person who during the whole of the period of two years ending with the death of the deceased was living in the same household as the deceased and as the civil partner of the deceased. The criteria applicable to such claims are similar to those applicable to the corresponding relationships defined by reference to marriage. The amendments were brought into force by the Civil Partnership (Commencement No 2) Order 2005, SI 2005/3175 (C.136) with effect from 5 December 2005.

III FMY [7.2]

Subsection 1(1)(a) – the spouse or civil partner of the deceased For void marriages, see sub-s 25(4). For void civil partnerships see sub-s 25(4A) (para **III FMY [20]**). For polygamous marriages, see *Re Sehota, Kaur v Kaur* [1978] 3 All ER 385, [1978] 1 WLR 1506.

III FMY [7.3]

Subsection 1(1)(b) – a former spouse or former civil partner of the deceased See the definitions of "former spouse" and "former civil partner" in sub-s 25 (1) (para **III FMY [20]**). For void marriages, see sub-s 25(4). For void civil partnerships see sub-s c 25(4A) (para **III FMY [20]**). Where a subsequent marriage or civil partnership is void or voidable, see sub-s 25 (5) (para **III FMY [20]**). Where a marriage or civil partnership was preceded by a marriage or civil partnership which was void or voidable, see sub-s 25 (5A) (para **III FMY [20]**). For special provisions relating to the separation of spouses and civil partners and the dissolution of marriages and civil partnerships, see sections 14 to 18A (paras **III FMY [17]–III FMY[17E]**).

A former spouse who is precluded by an order under sub-s 15(1) from bringing a claim under sub-s 1(1)(b) is not precluded by that order from bringing a claim under sub-s 1(1)(ba): *Chekov v Fryer* [2015] EWHC 1642 (Ch) (Deputy Master Matthews): see para **III FMY [17E.1]**.

III FMY [7.4]

Subsection 1(1)(ba) – unmarried partners Sub-s 1(1)(ba) and sub-s (1A) were inserted by the Law Reform (Succession) Act 1995. They apply if the deceased died after 1 January 1996. Sub-s 1(1B) was inserted by the Civil Partnership Act 2004 (see para **III FMY [7.1]**).

A claimant may claim under sub-s 1(1)(ba) even if precluded by an order under sub-s 15(1) from bringing a claim under sub-s 1(1)(b): *Chekov v Fryer* [2015] EWHC 1642 (Ch), [2015] All ER (D) 303 (Jun) (Deputy Master Matthews): see **III FMY [17E.1]**.

III FMY [7.4A]

"During the whole of the period of two years ending immediately before the deceased died" The requirements of s 1A of the Act may be satisfied notwithstanding that the parties were living apart at the time of the deceased's death. In determining whether the requirements are satisfied, regard is to be had to the settled state of affairs existing during the relationship and not to the immediate situation at the moment of death. Accordingly, if the parties, although living apart, are still tied by the relationship, neither having demonstrated a settled acceptance or recognition that it is at an end, they may still be regarded as living "in the same household". It is otherwise if there has been an irretrievable breakdown of the relationship: *Re Dix decd* [2004] EWCA Civ 139, [2004] 1 WLR 1399. For an application of these principles, see *Kaur v Dhaliwal* [2014] EWHC 1991 (Ch), [2014] Fam Law 1241, [2014] WTLR 1381.

III FMY [7.4B]

"in the same household as the deceased" Living in the same household "seems to me to have elements of permanence, to involve a consideration of the frequency and intimacy of contact, to contain an element of mutual support, to require some consideration of the degree of voluntary restraint upon personal freedom which each party undertakes, and to involve an element of community of resources. None of these factors of itself is sufficient, but each may provide an indicator": *Churchill v Roach* [2002] EWHC 3230 (Ch), [2004] 2 FLR 989, Judge Norris QC, followed in *Baynes v Hedger* [2008] EWHC 1587 (Ch), [2008] 2 FLR 1805 Lewison J at [117], affd [2009] EWCA Civ 374, [2009] 2 FLR 767. See too *Lindsop v Agus* [2009] EWHC 1795 (Ch), [2009] WTLR 1175.

III FMY [7.4C]

"as the husband or wife of the deceased" It is wrong to conclude that two people were living together as husband and wife simply because their relationship was one which a husband and wife could have. The court should ask whether, in the opinion of a reasonable person with normal perceptions, it could be said that they were living together as husband and wife. But the court should not ignore the multifarious nature of marital relationships: *Re Watson* [1999] 3 FCR 595, [1999] 1 FLR 878.

A test of whether two persons were living as husband and wife is (a) whether the relationship is an emotional one of mutual lifetime commitment rather than simply one of convenience, friendship or the living together of lovers and (b) whether the relationship has been presented to the outside world openly and unequivocally, so that society considers it to be of permanent intent: *Southern Housing Group Ltd v Nutting* [2004] EWHC 2982 (Ch), [2005] 2 P & CR 14, Evans-Lombe J, followed in *Baynes v Hedger* [2008] EWHC 1587 (Ch), [2008] 2 FLR 1805 Lewison J at [123]–[125], affd [2009] EWCA Civ 374, [2009] 2 FLR 767. See too *Lindsop v Agus* [2009] EWHC 1795 (Ch), [2009] WTLR 1175.

III FMY [7.4D]

"as the civil partner of the deceased" See *Baynes v Hedger* [2008] EWHC 1587 (Ch), [2008] 2 FLR 1805 Lewison J at [117]–[125], affd [2009] EWCA Civ 374, [2009] 2 FLR 767.

III FMY [7.5]

Subsection 1(1)(c) – a child of the deceased See the definition of "child" in sub-s 25(2) (para **III FMY [20]**). A child of the deceased who has been adopted by others under the Adoption Act 1976 is in law the child of the adopters and not of the deceased: *Re Collins* [1990] Fam 56, [1990] 2 All ER 47.

III FMY [7.6]

Subsection 1(1)(d) – a person treated by the deceased as a child of the family This category is not limited to minor children: see *Re Callaghan* [1985] Fam 1, [1984] 3 All ER 790; *Re Leach* [1986] Ch 226, [1985] 2 All ER 754, CA.

Sub-s 1(1)(d) formerly extended only to any person who was treated by the deceased as a child of the family in relation to a marriage or civil partnership to which the deceased was at any time a party. This provision was amended by the Inheritance and Trustees' Powers Act 2014 to include any person who was treated by the deceased as a child of the family in relation to any other family in which the deceased stood in the role of a parent. The requirement that the deceased stood in the role of a parent in that family means that the relationship between the deceased and the applicant needs to have been akin to that between a parent and a child. Other family members who form part of the deceased's family, but in relation to whom the deceased did not stand in in the role of a parent, are not within this category of claimant.

Sub-s 1(2A) provides that an applicant can be treated as a child of a family in which the deceased stood in the role of a parent even if that family only existed in the relationship between the deceased and the applicant. Thus, a 'single parent family' is included within the scope of sub-s 1(1)(d).

III FMY [7.7]

Subsection 1(1)(e) – a person who was being maintained by the deceased Where the deceased died on or after 1 January 1996, many claimants who would formerly have had to bring themselves within sub-s 1(1)(e) will now fall within sub-s 1(1)(ba). If a claimant falls within sub-s 1(1)(ba) he does not fall within sub-s 1(1)(e): see sub-s 1(1)(e).

Sub-s 1(3) exhaustively defines what is meant by "being maintained": *Re Beaumont* [1980] Ch 444, [1980] 1 All ER 266; *Jelley v Iliffe* [1981] Fam 128, [1981] 2 All ER 29, CA.

Sub-s 1(3) was amended by the Inheritance and Trustees' Powers Act 2014. Formerly, sub-s 1(3) required the court to balance the contribution made by the deceased towards the needs of the applicant against any benefits the applicant provided to the deceased. This was the case even if the applicant and the deceased were living in an interdependent domestic relationship, with no commercial aspect. If the 'balance sheet' showed that the applicant contributed more to the deceased than vice versa, the applicant was not considered to have been maintained by the deceased, and could not apply under sub-s 1(1)(e).

As amended, sub-s 1(3) requires the deceased to have been making a substantial contribution towards the reasonable needs of the applicant, but in deciding whether that requirement is met the only benefits provided by the applicant to the deceased that are taken into account are those provided for full valuable consideration pursuant to an arrangement of a commercial nature. This means that contributions made between people in a domestic context should not be weighed against one another for these purposes.

III FMY [7.8]

Immediately before the death of the deceased When deciding whether the claimant was being maintained by the deceased "immediately before the death of the deceased" the court has to look at the settled basis or general arrangement between the parties, not the actual, perhaps fluctuating, variation of it which existed at the precise moment of death: *Re Beaumont* [1980] Ch 444, [1980] 1 All ER 266; *Jelley v Iliffe* [1981] Fam 128, [1981] 2 All ER 29, CA; *Re Dix decd* [2004] EWCA Civ 139, [2004] 1 WLR 1399. Contrast *Kourkby v Lusher* (1981) 4 FLR 65, 12 Fam Law 86 (claimant and deceased separated a few days before the deceased's death; claimant not being maintained "immediately before" deceased's death).

The provision of financial assistance is not be equated with assuming responsibility for maintenance and setting up a trust fund years before the death does not amount to providing maintenance "immediately before the death": *Baynes v Hedger* [2009] EWCA Civ 374, [2009] FLR 767.

III FMY [7.9]

That person may apply The claim is personal to the claimant and does not pass to his personal representatives on his death: *Whyte v Ticehurst* [1986] Fam 64, [1986] 2 All ER 158; *Re R, R v O* [1986] Fam Law 58; *Re Bramwell* [1988] 2 FLR 263; *Roberts v Fresco* [2017] EWHC 283 (Ch), [2017] Ch 433.

III FMY [7.10]

Law relating to intestacy For succession on intestacy see the Administration of Estates Act 1925 s 46 as amended. The provisions of that section relating to bona vacantia take effect subject to the provisions of this Act: s 24 of this Act (see para **III FMY [19B]**).

III FMY [7.11]

Failure to make reasonable financial provision The condition for making an order under the Act is that the will, or the intestacy regime, as the case may be, does not "make reasonable financial provision" for the claimant: s 1(1). Reasonable financial provision is, by s 1(2), what it is "reasonable for [the claimant] to receive", either for maintenance or without that limitation, according to the class of claimant. These words connote an objective standard of financial provision, to be determined by the court. The Act does not say that the court may make an order when it judges that the deceased acted unreasonably. There can be a failure to make reasonable financial provision when the deceased's conduct cannot be said to be unreasonable. Conversely, the deceased may have acted unreasonably towards a claimant, but it may not follow that his dispositions fail to make reasonable financial provision for that claimant: *Ilott v Mitson (No 2)* [2017] UKSC 17, [2018] AC 545, [2017] 4 All ER 545 at [16], approving *Re Coventry, decd* [1980] Ch 461, [1979] 2 All ER 408, [1979] 3 All ER 815.

III FMY [7.12]

Maintenance The concept of maintenance is broad, but does not extend to everything which it would be desirable for the claimant to have. It must import provision to meet the everyday expenses of living. The level at which maintenance may be provided for is flexible and falls to be assessed on the facts of each case. It is not limited to subsistence level. Although maintenance is by definition the provision of income rather than capital, it need not necessarily be provided for by periodical payments. It will very often be more appropriate for provision to be made by a lump sum: *Ilott v Mitson (No 2)* [2017] UKSC 17, [2018] AC 545, [2017] 4 All ER 545 at [14]–[15], approving *Re Dennis, decd* [1981] 2 All ER 140, 145–146. See too *Re Jennings* [1994] Ch 286 at 297; *Negus v Bahouse* [2007] EWHC 2628 (Ch), [2008] 1 FLR 381.

A sum awarded to pay a claimant's debts will not fall within the concept of "maintenance" unless the payment of those debts enables the claimant to derive a future income which he or she could not do if the debts remain unpaid; or the debts represent living expenses incurred since the date of death of the deceased: *Baynes v Hedger* [2008] EWHC 1587 (Ch), [2008] 2 FLR 1805 Lewison J at [147], affd [2009] EWCA Civ 374, [2009] 2 FLR 767.

'Maintenance' can exceptionally encompass an arrangement for full consideration. Accordingly, where the deceased owned a house in which she and the elderly and infirm claimant had lived as husband and wife for 20 years, her Will, in leaving her entire estate to her daughter, failed to make reasonable provision for the claimant's maintenance, notwithstanding that he had sufficient funds to buy another house for himself. In the circumstances, reasonable financial provision for the claimant's maintenance consisted of the grant of an option for the claimant to buy the house from the deceased's executors at full market value: *Lewis v Warner* [2016] EWCA Civ 2182, [2018] Ch 450, [2017] All ER (D) 116 (Dec).

III FMY [7.13]

Reasonable financial provision for a spouse or civil partner In a claim by a surviving spouse or civil partner, "reasonable financial provision" is what it would be reasonable for the claimant to receive, whether or not that provision is needed for his or her maintenance: see s 1(2)(a). The mischief at which this provision is directed is the risk of a surviving spouse or civil partner being in a worse provision if the relationship were terminated by death than by divorce: *Ilott v Mitson (No 2)* [2017] UKSC 17, [2018] AC 545, [2017] 4 All ER 545 at [13].

Where a party to a marriage dies within 12 months from the date on which a decree of divorce or nullity of marriage has been made absolute or a decree of judicial separation has been granted, see s 14 of the Act (**III FMY [17]**). Where a party to a civil partnership dies within 12 months from the date of a dissolution order, nullity order, separation order or presumption of death order under Chapter 2 of Part 2 of the Civil Partnership Act 2004, see s 14A of the Act (**III FMY [17]**).

The provision which the claimant might reasonably have expected to receive if the marriage had been terminated by a decree of divorce instead of by death is only one of the factors, although an important one, to which the court is required to have regard. The court should not take that provision as a starting point: *Re Krubert* [1997] Ch 97, CA, preferring the approach of Oliver LJ in *Re Besterman* [1984] Ch 458, [1984] 2 All ER 656, CA to the approach of the Court of Appeal in *Moody v Stevenson* [1992] Ch 486, [1992] 2 All ER 524, CA.

For the approach to be taken in a "big money, short marriage" case, see *Cunliffe v Fielden* [2005] EWCA Civ 1508, [2006] Ch 361, [2006] 2 All ER 115; *Lilleyman v Lilleyman* [2012] EWHC 821 (Ch), [2013] Ch 225, [2013] 1 All ER 302.

For a claim by a disabled spouse, resulting in her being awarded a life but not an absolute interest in the half share of the former matrimonial home comprised in the deceased's estate, see *Moore v Holdsworth* [2010] EWHC 683 (Ch), [2010] 2 FLR 1501, [2010] Fam Law 701. For a claim by a surviving spouse against a small estate, see *Iqbal v Ahmed* [2011] EWCA Civ 900, [2011] 3 FCR 1, [2012] 1 FLR 31.

III FMY [7.14]

Reasonable financial provision for a former spouse or civil partner The will be slow to find it unreasonable to make no financial provision for a former wife, or husband, where financial provision on divorce has been settled by agreement: *Re Fullard* [1982] Fam 42, [1981] 2 All ER 796, CA; *Brill v Proud* [1984] Fam Law 59, CA. See too *Cameron v Treasury Solicitor* [1996] 2 FLR 216: spouses divorced 19 years before death of former husband, financial obligations of husband on divorce settled by lump sum paid as part of clean break settlement, surviving spouse in necessitous circumstances; claim failed. Discussed in *Ilott v Mitson (No 2)* [2017] UKSC 17, [2018] AC 545, [2017] 4 All ER 545 at [21].

On the other hand, it may be unreasonable to make no such provision where periodical payments cease on death or a large capital sum becomes available, although the reasonable expectations of surviving relatives need also to be weighed. See *Talbot v Talbot* [1962] 3 All ER 174, [1962] 1 WLR 1113; *Re Harker-Thomas's Application, Harker-Thomas v Harker-Thomas* [1969] P 28, [1968] 3 All ER 17, CA; *Re Crawford* (1982) 4 FLR 273; *Re Farrow* [1987] 1 FLR 205, [1987] Fam Law 14.

III FMY [7.15]

Reasonable financial provision for a child There is no requirement for a moral claim as a sine qua non for all applications under the 1975 Act. But in the case of an adult child well capable of living independently, something more than the qualifying relationship is needed to found a claim; hence the presence or absence of a moral claim will often be at the centre of the decision under the 1975 Act: *Ilott v Mitson (No 2)* [2017] UKSC 17, [2018] AC 545, [2017] 4 All ER 545 at [20] ((estranged adult daughter in straitened circumstances, claim succeeded).

For other examples of claims by adult children see *Re Coventry* [1980] Ch 461, [1979] 3 All ER 815, CA (adult son, claim failed); *Re Wood* [1982] LS Gaz R 774 (adult disabled daughter, claim succeeded); *Re Jennings* [1994] Ch 286, [1994] 3 All ER 27, CA (adult son, deceased failed to honour obligations to claimant in childhood, claimant now affluent, claim failed); *Re Goodchild* [1997] 3 All ER 63, [1997] 1 WLR 1216, CA (adult son, claim succeeded): *Snapes v Aram* [1998] 20 LS Gaz R 35, CA; *Re Hancock* [1999] 1 FCR 500, [1998] 2 FLR 346, CA (adult daughter, claim succeeded); *Re Pearce* [1999] 2 FCR 179, [1998] 2 FLR 705, CA (adult son, claim succeeded); *Espinosa v Bourke* [1999] 3 FCR 76, [1999] 1 FLR 747, CA (adult daughter, claim succeeded); *Robinson v Fernsby* [2003] EWCA Civ 1820, (2003) 148 Sol Jo LB 59 (adult daughter, claim failed); *Myers v Myers* [2004] EWHC 1944 (Fam) (adult daughter, claim succeeded); *Gold v Curtis* [2005] WTLR 673 (adult son, claim succeeded); *Challinor v Challinor* [2009] EWHC 180 (Ch), [2009] WTLR. 931 (adult disabled daughter, claim succeeded).

III FMY [7.15A]

Reasonable financial provision for a person living in the same household and as the husband or wife of the deceased See *Saunders v Garrett* [2005] WTLR 749.

See *Lewis v Warner* [2017] EWCA (Civ) 2182, [2018] Ch 450, [2017] All ER (D) 116 (Dec) (para **III FMY [7.12]**): reasonable financial provision for an elderly, infirm but wealthy claimant under sub-s 1(1)(ba) consisted of the grant of an option to buy a house in which the claimant and the deceased had lived for its full market value; *Thompson v Ragget* [2018] EWHC 688 (Ch): reasonable financial provision for a 79-year-old woman who had lived with the deceased for 42 years consisted of the outright transfer of a cottage and financial provision.

III FMY [7.16]

Reasonable financial provision for a person maintained by the deceased See the cases cited at para **III FMY [7.7]**. For further examples of claims under sub-s 1(1)(e) see *Malone v Harrison* [1979] 1 WLR 1353 (mistress); *Re Wilkinson* [1978] Fam 22, [1978] 1 All ER 221 (sisters).

III FMY [8]

2. Powers of court to make orders

(1) Subject to the provisions of this Act, where an application is made for an order under this section, the court may, if it is satisfied that the disposition of the deceased's estate effected by his will or the law relating to intestacy, or the combination of his will and that law, is not such as to make reasonable financial provision for the applicant, make any one or more of the following orders—

(a) an order for the making to the applicant out of the net estate of the deceased of such periodical payments and for such term as may be specified in the order;

(b) an order for the payment to the applicant out of that estate of a lump sum of such amount as may be so specified;

(c) an order for the transfer to the applicant of such property comprised in that estate as may be so specified;

(d) an order for the settlement for the benefit of the applicant of such property comprised in that estate as may be so specified;

(e) an order for the acquisition out of property comprised in that estate of such property as may be so specified and for the transfer of the property so acquired to the applicant or for the settlement thereof for his benefit;

(f) an order varying any ante-nuptial or post-nuptial settlement (including such a settlement made by will) made on the parties to a marriage to which the deceased was one of the parties, the variation being for the benefit of the surviving party to that marriage, or any child of that marriage, or any person who was treated by the deceased as a child of the family in relation to that marriage.

(g) an order varying any settlement made—

(i) during the subsistence of a civil partnership formed by the deceased, or

(ii) in anticipation of the formation of a civil partnership by the deceased,

on the civil partners (including such a settlement made by will), the variation being for the benefit of the surviving civil partner, or any child of both the civil partners, or any person who was treated by the deceased as a child of the family in relation to that civil partnership.

(h) an order varying for the applicant's benefit the trusts on which the deceased's estate is held (whether arising under the will, or the law relating to intestacy, or both).

(2) An order under subsection (1)(a) above providing for the making out of the net estate of the deceased of periodical payments may provide for—

(a) payments of such amount as may be specified in the order,

(b) payments equal to the whole of the income of the net estate or of such portion thereof as may be so specified,

(c) payments equal to the whole of the income of such part of the net estate as the court may direct to be set aside or appropriated for the making out of the income thereof of payments under this section,

or may provide for the amount of the payments or any of them to be determined in any other way the court thinks fit.

(3) Where an order under subsection (1)(a) above provides for the making of payments of an amount specified in the order, the order may direct that such part of the net estate as may be so specified shall be set aside or appropriated for the making out of the income thereof of those payments; but no larger part of the net estate shall be so set aside or appropriated than is sufficient, at the date of the order, to produce by the income thereof the amount required for the making of those payments.

(3A) In assessing for the purposes of an order under this section the extent (if any) to which the net estate is reduced by any debts or liabilities (including any inheritance tax paid or payable out of the estate), the court may assume that the order has already been made.

(4) An order under this section may contain such consequential and supplemental provisions as the court thinks necessary or expedient for the purpose of giving effect to the order or for the purpose of securing that the order operates fairly as between one beneficiary of the estate of the deceased and another and may, in particular, but without prejudice to the generality of this subsection—

(a) order any person who holds any property which forms part of the net estate of the deceased to make such payment or transfer such property as may be specified in the order;

(b) varying the disposition of the deceased's estate effected by the will or the law relating to intestacy, or by both the will and the law relating to intestacy, in such manner as the court thinks fair and reasonable having regard to the provisions of the order and all the circumstances of the case;

(c) confer on the trustees of any property which is the subject of an order under this section such powers as appear to the court to be necessary or expedient.

III FMY [8.1]

Orders the court can make Where there are alternative ways of providing for the applicant, the court is justified in taking the course which least disturbs the testator's wishes: *Stead v Stead* [1985] FLR 16, [1985] Fam Law 154, CA.

For an order consisting of the grant an option to purchase an asset at its full market value, see *Lewis v Warner* [2017] EWCA Civ 2182, [2018] Ch 450, [2017] All ER (D) 116 (Dec) (para **III FMY [7.12]**).

III FMY [8.1A]

Periodical payments For periodical payment orders, see further s 19 of the Act (para **III FMY [18]**). For variation and discharge of orders for periodical payments see s 6 of the Act (para **III FMY [12]**).

III FMY [8.2]

Lump sum For the court's power to order payment of lump sums by instalments see s 7 of the Act (para **III FMY [13]**).

III FMY [8.3]

Ante-nuptial settlement See *Brooks v Brooks* [1996] AC 375, [1995] 3 All ER 257, HL.

III FMY [8.4]

Certificate to defer enforcement of Legal Aid Charge Where a legally aided applicant is awarded a lump sum to buy property for use as a home, a certificate to this effect should be included in the order in the terms recommended in *Practice Direction* [1991] 3 All ER 896, [1991] 1 WLR 955. This will assist on an application to the Legal Aid Agency for deferment of enforcement of the statutory charge. For the statutory charge, see the Access to Justice Act 1999, s 10(7), (8) (para **III FUND [16]**).

III FMY [8.5]

Orders varying the disposition of the deceased's estate Where the effect of an order under sub-s 2(4) of the Act is to confer substantial advantage on the parties at the expense of the revenue the court must satisfy itself not only that the order is within its jurisdiction but is one which may properly be made: *Re Goodchild* [1997] 3 All ER 63, [1997] 1 WLR 1216, CA.

For the form of consent orders under the Act in the Chancery Division, see the Chancery Guide (para **CHG 29.65**).

III FMY [9]

3. Matters to which court is to have regard in exercising powers under s 2

(1) Where an application is made for an order under section 2 of this Act, the court shall, in determining whether the disposition of the deceased's estate effected by his will or the law relating to intestacy, or the combination of his will and that law, is such as to make reasonable financial provision for the applicant and, if the court considers that reasonable financial provision has not been made, in determining whether and in what manner it shall exercise its powers under that section, have regard to the following matters, that is to say—

(a) the financial resources and financial needs which the applicant has or is likely to have in the foreseeable future;

(b) the financial resources and financial needs which any other applicant for an order under section 2 of this Act has or is likely to have in the foreseeable future;

(c) the financial resources and financial needs which any beneficiary of the estate of the deceased has or is likely to have in the foreseeable future;

(d) any obligations and responsibilities which the deceased had towards any applicant for an order under the said section 2 or towards any beneficiary of the estate of the deceased;

(e) the size and nature of the net estate of the deceased;

(f) any physical or mental disability of any applicant for an order under the said section 2 or any beneficiary of the estate of the deceased;

(g) any other matter, including the conduct of the applicant or any other person, which in the circumstances of the case the court may consider relevant.

(2) This subsection applies, without prejudice to the generality of paragraph (g) of subsection (1) above, where an application for an order under section 2 of this Act is made by virtue of section 1(1)(a) or (b) of this Act.

The court shall, in addition to the matters specifically mentioned in paragraphs (a) to (f) of that subsection, have regard to—

(a) the age of the applicant and the duration of the marriage or civil partnership;

(b) the contribution made by the applicant to the welfare of the family of the deceased, including any contribution made by looking after the home or caring for the family.

In the case of an application by the wife or husband of the deceased, the court shall also, unless at the date of death a *decree of judicial separation* [separation order under the Family Law Act 1996] was in force and the separation was continuing, have regard to the provision which the applicant might reasonably have expected to receive if on the day on which the deceased died the marriage, instead of being terminated by death, had been terminated by *a decree of divorce* [a divorce order]; but nothing requires the court to treat such provision as setting an upper or lower limit on the provision which may be made by an order under section 2.

In the case of an application by the civil partner of the deceased, the court shall also, unless at the date of the death a separation order under Chapter 2 of Part 2 of the Civil Partnership Act 2004 was in force and the separation was continuing, have regard to the provision which the applicant might reasonably have expected to receive if on the day on which the deceased died the civil partnership, instead of being terminated by death, had been terminated by a dissolution order; but nothing requires the court to treat such provision as setting an upper or lower limit on the provision which may be made by an order under section 2.

(2A) Without prejudice to the generality of paragraph (g) of subsection (1) above, where an application for an order under section 2 of this Act is made by virtue of section 1(1)(ba) of this Act, the court shall, in addition to the matters specifically mentioned in paragraphs (a) to (f) of that subsection, have regard to—

- (a) the age of the applicant and the length of the period during which the applicant lived as the husband or wife or civil partner of the deceased and in the same household as the deceased;
- (b) the contribution made by the applicant to the welfare of the family of the deceased, including any contribution made by looking after the home or caring for the family.

(3) Without prejudice to the generality of paragraph (g) of subsection (1) above, where an application for an order under section 2 of this Act is made by virtue of section 1(1)(c) or 1(1)(d) of this Act, the court shall, in addition to the matters specifically mentioned in paragraphs (a) to (f) of that subsection, have regard to the manner in which the applicant was being or in which he might expect to be educated or trained, and where the application is made by virtue of section 1(1)(d) the court shall also have regard—

- (a) to whether the deceased maintained the applicant and, if so, to the length of time for which and basis on which the deceased did so, and to the extent of the contribution made by way of maintenance;
- (aa) to whether and, if so, to what extent the deceased assumed responsibility for the maintenance of the applicant;
- (b) to whether in maintaining or assuming responsibility for maintaining the applicant the deceased did so knowing that the applicant was not his own child;
- (c) to the liability of any other person to maintain the applicant.

(4) Without prejudice to the generality of paragraph (g) of subsection (1) above, where an application for an order under section 2 of this Act is made by virtue of section 1(1)(e) of this Act, the court shall, in addition to the matters specifically mentioned in paragraphs (a) to (f) of that subsection, have regard—

- (a) to the length of time for which and basis on which the deceased maintained the applicant, and to the extent of the contribution made by way of maintenance;
- (b) to whether and, if so, to what extent the deceased assumed responsibility for the maintenance of the applicant.

(5) In considering the matters to which the court is required to have regard under this section, the court shall take into account the facts as known to the court at the date of the hearing.

(6) In considering the financial resources of any person for the purposes of this section the court shall take into account his earning capacity and in considering the financial needs of any person for the purposes of this section the court shall take into account his financial obligations and responsibilities.

Amendment *Text in italic is deleted and subsequent text in square brackets is inserted by the Family Law Act 1996, with effect from a date to be appointed.*

III FMY [9.1]

Subsection 3(1)(a) – financial resources and financial needs "Financial needs" means "reasonable requirements": *Harrington v Gill* (1983) 4 FLR 265, CA. See further s 3(6).

For the position of charities as beneficiaries under wills see *Ilott v Mitson (No 2)* [2017] UKSC 17, [2018] AC 545, [2017] 4 All ER 545, esp at [46].

III FMY [9.2]

Social security benefits For the relevance of the claimant being in receipt of social security benefits see *Re Collins* [1990] Fam 56, [1990] 2 All ER 47; *Ilott v Mitson (No 2)* [2017] UKSC 17, [2018] AC 545, [2017] 4 All ER 545, esp at [36]–[47].

III FMY [9.3]

Subsection 3(1)(c) – beneficiary of the estate See the definition in sub-s 25(1) of the Act (para **III FMY [20]**).

III FMY [9.4]

Subsection 3(1)(d) – obligations and responsibilities of the deceased As a general rule these are limited to obligations and responsibilities which the deceased had immediately before his death: *Re Jennings* [1994] Ch 286, [1994] 3 All ER 27, CA.

III FMY [9.5]

Sub-s 3(1)(e) – size and nature of the net estate See the definition of "net estate" in s 25(1) of the Act (para **III FMY [20]**). Changes in the value of the net estate between the date of death and the date of the hearing must be taken into account by virtue of s 3(5): *Re Jennings* [1984] Ch 286, [1984] 3 All ER 27.

III FMY [9.6]

Subsection 3(1)(g) – Any other matter For the relevance of the deceased's wishes see *Rees v Newbury and Institute of Cancer Research* [1998] 1 FLR 1041; *Re Goodchild* [1997] 3 All ER 63, [1997] 1 WLR 1216; *Re Hancock* [1998] 2 FLR 346 at 353; *Espinosa v Bourke* [1999] 3 FCR 76, [1999] 1 FLR 747, CA; *Robinson v Bird* [2003] EWHC 30 (Ch) (Blackburne J) at para 114; on appeal *Robinson v Fernsby* [2003] EWCA Civ 1820, (2003) 148 Sol Jo LB 59; *Ilott v Mitson (No 2)* [2017] UKSC 17, [2018] AC 545, [2017] 4 All ER 545.

III FMY [9.7]

Conduct of the appellant Where the applicant has killed the deceased, see the Forfeiture Act 1982 (para **III TRU [39]**).

III FMY [9.8]

Sub-section 3(4) Sub-section 3(4) does not add to the threshold conditions in sub-ss 1(1)(e) and (3): *Re B* [2000] Ch 662, [2000] 1 All ER 665, CA.

III FMY [9.9]

Sub-section 3(5) The facts are to be assessed as at the date of the hearing. For the approach on appeal, see *Ilott v Mitson (No 2)* [2017] UKSC 17, [2018] AC 545, [2017] 4 All ER 545 at [25].

III FMY [10]

4. Time-limit for applications

An application for an order under section 2 of this Act shall not, except with the permission of the court, be made after the end of the period of six months from the date on which representation with respect to the estate of the deceased is first taken out (but nothing prevents the making of an application before such representation is first taken out).

III FMY [10.1]

Making an application out of time An application for permission to bring a claim out of time should be made in the claim form by which the claim is commenced. If is contested it may be convenient for it to be decided as a preliminary issue.

In *Re Salmon* [1981] Ch 167, [1980] 3 All ER 532 Sir Robert Megarry V-C laid down guidelines for the exercise of the discretion under this section. These can be summarised as follows:

(a) the discretion in unfettered;
(b) the onus is on the applicant to make out a substantial case for it being proper for the court to extend time;
(c) it is material in what circumstances and how promptly the applicant has sought the permission of the court after the time limit has expired;
(d) it is material whether negotiations were commenced within the time limit;
(e) it is material whether the estate has been distributed before notification of the claim; and
(f) it is material whether, if permission were refused, the applicant would have redress against anybody else.

For the relevance of a remedy against solicitors see *Adams v Schofield* [2004] WTLR 1049.

For other examples of decisions on applications to extend time, see *Re Dennis* [1981] 2 All ER 140 (19 months, application refused); *Escritt v Escritt* (1982) 3 FLR 280 (three years, application refused); *Stock v Brown* [1994] 2 FCR 1125, [1994] 1 FLR 840 (five years, application granted); *Re B* [2000] Ch 662, [2000] 1 All ER 665, CA (16 months, application granted); *Re McNulty (dec'd)* [2002] WTLR 737 (four years, application granted); *Berger v Berger* [2013] EWCA Civ 1305, [2014] WTLR 35 (6 years, application refused); *Sargeant v Sargeant* [2018] EWHC 8 (Ch) (10 years, application refused)..

III FMY [10.2]

The date on which representation with respect to the estate of the deceased is first taken out The final day for issue of the application is the same day of the month as the day of the grant six months before. See the notes to s 23 of the Act, para **III FMY [19A]**.

III FMY [10.3]

Date of the application The application is "made" on the date of issue or earlier receipt by the court of the claim form: see CPR Part 7 r 7.2 (para **CPR 7.2**) and CPR PD 7A, para 5 (para **CPR PD 7A**), and *Re Chittenden, Chittenden v Doe* [1970] 3 All ER 562, [1970] 1 WLR 1618, Ch D.

III FMY [10.4]

Searching for a grant An intending claimant who wishes to be notified of the issue of a grant of representation can enter a standing search: see the Non-Contentious Probate Rules 1987 r 43. It is inappropriate to lodge a caveat unless the intending claimant wishes to challenge the issue of a grant.

III FMY [10.5]

Application before grant Section 4 was amended by the Inheritance and Trustees' Powers Act 2014 to permit an application to be made before a grant of representation is taken out. CPR 57.16(3A) specifies the procedure to be followed when a claim under the Act is commenced before a grant of representation has been issued.

III FMY [11]

5. Interim orders

(1) Where an application for an order under section 3 of this Act it appears to the court-

(a) that the applicant is in immediate need of financial assistance, but it is not yet possible to determine what order (if any) should be made under that section; and

(b) that property forming part of the net estate of the deceased is or can be made available to meet the need of the applicant;

the court may order that, subject to such conditions or restrictions, if any, as the court may impose and to any further order of the court, there shall be paid to the applicant out of the net estate of the deceased such sum or sums and (if more than one) at such intervals as the court thinks reasonable; and the court may order that, subject to the provisions of this Act, such payments are to be made until such date as the court may specify, not being later than the date on which the court either makes an order under the said section 2 or decides not to exercise its powers under that section.

(2) Subsections (2), (3) and (4) of section 2 of this Act shall apply in relation to an order under this section as they apply in relation to an order under that section.

(3) In determining what order, if any, should be made under this section the court shall, so far as the urgency of the case admits, have regard to the same matters as those to which the court is required to have regard under section 3 of this Act.

(4) An order made under section 2 of this Act may provide that any sum paid to the applicant by virtue of this section shall be treated to such an extent and in such manner as may be provided by that order as having been paid on account of any payment provided for by that order.

III FMY [11.1]

Interim orders A claimant who wishes to apply for an interim order at the inception of the claim should claim it as a separate head of relief in the claim form and seek directions for it to be tried as a preliminary issue. A claimant who decides in the course of proceedings to apply for an interim order should apply by application notice under CPR Part 23 (see para **CPR 23**). The powers of the court under this section extend only to the making of orders for the payment of sums of money. A claimant who urgently needs some other form of relief should press for an early hearing of the full claim.

III FMY [12]

6. Variation, discharge, etc of orders for periodical payments

(1) Subject to the provisions of this Act, where the court has made an order under section 2(1)(a) of this Act (in this section referred to as "the original order") for the making of periodical payments to any person (in this section referred to as "the original recipient"), the court, on an application under this section, shall have power by order to vary or discharge the original order or to suspend any provision of it temporarily and to revive the operation of any provision so suspended.

(2) Without prejudice to the generality of subsection (1) above, an order made on an application for the variation of the original order may—

(a) provide for the making out of any relevant property of such periodical payments and for such term as may be specified in the order to any person who has applied, or would but for section 4 of this Act be entitled to apply, for an order under section 2 of this Act (whether or not, in the case of any application, an order was made in favour of the applicant);

(b) provide for the payment out of any relevant property of a lump sum of such amount as may be so specified to the original recipient or to any such person as is mentioned in paragraph (a) above;

(c) provide for the transfer of the relevant property, or such part thereof as may be so specified, to the original recipient or to any such person as is so mentioned.

(3) Where the original order provides that any periodical payments payable thereunder to the original recipient are to cease on the occurrence of an event specified in the order (other than the formation of a subsequent marriage or civil partnership by a former spouse or former civil partner) or on the expiration of a period so specified, then, if, before the end of the period of six months from the date of the occurrence of that event or of the expiration of that period, an application is made for an order under this section, the court shall have power to make any order which it would have had power to make if the application had been made before the date (whether in favour of the original recipient or any such person as is mentioned in subsection (2)(a) above and whether having effect from that date or from such later date as the court may specify).

(4) Any reference in this section to the original order shall include a reference to an order made under this section and any reference in this section to the original recipient shall include a reference to any person to whom periodical payments are required to be made by virtue of an order under this section.

(5) An application under this section may be made by any of the following persons, that is to say—

(a) any person who by virtue of section 1(1) of this Act has applied, or would but for section 4 of this Act be entitled to apply, for an order under section 2 of this Act,

(b) the personal representatives of the deceased,

(c) the trustees of any relevant property, and

(d) any beneficiary of the estate of the deceased.

(6) An order under this section may only affect—

(a) property the income of which is at the date of the order applicable wholly or in part for the making of periodical payments to any person who has applied for an order under this Act, or

(b) in the case of an application under subsection (3) above in respect of payments which have ceased to be payable on the occurrence of an event or the expiration of a period, property the income of which was so applicable immediately before the occurrence of that event or the expiration of that period, as the case may be,

and any such property as is mentioned in paragraph (a) or (b) above is in subsections (2) and (5) above referred to as "relevant property".

(7) In exercising the powers conferred by this section the court shall have regard to all circumstances of the case, including any change in any of the matters to which the court was required to have regard when making the order to which the application relates.

(8) Where the court makes an order under this section, it may give such consequential directions as it thinks necessary or expedient having regard to the provisions of the order.

(9) No such order as is mentioned in section 2(1)(d), (e) or (f), 9, 10 or 11 of this Act shall be made on an application under this section.

(10) For the avoidance of doubt it is hereby declared that, in relation to an order which provides for the making of periodical payments which are to cease on the occurrence of an event specified in the order (other than the formation of a subsequent marriage or civil partnership by a former spouse or former civil partner) or on the expiration of a period so specified, the power to vary an order includes power to provide for the making of periodical payments after the expiration of that period or the occurrence of that event.

III FMY [13]

7. Payment of lump sums by instalments

(1) An order under section 2(1)(b) or 6(2)(b) of this Act for the payment of a lump sum may provide for the payment of that sum by instalments of such amount as may be specified in the order.

(2) Where an order is made by virtue of subsection (1) above, the court shall have power, on an application made by the person to whom the lump sum is payable, by the personal representatives of the deceased or by the trustees of the property out of which the lump sum is payable, to vary that order by varying the number of instalments payable, the amount of any instalment and the date on which any instalment becomes payable.

III FMY [14]

8. Property treated as part of "net estate"

(1) Where a deceased person has in accordance with the provisions of any enactment nominated any person to receive any sum of money or other property on his death and that nomination is in force at the time of his death, that sum of money, after deducting therefrom any inheritance tax payable in respect thereof, or that other property, to the extent of the value thereof at the date of the death of the deceased after deducting therefrom any inheritance tax so payable, shall be treated for the purposes of this Act as part of the net estate of the deceased; but this subsection shall not render any person liable for having paid that sum or transferred that other property to the person named in the nomination in accordance with the directions given in the nomination.

(2) Where any sum of money or other property is received by any person as a donatio mortis causa made by a deceased person, that sum of money, after deducting therefrom any inheritance tax payable thereon, or that other property, to the extent of the value thereof at the date of the death of the deceased after deducting therefrom any inheritance tax so payable, shall be treated for the purposes of this Act as part of the net estate of the deceased; but this subsection shall not render any person liable for having paid that sum or transferred that other property in order to give effect to that donatio mortis causa.

(3) The amount of inheritance tax to be deducted for the purposes of this section shall not exceed the amount of that tax which has been borne by the person nominated by the deceased or, as the case may be, the person who has received a sum of money or other property as a donatio mortis causa.

III FMY [14.1]

"in accordance with the provisions of any enactment" The term "enactment" includes subordinate legislation: *Goenka v Goenka* [2014] EWHC 2966 (Ch), [2016] Ch 267. Accordingly, where a deceased was at his death a member of a pension scheme established by statute and had exercised a right conferred by rules made in accordance with a statutory instrument to nominate a person to receive a lump sum death benefit payable under the terms of the scheme, which nomination was in force at the date of his death, the property affected by that nomination was to be treated as part of his net estate for the purposes of this Act.

III FMY [15]

9. Property held on a joint tenancy

(1) Where a deceased person was immediately before his death beneficially entitled to a joint tenancy of any property, then, if an application is made for an order under section 2 of this Act, the court for the purpose of facilitating the making of financial provision for the applicant under this Act may order that the deceased's severable share of that property shall, to such extent as appears to the court to be just in all the circumstances of the case, be treated for the purposes of this Act as part of the net estate of the deceased.

(1A) Where an order is made under subsection (1) the value of the deceased's severable share of the property concerned is taken for the purposes of this Act to be the value that the share would have had at the date of the hearing of the application for an order under section 2 had the share been severed immediately before the deceased's death, unless the court orders that the share is to be valued at a different date.

(2) In determining the extent to which any severable share is to be treated as part of the net estate of the deceased by virtue of an order under subsection (1) above, the court shall have regard to any inheritance tax payable in respect of that severable share.

(3) Where an order is made under subsection (1) above, the provisions of this section shall not render any person liable for anything done by him before the order was made.

(4) For the avoidance of doubt it is hereby declared that for the purposes of this section there may be a joint tenancy of a chose in action.

III FMY [15.1]

Joint tenancy of any property "for the purpose of facilitating the making of financial provision for the applicant under this Act"

Notwithstanding these words, the discretion conferred by this section is to be exercised both when deciding whether to make an award to the claimant and in deciding what award to make. It is not limited to the second stage only. These words do not narrow the broad discretionary power given by sub-s 9(1): *Kourkgy v Lusher* (1981) 4 FLR 65; *Jessop v Jessop* [1992] 1 FLR 591; [1993] 1 FCR 253.

III FMY [15.2]

Valuation of property For the approach to the treatment, for the purposes of s 9(1), of the deceased's severable share in a terminal illness benefit payable under a joint lives insurance policy, see *Lim (an infant) v Walia* [2014] EWCA Civ 1076, [2015] Ch 375, [2014] All ER (D) 55 (Aug).

Powers of court in relation to transactions intended to defeat applications for financial provision

III FMY [16]

10. Dispositions intended to defeat applications for financial provision

(1) Where an application is made to the court for an order under section 2 of this Act, the applicant may, in the proceedings on that application, apply to the court for an order under subsection (2) below.

(2) Where on an application under subsection (1) above the court is satisfied—

(a) that, less than six years before the date of the death of the deceased, the deceased with the intention of defeating an application for financial provision under this Act made a disposition, and

(b) that full valuable consideration for that disposition was not given by the person to whom or for the benefit of whom the disposition was made (in this section referred to as "the donee") or by any other person, and

(c) that the exercise of the powers conferred by this section would facilitate the making of financial provision for the applicant under this Act,

then, subject to the provisions of this section and of sections 12 and 13 of this Act, the court may order the donee (whether or not at the date of the order he holds any interest in the property disposed of to him or for his benefit by the deceased) to provide, for the purpose of the making of that financial provision, such sum of money or other property as may be specified in the order.

(3) Where an order is made under subsection (2) above as respects any disposition made by the deceased which consisted of the payment of money to or for the benefit of the donee, the amount of any sum of money or the value of any property ordered to be provided under that subsection shall not exceed the amount of the payment made by the deceased after deducting therefrom any inheritance tax borne by the donee in respect of that payment.

(4) Where an order is made under subsection (2) above as respects any disposition made by the deceased which consisted of the transfer of property (other than a sum of money) to or for the benefit of the donee, the amount of any sum of money or the value of any property ordered to be provided under that subsection shall not exceed the value at the date of the death of the deceased of the

property disposed of by him to or for the benefit of the donee (or if that property has been disposed of by the person to whom it was transferred by the deceased, the value at the date of that disposal thereof) after deducting therefrom any inheritance tax borne by the donee in respect of the transfer of that property by the deceased.

(5) Where an application (in this subsection referred to as "the original application") is made for an order under subsection (2) above in relation to any disposition, then, if on an application under this subsection by the donee or by any applicant for an order under section 2 of this Act the court is satisfied—

- (a) that, less than six years before the date of the death of the deceased, the deceased with the intention of defeating an application for financial provision under this Act made a disposition other than the disposition which is the subject of the original application, and
- (b) that full valuable consideration for that other disposition was not given by the person to whom or for the benefit of whom that other disposition was made or by any other person,

the court may exercise in relation to the person to whom or for the benefit of whom that other disposition was made the powers which the court would have had under subsection (2) above if the original application had been made in respect of that other disposition and the court had been satisfied as to the matters set out in paragraphs (a), (b) and (c) of that subsection; and where any application is made under this subsection, any reference in this section (except in subsection (2)(b)) to the donee shall include a reference to the person to whom or for the benefit of whom that other disposition was made.

(6) In determining whether and in what manner to exercise its powers under this section, the court shall have regard to the circumstances in which any disposition was made and any valuable consideration which was given therefor, the relationship, if any, of the donee to the deceased, the conduct and financial resources of the donee and all the other circumstances of the case.

(7) In this section "disposition" does not include—

- (a) any provision in a will, any such nomination as is mentioned in section 8(1) of this Act or any donatio mortis causa, or
- (b) any appointment of property made, otherwise than by will, in the exercise of a special power of appointment,

but, subject to these exceptions, includes any payment of money (including the payment of a premium under a policy of assurance) and any conveyance, assurance, appointment or gift of property of any description, whether made by an instrument or otherwise.

(8) The provisions of this section do not apply to any disposition made before the commencement of this Act.

III FMY [16A]

11. Contracts to leave property by will

(1) Where an application is made to a court for an order under section 2 of this Act, the applicant may, in the proceedings on that application, apply to the court for an order under this section.

(2) Where on an application under subsection (1) above the court is satisfied—

- (a) that the deceased made a contract by which he agreed to leave by his will a sum of money or other property to any person or by which he agreed that a sum of money or other property would be paid or transferred to any person out of his estate, and
- (b) that the deceased made that contract with the intention of defeating an application for financial provision under this Act, and
- (c) that when the contract was made full valuable consideration for that contract was not given or promised by the person with whom or for the

benefit of whom the contract was made (in this section referred to as "the donee") or by any other person, and

(d) that the exercise of the powers conferred by this section would facilitate the making of financial provision for the applicant under this Act,

then, subject to the provisions of this section and of sections 12 and 13 of this Act, the court may make any one or more of the following orders, that is to say—

(i) if any money has been paid or any other property has been transferred to or for the benefit of the donee in accordance with the contract, an order directing the donee to provide, for the purpose of the making of that financial provision, such sum of money or other property as may be specified in the order;

(ii) if the money or all the money has not been paid or the property or all the property has not been transferred in accordance with the contract, an order directing the personal representatives not to make any payment or transfer any property, or not to make any further payment or transfer any further property, as the case may be, in accordance therewith or directing the personal representatives only to make such payment or transfer such property as may be specified in the order.

(3) Notwithstanding anything in subsection (2) above, the court may exercise its powers thereunder in relation to any contract made by the deceased only to the extent that the court considers that the amount of any sum of money paid or to be paid or the value of any property transferred or to be transferred in accordance with the contract exceeds the value of any valuable consideration given or to be given for that contract, and for this purpose the court shall have regard to the value of property at the date of the hearing.

(4) In determining whether and in what manner to exercise its powers under this section, the court shall have regard to the circumstances in which the contract was made, the relationship, if any, of the donee to the deceased, the conduct and financial resources of the donee and all the other circumstances of the case.

(5) Where an order has been made under subsection (2) above in relation to any contract the rights of any person to enforce that contract or to recover damages or to obtain other relief for the breach thereof shall be subject to any adjustment made by the court under section 12(3) of this Act and shall survive to such extent only as is consistent with giving effect to the terms of that order.

(6) The provisions of this section do not apply to a contract made before the commencement of this Act.

III FMY [16B]

12. Provisions supplementary to ss 10 and 11

(1) Where the exercise of any of the powers conferred by section 10 or 11 of this Act is conditional on the court being satisfied that a disposition or contract was made by a deceased person with the intention of defeating an application for financial provision under this Act, that condition shall be fulfilled if the court is of the opinion that, on a balance of probabilities, the intention of the deceased (though not necessarily his sole intention) in making the disposition or contract was to prevent an order for financial provision being made under this Act or to reduce the amount of the provision which might otherwise be granted by an order thereunder.

(2) Where an application is made under section 11 of this Act with respect to any contract made by the deceased and no valuable consideration was given or promised by any person for that contract then, notwithstanding anything in subsection (1) above, it shall be presumed, unless the contrary is shown, that the deceased made that contract with the intention of defeating an application for financial provision under this Act.

(3) Where the court makes an order under section 10 or 11 of this Act it may give such consequential directions as it thinks fit (including directions requiring the making of any payment or the transfer of any property) for giving effect to the order or for securing a fair adjustment of the rights of the persons affected thereby.

(4) Any power conferred on the court by the said section 10 or 11 to order the donee, in relation to any disposition or contract, to provide any sum of money or other property shall be exercisable in like manner in relation to the personal representative of the donee, and—

- (a) any reference in section 10(4) to the disposal of property by the donee shall include a reference to disposal by the personal representative of the donee, and
- (b) any reference in section 10(5) to an application by the donee under that subsection shall include a reference to an application by the personal representative of the donee;

but the court shall not have power under the said section 10 or 11 to make an order in respect of any property forming part of the estate of the donee which has been distributed by the personal representative; and the personal representative shall not be liable for having distributed any such property before he has notice of the making of an application under the said section 10 or 11 on the ground that he ought to have taken into account the possibility that such an application would be made.

III FMY [16C]

13. Provisions as to trustees in relation to ss 10 and 11

(1) Where an application is made for—

- (a) an order under section 10 of this Act in respect of a disposition made by the deceased to any person as a trustee, or
- (b) an order under section 11 of this Act in respect of any payment made or property transferred, in accordance with a contract made by the deceased, to any person as a trustee,

the powers of the court under the said section 10 or 11 to order that trustee to provide a sum of money or other property shall be subject to the following limitation (in addition, in a case of an application under section 10, to any provision regarding the deduction of inheritance tax) namely, that the amount of any sum of money or the value of any property ordered to be provided—

- (i) in the case of an application in respect of a disposition which consisted of the payment of money or an application in respect of the payment of money in accordance with a contract, shall not exceed the aggregate of so much of that money as is at the date of the order in the hands of the trustee and the value at that date of any property which represents that money or is derived therefrom and is at that date in the hands of the trustee;
- (ii) in the case of an application in respect of a disposition which consisted of the transfer of property (other than a sum of money) or an application in respect of the transfer of property (other than a sum of money) in accordance with a contract, shall not exceed the aggregate of the value at the date of the order of so much of that property as is at that date in the hands of the trustee and the value at that date of any property which represents the first mentioned property or is derived therefrom and is at that date in the hands of the trustee.

(2) Where any such application is made in respect of a disposition made to any person as a trustee or in respect of any payment made or property transferred in pursuance of a contract to any person as a trustee, the trustee shall not be liable for having distributed any money or other property on the ground that he ought to have taken into account the possibility that such an application would be made.

(3) Where any such application is made in respect of a disposition made to any person as a trustee or in respect of any payment made or property transferred in accordance with a contract to any person as a trustee, any reference in the said section 10 or 11 to the donee shall be construed as including a reference to the trustee or trustees for the time being of the trust in question and any reference in subsection (1) or (2) above to a trustee shall be construed in the same way.

III FMY [16C.1]

Powers of the court in relation to transactions intended to defeat applications for financial provision For a description of what is required to obtain an order under s 10 of the Act see *Dellal v Dellal* [2015] EWHC 907 (Fam), [2015] WTLR 1137. See further as to s 10: *Re Kennedy, Kennedy v Official Solicitor* [1980] CLY 2820; *Re Dawkins, Dawkins v Judd* [1986] 2 FLR 360, [1986] Fam Law 295.

For a comparison of the effects of an order under s 10 of the Act and an order under s 37 of the Matrimonial Causes Act 1973 see *AC v DC (Financial Remedy: Effect of section 37 Avoidance Orders)* [2012] EWHC 2032 (Fam), [2013] 2 FLR 1483 (Mostyn J).

In addition to a remedy under s 10, an applicant may also have a remedy under the Insolvency Act 1986, s 423 (transactions defrauding creditors). The remedies may be pursued together. For a comparison of the two sections, see *B v IB* [2013] EWHC 3755 (Fam), [2014] 2 FLR 273.

Special provisions relating to cases of divorce, separation etc

III FMY [17]

14. Provision as to cases where no financial relief was granted in divorce proceedings, etc

(1) Where, within twelve months from the date on which a decree of divorce or nullity of marriage has been made absolute or a decree of judicial separation has been granted, a party to the marriage dies and—

(a) an application for a financial provision order under section 23 of the Matrimonial Causes Act 1973 or a property adjustment order under section 24 of that Act has not been made by the other party to that marriage, or

(b) such an application has been made but the proceedings thereon have not been determined at the time of the death of the deceased,

then, if an application for an order under section 2 of this Act is made by that other party, the court shall, notwithstanding anything in section 1 or section 3 of this Act, have power, if it thinks it just to do so, to treat that party for the purposes of that application as if *the decree of divorce or nullity of marriage had not been made absolute or the decree of judicial separation had not been granted, as the case may be* [, as the case may be, the divorce order or separation order had not been made or the decree of nullity had not been made absolute].

(2) This section shall not apply in relation to a *decree of judicial separation* [separation order] unless at the date of the death of the deceased *the decree* [the order] was in force and the separation was continuing.

Amendment *Text in italic is deleted and text in square brackets is inserted by the Family Law Act 1996 with effect from a date to be appointed.*

III FMY [17AA]

14A. Provision as to cases where no financial relief was granted in proceedings for the dissolution etc of a civil partnership

(1) Subsection (2) below applies where—

(a) a dissolution order, nullity order, separation order or presumption of death order has been made under Chapter 2 of Part 2 of the Civil Partnership Act 2004 in relation to a civil partnership,

(b) one of the civil partners dies within twelve months from the date on which the order is made, and

(c) either—

(i) an application for a financial provision order under Part 1 of Schedule 5 to that Act or a property adjustment order under Part 2 of that Schedule has not been made by the other civil partner, or

(ii) such an application has been made but the proceedings on the application have not been determined at the time of the death of the deceased.

(2) If an application for an order under section 2 of this Act is made by the surviving civil partner, the court shall, notwithstanding anything in section 1 or section 3 of this Act, have power, if it thinks it just to do so, to treat the surviving civil partner as if the order mentioned in subsection (1)(a) above had not been made.

(3) This section shall not apply in relation to a separation order unless at the date of the death of the deceased the separation order was in force and the separation was continuing.

III FMY [17A]

15. Restriction imposed in divorce proceedings, etc on application under this Act

(1) *On the grant of a decree of divorce, a decree of nullity of marriage or a decree of judicial separation or at any time thereafter* [At any time when the court—

(a) has jurisdiction under section 23A or 24 of the Matrimonial Causes Act 1973 to make a property adjustment order in relation to a marriage; or

(b) would have such jurisdiction if either the jurisdiction had not already been exercised or an application for such an order were made with the leave of the court,]

the court, if it considers it just to do so, may, on the application of either party to the marriage, order that the other party to the marriage shall not on the death of the applicant be entitled to apply for an order under section 2 of this Act.

In this subsection "the court" means the High Court or, where a county court has jurisdiction by virtue of Part V of the Matrimonial and Family Proceedings Act 1984, a county court.

(2) In the case of a decree of divorce or nullity of marriage an order may be made under subsection (1) above before or after the decree is made absolute, but if it is made before the decree is made absolute it shall not take effect unless the decree is made absolute.

[(2) An order made under subsection (1) above with respect to any party to a marriage has effect in accordance with subsection (3) below at any time—

(a) after the marriage has been dissolved;

(b) after a decree of nullity has been made absolute in relation to the marriage; and

(c) while a separation order under the Family Law Act 1996 is in force in relation to the marriage and the separation is continuing.]

(3) Where an order made under subsection (1) above on the grant of a decree of divorce or nullity of marriage has come into force with respect to a party to a marriage, then, on the death of the other party to that marriage, the court shall not entertain any application for an order under section 2 of this Act made by the first-mentioned party.

[(3) If at any time when an order made under subsection (1) above with respect to any party to a marriage has effect the other party to the marriage dies, the court shall not entertain any application made by the surviving party to the marriage for an order under section 2 of this Act.]

(4) Where an order made under subsection (1) above on the grant of a decree of judicial separation has come into force with respect to any party to a marriage, then, if the other party to that marriage dies while the decree is in force and the separation is continuing, the court shall not entertain any application for an order under section 2 of this Act made by the first-mentioned party.

Amendment *Text in italic is deleted and text in square brackets is inserted by the Family Law Act 1996 with effect from a date to be appointed.*

Cohabitation after the ending of the marriage Sub-section (3) does not prevent a former wife from making an application under section 2 in her capacity as a cohabitant within section 1(1)(ba) and (1A): *Chekov v Fryer* [2015] EWHC 1642 (Ch), [2015] All ER (D) 303 (Jun).

III FMY [17AB]

15ZA. Restriction imposed in proceedings for the dissolution etc of a civil partnership on application under this Act

(1) On making a dissolution order, nullity order, separation order or presumption of death order under Chapter 2 of Part 2 of the Civil Partnership Act 2004, or at any time after making such an order, the court, if it considers it just to do so, may, on the application of either of the civil partners, order that the other civil partner shall not on the death of the applicant be entitled to apply for an order under section 2 of this Act.

(2) In subsection (1) above "the court" means the High Court or the family court.

(3) In the case of a dissolution order, nullity order or presumption of death order ("the main order") an order may be made under subsection (1) above before (as well as after) the main order is made final, but if made before the main order is made final it shall not take effect unless the main order is made final.

(4) Where an order under subsection (1) above made in connection with a dissolution order, nullity order or presumption of death order has come into force with respect to a civil partner, then, on the death of the other civil partner, the court shall not entertain any application for an order under section 2 of this Act made by the surviving civil partner.

(5) Where an order under subsection (1) above made in connection with a separation order has come into force with respect to a civil partner, then, if the other civil partner dies while the separation order is in force and the separation is continuing, the court shall not entertain any application for an order under section 2 of this Act made by the surviving civil partner.

III FMY [17B]

15A. Restriction imposed in proceedings under Matrimonial and Family Proceedings Act 1984 on application under this Act

(1) On making an order under section 17 of the Matrimonial and Family Proceedings Act 1984 (orders for financial provision and property adjustment following overseas divorces, etc) the court, if it considers it just to do so, may, on the application of either party to the marriage, order that the other party to the marriage shall not on the death of the applicant be entitled to apply for an order under section 2 of this Act.

In this subsection "the court" means the High Court or the family court.

(2) Where an order under subsection (1) above has been made with respect to a party to a marriage which has been dissolved or annulled, then, on the death of the other party to that marriage, the court shall not entertain an application under section 2 of this Act made by the first-mentioned party.

(3) Where an order under subsection (1) above has been made with respect to a party to a marriage the parties to which have been legally separated, then, if the other party to the marriage dies while the legal separation is in force, the court shall not entertain an application under section 2 of this Act made by the first-mentioned party.

III FMY [17BA]

15B. Restriction imposed in proceedings under Schedule 7 to the Civil Partnership Act 2004 on application under this Act

(1) On making an order under paragraph 9 of Schedule 7 to the Civil Partnership Act 2004 (orders for financial provision, property adjustment and pension-sharing following overseas dissolution etc of civil partnership) the court, if it considers it just to do so, may, on the application of either of the civil partners, order that the other civil partner shall not on the death of the applicant be entitled to apply for an order under section 2 of this Act.

(2) In subsection (1) above "the court" means the High Court or the family court.

(3) Where an order under subsection (1) above has been made with respect to one of the civil partners in a case where a civil partnership has been dissolved or annulled, then, on the death of the other civil partner, the court shall not entertain an application under section 2 of this Act made by the surviving civil partner.

(4) Where an order under subsection (1) above has been made with respect to one of the civil partners in a case where civil partners have been legally separated, then, if the other civil partner dies while the legal separation is in force, the court shall not entertain an application under section 2 of this Act made by the surviving civil partner.

III FMY [17C]

16. Variation and discharge of secured periodical payments orders made under Matrimonial Causes Act 1973

(1) Where an application for an order under section 2 of this Act is made to the court by any person who was at the time of the death of the deceased entitled to payments from the deceased under a secured periodical payments order made under the Matrimonial Causes Act 1973 or Schedule 5 to the Civil Partnership Act 2004, then, in the proceedings on that application, the court shall have power, if an application is made under this section by that person or by the personal representative of the deceased, to vary or discharge that periodical payments order or to revive the operation of any provision thereof which has been suspended under section 31 of that Act of 1973 or Part 11 of that Schedule.

(2) In exercising the powers conferred by this section the court shall have regard to all the circumstances of the case, including any order which the court proposes to make under section 2 or section 5 of this Act and any change (whether resulting from the death of the deceased or otherwise) in any of the matters to which the court was required to have regard when making the secured periodical payments order.

(3) The powers exercisable by the court under this section in relation to an order shall be exercisable also in relation to any instrument executed in pursuance of the order.

III FMY [17D]

17. Variation and revocation of maintenance agreements

(1) Where an application for an order under section 2 of this Act is made to the court by any person who was at the time of the death of the deceased entitled to payments from the deceased under a maintenance agreement which provided for the continuation of payments under the agreement after the death of the deceased, then, in the proceedings on that application, the court shall have power, if an application is made under this section by that person or by the personal representative of the deceased, to vary or revoke that agreement.

(2) In exercising the powers conferred by this section the court shall have regard to all the circumstances of the case, including any order which the court proposes to make under section 2 or section 5 of this Act and any change (whether resulting from the death of the deceased or otherwise) in any of the circumstances in the light of which the agreement was made.

(3) If a maintenance agreement is varied by the court under this section the like consequences shall ensue as if the variation had been made immediately before the death of the deceased by agreement between the parties and for valuable consideration.

(4) In this section "maintenance agreement", in relation to a deceased person, means any agreement made, whether in writing or not and whether before or after the commencement of this Act, by the deceased with any person with whom he formed a marriage or civil partnership, being an agreement which contained provisions governing the rights and liabilities towards one another when living separately of the parties to that marriage or of the civil partners (whether or not the marriage or civil partnership has been dissolved or annulled) in respect of the making or securing of payments or the disposition or use of any property, including such rights and liabilities with respect to the maintenance or education of any child, whether or not a child of the deceased or a person who was treated by the deceased as a child of the family in relation to that marriage or civil partnership.

III FMY [17E]

18. Availability of court's powers under this Act in applications under ss 31 and 36 of the Matrimonial Causes Act 1973

(1) Where—

- (a) a person against whom a secured periodical payments order was made under the Matrimonial Causes Act 1973 has died and an application is made under section 31(6) of that Act for the variation or discharge of that order or for the revival of the operation of any provision thereof which has been suspended, or
- (b) a party to a maintenance agreement within the meaning of section 34 of that Act has died, the agreement being one which provides for the continuation of payments thereunder after the death of one of the parties, and an application is made under section 36(1) of that Act for the alteration of the agreement under section 35 thereof.

the court shall have power to direct that the application made under the said section 31(6) or 36(1) shall be deemed to have been accompanied by an application for an order under section 2 of this Act.

(2) Where the court gives a direction under subsection (1) above it shall have power, in the proceedings on the application under the said section 31(6) or 36(1), to make any order which the court would have had power to make under the provisions of this Act if the application under the said section 31(6) or 36(1), as the case may be, had been made jointly with an application for an order under the

said section 2; and the court shall have power to give such consequential directions as may be necessary for enabling the court to exercise any of the powers available to the court under this Act in the case of an application for an order under section 2.

(3) Where an order made under section 15(1) of this Act is in force with respect to a party to a marriage, the court shall not give a direction under subsection (1) above with respect to any application made under the said section 31(6) or 36(1) by that party on the death of the other party.

III FMY [17EA]

18A. Availability of court's powers under this Act in applications under paragraphs 60 and 73 of Schedule 5 to the Civil Partnership Act 2004

(1) Where—

(a) a person against whom a secured periodical payments order was made under Schedule 5 to the Civil Partnership Act 2004 has died and an application is made under paragraph 60 of that Schedule for the variation or discharge of that order or for the revival of the operation of any suspended provision of the order, or

(b) a party to a maintenance agreement within the meaning of Part 13 of that Schedule has died, the agreement being one which provides for the continuation of payments under the agreement after the death of one of the parties, and an application is made under paragraph 73 of that Schedule for the alteration of the agreement under paragraph 69 of that Schedule,

the court shall have power to direct that the application made under paragraph 60 or 73 of that Schedule shall be deemed to have been accompanied by an application for an order under section 2 of this Act.

(2) Where the court gives a direction under subsection (1) above it shall have power, in the proceedings on the application under paragraph 60 or 73 of that Schedule, to make any order which the court would have had power to make under the provisions of this Act if the application under that paragraph had been made jointly with an application for an order under section 2 of this Act; and the court shall have power to give such consequential directions as may be necessary for enabling the court to exercise any of the powers available to the court under this Act in the case of an application for an order under section 2.

(3) Where an order made under section 15ZA(1) of this Act is in force with respect to a civil partner, the court shall not give a direction under subsection (1) above with respect to any application made under paragraph 60 or 73 of that Schedule by that civil partner on the death of the other civil partner.

III FMY [17E.1]

Court's powers in matrimonial cases Section 14 of the Act applies where a party to a marriage dies within 12 months of the date on which a decree of divorce or nullity is made absolute or a decree of judicial separation has been granted and an application for a financial provision order or a property adjustment order has not been made by the other party to the marriage, or has been made and not determined. On an application made by the other party under this Act, the court has power to treat that party for the purpose of the application as if the decree of divorce or nullity had not been made absolute or a decree of judicial separation had not been granted.

Sections 15 and 15A of the Act give the court powers in matrimonial proceedings to make orders restricting applications under this Act. Section 16 of the Act gives the court power on an application under this Act to vary or discharge secured periodical payment orders made under the Matrimonial Causes Act 1973. Section 17 of the Act gives the court power on an application under this Act to vary or revoke maintenance agreements. Section 18 of the Act makes the court's powers under this Act available on applications under ss 31 and 36 of the Matrimonial Causes Act 1973.

An order under s 15(1) that a party to a former marriage shall not be entitled to bring a claim against the estate of the other party only precludes the making of a claim on the basis that the claimant falls within sub-s 1(1)(b) of the Act, as a former spouse of the deceased. It does not preclude the making of a claim in another capacity. Thus where an order had been made on a divorce under s 15(1), and the parties to the former marriage subsequently resumed living together, the former wife was not precluded by the order from bringing a claim om the basis that she fell within sub-s 1(1)(ba) of the Act, as a person who during the period of two years ending with the deceased's death was living in the same household as the deceased and as his wife: *Chekov v Fryer* [2015] EWHC 1642 (Ch) (Deputy Master Matthews).

III FMY [17E.2]

Court's powers in civil partnership cases Section 14A gives the court a power to treat a civil partnership as continuing in similar circumstances to those provided for in matrimonial cases by s 14. Sections 15ZA and 15B give the court powers in proceedings between civil partners to make orders restricting applications by civil partners under this Act. Section 18A makes the court's powers under this Act available in applications under paras 60 and 73 of Schedule 5 to the Civil Partnership Act 2004.

Miscellaneous and supplementary provisions

III FMY [18]

19. Effect, duration and form of orders

(1) Where an order is made under section 2 of this Act then for all purposes, including the purposes of the enactments relating to inheritance tax, the will or the law relating to intestacy, or both the will and the law relating to intestacy, as the case may be, shall have effect and be deemed to have had effect as from the deceased's death subject to the provisions of the order.

(2) Any order made under section 2 or 5 of this Act in favour of—

(a) an applicant who was the former spouse or former civil partner of the deceased, or

(b) an applicant who was the husband or wife of the deceased in a case where *the marriage with the deceased was the subject of a decree of judicial separation and at the date of death the decree was in force* [, at the date of death, a separation order under the Family Law Act 1996 was in force in relation to the marriage with the deceased] and the separation was continuing, or

(c) an applicant who was the civil partner of the deceased in a case where, at the date of death, a separation order under Chapter 2 of Part 2 of the Civil Partnership Act 2004 was in force in relation to their civil partnership and the separation was continuing,

shall, in so far as it provides for the making of periodical payments, cease to have effect on the formation by the applicant of a subsequent marriage or civil partnership, except in relation to any arrears due under the order on the date of the formation of the subsequent marriage or civil partnership.

(3) A copy of every order made under this Act other than an order made under section 15(1) or 15ZA(1) of this Act shall be sent to the principal registry of the Family Division for entry and filing, and a memorandum of the order shall be endorsed on, or permanently annexed to, the probate or letters of administration under which the estate is being administered.

Amendment *Text in italic is deleted and text in square brackets is inserted by the Family Law Act 1996 with effect from a date to be appointed.*

III FMY [18.1]

Tax The inheritance tax consequences of an order under this Act are set out in more detail in the Inheritance Tax Act 1984, s 146. Sub-section 146(8) of that Act also provides that where an order is made staying or dismissing proceedings under this Act on terms set out in or scheduled to the order, s 146 has effect as if any of those terms which could have been included in an order under s 2 or s 10 of this Act were provisions of such an order. Where the court is asked to make or approve an order in a form which confers substantial tax advantages on the parties, see *Re Goodchild* [1997] 3 All ER 63, [1997] 1 WLR 1216, CA (para **III FMY [8.5]**).

III FMY [19]

20. Provisions as to personal representatives

(1) The provisions of this Act shall not render the personal representative of a deceased person liable for having distributed any part of the estate of the deceased, after the end of the period of six months from the date on which representation with respect to the estate of the deceased is first taken out, on the ground that he ought to have taken into account the possibility—

(a) that the court might permit the making of an application for an order under section 2 of this Act after the end of that period, or

(b) that, where an order has been made under the said section 2, the court might exercise in relation thereto the powers conferred on it by section 6 of this Act,

but this subsection shall not prejudice any power to recover, by reason of the making of an order under this Act, any part of the estate so distributed.

(2) Where the personal representative of a deceased person pays any sum directed by an order under section 5 of this Act to be paid out of the deceased's net estate, he shall not be under any liability by reason of that estate not being sufficient to make the payment, unless at the time of making the payment he has reasonable cause to believe that the estate is not sufficient.

(3) Where a deceased person entered into a contract by which he agreed to leave by his will any sum of money or other property to any person or by which he agreed that a sum of money or other property would be paid or transferred to any person out of his estate, then, if the personal representative of the deceased has reason to believe that the deceased entered into the contract with the intention of defeating an application for financial provision under this Act, he may, notwithstanding anything in that contract, postpone the payment of that sum of money or the transfer of that property until the expiration of the period of six months from the date on which representation with respect to the estate of the deceased is first taken out or, if during that period an application is made for an order under section 2 of this Act, until the determination of the proceedings on that application.

III FMY [19.1]

For the courses of action open to personal representatives after the six-month period has expired see further *Re Ralphs* [1968] 3 All ER 285, [1968] 1 WLR 1522.

III FMY [19A]

23. Determination of date on which representation was first taken out

(1) The following are to be left out of account when considering for the purposes of this Act when representation with respect to the estate of a deceased person was first taken out—

(a) a grant limited to settled land or to trust property,

(b) any other grant that does not permit any of the estate to be distributed,

(c) a grant limited to real estate or to personal estate, unless a grant limited to the remainder of the estate has previously been made or is made at the same time,

(d) a grant, or its equivalent, made outside the United Kingdom (but see subsection (2) below).

(2) A grant sealed under section 2 of the Colonial Probates Act 1892 counts as a grant made in the United Kingdom for the purposes of this section, but is to be taken as dated on the date of sealing.

III FMY [19A.1]

The date on which representation with respect to the estate of the deceased is first taken out The day on which representation is first taken out counts as the first day of the six-month period: *Re Kay, Kay v West* [1965] 3 All ER 724, [1965] 1 WLR 1463. Where a grant in common form is followed by a grant in solemn form, time runs from the date of the earlier grant: *Re Miller, Miller v de Courcey* [1968] 3 All ER 844, [1969] 1 WLR 583. Where a grant of probate is revoked and letters of administration are granted, time runs from the date of the latter: *Re Freeman* [1984] 3 All ER 906, [1984] 1 WLR 1419. Section 23 provides that a grant limited to settled land or to trust property should be left out of account and that a grant limited to real estate or to personal estate should also be left out of account unless a grant limited to the remainder of the estate has been previously made or is made at the same time. In *Re Johnson* [1987] CLY 3882 it was held, by analogy with s 23, that a grant to solicitors should also be left out of account where it was taken out for the limited purpose of pursuing a claim in negligence arising out of the deceased's fatal accident.

III FMY [19B]

24. Effect of this Act on s 46(1)(vi) of Administration of Estates Act 1925

Section 46(1)(vi) of the Administration of Estates Act 1925, in so far as it provides for the devolution of property on the Crown, the Duchy of Lancaster or the Duke of Cornwall as bona vacantia, shall have effect subject to the provisions of this Act.

III FMY [20]

25. Interpretation

(1) In this Act—

"beneficiary", in relation to the estate of a deceased person, means—

(a) a person who under the will of the deceased or under the law relating to intestacy is beneficially interested in the estate or would be so interested if an order had not been made under this Act, and

(b) a person who has received any sum of money or other property which by virtue of section 8(1) or 8(2) of this Act is treated as part of the net estate of the deceased or would have received that sum or other property if an order had not been made under this Act;

"child" includes an illegitimate child and a child en ventre sa mere at the death of the deceased;

"the court" unless the context otherwise requires means the High Court, or where the county court has jurisdiction by virtue of 25 of the County Courts Act 1984, the county court;

"former civil partner" means a person whose civil partnership with the deceased was during the lifetime of the deceased either—

(a) dissolved or annulled by an order made under the law of any part of the British Islands, or

(b) dissolved or annulled in any country or territory outside the British Islands by a dissolution or annulment which is entitled to be recognised as valid by the law of England and Wales;

"former spouse" means a person whose marriage with the deceased was during the lifetime of the deceased either—

(a) dissolved or annulled by an order or decree of divorce or a decree of nullity of marriage granted under the law of any part of the British Islands, or

(b) dissolved or annulled in any country or territory outside the British Islands by a divorce or annulment which is entitled to be recognised as valid by the law of England and Wales;

"net estate", in relation to a deceased person, means—

(a) all property of which the deceased had power to dispose by his will (otherwise than by virtue of a special power of appointment) less the amount of his funeral, testamentary and administration expenses, debts and liabilities, including any inheritance tax payable out of his estate on his death;

(b) any property in respect of which the deceased held a general power of appointment (not being a power exercisable by will) which has not been exercised;

(c) any sum of money or other property which is treated for the purposes of this Act as part of the net estate of the deceased by virtue of section 8(1) or (2) of this Act;

(d) any property which is treated for the purposes of this Act as part of the net estate of the deceased by virtue of an order made under section 9 of the Act;

(e) any sum of money or other property which is, by reason of a disposition or contract made by the deceased, ordered under section 10 or 11 of this Act to be provided for the purpose of the making of financial provision under this Act;

"property" includes any chose in action;

"reasonable financial provision" has the meaning assigned to it by section 1 of this Act;

"valuable consideration" does not include marriage or a promise of marriage;

"will" includes codicil.

(2) For the purposes of paragraph (a) of the definition of "net estate" in subsection (1) above a person who is not of full age and capacity shall be treated as having power to dispose by will of all property of which he would have had power to dispose by will if he had been of full age and capacity.

(3) Any reference in this Act to provision out of the net estate of a deceased person includes a reference to provision extending to the whole of that estate.

(4) For the purposes of this Act any reference to a spouse, wife or husband shall be treated as including a reference to a person who in good faith entered into a void marriage with the deceased unless either—

(a) the marriage of the deceased and that person was dissolved or annulled during the lifetime of the deceased and the dissolution or annulment is recognised by the law of England and Wales, or

(b) that person has during the lifetime of the deceased formed a subsequent marriage or civil partnership.

(4A) For the purposes of this Act any reference to a civil partner shall be treated as including a reference to a person who in good faith formed a void civil partnership with the deceased unless either—

(a) the civil partnership between the deceased and that person was dissolved or annulled during the lifetime of the deceased and the dissolution or annulment is recognised by the law of England and Wales, or

(b) that person has during the lifetime of the deceased formed a subsequent civil partnership or marriage.

(5) Any reference in this Act to the formation of, or to a person who has formed, a subsequent marriage or civil partnership includes (as the case may be) a reference to the formation of, or to a person who has formed, a marriage or civil partnership which is by law void or voidable.

(5A) The formation of a marriage or civil partnership shall be treated for the purposes of this Act as the formation of a subsequent marriage or civil partnership, in relation to either of the spouses or civil partners, notwithstanding that the previous marriage or civil partnership of that spouse or civil partner was void or voidable.

(6) Any reference in this Act to an order or decree made under the Matrimonial Causes Act 1973 or under any section of that Act shall be construed as including a reference to an order or decree which is deemed to have been made under that Act or under that section thereof, as the case may be.

(6A) Any reference in this Act to an order made under, or under any provision of, the Civil Partnership Act 2004 shall be construed as including a reference to anything which is deemed to be an order made (as the case may be) under that Act or provision.

(7) Any reference in this Act to any enactment is a reference to that enactment as amended by or under any subsequent enactment.

III FMY [20.1]

Void marriage A ceremony conducted in England and Wales which does not comply with the formal requirements contained in the Marriage Act 1949 is not a "void marriage": *Gandhi v Patel* [2002] 1 FLR 603, [2001] All ER (D) 436 (Jul), Laddie J.

FUNDING OF LEGAL SERVICES

TABLE OF CONTENTS

GENERAL NOTES ON THE FUNDING OF LEGAL SERVICES

III FUND [1]

The funding of litigation has substantially changed following the introduction of the Jackson reforms in April 2013. This Section seeks to accommodate those changes and the reader is advised to consult this same section in earlier editions of the Green Book for the statutory provisions and regulations pertaining to the pre-Jackson funding regime. The reader will find the relevant pre-1 April 2013 material in the 2014 edition – Funding of Legal Services Section (**III FUND**).

Traditionally there have been two methods under which funding for litigation services between a solicitor and his client has been provided for. Firstly, and most commonly, the solicitor can be retained under a privatc contract for a retainer. The terms of the contract, usually set out in a letter complying with what was formerly the Solicitors Practice Rules 1990, r 15 (often referred to as a "rule 15 letter"), the Solicitors Information Client Care Code 1999, the Solicitors Code of Conduct 2007 (replaced on 6 October 2011) and, now, the recently introduced SRA Handbook, provide the basis for the charging, and will set out the charging rates to be applied and any other matters required by those rules. Contractual retainers may also take the form of non-contentious business agreements, or contentious business agreements under the Solicitors Act 1974, ss 57 and 59 respectively (**III SOL [17]**, **III SOL [18]**). The Solicitors Act 1974 regulates the enforcement and reasonableness of private client retainers alongside considerations of public policy. Public policy considerations remain dominant in the area of contingency/conditional fee arrangements with the result that, save for those contingency/conditional fee agreements sanctioned by statute, all other forms of contingency/conditional fee agreements are contrary to public policy and are unenforceable (*Hollins v Russell* [2003] EWCA Civ 718, [2003] 4 All ER 590, [2003] 1 WLR 2487; *Awwad v Geraghty & Co* [2000] 1 All ER 608, [2000] 3 WLR 1014, CA). See also *R (on the application of Factortame) v Secretary of State for Transport Environment and the Regions (No 8)* [2002] EWCA Civ 932, [2003] QB 381, sub nom *Factortame Ltd v Secretary of State for the Environment, Transport and the Regions (No 2)* [2002] 4 All ER 97 as to the common law on champerty and public policy outside the statutory regime. In *Sibthorpe v Southwark London Borough Council (Law Society intervening)* [2011] EWCA Civ 25, [2011] 2 All ER 240, [2011] 1 WLR 2111 the Court of Appeal held that it was not champertous for a solicitor to represent clients under "no win no fee agreements" and provide funding in respect of the client's disbursements and in respect of any adverse costs ordered to be paid by the client to the Opponent. Note also that it is not champertous or improper for a solicitor to continue to act for a client in litigation although aware that the client could not afford to pay the costs involved, provided that there was a retainer letter under which the client had agreed to pay costs at the outset: *Burnstein v Times Newspapers Ltd (No 2)* (2002) Times, 6 December, CA.

Alongside the private client arrangements, the public funding of civil litigation has developed in the form of legal aid, most recently under the Access to Justice Act 1999 and previously under the Legal Aid Act 1988. A solicitor is bound at the outset to consider whether a client may be eligible for public funding, rather than continue to take instructions and run up costs while gathering information before considering public funding eligibility: *David Truex (a firm) v Kitchin* [2007] EWCA Civ 618, (2007) Times, 29 August.

The introduction of the Access to Justice Act 1999 brought about a wind of change to the funding of litigation services. Whereas hitherto the words "funding arrangements" would loosely encompass the range of funding possibilities that could be entered into between solicitor and client, in modern parlance those words take on a specific meaning. A "funding arrangement" became the statutory reference to an agreement where a person had:

(1) entered into a conditional fee agreement which provides for a success fee within the meaning of s 58(2) of the Courts and Legal Services Act 1990;
(2) taken out an insurance policy to which s 29 of the Access to Justice Act 1999 (recovery of insurance premiums by way of costs) applies; or
(3) made an agreement with a membership organisation to meet his legal costs.

Following further legislative changes on 1 April 2013 pursuant to the Legal Aid Sentencing and Punishment of Offenders Act 2012 (LASPO), the concept of 'funding arrangements' now only has relevance to conditional fee agreements and ATE insurance policies entered into before 1 April 2013. For agreements or policies incepted after 1 April 2013 a party may not recover any additional liabilities by way of costs save for remaining exceptions. The government announced in May 2012 that CFA success fees and ATE insurance premiums would continue to be recoverable in insolvency proceedings until April 2015, on the basis that such cases 'bring substantial revenue to the taxpayer, as well as other creditors, and encourage good business practice'. In fact that exception remained in place until April 2016.

There are also exceptions for:

(a) publication and privacy proceedings – ie claims for defamation, malicious falsehood, breach of confidence involving publication to the general public, misuse of private information, or (where the defendant is a news publisher) harassment – pending implementation of Lord Justice Leveson's recommendation that costs protection should be extended to such claims;
(b) claims for damages in respect of diffuse mesothelioma;
(c) in relation to ATE, premiums to cover the cost of expert reports on liability or causation in clinical negligence cases.

On 6 April 2019 the law will change again with the abolition of the publication and privacy exception save that after the event insurance premiums will remain recoverable in publication and privacy cases. This gives effect to legal obligations under the *MGN v UK* judgment of the European Court of Human Rights in 2011. In the MGN case, the court concluded that the obligation for the defendant to pay a 100% 'success fee' to the claimant was disproportionate, and that the conditional fee agreements regime was therefore in breach of the defendant's rights under Article 10 (freedom of expression) of the European Convention on Human Rights.

The introduction of the Jackson reforms recommended by Lord Justice Jackson in his Final Report 'Review of Civil Litigation Costs' changed the litigation landscape.

The main and most significant of the reforms are these:

(a) For all conditional fee agreements which provide for a success fee which are entered into after 1 April 2013 then the success fee will not be recoverable by way of costs from the opponent.
(b) For all after the event ("ATE") premiums taken out after 1 April 2013 the premiums will not be recoverable by way of costs.
(c) In all conditional fee agreements entered into after 1 April 2013 in respect of claims for damages for personal injury which provide for a success fee, the maximum success fee is capped as between solicitor and client at 25% of the damages. The damages being defined in the Conditional Fee Agreements Order 2013 as:
    (i) general damages for pain, suffering, and loss of amenity; and
    (ii) damages for pecuniary loss, other than future pecuniary loss, net of any sums recoverable by the Compensation Recovery Unit of the Department for Work and Pensions.
(d) In all other claims (not claims for damages for personal injury) and all appeals including those in respect of claims for damages for personal injury, the success fee is not limited by 25% of the damages but cannot exceed 100% of the basic charges on which the success fee is calculated.
(e) From 1 April 2013 a party may enter into a damages based agreement in all civil litigation subject to exceptions. Damages based agreements are addressed further at (**III FUND [5]** and **III FUND [27.7]** below)

PART I CIVIL LEGAL AID

III FUND [1.1]

General Overview Historically, the Civil Court Practice and its predecessor the County Court Practice (both known colloquially as the "Green Book"), devoted a good deal of commentary to the subject of Legal Aid and its substitute, Community Legal Service Funding. However,

Community Legal Service Funding has become less relevant to civil court practice over the past few years and as a consequence this Edition of the Civil Court Practice deliberately reduces the extent of coverage devoted to Community Legal Service Funding. Access to past editions will provide practitioners with the core statutory provisions and commentary: see the Legal Aid section in previous editions of Volume 2.

The Access to Justice Act 1999 received Royal Assent on 27 July 1999. The Act replaced the then existing legal aid system. The Legal Services Commission has replaced the Legal Aid Board and it secures the provision of civil legal services through the Community Legal Service. The Legal Services Commission manages the Community Legal Service Fund which replaced the Legal Aid fund in civil and family cases. Whether funding is granted is largely dictated by the Funding Code which sets out the criteria to be applied in deciding whether to grant funding in an individual case. The Funding Code is supplemented by the Lord Chancellor's Directions and Guidance given under ss 6(1) and 23 of the Access to Justice Act 1999. The Legal Services Commission funding framework is supported by subordinate legislation and many of the key provisions are referenced in earlier Editions of this work.

From 1 April 2013 the Ministry of Justice administer legal aid through the Legal Aid Agency, a new executive agency, which has responsibility for the administration of legal aid in England and Wales.

PART II FUNDING OF LEGAL SERVICES: ACCESS TO JUSTICE ACT 1999

III FUND [2]

Changes made by the Access to Justice Act 1999 The Access to Justice Act 1999 received Royal Assent on 27 July 1999. It has seven parts but Parts I and II brought about the major changes to litigation funding. Part I replaced the former legal aid system with the introduction of the Community Legal Service run by the Legal Services Commission. The Legal Services Commission, a non-departmental public body, replaced the Legal Aid Board. Part II of the Access to Justice Act 1999 introduced significant amendments to the Courts and Legal Services Act 1990 s 58. Under those amendments, the concept of conditional fee agreements was further extended to those cases in which no success fee is claimed (*Thai Trading* agreements – *Thai Trading Co v Taylor* [1998] QB 781, [1998] 3 All ER 65, CA), but which provides for the payment of fees and expenses, or any part of them, only in specified circumstances. The other significant changes brought about by the Access to Justice Act 1999 were in relation to the recovery of additional liabilities. Under the Access to Justice Act 1999 s 27, amendments to s 58 of the Courts and Legal Services Act 1990 enabled costs orders to provide for the recovery of success fees inter partes. Section 29 of the Access to Justice Act 1999 provides that a party may recover the cost of an insurance policy taken out against the risk of incurring a liability in those proceedings. These changes have now been reversed by the Legal Aid, Sentencing and Punishment of Offenders Act 2012 (LASPO). That Act abolishes the recovery of additional liabilities (success fees and insurance premiums) by way of costs.

III FUND [3]

The Community Legal Service Section 4 of the Access to Justice Act 1999 established the Community Legal Service and listed the services which were funded as part of it. These ranged from the provision of general information and the law and legal services to providing help towards preventing or resolving disputes and enforcing decisions which have been reached. The scheme encompassed advice, assistance and representation by lawyers and also the services of non-lawyers. The aim of the Community Legal Service was to promote the availability to individuals of those services and, in particular, to secure, within the resources available and the priorities set, that individuals have access to services that effectively meet their needs. However, from 1 April 2013 the CLS was abolished and replaced with the Legal Aid Agency which is an executive agency of the Ministry of Justice. This new agency will administer legal aid services in England and Wales.

III FUND [4]

The Legal Services Commission The Legal Services Commission was set up by s 1 of the Access to Justice Act 1999 and had two main duties. First, to manage the Community Legal Service fund, which replaced legal aid in civil and family cases and second, it established, developed and maintained the Community Legal Service which included the provision of services beyond those supported by the Community Legal Service fund. The Commission replaced the former Legal Aid Board. From 1 April 2013 the Commission was abolished and replaced with the Legal Aid Agency.

III FUND [4.1]

The Legal Aid Agency From 1 April 2013 the Ministry of Justice administers legal aid services via a new executive agency, called the Legal Aid Agency, which assumed

FUNDING

responsibility for the administration of legal aid in England and Wales from the Legal Services Commission. On 1 April 2013 the Legal Services Commission was abolished and the Lord Chancellor became responsible for securing that legal aid is made available in England and Wales, in line with the provisions contained in the Legal Aid, Sentencing and Punishment of Offenders Act 2012 (LASPO). That Act also contains the legislative provisions needed to abolish the Legal Services Commission. There is a Framework Document which details the governance arrangements between the Department and the Legal Aid Agency has been published. The Framework Document came into force on 1 April 2013. In line with the requirements for all executive agencies, the Framework Document sets out the overarching framework for the governance and accountability arrangements between the Department and the Agency. The Legal Aid, Sentencing and Punishment of Offenders Act 2012 also requires the Lord Chancellor to designate a civil servant as the Director of Legal Aid Casework. This is a statutory office, with the function of making independent decisions on whether to grant legal aid in individual cases. The Director assumed this function on 1 April 2013, following the abolition of the Legal Services Commission. Part 1 of the Legal Aid, Sentencing and Punishment of Offenders Act 2012, which was commenced on 1 April 2013, sets out the new framework for legal aid in England and Wales which, as well as the abolition of the Legal Services Commission, includes reforms to the scope of civil legal aid.

Copies of the Framework Document and code of conduct can be found on the Department's website at: www.justice.gov.uk. This document sets out the arrangements for the governance, accountability, financing, staffing and operation of the Legal Aid Agency, agreed between the Permanent Secretary and the Chief Executive of the Legal Aid Agency with the a pproval of the Lord Chancellor.

PART III CONDITIONAL FEE AGREEMENTS AND DAMAGES BASED AGREE- MENTS

III FUND [5]

Conditional fee agreements and success fees The framework for conditional fees has altered following the introduction of Part 2 of Legal Aid, Sentencing and Punishment of Offenders Act 2013. Section 58 of the Courts and Legal Services Act 1990 is the primary piece of legislation governing conditional fee agreements. Various amendments have been made over the past decade with the most recent being introduced via LASPO in April 2013. The requirements of an enforceable conditional fee agreement differ depending upon whether it was entered into before or after 1 November 2005 and now before or after 1 April 2013. Where it is entered into before 1 November 2005, it must comply with the Conditional Fee Agreements Regulations 2000, SI 2000/692, and the Conditional Fee Agreements Order 2000, SI 2000/823. Furthermore, if entered into after 1 April 2013 the agreement must comply with s 44 of Legal Aid, Sentencing and Punishment of Offenders Act 2012, which made further amendments to s 58 Courts and Legal Services Act 1990. It must also comply with the Conditional Fee Agreements Order 2013 which provides limitations on the level of chargeable success fee in specified proceedings. In order for the success fee payable under a conditional fee agreement to be recovered the CFA must have been entered into before 1 April 2013. Further, it will be necessary to comply with rules of court and the supporting Practice Direction about costs. Particular attention must be had to (pre-April 2013) CPR 44.3A, 44.3B and 44.15 to 44.17. Section 19 of the pre 1 April 2013 Costs Practice Direction (see para **CPR PD 44**) sets out the information to be provided to the opposing party as a pre-requisite to the recovery of any additional liability, such as a success fee.

In *Callery v Gray* [2001] EWCA Civ 1117, [2001] 3 All ER 833, [2001] 1 WLR 2112, the Court of Appeal was asked to consider the legitimacy and reasonableness of success fees in low value motor accident cases. The court held that whilst each case must be considered on its own merits, a 20% success fee on base costs would be reasonable in a simple motor accident claim where liability was not issue. Lord Woolf CJ postulated the concept of a two-stage success fee so as to provide for a low percentage success fee in those cases which settled before the conclusion of the pre-action protocol but to allow a success fee as high as 100% in those cases which were fought. It remains to be seen whether such arrangements become common or not. In *Atack v Lee* [2004] EWCA Civ 1712, (2004) 149 Sol Jo LB 60, further encouragement was given to the two stage success fee. See also *KU v Liverpool City Council* [2005] EWCA Civ 475.

The House of Lords upheld the decision of the Court of Appeal in *Callery v Gray (Nos 1 and 2)* [2002] UKHL 28, [2002] 3 All ER 417, [2002] 1 WLR 2000, declining to interfere in the policing and development of practice relating to conditional fees, which was best left in the hands of the Court of Appeal. See also *Julia Bensusan v Bernard Freedman* [2001] All ER (D) 212 (Oct) as to the assessment of the success fee in a clinical negligence case where liability was unlikely to be seriously in issue. In *Hollins v Russell* [2003] EWCA Civ 718, [2003] 4 All ER 590, [2003] 1 WLR 2487, the Court of Appeal heard five test cases as to the effect of non-compliance of conditional fee agreements with the statutory requirements (note the Conditional Fee Agreements Regulations 2000 which *Hollins v Russell* was principally concerned has been revoked from 1 November 2005. The Court held that defects which could not be said to have materially adversely affected the protection which is afforded to the client by the statutory regime or which have not materially adversely affected the administration of justice would not amount to defects capable of rendering the conditional fee agreement unenforceable under s 58(1) of the Courts and Legal Services Act 1990. The relevant law as to the enforceability of conditional fee agreements was the subject of much clarification in the case of *Garrett v Halton Borough Council; Myatt v National Coal Board* [2006] EWCA Civ 1017, [2007] 1 All ER 147. Leading Court of Appeal cases include *Kier Tankard (Appellant) v John Fredricks Plastics Ltd (Respondent): (1) Fawcett Old Ltd (2) Michael Jane Hair & Beauty (Appellants) v Yvonne Hibberd (Respondent): Mark Jones (Appellant) v Karl Joseph Attrill (Respondent) & Law Society (Intervener) (2008)* [2008] EWCA Civ 1375. See also *Jones v Wrexham Borough Council* [2007] EWCA Civ 1356, [2007] All ER (D) 300 (Dec) on the topic of the requirements of a Conditional Fee Agreement "Lite".

The fact that the claimant is comprehensively insured against the loss claimed and is suing at the instance of his, or her, insurers, is not a ground for refusing the recovery of a success fee: *Sousa v London Borough of Waltham Forest Council* [2011] EWCA Civ 194, [2011] NLJR 435, (2011) Times, 9 March, CA.

In *Hyde v Milton Keynes NHS Foundation Trust* [2017] EWCA Civ 399, Lord Justice Davis found that there was no period of time when the claimant solicitors were being paid both under the CFA, and by legal aid and therefore the CFA was enforceable; the legal aid certificate had not been discharged but funding under it had.

The Supreme Court has confirmed that the Access to Justice Act 1999 is compatible with the European Convention on Human Rights, although the decision was by a majority of 5-2: *Coventry v Lawrence* [2015] UKSC 50, 165 NLJ 7663, [2015] All ER (D) 234 (Jul). The court held that the key aims of the regime under the AJA were (1) to contain the rising cost of legal aid, (2) to improve access to justice for members of the public with meritorious claims and (3) to discourage weak claims. The decision of the European Court of Human Rights in *MGN v UK*, which held that the AJA scheme was incompatible with Article 10 of the Convention, concerned the balancing of the rights guaranteed by Article 10 with article 6 rights, and was therefore an exercise of a different character to the one concerning the court in *Coventry v Lawrence*. The scheme as a whole was held to be a rational and coherent scheme for providing access to justice and in the circumstances this led to the conclusion that the scheme was not incompatible with Article 6 or A1P1.

For all CFAs entered into after 1 April 2013, no success fee can be recovered by way of costs unless one of the statutory exemptions applies. The government announced in May 2012 that CFA success fees and ATE insurance premiums would continue to be recoverable in insolvency proceedings until April 2015, on the basis that such cases 'bring substantial revenue to the taxpayer, as well as other creditors, and encourage good business practice'. In fact that exception remained in place until April 2016.

There are also exceptions for:

(a) publication and privacy proceedings – ie claims for defamation, malicious falsehood, breach of confidence involving publication to the general public, misuse of private information, or (where the defendant is a news publisher) harassment – pending implementation of Lord Justice Leveson's recommendation that costs protection should be extended to such claims;
(b) claims for damages in respect of diffuse mesothelioma;
(c) in relation to ATE, premiums to cover the cost of expert reports on liability or causation in clinical negligence cases..

III FUND [6]–III FUND [25]

Success fees and freedom of expression The obligation of a defendant newspaper to pay the claimant's success fees in libel litigation has been held to infringe the newspaper's right to freedom of expression, in circumstances where the success fees far exceeded the damages and awarded. The aim of the success fee system was to increase access to justice but the costs burden was disproportionate to the aim and imposed a penalty on the media's freedom of expression, in breach of article 10: *MGN Ltd v United Kingdom (Application No 39401/04)* (2011) 53 EHRR 195, (2011) Times, 20 January, ECtHR. For a further discussion of the *MGN* case, see *Coventry v Lawrence* [2015] UKSC 50, 165 NLJ 7663, [2015] All ER (D) 234 (Jul).

FUNDING

COURTS AND LEGAL SERVICES ACT 1990

(c 41)

PART I
LEGAL SERVICES COMMISSION

CONDITIONAL FEE AND LITIGATION FUNDING AGREEMENTS

III FUND [26]–III FUND [27]

58. Conditional fee agreements

(1) A conditional fee agreement which satisfies all of the conditions applicable to it by virtue of this section shall not be unenforceable by reason only of its being a conditional fee agreement; but (subject to subsection (5)) any other conditional fee agreement shall be unenforceable.

(2) For the purposes of this section and section 58A—

(a) a conditional fee agreement is an agreement with a person providing advocacy or litigation services which provides for his fees and expenses, or any part of them, to be payable only in specified circumstances;

(b) a conditional fee agreement provides for a success fee if it provides for the amount of any fees to which it applies to be increased, in specified circumstances, above the amount which would be payable if it were not payable only in specified circumstances; and

(c) references to a success fee, in relation to a conditional fee agreement, are to the amount of the increase.

(3) The following conditions are applicable to every conditional fee agreement—

(a) it must be in writing;

(b) it must not relate to proceedings which cannot be the subject of an enforceable conditional fee agreement; and

(c) it must comply with such requirements (if any) as may be prescribed by the Lord Chancellor.

(4) The following further conditions are applicable to a conditional fee agreement which provides for a success fee—

(a) it must relate to proceedings of a description specified by order made by the Lord Chancellor;

(b) it must state the percentage by which the amount of the fees which would be payable if it were not a conditional fee agreement is to be increased; and

(c) that percentage must not exceed the percentage specified in relation to the description of proceedings to which the agreement relates by order made by the Lord Chancellor.

(4A) The additional conditions are applicable to a conditional fee agreement which—

(a) provides for a success fee; and

(b) relates to proceedings of a description specified by order made by the Lord Chancellor for the purposes of this subsection.

(4B) The additional conditions are that—

(a) the agreement must provide that the success fee is subject to a maximum limit;

(b) the maximum limit must be expressed as a percentage of the descriptions of damages awarded in the proceedings that are specified in the agreement;

(c) that percentage must not exceed the percentage specified by order made by the Lord Chancellor in relation to the proceedings or calculated in a manner so specified; and

(d) those descriptions of damages may only include descriptions of damages specified by order made by the Lord Chancellor in relation to the proceedings.

(5) If a conditional fee agreement is an agreement to which section 57 of the Solicitors Act 1974 (non-contentious business agreements between solicitor and client) applies, subsection (1) shall not make it unenforceable.

III FUND [27.1]

Conditions The formal and other requirements, as to the contents of the agreement, the information to be provided to the client and the need for signatures, were set out in the Conditional Fee Agreements Regulations 2000, SI 2000/692, the text of which can be found in earlier editions of this work. Those regulations do not apply to conditional fee agreement entered into after 1 November 2005. The only statutory requirements for agreements entered into after 1 November 2005 but before 1 April 2013 are the requirements of s 58 of the Courts and Legal Services Act and the Conditional Fee Agreements Order 2000. For those agreements entered into after 1 April 2013, it is necessary to comply with the Conditional Fee Agreements Order 2013.

Note that "conditional fee agreement" is confined to an agreement for the provision of litigation services and does not include an agreement to provide pre-litigation services, of advice and a letter of claim, on the terms that no charge will be made if the claim is disputed and the client decides to proceed no further: *Gaynor v Central West London Buses Ltd (t/a First Transforming Wave)* [2006] EWCA Civ 1120, [2007] 1 All ER 84, [2007] 1 WLR 1045.

Work undertaken outside the scope of the CFA (as defined by the CFA) will not be recoverable from the paying party: *Frade v Radford* [2017] EQCA Civ 1010. It is therefore important that consideration is given to the wording of the CFA such that it covers the correct opponent and the correct claims and proceedings.

In *Jenkins v Young Brothers Transport Ltd* [2006] EWHC 151 (QB), [2006] 2 All ER 798, [2006] 1 WLR 3189, it was held that the benefits and burdens of a compliant conditional fee agreement may be assigned by one firm to another, without the need for a novation, provided that the reason for the assignment is the trust and confidence of the client in the particular solicitor who has moved from the assignor firm to the assignee. However, the Court of Appeal in *Budana v The Leeds Teaching Hospital NHS Trust* [2017] EWCA Civ 180. Disagreed by majority that the burdens under the CFA could be assigned. With the agreement of all the parties the client who wishes to change solicitors may have the benefits and burdens of a CFA agreement transferred by novation from one firm to the next. Assignments were popular amongst solicitors in cases which transitioned the Jackson reforms so as to preserve the recoverable success fees under pre-Jackson CFAs. The Court of Appeal in *Budana* held that a novation of a CFA post Jackson in respect of a CFA entered into before 1 April 2013 kept alive the recoverable success fee by virtue of the transitional provisions of s 44(6) of the Legal Aid Sentencing and Punishment of Offenders Act 2012.

For agreements entered into after 1 April 2013, s 44 of LASPO further requirements must be met for the agreement to be enforceable. Section 58(4) has been added to by a new s 58(4A), and this now requires all post- April 2013 CFAs which provide for a success fee to:

(a) provide that the success fee is subject to a maximum limit;

(b) the maximum limit must be expressed as a percentage of the descriptions of damages awarded in the proceedings that are specified in the agreement;

(c) that percentage must not exceed the percentage specified by order made by the Lord Chancellor in relation to the proceedings or calculated in a manner so specified; and

(d) those descriptions of damages may only include descriptions of damages specified by order made by the Lord Chancellor in relation to the proceedings.

For all agreements entered into after 1 April 2013, the requirements of the Conditional Fee Agreements Order 2013 must all be met. This is particularly relevant to agreements covering claims for damages for personal injury as paragraph 5 of the Order limits the chargeable success fee to no more than 25% of the damages for pain, suffering and loss of amenity and past future loss net of any sums recoverable by the Compensation Recovery Unit of the Department for Work and Pensions.

III FUND [27.2]

Conditional fee agreements with no success fee Conditional fee agreements which do not provide for a success fee, but which provide only for "normal" fees to be paid by the client on success, and a lesser sum or nothing if the case is lost, are now covered by the s 58(2)(a) as amended. These agreements can loosely be described as *Thai Trading* agreements, after the case of *Thai Trading Co (a firm) v Taylor* [1998] QB 781, [1998] 3 All ER 65, CA.

III FUND [27.3]

Conditional fee agreements with a success fee For agreements entered into before 1 April 2013.

The Courts and Legal Services Act 1990, s 58(2)(b) enables a percentage "uplift" to be applied to the costs charged to the client in the event of success. The percentage uplift applies to the costs charged and not to the damages recovered. Agreements which provide for a share of the damages remain illegal and unenforceable as contingency fee agreements. See generally *Callery v Gray* [2001] EWCA Civ 1117, [2001] 3 All ER 833, [2001] 1 WLR 2112 and *Callery v Gray (No 2)* [2001] EWCA Civ 1246, [2001] 4 All ER 1, [2001] 1 WLR 2142 (see para **III FUND [28.4]**). See also *Callery v Gray (Nos 1 and 2)* [2002] UKHL 28, [2002] 3 All ER 417, [2002] 1 WLR 2000; *R (on the application of Factortame) v Secretary of State for Transport Environment and the Regions (No 8)* [2002] EWCA Civ 932, [2003] QB 381, sub nom *Factortame Ltd v Secretary of State for the Environment, Transport and the Regions (No 2)* [2002] 4 All ER 97.

Where success on the facts is a near certainty, a success fee should not exceed 15%: *Begum v Klarit* [2005] EWCA Civ 234, (2005) Times, 18 March, [2005] 3 Costs LR 452, a case where the success fees of 100% for counsel and 70% for solicitors were both reduced to 15%, following guidance given in *Atack v Lee* [2004] EWCA Civ 1712, [2005] 1 WLR 2643, [2006] RTR 127 and rejecting the suggestion that success fee remuneration should compensate for the those cases where no success fee was payable because the case was lost.

Where liability had been admitted in an action for personal injuries a judge had erred in allowing a success fee under a conditional fee agreement of 50%, the appropriate success fee in the circumstances was 20%: *C v W* [2008] EWCA Civ 1459, [2009] 4 All ER 1129, [2009] RTR 199.

In *Surrey v Barnet & Chase Farm Hospitals NHS Trust* [2018 EWCA Civ 451 the Court of Appeal considered the reasonableness of costs claimed when, after liability has been admitted by the Defendant, funding of the claim has changed from legal aid (LSC) to a conditional fee agreement (CFA) supplemented by after the event insurance (ATE). In these cases it was considered unreasonable and the Claimants could therefore recover base costs only.

A 100% success fee will not be justified inter partes where liability has already been admitted and where there is no Part 36 offer: *NJL v PTE* [2018] EWHC 3570 (QB) (20 December 2018)

For agreements entered into after 1 April 2013.

These must comply with both the amended version of s 58 of the Courts and Legal Services Act 1990, as amended by LASPO and the Conditional Fee Agreements Order 2013. For the Order see para **III FUND [54A]**.

III FUND [27.4]

Specified percentage The Conditional Fee Agreements Order 2000, SI 2000/823, art 4, specifies a percentage of 100% as the maximum percentage which may be agreed as a success fee. Where the success fee is stated to exceed 100% the agreement will be declared unenforceable: *Jones v Caradon Catnic Ltd* [2005] EWCA Civ 1821, [2006] 3 Costs LR 427. For agreements entered into after 1 April 2013, the Conditional Fee Agreements Order 2013 provides for a similar 100% limit. However, significantly the Order provides for the types of proceedings which are specified for the purposes of s 58(4)(c) of LASPO.

It has been held that where the agreement provides for a basic rate (chargeable in the event of success) and a discounted rate (chargeable in the event of failure) the success fee is compliant if it adds no more than 100% to the basic rate, although it would be in excess if applied to the discounted rate: *Gloucestershire County Council v Evans* [2008] EWCA Civ 21, [2008] 1 WLR 1883, [2008] NLJR 219.

The agreement must cover litigation and advocacy services. Anything short of that and the agreement will not be a CFA regulated by s 58: *Gaynor v Central West London Buses Ltd (t/a First Transforming Wave)* [2006] EWCA Civ 1120, [2007] 1 All ER 84, [2007] 1 WLR 1045.

The provisions limiting the specified percentage in the Conditional Fee Agreements Order

2013 in respect of personal injury claims are paragraphs 4 and 5 of the order:

4. Specified proceedings

A claim for personal injuries shall be proceedings specified for the purpose of section 58(4A)(b) of the Act.

5. Amount of success fee in specified proceedings

(1) In relation to the proceedings specified in article 4, the percentage prescribed for the purposes of section 58(4B)(c) of the Act is—

(a) in proceedings at first instance, 25%; and

(b) in all other proceedings, 100%.

(2) The descriptions of damages specified for the purposes of section 58(4B)(d) of the Act are—

(a) general damages for pain, suffering, and loss of amenity; and

(b) damages for pecuniary loss, other than future pecuniary loss,

net of any sums recoverable by the Compensation Recovery Unit of the Department for Work and Pensions.

III FUND [27.5]

Family proceedings The client care letter written in family proceedings should avoid ambiguous terms which could be construed as creating a conditional fee agreement, since such an agreement is excluded by s 58A(1)(b) from the validating provisions of s 58. In *Denton v Denton* [2004] EWHC 1308 (Fam), [2004] 2 FLR 594, [2005] Fam Law 353, the client care letter included a promise that "a claim for costs will not be made until money is received at the end of the case". This was held, on a purposive construction, to indicate that the client would be liable for her own costs but that they would not be claimed until the end of the case. The alternative construction, which the court rejected, was that it was an unenforceable conditional fee agreement.

III FUND [27.6]

Promise by claimant's solicitor of indemnity in respect of defendant's costs It may be contrary to public policy for an indemnity in respect of the other side's costs to be a term of the CFA. However such a term would contravene public policy only where it placed an unacceptable burden on the solicitor that might realistically cause an overriding of the client's interests. In cases of low risk, low quantum, low volume and low success fee such a provision would be enforced since it had the advantage of increasing access to justice without any serious disadvantages: *Sibthorpe v Southwark London Borough Council (Law Society intervening)* [2011] EWCA Civ 25, [2011] 2 All ER 240, [2011] 1 WLR 2111. The Court of Appeal refused to find that a solicitor had maintained an action in which he failed to secure after the event insurance having advised his client that it would be appropriate to do so: *Heron v TNT (UK) Ltd* [2013] EWCA Civ 469, [2013] 3 All ER 479, [2013] NLJR 21.

III FUND [27.7]

Damages Based Agreements Damages based agreements were first introduced into the litigation arena by the Coroners and Justice Act 2009. However, their scope was limited to employment matters. Following recommendations made by Lord Justice Jackson in his Review of Civil Costs, Parliament agreed to extend the operation of damages based agreements to the litigation arena generally with only limited exceptions. The exceptions are those same exceptions which cannot be the subject of an enforceable conditional fee agreement. Thus, where it is possible to enter into a conditional fee agreement, it is also now possible to enter into a damages based agreement. A damages based agreement provides that the sole mechanism for payment is the recovery of damages from which a specified percentage payment is made. It is for all intents and purposes a contingency fee agreement.

Taking into account both the changes brought about by the Coroners and Justice Act 2009, and the changes brought about by the Legal Aid, Sentencing and Punishment of Offenders Act 2012, s 45, section 5AA now reads as follows:

58AA. Damages-based agreements

(1) A damages-based agreement which satisfies the conditions in subsection (4) is not unenforceable by reason only of its being a damages-based agreement.

(2) But (subject to subsection (9)) a damages-based agreement which does not satisfy those conditions is unenforceable.

(3) For the purposes of this section—

(a) a damages-based agreement is an agreement between a person providing advocacy services, litigation services or claims management services and the recipient of those services which provides that—

FUNDING

(i) the recipient is to make a payment to the person providing the services if the recipient obtains a specified financial benefit in connection with the matter in relation to which the services are provided, and

(ii) the amount of that payment is to be determined by reference to the amount of the financial benefit obtained;

(b) ...

(4) The agreement—

(a) must be in writing;

(aa) must not relate to proceedings which by virtue of section 58A(1) and (2) cannot be the subject of an enforceable conditional fee agreement or to proceedings of a description prescribed by the Lord Chancellor;

(b) if regulations so provide, must not provide for a payment above a prescribed amount or for a payment above an amount calculated in a prescribed manner;

(c) must comply with such other requirements as to its terms and conditions as are prescribed; and

(d) must be made only after the person providing services under the agreement has complied with such requirements (if any) as may be prescribed as to the provision of information.

(5) Regulations under subsection (4) are to be made by the Lord Chancellor and may make different provision in relation to different descriptions of agreements.

(6) Before making regulations under subsection (4) the Lord Chancellor must consult—

(a) the designated judges,

(b) the General Council of the Bar,

(c) the Law Society, and

(d) such other bodies as the Lord Chancellor considers appropriate.

(7) In this section—

"payment" includes a transfer of assets and any other transfer of money's worth (and the reference in subsection (4)(b) to a payment above a prescribed amount, or above an amount calculated in a prescribed manner, is to be construed accordingly);

"claims management services" has the same meaning as in Part 2 of the Compensation Act 2006 (see section 4(2) of that Act).

(7A) In this section (and in the definitions of "advocacy services" and "litigation services" as they apply for the purposes of this section) "proceedings" includes any sort of proceedings for resolving disputes (and not just proceedings in a court), whether commenced or contemplated.

(8) Nothing in this section applies to an agreement entered into before the coming into force of the first regulations made under subsection (4).

(9) Where section 57 of the Solicitors Act 1974 (non-contentious business agreements between solicitor and client) applies to a damages-based agreement other than one relating to an employment matter, subsections (1) and (2) of this section do not make it unenforceable.

(10) For the purposes of subsection (9) a damages-based agreement relates to an employment matter if the matter in relation to which the services are provided is a matter that is, or could become, the subject of proceedings before an employment tribunal.

It is necessary for a damages based agreement to comply with the requirements of the Damages Based Agreements Regulations 2013. These contain complex provisions. For the 2013 Regulations see para **III FUND [69L]**.

PART III CONDITIONAL FEE AGREEMENTS

GENERAL NOTES ON CONDITIONAL FEE AGREEMENTS

III FUND [27A]

Legislation Conditional fee agreements first received statutory recognition by virtue of the Courts and Legal Services Act 1990 s 58 and by the subsequent introduction of the Conditional Fee Agreements Regulations 1995, SI 1995/1675 and the Conditional Fee Agreements Order 1995, SI 1995/1674. These provisions came into force on 5 July 1995. The 1995 Order specified only a limited number of categories of proceedings which could be the subject of a conditional fee agreement. In August 1998, the Conditional Fee Agreements

Order 1998, SI 1998/1860 opened up the categories of cases to which a conditional fee agreement could apply and practitioners became increasingly more familiar with them. Whilst practitioners saw the benefit of charging a success fee to their clients, clients did not. Why should the client pay his solicitor more if the case is bound to succeed in any event? Clients therefore began to take the initiative and variations to the conditional fee agreement were developed at common law. The most widely adopted of these was the *Thai Trading* agreement, named after the case of *Thai Trading Co (a firm) v Taylor* [1998] QB 781, [1998] 3 All ER 65. Such agreements provided for the payment by the client of the solicitor's normal costs if the case was won, but nothing if the case was lost. Alternatively, a discounted fee may have been payable if the case was not successful. The court of Appeal in *Awwad v Geraghty & Co* [2000] 1 All ER 608, [2000] 3 WLR 1041, CA found *Thai Trading* to have been decided *per incuriam* and held that Thai Trading agreements were unlawful to the extent that they did not comply with statute. However, with the advent of the Access to Justice Act 1999 on 1 April 2000, the future for conditional fee agreements of various sorts looks healthy. Thai Trading agreements were placed on a statutory footing and solicitors could be assured that if their agreements complied with the Access to Justice Act 1999 and the regulations made there under, their agreements would be enforceable by the court. The Conditional Fee Agreements Regulations 2000, SI 2000/692 and the Conditional Fee Agreements Order 2000, SI 2000/823 provided the new regulatory framework for conditional fee agreements. However, the regulations did not last and on 1 November 2005 they were revoked so that only those agreements entered into before 1 November 2005 are required to meet the requirements of those regulations. All agreements must however meet the requirements of s 58 of the Courts and Legal Services Act 1990 as amended by s 27 of the Access to Justice Act 1999 and now as amended by the Legal Aid, Sentencing and Punishment of Offenders Act 2012, s 45. Rules of court and the costs practice directions (see paras **CPR PD 44** to **CPR PD 48**) provide the mechanism for assessment of costs payable under a conditional fee agreement between both a solicitor and client and inter partes where they were entered into before 1 April 2013.

In exercise of powers conferred on the Lord Chancellor by ss 58(3)(c), 58A(3) and 119 of the Courts and Legal Services Act 1990, the Lord Chancellor made the Collective Conditional Fee Agreements Regulations 2000 (SI 2000/2988). The regulations, together with commentary are to be found at **III FUND [117]**.

FUNDING

III FUND [27A.1]

The agreement There are two types of conditional fee agreements. The first is an agreement with a person providing advocacy or litigation services which provides for his fees and expenses, or any part of them, to be payable only in specified circumstances. In this kind of conditional fee agreement, no success fee is chargeable. These agreements are provided for under the new s 58(2)(a) of the Courts and Legal Services Act 1990. The second kind of conditional fee agreement is one where a success fee is payable to the person providing the advocacy or litigation services under the Courts and Legal Services Act 1990, s 58(2)(b). A Conditional fee agreement provides for a success fee if it provides for the amount of any fees to which it applies to be increased, in specified circumstances, above the amount which would be payable if it were not payable only in specified circumstances. The increase is a percentage increase. The Conditional Fee Agreements Order 2000, SI 2000/823, provides that the percentage increase can be no higher than 100%. The Law Society had recommended under the 1995 and 1998 regime of conditional fee agreements that practitioners should voluntarily impose a cap on the success fee such that it does not seek more than 25% of the damages recovered. This cap has now found its way into the new form of conditional fee agreement entered into post-1 April 2013. For conditional fee agreements with a success fee entered into after 1 April 2013 there are further limitations on the chargeable success fee. Section 44 sets out the additional conditions as follows:

The additional conditions are applicable to a conditional fee agreement which—

(a) provides for a success fee, and

(b) relates to proceedings of a description specified by order made by the Lord Chancellor for the purposes of this subsection.

The additional conditions are that—

(a) the agreement must provide that the success fee is subject to a maximum limit,

(b) the maximum limit must be expressed as a percentage of the descriptions of damages awarded in the proceedings that are specified in the agreement,

(c) that percentage must not exceed the percentage specified by order made by the Lord Chancellor in relation to the proceedings or calculated in a manner so specified, and

(d) those descriptions of damages may only include descriptions of damages specified by order made by the Lord Chancellor in relation to the proceedings.

The Conditional Fee Agreements Order 2013 specifies the percentage limit and the "specified proceedings" to which the success fee limit is operative. The key provisions are regulations 3, 4 and and 5:

3. Amount of success fee

In relation to all proceedings specified in article 2, the percentage specified for the purposes of section 58(4)(c) of the Act is 100%.

4. Specified proceedings

A claim for personal injuries shall be proceedings specified for the purpose of section 58(4A)(b) of the Act.

5. Amount of success fee in specified proceedings

(1) In relation to the proceedings specified in article 4, the percentage prescribed for the purposes of section 58(4B)(c) of the Act is—

(a) in proceedings at first instance, 25%; and

(b) in all other proceedings, 100%.

(2) The descriptions of damages specified for the purposes of section 58(4B)(d) of the Act are—

(a) general damages for pain, suffering, and loss of amenity; and

(b) damages for pecuniary loss, other than future pecuniary loss,

net of any sums recoverable by the Compensation Recovery Unit of the Department for Work and Pensions.

III FUND [27A.2]

CFA "lite" The Conditional Fee Agreements (Miscellaneous Amendments) Regulations 2003, SI 2003/1240 came into force on 2 June 2003 that legitimised a further form of conditional fee agreement, known as the CFA Lite. These Regulations made amendments to the Conditional Fee Agreements Regulations 2000 and the Collective Conditional Fee Agreements Regulations 2000 to provide that a conditional fee agreement will be enforceable even though the client is liable to pay his legal representative's fees and expenses only if and to the extent that he recovers damages or costs in the proceedings. Amendments made to the Civil Procedure Rules 1998 provide that costs payable under such a conditional fee agreement are recoverable under Parts 44 to 48 of those Rules. However, the Miscellaneous Amendments Regulations were revoked along with the Conditional Fee Agreements Regulations 2000 on 1 November 2005, so that a CFA Lite, whilst still permissible, need now only comply with the requirements of s 58 of the Courts and Legal Services Act 1990 and the post-1 April 2013 Conditional Fee Agreements Order 2013, where it is entered into after 1 November 2005.

This in effect abrogates in relation to this type of conditional fee agreement the so-called indemnity principle – the principle that the amount which can be awarded to a party in respect of costs to be paid by him to his legal representatives is limited to what would have been payable by him to them if he had not been awarded costs. Solicitors will to this extent be able to agree lawfully with their clients not to seek to recover by way of costs anything in excess of what the court awards, or what it is agreed will be paid, and will no longer be prevented from openly contracting with their clients on such terms.

In considering whether a conditional fee agreement fell within the Conditional Fee Agreements Regulations 2000, reg 3A as amended by the Conditional Fee Agreements (Miscellaneous Amendments) Regulations 2003, the correct approach was to look at the whole package produced by the solicitor: the CFA agreement, the client care letter and the insurance policy, and to ask whether the solicitor had produced an arrangement under which the client would not be liable for any own-side costs or expenses other than those that were actually recovered from the other side or from insurers: *Jones v Wrexham Borough Council* [2007] EWCA Civ 1356, [2007] All ER (D) 300 (Dec).

In *Sharratt v London Central Bus Co (No 2)* [2003] NLJR 790 (a full transcript can also be found on the SCCO website), it was held that the CFA (Miscellaneous Amendments) Regulations 2003 (above) clarified existing law such that CFA Lites were permissible under the Conditional Fee Agreement Regulations 2000.

III FUND [27A.3]

Recovery of success fee The Access to Justice 1999 provided that a successful party to litigation could recover, subject to rules of court, the sums payable to his solicitor under a conditional fee agreement (Courts and Legal Services Act 1990 s 58A(6)). By amendments to the pre 1 April 2013 Civil Procedure Rules brought about the Civil Procedure (Amendment No 3) Rules 2000, SI 2000/1317, a conditional fee agreement which provided for a success fee was a "funding arrangement" (CPR 43.2(1)(k)(i) at para **CPR 43**). A success fee under a conditional fee agreement was defined as a "percentage increase" (CPR 43.2(1)(l) at para **CPR 43**), which itself fell into the definition of an "additional liability" (CPR 43.2(1)(o) at para **CPR 43**). Subject to restrictions imposed by CPR 44.3B (see para **CPR 44.3B**), the additional liability was recoverable inter partes subject to assessment. The recoverability of a success fee does not depend on the successful party's not having the means to fund litigation on a conventional basis. The use of conditional fee agreements and success fees for the purposes of bringing a libel claim may have a chilling effect on newspapers' rights under Art 10 but it does not contravene them: *Campbell v MGN Ltd* [2005] 4 All ER 793, [2005] All ER (D) 215 (Oct). See, however, the contrary view of the European Court of Human Rights in *MGN Ltd v United Kingdom (Application No 39401/04)* (2011) Times, 20 January, ECtHR.

From 1 April 2013 different rules apply. Save for some exceptions referred to below, in all conditional fee agreements which are entered into after 1 April 2013 there can be no recovery of the success fee by way of costs. This amendment was brought in by s 44(4) of LASPO.

The exceptions are:

• **Personal Injury Exceptions** Articles 4 and 5 do not apply to any Conditional Fee Agreement entered in to in relation to proceedings relating to a claim for damages in respect of diffuse mesothelioma. (Article 6(2)(a)) of this Order and Article 4(a) of The Legal Aid, Sentencing and Punishment of Offenders Act 2012 (Commencement No 5 and Saving Provision) Order 2013.

In such proceedings the success fee remains recoverable and is not limited by reference to damages.

• **Other Exceptions** In relation to the exceptions set out below, the success fee remains recoverable. In simple terms insolvency, defamation and privacy claims carry on as before.

Exempted from the scope of the Order are:

(a) defamation;
(b) malicious falsehood;
(c) breach of confidence involving publication to the general public;
(d) misuse of private information;
(e) harassment, where the defendant is a news publisher.

"News publisher" means a person who publishes a newspaper, magazine or website containing news or information about or comment on current affairs.

(Article 6(2)(b) and Article 1) of this Order and Article 4(b) of The Legal Aid, Sentencing and Punishment of Offenders Act 2012 (Commencement No 5 and Saving Provision) Order 2013.)

Also exempted, until 1 April 2016, are:

(a) proceedings in England and Wales brought by a person acting in the capacity of:
    (i) a liquidator of a company which is being wound up in England and Wales or Scotland under Parts IV or V of the 1986 Act; or
    (ii) a trustee of a bankrupt's estate under Part IX of the 1986 Act;
(b) proceedings brought by a person acting in the capacity of an administrator appointed pursuant to the provisions of Part II of the 1986 Act;
(c) proceedings in England and Wales brought by a company which is being wound up in England and Wales or Scotland under Part IV and V of the 1986 Act; or
(d) proceedings brought by a company which has entered administration under Part II of the 1986 Act.

(Article 6(2)(c)–(f) and Article 1) of this Order and Article 4(c)–(f) of The Legal Aid, Sentencing and Punishment of Offenders Act 2012 (Commencement No 5 and Saving Provision) Order 2013. References to the 1986 Act are to the Insolvency Act 1986.)

On 6 April 2019 the law will change again with the abolition of the publication and privacy exception save that after the event insurance premiums will remain recoverable in publication and privacy cases. This gives effect to legal obligations under the MGN v UK judgment of the European Court of Human Rights in 2011. In the *MGN* case, the court concluded that the obligation for the defendant to pay a 100% 'success fee' to the claimant was disproportionate, and that the conditional fee agreements regime was therefore in breach of the defendant's rights under Article 10 (freedom of expression) of the European Convention on Human Rights.

Under the terms of a collective conditional fee agreement solicitors acting for the claimant to a personal injury action had been entitled to a success fee in respect of work done by costs consultants instructed by the legal representative in costs only proceedings: *Crane v Cannons Leisure Centre* [2007] EWCA Civ 1352, [2008] 2 All ER 931, [2008] 1 WLR 2549 (May LJ, Maurice Kay LJ, Hallett LJ, Chief Master Hurst).

Where a CFA with a success fee is entered into before 1 April 2013, but novated post–1 April 2013, the success fee remains recoverable by virtue of the LASPO Transitional provisions contained within s 44(6) of LASPO: *Budana v Leeds Teaching Hospitals NHS Trust (Law Society intervening)* [2017] EWCA Civ 1980, 159 BMLR 50, (2018) Times, 19 January.

III FUND [27A.4]

Requirements imposed by the Access to Justice Act 1999 In order for a pre-1 April 2013 conditional fee agreement (both kinds see above) not to be unenforceable, it must comply with the following:

(1) It must be in writing

(2) It must not relate to proceedings which cannot be the subject of an enforceable conditional fee agreement

(3) It must comply with such requirements as are prescribed by the Lord Chancellor.

(See the Courts and Legal Services Act 1990 s 58 (3) as amended.)

For those conditional fee agreements under which a success fee is payable, the following additional conditions must be satisfied:

(1) It must relate to proceedings of a description specified by order made by the Lord Chancellor.

(2) It must state the percentage by which the amount of the fees, which would be payable if it were not a conditional fee agreement, is to be increased.

(3) The percentage must not exceed the percentage specified in relation to the description of proceedings to which the agreement relates by order made by the Lord Chancellor.

(See the Courts and Legal Services Act 1990 s 58(4) as amended.)

III FUND [27A.5]

Requirements imposed by the Conditional Fee Agreements Order 2013 For all conditional fee agreements which provide for a success fee entered into after 1 April 2013 the following conditions must be met:

(a) the agreement must provide that the success fee is subject to a maximum limit;

(b) the maximum limit must be expressed as a percentage of the descriptions of damages awarded in the proceedings that are specified in the agreement;

(c) that percentage must not exceed the percentage specified by order made by the Lord Chancellor in relation to the proceedings or calculated in a manner so specified; and

(d) those descriptions of damages may only include descriptions of damages specified by order made by the Lord Chancellor in relation to the proceedings.

By virtue of the Conditional Fee Agreements Order 2013, the maximum chargeable success fee is 100% of the basic charges but limited in all cases to no more than 25% of the damages. Regulations 3, 4 and 5 are set out below:

3. Amount of success fee

In relation to all proceedings specified in article 2, the percentage specified for the purposes of section 58(4)(c) of the Act is 100%.

4. Specified proceedings

A claim for personal injuries shall be proceedings specified for the purpose of section 58(4A)(b) of the Act.

5. Amount of success fee in specified proceedings

(1) In relation to the proceedings specified in article 4, the percentage prescribed for the purposes of section 58(4B)(c) of the Act is—

(a) in proceedings at first instance, 25%; and

(b) in all other proceedings, 100%.

(2) The descriptions of damages specified for the purposes of section 58(4B)(d) of the Act are—

(a) general damages for pain, suffering, and loss of amenity; and

(b) damages for pecuniary loss, other than future pecuniary loss,

net of any sums recoverable by the Compensation Recovery Unit of the Department for Work and Pensions.

III FUND [27A.6]

The effect on a conditional fee agreement of a failure to satisfy the conditions The statutory conditions of a conditional fee agreement should be regarded as satisfied when there has been substantial compliance with, or in other words no material departure from, what is required: *Hollins v Russell* [2003] EWCA Civ 718, [2003] 4 All ER 590, [2003] 1 WLR 2487. Whilst the cases addressing this issue were decided under the former CFA regime of the Conditional Fee Agreements Regulations 2000 there is no reason to suppose that a different approach would not be taken in respect of statutory conditions imposed under the new post 1 April 2013 regime.

In *Hollins v Russell* the Court suggested that, where there is an issue about non-compliance, the court should first consider whether, as between solicitor and client, the client would have just cause for complaint because some requirement introduced for his or her protection was not satisfied or because public policy was offended in some other way. If so, the non-compliance would probably result in the agreement being unenforceable by the solicitor and the indemnity principle would operate in favour of the paying party. Even then, however, the client should be able to recover disbursements and any ATE premium. But where the non-compliance did not involve a material departure the condition should be regarded as satisfied. Judges should be watchful to see that the parliamentary purpose of enhancing access to justice is not thwarted. The relevant law as to the enforceability of conditional fee agreements was clarified and reinforced in the case of *Garrett v Halton Borough Council; Myatt v National Coal Board* [2006] EWCA Civ 1017, [2007] 1 All ER 147.

The Court confirmed the decision at first instance that the responsibilities of the legal representative under reg 4 (information to be given) could be delegated to a lay representative, acting under proper supervision.

In *Myler v Williams* [2003] EWHC 1587, [2003] 4 Costs LR 566, it was held that the provision for hourly rates did not comply with regulation 2(1)(d) but that this did not render the agreement unenforceable, because it did not diminish the client's protection or affect the proper administration of justice. On the other hand, in *Spencer v Wood* [2004] EWCA Civ 352, [2004] All ER (D) 275 (Mar) it was held that a conditional fee agreement which did not specify how much of the percentage increase related to the cost of postponement of payment of fees and expenses did not comply with regulation 3(1)(b) and was therefore unenforceable.

In a case where the ATE insurance policy cost £798 and the damages were never going to exceed £2,000 it was held that the solicitor's failure to inquire about any insurance other than the client's motor insurance was a material breach of reg 4(2)(c), making the CFA unenforceable: *Samonini v London General Transport Services Ltd* [2005] PIQR P20.

Where an agreement has been backdated and the backdating had not been explained the agreement will still be enforceable if the backdating has no material effect on the protection offered to the client: *Holmes v Alfred McAlpine Homes (Yorkshire) Ltd* [2006] EWHC 110, [2006] 3 Costs LR 466.

III FUND [27A.7]

Proceedings The proceedings which cannot be the subject of an enforceable conditional fee agreement are as follows:

(1) Criminal Proceedings.
(2) Family Proceedings which include proceedings under:
  (a) Matrimonial Causes Act 1973,
  (b) Adoption Act 1976,
  (c) Domestic Proceedings and Magistrates Courts Act 1978,
  (d) Part III of the Matrimonial and Family Proceedings Act 1984,
  (e) Parts I, II, and IV of the Children Act 1989,
  (f) Part IV of the Family Law Act 1996,
  (g) Inherent jurisdiction of the High Court in relation to children.

(See the Courts and Legal Services Act 1990, s 58A(1), as amended.)

Proceedings are defined as including any sort of proceedings for resolving disputes and not just proceedings in a court, whether commenced or contemplated. In other words, conditional fee agreements can apply to arbitration proceedings and dispute resolution by mediation (Courts and Legal Services Act 1990, s 58A(4)).

III FUND [27A.8]

If it is intended to limit the coverage of the CFA to claims against a particular defendant, precision in drafting is required: *Malone v Birmingham NHS Trust* [2018] EWCA Civ 1376. Work undertaken in proceedings not covered by the CFA (as defined by the CFA) will not be recoverable from the paying party: *Frade v Radford* [2017] EQCA Civ 1010.

III FUND [27A.9]

The solicitor's equitable lien in respect of the fixed costs An element in every conditional fee agreement is the solicitor's right to the fixed costs that are recoverable from the defendant. The solicitor's equitable lien entitles the solicitor to recover those costs from the amount recovered for the client. If therefore a CFA claimant is persuaded by an insurance company, or other third party, to engage their services to recover a higher sum by cutting out the solicitor's costs, the equitable lien comes into play. It has been held that in those circumstances the CFA solicitors may recover their fixed costs from the sum recovered by the defendant's insurance company: *Haven Insurance v Gavin Edmondson Solicitors* [2018] UKSC 21.

FUNDING

GENERAL NOTES ON COLLECTIVE CONDITIONAL FEE AGREEMENTS

III FUND [27B]

Collective conditional fee agreements On 30 November 2000 the Collective Conditional Fee Agreements Regulations 2000 (CCFAR) came into force. These regulations were made under powers conferred upon the Lord Chancellor by ss 58(3)(c), 58A(3) and 119 of the Courts and Legal Services Act 1990. The regulations applied to agreements entered into on or after 30 November 2000 and agreements entered into before that date shall be treated as if the regulations had not come into force. However, like the Conditional Fee Agreements Regulations 2000 their days were numbered and on 1 November 2005 they were revoked: Conditional Fee Agreements (Revocation) Regulations 2005/2305. A collective conditional fee agreement is a conditional fee agreement which does not refer to specific proceedings but provides for fees to be payable on a common basis in relation to a class of proceedings or, if it refers to more than one class of proceedings, on a common basis in relation to each class. It is an agreement which, disregarding s 58(3)(c) of the Courts and Legal Services Act 1990, would be a conditional fee agreement. The Conditional Fee Agreements Regulations 2000 do not apply to collective conditional fee agreements. The collective conditional fee agreements are designed specifically for mass providers and purchasers of legal services such as trade unions, insurers or other commercial organisations. A collective conditional fee agreement will enable a trade union, for example, to enter into a single agreement with solicitors to govern the way in which cases for its members will be run and paid for.

Solicitors acting under a collective conditional fee agreement with an insurance company were entitled to claim a success fee against the defendant to a claim by the insured: *D'Sousa v Waltham Forest London Borough Council* (2010) CC (Leeds) (John Behrens) 12/1/2010.

III FUND [27B.1]

Revocation The Collective Conditional Fee Agreements Regulations 2000 were revoked on 1 November 2005: Conditional Fee Agreements (Revocation) Regulations 2005/2305.

III FUND [27B.2]

Terminology The Collective Conditional Fee Agreements Regulations 2000 introduce the concept of the "funder" into the conditional fee arena. The funder is the party to the agreement who, under the agreement, is liable to pay the legal representative's fees. The client is the person who receives the advocacy or litigation services to which the agreement relates. An agreement may be a collective conditional fee agreement whether or not the funder is a client or whether or not any clients are named in the agreement. It is not thought that the courts will wish to develop new terminology following the revocation of the Collective Conditional Fee Agreements 2000.

III FUND [27B.3]

Requirements A collective conditional fee agreement must be in writing and it must not relate to proceedings which cannot be the subject of an enforceable conditional fee agreement. It must be signed by the funder and by the legal representative unless the agreement is between a legal representative and an additional legal representative. It must specify the circumstances in which the legal representatives fees and expenses, or part of them, are payable. Save in relation to those agreements between a legal representative and an additional legal representative, the agreement must provide that when accepting instructions in relation to any specific proceedings the legal representative must inform the client as to the circumstances in which the client may be liable to pay the costs of the legal representative and, if the client requires any further explanation, advice or other information about the circumstances in which the client may be liable for those costs, provide such further information at it as the client may require. The agreement must also provide that after accepting instructions in relation to any specific proceedings, the legal representative must confirm his acceptance of instructions in writing to the client.

The indemnity principle is satisfied by the litigant's agreeing with the legal representative to permit the funder, such as a trade union, to instruct the solicitor in the intending litigants name. Provided that this requirement is satisfied and that there has been compliance with regulation 4, success fees ought normally to be recoverable: *Gliddon v Lloyd Maunder Ltd* [2003] NLJR 318; *Thornley v Lang* [2003] EWCA Civ 1484, [2004] 1 All ER 886, [2004] 1 WLR 378.

III FUND [27B.4]

Requirements where a success fee is payable Where a collective conditional fee agreement provides for a success fee the agreement must provide that when accepting instructions in relation to any specific proceedings, the legal representative must prepare and retain a writing statement containing the risk assessment, the assessment of the percentage increase, and the reasons for setting the percentage increase at the level chosen. Where the agreement relates to court proceedings similar requirements to reg 3(2) of the Conditional Fee Agreements Regulations 2000 (**III FUND [46]**). If on assessment of the fees claimed under the agreement, the amount of the percentage increase is disallowed on the ground that the level at which it was set was unreasonable in view of the facts which were or should have been known to the legal representative at the time it was set, that amount ceases to be payable under the agreement unless the court is satisfied that it should continue to be so payable. Similar consequences follow where a legal representative agrees with the paying party (inter partes) that the percentage increase should be reduced; the amount payable under the agreement is reduced accordingly unless the court directs otherwise.

III FUND [27B.5]

"CCFA Lite" A collective conditional fee agreement may provide that the legal representative's fees and expenses are payable only to the extent that sums are recovered in respect of proceedings, whether by way of costs or otherwise: Collective Conditional Fee Agreements (Miscellaneous Amendments) Regulations 2003 (**III FUND [64.1]**). Whilst the Collective Conditional Fee Agreements (Miscellaneous Amendments) Regulations 2003 were revoked from 1 November 2005, CCFA Lites remain permissible so long as they meet the requirements of s 58 Courts and Legal Services Act 1990.

III FUND [27B.6]

Percentage increase This bears the same definition as under reg 3(3) of the Conditional Fee Agreements Regulations 2000. It is the percentage by which the amount of the fees which would have been payable if the agreement were not a conditional fee agreement is to be increased under the agreement.

FUNDING

ACCESS TO JUSTICE ACT 1999

(c 22)

COSTS

III FUND [28]

29. Recovery of insurance premiums by way of costs

Repealed by the Legal Aid, Sentencing and Punishment of Offenders Act 2012.

III FUND [28.1]

Recovery of insurance premiums The Access to Justice Act 1999 s 29 provided that where an order for costs is made in any proceedings in favour of any party who has taken out an insurance policy against the risk of incurring a liability in those proceedings, the costs payable to him, subject to rules of court, may include costs in respect of the premium of the policy. Under section 9 of the Costs Practice Direction (see para **CPR PD 44**) an order for payment of "costs" was deemed to include an additional liability incurred under a funding arrangement. See also Section 2.1 of the Costs Practice Direction (see para **CPR PD 43**). Section 30 of the Access to Justice Act 1999 provides for the recovery of additional liabilities (such as a notional insurance premium). Where the insurance policy is entered into after 1 April 2013 then the premium cannot be recovered by way of costs. This is one of the consequences of LASPO 2013, s 46.

The Court of Appeal has considered the extent to which insurance premiums may be recoverable under s 29 of the Access to Justice Act. In *Callery v Gray* [2001] EWCA Civ 1117, [2001] 3 All ER 833, [2001] 1 WLR 2112, it was held that it was reasonable for a litigant to take out an insurance policy right at the outset of the solicitor and client retainer. The court held that s 29 did not prevent the recovery of an insurance premium simply because no proceedings were issued in the action itself. It was sufficient that the claim was compromised on terms that costs were paid. The premium could be recovered in default of agreement under a claim made pursuant to CPR Part 8 (see para **CPR 8**). In *Callery v Gray (No 2)* [2001] EWCA Civ 1246, [2001] 1 WLR 2142, the Court declined to give "guidance" as to the level of the reasonableness of insurance premiums. However, the court did provide guidance as to what a recoverable premium may consist of. The Court of Appeal held that the premium was recoverable in principle (subject to being reasonable) despite the fact that it may have provided cover for "own sides costs" and not just cover in respect of the other side's costs. The House of Lords upheld the decision of the Court of Appeal in *Callery v Gray (Nos 1 and 2)* [2002] UKHL 28, [2002] 3 All ER 417, [2002] 1 WLR 2000, declining to interfere in the policing and development of practice relating to conditional fees, which was best left in the hands of the Court of Appeal. More recent guidance was given in *Rogers v Merthyr Tydfil County Borough Council* [2006] EWCA Civ 1134, [2007] 1 All ER 354 regarding a staged policy of insurance. See also the *Claims Direct Test Cases* [2003] EWCA Civ 136, [2003] 4 All ER 508, [2003] 2 All ER (Comm) 788 where it was held that the money a claimant paid for the right to be included within the Claims Direct scheme was not all premium within the meaning of s 29 of the Access to Justice Act 1999. However part of the Claims Direct policy scheme was an insurance policy, the premium for which was recoverable, in so far as it had been reasonable. See also *Sharratt v London Central Bus Co (No 2)* [2004] 3 All ER 325, CA; [2003] NLJR 790; (a full transcript can also be found on the SCCO Web Site), where the Senior Costs Judge held that only parts of the sums payable for insurance under the TAG scheme was recoverable as premium under s 29 of the Access to Justice Act 1999. In *Sharratt v London Central Bus Co (No 2) The Accident Group Test Cases* [2004] EWCA Civ 575, [2004] 3 All ER 325, the Court of Appeal supported the conclusions on the judge below and dismissed the appeal. See also the decision of Master Hurst in the RSA Pursuit Test Cases at **III FUND [28.6]**. It matters not that the ATE premium may have been incepted very late in the proceedings; as a matter of principle subject to the qualifying tests of reasonableness and proportionality the ATE premium will be recoverable: *Kris Motor Spares Ltd v Fox Williams LLP* [2010] EWHC 1008. The Supreme Court upheld the compatibility of the 1999 costs regime with the Article 6 rights of parties to litigation arising under the European Convention of Human Rights in *Coventry v Lawrence* [2015] UKSC 50, [2015] 1 WLR 3485, [2016] 2 All ER 97, [2015] 4 Costs LO 507.

In *Sarwar v Alam* [2001] EWCA Civ 1401, [2001] 4 All ER 541, the Court of Appeal gave some guidance as to the extent to which solicitors were obliged to investigate the existence of alternative forms of funding before recommending to a client that he take out an after the event insurance policy (see CPR PD 44 para 11.10(3) (para **CPR PD 44**)). Ordinarily, a solicitor should enquire with the client whether he has any stand alone pre-event legal expense insurance or any legal expense insurance attached to his motor or household insurance policy. If he has, the solicitor will be required to consider the terms of the particular policy before deciding, in the light of that enquiry, whether or not to advise the client to take out an after the event policy. In *Sarwar* it was held that would be unreasonable to expect the claimant to rely on the defendant's legal expense insurance policy notwithstanding that cover under the policy may have covered the claimant's claim.

In *Pratt v Bull*, reported under *Hollins v Russell* [2003] EWCA Civ 718, [2003] 4 All ER 590, [2003] 1 WLR 2487, the legal representative had asked the client about household insurance without checking the terms of the policy. This was held to be sufficient by the Court of Appeal on the facts of the case where the elderly Claimant was seriously ill in hospital at the time the reg 4 advice was given.

Section 29 of the Access to Justice Act 1999 does not apply where the policy is taken out after 1 April 2013, subject to some minor exceptions relating to clinical negligence cases. This is because s 46 of LASPO repeals s 29 as from 1 April 2013:

46. Recovery of insurance premiums by way of costs

(1) In the Courts and Legal Services Act 1990, after section 58B insert—

58C Recovery of insurance premiums by way of costs

(1) A costs order made in favour of a party to proceedings who has taken out a costs insurance policy may not include provision requiring the payment of an amount in respect of all or part of the premium of the policy, unless such provision is permitted by regulations under subsection (2).

(2) The Lord Chancellor may by regulations provide that a costs order may include provision requiring the payment of such an amount where—

(a) the order is made in favour of a party to clinical negligence proceedings of a prescribed description,

(b) the party has taken out a costs insurance policy insuring against the risk of incurring a liability to pay for one or more expert reports in respect of clinical negligence in connection with the proceedings (or against that risk and other risks),

(c) the policy is of a prescribed description,

(d) the policy states how much of the premium relates to the liability to pay for an expert report or reports in respect of clinical negligence ("the relevant part of the premium"), and

(e) the amount is to be paid in respect of the relevant part of the premium.

(3) Regulations under subsection (2) may include provision about the amount that may be required to be paid by the costs order, including provision that the amount must not exceed a prescribed maximum amount.

(4) The regulations may prescribe a maximum amount, in particular, by specifying—

(a) a percentage of the relevant part of the premium;

(b) an amount calculated in a prescribed manner.

(5) In this section—

"clinical negligence" means breach of a duty of care or trespass to the person committed in the course of the provision of clinical or medical services (including dental or nursing services);

"clinical negligence proceedings" means proceedings which include a claim for damages in respect of clinical negligence;

"costs insurance policy", in relation to a party to proceedings, means a policy insuring against the risk of the party incurring a liability in those proceedings;

"expert report" means a report by a person qualified to give expert advice on all or most of the matters that are the subject of the report;

"proceedings" includes any sort of proceedings for resolving disputes (and not just proceedings in court), whether commenced or contemplated.

Section 46(2) and (3) provide:

> (2) In the Access to Justice Act 1999, omit section 29 (recovery of insurance premiums by way of costs).
>
> (3) The amendments made by this section do not apply in relation to a costs order made in favour of a party to proceedings who took out a costs insurance policy in relation to the proceedings before the day on which this section comes into force.

Accordingly, premiums incepted before 1 April 2013 remain recoverable.

III FUND [28.1A]

Recovery of insurance premiums in Clinical Negligence Cases The Recovery of Costs Insurance Premiums in Clinical Negligence Proceedings (No 2) Regulations 2013 enables a party to recover that part of a premium which relates to the risk of incurring a liability to pay for an expert report or reports relating to liability or causation in respect of clinical negligence in connection with the proceedings. The Court of Appeal held in *Peterborough & Stamford Hospitals NHS Trust v McMenemy* [2017] EWCA Civ 1941, 168 NLJ 7777, [2017] All ER (D) 69 (Dec) that it is appropriate for a claimant to take out an after the event policy when a conditional fee agreement was entered into. It rejected the argument that the reasonableness of this (timing issue) should be considered on a case by case basis. In this regard the court was not persuaded to depart from the policy decision taken in *Callery v Gray* (see para **III FUND [28.4]**) when examining the reasonableness of taking out an ATE insurance policy.

Recovery of Costs Insurance Premiums in Clinical Negligence Proceedings (No 2) Regulations 2013

1. Citation and commencement

(1) These Regulations may be cited as the Recovery of Costs Insurance Premiums in Clinical Negligence Proceedings (No 2) Regulations 2013 and shall come into force on 1st April 2013.

2. Revocation of the 2013 Regulations

The Recovery of Costs Insurance Premiums in Clinical Negligence Proceedings Regulations 2013 are revoked.

3. Costs order may require payment of an amount of the relevant part of the premium

(1) A costs order made in favour of a party to clinical negligence proceedings who has taken out a costs insurance policy may include provision requiring the payment of an amount in respect of all or part of the premium of that policy if—

(a) the financial value of the claim for damages in respect of clinical negligence is more than £1,000; and

(b) the costs insurance policy insures against the risk of incurring a liability to pay for an expert report or reports relating to liability or causation in respect of clinical negligence (or against that risk and other risks).

(2) The amount of the premium that may be required to be paid under the costs order shall not exceed that part of the premium which relates to the risk of incurring liability to pay for an expert report or reports relating to liability or causation in respect of clinical negligence in connection with the proceedings.

III FUND [28.2]

Assessment of the premium Where the policy was incepted in proceedings prior to 1 April 2013 in deciding whether the cost of insurance cover is reasonable, relevant factors to be taken into account include the following (Costs Practice Direction Section 11.10 at para **CPR PD 44**)—

(a) Where the insurance cover is not purchased in support a CFA with a success fee, how its cost compares with the likely cost of funding the case with a CFA agreement with a success fee and supporting insurance.
(b) The court can also take into account the level and extent of the cover
(c) The availability of any pre-existing insurance cover
(d) Whether any part of the premium would be rebated in the event of early settlement.
(e) The amount of commission payable to the receiving party or his legal representatives or other agents is also something which the courts will take into account.

III FUND [28.3]

Rules of Court For cases where the premium was taken out before 1 April 2013 the main relevant rules then in force were **CPR 44.3A**, **CPR 44.3B** and **CPR 44.15** and **CPR 44.16**. The Costs Practice Direction at Sections 9, 10, 11, 14, 19, 20, 55 should also be referred to (see paras **CPR PD 44**, **CPR PD 48**).

The commencement of s 29 (recovery of insurance premiums by way of costs) took effect on 1 April 2000 even though the relevant rules of court did not come into operation until 3 July 2000: *Inline Logistics Ltd v UCI Logistics Ltd* [2002] EWHC 519 (Ch), [2002] All ER (D) 435 (Mar), [2002] 19 LS Gaz R 28.

III FUND [28.4]

Callery v Gray See generally *Callery v Gray* [2001] EWCA Civ 1117, [2001] 3 All ER 833, [2001] 1 WLR 2112 and *Callery v Gray (No 2)* [2001] EWCA Civ 1246, [2001] 4 All ER 1. The House of Lords refused to interfere with the decisions of the Court of Appeal in *Callery v Gray (No 1) and (No 2)*: *Callery v Gray (Nos 1 and 2)* [2002] UKHL 28, [2002] 3 All ER 417, [2002] 1 WLR 2000. *Callery v Gray (No 1)* concerned the recovery of both insurance premiums under s.29 and the recovery of success fees claimed under a conditional fee agreement. In principle, it mattered not that the policy was taken out at the outset of the proceedings, nor that proceedings in the action had not in fact been commenced. The insurance premium could be claimed under s 29 within Pt 8 proceedings under CPR 44.12A. It was held that the jurisdiction to include an after the event insurance premium in an award of costs was conferred by s 29 of the Act. *Callery v Gray (No 2)* concerned the reasonableness of the level of after the event insurance premiums claimed under s 29. It was not in issue or doubt that the liability referred to in s 29 was restricted to liability for costs, but there was an issue as to whether or not the liability included "own sides costs". The primary liability covered by the claimant's policy was for the opponent's costs in the event of court order, withdrawal, discontinuance or settlement with the insurers' prior approval, all of which fell within the meaning of s 29. The court held that s 29 could and should be interpreted to treat the words "insurance against the risk of incurring a costs liability" as meaning "insurance against the risk of incurring a costs liability that could not be passed on to the opposing party". This is a wide definition. In the context of "own sides cover" it was held that the whole of the claimant's premium, including the small element of cover for own costs insurance, fell within the description of insurance against the risk of liability within s 29 and was recoverable. The court held that it was necessary, when considering whether or to what extent a premium was recoverable, to ask whether it was consideration paid for insurance against the risk of incurring a costs liability in the proceedings. The court recognised that it was important to distinguish contractual entitlement to benefits from the use made by the insurer of the premium. The court was only concerned with whether the premium was a reasonable price to pay for the benefits it purchased. However, a costs judge would not be required to "audit" an insurance premium. It was open to the insurer to place evidence before the court about the reasonableness of his premium but satellite litigation on the point was unsatisfactory and a judge could only be expected to give broad consideration to such evidence. No objection was taken to the parts of the premium that covered risk/profit cost, or administrative costs. The court also considered in detail the benefits provided in exchange for the premium paid. The court also had to consider whether the premium was reasonable in amount. Insofar as the court found that the premium was not reasonable it could be reduced. Master O'Hare had indicated in his report to the Court of Appeal that it would be reasonable to presume as a starting point that a premium was reasonable unless the contrary was shown; the Court of Appeal disagreed. The court had to consider the evidence of the relationship between the premium, the risk and the cost of alternative cover. In this case the premium was £350 and was allowed in full. There was no reason in principle why £7.50 insurance premium tax should not also be recoverable.

III FUND [28.5]

Insurance premiums and referral fees It was held in *Sharratt v London Central Bus Co (No 2)* [2003] NLJR 790, that only part of the sums payable for insurance under the TAG scheme were recoverable under s 29 of the Access to Justice Act 1999. It was further held that a sum payable to an associated company (AIL) was a referral fee and in breach of rule 2(3) of the Introduction and Referral Code. In *Sharratt v London Central Bus Co (No 2) The Accident Group Test Cases* [2004] EWCA Civ 575, [2004] 3 All ER 325 the Court supported the conclusions of the judge below and dismissed the appeal.

III FUND [28.6]

Master Hurst made a decision on 27 May 2005 regarding the recovery of insurance premiums in respect of an After The Event (ATE) insurance policy provided by Royal Sun & Alliance, (RSA) and known as the "Pursuit" policy. There is a 2 page article on it in the New Law Journal (2005) Vol 155, 15 July pp 1097-1098. The policy provided ATE insurance but required an escalating premium payable only in the event of success. The premium was geared to the amount of costs claimed by the claimant and in most of the test cases (eg *Baker v Addenbrooks*) it amounted to well over 100% of the claimant's solicitor's base costs, irrespective of assessment. Master Hurst held that the premium was recoverable in principal but the premiums were reduced in amount to reflect reasonableness and proportionality and to reflect the sums allowed on detailed assessment by way of base costs.

III FUND [29]–III FUND [30]

30. ***Recovery where a body undertakes to meet costs liabilities***

Repealed by the Legal Aid, Sentencing and Punishment of Offenders Act 2012.

III FUND [29.1]

Recovery where a body undertakes to meet costs liabilities Section 30 Access to Justice Act 1999 enabled specified bodies to recover by way of costs a sum equivalent to an after the event insurance premium. Section 30 was repealed as from 1 April 2013 by s 47 of LASPO.

Section 47 of the Legal Aid, Sentencing and Punishment of Offenders Act 2012 provides:

47. Recovery where body undertakes to meet costs liabilities

(1) In the Access to Justice Act 1999, omit section 30 (recovery where body undertakes to meet costs liabilities).

(2) The repeal made by subsection (1) does not apply in relation to a costs order made in favour of a person to whom a body gave an undertaking before the day on which this section comes into force if the undertaking was given specifically in respect of the costs of other parties to proceedings relating to the matter which is the subject of the proceedings in which the costs order is made.

Please consult the 2014 Edition of the Civil Court Practice for the relevant statutory and narrative guidance in respect of s 30 notional premiums (formerly **III FUND [29.A1]–III FUND [29.3]**).

III FUND [31]–III FUND [38]

Part IV – Orders for costs inter partes An order for costs will include an additional liability incurred under a funding arrangement where the funding agreement was entered into before 1 April 2013. There is therefore, no need for the order for costs to recite separately the entitlement to recover the additional liability incurred under a funding arrangement (**CPR PD 44**, Section 9).

The Conditional Fee Agreements Regulations 2000 were revoked in 2005. Furthermore, from 1 April 2013 the law prohibits the recovery of a success fee save in some limited circumstances.

The exceptions are:

Personal Injury Exceptions Articles 4 and 5 do not apply to any Conditional Fee Agreement entered in to in relation to proceedings relating to a claim for damages in respect of diffuse mesothelioma. (Article 6(2)(a)) of this Order and Article 4(a) of the Legal Aid, Sentencing and Punishment of Offenders Act 2012 (Commencement No 5 and Saving Provision) Order 2013.

FUNDING

In such proceedings the success fee remains recoverable and is not limited by reference to damages.

Other Exceptions In relation to the exceptions set out below, the success fee remains recoverable. In simple terms insolvency, defamation and privacy claims carry on as before. Exempted from the scope of the Order are:

(a) defamation;
(b) malicious falsehood;
(c) breach of confidence involving publication to the general public;
(d) misuse of private information;
(e) harassment, where the defendant is a news publisher.

"News publisher" means a person who publishes a newspaper, magazine or website containing news or information about or comment on current affairs.

(Article 6(2)(b) and Article 1) of this Order and Article 4(b) of the Legal Aid, Sentencing and Punishment of Offenders Act 2012 (Commencement No 5 and Saving Provision) Order 2013.)

On 6 April 2019 the law will change again with the abolition of the publication and privacy exception save that after the event insurance premiums will remain recoverable in publication and privacy cases.

Also exempted, until 1 April 2016, are:

(a) proceedings in England and Wales brought by a person acting in the capacity of:
   (i) a liquidator of a company which is being wound up in England and Wales or Scotland under Parts IV or V of the 1986 Act; or
   (ii) a trustee of a bankrupt's estate under Part IX of the 1986 Act;
(b) proceedings brought by a person acting in the capacity of an administrator appointed pursuant to the provisions of Part II of the 1986 Act;
(c) proceedings in England and Wales brought by a company which is being wound up in England and Wales or Scotland under Part IV and V of the 1986 Act; or
(d) proceedings brought by a company which has entered administration under Part II of the 1986 Act.

(Article 6(2)(c-f) and Article 1) of this Order and Article 4(c) to (f) of the Legal Aid, Sentencing and Punishment of Offenders Act 2012 (Commencement No 5 and Saving Provision) Order 2013.)

References to the 1986 Act are to the Insolvency Act 1986.

III FUND [39]

The assessment of the success fee Where the success fee is claimed under a conditional fee agreement entered into before 1 April 2013, then under CPR 44.3A the court will not assess any additional liability until the conclusion of the proceedings, or part of the proceedings, to which the funding arrangement relates. At that stage, the court may:

(1) make a summary assessment of all the costs, including any additional liability, or
(2) make an order for a detailed assessment of the additional liability but make a summary assessment of the other costs, or
(3) make an order for detailed assessment of all the costs (CPR 44.3A(2)).

A party may not recover as an additional liability any proportion of the percentage increase relating to the cost of the legal representative of the postponement of the payment of his fees and expenses. A failure to provide information about the funding arrangement in accordance with the rules or a practice direction or a court order will also prevent recovery of any additional liability for the period in the proceedings during which the information was not provided (**CPR 44.3B**). If a party fails to disclose in any assessment proceedings the reasons for setting the percentage increase at the level stated in the conditional fee agreement, contrary to a requirement in the costs practice directions (see paras **CPR PD 44–CPR PD 48**), or a court order, that party will be prevented from recovering any percentage increase (success fee). Provision is made for relief from these sanctions under Section 10 of the costs practice direction (see **CPR PD 44**). The application should be made under Part 23 as "quickly as possible". If counsel's fees are affected, the solicitor making the application must serve on counsel a copy of the application notice and notice of hearing as soon as practicable and in any event at least two days before the hearing. Where a court carries out a summary assessment of the base costs at the conclusion of the proceedings it may identify separately the amount allowed in respect of solicitors charges, counsel's fees, other disbursements and VAT. Where an order for the payment of base costs does not identify separately those items, the court which later makes an assessment of an additional liability may apportion the base costs previously ordered (**CPR PD 44**, Section 9).

III FUND [39A]

Reasonableness of success fees What is discussed below relates to the reasonableness of a success fee which is chargeable under a conditional fee agreement entered into before 1 April 2013.

In *Callery v Gray; Russell v Pal Pak Corrugated Ltd* [2001] 3 All ER 833, [2001] 1 WLR 2112, the Court of Appeal gave some indication as to the levels of success fees in simple and straightforward low value motor accident cases. In both appeals the claimants' solicitors reasonably concluded that the claims had every prospect of an early settlement of both liability and quantum. The vital issue was whether the court should allow recovery of an uplift in those circumstances or whether it should require all solicitors to defer agreeing an uplift until the defendant's response to the claim was known, so that the risk of failure could be assessed on an individual basis. It was held that if the latter approach was adopted, liability for success fees would be borne in much larger amounts by those unsuccessful defendants who persisted in contesting liability. This would not result in an equitable sharing of costs between unsuccessful defendants. Additionally, in claims arising out of road traffic accidents where defendants were insured, the same insurers would often be sharing the costs involved. It was recognised that insurance premiums also benefited defendants as they ensured payment of the defendant's costs when a claimant was unsuccessful. Premiums taken out at an early stage were substantially cheaper than when it was known if the defendant was going to contest liability. Further, it would assist access to justice for solicitors to offer legal services on terms that the claimant will not pay costs whatever the circumstances. Consequently, where at the outset a reasonable uplift was agreed and after the event insurance at a reasonable premium was taken out, the costs of each were recoverable from the defendant in the event that the claim succeeded or was settled on terms that the defendant pay the claimant's costs. Where a success fee was agreed at the outset in this category of claim, 20% was the maximum uplift that could reasonably be agreed. That figure assumed no special feature in the claim and the court's conclusion was based on very limited data at an early stage in the new costs regime. The court held that it would be desirable to review that conclusion once sufficient data was available to enable a fully informed assessment of the position. The House of Lords upheld the decision of the Court of Appeal in *Callery v Gray (Nos 1 and 2)* [2002] UKHL 28, [2002] 3 All ER 417, [2002] 1 WLR 2000, declining to interfere in the policing and development of practice relating to conditional fees, which was best left in the hands of the Court of Appeal. Further guidance on the appropriate level of success fees in road traffic accident cases was given by the Court of Appeal in *Atack v Lee*. Where liability had been admitted in an action for personal injuries a judge had erred in allowing a success fee under a conditional fee agreement of 50%, the appropriate success fee in the circumstances was 20%: *C (A Patient Acting By Her Litigation Friend Jocelyn Fox) v W* [2008] EWCA Civ 1459.

Where the court holds a success fee percentage to be reasonable at the time that it was agreed there is no power to reduce it to a lower percentage in respect of subsequent periods: *U (a child) v Liverpool City Council* [2005] EWCA Civ 475, (2005) Times, 16 May.

In a case where liability was admitted but quantum was disputed a success fee was held to be fairly assessed at 20% and it was added that a CFA might reasonably include a provision for reviewing the success fee on receipt of a Part 36 offer: *C v W* [2008] EWCA Civ 1459, [2008] All ER (D) 239 (Dec).

A 100% success fee will not be justified inter partes where liability has already been admitted and where there is no Part 36 offer: *NJL v PTE* [2018] EWHC 3570 (QB) (20 December 2018).

Cases falling within CPR 45.7 attract fixed success fees. For further details see para **CPR 45.7** in Volume 1.

Proceedings to enforce an award may be the subject of a CFA that provides for a success fee and ATE insurance. However courts should think long and hard about allowing a substantial CFA mark-up, particularly where an application is made for summary judgment. The same applies to the ATE premium. The assessment should not award more than was reasonable and proportionate, given the strong chances of successful enforcement: *Redwing Construction Ltd v Wishart* [2011] EWHC 19 (TCC), [2011] Lloyd's Rep IR 331, [2011] NLJR 137, Akenhead J.

Very often the court will defer to the use of a ready reckoner of the following kind:

Prospects of Success %	**Success Fee %**
100	0
90	11
80	25
75	33.3

70	43
65	54
60	67
50	100

III FUND [39B]

Disbursements The Court of Appeal has decided, Maurice Kay LJ dissenting, that where costs consultants are instructed by solicitors to conduct a detailed costs assessment under a collective conditional fee agreement and the solicitors remain responsible for the proper conduct of the work, the fees are base costs, not disbursements and a success fee is payable on them: *Crane v Canons Leisure Centre* (2008) Times, 10 January, CA.

III FUND [40]

The amount of the additional liability For pre 1 April 2013 conditional fee agreements the former CPR 44.5 (**CPR 44.5**) sets out the factors that the court will take into account in deciding the amount of costs. In deciding whether a percentage increase (success fee) is reasonable, the court will take into account the following:

(1) The risk that the circumstances in which the costs would be payable might or might not occur.
(2) The legal representative's liability for any disbursements.
(3) What other methods of financing the costs were available to the receiving party.

The **CPR PD 44**, Section 11.8 provides that the court has the power, when considering whether a percentage increase is reasonable, to allow different percentages for different items of costs or for different periods during which costs were incurred. See para **III FUND [39A]** above.

III FUND [41]

Proportionality A percentage increase will not be reduced simply on the ground that, when added to base costs which are reasonable and proportionate, the total appears disproportionate. But see per Lord Hope in *Campbell v MGN Ltd* [2005] UKHL 61, [2005] 4 All ER 793, [2005] 1 WLR 3394, para 47 for the suggestion that the success fee itself must be proportionate. As to the application of proportionality on pre Jackson 1 April 2013 CFAs where the success fee is being assessed on work undertaken post 1 April 2013, see: *BNM v MGN Ltd* [2017] EWCA Civ 1767, where the Court of Appeal held that a CFA entered into after 1 April 2013 with a success fee in publication and privacy proceedings was subject to the former pre-Jackson proportionality test. This decision overturned the earlier decision of the Senior Costs Judge: *BNM v MGN Ltd* [2016] EWHC B13 where the Senior Costs Judge held that the new test of proportionality applied. Accordingly the Court of Appeal has now clearly ruled that the new proportionality test in the CPR does not apply to additional liabilities in cases either which commenced before LASPO came into force on 1 April 2013 or which, although they commenced after 1 April 2013, are governed by the transitional provisions and exceptions to LASPO.

III FUND [42]

Provision of information A party who seeks to recover an additional liability must provide information about the funding arrangement to the court and to the other parties as required by a rule, practice direction or court order (**CPR 44.15 (1)**). Section 19 of **CPR PD 44** deals with the provision of such information. For section 19 see **CPR PD 44** (see also Form N251).

There is no requirement in the costs practice directions (see paras **CPR PD 44** to **CPR PD 48**) for the provision of information about funding arrangements before the commencement of proceedings although it is to be encouraged. See for example the Practice Direction — Pre-Action Conduct, para **PRO 1.4A**.

For the correct approach on an application for relief from sanction under CPR 3.9 see *Supperstone v Hurst* [2008] EWHC 735 (Ch), [2008] 4 Costs LR 572, [2008] BPIR 1134. Where the default occurred after 1 April 2013 the seminal case of *Mitchell (Andrew) v News Group Newspapers Ltd* provides the guiding principles: [2013] EWCA Civ 1537, [2013] 6 Costs LR 1008 as supplemented by *Denton v TH White Ltd; Decadent Vapours Ltd v Bevan; and Utilise TDS Ltd v Davies and another* [2014] EWCA Civ 906. There are essentially three stages for the court to consider.

1. The court should identify and assess the seriousness or significance of the 'failure to comply with any rule, practice direction, or court order' which engages CPR 3.9(1).

2. The court should consider why the default occurred.

3. The court should 'evaluate all the circumstances of the case, so as to enable it to deal justly with the application including factors in CPR 3.9(1)(a) and (b)' (which are set out above).

III FUND [43]–III FUND [53]

Solicitor and client liability The Conditional Fee Agreements Regulations 2000, SI 2000/692, reg 3(2)(b) provided that any amount of an agreed percentage increase which was disallowed on assessment inter partes, ceased to be payable under that agreement by the client unless the court was satisfied that it should continue to be payable. Where the agreement is one to which the Conditional Fee Agreements Regulations 2000 apply, and where disallowance of the percentage increase (success fee) is made on a summary assessment, the court will give directions to enable an application to be made by the legal representative for the disallowed amount to be payable by his client. However, the court may instead then and there decide the issue of whether the disallowance should continue to be payable by the client if the receiving party and all parties to the conditional fee agreement consent and if the receiving party is present in court. The court would also have to be satisfied that the issue could be fairly decided there and then. The procedure to be applied following detailed assessment is set out in the pre-1 April 2013 version of **CPR PD 44** at para **CPR PD 44**, Section 20.4.

III FUND [54]

Solicitor's success fees and protected parties CPR 21 makes provisions about the recovery of success fees from damages recovered by a child or protected party. The success fee can only be recovered if it is deemed to have been reasonably incurred and is reasonable. As much information as possible needs to be provided to the Court with the Application and supporting documents to justify the success fee: *A and M v Royal Mail Group* [2015] EW Misc B24 (CC) (14 August 2015). Where the claim is for damages for personal injury which do not exceed £25,000 the success fee is subject to a cap consistent with the Conditional Fee Agreements Order 2013.

CONDITIONAL FEE AGREEMENTS ORDER 2013

(SI 2013/689)

III FUND [54A]

1. Citation, commencement, interpretation and application

(1) This Order may be cited as the Conditional Fee Agreements Order 2013 and will come into force on 1st April 2013.

(2) In this Order—

"the 1986 Act" means the Insolvency Act 1986;

"the 1990 Act" means the Courts and Legal Services Act 1990;

"claim for personal injuries" has the same meaning as in Rule 2.3 of the Civil Procedure Rules 1998;

"company" means a company within the meaning of section 1 of the Companies Act 2006 or a company which may be wound up under Part V of the 1986 Act;

"diffuse mesothelioma" has the same meaning as in section 48(2) of the Legal Aid, Sentencing and Punishment of Offenders Act 2012;

"news publisher" means a person who publishes a newspaper, magazine or website containing news or information about or comment on current affairs;

"publication and privacy proceedings" means proceedings for—

(a) defamation;

(b) malicious falsehood;

(c) breach of confidence involving publication to the general public;

(d) misuse of private information; or

(e) harassment, where the defendant is a news publisher.

"representative" means the person or persons providing the advocacy services or litigation services to which the conditional fee agreement relates.

III FUND [54B]

2. Agreements providing for a success fee

All proceedings which, under section 58 of the Act, can be the subject of an enforceable conditional fee agreement, except proceedings under section 82 of the Environmental Protection Act 1990(a), are proceedings specified for the purpose of section 58(4)(a) of the Act.

III FUND [54C]

3. Amount of success fee

In relation to all proceedings specified in article 2, the percentage specified for the purposes of section 58(4)(c) of the Act is 100%.

III FUND [54D]

4. Specified proceedings

A claim for personal injuries shall be proceedings specified for the purpose of section 58(4A)(b) of the Act.

III FUND [54E]

5. Amount of success fee in specified proceedings

(1) In relation to the proceedings specified in article 4, the percentage prescribed for the purposes of section 58(4B)(c) of the Act is—

(a) in proceedings at first instance, 25%; and

(b) in all other proceedings, 100%.

(2) The descriptions of damages specified for the purposes of section 58(4B)(d) of the Act are—

(a) general damages for pain, suffering, and loss of amenity; and

(b) damages for pecuniary loss, other than future pecuniary loss,

net of any sums recoverable by the Compensation Recovery Unit of the Department for Work and Pensions.

III FUND [54F]

6. Transitional and saving provisions

(1) Articles 4 and 5 do not apply to a conditional fee agreement which is entered into before the date upon which this Order comes into force if—

(a) the agreement was entered into specifically for the purposes of the provision to a person ("P") of advocacy or litigation services in connection with the matter which is the subject of the proceedings; or

(b) advocacy or litigation services were provided to P under the agreement in connection with those proceedings before that date.

(2) Articles 4 and 5 do not apply to any conditional fee agreement entered into in relation to—

(a) proceedings relating to a claim for damages in respect of diffuse mesothelioma;

(b) publication and privacy proceedings;

(c) proceedings in England and Wales brought by a person acting in the capacity of—

(i) a liquidator of a company which is being wound up in England and Wales or Scotland under Parts IV or V of the 1986 Act; or

(ii) a trustee of a bankrupt's estate under Part IX of the 1986 Act;

(d) proceedings brought by a person acting in the capacity of an administrator appointed pursuant to the provisions of Part II of the 1986 Act;

(e) proceedings in England and Wales brought by a company which is being wound up in England and Wales or Scotland under Parts IV or V of the 1986 Act; or

(f) proceedings brought by a company which has entered administration under Part II of the 1986 Act.

III FUND [54G]–III FUND [69]

7. Revocation of 2000 Order

The Conditional Fee Agreements Order 2000 is revoked.

LEGAL AID, SENTENCING AND PUNISHMENT OF OFFENDERS ACT 2012 (COMMENCEMENT NO 5 AND SAVING PROVISION) ORDER 2013

(SI 2013/77)

III FUND [69A]

1. Citation and interpretation

(1) This Order may be cited as the Legal Aid, Sentencing and Punishment of Offenders Act 2012 (Commencement No 5 and Saving Provision) Order 2013.

(2) In this Order—

"the 1986 Act" means the Insolvency Act 1986;

"the 2012 Act" means the Legal Aid, Sentencing and Punishment of Offenders Act 2012;

"company" means a company within the meaning of section 1 of the Companies Act 2006 or a company which may be wound up under Part V of the 1986 Act;

"diffuse mesothelioma" has the same meaning as in section 48(2) of the 2012 Act;

"news publisher" means a person who publishes a newspaper, magazine or website containing news or information about or comment on current affairs;
"proceedings" has the same meaning as in section 58A(4) of the Courts and Legal Services Act 1990;
"publication and privacy proceedings" means proceedings for—

(a) defamation;
(b) malicious falsehood;
(c) breach of confidence involving publication to the general public;
(d) misuse of private information; or
(e) harassment, where the defendant is a news publisher.

III FUND [69B]

2. Provisions coming into force on 19th January 2013

(1) Subject to article 4, the following provisions of the 2012 Act come into force on 19th January 2013 for the purpose only of exercising any power to make orders, regulations or rules of court—

(a) section 44 (conditional fee agreements: success fees);
(b) section 45 (damages-based agreements), in so far as it is not already in force for that purpose; and
(c) section 46 (recovery of insurance premiums).

(2) Section 48 (sections 44 and 46 and diffuse mesothelioma proceedings) of the 2012 Act comes into force on 19th January 2013.

III FUND [69C]

3. Provisions coming into force on 1st April 2013

Subject to article 4, the following provisions come into force, in so far as they are not already in force, on 1st April 2013—

(a) section 44;
(b) section 45;
(c) section 46; and
(d) section 47 (recovery where a body undertakes to meet costs liabilities).

III FUND [69D]–III FUND [69K]

4. Saving provision

Article 2(1)(a) and (c) and article 3(a) and (c) do not apply to—

(a) proceedings relating to a claim for damages in respect of diffuse mesothelioma;
(b) publication and privacy proceedings;
(c) proceedings in England and Wales brought by a person acting in the capacity of—
  (i) a liquidator of a company which is being wound up in England and Wales or Scotland under Parts IV or V of the 1986 Act; or
  (ii) a trustee of a bankrupt's estate under Part IX of the 1986 Act;
(d) proceedings brought by a person acting in the capacity of an administrator appointed pursuant to the provisions of Part II of the 1986 Act;
(e) proceedings in England and Wales brought by a company which is being wound up in England and Wales or Scotland under Parts IV or V of the 1986 Act; or
(f) proceedings brought by a company which has entered administration under Part II of the 1986 Act.

DAMAGES-BASED AGREEMENTS REGULATIONS 2013

(SI 2013/609)

III FUND [69L]

1. Citation, commencement, interpretation and application

(1) These Regulations may be cited as the Damages-Based Agreements Regulations 2013 and come into force on 1st April 2013.

(2) In these Regulations—

"the Act" means the Courts and Legal Services Act 1990;

"claim for personal injuries" has the same meaning as in Rule 2.3 of the Civil Procedure Rules 1998;

"client" means the person who has instructed the representative to provide advocacy services, litigation services (within section 119 of the Act) or claims management services (within the meaning of section 4(2)(b) of the Compensation Act 2006) and is liable to make a payment for those services;

"costs" means the total of the representative's time reasonably spent, in respect of the claim or proceedings, multiplied by the reasonable hourly rate of remuneration of the representative;

"employment matter" means a matter that is, or could become, the subject of proceedings before an employment tribunal;

"expenses" means disbursements incurred by the representative, including the expense of obtaining an expert's report and, in an employment matter only, counsel's fees;

"payment" means that part of the sum recovered in respect of the claim or damages awarded that the client agrees to pay the representative, and excludes expenses but includes, in respect of any claim or proceedings to which these regulations apply other than an employment matter, any disbursements incurred by the representative in respect of counsel's fees;

"representative" means the person providing the advocacy services, litigation services or claims management services to which the damages-based agreement relates.

(3) Subject to paragraphs (4), (5) and (6), these Regulations shall apply to all damages-based agreements entered into on or after the date on which these Regulations come into force.

(4) Subject to paragraph (6), these Regulations shall not apply to any damages-based agreement to which section 57 of the Solicitors Act 1974 (non-contentious business agreements between solicitor and client) applies.

(5) In these Regulations—

(a) regulation 4 does not apply; and

(b) regulations 5, 6, 7 and 8 only apply,

to any damages-based agreement in respect of an employment matter.

(6) Where these Regulations relate to an employment matter, they apply to all damages-based agreements signed on or after the date on which these Regulations come into force.

III FUND [69M]

2. Revocation of 2010 Regulations and transitional provision

(1) Subject to paragraph (2), the Damages-Based Agreements Regulations 2010 ("the 2010 Regulations") are revoked.

(2) The 2010 Regulations shall continue to have effect in respect of any damages-based agreement to which those Regulations applied and which was signed before the date on which these Regulations come into force.

III FUND [69N]

3. Requirements of an agreement in respect of all damages-based agreements

The requirements prescribed for the purposes of section 58AA(4)(c) of the Act are that the terms and conditions of a damages-based agreement must specify—

(a) the claim or proceedings or parts of them to which the agreement relates;

(b) the circumstances in which the representative's payment, expenses and costs, or part of them, are payable; and

(c) the reason for setting the amount of the payment at the level agreed, which, in an employment matter, shall include having regard to, where appropriate, whether the claim or proceedings is one of several similar claims or proceedings.

III FUND [69O]

4. Payment in respect of claims or proceedings other than an employment matter

(1) In respect of any claim or proceedings, other than an employment matter, to which these Regulations apply, a damages-based agreement must not require an amount to be paid by the client other than—

(a) the payment, net of—

(i) any costs (including fixed costs under Part 45 of the Civil Procedure Rules 1998); and

(ii) where relevant, any sum in respect of disbursements incurred by the representative in respect of counsel's fees,

that have been paid or are payable by another party to the proceedings by agreement or order; and

(b) any expenses incurred by the representative, net of any amount which has been paid or is payable by another party to the proceedings by agreement or order.

(2) In a claim for personal injuries—

(a) the only sums recovered by the client from which the payment shall be met are—

(i) general damages for pain, suffering and loss of amenity; and
(ii) damages for pecuniary loss other than future pecuniary loss,

net of any sums recoverable by the Compensation Recovery Unit of the Department for Work and Pensions; and

(b) subject to paragraph (4), a damages-based agreement must not provide for a payment above an amount which, including VAT, is equal to 25% of the combined sums in paragraph (2)(a)(i) and (ii) which are ultimately recovered by the client.

(3) Subject to paragraph (4), in any other claim or proceedings to which this regulation applies, a damages-based agreement must not provide for a payment above an amount which, including VAT, is equal to 50% of the sums ultimately recovered by the client.

(4) The amounts prescribed in paragraphs (2)(b) and (3) shall only apply to claims or proceedings at first instance.

III FUND [69P]

5. Information to be given before an agreement is made in an employment matter

(1) In an employment matter, the requirements prescribed for the purposes of section 58AA(4)(d) of the Act are to provide—

(a) information to the client in writing about the matters in paragraph (2); and
(b) such further explanation, advice or other information about any of those matters as the client may request.

(2) Those matters are—

(a) the circumstances in which the client may seek a review of the costs and expenses of the representative and the procedure for doing so;
(b) the dispute resolution service provided by the Advisory, Conciliation and Arbitration Service (ACAS) in regard to actual and potential claims;
(c) whether other methods of pursuing the claim or financing the proceedings, including—
  (i) advice under arrangements made for the purposes of Part 1 (legal aid) of the Legal Aid, Sentencing and Punishment of Offenders Act 2012,
  (ii) legal expenses insurance,
  (iii) pro bono representation, or
  (iv) trade union representation,

are available, and, if so, how they apply to the client and the claim or proceedings in question;

(d) the point at which expenses become payable; and
(e) a reasonable estimate of the amount that is likely to be spent upon expenses, inclusive of VAT.

III FUND [69Q]

6. Additional causes of action

In an employment matter, any amendment to a damages-based agreement to cover additional causes of action must be in writing and signed by the client and the representative.

FUNDING

III FUND [69R]

7. Payment in an employment matter

In an employment matter, a damages-based agreement must not provide for a payment above an amount which, including VAT, is equal to 35% of the sums ultimately recovered by the client in the claim or proceedings.

III FUND [69S]–III FUND [125]

8. Terms and conditions of termination in an employment matter

(1) In an employment matter, the additional requirements prescribed for the purposes of section 58AA(4)(c) of the Act are that the terms and conditions of a damages-based agreement must be in accordance with paragraphs (2), (3) and (4).

(2) If the agreement is terminated, the representatives may not charge the client more than the representative's costs and expenses for the work undertaken in respect of the client's claim or proceedings.

(3) The client may not terminate the agreement—

(a) after settlement has been agreed; or

(b) within seven days before the start of the tribunal hearing.

(4) The representative may not terminate the agreement and charge costs unless the client has behaved or is behaving unreasonably.

(5) Paragraphs (3) and (4) are without prejudice to any right of either party under the general law of contract to terminate the agreement.

PART IV FURTHER RELEVANT STATUTORY MATERIAL

LEGAL AID, SENTENCING AND PUNISHMENT OF OFFENDERS ACT 2012

(c 10)

FUNDING

PART 1
LEGAL AID

PROVISION OF LEGAL AID

III FUND [126]

1 Lord Chancellor's functions

(1) The Lord Chancellor must secure that legal aid is made available in accordance with this Part.

(2) In this Part "legal aid" means—

(a) civil legal services required to be made available under section 9 or 10 or paragraph 3 of Schedule 3 (civil legal aid), and

(b) services consisting of advice, assistance and representation required to be made available under section 13, 15 or 16 or paragraph 4 or 5 of Schedule 3 (criminal legal aid).

(3) The Lord Chancellor may secure the provision of—

(a) general information about the law and the legal system, and

(b) information about the availability of advice about, and assistance in connection with, the law and the legal system.

(4) The Lord Chancellor may do anything which is calculated to facilitate, or is incidental or conducive to, the carrying out of the Lord Chancellor's functions under this Part.

(5) Nothing in this Part affects the powers that the Lord Chancellor has otherwise than under this Part.

III FUND [127]

2 Arrangements

(1) The Lord Chancellor may make such arrangements as the Lord Chancellor considers appropriate for the purposes of carrying out the Lord Chancellor's functions under this Part.

(2) The Lord Chancellor may, in particular, make arrangements by—

(a) making grants or loans to enable persons to provide services or facilitate the provision of services,

(b) making grants or loans to individuals to enable them to obtain services, and

(c) establishing and maintaining a body to provide services or facilitate the provision of services.

(3) The Lord Chancellor may by regulations make provision about the payment of remuneration by the Lord Chancellor to persons who provide services under arrangements made for the purposes of this Part.

(4) If the Lord Chancellor makes arrangements for the purposes of this Part that provide for a court, tribunal or other person to assess remuneration payable by the Lord Chancellor, the court, tribunal or person must assess the remuneration in accordance with the arrangements and, if relevant, with regulations under subsection (3).

(5) The Lord Chancellor may make different arrangements, in particular, in relation to—

(a) different areas in England and Wales,

(b) different descriptions of case, and

(c) different classes of person.

III FUND [128]

3 Standards of service

(1) The Lord Chancellor may set and monitor standards in relation to services made available under this Part.

(2) The Lord Chancellor may, in particular, make arrangements for the accreditation of persons providing, or wishing to provide, such services by—

(a) the Lord Chancellor, or

(b) persons authorised by the Lord Chancellor.

(3) Arrangements for accreditation must include—

(a) arrangements for monitoring services provided by accredited persons, and

(b) arrangements for withdrawing accreditation where the services provided are unsatisfactory.

(4) The Lord Chancellor may impose charges in connection with—

(a) accreditation,

(b) monitoring services provided by accredited persons, and

(c) authorising accreditation by others.

(5) Persons authorised by the Lord Chancellor may, in accordance with the terms of their authorisation, impose charges in connection with—

(a) accreditation, and

(b) monitoring services provided by accredited persons.

III FUND [129]

4 Director of Legal Aid Casework

(1) The Lord Chancellor must designate a civil servant as the Director of Legal Aid Casework ("the Director").

(2) The Lord Chancellor must make arrangements for the provision to the Director by civil servants or other persons (or both) of such assistance as the Lord Chancellor considers appropriate.

(3) The Director must—

(a) comply with directions given by the Lord Chancellor about the carrying out of the Director's functions under this Part, and

(b) have regard to guidance given by the Lord Chancellor about the carrying out of those functions.

(4) But the Lord Chancellor—

(a) must not give a direction or guidance about the carrying out of those functions in relation to an individual case, and

(b) must ensure that the Director acts independently of the Lord Chancellor when applying a direction or guidance under subsection (3) in relation to an individual case.

(5) The Lord Chancellor must publish any directions and guidance given under this section.

(6) Directions and guidance under this section may be revised or withdrawn from time to time.

III FUND [130]

5 Delegation

(1) The following functions of the Lord Chancellor may be exercised by, or by employees of, a person authorised by the Lord Chancellor for that purpose—

(a) securing the provision of information under section 1(3), and

(b) setting and monitoring standards under section 3.

FUNDING

(2) Regulations may provide for a function of the Lord Chancellor under regulations made under this Part to be exercisable by, or by employees of, a person authorised by the Lord Chancellor for that purpose.

(3) The functions conferred on the Director by this Part may be exercised by, or by employees of, a person authorised by the Director for that purpose.

(4) Regulations may provide for a function of the Director under regulations made under this Part to be exercisable by, or by employees of, a person authorised by the Director for that purpose.

(5) A direction given by the Lord Chancellor under section 4 about the carrying out of the Director's functions may, in particular, require the Director—

- (a) to authorise, or not to authorise, a person to carry out a function specified in the direction, or
- (b) to authorise, or not to authorise, a person specified, or of a description specified, in the direction to carry out such a function.

(6) Regulations under subsection (2) or (4) may provide that a function may be exercised—

- (a) wholly or to a limited extent;
- (b) generally or in particular cases or areas;
- (c) unconditionally or subject to conditions.

(7) An authorisation given for the purposes of this section or regulations under this section may provide that a function may be exercised—

- (a) wholly or to a limited extent;
- (b) generally or in particular cases or areas;
- (c) unconditionally or subject to conditions.

(8) In the case of an authorisation given for the purposes of regulations under this section, subsection (7) is subject to the provisions of the regulations.

III FUND [131]

6 Authorisations

(1) An authorisation given for the purposes of section 5 or regulations under that section—

- (a) may specify its duration,
- (b) may specify or describe the authorised person,
- (c) may be varied or revoked at any time by the person who gave it, and
- (d) does not prevent the Lord Chancellor, the Director or another person from exercising the function to which the authorisation relates.

(2) Anything done or omitted to be done by or in relation to a person authorised under section 5(1) or regulations under section 5(2) (or an employee of such a person) in, or in connection with, the exercise or purported exercise of the function concerned is to be treated for all purposes as done or omitted to be done by the Lord Chancellor.

(3) Anything done or omitted to be done by or in relation to a person authorised under section 5(3) or regulations under section 5(4) (or an employee of such a person) in, or in connection with, the exercise or purported exercise of the function concerned is to be treated for all purposes as done or omitted to be done by the Director.

(4) Subsections (2) and (3)—

- (a) do not affect the rights and liabilities of the authorised person or the Lord Chancellor under any arrangements made between them,
- (b) do not prevent any civil proceedings which could otherwise be brought by or against the authorised person (or an employee of that person) from being brought,

(c) do not apply for the purposes of criminal proceedings brought in respect of anything done or omitted to be done by the authorised person (or an employee of that person), and

(d) do not make the Lord Chancellor or the Director liable under section 6 of the Human Rights Act 1998 in respect of any act or omission of an authorised person if the act or omission is of a private nature.

(5) Where—

(a) an authorisation given for the purposes of section 5 or regulations under that section is revoked, and

(b) at the time of the revocation so much of any contract made between the authorised person and the Lord Chancellor as relates to the exercise of the function is subsisting,

the authorised person is entitled to treat the contract as repudiated by the Lord Chancellor (and not as frustrated by reason of the revocation).

(6) In this section "authorised person" means a person authorised for the purposes of section 5 or regulations under that section.

III FUND [132]

7 Annual report

(1) As soon as reasonably practicable after the end of each financial year, the Director must prepare an annual report for the financial year.

(2) The annual report must state how the Director has carried out the functions of the office in the financial year.

(3) The Director must send a copy of the report to the Lord Chancellor.

(4) The Lord Chancellor must—

(a) lay the copy of the report before Parliament, and

(b) arrange for it to be published.

(5) In this section "financial year" means—

(a) the period beginning on the day on which section 4 comes into force and ending on the following 31 March, and

(b) each successive period of 12 months.

Civil legal aid

III FUND [133]

8 Civil legal services

(1) In this Part "legal services" means the following types of services—

(a) providing advice as to how the law applies in particular circumstances,

(b) providing advice and assistance in relation to legal proceedings,

(c) providing other advice and assistance in relation to the prevention of disputes about legal rights or duties ("legal disputes") or the settlement or other resolution of legal disputes, and

(d) providing advice and assistance in relation to the enforcement of decisions in legal proceedings or other decisions by which legal disputes are resolved.

(2) The services described in subsection (1) include, in particular, advice and assistance in the form of—

(a) representation, and

(b) mediation and other forms of dispute resolution.

(3) In this Part "civil legal services" means any legal services other than the types of advice, assistance and representation that are required to be made available under sections 13, 15 and 16 (criminal legal aid).

FUNDING

III FUND [134]

9 General cases

(1) Civil legal services are to be available to an individual under this Part if—

- (a) they are civil legal services described in Part 1 of Schedule 1, and
- (b) the Director has determined that the individual qualifies for the services in accordance with this Part (and has not withdrawn the determination).

(2) The Lord Chancellor may by order—

- (a) add services to Part 1 of Schedule 1, or
- (b) vary or omit services described in that Part,

(whether by modifying that Part or Part 2, 3 or 4 of the Schedule).

III FUND [134.1]

The residence test A proposal to impose a requirement of 12 months' lawful residence by amendment to Part 2 of Schedule 1 was rejected by the Supreme Court as being ultra vires: *R (on the application of the Public Law Project v Lord Chancellor* [2016] UKSC 39.

III FUND [135]

10 Exceptional cases

(1) Civil legal services other than services described in Part 1 of Schedule 1 are to be available to an individual under this Part if subsection (2) or (4) is satisfied.

(2) This subsection is satisfied where the Director—

- (a) has made an exceptional case determination in relation to the individual and the services, and
- (b) has determined that the individual qualifies for the services in accordance with this Part,

(and has not withdrawn either determination).

(3) For the purposes of subsection (2), an exceptional case determination is a determination—

- (a) that it is necessary to make the services available to the individual under this Part because failure to do so would be a breach of—
  - (i) the individual's Convention rights (within the meaning of the Human Rights Act 1998), or
  - (ii) any rights of the individual to the provision of legal services that are enforceable EU rights, or
- (b) that it is appropriate to do so, in the particular circumstances of the case, having regard to any risk that failure to do so would be such a breach.

(4) This subsection is satisfied where—

- (a) the services consist of advocacy in proceedings at an inquest under the Coroners Act 1988 into the death of a member of the individual's family,
- (b) the Director has made a wider public interest determination in relation to the individual and the inquest, and
- (c) the Director has determined that the individual qualifies for the services in accordance with this Part,

(and neither determination has been withdrawn).

(5) For the purposes of subsection (4), a wider public interest determination is a determination that, in the particular circumstances of the case, the provision of advocacy under this Part for the individual for the purposes of the inquest is likely to produce significant benefits for a class of person, other than the individual and the members of the individual's family.

(6) For the purposes of this section an individual is a member of another individual's family if—

(a) they are relatives (whether of the full blood or half blood or by marriage or civil partnership),
(b) they are cohabitants (as defined in Part 4 of the Family Law Act 1996), or
(c) one has parental responsibility for the other.

III FUND [135.1]

The Exceptional Case Funding Scheme The Exceptional Case Funding Scheme was challenged successfully in an application for judicial review on grounds of complexity, narrowness and discrimination against those who lacked capacity: *IS v Director of Legal Casework* [2015] EWHC 1965 (Admin).

III FUND [136]

11 Qualifying for civil legal aid

(1) The Director must determine whether an individual qualifies under this Part for civil legal services in accordance with—
(a) section 21 (financial resources) and regulations under that section, and
(b) criteria set out in regulations made under this paragraph.
(2) In setting the criteria, the Lord Chancellor—
(a) must consider the circumstances in which it is appropriate to make civil legal services available under this Part, and
(b) must, in particular, consider the extent to which the criteria ought to reflect the factors in subsection (3).
(3) Those factors are—
(a) the likely cost of providing the services and the benefit which may be obtained by the services being provided,
(b) the availability of resources to provide the services,
(c) the appropriateness of applying those resources to provide the services, having regard to present and likely future demands for the provision of civil legal services under this Part,
(d) the importance for the individual of the matters in relation to which the services would be provided,
(e) the nature and seriousness of the act, omission, circumstances or other matter in relation to which the services are sought,
(f) the availability to the individual of services provided other than under this Part and the likelihood of the individual being able to make use of such services,
(g) if the services are sought by the individual in relation to a dispute, the individual's prospects of success in the dispute,
(h) the conduct of the individual in connection with services made available under this Part or an application for such services,
(i) the conduct of the individual in connection with any legal proceedings or other proceedings for resolving disputes about legal rights or duties, and
(j) the public interest.
(4) In setting the criteria, the Lord Chancellor must seek to secure that, in cases in which more than one form of civil legal service could be provided for an individual, the individual qualifies under this Part for the form of service which in all the circumstances is the most appropriate having regard to the criteria.
(5) The criteria must reflect the principle that, in many disputes, mediation and other forms of dispute resolution are more appropriate than legal proceedings.
(6) Regulations under subsection (1)(b) may provide that no criteria apply in relation to a prescribed description of individual or services.

III FUND [137]

12 Determinations

(1) A determination by the Director that an individual qualifies under this Part for civil legal services must specify—

(a) the type of services, and

(b) the matters in relation to which the services are to be available.

(2) Regulations may make provision about the making and withdrawal of determinations under sections 9 and 10.

(3) Regulations under subsection (2) may, in particular, include—

(a) provision about the form and content of determinations and applications for determinations,

(b) provision permitting or requiring applications and determinations to be made and withdrawn in writing, by telephone or by other prescribed means,

(c) provision setting time limits for applications and determinations,

(d) provision for a determination to be disregarded for the purposes of this Part if made in response to an application that is made otherwise than in accordance with the regulations,

(e) provision about conditions which must be satisfied by an applicant before a determination is made,

(f) provision about the circumstances in which a determination may or must be withdrawn,

(g) provision requiring information and documents to be provided,

(h) provision requiring individuals who are the subject of a determination to be informed of the reasons for making or withdrawing the determination, and

(i) provision for giving information to individuals who do not qualify for civil legal services under this Part about alternative ways of obtaining or funding civil legal services.

(4) The circumstances prescribed under subsection (3)(f) may, in particular, relate to whether the individual who is the subject of the determination has complied with requirements imposed by or under this Part.

(5) Regulations under subsection (2) must make provision establishing procedures for the review of determinations under sections 9 and 10 and of the withdrawal of such determinations.

(6) Regulations under subsection (2) may make provision for appeals to a court, tribunal or other person against such determinations and against the withdrawal of such determinations.

Financial resources

III FUND [138]

21 Financial resources

(1) A person may not make a relevant determination that an individual qualifies under this Part for services unless the person has determined that the individual's financial resources are such that the individual is eligible for the services (and has not withdrawn the determination).

(2) Regulations may—

(a) make provision about when an individual's financial resources are such that the individual is eligible under this Part for services, and

(b) make provision for exceptions from subsection (1).

(3) Regulations may provide that an individual is to be treated, for the purposes of regulations under subsection (2), as having or not having financial resources of a prescribed description.

(4) Regulations under subsection (3) may, in particular, provide that the individual is to be treated as having prescribed financial resources of a person of a prescribed description.

(5) Regulations may make provision about the making and withdrawal of determinations under this section.

(6) Regulations under subsection (5) may, in particular, include—

- (a) provision about the form and content of determinations,
- (b) provision permitting or requiring determinations to be made and withdrawn in writing, by telephone or by other prescribed means,
- (c) provision setting time limits for determinations,
- (d) provision about conditions which must be satisfied before a determination is made,
- (e) provision about the circumstances in which a determination may or must be withdrawn,
- (f) provision requiring information and documents to be provided,
- (g) provision requiring individuals who are the subject of a determination to be informed of the reasons for making or withdrawing the determination, and
- (h) provision for the review of a determination in respect of an individual's financial resources.

(7) The circumstances prescribed under subsection (6)(e) may, in particular, relate to whether the individual who is the subject of the determination has complied with requirements imposed by or under this Part.

(8) In this section "relevant determination" means a determination that is required to be carried out in accordance with this section by—

- (a) section 11 or 17, or
- (b) regulations under section 15 or paragraph 4 of Schedule 3.

III FUND [135.1]

Regulations providing for an individual's financial resources Regulations have been made under sub-s (2), namely the Civil Legal Aid (Financial Resources and Payment for Services) Regulations 2013, SI 2013/480, as amended by SI 2017/745.

III FUND [139]

22 Information about financial resources

(1) The relevant authority may make an information request to—

- (a) the Secretary of State,
- (b) a relevant Northern Ireland Department, or
- (c) the Commissioners for Her Majesty's Revenue and Customs ("the Commissioners").

(2) An information request may be made only for the purposes of facilitating a determination about an individual's financial resources for the purposes of this Part.

(3) An information request made to the Secretary of State or a relevant Northern Ireland Department under this section may request the disclosure of some or all of the following information—

- (a) a relevant individual's full name and any previous names;
- (b) a relevant individual's address and any previous addresses;
- (c) a relevant individual's date of birth;
- (d) a relevant individual's national insurance number;
- (e) a relevant individual's benefit status at a time specified in the request;

FUNDING

(f) information of a prescribed description.

(4) An information request made to the Commissioners under this section may request the disclosure of some or all of the following information—

(a) whether or not a relevant individual is employed or was employed at a time specified in the request;

(b) the name and address of the employer;

(c) whether or not a relevant individual is carrying on a business, trade or profession or was doing so at a time specified in the request;

(d) the name under which it is or was carried on;

(e) the address of any premises used for the purposes of carrying it on;

(f) a relevant individual's national insurance number;

(g) a relevant individual's benefit status at a time specified in the request;

(h) information of a prescribed description.

(5) The information that may be prescribed under subsections (3)(f) and (4)(h) includes, in particular, information relating to—

(a) prescribed income of a relevant individual for a prescribed period, and

(b) prescribed capital of a relevant individual.

(6) Information may not be prescribed under subsection (4)(h) without the Commissioners' consent.

(7) The Secretary of State, the relevant Northern Ireland Departments and the Commissioners may disclose to the relevant authority information specified in an information request made under this section.

(8) In this section—

"benefit status", in relation to an individual, means whether or not the individual is in receipt of a prescribed benefit or benefits and, if so—

(a) which benefit or benefits the individual is receiving,

(b) whether the individual is entitled to the benefit or benefits alone or jointly,

(c) in prescribed cases, the amount the individual is receiving by way of the benefit (or each of the benefits) ("the benefit amount"), and

(d) in prescribed cases, where the benefit consists of a number of elements, what those elements are and the amount included in respect of each element in calculating the benefit amount;

"the relevant authority" means—

(a) a prescribed person, or

(b) in relation to circumstances for which no person is prescribed, the Director;

"a relevant individual", in relation to an information request for the purposes of a determination about an individual's financial resources, means—

(a) that individual, and

(b) any other individual whose financial resources are or may be relevant for the purposes of the determination;

"relevant Northern Ireland Department" means the Department for Social Development in Northern Ireland or the Department of Finance and Personnel in Northern Ireland.

Contributions and costs

III FUND [140]

23 Payment for services

(1) An individual to whom services are made available under this Part is not to be required to make a payment in connection with the provision of the services, except where regulations provide otherwise.

(2) The regulations may, in particular, provide that in prescribed circumstances an individual must do one or more of the following—

(a) pay the cost of the services;

(b) pay a contribution in respect of the cost of the services of a prescribed amount;

(c) pay a prescribed amount in respect of administration costs.

(3) The regulations may, in particular, provide that where—

(a) civil legal services are provided to an individual under this Part in relation to a dispute, and

(b) prescribed conditions are met,

the individual must pay a prescribed amount which may exceed the cost of the civil legal services provided.

(4) The regulations may, in particular, make provision about the determination of the cost of services for the purposes of the regulations.

(5) The regulations may, in particular—

(a) provide for an individual's liability under the regulations to make a payment to change or cease in prescribed circumstances,

(b) provide for an individual's liability under the regulations to arise on a determination by a prescribed person,

(c) provide for such a determination to be varied or withdrawn by a prescribed person, and

(d) provide for the review of such a determination in respect of an individual's liability to make a payment.

(6) The regulations may, in particular, provide that an individual is to be treated, for the purposes of the regulations, as having or not having financial resources of a prescribed description.

(7) Regulations under subsection (6) may, in particular, provide that the individual is to be treated as having prescribed financial resources of a person of a prescribed description.

(8) The regulations may, in particular, include provision for an amount to be payable entirely or partly—

(a) by periodical payments;

(b) by one or more lump sums;

(c) out of income;

(d) out of capital.

(9) The regulations may, in particular, include—

(a) provision requiring information and documents to be provided,

(b) provision about the time and manner in which payments must be made,

(c) provision about the person to whom payments must be made, and

(d) provision about what that person must do with the payments.

(10) The regulations may, in particular, make provision for the payment by an individual of interest, on such terms as may be prescribed, in respect of—

(a) a loan made to the individual under this Part,

(b) a payment in connection with the provision of services which is not required by the regulations to be made by the individual until after the time when the services are provided, and

(c) so much of a payment as remains unpaid after the time when it is required by the regulations to be made by the individual.

(11) The regulations—

(a) must make provision for the repayment to an individual of any amount in excess of the individual's liability under the regulations or under section 24, and

FUNDING

(b) may make provision for the payment of interest on the excess.

(12) In this section—

"administration costs" means costs in connection with the administration of legal aid, including the administration of charges arising under section 25;

"prescribed amount" includes an amount calculated in a prescribed manner.

III FUND [141]

24 Enforcement

(1) Regulations may make provision about the enforcement of an obligation to make a payment imposed under section 23.

(2) The regulations may, in particular, make provision for costs incurred in connection with the enforcement of an individual's obligation to make a payment to be recovered from the individual.

(3) Regulations under this section may, in particular—

(a) provide that overdue amounts are recoverable summarily as a civil debt;

(b) provide that overdue amounts are recoverable as if they were payable under an order of the High Court or the county court, if the court in question so orders on the application of the person to whom the amounts are due.

(4) Regulations under this section may include provision requiring information and documents to be provided.

(5) Schedule 2 (criminal legal aid: motor vehicle orders) has effect.

III FUND [142]

25 Charges on property in connection with civil legal services

(1) Where civil legal services are made available to an individual under this Part, the amounts described in subsection (2) are to constitute a first charge on—

(a) any property recovered or preserved by the individual in proceedings, or in any compromise or settlement of a dispute, in connection with which the services were provided (whether the property is recovered or preserved for the individual or another person), and

(b) any costs payable to the individual by another person in connection with such proceedings or such a dispute.

(2) Those amounts are—

(a) amounts expended by the Lord Chancellor in securing the provision of the services (except to the extent that they are recovered by other means), and

(b) other amounts payable by the individual in connection with the services under section 23 or 24.

(3) Regulations may make provision for exceptions from subsection (1).

(4) Regulations may make provision about the charge under subsection (1) including, in particular—

(a) provision as to whether the charge is in favour of the Lord Chancellor or a person by whom the services were made available,

(b) provision modifying the charge for the purposes of its application in prescribed cases or circumstances, and

(c) provision about the enforcement of the charge.

(5) Regulations under subsection (4)(c) may, in particular, include—

(a) provision requiring amounts recovered by the individual in proceedings or as part of a compromise or settlement of a dispute, and costs payable to the individual, to be paid to the Lord Chancellor or a person by whom the services were made available,

(b) provision about the time and manner in which the amounts must be paid,
(c) provision about what the Lord Chancellor or the person by whom the services were made available must do with the amounts,
(d) provision for the payment of interest on all or part of the amounts,
(e) provision for the payment to the individual concerned of any amount in excess of the amounts described in subsection (2), and
(f) provision for the enforcement of requirements described in paragraph (a).

(6) Regulations under this section may include provision requiring information and documents to be provided.

III FUND [143]

26 Costs in civil proceedings

(1) Costs ordered against an individual in relevant civil proceedings must not exceed the amount (if any) which it is reasonable for the individual to pay having regard to all the circumstances, including—
(a) the financial resources of all of the parties to the proceedings, and
(b) their conduct in connection with the dispute to which the proceedings relate.

(2) In subsection (1) "relevant civil proceedings", in relation to an individual, means—
(a) proceedings for the purposes of which civil legal services are made available to the individual under this Part, or
(b) if such services are made available to the individual under this Part for the purposes of only part of proceedings, that part of the proceedings.

(3) Regulations may make provision for exceptions from subsection (1).

(4) In assessing for the purposes of subsection (1) the financial resources of an individual to whom civil legal services are made available, the following must not be taken into account, except so far as prescribed—
(a) the individual's clothes and household furniture, and
(b) the implements of the individual's trade.

(5) Subject to subsections (1) to (4), regulations may make provision about costs in relation to proceedings for the purposes of which civil legal services are made available under this Part.

(6) Regulations under subsection (5) may, in particular, make provision—
(a) specifying the principles to be applied in determining the amount of any costs which may be awarded against a party to whom civil legal services are made available under this Part,
(b) limiting the circumstances in which, or the extent to which, an order for costs may be enforced against such a party,
(c) as to the cases in which, and the extent to which, such a party may be required to give security for costs and the manner in which it is to be given,
(d) requiring the payment by the Lord Chancellor of the whole or part of any costs incurred by a party to whom civil legal services are not made available under this Part,
(e) specifying the principles to be applied in determining the amount of costs which may be awarded to a party to whom civil legal services are made available under this Part,
(f) as to the court, tribunal or other person by whom the amount of any costs is to be determined, and
(g) as to the extent to which any determination of that amount is to be final.

(7) Regulations may provide that an individual is to be treated, for the purposes of subsection (1) or regulations under subsection (3) or (5), as having or not having financial resources of a prescribed description (but such regulations have effect subject to subsection (4)).

(8) Regulations under subsection (7) may, in particular, provide that the individual is to be treated as having prescribed financial resources of a person of a prescribed description.

(9) Regulations under this section may include provision requiring information and documents to be provided.

PROVIDERS OF SERVICES ETC

III FUND [144]

27 Choice of provider of services etc

(1) The Lord Chancellor's duty under section 1(1) does not include a duty to secure that, where services are made available to an individual under this Part, they are made available by the means selected by the individual.

(2) The Lord Chancellor may discharge that duty, in particular, by arranging for the services to be provided by telephone or by other electronic means.

(3) The Lord Chancellor's duty under section 1(1) does not include a duty to secure that, where services are made available to an individual under this Part, they are made available by a person selected by the individual, subject to subsections (4) to (10).

(4) An individual who qualifies under this Part for representation for the purposes of criminal proceedings by virtue of a determination under section 16 may select any representative or representatives willing to act for the individual, subject to regulations under subsection (6).

(5) Where an individual exercises that right, representation by the selected representative or representatives is to be available under this Part for the purposes of the proceedings.

(6) Regulations may provide that in prescribed circumstances—

- (a) the right conferred by subsection (4) is not to apply in cases of prescribed descriptions,
- (b) an individual who has been provided with advice or assistance in accordance with section 13 or regulations under section 15 by a person selected by the individual is to be taken to have selected that person under subsection (4),
- (c) the right conferred by subsection (4) is not to include a right to select a representative of a prescribed description,
- (d) that right is to select only a representative located in a prescribed area or of a prescribed description,
- (e) that right is to select not more than a prescribed number of representatives to act at any one time, and
- (f) that right is not to include a right to select a representative in place of a representative previously selected.

(7) Regulations under subsection (6)(b) may prescribe circumstances in which an individual is to be taken to have selected a person to provide advice or assistance.

(8) Regulations may provide that in prescribed circumstances the Lord Chancellor is not required to make available representation for an individual by a prescribed representative.

(9) Provision made under subsection (8) does not prejudice any right of the individual to select another representative.

(10) The circumstances which may be prescribed under this section include that a determination has been made by a prescribed person.

III FUND [145]

28 Position of providers of services

(1) The fact that services provided for an individual are or could be provided under arrangements made for the purposes of this Part does not affect—

- (a) the relationship between the individual and the person by whom the services are provided,
- (b) any privilege arising out of that relationship, or
- (c) any right which the individual may have to be indemnified by another person in respect of expenses incurred by the individual,

except to the extent that regulations provide otherwise.

(2) A person who provides services under arrangements made for the purposes of this Part must not take any payment in respect of the services apart from—

- (a) payment made in accordance with the arrangements, and
- (b) payment authorised by the Lord Chancellor to be taken.

(3) Regulations may provide that the withdrawal of a determination that an individual qualifies for prescribed services under this Part does not affect the right of any person who has provided such services to the individual under arrangements made for the purposes of this Part to remuneration for work done before the date of the withdrawal.

FUNDING

III FUND [146]

29 Code of conduct

(1) The Lord Chancellor must publish a code of conduct to be observed by the following persons when providing services to an individual under arrangements made for the purposes of this Part—

- (a) civil servants, and
- (b) employees of a body established and maintained by the Lord Chancellor.

(2) The code must include—

- (a) duties to avoid discrimination,
- (b) duties to protect the interests of the individuals for whom services are provided,
- (c) duties to courts and tribunals,
- (d) duties to avoid conflicts of interest,
- (e) duties of confidentiality, and
- (f) duties on persons who are members of a professional body to comply with the rules of the body.

(3) The Lord Chancellor must lay the code, and any revision of the code, before Parliament.

(4) The persons described in subsection (1)(a) and (b) are not subject to the direction of the Lord Chancellor when providing services to an individual under arrangements made for the purposes of this Part.

III FUND [147]

30 Position of other parties, courts and tribunals

(1) Except as expressly provided by regulations, any rights conferred by or under this Part on an individual for whom services are provided under this Part for the purposes of proceedings do not affect—

- (a) the rights or liabilities of other parties to the proceedings, or
- (b) the principles on which the discretion of a court or tribunal is normally exercised.

(2) Regulations may make provision about the procedure of a court or tribunal in relation to services made available under this Part.

(3) Regulations under subsection (2) may, in particular, authorise the exercise of the functions of a court or tribunal by—

- (a) a member or officer of that court or tribunal, or
- (b) another court or tribunal.

SUPPLEMENTARY

III FUND [148]

31 Legal aid for legal persons

Schedule 3 (legal aid for legal persons) has effect.

III FUND [149]

32 Foreign law

(1) The civil legal services described in Part 1 of Schedule 1 do not include services relating to any law other than the law of England and Wales, except—

- (a) where express provision to the contrary is made by or under Part 1 of Schedule 1;
- (b) where such law is relevant for determining any issue relating to the law of England and Wales;
- (c) in other circumstances specified by the Lord Chancellor by order.

(2) A determination by the Director or a court under section 13, 15 or 16 that an individual qualifies for advice, assistance or representation under this Part does not impose a duty on the Lord Chancellor to secure that services relating to any law other than the law of England and Wales are made available, except—

- (a) where such law is relevant for determining any issue relating to the law of England and Wales;
- (b) in other circumstances specified by the Lord Chancellor by order.

(3) The Lord Chancellor may not make an order under subsection (1) or (2) unless the Lord Chancellor considers—

- (a) that it is necessary to make the order because failure to do so would result in a breach of—
  - (i) an individual's Convention rights (within the meaning of the Human Rights Act 1998), or
  - (ii) any rights of an individual to the provision of legal services that are enforceable EU rights, or
- (b) that it is appropriate to make the order having regard to any risk that failure to do so would result in such a breach.

III FUND [150]

33 Restriction on disclosure of information about financial resources

(1) A person to whom information is disclosed under section 22 or this subsection may disclose the information to any person to whom its disclosure is necessary or expedient in connection with facilitating a determination in respect of an individual's financial resources that is required under section 21.

(2) A person to whom such information is disclosed must not—

- (a) disclose the information other than in accordance with subsection (1), or
- (b) use the information other than for the purpose of facilitating a determination described in subsection (1).

(3) Subsection (2) does not prevent—

- (a) the disclosure of information in accordance with an enactment or an order of a court,

(b) the disclosure of information for the purposes of the investigation or prosecution of an offence (or suspected offence) under the law of England and Wales or Northern Ireland or any other jurisdiction, except where regulations otherwise provide,

(c) the disclosure of information for the purposes of instituting, or otherwise for the purposes of, proceedings before a court, or

(d) the disclosure of information which has previously been lawfully disclosed to the public.

(4) A person who discloses or uses information in contravention of this section is guilty of an offence and liable—

(a) on conviction on indictment, to imprisonment for a term not exceeding 2 years or a fine (or both);

(b) on summary conviction—

(i) in England and Wales, to imprisonment for a term not exceeding 12 months or a fine not exceeding the statutory maximum (or both), and

(ii) in Northern Ireland, to imprisonment for a term not exceeding 6 months or a fine not exceeding the statutory maximum (or both).

(5) It is a defence for a person charged with an offence under this section to prove that the person reasonably believed that the disclosure or use was lawful.

(6) In this section "enactment" includes—

(a) an enactment contained in subordinate legislation (within the meaning of the Interpretation Act 1978), and

(b) an enactment contained in, or in an instrument made under, an Act or Measure of the National Assembly for Wales or Northern Ireland legislation.

(7) In relation to an offence under this section committed before the commencement of section 154(1) of the Criminal Justice Act 2003, the reference in subsection (4)(b)(i) to 12 months has effect as if it were a reference to 6 months.

III FUND [151]

34 Restriction on disclosure of other information

(1) This section applies to information that is provided—

(a) to the Lord Chancellor, the Director, a court, a tribunal or any other person on whom functions are imposed or conferred by or under this Part, and

(b) in connection with the case of an individual seeking or receiving services provided under arrangements made for the purposes of this Part.

(2) Such information must not be disclosed, subject to the exceptions in section 35.

(3) A person who discloses information in contravention of this section is guilty of an offence and liable on summary conviction to a fine not exceeding level 4 on the standard scale.

(4) It is a defence for a person charged with an offence under this section to prove that the person reasonably believed that the disclosure was lawful.

(5) Proceedings for an offence under this section may not be brought without the consent of the Director of Public Prosecutions.

(6) Nothing in this section applies to information if—

(a) it is provided to a person providing services under arrangements made for the purposes of this Part, and

(b) it is provided by or on behalf of an individual seeking or receiving the services.

(7) Nothing in this section applies to information to which section 33 applies.

III FUND [152]

35 Exceptions from restriction under section 34

(1) Section 34(2) does not prevent the disclosure of information—

(a) for the purpose of enabling or assisting the Lord Chancellor or the Secretary of State for Justice to carry out their functions (whether conferred or imposed by an Act or otherwise),

(b) for the purpose of enabling or assisting the Director to carry out functions imposed or conferred on the Director by or under this Part, or

(c) for the purpose of enabling or assisting a court, tribunal or other person on whom functions are imposed or conferred by or under this Part to carry out those functions.

(2) Section 34(2) does not prevent—

(a) the disclosure of information in accordance with the law of England and Wales or an order of a court,

(b) the disclosure of information for the purposes of the investigation or prosecution of an offence (or suspected offence) under the law of England and Wales or any other jurisdiction, except where regulations otherwise provide,

(c) the disclosure of information for the purposes of instituting, or otherwise for the purposes of, proceedings before a court,

(d) the disclosure of information which has previously been lawfully disclosed to the public, or

(e) the disclosure of information for the purpose of facilitating the proper performance by a tribunal of disciplinary functions.

(3) Section 34(2) does not prevent the disclosure of—

(a) information in the form of a summary or collection of information that is framed so that information relating to an individual cannot be ascertained from it, or

(b) information about the amount of any grant, loan or other payment made to a person by the Lord Chancellor under arrangements made for the purposes of this Part.

(4) Section 34(2) does not prevent the disclosure of information for any purpose—

(a) with the consent of the individual in connection with whose case it was provided, and

(b) if the information was provided other than by that individual, with the consent of the person who provided the information.

(5) Section 34(2) does not prevent the disclosure of information after the end of the restricted period if—

(a) the disclosure is by a person who is a public authority for the purposes of the Freedom of Information Act 2000 or who is acting on behalf of such a person, and

(b) the information is not held by the public authority on behalf of another person.

(6) The restricted period is the period of 100 years beginning with the end of the calendar year in which a record containing the information was first created by a person to whom the information was provided in connection with a case described in section 34(1)(b).

III FUND [153]

36 Misrepresentation

(1) This section applies where a person—

(a) intentionally fails to comply with a requirement imposed by or under this Part to provide documents or information, or

(b) in providing documents or information in accordance with such a requirement, makes a statement or representation knowing or believing it to be false.

(2) The person is guilty of an offence and liable on summary conviction to a fine not exceeding level 4 on the standard scale.

(3) Proceedings in respect of an offence under this section may (despite anything in the Magistrates' Courts Act 1980) be brought at any time within the period of 6 months beginning with the date on which evidence sufficient in the opinion of the prosecutor to justify a prosecution comes to the prosecutor's knowledge.

(4) Subsection (3) does not authorise the commencement of proceedings for an offence more than 2 years after the date on which the offence was committed.

(5) The county court is to have jurisdiction to hear and determine an action brought by the Lord Chancellor to recover loss sustained by reason of—

(a) the failure by a person to comply with a requirement imposed by or under this Part to provide documents or information, or

(b) a false statement or false representation made by a person in providing documents or information in accordance with such a requirement.

FUNDING

III FUND [154]

37 Status of Director and Lord Chancellor

(1) The Director is to carry out the functions of the office on behalf of the Crown.

(2) Service as the Director is service in the civil service of the State.

(3) The Lord Chancellor is to be treated as a corporation sole—

(a) for all purposes relating to the acquisition, holding, management and disposal of property and interests in property under this Part, and

(b) for all other purposes relating to the Lord Chancellor's functions in connection with legal aid and other functions under this Part.

(4) An instrument in connection with the acquisition, holding, management or disposal by the Lord Chancellor of property or an interest in property under this Part or for a purpose mentioned in subsection (3)(b) may be executed on the Lord Chancellor's behalf by a person authorised by the Lord Chancellor for that purpose.

(5) Any such instrument purporting to have been executed by the Lord Chancellor or on the Lord Chancellor's behalf is to be received in evidence and, unless the contrary is proved, to be treated as having been so executed.

III FUND [155]

38 Abolition of Legal Services Commission

(1) The Legal Services Commission ceases to exist.

(2) Schedule 4 (transfer of employees and property etc of Legal Services Commission) has effect.

(3) The Lord Chancellor must, as soon as practicable after subsection (1) comes into force—

(a) prepare a report on how the Legal Services Commission has carried out its functions in the final period,

(b) lay a copy of the report before Parliament, and

(c) once it has been laid, publish the report.

(4) The Lord Chancellor must, as soon as practicable after subsection (1) comes into force—

- (a) prepare a statement of accounts for the Legal Services Commission for the final period, and
- (b) send a copy of the statement to the Comptroller and Auditor General.

(5) The Comptroller and Auditor General must—

- (a) examine, certify and report on the statement, and
- (b) arrange for a copy of the statement and the report to be laid before Parliament.

(6) In this section—

"the final period" means the period—

- (a) beginning with end of the last financial year for which the Legal Services Commission produced a report and accounts in accordance with paragraphs 14 and 16 of Schedule 1 to the Access to Justice Act 1999, and
- (b) ending immediately before the day on which subsection (1) comes into force;

"financial year" means a period of 12 months ending with 31 March.

III FUND [156]

39 Consequential and transitional provision

(1) Schedule 5 (legal aid: consequential amendments) has effect.

(2) Where the Lord Chancellor considers it appropriate as part of the arrangements for effecting the transition from the operation of Part 1 of the Access to Justice Act 1999 to the operation of this Part of this Act, the Lord Chancellor may by regulations make provision requiring or enabling prescribed 1999 Act services to be made available to individuals or other persons under this Part for a period specified or described in the regulations.

(3) In subsection (2) "1999 Act services" means services which, immediately before the day on which the first regulations under that subsection come into force, may be funded under Part 1 of the Access to Justice Act 1999.

(4) Where the Lord Chancellor considers it appropriate for the Legal Services Commission to cease to exist before this Part is brought fully into force, the Lord Chancellor may by regulations make provision for the purpose of requiring or enabling the Lord Chancellor and the Director, or persons authorised by the Lord Chancellor or the Director, to carry out LSC functions for a period specified or described in the regulations.

(5) In subsection (4) "LSC functions" means functions conferred or imposed on the Legal Services Commission by or under Part 1 of the Access to Justice Act 1999.

(6) Regulations under subsection (4) may not include provision requiring or enabling the Lord Chancellor—

- (a) to take decisions about whether services should be funded in individual cases, or
- (b) to give directions or guidance about the carrying out of functions under Part 1 of the Access to Justice Act 1999 in relation to individual cases.

(7) Regulations under this section—

- (a) may amend, repeal, revoke or otherwise modify Part 1 of the Access to Justice Act 1999, this Part of this Act, any other Act and any instrument made under an Act;
- (b) may describe a period, in particular, by reference to the coming into force of a provision of this Part of this Act or the repeal of a provision of Part 1 of the Access to Justice Act 1999.

(8) The requirement for regulations under this section to specify or describe a period does not prevent the making of further regulations under this section.

(9) The powers to make regulations under this section are without prejudice to the generality of the powers to make regulations under the other provisions of this Part and under section 149.

(10) In this section "Act" includes an Act or Measure of the National Assembly for Wales.

III FUND [157]

40 Northern Ireland: information about financial resources

Schedule 6 (Northern Ireland: information about financial resources) has effect.

III FUND [158]

41 Orders, regulations and directions

(1) Orders, regulations and directions under this Part—

- (a) may make different provision for different cases, circumstances or areas,
- (b) may make provision generally or only for specified cases, circumstances or areas, and
- (c) may make provision having effect for a period specified or described in the order, regulations or direction.

(2) They may, in particular, make provision by reference to—

- (a) services provided for the purposes of proceedings before a particular court, tribunal or other person,
- (b) services provided for a particular class of individual, or
- (c) services provided for individuals selected by reference to particular criteria or on a sampling basis.

(3) Orders and regulations under this Part—

- (a) may provide for a person to exercise a discretion in dealing with any matter,
- (b) may make provision by reference to a document produced by any person, and
- (c) may make consequential, supplementary, incidental, transitional or saving provision.

(4) Orders and regulations under this Part are to be made by statutory instrument.

(5) A statutory instrument containing an order or regulations under this Part is subject to annulment in pursuance of a resolution of either House of Parliament, unless it is an instrument described in subsection (6) or (9).

(6) A statutory instrument containing an order or regulations listed in subsection (7) (whether alone or with other provision) may not be made unless a draft of the instrument has been laid before, and approved by a resolution of, each House of Parliament.

(7) Those orders and regulations are—

- (a) orders under section 9;
- (b) regulations under section 11(1)(b), other than regulations in respect of which the Lord Chancellor has made an urgency statement;
- (c) regulations under section 13(8);
- (d) orders under section 17(3);
- (e) regulations under section 18(7);
- (f) regulations under section 19;
- (g) regulations under section 20;
- (h) regulations under section 22;

FUNDING

(i) regulations under section 26(3) or (6)(b) or (d);
(j) regulations under section 27(6)(a) or (8);
(k) regulations under section 39 that amend or repeal a provision of an Act (as defined in that section), other than regulations revoking such regulations or inserting or repealing provision previously repealed or inserted by such regulations;
(l) regulations under paragraph 5(9) of Schedule 3;
(m) regulations under paragraph 11 of Schedule 4 that amend or repeal a provision of an Act (as defined in that Schedule).

(8) An urgency statement is a statement that the Lord Chancellor considers that it is desirable for the regulations to come into force without delay for the reasons given in the statement.

(9) Where a statutory instrument contains regulations under section 11(1)(b) in respect of which the Lord Chancellor has made an urgency statement—
(a) the regulations may not come into force before the instrument and the statement are laid before Parliament, and
(b) the regulations cease to have effect at the end of the period of 120 days beginning with the day on which the instrument is made unless the instrument is approved by a resolution of each House of Parliament before the end of that period.

(10) In reckoning the period of 120 days no account is to be taken of any time—
(a) during which Parliament is dissolved or prorogued, or
(b) during which both Houses are adjourned for more than 4 days.

(11) Where regulations cease to have effect under subsection (9) that does not affect—
(a) anything previously done in reliance on the regulations, or
(b) the making of further regulations.

III FUND [159]

42 Interpretation

(1) In this Part—

"advocacy" means the exercise of a right of audience before a court, tribunal or other person;

"civil legal services" has the meaning given in section 8;

"civil servant" means an individual employed in the civil service of the State;

"criminal proceedings" has the meaning given in section 14;

"the Director" means the Director of Legal Aid Casework;

"functions" includes powers and duties;

"legal aid" has the meaning given in section 1;

"legal proceedings" means proceedings before a court or tribunal;

"legal services" has the meaning given in section 8;

"modify", in relation to an Act or instrument, includes amend, repeal or revoke and related terms are to be interpreted accordingly;

"prescribed" means prescribed by regulations (except in Schedule 6) and related terms are to be interpreted accordingly;

"regulations" means regulations made by the Lord Chancellor (except in Schedule 6);

"remuneration" includes disbursements;

"representation" means representation for the purposes of proceedings and includes—
(a) the advice and assistance which is usually given by a representative in the steps preliminary or incidental to proceedings, and

(b) subject to any time limits which may be prescribed, advice and assistance as to any appeal.

(2) In this Part references to proceedings are to be interpreted in accordance with section 20(3).

III FUND [160]

43 Crown application

This Part binds the Crown.

PART 2
LITIGATION FUNDING AND COSTS

PAYMENTS FOR LEGAL SERVICES IN CIVIL CASES

III FUND [161]

44 Conditional fee agreements: success fees

(1) In section 58 of the Courts and Legal Services Act 1990 (conditional fee agreements), in subsection (2)—

(a) omit "and" after paragraph (a), and

(b) after paragraph (b) insert

"and

(c) references to a success fee, in relation to a conditional fee agreement, are to the amount of the increase."

(2) After subsection (4) of that section insert—

"(4A) The additional conditions are applicable to a conditional fee agreement which—

(a) provides for a success fee, and

(b) relates to proceedings of a description specified by order made by the Lord Chancellor for the purposes of this subsection.

(4B) The additional conditions are that—

(a) the agreement must provide that the success fee is subject to a maximum limit,

(b) the maximum limit must be expressed as a percentage of the descriptions of damages awarded in the proceedings that are specified in the agreement,

(c) that percentage must not exceed the percentage specified by order made by the Lord Chancellor in relation to the proceedings or calculated in a manner so specified, and

(d) those descriptions of damages may only include descriptions of damages specified by order made by the Lord Chancellor in relation to the proceedings."

(3) In section 58A of that Act (conditional fee agreements: supplementary), in subsection (5) after "section 58(4)" insert ", (4A) or (4B)".

(4) For subsection (6) of that section substitute—

"(6) A costs order made in proceedings may not include provision requiring the payment by one party of all or part of a success fee payable by another party under a conditional fee agreement."

(5) In section 120(4) of that Act (regulations and orders subject to parliamentary approval) after "58(4)," insert "(4A) or (4B),".

(6) The amendment made by subsection (4) does not prevent a costs order including provision in relation to a success fee payable by a person ("P") under a conditional fee agreement entered into before the day on which that subsection comes into force ("the commencement day") if—

FUNDING

(a) the agreement was entered into specifically for the purposes of the provision to P of advocacy or litigation services in connection with the matter that is the subject of the proceedings in which the costs order is made, or

(b) advocacy or litigation services were provided to P under the agreement in connection with that matter before the commencement day.

III FUND [161.1]

Transitional provisions Parties who made conditional fee agreements before 1 April 2013, which provided for success fees and after the event insurance, were held to be entitled to retain the benefits of those provisions in relation to proceedings that continued after that date and were extended or varied to cover subsequent appeals, unless it was clear that the new arrangements were totally separate and distinct: *Plevin v Paragon Personal Finance Ltd (No 2)* (2017) Times, 6 April, Sup Court.

III FUND [162]

45 Damages-based agreements

(1) Section 58AA of the Courts and Legal Services Act 1990 (damages-based agreements) is amended as follows.

(2) In subsection (1) omit "relates to an employment matter and".

(3) In subsection (2)—

(a) after "But" insert "(subject to subsection (9))", and

(b) omit "relates to an employment matter and".

(4) Omit subsection (3)(b).

(5) After subsection (4)(a) insert—

"(aa) must not relate to proceedings which by virtue of section 58A(1) and (2) cannot be the subject of an enforceable conditional fee agreement or to proceedings of a description prescribed by the Lord Chancellor;".

(6) In subsection (4)(b), at the beginning insert "if regulations so provide,".

(7) In subsection (4)(d) for "has provided prescribed information" substitute "has complied with such requirements (if any) as may be prescribed as to the provision of information".

(8) After subsection (6) insert—

"(6A) Rules of court may make provision with respect to the assessment of costs in proceedings where a party in whose favour a costs order is made has entered into a damages-based agreement in connection with the proceedings."

(9) After subsection (7) insert—

"(7A) In this section (and in the definitions of "advocacy services" and "litigation services" as they apply for the purposes of this section) "proceedings" includes any sort of proceedings for resolving disputes (and not just proceedings in a court), whether commenced or contemplated."

(10) After subsection (8) insert—

"(9) Where section 57 of the Solicitors Act 1974 (non-contentious business agreements between solicitor and client) applies to a damages-based agreement other than one relating to an employment matter, subsections (1) and (2) of this section do not make it unenforceable.

(10) For the purposes of subsection (9) a damages-based agreement relates to an employment matter if the matter in relation to which the services are provided is a matter that is, or could become, the subject of proceedings before an employment tribunal."

(11) In the heading of that section omit "relating to employment matters".

(12) In section 120(4) of that Act (regulations and orders subject to parliamentary approval) for "58AA" substitute "58AA(4)".

(13) The amendments made by subsections (1) to (11) do not apply in relation to an agreement entered into before this section comes into force.

III FUND [163]

46 Recovery of insurance premiums by way of costs

(1) In the Courts and Legal Services Act 1990, after section 58B insert—

"58C Recovery of insurance premiums by way of costs

(1) A costs order made in favour of a party to proceedings who has taken out a costs insurance policy may not include provision requiring the payment of an amount in respect of all or part of the premium of the policy, unless such provision is permitted by regulations under subsection (2).

(2) The Lord Chancellor may by regulations provide that a costs order may include provision requiring the payment of such an amount where—

- (a) the order is made in favour of a party to clinical negligence proceedings of a prescribed description,
- (b) the party has taken out a costs insurance policy insuring against the risk of incurring a liability to pay for one or more expert reports in respect of clinical negligence in connection with the proceedings (or against that risk and other risks),
- (c) the policy is of a prescribed description,
- (d) the policy states how much of the premium relates to the liability to pay for an expert report or reports in respect of clinical negligence ("the relevant part of the premium"), and
- (e) the amount is to be paid in respect of the relevant part of the premium.

(3) Regulations under subsection (2) may include provision about the amount that may be required to be paid by the costs order, including provision that the amount must not exceed a prescribed maximum amount.

(4) The regulations may prescribe a maximum amount, in particular, by specifying—

- (a) a percentage of the relevant part of the premium;
- (b) an amount calculated in a prescribed manner.

(5) In this section—

"clinical negligence" means breach of a duty of care or trespass to the person committed in the course of the provision of clinical or medical services (including dental or nursing services);

"clinical negligence proceedings" means proceedings which include a claim for damages in respect of clinical negligence;

"costs insurance policy", in relation to a party to proceedings, means a policy insuring against the risk of the party incurring a liability in those proceedings;

"expert report" means a report by a person qualified to give expert advice on all or most of the matters that are the subject of the report;

"proceedings" includes any sort of proceedings for resolving disputes (and not just proceedings in court), whether commenced or contemplated."

(2) In the Access to Justice Act 1999, omit section 29 (recovery of insurance premiums by way of costs).

(3) The amendments made by this section do not apply in relation to a costs order made in favour of a party to proceedings who took out a costs insurance policy in relation to the proceedings before the day on which this section comes into force.

III FUND [163.1]

Transitional provisions Parties who made conditional fee agreements before 1 April 2013, which provided for success fees and after the event insurance, were held to be entitled to

FUNDING

retain the benefits of those provisions in relation to proceedings that continued after that date and were extended or varied to cover subsequent appeals, unless it was clear that the new arrangements were totally separate and distinct: *Plevin v Paragon Personal Finance Ltd (No 2)* (2017) Times, 6 April, Sup Court.

With the agreement of all the parties the client who wishes to change solicitors may have the benefits and burdens of a CFA agreement transferred by novation from one firm to the next: *Budana v Leeds Teaching Hospitals NHS Trust (Law Society intervening)* [2017] EWCA Civ 1980, 159 BMLR 50, (2018) Times, 19 January.

III FUND [164]

47 Recovery where body undertakes to meet costs liabilities

(1) In the Access to Justice Act 1999, omit section 30 (recovery where body undertakes to meet costs liabilities).

(2) The repeal made by subsection (1) does not apply in relation to a costs order made in favour of a person to whom a body gave an undertaking before the day on which this section comes into force if the undertaking was given specifically in respect of the costs of other parties to proceedings relating to the matter which is the subject of the proceedings in which the costs order is made.

III FUND [165]

48 Sections 44 and 46 and diffuse mesothelioma proceedings

(1) Sections 44 and 46 may not be brought into force in relation to proceedings relating to a claim for damages in respect of diffuse mesothelioma until the Lord Chancellor has—

- (a) carried out a review of the likely effect of those sections in relation to such proceedings, and
- (b) published a report of the conclusions of the review.

(2) In this section "diffuse mesothelioma" has the same meaning as in the Pneumoconiosis etc (Workers' Compensation) Act 1979.

III FUND [166]

49 Divorce etc proceedings: orders for payment in respect of legal services

(1) In section 22 of the Matrimonial Causes Act 1973 (maintenance pending suit)—

- (a) number the existing provision subsection (1), and
- (b) after that subsection insert—

"(2) An order under this section may not require a party to a marriage to pay to the other party any amount in respect of legal services for the purposes of the proceedings.

(3) In subsection (2) "legal services" has the same meaning as in section 22ZA."

(2) After that section insert—

"22ZA Orders for payment in respect of legal services

(1) In proceedings for divorce, nullity of marriage or judicial separation, the court may make an order or orders requiring one party to the marriage to pay to the other ("the applicant") an amount for the purpose of enabling the applicant to obtain legal services for the purposes of the proceedings.

(2) The court may also make such an order or orders in proceedings under this Part for financial relief in connection with proceedings for divorce, nullity of marriage or judicial separation.

(3) The court must not make an order under this section unless it is satisfied that, without the amount, the applicant would not reasonably be able to obtain appropriate legal services for the purposes of the proceedings or any part of the proceedings.

(4) For the purposes of subsection (3), the court must be satisfied, in particular, that—

- (a) the applicant is not reasonably able to secure a loan to pay for the services, and
- (b) the applicant is unlikely to be able to obtain the services by granting a charge over any assets recovered in the proceedings.

(5) An order under this section may be made for the purpose of enabling the applicant to obtain legal services of a specified description, including legal services provided in a specified period or for the purposes of a specified part of the proceedings.

(6) An order under this section may—

- (a) provide for the payment of all or part of the amount by instalments of specified amounts, and
- (b) require the instalments to be secured to the satisfaction of the court.

(7) An order under this section may direct that payment of all or part of the amount is to be deferred.

(8) The court may at any time in the proceedings vary an order made under this section if it considers that there has been a material change of circumstances since the order was made.

(9) For the purposes of the assessment of costs in the proceedings, the applicant's costs are to be treated as reduced by any amount paid to the applicant pursuant to an order under this section for the purposes of those proceedings.

(10) In this section "legal services", in relation to proceedings, means the following types of services—

- (a) providing advice as to how the law applies in the particular circumstances,
- (b) providing advice and assistance in relation to the proceedings,
- (c) providing other advice and assistance in relation to the settlement or other resolution of the dispute that is the subject of the proceedings, and
- (d) providing advice and assistance in relation to the enforcement of decisions in the proceedings or as part of the settlement or resolution of the dispute,

and they include, in particular, advice and assistance in the form of representation and any form of dispute resolution, including mediation.

(11) In subsections (5) and (6) "specified" means specified in the order concerned."

FUNDING

III FUND [167]

50 Divorce etc proceedings: matters to be considered by court making legal services order

After section 22ZA of the Matrimonial Causes Act 1973 insert—

"22ZB Matters to which court is to have regard in deciding how to exercise power under section 22ZA

(1) When considering whether to make or vary an order under section 22ZA, the court must have regard to—

- (a) the income, earning capacity, property and other financial resources which each of the applicant and the paying party has or is likely to have in the foreseeable future,
- (b) the financial needs, obligations and responsibilities which each of the applicant and the paying party has or is likely to have in the foreseeable future,
- (c) the subject matter of the proceedings, including the matters in issue in them,

(d) whether the paying party is legally represented in the proceedings,
(e) any steps taken by the applicant to avoid all or part of the proceedings, whether by proposing or considering mediation or otherwise,
(f) the applicant's conduct in relation to the proceedings,
(g) any amount owed by the applicant to the paying party in respect of costs in the proceedings or other proceedings to which both the applicant and the paying party are or were party, and
(h) the effect of the order or variation on the paying party.

(2) In subsection (1)(a) "earning capacity", in relation to the applicant or the paying party, includes any increase in earning capacity which, in the opinion of the court, it would be reasonable to expect the applicant or the paying party to take steps to acquire.

(3) For the purposes of subsection (1)(h), the court must have regard, in particular, to whether the making or variation of the order is likely to—
(a) cause undue hardship to the paying party, or
(b) prevent the paying party from obtaining legal services for the purposes of the proceedings.

(4) The Lord Chancellor may by order amend this section by adding to, omitting or varying the matters mentioned in subsections (1) to (3).

(5) An order under subsection (4) must be made by statutory instrument.

(6) A statutory instrument containing an order under subsection (4) may not be made unless a draft of the instrument has been laid before, and approved by a resolution of, each House of Parliament.

(7) In this section "legal services" has the same meaning as in section 22ZA."

III FUND [168]

51 Divorce etc proceedings: orders for sale of property

In section 24A(1) of the Matrimonial Causes Act 1973 (orders for sale of property), after "makes" insert "an order under section 22ZA or makes".

III FUND [169]

52 Dissolution etc proceedings: orders for payment in respect of legal services

(1) Part 8 of Schedule 5 to the Civil Partnership Act 2004 (maintenance pending outcome of dissolution etc proceedings) is amended as follows.

(2) In the heading of that Part after "Maintenance" insert "and other payments".

(3) Before paragraph 38 insert—

"*Maintenance orders*"

(4) In that paragraph—
(a) number the existing provision sub-paragraph (1), and
(b) after that sub-paragraph insert—

"(2) An order under this paragraph may not require one civil partner to pay to the other any amount in respect of legal services for the purposes of the proceedings.

(3) In sub-paragraph (2) "legal services" has the same meaning as in paragraph 38A."

(5) After that paragraph insert—

"38A Orders in respect of legal services

(1) In proceedings for a dissolution, nullity or separation order, the court may make an order or orders requiring one civil partner to pay to the other ("the applicant") an amount for the purpose of enabling the applicant to obtain legal services for the purposes of the proceedings.

(2) The court may also make such an order or orders in proceedings under this Schedule for financial relief in connection with proceedings for a dissolution, nullity or separation order.

(3) The court must not make an order under this paragraph unless it is satisfied that, without the amount, the applicant would not reasonably be able to obtain appropriate legal services for the purposes of the proceedings or any part of the proceedings.

(4) For the purposes of sub-paragraph (3), the court must be satisfied, in particular, that—

(a) the applicant is not reasonably able to secure a loan to pay for the services, and

(b) the applicant is unlikely to be able to obtain the services by granting a charge over any assets recovered in the proceedings.

(5) An order under this paragraph may be made for the purpose of enabling the applicant to obtain legal services of a specified description, including legal services provided in a specified period or for the purposes of a specified part of the proceedings.

(6) An order under this paragraph may—

(a) provide for the payment of all or part of the amount by instalments of specified amounts, and

(b) require the instalments to be secured to the satisfaction of the court.

(7) An order under this paragraph may direct that payment of all or part of the amount is to be deferred.

(8) The court may at any time in the proceedings vary an order made under this paragraph if it considers that there has been a material change of circumstances since the order was made.

(9) For the purposes of the assessment of costs in the proceedings, the applicant's costs are to be treated as reduced by any amount paid to the applicant pursuant to an order under this section for the purposes of those proceedings.

(10) In this paragraph "legal services", in relation to proceedings, means the following types of services—

(a) providing advice as to how the law applies in the particular circumstances,

(b) providing advice and assistance in relation to the proceedings,

(c) providing other advice and assistance in relation to the settlement or other resolution of the dispute that is the subject of the proceedings, and

(d) providing advice and assistance in relation to the enforcement of decisions in the proceedings or as part of the settlement or resolution of the dispute,

and they include, in particular, advice and assistance in the form of representation and any form of dispute resolution, including mediation.

(11) In sub-paragraphs (5) and (6) "specified" means specified in the order concerned."

FUNDING

III FUND [170]

53 Dissolution etc proceedings: matters to be considered by court making legal services order

After paragraph 38A of Schedule 5 to the Civil Partnership Act 2004 insert—

"38B

(1) When considering whether to make or vary an order under paragraph 38A, the court must have regard to—

(a) the income, earning capacity, property and other financial resources which each of the applicant and the paying party has or is likely to have in the foreseeable future,

(b) the financial needs, obligations and responsibilities which each of the applicant and the paying party has or is likely to have in the foreseeable future,

(c) the subject matter of the proceedings, including the matters in issue in them,

(d) whether the paying party is legally represented in the proceedings,

(e) any steps taken by the applicant to avoid all or part of the proceedings, whether by proposing or considering mediation or otherwise,

(f) the applicant's conduct in relation to the proceedings,

(g) any amount owed by the applicant to the paying party in respect of costs in the proceedings or other proceedings to which both the applicant and the paying party are or were party, and

(h) the effect of the order or variation on the paying party.

(2) In sub-paragraph (1)(a) "earning capacity", in relation to the applicant or the paying party, includes any increase in earning capacity which, in the opinion of the court, it would be reasonable to expect the applicant or the paying party to take steps to acquire.

(3) For the purposes of sub-paragraph (1)(h), the court must have regard, in particular, to whether the making or variation of the order is likely to—

(a) cause undue hardship to the paying party, or

(b) prevent the paying party from obtaining legal services for the purposes of the proceedings.

(4) The Lord Chancellor may by order amend this paragraph by adding to, omitting or varying the matters mentioned in sub-paragraphs (1) to (3).

(5) An order under sub-paragraph (4) must be made by statutory instrument.

(6) A statutory instrument containing an order under sub-paragraph (4) may not be made unless a draft of the instrument has been laid before, and approved by a resolution of, each House of Parliament.

(7) In this paragraph "legal services" has the same meaning as in paragraph 38A."

III FUND [171]

54 Dissolution etc proceedings: orders for sale of property

(1) Paragraph 10(1)(a) of Schedule 5 to the Civil Partnership Act 2004 (sale of property orders) is amended as follows.

(2) Omit the "or" at the end of sub-paragraph (i).

(3) After sub-paragraph (ii) insert—

"(iii) an order under paragraph 38A for a payment in respect of legal services, or".

Offers to settle

III FUND [172]

55 Payment of additional amount to successful claimant

(1) Rules of court may make provision for a court to order a defendant in civil proceedings to pay an additional amount to a claimant in those proceedings where—

(a) the claim is a claim for (and only for) an amount of money,

(b) judgment is given in favour of the claimant,

(c) the judgment in respect of the claim is at least as advantageous as an offer to settle the claim which the claimant made in accordance with rules of court and has not withdrawn in accordance with those rules, and

(d) any prescribed conditions are satisfied.

(2) Rules made under subsection (1) may include provision as to the assessment of whether a judgment is at least as advantageous as an offer to settle.

(3) In subsection (1) "additional amount" means an amount not exceeding a prescribed percentage of the amount awarded to the claimant by the court (excluding any amount awarded in respect of the claimant's costs).

(4) The Lord Chancellor may by order provide that rules of court may make provision for a court to order a defendant in civil proceedings to pay an amount calculated in a prescribed manner to a claimant in those proceedings where—

(a) the claim is or includes a non-monetary claim,

(b) judgment is given in favour of the claimant,

(c) the judgment in respect of the claim is at least as advantageous as an offer to settle the claim which the claimant made in accordance with rules of court and has not withdrawn in accordance with those rules, and

(d) any prescribed conditions are satisfied.

(5) An order under subsection (4) must provide for the amount to be calculated by reference to one or more of the following—

(a) any costs ordered by the court to be paid to the claimant by the defendant in the proceedings;

(b) any amount awarded to the claimant by the court in respect of so much of the claim as is for an amount of money (excluding any amount awarded in respect of the claimant's costs);

(c) the value of any non-monetary benefit awarded to the claimant.

(6) An order under subsection (4)—

(a) must provide that rules made under the order may include provision as to the assessment of whether a judgment is at least as advantageous as an offer to settle, and

(b) may provide that such rules may make provision as to the calculation of the value of a non-monetary benefit awarded to a claimant.

(7) Conditions prescribed under subsection (1)(d) or (4)(d) may, in particular, include conditions relating to—

(a) the nature of the claim;

(b) the amount of money awarded to the claimant;

(c) the value of the non-monetary benefit awarded to the claimant.

(8) Orders under this section are to be made by the Lord Chancellor by statutory instrument.

(9) A statutory instrument containing an order under this section is subject to annulment in pursuance of a resolution of either House of Parliament.

(10) Rules of court and orders made under this section may make different provision in relation to different cases.

(11) In this section—

"civil proceedings" means proceedings to which rules of court made under the Civil Procedure Act 1997 apply;

"non-monetary claim" means a claim for a benefit other than an amount of money;

"prescribed" means prescribed by order made by the Lord Chancellor.

Referral fees

III FUND [173]

56 Rules against referral fees

(1) A regulated person is in breach of this section if—

(a) the regulated person refers prescribed legal business to another person and is paid or has been paid for the referral, or

(b) prescribed legal business is referred to the regulated person, and the regulated person pays or has paid for the referral.

(2) A regulated person is also in breach of this section if in providing legal services in the course of prescribed legal business the regulated person—

(a) arranges for another person to provide services to the client, and

(b) is paid or has been paid for making the arrangement.

(3) Section 59 defines "regulated person".

(4) "Prescribed legal business" means business that involves the provision of legal services to a client, where—

(a) the legal services relate to a claim or potential claim for damages for personal injury or death,

(b) the legal services relate to any other claim or potential claim for damages arising out of circumstances involving personal injury or death, or

(c) the business is of a description specified in regulations made by the Lord Chancellor.

(5) There is a referral of prescribed legal business if—

(a) a person provides information to another,

(b) it is information that a provider of legal services would need to make an offer to the client to provide relevant services, and

(c) the person providing the information is not the client;

and "relevant services" means any of the legal services that the business involves.

(6) "Legal services" means services provided by a person which consist of or include legal activities (within the meaning of the Legal Services Act 2007) carried on by or on behalf of that person; and a provider of legal services is a person authorised to carry on a reserved legal activity within the meaning of that Act.

(7) "Client"—

(a) where subsection (4)(a) applies, means the person who makes or would make the claim;

(b) where subsection (4)(c) applies, has the meaning given by the regulations.

(8) Payment includes any form of consideration whether any benefit is received by the regulated person or by a third party (but does not include the provision of hospitality that is reasonable in the circumstances).

III FUND [174]

57 Effect of rules against referral fees

(1) The relevant regulator must ensure that it has appropriate arrangements for monitoring and enforcing the restrictions imposed on regulated persons by section 56.

(2) A regulator may make rules for the purposes of subsection (1).

(3) The rules may in particular provide for the relevant regulator to exercise in relation to anything done in breach of that section any powers (subject to subsections (5) and (6)) that the regulator would have in relation to anything done by the regulated person in breach of another restriction.

(4) Where the relevant regulator is the Financial Conduct Authority, section 58 applies instead of subsections (1) to (3) (and (7) to (9)).

(5) A breach of section 56—

- (a) does not make a person guilty of an offence, and
- (b) does not give rise to a right of action for breach of statutory duty.

(6) A breach of section 56 does not make anything void or unenforceable, but a contract to make or pay for a referral or arrangement in breach of that section is unenforceable.

(7) Subsection (8) applies in a case where—

- (a) a referral of prescribed legal business has been made by or to a regulated person, or
- (b) a regulated person has made an arrangement as mentioned in section 56(2)(a),

and it appears to the regulator that a payment made to or by the regulated person may be a payment for the referral or for making the arrangement (a "referral fee").

(8) Rules under subsection (2) may provide for the payment to be treated as a referral fee unless the regulated person shows that the payment was made—

- (a) as consideration for the provision of services, or
- (b) for another reason,

and not as a referral fee.

(9) For the purposes of provision made by virtue of subsection (8) a payment that would otherwise be regarded as consideration for the provision of services of any description may be treated as a referral fee if it exceeds the amount specified in relation to services of that description in regulations made by the Lord Chancellor.

FUNDING

III FUND [175]

58 Regulation by FCA

(1) The Treasury may make regulations to enable the Financial Conduct Authority, where it is the relevant regulator, to take action for monitoring and enforcing compliance with the restrictions imposed on regulated persons by section 56.

(2) The regulations may apply, or make provision corresponding to, any of the provisions of the Financial Services and Markets Act 2000 with or without modification.

(3) Those provisions include in particular—

- (a) provisions as to investigations, including powers of entry and search and criminal offences;
- (b) provisions for the grant of an injunction in relation to a contravention or anticipated contravention;
- (c) provisions giving Ministers or the Financial Conduct Authority powers to make subordinate legislation;
- (d) provisions for the Financial Conduct Authority to charge fees.

(4) The regulations may make provision corresponding to the provision that may be made by virtue of section 57(7) to (9) (but as if the reference to the Lord Chancellor were a reference to the Treasury).

(5) The power to make regulations under this section is subject to section 57(5) and (6).

III FUND [176]

59 Regulators and regulated persons

(1) In relation to a referral of business within section 56(4)(a)—

- (a) a regulator is any person listed in column 1 below;
- (b) a regulated person is any person listed in column 2;

(c) a regulator in column 1 is the relevant regulator in relation to the corresponding person in column 2.

1 Regulator	*2 Regulated person*
the Financial Conduct Authority	an authorised person (within the meaning of the Financial Services and Markets Act 2000) of a description specified in regulations made by the Treasury
the Claims Management Regulator	a person authorised by the Regulator under section 5(1)(a) of the Compensation Act 2006 to provide regulated claims management services
the General Council of the Bar	a person authorised by the Council to carry on a reserved legal activity within the meaning of the Legal Services Act 2007
the Law Society	a person authorised by the Society to carry on a reserved legal activity within the meaning of the Legal Services Act 2007
a regulatory body specified for the purposes of this subsection in regulations made by the Lord Chancellor	a person of a description specified in the regulations in relation to the body

(2) In relation to a referral of prescribed legal business of any other kind—

(a) a regulator is any person listed in column 1 below and specified in relation to business of that kind in regulations made by the Lord Chancellor;

(b) a regulated person is any person specified in accordance with column 2 in relation to business of that kind;

(c) a person specified under paragraph (a) in relation to business of that kind is the relevant regulator in relation to a person specified in accordance with the corresponding entry in column 2 in relation to business of that kind.

1 Regulator	*2 Regulated person*
the Financial Conduct Authority	an authorised person (within the meaning of the Financial Services and Markets Act 2000) of a description specified in regulations made by the Treasury
the Claims Management Regulator	a person who is authorised by the Regulator under section 5(1)(a) of the Compensation Act 2006 to provide regulated claims management services and is of a description specified in regulations made by the Lord Chancellor
an approved regulator for the purposes of Part 3 of the Legal Services Act 2007 (approved legal activities);	a person who is authorised by the regulator to carry on a reserved legal activity and is of a description specified in regulations made by the Lord Chancellor

a licensing authority for the purposes of Part 5 of that Act (alternative business structures)	a person who is licensed by the authority to carry on a reserved legal activity and is of a description specified in regulations made by the Lord Chancellor

III FUND [177]

60 Referral fees: regulations

(1) This section applies to any regulations under sections 56 to 59.

(2) The regulations are to be made by statutory instrument.

(3) The power to make the regulations includes power to make consequential, supplementary, incidental, transitional, transitory or saving provision.

(4) A statutory instrument containing the regulations may not be made unless a draft of the instrument has been laid before, and approved by a resolution of, each House of Parliament.

Pro bono representation

III FUND [178]

61 Payments in respect of pro bono representation before the Supreme Court

(1) In section 194 of the Legal Services Act 2007 (power for certain courts to order losing party to make payment to charity where other party is represented pro bono) in subsection (10) for the definition of "civil court" substitute—

""civil court" means—

(a) the Supreme Court when it is dealing with a relevant civil appeal,

(b) the civil division of the Court of Appeal,

(c) the High Court, or

(d) any county court;

"relevant civil appeal" means an appeal to the Supreme Court—

(a) from the High Court in England and Wales under Part 2 of the Administration of Justice Act 1969,

(b) from the Court of Appeal under section 40(2) of the Constitutional Reform Act 2005, or

(c) under section 13 of the Administration of Justice Act 1960 (appeal in cases of contempt of court) other than an appeal from an order or decision made in the exercise of jurisdiction to punish for criminal contempt of court;".

(2) This section applies in relation to appeals to the Supreme Court only where the decision, order or judgment that is the subject of the appeal is made or given on or after the day on which this section comes into force.

Costs in criminal cases

III FUND [179]

62 Costs in criminal cases

(1) Schedule 7 (costs in criminal cases) has effect.

(2) Schedule 8 (costs in criminal cases: service courts) has effect.

SCHEDULE 1
CIVIL LEGAL SERVICES

Section 9

PART 1
SERVICES

Care, supervision and protection of children

III FUND [180]

1 (1) Civil legal services provided in relation to—
(a) orders under section 25 of the Children Act 1989 ("the 1989 Act") (secure accommodation);
(b) orders under Part 4 of the 1989 Act (care and supervision);
(c) orders under Part 5 of the 1989 Act (protection of children);
(d) approval by a court under paragraph 19 of Schedule 2 to the 1989 Act (arrangements to assist children to live abroad);
(e) parenting orders under section 8 of the Crime and Disorder Act 1998 ("the 1998 Act");
(f) child safety orders under section 11 of the 1998 Act;
(g) orders for contact under section 26 of the Adoption and Children Act 2002 ("the 2002 Act");
(h) applications for leave of the court to remove a child from a person's custody under section 36 of the 2002 Act;
(i) placement orders, recovery orders or adoption orders under Chapter 3 of Part 1 of the 2002 Act (see sections 21, 41 and 46 of that Act);
(j) orders under section 84 of the 2002 Act (parental responsibility prior to adoption abroad);
(k) orders under section 119 of the Social Services and Well-being (Wales) Act 2014 ("the 2014 Act") (secure accommodation);
(l) approval by a court under section 124 of the 2014 Act (arrangements to assist children to live abroad).

(2) Civil legal services provided in relation to an order under an enactment made—
(a) as an alternative to an order mentioned in sub-paragraph (1), or
(b) in proceedings heard together with proceedings relating to such an order.

Exclusions

(3) Sub-paragraphs (1) and (2) are subject to the exclusions in Parts 2 and 3 of this Schedule.

Definitions

(4) In this paragraph "children" means persons under the age of 18.

Special educational needs

2 (1) Civil legal services provided in relation to—
(a) matters arising under *Part 4 of the Education Act 1996* [Part 2 of the Additional Learning Needs and Education Tribunal (Wales) Act 2018] or Part 3 of the Children and Families Act 2014 (special educational needs);
(b) *assessments relating to learning difficulties under section 140 of the Learning and Skills Act 2000.*

Exclusions

(2) Sub-paragraph (1) is subject to the exclusions in Parts 2 and 3 of this Schedule.

Abuse of child or vulnerable adult

3 (1) Civil legal services provided in relation to abuse of an individual that took place at a time when the individual was a child or vulnerable adult, but only where—

(a) the services are provided to the individual, or

(b) the individual has died and the services are provided—

(i) to the individual's personal representative, or

(ii) for the purposes of a claim under the Fatal Accidents Act 1976 for the benefit of the individual's dependants.

General exclusions

(2) Sub-paragraph (1) is subject to—

(a) the exclusions in Part 2 of this Schedule, with the exception of paragraphs 1, 2, 3, 8 and 12 of that Part, and

(b) the exclusion in Part 3 of this Schedule.

Specific exclusions

(3) The services described in sub-paragraph (1) do not include services provided in relation to clinical negligence.

(4) The services described in sub-paragraph (1) do not include services provided in relation to a matter arising under a family enactment.

Definitions

(5) In this paragraph—

"abuse" means physical or mental abuse, including—

(a) sexual abuse, and

(b) abuse in the form of violence, neglect, maltreatment and exploitation;

"child" means a person under the age of 18;

"clinical negligence" means breach of a duty of care or trespass to the person committed in the course of the provision of clinical or medical services (including dental or nursing services);

"family enactment" has the meaning given in paragraph 12;

"personal representative", in relation to an individual who has died, means—

(a) a person responsible for administering the individual's estate under the law of England and Wales, Scotland or Northern Ireland, or

(b) a person who, under the law of another country or territory, has functions equivalent to those of administering the individual's estate;

"vulnerable adult" means a person aged 18 or over whose ability to protect himself or herself from abuse is significantly impaired through physical or mental disability or illness, through old age or otherwise.

Working with children and vulnerable adults

4 (1) Civil legal services provided in relation to—

(a) the inclusion of a person in a barred list or the removal of a person from a barred list;

(b) a disqualification order under section 28, 29 or 29A of the Criminal Justice and Court Services Act 2000 (disqualification from working with children);

(c) a direction under section 142 of the Education Act 2002 (prohibition from teaching etc).

Exclusions

(2) Sub-paragraph (1) is subject to the exclusions in Parts 2 and 3 of this Schedule.

Definitions

(3) In this paragraph "barred list" means a list maintained under—

(a) section 2 of the Safeguarding Vulnerable Groups Act 2006 (persons barred from regulated activities relating to children or vulnerable adults);

(b) section 81 of the Care Standards Act 2000;

(c) section 1 of the Protection of Children Act 1999.

Mental health and mental capacity

5 (1) Civil legal services provided in relation to matters arising under—

(a) the Mental Health Act 1983;

(b) paragraph 5(2) of the Schedule to the Repatriation of Prisoners Act 1984;

(c) the Mental Capacity Act 2005.

General exclusions

(2) Sub-paragraph (1) is subject to the exclusions in Parts 2 and 3 of this Schedule.

Specific exclusion

(3) The services described in sub-paragraph (1) do not include services provided in relation to—

(a) the creation of lasting powers of attorney under the Mental Capacity Act 2005, or

(b) the making of advance decisions under that Act.

(4) Sub-paragraph (3) does not exclude services provided in relation to determinations and declarations by a court under the Mental Capacity Act 2005 as to the validity, meaning, effect or applicability of—

(a) a lasting power of attorney that has been created, or

(b) an advance decision that has been made.

Community care

6 (1) Civil legal services provided in relation to community care services.

Exclusions

(2) Sub-paragraph (1) is subject to the exclusions in Parts 2 and 3 of this Schedule.

Definitions

(3) In this paragraph—

"community care services" means services which a relevant person may provide or arrange to be provided under—

(a)–(d) . . .;

(e) section 117 of the Mental Health Act 1983 (after-care);

(f) section 17 of the Children Act 1989 ("the 1989 Act") (provision of services for children in need);

(g) section 20 of the 1989 Act (provision of accommodation for children);

(h) sections 22A, 22B and 22C of the 1989 Act (accommodation and maintenance for children in care and looked after children);

(i) sections 23B and 23C of the 1989 Act (local authority functions in respect of relevant children);

(j) sections 24, 24A and 24B of the 1989 Act (provision of services for persons qualifying for advice and assistance);

(k)–(m) . . .;

(n) Part 1 of the Care Act 2014 (local authority's functions of meeting adult's needs for care and support);

(o) section 15 of the Social Services and Well-being (Wales) Act 2014 ("the 2014 Act") (preventative services);

(p) Part 4 of the 2014 Act (local authority's functions of meeting a person's needs for care and support);

(q) section 76 of the 2014 Act (provision of accommodation for children);

(r) sections 79, 80 and 81 of the 2014 Act (accommodation and maintenance for children in care and looked after children);

(s) sections 105 to 116 of the 2014 Act (local authority support for certain children);

"relevant person" means—

(a) a district council;

(b) a county council;

(c) a county borough council;

(d) a London borough council;

(e) the Common Council of the City of London;

(f) a Primary Care Trust established under section 18 of the National Health Service Act 2006;

(g) a Local Health Board established under section 11 of the National Health Service (Wales) Act 2006;

(h) any other person prescribed for the purposes of this paragraph.

Facilities for disabled persons

7 (1) Civil legal services provided in relation to grants under Part 1 of the Housing Grants, Construction and Regeneration Act 1996 for the provision of facilities for disabled persons.

Exclusions

(2) Sub-paragraph (1) is subject to the exclusions in Parts 2 and 3 of this Schedule.

Definitions

(3) In this paragraph "disabled person" has the meaning given in section 100 of the Housing Grants, Construction and Regeneration Act 1996.

Appeals relating to welfare benefits

8 (1) Civil legal services provided in relation to an appeal on a point of law to the Upper Tribunal, the Court of Appeal or the Supreme Court relating to a benefit, allowance, payment, credit or pension under—

(a) a social security enactment,

(b) the Vaccine Damage Payments Act 1979, or

(c) Part 4 of the Child Maintenance and Other Payments Act 2008.

Exclusions

(2) Sub-paragraph (1) is subject to—

(a) the exclusions in Part 2 of this Schedule, with the exception of paragraphs 1 and 15 of that Part, and

(b) the exclusion in Part 3 of this Schedule.

Definitions

(3) In this paragraph "social security enactment" means—

(a) the Social Security Contributions and Benefits Act 1992,

(b) the Jobseekers Act 1995,

(c) the State Pension Credit Act 2002,

(d) the Tax Credits Act 2002,

(e) the Welfare Reform Act 2007,

(f) the Welfare Reform Act 2012, or

(g) any other enactment relating to social security.

Inherent jurisdiction of High Court in relation to children and vulnerable adults

9 (1) Civil legal services provided in relation to the inherent jurisdiction of the High Court in relation to children and vulnerable adults.

Exclusions

(2) Sub-paragraph (1) is subject to the exclusions in Parts 2 and 3 of this Schedule.

Definitions

(3) In this paragraph—

"adults" means persons aged 18 or over;

"children" means persons under the age of 18.

Unlawful removal of children

10 (1) Civil legal services provided to an individual in relation to the following orders and requirements where the individual is seeking to prevent the unlawful removal of a related child from the United Kingdom or to secure the return of a related child who has been unlawfully removed from the United Kingdom—

(a) a prohibited steps order or specific issue order (as defined in section 8(1) of the Children Act 1989);

(b) an order under section 33 of the Family Law Act 1986 for disclosure of the child's whereabouts;

(c) an order under section 34 of that Act for the child's return;

(d) a requirement under section 37 of that Act to surrender a passport issued to, or containing particulars of, the child.

(2) Civil legal services provided to an individual in relation to the following orders and applications where the individual is seeking to secure the return of a related child who has been unlawfully removed to a place in the United Kingdom—

(a) a prohibited steps order or specific issue order (as defined in section 8(1) of the Children Act 1989);

(b) an application under section 27 of the Family Law Act 1986 for registration of an order relating to the child;

(c) an order under section 33 of that Act for disclosure of the child's whereabouts;

(d) an order under section 34 of that Act for the child's return.

Exclusions

(3) Sub-paragraphs (1) and (2) are subject to the exclusions in Parts 2 and 3 of this Schedule.

Definitions

(4) For the purposes of this paragraph, a child is related to an individual if the individual is the child's parent or has parental responsibility for the child.

(5) In this paragraph "child" means a person under the age of 18.

Family homes and domestic violence

11 (1) Civil legal services provided in relation to home rights, occupation orders and non-molestation orders under Part 4 of the Family Law Act 1996.

(2) Civil legal services provided in relation to the following in circumstances arising out of a family relationship—

(a) an injunction following assault, battery or false imprisonment;

(b) the inherent jurisdiction of the High Court to protect an adult.

Exclusions

(3) Sub-paragraphs (1) and (2) are subject to—

(a) the exclusions in Part 2 of this Schedule, with the exception of paragraphs 3 and 11 of that Part, and

(b) the exclusion in Part 3 of this Schedule.

Definitions

(4) For the purposes of this paragraph—

(a) there is a family relationship between two people if they are associated with each other, and

(b) "associated" has the same meaning as in Part 4 of the Family Law Act 1996 (see section 62 of that Act).

(5) For the purposes of this paragraph, the Lord Chancellor may by regulations make provision about when circumstances arise out of a family relationship.

Victims of domestic violence and family matters

12 (1) Civil legal services provided to an adult ("A") in relation to a matter arising out of a family relationship between A and another individual ("B") where—

(a) there has been, or is a risk of, domestic violence between A and B, and

(b) A was, or is at risk of being, the victim of that domestic violence.

General exclusions

(2) Sub-paragraph (1) is subject to the exclusions in Part 2 of this Schedule, with the exception of paragraph 11 of that Part.

(3) But the exclusions described in sub-paragraph (2) are subject to the exception in sub-paragraph (4).

(4) The services described in sub-paragraph (1) include services provided in relation to conveyancing, but only where—

- (a) the services in relation to conveyancing are provided in the course of giving effect to a court order made in proceedings, and
- (b) services described in that sub-paragraph (other than services in relation to conveyancing) are being or have been provided in relation to those proceedings under arrangements made for the purposes of this Part of this Act.

(5) Sub-paragraph (1) is subject to the exclusion in Part 3 of this Schedule.

Specific exclusion

(6) The services described in sub-paragraph (1) do not include services provided in relation to a claim in tort in respect of the domestic violence.

Definitions

(7) For the purposes of this paragraph—

- (a) there is a family relationship between two people if they are associated with each other, and
- (b) "associated" has the same meaning as in Part 4 of the Family Law Act 1996 (see section 62 of that Act).

(8) For the purposes of this paragraph—

- (a) matters arising out of a family relationship include matters arising under a family enactment, and
- (b) (subject to paragraph (a)) the Lord Chancellor may by regulations make provision about when matters arise out of a family relationship.

(9) In this paragraph—

"adult" means a person aged 18 or over;

"domestic violence" means any incident, or pattern of incidents, of controlling, coercive or threatening behaviour, violence or abuse (whether psychological, physical, sexual, financial or emotional) between individuals who are associated with each other;

"family enactment" means—

- (a) section 17 of the Married Women's Property Act 1882 (questions between husband and wife as to property);
- (b) the Maintenance Orders (Facilities for Enforcement) Act 1920;
- (c) the Maintenance Orders Act 1950;
- (d) the Maintenance Orders Act 1958;
- (e) the Maintenance Orders (Reciprocal Enforcement) Act 1972;
- (f) Schedule 1 to the Domicile and Matrimonial Proceedings Act 1973 (staying of matrimonial proceedings) and corresponding provision in relation to civil partnerships made by rules of court under section 223 of the Civil Partnership Act 2004;
- (g) the Matrimonial Causes Act 1973;
- (h) the Inheritance (Provision for Family Dependants) Act 1975;
- (i) the Domestic Proceedings and Magistrates' Courts Act 1978;
- (j) Part 3 of the Matrimonial and Family Proceedings Act 1984 (financial relief after overseas divorce etc);
- (k) Parts 1 and 3 of the Family Law Act 1986 (child custody and declarations of status);
- (l) Parts 1 and 2 of the Children Act 1989 (orders with respect to children in family proceedings);
- (m) section 53 of, and Schedule 7 to, the Family Law Act 1996 (transfer of tenancies on divorce etc or separation of cohabitants);

(n) Chapters 2 and 3 of Part 2 of the Civil Partnership Act 2004 (dissolution, nullity and other proceedings and property and financial arrangements);

(o) section 54 of the Human Fertilisation and Embryology Act 2008 (applications for parental orders);

(p) section 51A of the Adoption and Children Act 2002 (post-adoption contact orders).

Protection of children and family matters

13 (1) Civil legal services provided to an adult ("A") in relation to the following orders and procedures where the child who is or would be the subject of the order is at risk of abuse from an individual other than A—

(a) orders under section 4(2A) of the Children Act 1989 ("the 1989 Act") (removal of father's parental responsibility);

(b) orders under section 6(7) of the 1989 Act (termination of appointment of guardian);

(c) orders mentioned in section 8(1) of the 1989 Act (child arrangements orders and other orders);

(d) special guardianship orders under Part 2 of the 1989 Act;

(e) orders under section 33 of the Family Law Act 1986 ("the 1986 Act") (disclosure of child's whereabouts);

(f) orders under section 34 of the 1986 Act (return of child).

(g) orders under section 51A of the Adoption and Children Act 2002 (post-adoption contact).

Exclusions

(2) Sub-paragraph (1) is subject to the exclusions in Parts 2 and 3 of this Schedule.

Definitions

(3) In this paragraph—

"abuse" means physical or mental abuse, including—

(a) sexual abuse, and

(b) abuse in the form of violence, neglect, maltreatment and exploitation;

"adult" means a person aged 18 or over;

"child" means a person under the age of 18.

Mediation in family disputes

14 (1) Mediation provided in relation to family disputes.

(2) Civil legal services provided in connection with the mediation of family disputes.

Exclusions

(3) Sub-paragraphs (1) and (2) are subject to the exclusions in Part 2 of this Schedule, with the exception of paragraph 11 of that Part.

(4) But the exclusions described in sub-paragraph (3) are subject to the exception in sub-paragraph (5).

(5) The services described in sub-paragraph (2) include services provided in relation to conveyancing, but only where—

(a) the services in relation to conveyancing are provided in the course of giving effect to arrangements for the resolution of a family dispute, and

(b) services described in that sub-paragraph or sub-paragraph (1) (other than services in relation to conveyancing) are being or have been provided in relation to the dispute under arrangements made for the purposes of this Part of this Act.

(6) Sub-paragraphs (1) and (2) are subject to the exclusion in Part 3 of this Schedule.

Definitions

(7) For the purposes of this paragraph—

(a) a dispute is a family dispute if it is a dispute between individuals about a matter arising out of a family relationship between the individuals,
(b) there is a family relationship between two individuals if they are associated with each other, and
(c) "associated" has the same meaning as in Part 4 of the Family Law Act 1996 (see section 62 of that Act).

(8) For the purposes of this paragraph—
(a) matters arising out of a family relationship include matters arising under a family enactment, and
(b) (subject to paragraph (a)) the Lord Chancellor may by regulations make provision about when matters arise out of a family relationship.

(9) In this paragraph—
"child" means a person under the age of 18;
"family enactment" has the meaning given in paragraph 12.

Children who are parties to family proceedings

15 (1) Civil legal services provided to a child in relation to family proceedings—
(a) where the child is, or proposes to be, the applicant or respondent;
(b) where the child is made a party to the proceedings by a court under rule 16.2 of the Family Procedure Rules;
(c) where the child is a party to the proceedings and is conducting, or proposes to conduct, the proceedings without a children's guardian or litigation friend in accordance with rule 16.6 of the Family Procedure Rules.

Exclusions

(2) Sub-paragraph (1) is subject to the exclusions in Parts 2 and 3 of this Schedule.

Definitions

(3) For the purposes of this paragraph—
(a) proceedings are family proceedings if they relate to a matter arising out of a family relationship,
(b) there is a family relationship between two individuals if they are associated with each other, and
(c) "associated" has the same meaning as in Part 4 of the Family Law Act 1996 (see section 62 of that Act).

(4) For the purposes of this paragraph—
(a) matters arising out of a family relationship include matters arising under a family enactment, and
(b) (subject to paragraph (a)) the Lord Chancellor may by regulations make provision about when matters arise out of a family relationship.

(5) In this paragraph—
"child" means a person under the age of 18;
"family enactment" has the meaning given in paragraph 12.

Female genital mutilation protection orders

15A (1) Civil legal services provided in relation to female genital mutilation protection orders under paragraph 1 of Schedule 2 to the Female Genital Mutilation Act 2003.

Exclusions

(2) Sub-paragraph (1) is subject to the exclusions in Parts 2 and 3 of this Schedule.

Forced marriage

16 (1) Civil legal services provided in relation to forced marriage protection orders under Part 4A of the Family Law Act 1996.

Exclusions

(2) Sub-paragraph (1) is subject to the exclusions in Parts 2 and 3 of this Schedule.

EU and international agreements concerning children

17 (1) Civil legal services provided in relation to—
(a) an application made to the Lord Chancellor under the 1980 European Convention on Child Custody for the recognition or enforcement in England and Wales of a decision relating to the custody of a child;
(b) an application made to the Lord Chancellor under the 1980 Hague Convention in respect of a child who is, or is believed to be, in England and Wales;
(c) the recognition or enforcement of a judgment in England and Wales in accordance with Article 21, 28, 41, 42 or 48 of the 2003 Brussels Regulation.

Exclusions

(2) Sub-paragraph (1) is subject to the exclusions in Parts 2 and 3 of this Schedule.

Definitions

(3) In this paragraph—

"the 1980 European Convention on Child Custody" means the European Convention on Recognition and Enforcement of Decisions concerning Custody of Children and on the Restoration of Custody of Children which was signed in Luxembourg on 20 May 1980;

"the 1980 Hague Convention" means the Convention on the Civil Aspects of International Child Abduction which was signed at The Hague on 25 October 1980;

"the 2003 Brussels Regulation" means Council Regulation (EC) No 2001/2003 of 27 November 2003 concerning jurisdiction and the recognition and enforcement of judgments in matrimonial matters and the matters of parental responsibility.

(4) For the purposes of this paragraph, an application is made to the Lord Chancellor if it is addressed to the Lord Chancellor or transmitted to the Lord Chancellor in accordance with section 3 or 14 of the Child Abduction and Custody Act 1985.

EU and international agreements concerning maintenance

18 (1) Civil legal services provided in relation to an application under the following for the recognition or enforcement in England and Wales of a maintenance order—
(a) the 1968 Brussels Convention;
(b) the 1973 Hague Convention;
(c) the 1989 Lugano Convention;
(d) the 2000 Brussels Regulation;
(e) the 2007 Lugano Convention.

(2) Civil legal services provided in relation to an application under Article 56 of the EU Maintenance Regulation (applications relating to maintenance decisions).

(3) Civil legal services provided to an individual in relation to proceedings in England and Wales relating to the recognition, enforceability or enforcement of a maintenance decision in circumstances in which the individual falls within Article 47(2) or (3) of the EU Maintenance Regulation (parties who benefited from free legal aid etc in Member State of origin).

(3A) Civil legal services provided in relation to an application under Article 10 of the 2007 Hague Convention (applications relating to maintenance decisions).

(3B) Civil legal services provided to an individual in relation to proceedings in England and Wales relating to the recognition or enforcement of a maintenance decision in circumstances in which—
(a) Article 17(b) of the 2007 Hague Convention (free legal assistance for persons who benefited from such assistance in State of origin) applies to the proceedings by virtue of Article 37(2) of that Convention (direct request to competent authority of Contracting State), and
(b) the individual falls within Article 17(b) as so applied.

Exclusions

(4) Sub-paragraphs (1) to (3B) are subject to—

(a) the exclusions in Part 2 of this Schedule, with the exception of paragraph 11 of that Part, and

(b) the exclusion in Part 3 of this Schedule.

Definitions

(5) In this paragraph—

"the 1968 Brussels Convention" means the Convention on jurisdiction and the enforcement of judgments in civil and commercial matters (including the Protocol annexed to that Convention) signed at Brussels on 27 September 1968;

"the 1973 Hague Convention" means the Convention on the recognition and enforcement of decisions relating to maintenance obligations concluded at The Hague on 2 October 1973;

"the 1989 Lugano Convention" means the Convention on jurisdiction and the enforcement of judgments in civil and commercial matters (including the Protocols annexed to that Convention) opened for signature at Lugano on 16 September 1988 and signed by the United Kingdom on 18 September 1989;

"the 2000 Brussels Regulation" means Council Regulation (EC) No 44/2001 of 22 December 2000 on jurisdiction and the recognition and enforcement of judgments in civil and commercial matters;

"the 2007 Hague Convention" means the Convention on the international recovery of child support and other forms of family maintenance concluded at The Hague on 23 November 2007;

"the 2007 Lugano Convention" means the Convention on jurisdiction and enforcement of judgments in civil and commercial matters, between the European Community and the Republic of Iceland, the Kingdom of Norway, the Swiss Confederation and the Kingdom of Denmark signed on behalf of the European Community on 30 October 2007;

"the EU Maintenance Regulation" means Council Regulation (EC) No 4/2009 of 18 December 2008 on jurisdiction, applicable law, recognition and enforcement of decisions and co-operation in matters relating to maintenance obligations;

"maintenance order", in relation to a convention or regulation listed in this paragraph, means a maintenance judgment within the meaning of that convention or regulation.

Judicial review

19 (1) Civil legal services provided in relation to judicial review of an enactment, decision, act or omission.

General exclusions

(2) Sub-paragraph (1) is subject to—

(a) the exclusions in Part 2 of this Schedule, with the exception of paragraphs 1, 2, 3, 4, 5, 6, 8, 12, 15, 16 and 18 of that Part, and

(b) the exclusion in Part 3 of this Schedule.

Specific exclusion: benefit to individual

(3) The services described in sub-paragraph (1) do not include services provided to an individual in relation to judicial review that does not have the potential to produce a benefit for the individual, a member of the individual's family or the environment.

(4) Sub-paragraph (3) does not exclude services provided in relation to a judicial review where the judicial review ceases to have the potential to produce such a benefit after civil legal services have been provided in relation to the judicial review under arrangements made for the purposes of this Part of this Act.

Specific exclusions: immigration cases

(5) The services described in sub-paragraph (1) do not include services provided in relation to judicial review in respect of an issue relating to immigration where—

(a) the same issue, or substantially the same issue, was the subject of a previous judicial review or an appeal to a court or tribunal,

(b) on the determination of the previous judicial review or appeal (or, if there was more than one, the latest one), the court, tribunal or other person hearing the case found against the applicant or appellant on that issue, and

FUNDING

(c) the services in relation to the new judicial review are provided before the end of the period of 1 year beginning with the day of that determination.

(6) The services described in sub-paragraph (1) do not include services provided in relation to judicial review of removal directions in respect of an individual where the directions were given not more than 1 year after the latest of the following—

(a) the making of the decision (or, if there was more than one, the latest decision) to remove the individual from the United Kingdom by way of removal directions;

(b) the refusal of leave to appeal against that decision;

(c) the determination or withdrawal of an appeal against that decision.

(7) Sub-paragraphs (5) and (6) do not exclude services provided to an individual in relation to—

(a) judicial review of a negative decision in relation to an asylum application (within the meaning of the EU Procedures Directive) where there is no right of appeal to the First-tier Tribunal against the decision;

(b) judicial review of certification under section 94 or 96 of the Nationality, Immigration and Asylum Act 2002 (certificate preventing or restricting appeal of immigration decision).

(8) Sub-paragraphs (5) and (6) do not exclude services provided in relation to judicial review of removal directions in respect of an individual where prescribed conditions relating to either or both of the following are met—

(a) the period between the individual being given notice of the removal directions and the proposed time for his or her removal;

(b) the reasons for proposing that period.

Definitions

(9) For the purposes of this paragraph an individual is a member of another individual's family if—

(a) they are relatives (whether of the full blood or half blood or by marriage or civil partnership),

(b) they are cohabitants (as defined in Part 4 of the Family Law Act 1996), or

(c) one has parental responsibility for the other.

(10) In this paragraph—

"EU Procedures Directive" means Council Directive 2005/85/EC of 1 December 2005 on minimum standards on procedures in Member States for granting and withdrawing refugee status;

"an issue relating to immigration" includes an issue relating to rights described in paragraph 30 of this Part of this Schedule;

"judicial review" means—

(a) the procedure on an application for judicial review (see section 31 of the Senior Courts Act 1981), but not including the procedure after the application is treated under rules of court as if it were not such an application, and

(b) any procedure in which a court, tribunal or other person mentioned in Part 3 of this Schedule is required by an enactment to make a decision applying the principles that are applied by the court on an application for judicial review;

"removal directions" means directions under—

(a) paragraphs 8 to 10A of Schedule 2 to the Immigration Act 1971 (removal of persons refused leave to enter and illegal entrants);

(b) paragraphs 12 to 14 of Schedule 2 to that Act (removal of seamen and aircrew);

(c) paragraph 1 of Schedule 3 to that Act (removal of persons liable to deportation);

(d) section 10 of the Immigration and Asylum Act 1999 (removal of certain persons unlawfully in the United Kingdom);

(e) . . .

Habeas corpus

20 (1) Civil legal services provided in relation to a writ of habeas corpus ad subjiciendum.

Exclusions

(2) Sub-paragraph (1) is subject to the exclusions in Parts 2 and 3 of this Schedule.

Abuse of position or powers by public authority

21 (1) Civil legal services provided in relation to abuse by a public authority of its position or powers.

General exclusions

(2) Sub-paragraph (1) is subject to—

(a) the exclusions in Part 2 of this Schedule, with the exception of paragraphs 1, 2, 3, 4, 5, 6, 8 and 12 of that Part, and

(b) the exclusion in Part 3 of this Schedule.

Specific exclusion

(3) The services described in sub-paragraph (1) do not include services provided in relation to clinical negligence.

Definitions

(4) For the purposes of this paragraph, an act or omission by a public authority does not constitute an abuse of its position or powers unless the act or omission—

(a) is deliberate or dishonest, and

(b) results in harm to a person or property that was reasonably foreseeable.

(5) In this paragraph—

"clinical negligence" means breach of a duty of care or trespass to the person committed in the course of the provision of clinical or medical services (including dental or nursing services);

"public authority" has the same meaning as in section 6 of the Human Rights Act 1998.

Breach of Convention rights by public authority

22 (1) Civil legal services provided in relation to—

(a) a claim in tort, or

(b) a claim for damages (other than a claim in tort),

in respect of an act or omission by a public authority that involves a significant breach of Convention rights by the authority.

General exclusions

(2) Sub-paragraph (1) is subject to—

(a) the exclusions in Part 2 of this Schedule, with the exception of paragraphs 1, 2, 3, 4, 5, 6, 8 and 12 of that Part, and

(b) the exclusion in Part 3 of this Schedule.

Specific exclusion

(3) The services described in sub-paragraph (1) do not include services provided in relation to clinical negligence.

Definitions

(4) In this paragraph—

"clinical negligence" means breach of a duty of care or trespass to the person committed in the course of the provision of clinical or medical services (including dental or nursing services);

"Convention rights" has the same meaning as in the Human Rights Act 1998;

"public authority" has the same meaning as in section 6 of that Act.

Clinical negligence and severely disabled infants

23 (1) Civil legal services provided in relation to a claim for damages in respect of clinical negligence which caused a neurological injury to an individual ("V") as a

result of which V is severely disabled, but only where the first and second conditions are met.

(2) The first condition is that the clinical negligence occurred—

(a) while V was in his or her mother's womb, or

(b) during or after V's birth but before the end of the following period—

(i) if V was born before the beginning of the 37th week of pregnancy, the period of 8 weeks beginning with the first day of what would have been that week;

(ii) if V was born during or after the 37th week of pregnancy, the period of 8 weeks beginning with the day of V's birth.

(3) The second condition is that—

(a) the services are provided to V, or

(b) V has died and the services are provided to V's personal representative.

General exclusions

(4) Sub-paragraph (1) is subject to—

(a) the exclusions in Part 2 of this Schedule, with the exception of paragraphs 1, 2, 3 and 8 of that Part, and

(b) the exclusion in Part 3 of this Schedule.

Definitions

(5) In this paragraph—

"birth" means the moment when an individual first has a life separate from his or her mother and references to an individual being born are to be interpreted accordingly;

"clinical negligence" means breach of a duty of care or trespass to the person committed in the course of the provision of clinical or medical services (including dental or nursing services);

"disabled" means physically or mentally disabled;

"personal representative", in relation to an individual who has died, means—

(a) a person responsible for administering the individual's estate under the law of England and Wales, Scotland or Northern Ireland, or

(b) a person who, under the law of another country or territory, has functions equivalent to those of administering the individual's estate.

Special Immigration Appeals Commission

24 (1) Civil legal services provided in relation to proceedings before the Special Immigration Appeals Commission.

Exclusions

(2) Sub-paragraph (1) is subject to the exclusions in Parts 2 and 3 of this Schedule.

Immigration: detention

25 (1) Civil legal services provided in relation to—

(a) detention under the authority of an immigration officer;

(b) detention under Schedule 3 to the Immigration Act 1971;

(c) detention under section 62 of the Nationality, Immigration and Asylum Act 2002;

(d) detention under section 36 of the UK Borders Act 2007.

Exclusions

(2) Sub-paragraph (1) is subject to the exclusions in Parts 2 and 3 of this Schedule.

Immigration: *temporary admission* [conditions of immigration bail: persons liable to examination or removal]

26 (1) *Civil legal services provided in relation to temporary admission to the United Kingdom under—* [Civil legal services provided in relation to conditions of

immigration bail where the services are provided to a person who is liable to detention under—

(a) *paragraph 21 of Schedule 2 to the Immigration Act 1971;* [paragraph 16(1), (1A) or (2) of Schedule 2 to the Immigration Act 1971 (detention of persons liable to examination or removal);]

(b) *section 62 of the Nationality, Immigration and Asylum Act 2002.* [section 62 of the Nationality, Immigration and Asylum Act 2002 (detention by Secretary of State of persons liable to examination or removal).]

Exclusions

(2) Sub-paragraph (1) is subject to the exclusions in Parts 2 and 3 of this Schedule.

Immigration: *residence etc restrictions* [conditions of immigration bail (deportation)]

27 (1) *Civil legal services provided in relation to restrictions imposed under—* [Civil legal services provided in relation to conditions of immigration bail where the services are provided to a person who is liable to detention under—]

(a) *paragraph 2(5) or 4 of Schedule 3 to the Immigration Act 1971 (residence etc restrictions pending deportation);* [paragraph 2(1), (2) or (3) of Schedule 3 to the Immigration Act 1971 (detention or control pending deportation);]

(b) *section 71 of the Nationality, Immigration and Asylum Act 2002 (residence etc restrictions on asylum-seekers).* [section 36(1) of the UK Borders Act 2007 (detention pending deportation of criminals).]

(2) Sub-paragraph (1) is subject to the exclusions in Parts 2 and 3 of this Schedule.

[Immigration: conditions imposed under other provisions

27A (1) Civil legal services provided in relation to—

(a) conditions imposed on a person released on bail under paragraph 2(1A) of Schedule 3 to the Immigration Act 1971 (detention or control pending deportation);

(b) conditions imposed on a person under section 71(2) of the Nationality, Immigration and Asylum Act 2002 (asylum-seeker: residence, &c restriction).

Exclusions

(2) Sub-paragraph (1) is subject to the exclusions in Parts 2 and 3 of this Schedule.]

Immigration: victims of domestic violence and indefinite leave to remain

28 (1) Civil legal services provided to an individual ("V") in relation to an application by V for indefinite leave to remain in the United Kingdom on the grounds that—

(a) V was given leave to enter or remain in the United Kingdom for a limited period as the partner of another individual present and settled in the United Kingdom, and

(b) V's relationship with the other individual broke down permanently because V was the victim of domestic violence.

General exclusions

(2) Sub-paragraph (1) is subject to the exclusions in Parts 2 and 3 of this Schedule.

Specific exclusion

(3) The services described in sub-paragraph (1) do not include attendance at an interview conducted on behalf of the Secretary of State with a view to reaching a decision on an application.

Definitions

(4) For the purposes of this paragraph, one individual is a partner of another if—

(a) they are married to each other,

(b) they are civil partners of each other, or
(c) they are cohabitants.

(5) In this paragraph—

"cohabitant" has the same meaning as in Part 4 of the Family Law Act 1996 (see section 62 of that Act);

"domestic violence" means any incident, or pattern of incidents, of controlling, coercive or threatening behaviour, violence or abuse (whether psychological, physical, sexual, financial or emotional) between individuals who are associated with each other (within the meaning of section 62 of the Family Law Act 1996);

"indefinite leave to remain in the United Kingdom" means leave to remain in the United Kingdom under the Immigration Act 1971 which is not limited as to duration;

"present and settled in the United Kingdom" has the same meaning as in the rules made under section 3(2) of the Immigration Act 1971.

Immigration: victims of domestic violence and residence cards

29 (1) Civil legal services provided to an individual ("V") in relation to a residence card application where V—

(a) has ceased to be a family member of a qualified person on the termination of the marriage or civil partnership of the qualified person,
(b) is a family member who has retained the right of residence by virtue of satisfying the conditions in regulation 10(5) of the Immigration (European Economic Area) Regulations 2006 (SI 2006/1003) ("the 2006 Regulations"), and
(c) has satisfied the condition in regulation 10(5)(d)(iv) of the 2006 Regulations on the ground that V or a family member of V was the victim of domestic violence while the marriage or civil partnership of the qualified person was subsisting.

General exclusions

(2) Sub-paragraph (1) is subject to the exclusions in Parts 2 and 3 of this Schedule.

Specific exclusion

(3) The services described in sub-paragraph (1) do not include attendance at an interview conducted on behalf of the Secretary of State with a view to reaching a decision on an application.

Definitions

(4) In this paragraph—

"domestic violence" means any incident, or pattern of incidents, of controlling, coercive or threatening behaviour, violence or abuse (whether psychological, physical, sexual, financial or emotional) between individuals who are associated with each other (within the meaning of section 62 of the Family Law Act 1996);

"family member" has the same meaning as in the 2006 Regulations (see regulations 7 and 9);

"family member who has retained the right of residence" has the same meaning as in the 2006 Regulations (see regulation 10);

"qualified person" has the same meaning as in the 2006 Regulations (see regulation 6);

"residence card application" means—

(a) an application for a residence card under regulation 17 of the 2006 Regulations, or
(b) an application for a permanent residence card under regulation 18(2) of the 2006 Regulations.

Immigration: rights to enter and remain

30 (1) Civil legal services provided in relation to rights to enter, and to remain in, the United Kingdom arising from—

(a) the Refugee Convention;
(b) Article 2 or 3 of the Human Rights Convention;
(c) the Temporary Protection Directive;

(d) the Qualification Directive.

General exclusions

(2) Sub-paragraph (1) is subject to the exclusions in Parts 2 and 3 of this Schedule.

Specific exclusion

(3) The services described in sub-paragraph (1) do not include attendance at an interview conducted on behalf of the Secretary of State with a view to reaching a decision on a claim in respect of the rights mentioned in that sub-paragraph, except where regulations provide otherwise.

Definitions

(4) In this paragraph—

"the Human Rights Convention" means the Convention for the Protection of Human Rights and Fundamental Freedoms, agreed by the Council of Europe at Rome on 4 November 1950 as it has effect for the time being in relation to the United Kingdom;

"the Qualification Directive" means Council Directive 2004/83/EC of 29 April 2004 on minimum standards for the qualification and status of third country nationals or stateless persons as refugees or as persons who otherwise need international protection and the content of the protection granted;

"the Refugee Convention" means the Convention relating to the Status of Refugees done at Geneva on 28 July 1951 and the Protocol to the Convention;

"the Temporary Protection Directive" means Council Directive 2001/55/EC of 20 July 2001 on minimum standards for giving temporary protection in the event of a mass influx of displaced persons and on measures promoting a balance of efforts between Member States in receiving such persons and bearing the consequences thereof.

Immigration: accommodation for asylum-seekers etc

31 (1) Civil legal services provided in relation to the Secretary of State's powers to provide, or arrange for the provision of, accommodation under—

(a) section *4 or* 95 of the Immigration and Asylum Act 1999 (accommodation for *persons temporarily admitted and* asylum-seekers);

(b) section 17 of the Nationality, Immigration and Asylum Act 2002 (support for destitute asylum-seekers).

Exclusions

(2) Sub-paragraph (1) is subject to the exclusions in Parts 2 and 3 of this Schedule.

Victims of trafficking in human beings

32 (1) Civil legal services provided to an individual in relation to an application by the individual for leave to enter, or to remain in, the United Kingdom where—

(a) there has been a conclusive determination that the individual is a victim of trafficking in human beings, or

(b) there are reasonable grounds to believe that the individual is such a victim and there has not been a conclusive determination that the individual is not such a victim.

(2) Civil legal services provided in relation to a claim under employment law arising in connection with the exploitation of an individual who is a victim of trafficking in human beings, but only where—

(a) the services are provided to the individual, or

(b) the individual has died and the services are provided to the individual's personal representative.

(3) Civil legal services provided in relation to a claim for damages arising in connection with the trafficking or exploitation of an individual who is a victim of trafficking in human beings, but only where—

(a) the services are provided to the individual, or

(b) the individual has died and the services are provided to the individual's personal representative.

Exclusions

(4) Sub-paragraph (1) is subject to the exclusions in Parts 2 and 3 of this Schedule.

(5) Sub-paragraphs (2) and (3) are subject to—

(a) the exclusions in Part 2 of this Schedule, with the exception of paragraphs 1, 2, 3, 4, 5, 6 and 8 of that Part, and

(b) the exclusion in Part 3 of this Schedule.

Definitions

(6) For the purposes of sub-paragraph (1)(b) there are reasonable grounds to believe that an individual is a victim of trafficking in human beings if a competent authority has determined for the purposes of Article 10 of the Trafficking Convention (identification of victims) that there are such grounds.

(7) For the purposes of sub-paragraph (1) there is a conclusive determination that an individual is or is not a victim of trafficking in human beings when, on completion of the identification process required by Article 10 of the Trafficking Convention, a competent authority concludes that the individual is or is not such a victim.

(8) In this paragraph—

"competent authority" means a person who is a competent authority of the United Kingdom for the purposes of the Trafficking Convention;

"employment" means employment under a contract of employment or a contract personally to do work and references to "employers" and "employees" are to be interpreted accordingly;

"employment law" means an enactment or rule of law relating to employment, including in particular an enactment or rule of law conferring powers or imposing duties on employers, conferring rights on employees or otherwise regulating the relations between employers and employees;

"exploitation" means a form of exploitation described in section 3 of the Modern Slavery Act 2015 (meaning of exploitation for purposes of human trafficking offence in section 2 of that Act);

"personal representative", in relation to an individual who has died, means—

(a) a person responsible for administering the individual's estate under the law of England and Wales, Scotland or Northern Ireland, or

(b) a person who, under the law of another country or territory, has functions equivalent to those of administering the individual's estate;

"the Trafficking Convention" means the Council of Europe Convention on Action against Trafficking in Human Beings (done at Warsaw on 16 May 2005);

"trafficking in human beings" has the same meaning as in the Trafficking Convention.

Victims of slavery, servitude or forced or compulsory labour

32A (1) Civil legal services provided to an individual in relation to an application by the individual for leave to enter, or to remain in, the United Kingdom where—

(a) there has been a conclusive determination that the individual is a victim of slavery, servitude or forced or compulsory labour, or

(b) there are reasonable grounds to believe that the individual is such a victim and there has not been a conclusive determination that the individual is not such a victim.

(2) Civil legal services provided in relation to a claim under employment law arising in connection with the conduct by virtue of which an individual who is a victim of slavery, servitude or forced or compulsory labour is such a victim, but only where—

(a) the services are provided to the individual, or

(b) the individual has died and the services are provided to the individual's personal representative.

(3) Civil legal services provided in relation to a claim for damages arising in connection with the conduct by virtue of which an individual who is a victim of slavery, servitude or forced or compulsory labour is such a victim, but only where—

(a) the services are provided to the individual, or

(b) the individual has died and the services are provided to the individual's personal representative.

Exclusions

(4) Sub-paragraph (1) is subject to the exclusions in Parts 2 and 3 of this Schedule.

(5) Sub-paragraphs (2) and (3) are subject to—

(a) the exclusions in Part 2 of this Schedule, with the exception of paragraphs 1, 2, 3, 4, 5, 6 and 8 of that Part, and

(b) the exclusion in Part 3 of this Schedule.

Definitions

(6) For the purposes of sub-paragraph (1)(b) there are reasonable grounds to believe that an individual is a victim of slavery, servitude or forced or compulsory labour if a competent authority has determined that there are such grounds.

(7) For the purposes of sub-paragraph (1) there is a conclusive determination that an individual is or is not a victim of slavery, servitude or forced or compulsory labour when a competent authority concludes that the individual is or is not such a victim.

(8) For the purposes of this paragraph "slavery", "servitude" and "forced or compulsory labour" have the same meaning as they have for the purposes of article 4 of the Human Rights Convention.

(9) The "Human Rights Convention" means the Convention for the Protection of Human Rights and Fundamental Freedoms, agreed by the Council of Europe at Rome on 4 November 1950, as it has effect for the time being in relation to the United Kingdom.

(10) The definitions of "competent authority", "employment", "employment law" and "personal representative" in paragraph 32(8) also apply for the purposes of this paragraph.

Loss of home

33 (1) Civil legal services provided to an individual in relation to—

(a) court orders for sale or possession of the individual's home, or

(b) the eviction from the individual's home of the individual or others.

(2) Civil legal services provided to an individual in relation to a bankruptcy order against the individual under Part 9 of the Insolvency Act 1986 where—

(a) the individual's estate includes the individual's home, and

(b) the petition for the bankruptcy order is or was presented by a person other than the individual,

including services provided in relation to a statutory demand under that Part of that Act.

General exclusions

(3) Sub-paragraphs (1) and (2) are subject to the exclusions in Part 2 of this Schedule, with the exception of paragraph 14 of that Part.

(4) But the exclusions described in sub-paragraph (3) are subject to the exceptions in sub-paragraphs (5) and (6).

(5) The services described in sub-paragraph (1) include services provided in relation to proceedings on an application under the Trusts of Land and Appointment of Trustees Act 1996 to which section 335A of the Insolvency Act 1986 applies (application by trustee of bankrupt's estate).

(6) The services described in sub-paragraph (1) include services described in any of paragraphs 3 to 6 or 8 of Part 2 of this Schedule to the extent that they are—

(a) services provided to an individual in relation to a counterclaim in proceedings for a court order for sale or possession of the individual's home, or

(b) services provided to an individual in relation to the unlawful eviction from the individual's home of the individual or others.

FUNDING

(7) Sub-paragraphs (1) and (2) are subject to the exclusion in Part 3 of this Schedule.

Specific exclusion

(8) The services described in sub-paragraph (1) do not include services provided in relation to—

(a) proceedings under the Matrimonial Causes Act 1973;

(b) proceedings under Chapters 2 and 3 of Part 2 of the Civil Partnership Act 2004 (dissolution, nullity and other proceedings and property and financial arrangements).

Definitions

(9) In this paragraph "home", in relation to an individual, means the house, caravan, houseboat or other vehicle or structure that is the individual's only or main residence, subject to sub-paragraph (10).

(10) References in this paragraph to an individual's home do not include a vehicle or structure occupied by the individual if—

(a) there are no grounds on which it can be argued that the individual is occupying the vehicle or structure otherwise than as a trespasser, and

(b) there are no grounds on which it can be argued that the individual's occupation of the vehicle or structure began otherwise than as a trespasser.

(11) In sub-paragraphs (9) and (10), the references to a caravan, houseboat or other vehicle include the land on which it is located or to which it is moored.

(12) For the purposes of sub-paragraph (10) individuals occupying, or beginning occupation, of a vehicle or structure as a trespasser include individuals who do so by virtue of—

(a) title derived from a trespasser, or

(b) a licence or consent given by a trespasser or a person deriving title from a trespasser.

(13) For the purposes of sub-paragraph (10) an individual who is occupying a vehicle or structure as a trespasser does not cease to be a trespasser by virtue of being allowed time to leave the vehicle or structure.

Homelessness

34 (1) Civil legal services provided to an individual who is homeless, or threatened with homelessness, in relation to the provision of accommodation and assistance for the individual under—

(a) Part 6 of the Housing Act 1996 (allocation of housing accommodation);

(b) Part 7 of that Act (homelessness).

(c) Part 2 of the Housing (Wales) Act 2014 (homelessness).

Exclusions

(2) Sub-paragraph (1) is subject to the exclusions in Parts 2 and 3 of this Schedule.

Definitions

(3) In this paragraph "homeless" and "threatened with homelessness" have the same meaning—

(a) as in section 175 of the Housing Act 1996 in cases where sub-paragraph (1) applies in relation to the provision of accommodation and assistance under—

(i) Part 6 of that Act as it relates to England;

(ii) Part 7 of that Act;

(b) as in section 55 of the Housing (Wales) Act 2014 in cases where sub-paragraph (1) applies in relation to the provision of accommodation and assistance under—

(i) Part 6 of the Housing Act 1996 as it relates to Wales;

(ii) Part 2 of the Housing (Wales) Act 2014.

Risk to health or safety in rented home

35 (1) Civil legal services provided to an individual in relation to the removal or reduction of a serious risk of harm to the health or safety of the individual or a relevant member of the individual's family where—

(a) the risk arises from a deficiency in the individual's home,

(b) the individual's home is rented or leased from another person, and

(c) the services are provided with a view to securing that the other person makes arrangements to remove or reduce the risk.

Exclusions

(2) Sub-paragraph (1) is subject to—

(a) the exclusions in Part 2 of this Schedule, with the exception of paragraphs 6 and 8 of that Part, and

(b) the exclusion in Part 3 of this Schedule.

Definitions

(3) For the purposes of this paragraph—

(a) a child is a relevant member of an individual's family if the individual is the child's parent or has parental responsibility for the child;

(b) an adult ("A") is a relevant member of an individual's family if—

(i) they are relatives (whether of the full blood or half blood or by marriage or civil partnership) or cohabitants, and

(ii) the individual's home is also A's home.

(4) In this paragraph—

"adult" means a person aged 18 or over;

"building" includes part of a building;

"child" means a person under the age of 18;

"cohabitant" has the same meaning as in Part 4 of the Family Law Act 1996 (see section 62(1) of that Act);

"deficiency" means any deficiency, whether arising as a result of the construction of a building, an absence of maintenance or repair, or otherwise;

"harm" includes temporary harm;

"health" includes mental health;

"home", in relation to an individual, means the house, caravan, houseboat or other vehicle or structure that is the individual's only or main residence, together with any garden or ground usually occupied with it.

Anti-social behaviour

36 (1) Civil legal services provided to an individual in relation to an application for, or proceedings in respect of, an injunction against the individual under section 1 of the Anti-social Behaviour, Crime and Policing Act 2014.

Exclusions

(2) Sub-paragraph (1) is subject to the exclusions in Parts 2 and 3 of this Schedule.

Protection from harassment

37 (1) Civil legal services provided in relation to—

(a) an injunction under section 3 or 3A of the Protection from Harassment Act 1997;

(b) the variation or discharge of a restraining order under section 5 or 5A of that Act.

Exclusions

(2) Sub-paragraph (1) is subject to the exclusions in Parts 2 and 3 of this Schedule.

Gang-related violence and drug-dealing activity

38 (1) Civil legal services provided in relation to injunctions under Part 4 of the Policing and Crime Act 2009 (injunctions to prevent gang-related violence and drug-dealing activity).

Exclusions

(2) Sub-paragraph (1) is subject to the exclusions in Parts 2 and 3 of this Schedule.

FUNDING

Sexual offences

39 (1) Civil legal services provided in relation to a sexual offence, but only where—

(a) the services are provided to the victim of the offence, or

(b) the victim of the offence has died and the services are provided to the victim's personal representative.

Exclusions

(2) Sub-paragraph (1) is subject to—

(a) the exclusions in Part 2 of this Schedule, with the exception of paragraphs 1, 2, 3, 8 and 12 of that Part, and

(b) the exclusion in Part 3 of this Schedule.

Definitions

(3) In this paragraph—

"personal representative", in relation to an individual who has died, means—

(a) a person responsible for administering the individual's estate under the law of England and Wales, Scotland or Northern Ireland, or

(b) a person who, under the law of another country or territory, has functions equivalent to those of administering the individual's estate;

"sexual offence" means—

(a) an offence under a provision of the Sexual Offences Act 2003 ("the 2003 Act"),

(b) an offence under section 1 of the Protection of Children Act 1978 ("the 1978 Act") (indecent photographs of children), and

(c) an offence under section 2 of the Modern Slavery Act 2015 (human trafficking) committed with a view to exploitation that consists of or includes behaviour within section 3(3) of that Act (sexual exploitation).

(4) The references in sub-paragraph (1) to a sexual offence include—

(a) incitement to commit a sexual offence,

(b) an offence committed by a person under Part 2 of the Serious Crime Act 2007 (encouraging or assisting crime) in relation to which a sexual offence is the offence which the person intended or believed would be committed,

(c) conspiracy to commit a sexual offence, and

(d) an attempt to commit a sexual offence.

(5) In this paragraph references to a sexual offence include conduct which would be an offence under a provision of the 2003 Act or section 1 of the 1978 Act but for the fact that it took place before that provision or section came into force.

(6) Conduct falls within the definition of a sexual offence for the purposes of this paragraph whether or not there have been criminal proceedings in relation to the conduct and whatever the outcome of any such proceedings.

Proceeds of crime

40 (1) Civil legal services provided in relation to—

(a) restraint orders under section 41 of the Proceeds of Crime Act 2002 ("the 2002 Act") including orders under section 41(7) of that Act (orders for ensuring that restraint order is effective);

(b) orders under section 47M of the 2002 Act (detention of property);

(c) directions under section 54(3) of the 2002 Act (distribution of funds in the hands of a receiver);

(d) directions under section 62 of the 2002 Act (action to be taken by receiver);

(e) orders under section 67A of the 2002 Act (realising property), including directions under section 67D of that Act (distribution of proceeds of realisation);

(f) orders under section 72 or 73 of the 2002 Act (compensation);
(g) applications under section 351 of the 2002 Act (discharge or variation of a production order or order to grant entry);
(h) applications under section 362 of the 2002 Act (discharge or variation of disclosure order);
(i) applications under section 369 of the 2002 Act (discharge or variation of customer information order);
(j) applications under section 375 of the 2002 Act (discharge or variation of account monitoring orders).

General exclusions

(2) Sub-paragraph (1) is subject to—
(a) the exclusions in Part 2 of this Schedule, with the exception of paragraph 14 of that Part, and
(b) the exclusion in Part 3 of this Schedule.

Specific exclusions

(3) Where a confiscation order has been made under Part 2 of the 2002 Act against a defendant, the services described in sub-paragraph (1) do not include services provided to the defendant in relation to—
(a) directions under section 54(3) of that Act (distribution of funds in the hands of a receiver), or
(b) directions under section 67D of that Act (distribution of proceeds of realisation),

that relate to property recovered pursuant to the order.

(4) Where a confiscation order has been made under Part 2 of the 2002 Act against a defendant and varied under section 29 of that Act, the services described in sub-paragraph (1) do not include services provided in relation to an application by the defendant under section 73 of that Act (compensation).

Inquests

41 (1) Civil legal services provided to an individual in relation to an inquest under the Coroners Act 1988 into the death of a member of the individual's family.

Exclusions

(2) Sub-paragraph (1) is subject to—
(a) the exclusions in Part 2 of this Schedule, with the exception of paragraph 1 of that Part, and
(b) the exclusion in Part 3 of this Schedule.

Definitions

(3) For the purposes of this paragraph an individual is a member of another individual's family if—
(a) they are relatives (whether of the full blood or half blood or by marriage or civil partnership),
(b) they are cohabitants (as defined in Part 4 of the Family Law Act 1996), or
(c) one has parental responsibility for the other.

Environmental pollution

42 (1) Civil legal services provided in relation to injunctions in respect of nuisance arising from prescribed types of pollution of the environment.

Exclusions

(2) Sub-paragraph (1) is subject to the exclusions in Parts 2 and 3 of this Schedule.

Equality

43 (1) Civil legal services provided in relation to contravention of the Equality Act 2010 or a previous discrimination enactment.

Exclusions

(2) Sub-paragraph (1) is subject to—

FUNDING

(a) the exclusions in Part 2 of this Schedule, with the exception of paragraph 15 of that Part, and
(b) the exclusion in Part 3 of this Schedule.

Definitions

(3) In this paragraph "previous discrimination enactment" means—
(a) the Equal Pay Act 1970;
(b) the Sex Discrimination Act 1975;
(c) the Race Relations Act 1976;
(d) the Disability Discrimination Act 1995;
(e) the Employment Equality (Religion or Belief) Regulations 2003 (SI 2003/1660);
(f) the Employment Equality (Sexual Orientation) Regulations 2003 (SI 2003/1661);
(g) the Equality Act 2006;
(h) the Employment Equality (Age) Regulations 2006 (SI 2006/1031);
(i) the Equality Act (Sexual Orientation) Regulations 2007 (SI 2007/1263).

(4) The reference in sub-paragraph (1) to contravention of the Equality Act 2010 or a previous discrimination enactment includes—
(a) breach of a term modified by, or included by virtue of, a provision that is an equality clause or equality rule for the purposes of the Equal Pay Act 1970 or the Equality Act 2010, and
(b) breach of a provision that is a non-discrimination rule for the purposes of the Equality Act 2010.

Cross-border disputes

44 (1) Civil legal services provided in relation to proceedings in circumstances in which the services are required to be provided under Council Directive 2002/8/EC of 27 January 2003 to improve access to justice in cross-border disputes by establishing minimum common rules relating to legal aid for such disputes.

No exclusions

(2) Sub-paragraph (1) is not subject to the exclusions in Parts 2 and 3 of this Schedule.

Terrorism prevention and investigation measures etc

45 (1) Civil legal services provided to an individual in relation to a TPIM notice relating to the individual.

(2) Civil legal services provided to an individual in relation to control order proceedings relating to the individual.

Exclusions

(3) Sub-paragraphs (1) and (2) are subject to the exclusions in Parts 2 and 3 of this Schedule.

(4) In this paragraph—

"control order proceedings" means proceedings described in paragraph 3(1)(a) to (e) of Schedule 8 to the Terrorism Prevention and Investigation Measures Act 2011 ("the 2011 Act");

"TPIM notice" means a notice under section 2(1) of the 2011 Act.

Extension of time for retention of travel documents

45A (1) Civil legal services provided in relation to proceedings under paragraph 8 of Schedule 1 to the Counter-Terrorism and Security Act 2015.

Exclusions

(2) Sub-paragraph (1) is subject to the exclusions in Parts 2 and 3 of this Schedule.

Connected matters

46 (1) Prescribed civil legal services provided, in prescribed circumstances, in connection with the provision of services described in a preceding paragraph of this Part of this Schedule.

Exclusions

(2) Sub-paragraph (1) is subject to—

(a) the exclusions in Parts 2 and 3 of this Schedule, except to the extent that regulations under this paragraph provide otherwise, and

(b) any other prescribed exclusions.

Amendment *In para 2, text in italic is deleted and text in square brackets is inserted by the Additional Learning Needs and Education Tribunal (Wales) Act 2018 with effect from a date to be appointed.*

In paras 26, 27 and 27A, text in italic is deleted and text in square brackets is inserted by the Immigration Act 2016 (Consequential Amendments) (Biometrics and Legal Aid) Regulations 2017, SI 2017/617, with effect from a date to be appointed.

Text in italic in para 31 is deleted by the Immigration Act 2016 with effect from a date to be appointed.

PART 2
EXCLUDED SERVICES

The services described in Part 1 of this Schedule do not include the services listed in this Part of this Schedule, except to the extent that Part 1 of this Schedule provides otherwise.

1 Civil legal services provided in relation to personal injury or death.

2 Civil legal services provided in relation to a claim in tort in respect of negligence.

3 Civil legal services provided in relation to a claim in tort in respect of assault, battery or false imprisonment.

4 Civil legal services provided in relation to a claim in tort in respect of trespass to goods.

5 Civil legal services provided in relation to a claim in tort in respect of trespass to land.

6 Civil legal services provided in relation to damage to property.

7 Civil legal services provided in relation to defamation or malicious falsehood.

8 Civil legal services provided in relation to a claim in tort in respect of breach of statutory duty.

9 Civil legal services provided in relation to conveyancing.

10 Civil legal services provided in relation to the making of wills.

11 Civil legal services provided in relation to matters of trust law.

12 (1) Civil legal services provided in relation to a claim for damages in respect of a breach of Convention rights by a public authority to the extent that the claim is made in reliance on section 7 of the Human Rights Act 1998.

(2) In this paragraph—

"Convention rights" has the same meaning as in the Human Rights Act 1998;

"public authority" has the same meaning as in section 6 of that Act.

13 Civil legal services provided in relation to matters of company or partnership law.

14 Civil legal services provided to an individual in relation to matters arising out of or in connection with—

(a) a proposal by that individual to establish a business,

(b) the carrying on of a business by that individual (whether or not the business is being carried on at the time the services are provided), or

FUNDING

(c) the termination or transfer of a business that was being carried on by that individual.

15 (1) Civil legal services provided in relation to a benefit, allowance, payment, credit or pension under—

(a) a social security enactment,
(b) the Vaccine Damage Payments Act 1979, or
(c) Part 4 of the Child Maintenance and Other Payments Act 2008.

(2) In this paragraph "social security enactment" means—

(a) the Social Security Contributions and Benefits Act 1992,
(b) the Jobseekers Act 1995,
(c) the State Pension Credit Act 2002,
(d) the Tax Credits Act 2002,
(e) the Welfare Reform Act 2007,
(f) the Welfare Reform Act 2012, or
(g) any other enactment relating to social security.

16 Civil legal services provided in relation to compensation under the Criminal Injuries Compensation Scheme.

17 Civil legal services provided in relation to changing an individual's name.

18 (1) Civil legal services provided in relation to judicial review of an enactment, decision, act or omission.

(2) In this paragraph "judicial review" means—

(a) the procedure on an application for judicial review (see section 31 of the Senior Courts Act 1981), but not including the procedure after the application is treated under rules of court as if it were not such an application, and
(b) any procedure in which a court, tribunal or other person mentioned in Part 3 of this Schedule is required by an enactment to make a decision applying the principles that are applied by the court on an application for judicial review.

PART 3
ADVOCACY: EXCLUSION AND EXCEPTIONS

The services described in Part 1 of this Schedule do not include advocacy, except as follows—

(a) those services include the types of advocacy listed in this Part of this Schedule, except to the extent that Part 1 of this Schedule provides otherwise;
(b) those services include other types of advocacy to the extent that Part 1 of this Schedule so provides.

Exceptions: courts

1 Advocacy in proceedings in the Supreme Court.

2 Advocacy in proceedings in the Court of Appeal.

3 Advocacy in proceedings in the High Court.

4 Advocacy in proceedings in the Court of Protection to the extent that they concern—

(a) a person's right to life,
(b) a person's liberty or physical safety,
(c) a person's medical treatment (within the meaning of the Mental Health Act 1983),

(d) a person's capacity to marry, to enter into a civil partnership or to enter into sexual relations, or

(e) a person's right to family life.

5 Advocacy in proceedings in the county court.

5A Advocacy in proceedings in the family court.

6 Advocacy in the following proceedings in the Crown Court—

(a) proceedings for the variation or discharge of an order under section 5 or 5A of the Protection from Harassment Act 1997 . . .

(aa) proceedings on an appeal under section 10(1)(b) of the Crime and Disorder Act 1998 against the making of a parenting order where an injunction is granted under section 1 of the Anti-social Behaviour, Crime and Policing Act 2014,

(b) proceedings under the Proceeds of Crime Act 2002 in relation to matters listed in paragraph 40 of Part 1 of this Schedule,

(c) proceedings on an appeal under section 46B of the Policing and Crime Act 2009,

(d) proceedings on an appeal under section 15 of the Anti-social Behaviour, Crime and Policing Act 2014, and

(e) proceedings for the variation or discharge of an order under paragraph 1 of Schedule 2 to the Female Genital Mutilation Act 2003.

7 Advocacy in a magistrates' court that falls within the description of civil legal services in any of the following provisions of Part 1 of this Schedule—

(a) paragraph 1(1)(e),

(b) paragraph 1(2) so far as relating to paragraph (1)(1)(e), and

(b) paragraphs 11(2), 12, 13(1)(e), 15, 17 (1)(a) and (b), 36 and 38.

8 Advocacy in the following proceedings in a magistrates' court—

(a) . . .

(b) *proceedings in relation to—*

(i) *bail under Schedule 2 to the Immigration Act 1971, or*

(ii) *arrest under Schedule 2 or 3 to that Act,*

(c) proceedings for the variation or discharge of an order under section 5 or 5A of the Protection from Harassment Act 1997,

(d) proceedings under the Proceeds of Crime Act 2002 in relation to matters listed in paragraph 40 of Part 1 of this Schedule, and

(e) proceedings for the variation or discharge of an order under paragraph 1 of Schedule 2 to the Female Genital Mutilation Act 2003.

Exceptions: tribunals

9 Advocacy in proceedings in the First-tier Tribunal under—

(a) the Mental Health Act 1983, or

(b) paragraph 5(2) of the Schedule to the Repatriation of Prisoners Act 1984.

10 Advocacy in proceedings in the Mental Health Review Tribunal for Wales.

11 Advocacy in proceedings in the First-tier Tribunal under—

(a) *Schedule 2 to the Immigration Act 1971, or*

(b) Part 5 of the Nationality, Immigration and Asylum Act 2002 [;

(c) Schedule 10 to the Immigration Act 2016].

12 Advocacy in proceedings in the First-tier Tribunal under—

(a) section 40A of the British Nationality Act 1981, or

(b) regulation 26 of the Immigration (European Economic Area) Regulations 2006 (SI 2006/1003),

FUNDING

but only to the extent that the proceedings concern contravention of the Equality Act 2010.

13 Advocacy in the First-tier Tribunal that falls within the description of civil legal services in paragraph 28, 29, 32(1) or 32A(1) of Part 1 of this Schedule.

14 Advocacy in proceedings in the First-tier Tribunal under—
- (a) section 4 or 4A of the Protection of Children Act 1999 (appeals and applications relating to list of barred from regulated activities with children or vulnerable adults),
- (b) section 86 or 87 of the Care Standards Act 2000 (appeals and applications relating to list of persons unsuitable to work with vulnerable adults),
- (c) section 32 of the Criminal Justice and Court Services Act 2000 (applications relating to disqualification orders), or
- (d) section 144 of the Education Act 2002 (appeals and reviews relating to direction prohibiting person from teaching etc).

15 Advocacy in proceedings in the Upper Tribunal arising out of proceedings within any of paragraphs 9 to 14 of this Part of this Schedule.

16 Advocacy in proceedings in the Upper Tribunal under section 4 of the Safeguarding Vulnerable Groups Act 2006.

17 Advocacy in proceedings in the Upper Tribunal under section 11 of the Tribunals, Courts and Enforcement Act 2007 (appeals on a point of law) from decisions made by the First-tier Tribunal or the *Special Educational Needs* [Education] Tribunal for Wales in proceedings under—
- (a) *Part 4 of the Education Act 1996 (special educational needs),* [Part 2 of the Additional Learning Needs and Education Tribunal (Wales) Act 2018,]
- (b) the Equality Act 2010, or
- (c) Part 3 of the Children and Families Act 2014 (children and young people in England with special educational needs or disabilities).

18 Advocacy in proceedings which are brought before the Upper Tribunal (wholly or primarily) to exercise its judicial review jurisdiction under section 15 of the Tribunals, Courts and Enforcement Act 2007.

19 Advocacy where judicial review applications are transferred to the Upper Tribunal from the High Court under section 31A of the Senior Courts Act 1981.

20 Advocacy in proceedings in the Employment Appeal Tribunal, but only to the extent that the proceedings concern contravention of the Equality Act 2010.

Other exceptions

21 Advocacy in proceedings in the Special Immigration Appeals Commission.

22 Advocacy in proceedings in the Proscribed Organisations Appeal Commission.

22A Advocacy in proceedings before a District Judge (Magistrates' Courts) under paragraph 8 of Schedule 1 to the Counter-Terrorism and Security Act 2015.

23 Advocacy in legal proceedings before any person to whom a case is referred (in whole or in part) in any proceedings within any other paragraph of this Part of this Schedule.

24 Advocacy in bail proceedings before any court which are related to proceedings within any other paragraph of this Part of this Schedule.

25 Advocacy in proceedings before any person for the enforcement of a decision in proceedings within any other paragraph of this Part of this Schedule.

Amendment *In paras 8 and 11, text in italic is deleted and text in square brackets is inserted by the Immigration Act 2016 (Consequential Amendments) (Biometrics and Legal Aid) Regulations 2017, SI 2017/617, with effect from a date to be appointed.*

In para 17, text in italic is deleted and text in square brackets is inserted by the Additional Learning Needs and Education Tribunal (Wales) Act 2018, with effect from a date to be appointed.

PART 4
INTERPRETATION

1 For the purposes of this Part of this Act, civil legal services are described in Part 1 of this Schedule if they are described in one of the paragraphs of that Part (other than in an exclusion), even if they are (expressly or impliedly) excluded from another paragraph of that Part.

2 References in this Schedule to an Act or instrument, or a provision of an Act or instrument—

(a) are references to the Act, instrument or provision as amended from time to time, and

(b) include the Act, instrument or provision as applied by another Act or instrument (with or without modifications).

3 References in this Schedule to services provided in relation to an act, omission or other matter of a particular description (however expressed) include services provided in relation to an act, omission or other matter alleged to be of that description.

4 References in this Schedule to services provided in relation to proceedings, orders and other matters include services provided when such proceedings, orders and matters are contemplated.

5 (1) Where a paragraph of Part 1 or 2 of this Schedule describes services that consist of or include services provided in relation to proceedings, the description is to be treated as including, in particular—

(a) services provided in relation to related bail proceedings,

(b) services provided in relation to preliminary or incidental proceedings,

(c) services provided in relation to a related appeal or reference to a court, tribunal or other person, and

(d) services provided in relation to the enforcement of decisions in the proceedings.

(2) Where a paragraph of Part 3 of this Schedule describes advocacy provided in relation to particular proceedings in or before a court, tribunal or other person, the description is to be treated as including services provided in relation to preliminary or incidental proceedings in or before the same court, tribunal or other person.

(3) Regulations may make provision specifying whether proceedings are or are not to be regarded as preliminary or incidental for the purposes of this paragraph.

6 For the purposes of this Schedule, regulations may make provision about—

(a) when services are provided in relation to a matter;

(b) when matters arise under a particular enactment;

(c) when proceedings are proceedings under a particular enactment;

(d) when proceedings are related to other proceedings.

7 In this Schedule "enactment" includes—

(a) an enactment contained in subordinate legislation (within the meaning of the Interpretation Act 1978), and

FUNDING

(b) an enactment contained in, or in an instrument made under, an Act or Measure of the National Assembly for Wales.

SCHEDULE 3
LEGAL AID FOR LEGAL PERSONS

Section 31

Legal persons

III FUND [181]

1 In this Schedule "legal person" means a person other than an individual.

Exceptional case determinations

2 (1) For the purposes of this Schedule, in relation to a legal person and civil legal services, advice, assistance or representation for the purposes of criminal proceedings, an exceptional case determination is a determination that sub-paragraph (2) or (3) is satisfied.

(2) This sub-paragraph is satisfied if it is necessary to make the services available to the legal person under this Part because failure to do so would be a breach of—

(a) the person's Convention rights (within the meaning of the Human Rights Act 1998), or

(b) any rights of the person to the provision of legal services that are enforceable EU rights.

(3) This sub-paragraph is satisfied if it is appropriate to make the services available to the legal person under this Part, in the particular circumstances of the case, having regard to any risk that failure to do so would be such a breach.

Civil legal aid

3 (1) Civil legal services are to be available to a legal person under this Part only if the Director—

(a) has made an exceptional case determination in relation to the person and the services, and

(b) has determined that the person qualifies for the services in accordance with this Part,

(and has not withdrawn either determination).

(2) Sections 11 and 12(1) apply in relation to a determination under sub-paragraph (1)(b) as they apply in relation to a determination under section 10(2)(b).

(3) Subsections (2) to (6) of section 12 apply in relation to a determination under this paragraph as they apply in relation to a determination under section 10.

(4) In sections 11 and 12 as applied by this paragraph, references to an individual include a legal person.

Advice and assistance for criminal proceedings

4 (1) Regulations may provide that prescribed advice and assistance is to be available under this Part to a legal person described in sub-paragraph (2) if—

(a) prescribed conditions are met,

(b) the Director has made an exceptional case determination in relation to the person and the advice and assistance (and has not withdrawn that determination), and

(c) the Director has determined that the legal person qualifies for such advice and assistance in accordance with the regulations (and has not withdrawn that determination).

(2) Those legal persons are—

(a) legal persons who are involved in investigations which may lead to criminal proceedings, and

(b) legal persons who are before a court, tribunal or other person in criminal proceedings.

(3) Subsections (3) to (9) of section 15 apply in relation to regulations under this paragraph (and decisions made under such regulations) as they apply in relation to regulations under that section (and decisions made under such regulations).

(4) In those subsections as applied by this paragraph, references to an individual include a legal person.

(5) In this paragraph "assistance" includes, in particular, assistance in the form of advocacy.

Representation for criminal proceedings

5 (1) Representation for the purposes of criminal proceedings is to be available under this Part to a legal person if—

(a) the person is a specified legal person in relation to the proceedings, or

(b) the proceedings involve the person resisting an appeal to the Crown Court otherwise than in an official capacity,

and the conditions in sub-paragraph (2) are met.

(2) Those conditions are that the Director—

(a) has made an exceptional case determination in relation to the legal person and representation for the purposes of the proceedings, and

(b) has determined (provisionally or otherwise) that the legal person qualifies for such representation in accordance with this Part,

(and has not withdrawn either determination).

(3) Where a legal person qualifies under this Part for representation for the purposes of criminal proceedings, representation is also to be available to the legal person for the purposes of any preliminary or incidental proceedings.

(4) Regulations under section 16(4) and (5) apply for the purposes of sub-paragraph (3) as they apply for the purposes of section 16(3), except to the extent that the regulations provide otherwise.

(5) Section 17(1)(b) applies in relation to an exceptional case determination under sub-paragraph (2)(a) as it applies in relation to a determination under section 16.

(6) Paragraphs (a) and (b) of section 17(1) apply in relation to a determination under sub-paragraph (2)(b) as they apply in relation to a determination under section 16.

(7) Subsections (2) to (7) of section 18 apply in relation to a determination under sub-paragraph (2) (and a decision in relation to the interests of justice for the purposes of such a determination) as they apply in relation to a determination under section 16 (and a decision for the purposes of such a determination).

(8) The Director may not make a provisional determination under sub-paragraph (2)(b) unless authorised to do so by regulations under sub-paragraph (9).

(9) Regulations may provide that the Director may make a provisional determination that a legal person qualifies under this Part for representation for the purposes of criminal proceedings where—

(a) the legal person is involved in an investigation which may result in criminal proceedings,

(b) the determination is made for the purposes of criminal proceedings that may result from the investigation, and

(c) any prescribed conditions are met.

(10) Subsections (2) and (3) of section 20 apply in relation to regulations under sub-paragraph (9) (and determinations and decisions made under such regulations) as they apply in relation to regulations under that section (and determinations and decisions made under such regulations).

(11) In sections 17, 18 and 20 as applied by this paragraph—

(a) references to an individual include a legal person,

(b) references to the relevant authority have effect as if they were references to the Director, and

(c) the reference in section 20(2)(d) to a determination made by the Director or a court in reliance on section 18 or 19 has effect as if it were a reference to a determination by the Director under sub-paragraph (2)(b) made otherwise than in reliance on regulations under sub-paragraph (9).

(12) Regulations may prescribe circumstances in which making representation available to a legal person for the purposes of criminal proceedings is to be taken to be in the interests of justice for the purposes of a determination under this paragraph.

(13) In this paragraph "specified legal person", in relation to criminal proceedings, means a description of legal person specified in regulations in relation to those proceedings.

Financial resources

6 Section 21 applies for the purposes of a determination under paragraph 3(1)(b) or 5(2)(b), or under regulations under paragraph 4 or 5(9), as if the references to an individual included a legal person.

Contributions and costs

7 In sections 23, 24, 25 and 26 and Schedule 2, references to an individual include a legal person to whom services are made available under this Part in accordance with this Schedule or regulations under this Schedule.

8 In Schedule 2, references to criminal legal aid include advice, assistance and representation required to be made available under paragraph 4 or 5 of this Schedule.

Providers of services etc

9 (1) Section 27 applies in relation to the provision of services to a legal person in accordance with this Schedule or regulations under this Schedule as it applies in relation to the provision of services to an individual under this Part.

(2) In that section as applied by this paragraph—

(a) references to an individual include a legal person,

(b) the reference to a determination under section 16 includes a determination under paragraph 5(2)(b) of this Schedule, and

(c) the reference to regulations under section 15 includes regulations under paragraph 4 of this Schedule.

(3) In sections 28, 29 and 30, references to an individual include a legal person to whom services are made available under this Part in accordance with this Schedule or regulations under this Schedule.

Supplementary matters

10 In sections 34, 35 and 41(2), references to an individual include a legal person to whom services are made available under this Part in accordance with this Schedule or regulations under this Schedule or who is seeking the provision of such services.

CIVIL LEGAL AID (PROCEDURE) REGULATIONS 2012

SI 2012/3098

III FUND [182]

1 Citation and commencement

These Regulations may be cited as the Civil Legal Aid (Procedure) Regulations 2012 and come into force on 1st April 2013.

PART 1
INTERPRETATION AND GENERAL

III FUND [183]

2 Interpretation

In these Regulations—

"the Act" means the Legal Aid, Sentencing and Punishment of Offenders Act 2012;

"adjudicator" means an independent funding adjudicator appointed by the Lord Chancellor under section 2 of the Act;

"business day" means any day except Saturday, Sunday, a bank holiday, Good Friday or Christmas Day;

"child" means an individual under the age of 18;

"children's guardian" has the meaning given in rule 2.3 of the Family Procedure Rules 2010;

"Controlled Work" has the meaning given in regulation 21(2);

"costs" means the fees payable to any provider calculated by reference to remuneration rates set out in arrangements made by the Lord Chancellor under section 2(1) of the Act or in regulations under section 2(3) of the Act, including (but not limited to)—

(a) counsel's fees;

(b) disbursements; and

(c) any fees paid to providers at an enhanced rate,

but not including Value Added Tax;

"cost benefit criteria" means the criteria of that name which the Director must apply when determining whether an individual qualifies for full representation in accordance with regulations made under section 11 of the Act;

"the effective administration of justice test" has the meaning given in regulation 31(5);

"emergency representation" means legal representation (that is not Controlled Work) or family help (higher) provided following a determination made on an urgent application;

"face-to-face provider" means a provider with whom the Lord Chancellor has made an arrangement under section 2(1) of the Act for the provision of civil legal services to an individual in person;

"family dispute" means any matter which is described in any of the following paragraphs of Part 1 of Schedule 1 to the Act—

(a) paragraph 1 (care, supervision and protection of children);

(b) paragraph 9 (inherent jurisdiction of the High Court in relation to children and vulnerable adults), to the extent that it relates to—

(i) a child; or

(ii) a vulnerable adult, but only in so far as such matters arise out of a family relationship within the meaning of paragraph 14(7) of Part 1 of Schedule 1 to the Act;

(c) paragraph 10 (unlawful removal of children);

(d) paragraph 11 (family homes and domestic violence);

(e) paragraph 12 (victims of domestic violence and family matters);

(f) paragraph 13 (protection of children and family matters);

(g) paragraph 14 (mediation in family disputes);

(h) paragraph 15 (children who are parties to family proceedings);

(ha) paragraph 15A (female genital mutilation protection orders);

(i) paragraph 16 (forced marriage);

(j) paragraph 17 (EU and international agreements concerning children); or

(k) paragraph 18 (EU and international agreements concerning maintenance);

"individual case contract" means an arrangement between the Lord Chancellor and a provider under section 2(1) of the Act for the provision of civil legal services in an individual case;

"Licensed Work" has the meaning given in regulation 29(2);

"litigation friend" has the meaning given in Part 21 of the Civil Procedure Rules 1998 and rule 2.3 of the Family Procedure Rules 2010;

"parental order reporter" has the meaning given in rule 13.1 of the Family Procedure Rules 2010;

"prospects of success" means the prospects of success as assessed by the Director in accordance with regulations made under section 11 of the Act;

"protected party" means a party or a proposed party who lacks capacity (within the meaning of the Mental Capacity Act 2005) to conduct proceedings;

"provider" means a person who provides civil legal services under Part 1 of the Act;

"revocation" means the withdrawal of a determination which has the consequences described in regulations made under section 23 and 26 of the Act (and "revoked" and "revoke" have equivalent meanings);

"Special Case Work" means civil legal services provided under an individual case contract in the circumstances described in regulation 54(3);

"specialist telephone provider" means a provider with whom the Lord Chancellor has made an arrangement under section 2(1) of the Act for the provision of civil legal services by telephone or other means that do not require the attendance in person of the individual to whom the services are provided; and

"2010 Standard Civil Contract", "2013 Standard Civil Contract", "2013 CLA Contract", "2014 Standard Civil Contract", "2015 Standard Civil Contract", "2018 Standard Civil Contract" and "2018 CLA Contract" mean the contracts so named between the Lord Chancellor and a provider for the provision of civil legal services.

III FUND [184]

3 Form of civil legal services

"Form of civil legal services" means—

(a) legal help;
(b) help at court;
(c) family help;
(d) family mediation;
(e) help with family mediation;
(f) legal representation; and
(g) other legal services,

which are further defined in regulations 4 to 10.

III FUND [185]

4 Legal help

"Legal help" means the provision of civil legal services other than—

(a) acting as a mediator or arbitrator;
(b) issuing or conducting court proceedings;
(c) instructing an advocate in proceedings;
(d) preparing to provide advocacy in proceedings; or
(e) advocacy in proceedings.

III FUND [186]

5 Help at court

"Help at court" means the provision of any of the following civil legal services at a particular hearing—

(a) instructing an advocate;
(b) preparing to provide advocacy; or
(c) advocacy.

III FUND [187]

6 Family help

(1) Family help may be provided in a family dispute as either family help (lower) or family help (higher).

(2) "Family help (lower)" means—

(a) civil legal services provided in relation to the negotiation of a family dispute before the issuing of proceedings; or
(b) civil legal services provided in relation to the issuing of proceedings in order to obtain a consent order following the settlement of a family dispute.

(3) "Family help (higher)" means such civil legal services as are available under legal representation but does not include preparation for, or representation at, a contested final hearing or appeal.

III FUND [188]

7 Family mediation

"Family mediation" means the provision of any of the following civil legal services in a family dispute—

(a) an assessment by a mediator of whether, in light of all the circumstances, a case is suitable for mediation; or

(b) acting as a mediator.

III FUND [189]

8 Help with family mediation

"Help with family mediation" means the provision of any of the following civil legal services, in relation to a family dispute—

(a) civil legal services provided in relation to family mediation; or

(b) civil legal services provided in relation to the issuing of proceedings to obtain a consent order following the settlement of the dispute following family mediation.

III FUND [190]

9 Legal representation

(1) Legal representation may be provided as either investigative representation or full representation.

(2) "Legal representation" means the provision of civil legal services, other than acting as a mediator or arbitrator, to an individual or legal person in particular proceedings where that individual or legal person—

(a) is a party to those proceedings;

(b) wishes to be joined as a party to those proceedings; or

(c) is contemplating issuing those proceedings.

(3) "Investigative representation" means legal representation which is limited to the investigation of the strength of the contemplated proceedings and includes the issuing and conducting of proceedings but only so far as necessary—

(a) to obtain disclosure of information relevant to the prospects of success of the proceedings;

(b) to protect the position of the individual or legal person applying for investigative representation in relation to an urgent hearing; or

(c) to protect the position of the individual or legal person applying for investigative representation in relation to the time limit for the issue of the proceedings.

(4) "Full representation" means legal representation other than investigative representation.

III FUND [191]

10 Other legal services

"Other legal services" means the provision of any of the following civil legal services—

(a) instructing an advocate;

(b) preparing to provide advocacy; or

(c) advocacy,

in proceedings in relation to which the Director, having applied the relevant merits criteria in accordance with regulations made under section 11 of the Act, has made a determination under section 10(2)(b) or (4)(c) of the Act.

III FUND [192]

11 Notification

(1) Where these Regulations provide for notice to be given, one or more of the following methods of delivery must be used—

- (a) personal service;
- (b) first class post, document exchange or other service which provides for delivery on the next business day;
- (c) fax or other means of electronic communication; or
- (d) any method authorised in writing by the Director.

(2) Where the intended recipient is represented by a provider, notice must be delivered to the business address of the provider.

(3) Where the intended recipient is not represented by a provider, notice must be delivered to that person's usual or last known residence or, for legal persons, business address.

III FUND [193]

12 Delegation

Except as provided in regulation 39(3), a function of the Lord Chancellor or Director under these Regulations may be exercised by, or by an employee of, a person authorised for that purpose by the Lord Chancellor or Director respectively.

III FUND [194]

13 Disregarding determinations

The Director may disregard a determination about whether an individual qualifies for civil legal services under Part 1 of the Act if the determination was made—

- (a) by a person to whom the Director has delegated that function; and
- (b) in response to an application made otherwise than in accordance with these Regulations.

III FUND [195]

14 Duty Scheme

These Regulations do not apply to civil legal services which are—

- (a) provided under the Housing Possession Court Duty Scheme (as described in the Specification to the 2013 Standard Civil Contract); or
- (b) required by the Specification to the 2013 Standard Civil Contract to be treated as services described in sub-paragraph (a).

III FUND [196]

15 Applications by legal persons

(1) An application by a legal person for a determination under paragraph 3 of Schedule 3 to the Act must be made in a form specified by the Lord Chancellor.

(2) The legal person must provide any additional information and documents requested by the Director in order to make a determination in relation to the application.

(3) A determination that a legal person qualifies for civil legal services must specify any limitation or condition to which the determination is subject.

(4) Where the Director—

- (a) does not make the determination for which the legal person has applied; or

(b) withdraws a determination that the legal person qualifies for civil legal services,

the Director must notify the legal person, giving written reasons and notice of the right of review.

(5) Within fourteen days of receipt of the notification described in paragraph (4), the legal person may—

(a) apply to the Director in a form specified by the Lord Chancellor for a review of the determination or the withdrawal of a determination; and

(b) include written representations supporting that application.

(6) The Director must—

(a) consider the application for review and any written representations;

(b) confirm or amend the determination or withdrawal or substitute a new determination; and

(c) notify the legal person of the determination or withdrawal following the review.

PART 2
GATEWAY WORK

FUNDING

III FUND [197]

16 General

(1) This Part makes provision about the making and withdrawal of determinations under section 9 of the Act about Gateway Work.

(2) Except as specifically provided in this Part, Part 3 (Controlled Work) applies to Gateway Work.

(3) Regulations 22(1) and 23(1)(d) do not apply to Gateway Work.

III FUND [198]

17 Applicants

(1) An individual, other than an exempted person, must apply to the Gateway (established by the Lord Chancellor under section 2 of the Act) for a determination by the Director about Gateway Work.

(2) An exempted person may apply for a determination by the Director about Gateway Work to—

(a) the Gateway; or

(b) a face-to-face provider.

III FUND [199]

18 The application

An application to the Gateway may be made by—

(a) telephone;

(b) email;

(c) electronic format made available by the Lord Chancellor for the purpose of such applications; or

(d) post.

III FUND [200]

19 Determinations

(1) Where a determination is made that an individual qualifies for Gateway Work, the determination must specify whether the services are to be provided by—

(a) a specialist telephone provider; or

(b) a face-to-face provider.

(2) A determination described in paragraph (1) may be amended to change the description of the provider specified in the determination.

III FUND [201]

20 Interpretation

In this Part—

"debt matter" means—

(a) a matter described in paragraph 33(1)(a) of Part 1 of Schedule 1 to the Act that relates to a court order for sale of the individual's home;

(b) a matter described in paragraph 33(1)(a) of Part 1 of Schedule 1 to the Act that relates to a court order for possession of the individual's home arising out of a failure to make payments due under a mortgage; or

(c) a matter described in paragraph 33(2) of Part 1 of Schedule 1 to the Act;

"exempted person" means an individual who—

(a) has been deprived of their liberty;

(b) is a child; or

(c) is a previously assessed person with a linked problem;

"Gateway discrimination matter" means a matter described in paragraph 43 of Part 1 of Schedule 1 to the Act, except where the matter to which the alleged contravention of the Equality Act 2010 or previous discrimination enactment relates is a matter described in a relevant category;

"Gateway Work" means the provision of legal help by a specialist telephone provider or a face-to-face provider in—

(a) a matter described in paragraph 2 of Part 1 of Schedule 1 to the Act;

(b) a debt matter; or

(c) a Gateway discrimination matter;

"linked problem" means a matter arising out of or related to a matter in relation to which Gateway Work was provided by a face-to-face provider;

"previously assessed person" means an individual—

(a) in respect of whom a determination has been made within the previous twelve months that the individual qualifies for Gateway Work to be provided by a face-to-face provider; and

(b) who is applying for Gateway Work from the same face-to-face provider in relation to a linked problem; and

"relevant category" means any of the following categories in the Category Definitions that form part of the 2010 Standard Civil Contract, 2013 Standard Civil Contract, 2014 Standard Civil Contract, 2015 Standard Civil Contract or 2018 Standard Civil Contract: Actions Against the Police; Clinical Negligence; Community Care; Family; Housing; Immigration and Asylum; Mental Health; Public Law; or Welfare Benefits.

PART 3
CONTROLLED WORK

III FUND [202]

21 General

(1) This Part makes provision in relation to the making and withdrawal of determinations under section 9 of the Act about Controlled Work.

(2) In this Part, "Controlled Work" means the provision of any of the following forms of civil legal services—

(a) legal help;

(b) help with family mediation;

(c) help at court;

(d) family help (lower); or

(e) legal representation for proceedings in—

(i) the Health, Education and Social Care Chamber of the First-tier Tribunal under the Mental Health Act 1983 or paragraph 5(2) of the Schedule to the Repatriation of Prisoners Act 1984;

(ii) the Mental Health Review Tribunal for Wales; or

(iii) the Immigration and Asylum Chamber of the First-tier Tribunal, other than in relation to an application for permission to appeal to the Immigration and Asylum Chamber of the Upper Tribunal.

(iv) ...

III FUND [203]

22 Applicants

(1) An individual applying for Controlled Work must attend the proposed provider's premises in person unless—

(a) the proposed provider decides that attendance in person is not necessary in accordance with the provider's arrangement with the Lord Chancellor under section 2(1) of the Act;

(b) the individual—

(i) resides, or is present, in the European Union;

(ii) cannot attend in person for good reason; and

(iii) authorises another person to attend on their behalf; or

(c) the individual is applying for Controlled Work to be provided by a specialist telephone provider.

(2) A child may make an application for Controlled Work if—

(a) the civil legal services which are the subject of the application are in relation to proceedings or proposed proceedings which the child may conduct without—

(i) a children's guardian or litigation friend in accordance with rule 16.6 of the Family Procedure Rules 2010; or

(ii) a litigation friend in accordance with rule 21.2 of the Civil Procedure Rules 1998; or

(b) there is good reason why none of the persons described in paragraph (3)(a) or (b) can make the application on behalf of the child and the provider considers that child is able, having regard to the child's understanding, to give instructions.

(3) The following persons may make an application for Controlled Work on behalf of a child—

(a) the child's parent, guardian or other person who has care of the child;

(b) a person acting or proposing to act as the child's professional children's guardian or litigation friend; or

(c) any other person where there is good reason why none of the persons described in sub-paragraph (a) or (b) can make the application.

(4) The following persons may make an application for Controlled Work on behalf of a protected party—

(a) a person acting or proposing to act as the protected party's litigation friend; or

(b) any other person where there is good reason why a litigation friend or proposed litigation friend cannot make the application.

(5) The proposed provider may not make an application for Controlled Work on behalf of a child or protected party.

III FUND [204]

23 The application

(1) An application for Controlled Work must be in a form specified by the Lord Chancellor and must specify—

(a) the form of civil legal services to which the application relates;

(b) the matter to which the application relates;

(c) the category within which the civil legal services fall (as described in the Category Definitions that form part of the 2010 Standard Civil Contract, 2013 Standard Civil Contract, 2014 Standard Civil Contract, 2015 Standard Civil Contract or 2018 Standard Civil Contract); and

(d) a proposed provider with whom the Lord Chancellor has made an arrangement under section 2(1) of the Act for the provision of the services which are the subject of the application (unless the Director has waived this requirement under paragraph (1A)).

(1A) The Director may waive the requirement in regulation 23(1)(d) if—

(a) the application is for civil legal services described in paragraph 41 of Part 1 of Schedule 1 to the Act in the form of legal help;

(b) the Director has determined that civil legal services in the same matter are to be made available to the individual under section 10 of the Act, and

(c) the effective administration of justice test is satisfied.

(1B) If the Director, having waived the requirement in regulation 23(1)(d), determines that an individual qualifies for Controlled Work—

(a) the Director may make the determination conditional upon the proposed provider entering into an individual case contract with the Lord Chancellor, and

(b) the determination may specify that the determination is to be treated as having effect from a date earlier than the date of the determination.

(2) An application for civil legal services described in paragraph 12 of Part 1 of Schedule 1 to the Act to be provided as Controlled Work must include evidence of the domestic violence or risk of domestic violence and regulation 33 applies to such an application.

(3) An application for civil legal services described in paragraph 13 of Part 1 of Schedule 1 to the Act to be provided as Controlled Work must include evidence that the child who is or would be the subject of the order to which the application relates is at risk of abuse from an individual other than the applicant for civil legal services and regulation 34 applies to such an application.

(3A) An application for civil legal services described in paragraph 32(1) of Part 1 of Schedule 1 to the Act to be provided as Controlled Work to an individual must be made—

(a) where a conclusive determination described in paragraph 32(1)(a) of Part 1 of Schedule 1 to the Act has been made in relation to that individual, within twelve months of the date of that determination;

(b) where a determination by a competent authority described in paragraph 32(6) of Part 1 of Schedule 1 to the Act has been made in relation to that individual and the individual has been given—

(i) leave to remain in the United Kingdom outside the rules made under section 3(2) of the Immigration Act 1971, or

(ii) immigration bail under paragraph 1 of Schedule 10 to the Immigration Act 2016),

on or before the latest date on which that leave or immigration bail comes to an end,

(and in any case where both sub-paragraphs (a) and (b) apply, the application must be made by the latest date specified by those sub-paragraphs).

(3B) An application for civil legal services described in paragraph 32A(1) of Part 1 of Schedule 1 to the Act to be provided as Controlled Work to an individual must be made—

(a) where a conclusive determination described in paragraph 32A(1)(a) of Part 1 of Schedule 1 to the Act has been made in relation to that individual, within twelve months of the date of that determination;

(b) where a determination by a competent authority described in paragraph 32A(6) of Part 1 of Schedule 1 to the Act has been made in relation to that individual and the individual has been given—

(i) leave to remain in the United Kingdom outside the rules made under section 3(2) of the Immigration Act 1971, or

(ii) immigration bail under paragraph 1 of Schedule 10 to the Immigration Act 2016,

on or before the latest date on which that leave or immigration bail comes to an end,

(and in any case where both sub-paragraphs (a) and (b) apply, the application must be made by the latest date specified by those sub-paragraphs).

(4) Where a determination has been made that an individual qualifies for legal help in a particular matter (the "initial determination"), the individual may not, within the six month period following the last provision of services pursuant to that determination, make an application for legal help in the same matter which proposes a different provider unless—

(a) there has been a material change in relevant circumstances since the initial determination;

(b) the individual has reasonable cause to be dissatisfied with the services provided under the initial determination;

(c) the individual's usual residence has changed since the initial determination and, as a result, effective communication between the individual and the provider is not practicable; or

(d) the provider named in the initial determination has confirmed in writing that no remuneration will be claimed under arrangements made by the Lord Chancellor under section 2(1) of the Act in respect of any services provided under the initial determination.

(5) An application for help with family mediation in relation to the issuing of proceedings to obtain a consent order following the settlement of a family dispute must be made within three months of the final family mediation session at which the dispute was settled.

(6) The individual must provide any additional information and documents requested by the Director in order to make a determination in relation to the application.

III FUND [205]

24 Position of providers

(1) Notwithstanding the relationship between an individual and the provider or any privilege arising out of that relationship, where the provider knows or suspects that the individual—

(a) has failed without good reason to comply with a requirement to provide information or documents; or

FUNDING

(b) in providing required information or documents has made a statement or representation knowing or believing it to be false,

the provider must immediately report the relevant circumstances to the Director.

(2) A provider's retainer terminates upon the withdrawal of a determination that an individual qualifies for Controlled Work following the conclusion of any review or appeal for which provision is made in these Regulations.

(3) Where an authorised person within the meaning of the Legal Services Act 2007 has been instructed (by a provider with whom the Lord Chancellor has made an arrangement under section 2(1) of the Act) to provide civil legal services in relation to a determination, the reporting requirement described in paragraph (1) also applies to that authorised person.

III FUND [206]

25 Reasons

(1) Where the Director has—

(a) made a determination that the services which are the subject of the application are not civil legal services described in Part 1 of Schedule 1 to the Act;

(b) made a determination that an individual does not qualify for Controlled Work; or

(c) withdrawn a determination that an individual qualifies for Controlled Work,

the Director must notify the individual.

(2) The Director must also provide—

(a) reasons for the determination or withdrawal of a determination; and

(b) notice of the right to a review of the determination or withdrawal of a determination,

and may provide information about alternative ways of obtaining or funding civil legal services.

III FUND [207]

26 Withdrawal of determinations

The Director may withdraw a determination about Controlled Work where—

(a) the individual no longer qualifies for the services to be made available by the determination in accordance with—

(i) the criteria set out in regulations made under section 11 of the Act; or

(ii) regulations made under section 21 of the Act;

(b) the services made available by the determination have been provided;

(c) the proceedings to which the determination relates have been concluded;

(d) the individual consents;

(e) the individual has died;

(f) a bankruptcy order has been made against the individual; or

(g) the individual has failed without good reason to comply with a requirement to provide information or documents or, in providing required information or documents, has made a statement or representation knowing or believing it to be false.

III FUND [208]

27 Review

(1) An individual may apply to the Director for a review of—

(a) a determination that an individual does not qualify for Controlled Work; or

(b) a withdrawal of a determination in the circumstances described in regulation 26(a)(i) and (g),

within fourteen days of receipt of the determination or withdrawal ("the original decision").

(2) The Director must consider the application and may confirm the original decision or substitute a new determination.

(3) Where the original decision was the withdrawal of a determination and, following the review, the Director substitutes a determination for that withdrawal, the determination takes effect (unless the Director directs otherwise) as if the original decision had not been made.

(4) The Director must notify the individual of—

(a) the determination or withdrawal following the review; and

(b) any right of appeal described in regulation 28.

III FUND [209]

28 Appeal

(1) Following the conclusion of a review, an individual may appeal to an adjudicator against—

(a) a determination that an individual does not qualify for legal representation that is Controlled Work; or

(b) a withdrawal of a determination that an individual qualifies for legal representation that is Controlled Work.

(2) The provisions about appeals in Part 4 (Licensed Work) apply to an appeal under paragraph (1).

PART 4
LICENSED WORK

III FUND [210]

29 General

(1) This Part makes provision in relation to the making and withdrawal of determinations under section 9 of the Act about Licensed Work.

(2) In this Part, "Licensed Work" means the provision of any of the following forms of civil legal services—

(a) family help (higher); or

(b) legal representation that is not Controlled Work or Special Case Work.

III FUND [211]

30 Applicants

(1) An individual applying for Licensed Work must be—

(a) a party to the proceedings to which the application relates;

(b) proposing to be joined as a party to those proceedings; or

(c) contemplating issuing those proceedings.

(2) An application on behalf of a child must be made by—

(a) a person who is, or proposes to be, the child's litigation friend, professional children's guardian or parental order reporter;

(b) the proposed provider if the application is made in relation to proceedings which the child may conduct without—

(i) a children's guardian or litigation friend in accordance with rule 16.6 of the Family Procedure Rules 2010; or

FUNDING

(ii) a litigation friend in accordance with rule 21.2 of the Civil Procedure Rules 1998; or

(c) the proposed provider if the application is made in relation to proceedings in the youth court for civil legal services in circumstances where a child is permitted to conduct proceedings on the child's own behalf.

(3) An individual acting as a professional children's guardian or parental order reporter may not make an application other than on behalf of a child.

(4) An application on behalf of a protected party must be made by a person who is, or proposes to be, the protected party's litigation friend.

(5) The Director may waive any or all of the requirements of this regulation if the application otherwise satisfies the requirements of these Regulations.

III FUND [212]

31 The application

(1) An application for Licensed Work must be made in writing in a form specified by the Lord Chancellor and signed by the individual and proposed provider.

(2) Except as provided in paragraph (3), the application must be in English unless—

(a) the individual resides in or is present in Wales; or

(b) the application relates to proceedings which may be heard in Wales,

in which case the application may be in English or Welsh.

(3) Where the individual resides outside the European Union and is not present in England and Wales when the application is made, the application must—

(a) be in English or French;

(b) include a written statement of the individual's financial resources; and

(c) be verified by a statement that the individual believes that the facts stated in the application are true.

(4) The application must specify—

(a) the form of civil legal services to which the application relates;

(b) the matter to which the application relates;

(c) the category within which the civil legal services fall (as described in the Category Definitions that form part of the 2010 Standard Civil Contract, 2013 Standard Civil Contract, 2014 Standard Civil Contract, 2015 Standard Civil Contract or 2018 Standard Civil Contract); and

(d) a proposed provider with whom the Lord Chancellor has made an arrangement under section 2(1) of the Act for the provision of the services which are the subject of the application (unless the effective administration of justice test described in paragraph (5) is satisfied).

(5) The effective administration of justice test is satisfied if the Director decides that it is necessary for a provider to provide the services which are the subject of the application under an individual case contract having considered—

(a) the provider's knowledge of the particular proceedings or dispute and expertise in providing the civil legal services which are the subject of the application;

(b) the nature and likely length of the particular proceedings or dispute;

(c) the complexity of the issues; and

(d) the circumstances of the individual making the application.

(6) The individual must provide any additional information or documents requested by the Director in order to make a determination in relation to the application.

(7) Where additional information or documents are requested in accordance with paragraph (6), the application may not be considered until the requested information or documents are provided.

(7A) Regulations 33 and 34 do not apply to an application for legal representation for an individual where a determination has already been made that the individual qualifies for family help (higher) ("the initial determination") and—

- (a) the initial determination has not been withdrawn by the Director under regulation 42(1); and
- (b) the application is for legal representation in the same proceedings as those for which the initial determination was made.

(8) An application for civil legal services described in paragraph 32(1) of Part 1 of Schedule 1 to the Act to be provided to an individual must be made—

- (a) where a conclusive determination described in paragraph 32(1)(a) of Part 1 of Schedule 1 to the Act has been made in relation to that individual, within twelve months of the date of that determination;
- (b) where a determination by a competent authority described in paragraph 32(6) of Part 1 of Schedule 1 to the Act has been made in relation to that individual and the individual has been given—
  - (i) leave to remain in the United Kingdom outside the rules made under section 3(2) of the Immigration Act 1971, or
  - (ii) immigration bail under paragraph 1 of Schedule 10 to the Immigration Act 2016,

  on or before the latest date on which that leave or immigration bail comes to an end,

(and in any case where both sub-paragraphs (a) and (b) apply, the application must be made by the latest date specified by those sub-paragraphs).

(9) An application for civil legal services described in paragraph 32A(1) of Part 1 of Schedule 1 to the Act to be provided to an individual must be made—

- (a) where a conclusive determination described in paragraph 32A(1)(a) of Part 1 of Schedule 1 to the Act has been made in relation to that individual, within twelve months of the date of that determination;
- (b) where a determination by a competent authority described in paragraph 32A(6) of Part 1 of Schedule 1 to the Act has been made in relation to that individual and the individual has been given—
  - (i) leave to remain in the United Kingdom outside the rules made under section 3(2) of the Immigration Act 1971, or
  - (ii) immigration bail under paragraph 1 of Schedule 10 to the Immigration Act 2016,

  on or before the latest date on which that leave or immigration bail comes to an end,

(and in any case where both sub-paragraphs (a) and (b) apply, the application must be made by the latest date specified by those paragraphs).

III FUND [213]

32 Supporting documents: damages

(1) Where an application for Licensed Work requires the Director to consider likely damages (in accordance with regulations made under section 11 of the Act), the application must include—

- (a) an estimate of likely damages; and
- (b) an explanation of the estimate, including the calculations required by paragraph (2).

(2) An estimate of likely damages must take into account—

- (a) any likely reduction in the damages or other sum of money contested in the case through contributory negligence, set-off or otherwise;

FUNDING

(b) any amount of damages the individual is likely to receive in addition to any amount that is offered by way of settlement;

(c) any likely reduction in damages or other sum of money contested in the case to take account of any amount which is recoverable under the Social Security (Recovery of Benefits) Act 1997; and

(d) the ability of the other party to the proceedings to pay any damages or other sum of money contested in the case.

III FUND [214]

33 Supporting documents: domestic violence

(1) An application for civil legal services described in paragraph 12 of Part 1 of Schedule 1 to the Act must include evidence of the domestic violence or the risk of domestic violence.

(2) For the purpose of paragraph (1), the evidence of domestic violence or risk of domestic violence must be provided in one or more of the forms that is described in Schedule 1 to these Regulations.

(3) ...

(4) ...

(5) In relation to Licensed Work, this regulation applies subject to regulation 31(7A).

III FUND [214.1]

Invalidity of certain provisions Regulation 33 in its original form was declared invalid insofar as it (i) requires verification of domestic violence to be given within a 24-month period before any application for legal aid; and (2) did not cater for the victims of domestic violence who had suffered from financial abuse: *R (on the application of Rights of Women) v Lord Chancellor* [2016] EWCA Civ 91, [2016] All ER (D) 177 (Feb). The Lord Chancellor responded by amending regulation 33(2) and also expanding the scope of reg 33(3) (protective injunctions). The amendments made by the amending instrument, the Civil Legal Aid (Procedure)(Amendment) Regulations 2016, SI 2016/516, have been incorporated into the regulation above.

III FUND [215]

34 Supporting documents: protection of children

(1) An application for civil legal services described in paragraph 13 of Part 1 of Schedule 1 to the Act must include evidence that the child who is or would be the subject of the order to which the application relates is at risk of abuse from an individual ("B") other than the applicant for civil legal services ("A") against which risk of abuse the order is to provide protection.

(2) For the purpose of paragraph (1), evidence of the risk of abuse must be provided in one or more of the forms that is described in Schedule 1 to these Regulations.

(3) ...

(4) In relation to Licensed Work, this regulation applies subject to regulation 31(7A).

III FUND [216]

35 Determinations: general

(1) A determination that an individual qualifies for Licensed Work must specify—

(a) the maximum costs which may be incurred in providing the services to which the determination relates; and

(b) any other limitations and conditions to which the determination is subject.

(2) Where a limitation is exceeded or a condition is breached, the Director may—

(a) withdraw the determination; or
(b) amend the relevant limitation or condition.

III FUND [217]

36 Determinations: contributions

(1) Where an individual is required to make a contribution in respect of the cost of the civil legal services in accordance with regulations made under section 23 of the Act, a determination that an individual qualifies for Licensed Work must be made subject to a condition that the individual pays, or arranges payment of, the required contribution.

(2) The determination must specify—
(a) the amount of any contribution;
(b) whether the individual is required to pay, or arrange payment of, the contribution—
(i) by periodical payments;
(ii) by one or more lump sums;
(iii) out of income;
(iv) out of capital; and
(c) any time limit about payment.

(3) The individual must—
(a) complete and return the form specified by the Lord Chancellor to indicate acceptance of a condition; and
(b) pay any contribution required by the determination,
within any time limit specified in the determination.

(4) If the individual fails to comply with the obligation in paragraph (3), the determination may be withdrawn.

III FUND [218]

37 Certificates

(1) When the Director makes a determination that an individual qualifies for Licensed Work, the Director must—
(a) issue a certificate recording the determination and send the certificate to the provider; and
(b) send a copy of the certificate to the individual.

(2) A certificate issued by the Director must specify—
(a) the name and address of—
(i) the individual;
(ii) where an application was made on behalf of a child or protected party, the person who is acting on behalf of the child or protected party; and
(iii) the provider;
(b) the date of the determination;
(c) the form of civil legal services to which the determination relates;
(d) the matter in relation to which the civil legal services are to be available;
(e) the proceedings to which the determination relates;
(f) the parties to any proceedings to which the determination relates (except to the extent that the Director considers it inappropriate to name any of the parties); and
(g) any limitation or condition to which the determination is subject.

(3) Except as provided in paragraph (4), the Director must issue a separate certificate for each—
(a) form of civil legal services for which the individual qualifies; and

FUNDING

(b) set of proceedings to which a determination relates, unless the Director decides that the proceedings are so closely connected that they should be covered by a single certificate.

(4) The Director may amend a certificate for—

(a) family help (higher) to record a subsequent determination that the individual qualifies for legal representation in family proceedings which arose out of the dispute which was the subject of the initial determination in relation to family help (higher); or

(b) investigative representation to record a subsequent determination that the individual qualifies for full representation in the same proceedings.

(5) The Director may amend a certificate to ensure that it accurately records a determination either—

(a) upon the application of the individual in a form specified by the Lord Chancellor; or

(b) of the Director's own volition.

(6) The Director must amend a certificate to record an amendment of a limitation or condition to which the determination is subject.

(7) When the Director amends a certificate, the Director must send—

(a) the amended certificate to the provider; and

(b) a copy of the amended certificate to the individual.

(8) Where the Director withdraws a determination, the Director must withdraw the certificate recording that determination and notify the provider.

III FUND [219]

38 Notice of determinations

(1) Where the Director issues a certificate in relation to proceedings that have been issued, the provider must—

(a) send a copy of the certificate to the court or tribunal, and

(b) give notice of the determination in a form specified by the Lord Chancellor to all parties to the proceedings.

(2) Where the Director issues a certificate before proceedings are issued, the provider must—

(a) give notice of the determination in a form specified by the Lord Chancellor to any proposed party to those proceedings except in proceedings relating to a family dispute; and

(b) when proceedings are issued—

(i) send a copy of the certificate to the court or tribunal, and

(ii) give notice of the determination in a form specified by the Lord Chancellor to all parties to the proceedings.

(3) The provider must give notice of a determination in accordance with paragraph (1)(b) to any person subsequently joined as a party to the proceedings.

(4) Where, in relation to proceedings which have been issued, the Director amends a certificate to alter the description of the proceedings or the form of civil legal services to which the determination relates, the provider must—

(a) send a copy of the amended certificate to the court or tribunal; and

(b) give notice of the new or amended determination in a form specified by the Lord Chancellor to all parties to the proceedings, unless the Director directs otherwise.

(5) Nothing in this regulation entitles a party or proposed party to the proceedings to which the determination relates to see the certificate recording the determination.

III FUND [220]

39 Authorised representation

(1) Where the Director has authorised a provider to make a determination under section 9 of the Act that an individual qualifies for legal representation that is Licensed Work ("authorised representation"), the provider must, within 5 business days of making a determination, notify the Director in a form specified by the Lord Chancellor.

(2) The Director may remove or amend any limitation or condition to which a determination about authorised representation is subject or impose a new limitation or condition on such a determination.

(3) The following functions of the Director may not be delegated to the provider—

- (a) issuing a certificate recording the determination in relation to authorised representation;
- (b) amending a limitation or condition to which the determination is subject (unless the determination relates to emergency representation);
- (c) the withdrawal of the determination; and
- (d) conducting a review in relation to authorised representation under regulation 44.

(4) Where, following a review in relation to authorised representation under regulation 44, the Director makes a determination that an individual qualifies for the legal representation which was the subject of the application, the individual may choose a different authorised provider from the provider named on the original application.

III FUND [221]

40 Reporting duties

(1) The individual (or the person acting on behalf of the individual) must—

- (a) immediately notify the provider of any change in circumstances which might affect a determination that the individual qualifies for civil legal services; and
- (b) attend a meeting with the Director if requested to do so.

(2) The provider must report to the Director any change in the individual's circumstances which become known to the provider and which might affect a determination that an individual qualifies for civil legal services.

(3) The provider must report to the Director—

- (a) a refusal by the individual (or the person acting on behalf of the individual) to accept—
  - (i) an offer to settle;
  - (ii) an offer to mediate any issue in the proceedings;
  - (iii) an offer to use an alternative dispute resolution procedure; or
  - (iv) any other offer of settlement which the provider considers to be reasonable;
- (b) any aspect of the conduct of the individual (or the person acting on behalf of the individual) which the provider considers relevant to the determination that the individual qualifies for civil legal services;
- (c) notice of any other party to the proceedings to which the determination relates qualifying for civil legal services;
- (d) any other information which might affect a determination that an individual qualifies for civil legal services; or
- (e) the fact that the provider has concluded that it is no longer possible to act for the individual, together with reasons for the provider's conclusion.

(4) Where an authorised person within the meaning of the Legal Services Act 2007 has been instructed by the provider to provide civil legal services in relation to a determination, the reporting requirements described in paragraphs (2) and (3) also apply to that person.

III FUND [222]

41 Position of providers

(1) Notwithstanding the relationship between an individual and the provider or any privilege arising out of that relationship, where the provider knows or suspects that the individual (or the person acting on behalf of the individual)—

- (a) has failed without good reason to comply with a requirement to provide information or documents; or
- (b) in providing required information or documents has made a statement or representation knowing or believing it to be false,

the provider must immediately report the relevant circumstances to the Director.

(2) A provider's retainer terminates upon the withdrawal of a determination that an individual qualifies for Licensed Work but that termination does not take effect until—

- (a) the conclusion of any review or appeal for which provision is made in this Part; and
- (b) the provider has complied with any obligation to give notice of the withdrawal of the determination.

(3) Where an authorised person within the meaning of the Legal Services Act 2007 has been instructed (by a provider with whom the Lord Chancellor has made an arrangement under section 2(1) of the Act) to provide civil legal services in relation to a determination, the reporting requirement described in paragraph (1) also applies to that authorised person.

III FUND [223]

42 Withdrawal of determinations

(1) The Director may withdraw a determination where—

- (a) the individual no longer qualifies for the services to be made available by the determination in accordance with—
  - (i) the criteria set out in regulations made under section 11 of the Act; or
  - (ii) regulations made under section 21 of the Act;
- (b) the services made available by the determination have been provided;
- (c) the proceedings to which the determination relates have been concluded;
- (d) the service made available by the determination was investigative representation and sufficient work has been carried out to determine the prospects of success and the cost benefit criteria;
- (e) the individual consents;
- (f) the individual has died;
- (g) a bankruptcy order has been made against the individual;
- (h) the individual has—
  - (i) failed without good reason to comply with a requirement to provide information or documents;
  - (ii) failed without good reason to attend a meeting with the Director; or
  - (iii) in providing required information or documents, made a statement or representation knowing or believing it to be false;

(i) an order has been made under section 42 of the Senior Courts Act 1981 or section 33 of the Employment Tribunals Act 1996 (restriction of vexatious proceedings) in relation to the individual;

(j) the Director is satisfied that the individual has required the proceedings to be conducted unreasonably so as to incur unjustifiable expense; or

(k) in relation to services described in paragraphs 12 and 13 of Part 1 of Schedule 1 to the Act, the evidence included with the application was—

(i) a conviction for an offence and that conviction has subsequently been quashed;

(ii) evidence of ongoing criminal proceedings and those proceedings have subsequently been concluded without a conviction;

(iii) evidence described in paragraph 7 of Schedule 1 or paragraph 5 of Schedule 2 where—

(a) the order was obtained without notice to the respondent; and

(b) that order has subsequently been set aside by the court;

(iv) evidence described in paragraph 7 of Schedule 1 where the application for a domestic violence protection order has been made under section 27 of the Crime and Security Act 2010 but has been unsuccessful on account of the conditions set out in section 28 of that Act not having been satisfied;

(v) evidence described in paragraph 1 of Schedule 1 where no charge is brought for the domestic violence offence (within the meaning of Schedule 1) and the Director is satisfied that it is unlikely that such a charge will be brought;

(vi) evidence described in paragraphs 16 to 18 of Schedule 1 and a public authority has confirmed in writing that it is satisfied—

(a) there has not been domestic violence between A and B; or

(b) A was not at any time at risk of being the victim of domestic violence

and in this sub-paragraph "public authority" has the meaning given by Schedule 1 to these Regulations;

(vii) evidence described in paragraph 1 of Schedule 2 where no charge is brought for the child abuse offence (within the meaning of Schedule 2) and the Director is satisfied that it is unlikely that such a charge will be brought;

(viii) evidence of an application described in paragraph 9 of Schedule 2 and that application has subsequently been withdrawn or refused,

unless the individual provides another form of evidence (excluding evidence described in paragraphs (i) to (viii)) which would have been permitted in accordance with these Regulations at the date of the application.

(2) In any of the circumstances described in paragraph (1)(h) to (j) the Director may—

(a) revoke the determination; and

(b) withdraw any other determination that the individual qualifies for civil legal services.

(3) Except in the circumstances described in paragraph (1)(a)(ii), (b), (e) and (f), before withdrawing a determination, the Director must—

(a) notify the individual of the intention to withdraw the determination;

(b) invite written representations within a specified time limit;

(c) upon the expiry of the time limit specified under sub-paragraph (b)—

(i) consider the written representations;

(ii) decide whether to withdraw the determination; and

(iii) notify the individual of the decision as to whether to withdraw the determination.

FUNDING

(4) The withdrawal is to be treated as having effect from the date of the notification described in paragraph (3)(a).

(5) The withdrawal of a determination does not affect the provider's right to remuneration for work done prior to the date of the withdrawal unless the provider failed without good reason to comply with the reporting requirements in regulations 40(2) and (3) and 41(1).

(6) Where the Director has withdrawn a determination, the Director may subsequently determine that the withdrawal is to be treated as a revocation following the provision of new information which demonstrates that the circumstances described in paragraph (1)(h) to (j) were present at the time of withdrawal.

III FUND [224]

43 Reasons

(1) Where the Director has—

- (a) determined that the services which are the subject of the application are not civil legal services described in Part 1 of Schedule 1 to the Act;
- (b) determined that an individual does not qualify for particular services;
- (c) determined that an individual does qualify but not on the terms requested in the application (whether because of a limitation or condition to which the determination has been made subject or otherwise);
- (d) amended a limitation or condition to which the determination is subject; or
- (e) withdrawn a determination,

the Director must notify the individual.

(2) In the circumstances described in paragraph (1), the Director must send to the individual and provider or proposed provider—

- (a) written notice of the determination, amendment or withdrawal of a determination in a form specified by the Lord Chancellor;
- (b) written reasons for the determination, amendment or withdrawal of a determination; and
- (c) notice of the right to a review of the determination, amendment or withdrawal of a determination,

and may provide information about alternative ways of obtaining or funding civil legal services.

III FUND [225]

44 Review

(1) An individual may apply for a review by the Director of any of the following—

- (a) a determination that the services which are the subject of the application are not civil legal services described in Part 1 of Schedule 1 to the Act;
- (b) a determination that an individual does not qualify for the civil legal services which are the subject of the application;
- (c) a determination that an individual qualifies for civil legal services but not on the terms requested in the application (whether because of a limitation or condition to which the determination has been made subject or otherwise);
- (d) an amendment of, or refusal to amend, a limitation or condition to which the determination is subject; or
- (e) a withdrawal of a determination,

within fourteen days of receipt of the notice of the determination, amendment or withdrawal ("the original decision").

(2) The application for review must be in a form specified by the Lord Chancellor and must include any written representations supporting the application.

(3) The Director must consider the application and any written representations and may confirm or amend the original decision or substitute a new determination, amendment or withdrawal.

(4) Where the original decision was the withdrawal of a determination and, following the review, the Director substitutes a determination for that withdrawal, the determination takes effect (unless the Director directs otherwise) as if the original decision had not been made.

(5) The Director must ensure that a certificate accurately records the civil legal services for which an individual qualifies following the review.

(6) The Director must notify the individual and the provider or proposed provider identified in the individual's application of—

- (a) the decision following the review; and
- (b) any right of appeal to an adjudicator.

III FUND [226]

45 Appeal: general

(1) Where an individual remains dissatisfied following a review, the individual may appeal to an adjudicator unless the determination in question is—

- (a) a determination under section 21 of the Act; or
- (b) a determination that the services which are the subject of the application are not civil legal services described in Part 1 of Schedule 1 to the Act.

(2) An appeal must be considered without a hearing unless the adjudicator considers that it is in the interests of justice for the individual or a person acting on their behalf to make oral representations.

(3) Where the Director or adjudicator considers that the appeal is of exceptional complexity or importance, the Director or adjudicator may refer the appeal to a panel of two or more adjudicators.

III FUND [227]

46 Appeal: power to refer for reconsideration

(1) The adjudicator may do one or more of the following—

- (a) decide certain issues in accordance with regulation 47; and
- (b) consider whether the determination, amendment or withdrawal under appeal ("the decision under appeal") was unlawful or unreasonable.

(2) Where the adjudicator decides that the decision under appeal was not unlawful or unreasonable—

- (a) the adjudicator must confirm the decision under appeal, giving written reasons; and
- (b) the Director must notify the individual.

(3) Where the adjudicator decides that the decision under appeal was unlawful or unreasonable—

- (a) the adjudicator must refer the decision under appeal to the Director for reconsideration, giving written reasons; and
- (b) the Director must notify the individual.

(4) Where new information relevant to the decision under appeal is provided by the individual following the review, the adjudicator may refer the decision under appeal to the Director for reconsideration instead of determining the appeal.

III FUND [228]

47 Appeal: power to decide certain issues

(1) The adjudicator may decide any of the following issues on appeal and the decision of the adjudicator on any such issue is binding on the Director—

(a) the prospects of success;

(b) the cost benefit criteria;

(c) whether a case has overwhelming importance to the individual; and

(d) whether a determination should be made, withdrawn or revoked in light of the individual's conduct.

(2) Where the adjudicator confirms the Director's assessment of any of the issues described in paragraph (1)—

(a) the adjudicator must give written reasons, and

(b) the Director must notify the individual.

(3) Where the adjudicator disagrees with the Director's assessment of any of the issues described in paragraph (1), the adjudicator must—

(a) refer the determination, amendment or withdrawal under appeal to the Director for reconsideration, giving written reasons; and

(b) the Director must notify the individual.

(4) In this regulation, "case with overwhelming importance to the individual" means a case which is not primarily a claim for damages or other sum of money and which relates to one or more of the following—

(a) the life, liberty or physical safety of the individual or a member of that individual's family (an individual is a member of another individual's family if the requirements of section 10(6) of the Act are met); or

(b) the immediate risk that the individual may become homeless.

III FUND [229]

48 Appeal: reconsideration by the Director

(1) Where a determination, amendment or withdrawal ("the decision under appeal") is referred to the Director by the adjudicator under regulation 46 or 47, the Director must reconsider that decision taking into account—

(a) the adjudicator's decision and written reasons; and

(b) any new information provided by the individual following the review.

(2) After reconsidering the decision under appeal, the Director may confirm or amend that decision or substitute a new determination, amendment or withdrawal.

(3) The Director must notify the individual and the provider or proposed provider identified in the individual's application of the decision following the appeal, giving written reasons.

(4) Where the Director confirms the decision under appeal but for reasons that are materially different from the reasons for the decision under appeal, the individual may make a further appeal to the adjudicator (using the appeal provisions in this Part), following which there is no further review or appeal under these Regulations.

(5) Where the decision under appeal was the withdrawal of a determination and, following the appeal, the Director substitutes a determination for that withdrawal, the determination takes effect (unless the Director directs otherwise) as if the original withdrawal had not been made.

(6) The Director must ensure that a certificate accurately records the civil legal services for which an individual qualifies following the appeal.

III FUND [230]

49 Notice to third parties

Where the Director withdraws a determination and the proceedings to which the determination related have not been concluded, the provider must give notice of the withdrawal in a form specified by the Lord Chancellor to—

(a) the court or tribunal; and

(b) any parties to the proceedings who were given notice of the determination under regulation 38.

PART 5
EMERGENCY REPRESENTATION

III FUND [231]

50 General

(1) This Part makes provision about the making and withdrawal of determinations under section 9 of the Act about emergency representation.

(2) Except as specifically provided in this Part, determinations about emergency representation must be made and withdrawn in accordance with the provisions of these Regulations which would have applied had the application not been made on an urgent basis.

(3) Regulation 42(3) does not apply in relation to emergency representation.

III FUND [232]

51 The application

(1) An individual may make an application for emergency representation by such method (including by fax, telephone or e-mail) as the Director has agreed to accept given the urgency of the particular circumstances.

(2) The application must specify whether the emergency representation is to be provided as Licensed Work or under an individual case contract.

III FUND [233]

52 Determinations

(1) A determination that an individual qualifies for emergency representation—

(a) must be made subject to a specified time limit; and

(b) may be made on the basis of limited information and documents if the Director considers that it would be in the interests of justice to do so.

(2) A determination made on the basis of limited information and documents—

(a) must be made conditional upon the provision, within a specified time limit, of the information and documents which would have been required had the application not been made on an urgent basis;

(b) may be disregarded if the condition is not satisfied within the specified time limit; and

(c) must be revoked where, following the provision of further information and documents, the Director determines that the individual does not qualify for legal representation or family help (higher) in accordance with section 21 of the Act and regulations made under that section.

(3) Where, following the provision of further information and documents—

(a) the Director determines that the individual qualifies for legal representation subject to a condition requiring the payment of a contribution in accordance with regulation 36; and

(b) the individual does not agree to pay, or arrange payment of, the contribution described in sub-paragraph (a),

FUNDING

the determination in relation to emergency representation may be revoked or withdrawn.

III FUND [234]

53 Appeal

(1) An individual may not appeal—

(a) against a determination that the individual does not qualify for emergency representation made on the basis of limited information and documents; or

(b) the withdrawal of a determination about emergency representation on the basis only of the expiry of a time limit.

PART 6
SPECIAL CASE WORK

III FUND [235]

54 General

(1) This Part makes provision about the making and withdrawal of determinations about Special Case Work.

(2) An application for—

(a) a determination that an individual qualifies for a form of civil legal services; or

(b) an amendment of a determination,

may be treated by the Director as an application for Special Case Work in the circumstances described in paragraph (3).

(3) The circumstances mentioned in paragraph (2) are where the Director has reasonable grounds to believe that—

(a) the actual or likely costs of the case exceed £25,000;

(b) if the case were to proceed to—

(i) a trial or final hearing; or

(ii) in the case of appeal proceedings before the Court of Appeal, the conclusion of that appeal,

the likely costs would exceed £75,000;

(c) the application relates to a multi-party action or potential multi-party action;

(d) the application relates to an appeal or proposed appeal to the Supreme Court;

(e) it is necessary to decide whether—

(i) the case is of significant wider public interest; or

(ii) the substance of the case relates to a breach of Convention rights (within the meaning of the Human Rights Act 1998),

in order to determine whether the individual qualifies for civil legal services in accordance with the criteria set out in regulations made under section 11 of the Act;

(f) the application relates to a case which satisfies the effective administration of justice test; or

(g) the application relates to a community action.

(4) Different proceedings may be treated as if they were a single case for the purpose of paragraph (2) if the Director decides that the proceedings are closely connected or are being heard together by the court or tribunal.

(5) Except as provided in this Part, Part 4 (Licensed Work) applies to Special Case Work.

(6) In this Part—

"community action" means proceedings proposed, begun or continued by or against one or more individuals who belong to an identifiable geographic community the members of which have a common interest in the proceedings;

"likely costs" means the total costs likely to have been incurred on behalf of the applicant for civil legal services at final judgment or settlement of the proceedings—

(a) calculated on the basis that the proceedings fail to obtain a successful outcome or costs are not recovered from another party to the proceedings; and

(b) taking into account the prospects of the proceedings settling before trial or other final hearing;

"multi-party action" means proceedings in which a number of individuals have a cause of action which involves common or related issues of fact or law; and

"significant wider public interest" has the meaning given in regulations made under section 11 of the Act.

III FUND [236]

55 Conditions

(1) The Director may make a determination about Special Case Work conditional upon the proposed provider entering into an individual case contract with the Lord Chancellor.

(2) The Director may make a determination about Special Case Work conditional upon the proposed provider submitting a costed case plan in a form specified by the Lord Chancellor which—

(a) sets out proposals for progressing the Special Case Work; and

(b) identifies—

(i) the key stages of the case;

(ii) the form of civil legal services likely to be needed at each key stage;

(iii) the likely costs at each key stage; and

(iv) appropriate intervals for the plan to be checked and adjusted by the provider with the agreement of the Director to reflect the progress of the Special Case Work.

(3) The Director may make a determination about a case which is of significant wider public interest conditional upon the individual agreeing not to settle the proceedings without the prior written consent of the Director.

III FUND [237]

56 Determinations affecting several cases

(1) A determination ("a determination of principle") about Special Case Work which appears likely to affect a group of cases or cases of a particular description may specify that it applies generally to the cases which appear likely to be affected.

(2) A determination of principle must specify—

(a) the group of cases or the particular description of cases to which it applies;

(b) the date on which it takes effect and, if relevant, ceases to have effect;

(c) whether the cases are being treated as a multi-party action.

(3) An application for a determination about Special Case Work may include a request, with written reasons, for the case to be covered by a determination of general principle.

III FUND [238]

57 Multi-party actions

(1) An application for a determination in relation to a multi-party action must name a lead provider.

(2) Applications from different individuals in the same multi-party action may be treated as a single application.

(3) The Director must specify in a determination in relation to a multi-party action—

- (a) the identity of the lead provider;
- (b) whether the civil legal services to be made available are limited to an issue which is common to all parties or a particular group of parties (a "generic issue"); and
- (c) if the civil legal services do relate to a generic issue, whether the services include or are limited to—
  - (i) the selection, preparation and trial of lead issues and lead cases;
  - (ii) the co-ordination of the action; and
  - (iii) any other civil legal services which the Director considers necessary for the action to be progressed as a multi-party action.

(4) The Director may send any notices in relation to a multi-party action to the lead provider who must communicate the information in those notices to the parties for whom that provider is the lead provider.

(5) The Director may waive any of the requirements of regulations 37 and 49 in relation to a multi-party action.

(6) A certificate recording a determination in relation to a multi-party action must be amended to record a change in the identity of the lead provider.

III FUND [239]

58 Special controls

(1) Special Case Work to be provided in the circumstances described in—

- (a) regulation 54(3)(c), (d), (e) and (g); and
- (b) regulation 54(3)(b) where the Director has reasonable grounds to believe that the likely costs would exceed £250,000,

is subject to special controls.

(2) The provisions about appeals in Part 4 (Licensed Work) do not apply to Special Case Work subject to special controls.

(3) Where the individual remains dissatisfied following a review about Special Case Work subject to special controls, the individual may appeal to the Special Controls Review Panel appointed by the Lord Chancellor ("the Panel") under section 2 of the Act unless the determination in question is—

- (a) a determination under section 21 of the Act; or
- (b) a determination that the services which are the subject of the application are not civil legal services described in Part 1 of Schedule 1 to the Act.

(4) The Director may refer to the Panel any issue which is relevant to a determination or the withdrawal of a determination about Special Case Work subject to special controls.

(5) Appeals and issues referred to the Panel must be considered without a hearing unless the Panel considers that it is in the interests of justice for the individual, the Director or any person authorised by the individual or the Director to make oral representations before the Panel.

(6) The Panel may—

- (a) confirm the determination or withdrawal of a determination; or

(b) report to the Director its views on the case and any issues referred by the Director.

(7) The Panel must—

(a) give written reasons for its findings; and

(b) send a copy of the confirmation or report to the Director and the individual.

(8) The individual or any person authorised by the individual may make further written representations to the Director about the Panel's findings or any issue addressed in the Panel's report.

(9) The Director must—

(a) consider the Panel's report and any further representations;

(b) make a determination on the issues raised in the report;

(c) give written reasons for any determination;

(d) send a copy of the determination with written reasons to the individual; and

(e) ensure that any certificate accurately records the civil legal services for which an individual qualifies following an appeal.

(10) A determination by the Panel about the prospects of success made in accordance with the criteria set out in regulations made under section 11 of the Act is binding on the Director.

FUNDING

III FUND [240]

59 Appeals

Where an adjudicator is considering an appeal in relation to Special Case Work, regulation 47(1)(b) does not apply but the adjudicator must instead consider the likely damages or any other benefit or remedy which the individual is likely to receive.

PART 7
FAMILY MEDIATION

III FUND [241]

60 General

This Part makes provision about the making and withdrawal of determinations under section 9 of the Act about family mediation.

III FUND [242]

61 The application

An individual applying for family mediation must—

(a) attend the mediator's premises in person;

(b) complete the application form specified by the Lord Chancellor; and

(c) provide any additional information and documents requested by the Director in order to make a determination in relation to the application.

III FUND [242A]

61A Determinations relating to Mediation Information and Assessment meetings

(1) A determination that an individual "A" qualifies for the form of civil legal services described in regulation 5(1)(ga) of the Civil Legal Aid (Financial Resources and Payment for Services) Regulations 2013(c)(such family mediation

as is a Mediation Information and Assessment meeting) may specify that the determination is to be treated as having effect from a date earlier than the date of determination where—

(a) those civil legal services were provided to A before the date of the determination, and

(b) after those civil legal services were provided to A, the Director made a determination that the financial resources of another individual who is a party to that Mediation Information and Assessment meeting ("B") are such that B is eligible, for that meeting, for such family mediation as is a Mediation Information and Assessment meeting.

(2) In this regulation—

"Mediation Information and Assessment meeting" means an assessment by a mediator of whether, in light of all the circumstances, a case is suitable for mediation;

"mediator" means a mediator with whom the Lord Chancellor has made an arrangement under section 2(1) of the Act (arrangements)."

III FUND [242A.1

The new r 61A does not apply to a determination that an individual qualifies for civil legal services provided to that individual on or before 30 May 2016.

III FUND [243]

62 Mediators

The individual must propose a mediator with whom the Lord Chancellor has made an arrangement under section 2(1) of the Act for the mediator to provide family mediation in accordance with a code of practice approved by the Lord Chancellor.

III FUND [244]

63 Reasons

(1) Where the Director—

(a) determines that an individual does not qualify for family mediation; or

(b) withdraws a determination in relation to family mediation,

the Director must notify the individual.

(2) In the circumstances described in paragraph (1), the Director must send to the individual—

(a) written notice of the determination or withdrawal in a form specified by the Lord Chancellor;

(b) written reasons for the determination or withdrawal; and

(c) notice of the right to a review of the determination or withdrawal,

and may provide information about alternative ways of obtaining or funding civil legal services.

(3) The withdrawal of a determination does not affect the right of the mediator to remuneration for work done before the date of withdrawal.

III FUND [245]

64 Withdrawal of determinations

The Director may withdraw a determination where—

(a) the individual no longer qualifies for the services made available by the determination in accordance with section 21 of the Act and regulations made under that section;

(b) the services made available by the determination have been provided;

(c) the Director is satisfied that continuing to act would breach the mediator's code of practice referred to in regulation 62;

(d) the individual consents;
(e) the individual has died;
(f) a bankruptcy order has been made against the individual; or
(g) the individual has failed without good reason to comply with a requirement to provide information or documents or in providing required information or documents has made a statement or representation knowing or believing it to be false.

III FUND [246]

65 Review

(1) An individual may apply to the Director for a review of a determination or withdrawal of a determination about family mediation, making written representations supporting the application.

(2) The Director must—
(a) consider the application and any written representations;
(b) confirm the determination or withdrawal or substitute a new determination or withdrawal; and
(c) notify the individual of the determination or withdrawal following the review.

PART 8
EXCEPTIONAL CASES

III FUND [247]

66 General

(1) This Part makes provision about the making and withdrawal of determinations under section 10 of the Act about exceptional cases.

(2) Except as provided in this Part—
(a) determinations under section 10 of the Act must be made and withdrawn in accordance with the provisions of these Regulations which apply to the form of civil legal services which is the subject of the application; and
(b) Part 4 (Licensed Work), applies to other legal services.

(3) The provisions in these Regulations about—
(a) appeals;
(b) review (other than in this Part); and
(c) emergency representation,

do not apply to the making and withdrawal of determinations under section 10 of the Act.

(4) Regulations 23(1)(c) and (d) and 31(4)(c) and (d) do not apply to the making and withdrawal of determinations under section 10 of the Act.

III FUND [248]

67 The application

(1) Where the civil legal services which are the subject of an application are described in a category in the Category Definitions that form part of the 2010 Standard Civil Contract, 2013 Standard Civil Contract, 2014 Standard Civil Contract, 2015 Standard Civil Contract or 2018 Standard Civil Contract, the application must specify—
(a) the category within which the civil legal services are described; and
(b) if the individual has identified a proposed provider, a provider with whom the Lord Chancellor has made an arrangement under

FUNDING

section 2(1) of the Act for the provision of services which fall within the category specified in the application (unless the effective administration of justice test is satisfied).

(2) An application for a determination under section 10 of the Act must—

(a) be made to the Director in writing in a form specified by the Lord Chancellor and signed by the individual and any proposed provider; and

(b) state whether it is proposed that the services should be provided as Controlled Work, Licensed Work or under an individual case contract.

III FUND [249]

68 Determinations

(1) A determination under section 10 of the Act may specify that the determination is to be treated as having effect from a date earlier than the date of the determination.

(2) Where the Director makes—

(a) an exceptional case determination under section 10(2)(a) of the Act; or

(b) a wider public interest determination under section 10(4)(b) of the Act,

the Director must provide written reasons for the determination and notice of any right of review.

III FUND [250]

69 Review

(1) The individual may, in accordance with paragraph (2), apply for a review of—

(a) a refusal to make a determination under section 10(2)(a) or 10(4)(b) of the Act;

(b) a determination that an individual does not qualify for the services under section 10(2)(b) or 10(4)(c) of the Act;

(c) an amendment of, or refusal to amend, a limitation or condition to which a determination under section 10(2)(b) or 10(4)(c) of the Act is subject; or

(d) a withdrawal of a determination.

(2) Within fourteen days of receipt of a refusal, determination, amendment, or withdrawal described in paragraph (1) (a "decision"), the individual may—

(a) apply to the Director for a review of the decision in a form specified by the Lord Chancellor; and

(b) include written representations supporting that application.

(3) The Director must consider the application and any written representations and may—

(a) confirm or amend the decision which is the subject of the review; or

(b) substitute a new decision.

(4) Where the decision which is the subject of the review was the withdrawal of a determination and, following the review, the Director substitutes a determination for that withdrawal, the determination takes effect (unless the Director directs otherwise) as if the original decision had not been made.

(5) The Director must ensure that a certificate accurately records the civil legal services for which the individual qualifies following the review (unless the services are to be provided as Controlled Work).

(6) The Director must notify the individual and the provider or proposed provider identified in the individual's application of the decision following the review.

SCHEDULE 1
SUPPORTING DOCUMENTS: DOMESTIC VIOLENCE

III FUND [250A]

1 Evidence that B has been arrested for a relevant domestic violence offence.

2 A relevant police caution for a domestic violence offence.

3 Evidence of relevant criminal proceedings for a domestic violence offence which have not concluded.

4 A relevant conviction for a domestic violence offence.

5 Evidence of a court order binding over B in connection with a domestic violence offence.

6 A domestic violence protection notice issued under section 24 of the Crime and Security Act 2010 against B.

7 A relevant protective injunction.

8 An undertaking given in England and Wales under section 46 or 63E of the Family Law Act 1996 (or given in Scotland or Northern Ireland in place of a protective injunction) by B provided that a cross-undertaking relating to domestic violence was not given by A.

9 A copy of a finding of fact, made in proceedings in the United Kingdom, that there has been domestic violence by B.

10 An expert report produced as evidence in proceedings in the United Kingdom for the benefit of a court or tribunal confirming that a person with whom B is or was in a family relationship, was assessed as being, or at risk of being, a victim of domestic violence by B.

11 A letter or report from an appropriate health professional confirming that that professional, or another appropriate health professional—

(a) has examined A in person; and

(b) in the reasonable professional judgement of the author or the examining appropriate health professional A has, or has had, injuries or a condition consistent with being a victim of domestic violence.

12 A letter or report from—

(a) the appropriate health professional who made the referral described below;

(b) an appropriate health professional who has access to the medical records of A; or

(c) the person to whom the referral described below was made;

confirming that there was a referral by an appropriate health professional of A to a person who provides specialist support or assistance for victims of, or those at risk of, domestic violence.

13 A letter from any person who is a member of a multi-agency risk assessment conference (or other suitable local safeguarding forum) confirming that A, or a person with whom A is in a family relationship, is or has been at risk of harm from domestic violence by B.

14 A letter from an independent domestic violence advisor confirming that they are providing support to A.

15 A letter from an independent sexual violence advisor confirming that they are providing support to A relating to sexual violence by B.

16 A letter from an officer employed by a local authority or housing association (or their equivalent in Scotland or Northern Ireland) for the purpose of supporting tenants containing—

(a) a statement to the effect that, in their reasonable professional judgment, a person with whom B is or has been in a family relationship is, or is at risk of being, a victim of domestic violence by B;

(b) a description of the specific matters relied upon to support that judgment; and

(c) a description of the support they provided to the victim of domestic violence or the person at risk of domestic violence by B.

17 (1) A letter from an organisation providing domestic violence support services.

(2) The letter must confirm that it—

(a) is situated in England and Wales;

(b) has been operating for an uninterrupted period of six months or more; and

(c) provided A with support in relation to A's needs as a victim, or person at risk, of domestic violence.

(3) The letter must contain—

(a) a statement to the effect that, in the reasonable professional judgment of the author of the letter, A is, or is at risk of being, a victim of domestic violence;

(b) a description of the specific matters relied upon to support that judgment;

(c) a description of the support provided to A; and

(d) a statement of the reasons why A needed that support.

18 A letter or report from an organisation providing domestic violence support services in the United Kingdom confirming—

(a) that a person with whom B is or was in a family relationship was refused admission to a refuge;

(b) the date on which they were refused admission to the refuge; and

(c) they sought admission to the refuge because of allegations of domestic violence by B.

19 A letter from a public authority confirming that a person with whom B is or was in a family relationship, was assessed as being, or at risk of being, a victim of domestic violence by B (or a copy of that assessment).

20 A letter from the Secretary of State for the Home Department confirming that A has been granted leave to remain in the United Kingdom under paragraph 289B of the Immigration Rules.

21 Evidence which the Director is satisfied demonstrates that A has been, or is at risk of being, the victim of domestic violence by B in the form of abuse which relates to financial matters.

22 For the purpose of this Schedule—

"A" means the applicant for civil legal services;

"appropriate health professional" means—

(a) a medical practitioner licensed to practise by the General Medical Council; or

(b) a health professional who is registered to practise in the United Kingdom by—

(i) the Nursing and Midwifery Council;

(ii) the General Dental Council; or

(c) a paramedic, practitioner psychologist, radiographer or social worker registered to practise in the United Kingdom by the Health and Care Professions Council;

"B" means the individual with whom A was in a family relationship giving rise to the need for the civil legal services that are the subject of the application;

"domestic violence offence" has the meaning given in the document published by the Lord Chancellor for that purpose under section 2 of the Act;

"expert report" means a report by a person qualified to give expert advice on all or most of the matters that are the subject of the report;

"housing association" has the same meaning as in subsection 1(1) of the Housing Associations Act 1985;

"Immigration Rules" means rules made by the Secretary of State under section 3(3) of the Immigration Act 1971;

"local authority" means a county council, a district council, a London borough council or a parish council but, in relation to Wales, means a county council, county borough council or community council;

"protective injunction" means an order made by the court—

(a) in respect of persons who are in a family relationship with each other, containing any of the following provisions—

(i) protecting a person from harm, intimidation, threats or harassment;

(ii) protecting a person from being forced into a marriage or from any attempt to be forced into a marriage;

(iii) prohibiting a person from contacting, or communicating with, another;

(iv) concerning entry or access to, or the use or occupation of, property;

(b) for the protection from female genital mutilation under paragraph 1 or 18 of Schedule 2 to the Female Genital Mutilation Act 2003; or

(c) in respect of a violent offender within the meaning of section 98 of the Criminal Justice and Immigration Act 2008;

but does not include an order made without notice to the respondent that was subsequently set aside by the court;

"public authority" has the same meaning as in section 6 of the Human Rights Act 1998;

"refuge" means—

(a) a refuge established for the purpose of providing accommodation for victims of, or those at risk of, domestic violence; or

(b) a residential home established and maintained by a public body for any other purpose that also provides accommodation to the victims of, or those at risk of, domestic violence;

"relevant" means that the evidence—

(a) identifies a person with whom B is or was in a family relationship as being, or at risk of being, the victim of domestic violence; or

(b) is—

(i) in a form described in paragraphs 1 to 4 of this Schedule;

(ii) identifies B as the person arrested for, cautioned with, charged with, or convicted of the domestic violence offence; and

(iii) relates to a domestic violence offence which does not identify the victim.

FUNDING

SCHEDULE 2
SUPPORTING DOCUMENTS: PROTECTION OF CHILDREN

III FUND [250B]

1 Evidence that B has been arrested for a child abuse offence.

2 A relevant police caution for a child abuse offence.

3 Evidence of relevant criminal proceedings for a child abuse offence which have not concluded.

4 A relevant conviction for a child abuse offence.

5 A relevant protective injunction.

6 A copy of a finding of fact made in proceedings in the United Kingdom of abuse of a child by B.

7 A letter from a social services department in England and Wales (or its equivalent in Scotland or Northern Ireland) confirming that the child was assessed as being, or at risk of being, a victim of child abuse by B (or a copy of that assessment).

8 A letter from a social services department in England and Wales (or its equivalent in Scotland or Northern Ireland) confirming that a child protection plan was put in place to protect the child from abuse or a risk of abuse by B (or a copy of that plan).

9 An application for an injunction described in paragraph 5 of this Schedule made with an application for a prohibited steps order against B under section 8 of the Children Act 1989 which has not, at the date of the application for civil legal services, been decided by the court.

10 For the purpose of this Schedule—
"child abuse offence" has the meaning given in the document published by the Lord Chancellor for that purpose under section 2 of the Act;
"protective injunction" has the same meaning given in Schedule 1 to these Regulations;
"relevant" means—

(a) for the purpose of paragraphs 1 to 4 of this Schedule that the arrest, caution, criminal proceedings or conviction identifies B as being arrested for, cautioned for, charged with, or convicted of, the child abuse offence; and

(b) for the purpose of paragraph 5 of this Schedule, that the protective injunction—

(i) identifies B as the respondent; and

(ii) is made for the protection of the child who is or would be the subject of the order to which the application relates.

CIVIL LEGAL AID (MERITS CRITERIA) REGULATIONS 2013

SI 2013/104

FUNDING

PART 1
INTERPRETATION AND GENERAL

III FUND [251]

1 Citation and commencement

These Regulations may be cited as the Civil Legal Aid (Merits Criteria) Regulations 2013 and come into force on 1st April 2013.

III FUND [252]

2 Interpretation

In these Regulations—

"the 1990 Act" means the Courts and Legal Services Act 1990;

"the Act" means the Legal Aid, Sentencing and Punishment of Offenders Act 2012;

"advocate" means a person who exercises a right of audience before a court, tribunal or other person;

"case with overwhelming importance to the individual" means a case which is not primarily a claim for damages or other sum of money and which relates to one or more of the following—

(a) the life, liberty or physical safety of the individual or a member of that individual's family (an individual is a member of another individual's family if the requirements of section 10(6) are met); or

(b) the immediate risk that the individual may become homeless;

"conditional fee agreement" means an enforceable agreement which satisfies the conditions in—

(a) section 58 of the 1990 Act (conditional fee agreements);

(b) section 58AA of the 1990 Act (damages-based agreements); or

(c) section 58B of the 1990 Act (litigation funding agreements);

"Convention rights" has the same meaning as in section 1 of the Human Rights Act 1998;

"domestic violence case" means any matter which is described in either of the following paragraphs of Part 1 of Schedule 1 to the Act (civil legal services)—

(a) paragraph 11 (family homes and domestic violence);
(ab) paragraph 15A (female genital mutilation protection orders); or
(b) paragraph 16 (forced marriage);

"Dublin III claim" means any matter described in paragraph 19(1) of Part 1 of Schedule 1 to the Act (judicial review) in relation to a transfer decision within the meaning of Regulation (EU) No 604/2013 of the European Parliament and of the Council of 26 June 2013 establishing the criteria and mechanisms for determining the Member State responsible for examining an application for international protection lodged in one of the Member States by a third-country national or a stateless person;

"emergency representation" means the provision of civil legal services following an urgent application made in accordance with regulations made under section 12 (determinations) of the Act;

"family dispute" means any matter which is described in any of the following paragraphs of Part 1 of Schedule 1 to the Act (civil legal services)—

(a) paragraph 1 (care, supervision and protection of children);
(b) paragraph 9 (inherent jurisdiction of High Court in relation to children and vulnerable adults), to the extent that the matter relates to—
  (i) a child; or
  (ii) a vulnerable adult, but only to the extent that the matter arises out of a family relationship within the meaning of paragraph 14(7)(b) and (c) of Part 1 of Schedule 1 to the Act;
(c) paragraph 10 (unlawful removal of children);
(d) paragraph 11 (family homes and domestic violence);
(e) paragraph 12 (victims of domestic violence and family matters);
(f) paragraph 13 (protection of children and family matters);
(g) paragraph 14 (mediation in family disputes);
(h) paragraph 15 (children who are parties to family proceedings);
(ha) paragraph 15A (female genital mutilation protection orders);
(i) paragraph 16 (forced marriage);
(j) paragraph 17 (EU and international agreements concerning children); or
(k) paragraph 18 (EU and international agreements concerning maintenance);

"general merits criteria" means the criteria set out in Part 4 (general merits criteria);

"lead claim" means the claim in a multi-party action which the Director has identified as being the appropriate claim to be a test case for common or related issues of fact or law;

"merits criteria" means the general merits criteria and the specific merits criteria;

"multi-party action" means proceedings in which a number of individuals have a cause of action which involves common or related issues of fact or law;

"private law children case" means any matter which is described in any of the following paragraphs of Part 1 of Schedule 1 to the Act (civil legal services)—

(a) paragraph 10 (unlawful removal of children);
(b) paragraph 12 (victims of domestic violence and family matters) [or paragraph 15 (children who are parties to family proceedings), to the extent such provisions relate to—

(i) Part 1 or 3 of the Family Law Act 1986 (child custody and declarations of status); or

(ii) any provision of Part 1 or 2 of the Children Act 1989 (orders with respect to children in family proceedings), other than section 15 of, and Schedule 1 to, that Act; or

(c) paragraph 13 (protection of children and family matters);

"provider" means a person who provides civil legal services under Part 1 of the Act (legal aid);

"public law children case" means any matter which is described in either of the following paragraphs of Part 1 of Schedule 1 to the Act (civil legal services)—

(a) paragraph 1 (care, supervision and protection of children), to the extent that the matter is not a "special Children Act 1989 case"; or

(b) paragraph 9 (inherent jurisdiction of High Court in relation to children and vulnerable adults), to the extent that the matter relates to a child;

"public law claim" means any matter which is described in any of the following paragraphs of Part 1 of Schedule 1 to the Act (civil legal services)—

(a) paragraph 19 (judicial review) other than a Dublin III claim;

(b) paragraph 20 (habeas corpus); or

(c) paragraph 34 (homelessness);

"small claims track" means the small claims track for which provision is made in Part 27 of the Civil Procedure Rules, which are made in exercise of the power conferred by section 2 of the Civil Procedure Act 1997 to make rules of court under section 1 of that Act;

"special Children Act 1989 case" means any matter described in paragraph 1(1)(a), (b) or (c) of Part 1 of Schedule 1 to the Act (care, supervision and protection of children), to the extent that it relates to any of the following provisions of Children Act 1989 or, where specified, the Social Services and Well-being (Wales) Act 2014—

(a) section 25 (use of accommodation for restricting liberty), to the extent that the individual to whom civil legal services may be provided is the child who is or would be the subject of the order;

(aa) section 119 of the Social Services and Well-being (Wales) Act 2014 (use of accommodation for restricting liberty), to the extent that the individual to whom civil legal services may be provided is the child who is or would be the subject of the order;

(b) section 31 (care and supervision orders), to the extent that the individual to whom civil legal services may be provided is the child who is or would be the subject of the order, that child's parent or other person with parental responsibility for that child;

(c) section 43 (child assessment orders), to the extent that the individual to whom civil legal services may be provided is the child who is or would be the subject of the order, that child's parent or other person with parental responsibility for that child;

(d) section 44 (orders for emergency protection of children), to the extent that the individual to whom civil legal services may be provided is the child who is or would be the subject of the order, that child's parent or other person with parental responsibility for that child; or

(e) section 45 (duration of emergency protection orders and other supplemental provisions), to the extent that the individual to whom civil legal services may be provided is the child who is or would be the subject of the order, that child's parent or other person with parental responsibility for that child,

but does not include appeals from final orders made under any of those provisions of the Children Act 1989 or, as the case may be, the Social Services and Well-being (Wales) Act 2014; and

"specific merits criteria" means the criteria set out in Part 6 (specific merits criteria).

III FUND [253]

3 Delegation

A function of the Director under these Regulations may be exercised by a person authorised for that purpose by the Director, or by an employee of that person.

III FUND [254]

4 Prospects of success

(1) In these Regulations, "prospects of success" means the likelihood that an individual who has made an application for civil legal services will obtain a successful outcome at a trial or other final hearing in the proceedings to which the application relates, as assessed by the Director in accordance with regulation 5 (prospects of success test).

(2) When the Director assesses the prospects of success, the Director must not have regard to—

(a) the possibility of settling the proceedings to which the application relates; or

(b) subject to paragraph (3), the prospects of success in any appeal or possible appeal.

(3) If the application for civil legal services is in relation to an appeal, then the prospects of success are the prospects of success in relation to that appeal.

(4) "Successful outcome" means the outcome a reasonable individual would intend to achieve in the proceedings in all the circumstances of the case.

III FUND [255]

5 Prospects of success test

(1) Where the Director assesses, for the purposes of these Regulations, the prospects of success of a matter to which an application for civil legal services relates, the Director must classify the prospects of that matter as follows—

(a) "very good", which means an 80% or more chance of obtaining a successful outcome;

(b) "good", which means a 60% or more chance, but less than an 80% chance, of obtaining a successful outcome;

(c) "moderate", which means a 50% or more chance, but less than a 60% chance, of obtaining a successful outcome;

(d) "borderline", which means that the case is not "unclear" but that it is not possible, by reason of disputed law, fact or expert evidence, to—

(i) decide that the chance of obtaining a successful outcome is 50% or more; or

(ii) classify the prospects as marginal or poor . . .;

(da) "marginal", which means a 45% or more chance, but less than a 50% chance, of obtaining a successful outcome;

(e) "poor", which means less than a 45% chance of obtaining a successful outcome; or

(f) "unclear", which has the meaning given in paragraph (2).

(2) "Unclear" means the Director cannot put the case into any of the categories in paragraph (1)(a) to (e) because, in all the circumstances of the case, there are identifiable investigations which could be carried out, after which it should be possible for the Director to make a reliable estimate of the prospects of success.

III FUND [256]

6 Public interest

(1) For the purposes of these Regulations, a case is of significant wider public interest if the Director is satisfied that the case is an appropriate case to realise—

(a) real benefits to the public at large, other than those which normally flow from cases of the type in question; and

(b) benefits for an identifiable class of individuals, other than the individual to whom civil legal services may be provided or members of that individual's family.

(2) In paragraph (1), an individual is a member of another individual's family if the requirements of section 10(6) are met.

III FUND [257]

7 Reasonable private paying individual test

For the purposes of these Regulations, the reasonable private paying individual test is met if the Director is satisfied that the potential benefit to be gained from the provision of civil legal services justifies the likely costs, such that a reasonable private paying individual would be prepared to start or continue the proceedings having regard to the prospects of success and all the other circumstances of the case.

III FUND [258]

8 Proportionality test

For the purposes of these Regulations, the proportionality test is met if the Director is satisfied that the likely benefits of the proceedings to the individual and others justify the likely costs, having regard to the prospects of success and all the other circumstances of the case.

III FUND [259]

9 Likely damages

"Likely damages" means the amount of any damages or other sum of money contested in the case that the individual who is applying for civil legal services is likely to receive if substantially successful at trial or other final hearing, calculated in accordance with regulations made under section 12 of the Act (determinations).

III FUND [260]

10 Likely costs

(1) For the purposes of these Regulations, "likely costs" means the total costs likely to have been incurred on behalf of an applicant for civil legal services at final judgment or settlement of the proceedings—

(a) calculated on the basis that the proceedings fail to obtain a successful outcome, or costs are not recovered from another party to the proceedings; and

(b) taking into account the prospects of the proceedings settling before trial or other final hearing.

(2) In paragraph (1), "costs" means the fees payable to any provider, calculated by reference to remuneration rates set out in arrangements made by the Lord Chancellor under section 2(1) of the Act or in regulations under section 2(3) of the Act, including (but not limited to)—

(a) counsel's fees;

(b) disbursements; and

(c) any fees payable at an enhanced rate,

but not including Value Added Tax.

III FUND [261]

11 Qualifying for civil legal services

(1) These Regulations apply for the purposes of determining whether an individual or a legal person qualifies for civil legal services under Part 1 of the Act in accordance with section 11(1)(b).

(2) In determining whether an individual qualifies for civil legal services under Part 1 of the Act, the Director must apply the general merits criteria, except to the extent that they are disapplied, modified or supplemented by the specific merits criteria.

(3) The Director must apply the merits criteria which are appropriate in each case in accordance with Part 5 (application of the merits criteria), to the extent that it is relevant.

(4) Subject to paragraph (9), an individual or legal person may qualify for civil legal services in accordance with Part 1 of the Act only if the Director is satisfied that—

(a) the general merits criteria and, to the extent that they are relevant, the specific merits criteria are met;

(b) the criterion in paragraph (6) is met; and

(c) the criterion in paragraph (8) is met, to the extent that it is relevant.

(5) When determining whether an individual qualifies for civil legal services under Part 1 of the Act, the Director must apply the merits criteria which are relevant to the forms of civil legal services set out in Part 2 (form of civil legal services) and must consider which form of civil legal services is appropriate in accordance with Part 3 (availability of forms of civil legal services).

(6) An individual or legal person may qualify for civil legal services only if the Director is satisfied that it would be reasonable to provide those services in the light of the conduct of that individual or legal person in connection with—

(a) any civil legal services made available under Part 1 of the Act;

(b) any application for civil legal services under Part 1 of the Act; or

(c) any civil proceedings for resolving disputes about legal rights or duties.

(7) If the Director is satisfied that—

(a) the case is not a case which relates to the life or liberty of the individual or their family (an individual is a member of another individual's family if the requirements of section 10(6) are met);

(b) the case is not a public law children case; and

(c) the likely costs of the case exceed £250,000 or, if the case forms part of a multi-party action, the likely costs of the multi-party action exceed £1,000,000,

the criterion in paragraph (8) applies.

(8) An individual or legal person may qualify for civil legal services only if the Director is satisfied that, having had regard to the present and likely future demands for the provision of civil legal services under Part 1 of the Act, it is reasonable to provide the individual or legal person with civil legal services in all the circumstances of the case including, but not limited to, the particular circumstances of the individual or legal person.

(9) No merits criteria apply to civil legal services provided—

(a) in relation to an assessment by a mediator of whether, in the light of all the circumstances, a case is suitable for mediation;

(b) in relation to any matter described in paragraph 18(2) of Part 1 of Schedule 1 to the Act (EU and international agreements concerning maintenance), to the extent that it—

(i) relates to any application under Article 56(1)(a) or (b) of the EU Maintenance Regulation; and

(ii) concerns maintenance obligations arising from a parent-child relationship towards a person under the age of 21;

(c) in relation to any matter described in paragraph 17(1)(b) of Part 1 of Schedule 1 to the Act (an application made to the Lord Chancellor under the 1980 Hague Convention in respect of a child who is, or is believed to be, in England and Wales), to the extent that it relates to an applicant under the 1980 Hague Convention; or

(d) in relation to any matter described in paragraph 18(3A) of Part 1 of Schedule 1 to the Act (application made under Article 10 of the 2007 Hague Convention) to the extent that it—

(i) relates to any application under Article 10(1)(a) or (b) of the 2007 Hague Convention; and

(ii) is an application made by a creditor under the 2007 Hague Convention concerning maintenance obligations arising from a parent-child relationship towards a person under the age of 21.

FUNDING

PART 2
FORM OF CIVIL LEGAL SERVICES

III FUND [262]

12 Form of civil legal services

(1) Subject to Part 3 (availability of forms of civil legal services), when determining whether an individual qualifies for civil legal services under Part 1 of the Act, the Director must apply the merits criteria which are relevant to each form of civil legal services set out in paragraph (3).

(2) Subject to Part 3 (availability of forms of civil legal services), when determining whether a legal person qualifies for civil legal services under Part 1 of the Act by virtue of the criteria in Chapter 8 of Part 6, the Director must apply the merits criteria which are relevant to each of the forms of civil legal services set out in paragraph (3)(a) or (f).

(3) "Form of civil legal services" means—

(a) legal help;

(b) help at court;

(c) family help;

(d) family mediation;

(e) help with family mediation;

(f) legal representation; and

(g) other legal services,

which are further defined in regulations 13 to 19.

III FUND [263]

13 Legal help

"Legal help" means the provision of civil legal services other than—

(a) acting as a mediator or arbitrator;

(b) issuing or conducting court proceedings;
(c) instructing an advocate in proceedings;
(d) preparing to provide advocacy in proceedings; or
(e) advocacy in proceedings.

III FUND [264]

14 Help at court

"Help at court" means the provision of any of the following civil legal services at a particular hearing—

(a) instructing an advocate;
(b) preparing to provide advocacy; or
(c) advocacy.

III FUND [265]

15 Family help

(1) Family help may be provided in a family dispute as either family help (lower) or family help (higher).

(2) "Family help (lower)" means—

(a) civil legal services provided in relation to the negotiation of a family dispute before the issuing of proceedings; or
(b) civil legal services provided in relation to the issuing of proceedings in order to obtain a consent order following the settlement of a family dispute.

(3) "Family help (higher)" means such civil legal services as are available under legal representation but does not include preparation for, or representation at, a contested final hearing or appeal.

III FUND [266]

16 Family mediation

(1) "Family mediation" means the provision of any of the following civil legal services, in a family dispute—

(a) an assessment by a mediator of whether, in the light of all the circumstances, a case is suitable for mediation; or
(b) acting as a mediator.

(2) In this regulation, "mediator" means a mediator with whom the Lord Chancellor has made an arrangement under section 2(1) of the Act (arrangements).

III FUND [267]

17 Help with family mediation

"Help with family mediation" means the provision of any of the following civil legal services, in relation to a family dispute—

(a) civil legal services provided in relation to family mediation; or
(b) civil legal services provided in relation to the issuing of proceedings to obtain a consent order following the settlement of the dispute following family mediation.

III FUND [268]

18 Legal representation

(1) Legal representation may be provided as either investigative representation or full representation.

(2) "Legal representation" means the provision of civil legal services, other than acting as a mediator or arbitrator, to an individual or legal person in particular proceedings where that individual or legal person—

(a) is a party to those proceedings;

(b) wishes to be joined as a party to those proceedings; or

(c) is contemplating issuing those proceedings.

(3) "Investigative representation" means legal representation which is limited to the investigation of the strength of the contemplated proceedings and includes the issuing and conducting of proceedings but only so far as necessary—

(a) to obtain disclosure of information relevant to the prospects of success of the proceedings;

(b) to protect the position of the individual or legal person applying for investigative representation in relation to an urgent hearing; or

(c) to protect the position of the individual or legal person applying for investigative representation in relation to the time limit for the issue of the proceedings.

(4) "Full representation" means legal representation other than investigative representation.

III FUND [269]

19 Other legal services

"Other legal services" means the provision of any of the following civil legal services—

(a) instructing an advocate;

(b) preparing to provide advocacy; or

(c) advocacy,

in proceedings in relation to which the Director, having applied the relevant merits criteria in accordance with regulations 48 to 50 (application of the merits criteria in exceptional cases), has made a determination under section 10(2)(b) or (4)(c)(exceptional cases) of the Act.

PART 3

AVAILABILITY OF FORMS OF CIVIL LEGAL SERVICES

III FUND [270]

20 Provision of the most appropriate form of civil legal services

(1) Where the Director determines in accordance with regulations 21 to 31 that—

(a) an individual or a legal person qualifies for civil legal services under Part 1 of the Act; and

(b) that more than one form of civil legal services could be provided for that individual or legal person,

the services provided must be those the Director considers most appropriate in all the circumstances.

(2) Regulations 21 to 31 apply, in relation to any matter referred to in those regulations, for the purpose of determining which form of civil legal services is most appropriate in relation to that matter.

III FUND [271]

21 Mental Health

Investigative representation is not appropriate in relation to any matter described in paragraph 5(1)(a) or (b) of Part 1 of Schedule 1 to the Act (mental health), to the extent that it relates to proceedings before the First-tier Tribunal or the Mental Health Review Tribunal for Wales.

III FUND [272]

22 Immigration and terrorism prevention and investigation measures etc

Help at court and investigative representation are not appropriate in relation to any matter described in any of the following paragraphs of Part 1 of Schedule 1 to the Act (civil legal services)—

(a) paragraphs 25 to 30 of Part 1 of Schedule 1 to the Act (immigration), to the extent they relate to proceedings before the First-tier Tribunal or the Upper Tribunal;

(b) paragraphs 32(1) (victims of trafficking in human beings) and 32A(1) (victims of slavery, servitude or forced or compulsory labour); and

(c) paragraph 45 of Part 1 of Schedule 1 to the Act (terrorism prevention and investigation measures etc).

III FUND [273]

23 Special Immigration Appeals Commission, immigration: accommodation for asylum-seekers etc and victims of trafficking in human beings

Help at court is not appropriate in relation to any matter described in any of the following paragraphs of Part 1 of Schedule 1 to the Act (civil legal services)—

(a) paragraph 24 (Special Immigration Appeals Commission); and

(b) paragraph 31 (immigration: accommodation for asylum-seekers etc).

III FUND [274]

24 Family disputes

(1) Help at court and investigative representation are not appropriate in relation to a family dispute.

(2) Full representation is not appropriate in relation to any matter described in paragraph 14 of Part 1 of Schedule 1 to the Act (mediation in family disputes).

III FUND [275]]

25 Victims of domestic violence and family matters: family help (lower)

Family help (lower) is not appropriate in relation to any matter described in paragraph 12 of Part 1 of Schedule 1 to the Act (victims of domestic violence and family matters) to the extent that it relates to a petition for divorce under section 1 of the Matrimonial Causes Act 1973 or an application for a dissolution order under section 44 of the Civil Partnership Act 2004.

III FUND [276]

26 Public law children cases and special Children Act 1989 cases

Family help (higher) is not appropriate in public law children cases or special Children Act 1989 cases.

III FUND [277]

27 Victims of domestic violence and family matters: help with family mediation
Help with family mediation described in regulation 17(b) is not appropriate in relation to any matter arising under an enactment specified in paragraph (e), (i), (k), (l) or (o) of the definition of "family enactment" in paragraph 12(9) (victims of domestic violence and family matters) of Part 1 of Schedule 1 to the Act (civil legal services).

III FUND [278]

28 Emergency representation
Legal representation and family help (higher) are the only forms of civil legal services which are appropriate for an individual who qualifies for emergency representation.

III FUND [279]

29 Civil legal services which do not include advocacy
Legal representation, family help (higher) and help at court are not appropriate forms of civil legal services in relation to any matter in which the civil legal services available under Part 1 of the Act do not include advocacy.

III FUND [280]

30 Inquests
Legal help is the only form of civil legal services which is appropriate in relation to any matter described in paragraph 41 of Part 1 of Schedule 1 to the Act (inquests).

III FUND [281]

31 Cross-border disputes
Legal help and legal representation are the only forms of civil legal services which are appropriate in relation to any matter described in paragraph 44 of Part 1 of Schedule 1 to the Act (cross-border disputes).

PART 4
GENERAL MERITS CRITERIA

III FUND [282]

32 Criteria for determinations for legal help
An individual may qualify for legal help only if the Director is satisfied that the following criteria are met—

(a) it is reasonable for the individual to be provided with legal help, having regard to any potential sources of funding for the individual other than under Part 1 of the Act; and

(b) there is likely to be sufficient benefit to the individual, having regard to all the circumstances of the case, including the circumstances of the individual, to justify the cost of provision of legal help.

III FUND [283]

33 Criteria for determinations for help at court
An individual may qualify for help at court only if the Director is satisfied that the following criteria are met—

FUNDING

(a) it is reasonable for the individual to be provided with help at court having regard to any potential sources of funding for the individual, other than under Part 1 of the Act;

(b) there is likely to be sufficient benefit to the individual, having regard to all the circumstances of the case, including the circumstances of the individual, to justify the cost of provision of help at court; and

(c) the nature and circumstances of—

(i) the proceedings;

(ii) the particular hearing; and

(iii) the individual,

are such that advocacy is appropriate and will be of real benefit to that individual.

III FUND [284]

34 Criterion for determinations for family help

An individual may qualify for family help only if the Director is satisfied that the reasonable private paying individual test is met.

III FUND [285]

35 Criteria for determinations for family help (lower)

An individual may qualify for family help (lower) only if the Director is satisfied that the criterion in regulation 34 (criterion for determinations for family help) is met and that the provision of family help (lower) would help to avoid the issue of contested proceedings.

III FUND [286]

36 Criteria for determinations for family help (higher)

(1) An individual may qualify for family help (higher) only if the Director is satisfied that the criterion in regulation 34 (criterion for determinations for family help) is met and that the individual has exhausted all reasonable alternatives to bringing proceedings.

(2) Alternatives to bringing proceedings include, but are not limited to, mediation and negotiation.

III FUND [287]

37 Criteria for determinations for family mediation

An individual may qualify for family mediation under regulation 16(1)(b) (mediation) only if the Director is satisfied that the mediator has assessed that, in all the circumstances of the case, the case is suitable for mediation.

III FUND [288]

38 Criteria for determinations for help with family mediation

An individual may qualify for help with family mediation only if the Director is satisfied that the following criteria are met—

(a) the individual is participating, or has participated in, family mediation (other than attending an assessment of the kind referred to in regulation 16(1)(a)); and

(b) there is sufficient benefit to the individual, having regard to all the circumstances of the case, including the circumstances of the individual, to justify the cost of provision of help with family mediation.

III FUND [289]

39 Standard criteria for determinations for legal representation

An individual may qualify for legal representation only if the Director is satisfied that the following criteria are met—

(a) the individual does not have access to other potential sources of funding (other than a conditional fee agreement) from which it would be reasonable to fund the case;

(b) the case is unsuitable for a conditional fee agreement;

(c) there is no person other than the individual, including a person who might benefit from the proceedings, who can reasonably be expected to bring the proceedings;

(d) the individual has exhausted all reasonable alternatives to bringing proceedings including any complaints system, ombudsman scheme or other form of alternative dispute resolution;

(e) there is a need for representation in all the circumstances of the case including—

(i) the nature and complexity of the issues;

(ii) the existence of other proceedings; and

(iii) the interests of other parties to the proceedings; and

(f) the proceedings are not likely to be allocated to the small claims track.

III FUND [290]

40 Criteria for determinations for investigative representation

(1) An individual may qualify for investigative representation only if the Director is satisfied that the criteria in regulation 39 (standard criteria for determinations for legal representation) and the following criteria are met—

(a) the prospects of success of the case are unclear and substantial investigative work is required before those prospects can be determined;

(b) the Director has reasonable grounds for believing that, once the investigative work to be carried out under investigative representation is completed, the case will satisfy the criteria for full representation and, in particular, will meet the cost benefit criteria in regulation 42 and the prospects of success criterion in regulation 43; and

(c) subject to paragraph (2), if the individual's claim is primarily a claim for damages or other sum of money in which the likely damages do not exceed £5,000, the case must be of significant wider public interest.

(2) For the purposes of paragraph (1)(c), if the claim forms part of a multi-party action only the lead claim within that action is capable of being a case of significant wider public interest.

III FUND [291]

41 Criteria for determinations for full representation

An individual may qualify for full representation only if the Director is satisfied that the criteria in regulation 39 (standard criteria for determinations for legal representation) and the following criteria are met——

(a) the cost benefit criteria in regulation 42;

(b) the prospects of success criterion in regulation 43; and

(c) if the individual's claim forms part of a multi-party action and is primarily a claim for damages or other sum of money in which the likely damages do not exceed £5,000, the multi-party action damages criterion in regulation 44.

FUNDING

III FUND [292]

42 Cost benefit criteria for determinations for full representation

(1) The cost benefit criteria are as follows.

(2) If the case is primarily a claim for damages or other sum of money and is not of significant wider public interest—

(a) if the prospects of success of the case are very good, the Director must be satisfied that the likely damages exceed likely costs;

(b) if the prospects of success of the case are good, the Director must be satisfied that the likely damages exceed likely costs by a ratio of two to one; or

(c) if the prospects of success of the case are moderate . . ., the Director must be satisfied that the likely damages exceed likely costs by a ratio of four to one.

(3) If the case is—

(a) not primarily a claim for damages or other sum of money; and

(b) not of significant wider public interest,

the Director must be satisfied that the reasonable private paying individual test is met.

(4) If the case is of significant wider public interest, the Director must be satisfied that the proportionality test is met.

III FUND [293]

43 Prospects of success criterion for determinations for full representation

The prospects of success criterion is only met if the Director is satisfied that the prospects of success are—

(a) very good, good or moderate; or

(b) borderline or marginal, and the case is—

(i) of significant wider public interest; or

(ii) a case with overwhelming importance to the individual.

III FUND [294]

44 Multi-party action damages criterion for determinations for full representation

The multi-party action damages criterion is only met if—

(a) the individual's claim is the lead claim, and

(b) the Director is satisfied that the case is of significant wider public interest.

III FUND [295]

45 Criterion for determinations for other legal services

An individual may qualify for other legal services only if the Director is satisfied that it would be reasonable in all the circumstances of the case for the individual to be provided with other legal services.

III FUND [296]

46 Criteria for determinations for family help (higher) or legal representation provided as emergency representation

An individual may qualify, in relation to an application for emergency representation for family help (higher) or legal representation, only if the Director is satisfied that—

(a) the merits criteria which apply to that application are met; and

(b) it is in the interests of justice to provide emergency representation.

PART 5
APPLICATION OF THE MERITS CRITERIA

III FUND [297]

47 Application of the merits criteria in cases described in more than one paragraph of Part 1 of Schedule 1 to the Act

Where more than one set of merits criteria could be applied to a case because it is described in more than one paragraph of Part 1 of Schedule 1 to the Act (civil legal services), the Director must apply the merits criteria which are, in the opinion of the Director, most appropriate in all the circumstances of the case.

III FUND [298]

48 Application of the merits criteria in exceptional inquest cases

The Director must apply the criterion in regulation 45 (criterion for determinations for other legal services) for the purposes of a determination under—

(a) section 10(2)(b) of the Act, to the extent to that it relates to services which consist of advocacy in proceedings at an inquest under the Coroners Act 1988 into the death of a member of the family of the individual who has made an application for civil legal services; or

(b) section 10(4)(c) of the Act.

III FUND [299]

49 Application of the merits criteria in cases which are exceptional cases excluded from Part 1 of Schedule 1 to the Act

(1) The Director must apply the merits criteria in paragraph (2) for the purpose of making a determination under section 10(2)(b) of the Act (exceptional cases) in relation to civil legal services in any matter which would fall within a description in Part 1 of Schedule 1 to the Act, but for an exclusion in Part 2 (excluded services) or Part 3 (advocacy: exclusions and exceptions) of that Schedule.

(2) The criteria referred to in paragraph (1) are the merits criteria which would have applied in relation to that matter had it not been subject to that exclusion.

III FUND [300]

50 Application of the merits criteria in cases which are exceptional cases other than by virtue of the exclusions in Part 2 or 3 of Schedule 1 to the Act

(1) To the extent that regulation 49 does not apply, the Director must apply the merits criteria in paragraph (2) for the purpose of making a determination under section 10(2)(b) of the Act (exceptional cases) in relation to any matter in which civil legal services are not otherwise available because they are not described in Part 1 of Schedule 1 to the Act.

(2) The criteria referred to in paragraph (1) are the merits criteria which appear to the Director to be most appropriate in all the circumstances of the case.

PART 6
SPECIFIC MERITS CRITERIA

CHAPTER 1 MENTAL HEALTH AND MENTAL CAPACITY

III FUND [301]

51 Criteria for determinations for full representation in relation to mental health proceedings

(1) For the purposes of a determination for full representation in relation to any matter described in paragraph 5(1)(a) or (b) of Part 1 of Schedule 1 to the Act (mental health and the repatriation of prisoners), to the extent that it relates to proceedings before the First-tier Tribunal or the Mental Health Review Tribunal for Wales—

(a) the criteria in regulations 39 (standard criteria for determinations for legal representation) and 41 to 44 (criteria for determinations for full representation) do not apply; and

(b) the criterion in paragraph (2) applies.

(2) The Director must be satisfied that it would be reasonable in all the circumstances of the case for the individual to be provided with full representation.

III FUND [302]

52 Criteria for determinations for full representation in relation to mental capacity proceedings

(1) For the purposes of a relevant determination the criteria in—

(a) regulation 39 (standard criteria for determinations for legal representation) and regulations 41(a) and (b), 42 and 43 (criteria for determinations for full representation) apply;

(b) regulations 41(c) and 44 (multi-party action damages criterion) do not apply; and

(c) paragraph (2) apply.

(2) The Director must be satisfied that—

(a) the Court of Protection has ordered, or is likely to order, an oral hearing; and

(b) it is necessary for the individual to be provided with full representation in the proceedings.

(3) In this regulation, a relevant determination is a determination for full representation in relation to any matter described in paragraph 5(1)(c) of Part 1 of Schedule 1 to the Act (mental capacity) in proceedings before the Court of Protection to the extent that they relate to—

(a) a person's right to life;

(b) a person's liberty or physical safety;

(c) a person's medical treatment (within the meaning of the Mental Health Act 1983);

(d) a person's capacity to marry, to enter into a civil partnership or to enter into sexual relations; or

(e) a person's right to family life.

CHAPTER 2 PUBLIC LAW

III FUND [303]

53 Standard criteria for determinations for legal representation in relation to public law claims

For the purposes of a determination for legal representation in relation to a public law claim, the Director must be satisfied that the criteria in regulation 39 (standard criteria for determinations for legal representation) are met and that—

(a) the act, omission or other matter complained of in the proposed proceedings appears to be susceptible to challenge; and

(b) there are no alternative proceedings before a court or tribunal which are available to challenge the act, omission or other matter, except where the Director considers that such proceedings would not be effective in providing the remedy that the individual requires.

III FUND [304]

54 Standard criteria for determinations for investigative representation in relation to public law claims

For the purposes of a determination for investigative representation in relation to a public law claim, the Director must be satisfied that—

(a) the criteria in regulation 53 (standard criteria for determinations for legal representation in relation to public law claims) are met; and

(b) the individual has—

(i) notified the proposed defendant of the individual's potential challenge and given a reasonable time for the proposed defendant to respond; or

(ii) shown that doing so would be impracticable.

III FUND [305]

55 Criteria for determinations for investigative representation in relation to public law claims

For the purposes of a determination for investigative representation in relation to a public law claim the criteria in regulation 40(1)(a) and (b) (investigative representation) and 54 (standard criteria for determinations for investigative representation in relation to public law claims) apply and the criteria in regulation 40(1)(c) and (2) (investigative representation: minimum damages rule) do not apply.

III FUND [306]

56 Criteria for determinations for full representation in relation to public law claims

(1) For the purposes of a determination for full representation in relation to a public law claim—

(a) the criteria in regulations 41 to 44 (criteria for determinations for full representation) do not apply;

(b) the Director must be satisfied that the criteria in regulation 53 (standard criteria for determinations for legal representation in relation to public law claims) are met; and

(c) the criteria in paragraphs (2) and (3) apply.

(2) An individual may qualify for full representation in relation to a public law claim only if the Director is satisfied that—

(a) the individual has sent a letter before claim to the proposed defendant (except where this is impracticable), and where such a letter has been

FUNDING

sent, the proposed defendant has been given a reasonable time to respond;

(b) the proportionality test is met; and

(c) the criterion in paragraph (3) is met.

(3) The Director must be satisfied that the prospects of successfully obtaining the substantive order sought in the proceedings are—

(a) very good, good or moderate; or

(b) borderline or marginal, and—

(i) the case is of significant wider public interest;

(ii) the case is one with overwhelming importance to the individual; or

(iii) the substance of the case relates to a breach of Convention rights.

III FUND [306A]

56A Criteria for determinations in relation to Dublin III claims

(1) For the purposes of a determination for any form of civil legal services in relation to a Dublin III claim, the general merits criteria do not apply and paragraph (2) applies.

(2) An individual may qualify for civil legal services only if the Director is satisfied that the individual's case has a tangible prospect of success.

CHAPTER 3 CLAIMS AGAINST PUBLIC AUTHORITIES

III FUND [307]

57 Criteria for determinations for investigative representation in relation to claims against public authorities

(1) For the purposes of a determination for investigative representation in relation to any matter described in paragraph 21 (abuse of position or powers by public authority) or 22 (breach of Convention rights by public authority) of Part 1 of Schedule 1 to the Act the criteria in—

(a) regulations 39 (standard criteria for determinations for legal representation) and 40(1)(a) and (b) (criteria for determinations for investigative representation) apply; and

(b) regulation 40(1)(c) and (2) apply, subject to paragraph (2).

(2) The criteria in regulation 40(1)(c) and (2) (investigative representation: minimum damages rule) only apply to the extent that such a matter—

(a) is part of a multi-party action; and

(b) does not relate to—

(i) the abuse of a child or a vulnerable adult; or

(ii) a contravention of the Equality Act 2010 or of a previous discrimination enactment.

(3) In this regulation and in regulation 59—

(a) "abuse", "child" and "vulnerable adult" have the meaning given by paragraph 3(5) of Part 1 of Schedule 1 to the Act (abuse of child or vulnerable adult); and

(b) "previous discrimination enactment" has the meaning given by paragraph 43(3) of Part 1 of Schedule 1 to the Act (equality).

III FUND [308]

58 Criteria for determinations for full representation in relation to claims against public authorities

(1) For the purposes of a determination for full representation in relation to any matter described in paragraph 21 (abuse of position or powers by public authority) or 22 (breach of Convention rights by public authority) of Part 1 of Schedule 1 to the Act, the criteria in—

(a) regulation 39 (standard criteria for determinations for legal representation) . . . apply;

(b) regulation 41(a) and (b) (criteria for determinations for full representation), regulation 42 (cost benefit criteria) and regulation 43 (prospects of success criterion) do not apply; and

(c) paragraphs (2) and (3) apply.

(2) An individual may qualify for full representation in relation to any matter described in paragraph 21 (abuse of position or powers by public authority) or 22 (breach of Convention rights by public authority) of Part 1 of Schedule 1 to the Act only if the Director is satisfied that—

(a) the proportionality test is met; and

(b) the criterion in paragraph (3) is met.

(3) The Director must be satisfied that the prospects of success are—

(a) very good, good or moderate; or

(b) borderline or marginal, and—

(i) the case is of significant wider public interest;

(ii) the case is one with overwhelming importance to the individual; or

(iii) the substance of the case relates to a breach of Convention rights.

III FUND [309]

59 Criteria for determinations for full representation in relation to claims against public authorities: multi-party action damages criterion

For the purposes of a determination for full representation in relation to any matter described in paragraph 21 (abuse of position or powers by public authority) or paragraph 22 (breach of Convention rights by public authority) of Part 1 of Schedule 1 to the Act, the criteria in regulation 41(c) and 44 (multi-party action damages criterion) only apply to the extent that such a matter does not relate to—

(a) the abuse of a child or a vulnerable adult; or

(b) a contravention of the Equality Act 2010 or of a previous discrimination enactment.

CHAPTER 4 IMMIGRATION

III FUND [310]

60 Criteria for determinations for full representation in relation to immigration

(1) For the purposes of a determination for full representation in relation to any matter described in paragraphs 25 to 30 (immigration), 32(1) (victims of trafficking in human beings) or 32A(1) (victims of slavery, servitude or forced or compulsory labour) of Part 1 of Schedule 1 to the Act, to the extent that it relates to proceedings before the First-tier Tribunal or Upper Tribunal, the criteria in—

(a) regulation 39(a) to (e) (standard criteria for determinations for legal representation) apply;

FUNDING

(b) regulations 39(f) and 41 to 44 (criteria for determinations for full representation) do not apply; and
(c) paragraphs (2) and (3) apply.

(2) An individual may qualify for full representation in relation to any matter described in paragraphs 25 to 30 (immigration), 32(1) (victims of trafficking in human beings) or 32A(1) (victims of slavery, servitude or forced or compulsory labour) of Part 1 of Schedule 1 to the Act only if the Director is satisfied that—
(a) if the case is not of significant wider public interest, the reasonable private paying individual test is met;
(b) if the case is of significant wider public interest, the proportionality test is met; and
(c) the criterion in paragraph (3) applies.

(3) The Director must be satisfied that the prospects of success are—
(a) very good, good or moderate; or
(b) borderline or marginal, and—
(i) the case is of significant wider public interest;
(ii) the case is one with overwhelming importance to the individual; or
(iii) the substance of the case relates to a breach of Convention rights.

CHAPTER 5 HOUSING

III FUND [311]

61 Criteria for determinations for full representation in relation to court orders for possession

(1) For the purposes of a determination for full representation in relation to any matter described in paragraph 33(1)(a) of Part 1 of Schedule 1 to the Act (court orders for sale or possession of the individual's home), to the extent that it relates to court orders for possession of the individual's home, the criteria in—
(a) regulation 39 (standard criteria for determinations for legal representation) apply;
(b) regulations 41 to 44 (criteria for determinations for full representation) do not apply; and
(c) paragraph (2) apply.

(2) The Director must be satisfied that the following criteria are met—
(a) if the individual is the defendant to a claim for possession, the individual has a defence to the claim; . . .
(b) the prospects of success are very good, good, moderate, borderline or marginal; and
(c) the proportionality test is met.

III FUND [312]

62 Criteria for determinations for full representation in relation to other housing matters to which specific merits criteria apply

(1) For the purposes of a relevant determination the criteria in—
(a) regulations 39 (standard criteria for determinations for legal representation), 41(b) and 43 apply (prospects of success criterion);
(b) regulations 41(a) and (c) (criteria for determinations for full representation), 42 (costs benefit criteria) and 44 (multi-party action damages criterion) do not apply; and
(c) paragraph (2) apply.

(2) The Director must be satisfied that—

(a) the proportionality test is met; and

(b) the landlord or other person responsible for the matter complained of has been notified of the individual's complaint (except where this is impracticable) and, where such notice has been given, the landlord or other person has had a reasonable opportunity to resolve the matter.

(3) In this regulation, a relevant determination is a determination for full representation in relation to any matter described in—

(a) paragraph 33(1)(b) of Part 1 of Schedule 1 to the Act (the eviction from the individual's home of the individual or others), to the extent that it relates to services provided to an individual in relation to the unlawful eviction from the individual's home of the individual or others;

(b) paragraph 35 of Part 1 of Schedule 1 to the Act (risk to health or safety in rented home); or

(c) paragraph 37 of Part 1 of Schedule 1 to the Act (protection from harassment), to the extent that it relates to the interference with an individual's enjoyment of their home (within the meaning of paragraph 35(4) of Part 1 of Schedule 1 to the Act) by a landlord or other person.

III FUND [313]

63 Criteria for determinations for investigative representation in relation to unlawful eviction cases

(1) For the purposes of a determination for investigative representation in relation to any matter described in paragraph 33(1)(b) of Part 1 of Schedule 1 to the Act (the eviction from the individual's home of the individual or others), to the extent that it relates to services provided to an individual in relation to the unlawful eviction from the individual's home of the individual or others, the criteria in—

(a) regulations 39 (standard criteria for determinations for legal representation) and 40(1)(a) and (b) (criteria for determinations for investigative representation) apply;

(b) regulation 40(1)(c) and (2) do not apply; and

(c) paragraphs (2) and (3) apply.

(2) Subject to paragraph (3), if the individual's claim is primarily a claim for damages or other sum of money in which the likely damages do not exceed £1,000, the case must be of significant wider public interest.

(3) For the purposes of paragraph (2), if the claim forms part of a multi-party action, only the lead claim within that action is capable of being a case of significant wider public interest.

CHAPTER 6 FAMILY

III FUND [314]

64 Standard criteria for determinations for full representation in relation to certain family disputes

(1) For the purposes of a relevant determination the criteria in—

(a) regulation 39(a) and (c) to (e) (standard criteria for determinations for legal representation) apply; and

(b) regulations 39(b) and (f) (standard criteria for determinations for full representation) and 41 to 44 (criteria for determinations for full representation) do not apply.

(2) In this regulation, a relevant determination is a determination for full representation in relation to—

(a) a domestic violence case;
(b) a private law children case;
(c) . . .
(d) any matter described in paragraph 17(1)(EU and international agreements concerning children) of Part 1 of Schedule 1 to the Act, to the extent that regulations 11(9)(c) or 65 do not apply; or
(e) any matter described in paragraph 18(1)(EU and international agreements concerning maintenance) of Part 1 of Schedule 1 to the Act, to the extent that regulation 65 does not apply.

III FUND [315]

65 Criteria for determinations for full representation in relation to special Children Act 1989 cases and certain cases relating to EU and international agreements

(1) For the purposes of a determination for full representation in relation to a relevant determination, the criteria in—
(a) regulation 39(e) apply (standard criteria for determinations for legal representation); and
(b) regulations 39(a) to (d) and (f) (standard criteria for determinations for legal representation) and 41 to 44 (criteria for determinations for full representation) do not apply.

(2) In this regulation, a relevant determination is—
(a) a determination for full representation in relation to a special Children Act 1989 case; or
(b) a determination for full representation in a case in which the applicant is an individual who, in the State of origin, has benefited from complete or partial legal aid in relation to any matter described in—
(i) paragraph 17(1)(c)(EU and international agreements concerning children) of Part 1 of Schedule 1 to the Act;
(ii) paragraph 18(1)(EU and international agreements concerning maintenance) of that Part;
(iii) paragraph 18(3)(parties who benefited from free legal aid etc in the Member State of origin) of that Part;
(iv) paragraph 18(3A)(applications under Article 10 of the 2007 Hague Convention) of that Part, to the extent that Article 17(b) of that Convention applies; or
(v) paragraph 18(3B)(applications under Article 17(b) of the 2007 Hague Convention which is applied by virtue of Article 37(2)) of that Part.

III FUND [316]

66 Criteria for determinations for full representation in relation to public law children cases

(1) For the purposes of a determination for full representation in relation to a public law children case—
(a) the criteria in regulations 39(b) to (d) and (f) (standard criteria for determinations for legal representation) and 41 to 44 (criteria for determinations for full representation) do not apply;
(b) the criteria in regulation 39(a) and (e) apply; and
(c) paragraph (2) applies.

(2) An individual may qualify for full representation in a public law children case only if the Director is satisfied that the criterion in paragraph (3) and, where applicable, paragraph (4) are met.

(3) It is reasonable for full representation to be provided, having regard to the importance of the case to the individual.

(4) If the individual is making or supporting an appeal or application, the prospects of success of that appeal or application are very good, good, moderate, borderline or marginal.

III FUND [317]

67 Criteria for determinations for full representation in relation to domestic violence cases

(1) For the purposes of a determination for full representation in relation to a domestic violence case, regulation 64 (standard criteria for determinations for full representation in relation to certain family disputes) applies in addition to the criteria in paragraphs (2) and (3).

(2) An individual may qualify for full representation in a domestic violence case only if the Director is satisfied that the prospects of success are very good, good, moderate, borderline or marginal.

(3) An individual may qualify for full representation in a domestic violence case only if the Director is satisfied that the proportionality test is met.

III FUND [318]

68 Criteria for determinations for full representation in relation to private law children cases and certain cases relating to EU and international agreements

(1) For the purposes of a relevant determination the criteria in regulation 64 (standard criteria for determinations for full representation in relation to certain family disputes) apply in addition to the criteria in paragraphs (2) and (2A).

(2) The Director is satisfied that the prospects of success are very good, good, moderate, borderline or marginal.

(2A) The Director is satisfied that the reasonable private paying individual test is met.

(3) In this regulation, a relevant determination is a determination for full representation in relation to—

- (a) a private law children case;
- (b) any matter described in paragraph 17(1) (EU and international agreements concerning children) of Part 1 of Schedule 1 to the Act, to the extent that regulations 11(9)(c) and 65 do not apply; or
- (c) any matter described in paragraph 18(1) (EU and international agreements concerning maintenance) of Part 1 of Schedule 1 to the Act, to the extent that regulation 65 does not apply.

III FUND [319]

69 Criteria for determinations for full representation in relation to other family cases to which specific merits criteria apply

(1) For the purposes of a relevant determination the criteria in—

- (a) regulations 39(a) to (e) (criteria for determinations for legal representation) apply;
- (b) regulations 39(f), 41, 42 (cost benefit criteria), 43 (prospects of success criterion) and 44 (multi-party) do not apply; and
- (c) paragraphs (2) and (3) apply.

(2) The Director must be satisfied that—

- (a) the reasonable private paying individual test is met; and
- (b) the criterion in paragraph (3) is met.

(3) The Director must be satisfied that the prospects of success are—

- (a) very good, good or moderate;

FUNDING

(b) borderline, marginal or unclear, and—
(i) the case is of significant wider public interest;
(ii) the case is one with overwhelming importance to the individual; or
(iii) the substance of the case relates to a breach of Convention rights.

(4) In this regulation, a relevant determination is—
(a) a determination for full representation in relation to any matter described in paragraph 12 of Part 1 of Schedule 1 to the Act (victims of domestic violence and family matters) to the extent that it does not relate—
(i) to Part 1 or 3 of the Family Law Act 1986 (child custody and declarations of status);
(ii) subject to sub-paragraph (b), to any provision of Part 1 or 2 of the Children Act 1989 (orders with respect to children in family proceedings); or
(iii) to section 51A of the Adoption and Children Act 2002 (post-adoption contact orders);
(b) a determination for full representation in relation to any matter described in paragraph 12 of Part 1 of Schedule 1 to the Act (victims of domestic violence and family matters) to the extent that it relates an order made under section 15 of, and Schedule 1 to, the Children Act 1989;
(ba) a determination for full representation in relation to any matter described in paragraph 15 of Part 1 of Schedule 1 to the Act (children who are parties to family proceedings), to the extent that regulations 64 and 68 do not apply;
(c) a determination for full representation in relation to any matter described in paragraph 18(2) of Part 1 of Schedule 1 to the Act (applications in relation to maintenance decisions), to the extent that regulations 11(9)(b) or 70 do not apply; or
(d) any matter described in paragraph 18(3A) of Part 1 of Schedule 1 to the Act (applications under Article 10 of the 2007 Hague Convention), to the extent that article 17(a) of the 2007 Hague Convention applies.

III FUND [320]

70 Criteria for determinations in relation to the EU Maintenance Regulation

(1) For the purposes of a determination for any form of civil legal services in relation to any matter described in paragraph 18(2) of Part 1 of Schedule 1 to the Act (applications relating to maintenance decisions), to the extent that it—
(a) is an application under Article 56(1)(c) to (f) of the EU Maintenance Regulation; and
(b) concerns maintenance obligations arising from a parent-child relationship towards a person under the age of 21,

the general merits criteria do not apply and paragraph (2) applies.

(2) An individual may qualify for civil legal services only if the Director is satisfied that the application is not manifestly unfounded.

III FUND [321]

71 Criteria for determinations in relation to the 2007 Hague Convention

(1) For the purposes of a determination for any form of civil legal services in relation to any matter described in paragraph 18(3A) (applications under Article 10 of the 2007 Hague Convention), to the extent that it—
(a) does not relate to an application under Article 10(1)(a) or (b) of the 2007 Hague Convention; and

(b) is an application by a creditor under the 2007 Hague Convention concerning maintenance obligations arising from a parent-child relationship towards a person under the age of 21,

the general merits criteria do not apply and paragraph (2) applies.

(2) The individual may qualify for civil legal services only if the Director is satisfied that the application is not manifestly unfounded.

CHAPTER 7 CROSS-BORDER DISPUTES

III FUND [322]

72 Criteria for determinations in relation to cross-border disputes

(1) For the purposes of a determination for legal help in relation to any matter described in paragraph 44 of Part 1 of Schedule 1 to the Act (cross-border disputes), regulation 32 (criteria for determinations for legal help) does not apply and the criterion in paragraph (2) applies.

(2) An individual may qualify for legal help only if the Director is satisfied that the application is not manifestly unfounded.

(3) For the purposes of a determination for legal representation in relation to any matter described in paragraph 44 of Part 1 of Schedule 1 to the Act (cross-border disputes)—

(a) the general merits criteria apply; and

(b) if the general merits criteria are not met the Director must then consider whether legal representation should be granted in any event—

(i) in order to guarantee access to justice;

(ii) in order to ensure equality of parties; or

(iii) in view of the complexity of the case,

and taking into account the importance of the case to the individual.

CHAPTER 8 LEGAL PERSONS

III FUND [323]

73 Criteria for determinations in relation to legal persons

For the purposes of a determination in relation to an application for civil legal services by a legal person—

(a) to the extent that it relates to legal help, regulation 32 (criteria for determinations for legal help) does not apply and the criteria in regulation 74 apply;

(b) to the extent that it relates to legal representation, regulations 39 (standard criteria for legal representation), 40 (criteria for determinations for investigative representation) and 41 to 44 (criteria for determinations for full representation) do not apply and the criteria in regulations 74 and 75 apply.

III FUND [324]

74 Standard criteria for legal help and legal representation in relation to legal persons

(1) A legal person may qualify for legal help or legal representation only if the Director is satisfied that it is reasonable, in all the circumstances of the case, for the legal person to be provided with legal help or legal representation.

(2) It is reasonable for the legal person to be provided with legal help or legal representation only if the Director is satisfied that—

FUNDING

(a) the legal person does not have access to other potential sources of funding (other than a conditional fee agreement) from which it would be reasonable to fund the provision of legal help or legal representation, including, but not limited to, taking into account the financial capacity of the legal person's shareholders, partners or members;

(b) there are no other persons, other than the legal person, including those who might benefit from the provision of legal help or the proceedings, who can reasonably be expected to be provided with legal help or to bring the case;

(c) there is a need for legal help or legal representation in all the circumstances of the case; and

(d) there is sufficient benefit to the legal person, having regard to all the circumstances of the case, to justify the provision of legal help or legal representation.

III FUND [325]

75 Criteria for determinations for legal representation in relation to legal persons

(1) A legal person may qualify for legal representation only if the Director is satisfied that the following criteria are met—

(a) the case is unsuitable for a conditional fee agreement;

(b) the legal person has exhausted all reasonable alternatives to bringing proceedings including any complaints system, ombudsman scheme or other form of alternative dispute resolution; and

(c) the proceedings are not likely to be allocated to the small claims track.

(2) A legal person may qualify for investigative representation only if the Director is satisfied that—

(a) the criteria in paragraph (1) are met;

(b) the prospects of success of the case are unclear and substantial investigative work is required before those prospects can be determined; and

(c) the Director has reasonable grounds for believing that once the investigative work to be carried out under investigative representation is completed the case will satisfy the criteria in paragraphs (3)(b) and (3A).

(3) A legal person may qualify for full representation only if the Director is satisfied that—

(a) the criteria in paragraphs (1) and (3A) are met; and

(b) the likely benefit of the proceedings to the legal person and others justify the likely costs, having regard to the prospects of success and all the other circumstances of the case; . . .

(c) . . .

(3A) The Director must be satisfied that the prospects of success of the case are—

(a) very good, good or moderate; or

(b) borderline or marginal, and the case is of significant wider public interest.

(4) For the purposes of this regulation, regulations 4 (prospects of success) and 5 (prospects of success test) apply as if the references in them to individuals were references to legal persons.

III FUND [325.1]

Lawfulness of merits criteria The merits criteria set by the regulations have been held, by the Court of Appeal, to be lawful, reversing the contrary decision of Collins J: *Director of Legal Aid Casework v IS (a protected party, by his litigation friend the Official Solicitor)* [2016] EWCA Civ 464.

CIVIL LEGAL AID (REMUNERATION) REGULATIONS 2013

SI 2013/422

FUNDING

III FUND [326]

1 Citation and commencement

These Regulations may be cited as the Civil Legal Aid (Remuneration) Regulations 2013 and come into force on 1st April 2013.

III FUND [327]

2 Interpretation

(1) In these Regulations—

"the Act" means the Legal Aid, Sentencing and Punishment of Offenders Act 2012;

"1981 Act" means the Senior Courts Act 1981;

"1984 Act" means the Matrimonial and Family Proceedings Act 1984;

"2003 Act" means the Courts Act 2003;"

"advocate" means a person who exercises a right of audience before a court, tribunal or other person and "advocacy" means the exercise of such a right;

"advocates' meeting" means an advocates' meeting directed by the court pursuant to the outline set out in the table following paragraph 1.3 of Practice Direction 12A (Care, Supervision and other Part 4 Proceedings: Guide to Case Management) to the Family Procedure Rules 2010;

"advocacy services" means work done—

(a) by an advocate at a court hearing;
(b) by an advocate, as such, in connection with an advocates' meeting;
(c) by counsel in connection with a conference; and
(d) by counsel in connection with an opinion,

and fees and rates for advocacy services include, unless different provision is made in these Regulations, remuneration for preparatory work, attendances, travelling and waiting in relation to those services;

"assistant to a justices' clerk" has the meaning given in section 27(5) of the 2003 Act;

"authorised" means authorised by the President of the Family Division, or nominated by or on behalf of the Lord Chief Justice to conduct particular business, under powers granted by rules made under section 31D of the 1984 Act;

"Category Definition" means one of the Category Definitions that form part of the 2010 Standard Civil Contract, the 2013 Standard Civil Contract, the 2014 Standard Civil Contract, the 2015 Standard Civil Contract or the 2018 Standard Civil Contract;

"Controlled Work" has the same meaning as in regulation 21(2) of the Civil Legal Aid (Procedure) Regulations 2012;

"costs judge" means—
(a) the Chief Taxing Master;
(b) a taxing master of the Senior Courts; or
(c) a person appointed to act as deputy for the person holding office referred to in sub-paragraph (b) or to act as a temporary additional officer for any such office;

"counsel" means—
(a) a barrister in independent practice; and
(b) a solicitor or Fellow of the Institute of Legal Executives who does not work in a partnership and who is not a party to the relevant contract;

"family proceedings" means proceedings which arise out of family relationships, and includes proceedings in which the welfare of children is determined, and includes proceedings under the following—
(a) the Matrimonial Causes Act 1973;
(b) the Adoption Act 1976;
(c) the Domestic Proceedings and Magistrates' Courts Act 1978;
(d) Part III (financial relief in England and Wales after overseas divorce etc) of the Matrimonial and Family Proceedings Act 1984;
(e) Parts I to V (introductory, orders with respect to children in family proceedings, local authority support for children and families, care and supervision, protection of children) of the Children Act 1989;
(ea) section 119 and section 124 of the Social Services and Well-being (Wales) Act 2014 (use of accommodation for restricting liberty);
(f) Part IV (family homes and domestic violence) of the Family Law Act 1996;
(g) the Adoption and Children Act 2002;
(h) the Civil Partnership Act 2004; and
(i) the inherent jurisdiction of the High Court in relation to children,

but does not include judicial review proceedings, proceedings under the Inheritance (Provision for Family and Dependants) Act 1975 or proceedings under the Trusts of Land and Appointment of Trustees Act 1996;

"judge of circuit judge level" means—

(a) a circuit judge who is authorised, where applicable;

(b) a Recorder who is authorised, where applicable; or

(c) any other judge of the family court authorised to sit as a judge of circuit judge level in the family court;

"judge of district judge level" means—

(a) the Senior District Judge of the Family Division;

(b) a district judge of the Principal Registry of the Family Division;

(c) a person appointed to act as deputy for the person holding office referred to in sub-paragraph (b) or to act as a temporary additional officer for any such office;

(d) a district judge who is authorised, where applicable;

(e) a deputy district judge appointed under section 102 of the 1981 Act or section 8 of the County Courts Act 1984 who is authorised, where applicable;

(f) an authorised District Judge (Magistrates' Courts); or

(g) any other judge of the family court authorised to sit as a judge of district judge level in the family court;

"judge of High Court judge level" means—

(a) a deputy judge of the High Court;

(b) a puisne judge of the High Court;

(c) a person who has been a judge of the Court of Appeal or a puisne judge of the High Court who may act as a judge of the family court by virtue of section 9 of the 1981 Act;

(d) the Senior President of Tribunals;

(e) the Chancellor of the High Court;

(f) an ordinary judge of the Court of Appeal (including the vice-president, if any, of either division of that court);

(g) the President of the Queen's Bench Division;

(h) the President of the Family Division;

(i) the Master of the Rolls; or

(j) the Lord Chief Justice;

"judge of the family court" means a judge referred to in section 31C(1) of the 1984 Act;

"justices' clerk" has the meaning given in section 27(1) of the 2003 Act;

"lay justice" means an authorised justice of the peace who is not a District Judge (Magistrates' Courts);

"legally aided person" means a person for whom civil legal services are made available under arrangements made for the purposes of Part 1 of the Act and "client" has the same meaning;

"provider" means a party, other than the Lord Chancellor, to the relevant contract;

"the relevant contract" means whichever of the 2010 Standard Civil Contract, the 2010 Standard Crime Contract, the 2013 Standard Civil Contract, the 2013 Individual Case Contract (Civil), the 2014 Standard Civil Contract, the 2014 Standard Civil Contract (Welfare Benefits), the 2015 Standard Civil Contract, the 2016 Standard Civil Contract (Welfare Benefits) or the 2018 Standard Civil Contract governs the provision of civil legal services for which remuneration is claimed; and

"the 2010 Standard Civil Contract", "the 2010 Standard Crime Contract", "the 2013 Standard Civil Contract", the "2013 Individual Case Contract (Civil)", "the 2013 Individual Case Contract (High Cost Civil)", the 2014 Standard Civil Contract, "the 2014 Standard Civil Contract (Welfare Benefits)"[, "the 2015 Standard Civil Contract", "the 2016 Standard

FUNDING

Civil Contract (Welfare Benefits)" and "the 2018 Standard Civil Contract" mean the contracts so named between the Lord Chancellor and a provider of civil legal services under Part 1 of the Act (legal aid).

(2) A reference in these Regulations to the following forms of civil legal services—

(a) legal help;
(b) help at court;
(c) family help;
(d) family mediation;
(e) help with family mediation;
(f) legal representation; and
(g) other legal services,

is to the provision of those forms of service as defined in Part 2 of the Civil Legal Aid (Merits Criteria) Regulations 2013.

III FUND [328]

3 Value Added Tax

All rates and fees set out in the Schedules are exclusive of value added tax.

III FUND [329]

4 Delegation

A function of the Lord Chancellor under these Regulations may be exercised by, or by an employee of, a person authorised for that purpose by the Lord Chancellor.

III FUND [330]

5 Non application to civil legal services provided under certain contracts

(1) Regulations 5A to 11 are subject to this regulation.

(2) These Regulations do not apply to the payment of remuneration by the Lord Chancellor to persons who provide civil legal services where the provision of those services is governed by a contract between a person and the Lord Chancellor which has been awarded as part of any pilot which provides for remuneration by way of one or more standard fees.

(3) With the exception of regulations 5A, 7 and 10, these Regulations do not apply to the payment of remuneration by the Lord Chancellor to persons who provide civil legal services where the provision of those services is governed by a contract between a person and the Lord Chancellor which has been awarded after competitive tendering as to price has taken place.

(4) With the exception of regulations 5A and 10,, these Regulations do not apply to the payment of remuneration by the Lord Chancellor to persons who provide civil legal services where the provision of those services is governed by the Individual Case Contract (High Cost Civil).

(5) Where paragraph (3) applies, the reference in regulation 10(a) to "the relevant contract" is to the contract between a person and the Lord Chancellor which has been awarded after competitive tendering as to price has taken place.

(6) Where paragraph (4) applies, the reference in regulation 10(a) to "the relevant contract" is to the Individual Case Contract (High Cost Civil).

III FUND [330A]

5A Remuneration for civil legal services: judicial review

(1) Where an application for judicial review is issued, the Lord Chancellor must not pay remuneration for civil legal services consisting of making that application unless either the court—

(a) gives permission to bring judicial review proceedings; or

(b) neither refuses nor gives permission and the Lord Chancellor considers that it is reasonable to pay remuneration in the circumstances of the case, taking into account, in particular—

(i) the reason why the provider did not obtain a costs order or costs agreement in favour of the legally aided person;

(ii) the extent to which, and the reason why, the legally aided person obtained the outcome sought in the proceedings; and

(iii) the strength of the application for permission at the time it was filed, based on the law and on the facts which the provider knew or ought to have known at that time.

(2) Nothing in this regulation affects any payment—

(a) by the Lord Chancellor of disbursements incurred by a provider in accordance with the relevant contract; or

(b) on account by the Lord Chancellor to a provider in accordance with the relevant contract.

(3) In this regulation—

(a) . . .

(b) "2013 CLA Contract" and "2018 CLA Contract" mean the contracts so named between the Lord Chancellor and a provider for the provision of civil legal services under Part 1 of the Legal Aid, Sentencing and Punishment of Offenders Act 2012;

(c) "2013 CLA Contract" means the contract so named between the Lord Chancellor and a provider for the provision of civil legal services under Part 1 of the Legal Aid, Sentencing and Punishment of Offenders Act 2012;

(i) Part 54 of the Civil Procedure Rules 1998; or

(ii) Part 4 of the Tribunal Rules;

and includes bringing a relevant appeal and making an application for permission to bring a relevant appeal, but does not include a relevant application for interim relief;

(d) "costs agreement" and "costs order" mean, respectively, an agreement or an order that another party to the proceedings pay all, or part of, the costs of the legally aided person;

(e) "court" includes the Upper Tribunal established under section 3 of the Tribunals, Courts and Enforcement Act 2007;

(f) "issued" includes—

(i) the sending of the application by the Upper Tribunal under rule 28(8) of the Tribunal Rules; or

(ii) the provision of the application by the applicant under rule 28A(2)(a) of the Tribunal Rules,

to each person named in the application as a respondent or interested party;

(g) "Procedure Rules" means the Civil Procedure Rules 1998;

(h) "relevant appeal" means an appeal against a decision to refuse permission to bring judicial review proceedings under—

(i) Part 52 of the Procedure Rules, or

(ii) Part 7 of the Tribunal Rules;

(i) "relevant application for interim relief" means application for an interim remedy under—

(i) Part 25 of the Procedure Rules, or

(ii) Part 4 of the Tribunal Rules;

(j) "relevant contract" means whichever of the 2010 Standard Civil Contract, the 2010 Standard Crime Contract, the 2013 Standard Civil Contract, the 2013 Individual Case Contract (Civil), the 2013

Individual Case Contract (High Cost Civil), the 2013 CLA Contract, the 2014 Standard Civil Contract, the 2014 Standard Civil Contract (Welfare Benefits), the 2015 Standard Civil Contract, the 2018 Standard Civil Contract or the 2018 CLA Contract governs the provision of the civil legal services for which remuneration is claimed;

(k) "rolled-up hearing" means a hearing at which the court considers the application for judicial review (including whether to give permission to bring judicial review proceedings);

(l) "Tribunal Rules" means the Tribunal Procedure (Upper Tribunal) Rules 2008.

III FUND [331]

6 Remuneration for civil legal services: general

(1) This regulation applies to the payment by the Lord Chancellor of remuneration to providers of civil legal services other than—

(a) advocacy services in family proceedings; or

(b) civil legal services in relation to inquests.

(2) Subject to regulation 5A, the Lord Chancellor must pay remuneration to a provider of civil legal services in accordance with—

(a) the relevant contract; and

(b) subject to paragraph (3), the fees and rates set out in Schedule 1.

(3) The Lord Chancellor may pay a percentage enhancement to the hourly rates set out in Schedule 1, but the percentage enhancement must not exceed—

(a) 100% for proceedings in the Upper Tribunal, High Court, Court of Appeal or the Supreme Court; and

(b) 50% for all other proceedings.

III FUND [332]

7

(1) This regulation applies to the payment by the Lord Chancellor of remuneration for civil legal services provided by barristers in independent practice where the civil legal services—

(a) are in relation to work that is not Controlled Work; and

(b) are not—

(i) advocacy services in family proceedings; or

(ii) other legal services in relation to inquests.

(2) Subject to regulation 5A and paragraphs (3) and (4) of this regulation,, the Lord Chancellor must pay remuneration for civil legal services to which this regulation applies in accordance with the rates set out in Schedule 2.

(3) The Lord Chancellor may pay an enhancement to the hourly rates set out in Table 1 of Schedule 2 where—

(a) the work was done with exceptional competence, skill or expertise;

(b) the work was done with exceptional speed; or

(c) the case involved exceptional circumstances or complexity.

(3A) Subject to paragraph (3B), when calculating the percentage by which the hourly rates may be enhanced under paragraph (3), the Lord Chancellor must have regard to the—

(a) degree of responsibility accepted by the barrister;

(b) care, speed and efficiency with which the barrister prepared the case; and

(c) novelty, weight and complexity of the case.

(3B) The Lord Chancellor must not pay an enhancement which exceeds—

(a) 100% for proceedings in the Upper Tribunal or High Court; or

(b) 50% for all other proceedings.

(4) Where a barrister in independent practice who is not a Queen's Counsel provides civil legal services in a category not listed in Table 1 or Table 2 in Schedule 2, in considering the rate at which to remunerate the barrister for the services provided, the Lord Chancellor must have regard to the rates set out in Table 1 and the provisions relating to enhancement under paragraphs (3) to (3B).

(4A) Where a barrister in independent practice who is a Queen's Counsel provides civil legal services in a category not listed in Table 2 in Schedule 2, in considering the rate at which to remunerate the barrister for the services provided, the Lord Chancellor must have regard to the rates set out in that Table.

(5) For the purpose of this regulation—

- (a) in determining what is exceptional, the Lord Chancellor may have regard to the generality of proceedings to which the relevant rates apply;
- (b) "care" includes the skill with which the barrister has carried out the work and, in particular, the care with which the barrister has dealt with a vulnerable client; and
- (c) "weight" means the—
  - (i) volume of documentation or other material in a case;
  - (ii) number of issues arising in a case; or
  - (iii) importance of the case to the client.

III FUND [333]

8 Remuneration: advocacy services in family proceedings

(1) This regulation applies to the payment by the Lord Chancellor of remuneration for the provision of advocacy services in family proceedings.

(2) Subject to paragraph (3), the Lord Chancellor must pay remuneration for advocacy services in family proceedings in accordance with—

- (a) the relevant contract; and
- (b) the provisions of Schedule 3.

(3) The Lord Chancellor must pay remuneration, other than to counsel, for advocacy services in family proceedings provided in the circumstances described in paragraph (4) in accordance with—

- (a) the relevant contract; and
- (b) the relevant hourly rates set out in Schedule 1.

(4) The circumstances referred to in paragraph (3) are where advocacy services are provided—

- (a) to any party in child abduction proceedings;
- (aa) in proceedings under paragraph 1 of Schedule 2 to the Female Genital Mutilation Act 2003;
- (b) in proceedings under Part IVA (forced marriage) of the Family Law Act 1996;
- (c) in defended proceedings for divorce or judicial separation, for dissolution of a civil partnership or the legal separation of civil partners;
- (d) in proceedings for the nullity of marriage or annulment of a civil partnership;
- (e) in applications for a parental order under the Human Fertilisation and Embryology Act 2008;
- (f) in proceedings under the inherent jurisdiction of the High Court in relation to children;
- (g) where the advocate separately represents a child in proceedings which are neither specified proceedings within the meaning of section 41(6) of the Children Act 1989 nor are heard together with such proceedings;

(h) in proceedings in the Court of Appeal or the Supreme Court;
(i) in a final appeal; or
(j) by Queen's Counsel acting as such under a prior authority given by the Lord Chancellor under the relevant contract.

(5) In paragraph (4), "final appeal" means any appeal against a final order in family proceedings but does not include—
(a) an application to the court of first instance for permission to appeal; and
(b) advice on the merits of appealing against a final order.

(6) Where advocacy services in the circumstances described in paragraph (4) are provided by counsel, the Lord Chancellor must pay remuneration to counsel in accordance with the relevant contract.

(7) In circumstances where the relevant contract requires the amount of remuneration payable to counsel to be determined having regard to matters including the remuneration that would have been payable had the services been remunerated under the provisions of the Community Legal Service (Funding) (Counsel in Family Proceedings) Order 2001, in deciding the amount of remuneration to pay to counsel under paragraph (6) the Lord Chancellor must reduce by 10% the remuneration that would have been payable under that Order.

III FUND [334]

9 Remuneration for civil legal services: inquests

(1) This regulation applies to the payment by the Lord Chancellor of remuneration for civil legal services provided in relation to inquests.

(2) The Lord Chancellor must pay remuneration to the provider of civil legal services in relation to an inquest in the form of legal help in accordance with—
(a) the relevant contract; and
(b) the fees and rates in Part 1 and Part 2 of Schedule 1 that are applicable to the Category Definition most relevant to the circumstances giving rise to the inquest.

(3) The Lord Chancellor must pay remuneration for civil legal services provided in relation to an inquest in the form of other legal services in accordance with—
(a) the relevant contract; and
(b) subject to paragraph (4), the rates set out in Schedule 4.

(4) If, due to exceptional circumstances, the Lord Chancellor considers it reasonable to do so, instead of paying remuneration in accordance with the rates set out in Schedule 4, the Lord Chancellor may pay remuneration in accordance with the payment rates set out in Part 2 of Schedule 2 to the Criminal Defence Service (Very High Cost Cases) (Funding) Order 2013.

(5) In paragraph (4), "exceptional circumstances" must relate to one or more of the following—
(a) the unusual length of the inquest;
(b) the volume of material; or
(c) the complexity of the issues.

(6) [...]

III FUND [335]

10 Remuneration: expert services

The Lord Chancellor must pay remuneration to a provider in relation to expert services incurred as a disbursement by the provider in accordance with—
(a) the relevant contract; and
(b) the provisions of Schedule 5.

III FUND [336]

11 Payments on account by the Lord Chancellor direct to barristers in independent practice

(1) Subject to paragraphs (5) and (6), where a provider has instructed a barrister in independent practice to carry out work that is not Controlled Work, the barrister may apply to the Lord Chancellor on a form approved by the Lord Chancellor for payment on account of remuneration for the civil legal services provided by the barrister where any of the conditions in paragraphs (2) to (4) apply.

(2) The first condition is that a period of 12, 24 or 36 months has elapsed since the date that the Director determined under section 9 of the Act that the legally aided person qualified for civil legal services.

(3) The second condition is that—

(a) the determination referred to in paragraph (2) related to proceedings that have continued for more than 12 months;

(b) it appears unlikely that an order will be made for the costs of the case to be assessed within the next 12 months; and

(c) delay in the assessment of costs will cause hardship to the barrister.

(4) The third condition is that the proceedings to which the determination referred to in paragraph (2) related have concluded or the provider is otherwise entitled to have the costs of the case assessed but the barrister has not been paid for at least six months since the provider was first so entitled.

(5) An application under paragraph (2) must be made within the period—

(a) beginning two months before one of the periods of time referred to in paragraph (2); and

(b) ending two months after that period.

(6) An application under paragraph (1) may not be made in respect of advocacy services in family proceedings.

III FUND [337]

12

(1) Where an application is made in accordance with regulation 11, the Lord Chancellor may pay the barrister up to 75% of the amount that the Lord Chancellor considers to be the barrister's reasonable fees.

(2) In deciding how much to pay under paragraph (1), the Lord Chancellor must take into account—

(a) any amounts that the Lord Chancellor has previously paid on account to the barrister; and

(b) any cost limitation to which the determination referred to in regulation 11(2) is subject.

(2A) Where an application for judicial review is issued and none of sub-paragraphs (a) to (e) of regulation 5A(1) applies, the barrister must repay to the Lord Chancellor any amount paid on account under paragraph (1) of this regulation for civil legal services consisting of making that application.

(3) If a barrister's final fees are assessed at an amount less than the amount that the Lord Chancellor has paid to the barrister on account, the barrister must pay the difference to the Lord Chancellor.

SCHEDULE 1

Regulations 6, 8(3) and 9(2)

III FUND [338]

1 Interpretation

(1) Unless different provision is made, words and expressions used in this Schedule have the same meaning as in the relevant contract.

(2) In this Schedule, "Mental Health Proceedings" means proceedings or potential proceedings before the First-tier Tribunal or the Mental Health Review Tribunal for Wales under any provision of the Mental Health Act 1983 or paragraph 5(2) of the Schedule to the Repatriation of Prisoners Act 1984.

(3) In Part 3 of this Schedule (Hourly Rates—Licensed Work) "Higher Courts" means as appropriate the Court of Protection, the Crown Court, the Employment Appeal Tribunal, the Upper Tribunal, the High Court other than a judge of High Court judge level acting as a judge of the family court, the Court of Appeal and the Supreme Court.

PART 1
CIVIL STANDARD AND GRADUATED FEES

2 Legal help and help at court

The fees in Table 1 for Housing do not apply to the Housing Possession Court Duty Scheme. The fees for that Scheme are contained in Table 6 in this Part.

2A The fees in Table 1 for Welfare Benefits do not apply to the payment of remuneration by the Lord Chancellor to providers of civil legal services where the provision of those services is governed by the 2014 Standard Civil Contract (Welfare Benefits) or the 2016 Standard Civil Contract (Welfare Benefits). The fee for the payment of remuneration by the Lord Chancellor to those persons is contained in Table 7 in this Part.

3 In Table 1, "consumer general contract", "employment" and "personal injury" have the same meanings as in the category definitions of the 2010 Standard Civil Contract in force on 31st March 2013.

Table 1

Category Definition	*. . . Standard Fee*	*. . . Escape Fee Threshold*
Actions Against the Police	£239	£717
Clinical Negligence	£195	£585
Community Care	£266	£798
Debt	£180	£540
Education	£272	£816
Housing	£157	£471
Miscellaneous	£159 (consumer general contract) £207 (employment) £157 (injunctions under Part 1 of the Anti-social Behaviour, Crime and Policing Act 2014 and related parenting orders) £203 (personal injury)	£477 (consumer general contract) £621 (employment) £471 (injunctions under Part 1 of the Anti-social Behaviour, Crime and Policing Act 2014 and related parenting orders) £609 (personal injury)

	£79 (all other matters)	£237 (all other matters)
Public Law	£259	£777
Welfare Benefits	£150	£450

Table 2(a): Legal help

Family Public Law

Region	*Fee*
National	£132

Table 2(b): Family help (lower)—section 31 Children Act 1989 Care or Supervision proceedings only

Region	*Fee*
National	£365

Table 2(c): Legal representation—section 31 Children Act 1989 Care or Supervision proceedings only

Party	*Person before whom proceedings are heard*	*Number of clients*	*Midlands*	*North*	*London and South*	*Wales*
Child	Assistant to a justices' clerk, justices' clerk, lay justice, judge of district judge level, judge of circuit judge level or costs judge	1	£1,754	£1,438	£2,013	£1,965
Child	Assistant to a justices' clerk, justices' clerk, lay justice, judge of district judge level, judge of circuit judge level or costs judge	2 or more	£2,630	£2,156	£3,020	£2,948
Child	Judge of High Court judge level	1	£2,332	£1,913	£2,678	£2,613

FUNDING

Child	Judge of High Court judge level	2 or more	£3,498	£2,869	£4,015	£3,919
Joined Party	Assistant to a justices' clerk, justices' clerk, lay justice, judge of district judge level, judge of circuit judge level or costs judge		£930	£718	£1,081	£1,171
Joined Party	Judge of High Court judge level		£1,237	£956	£1,437	£1,557
Parent	Assistant to a justices' clerk, justices' clerk, lay justice, judge of district judge level, judge of circuit judge level or costs judge	1	£2,300	£1,911	£2,616	£2,370
Parent	Assistant to a justices' clerk, justices' clerk, lay justice, judge of district judge level, judge of circuit judge level or costs judge	2	£2,876	£2,388	£3,270	£2,962
Parent	Judge of High Court judge level	1	£3,059	£2,541	£3,479	£3,152
Parent	Judge of High Court judge level	2	£3,824	£3,177	£4,349	£3,940

Table 3(a): Legal help

Family Private Law

Region	*Fee*
National	£86

Table 3(b): Legal help—Divorce petition only

Region	*Fee*
National	£146

Table 3(c): Family help (lower)—Children

Region	*Fee*	*Settlement Fee*
London	£230	£138
Non-London	£199	£119

Table 3(d): Family help (lower)—Finance

Region	*Fee*	*Settlement Fee*
London	£241	£145
Non-London	£208	£125

Table 3(e): Help with family mediation

Activity	*Fee*
Mediation Advice	£150
Mediation Consent Order (Finance)	£200

Table 3(f): Higher Standard Fee Scheme—Children

Region	*Person or court before whom proceedings are heard*	*Family help (higher) Standard Fee*	*Legal representation Standard Fee*
London	Assistant to a justices' clerk, justices' clerk, lay justice, judge of district judge level, judge of circuit judge level or costs judge	£424	£302
London	Judge of High Court judge level or Court of Protection	£509	£362
Non-London	Assistant to a justices' clerk, justices' clerk, lay justice, judge of district judge level,	£353	£251

FUNDING

	judge of circuit judge level or costs judge		
Non-London	Judge of High Court judge level or Court of Protection	£424	£302

Table 3(g): Higher Standard Fee Scheme—Finance

Region	*Person or court before whom proceedings are heard*	*Family help (higher) Standard Fee*	*Family help (higher) Standard Fee*	*Legal representation Standard Fee*
London	Assistant to a justices' clerk, justices' clerk, lay justice, judge of district judge level, judge of circuit judge level or costs judge	£471	£95	£374
London	Judge of High Court judge level or Court of Protection	£565	£113	£449
Non-London	Assistant to a justices' clerk, justices' clerk, lay justice, judge of district judge level, judge of circuit judge level or costs judge	£392	£78	£311
Non-London	Judge of High Court judge level or Court of Protection	£471	£95	£374

Table 3(h): Higher Standard Fee Scheme—Domestic Abuse Proceedings

Region	*Person or court before whom proceedings are heard*	*Legal representation Standard Fee*
London	Assistant to a justices' clerk, justices' clerk, lay justice, judge of district judge level, judge of circuit judge level or costs judge	£608
London	Judge of High Court judge level or Court of Protection	£729
Non-London	Assistant to a justices' clerk, justices' clerk, lay	£507

	justice, judge of district judge level, judge of circuit judge level or costs judge	
Non-London	Judge of High Court judge level or Court of Protection	£608

Table 4(a): Immigration and Asylum Standard Fees

Immigration and Asylum

Type of matter	*Stage 1 (legal help)*	*Stage 2a (controlled legal representation)*	*Stage 2b (controlled legal representation)*
Asylum	£413	£227	£567
Immigration—non-asylum	£234	£227	£454

Table 4(b): Additional Payment—UKBA Interview

Representation at UKBA Interview	£266

Table 4(c): Additional Payments for Advocacy Services

Oral Case Management Review Hearing	£166
Telephone Case Management Review Hearing	£90
Substantive Hearing in the Immigration and Asylum Chamber of the First-tier Tribunal	Asylum—£302 Immigration—£ 237
Additional Day Substantive Hearing	Asylum—£161 Immigration—£161

Table 4(d): Immigration Removal Centres Standard Fees (for Exclusive Schedule Holders only)

On Site Surgery—advising 5 or more clients	£360
On Site Surgery—advising 4 clients or less	£180
Fast Track Standby Payment	£34.02

FUNDING

Table 5(a): Basic Fees

Mental Health

Basic Fees	*Value*
Mental Health: non-Tribunal	£253
Level 1 (Mental Health Proceedings)	£129
Level 2 (Mental Health Proceedings)	£321
Level 3 (Mental Health Proceedings)	£294

Table 5(b): Additional Fees

Additional Fees	*Value*
Adjourned Hearing Fee	£117
Remote Travel Payment: Level 1 (Mental Health Proceedings)	£69
Remote Travel Payment: Non-Tribunal, Level 2 (Mental Health Proceedings), Level 3 (Mental Health Proceedings)	£138

Table 6: Standard Fee

Housing Possession Court Duty Scheme

Region	*Standard Fee*
London	£75.60
Non-London	£71.55

Table 7: Standard Fee

2014 Standard Civil Contract (Welfare Benefits) and 2016 Standard Civil Contract (Welfare Benefits)

Standard Fee	£208

PART 2
HOURLY RATES—CONTROLLED WORK

Table 7(a): Immigration and Asylum Escape Fee cases, Mental Health, Actions Against the Police, Public Law, Education and Community Care

Legal help, help at court and family help (lower)

Activity	*London Rate*	*Non-London Rate*
Preparation, Attendance and Advocacy	£52.65 per hour	£48.24 per hour

Travel and Waiting Time	£27.81 per hour	£27.00 per hour
Routine Letters Out and Telephone Calls	£4.05 per item	£3.78 per item

Table 7(b): Family and Housing (except as in Table 7(c)) and Miscellaneous (employment)

Activity	*London Rate*	*Non-London Rate*
Preparation, Attendance and Advocacy	£48.74 per hour	£45.95 per hour
Travel and Waiting Time	£25.74 per hour	£25.74 per hour
Routine Letters Out and Telephone Calls	£3.78 per item	£3.65 per item

Table 7(c): Legal help or help at court provided in relation to a review under section 202 of the Housing Act 1996 and to a defendant to a possession claim in the County Court, family help (lower) and related legal help in relation to section 31 of the Children Act 1989

Activity	*London Rate*	*Non-London Rate*
Preparation, Attendance and Advocacy	£56.16 per hour	£52.56 per hour
Travel and Waiting Time	£27.81 per hour	£27.05 per hour
Routine Letters Out and Telephone Calls	£4.05 per item	£3.78 per item

Table 7(d): Immigration and Asylum hourly rates cases

Activity	*London Rate*	*Non-London Rate*
Preparation, Attendance and Advocacy	£51.62 per hour	£47.30 per hour
Travel and Waiting Time	£27.27 per hour	£26.51 per hour
Routine Letters Out and Telephone Calls	£3.96 per item	£3.69 per item

Table 7(e): All other categories

Activity	*London Rate*	*Non-London Rate*
Preparation, Attendance and Advocacy	£46.53 per hour	£43.88 per hour
Travel and Waiting Time	£24.62 per hour	£24.62 per hour
Routine Letters Out and Telephone Calls	£3.60 per item	£3.47 per item

FUNDING

Table 8(a): Immigration and Asylum—Escape Fee Cases Controlled Legal Representation

Activity	*London Rate*	*Non-London Rate*
Preparation and Attendance	£57.83 per hour	£54.09 per hour
Travel and Waiting Time	£28.62 per hour	£27.81 per hour
Routine Letters Out and Telephone Calls	£4.14 per item	£3.87 per item
Advocacy	£65.79 per hour	£65.79 per hour

Table 8(b): Immigration and Asylum Chamber of the Upper Tribunal cases where permission granted to Client (non Fast Track)

Revoked by the Civil Legal Aid (Remuneration) (Amendment) Regulations 2013 with effect from 2 December 2013.

Table 8(c): Controlled Legal Representation—Immigration and Asylum hourly rates cases

Activity	*London Rate*	*Non-London Rate*
Preparation and Attendance	£55.08 per hour	£51.53 per hour
Travel and Waiting Time	£27.27 per hour	£26.51 per hour
Routine Letters Out and Telephone Calls	£3.96 per hour	£3.69 per hour
Advocacy	£62.64 per hour	£62.64 per hour

Table 8(d): Representation in Mental Health Proceedings

Activity	*London Rate*	*Non-London Rate*
Preparation, Attendance and Advocacy	£57.83 per hour	£54.09 per hour
Travel and Waiting Time	£28.62 per hour	£27.81 per hour
Routine Letters Out and Telephone Calls	£4.14 per item	£3.87 per item
Advocacy	£65.79 per item	£65.79 per item
Attending Tribunal with Counsel	£30.78 per hour	£30.78 per hour

PART 3
HOURLY RATES—LICENSED WORK

Table 9(a): Proceedings under Parts IV or V of the Children Act 1989, including proceedings under section 25 of that Act, or as the case may be, section 119 of the Social Services and Well-being (Wales) Act 2014 but excluding proceedings under section 31 of the Children Act 1989

Family Prescribed Rates

Activity	*Judge of High Court judge level (acting as a judge of the family court) or Higher Courts*	*Assistant to a justices' clerk, justices' clerk, lay justice, judge of district judge level, judge of circuit judge level or costs judge*
Writing routine letters	£4.23 per item	£3.69 per item
Receiving routine letters	£2.12 per item	£1.85 per item
Routine telephone calls	£4.23 per item	£3.69 per item
Preparation and attendance	£70.07 per hour (London rate) £65.84 per hour (Non-London rate)	£61.38 per hour (London rate) £58.41 per hour (Non-London rate)
Attendance at court or conference with counsel	£37.13 per hour	£32.67 per hour
Advocacy	£70.07 per hour (London rate) £65.84 per hour (Non-London rate)	£64.35 per hour
Travelling and waiting time	£32.18 per hour	£29.21 per hour

Table 9(aa): Legal representation—section 31 Children Act 1989 Care or Supervision proceedings only

Family Prescribed Rates

Activity	*Judge of High Court judge level (acting as a judge of the family court) or Higher Courts*	*Assistant to a justices' clerk, justices' clerk, lay justice, judge of district judge level, judge of circuit judge level or costs judge*
Writing routine letters	£4.23 per item	£3.69 per item
Receiving routine letters	£2.12 per item	£1.85 per item
Routine telephone calls	£4.23 per item	£3.69 per item
Preparation and attendance	£63.06 per hour (London rate) £59.26 per hour (Non-London rate)	£55.24 per hour (London rate) £52.57 per hour (Non-London rate)
Attendance at court or conference with counsel	£33.42 per hour	£29.40 per hour
Travelling and waiting time	£28.96 per hour	£26.29 per hour

FUNDING

Table 9(b): Other Family Proceedings

Activity	*Judge of High Court judge level (acting as a judge of the family court) or Higher Courts*	*Assistant to a justices' clerk, justices' clerk, lay justice, judge of district judge level, judge of circuit judge level or costs judge*
Routine letters out	£6.35 per item	£5.40 per item
Receiving routine letters	£3.15 per item	£2.70 per item
Routine telephone calls	£6.35 per item	£5.40 per item
Preparation and attendance	£70.56 per hour (London rate) £65.75 per hour (Non-London rate)	£59.40 per hour (London rate) £54.90 per hour (Non-London rate)
Attending court or conference with Counsel	£37.13 per hour	£32.40 per hour
Advocacy	£70.56 per hour (London rate) £65.75 per hour (Non-London rate)	£59.40 per hour (London rate) £56.70 per hour (Non-London rate)
Travelling and waiting time	£32.18 per hour	£28.80 per hour (London rate) £27.90 per hour (Non-London rate)

Table 10(a): Higher Courts, County Courts and Magistrates' Courts for work carried out with Schedule Authorisation or injunctions under Part 1 of the Anti-social Behaviour, Crime and Policing Act 2014 and related parenting orders

Non Family Prescribed Rates

Activity	*Higher Courts*	*County Court and Magistrates' Courts*
Routine letters out	£6.75 per item	£5.94 per item
Routine telephone calls	£3.74 per item	£3.29 per item
Preparation and attendance	£71.55 per hour (London rate) £67.50 per hour (Non-London rate)	£63.00 per hour (London rate) £59.40 per hour (Non-London rate)
Attendance at court or conference with Counsel	£33.30	£29.25
Advocacy	£67.50 per hour	£59.40 per hour
Travelling and waiting time	£29.93 per hour	£26.28 per hour

Table 10(b): Higher Courts, County Courts and Magistrates' Courts for work not carried out with Schedule Authorisation (except as in Table 10(a))

Activity	*Higher Courts*	*County Court and Magistrates' Courts*
Routine letters out	£6.66 per item	£5.85 per item

Routine telephone calls	£3.69 per item	£3.24 per item
Preparation and attendance	£70.65 per hour (London rate) £66.60 per hour (Non-London rate)	£62.10 per hour (London rate) £58.50 per hour (Non-London rate)
Attendance at court or conference with Counsel	£32.76 per hour	£28.80 per hour
Advocacy	£66.60 per hour	£58.50 per hour
Travelling and waiting time	£29.43 per hour	£25.88 per hour

Table 10(c): First-tier Tribunal

Activity	*London Rate*	*Non-London Rate*
Preparation and attendance	£55.08 per hour	£51.53 per hour
Routine letters out and telephone calls	£3.96 per item	£3.69 per item
Attending tribunal or conference with counsel	£29.30 per hour	£29.30 per hour
Advocacy	£62.64 per hour	£62.64 per hour
Travelling and waiting time	£27.27 per hour	£26.51 per hour

FUNDING

PART 4
FAMILY MEDIATION FEES

Table 11(a): Assessment Meetings

Activity	*Fee*
Assessment alone	£87
Assessment separate	£87
Assessment together	£130

Table 11(b): Mediation Fees

Category of Work	*Single Session*	*Multi Session*	*Agreed Proposal*
All Issues of Sole Mediation	£168	£756	£252
All Issues Co-Mediation	£230	£1,064	£252
Property and Finance Sole Mediation	£168	£588	£189
Property and Finance Co-Mediation	£230	£834	£189

Child Sole Mediation	£168	£462	£126
Child Co-Mediation	£230	£647	£126

SCHEDULE 2
REMUNERATION OF BARRISTERS IN INDEPENDENT PRACTICE IN RELATION TO WORK THAT IS NOT CONTROLLED WORK, ADVOCACY SERVICES IN FAMILY PROCEEDINGS OR OTHER LEGAL SERVICES IN RELATION TO INQUESTS

Regulation 7

III FUND [339]

1 Interpretation

For the purpose of this Schedule—

"junior counsel" means a barrister in independent practice of less than 10 years call; and

"senior counsel" means a barrister in independent practice of 10 years call or more.

Table 1: Rates in the County Court, High Court or Upper Tribunal other than for Queen's Counsel

Category	*Hourly Rate*
Preparation and attendance in the High Court or Upper Tribunal	£71.55 (London rate) £67.50 (Non-London rate)
Preparation and attendance in the County Court	£63.00 (London rate) £59.40 (Non-London rate)
Attendance at court or conference in the High Court or Upper Tribunal	£33.30
Attendance at court or conference in the County Court	£29.25
Advocacy in the High Court or Upper Tribunal	£67.50
Advocacy in the County Court	£59.40
Travel and waiting in the High Court or Upper Tribunal	£29.93
Travel and waiting in the County Court	£26.28

Table 2: Rates in the Court of Appeal or Supreme Court and for Queen's Counsel (in any court)

Category	*Hourly Rate*
Led junior counsel in the Court of Appeal or the Supreme Court	£112.50
Leading senior counsel in the Court of Appeal	£157.50

Queen's Counsel (where approved for briefing or instruction by the Lord Chancellor) in the High Court or Court of Appeal	£180
Leading senior counsel in the Supreme Court	£180
Queen's Counsel (where approved for briefing or instruction by the Lord Chancellor) in the Supreme Court	£225
Noter/Pupil/2nd led junior counsel in the Court of Appeal or Supreme Court	£36

SCHEDULE 3
FAMILY ADVOCACY SCHEME: FEES AND RATES

Regulation 8(2)

FUNDING

III FUND [340]

1 Interpretation

Unless different provision is made, words and expressions used in this Schedule have the same meaning as in the relevant contract.

2 Bolt on fees—advocate's bundle

(1) The Lord Chancellor must pay a bolt-on fee at the rates set out in tables 1(d) (Public Law—bolt-on fee—advocate's bundle payments) or 2(e) (Private Law Children and finance—bolt-on fees—advocate's bundle payment) as applicable to an advocate providing advocacy services in family proceedings where—

(a) the advocate's bundle for a hearing exceeds 350 pages; and

(b) the advocate submits a claim on a form specified by the Lord Chancellor.

(2) An advocate must provide any additional information or documents requested by the Lord Chancellor as evidence that paragraph 2(1)(a) is satisfied.

(3) For the purposes of this paragraph the advocate's bundle—

(a) may only include—

(i) those documents relevant to the case which have been served by the parties to the proceedings to which the hearing relates; and

(ii) notes of contact visits if included in the court bundle; and

(b) must include a paginated index agreed by the parties to those proceedings.

(4) In this paragraph, "court bundle" means the bundle prepared for the hearing to which the claim relates in accordance with Practice Direction 27A—Family Proceedings: Court Bundles (universal practice to be applied in the High Court and Family Court) to the Family Procedure Rules 2010.

PART 1
PUBLIC LAW ADVOCACY FEES

Table 1(a): Care or supervision proceedings under section 31 of the Children Act 1989—graduated fees

Person before whom proceedings are heard	*Hearing Unit 1 (up to 1 hour)*	*Hearing Unit 2 (up to 2.5 hours)*	*Conference fee*	*Opinion fee*	*Advocates' Meeting Fee*	*Final Hearing Fee (per day)*
Assistant to a justices' clerk, justices' clerk or lay justices	£86.72	£216.81	£127.71	£105.66	£128.16	£506.25
Judge of district judge level, judge of circuit judge level or costs judge	£95.40	£238.46	£127.71	£105.66	£140.99	£556.88
Judge of High Court judge level	£114.48	£286.16	£127.71	£105.66	£169.20	£668.25

Table 1(b): Other Public Law Case—graduated fees

Person before whom proceedings are heard	*Hearing Unit 1 (up to 1 hour)*	*Hearing Unit 2 (up to 2.5 hours)*	*Conference fee*	*Opinion fee*	*Advocates' Meeting Fee*	*Final Hearing Fee (per day)*
Assistant to a justices' clerk, justices' clerk or lay justices	£75.83	£189.59	£127.71	£105.66	£128.16	£464.31
Judge of district judge level, judge of circuit judge level or costs judge	£83.39	£208.53	£127.71	£105.66	£140.99	£510.75
Judge of High Court judge level	£100.08	£250.20	£127.71	£105.66	£169.20	£612.90

Table 1(c): Public Law—bolt-on fees

Category	*Payable For*	*Fee Payable*

Client—Allegations of Harm	Hearings	25% of Hearing Unit Fee
Client—Lack of understanding etc	Hearings	25% of Hearing Unit Fee
Expert's cross examination	Hearings	25% of Hearing Unit Fee
Exceptional travel fee	Hearings, Advocates' Meetings and Conferences	£32.04

Table 1(d): Public Law—bolt-on fee—advocate's bundle payments

Hearing type	*ABP1 (351–700 pages)*	*ABP2 (701–1,400 pages)*	*ABP3 (over 1,400 pages)*
Interim Hearing	£59.40	£89.10	£89.10
Final Hearing	£159.30	£239.40	£318.60

PART 2

PRIVATE LAW ADVOCACY FEES

Table 2(a): Private Law Children—Graduated Fees

Person before whom proceedings are heard	*Hearing Unit 1 (up to 1 hour)*	*Hearing Unit 2 (up to 2.5 hours)*	*Conference fee*	*Opinion fee*	*Final hearing fee (per day)*
Assistant to a justices' clerk, justices' clerk or lay justices	£62.69	£156.74	£125.37	£94.05	£397.04
Judge of district judge level, judge of circuit judge level or costs judge	£68.94	£172.40	£125.37	£94.05	£436.73
Judge of High Court judge level	£82.76	£206.87	£125.37	£94.05	£524.07

Table 2(b): Domestic Abuse—Graduated Fees

Person before whom proceedings are heard	*Hearing Unit 1 (up to 1 hour)*	*Hearing Unit 2 (up to 2.5 hours)*	*Final hearing fee (per day)*
Assistant to a justices' clerk, jus-	£81.50	£203.76	£361.17

tices' clerk or lay justices			
Judge of district judge level, judge of circuit judge level or costs judge	£81.50	£203.76	£361.17
Judge of High Court judge level	£81.50	£203.76	£361.17

Table 2(c): Private Law Finance—Graduated Fees

Person before whom proceedings are heard	*Hearing Unit 1(up to 1 hour)*	*Hearing Unit 2 (up to 2.5 hours)*	*Financial Dispute Resolution Hearing Unit 1*	*Financial Dispute Resolution Hearing Unit 2*	*Early resolution fee*	*Conference fee*	*Opinion Fee*	*Final hearing fee (per day)*
Assistant to a justices' clerk, justices' clerk, lay justice, judge of district judge level, judge of circuit judge level or costs judge	£63.18	£157.95	£101.07	£252.72	£126.36	£126.36	£94.77	£443.70
Judge of High Court judge level	£75.83	£189.54	£121.32	£303.26	£151.65	£126.36	£94.77	£532.44

Table 2(d): Private Law—bolt-on fees

Bolt-on Fee	*Payable For*	*Fee Payable*
Client—Allegations of Harm	Private Law Children Hearings	25% of Hearing Unit Fee
Expert's cross examination	Private Law Children Hearings	20% of Hearing Unit Fee
Exceptional travel fee	Hearings and Conferences	£32.04

Table 2(e): Private Law Children and Finance—bolt-on fees—advocate's bundle payment

Hearing type	*ABP1 (351–700 pages)*	*ABP2 (701–1,400 pages)*	*ABP3 (over 1,400 pages)*
Interim hearing	£59.40	£89.10	£89.10
Final hearing	£159.30	£239.40	£318.60

SCHEDULE 4
INQUESTS

Regulation 9(3) and (4)

III FUND [341]

1 Interpretation

(1) Unless different provision is made, words and expressions used in this Schedule have the same meaning as in the relevant contact.

(2) In this Schedule, "Senior Solicitor" means a solicitor with over eight years' qualified experience.

FUNDING

Table 1: Provider Hourly Rates

Item	*Grade*	*Inside London (hourly rate)*	*Outside London (hourly rate)*
Preparation	Senior Solicitor	£75.27	£71.55
	Other Solicitor	£63.80	£60.75
	Trainee Solicitor	£45.90	£40.17
Conference with counsel	Senior Solicitor	£75.27	£71.55
	Other Solicitor	£63.80	£60.75
	Trainee Solicitor	£45.90	£40.17
Attendance at hearing	Senior Solicitor	£57.05	£57.05
	Other Solicitor	£45.90	£45.90
	Trainee Solicitor	£27.68	£27.68
Advocacy (by solicitor)	Senior Solicitor	£87.08	£87.08
	Other Solicitor	£75.60	£75.60
Travel and waiting	Senior Solicitor	£22.28	£22.28
	Other Solicitor	£22.28	£22.28
	Trainee Solicitor	£11.25	£11.25

Table 2: Barrister rates

Item	*Category*	*Fixed rate*
Brief fee	Junior Counsel	£900
	Queen's Counsel	£1800

Refresher fee	Junior Counsel	£450
	Queen's Counsel	£630

SCHEDULE 5
EXPERTS' FEES AND RATES

Regulation 10

III FUND [342]

1 Subject to paragraph 2, where the expert service is of a type listed in the Table, the Lord Chancellor must pay remuneration to the provider for the expert service at the fixed fees or at rates not exceeding the rates set out in the Table.

Table

Expert	*Non-London—Hourly Rate unless stated to be a fixed fee*	*London—Hourly Rate unless stated to be a fixed fee*	*Comments*
A&E consultant	£100.80	£108	
Accident reconstruction	£72	£54.40	
Accountant	£64	£64	
Accountant (general staff)	£40	£40	
Accountant (manager)	£86.40	£86.40	
Accountant (partner)	£108	£115.20	
Anaesthetist	£108	£108	
Architect	£79.20	£72	
Cardiologist	£115.20	£115.20	
Cell telephone site analysis	£72	£72	
Child psychiatrist	£108	£108	
Child psychologist	£100.80	£100.80	
Computer expert	£72	£72	
Consultant engineer	£72	£54.40	
Dentist	£93.60	£93.60	
Dermatologist	£86.40	£86.40	
Disability consultant	£54.40	£54.40	
DNA (testing of sample)	£252 per test	£252 per test	
DNA (preparation of report)	£72	£72	
Doctor (GP)	£79.20	£72	
Employment consultant	£54.40	£54.40	
Enquiry agent	£25.60	£18.40	

ENT surgeon	£100.80	£100.80
General surgeon	£108	£72
Geneticist	£86.40	£86.40
GP (records report)	£50.40 fixed fee	£72 fixed fee
Gynaecologist	£108	£72
Haematologist	£97.60	£72
Handwriting expert	£72	£72
Interpreter	£28	£25
Lip reader/Signer	£57.60	£32.80
Mediator	£100.80	£100.80
Medical consultant	£108	£72
Medical microbiologist	£108	£108
Meteorologist	£100.80	£144 fixed fee
Midwife	£72	£72
Neonatologist (non-clinical negligence cerebral palsy case)	£108	£108
Neonatologist (clinical negligence cerebral palsy case)	£180	£180
Neurologist (non-clinical negligence cerebral palsy case)	£122.40	£72
Neurologist (clinical negligence cerebral palsy case)	£200	£200
Neuropsychiatrist	£126.40	£72
Neuroradiologist (non-clinical negligence cerebral palsy case)	£136.80	£136.80
Neuroradiologist (clinical negligence cerebral palsy case)	£180	£180
Neurosurgeon	£136.80	£72
Nursing expert	£64.80	£64.80
Obstetrician	£108	£108
Occupational therapist	£54.40	£54.40
Oncologist	£112	£112
Orthopaedic surgeon	£115.20	£115.20
Paediatrician	£108	£72
Pathologist	£122.40	£432 fixed fee
Pharmacologist	£97.60	£97.60
Photographer	£25.60	£18.40
Physiotherapist	£64.80	£64.80
Plastic surgeon	£108	£108
Process server	£25.60	£18.40
Psychiatrist	£108	£108
Psychologist	£93.60	£93.60

Radiologist	£108	£108
Rheumatologist	£108	£108
Risk assessment expert	£50.40	£50.40
Speech therapist	£79.20	£79.20
Surveyor (housing disrepair)	£85	£115
Surveyor (non-housing disrepair)	£40	£40
Telecoms expert	£72	£72
Toxicologist	£108	£108
Urologist	£108	£108
Vet	£72	£72
Voice recognition	£93.60	£72

2 Exceptional circumstances

(1) The Lord Chancellor may increase the fixed fees or rates set out in the Table after paragraph 1 if the Lord Chancellor considers it reasonable to do so due to exceptional circumstances.

(2) In sub-paragraph (1), "exceptional circumstances" mean that the expert's evidence is key to the client's case and either—

(a) the complexity of the material is such that an expert with a high level of seniority is required; or

(b) the material is of such a specialised and unusual nature that only very few experts are available to provide the necessary evidence.

3 Payment of expert services of a type not listed in the Table after Part 1

Where the expert service is of a type not listed in the Table after paragraph 1, in considering the rate at which to fund the expert service the Lord Chancellor—

(a) must have regard to the rates set out in the Table after paragraph 1; and

(b) may require a number of quotes for provision of the service to be submitted to the Lord Chancellor.

4 General provisions relating to experts

(1) The costs and expenses relating to experts listed at sub-paragraph (2) are not payable by the Lord Chancellor.

(2) The costs and expenses are—

(a) any administration fee charged by an expert, including (but not limited to)—

(i) a fee in respect of office space or provision of a consultation room;

(ii) a fee in respect of administrative support services, such as typing services;

(iii) a fee in respect of courier services;

(iv) a subsistence fee; and

(b) any cancellation fee charged by an expert, where the notice of cancellation was given to the expert more than 72 hours before the relevant hearing or appointment.

5 The maximum amount that the Lord Chancellor may pay as a disbursement in respect of an expert's vehicle mileage is £0.45 per mile.

6 The maximum amount that the Lord Chancellor may pay as a disbursement in respect of an expert's travel time is £40 per hour.

FUNDS IN COURT

TABLE OF CONTENTS

GENERAL NOTE ON FUNDS IN COURT

III FUN [1]

Part VI of the Administration of Justice Act 1982 provides the statutory powers for the administration of funds in court. The Court Funds Rules 2011, SI 2011/1734 made under s 38(7) provide a common code for the regulation of the Court Funds Office and for the administration of money paid into court, or effects deposited, in the High Court, the Family Court and in the County Court.

ADMINISTRATION OF JUSTICE ACT 1982

(c 53)

FUNDS IN COURT

III FUN [2]

38. Management and investment of funds in court

(1) Subject to rules made under subsection (7) below, all sums of money, securities and effects paid and deposited in, or under the custody of—

(a) the High Court;

(aa) the family court;

(b) the county court; or

(c) such other courts and tribunals as the Lord Chancellor may by rules made under that subsection prescribe,

shall be vested in the Accountant General.

(2) One or more accounts shall be opened and kept in the name of the Accountant General at such bank or banks as may be designated by the Lord Chancellor with the concurrence of the Treasury.

(3) Money and securities held by the Accountant General shall vest in his successor in office without any assignment or transfer.

(4) A sum of money paid and deposited in court may, [. . .] be invested and reinvested by the Accountant General in any manner authorised by rules made under subsection (7) below.

(5) [. . .]

(6) The Accountant General may, in such cases as the Lord Chancellor may by rules made under subsection (7) below prescribe, apply to the court for an order for directions as to the manner in which a particular fund in court is to be dealt with.

(7) The Lord Chancellor, with the concurrence of the Treasury, may make provision as to the payment of interest on funds in court and may make rules as to the administration and management of funds in court including the deposit, payment, delivery and transfer in, into and out of any court of funds in court and regulating the evidence of such deposit, payment, delivery or transfer.

(8) Rules made under subsection (7) above may—

(a) provide for the discharge of the functions of the Accountant General under the rules by a person or persons appointed by him;

(b) provide for the transfer of money in court to and from the Commissioners;

(c) provide for money paid and deposited in the county court to be vested in, and accounted for by, a person other than the Accountant General;

(d) prescribe cases in which interest is to be paid on funds in court;

(e) prescribe cases in which funds in court are to be invested;

(f) make provision for the transfer of funds in court from one court to another; and

(g) prescribe cases in which moneys payable under a judgment or order shall be paid into court.

(9) Any such rules may make different provision for different cases.

III FUN [2.1]

Rules The rules made under sub-s (7) are the Court Funds Rules 2011, SI 2011/1734; for the main ones see para **III FUN [9]**. The forms used to effect transactions may be obtained from any legal stationer or any county court. The main forms may also be found via http://www.gov.uk, under Court Funds Office forms.

III FUN [2.2]

Accountant General See Senior Courts Act 1981 s 97 (see para **II SCA [64A]**).

III FUN [2A]

39. Investment of money transferred to National Debt Commissioners

(1) The Commissioners may invest, in such manner as may be prescribed by regulations made by the Treasury, money transferred to them in pursuance of rules made under section 38(7) above or section 82(1) of the Judicature (Northern Ireland) Act 1978 and the interest or dividends accruing on investments made under this subsection.

(2) If in any accounting year the aggregate of the sums of money received by the Commissioners by way of interest and dividends on investments made by them under subsection (1) above, after deduction of—

(a) any sum required by the Treasury to be set aside to provide for depreciation in the value of investments so made; and

(b) such sum as the Lord Chancellor may with the concurrence of the Treasury direct to be paid to him in respect of the cost to him in that year of administering funds in court, and

(c) an amount equal to the expenses incurred by the Commissioners in that year in making investments under subsection (1) above and disposing of investments so made exceeds the aggregate of the sums due to be paid or credited in respect of that year by way of interest on funds in courts, the excess shall be paid into the Consolidated Fund.

(3) If in any accounting year the aggregate of the sums of money received as mentioned in subsection (2) above, after deduction of the sum or sums falling to be deducted under paragraphs (a)–(c) of that subsection, is less than the aggregate of the sums due as mentioned in that subsection, the deficiency shall be made good out of the Consolidated Fund.

(4) The Commissioners shall pay to the Lord Chancellor any sum deducted by them under subsection (2)(b) above; and any sum received by the Lord Chancellor under this subsection shall be paid into the Consolidated Fund.

(4A) Any sum deducted by the Commissioners under subsection (2)(c) above shall be applied as an appropriation in aid of moneys provided by Parliament for the expenses of the National Debt Commissioners; and, so far as not so applied, shall be paid into the Consolidated Fund.

(5) If at any time the Commissioners are unable to pay—

(a) to the Accountant General a sum due from them to him under rules made under section 38(7) above; or

(b) to the Accountant General of the Court of Judicature of Northern Ireland a sum due from them to him under rules made under section 82(1) of the Judicature (Northern Ireland) Act 1978,

the Treasury shall provide them with it out of the Consolidated Fund.

III FUN [3]

40. Statutory deposits

(1) Where money or securities are deposited with the Accountant General under any enactment or subordinate legislation, whether passed or made before or after the commencement of this Part of this Act, they shall for the purposes of this Part of this Act be treated as if they were funds in court except in so far as—

(a) the enactment; or

(b) the subordinate legislation; or

(c) rules made under section 38 (7) above,

provide to the contrary.

(2) In subsection (1) above "subordinate legislation" means Orders in Council, orders, rules, regulations and other instruments made or to be made under any Act.

III FUN [3.1]

Statutory deposits Deposits may be made under several statutes such as s 3 of the Life Assurance Companies (Payment into Court) Act 1896, s 63 of the Trustee Act 1925 and ss 84 and 136 of the Law of Property Act 1925. The procedure for paying in is regulated by CPR 37.4 and CPR PD 37. These payments are made generally where trustees or other statutory depositors cannot obtain a good discharge from beneficiaries.

III FUN [3.2]

Forms For deposits under the Life Assurance Companies Act a witness statement or affidavit must be filed with Chancery Chambers in the Royal Courts of Justice with a CFO Form 106. The Court Funds Office will receive a copy of the F106 and witness statement or affidavit and will issue directions to deposit.

For deposits under the Trustee Act 1925 a CFO Form 103 in duplicate is required together with an affidavit or witness statement. The Forms 103 and affidavit/witness statement should then be filed with Chancery Chambers or local District Registry who send one copy of the Form 103 to the Court Funds Office who will issue deposit directions.

Deposits made under other Acts may be made by way of CFO Form 102 (Compulsory Purchase Act deposits) or Form 105 (Rent Redemption Act deposits) or by way of a Form 101 (general deposit schedule) authenticated by the relevant court.

All these forms may be found via http://www.gov.uk, under Court Funds Office forms, or at legal stationers.

III FUN [3A]

41. Transfer of funds in Court to Official Custodian for Charities and appropriate authority

(1) Any funds for the time being vested in the Accountant General and held by him in trust for any charity or in trust for any ecclesiastical corporation in the Church of England may, if the Accountant General on an application made in that behalf to him by the Charity Commission or the appropriate authority thinks fit so to direct, be transferred to the Official Custodian for Charities or the appropriate authority, as the case may be.

(2) Any funds transferred by virtue of a direction given under subsection (1) above shall be vested in and held by the Official Custodian for Charities or the appropriate authority respectively in trust for the charity or ecclesiastical corporation upon the trusts upon which the funds were held before the transfer.

(3) In this section "ecclesiastical corporation" means a capitular body within the meaning of the Cathedrals Measure 1963 or the incumbent of a benefice and "appropriate authority" means, in the case of funds held in trust for a cathedral, the corporate body of that cathedral established under section 9(1)(a) of the Cathedrals Measure 1999 and in the case of funds held in trust for a benefice the Diocesan Board of Finance for the diocese in which that benefice is situated.

III FUN [4]

42. Common investment schemes

(1) The Lord Chancellor may continue to make schemes ("common investment schemes") establishing common investment funds for the purpose of investing funds in court and money held by any person who in accordance with subsection (5)(b) below may hold shares in common investment funds.

(2) A common investment scheme shall provide for the fund thereby established to be under the management and control of an investment manager appointed by the Lord Chancellor.

(3) A common investment scheme shall make provision for the investment by its investment manager in accordance with the provisions of this section of funds in court transferred to the fund under rules made by virtue of section 38 (7) above and of any sums of money transferred to the fund by persons who in accordance with subsection (5)(b) below may hold shares in the fund.

(4) A common investment scheme shall make provision—

- (a) for treating the fund established by it as being divided into shares; and
- (b) for treating a sum invested in the fund as being represented by a number of shares determined by reference to that sum and the value of the fund at the time the investment was made.

(5) Shares in a common investment fund—

- (a) shall be allotted to and held by the Accountant General; and
- (b) may be allotted to and held by the Accountant General of the Court of Judicature of Northern Ireland and any other person authorised by the Lord Chancellor.

(6) Where a person is authorised under subsection (5) above to hold shares in a common investment fund—

- (a) he may invest trust money in shares in the fund without obtaining and considering advice on whether to make such an investment; and
- (b) he may invest trust money in a common investment fund of which he is the investment manager.

(7) Moneys comprised in the fund established by a common investment scheme may, subject to the provisions of the scheme, be invested by the investment manager of the fund in any way in which he thinks fit, whether or not authorised by the general law in relation to trust funds.

(8) [. . .]

(9) The investment manager of a fund established by a common investment scheme shall not be required or entitled to take account of any trusts or equities affecting any share in the fund whether or not he is also a trustee of any such trust.

(10) The investment manager of a fund established by a common investment scheme shall be remunerated at such rates and in such manner as the Lord Chancellor shall with the concurrence of the Treasury determine.

(11) The salary or remuneration of an investment manager and his officers and such other expenses of executing his office or otherwise carrying this Part of this Act into effect as may be sanctioned by the Treasury shall be paid out of moneys provided by Parliament.

(12) There shall be charged in respect of the running of a common investment scheme such fees, whether by way of percentage or otherwise, as the Lord Chancellor shall with the concurrence of the Treasury fix and such fees shall be collected and accounted for by such persons, and in such manner, and shall be paid to such account, as the Treasury direct.

(13) There shall be retained or paid out of a fund established by a common investment scheme any expenses which could be so retained or paid out of trust property if the investment manager of the fund were a trustee and such expenses shall be retained or paid in the same way as and in addition to fees charged in respect of the running of the scheme.

(14) Fees and expenses recovered under this section shall be paid into the Consolidated Fund.

(15) Money and securities held by an investment manager of a fund established by a common investment scheme shall vest in his successor in office without any assignment or transfer.

(16) The power conferred by subsection (1) above to make a common investment scheme shall include the power to vary or revoke such a scheme.

III FUN [4.1]

Common investment scheme The Common Investment Scheme 2004, SI 2004/266 came into force on 27 February 2004 in place of the Common Investment Scheme 1991 and was amended by the Common Investment (Amendment) Scheme 2007, SI 2007/1095.

FUNDS IN COURT

III FUN [5]

43. Provision for making good defaults

If the Lord Chancellor, whether on a recommendation made to him by any person interested or not, certifies—

(a) that the Accountant General; or

(b) that the manager of a common investment fund,

has been guilty of any default with respect to any money, securities and effects for which he is responsible under this Part of this Act, such sum as may be certified by the Lord Chancellor to be necessary for making good the default shall be paid out of moneys provided by Parliament or, if and so far as it is not so paid, shall be charged on and issued out of the Consolidated Fund.

III FUN [6]

44. Power to repeal and modify ss 42 and 43

(1) Her Majesty may by Order in Council—

(a) repeal subsections (8), (10), (12), (14) and (15) of section 42 above and section 43 above; or

(b) make such modifications to those enactments as Her Majesty considers appropriate.

(2) Any Order in Council made under subsection (1) above shall be subject to annulment in pursuance of a resolution of either House of Parliament.

III FUN [7]

45. Accounts

(1) Accounts shall be prepared and shall at such times as the Treasury shall direct be sent to the Comptroller and Auditor General—

(a) in respect of his transactions under section 38 above, by the Accountant General;

(b) in respect of their transactions under section 39 above, by the Commissioners; and

(c) in respect of transactions in a fund established by a common investment scheme, by the investment manager.

(2) The accounts shall be in such form and shall be prepared in respect of such periods as the Treasury may direct.

(3) The Comptroller and Auditor General shall examine, certify and report on accounts sent to him under subsection (1) above and lay copies of them and his report on them before each House of Parliament.

III FUN [8]

46. Supplemental

(1) Any power conferred by this Part of this Act to make a scheme or rules or regulations shall be exercisable by statutory instrument which shall be subject to annulment in pursuance of a resolution of either House of Parliament (subject to subsection (1A)).

(1A) Where the power is exercisable by a Northern Ireland department it shall be exercisable by statutory rule for the purposes of the Statutory Rules (Northern Ireland) Order 1979 subject to negative resolution (within the meaning of section 41(6) of the Interpretation Act (Northern Ireland) 1954).

(2) The following amendments shall have effect—

(a) the words "invested under section 38 of the Administration of Justice Act 1982" shall be substituted for the words "dealt with under section 6 of the Administration of Justice Act 1965" in each case where they occur in the following enactments—

(i) section 46 of the Chelsea and Kilmainham Hospitals Act 1826;

(ii) ...

(iii) sections 70, 78 and 86 of the Land Clauses Consolidation Act 1845; and

(iv) ...

(b)–(g) ...

III FUN [8A]

47. Interpretation

In this Part

"Accountant General" means in relation to England and Wales, the Accountant General of the Senior Courts and, in relation to Northern Ireland, the Accountant General of the Court of Judicature;

"the Commissioners" means the National Debt Commissioners;

"a common investment scheme" means a scheme made under section 42 above;

"funds" or "funds in court" means—

(i) a county court;
(ii) the High Court;
(iii) the Civil Division of the Court of Appeal;
(iv) the Court of Protection; or
(v) the family court

III FUN [12]

3. Interpretation

(1) Expressions used in these Rules that are also used in the Civil Procedure Rules 1998 shall have the same meaning as they have in those Rules.

(2) In these Rules:

"Accountant General" means the Accountant General of the Senior Courts or a person appointed under rule 5;

"Authenticated" means authenticated with a stamp issued by the Accountant General;

"Child" means a person under 18;

"Common investment fund" means a fund established by a scheme made under section 42 of the Administration of Justice Act 1982;

"Court" means any court listed in rule 2(b);

"CPR" means the Civil Procedure Rules 1998;

"Deposit schedule" means a schedule to an order directing that a fund be deposited in court;

"Deputy" means a person who makes decisions on behalf of a person who lacks capacity and who has been:

(a) appointed by a court under section 16(2)(b) of the Mental Capacity Act 2005; or
(b) deemed to be so appointed by virtue of paragraph 1 of schedule 5 to that Act;

"Foreign currency" means currency other than sterling;

"Fund" means money (including foreign currency), securities or effects;

"Fund in court" means a fund deposited in court in accordance with Part 2 of these Rules;

"Investment manager" means a person appointed by a deputy to make decisions as to the investment of a fund in court on behalf of a person who lacks capacity;

"Order" means an order or direction made under the seal of a court;

"Payment schedule" means a schedule to an order directing a payment from, or a dealing with, a fund in court;

"Person who lacks capacity" means a person who:

(a) immediately before 1st October 2007 was a patient within the meaning of Part VII of the Mental Health Act 1983; or
(b) a court has found lacks capacity within the meaning of the Mental Capacity Act 2005 in relation to a fund in court held or to be held on that person's behalf; and

"Written request" means a request made on a form approved by the Accountant General to:

(a) deposit funds in court;
(b) deal with a fund in court; or
(c) receive payment from a fund in court.

(3) In these Rules, where two or more deputies are appointed in relation to a person who lacks capacity:

FUNDS IN COURT

(a) the word "deputy" refers to those deputies acting jointly if and to the extent that joint action is required by the terms of their appointment; and
(b) any rule permitting the Accountant General to refuse to:
  (i) follow a direction given by a deputy; or
  (ii) undertake any other act at the request of a deputy,

includes a power to refuse to do so on the ground that, while the terms of appointment require the deputies to act jointly, the direction or request was not jointly made.

III FUN [13]

4. Court Funds Office
The office of the Accountant General shall continue to be known as the Court Funds Office.

III FUN [14]

5. Discharge of Accountant General's functions
The Accountant General may appoint one or more persons to do anything that may be done by the Accountant General under these Rules.

PART 2
DEPOSIT OF FUNDS IN COURT

III FUN [15]

6. Documents accompanying deposit of funds in court
(1) The general rule is that the Accountant General shall only accept a deposit of a fund if provided with:
(a) a deposit schedule signed and authenticated by a court; or
(b)
  (i) a written request; and
  (ii) a sealed copy of the court order authorising the deposit.

(2) The general rule does not apply if a fund is deposited in court under one of the following paragraphs in this rule.
(3) Where the deposit is made under CPR rule 37.2 (which provides that there must be a payment into court where a defendant wishes to rely on a defence of tender before claim) the Accountant General shall only accept the deposit if provided with:
(a) a written request;
(b) a sealed copy of the claim form; and
(c) a copy of the defence.

(4) Where the deposit is made under CPR rule 61.11(18) (which provides that the claimant may constitute a limitation fund by making a payment into court) the Accountant General shall only accept the deposit if provided with a written request sealed by a court.
(5) Where the deposit is made under the Life Assurance Companies (Payment into Court) Act 1896, the Accountant General shall only accept the deposit if provided with:
(a) a deposit schedule signed and authenticated by a court; and
(b) a copy of the witness statement or affidavit filed in accordance with CPR rule 37.4 (which relates to payment into court under enactments).

(6) Where the deposit is made under the Trustee Act 1925, the Accountant General shall only accept the deposit if provided with:

(a)

(i) a deposit schedule signed and authenticated by a court; and

(ii) a copy of the witness statement or affidavit filed in accordance with CPR rule 37.4; or

(b)

(i) a written request; and

(ii) a sealed copy of the court order authorising the deposit.

(7) Where the deposit is made under any other enactment that requires specific authority for a fund to be deposited in court, the Accountant General shall only accept the deposit if provided with:

(a) a written request; and

(b) the document authorising the deposit.

(8) Where the deposit is made by a deputy, the Accountant General shall only accept the deposit if provided with:

(a) a written request; and

(b) a sealed copy of the order appointing the deputy.

(9) The Accountant General shall only accept the deposit of foreign currency in court if provided with:

(a) a deposit schedule signed and authenticated by a court authorising the deposit of that currency; or

(b)

(i) a written request; and

(ii) a sealed copy of the court order authorising the deposit of that currency.

(10) A sealed copy of a court order is not required where the written request is made by the Admiralty Marshal.

(11) A sealed copy of a court order is not required where the written request has been sealed by the court that made the order.

III FUN [15.1]

The Court Funds Office requires that a deposit form is submitted when making a deposit into court. The relevant form is the written request referred to in the Rule above. Generally speaking the correct form to use is the form 100. However, where a deposit schedule is provided by the court this is by way of a form 101. Different forms are required for Chancery cases. Where a deputy wishes to deposit funds into court on behalf of a Court of Protection client a form L is generally required, although this may be dispensed with where a fund in court is already held. All forms are available via http://www.gov.uk, under Court Funds Office forms.

III FUN [16]

7. Deposit of funds

(1) Where a fund is to be deposited in court, it shall be sent to the Court Funds Office unless:

(a) it is deposited in accordance with rule 8; or

(b) the Accountant General directs otherwise.

(2) Where the fund to be deposited at the Court Funds Office is money, it shall be deposited by means of a cheque or bankers' draft unless the Accountant General directs otherwise.

(3) Any cheque or banker's draft shall be made payable to the Accountant General of the Senior Courts.

FUNDS IN COURT

III FUN [17]

8. Deposit of funds at a District Registry or county court or the Mayor's and City of London Court

(1) A fund may be deposited at a District Registry or county court or the Mayor's and City of London Court in accordance with this rule.

(2) A fund may be deposited at a District Registry or county court:

(a) in respect of proceedings at that District Registry or county court by a litigant in person without a current account; or

(b) where an enactment authorises a deposit at a District Registry or county court.

(3) A fund may only be deposited under paragraph (2)(a) as cash.

(4) A fund may only be deposited under paragraph (2)(b):

(a) by means of a cheque or banker's draft made payable to the Accountant General of the Senior Courts;

(b) as securities; or

(c) as cash, if deposited by a person without a current account.

(5) In addition, a fund may be deposited as cash at the Mayor's and City of London Court:

(a) in respect of proceedings at the Royal Courts of Justice, by a litigant in person without a current account; or

(b) by a person who is required by or under an enactment to give security for costs in respect of proceedings for an election petition.

(6) The Accountant General shall only accept a deposit made under this rule if the documents required under rule 6 are provided with the deposit.

(7) The District Registry, county court or the Mayor's and City of London Court, as the case may be, shall forward the deposit to the Accountant General within one working day of receipt, together with:

(a) any document provided to comply with rule 6; and

(b) confirmation of the date of receipt.

III FUN [17.1]

Deposits made under rule 8(5) may also be made at the county court at Central London, Thomas More Building, Strand, London WC2A 2LL.

III FUN [18]

9. Promissory notes

A fund may not be deposited by way of a promissory note.

III FUN [19]

10. Refusal to accept a deposit

The Accountant General shall refuse to accept a deposit if:

(a) the person requesting the deposit has not complied with these Rules; or

(b) there is any other good reason to do so.

PART 3
ACCOUNTS AND INVESTMENTS

III FUN [20]

11. Interest bearing accounts

(1) The Accountant General shall maintain two interest bearing accounts; a basic account and a special account.

(2) The Accountant General shall invest money in a basic account unless:

(a) a court directs otherwise;
(b) it is invested in a special account;
(c) it is transferred to an account of unclaimed funds; or
(d) it amounts to less than £10.

(3) Subject to rule 12(2), the Accountant General shall invest money to which a child or person who lacks capacity is entitled in a special account unless:
(a) a court directs otherwise;
(b) a deputy or investment manager directs otherwise;
(c) it is transferred to an account of unclaimed funds; or
(d) it amounts to less than £10.

(4) If the Accountant General appoints the Director of Savings under rule 5, from the date of the appointment paragraphs (2)(d) and (3)(d) shall cease to have effect.

III FUN [20.1]

The Accountant General appointed the Director of Savings to act on 5th December 2011, on which date Rule 11(4) came into effect.

III FUN [21]

12. Transfer between accounts

(1) Paragraph (2) applies where a child or person who lacks capacity has become entitled to money held in a basic account.

(2) The Accountant General shall only transfer the money to a special account if provided with a payment schedule signed and authenticated by the court directing such transfer.

(3) The transfer under paragraph (2) shall only take effect from the date on which the payment schedule is received by the Court Funds Office.

(4) Paragraph (5) applies where a person who is entitled to money in a special account:
(a) dies;
(b) ceases to be a child; or
(c) ceases to be a person who lacks capacity.

(5) The Accountant General shall transfer the money to a basic account.

(6) The transfer under paragraph (5) shall take effect from the date on which the person died or ceased to be a child or a person who lacks capacity.

III FUN [22]

13. Accrual of interest

(1) In this rule, the effective date means:
(a) in the case of a deposit made by cheque or banker's draft, the date on which the cheque or bankers' draft is received by the Court Funds Office;
(b) where the Accountant General has directed under rule 7(1)(b) that the deposit is to be made at a bank, the date on which the deposit is credited to the Accountant General's account;
(c) in the case of a deposit made under rule 8, the date of its receipt in the court office; or
(d) such other date as the Accountant General may determine.

(2) Subject to paragraph (3) and rule 16(2), interest shall accrue on a daily basis from the effective date until the day before money is withdrawn from the account.

(3) Interest shall cease to accrue from the date on which a claimant accepts an offer under CPR Part 36.

(4) Unless the Accountant General directs otherwise, accrued interest shall be credited:

(a) to a basic account, on the last Friday in March and September;
(b) to a special account, on the last Friday in May and November;
(c) when money is withdrawn from an account;
(d) when money is transferred from a basic account to a special account;
(e) when money is transferred from a special account to a basic account; and
(f) when an account is closed.

(5) The Accountant General shall credit accrued interest without deducting income tax.

(6) If the Accountant General appoints the Director of Savings under rule 5, from the date of the appointment:

(a) paragraph (4)(a), (b) and (c) shall cease to have effect;
(b) accrued interest shall be credited to a basic account on 31 March and 30 September; and
(c) accrued interest shall be credited to a special account on 31 May and 30 November.

III FUN [22.1]

The Accountant General appointed the Director of Savings to act on 5th December 2011, on which date Rule 13(6) came into effect.

III FUN [23]

14. Investment

(1) Except where rule 15 applies, the Accountant General may only invest or reinvest a fund in court in:

(a) a basic account;
(b) a special account; or
(c) a common investment fund.

(2) Except where rule 15 applies, the Accountant General may only invest money in a common investment fund if it:

(a) amounts to £10,000 or more; and
(b) is held on behalf of:
  (i) a child who, on the date on which the investment policy is approved by a court, has 5 years or more until their 18th birthday; or
  (ii) a person who lacks capacity who a court, deputy or investment manager has reason to believe will require the investment to be held for 5 years or more.

III FUN [24]

15. Investment in securities

(1) This rule applies where a fund in court was invested by the Accountant General in any of the following ways before 3rd October 2011 and remained so invested immediately before that date:

(a) in any manner specified in Part I, paragraphs 1 to 10 and 12 of Part II and paragraphs 2, 2A and 3 of Part III of schedule 1 to the Trustee Act 1961, as supplemented by the provisions of Part IV of that schedule;
(b) in investment trust ordinary shares;
(c) in securities (other than common investment fund units) where the person entitled to the securities is subject to an order of the Court of Protection; or
(d) in a common investment fund.

(2) The Accountant General may continue to invest or reinvest the fund in court in the ways mentioned in paragraph (1).

(3) The Accountant General may not invest or reinvest the fund in court in accordance with paragraph (2) if the cost would be disproportionate to the amount to be invested or reinvested.

III FUN [24.1]

Investment of damages awarded to children The investment media available are:

- **A: Special Account (formerly Short Term Investment Account)** This is an account operated by the Accountant General in conjunction with the National Investment and Loans Office. It pays interest without deduction of tax on money invested on a day to day basis. One would normally expect all funds to have some capital on the Special Account to ensure that some cash is readily and quickly available. The account is not normally suitable for long term investment (over five years) or the investment of larger sums, because there is no increase in value of the capital to guard against inflation.
- **B: Common Investment Funds** Common Investment Funds are Unit Trusts available only for the use of clients of the Accountant General, the Court of Protection and the Official Solicitor and Public Trustee Office or, in certain circumstances, former clients of these organisations. They were set up in 1965 and are now under commercial management and are operated under the Common Investment Scheme 2004, SI 2004/266 as amended by SI 2007/1095 which allowed for investment in the Fund by the Accountant General of Northern Ireland. There is one fund:

The Equity Index Tracker Fund— to provide a low-risk opportunity for capital growth, with some income, by tracking a partially UK, partially foreign-based index.

In general the only way in which a child's damages may be invested in equities (that is company shares) is by the purchase of units in the Common Investment Funds. It is inappropriate to purchase units in equity-based investments for children's funds which will remain in court for less than five years. It is also unwise to commit the whole fund to the purchase of units because sometimes some money will be needed to be paid before the child reaches the age of 18 and the purchase and sale of units within a short time span can result in capital loss. These units can now be transferred to a child on attaining majority or to a client of the Court of Protection in certain circumstances. They cannot, however, be transferred to an estate should the child or person who lacks capacity die whilst the fund is held in court. Other investment holdings can be transferred to the beneficiaries on closure of a fund.

III FUN [24.2]

Management of damages awarded to children See also CPR 21.11(1) (see para **CPR 21.11**). The judge or district judge is responsible for approving awards of damages, directing their payment into and out of court and deciding what is to be achieved by investment, that is to say whether capital appreciation, income or an element of both is appropriate to a child's needs. Currently the Form 320 advises litigants and/or their advisers what the court needs to be told to enable it to decide what return a child desires from the investment of damages awarded. A copy of the form should be issued to the litigant/adviser when an application to approve agreed damages is made in accordance with CPR 21.10 (see para **CPR 21.10**) and CPR 21.11 (see para **CPR 21.11**). At the hearing provision is made for completion of the CFO Form 320 by the district judge with investment decisions in such a way that court staff can complete CFO Form 212, which is the authorised schedule and is sent to the Court Funds Office for implementation.

III FUN [24.3]

Investment of monies for persons who lack capacity The implementation of the Mental Capacity Act 2005 in October 2007 has changed the way that monies may be invested for Court of Protection clients. It is now the responsibility of the deputy to decide how best to invest the monies on behalf of the person who lacks capacity for whom they act, subject to any restrictions imposed by the Court. However, the Court Funds Office can only release monies held in court to the deputy direct, unless a specific direction from the Court of Protection allowing monies to be paid to a third party is received. Where a Fund Manager has been appointed, and the investments are held in court, the Court Funds Office will continue to act on the instructions of the Fund Manager with regard to sales and purchases of investments as long as the instructions are within the terms of the order appointing the deputy and the deputy's agreement with the Fund Manager. It is advisable that the deputy contacts the Securities Section of the Court Funds Office prior to embarking on any new investment management scheme to ensure that the scheme is within the terms of the order and that the Court Funds Office can release the required funds or effect the required investments.

III FUN [25]

16. Foreign currency

(1) The Accountant General shall invest or reinvest foreign currency in an interest bearing account in such currency if provided with:

- (a) a payment schedule signed and authenticated by a court directing the investment or reinvestment of the foreign currency; or
- (b) written directions in accordance with rule 17(2) directing the investment or reinvestment of the foreign currency.

(2) Interest shall accrue on money invested or reinvested under paragraph (1) from the date on which the Accountant General is provided with either the payment schedule or written directions directing the investment or reinvestment of the foreign currency.

(3) The Accountant General shall pay any charge incurred in placing foreign currency into a foreign currency account from the account in which the foreign currency is held.

(4) Unless a court, deputy or investment manager directs otherwise, the Accountant General shall convert dividend payments received in a foreign currency into sterling and invest the proceeds in accordance with this Part.

III FUN [26]

17. Authority to direct investment

(1) Subject to paragraph (2), the Accountant General shall invest or reinvest a fund in court in accordance with a written request from a court.

(2) The Accountant General shall invest or reinvest a fund in court that is subject to an order of the Court of Protection in accordance with written directions from:

- (a) the Court of Protection;
- (b) a deputy; or
- (c) an investment manager.

(3) If a deputy appoints an investment manager, the deputy must send in writing to the Accountant General:

- (a) authority for the investment manager to give directions for the investment of a fund in court; and
- (b) contact details of the investment manager.

(4) The Accountant General may not comply with a direction given under paragraph (2)(b) if:

- (a) the deputy gave the direction without authority to do so;
- (b) the Court of Protection has made a contrary direction; or
- (c) there is any other good reason for not complying.

(5) The Accountant General may not comply with a direction given under paragraph (2)(c) if:

- (a) a deputy appointed the investment manager without authority to do so;
- (b) the deputy has not complied with paragraph (3);
- (c) the investment manager gave the direction without authority to do so;
- (d) the Court of Protection has made a contrary direction; or
- (e) there is any other good reason for not complying.

III FUN [27]

18. Timing of investment

The Accountant General shall comply with any order, direction or request for investment as soon as is practicable.

III FUN [28]

19. Payment of charges when dealing with securities

Unless a court directs otherwise, the Accountant General shall pay any charge incurred when dealing with securities from the fund in court of the person on whose behalf the Accountant General is dealing.

III FUN [29]

20. Conversion and allotment of securities

(1) Where nobody else is able to give directions, the Accountant General may apply to the appropriate court for directions on how to deal with a conversion or allotment of securities.

(2) Where a security in court has been converted into another security, the Accountant General shall write off the original security and replace it with the whole, or where appropriate a proportionate part, of the substituted security.

(3) Unless the court directs otherwise, the Accountant General shall deal with any substituted security and dividends, so far as is practicable, in the same manner as the original security and dividends.

(4) Where an allotment is made in respect of a security in court the Accountant General shall:

- (a) credit the whole, or a proportionate part, of the allotment to the account of the original security if the allotment is fully paid;
- (b) sell the allotment and credit the whole, or a proportionate part, of the proceeds of sale to the appropriate account or otherwise as the court may direct if the allotment is not fully paid; or
- (c) sell any non-apportionable security and credit the proceeds to the appropriate account.

III FUN [30]

21. Securities of a dissolved company

The Accountant General shall write off the securities of any company that has been struck off the company register in the country in which the company is incorporated.

PART 4
PAYMENT OUT FROM A FUND IN COURT

III FUN [31]

22. Documents required for payment

(1) The general rule is that the Accountant General shall make a payment from a fund in court if provided with a payment schedule signed and authenticated by a court.

(2) The general rule does not apply if a payment is made under one of the following paragraphs in this rule.

(3) Subject to paragraphs (6) and (7), where a deputy has been appointed, the Accountant General shall only make a payment from a fund in court if provided with:

- (a) a written request from the deputy; and
- (b) a sealed copy of the court order authorising the payment.

(4) Where an enactment requires specific authority for payment, the Accountant General shall only make a payment from a fund in court if provided with:

- (a) a written request; and
- (b) any authority required to permit payment under the enactment.

(5) Where a court has ordered that a person may apply directly to the Court Funds Office for payment of a fund in court on or after reaching their majority, the Accountant General shall only make a payment from the fund in court if provided with a written request from that person.

(6) Where the Court of Protection is satisfied that a person no longer lacks capacity in relation to a fund in court to which that person is entitled, the Accountant General shall only make a payment from the fund in court if provided with:

(a) a written request; and
(b) a sealed copy of the court order.

(7) Where the Court of Protection has ordered a payment from a fund in court be made to a person other than the person entitled to the fund in court or a deputy, the Accountant General shall only make a payment from the fund in court if provided with:

(a) a payment schedule signed and authenticated by the court; or
(b)
 (i) a written request; and
 (ii) a sealed copy of the court order authorising the payment.

III FUN [31.1]

Generally speaking the payment schedule required is a form 200. However, payments under Rule 22(3) are by way of a form P. Payments under Rule 22(4), (6) and (7) are by way of a form 205 and payments under Rule 22(5) are by way of form 203. All forms apart from the form 203 are available via http://www.gov.uk, under Court Funds Office forms. The form 203 is only available on application to the Court Funds Office.

III FUN [32]

23. Interest on payments

Where rule 22 applies, the Accountant General shall deal with any interest in accordance with:

(a) the payment schedule; or
(b) the other authority for payment.

III FUN [33]

24. Payment to a representative of a deceased person

(1) This rule applies where a person entitled to a fund in court dies.

(2) Where a grant of representation has been obtained, the Accountant General shall pay out the fund in court to the personal representative of the deceased if provided with:

(a) a written request; and
(b) a sealed copy of the grant of representation.

(3) Where a grant of representation has been obtained by two or more persons, the Accountant General shall only pay out the fund in court if provided with:

(a) the documents required under paragraph (2);
(b) the written consent of each living person named as a personal representative in the grant of representation; and
(c) a copy of the death certificate of any deceased person who was named as a personal representative in the grant of representation.

(4) Where the value of the estate is less than £5,000 and the person dies testate, the Accountant General shall pay out the fund in court to the person who claims to have the right to a grant of probate if provided with:

(a) a written request;
(b) a copy of the will of the deceased; and
(c) a copy of the death certificate of the deceased.

(5) Where the value of the estate is less than £5,000 and two or more persons have a right to a grant of probate, the Accountant General shall only pay out the fund in court if provided with:

(a) the documents required under paragraph (4);

(b) the written consent of each living person who has been named as an executor in the deceased's will; and

(c) a copy of the death certificate of any deceased person who was named as an executor in the deceased's will.

(6) Where the value of the estate is less than £5,000 and the person dies intestate, the Accountant General shall pay out the fund in court to the person who claims to have a prior right to a grant of letters of administration if provided with:

(a) a written request;

(b) a written declaration of kinship; and

(c) a copy of the death certificate of the deceased.

(7) Where the value of the estate is less than £5,000 and two or more persons claim to have a prior right to a grant of letters of administration, the Accountant General shall only pay out the fund in court if provided with:

(a) the documents required under paragraph (6);

(b) the written consent of each person who appears to have a prior right to a grant of letters of administration; and

(c) a written declaration of kinship of each such person.

III FUN [33.1]

Where an estate is valued at £5,000 or more a form 209 is required. For estates valued at less than £5,000 a form 210 is required.

III FUN [34]

25. Payment of funeral expenses

(1) This rule applies where a person who is entitled to a fund in court and subject to an order of the Court of Protection dies.

(2) The Accountant General shall make a payment from the fund in court of the deceased to a funeral director in respect of reasonable funeral expenses if provided with:

(a) a funeral invoice; and

(b) a written request from:

(i) an executor of the deceased's estate; or

(ii) the person who arranged the funeral if the deceased died intestate.

III FUN [34.1]

Funds may only be released to pay the cost of the funeral itself. The cost of refreshments after the funeral, or the cost of the headstone cannot be included. The correct form to apply for payment of funeral expenses is a form FE.

III FUN [35]

26. Payment of inheritance tax

(1) This rule applies where a person who is entitled to a fund in court and subject to an order of the Court of Protection dies.

(2) The Accountant General shall make a payment from the fund in court of the deceased to Her Majesty's Revenue and Customs in respect of all or part of the inheritance tax due on the deceased's estate if provided with:

(a) the completed relevant form from Her Majesty's Revenue and Customs; and

(b) a written request from:

(i) an executor of the deceased's estate; or

FUNDS IN COURT

(ii) a person who appears to have a prior right to a grant of letters of administration of the estate if the deceased died intestate.

III FUN [35.1]

The written request required is a form IHT.

III FUN [36]

27. Payment in respect of CPR Part 36 (offers to settle)

(1) This rule applies where:

(a) a payment is to be made to a claimant out of a fund in court under CPR Part 36; and

(b) the permission of a court is not required for the payment.

(2) Subject to rule 28(3), where a defendant has deposited money under a court order or in support of a defence of tender before claim and a CPR Part 36 offer is subsequently accepted, the Accountant General shall make a payment from a fund in court if provided with:

(a) a written request from the claimant; and

(b) written confirmation from the defendant that all, or part, of the fund in court may be used to satisfy the offer (in whole or in part).

(3) Subject to rule 28(3), where a CPR Part 36 deposit has been made and the CPR Part 36 offer has been accepted, the Accountant General shall make a payment from a fund in court if provided with a written request from the claimant.

(4) The Accountant General shall pay any accrued interest remaining in court following a payment under paragraph (2) or (3) or rule 28(2) to the defendant.

(5) The Accountant General may not make any payment under this rule where more than one defendant is sued jointly and not all of the defendants have deposited money in court unless:

(a) the claimant has also discontinued the claim against the defendants who have not deposited money in court; and

(b) the Accountant General is provided with a copy of:

(i) the notice of discontinuance; and

(ii) the written consent to the discontinuance of each of those defendants.

III FUN [36.1]

Where funds are requested under Rule 27(2) a form 201 completed by the claimant and a form 202 completed by the defendant are required. If the sum required to settle the offer is less than the capital amount held in court the balance of capital held may only be released on the direction of the court by way of form 200. For payment out under Rule 27(3) a form 201 only is required.

III FUN [37]

28. Payment where the claimant's legal representation has been funded by the Legal Services Commission or provided under arrangements made for the purposes of Part 1 of the Legal Aid, Sentencing and Punishment of Offenders Act 2012

(1) This rule applies where:

(a) a payment is to be made to a claimant out of a fund in court under CPR Part 36;

(b) the claimant's legal representation has been funded by the Legal Services Commission or provided under arrangements made for the purposes of Part 1 of the Legal Aid, Sentencing and Punishment of Offenders Act 2012; and

(c) regulation 18(1) of the Community Legal Services (Costs) Regulations 2000 or regulation 13(1) of the Civil Legal Aid (Statutory Charge) Regulations 2013 applies to the fund in court.

(2) Where the claimant is legally represented, the Accountant General shall pay the amount to be paid out under rule 27(2) or (3) to the claimant's legal representative.

(3) Where the claimant is no longer legally represented, the Accountant General shall only make a payment from a fund in court if provided with a payment schedule signed and authenticated by a court.

III FUN [37.1]

This section has been amended by the Legal Aid, Sentencing and Punishment of Offenders Act 2012 (Consequential, Transitional and Savings provisions) Regulations 2013, SI 2013/534, Sch 1, para 9 with effect from April 2013.

III FUN [38]

29. Remaining balance

The remaining balance of a fund in court (if any) after a payment under rule 27 or 28(2) shall be paid out in accordance with rule 22.

III FUN [39]

30. Time for making payments

The Accountant General shall make any payment as soon as practicable after receipt of:

(a) the payment schedule; or

(b) the other authority for payment.

III FUN [40]

31. Regular payments

Where a payment schedule directs that regular payments are to be made, the payment schedule shall state the dates on which the payments shall be made.

III FUN [41]

32. Method of payment

(1) In this rule:

"BACS" means the method of payment known as "Banks Automated Clearing System" by which money is transferred from one bank in the United Kingdom to another; and

"International money transfer" means a method of payment in which money is transferred from a bank in the United Kingdom to a bank outside the United Kingdom by means of an automated system.

(2) Unless the Accountant General directs otherwise, payment out from a fund in court shall be made by:

(a) BACS;

(b) international money transfer;

(c) cheque; or

(d) warrant.

(3) The Accountant General may deduct any charges incurred in paying money out of court from the fund in court from which the payment was made.

III FUN [42]

33. Dealing with a fund in court before the receipt of a payment schedule

(1) Paragraph 2 applies where the Accountant General has dealt with a fund in court after the date of a court order but before the receipt of the related payment schedule.

(2) The Accountant General shall, if reasonably practicable, deal with an asset that is not mentioned in the payment schedule in accordance with the payment schedule.

III FUN [43]

34. Refusal to make a payment

The Accountant General may not make a payment if:

(a) the identity or entitlement of a person claiming to be entitled to a payment is in doubt;

(b) the request for payment is outside the scope of a deputy's power;

(c) the person requesting payment has not complied with these Rules; or

(d) there is any other good reason not to do so.

III FUN [44]

35. Identification of payees

(1) If the Accountant General, in accordance with rule 34(a), does not make a payment, the Accountant General may require the personal attendance of the person claiming to be entitled to the payment at a court in order to provide evidence of their identity or entitlement.

(2) The Accountant General may not pay a person who changes their name before a fund in court has been paid, unless that person provides the Accountant General with evidence of their change of name.

PART 5
UNCLAIMED FUNDS IN COURT

III FUN [45]

36. Transfer to the unclaimed funds account

(1) The Accountant General may transfer an unclaimed fund in court to an account of unclaimed funds.

(2) Subject to paragraph (3), a fund in court shall be treated as unclaimed if:

(a) it has not been dealt with for ten years other than:

(i) being credited with accrued interest or dividends; or

(ii) by a compulsory dealing in securities; or

(b) the Accountant General is, at any time, satisfied that all reasonable steps have been taken to trace the person entitled to the fund in court and that person cannot be traced.

(3) Where a fund in court is held on behalf of a child and the child's date of birth is known, paragraph (2)(a) shall not apply until the child's 18th birthday.

III FUN [46]

37. Disposal of unclaimed securities and effects

(1) The Accountant General may sell any unclaimed securities (including common investment fund units) or effects to be transferred under rule 36 and pay the proceeds into an account of unclaimed funds.

(2) The Accountant General shall write off any securities or effects transferred under rule 36 which have no value.

III FUN [47]

38. Converting unclaimed foreign currency

The Accountant General shall convert any foreign currency to be transferred under rule 36 into sterling and pay the proceeds into an account of unclaimed funds.

III FUN [48]

39. Unclaimed county court money

(1) Money paid into a county court other than under rule 8 may be treated as unclaimed if it has not been dealt with for a period of one year immediately before 1st March in any year.

(2) The Accountant General shall accept a deposit of money treated by a county court as unclaimed under paragraph (1) if provided with a written request from an officer of that court.

(3) The Accountant General shall place money that has been deposited under paragraph (2) to an account of unclaimed funds.

(4) Each county court shall maintain a list of monies deposited under paragraph (2), which may be inspected at that court's office.

III FUN [49]

40. List of unclaimed funds in court and money

The Accountant General shall maintain a list of funds in court transferred under rule 36(1) and of money deposited under rule 39(2).

III FUN [50]

41. Payment out of an unclaimed funds account

(1) The Accountant General shall make a payment out of an account of unclaimed funds if provided with a payment schedule signed and authenticated by a court.

(2) Subject to paragraph (3), money paid out of an account of unclaimed funds shall be credited with simple interest at the rate of interest payable on a basic account at the date of payment, from the date on which the money was transferred to an account of unclaimed funds.

(3) The Accountant General may not credit any interest to unclaimed money deposited under rule 39(2).

PART 6
MISCELLANEOUS PROVISIONS

III FUN [51]

42. Information about a fund in court

The Accountant General shall, on receipt of a request in writing, provide information about a fund in court to:

(a) a person who is entitled to the fund in court; or

(b) a person who the Accountant General considers to have a valid reason for requesting the information.

III FUN [52]

43. Statement of account

(1) Paragraph (2) applies where a child or a person who lacks capacity is entitled to a fund in court.

(2) The Accountant General shall send a statement of account to the child or person who lacks capacity:

(a) on an annual basis; and

(b) at such other times as the Accountant General considers appropriate.

III FUN [53]

44. Court's obligations in respect of deposit and payment schedules

(1) Where an order has been made in respect of a fund in court, an officer of the court which made the order shall:

(a) sign and authenticate the deposit schedule or payment schedule, as the case may be; and

(b) send it to the Accountant General.

(2) Where the court amends a deposit schedule or payment schedule, an officer of the court which made the order shall:

(a) sign and seal the amendment; and

(b) send it to the Accountant General.

III FUN [54]

45. Transfer between courts

Where proceedings in which a fund has been deposited in court are transferred to another court, the court to which the proceedings are transferred must notify the Accountant General of the transfer.

III FUN [54.1]

Such notification must be made by way of a form 211.

III FUN [55]

46. National Debt Commissioners

(1) The Accountant General shall transfer to the National Debt Commissioners:

(a) money held in the account of the Accountant General (the "operational account") that exceeds the amount reasonably required to satisfy current demands; and

(b) non-apportionable sums received in respect of securities.

(2) The National Debt Commissioners shall transfer to the Accountant General such amount as the Accountant General may request in writing if the balance of the operational account is less than the amount reasonably required to satisfy current demands.

(3) As soon as is practicable after half-yearly interest accruing on money invested in a basic or special account has been credited to the appropriate accounts the Accountant General shall certify to the National Debt Commissioners the amount required to credit interest on those accounts.

(4) When the Accountant General has informed the National Debt Commissioners of the amount required in paragraph (3), the National Debt Commissioners shall credit that amount to the account into which the money transferred under paragraph (1) was invested.

HARASSMENT

TABLE OF CONTENTS

GENERAL NOTES ON HARASSMENT

III HAR [1]

Scope and effect of the legislation The Protection from Harassment Act 1997 came into force on 16 June 1997 (Protection from Harassment Act 1997 (Commencement) (No 1) Order 1997, SI 1997/1418 and Protection from Harassment Act 1997 (Commencement) (No 2) Order 1997, SI 1997/1498) except as regards the arrest provisions in s 3 which were brought into force on 1 September 1998 (Protection from Harassment Act 1997 (Commencement) (No 3) Order 1998, SI 1998/1902). It provides both civil and criminal remedies for acts of harassment (as defined by ss 1, 7 of the Act). The breadth of the definition of harassment and the absence (to date) of special rules to govern the bringing of claims in respect of harassment mean that it is advisable to include such a claim in addition to other similar claims such as in nuisance, intimidation, wrongful eviction or breach of the covenant of quiet enjoyment. There may be advantages in using the Protection from Harassment Act in some domestic situations instead of the provisions to combat domestic violence set out at para **III FAM [93]**). The jurisdiction under Part IV of the Family Law Act 1996 is confined to the Family Court, requires the use of detailed prescribed forms and is governed by the legal aid rates for family work. Also "molestation" has been given a narrow construction in *C v C (non-molestation order jurisdiction)* [1998] Fam 70, [1998] 1 FCR 11, Sir Stephen Brown, P.

It should be noted that there is no tort of harassment at common law (*Wong v Parkside Health NHS Trust* [2001] EWCA Civ 721, [2003] 3 All ER 932) nor of invasion of privacy (*Wainwright v Home Office* [2001] EWCA Civ 2081, [2002] QB 1334, [2003] 3 All ER 943; affd [2003] UKHL 53, [2004] 2 AC 406, [2003] 4 All ER 969.

III HAR [2]

Particular points Points to note about the Act are:

- Damages may not be claimed for harassment which precedes 16 June 1997.
- It is necessary to show that the defendant knew or ought to have known that his conduct amounted to harassment see s 1(1)(b). See also s 7(2) for the significance of alarm, anxiety and distress as elements in the civil wrong of harassment.
- CPR 65 applies to proceedings under this Act and the claim must be brought using the Part 8 procedure.
- Injunctions granted on or after 1 September 1998 must be in Form N138. The procedure for the issue of a warrant for arrest is set out in CPR 65.29 and CPR 65.30 (see para **CPR 65.29** and **CPR 65.30**). In other respects the usual rule provisions relating to particulars of claim, applications for injunction etc apply. This means that CPR 25.2 enables claimants to apply for an interim injunction and to make such an application without notice, even before the issue of proceedings (see para **CPR 25.2**). For a precedent see **BCCP C[16]**.
- There is no reason why a claim for harassment cannot be allocated to the small claims track if the amount of damages claimed is limited, but see **CPR 26.7** (4) (claims against landlords for harassment will not be allocated to the small claims track) and para **CPR 26.7 [2]**.

III HAR [3]

Jurisdiction The High Court and county courts have concurrent jurisdiction.

III HAR [4]

Legal aid A legal services commission funding certificate must actually state that proceedings under the Act are covered.

III HAR [5]

Precedents For a precedent for particulars of claim for harassment and for an injunction see **BCCP L[901]**, **BCCP L[902]**. See **BCCP C[503]** for an application for an injunction in default of appearance; **BCCP C[813]** (order by consent) and **BCCP G[243]** and **BCCP G[245]** for compromises on undertakings.

PROTECTION FROM HARASSMENT ACT 1997

(c 40)

III HAR [6]

1. Prohibition of harassment

(1) A person must not pursue a course of conduct—

(a) which amounts to harassment of another, and

(b) which he knows or ought to know amounts to harassment of the other.

(1A) A person must not pursue a course of conduct—

(a) which involves harassment of two or more persons, and

(b) which he knows or ought to know involves harassment of those persons, and

(c) by which he intends to persuade any person (whether or not one of those mentioned above)—

(i) not to do something that he is entitled or required to do, or

(ii) to do something that he is not under any obligation to do.

(2) For the purposes of this section, the person whose course of conduct is in question ought to know that it amounts to [or involves] harassment of another if a reasonable person in possession of the same information would think the course of conduct amounted to or involved harassment of the other.

(3) Subsection (1) or (1A) does not apply to a course of conduct if the person who pursued it shows—

(a) that it was pursued for the purpose of preventing or detecting crime,

(b) that it was pursued under any enactment or rule of law or to comply with any condition or requirement imposed by any person under any enactment, or

(c) that in the particular circumstances the pursuit of the course of conduct was reasonable.

III HAR [6.1]

Harassment and public demonstrations In *Huntingdon Life Sciences Ltd v Curtin* (1997) Times, 11 December, Eady J observed that the Act was not intended to be used to clamp down on the discussion of matters of public interest or upon the rights of political protest and public demonstration which are so much a part of our democratic tradition. He added that "the courts would resist any wide interpretation of the Act".

On the other hand, a campaign against a local councillor which involved flying abusive banners from aircraft, dropping leaflets and arranging secret surveillance has been held to be harassment within the Act. As an exercise of the right of free speech under article 10, the banners and leaflets caused anguish that was out of all proportion to the value of the right. As regards the private surveillance, the distress caused by the knowledge that it could take place at any time was a sufficient basis for granting an injunction; and it was not open to a private citizen to justify private surveillance as being "for the purpose of preventing or detecting crime" within sub-s (3): *Howlett v Holding* [2006] EWHC 3758 (QB), (2006) Times, 8 February, 150 Sol Jo LB 161, Eady J.

III HAR [6.1A]

Harassment of corporate bodies 'A person' under the Act does not include a corporate entity and thus a corporate employer could not be a proper claimant under the Act although a named individual could bring proceedings on behalf of fellow employees on a representative basis within CPR 19.6: *Daiichi UK Ltd v Stop Huntingdon Animal Cruelty* [2003] EWHC 2337 (QB), [2004] 1 WLR 1503, (2003) Times, 22 October; *Huntingdon Life Sciences Ltd v Stop Huntingdon Animal Cruelty* [2003] All ER (D) 280 (Jun).

In *Emerson Developments v Avery* [2004] EWHC 194 (QB) the court granted an injunction in favour of a company and a director representing himself and the employees of the company, but only after taking account of the effect of the order on the defendant's rights under Arts 10 and 11.

The Criminal Division of the Court of Appeal has now ruled that there is no reason in principle why a restraining order should not be made to protect a company or a group of persons from harassment: *R v Buxton* [2010] EWCA Crim 2923, [2011] 2 Cr App Rep (S) 121, [2011] Crim LR 332.

III HAR [6.1B]

Harassment by corporate bodies In contrast with the line taken in some of the cases cited under the preceding note, it has been held that a claim for harassment may be brought against a corporate body where the harassment is carried out by the company or, alternatively, where the company is vicariously liable for harassment by others in the course of employment. An individual may, therefore, bring a claim against his or her employing company on the ground of harassment by another individual in the course of employment: *Majrowski v Guy's and St Thomas's NHS Trust* [2005] EWCA Civ 251, (2005) Times, 21 March, applying the doctrine of vicarious liability as propounded by Lord Millett in *Lister v Hesley Hall Ltd* [2001] UKHL 22, [2002] 1 AC 215, 245-249 (appeal dismissed by the House of Lords in *Majirowski v Guy's and St Thomas's NHS Trust* [2006] UKHL 34, [2006] 4 All ER 395, (2006) Times, 13 July). This approach was followed in *Green v DB Group Services (UK) Ltd* [2006] EWHC 1898 (QB), [2006] IRLR 764 where the employer was held to be vicariously liable for a concerted campaign of harassment by fellow employees where such acts of harassment were carried out within the scope of their employment. On the other hand, a claim is not sustainable against the employer on the basis of a single incident since this is not enough to constitute harassment within the Act: *Banks v Ablex Ltd* [2005] EWCA Civ 173, [2005] ICR 819.

In the context of abuse by priests it has been held that a Diocesan Trust of the Roman Catholic Church may be liable vicariously for the improper acts of a priest who was not employed by them. The basis of the liability has been held to be the empowerment and granting of authority: *JGE v English Province of Our Lady of Charity* ([2011] EWHC 2871 (QB), [2012] 1 All ER 723, [2012] 2 WLR 709, MacDuff J.

III HAR [6.1C]

Harassment by an unincorporated association A claim for injunctive relief under the Act to govern the future conduct of an unincorporated association by its representative is justifiable on the basis that those represented by the representative have similar interests to satisfy CPR 19.6. However, insofar as a claim for damages in tort is concerned, those represented by the representative may be expected to have widely divergent interests and thus the claim is likely to fail unless made against named individuals: *Huntingdon Life Sciences Group v Stop Huntingdon Animal Cruelty* [2007] EWHC 522 (QB), [2007] All ER (D) 506 (Mar). An injunction preventing harassment will be binding against protesters within the ambit of the unincorporated association but will not be enforceable against such individuals pursuant to CPR 19.6 without permission of the court: *Smithkline Beecham plc v Avery* [2007] EWHC 948 (QB), [2007] All ER (D) 249 (Apr).

It has been held that a partnership, such as a firm of solicitors, may be defendant for the purposes of the Act: *Iqbal v Dean Manson Solicitors* [2011] EWCA Civ 123, [2011] IRLR 428, [2011] NLJR 288.

III HAR [6.1D]

Bullying at work It is settled that an employer may be civilly liable under the Act for a concerted campaign of bullying by fellow employees: see the note at **III HAR [6.1B]**. However, the Court of Appeal noted that to amount to harassment the conduct had to be repetitive and

HARASSMENT

also "oppressive and unacceptable" and that the facts of the case were "extraordinary". As a general rule the Employment Tribunal is a more appropriate forum for cases based on discrimination or high-handed misconduct: *Veakins v Kier Islington Ltd* [2010] EWCA Civ 1288, [2010] IRLR 132, (2010) Times, 13 January.

III HAR [6.2]

Reasonable conduct Harassment in breach of a court injunction (even when granted without notice) cannot be justified on the ground that it is reasonable. The proper course is to seek to set the injunction aside: *DPP v Selvanayagam* (1999) Times, 23 June.

III HAR [6.3]

Nature and frequency of incidents There need not be more than two incidents to constitute harassment, but the fewer there are and the further apart, if irregular, then the less likely they are to be reasonably thought of as a course of conduct amounting to harassment: *Lau v DPP* [2000] 1 FLR 799, [2000] Fam Law 610, DC.

The Court of Appeal held that the conviction of a husband for harassment based on two incidents of aggressive behaviour three months apart was "close to the borderline" of what could constitute the offence of harassment: *Pratt v DPP* [2001] EWHC Admin 483, (2001) 165 JP 800. It has been held in the criminal courts that a person may be harassed by threats to her dog (*R (A Child) v DPP* [2001] Crim LR 396) and by malicious calls to her employer (*Kellet v DPP* [2001] EWHC Admin 107, [2001] All ER (D) 124 (Feb)).

The harassment must be targeted at the claimant but others who are foreseeably and directly harmed by the conduct, may be able to claim too, to the extent that could properly be described as victims of it: *Levi v Bates* [2015] EWCA Civ 206, 165 NLJ 7646, [2015] All ER (D) 139 (Mar).

III HAR [6.4]

Definition of harassment Whilst the Act offered no definition of harassment, it was directed at the prevention of stalking, anti-social behaviour by neighbours and racial harassment. It was not intended to cover alleged oppressive litigation: *Turner v Microsoft Corpn Ltd* (2000) Times, 15 November, CA. It was held in *Thomas v News Group Newspapers Ltd* [2001] EWCA Civ 1233, [2001] 34 LS Gaz R 43, that the publication of a series of articles calculated to incite racial hatred of an identifiable individual could be within the definition of harassment. The publishers' right of freedom of expression under the European Convention on Human Rights did not extend to protect remarks against the Convention's underlying values.

Repeated mocking by a national newspaper of a person by reference to their sexual orientation would almost inevitably be so oppressive as to amount to harassment; but articles about a public figure that described her as 'lesbian' and 'bisexual' were held to be reasonable in the *Thomas* context: *Trimingham v Associated Newspapers Ltd* [2012] EWHC 1296 (QB), [2012] 4 All ER 717, [2013] IP & T 43, where it was held that the word 'reasonable' in s 1(3)(c) had to be read compatibly with the right to freedom of expression under Article 10.

There are genuine doubts about the limits of the new civil wrong of harassment and courts should therefore be slow to deprive a claimant of a hearing, particularly a litigant in person: *Merelie v Newcastle Primary Care Trust* [2004] EWHC 2554 (QB), (2004) Times, 1 December, Eady J.

The touchstone as to whether the facts of a particular case cross the boundary from the regrettable to the unacceptable is to ask whether the gravity of the conduct was of an order which would sustain criminal liability under s 1 of the Act: *Conn v Sunderland City Council* (2007) 1 November, CA. This was an employment case of bullying at work for which the employer was being held vicariously liable. While the Court of Appeal concluded that the employer could be held vicariously liable, on the facts of the case the alleged conduct did not amount to harassment.

It has been held that a gas company's unjustified demands for payment which induced a state of anxiety in the householder could be characterised as harassment, although the demands were sent as a result of computer error: *Ferguson v British Gas Trading Ltd* [2009] EWCA Civ 46, [2009] 3 All ER 304, [2009] 8 LS Gaz R 18. The issue is not whether a criminal offence has been committed but whether the conduct has crossed the line by being "oppressive and unreasonable": *Allen v Southwark London Borough Council* [2008] EWCA Civ 1478. [2008] All ER (D) 113 (Nov).

A sustained attack on a professional person's integrity is an attack on the lifeblood of his, or her, vocation and is capable of causing alarm and distress: *Iqbal v Dean Manson Solicitors* [2011] EWCA Civ 123, [2011] IRLR 428, [2011] NLJR 288.

The bringing of unjustified claims in court might amount to harassment: *Allen v Southwark London Borough Council* [2008] EWCA Civ 1478, [2008] All ER (D) 113 (Nov); *Fox v Hall* [2014] EWHC 2747 (QB), [2014] All ER (D) 78 (Aug).

III HAR [6.5]

Mental disorder not a defence The test for liability is objective and it is not a defence that the defendant's course of conduct was the result of, or affected by, mental disorder: *R v Colohan* [2001] EWCA Crim 1251, [2001] 3 FCR 409, [2001] 2 FLR 757 (Criminal Division).

III HAR [6.6]

Conduct pursued for the purpose of preventing or detecting crime Conduct cannot be justified as being for the purpose of preventing or detecting crime if it had some other purpose as well: *Hayes v Willoughby* [2011] EWCA Civ 1541, [2012] 1 WLR 1510, (2011) Times, 13 January, CA.

III HAR [6.7]

Prevention of harassment letters The police practice of issuing a Prevention of Harassment letter in what they judge to be an appropriate case stems from their wide discretion in enforcing the law. It may be particularly useful where the recipient appears to be unaware that their conduct might be classed as harassment. Although not a procedural requirement it is good practice for the police to speak to the person concerned before sending the letter, where this is possible. In a case where the alleged harassment involved posts on Twitter, it was held that the issue of the letter interfered with the recipient's Article 8 rights, but that it was a proportionate response in the circumstances: *R (on the application of Hewson) v Metropolitan Police Comr* (2018) Times, 23 April, QBD.

III HAR [7]

3. Civil remedy

(1) An actual or apprehended breach of section 1(1) may be the subject of a claim in civil proceedings by the person who is or may be the victim of the course of conduct in question.

(2) On such a claim, damages may be awarded for (among other things) any anxiety caused by the harassment and any financial loss resulting from the harassment.

(3) Where—

- (a) in such proceedings the High Court or the county court grants an injunction for the purpose of restraining the defendant from pursuing any conduct which amounts to harassment, and
- (b) the plaintiff considers that the defendant has done anything which he is prohibited from doing by the injunction,

the plaintiff may apply for the issue of a warrant for the arrest of the defendant.

(4) An application under subsection (3) may be made—

- (a) where the injunction was granted by the High Court, to a judge of that court, and
- (b) where the injunction was granted by the county court, to a judge of that court.

(5) The judge to whom an application under subsection (3) is made may only issue a warrant if—

- (a) the application is substantiated on oath, and
- (b) the judge has reasonable grounds for believing that the defendant has done anything which he is prohibited from doing by the injunction.

(6) Where—

- (a) the High Court or the county court grants an injunction for the purpose mentioned in subsection (3)(a), and
- (b) without reasonable excuse the defendant does anything which he is prohibited from doing by the injunction,

he is guilty of an offence.

(7) Where a person is convicted of an offence under subsection (6) in respect of any conduct, that conduct is not punishable as a contempt of court.

(8) A person cannot be convicted of an offence under subsection (6) in respect of any conduct which has been punished as a contempt of court.

HARASSMENT

(9) A person guilty of an offence under subsection (6) is liable—

(a) on conviction on indictment, to imprisonment for a term not exceeding five years, or a fine, or both, or

(b) on summary conviction, to imprisonment for a term not exceeding six months, or a fine not exceeding the statutory maximum, or both.

III HAR [7.1]

Procedure An application for an interim injunction may be made before the claim has been issued if the case is one of urgency: CPR 25.2 (2)(b) (see para **CPR 25.2**). For precedents see **BCCP C[16]**, **BCCP L[901]** and **BCCP L[902]**.

A claim under the Act is subject to the Part 8 procedure and must be commenced in the Queen's Bench Division of the High Court or in the court for the district where either the claimant or the defendant resides or carries on business: **CPR 65.28**. The rules for applying, in accordance with Part 23, for the issue of a warrant under s 3(3) are in **CPR 65.29** and those governing proceedings following arrest are in **CPR 65.30**.

Unlike antisocial behaviour orders, which are civil remedies for the benefit of the community, the criminal standard of proof is not applicable to remedies under the Harassment Act, since they are for the protection of rights of individuals. However, the civil standard of proof would require strictness of proof appropriate to the seriousness of the matters to be proved: *Hipgrave v Jones* [2004] EWHC 2901 (QB), (2005) Times, 11 January.

Where a restraining order is made the judge should state the factual basis for imposing the order, otherwise it may be quashed on appeal: *R v Major* [2010] EWCA Crim 3016, [2011] 1 Cr App Rep 322, [2011] 2 Cr App Rep (S) 139 (a Crown Court case on the exercise of powers under s 5A).

III HAR [7.2]

Enforcement An injunction granted after 1 September 1998 may be enforced by the issue of a warrant of arrest. The warrant should be in Form N140 and the application for it in Form N139. As an alternative to a warrant, an applicant may apply for the defendant to be committed for contempt. For a precedent for an application for an order of committal see **BCCP H[602]**. Civil means of enforcement are not available if criminal proceedings have resulted in a conviction: s 3(7).

Breach of an injunction against molestation, whether granted under the Protection from Harassment Act 1997 or under the Family Law Act 1996 may be punished by committal to prison for contempt of court or it may be the subject of criminal proceedings leading to higher penalties. The courts regard domestic and other violence associated with harassment and molestation as demanding rather more condign deterrent punishment: *Robinson v Murray* [2005] EWCA Civ 935, (2005) Times, 19 August, applying the principles in *H v O (Contempt of Court: Sentencing)* [2004] EWCA Civ 1691, [2005] 2 FLR 329.

Where an injunction was sought against an unincorporated association the court made an order against nominated representatives of the association which was binding on protesters who were members of the association although they were not named in the proceedings. Those protesters did not become parties to the proceedings and there should be no enforcement against them without the permission of the court: *Astellas Pharma Ltd v. Stop Huntingdon Animal Cruelty* [2011] EWCA Civ 752, [2011] All ER (D) 169 (Jul).

III HAR [7.3]

The position at common law As regards civil remedies for acts of harassment before 16 June 1997, the tort of inflicting intentional harm requires the proof of injury: *Wong v Parkside Health NHS Trust* [2001] EWCA Civ 1721, [2003] 3 All ER 932, (2001) Times, 7 December. See also the cases referred to at para **II CCA [21.5]**.

III HAR [7.4]

Injunctive relief to be no wider than necessary for the protection of the protected persons Various points arose for consideration in *Hall v Save Newchurch Guinea Pigs (Campaign)* [2005] EWHC 372 (QB), (2005) Times, 7 April. Because of the defendants' guerrilla tactics, involving criminal damage, intimidation and arson, the applicant farmers sought an injunction in the form of an exclusion zone of an area of approximately 200 square kilometres. This was refused on the ground that it was wider than necessary for the protection of those to be protected; and an injunction prohibiting the harassment of those individuals was continued instead. But the court indicated that if the more limited order was not effective to stop the harassment the matter could be restored and the probable outcome would be the grant of an exclusion zone.

It is not necessary to prove that the civil wrong of harassment has already taken place. An injunction may be granted where there is a reasonable apprehension that it is about to take place: *Iqbal v Dean Manson Solicitors* [2011] EWCA Civ 123, [2011] IRLR 428, [2011] NLJR 288.

III HAR [7.5]

Damages Where harassment has caused psychiatric harm as well as injury to feelings it may be appropriate to separate the award for psychiatric injury from the award for injury to feelings in which an element of aggravated damages may be included; but the court should guard against duplication leading to double recovery: *Choudhary v Martins* (2008) Times, 2 January, CA.

Financial loss resulting from harassment is recoverable. There is no requirement that the loss should be foreseeable: *Jones v Ruth* [2011] EWCA Civ 804, [2011] NLJR 1027.

The Court of Appeal upheld an award of £7,500 in a case where a bank customer received 547 telephone calls from the bank to which she owed money, although she made it clear at the outset that she did not wish to discuss the indebtedness: *Roberts v Bank of Scotland plc* [2013] EWCA Civ 882, [2013] All ER (D) 88 (Jun).

III HAR [7.6]

Victims of harassment The harassment need not be targeted at the claimant. Others who are foreseeably and directly harmed by the conduct, may be able to claim to the extent that they could properly be described as victims of it: *Levi v Bates* [2015] EWCA Civ 206, 165 NLJ 7646, [2015] All ER (D) 139 (Mar).

III HAR [7A]

3A. Injunctions to protect persons from harassment within section 1(1A)

(1) This section applies where there is an actual or apprehended breach of section 1(1A) by any person ("the relevant person").

(2) In such a case—

(a) any person who is or may be a victim of the course of conduct in question, or

(b) any person who is or may be a person falling within section 1(1A)(c),

may apply to the High Court or the county court for an injunction restraining the relevant person from pursuing any conduct which amounts to harassment in relation to any person or persons mentioned or described in the injunction.

(3) Section 3(3) to (9) apply in relation to an injunction granted under subsection (2) above as they apply in relation to an injunction granted as mentioned in section 3(3)(a).

III HAR [7A.1]

New provisions This section was inserted, with effect from 1 July 2005, by s 125 of the Serious Organised Crime and Police Act 2005. One of its purposes is to enable a person to seek an injunction to stop the harassment of others as a way of dissuading that person from carrying out lawful activities.

III HAR [8]

7. Interpretation of this group of sections

(1) This section applies for the interpretation of sections 1 to 5A.

(2) References to harassing a person include alarming the person or causing the person distress.

(3) A "course of conduct" must involve—

(a) in the case of conduct in relation to a single person (see section 1(1)), conduct on at least two occasions in relation to that person, or

(b) in the case of conduct in relation to two or more persons (see section 1(1A)), conduct on at least one occasion in relation to each of those persons.

(3A) A person's conduct on any occasion shall be taken, if aided, abetted, counselled or procured by another—

(a) to be conduct on that occasion of the other (as well as conduct of the person whose conduct it is); and

(b) to be conduct in relation to which the other's knowledge and purpose, and what he ought to have known, are the same as they were in relation to what was contemplated or reasonably foreseeable at the time of the aiding, abetting, counselling or procuring.

(4) "Conduct" includes speech.

(5) References to a person, in the context of the harassment of a person, are references to a person who is an individual.

III HAR [8.1]

Course of conduct A course of conduct, involving at least two occasions, could amount overall to harassment although the individual occasions, taken in isolation, might not amount to harassment: *Iqbal v Dean Manson Solicitors* [2011] EWCA Civ 123, [2011] IRLR 428, [2011] NLJR 288.

HUMAN RIGHTS

TABLE OF CONTENTS

HUMAN RIGHTS ACT 1998

(c 42)

TABLE OF CONTENTS

GENERAL NOTES ON HUMAN RIGHTS ACT 1998

III HUM [1]

Human Rights and the Administrative Court The Human Rights Act 1998 incorporates into domestic law the rights (and fundamental freedoms) of individuals arising under certain provisions in the Convention for the Protection of Human Rights and Fundamental Freedoms, agreed by the Council of Europe at Rome on 4 November 1950. The provisions covered by the Act are those in Arts 2–12 and 14 of the Convention; Arts 1–3 of the First Protocol; and Art 1 of the Thirteenth Protocol as read with Arts 16–18 of the Convention. They were brought into force on 2 October 2000, on the same day as the Crown Office List was re-named the Administrative Court, part of the Queen's Bench Division of the High Court. Challenges to legislation under s 4 (declarations of incompatibility) will normally proceed in this court as applications for judicial review. They will then be subject to **CPR 54** and the supporting Practice Direction at **CPR PD 54** as well as having to be served on the Crown in accordance with **CPR 19.4** and para 6 of the supporting Practice Direction at **CPR PD 19A**.

III HUM [2]

Derogations and reservations The United Kingdom made a formal derogation from Art 5(3) in the context of the detention of terrorists which has since been withdrawn, following the implementation of Sch 8 to the Terrorism Act 2000. The United Kingdom also made a reservation in relation to Art 2 of the First Protocol (right to education). This reservation is still effective and its terms are set out at para **III HUM [40.2]** in the notes on that Protocol. In addition, the United Kingdom designated a derogation from Art 5(1) as regards detention under the Anti-terrorism, Crime and Security Act 2001, see the Human Rights Act 1998 (Designated Derogation) Order 2001 (SI 2001/3644). The designation order was quashed and a declaration of incompatibility made in respect of s 23 of the 2001 Act by the House of Lords: *A v Secretary of State for the Home Department* [2004] UKHL 56, [2005] 2 AC 68, [2005] 3 All ER 169. The derogation was formally withdrawn by the Human Rights Act 1998 (Amendment) Order 2005, SI 2005/1071 with effect from 8 April 2005.

III HUM [3]

Interpretation of the Convention The Convention will have to be interpreted in accordance with its own jurisprudence, for example, the doctrine that the Convention is a "living instrument" to be interpreted in a generous way and in the light of developing social conditions. Domestic courts must take into account the decisions of the European Court of Human Rights (ECHR) and the European Commission of Human Rights (which existed until 1998): s 2. However, the case law from those institutions is not binding on the courts of this country. The Supreme Court should not necessarily follow a decision of a chamber of the ECHR if it considers that the chamber has misunderstood the effect of domestic law and that the decision of the Grand Chamber may be different. In such circumstances the Supreme Court could decide not to follow the ECHR decision, giving reasons for adopting that course: *R v Horncastle* [2009] UKSC 14, [2010] 2 WLR 47, (2009) Times, 10 December. However, the Courts have held that ECHR case law should be followed where "there is a clear and constant line of decisions whose effect is not inconsistent with some fundamental substantive or procedural aspect of our law, and whose reasoning does not appear to overlook or misunderstand some argument or point of principle" (*Manchester City Council v Pinnock (No 2)* [2011] 2 AC 104, [2011] 2 WLR 220, [2011] All ER (D) 93 (Feb), para 48). For the position where the ECHR's jurisprudence is developing alongside parallel developments at domestic level see *Moohan v The Lord Advocate* [2014] UKSC 67, [2015] AC 901, per Lord Wilson at para 104. Paragraph 8 of the Practice Direction—Miscellaneous Provisions Relating to Hearings (at **CPR PD 39A**) provides that only authoritative and complete reports of ECHR cases may be put in evidence and that the court and other parties must be given a list of authorities at least three days before the hearing. Copies of the complete original texts may be obtained from the ECHR database (HUDOC) online. Where the Court of Appeal or House of Lords has interpreted provisions of the Convention it is not open to lower courts to depart from those decisions: *R v Central Criminal Court, ex p Bright* [2001] 2 All ER 244, [2001] 1 WLR 662; approved after the entry into force of the HRA in *Ghaidan v Godin-Mendoza* [2002] EWCA Civ 1533, [2003] Ch 380, [2002] 4 All ER 1162, para 6. See now *Ghaidan v Godin-Mendoza* [2004] UKHL 30, [2004] 2 AC 557, [2004] 3 All ER 411. The judicial approach to legislation which borders on incompatibility is considered at para **III HUM [9.3]**.

III HUM [4]

Interpretation of UK legislation As with the law of the European Community, the courts must, so far as possible, interpret domestic legislation in a way compatible with incorporated provisions of the Convention: s 3. But, unlike the position in relation to EC law, incompatible primary legislation must be given effect; so too must incompatible subordinate legislation if primary legislation prevents removal of the incompatibility; other secondary legislation is void in so far as it is incompatible with a Convention right and to that extent should not be given effect. Certain courts, but not county courts, are empowered by s 4 to grant a declaration of incompatibility in respect of legislation which is incompatible with a Convention right but must be given effect: this will usually be primary legislation. The Crown has the right, under s 5, to intervene and be heard if the court is considering the grant of such a declaration.

III HUM [5]

Proceedings against public authorities Section 6 makes it unlawful for a court, tribunal or "person . . . whose functions are functions of a public nature" to "act in way which is incompatible" with the rights under the Convention unless UK legislation makes it impossible to do otherwise. Normally the unlawfulness will be established in proceedings by judicial review. In addition the victim of an unlawful act may bring proceedings against the offending authority in "the appropriate court" and rely on the unlawfulness as a defence to proceedings in any court at all: s 7(1)(a) and (b). The court may grant appropriate relief against the illegality, including an award of damages: s 8.

III HUM [5A]

Precedents Reliance on the Human Rights Act 1998 in proceedings for judicial review has drafting implications which are discussed at **BCCP J[23]–BCCP J[25]**. Illustrative precedents are provided at **BCCP J[102]** onwards, alleging contravention of Arts 2, 6 and 8 in particular. In addition, the pleading of Convention rights in other kinds of proceedings is discussed at **BCCP L[10]–BCCP L[14]**; and a wide range of precedents for claims and defences under the Convention is provided at **BCCP L[351]–BCCP L[381]**.

III HUM [6]

Commencement The Act was brought fully into force on 2 October 2000 by SI 2000/1851. Subsequent amendments are noted below.

III HUM [6A]

Retrospectivity The HRA does not have retrospective effect except to the extent provided for by s 22(4), that is where proceedings are brought by or at the instigation of a public authority. In *R (on the application of Mahmood) v Secretary of State for the Home Department* [2001] 1 WLR 840, (2001) Times, 9 January, CA the Court of Appeal held, by a majority, that the Act was not to be applied to decision-making before the Act was in force, even though the implementation of the decision would take place after. A pre-commencement conviction may not be appealed on the ground that the Convention was breached: *R v Lambert* [2001] UKHL 37, [2002] 2 AC 545, [2001] 3 All ER 577, followed in *R v Kansal (No 2)* [2001] UKHL 62, [2002] 2 AC 69, [2002] 1 All ER 257, although a majority of their Lordships doubted the correctness of the earlier decision. It is clear that a claim for damages for pre-commencement acts must be based on the pre-existing law: *Wainwright v Home Office* [2001] EWCA Civ 2081, [2002] QB 1334, [2003] 3 All ER 943; affirmed by the House of Lords [2003] UKHL 53, [2003] 4 All ER 969. Redress was subsequently obtained in the European Court of Human Rights: *Wainwright v United Kingdom Application No 12350/04* [2006] All ER (D) 125 (Sep).

In construing a provision in a pre-1948 settlement for "statutory next of kin" the exclusion of adopted children by s 5 of the Adoption of Children Act 1926 has been held to be discriminatory and contrary to Art 14. In that case the court found that the Act could be applied retrospectively without unfairness so that adopted children were, in the instant case, included: *Re Erskine 1948 Trust, Gregg v Pigott* [2012] EWHC 732 (Ch), [2012] 3 All ER 532, [2012] 3 WLR 913.

For the application of the non-retrospectivity principle in cases where the right in question includes separable duties (such as the right to investigate arising under Art 2), see *Re McKerr* [2004] UKHL 12, [2004] NI 212, [2004] 2 All ER 409; *Re McCaughey'* [2011] UKSC 20, [2012] AC 725, [2011] All ER (D) 163 (May); and *Keyu v Secretary of State for Foreign and Commonwealth Affairs* [2015] UKSC 69, [2015] All ER (D) 223 (Nov).

For the substantive law see *Halsbury's Laws* title RIGHTS AND FREEDOMS. See also Lester, Pannick and Herberg *Human Rights Law and Practice* (3rd edn, 2009).

III HUM [7]

1. The Convention Rights

(1) In this Act "the Convention rights" means the rights and fundamental freedoms set out in—

(a) Articles 2 to 12 and 14 of the Convention,

(b) Articles 1 to 3 of the First Protocol, and

(c) Article 1 of the Thirteenth Protocol,

as read with Articles 16–18 of the Convention.

(2) Those Articles are to have effect for the purposes of this Act subject to any designated derogation or reservation (as to which see sections 14, 15).

(3) The Articles are set out in Schedule 1.

(4) The Secretary of State may by order make such amendments to this Act as he considers appropriate to reflect the effect, in relation to the United Kingdom, of a protocol.

(5) In subsection (4) "protocol" means a protocol to the Convention—

(a) which the United Kingdom has ratified; or

(b) which the United Kingdom has signed with a view to ratification.

(6) No amendment may be made by an order under subsection (4) so as to come into force before the protocol concerned is in force in relation to the United Kingdom.

III HUM [7.1]

Incorporation This section identifies the provisions in the Convention and First and Thirteenth Protocols which are incorporated into UK law, subject to any designated derogation (of which there are none currently in force) and a reservation regarding the right to education (see para **III HUM [40.2]**): they are set out in schedule 1 below. The power, under sub-s (4), to amend the provisions has been exercised to include Art 1 of the Thirteenth Protocol, which replaced the Sixth Protocol.

III HUM [7.2]

Article 13 Article 13 of the Convention has not been carried into domestic law because it promises the very thing which the Act is intended to provide. Article 13 may, however, still need to be relied on in the European Court of Human Rights where Convention rights have been infringed before the coming into force of the Act or without there being an adequate right of redress under the Act: *Lustig-Prean and Beckett v United Kingdom* (1999) 29 EHRR 548, ECtHR; *Smith and Grady v United Kingdom* [1999] IRLR 734, ECtHR; *DP and JC v United Kingdom (Application 38719/97)* [2002] 3 FCR 385, ECtHR.

In *Bubbins v United Kingdom (Application No 50196/00)* (2005) Times, 30 March ECHR it was held that Mrs Bubbins should be compensated for the non-availability of a civil remedy for the shooting by the police of her brother, although the shooting was held in the circumstances to have been justified (in terms of Art 2) and had been thoroughly investigated at the inquest.

Where the police forcibly enter a dwelling house at night, under a search warrant, there may be a breach of Art 8 although they acted without malice. The requirement of the common law that malice must be proved has been held to be unjustified and not necessary in a democratic society with the result that a remedy should be provided where the police action could have been avoided by taking reasonable steps: *Keegan v United Kingdom (Application No 28867/03)* (2006) Times, 9 August, ECtHR. In a similar case involving a strip search of relatives visiting a prisoner, it was held that although it complied with the domestic law and did not breach Art 3 (degrading treatment) it was a breach of the Art 8 right to privacy because it was a disproportionate response to the legitimate aim of preventing drugs being smuggled into the prison. Since redress was not available under UK law the European Court awarded damages: *Wainwright v United Kingdom (Application No 12350/04)* [2006] All ER (D) 125 (Sep).

Similarly, a father wrongly excluded by a local authority from contact with his daughter because of suspected child abuse received compensation from the ECtHR for breaches of Arts 8 and 13 of the Convention where he could not succeed in negligence because of the absence of a duty of care and the relevant acts occurred before the Human Rights Act came into force: *MAK v United Kingdom (Application Nos 45901/05 and 40146/06)* [2010] 2 FLR 451, [2010] Fam Law 582, ECtHR.

In *Reynolds v United Kingdom (Application No 2694/2008)* [2012] All ER (D) 176 (Mar) where the ECtHR awarded compensation for breaches of Arts 2 and 13 where the non-dependant mother of an adult son could not claim damages for non-pecuniary damage following his death while in the care of an NHS hospital.

In *R (on the application of Byndloss) v Secretary of State for the Home Department* [2017] UKSC 42, [2017] 1 WLR 2380 the Supreme Court held that certificates issued by the Secretary of State under the Nationality, Immigration and Asylum Act 2002, s 94B requiring that a human rights challenge could only be brought from abroad following deportation were inconsistent with Arts 8 and 13 because an 'out-of-county' appeal would not be effective.

The ECtHR also made an award of compensation in *Hammerton v United Kingdom (Application No 6287/10)* (2016) 63 EHRR 23 in respect of a breach of Art 6 which resulted in a defendant serving longer in prison than might otherwise have been the case. Finding a violation of Art 13, the Court held that the domestic courts' acknowledgment of the breach of Art 6 had been insufficient.

III HUM [7.3]

Article 1 of the 13th Protocol Section 1(1)(c) was amended by the Human Rights Act 1998 (Amendment) Order 2004, SI 2004/1574, with effect from 22 June 2004, so as to delete the reference to Arts 1 and 2 of the Sixth Protocol and to refer instead to Art 1 of the Thirteenth Protocol. Article 1 abolishes the death penalty in all circumstances, whereas the former had preserved the power of states to retain it in time of war. The Thirteenth Protocol means the protocol to the Convention agreed at Vilnius on 3 May 2002.

III HUM [8]

2. Interpretation of Convention rights

(1) A court or tribunal determining a question which has arisen in connection with a Convention right must take into account any—

- (a) judgment, decision, declaration or advisory opinion of the European Court of Human Rights,
- (b) opinion of the Commission given in a report adopted under Article 31 of the Convention,
- (c) decision of the Commission in connection with Article 26 or 27 (2) of the Convention, or
- (d) decision of the Committee of Ministers taken under Article 46 of the Convention,

whenever made or given, so far as, in the opinion of the court or tribunal, it is relevant to the proceedings in which that question has arisen.

(2) Evidence of any judgment, decision, declaration or opinion of which account may have to be taken under this section is to be given in proceedings before any court or tribunal in such manner as may be provided by rules.

(3) In this section "rules" means rules of court or, in the case of proceedings before a tribunal, rules made for the purposes of this section—

- (a) by the Lord Chancellor or the Secretary of State, in relation to any proceedings outside Scotland;
- (b) by the Secretary of State, in relation to proceedings in Scotland; or
- (c) by a Northern Ireland department, in relation to proceedings before a tribunal in Northern Ireland–
  - (i) which deals with transferred matters; and
  - (ii) for which no rules made under paragraph (a) are in force.

III HUM [8.1]

Citation of authorities Paragraph 8 of the Practice Direction—Miscellaneous Provisions Relating to Hearings (at **CPR PD 39A**) provides that only authoritative and complete reports of ECHR cases may be put in evidence and that the court and other parties must be given a list of authorities at least three days before the hearing. Copies of the complete original texts may be obtained from the ECHR database (HUDOC) online. The relationship between Strasbourg case law and the domestic law doctrine of precedent was authoritatively considered by the House of Lords in *Lambeth London Borough Council v Kay* [2006] UKHL 10, [2006] 2 AC 465. It was held that, although domestic courts are not strictly required to follow the rulings of the Strasbourg court, they are obliged to give practical effect to the principles it has expounded; it is for the domestic courts to determine initially how those principles are to be applied in the domestic context; the doctrine of precedent is a cornerstone of the domestic legal system; therefore domestic courts could give permission to appeal where they consider a binding precedent to be inconsistent with Strasbourg authority but generally they should follow a binding precedent save in an extreme case where the decision of a superior court could not survive the introduction of the Human Rights Act 1998. However, the Supreme Court should not necessarily follow a decision of a chamber of the ECtHR if it considers that the chamber has misunderstood the effect of domestic law and that the decision of the Grand Chamber may be different. In such circumstances the Supreme Court could decide not to follow the ECHR decision, giving reasons for adopting that course: *R v Horncastle* [2009] UKSC 14, [2010] 2 WLR 47, (2009) Times, 10 December. See also *Manchester City Council v Pinnock* [2010] UKSC 45, [2010] 3 WLR 1441, [2010] 44 LS Gaz R 16 paragraph 48 per Lord Neuberger affirming this approach but emphasising that a 'clear and constant line of decisions' by the ECtHR will usually be followed. In *R (on the application of Chester) v Secretary of State for Justice* [2013] UKSC 63, [2014] AC 271, Lord Mance (at para 27) said that 'it would have then to involve some truly fundamental principle of our law or some most egregious oversight or misunderstanding before it could be appropriate for this court to contemplate an outright refusal to follow Strasbourg authority at the Grand Chamber level'. See also *R (on the application of Haney) v Secretary of State for Justice* [2014] UKSC 66, [2015] 2 WLR 76, (2014) Times, 15 December where the Supreme Court decided that it could not follow the reasoning of the ECtHR, which it considered illogical, in *James, Wells and Lee v UK* (2013) 56 EHRR 12 relating to the lawfulness of the continued imprisonment of prisoners serving indeterminate sentences who were not being enabled to progress towards release, and also the helpful summary of the applicable principles, as they have developed, set out in the judgment of Lord Wilson in *Moohan v The Lord Advocate* [2014] UKSC 67, [2015] AC 901 at para 104. But see *Brown v Parole Board for Scotland* [2017] UKSC 69, [2018] AC 1, para 44, superseding *Haney* and reverting to the ECtHR's approach in *James* 'on the basis that it is no longer possible to deny that the analysis in the James case forms part of a clear and constant line of decisions' that the domestic courts should follow (Lord Reed, para 38).

The Supreme Court may also decline to reconsider an earlier domestic decision in light of a subsequent ECtHR Chamber decision if it appears that it is 'unlikely to be the last word', in which case Lord Carnwath said '[i]t is appropriate that we should await a full consideration by a Grand Chamber before considering whether (and if so how) to modify our own position': *Poshteh v Kensington and Chelsea Royal London Borough Council* [2017] UKSC 36, [2017] AC 624, para 37.

In *R (on the application of RJM) v Secretary of State for Work and Pensions* [2008] 3 WLR 1023, HL the House of Lords further ruled that if the Court of Appeal considered that a decision of the House of Lords was inconsistent with a subsequent decision of the ECtHR, then save in wholly exceptional circumstances it should follow the House of Lords' decision. However, where it concluded that one of its own previous decisions was inconsistent with a subsequent decision of the ECtHR, it was free, but not obliged, to depart from that decision. See, for example the Supreme Court departing from a previous decision in *Brown v Parole Board for Scotland* [2017] UKSC 69, [2018] AC 1, paras 38-45 on this basis, but declining to do so in *Poshteh v Kensington and Chelsea Royal London Borough Council* [2017] UKSC 36, [2017] AC 624.

III HUM [9]

3. Legislation

(1) So far as it is possible to do so, primary legislation and subordinate legislation must be read and given effect in a way which is compatible with the Convention rights.

(2) This section—

(a) applies to primary legislation and subordinate legislation whenever enacted;

(b) does not affect the validity, continuing operation or enforcement of any incompatible primary legislation; and

(c) does not affect the validity, continuing operation or enforcement of any incompatible subordinate legislation if (disregarding any possibility of revocation) primary legislation prevents removal of the incompatibility.

III HUM [9.1]

Definitions "Primary" and "subordinate" legislation are each defined in s 21(1) see para **III HUM [22]**.

III HUM [9.2]

Giving effect to legislation in a way which is compatible The judicial approach to the interpretation of legislation which borders on incompatibility was first considered by the House of Lords in *R v A (No 2)* [2001] UKHL 25, [2002] 1 AC 45, [2001] 3 All ER 1, a case about the statutory restraints on cross-examining the complainant in a rape case. Lord Steyn, giving the leading judgment, stated that a declaration of incompatibility was a "measure of last resort". It must be avoided unless it is "plainly impossible to do so". His Lordship's test for incompatibility was to treat the legislation in question as "subject to the implied provision that evidence or questioning which is required to ensure a fair trial under Art 6 of the Convention should not be treated as admissible. On this basis a declaration of incompatibility can be avoided." Lord Hope expressly rejected the "implied provision" approach and there is some doubt as to whether it had majority support. See also the narrower approach taken by Lord Hope in *R v Lambert* [2001] UKHL 37, [2002] 2 AC 545, [2001] 3 All ER 577.

In *Goode v Martin* [2001] EWCA Civ 1899, [2002] 1 All ER 620, (2002) Times, 24 January, the Court of Appeal adopted the approach recommended by Lord Steyn in *R v A (No 2)* [2001] UKHL 25, [2002] 1 AC 45, [2001] 3 All ER 1. In applying s 3(1) of the Human Rights Act 1998 (see para **III HUM [9]**), the Court held that the reference to a new claim which arises "out of the same facts or substantially the same facts as a claim" in para (2) of **CPR 17.4** should be construed widely, as if the text included the words "*are already in issue in*" before the words "a claim". In *Re S (minors) (Care Plan)* [2002] UKHL 10, [2002] 2 AC 291, [2002] 2 All ER 192, at paras 39–41, Lord Nicholls stressed that s 3 does not permit judicial amendment of legislation, only interpretation of it.

The interpretation obligation under s 3 is a strong one and may require the court to read in or out words which change the meaning or depart from the intention of the enacting Parliament. This obligation reaches its limit only where a compatible interpretation is inconsistent with a fundamental feature or the underlying thrust of the legislation: *Ghaidan v Godin-Mendoza* [2004] UKHL 30, [2004] 2 AC 557, [2004] 3 All ER 411, in which the court read "spouse" in the Rent Act 1977 as including persons of the same sex. *Ghaidan* may now be regarded as the leading authority on the approach to be taken under s 3. See also its application in *Secretary of State for Work and Pensions v M* [2006] UKHL 11, [2006] 2 AC 91, [2006] 4 All ER 929, at paragraph 117 per Baroness Hale.

In *Smith (suing in her own right and as the surviving partner of Bulloch, deceased) v Lancashire Teaching Hospitals NHS Foundation Trust* [2017] EWCA Civ 1916, (2018) Times, 08 January, [2017] All ER (D) 11 (Dec) the Court of Appeal emphasised that a s 4 declaration of incompatibility may only be made it if would be impossible to use the interpretive power in s 3. This is the situation if attempting to reinterpret it would be inconsistent with a fundamental feature of the legislation. In the instant case, s 1A of the Fatal Accidents Act 1976 provided for bereavement damages for spouses, civil partners and parents but not for cohabiting couples who had been living together for more than two years. This was incompatible with Art 8 in conjunction with Art 14 but it could not be interpreted down as the non-inclusion of cohabiting couples 'is clear, express and intentional and is an ingrained feature of the legislation' (para 97).

A court is a public authority for the purpose of the Human Rights Act 1998 and must act compatibly with Convention rights unless precluded from doing so by primary legislation which cannot be read in any other way. Therefore in proceedings relating to non-derogating control orders under the Prevention of Terrorism Act 2005, the provisions of the Act and the CPR were read and given effect so as to empower the court to direct that the Secretary of State could not rely upon material which was withheld from disclosure in the public interest where the non-disclosure would prevent the person subject to the order from having a fair hearing and, if necessary, to quash orders in cases where the material was crucial to the decision: *Secretary of State for the Home Department v MB, Secretary of State for the Home Department v AF* [2007] UKHL 46, [2008] 1 AC 440.

The reading down of the provisions of s 3(10) of the Prevention of Terrorism Act 2005, to make them compatible with the Convention rights under Arts 5 and 6, was approved by the House of Lords on the further appeal in *Secretary of State for the Home Department v AF (No 3)* [2009] UKHL 28, [2009] 3 All ER 643, [2009] 3 WLR 74. On the other hand, their Lordships ordered a reconsideration of the fairness issue in the cases before them, on the ground that a judge holding a section 3(10) hearing should consider not merely the allegations to be disclosed but also whether there was any other matter whose disclosure was essential to the fairness of the trial. Lord Phillips observed that there were strong policy considerations supporting a rule that a trial procedure could never be considered fair if a party was kept in ignorance of the case against him, or her.

On the other hand, the Supreme Court in *Kennedy v Charity Commission* [2014] UKSC 40, [2015] AC 455, concluded that ECHR Art 10 did not require s 32(2) of the Freedom of Information Act 2000 (which exempts from disclosure any information held by persons conducting an inquiry or arbitration) to be read down so as to apply only during the lifetime of the inquiry or arbitration, applying *Sugar v British Broadcasting Corpn* [2012] UKSC 4, [2012] 2 All ER 509, [2012] 1 WLR 439. The 2000 Act did not provide an exhaustive scheme for disclosure in those circumstances, and attention should be directed to whether disclosure could take place pursuant to the Charities Act 1993 (as amended).

In *R (on the application of Chester) v Secretary of State for Justice* [2013] UKSC 63, [2014] AC 271, Baroness Hale recognised that s 4(2) of the Human Rights Act 1998 left open the possibility of a declaration in abstracto irrespective of whether the provision was incompatible with the right of the individual litigant. She held that the Court "should be extremely slow" to make a declaration where the relevant provision was not incompatible with the litigant in question's rights: "Any other approach is to invite a multitude of unmeritorious claims" (para 102). See also per Lord Wilson in *R (on the application of T) v Chief Constable of Greater Manchester Police* [2014] UKSC 35, [2015] AC 49, [2014] 4 All ER 159 at para 51, and *Secretary of State for Defence v Nicholas* [2015] EWCA Civ 53, [2015] 1 WLR 2116, [2015] All ER (D) 53 (Feb) per Lewison LJ at paras 21–23.

III HUM [9.3]

Pre-commencement conduct In a claim based on pre-commencement conduct, the court must apply the pre-commencement law since s 3 is not given retrospective effect by s 22(4) (at para **III HUM [23]**): *Wainwright v Home Office* [2001] EWCA Civ 2081, [2002] QB 1334, [2003] 3 All ER 943; affirmed in the House of Lords [2003] UKHL 53, [2004] 2 AC 406, [2003] 4 All ER 969.

Similarly s 3 does not require inquests to comply with the UK's Convention obligations no matter when the death occurred. The Convention rights apply only to deaths occurring after the 1998 Act came into force: *R (on the application of Hurst) v Northern District of*

London Coroner [2007] UKHL 13, [2007] 2 All ER 1025. However, if the state decides to hold an inquest in relation to such a death which occurred before commencement of the HRA, it may have a freestanding obligation to ensure that it complies with the procedural obligations of Art 2 of the Convention: *Re McCaughey And Quinn's Application For Leave To Apply For Judicial Review* [2011] UKSC 20, [2011] 3 All ER 607, (2011) UKHRR 720, (2011) HRLR 25, (2011) Times, 20 May. See also the analysis in and *Keyu v Secretary of State for Foreign and Commonwealth Affairs* [2015] UKSC 69, [2015] 3 WLR 1665.

III HUM [10]

4. Declaration of incompatibility

(1) Subsection (2) applies in any proceedings in which a court determines whether a provision of primary legislation is compatible with a Convention right.

(2) If the court is satisfied that the provision is incompatible with a Convention right, it may make a declaration of that incompatibility.

(3) Subsection (4) applies in any proceedings in which a court determines whether a provision of subordinate legislation, made in the exercise of a power conferred by primary legislation, is compatible with a Convention right.

(4) If the court is satisfied—

- (a) that the provision is incompatible with a Convention right, and
- (b) that (disregarding any possibility of revocation) the primary legislation concerned prevents removal of the incompatibility,

it may make a declaration of that incompatibility.

(5) In this section "court" means—

- (a) the Supreme Court;
- (b) the Judicial Committee of the Privy Council;
- (c) the Court Martial Appeal Court;
- (d) in Scotland, the High Court of Justiciary sitting otherwise than as a trial court or the Court of Session;
- (e) in England and Wales or Northern Ireland, the High Court or the Court of Appeal;
- (f) the Court of Protection, in any matter being dealt with by the President of the Family Division, the Chancellor of the High Court or a puisne judge of the High Court.

(6) A declaration under this section ("a declaration of incompatibility")—

- (a) does not affect the validity, continuing operation or enforcement of the provision in respect of which it is given; and
- (b) is not binding on the parties to the proceedings in which it is made.

III HUM [10.1]

Procedure for giving notice to the Crown **CPR 19.4A** requires notice to be given to the Crown and the procedure for giving notice is set out in paras 6.1–6.5 of the Practice Direction—Addition and Substitution of Parties at **CPR PD 19A**.

III HUM [10.2]

Circumstances where declarations may be made A number of declarations of incompatibility have been made but not all have been upheld on appeal.

In *A v Secretary of State for the Home Department* a declaration of incompatibility was made by the Special Immigration Appeals Commission in relation to s 23 of the Anti-terrorism, Crime and Security Act 2001 but reversed by the Court of Appeal: [2002] EWCA Civ 1502, [2003] 1 All ER 816. The House of Lords allowed the appeal (by a majority of 8 to 1) and made a declaration that s 23 is incompatible with Arts 5 and 14 of the Convention: [2004] UKHL 56, ([2005] 2 AC 68.

However, the House of Lords refused a declaration in *R (on the application of Animal Defenders International) v Secretary of State for Culture, Media and Sport* [2008] UKHL 15, [2008] 1 AC 1312 in relation to the ban on political advertising imposed by the Communications Act 2003, holding that the restriction was necessary and proportionate notwithstanding that different states took different views on the measures necessary to achieve a level playing field in political debate.

Sections 1 and 3 of the Civil Partnerships Act 2004 have been held by the Supreme Court to contravene Art 14 (read with Art 8) of the Convention by confining the opportunity for a civil partnership to couples of the same gender: *R (on the application of Steinfeld) v Secretary of State for International Development* [2018] UKSC 32, [2018] 3 WLR 415.

In a similar vein the Supreme Court has held entitlement to widowed parent's allowance is discriminatory to the extent that it requires the parent to be married: *Re McLaughlin* [2018] UKSC 48, [2018] 1 WLR 4250.

In *R (on the application of Hooper) v Secretary of State for Work and Pensions* [2003] EWCA Civ 813, [2003] 3 All ER 673, [2003] 1 WLR 2623 the Court of Appeal discharged a declaration of incompatibility made by Moses J in relation to s 36 of the Social Security (Contributions and Benefits) Act 1992, which distinguished between widows and widowers. The Court held that the Secretary of State had acted unlawfully and the primary legislation was not incompatible with the Convention. In the related case of *R (on the application of Wilkinson) v IRC* [2003] EWCA Civ 814, [2003] 3 All ER 719, [2003] 1 WLR 2683, a declaration of incompatibility was made by Moses J in relation to s 262 of the Income and Corporation Taxes Act 1988 and the appeal dismissed. The House of Lords held in both cases that there was no incompatibility with the Convention: *R (on the application of Hooper) v Secretary of State for Work and Pensions* [2005] 1 WLR 1681; *R (on the application of Wilkinson) v IRC* [2005] 1 WLR 1718.

In *R (on the application of Wright) v Secretary of State for Health and Secretary of State for Education and Skills* [2009] UKHL 3, [2009] 1 AC 739, [2009] 2 All ER 129 the House of Lords declared that the provision in the Care Standards Act 2000 for care workers to be placed provisionally on a list of persons unsuitable to work with vulnerable adults with no power to apply to the Care Standards Tribunal to be removed from the list until some months had passed was incompatible with the right of access to a court under Art 6, restoring the order of the High Court (*R (Wright) v Secretary of State for Health and Secretary of State for Education and Skills* [2006] EWHC 2886 (Admin), [2007] 1 All ER 825, [2007] IRLR 507) but overturning the Court of Appeal, which had held that s 82(4)(b) should be interpreted as requiring the Secretary of State to give the worker an opportunity to make representations before being included in the list, unless the resultant delay would expose vulnerable adults to the risk of harm (*R (Wright) v Secretary of State for Health and Secretary of State for Education and Skills* [2007] EWCA Civ 999, [2007] QB 422). See also *R (on the application of the Royal College of Nursing) v Secretary of State for the Home Department* [2010] EWHC 2761 (Admin), 154 Sol Jo (no 46) 30 where the reasoning in *Wright* was applied, issuing a declaration of incompatibility in respect of a scheme whereby a person convicted or cautioned of certain offences was automatically placed on a list barring them from working with children or vulnerable adults without first having the opportunity to make representations.

A declaration was also made in relation to the provisions of ss 72 and 73 of the Mental Health Act 1983, which placed the burden on a person detained in a secure hospital to satisfy the Tribunal that he, or she, should be released: *R (on the application of H) v London North and East Regional Mental Health Tribunal* [2001] EWCA Civ 415, [2002] QB 1, [2001] 3 WLR 512. This declaration was not appealed against; instead, the Act was amended by way of a remedial order under s 10 and Sch 2 (below). Another declaration that was not appealed against was made by the Court of Appeal in *International Transport Roth GmbH v Secretary of State for the Home Department* [2002] EWCA Civ 158, [2003] QB 728. The incompatibility in the immigration legislation relating to the liability of hauliers was removed by primary legislation in 2002. Some declarations made by the House of Lords have also prompted primary legislation rather than remedial orders. See *R (on the application of Anderson) v Secretary of State for the Home Department* [2002] UKHL 46, [2003] 1 AC 837, [2002] 4 All ER 1089; and *Bellinger v Bellinger* [2003] UKHL 21, [2003] 2 AC 467, [2003] 2 All ER 593. There was also primary legislation in response to the declaration of incompatibility made by the House of Lords in respect of s 23 of the Anti-terrorism, Crime and Security Act 2001: *A v Secretary of State for the Home Department* [2004] UKHL 56, [2005] 2 AC 68: the Prevention of Terrorism Act 2005, which repealed Part 4 of the 2001 Act and introduced the system of "control orders" which may be imposed on suspected terrorists.

A declaration of incompatibility was made in respect of s 82(1) of the Sexual Offences Act 2003. The absence of a right of review at any time of notification requirements imposed upon offenders who had been placed on the sex offenders register indefinitely was a disproportionate interference with the right to respect for private and family life. The case for granting a declaration of incompatibility was even stronger in the case of young offenders than of adult offenders: *R (on the application by JF (by his litigation friend OF)) v Secretary of State for the Home Department* [2010] UKSC 17, [2010] 2 All ER 707, [2010] 2 WLR 992.

A declaration of incompatibility was also made in respect of s 19(3) of the Land Compensation Act 1973 which excludes compensation claims by property owners affected by a new road that is not adopted by a local authority within three years of its opening date. This was held incompatible with the right to peaceful enjoyment of possessions Under Art 1 of Protocol 1: *Thomas v Bridgend County Borough Council* [2011] EWCA Civ 862, [2011] RVR 241, [2011] All ER (D) 234 (Jul).

In *R (on the application of GC) v Metropolitan Police Comr; R (on the Application of C) v Metropolitan Police Comr* [2011] UKSC 21, [2011] 3 All ER 859, [2011] 1 WLR 1230, (2011) Times, 19 May the Supreme Court held that although the provision in s 64(1A) of the Police and Criminal Evidence Act 1984 for the indefinite retention of the biometric data of all suspects breached individuals' rights under Art 8, the section could be read so as not to require indefinite retention and no declaration of incompatibility was required.

Similarly s 115(7) of the Police Act 1997, dealing with material to be included in an enhanced criminal records check, was not incompatible with Art 8 as long as the words 'ought to be included' were given their full weight, so that in exercising his discretion the chief police officer had to give proper consideration to a person's right to respect for his private life: *R (on the application of L) v Metropolitan Police Comr* [2009] UKSC 3, [2010] 1 AC 410, [2010] 1 All ER 113. However, in *R (on the application of T) v Chief Constable of Greater Manchester* [2014] UKSC 35, [2015] AC 49 the Supreme Court upheld a declaration of incompatibility made in respect of the disclosure provisions of the Police Act 1997 because they imposed a blanket statutory requirement of disclosure of cautions held on the police national computer which was disproportionate and exceeded the legitimate aims of protecting employers and vulnerable individuals.

Police stop and search authorisations pursuant to s 60 of the Criminal Justice and Public Order Act 1994 were challenged in *R (on the application of Roberts) v Metropolitan Police Comr* [2015] UKSC 79, [2016] 1 WLR 210. The Supreme Court declined to make a declaration of incompatibility because the legal framework within which that power was operated, and the standard police operating procedures in force, should make it possible to judge whether an individual stop and search was necessary in a democratic society for the prevention of disorder or crime.

The same result can be seen in *Coventry v Lawrence* [2015] UKSC 50, 165 NLJ 7663, [2015] All ER (D) 234 (Jul), where the Supreme Court rejected a challenge on grounds of incompatibility with Art 6 and Art 1 of Protocol 1 ECHR of the pre-April 2013 conditional fee agreement regime introduced by s 58 of the Courts and Legal Services Act 1990, as substituted by s 27 of the Access to Justice Act 1999. Claimants in a successful nuisance claim incurred a liability for costs and an after the event insurance premium exceeding £800,000 in respect of a claim worth nearly £21,000 and, upon success, sought an order that the defendant pay those costs. The Supreme Court considered that success fees and ATE premiums were integral to the scheme of the 1999 Act and had a legitimate aim: they sought to maintain access to justice for litigants no longer entitled to legal aid. Whilst the scheme was open to objections, the issue was not whether it was unfair, but whether it was disproportionate and the Court held it was not.

In *R (on the application of Johnson) v Secretary of State for the Home Department* [2016] UKSC 56, [2016] 3 WLR 1267 the Supreme Court declared that para 70 of Sch 9 to the Immigration Act 2014 (which amended s 41A(1) of the British Nationality Act 1981 Act by introducing an additional requirement that an applicant for British citizenship who, but for his parents' marital status, would have automatically acquired citizenship at birth be also of good character) was incompatible with Art 8 (taken with Art 14) of the Convention.

In *Benkharbouche v Embassy of the Republic of Sudan (Secretary of State for Foreign and Commonwealth Affairs)* [2015] EWCA Civ 33, [2015] 3 WLR 301, [2015] All ER (D) 51 (Feb), the Court of Appeal made a declaration of incompatibility in respect of ss 16(1)(a) and 4(2) of the State Immunity Act 1978, which, respectively, (i) imposed a blanket exclusion on 'members of a mission' from protections that would otherwise be afforded to employees, and (ii) did not remove state immunity from employees inter alia those who were not habitually resident in the UK. The Court considered these provisions breached Art 6 ECHR and could not be read down. The Employment Appeal Tribunal had granted permission to appeal because it did not have jurisdiction to grant the declaration under s 4 Human Rights Act 1998: [2014] ICR 169. The incompatibility was upheld by the Supreme Court: *Benkharbouche v Secretary of State for Foreign and Commonwealth Affairs* [2017] UKSC 62, [2017] All ER (D) 84 (Oct).

In *R (on the application of Nicklinson) v Ministry of Justice* [2014] UKSC 38, [2015] AC 657, a plurality of Lord Neuberger, Lord Mance and Lord Wilson held that it would be institutionally inappropriate to grant a declaration of incompatibility relating to the Suicide Act 1961, s 2(1) because Parliament should first be given the opportunity to consider changing the law. In light of Parliament's decision not to amend s 2(1), however, the Court of Appeal in *R (on the application of Conway) v Secretary of State for Justice* [2017] EWCA Civ 275 held that an applicant could be given permission to apply for judicial review on the same grounds as those in *Nicklinson*. When that case proceeded, the Court of Appeal rejected the argument that s 2(1) of the Suicide Act 1961 imposes a disproportionate ban on suicide, when physician assisted. Whether the argument is put under Art 2 or Art 8 the law is not incompatible, for the purpose of s 4, with the provisions of the Convention: *R (on the application of Conway) v Secretary of State for Justice* [2018] EWCA Civ 1431, [2018] 3 WLR 925.

The judicial approach to legislation which borders on incompatibility is considered above at para **III HUM [9.2]**.

In *R (on the application of M) v Secretary of State for Health* [2003] EWHC 1094 (Admin), [2003] 3 All ER 672, (2003) Times, 25 April, a declaration of incompatibility was granted as regards ss 26 and 29 of the Mental Health Act 1983. This was on the ground that Art 8 was contravened by denying the patient the right to apply to replace the 'nearest relative'. The court exercised its discretion to grant the declaration although the Government had previously agreed to put amending legislation before Parliament: see **III MEN [8A.1]**.

It was held by the Court of Appeal that s 2 of the Mental Health Act 1983 is incompatible with Art 5.4 in that it does not provide adequate access to the Mental Health Tribunal for patients detained under s 2 who lack capacity to exercise those rights of access: *R (on the application of MH) v Secretary of State for Health* [2004] EWCA Civ 1609, (2004) Times, 8 December. It was further declared in that case that s 29(4) of the same Act was also incompatible because it denied the detained patient access to a court, or tribunal, during the period of extended detention which arose under that sub-section. However, the House of Lords reversed the Court of Appeal and discharged the declaration of incompatibility: [2005] 3 WLR 867.

The Court has also emphasised that declarations of incompatibility only apply to legislation. So in applying the Immigration Rules, which are a statement of policy, the Home Secretary had to respect Convention rights but there was no requirement to read down the wording of the Rules so as to be compliant with the Convention: *R (on the application of Syed) v Home Secretary* [2011] EWCA Civ 1059. Nonetheless, it is possible, in an appropriate case, to invite the Court to rule on whether a requirement in the Immigration Rules (or guidance as to how those rules will be operated) will inevitably be unlawful. In *R (on the application of Ali) v Secretary of State for the Home Department* [2015] UKSC 68, [2015] All ER (D) 150 (Nov), the Supreme Court considered that a requirement in the Immigration Rules for the foreign spouse or partner of a British citizen to produce a test of competence in English before entering the UK was capable of being operated compatibly with Arts 8 and 14 ECHR. However, the Court was concerned about guidance accompanying the Rules and its potential incompatibility with Art 8. Further submissions as to whether the Court should make such a ruling were invited as it had not been part of the remedy Initially sought.

III HUM [10.2A]

Data Retention and Investigatory Powers Act 2014 The High Court granted a declaration that s 1 of the Data Retention and Investigatory Powers Act 2014 was inconsistent with EU law, and in particular Art 8 of the Convention on Human Rights: *R (on the application of Davis MP) v Secretary of State for the Home Department (Open Rights Group and others intervening)* [2015] EWHC 2092 (Admin), 165 NLJ 7663, [2015] All ER (D) 180 (Jul). This followed a decision to similar effect by the Court of Justice of the European Union in regard to the Data Retention Directive, reported as *Digital Rights Ireland Ltd v Minister for Communications, Marine and Natural Resources and others; Re Landesregierung* case: [2014] 2 All ER (Comm) 1.

III HUM [10.2B]

The right to bereavement damages It has been held that the restriction (in s 1A of the Fatal Accidents Act 1976) of the right to damages for bereavement to those who are married to the deceased at the time of death (thereby excluding those who are living as husband and wife but without being married) is incompatible with Art 14 read with Art 8 of the Human Rights Convention: *Smith (suing in her own right and as the surviving partner of Bulloch, deceased) v Lancashire Teaching Hospitals NHS Foundation Trust* [2017] EWCA Civ 1916, (2018) Times, 08 January, [2017] All ER (D) 11 (Dec). See **III PID [11.1]**.

III HUM [10.3]

Precedents A precedent for judicial review proceedings for, amongst other things, a declaration of incompatibility is provided at **BCCP J[105]**.

III HUM [11]

5. Right of Crown to intervene

(1) Where a court is considering whether to make a declaration of incompatibility, the Crown is entitled to notice in accordance with rules of court.

(2) In any case to which subsection (1) applies—

(a) a Minister of the Crown (or a person nominated by him),

(b) a member of the Scottish Executive,

(c) a Northern Ireland Minister,

(d) a Northern Ireland department,

is entitled, on giving notice in accordance with rules of court, to be joined as a party to the proceedings.

(3) Notice under subsection (2) may be given at any time during the proceedings.

(4) A person who has been made a party to criminal proceedings (other than in Scotland) as the result of a notice under subsection (2) may, with leave, appeal to the Supreme Court against any declaration of incompatibility made in the proceedings.

(5) In subsection (4)—

"criminal proceedings" includes all proceedings before the Court Martial Appeal Court; and

"leave" means leave granted by the court making the declaration of incompatibility or by the Supreme Court.

III HUM [11.1]

County court exclusion It will be noted that county courts are not included in the definition of "court" in s 4(5) and are therefore not competent to grant declarations of incompatibility. This does not mean that the county court can avoid deciding whether legislation can be read and given effect in a way which is compatible with Convention rights – if a question of statutory interpretation arises, that is how the court must read legislation, so far as possible: s 3. However, if the county court reaches the conclusion that primary legislation cannot be read in a way which is compatible with Convention rights, it should say so in its judgment while not being able to make a formal declaration of incompatibility. The court must have regard to the question of whether the making of a declaration of incompatibility has arisen or may arise when considering whether to transfer a claim from the county court to the High Court: CPR 30.3.2(g). On any appeal from a county court, the Court of Appeal can make such a formal declaration if one is appropriate.

III HUM [11.2]

Rules of court **CPR 19.4A** requires notice to be given to the Crown and the procedure for giving notice is set out in paras 6.1–6.5 of the Practice Direction—Addition and Substitution of Parties at **CPR PD 19A**.

III HUM [11.3]

Crown application to be joined The appropriate Minister may be joined by the court before a declaration of incompatibility is under consideration if the issue of incompatibility is likely to arise: *R v A (Joinder of appropriate Minister)* (2001) Times, 21 March, HL. It was also decided in that case that the fact that the Crown Prosecution Service was already a party was not a reason for not joining the Home Secretary, seeing that he was the Minister with responsibility for the relevant legislation. See also *Benkharbouche v Secretary of State for Foreign and Commonwealth Affairs* [2017] UKSC 62, [2017] All ER (D) 84 (Oct).

III HUM [11.4]

Declaration of Incompatibility only where Convention rights infringed In *R (on the application of Nasseri) v Secretary of State for the Home Department* [2009] UKHL 23, [2009] 3 All ER 774, [2009] 2 WLR 1190 the HL discharged a declaration of incompatibility made by the Court of Appeal in relation to paragraph 3(2)(b) of Part 2 of Sch 3 to the Asylum and Immigration (Treatment of Claimants, etc) Act 2004. That provision prevented the Secretary of State from considering whether the applicant's enforced return to Greece would result in treatment infringing his Art 3 rights. However, on the facts there was no risk of such an infringement. Therefore any failure to investigate whether there was such a risk was not a breach of the Convention. A declaration of incompatibility would usually not be made in a hypothetical case where there would be no actual infringement of Convention rights.

The Court of Appeal has also emphasised that a person is not entitled to apply for a declaration of incompatibility if he is not adversely affected by the legislation in question: *Lancashire County Council v Taylor (Secretary of State for the Environment, Food and Rural Affairs intervening)* [2005] EWCA Civ 284, [2005] 1 WLR 2668, [2005] 2 EGLR 17.

In *Coventry v Lawrence* [2014] UKSC 46, [2015] AC 106, [2014] 2 P & CR 304, having determined liability in a nuisance claim, the Supreme Court considered that the costs effect on a party of a conditional fee agreement under the Access to Justice Act 1999 and the Courts and Legal Services Act 1990 might be inconsistent with the party's rights under ECHR Art 6 and Art 1 Protocol 1. However, a decision to make a declaration of incompatibility could be questionable given that the relevant provisions had already been repealed and replaced. The Court decided that if the parties affected wished to pursue the matter, they would need to have the case relisted with notice given to the Attorney General and the Secretary of State for Justice. This was done and, as noted above at para **III HUM [10.2]**, the Court ultimately found no incompatibility: [2015] UKSC 50, 165 NLJ 7663, [2015] All ER (D) 234 (Jul).

III HUM [11.5]

Supreme Court In the Supreme Court, if a Minister or other person has already been joined to proceedings in the court below in accordance with the provisions of s 5 of the Human Rights Act 1998, the permission of the Court is not required for the continued intervention of the Crown (Supreme Court PD 9, paragraph 9.1.4.).

Where an appeal raises a question of incompatibility under s 4 of the Human Rights Act 1998 and the Crown is not already a party to the appeal, the Registrar shall give 21 days' notice of the question to the Crown (Supreme Court Rules 2009, r 40(1); Supreme Court PD 9 para 9.1.2, 9.1.3.). If notice is given that the Crown wishes to be joined, the appropriate Minister or person shall be joined accordingly (Supreme Court Rules 2009, r 40(2)). If such a question arises for the first time during the course of an appeal hearing the Court will if necessary adjourn the proceedings to enable the Registrar to give notice (Supreme Court Rules 2009, r 40(3); Supreme Court PD 9 para. 9.1.6).

III HUM [12]

6. Acts of public authorities

(1) It is unlawful for a public authority to act in a way which is incompatible with a Convention right.

(2) Subsection (1) does not apply to an act if—

(a) as the result of one or more provisions of primary legislation, the authority could not have acted differently; or

(b) in the case of one or more provisions of, or made under, primary legislation which cannot be read or given effect in a way which is compatible with the Convention rights, the authority was acting so as to give effect to or enforce those provisions.

(3) In this section "public authority" includes—

(a) a court or tribunal, and

(b) any person certain of whose functions are functions of a public nature,

but does not include either House of Parliament or a person exercising functions in connection with proceedings in Parliament.

(4) . . .

(5) In relation to a particular act, a person is not a public authority by virtue only of subsection (3)(b) if the nature of the act is private.

(6) "An act" includes a failure to act but does not include a failure to—

(a) introduce in, or lay before, Parliament a proposal for legislation; or

(b) make any primary legislation or remedial order

III HUM [12.1]

Public authority The definition in sub-s (3) of "public authority" includes the courts. A decision of a county court, for example, to commit an individual to prison, is unlawful if the individual is denied his or her rights under Arts 5 or 6, in particular. Public authorities which appear regularly as claimants in the county court include local authorities and government departments; if their claims are founded on acts which are incompatible with the Convention this issue may be raised by way of defence, under s 7(1)(b) below. "Tribunal" is given a broad definition in s 21(1) see para **III HUM [22]**.

An NHS Trust has been held to be a public authority for the purposes of s 6: *Frame v Grampian University Hospitals NHS Trust* [2004] HRLR 18, (2004) Times, 2 March, Court of Criminal Appeal in Scotland.

The Asylum and Immigration Tribunal is a public body which must exercise its appellant function in accordance with the Convention. The decision of the immigration officer is relevant but the Tribunal's role is not merely to review: it must establish the relevant facts which may well have changed since the original decision and then decide whether the impugned decision is lawful: *Huang v Secretary of State for the Home Department, Kashmiri v Same* [2007] 2 AC 167, [2007] 4 All ER 15, HL.

III HUM [12.1A]

Public authorities with private functions In *Aston Cantlow and Wilmcote with Billesley Parochial Church Council v Wallbank* [2003] UKHL 37, [2004] 1 AC 546, [2003] 3 All ER 1213 the House of Lords held, reversing the Court of Appeal, that a parochial church council was not a public authority since it was no different in substance from other private religious bodies although it was part of the established Church of England. The House of Lords approved the classification of bodies into pure or obvious public authorities, which are bound by the Human Rights Act in relation to all of their functions; and hybrid or functional public authorities, which are bound by the Act in relation to their public functions but not their private functions because of s 6(5).

A registered social landlord has been held to be a hybrid public authority and amenable to judicial review. The termination of a tenancy by such a body was not an act of private nature under the Human Rights Act 1998, s 6(5) and was in principle subject to human rights considerations: *R (on the application of Weaver) v London and Quadrant Housing Trust (Equality and Human Rights Commission intervening)* [2009] EWCA Civ 587, [2009] 4 All ER 865, [2009] 25 EG 137 (CS).

III HUM [12.1B]

Private and voluntary bodies with public functions A Housing Association which is set up by a local authority for the accommodation of homeless people may be a public authority to the extent that its functions include functions of a public nature. But the grant of a tenancy by a Housing Association is not necessarily a function of a public nature. A Housing Association's decision to seek a possession order under the Housing Act 1988 s 21(4) was held, in *Poplar Housing and Regeneration Community Association Ltd v Donoghue* [2001] EWCA Civ 595, [2002] QB 48, [2001] 4 All ER 604 to be an act of a public authority, on the facts of that case.

It was held, in *R (on the application of A) v Partnerships in Care Ltd* [2002] EWHC 529 (Admin), [2002] 1 WLR 2611, (2002) Times, 23 April, that a private psychiatric hospital performed public functions in relation to compulsory admissions under s 3 of the Mental Health Act 1983. The court had regard also to the hospital's statutory duty on registration to provide adequate professional staff and treatment facilities and to the public concern and interest in restoring patients to the community.

In *R (on the application of Heather) v Leonard Cheshire Foundation* [2002] EWCA Civ 366, [2002] 2 All ER 936, [2002] All ER (D) 326 (Mar), the Court considered whether a charitable foundation which ran a home for residents funded under the National Assistance Act 1948, ss 21(1) and 26(1) was a body performing public functions. The conclusion was that the foundation was not, although it was receiving public money. The local authority, on the other hand, owed the funded residents certain statutory duties and duties to respect their Convention rights.

III HUM [12.1C]

The provision of services by a private body under a contract made with a local authority Where a local authority is required, by s 21 of the National Assistance Act 1948, as amended, to arrange the provision of care and accommodation for an elderly person, and arranges for its provision under by a contract with a private care home, the functions performed by the care home have been held, by a majority decision of the House of Lords, not to be of a public nature: *YL v Birmingham City Council* [2007] UKHL 27, [2007] 3 All ER 957, (2007) Times, 21 June, Lord Bingham and Lady Hale dissenting).

III HUM [12.2]

Acts saved from illegality by sub-s (2) For an example of an act saved from illegality by sub-s (2) see the decision of the High Court in *R (on the application of Hooper) v Secretary of State for Work and Pensions* [2002] EWHC 191 (Admin) but note that on this point the Court of Appeal disagreed and set out the approach to be used in applying s 6(2)(a) and (b): [2003] EWCA Civ 813, [2003] 3 All ER 673, [2003] 1 WLR 2623, paras 109–119 and 136–137. The House of Lords held that there was no incompatibility in any event with the Convention: [2005] 1 WLR 1681.

Compliance with subordinate legislation does not save an act from illegality if the enabling powers under primary legislation could have been exercised in a way which did not infringe Convention rights: *R (on the application of Bono) v Harlow District Council* [2002] EWHC 423 (Admin), [2002] 1 WLR 2475, (2002) Times, 23 April.

Where a local authority has decided to claim possession of land within its caravan site and the site is excluded from the definition of "protected site" in s 5(1) of the Mobile Homes Act 1983, s 6(2)(b) saves the authority's decision from being unlawful under the Human Rights Act 1998. However, the judge hearing the claim for possession should refuse to make the order if satisfied that the authority's decision to evict was unreasonable in the *Wednesbury* (*Associated Provincial Picture Houses Ltd v Wednesbury Corpn* [1948] 1 KB 223) sense: *Doherty v Birmingham City Council* [2008] UKHL 57, [2008] 3 WLR 636.

III HUM [12.3]

Failure to introduce a proposal for legislation Where a provision has been held to be incompatible, a failure to introduce remedial legislation is excluded from illegality by sub-s (6): *R (on the application of Chester) v Secretary of State for Justice* (2009) Times, 3 November, [2009] All ER (D) 279 (Oct). The Court of Appeal in the same case stated that the Court would not give an opinion as to the legally proper content of the remedial legislation other than in very carefully controlled circumstances: [2011] 1 WLR 1436, (2011) Times, 17 January. The Supreme Court, dismissing a further appeal, emphasised that it was now for Parliament to consider the position and there was no further role for the court: [2013] UKSC 63, [2013] 3 WLR 1076.

III HUM [13]

7. Proceedings

(1) A person who claims that a public authority has acted (or proposes to act) in a way which is made unlawful by section 6 (1) may—

(a) bring proceedings against the authority under this Act in the appropriate court or tribunal, or

(b) rely on the Convention right or rights concerned in any legal proceedings,

but only if he is (or would be) a victim of the unlawful act.

(2) In subsection (1)(a) "appropriate court or tribunal" means such court or tribunal as may be determined in accordance with rules; and proceedings against an authority include a counterclaim or similar proceeding.

(3) If the proceedings are brought on an application for judicial review, the applicant is to be taken to have a sufficient interest in relation to the unlawful act only if he is, or would be, a victim of that act.

(4) If the proceedings are made by way of a petition for judicial review in Scotland, the applicant shall be taken to have title and interest to sue in relation to the unlawful act only if he is, or would be, a victim of that act.

(5) Proceedings under subsection (1)(a) must be brought before the end of—

(a) the period of one year beginning with the date on which the act complained of took place; or

(b) such longer period as the court or tribunal considers equitable having regard to all the circumstances,

but that is subject to any rule imposing a stricter time limit in relation to the procedure in question.

(6) In subsection (1)(b) "legal proceedings" includes—

(a) proceedings brought by or at the instigation of a public authority; and

(b) an appeal against the decision of a court or tribunal.

(7) For the purposes of this section, a person is a victim of an unlawful act only if he would be a victim for the purposes of Article 34 of the Convention if proceedings were brought in the European Court of Human Rights in respect of that act.

(8) Nothing in this Act creates a criminal offence.

(9) In this section "rules" means—

(a) in relation to proceedings before a court or tribunal outside Scotland, rules made by the Lord Chancellor or the Secretary of State for the purposes of this section or rules of court,

(b) in relation to proceedings before a court or tribunal in Scotland, rules made by the Secretary of State for those purposes,

(c) in relation to proceedings before a tribunal in Northern Ireland—

(i) which deals with transferred matters; and

(ii) for which no rules made under paragraph (a) are in force,

rules made by a Northern Ireland department for those purposes,

and includes provision made by order under section 1 of the Courts and Legal Services Act 1990.

(10) In making rules, regard must be had to section 9.

(11) The Minister who has power to make rules in relation to a particular tribunal may, to the extent he considers it necessary to ensure that the tribunal can provide an appropriate remedy in relation to an act (or proposed act) of a public authority which is (or would be) unlawful as a result of section 6 (1), by order add to—

(a) the relief or remedies which the tribunal may grant; or

(b) the grounds on which it may grant any of them.

(12) An order made under subsection (11) may contain such incidental, supplemental, consequential or transitional provision as the Minister making it considers appropriate.

(13) "The Minister" includes the Northern Ireland department concerned.

III HUM [13.1]

Appropriate court **CPR 7.11** provides that a claim under s 7(1)(a) in respect of a judicial act may be brought only in the High Court, whereas any other claim under s 7(1)(a) may be brought in any court. The implication is that damages for an unlawful *judicial* act by a county court district judge may not be sought by appeal to the circuit judge, but only by initiating a claim for damages in the High Court.

III HUM [13.1A]

Proceedings by a victim of the unlawful act A person is a "victim" under Art 34 of the Convention (and therefore under s 7(1) of the 1998 Act) only if directly and personally affected: *Norris v Ireland* (1988) 13 EHRR 186, ECtHR, (1998) Series A No 142, p 16, para 13; *Bowman v United Kingdom* (1998) 26 EHRR 1 (Case No 141/1996/762/959), ECtHR, decided 19 February 1998. Accordingly a representative body is not entitled to claim relief on behalf of its members, in the absence of a representative order by the court: *Re Medicaments and Related Classes of Goods (No 4)* [2001] 34 LS Gaz R 37, 145 Sol Jo LB 209, CA. It has been held that an NHS Trust cannot claim breach of its human rights since it falls outside the definition in Art 34 of a "victim": *Frame v Grampian University Hospitals NHS Trust* (2004) Times, 2 March, Court of Criminal Appeal in Scotland. It is not the intention of the Act that members of the public should use the provisions if they were not adversely affected: *Taylor v Lancashire County Council* [2005] EWCA Civ 284, [2005] HRLR 17. In *Savage v South East NHS Partnership NHS Foundation Trust* [2008] UKHL 74, [2009] 1 AC 681, [2009] 1 All ER 1053, where hospital authorities failed to prevent a patient's suicide, Lord Scott considered (*obiter*) that the daughter of the deceased could not properly be regarded as a 'victim' in relation to a breach of Art 2(1). In *Bank Mellat v Her Majesty's Treasury* [2015] EWHC 1258 (Comm), [2015] All ER (D) 112 (May) while the bank was a 'victim' when shut out of the UK financial sector by the Financial Restrictions (Iran) Order 2009, a UK subsidiary was only a secondary victim in the sense of being a 'relevant person' under the scheme who was directed not to do business with the bank (para 33; an appeal to the Court of Appeal is outstanding at time of writing).

III HUM [13.2]

Proceedings against the victim of the unlawful act It is already established in *Wandsworth London Borough Council v Winder* [1985] AC 461, [1984] 3 All ER 976, HL that a defendant may rely on a defence of ultra vires in relation to the acts on which the claimant's case is founded. Section 7(1)(b) extends the same principle to defending claims which are founded on acts which are incompatible with the Convention.

III HUM [13.3]

Disclosure in judicial review claims Where a judicial review claim on human rights grounds raises an issue of proportionality, the need for disclosure of documents may be greater than in other judicial review claims. However, there is no general proposition that there will be orders for disclosure in such cases. Disclosure will be ordered only where necessary, and even in proportionality cases this is likely to occur only in exceptional cases: *Tweed v Parades Commission for Northern Ireland* [2006] UKHL 53, [2007] 2 All ER 273.

III HUM [13.4]

Proceedings to be brought within one year The time limit in s 7(5)(a) is one year from the date of the act complained of. In a case where the act complained of was deprivation of possessions without compensation, the court rejected the argument that the failure to compensate was a continuing act so that the year never started to run: *Jeffrey v Secretary of State for Transport* [2004] EWHC 2772, [2005] UKHRR 154. But an extension was granted under s 7(5)(b) seeing that there had been no serious prejudice resulting from the delay.

The time limit in section 7(5) is a time limit of the same kind as in the Limitation Act 1980; a defence that the time limit has been exceeded is not a challenge to the jurisdiction and a claimant who seeks an extension under sub-sub-section (b) has the normal burden of proving supporting circumstances: *M (a minor by his litigation friend LT) v Ministry of Justice* [2009] EWCA Civ 419, [2009] NLJR 860.

Although the court has power to grant an extension of the time limit without a formal application being made, the norm is for extension to be granted only after consideration of an application to the court, on notice, that explains what is sought and why and exhibits the evidence relied upon: *O'Connor v Bar Standards Board* [2016] EWCA Civ 775, [2016] 1 WLR 4085. The Supreme Court did not address this aspect of the Court of Appeal's decision. The Supreme Court held that where the act complained of was a course of conduct, the one year time limit only began to run when that course of conduct had ended: *O'Connor v Bar Standards Board* [2017] UKSC 78, [2017] 1 WLR 4833.

An extension of three years was granted in *R (on the application of D) v Metropolitan Police Comr* [2012] EWHC 309 (QB), [2012] All ER (D) 162 (Feb), where the claim raised serious questions about the Police's failure to investigate a rape complaint and where the delay was caused by waiting for a funding decision from the Legal Services Commission which was necessary to enable the complainant to apply for anonymity before issuing her claim.

III HUM [14]

8. Judicial remedies

(1) In relation to any act (or proposed act) of a public authority which the court finds is (or would be) unlawful, it may grant such relief or remedy, or make such order, within its powers as it considers just and appropriate.

(2) But damages may be awarded only by a court which has power to award damages, or to order the payment of compensation, in civil proceedings.

(3) No award of damages is to be made unless, taking account of all the circumstances of the case, including—

- (a) any other relief or remedy granted, or order made, in relation to the act in question (by that or any other court), and
- (b) the consequences of any decision (of that or any other court) in respect of that act,

the court is satisfied that the award is necessary to afford just satisfaction to the person in whose favour it is made.

(4) In determining—

- (a) whether to award damages, or
- (b) the amount of an award,

the court must take into account the principles applied by the European Court of Human Rights in relation to the award of compensation under Article 41 of the Convention.

(5) A public authority against which damages are awarded is to be treated—

- (a) in Scotland, for the purposes of section 3 of the Law Reform (Miscellaneous Provisions) (Scotland) Act 1940 as if the award were made in an action of damages in which the authority has been found liable in respect of loss or damage to the person to whom the award is made;
- (b) for the purposes of the Civil Liability (Contribution) Act 1978 as liable in respect of damage suffered by the person to whom the award is made.

(6) In this section—

"court" includes a tribunal;

"damages" means damages for an unlawful act of a public authority; and "unlawful" means unlawful under section 6 (1).

III HUM [14.1]

A court which has power to award damages The county court has power, like the High Court, to award damages and is therefore competent to award damages for breach of the Convention under this section. But proceedings for damages in respect of a judicial act must be started in the High Court: see para **III HUM [15.1]** and **CPR 7.11**.

III HUM [14.2]

Awards of damages In *Marcic v Thames Water Utilities Ltd* [2001] 3 All ER 698, the defendant's decision to give a low priority to alleviating the recurrent flooding of the claimant's premises was held at first instance to be a continuing contravention of his right under Art 8(1) to respect for his home. The court further held that the measure of damage was the added value which the house would have gained if the defendant had put the necessary work in hand on 2 October 2000 when the Act came into force. The valuation should be made as at the notional date of completion of the work and interest awarded on the added value from that date down to the date of the award, if appropriate: *Marcic v Thames Water Utilities Ltd (No 2)* [2002] QB 1003, [2001] 4 All ER 326, [2001] 10 July, TCC 1998/224.

The Court of Appeal held that the common law right to damages for nuisance displaced the right under the Act to respect for one's home: *Marcic v Thames Water Utilities Ltd* [2002] EWCA Civ 65, [2002] QB 929, [2002] 2 All ER 55. The House of Lords reversed the lower courts and held that there was no breach. It held in particular that the statutory regime enacted by Parliament in the Water Industry Act 1991 was compatible with Art 8 and that no independent cause of action arose under the Human Rights Act: [2003] UKHL 66, [2004] 1 All ER 135, [2003] 3 WLR 1603. Note, however, that the Act may provide a right to damages for nuisance where the common law requirement of a proprietary interest is not satisfied: *McKenna v British Aluminium Ltd* (2002) Times, 25 April.

Where the defendant's activities amount to a common law nuisance which damages the interests of the proprietor of neighbouring land, the damages available to the proprietor at common law will almost invariably be just satisfaction of a claim for breach of Art 8. On the other hand, other persons who are in lawful occupation of the land but who have no right to damages at common law may, in some circumstances, show that an award to the proprietor together with a declaration of infringement will not be just satisfaction unless they too are awarded compensation: *Dobson v Thames Water Utilities Ltd* [2009] EWCA Civ 28, [2009] 3 All ER 319, 122 Con LR 32.

In *R (on the application of Bernard) v Enfield London Borough Council* [2003] EWHC 2282 (Admin), [2002] All ER (D) 383 (Oct), (2002) Times, 8 November, Sullivan J held that awards for distress and inconvenience caused by maladministration on the part of a local authority should be in line with awards by local government ombudsmen and that £10,000 was appropriate in a bad case. On the other hand where an interference by prison officers with a prisoner's correspondence with his solicitor is a breach of his human rights but causes no financial loss or substantial distress and inconvenience, there is no cause of action for misfeasance in office, nor is there any legal basis for awarding exemplary (as opposed to nominal) damages: *Watkins v Secretary of State for the Home Department* [2006] UKHL 17, [2006] 2 All ER 353, HL.

The power to award damages for breach of Convention rights is not limited by decisions before 1998 on remedies available at common law: *R (on the application of N) v Secretary of State for the Home Department* (2003) Times, 7 March, Silber J. This and related cases were considered in *Anufrijeva v London Borough of Southwark* [2003] EWCA Civ 1406, [2003] 3 FCR 673, (2003) Times, 17 October, in which the Court of Appeal set out guidelines for the award of damages for maladministration under the Human Rights Act. The Court stressed in particular the need to maintain a sense of proportion as between the damages likely to be awarded and the costs of litigation and that damages should not be awarded on the sole ground of delay. A breach would be more easily made out where the welfare of a child was at stake and had been prejudiced by the failure to provide welfare support.

A remedy in damages may lie where an authority refuses prior approval for planning permission but fails to serve the necessary notification and thereby deprives interested members of the public of the right to make representations: *R (on the application of Nunn) v First Secretary of State* [2005] EWCA Civ 101, (2005) Times, 23 February, CA.'

It has been held that damages may not be awarded to a doctor who has been improperly suspended from inclusion in a primary care trust's performers' list. The court rejected an argument that inclusion in the list was akin to a licence and constituted a possession within

Art 1 of the First Protocol. Nor was a livelihood a possession. Nor was the doctor's clientele a "possession", because the effect of statute was that this form of goodwill was not marketable: *R (on the application of Malik) v Waltham Forest Primary Care Trust* [2007] EWCA Civ 265, [2007] 4 All ER 832 CA.

In *R (on the application of MK Iran) v Secretary of State for the Home Department* [2010] EWCA Civ 115, [2010] 4 All ER 892, [2010] 1 WLR 2059 the Court of Appeal held that an asylum seeker could not claim damages for the unreasonable delay in the processing of his asylum application because asylum decisions do not engage Art 6 of the ECHR.

Damages should not be awarded on a tort basis but on the same 'just and equitable' basis as remedies in ECtHR: *R (on the application of Greenfield) v Secretary of State for the Home Department* [2005] UKHL 14, [2005] 1 WLR 673, which should be regarded as the leading domestic authority on damages for breach of Convention rights and in the light of which the earlier cases referred to above should be seen.

In *R (on the application of Infinis Plc) v Gas and Electricity Marketing Authority* [2013] EWCA Civ 70, , [2013] All ER (D) 152 (Feb), the Court of Appeal held that where the breach of a Convention right had clearly caused significant pecuniary loss that was readily calculable, that would usually be assessed and awarded. In that case restitution in integrum was appropriate.

In *R (on the application of Degainis) v Secretary of State for Justice* [2010] EWHC 137 (Admin), [2010] All ER (D) 35 (Feb) the claimant could not recover damages where there had been an unreasonable delay in securing a review of his release from prison, at least without evidence of his having suffered a sufficient degree of frustration and anxiety or of the delay extending the period spent in custody. An apology and acceptance of his complaint was held to be a sufficient remedy.

Similarly, Art 5 will not have been breached if a detainee is detained beyond the proper length of his sentence, provided it was done in accordance with proper procedures (*R (on the application of Brooks) v The Independent Adjudicator* [2016] EWCA Civ 1033).

III HUM [14.2A]

Necessary to afford just satisfaction 'Just satisfaction' refers to Art 41 (see s 8(4)) and the concept that an award of damages is not always necessary for the purpose of affording just satisfaction. Not every feeling of frustration and distress is to be compensated by damages; and awards in discrimination cases do not provide a reliable analogy. In *R (on the application of KB) v Mental Health Review Tribunal* [2003] EWHC 193 (Admin), [2004] QB 936, [2003] 2 All ER 209, claims were made in respect of delays in the hearing of applications under the Mental Health Act 1983 which should have been heard speedily as required by Art 5.4. Stanley Burnton J made awards of between £750 and £4,000 but in two cases made no awards in addition to the findings of infringement.

Where a patient is detained in breach of Art 5 but in accordance with domestic law (lawful authority) the compensation under Art 5.5 is not the sum which would be awarded in a case of false imprisonment: *R (on the application of W) v Doncaster Metropolitan Borough Council* [2003] EWHC 192 (Admin), (2003) Times, 12 March, Stanley Burnton J. See *Lee-Hirons v Secretary of State for Justice* [2016] UKSC 46, [2017] AC 52 where no damages were payable.

In *R (on the application of Faulkner) v Secretary of State for Justice and the Parole Board* [2011] EWCA Civ 349, [2011] HRLR 23, [2011] 05 LS Gaz R 20, the Supreme Court dealt with remedies issues following the Court of Appeal's finding that unlawful delays in dealing with a parole application had probably prolonged the claimant's detention by ten months. Continued detention contrary to Art 5(4), unlike false imprisonment, involved only the loss of the opportunity to be granted conditional liberty within the currency of a lawful custodial sentence. The claimant's award was reduced from £10,000 to £6,500. Another appellant, who on the balance of probabilities would not have been released earlier but who suffered stress and anxiety during a delay of 6 months, was awarded £300. The Supreme Court also gave guidance on the citation of ECtHR authorities in such cases: *R (on the application of Faulkner) v Secretary of State for Justice; R (on the application of Sturnham) v Parole Board* [2013] UKSC 23, [2013] 2 All ER 1013, [2013] 2 WLR 1157.

In a case where a claimant who has been granted entry clearance has sustained financial loss as the foreseeable consequence of immigration officers mistakenly imposing conditions, contrary to the established practice, the court may properly conclude that it is necessary to award damages in order to provide just satisfaction for the loss caused by a breach of duty which it would be just, fair and reasonable to impose: *R (on the application of A) v Secretary of State for the Home Department* [2004] EWHC 1585 (Admin), [2004] All ER (D) 91 (Jul).

In *Whitfield v United Kingdom (Application Nos 46387/99, 48906/99, 57410/00 and 57419/00)* (2005) Times, 27 April, ECtHR, the European Court of Human Rights determined that disciplinary proceedings against various prisoners for breach of the Prison Rules contravened Art 6 by not allowing legal representation or providing an independent and impartial tribunal. But in all cases save one the Court concluded that the findings of violation constituted sufficient just satisfaction; so damages were not awarded. There was a similar outcome in *R (on the application of Greenfield) v Secretary of State for the Home Department* [2005] UKHL 14, [2005] 2 All ER 240.

In the case of a breach of Art 8 by a local authority, in failing to consult the mother before abandoning a care plan for her rehabilitation with her only child, the court granted a declaration of breach but refused monetary compensation as unnecessary to afford just satisfaction, seeing that the breach was no more than a procedural failure and she had not lost any real opportunity to change the decision: *Re P* [2007] EWCA Civ 2, (2007) HRLR 14, (2007) Times, 1 February.

III HUM [14.3]

No power to award damages where procedural breach prevented Where the Court of Appeal prevents a breach of Art 6 by upholding a decision of the court below to abandon a hearing because of apparent bias, there is no power to order the Lord Chancellor to pay the wasted costs under s 8 of the Human Rights Act 1998: *Re Medicaments and Related Classes of Goods (No 4)* [2001] EWCA Civ 1217, [2002] 1 WLR 269; *Director General of Fair Trading v Proprietary Association of Great Britain* [2001] EWCA Civ 1217, [2002] 1 All ER 843.

III HUM [14.4]

Damages claimed in an application for judicial review If a claim for judicial review includes a claim for damages for breach of the Human Rights Act 1998 the claim must be properly pleaded and particularised and should set out the principles applied by the ECHR in relation to awards of compensation under Art 41 of the Convention which are said to be relevant (s 8(4) of the Human Rights Act 1998): *R (on the application of Fayad) v Secretary of State for Home Department* [2018] EWCA Civ 54, (2018) Times, 8 February.

III HUM [15]

9. Judicial acts

(1) Proceedings under section 7(1)(a) in respect of a judicial act may be brought only—

- (a) by exercising a right of appeal;
- (b) on an application (in Scotland a petition) for judicial review; or
- (c) in such other forum as may be prescribed by rules.

(2) That does not affect any rule of law which prevents a court from being the subject of judicial review.

(3) In proceedings under this Act in respect of a judicial act done in good faith, damages may not be awarded otherwise than to compensate a person to the extent required by Article 5(5) of the Convention.

(4) An award of damages permitted by subsection (3) is to be made against the Crown; but no award may be made unless the appropriate person, if not a party to the proceedings, is joined.

(5) In this section—

"appropriate person" means the Minister responsible for the court concerned, or a person or government department nominated by him;

"court" includes a tribunal;

"judge" includes a member of a tribunal, a justice of the peace (or, in Northern Ireland, a lay magistrate) and a clerk or other officer entitled to exercise the jurisdiction of a court;

"judicial act" means a judicial act of a court and includes an act done on the instructions, or on behalf, of a judge; and

"rules" has the same meaning as in section 7(9).

III HUM [15.1]

Proceedings under section 7(1)(a) Proceedings under s 7(1)(a) in respect of a judicial act may be brought only in the High Court and not in the county court: see **CPR 7.11**. Notice has to be given to the Crown in accordance with **CPR 19.4A** and para 6.6 of the Practice Direction—Addition and Substitution of Parties at **CPR PD 19A**. Any other claim may be brought in any court, including the county court: see **CPR 7.11**. This means that the county court may be able to rule on, for example, the lawfulness of decisions by local authorities, the police or central government and to award damages in accordance with s 8.

III HUM [15.2]

Damages for unlawful detention for contempt In *LL v Lord Chancellor (Liability)* [2017] EWCA Civ 237, [2017] 4 WLR 162 the Court of Appeal allowed a claim for damages for breach of Art 5 brought by a father who had been wrongly committed to prison for contempt of court by a High Court Judge. Errors made by the Judge, when viewed cumulatively, amounted to a 'gross and obvious procedural irregularity' which could not be justified.

III HUM [16]

10. Power to take remedial action

(1) This section applies if—

(a) a provision of legislation has been declared under section 4 to be incompatible with a Convention right and, if an appeal lies—

(i) all persons who may appeal have stated in writing that they do not intend to do so;

(ii) the time for bringing an appeal has expired and no appeal has been brought within that time; or

(iii) an appeal brought within that time has been determined or abandoned; or

(b) it appears to a Minister of the Crown or Her Majesty in Council that, having regard to a finding of the European Court of Human Rights made after the coming into force of this section in proceedings against the United Kingdom, a provision of legislation is incompatible with an obligation of the United Kingdom arising from the Convention.

(2) If a Minister of the Crown considers that there are compelling reasons for proceeding under this section, he may by order make such amendments to the legislation as he considers necessary to remove the incompatibility.

(3) If, in the case of subordinate legislation, a Minister of the Crown considers—

(a) that it is necessary to amend the primary legislation under which the subordinate legislation in question was made, in order to enable the incompatibility to be removed, and

(b) that there are compelling reasons for proceeding under this section,

he may by order make such amendments to the primary legislation as he considers necessary.

(4) This section also applies where the provision in question is in subordinate legislation and has been quashed, or declared invalid, by reason of incompatibility with a Convention right and the Minister proposes to proceed under paragraph 2 (b) of Schedule 2.

(5) If the legislation is an Order in Council, the power conferred by subsection (2) or (3) is exercisable by Her Majesty in Council.

(6) In this section "legislation" does not include a Measure of the Church Assembly or of the General Synod of the Church of England.

(7) Schedule 2 makes further provision about remedial orders.

III HUM [16.1]

Remedial orders A number of remedial orders have been made. The first was the Mental Health Act 1983 (Remedial) Order 2001 (SI 2001/3712), which was enacted in response to the declaration of incompatibility made in *R (on the application of H) v London North and East Regional Mental Health Review Tribunal* [2001] EWCA Civ 415, [2002] QB 1 and amended ss 72 and 73 of the Mental Health Act 1983. The next was the Naval Discipline Act 1957 (Remedial) Order 2004 (SI 2004/66), which made various amendments in response to the decision of the European Court of Human Rights in *Grieves v United Kingdom* (Application 57067/00), (2004) Times, 12 January, which held that there had been a breach of Art 6(1) of the Convention because the position of the judge advocate in a court-martial was not sufficiently independent. The Marriage Act 1949 (Remedial) Order 2007, SI 2007/438 repealed provisions which prohibited marriages between a person and a parent of their former spouse or the former spouse of the person's child, following the decision of the European Court of Human Rights in *B and L v UK* [2006] 42 EHRR 11. More recently the Terrorism Act 2000 (Remedial) Order 2011 (SI 2011/631) repealed and amended stop and search powers under ss 44-47 of the Terrorism Act 2000, and the Sexual Offences Act 2003 (Remedial) Order 2012 amended the indefinite notification requirements of s 82 of the 2003 Act following *R (on the application by JF (by his litigation friend OF)) v Secretary of State for the Home Department* [2010] UKSC 17, [2010] 2 All ER 707, [2010] 2 WLR 992.

III HUM [17]

11. Safeguard for existing human rights

A person's reliance on a Convention right does not restrict–

(a) any other right or freedom conferred on him by or under any law having effect in any part of the United Kingdom; or

(b) his right to make any claim or bring any proceedings which he could make or bring apart from sections 7–9.

III HUM [18]

12. Freedom of expression

(1) This section applies if a court is considering whether to grant any relief which, if granted, might affect the exercise of the Convention right to freedom of expression.

(2) If the person against whom the application for relief is made ("the respondent") is neither present nor represented, no such relief is to be granted unless the court is satisfied—

(a) that the applicant has taken all practicable steps to notify the respondent; or

(b) that there are compelling reasons why the respondent should not be notified.

(3) No such relief is to be granted so as to restrain publication before trial unless the court is satisfied that the applicant is likely to establish that publication should not be allowed.

(4) The court must have particular regard to the importance of the Convention right to freedom of expression and, where the proceedings relate to material which the respondent claims, or which appears to the court, to be journalistic, literary or artistic material (or to conduct connected with such material), to—

(a) the extent to which—

(i) the material has, or is about to, become available to the public; or

(ii) it is, or would be, in the public interest for the material to be published;

(b) any relevant privacy code.

(5) In this section—

"court" includes a tribunal; and

"relief" includes any remedy or order (other than in criminal proceedings).

III HUM [18.1]

The Convention right to freedom of expression The right to freedom of expression is set out in Art 10. For the text of the article and discussion of cases see **III HUM [32]**.

III HUM [18.2]

Publication of confidential material The requirements of sub-s (2) are mandatory. Relief will be refused if the respondent is neither present nor represented – unless the applicant submits cogent evidence which satisfies the requirements of paragraph (a) or (b). The applicant must show that all practicable steps have been taken to notify the respondent of the application or, alternatively, that compelling reasons exist why the respondent should not be so notified. The applicant must not overlook these requirements. *Kerner v WX* [2015]

EWHC 128 (QB), [2015] All ER (D) 214 (Jan) is an example where an injunction was not granted restraining publication of photographs as there had been no notice given to the media, against whom it was sort (although an injunction restraining harassment was granted against 'persons unknown').

III HUM [18.3]

Satisfying the court that relief should be granted The HL allowed an appeal against the grant of an interim injunction in *Cream Holdings Ltd v Banerjee* [2004] UKHL 44, [2004] 4 All ER 617, (2004) Times 15 October. They held the test to be a broad one of "sufficiently likely [to succeed at the trial] to justify making an interim restraint order". They added that this test would generally require an applicant to cross the "more likely than not" threshold, but that a lower degree of likelihood might suffice where the adverse consequences of disclosure were particularly grave or where a short-lived injunction was sought pending the hearing of an application for relief or an appeal. On the facts they concluded that the threshold had not been crossed and that the public interest clearly supported disclosure.

In *John v Associated Newspapers Ltd* [2006] EWHC 1611, (QB), [2006] EMLR 772, the court refused an application for an interim injunction to restrain publication of a photograph of Elton John outside his house, taken without his permission: the court applied the principles in *Cream Holdings v Banerjee*. See, more recently, *CSC Computer Sciences Limited v Price* [2015] EWHC 2438 where Kerr J followed *Cream Holdings* and restrained an ex-employee from threatening individuals working for an employer despite the impact on his freedom of expression.

On the other hand, where a claimant had had an adulterous relationship with the defendant's wife the court held on the particular facts of the case that, in order to protect the claimant's family life an interim injunction should be granted restraining the defendant from publicising the adultery in the media for no better reason than spite, money-making and tittle-tattle: *CC v AB* [2006] EWHC 3083 (QB), [2007] EMLR 312, Eady J, QBD. Similarly, in *AMM v HXW* [2010] EWHC 2457 (QB), [2010] NLJR 1425 an injunction was granted to prohibit the disclosure of information by an alleged blackmailer about the marriage and sexual relationships of a television star. See, too, *AMC v News Group Newspapers* [2015] EWHC 2361 (QB), [2015] All ER (D) 38 (Aug): an injunction was granted to restrain publication about a sportsman's affair after a relationship with his future wife was ongoing, but before the marriage. The fact of a person being a public figure did not of itself make that person's sexual history public property.

See also *Boehringer Ingelheim Ltd v Vetplus Ltd* [2007] EWCA Civ 583, (2007) Times, 27 June, in which the Court of Appeal ruled that the *Cream* test applies to a case of trademark infringement in a comparative advertising case, refusing to grant an interim injunction because the claimant had not shown that it was more likely than not to obtain a final injunction at trial.

"Any relevant privacy code" in s 12(4) will include the Codes of Practice established by the Press Complaints Commission or Ofcom: *Douglas v Hello! Ltd* [2001] QB 967, [2001] 2 All ER 289, CA. It is submitted that it should also include the BBC's Producer Guidelines as well as any "in house" code on privacy.

In *Mills v News Group Newspapers Ltd* [2001] EMLR 957, the court considered not only the PCC's Code of Practice but also its adjudications under Clause 3 (Privacy) of the PCC Code.

It has been held that there is no confidentiality in the outcome of complaints to the Law Society and accordingly no basis for granting an interim injunction against publication: *Napier v Pressdram Ltd* [2009] EWCA Civ 443, [2009] NLJR 859, (2009) Times, 2 June.

In *Ashworth v Royal National Theatre* [2014] EWHC 1176 (QB), [2014] 4 All ER 238, 164 NLJ 7604, the Court refused an application for specific performance of musicians' contracts of employment or mandatory injunction requiring the theatre to re-engage them. Inter alia, granting the applications would interfere with the theatre's Art 10 rights to stage the play as it considered artistically preferable and was not necessary or proportionate to protect the musicians' rights.

III HUM [18.4]

The public interest It was held, in *A v B (a company)* [2002] EWCA Civ 337, [2003] QB 195, [2002] 2 All ER 545, that it is not for a newspaper to demonstrate the public interest in disclosure but for the claimant to justify restraining the exercise of free expression. On the facts the case for privacy was not strong given that the relationships were transitory and the other parties favoured disclosure. Note that the 'supermodel' Naomi Campbell was successful in the House of Lords mainly because of the importance of protecting privacy in matters of health and addiction: *Campbell v Mirror Group Newspapers plc* [2004] UKHL 22, [2004] 2 AC 457, [2004] 2 All ER 995. Similarly in a documentary broadcast about the adoption process the right of a particular mother and daughter to privacy was held to outweigh the BBC's freedom of expression in the public interest: *T v BBC* [2007] EWHC 1683 (QB), [2008] 2 FCR 497, [2008] 1 FLR 281, Eady J, QBD. More recently, in *Khuja v Times*

Newspapers Ltd [2017] UKSC 49, [2017] 3 WLR 351 the Supreme Court held that the balance between Arts 8 and 10 was fact specific, neither right being in principle stronger than the other, and that in striking the balance, regard should be had to their comparative importance in the particular circumstances. There, the publication of the name of a person suspected of involvement in (but not charged with) a serious crime could be published. Members of the public could be expected not to equate suspicion with guilt when assessing reports of arrest without charge. In *PJS v News Group Newspapers Ltd* [2016] UKSC 26, [2016] AC 1081 the Supreme Court held that engaging in adultery involving more than one person at the same time did not, without more, give rise to public interest in the legal sense, however much it might interest the public.

In another case, where a well-known television presenter had sex with a prostitute, there was held to be a public interest in making it public, because of his portrayal as an appropriate person to present programmes aimed at young viewers: *Theakston v MGN Ltd* [2002] EWHC 137 (QB), [2002] All ER (D) 182 (Feb). In a case about the captain of the England football team, who had written about himself as a faithful family man, the court favoured the newspaper's right to publicise his affair with another woman as having greater force than his right to protect his private life: *Ferdinand v MGN Ltd* [2011] EWHC 2454 (QB), [2011] All ER (D) 04 (Oct).

In *Mills v News Group Newspapers Ltd* [2001] EMLR 957, the court refused to continue an injunction to restrain a newspaper from publishing the newly acquired address of a well-known model; the evidence of potential harm resulting from disclosure was not sufficiently cogent.

It was observed in *Prudential Assurance Co Ltd v Prudential Insurance Co of America* [2002] EWHC 2809 (Ch), [2002] All ER (D) 337 (Dec), (2003) Times, 2 January by Sir Andrew Morritt V-C that there was a need to apply the without prejudice rule with restraint and only in cases to which the public interests underlying the rule were plainly applicable. This is because the Art 10 right to receive and impart information is engaged.

It was held in *Tillery Valley Foods Ltd v Channel Four Television Corpn* [2004] EWHC 1075 (Ch), (2004) Times, 21 May that where the publication of confidential information was justified in the public interest the publisher was not obliged to give the owner of the information a right to respond or reply before publication.

Where the information has obviously been imparted subject to a duty of confidentiality there is a public interest in upholding the duties of confidence, this being a factor that Art 10.2 recognises as capable of justifying restriction on freedom of expression: *HRH Prince of Wales v Associated Newspapers Ltd* [2006] EWCA Civ 1776, [2007] 2 All ER 139, (2006) Times, 28 December.

It has been held that it is not for the media to expose sexual conduct which does not involve a significant breach of the law and that the public interest may not be relied on in support of publication unless exposure of the conduct prevents the public from being misled or calls into question the fitness of the individuals concerned for a responsible role in their organisation: *Mosley v News Group Newspapers Ltd* [2008] EWHC 1777 QB, (2008) Times, 30 July, Eady J.

In *R (on the application of Core Issues Trust) v Transport for London* [2014] EWCA Civ 34, [2014] PTSR 785, [2014] EqLR 164 it was held that a decision by TFL to refuse to accept advertising by a Christian organisation on London buses did not infringe Art 10 because it pursued the legitimate aims of avoiding causing serious offence to the public, protecting the rights of others, and complying with statutory duties under section 149 of the Equality Act 2010, having regard also to the fact that there were many other ways in which the advertiser could express its opinions and to the impact on the Art 8 rights of gay people who would be offended by the proposed advertisement.

III HUM [18.5]

Restraining publicity Where a child will suffer as a result of newspaper publicity given to a parent's criminal trial, Art 8 is engaged. But Art 10 is also engaged because full contemporaneous reporting of criminal trials in progress promotes public confidence in the administration of justice and promotes the values of the rule of law. An injunction to protect the child (or indeed an adult) by preventing the publication of the defendant's name during the trial would have a chilling effect on reporting by local and regional newspapers which would impoverish public discussion of criminal justice; for this reason in particular an injunction was refused in *Re S (a Child) (Identification: Restrictions on publication)* [2004] UKHL 47, [2004] 4 All ER 883, (2004) Times, 29 October. Where information that a convicted paedophile is the sole carer of vulnerable young children has already been in the public domain the court may nevertheless grant an injunction with a qualified open court reporting proviso as regards the reporting of proceedings for child sex offences against another member of the family: *F v Newsquest Ltd* [2004] EWHC 762, [2004] EMLR 29. An injunction to restrain the identification of parents in criminal proceedings was granted for the protection of the privacy of the children in *Re W (Children) (Identification: Restrictions on Publication)* (2005) Times, 21 July, CA. See also the President of the Family Division's *Practice Direction: Applications for reporting Restriction Orders, 18 March 2005.*

However, the BBC's Art 10 rights to broadcast the circumstances of an acquittal outweighed the Art 8 rights of a criminal defendant acquitted of rape: *Re S (a child) (identification: restrictions on publication)* [2004] UKHL 47, [2005] 1 AC 593, [2004] 4 All ER 683; *A-G's Reference (No 3 of 1999), Re British Broadcasting Corpn* [2009] UKHL 34, [2010] 1 All ER 235, [2009] 3 WLR 142.

In *Spelman (by his litigation friends) v Express Newspapers* [2012] EWHC 239 (QB), [2012] 09 LS Gaz R 18 the court granted an injunction prohibiting publication of a story about the 17-year-old son of a Cabinet minister where he had a reasonable expectation of privacy and it was probable that publication would have a very significant harmful effect on him.

The striking of a balance between the right to freedom of expression and an individual's right to private or family life under Art 8 will be fact-specific in every case: *Hutcheson v News Group Newspapers Ltd* [2011] EWCA Civ 808, [2012] EMLR 38. See also now *Khuja v Times Newspapers Ltd* [2017] UKSC 49, [2017] 3 WLR 351.

The court may properly publicise a decision in family proceedings heard in private where the issues are already being reported on in the public domain but inaccurately: *Blunkett v Quinn* [2004] EWHC 2816 (Fam), [2004] All ER (D) 49 (Dec), (2004) Times, 7 December, Ryder J.

The court is also empowered to make an order prohibiting the identification of a child for a period beyond the end of the proceedings in order to protect his Art 8 rights: *Clayton v Clayton* [2006] EWCA Civ 878, [2007] 1 All ER 1197.

Proceedings in the Court of Protection are normally heard in private since this is required by r 90 of the Court of Protection Rules 2007 (SI 2007/1744), made under the Mental Capacity Act 2005. However, the Court has the power, on an application under r 93(1)(a), to allow media representatives to attend and to authorise publication, if there is a good reason for doing so. Article 10 of the Convention is engaged when an application is made. The court must decide whether good reason is made out and if so must then conduct a balancing exercise weighing the competing policies under Art 10 and Art 8: *Independent News and Media Ltd v A* [2010] EWCA Civ 343, [2010] 3 All ER 32, [2010] 2 FCR 187. Previous press interest in a case and the legitimate public interest in the court's powers amounted to a good reason which was not outweighed by an incapacitated person's Art 8 rights in *P (by his litigation friend the Official Solicitor) v Independent Print Ltd* [2011] EWCA Civ 756, [2011] Fam Law 1081, [2011] All ER (D) 36 (Jul). For the relevant factors in the balancing exercise see also *W (by her litigation friend B) v M (by her litigation friend, the Official Solicitor)* [2012] 1 FCR 1.

III HUM [18.5A]

Anonymity Orders The court's decision whether or not to grant anonymity to a party or witness to proceedings is a matter of obligation, not discretion, based on a balancing of the Art 8 and Art 10 factors: *AMM v HXW* [2010] EWHC 2457 (QB), [2010] All ER (D) 48 (Oct) per Tugendhat J at paragraphs 31, 34-35, in which an injunction was granted to prohibit publication which had been threatened by a blackmailer and an anonymity order was made as well.

In contrast an anonymity order was refused in a case where the claimant had not shown to the high standard required by Art 6 that the objective of achieving justice in the case would be rendered doubtful if the anonymity order were not made: *JIH v News Group Newspapers Ltd* [2011] EWCA Civ 42, [2011] 2 All ER 324, [2011] 1 WLR 1645, in which it was also said that the general rule that parties to civil proceedings should be named is based on open justice and the Art 10 rights of the public; there is no general exception for privacy cases and no special treatment for celebrities. Any application for anonymity or a restriction on normally reportable details of the case should be made on notice, unless good reasons are advanced for not doing so, and should not be ordered by reason only of the consent of the parties. The issue for decision on such an application is whether there is sufficient general, public interest in publishing a party's name and/or the normally reportable details to justify the curtailment of that party's Art 8 rights. Whether or not an anonymity order is made, a publicly available judgment should normally be given and a copy of the consequential court order should also be publicly available, although some editing of the judgment or order may be necessary. Any order restricting publication of a name or case details should be limited in time to a return date.

In *Spelman (by his litigation friends) v Express Newspapers* [2012] EWHC 239 (QB), [2012] 09 LS Gaz R 18 (see **III HUM [18.5]**) although publication was restrained, anonymisation of the court proceedings was not considered necessary.

III HUM [18.5B]

Information in the public domain A court should not grant an injunction to restrain the publication of information on the ground of confidentiality once that information has become so generally accessible within the public domain that it has lost its confidential character: *BBC v HarperCollins Ltd* [2010] EWHC 2424 (Ch), [2010] NLJR 1426.

III HUM [18.5C]

Order against unknown persons The Court may grant relief against persons unknown in an appropriate case: see eg *Bloomsbury Publishing Group plc v New Group Newspapers Ltd* [2003] 1 WLR 1633 in which the Court held that the description of the persons concerned was sufficiently certain. See also *Middleton v Persons Unknown* [2016] EWHC 2354 in which the Court granted an injunction against persons unknown in a case where private information was obtained by hacking into the claimant's iCloud account.

III HUM [18.6]

Libel Where a defendant maintains a defence of justification, the court should not grant an interim injunction against publication unless it is plain that the defence will fail: *Bonnard v Perryman* [1891] 2 Ch 269, CA. This proposition has been approved and applied by the Court of Appeal as not having been affected by the enactment of s 12(3) of the Human Rights Act 1998: *Greene v Associated Newspapers Ltd* [2004] EWCA Civ 1462, [2005] 1 All ER 30, (2004) Times, 10 November. See also *Francotyp-Postalia Ltd v Mailing Room Ltd (formerly FP Mailing (North West) Ltd* [2015] EWCA Civ 1167, [2015] All ER (D) 246 (Nov).

The common law rule that a libel does not require proof of damage is not incompatible with Art 10. However, where a trading company had suffered no actual financial loss as a result of a defamatory statement any damages awarded should be kept strictly within modest bounds: *Jameel and Jameel v Wall Street Journal Europe SPRL* [2006] UKHL 44, [2006] 4 All ER 1279, CA.

III HUM [19]

13. Freedom of thought, conscience and religion

(1) If a court's determination of any question arising under this Act might affect the exercise by a religious organisation (itself or its members collectively) of the Convention right to freedom of thought, conscience and religion, it must have particular regard to the importance of that right.

(2) In this section "court" includes a tribunal.

III HUM [19.1]

The Convention right to freedom of thought The Convention right to freedom of thought, conscience and religion is set out in Art 9. For the text of the article and discussion of cases see **III HUM [31]**. The s 13 duty was applied by the court in *City of London v Samede* [2012] EWHC 34 (QB), [2012] 05 LS Gaz R 21, (2012) Times, 27 January in which the Art 9 rights of worshippers at St Paul's Cathedral prevailed over the rights under Arts 10 and 11 of those wishing to maintain a protest camp outside the cathedral. Compare *R (on the application of Gallastegui) v Westminster City Council and Comr of the Police for the Metropolis and Secretary of State for the Home Department* [2012] EWHC 1123 (Admin), [2012] 4 All ER 401, [2012] LGR 789, in which the rights of protesters were not infringed by legislation empowering the authorities to stop them erecting and using tents in Parliament Square.

III HUM [20]

19. Statements of compatibility

(1) A Minister of the Crown in charge of a Bill in either House of Parliament must, before Second Reading of the Bill—

(a) make a statement to the effect that in his view the provisions of the Bill are compatible with the Convention rights ("a statement of compatibility"); or

(b) make a statement to the effect that although he is unable to make a statement of compatibility the government nevertheless wishes the House to proceed with the Bill.

(2) The statement must be in writing and be published in such manner as the Minister making it considers appropriate.

III HUM [21]

20. Orders etc under this Act

(1) Any power of a Minister of the Crown to make an order under this Act is exercisable by statutory instrument.

(2) The power of the Lord Chancellor or the Secretary of State to make rules (other than rules of court) under section 2 (3) or 7 (9) is exercisable by statutory instrument.

(3) Any statutory instrument made under section 14, 15 or 16 (7) must be laid before Parliament.

(4) No order may be made by the Lord Chancellor or the Secretary of State under section 1 (4), 7 (11) or 16 (2) unless a draft of the order has been laid before, and approved by, each House of Parliament.

(5) Any statutory instrument made under section 18 (7) or Schedule 4, or to which subsection (2) applies, shall be subject to annulment in pursuance of a resolution of either House of Parliament.

(6) The power of a Northern Ireland department to make—

(a) rules under section 2 (3)(c) or 7 (9)(c), or

(b) an order under section 7 (11), is exercisable by statutory rule for the purposes of the Statutory Rules (Northern Ireland) Order 1979.

(7) Any rules made under section 2 (3)(c) or 7 (9)(c) shall be subject to negative resolution; and section 41 (6) of the Interpretation Act Northern Ireland) 1954 (meaning of "subject to negative resolution") shall apply as if the power to make the rules were conferred by an Act of the Northern Ireland Assembly.

(8) No order may be made by a Northern Ireland department under section 7 (11) unless a draft of the order has been laid before, and approved by, the Northern Ireland Assembly.

III HUM [22]

21. Interpretation etc

(1) In this Act—

"amend" includes repeal and apply (with or without modifications);

"the appropriate Minister" means the Minister of the Crown having charge of the appropriate authorised government department (within the meaning of the Crown Proceedings Act 1947);

"the Commission" means the European Commission of Human Rights;

"the Convention" means the Convention for the Protection of Human Rights and Fundamental Freedoms, agreed by the Council of Europe at Rome on 4th November 1950 as it has effect for the time being in relation to the United Kingdom;

"declaration of incompatibility" means a declaration under section 4;

"Minister of the Crown" has the same meaning as in the Ministers of the Crown Act 1975;

"Northern Ireland Minister" includes the First Minister and the deputy First Minister in Northern Ireland;

"primary legislation" means any—

(a) public general Act;

(b) local and personal Act;

(c) private Act;

(d) Measure of the Church Assembly;

(e) Measure of the General Synod of the Church of England;

(f) Order in Council—

(i) made in exercise of Her Majesty's Royal Prerogative;

(ii) made under section 38(1)(a) of the Northern

Ireland Constitution Act 1973 or the corresponding provision of the Northern Ireland Act 1998; or

(iii) amending an Act of a kind mentioned in paragraph (a), (b) or (c);

and includes an order or other instrument made under primary legislation (otherwise than by the Welsh Ministers, the First Minister for Wales, the Counsel General to the Welsh Assembly Government, a member of the Scottish Executive, a Northern Ireland Minister or a Northern Ireland department) to the extent to which it operates to bring one or more provisions of that legislation into force or amends any primary legislation;

"the First Protocol" means the protocol to the Convention agreed at Paris on 20th March 1952;

"the Eleventh Protocol" means the protocol to the Convention (restructuring the control machinery established by the Convention) agreed at Strasbourg on 11th May 1994;

"the Thirteenth Protocol" means the protocol to the Convention (concerning the abolition of the death penalty in all circumstances) agreed at Vilnius on 3rd May 2002;

"remedial order" means an order under section 10;

"subordinate legislation" means any—

(a) Order in Council other than one—

(i) made in exercise of Her Majesty's Royal Prerogative;

(ii) made under section 38(1)(a) of the Northern Ireland Constitution Act 1973 or the corresponding provision of the Northern Ireland Act 1998; or

(iii) amending an Act of a kind mentioned in the definition of primary legislation;

(b) Act of the Scottish Parliament;

(ba) Measure of the National Assembly for Wales;

(bb) Act of the National Assembly for Wales;

(c) Act of the Parliament of Northern Ireland;

(d) Measure of the Assembly established under section 1 of the Northern Ireland Assembly Act 1973;

(e) Act of the Northern Ireland Assembly;

(f) order, rules, regulations, scheme, warrant, byelaw or other instrument made under primary legislation (except to the extent to which it operates to bring one or more provisions of that legislation into force or amends any primary legislation);

(g) order, rules, regulations, scheme, warrant, byelaw or other instrument made under legislation mentioned in paragraph (b), (c), (d) or (e) or made under an Order in Council applying only to Northern Ireland;

(h) order, rules, regulations, scheme, warrant, byelaw or other instrument made by a member of the Scottish Executive, Welsh Ministers, the First Minister for Wales, the Counsel General to the Welsh Assembly Government, a Northern Ireland Minister or a Northern Ireland department in exercise of prerogative or other executive functions of Her Majesty which are exercisable by such a person on behalf of Her Majesty;

"transferred matters" has the same meaning as in the Northern Ireland Act 1998; and

"tribunal" means any tribunal in which legal proceedings may be brought.

(2) The references in paragraphs (b) and (c) of section 2(1) to Articles are to Articles of the Convention as they had effect immediately before the coming into force of the 11th Protocol.

(3) The reference in paragraph (d) of section 2(1) to Article 46 includes a reference to Articles 32 and 54 of the Convention as they had effect immediately before the coming into force of the 11th Protocol.

(4) The references in section 2(1) to a report or decision of the Commission or a decision of the Committee of Ministers include references to a report or decision made as provided by paragraphs 3, 4 and 6 of Article 5 of the 11th Protocol (transitional provisions).

(5) . . .

III HUM [23]

22. Short title, commencement, application and extent

(1) This Act may be cited as the Human Rights Act 1998.

(2) Sections 18 and 20 and this section come into force on the passing of this Act.

(3) The other provisions of this Act come into force on such day as the Secretary of State may by order appoint; and different days may be appointed for different purposes.

(4) Paragraph (b) of subsection (1) of section 7 applies to proceedings brought by or at the instigation of a public authority whenever the act in question took place; but otherwise that subsection does not apply to an act committed before the coming into force of that section.

(5) This Act binds the Crown.

(6) This Act extends to Northern Ireland.

(7) . . .

III HUM [23.1]

Commencement The Act was brought fully into force on 2 October 2000 by SI 2000/1851, although certain provisions, such as section 19, had been brought into force earlier.

III HUM [23.2]

Proceedings brought by or at the instigation of a public authority The Court of Appeal has held that applications for judicial review are proceedings brought by the applicant, not "proceedings brought by or at the instigation of a public authority": *R (on the application of Ben-Abdelaziz) v Haringey London Borough Council* [2001] EWCA Civ 803, [2001] 1 WLR 1485, [2001] 26 LS Gaz R 44; see also *R v Secretary of State for the Environment* [2001] EWHC Admin 100, 7 February. The issue of an enforcement notice by a planning authority does not amount to "proceedings" but the issue of a magistrates' court summons to ensure compliance would: *Mabey v Secretary of State for the Environment, Transport and the Regions* [2001] PLCR 417.

III HUM [23.3]

Appeals against pre-commencement convictions The majority decision in *R v Lambert* [2001] UKHL 37, [2002] 2 AC 545, [2001] 3 All ER 577 was that "proceedings brought by or at the instigation of a public authority" did not include appeals against conviction. This decision was followed (in the interests of legal certainty) by a majority in *R v Kansal (No 2)* [2001] UKHL 62, [2002] 2 AC 69, [2002] 1 All ER 257 although only two out of five Law Lords considered the earlier interpretation to be correct.

III HUM [23.4]

Civil claims based on pre-commencement conduct In a claim based on pre-commencement conduct, the court must apply the pre-commencement law since s 3, at para **III HUM [9]**, is not given retrospective effect by s 22(4): *Wainwright v Home Office* [2001] EWCA Civ 2081, [2002] QB 1334, [2003] 3 All ER 943; affirmed by the House of Lords [2003] UKHL 53, [2004] 2 AC 406, [2003] 4 All ER 969.

However, the conduct of an inquest after commencement may be subject to the requirements of Art 2 although the death was before the Act came into force: *Re McCaughey* [2011] UKSC 20, (2011) Times, 20 May. See now also the analysis in *Keyu v Secretary of State for Foreign and Commonwealth Affairs* [2015] UKSC 69, [2015] 3 WLR 1665.

A provision in a pre-1948 settlement for 'statutory next of kin' which excluded adopted children was held to be discriminatory and contrary to Art 14 in circumstances where the Act could be applied retrospectively without unfairness: *Re Erskine 1948 Trust, Gregg v Pigott* [2012] EWHC 732 (Ch), [2012] 3 All ER 532, [2012] 3 WLR 913.

III HUM [23.5]

Application and extent The enforcement of Convention rights by the domestic courts of the United Kingdom does not normally extend to persons outside the jurisdiction: *Re J (a Child) (Child returned abroad: Convention rights)* [2004] EWCA Civ 417, [2004] 2 FCR 337. However, it has been held that the duty in s 6 to act compatibly with Convention rights will apply to UK public authorities if and in so far as they exercise "jurisdiction" overseas within the meaning of Art 1 of the Convention. That jurisdiction should be understood as extending to the activities of embassy and consular officials abroad when exercising the authority of the sending state. However it would be contrary to international law for such officials to grant asylum to fugitives from the host state except in circumstances of immediate and severe threat to their life or physical safety: *R (on the application of B) v Secretary of State for the Foreign and Commonwealth Office* [2004] EWCA Civ 1344, (2004) Times, 25 October.

In *R (on the application of Al-Skeini) v Secretary of State for Defence* [2005] EWCA Civ 1609, [2006] 3 WLR 508 the Court of Appeal definitively held that the Human Rights Act is capable in principle of applying to UK public authorities outside the territory of the UK where there is the exercise of jurisdiction within the meaning of the Convention. The Court also held that there could be such jurisdiction where a person was detained, even if not in a prison; and where there was effective control of an area even if that area was outside the Council of Europe but that effective control was not synonymous with the concept of occupation in international humanitarian law. The decision of the Court of Appeal was upheld by a majority of the House of Lords: *R (on the application of Al-Skeini) v Secretary of State for Defence* [2007] UKHL 26, [2007] 3 All ER 685, Lord Bingham dissenting.

In *Smith v Ministry of Defence* [2013] UKSC 41, [2013] 4 All ER 794, [2013] 3 WLR 69 the Supreme Court held that British troops serving overseas were within the jurisdiction of the United Kingdom for the purposes of securing to them the protection of Art 2 under the Human Rights Act 1998 save where this was impossible or inappropriate. Accordingly the application of substantive obligations under Art 2 would vary from case to case. This decision followed that of the Grand Chamber of the ECtHR in *Al-Skeini v United Kingdom* [2011] ECHR 1093, (2011) 53 EHRR 18 holding that where an occupying State overseas assumes the exercise of public powers normally to be exercised by a sovereign government, it may thereby exercise authority and control over individuals such as those killed in the course of such security operations, so as to establish a jurisdictional link between the deceased and the United Kingdom for the purposes of Art 1. The Supreme Court therefore overruled its earlier decision to the contrary in *R (on the application of Smith) v Secretary of State for Defence* [2010] UKSC 29, [2011] 1 AC 1, [2010] 3 All ER 1067, [2010] 2 WLR 334.

If a state is to exercise Art 1 jurisdiction outside its own territory it must have the legal power to fulfil substantial governmental functions of a sovereign state, for example in an embassy, consulate, military base or prison. The jurisdiction has been held not to exist in a case where Iraqi prisoners were being detained by the British forces as agents for the Iraqi authorities: *R (on the application of Al-Saadoon) v Secretary of State for Defence* [2009] EWCA Civ 7, [2010] 1 All ER 271, [2009] 3 WLR 957 and *Al-Saadoon and Mufdhi v United Kingdom (Admissibility)* (2009) 49 EHRR SE 95.

Nor was it possible to identify any relevant exercise of authority or control where a UK national had been sentenced to death by a court in Indonesia for drug trafficking and the UK Government declined to pay for legal representation by which she could apply to the Indonesian Supreme Court to re-open her case and to the President for clemency, relying on its blanket policy in relation to British nationals facing criminal proceedings abroad. The UK national was under the authority and control of the Indonesian authorities and it was they who were under a duty to ensure her fair trial: *R (on the application of Sandiford) v Secretary of State for Foreign and Commonwealth Affairs* [2014] UKSC 44, [2014] 4 All ER 843, [2014] 1 WLR 2697.

In *Keyu v Secretary of State for Foreign and Commonwealth Affairs* [2015] UKSC 69, [2015] 3 WLR 1665, the Supreme Court considered that British troops deployed in the State of Selangor in the Federation of Malaya prior to independence (where the UK had been in complete control of defence and external affairs) were acting in the interests of the UK Government that and those under their control fell within the jurisdiction of the UK for the purposes of a claim based on Art 2 of the ECHR.

Schedules

SCHEDULE 1
THE ARTICLES

PART I
THE CONVENTION RIGHTS AND FREEDOMS

III HUM [24]

Article 2 Right to life

1. Everyone's right to life shall be protected by law. No one shall be deprived of his life intentionally save in the execution of a sentence of a court following his conviction of a crime for which this penalty is provided by law.

2. Deprivation of life shall not be regarded as inflicted in contravention of this Article when it results from the use of force which is no more than absolutely necessary:

(a) in defence of any person from unlawful violence;

(b) in order to effect a lawful arrest or to prevent the escape of a person lawfully detained;

(c) in action lawfully taken for the purpose of quelling a riot or insurrection.

III HUM [24.1]

Medical treatment It was held by Cazalet J, in *A National Health Service Trust v D* [2000] 2 FCR 577, 19 July, that the court could and should declare restricted treatment to be in the child's best interests and lawful in the event of respiratory or cardiac failure. The foreseeable consequence was that the child would be allowed to die peacefully and with dignity, but this did not involve a breach of Convention rights under either Art 2 or Art 3.

In *Great Ormond Street Hospital for Children NHS Foundation Trust v Yates* [2017] EWCA Civ 410, [2018] 1 All ER 596, the Court of Appeal held that the court's task was purely to determine the baby's best interests in circumstances where the parents of a terminally ill baby sought for him to have experimental untested treatment in the US whereas the hospital considered withdrawal of life support was in his best interests. Such an approach did not breach article 8: see the decision of the Supreme Court refusing permission to appeal, and the ECtHR's admissibility decision: (2017] 65 EHRR SE9. See further *Re E (a child)* [2018] EWCA Civ 550, [201] 1 WLR 594.

In *NHS Trust A v M* [2000] All ER (D) 1522, (2000) Times, 29 November the President of the Family Division held that there was no breach of Art 3 in withholding treatment from a person in a persistent vegetative state since there was no legal obligation to provide treatment. In the case of conjoined twins, an operation to separate them which was not in the best interests of one might nevertheless be lawful, and not contravening Art 2, if necessary to save the life of the other: *Re A (children) (conjoined twins; surgical separation)* [2001] Fam 147, [2000] 3 FCR 577, CA. Treatment may lawfully be withdrawn without contravening a patient's Convention rights where he, or she, has communicated a clear wish for this to happen: *Re AK (Adult Patient) (Medical Treatment: Consent)* [2001] 2 FCR 35, [2001] 1 FLR 129. Where a claimant was in a persistent vegetative state so that it was not in her best interests to be given life-sustaining medical treatment, the withdrawal of treatment did not contravene her Convention rights: *A Hospital v SW and a PCT* [2007] EWHC 425 (Fam). In *W (by her litigation friend B) v M (by her litigation friend the Official Solicitor)* [2011] EWHC 2443 (Fam), (2011) Times, 1 December the Court of Protection explained that where the issue was whether artificial nutrition and hydration was to be withdrawn from a patient in a minimally conscious state, the court had to identify and weigh the factors on each side which were relevant to the patient's best interests.

See also *An NHS Trust v Y* [2018] UKSC 46, [2018] 3 WLR 751: it was not necessary for a court order to be obtained in every case before clinically assisted nutrition and hydration could be withdrawn from a person with prolonged disorder of consciousness. In both domestic and Strasbourg jurisprudence, there was an important distinction between the intentional taking of live, and the abstention from treatment.

III HUM [24.1A]

Suicide The Convention does not confer a right to die or a right to assisted suicide; and accordingly s 2(1) of the Suicide Act 1961 (unlawful to assist suicide) is compatible with it: *R (on the application of Pretty) v DPP* [2001] UKHL 61, [2002] 1 AC 800, [2002] 1 All ER 1; *Pretty v United Kingdom (Application 2346/02)* [2002] 2 FCR 97, [2002] 2 FLR 45, ECtHR. Section 2(1) does not impose what the ECtHR would regard as an impermissible blanket ban on suicide and therefore is within the UK's margin of appreciation, although the policy of the DPP on prosecution required clarification: *R (on the application of Nicklinson) v Ministry of Justice (CNK Alliance Ltd and British Humanist Association intervening); R (on the application of AM) v DPP* [2014] UKSC 38, [2014] 3 All ER 843, (2013) Times, 08 October. In light of Parliament's decision not to amend s 2(1) following *Nicklinson*, however, the Court of Appeal in *R (on the application of Conway) v Secretary of State for Justice* [2017] EWCA Civ 275 held that an applicant could be given permission to apply for judicial review on the same grounds as those in *Nicklinson*. Upon that judicial review, the Court rejected the argument that s 2(1) of the Suicide Act 1961 imposes a disproportionate ban on suicide, when physician assisted. Whether the argument is put under Art 2 or Art 8 the law is not incompatible, for the purpose of section 4, with the provisions of the Convention: *R (on the application of Conway) v Secretary of State for Justice* [2018] EWCA Civ 1431, [2018] 3 WLR 925.

III HUM [24.2]

Parental wishes When considering the lawfulness of a proposed operation on conjoined twins the Court of Appeal held that the duty to weigh the welfare of each child took precedence over the wishes of the parents: *Re A (children) (conjoined twins: surgical separation)* [2001] Fam 147, [2000] 3 FCR 577, CA.

III HUM [24.3]

Injunction to prevent publication of identity and other confidential information which might endanger individuals In *Venables v News Group Newspapers* [2001] 1 All ER 908, the President of the Family Division granted injunctions, based on the right to life of two 18-year-olds being released from prison, to prevent publication by anyone of confidential information about them. In making the order, the court had regard to the matters set out in Art 10(2) at para **III HUM [32]**. In *A-G v Greater Manchester Newspapers Ltd* (2001) 145 Sol Jo LB 279, Butler-Sloss P decided that the defendants had broken the injunction by publishing information likely to lead to the identification of the whereabouts of the individuals concerned. The risk of danger to life need not be direct or immediate or limited to specified individuals: *R (on the application of A) v Lord Saville of Newdigate (Bloody Sunday Inquiry)* [2001] EWHC Admin 888, (2001) 145 Sol Jo LB 262. For a case where anonymity was granted to inquest witnesses on the ground of threats to their lives see *R (on the application of A) v Inner South London Coroner* (2004) Times, 11 November, CA. The positive obligation on the state to take action such as allowing evidence to be given anonymously arose only when the risk was real, objectively verified and present and continuing. The threshold was high and the standard constant; it was not variable with the type of action in contemplation. The degree of stringency imposed on state authorities in the level of precautions which they had to take was based on reasonableness, bringing in consideration of the circumstances of the case, the ease or difficulty of taking precautions and the resources available: *Re Officer L* [2007] UKHL 36, [2007] 4 All ER 965.

III HUM [24.4]

Implied duty to investigate killings The right to life, coupled with the general duty under Art 1 to secure everyone's Convention rights and freedoms, means that there has to be some form of effective official investigation when individuals have been killed as a result of the use of force: *Jordan v United Kingdom* (2001) Times, 18 May, ECtHR. The obligation to investigate also applies if the state is arguably culpable in some other way, where for example one detained person kills another; and a private investigation which is unable to compel evidence from the most important witnesses does not meet the requirements of Art 2: *Edwards v United Kingdom (Application 46477/99)* (2002) Times, 1 April, ECtHR. The leading domestic authority is *R (on the application of Amin) v Secretary of State for the Home Department* [2003] UKHL 51, [2004] 1 AC 653, [2003] 4 All ER 1264, in which the House of Lords reversed the Court of Appeal and ordered a public inquiry to take place into the killing of a person held at a Young Offender's Institute by his cellmate. See also *R (on the application of Khan) v Secretary of State for Health* [2003] EWCA Civ 1129, [2003] 4 All ER 1239. The coronial system of inquests was held to be inadequate in *R (on the application of Middleton) v West Somerset Coroner* [2004] UKHL 10. To meet the procedural requirement of Art 2 the inquest ought ordinarily to culminate in an expression, however brief, of the jury's conclusion on the disputed factual issues at the heart of the case. A jury should be summoned where a death has occurred in prison or in police custody or from an injury caused by a police officer. The inquest hearing should be independent and public, involving the deceased's family, and enough evidence should be called properly to investigate the circumstances and the means by which the deceased died.

Although the death of a hospital patient does not necessarily require an investigation, in the way that the death of a prisoner in custody does, if there is an investigation by a coroner it should be a full and sufficient one covering any questions arising as to the hospital's systems for looking after patients whose lives may be at risk: *R (on the application of Takoushis) v HM Coroner for Inner North London* [2005] EWCA Civ 1440, (2005) Times, 8 December. The duty to investigate in the case of a prisoner in custody applies also to circumstances where the individual does not die but sustains life-threatening injuries: *R (on the application of D) v Secretary of State for the Home Department* [2006] EWCA Civ 143, [2006] 3 All ER 946.

An investigation satisfying Art 2 is required where the death of a patient detained under the Mental Health Act 1983 raised issues as to whether the medical authorities had failed in their obligation to take general measures to save her from dying and whether the death was so caused: *R (on the application of Allen) v HM Coroner for Inner North London* [2009] EWCA Civ 623, [2009] All ER (D) 287 (Jun). A Heath Trust owes a duty under Art 2 to a voluntary patient suffering from physical or mental illness where there was a real and immediate risk of death. Accordingly the family of a depressed patient who committed suicide while on home leave were awarded damages in *Rabone v Pennine Care NHS Trust* [2012] UKSC 2, [2012] 2 AC 72, [2012] 2 All ER 381. The relatives had a claim in their own right for a breach of the investigative duty and/or the substantive duty and these could be pursued notwithstanding settlement of a negligence claim. However, the investigative obligation does not require an inquiry to take place prior to an inquest: *R (on the application of Antoniou) v Central and North West London NHS Foundation Trust* [2013] EWHC 3055 (Admin), [2013] Med LR 536.

The implied duty to investigate deaths does not extend to deaths beyond national boundaries, where the death occurred in the territory of another Contracting State: *Al Fayed v Lord Advocate* (2004) Times, 23 March, Ct of Session, Outer House. This can be contrasted with the case of *R (on the application of Al-Skeini) v Secretary of State for Defence* [2004] EWHC 2911 (Admin), (2004) Times, 20 December, in which the Divisional Court held that the duty to investigate (under both Arts 2 and 3) did arise and had been breached where British forces held a person in detention at a prison in Iraq: in such circumstances they were exercising "jurisdiction" within the meaning of Art 1 of the Convention even though the events took place outside the territory of the UK. The Court of Appeal upheld the Divisional Court on this aspect of the case, except that it considered that, in the light of more recent developments, in particular the institution of criminal proceedings, it would be premature to hold that there had been a violation of the procedural obligation and that this issue should be stayed pending the outcome of courts martial [2005] EWCA Civ 1609, [2006] 3 WLR 508. The decision of the Court of Appeal was upheld by a majority of the House of Lords: *R (on the application of Al-Skeini) v Secretary of State for Defence* [2007] UKHL 26, [2007] 3 All ER 685, Lord Bingham dissenting. However, the Grand Chamber of the ECtHR in *Al-Skeini v United Kingdom* [2011] ECHR 1093, (2011) 53 EHRR 18 has subsequently held that because UK forces assumed the exercise of public powers in Iraq normally to be exercised by a sovereign government, it exercised authority and control over individuals such as those killed in the course of such security operations, so as to establish a jurisdictional link between the deceased and the United Kingdom for the purposes of Art 1 (a decision followed by the Supreme Court in *Smith v Ministry of Defence* [2013] UKSC 41, [2013] 4 All ER 794, [2013] 3 WLR 69). Accordingly the procedural duty under Art 2 arose and had not been satisfied. These decisions overrule the earlier decision of the Supreme Court in *R (on the application of Smith) v Secretary of State for Defence* [2010] UKSC 29, [2011] 1 AC 1, [2010] 3 WLR 223. The position of British forces operating under the constitutional arrangements in Selangor in pre-independence Malaya was considered in *Keyu v Secretary of State for Foreign and Commonwealth Affairs* [2015] UKSC 69, [2015] 3 WLR 1665. The Supreme Court considered that the troops were in the service of His Majesty and acting in the interests of the UK. The deceased were within the British army's control such that had the ECHR been in force at the time, the killings would have occurred within the UK's jurisdiction.

Contrast the position of Iraqi prisoners detained by the British forces as agents for the Iraqi authorities *R (on the application of Al-Saadoon) v Secretary of State for Defence* [2009] EWCA Civ 7, [2009] 1 All ER 271, [2009] 3 WLR 957.

For a case about the duty to investigate deaths of soldiers on active service, where the Royal Military Police patrols were not provided with iridium phones as orders required, see *R (on the application of Long) v Secretary of State for Defence* [2015] EWCA Civ 770, [2016] 1 WLR 5006, [2015] All ER (D) 206 (Jul). In that case the inquest and other inquiries had revealed the reasons for the lack of phones and an investigation was refused on the ground that there was little more information that an investigation could discover. (See also the views of Baroness Hale in *Keyu* (above) that an inquest to establish historical truth (as opposed to 'acts undertaken in the framework of criminal, civil, administrative or disciplinary proceedings which are capable of leading to the identification and punishment of those responsible or to an award of compensation to the injured party', citing *Labita v Italy* (2000) 46 EHRR 50) falls outside Art 2 (see para 300).)

A refusal by the Home Secretary to order a public inquiry into matters of sentencing policy, available facilities and resources, requested by a coroner at the conclusion of an inquest, has been held not to violate Art 2 in a case where there was evidence that the Home Secretary was confronting those issues which had been the subject of a substantial public debate: *R (on the application of Scholes) v Secretary of State for the Home Department* (2006) Times, 10 November, CA.

The obligation to investigate killings does not go as far as to require a public inquiry into questions of international law or questions of policy which were as a general rule non-justiciable: *R (on the application of Gentle) v Prime Minister* [2008] UKHL 20, [2008] 1 AC 1356.

In order to comply with Art 2 authorities may in some circumstances be obliged to re-open a case and make further investigations in the light of new evidence: *Brecknell v United Kingdom (Application No 32457/04)* (2007) Times, 7 December, ECtHR. With regard to near-suicide cases resulting in lasting serious injury, investigations are required which include an independent element and engage the person who has been harmed and/or their family: *R (on the application of JL) v Secretary of State for the Home Department* [2008] UKHL 68, [2009] 1 AC 588, [2009] 2 All ER 521.

There is no investigative right in respect of deaths occurring before the entry into force of the Human Rights Act 1998: *Re McKerr* [2004] UKHL 12, [2004] NI 212, [2004] 2 All ER 409. However, where the state decides to hold an inquest in relation to a death which occurred before commencement of the HRA, it may have a freestanding obligation to ensure that it complies with the procedural obligations of Art 2 of the Convention: *Re McCaughey and Quinn's Application For Leave To Apply For Judicial Review* [2011] UKSC 20, [2011] 3 All ER 607, (2011) UKHRR 720, (2011) HRLR 25, (2011) Times, 20 May. The ECtHR has ruled that the UK was in breach of this obligation by permitting an excessive delay in the investigation of the killings of three Irish nationals by members of the British Army and the RUC: *McCaughey v United Kingdom (Application No 43098/09)* (2013) 163 (7572) NLJ 20, (2013) Times, 4 October. However, in *Keyu v Secretary of State for Foreign and Commonwealth Affairs* [2015] UKSC 69, [2015] 3 WLR 1665, the Supreme Court declined to overrule *Re McKerr*. In *Keyu* the Court was faced with deaths which occurred in 1948 and therefore preceded the ECHR of 1950, the date when the UK extended it to the Federation of Malaya in 1953, and the date on which the UK granted a right of individual petition to the ECtHR in 1969. Applying *Šilih v Slovenia (Application No 71463/01)* (2009) 49 EHRR 996, [2009] ECHR 71 and *Janowiec v Russia* (2013) 58 EHRR 792, and by a majority, the Court held that the 1969 date was the 'critical date' for the purposes of discovering whether there existed a genuine connection between the death and the critical date. The majority concluded that as the deaths occurred more than ten years before the critical date, no genuine connection could be established. Accordingly, no separable Art 2 duty to investigate arose.

III HUM [24.4A]

Duty to protect life of persons detained The obligation to protect life includes an obligation to take reasonable steps to protect one individual from being killed by another, as in *Edwards v United Kingdom (Application 46477/99)* (2002) Times, 1 April, ECtHR; and *R (on the application of Amin) v Secretary of State for the Home Department* [2003] UKHL 51, [2004] 1 AC 653, [2003] 4 All ER 1264. The article also places a duty on the police to protect the lives of witnesses who have received threats: *Van Colle v Chief Constable of Hertfordshire* [2006] EWHC 360 (QB), [2006] 3 All ER 963, [2006] 1 FCR 755, QBD. Although allowing an appeal on the facts of the case, the House of Lords concluded that witnesses and others would have a claim under Art 2 if they could show that the authorities had not done all that could reasonably be expected of them to avoid a real and immediate risk to life of which they had or ought to have had knowledge: *Van Colle v Chief Constable of Hertfordshire Constabulary* [2008] UKHL 50, [2008] 3 All ER 977, (2008) Times, 1 August, HL *per* Lord Bingham.

In *R (on the application of L) v Secretary of State for Justice* [2008] UKHL 68, [2008] 3 WLR 1325, the House of Lords held that since prisoners presented a particular risk of suicide, the state's positive obligation under Art 2 to protect life had special application. This required prison authorities to put in place systemic measures to prevent suicide and to take operational measures when they knew or ought to have known of a real and immediate risk of a suicide. The obligation to hold an investigation under the procedural duty imposed by Art 2 was triggered automatically by an attempted suicide causing long-term injury. The investigative duty might be discharged in different ways but must meet the basic requirements of Art 2, in particular by being promptly and expeditiously conducted by a person who was independent of those implicated in the relevant events, involving the victim's family and making sufficient provision for public scrutiny.

A health authority has similar obligations to prevent patients detained in hospital under the Mental Health Act 1983, s 3 from committing suicide. As well as requiring the authority to employ competent staff and to adopt appropriate systems of work, Art 2 imposes an "operational" obligation on authorities and staff to do all that could be reasonably expected to prevent the patient committing suicide where they know or ought to know that that patient presents a real and immediate risk of suicide: *Savage v South Essex Partnership NHS Trust* [2008] UKHL 74, [2009] 1 AC 681. For the position of an informal patient not detained under s 3, see *Rabone v Pennine Care NHS Trust* [2012] UKSC 2, [2012] 2 AC 72, [2012] 2 All ER 381: **III HUM [24.4]**.

III HUM [24.4B]

Duty to warn persons at risk A duty to warn a person that he was at risk of loss, injury or damage as the result of the criminal act of a third party would arise only where the defendant had by words or conduct assumed responsibility for the other person's safety, and therefore a local authority was not under a duty to warn a tenant that his neighbour might respond violently after being told of possible eviction: *Mitchell v Glasgow City Council* [2009] UKHL 11, [2009] 1 AC 874, [2009] 3 All ER 205.

III HUM [24.4C]

Frozen embryos Embryos fertilised outside the womb with a view to implantation do not have a right to life: *Evans v United Kingdom (Application No 6339/05)* (2007) Times, 2 May, ECtHR.

III HUM [24.4D]

Duty to protect members of the Armed Forces The duty to protect the right to life extends to members of the Armed Forces: a failure by the State to provide its soldiers with adequate equipment and vehicles may amount not only to negligence at common law but also a breach of the human right established by this article: *Smith v Ministry of Defence* [2013] UKSC 41, [2013] 4 All ER 794, [2013] 3 WLR 69 (the Snatch Land Rover case).

III HUM [24.5]

Precedents See **BCCP J[102]** for a precedent which sets out claims in judicial review proceedings for a quashing order, an injunction and other relief in protection of the claimant's right to life.

III HUM [25]

Article 3 Prohibition of torture

No one shall be subjected to torture or to inhuman or degrading treatment or punishment.

III HUM [25.1]

Prisoners' rights The imposition of a whole life sentence was found to be compatible with Article 3 by the Grand Chamber in *Hutchinson v United Kingdom (Application 57592/08)* [2017] ECHR 65.

A punishment which involves denying a prisoner adequate food is in breach of r 24 of the Prison Rules 1999, SI 1999/728, and potentially in breach of Art 3: *R v Governor of Frankland Prison, ex p Russell (Right to Meals)* [2000] 1 WLR 2027.

In *Keenan v United Kingdom (Application 27229/95)* (2001) Times, 18 April, ECtHR, the court held that the segregation and punishment of a mentally ill prisoner who was known to be a suicide risk was, in the circumstances, inhuman and degrading treatment. A similar conclusion was reached in *Price v United Kingdom (Application 33394/96)* (2001) Times, 13 August, ECtHR, in the case of a severely disabled person detained in conditions unsuitable to her needs; and see *Napier v Scottish Ministers* (2001) Times, 15 November, regarding cells without toilets. Similarly, in *McGlinchey v United Kingdom (Application 50390/99)* (2003) Times, 1 May, ECHR, it was held that the failure by prison authorities to provide a detained person with the requisite medical care was a breach of the duty under Art 3. It was further held that the absence of an appropriate remedy was a breach of Art 13.

In *Shahid v Scottish Ministers* [2015] UKSC 58, [2015] 3 WLR 58, 165 NLJ 7673, [2015] All ER (D) 109 (Oct), a prisoner had been segregated for a period of around 56 months. In the circumstances, this did not meet the minimum level of severity required to breach Art 3, although a violation of Art 8 was made out. In *R (on the application of AB (a child)) v Secretary of State for Justice* [2019] EWCA Civ 9, the Court of Appeal rejected a claim that a special detention regime in a young offender institution breached Art 3 where the regime consisted of solitary confinement of 8 weeks for a 15 year old offender.

In *Grant and Gleaves v Ministry of Justice* [2011] EWHC 3379 (QB) it was held that Art 3 was not violated by prison conditions where prisoners occasionally, if a call system for night-time sanitation was not working, had to use a bucket in the cell and 'slop out' the next day.

The handcuffing of a prisoner during chemotherapy treatment breached his Convention rights because he represented no risk to the public and there was no risk of his escape: *R (on the application of Graham) v Secretary of State for Justice* [2007] EWHC 2940 (Admin). Contrast *R (on the application of Faizovas) v Secretary of State for Justice* [2008] EWHC 1197 (Admin), (2008) ACD 82 in which similar treatment was held not to breach Convention rights because such risks did exist. An appeal against the latter decision was dismissed but the Court of Appeal observed that the use of handcuffs during particular types of medical treatment might be disproportionate if there was a practical alternative: *R (on the application of Faizovas) v Secretary of State for Justice* [2009] EWCA Civ 373, 109 BMLR 15, (2009) Times, 25 May. Where a severely disabled prisoner received medical treatment in prison of a lower standard than that to which he was accustomed but his symptoms were caused by his condition, not the treatment, there was no breach of Art 3 (or Arts 2 or 8): *R (on the application of Hall (Roque)) v University College London Hospitals NHS Foundation Trust* [2013] EWHC 198 (Admin), [2013] NLJR 208, [2013] ACD 55.

As regards the detention of persons by other States, for example in Guantanamo Bay, a contracting state has no obligation under the Convention to take up complaints of any individual within its territory touching the acts of another sovereign state: *R (on the application of Al Rawi) v Secretary of State for Foreign and Commonwealth Affairs* [2006] EWCA Civ 1279, [2008] QB 289, adopting the reasoning in *Bertrand Russell Peace Foundation v United Kingdom* (1978) 14 Decisions and Reports 117.

However, the UK would not extradite an offender to Romania without an undertaking that he would serve his sentence in a cell where he would have more than two metres of personal space, failing which the extradition would infringe Art 3: *Florea v Judicial Authority Carei Courthouse, Satu Mare County, Romania* [2014] EWHC 2528 (Admin), (2014) Times, 14 August, Div Ct.

III HUM [25.2]

Stopping treatment It has been suggested that stopping treatment in the case of a person in a persistent vegetative state is not "inhuman or degrading treatment" for the purpose of Art 3, since the individual concerned is not aware of what is happening: *NHS Trust A v M* [2000] All ER (D) 1522, (2000) Times, 29 November. However, subsequently it was suggested that stopping treatment of a person in a persistent vegetative state might be degrading if it would be seen by right-thinking bystanders as debasing the victim or showing a lack of respect or diminishing his or her human dignity: *R (on the application of Burke) v General Medical Council* [2004] EWHC 1879 (Admin), [2004] 3 FCR 579, (2004) Times, 6 August, Munby J. Note that the decision of Munby J was reversed, with strong disapproval, by the Court of Appeal in *R (on the application of Burke) v General Medical Council (Official Solicitor and Others intervening)* [2005] EWCA Civ 1003, [2006] QB 273. The Court confirmed the lawfulness of the GMC guidance on the withdrawal of life-prolonging treatment and emphasised that although it might be appropriate to seek a declaration of lawfulness, for example where the legality of the proposed treatment was in doubt, this was not required as a matter of law. Where a claimant was in a persistent vegetative state so that it was not in her best interests to be given life-sustaining medical treatment, it was held that the withdrawal of treatment did not contravene her Art 2 or Art 3 rights: *A Hospital v SW and a PCT* [2007] EWHC 425 (Fam). In *Re OT* [2009] EWHC 633 (Fam) it was reiterated that withdrawal of life sustaining treatment which is no longer in a patient's best interests is not a breach of Art 2 or Art 8. On the basis of medical evidence showing that a seriously ill nine-month-old child was experiencing distress and that long-term paediatric care would not be in his best interests, the court granted orders and declarations allowing withdrawal of ventilation with palliative care to allow the child to die with as little distress as possible.

III HUM [25.2A]

Failure to provide support In *R (on the application of Q) v Secretary of State for the Home Department* [2003] EWCA Civ 364, [2004] QB 36, [2003] 2 All ER 905, it was held that the refusal by the State to provide support to those in need could, in certain circumstances, amount to inhuman or degrading treatment.

To require an asylum seeker to sleep rough in winter was held, in *R (on the application of Limbuela) v Secretary of State for the Home Department* [2004] EWHC 219 (Admin), [2004] All ER (D) 56 (Feb), Collins J, to breach his rights under Art 3. The decision in this and similar cases was upheld on appeal, by a 2–1 majority: *R (on the application of Limbuela) v Secretary of State for the Home Department, R (on the application of Tesema) v Secretary of State for the Home Department, R (on the application of Adam) v Secretary of State for the Home Department* [2004] EWCA Civ 540, [2004] QB 1440, [2004] All ER (D) 323 (May). The House of Lords upheld the majority of the Court of Appeal but went further, by re-affirming the reasoning of the Court of Appeal in *Q*: [2005] UKHL 66, [2006] 1 AC 396, [2005] 3 All ER 29.

A decision on the eve of trial to discontinue a prosecution for a serious assault on the ground that the victim, whose account was prima facie credible, suffered from a mental disorder and would therefore be an unreliable witness has been held to be an irrational decision, having regard to the terms of the medical report and a breach of the victim's rights under Art 3 which would add insult to injury: *R (on the application of B) v DPP (Equality and Human Rights Commission intervening)* [2009] EWHC 106 (Admin), [2009] 1 WLR 2072, [2009] 1 Cr App Rep 580.

It has been held to be a breach of Art 3 to detain a mentally disordered person who has been arrested under s 136 of the Mental Health Act 1983 to a police station for 4 days before transfer to a clinic: *MS v United Kingdom (Application No 24527/08)* [2012] ECHR 804, (2012) 126 BMLR 168, ECtHR.

III HUM [25.3]

Repatriating the mentally ill It was held in *R v Secretary of State for the Home Department, ex p X* [2001] 1 WLR 740, CA that the fact that an illegal immigrant was protected by the provisions of the Mental Health Act 1983 did not make repatriation under the Immigration Act 1971 a breach of Art 3. Where a deportee presents a risk of suicide if returned to a non-Convention state, Art 3 may be engaged if there is shown to be a real increased risk of suicide compared to the risk which would be faced on release in the UK: *J v Secretary of State for the Home Department* [2005] EWCA Civ 629, [2005] All ER (D) 359 (May), in which the Court listed the relevant factors to be considered in assessing the risk of suicide in such a case.

III HUM [25.3A]

Using forcible restraints on protected persons It has been held that the forcible restraint, with handcuffs and leg restraints, of a vulnerable teenage boy who was autistic, epileptic and lacked understanding, was in the particular circumstances of the case a breach of arts 3 and 5 and not in his best interests. An award of £28,250 for false imprisonment was upheld by the Court of Appeal: *ZH (by his litigation friend) v Metropolitan Police Comr* [2013] EWCA Civ 69, [2013] 3 All ER 113, [2013] 1 WLR 3021.

III HUM [25.4]

Child abuse and violent and indecent assault The failure of a social services department to protect children from inhuman and degrading forms of child abuse may constitute infringement of their rights under Art 3. It was held in *Z v United Kingdom (Application 29392/95)* [2001] 2 FCR 246, (2001) Times 31 May, ECtHR, that the absence of a legal remedy for such a failure was a breach of Art 13.

A failure by the police to investigate complaints of violent and indecent assaults may be a breach of the implied duty in Art 3 to protect the public from degrading physical attack for which the complainants may be awarded damages for breach of the Convention: *DSD v Metropolitan Police Comr; Koraou v Chief Constable of Greater Manchester Police* [2015] EWCA Civ 646, [2015] 3 WLR 966, [2015] All ER (D) 21 (Jul). Accordingly, in *Metropolitan Police Comr v DSD* [2018] UKSC 11, [2018] 2 WLR 895, the Supreme Court held the police liable in damages for serious defects in the police investigation into black cab assaults by John Worboys. Article 3 obliged the state to conduct an effective investigation into crimes involving serious violence to the person even where that was carried out by individual criminals.

III HUM [25.5]

Repatriation of person in need of health care The fact that a deportee needs medical care which he cannot afford in his home country does not mean that a refusal of asylum would infringe Art 3: *K v Secretary of State for the Home Department* [2001] Imm AR 11, CA. See now the leading authority of *N v Secretary of State for the Home Department* [2005] UKHL 31, [2005] 2 AC 296.

III HUM [25.5A]

Breach of implied positive obligation Where the Home Secretary is, or should be, aware that an individual is suffering or at risk of treatment of the kind necessary to engage Art 3 or of harm necessary to engage Art 8 but does not take reasonable steps to prevent or reduce this risk a finding of breach of implied obligation may be made: *E v United Kingdom (Application 33218/96)* (2002) Times, 4 December, ECtHR. In mental health cases, a failure to adhere to the Code of Practice (HSC 1999/50) issued under s 118 of the Mental Health Act 1983 was thought by the Court of Appeal as giving rise to a potential breach of Arts 3, 5 or 8: *R (on the application of Munjaz) v Mersey Care NHS Trust* [2003] EWCA Civ 1036, [2004] QB 395, [2003] 3 WLR 1505. However, the House of Lords, by a majority, held the Code to be guidance rather than instruction and that a Trust could depart from it if there were cogent reasons for doing so, as there were in that case: *R (on the application of Munjaz) v Mersey Care NHS Trust* [2005] UKHL 58, [2005] 3 WLR 793.

The positive obligation to prevent inhuman treatment is not absolute; as in the case of Art 2 the obligation is to do all that can be reasonably expected to avoid a real and immediate risk of such treatment being inflicted: *E v Chief Constable of the Royal Ulster Constabulary (Northern Ireland Human Rights Commission intervening)* [2008] UKHL 66, [2009] 1 AC 536, [2009] NI 141. Note also that the duty to investigate allegations of degrading treatment depends on the allegations reaching the Government before it is too late for the duty to be given effect (although the Court did not agree that this had occurred on the facts of the case): *R (on the application of AM) v Secretary of State for the Home Department* [2009] EWCA Civ 219, (2009) Times, 20 March.

As with Art 2 there is also a positive obligation to investigate possible breaches of Art 3. In *R (on the application of Mousa) v Secretary of State for Defence* [2011] EWCA Civ 1334, (2011) Times, 28 December the Court of Appeal held that the Iraq Historic Allegations Team, set up to investigate allegations that detainees in Iraq had been ill-treated by British armed forces, lacked the necessary independence for an effective investigation because of the involvement of members of the Royal Military Police. Following the reconstitution of IHAT with members of the Royal Navy Police instead of the RMP, its independence was accepted in *R (on the application of Mousa) v Secretary of State for Defence (No 2)* [2013] EWHC 1412 (Admin), [2013] HRLR 32. See also *R (on the application of AB) v Secretary of State for Defence* [2013] EWHC 3908 (Admin), [2014] ACD 46 in which the Divisional Court ruled that the Special Investigations Branch of the Royal Military Police was sufficiently independent to conduct an investigation compliant with Arts 2 and 3 into an incident in Afghanistan in which men were shot and killed during an operation involving British and Afghan soldiers.

However, there would not routinely be a requirement for an independent investigation upon the occurrence of events such as a disturbance in an immigration detention centre, even if children were involved. Applications would be considered on their merits, having regard to the nature, scale and consequences of the incident, the likelihood of recurrence, and the existence of other investigations conducted or available. The costs involved in a further investigation could also be a relevant consideration: *R (on the application of MM and AO) v Secretary of State for the Home Department* [2012] EWCA Civ 668.

III HUM [25.5B]

Extradition The HL held in *R (on the application of Wellington) v Secretary Of State for the Home Department* [2008] UKHL 72, [2009] 1 AC 335, [2009] 2 All ER 436, that whether a criminal sentence faced by a person at risk of extradition amounts to inhuman or degrading treatment depends upon all the circumstances of the case. The desirability of extradition is a factor to be taken into account in deciding whether the punishment likely to be imposed in the receiving state attains the level of severity to make it inhuman and degrading. Punishment viewed as inhuman and degrading in the UK will not necessarily be so regarded in an extradition case but will do so only if the sentence was likely to be clearly disproportionate for the offence in question. On the facts, a sentence of life without parole would not be so grossly disproportionate to the offence as to meet the heightened standard for contravention of Art 3 in its application to extradition cases.

Although an individual with Asperger's Syndrome would be likely to suffer a serious deterioration in his mental health if he was extradited to the USA on charges of computer hacking, his case did not approach the severity required to infringe Art 3 and the Secretary of State was entitled to order his extradition: *R (on the application of McKinnon) v Secretary of State for Home Affairs* [2009] EWHC 2021 (Admin), [2009] All ER (D) 01 (Aug), DC. But a contrary conclusion was arrived at in a case where the individual's mental health condition was more severe: *Aswat v United Kingdom (Application No 17299/12)* (2013) Times, 24 April, 34 BHRC 656, ECtHR.

The extradition of suspected terrorists facing life sentences in the USA's maximum security prison 'ADX' has been held not to contravene Art 3: *Babar Ahmad v United Kingdom (Application Nos 24027/07, 11949/08, 36742/08, 66911/09 and 67354/09)* (2012) Times, 12 April, ECtHR.

However, the UK would not extradite an offender to Romania without an undertaking that he would serve his sentence in a cell where he would have more than two metres of personal space, failing which the extradition would infringe Art 3: *Florea v Judicial Authority Carei Courthouse, Satu Mare County, Romania* [2014] EWHC 2528 (Admin), (2014) Times, 14 August, Div Ct. An example of a case where assurances were sufficient to permit extradition is *Donald v Republic of South Africa* [2017] EWHC 2580 (Admin).

III HUM [25.5C]

Abortion law In *Re Northern Ireland Human Rights Commission's Application for Judicial Review* [2018] UKSC 27, [2019] 1 All ER 173, the Supreme Court held that the NI Human Rights Commission had no standing to seek a declaration that abortion law in Northern Ireland was incompatible with Arts 3 and 8. Even though the Supreme Court therefore lacked jurisdiction to make a declaration of incompatibility, it observed that the absolute rights contained in article 3 would not bound to be infringed by operation of Northern Ireland law; it

III HUM [27.2D]

Patient under a sentence of discretionary life imprisonment A prisoner suffering from a mental disorder who has been detained in hospital after being sentenced to a term of discretionary life imprisonment is entitled to have the question of his release decided by an independent tribunal, not by the Secretary of State. This was held, in *Benjamin v United Kingdom (Application 28212/95)* [2002] All ER (D) 160 (Sep), (2002) Times, 9 October, ECtHR, to contravene Art 5(4).

III HUM [27.2E]

Patient's right of access to the Tribunal when detained under s 2 It was held by the Court of Appeal that s 2 of the Mental Health Act 1983 is incompatible with Art 5.4 in that it does not provide adequate access to the Mental Health Tribunal for patients detained under s 2 who lack capacity to exercise those rights of access: *R (on the application of MH) v Secretary of State for Health* [2004] EWCA Civ 1690, (2004) Times, 8 December, CA. It was further declared in that case that s 29(4) of the same Act was also incompatible because it denied the detained patient access to a court, or tribunal, during the period of extended detention which arose under that sub-section. However, the House of Lords reversed the Court of Appeal and discharged the declaration of incompatibility: [2005] 3 WLR 867.

III HUM [27.2F]

Detention by British forces overseas British forces in Iraq exercising a power to detain under the relevant United Nations Security Council Resolutions had to ensure that the detainee's rights under Art 5 were not infringed beyond what was inherent in any such detention: *R (on the application of Al-Jedda) v Secretary of State for Defence* [2007] UKHL 58, [2008] 1 AC 332, [2008] 3 All ER 28. Resolution 1546 of the UN Security Council authorised the British and other forces to take necessary measures to contribute to the maintenance of security and stability but this did not authorise the breach of Art 5.1 by detaining suspects for long periods without charge: *Al-Jedda v United Kingdom* [2011] ECHR 27021/08, 20 BHRC 637.

In a private law claim for unlawful detention by HM armed forces, contrary to Afghan law, the Supreme Court held that the UK government could rely on the doctrine of Crown act of state to preclude the court passing judgment on a tort claim. The defence arose if the acts were 'by their nature sovereign acts, acts which are inherently governmental, committed in the conduct of the foreign relations of the Crown'. By virtue of the acts needing to be 'inherently governmental', the defence would not apply to torture, maltreatment of prisoners or some expropriation of property: *Iraqi Civilians v Ministry of Defence* [2017] UKSC 1, [2017] 2 WLR 287, para 36.

III HUM [27.2G]

Continued detention on the decision of the Parole Board It has been declared that the sponsorship of the Parole Board by the Home Office created an appearance of a lack of independence in its decision-making regarding the detention of prisoners, which meant that the Board did not qualify as a court to meet the requirements of Art 5(4): *R (on the application of Brooke) v Parole Board* (2007) Times, 18 October, QB Div Ct. This finding has been upheld by the Court of Appeal which gave guidance to the Secretary of State on how to place the Board within the sponsorship responsibility of the Ministry so that its independence would not be open to question: [2008] EWCA Civ 29, [2008] 3 All ER 289.

In *Black v Secretary of State for Justice* [2008] EWCA Civ 359, [2008] 4 All ER 151 the Court of Appeal declared that s 35 of the Criminal Justice Act 1991, as applied to prisoners serving 15 years or more, was incompatible with Art 5(4) because it left the decision as to release in the hands of the executive (the Secretary of State, on the recommendation of the Parole Board) and was therefore capable of being applied arbitrarily, which was the mischief at which Art 5(4) was directed.

Article 5(4) will require the Parole Board to hold an oral hearing whenever fairness makes this necessary, and this will include cases in which (a) important facts are in dispute or the prisoner has advanced significant explanation or mitigation of which the credibility must be determined, (b) it is maintained on tenable grounds that an oral hearing is necessary for the prisoner to put his case effectively, (c) a decision on the papers would be unfair and (d) the board could not otherwise fairly make an independent assessment of risk or the means by which to manage risk: *Osborn and Booth v Parole Board, Re Reilly* [2013] UKSC 61, [2014] 1 All ER 369, [2013] 3 WLR 1020. In *R (on the application of DSD, Mayor of London, News Group Newspapers Ltd) v Parole Board* [2018] EWHC 694 (Admin), [2018] 3 WLR 829, the Divisional Court held that the rule which prohibited making information public about parole board proceedings (Parole Board Rules 2016, r 25(1)) was ultra vires.

As to the scope of review of a decision of the parole board, see *Browne v Parole Board* [2018] EWCA Civ 2024, holding that there was no basis to introduce proportionality review in place of the anxious scrutiny rationality review.

2. Everyone charged with a criminal offence shall be presumed innocent until proved guilty according to law.
3. Everyone charged with a criminal offence has the following minimum rights:
   (a) to be informed promptly, in a language which he understands and in detail, of the nature and cause of the accusation against him;
   (b) to have adequate time and facilities for the preparation of his defence;
   (c) to defend himself in person or through legal assistance of his own choosing or, if he has not sufficient means to pay for legal assistance, to be given it free when the interests of justice so require;
   (d) to examine or have examined witnesses against him and to obtain the attendance and examination of witnesses on his behalf under the same conditions as witnesses against him;
   (e) to have the free assistance of an interpreter if he cannot understand or speak the language used in court.

III HUM [28.1]

Civil Rights It has been held that a civil servant's rights in respect of recruitment, career and termination of service are not "civil rights" for the purposes of this article: *Huber v France* (1998) 26 EHRR 457, ECtHR. In *Pellegrin v France (Application 28541/95)* (1999) 31 EHRR 651 the European Court of Human Rights clarified its case law and established that: (1) disputes relating to civil service pensions are within the scope of Art 6(1); (2) disputes relating to the recruitment, career and termination of service of public servants who do not exercise powers conferred by public law are also within the scope of Art 6(1); but (3) such disputes are outside the scope of Art 6(1) where they relate to public servants who do exercise powers conferred by public law. These are difficult concepts derived to some extent from the distinction between public law and private law to be found more markedly in continental legal systems than in the United Kingdom.

Article 6.1 applies only to civil rights which can be said on arguable grounds to be recognised under domestic law: *Matthews v Ministry of Defence* [2003] UKHL 4, [2003] 1 AC 1163, [2003] 1 All ER 689. Proceedings under s 34 of the Policing and Crime Act 2009 and s 1 of the Anti-social Behaviour, Crime and Policing Act 2014 concerning gang-related injunctions were not criminal proceedings engaging the criminal protections of Art 6: *Jones v Birmingham City Council* [2018] EWCA Civ 1189, [2018] 3 WLR 1695.

In *R (on the application of A) v Croydon London Borough Council and R (on the application of M) v Lambeth London Borough Council* [2009] UKSC 8, [2009] 1 WLR 2557, [2009] 3 FCR 607, the SC declined to decide whether the right of a child in need to be accommodated by a local authority under s 20 of the Children Act 1989 is a civil right (though Lord Hope expressed the view that it was not) but held that even if it is, the local authority's decision-making processes combined with judicial review satisfy the requirements of Art 6).

The provision of accommodation for homeless people under the Housing Act 1996 has been held not to be a civil right for the purposes of Art 6: *Tomlinson v Birmingham City Council and Ali v Birmingham City Council* [2010] UKSC 8, [2010] 2 AC 39, [2010] 2 All ER 175, affirmed in *Poshteh v Kensington and Chelsea Royal London Borough Council* [2017] UKSC 36, [2017] AC 624.

It was held in *R (on the application of Thompson) v Law Society* [2004] EWCA Civ 167, [2004] 2 All ER 113, (2004) Times, 1 April, that decisions under the authority of the Law Society to reprimand a solicitor and to impose a fine do not determine that person's civil rights.

Where an employee was refused legal representation for a disciplinary hearing at the school where he was employed, his civil right to practise his profession was not engaged because it would be directly determined by a separate decision of the Independent Safeguarding Authority. The test was whether the disciplinary proceedings would directly determine or exert a substantial influence over that subsequent decision: *R (on the application of G) v X School Governors and Y City Council* [2011] UKSC 30, [2011] 4 All ER 625, [2011] 3 WLR 237, [2011] IRLR 756, (2011) Times, 4 July.

Where a disciplinary finding against a prisoner involves additional days of detention the prisoner is entitled to a fair hearing: *R (on the application of Napier) v Secretary of State for the Home Department* [2004] EWHC 936 (Admin), [2005] 3 All ER 76.

Decisions by prison governors or segregation review boards on segregation and cellular confinement are not determinations of civil rights: *R (on the application of King) v Secretary of State for Justice; R (on the application of Bourgass and Hussain) v Secretary of State for Justice* [2012] EWCA Civ 376, [2012] 4 All ER 44, [2012] 1 WLR 3602.

Where after deportation an alien will face a trial in the receiving country which would not satisfy Art 6 in a domestic case, the deportation will infringe Art 6 only if the defect would lead to a miscarriage of justice which itself constitute a flagrant breach of Art 6: *RB (Algeria) v Secretary of State for the Home Department* [2009] UKHL 10, [2009] 3 All ER 643, [2009] 2 WLR 512.

Tax disputes fall outside the scope of Art 6 because they are not included within the concept of 'civil rights and obligations' despite the pecuniary effects which they produce for the taxpayer: *Ferrazzini v Italy* (2001) 34 EHRR 1068, [2001] STC 1314, [2001] ECHR 44759/98, followed in *R (on the application of APVCO 19 Ltd) v HM Treasury* [2015] EWCA Civ 648, 165 NLJ 7661, [2015] All ER (D) 12 (Jul).

III HUM [28.2]

Fair hearing The Convention does not lay down rules of evidence as such, but Art 6 requires fairness in adversarial litigation, as a matter of general principle. Procedures held to be unfair and in breach of Art 6 include the reception by the court of external advice (eg from the Attorney General or a court-appointed expert) where the parties themselves had not had the opportunity to comment: *McMichael v United Kingdom* (1995) 20 EHRR 205, ECtHR; *Lobo Machado v Portugal* (1996) 23 EHRR 79, ECtHR; *Mantovanelli v France* (1996) 24 EHRR 370, ECtHR.

In *Re W (A Child) (Care Proceedings: Non Party Appeal)* [2016] EWCA Civ 1140, [2017] 1 WLR 2415, the Court of Appeal found violations of both Art 6 and Art 8. The judge had made serious criticisms of two witnesses in his judgment and the Court of Appeal found he had conducted the trial in an 'intrinsically unfair' manner 'by keeping these matters to himself during the four week hearing, and failing to arrange for the witnesses to have any opportunity to know of the critical points and to offer any answer to them' before including the criticisms in his judgment.

Where a judge seeks the advice of nautical assessors it should, as a matter of fairness, be disclosed to the parties, except where unnecessary in the light of submissions made earlier: *Owners of Bow Spring v Owners of Manzanillo II* [2004] EWCA Civ 1007, [2005] 1 WLR 144, (2004) Times, 19 August.

Also the failure to conduct an oral hearing at some stage in care proceedings has been held to be a breach of Art 6(1): *L v Finland* [2000] 2 FLR 118, ECtHR.

The Civil Procedure Rules lay down as an overriding objective that cases should be dealt with justly and may not be challenged as defective because they provide for judicial discretion which is capable of being exercised unfairly: *Daniels v Walker* [2000] 1 WLR 1382, CA. Similarly, the court's power, under Children Act 1989 s 34 to allow a local authority to refuse contact with children in its care was not in breach of Arts 6 or 8 if used fairly in appropriate circumstances: *Re F (care: termination of contact)* [2000] 2 FCR 481, [2000] Fam Law 708.

Evidence may be excluded on the ground of public interest on the judge's decision, without the contents being disclosed to the defence, so long as the defence has been kept informed, so far as possible without revealing the material: *Fitt v United Kingdom (Application 29777/96)* [2000] Crim LR 586, ECtHR. The European Court of Human Rights has confirmed that procedures for deciding questions of public interest immunity without giving the defendant a right to be heard are justifiable only where they are strictly necessary: *Edwards and Lewis v United Kingdom* (2003) Times, 29 July, a criminal case where entrapment was raised as a defence. The Court of Appeal has since ruled that there is no material difference between English law and that of the ECHR regarding entrapment: *R v Syed (Haroon Ali)* [2019] EWCA Crim 2809.

A departure from the principle of open justice may be justified by the danger to life that publicity might cause to the main party: see *A v British Broadcasting Corpn* [2014] UKSC 25, [2015] AC 588 in the context of a deportation of a sex-offender who had been granted anonymity to safeguard against risks of violence or death that might be faced when deported.

The failure to disclose material evidence to a defendant in a criminal trial might infringe Art 6; although an appeal court would find a trial unfair only if it found a real possibility that the jury would have arrived at a different verdict if the disclosure had been made: see *McInnes v HM Advocate* [2010] UKSC 7, [2010] SLR 266, [2010] All ER (D) 101 (Feb) and *Macklin v Her Majesty's Advocate (Scotland)* [2015] UKSC 77, [2016] SLT 1, [2015] All ER (D) 154 (Dec). See also *R (on the application of Wang Yam) v Central Criminal Court* [2015] UKSC 76, [2016] 2 WLR 19, (2015) Times, 31 December, [2015] All ER (D) 153 (Dec) in which the Supreme Court upheld a decision to refuse permission to disclosure material heard in camera during a murder trial to the ECtHR for the purposes of a complaint that he had not had a fair trial. There was no breach of domestic or international law obligations. See *R (on the application of Haralambous) v St Albans Crown Court* [2018] UKSC 1, [2018] AC 236 for the ability of magistrates to take into account closed material when issuing search and seizure warrants under s 8 of the Police and Criminal Evidence Act 1984, the Crown Court when authorising retention of seized material under s 59 of the Criminal Justice and Police Act 2001, and upon a judicial review from either decision.

Government guidance was held unlawful where it indicated that civil legal aid in immigration cases under s 10 of the Legal Aid, Sentencing and Punishment of Offenders Act 2012 would be granted only in rare and extreme cases: *G v Director of Legal Aid Casework (British Red Cross Society intervening)* [2014] EWCA Civ 1622, 2015] 1 WLR 2247. To decide whether Art 6 (and also the procedural requirements of Art 8) mandated a grant of legal aid, the key question was whether an unrepresented litigant could present his case effectively and without obvious unfairness. This depended on the facts of the case, including the importance and complexity of the issues and the litigant's ability to represent himself without assistance. Similarly, there was a potential breach of Art 6 where the complexity of the process of obtaining legal aid in child care proceedings was beyond the capabilities of parents, one of whom lacked capacity and the other had learning difficulties: *Re D (a child) (No 2)* [2015] EWFC 2, [2015] 1 FLR 1247 per Sir James Munby PFD; see also *Re K and H (Children)* [2015] EWCA Civ 543, [2015] 1 WLR 3801, [2015] All ER (D) 230 (May).

Where an employee was refused legal representation for a disciplinary hearing at the school where he was employed, his civil right to practise his profession was not engaged because it would be directly determined by a separate decision of the Independent Safeguarding Authority. The test was whether the disciplinary proceedings would directly determine or exert a substantial influence over that subsequent decision: *R (on the application of G) v X School Governors and Y City Council* [2011] UKSC 30, [2011] 4 All ER 625, [2011] 3 WLR 237, [2011] IRLR 756, (2011) Times, 4 July.

Legal representation by the Medical Protection Society has been held to meet the requirements of Art 6 in disciplinary proceedings where it would have been a breach to deny a doctor any legal representation at all: *Kulkarni v Milton Keynes Hospital NHS Foundation Trust* [2009] EWCA Civ 789, [2010] ICR 101, [2009] IRLR 829.

III HUM [28.2AA]

Conditional fee agreements In a nuisance claim, after determining issues of liability, the Supreme Court in *Coventry v Lawrence* [2014] UKSC 46, [2015] AC 106, [2014] 2 P & CR 304, considered that the costs effect on a party of a conditional fee agreement under the Access to Justice Act 1999 and the Courts and Legal Services Act 1990 might potentially be inconsistent with the party's rights under ECHR, Art 6. The Court also provisionally questioned whether a declaration of incompatibility could be made given that the relevant provisions had already been repealed and replaced. After notice was given to the Attorney General and the Secretary of State for Justice, and full argument on the point had taken place, the Supreme Court ultimately decided (*Coventry v Lawrence* [2015] UKSC 50, 165 NLJ 7663, [2015] All ER (D) 234 (Jul)) that there was no incompatibility with Art 6 (or Art 1 Protocol 1). The success fees and ATE premiums (although well in excess of the value of the claim) were integral to the scheme of the 1999 Act and had a legitimate aim: they sought to maintain access to justice for litigants no longer entitled to legal aid. Whilst the scheme was open to objections, the issue was not whether it was unfair, but whether it was disproportionate and the Court held it was not.

III HUM [28.2B]

Appeal on law but not on fact The question has arisen whether an appeal on law under s 204 of the Housing Act 1996 provides a fair hearing for the determination of civil rights. It has been held that, since the court does not have power to decide disputes of fact it is not fully competent for the purposes of Art 6 of the Human Rights Convention: *Adan v Newham London Borough Council* [2002] EWCA Civ 1916, [2002] 1 All ER 931. But a slightly different conclusion was reached in *Runa Begum v Tower Hamlets London Borough Council* [2003] UKHL 5, [2003] 2 AC 430, [2003] 1 All ER 731, where the House of Lords held that although the judge hearing the appeal does not have power to make fresh determinations on issues of fact the jurisdiction to allow appeals on questions of law meets the requirements of Art 6. This is because the first tier decision-making is conducted at a senior administrative level and is subject to detailed statutory rules to ensure fair decision making so that the context did not require a full fact-finding jurisdiction on appeal.

In *Fazia Ali v Birmingham City Council* [2008] EWCA Civ 1228, [2009] 2 All ER 601, the Court of Appeal applied the *Begum* reasoning to a determination where the sole issue for the reviewing officer was a simple issue of primary fact as well as where the reviewing officer had to use specialist knowledge or have regard to policy considerations. The decision was affirmed in *Tomlinson v Birmingham City Council and Ali v Birmingham City Council* [2010] UKSC 8, [2010] 2 AC 39, [2010] 2 All ER 175.

III HUM [28.2C]

Informal discussions with the judge Under Art 6, as at common law, there is a right to an impartial tribunal. This precludes not only actual bias but also apparent bias. The test is whether a fair-minded and informed observer would conclude that there was a real possibility of bias: *Porter v Magill* [2002] 2 AC 357.

In *Hart v Relentless Records Ltd* (2002) Times, 8 October, Jacob J called an informal meeting with counsel when an application was part heard. He then gave the parties an indication that the applicant's case seemed weak and that it would be in the interests of the parties to settle. He refused a subsequent application to recuse himself for apparent bias. He held that there was no breach of Art 6: a judge was under a duty to help parties to settle a case, the informal meeting was not part of the trial and a fair-minded and informed observer would not have concluded that there was a real possibility of bias. Similarly, a throwaway remark by the chair of a planning committee that "he was going to go with the inspector's report", made to an objector at an unexpected meeting before the hearing, was held by the Court of Appeal to indicate no more than a predisposition. The hearing which followed was unusually prolonged and the members explored the issues fully so that an impartial observer would not have believed that the committee had approached the task with a closed mind: *National Assembly for Wales v Condron* [2006] EWCA Civ 1573, (2006) Times, 13 December, CA.

In *Bubbles & Wine Ltd v Lusha* [2018] EWCA Civ 468, the Court of Appeal gave a strong warning that for the judge to have an informal discussion with one counsel in the absence of the other counsel created an appearance of bias.

III HUM [28.3]

Independent and impartial tribunal In Scotland the High Court of Justiciary has held that a judge who has no security of tenure and whose appointment was subject to annual renewal was not independent for the purposes of Art 6: *Starrs v Procurator Fiscal, Linlithgow* (1999) Times, 17 November. The defendant may waive this ground of objection but only where he, or she, is aware of it. Otherwise it may be taken at a later stage on appeal: *Millar v Dickson (Procurator Fiscal, Elgin)* [2001] UKPC D4, [2002] 3 All ER 1041.

Further, in *McGonnell v United Kingdom* (Application 28488/95) (2000) 30 EHRR 289, ECtHR it was held that any direct involvement in the passage of legislation or of executive rules was likely to cast doubt on the judicial impartiality of a person who subsequently determined a dispute over whether reasons existed to permit a variation from the wording of the legislation or rules at issue. The case concerned the position of the Deputy Bailiff of Guernsey but could have implications for the district judge's role in interpleader under execution.

It is well established that the judge must be independent of the executive and legislative powers of the state as well as the parties to the case. In determining the degree of independence regard should be had to (a) the manner of appointment (b) the duration of the term of office (c) the conditions of the office (d) the provisions for removability and (e) the existence of guarantees against outside pressure. It has to be shown, on an objective basis, that there is an appearance of independence and impartiality: *R (on the application of Barclay) v Secretary of State* [...] EWHC 1183 (Admin), [2014] 1 WLR [...]15 (the order of the [...] set aside for other reasons, see *R (on the application of* [...] *Justice* [2015] UKSC 54, [2015] AC 276). [...] maker is not an independent and impartial tribunal, [...] Minister, the [...] not be challenged on this ground if an appeal lies to [...] independent and [...] tribunal with full jurisdiction. As to the last three words see [...] decision in *Bryan v United Kingdom* (1995) 21 EHRR 342, ECtHR; applied in *R (on the application of Alconbury Developments Ltd) v Secretary of State for the Environment*, [...] *Transport and the Regions* [2001] UKHL 23, [2003] 2 AC 295. See also the decision of [...] European Court of Human Rights in *Chapman v United Kingdom* (Application 27238/9[...]1) Times, 30 January that decisions by planning authorities complied with Art 6.1 [...] of the availability of judicial review after a public procedure before an inspector. [...] that the Administrative Court has been held not to have "full jurisdiction" to do ju[...] the case of a decision by a biased authority if it cannot either substitute its own dec[...] remit the decision-making to another body: *Kingsley v United Kingdom (Application* [...]) (2001) Times, 9 January.

On the other hand, an objection that the d[...]er is not independent may be cured by the court's decision on judicial review. [...] held in *R (on the application of Beeson) v Dorset County Council* [2002] EWCA [...] [2003] HLR 550, (2003) Times, 2 January that, there being no reason to cha[...] objective integrity of the first instance process (although persons were involve[d in the dec]ision-making who were not 'independent'), the panel on whose report the [...]ty acted had arrived at a fair and reasonable recommendation.

The fact that a person [...] High Court Judge lacks the necessary authority does not mean that he is not [...] law where he and all those involved honestly believe that he has that auth[ority ...] v *Customs and Excise Comrs* [2003] EWCA Civ 511, [2003] QB 142[...] ER 351.

In *Cooper v* [...] *(Application No 48843/00)* (2004) Times, 12 January, ECtHR, the inden[...] Royal Air Force courts martial was held to be secured by appoint[...]n judge advocate by a civilian Lord Chancellor and a civilian Judge

Advocate General. A contrary conclusion was reached in relation to a Royal Navy court martial because the judge advocate was a serving naval officer in *Grieves v United Kingdom (Application 570567/00)* (2004) Times, 12 January, ECtHR.

It has been held that disciplinary proceedings before an adjudicating body for breach of the Prison Rules do not satisfy the requirement of Art 6.1 that the adjudicating body should be independent and impartial: *Whitfield v United Kingdom (Application Nos 46387/99, 48906/99, 57410/00 and 57419/00)* (2005) Times, 27 April, ECtHR. See also *R (on the application of Al-Hasan) v Secretary of State for the Home Department* [2005] UKHL 13, [2005] 1 All ER 927, HL, in which it was held that a decision of a deputy governor, that an order for a squat search was a lawful order which the applicants had committed an offence by disobeying, should be set aside for bias, on the ground that the decision-maker had known about and approved the making of the order in question.

A hearing by a prison governor of a disciplinary matter which could result in a sentence of additional days' detention is in breach of Art 6: *Young v United Kingdom (60682/00)* (2007) 45 EHRR 29, ECHR. The same applies to a summary trial of a soldier by his commanding officer on a charge of using insubordinate language to a superior officer: *Bell v United Kingdom (41534/98)* (2007) 45 EHRR 24, ECHR.

However, in *R (on the application of King) v Secretary of State for Justice* [2010] EWHC 2522 (Admin), [2010] NLJR 1458 it was held that whilst a prison governor adjudicating a disciplinary charge against an inmate resulting in cellular confinement was not an 'independent tribunal' for the purposes of Art 6, the availability of judicial review meant that the process as a whole satisfied the requirements of Art 6.

III HUM [28.3A]

Setting aside for bias Before setting aside for bias, the court has first to ascertain all the circumstances which have a bearing on the suggestion of bias and then to decide whether they would lead a fair-minded and informed observer to conclude that there was a real possibility that the tribunal was biased: *Director General of Fair Trading v Proprietary Association of Great Britain* [2001] NLJR 17, CA (also reported as *Re Medicaments and Related Classes of Goods (No 2)* [2001] 1 WLR 700, [2000] All ER (D) 2425). Where the Court of Appeal prevents a violation of Art 6 by upholding a decision of the court below to abandon a hearing because of apparent bias, there is no power to order the Lord Chancellor to pay the wasted costs under s 8 of the Human Rights Act 1998: *Re Medicaments and Related Classes of Goods (No 4)* [2001] EWCA Civ 1217, [2002] 1 WLR 269. A family judge who is invited to take part in inter-disciplinary conferences, committees and projects, needs to consider whether a fair-minded observer might conclude that there was a real possibility of being influenced, by such involvement ... the ... relevant to the outcome of a case before him. Applying this test ... should not proceed to try it: *M v Islington London Borough* ... NLJR ... Med 665, applying *Re Medicaments (No 2)* [2001] 1 WLR 700, [2002] 2 AC ... Senguents approach was approved in *Porter v Magill* [2002] ... *v Holmes (Lord Chancellor Intervening)* (2002) Times, 19 August, CA.

In *Harb v Prince Abdul Aziz Bin Fahd Bin Abdul Aziz* [2016] EWCA Civ 556, the Court of Appeal held ... judicial irritation and hostility towards an advocate does not necessarily entail a real possibility of bias against a litigant, even if the conduct of the judge was deplorable. ... court said:

> 'From time ... the patience of judges can be sorely tested by the behaviour of advocates. So ... a judge will overreact and unwisely make an intemperate comment. But judges ... expected to be true to their judicial oaths and not allow their feelings about an advocate to affect their determination of the case they are hearing. The informed and fair-minded observer is to be assumed to know this.'

III HUM [28.3B]

Judicial self-recusal A judge should not necessarily recuse himself because he has seen correspondence which was written ... prejudice. The question whether he can proceed to act impartially depends on whether, in all the circumstances, a fair-minded and informed observer would conclude that there was a real possibility that there could not, or would not, be a fair trial: *Berg v IML London Ltd* [2002] ... 17. On the other hand, the requirement that a judge should be free from any actual ... bias does not apply to counsel. Where an advocate has a connection with a party ... on the other side, the court may prevent the advocate from acting where there would be ... disclosure of relevant confidential information or of irregularity which would ... ordering a re-trial: *Geveran Trading Co Ltd v Skjevesland* [2002] EWCA Civ 1... All ER 1, (2002) Times, 13 November. In *Taylor v Williamsons (a firm)* (2002) ... CA, the trial judge had, because of a lapse of memory, sent the parties his draft ... before he had considered their written submissions. He recalled the judgment as soon as the error was pointed out and the Court held that his conduct did not disclose a real possibility of bias and that it was therefore not appropriate for him to recuse himself or for there to be a re-trial.

The fact that the judge has made adverse comments about a party in previous litigation or adverse findings is not, by itself, sufficient to require judicial self-recusal. On the other hand, the fact that only one out of three members of a tribunal raises perceptions of bias is not, by itself, a sufficient reason for not standing down. The question whether a case for recusal is made out is one of law in the context of the proceedings as a whole. It may be appropriate that a court hearing an appeal against a judge's refusal to recuse himself, or herself, should look at witness statements as to how the issue was raised and determined, together with observations on the witness statements by members of the original tribunal or court. See *Lodwick v Southwark London Borough Council* [2004] EWCA Civ 306, [2004] ICR 884, [2004] All ER (D) 349 (Mar).

A judge should not cease hearing a case, or application, where a party appearing in person has asserted that judges in general, including those listed to hear his case, were likely to favour submissions by members of the legal profession over those of a lay litigant. Nor should such an assertion by itself justify the court in urging the Legal Services Commission to grant legal aid. Both points were made by the Court of Appeal in *Triados Bank NV v Dobbs* (2005) Times, 11 May, CA.

If a judge has a long-standing friendship with an individual who is involved in the case he should recuse himself on *Locabail* principles even where the individual is not going to be called as a witness; and it should not be a matter of weighing the danger of apparent bias against the disruption caused by withdrawing from the case at a late stage: *AWG Group Ltd v Morrison* [2006] EWCA Civ 6, [2006] 1 All ER 967.

It is invidious for a judge to sit in judgment of his own conduct; so, where circumstances permit (which will not always be the case). First an informal approach should be made by letter to the judge inviting recusal. He, or she, might with honour deny the complaint but still pass the case to a colleague, or invite another judge to take the decision: *El Farargy v El Farargy* (2007) Times 23 November, CA.

A judge did not err in declining to recuse himself as trial judge following his finding of contempt against a defendant. That decision, made on a proper objective basis, did not create a real possibility of bias and the defendant had made an unequivocal and informed decision not to make a recusal application earlier in the proceedings: *JSC BTA Bank v Mukhtar Ablyazov* [2012] EWCA Civ 1551, [2012] NLJR 1536.

III HUM [28.3C]

Bias in specific contexts In *R v Spear* (2001) Times, 30 January, the Courts-Martial Appeal Court held that there was no real possibility of a judge being biased in favour of a Government Department because of having acted for the Government as Treasury counsel. Upon appointment to the bench connections with previous government clients became historic only. See also the conclusions in *R v Williams* [2001] 38 LS Gaz R 37, C-Mac, that the court martial procedures do not give rise to apparent bias and are Convention compatible. In *R v Spear* [2002] UKHL 31, [2003] 1 AC 734, [2002] 3 All ER 1074, the House of Lords held, following *Morris v United Kingdom (Application 34784/97)* (2002) 34 EHRR 52, that a trial by court martial does not infringe an accused's rights under Art 6. Where a soldier chooses to be tried by his commanding officer, rather than to be tried by a district court martial, but has a right of appeal by way of rehearing before an independent tribunal, the summary trial, although not itself a trial by an independent tribunal, is Convention compliant: *Baines v Army Prosecuting Authority* [2005] EWHC 1339 (Admin), in which the view was also expressed that the accused had, by his election for summary trial, waived his right to challenge the process for breach of Art 6(1) and (3).

An allegation of bias is not sustainable if based solely on the religion, ethnic or national origin, gender, age, class, means or sexual orientation of the judge hearing the case: *Seer Technologies Ltd v Abbas* [2000] 07 LS Gaz R 40.

On the other hand, evidence of racial bias in the course of a jury's deliberations may be a ground for concluding that the trial was unfair, even though the judge may have addressed the issue in a special direction: *Sanders v United Kingdom (Application 34129/96)* (2000) Times, 12 May, ECtHR.

The House of Lords reversed the Court of Appeal decision in *Lawal v Northern Spirit Ltd* [2003] UKHL 35, [2004] 1 All ER 187, (2003) Times, 27 June. It was decided that apparent bias could arise sufficient to require self-recusal where a QC who had sat as a part-time judge in the Employment Appeal Tribunal appeared before the same lay member or members when acting for a party in a different case.

In *R (on the application of PD) v West Midlands and North West Mental Health Review Tribunal* (2003) Times, 31 October, CA, it was held that the fact that a medical member of a mental health review tribunal was employed as a consultant by the NHS trust responsible for the claimant's detention was not a breach of Art 6. The consultant had no connections with any hospital run by the trust and there were sufficient guarantees to exclude any legitimate doubt about his independence.

The fact that a court or tribunal expresses a preliminary view prior to hearing all the evidence does not by itself suggest bias. But the strength of any wording used and it is good practice to make clear that views expressed before the conclusion are only provisional and that the court or tribunal remains open to persuasion: *Southwark London Borough Council v Jiminez* [2003] EWCA Civ 502, [2003] ICR 1176. Where a judge calls counsel into his room half way through the trial and indicates that he believes the claimant whereas the defendant (who had not given evidence) had a police background which meant he would be less likely to admit he was wrong, this could give a indication of a prematurely closed mind ie bias: *Steadman-Byrne v Amjad* [2007] EWCA Civ 625, [2007] 1 WLR 2484.

The fact that a medical member of a disability appeal tribunal had for a number of years provided reports for the Benefits Agency as an examining medical practitioner did not give rise to a reasonable apprehension of bias. A fair-minded observer who had considered the facts properly would appreciate that professional detachment and the ability to exercise her own independent judgment on medical issues lay at the heart of her relationship with the agency and that she was just as capable of exercising those qualities when sitting as the medical member of a tribunal: *Gillies v Secretary of State for Work and Pensions* [2006] UKHL 2, [2006] 1 All ER 731, (2006) Times, 30 January.

On the other hand where the judge's circumstances (such as close relationship with the advocates or the litigants) entitle a party to object the decision whether to waive the right to object should be taken by the litigant on the basis of objective advice as to the implications of the decision either way and counsel should not seek to influence the decision by recommendations based on personal knowledge of the individuals concerned or make strong recommendations for the objection to be waived: *Smith v Kvaerner Cementation Foundations Ltd* [2006] EWCA Civ 242, [2006] 3 All ER 593, (2006) Times, 11 April.

The European Court of Human Rights has held that, in the absence of special circumstances, the trial of a civilian by a military court martial would offend the right to a fair trial and was held to do so in the instant case: *Martin v United Kingdom (Application No 40426/98)* (2006) Times, 27 November, ECtHR.

Where one member of a tribunal has had to stand down because of apparent bias it does not necessarily follow that the other members should have to stand down too although this may be appropriate depending on the circumstances of the case: *ASM Shipping Ltd of India v Harris* (2007) Times, 6 August, [2008] 1 Lloyd's Rep 61, QBD.

III HUM [28.3D]

Prejudicial publicity There is no absolute rule that knowledge of prejudicial publicity is fatal to the fairness of proceedings. Its effect has to be considered in the context of the proceedings as a whole, including the likely impact of the oral evidence and the legal advice available: *R (on the application of Mahfouz) v General Medical Council* [2004] EWCA Civ 233, (2004) 80 BMLR 113, [2004] All ER (D) 114 (Mar). In that case the Court of Appeal held that the General Medical Council's professional conduct committee should have allowed a short adjournment to enable the respondent to apply for judicial review of their decision to proceed despite the prejudicial publicity in the press.

III HUM [28.3E]

Declaring an interest An unsuccessful litigant sought to have a decision set aside on the ground that the chairman's husband was occasionally instructed by the respondents. The Court of Appeal held that these circumstances were not grounds for presuming bias and that, in any case, they had been disclosed at the outset and the litigant had not objected, thereby waiving his right to object at a later stage: *Jones v DAS Legal Expenses Insurance Co Ltd* [2003] EWCA Civ1071, [2004] IRLR 218.

III HUM [28.4]

Absolute bar An absolute bar on negligence claims against the police has been held to prevent access to a fair trial of civil rights, in breach of Art 6(1): *Osman v United Kingdom* [1999] 1 FLR 193, ECtHR. But the ECtHR took a different view in *Z v United Kingdom* (2001) Times, 1 June, ECtHR: they concluded that it was not a case of immunity but there was a breach of Art 13 because the domestic law provided no remedy for a breach of Art 3 (by permitting flagrant abuse of children in care in a local authority home). Awards were made for breach of Art 3 in *E v United Kingdom (Application 33218/96)* [2002] 3 FCR 700, (2002) Times, 4 December, ECtHR. In *JD v East Berkshire Community NHS Trust* [2003] EWCA Civ 1151, [2004] QB 558, [2003] 4 All ER 796, it was held that public policy objections to the recognition of a duty of care on the part of local authorities as regards children in their care were no longer sustainable. However, it was held that no duty was owed to the parents, a conclusion upheld in the House of Lords: [2005] UKHL 23, [2005] 2 AC 373, [2005] 2 All ER 443.

The lodging of a public safety certificate under s 42 of the Fair Employment (Northern Ireland) Act 1976 was held to be a disproportionate denial of access to the tribunal: *Devenney v United Kingdom (Application No 24265/94)* (2002) Times, 11 April, ECtHR.

In *Iraqi Civilians v Ministry of Defence* [2017] UKSC 1, [2017] 2 WLR 287 the Supreme Court held that the UK government could rely on the doctrine of Crown act of state to preclude the court passing judgment on a tort claim. The defence was one of the substantive law and did not amount to a breach of Art 6. In *Belhaj v Straw* [2017] UKSC 3, [2017] AC 964 the Supreme Court held that the state immunity defence, however, could not apply in proceedings against the United Kingdom where a foreign state was not facing liability.

The barring of a civil claim by State immunity had been held not to be in conflict with Art 6, see *Holland v Lampen-Wolfe* [2000] 3 All ER 833, [2000] 1 WLR 1573, HL. See also *Jones v Ministry of the Interior of the Kingdom of Saudi Arabia* [2006] UKHL 26, [2007] 1 All ER 113 in which the sovereign immunity from suit of a foreign state under the State Immunity Act 1978, which barred claims by individuals that they had been systematically tortured by State officials, was found not disproportionate and therefore not to infringe Art 6. See also *Jones v United Kingdom (Application 34356/06)* (2014) 59 EHRR 1 in which the ECtHR held that state immunity for state officials reflected generally recognised rules of public international law and did not amount to an unjustified restriction on access to the court. The matter would, however, be kept under review.

However, in *Benkharbouche v Embassy of the Republic of Sudan* [2017] UKSC 62, [2017] All ER (D) 84 (Oct), the Supreme Court noted that such domestic authority was in conflict with the jurisprudence of ECtHR in *Al-Adsani v UK (Application 35763/97)* (2002) 34 EHRR 11 and subsequent cases. The Court held that ss 16(1)(a) and 4(2) of the State Immunity Act 1978, which, respectively, (i) imposed a blanket exclusion on 'members of a mission' from protections that would otherwise be afforded to employees, and (ii) did not remove state immunity from employees inter alia those who were not habitually resident in the UK, breached ECHR, Art 6. Furthermore the Court found that Art 47 of the Charter of Fundamental Rights of the European Union (the content of which it said was not identical to Art 6) had also been violated on the basis that the Secretary of State had agreed that it was coextensive with Art 6 ECHR on the facts of this case.

In *A v United Kingdom (Application 35373/97)* (2002) Times, 28 December, ECtHR, the European Court held that the absolute privilege attaching to statements made by MPs in the course of parliamentary debates was not disproportionate and did not exceed the margin of appreciation afforded to individual member states.

There is no breach of Art 6 where a person is prevented, by anti-suit injunction, from litigating in one forum because the contract provides for proceedings to be brought in another: *OT Africa Line Ltd v Fayad Hijazy* [2001] 1 Lloyd's Rep 76. Limitation periods may be justified as part of the margin of appreciation: *Stubbings v United Kingdom* (1996) 23 EHCR 213, ECtHR.

In *A v United Kingdom (Application 35373/97)* (2003) 36 EHRR 51, (2002) Times, 28 December, ECtHR, the European Court held that the absolute privilege attaching to statements made by MPs in the course of parliamentary debates was not disproportionate and did not exceed the margin of appreciation afforded to individual member states.

III HUM [28.5]

Within a reasonable time Unacceptable delays may be a denial of the litigant's right to justice: *H v France* (Case No 6/1988/150/204) (1989) 12 EHRR 74, ECtHR; *Robins v United Kingdom* (Case No 118/1996/737/936), (1997) 26 EHRR 527, ECtHR. See also *Steedman v BBC* [2001] EWCA Civ 1534, [2001] 47 LS Gaz R 27 and *Loutchansky v Times Newspapers Ltd (No 2)* [2001] EMLR 876 (at para **III HUM [32.5A]** (libel proceedings)). In *Davies v United Kingdom (Application 42007/98)* (2002) 35 EHRR 720, Times, 1 August, ECtHR, the European Court of Human Rights awarded the claimant damages for distress, anxiety and frustration caused by unreasonable delay by the Secretary of State in the progress of proceedings under the Directors Disqualification Act 1986. The Court reached substantially the same conclusion as in *Davies* in *Eastaway v United Kingdom (Application 74976/01)* [2004] All ER (D) 347 (Jul), (2004) Times, 9 August, ECtHR.

In *Obasa v United Kingdom (Application 50034/99)* it was held by the ECHR that seven years was an unreasonably long time to bring an employment case to a conclusion, following a hold-up of 14 months before the Court of Appeal and 13 months before the House of Lords. Litigation to prevent a spy, George Blake, from receiving royalties form his book took over nine years before a ruling of the House of Lords was obtained and this was held to have been in breach of Art 6 rights, for which compensation was awarded: *Blake v United Kingdom (Application No 68890/01)* (2006) Times, 11 October, ECtHR.

Three periods of delay by the State, accounting for 43 months out of 66 were held unreasonable delay in a confiscation case: *Bullen and Soneji v United Kingdom (Application No 3383/06)* (2009) Times, 2 February, ECtHR. See also the decision of the European Court that the waiting time, of four years seven months, for an appeal against a confiscation order was excessive and contrary to Art 6, attracting an award of 2,000 euros: *Minshall v United Kingdom (Application No 7350/06)* [2012] STC 731, (2012) Times, 24 January, ECtHR.

III HUM [28.5A]

Judgment to be pronounced publicly and Court Records Judgment may be pronounced privately, where a private hearing was justified in the interests of justice. The availability of copies of the judgment, in accordance with CPR 5.4(2)(c) (see **CPR 5.4**), saves the private pronouncement from breaching Art 6: *Re Trusts of X Charity* [2003] EWHC 1462 (Ch), [2003] 3 All ER 860, [2003] 1 WLR 2751.

As to a non-party's right to obtain copies of documents filed in Court proceedings, see CPR Part 5 and *Cape Intermediate Holdings Ltd v Dring* [2018] EWCA Civ 1795, [2019] 1 WLR 479.

III HUM [28.6]

Disclosure of relevant records It could be a breach of Art 6 for a government to withhold medical and radiation records without which the claimant could not obtain justice regarding his claim for compensation. On the face of it, however, the availability of disclosure of documents is a good answer to such a complaint: *McGinley and Egan v United Kingdom* (Case No 10/1997/794/995-996) (1998) 27 EHRR 1, ECtHR.

On a similar point it was held in *McElduff v United Kingdom* (Case No 62/1997/846/1052-1053) (1998) 4 BHRC 393, ECtHR, that the use by the Government of s 42 of the Fair Employment (Northern Ireland) Act 1976 to withhold documents which might show discrimination because of religious beliefs was effectively to deny the persons concerned access to a fair hearing by a court which could compensate them and was therefore a breach of Art 6(1).

III HUM [28.7]

Denial of access to the courts for vexatious litigation The inherent power of the High Court to prevent a litigant from starting proceedings without leave (so as to prevent abuse) is not a breach of Art 6, nor is the statutory power under the Vexatious Actions Act 1896: *Ebert v Birch* [2000] Ch 484, [1999] 3 WLR 670, CA. Also an order for the stay to proceedings, conditional on the payment of costs arising in other proceedings, has been held not to contravene the requirements of Art 6.1: *Stevens v School of Oriental and African Studies* (2001) Times, 2 February.

The fact that the Attorney General may exercise an advisory role in the selection and appointment of judges does not compromise the impartiality of the judges once appointed: *A-G v Covey; A-G v Matthews* [2001] EWCA Civ 254, (2001) Times, 2 March. It was held in the same case: (a) that the denial of access in the case of a vexatious litigant was not a breach of Art 6.1 where it pursued a legitimate aim; and (b) that, by allowing the litigant to seek permission or to seek a variation of the order, the court was ensuring that the restriction was not out of proportion. It was also held that there was no breach in failing to disclose a bench memorandum provided that the litigant was not prejudiced by it.

III HUM [28.7A]

Lack of direct access for child support The fact that a parent has no route to insist on the enforcement of child maintenance assessments made by the Child Support Agency does not mean a breach of Art 6. The parent has the right to apply for judicial review and for damages under s 7: *R (on the application of Kehoe) v Secretary of State for Work and Pensions* [2003] EWHC 1021 (Admin), [2003] 3 FCR 481, [2003] 2 FLR 578. An appeal to the House of Lords was dismissed, Lady Hale dissenting: *R (on the application of Kehoe) v Secretary of State for Work and Pensions* (2005) Times, 15 July, HL.

III HUM [28.7B]

Delayed access to court under Care Standards Act 2000 The provision in the Care Standards Act 2000 for care workers to be placed provisionally on a list of persons unsuitable to work with vulnerable adults with no power to apply to the Care Standards Tribunal to be removed from the list until some months had passed was held incompatible with the right of access to a court under Art 6: *R (on the application of Wright) v Secretary of State for Health and Secretary of State for Education and Skills* [2009] UKHL 3, [2009] 1 AC 739, [2009] 2 All ER 129.

III HUM [28.7C]

Arbitration agreements Where parties have voluntarily entered into an arbitration agreement they are to be treated as waiving their rights under Art 6, but the agreement must be made without constraint and must not run counter to any important public interest: *Stretford v Football Association* [2007] EWCA Civ 238, [2007] All ER (D) 346 (Mar). Similarly it has been held that a voluntary agreement, under s 69(1) of the Arbitration Act 1996, that there should be no right of appeal to the courts has been held not to infringe Art 6: *Sumukan Ltd v Commonwealth Secretariat* [2007] EWCA Civ 243, [2007] All ER (D) 341 (Mar).

III HUM [28.7D]

Tribunal Fees The right of access to justice in the Employment Tribunal was considered by the Supreme Court in *R(Unison) v Lord Chancellor (EHRC intervening)* [2017] UKSC 51, [2017] 3 WLR 409. The case concerned the lawfulness of fees imposed in order to issue claims and to have a hearing. Although the proceedings were not based under the HRA, the Supreme Court drew an analogy with the law of the ECtHR concerning access to justice: even an interference with access to the courts which is not unsurmountable will be unlawful unless it can be justified as reasonably necessary to meet a legitimate objective.

III HUM [28.8]

State Immunity Act 1978 The immunity which the State Immunity Act 1978 confers on foreign states, in respect of litigation within the United Kingdom, reflects accepted principles of international law and is not in breach of Art 6: *McElhinney v Ireland (Application 31253/96) Al-Adsani v United Kingdom (Application 35763/97) and Fogarty v United Kingdom (Application 37112/97)* (2001) Times, 26 November, ECtHR. See also *Jones v Ministry of the Interior of the Kingdom of Saudi Arabia* [2006] UKHL 26, [2007] 1 All ER 113, the ruling in which was upheld by the ECtHR in *Jones v United Kingdom (Applications 34356/06 and 40528/06)* (2014) 59 EHRR 1, (2014) Times, 18 January, ECtHR. See now also *Benkharbouche v Embassy of the Republic of Sudan* [2015] EWCA Civ 33, [2015] 3 WLR 301, noted above at para **III HUM [28.4]**. The Supreme Court has held that the immunity conferred by s 4(2)(b) of the State Immunity Act 1978 in respect of State employees who are not citizens of the United Kingdom or settled here is incompatible with article 6 of the Human Rights Convention and so is the immunity conferred by s 16(1)(a) in respect of civil claims by embassy staff: *Benkharbouche v Secretary of State for Foreign and Commonwealth Affairs* [2017] UKSC 62, [2017] All ER (D) 84 (Oct).

III HUM [28.8A]

Restraining the bringing of proceedings in a foreign court which may be conducted unfairly It is not appropriate for an English court to restrain a party in proceedings before it from suing in another jurisdiction merely because of concerns about possible unfairness, although proved unfairness would be a ground for refusing to recognize a judgment so obtained: *Al-Bassam v Al-Bassam* [2004] EWCA Civ 857, (2004) 148 Sol Jo LB 826, (2004) Times, 22 July.

III HUM [28.8B]

Injunctions to restrain gang violence and other anti-social behaviour It has been held that proceedings under Part 4 of the Policing and Crime Act 2009, to restrain gang violence, are essentially civil proceedings to which the standard burden of proof, on the balance of probabilities, applies; and that they do not involve the bringing of a criminal charge, for the purposes of Article 6 of the Convention: *Jones v Birmingham City Council* [2018] EWCA Civ 1189, [2018] All ER (D) 129 (May).

III HUM [28.9]

Enforcement of orders by committal to prison Enforcement by committal involves the presumption of innocence and the proof to a criminal standard of non-compliance and the mental element in the offence. Proceedings by judgment summons, for example, must comply with Art 6, in its applications to criminal offences, and this means compliance with the Practice Direction on Committal at **CPR PD 52**: *Mubarak v Mubarak* [2000] All ER (D) 2303, CA and *Quinn v Cuff* [2001] EWCA Civ 36, [2001] All ER (D) 49 (Jan). In these cases the court failed to treat the summons for failure to pay as a criminal charge. The court should have applied a presumption of innocence and required proof, to a criminal standard of a wilful refusal to pay before making any committal order, or instalment order backed by a suspended committal. It would be inconsistent with the rights in Art 6(3) for a judge to proceed with an effective hearing of an application to commit to prison knowing that the prisoner wished to be heard in person but was prevented from doing so by matters over which he had no control: *Raja v Van Hoogstraten* [2004] EWCA Civ 968, [2004] 4 All ER 793, (2004) Times, 27 July.

But, so long as the overall trial is fair, Art 6(3)(d) does not preclude the admission of hearsay evidence which is primarily a matter for national law: *Daltel Europe Ltd (in liquidation) v Makki (Committal for contempt)* [2006] EWCA Civ 94, (2006) Times, 8 March.

It has been held by the European Court of Human Rights that the jailing of council tax and fine defaulters who were unrepresented at the hearing was a breach of their rights under Art 6.3: *Beet v United Kingdom (Application Nos 47676/99 etc)* (2005) Times, 10 March, ECHR.

III HUM [28.10]

Penalties and confiscation Paragraphs 2 and 3 of Art 6 come into play when a person is charged with a criminal offence. This has been held to apply to the imposition of a tax penalty: *King v Walden (Inspector of Taxes)* [2001] STC 822, following *Georgiou v United Kingdom (Application 40042/98)* [2001] STC 80, ECtHR). Conversely it has been held that the forfeiture of goods for a failure to pay duty does not involve a criminal charge: *Goldsmith v Customs and Excise Comrs* [2001] EWHC Admin 285, [2001] 1 WLR 1673. This decision followed the reasoning in *R (on the application of McCann) v Manchester Crown Court* [2001] EWCA Civ 281, [2001] 4 All ER 264 for classing proceedings for an anti-social behaviour order as civil rather than criminal; an approach confirmed by the House of Lords: [2002] UKHL 39. On the other hand, the statutory imposition of heavy fixed penalties on lorry drivers under the Immigration and Asylum Act 1999, coupled with detention of the vehicle, has been held to infringe Art 6 as being unfair and disproportionate whether or not it was classified as criminal or civil: *International Transport Roth GmbH v Secretary of State for the Home Department* [2002] EWCA Civ 158, [2003] QB 728, [2002] 3 WLR 344.

III HUM [28.10A]

Compensation for miscarriages of justice The Supreme Court has held that the rule (see Criminal Justice Act 1988, s 133(1ZA)) that compensation for a miscarriage of justice is only payable if the evidence which caused the conviction to be quashed demonstrated innocence 'beyond reasonable doubt' was not incompatible with Art 6(2): see *R (on the application of Hallam) v Secretary of State for Justice* [2019] UKSC 2.

III HUM [28.11]

Precedents Precedents for judicial review proceedings based on Art 6 are provided at **BCCP J[104]** and **BCCP J[105]**. Precedents for Part 7 claims based on Art 6 are provided at **BCCP L[358]** and **BCCP L[359]**.

III HUM [29]

Article 7 No punishment without law

1. No one shall be held guilty of any criminal offence on account of any act or omission which did not constitute a criminal offence under national or international law at the time when it was committed. Nor shall a heavier penalty be imposed than the one that was applicable at the time the criminal offence was committed.
2. This Article shall not prejudice the trial and punishment of any person for any act or omission which, at the time when it was committed, was criminal according to the general principles of law recognised by civilised nations.

III HUM [30]

Article 8 Right to respect for private and family life

1. Everyone has the right to respect for his private and family life, his home and his correspondence.
2. There shall be no interference by a public authority with the exercise of this right except such as is in accordance with the law and is necessary in a democratic society in the interests of national security, public safety or the economic well-being of the country, for the prevention of disorder or crime, for the protection of health or morals, or for the protection of the rights and freedoms of others.

III HUM [30.1]

Family proceedings The provisions of Art 8 have been litigated in the ECtHR in the context of adoption against the will of the parent and in denial of access to children: *B v United Kingdom* (Case No 5/1986/103/151) (1987) 10 EHRR 87, ECtHR; *H v United Kingdom*

(Case No 3/1986/10/149) (1987) 10 EHRR 95, ECtHR and *W v United Kingdom* (Case No 4/1986/102/150) (1987) 10 EHRR 29. In *Soderbank v Sweden* (22 October 1997, unreported) Case No 33/24/96, ECtHR, it was held that the consent of the natural father to adoption by the mother and her husband could be dispensed with only in exceptional circumstances.

Dispensing with parental consent was held not to contravene Arts 6 or 8 in *Irene Scott v United Kingdom* [2000] 2 FCR 560, [2000] 1 FLR 958, ECtHR (Case 34745/97) and *GHB v United Kingdom (Application 42455/98)* (4 May 2000, unreported), ECtHR. Similarly, the court's power, under the Children Act 1989 s 34 to allow a local authority to refuse contact with children in its care was not in breach of Arts 6 or 8 if used fairly in appropriate circumstances: *Re F (care: termination of contact)* [2000] 2 FCR 481, [2000] Fam Law 708. But in *K and T v Finland* [2000] 3 FCR 248, [2000] 2 FLR 79, ECtHR, the court held that the care orders went beyond the wide margin for assessing the necessity for taking children away from their mother. As regards freeing for adoption, it has been held that Art 8 does not impose an absolute duty on the local authority to inform or investigate members of the child's extended family: *Re R (a child) (adoption: duty to investigate)* (2001) Times, 13 February.

A failure to involve a mother in the decision-making process concerning her child's care may, however, infringe Convention rights under Art 8: *TP and KM v United Kingdom* [2001] 2 FCR 289, [2001] 2 FLR 549, ECtHR, a case brought after the courts had struck out a domestic claim for damages for negligence and breach of statutory duty: *M (A minor) v Newham London Borough Council* [1995] 2 AC 633, HL. A local authority's decision to remove a child from the mother's care at birth has been held to fall outside the "necessary" exceptions in para 2: *P, C & S v United Kingdom (Application 56547/00)* [2002] 3 FCR 1, (2002) Times, 16 August, ECtHR.

In *Glaser v United Kingdom (Minors: Right of Contact)* [2000] 3 FCR 193, ECtHR it was held that the courts were not in breach of Art 8 by failing to compel contact after divorce by a non-custodial parent with a child, as long as they made orders which facilitated it.

It was contrary to Art 8, read in conjunction with Art 14, for secondary legislation in Northern Ireland to prohibit adoption by unmarried couples: *Re P (adoption: unmarried couple)* [2008] UKHL 38, [2008] NI 310, [2008] 2 FCR 366.

In *Sheffield City Council v Personal Representative of June Wall* [2010] EWCA Civ 922, (2010) Times, 9 September it was held that a foster child was not a member of the family for the purposes of succeeding to a secure tenancy under the Housing Act 1985, s 113 and that this exclusion was objectively justified and did not infringe Art 8.

III HUM [30.1A]

Natural father's right to family life Where the natural father of an illegitimate child has close family ties with the child, his rights under Arts 6 and 8 entitle him to be given notice of adoption proceedings: *Re A (a Child) (Adoption Disclosure)* (2001) Times, 5 January. In a case where the natural father opposed an adoption by foster parents because of his close family relationship with the child the Court of Appeal set aside the adoption order made at first instance. They did so on the ground that the judge had not considered sufficiently the father's Convention rights under Art 8*: Re B (A Child: Adoption order)* [2001] EWCA Civ 347, [2001] 2 FCR 89, [2001] 2 FLR 26.

Conversely the Art 8 rights of a would-be mother to have her fertilised embryo implanted do not outweigh the would-be father's right to withhold his consent: *Evans v United Kingdom (Application No 6339/05)* (2007) Times, 2 May, ECtHR.

A local authority was not compelled under the Adoption and Children Act 2002 to disclose the existence and identity of a child to the mother's family and, if he could be identified, the father and his extended family, contrary to the wishes of the mother who wished to place the child for adoption: *Re C, a child v XYZ County Council* [2007] EWCA Civ 1206, [2008] 3 WLR 445,(2007) Times, 5 December.

An unmarried father who does not have parental responsibility according to the statute may have rights under Art 8 of the Convention if he has established family life with his child. He should be given notice of, and allowed to participate in, any proceedings in relation to the child which engage his Art 8 rights: *Principal Reporter v K* [2010] UKSC 56, [2011] 01 LS Gaz R 15, [2011] NLJR 63.

III HUM [30.1B]

Children born by artificial insemination Respect for private and family life includes the concept of personal identity: *Gaskin v United Kingdom (Application No 10454/83* (1989) 12 EHRR 36, ECtHR. It therefore includes the right of a child conceived by artificial insemination to obtain information about a biological parent who would have contributed to that identity: *R (on the application of Rose) v Secretary of State for Health* [2002] EWHC 1593 (Admin), [2002] 3 FCR 731, (2002) Times, 22 August. The court left open the question of whether information which identified the donor should be withheld on grounds within para 2.

It has been held to be lawful for sperm taken from a woman's husband prior to his death to be stored by a fertility clinic beyond the period permitted by the Human Fertilisation and Embryology Act 1990 and regulations. Refusal to allow her to use it in this way to conceive a child in accordance with the husband's wishes and written consent would constitute a disproportionate interference with her Art 8 rights: *Warren v Care Fertility (Northampton) Ltd* [2014] EWHC 602 (Fam), [2015] Fam 1, [2014] 3 WLR 1310.

III HUM [30.1C]

Transsexuals Laws which treat people as continuing to have the same gender as at birth notwithstanding gender reassignment surgery are in breach of Art 8 because they do not respect human dignity: *Goodwin v United Kingdom (Application 28957/95)* [2002] 2 FCR 577, ECtHR. However, pre-transition records relating to gender are allowed to be retained provided this is done subject to a policy that is sufficiently precise as to be in accordance with law: *R (on the application of C) v Secretary of State for Work and Pensions* [2017] UKSC 72.

The law which denies legal validity to a marriage of a male to a female who was born a male is incompatible with the Convention: *Bellinger v Bellinger* [2003] UKHL 21, [2003] 2 AC 467, [2003] 2 All ER 593. Primary legislation has been introduced to remove the incompatibility: see the Gender Recognition Act 2004.

However, a primary care trust was entitled to apply its gender dysphoria policy by refusing to fund breast augmentation surgery for a male to female transsexual on the basis that there was limited evidence that it would provide any clinical benefit: *R (on the application of C) v Berkshire West PCT* [2011] EWCA Civ 247, [2011] Eq LR 499.

III HUM [30.1D]

Physical and psychological integrity Respect for private life includes respect for 'a person's physical and psychological integrity': *Botta v Italy (Application 21439/93)* (1998) 26 EHRR 241, para 32. Further, mental health must also be regarded as a crucial part of private life associated with the aspect of moral integrity: *Bensaid v United Kingdom (Application 44599/98)* (2001) 33 EHRR 205, para 47: *R (on the application of Razgar) v Secretary of State for the Home Department* [2004] UKHL 27, [2004] 2 AC 368, [2004] 3 All ER 821.

III HUM [30.1E]

Foreign laws which discriminate against mothers It has been held that a mother should not be returned to a country where the law gives the father an absolute and exclusive right to have a child of the family live with him, since such a law discriminated against women and denied and nullified a mother's right to respect for family life: *EM (Lebanon) v Secretary of State for the Home Department* [2008] UKHL 64; (2008) Times, 24 October.

III HUM [30.1F]

Enhanced criminal record certificates Regulations under the Police Act 1997 and the Rehabilitation of Offenders Act 1975 have been held to contravene the right to respect for private and family life, by requiring disclosure of all spent convictions or cautions regardless of relevance. The Supreme Court held that such provisions were not 'necessary in a democratic society': *R (on the application of T) v Chief Constable of Greater Manchester Police; R (on the application of B) v Secretary of State for the Home Department* [2014] UKSC 35, [2015] AC 49.

Following *R (on the application of T)* the scheme was revised under the Police Act 1997 (Criminal Record Certificates: Relevant Matters) (Amendment) (England and Wales) Order 2013. Under the revised scheme spent convictions ordinarily did not need to be disclosed unless they were for serious offences or the offender had multiple convictions. The Court of Appeal, in *R (on the application of P) v The Secretary of State for the Home Department* [2017] EWCA Civ 321, [2017] 2 Cr App Rep 12, held that the revised scheme remained inconsistent with Art 8 because it could be applied in an indiscriminate manner by not accounting for the circumstances of the offences. However, on appeal to the Supreme Court (see *Re Gallagher's Application for Judicial Review* [2019] UKSC 3), it was held that the revised statutory scheme were, for the purposes of Art 8, in accordance with law and not disproportionate, albeit with the exception of the multiple conviction rule, and warnings and reprimands issued to young offenders.

In *R (on the application of R) v Chief Constable of Greater Manchester* [2018] UKSC 47, [2018] 1 WLR 4079, the Supreme Court held that the inclusion of an acquittal on a charge of rape on an enhanced criminal record certificate was a proportionate interference with Art 8 rights. It was not necessary or appropriate for those responsible for producing an ECRC to conduct a detailed analysis of the evidence at trial.

III HUM [30.1G]

Provision of abortion services Although the Secretary of State for Health (who was obliged to provide abortion services for women resident in England) had a power to require the same abortion services to be provided in England for women from Northern Ireland. He refused to do so on the basis that the NHS should not fund services for residents of Northern Ireland which the Northern Ireland Assembly had deliberately decided not to legislate to provide and which would be unlawful in Northern Ireland. In *R (on the application of A) v Secretary of State for Health* [2017] UKSC 41, [2017] 1 WLR 2492, the Supreme Court held that the decision involved no breach of Art 8, read with Art 14. The decision to treat women from England differently was justified. No less intrusive decision could have been reached, and the decision struck a fair balance between the rights of the women and the interests of the UK as a whole.

In *Re Northern Ireland Human Rights Commission's Application for Judicial Review* [2018] UKSC 27, [2019] 1 All ER 173, the Supreme Court held that the NI Human Rights Commission had no standing to seek a declaration that abortion law in Northern Ireland was incompatible with Arts 3 and 8. Even though the Supreme Court therefore lacked jurisdiction to make a declaration of incompatibility, it observed that Northern Ireland law was disproportionate and incompatible with Art 8 insofar as it prevented abortions in cases of fatal foetal abnormality and where pregnancy resulted from rape or incest. In relation to Art 3, see **III HUM [25.5C]**.

III HUM [30.2]

Respect for private life It is arguable that Art 8 is concerned with the privacy of individuals, not companies, although a company may have a statutory right to complain about invasion of privacy, for example, under the Broadcasting Act 1996, ss 110, 111: *R v Broadcasting Standards Commission, ex p BBC* [2001] QB 885, [2000] 3 All ER 989, CA.

Article 8 has been relied on successfully in support of an individual having access to local authority files regarding his time in local authority care: *Gaskin v United Kingdom* (Case No 2/1988/146/200) (1989) 12 EHRR 36, ECtHR; *MG v United Kingdom (Application 39393/98)* [2002] 3 FCR 289, (2002) Times, 11 October, ECtHR. Also the Ministry of Defence's policy of interrogating as to homosexual practices with a view to excluding homosexuals from the armed forces in all circumstances was held to be a serious invasion of the right to respect for private life: *Lustig-Prean and Beckett v United Kingdom* (1999) 29 EHRR 548, ECtHR.

Restrictions on child visits to patients at high security hospitals who had committed murder, manslaughter or sexual offences were held to be compatible with Art 8 in *R v Secretary of State for Health, ex p ML* (2000) Times, 26 October.

A high security hospital's policy on secluding patients in certain circumstances is not in breach of Art 5 or Art 8. In *R (on the application of Munjaz) v Mersey Care NHS Trust* [2005] UKHL 58, [2006] 2 AC 148, [2006] 4 All ER 736 the House of Lords found that a hospital could depart from the Code of Practice but, for that departure to be lawful, it had to be justified by cogent reasons. In *Munjaz v United Kingdom (Application No 2913/06)* (2012) Times, 9 October the ECtHR held that the House of Lords had struck the right balance between recognising the status of mental patients as particularly vulnerable detainees and deferring to the advice of expert mental health practitioners, thereby meeting the requirement of foreseeability.

A ban on the consumption of alcohol as a condition of a doctor's continued right to practice has been held to be justified by the terms of para 2: *Whitefield v General Medical Council* [2002] UKPC 62, [2003] IRLR 39, (2002) Times, 29 November.

Where there are grounds for believing that a story may be passed to the newspapers and that publication would be in breach of confidence and in breach of Art 8, the court may grant an injunction against persons unknown (a "John Doe" injunction), for service on newspaper groups; and where some of the story is already in the public domain a proviso may be added, excepting those aspects from the scope of the injunction: *X v Unnamed Persons* [2006] EWHC 2783, [2007] HRLR 4, Eady J.

There is a reasonable expectation of privacy in relation to the sexual activities, even unconventional, of consenting adults on private property. The exposure by a newspaper of sado-masochistic and sexual activities between the claimant and other consenting adults was not justified on grounds of public interest and had been in breach of confidence and the claimant's rights under Art 8: *Mosley v News Group Newspapers Ltd* [2008] EWHC 1777, (2008) Times, 30 July, Eady J. See also *PJS v News Group Newspapers Ltd* [2016] UKSC 26,

[2016] AC 1081 in which the Supreme Court upheld an injunction in respect of extra marital activities by a famous claimant who had 2 small children. The Court held that neither Art 8 or Art 10 trumped the other, but instead an intense focus on the comparative importance of the rights was required, with the justifications for interfering being taken into account, and a proportionality test applied.

A boyfriend of a claimant with a high public profile was restrained by injunction from publicising confidential information and pictures regarding the claimant's adulterous relationship with another high profile person. Her right to respect for her private life weighed more heavily in the balance than the defendant's freedom of expression: *CHS v DNH* [2015] EWHC 1214 (Ch), 165 NLJ 7655, [2015] All ER (D) 212 (May).

The ban on some types of hunting under the Hunting Act 2004 did not infringe the right to respect for private life. It was far removed from the values that Art 8 existed to protect, hunting being a very public activity. Even were Art 8 were engaged, the interference would be justified since it was in accordance with the law, was for the protection of morals and was necessary in a democratic society. The Act was proportionate to the end that it sought to achieve and had the approval of a majority of the democratically elected representatives of the public in Parliament: *R (on the application of Countryside Alliance) v Attorney General* [2007] UKHL 52, [2008] 1 AC 719, [2008] 2 All ER 95.

In *R (on the application of N) v Secretary of State for Health; R (on the application of E) v Nottinghamshire Healthcare NHS Trust (Equality and Human Rights Commission intervening)* [2009] EWCA Civ 795,110 BMLR 87, a ban on smoking in mental health units under the Smoke-free (Exemptions and Vehicles) Regulations 2007, reg 10(3) was held not to adversely affect the rights of detained patients under Art 8 in all the circumstances including the public nature of hospitals and the limited significance to the integrity of a person's identity of the right to smoke.

The requirements under Art 8 of accessibility and foreseeability in assessing how prosecutorial discretion was likely to be exercised in cases of assisted suicide under the Suicide Act 1961, s 2(1) required the Director of Public Prosecutions to promulgate an offence-specific policy identifying the facts and circumstances that he would take into account in deciding whether to consent to a prosecution under s 2(1): *R (on the application of Purdy) v DPP* [2009] UKHL 45, [2009] 4 All ER 1147, [2009] 3 WLR 403.

Section 2(1) does not impose what the ECtHR would regard as an impermissible blanket ban on suicide and therefore is within the UK's margin of appreciation: *R (on the application of Nicklinson v Ministry of Justice (CNK Alliance Ltd and British Humanist Association intervening); R (on the application of AM) v DPP* [2014] UKSC 38, [2014] 3 All ER 843. In light of Parliament's decision not to amend s 2(1) following *Nicklinson*, however, the Court of Appeal in *R (on the application of Conway) v Secretary of State for Justice* [2017] EWCA Civ 275 held that an applicant could be given permission to apply for judicial review on the same grounds as those in *Nicklinson*. Upon that judicial review, the Court rejected the argument that s 2(1) of the Suicide Act 1961 imposes a disproportionate ban on suicide, when physician assisted. Whether the argument is put under Art 2 or Art 8 the law is not incompatible, for the purpose of s 4, with the provisions of the Convention: *R (on the application of Conway) v Secretary of State for Justice* [2018] EWCA Civ 1431, [2018] 3 WLR 925.

The law of the United Kingdom is not in breach of Art 8 in allowing newspapers to publish stories exposing the private lives of individuals without notifying the individuals concerned and giving them an opportunity to apply for an injunction: *Mosley v United Kingdom* [2011] ECHR 774, [2011] NLJR 703, ECtHR.

In a case brought under the Human Rights Act 1998 and the Data Protection Act 1998 it was held that Sir Cliff Richard had a reasonable expectation of privacy during the police investigation of allegations of historic sexual abuse and that the argument by the BBC that they had the right to inform the public by televised reportage of the search of his flat was of much less weight than his entitlement to privacy. His article 8 rights were more potent than their rights under Art 10, so substantial damages were awarded: *Richard v British Broadcasting Corporation and South Yorkshire Police* [2018] EWHC 1837 (Ch), [2018] 3 WLR 1715.

III HUM [30.2A]

Decision to prosecute The institution of criminal proceedings for a matter that is properly the subject of the criminal law may not be challenged on Art 8 grounds. This is because the institution of proceedings places the matter before a court. A decision to prosecute does not of itself involve a lack of respect for the autonomy of the defendant but places the questions of guilt, innocence, bail etc before the court for its determination by a process that complies with Art 6: *SXH v Crown Prosecution Service* (2017) Times, 19 April, Sup Ct. See *Khuja v Times Newspapers Ltd* [2017] UKSC 49, [2017] 3 WLR 351 in respect of the relationship between Arts 8 and 10 in the context of a person who was arrested but then not charged.

III HUM [30.3]

Implications for court procedures It is necessary for procedures to ensure that Art 8 rights are practical and effective. In *G v Director of Legal Aid Casework (British Red Cross Society intervening)* [2014] EWCA Civ 1622, [2015] 1 WLR 2247, 165 NLJ 7636 it was held that this precluded Government guidance which indicated that civil legal aid in immigration cases under s 10 of the Legal Aid, Sentencing and Punishment of Offenders Act 2012 would be granted only in rare and extreme cases. Instead, both Art 6 and Art 8 required a decision whether an unrepresented litigant could present his case effectively and without obvious unfairness. This depended on the facts of the case, including the importance and complexity of the issues and the litigant's ability to represent himself without assistance.

In disclosure applications the courts may need to weigh respect for private and home life in the balance when determining whether to order the disclosure of documents or information of a private nature is "necessary": see *MS v Sweden* (1997) 3 BHRC 248, ECtHR. It may also be a factor in determining the admissibility of evidence (eg evidence obtained by unauthorised invasion of privacy); see ss 17 and 18 of the Regulation of Investigatory Powers Act 2000 and the phone-tapping cases *Malone v United Kingdom* (Case No 4/1983/80/94) (1984) 7 EHRR 14, ECtHR; *Halford v United Kingdom* (73/1996/692/884) [1997] IRLR 471, ECtHR. It may also be a reason for limiting cross-examination as to credit.

In *Dunn v Durham County Council* [2012] EWCA Civ 1654, [2013] 2 All ER 213, [2013] 1 WLR 2305 the Court of Appeal explained that the court can excuse disclosure or inspection under CPR 31 on public interest grounds. Whilst it might be misleading to describe any such issue as one of public interest immunity, it would be necessary to balance the Art 6 rights of the party seeking disclosure against the Art 8 rights to privacy or confidentiality, though disclosure or inspection would be denied only where this was strictly necessary.

The court is not bound to reject video evidence which has been obtained in breach of art 8.1 but has a discretion to do so, depending on the seriousness of the breach and the over-riding objective to deal with the case justly: *Jones v University of Warwick* [2003] EWCA Civ 151, [2003] 3 All ER 760, [2003] 1 WLR 954. Similarly in *Martin v McGuiness* 2003 SLT 1136, (2003) Times, 21 April, Ct of Sess (Outer House) infringing evidence was admitted because it was admissible under Art 8.2.

III HUM [30.3A]

Spousal rights of confidence Each spouse is entitled to confidence in respect of his or her private life and may assert this right against the other spouse, except as regards their shared married life. Where a spouse infringes the other's right to confidence, for example by copying documents relating to the other's private businesses for use in proceedings for financial provision, the spouse in breach must disclose the facts promptly and may be enjoined by the court against using or retaining the documents or passing them on to professional advisers: *Imerman v Tchenguiz* [2010] EWCA Civ 908, [2011] Fam 116, [2011] 1 All ER 555 (applied in *Arbili v Arbili* [2015] EWCA Civ 542, [2015] Fam Law 882, [2015] All ER (D) 228 (May)), disapproving the so-called rule to the contrary effect in *Hildebrand v Hildebrand* [1992] 1 FLR 244, [1992] Fam Law 235.

III HUM [30.4]

Privacy of medical reports Disclosure of medical records may be a breach of a person's Art 8 right to respect for their private life but the disclosure may be justified as necessary in a democratic society, for example, to check accuracy of information received: *MS v Sweden* (1997) 3 BHRC 248, ECtHR. The disclosure of dental records of patients to the General Dental Council, in connection with issues of competence, have been held to be justified under Art 8(2): *Re General Dental Council's application (Savery)* [2011] EWHC 3011 (Admin), (2011) Times, 10 December, [2012] Med LR 204.

The High Court permitted the Secretary of the Department of Health and Human Services of the United States of America permission under the CPR 5.4C(2) to obtain from the court records copies of expert reports filed by the defendants in the MMR/MR vaccine litigation for use in litigation in the USA but ordered that the reports must be redacted so as to prevent identification of those from whom medical specimens had been taken: *Sayers v Smithkline Beecham plc* [2007] EWHC 1346 (QB), [2007] All ER (D) 30 (Jun).

III HUM [30.4A]

Use of electoral register for direct marketing An electoral registration officer must allow an elector to have his name removed from an electoral register before it is sold to a commercial concern for marketing purposes. A refusal to do so is in breach of s 11 of the Data Protection Act 1998 (at para **III PAT [61]**) and also contravenes the elector's Convention rights under Art 8: *R (on the application of Robertson) v Wakefield Metropolitan District Council* [2001] EWHC Admin 915, [2002] QB 1052.

III HUM [30.4B]

DNA samples The UK courts had held that retention by the police of DNA samples of persons suspected but not subsequently convicted of offences was justified by para 2 of Art 8, provided that the terms of s 64 of the Criminal Justice and Police Act 2001 were satisfied; and that s 64 itself was compatible with Art 8: *R (on the application of S and Marper) v Chief Constable of South Yorkshire Police*: [2004] UKHL 39, [2004] 4 All ER 193, [2004] 1 WLR 2196. However, the Grand Chamber of the European Court subsequently ruled that the blanket and indiscriminate nature of the powers of retention failed to strike a fair balance between the competing public and private interests, and the state had overstepped any acceptable margin of appreciation. Therefore there was a disproportionate interference with the complainants' right to respect for private life which could not be regarded as necessary in a democratic society, and so there had been a violation of Art 8: *S and Marper v United Kingdom* (Application No: 00030562/04: 00030566/04).

In *R (on the application of GC) v Metropolitan Police Comr: R (on the application of C) V Metropolitan Police Comr* [2011] UKSC 21, [2011] 3 All ER 859, [2011] 1 WLR 1230, (2011) Times, 19 May the Supreme Court held that although the provision in s 64(1A) of the Police and Criminal Evidence Act 1984 for the indefinite retention of the biometric data of all suspects breached individuals' rights under Art 8, the section could be read so as not to require indefinite retention and no declaration of incompatibility was required.

Furthermore, the policy of retaining indefinitely the DNA profile, fingerprints and photographs of a person convicted of a recordable offence has been held to be within the UK's margin of appreciation under Art 8: *Gaughran v Chief Constable of the Police Service of Northern Ireland* [2015] UKSC 29, [2015] 2 WLR 1303, 165 NLJ 7653.

III HUM [30.4C]

Disclosure of convictions A local authority infringed Art 8 by maintaining a blanket policy pursuant to which it disclosed a sex offender's previous conviction for indecent assault of a child to charitable organisations and public bodies in which he was involved, determining any future disclosures on a case-by-case basis. The offender in question did not work with children and the policy was held not to be fair, balanced or proportionate: *R (on the application of H) v A City Council* [2011] EWCA Civ 403, [2011] LGR 590, [2011] All ER (D) 143 (Apr), applied in *R (on the application of B) v Chief Constable of Derbyshire Constabulary* [2011] EWHC 2362 (Admin), [2011] All ER (D) 75 (Sep).

In *R (on the application of T) v Secretary of State for the Home Department* [2014] UKSC 35, [2015] AC 49, [2014] 4 All ER 159 the Supreme Court held that the disclosure provisions of the Police Act 1997, ss 113A and 113B, prior to amendments made with a view to eliminating any incompatibility, infringed the Art 8 rights of a claimant who had received police warnings at age 11 and another who had received a police caution in her 40s, by requiring these matters to be disclosed to employers on Enhanced Criminal Record Certificates. The interference with Art 8 rights was not 'in accordance with the law' because no regard was had to the nature of the offence, the disposal in the case, the time elapsed since the offences or the relevance of the data to the employment sought, and there was no mechanism for independent review of a decision to disclose the data. The legislation required indiscriminate disclosure by the state of personal data without adequate safeguards. The disclosure of T's warnings bore no rational relationship to the aim of protecting the safety of children with whom he might come into contact. The impact on B's private life of the disclosure of her caution for minor dishonesty many years earlier was disproportionate to the aim of protecting people who were receiving care.

Following *R (on the application of T)* the scheme was revised under the Police Act 1997 (Criminal Record Certificates: Relevant Matters) (Amendment) (England and Wales) Order 2013. Under the revised scheme spent convictions ordinarily did not need to be disclosed unless they were for serious offences or the offender had multiple convictions. The Court of Appeal, in *R (on the application of P) v The Secretary of State for the Home Department* [2017] EWCA Civ 321, [2017] 2 Cr App Rep 12, held that the revised scheme remained inconsistent with Art 8 because it could be applied in an indiscriminate manner by not accounting for the circumstances of the offences.

III HUM [30.4D]

Records of other activity In *R (on the application of Catt) v Association of Chief Police Officers of England, Wales and Northern Ireland; R (on the application of T) v Metropolitan Police Comr* [2015] UKSC 9, [2015] AC 1065, the Supreme Court (reversing the finding of the Court of Appeal) held that the retention of data on the National Domestic Extremism Database about the attendance of an elderly and non-violent man at demonstrations organised by an extremist protest group was proportionate under ECHR, Art 8. Furthermore, in the second case, it was also proportionate for information about a warning letter sent concerning possible harassment to be kept for a period of years as set out in standard practice, provided the policy was flexible enough to allow for deletion when the information was no longer required.

In the earlier decision of the Court of Appeal in *R (on the application of TD) v Metropolitan Police Comr* [2014] EWCA Civ 585, the Court held that the retention of police records regarding an unfounded allegation of sexual assault from nine years earlier where these were not disclosable to the public but were of use in the investigation of crime were of utility and did not need to be destroyed. However, the Court was troubled by the lack of policy for systematic review and that the policy of retention for 100 years appeared over-rigid and not demonstrably proportionate.

The regimes for intercepting communications and acquiring data under s 8(4) of the Regulation of Investigatory Powers Act 2000 have been held by the European Court of Human Rights to violate Arts 8 and 10: *Big Brother Watch v United Kingdom* [2018] ECHR 58170/13, 62322/14 and 24960/15, [2018] All ER (D) 22 (Sep).

III HUM [30.5]

Respect for home Article 8(1) entitles everyone to respect for their home, a consideration which is important in the determination of applications for possession and the processes of enforcement. *See Gillow v United Kingdom* (Case No 13/1984/85/132) (1986) 11 EHRR 335 in relation to the residence laws of Guernsey. In *Camenzind v Switzerland* (1997) 28 EHRR 458, ECtHR it was held that a search of a home under a warrant was 'necessary within a democratic society' seeing that its purpose was preventing crime and the interference was not out of proportion.

In *Birse v HM Advocate* 2000 SLT 869, the High Court of Justiciary in Scotland concluded that the grant of a search warrant by a justice of the peace who had considered the merits of the application properly was not in breach of Art 8; nor was the failure to keep a record of the proceeding a breach of Convention rights.

There is no unlawful interference with the Art 8 rights of registered sex offenders by the practice of police officers making visits to their homes to monitor their behaviour under arrangements made pursuant to s 325 of the Criminal Justice Act 2003: *R (on the application of M) v Chief Constable of Hampshire Constabulary (Secretary of State for the Home Department intervening)* [2014] EWCA Civ 1651, [2015] 1 WLR 1176. Nor is Art 8 infringed by a requirement that a person subject to a sexual offences prevention order wear an electronic tag, even though the 2003 Act does not expressly authorise the use of tagging: *R (on the application of Richards) v Teesside Magistrates Court and Chief Constable of Cleveland* [2015] EWCA Civ 7, [2015] 1 WLR 1695.

In *Shlosberg v Avonwick Holdings Ltd* [2016] EWCA Civ 1138 the Court of Appeal (affirming the decision of the High Court [2016] EWHC 1001 (Ch), [2016] 3 WLR 1330) held that legal professional privilege afforded to a bankrupt's documents was a personal right, protected under Arts 6 and 8; it did not devolve to the trustees in bankruptcy.

III HUM [30.5A]

Possession proceedings Where possession is sought by a private landlord, even though Art 8 might be engaged were the judge to make an order for possession of a tenant's home, the tenant's Art 8 rights could not compel a different outcome from that which would result from the contractual relationship between the parties in a case where legislative protections (such as s 21(4) of the Housing Act 1988 and s 89(1) of the Housing Act 1980) apply. Thus held the Supreme Court in *McDonald v McDonald* [2016] UKSC 28, [2016] 3 WLR 45. The democratically elected legislature had properly balanced the competing interests when enacting the legislation, including Convention rights of private sector landlords and residential tenants. There was therefore no need for a judge asked to make a possession order to consider the proportionality of that order. To decide otherwise would render the convention directly enforceable horizontally between private citizens.

The decision by a public body such as a housing authority to take proceedings for possession is judicially reviewable if Convention rights are breached, but normally the requirements of para (2) of Art 8 are satisfied where the authority acts fairly and reasonably in accordance with a statutory scheme: *Sheffield City Council v Smart* [2002] EWCA Civ 04, [2002] LGR 468, [2002] HLR 639.

The definition of 'protected site' in s 5 of the Mobile Homes Act 1983 excludes land occupied by a local authority as a caravan site providing accommodation for gypsies. This means that gypsy occupiers of such a site are vulnerable to summary eviction for reasons which they cannot challenge. It was held in *Connors v United Kingdom (Application 66746/01)* (2004) 40 EHRR 189, [2004] HLR 991 that such an interference with family life could not be justified within the appropriate margin of appreciation and that Convention rights under Art 8 had been violated. Where the owners of land establish their homes on it in caravans without obtaining planning permission it may be a disproportionate response, in breach of Art 8, to take enforcement proceedings for their removal: *Chichester District Council v First Secretary of State* [2004] EWCA Civ 1248, [2005] 1 WLR 279, [2005] LGR 427. The possession of temporary accommodation provided by a housing authority under ss 188 or 190 of the Housing Act 1996 may be recovered without a court order. This is because the premises are not 'occupied as a dwelling under a licence' for the purposes of s 3(2B) of the Protection from

Eviction Act 1997, at **III L&T [90]**, and although eviction without a court order could interfere with the occupier's right to respect for his home, under Art 8 of the Convention, such interference has been held to be necessary, within Art 8.2: *Desnousse v Newham London Borough Council* [2006] EWCA Civ 547, [2006] QB 831, [2007] 2 All ER 218 and *R (on the application of ZH and CN) v London Borough of Newham* [2014] UKSC 62, [2014] 3 WLR 1548, [2014] LGR 842.

Mandatory possession orders under Housing Act 1988, s 21(4) do not infringe Convention rights under Art 8. A procedure for the recovery of possession is necessary in a democratic society and the terms of s 21(4), expressing the will of Parliament, should be accepted as legitimate and proportionate: *Poplar Housing and Regeneration Community Association Ltd v Donoghue* [2001] EWCA Civ 595, [2002] QB 48, [2001] 4 All ER 604.

In *Lambeth London Borough Council v Kay* [2006] UKHL 10, [2006] 2 AC 465, [2006] 4 All ER 128 the House of Lords held that: the right of a public authority to possession of premises under domestic law would normally provide the justification needed under Art 8(2) and domestic courts were to assume that the domestic legislation struck the relevant balance of competing interests under Art 8(2); that a challenge to the making of a possession order could be raised in county court proceedings so far as its jurisdictional limits permitted if the defendant could exceptionally show a seriously arguable case that the domestic law was incompatible with the Convention (raising either issues of interpretation under s 3 of the Human Rights Act 1998 or a question of transfer to the High Court for consideration of a declaration of incompatibility); but that (by a majority) where the requirements of the law had been satisfied and the right to possession was unqualified no challenge based on a defendant's individual circumstances was permissible. However, the order would not have to be made if the defendant could show that the decision of the authority to seek it was an improper exercise of its powers on conventional judicial review grounds.

This last point was further explained by Lord Hope in *Doherty v Birmingham City Council* [2008] UKHL 57, [2008] 3 WLR 636 (at paragraphs 45–56), emphasising that the judge hearing the claim for possession should refuse to make the order if satisfied that the authority's decision to evict was unreasonable in the *Wednesbury* (*Associated Provincial Picture Houses Ltd v Wednesbury Corpn* [1948] 1 KB 223) sense. So where domestic legislation providing for summary possession orders against gypsies could not be read in a way which was compatible with Convention rights by providing proper procedural protection to the defendant, such protection was provided by enabling the grounds upon which the authority reached its decision to be scrutinised.

The approach in *Kay* and *Doherty* was considered by the ECtHR in *Kay v United Kingdom (Application No 37341/06)* [2010] NLJR 1346, (2010) Times, 18 October where it was held that a tenant wishing to challenge the grant of a possession order ought to be able to rely on Art 8 to test whether the orders were proportionate to the legitimate aim which they sought to achieve. This approach was followed by the UK Supreme Court in *Manchester City Council v Pinnock* [2010] UKSC 45. Departing from the previous approach in *Kay* and *Doherty*, the Court held that Art 8 is engaged in the context of an order for possession under the Housing Act, s 143D(2). Thus, a person at risk of being dispossessed of his home pursuant to an order for possession was entitled to raise questions under Art 8, even if his right of occupation in the premises had ended.

Where a housing authority takes a series of decisions regarding the eviction of an unlawful occupier from his or her home, each decision has to be reasonable to satisfy the requirements of Art 8 and, following *Doherty* (above) reasonableness connotes something wider than rationality (eg having regard to the aim which the authority was pursuing and to the length of time that the occupiers had resided on the site). The authority should take account of the personal circumstances of the occupiers since they might be relevant to deciding whether and for how long to postpone execution of an order for possession; but such circumstances could not make it unreasonable to decide to take possession proceedings: *Central Bedfordshire Council v Taylor (Secretary of State for Communities and Local Government intervening)* [2009] EWCA Civ 613, [2009] LGR 773, [2010] 1 P&CR 19.

Accordingly Art 8 can be relied on to resist enforcement of a possession order in the same way as it can be cited as a defence to the claim for the possession order: *R (on the application of JL) v Secretary of State for Defence* [2013] EWCA Civ 449, [2013] PTSR 1014, [2013] HLR 359.

In *Hounslow London Borough Council v Powell, Leeds City Council v Hall and Birmingham City Council v Frisby* [2011] UKSC 8, [2011] 2 All ER 129, [2011] 2 WLR 287, [2011] HRLR 18, (2011) Times, 1 March, the Supreme Court considered possession proceedings brought against tenants occupying premises under introductory tenancies and against a person with a licence to occupy a property under the homelessness regime in Part VII of the Housing Act 1996. It ruled that the statutory schemes did not prevent the court from refusing to make an order for possession if it considered that the order would not be proportionate. However, most cases would turn on the two legitimate aims identified in *Pinnock*, ie vindication of the landlord's ownership rights and enabling it to comply with public duties in relation to its housing stock. It would not be necessary to adjourn for further consideration of lawfulness or proportionality unless the defence was seriously arguable. The threshold for an arguable case on proportionality was a high one which would be reached in only a small proportion of cases.

Where the defendant to a possession claim has no right to occupy the premises under domestic law, Art 8 can be invoked as a defence only in highly exceptional circumstances: *Birmingham City Council v Lloyd* [2012] EWCA Civ 969, [2012] 2 P&CR DG 18, [2012] HLR 44.

In *Malik v Fassenfelt (since dec'd)* [2013] EWCA Civ 798, [2013] All ER (D) 44 (Jul) the Court of Appeal said that it would be difficult to imagine circumstances in which it would not be proportionate to grant and enforce a possession order against squatters but that Art 8 required that question to be asked. The majority declined to decide whether the rule in *McPhail v Persons, Names Unknown* [1973] Ch 447, [1973] 3 All ER 393, CA that there was no discretion to suspend a possession order against squatters therefore now had to be relaxed.

The rule that a periodic joint tenancy is terminated automatically if one joint tenant serves notice to quit on the landlord is not incompatible with the Art 8 rights of the other joint tenant, who in such a case has no right to remain as a sole tenant of the local authority: *Sims v Dacorum Borough Council* [2014] UKSC 63, [2014] 3 WLR 1600, [2014] LGR 898.

An Art 8 proportionality defence must demonstrate that it reaches the high threshold of being seriously arguable and the court must at the earliest opportunity summarily consider whether the defence reaches that high threshold; and, if not, the defence must be struck out or dismissed: *Thurrock Borough Council v West* [2012] EWCA Civ 1435, [2013] 1 P & CR 175, [2013] HLR 69.

III HUM [30.5B]

Aircraft noise It was held by a Chamber of the Court in *Hatton v United Kingdom* (2001) Times, 8 October, ECtHR, that the United Kingdom was in breach of the fundamental freedoms of residents living near Heathrow by not exercising sufficient control over the take-off and landing of aircraft to prevent excessive noise and disturbance. The case was referred to the Grand Chamber, which held that there was no violation of Art 8, bearing in mind the margin of appreciation to be afforded to the state in striking a fair balance between economic policies and the rights of individual homeowners: (2003) Times, 10 July.

In *Dennis v Ministry of Defence* [2003] EWHC 793 (QB), [2003] NLJR 634, Times, 6 May, Buckley J awarded substantial damages to compensate for past and future noise from an RAF training base. The damages were awarded for nuisance at common law and the award was held to provide just satisfaction for infringement of rights under Art 8 and Art 1 of the First Protocol.

III HUM [30.5C]

Searches and surveillance The powers contained in the Terrorism Act 2000 Schedule 7 to search at ports and borders was found not to be incompatible with Art 8 in *Beghal v DPP* [2015] UKSC 49, [2016] AC 88; but contrast *R (on the application of Miranda) v Secretary of State for the Home Department* [2016] EWCA Civ 6, which concerned journalistic material.

Police surveillance devices will be unlawful in certain circumstances, either because they are 'not in accordance with law' or because the degree of interference with Art 8 rights violates the principle of proportionality: *Khan v United Kingdom (Application No 35394/97)* [2000] Crim LR 684, ECtHR, in *Armstrong v United Kingdom (Application 49521/99)* (2002) Times, 6 August, ECtHR and in *Allan v United Kingdom (Application 48539/99)* (2002) Times, 12 November, ECtHR. Note also that although police interception by private radio of an individual's pager messages may be outside the Interception of Communications Act 1985, it has been held to infringe Art 8: *Taylor-Sabori v United Kingdom (Application 47114/99)* (2002) Times, 31 October, ECtHR. See also a case on covert cell recording, *Wood v UK (Application 23414/02)* (2004) Times, 23 November, ECtHR, which reached the same result as in *Khan*.

On the other hand, it was held in *R v Ashworth Special Hospital Authority, ex p N* (2001) Times, 26 June, QBD that random monitoring of telephone calls made by high risk patients did not infringe their rights under Art 8. Calls to legal advisers were not monitored. The court accepted that some monitoring was necessary for security reasons and that the level of monitoring was proportionate to the risks and within the permitted margin of appreciation.

As regards lawful surveillance, orders have been made under s 47 of the Regulation of Investigatory Powers Act 2000 in relation to surveillance of TV reception without a licence (SI 2001/1057) and under s 41 in relation to the surveillance of prisoners (SI 2001/1126).

Media publication of extracts from CCTV footage obtained, and released, by a local authority was held in *Peck v United Kingdom (Application 44647/98)* (2003) 36 EHRR 719, Times, 3 February, ECHR to be a serious interference with the privacy of the individual portrayed: no adequate steps had been taken to mask his identity.

Monitoring by a public authority of an employee's use of telephone, email or internet at the place of work has been held to be a breach of Art 8: *Copland v United Kingdom (Application No 62617/00)* (2007) Times, 24 April, ECtHR. But the Telecommunications (Lawful Business Practice) Regulations 2000 (SI 2000/2699) were not in force at the time. In *Barbulescu v Romania (Application No 61496/08)* [2017] ECHR 754 monitoring of Yahoo Messenger communications by an employer was found to be a breach of Art 8. The notion of private life included professional activities and the employer could not reduce private social life in the workplace to zero by restrictive regulations. In *Lopez Ribalda v Spain (Applications 1874/13 and 8567/13)* (2018) the ECtHR found a breach of Art 8 where surveillance cameras had been installed in a supermarket in response to suspected theft. Workers had been told about visible cameras, but not others which were covertly mounted. Images from the covertly mounted cameras were used to dismiss several workers. The Court held that covert video surveillance of an employee at his or her workplace was a considerable intrusion into his/her private life. A fair balance between the parties' rights had not been struck taking into account the generalised nature of the suspicion and the wide ranging monitoring conducted without time limit. See also *Antovic and Mirkovic v Montenegro (Application No 70838/13)* [2017] ECHR 1068 in which video surveillance of a university lecture hall introduced to ensure the safety of people and property was found to violate a professor's article 8 rights: even though the university was a public sphere, private life includes business and professional activities and the surveillance here could not be justified.

III HUM [30.5D]

Photographs In the case of unauthorised photographs the right to respect for private life does not stop at the front door. In *Von Hannover v Germany* Application No 59320/00 [2005] 40 EHRR 1 the European Court of Human Rights concluded that the publication of unauthorised photographs of Princess Caroline of Monaco was a breach of Art 8, outside the protection of Art 10. The presiding judge stated 'In my view, whenever a public figure has a 'legitimate expectation' of being safe from the media his or her right to private life prevails over the right of freedom of expression or the right to be informed.' The Court of Appeal expressed similar views in *Douglas v Hello! Ltd* [2005] EWCA Civ 595, [2006] QB 125 to the effect that where a celebrity has private information to which he or she cannot deny access, use of such information by a third party can constitute a breach of confidence and the right to privacy will prevail unless the intrusion can be justified. See also *McKennitt v Ash* [2005] EWHC 3003 (QB), [2006] All ER (D) 02 (Feb), where an injunction was granted restraining the publication of a book about a famous singer by her former friend, because the inclusion of private information about her health and home were intrusive and could not be justified in the public interest, applying the test in *Von Hannover v Germany*. But this is not to entitle a celebrity to a press-free zone at all times for all activities.

The Court of Appeal decided that a claim to prevent the use of a photograph of JK Rowling's young son when out shopping with his parents was arguable and should proceed to trial: *Murray v Express Newspapers* [2008] EWCA Civ 446, [2008] 3 WLR 1360, (2008) Times 12 May. It was necessary to ask whether there was a reasonable expectation of privacy on a broad basis taking account of all the circumstances (for example that the claimant was a child, the photograph was taken clandestinely and the parents would not have consented to publication) and if so, how to strike a fair balance between the claimant's right to privacy and the publisher's right to publish. To this extent it was necessary for the law to protect children from intrusive media attention.

The police interfered with Art 8 rights to respect for private life by taking and retaining photographs of a person connected with a group opposed to the arms industry as he left a shareholders' meeting of a company which organised arms trade fairs because this was a disproportionate response by the police to the need to protect the community from disorder and low level offences: *R (on the application of Wood) v Metropolitan Police Comr* [2009] EWCA Civ 414, [2010] 1 WLR 123, [2009] 4 All ER 951, (2009) Times, 1 June. (See also the cases referred to at para **III HUM [30.4D]**.) Contrast *Re An application by JR38 for Judicial Review (Northern Ireland)* [2015] UKSC 42, [2015] 3 WLR 155, [2015] All ER (D) 11 (Jul) where the Supreme Court held that the publication (for the purposes of identification) of images of a 14 year old boy seeming to commit public order offences during a riot were not in breach of Art 8: there was no reasonable expectation of privacy in the circumstances.

It has been held to be breach of this article for a health authority to take a blood sample and intimate photographs of a nine-year old girl against the express wishes of both her parents in the absence of evidence of her being in pain or a critical condition: *MAK v United Kingdom (Application Nos 45901/05 and 40146/06)* [2010] 2 FLR 451, [2010] Fam Law 582, ECtHR.

III HUM [30.5E]

Redundancy It has been held that although park police were denied access to Employment tribunals by s 200 of the Employment Rights Act 1996, their rights under Art 8 or Art 14 were not engaged: *Wandsworth London Borough Council v Vining* [2017] EWCA Civ 1092, [2018] ICR 499.

III HUM [30.6]

Necessary in a democratic society In *Silver v United Kingdom (Case No 2/1981/41/60–66)* (1983) 5 EHRR 347, ECtHR the court enunciated the following principles:

"(a) this adjective 'necessary' is not synonymous with 'indispensable', neither has it the flexibility of such expressions as 'admissible', 'ordinary', 'useful', 'reasonable' or 'desirable';

(b) the Contracting States enjoy a certain but not unlimited margin of appreciation in the matter of the imposition of restrictions, but it is for the Court to give the final ruling on whether they are compatible with the Convention;

(c) the phrase "necessary in a democratic society" means that, to be compatible with the Convention, the interference must, *inter alia*, correspond to a pressing social need and be proportionate to the legitimate aim pursued . . . "

See also *Foxley v United Kingdom* (2000) 31 EHRR 637, Times, 4 July, ECtHR, considered below at para **III HUM [30.8]** and the observations in *Handyside v United Kingdom* (1976) 1 EHRR 737, 754 that features of a "democratic society" are "pluralism, tolerance and broadmindedness".

Where the police forcibly enter a dwelling house at night, under a search warrant, there may be a breach of Art 8 although they acted without malice. The requirement of the common law that malice must be proved has been held to be unjustified and not necessary in a democratic society with the result that a remedy should be provided where the police action could have been avoided by taking reasonable steps: *Keegan v United Kingdom (Application No 28867/03)* (2006) Times, 9 August, ECtHR.

It was not necessary, and therefore was unlawful, for the police to prevent a bus carrying demonstrators from completing its journey to the scene of a proposed demonstration where no breach of the peace could be thought to be imminent: see the note of *R (on the application of Laporte) v Chief Constable of Gloucestershire Constabulary* [2006] UKHL 55, [2007] 2 AC 105, [2007] 2 All ER 529 at **III HUM [33.3]** below. However, in *Howarth v Metropolitan Police Comr* [2011] EWHC 2818 (QB) there was no breach of Art 8 where a group of protestors was searched on their way to an anti-oil industry demonstration. The Police had intelligence that they were equipped with items which had been used to cause criminal damage at previous demonstrations. Indeed, there is a positive duty under Arts 2 and 3 for police to avert a risk to life and protect individuals from physical violence, even if the incident in question has already started and the identity of potential victims is not known: *Sarjantson v Humberside Police Chief Constable* [2013] EWCA Civ 1252, [2013] 3 WLR 1540.

The police, when deciding whether to include information in an enhanced criminal record certificate under s 115 of the Police Act 1997, must consider whether the resulting interference with the subject's Art 8 rights is justified as being proportionate and in cases of doubt should receive representations: *R (on the application of L) v Metropolitan Police Comr* [2009] UKSC 3, [2010] 1 All ER 113, [2009] 3 WLR 1056. In *R (on the application of T) v Chief Constable of Greater Manchester Police (Liberty intervening)* [2014] UKSC 35, [2015] AC 49 the disclosure provisions of the Police Act 1997 were found to impose a blanket statutory requirement of disclosure of cautions held on the police national computer which was disproportionate and exceeded the legitimate aims of protecting employers and vulnerable individuals. Following the introduction of a revised scheme under the Police Act 1997 (Criminal Record Certificates: Relevant Matters) (Amendment) (England and Wales) Order 2013 that still allowed for some disclosure of spent convictions and cautions, the Court of Appeal in *R (on the application of P) v The Secretary of State for the Home Department* [2017] EWCA Civ 321, [2017] 2 Cr App Rep 12, held that it was a disproportionate interference with Art 8 rights.

In *R (on the application of Roberts) v Metropolitan Police Comr* [2015] UKSC 79, [2016] 1 WLR 210 the Supreme Court considered the legal framework within which stop and search authorisations operated, and the standard police operating procedures in force, made it possible to judge whether an individual stop and search was necessary in a democratic society for the prevention of disorder or crime. There was therefore no basis for a declaration of incompatibility.

In *R (on the application of Condliff) v North Staffordshire PCT* [2011] EWCA Civ 910, [2011] Med LR 572, (2011) 121 BMLR 192 the Court of Appeal held that a primary care trust's funding policy which focused only on clinical need and not on non-clinical, social factors did not breach Art 8. Such decisions require a balance between the competing interests of the individual and of the community as a whole and states are allowed a wide margin of appreciation. The trust was entitled to refuse funding for gastric bypass for a morbidly obese patient.

A local authority's decision to withdraw the provision of an overnight carer from a person with limited mobility who suffered from bladder problems did not infringe Art 8 where it was based on an assessment that her needs could equally be met in other ways. The decision was proportionate and in the interests of other service users: *R (on the application of Elaine Mcdonald) v Kensington & Chelsea Royal London Borough Council* [2011] UKSC 33, [2011] 4 All ER 881, (2011) Times, 7 July.

An information-sharing system relating to children in Scotland was in violation of Art 8 for not being 'in accordance with the law' because it was based on unclear rules and contained insufficient safeguards, such as requiring consent. It was also not necessary and would lead to disproportionate interference with privacy: *The Christian Institute v Lord Advocate* [2016] UKSC 51.

The questions whether and for how long personal data retention is 'necessary' for the purpose of the Data Protection principles needs to be seen in the context of Art 8.2 of the Convention. It has been held that details of personal attendances at political protest meetings may be retained on a "domestic extremism" data-base for a number of years: *R (on the application of Catt) v Association of Chief Police Officers of England, Wales and Northern Ireland* [2015] UKSC 9, [2015] 2 All ER 727, [2015] 2 WLR 664. Similarly, the retention on a police database, for seven or twelve years, of a 'prevention of harassment' warning may be justified: *R (on the application of T) v Metropolitan Police Comr* [2015] UKSC 9, [2015] 2 All ER 727, [2015] 2 WLR 664. See **III DAT [46.2]**.

III HUM [30.7]

Inland Revenue requirements Notices from the Inland Revenue requiring documents and information under s 20 of the Taxes Management Act 1970 and s 767 of the Income and Corporation Taxes Act 1988 have been held to be necessary in a democratic society: *R v IRC, ex p Banque Internationale à Luxembourg SA* [2000] STC 708. The House of Lords has held that the statutory provisions in question did not remove the right to claim professional privilege: *R (on the application of Morgan Grenfell & Co Ltd) v Special Comr of Income Tax* [2002] UKHL 21, [2003] 1 AC 563.

III HUM [30.8]

Conduct of trustee in bankruptcy In *Foxley v United Kingdom* (2000) 31 EHRR 637, Times, 4 July, ECtHR, the court held that there was a breach by the trustee in bankruptcy in intercepting and copying the correspondence of the bankrupt. The actions were, up to a point, justified as being "in accordance with the law" and "necessary in a democratic society" to the extent that they were authorised by a court order under Insolvency Act 1986 s 371. The court had regard to the State's margin of appreciation, in accordance with *Campbell v United Kingdom* (1992) 15 EHRR 137, ECtHR, [1992] Series A No 233, p18, para 44. Mr Foxley, the bankrupt, had been convicted of corruption while working at the Ministry of Defence and the criminal court had made a confiscation order for over £1m. However, the intervention was in breach when it involved reading and copying privileged communications between solicitor and client and when it continued beyond the period authorised by the court order.

III HUM [30.9]

Planning controls The refusal of planning permission for a caravan site for gypsies was held to fall within the exception in Art 8.2 where it pursued the legitimate aim of protecting the rights of others through preservation of the environment: *Chapman v United Kingdom (Application 27238/95)* (2001) Times, 30 January, ECtHR. This factor also saved it from breach of Art 14 (discrimination) and Arts 1 and 2 of Protocol No 1(enjoyment of property; right to education).

The Town and Country Planning Act 1990 s 183(4) by providing for "stop notices" against caravans but not dwelling houses was indirectly discriminatory against Gypsies, but the discrimination could be objectively justified by the legitimate aim of protecting the environment and was not therefore incompatible with Convention Rights under Art 8 in conjunction with Art 14: *R (on the application of Wilson) v Wychavon District Council* [2007] EWCA Civ 52, [2007] QB 801.

III HUM [30.10]

Immigration controls Where, in the case of an illegal immigrant, an order for deportation would affect his, or her, family life, the decision-maker must respect the fundamental rights of the immigrant and must show that considerations exist which objectively justify any interference with them. The function of the court, on judicial review, is to see whether the decision maker has exceeded the discretion given to him: *R v Secretary of State for the Home*

Department, ex p Isiko [2001] 1 FCR 633, [2001] 1 FLR 930, CA, adopting the approach taken in *R (on the application of Mahmood) v Secretary of State for the Home Department* [2001] 1 WLR 840, CA, noted at para **III HUM [6A]**. However, these cases should be read in the light of the House of Lords decision in *R (on the application of Daly) v Secretary of State for the Home Department* [2001] UKHL 26, [2001] 2 AC 532, [2001] 3 All ER 433, especially Lord Steyn's opinion at paras 27–28, in which it was stressed that the test of proportionality is more stringent than the traditional test of irrationality.

In *Huang v Secretary of State for the Home Department* [2007] UKHL 11, [2007] 4 All ER 15 the House of Lords held that in an Art 8 case where the question of proportionality was reached, the ultimate question for the appellate immigration authority was whether the refusal of leave to enter or remain in circumstances where the life of the family could not reasonably be expected to be enjoyed elsewhere, taking full account of all considerations weighing in favour of the refusal, prejudiced the family life of the applicant in a manner sufficiently serious to amount to a breach of the fundamental right protected by Art 8. If the answer to that question was in the affirmative, the refusal was unlawful and the authority had so to decide. It was not necessary for the appellate authority to ask in addition whether the case met a test of exceptionality.

In normal circumstances interference with family life would be justified by the requirements of immigration control, as was observed by Carnwath LJ in *Mukarkar v Secretary of State for the Home Department* [2006] EWCA Civ 1045, [2006] All ER (D) 367 (Jul), but this is not to treat exceptionality as the yardstick for success. What matters is that the courts and tribunals should have proper and visible regard to relevant principles in making a structured decision, case by case: *AG (Eritrea) v Secretary of State for the Home Department* [2007] EWCA Civ 801, [2008] 2 All ER 28 per Sedley LJ.

In determining whether a person's removal will amount to a disproportionate interference with Art 8 rights, the authorities must have regard to the effect of removal on all members of the family unit: *Beoku-Betts v Secretary of State for the Home Department* [2008] UKHL 39, [2008] 4 All ER 1146.

Family life for Art 8 purposes will not normally exist between parents and adult children in the absence of elements of dependency going beyond normal emotional ties. Financial dependency by itself was not sufficient: *Amina Ali Odawey v Entry Clearance Officer* [2011] EWCA Civ 840.

In a case where there has been culpable delay in handling an application for leave to remain, amounting to an interference with family life (Art 8), a proportionate response may be to allow the application, even though it would have been rightly rejected if dealt with in time: *Akaeke v Secretary of State for the Home Department* (2005) Times, 23 September, CA. However, there is no entitlement to claim damages for an unreasonable delay in the processing of an asylum application because asylum applications do not engage Art 6: *R (on the application of MK) v Secretary of State for the Home Department* [2010] EWCA Civ 115, [2010] 4 All ER 892, [2010] 1 WLR 2059.

In principle, an alien resisting removal from the United Kingdom may, in exceptional circumstances, rely on provisions of the European Convention other than Art 3 to challenge a decision to remove. But the facts relied on for other articles, such as Arts 2, 4, 5, 6, 8 or 9 to be engaged would need, according to Strasbourg jurisprudence, which should be followed, to be very strong, in other words "a flagrant breach": *R (on the application of Ullah) v Special Adjudicator; R (on the application of Ullah) v Immigration Appeal Tribunal* [2004] UKHL 26, [2004] 2 AC 323, [2004] 3 All ER 785.

The threshold of reliance on Art 8 as a ground for challenging removal from the United Kingdom is high; but "private life" is a broad term and if the facts are strong enough Art 8 may be invoked successfully: *R (on the application of Razgar) v Secretary of State for the Home Department* [2004] UKHL 27, [2004] 2 AC 368, [2004] 3 All ER 821. In that case the applicant relied on his need for psychiatric treatment which was being provided in the United Kingdom and would not be available in the country to which he would be returned, with the probable consequence that he would commit suicide. Lord Bingham listed five questions for a reviewing court hearing applications for judicial review in cases where reliance was placed on Art 8:

(1) Would the proposed removal be an interference by a public authority with the exercise of the applicant's right to respect for his private, or as the case might be, family life?
(2) If so, would such interference have consequences of such gravity as potentially to engage the operation of Art 8?
(3) If so, was such interference in accordance with the law?
(4) If so, was such interference necessary in a democratic society in the interests of national security, public safety or the economic well being of the country, for the prevention of disorder or crime, for the protection of health or morals, or for the protection of the rights and freedoms of others?
(5) If so, was such interference proportionate to the legitimate public end sought to be achieved?

In *RA (Sri Lanka) v Secretary of State for the Home Department* [2008] EWCA Civ 1210 the Court of Appeal ruled that the same principles are to be applied in such cases whether they involve physical illness or mental illness, applying *N v United Kingdom (26565/05)* (2008) 47 EHRR 39.

When considering the removal of the parent of a British child from the United Kingdom, the best interests of the child have to be a primary consideration in making the proportionality decision. Nationality of the child is not a "trump card" but the best interests of children who have lived here all their lives may not be served by expecting them to go to a foreign country with the immigrant parent and to be separate from the British one: *ZH (Tanzania) v Secretary of State for the Home Department* [2011] UKSC 4, [2011] 2 AC 166, [2011] 2 All ER 783, [2011] 1 FCR 221. However, it is necessary for the court carefully to balance all factors for and against removal: *ZS (Jamaica) v Secretary of State for the Home Department* [2012] EWCA Civ 1639, [2012] All ER (D) 144 (Dec). The Supreme Court in *Zoumbas v Secretary of State for the Home Department* [2013] UKSC 74, [2013] 1 WLR 3690, (2014) Times, 13 January has now listed the relevant principles to be applied: (a) the child's best interests were an integral part of the proportionality assessment; (b) in making the assessment those best interests were a primary consideration but were not always the only primary consideration and were not a paramount consideration; (c) although the child's best interests could be outweighed by the cumulative effect of other considerations, no other consideration could be treated as inherently more significant; (d) it was important to ask the right questions in an orderly manner to avoid undervaluing the child's best interests relevant to other important considerations; (e) the child's circumstances and what was in his or her best interests had to be clearly identified before considering whether those interests were outweighed by other considerations; (f) there was therefore no substitute for a careful examination of all relevant factors as to the interests of a child; (g) the child must not be blamed for matters for which he or she was not responsible, such as the conduct of a parent. Proportionality was to be assessed in the particular circumstances of each case. The child's best interests might point only marginally in one, rather than another, direction, and in some cases the weight of another primary consideration could tip the balance and make the interference proportionate even where it had very severe consequences for children. However, a court would not be likely to reach the 'firm if bleak' conclusion that young children should be separated from their parents.

The Supreme Court has ruled that a policy of refusing to grant a marriage visa to a foreign national, as a spouse of a person settled in the United Kingdom, where either person was aged under 21, interfered with their Art 8 rights and there was insufficient evidence to show that the interference was justified: *R (on the application of Aguilar Quila) v Secretary of State for the Home Department* [2011] UKSC 45, [2011] 3 WLR 836, [2011] 3 FCR 575, [2011] NLJR 1449.

However, a rule requiring foreign spouses and partners of British citizens or those settled in the UK to produce a certificate of knowledge of English when seeking leave to enter with a view to settlement did not infringe inter alia Art 8: *R (on the application of Bibi) v Secretary of State for the Home Department (Liberty and Joint Council for the Welfare of Immigrants, intervening)* [2015] UKSC 68, [2015] 1 WLR 5055; albeit the Supreme Court commented that the guidance accompanying the rule might be incompatible with Art 8 (as to which further submissions were required). See also *MM (Lebanon) v Secretary of State for the Home Department* [2017] UKSC 10, [2017] 1 WLR 771 in relation to minimum income requirements on those with the right to live in the UK who wish to bring non-EEA citizen spouses to live in the UK.

The refusal of a holiday visa to a foreign sister of a UK citizen was not an interference with the non-national's Art 8 family life as this right did not ordinarily extent to non-cohabiting and non-dependant relations. It was also not a violation of her right to respect for family life: *Secretary of State for the Home Department v Onuorah* [2017] EWCA Civ 1757.

The approach to Art 8 rights (eg in relation to separating a child from a parent) is not radically different as between extradition and expulsion cases. A child's best interests would be a primary consideration but it might be outweighed by countervailing factors: *HH v Deputy Prosecutor of the Italian Republic* [2012] UKSC 25, [2012] 3 WLR 90, [2012] 4 All ER 539.

The deportation of foreign criminals requires the court to balance the powerful public interest in deportation as against any Art 8 rights that are in play. When doing so, the Court should have regard to the factors outlined in *Maslov v Austria (Application No 1638/03)* [2008] ECHR 1638/03 and other ECtHR cases summarised *Hesham Ali v Secretary of State for the Home Department* [2016] UKSC 60, [2016] 1 WLR 4799. The ECtHR has, for example, held that the deportation of a drug dealer who had lived in the United Kingdom since he was three years old was a proportionate response and not in breach of Art 8: *Balogun v United Kingdom (Application No 60286/09)* (2012) Times, 13 April, ECtHR. Conversely, the deportation of a convicted juvenile rapist may be in breach of Art 8 where a settled immigrant has, during the nine years since his conviction, developed social ties with his community although not family ties as such: *AA v United Kingdom No 8000/08* [2011] All ER (D) 112 (Sep).

The Court of Appeal had decided that the relevant immigration rules, introduced in 2012 and updated in 2014, provided a complete code for the assessment of Art 8 arguments: see *MF (Nigeria v Secretary of State for the Home Department* [2013] EWCA Civ 1192, [2014] 1 WLR 544, [2013] All ER (D) 78 (Oct); *YM (Uganda) v Secretary of State for the Home Department* [2014] EWCA Civ 1292, [2014] All ER (D) 148 (Oct); *LC (China) v Secretary of State for the Home Department* [2014] EWCA Civ 1210; and *Secretary of State for the Home Department v AJ (Angola)* [2014] EWCA Civ 1636. In *Hesham Ali v Secretary of State for the Home Department* [2016] UKSC 60, [2016] 1 WLR 4799, however, the Supreme Court held that the rules should no longer be treated as a complete code. Nonetheless, they were an important consideration given the margin of appreciation that applied and because they constituted the Home Secretary's policy which had been endorsed by Parliament. The critical issue for the tribunal would generally be whether, giving due weight to the strength of the public interest in the deportation of the offender in the case before it, the Art 8 claim was sufficiently strong to outweigh it. The Court of Appeal has since underlined that the strength of the public interest in deportation has not diminished since *Ali*: *Assad v Secretary of State for the Home Department* [2017] EWCA Civ 10. In *NE-A (Nigeria) v Secretary of State for the Home Department* [2017] EWCA Civ 239, [2017] Imm AR 1077 the Court of Appeal described the focus in *Ali* as having been on the immigration rules, whereas in subsequent cases to which Part 5A of the Nationality, Immigration and Asylum Act 2002 applied, there was a statutory underpinning for the applicable considerations. In *KO (Nigeria) v Secretary of State for the Home Department* [2018] UKSC 53, [2018] 1 WLR 5273, the Supreme Court held that Part 5A of the 2002 Act was intended to produce a straightforward set of rules, which narrowed rather than widen the residual area of discretionary judgment for the court to take account of public interest or other factors not reflected in the wording of the statute.

The Supreme Court in *Hesham Ali* encouraged Tribunals conducting proportionality assessments in the context of foreign criminal deportations to follow a balance sheet approach: weighing up expressly the factors that speak in favour of and against deportation (the Court of Appeal has subsequently described this approach as constituting a 'good discipline' for Tribunals: see *Secretary of State for the Home Department v Quarey* [2017] EWCA Civ 47).

See also *Makhlouf v Secretary of State for the Home Department (Northern Ireland)* [2016] UKSC 59 which was determined by the Supreme Court together with *Ali*.

In *KO (Nigeria)* the Supreme Court held that when deciding whether the deportation of a foreign criminal would be 'unduly harsh' on a qualifying child (under s 117C(5) of the 2002 Act), it was not necessary to consider the nature of the foreign criminal's offending or immigration history. The same applied when assessing the reasonableness of expecting a child to leave the UK for the purposes of s 117B(6).

In *Rhuppiah v Secretary of State for the Home Department* [2018] UKSC 58, [2018] 1 WLR 5536, the Supreme Court held that a non-UK citizen without indefinite leave to remain had a precarious immigration status for the purposes of s 117B(5) of the 2002 Act, with the consequence that little weight should be given to private live established during that time.

In *Kiarie v Secretary of State for the Home Department; R (on the application of Byndloss) v Secretary of State for the Home Department* [2017] UKSC 42, [2017] 1 WLR 2380 the Supreme Court held that certificates issued by the Secretary of State under the Nationality, Immigration and Asylum Act 2002, s 94B requiring that a human rights challenge could only be brought from abroad following deportation were inconsistent with Arts 8 and 13 because an 'out-of-county' appeal would not be effective. The public interest in a foreign criminal's removal in advance of an arguable appeal was outweighed by the wider public interest that an arguable appeal should remain effective even if brought from abroad.

III HUM [30.11]

Prisoners' rights An unqualified right to search prisoners' cells and possessions contravenes Art 8 to the extent that it allows prison officers to examine the prisoner's legally privileged communications in his, or her, absence: *R (on the application of Daly) v Secretary of State for the Home Department* [2001] UKHL 26, [2001] 2 AC 532, [2001] 3 All ER 433. Conversely, the separation of a female prisoner from her 18-month-old child does not necessarily infringe Convention rights to respect for family life but the application of such a policy must not be rigid and must have regard to all the facts of the individual case: *R (on the application of P) v Secretary of State for the Home Department* [2001] EWCA 1151, [2002] 1 WLR 2002.

Where a prisoner obviously requires treatment in a mental hospital, a failure to arrange for a transfer may be a breach of the prisoner's rights under Art 8 and, in an extreme case, Art 3: *D v Secretary of State for the Home Department* (2004) Times, 27 December, QBD.

A policy barring prisoners from the use of artificial insemination facilities save in exceptional circumstances was a disproportionate interference with their rights under Art 8. Prisoners do not forfeit their Convention rights apart from the necessary and inevitable consequences of imprisonment or by an adequate link between a restriction and the circumstances of the prisoner in question. In this case the policy was not justified by security issues or by administrative and financial demands on the State. A proper weighing of the competing individual and public interests is required in each case: *Dickson v United Kingdom (Application 44362/04)* [2007] 3 FCR 877, ECtHR.

Article 8 was not breached by decisions to separate prisoners who were in long-term same sex relationships, or by a failure to publish a policy explaining whether same sex relationships were to be facilitated or restricted: *R (on the application of B) v Secretary of State for Justice* [2014] EWCA Civ 1628.

A judge sentencing a mother to imprisonment for contempt of court was required to consider whether the resulting grave interference with the Art 8 rights of her baby was proportionate and justified: *B v S (contempt: imprisonment of mother)* [2009] EWCA Civ 548, [2009] 2 FLR 1005, [2009] Fam Law 1028.

The Court of Appeal held that there was no breach of Art 8 where a prisoner, detained in segregation at his own request, was provided with only 30 minutes each day in the open air contrary to a Prison Service Order requiring that such prisoner have at least one hour each day in the open air: *Malcolm v Ministry of Justice* [2011] EWCA Civ 1538. Compare *Shahid v Scottish Ministers* [2015] UKSC 58, [2015] 3 WLR 58, 165 NLJ 7673, [2015] All ER (D) 109 (Oct), in which segregating a prisoner for a period of around 56 months was found to amount to a violation of Art 8.

III HUM [30.11A]

Correspondence The monitoring by the prison authorities of medical correspondence between a convicted prisoner and his external specialist doctor has been held to contravene Art 8, although the issue is essentially one of striking a proper balance in the circumstances: *Szuluk v United Kingdom (Application No 36936/05)* (2009) 108 BMLR 190, (2009) Times, 17 June, ECtHR.

III HUM [30.12]

Precedents Precedents for judicial review proceedings based on Art 8 are provided at **BCCP J[103]** and **BCCP J[104]**; precedents for Part 7 claims based on this article are at **BCCP L[356]**, **BCCP L[361]**, **BCCP L[362]**, **BCCP L[362.1]** and **BCCP L[363]** and precedents for Part 8 claims are at **BCCP L[370]** and **BCCP L[371]**.

III HUM [31]

Article 9 Freedom of thought, conscience and religion

1. Everyone has the right to freedom of thought, conscience and religion; this right includes freedom to change his religion or belief and freedom, either alone or in community with others and in public or private, to manifest his religion or belief, in worship, teaching, practice and observance.
2. Freedom to manifest one's religion or beliefs shall be subject only to such limitations as are prescribed by law and are necessary in a democratic society in the interests of public safety, for the protection of public order, health or morals, or for the protection of the rights and freedoms of others.

III HUM [31.1]

Scope of the freedom See the provisions of s 13, at para **III HUM [19]**, regarding the grant of relief.

The Convention right to believe in the virtue of assisted suicide is not infringed by the risk of prosecution under the Suicide Act 1961, s 2(1) for giving such assistance: *R (on the application of Pretty) v DPP* [2001] UKHL 61, [2001] 1 All ER 1, [2001] 3 WLR 1598. Similarly, s 2(1) does not impose what the ECtHR would regard as an impermissible blanket ban on suicide and therefore is within the UK's margin of appreciation: *R (on the application of Nicklinson v Ministry of Justice (CNK Alliance Ltd and British Humanist Association intervening); R (on the application of AM) v DPP* [2014] UKSC 38, [2014] 3 All ER 843.

Article 9 rights were engaged where prison authorities sought to require a devout Muslim to drink water during a period of fasting so as to provide a urine sample for a drug test although the fasting was a personal discipline not required by his religion: *R (on the application of Bashir) v Independent Adjudicator* [2011] EWHC 1108 (Admin), [2011] NLJR 812, 175 CL&J 374. However, this does not mean that a prisoner can refuse to provide a sample for drug testing in such circumstances: *R (on the application of Eguakhide) v Governor of HMP Gartree* [2014] EWHC 1328 (Admin).

III HUM [31.2]

Discrimination in the receiving state as a ground for granting asylum In *R (on the application of Ullah) v Special Adjudicator* [2004] UKHL 26, [2004] 2 AC 323, [2004] 3 All ER 785 the House of Lords dismissed the appeal on the facts but took a broader view about the principles involved than the Court of Appeal had done. In principle, an alien resisting removal from the United Kingdom may, in exceptional circumstances, rely on provisions of the European Convention other than Art 3 to challenge a decision to remove. But the facts relied on for other articles, such as Arts 2, 4, 5, 6, 8 or 9 to be engaged would need, according to Strasbourg jurisprudence, which should be followed, to be very strong, in other words "a flagrant breach".

Article 9 protects the right to hold, or not to hold, political beliefs as well as religious ones. Nobody ought to be forced to have or express a political opinion in which he did not believe: *RT (Zimbabwe) v Secretary of State for the Home Department* [2012] UKSC 38, [2012] 4 All ER 843, applying the principle in *Kokkinakis v Greece* (1993) 17 EHRR 397.

III HUM [31.3]

School uniform Article 9.1 of the Convention on Human Rights may be engaged where a school pupil is turned away from school because he or she is wearing religious clothing which is not allowed by the school's rules regarding school uniform. However, the decision of the Court of Appeal was overturned in the House of Lords where it was held that since the claimant could have changed to another school where the rules on uniform suited her better she was not being excluded from education and that the insistence on the uniform was, on the facts of the case, justified: *R (on the application of Begum) v Headteacher and Governors of Denbigh High School* [2006] UKHL 15, [2006] 2 All ER 487.

Similarly, a school was entitled to refuse to permit a pupil to wear a purity ring as an expression of her Christian faith and sign of her belief in celibacy before marriage. The pupil voluntarily accepted the school's uniform policy which did not allow the wearing of the ring and there were other means open to her to practise her belief without undue hardship or inconvenience. The uniform policy was prescribed by law and served important functions ie fostering the identity of the school and an atmosphere of allegiance, discipline, equality and cohesion which allowed pupils to learn in an environment which minimised pressures from signs of wealth and status: *R (on the application of Playfoot) v Millais School Governing Body* [2007] EWHC 1698 (Admin), (2007) Times, 23 July.

As for work uniform, see *Eweida v United Kingdom (48420/10)* (2013) 57 EHRR 8 at para **III HUM [31.5]**.

III HUM [31.4]

Corporal punishment and parental beliefs In a case where parents' religious beliefs included the administration of corporal punishment and authorised the school to discipline their children accordingly, it was held that the ban imposed by s 548 of the Education Act 1996 interfered with the parents' rights under Art 9, but that the interference was justified within the terms of the second paragraph of the article: *R (on the application of Williamson) v Secretary of State for Education and Employment* [2005] UKHL 15, [2005] 2 All ER 1, (2005) Times, 25 February, dismissing an appeal against the decision of the Court of Appeal.

III HUM [31.5]

Discrimination and religious beliefs In *Eweida v United Kingdom (Application No 48420/10)* (2013) 57 EHRR 8, the ECtHR considered four joined cases of in which workplace policies restricted Art 9 rights. Ms Eweida was a Christian member of the check-in staff for British Airways and wanted to wear a cross visibly contrary to a uniform policy (which was in fact relaxed before the ECtHR's decision). The English Courts had found no indirect discrimination: *Eweida v British Airways Plc* [2010] EWCA Civ 80, [2010] ICR 890). Ms Chaplin also wanted to wear a visible cross in her work as a geriatric nurse at an NHS hospital. A policy restricted the wearing of necklaces to minimise infection and injury risks when handling patients. It was found she had not been discriminated against by a Tribunal at first instance. Ms Ladele was the third applicant (see *Ladele v Islington London Borough Council* [2009] EWCA Civ 1357, [2010] 1 WLR 955, [2010] LGR 690). She was a registrar of births, deaths and marriages who, as a result of her Christian beliefs refused to conduct civil partnership ceremonies but this was found not to amount to discrimination. Finally, Mr McFarlane was a counsellor for a sex therapy and relationship counselling service. He refused to provide services to homosexual couples because of his religious beliefs and was dismissed. No discrimination was found by the domestic Court (*McFarlane v Relate Avon Ltd* [2010] EWCA Civ 880, [2010] IRLR 872, 29 BHRC 249).

The ECtHR held that manifesting one's religious – and also non-religious – beliefs were covered by Art 9 and this extended to manifestations in public or at work. Not every act influenced by a belief will amount to a manifestation, eg where they are only remotely connected. Such acts would fall outside Art 9. Manifestations may impact on others, and accordingly restrictions were permissible under Art 9(2). In the employment field, the possibility of choosing to leave the employment in question would be a factor to weigh in the balance. A fair balance had not been struck by the refusal in Ms Eweida's case: BA's aim of wishing to project a corporate image was legitimate but had been given too much weight. In the other cases, however, the restriction on Art 9 rights were all justified and proportionate and the domestic courts were found to have struck the correct balance.

In *Belcacemi & Oussar v Belgium (Application No 37798/13)* [2017] ECHR 655 and *Dakir v Belgium (Application 4619/12)* [2017] ECHR 656, the ECtHR rejected complaints of breaches of Arts 8 and 9 by women who had been affected by restrictions on the ability to wear a niqab. The Court emphasised the width of the margin of appreciation possessed by the state and accepted that the restrictions were proportionate to the aim of promoting social cohesion by protecting the rights and freedoms of others.

See also the earlier case of *MBA v Mayor and Burgesses of the London Borough of Merton* [2013] EWCA Civ 1562, 157 (48) Sol Jo LB 37 in which a local authority's requirement that a care home worker be available to work on Sunday despite her religious belief that Sunday should be a day of rest was held to constitute a proportionate interference with the worker's Art 9 rights.

The prospect of religious rights covered by Art 9 clashing with rights held by others has caused the Courts to draw a distinction clearly expressed by Laws LJ in *McFarlane v Relate Avon Ltd* [2010] EWCA Civ 880, [2010] IRLR 872, 29 BHRC 249 (para 22):

> 'In a free constitution such as ours there is an important distinction to be drawn between the law's protection of the right to hold and express a belief and the law's protection of that belief's substance or content. The common law and ECHR Article 9 offer vigorous protection of the Christian's right (and every other person's right) to hold and express his or her beliefs. And so they should. By contrast they do not, and should not, offer any protection whatever of the substance or content of those beliefs on the ground only that they are based on religious precepts. These are twin conditions of a free society.'

The Equality Act (Sexual Orientation) Regulations 2007 were found to be infringed by hoteliers who refused to let double rooms to a gay couple on religious grounds: *Hall v Bull (Liberty intervening)* [2013] UKSC 73, [2013] 1 WLR 3741, (2014) Times, 09 January. Compare the similar decision of the Court of Appeal in *Black v Wilkinson* [2013] EWCA Civ 820, [2013] 4 All ER 1053, [2013] 1 WLR 2490.

Permission to apply for judicial review was refused to applicants for local authority approval as foster carers who claimed that their religious views on sexuality were not a legitimate fostering concern for the local authority: *R (on the application of Johns) v Derby City Council and Equality and Human Rights Commission* [2011] EWHC 375, [2011] 1 FCR 493, [2011] HRLR 20.

The refusal to accept advertising by a religious organisation on the basis that it pursues the legitimate aim of avoiding serious offence to the public, protecting the rights of others, and complying with statutory duties, can be a proportionate interference: see *R (on the application of Core Issues Trust) v Transport for London* [2014] EWCA Civ 34, [2014] PTSR 785, [2014] EqLR 164 (a case concerning interferences with Art 10).

Had Northern Ireland law prohibited the appointment of a humanist celebrant to solemnise a marriage, that would have constituted discrimination under Arts 9 and 14. However, the Marriage (Northern Ireland) Order 2003 provided a basis for a humanist celebrant to solemnise the marriage and the fact that that method of appointment was different when compared to religious bodies did not give rise to an actionable difference in treatment: *Re Smyth's Application for Judicial Review* [2018] NICA 25.

III HUM [31.6]

Funeral rites In *Ghai v Newcastle City Council (Ramgharia Gurdwara, Hitchin intervening)* [2009] EWHC 978 (Admin), [2009] NLJR 713, (2009) Times, 18 May the High Court decided that the burning of human remains other than in a building, such as on an open-air funeral pyre, was an offence. The failure to provide land for an open air funeral in accordance with orthodox Hindu beliefs amounted to an interference with the right to manifest religious belief under Art 9, but such interference was justified where a significant number of people would be offended by both the principle and the reality of cremation by means of open air pyres. However, on appeal it was held that the claimants' beliefs could be accommodated under the UK legislation. If the cremation, despite being by traditional rather than electric fire and with sunlight shining directly on the body, took place in a relatively permanent and substantial structure, this would satisfy the requirement for a "building": *Ghai v Newcastle City Council* [2010] EWCA Civ 59, [2010] All ER (D) 106 (Feb).

The Divisional Court has held that a coroner's declared policy of not prioritising a death because of the religion of the deceased or family breached Arts 9 and 14: *R (on the application of Adath Yisroel Burial Society) v Inner North London Coroner* [2018] EWHC 969 (Admin), [2018] 3 WLR 1354.

III HUM [32]

Article 10 Freedom of expression

1. Everyone has the right to freedom of expression. This right shall include freedom to hold opinions and to receive and impart information and ideas without interference by public authority and regardless of frontiers. This Article shall not prevent States from requiring the licensing of broadcasting, television or cinema enterprises.

2. The exercise of these freedoms, since it carries with it duties and responsibilities, may be subject to such formalities, conditions, restrictions or penalties as are prescribed by law and are necessary in a democratic society, in the interests of national security, territorial integrity or public safety, for the prevention of disorder or crime, for the protection of health or morals, for the protection of the reputation or rights of others, for preventing the disclosure of information received in confidence, or for maintaining the authority and impartiality of the judiciary.

III HUM [32.1]

Election expenses The statutory limit on the amount that an unauthorised person can spend on issuing publications to promote a candidate was held to be a breach of Art 10: *Bowman v United Kingdom* (1998) 26 EHRR 1, ECtHR.

III HUM [32.2]

Binding over A bind-over to keep the peace, where a breach of the peace has been proved to have occurred, is a 'restriction prescribed by law' and therefore not in principle a breach of Art 10(2): *Steel v United Kingdom* [1998] Crim LR 893, ECtHR. However, it has been held to breach Art 10(2) to bind an individual over where he has not been found to have broken the peace and where the threatened behaviour is not contrary to law, as such, but 'wrong rather than right in the judgment of the majority of contemporary fellow citizens': *Hashman and Harrup v United Kingdom* (1999) 30 EHRR 241, ECtHR. This is because the domestic law concept of being of 'good behaviour' was too uncertain to qualify as "law" within the meaning of the Convention.

III HUM [32.3]

Scope of the freedom It has been held that 'freedom of expression is one of the essential foundations of a democratic society and one of the basic conditions for its progress and for each individual's self-fulfilment': *Lingens v Austria* (1986) 8 EHRR 407, 418–419. The court is 'faced not with a choice between two conflicting principles but with a principle of freedom of expression that is subject to a number of exceptions which must be narrowly interpreted': *Sunday Times v United Kingdom* (1979) 2 EHRR 245. 'Exceptions to freedom of expression must be justified as being necessary in a democracy. In other words, freedom of expression is the rule and regulation of speech is the exception requiring justification . . . Any exceptions can only be justified if . . . underpinned by a pressing social need': *Reynolds v Times Newspapers Ltd* [2001] 2 AC 127, [1999] 4 All ER 609, HL. 'To be justified, any curtailment of freedom of expression must be convincingly established by compelling countervailing consideration, and the means employed must be proportionate to the end sought to be achieved': *Reynolds v Times Newspapers* [2001] 2 AC 127, [1999] 4 All ER 609, HL. See also the provisions of s 12 (at para **III HUM [18]**), regarding the grant of relief.

It was held in *A-G v Punch Ltd, sub nom Steen v A-G* [2001] EWCA Civ 403, [2001] QB 1028, [2001] 2 All ER 655 that an injunction against publishing any information obtained in the employment of the Security Service, except with the consent of the Attorney-General, was disproportionate as to any public interest and contrary to Art 10. But it does not expand the defence of qualified privilege, on the part of the press, to allow reliance on factors unknown to the publisher at the time of publication: *Loutchansky v Times Newspapers Ltd* [2001] EWCA Civ 536, [2002] QB 321, [2001] 4 All ER 115; but on qualified privilege and reporting by the press of matters of public interest now see *Jameel v Wall Street Journal Europe SprL*

[2006] UKHL 44, [2006] 3 WLR 642 The scope of the Convention right must be considered in the context provided by s 12 at para **III HUM [18]**. Cases on the grant or refusal of injunctions to restrain the publication of confidential material are noted at para **III HUM [18.2]**.

Where a defendant relied upon the defence of qualified privilege in respect of a report on a dispute airing the allegations made by one party against the other, provided the paper did not adopt the allegations as true, the defence of qualified privilege was available to the defendant, notwithstanding the allegations had not been verified: *Al-Fagih v HH Saudi Research & Marketing UK Ltd* [2001] EWCA Civ 1634, [2002] EMLR 215.

It has also been held that where a defendant pleads justification based on reasonable grounds for suspecting that the claimant had committed the offence, the common law restrictions (for example excluding post-publication evidence) do not contravene Art 10: *Chase v News Group Newspapers Ltd* [2002] EWCA Civ 1772, [2002] All ER (D) 20 (Dec), (2002) Times, 31 December. It has been held that s 10 of the Defamation Act 1952 does not impinge on the defence of qualified privilege in the context of election publications and it is therefore compatible with Arts 6 and 10 of the Convention: *Culnane v Morris* [2005] EWHC 2438 (QB), [2006] 2 All ER 149.

Where a publisher of a libel is ordered to pay costs, Art 10 may not be relied on as a reason for not paying the success fee and after the event insurance: *Times newspapers Ltd v Flood, Miller v Associated Newspapers* [2017] UKSC 33.

III HUM [32.3A]

Relative weight of right to freedom of expression In assessing the proportionality of an interference with the exercise of the right to freedom of speech, it is necessary to consider the context in which an applicant seeks to exercise the right. Arguably the right of the media to freedom of expression in the field of political discussion is of a higher order than the individual right to a good reputation. It has also been held by the Court of Appeal that the exercise of the right is of exceptionally high value in the case of Parliamentarians seeking to exercise it in Parliament on matters of public interest: *R (on the application of Lord Carlile of Berriew QC) v Secretary of State for the Home Department* [2013] EWCA Civ 199, [2013] NLJR 26. However, the Supreme Court on appeal held that an interference with Art 10 rights by exclusion from the UK of a dissident Iranian politician who wished to address meetings in Westminster could be justified by the need to guard against the potential adverse reaction by the Iranian state, even though Iran did not share the UK's values in respect of free speech, and held also that special weight must be attached to policy choices made by decision makers with special institutional competence: [2014] UKSC 60, [2014] 3 WLR 1404.

The right to freedom of expression should not be presumed to rank higher than other basic human rights, such as those under Art 8: *Cream Holdings Ltd v Banerjee* [2004] UKHL 44, [2005] 1 AC 253, [2004] 4 All ER 617. See also *Re W (Children) (Identification: Restrictions on publication)* (2005) Times, 21 July, holding that the exercise to be performed is one of parallel analysis in which the starting point is presumptive parity between the competing rights and not priority for freedom of expression. See also *Khuja v Times Newspapers Ltd* [2017] UKSC 49, [2017] 3 WLR 351: neither Art 8 or Art 10 was in principle stronger than the other. In *Re X and Y (children) (executive summary of serious case review: reporting restrictions)* [2012] EWCA Civ 1500, [2013] 1 FCR 1, [2012] NLJR 1503 it was held that the balance had been wrongly struck: a public report produced by a local authority in relation to child abuse should have been subject to drastic redaction so as to protect a child's rights under Art 8.

Where individuals challenged anti-terrorism asset-freezing orders, the general public interest in publishing a report of the proceedings in which they were named justified curtailing their rights to private life: *Guardian News and Media Ltd, Re* [2010] UKSC 1, [2010] 2 All ER 799, [2010] 2 WLR 325. But the public importance in publishing a full report of control order proceedings identifying a suspected terrorist may be outweighed by the need to protect that person, by anonymity, from violence and racist attacks: *Secretary of State for the Home Department v AP (No 2)* [2010] UKSC 26, [2010] 4 All ER 259, [2010] 1 WLR 1652.

III HUM [32.3B]

The open justice principle In a case where documents are put before a judge and referred to in the course of proceedings, the default position should be that access to the documents, for example by journalists, should be permitted, although countervailing considerations might prevail. The open justice principle is a principle of the common law and does not derive from Art 10 of the Convention: *R (on the application of Guardian News and Media Ltd) v City of Westminster Magistrates' Court* [2012] EWCA Civ 420, [2012] 3 All ER 551, [2012] 3 WLR 1343, a case about the disclosure of documents put in evidence in extradition proceedings.

III HUM [32.4]

Copyright Rare circumstances may arise where the right to freedom of expression would come into conflict with the rights granted by the Copyright, Designs & Patents Act 1988. There were circumstances in which the public interest in the right to freedom of expression might override copyright. In such instances, s 171(3) of the 1988 Act permitted the defence of public interest to be raised. While rare, such cases were not capable of categorisation or definition, each case depends on its facts. The tight circumscribing of the public interest defence in *Hyde Park Residence Ltd v Yelland* [2001] Ch 143, [2000] 3 WLR 215 by Aldous LJ was not justified: *Ashdown v Telegraph Group Ltd* [2001] EWCA Civ 1142, [2002] Ch 149, [2001] 4 All ER 666.

III HUM [32.5]

Publication of information relating to proceedings in private The restrictions, under s 12 of the Administration of Justice Act 1960, on publishing information relating to proceedings in private (for example proceedings about the upbringing of a child) do not infringe Convention rights under Art 10 where privacy is compatible with Art 6(1): *B v United Kingdom, P v United Kingdom (Application Nos 36337/97, 35974/97)* [2001] 2 FLR 261. On the other hand, the mere fact that proceedings under Part IV of the Family Law Act 1996 were heard in chambers does not by itself justify an injunction to restrain publication of extracts from the affidavits used: *Clibbery v Allan* [2001] 2 FCR 577; upheld by the Court of Appeal: [2002] EWCA Civ 45, [2002] Fam 261.

The court may properly publicise a decision in family proceedings heard in private where the issues are already being reported on in the public domain but inaccurately: *Blunkett v Quinn* [2004] EWHC 2816 (Fam), [2004] All ER (D) 49 (Dec), (2004) Times, 7 December, Ryder J.

Proceedings in the Court of Protection will normally be held in private in accordance with rr 90 to 93 of the Court of Protection Rules 2007, SI 2007/1744 and the Practice Direction PD 13A Court of Protection Reporting Restrictions. However, they may be held in public if 'good reason' is established. The existence of good reason does not automatically lift the requirement of privacy, but Arts 10 and 8 are then engaged and a balance must be struck: *Independent News and Media Ltd v A* (2009) Times, 17 November (affirmed by the Court of Appeal at [2010] EWCA Civ 343, [2010] 1 WLR 2262) in which Hedley J decided, on balance that the media should be allowed to attend on the grounds that (1) issues concerning the particular individual were already in the public domain (2) the court retained power to preserve privacy while addressing the issues and (3) it was in the public interest that the general public should understand the jurisdiction and how it was exercised in such cases. Previous press interest in a case and the legitimate public interest in the court's powers amounted to a good reason which was not outweighed by an incapacitated person's Art 8 rights in *P (by his Litigation Friend The Official Solicitor) v Independent Print Ltd* [2011] EWCA Civ 756. For the relevant factors in the balancing exercise see also *W (by her litigation friend B) v M (an adult patient, by her litigation friend the Official Solicitor)* [2011] EWHC 1197, (Fam) [2011] 4 All ER 1295, (2011) 2 FLR 1143.

The right to report matters stated in open court is not a civil right but it is a breach of Art 10 to deny the Press an opportunity to apply to the court to argue against an order prohibiting publication: *Mackay and BBC Scotland v United Kingdom (Application No 10734/05)* (2011) Times, 4 January, ECtHR.

Where reporting restrictions were necessary to protect a child sex offender from facing infringement of his Art 3 rights on his return to his home country, the restrictions did not contravene Art 10 (or Art 6): *A v British Broadcasting Corpn* [2014] UKSC 25, [2014] 2 All ER 1037, [2014] 2 WLR 1243.

III HUM [32.5A]

Libel Where a claimant brought libel proceedings in respect of an advertisement featuring a woman who was a look-alike of the claimant, it would place an impossible burden on a publisher to check if a true picture of one person resembled a third party who might be defamed by the publication. To apply a strict liability rule in such circumstances would be an unjustified interference with freedom of expression disproportionate to the legitimate aim of protecting the reputations of look-alikes: *O'Shea v MGN Ltd* [2001] EMLR 943. The imposition of a single publication rule in respect of a publication of a newspaper article on a web site would be more restrictive than the proportionate one-year limitation rule and would therefore be disproportionate and an unjustified restriction on the claimant's right of access to the court under Art 6: *Loutchansky v Times Newspapers Ltd (No 2)* [2001] EMLR 876; approved by the Court of Appeal [2001] EWCA Civ 1805, [2002] QB 783.

The common law rule that a libel does not require proof of special damage is not incompatible with Art 10: *Jameel v Dow Jones & Co Inc* [2005] EWCA Civ 75, (2005) Times, 14 February, also *Jameel v Wall Street Journal Europe Sprl* (2005) Times, 14 February, CA (as regards libel of a corporation), upheld by a majority of the House of Lords [2006] UKHL 44, [2006] 3 WLR 642. On the other hand it has been held that the bringing of libel proceedings for substantial damages against defendants who were denied access to legal aid and who nevertheless proved the truth of many of their allegations contravened their human right to freedom of expression: *Steel v United Kingdom (Application No 68416/01)* (2005) Times, 16 February, ECtHR.

The obligation of a defendant newspaper to pay the claimant's success fees in libel litigation has been held to infringe the newspaper's right to freedom of expression, in circumstances where the success fees far exceeded the damages awarded. The aim of the success fee system was to increase access to justice but the costs burden was disproportionate to the aim and imposed a penalty on the media's freedom of expression, in breach of Art 10: *MGN Ltd v United Kingdom (Application No 39401/04)* (2011) Times, 20 January, ECtHR. However, the Supreme Court declined to apply *MGN Ltd v United Kingdom* as a general rule of domestic law in *Times Newspapers Ltd v Flood* [2017] UKSC 33, [2017] 1 WLR 1415. This is consistent with *Coventry v Lawrence* [2015] UKSC 50, 165 NLJ 7663, [2015] All ER (D) 234 (Jul) in which no violation was found in respect of a requirement to pay a success fee and ATE insurance premium in a nuisance case where the allegations of infringement concerned Art 6 and Art 1 protocol 1.

III HUM [32.5B]

Protection of health In *H (a healthcare worker) v N (a Health Authority)* [2002] EWCA Civ 195, [2002] All ER (D) 371, (Feb), (2002) Times, 19 March, an HIV positive healthcare worker had sought a declaration that a look-back exercise by the health authority would breach the confidentiality of patients including the claimant. The Court of Appeal held that, in the circumstances, the court could properly restrain the publication of information made available in the course of or as a result of those proceedings which, if disclosed, would pre-empt the decision of the court on the issues before it. The situation was covered by para 2 of Art 10 and the court's power to make such an order was recognised by **CPR 39.2**.

In *O (a child) v Rhodes* [2015] UKSC 32, [2015] 2 WLR 1373, the Supreme Court held that there was no basis for an injunction preventing a well-known concert pianist father from publishing a book in which he described his experiences of sexual abuse as a boy. Whilst his son was psychologically vulnerable, the book was not directed at him, but rather aimed at a wide audience and the tort of intentionally causing physical or intentional harm could not be made out, and should not be developed to interfere with free speech.

III HUM [32.5C]

Restrictions necessary in a democratic society In *R (on the application of Nilsen) v Governor of Full Sutton Prison* [2003] EWHC 3160 (Admin), (2004) Times, 2 January, it was held that a decision by a prison governor and by the Home Secretary not to return a murderer's autobiography manuscript was in accordance with the Prison Rules 1999 and those rules did not contravene Art 10 because they were justified as being necessary in a democratic society under para 2. The decision in Nilsen's case was upheld on appeal in *Nilsen v Governor of Full Sutton Prison* [2004] EWCA Civ 1540, [2004] NLJR 1788, (2004) Times, 23 November in which the Master of the Rolls considered that some restriction, by Prison Rules, on the freedom of prisoners to publish was proportionate and consistent with public expectations of punishment. The Court also upheld the decision that the applicant should not be allowed access to the typescript of the book he was rightly prohibited from publishing.

The controls on political broadcast advertising in ss 319-321 of the Communications Act 2003 were an interference with Art 10 rights which is justified in the public interest: *R (on the application of Animal Defenders International) v Secretary of State for Culture, Media and Sport* [2008] UKHL 15, [2008] 1 AC 1312, [2008] 3 All ER 193 and see also *R (on the application of London Christian Radio Ltd and Christian Communications Partnerships Ltd) v Radio Advertising Clearance Centre and Secretary of State for Culture, Olympics, Media and Sport* [2013] EWCA Civ 1495, 157 (45) Sol Jo LB 37.

The Court of Appeal upheld as lawful the exclusion of an Indian Muslim public speaker from entering the United Kingdom after he made statements which breached the Home Office's 'unacceptable behaviours policy'. The resulting interference with his Art 10 rights and those of his followers was justified: *R (on the application of Naik) v Home Secretary* [2011] EWCA Civ 1546.

The Secretary of State for Justice's refusal to permit the BBC to conduct and broadcast a face-to-face interview with a prisoner was held to amount to a disproportionate interference with Art 10 rights where the prisoner's case was highly exceptional and there was a strong public interest in making the programme: *R (on the application of British Broadcasting Corpn and Casciani) v Secretary of State for Justice and Babar Ahmad* [2012] EWHC 13 (Admin), [2012] 2 All ER 1089, [2012] IP & T 606.

In *R (on the application of Calver) v Adjudication Panel for Wales* [2012] EWHC 1172 (Admin), [2012] NLJR 714 it was held that a decision by a local authority standards committee that comments by a councillor on his website ridiculing other councillors was a disproportionate interference with his Art 10 rights, having regard to the nature of the comments and the need for politicians to have 'thicker skins'. *Calver* was followed in *Heesom v Public Services Ombudsman for Wales* [2014] EWHC 1504 (Admin), [2014] 4 All ER 269, [2014] LGR 509.

III HUM [32.6]

Disclosure of information received in confidence When considering an application, under s 10 of the Contempt of Court Act 1981, for the disclosure of journalistic sources, the court should equate the requirements of the Act with those of Art 10 and apply the same test of necessity as applied when considering Art 10. In a case where confidential medical records were disclosed to the press, it was held that there had been misconduct by the informant whose identity should be disclosed: *Ashworth Hospital Authority v MGN Ltd* [2001] 1 All ER 991, [2001] EMLR 301 (followed in *Interbrew SA v Financial Times Ltd* [2001] All ER (D) 313 (Dec), (2002) Times, 4 January). The House of Lords dismissed an appeal in *Ashworth Hospital Authority v MGN Ltd* [2002] UKHL 29, [2002] 4 All ER 193, [2002] 1 WLR 2033. Their Lordships held the order to be justified although the defendant company was not itself a wrongdoer and the purpose of the order was to identify and discipline the employee who had made the unauthorised disclosure, not to bring civil proceedings. The opposite conclusion was reached in follow-up proceedings against the journalist identified under court order in the first proceedings: *Mersey Care NHS Trust v Ackroyd* [2007] EWCA Civ 101, (2007) Times, 26 February. Factors contributing to the refusal of an order in the second case included the unlikelihood of further disclosures, the high turnover of staff, the absence of a finding that the patient had not consented and the responsible attitude shown by the defendant.

In *R (on the application of Miranda) v Secretary of State for the Home Department* [2016] EWCA Civ 6, the power in the Terrorism Act 2000 Schedule 7 to stop and question a person at a port or border was found to be incompatible with Art 10 in respect of journalistic material because there were insufficient safeguards against its arbitrary exercise. The Court contrasted the position where only Art 8 was engaged.

There is no confidentiality in a transitory sexual relationship with a prostitute. A brothel is not a private place for the purposes of the PCC Code: *Theakston v MGN Ltd* [2002] EWHC 137, [2002] All ER (D) 182 (Feb), QBD. It is not necessarily in the public interest that an individual who has been adopted as a role model, without seeking that distinction, should be demonstrated to have feet of clay. But it will normally be in the public interest to put the record straight where a public figure chooses to make untrue pronouncements about his, or her, private life: *Campbell v Mirror Group Newspapers plc* [2002] EWCA Civ 1373, [2003] 1 All ER 224, [2003] 2 WLR 80. Note that Ms Campbell was successful in the House of Lords, mainly because of the importance of protecting privacy in matters of health and addiction: *Campbell v MGN Ltd* [2004] UKHL 22, [2004] 2 AC 457, [2004] 2 All ER 995.

It was held in *Tillery Valley Foods Ltd v Channel Four Television Corpn* [2004] EWHC 1075 (Ch), [2004] All ER (D) 133 (May) that where the publication of confidential information was justified in the public interest the publisher was not obliged to give the owner of the information a right to respond or reply before publication.

The disclosure of medical records to the press does not automatically justify an order for the informant to be identified. Where the journalist has a real, even though difficult, prospect of defending the case it should not be decided in the claimant's favour under CPR Part 24: *Mersey Care NHS Trust v Ackroyd* (2003) Times, 21 May, CA.

Where the information has obviously been imparted subject to a duty of confidentiality there is a public interest in upholding the duties of confidence, this being a factor that Art 10.2 recognises as capable of justifying restriction on freedom of expression: *Prince of Wales v Associated Newspapers Ltd* (2006) Times, 28 December, CA.

As regards sexual activity involving consenting adults, the duty of confidentiality should be upheld and may not be over-ridden in the public interest except in cases where exposure of the conduct prevents the public from being misled or calls in question the fitness of the individuals concerned for a responsible role in their organisation: *Mosley v News Group Newspapers Ltd* (2008) Times, 30 July, Eady J.

A boyfriend of a claimant with a high public profile was restrained by injunction from publicising confidential information and pictures regarding the claimant's adulterous relationship with another high profile person. Her right to respect for her private life weighed more heavily in the balance than the defendant's freedom of expression: *CHS v DNH* [2015] EWHC 1214 (Ch), [2015] All ER (D) 212 (May).

The fact that a 'kiss and tell' story has been published over the Internet is not by itself a sufficient reason for refusing an injunction to stop publication within the United Kingdom where there is no public interest in favour of further publication. The children of those concerned have an independent right to have their family life protected: *PJS v News Group Newspapers Ltd* (2016) Times, 23 May, Sup Ct.

III HUM [32.6A]

Without prejudice correspondence It was observed in *Prudential Assurance Co Ltd v Prudential Insurance Co of America* [2002] EWHC 2809 (Ch), [2002] All ER (D) 337, (2003) Times, 2 January by Sir Andrew Morritt V-C that there was a need to apply the without prejudice rule with restraint and only in cases to which the public interests underlying the rule were plainly applicable. This is because the Art 10 right to receive and impart information is engaged; see also s 12(4) of the Human Rights Act 1998 at para **III HUM [18]**.

III HUM [32.6B]

Contempt of court A dissenting juror has the right to bring his concerns about the jury's deliberations to the attention of the court or the Court of Appeal, either directly or through an appropriate agency such as the jury bailiff or the clerk of the court. But a disclosure to the mother of a defendant is a contempt, in breach of s 8 of the Contempt of Court Act 1981, which cannot be justified by reference to the fundamental freedom of expression secured by Art 10 of the Convention: *A-G v Scotcher* [2005] UKHL 36, [2005] 3 All ER 1.

III HUM [32.7]

Advertising The adjudications of the Advertising Standards Authority, published under Codes recognised by the Control of Misleading Advertisements Regulations 1988, have been held to fall within the words "prescribed by law" although not having direct statutory effect and also, in the instant case "necessary for the protection of health": *R v Advertising Standards Authority Ltd, ex p Matthias Rath BV* [2001] EMLR 581.

In *R (on the application of Core Issues Trust) v Transport for London* [2014] EWCA Civ 34, [2014] PTSR 785, [2014] EqLR 164 it was held that a decision by TFL to refuse to accept advertising by a Christian organisation on London buses did not infringe Art 10 because it pursued the legitimate aims of avoiding causing serious offence to the public, protecting the rights of others, and complying with statutory duties under s 149 of the Equality Act 2010, having regard also to the fact that there were many other ways in which the advertiser could express its opinions and to the impact on the Art 8 rights of gay people who would be offended by the proposed advertisement.

III HUM [32.7A]

Broadcasting Code In *R (on the application of Jon Gaunt) v Office of Communications* [2011] EWCA Civ 692, [2011] 1 WLR 2355, the Court of Appeal held that a finding by OFCOM that a radio presenter had breached the Broadcasting Code by hectoring and insulting an interviewee was not a disproportionate interference with his Art 10 rights.

III HUM [32.8]

Official Secrets Act 1989 The sanctions provided by ss 1 and 4 of the Official Secrets Act 1989 are Convention compliant: *R v Shayler* [2002] UKHL 11, [2003] 1 AC 247, [2002] 2 All ER 477.

III HUM [32.8A]

Freedom of information Article 10 imposes no positive obligation on government to provide information by means of an open forum. Therefore, a decision to hold an inquiry in private does not violate the article, although it may be open to challenge on other grounds, depending on the circumstances of the case: *R (on the application of Persey) v Secretary of State for Environment, Food and Rural Affairs* [2002] EWHC 371, [2003] QB 794, [2002] 3 WLR 704, distinguishing the decision in *R (on the application of Wagstaff) v Secretary of State for Health* [2001] 1 WLR 292. From 1 January 2005, however, the provisions of the Freedom of Information Act 2000 have provided effective access to information subject only to statutory categories of exemption.

In *Sugar v British Broadcasting Corp* [2012] UKSC 4, [2012] 2 All ER 509, [2012] 1 WLR 439 Lord Brown said at paragraph 94 that Art 10 creates no general right to freedom of information so that where the legislation expressly limits such right to information eg by the exemption for documents held by the BBC otherwise than for the purposes of journalism, it would not be interfered with when access was refused on that ground.

In *Kennedy v Charity Commission* [2014] UKSC 20, [2014] 2 All ER 847 the Supreme Court similarly ruled that s 32(2) of the Freedom of Information Act 2000 provided an absolute exemption from any duty under that Act to disclose documents created or held by a public body for the purposes of conducting an inquiry, and that Art 10 did not require this section to be read differently, in particular where other disclosure rights existed under the Charities Act 2011.

III HUM [32.9]

The importance of the right to freedom of expression See also the reference to cases on s 12 of the Human Rights Act 1998 at **III HUM [18.1]–III HUM [18.6]**.

III HUM [32.10]

Precedents A precedent for particulars of a Part 7 claim based on Art 10 is provided at **BCCP L[365]**.

III HUM [33]

Article 11 Freedom of assembly and association

1. Everyone has the right to freedom of peaceful assembly and to freedom of association with others, including the right to form and to join trade unions for the protection of his interests.

2. No restrictions shall be placed on the exercise of these rights other than such as are prescribed by law and are necessary in a democratic society in the interests of national security or public safety, for the prevention of disorder or crime, for the protection of health or morals or for the protection of the rights and freedoms of others. This Article shall not prevent the imposition of lawful restrictions on the exercise of these rights by members of the armed forces, of the police or of the administration of the State.

III HUM [33.1]

Membership of a charitable body Article 11 entitles a charitable body to exclude from membership those whose membership would, it believes, be damaging to its interests. However, applicants for membership should be made aware of any arbitrary policy of exclusion and be given an opportunity to make representations in favour of admission: *RSPCA v A-G* [2001] 3 All ER 530.

III HUM [33.1A]

Refusal of consent to enter a town centre shopping mall It was held in *Appleby v United Kingdom (Application 44306/98)* (2003) Times, 13 May, ECtHR, that UK law was not defective in permitting the private owners of a shopping mall to exclude campaigners on a local issue from entering in order to collect signatures from customers. There was on the facts no breach by the state of Art 10 or Art 11.

III HUM [33.1B]

Dismissal of an employee because of political opinions The claimant was dismissed within a year from his job as bus driver for a company whose passengers were mainly Asian. The employers dismissed him because he was elected as a local councillor standing for the British National Party. The ECHR held, by a majority that his dismissal was a breach of his right of association and that the law of the United Kingdom was defective in not providing a remedy for discrimination on the grounds of political opinion or affiliation: *Redfearn v United Kingdom (Application No 47335/06)* [2013] IRLR 51, [2012] NLJR 1466.

III HUM [33.2]

Precedents A precedent for particulars of a Part 7 claim based on Art 11 is provided at **BCCP L[366]**.

III HUM [33.3]

Protests and demonstrations Although the police are entitled to intervene and make arrests where the threat of a breach of the peace is imminent, there is no legal justification for preventing a bus carrying demonstrators from completing its journey to the scene of the proposed demonstration. Since there is no prescribed justification at common law or by statute, such an act is an unjustifiable breach of Arts 10 and 11: *R (on the application of Laporte) v Chief Constable of Gloucestershire Constabulary* [2006] UKHL 55, [2007] 2 AC 105, [2007] 2 All ER 529.

However, there is a positive duty under Arts 2 and 3 for police to act so as to avert a risk to life and protect individuals from physical violence, even if the incident in question has already started and the identity of potential victims is not known: *Sarjantson v Humberside Police Chief Constable* [2013] EWCA Civ 1252, [2013] 3 WLR 1540.

In a case concerning bye-laws made to prohibit camping at Aldermaston by the Women's Peace Camp it was held that the interference with their freedom to express their views on nuclear weapons was, in the circumstances, an unjustified breach of that right under Art 10 and of the right of assembly conferred by Art 11: *Tabernacle v Secretary of State for Defence* [2009] EWCA Civ 23, (2009) Times, 25 February.

However, the court was justified in ordering the removal of a protest camp next to St Paul's Cathedral in *City of London v Samede* [2012] EWCA Civ 160, [2012] 2 All ER 1039 in which the Art 9 rights of worshippers at St Paul's Cathedral prevailed over the rights under Arts 10 and 11 of those wishing to protest.

Similarly the provisions in the Police Reform and Social Responsibility Act 2011, Part 3 empowering police and local authority officers to stop protesters erecting and using tents in Parliament Square did not infringe the protesters' rights under Arts 10 and 11: *R (on the application of Gallastegui) v Westminster City Council* [2012] EWHC 1123 (Admin), [2012] 4 All ER 401, [2012] LGR 789.

In *R (on the application of Hicks) v Metropolitan Police Comr* [2012] EWHC 1947 (Admin), [2012] All ER (D) 232 (Jul) it was held that the police had not operated an unlawful policy or practice with an impermissibly low threshold of tolerance for public protest in relation to the Royal wedding, and arrests and searches of property under the policy were lawful.

Article 11 did not oblige the police to facilitate peaceful un-notified protests: see *DB v Chief Constable of Police of Northern Ireland* [2017] UKSC 7, [2017] NI 301.

III HUM [33.4]

Ban on hunting The ban on some types of hunting under the Hunting Act 2004 did not infringe the right to freedom of assembly. See the note of *R (on the application of the Countryside Alliance) v A-G* [2007] UKHL 52, [2008] 1 AC 719, [2008] 2 All ER 95 at **III HUM [30.2]**.

III HUM [33.5]

Trade Union rights Article 11 has been found to include a number of trade union rights. Thus the ECtHR has recognised the right to form and join a trade union (*Tüm Haber Sen v Turkey (Application 28602/95)* (2008) 46 EHRR 19), the prohibition of closed-shop agreements (see, for example, *Sørensen and Rasmussen v Denmark (Application 52562/99)* (2008) 46 EHRR 29, 20 BHRC 258, IHRL 2988) and the right for a trade union to seek to persuade the employer to hear what it has to say on behalf of its members (*Wilson, National Union of Journalists v United Kingdom (Application 30668/96)* (2002) 35 EHRR 20). More recently, the Grand Chamber has recognised the right to bargain collectively with the employer as one of the 'essential elements' of the right to form and join a trade union: *Demir v Turkey (Application 34503/97)* (2008) 48 EHRR 1272, [2009] IRLR 766, [2008] ECHR 34503/97. More controversially, the Court has also recognised right to strike: *Enerji Yapi-Yol Sen v Turkey (Application 68959/01)* Unreported, although the Court of Appeal in *Metrobus Ltd v Unite the Union* [2009] EWCA Civ 829, [2009] IRLR 851, [2009] All ER (D) 03 (Aug) considered that this was found too summarily for one to conclude that the right to strike is now established as an essential element of Art 11 (see per Lloyd LJ at para 35). The ECtHR had itself also seemed to proceed more cautiously in *Unison v United Kingdom (Application 53574/99)* [2002] IRLR 497 (para 35). Contrast the warmer reception of Elias LJ in *London Midland v ASLEF; Serco v RMT* [2011] EWCA Civ 226, [2011] 3 All ER 913, [2011] ICR 848 (para 8).

In *National Union of Rail, Maritime and Transport Workers v United Kingdom (Application 31045/10)* (2014) 60 EHRR 10, [2014] IRLR 467, [2014] All ER (D) 101 (Jun) the ECtHR held, in the context of considering whether a ban on secondary action in UK law infringed Art 11 rights, that secondary action constituted an 'accessory rather than a core aspect of trade union freedom' (para 77) but considered that taking secondary industrial action – including strike action – must be regarded as part of trade union activity under Art 11 (para 77). It held that strike action was 'clearly protected by article 11' (see para 84). Any restriction imposed on that right can be justified by application of Art 11(2). In *RMT* the ban on secondary action was justified.

It has been held that s 280 of the Trade Union and Labour Relations (Consolidation) Act 1992 should not be interpreted as excluding park police from redundancy consultations since this may be a breach of their rights under Art 11: *Wandsworth London Borough Council v Vining* [2017] EWCA Civ 1092, [2017] IRLR 1140.

The dismissal of an application for recognition by an independent union under the statutory scheme which allowed a 'sweetheart deal' recognition agreement with a non-independent union to prevent recognition was found not to involve a breach of Art 11 rights in *Pharmacists' Defence Association Union v Boots* [2017] EWCA Civ 66, [2017] IRLR 355.

III HUM [34]

Article 12 Right to marry

Men and women of marriageable age have the right to marry and to found a family, according to the national laws governing the exercise of this right.

III HUM [34.1]

Right to marry The right to marry does not include an implied right to divorce: *Johnston v Ireland* (1987) 9 EHRR 203.

The question of whether there is a right for same sex couples to marry has been left to national law and is not compelled by the ECHR (whether under Art 12 or under Art 12 or 8 taken in conjunction with Art 14). The wording of Art 12 refers to 'men and women' rather than 'everyone': see *Schalk v Austria (Application No 30141/04)* (2010) 53 EHRR 683, [2011] 2 FCR 650, [2010] EqLR 194. That said, same sex couples cannot be excluded from rights given to cohabiting couples in civil unions outside of marriage by virtue of Art 14 taken with Art 8: *Vallianatos v Greece (29381/09)* (2014) 59 EHRR 12.

Potter P declined to make a declaration of incompatibility in respect of the provisions of the Civil Partnership Act 2004 which accorded same sex relationships all the rights, responsibilities, benefits and advantages of civil marriage except the name. At that time, Parliament had declined to alter the conception of marriage as a relationship between a man and woman (see now the Marriage (Same Sex Couples) Act 2013), but without interfering with or failing to recognise the right of same sex couples to respect for their private or family life. Any such discrimination against same sex partners had a legitimate aim, was reasonable and proportionate and fell within the margin of appreciation accorded to Convention States: *Wilkinson v Kitzinger* [2006] EWHC 2022 (Fam), (2006) Times, 21 August. A challenge to the Civil Partnership Act 2004 brought by a heterosexual couple on the basis that, while same sex couples can now marry or have a civil partnership, heterosexuals can only choose to marry, succeeded before the Supreme Court in *R (on the application of Steinfeld) v Secretary of State for International Development* [2018] UKSC 32, [2018] 3 WLR 415: s 1 and s 3 of the Civil Partnership Act 2004 were incompatible with ECHR Art 14 read with Art 8.

Although the right to marry applies only to persons of the opposite sex, the rule which prohibited a transsexual from being recognised in his or her new gender for this purpose has been held to be incompatible with Art 12: *Goodwin v United Kingdom* (2002) 35 EHRR 447; and *Bellinger v Bellinger* [2003] UKHL 21, [2003] 2 AC 467, [2003] 2 All ER 593. This incompatibility has been removed by the Gender Recognition Act 2004.

The Home Office regime for determining whether permission to be married by a registrar should be granted under s 19(3) of the Asylum and Immigration (Treatment of Claimants etc) Act 2004 has been held to contravene Convention rights under Art 12 (right to marry) because it operates a blanket presumption that certain marriages are likely to be sham marriages without proper investigation of individual cases: *R (on the application of Baiai) v Secretary of State for the Home Department* [2008] UKHL 53, [2008] 3 All ER 1094. The European Court reached the same conclusion as the House of Lords, that the regime contravened the right to marry (Art 12) and also that the preferential treatment of marriage according to the rites of the Church of England was discriminatory and in breach of Arts 9 and 14: *O'Donoghue v United Kingdom (Application No 34848/07)* (2010) Times, 31 December, ECtHR.

However, a rule requiring foreign spouses and partners of British citizens or those settled in the UK to produce a certificate of knowledge of English when seeking leave to enter with a view to settlement did not infringe Art 8 or Art 12 or Art 14: *R (on the application of Bibi) v Secretary of State for the Home Department (Liberty and Joint Council for the Welfare of Immigrants, intervening)* [2013] EWCA Civ 322, [2013] 3 All ER 778, (2013) Times, 05 June, upheld by the Supreme Court [2015] UKSC 68, [2015] 1 WLR 5055 albeit with comments that the guidance accompanying the rule might be incompatible with Art 8 (as to which further submissions were required).

III HUM [34.2]

Right to found a family The right to found a family does not mean that an individual is guaranteed the right at all times to conceive children: *X v United Kingdom* (1975) 2 DR 105, EComHR. Similarly there is no right in a husband serving a prison sentence to insist on the artificial impregnation of his wife and in *R v Secretary of State for the Home Department, ex p Mellor* [2000] 3 FCR 148, [2000] 2 FLR 951 it was further held that there were valid public policy grounds for the Home Secretary's refusal of permission in such a situation. However, the ECtHR has now ruled that this policy infringes Art 8: see the note of *Dickson v UK* at **III HUM [30.11]** above.

III HUM [35]

Article 14 Prohibition of discrimination

The enjoyment of the rights and freedoms set forth in this Convention shall be secured without discrimination on any ground such as sex, race, colour, language, religion, political or other opinion, national or social origin, association with a national minority, property, birth or other status.

III HUM [35.1]

Scope of Art 14 It should be noted that Art 14 is not a freestanding right to equality. It applies only to the enjoyment of other Convention rights. It should also be noted that the grounds on which it prohibits discrimination are not exhaustively listed and have been held to include, for example, sexual orientation: *Salgueiro da Silva Mouta v Portugal* (1999) 31 EHRR 1055, ECtHR. However, in the absence of any ECHR right to a state-funded abortion, there could be no challenge under Art 14 to the policy of the Secretary of State for Health for England that the NHS should not provide state-funded abortions in England to Northern Ireland residents: *R (on the application of A) v Secretary of State for Health* [2014] EWHC 1364 (Admin), [2014] Med LR 246, subsequently upheld by the Court of Appeal [2015] EWCA Civ 771, [2016] 1 WLR 331 and the Supreme Court [2017] UKSC 41, [2017] 1 WLR 2492.

In *Wandsworth London Borough Council v Michalak* [2002] EWCA Civ 271, [2003] 1 WLR 617 the Court of Appeal set out guidance. At para 20 Brooke LJ suggested that four questions should be asked in a case under Art 14: (1) Do the facts fall within the ambit of one or more of the substantive Convention provisions? (2) If so, was there different treatment as between the complainant and the chosen comparators? (3) Were the chosen comparators in an analogous situation to the complainant? (4) If so, did the difference in treatment have an objective and reasonable justification, in other words did it pursue a legitimate aim and did it bear a reasonable relationship of proportionality to that aim? In *R (on the application of Carson) v Secretary of State for Work and Pensions* [2003] EWCA Civ 797, [2003] 3 All ER 577, at para 61, Laws LJ said that the third question should be modified as follows: are the circumstances of X and Y so similar as to call (in the mind of a rational and fair-minded person) for a positive justification of the less favourable treatment of Y as compared with X? In *R (on the application of Purja) v Ministry of Defence* [2003] EWCA Civ 1345, [2004] 1 WLR 289, (2003) Times, 16 October, at paragraph 70, Simon Brown LJ stressed that the questions were not intended to be rigidly applied and may well merge into one another. In that case the Court of Appeal held that differences in the pay and conditions of Gurkhas as compared with other soldiers in the British Army were not unlawful under Art 14 because they were not in an analogous situation and the differences were in any event justified as being objective and reasonable. See also *R (on the application of the British Gurkha Welfare Society) v Ministry of Defence* [2010] EWCA Civ 1098, [2010] All ER (D) 131 (Oct). The approach in *Michalak* was approved by the House of Lords with an additional question inserted between (2) and (3): was the difference in treatment on a prohibited ground? The five questions were endorsed and followed in *Ghaidan v Godin-Mendoza* [2004] UKHL 30, [2004] 2 AC 557; *R (on the application of S and Marper) v Chief Constable of South Yorkshire Police* [2004] UKHL 39, [2004] 4 All ER 193, [2004] 1 WLR 2196; and *A v Secretary of State for the Home Department* [2005] 2 AC 68. However, the leading authority now is *R (on the application of Carson) v Secretary of State for Work and Pensions* in the House of Lords, which disapproved the "*Michalak* catechism" and suggested that just one question should be asked, whether there has been unjustifiable discrimination on a ground contrary to Art 14: [2005] 2 WLR 1369. The Divisional Court has held that a coroner's declared policy of not prioritising a death because of the religion of the deceased or family breached Arts 9 and 14: *R (Adath Yisroel Burial Society) v Inner North London Coroner* [2018] EWHC 969 (Admin), [2018] 3 WLR 1354.

III HUM [35.2]

Unmarried fathers The difference in treatment of a father with parental responsibility and one without is justifiable objectively and does not amount to discrimination: *B v United Kingdom* [2000] 1 FCR 289, [2000] 1 FLR 1, ECtHR. A similar conclusion was reached in *R (on the application of Montana) v Secretary of State for the Home Department* [2001] 1 WLR 552, CA regarding the registration of an illegitimate child under ss 2(1) or 3(1) of the British Nationality Act 1981. On the other hand the legal right of a divorced father to deduct payments for his child from his liability for tax is not available to an unmarried father and this has been held to be discriminatory in violation of Art 14: *M v United Kingdom (Application No 6638/03)* (2005) Times, 15 September, ECtHR.

III HUM [35.2A]

Student loans In *R (on the application of Douglas) v North Tyneside Metropolitan Borough Council* [2003] EWCA Civ 1847, [2004] 1 WLR 2363, it was held that Art 2 applies to tertiary education but that arrangements relating to student loans were outside the ambit of Art 2. Accordingly, alleged discrimination on grounds such as age fell outside the scope of Art 14.

In *R (on the application of Tigere) v Secretary of State for Business, Innovation and Skills* [2015] UKSC 57, [2015] 1 WLR 3820, [2015] All ER (D) 304 (Jul) the Supreme Court considered that a requirement that an applicant for a student loan be 'settled' in the UK was incompatible with Art 14 taken with Art 2 of Protocol 1.

III HUM [35.2B]

Priority need of parent with a dependent child The fact that a dependent child is subject to immigration control does not affect the priority need of the parent and provisions to the contrary in s 185(4) have been declared to be incompatible with Art 14: *Westminster City Council v Morris* [2005] EWCA Civ 1184, [2006] 1 WLR 505.

III HUM [35.2C]

Planning controls The Town and Country Planning Act 1990 s 183(4) by providing for "stop notices" against caravans but not dwelling houses was indirectly discriminatory against Gypsies, but the discrimination could be objectively justified by the legitimate aim of protecting the environment and was not therefore incompatible with Convention Rights under Art 8 in conjunction with Art 14: *R (on the application of Wilson) v Wychavon District Council* [2007] EWCA Civ 52, [2007] QB 801.

III HUM [35.2D]

Immigration controls The differences between the immigration controls applied to families with children and those applied to single young adults have been held to be justified: *AL (Serbia) v Secretary of State for the Home Department* [2008] UKHL 42, [2008] 4 All ER 1127, [2008] 1 WLR 1434.

A condition of entry on an African passport preventing the holder from having access to public funds and social housing was held not to discriminate on the ground of race: *Bah v United Kingdom (Application No 56328/07)* (2011) 54 EHRR 773, [2011] 39 LS Gaz R 19.

III HUM [35.2E]

Foreign laws which discriminate against mothers It has been held that a mother should not be returned to a country where the law gives the father an absolute and exclusive right to have a child of the family live with him, since such a law discriminated against women and denied and nullified a mother's right to respect for family life: *EM (Lebanon) v Secretary of State for the Home Department* [2008] UKHL 64, (2008) Times, 24 October.

III HUM [35.2F]

Adoption by unmarried couples It was contrary to Art 8, read in conjunction with Art 14, for secondary legislation in Northern Ireland to prohibit adoption by unmarried couples: *Re P and others* [2008] UKHL 38, [2009] 1 AC 273.

III HUM [35.2G]

Couples receiving Child Support Contributions In *JM v United Kingdom (Application No 37060/06)* [2010] 3 FCR 648, [2010] Fam Law 1270, ECtHR the ECtHR held that the UK was in breach of Art 14 and Protocol 1 Art 1 when assessing child support contributions of a divorced parent living with a same sex partner differently from those of a divorced parent who was in a new heterosexual relationship.

III HUM [35.2H]

The discharge of a restricted patient If a restricted patient is discharged in order to allow him, or her, to live in a residential care home instead of in hospital, the discharge may not be made subject to restrictions on liberty since this would discriminate, by subjecting that person to disadvantages not applicable to other people with the status of a discharged patient who were to remain in hospital: *Secretary of State for Justice v RB and Lancashire Care NHS Foundation Trust* [2011] EWCA Civ 1608, [2012] 1 WLR 2043, Times, 19 January.

III HUM [35.2I]

Business rates It has been held that, since only a select group of the most devout Mormons have access to their temple, it did not qualify as a 'place of public religious worship' and so business rates were payable. The European Court of Human Rights concluded that there was no discrimination since the law applied in the same way to places of private religious worship in all religions and the line drawn between public and non-public religious worship was justified: *Church of Jesus Christ of Latter-day Saints v United Kingdom (Application No 7552/09)* (2014) 59 EHRR 18, in line with the earlier decision of the House of Lords: [2008] 1 WLR 1852.

III HUM [35.2J]

Needs of disabled children In *Mathieson v Secretary of State for Work and Pensions* [2015] UKSC 47, [2015] 1 WLR 3250, [2015] All ER (D) 90 (Jul), the Supreme Court held that the withdrawal of disability living allowance under the Social Security (Disability Living Allowance) Regulations 1991 because the disabled child required hospitalisation for more than 84 days was a violation of Art 14, taken with Art 1 protocol 1. Discrimination between disabled persons with different needs engaged Art 14 as much as discrimination between the disabled and able-bodied and the policy for the 84 day rule could not be justified.

III HUM [35.2K]

Heterosexual couples and civil partnerships A challenge based on Art 8 taken in conjunction with Art 14, to the position whereby heterosexual couples cannot choose to have civil partnerships under the Civil Partnership Act 2004 (whereas same-sex couples may choose marriage or a civil partnership) succeeded: see *R (on the application of Steinfeld) v Secretary of State for International Development* [2018] UKSC 32, [2018] 3 WLR 415.

III HUM [35.2L]

Pension rights of cohabitants As with a surviving spouse, a surviving cohabitant is eligible for pension scheme benefits, which qualify as "property". But, in the instant case there was a requirement that the deceased partner must have completed and submitted a nomination form identifying the surviving partner as the intended beneficiary. This additional requirement has been held to discriminate, contrary to Art 14, as it deprived the applicant of her property contrary to Art 1 of the Protocol: *Re an application by Denise Brewster for Judicial Review* [2017] UKSC 8, [2017] 2 All ER 1001, [2017] 1 WLR 519.

III HUM [35.3]

Justification Discrimination which would otherwise infringe Art 14 may be justified if it is a proportionate means of pursuing a legitimate aim: see *R (on the application of RJM) v Secretary of State for Work and Pensions* (2007) Times, 27 October, HL, [2008] 3 WLR 1023 per Lord Neuberger at para 48, applying *Stec v UK* (2006) 43 EHRR 1017. The court held that the exclusion, under the Income Support (General) Regulations 1987 Sch 7, of disabled persons without accommodation from the disability premium element of income support was justified although homelessness is a 'status' for the purpose of Art 14.

In *Humphreys v Revenue and Customs Comrs* [2012] UKSC 18, [2012] 4 All ER 27, [2012] 1 WLR 1545 it was held that whilst the system of single payment of child tax credit to the person mainly responsible for a child was indirectly discriminatory against men, it was justified as a proportionate means of pursuing a legitimate aim of social policy.

In *Swift v Secretary of State for Justice* [2013] EWCA Civ 193, [2013] 3 WLR 1151, [2013] 2 FCR 1 the Court of Appeal held that the Fatal Accidents Act 1976, s 1(3)(b), which disentitles cohabitees who had been living with the deceased for less than two years from claiming damages for loss of dependency, was not incompatible with Art 14 in conjunction with Art 8 because it was a proportionate means of pursuing the legitimate aim of conferring a right of action on dependants of victims of fatal wrongdoing while confining that right to those who had relationships of some degree of permanence and dependence.

Similarly, a requirement in the Housing Act 1985, s 87(b) of 12 months cohabitation in order to obtain a secure tenancy on the death of the original tenant was proportionate and justified and thus not a breach of Art 8 in conjunction with Art 14 (*R (Turley) v Wandsworth London Borough Council* [2017] EWCA Civ 189, [2017] HLR 21).

However, Art 14 was infringed by statutory criteria for assessment of housing benefit payable to disabled claimants in the private rented sector where these amounted to unjustified disability discrimination: *Burnip v Birmingham City Council* [2012] EWCA Civ 629, [2012] HRLR 20, [2012] Eq LR 701.

The Benefit Cap (Housing Benefit) Regulations 2012 were found not to be incompatible with Art 14 in *R (on the application of SG) v Secretary of State for Work and Pensions* [2015] UKSC 16, [2015] 1 WLR 1449, [2015] All ER (D) 90 (Jul): while they affected a greater number of women and men, there was objective and reasonable justification.

III HUM [35.4]

Precedents Precedent for particulars of Part 7 claims based on Art 14 are provided at **BCCP L[356]** and **BCCP L[367]**.

III HUM [36]

Article 16 Restrictions on political activity of aliens

Nothing in Articles 10, 11 and 14 shall be regarded as preventing the High Contracting Parties from imposing restrictions on the political activity of aliens.

III HUM [37]

Article 17 Prohibition of abuse of rights

Nothing in this Convention may be interpreted as implying for any State, group or person any right to engage in any activity or perform any act aimed at the destruction of any of the rights and freedoms set forth herein or at their limitation to a greater extent than is provided for in the Convention.

III HUM [38]

Article 18 Limitation on use of restrictions on rights

The restrictions permitted under this Convention to the said rights and freedoms shall not be applied for any purpose other than those for which they have been prescribed.

PART II
THE FIRST PROTOCOL

III HUM [39]

Article 1 Protection of property

Every natural or legal person is entitled to the peaceful enjoyment of his possessions. No one shall be deprived of his possessions except in the public interest and subject to the conditions provided for by law and by the general principles of international law.

The preceding provisions shall not, however, in any way impair the right of a State to enforce such laws as it deems necessary to control the use of property in accordance with the general interest or to secure the payment of taxes or other contributions or penalties.

III HUM [39.1]

Protection of property A claim that leasehold enfranchisement infringed Art 1 of the First Protocol was rejected in *James v United Kingdom (Application 8793/79)* (1986) 8 EHRR 123, ECtHR. An applicant company claimed unsuccessfully that the ban on handguns deprived it of business income for which it had not been compensated. It was held that the loss of future income fell outside Art 1 because it amounted to "control of use" rather than "deprivation of possessions" and that the company could not be said to have suffered an individual and excessive burden from the impact on one part of its business: *Ian Edgar (Liverpool) Ltd v United Kingdom (Application 37683/97)* (25 January 2000, unreported), ECtHR.

The compulsory purchase of a person's property engages his rights under this article and under Art 8. However, those rights are not absolute, and the taking of a person's property in the public interest will not contravene those articles if there are provisions to give reasonable compensation: *Mortell v Secretary of State for Communities and Local Government and Oldham Metropolitan Borough Council* [2009] EWCA Civ 1274 applying *James v United Kingdom* (A/98) (1986) 8 EHRR 123 ECHR.

It has been held that a mortgagee's statutory power under s 101 of the Law of Property Act 1925 to sell the mortgaged property without first obtaining orders for possession or sale does not engage Art 1 of the First Protocol because it serves to implement rather than override the private bargain between mortgagor and mortgagee: *Horsham Properties Group Ltd v Clark* [2008] EWHC 2327 (Ch), [2009] 1 All ER (Comm) 745, [2009] 1 WLR 1255, Briggs J.

In considering whether property, such as a car, is liable to forfeiture under s 139 of the Customs and Excise Management Act 1979, the court should consider whether forfeiture would be a disproportionate sanction, having regard to the owner's right to the protection of property: *Customs and Excise Comrs v Newbury* [2003] EWHC 702 (Admin), [2003] 1 WLR 2131, Times, 18 April.

In *Stretch v United Kingdom (Application 44277/98)* [2004] 03 EG 100, (2003) Times, 3 July, ECtHR, the applicant claimed successfully under this article when the local authority refused to allow him to exercise his option to renew a lease. They refused to renew because they had discovered that they had no power to grant the option; but he succeeded because their refusal deprived him of his legitimate expectation of obtaining effective enjoyment of a property right.

The Court of Appeal has held that the personal right of a doctor to practise in the NHS, flowing from his inclusion in the performers list, is not a possession for the purposes of this article and therefore that the suspension of that right, unlawfully, did not involve a breach of Convention rights: *R (on the application of Malik) v Waltham Forest Primary Care Trust* [2007] 4 All ER 832, (2007) Times, 10 April, CA.

A legally enforceable right to a social security benefit is a "possession" for the purposes of this article whether the benefit in question is contributory or non-contributory: *R (on the application of RJM) v Secretary of State for Work and Pensions* [2008] UKHL 63, [2008] 3 WLR 1023. Equally, entitlement to compensation under the Civil Service Compensation Scheme constituted a 'possession' for the purposes of this article: *Public & Commercial Services Union v Minister for the Cabinet Office* [2017] EWHC 1787 (Admin), [2018] 1 All ER 142.

Where a claimant had obtained judgment on liability, with damages to be assessed, that was a possession for the purposes of Art 1 of the First Protocol. Depriving him of that possession by striking out his claim was only permissible if it was in the public interest and was a proportionate response. The public interest required a power to strike out a statement of case for abuse of process, but only in the very exceptional case would it be just and proportionate for the court to strike out an action after a trial. Such an order might be justified if there had been a massive attempt to deceive the court and the award of damages would be very small: *Fairclough Homes Ltd v Summers* [2012] UKSC 26, [2012] 4 All ER 317, [2012] 1 WLR 2004.

The ban on certain types of hunting in the Hunting Act 2004 affected the use to which property could be put, but any interference with Convention rights was justifiable: *R (on the application of Countryside Alliance) v Attorney General* [2007] UKHL 52, (2007) Times, 29 November.

Where the Environmental Agency renewed a salmon fishing licence subject to conditions that effectively destroyed the livelihood of a putcher rank fisherman it was held that the disproportionate impact of the conditions breached Article 1 of the First Protocol and was not justified by the need to protect the environment: *R (on the application of Mott) v Environment Agency* [2018] UKSC 10, [2018] 1 WLR 1022.

III HUM [39.2]

Title acquired by adverse possession It was held in *J A Pye (Oxford) Ltd v Graham* [2001] EWCA Civ 117, [2001] Ch 804, [2001] 2 WLR 1293 that the acquisition of land from the legal owner by adverse possession would not, if established on the facts, infringe property rights protected by this article. In the House of Lords, however, the Convention issue did not arise because it was conceded that the Human Rights Act did not have retrospective effect in the circumstances of the case: [2002] UKHL 30, [2003] 1 AC 419. The Grand Chamber of the European Court of Human Rights held that there was no breach of this article because the operation of a limitation provision generally barred a remedy rather than a right and the termination of the title of the paper owner did little more than regularise the positions of the paper owner and the person who had acquired title: *J A Pye (Oxford) Ltd v United Kingdom (Application 44302/02)* [2007] RVR 302, [2007] All ER (D) 177 (Aug). This rule applies to all cases of adverse possession and it is not open to the court not to follow it because a case is distinguishable on its facts: *Ofulue v Bossert* [2008] EWCA Civ 7, [2008] 3 WLR 1253, (2008) Times, 11 February.

III HUM [39.2A]

Confidentiality of commercial information Confidentiality of commercial information could be seen as a possession. When balancing the public interest in transparency and the public interest in maintaining commercial confidentiality (on an application for disclosure of information under the Audit Commission Act 1998), the court has to apply a proportional nuanced approach to individual cases on the facts: *R (on the application of Veolia ES Nottinghamshire Ltd) v Nottinghamshire County Council* [2010] EWCA Civ 1214, [2010] 44 LS Gaz R 18, (2010) Times, 9 November.

III HUM [39.2B]

Tax legislation Where tax legislation clarifies earlier provisions on the efficacy of tax avoidance schemes it is not retrospectively removing a 'possession' in the form of the benefit of a scheme that, but for the clarification, was arguably valid: *R (on the application of St Matthews (West) Ltd) v HM Treasury* [2015] EWCA Civ 648, [2015] STC 2272.

In *JP Whitter (Waterwell Engineers Ltd) v Revenue and Customs Comrs* [2018] UKSC 31, [2018] 1 WLR 3117, the Supreme Court has held that HMRC's discretionary power to cancel a taxpayer's registration under the Construction Industry Scheme (see Finance Act 2004, s 66) was a proportionate interference with rights under Art 1 of the first protocol even though the statutory discretion did not require HMRC to take into account the likely effect of cancellation on the taxpayer's business.

III HUM [39.3]

Precedents A precedent for particulars of a Part 7 claim based on Art 1 of the First protocol is provided at **BCCP L[368]**.

III HUM [40]

Article 2 Right to education

No person shall be denied the right to education. In the exercise of any functions which it assumes in relation to education and to teaching, the State shall respect the right of parents to ensure such education and teaching in conformity with their own religious and philosophical convictions.

III HUM [40.1]

"Respect the right of parents" The requirement of "respect" in Art 2 implies some positive obligation on the part of the state: *Campbell and Cosans v United Kingdom* (Series A, No 48) (1982) 4 EHRR 293, ECtHR.

III HUM [40.1A]

Immigration controls The right of a child to education while in this country does not carry with it the right to stay here; the Convention does not confer a right to education in any particular country: *R v Secretary of State for the Home Department, ex p Holub* [2001] 1 WLR 1359, CA.

III HUM [40.2]

Reservation on the right to education The second sentence of Art 2 is subject to a reservation, set out in Part II of Schedule 3 to the Act, as required by s 15, in the following terms:

'Reservation

At the time of signing the present (First) Protocol, I declare that, in view of certain provisions of the Education Acts in the United Kingdom, the principle affirmed in the second sentence of Art 2 is accepted by the United Kingdom only so far as it is compatible with the provision of efficient instruction and training, and the avoidance of unreasonable public expenditure.

Dated 20 March 1952. Made by the United Kingdom Permanent Representative to the Council of Europe.'

III HUM [40.2A]

Fees Allowing institutes of higher education to increase fees under the Higher Education (Basic Amount) (England) Regulations 2010 and the Higher Education (Higher Amount) (England) Regulations 2010 was not contrary to Protocol 1 art 2: *R (on the application of Hurley and Moore) v Secretary of State for Business Innovation and Skills* [2012] EWHC 201 (Admin), [2012] Eq LR 447, [2012] ELR 297.

III HUM [40.2B]

Student loans In *R (on the application of Douglas) v North Tyneside Metropolitan Borough Council* [2003] EWCA Civ 1847, [2004] 1 All ER 709, (2004) Times, 22 January, it was held that Art 2 applies to tertiary education but that arrangements relating to student loans were outside the ambit of Art 2. Accordingly, alleged discrimination on grounds such as age fell outside the scope of Art 14.

III HUM [40.2C]

Wrongful exclusion from school The wrongful exclusion of a pupil from school may amount to a denial of the right to education, in breach of Art 2, even where self-assessed revision work is provided for doing at home: *A v Head Teacher and Governors of Lord Grey School* [2004] EWCA Civ 382, [2004] QB 1231, [2004] 4 All ER 628. However, the House of Lords concluded, by majority, that an exclusion of a pupil in contravention of domestic law was not necessarily a denial of the right to education. The convention right did not guarantee education at or by a particular institution and their Lordships decided that the claimant pupil who was excluded from one institution while a prosecution was in progress, was not denied access to such other educational facilities as the state provided: *Ali v Head and Governors of Lord Grey School* [2006] UKHL 14, (2006) Times, 27 March.

Article 9.1 of the Convention on Human Rights may be engaged where a school pupil is turned away from school because he or she is wearing religious clothing which is not allowed by the school's rules regarding school uniform. The House of Lords reversed the Court of Appeal and held that since the claimant could have changed to another school where the rules on uniform suited her better she was not being excluded from education and that the insistence on the uniform was, on the facts of the case, justified: *R (on the application of Begum) v Headteacher and Governors of Denbigh High School* [2006] UKHL 15, (2006) Times, 23 March.

III HUM [40.2D]

Special needs A local authority's failure to provide for a child's special educational needs for 18 months was not a denial of the child's right to education under Protocol 1 Art 2: *A v Essex County Council and National Autistic Society* [2010] UKSC 33, [2011] 1 AC 280, [2010] 4 All ER 199. Applying *A v Head Teacher and Governors of Lord Grey School* (**III HUM [40.2C]**), it was not a denial of the very essence of his right to education.

III HUM [40.3]

Precedents A precedent for particulars of a Part 7 claim based on Art 2 of the First Protocol is provided at **BCCP L[369]**.

III HUM [41]

Article 3 Right to free elections

The High Contracting Parties undertake to hold free elections at reasonable intervals by secret ballot, under conditions which will ensure the free expression of the opinion of the people in the choice of the legislature.

III HUM [41.1]

Prisoners' voting rights The prohibition on voting by convicted prisoners during the period of their detention, under s 3(1) of the Representation of the People Act 1983 was held by the Divisional Court not to infringe Convention rights: *R (on the application of Pearson) v Secretary of State for the Home Department* [2001] EWHC Admin 239, [2001] All ER (D) 22 (Apr), (2001) Times, 17 April.

However, the European Court has ruled, unanimously that the disenfranchisement of a prisoner does breach this article; *Hirst v United Kingdom (No 2) (Application 74025/01)* (2004) 16 BHRC 409, ECtHR. The case was referred to the Grand Chamber, which by a majority confirmed that the present legislation in the UK is incompatible with this article because it applies to all convicted prisoners during their incarceration and so breaches the principle of proportionality: *Hirst v United Kingdom (No 2) (Application No 74035/01)* (2005) Times, 10 October, ECtHR (Grand Chamber). A declaration of incompatibility was made by the Registration Appeal Court under the Human Rights Act 1998, s 4(5) because, despite the ruling in *Hirst*, the Representation of the People Act 1983, s 3(1) could not be read down so as to make it compatible with Art 3: *Smith v Scott* [2007] CSIH 9, (2007) Times, 5 February. However, in *R (on the application of Chester) v Secretary of State for Justice* [2010] EWCA Civ 1439, (2011) 1 WLR 1436, (2011) Times, 17 January the Court of Appeal held that the nature and scope of amendment and replacement of the legislation was likely to be acutely sensitive and a matter for Parliament to determine. The Supreme Court, dismissing a further appeal, emphasised that it was now for Parliament to consider the position and there was no further role for the court: [2013] UKSC 63, [2013] 3 WLR 1076.

The Supreme Court has also ruled that the blanket ban on prisoners voting in the Scottish independence referendum was not unlawful: *Moohan v Lord Advocate* [2014] UKSC 67, [2015] AC 901, [2015] 2 WLR 141, 165 NLJ 7636.

In *McHugh v United Kingdom (Application No 51987/08)* (2015) 165 NLJ 7641, [2015] ECHR 51987/08, [2015] All ER (D) 95 (Feb) the ECtHR held that a declaration that the automatic ban on voting by prisoners was a violation of rights under Art 3 was sufficient redress for non-pecuniary loss and there was no entitlement to a further remedy.

III HUM [41.2]

Use of electoral register for direct marketing An electoral registration officer must allow an elector to have his name removed from an electoral register before it is sold to a commercial concern for marketing purposes. A refusal to do so is in breach of s 11 and also contravenes the elector's Convention rights under Art 8 (see para **III HUM [30]**) and, to the extent that it inhibits the right to take part in elections, Art 3 of the First Protocol: *R (on the application of Robertson) v City of Wakefield Metropolitan District Council* [2001] EWHC Admin 915, [2002] QB 1052, [2002] 2 WLR 889.

III HUM [41.3]

Sanctions for electoral misconduct Voters are entitled to be told true facts and political arguments rather than personal attacks which are without factual foundation. The sanctions provided by s 160 of the Representation of the People Act 1983 are required, as a pressing social need, to underpin the right to vote. Also electoral addresses which include false statements about a candidate's private life are in breach of Art 8. The interference with freedom of expression, as provided in s 160, is proportionate and justified: *Watkins v Woolas (In the matter of the Representation of the People Act 1983)* [2010] EWHC 2702 (QB), [2010] 45 LS Gaz R 20, (2010) Times, 16 November.

PART III
ARTICLE 1 OF THE THIRTEENTH PROTOCOL

III HUM [42]–III HUM [43]

Article 1 Abolition of the death penalty

The death penalty shall be abolished. No one shall be condemned to such penalty or executed.

III HUM [42.1]

Extradition for murder to a country which retains the death penalty Where a person is committed in custody pending a decision by the Home Secretary regarding extradition for murder a ruling on Art 1 should be deferred until a decision on the question of extradition is made: *St John v United States of America* (2001) Times, 10 August, QBD (a habeas corpus case).

However, in *R (on the application of Al-Saadoon) v Secretary of State for Defence* [2009] EWCA Civ 7, [2010] QB 486, [2010] 1 All ER 271 a proposed transfer of Iraqi nationals from the custody of British forces in Iraq to the Iraqi High Tribunal with a view to trial was held to be lawful although they would face the death penalty if convicted. The prisoners' Convention rights applied because they remained under the jurisdiction of the United Kingdom but the rights were qualified by the requirements of public international law. Although the death penalty was repugnant under UK law and the Convention, it did not infringe international law. The possibility that the prisoners could be subject to the death penalty did not relieve the UK of its obligation to transfer them into the custody of the Iraqi court.

III HUM [42.2]

Substitution of a new Part III Articles 1 and 2 of the Sixth Protocol were replaced by the new Art 1 of the Thirteenth Protocol which was agreed at Vilnius on 3 May 2002. Part III was accordingly modified by the Human Rights Act 1998 (Amendment) Order 2004, SI 2004/1574. The new Art 1 is in the same terms as the old, but the omitting of the old Art 2 removes the exception which allowed the death penalty in time of war.

SCHEDULE 2
REMEDIAL ORDERS

III HUM [44]–III HUM [44.1]

Orders

1 (1) A remedial order may—

(a) contain such incidental, supplemental, consequential or transitional provision as the person making it considers appropriate;

(b) be made so as to have effect from a date earlier than that on which it is made;

(c) make provision for the delegation of specific functions;

(d) make different provision for different cases.

(2) The power conferred by sub-paragraph (1)(a) includes—

(a) power to amend primary legislation (including primary legislation other than that which contains the incompatible provision); and

(b) power to amend or revoke subordinate legislation (including subordinate legislation other than that which contains the incompatible provision).

(3) A remedial order may be made so as to have the same extent as the legislation which it affects.

(4) No person is to be guilty of an offence solely as a result of the retrospective effect of a remedial order.

III HUM [44.2]

Procedure

2. No remedial order may be made unless—

(a) a draft of the order has been approved by a resolution of each House of Parliament made after the end of the period of 60 days beginning with the day on which the draft was laid; or

(b) it is declared in the order that it appears to the person making it that, because of the urgency of the matter, it is necessary to make the order without a draft being so approved.

III HUM [44.3]

Orders laid in draft

3 (1) No draft may be laid under paragraph 2 (a) unless—

(a) the person proposing to make the order has laid before Parliament a document which contains a draft of the proposed order and the required information; and

(b) the period of 60 days, beginning with the day on which the document required by this sub-paragraph was laid, has ended.

(2) If representations have been made during that period, the draft laid under paragraph 2 (a) must be accompanied by a statement containing—

(a) a summary of the representations; and

(b) if, as a result of the representations, the proposed order has been changed, details of the changes.

III HUM [44.4]

Urgent cases

4 (1) If a remedial order ("the original order") is made without being approved in draft, the person making it must lay it before Parliament, accompanied by the required information, after it is made.

(2) If representations have been made during the period of 60 days beginning with the day on which the original order was made, the person making it must (after the end of that period) lay before Parliament a statement containing—

(a) a summary of the representations; and

(b) if, as a result of the representations, he considers it appropriate to make changes to the original order, details of the changes.

(3) If sub-paragraph (2)(b) applies, the person making the statement must—

(a) make a further remedial order replacing the original order; and

(b) lay the replacement order before Parliament.

(4) If, at the end of the period of 120 days beginning with the day on which the original order was made, a resolution has not been passed by each House approving the original or replacement order, the order ceases to have effect (but without that affecting anything previously done under either order or the power to make a fresh remedial order).

III HUM [44.4A]

Two of the remedial orders made to date were made under this urgent procedure: the Mental Health Act 1983 (Remedial) Order 2001 (SI 2001/3712); the Naval Discipline Act 1957 (Remedial) Order 2004 (SI 2004/66); compare the Marriage Act 1949 (Remedial) Order 2007, SI 2007/438.

III HUM [44.5]

Definitions

5. In this Schedule—

"representations" means representations about a remedial order (or proposed remedial order) made to the person making (or proposing to make) it and includes any relevant Parliamentary report or resolution; and

"required information" means—

(a) an explanation of the incompatibility which the order (or proposed order) seeks to remove, including particulars of the relevant declaration, finding or order; and

(b) a statement of the reasons for proceeding under section 10 and for making an order in those terms.

III HUM [44.6]

Calculating periods

6. In calculating any period for the purposes of this Schedule, no account is to be taken of any time during which—

(a) Parliament is dissolved or prorogued; or

(b) both Houses are adjourned for more than four days.

LANDLORD & TENANT AND HOUSING

TABLE OF CONTENTS

LANDLORD & TENANT AND HOUSING

GENERAL NOTE ON LANDLORD & TENANT AND HOUSING

III L&T [1]

The focus of this title is on the statutes which confer jurisdiction on the civil courts in relation to housing, in the landlord and tenant context. It is not, however, limited to residential premises: it includes business premises too. Nor is it limited to matters of landlord and tenant: it also covers licensed occupancy and homelessness appeals. On the other hand it does not include mobile homes, which have a title of their own (see **III MOB [1]**) nor mortgage enforcement; The eviction of trespassers is dealt with at para **CPR 55[2]** and interim possession orders against trespassers at paras **CCR 24r15 [1]–CCR 24r15 [4]**. The relevant provisions in the Supreme Court Act 1981 and the County Courts Act 1984 are set out elsewhere, eg in relation to relief against forfeiture: see para **II SCA [39]** and see para **II CCA [133]**.

For the substantive law see 22 *Halsbury's Laws* (4th edition, reissue) title HOUSING, para 1 and 27(1) *Halsbury's Laws* (4th edition, reissue) title LANDLORD AND TENANT, para 1.

LAW OF PROPERTY ACT 1925

(c 20)

III L&T [2]

146. Restrictions on and relief against forfeiture of leases and underleases

(1) A right of re-entry or forfeiture under any proviso or stipulation in a lease for a breach of any covenant or condition in the lease shall not be enforceable, by action or otherwise, unless and until the lessor serves on the lessee a notice—

(a) specifying the particular breach complained of; and

(b) if the breach is capable of remedy, requiring the lessee to remedy the breach; and

(c) in any case, requiring the lessee to make compensation in money for the breach;

and the lessee fails, within a reasonable time thereafter, to remedy the breach, if it is capable of remedy, and to make reasonable compensation in money, to the satisfaction of the lessor, for the breach.

(2) Where a lessor is proceeding, by action or otherwise, to enforce such a right of re-entry or forfeiture, the lessee may, in the lessor's action, if any, or in any action brought by himself, apply to the court for relief; and the court may grant or refuse relief, as the court, having regard to the proceedings and conduct of the parties under the foregoing provisions of this section, and to all the other circumstances, thinks fit; and in case of relief may grant it on such terms, if any, as to costs, expenses, damages, compensation, penalty, or otherwise, including the granting of an injunction to restrain any like breach in the future, as the court, in the circumstances of each case, thinks fit.

(3) A lessor shall be entitled to recover as a debt due to him from a lessee, and in addition to damages (if any), all reasonable costs and expenses properly incurred by the lessor in the employment of a solicitor and surveyor or valuer, or otherwise, in reference to any breach giving rise to a right of re-entry or forfeiture which, at the request of the lessee, is waived by the lessor, or from which the lessee is relieved, under the provisions of this Act.

(4) Where a lessor is proceeding by action or otherwise to enforce a right of re-entry or forfeiture under any covenant, proviso, or stipulation in a lease, or for non-payment of rent, the court may, on application by any person claiming as under-lessee any estate or interest in the property comprised in the lease or any part thereof, either in the lessor's action (if any) or in any action brought by such person for that purpose, make an order vesting, for the whole term of the lease or any less term, the property comprised in the lease or any part thereof in any person entitled as under-lessee to any estate or interest in such property upon such conditions as to execution of any deed or other document, payment of rent, costs, expenses, damages, compensation, giving security, or otherwise, as the court in the circumstances of each case may think fit, but in no case shall any such under-lessee be entitled to require a lease to be granted to him for any longer term than he had under his original sub-lease.

(5) For the purposes of this section—

(a) "Lease" includes an original or derivative under-lease; also an agreement for a lease where the lessee has become entitled to have his lease granted; also a grant at a fee farm rent, or securing a rent by condition;

(b) "Lessee" includes an original or derivative under-lessee, and the persons deriving title under a lessee; also a grantee under any such grant as aforesaid and the persons deriving title under him;

(c) "Lessor" includes an original or derivative under-lessor, and the persons deriving title under a lessor; also a person making such grant as aforesaid and the persons deriving title under him;

(d) "Under-lease" includes an agreement for an underlease where the underlessee has become entitled to have his underlease granted;

(e) "Underlessee" includes any person deriving title under an underlessee.

(6) This section applies although the proviso or stipulation under which the right of re-entry or forfeiture accrues is inserted in the lease in pursuance of the directions of any Act of Parliament.

(7) For the purposes of this section a lease limited to continue as long only as the lessee abstains from committing a breach of covenant shall be and take effect as a lease to continue for any longer term for which it could subsist, but determinable by a proviso for re-entry on such a breach.

(8) This section does not extend—

(i) To a covenant or condition against assigning, underletting, parting with the possession, or disposing of the land leased where the breach occurred before the commencement of this Act; or

(ii) In the case of a mining lease, to a covenant or condition for allowing the lessor to have access to or inspect books, accounts, records, weighing machines or other things, or to enter or inspect the mine or the workings thereof.

(9) This section does not apply to a condition for forfeiture on the bankruptcy of the lessee or on taking in execution of the lessee's interest if contained in a lease of—

(a) Agricultural or pastoral land;

(b) Mines or minerals;

(c) A house used or intended to be used as a public-house or beershop;

(d) A house let as a dwelling-house, with the use of any furniture, books, works of art, or other chattels not being in the nature of fixtures;

(e) Any property with respect to which the personal qualifications of the tenant are of importance for the preservation of the value or character of the property, or on the ground of neighbourhood to the lessor, or to any person holding under him.

(10) Where a condition of forfeiture on the bankruptcy of the lessee or on taking in execution of the lessee's interest is contained in any lease, other than a lease of any of the classes mentioned in the last subsection, then—

(a) if the lessee's interest is sold within one year from the bankruptcy or taking in execution, this section applies to the forfeiture condition aforesaid;

(b) if the lessee's interest is not sold before the expiration of that year, this section only applies to the forfeiture condition aforesaid during the first year from the date of the bankruptcy or taking in execution.

(11) This section does not, save as otherwise mentioned, affect the law relating to re-entry or forfeiture or relief in case of non-payment of rent.

(12) This section has effect notwithstanding any stipulation to the contrary.

(13) The county court has jurisdiction under this section [. . .]

III L&T [2.1]

Jurisdiction The High Court and county courts have concurrent, and unlimited, jurisdiction under the Law of Property Act 1925 ss 146 and 147 (see paras **III L&T [2]** and **III L&T [3]**).

III L&T [2.1A]

Remediable and irremediable breaches In *Akici v Butlin* [2005] EWCA Civ 1296, [2006] 2 All ER 872, [2006] 1 WLR 201 the Court of Appeal cautioned against an over technical approach to the question whether a breach was capable of remedy and was of the view that, in principle, the great majority of breaches of covenant should be capable of remedy including, as in *Akici*, a breach consisting of parting with possession or sharing possession, falling short of creating or transferring a legal interest. The court concluded that, on the authorities, the only breaches that are, in principle, incapable of remedy are subletting (*Scala House Limited v Forbes* [1974] QB 575) and illegal or immoral use (*Rugby School (Governors) v Tannahill* [1935] 1 KB 87).

LANDLORD & TENANT AND HOUSING

III L&T [2.1B]

Entitlement to serve s 146 notice A s 146 notice can only be validly served if a right of re-entry to leasehold premises has arisen; there is no authority for the proposition that such a notice can be served before the relevant right to re-entry had occurred, on the basis of an anticipated breach: *Toms v Ruberry* [2019] EWCA Civ 128.

III L&T [2.2]

The court may grant relief For a consideration of the principles applicable to the grant of relief for wilful breach of covenants other than to pay rent see *Shiloh Spinners Ltd v Harding* [1973] AC 691, [1973] 1 All ER 90, HL. In *Khar v Delbounty Ltd* [1996] NPC 163, CA, relief was granted on terms that the lease should be sold, so that the lessee could benefit from its value and the lessor could recover the outstanding sums. *Khar v Delbounty Ltd* was considered in *Freifeld v West Kensington Court Ltd* [2015] EWCA Civ 806, [2015] All ER (D) 37 (Aug) where the court held that relief could be granted even in the case of a wilful breach (in that case deliberate sub-letting in breach of covenant). The value of the leasehold interest is relevant but, without more, it is not enough (for forfeiture to be avoided) that forfeiture will put a large windfall into the hands of the landlord: see *Ul-Hassan v Magnic Ltd* [2015] EWCA Civ 224, [2015] All ER (D) 220 (Mar). The proportionality of forfeiture must be examined and, in every case, a balance is to be struck; moreover, as the court in *Freifeld* observed, the decision in that case should not be regarded as conferring carte blanche on tenants, who happen to have a valuable leasehold interest, to disregard their covenant.

Note that a tenant, or mortgagee, who has been served with a s 146 notice will rarely be allowed to apply for relief once possession has been regained: *Rogers v Rice* [1892] 2 Ch 170, CA; *Billson v Residential Apartments Ltd* [1992] 1 AC 494, [1992] 1 All ER 141; *Rexhaven Ltd v Nurse* (1995) 28 HLR 241, [1995] EGCS 125. A mortgagee may be entitled to relief under the Law of Property Act 1925 s 146(4) on the bankruptcy of the leaseholder: *Barclays Bank plc v Prudential Assurance Co Ltd* [1998] 1 EGLR 44. See also *Croydon (Unique) Ltd v Wright* (see para **III L&T [2.3]**). A tenant's denial of the landlord's title gives the landlord a claim in forfeiture (thereby attracting the operation of s 146), but is not a repudiation of the lease. A s 146 notice is therefore required, see *Abidogun v Frolan Health Care Ltd* [2001] 45 EG 138 (CS), CA. A mortgagee in possession of a leasehold interest is not a "lessee" for the purposes of s 146 and is not entitled to receive notice or serve counter-notice thereunder: *Smith v Spaul* [2002] EWCA Civ 1830, [2003] QB 983, [2003] 1 All ER 509.

Relief from forfeiture may be granted in respect of a finance lease, but not after the applicant for relief has sold the subject matter: *On Demand Information plc v Michael Gerson Finance plc* [2000] 4 All ER 734, [2001] 1 WLR 155, CA.

Relief may even be given where the breach consists of immoral user of the demised premises: see *Patel v K & J Restaurants Ltd* [2010] EWCA Civ 1211, [2010] AlL ER (D) 278 (Oct) where the breach was not wilful and the grant of vacant possession would have been out of all proportion to the breach and resulting damage.

The procedure on a tenant's claim for relief from forfeiture is governed by CPR Pt 55 (see CPR 55.2(1)(c) at para **CPR 55.2**). In particular, the claimant for relief should use Form N5A.

Where a company buys a lease, grants subleases and then sells its interest to an enterprise which becomes insolvent, and the head landlord then seeks to forfeit the lease for non-payment of rent, the sub-lessees may have to pay off the arrears on the lease and enter fresh agreements with the head landlord as terms of being granted relief: *London Diocesan Funds v Phithwa* [2005] UKHL 70, [2006] 1 All ER 127. In the same case it was held, by a majority, that the original landlord was not liable for the rent under the lease or for the consequences of non-payment because agreements made with the sub-lessees excluded liability and the agreements were valid under the Landlord and Tenant (Covenants) Act 1995.

III L&T [2.2A]

Relief in relation to consent orders In *Crawford v Clark* [2000] EGCS 33, CA, the parties agreed in a consent order that a lease be forfeit with relief from forfeiture upon compliance by the tenant with an agreed schedule of works, but the tenant failed to comply. The Court of Appeal doubted that the court could entertain a further application for relief because the consent order constituted a bargain made between the parties and, as such, was not open to variation by the court. Similarly, in *Ropac Ltd v Inntrepreneur Pub Co* [2000] 26 LS Gaz R 36, Ch D, the court, while noting that it has wider and more flexible powers under the Civil Procedure Rules in relation to interfering with consent orders, held that it should be slow to interfere with what the parties had agreed and declined to extend the agreed time for payment of arrears.

III L&T [2.3]

Forfeiture in the case of non-payment of rent See the County Courts Act 1984 s 138 (see para **III CCA [133]**). A person with the benefit of a charging order over leasehold land is entitled to seek relief under s 138(9C): *Croydon (Unique) Ltd v Wright* [2001] Ch 318, [1999] 4 All ER 257, CA. In order to obtain relief, the tenant must show an ability to pay the arrears within a reasonable time: *Inntrepreneur Pub Co (CPC) Ltd v Langton* [1999] 44 LS Gaz R 39, Ch D. For the position with consent orders in relation to arrears, see para **III L&T [2.2A]** above.

A creditor of a lessee who has a charging order against the leasehold estate is not entitled to claim relief in his own name as a person with an interest in the lease but may claim indirectly, by claiming on behalf of the lessee as a beneficiary under the trust on which the lessee holds the estate. The lessee may be joined by the chargee as a defendant to the application for relief: *Bland v Ingram's Estates Ltd* [2001] Ch 767, [2002] 1 All ER 221, CA. Where, following re-entry, the lessor granted a lease to a third person who took with notice of the right to relief, the applicant was liable to pay (as a condition of obtaining relief) arrears of rent but, for the period after re-entry, was entitled to credit for a full occupation rent, being at least the amount of contractual rent paid or payable by the third person. This is because the lessor is required to bring into account the benefits he enjoys as a consequence of his re-entry: *Bland v Ingram's Estates Ltd (No 2)* [2001] EWCA Civ 1088, [2002] Ch 177, [2002] 1 All ER 244.

Section 167 of the Commonhold and Leasehold Reform Act 2002 provides that a landlord is not entitled to forfeit a long lease of a dwelling for non payment of rent unless the unpaid amount exceeds the prescribed sum (which is £350) or has remained unpaid for longer than the prescribed period (which is 3 years): see the Rights of Re-entry and Forfeiture (Prescribed Sum and Period) (England) Regulations 2004 SI 2004/3086. Section 166 of the 2002 Act provides that a tenant under a long lease of a dwelling is not liable to pay ground rent unless the landlord has given notice (in a prescribed form) of the amount due and the date it is due to be paid. It follows that a risk of forfeiture in relation to unpaid ground rent will not be incurred unless and until notice in proper form has been served and not complied with. For ss 166 and 167 of the 2002 Act, see paras **III L&T [316]–III L&T [317]**. For the prescribed information and form of notice for s 166, see the Landlord and Tenant (Notice of Rent) (England) Regulations 2004, SI 2004/3096.

III L&T [2.3A]

Forfeiture for non-repair For the restrictions on forfeiture of long leases for disrepair, see **III L&T [8]–III L&T[10]**. A writ based upon a defective s 146 notice alleging disrepair is not a defect which excuses a leaseholder from failing to complete a sale of the lease: *Lambeth London Borough Council v Vincent* [2000] 2 EGLR 73, Ch D. A landlord is not entitled to serve a s 146 notice in relation to a long lease of a dwelling unless the breach in question (i) has been admitted by the tenant or (ii) has been found to have occurred by a court/tribunal. In practice, it seems that (unless an arbitration agreement applies or there has already been a determination by the court) a landlord who desires to serve a s 146 notice will first have to apply to the LVT for a determination that the breach has occurred. For s 168 of the 2002 Act, see para **III L&T [318]**.

III L&T [2.3B]

Forfeiture for nuisance Where a lessee granted a sub-lease without a covenant, in line with the head lease, to prevent a nuisance, the Court of Appeal held that the lessee could not raise his inability to abate nuisance on the part of the sub-tenant as a defence to forfeiture proceedings. On the other hand, the Court held that he was entitled to a reasonable period in which to use influence over the sub-tenant to stop the nuisance and that four working days to respond to the section 146 notice was not a reasonable period: *Courtney Lodge Managements Ltd v Blake* [2004] EWCA Civ 975, (2004) Times 15 July.

III L&T [2.4]

Service charges See the Housing Act 1996 ss 81, 82 (see para **III L&T [276]** and **III L&T [277]**) regarding forfeiture for non-payment of service charge. By virtue of s 167 of the Commonhold and Leasehold Reform Act 2002 a landlord is not entitled to forfeit a long lease of a dwelling for non payment of service charges or "administration charges" (a newly defined expense brought expressly within the service charge regime) unless the unpaid amount exceeds the prescribed sum (which is £350) or has remained unpaid for longer than the prescribed period (which is 3 years): see the Rights of Re-entry and Forfeiture (Prescribed Sum and Period) (England) Regulations 2004, SI 2004/3086.

Where service charges are recoverable as rent there is no requirement to serve a s 146 notice before starting proceedings to forfeit the lease: *419 Archway Road Freehold Co Ltd v Ennison* [2012] EWCA Civ 831, the court holding that the tenant's Article 8 rights were protected by her entitlement to apply to a county court for relief from forfeiture.

III L&T [2.5]

Proceedings by paying tenants to forfeit leases of non-paying In *Britel Corpn NV v Orbach Chani* (1997) 29 HLR 883, CA, tenants who paid their service charges to a management company obtained an injunction to compel the landlord to forfeit the leases of the non-paying tenants and to have the management company appointed to sue the non-paying tenants in the landlord's name.

III L&T [2.5A]

Breach capable of remedy If the breach complained of is capable of remedy the s 146 notice must require the lessee to remedy the breach. Breach of covenant by unlawful subletting is not capable of remedy: see *Scala House and District Property Co Ltd v Forbes* [1974] QB 575. However, in the absence of special circumstances, a breach of covenant against parting with possession or sharing possession, falling short of creating or transferring a legal interest, is capable of remedy within the meaning of s 146: *Akici v Butlin* [2005] EWCA Civ 1296, [2006] 2 All ER 872, [2006] 1 WLR 201.

III L&T [2.6]

Precedents See **BCCP 0[49]** and **BCCP 0[50]** for specimen s 146 notices. See also Form N5A which should be used in a claim for relief against forfeiture. For a specimen, see **BCCP 0[50.1]**.

III L&T [3]

147. Relief against notice to effect decorative repairs

(1) After a notice is served on a lessee relating to the internal decorative repairs to a house or other building, he may apply to the court for relief, and if, having regard to all the circumstances of the case (including in particular the length of the lessee's term or interest remaining unexpired), the court is satisfied that the notice is unreasonable, it may, by order, wholly or partially relieve the lessee from liability for such repairs.

(2) This section does not apply:

- (i) where the liability arises under an express covenant or agreement to put the property in a decorative state of repair and the covenant or agreement has never been performed;
- (ii) to any matter necessary or proper—
  - (a) for putting or keeping the property in a sanitary condition; or
  - (b) for the maintenance or preservation of the structure;
- (iii) to any statutory liability to keep a house in all respects reasonably fit for human habitation;
- (iv) to any covenant or stipulation to yield up the house or other building in a specified state of repair at the end of the term.

(3) In this section "lease" includes an underlease and an agreement for a lease, and "lessee" has a corresponding meaning and includes any person liable to effect the repairs.

(4) This section applies whether the notice is served before or after the commencement of this Act, and has effect notwithstanding any stipulation to the contrary.

(5) The county court has jurisdiction under this section [. . .]

III L&T [3A]

196. Regulations respecting notices

(1) Any notice required or authorised to be served or given by this Act shall be in writing.

(2) Any notice required or authorised by this Act to be served on a lessee or mortgagor shall be sufficient, although only addressed to the lessee or mortgagor by that designation, without his name, or generally to the persons interested, without any name, and notwithstanding that any person to be affected by the notice is absent, under disability, unborn, or unascertained.

(3) Any notice required or authorised by this Act to be served shall be sufficiently served if it is left at the last-known place of abode or business in the United Kingdom of the lessee, lessor, mortgagee, mortgagor, or other person to be served,

or, in case of a notice required or authorised to be served on a lessee or mortgagor, is affixed or left for him on the land or any house or building comprised in the lease or mortgage, or, in case of a mining lease, is left for the lessee at the office or counting-house of the mine.

(4) Any notice required or authorised by this Act to be served shall also be sufficiently served, if it is sent by post in a registered letter addressed to the lessee, lessor, mortgagee, mortgagor, or other person to be served, by name, at the aforesaid place of abode or business, office, or counting-house, and if that letter is not returned by the postal operator (within the meaning of the Postal Services Act 2000) concerned undelivered; and that service shall be deemed to be made at the time at which the registered letter would in the ordinary course be delivered.

(5) The provisions of this section shall extend to notices required to be served by any instrument affecting property executed or coming into operation after the commencement of this Act unless a contrary intention appears.

(6) This section does not apply to notices served in proceedings in the court.

III L&T [3A.1]

Generally A notice to quit is not a notice required or authorised by s 196; accordingly, the deeming provisions as to service contained in s 196 do not apply to such a notice: *Wandsworth London Borough Council v Attwell* [1996] 1 EGLR 57 and *Enfield London Borough Council v Devonish* (1996) 28 HLR 641. Where the section applies, a notice, once served, cannot be withdrawn even if it has not come to the attention of the recipient: *Kinch v Bullard* [1999] 1 WLR 423. "Ordinary course" in s 196(4) means ordinary course of post, and the deeming provision connotes an imaginary state of affairs and produces a presumed date of delivery regardless of when delivery of a registered letter or recorded delivery actually takes place: *WX Investments Ltd v Begg* [2002] EWHC 925 (Ch), [2002] 1 WLR 2849, and see also *Holwell Securities Ltd v Hughes* [1974] 1 WLR 155. A recorded delivery letter is a valid alternative to a registered letter: s 1 of the Recorded Delivery Service Act 1962.

LANDLORD AND TENANT ACT 1927

(c 36)

GENERAL NOTES ON PART I OF THE ACT

III L&T [4]

Jurisdiction Claims under the Landlord and Tenant Act 1927 Pt I are landlord and tenant claims within the meaning of CPR 56. Accordingly, although the High Court and county courts have concurrent, and unlimited, jurisdiction to entertain such claims (Landlord and Tenant Act 1954 s 63 (see para **III L&T [36]**) (as applied by the Landlord and Tenant Act 1927 s 21)), such claims should be started in the county court unless the claimant can certify (and verify with a statement of truth (see CPR PD 22 para 1.1(5); para **CPR PD 22**)) that there are complicated disputes of fact or points of law of general importance: see CPR 55.2 (para **CPR 55.2**) and the Practice Direction to CPR Pt 56 para 2 (para **CPR PD 56**). If in exceptional circumstances a claim is made in the High Court, a master or district judge in the Chancery Division may not, without the consent of the Vice-Chancellor, make final orders under the Act except by consent. In the county court a district judge has no jurisdiction to hear claim under Pt I of the 1927 Act, see CPR PD 2B para 11.1(a)(i) (para **CPR PD 2B**). With effect from 2 December 2002, CPR PD 56 para 2.6 (para **CPR PD 56**) makes clear that a landlord and tenant claim started in the High Court must be brought in the Chancery Division.

III L&T [5]

Claims under Part I The Landlord and Tenant Act 1927 s 1 gives the business tenant the right, on quitting the premises, to compensation for improvements made after notice to the landlord under Landlord and Tenant Act 1927 s 3. Applications may be made for a determination by the court if the landlord objects or disputes the improvements or their value.

Where the landlord has responded to a tenant's notice by stating his intention to carry out the improvements himself, the landlord cannot force the tenant to give access for the improvements to be carried out after the tenant has withdrawn his original notice: *Norfolk Capital Group Ltd v Cadogan Estates Ltd* [2004] EWHC 384 (Ch), [2004] 3 All ER 889, [2004] 1 WLR 1458, Etherton J.

III L&T [6]

Procedure Claims started under the Landlord and Tenant Act 1927 Pt I are governed by CPR Pt 56. The appropriate court will generally be the county court (see para **III L&T [4]**) for the district in which the land is situated. For the required procedure, see CPR PD 56 paras 5.1 to 5.9 (para **CPR PD 56**) and the notes set out at para **CPR 56.1[1]**. Note also that on 15 October 2001, RSC Order 97 and CCR Order 43 were revoked and that, by the Civil Procedure (Modification of Enactments Order)2001 (SI 2001/2717), s 25(1) of the 1927 Act was amended so as to remove references to the old rules.

III L&T [6A]

18. Provisions as to covenants to repair

(1) Damages for a breach of a covenant or agreement to keep or put premises in repair during the currency of a lease, or to leave or put premises in repair at the termination of a lease, whether such covenant or agreement is expressed or implied, and whether general or specific, shall in no case exceed the amount (if any) by which the value of the reversion (whether immediate or not) in the premises is diminished owing to the breach of such covenant or agreement as aforesaid; and in particular no damage shall be recovered for a breach of any such covenant or agreement to leave or put premises in repair at the termination of a lease, if it is shown that the premises, in whatever state of repair they might be, would at or shortly after the termination of the tenancy have been or be pulled down, or such structural alterations made therein as would render valueless the repairs covered by the covenant or agreement.

(2) A right of re-entry or forfeiture for a breach of any such covenant or agreement as aforesaid shall not be enforceable, by action or otherwise, unless the lessor proves that the fact that such a notice as is required by section one hundred and forty-six of the law of Property Act 1925, has been served on the lessee was known either -

- (a) to the lessee; or
- (b) to an under-lessee holding under an under-lease which reserved a nominal reversion only to the lessee; or
- (c) to the person who last paid the rent due under the lease either on his own behalf or as agent for the lessee or under-lessee,

and that a time reasonably sufficient to enable the repairs to be executed had elapsed since the time when the fact of the service of the notice came to the knowledge of any such person.

Where a notice has been sent by registered post addressed to a person at his last known place of abode in the United Kingdom, then, for the purposes of this subsection, that person shall be deemed, unless the contrary is proved, to have had knowledge of the fact that the notice had been served as from the time at which the letter would have been delivered in the ordinary course of post.

This subsection shall be construed as one with section one hundred and forty-six of the Law of Property Act 1925.

(3) This section applies whether the lease was created before or after the commencement of the Act.

III L&T [6A.1]

Measure of damages It is first necessary to assess the damages at common law which is the cost of putting the premises in repair. The statutory cap, which limits the damages to the diminution in the value of the reversion, must then be applied: *Joyner v Weeks* (1891) 2 QB 31, CA. If repairs are actually carried out, then the cost of those repairs may well be a good indication of the diminution on value of the reversion by reason of the disrepair in question: *Jones v Herxheimer* [1950] 2 KB 106, [1950] 1 All ER 323, CA; and see also *Sunlife Europe Properties Ltd v Tiger Aspect Holdings Ltd* [2013] EWCA Civ 1656, [2013] All ER (D) 163 (Dec) where the Court of Appeal held that, on the facts, the trial judge had been entitled to conclude that the amount of the diminution in value could be inferred from the cost of the necessary repairs.

Where, however, there is little or no likelihood of the landlord doing the repairs the estimated cost of them provides very little evidence of the existence of damage or its amount and evidence must be given of an actual diminution in the value of the premises through being out of repair in order to entitle the landlord to damages. For a recent statement of what constitutes diminution in value of the reversion see *Van Dal Footwear Ltd v Ryman Ltd* [2009] EWCA Civ 1478, [2010] 1 All ER 883, [2010] 1 WLR 2015. It is necessary to look at the value of the property which has reverted at the moment that it reverts to the landlord ("the valuation date"). The value of the reversion on the valuation date is then valued on the basis of two hypotheses. The first is that the reversion is sold in its actual condition. The second is that the reversion is sold in the condition in which it would have been if the tenant's covenants had been performed. No other hypotheses are required or permitted. The need for two valuations was adopted in *Re Teathers Ltd, Baroque Investments Ltd v Heis* [2012] EWHC 2886 (Ch), [2013] 1 P & CR 168, [2012] 3 EGLR 30. In that case, the tenant's obligation to reinstate at the end of the term had been released by an earlier surrender. In approaching the dilapidations claim by reference to the tenant's covenant to keep the demised premise in good repair during the term, the court observed that the valuations must assume that a purchaser would take the reversion subject to the lease, with the benefit and burden of the covenants and stipulations it contained for the rest of the term.

III L&T [7]

19. Provisions as to covenants not to assign, etc without licence or consent

(1) In all leases whether made before or after the commencement of this Act containing a covenant condition or agreement against assigning, under-letting, charging or parting with the possession of demised premises or any part thereof without licence or consent, such covenant condition or agreement shall, notwithstanding any express provision to the contrary, be deemed to be subject—

(a) to a proviso to the effect that such licence or consent is not to be unreasonably withheld, but this proviso does not preclude the right of the landlord to require payment of a reasonable sum in respect of any legal or other expenses incurred in connection with such licence or consent; and

(b) (if the lease is for more than forty years, and is made in consideration wholly or partially of the erection, or the substantial improvement, addition or alteration of buildings, and the lessor is not a Government department or local or public authority, or a statutory or public utility company) to a proviso to the effect that in the case of any assignment, under-letting, charging or parting with the possession (whether by the holders of the lease or any under-tenant whether immediate or not) effected more than seven years before the end of the term no consent or licence shall be required, if notice in writing of the transaction is given to the lessor within six months after the transaction is effected.

(1A) Where the landlord and the tenant under a qualifying lease have entered into an agreement specifying for the purposes of this subsection—

(a) any circumstances in which the landlord may withhold his licence or consent to an assignment of the demised premises or any part of them, or

(b) any conditions subject to which any such licence or consent may be granted,

then the landlord—

(i) shall not be regarded as unreasonably withholding his licence or consent to any such assignment if he withholds it on the ground (and it is the case) that any such circumstances exist, and

(ii) if he gives any such licence or consent subject to any such conditions, shall not be regarded as giving it subject to unreasonable conditions;

and section 1 of the Landlord and Tenant Act 1988 (qualified duty to consent to assignment etc) shall have effect subject to the provisions of this subsection.

(1B) Subsection (1A) of this section applies to such an agreement as is mentioned in that subsection—

(a) whether it is contained in the lease or not, and

(b) whether it is made at the time when the lease is granted or at any other time falling before the application for the landlord's licence or consent is made.

(1C) Subsection (1A) shall not, however, apply to any such agreement to the extent that any circumstances or conditions specified in it are framed by reference to any matter falling to be determined by the landlord or by any other person for the purposes of the agreement, unless under the terms of the agreement—

(a) that person's power to determine that matter is required to be exercised reasonably, or

(b) the tenant is given an unrestricted right to have any such determination reviewed by a person independent of both landlord and tenant whose identity is ascertainable by reference to the agreement,

and in the latter case the agreement provides for the determination made by any such independent person on the review to be conclusive as to the matter in question.

(1D) In its application to a qualifying lease, subsection (1) (b) of this section shall not have effect in relation to any assignment of the lease.

(1E) In subsections (1A) and (1D) of this section—

(a) "qualifying lease" means any lease which is a new tenancy for the purposes of section 1 of the Landlord and Tenant (Covenants) Act 1995 other than a residential lease, namely a lease by which a building or part of a building is let wholly or mainly as a single private residence; and

(b) references to assignment include parting with possession on assignment.

(2) In all leases whether made before or after the commencement of this Act containing a covenant condition or agreement against the making of improvements without licence or consent, such covenant condition or agreement shall be deemed, notwithstanding any express provision to the contrary, to be subject to a proviso that such licence or consent is not to be unreasonably withheld; but this proviso does not preclude the right to require as a condition of such licence or consent the payment of a reasonable sum in respect of any damage to or diminution in the value of the premises or any neighbouring premises belonging to the landlord, and of any legal or other expenses properly incurred in connection with such licence or consent nor, in the case of an improvement which does not add to the letting value of the holding, does it preclude the right to require as a condition of such licence or consent, where such a requirement would be reasonable, an undertaking on the part of the tenant to reinstate the premises in the condition in which they were before the improvement was executed.

(3) In all leases whether made before or after the commencement of this Act containing a covenant condition or agreement against the alteration of the user of the demised premises, without licence or consent, such covenant condition or agreement shall, if the alteration does not involve any structural alteration of the premises, be deemed, notwithstanding any express provision to the contrary, to be

subject to a proviso that no fine or sum of money in the nature of a fine, whether by way of increase of rent or otherwise, shall be payable for or in respect of such licence or consent; but this proviso does not preclude the right of the landlord to require payment of a reasonable sum in respect of any damage to or diminution in the value of the premises or any neighbouring premises belonging to him and of any legal or other expenses incurred in connection with such licence or consent. Where a dispute as to the reasonableness of any such sum has been determined by a court of competent jurisdiction, the landlord shall be bound to grant the licence or consent on payment of the sum so determined to be reasonable.

(4) This section shall not apply to leases of agricultural holdings within the meaning of the Agricultural Holdings Act 1986 which are leases in relation to which that Act applies, or to farm business tenancies within the meaning of the Agricultural Tenancies Act 1995, and paragraph (b) of subsection (1), subsection (2) and subsection (3) of this section shall not apply to mining leases.

LANDLORD & TENANT AND HOUSING

III L&T [7.1]

Jurisdiction The High Court and county courts have concurrent, and unlimited, jurisdiction by operation of Landlord and Tenant Act 1954 s 53. A claim for a declaration that a landlord has unreasonably withheld his consent to a proposed assignment etc would appear to be a claim under the Landlord and Tenant Act 1927 and thus a landlord and tenant claim within the meaning of CPR Pt 56 (see para **CPR 56**). Accordingly, the usual court for bringing proceedings will be the county court for the district in which the land is situated unless the claimant can certify (and verify with a statement of truth (see CPR PD 22 para 1.1(5); para **CPR PD 22**)) that there are complicated disputes of fact or points of law of general importance: see para **CPR 55.2** and CPR PD 56 para 2 (para **CPR PD 56**). If the claim is brought in the High Court CPR PD 56 para 2.6 (para **CPR PD 56**) makes clear that the claim must be brought in the Chancery Division.

III L&T [7.2]

Procedure The claimant in a landlord and tenant claim must use the Pt 8 procedure as modified by CPR Pt 56: see para **CPR 56** and CPR PD 56 para 2.1 (para **CPR PD 56**). In contrast with the position for claims for compensation under Pt I of the Act, the Practice Direction to CPR Pt 56 contains no specific procedure for claims for a declaration under s 19 of the Landlord and Tenant Act 1927. The claimant should therefore follow the Pt 8 procedure.

III L&T [7.3]

Unreasonable refusal of consent to assign See *International Drilling Fluids Ltd v Louisville Investments (Uxbridge) Ltd* [1986] Ch 513, [1986] 1 All ER 321, CA for a review of the authorities. Where the proposed assignee's intended user will possibly (but not necessarily) involve a breach of covenant, refusal of consent will rarely be unreasonable: see *Ashworth Frazer Ltd v Gloucester City Council* [2001] UKHL 59, [2001] 1 WLR 2180 (overruling the Court of Appeal on this point, and also the case of *Killick v Second Covent Garden Property Co Ltd* [1973] 1 WLR 658, on which the Court of Appeal's decision had been based). Consent was held to be unreasonably refused where the landlord insisted on having the guarantee of a parent company of the obligations of a subsidiary: *Storehouse Properties Ltd v Ocobase Ltd* (1998) Times, 3 April. Where a tenant's use of a proposed building extension might detrimentally affect the landlord's business interests, the landlord could legitimately refuse consent unless a condition restricting the future use of the extension was inserted into the lease. However, if the condition would preclude the tenant from carrying on some of his existing business activities that was unreasonable *Sargeant v Macepark (Whittlebury) Ltd* [2004] EWHC 1333 (Ch), [2004] 4 All ER 662, (2004) Times, 6 July.

In *Royal Bank Of Scotland Plc v Victoria Street (No 3) Ltd* [2008] EWHC 3052 (Ch), [2008] All ER (D) 280 (Oct) (Morgan J), the Court, applying *Ashworth Frazer Ltd v Gloucester City Council* (above), confirmed that the reasonableness of the landlord's decision is a question of fact, and further held that a landlord's entitlement to refuse consent is not limited to where the reversion would, if the assignment proceeded, in some way be damaged or diminished.

Where the covenant against sub-letting or assignment is absolute s 1 of the Act of 1988 has no application: *Crestford Ltd v Tesco Stores Ltd* [2005] EWHC 805, [2005] 37 EG 148.

In *Landlord Protect Ltd v St Anselm Development Co Ltd* [2009] EWCA Civ 99, [2009] 2 P&CR 150, [2009] 19 EG 112, it was held that it is for the landlord to show that a refusal of consent is reasonable, in accordance with section 1(6)(b) of the Landlord and Tenant Act 1988. It was further held that it will normally be reasonable for a landlord to refuse consent or impose a condition to prevent prejudice to the landlord's contractual rights under the head lease. Conversely it will not normally be reasonable for a landlord to impose a condition designed to increase or enhance the rights enjoyed under the head-lease.

III L&T [7.3A]

Expense in connection with licence or consent For consideration and application of s 19(1)(a), and determination that a landlord's reasonable charge for the cost and expense incurred in giving his consent is an 'administration charge' under Sch 11 to the Commonhold and Leasehold Reform Act 2002, see *Freehold Managers (Nominees) Ltd v Piatti* [2012] UKUT 241 (LC) and *Holding & Management (Solitaire) Ltd v Norton* [2012] UKUT 1 (LC), [2012] 26 Estates Gazette 98, [2012] 07 EG 91 (CS).

III L&T [7.4]

Statutory duty under Landlord and Tenant Act 1988 The Landlord and Tenant Act 1988 (**III L&T [209.2]**) imposes statutory duties in connection with covenants to which the Landlord and Tenant Act 1927 s 19(1) applies. A landlord must give his reasons for refusing consent in writing and is confined to his written reasons: *Norwich Union Life Assurance v Shopmoor Ltd* [1998] 3 All ER 32, [1999] 1 WLR 531; *Footwear Corpn Ltd v Amplight Properties Ltd* [1998] 3 All ER 52, [1999] 1 WLR 551. The landlord should give reasons for refusing consent within a reasonable time of the application for it and should not be permitted to rely on other reasons at a later stage: *London & Argyll Developments Ltd v Mount Cook Land Ltd* [2002] All ER (D) 06 (Oct).

The service of the written notice of refusal brings the process to an end: *Go West Ltd v Spigaloro* [2003] EWCA Civ 17, [2003] QB 1140, [2003] 2 All ER 141.

Where a landlord breaks his statutory obligation, under s 1, to respond to a written request for consent to assign, and does so in a cynical way with a view to making a profit for himself, an award of exemplary damages may be appropriate, as was made in *Design Progression Ltd v Thurloe Properties Ltd* [2004] EWHC 324 (Ch), [2004] 10 EG 184 (CS), (2004) Times, 2 March, Peter Smith J.

III L&T [7.5]

Covenants In the case of non-residential premises the Landlord and Tenant Act 1927 s 19 (1A)–(1E) enables a lease granted on or after 1 January 1996 to specify the circumstances in which any consent to an assignment may be withheld, thus in effect empowering the parties to define the terms on which the landlord will be deemed to be acting reasonably for the purposes of the Landlord and Tenant Act 1927. Landlord and Tenant (Covenants) Act 1995 s 8 also enables a county court to override an objection by the tenant to an application by the landlord or former landlord to be released from the landlord covenants on an assignment of the reversion. Landlord and Tenant (Covenants) Act 1995 s 10 confers similar jurisdiction where there is an objection to an apportionment of liability under a tenant or landlord covenant on an assignment of part only of the demised premises or the reversion in part. These provisions apply only to new tenancies but are not confined to business premises. It was held in *BHP Petroleum Great Britain Ltd v Chesterfield Properties Ltd* [2002] Ch 12, [2001] 2 All ER 914 (and upheld by the Court of Appeal: [2001] EWCA Civ 1797, [2002] Ch 194, [2002] 1 All ER 821) that a personal covenant, which was not transmissible, was outside the definition of a landlord covenant in s 28 and thus the landlord could not obtain release by means of an application under s 8. For notices to be used under the Landlord and Tenant (Covenants) Act 1995, see the Landlord and Tenant (Covenants) Act 1995 (Notices) Regulations 1995, SI 1995/2964.

III L&T [7.6]

Unreasonable refusal of consent to improvements Note that the effect of s 19(2) is that a landlord cannot object to a proposed alteration on the ground that it may diminish the value of his neighbouring property or reversion. An objection by the landlord on the ground of pecuniary damage only is not a reasonable ground for refusing consent. If the landlord has such a concern his entitlement is to stipulate, as a condition of his consent, payment of a reasonable sum as compensation. The landlord may thus object, for example, on grounds based on aesthetic, artistic, historic or sentimental considerations. The landlord may also object where he is concerned about the structural effect of the tenant's proposed works and where the tenant has not provided sufficient information to enable the landlord to make an informed decision.

It is not necessary that the conclusions which led the landlord to refuse consent are justified, if they are conclusions which might be reached by a reasonable landlord in the particular circumstances: see *Iqbal v Thakrah* [2004] 3 EGLR 21; and see also *Sargeant v Macepark (Whittlebury) Ltd* [2004] EWHC 1333 (Ch): the landlord does not have to show that his conclusions are right or justifiable, but simply that they are conclusions that might be reached by a reasonable person in the circumstances.

III L&T [7.7]

Landlord's entitlement to information The tenant must make sufficiently clear what his proposals are, so that the landlord knows whether he should refuse or give consent to the proposed alterations or additions: see *Iqbal v Thakrah* [2004] 3 EGLR 21. The importance of the landlord's entitlement to plans and specifications (particularly where the covenant expressly requires the tenant to carry out the works in accordance with them) was made clear in *Kalford Ltd v Peterborough City Council* [2001] EGCS 42: once approved, the plans and specifications define the nature of the obligation to be performed and provide the yardstick by which an order for specific performance of the obligation would be defined, or by which any deficiency of performance on the tenant's part would be measured.

III L&T [7.8]

More than one reason A landlord may seek to rely upon more than one reason for withholding consent to a proposed assignment etc. or proposed alterations. If the landlord has a good and a bad reason for withholding consent, consent may nevertheless have been reasonably withheld if the good reason is a sufficient reason and is not otherwise vitiated by the bad reason: *BRS v Templeheights* [1998] 2 EGLR 182. The approach in *BRS v Templeheights* was approved by the Court of Appeal in *No 1 West India Quay v (Residential) Ltd v East Tower Apartments Ltd* [2018] HLR 20: 'If the decision would have been the same without reliance on the bad reason, then the decision (looked at overall) is good. In that situation the bad reason will not have vitiated or infected the good one'. The question is 'whether the decision to refuse consent was reasonable; not whether all the reasons for the decision were reasonable'.

LANDLORD & TENANT AND HOUSING

LEASEHOLD PROPERTY (REPAIRS) ACT 1938

(c 34)

GENERAL NOTES ON LEASEHOLD PROPERTY (REPAIRS) ACT 1938

III L&T [8]

Jurisdiction Leasehold Property (Repairs) Act 1938 s 6 provides that proceedings should be brought in the county court except in the very rare case where the main action, for which leave under the Act was required, "would have to be taken in a court other than the county court" Claims under the 1938 Act are landlord and tenant claims within the meaning of CPR Pt 56. Accordingly, the usual court for bringing proceedings will be the county court for the district in which the land is situated unless the claimant can certify (and verify with a statement of truth (see CPR PD 22 para 1.1(5); para **CPR PD 22**)) that there are complicated disputes of fact or points of law of general importance: see para **CPR 55.2** and CPR PD 56 para 2 (para **CPR PD 56**). If the claim is brought in the High Court CPR PD 56 para 2.6 (para **CPR PD 56**) makes clear that the claim must be brought in the Chancery Division.

III L&T [9]

Restriction on enforcement of repairing covenants in long leases In the case of a lease of at least seven years with three still to run, the lessee who is served with a notice under Law of Property Act 1925 s 146 (see para **III L&T [2]**) relating to a repair covenant has 28 days in which to serve a counter-notice claiming the benefit of the Act; and the lessor cannot start an action for damages without serving a s 146 notice (Leasehold Property (Repairs) Act 1938 s 1), which must explain the right to serve a counter-notice. The relevant date for an applicant to prove the matters he relies upon in an application under s 1 is the date of the hearing: *Landmaster Properties Ltd v Thackeray Property Service Ltd* [2003] EWHC 959 (QB), [2003] 35 EG 83. Once a counter-notice is served the lessor may not sue for damages, or enforce the right of re-entry, without the leave of the court. But the lessor may sue to recover any liquidated sum representing the costs of repairs carried out because of the lessee's default: *Jervis v Harris* [1996] Ch 195, [1996] 1 All ER 303, CA. A mortgagee in possession of a leasehold interest is not a "lessee" for the purposes of s 1 (or s 146 of the 1925 Act) and is not entitled to receive notice or serve counter-notice thereunder: *Smith v Spaul* [2003] QB 983.

III L&T [10]

Procedure An application to the county court for leave, on the grounds in Leasehold Property (Repairs) Act 1938 s 1(5), is a landlord and tenant claim (see para **CPR 56.1**). The claimant in a landlord and tenant claim must use the Pt 8 procedure as modified by CPR Pt 56 and the Practice Direction to CPR Pt 56 para 2.1 (see para **CPR PD 56**). CPR PD 56 contains no specific procedure for claims under the 1938 Act. The claimant should therefore follow the Pt 8 procedure.

LANDLORD AND TENANT ACT 1954

(c 56)

GENERAL NOTES ON LANDLORD AND TENANT ACT 1954

III L&T [11]

Jurisdiction The Landlord and Tenant Act 1954 Pt I conferred security of tenure on tenancies of over 21 years at a low rent. Although it does not apply to leases granted on or after 1 April 1990 it continues to apply to leases ending before 15 January 1999. Security is provided thereafter by the creation of an assured tenancy under the Local Government and Housing Act 1989 s 186, Sch 10. Jurisdiction under the Landlord and Tenant Act 1954 Pt I is exercised by the county court. A claim under Pt I of the 1954 Act is a landlord and tenant claim as defined by CPR 56.1 (see para **CPR 56.1**). Save in exceptional circumstances therefore (as to which see CPR PD 56 paras 2.1 to 2.5 (para **CPR PD 56**)), the claim must be brought in the county court for the district in which the land is situated. The Landlord and Tenant Act 1954 Pt II enables tenants of business premises to obtain new leases in the circumstances set out in the Act. The Landlord and Tenant Act 1954 s 63 (see para **III L&T [36]**) confers jurisdiction in relation to Pt II on the High Court and county courts, without limit. Claims under Pt II are also landlord and tenant claims as defined by CPR 56.1. Such claims must, save in exceptional circumstances (as to which see CPR PD 56 paras 2.1 to 2.5), be brought in the county court for the district in which the land is situated. A joint claim by a landlord and tenant to authorise an agreement under s 38(4) of the Landlord and Tenant Act 1954 (see para **III L&T [31]**) may, however, be started in the High Court or any county court: see CPR 56.2(4) (para **CPR 56.2**). If (in exceptional circumstances) the claim is brought in the High Court, it must be brought in the Chancery Division (CPR PD 56 para 2.6) and a master or district judge in the Chancery Division may not, without the consent of the Vice-Chancellor, make final orders under the 1954 Act except (i) by consent, (ii) for interim rent or (iii) for authorisation under s 38(4) (CPR PD 2B para 5.1(j) (see para **CPR PD 2B**)). In the county court, a district judge has no jurisdiction to hear a claim for a new business tenancy under s 24: CPR PD 2B para 11.1(a)(ii) (see para **CPR PD 2B**).

III L&T [12]

Procedure All claims under Pts I and II of the Landlord and Tenant Act 1954 must follow the Pt 8 procedure as modified by CPR Part 56 and the Practice Direction to CPR PD 56 para 2.1 (see para **CPR PD 56**). No specific modifications are prescribed for claims under Part I of the Act. The general Pt 8 procedure should therefore be followed on such claims. Specific and detailed provision is, however, made for claims under Pt II of the Act (i) by a landlord or a tenant for a new business tenancy, (ii) by a landlord for termination of a tenancy and (iii) by a landlord or a tenant for interim rent (see para **CPR 56.3** and CPR PD 56 paras 2.1 and 3.1 to 3.19 (para **CPR PD 56**)). The practitioner should therefore refer to CPR 56.3 and CPR PD 56 and the notes at para **CPR 56 [4]** for the extensive requirements in relation to: (1) the contents of the claim form; (2) service of the claim form; (3) the appropriate defendant; (4) the filing, service and contents of the defendant's acknowledgment of service; and (5) the filing and service of evidence.

III L&T [13]

Precedents and Forms For precedents for court proceedings under both Pt I and Pt II of the 1954 Act, see **BCCP O[601]–BCCP O[606]**.

PART II
SECURITY OF TENURE FOR BUSINESS, PROFESSIONAL AND OTHER TENANTS

TENANCIES TO WHICH PART II APPLIES

III L&T [14]

23. Tenancies to which Part II applies

(1) Subject to the provisions of this Act, this Part of this Act applies to any tenancy where the property comprised in the tenancy is or includes premises which are occupied by the tenant and are so occupied for the purposes of a business carried on by him or for those and other purposes.

(1A) Occupation or the carrying on of a business—

(a) by a company in which the tenant has a controlling interest; or

(b) where the tenant is a company, by a person with a controlling interest in the company,

shall be treated for the purposes of this section as equivalent to occupation or, as the case may be, the carrying on of a business by the tenant.

(1B) Accordingly references (however expressed) in this Part of this Act to the business of, or to use, occupation or enjoyment by, the tenant shall be construed as including references to the business of, or to use, occupation or enjoyment by, a company falling within subsection (1A)(a) above or a person falling within subsection (1A)(b) above.

(2) In this Part of this Act the expression "business" includes a trade, profession or employment and includes any activity carried on by a body of persons, whether corporate or unincorporate.

(3) In the following provisions of this Part of this Act the expression "the holding", in relation to a tenancy to which this Part of this Act applies, means the property comprised in the tenancy, there being excluded any part thereof which is occupied neither by the tenant nor by a person employed by the tenant and so employed for the purposes of a business by reason of which the tenancy is one to which this Part of this Act applies.

(4) Subject to subsection (5), where the tenant is carrying on a business, in all or any part of the property comprised in a tenancy, in breach of a prohibition (however expressed) of use for business purposes which subsists under the terms of the tenancy and extends to the whole of that property, this Part of this Act shall not apply to the tenancy unless the immediate landlord or his predecessor in title has consented to the breach or the immediate landlord has acquiesced therein.

In this subsection the reference to a prohibition of use for business purposes does not include a prohibition of use for the purposes of a specified business, or of use for purposes of any but a specified business, but save as aforesaid includes a prohibition of use for the purposes of some one or more only of the classes of business specified in the definition of that expression in subsection (2) of this section.

(5) Where the tenant's breach of a prohibition (however expressed) of use for business purposes which subsists under the terms of the tenancy and extends to the whole of that property consists solely of carrying on a home business, this Part of this Act does not apply to the tenancy, even if the immediate landlord or the immediate landlord's predecessor in title has consented to the breach or the immediate landlord has acquiesced in the breach.

(6) In subsection (5) "home business" has the same meaning as in section 43ZA.

III L&T [14.1]

"Subject to the provisions of this Act" For tenancies to which this Part of the Act does not apply, see the Landlord and Tenant Act 1954 ss 28, 36(2), 43 (see paras **III L&T [20]**, **III L&T [29]**, **III L&T [32]**). The Crown is included by the Landlord and Tenant Act 1954 s 56, but

Government departments, local authorities and certain others have an overriding right to insist on a change of user, subject to certain qualifications in the Landlord and Tenant Act 1954 ss 57–60, including the duty to compensate the tenant. Special provision is made for the application of the Act to derelict land (Landlord and Tenant Act 1954 s 54). The application of a local Act such as the Huddersfield Waterworks and Improvement Act 1876 to the tenancy does not take it out of the jurisdiction of the Landlord and Tenant Act 1954 Pt II: *R v Huddersfield County Court Judge, ex p Beaumont Ashton Ltd* (1967) 19 P & CR 62.

III L&T [14.1A]

Person with controlling interest An individual and any company he controls are treated as one and the same for the purpose of Part II of the 1954 Act.

III L&T [14.2]

Tenancy For the meaning of "tenancy", see the Landlord and Tenant Act 1954 s 69(1) (see para **III L&T [41]**). An agreement whereby the applicant was granted the saloon and refreshment bars and cloakroom in a theatre, with the sole right to sell alcoholic drinks, refreshments and programmes, was held to confer a mere licence: *Payne-Jennings and Killick Ltd v Bright Enterprises Ltd* (1959) 173 Estates Gazette 917, so also was an agreement, described as a licence, whereby an oil company granted to the licensee the right to use premises as a filling station but retained rights of possession and control and could visit the premises whenever they liked for alteration of the equipment: *Shell–Mex and BP Ltd v Manchester Garages Ltd* [1971] 1 All ER 841, [1971] 1 WLR 612, CA; *Esso Petroleum Co Ltd v Fumegrange* [1994] 2 EGLR 90, [1994] 46 EG 199, CA; an agreement for the use of land as a car park between certain hours: *Manchester City Council v National Car Parks Ltd* [1982] 1 EGLR 94, CA, and *National Car Parks Ltd v Trinity Development Co (Banbury) Ltd* [2001] 2 EGLR 43, [2001] 28 EG 144; and also an agreement for a person to occupy a shop unit for a year as a licensee with an option to take a 30 year lease from the commencement of the licence, the owner meanwhile retaining possession of the premises subject to the licence: *Essex Plan Ltd v Broadminster Ltd* [1988] 2 EGLR 73, [1988] 43 EG 84. A right to place advertising hoardings does not amount to a lease: *Kewal Investments Ltd v Arthur Maiden Ltd* [1990] 1 EGLR 193, [1990] 15 EG 58, nor does a right to deposit refuse: *Hunts Refuse Disposals Ltd v Norfolk Environmental Waste Services Ltd* [1997] 1 EGLR 16, [1997] 03 EG 139, CA. An agreement under which an advertising company obtained the right to put up hoardings for advertisements at certain locations owned by the local authority conferred a licence but not a tenancy of the premises in question: *Clear Channel UK Ltd v Manchester City Council* [2005] EWCA Civ 1304, [2006] 1 EGLR 27. But a lease of gallops for training and exercising racehorses on downland was held to create a tenancy: *Bracey v Read* [1963] Ch 88, [1962] 3 All ER 472. It was thought doubtful whether the mere letting of an incorporeal hereditament could be occupation such as to be the subject of a new tenancy within the Landlord and Tenant Act 1954: *Jones v Christy* (1963) 107 Sol Jo 374, CA; and it has now been confirmed that the Act has no application to an easement such as a right of way, because of itself such a right is not property capable of being occupied for the purposes of a business: *Land Reclamation Co Ltd v Basildon District Council* [1979] 2 All ER 993, [1979] 1 WLR 767, CA. It is otherwise where a right of way over adjoining property of the landlord is included in a lease of business premises, even if the reversions are subsequently severed: *Nevill Long & Co (Boards) v Firmenich & Co* (1983) 47 P & CR 59, CA.

III L&T [14.3]

"Premises" This word is not to be construed in the restricted sense of buildings or buildings with land immediately adjoining them but covers any kind of property of which a lease is granted: *Bracey v Read* [1963] Ch 88, [1962] 3 All ER 472. An incorporeal hereditament can constitute premises for the purpose of s 23; see *Pointon York Group plc v Poulton* [2006] EWCA Civ 1001, [2006] 38 EG 192 where a right to use parking spaces was held to constitute premises.

III L&T [14.4]

Business The definition of "business" in the Landlord and Tenant Act 1954 s 23(2) brings within the Act a much wider range of activities than that covered by the Landlord and Tenant Act 1927. Occupation of premises for the purposes of a Government department is equivalent to the carrying on of a business therein: Landlord and Tenant Act 1954 s 56(3). Similarly, the activity of a tennis club registered as a society under the Industrial and Provident Societies Act 1965 is a business within the Act: *Addiscombe Garden Estates Ltd v Crabbe* [1958] 1 QB 513, [1957] 3 All ER 563, CA. So also is the activity of a local authority in maintaining an open space for the leisure use of local inhabitants: *Wandsworth London Borough Council v Singh* [1991] 2 EGLR 75, 62 P & CR 219, CA. A non-profit-making company limited by guarantee and formed for the purpose of leasing and managing sports grounds and social clubs has been held to be carrying on a business: *Hawkesbrook Leisure Ltd v Reece-Jones Partnership* [2003] EWHC 3333, [2004] 25 EG 172, Ch D. But the subletting of the demised premises into flats is not within the Act: *Bagettes Ltd v GP Estates Co Ltd* [1956] Ch

LANDLORD & TENANT AND HOUSING

290, [1965] 1 All ER 729, CA (followed in *Horford Investments Ltd v Lambert* [1976] Ch 39, [1974] 1 All ER 131, CA), nor is the carrying on of a Sunday school by an individual tenant without charge: *Abernethie v A M & J Kleiman Ltd* [1970] 1 QB 10, [1969] 2 All ER 790, CA, nor the taking in of lodgers simply as a domestic activity: *Lewis v Weldcrest Ltd* [1978] 3 All ER 1226, [1978] 1 WLR 1107, CA, nor the use of the premises for dumping spoil from neighbouring shops which the tenants are having altered: *Hillil Property and Investment Co Ltd v Naraine Pharmacy Ltd* (1979) 39 P & CR 67, [1979] 2 EGLR 65, CA. If residential premises are used for a business, the question is whether the business activity is a significant purpose of the occupation and not merely incidental to the occupation of the premises as a home: *Cheryl Investments Ltd v Saldanha* [1979] 1 All ER 5, [1978] 1 WLR 1329, CA. See also *Durman v Bell* (1998) 20 HLR 340, [1988] 2 EGLR 117, CA; *Gurton v Parrott* [1991] 1 EGLR 98, 23 HLR 418, CA and *Wright v Mortimer* (1996) 28 HLR 719, CA. Premises consisting of a shop with a residential flat above are wholly within the Landlord and Tenant Act 1954 Pt II, since the property includes premises occupied for the purposes of a business: *Kent Coast Property Investments Ltd v Ward* [1990] 2 EGLR 86, [1990] 45 EG 107, CA; see also *Broadway Investments Hackney Ltd v Grant* [2006] EWCA Civ 1709, [2006] All ER (D) 304 (Dec). Premises let for business purposes cannot, without the landlord's concurrence, be taken out of the Landlord and Tenant Act 1954 Pt II and brought under the Rent Acts by the tenant's ceasing the business user: *Wagle v Trustees of Henry Smith's Charity Kensington Estate* [1990] QB 42, CA, applied in *Webb v Barnet London Borough Council* (1988) 21 HLR 228, [1989] 1 EGLR 49, CA. In relation to mixed premises to which the Landlord and Tenant Act 1954 Pt II applies the effect of the Rent Act 1977 s 137(3) (see para **III L&T [76]**), is that a lawful sub-tenant of the residential part may become a protected tenant on the surrender of the head lease: *Wellcome Trust Ltd v Hamad* [1998] QB 638, [1998] 1 All ER 657, CA, in which the court declined to follow *Pittalis v Grant* [1989] QB 605, [1989] 2 All ER 622, CA. Where a local authority landlord takes a surrender of business premises, a sub-tenant of part of the premises unlawfully converted into a flat becomes a secure tenant of the authority: *Basingstoke and Deane Borough Council v Paice* (1995) 27 HLR 433, [1995] 2 EGLR 9, CA.

III L&T [14.5]

Continuity of business Where a tenant had, at the material date, gone to live elsewhere and had, in return for a fixed sum, granted to a so-called manager the right to carry on the business at the premises as he considered fit without interference from the tenant, it was held that the tenant was not occupying the premises for the purposes of a business carried on by him: *Teasdale v Walker* [1958] 3 All ER 307, [1958] 1 WLR 1076, CA. But a tenant does not lose the protection of the Act simply by ceasing physically to occupy the premises if the thread of continuity of business user by him is not broken: *I and H Caplan Ltd v Caplan (No 2)* [1963] 2 All ER 930, [1963] 1 WLR 1247. Whether business user has ceased is a question of fact for the judge: *Pulleng v Curran* (1980) 44 P & CR 58, CA. The thread of continuity was held to be broken where the tenant had granted a six-months' licence for the exclusive occupation of the premises by the licensee subject to the tenant's right to use a wine cellar and to hold staff lunches twice a month in the dining area of the premises: *Hancock and Willis v GMS Syndicate Ltd* (1982) 265 Estates Gazette 473, CA, and where the tenant had moved his gaming club to other premises, intending to return when another gaming licence could be obtained for the demised premises: *Aspinall Finance Ltd v Viscount Chelsea* [1989] 1 EGLR 103, [1989] 09 EG 77. A part of the premises sub-let by the tenant as a furnished flat is occupied by the sub-tenant and not by the tenant: *Narcissi v Wolfe* [1960] Ch 10, [1959] 3 All ER 71. Occupation by an employee of the tenant is not occupation for the purposes of the tenant's business unless it is necessary, and not merely convenient, for the employee to live in the property so as to carry out his duties in relation to the business: *Chapman v Freeman* [1978] 3 All ER 878, [1978] 1 WLR 1298, CA. Where a flat let to a medical school was used to house students with a view to fostering a corporate spirit and thereby advancing the educational process, the flat was held to be occupied by the school for the purposes of its business: *Groveside Properties Ltd v Westminster Medical School* (1983) 47 P & CR 507, [1983] 2 EGLR 68, CA.

III L&T [14.6]

Company Special provision is made in the Landlord and Tenant Act 1954 s 42 for cases where the tenancy is held by one member of a group of companies but the premises are occupied or the business carried on by another member of the group. Cases may also arise where the tenancy is vested in an individual but the premises are occupied or the business carried on by a company of which he is a member, and perhaps the majority shareholder: see *Tunstall v Steigmann* [1962] 2 QB 593, [1962] 2 All ER 417, CA; *Cristina v Seear* [1985] 2 EGLR 128, 275 Estates Gazette 898, CA and *Nozari-Zadeh v Pearl Assurance plc* [1987] 2 EGLR 91, 283 Estates Gazette 457, CA. Note, however, that ss (1A) and (1B) have the effect that an individual and any company he controls are treated as one and the same for the purpose of Part II of the 1954 Act.

Trusts Where the tenancy is held on trust the broad effect of the Landlord and Tenant Act 1954 s 41 is to treat the business occupation and activities of beneficiaries as those of the tenant.

III L&T [14.7]

"Occupied" Whereas the Landlord and Tenant Act 1954 Pt II applies where the property comprised in the tenancy is or includes premises occupied by the tenant for the purposes of his business, the "holding" of which a new tenancy may be granted means only such part of the property as is occupied by the tenant or his employee (Landlord and Tenant Act 1954 s 23(1), (3)). "Occupation" connotes some physical use of the property for the purposes of the tenant's business. It is a question of degree dependent on the facts of the particular case, but two persons cannot each occupy the same premises for business purposes at the same time. The fact that the tenant provides management services or the like does not enable him to be treated as occupying part of the premises let by him to a business sub-tenant. It follows that if, because of the exclusion of the sub-let accommodation, the tenant can no longer carry on his business in the retained part, there ceases to be a holding for the purposes of the Landlord and Tenant Act 1954 s 23(3): *Graysim Holdings Ltd v P & O Property Holdings Ltd* [1996] AC 329, [1995] 4 All ER 831, HL, disapproving dicta in *Lee-Verhulst (Investments) Ltd v Harwood Trust* [1973] QB 204, [1972] 3 All ER 619, CA and *William Boyer & Sons v Adams* (1975) 32 P & CR 89. See also *Bagettes Ltd v GP Estates Co Ltd* [1956] Ch 290, [1956] 1 All ER 729, CA and *Bassairi v London Borough of Camden* [1999] L & TR 45, CA. A local authority tenant of a small open space which it maintained for the recreation of local inhabitants was held to be in occupation of it for the purpose of its business although the horticultural care of the land was contracted out, since it was regularly inspected by the council's employees and the contractor was not a sub-tenant or licensee: *Wandsworth Borough Council v Singh* (1991) 62 P & CR 219, [1991] 2 EGLR 75, CA. On the other hand, where the premises were sub let as lock-up garages and the tenant merely inspected the site twice-monthly and carried out cleaning and maintenance although not obliged by the subletting to do so, it was held that he did not occupy the premises for the purposes of his business: *Trans-Britannia Properties Ltd v Darby Properties* [1986] 1 EGLR 151, 278 Estates Gazette 1254, CA. A tenant may occupy premises without being physically present in them so long as the tenant is using the premises as an incident in the ordinary course or conduct of the tenant's business life: *Pointon York Group plc v Poulton* [2006] EWCA Civ 1001, [2006] 38 EG 192.

Where the tenant, after issuing an originating application for a new tenancy, ceases to occupy the premises, the application will be struck out as an abuse of the process of the court: *Domer v Gulf Oil (Great Britain) Ltd* (1975) 119 Sol Jo 392. Likewise, if the tenant has voluntarily moved to other premises, albeit under an agreement with his landlord to give him temporary accommodation during the reconstruction of the demised premises, he cannot apply for a new tenancy, although he may have a remedy against his landlord for breach of contract: *Aireps Ltd v City of Bradford Metropolitan Council* [1985] 2 EGLR 143, 276 Estates Gazette 1067, CA. In order to apply for a new tenancy the tenant must show either that he is continuing in occupation of the premises for the purposes of a business carried on by him or, if events over which he has no control (eg a disastrous fire) have led him to absent himself from the premises, he continues to exert and claim his right to occupancy: *Morrison Holdings Ltd v Manders Property (Wolverhampton) Ltd* [1976] 2 All ER 205, [1976] 1 WLR 533, CA; compare *Demetriou v Robert Andrews (Estate Agencies)* (1990) 62 P & CR 536, sub nom *Demetriou v Poolaction Ltd* [1991] 1 EGLR 100, CA, where the tenant's allegation that he was unable to carry on his business of subletting the premises because of the landlord's failure to carry out his repairing obligations was rejected. If a landlord gives notice under the Landlord and Tenant Act 1954 s 25 (see para **III L&T [17]**) or a tenant requests a new tenancy under the Landlord and Tenant Act 1954 s 26 (see para **III L&T [18]**), the question whether the tenant is in occupation of the premises at the relevant time may be the subject of an agreement or estoppel: *Benedictus v Jalaram Ltd* (1988) 58 P & CR 330, CA. In a case where a ground floor shop and basement were sublet to a person who used them as a restaurant and the tenant did not begin to occupy the upper floors for a business of his until after the date of his application for a new lease, the Court of Appeal refused to upset the judge's findings that neither part of the premises was occupied by the tenant for the purpose of his business at the relevant time: *Latif v Hillside Estates (Swansea) Ltd* [1992] EGCS 75, CA.

Note that new sub-ss (1A) and (1B) have the effect that occupation by an individual and any company he controls are treated as one and the same for the purpose of Part II of the 1954 Act.

A tenant is not occupying for the purposes of his business when it is his wife who is in occupation for the purposes of a different business from the tenant's: *Zafiris v Liu* (2005) Times, 3 March, CA.

In determining whether the contract under which a managing agent occupies the tenant's premises is in reality a sub-tenancy the court may have to decide whether the agreement is a sham. See *Brumwell v Powys County Council* [2011] EWCA Civ 1613, [2012]

P & CR D46. Cases where a management agreement was held to confer a sub-tenancy include *Cafeteria (Keighley Ltd v Harrison* (1956) 168 EG 668, [1956] EGD 200; *Chez Gerard v Greene Ltd* [1983] 2 EGLR 79, 268 Estates Gazette 575, CA and *Teesside Indoor Bowls Ltd v Stockton on Tees Borough Council* [1990] 2 EGLR 87, [1990] 46 EG 116.

III L&T [14.8]

"Holding" Where the property comprised in the tenancy includes buildings, the landlord cannot succeed under the Landlord and Tenant Act 1954 s 30(1)(g) (see para **III L&T [22]**), by showing that he intends to demolish the buildings and use the land for some other purpose: *Nursey v P Currie (Dartford) Ltd* [1959] 1 All ER 497, [1959] 1 WLR 273, CA. It is otherwise where the holding consists of a vacant site used as a car park and the landlord intends to use it as a car testing centre and to build on part of it, since the fact that he will be occupying the holding comprised in the tenancy plus the building does not mean that he intends to occupy a different holding: *Cam Gears Ltd v Cunningham* [1981] 2 All ER 560, [1981] 1 WLR 1011, CA. So long as the tenant's occupation is not simply colourable, it is immaterial that his main object in using part of the premises is to secure its inclusion in a new lease granted under the Act; but semble occupation cannot be based on a user which is in breach of a covenant in the existing lease: *Narcissi v Wolfe* [1960] Ch 10, [1959] 3 All ER 71.

III L&T [14.9]

Prohibition of use for business Acquiescence for the purposes of the Landlord and Tenant Act 1954 s 23(4) means more than mere knowledge of the breach by an employee of the landlord who has no authority to do anything about it; there must be such knowledge and acquiescence that concurrence on the part of the landlord can be inferred: *Real and Leasehold Estates Investment Society Ltd v Medina Shipping Ltd* (1968) 112 Sol Jo 862, CA. Whereas it is sufficient to show acquiescence on the part of the immediate landlord, it is necessary in the case of a predecessor in title to show that he consented to the breach; for this purpose acquiescence is a passive failure to do anything in the face of knowledge of the breach while consent involves something of a positive kind, either in words or deed, which amounts to an express affirmation of what is being done: *Bell v Alfred Franks and Bartlett Co Ltd* [1980] 1 All ER 356, [1980] 1 WLR 340, CA. The subsection applies only where there is a breach, by the person who is in occupation and is using the premises for business purposes, of some prohibition which is immediately binding on him. If an under-lease is granted without the consent of the superior landlord to the use of the premises for business purposes as required by the head lease, the under-tenant's use of the premises for such purposes will not disentitle him to the protection of the Landlord and Tenant Act 1954 Pt II, since there is no prohibition binding as between him and his immediate landlord and he is not in breach of the covenant in the head lease as he is not a party to it: *D'Silva v Lister House Development Ltd* [1971] Ch 17, [1970] 1 All ER 858. A covenant to use a dwelling-house adjoining a school as a private residence only was held to be broken by allowing the house to be occupied by a school caretaker who had to be on call to carry out the duties of his employment during non-working hours, and in the absence of knowledge there was no acquiescence by the landlord: *Methodist Secondary Schools Trust Deed (Trustees) v O'Leary* (1992) 66 P & CR 364, [1993] 1 EGLR 105, CA.

CONTINUATION AND RENEWAL OF TENANCIES

III L&T [15]

24. Continuation of tenancies to which Part II applies and grant of new tenancies

(1) A tenancy to which this Part of this Act applies shall not come to an end unless terminated in accordance with the provisions of this Part of this Act; and, subject to the following provisions of the Act either the tenant or the landlord under such a tenancy may apply to the court for an order for the grant of a new tenancy—

- (a) if the landlord has given notice under section 25 of this Act to terminate the tenancy, or
- (b) if the tenant has made a request for a new tenancy in accordance with section twenty-six of this Act.

(2) The last foregoing subsection shall not prevent the coming to an end of a tenancy by notice to quit given by the tenant, by surrender or forfeiture, or by the forfeiture of a superior tenancy unless—

- (a) in the case of a notice to quit, the notice was given before the tenant had been in occupation in right of the tenancy for one month;

(b) ...

(2A) Neither the tenant nor the landlord may make an application under subsection (1) above if the other has made such an application and the application has been served.

(2B) Neither the tenant nor the landlord may make such an application if the landlord has made an application under section 29(2) of this Act and the application has been served.

(2C) The landlord may not withdraw an application under subsection (1) above unless the tenant consents to its withdrawal.

(3) Notwithstanding anything in subsection (1) of this section—

(a) where a tenancy to which this Part of this Act applies ceases to be such a tenancy, it shall not come to an end by reason only of the cesser, but if it was granted for a term of years certain and has been continued by subsection (1) of this section then (without prejudice to the termination thereof in accordance with any terms of the tenancy) it may be terminated by not less than three nor more than six months' notice in writing given by the landlord to the tenant;

(b) where, at a time when a tenancy is not one to which this Part of this Act applies, the landlord gives notice to quit, the operation of the notice shall not be affected by reason that the tenancy becomes one to which this Part of this Act applies after the giving of the notice.

III L&T [15.1]

Tenancy For the definition of "tenancy", see the Landlord and Tenant Act 1954 s 69(1) (see para **III L&T [41]**). It is a continuing condition of the tenant's right to a new tenancy that he should be, throughout the proceedings, tenant under a tenancy to which the Landlord and Tenant Act 1954 Pt II applies: *I and H Caplan Ltd v Caplan (No 2)* [1963] 2 All ER 930, [1963] 1 WLR 1247. A tenancy by estoppel is included: *Bell v General Accident Fire & Life Assurance Corpn Ltd* [1998] 1 EGLR 69, [1998] 17 EG 144, CA. There is no continuation if the tenant has ceased to occupy the premises for business purposes before the expiry of the contractual term: *Esselte AB v Pearl Assurance plc* [1997] 2 All ER 41, [1997] 1 WLR 891, CA, followed in *Surrey County Council v Single Horse Properties Ltd* [2002] EWCA Civ 367, [2002] 4 All ER 143, [2002] 1 WLR 2106.

III L&T [15.1A]

Notice to quit Section 24(2) allows for termination of the tenancy by tenant's notice to quit. In *Siemens Hearing Instruments Ltd v Friends Life Ltd* [2014] EWCA Civ 382, [2014] 2 P & CR 95 a tenant's break clause stated that the notice must be expressed to be given under s 24(2). The tenant's notice exercising the break was held to be invalid because it was not expressed to be given under s 24(2); compliance with the substantive provisions of s 24(2) did not save the notice.

III L&T [15.1B]

Application by landlord or tenant An application to the court for a new tenancy may be made by either the tenant or the landlord. Such applications are "unopposed claims" for the purpose of CPR PD 56: see para **CPR 56.3**. Note also that, under the new s 29(2), the landlord may apply to the court for an order for the termination of a tenancy without the grant of a new tenancy if he has given notice of his opposition to the grant of a new tenancy by means of his s 25 notice or by means of a s 26(6) counter notice.

III L&T [15.2]

Partnership The Landlord and Tenant Act 1954 s 41A distinguishes between business partners who have the benefit of the Act and non-business partners who do not.

III L&T [15.3]

Procedure and precedents A claim under s 24 for a new business tenancy which is unopposed must follow the Part 8 procedure, as modified by CPR 56.3 and CPR PD 56. CPR PD 56 sets out extensive requirements for the contents of claim forms and acknowledgments of service and for the filing of evidence. The practitioner should therefore refer to paras **CPR 56.3** and **CPR PD 56** and the notes at para **CPR 56 [4]** for the requirements in relation to:

(1) the contents of the claim form; (2) service of the claim form; (3) the appropriate defendant; (4) the filing, service and contents of the defendant's acknowledgment of service; and (5) the filing and service of evidence.

The 1954 Act has been held to be an enactment which allows a change of parties after the end of a relevant period, within CPR 19.5(1)(c). CPR 19.5 is therefore engaged and the court may allow a substitution outside the limitation period in cases of genuine mistake: *Parsons v George* [2004] EWCA Civ 912, [2004] 3 All ER 633, [2004] 1 WLR 3264.

For precedents for a claim form and acknowledgment of service under CPR Pt 56, see **BCCP O[601]** and **BCCP O[602]**.

III L&T [15.3A]

Evidence in support In claims by either a landlord or a tenant for the grant of a new tenancy, no evidence need be filed unless and until the court directs it to be filed; see CPR PD 56 paragraph 3.14(see para **CPR PD 56**).

III L&T [15.4]

Continuation of tenancy The effect of the Landlord and Tenant Act 1954 s 24(1) is to continue the tenant's common law tenancy with a statutory variation as to the mode of determination: *H L Bolton (Engineering) Co Ltd v T J Graham & Sons Ltd* [1957] 1 QB 159, [1956] 3 All ER 624, CA, per Lord Denning. But where a guarantor has covenanted that the tenant will pay the rent reserved by a lease, the guarantee will apply only to the rent payable during the contractual term and not the statutory extension: *Junction Estates Ltd v Cope* (1974) 27 P & CR 482; *A Plesser & Co Ltd v Davis* [1983] 2 EGLR 70. So, too, the tenant is not liable for arrears of rent by an assignee after the end of the contractual term, unless he has expressly agreed to pay during any statutory extension, in which case he will be liable for the contractual rent but not any interim rent fixed under the Landlord and Tenant Act 1954 s 24A: *City of London Corpn v Fell, Herbert Duncan Ltd v Cluttons* [1993] QB 589, [1993] 2 All ER 449, CA; affd on the first point, sub nom *City of London Corpn v Fell* [1994] 1 AC 458, [1993] 4 All ER 968, HL.

A landlord whose own tenancy is continued under the Act remains the landlord of any sub-tenant to whom he has let the premises: *Cornish v Brook Green Laundry Ltd* [1959] 1 QB 394, [1959] 1 All ER 373, CA, applied in *Bowes-Lyon v Green* [1963] AC 420, [1961] 3 All ER 843, HL. An underlease expressed to be for longer than the underlessor's own term will not operate as an assignment if the underlessor's term will last indefinitely by virtue of the Landlord and Tenant Act 1954 s 24(1): *William Skelton & Son Ltd v Harrison and Pinder Ltd* [1975] QB 361, [1975] 1 All ER 182, and an underlessee whose tenancy has not yet been terminated in accordance with the Landlord and Tenant Act 1954 Pt II can, on forfeiture of the superior lease, apply under the Law of Property Act 1925 s 146(4) (see para **III L&T [2]**) for the property to be vested in him, even after the date when the underlease would otherwise have expired: *Cadogan v Dimovic* [1984] 2 All ER 168, [1984] 1 WLR 609, CA. Where a tenant remains in possession of business premises at the expiry of the contractual term under a tenancy subject to the Landlord and Tenant Act 1954 Pt II, the prima facie inference is not that a new yearly tenancy has been created by the parties but that the tenant's continuance in possession is attributable only to the statutory extension of his tenancy: *Rainsbury v Bass* (1961) 105 Sol Jo 1009, CA; *Thorne (Sandown Lodge) v New Sherwood School* (1962) 181 Estates Gazette 859; *Lewis v MTC (Cars) Ltd* [1975] 1 All ER 874, [1975] 1 WLR 457, CA; see *Winter v Mobil Oil Co Ltd* (1975) 119 Sol Jo 398 (county court), also cited in 119 Sol Jo 398. If a tenancy continued by the Landlord and Tenant Act 1954 is surrendered by operation of law on the grant of a new tenancy by agreement, the tenant does not, in the absence of any provision to the contrary, lose his right to remove tenant's fixtures annexed during the original tenancy: *New Zealand Government Property Corpn v HM & S Ltd* [1982] QB 1145, [1982] 1 All ER 624, CA. A landlord's right to remove buildings on the demised premises at the end of his own term cannot be exercised while a sub-tenancy is continued under sub-s (1): *Poster v Slough Estates Ltd* [1969] 1 Ch 495, [1968] 3 All ER 257. Nor can a rent review clause be operated during the statutory continuation of the original tenancy after it has been determined pursuant to a break clause: *Willison v Cheverell Estates Ltd* [1995] NPC 101, [1996] 1 EGLR 116, CA.

III L&T [15.5]

Forfeiture For the purposes of the Landlord and Tenant Act 1954 s 24(2), a tenancy is not to be regarded as coming to an end by forfeiture if there is a subsisting claim by the tenant to relief, even though a judgment for forfeiture has been given: *Meadows v Clerical, Medical and General Life Assurance Society* [1981] Ch 70, [1980] 1 All ER 454. Similarly a subtenancy will not be regarded as coming to an end by forfeiture of the superior tenancy if the subtenant could be granted relief against forfeiture by way of a vesting order under the Law of Property Act 1925 s 146(4) (see para **III L&T [2]**), and therefore, by virtue of sub-s (1) above, the subtenancy will continue until terminated in accordance with the Landlord and Tenant Act 1954 Pt II: *Cadogan v Dimovic* [1984] 2 All ER 168, [1984] 1 WLR 609, CA; *Hill v Griffin* [1987] 1 EGLR 81, 282 Estates Gazette 85, CA.

III L&T [15.6]

"Ceases to be such a tenancy" The Landlord and Tenant Act 1954 s 24(3)(a) is applicable only where the tenancy ceases to be one to which Part II of the Act applies before an application for a new tenancy is made: *I and H Caplan Ltd v Caplan (No 2)* [1963] 2 All ER 930, [1963] 1 WLR 1247. If a reversionary lease granted to the tenant severs the reversion expectant on the landlord's own lease so that he ceases to occupy the severed part for the purposes of his business, the landlord is no longer protected by the Landlord and Tenant Act 1954 Pt II and the tenant can serve notice under the Landlord and Tenant Act 1954 s 24(3)(a) terminating the landlord's interest in that part: *William Skelton & Son Ltd v Harrison and Pinder Ltd* [1975] QB 361, [1975] 1 All ER 182. Where a landlord serves notice under s 24(3) on the basis that a tenants company, which has been struck-off the Register of Companies, is no longer trading the landlord may, as a person directly affected, intervene in any application by the tenant's company to be restored to the Register: *Re Blenheim Leisure (Restaurants) Ltd* [1999] 33 LS Gaz R 29, CA.

LANDLORD & TENANT AND HOUSING

III L&T [16]

24A. Applications for determination of interim rent while tenancy continues

(1) Subject to subsection (2) below, if—

(a) the landlord of a tenancy to which this Part of this Act applies has given notice under section 25 of this Act to terminate the tenancy; or

(b) the tenant of such a tenancy has made a request for a new tenancy in accordance with section 26 of this Act,

either of them may make an application to the court to determine a rent (an "interim rent") which the tenant is to pay while the tenancy ("the relevant tenancy") continues by virtue of section 24 of this Act and the court may order payment of an interim rent in accordance with section 24C or 24D of this Act.

(2) Neither the tenant nor the landlord may make an application under subsection (1) above if the other has made such an application and has not withdrawn it.

(3) No application shall be entertained under subsection (1) above if it is made more than six months after the termination of the relevant tenancy.

III L&T [16.1]

Interim rent Under ss 24A to 24D, tenants as well as landlords are entitled to apply to the court for interim rent. The date from which any interim rent is payable is the earliest date for renewal of the tenancy which could have been specified in the statutory notice served by the landlord or tenant. Where the landlord does not oppose renewal the interim rent is set at the same level as the rent for the new tenancy (usually the open market rent), but subject to adjustment where market conditions or the occupational terms of the tenancy change significantly during the interim period. In other circumstances, the rules for calculation of interim rent contained in s 24D(2)) apply.

III L&T [16.2]

Amount of rent Detailed provisions for the assessment of the amount of interim rent are contained in s 24C (new tenancy not opposed) and s 24D (any other case) (see paras **III L&T [16B]** and **[16C]**).

III L&T [16.2A]

Date from which interim rent is payable. Interim rent is payable from the "appropriate date": see s 24B (see para **III L&T [16A]**).

III L&T [16.3]

Procedure The procedure for applying for interim rent is contained in CPR PD 56 paras 3.17 to 3.19 (see para **CPR PD 56**). Where proceedings have already been commenced for the grant of a new tenancy or the termination of an existing tenancy, the claim for interim rent should made in those proceedings by (1) the claim form, (2) the acknowledgment of service or defence or (3) an application notice under Part 23. Where no proceedings have been commenced for the grant of a new tenancy or termination of an existing tenancy, or where such proceedings have been disposed of, an application for interim rent must be made under the procedure in Part 8 and the claim form must include the details prescribed by CPR PD 56 para. 3.19. Under the old law, where an application was not served until more than a year after it had been issued, by which time the tenant had withdrawn his application for a new lease, it was held to be invalid: *Texaco Ltd v Benton and Bowles (Holdings) Ltd* (1983) 127 Sol Jo 307; see also *Coates Bros plc v General Accident Life Assurance Ltd* [1991] 3 All ER 929, [1991] 1 WLR 712, where the practice of issuing an application for a day to be fixed was approved, but it was held that, since the application was in essence an originating process, it had to be served within the period prescribed for originating applications. An application for an interim rent may be struck out for want of prosecution where the landlord has been guilty of inordinate and inexcusable delay, and in any event the six-year limitation period under the Limitation Act 1980 s 9 (see para **III LIM [11]**) applies as from the date of the notice or request mentioned in the Landlord and Tenant Act 1954 s 24A(1): *Morris and Morris v Royel Properties* [1995] CLY 2963.

III L&T [16.3A]

Time limit No application for interim rent will be entertained if it is made more than six months after the termination of the relevant tenancy: s 24A(3).

III L&T [16.4]

Precedents See **BCCP O[603]** for a precedent for a landlord's application, under CPR Pt 23, for determination of an interim rent.

III L&T [16.5]

Assignment of reversion Since an order under this section is not an order for the payment of money but merely fixes the amount of interim rent payable to the landlord for the time being, the court has jurisdiction to entertain an application by a landlord who, during the pendency of the proceedings, has assigned his interest to a person who is joined as a party: *Bloomfield v Ashwright Ltd* (1983) 47 P & CR 78, 266 Estates Gazette 1095, CA.

III L&T [16.6]

Estoppel An order for payment of an interim rent under this section will estop the tenant from subsequently contending that the Landlord and Tenant Act 1954 Pt II does not apply and that he is protected by the Rent Acts as a residential tenant: *De Vere Hotels and Restaurants Ltd v Culshaw* (1972) 116 Sol Jo 681, CA.

III L&T [16A]

24B. Date from which interim rent is payable

(1) The interim rent determined on an application under section 24A(1) of this Act shall be payable from the appropriate date.

(2) If an application under section 24A(1) of this Act is made in a case where the landlord has given a notice under section 25 of this Act, the appropriate date is the earliest date of termination that could have been specified in the landlord's notice.

(3) If an application under section 24A(1) of this Act is made in a case where the tenant has made a request for a new tenancy under section 26 of this Act, the appropriate date is the earliest date that could have been specified in the tenant's request as the date from which the new tenancy is to begin.

III L&T [16B]

24C. Amount of interim rent where new tenancy of whole premises granted and landlord not opposed

(1) This section applies where—

(a) the landlord gave a notice under section 25 of this Act at a time when the tenant was in occupation of the whole of the property comprised in the relevant tenancy for purposes such as are mentioned in section 23(1) of this Act and stated in the notice that he was not opposed to the grant of a new tenancy; or

(b) the tenant made a request for a new tenancy under section 26 of this Act at a time when he was in occupation of the whole of that property

(b) for such purposes and the landlord did not give notice under subsection (6) of that section,

and the landlord grants a new tenancy of the whole of the property comprised in the relevant tenancy to the tenant (whether as a result of an order for the grant of a new tenancy or otherwise).

(2) Subject to the following provisions of this section, the rent payable under and at the commencement of the new tenancy shall also be the interim rent.

(3) Subsection (2) above does not apply where—

(a) the landlord or the tenant shows to the satisfaction of the court that the interim rent under that subsection differs substantially from the relevant rent; or

(b) the landlord or the tenant shows to the satisfaction of the court that the terms of the new tenancy differ from the terms of the relevant tenancy to such an extent that the interim rent under that subsection is substantially different from the rent which (in default of such agreement) the court would have determined under section 34 of this Act to be payable under a tenancy which commenced on the same day as the new tenancy and whose other terms were the same as the relevant tenancy.

(4) In this section "the relevant rent" means the rent which (in default of agreement between the landlord and the tenant) the court would have determined under section 34 of this Act to be payable under the new tenancy if the new tenancy had commenced on the appropriate date (within the meaning of section 24B of this Act).

(5) The interim rent in a case where subsection (2) above does not apply by virtue only of subsection (3)(a) above is the relevant rent.

(6) The interim rent in a case where subsection (2) above does not apply by virtue only of subsection (3)(b) above, or by virtue of subsection (3)(a) and (b) above, is the rent which it is reasonable for the tenant to pay while the relevant tenancy continues by virtue of section 24 of this Act.

(7) In determining the interim rent under subsection (6) above the court shall have regard—

(a) to the rent payable under the terms of the relevant tenancy; and

(b) to the rent payable under any sub-tenancy of part of the property comprised in the relevant tenancy,

but otherwise subsections (1) and (2) of section 34 of this Act shall apply to the determination as they would apply to the determination of a rent under that section if a new tenancy of the whole of the property comprised in the relevant tenancy were granted to the tenant by order of the court and the duration of that new tenancy were the same as the duration of the new tenancy which is actually granted to the tenant.

(8) In this section and section 24D of this Act "the relevant tenancy" has the same meaning as in section 24A of this Act.

III L&T [16B.1]

Assessment of interim rent where new tenancy is not opposed If the landlord does not oppose the grant of a new tenancy and grants a new tenancy to the tenant (whether as a result of an order for the grant of a new tenancy or otherwise) there is, in effect a statutory presumption that the interim rent will be the same as the rent payable under (and at the commencement of) the new tenancy. Either the landlord or tenant may, however, seek to rebut this presumption. If it is established that such rent differs substantially from the relevant rent (ie the rent which the court would have determined under s 34 to be payable under the new tenancy if the new tenancy had commenced on the appropriate date), the interim rent will be the relevant rent. Alternatively, the landlord or tenant may seek to establish that the terms of the new tenancy differ from the terms of the relevant tenancy to such an extent that rent payable under the new tenancy is substantially different from the rent which the court would have determined under s 34 to be payable under a tenancy which commenced on the same day as the new tenancy and whose other terms were the same as the relevant tenancy. In these circumstances, the interim rent is the rent which it is reasonable for the tenant to pay while the relevant tenancy continues by virtue of s 24 of this Act. The same principles of assessment apply as where the landlord opposes the grant of a new tenancy (as to which see s 24D).

III L&T [16C]

24D. Amount of interim rent in any other case

(1) The interim rent in a case where section 24C of this Act does not apply is the rent which it is reasonable for the tenant to pay while the relevant tenancy continues by virtue of section 24 of this Act.

(2) In determining the interim rent under subsection (1) above the court shall have regard—

(a) to the rent payable under the terms of the relevant tenancy; and

(b) to the rent payable under any sub-tenancy of part of the property comprised in the relevant tenancy,

but otherwise subsections (1) and (2) of section 34 of this Act shall apply to the determination as they would apply to the determination of a rent under that section if a new tenancy from year to year of the whole of the property comprised in the relevant tenancy were granted to the tenant by order of the court.

(3) If the court—

(a) has made an order for the grant of a new tenancy and has ordered payment of interim rent in accordance with section 24C of this Act, but

(b) either—

(i) it subsequently revokes under section 36(2) of this Act the order for the grant of a new tenancy; or

(ii) the landlord and tenant agree not to act on the order,

the court on the application of the landlord or the tenant shall determine a new interim rent in accordance with subsections (1) and (2) above without a further application under section 24A(1) of this Act.

III L&T [16C.1]

Assessment of interim rent in other cases The basis of assessment remains substantially the same as under the old law. The interim rent is the rent (assessed by reference to the criteria in sub-ss 34(1) and (2) of the Act) which it is reasonable for the tenant to pay while the relevant tenancy continues by virtue of s 24, having regard to the rent payable under the terms of the relevant tenancy.

For a detailed analysis of the principal elements involved in the test for assessing interim rent payable under s 24D, see *Humber Oil Terminal Trustee Ltd v Associated British Ports* [2012] EWHC 1336 (Ch), [2012] 2 P & CR D27.

Section 24D(2)(a) directs the court to have regard also to the rent payable under any sub-tenancy of part of the property comprised in the relevant tenancy. The court is not precluded from having regard to the existing rent in cases where it is a relevant element in determining the rent at which the holding might reasonably be expected to be let on a tenancy from year to year, but the court is not bound to take the existing rent into account where it is not relevant: *Regis Property Co Ltd v Lewis and Peat Ltd* [1970] Ch 695, [1970] 3 All ER 227. The Landlord and Tenant Act 1954 s 34 (see para **III L&T [27]**) should, however, be applied in the same way as to a hypothetical new tenancy from year to year. The market rent at the beginning of the interim period (or at the hearing: *Lovely and Orchard Services Ltd v Daejan Investments (Grove Hall) Ltd* (1977) 121 Sol Jo 711) should be applied and tempered, where appropriate, by reference to the existing rent: *English Exporters (London) Ltd v Eldonwall Ltd* [1973] Ch 415, [1973] 1 All ER 726, and see *Janes (Gowns) Ltd v Harlow Development Corpn* [1980] 1 EGLR 52, 253 Estates Gazette 799 and *Charles Follett Ltd v Cabtell Investments Co Ltd* (1987) 55 P & CR 36, CA. Account should be taken of a reduction in turnover caused by the removal of a local supermarket: *French v Commercial Union Life Assurance Co plc* [1993] 1 EGLR 113, CA. The interim rent should not be fixed at a figure so close to the new rent as to be in excess of the market value for the earlier part of the interim period: *Conway v Arthur* [1988] 2 EGLR 113, [1988] 40 EG 120, CA. The court has jurisdiction to determine a differential rent by reason of want of repair, but only in very exceptional circumstances: *Fawke v Viscount Chelsea* [1980] QB 441, [1979] 3 All ER 568, CA. On appeal the parties will not be put to the delay and expense of a new trial unless the figure estimated by the judge who has seen the property and seen and heard the expert evidence is so obviously wrong that some substantial wrong or miscarriage has been thereby occasioned: *Halberstam v Tandalco Corpn NV* [1985] 1 EGLR 90, 274 Estates Gazette 393, CA. As to the granting of a stay of execution pending appeal, see *Linotype-Hell Finance Ltd v Baker* [1992] 4 All ER 887, [1993] 1 WLR 321, CA; *Simonite v Sheffield City Council* (1993) Times, 12 January and *Winchester Cigarette Machinery Ltd v Payne (No 2)* (1993) Times, 15 December, CA.

III L&T [17]

25. Termination of tenancy by the landlord

(1) The landlord may terminate a tenancy to which this Part of this Act applies by a notice given to the tenant in the prescribed form specifying the date at which the tenancy is to come to an end (hereinafter referred to as "the date of termination"):

Provided that this subsection has effect subject to [the provisions of section 29B(4) of this Act and] the provisions of Part IV of this Act as to the interim continuation of tenancies pending the disposal of applications to the court.

(2) Subject to the provisions of the next following subsection, a notice under this section shall not have effect unless it is given not more than twelve nor less than six months before the date of termination specified therein.

(3) In the case of a tenancy which apart from this Act could have been brought to an end by notice to quit given by the landlord—

- (a) the date of termination specified in a notice under this section shall not be earlier than the earliest date on which apart from this Part of this Act the tenancy could have been brought to an end by notice to quit given by the landlord on the date of the giving of the notice under this section; and
- (b) where apart from this Part of this Act more than six months' notice to quit would have been required to bring the tenancy to an end, the last foregoing subsection shall have effect with the substitution for twelve months of a period six months longer than the length of notice to quit which would have been required as aforesaid.

(4) In the case of any other tenancy, a notice under this section shall not specify a date of termination earlier than the date on which apart from this Part of this Act the tenancy would have come to an end by effluxion of time.

(6) A notice under this section shall not have effect unless it states whether the landlord is opposed to the grant of a new tenancy to the tenant.

(7) A notice under this section which states that the landlord is opposed to the grant of a new tenancy to the tenant shall not have effect unless it also specifies one or more of the grounds specified in section 30(1) of this Act as the ground or grounds for his opposition.

(8) A notice under this section which states that the landlord is not opposed to the grant of a new tenancy to the tenant shall not have effect unless it sets out the landlord's proposals as to—

- (a) the property to be comprised in the new tenancy (being either the whole or part of the property comprised in the current tenancy);
- (b) the rent to be payable under the new tenancy; and
- (c) the other terms of the new tenancy.

III L&T [17.1]

Landlord's proposals for a new tenancy Where the landlord states in his notice that he is not opposed to the grant of a new tenancy, the landlord must set out in his s 25 notice his proposals as to the terms of a new tenancy

III L&T [17.1A]

Tenant's response to a section 25 notice By virtue of the deletion of sub-s 25(5), the requirement for a tenant to serve a counter notice to a landlord's notice of termination is abolished.

III L&T [17.1B]

"Prescribed form" The forms of notice to be given by a landlord under the Landlord and Tenant Act 1954 s 25(1) are those prescribed in Schedule 2 to the Landlord and Tenant Act 1954, Part 2 (Notices) Regulations 2004, SI 2004/1005. Form 1 in Schedule 2 is to be used where the landlord is not opposed to the grant of a new tenancy. Where the landlord is so opposed, and also in the various circumstances provided for in Schedule 2, the landlord should use Form 2 or one of Forms 7 to 17 as may be appropriate. For precedents, see **BCCP O[600]** and **[600.1]**. A notice in a form previously prescribed but subsequently amended or replaced has been held to be substantially to the like effect as the amended or substituted form of notice: *Sun Alliance and London Assurance Co Ltd v Hayman* [1975] 1 All ER 248, [1975] 1 WLR 177, CA; *Morris v Patel* [1987] 1 EGLR 75, 281 Estates Gazette 419, CA, and therefore to be valid although referring to "receiving" instead of "the giving of" the notice: *Snook v Schofield* [1975] 1 EGLR 69, 234 Estates Gazette 197, CA. The same conclusion was reached in the case of a notice containing an out-of-date note about the county court limit of rateable value, where the rateable value of the premises was within both the limit quoted and the actual limit: *Bond v Graham* [1975] 2 EGLR 63, and see *British Railways Board v A J A Smith Transport Ltd* [1981] 2 EGLR 69, 259 Estates Gazette 766. Leaving a blank when completing the prescribed form will not render the notice invalid if the blank can be filled in by reference to the notes on the form. So where the date of termination was given simply as "15th July" but the year was clear from note 1, the notice was held to be valid: *Sunrose Ltd v Gould* [1961] 3 All ER 1142, [1962] 1 WLR 20, CA. Failure to insert, in the space provided, the date on which the notice is signed is not a material omission: *Falcon Pipes Ltd v Stanhope Gate Property Co Ltd* (1967) 204 Estates Gazette 1243. So, too, failure to state positively that the grant of a new tenancy will be opposed, neither of the alternative sentences in the prescribed form being struck out, will not invalidate the notice if the landlord has inserted in the space provided his reason for opposing the grant: *Lewis v MTC (Cars) Ltd* [1974] 3 All ER 423, [1974] 1 WLR 1499 (affd on different grounds, [1975] 1 All ER 874, [1975] 1 WLR 457, CA). Similarly, the omission of notes which in the circumstances are immaterial, eg a note relevant only where the landlord wishes to oppose the grant of a new tenancy when the landlord is in fact willing to grant one, can be disregarded: *Tegerdine v Brooks* (1977) 36 P & CR 261, CA; and a notice in the then prescribed form requiring the tenant to inform the landlord if he was not willing to give up possession was held to be valid notwithstanding its failure to require him, pursuant to the Landlord and Tenant Act 1954 s 25(4), to state whether or not he was willing to do so: *Baglarbasi v Deedmethod Ltd* [1991] 2 EGLR 71, [1991] 29 EG 137; *Bridgers and Hamptons Residential v Stanford* (1991) 63 P & CR 18, CA. But although omissions taken separately may be insignificant, together they may make a notice invalid: *Montgomery v Sabella Ltd* [1997] EGCS 15, affirmed on appeal in *Montgomery v Sabella Ltd* [1998] 1 EGLR 65, [1997] 09 EG 153, CA. However, an invalid notice may be made effective by the subsequent actions of the tenant: *Keepers and Governors of the Free Grammar School of John Lyon v Mayhew* [1997] 1 EGLR 88, [1997] 17 EG 163, CA. The court will have regard to the contextual background and the response of the reasonable recipient: see *Barclays Bank plc v Bee* [2001] EWCA Civ 1126, [2002] 1 WLR 332, [2002] 1 P & CR 321, where an otherwise valid s 25 notice stating that the landlord did not object to a new tenancy was ignored by the court where the landlord's true intention (which was to develop the property) was quite apparent and was confirmed in a further s 25 notice, setting out grounds of opposition, served 6 days later.

III L&T [17.1C]

Service In *Beanby Estates Ltd v Egg Stores (Stamford Hill) Ltd* [2003] EWHC 1252 (Ch), [2003] 1 WLR 2064, [2004] 3 All ER 184 the court held that a notice under s 25 of the Landlord and Tenant Act 1954 sent by recorded delivery was deemed (by virtue of the operation of s 23 of the Landlord and Tenant Act 1927) to have been served when posted rather than when received by the addressee. This principle is not incompatible with Art 6 and Protocol 1, Art 1 of the European Convention on Human Rights: *CA Webber (Transport) Ltd v Network Rail Infrastructure Ltd* [2003] EWCA Civ 1167, [2004] 3 All ER 202, (2003) Times, 5 August.

III L&T [17.2]

Defective form cured by letter It has previously been held that the prescribed form is not mandatory to the extent that every detail must be filled in. If the form or a covering letter gives the required information to the tenant and is sufficiently authenticated, the notice will be valid. So where the form was unsigned but was accompanied by a letter showing from whom it came, the notice was held to be effective even though the tenant alleged that he did not see the letter in the envelope: *Stidolph v American School in London Educational Trust Ltd* (1969) 20 P & CR 802, CA. The test is whether the notice would be clear to a reasonable tenant and whether it is plain enough not to mislead the tenant: *Carradine Properties Ltd v*

Aslam [1976] 1 All ER 573, [1976] 1 WLR 442. Accordingly, where the date of termination was wrongly given in the notice but it was clear from the covering letter what date was intended, the notice was held to be valid: *Germax Securities Ltd v Spiegal* (1978) 37 P & CR 204, CA.

III L&T [17.3]

Material omissions Similarly, a notice which failed to describe the premises as including a garage site outside was held to be good since the tenant could not have been misled by it: *Safeway Food Stores Ltd v Morris* [1980] 1 EGLR 59, 254 Estates Gazette 1091; so too, was a notice which, while not naming the tenant with complete accuracy, sufficiently identified him: *Bridgers and Hamptons Residential v Stanford* (1991) 63 P & CR 18, [1991] 2 EGLR 265 CA. On the other hand, where the tenancy was of part of a building comprising office accommodation on one floor and storage premises and parking spaces on two other floors, a notice mentioning only the office accommodation was held to be invalid, since a reasonable tenant might have thought that this was all the landlord wanted to take back: *Herongrove Ltd v Wates City of London Properties plc* [1988] 1 EGLR 82, [1998] 24 EG 108.

Subject to the Landlord and Tenant Act 1954 s 41A a notice addressed to only one of two joint tenants is bad, although the irregularity can be waived: *Norton v Charles Deane Productions Ltd* (1969) 214 Estates Gazette 559; but where one of two joint landlords was principal shareholder and managing director of the tenant company, a notice given by the other landlord without his concurrence was held to be valid: *Leckhampton Dairies Ltd v Artus Whitfield Ltd* (1986) 130 Sol Jo 225. A notice which fails to specify or misstates the landlord's name and address is invalid although there might perhaps be an exceptional case in which any reasonable tenant would have appreciated the mistake and known clearly what was intended: *Morrow v Nadeem* [1987] 1 All ER 237, [1986] 1 WLR 1381, CA. So in that case a notice which did not include the name or address of the landlord company but implied that the landlord was a person in fact only the sole director was held not to comply with the statutory requirements. So also was a notice which named only one of two joint landlords, even though they were husband and wife: *Pearson v Alyo* (1989) 60 P & CR 56[1990] 1 EGLR 114, CA. Where, in response to a landlord's notice under the Landlord and Tenant Act 1954 s 25 naming only two of three joint landlords, the tenant gave a counter-notice and applied to the court for a new tenancy but later, in response to a further s 25 notice naming all three landlords, gave another counter-notice but failed to file a second application in the court, it was held that, the first s 25 notice being invalid and the tenant being out of time for making a second application, he could not resist a claim for possession: *Smith v Draper* (1990) 60 P & CR 252, [1990] 2 EGLR 69, CA.

III L&T [17.4]

Legal effect of invalid notice A notice which is not in the prescribed form will, if otherwise valid, operate to terminate the contractual demise and thereafter the tenancy will continue solely by virtue of the Landlord and Tenant Act 1954 s 24(1) (see para **III L&T [15]**), consequently, if a subsequent notice is served in the prescribed form, the date of termination specified therein may, for the purposes of the Landlord and Tenant Act 1954 s 25(3) or (4), be any date not earlier than the date specified in the original notice: *Castle Laundry (London) Ltd v Read* [1955] 1 QB 586, [1955] 2 All ER 154. Likewise a landlord's notice purporting to exercise an option to determine the lease, although not in the prescribed form, will be effective to break the term and the tenancy will then continue in accordance with the Act: *Castle Laundry (London) Ltd v Read* [1955] 1 QB 586, [1955] 2 All ER 154. and *Weinbergs Weatherproofs Ltd v Radcliffe Paper Mill Co Ltd* [1958] Ch 437, sub nom *Re Bleachers' Association Ltd's Leases* [1957] 3 All ER 663. If the notice is in the prescribed form and specifies a date of termination not earlier than the date when the lease can be determined in accordance with the option, the notice will operate as an exercise of the option without a separate notice for that purpose: *Scholl Manufacturing Co Ltd v Clifton (Slim-Line) Ltd* [1967] Ch 41, [1966] 3 All ER 16, CA; *Rene Claro (Haute Coiffure) Ltd v Hallé Concerts Society* [1969] 2 All ER 842, [1969] 1 WLR 909, CA.

III L&T [17.4A]

Estoppel Service of a s 25 notice will not necessarily estop the landlord from contending at trial that the premises were held under a mere licence; see *Wroe (t/a Telepower) v Exmos Cover Ltd* [2000] 1 EGLR 66, [2000] 15 EG 155, CA.

III L&T [17.5]

Date of termination The date of termination specified in the notice need not be one on which the contractual tenancy could be brought to an end, provided that the Landlord and Tenant Act 1954 s 25(2)–(4) are complied with: *Commercial Properties Ltd v Wood* [1968] 1 QB 15, [1967] 2 All ER 916, CA. Where a tenancy ran for three years from a certain day but the rent was payable in advance and the first payment was to be made on that day, it was held that a notice terminating the tenancy on the third anniversary of the previous day was valid, as the presumption that "from" meant beginning at the first moment of the following day was rebutted: *Ladyman v Wirral Estates Ltd* [1968] 2 All ER 197. The fact that the tenancy was granted from the day after the expiry of a previous term will also serve to rebut the presumption, the inference being that the new lease was to commence at the very moment the old one terminated: *Whelton Sinclair v Hyland* [1992] 2 EGLR 158, [1992] 41 EG 112, CA. A notice specifying the last day of the contractual term is good, since that is the day on which the tenancy would come to an end by effluxion of time: *Re Crowhurst Park, Sims-Hilditch v Simmons* [1974] 1 All ER 991, [1974] 1 WLR 583. On the other hand, where a lease for 14 years from 25 March 1953 enabled the tenant to terminate, after seven years, on 25 March 1960, that date was held to be within the lease period so that a notice under the present section purporting to bring the tenancy to an end on 24 March 1967 was invalid: *Central Estates (Belgravia) Ltd v Webster* (1969) 209 Estates Gazette 1319.

A notice served by a head landlord on a sub-tenant terminating his business tenancy on a date after the expiration of the sub-tenancy but before the expiration of the mesne landlord's contractual tenancy is valid if the head landlord is the competent landlord: *Lewis v MTC (Cars) Ltd* [1975] 1 All ER 874, [1975] 1 WLR 457, CA.

III L&T [17.6]

Signature by agent It is not necessary that a notice under the Landlord and Tenant Act 1954 s 25 should be signed by the landlord himself; it will be a good notice if it is signed by the landlord's duly authorised agent or if the landlord's or the agent's name is affixed to the notice by someone writing the landlord's or the agent's signature for him with due authority per procurationem: *Tennant v LCC* (1957) 121 JP 428, CA, but the landlord must be named, and named correctly, in the notice: *Morrow v Nadeem* [1987] 1 All ER 237, [1986] 1 WLR 1381, CA. A notice given on behalf of the London County Council by a person described as their agent was held to be invalid in the absence of a statement therein that he was duly authorised by them to sign it on their behalf or evidence to show that he was authorised in fact: *LCC v Farren* [1956] 3 All ER 401, [1956] 1 WLR 1297, CA.

III L&T [17.6A]

The landlord See s 44, at **III L&T [34]** for the meaning of "the landlord".

III L&T [17.7]

Forfeiture A landlord may serve a notice under this section notwithstanding that he has already brought forfeiture proceedings: *Baglarbasi v Deedmethod Ltd* [1991] 2 EGLR 71, [1991] 29 EG 137.

III L&T [17.8]

Acceptance of rent The acceptance of rent after service of a landlord's notice will not be regarded as creating a new tenancy where the tenant has maintained throughout that the notice is a bad one and has made the payments on the footing that he is a statutory tenant: *Lewis v MTC (Cars) Ltd* [1975] 1 All ER 874, [1975] 1 WLR 457, CA. So, too, if negotiations have been taking place between the parties and the tenant has been holding over pending agreement on a new lease, the landlord may be estopped from denying the tenant's status as a tenant, so as to enable him to apply for a new tenancy although he would otherwise be out of time: *Winter v Mobil Oil Co Ltd* [1975] CLY 1878, and cited in 119 Sol Jo 398. On the other hand the acceptance of proffered rent without explanation will not create a new tenancy where the acceptance of the money is consistent with the landlord's stated aim of not creating a new tenancy but of redeveloping the site: *London Baggage Co (Charing Cross) Ltd v Railtrack plc* [2000] L & T R 439.

III L&T [17.9]–III L&T [17.10]

Notice to quit This expression in the Landlord and Tenant Act 1954 s 25(3) means a notice to quit given by the immediate landlord: Landlord and Tenant Act 1954 s 44(2) (see para **III L&T [34]**). Where that landlord could not give a notice to quit because his own interest is about to expire, the date of termination specified in a notice under this section must comply with the Landlord and Tenant Act 1954 s 25(4) on the footing that, apart from the Act, the tenant's tenancy will come to an end at the same time: *Westbury Property and Investment Co Ltd v Carpenter* [1961] 1 All ER 481. The Landlord and Tenant Act 1954 s 25(3)(a) deals only with the case in which at common law a notice to quit is required but has not been served: *Jones v Daniels and Davidson (Holdings)* [1981] CLY 1513.

III L&T [17.11]

Property comprised in the tenancy Where two properties are demised by the same instrument for different terms at different rents, it is a question of law and construction whether there is a single tenancy or there are two tenancies. If there is a single tenancy, the landlord cannot serve a notice under this section in respect of one of the properties comprised in the tenancy, even though the reversion is severed between the two properties: *Dodson Bull Carpet Co Ltd v City of London Corpn* [1975] 2 All ER 497, [1975] 1 WLR 781. Similarly, where a lease of two properties under a single tenancy gives the landlord a right to determine the tenancy as to one property only, a s 25 notice cannot be served in respect of that property alone and the exercise of the contractual break clause will not prevent the statutory tenancy of the entire holding from continuing: *Southport Old Links Ltd v Naylor* [1985] 1 EGLR 66, CA. So also where five buildings had been let by four landlords under a single tenancy, it was held that four s 25 notices, each served by a landlord in respect of his building or buildings, could not be treated as a single notice in respect of them all, as the tenant might think that he was being invited to consider the buildings separately and to apply, if he wished, in respect of one only, which he could not do; but the notices could be treated as a valid reply to a s 26 (see para **III L&T [16]**) notice previously served by the tenant so as to enable the landlords to rely on s 30(1)(g) (see para **III L&T [22]**): *M & P Enterprises (London) Ltd v Norfolk Square Hotels Ltd* [1994] 1 EGLR 129, [1994] 14 EG 128. It is otherwise if on its proper construction the lease creates two separate demises: *Moss v Mobil Oil Co Ltd* [1988] 1 EGLR 71, [1988] 06 EG 109, CA. See also *Latif v Hillside Estates (Swansea) Ltd* [1992] EGCS 75, CA.

III L&T [17.12]

Grounds of opposition Where a landlord has given notice under this section but the tenant has failed to apply for a new tenancy, the court will not consider, on a subsequent claim for possession, whether the ground stated in the landlord's notice was such that, if the tenant had applied for a new tenancy, it would have enabled the landlord successfully to oppose the application: *Cope v Brandon* [1956] CLY 4867. As to the sufficiency of a statement under the Landlord and Tenant Act 1954 s 25(6), see notes to the Landlord and Tenant Act 1954 s 30: (see para **III L&T [22.1]**).

III L&T [17.13]

Severed reversion A section 25 notice must be given in respect of the whole of the land comprised in the tenancy; so a notice which related to only part of the land and was given by only one of the three severed reversioners on the lease was ineffective: see *EDF Energy Networks (EPN) Plc v BOH Ltd* [2009] EWHC 3193 (Ch), [2009] 49 EG 71 (CS).

III L&T [18]

26. Tenant's request for a new tenancy

(1) A tenant's request for a new tenancy may be made where the tenancy under which he holds for the time being (hereinafter referred to as "the current tenancy") is a tenancy granted for a term of years certain exceeding one year, whether or not continued by section twenty-four of this Act, or granted for a term of years certain and thereafter from year to year.

(2) A tenant's request for a new tenancy shall be for a tenancy beginning with such date, not more than twelve nor less than six months after the making of the request, as may be specified therein;

Provided that the said date shall not be earlier than the date on which apart from this Act the current tenancy would come to an end by effluxion of time or could be brought to an end by notice to quit given by the tenant.

(3) A tenant's request for a new tenancy shall not have effect unless it is made by notice in the prescribed form given to the landlord and sets out the tenant's proposals as to the property to be comprised in the new tenancy (being either the whole or part of the property comprised in the current tenancy), as to the rent to be payable under the new tenancy and as to the other terms of the new tenancy.

(4) A tenant's request for a new tenancy shall not be made if the landlord has already given notice under the last foregoing section to terminate the current tenancy, or if the tenant has already given notice to quit or notice under the next following section; and no such notice shall be given by the landlord or the tenant after the making by the tenant of a request for a new tenancy.

(5) Where the tenant makes a request for a new tenancy in accordance with the foregoing provisions of this section, the current tenancy shall, subject to the provisions of sections 29B(4) and 36(2) of this Act and the provisions of Part IV of this Act as to the interim continuation of tenancies, terminate immediately before the date specified in the request for the beginning of the new tenancy.

(6) Within two months of the making of a tenant's request for a new tenancy the landlord may give notice to the tenant that he will oppose an application to the court for the grant of a new tenancy, and any such notice shall state on which of the grounds mentioned in section thirty of this Act the landlord will oppose the application.

III L&T [18.1]

"Prescribed form" The form of notice to be given by a tenant under the Landlord and Tenant Act 1954 s 26 is prescribed as Form 3 in Schedule 2 to the Landlord and Tenant Act 1954, Part 2 (Notices) Regulations 2004, SI 2004/1005. For a precedent, see **BCCP 0[600.3]**.

III L&T [18.1A]

Tenant's motive for requesting a new tenancy The Court of Appeal has held, reversing the decision at first instance, that a tenant's motive for requesting a new tenancy is irrelevant and that a request is therefore not invalidated by a lack of intention to obtain a further lease: *Sun Life Assurance v Thales Tracs Ltd* [2001] EWCA Civ 704, [2002] 1 All ER 64, [2001] All ER (D) 141.

III L&T [18.2]

Length of term Although a tenant's request must specify the duration proposed for the new tenancy, this may be done by implication, eg by asking for a new lease upon the terms of the existing tenancy. Evidence is not admissible to show that the proposal was made under a mistake and therefore the request is invalid: *Sidney Bolsom Investment Trust Ltd v E Karmios & Co (London) Ltd* [1956] 1 QB 529, [1956] 1 All ER 536, CA. Where a tenant's request gave the wrong date for the commencement of a new tenancy but the landlord indicated that he would not oppose the request and gave no notice under the Landlord and Tenant Act 1954 s 26(6) but applied to the court for an interim rent under the Landlord and Tenant Act 1954 s 24A (see para **III L&T [16]**), it was held that the landlord's assignee, who had continued the negotiations for an interim rent, was estopped from denying the validity of the tenant's request and any defect in it had been waived: *Bristol Cars Ltd v R K H (Hotels) Ltd* (1979) 38 P & CR 411, CA. In *Garston v Scottish Widows' Fund and Life Assurance Society* [1998] 3 All ER 596, [1998] 1 WLR 1583, CA, the court applied the "reasonable recipient" test in *Mannai Investment Co Ltd v Eagle Star Life Assurance Co Ltd* [1997] AC 749, [1997] 3 All ER 352, HL, to a request which made an obvious mistake over the start date.

III L&T [18.3]

Application to the court The tenant has until the end of the "statutory period" to apply to the court (see s 29A (see para **III L&T [21A]**)).

The 1954 Act has been held to be an enactment which allows a change of parties after the end of a relevant period, within CPR 19.5(1)(c). CPR 19.5 is therefore engaged and the court may allow a substitution outside the limitation period in cases of genuine mistake: *Parsons v George* [2004] EWCA Civ 912, [2004] 3 All ER 633, [2004] 1 WLR 3264.

III L&T [18.4]

Landlord's notice The landlord giving notice of opposition under the Landlord and Tenant Act 1954 s 26(6) may, if he has acquired the reversion since the date of the tenant's request, be a different person from the landlord at the date of the request: *XL Fisheries Ltd v Leeds Corpn* [1955] 2 QB 636, [1955] 2 All ER 875, CA. The notice will not be bad merely because it describes the premises as "the building" instead of "the holding": *McMullen v Great Southern Cemetery and Crematorium Co* (1958) 172 Estates Gazette 855. Although separate notices given by the landlords of several buildings let under a single tenancy may be invalid under the Landlord and Tenant Act 1954 s 25 (see para **III L&T [17]**) they may constitute a sufficient counter-notice under the Landlord and Tenant Act 1954 s 26(6) to enable them to rely on the Landlord and Tenant Act 1954 s 30(1)(g) (see para **III L&T [22]**): *M & P Enterprises (London) Ltd v Norfolk Square Hotels* [1994] 1 EGLR 129, [1994] 14 EG 128. See also notes to the Landlord and Tenant Act 1954 s 30 (see para **III L&T [22.1]** onwards). Where, nine months after the landlord borough council had served a counter-notice relying on the Landlord and Tenant Act 1954 s 30(1)(a), (c) and (g), the tenant applied for judicial review on the ground that, as a result of a previous resolution of the council, he had a reasonable expectation that a new lease would be granted, the application was refused as being out of time which there was no good reason for extending: *R v Bexley London Borough, ex p Barnehurst Golf Club* [1992] NPC 43.

If the landlord does not give notice under s 26(6) he can neither oppose the grant of a new tenancy (see s 30(1)) nor apply for termination of the tenancy (see s 29(2)(b)).

III L&T [19]

27. Termination by tenant of tenancy for fixed term

(1) Where the tenant under a tenancy to which this Part of this Act applies, being a tenancy granted for a term of years certain, gives to the immediate landlord, not later than three months before the date on which apart from this Act the tenancy would come to an end by effluxion of time, a notice in writing that the tenant does not desire the tenancy to be continued, section twenty-four of this Act shall not have effect in relation to the tenancy unless the notice is given before the tenant has been in occupation in right of the tenancy for one month.

(1A) Section 24 of this Act shall not have effect in relation to a tenancy for a term of years certain where the tenant is not in occupation of the property comprised in the tenancy at the time when, apart from this Act, the tenancy would come to an end by effluxion of time.

(2) A tenancy granted for a term of years certain which is continuing by virtue of section twenty-four of this Act shall not come to an end by reason only of the tenant ceasing to occupy the property comprised in the tenancy but may be brought to an end on any day by not less than three months' notice in writing given by the tenant to the immediate landlord, whether the notice is given [. . .] after the date on which apart from this Act the tenancy could have come to an end or before that date, but not before the tenant has been in occupation in right of the tenancy for one month.

(3) Where a tenancy is terminated under subsection (2) above, any rent payable in respect of a period which begins before, and ends after, the tenancy is terminated shall be apportioned, and any rent paid by the tenant in excess of the amount apportioned to the period before termination shall be recoverable by him.

III L&T [19.1]

Notice by tenant In the Landlord and Tenant Act 1954 s 27(1) the words "a tenancy to which this Part of the Act applies" refer to the current situation; if the tenant has ceased to occupy the premises for business purposes before the expiration of the contractual term, any notice subsequently served will be of no effect, so that the tenancy will come to an end on the contractual date and not on any later date specified in the notice: *Esselte AB v Pearl Assurance plc* [1997] 2 All ER 41, [1997] 1 WLR 891, CA, not following *Long Acre Securities Ltd v Electro Acoustic Industries Ltd* (1990) 61 P & CR 177, [1990] 1 EGLR 91, CA. New s 27(1A) gives statutory effect to the decision in *Esselte AB v Pearl Assurance plc* (supra).

III L&T [20]

28. Renewal of tenancies by agreement

Where the landlord and tenant agree for the grant to the tenant of a future tenancy of the holding, or of the holding with other land, on terms and from a date specified in the agreement, the current tenancy shall continue until that date but no longer, and shall not be a tenancy to which this Part of this Act applies.

III L&T [20.1]

Landlord "Landlord" has the meaning assigned to it by the Landlord and Tenant Act 1954 s 44(1) (see para **III L&T [34]**), and therefore does not include a superior landlord where the immediate landlord's own tenancy has been continued under the Landlord and Tenant Act 1954 s 24(1) (see para **III L&T [15]**): *Bowes-Lyon v Green* [1963] AC 420, [1961] 3 All ER 843, HL.

III L&T [20.2]

"Agree" To come within this section the agreement must be in writing; see the Landlord and Tenant Act 1954 s 69(2) (see para **III L&T [41]**). But it need not be made with any particular formality provided it is a binding contractual agreement enforceable at law between the parties; it is immaterial therefore that the agreement is not binding on a subsequent assignee of the landlord because of failure to register it as an estate contract: *RJ Stratton Ltd v Wallis Tomlin & Co Ltd* [1986] 1 EGLR 104, 277 Estates Gazette 409, CA.

III L&T [20.3]

Future tenancy There is no distinction between the agreement for a future tenancy referred to in this section and the reversionary tenancy mentioned in s 65(3) (see para **III L&T [38]**): *Bowes-Lyon v Green* [1963] AC 420, [1961] 3 All ER 843, HL, per Lord Hodson.

III L&T [20.4]

Precedent For a precedent for a joint application for court approval of exclusion of ss 24–28, see **BCCP 0[604]**. Such a claim may be started in the High Court or any county court: CPR 56.2(4) (see para **CPR 56.2**).

APPLICATIONS TO COURT FOR NEW TENANCIES

III L&T [21]

29. Order by court for grant of a new tenancy or termination of current tenancy

(1) Subject to the provisions of this Act, on an application under section 24(1) of this Act, the court shall make an order for the grant of a new tenancy and accordingly for the termination of the current tenancy immediately before the commencement of the new tenancy.

(2) Subject to the following provisions of this Act, a landlord may apply to the court for an order for the termination of a tenancy to which this Part of this Act applies without the grant of a new tenancy—

(a) if he has given notice under section 25 of this Act that he is opposed to the grant of a new tenancy to the tenant; or

(b) if the tenant has made a request for a new tenancy in accordance with section 26 of this Act and the landlord has given notice under subsection (6) of that section.

(3) The landlord may not make an application under subsection (2) above if either the tenant or the landlord has made an application under section 24(1) of this Act.

(4) Subject to the provisions of this Act, where the landlord makes an application under subsection (2) above—

(a) if he establishes, to the satisfaction of the court, any of the grounds on which he is entitled to make the application in accordance with section 30 of this Act, the court shall make an order for the termination of the current tenancy in accordance with section 64 of this Act without the grant of a new tenancy; and

(b) if not, it shall make an order for the grant of a new tenancy and accordingly for the termination of the current tenancy immediately before the commencement of the new tenancy.

(5) The court shall dismiss an application by the landlord under section 24(1) of this Act if the tenant informs the court that he does not want a new tenancy.

(6) The landlord may not withdraw an application under subsection (2) above unless the tenant consents to its withdrawal.

III L&T [21.1]

Landlord's application for termination order The landlord may apply to the court for an order for the termination of a tenancy without the grant of a new tenancy if he has given notice of his opposition to the grant of a new tenancy by means of his s 25 notice or by means of a s 26(6) counter notice. Such an application constitutes an opposed claim: see CPR 53.3(2)(c)(ii). Accordingly, the landlord must use the Part 7 procedure and comply with the requirements of CPR PD 56, paras 3.4 and 3.9. Evidence in an opposed claim (including expert evidence) must be filed by the parties as the court directs and the landlord shall be required to file his evidence first (see CPR PD 56, para 3.15) and, unless in the circumstances of the case it is unreasonable to do so, any grounds of opposition shall be tried as a preliminary issue (see CPR PD 56 paragraph 3.16).

III L&T [21.1A]

Wrong person made respondent It was held in *Re Nos 55 and 57, Holmes Road, Kentish Town* [1959] Ch 298, [1958] 2 All ER 311, that where the wrong person had been made respondent to a tenant's application for a new tenancy and it was not a case of mere misnomer or misdescription, no amendment would be allowed after the period mentioned in the Landlord and Tenant Act 1954 s 29(3) had expired. But where it transpired at the hearing of an application that a company and not an individual was the landlord and the company was thereupon substituted as respondent, it was held that, the company being estopped on the facts from denying that the individual was the landlord during the relevant period, the application was not out of time although the period of four months mentioned in the Landlord and Tenant Act 1954 s 29(3) had elapsed: *Garner v Heath Park Engineering Co* [1975] CLY 1872. So, too, if in ignorance of the fact that the landlord has assigned his interest the tenant names him as respondent, the mistake will be treated as a misnomer which can be corrected by amendment notwithstanding that the period mentioned in the Landlord and Tenant Act 1954 s 29(3) has elapsed: *S W Eburne Ltd v Toome Investments* [1977] CLY 445. These cases were decided before the making of CCR Ord 15 r 1 which, by applying RSC Ord 20 r 5(3) (see now CPR 17.4, para **CPR 17.4**), enabled the substitution of a new party to be allowed in certain circumstances even after the expiry of a relevant period of limitation.

So, where the original reversion had been assigned by company A to company B in the same group but company A continued to manage the property on behalf of company B and the tenant mistakenly named company A as landlord in his application for a new tenancy, he was given leave to correct the name by substituting company B, even though the time for making a fresh application had expired, since the mistake was a genuine one and no one had been misled as to the identity of the person intended to be sued: *Evans Constructions Co Ltd v Charrington & Co Ltd* [1983] QB 810, [1983] 1 All ER 310, CA, followed in *Thistle Hotels v Sir Robert McAlpine & Sons Ltd* (1989) Times, 11 April, CA, and *The Sardinia Sulcis and the Al Tawwab* [1991] 1 Lloyd's Rep 201, CA. But see the comments on these cases in *Payabi v Armstel Shipping Corpn, The Jay Bola* [1992] QB 907, [1992] 3 All ER 329, where RSC Ord 20 r 5 (3) (see now CPR 17.4, para **CPR 17.4**), was held to have no application to a substantive as distinct from procedural time bar, and see *Bank of America National Trust and Savings Association v Chrismas, The Kyriaki* [1994] 1 All ER 401, where, in a case to which RSC Ord 20 r 5(3) (see now CPR 17.4, para **CPR 17.4**) did not apply, it was held that a new respondent did not become a party for limitation purposes until served with the originating process. The new rules on amending or adding parties outside the limitation period are in CPR 17.4, (see para **CPR 17.4**) (which has replaced RSC Ord 20 r 5(2)–(5)) and CPR 19.4 (see para **CPR 19.4**) (which has replaced RSC Ord 15 r 6(5) and (6)). The 1954 Act has been held to be an enactment which allows a change of parties after the end of a relevant period, within CPR 19.5(1)(c). CPR 19.5 is therefore engaged and the court may allow a substitution outside the limitation period in cases of genuine mistake: *Parsons v George* [2004] EWCA Civ 912, [2004] 3 All ER 633, [2004] 1 WLR 3264.

III L&T [21.2]

Misdescription of premises Where an originating application refers to part only of the premises comprised in the lease and landlord's notice, the court has power to allow the application to be amended so as to include the remainder of the holding, notwithstanding that the period mentioned in the Landlord and Tenant Act 1954 s 29(3) has expired: *Bar v Pathwood Investments Ltd* (1987) 54 P & CR 178, [1987] 1 EGLR 90, CA.

III L&T [21.3]–III L&T [21.7]

Order For the limitation in the High Court on a Chancery Master or district judge's powers in relation to making final orders under the 1954 Act, see CPR PD 2B para 5.1(j) (para **CPR PD 2B**). The former practice whereby on the grant of a new lease each side was often left to pay his own costs should no longer be followed; costs should be in the discretion of the county court judge to do as he thinks just: *Decca Navigator Co Ltd v Greater London Council* [1974] 1 All ER 1178, [1974] 1 WLR 748, CA.

III L&T [21.8]

Extension of time By CPR 56.3(3) (see para **CPR 56.3**), the claim form for a new tenancy under s 24 must be served within two months of the date of issue and CPR 7.5 (see para **CPR 7.5**) and r 7.6 (see para **CPR 7.6**) are modified accordingly. CPR 7.6 enables a claimant to apply for an order extending the time for serving the claim form. In *Chabba v Turbogame Ltd* (2001) Independent, 15 October, CA, the court was concerned with the question of extension

LANDLORD & TENANT AND HOUSING

of time for serving a claim for a new tenancy under Pt II of the 1954 Act. CCR Ord 43 had not yet been revoked but the court was mindful of the forthcoming impact of CPR 56. The court held that CPR 7.6(2) and (3) (see para **CPR 7.6**) applied to cases where extension of time was sought in Pt II claims but warned that the profession should be aware of the time limits for service and should serve proceedings promptly within the relevant time limits.

The time for making an application for a new tenancy can be extended by agreement; see *Kammins Ballrooms Co Ltd v Zenith Investments (Torquay) Ltd* [1971] AC 850, [1970] 2 All ER 871, HL. For a suggested form of agreement, see (1981) 78 Law Society's Gazette 853. In the absence of special circumstances, negotiations "subject to contract" for a new lease will not be construed as a waiver or estoppel preventing the landlord relying on expiry of the time limit: *Akiens v Salomon* (1992) 65 P & CR 364, sub nom *Salomon v Akiens* [1993] 1 EGLR 101, CA.

The landlord and tenant are entitled to agree extensions to the statutory period within which an application must be made: see s 29B (see para **III L&T [21B]**).

III L&T [21.9]

Withdrawal of application By CPR 38.2 (see para **CPR 38.2**), a claimant may (save in the prescribed cases) discontinue a claim without permission. The procedure for discontinuing is set out at para **CPR 38.3**. The defendant may apply for the notice of discontinuance to be set aside (see para **CPR 38.4**). On discontinuance the normal rule about costs applies and the tenant has to pay the landlord's costs of the whole proceedings: *Lay v Drexler* [2007] EWCA Civ 464, (2007) Times 20 June, [2007] All ER (D) 318 (May).

Where a tenant's request for a new tenancy has been duly made, it cannot be treated as withdrawn so as to enable an application based on a second request to be made in time: *Polyviou v Seeley* [1979] 3 All ER 853, [1980] 1 WLR 55, CA. On the other hand, where the tenant withdraws his application and yields physical possession of the premises under a purported agreement that in return the landlord will grant him an option to take a lease of part of the premises when they have been reconstructed, the court will not regard the agreement as void simply because it does not specify the commencement date, rent or conditions of the term to be granted if these can be spelled out with sufficient certainty: *Trustees of National Deposit Friendly Society v Beatties of London Ltd* [1985] 2 EGLR 59, 275 Estates Gazette 54.

For the effect of discontinuance on compensation, see para **III L&T [30.2]**.

III L&T [21A]

29A. Time limits for applications to court

(1) Subject to section 29B of this Act, the court shall not entertain an application—

(a) by the tenant or the landlord under section 24(1) of this Act; or

(b) by the landlord under section 29(2) of this Act,

if it is made after the end of the statutory period.

(2) In this section and section 29B of this Act "the statutory period" means a period ending—

(a) where the landlord gave a notice under section 25 of this Act, on the date specified in his notice; and

(b) where the tenant made a request for a new tenancy under section 26 of this Act, immediately before the date specified in his request.

(3) Where the tenant has made a request for a new tenancy under section 26 of this Act, the court shall not entertain an application under section 24(1) of this Act which is made before the end of the period of two months beginning with the date of the making of the request, unless the application is made after the landlord has given a notice under section 26(6) of this Act.

III L&T [21A.1]

Time limit for applications to the court Applications to the court under s 24(1) for a new tenancy or (by the landlord) under s 29(2) for an order for the termination of a tenancy must be made before the end of the statutory period as defined in sub-s (2). New s 29B provides that the landlord and tenant may agree to extend the time limit for making an application under s 29A(1). Note that by, virtue of s 69(2) of the Act, the agreement must be in writing.

simply because it does not say that the work could not reasonably be done without obtaining possession of the holding: *Bolton's (House Furnishers) Ltd v Oppenheim* [1959] 3 All ER 90, [1959] 1 WLR 913, CA. The question for the court to consider is whether the landlord's notice has given such information to the tenant as will enable him to deal properly with the situation arising from it: per Hodson LJ. It was held that this test was not satisfied where a landlord's notice stated that he would not oppose an application for a new tenancy if payment of the rent and performance of the covenants were guaranteed by a person approved by him. The corollary was that the landlord would oppose an application if such a guarantor were not found and this was not a ground of opposition specified in the Landlord and Tenant Act 1954 s 30(1): *Barclays Bank Ltd v Ascott* [1961] 1 All ER 782, [1961] 1 WLR 717. On the other hand, where the wording of the notice differed in minor respects only from the language of the Act and referred in one case to "substantial work for reconstruction" and in another case to "substantial works of redecoration", it was held to be sufficient: *Housleys Ltd v Bloomer-Holt Ltd* [1966] 2 All ER 966, [1966] 1 WLR 1244, CA; *Philipson-Stow v Trevor Square Ltd* [1981] 1 EGLR 56, 257 Estates Gazette 1262. So, too, where (before the Landlord and Tenant Act 1954 s 30(3) was added by the Law of Property Act 1969 s 6) the notice said that the landlord intended to occupy the premises for the purposes of a business to be carried on by him, whereas (as his answer clearly showed) the business was to be carried on by a company for which he was trustee, it was held that the notice was not misleading and was therefore valid: *Sevenarts Ltd v Busvine* [1969] 1 All ER 392, [1968] 1 WLR 1929, CA. There is no power to amend a ground stated in a landlord's notice: *Nursey v P Currie (Dartford) Ltd* [1959] 1 All ER 497, [1959] 1 WLR 273, CA. A break clause entitling the landlord to determine the term at the end of a particular year for the purpose of revising the principal rent reserved does not confer on the tenant an option for a new term equivalent to the residue of the original term and on the same covenants but simply prevents the landlord from refusing a new tenancy on a ground mentioned in s 30: *Safeway Food Stores Ltd v Morris* [1980] 1 EGLR 59, 254 Estates Gazette 1091.

LANDLORD & TENANT AND HOUSING

III L&T [22.2]

Landlord's dishonesty If the landlord has no honest belief in the grounds stated in his notice and it is simply designed to harass the tenant and put pressure on him to give up possession, the notice will be treated as a nullity: *Rous v Mitchell* [1991] 1 All ER 676, [1991] 1 WLR 469, CA, where *Betty's Cafés Ltd v Phillips Furnishing Stores Ltd* [1959] AC 20, [1958] 1 All ER 607, HL and *Marks v British Waterways Board* [1963] 3 All ER 28, [1963] 1 WLR 1008, CA were regarded as establishing that a landlord's notice under s 26(6) (see para **III L&T [18]**), is invalid and of no effect if the statement contained in it of the landlord's intention is fraudulent, not honestly made, whether or not the tenant is in fact deceived.

III L&T [22.3]

"Ought not to be granted" These words in the Landlord and Tenant Act 1954 s 30(1)(a) give the court a discretion to refuse a new tenancy where the tenant has failed to comply with his repairing obligations; the court has to ask itself whether it would be unfair to the landlord, having regard to the tenant's conduct as a tenant, to grant a new tenancy, but the fact that the tenant has contracted to sell his interest and any new tenancy would be for the benefit of the purchaser is irrelevant: *Lyons v Central Commercial Properties Ltd* [1958] 2 All ER 767, [1958] 1 WLR 869, CA. So, too, where the court is satisfied that there has been a substantial breach by the tenant of his obligations under the tenancy, the court can for the purposes of the Landlord and Tenant Act 1954 s 30(1)(c) look at all the circumstances in connection with that breach and consider the conduct of the tenant as a whole with regard to his obligations under the tenancy, whether mentioned in the landlord's notice or not: *Eichner v Midland Bank Executor and Trustee Co Ltd* [1970] 2 All ER 597, [1970] 1 WLR 1120, CA. See also *Yossefi v Mussellwhite* [2014] EWCA Civ 885, [2014] 2 P & CR 228: in considering an objection under s 30(1)(a) the court has to ask itself whether, in view of the state of repair of the holding brought about by the tenant's breach, the tenant ought not to be granted a new tenancy. That involves the court focusing exclusively on the state of repair and asking itself whether, looking forward to the hypothetical new term, 'the proper interests of the landlord would be prejudiced'.

Breaches of covenant against nuisance and annoyance, although not serious enough to justify forfeiture of the lease, may afford sufficient reason for refusing a new tenancy: *Norton v Charles Deane Productions Ltd* (1969) 214 Estates Gazette 559. Where the lease provides that the tenant shall not live on the land, the court can take into account under the Landlord and Tenant Act 1954 s 30(1)(c) the fact that the tenant is living precariously in a van parked near the premises, but nevertheless in exercising its discretion the court must ask itself whether the landlord's interest is likely to be prejudiced by the tenant's conduct: *Beard (formerly Coleman) v Williams* [1986] 1 EGLR 148, 278 Estates Gazette 1087, CA. Where a landlord opposed an application for a new tenancy on unanswerable evidence of arrears of rent and breach of user covenant by the tenant but was irregularly allowed at the hearing to amend his grounds of opposition so as to rely in addition on nuisance caused by the tenant, it was held that the judge was nevertheless entitled to hear evidence of nuisance on the issue of discretion: *Hutchinson v Lamberth* [1984] 1 EGLR 75, 270 Estates Gazette 545, CA.

III L&T [22.4]

Persistent delay in paying rent It is not necessary for the purposes of the Landlord and Tenant Act 1954 s 30(1)(b) that the rent should be substantially in arrear or that the arrears should have lasted for a long time; a landlord is not expected to be subjected to the work and irritation of dunning the tenant for his rent: *Horowitz v Ferrand* [1956] CLY 4843. Where the tenant had occupied the premises for 20 years but over the last two years had been constantly in arrear with rent, once having paid nothing for five months, and had made no offer thereafter to pay in advance or to give security, it was held that the judge was amply justified in refusing a new lease: *Hopcutt v Carver* (1969) 209 Estates Gazette 1069, CA. Regular late payment of rent, tolerated by the landlord over a period of years, may estop the landlord from relying on that persistent late payment under s 30(1)(b) until reasonable notice has been given to the tenant that strict compliance with the lease is required and, following such notice, the tenant persists in making late payment: *Hazel v Hassan Akhtar* [2001] EWCA Civ 1883, [2002] 2 P & CR 240, (2002) Times, 7 January. The Court of Appeal will not interfere with a judge's finding, justified by the evidence before him, that there will be no recurrence of late payment of rent: *Hurstfell Ltd v Leicester Square Property Co Ltd* [1988] 2 EGLR 105, [1988] 37 EG 109, CA.

III L&T [22.5]

Breach of tenancy obligations Under the Leasehold Property (Temporary Provisions) Act 1951 s 12, it was held that, where the landlord opposed the grant of a new tenancy on the ground that the tenant had broken the terms of his expiring tenancy, the breach must be such that, if the tenancy were extended as suggested, it would really prejudice the proper interests of the landlord: *John Kay Ltd v Kay and Levy* [1952] 2 QB 258 at 272, [1952] 1 All ER 813 at 818. Where the tenant had used the premises for a translation agency in breach of a covenant in the lease and had been an unsatisfactory tenant, indulging in litigation with the landlord and causing difficulties over the payment of rent, for at least 11 years, the Court of Appeal declined to interfere with the judge's refusal of a new tenancy: *Eichner v Midland Bank Executor and Trustee Co Ltd* [1970] 2 All ER 597, [1970] 1 WLR 1120, CA. Similarly, in *Fowles v Heathrow Airport Ltd* (2008) 16 October, (Lawtel Doc No AC9300858), the Court of Appeal held that there was no flaw in the exercise of the judge's discretion under s 30(1)(c) where the tenant had continually flouted planning controls in his user of the holding and it was clear that the tenant would continue to act unlawfully if granted a new lease. Where the tenant of a lodge and grounds with the option of taking certain fishing rights let the rights year after year at a profitable rate, making a room in the premises available as a drying room in breach of a covenant not to use the premises or any part of them otherwise than as a private residence or for the profession of a veterinary surgeon, it was held that, since the breach was a continuing one, no waiver was to be inferred from the landlord's past acquiescence and in the circumstances the tenant ought not to be granted a new tenancy: *Jones v Christy* (1963) 107 Sol Jo 374, CA. If the tenant alleges that the landlord has consented to or acquiesced in a breach of the tenant's covenant to use the premises as a private dwelling-house only, the onus of proof is on the tenant and a strong case must be made out, something more than mere waiver. The fact that the landlord had bought the premises as an "apartment house" and his predecessor in title was aware that there were six weekly sub-tenancies of furnished rooms was held insufficient to establish that the landlord knew that the tenant was carrying on the business of a lodging-house keeper in breach of covenant: *Bigos v Trustee of JSSRT Charitable Trust* (1965) 109 Sol Jo 273, CA. Where, without regard to legal advice, the tenants pursued a campaign of litigation against the landlord in respect of alleged obstruction of rights of way, thereby exposing the landlord to unreasonable and unnecessary proceedings, that was a 'reason connected with the tenant's use or management of the holding' within s 30(1)(c) entitling the landlord to refuse a new tenancy: see *Horne & Meredith Properties Ltd v Cox* [2014] EWCA Civ 423, [2014] 2 P & CR 297, [2014] 2 P & CR 18.

The landlord is entitled to an order for discovery of the tenant's balance sheets and profit and loss accounts for the period of his current tenancy, as they are relevant to his ability to perform the covenants in the new lease, particularly if the tenant is a limited company and there have been breaches of covenant under the current tenancy: *Re St Martin's Theatre, Bright Enterprises v Lord Willoughby de Broke* [1959] 3 All ER 298, [1959] 1 WLR 872.

III L&T [22.6]

Landlord's intention In determining whether the landlord has the intention required for the purposes of the Landlord and Tenant Act 1954 s 30(1)(f) or (g), the test laid down in *Cunliffe v Goodman* [1950] 2 KB 237, [1950] 1 All ER 720, CA, still affords guidance. "An 'intention' . . . connotes a state of affairs which the party 'intending' . . . does more than merely contemplate. It connotes a state of affairs which, on the contrary, he decides, so far as in him lies, to bring about, and which, in point of possibility, he has a reasonable prospect of being able to bring about by his own act or volition": per A SQUITH LJ, cited with approval in *Betty's Cafés Ltd v Phillips Furnishing Stores Ltd* [1959] AC 20, [1958] 1 All ER 607, HL. See also *Patel v Keles* [2009] EWCA Civ 1187, (2009) Times, 8 December: there has to be some substance in the intended occupation and the occupation has to be more than short-term and see **III L&T [22.9]**. Where the landlord's real purpose is to obtain possession for his own business, he cannot escape the provisions of the Landlord and Tenant Act 1954 s 30(2) by putting forward a flimsy case of reconstruction: *Atkinson v Bettison* [1955] 3 All ER 340, [1955] 1 WLR 1127, CA. Where, however, the landlord has a genuine intention to reconstruct the premises, the fact that he also intends to occupy the rebuilt premises for his own business and could not make that the ground for opposing the tenant's application because he has not been landlord for the requisite period of five years will not debar him from obtaining possession: *Fisher v Taylors Furnishing Stores Ltd* [1956] 2 QB 78, [1956] 2 All ER 78, CA. "The court must be satisfied that the intention to reconstruct is genuine and not colourable; that it is a firm and settled intention, not likely to be changed; that the reconstruction is of a substantial part of the premises, indeed so substantial that it cannot be thought to be a device to get possession; that the work is so extensive that it is necessary to get possession of the holding in order to do it; and that it is intended to do the work at once and not after a time": per Denning LJ. Similarly, where the landlord bona fide intends to demolish the premises, the fact that his main object is to let the land as part of an agricultural holding will not prevent him from relying on the Landlord and Tenant Act 1954 s 30(1)(f): *Craddock v Hampshire County Council* [1958] 1 All ER 449, [1958] 1 WLR 202, CA. Compare, however, *S Franses Ltd v Cavendish Hotel (London) Ltd* [2018] UKSC 62, where the Supreme Court held that a landlord's intention to demolish or reconstruct the subject premises could not be conditional on whether the tenant chose to assert his claim to a new tenancy. The landlord could not oppose a new tenancy under s 30(1)(f) if the proposed works, even if genuinely intended, had no practical utility and the sole purpose of the works was to obtain vacant possession.

In *Dolgellau Golf Club v Hett* (1998) 76 P & CR 526, [1998] 2 EGLR, 75, CA, the court accepted that the case under the Landlord and Tenant Act 1954 s 30(1)(f) was made out even though the details of the scheme, the planning consents and the financial wisdom of the of the project was not clearly established. See, however, *Coppein v Bruce-Smith* (1998) 77 P & CR 239, CA for the position where planning permission has been refused.

In *Ambrose v Kaye* [2002] EWCA Civ 91, [2002] 15 EG 134 it was considered permissible, and in accordance with the overriding objective, to adjourn proceedings after closing submissions so that a transfer of shares, sufficient to give the landlord a controlling interest, could be arranged and proved, thereby enabling the landlord to establish his intention for the purpose of s 30(1)(g).

III L&T [22.7]

Corporate landlord Where the landlord is a limited company, then, unless its functions can be exercised by means of some agent: *H L Bolton (Engineering) Co Ltd v T J Graham & Sons Ltd* [1957] 1 QB 159, [1956] 3 All ER 624, CA, its intention should be shown by a resolution of the directors as recorded in the minutes: *Betty's Cafés Ltd v Phillips Furnishing Stores (No 2)* [1957] Ch 67, [1957] 1 All ER 1, CA (affd [1959] AC 20, [1958] 1 All ER 607, HL), followed in *London Hilton Jewellers Ltd v Hilton International Hotels Ltd* [1990] 1 EGLR 112, [1990] 20 EG 69, CA, or, if the matter is beyond their powers, by a resolution of the company in general meeting: *A and W Birch Ltd v P B (Sloane) Ltd and Cadogan Settled Estates Co* (1956) 106 L Jo 204. See also *Europark (Midlands) Ltd v Town Centre Securities plc* [1985] 1 EGLR 88, where the landlord successfully relied on board minutes, quotations from suppliers and potential suppliers of equipment and an affidavit sworn by the landlord's property director on which he had been cross-examined. The intention may be that of an agent (eg the regional manager of a company) if the contemplated act is within his authority and is not inconsistent with the intention of a superior authority: *Manchester Garages v Petrofina (UK)* (1974) 233 Estates Gazette 509, CA. In the case of a local authority or other corporation a resolution passed by the body is not essential, for its intention can be established by any relevant evidence: *Poppett's (Caterers) Ltd v Maidenhead Borough Council* [1970] 3 All ER 289, [1971] 1 WLR 69, CA. The intention must exist at the date of the hearing of the application but need not have existed when the landlord's notice was given: *Betty's Cafés Ltd v Phillips Furnishing Stores Ltd* [1959] AC 20, [1958] 1 All ER 607, HL. So in that case a resolution passed by the respondent company during the hearing of the application, coupled with an authority to counsel to give an undertaking that the proposed works would be carried out as soon as practicable, was held to be sufficient: *Betty's Cafés Ltd v Phillips Furnishing Stores Ltd* [1957] 2 All ER 223n, [1957] 1 WLR 799; but where a resolution was sought to be put in evidence after both counsel had made their closing speeches, the county court judge refused to accept it: *A and B Gallant Ltd v British Home Stores Ltd* (1957) 107 L Jo 556. Since the time at which the landlord's intention must be shown to exist is the date of the hearing, little weight will be attached to the fact that he then puts forward a revision of the scheme he originally proposed: *J W Thornton Ltd v Blacks Leisure Group plc* (1986) 53 P & CR 223, [1986] 2 EGLR 61, CA. See also *Spook*

Erection Ltd v British Railways Board [1988] 1 EGLR 76, [1988] 21 EG 73, CA. The use of the present tense 'is opposed' in the landlord's section 25 notice, as required by s 25(6), does not affect the rule that the relevant time for having the requisite intention is the date of the hearing: *Hough v Greathall Ltd* [2015] EWCA Civ 23, [2015] 3 WLR 587, [2015] All ER (D) 219 (Jan).

III L&T [22.8]

Preliminary issue For the court's power to direct trial of a preliminary issue, see para **CPR 3.1**. CPR PD 56 para 3.16 provides that, unless in the circumstances of the case it is unreasonable to do so, any grounds of opposition shall be tried as a preliminary issue.

Where the landlord opposes an application under the Landlord and Tenant Act 1954, s 30(1)(f), if it will normally be convenient to try that question first, possibly as a preliminary issue, and postpone to a subsequent occasion the question of the terms of any new tenancy. If a preliminary issue is directed it will provide the hearing at which the landlord's intention must be established: *Dutch Oven Ltd v Egham Estate and Investment Co Ltd* [1968] 3 All ER 100, [1968] 1 WLR 1483. Note, however, that it is not appropriate to dispose of the issue of a landlord's s 30(1)(f) intention on an application for summary judgment where, looking forward to the anticipated date of trial, the landlord can show a real prospect of being able to establish the necessary intention at that future date: *Somerfield Store Ltd v Spring (Sutton Coldfield) Ltd (in administration)* [2010] EWHC 2084 (Ch), [2010] 33 EG 71 (CS), (2010) Times 15 September, Ch D.

III L&T [22.9]

Proof of intention The landlord need not intend to do the work of demolition or reconstruction himself or by his immediate servants or agents; it is sufficient if he proposes to have it done by a building lessee under a firm agreement: *Gilmour Caterers Ltd v Governors of St Bartholomew's Hospital* [1956] 1 QB 387, [1956] 1 All ER 314, CA; *Sheil v St Helens Metropolitan Borough Council* [1997] CLY 3266 but not if he proposes to have it done by a development company and the arrangements are purely tentative: *Reohorn v Barry Corpn* [1956] 2 All ER 742, [1956] 1 WLR 845, CA. See also *P F Ahern & Sons Ltd v Hunt* [1988] 1 EGLR 74, [1988] 21 EG 69, CA; *Spook Erection Ltd v British Railways Board* [1988] 1 EGLR 76, [1988] 21 EG 73, CA; and *Turner v Wandsworth London Borough Council* (1994) 69 P & CR 433, CA. Where a landlord had accepted an estimate of the cost of demolition but had had his outline application for planning permission refused, it was held that he had not proved an intention to demolish within the meaning of the Landlord and Tenant Act 1954 s 30(1)(f): *Joss v Bennett* [1956] CLY 1654, 4858. When planning permission is yet to be applied for, the landlord must show that there is a reasonable prospect, in the sense of a real chance, of its being granted; the test is not whether permission is more likely than not to be granted: *Cadogan v McCarthy and Stone Developments Ltd* [1996] NPC 77, CA. Similarly, the necessary intention was held not to be proved where the development of the premises was dependent on completion of a larger development for which there was no firm arrangement: *Edwards v Thompson* (1990) 60 P & CR 222, CA; but if there is clear evidence of the landlord's intention, the fact that he has not actually entered into a building contract is irrelevant: *A J A Smith Transport Ltd v British Railways Board* [1981] 1 EGLR 54, CA; see also *Capocci v Goble* [1987] 2 EGLR 102, CA, and *A Levy & Son Ltd v Martin Brent Developments Ltd* [1987] 2 EGLR 93. So, too, is the fact that he has not produced the kind of detailed scheme which would enable him to obtain a loan from a finance company, if there is sufficient other material to demonstrate the financial feasibility of his plan: *DAF Motoring Centre (Gosport) v Hatfield and Wheeler Ltd* [1982] 2 EGLR 59, CA. There is no absolute rule that any prospective illegality will prevent a landlord from establishing the requisite intention; it is relevant only to the question whether he has a reasonable prospect of carrying it out. So where the landlord proposed to demolish the premises before putting the development contract out to tender, in breach of a planning condition not to undertake the demolition before a contract for redeveloping the site had been made, it was held that the landlord had nevertheless established a genuine intention to demolish and reconstruct, since there was a reasonable prospect of his getting over the technical difficulty by renegotiating the planning condition or altering his proposed programme of work: *Palisade Investments Ltd v Collin Estates Ltd* [1992] 2 EGLR 94, [1992] 27 EG 134, CA. If the landlord has a genuine intention to reconstruct the premises, his motive in wishing eventually to sell them is irrelevant. *Turner v Wandsworth London Borough Council* (1994) 69 P & CR 433, [1994] 1 EGLR 134, CA. Nor will an intention to occupy the premises for the landlord's own business be defeated by the fact that he has been exploring the possibility of obtaining a tenancy of other premises: *Espresso Coffee Machine Co Ltd v Guardian Assurance Co* [1958] 2 All ER 692, [1958] 1 WLR 900.

An intention by the landlord to occupy the premises for even a short time will suffice for the Landlord and Tenant Act 1954 s 30(1)(g) if, for example, he intends at the end of that time to transfer the business to a member of his family but not if he intends to transfer it to a purchaser for cash. In the latter case the paragraph will not be satisfied if the intended transfer is one which, had it been made before the hearing, would have fallen within the

Landlord and Tenant Act 1954 s 30 (2): *Willis v Association of Universities of the British Commonwealth* [1965] 1 QB 140, [1964] 2 All ER 39, CA. Where the landlord opposed the tenant's application on the ground that he required the premises for use as a garage and for storage purposes in connection with his neighbouring business but in fact wanted the premises so as to be able to include them in the sale of his business, it was held that he had not established the intention requisite for s 30(1)(g): *Honey v Clarke* (1960) 110 L Jo 352. The same conclusion was reached where the landlord of a restaurant said that he intended to occupy the premises for his business as a solicitor, but it was found that the premises were unsuitable for that purpose without reconstruction and he had not applied for planning permission or obtained estimates for the necessary work: *Aperebar v German* (1960) 177 Estates Gazette 197. The fact that the landlord proposes to remove partitions previously separating the demised premises from the rest of the ground floor which he occupies, so that the premises lose their identity, will not negative an intention by the landlord to use the premises for his own business: *J W Thornton Ltd v Blacks Leisure Group plc* (1986) 53 P & CR 223, [1986] 2 EGLR 61, CA.

Although section 30(1)(g) does not require that the landlord should intend to occupy the premises for any particular length of time, there has to be some substance in the intended occupation and the occupation has to be more than short-term. What is short-term will depend on the facts of the case. If it is established that the landlord intends to sell the premises within five years he will be treated as not having the requisite intention to occupy: see *Patel v Keles* [2009] EWCA Civ 1187, (2009) Times 8 December.

LANDLORD & TENANT AND HOUSING

III L&T [22.10]

Demolition or reconstruction "Premises" in the Landlord and Tenant Act 1954 s 30(1)(f) means that part of the holding which is capable of being demolished and of being reconstructed, such as a garage and wall occupying about one-third of a holding which is otherwise unbuilt on: *Housleys Ltd v Bloomer-Holt Ltd* [1966] 2 All ER 966, [1966] 1 WLR 1244, CA. So the excavation and refilling of a site without buildings, used by a local gun club, does not represent reconstruction: *Botterill and Cheshire v Bedfordshire County Council* [1985] 1 EGLR 82, CA. The word "reconstruct" means, in the first place, a substantial interference with the structure of the premises and then a rebuilding, in probably a different form, of such part of the premises as has been demolished by reason of the interference with the structure: *Percy E Cadle & Co Ltd v Jacmarch Properties Ltd* [1957] 1 QB 323, [1957] 1 All ER 148, CA. "It would be difficult to reconstruct something unless first of all there was a construction that was wholly or partially demolished": per O RMEROD LJ, in *Cook v Mott* (1961) 178 Estates Gazette 637, CA. The work should involve the structure of the building in some way and therefore the mere refurbishment or improvement of the interior as by rewiring the electricity supply, installing partitions and new central heating and re-siting toilets does not amount to substantial work of construction: *Barth v Prichard* [1990] 1 EGLR 109, [1990] 20 EG 65, CA. However, it is not necessary that there should be demolition or reconstruction of structural or load bearing features; extensive refurbishment, including the demolition of internal partitions and their reconstruction in different places, was held to suffice in *Ivorygrove Ltd v Global Grange Ltd* [2003] EWHC 1409 (Ch), [2004] 4 All ER 144, [2003] 1 WLR 2090. The court should consider the effect of the work as a whole and not merely whether each item taken individually constitutes work of reconstruction: *Joel v Swaddle* [1957] 3 All ER 325, [1957] 1 WLR 1094, CA; *Barth v Prichard* [1990] 1 EGLR 109, [1990] 20 EG 65, CA. If the work to be done involves some demolition and also some construction or reconstruction, the court should not consider the two elements separately but should look at the totality of what is proposed to be done: *Bewlay (Tobacconists) Ltd v British Bata Shoe Co Ltd* [1958] 3 All ER 652, [1959] 1 WLR 45, CA. The making of a road and the laying of cables, pipes and drains may be "work of construction" according to the circumstances of the particular case: *Cook v Mott* (1961) 178 Estates Gazette 637, CA. So also may be the laying of concrete, eg for the purpose of a runway: *Housleys Ltd v Bloomer-Holt Ltd* [1966] 2 All ER 966, [1966] 1 WLR 1244, CA. The question what is "substantial" is one of degree and therefore of fact. Accordingly, the Court of Appeal will not upset the county court judge's conclusion unless it was clearly wrong or no reasonable man could have come to it: *Atkinson v Bettison* [1955] 3 All ER 340, [1955] 1 WLR 1127, CA. In that case the installation of a new arcaded shop front and the removal of a back wall was held not to be a reconstruction of a substantial part of a building on three floors. See also *Barth v Prichard* [1990] 1 EGLR 109, [1990] 20 EG 65, CA. The decision was otherwise where the greater part of the interior of the whole premises was affected: *Betty's Cafés Ltd v Phillips Furnishing Stores Ltd* [1956] 2 All ER 497, [1956] 1 WLR 678. See also *Bewlay (Tobacconists) Ltd v British Bata Shoe Co Ltd* [1958] 3 All ER 652, [1959] 1 WLR 45, CA; *Whittingham v Davies* [1962] 1 All ER 195, [1962] 1 WLR 142, CA; *Fernandez v Walding* [1968] 2 QB 606, [1968] 1 All ER 994, CA; *Romulus Trading Co Ltd v Trustees of Henry Smith's Charity* (1989) 60 P & CR 62, [1990] 2 EGLR 75, CA; and *Graysim Holdings Ltd v P & O Property Holdings Ltd* [1993] 1 EGLR 96. It is not for the judge to consider objectively whether the premises are ripe for development; it is a question of what the landlord bona fide wants to do: *Becker v Hill Street Properties Ltd* [1990] 2 EGLR 78, [1990] 38 EG 107, CA. The words "could not reasonably do [the work] without obtaining possession of the holding" mean "could not reasonably carry out [the work] without putting an end to such rights of occupation as are vested in the tenant under his current tenancy". If those terms enable the landlord to carry out the work, it is immaterial that the tenant would be prevented from having access to the premises for his business while the work is in progress: *Heath v Drown* [1973] AC 498, [1972] 2 All ER 561, HL. The test is whether the landlord could under the existing tenancy enter the premises to do the work without getting possession or terminating the lease: *Leathwoods v Total Oil (Great Britain) Ltd* (1986) 51 P & CR 20, CA. As to the position where the tenant is prepared to take a new lease on terms giving the landlord access to do the proposed work or a new lease of part of the premises which the landlord does not require for the work, see the Landlord and Tenant Act 1954 s 31A, post. If the landlord shows that the only economic and practical way of getting the work done is for him to do it himself in his spare time and he requires possession for that purpose, he will satisfy the Landlord and Tenant Act 1954 s 30 (1)(f) although contractors might be able to do the work expeditiously without interfering with the tenant's possession: *Jones v Thomas* (1963) 107 Sol Jo 395, CA.

III L&T [22.10A]

Demolition of tenant's fixtures The landlord's intention to demolish tenant's fixtures is not a sufficient ground of opposition if the tenant intends to remove the fixtures at the end of the term: *Wessex Reserve Forces and Cadets Association v White* [2005] EWHC 983 (QB), [2005] 3 EGLR 127, QBD, Michael Harvey QC. Appeal dismissed in *Wessex Reserve Forces and Cadets Association v White* [2005] EWCA Civ 1744, [2006] 13 EG 142.

III L&T [22.11]

Occupation by landlord Where the reversion of the lease is vested in the board of governors of a teaching hospital, an intention by them to sell the freehold to the Minister of Health and to use the premises for the purposes of the hospital is sufficient to satisfy the Landlord and Tenant Act 1954 s 30(1)(g) of the present section: *Hills (Patents) Ltd v Board of Governors of University College Hospital* [1956] 1 QB 90, [1955] 3 All ER 365, CA. So also is the intention of a non-profit-making company in liquidation to occupy the premises until they are transferred to a new chartered company formed to take over its activities: *Willis v Association of Universities of the British Commonwealth* [1965] 1 QB 140, [1964] 2 All ER 39, CA, and similarly the intention of a trustee company, formed to execute trusts for the Roman Catholic Church, that the local parish priest acting as their agent should run the premises as a community centre and church meeting room for members of the congregation: *Parkes v Westminster Roman Catholic Diocese Trustee* (1978) 36 P & CR 22, CA. An intention by an individual landlord that the premises should be used for the purposes of a business to be carried on by a limited company for which he holds the reversion as trustee is sufficient because, by virtue of the Landlord and Tenant Act 1954 s 41(2), the reference in the Landlord and Tenant Act 1954 s 30 (1)(g) to a landlord who is a trustee is to be construed as including references to all or any of the beneficiaries: *Sevenarts Ltd v Busvine* [1969] 1 All ER 392, [1968] 1 WLR 1929, CA.

III L&T [22.12]

Intention to occupy Where the property comprised in the tenancy includes buildings, the landlord cannot succeed under the Landlord and Tenant Act 1954 s 30(1)(g) by showing that he intends to demolish the buildings and use the land for some other purpose: *Nursey v P Currie (Dartford) Ltd* [1959] 1 All ER 497, [1959] 1 WLR 273, CA. It is otherwise where the holding is a vacant site used as a car-park and the landlord intends to occupy it as a car testing centre and to erect a building for that purpose on part of the site: *Cam Gears Ltd v Cunningham* [1981] 2 All ER 560, [1981] 1 WLR 1011, CA. The landlord must intend at the termination of the lease (that is within a reasonable time from the date of its termination) to enter into occupation of *all* the holding but he need not intend to use more than a substantial part for the purposes of his business: *Method Developments Ltd v Jones* [1971] 1 All ER 1027, [1971] 1 WLR 168, CA, commenting on *Nursey v P Currie (Dartford) Ltd* [1959] 1 All ER 497, [1959] 1 WLR 273, CA. See also *J W Thornton Ltd v Blacks Leisure Group plc* (1986) 53 P & CR 223, CA. The intention must be unconditional: *S Franses Ltd v Cavendish Hotel (London) Ltd* [2017] EWHC 1670 (QB), where, following Method Developments, the court held that a period of 12 months from the date of obtaining vacant possession was unreasonable.

In *Cox v Binfield* [1989] 1 EGLR 97, [1989] 01 EG 69, CA, an intention to occupy the premises partly to carry on a business of the landlord's own and partly as a residence was held sufficient, even though the landlord's plans were ill thought out and likely to fail. An intention to use the premises for the business of letting parts as residential flats is not, however, sufficient, as such use could not amount to occupation by the landlord and the objection could not be overcome by the landlord's occupying the premises for a short period during conversion and redecoration: *Jones v Jenkins* [1986] 1 EGLR 113, CA. The judge should consider whether planning permission is necessary for the proposed user by the landlord, and, if so, whether, looking at the matter objectively, there is a reasonable prospect of its being granted: *Gregson v Cyril Lord Ltd* [1962] 3 All ER 907, [1963] 1 WLR 41, CA, and *Cadogan v McCarthy and Stone Developments Ltd* [1996] NPC 77, CA, if not by the planning authority, then on appeal to the Secretary of State acting judicially: *Westminster City Council v British Waterways Board* [1985] AC 676, [1984] 3 All ER 737, HL.

Westminster City Council v British Waterways Board was followed in *Humber Oil Terminals Trustee Ltd v Associated British Ports* [2012] EWCA Civ 596, [2012] 2 EGLR 59, where the Court held that the judge had to assess the objective element of the landlord's stated intention by making the required statutory assumption that it was the landlord and not the tenant that was in possession of the premises, and on the assumption that the tenant's tenancy had determined. See also *Gatwick Parking Services Ltd v Sargent* [2000] 2 EGLR 45, CA: the test is whether the landlord has a real as opposed to fanciful chance of obtaining permission. See *Palisade Investments Ltd v Collin Estates Ltd* [1992] 2 EGLR 94, [1992] 27 EG 134, CA, as to conditional planning permission. In a suitable case the court will accept an undertaking by a responsible landlord, such as a company of standing, to occupy the premises if given possession; the undertaking should then be incorporated in the court's order: *Espresso Coffee Machine Co Ltd v Guardian Assurance Co Ltd* [1959] 1 All ER 458, [1959] 1 WLR 250, CA. For subsequent proceedings in this case see (1961) 177 Estates Gazette 9. But an undertaking will not avail if the landlord has no present fixed and genuine intention to use the land for the purposes of his business. So where the landlord said that he intended to use the land for his business as a farmer but his existing land was only farmed to a 50% capacity, the Court of Appeal refused to disturb the judge's decision that the landlord had not made out his case: *Lightcliffe and District Cricket and Lawn Tennis Club v Walton* [1978] 1 EGLR 35, CA. On the other hand, inability, pending an appeal, to obtain possession of neighbouring property which he plans to include in his scheme will not frustrate the landlord's intention if he can proceed with that part of his scheme which relates to the applicant's premises: *London Hilton Jewellers Ltd v Hilton International Hotels Ltd* [1990] 1 EGLR 112, [1990] 20 EG 69, CA.

A landlord who opposes the grant of a new tenancy on the ground that he intends to occupy the premises for his own business purposes may fail if he does not adduce evidence of the financial viability of his plans. This was the outcome in *Zarvos v Pradhan* [2003] EWCA Civ 208, [2003] 2 P & CR 122, (2003) Times, 4 April. The application to put in fresh evidence of financial viability was rejected on the ground that it could have been adduced at the original hearing. It was further held in that case that it is not necessary for the court to consider first whether there is a genuine bona fide intention before considering whether the landlord has a reasonable prospect of bringing it about.

LANDLORD & TENANT AND HOUSING

III L&T [22.13]

Landlord by recent purchase A freeholder who has, within the five-year period mentioned in the Landlord and Tenant Act 1954 s 30 (2), accepted a surrender of the interest of the tenant's lessor is not precluded from relying on the Landlord and Tenant Act 1954 s 30(1)(g) if the interest would have had less than fourteen months to run at the relevant time and therefore its owner would not have been the landlord within the meaning of s 44 (see para **III L&T [34]**): *Diploma Laundry Ltd v Surrey Timber Co Ltd* [1955] 2 QB 604, [1955] 2 All ER 922, CA (but compare *George Akin Ltd v Ward* [1981] CLY 1510, where the respondent himself had, as head lessee granted the tenant's lease and subsequently within the five-year period purchased the freehold). Indeed, if the surrender was by operation of law, the superior landlord cannot be said to have "purchased" the interest of the tenant's lessor, since the word "purchase" is here used in the same sense as in the Rent Act, namely buying for money: *H L Bolton (Engineering) Co Ltd v T J Graham & Sons Ltd* [1957] 1 QB 159, [1956] 3 All ER 624, CA. The whole transaction should be considered and not merely the consideration for the landlord's interest in the premises to which the application relates: *Frederick Lawrence Ltd v Freeman Hardy and Willis Ltd* [1959] Ch 731, [1959] 3 All ER 77, CA. The fact that during the five-year period the landlord has declared himself to hold the premises in trust for his children does not bring him within the Landlord and Tenant Act 1954 s 30 (2): *Morar v Chauhan* [1985] 3 All ER 493, [1985] 1 WLR 1263, CA. Where there is a contract of sale, the five-year period runs from the signing of the contract: *Frederick Lawrence Ltd v Freeman Hardy and Willis Ltd* [1959] Ch 731, [1959] 3 All ER 77, CA. Where a landlord has died, the interest of a beneficiary under his will is created not on the death of the testator but on the date when the testator became the tenant's landlord: *Gundry v Stewart* [1959] CLY 1818, and see the Landlord and Tenant Act 1954 s 41(2). If the landlord's interest is vested in two persons in equal shares and the interest of one is to be conveyed to the other for consideration, the other cannot rely on the Landlord and Tenant Act 1954 s 30(1)(g) by virtue of the Landlord and Tenant Act 1954 s 41 (2), because half his interest will be by recent purchase contrary to the Landlord and Tenant Act 1954 s 30(2): *Carshalton Beeches Bowling Club Ltd v Cameron* [1979] 1 EGLR 80, CA. A transfer within the five-year period by a holding company to a member within the same group has been held not to fall foul of s 30(2) as the transfer was within the same group of companies: *VCS Car Park Management Ltd v Regional Rlys North East Ltd* [2000] 1 All ER 403, [2000] 3 WLR 370, CA.

A landlord whose own lease has expired during the five-year period but who has remained in possession under a conditional agreement for a new lease cannot, if the condition has not been fulfilled, be regarded as having a new equitable lease under the doctrine in *Walsh v Lonsdale* (1882) 21 Ch D 9, CA, and is therefore not disqualified by the Landlord and Tenant Act 1954 s 30 (2) from relying on the Landlord and Tenant Act 1954 s 30(1)(g): *Cornish v Brook Green Laundry Ltd* [1959] 1 QB 394, [1959] 1 All ER 373, CA. In *Artemiou v Procopiou* [1966] 1 QB 878, [1965] 3 All ER 539, CA, the Court of Appeal held by a majority that the latter part of this decision (namely, that the landlord would have been disqualified if he had had a new lease) was obiter and that "the interest of the landlord" covered not only an interest under one lease but also an interest under a series of leases. For the purposes of the Landlord and Tenant Act 1954 s 30 (2) the termination of the current tenancy is to be ascertained without regard to any interim continuation under the Landlord and Tenant Act 1954 s 64 (see **III L&T [37]**): *Frederick Lawrence Ltd v Freeman Hardy and Willis Ltd* [1959] Ch 731, [1959] 3 All ER 77, CA. The phrase "tenancy or successive tenancies" refers only to tenancies of the tenant: *Artemiou v Procopiou* [1966] 1 QB 878, [1965] 3 All ER 539, CA. A landlord who intends to sell the premises cannot evade the consequences of the Landlord and Tenant Act 1954 s 30(2) by postponing the sale until after the hearing: *Willis v Association of Universities of the British Commonwealth* [1965] 1 QB 140, [1964] 2 All ER 39, CA. Where the applicant had become a sub-tenant of the landlord on the day when the landlord's own tenancy commenced under a lease executed six days previously, it was held that the holding had not been comprised in a business tenancy since the creation of the landlord's interest and therefore, although he had been the landlord for less than five years, he was not precluded from relying on the Landlord and Tenant Act 1954 s 30(1)(g): *Northcote Laundry Ltd v Frederick Donnelly Ltd* [1968] 2 All ER 50, [1968] 1 WLR 562, CA.

A landlord whose status as competent landlord has been interrupted by the operation of s 44(1) cannot aggregate his successive leases in order to satisfy the five-year rule: see *Frozen Value Ltd v Heron Foods Ltd* [2012] EWCA Civ 473, [2012] 3 All ER 1328, [2012] 3 WLR 437.

III L&T [23]

31. Dismissal of application for new tenancy where landlord successfully opposes

(1) If the landlord opposes an application under subsection (1) of section twenty-four of this Act on grounds on which he is entitled to oppose it in accordance with the last foregoing section and establishes any of those grounds to the satisfaction of the court, the court shall not make an order for the grant of a new tenancy.

(2) Where the landlord opposes an application under section 24(1) of this Act, or makes an application under section 29(2) of this Act, on one or more of the grounds specified in section 30(1)(d) to (f) of this Act but establishes none of those grounds, and none of the other grounds specified in section 30(1) of this Act, to the satisfaction of the court, then if the court would have been satisfied on any of the grounds specified in section 30(1)(d) to (f) of this Act if the date of termination specified in the landlord's notice or, as the case may be, the date specified in the tenant's request for a new tenancy as the date from which the new tenancy is to begin, had been such later date as the court may determine, being a date not more than one year later than the date so specified,—

(a) the court shall make a declaration to that effect, stating of which of the said grounds the court would have been satisfied as aforesaid and specifying the date determined by the court as aforesaid, but shall not make an order for the grant of a new tenancy;

(b) if, within fourteen days after the making of the declaration, the tenant so requires the court shall make an order substituting the said date for the date specified in the said landlord's notice or tenant's request, and thereupon that notice or request shall have effect accordingly.

III L&T [23.1]

Form of order Formerly (and by virtue of RSC Ord 97 r9 and CCR Ord 43 r8), where the court was precluded from making an order for the grant of a new tenancy on any grounds specified in the Landlord and Tenant Act 1954 s 30 (see para **III L&T [22]**), the order dismissing the application had to state all the grounds on which the court was so precluded. RSC Ord 97 and CCR Ord 43 have now been revoked. Having regard, however, to the provision in s 37(4) (see para **III L&T [30]**) for the certification by the court of grounds precluding renewal, and the relevance of the grounds to the tenant's entitlement to compensation, it is suggested that the practice contained in the revoked rules should still apply as part of case management.

III L&T [23.2]

Declaration For an example of a declaration made under the Landlord and Tenant Act 1954 s 31(2)(a), see *Adams v Astburys (Chester) Ltd* (1955) 105 L Jo 748, in which the date specified was the date on which the landlord would be ready to begin his intended work of reconstruction. Where events had occurred making it unlikely that planning permission would be granted by the date determined by the judge under the Landlord and Tenant Act 1954 s 31 (2)(a), which was six months after the date of termination specified in the landlord's notice, the Court of Appeal varied the date to three months later: *Accountancy Personnel Ltd v Worshipful Co of Salters* (1972) 116 Sol Jo 240, CA. If a declaration has been made, an application by the tenant for an order under the Landlord and Tenant Act 1954 s 31(2)(b) may be made, presumably by means of an application under CPR Pt 23 (see para **CPR 23**). Following the revocation of RSC Ord 97 and CCR Ord 43, it is not yet clear whether the application is to be made with or without notice.

III L&T [23.3]

Compensation for possession obtained by misrepresentation A landlord who successfully opposes a new tenancy or obtains an order for termination of a tenancy by misrepresentation or concealment of material facts may be liable to compensate the tenant under the Landlord and Tenant Act 1954 s 37A (see para **III L & T [30A]**).

LANDLORD & TENANT AND HOUSING

III L&T [24]

31A. Grant of new tenancy in some cases where section 30(1)(f) applies

(1) Where the landlord opposes an application under section 24 (1) of this Act on the ground specified in paragraph (f) of section 30 (1) of this Act, or makes an application under section 29(2) of this Act on that ground, the court shall not hold that the landlord could not reasonably carry out the demolition, reconstruction or work of construction intended without obtaining possession of the holding if—

(a) the tenant agrees to the inclusion in the terms of the new tenancy of terms giving the landlord access and other facilities for carrying out the work intended and, given that access and those facilities, the landlord could reasonably carry out the work without obtaining possession of the holding and without interfering to a substantial extent or for a substantial time with the use of the holding for the purposes of the business carried on by the tenant; or

(b) the tenant is willing to accept a tenancy of an economically separable part of the holding and either paragraph (a) of this section is satisfied with respect to that part or possession of the remainder of the holding would be reasonably sufficient to enable the landlord to carry out the intended work.

(2) For the purposes of subsection (1)(b) of this section a part of a holding shall be deemed to be an economically separable part if, and only if, the aggregate of the rents which, after the completion of the intended work, would be reasonably obtainable on separate lettings of that part and the remainder of the premises affected by or resulting from the work would not be substantially less than the rent which would then be reasonably obtainable on a letting of those premises as a whole.

III L&T [24.1]

Possession for demolition or reconstruction This section, which was inserted by the Law of Property Act 1969 s 7 to obviate the difficulties shown by such cases as *Whittingham v Davies* [1962] 1 All ER 195, [1962] 1 WLR 142, CA, and *Fernandez v Walding* [1968] 2 QB 606, [1968] 1 All ER 994, CA, prevents the landlord from relying on the Landlord and Tenant Act 1954 s 30(1)(f) (see para **III L&T [22]**) if the tenant is prepared to take a new lease on terms enabling the landlord to exercise such rights over the premises as are necessary for carrying out the proposed work or a new lease of an economically severable part of the holding which is not required by the landlord for the purpose. In an appropriate case it may be desirable for the tenant to indicate his preparedness in his originating application with a view to saving costs, but the tenant is not obliged to make an advance election as to which paragraph of the Landlord and Tenant Act 1954 s 31A(1)(a) or (b), he relies on: *Romulus Trading Co Ltd v Henry Smith's Charity Trustees (No 2)* [1991] 1 EGLR 95, [1991] 11 EG 112, CA. The Landlord and Tenant Act 1954 s 31A is material only where the current lease does not incorporate a right of entry adequate for the landlord's purposes; see *Heath v Drown*

[1973] AC 498, [1972] 2 All ER 561, HL; *Redfern v Reeves* (1978) 37 P & CR 364, CA; and *Leathwoods v Total Oil Great Britain Ltd* (1985) 51 P & CR 20, CA: compare *Price v Esso Petroleum Co Ltd* [1980] 2 EGLR 58, CA. In *Pumperninks of Piccadilly Ltd v Land Securities plc* [2002] EWCA Civ 621, [2002] Ch 332, [2002] 3 All ER 609 the Court held that it is possible, for the purpose of s 30(1)(f) for a landlord to intend to demolish or reconstruct premises which are the subject of an "eggshell" tenancy (ie the demised premises consist merely of an internal non-structural skin) and that, on the facts, s 31A did not assist the tenant.

III L&T [24.2]

Substantial interference The tenant can invoke the Landlord and Tenant Act 1954 s 31A (1)(a) if and only if, with the facilities offered by the tenant, the landlord could reasonably carry out the proposed work (or such part of it as is not covered by a power of entry in the existing lease) without substantial interference with the use of the holding for the purposes of the tenant's business having regard to the extent and length of time of such interference: *Cerex Jewels Ltd v Peachey Property Corpn plc* (1986) 52 P & CR 127, CA. The test was held to be satisfied where the work which could not be carried out under an existing power of entry for repair would take only two weeks: *Cerex Jewels Ltd v Peachey Property Corpn plc* (1986) 52 P & CR 127, CA, but not where premises used for keeping dogs and clipping poodles were so dilapidated that the landlord would have to clear the whole site in order to carry out the proposed work of reconstruction and, even with the facilities offered by the tenant, the landlord could not do this without obtaining possession and interfering for a substantial time or to a substantial extent with the tenant's business: *Mularczyk v Azralnove Investments Ltd* [1985] 2 EGLR 141, CA. See also *Blackburn v Hussain* [1988] 1 EGLR 77, CA, and *Graysim Holdings Ltd v P & O Property Holdings Ltd* [1993] 1 EGLR 96.

III L&T [24.3]

Intended work The "demolition, reconstruction or work of construction intended" is the work of demolition etc referred to in the Landlord and Tenant Act 1954 s 30(1)(f) (see para **III L&T [22]**): *Romulus Trading Co Ltd v Henry Smith's Charity* (1989) 60 P & CR 62, [1990] 2 EGLR 75, CA. The "intended work" in the Landlord and Tenant Act 1954 s 31A(1)(b) means the work which the landlord in fact intends to do. If he bona fide intends to do work which will occupy the whole of the holding, he is entitled to possession and the court cannot inquire whether it would be reasonable for him to achieve his purpose by doing different work occupying only part of the holding: *Decca Navigator Co Ltd v Greater London Council* [1974] 1 All ER 1178, [1974] 1 WLR 748, CA.

III L&T [25]

32. Property to be comprised in new tenancy

(1) Subject to the following provisions of this section, an order under section twenty-nine of this Act for the grant of a new tenancy shall be an order for the grant of a new tenancy of the holding; and in the absence of agreement between the landlord and the tenant as to the property which constitutes the holding the court shall in the order designate that property by reference to the circumstances existing at the date of the order.

(1A) Where the court, by virtue of paragraph (b) of section 31A (1) of this Act, makes an order under section 29 of this Act for the grant of a new tenancy in a case where the tenant is willing to accept a tenancy of part of the holding, the order shall be an order for the grant of a new tenancy of that part only.

(2) The foregoing provisions of this section shall not apply in a case where the property comprised in the current tenancy includes other property besides the holding and the landlord requires any new tenancy ordered to be granted under section twenty-nine of this Act to be a tenancy of the whole of the property comprised in the current tenancy; but in any such case—

- (a) any order under the said section twenty-nine for the grant of a new tenancy shall be an order for the grant of a new tenancy of the whole of the property comprised in the current tenancy, and
- (b) references in the following provisions of this Part of this Act to the holding shall be construed as references to the whole of that property.

(3) Where the current tenancy includes rights enjoyed by the tenant in connection with the holding, those rights shall be included in a tenancy ordered to be granted under section twenty-nine of this Act except as otherwise agreed between the landlord and the tenant or, in default of such agreement, determined by the court.

III L&T [25.1]

Designation of holding "Holding" is defined in the Landlord and Tenant Act 1954 s 23(3) (see para **III L&T [14]**). An order for the grant of a new tenancy must designate the holding as at the date of the order, even if the application has been partly determined on a previous occasion: *I and H Caplan Ltd v Caplan* [1961] 3 All ER 1174, [1962] 1 WLR 55, HL. Where an order for a new tenancy and the lease giving effect to it referred to a shop only, whereas the intention of the parties was that an adjoining store-room granted to the tenant under a subsequent tenancy should be included, it was held that extrinsic evidence was admissible to identify the parcels and a declaration was granted that the storeroom passed under the lease: *I S Mills (Yardley) Ltd v Curdworth Investments Ltd* (1975) 119 Sol Jo 302, CA.

III L&T [25.2]

Tenancy of whole property The landlord must state in his acknowledgment of service if he requires that any tenancy ordered to be granted shall be a tenancy of the whole of the property comprised in the applicant's current tenancy: CPR PD 56 para 3.6(5) (see para **CPR PD 56**). In the county court case of *Atkey v Collman* (1955) 105 L Jo 396, it was held that a landlord was entitled under the Landlord and Tenant Act 1954 s 32 (2) to require that any new tenancy should be a tenancy of the whole of the property although part of it had been sub-let by the tenant with the landlord's consent.

LANDLORD & TENANT AND HOUSING

III L&T [26]

33. Duration of new tenancy

Where on an application under this Part of this Act the court makes an order for the grant of a new tenancy, the new tenancy shall be such tenancy as may be agreed between the landlord and the tenant, or, in default of such an agreement, shall be such a tenancy as may be determined by the court to be reasonable in all the circumstances, being, if it is a tenancy for a term of years certain, a tenancy for a term not exceeding fifteen years, and shall begin on the coming to an end of the current tenancy.

III L&T [26.1]

"Such tenancy as may be agreed" This means a tenancy agreed for the purposes of the tenant's application for a new lease. The agreement must be final and not subject to any suspensive or other condition. So the landlord cannot insist on the grant of a tenancy in terms agreed subject to contract and without prejudice to the tenant's rights under the Act where the negotiations have broken down: *Derby & Co Ltd v ITC Pension Trust Ltd* [1977] 2 All ER 890, nor, where the tenant has failed to apply for a new lease within the time prescribed by the Landlord and Tenant Act 1954 s 29(3) (see para **III L&T [21]**), can he rely on an agreement for a new lease made "subject to contract" in negotiations before and after that deadline: *Akiens v Salomon* (1992) 65 P & CR 364, sub nom *Salomon v Akiens* [1993] 1 EGLR 101, CA. Where an application is settled on terms that a new lease be granted from the date of expiration of the original term at a specified rate, there is no reason why, if the proper construction of the new lease so requires, the rent should not be payable at that rate although the new term cannot begin until the date when the lease is executed: *Bradshaw v Pawley* [1979] 3 All ER 273, [1980] 1 WLR 10. If a tenant's counsel has said in opening his case that the parties have agreed on the grant to his client of a lease for a specified number of years, he cannot, much later in the hearing, indicate that the tenant now desires only a considerably shorter lease, since counsel's opening statement must have either reflected an agreement for a lease for the stated term from which the tenant cannot resile without the landlord's concurrence or amounted to a concession by the tenant which he cannot withdraw without the leave of the court: *Boots the Chemists Ltd v Pinkland Ltd* [1992] 2 EGLR 98, [1992] 28 EG 118.

III L&T [26.2]

"Reasonable in all the circumstances" These words enable the court to consider, when settling the terms (and in particular the duration) of the new tenancy, the fact that the landlord wishes to occupy the premises for his own business although he cannot oppose the application on that ground because he has not been landlord for five years, the question of greater hardship, the risk that the landlord may have to vacate his own premises in the near future and the fact that the tenant is a large and powerful company with many branches in contrast to the landlord who has only one shop: *Upsons Ltd v E Robins Ltd* [1956] 1 QB 131, [1955] 3 All ER 348, CA. The court can also take into account the fact that the landlord wishes to occupy the premises for his business although he cannot at present maintain this ground of opposition under the Landlord and Tenant Act 1954 s 30(1)(g) (see para **III L&T [22]**): *Chipperfield v Shell UK Ltd* (1980) 42 P & CR 136, CA. Where the premises are ripe for development and the work is obviously desirable, the terms of the new tenancy should not impede that development as and when the landlord has the necessary intention and ability: *Reohorn v Barry Corpn* [1956] 2 All ER 742, [1956] 1 WLR 845, CA. If the judge fails to take this factor into account in settling the duration of the new tenancy, his order will be set aside or varied on appeal: *London and Provincial Millinery Stores Ltd v Barclays Bank Ltd* [1962] 2 All ER 163, [1962] 1 WLR 510, CA. The court's discretion is wider than its discretion under the Landlord and Tenant Act 1954 s 30(1)(a), (b) or (c), to refuse a new tenancy and it can therefore take into account the fact that the tenant has contracted to sell his interest and is a mere trustee for the purchaser: *Lyons v Central Commercial Properties Ltd* [1958] 2 All ER 767 at 775, per Harman LJ. Regard should also be had to the length of the previous term or terms on which the tenant has held the premises: *Betty's Cafés Ltd v Phillips Furnishing Stores Ltd* [1957] Ch 67, [1957] 1 All ER 1, CA, affd on a different point [1959] AC 20, [1958] 1 All ER 607, HL, and to the length of time since the expiry of his contractual tenancy: *Frederick Lawrence Ltd v Freeman Hardy and Willis Ltd* (1960) 176 Estates Gazette 11; *London and Provincial Millinery Stores Ltd v Barclays Bank Ltd* [1962] 2 All ER 163, [1962] 1 WLR 510, CA. The landlord is not entitled to insist on the new tenancy being granted for longer than the period which the tenant desires, but where that period is short the court may, in view of the Landlord and Tenant Act 1954 s 36(2) (see para **III L&T [29]**), extend it for a reasonable time to enable the landlord to arrange for the reletting of the premises after the duration of the new lease is known: *Re Sunlight House* (1959) 173 Estates Gazette 311. Even if the landlord does not state in his answer that he objects to a new tenancy being granted on the terms proposed by the tenant, the court must decide on evidence whether those terms are reasonable in all the circumstances: *Morgan v Jones* [1960] 3 All ER 583, [1960] 1 WLR 1220, CA. There is no rule that in normal circumstances the court is unlikely to order the grant of a new tenancy for a term longer than that for which the tenant contends: *Ganton House Investments v Crossman Investments* [1993] CLY 2452. The court has power to insert a "break clause" enabling the new tenancy to be determined during its term: *McCombie v Grand Junction Co Ltd* [1962] 2 All ER 65n, [1962] 1 WLR 581, CA, and should do so where there is a real possibility that the premises will be required for reconstruction during the continuance of the new tenancy: *National Car Parks Ltd v Paternoster Consortium Ltd* [1990] 1 EGLR 99, [1990] 15 EG 53.

III L&T [26.3]

Term not exceeding 15 years As the court may order the grant of a new tenancy for a term not exceeding 15 years, the parties are required to state if there is anyone else who has an interest in reversion in the premises expectant (whether immediately or in not more than 14 years) on the termination of the current tenancy. For the claimant's obligation, see CPR PD 56 para 3.2(7) and for the defendant's obligation, see CPR PD 56 para 3.6(3) (at para **CPR PD 56**). Any such person may apply to the court to be made a party to the proceedings or the court may, if necessary, of its own motion order notice of the proceedings to be given to any such person or order him to be made a party: CPR 19.1(2) (see para **CPR 19.1**).

III L&T [26.4]

Coming to an end of the current tenancy Having regard to the Landlord and Tenant Act 1954 ss 25(1) and 64(1) (see paras **III L&T [17]** and **III L&T [37]**), this means the expiration of the day specified in the landlord's notice or tenant's request or the expiration of three months from the date on which the application is finally disposed of, whichever is the later: *Re No 88, High Road, Kilburn* [1959] 1 All ER 527, [1959] 1 WLR 279. As this date may be uncertain when a new tenancy is ordered, the court in determining the duration of the new tenancy should, rather than nominate the number of years, express the tenancy as being for a term expiring on a specified date: *Chipperfield v Shell UK Ltd* (1980) 42 P & CR 136, CA.

III L&T [27]

34. Rent under new tenancy

(1) The rent payable under a tenancy granted by order of the court under this Part of this Act shall be such as may be agreed between the landlord and the tenant or as, in default of such agreement, may be determined by the court to be that at which, having regard to the terms of the tenancy (other than those relating to rent), the holding might reasonably be expected to be let in the open market by a willing lessor, there being disregarded—

(a) any effect on rent of the fact that the tenant has or his predecessors in title have been in occupation of the holding;

(b) any goodwill attached to the holding by reason of the carrying on thereat of the business of the tenant (whether by him or by a predecessor of his in that business);

(c) any effect on rent of any improvement to which this paragraph applies;

(d) in the case of a holding comprising licensed premises, any addition to its value attributable to the licence, if it appears to the court that having regard to the terms of the current tenancy and any other relevant circumstances the benefit of the licence belongs to the tenant.

(2) Paragraph (c) of the foregoing subsection applies to any improvement carried out by a person who at the time it was carried out was the tenant, but only if it was carried out otherwise than in pursuance of an obligation to his immediate landlord, and either it was carried out during the current tenancy or the following conditions are satisfied, that is to say,—

(a) that it was completed not more than twenty-one years before the application to the court was made; and

(b) that the holding or any part of it affected by the improvement has at all times since the completion of the improvement been comprised in tenancies of the description specified in section 23 (1) of this Act; and

(c) that at the termination of each of those tenancies the tenant did not quit.

(2A) If this Part of this Act applies by virtue of section 23(1A) of this Act, the reference in subsection (1)(d) above to the tenant shall be construed as including—

(a) a company in which the tenant has a controlling interest, or

(b) where the tenant is a company, a person with a controlling interest in the company.

(3) Where the rent is determined by the court the court may, if it thinks fit, further determine that the terms of the tenancy shall include such provision for varying the rent as may be specified in the determination.

(4) It is hereby declared that the matters which are to be taken into account by the court in determining the rent include any effect on rent of the operation of the provisions of the Landlord and Tenant (Covenants) Act 1995.

III L&T [27.1]

Having regard to other terms Where the tenant asked for a new tenancy on the same terms as his current tenancy, which contained a clause restricting the use of the premises, it was held that the new rent should be fixed on the basis of that use, although the landlord would be able to put the premises to a more profitable use at a future date: *Gorleston Golf Club v Links Estate (Gorleston) Ltd* [1959] CLY 1830. The court will not, however, impose a fresh restriction at the instance of the tenant solely for the purpose of reducing the rent payable under the new tenancy: *Aldwych Club Ltd v Copthall Property Co Ltd* (1962) 185 Estates Gazette 219. In having regard to the other terms of the tenancy the court must take into account any special legislation, such as a local Act, which affects the rights of the landlord and tenant: *R v Huddersfield County Court Judge, ex p Beaumont Ashton Ltd* (1967) 19 P & CR 62, DC. The rent should not be fixed until the other terms of the new tenancy have been settled: *Cardshops Ltd v Davies* [1971] 2 All ER 721, [1971] 1 WLR 591, CA. See also s 35 (see para **III L&T [28]**). Where the rent under the current tenancy of part of a building includes a service charge, it is desirable that the new tenancy should provide for a separate service charge proportionate to the extent of the tenant's occupation of the whole building: *Hyams v Titan Properties Ltd* (1972) 24 P & CR 359, CA. Similarly, where the premises form part of a parade, it may be more appropriate for the tenant to contribute to a service charge referable to the whole parade rather than one referable only to his and the immediately adjoining premises: *Amarjee v Barrowfen Properties Ltd* [1993] 2 EGLR 133, [1993] 30 EG 98.

III L&T [27.2]

Statutory sub-tenancy In determining the rent at which the holding might reasonably be expected to be let in the open market, the existence of a statutory sub-tenancy of a residential part of the premises should be taken into account: *Oscroft v Benabo* [1967] 2 All ER 548, [1967] 1 WLR 1087, CA.

III L&T [27.3]

Differential rent Under the Landlord and Tenant Act 1954 s 34(1) the court has power to determine a differential rent, that is one which varies from time to time during the new tenancy according to the state of repair of the premises: *Fawke v Viscount Chelsea* [1980] QB 441, [1979] 3 All ER 568, CA.

III L&T [27.4]

Open market Although a market can still be an open market even though most of the persons occupying premises there belong to a particular profession or engage in a particular trade, an open market does not operate in Gray's Inn: *Baptist v Gray's Inn (Master of the Bench and Trustees)* [1993] 2 EGLR 136, [1993] 42 EG 287. The court should take the passing rent of the property and the rent of the comparable adjoining property into account unless evidence is adduced to show that these rents should not be treated as relevant factors: *Trans-World Investments Ltd v Dadarwalla* [2008] EWCA Civ 480, [2008] 1 P&CR 18.

III L&T [27.5]

Willing lessor The fact that it would be very expensive for the tenant to move is not a consideration. The requirement of a *willing* lessor excludes forcing the rent up on such grounds: *Northern Electric plc v Addison* (1997) 77 P & CR 168, [1997] 39 EG 175, CA.

III L&T [27.6]

Market rents In assessing the rent to be paid for a cattle market a percentage of the auctioneer's gross commission is a more reasonable basis than a percentage of turnover: *Naylor v Uttoxeter UDC* (1974) 231 Estates Gazette 619. As to the rent payable for a stall in a covered market, see *Simonite v Sheffield City Council* [1992] 1 EGLR 105, [1992] 24 EG 134, where it was held that normally a three-year term would command more rent than a quarterly tenancy and a tenancy with a right to assign more than a non-assignable one, but no assessment should be based simply on a belief in future inflation.

III L&T [27.7]

Evidence of tenant's accounts Evidence of the financial results of the tenant's business is admissible with a view to showing what rent could reasonably be expected to be obtained for the premises in the open market but not for the purpose of showing what the tenant can afford to pay: *Harewood Hotels Ltd v Harris* [1958] 1 All ER 104, [1958] 1 WLR 108, CA. This principle applies only to such premises as hotels, petrol filling stations, theatres or racecourses; in the ordinary case of a shop where there are plenty of comparable premises in the neighbourhood from which the open market rent of the premises in suit can be deduced, evidence of the successful or unsuccessful nature of the particular tenant's business is irrelevant and discovery of his trading accounts will be refused: *W J Barton Ltd v Long Acre Securities Ltd* [1982] 1 All ER 465, [1982] 1 WLR 398, CA. A fortiori, the trading accounts of a similar business carried on by the tenant in a totally different area cannot be a guide to the market rent of the premises in question: *W J Barton Ltd v Long Acre Securities Ltd* [1982] 1 All ER 465, [1982] 1 WLR 398, CA.

III L&T [27.8]

Review of rent The Landlord and Tenant Act 1954 s 34 (3), which was added by the Law of Property Act 1969 s 2, makes it clear that the court may include a rent review clause in the terms of the new tenancy, as was done *in Re No 88, High Road, Kilburn* [1959] 1 All ER 527, [1959] 1 WLR 279. In *Janes (Gowns) Ltd v Harlow Development Corpn* [1980] 1 EGLR 52, a rent review clause was ordered, five-yearly, upwards or downwards. See also *Forbuoys plc v Newport Borough Council* [1994] 1 EGLR 138, [1994] 24 EG 156 and the other county court cases there cited, where rent review clauses were ordered, upwards or downwards, although the current tenancies did not contain such a clause, and compare *Blythewood Plant Hire Ltd v Spiers Ltd* [1992] 2 EGLR 103, [1992] 48 EG 117, where an upwards only review clause was ordered. From these cases it seems unlikely that an upwards only review clause will be ordered unless it is clear that market rents have reached rock bottom in the locality. Where there is no realistic possibility of a rental value rising to a level which would justify the cost of a rent review, the court should not include a rent review clause, but may adjust the rent to reflect the accelerated receipt of any increase which might otherwise have been obtained on review: *Northern Electric plc v Addison* (1997) 77 P & CR 168, [1997] 39 EG 175, CA.

III L&T [27.9]

Landlord and Tenant (Covenants) Act 1995 This Act, which inserted the Landlord and Tenant Act 1954 s 34(4), provides for the release of the tenant and the landlord from their respective covenants on an assignment of the lease or the reversion. See the General Notes to the Landlord and Tenant Act 1927: see para **III L&T [4]**.

III L&T [27.10]

Tenant's Improvements By s 34(2) the effect on rent of any improvement carried out by the tenant is disregarded; this will include improvements carried out by a third party provided that the works were arranged, supervised and financed by the tenant: *Durley House Ltd v Cadogan* [2000] 1 WLR 246, Neuberger J.

III L&T [28]

35. Other terms of new tenancy

(1) The terms of a tenancy granted by order of the court under this Part of this Act (other than terms as to the duration thereof and as to the rent payable thereunder), including, where different persons own interests which fulfil the conditions specified in section 44(1) of this Act in different parts of it, terms as to the apportionment of the rent, shall be such as may be agreed between the landlord and the tenant or as, in default of such agreement, may be determined by the court; and in determining those terms the court shall have regard to the terms of the current tenancy and to all relevant circumstances.

(2) In subsection (1) of this section the reference to all relevant circumstances includes (without prejudice to the generality of the reference) a reference to the operation of the provisions of the Landlord and Tenant (Covenants) Act 1995.

III L&T [28.1]

Terms of tenancy The intention of Parliament was to protect the tenant in his business and it would be most unusual to grant a new tenancy preventing him from carrying on an important part of it. So, where a tenant who had been carrying on business as a dealer in new and second-hand clothes had been granted a new lease which excluded dealing in second-hand clothes, the Court of Appeal held that there was no evidence to justify this restriction: *Gold v Brighton Corpn* [1956] 3 All ER 442, [1956] 1 WLR 1291, CA. There must be a good reason for any material departure from the terms of the current tenancy. So, where the tenant's existing lease contained a covenant not to assign without consent, the addition in the new lease of a condition requiring him first to offer to surrender the tenancy to the landlord was held to be burdensome and unwarranted: *Cardshops Ltd v Davies* [1971] 2 All ER 721, [1971] 1 WLR 591, CA. Where a lease contained a restriction on the use of the premises except for the purpose of a club without the landlord's permission but the premises were suitable for use as offices and planning permission had been obtained for that purpose, it was decided that, since the landlord could not reasonably refuse consent to such use, the new tenancy should permit the premises to be used as a club or offices without any exception on the part of the landlord: *Aldwych Club Ltd v Copthall Property Co Ltd* (1962) 185 Estates Gazette 219. In the absence of any special reason a covenant in the current lease against use of the premises except for a specified business without the landlord's consent will not be modified in the new lease by adding the words "such consent not to be unreasonably withheld", if the modification is likely substantially to increase the rent and is opposed by the tenant: *Charles Clements (London) Ltd v Rank City Wall Ltd* [1978] 1 EGLR 47. The burden of persuading the court to change the terms of the current lease rests on the party proposing the change; a small reduction in the basic rent is not sufficient to justify transferring to the tenant of an office block, through a variable service rent, the whole financial risk of maintaining the premises which has previously been borne by the landlord and reflected to a finite extent in the basic rent: *O'May v City of London Real Property Co Ltd* [1983] 2 AC 726, [1982] 1 All ER 660, HL. If it is fair and reasonable having regard to the existing lease and all the circumstances, a term may be imposed that the tenant shall provide guarantors for the due observance of his obligations under the new lease: *Cairnplace Ltd v CBL (Property Investment) Co Ltd* [1984] 1 All ER 315, [1984] 1 WLR 696, CA, but the fact that the existing lease, having been granted before the Costs of Leases Act 1958, required the tenant to pay the landlord's costs of the lease and counterpart does not justify the imposition of a similar term in a new lease ordered after that Act: *Cairnplace Ltd v CBL (Property Investment) Co Ltd* [1984] 1 All ER 315, [1984] 1 WLR 696, CA.

III L&T [28.2]

Court's discretion This section gives the court the widest possible discretion as to the terms of the new tenancy and it can therefore include purely personal rights conferred by the tenant's existing lease, such as the right to exhibit advertising signs outside the building of which the demised premises form part, even though they are not "rights enjoyed by the tenant in connection with the holding" within the meaning of the Landlord and Tenant Act 1954 s 32(3) (see para **III L&T [25]**): *Re No 1, Albemarle Street, W1* [1959] Ch 531, [1959] 1 All ER 250. But the court cannot enlarge the holding by including rights not possessed by the tenant under the current lease: *G Orlik (Meat Products) Ltd v Hastings and Thanet Building Society* (1974) 29 P & CR 126, CA. So, where the original lease contained an option to purchase the freehold which has expired, the court cannot, when granting a new lease, order the insertion of a fresh option: *Kirkwood v Johnson* (1979) 38 P & CR 392, CA. It may possibly be within the court's discretion to include a term that in certain circumstances the landlord may give notice to recover a specified part of the premises: per DANCKWERTS J in *Re No 5, Panton Street, Haymarket* (1959) 175 Estates Gazette 49.

In *Wallis Fashion Group Ltd v CGU Life Assurance Ltd* [2000] 2 EGLR 49, [2000] 27 EG 145 the court, exercising its discretion under s 35, held that a landlord was not entitled to have included, in the covenant against alienation in the new lease, the right to insist upon the tenant entering into an authorised guarantee agreement as a condition of its consent to any assignment.

III L&T [28.3]

Alteration of terms Where the judge in granting a new tenancy for seven years directed that the tenant should be liable for internal repairs and the landlord for external repairs but the order as drawn up by the district judge on the judge's instructions imposed on the landlord a liability for structural repairs also, it was held that the judge should not have altered his decision without reference to the parties and that the reference to structural repairs, which was inappropriate in a short tenancy of seven years, should be omitted: *Bullen v Goodland* (1961) 105 Sol Jo 231, CA.

III L&T [29]

36. Carrying out of order for new tenancy

(1) Where under this Part of this Act the court makes an order for the grant of a new tenancy, then, unless the order is revoked under the next following subsection or the landlord and the tenant agree not to act upon the order, the landlord shall be bound to execute or make in favour of the tenant, and the tenant shall be bound to accept, a lease or agreement for a tenancy of the holding embodying the terms agreed between the landlord and the tenant or determined by the court in accordance with the foregoing provisions of this Part of this Act; and where the landlord executes or makes such a lease or agreement the tenant shall be bound, if so required by the landlord, to execute a counterpart or duplicate thereof.

(2) If the tenant, within fourteen days after the making of an order under this Part of this Act for the grant of a new tenancy, applies to the court for the revocation of the order the court shall revoke the order; and where the order is so revoked, then, if it is so agreed between the landlord and the tenant or determined by the court, the current tenancy shall continue, beyond the date at which it would have come to an end apart from this subsection, for such period as may be so agreed or determined to be necessary to afford to the landlord a reasonable opportunity for reletting or otherwise disposing of the premises which would have been comprised in the new tenancy; and while the current tenancy continues by virtue of this subsection it shall not be a tenancy to which this Part of this Act applies.

(3) Where an order is revoked under the last foregoing subsection any provision thereof as to payment of costs shall not cease to have effect by reason only of the revocation; but the court may, if it thinks fit, revoke or vary any such provision or, where no costs have been awarded in the proceedings for the revoked order, award such costs.

(4) A lease executed or agreement made under this section, in a case where the interest of the lessor is subject to a mortgage, shall be deemed to be one authorised by section ninety-nine of the Law of Property Act, 1925 (which confers certain powers of leasing on mortgagors in possession), and subsection (13) of that section (which allows those powers to be restricted or excluded by agreement) shall not have effect in relation to such a lease or agreement.

III L&T [29.1]

Revocation of order An application under the Landlord and Tenant Act 1954 s 36(2) for the revocation of an order for the grant of a new tenancy should be made in accordance with CPR Pt 23 (see para **CPR 23**). For a case in which the court revoked its grant of a new tenancy but ordered the tenant under the Landlord and Tenant Act 1954 s 36(3) to pay the whole of the landlord's costs, including the costs of the application for revocation, see *Re No 88, High Road, Kilburn, Meakers, Ltd v DAW Consolidated Properties Ltd* [1959] 1 All ER 527, [1959] 1 WLR 279. Where, on an application in respect of two adjoining properties, an order was made for the grant of a new lease of each, it was held that the order could be revoked as to one of the properties only: *Broadmead Ltd v Corben-Brown* (1966) 201 Estates Gazette 111.

III L&T [30]

37. Compensation where order for new tenancy precluded on certain grounds

(1) Subject to the provisions of this Act, in a case specified in subsection (1A), (1B) or (1C) below (a "compensation case") the tenant shall be entitled on quitting the holding to recover from the landlord by way of compensation an amount determined in accordance with this section.

(1A) The first compensation case is where on the making of an application by the tenant under section 24(1) of this Act the court is precluded (whether by subsection (1) or subsection (2) of section 31 of this Act) from making an order for the grant of a new tenancy by reason of any of the grounds specified in paragraphs (e), (f) and (g) of section 30(1) of this Act (the "compensation grounds") and not of any grounds specified in any other paragraph of section 30(1).

(1B) The second compensation case is where on the making of an application under section 29(2) of this Act the court is precluded (whether by section 29(4)(a) or section 31(2) of this Act) from making an order for the grant of a new tenancy by reason of any of the compensation grounds and not of any other grounds specified in section 30(1) of this Act.

(1C) The third compensation case is where—

(a) the landlord's notice under section 25 of this Act or, as the case may be, under section 26(6) of this Act, states his opposition to the grant of a new tenancy on any of the compensation grounds and not on any other grounds specified in section 30(1) of this Act; and

(b) either—

(i) no application is made by the tenant under section 24(1) of this Act or by the landlord under section 29(2) of this Act; or

(ii) such an application is made but is subsequently withdrawn.

(2) Subject to the following provisions of this section, compensation under this section shall be as follows, that is to say,—

(a) where the conditions specified in the next following subsection are satisfied in relation to the whole of the holding it shall be the product of the appropriate multiplier and twice the rateable value of the holding;

(b) in any other case it shall be the product of the appropriate multiplier and the rateable value of the holding.

(3) The said conditions are—

(a) that, during the whole of the fourteen years immediately preceding the termination of the current tenancy, premises being or comprised in the holding have been occupied for the purposes of a business carried on by the occupier or for those and other purposes;

(b) that, if during those fourteen years there was a change in the occupier of the premises, the person who was the occupier immediately after the change was the successor to the business carried on by the person who was the occupier immediately before the change.

(3A) If the conditions specified in subsection (3) above are satisfied in relation to part of the holding but not in relation to the other part, the amount of compensation shall be the aggregate of sums calculated separately as compensation in respect of each part, and accordingly, for the purpose of calculating compensation in respect of a part any reference in this section to the holding shall be construed as a reference to that part.

(3B) Where section 44(1A) of this Act applies, the compensation shall be determined separately for each part and compensation determined for any part shall be recoverable only from the person who is the owner of an interest in that part which fulfils the conditions specified in section 44(1) of this Act.

(4) Where the court is precluded from making an order for the grant of a new tenancy under this Part of this Act in a compensation case, the court shall on the application of the tenant certify that fact.

(5) For the purposes of subsection (2) of this section the rateable value of the holding shall be determined as follows:—

- (a) where in the valuation list in force at the date on which the landlord's notice under section twenty-five or, as the case may be, subsection (6) of section twenty-six of this Act is given a value is then shown as the annual value (as hereinafter defined) of the holding, the rateable value of the holding shall be taken to be that value;
- (b) where no such value is so shown with respect to the holding but such a value or such values is or are so shown with respect to premises comprised in or comprising the holding or part of it, the rateable value of the holding shall be taken to be such value as is found by a proper apportionment or aggregation of the value or values so shown;
- (c) where the rateable value of the holding cannot be ascertained in accordance with the foregoing paragraphs of this subsection, it shall be taken to be the value which, apart from any exemption from assessment to rates, would on a proper assessment be the value to be entered in the said valuation list as the annual value of the holding;

and any dispute arising, whether in proceedings before the court or otherwise, as to the determination for those purposes of the rateable value of the holding shall be referred to the Commissioners of Inland Revenue for decision by a valuation officer.

An appeal shall lie to the Upper Tribunal from any decision of a valuation officer under this subsection, but subject thereto any such decision shall be final.

(5A) If part of the holding is domestic property, as defined in section 66 of the Local Government Finance Act 1988,—

- (a) the domestic property shall be disregarded in determining the rateable value of the holding under subsection (5) of this section; and
- (b) if, on the date specified in subsection (5)(a) of this section, the tenant occupied the whole or any part of the domestic property, the amount of compensation to which he is entitled under subsection (1) of this section shall be increased by the addition of a sum equal to his reasonable expenses in removing from the domestic property.

(5B) Any question as to the amount of the sum referred to in paragraph (b) of subsection (5A) of this section shall be determined by agreement between the landlord and the tenant or, in default of agreement, by the court.

(5C) If the whole of the holding is domestic property, as defined in section 66 of the Local Government Finance Act 1988, for the purposes of subsection (2) of this section the rateable value of the holding shall be taken to be an amount equal to the rent at which it is estimated the holding might reasonably be expected to let from year to year if the tenant undertook to pay all usual tenant's rates and taxes and to bear the cost of the repairs and insurance and the other expenses (if any) necessary to maintain the holding in a state to command that rent.

(5D) The following provisions shall have effect as regards a determination of an amount mentioned in subsection (5C) of this section—

- (a) the date by reference to which such a determination is to be made is the date on which the landlord's notice under section 25 or, as the case may be, subsection (6) of section 26 of this Act is given;
- (b) any dispute arising, whether in proceedings before the court or otherwise, as to such a determination shall be referred to the Commissioners of Inland Revenue for decision by a valuation officer;

of material facts, the court may order the landlord to pay to the tenant such sum as appears sufficient as compensation for damage or loss sustained by the tenant as the result of the order or refusal.

(2) Where—

(a) the tenant has quit the holding—

(i) after making but withdrawing an application under section 24(1) of this Act; or

(ii) without making such an application; and

(b) it is made to appear to the court that he did so by reason of misrepresentation or the concealment of material facts,

the court may order the landlord to pay to the tenant such sum as appears sufficient as compensation for damage or loss sustained by the tenant as the result of quitting the holding.

III L&T [31]

38. Restriction on agreements excluding provisions of Part II

(1) Any agreement relating to a tenancy to which this Part of this Act applies (whether contained in the instrument creating the tenancy or not) shall be void (except as provided by section 38A of this Act) in so far as it purports to preclude the tenant from making an application or request under this Part of this Act or provides for the termination or the surrender of the tenancy in the event of his making such an application or request or for the imposition of any penalty or disability on the tenant in that event.

(2) Where—

(a) during the whole of the five years immediately preceding the date on which the tenant under a tenancy to which this Part of this Act applies is to quit the holding, premises being or comprised in the holding have been occupied for the purposes of a business carried on by the occupier or for those and other purposes, and

(b) if during those five years there was a change in the occupier of the premises, the person who was the occupier immediately after the change was the successor to the business carried on by the person who was the occupier immediately before the change,

any agreement (whether contained in the instrument creating the tenancy or not and whether made before or after the termination of that tenancy) which purports to exclude or reduce compensation under the last foregoing section shall to that extent be void, so however that this subsection shall not affect any agreement as to the amount of any such compensation which is made after the right to compensation has accrued.

(3) In a case not falling within the last foregoing subsection the right to compensation conferred by the last foregoing section may be excluded or modified by agreement.

III L&T [31.1]

Contracting out The landlord is required to serve a prescribed form of notice on the tenant at least 14 days before the parties enter into such an agreement. The tenant may then sign a simple declaration that he has received and accepted the consequences of the notice. If the parties wish to waive the 14 day period, the tenant must sign a statutory declaration rather than the simple declaration. In the case of an agreement to exclude security of tenure, the declaration must be made before the tenant enters into the tenancy or becomes contractually bound to do so. In the case of an agreement to surrender, the declaration must be made before the agreement is entered into. The prescribed forms of the notice, the simple declaration and the statutory declaration are set out in full in Schedules 1 to 4 to the Regulatory Reform (Business Tenancies)(England and Wales) Order 2003, SI 2003/3096.

LANDLORD & TENANT AND HOUSING

(ii) permit a home business to be carried on in the dwelling-house, or permit the immediate landlord to give consent for a home business to be carried on in the dwelling-house, and

(iii) do not permit a business other than a home business to be carried on in the dwelling-house.

(3) The terms of a tenancy permit the carrying on of a home business if they permit the carrying on of a particular home business, a particular description of home business or any home business.

(4) A "home business" is a business of a kind which might reasonably be carried on at home.

(5) A business is not to be treated as a home business if it involves the supply of alcohol for consumption on licensed premises which form all or part of the dwelling-house.

(6) The appropriate national authority may by regulations prescribe cases in which businesses are, or are not, to be treated as home businesses.

(7) Regulations under this section—

(a) may include transitional or saving provision,

(b) may make different provision for different purposes,

(c) are to be made by statutory instrument,

(d) may not be made unless—

(i) in the case of regulations made by the Secretary of State, a draft of the statutory instrument containing the regulations has been laid before Parliament and approved by a resolution of each House of Parliament,

(ii) in the case of regulations made by the Welsh Ministers, a draft of the statutory instrument containing the regulations has been laid before, and approved by a resolution of, the National Assembly for Wales.

(8) For the purposes of this section, a dwelling-house which is let for mixed residential and business use is capable of being let as a dwelling.

(9) If, under a tenancy, a dwelling-house is let together with other land, then, for the purposes of this section—

(a) if the main purpose of the letting is the provision of a home for the tenant, the other land is to be treated as part of the dwelling-house, and

(b) if the main purpose of the letting is not as mentioned in paragraph (a), the tenancy is to be treated as not being one under which a dwelling-house is let as a separate dwelling.

(10) In this section—

"the appropriate national authority" means—

(a) in relation to England, the Secretary of State, and

(b) in relation to Wales, the Welsh Ministers;

"dwelling-house" may be a house or part of a house;

"let" includes sub-let;

"licensed premises" has the same meaning as in the Licensing Act 2003 (see section 193 of that Act);

"supply of alcohol" has the same meaning as in the Licensing Act 2003 (see section 14 of that Act).

III L&T [33]

43A. Jurisdiction of county court to make declaration

Where the rateable value of the holding is such that the jurisdiction conferred on the court by any other provision of this Part of this Act is, by virtue of section 63 of this Act, exercisable by the county court, the county court shall have jurisdiction (but without prejudice to the jurisdiction of the High Court) to make any declaration as to any matter arising under this Part of this Act, whether or not any other relief is sought in the proceedings.

III L&T [34]

44. Meaning of "the landlord" in Part II, and provisions as to mesne landlords, etc

(1) Subject to subsections (1A) and (2) below, in this Part of this Act the expression "the landlord", in relation to a tenancy (in this section referred to as "the relevant tenancy"), means the person (whether or not he is the immediate landlord) who is the owner of that interest in the property comprised in the relevant tenancy which for the time being fulfils the following conditions, that is to say—

(a) that it is an interest in reversion expectant (whether immediately or not) on the termination of the relevant tenancy, and

(b) that it is either the fee simple or a tenancy which will not come to an end within fourteen months or less by effluxion of time, and, if it is such a tenancy, that no notice has been given by virtue of which it will come to an end within fourteen months or any further time by which it may be continued under section 36 (2) or section 64 of this Act,

and is not itself in reversion expectant (whether immediately or not) on an interest which fulfils those conditions.

(1A) The reference in subsection (1) above to a person who is the owner of an interest such as is mentioned in that subsection is to be construed, where different persons own such interests in different parts of the property, as a reference to all those persons collectively.

(2) References in this Part of this Act to a notice to quit given by the landlord are references to a notice to quit given by the immediate landlord.

(3) The provisions of the Sixth Schedule to this Act shall have effect for the application of this Part of this Act to cases where the immediate landlord of the tenant is not the owner of the fee simple in respect of the holding.

III L&T [34.1]

Tenancy A tenancy for the purposes of the Landlord and Tenant Act 1954 s 44(1)(b) includes a tenancy continuing by virtue of the Landlord and Tenant Act 1954 s 24(1) (see para **III L&T [15]**), after the expiry of the landlord's contractual term: *Cornish v Brook Green Laundry Ltd* [1959] 1 QB 394, [1959] 1 All ER 373, CA, applied in *Bowes-Lyon v Green* [1963] AC 420, [1961] 3 All ER 843, HL. Formerly the Landlord and Tenant Act 1954 s 44(1)(b) referred to a tenancy which would not come to an end within 14 months or less by effluxion of time "or by virtue of a notice to quit already given by the landlord". It was held that a mesne landlord who had received notice under the Landlord and Tenant Act 1954 s 25(1) (see para **III L&T [17]**), terminating his own tenancy within 14 months was not within the definition of "landlord", since a notice under the Landlord and Tenant Act 1954 s 25 was a notice to quit for the purposes of this provision: *Rene Claro (Haute Coiffure) Ltd v Hallé Concerts Society* [1969] 2 All ER 842, [1959] 1 WLR 909, CA. The Law of Property Act 1969 s 14 substituted for the words quoted above the words "and, if it is such a tenancy" to the end of the paragraph. The effect is to make a superior landlord the competent landlord of a sub-tenant not only where the superior landlord gives notice under the Landlord and Tenant Act 1954 s 25(1), to the mesne landlord, but also where the mesne landlord serves on the superior landlord a request for a new tenancy under the Landlord and Tenant Act 1954 s 26(1) (see para **III L&T [18]**). See *Shelley v United Artists Corpn Ltd* (1990) 60 P & CR 241, [1990] 1 EGLR 103, CA.

III L&T [34.1A]

Competent landlord For the purposes of s 25 of the Landlord and Tenant Act 1954, the registered proprietor of the lease must be treated as the competent landlord by virtue of the Land Registration Act 1925 ss 9 and 69: *Prudential Assurance Co Ltd v Eden Restaurants (Holborn) Ltd* [2000] L & TR 480, CA.

III L&T [34.2]

Transfer of reversion It is not necessary that the landlord should be the same person throughout the whole period after the machinery of the Act has been set in motion: *X L Fisheries Ltd v Leeds Corpn*, [1955] 2 QB 636, [1955] 2 All ER 875, CA, followed in *A D Wimbush & Son Ltd v Franmills Properties Ltd* [1961] Ch 419, [1961] 2 All ER 197.

III L&T [34.3]

Estoppel Where, between service by a landlord of a notice under the Landlord and Tenant Act 1954 s 25 (see para **III L&T [17]**), terminating the tenant's current tenancy and service of the tenant's counter-notice under the Landlord and Tenant Act 1954 s 26 (see para **III L&T [18]**), claiming a new lease, the landlord had, without telling the tenant, served on his superior landlord a notice under the Landlord and Tenant Act 1954 s 26, which would have made the latter the tenant's competent landlord, and had at the same time exercised an option for a new 14 year lease which was subsequently granted to him, it was held that he had remained the tenant's competent landlord and was in any event estopped from asserting that the tenant's application against him for a new tenancy was improperly constituted: *Shelley v United Artists Corpn Ltd* (1990) 60 P & CR 241, [1990] 1 EGLR 103, CA.

III L&T [35]

46. Interpretation of Part II

(1) In this Part of this Act:—

"business' has the meaning assigned to it by subsection (2) of section twenty-three of this Act;

"current tenancy" has the meaning assigned to it by subsection (1) of section twenty-six of this Act;

"date of termination" has the meaning assigned to it by subsection (1) of section twenty-five of this Act;

subject to the provisions of section thirty-two of this Act, "the holding" has the meaning assigned to it by subsection (3) of section twenty-three of this Act;

"mining lease" has the same meaning as in the Landlord and Tenant Act 1927.

(2) For the purposes of this Part of this Act, a person has a controlling interest in a company, if, had he been a company, the other company would have been its subsidiary; and in this Part—

"company" has the meaning given by section 1(1) of the Companies Act 2006; and

"subsidiary" has the meaning given by section 1159 of that Act.

PART IV
MISCELLANEOUS AND SUPPLEMENTARY

III L&T [36]

63. Jurisdiction of court for purposes of Parts I and II and of Part I of Landlord and Tenant Act 1927

(1) Any jurisdiction conferred on the court by any provision of Part I of this Act shall be exercised by the county court.

(2) Any jurisdiction conferred on the court by any provision of Part II of this Act or conferred on the tribunal by Part I of the Landlord and Tenant Act 1927, shall, subject to the provisions of this section, be exercised by the High Court or the county court.

(3) [. . .]

(4) The following provisions shall have effect as respects transfer of proceedings from or to the High Court or the county court, that is to say—

(a) where an application is made to the one but by virtue of an Order under section 1 of the Courts and Legal Services Act 1990 cannot be entertained except by the other, the application shall not be treated as improperly made but any proceedings thereon shall be transferred to the other court;

(b) any proceedings under the provisions of Part II of this Act or of Part I of the Landlord and Tenant Act 1927, which are pending before one of those courts may by order of that court made on the application of any person interested be transferred to the other court, if it appears to the court making the order that it is desirable that the proceedings and any proceedings before the other court should both be entertained by the other court.

(5) In any proceedings where in accordance with the foregoing provisions of this section the county court exercises jurisdiction the powers of the judge of summoning one or more assessors under subsection (1) of section eighty-eight of the County Courts Act 1934, may be exercised notwithstanding that no application is made in that behalf by any party to the proceedings.

(6) Where in any such proceedings an assessor is summoned by a judge under the said subsection (1),—

(a) he may, if so directed by the judge, inspect the land to which the proceedings relate without the judge and report to the judge in writing thereon;

(b) the judge may on consideration of the report and any observations of the parties thereon give such judgment or make such order in the proceedings as may be just;

(c) the remuneration of the assessor shall be at such rate as may be determined by the Lord Chancellor with the approval of the Treasury and shall be defrayed out of moneys provided by Parliament.

(7) In this section the expression "the holding"—

(a) in relation to proceedings under Part II of this Act, has the meaning assigned to it by subsection (3) of section twenty-three of this Act;

(b) in relation to proceedings under Part I of the Landlord and Tenant Act 1927, has the same meaning as in the said Part I.

(8) [. . .]

(9) Nothing in this section shall prejudice the operation of section 41 of the County Courts Act 1984 (which relates to the removal into the High Court of proceedings commenced in the county court).

(10) [. . .]

III L&T [37]

64. Interim continuation of tenancies pending determination by court

(1) In any case where—

(a) a notice to terminate a tenancy has been given under Part I or Part II of this Act or a request for a new tenancy has been made under Part II thereof; and

(b) an application to the court has been made under the said Part I or the said Part II, as the case may be; and

(c) apart from this section the effect of the notice or request would be to terminate the tenancy before the expiration of the period of three months beginning with the date on which the application is finally disposed of,

the effect of the notice or request shall be to terminate the tenancy at the expiration of the said period of three months and not at any other time.

(2) The reference in paragraph (c) of subsection (1) of this section to the date on which an application is finally disposed of shall be construed as a reference to the earliest date by which the proceedings on the application (including any

proceedings on or in consequence of an appeal) have been determined and any time for appealing or further appealing has expired, except that if the application is withdrawn or any appeal is abandoned the reference shall be construed as a reference to the date of the withdrawal or abandonment.

III L&T [37.1]

Termination of current tenancy Where an application for a new tenancy is made under the Landlord and Tenant Act 1954 Pt II, this section has the effect of postponing the termination of the current tenancy for relevant purposes, which include the commencement under the Landlord and Tenant Act 1954 s 33 (see para **III L&T [26]**), of any new lease that may be granted: *Re No 88, High Road, Kilburn* [1959] 1 All ER 527, [1959] 1 WLR 279, but not the ascertainment of the period specified in the Landlord and Tenant Act 1954 s 30(2) (see para **III L&T [22]**): *Frederick Lawrence Ltd v Freeman Hardy and Willis Ltd* [1959] Ch 731, [1959] 3 All ER 77, CA. An application for the purposes of the Landlord and Tenant Act 1954 s 64(1)(b) includes an application which is invalid because it has been made prematurely, since the requirements of the Landlord and Tenant Act 1954 s 29(3) (see para **III L&T [21]**), are procedural only: *Zenith Investments (Torquay) Ltd v Kammins Ballrooms Co Ltd (No 2)* [1971] 3 All ER 1281, [1951] 1 WLR 1751, CA; but it does not include an application made after the tenancy has terminated by virtue of the Landlord and Tenant Act 1954 s 26(5) (see para **III L&T [18]**): *Meah v Sector Properties Ltd* [1974] 1 All ER 1074, [1974] 1 WLR 547, CA. Where the tenant goes out of occupation before the expiry of the term, there is no three-month extension because the terms of s 64(1) are not satisfied: *Surrey County Council v Single Horse Properties Ltd* [2002] EWCA Civ 367, [2002] 4 All ER 143, (2002) Times, 12 April.

III L&T [37.2]

Dismissal for want of prosecution In view of the fact that under this section the mere issue of proceedings extends the tenant's current tenancy until three months after the proceedings are disposed of, the landlord is entitled, if nothing further is done, to apply for the dismissal of the proceedings for want of prosecution, even though he has not been served with the application: *Pike v Michael Nairn & Co Ltd* [1960] Ch 553, [1960] 2 All ER 184. If, however, the claim form is not served within the two-month period prescribed by CPR 56.3(3), the proceedings will in any event be effectively at an end unless an extension of time is granted (as to which see para **III L&T [21.8]**).

III L&T [37.3]

"Finally disposed of" The Court of Appeal has power to strike out a notice of appeal where the appeal is plainly incompetent: *Aviagents Ltd v Balstravest Investments Ltd* [1966] 1 All ER 450, [1966] 1 WLR 150, CA, or is clearly and obviously an abuse of the process of the court: *Burgess v Stafford Hotel Ltd* [1990] 3 All ER 222, [1990] 1 WLR 1215, CA, as where it is being brought in order to obtain some collateral advantage, such as the continuation of a business tenancy under this section: *James v Barclays Bank plc* (1994) 138 Sol Jo LB 222, CA. If the Court of Appeal refuses leave to appeal to the House of Lords, the proceedings are finally disposed of, not on the date when the Court of Appeal refuses leave, but on the last day for lodging a petition to the House of Lords for leave to appeal: *Re 20, Exchange Street, Manchester (No 2)* [1956] 3 All ER 490, [1956] 1 WLR 1339. Likewise in *Shotley Point Marina (1986) Ltd v Spalding* [1997] 1 EGLR 233, CA it was held that unsuccessful proceedings to extend the time for appealing to the Court of Appeal could not be regarded as "proceedings on or in consequence of an appeal".

Interim rent Where a tenancy continues by virtue of the Landlord and Tenant Act 1954 s 24 (see para **III L&T [15]**), and this section, the court has power on the application of the landlord to determine a reasonable rent for the tenant to pay in the meantime: Landlord and Tenant Act 1954 s 24A (see para **III L&T [16]**). The application for an order that the tenant pay an interim rent may be included in or accompany the landlord's acknowledgment of service: CPR PD 56 para 3.7 (see para **CPR PD 56**).

III L&T [38]

65. Provisions as to reversions

(1) Where by virtue of any provision of this Act a tenancy (in this subsection referred to as "the inferior tenancy") is continued for a period such as to extend to or beyond the end of the term of a superior tenancy, the superior tenancy shall, for the purposes of this Act and of any other enactment and of any rule of law, be deemed so long as it subsists to be an interest in reversion expectant upon the termination of the inferior tenancy and, if there is no intermediate tenancy, to be the interest in reversion immediately expectant upon the termination thereof.

(2) In the case of a tenancy continuing by virtue of any provision of this Act after the coming to an end of the interest in reversion immediately expectant upon the termination thereof, subsection (1) of section one hundred and thirty-nine of the Law of Property Act 1925 (which relates to the effect of the extinguishment of a reversion) shall apply as if references in the said subsection (1) to the surrender or merger of the reversion included references to the coming to an end of the reversion for any reason other than surrender or merger.

(3) Where by virtue of any provision of this Act a tenancy (in this subsection referred to as "the continuing tenancy") is continued beyond the beginning of a reversionary tenancy which was granted (whether before or after the commencement of this Act) so as to begin on or after the date on which apart from this Act the continuing tenancy would have come to an end, the reversionary tenancy shall have effect as if it had been granted subject to the continuing tenancy.

(4) Where by virtue of any provision of this Act a tenancy (in this subsection referred to as "the new tenancy") is granted for a period beginning on the same date as a reversionary tenancy or for a period such as to extend beyond the beginning of the term of a reversionary tenancy, whether the reversionary tenancy in question was granted before or after the commencement of this Act, the reversionary tenancy shall have effect as if it had been granted subject to the new tenancy.

III L&T [38.1]

Law of Property Act 1925 The Law of Property Act 1925 s 139(1) provides that where a reversion expectant on a lease of land is surrendered or merged, the estate or interest which as against the lessee for the time being confers the next vested right to the land, shall be deemed the reversion for the purpose of preserving the same incidents and obligations as would have affected the original reversion had there been no surrender or merger thereof. Thus, where a sub-tenant's tenancy is continued by the Landlord and Tenant Act 1954 beyond the termination of the head lease, the superior landlord is entitled by virtue of the Landlord and Tenant Act 1954 s 65(2) to sue the sub-tenant direct on the covenants in the underlease: *Electricity Supply Nominees Ltd v Thorn EMI Retail Ltd* (1991) 63 P & CR 143, [1991] 2 EGLR 46, CA.

III L&T [39]

66. Provisions as to notices

(1) Any form of notice required by this Act to be prescribed shall be prescribed by regulations made by the Secretary of State by statutory instrument.

(2) Where the form of a notice to be served on persons of any description is to be prescribed for any of the purposes of this Act, the form to be prescribed shall include such an explanation of the relevant provisions of this Act as appears to the Secretary of State requisite for informing persons of that description of their rights and obligations under those provisions.

(3) Different forms of notice may be prescribed for the purposes of the operation of any provision of this Act in relation to different cases.

(4) Section twenty-three of the Landlord and Tenant Act 1927 (which relates to the service of notices) shall apply for the purposes of this Act.

(5) Any statutory instrument under this section shall be subject to annulment in pursuance of a resolution of either House of Parliament.

III L&T [39.1]

Service of notices The relevant section of the Landlord and Tenant Act 1927 provides as follows:

23 (1)

(1) Any notice, request, demand or other instrument under this Act shall be in writing and may be served on the person on whom it is to be served either personally, or by leaving it for him at his last known place of abode in England or Wales, or by sending it through the post in a registered letter addressed to him there, or, in the case of a local or public authority or a statutory or a public utility company, to the secretary or other proper officer at the principal

office of such authority or company, and in the case of a notice to a landlord, the person on whom it is to be served shall include any agent of the landlord duly authorised in that behalf.

(2) Unless or until a tenant of a holding shall have received notice that the person theretofore entitled to the rents and profits of the holding (hereinafter referred to as the original landlord) has ceased to be so entitled, and also notice of the name and address of the person who has become entitled to such rents and profits, any claim, notice, request, demand, or other instrument which the tenant shall serve upon or deliver to the original landlord shall be deemed to have been served upon or delivered to the landlord of such holding.

III L&T [39.2]

"Place of abode" For the purposes of the Landlord and Tenant Act 1954 Pt II, "place of abode" includes the business address of the person to be served: *Price v West London Investment Building Society Ltd* [1964] 2 All ER 318, [1964] 1 WLR 616, CA, applied in *Italica Holdings SA v Bayadea* [1985] 1 EGLR 70, 273 Estates Gazette 888, where sending a notice by registered post to a business tenant at the demised premises was held to be good service.

III L&T [39.3]

Mode of service Sending a notice to a person in a letter which is delivered at his last-known place of abode is equivalent to leaving it for him there, even if the letter was wrongly addressed and re-directed by the post office: *Stylo Shoes Ltd v Prices Tailors Ltd* [1960] Ch 396, [1959] 3 All ER 901. Service by recorded delivery has been held to be effective even where the letter is returned to the sender, undelivered: *Blunden v Frogmore Investments Ltd* [2002] EWCA Civ 573, [2003] 2 P & CR 84, [2002] 29 EG 153. Where the person to be served resides in only part of a building, service of a notice is duly effected by leaving it at the nearest place to which a member of the public or postman can go, eg in the letter box of the hall: *Trustees of Henry Smith's Charity v Kyriakou* (1989) 22 HLR 66, CA. In any event, the modes of service set out in s 23(1) of the 1927 Act are not exhaustive and it is sufficient if the notice is sent to and in fact received by person to be served: *Trustees of Henry Smith's Charity v Kyriakou* (1989) 22 HLR 66, CA. Service of a notice on a tenant's solicitor is good, whether or not the tenant in fact receives it: *Galinski v McHugh* (1988) 57 P & CR 359, 21 HLR 47, CA. A notice under the provisions of the Landlord and Tenant Act 1927 or the Landlord and Tenant Act 1954 Act is both given and received when it is served in accordance with the Landlord and Tenant Act 1927 s 23(1): *Sun Alliance and London Assurance Co Ltd v Hayman* [1975] 1 All ER 248, [1975] 1 WLR 177, CA. Generally speaking, a document other than one initiating legal proceedings can be served by fax provided it is proved that a legible copy of the document has in fact been received by the person to be served: *Hastie and Jenkerson v McMahon* [1991] 1 All ER 255, [1990] 1 WLR 1575, CA. As to service by fax of documents see CPR 6.2 (1), 6.5, 6.7 (see paras **CPR 6.2**, **CPR 6.5** and **CPR 6.7**) and the Practice Direction which supplements CPR Pt 6. As regards service on a deceased landlord, service on the agent of the landlord when alive was held invalid in *Lodgepower Ltd v Taylor* [2004] EWCA Civ 1367, [2004] All ER (D) 328 (Oct), (2004) Times, 3 November (a case concerning service under s 93 of the Agricultural Holdings Act 1986).

III L&T [39.4]

Service by recorded delivery It seems that service by a mode within s 23 of the 1927 Act (such as recorded delivery) is deemed effective even though there may be evidence to the contrary: *Commercial Union Life Assurance Co Ltd v Moustafa* [1999] 2 EGLR 44, following *Galinski v McHugh* [1989] 1 EGLR 109, CA.

It was held in *Beanby Estates Ltd v Egg Stores (Stamford Hill) Ltd* [2003] EWHC 1252 (Ch), [2004] 3 All ER 184, [2003] 1 WLR 2064 that a notice sent by recorded delivery is to be treated as served on the day of posting, as this is the effect of s 23(1) of the 1927 Act. It was further held that this provision is not to be read subject to the provisions of s 7 of the Interpretation Act 1978. This view was confirmed in *CA Webber (Transport) Ltd v Network Rail Infrastructure Ltd* [2003] EWCA Civ 1167, [2004] 3 All ER 202, [2004] 1 WLR 320.

III L&T [40]

67. Provisions as to mortgagees in possession

Anything authorised or required by the provisions of this Act, other than subsection (2) or (3) of section forty, to be done at any time by, to or with the landlord, or a landlord of a specified description, shall, if at that time the interest of the landlord in question is subject to a mortgage and the mortgagee is in

possession or a receiver appointed by the mortgagee or by the court is in receipt of the rents and profits, be deemed to be authorised or required to be done by, to or with the mortgagee instead of that landlord.

III L&T [40.1]

Mortgage of landlord's interest Where the landlord's interest is subject to a mortgage and the mortgagee is in possession or a receiver has been appointed, the mortgagee is the proper person to give notice under the Landlord and Tenant Act 1954 s 25 (see para **III L&T [17]**) or to receive notice under the Landlord and Tenant Act 1954 s 29 (see para **III L&T [21]**) or the other relevant provisions of the Act, and he is the person who should be named as respondent to an application by the tenant for a new tenancy under the Landlord and Tenant Act 1954 Pt II: *Meah v Mouskos* [1964] 2 QB 23, [1963] 3 All ER 908, CA.

III L&T [41]

69. Interpretation

(1) In this Act the following expressions have the meanings hereby assigned to them respectively, that is to say:—

"agricultural holding" has the same meaning as in the Agricultural Holdings Act 1986;

"development corporation" has the same meaning as in the New Towns Act 1946;

"farm business tenancy" has the same meaning as in the Agricultural Tenancies Act 1995;

"local authority" means any local authority within the meaning of the Town and Country Planning Act 1990, any National Park authority, the Broads Authority, the London Fire Commissioner, a joint authority established by Part 4 of the Local Government Act 1985, an economic prosperity board established under section 88 of the Local Democracy, Economic Development and Gonstruction Act 2009, a combined authority established under section 103 of that Act or a fire and rescue authority created by an order under section 4A of the Fire and Rescue Services Act 2004;

"mortgage" includes a charge or lien and "mortgagor" and "mortgagee" shall be construed accordingly;

"notice to quit" means a notice to terminate a tenancy (whether a periodical tenancy or a tenancy for a term of years certain) given in accordance with the provisions (whether express or implied) of that tenancy;

"repairs" includes any work of maintenance, decoration or restoration, and references to repairing, to keeping or yielding up in repair and to state of repair shall be construed accordingly;

"statutory undertakers" has the same meaning as in the Town and Country Planning Act 1947 [. . .];

"tenancy" means a tenancy created either immediately or derivatively out of the freehold, whether by a lease or underlease, by an agreement for a lease or underlease or by a tenancy agreement or in pursuance of any enactment (including this Act), but does not include a mortgage term or any interest arising in favour of a mortgagor by his attorning tenant to his mortgagee, and references to the granting of a tenancy and to demised property shall be construed accordingly;

"terms", in relation to a tenancy, includes conditions.

(2) References in this Act to an agreement between the landlord and the tenant (except in section seventeen and subsections (1) and (2) of section thirty-eight thereof) shall be construed as references to an agreement in writing between them.

(3) References in this Act to an action for any relief shall be construed as including references to a claim for that relief by way of counterclaim in any proceedings.

III L&T [41.1]

Notice to quit This includes a notice given under the Landlord and Tenant Act 1954 s 25(1) (see para **III L&T [17]**): *Rene Claro (Haute Coiffure) Ltd v Hallé Concerts Society* [1969] 2 All ER 842, [1969] 1 WLR 909, CA, overruling *Westbury Property and Investment Co Ltd v Carpenter* [1961] 1 All ER 481, [1961] 1 WLR 272, and also a notice exercising an option to determine the tenancy: *Scholl Manufacturing Co Ltd v Clifton (Slim-Line) Ltd* [1967] Ch 41, [1966] 3 All ER 16, CA.

III L&T [41.2]

Statutory undertakers The definition of "statutory undertakers" was amended successively by the Coal Industry Act 1987 s 1 (2), Sch 1 para 4, and the Coal Industry Act 1994 s 67, Sch 9, para 11. The authority established by the Post Office Act 1969 s 6 (1) is to be deemed to be a statutory undertaker for the purposes of the Landlord and Tenant Act 1954: Post Office Act 1969 s 76, Sch 4 para 93 (1)(xii). So also are the Civil Aviation Authority (Civil Aviation Act 1982 s 19 (2), Sch 2 para 4).

III L&T [41.3]

Tenancy A tenancy at will is not a tenancy within the definition in the Landlord and Tenant Act 1954 s 69 (1), whether it arises by implication of law: *Wheeler v Mercer* [1957] AC 416, [1956] 3 All ER 631, HL, or by express agreement: *Manfield & Sons Ltd v Botchin* [1970] 2 QB 612, [1970] 3 All ER 143 (approved in *Hagee (London) Ltd v A B Erikson and Larson* [1976] QB 209, [1975] 3 All ER 234, CA). See also *Cricket Ltd v Shaftesbury plc* [1999] 3 All ER 283. Where a person is let into possession and pays rent on a periodic basis while ultimately abortive negotiations are proceeding for the grant of a lease to him, it depends on the surrounding circumstances whether a tenancy has been created; the fact that the parties have not yet agreed terms will readily justify an inference that the person let into possession is only a tenant at will: *Javad v Aqil* [1991] 1 All ER 243, [1991] 1 WLR 1007, CA. So in *Brent London Borough Council v O'Bryan* (1992) 65 P & CR 258, [1993] 1 EGLR 59, CA, a letter from a local authority agreeing to the monthly letting of non-residential premises on terms to be laid down by valuers was held to be no more than a statement of willingness by the local authority to offer to let the property to the occupier on a monthly basis when the valuer had decided what the rent should be. See also *Dean and Chapter of the Cathedral of Canterbury v Whitbread plc* (1995) 72 P & CR 9, [1995] 1 EGLR 82. A sub-tenancy granted without the head landlord's consent to the proposed user, as required by the head lease, is valid as between the sub-tenant and his immediate landlord so that he is entitled to the protection of the Landlord and Tenant Act 1954 Pt II: *D'Silva v Lister House Development Ltd* [1971] Ch 17, [1970] 1 All ER 858. A tenancy continuing by virtue of the Landlord and Tenant Act 1954 s 24(1) (see para **III L&T [15]**) after the expiry of the contractual term is within the definition: *Cornish v Brook Green Laundry Ltd* [1959] 1 QB 394, [1959] 1 All ER 373, CA, applied in *Bowes-Lyon v Green* [1963] AC 420, [1961] 3 All ER 843, HL.

The grant of a sub-tenancy for not less than the rest of the term takes effect not as a sub-tenancy but as an assignment of the term: *Milmo v Carreras* [1946] KB 306, [1946] 1 All ER 288, CA. This is so where the grant is not in writing as required by the Law of Property Act 1925 s 53(1)(a). The assignment takes effect by operation of law. Where, therefore, the lease excluded ss 24–28 of the Act, the assignee was not protected: *Parc (Battersea) Ltd v Hutchinson* [1999] 2 EGLR 33, [1999] 22 EG 149.

III L&T [41.4]

Mere licences The question whether an agreement creates a tenancy or a mere licence depends on the effect in law of the document as a whole and not on the way in which it describes the interest created. The test is whether the occupier has been granted exclusive possession for a fixed or periodic term at a stated rent; if he has, then, save in exceptional circumstances such as the absence of any intention to create legal relations, the result will be a tenancy: *Street v Mountford* [1985] AC 809, [1985] 2 All ER 289, HL. See also *A G Securities v Vaughan* [1990] 1 AC 417, [1988] 3 All ER 1058, HL; *Estavest Investments Ltd v Commercial Express Travel Ltd* (1987) 21 HLR 106, [1988] 2 EGLR 91, CA; *Stribling v Wickham* (1989) 21 HLR 381, [1989] 2 EGLR 35, CA; *Aslan v Murphy* [1989] 3 All ER 130, [1990] 1 WLR 766, CA; *Nunn v Dalrymple* [1990] Fam Law 65, 59 P & CR 231, CA; *Venus Investments Ltd v Stocktop Ltd* [1996] EGCS 173, *National Car Parks Ltd v Trinity Development Co (Banbury) Ltd* [2001] 2 EGLR 43, [2001] 28 EG 144, CA and the statutes relating to residential premises. But the indicia, which may make it more apparent in the case of a residential tenant or occupier that he is indeed a tenant, may be less applicable or less likely to have effect in the case of some business tenancies: *Dresden Estates Ltd v Collinson* (1987) 55 P & CR 47, [1987] 1 EGLR 45, CA.

III L&T [41.5]

Exclusive possession An agreement purporting to be a mere management agreement conferring only a licence on the manager may, on examination, prove to be a sham and to

create a tenancy to which the Landlord and Tenant Act 1954 Pt II applies: *Wang v Wei* (1975) 119 Sol Jo 492; *Dellneed Ltd v Chin* (1986) 53 P & CR 172, [1987] 1 EGLR 75; likewise a document described as a licence which confers the right to use land as gallops but is in material respects similar to a lease: *University of Reading v Johnson-Houghton* [1985] 2 EGLR 113, 276 Estates Gazette 1353. If a person has been granted exclusive possession for a term at a rent, the fact that he entered with the intention of purchasing the property does not displace the inference that he is a tenant and not a mere licensee: *Bretherton v Paton* (1986) 18 HLR 257, [1986] 1 EGLR 172, CA. So, too, where the defendants had gone into occupation of office accommodation under a proposed sub-underlease for five years on similar terms to the underlease but no sub-underlease was in fact granted, it was held that there was a tenancy and not a licence and on the defendants quitting the premises after nearly four years' occupation they were liable for rent for the remainder of the term: *London & Associated Investment Trust plc v Calow* (1986) 53 P & CR 340, [1986] 2 EGLR 80. Although exclusive possession may be consistent with relationships other than that of landlord and tenant, eg where a purchaser is let into possession before completion, this is not so in the case of a purchaser of goodwill, since goodwill confers no rights of occupation; so, if such a person is in fact given exclusive possession, he will be a tenant and not a mere licensee: *Vandersteen v Agius* (1992) 65 P & CR 266, CA. Where the landlord of a workshop and store was entitled to require the occupier to transfer to other premises of the landlord, it was held that this was inconsistent with exclusive occupation and the arrangement was therefore a licence and not a tenancy: *Dresden Estates Ltd v Collinson* (1987) 55 P & CR 47, [1987] 1 EGLR 45, CA. Similarly, the grant of five stalls in a market was held to be a licence and not a lease notwithstanding that they had been shop-fitted to the grantees' own liking and three had been knocked into one to form a substantial shop: *Wigan Borough Council v Green & Son (Wigan) Ltd* [1985] 2 EGLR 242, CA; so also was an agreement for a person to occupy a shop unit as a licensee for a year with an option to take a 30-year lease from the commencement of the licence, the owner meanwhile retaining possession of the premises subject to the licence: *Essex Plan Ltd v Broadminster* (1988) 56 P & CR 353, [1988] 2 EGLR 73.

Schedule

SCHEDULE 6

PROVISIONS FOR PURPOSES OF PART II WHERE IMMEDIATE LANDLORD IS NOT THE FREEHOLDER

Section 44

III L&T [42]

Definitions

1. In this Schedule the following expressions have the meanings hereby assigned to them in relation to a tenancy (in this Schedule referred to as "the relevant tenancy"), that is to say:—

"the competent landlord" means the person who in relation to the tenancy is for the time being the landlord (as defined by section forty-four of this Act) for the purposes of Part II of this Act;

"mesne landlord" means a tenant whose interest is intermediate between the relevant tenancy and the interest of the competent landlord; and

"superior landlord" means a person (whether the owner of the fee simple or a tenant) whose interest is superior to the interest of the competent landlord.

Power of court to order reversionary tenancies

2. Where the period for which in accordance with the provisions of Part II of this Act it is agreed or determined by the court that a new tenancy should be granted thereunder will extend beyond the date on which the interest of the immediate landlord will come to an end, the power of the court under Part II of this Act to order such a grant shall include power to order the grant of a new tenancy until the expiration of that interest and also to order the grant of such a reversionary tenancy or reversionary tenancies as may be required to secure that the combined

LANDLORD & TENANT AND HOUSING

effects of those grants will be equivalent to the grant of a tenancy for that period; and the provisions of Part II of this Act shall, subject to the necessary modifications, apply in relation to the grant of a tenancy together with one or more reversionary tenancies as they apply in relation to the grant of one new tenancy.

Acts of competent landlord binding on other landlords

3.—(1) Any notice given by the competent landlord under Part II of this Act to terminate the relevant tenancy, and any agreement made between that landlord and the tenant as to the granting, duration, or terms of a future tenancy, being an agreement made for the purposes of the said Part II, shall bind the interest of any mesne landlord notwithstanding that he has not consented to the giving of the notice or was not a party to the agreement.

(2) The competent landlord shall have power for the purposes of Part II of this Act to give effect to any agreement with the tenant for the grant of a new tenancy beginning with the coming to an end of the relevant tenancy, notwithstanding that the competent landlord will not be the immediate landlord at the commencement of the new tenancy, and any instrument made in the exercise of the power conferred by this sub-paragraph shall have effect as if the mesne landlord had been a party thereto.

(3) Nothing in the foregoing provisions of this paragraph shall prejudice the provisions of the next following paragraph.

Provisions as to consent of mesne landlord to acts of competent landlord

4.—(1) If the competent landlord, not being the immediate landlord, gives any such notice or makes any such agreement as is mentioned in sub-paragraph (1) of the last foregoing paragraph without the consent of every mesne landlord, any mesne landlord whose consent has not been given thereto shall be entitled to compensation from the competent landlord for any loss arising in consequence of the giving of the notice or the making of the agreement.

(2) If the competent landlord applies to any mesne landlord for his consent to such a notice or agreement, that consent shall not be unreasonably withheld, but may be given subject to any conditions which may be reasonable (including conditions as to the modification of the proposed notice or agreement or as to the payment of compensation by the competent landlord).

(3) Any question arising under this paragraph whether consent has been unreasonably withheld or whether any conditions imposed on the giving of consent are unreasonable shall be determined by the court.

Consent of superior landlord required for agreements affecting his interest

5. An agreement between the competent landlord and the tenant made for the purposes of Part II of this Act in a case where—

(a) the competent landlord is himself a tenant, and

(b) the agreement would apart from this paragraph operate as respects any period after the coming to an end of the interest of the competent landlord,

shall not have effect unless every superior landlord who will be the immediate landlord of the tenant during any part of that period is a party to the agreement.

Withdrawal by competent landlord of notice given by mesne landlord

6. Where the competent landlord has given a notice under section 25 of this Act to terminate the relevant tenancy and, within two months after the giving of the notice, a superior landlord—

(a) becomes the competent landlord; and

(b) gives to the tenant notice in the prescribed form that he withdraws the notice previously given,

the notice under section 25 of this Act shall cease to have effect, but without prejudice to the giving of a further notice under that section by the competent landlord.

Duty to inform superior landlords

7. If the competent landlord's interest in the property comprised in the relevant tenancy is a tenancy which will come or can be brought to an end within sixteen months (or any further time by which it may be continued under section 36 (2) or section 64 of this Act) and he gives to the tenant under the relevant tenancy a notice under section 25 of this Act to terminate the tenancy or is given by him a notice under section 26 (3) of this Act:—

(a) the competent landlord shall forthwith send a copy of the notice to his immediate landlord; and

(b) any superior landlord whose interest in the property is a tenancy shall forthwith send to his immediate landlord any copy which has been sent to him in pursuance of the preceding sub-paragraph or this sub-paragraph.

III L&T [42.1]

Prescribed form The prescribed form referred to in paragraph 6 is Form 6 in Schedule 2 to the Landlord and Tenant Act 1954, Part 2 (Notices) Regulations 2004/1005.

LEASEHOLD REFORM ACT 1967

(c 88)

GENERAL NOTES ON LEASEHOLD REFORM ACT 1967

III L&T [43]

Scope and jurisdiction Part I of the Leasehold Reform Act 1967 enables a resident tenant of a leasehold house to acquire the freehold or an extended lease where the premises are within the appropriate rateable value limits and the tenancy is a long tenancy at a low rent. Special provision is made for cases in which a mortgagee of the landlord is in possession (s 25) or the landlord is a custodian trustee or a mental patient (s 26) or the landlord is a public authority which will shortly require the site for redevelopment (s 28) or the land is ecclesiastical property (s 31) or Crown land (s 33). Where the landlord's interest is subject to a mortgage the court may in certain circumstances discharge or modify the mortgage (s 36). The county court has exclusive jurisdiction (s 20, see para **III L&T [59]**).

III L&T [44]

Procedure Provision is made in the Practice Direction to CPR Pt 56 (see para **CPR PD 56**) with regard to claims under the Leasehold Reform Act 1967. In summary, the provisions are as follows: CPR PD 56 para 13.2 sets out the procedure which a tenant must follow if he wishes to pay money into court under ss 11(4), 13(1) or 13(3) of the Act; CPR PD 56 para 13.3 sets out the procedure on transfer of an application to the Leasehold Valuation Tribunal; CPR PD 56 para 13.4 states that a claim under ss 17 or 18 for an order for possession must be made in accordance with CPR Pt 55; and CPR PD 56 para 13.5 sets out the obligations of the defendant when served with a claim form under ss 17 or 18. CPR PD para 13.6 provides that an application made to the High Court under s 19 or s 27 shall be assigned to the Chancery Division. Other points of procedure are covered in Sch 3 to the Leasehold Reform Act 1967 (see para **III L&T [64]**).

For the conditions binding upon landlords and tenants (unless they otherwise agree) in any transactions undertaken to give effect to a tenant's notice, see the Leasehold Reform (Enfranchisement and Extension) Regulations 1967, SI 1967/1879 as amended (with effect from 30 September 2003) by the Leasehold Reform (Enfranchisement and Extension) (Amendment) (England) Regulations 2003, SI 2003/1989. For amendments effective in Wales as from 31 March 2004 see the Leasehold Reform (Enfranchisement and Extension) (Amendment) (Wales) Regulations 2004 SI 2004/ 699.

III L&T [45]

Precedents See **BCCP O[1101]** for a Pt 8 claim form for a declaration of entitlement and **BCCP O[1101.1]** for a claim form for relief under s 27 where the landlord cannot be found.

III L&T [45A]

Repeals and amendments The sections of the Leasehold Reform Act 1967 reproduced in this Volume are as repealed and amended (so as to abolish the low rent test) with effect from 7th September 2009, by section 300 of the Housing and Regeneration Act 2008 and the Housing and Regeneration Act 2008 (Commencement No. 6 and Transitional and Savings Provisions) Order 2009. Note, however, that the changes (and, in particular, the repeals of ss 1A(2), 1AA and 4A) do not have effect as regards any long tenancy granted before 7th September 2009 (or granted pursuant to a written agreement made before that date). Also, s 1AA of the 1967 Act continues to have effect as regards a tenancy granted before 7th September 2009 and in respect of a house that is within an area described in the Housing (Right to Enfranchise) (Designated Protected Areas) (England) Order 2009.

PART I
ENFRANCHISEMENT AND EXTENSION OF LONG LEASEHOLDS

RIGHT TO ENFRANCHISEMENT OR EXTENSION

III L&T [46]

1. Tenants entitled to enfranchisement or extension

(1) This Part of this Act shall have effect to confer on a tenant of a leasehold house, a right to acquire on fair terms the freehold or an extended lease of the house and premises where—

(a) his tenancy is a long tenancy;

(aa) in the case of a right to acquire an extended lease, his long tenancy is a tenancy at a low rent; and,—

(i) if the tenancy was entered into before 1 April 1990, or on or after 1 April 1990 in pursuance of a contract made before that date, and the house and premises had a rateable value at the date of commencement of the tenancy or else at any time before 1 April 1990, subject to subsections (5) and (6) below, the rateable value of the house and premises on the appropriate day was not more than £200 or, if it is in Greater London, than £400; and

(ii) if the tenancy does not fall within sub-paragraph (i) above, on the date the contract for the grant of the tenancy was made or, if there was no such contract, on the date the tenancy was entered into R did not exceed £25,000 under the formula—

R = (P x I) divided by (1 – (1 + I) to the power of –T)

where—

P is the premium payable as a condition of the grant of the tenancy (and includes a payment of money's worth) or, where no premium is so payable, zero,

I is 0.06, and

T is the term, expressed in years, granted by the tenancy (disregarding any right to terminate the tenancy before the end of the term or to extend the tenancy); and

(b) at the relevant time (that is to say, at the time when he gives notice in accordance with this Act of his desire to have the freehold or to have an extended lease, as the case may be) he has

(i) in the case of a right to acquire the freehold, been tenant of the house under a long tenancy for the last two years; and

(ii) in the case of a right to acquire an extended lease, been a tenant of the house under a long tenancy at a low rent for the last two years;

and to confer the like right in the other cases for which provision is made in this Part of this Act.

(1ZA) Where a house is for the time being let under two or more tenancies, a tenant under any of those tenancies which is superior to that held by any tenant on whom this Part of this Act confers a right does not have any right under this Part of this Act.

(1ZB) Where a flat forming part of a house is let to a person who is a qualifying tenant of the flat for the purposes of Chapter 1 or 2 of Part 1 of the Leasehold Reform, Housing and Urban Development Act 1993 (c 28), a tenant of the house does not have any right under this Part of this Act unless, at the relevant time, he has been occupying the house, or any part of it, as his only or main residence (whether or not he has been using it for other purposes)—

(a) for the last two years; or

(b) for periods amounting to two years in the last ten years.

(1ZC) The references in subsection (1)(a) and (b) to a long tenancy do not include a tenancy to which Part 2 of the Landlord and Tenant Act 1954 (business tenancies) applies unless—

(a) it is granted for a term of years certain exceeding thirty-five years, whether or not it is (or may become) terminable before the end of that term by notice given by or to the tenant or by re-entry, forfeiture or otherwise,

(b) it is for a term fixed by law under a grant with a covenant or obligation for perpetual renewal, unless it is a tenancy by sub-demise from one which is not a tenancy which falls within any of the paragraphs in this subsection,

(c) it is a tenancy taking effect under section 149(6) of the Law of Property Act 1925 (c 20) (leases terminable after a death or marriage or the formation of a civil partnership), or

(d) it is a tenancy which—

(i) is or has been granted for a term of years certain not exceeding thirty-five years, but with a covenant or obligation for renewal without payment of a premium (but not for perpetual renewal), and

(ii) is or has been once or more renewed so as to bring to more than thirty-five years the total of the terms granted (including any interval between the end of a tenancy and the grant of a renewal).

(1ZD) Where this Part of this Act applies as if there were a single tenancy of property comprised in two or more separate tenancies, then, if each of the separate tenancies falls within any of the paragraphs of subsection (1ZC) above, that subsection shall apply as if the single tenancy did so.

(1A) The references in subsection (1) to a long tenancy do not include a tenancy excluded from the operation of this Part by section 33A of and Schedule 4A to this Act.

(1B) This Part of this Act shall not have effect to confer any right on the tenant of a house under a tenancy to which Part 2 of the Landlord and Tenant Act 1954 (c 56) (business tenancies) applies unless, at the relevant time, the tenant has been occupying the house, or any part of it, as his only or main residence (whether or not he has been using it for other purposes)—

(a) for the last two years; or

(b) for periods amounting to two years in the last ten years.

(2) . . .

(3) This Part of this Act shall not confer on the tenant of a house any right by reference to his being a tenant of it at any time when—

(a) it is let to him with other land or premises to which it is ancillary; or

(b) it is comprised in—

(i) an agricultural holding within the meaning of the Agricultural Holdings Act 1986 held under a tenancy in relation to which that Act applies, or

(ii) the holding held under a farm business tenancy within the meaning of the Agricultural Tenancies Act 1995,

or, in the case of any right to which subsection (3A) below applies, at any time when the tenant's immediate landlord is a charitable housing trust and the house forms part of the housing accommodation provided by the trust in the pursuit of its charitable purposes.

(3A) For the purposes of subsection (3) above this subsection applies as follows—

(a) where the tenancy was created after the commencement of Chapter III of Part I of the Leasehold Reform, Housing and Urban Development Act 1993, this subsection applies to any right to acquire the freehold of the house and premises; but

(b) where the tenancy was created before that commencement, this subsection applies only to any such right exercisable by virtue of any one or more of the provisions of sections 1A and 1B below;

and in that subsection "charitable housing trust" means a housing trust within the meaning of the Housing Act 1985 which is a charity within the meaning of the Charities Act 1993.

(4) In subsection (1)(a) above, "the appropriate day", in relation to any house and premises, means the 23rd March 1965 or such later day as by virtue of section 25 (3) of the Rent Act 1977 would be the appropriate day for purposes of that Act in relation to a dwelling house consisting of that house.

(4A) Schedule 8 to the Housing Act 1974 shall have effect to enable a tenant to have the rateable value of the house and premises reduced for purposes of this section in consequence of tenant's improvements.

(5) If, in relation to any house and premises, the appropriate day for the purposes of subsection (1)(a) above falls on or after 1st April 1973 that subsection shall have effect in relation to the house and premises,—

- (a) in a case where the tenancy was created on or before 18th February 1966, as if for the sums of £200 and £400 specified in that subsection there were substituted respectively the sums of £750 and £1500; and
- (b) in a case where the tenancy was created after 18th February 1966, as if for those sums of £200 and £400 there were substituted respectively the sums of £500 and £1000.

(6) If, in relation to any house and premises,—

- (a) the appropriate day for the purposes of subsection (1)(a) above falls before 1st April 1973, and
- (b) the rateable value of the house and premises on the appropriate day was more than £200 or, if it was then in Greater London, £400, and
- (c) the tenancy was created on or before 18th February 1966,

subsection (1)(a) above shall have effect in relation to the house and premises as if for the reference to the appropriate day there were substituted a reference to 1st April 1973 and as if for the sums of £200 and £400 specified in that subsection there were substituted respectively the sums of £750 and £1500.

(7) The Secretary of State may by order replace the amount referred to in subsection (1)(a)(ii) above and the number in the definition of "I" in that subsection by such amount or number as is specified in the order; and such an order shall be made by statutory instrument which shall be subject to annulment in pursuance of a resolution of either House of Parliament.

LANDLORD & TENANT AND HOUSING

III L&T [46.1]

Right to acquire freehold A sub-lessee who owns the freehold already may not use the Act as a means of acquiring the intermediate lease: *Gratton-Storey v Lewis* (1987) 55 P & CR 326, 19 HLR 546, CA.

III L&T [46.2]

Definitions For the meaning of "house", see Leasehold Reform Act 1967 s 2 (see para **III L&T [50]**); for "tenancy", see Leasehold Reform Act 1967 s 37 (1)(f) (see para **III L&T [63]**); for "long tenancy", see Leasehold Reform Act 1967 s 3 (see para **III L&T [51]**); for "low rent", see Leasehold Reform Act 1967 s 4 (see para **III L&T [52]**).

III L&T [46.3]

Exclusions from enfranchisement There are various categories of exclusion from enfranchisement in Leasehold Reform Act 1967 ss 31 onwards:

National Trust property (Leasehold Reform Act 1967 s 32).

Property transferred for public benefit (Leasehold Reform Act 1967 s 32A).

Crown land (Leasehold Reform Act 1967 s 33).

Shared ownership leases (Leasehold Reform Act 1967 s 33A and Sch 4A).

Also, right-to-buy leases are excluded by Housing Act 1985 ss 172–175.

III L&T [46.4]

"Occupying a house as his residence" This does not extend to any occupation of a company or other artificial person, nor, where the tenant is a corporation sole, is the corporator, while in occupation, to be treated as occupying as tenant: Leasehold Reform Act 1967 s 37 (5) post. Nor does it extend to a tenant who is a trustee of the lease for a company and accordingly occupying as a licensee of the company: *Duke of Westminster v Oddy* (1984) 15 HLR 80, [1984] 1 EGLR 83, CA. Where a tenant became bankrupt, his entire interest vested in his trustee; accordingly, a notice claiming the right to enfranchise served by receivers subsequently appointed was invalid as, at the time of the notice, the tenant had not been tenant for the last two years: *Governors of the Free Grammar School of John Lyon v Helman* [2014] EWCA Civ 17. A house is occupied by a tenant as his residence not only when he occupies the whole of it, but also when he occupies a part only and sublets other parts: *Harris v Swick Securities Ltd* [1969] 3 All ER 1131, [1969] 1 WLR 1604, CA. On the other hand a house is not occupied by a tenant as his residence while he is abroad and the property is in the hands of estate agents with instructions to sublet; nor where mortgagees have taken possession following the tenant-mortgagor's default: *Poland v Earl Cadogan* [1980] 3 All ER 544, CA. A person may be treated as occupying a house during a period when fire damage has rendered it uninhabitable, if he has a real hope of returning and it is a practical possibility that he may be able to do so within a reasonable time: *Bolhah v Jigwood Securities Continuation* [1987] CLY 2170. Note that the amendments introduced, with effect from 26 July 2002, by the Commonhold and Leasehold Reform Act 2002 have the effect of removing the residency qualification.

In *Cadogan v Search Guarantees plc* [2004] EWCA Civ 969, [2004] 1 WLR 2768, (2004) Times, 3 August, the court held that the purpose of retaining the residence requirement in s 1(1ZB) was to resolve who should have the right to enfranchise when the tenant of a house and the tenant of a flat forming part of the house were different persons. The tenant of a house which he had sublet into flats was not prevented by s 1(1ZB) from applying to enfranchise, so long as the sub-tenants were not "qualifying" tenants.

III L&T [46.5]

Main residence A husband and wife may each have their own main residences: *Fowell v Radford* (1969) 21 P & CR 99, CA. What is a man's main residence is essentially a question of fact and degree which must be looked at in a common-sense way: *Byrne v Rowbotham* (1969) 210 Estates Gazette 823, CA; *Dymond v Arundel-Timms* (1990) 23 HLR 397, [1991] 1 EGLR 109, CA.

III L&T [46.6]

Effect of forfeiture Although the right to enfranchisement may be forfeited along with the lease, it is restored if possession proceedings are dismissed: *Twinsectra Ltd v Hynes* (1995) 71 P & CR 145, CA.

III L&T [46.7]

Mortgage term This should be read as "term under a subsisting mortgage" and not as extending to a term created by a mortgage which no longer affects it; see *Re Fairview, Church Street, Bromyard* [1974] 1 All ER 1233, [1974] 1 WLR 579 (MEGARRY J).

III L&T [46.8]

Reduction of rateable value Where the rateable value is reduced, the reduction takes effect from the first day of the period in which the application was made: *Gwynne Trusts Ltd v Rodwell* [1969] 2 All ER 435, [1969] 1 WLR 740, CA; *Rendall v Duke of Westminster* (1987) 19 HLR 345, CA. But where the reduction has retrospective effect to an earlier date it has like effect for the purposes of Leasehold Reform Act 1967 s 1(6): *Macfarquhar v Phillimore* (1986) 53 P & CR 44, 18 HLR 397, CA. Further, where a tenant seeks a reduction of the rateable value by a notice under the Housing Act 1974 Sch 8 (tenant's improvements) after giving a Leasehold Reform Act 1967 Sch 3 (see para **III L&T [64]**) notice of his desire to acquire the freehold (or an extension), the notional rateable value when determined may date back to the giving of the Leasehold Reform Act 1967 Sch 3 notice: This was the view expressed *obiter* in *Duke of Westminster v Oddy* (1984) 15 HLR 80, [1984] 1 EGLR 83, CA. The opposite view was taken in *Free Grammar School of John Lyon v Vignaud* [1993] 2 EGLR 122, [1993] 26 EG 128.

III L&T [46.9]

Adjustment for tenant's improvements Rateable values may be adjusted downwards to take account of the value of tenant's improvements, such as the installation of a new central heating system: *Pearlman v Keepers and Governors of Harrow School* [1979] QB 56, [1979] 1 All ER 365, CA. Adjustments are required to be made by the Housing Act 1974 Sch 8, as amended by the Housing Act 1980 Sch 21. In *Shalson v Keepers and Governors of the Free Grammar School of John Lyon* [2003] UKHL 32, [2004] 1 AC 802, [2003] 3 All ER 975 it was held that an improvement was a physical and not an economic concept and that a diminution in the open market value of the property in question was to be allowed only by the extent to which that value was increased by any improvement carried out by the tenant or his predecessors at their own expense; that the tenant was required both to identify the improvement relied upon and to show that, but for the improvement, the house would have been worth less. Where the tenant has made improvements the valuation should be on the basis that the improvements had not been made but that the property had potential for improvement. The significance of the tenant's improvements is therefore the amount by which they increased the value, ie the difference between the value of the improved property and the value of the property without the improvements but with the potential to add them: *Fattal v Keepers and Governors of the Free Grammar School of John Lyon* [2004] EWCA Civ 1530, [2004] NLJR 1861, (2004) Times, 2 December, CA.

III L&T [46.10]

Schedule 8 The Housing Act 1974 Sch 8 para 2(2) provides that, in the absence of agreement, a tenant may apply to the county court to determine whether the schedule applies and the contribution made by the improvement.

The timetable laid down by the Housing Act 1974 Sch 8 is mandatory and may not be exceeded without the consent of the county court judge: *Pollock v Brook-Shepherd* (1982) 45 P & CR 357, 266 Estates Gazette 214, CA. A tenant who is out of time and has been refused an extension may not start again with a second notice: *Mayhew v Free Grammar School of John Lyon* (1991) 63 P & CR 53, 23 HLR 479, CA. On the other hand, an application under the Housing Act 1974 Sch 8 para 2(3) for a longer period than six weeks may be made to the county court even where the six weeks have already elapsed: *Arieli v Duke of Westminster* [1984] 1 EGLR 81, 269 Estates Gazette 535, CA. And an extension may be granted as a matter of discretion although the circumstances are not exceptional: *Johnston v Duke of Devonshire* [1984] 2 EGLR 112, 272 Estates Gazette 661, CA; *Johnston v Duke of Westminster* (1984) 17 HLR 136, CA.

III L&T [47]

1A. Right to enfranchisement only in case of houses whose value or rent exceeds limit under s 1 or 4

(1) Where subsection (1) of section 1 above would apply in the case of the tenant of a house but for the fact that the applicable financial limit specified in subsection (1)(a)(i) or (ii) or (as the case may be) subsection (5) or (6) of that section is exceeded, this Part of this Act shall have effect to confer on the tenant the same right to acquire the freehold of the house and premises as would be conferred by subsection (1) of that section if the limit were not exceeded.

(2) . . .

III L&T [48]

1AA. ***Additional right to enfranchisement only in case of houses whose rent exceeds applicable limit under section 4***

(1) Where

(a) section 1(1) above would apply in the case of the tenant of a house but for the fact that the tenancy is not a tenancy at a low rent, and.

(b) the tenancy . . . is not an excluded tenancy,

this Part of this Act shall have effect to confer on the tenant the same right to acquire the freehold of the house and premises as would be conferred by section 1(1) above if it were a tenancy at a low rent.

(2) . . .

(3) A tenancy is an excluded tenancy for the purposes of subsection (1) above if:

(a) the house which the tenant occupies under the tenancy is in an area designated for the purposes of this provision as a rural area by order made by the Secretary of State.

(b) the freehold of that house is owned together with adjoining land which is not occupied for residential purposes and has been owned together with such land since [1st April 1997 (the date on which section 106 of the Housing Act 1996 came into force)], and

(c) the tenancy either—

(i) was granted on or before that date, or.

(ii) was granted after that date, but on or before the coming into force of section 141 of the Commonhold and Leasehold Reform Act 2002, for a term of years certain not exceeding thirty-five years.

(4) . . .

(5) The power to make an order under subsection (3) above shall be exercisable by statutory instrument which shall be subject to annulment in pursuance of a resolution of either House of Parliament.

III L&T [48.1]

Adjoining land In s 1AA(3) the word 'house' means the house alone and the words 'adjoining land' mean neighbouring land that either might or might not touch, or physically adjoin, the house: *Hertsmere BC v Lovat* [2011] EWCA Civ 1185.

III L&T [49]

1B. Right to enfranchisement only in case of certain tenancies terminable after death or marriage

Where a tenancy granted so as to become terminable by notice after a death, a marriage or the formation of a civil partnership—

(a) is (apart from this section) a long tenancy in accordance with section 3 (1) below, but

(b) was granted before 18th April 1980 or in pursuance of a contract entered into before that date,

then (notwithstanding section 3 (1)) the tenancy shall be a long tenancy for the purposes of this Part of this Act only so far as this Part has effect for conferring on any person a right to acquire the freehold of a house and premises.

III L&T [50]

2. Meaning of "house" and "house and premises", and adjustment of boundary

(1) For purposes of this Part of this Act, "house" includes any building designed or adapted for living in and reasonably so called, notwithstanding that the building is not structurally detached, or was or is not solely designed or adapted for living in, or is divided horizontally into flats or maisonettes; and—

(a) where a building is divided horizontally, the flats or other units into which it is so divided are not separate "houses", though the building as a whole may be; and

(b) where a building is divided vertically the building as a whole is not a "house" though any of the units into which it is divided may be.

(2) References in this Part of this Act to a house do not apply to a house which is not structurally detached and of which a material part lies above or below a part of the structure not comprised in the house.

(3) Subject to the following provisions of this section, where in relation to a house let to a tenant reference is made in this Part of this Act to the house and premises, the reference to premises is to be taken as referring to any garage, outhouse, garden, yard and appurtenances which at the relevant time are let to him with the house.

(4) In relation to the exercise by a tenant of any right conferred by this Part of this Act there shall be treated as included in the house and premises any other premises let with the house and premises but not at the relevant time subject to a tenancy vested in him (whether in consequence of an assignment of the term therein or otherwise), if—

(a) the landlord at the relevant time has an interest in the other premises and, not later than two months after the relevant time, gives to the tenant written notice objecting to the further severance of them from the house and premises; and

(b) either the tenant agrees to their inclusion with the house and premises or the court is satisfied that it would be unreasonable to require the landlord to retain them without the house and premises.

(5) In relation to the exercise by a tenant of any right conferred by this Part of this Act there shall be treated as not included in the house and premises any part of them which lies above or below other premises (not consisting only of underlying mines or minerals), if—

(a) the landlord at the relevant time has an interest in the other premises and, not later than two months after the relevant time, gives to the tenant written notice objecting to the further severance from them of that part of the house and premises; and

(b) either the tenant agrees to the exclusion of that part of the house and premises or the court is satisfied that any hardship or inconvenience likely to result to the tenant from the exclusion, when account is taken of anything that can be done to mitigate its effects and of any undertaking of the landlord to take steps to mitigate them, is outweighed by the difficulties involved in the further severance from the other premises and any hardship or inconvenience likely to result from that severance to persons interested in those premises.

(6) The rights conferred on a tenant by this Part of this Act in relation to any house and premises shall not extend to underlying minerals comprised in the tenancy if the landlord requires that the minerals be excepted, and if proper provision is made for the support of the house and premises as they have been enjoyed during the tenancy and in accordance with its terms.

(7) Where by virtue of subsection (4) above a tenant of a house acquiring the freehold or an extended lease is required to include premises of which the tenancy is not vested in him, this Part of this Act shall apply for the purpose as if in the case of those premises a tenancy on identical terms were vested in him and the holder of the actual tenancy were a sub-tenant; and where by virtue of subsection (5) or (6) above a tenant of a house acquiring the freehold or an extended lease is required to exclude property of which the tenancy is vested in him, then unless the landlord and the tenant otherwise agree or the court for the protection of either of them from hardship or inconvenience otherwise orders, the grant to the tenant shall operate as a surrender of the tenancy in that property and the provision to be made by the grant shall be determined as if the surrender had taken place before the relevant time.

III L&T [50.1]

House A building may be a house "reasonably so called" although the ground floor is let as a shop: *Lake v Bennett* [1970] 1 QB 663, [1970] 1 All ER 457, CA, even where the building is a purpose built shop, in a parade of shops, with a modest flat above: *Tandon v Trustees of Spurgeon's Homes* [1982] AC 755, [1982] 1 All ER 1086, HL. A building does not cease to be a house merely because it has been connected to an adjoining shop or house: *Gaidowski v Gonville and Caius College, Cambridge* [1975] 2 All ER 952, [1975] 1 WLR 1066, CA. Nor does a flat above a ground floor shop cease to be a house "reasonably so called" because it is not linked internally to the remainder of the building: see *Jewelcraft Ltd v Pressland* [2015] EWCA Civ 1111, [2015] All ER (D) 278 (Oct). A building which had been designed as a house and resembled a house, but which was required to be used predominantly as offices by the terms of a lease, was held not to be a house "reasonably so called" within the meaning of s 2(1). The prescribed and predominant use of the building, not its design and appearance, was the overwhelmingly significant factor in the decision: *Prospect Estates Ltd v Grosvenor Estates Ltd* [2008] EWCA Civ 1281.

In conjoined appeals in *Day v Hosebay Ltd and Howard de Walden Estates Ltd v Lexgorge Ltd* [2012] UKSC 41, [2012] 1 WLR 2884, [2012] 4 All ER 1347 the Supreme Court, reviewing the authorities, explaining *Tandon* and approving *Prospect Estates*, held that a property used entirely for commercial purposes was not a house reasonably so called, whatever its original design or current appearance, or the fact that it might look like a house and might be referred to as such for some purposes. However, in *Grosvenor (Mayfair) Estate v Merix International Ventures Ltd* [2017] EWCA Civ 190, the Court of Appeal held, following Boss Holdings (see **III L&T [50.1A]**), that the trial judge had been entitled to find that a townhouse with past mixed residential and office use and no current use at all, was a 'house'.

A purpose-built block of seven flats was held not to be a 'house' in *Magnohard Ltd v Earl Cadogan and Cadogan Estates* [2012] EWCA Civ 594, [2013] 1 WLR 24, [2012] HLR 495. In *Malekshad v Howard de Walden Estates Ltd* [2002] UKHL 49, [2003] 1 AC 1013, [2003]

1 All ER 193, the House of Lords, reversing the Court of Appeal decision, held that two houses (the main house and a mews house linked by an underground basement) did not constitute a single house and that the Court of Appeal had been wrong to apply the guidance given in *Tandon* because the question of whether it was reasonable to call the building a house did not arise on the facts. Compare, however, *Collins v Howard de Walden Estates Ltd* [2003] EWCA Civ 545, [2003] HLR 1083 where the court held that a property comprising two linked mews houses was a house; that the vertical division referred to in s 2(1)(b) contemplated separate residential units being produced, not parts of units as in the instant case. Where appropriate it is necessary first to identify the building held by the tenant, then to decide whether it is excluded from enfranchisement by Leasehold Reform Act 1967 s 2(2) and finally whether it is occupied by the tenant as a residence, as required by Leasehold Reform Act 1967 s 1(1) (see para **III L&T [46]**): *Duke of Westminster v Birrane* [1995] QB 262, [1995] 3 All ER 416, CA, rejecting the view that the three questions should be rolled together as held by Lord Denning MR in *Peck v Anicar Properties Ltd* [1971] 1 All ER 517, CA, and *Wolf v Crutchley* [1971] 1 All ER 520, [1971] 1 WLR 99, CA. In *Dugan-Chapman v Grosvenor Estates* [1997] 1 EGLR 96, [1997] 10 EG 152 the lease comprised two buildings separated by a garden. One of the buildings was the main residence and the other comprised a garage with a flat above. It was held that the garage was part of the "house and premises" but that the flat was not.

The Supreme Court has now ruled that whatever its design a building used solely for commercial purposes does not constitute a house: *Day v Hosebay Ltd; Howard de Walden Estates Ltd v Lexgorge Ltd* [2012] UKSC 41, [2012] 4 All ER 1347, [2012] 1 WLR 2884.

III L&T [50.1A]

Designed or adapted for living in The words "designed or adapted for living in" in s 2(1) involve the court in considering the property as it was initially built, considering the purpose for which it was originally designed and whether any work has subsequently been done so that the original design has been changed. Where a property had been unoccupied for a number of years and had become internally dilapidated but had nevertheless been originally designed for living in it was, in the circumstances, a house within the meaning of s 2 of the Act: see *Boss Holdings Ltd v Grosvenor West End Properties* [2008] UKHL 5, [2008] 2 All ER 759, [2008] 1 WLR 289. Note, however, that in *Day v Hosebay Ltd and Howard de Walden Estates Ltd v Lexgorge Ltd* [2012] UKSC 41, [2012] 4 All ER 1347, [2012] 1 WLR 2884, the Supreme Court, while not calling into question the actual decision in *Boss Holdings*, preferred the revised view of Lord Neuberger in the Court of Appeal in the instant case — that a building originally designed for living in, but adapted for some other purpose, was not 'designed or adapted for living in', unless subsequently re-adapted for that purpose — to the view he had previously expressed in *Boss Holdings*.

A building may be designed or adapted for living in, yet not be a house reasonably so called. Where the tenant converted a shop storeroom into a residence in breach of a covenant in the lease, the tenant was not entitled to rely on the unauthorised conversion work; it was unacceptable to enforce a right to acquire a property compulsorily where the applicant had deliberately done something wrongful that was necessary to found the claim: see *Henley v Cohen* [2013] EWCA Civ 480, [2013] 2 P & CR 201, [2013] HLR 376. In *Brightbest Ltd v Meyrick* (2014) it was held in the county court (Winchester), following *Day v Hosebay Ltd* and *Henley v Cohen*, that two derelict buildings, comprising a main building and a cottage, which had been converted into bedsits and flats were not 'houses' within the meaning of s 2(1). Note that, in *Jewelcraft Ltd v Pressland* [2015] EWCA Civ 1111, [2015] All ER (D) 278 (Oct), *Henley v Cohen* was regarded as an exceptional case, and its correctness was doubted.

III L&T [50.2]

Horizontal division Where a building originally comprised two flats, one on each floor, but was later owned and occupied as a single dwelling with an internal connecting door it was held to have become a house which was divided horizontally within, notwithstanding the vertical division created by the stairway to the upper floor: *Sharpe v Duke Street Securities NV* (1987) 55 P & CR 331, 19 HLR 506, CA. Likewise, it was held in *Malpas v St Ermin's Property Co Ltd* (1992) 24 HLR 537, [1992] 2 EGLR 109, CA that a building divided into maisonettes is still a house.

III L&T [50.3]

Not structurally detached "Structurally detached" means detached from any other structure, see *Parsons v Viscount Gage (Trustees of Henry Smith's Charity)* [1974] 1 All ER 1162, [1974] 1 WLR 435, HL.

III L&T [50.4]

Material part Whether, in any case, a part is material is a matter for the judge. The issue must be largely factual and one of common sense, see *Parsons v Viscount Gage (Trustees of Henry Smith's Charity)* [1974] 1 All ER 1162, [1974] 1 WLR 435, HL. Compare *Duke of*

Westminster v Birrane [1995] QB 262, [1995] 3 All ER 416, CA. In *Malekshad v Howard de Walden Estates Ltd* [2002] UKHL 49, [2003] 1 All ER 193, (2002) Times, 6 December, the House of Lords held by a majority, that the purpose of s 2(2) is to ensure that the right of enfranchisement is not lost because a trivial or unimportant part of the house in question overhangs or underlays another part of the structure to which it is attached, and that the test of materiality depends on the relationship between the part in question and the house as a whole and is not linked to the use made of the part in question by the tenant. For an application of *Malekshad* see *West End Investments (Cowell Group) Ltd v Birchlea Ltd* [2015] EWHC 3381 (Ch), [2015] All ER (D) 15 (Dec), where the court held that the vertical division of a party wall did not create a material overhang into adjoining property sufficient to disqualify a house from enfranchisement.

III L&T [50.5]

Part of the structure not comprised in the house In the case of a house with an arched tunnel through it, it was held that the arch was part of the structure comprised in the house and that the house was not excepted by s 2(2): *Cresswell v Duke of Westminster* [1985] 2 EGLR 151, CA.

III L&T [50.6]

"Appurtenant" This means incorporeal rights appurtenant to the land and not corporeal rights: *Methuen-Campbell v Walters* [1979] QB 525, [1979] 1 All ER 606, CA, in which it was held that the applicant had no right to have a separate paddock conveyed together with an adjoining house. A more liberal meaning is given to the word in the context of enfranchisement of flats under the Leasehold Reform, Housing and Urban Development Act 1993 (see para **III L&T [247]**).

III L&T [50.7]

"Relevant time" This means, in relation to a person's claim to acquire the freehold or an extended lease under Part I, the time when he gives notice of his desire to have it: Leasehold Reform Act 1967 s 37(1)(d) (see para **III L&T [63]**).

III L&T [51]

3. Meaning of "long tenancy"

(1) In this Part of this Act "long tenancy" means, subject to the provisions of this section, a tenancy granted for a term of years certain exceeding twenty-one years, whether or not the tenancy is (or may become) terminable before the end of that term by notice given by or to the tenant or by re-entry, forfeiture or otherwise, and includes both a tenancy taking effect under section 149 (6) of the Law of Property Act 1925 (leases terminable after a death or marriage or the formation of a civil partnership) and a tenancy for a term fixed by law under a grant with a covenant or obligation for perpetual renewal unless it is a tenancy by sub-demise from one which is not a long tenancy:

Provided that a tenancy granted so as to become terminable by notice after a death, a marriage or the formation of a civil partnership is not to be treated as a long tenancy if—

- (a) the notice is capable of being given at any time after the death or marriage of or the formation of a civil partnership by the tenant;
- (b) the length of the notice is not more than three months; and
- (c) the terms of the tenancy preclude both—
  - (i) its assignment otherwise than by virtue of section 92 of the Housing Act 1985 (assignments by way of exchange), and
  - (ii) the sub-letting of the whole of the premises comprised in it.

(2) Where the tenant of any property under a long tenancy at a low rent (other than a lease excluded from the operation of this Part by section 33A of and Schedule 4A to this Act), on the coming to an end of that tenancy, becomes or has become tenant of the property or part of it under another tenancy (whether by express grant or by implication of law), then the later tenancy shall be deemed for the purposes of this Part of this Act, including any further application of this subsection, to be a long tenancy irrespective of its terms.

(3) Where the tenant of any property under a long tenancy, on the coming to an end of that tenancy, becomes or has become tenant of the property or part of it under another long tenancy, then in relation to the property or that part of it this Part of this Act, shall apply as if there had been a single tenancy granted for a term beginning at the same time as the term under the earlier tenancy and expiring at the same time as the term under the later tenancy.

(4) Where a tenancy is or has been granted for a term of years certain not exceeding twenty-one years, but with a covenant or obligation for renewal without payment of a premium (but not for perpetual renewal), and the tenancy is or has been once or more renewed so as to bring to more than twenty-one years the total of the terms granted (including any interval between the end of a tenancy and the grant of a renewal), then this Part of this Act shall apply as it would apply if the term originally granted had been one exceeding twenty-one years.

(5) References in this Part of this Act to a long tenancy include any period during which the tenancy is or was continued under Part I or II of the Landlord and Tenant Act 1954 under Schedule 10 to the Local Government and Housing Act 1989 or under the Leasehold Property (Temporary Provisions) Act 1951.

(6) Where at any time there are separate tenancies, with the same landlord and the same tenant, of two or more parts of a house, or of a house or part of it and land or other premises occupied therewith, then in relation to the property comprised in such of those tenancies as are long tenancies this Part of this Act shall apply as it would if at that time there were a single tenancy of that property and the tenancy were a long tenancy, and for that purpose references in this Part of this Act to the commencement of the term or to the term date shall, if the separate tenancies commenced at different dates or have different term dates, have effect as references to the commencement or term date, as the case may be, of the tenancy comprising the house (or the earliest commencement or earliest term date of the tenancies comprising it):

Provided that this subsection shall have effect subject to the operation of subsections (2) to (5) above in relation to any of the separate tenancies.

III L&T [51.1]

Definitions For the meaning of "tenancy" and "term date", see Leasehold Reform Act 1967 s 37(1)(f), (g) (see para **III L&T [63]**).

III L&T [51.2]

Long tenancy To have a long tenancy a tenant must be, or have been, in a position to say that, subject to options to determine, rights of entry and so on, he is entitled to remain a tenant for the next 21 years, whether in law or equity. It is not sufficient merely to have successive periods of right as tenant amounting to 21 years. The subsequent periods must stem from a right of renewal or extension; *see Roberts v Church Comrs for England* [1972] 1 QB 278, [1971] 3 All ER 703, CA. Where Leasehold Reform Act 1967 s 3(2) applies, the second tenancy will be a long tenancy in the hands of any tenant in whom it becomes vested: *Austin v Dick Richards Properties Ltd* [1975] 2 All ER 75, [1975] 1 WLR 1033, CA. In *Eton College v Bard* [1983] Ch 321, [1983] 2 All ER 961, CA, it was held that a 94-year lease, granted by a housing association, was a long tenancy within Leasehold Reform Act 1967 s 3(1) (see para **III L&T [51]**) despite a provision that the lease would come to an end if it ceased to be vested in a member of the housing association (otherwise than by death or bankruptcy). Where an underlease is granted after 18 April 1980, in accordance with the terms of a head lease which was created before that date, it is not necessarily granted "in pursuance of a contract entered into before that date" for the purposes of para (a) of the proviso to Leasehold Reform Act 1967 s 3(1) (see para **III L&T [51]**). In order to come within the proviso the lessee would have to be under an obligation to grant the underlease: *Proma Ltd v Curtis* (1990) 59 P & CR 242, [1990] 1 EGLR 117, CA. Where the landlord or the tenant's estate was entitled to terminate a tenancy by giving not less than one month's notice on the death of the tenant, the proviso to s 3(1) was satisfied and the tenancy was not a long tenancy: *Skinns v Greenwood* [2002] EWCA Civ 424, [2002] HLR 906, [2002] 22 EG 137.

III L&T [51.3]

Term certain In *Re 51 Bennington Road, Aston* (1993) Times, 21 July it was held that the tenants of the residue of "the term or several terms of 500 years" dating from 20 October 1563 had a "term certain" within the definition of a "long tenancy" in Leasehold Reform Act 1967 s 5(1) (see para **III L&T [54]**).

III L&T [52]

4. Meaning of "low rent"

(1) For purposes of this Part of this Act a tenancy of any property is a tenancy at a low rent at any time when rent is not payable under the tenancy in respect of the property at a yearly rate—

- (i) if the tenancy was entered into before 1st April 1990, or on or after 1st April 1990 in pursuance of a contract made before that date, and the property had a rateable value other than nil at the date of the commencement of the tenancy or else at any time before 1st April 1990, equal to or more than two-thirds of the rateable value of the property on the appropriate day or, if later, the first day of the term;
- (ii) if the tenancy does not fall within paragraph (i) above, more than £1,000 if the property is in Greater London and £250 if the property is elsewhere:

Provided that a tenancy granted between the end of August 1939 and the beginning of April 1963 otherwise than by way of building lease (whether or not it is, by virtue of section 3(3) above, to be treated for other purposes as forming a single tenancy with a previous tenancy) shall not be regarded as a tenancy at a low rent if at the commencement of the tenancy the rent payable under the tenancy exceeded two-thirds of the letting value of the property (on the same terms).

For the purpose of this subsection—

- (a) "appropriate day" means 23rd March 1965 or such later day as by virtue of section 25(3) of the Rent Act 1977 would be the appropriate day for purposes of that Act in relation to a dwelling-house consisting of the house in question if the reference in paragraph (a) of that provision to a rateable value were to a rateable value other than nil]; and
- (b) "rent" means rent reserved as such, and there shall be disregarded any part of the rent expressed to be payable in consideration of services to be provided, or of repairs, maintenance or insurance to be effected by the landlord, or to be payable in respect of the cost thereof to the landlord or a superior landlord; and
- (c) there shall be disregarded any term of the tenancy providing for suspension or reduction of rent in the event of damage to property demised, or for any penal addition to the rent in the event of a contravention of or non-compliance with the terms of the tenancy or an agreement collateral thereto; and
- (d) "building lease" means a lease granted in pursuance or in consideration of an agreement for the erection or the substantial re-building or reconstruction of the whole or part of the house in question or a building comprising it.

(2) Where on a claim by the tenant of a house to exercise any right conferred by this Part of this Act a question arises under section 1(1) above whether his tenancy of the house is or was at any time a tenancy at a low rent, the question shall be determined by reference to the rent and rateable value of the house and premises as a whole, and in relation to a time before the relevant time shall be so determined whether or not the property then occupied with the house or any part of it was the same in all respects as that comprised in the house and premises for purposes of

the claim; but in a case where the tenancy derives (in accordance with section 3(6) above) from one or more than one separate tenancy, the proviso to subsection (1) above shall have effect if, but only if, it applies to one of the separate tenancies which comprises the house or part of it.

(3) Where on a claim by the tenant of a house to exercise any right conferred by this Part of this Act a question arises under section 3(2) above whether a tenancy is or was a long tenancy by reason of a previous tenancy having been a long tenancy at a low rent, the question whether the previous tenancy was one at a low rent shall be determined in accordance with subsection (2) above as if it were a question arising under section 1(1), and shall be so determined by reference to the rent and rateable value of the house and premises or the part included in the previous tenancy, exclusive of any other land or premises so included:

Provided that where an apportionment of rent or rateable value is required because the previous tenancy did not include the whole of the house and premises or included other property, the apportionment shall be made as at the end of the previous tenancy except in so far as, in the case of rent, an apportionment falls to be made at an earlier date under subsection (6) below.

(4) For purposes of subsection (2) or (3) above a house and premises shall be taken as not including any premises which are to be or may be included under section 2(3) above in giving effect to the tenant's claim, and as including any part which is to be or may be excluded under section 2(5) or (6).

(5) Where on a claim by the tenant of a house to exercise any right conferred by this Part of this Act a question arises whether a tenancy granted as mentioned in the proviso to subsection (1) above is or was at any time a tenancy at a low rent, it shall be presumed until the contrary is shown that the letting value referred to in that proviso was such that the proviso does not apply.

(6) Any entire rent payable at any time in respect of both a house and premises or part thereof and of property not included in the house and premises shall for purposes of this section be apportioned as may be just according to the circumstances existing at the date of the severance giving rise to the apportionment, and references in this section to the rent of a house and premises or of part thereof shall be construed accordingly.

(7) Section 1(7) above applies to any amount referred to in subsection (1)(ii) above as it applies to the amount referred to in subsection (1)(a)(ii) of that section.

III L&T [52.1]

Letting value The rent restrictions which were in force at the commencement of the tenancy must be taken into account in ascertaining the letting value and so must the decapitalised value of any lawfully obtainable premium: *Manson v Duke of Westminster* [1981] QB 323, [1981] 2 All ER 40, CA; *Johnston v Duke of Westminster* [1986] AC 839, [1986] 2 All ER 613, HL. The true annual letting value may reasonably be inferred from the premium paid on an assignment of the lease a week later: *McDonald v Trustees of Henry Smith's Charity* (1987) Times, 30 July, CA.

III L&T [52.2]

Lease of two cottages later converted into a single dwelling Where a lease was granted of two cottages which were later converted into a single dwelling, the rateable value of the dwelling at the date of the grant was taken to be the aggregate of the rateable values of the two cottages: *Neville v Cowdray Trust Ltd* [2006] EWCA Civ 709, [2006] 1 WLR 2097.

III L&T [53]

4A. *Repealed*

III L&T [54]

5. General provisions as to claims to enfranchisement or extension

(1) Where under this Part of this Act a tenant of a house has the right to acquire the freehold or an extended lease and gives notice of his desire to have it, the rights and obligations of the landlord and the tenant arising from the notice shall inure for the benefit of and be enforceable against them, their executors, administrators and assigns to the like extent (but no further) as rights and obligations arising under a contract for a sale or lease freely entered into between the landlord and tenant; and accordingly, in relation to matters arising out of any such notice, references in this Part of this Act to the tenant and the landlord shall, in so far as the context permits, include their respective executors, administrators and assigns.

(2) Notwithstanding anything in subsection (1) above, the rights and obligations there referred to of a tenant shall be assignable with, but not capable of subsisting apart from, the tenancy of the entire house and premises; and if the tenancy is assigned without the benefit of the notice, or if the tenancy of one part of the house and premises is assigned to or vests in any person without the tenancy of another part, the notice shall accordingly cease to have effect, and the tenant shall be liable to make such compensation as may be just to the landlord in respect of the interference (if any) by the notice with the exercise by the landlord of his power to dispose of or deal with the house and premises or any neighbouring property.

(3) In the event of any default by the landlord or the tenant in carrying out the obligations arising from any such notice, the other of them shall have the like rights and remedies as in the case of a contract freely entered into.

(4) The provisions of Schedule 1 to this Act shall have effect in relation to the operation of this Part of this Act where a person gives notice of his desire to have the freehold or an extended lease of a house and premises, and either he does so in respect of a sub-tenancy or there is a tenancy reversionary on his tenancy; but any such notice given in respect of a tenancy granted by sub-demise out of a superior tenancy other than a long tenancy at a low rent shall be of no effect if the grant was made in breach of the terms of the superior tenancy and there has been no waiver of the breach by the superior landlord.

(5) A tenant's notice of his desire to have an extended lease under this Part of this Act shall cease to have effect if afterwards (being entitled to do so) he gives notice of his desire to have the freehold.

LANDLORD & TENANT AND HOUSING

III L&T [54.1]

Tenant's notice For procedural provisions with regard to a tenant's notice, see the Leasehold Reform Act 1967 Sch 3 Pt II (see paras **III L&T [64]** and **III L&T [64.4]**). The notice must be unequivocal and cannot be in the alternative: *Byrnlea Property Investment Ltd v Ramsay* [1969] 2 QB 253, sub nom *Re 33, Byrne Road, Balham, Byrnlea Property Investments Ltd v Ramsay* [1969] 2 All ER 311, CA. For form of notice, see the Leasehold Reform (Notices) Regulations 1997, SI 1997/640. In the case of notices given after 26 July 2002, Forms 1 and 2 in the Schedule to the 1997 Regulations are, to the extent of England only, replaced by Forms 1 and 2 in the Schedule to the Leasehold Reform (Notices) (Amendment) (England) Regulations 2002, SI 2002/1715. For Wales, from 1 January 2003 Forms 1 and 2 are as in the Schedule to the Leasehold Reform (Notices) (Amendment) (Wales) Regulations 2002, SI 2002/3187. See also SI 2002/3209 for the Form 3 to be used as from 10 April 2003.

III L&T [54.2]

Tenant of a house Provision is made in the Leasehold Reform Act 1967 s 6 (rights of trustees) for circumstances where the tenant was at an earlier time sole tenant for life or beneficially interested in the trust in which the tenancy was vested. Where the tenant of a house dies and a resident member of the family succeeds to the tenancy the Leasehold Reform Act 1967 s 7 provides for the rights under the Act to be exercisable by the successor.

III L&T [54.2A]

Assignment of the benefit of a notice Section 5(2) provides that, if a tenancy is assigned without the benefit of the tenant's notice, the notice shall cease to have effect. However, an assignment of the benefit of the notice which was made independently of or before an assignment of the tenancy is of no effect and does not serve to deprive the tenant of the right to enfranchise: *South v Chamberlayne* [2001] 43 EG 190.

III L&T [54.3]

Sub-tenants Detailed provision is made in the Leasehold Reform Act 1967 Sch 1 for enfranchisement or extension by sub-tenants.

III L&T [54.4]

Limitation period The tenant's cause of action derives from Leasehold Reform Act 1967 s 8 (see para **III L&T [55]**) and, to the extent that the Limitation Act 1980 is applicable, it allows 12 years in which to bring proceedings on the cause of action, not six years from the date when proceedings could have been taken after the service of notice under the Leasehold Reform Act 1967 s 5 (see para **III L&T [54]**): *Collin v Duke of Westminster* [1985] QB 581, [1985] 1 All ER 463, CA.

ENFRANCHISEMENT

III L&T [55]

8. Obligation to enfranchise

(1) Where a tenant of a house has under this Part of this Act a right to acquire the freehold, and gives to the landlord written notice of his desire to have the freehold, then except as provided by this Part of this Act the landlord shall be bound to make to the tenant, and the tenant to accept, (at the price and on the conditions so provided) a grant of the house and premises for an estate in fee simple absolute, subject to the tenancy and to tenant's incumbrances, but otherwise free of incumbrances.

(2) For purposes of this Part of this Act "incumbrances" includes rentcharges and, subject to subsection (3) below, personal liabilities attaching in respect of the ownership of land or an interest in land though not charged on that land or interest; and "tenant's incumbrances" includes any interest directly or indirectly derived out of the tenancy, and any incumbrance on the tenancy or any such interest (whether or not the same matter is an incumbrance also on any interest reversionary on the tenancy).

(3) Burdens originating in tenure, and burdens in respect of the upkeep or regulation for the benefit of any locality of any land, building, structure, works, ways or watercourse shall not be treated as incumbrances for purposes of this Part of this Act, but any conveyance executed to give effect to this section shall be made subject thereto as otherwise provided by section 11 below.

(4) A conveyance executed to give effect to this section—

- (a) shall have effect under section 2 (1) of the Law of Property Act 1925 to overreach any incumbrance capable of being overreached under that section as if, where the interest conveyed is settled land, the conveyance were made under the powers of the Settled Land Act 1925 and as if the requirements of section 2 (1) as to payment of the capital money allowed any part of the purchase price paid or applied in accordance with sections 11 to 13 below to be so paid or applied;
- (b) shall not be made subject to any incumbrance capable of being overreached by the conveyance, but shall be made subject (where they are not capable of being overreached) to rentcharges redeemable under sections *8* [7A] to 10 of the Rentcharges Act 1977 and those falling within paragraphs (c) and (d) of section 2(3) of that Act (estate rentcharges and rentcharges imposed under certain enactments), except as otherwise provided by section 11 below.

(5) Notwithstanding that on a grant to a tenant of a house and premises under this section no payment or a nominal payment only is required from the tenant for the price of the house and premises, the tenant shall nevertheless be deemed for all purposes to be a purchaser for a valuable consideration in money or money's worth.

Amendment *Text in italic is deleted and text in square brackets is inserted by the Housing and Planning Act 2016, with effect from a date to be appointed.*

III L&T [55.1]

"Written notice" A tenant's notice must be in the prescribed form (see the Leasehold Reform (Notices) Regulations 1997, SI 1997/640) and contain the particulars set out in the Leasehold Reform Act 1967 Sch 3 para 6(1) (see paras **III L&T [64]** and **III L&T [64.4]**). In the case of notices given after 26 July 2002, Forms 1 and 2 in the Schedule to the 1997 Regulations are, to the extent of England only, replaced by Forms 1 and 2 in the Schedule to the Leasehold Reform (Notices) (Amendment) (England) Regulations 2002, SI 2002/1715. For Wales, from 1 January 2003 Forms 1 and 2 are as in the Schedule to the Leasehold Reform (Notices) (Amendment) (Wales) Regulations 2002, SI 2002/3187. See also SI 2002/3209 for the Form 3 to be used as from 10 April 2003. Joint tenants must join the giving of the notice or one may act with the authority of the other: *Wax v Viscount Chelsea* [1996] 2 EGLR 80, [1996] 41 EG 169.

III L&T [55.2]

Enfranchisement where landlord cannot be found Where the tenant is prevented from giving notice of his desire to have the freehold because the person to be served with the notice cannot be found or his identity cannot be ascertained the Leasehold Reform Act 1967 s 27 enables the High Court, on an application by the tenant, to make such order as the court thinks fit with a view to the house being vested in him for the like estate and on the like terms as if he had given notice of his desire to have the freehold.

III L&T [55.3]

Rights and incumbrances Detailed provision is made in the Leasehold Reform Act 1967 s 10 for the rights to be conveyed on enfranchisement and in the Leasehold Reform Act 1967 ss 12 and 13 for the discharge of mortgages and the circumstances in which the mortgage money is to be paid into the county court. The Leasehold Reform Act 1967 s 36 provides relief in respect of mortgages on the landlord's estate.

It has been held that where the tenancies were granted under a building scheme under which the tenants of each plot had rights of way over the adjacent plot the enfranchisement of the lease in effect enfranchised the easements too, so that they subsisted for the benefit/burden of the respective freehold interests: *Kent v Kavanagh* [2006] EWCA Civ 162, (2006) Times, 24 March.

III L&T [55.4]

Costs The fact that the tenant's acquisition of the freehold may be highly profitable is not a reason for ordering him to bear his own costs: *Lawlor v Hannon* [1981] CA Transcript 338.

III L&T [55.5]

Prior service of notice under s 42 of LRHUDA 1993 Where the tenant held a long lease of a building, which comprised five flats, one of which the tenant occupied and, shortly before the expiry date of the lease of the building, the tenant served a notice under s 42 of Leasehold Reform Housing and Urban Development Act 1993 claiming to exercise the right to acquire a new lease of that flat only, service of the s 42 notice severed the lease of the flat from the lease of the rest of the property. Schedule 12 para 5 of LHRUDA 1993 did not provide for continuation of the lease of the whole property following service of the s 42 notice. Accordingly a claim by the tenant, under s 8 of the 1967 Act to acquire the freehold of the building failed because the lease of the building had expired on its expiry date: *Ackerman v Lay* [2008] EWCA Civ 1428.

III L&T [55.6]

Marriage value and hope value Combining the leasehold and freehold interests releases a "marriage value" which is required by s 9(1D) to be split between the landlord and the tenant when assessing the price to be paid for enfranchisement. In circumstances where marriage value arises as between landlord and participating tenants nothing extra can be claimed as "hope value". But "hope value" does arise as between landlord and non-participating tenants: *Earl Cadogan v Sportelli* (2008) Times, 17 December, CA.

See now the decisions of the House of Lords in *Cadogan v Pitts* [2008] UKHL 71, [2009] 3 All ER 365, [2009] 2 WLR 12 (i) that s 9(1) excludes hope value as well as marriage value, (ii) that s 9(1A) does not allow hope value to be added to marriage value, (iii) that Sch 13, para 3(2) bars the inclusion of hope value as well as marriage value, but (4) that under Sch 6, para 3 hope value may be taken into account so far as attributable to the possibility of non-participating tenants seeking leases by negotiation, not as of right.

EXTENSION

III L&T [56]

14. Obligation to grant extended lease

(1) Where a tenant of a house has under this Part of this Act a right to an extended lease, and gives to the landlord written notice of his desire to have it, then except as provided by this Part of this Act the landlord shall be bound to grant to the tenant and the tenant to accept, in substitution for the existing tenancy a new tenancy of the house and premises for a term expiring fifty years after the term date of the existing tenancy.

(2) Where a person gives notice of his desire to have an extended lease of a house and premises under this Part of this Act, then unless the notice lapses under any provision of this Act excluding his liability, there shall be borne by him (so far as they are incurred in pursuance of the notice) the reasonable costs of or incidental to any of the following matters—

- (a) any investigation by the landlord of that person's right to an extended lease;
- (b) any lease granting the new tenancy;
- (c) any valuation of the house and premises obtained by the landlord before the grant of the new tenancy for the purpose of fixing the rent payable under it in accordance with section 15 below.

(2A) Subsection (2) above does not require a person to bear the costs of another person in connection with an application to the appropriate tribunal.

(3) A tenant shall not be entitled to require the execution of a lease granting a new tenancy under this section otherwise than on tender of the amount, so far as ascertained,—

- (a) of any sums payable by way of rent or recoverable as rent in respect of the house and premises up to the date of tender; and
- (b) of any sums for which at that date the tenant is liable under subsection (2) above; and
- (c) of any other sums due and payable by him to the landlord under or in respect of the existing tenancy or any agreement collateral thereto;

and, if the amount of any such sums is not or may not be fully ascertained, on offering reasonable security for the payment of such amount as may afterwards be found to be payable in respect of them.

(4) This section shall have effect notwithstanding that the grant of the existing tenancy was subsequent to the creation of a charge on the landlord's estate and not authorised as against the persons interested in the charge; and a lease executed to give effect to this section shall be deemed to be authorised as against the persons interested in any charge on the landlord's estate, however created or arising, and shall be binding on them:

Provided that, where the existing tenancy is granted after the commencement of this Part of this Act (whether or not it is, by virtue of section 3 (3) above, to be treated for other purposes as forming a single tenancy with a previous tenancy) and, the grant being subsequent to the creation of the charge on the landlord's estate, the existing tenancy is not binding on the persons interested in the charge, a lease executed to give effect to this section shall not by virtue of this subsection be binding on those persons.

(5) Where a lease is executed to give effect to this section, and any person having a charge on the landlord's estate is by reason thereof entitled to possession of the documents of title relating to that estate, the landlord shall within one month after execution of the lease deliver to that person a counterpart of it duly executed by the tenant, and the instrument creating or evidencing the charge shall apply in the event of his failing to deliver a counterpart in accordance with this subsection as if the obligation to do so were included in the terms of the charge as set out in that instrument.

(6) Where under a lease executed to give effect to this section the new tenancy takes effect subject to a subsisting charge on the existing tenancy, and at the time of its execution the person having the charge is by reason thereof entitled to possession of the documents of title relating to the existing tenancy, then he shall be similarly entitled to possession of the documents of title relating to the new tenancy and the tenant shall within one month of the execution of the lease deliver it to him, and the instrument creating or evidencing the charge shall apply in the event of the tenant failing to deliver the lease in accordance with this subsection as if the obligation to do so were included in the terms of the charge as set out in that instrument.

(7) A landlord granting a lease under this section shall be bound to take such steps as may be necessary to secure that it is not liable in accordance with the proviso to subsection (4) above to be defeated by persons interested in a charge on his estate; but a landlord is not obliged, in order to grant a lease under this section, to acquire a better title than he has or could require to be vested in him.

III L&T [56.1]

"Written notice" A tenant's notice must be in the prescribed form (see the Leasehold Reform (Notices) Regulations 1997, SI 1997/640) and contain the particulars set out in the Leasehold Reform Act 1967 Sch 3 para 6(1) (see para **III L&T [64]** and para **III L&T [64.4]**). In the case of notices given after 26 July 2002, Forms 1 and 2 in the Schedule to the 1997 Regulations are, to the extent of England only, replaced by Forms 1 and 2 in the Schedule to the Leasehold Reform (Notices) (Amendment) (England) Regulations 2002, SI 2002/1715. For Wales, from 1 January 2003 Forms 1 and 2 are as in the Schedule to the Leasehold Reform (Notices) (Amendment) (Wales) Regulations 2002, SI 2002/3187. See also SI 2002/3209 for Form 3 to be used as from 10 April 2003.

III L&T [56.2]

County court jurisdiction The county court has jurisdiction to determine what provisions ought to be contained in a lease granting a new tenancy under this section: Leasehold Reform Act 1967 s 20(2)(b) (see para **III L&T [59]**).

III L&T [56.3]

Terms and exclusion of further rights The Leasehold Reform Act 1967 s 15 specifies the terms of the tenancy to be granted on extension and the Leasehold Reform Act 1967 s 16 provides for the exclusion of further rights after extension. For amendments to prescribed forms, following the amendment of s 16 of the Act by s 143 of the Commonhold and Leasehold Reform Act 2002, see the Long Residential Tenancies (Principal Forms) (Amendment) (England) Regulations 2002, SI 2002/2227.

LANDLORD'S OVERRIDING RIGHTS

III L&T [57]

17. Redevelopment rights (exclusion or termination of extension)

(1) Where a tenancy of a house and premises has been extended under section 14 above, the landlord may, at any time not earlier than twelve months before the original term date of the tenancy, apply to the court for an order that he may resume possession of the property on the ground that for purposes of redevelopment he proposes to demolish or reconstruct the whole or a substantial part of the house and premises.

(2) If on an application under subsection (1) above the court is satisfied that the landlord has established the ground mentioned in that subsection, then subject to the provisions of this section the court shall by order declare that the landlord is entitled as against the tenant to obtain possession of the house and premises and the tenant is entitled to be paid compensation by the landlord for the loss of the house and premises.

(3) Where an order is made under subsection (2) above, the tenancy shall determine and the compensation become payable in accordance with Schedule 2 to this Act; and the provisions of that Schedule shall have effect as regards the measure of compensation under any such order and the effects of the order where there are sub-tenancies, and as regards other matters relating to applications and orders under this section.

(4) Where the tenancy of a house and premises has not been extended under section 14 above, but the tenant has a right to an extended lease and gives notice of his desire to have one, then this section shall apply as if the lease had been extended under section 14; and—

(a) on the making by the landlord of an application under this section, the notice shall be suspended until the time when an order under subsection (2) or an order dismissing the application becomes final or the application is withdrawn; and

(b) on an order under subsection (2) becoming final, the notice shall cease to have effect, but section 14 (2) above shall not apply to require the tenant to make any payment to the landlord in respect of costs incurred by reason of the notice.

(5) For purposes of subsection (4) above, the reference in subsection (1) to the original term date shall have effect as a reference to the term date or, in a case where before the relevant time the landlord had given notice to quit terminating the tenancy at a date earlier than the term date, as a reference to the date specified in the notice to quit.

(6) Where a landlord makes an application under subsection (1) above, then—

(a) if the tenant afterwards gives notice of his desire to have the freehold of the house and premises under this Part of this Act, that notice shall be of no effect if it is not given before the date of the order fixing the date for the termination of the tenancy (in accordance with Schedule 2 to this Act), or if the tenant's notice of his desire to have an extended lease was given within twelve months before the making of the landlord's application; and

(b) if a notice given by the tenant (before or after the making of the landlord's application) of his desire to have the freehold has effect, no order or further order shall be made on the landlord's application except as regards costs, but without prejudice to the making of a further application by the landlord if the tenant's notice lapses without effect being given to it.

III L&T [57.1]

"Term date" For the meaning of this expression, see the Leasehold Reform Act 1967 s 37(1)(g), (3) (see para **III L&T [63]**).

III L&T [57.2]

"Apply to the court" An application under the Leasehold Reform Act 1967 s 17(1) (see para **III L&T [57]**) must be made to the county court: Leasehold Reform Act 1967 s 20(1) (see para **III L&T [59]**). The claim under s 17 must be made in accordance with CPR Pt 55 (see CPR PD 56 para 13.4 (para **CPR PD 56**)). The defendant must, immediately after being served with the claim form, serve on every person in occupation of the property, or part of it under an immediate or derivative sub-tenancy, a notice informing him of the claim and of his right under para 3(4) of Sch 2 to the 1967 Act to take part in the hearing of the claim with the permission of the court. He must also, within 14 days after being served with the claim form, file a defence stating the ground, if any, on which he intends to oppose the claim and giving particulars of every such sub-tenancy (see CPR PD 56 para 13.4).

III L&T [57.3]

Special cases Special provision is made for cases in which the landlord's interest is subject to a mortgage (Leasehold Reform Act 1967 s 25(2), (5)(b)) or the landlord is a custodian trustee (Leasehold Reform Act 1967 s 26(1)) or a mental patient (Leasehold Reform Act 1967 s 26 (2)) or the house is ecclesiastical property (Leasehold Reform Act 1967 s 31(2)(b)).

III L&T [57.4]

"Demolish or reconstruct" Compare the similar ground on which an application for a new business tenancy may be opposed under the Landlord and Tenant Act 1954 s 30(1)(f) (see para **III L&T [22]**). Where the landlord is one of certain public bodies a certificate given by a Minister of the Crown is conclusive evidence that the ground specified in the Leasehold Reform Act 1967 s 17(1) is established: Leasehold Reform Act 1967 s 28(1)(c).

III L&T [57.5]

"Has not been extended" Where the tenant gives notice of his desire to have an extended lease and the landlord intends to apply for possession of the house under this section, the landlord's notice in reply must state this intention: Leasehold Reform Act 1967 Sch 3 para 7(3) (see para **III L&T [64]**).

III L&T [57.6]

"Becomes final" As to the circumstances in which an order of a court is to be treated as becoming final, see the Leasehold Reform Act 1967 s 37(7) (see para **III L&T [63]**).

LANDLORD & TENANT AND HOUSING

III L&T [58]

18. Residential rights (exclusion of enfranchisement or extension)

(1) Subject to subsection (2) below, where the tenancy of a house and premises has not been extended under section 14 above, but the tenant has a right to acquire the freehold or an extended lease and has given notice of his desire to have it, the landlord may, at any time before effect is given to the notice, apply to the court for an order that he may resume possession of the property on the ground that it or part of it is or will be reasonably required by him for occupation as the only or main residence of the landlord or of a person who is at the time of the application an adult member of the landlord's family.

(2) A landlord shall not be entitled to apply to the court under this section if his interest in the house and premises, or an interest which has merged in that interest but would otherwise have had a duration extending at least five years longer than that of the tenancy, was purchased or created after the 18th February 1966; and for purposes of this subsection the duration of any interest in the house and premises (including the tenancy) shall be taken to be the period until it is due to expire or, if capable of earlier determination by notice given by a person as landlord, the date or earliest date which has been or could be specified in such a notice.

(3) Where the landlord's interest is held on trust, subsection (1) above shall apply as if the reference to occupation as the residence of the landlord were a reference to the like occupation of a person having an interest under the trust (whether or not also a trustee), and the reference to a member of the landlord's family were a reference to the like member of such a person's family; and for purposes of subsection (1) a person is an adult member of another's family if that person is—

(a) the other's spouse or civil partner; or

(b) a son or daughter or a son-in-law or daughter-in-law of the other, or of the other's spouse or civil partner, who has attained the age of eighteen; or

(c) the father or mother of the other, or of the other's spouse or civil partner.

In paragraph (b) above any reference to a person's son or daughter includes a reference to any stepson or stepdaughter, any illegitimate son or daughter, [. . .] of that person, and "son-in-law" and "daughter-in-law" shall be construed accordingly.

(4) If on an application under subsection (1) above the court is satisfied that the landlord has established the ground mentioned in that section and is not disentitled by subsection (2), the court shall by order declare that the landlord is entitled as against the tenant to obtain possession of the house and premises and the tenant is entitled to be paid compensation by the landlord for the loss of the house and premises:

Provided that the court shall not make an order under this subsection if the court is satisfied that having regard to all the circumstances of the case, including the question whether other accommodation is available for the landlord or the tenant, greater hardship would be caused by making the order than by refusing to make it.

(5) Where an order is made under subsection (4) above, the tenancy shall determine and the compensation become payable in accordance with Schedule 2 to this Act; and the provisions of that Schedule shall have effect as regards the measure of compensation under any such order and the effects of the order where there are sub-tenancies, and as regards other matters relating to applications and orders under this section.

(6) Where a landlord makes an application under this section,—

- (a) any notice previously given by the tenant of his desire to have the freehold or an extended lease of the house and premises under this Part of this Act shall be suspended until the time when an order under subsection (4) or an order dismissing the application becomes final or the application is withdrawn; and
- (b) on an order under subsection (4) becoming final, the notice shall cease to have effect, but section 9 (4) or 14 (2) above shall not apply to require the tenant to make any payment to the landlord in respect of costs incurred by reason of the notice;

and a notice of the tenant's desire to have the freehold shall be of no effect if given after the making of the application and before the time referred to in paragraph (a) above or after an order under subsection (4) above has become final.

III L&T [58.1]

Notice Where a tenant gives notice of his desire to have the freehold or an extended lease and the landlord intends to apply for possession of the house under this section, the landlord's notice in reply must state this intention: Leasehold Reform Act 1967 Sch 3 para 7(3) (see para **III L&T [64]**).

III L&T [58.2]

"Apply to the court" An application under this provision must be made to the county court: Leasehold Reform Act 1967 s 20(1) (see para **III L&T [59]**). The claim under s 18 must be made in accordance with CPR Pt 55 (see CPR PD 56 para 13.4 (para **CPR PD 56**)). The defendant must, immediately after being served with the claim form, serve on every person in occupation of the property or part of it under an immediate or derivative sub-tenancy, a notice informing him of the claim and of his right under para 3(4) of Sch 2 to the 1967 Act to take part in the hearing of the claim with the permission of the court. He must also, within 14 days after being served with the claim form, file a defence stating the ground, if any, on which he intends to oppose the claim and giving particulars of every such sub-tenancy (see CPR PD 56 para 13.4 (para **CPR PD 56**)).

III L&T [58.3]

Landlord mortgagor Where the landlord's interest is subject to a mortgage and a receiver has been appointed, an application cannot be made under this section without the consent of the mortgagee: Leasehold Reform Act 1967 s 25 (5)(a).

III L&T [58.4]

Own use The landlord's requirement of the premises for his own use must relate to the date when the lease ends and must be a definite one. A nebulous possibility is insufficient and the burden of establishing the requirement is difficult where the lease will end several years ahead: *Gurvidi v Mangat* (1972) 116 Sol Jo 255, CA.

III L&T [58.5]

"Becomes final" As to the circumstances in which an order of a court is to be treated as becoming final, see Leasehold Reform Act 1967 s 37(7) (see para **III L&T [63]**).

DETERMINATION OF QUESTIONS, PROCEDURE, ETC.

III L&T [59]

20. Jurisdiction and special powers of county court

(1) Subject to section 115 of the County Courts Act 1959, any jurisdiction expressed to be conferred on the court by this Part of this Act shall, unless the contrary intention appears, be exercised by the county court.

(2) Except as provided by this section and section 21 below, there shall also be brought in the county court any proceedings under this Part of this Act of the following descriptions:—

- (a) proceedings for determining whether a person is entitled to acquire the freehold or an extended lease of a house and premises, or to what property his right extends;
- (b) proceedings for determining what provisions ought to be contained in a conveyance in accordance with section 10 or 29 (1), or in a lease granting a new tenancy under section 14;
- (c) any other proceedings relating to the performance or discharge of obligations arising out of a tenant's notice of his desire to have the freehold or an extended lease, including proceedings for the recovery of damages or compensation in the event of the obligations not being performed;
- (d) any proceedings for determining the amount of a sub-tenant's share under Schedule 2 to this Act in compensation payable to a tenant under section 17 or 18, or for establishing or giving effect to his right to it.

(3) Where in connection with any acquisition by a tenant of the freehold or an extended lease under this Part of this Act it is necessary to apportion between the house and premises (or part of them) and other property the rent payable under his tenancy or any superior or reversionary tenancy, then, subject to section 115 of the County Courts Act 1959 and to section 21 below, the apportionment shall be made by the county court.

(4) Where it is made to appear to the court that the landlord or the tenant has been guilty of any unreasonable delay or default in the performance of obligations arising from a tenant's notice of his desire to have the freehold or an extended lease under this Part of this Act, then (without prejudice to any right to damages) the court may—

- (a) by order revoke or vary, and direct repayment of sums paid under, any provision made by a previous order as to payment of the costs of proceedings in the court in relation to the matter, or, where costs have not been awarded, award costs;
- (b) certify particulars of the delay or default to the Upper Tribunal with a view to enabling the Tribunal to exercise a like discretion in relation to costs of proceedings before the Tribunal.

LANDLORD & TENANT AND HOUSING

(4A) Where the court certifies particulars of delay or default to the Upper Tribunal under subsection (4)(b) above, the Lands Tribunal may make any order as to costs of proceedings before the Lands Tribunal which the court may make in relation to proceedings in the court.

(5) Where a person gives notice of his desire to have the freehold or to have an extended lease of a house and premises under this Part of this Act, and the notice either is set aside by the court or withdrawn, or ceases to have effect, or would, if valid, cease to have effect, then if it is made to appear to the court—

(a) that the notice was not given in good faith; or

(b) that the person giving the notice attempted in any material respect to support it by misrepresentation or the concealment of material facts;

the court may, on the application of the landlord, order that person to pay to the landlord such sum as appears sufficient as compensation for damage or loss sustained by the landlord as the result of the giving of the notice.

(6) In any case where under subsection (5) above the court has power, on the application of the landlord, to order a person to make a payment to the landlord, the court (whether or not it makes an order under that subsection) may, on the application of the landlord, order that any further notice given by that person under this Part of this Act of his desire to have the freehold or an extended lease of the same house or any part of it, with or without other property, shall be void if given within the five years beginning with the date of the order.

(7) Subsection (2)(c) above shall not prevent the bringing of proceedings in a court other than the county court where the claim is for damages or pecuniary compensation only.

III L&T [59.1]

County Courts Act 1959 County Courts Act 1959 s 115, which provided for the removal of proceedings into the High Court where it was desirable that they should be heard and determined there has been repealed and replaced by the County Courts Act 1984 s 41 (see para **II CCA [23]**). In *South v Chamberlayne* [2001] 43 EG 190, the High Court judge confirmed that s 20 of the Leasehold Reform Act 1967 gives the county court exclusive jurisdiction. The judge was therefore bound to transfer a claim under the Act to the county court under s 40 of the 1984 Act. However, as the matter was suitable for determination in the High Court, the judge thereupon transferred the claim back to his court pursuant to s 41 of the 1984 Act.

III L&T [59.2]

Procedure Procedure under the Leasehold Reform Act 1967 is now regulated by CPR 56.4 (see para **CPR 56.4**) and CPR PD 56 paras 13.1 to 13.5 (see para **CPR PD 56**). For a general summary see para **III L&T [44]**, for procedure on claims under s 17 see para **III L&T [57.2]** and for procedure on claims under s 18 see para **III L&T [58.2]**.

III L&T [59.3]

Tenant's concealment of material facts In *Dymond v Arundel-Timms* (1990) 23 HLR 397, [1991] 1 EGLR 109 the Court of Appeal refused to disturb county court findings that a tenant's failure to disclose another residence, in breach of Leasehold Reform Act 1967 Sch 3 para 6 (1)(ii) (see para **III L&T [64]**) was a "misrepresentation or concealment of material facts" within Leasehold Reform Act 1967 s 20(5)(b) and that the tenant was, for this reason, not entitled to buy the freehold.

III L&T [59.4]

Enforcement of tenant's rights Proceedings cannot be instituted by a tenant with a view to the enforcement of his right to have the freehold or an extended lease before the landlord has given his notice in reply to the tenant's notice or two months have elapsed without his doing so since the giving of the tenant's notice: Leasehold Reform Act 1967 Sch 3 para 7(5) (see para **III L&T [64]**).

III L&T [59.5]

Special cases Leasehold Reform Act 1967 ss 25, 26 and 28 make special provision for cases in which the landlord is a mortgagee in possession, a custodian trustee or person under disability or a public body.

III L&T [60]

21. Jurisdiction of tribunals

(1) The following matters shall, in default of agreement, be determined by the appropriate tribunal namely,—

(a) the price payable for a house and premises under section 9 above;

(b) the amount of the rent to be payable (whether originally or on a revision) for a house and premises in accordance with section 15 (2);

(ba) the amount of any costs payable under section 9 (4) or 14 (2);

(c) the amount of any compensation payable to a tenant under section 17 or 18 for the loss of a house and premises;

(cza) the amount of the appropriate sum to be paid into court under section 27(5);

(ca) the amount of any compensation payable under section 27A.

(1A) . . .

(1B) No application may be made to the appropriate tribunal under subsection (1) above to determine the price for a house and premises unless either—

(a) the landlord has informed the tenant of the price he is asking; or

(b) two months have elapsed without his doing so since the tenant gave notice of his desire to have the freehold under this Part of this Act.

(2) Notwithstanding section 20 (2) or (3) above, the appropriate tribunal shall have jurisdiction, either by agreement or in a case where an application is made to a tribunal under subsection (1) above with reference to the same transaction,—

(a) to determine what provisions ought to be contained in a conveyance in accordance with section 10 or 29 (1) of this Act, or in a lease granting a new tenancy under section 14; or

(b) to apportion between the house and premises (or part of them) and other property the rent payable under any tenancy; or

(c) to determine the amount of a sub-tenant's share under Schedule 2 to this Act in compensation payable to a tenant under section 17 or 18.

(2A) For the purposes of this Part of this Act a matter is to be treated as determined by (or on appeal from) the appropriate tribunal—

(a) if the decision on the matter is not appealed against, at the end of the period for bringing an appeal; or

(b) if that decision is appealed against, at the time when the appeal is disposed of.

(2B) An appeal is disposed of—

(a) if it is determined and the period for bringing any further appeal has ended; or

(b) if it is abandoned or otherwise ceases to have effect.

(3), (4), (4A), (5) [. . .]

III L&T [60.1]

Price payable For a case where the price for a house and premises was fixed at site value see *British Petroleum Pension Trust v Blake* [1982] 2 EGLR 225, (Lands Tribunal).

III L&T [61]

22. Validity of tenants' notices, effect on Landlord and Tenant Act 1954 and on notices to quit, etc., and procedure generally

(1) The provisions of Schedule 3 to this Act shall have effect—

(a) to exclude a tenant's right to acquire the freehold or an extended lease under this Part of this Act if a notice of his desire to have it is given too late; and

(b) to make a notice of a person's desire to have the freehold or an extended lease under this Part of this Act effectual where apart from the notice the tenancy would or might terminate by forfeiture or otherwise; and

(c) for adapting the procedure under Parts I and II of the Landlord and Tenant Act 1954, and for relating to one another proceedings under that Act and proceedings under this Part of this Act; and

(cc) for adapting the procedure under Schedule 10 to the Local Government and Housing Act 1989, and for relating to one another proceedings under that Schedule and proceedings under this Part of this Act; and

(d) generally for regulating the procedure under this Part of this Act.

(2) Where a tenant having a right under this Part of this Act to acquire the freehold or an extended lease gives the landlord notice in accordance with this Part of this Act of his desire to have it, then except as otherwise provided by this Act the procedure for giving effect to the notice, and the rights and obligations of all parties in relation to the investigation of title and other matters arising in giving effect to the notice, shall be such as may be prescribed by regulations made by the Secretary of State by statutory instrument (which shall be subject to annulment in pursuance of a resolution of either House of Parliament), and subject to or in the absence of provision made by any regulations as regards any matter shall be as nearly as may be the same as in the case of a contract of sale or leasing freely negotiated between the parties.

(5) Section 66 of the Landlord and Tenant Act 1954 (which requires the prescribed form for a notice to be prescribed by regulations of the Secretary of State, and makes provisions as to the contents of prescribed forms and as to the service of notices) shall have effect as if any reference therein to that Act were a reference also to this Part of this Act.

III L&T [61.1]

Regulations For regulations made under sub-s (2), see the Leasehold Reform (Notices) Regulations 1997, SI 1997/640. In the case of notices given after 26 July 2002, Forms 1 and 2 in the Schedule to the 1997 Regulations are, to the extent of England only, replaced by Forms 1 and 2 in the Schedule to the Leasehold Reform (Notices) (Amendment) (England) Regulations 2002, SI 2002/1715. For Wales, from 1 January 2003 Forms 1 and 2 are as in the Schedule to the Leasehold Reform (Notices) (Amendment) (Wales) Regulations 2002, SI 2002/3187. See also SI 2002/3209 for Form 3 for use as from 10 April 2003. For the form to be used in Wales from 10 April 2003 by landlords replying to claims for enfranchisement and extension of long leaseholds see the Leasehold Reform (Notices) (Amendment) (Wales) Regulations 2003, SI 2003/991.

For the conditions binding upon landlords and tenants (unless they otherwise agree) in any transactions undertaken to give effect to a tenant's notice, see the Leasehold Reform (Enfranchisement and Extension) Regulations 1967, SI 1967/1879 as amended (with effect from 30 September 2003) by the Leasehold Reform (Enfranchisement and Extension) (Amendment) (England) Regulations 2003, SI 2003/1989.

SUPPLEMENTARY

III L&T [62]

23. Agreements excluding or modifying rights of tenant

(1) Except as provided by this section, any agreement relating to a tenancy (whether contained in the instrument creating the tenancy or not and whether made before the creation of the tenancy or not) shall be void in so far as it purports to exclude or modify any right to acquire the freehold or an extended lease or right to compensation under this Part of this Act, or provides for the termination or surrender of the tenancy in the event of a tenant acquiring or claiming any such right or for the imposition of any penalty or disability on the tenant in that event.

the New Towns Act 1981 (and references to the "Welsh new towns residuary body" shall be construed accordingly);

(c) "notice to quit" means a notice to terminate a tenancy (whether a periodical tenancy or a tenancy for a term of years certain) given in accordance with the provisions (whether express or implied) of that tenancy;

(d) "relevant time" means, in relation to a person's claim to acquire the freehold or an extended lease under this Part of this Act, the time when he gives notice in accordance with this Act of his desire to have it;

(e) . . . ;

(f) "tenancy" means a tenancy at law or in equity, but does not include a tenancy at will, nor any interest created by way of security and liable to termination by the exercise of any right of redemption or otherwise, nor any interest created by way of trust under a settlement, and "demise" shall be construed accordingly;

(g) "term date", in relation to a tenancy granted for a term of years certain, means the date of expiry of that term, and "extended term date" and "original term date" mean respectively the term date of a tenancy with and without an extension under this Part of this Act.

(2) A tenancy to which section 19 (2) of the Landlord and Tenant Act 1954 applies or paragraph 16 (2) of Schedule 10 to the Local Government and Housing Act 1989 applies shall be treated for purposes of this Part of this Act as granted to expire at the date which is the term date for purposes of the said Act of 1954 or, as the case may be, the said Schedule 10 (that is to say, the first date after the commencement of the said Act of 1954 or, as the case may be, the coming into force of the said Schedule 10 on which, apart from the said Act of 1954 or, as the case may be, the said Schedule 10, the tenancy could have been brought to an end by notice to quit given by the landlord).

(3) Subject to subsection (2) above, where under section 3 (2) of this Act a tenancy created or arising as a tenancy from year to year or other periodical tenancy is to be treated as a long tenancy, the term date of that tenancy shall be taken to be the date (if any) at which the tenancy is to terminate by virtue of a notice to quit given by the landlord before the relevant time, or else the earliest date at which it could at that time (in accordance with its terms and apart from any enactment) be brought to an end by a notice to quit given by the landlord.

(4) Subject to subsection (2) above, in the case of a tenancy granted to continue as a periodical tenancy after the expiration of a term of years certain, or to continue as a periodical tenancy if not terminated at the expiration of such a term, any question whether the tenancy is at any time to be treated for purposes of this Part of this Act, as a long tenancy, and (if so) with what term date, shall be determined as it would be if there had been two tenancies, as follows—

(a) one granted to expire at the earliest time (at or after the expiry of the said term of years) at which the tenancy could (in accordance with its terms and apart from any enactment) be brought to an end by notice to quit given by the landlord; and

(b) the other granted to commence at the expiration of the first (and not being one to which subsection (2) above applies).

(5) . . . no reference in this Part of this Act to a person occupying property as his residence shall be taken to extend to any occupation of a company or other artificial person nor, where the tenant is a corporation sole, shall the corporator while in occupation, be treated as occupying as tenant.

(6) Sections 25 (1), (2) and (4) of the Rent Act 1977 shall apply to the ascertainment for purposes of this Part of this Act of the rateable value of a house and premises or any other property as they apply to the ascertainment of that of a dwelling-house for purposes of that Act.

(7) For purposes of this Part of this Act an order of a court is to be treated as becoming final—

(a) if not appealed against, on the expiration of the time for bringing an appeal; or

(b) if appealed against and not set aside in consequence of the appeal, at the time when the appeal and any further appeal is disposed of by the determination of it and the expiration of the time for bringing a further appeal (if any) or by its being abandoned or otherwise ceasing to have effect.

Schedule

SCHEDULE 3

VALIDITY OF TENANT'S NOTICES, EFFECT ON LANDLORD AND TENANT ACT 1954 ETC. AND PROCEDURE GENERALLY

Sections 22 and 34

PART I

RESTRICTIONS ON CLAIMS BY TENANT, AND EFFECT OF CLAIMS ON OTHER NOTICES, FORFEITURES, ETC.

III L&T [64]

1.—(1) A claim to acquire the freehold or an extended lease of any property shall be of no effect if made after the tenant has given notice terminating the tenancy of that property (not being a notice that has been superseded by the grant, express or implied, of a new tenancy), or if made during the subsistence of an agreement for a future tenancy to which section 28 of the Landlord and Tenant Act 1954 or paragraph 17 of Schedule 10 to the Local Government and Housing Act 1989 applies.

(2) A tenant's notice terminating the tenancy of any property shall be of no effect if given during the currency of a claim made in respect of the tenancy to acquire the freehold or an extended lease of that property.

(3) In sub-paragraphs (1) and (2) above references to a notice terminating a tenancy include a tenant's request for a new tenancy under section 26 of the Landlord and Tenant Act 1954, and a tenant's notice under section 27 (1) of that Act that he does not desire the tenancy to be continued.

2.—(1) A claim to acquire the freehold or an extended lease of any property shall be of no effect if made more than two months after a landlord's notice terminating the tenancy of that property has been given under section 4 or 25 of the Landlord and Tenant Act 1954 or served under paragraph 4 (1) of Schedule 10 to the Local Government and Housing Act 1989 (whether or not that notice has effect to terminate the tenancy):

Provided that—

(a) this sub-paragraph shall not apply where the landlord gives his written consent to a claim being made after the end of those two months; and

(b) where a tenant, having given or served notice of his desire to have the freehold, gives after the end of those two months a further notice under section 9 (3) of this Act of his inability or unwillingness to acquire the house and premises at the price he must pay, he may with the notice under section 9 (3) give a notice of his desire to have an extended lease (if he then has a right thereto).

(2) A landlord's notice terminating a tenancy of any property under section 4 or 25 of the Landlord and Tenant Act 1954 or under paragraph 4 (1) of Schedule 10 to the Local Government and Housing Act 1989 shall be of no effect if given or

served during the currency of a claim made in respect of the tenancy to acquire the freehold or an extended lease of that property, and shall cease to have effect on the making of such a claim.

(3) Where any such landlord's notice ceases (by virtue of sub-paragraph (2) above[. . .]) to have effect on the making of a claim, but the claim is not effective, then if within one month after the period of currency of that claim (or any subsequent claim made by virtue of the proviso to sub-paragraph (1) above) a landlord's notice terminating the tenancy is given under section 4 or 25 of the Landlord and Tenant Act 1954 or served under paragraph 4 (1) of Schedule 10 to the Local Government and Housing Act 1989, the earliest date which may be specified therein as the date of termination shall be—

- (i) in the case of a notice given under the said Act of 1954 the date of termination specified in the previous notice or the expiration of three months from the giving of the new notice, whichever is the later;
- (ii) in the case of a notice served under the said Schedule 10, the date of termination specified in the previous notice or the expiration of the period of four months beginning on the date of service of the new notice, whichever is the later.

(4) Where by virtue of sub-paragraph (3) above a landlord's notice specifies as the date of termination of a tenancy a date earlier than six months after the giving of the notice, then—

- (a) if it is a notice proposing a statutory tenancy, section 7 (2) of the Landlord and Tenant Act 1954 shall apply in relation to the notice with the substitution, for references to the period of two months ending with the date of termination specified in the notice and the beginning of that period, of references to the period of three months beginning with the giving of the notice and the end of that period; and
- (b) if it is a notice under section 25 of that Act, an application under section 24 for a new tenancy shall not be entertained unless it is made within three months after the giving of the notice.

3.—(1) Where a tenant makes a claim to acquire the freehold or an extended lease of any property, then during the currency of the claim and for three months thereafter the tenancy in that property shall not terminate either by effluxion of time or in pursuance of a notice to quit given by the landlord or by the termination of a superior tenancy; but if the claim is not effective, and but for this sub-paragraph the tenancy would have so terminated before the end of those three months, the tenancy shall so terminate at the end of the three months.

(2) Sub-paragraph (1) above shall not be taken to prevent an earlier termination of the tenancy in any manner not there mentioned, nor affect the power under section 146 (4) of the Law of Property Act 1925 to grant a tenant relief against the termination of a superior tenancy, or any right of the tenant to relief under section 16 (2) of the Landlord and Tenant Act 1954 or under paragraph 9 of Schedule 5 to that Act.

(3) The reference in sub-paragraph (2) above to section 16 (2) of, and paragraph 9 of Schedule 5 to, the Landlord and Tenant Act 1954 includes a reference to those provisions as they apply in relation to Schedule 10 to the Local Government and Housing Act 1989.

4.—(1) Where a tenant makes a claim to acquire the freehold or an extended lease of any property, then during the currency of the claim no proceedings to enforce any right of re-entry or forfeiture terminating the tenancy shall be brought in any court without the leave of that court, and leave shall not be granted unless the court is satisfied that the claim was not made in good faith; but where leave is granted, the claim shall cease to have effect.

(2) Where a claim is made to acquire the freehold or an extended lease of property comprised in a tenancy, the tenancy shall be deemed for purposes of the claim to be a subsisting tenancy notwithstanding that the claim is made when

LANDLORD & TENANT AND HOUSING

proceedings are pending to enforce a right of re-entry or forfeiture terminating the tenancy and notwithstanding any order made afterwards in those proceedings, and if the claim is effective, the court in which the proceedings were brought may set aside or vary any such order to such extent and on such terms as appear to that court to be appropriate:

Provided that if it appears to that court that the claim is not made in good faith, or there has been unreasonable delay in making it, and that apart from the claim effect should be given to the right of re-entry or forfeiture, the court shall order that the tenancy shall not be treated as subsisting nor the claim as valid by virtue of this sub-paragraph.

(3) Where a court other than the county court—

(a) grants leave under sub-paragraph (1) above; or

(b) makes an order under the proviso to sub-paragraph (2) above on the ground that a claim was not made in good faith;

the court may make any such order as the county court is authorised to make by section 20 (5) or (6) of this Act.

5.—(1) For purposes of this Part of this Schedule—

(a) references to a claim to acquire the freehold or an extended lease shall be taken as references to a notice of a person's desire to acquire it under Part I of this Act and, except in so far as the contrary intention appears, as including a claim made by a tenant not entitled to acquire it and a claim made by a person who is not a tenant; and

(b) references to a claim being effective shall be taken as references to the freehold or an extended lease being acquired in pursuance of the claim; and

(c) references to the currency of a claim shall be taken as references to the period from the giving of a notice which has effect or would, if valid, have effect to the time when the notice is effective or ceases to have effect, or (not being a valid notice) is set aside by the court or withdrawn or would, if valid, cease to have effect, and those references shall include any period when the notice is suspended.

(2) For purposes of sub-paragraph (1)(c) above the date when a notice ceases to have effect or is set aside or would, if valid, cease to have effect in consequence of an order of a court shall be taken to be the date when the order becomes final.

PART II
PROCEDURAL PROVISIONS

6—(1) A tenant's notice under Part I of this Act of his desire to have the freehold or an extended lease of a house and premises shall be in the prescribed form, and shall contain the following particulars:—

(a) the address of the house, and sufficient particulars of the house and premises to identify the property to which the claim extends;

(b) such particulars of the tenancy and[, in the case of a tenancy falling within section 4(1)(i) of this Act,] of the rateable value of the house and premises as serve to identify the instrument creating the tenancy and show that

(i) (apart from the operation, if any, of the proviso to section 4(1) of this Act) the tenancy is and has at the material times been a long tenancy at a low rent;

(ii) at the material time the rateable value was within the limits specified for the purpose of section 1;

(c) the date on which the tenant acquired the tenancy;

(d) . . .

(e) in the case of a tenancy falling within section 1(1)(a)(ii) of this Act, the premium payable as a condition of the grant of the tenancy.

(1A) . . .

(2) Where the tenant gives the notice by virtue of section 6, 6A or 7 of this Act, sub-paragraph 1(c) above shall apply with the appropriate modifications of references to the tenant, so that the notice shall show the particulars bringing the case within section 6, 6A or 7.

(3) The notice shall not be invalidated by any inaccuracy in the particulars required by this paragraph or any misdescription of the property to which the claim extends; and where the claim extends to property not properly included in the house and premises, or does not extend to property that ought to be so included, the notice may with the leave of the court, and on such terms as the court may see fit to impose, be amended so as to exclude or include that property.

7—(1) Where a tenant of a house gives the landlord notice in accordance with Part I of this Act of the tenant's desire to have the freehold or an extended lease, the landlord shall within two months give the tenant a notice in reply in the prescribed form stating whether or not the landlord admits the tenant's right to have the freehold or extended lease (subject to any question as to the correctness of the particulars given in the tenant's notice of the house and premises); and if the landlord does not admit the tenant's right, the notice shall state the grounds on which it is not admitted.

(2) Subject to sub-paragraph (3) below, where under Part I of this Act the landlord may object to the inclusion of any part of the house and premises as described in the tenant's notice, or may object to the exclusion of other property, the notice of his objection shall be given with or before his notice in reply, unless the right to give it later is reserved by the notice in reply.

(3) If (on the assumption, where it is not admitted, that the tenant has the right claimed) it is intended to apply to the court for possession of the house and premises under section 17 or 18 of this Act, the notice in reply shall state that it is the intention to do so, and sub-paragraph (2) above shall not apply.

(4) Where a landlord's notice in reply admits the tenant's right to have the freehold or extended lease of a house and premises, the admission shall be binding on the landlord, so far as relates to the matters relevant to the existence of that right, unless the landlord shows that he was induced to make the admission by misrepresentation or the concealment of material facts; but the admission shall not conclude any question whether the particulars of the house and premises in the tenant's notice are correct.

(5) The tenant shall not institute proceedings in the court with a view to the enforcement of his right to have the freehold or an extended lease before the landlord has given his notice in reply or two months have elapsed without his doing so since the giving of the tenant's notice.

8—(1) Where a person ("the claimant") gives notice as tenant of a house of his desire to have the freehold or an extended lease under Part I of this Act,—

(a) the notice shall be regarded as served on the landlord if it is served on any of the persons having an interest in the house and premises superior to the claimant's tenancy and references to the relevant time shall be construed accordingly;

(b) copies of the notice shall be served by the claimant on any other persons known or believed by him to have such an interest;

(c) the notice shall state whether copies are being served in accordance with paragraph (b) above on anyone other than the recipient and, if so, on whom;

(d) a recipient of the notice or a copy of it (including a person receiving a copy under this paragraph), unless he is a person having no such interest, shall forthwith serve a copy on any person who is known or believed by him to have such an interest and is not stated in the recipient's copy of the notice or known by him to have received a copy;

(e) a recipient of the notice or a copy of it shall, in any further copies served by him in accordance with paragraph (d) above, supplement the

LANDLORD & TENANT AND HOUSING

statement under paragraph (c) by adding any further persons on whom he is serving copies or who are known by him to have received one.

(2) Any recipient of any such notice or a copy of it—

(a) if he serves further copies of it on other persons in accordance with sub-paragraph (1)(d) above, shall notify the claimant of the persons added by him to the statement under sub-paragraph (1)(c); and

(b) if he knows who is, or believes himself to be, the person designated as the reversioner by paragraph 2 of Schedule 1 to this Act, shall give written notice to the claimant stating who is thought by him to be the reversioner, and shall serve copies of it on all persons known or believed by him to have an interest superior to the claimant's tenancy.

(3) Any person who fails without reasonable cause to comply with sub-paragraph (1) or (2) above, or is guilty of any unreasonable delay in doing so, shall be liable for any loss thereby occasioned to the claimant or to any person having an interest superior to the claimant's tenancy.

(4) In this paragraph references to an interest superior to the claimant's tenancy mean the estate in fee simple and any tenancy superior to the claimant's tenancy, but shall apply also to a tenancy reversionary on the claimant's tenancy.

9—(1) Where the interest of a landlord is subject to a charge, and the person entitled to the benefit of the charge is in possession or a receiver appointed by him or by the court is in receipt of the rents and profits, a notice by a tenant of his desire to have the freehold or an extended lease under Part I of this Act shall be duly given if served either on the landlord or on that person or any such receiver; but the landlord or that person, if not the recipient of the notice, shall forthwith be sent the notice or a copy of it by the recipient:

Provided that in the case of a debenture-holders' charge within the meaning of section 12(5) of this Act this sub-paragraph shall not authorise the service of a notice on, or require a notice or copy to be sent to, the persons entitled to the benefit of the charge, other than trustees for the debenture-holders, but where the notice is served on the landlord and there is no trustee for the debenture-holders, he shall forthwith send it or a copy of it to any receiver appointed by virtue of the charge.

(2) Where a tenant of a house gives notice of his desire to have the freehold or an extended lease under Part I of this Act, and the interest of the person to whom the notice is given, or of any person receiving a copy of it under paragraph 8 above, is subject to a charge to secure the payment of money, then subject to sub-paragraph (3) below the recipient of the notice or copy shall forthwith inform the person entitled to the benefit of the charge (unless the notice was served on him or a receiver appointed by virtue of the charge) that the notice has been given, and shall give him such further information as may from time to time be reasonably required from the recipient by him.

(3) References in sub-paragraph (2) above to a charge shall not include a charge falling within section 11 of this Act or a debenture-holders' charge within the meaning of section 12(5) of this Act.

10—(1) This paragraph shall have effect in relation to a landlord's notice terminating a tenancy of a house under section 4 or 25 of the Landlord and Tenant Act 1954 or under paragraph 4(1) of Schedule 10 to the Local Government and Housing Act 1989 if—

(a) no previous notice terminating the tenancy has been given under any of those provisions; and

(b) in the case of a notice under section 25, the tenancy is a long tenancy at a low rent, and the tenant is not a company or other artificial person.

(2) The landlord's notice shall not have effect unless it states—

(a) that, if the tenant has a right under Part I of this Act to acquire the freehold or an extended lease of property comprised in the tenancy, notice of his desire to have the freehold or an extended lease cannot be given more than two months after the service of the landlord's notice; and

(b) that, in the event of a tenant having that right and giving such a notice within those two months, the landlord's notice will not operate; and

(c) that, in the event of the tenant giving such a notice within those two months, the landlord will be entitled to apply to the court under section 17 or 18 of this Act and proposes to do so or, as the case may be, will not be entitled or does not propose to do so.

(3) The landlord shall also in the notice give the names and addresses of any other persons known or believed by him to have an interest superior to the tenancy terminated by the notice or to be the agent concerned with the property on behalf of a person having such an interest; and for this purpose "an interest superior to the tenancy terminated by the notice" means the estate in fee simple and any tenancy superior to that tenancy, but includes also a tenancy reversionary on that tenancy.

(4) Where a tenant's notice of his desire to have the freehold or an extended lease of a house and premises under Part I of this Act is given after the service of a landlord's notice terminating the tenancy under section 4 or section 25 of the Landlord and Tenant Act 1954 or under paragraph 4(1) of Schedule 10 to the Local Government and Housing Act 1989, and the landlord's notice does not comply with sub-paragraph (2) above, no application made under section 17 or 18 of this Act with respect to the house and premises by the landlord giving the notice shall be entertained by the court (other than an application under section 17 after the grant of an extended lease).

(5) This paragraph shall not apply, < . . . >, to a landlord's notice given before the appointed day.

III L&T [64.1]

Leave to bring proceedings An application to a county court for leave to bring proceedings under the Leasehold Reform Act 1967 Sch 3 para 4(1) should be made by application in accordance with CPR Pt 23 (see para **CPR 23**).

III L&T [64.2]

Good faith A claim to a freehold or an extended lease is made in good faith when it is made honestly and without any ulterior motive, see *Central Estates (Belgravia) Ltd v Woolgar* [1972] 1 QB 48, [1971] 3 All ER 647, CA, and *Liverpool Corpn v Husan* [1972] 1 QB 48, [1971] 3 All ER 651, CA.

III L&T [64.3]

"Order becomes final" For the meaning of this expression, see the Leasehold Reform Act 1967 s 37(7) (see para **III L&T [63]**).

III L&T [64.4]

Notice in prescribed form A tenant's notice under Leasehold Reform Act 1967 Sch 3 para 6(1) and a landlord's notice in reply under Leasehold Reform Act 1967 Sch 3 para 7(1) must be in the form prescribed by the Leasehold Reform (Notices) Regulations 1997, SI 1997/640. In the case of notices given after 26 July 2002, Forms 1 and 2 in the Schedule to the 1997 Regulations are, to the extent of England only, replaced by Forms 1 and 2 in the Schedule to the Leasehold Reform (Notices) (Amendment) (England) Regulations 2002, SI 2002/1715. For Wales, from 1 January 2003 Forms 1 and 2 are as in the Schedule to the Leasehold Reform (Notices) (Amendment) (Wales) Regulations 2002, SI 2002/3187. See also SI 2002/3209 for Form 3 for use as from 10 April 2003. For the form to be used in Wales from 10 April 2003 by landlords replying to claims for enfranchisement and extension of long leaseholds see the Leasehold Reform (Notices) (Amendment) (Wales) Regulations 2003, SI 2003/991. A tenant's notice must indicate unequivocally whether he desires to have the freehold or an extended lease. Where the tenant left both of these alternatives in the form and failed to delete the one which he did not want, it was held that the notice was invalid and the defect could not be cured under the Leasehold Reform Act 1967 Sch 3 para 6(3): *Byrnlea Property Investments Ltd v Ramsay* [1969] 2 QB 253, sub nom *Re 33, Byrne Road, Balham, Byrnlea Property Investments Ltd v Ramsay* [1969] 2 All ER 311, CA. An accidental failure to delete an alternative in one paragraph of the form will not however vitiate the notice where a deletion in another paragraph makes the tenant's intention plain, see *Lewis v Harries* (1971) 22 P & CR 905, 115 Sol Jo 508, CA. In *Speedwell Estates Ltd v Dalziel* [2001] EWCA Civ 1277, [2002] HLR 813, a notice failed in material respects to satisfy the prescribed requirements. The Court held that provision of the prescribed information was not optional, that the omissions and errors could not be characterised as mere excusable inaccuracies and that the notice could not be not rescued by the benevolent approach to construction adopted in *Mannai Investment Co Ltd v Eagle Star Life Assurance Co Ltd* [1997] AC 749, [1997] 3 All ER 352, HL. The notice was therefore invalid.

For the conditions binding upon landlords and tenants (unless they otherwise agree) in any transactions undertaken to give effect to a tenant's notice, see the Leasehold Reform (Enfranchisement and Extension) Regulations 1967, SI 1967/1879 as amended (with effect from 30 September 2003) by the Leasehold Reform (Enfranchisement and Extension) (Amendment) (England) Regulations 2003, SI 2003/1989.

Paragraph 6(3) will save any non-compliant notice where there has been an honest mistake unless fundamental. In *Earl Cadogan v Strauss* [2004] EWCA Civ 211, [2004] 2 P & CR 295, (2004) Times, 11 March it was held that a tenant's failure to list all previous leases linked to the current lease did not invalidate the notice.

III L&T [64.5]

Leave to amend tenant's notice The court having jurisdiction to give leave to amend a tenant's notice under the Leasehold Reform Act 1967 Sch 3 para 6(3) is the county court: Leasehold Reform Act 1967 s 20(1) (see para **III L&T [59]**).

Unconditional leave to amend an invalid notice was granted in *Malekshad v Howard de Walden Estates Ltd (No 2)* [2003] EWHC 3106 (Ch), [2004] 4 All ER 162, [2004] 1 WLR 862 and Neuberger J indicated in that case that leave would normally be granted in the absence of dishonesty and that conditions should not be imposed except to compensate for relevant prejudice suffered by the landlord.

III L&T [64.6]

Service of notice after expiry of lease A notice is invalid if served after the expiry of the lease: *Duke of Westminster v Oddy* (1984) 15 HLR 80, [1984] 1 EGLR 83, CA.

Notice served after the expiry of the contractual term may nevertheless be valid during the period that the lease is continued by the provisions of paragraph 3 (1): *Malekshad v Howard de Walden Estates Ltd (No 2)* [2003] EWHC 3106 (Ch), [2004] 4 All ER 162, [2004] 1 WLR 862, Neuberger J

RENT ACT 1977

(c 42)

III L&T [68.3]

Hotel accommodation Arrangements for renting rooms in a hotel have been held not to create tenancies although conferring exclusive rights to possession: *Lugande v Service Hotels Ltd* [1969] 2 Ch 209, [1969] 2 All ER 692, CA, followed in *Mehta v Royal Bank of Scotland plc* (1999) 32 HLR 45, [1999] 3 EGLR 153. In *Uratemp Ventures Ltd v Collins* [2001] UKHL 43, [2002] 1 All ER 46, [2002] 1 All ER 46, it was held that a single hotel room was capable of constituting a "separate dwelling" and if the occupant had exclusive possession he occupied by virtue of an assured tenancy not a licence; the presence or absence of cooking facilities was irrelevant to the issue of exclusive occupation.

III L&T [68.4]

Family arrangement An oral agreement between members of a family for some to occupy part of a house belonging to others may be no more than a family arrangement, which does not create a legal relationship. But where the agreement is for the incoming members to have exclusive possession and to pay rent there is a rebuttable presumption that a tenancy is being created: *Nunn v Dalrymple* (1989) 21 HLR 569, CA. The presumption is not necessarily rebutted by the owner's retention of keys and occasionally coming to stay: *Ward v Warnke* (1990) 22 HLR 496, CA.

III L&T [68.5]

Dwelling house There is no definition of this expression except that it may be "a house or part of a house". A flat or a bed-sitting room is a dwelling house: see *Langford Property Co Ltd v Goldrich* [1949] 1 KB 511 at 517, [1949] 1 All ER 402 at 404, CA. In *Curl v Angelo* [1948] 2 All ER 189 at 190, LORD GREENE MR described the test as "On the facts as found by the judge can it be said, as a matter of fair and reasonable construction of simple words in the English language, that these premises were the 'home' of anybody?" So, an annexe to a hotel was not a dwelling: *Curl v Angelo* [1948] 2 All ER 189, CA. In *Wright v Howell* (1947) 92 Sol Jo 26, CA it was held that a room was not a dwelling house where the room was devoid of cooking facilities and a water supply and which was not used for one of the major activities of life (eg sleeping, cooking and eating); see also *Wimbush v Cibulia* [1949] 2 KB 564, [1949] 2 All ER 432, CA. A servant's bedroom was held not to be a dwelling house in *Metropolitan Properties Co (FGC) Ltd v Barder* [1968] 1 All ER 536, [1968] 1 WLR 286, CA. A caravan has been held not to be within the Rent Acts (see *Morgan v Taylor* (1948) 99 L Jo 290) but is capable of being a house if permanently sited: *R v Rent Officer of Nottingham Registration Area, ex p Allen* (1985) 52 P & CR 41, 17 HLR 481 and a beach hut with bunks, electric light and water supply has been held to be a house for the purposes of the Acts: *Spraggs v Prentice* (1950) 156 Estates Gazette 346. On the other hand, chalets which are not fixtures and are let under annual licences have been held not to be dwelling houses: *Davies v Elitestore* [1995] NPC 142. A different result was arrived at in *Elitestone Ltd v Morris* [1997] 2 All ER 513, [1997] 1 WLR 687, HL, where the chalet was held to be a bungalow and to be part and parcel of the land itself. See also the decision of *Chelsea Yacht and Boat Co v Pope* [2001] 2 All ER 409, [2000] 1 WLR 1941, CA, where it was held that a houseboat was not capable of being the subject of an assured tenancy; similarly, it has been held that a houseboat resting on wooden platforms, supported by piles driven into a plot of land (the bed of a harbour), may not be treated as part of the plot. Such a construction is not affixed to the land and remains a chattel which, as designed, is moveable and may not be classed as a dwelling-house. The occupier is a licensee not a tenant: *Tristmire Ltd v Mew* [2011] EWCA Civ 912, [2011] All ER (D) 278 (Jul).

Where two or more distinct units of accommodation are let to a tenant, they may constitute a dwelling house if they are let together on a single letting to one tenant for joint occupation as his home; see *Langford Property Co Ltd v Goldrich* [1949] 1 KB 511 at 517, [1949] 1 All ER 402 at 404, CA (two flats not contiguous); *Whitty v Scott-Russell* [1950] 2 KB 32, [1950] 1 All ER 884, CA (a house and cottage); and the criticisms of *Kavanagh v Lyroudias* [1985] 1 All ER 560, CA, in *Hampstead Way Investments Ltd v Lewis-Weare* [1985] 1 All ER 564, [1985] 1 WLR 164, HL.

III L&T [68.6]

Let as a dwelling In determining whether a house is let as a dwelling "it is necessary to look at the purpose of the letting. If the lease contains an express provision as to the purpose of the letting, it is not necessary to look further, but, if there is no express provision, it is open to the court to look at the circumstances of the letting. If the house is constructed for use as a dwelling, it is reasonable to infer that the purpose was to let it as a dwelling, but if it is constructed for use as a lock up shop, the reasonable inference is that it was let for business purposes. If the position were neutral, it would be proper to look at the actual use": *Wolfe v Hogan* [1949] 2 KB 194 at 205, [1949] 1 All ER 570 at 575, CA, per DENNING LJ.

A house originally let for business purposes may become let as a dwelling if it can be inferred from the acceptance of rent or otherwise that the landlord has affirmatively consented to the change of use: *Wolfe v Hogan* [1949] 2 KB 194, [1949] 1 All ER 570, CA, per DENNING LJ. If a tenancy provides for a particular use but, by the time proceedings are begun, that agreement has been superseded by a subsequent contract providing for a different use, the court may look at the later contract; if the tenant changes the use and the landlord knows and accepts these changes, it may be sufficient to infer a subsequent contract but otherwise a mere unilateral change of use will not enable a tenant to claim the protection of the Rent Acts where the lease provides for a use not attracting the protection of the Acts: see *Russell v Booker* (1982) 5 HLR 10, [1982] 2 EGLR 86, CA; *Wagle v Henry Smith's Charity Trustees* [1990] QB 42, [1989] 2 WLR 669, CA. In construing the covenant the court is entitled to pay regard to the surrounding circumstances with reference to which the lease was entered into and to look at the nature of the subject matter of the letting: *Levermore v Jobey* [1956] 2 All ER 362, [1956] 1 WLR 697, CA. See also *R v Brighton and Area Rent Tribunal, ex p Slaughter* [1954] 1 QB 446, [1954] 1 All ER 423 where premises were held to be let partly as a dwelling, notwithstanding a covenant that the tenant would not permit the premises to be used otherwise than for the business of a greengrocer. Residential use need not be the only use, premises have been held to be let as a dwelling where more than one use (including residential use) was permitted by the lease: see, for example, *Colls v Parnham* [1922] 1 KB 325; *Vickery v Martin* [1944] KB 679, [1944] 2 All ER 167, CA.

If houses are let for mixed business and residential use (so as not to fall within the 1954 Act) they are not brought within the Rent Act 1977 by the tenant's ceasing to carry on the business: *Tan v Sitkowski* [2007] EWCA Civ 30, [2007] 1 WLR 1628, [2007] All ER (D) 16 (Feb).

III L&T [68.7]

Separate dwelling In this context "dwelling" must be read in the singular only: *Horford Investments Ltd v Lambert* [1976] Ch 39, [1974] 1 All ER 131, CA where a tenancy of a house divided into a number of single rooms and a flat sub-let for multiple residential occupation was held not to be a protected tenancy because it was a letting as several dwellings rather than as a single dwelling. A tenancy granted to an educational institution of a house containing units of accommodation to be sub-let to students was held not to be a protected tenancy because the arrangement envisaged under the tenancy was inconsistent with the concept of a building let as a separate dwelling: *St Catherine's College v Dorling* [1979] 3 All ER 250, [1980] 1 WLR 66, CA. On the other hand, agreements which purport to give a number of individuals non-exclusive rights of occupation in the same premises may, on a proper construction, create joint tenancies: *Markou v Da Silvaesa* (1986) 52 P & CR 204, sub nom *Crancour Ltd v Da Silvaesa* [1986] 1 EGLR 80, CA, and *Hadjiloucas v Crean* [1987] 3 All ER 1008, [1988] 1 WLR 1006, CA, but not where the agreements with the occupants provide for different monthly payments and different starting dates: *A G Securities v Vaughan* [1990] 1 AC 417, [1988] 3 All ER 1058, HL. In *Mikeover Ltd v Brady* [1989] 3 All ER 618, CA separate agreements in respect of a two-roomed flat were held not to give rise to a joint tenancy although each of the two occupants had agreed to pay the same sum each month.

III L&T [68.8]

Sharing The requirement of a *separate* dwelling is relevant where the tenant shares part of the demised premises; it must however be considered subject to the Rent Act 1977 ss 21 and 22, which contain special provisions regulating the position where the tenant shares with his landlord or with persons other than his landlord. It has been held that in order for there to be a letting of a separate dwelling, there must be no sharing of essential accommodation. Where the tenant has the exclusive use of some rooms and shares certain accommodation with others "there is a letting of a part of a house as a separate dwelling, within the meaning of the Acts, if, and only if, the accommodation which is shared with others does not comprise any of the rooms which may fairly be described as 'living rooms', or 'dwelling rooms'": *Cole v Harris* [1945] KB 474 at 485, [1945] 2 All ER 146 at 152 per MORTON LJ. There must be an "agreement by which the occupier has the exclusive use of the essential living rooms of a separate dwelling-house. After all, a dwelling-house is that in which a person dwells or lives, and it seems reasonable that a separate dwelling should be one containing essential living room. A WC may be essential in modern days, but I do not think it is a living room, whereas a kitchen, I think is": *Cole v Harris* [1945] KB 474 at 479, [1945] 2 All ER 146 at 148, per MACKINNON LJ. See also *Neale v Del Soto* [1945] KB 144, [1945] 1 All ER 191, CA. Note, however, that in *Uratemp Ventures Ltd v Collins* [2001] UKHL 43, [2002] 1 AC 301, [2002] 1 All ER 46, the presence or absence of cooking facilities was regarded as irrelevant to the issue of exclusive occupation. The relevant time at which to determine whether there is sharing is the date of the commencement of the proceedings: *Baker v Turner* [1950] AC 401, [1950] 1 All ER 834, HL.

III L&T [68.9]

Human rights A former joint tenant who remains in occupation after termination of the tenancy by the other has a Convention right under Art 8 to respect for his home. However, Art 8 cannot be relied on to defeat proprietary or contractual rights to possession. Accordingly, a public authority landlord was entitled to claim possession; but an unfair exercise of the right may be capable of challenge by judicial review; see the majority decision in *Harrow London Borough Council v Qazi* [2003] UKHL 43, [2004] 1 AC 983, [2003] 4 All ER 461. Note, however, the decision in *Kay v Lambeth London Borough Council* [2006] UKHL 10, [2006] 2 AC 465, [2006] 2 WLR 570, [2006] 4 All ER 128 that, in so far as *Harrow London Borough Council v Qazi* decided that the enforcement of a right to possession in accordance with the domestic law of property could never be incompatible with the Art 8 of the Convention, that had to be modified in the light of *Connors v United Kingdom* (66746/01) [2005] 40 EHRR 9; moreover, that it was open to an occupier to raise an Art 8 defence to possession proceedings in the county court rather than by way of judicial review (a point subsequently emphasised in *Manchester City Council v Pinnock* [2010] UKSC 45, [2010] 3 WLR 1441, [2010] 44 LS Gaz R 16 (see para **III L&T [103.6]**)).

III L&T [69]

2. Statutory tenants and tenancies

(1) Subject to this Part of this Act—

(a) after the termination of a protected tenancy of a dwelling-house the person who, immediately before that termination, was the protected tenant of the dwelling-house shall, if and so long as he occupies the dwelling-house as his residence, be the statutory tenant of it; and

(b) Part I of Schedule 1 to this Act shall have effect for determining what person (if any) is the statutory tenant of a dwelling-house or, as the case may be, is entitled to an assured tenancy of a dwelling-house by succession at any time after the death of a person who, immediately before his death, was either a protected tenant of the dwelling-house or the statutory tenant of it by virtue of paragraph (a) above.

(2) In this Act a dwelling-house is referred to as subject to a statutory tenancy when there is a statutory tenant of it.

(3) In subsection (1)(a) above and in Part I of Schedule 1, the phrase "if and so long as he occupies the dwelling-house as his residence" shall be construed as it was immediately before the commencement of this Act (that is to say, in accordance with section 3 (2) of the Rent Act 1968).

(4) A person who becomes a statutory tenant of a dwelling-house as mentioned in subsection (1) (a) above is, in this Act, referred to as a statutory tenant by virtue of his previous protected tenancy.

(5) A person who becomes a statutory tenant as mentioned in subsection 1 (b) above is, in this Act, referred to as a statutory tenant by succession.

III L&T [69.1]

After the termination of a protected tenancy In order that a statutory tenancy may arise, it is first necessary that there be a protected tenancy. That tenancy must then come to an end by one of the normal methods of termination, eg effluxion of time, notice to quit, forfeiture. In the case of a notice to quit to end a protected tenancy, it must comply with the Protection from Eviction Act 1977 s 5. It is not necessarily terminated by the death of the tenant and may pass to the tenant's successor: see *Trustees of the Gift of Thomas Pocklington v Hill* (1989) 21 HLR 391, CA. At common law, where a tenant holds over and rent is accepted a new tenancy may be created by the acceptance of rent. However, where a protected tenant holds over, he usually does so by virtue of the Acts and the mere acceptance of rent will not create a new tenancy: see *Morrison v Jacobs* [1945] KB 577, [1945] 2 All ER 430, CA; *Marcroft Wagons Ltd v Smith* [1951] 2 KB 496, [1951] 2 All ER 271, CA.

III L&T [69.2]

Agreement reached after the making of a possession order Where the landlord makes an agreement with the tenant after obtaining a possession order this may create a fresh tenancy but the occupier must be more than a tolerated trespasser: *Burrows v Brent London Borough Council* [1996] 4 All ER 577, [1996] 1 WLR 1448, HL. But all the elements of a fresh contract must be present: *Southwark London Borough Council v Logan* (1995) 29 HLR 40, Times, 3 November, CA.

III L&T [69.3]

Protected tenants and companies One of two or more joint protected tenants may become a statutory tenant: *Lloyd v Sadler* [1978] QB 774, [1978] 2 All ER 529, CA, followed in *Featherstone v Staples* (1984) 49 P & CR 273, [1985] 1 EGLR 1. A company cannot become

LANDLORD & TENANT AND HOUSING

a statutory tenant as it cannot occupy premises as its residence: *Hiller v United Dairies (London) Ltd* [1934] 1 KB 57, CA. If a tenancy is granted to one person (eg a company) on terms that another person (eg a director) is to reside in the dwelling there will be no statutory tenancy in favour of that other person: *SL Dando Ltd v Hitchcock* [1954] 2 QB 317, [1954] 2 All ER 335, CA; *Firstcross Ltd v East-West (Export/Import) Ltd* (1980) 41 P & CR 145, CA. Where the parties agree on a "company let" which provides a residence for the managing director of the company, the transaction is not a sham merely because the possibility of a statutory tenancy is avoided thereby: *Hilton v Plustitle Ltd* [1988] 3 All ER 1051, [1989] 1 WLR 149, CA; *Estavest Investments Ltd v Commercial Express Travel* (1987) 21 HLR 106, [1988] 2 EGLR 91, CA; *Kaye v Massbetter Ltd and Kanter* (1990) 62 P & CR 558, [1991] 2 EGLR 97, CA.

See also *Eaton Square Properties Ltd v O'Higgins* (2000) 33 HLR 771, CA, where it was held that the fact that a tenancy was granted to a company solely for tax purposes did not render the tenancy a sham.

III L&T [69.4]

Effect of bankruptcy If the tenant is a *statutory* tenant before bankruptcy, the statutory tenancy does not pass to the trustee in bankruptcy because of the personal nature of such a tenancy: *Sutton v Dorf* [1932] 2 KB 304. Contrast, however, a continuation tenancy under the Landlord and Tenant Act 1954 Part I which constitutes 'property' and will therefore vest in the tenant's trustee in bankruptcy: *De Rothschild v Bell* [2000] 1 QB 33, [1999] 2 All ER 722, CA. A *protected* tenancy, on the other hand, is capable of forming part of the estate, but will be excluded by the Insolvency Act 1986 s 283(3A), unless the terms of the Rent Act 1977 s 127, allow it to be assigned for a premium. The same statutory exclusion applies to an assured tenancy, a tenancy of a dwelling house protected by the Rent (Agriculture) Act 1976 and an assured agricultural occupancy, provided in each case that it is not allowed to be assigned for a premium, as mentioned in the Rent Act s 127(5). Also excluded is a secure tenancy which is not capable of being assigned except as provided in the Housing Act 1985 s 91(3). As long as the protected tenancy is not part of the bankrupt's estate the protection given by the Act continues. However, the trustee in bankruptcy may, by service of a notice under the Insolvency Act 1986 s 308A, vest the tenancy in the trustee with effect from the commencement of the bankruptcy. In the exceptional circumstances where a protected tenancy vests in the trustee, the consequence of a disclaimer by the trustee or the tenancy ending in some other way is that the landlord may recover possession from the bankrupt: *Eyre v Hall* (1986) 18 HLR 509, CA. Note that, where the lease contains a proviso for re-entry in the case of bankruptcy, a statutory tenant who is made bankrupt is thereby in breach of an obligation for the purpose of Sch 15, Case 1 (see para **III L&T [82]**): *Cadogan Estates Ltd v McMahon* [2001] 1 AC 378, [2000] 4 All ER 897, HL.

III L&T [69.5]

If and so long as he occupies the dwelling house as his residence This requirement was not originally in the Acts but was developed by the courts. If the tenant does not satisfy this requirement at the end of the protected tenancy, or if thereafter he ceases to satisfy it, he will lose the protection of the Acts. The requirement derives from the "principle . . . governing the Acts, namely that they were passed during wartime owing to the scarcity of homes, and the fact that very high rents were being claimed by landlords from tenants led to the intervention by Parliament, which fixed the rents which could be exacted and in effect enacted that the Acts do not apply to a person who is not personally occupying the house and who has no intention of returning to it": *Skinner v Geary* [1931] 2 KB 546 at 560 per Scrutton LJ. Where a tenant is absent from the house, the proper approach to decide if he retains the protection of the Acts is as follows: (1) it is a question of fact and degree as to whether the absence is sufficiently prolonged to infer cesser of occupation, the burden of proof being on the landlord; (2) if so, the burden is on the tenant to show that his residence has not ceased by establishing, (a) a de facto intention to return and, (b) some outward sign of that intention, eg leaving furniture and effects on the premises; (3) if there is no such intention or sign, the tenant's protection ceases; (4) if there is such an intention and sign but one subsequently ceases, the tenant's protection ceases: see *Brown v Brash and Ambrose* [1948] 2 KB 247 at 252, [1948] 1 All ER 922 at 925, CA, per Asquith LJ. For a case where a second action on this ground succeeded although the first had failed see *Duke v Porter* (1986) 19 HLR 1, [1986] 2 EGLR 101, CA. If the tenant satisfies these requirements he may remain a statutory tenant notwithstanding substantial absences from the dwelling: see, for example, *Gofor Investments Ltd v Roberts* (1975) 29 P & CR 366, CA (tenant leaving dwelling in 1970 to go abroad but intending to return permanently in 8 to 10 years' time when children's education completed held still protected); *Bevington v Crawford* (1974) 232 Estates Gazette 191, CA (tenant absent in France for all but two to three months each year held not to have lost protection). However, in a case where a tenant moved into alternative accommodation, in order for repairs to be carried out, and raised objections to moving back afterwards, she was held to have lost the necessary *animus revertendi*: *Robert Thackray's Estates Ltd v Kaye* (1988) 21 HLR 160, [1989] 1 EGLR 127, CA. In any case, the question of occupation as a residence is one of fact for the county court judge and other decisions may be of limited, if any, assistance: see *Gofor Investments Ltd v Roberts* (1975) 29 P & CR 366, CA per LAWTON LJ and *Richards v Green* (1983) 11 HLR 1, [1983] 2 EGLR 104, CA per PURCHAS LJ.

III L&T [69.6]

Tenant with two houses In certain circumstances a person may have two homes: see, for example, *Langford Property Co Ltd v Tureman* [1949] 1 KB 29, [1948] 2 All ER 722, CA and *Blanway Investments Ltd v Lynch* (1993) 25 HLR 378, [1993] NPS 14, CA. However, in some cases the courts have been reluctant to find that people are "two homes" men; see *Beck v Scholz* [1953] 1 QB 570, [1953] 1 All ER 814, CA; *Walker v Ogilvy* (1974) 28 P & CR 288, CA; *Regalian Securities Ltd v Scheuer* (1982) 47 P & CR 362, 5 HLR 48, CA; *Hampstead Way Investments Ltd v Lewis-Weare* [1985] 1 All ER 564, [1985] 1 WLR 164, HL; and *Brickfield Properties Ltd v Hughes* (1988) 20 HLR 108, CA. In order for both of two residences to qualify for protection the tenant must occupy each residence separately from the other as a complete home: *Kavanagh v Lyroudias* [1985] 1 All ER 560, CA, unless the two premises are close enough to each other to make a composite home, as to which see the notes to Rent Act 1977 s 1 at para **III L&T [68.5]**.

III L&T [69.7]

The statutory tenant The expressions statutory tenancy and statutory tenant first appeared in the Rent Acts in the Housing Repairs and Rents Act 1954. Prior to that the precise nature of a statutory tenancy had been (and is still being) worked out by the courts "slowly and with extreme caution": *Skinner v Geary* [1931] 2 KB 546 at 558, CA per SCRUTTON LJ. The existence of a statutory tenancy may be assumed from the tenant having been a monthly tenant for years: *White v Wareing* [1992] 1 EGLR 271, CA. A statutory tenant has no estate or property as tenant but only a personal right to retain possession of the dwelling house: *Roe v Russell* [1928] 2 KB 117 at 131, CA per SARGANT LJ. He has a "status of irremoveability": see *Keeves v Dean* [1924] 1 KB 685, CA at 686 per LUSH J. Except as is provided in the Rent Act 1977 Sch 1 Pt II, the statutory tenant cannot assign his right: see *Keeves v Dean* [1924] 1 KB 685, CA. Similarly, he cannot transmit it by will (*John Lovibond & Sons Ltd v Vincent* [1929] 1 KB 687, CA) nor will it pass to his trustee in bankruptcy: *Sutton v Dorf* [1932] 2 KB 304. However, the statutory tenant can bring an action for trespass against a third party: *Keeves v Dean* [1924] 1 KB 685, CA. Also, he may sub-let part of the dwelling house and still remain statutory tenant of the whole if he intends to return to that part: see *Berkeley v Papadoyannis* [1954] 2 QB 149, [1954] 2 All ER 409, CA; *Regalian Securities Ltd v Ramsden* [1981] 2 All ER 65, [1981] 1 WLR 611, HL. Where the statutory tenant has no intention to return to the sub-let parts he will cease to be tenant of them: *Crowhurst v Maidment* [1953] 1 QB 23, [1952] 2 All ER 808, CA, applied in *Baron v Phillips* (1978) 38 P & CR 91, 247 Estates Gazette 1079, CA. A sub-letting of the whole of a dwelling house by a statutory tenant who has no intention to return deprives him of protection: see *Roe v Russell* [1928] 2 KB 117, CA. However, it may be that the sub-tenant is protected as against the landlord by the Rent Act 1977 s 137 (2): see *Trustees of Henry Smith's Charity v Willson* [1983] QB 316 at 333, [1983] 1 All ER 73 at 87, CA per ORMROD LJ but compare per SLADE LJ. As regards the effect of sub-letting by a statutory tenant see also *Haskins v Lewis* [1931] 2 KB 1, CA, where an order for possession of the whole of certain premises was made against a tenant who had sub-let parts for residential use and the rest of the premises was used by persons other than the tenant for business purposes.

III L&T [69.8]

Statutory tenancy by estoppel Where a landlord represents to members of a deceased statutory tenant's family that they are joint statutory tenants the effect may be that a joint statutory tenancy arises by estoppel: *Daejan Properties Ltd v Mahoney* (1995) 28 HLR 498, [1995] NPC 7, CA.

III L&T [69.9]

Destruction of dwelling house Where the dwelling house is destroyed or substantially damaged so that it ceases to exist, there cannot be a statutory tenancy: see *Ellis & Sons Amalgamated Properties Ltd v Sisman* [1948] 1 KB 653, [1948] 1 All ER 44, CA; *East End Dwellings Co Ltd v Finsbury Borough Council* [1952] AC 109, [1951] 2 All ER 587, HL. Partial destruction may not however bring a statutory tenancy to an end: see *Morleys (Birmingham) Ltd v Slater* [1950] 1 KB 506, [1950] 1 All ER 331, CA.

III L&T [69.10]

Rescission for fraud A protected tenancy may be rescinded for fraud after it has expired and in such a case the rescission prevents a statutory tenancy from coming into operation: *Killick v Roberts* [1991] 4 All ER 289, [1991] 1 WLR 1146, CA.

III L&T [69.11]

Possessory title A statutory tenant may acquire a possessory title as against his immediate landlord by ceasing to pay rent: *Price v Hartley* [1995] NPC 80, [1995] EGCS 74, CA. However, by doing so he does not lose his statutory tenancy as against the freeholder: *Jessamine Investments Co v Schwartz* [1978] QB 264, [1976] 3 All ER 521, CA.

III L&T [70]

3. Terms and conditions of statutory tenancies

(1) So long as he retains possession, a statutory tenant shall observe and be entitled to the benefit of all the terms and conditions of the original contract of tenancy, so far as they are consistent with the provisions of this Act.

(2) It shall be a condition of a statutory tenancy of a dwelling-house that the statutory tenant shall afford to the landlord access to the dwelling-house and all reasonable facilities for executing therein any repairs which the landlord is entitled to execute.

(3) Subject to section 5 of the Protection from Eviction Act 1977 (under which at least 4 weeks' notice to quit is required), a statutory tenant of a dwelling-house shall be entitled to give up possession of the dwelling-house if, and only if, he gives such notice as would have been required under the provisions of the original contract of tenancy, or, if no notice would have been so required, on giving not less than 3 months' notice.

(4) Notwithstanding anything in the contract of tenancy, a landlord who obtains an order for possession of a dwelling-house as against a statutory tenant shall not be required to give to the statutory tenant any notice to quit.

(5) Part II of Schedule 1 to this Act shall have effect in relation to the giving up of possession of statutory tenancies and the changing of statutory tenants by agreement.

III L&T [70.1]

The original contract of tenancy These words refer to the tenancy under which the tenant held immediately before he became a statutory tenant: *Oxley v Regional Properties Ltd* [1944] 1 KB 733n, [1944] 2 All ER 510, CA (reversed on a different point, [1945] AC 347, [1945] 2 All ER 418, HL). Note that a proviso in the lease for re-entry in the event of bankruptcy is a term which binds a statutory tenant whose bankruptcy is a breach of an obligation for the purpose of Sch 15, Case 1: *Cadogan Estates Ltd v McMahon* [2001] 1 AC 378, [2000] 4 All ER 897, HL.

III L&T [70.2]

So far as they are consistent with the provisions of this Act The right to assign a tenancy does not pass into the statutory tenancy for it is a natural incident of property and not a term or condition and is inconsistent with a statutory tenancy: *Keeves v Dean* [1924] 1 KB 685 at 691, 698, CA. A term allowing the tenant to make an exchange of properties with the landlord's consent is not carried into the statutory tenancy: *Cripps v Britpal Ltd* [1951] EGD 308, CA.

III L&T [70.2A]

Landlord's right of access The landlord's right of access to do necessary repairs does not include access to convert the tenant's room into a self-contained unit. The statutory rights of access to do work under s 116 do not arise unless the work is specified in a statutory grant which has been approved: *Akram v Adam* [2002] EWCA Civ 1679, [2003] HLR 381, [2002] All ER (D) 68 (Nov).

III L&T [70.3]

Termination of a statutory tenancy A statutory tenancy may end if: (1) the dwelling house ceases to exist: *Ellis & Sons Amalgamated Properties Co Ltd v Sisman* [1948] 1 KB 653, [1948] 1 All ER 44, CA; (2) the tenant ceases to occupy the house as his residence (but his liability to pay rent will continue unless he gives the requisite notice under the Rent Act 1977 s 3 (3)); (3) the tenant surrenders possession to the landlord who accepts it: *King's College, Cambridge v Kershman* (1948) 64 TLR 547, CA; (4) the tenant enters into a new arrangement the effect of which is to deprive him of the protection of the Acts: *J & F Stone Lighting and Radio Ltd v Levitt* [1947] AC 209, [1946] 2 All ER 653, HL (rent reduced to a low rent); *Foster v Robinson* [1951] 1 KB 149, [1950] 2 All ER 342, CA (tenancy replaced by licence);

Scrimgeour v Waller (1980) 257 Estates Gazette 61, CA (tenancy replaced by licence); but see *Newham London Borough Council v Phillips* [1998] 1 FLR 613, [1998] Fam Law 140, CA in which an agreement to add another person's name to the rent book was held not to involve a surrender of a statutory tenancy; (5) an order for possession is made: *Brown v Draper* [1944] KB 309 at 713, [1944] 1 All ER 246 at 248, CA. Although it is theoretically possible for a tenant to surrender the statutory tenancy and to be granted a new tenancy on different terms the acts of surrender and grant need to be unambiguously evidenced, preferably including a going out of possession and subsequent return on the grant of a new tenancy in writing: *Andre v Robinson* [2007] EWCA Civ 1449.

PART VII
SECURITY OF TENURE

LIMITATIONS ON RECOVERY OF POSSESSION OF DWELLING-HOUSES LET ON PROTECTED TENANCIES OR SUBJECT TO STATUTORY TENANCIES

III L&T [71]

98. Grounds for possession of certain dwelling-houses

(1) Subject to this Part of this Act, a court shall not make an order for possession of a dwelling-house which is for the time being let on a protected tenancy or subject to a statutory tenancy unless the court considers it reasonable to make such an order and either—

(a) the court is satisfied that suitable alternative accommodation is available for the tenant or will be available for him when the order in question takes effect, or

(b) the circumstances are as specified in any of the Cases in Part I of Schedule 15 to this Act.

(2) If, apart from subsection (1) above, the landlord would be entitled to recover possession of a dwelling-house which is for the time being let on or subject to a regulated tenancy, the court shall make an order for possession if the circumstances of the case are as specified in any of the Cases in Part II of Schedule 15.

(3) Part III of Schedule 15 shall have effect in relation to Case 9 in that Schedule and for determining the relevant date for the purposes of the Cases in Part II of that Schedule.

(4) Part IV of Schedule 15 shall have effect for determining whether, for the purposes of subsection (1) (a) above, suitable alternative accommodation is or will be available for a tenant.

(5) Part V of Schedule 15 shall have effect for the purpose of setting out conditions which are relevant to Cases 11 and 12 of that Schedule.

III L&T [71.1]

A court Although the High Court does have jurisdiction, proceedings for the recovery of possession of dwelling houses subject to the Rent Acts should, save in exceptional circumstances, be brought in the county court for the district in which the dwelling house is situated: see generally para **CPR 55.3** and the Practice Direction to CPR Pt 55 paras 1.1 to 1.4 (para **CPR PD 55**).

III L&T [71.2]

Proceedings for possession In order to recover possession of a dwelling house subject to the Rent Acts, the landlord must show that: (1) the contractual tenancy has ended; (2) one or more of the grounds in Rent Act 1977 s 98(1) and (2) is made out; and (3) in the case of a ground in Rent Act 1977 s 98(1) (see para **III L&T [71]**), it is reasonable to make a possession order. For possession proceedings in the county court generally, see paras **III L&T [65]–III L&T [67]**. The proceedings should be brought against the tenant unless it is clear that he no longer has or claims any interest in the property. If the tenant has left the dwelling house but his wife remains, both tenant and wife should be joined as defendants: see *Middleton v Baldock* [1950] 1 KB 657 at 661, [1950] 1 All ER 708 at 710, CA per EVERSHED MR.

III L&T [71.3]

Mortgage action The protection conferred on the tenant by the Rent Act 1977 s 98(1) is not normally effective vis-à-vis tenants let in by the mortgagor after creation of the mortgage: *Dudley and District Benefit Building Society v Emerson* [1949] Ch 707, [1949] 2 All ER 252, CA. But the Rent Act 1977 s 98(1) may well protect tenancies (contractual or statutory) which predate registration of the mortgage: *Pourdanay v Barclays Bank plc* (1996) Times, 12 November. Also it may remain effective against the landlord's subsequent mortgagee even where the tenant has signed a letter of consent agreeing that the tenant's rights are subordinate to those of the mortgagee: *Woolwich Building Society v Dickman* [1996] 3 All ER 204, CA.

III L&T [71.4]

Rent arrears Where, in a possession claim, one of the grounds is non-payment of rent, particulars of claim in Form N119 should be used and attached to claim form N5. Specimens of these forms can be found in the Forms supplement, the FORMS section on your CD-ROM and at **BCCP O[80]** and **BCCP O[83]**.

The landlord may not rely on rent arrears if he has not supplied an address as required by the Landlord and Tenant Act 1987 s 48: *Hussain v Singh* [1993] 2 EGLR 70, [1993] 31 EG 75, CA. But the supply of an address enables the landlord to rely on earlier non-payment: *Lindsey Trading Properties Inc v Dallhold Estates (UK) Pty Ltd* (1993) 70 P & CR 332, CA.

III L&T [71.5]

Possession order by consent An order for possession may not be made by consent against someone whose tenancy appears to be protected or statutory without a concession by the tenant or his representative that he is not entitled to the protection of the Rent Acts: *R v Bloomsbury and Marylebone County Court, ex p Blackburne* (1985) 14 HLR 56, [1985] 2 EGLR 157, CA. But where such a concession is made an order may be made by consent without the court's considering the facts: *Syed Hussain bin Abdul Rahman bin Shaikh Alkaff v AM Abdullah Sahib & Co* [1985] 1 WLR 1392, PC; *R v Newcastle upon Tyne County Court, ex p Thompson* (1988) 20 HLR 430. See, too, the circumstances in which an order may be made by consent under the Housing Act 1985 s 84 (see para **III L&T [109]**). On the other hand, where the landlord agrees to sell and the tenant agrees with the purchaser not to claim the protection of the Act, possession may not be ordered unless the conditions of the Rent Act 1977 s 98 (1) are satisfied: *Appleton v Aspin* [1988] 1 All ER 904, [1988] 1 WLR 410, CA.

III L&T [71.6]

Rescission for fraud A protected tenancy may be rescinded for fraud after it has expired and in such a case the rescission prevents a statutory tenancy from coming into operation: *Killick v Roberts* [1991] 4 All ER 289, [1991] 1 WLR 1146, CA.

III L&T [71.7]

Sub-tenants If there are any sub-tenants, they should be joined as defendants if the landlord wishes to obtain possession against them: if they are not joined as defendants the court may make an order for possession against the tenant of the parts sub-let; see *Crowhurst v Maidment* [1953] 1 QB 23, [1952] 2 All ER 808, CA. Such an order will only be enforceable against the tenant; as to the effect on the sub-tenant: see the Rent Act 1977 s 137(1), (2) (see para **III L&T [76]**). If the landlord does not join the sub-tenants in the proceedings but claims an order for possession against the tenant alone he will have to start separate proceedings against the sub-tenant: *Lord Hylton v Heal* [1921] 2 KB 438 at 449, per Rowlatt J. Alternatively, if the landlord joins the sub-tenants as a party to the proceedings, the court must consider whether the ground for possession relied upon against the tenant is also a ground against the sub-tenant: *Enniskillen UDC v Bartley and Lynch* [1947] NI 177; *Leith Properties Ltd v Byrne* [1983] QB 433, [1982] 3 All ER 731, CA. In certain of the cases in the Rent Act 1977 Sch 15 Pt I (see para **III L&T [82]**), the term "tenant" must be read as referring simply to the last immediate tenant and not as including a sub-tenant or an assignee; thus the landlord may rely on such a case to recover possession against the sub-tenant as well as the tenant provided it is reasonable to make an order against the sub-tenant: *Lord Hylton v Heal* [1921] 2 KB 438, *Leith Properties Ltd v Byrne* [1983] QB 433, [1982] 3 All ER 731, CA. The cases in the Rent Act 1977 Sch 15 in which it has been held that the word "tenant" has such a meaning are Case 5 (see *Lord Hylton v Heal* [1921] 2 KB 438) and Case 8 (*Leith Properties Ltd v Byrne* [1983] QB 433, [1982] 3 All ER 731, CA). In *Lord Hylton v Heal* [1921] 2 KB 438, Rowlatt J said obiter that the same meaning applied to Cases 1 and 2 also.

III L&T [71.8]

The court considers it reasonable The burden of proof is on the landlord: *Nevile v Hardy* [1921] 1 Ch 404. "The duty of the judge is to take into account all relevant circumstances as they exist at the date of the hearing. That he must do in what I venture to call a broad common-sense way giving weight as he thinks right to the various factors in the situation. Some factors may have little or no weight, others may be decisive": *Cumming v Danson* [1942] 2 All ER 653 at 655, CA, per Lord Greene MR. Even if the case in the Rent Act 1977 Sch 15 has an element of reasonableness, the court must still consider whether it is reasonable to order possession: *Shrimpton v Rabbits* [1924] All ER Rep 694. A failure to consider this requirement and the other requirements of this section will make any judgment a nullity: *Peachey Property Corpn Ltd v Robinson* [1967] 2 QB 543, [1966] 2 All ER 981; *Minchburn Ltd v Fernandez* (1986) 19 HLR 29, [1986] 2 EGLR 103, CA.

When deciding whether it is reasonable to order possession, the judge should follow the guidance in *Cresswell v Hodgson* [1951] 2 KB 92, [1951] 1 All ER 710, look at the question from all angles and consider the effect on the parties not just if an order was made, but also if it was not: *Whitehouse v Loi Lee* [2009] EWCA Civ 375, [2009] 31 EG 74, [2009] 20 EG 103 (CS).

Examples of what courts have taken into account in considering reasonableness are: the perjury of one party: *Yelland v Taylor* [1957] 1 All ER 627, [1957] 1 WLR 459, CA; the loss of goodwill and financial hardship to the tenant: *Williamson v Pallant* [1924] 2 KB 173, DC; the landlord's desire to have relations living with him: *Cumming v Danson* [1942] 2 All ER 653, CA; persistent delay in paying rent: *Dellenty v Pellow* [1951] 2 KB 858, [1951] 2 All ER 716, CA: the tenant's intention to continue a breach of covenant: *Bell London and Provincial Properties Ltd v Reuben* [1947] KB 157, [1946] 2 All ER 547, CA. In considering reasonableness the court should have regard only to matters which have been pleaded: *Raeuchle v Laimond Properties Ltd* (2000) 79 P & CR D40, CA.

Absence of personal fault on the part of the tenant may be a relevant consideration when the court considers whether it would be reasonable to make a possession order and whether to suspend the order: *Portsmouth City Council v Bryant* (2000) 32 HLR 906, CA (a case concerned with Ground 2 in Sch 2 of the Housing Act 1985).

LANDLORD & TENANT AND HOUSING

III L&T [71.8A]

Suitable alternative accommodation Section 98(1)(a) requires that suitable alternative accommodation is available at the date of the order for possession or would be available when the order is effected. Accordingly, where a landlord sought vacant possession of demised premises in order to refurbish them and then make them available to the tenant as suitable alternative accommodation, the court could not make order under s 98(1)(a) as it was the works themselves which were to achieve the suitable alternative accommodation: *Akram v Adam* [2002] All ER (D) 68 (Nov), (2002) Times, 19 November, CA. Where suitable alternative accommodation existed, but the tenant would have to rearrange his affairs in order to make it available, the court held that the landlord had to show that it was reasonable to require the tenant to do so: *Amrit Holdings Co Ltd v Shahbakhti* [2005] EWCA Civ 339, (2005) HLR 474.

III L&T [71.9]

Costs Costs in county court proceedings for possession of premises subject to the Rent Acts are in the discretion of the court; the discretion must be exercised judicially: *Ottway v Jones* [1955] 2 All ER 585, [1955] 1 WLR 706, CA. In that case, the landlord succeeded in establishing a ground for possession (nuisance) but failed on reasonableness due to matters unknown to him; the Court of Appeal declined to interfere with an order that the successful tenant should pay the landlord's costs. The court should consider the question of costs in each case and not leave them to follow the event automatically: *Bensusan v Bustard* [1920] 3 KB 654. Greater hardship cases may, depending on the facts in each case, warrant no order as to costs.

III L&T [71.10]

Precedents Precedents for particulars of claim for possession on various grounds not involving rent arrears can be found at **BCCP O[101]–BCCP O[105]**. These are suitable for attachment to Form N5. Where the claim includes a claim for non-payment of rent particulars of claim in Form N119 should be used.

III L&T [72]

99. Grounds for possession of certain dwelling-houses let to agricultural workers, etc

(1) This section applies to any protected or statutory tenancy which—

(a) if it were a tenancy at a low rent, and

(b) if (where relevant) any earlier tenancy granted to the tenant, or to a member of his family, had been a tenancy at a low rent, would be a protected occupancy or statutory tenancy as defined in the Rent (Agriculture) Act 1976.

(2) Notwithstanding anything in section 98 of this Act, the court shall not make an order for possession of a dwelling-house which is for the time being let on or subject to a tenancy to which this section applies unless the court considers it reasonable to make such an order and the circumstances are as specified in any of the Cases (except Case 8) in Part I of Schedule 15 to this Act or in either of the Cases in Schedule 16 to this Act.

(3) If, apart from subsection (2) above, the landlord would be entitled to recover possession of a dwelling-house which is for the time being let on or subject to a tenancy to which this section applies, the court shall make an order for possession if the circumstances are as specified in any of the Cases (except Cases 16 to 18) in Part II of Schedule 15 to this Act.

III L&T [72.1]

The Rent (Agriculture) Act 1976 The Rent (Agriculture) Act 1976 gives security of tenure to agricultural workers housed, or agreed to be housed, by their employers before the coming into force of the Housing Act 1988 Pt I, on 15 January 1989. The protection is similar to that given by the Rent Act 1977. An employee protected by the Act may become a statutory tenant after his contractual right to occupy ends: Rent (Agriculture) Act 1976 s 4. There are provisions for succession: Rent (Agriculture) Act 1976 ss 3 and 4. The landlord cannot recover possession of a dwelling-house occupied by a protected occupier or statutory tenant unless he establishes one of the specified cases for possession: Rent (Agriculture) Act 1976 s 6, Sch 4. Possession proceedings will normally be brought in the county court: Rent (Agriculture) Act 1976 s 26. Some grounds for possession are discretionary (Rent (Agriculture) Act 1976 Sch 4 Pt I) while others are mandatory (Rent (Agriculture) Act 1976 Sch 4 Pt II). Certain basic terms for statutory tenancies are prescribed by Rent (Agriculture) Act 1976 s 10, Sch 5. There is a system of rent control: Rent (Agriculture) Act 1976 ss 11–17. If the tenant pays rent which is irrecoverable by the landlord, he may bring proceedings in the county court to recover it: Rent (Agriculture) Act 1976 s 21.

The Rent (Agriculture) Act 1976 Pt IV deals with the obligation of housing authorities to rehouse those protected by the Act where the dwelling is required to house another agricultural employee but is not set out below; nor is the Rent (Agriculture) Act 1976 Part V about power to obtain information.

No security is given under Rent (Agriculture) Act 1976 to tenancies created after 15 January 1989, unless contracted before that date: subsequent tenancies are protected, if protected at all, as "assured agricultural occupancies" within the Housing Act 1988 ss 24, 25 (see paras **III L&T [230]**, **III L&T [231]**) and 26. Because the old law now has diminishing practical relevance the text of the 1976 Act is no longer printed in the *Practice*; but it will be found in editions for 1992 and earlier.

III L&T [72.2]

Precedent A precedent for a claim for possession under the Rent (Agriculture) Act 1976 is given at **BCCP O[106]**. The precedent may be adopted for attachment to Form N5.

III L&T [73]

100. Extended discretion of court in claims for possession of certain dwelling-houses

(1) Subject to subsection (5) below, a court may adjourn, for such period or periods as it thinks fit, proceedings for possession of a dwelling-house which is let on a protected tenancy or subject to a statutory tenancy.

(2) On the making of an order for possession of such a dwelling-house, or at any time before the execution of such an order (whether made before or after the commencement of this Act), the court, subject to subsection (5) below, may—

(a) stay or suspend execution of the order, or

(b) postpone the date of possession,

for such period or periods as the court thinks fit.

(3) On any such adjournment as is referred to in subsection (1) above or any such stay, suspension or postponement as is referred to in subsection (2) above, the court shall, unless it considers that to do so would cause exceptional hardship to

the tenant or would otherwise be unreasonable, impose conditions with regard to payment by the tenant of arrears of rent (if any) and rent or payments in respect of occupation after termination of the tenancy (mesne profits) and may impose such other conditions as it thinks fit.

(4) If any such conditions as are referred to in subsection (3) above are complied with, the court may, if it thinks fit, discharge or rescind any such order as is referred to in subsection (2) above.

(4A) Subsection (4B) below applies in any case where—

(a) proceedings are brought for possession of a dwelling-house which is let on a protected tenancy or subject to a statutory tenancy;

(b) the tenant's spouse or former spouse, having rights of occupation under the Matrimonial Homes Act 1967, is then in occupation of the dwelling-house; and

(c) the tenancy is terminated as a result of those proceedings.

(4B) In any case to which this subsection applies, the spouse or former spouse shall, so long as he or she remains in occupation, have the same rights in relation to, or in connection with, any such adjournment as is referred to in subsection (1) above or any such stay, suspension or postponement as is referred to in subsection (2) above, as he or she would have if those rights of occupation were not affected by the termination of the tenancy.

(5) This section shall not apply if the circumstances are as specified in any of the Cases in Part II of Schedule 15.

III L&T [73.1]

On the making of an order In addition to the powers under the Rent Act s 100 (2), the court has an inherent power when making a possession order to postpone the date for possession for a limited period: *Sheffield Corpn v Luxford* [1929] 2 KB 180. An order for possession will normally be either absolute or suspended. An absolute order for possession is an order that the tenant give up possession forthwith or on a later, fixed date; it is not subject to any conditions performance of which would render the order inoperative: see *Haymills Houses Ltd v Blake* [1955] 1 All ER 592, [1955] 1 WLR 237, CA. Where an absolute order is made but the date for possession is postponed and the tenant dies in the period of postponement, there can be no transmission under the Rent Act 1977 Sch 1 (see para **III L&T [81]**); see *American Economic Laundry Ltd v Little* [1951] 1 KB 400, [1950] 2 All ER 1186, CA. See also the notes at paras **III L&T [110.1]–III L&T [110.1C]**.

III L&T [73.2]

Suspended order A suspended order for possession is one where the operation of the order is suspended so long as the tenant complies with certain terms or conditions specified in the order, eg paying the current rent and a sum off the arrears, not committing any further nuisance: *Yates v Morris* [1951] 1 KB 77, [1950] 2 All ER 577, CA. Provided the tenant complies with the conditions he will not have to give up possession. (An order like this is sometimes called a conditional order instead of a suspended order.) Care must be taken in framing the conditions: where in a claim for possession under Case 9, the court made an order for possession in three months subject to a provision that the warrant was to lie in the court office until the death of the landlord's mother, it was held that the form of order was open to objection as being indeterminate and the Court of Appeal substituted a proviso that the warrant was to issue on the death of the landlord's mother if that occurred within 12 months of the date of the county court hearing but otherwise was to lapse: *Kidder v Birch* (1982) 46 P & CR 362, 5 HLR 28, CA. The Court of Appeal has reiterated (in a rent arrears case) that a suspended order should not be made to extend to an almost indefinite period; in the absence of sensible terms as to payment of the substantial arrears, an immediate possession order was substituted in place of the suspended order made by the trial judge: *Taj v Ali* [2000] 17 LS Gaz R 36, CA. A revised Form N28 has been produced for use in the county court for suspended possession orders.

III L&T [73.3]

Discharge or rescind an order In *Goldthorpe v Bain* [1952] 2 QB 455, [1952] 2 All ER 23, CA, it was doubted whether an absolute order for possession could be varied into a suspended order. However, in *Payne v Cooper* [1958] 1 QB 174, [1957] 3 All ER 335, CA, it was held that in a case where an order for possession on a fixed date had been made but not executed, the court had power to vary the order and make an order for possession postponing the date of possession subject to conditions and, if the conditions were performed, to discharge the order. Moreover, the terms of the Rent Act 1977 s 100 (2) do not prevent a court from setting aside an order for possession after it has been executed: *Governors of Peabody Donation Fund v Hay* (1986) 19 HLR 145, CA. But see *Scott-James v Bass Chebab* [1985] 2 EGLR 61, [1988] 41 EG 75, CA.

III L&T [73.4]

Forfeiture for non-payment of rent Where proceedings are brought to forfeit a protected tenancy for non-payment of rent, Form N5 should be used with particulars of claim in Form N119. The County Courts Act 1984 s 138 (see para **II CCA [133]**) will apply. The court must therefore first consider the requirements of that provision and then consider whether to make an order for possession under the Rent Acts. The relevant forms are: N27 (Order for possession on forfeiture for rent arrears) and N27(2) (Order for possession on forfeiture for rent arrears (suspended)). By virtue of s 167 of the Commonhold and Leasehold Reform Act 2002 a landlord is not be entitled to forfeit a long lease of a dwelling for non payment of rent unless the unpaid amount exceeds the prescribed sum (which is £350) or has remained unpaid for longer than the prescribed period (which is 3 years): see the Rights of Re-entry and Forfeiture (Prescribed Sum and Period) (England) Regulations 2004 SI 2004/3086. Section 166 of the 2002 Act also came into force, subject to savings, on 28 February 2005. A tenant under a long lease of a dwelling is not be liable to pay ground rent unless the landlord has given notice (in a prescribed form) of the amount due and the date it is due to be paid. It follows that a risk of forfeiture in relation to unpaid ground rent will not be incurred unless and until notice in proper form has been served and not complied with. For ss 166 and 167 of the 2002 Act, see para **III L&T [316]–III L&T [317]**. For the prescribed information and form of notice under s 166, see the Landlord and Tenant (Notice of Rent) (England) Regulations 2004, SI 2004/3096.

III L&T [74]

106A. Discretion of court in certain proceedings for possession

(1) This section applies to any dwelling-house which is the subject of a restricted contract entered into after the commencement of section 69 of the Housing Act 1980.

(2) On the making of an order for possession of such a dwelling-house, or at any time before the execution of such an order, the court may—

(a) stay or suspend execution of the order, or

(b) postpone the date of possession,

for such period or periods as, subject to subsection (3) below, the court thinks fit.

(3) Where a court makes an order for possession of such a dwelling-house, the giving up of possession shall not be postponed (whether by the order or any variation, suspension or stay of execution) to a date later than 3 months after the making of the order.

(4) On any such stay, suspension or postponement as is referred to in subsection (2) above, the court shall, unless it considers that to do so would cause exceptional hardship to the lessee or would otherwise be unreasonable, impose conditions with regard to payment by the lessee of arrears of rent (if any) and rent or payments in respect of occupation after termination of the tenancy (mesne profits) and may impose such other conditions as it thinks fit.

(5) Subsection (6) below applies in any case where—

(a) proceedings are brought for possession of such a dwelling-house;

(b) the lessee's spouse or former spouse, having rights of occupation under the Matrimonial Homes Act 1967, is then in occupation of the dwelling-house; and

(c) the restricted contract is terminated as a result of those proceedings.

(6) In any case to which this subsection applies, the spouse or former spouse shall, so long as he or she remains in occupation, have the same rights in relation to, or in connection with, any such stay, suspension or postponement as is referred to in subsection (2) above, as he or she would have if those rights of occupation were not affected by the termination of the restricted contract.

MISCELLANEOUS

III L&T [75]

107. Interpretation of Part VII

(1) In this Part of this Act, except where the context otherwise requires—

"appropriate tribunal" means—

(a) in relation to a dwelling in England, the First-tier Tribunal or, where determined by or under Tribunal Procedure Rules, the Upper Tribunal; and

(b) in relation to a dwelling in Wales, a rent assessment committee;

"dwelling" means a house or part of a house;

"lessee" means the person to whom is granted, under a restricted contract, the right to occupy the dwelling in question as a residence and any person directly or indirectly deriving title from the grantee; and

"lessor" means the person who, under a restricted contract, grants to another the right to occupy the dwelling in question as a residence and any person directly or indirectly deriving title from the grantor.

(2) References in this Part of this Act to a party to a contract include references to any person directly or indirectly deriving title from such a party.

PART XI
GENERAL

SUBLETTINGS

III L&T [76]

137. Effect on sub-tenancy of determination of superior tenancy

(1) If a court makes an order for possession of a dwelling-house from—

(a) a protected or statutory tenant, or

(b) a protected occupier or statutory tenant as defined in the Rent (Agriculture) Act 1976,

and the order is made by virtue of section 98 (1) or 99 (2) of this Act or, as the case may be, under Part I of Schedule 4 to that Act, nothing in the order shall affect the right of any sub-tenant to whom the dwelling-house or any part of it has been lawfully sublet before the commencement of the proceedings to retain possession by virtue of [. . .] this Act, nor shall the order operate to give a right to possession against any such sub-tenant.

(2) Where a statutorily protected tenancy of a dwelling-house is determined, either as a result of an order for possession or for any other reason, any sub-tenant to whom the dwelling-house or any part of it has been lawfully sublet shall, subject to this Act, be deemed to become the tenant of the landlord on the same terms as if the tenant's statutorily protected tenancy has continued.

(3) Where a dwelling-house—

(a) forms part of premises which have been let as a whole on a superior tenancy but do not constitute a dwelling-house let on a statutorily protected tenancy; and

(b) is itself subject to a protected or statutory tenancy.

then, from the coming to an end of the superior tenancy, this Act shall apply in relation to the dwelling-house as if, in lieu of the superior tenancy, there had been separate tenancies of the dwelling-house and of the remainder of the premises, for the like purposes as under the superior tenancy, and at rents equal to the just proportion of the rent under the superior tenancy.

In this subsection "premises" includes, if the sub-tenancy in question is a protected or statutory tenancy to which section 99 of this Act applies, an agricultural holding within the meaning of the [Agricultural Holdings Act 1986 held under a tenancy to which that Act applies and land comprised in a farm business tenancy within the meaning of the Agricultural Tenancies Act 1995.

(4) In subsections (2) and (3) above "statutorily protected tenancy" means—

- (a) a protected or statutory tenancy;
- (b) a protected occupancy or statutory tenancy as defined in the Rent (Agriculture) Act 1976; or
- (c) if the sub-tenancy in question is a protected or statutory tenancy to which section 99 of this Act applies—
  - (i) a tenancy of an agricultural holding within the meaning of the Agricultural Holdings Act 1986 which is a tenancy in relation to which that Act applies, or
  - (ii) a farm business tenancy within the meaning of the Agricultural Tenancies Act 1995.

(5) Subject to subsection (6) below, a long tenancy of a dwelling-house which is also a tenancy at a low rent but which, had it not been a tenancy at a low rent, would have been a protected tenancy or an assured tenancy within the meaning of Part I of the Housing Act 1988, shall be treated for the purposes of subsection (2) above as a statutorily protected tenancy.

(6) Notwithstanding anything in subsection (5) above, subsection (2) above shall not have effect where the sub-tenancy in question was created (whether immediately or derivately) out of a long tenancy falling within subsection (5) above and, at the time of the creation of the sub-tenancy—

- (a) a notice to terminate the long tenancy had been given under section 4 (1) of the Landlord and Tenant Act 1954 or, as the case may be, served under paragraph 4 (1) of Schedule 10 to the Local Government and Housing Act 1989; or
- (b) the long tenancy was being continued by section 3 (1) of [the said Act of 1954 or, as the case may be, paragraph 3 of the said Schedule 10;

unless the sub-tenancy was created with the consent in writing of the person who at the time when it was created was the landlord, within the meaning of Part I of the said Act of 1954 or, as the case may be, the said Schedule 10.

(7) This section shall apply equally where a protected occupier of a dwelling-house, or part of a dwelling-house, has a relevant licence as defined in the Rent (Agriculture) Act 1976, and in this section "tenancy" and all cognate expressions shall be construed accordingly.

III L&T [76.1]

Lawfully sublet The onus of proving the subletting to be lawful is on the sub-tenant: *Trustees of Henry Smith's Charity v Willson* [1983] QB 316 at 333, [1983] 1 All ER 73 at 86, CA per Slade LJ. A sub-letting is unlawful if it is contrary to the terms of the tenancy: *Maley v Fearn* [1946] 2 All ER 583, CA. If subletting is permitted provided that a substantial part of the rent represents payment for the use of furniture and the terms of the sublease are "otherwise consistent with the use of high-class furnished accommodation" a subletting with a carpet, curtains and one chair only is unlawful: *Patoner Ltd v Alexandratis* [1984] 2 EGLR 124, CA. Where there is no term restricting alienation, the subletting will be lawful; the Rent Act 1977 Sch 15 Case 6 (see para **III L&T [82]**) does not implicitly prohibit a subletting of the whole dwelling house without the consent of the landlord: *Leith Properties Ltd v Byrne* [1983] QB 433, [1982] 3 All ER 731, CA. The question of lawfulness must be determined as at the date of determination of the intermediate tenancy unless the intermediate tenant is a statutory tenant in which case it must be determined as at the date of issue of the proceedings: *Oak Property Co Ltd v Chapman* [1947] KB 886, [1947] 2 All ER 1, CA. An unlawful subletting may be rendered unlawful by waiver. However for the purpose of the Rent Act 1977 s 137 whether the acceptance of rent amounts to a waiver is a question of fact and not of law; there has to be such a degree of acquiescence that a consent to a subletting can be inferred: *Muspratt v Johnston* [1963] 2 QB 383 at 393, [1963] 2 All ER 339 at 341, CA, per Lord Denning MR; *Trustees of Henry Smith's Charity v Willson* [1983] QB 316, [1983]

1 All ER 73, CA, explaining *Oak Property Co Ltd v Chapman* [1947] KB 886, [1947] 2 All ER 1, CA; *Chrisdell Ltd v Johnson and Tickner* (1987) 19 HLR 406, [1987] 2 EGLR 123, CA. The knowledge of a porter employed in a block of flats may be imputed to the landlord and support a waiver: *Metropolitan Properties Co Ltd v Cordery* (1979) 39 P & CR 10, CA. A waiver only renders the subletting lawful from the date of the waiver: *Muspratt v Johnson* [1963] 2 QB 383, [1963] 2 All ER 339, CA.

III L&T [76.2]

Nor shall the order operate to give a right of possession against any such sub-tenant This means that where there is a sub-tenant lawfully and de facto in possession of the house or part of it, the landlord who desires to recover possession cannot avail himself as against the sub-tenant of any order or judgment which he has obtained against the tenant but must commence separate proceedings against the sub-tenant: *Lord Hylton v Heal* [1921] 2 KB 438 at 449 per Rowlatt J. Alternatively, the landlord may join the sub-tenant as a party to proceedings against the tenant in which case the court must address itself separately to the question of the sub-tenant and consider whether the ground on which possession is claimed can be relied upon against the sub-tenant and, if so, whether it is reasonable to make an order for possession against him: *Enniskillen UDC v Bartley and Lynch* [1947] NI 177; *Leith Properties Ltd v Byrne* [1983] QB 433, [1982] 3 All ER 731, CA. See also the notes to the Rent Act s 98 (see para **III L&T [71.1]** onwards).

III L&T [76.3]

Or for any other reason Examples of other reasons are: the tenant abandoning the premises and giving the key to the landlord: *Standingford v Bruce* [1926] 1 KB 466; the death of a statutory tenant: *Lewis v Reeves* [1952] 1 KB 19, [1951] 2 All ER 855, CA; forfeiture: *Ward v Larkins* (1923) 130 LT 184; surrender: *Barton v Fincham* [1921] 2 KB 291 at 297, CA. The rule at common law is that an upward notice from the mesne landlord to the head landlord ends the sub-lease, whereas a surrender does not prejudice the sub-lessee's rights of occupation: *Pennell v Payne* [1995] QB 192, [1995] 2 All ER 592, CA, followed in *Barrett v Morgan* [2000] 2 AC 264, [2000] 1 All ER 481, HL in which it was held that a notice to quit served on the tenant by the landlord terminated a sub-lease and that the tenant's agreement not to serve a counter-notice did not render the transaction between the landlord and the tenant a surrender. See also *PW & Co v Milton Gate Investments Ltd* [2003] EWHC 1994 (Ch), [2004] Ch 142 where the court held that, as a matter of law, it was not possible to contract out of the general rule in *Pennell v Payne* (above) that a sub-tenancy came to an end on determination of the head-tenancy.

III L&T [76.4]

Any sub-tenant to whom the dwelling-house has been lawfully sublet The wording of the Rent Act 197 s 137(2) may be sufficiently wide to give protection to a person who takes a subletting of the whole of the dwelling house from a statutory tenant: see *Trustees of Henry Smith's Charity v Willson* [1983] QB 316 at 333, [1983] 1 All ER 73 per Ormrod LJ; but see per Slade LJ for the contrary view.

Note also the decision in *Moreland Properties (UK) Ltd v Dhokia* [2003] EWCA Civ 1639, [2004] 1 P & CR D34 that where a tenant sublets the whole and goes out of possession his tenancy ceased to be protected and that, in any case, a statutory tenant has no right to sublet the whole so the sub-letting is unlawful. The result is that s 137(2) cannot apply.

III L&T [76.5]

On the same terms as if the tenant's statutorily protected tenancy had continued This appears to mean that if the sub-tenant was a contractual sub-tenant he becomes a contractual tenant of the landlord whereas if he was a statutory sub-tenant he becomes a statutory tenant: *Stanley v Compton* [1951] 1 All ER 859 at 863, CA, per Denning LJ. See, to the same effect, *Keepers and Governors of the Free Grammar School of John Lyon v James* [1996] QB 163, [1995] 4 All ER 740, CA.

III L&T [76.6]

Subsection (3) This subsection deals with the problems exposed by *Cow v Casey* [1949] 1 KB 474, [1949] 1 All ER 197, CA (head tenancy comprising premises the rateable value of which exceeded the Rent Act limits) and *Knightsbridge Estates Trust Ltd v Deeley* [1950] 2 KB 228, [1950] 1 All ER 577, CA (head tenancy at a low rent). However, the Rent Act 1977 s 137 (3) is not confined to cases where the superior tenancy is of residential premises. It was decided in *Wellcome Trust Ltd v Hamad* [1998] QB 638, [1998] 1 All ER 657, CA, that the subsection applies even where the superior tenancy is of business premises within the Landlord and Tenant Act 1954 Pt II (see para **III L&T [14]**). The court noted, in this connection, the words of qualification in the Rent Act 1977 s 24 (3). The court further held that a line of

LANDLORD & TENANT AND HOUSING

contrary cases, including *Pittalis v Grant* [1989] QB 605, [1989] 2 All ER 622, CA and the observations of LORD WILBERFORCE in *Maunsell v Olins* [1975] AC 373, [1975] 1 All ER 16, HL, were arrived at *per incuriam* and should no longer be followed.

III L&T [76.7]

Disclaimer of head-lease by landlord's liquidator A statutory tenant may apply, under Insolvency Act 1986 s 181, to have a lease vested in him upon the disclaimer of the head-lease, under Insolvency Act 1986 s 178, by the liquidator of the landlord; but the tenant's status of irremovability is not lost by his declining to accept a vesting order: *Re Vedmay Ltd* [1994] 1 BCLC 676, 26 HLR 70.

III L&T [77]

138. Effect on furnished sub-tenancy of determination of superior unfurnished tenancy

(1) If, in a case where section 137 (2) of this Act applies the conditions mentioned in subsection (2) below are fulfilled, the terms on which the sub-tenant is, by virtue of section 137 (2), deemed to become the tenant of the landlord shall not include any terms as to the provision by the landlord of furniture or services.

(2) The conditions are:—

(a) that the statutorily protected tenancy which is determined as mentioned in section 137 (2) was neither a protected furnished tenancy nor a statutory furnished tenancy; and

(b) that, immediately before the determination of that statutorily protected tenancy, the sub-tenant referred to in section 137 (2) was the tenant under a protected furnished tenancy or a statutory furnished tenancy; and

(c) that the landlord, within the period of 6 weeks beginning with the day on which the statutorily protected tenancy referred to in section 137 (2) is determined, serves notice on the sub-tenant that this section is to apply to his tenancy or statutory tenancy.

(3) In this section "statutorily protected tenancy" has the [same meaning as it has for the purposes of section 137 (2) of this Act].

JURISDICTION AND PROCEDURE

III L&T [78]

141. County court jurisdiction

(1) The county court shall have jurisdiction either in the course of any proceedings relating to a dwelling or on an application made for the purpose by the landlord or the tenant, to determine any question—

(a) as to whether a tenancy is a protected tenancy or whether any person is a statutory tenant of a dwelling-house, [. . .]; or

(b) as to the rent limit; or

(c) . . .

(d) as to the application of Part V and sections 103 to 106 of this Act to a contract; or

(e) as to whether a protected, statutory or regulated tenancy is a protected, statutory or regulated furnished tenancy;

or as to any matter which is or may become material for determining any such question.

(2) . . .

(3) The county court shall have jurisdiction to deal with any claim or other proceedings arising out of any of the provisions of this Act specified in subsection (5) below, notwithstanding that by reason of the amount of the claim or otherwise the case would not, apart from this subsection, be within the jurisdiction of the county court.

(4) If, under any of the provisions of this Act specified in subsection (5) below, a person takes proceedings in the High Court which he could have taken in the county court, he shall not be entitled to recover any costs.

(5) The provisions referred to in subsections (3) and (4) above are—

(a) . . .

(b) in Part III, section 57;

(c) in Part VII, except sections 98 (2) and 101;

(d) in Part IX, section 125 and 126;

(e) in Part X, sections 133 (1), 134 and 135; and

(f) in this Part of this Act, section 145.

Amendment *Sub-ss (4) and (5) are repealed by the Courts and Legal Services Act 1990, with effect from a date to be appointed.*

III L&T [78.1]

An application made for the purpose The Rent (County Court Proceedings) Rules 1970, SI 1970/1851 r 3(1) required an originating application. By virtue of CPR Pt 8 Practice Direction 8B paras B.1.3.c and B.8.(3) (see para **CPR PD 8B**) the application should now be by Pt 8 claim form.

III L&T [78.2]

Any question as to the rent limit The jurisdiction of the county court under the Rent Act 1977 s 141(1)(b) is to determine what the limit is according to the applicable part of the Act, but the court has no power to alter the registered rent or to do the rent officer's job by fixing the rent: *Tingey v Sutton* [1984] 3 All ER 561, [1984] 1 WLR 1154, CA.

III L&T [78.3]

Any claim or other proceedings arising out of A claim for possession of premises subject to the Rent Acts is a claim or proceeding "arising out of" the specified provision: *Russoff v Lipovitch* [1925] 1 KB 628, CA. An action for breach of the terms of a statutory tenancy is a claim or proceeding because the rights and duties of a statutory tenant arise out of the Acts: *Wolfe v Clarkson* [1950] 2 All ER 529, CA; *Wolff v Smith* [1923] 2 Ch 393. However, a claim for arrears of rent due under a protected tenancy has been held not to be a claim or proceeding "arising out of" the specified provision because it is a claim arising out of the contract: *A J Smith & Co Ltd v Kirby* [1947] 1 All ER 459.

III L&T [79]

142. *Rules as to procedure*
Repealed.

III L&T [79.1]

Rules and directions The Rent (County Court Proceedings) Rules 1970, SI 1970/1851 and the Rent Act (County Court Proceedings for Possession) Rules 1981, SI 1981/139, have been made under this power.

III L&T [80]

147. *Restriction on levy of distress for rent*
Repealed.

III L&T [80.1]

Leave of the county court Application for leave was formerly made by way of an originating application: Rent (County Court Proceedings) Rules 1970, SI 1970/1851 r 3(1). By virtue, therefore, of CPR Pt 8 Practice Direction 8B paras B.1.3.c and B.8.(3) (see para **CPR PD 8B**) the application should now be by Pt 8 claim form. If there is a dispute as to the rent payable, the court should not normally grant leave: *Townsend v Charlton* [1922] 1 KB 700 at 703, DC.

Schedules

SCHEDULE 1
STATUTORY TENANCIES

Sections 2, 3

PART I
STATUTORY TENANTS BY SUCCESSION

III L&T [81]

1. Paragraph 2 [. . .] below shall have effect, subject to section 2 (3) of this Act, for the purpose of determining who is the statutory tenant of a dwelling-house by succession after the death of the person (in this Part of this Schedule referred to as "the original tenant") who, immediately before his death, was a protected tenant of the dwelling-house or the statutory tenant of it by virtue of his previous protected tenancy.

2. (1) The surviving spouse or surviving civil partner (if any) of the original tenant, if residing in the dwelling-house immediately before the death of the original tenant, shall after the death be the statutory tenant if and so long as he or she occupies the dwelling-house as his or her residence.

(2) For the purposes of this paragraph-

(a) a person who was living with the original tenant as his or her wife or husband shall be treated as the spouse of the original tenant, and

(b) a person who was living with the original tenant as if they were civil partners shall be treated as the civil partner of the original tenant.

(3) If, immediately after the death of the original tenant, there is, by virtue of sub-paragraph (2) above, more than one person who fulfils the conditions in sub-paragraph (1) above, such one of them as may be decided by agreement or, in default of agreement, by the county court shall for the purposes of this paragraph be treated as the tenant's spouse, or if that person is the same sex as the tenant, and falls within paragraph 2(2)(b) of this Schedule, as the tenant's civil partner.

3.(1) Where paragraph 2 above does not apply, but a person who was a member of the original tenant's family was residing with him in the dwelling-house at the time of and for the period of 2 years immediately before his death then, after his death, that person or if there is more than one such person such one of them as may be decided by agreement, or in default of agreement by the county court, shall be entitled to an assured tenancy of the dwelling-house by succession.

(2) If the original tenant dies within the period of 18 months beginning on the operative date, then, for the purposes of this paragraph, a person who was residing in the dwelling-house with the original tenant at the time of his death and for the period which began 6 months before the operative date and ended at the time of his death shall be taken to have been residing with the original tenant for the period of 2 years immediately before his death.

4. A person who becomes the statutory tenant of a dwelling-house by virtue of paragraph 2 . . . above is in this Part of this Schedule referred to as "the first successor".

5. If, immediately before his death, the first successor was still a statutory tenant, paragraph 6 below shall have effect, for the purpose of determining who is who is entitled to an assured tenancy of the dwelling-house by succession after the death of the first successor.

6.—(1) Where a person who—

(a) was a member of the original tenant's family immediately before that tenant's death, and

(b) was a member of the first successor's family immediately before the successor's death,

was residing in the dwelling-house with the first successor at the time of, and for a period of 2 years immediately before, the first successor's death, that person or, if there is more than one such person,, such one of them as may be decided by agreement or, in default of agreement, by the county court shall be entitled to an assured tenancy of the dwelling-house by succession.

(2) If the first successor died within the period of 18 months beginning on the operative date, then, for the purposes of this paragraph, a person who was residing in the dwelling-house with the first successor at the time of his death and for the period which began 6 months before the operative date and ended at the time of his death shall be taken to have been residing with the first successor for the period of 2 years immediately before his death.]

7. [*Repealed by the Housing Act 1988 s 39(2), (3), 140(2), Sch 4 Pt 1, Sch 18*.]

8. [*Repealed by the Housing Act 1980 s 152 and Sch 26*.]

9. Paragraphs 5 to 8 above do not apply where the statutory tenancy of the original tenant arose by virtue of section 4 of the Requisitioned Houses and Housing (Amendment) Act 1955 or section 20 of the Rent Act 1965.

10. (1) Where after a succession the successor becomes the tenant of the dwelling-house by the grant to him of another tenancy, "the original tenant" and "the first successor" in this Part of this Schedule shall, in relation to that other tenancy, mean the persons who were respectively the original tenant and the first successor at the time of the succession, and accordingly—

(a) if the successor was the first successor, and, immediately before his death he was still the tenant (whether protected or statutory), paragraph 6 above shall apply on his death,

(b) if the successor was not the first successor, no person shall become a statutory tenant on his death by virtue of this Part of this Schedule.

(2) Sub-paragraph (1) above applies—

(a) even if a successor enters into more than one other tenancy of the dwelling-house, and

(b) even if both the first successor and the successor on his death enter into other tenancies of the dwelling-house.

(3) In this paragraph "succession" means the occasion on which a person becomes the statutory tenant of a dwelling-house by virtue of this Part of this Schedule and "successor" shall be construed accordingly.

(4) This paragraph shall apply as respects a succession which took place before 27th August 1972 if, and only if, the tenancy granted after the succession, or the first of those tenancies, was granted on or after that date, and where it does not apply as respects a succession, no account should be taken of that succession in applying this paragraph as respects any later succession.

11. (1) Paragraphs 5 to 8 above do not apply where—

(a) the tenancy of the original tenant was granted on or after the operative date within the meaning of the Rent (Agriculture) Act 1976, and

(b) both that tenancy and the statutory tenancy of the first successor were tenancies to which section 99 of this Act applies.

(2) If the tenants under both of the tenancies falling within sub-paragraph (1) (b) above were persons to whom Paragraph 7 of Schedule 9 to the Rent (Agriculture) Act 1976 applies, the reference in sub-paragraph (1)(a) above to the operative date shall be taken as a reference to the date of operation for forestry workers within the meaning of that Act.

11A. In this Part of this Schedule "the operative date" means the date on which Part I of the Housing Act 1988 came into force.

LANDLORD & TENANT AND HOUSING

III L&T [81.1]

Who is the statutory tenant by succession Only one person can be a statutory tenant by succession: *Dealex Properties Ltd v Brooks* [1966] 1 QB 542, [1965] 1 All ER 1080, CA, followed in *Newham London Borough Council v Phillips* [1998] 1 FLR 613, [1998] Fam Law, CA. Where the original tenant was a protected tenant, if the contractual tenancy devolves by will or intestacy on someone other than the statutory tenant by succession then the contractual tenancy is not destroyed but the rights and obligations under it are suspended so long as the statutory tenant by succession retains possession of the dwelling-house; that is the rights of the statutory tenant by succession take precedence over the rights of the person on whom the contractual tenancy devolves: *Moodie v Hosegood* [1952] AC 61, [1951] 2 All ER 582, HL, applied in *Mills v Allen* [1953] 2 QB 341, [1953] 2 All ER 534, CA.

III L&T [81.2]

Surviving spouse Prior to 28 November 1980, paras 2 and 6 applied only to widows; now it applies to a "surviving spouse" irrespective of the sex of the spouse. In *Fitzpatrick v Sterling Housing Association Ltd* [2001] 1 AC 27, [1999] 4 All ER 705, HL it was held that the extended meaning of the word spouse in para 2(2) did not apply to same sex partners; such partners could not, therefore, take a statutory tenancy (though, as a member of the original tenant's family, they could take an assured tenancy under para 3 (see para **III L&T [81.3]**)). The Court of Appeal decided (in *Ghaidan v Godin-Mendoza* [2002] EWCA Civ 1533, [2003] Ch 380, [2002] 4 All ER 1162) that para 2(2), as construed in *Fitzpatrick*, violates the provisions of Art 14 of the Convention on Human Rights as being discriminatory. Accordingly, the words "as his or her wife or husband" had to be read as meaning "as if they were his or her wife or husband". The same sex partner therefore succeeded to a statutory tenancy. The House of Lords held, dismissing the appeal, that it was possible to interpret Sch 1 para 2 so that it was compliant with the Convention. The court was required to depart from the interpretation of para 2 in *Fitzpatrick v Sterling Housing Association* (supra) and held that paragraph 2 should be read, and given effect, as if the survivor of a homosexual couple living together was the surviving spouse of the original tenant: *Ghaidan v Godin-Mendoza* [2004] UKHL 30, [2004] 2 AC 557, [2004] 3 All ER 411. Note that, in a decision as to whether the claimant was entitled to succeed to an assured tenancy under s 17 of the Housing Act 1988, the court held that, to be treated as the spouse when of the same gender as the deceased, the survivor would have to demonstrate a lifetime emotional commitment which was openly and unequivocally displayed to the whole world: *Southern Housing Group Ltd v Nuting* [2004] EWHC 2982 (Ch), [2004] All ER (D) 347 (Dec), (2005) Times, 5 January.

For a spouse to qualify as a surviving spouse, the marriage must not only be recognised as valid by the law of the domicil of the parties but it must also comply with the requirements of the Marriage Acts 1949 to 1986 if taking place in the United Kingdom: *Northumberland and Durham Property Trust Ltd v Ouaha* [2014] EWCA Civ 571, [2014] HLR 467 (an Islamic ceremony in a London Mosque).

III L&T [81.3]

Member of the original tenant's family The test, which must be applied at the date of the death, is whether an ordinary man would say that the person claiming to succeed is a member of the tenant's family: *Brock v Wollams* [1949] 2 KB 388 at 395, [1949] 1 All ER 715 at 718, CA per Cohen LJ; *Dyson Holdings Ltd v Fox* [1976] QB 503 at 508, [1975] 3 All ER 1030 at 1032, CA per Lord Denning MR; *Carega Properties SA v Sharratt* [1979] 2 All ER 1084, [1979] 1 WLR 928, HL. The word "family" is used as a popular, loose and flexible expression and not as a technical term: *Price v Gould* (1930) 143 LT 333 at 334, per Wright J. However, there must be a broadly recognisable *de facto familial nexus* recognisable as such by the ordinary man: *Ross v Collins* [1964] 1 All ER 861 at 866, [1964] 1 WLR 425 at 432, CA, per Russell LJ. A child of 16 is competent to succeed since a statutory tenancy is not a legal estate and lodgings are "necessaries": *Portman Registrars and Nominees v Latif* [1987] CLY 2239.

Examples of those held to be members of the tenant's family are: a husband, *Salter v Lask* [1925] 1 KB 584; a child or grandchild, *Collier v Stoneman* [1957] 3 All ER 20, [1957] 1 WLR 1108, CA; an illegitimate child, step-child or adoptive child, *Brock v Wollams* [1949] 2 KB 388, [1949] 1 All ER 715, CA; someone taken into the tenant's family by *de facto* adoption, unless already adult at the time, *Sefton Holdings Ltd v Cairns* (1988) 20 HLR 124, CA; a brother or sister, *Price v Gould* (1930) 143 LT 333; a woman who bears the tenant's children and lives with him but does not marry him, *Hawes v Evenden* [1953] 2 All ER 737, [1953] 1 WLR 1169, CA (compare *Gammans v Ekins* [1950] 2 KB 328, [1950] 2 All ER 140, CA); a woman who lived with the tenant as his wife for many years: *Dyson Holdings Ltd v Fox* [1976] QB 503, [1975] 3 All ER 1030, CA. Exceptionally a woman who lives with the tenant, in a stable relationship, for no more than two years may be regarded as a member of his family: *Chios Investment Property Co Ltd v Lopez* (1988) 20 HLR 120, [1988] 1 EGLR 98, CA. In the case of more distant relationships by marriage or blood the question becomes difficult and evidence of filial conduct may be necessary to establish that the would-be successor was a member of the deceased tenant's family: see, for example, *Jones v Whitehill* [1950] 2 KB

204, [1950] 1 All ER 71, CA (niece by marriage who looked after the tenant held to be a member of his family). It has now been held by the House of Lords that the surviving member of a stable and permanent homosexual relationship is a member of the deceased tenant's family: see *Fitzpatrick v Sterling Housing Association Ltd* [2000] 1 AC 27, [1999] 4 All ER 705, HL.

Examples of those held not to be members of the tenant's family are: a man who had cohabited with the tenant for three years: *Helby v Rafferty* [1978] 3 All ER 1016, [1979] 1 WLR 13, CA; a housekeeper: *Ross v Collins* [1964] 1 All ER 861, [1964] 1 WLR 425, CA; an adult living together with the tenant in a platonic relationship: *Carrega Properties SA v Sharatt* [1979] 2 All ER 1084, [1979] 1 WLR 928, HL, followed in *Sefton Holdings Ltd v Cairns* (1988) 20 HLR 124, CA.

III L&T [81.4]

Was residing with him A person can "reside" at a house even though he is physically absent at the relevant time: see *Middleton v Bull* [1951] 2 TLR 1010, CA. If the claimant is a sub-tenant of part of the house with joint use of the kitchen, he will not be "residing with" the tenant: *Edmunds v Jones* [1957] 3 All ER 23n, [1957] 1 WLR 1118n, CA. However, provided there is no such sub-tenancy, it need not be shown that the claimant used in common with the tenant every room in the house and there may be a "residing with" notwithstanding that each party had considerable independence of the other in domestic matters such as eating, cooking, etc: *Collier v Stoneman* [1957] 3 All ER 20, [1959] 1 WLR 1108, CA explaining *Edmunds v Jones* [1957] 3 All ER 23n, [1957] 1 WLR 1118n, CA. See also *Morgon v Murch* [1970] 2 All ER 100, [1970] 1 WLR 778, CA and *Foreman v Beagley* [1969] 3 All ER 838, [1969] 1 WLR 1387, CA. A person may "reside with" a tenant whilst owning another abode, but only if intending not to return to it: *Swanbrae Ltd v Elliott* (1986) 131 Sol Jo 410, 19 HLR 86, CA. A similar conclusion was reached by the Court of Appeal in *Hildebrand v Moon* (1989) 22 HLR 1, [1989] 2 EGLR 100, CA where a daughter took up residence with the tenant, moving from her own flat, which she had it in mind to sell. The quality of the residence is important: *Hedgedale Ltd v Hards* (1990) 23 HLR 158, CA in which a grandson was held to be residing with the tenant, because he moved in to look after her, although she was being cared for elsewhere by others during much of the relevant period.

III L&T [81.5]

Decided by agreement An agreement may arise from a sufficient period of acquiescence: *Trayfoot v Lock* [1957] 1 All ER 423 at 425 per DENNING LJ. The landlord need not be a party to the agreement: *General Management Ltd v Locke* [1980] 2 EGLR 83, CA.

III L&T [81.6]

In default by the county court Application was formerly made by way of originating application: Rent (County Court Proceedings) Rules 1970, SI 1970/1851 r 3(1). By virtue, therefore, of CPR Pt 8 Practice Direction 8B paras B.1.3.c and B.8.(3) (see para **CPR PD 8B**) the application should now be by Pt 8 claim form. The county court has a complete discretion as to the choice. For an example see *Williams v Williams* [1970] 3 All ER 988, [1970] 1 WLR 1530, CA where the needs of one party were balanced against the more meritorious conduct of the other and the needy party was declared to be the successor.

III L&T [81.7]

Section 20 of the Rent Act 1965 This contained transitional provisions whereby deemed statutory tenancies arose in respect of tenancies which had terminated before the commencement of the 1965 Act (8 December 1965) and which would otherwise have been regulated tenancies as a result of the 1965 Act.

III L&T [81.8]

Amendment by Housing Act 1988 By the Housing Act 1988 s 39 (2), (3) (see para **III L&T [236]**), the amendments set out below do not apply where the original tenant died before the commencement of that Act on 15 January 1989.

Amendments of Schedule 1 to Rent Act 1977

1. In paragraph 1 the words 'or, as the case may be, paragraph 3' shall be omitted.
2. At the end of paragraph 2 there shall be inserted the following sub-paragraphs—

   (2) For the purposes of this paragraph, a person who was living with the original tenant as his or her wife or husband shall be treated as the spouse of the original tenant.

   (3) If, immediately after the death of the original tenant, there is, by virtue of sub-paragraph (2) above, more than one person who fulfils the conditions

in sub-paragraph (1) above, such one of them as may be decided by agreement or, in default of agreement, by the county court shall be treated as the surviving spouse for the purposes of this paragraph.'

3. In paragraph 3—

(a) after the words 'residing with him' there shall be inserted 'in the dwelling-house';

(b) for the words 'period of 6 months' there shall be substituted 'period of 2 years'; and

(c) for the words from 'the statutory tenant' onwards there shall be substituted 'entitled to an assured tenancy of the dwelling-house by succession'; and

(d) at the end there shall be added the following sub-paragraph—

'(2) If the original tenant died within the period of 18 months beginning on the operative date, then, for the purposes of this paragraph, a person who was residing in the dwelling-house with the original tenant at the time of his death and for the period which began 6 months before the operative date and ended at the time of his death shall be taken to have been residing with the original tenant for the period of 2 years immediately before his death.'

4. In paragraph 4 the words 'or 3' shall be omitted.

SCHEDULE 15

GROUNDS FOR POSSESSION OF DWELLING-HOUSES LET ON OR SUBJECT TO PROTECTED OR STATUTORY TENANCIES

Section 98

PART I

CASES IN WHICH COURT MAY ORDER POSSESSION

CASE 1

III L&T [82]

Where any rent lawfully due from the tenant has not been paid, or any obligation of the protected or statutory tenancy which arises under this Act, or—

(a) in the case of a protected tenancy, any other obligation of the tenancy, in so far as is consistent with the provisions of Part VII of this Act, or

(b) in the case of a statutory tenancy, any other obligation of the previous protected tenancy which is applicable to the statutory tenancy,

has been broken or not performed.

CASE 2

Where the tenant or any person residing or lodging with him or any sub-tenant of his has been guilty of conduct which is a nuisance or annoyance to adjoining occupiers, or has been convicted of using the dwelling-house or allowing the dwelling-house to be used for immoral or illegal purposes.

CASE 3

Where the condition of the dwelling-house has, in the opinion of the court, deteriorated owing to acts of waste by, or the neglect or default of, the tenant or any person residing or lodging with him or any sub-tenant of his and, in the case of any act of waste by, or the neglect or default of, a person lodging with the tenant or a sub-tenant of his, where the court is satisfied that the tenant has not, before the making of the order in question, taken such steps as he ought reasonably to have taken for the removal of the lodger or sub-tenant, as the case may be.

CASE 4

Where the condition of any furniture provided for use under the tenancy has, in the opinion of the court, deteriorated owing to ill-treatment by the tenant or any person residing or lodging with him or any sub-tenant of his and, in the case of any ill-treatment by a person lodging with the tenant or a sub-tenant of his, where the court is satisfied that the tenant has not, before the making of the order in question, taken such steps as he ought reasonably to have taken for the removal of the lodger or sub-tenant, as the case may be.

CASE 5

Where the tenant has given notice to quit and, in consequence of that notice, the landlord has contracted to sell or let the dwelling-house or has taken any other steps as the result of which he would, in the opinion of the court, be seriously prejudiced if he could not obtain possession.

CASE 6

Where, without the consent of the landlord, the tenant has, at any time after—

(a) [*Repealed by the Housing Act 1980 s 152 and Sch 26*.]

(b) 22nd March 1973, in the case of a tenancy which became a regulated tenancy by virtue of section 14 of the Counter-Inflation Act 1973;

(bb) the commencement of section 73 of the Housing Act 1980, in the case of a tenancy which became a regulated tenancy by virtue of that section.

(c) 14th August 1974, in the case of a regulated furnished tenancy; or

(d) 8th December 1965, in the case of any other tenancy,

assigned or sublet the whole of the dwelling-house or sublet part of the dwelling-house the remainder being already sublet.

CASE 7

[*Repealed by the Housing Act 1980 s 152 and Sch 26*.]

CASE 8

Where the dwelling-house is reasonably required by the landlord for occupation as a residence for some person engaged in his whole-time employment, or in the whole-time employment of some tenant from him or with whom, conditional on housing being provided, a contract for such employment has been entered into, and the tenant was in the employment of the landlord or a former landlord, and the dwelling-house was let to him in consequence of that employment and he has ceased to be in that employment.

CASE 9

Where the dwelling-house is reasonably required by the landlord for occupation as a residence for—

(a) himself, or

(b) any son or daughter of his over 18 years of age, or

(c) his father or mother, or

(d) if the dwelling-house is let on or subject to a regulated tenancy, the father or mother of his spouse or civil partner,

and the landlord did not become landlord by purchasing the dwelling-house or any interest therein after—

(i) 7th November 1956, in the case of a [tenancy which was then a controlled tenancy;

(ii) 8th March 1973, in the case of a tenancy which became a regulated tenancy by virtue of section 14 of the Counter-Inflation Act 1973;

(iii) 24th May 1974, in the case of a regulated furnished tenancy; or
(iv) 23rd March 1965, in the case of any other tenancy.

CASE 10

Where the court is satisfied that the rent charged by the tenant—

(a) for any sublet part of the dwelling-house which is a dwelling-house let on a protected tenancy or subject to a statutory tenancy is or was in excess of the maximum rent for the time being recoverable for that part, having regard to [. . .] Part III of this Act, or

(b) for any sublet part of the dwelling-house which is subject to a restricted contract is or was in excess of the maximum (if any) which it is lawful for the lessor, within the meaning of Part V of this Act to require or receive having regard to the provisions of that Part.

CASE 10A

Both of the following conditions are met in relation to a dwelling-house in England.

Condition 1 is that the Secretary of State has given a notice in writing to the landlord or, in the case of joint landlords, one or more of them which identifies—

(a) the tenant or, in the case of joint tenants, one or more of them, or

(b) one or more other persons aged 18 or over who are occupying the dwelling-house,

as a person or persons disqualified as a result of their immigration status from occupying the dwelling-house under the tenancy.

Condition 2 is that the person or persons named in the notice—

(a) fall within paragraph (a) or (b) of condition 1, and

(b) are disqualified as a result of their immigration status from occupying the dwelling-house under the tenancy.

For the purposes of this case a person ("P") is disqualified as a result of their immigration status from occupying the dwelling-house under the tenancy if—

(a) P is not a relevant national, and

(b) P does not have a right to rent in relation to the dwelling-house.

P does not have a right to rent in relation to the dwelling-house if—

(a) P requires leave to enter or remain in the United Kingdom but does not have it, or

(b) P's leave to enter or remain in the United Kingdom is subject to a condition preventing P from occupying the dwelling-house.

But P is to be treated as having a right to rent in relation to a dwelling-house if the Secretary of State has granted P permission for the purposes of this case to occupy a dwelling-house which is for the time being let on a protected tenancy or subject to a statutory tenancy.

In this case "relevant national" means—

(a) a British citizen,

(b) a national of an EEA State other than the United Kingdom, or

(c) a national of Switzerland.

CASE 1

III L&T [82.1]

Any rent lawfully due A possession claim where one of the grounds is non-payment of rent should be brought by particulars of claim in Form N119 attached to Form N5: see generally para **CPR 55.4** and the Practice Direction to CPR Pt 55 paras 2.1 to 2.3 (para **CPR PD 55**). Rent is "lawfully due" when the proper date for payment has arrived; the material time for the court to consider whether rent is "lawfully due and has not been paid" is the date of commencement of the proceedings: *Bird v Hildage* [1948] 1 KB 91, [1947] 2 All ER 7, CA. If the rent has been tendered, even after the due date, then provided time is not made of the essence, it is not "lawfully due" and the condition precedent "has not been paid" is not fulfilled: *Bird v Hildage* [1948] 1 KB 91, [1947] 2 All ER 7, CA. If the tenant pays the rent into court or tenders it after the proceedings are commenced but before judgment, the court may still make an order for possession but should not normally do so unless there are special circumstances, such as a long history of default on the part of the tenant making it necessary for the landlord to issue summonses to extract the rent, which make it reasonable to make the order: *Dellenty v Pellow* [1951] 2 KB 858, [1951] 2 All ER 716, CA applied in *Grimshaw v Dunbar* [1953] 1 QB 408, [1953] 1 All ER 350, CA. Default in paying rent by a predecessor in title of a tenant is not a ground for possession against that tenant: *Tickner v Clifton* [1929] 1 KB 207, CA. A tenant who has stopped paying rent but is still receiving housing benefit in this respect may properly be ordered to pay the benefit into court pending the trial of the action: *Berg v Markhill* (1985) 17 HLR 455, CA.

The rent arrears of the outgoing husband may be relied on against the statutory tenant wife in occupation: but if she fails to comply with the terms of the suspended possession order made against her husband fresh proceedings would have to be taken in order to recover possession from her: *Church Comrs for England v Al-Emarah* [1997] Fam 34, [1996] 3 WLR 633, CA.

Failure by the landlord to supply a rent book containing the prescribed information required by the Landlord and Tenant Act 1985 s 4 does not prevent him recovering the rent: *Shaw v Groom* [1970] 2 QB 504, [1970] 1 All ER 702, CA. But the Landlord and Tenant Act 1987 ss 47, 48 (see paras **III L&T [203]**, **III L&T [204]**), which have effect from 1 February 1988 (Landlord and Tenant Act 1987 (Commencement No 1) Order 1987, SI 1987/2177), require a landlord to notify the tenant of his address for service in England and Wales and to state his name and address in any demand for rent; rent is not recoverable as due until these requirements are met: *Hussain v Singh* [1993] 2 EGLR 70, [1993] 31 EG 75, CA.

III L&T [82.2]

Any obligation The case covers implied obligations: *Williams Deacon's Bank Ltd v Catlow* [1928] EGD 286, DC. However, a personal obligation (eg a provision in a tenancy agreement that it is conditional on the tenant's remaining in his existing employment) is not an "obligation of the tenancy" and cannot form the basis of a claim under Case 1: *RMR Housing Society Ltd v Combs* [1951] 1 KB 486, [1951] 1 All ER 16, CA. It is not a breach of residential letting to allow members of the extended family into occupation: *Blanway Investments Ltd v Lynch* (1993) 25 HLR 378, CA. The court has jurisdiction to make an order for possession if it is established that there has been a breach of obligation notwithstanding that there is no breach on the date of the hearing: *Brown v Davies* [1958] 1 QB 117 at 122, 131, [1957] 3 All ER 401 at 403, 409, CA. Case 1 does not extend to obligations inconsistent with the provisions of the Rent Act Pt VII, eg a covenant to give up possession at the end of the term: *Artizans Labourers and General Dwellings Co Ltd v Whitaker* [1919] 2 KB 301. The fact that the breach might justify proceedings for possession is not by itself a sufficient reason for refusing an injunction to restrain a repetition or continuation of the breach: *Sutton Housing Trust v Lawrence* (1987) 19 HLR 520, CA. The obligation to give access for repairs (see the Rent Act 1977 ss 3, 148) is not necessarily broken by a refusal to move out of the premises: *Empson v Forde* [1990] 1 EGLR 131, [1990] 18 EG 99, CA. In *Cadogan Estates Ltd v McMahon* [2001] 1 AC 378, [2000] 4 All ER 897, [2000] 3 WLR 1555, HL, the House of Lords, upholding the Court of Appeal, held that where the lease contained a proviso for re-entry in the event of bankruptcy, a statutory tenant who became bankrupt was in breach of an obligation for the purpose of this case.

CASE 2

III L&T [82.3]

Nuisance or annoyance The word "nuisance" was defined in *Walter v Selfe* (1851) 4 De G & Sm 315 at 322 per Knight-Bruce VC as "an inconvenience materially interfering with the ordinary comfort physically of human existence, not merely according to elegant or dainty modes and habits of living, but according to plain and sober and simple notions among the English people". An "annoyance" is "a wider term than nuisance, and if you find a thing which reasonably troubles the mind and pleasure . . . of the ordinary sensible English inhabitants of a house . . . that seems to me an annoyance, although it may not appear to amount to physical detriment to comfort": *Tod-Heatly v Benham* (1888) 40 Ch D 80 at 98, CA, per Bowen LJ.

Examples of conduct held to be nuisance are: use of the house for prostitution: *Frederick Platts Co Ltd v Grigor* [1950] 1 All ER 941n, CA; *Yates v Morris* [1951] 1 KB 77, [1950] 2 All ER 577, CA; acts of destruction by the tenant's child tolerated by the tenant: *Wrigglesworth v Rose* (1951) 158 Estates Gazette 421; abuse to a neighbour's visitors: *Shine v Freedman* [1926] EGD 376, DC. In *Woking Borough Council v Bystram* [1993] EGCS 208, CA, the Court of Appeal held that a continuing pattern of verbal abuse of neighbours was so bad that it was unreasonable to refuse an order for possession.

III L&T [82.4]

To adjoining occupier In certain circumstances nuisance to adjoining occupiers may be inferred without the need for evidence from them: *Frederick Platts Co Ltd v Grigor* [1950] 1 All ER 941n, CA. The word "adjoining" does not necessarily connote premises which touch those of the tenant so long as they are sufficiently near for the occupiers to be affected by the tenant's conduct: *Cobstone Investments Ltd v Maxim* [1985] QB 140, [1984] 2 All ER 635, CA.

III L&T [82.5]

Or has been convicted An isolated incident will suffice, there need not be continuous or frequent use: *S Schneiders & Sons Ltd v Abrahams* [1925] 1 KB 301, CA. Use of the house does not have to be an essential part of the crime: however the house must have been used for committing the offence: *S Schneiders & Sons Ltd v Abrahams* [1925] 1 KB 301, CA; *Abrahams v Wilson* [1971] 2 QB 88, [1971] 2 All ER 1114, CA. In a decision relating to Ground 2 under the Housing Act 1985 (see para **III L&T [157]**), where the tenant had been convicted of handling stolen goods, the court held that it might be appropriate to make a suspended possession order on condition that the tenant committed no further breaches of his tenancy; see *Greenwich London Borough Council v Grogan* (2000) 33 HLR 140, CA.

CASE 3

III L&T [82.6]

Waste by, or the neglect or default of the tenant The word "neglect" is used in the context of tenant-like conduct. It need not amount to a breach of any obligation: *Lowe v Londrum* (1950) 156 Estates Gazette 423, CA per SOMERVELL LJ. Where a garden for which the tenant is responsible is in a state of deterioration following a substantial period of neglect, this may be a ground for ordering possession, although the garden may then be in no worse state than when he took over the tenancy: *Holloway v Povey* (1984) 49 P & CR 196, 15 HLR 104, CA.

CASE 4

III L&T [82.7]

This case was introduced by the Rent Act 1974 when furnished tenancies were given full Rent Act protection.

CASE 5

III L&T [82.8]

Notice to quit The requirement of notice to quit is not satisfied by the tenant merely going out of possession (*Standingford v Bruce* [1926] 1 KB 466) nor by his entering into an agreement to give up possession: *De Vries v Sparks* (1927) 137 LT 441, DC, where SALTER J said that there must be an act by the tenant which ends the tenancy "whether the other party likes it or not".

III L&T [82.9]

Seriously prejudice This element is essential to establish the ground: *Barton v Fincham* [1921] 2 KB 291, CA. Where the landlord enters into a contract of sale conditional on his obtaining vacant possession, it may be held that he is not seriously prejudiced if no order for possession is made: see *Hunt v Bliss* (1919) 89 LJKB 174, DC.

III L&T [82.10]

Effect on sub-tenants It appears that this case may be used against both a tenant and a sub-tenant providing the requirement of reasonableness is satisfied as regards both of them: *Lord Hylton v Heal* [1921] 2 KB 438, DC.

CASE 6

III L&T [82.11]

Without the consent of the landlord These words mean "without actual consent given by the landlord either expressly or by implication": *Regional Properties Co Ltd v Frankenschwerth and Chapman* [1951] 1 KB 631 at 638, [1951] 1 All ER 178 at 182, CA.

The conduct of the landlord (eg continued acceptance of rent with knowledge) may be sufficient consent: *Hyde v Pimley* [1952] 2 QB 506 at 512, [1952] 2 All ER 102 at 105, CA. Consent is sufficient if given at any time before the issue of proceedings though it need not precede the sub-letting: *Hyde v Pimley* [1952] 2 QB 506 at 512, [1952] 2 All ER 102 at 105, CA. Where there is no restriction in the lease on alienation, this does not amount to a consent: *Regional Properties Co Ltd v Frankenschwerth and Chapman* [1951] 1 KB 631 at 638, [1951] 1 All ER 178 at 182, CA. Acquiescence in an unlawful assignment, but without accepting rent, will not necessarily debar the landlord from relying on Case 6: *Pazgate Ltd v McGrath* [1984] 2 EGLR 130, CA.

The court may make an order under this ground where the sub-letting was of the whole even though the whole of the premises were not sub-let at the date the action was begun and although the time for which the whole was sub-let was only of limited duration: see *Finkle v Strzelczyk* [1961] 3 All ER 409, [1961] 1 WLR 1201, CA.

III L&T [82.12]

The tenant These words refer to the immediate tenant of the landlord rather than an assignee or sub-tenant against whom possession is sought: this case may be relied upon by a landlord against a sub-tenant but the court must consider whether it is reasonable to make an order for possession against the sub-tenant: *Leith Properties Ltd v Byrne* [1983] QB 433, [1982] 3 All ER 731, CA.

III L&T [82.13]

Counter-Inflation Act 1973 section 14 Repealed by the Rent Act 1977 s 155(5), Sch 25, and partly replaced by the Rent Act 1977 s 4(2), (3).

CASE 8

III L&T [82.14]

Engaged The material time at which it must be established that a person is engaged by the landlord is the date of the hearing: *Benninga (Mitcham) Ltd v Bijstra* [1946] KB 58, [1945] 2 All ER 433, CA. Engaged means actually in employment and not engaged to work at a future date: *Benninga (Mitcham) Ltd v Bijstra* [1946] KB 58, [1945] 2 All ER 433, CA. However, it is sufficient to show that the date for the employee to start work under the contract has arrived before the hearing and it is immaterial that by reason of, say, holiday or illness, he has not started to work when the hearing takes place: *R F Fuggle Ltd v Gadsden* [1948] 2 KB 236, [1948] 2 All ER 160, CA.

III L&T [82.15]

The tenant This refers to the original tenant and not to a successor: *Bolsover Colliery Co Ltd v Abbott* [1946] KB 8, CA.

III L&T [82.16]

Let to him in consequence of that employment The material time for deciding if this requirement is satisfied is the end of the contractual tenancy: *Read v Gordon* [1941] 1 KB 495, [1941] 1 All ER 222, CA. So, if the employment ends and a new tenancy is then granted, this condition will not be fulfilled: *Read v Gordon* [1941] 1 KB 495, [1941] 1 All ER 222, CA; *Murton v Aldis* (1929) 141 LT 168. In order to establish the link ("in consequence etc") it is necessary to consider the landlord's motive in granting the tenancy; it is immaterial what the tenant knew or thought: *Braithwaite & Co Ltd v Elliot* [1947] KB 177, [1946] 2 All ER 537, CA. The link need not be expressed in any agreement. It need not be shown that the nature of the employment made the letting necessary: *Munro v Daw* [1948] 1 KB 125, [1947] 2 All ER 360, CA; *Duncan v Hay* [1956] 3 All ER 555, [1956] 1 WLR 1329, CA.

CASE 9

III L&T [82.17]

Reasonably required The relevant time for evaluating the landlord's requirements is the date of the hearing, not, for example, the date of issue of proceedings: *Alexander v Mohamadzadeh* (1985) 51 P & CR 41, 276 Estates Gazette 1258, CA. The onus of proof is on the landlord: *Epsom Grand Stand Association Ltd v Clarke* (1919) 35 TLR 525, CA. This issue is a question of fact for the trial judge: *Chandler v Strevett* [1947] 1 All ER 164, CA. In *Aitken v Shaw* 1933 SLT (Sh Ct) 21 at 22 it was said that the landlord must show a "genuine present need . . . something more than desire although something less than absolute necessity will do". However in *Kidder v Birch* (1982) 46 P & CR 362, 5 HLR 28, CA, it was held that an order may be made where there is no present need but where the need for the accommodation is in the "ascertainable and not distant future". In a case where the court is satisfied that there is a need in the ascertainable future, the court should not make an indeterminate order but should limit it; so, where the court made an order subject to a proviso that the warrant was to lie in the office until the death of the landlord's mother, the Court of Appeal altered the order so that the warrant was to issue on the death of the mother if that occurred within 12 months but otherwise it was not to issue at all: *Kidder v Birch* (1982) 46 P & CR 362, 5 HLR 28, CA. Where the landlord really required the dwelling to sell it and discharge his debts, it was held that he did not "reasonably require" it: *Rowe v Truelove* [1977] 1 EGLR 46, CA. The landlord may reasonably require the whole of the dwelling even if he intends to occupy only a part of it: *Kelley v Goodwin* [1947] 1 All ER 810, CA.

III L&T [82.18]

Landlord Where the "landlord" comprises two or more people, all must reasonably require the dwelling house: *McIntyre v Hardcastle* [1948] 2 KB 82, [1948] 1 All ER 696, CA. Where the landlords are personal representatives, they will not normally be able to rely on Case 9 because it will be a breach of trust to claim possession for themselves; however, where that is not the case they can rely on Case 9: see *Sharpe v Nicholls* [1945] KB 382, [1945] 2 All ER 55, CA; *Parker v Rosenberg* [1947] KB 371, [1947] 1 All ER 87, CA, explained in *Patel v Patel* [1982] 1 All ER 68, [1981] 1 WLR 1342, CA where the personal representatives were trustees for children who were beneficial owners of the house and were also parents by adoption of them and so were not acting in breach of trust in claiming possession to live in the house with the children. A court may make an order for possession under Case 9 where the landlord reasonably requires the accommodation for an adult daughter even though that daughter has a beneficial interest as an equitable tenant in common: *Bostock v Tacher de la Pagerie* (1987) 19 HLR 358, [1987] 1 EGLR 104, CA.

III L&T [82.19]

Himself Where the landlord claims possession for "himself", it includes all his "normal emanations" such as his wife and children under 18: see *Richter v Wilson* [1963] 2 QB 426 at 430, [1963] 2 All ER 335 at 336, CA, per WILMER LJ. An order for possession under this case was made in favour of a landlord who was to live elsewhere due to his work but who wanted the house for the occupation of his children and housekeeper in *Smith v Penny* [1947] KB 230, [1946] 2 All ER 672, CA. Where the landlord requires possession for himself and for others, the test is whether, if he recovered possession, there would be a joint or separate household. If there is to be a joint household the court may consider all the proposed occupiers' needs and, if it thinks fit, make an order. If there are to be separate households then it cannot be said that the landlord requires the house as a residence for himself: *Richter v Wilson* [1963] 2 QB 426, [1963] 2 All ER 335, CA.

III L&T [82.20]

Son or daughter Joint landlords may recover possession of premises for a child who is the son of one and stepson of the other: *Potsos and Potsos v Theodotou* (1991) 23 HLR 356, [1991] 2 EGLR 93, CA.

III L&T [82.21]

Personal representatives Personal representatives of the deceased landlord may properly claim possession under Case 9 as long as this is consistent with their obligations to the beneficiaries of the estate: *Patel v Patel* [1982] 1 All ER 68, [1981] 1 WLR 1342, CA.

III L&T [82.22]

Landlord by purchase A landlord by purchase is one who buys the dwelling house subject to an existing tenancy and not one who buys with vacant possession and then lets the house: *Epps v Rothnie* [1945] KB 562, [1946] 1 All ER 146, CA; *Fowle v Bell* [1947] KB 242, [1946] 2 All ER 668, CA. A disposition by will is not a purchase, nor is it a gift: *Baker v Lewis* [1947] KB 186, [1946] 2 All ER 592, CA. An acquisition under a family arrangement is not a purchase: *Thomas v Fryer* [1970] 2 All ER 1, [1970] 1 WLR 845, CA. This is so even where the transferee members of the family agree to take over the mortgage: *Mansukhani v Sharkey* (1992) 24 HLR 600, CA. The creation of a tenancy of the reversion without a premium is not a purchase: *Powell v Cleland* [1948] 1 KB 262, [1947] 2 All ER 672, CA; *Lucas v Lineham* [1950] 1 KB 548 at 552, [1950] 1 All ER 586 at 588, CA. A landlord who obtains a possession order against a tenant and thereby becomes the landlord of a sub-tenant is not a landlord by purchase: *Cairns v Piper* [1954] 2 QB 210, [1954] 2 All ER 611, CA. If a tenant has granted a sub-tenancy, the later acquisition of the freehold by the tenant does not prevent him relying on this case: *Turney v Hammond* (1952) 160 Estates Gazette 582, CA. This was held to apply in *Amaddio v Dalton* (1991) 23 HLR 332, [1992] CLY 2686, CA even where the reversioner had given money with which the purchase was effected. The proviso protects a statutory tenant by succession (*Littlechild v Holt* [1950] 1 KB 1, [1949] 1 All ER 933, CA; *Wright v Walford* [1955] 1 QB 363, [1955] 1 All ER 207, CA) but probably not an assignee of the tenancy: *Wright v Walford* [1955] 1 QB 363, [1955] 1 All ER 207, CA. A successor in title to the reversion from a landlord by purchase will be unable to rely on Case 9 even if he is not a purchaser: *Littlechild v Holt* [1950] 1 KB 1, [1949] 1 All ER 933, CA. The relevant time is the date of the contract of sale and not the conveyance: *Emberson v Robinson* [1953] 2 All ER 755, [1953] 1 WLR 1129, CA. In exceptional circumstances the court may pierce the corporate veil to ascertain the true nature of a transaction in deciding if a landlord is a landlord by purchase: *Evans v Engelson* [1980] 1 EGLR 62, CA.

III L&T [82.23]

Greater hardship Under Case 9, the court must decide whether greater hardship would be caused by granting the order than by refusing to grant it: see the Rent Act 1977 Sch 15 Part III para 1 (see para **III L&T [84]**).

III L&T [82.24]

Counter-Inflation Act 1973 section 14 Repealed by the Rent Act 1977 s 155 (5), Sch 25, and partly replaced by the Rent Act 1977 s 4 (2), (3).

PART II

CASES IN WHICH COURT MUST ORDER POSSESSION WHERE DWELLING-HOUSE SUBJECT TO REGULATED TENANCY

CASE 11

III L&T [83]

Where a person (in this Case referred to as "the owner-occupier") who let the dwelling-house on a regulated tenancy had, at any time before the letting, occupied it as his residence and—

(a) not later than the relevant date the landlord gave notice in writing to the tenant that possession might be recovered under this Case, and

(b) the dwelling-house has not, since—

  (i) 22nd March 1973, in the case of a tenancy which became a regulated tenancy by virtue of section 14 of the Counter-Inflation Act 1973;

  (ii) 14th August 1974, in the case of a regulated furnished tenancy; or

  (iii) 8th December 1965, in the case of any other tenancy,

been let by the owner-occupier on a protected tenancy with respect to which the condition mentioned in paragraph (a) above was not satisfied, and

(c) the court is of the opinion that of the conditions set out in Part V of this Schedule one of those in paragraphs (a) and (c) to (f) is satisfied.

If the court is of the opinion that, notwithstanding that the condition in paragraph (a) or (b) above is not complied with, it is just and equitable to make an order for possession of the dwelling-house, the court may dispense with the requirements of either or both of those paragraphs, as the case may require.

The giving of a notice before 14th August 1974 under section 79 of the Rent Act 1968 shall be treated, in the case of a regulated furnished tenancy, as compliance with paragraph (a) of this Case.

Where the dwelling-house has been let by the owner-occupier on a protected tenancy (in this paragraph referred to as "the earlier tenancy") granted on or after 16th November 1984 but not later than the end of the period of two months beginning with the commencement of the Rent (Amendment) Act 1985 and either—

(i) the earlier tenancy was granted for a term certain (whether or not to be followed by a further term or to continue thereafter from year to year or some other period) and was during that term a protected shorthold tenancy as defined in section 52 of the Housing Act 1980, or

(ii) the conditions mentioned in paragraphs (a) to (c) of Case 20 were satisfied with respect to the dwelling-house and the earlier tenancy,

LANDLORD & TENANT AND HOUSING

then for the purposes of paragraph (b) above the condition in paragraph (a) above is to be treated as having been satisfied with respect to the earlier tenancy].

CASE 12

Where the landlord (in this Case referred to as "the owner") intends to occupy the dwelling-house as his residence at such time as he might retire from regular employment and has let it on a regulated tenancy before he has so retired and—

(a) not later than the relevant date the landlord gave notice in writing to the tenant that possession might be recovered under this Case; and

(b) the dwelling-house has not, since 14th August 1974, been let by the owner on a protected tenancy with respect to which the condition mentioned in paragraph (a) above was not satisfied; and

(c) the court is of the opinion that of the conditions set out in Part V of this Schedule one of those in paragraphs (b) to (e) is satisfied.

If the court is of the opinion that, notwithstanding that the condition in paragraph (a) or (b) above is not complied with, it is just and equitable to make an order for possession of the dwelling-house, the court may dispense with the requirements of either or both of those paragraphs, as the case may require.

CASE 13

Where the dwelling-house is let under a tenancy for a term of years certain not exceeding 8 months and—

(a) not later than the relevant date the landlord gave notice in writing to the tenant that possession might be recovered under this Case; and

(b) the dwelling-house was, at some time within the period of 12 months ending on the relevant date, occupied under a right to occupy it for a holiday.

For the purposes of this Case a tenancy shall be treated as being for a term of years certain notwithstanding that it is liable to determination by re-entry or on the happening of any event other than the giving of notice by the landlord to determine the term.

CASE 14

Where the dwelling-house is let under a tenancy for a term of years certain not exceeding 12 months and—

(a) not later than the relevant date the landlord gave notice in writing to the tenant that possession might be recovered under this Case; and

(b) at some time within the period of 12 months ending on the relevant date, the dwelling-house was subject to such a tenancy as is referred to in section 8 (1) of this Act.

For the purposes of this Case a tenancy shall be treated as being for a term of years certain notwithstanding that it is liable to determination by re-entry or on the happening of any event other than the giving of notice by the landlord to determine the term.

CASE 15

Where the dwelling-house is held for the purpose of being available for occupation by a minister of religion as a residence from which to perform the duties of his office and—

(a) not later than the relevant date the tenant was given notice in writing that possession might be recovered under this Case, and

(b) the court is satisfied that the dwelling-house is required for occupation by a minister of religion as such a residence.

CASE 16

Where the dwelling-house was at any time occupied by a person under the terms of his employment as a person employed in agriculture, and

(a) the tenant neither is nor at any time was so employed by the landlord and is not the widow of a person who was so employed, and

(b) not later than the relevant date, the tenant was given notice in writing that possession might be recovered under this Case, and

(c) the court is satisfied that the dwelling-house is required for occupation by a person employed, or to be employed, by the landlord in agriculture.

For the purposes of this Case "employed", "employment" and "agriculture" have the same meanings as in the Agricultural Wages Act 1948.

CASE 17

Where proposals for amalgamation, approved for the purposes of a scheme under section 26 of the Agriculture Act 1967, have been carried out and, at the time when the proposals were submitted, the dwelling-house was occupied by a person responsible (whether as owner, tenant, or servant or agent of another) for the control of the farming of any part of the land comprised in the amalgamation and—

(a) after the carrying out of the proposals, the dwelling-house was let on a regulated tenancy otherwise than to, or to the widow of, either a person ceasing to be so responsible as part of the amalgamation or a person who is, or at any time was, employed by the landlord in agriculture, and

(b) not later than the relevant date the tenant was given notice in writing that possession might be recovered under this Case, and

(c) the court is satisfied that the dwelling-house is required for occupation by a person employed, or to be employed, by the landlord in agriculture, and

(d) the proceedings for possession are commenced by the landlord at any time during the period of 5 years beginning with the date on which the proposals for the amalgamation were approved or, if occupation of the dwelling-house after the amalgamation continued in, or was first taken by, a person ceasing to be responsible as mentioned in paragraph (a) above or his widow, during a period expiring 3 years after the date on which the dwelling-house next became unoccupied.

For the purposes of this Case "employed" and "agriculture" have the same meanings as in the Agricultural Wages Act 1948 and "amalgamation" has the same meaning as in Part II of the Agriculture Act 1967.

CASE 18

Where—

(a) the last occupier of the dwelling-house before the relevant date was a person, or the widow of a person, who was at some time during his occupation responsible (whether as owner, tenant, or servant or agent of another) for the control of the farming of land which formed, together with the dwelling-house, an agricultural unit within the meaning of the Agriculture Act 1947, and

(b) the tenant is neither—

(i) a person or the widow of a person, who is or has at any time been responsible for the control of the farming of any part of the said land, nor

(ii) a person, or the widow of a person, who is or at any time was employed by the landlord in agriculture, and

(c) the creation of the tenancy was not preceded by the carrying out in connection with any of the said land of an amalgamation approved for the purposes of a scheme under section 26 of the Agriculture Act 1967, and

(d) not later than the relevant date the tenant was given notice in writing that possession might be recovered under this Case, and

(e) the court is satisfied that the dwelling-house is required for occupation either by a person responsible or to be responsible (whether as owner, tenant, or servant or agent of another) for the control of the farming of any part of the said land or by a person employed or to be employed by the landlord in agriculture, and

(f) in a case where the relevant date was before 9th August 1972, the proceedings for possession are commenced by the landlord before the expiry of 5 years from the date on which the occupier referred to in paragraph (a) above went out of occupation.

For the purposes of this Case "employed" and "agriculture" have the same meanings as in the Agricultural Wages Act 1948 and "amalgamation" has the same meaning as in Part II of the Agriculture Act 1967.

CASE 19

Where the dwelling-house was let under a protected shorthold tenancy (or is treated under section 55 of the Housing Act 1980 as having been so let) and—

(a) there either has been no grant of a further tenancy of the dwelling-house since the end of the protected shorthold tenancy or, if there was such a grant, it was to a person who immediately before the grant was in possession of the dwelling-house as a protected or statutory tenant; and

(b) the proceedings for possession were commenced after appropriate notice by the landlord to the tenant and not later than 3 months after the expiry of the notice.

A notice is appropriate for this Case if—

(i) it is in writing and states that proceedings for possession under this Case may be brought after its expiry; and

(ii) it expires not earlier than 3 months after it is served nor, if, when it is served, the tenancy is a periodic tenancy, before that periodic tenancy could be brought to an end by a notice to quit served by the landlord on the same day;

(iii) it is served—

(a) in the period of 3 months immediately preceding the date on which the protected shorthold tenancy comes to an end; or

(b) if that date has passed, in the period of 3 months immediately preceding any anniversary of that date; and

(iv) in a case where a previous notice has been served by the landlord on the tenant in respect of the dwelling-house, and that notice was an appropriate notice, it is served not earlier than 3 months after the expiry of the previous notice.

CASE 20

Where the dwelling-house was let by a person (in this Case referred to as "the owner") at any time after the commencement of section 67 of the Housing Act 1980 and—

(a) at the time when the owner acquired the dwelling-house he was a member of the regular armed forces of the Crown;

(b) at the relevant date the owner was a member of the regular armed forces of the Crown;

(c) not later than the relevant date the owner gave notice in writing to the tenant that possession might be recovered under this Case;

(d) the dwelling-house has not, since the commencement of section 67 of the Act of 1980 been let by the owner on a protected tenancy with respect to which the condition mentioned in paragraph (c) above was not satisfied; and

(e) the court is of the opinion that—

(i) the dwelling-house is required as a residence for the owner; or

(ii) of the conditions set out in Part V of this Schedule one of those in paragraphs (c) to (f) is satisfied.

If the court is of the opinion that, notwithstanding that the condition in paragraph (c) or (d) above is not complied with, it is just and equitable to make an order for possession of the dwelling-house, the court may dispense with the requirements of either or both of these paragraphs, as the case may require.

For the purposes of this Case "regular armed forces of the Crown" has the same meaning as in section 1 of the House of Commons Disqualification Act 1975.]

III L&T [83.1]

Procedure Proceedings under Cases 11 to 20 were formerly brought by way of originating application under the Rent Act (County Court Proceedings for Possession) Rules 1981, SI 1981/139. All such proceedings, being possession claims, should now be brought under CPR Pt 55 (see para **CPR 55**).

III L&T [83.2]

Notice of recovery under Cases in Part II Each of the Cases in Part II requires notice in writing to have been given to the tenant that possession might be recovered under that Case. It was held in *Fowler v Minchin* (1987) 19 HLR 224, [1987] 1 EGLR 108, CA, that written notice that the tenant would have to vacate on 28 days' notice if the landlord required the cottage for a farmworker did not meet the Case 16 requirement of notice that possession might be recovered under that Case. On the other hand notice was held to have been validly given when included in a Rent Officer's certificate: *Springfield Investments Ltd v Bell* (1990) 22 HLR 440, [1991] 1 EGLR 115, CA. These decisions have implications for all Cases in Part II.

CASE 11

III L&T [83.3]

The owner-occupier One of two joint owners may be the owner-occupier for the purposes of Case 11: *Tilling v Whiteman* [1980] AC 1, [1979] 1 All ER 737, HL. The amendments made to the opening words of Case 11 by the Rent (Amendment) Act 1985 s 1(1) reverse retrospectively the decision of the Court of Appeal in *Pocock v Steel* [1985] 1 All ER 434, [1985] 1 WLR 229, CA that the Case, as enacted, required the owner-occupier to be in possession immediately before the letting. Moreover they appear to be consistent with the decision of the Court of Appeal in *Naish v Curzon* (1984) 51 P & CR 229, 17 HLR 220, CA, that the requirement of occupation may be satisfied although temporary or intermittent, for example where the owner spends most of his time abroad. For a case where the landlord's temporary residence sufficed, see *Mistry v Isidore* (1990) 22 HLR 281, [1990] 2 EGLR 97, CA.

III L&T [83.4]

Long-term intention to sell The fact that the owner-occupier intends ultimately to sell does not defeat a claim under Case 11 if he needs the house to live in as a residence in the meantime: *Lipton v Whitworth* (1993) 26 HLR 293, CA.

III L&T [83.5]

Dispense with the requirements In *Fernandes v Parvardin* (1982) 5 HLR 33, [1982] 2 EGLR 104, the Court of Appeal upheld a decision to dispense with the requirement that notice be in writing where the tenant had oral notice that possession would be required under this case; the trial judge adopted a broad approach considering all the circumstances but DONALDSON LJ suggested, without deciding the point, that a narrower test may be appropriate, namely what injustice or inequity flows from the failure to comply precisely with the terms of the Case. In *Davies v Peterson* (1988) 21 HLR 63, [1989] 1 EGLR 121, CA an oral notice was one of the factors which led to the Court of Appeal's upholding a possession order under Case 11, although there had been no notice in writing. The power to dispense with notice is not limited to cases where written notice was given late or oral notice was given but it applies also to cases where no notice was given: *Minay v Sentongo* (1983) 45 P & CR 190, 6 HLR 79. However, it would not be just and equitable to dispense with the requirement of a notice if the landlord's original intention was to create an ordinary, secure, regulated tenancy: *Bradshaw* *v Baldwin-Wiseman* (1985) 49 P & CR 382, [1985] 1 EGLR 123, CA. Nor would it be just and equitable to dispense with the requirement of notice merely because the tenancy had been styled, and signed by the tenant, as a "licence agreement": *Ibie v Trubshaw* (1990) 22 HLR 191, CA. In *Jones v White* [1993] NPC 139, [1993] EGCS 178, CA, an oral notice was given but the Court of Appeal decided against dispensing with the requirement of written notice because of the very long period that the tenant had been in occupation and the severe hardship in having to move out as against the relatively minor hardship on the landlord's side.

CASE 16

III L&T [83.6]

Employed in agriculture Part-time employment in trimming hedges, coppicing and haymaking was held to be employment in agriculture in *Harley v Hood* [1981] 2 EGLR 84, CA. In *Springfield Investments Ltd v Bell* (1990) 22 HLR 440, [1991] 1 EGLR 115, CA, the Court of Appeal held that a certificate of fair rent which stated that the letting was to be one pursuant to Case 16 and which was handed to the tenant by the landlord immediately before commencement of the tenancy satisfied the Case 16 requirement as to notice.

CASE 19

III L&T [83.7]

Service of notice A notice which the landlord put through the letter-box of the locked front door was held in *Trustees of Henry Smith's Charity v Kyriakou* [1989] RVR 106, [1989] 2 EGLR 110, CA, to be served thereby on a tenant of a room on the third floor.

III L&T [83.8]

Dispensing with requirements In proceedings for possession under Case 19, if the court is of the opinion that, notwithstanding that the condition in the Housing Act 1980 s 52 (1)(b) (requirement of giving notice) is not satisfied, it is just and equitable to make an order for possession, it may treat the tenancy under which the dwelling house was let as a protected shorthold tenancy: see the Housing Act 1980 s 55 (2). A case may fall within Case 19 although not necessarily within the Housing Act 1980 s 52 (2): *Gent v de la Mare* (1987) 20 HLR 199, [1998] 1 EGLR 104, CA. However the court may not dispense with the requirement that proceedings must be started not later than three months from the expiry of the notice: *Ridehalgh v Horsefield* (1992) 24 HLR 453, [1992] NPC 46, CA.

CASE 20

III L&T [83.9]

Regular armed forces This expression means: "the Royal Navy, the regular forces as defined by the Army Act 1955 s 228, the regular air force as defined by the Air Force Act 1955 s 223, the Women's Royal Naval Service, Queen Alexandra's Royal Naval Nursing Service and Voluntary Aid Detachments serving in the Royal Navy": House of Commons Disqualification Act 1975 s 1.

PART III
PROVISIONS APPLICABLE TO CASE 9 AND PART II OF THIS SCHEDULE

PROVISION FOR CASE 9

III L&T [84]

1. A court shall not make an order for possession of a dwelling-house by reason only that the circumstances of the case fall within Case 9 in Part I of this Schedule if the court is satisfied that, having regard to all the circumstances of the case, including the question whether other accommodation is available for the landlord or the tenant, greater hardship would be caused by granting the order than by refusing to grant it.

PROVISION FOR PART II

2. Any reference in Part II of this Schedule to the relevant date shall be construed as follows—

(a) except in a case falling within paragraph (b) or (c) below, if the protected tenancy, or, in the case of a statutory tenancy, the previous contractual tenancy, was created before 8th December 1965, the relevant date means 7th June 1966; and

(b) except in a case falling within paragraph (c) below, if the tenancy became a regulated tenancy by virtue of section 14 of the Counter-Inflation Act 1973 and the tenancy or, in the case of a statutory tenancy, the previous contractual tenancy, was created before 22nd March 1973, the relevant date means 22nd September 1973; and

(c) in the case of a regulated furnished tenancy, if the tenancy or, in the case of a statutory furnished tenancy, the previous contractual tenancy was created before 14th August 1974, the relevant date means 13th February 1975; and

(d) in any other case, the relevant date means the date of the commencement of the regulated tenancy in question.

III L&T [84.1]

The court is satisfied The onus of proof is on the tenant: *Sims v Wilson* [1946] 2 All ER 261, CA; *Smith v Penny* [1947] KB 230, [1946] 2 All ER 672, CA.

III L&T [84.2]

Greater hardship The court must consider the circumstances existing at the time of the hearing: *Bumstead v Wood* (1946) 175 LT 149, CA.

The court must consider all the circumstances which may include: the financial position of the parties, the time they have been landlord and tenant, the efforts made by the tenant to find accommodation: *Kelley v Goodwin* [1947] 1 All ER 810, CA; the effect on a party's mental health: *Thomas v Fryer* [1970] 2 All ER 1, [1970] 1 WLR 845, CA; the position of others, such as family, lodgers, dependants, affected by the order: *Harte v Frampton* [1948] 1 KB 73, [1947] 2 All ER 604, CA. The longer term effects of making, or refusing, an order for possession must be considered as well as the short term: *Manaton v Edwards* (1985) 18 HLR 116, [1985] 2 EGLR 159, CA. The hardship caused may be mitigated or avoided by the imposition of conditions to an order for possession such as a lengthy postponement of the date for giving possession: *Wheeler v Evans* [1948] 1 KB 459, [1947] 2 All ER 740, CA. The principle of *res judicata* does not apply to a finding of greater hardship and a fresh application may be made if circumstances change: *Burman v Woods* [1948] 1 KB 111, CA. The question is primarily one of fact for the trial judge and on appeal the court will not interfere unless there is a misdirection or the judgment is based on a finding of fact of which there was no evidence: *Smith v Penny* [1947] KB 230 at 233, [1946] 2 All ER 672 at 673, CA per S OMERVELL LJ.

PART IV
SUITABLE ALTERNATIVE ACCOMMODATION

III L&T [85]

3. For the purposes of section 98 (1)(a) of this Act, a certificate of the local housing authority for the district in which the dwelling-house in question is situated, certifying that the authority will provide suitable alternative accommodation for the tenant by a date specified in the certificate, shall be conclusive evidence that suitable alternative accommodation will be available for him by that date.

4.—(1) Where no such certificate as is mentioned in paragraph 3 above is produced to the court, accommodation shall be deemed to be suitable for the purposes of section 98 (1)(a) of this Act if it consists of either—

(a) premises which are to be let as a separate dwelling such that they will then be let on a protected tenancy (other than one under which the landlord might recover possession of the dwelling-house under one of the Cases in Part II of this Schedule), or

(b) premises to be let as a separate dwelling on terms which will, in the opinion of the court, afford to the tenant security of tenure reasonably equivalent to the security afforded by Part VII of this Act in the case of a protected tenancy of a kind mentioned in paragraph (a) above,

and, in the opinion of the court, the accommodation fulfils the relevant conditions as defined in paragraph 5 below.

(2) [*Repealed by the Housing Act 1988.*]]

5.—(1) For the purposes of paragraph 4 above, the relevant conditions are that the accommodation is reasonably suitable to the needs of the tenant and his family as regards proximity to place of work, and either—

(a) similar as regards rental and extent to the accommodation afforded by dwelling-houses provided in the neighbourhood by any local housing authority for persons whose needs as regards extent are, in the opinion of the court, similar to those of the tenant and of his family; or

(b) reasonably suitable to the means of the tenant and to the needs of the tenant and his family as regards extent and character; and

that if any furniture was provided for use under the protected or statutory tenancy in question, furniture is provided for use in the accommodation which is either similar to that so provided or is reasonably suitable to the needs of the tenant and his family.

(2) For the purposes of sub-paragraph (1)(a) above, a certificate of a [local housing authority] stating—

(a) the extent of the accommodation afforded by dwelling-houses provided by the authority to meet the needs of tenants with families of such number as may be specified in the certificate, and

(b) the amount of the rent charged by the authority for dwelling-houses affording accommodation of that extent,

shall be conclusive evidence of the facts so stated.

6. Accommodation shall not be deemed to be suitable to the needs of the tenant and his family if the result of their occupation of the accommodation would be that it would be an overcrowded dwelling-house for the purposes of Part X of the Housing Act 1985.

7. Any document purporting to be a certificate of a local housing authority named therein issued for the purposes of this Schedule and to be signed by the proper officer of that authority shall be received in evidence and, unless the contrary is shown, shall be deemed to be such a certificate without further proof.

8. In this Part "local housing authority" and "district" in relation to such an authority have the same meaning as in the Housing Act 1985.

III L&T [85.1]

Housing authority's certificate The certificate must represent a definite offer of accommodation (*Hill v Rochard* [1983] 2 All ER 21, [1983] 1 WLR 478, CA) in the same district (*Sills v Watkins* [1956] 1 QB 250, [1955] 3 All ER 319, CA): as to formal requirements, see the Rent Act 1977 Sch 15 Pt IV paras 7, 8. Before ordering possession on the basis of a housing authority's certificate that alternative accommodation will be provided, the judge must be satisfied that the alternative accommodation will be suitable: *Jones v Cook* [1990] 2 EGLR 108, [1990] 42 EG 129, CA.

III L&T [85.2]

Deemed to be suitable It is not clear whether the provisions of the Rent Act 1977 Sch 15 Pt IV are exhaustive or merely indicative of what is suitable alternative accommodation. In *Barnard v Towers* [1953] 2 All ER 877, [1953] 1 WLR 1203, CA the provisions were said to be indicative and not exhaustive. In contrast, in *Standingford v Probert* [1950] 1 KB 377, [1949] 2 All ER 861, CA it was said that the Act lays down the conditions which must be satisfied, suggesting that they are exhaustive.

III L&T [85.3]

Security of tenure reasonably equivalent This requirement may be satisfied by the grant of an assured tenancy: *Laimond Properties Ltd v Al-Shakarchi* (1998) 30 HLR 1099, CA. However, a weekly tenancy outside the Acts will not suffice: *Scrace v Windust* [1955] 2 All ER 104, [1955] 1 WLR 475, CA.

III L&T [85.4]

Needs of the tenant In determining if accommodation is suitable to a tenant's needs as regards character, the court can only have regard to the housing needs of the particular tenant (that is his need for accommodation for habitation) which do not include his ability to enjoy the life-style and amenities which he enjoys in his existing accommodation: *Hill v Rochard* [1983] 2 All ER 21, [1983] 1 WLR 478, CA; *Gladyric Ltd v Collinson* (1983) 11 HLR 12, [1983] 2 EGLR 98, CA. But see *Enfield London Borough Council v French* (1984) 49 P & CR 223, CA, regarding the keen gardener's need for a garden.

III L&T [85.5]

Family There is no definition. The word probably has the same meaning as in the Rent Act 1977 Sch 1 (see para **III L&T [81]**): see *Standingford v Probert* [1950] 1 KB 377, [1949] 2 All ER 861, CA.

III L&T [85.6]

Place of work "Work" includes voluntary work: *Dakyns v Pace* [1948] 1 KB 22. The "place" need not be a building but may be an area: *Yewbright Properties Ltd v Stone* (1980) 40 P & CR 402, CA.

III L&T [85.7]

Reasonably suitable In determining the issue of suitability, the court can take into account not only the physical character of the accommodation, but also environmental matters, such as traffic noise, smells and noises generated by nearby premises: *Redspring Ltd v Francis* [1973] 1 All ER 640, [1973] 1 WLR 134, CA. However, the term "character" does not extend to matters such as the loss of the society of friends or cultural interests, although these are matters relevant to reasonableness: *Siddiqui v Rashid* [1980] 3 All ER 184, [1980] 1 WLR 1018, CA. The standard to be applied is that of an ordinary tenant and not one which will gratify to the full "all the fads and fancies and preferences of the tenant": *Christie v MacFarlane* 1930 SLT (Sh Ct) 5 at 10, although it is proper to take into account the reluctance of an elderly widow to leave accommodation which had been her home for 35 years and had pleasant memories for her: *Battlespring Ltd v Gates* (1983) 11 HLR 6, [1983] 2 EGLR 103, CA. Factors which the court will consider include: whether there is sufficient room for the tenant's furniture: *McIntyre v Hardcastle* [1948] 2 KB 82, [1948] 1 All ER 696, CA, although this will not render the premises unsuitable if the tenant has no foreseeable need for the extra furniture: *Mykolyshyn v Noah* [1971] 1 All ER 48, [1970] 1 WLR 1217, CA; the tenant's business needs: *MacDonnell v Daly* [1969] 3 All ER 851, [1969] 1 WLR 1482, CA; whether the accommodation will be shared: *Barnard v Towers* [1953] 2 All ER 877, [1953] 1 WLR 1203, CA: the state of repair of the alternative premises: *Yewbright Properties Ltd v Stone* (1980) 40 P & CR 402, CA; lack of a garden for a child to play in: *De Markozoff v Craig* (1949) 93 Sol Jo 693, CA; if the accommodation is too large: *Macey v Dolphin* (1950) 156 Estates Gazette 422, CA; or if the premises lack bathroom and lavatory facilities: *Esposito v Ware* (1950) 155 Estates Gazette 383, CA.

Suitable alternative accommodation can consist of part of the dwelling house let to the tenant, eg where he has sub-let part and resides in the rest, the landlord may be able to rely on the rest as the alternative: *Thompson v Rolls* [1926] 2 KB 426, DC; *Parmee v Mitchell* [1950] 2 KB 199, [1950] 1 All ER 872, CA. In such a case the order should be for possession of the whole conditional on the landlord offering the tenant a tenancy of the rest. An order may also be made conditional on the carrying out of work to the alternative accommodation within a stated time (*Yewbright Properties Ltd v Stone* (1980) 40 P & CR 402, CA) or conditional on the landlord getting planning permission as where it is needed to create a room to be offered to the tenant: *Schaffer v Griffiths* (1955) 105 L Jo 188. Where the rent of the alternative accommodation is beyond what the tenant can afford but the landlord offers to accept less than the recoverable rent, the order should include an undertaking by the landlord restricting his right to increase the rent: *Strutt v Panter* [1953] 1 QB 397 at 400, [1953] 1 All ER 445 at 446, CA.

III L&T [85.8]

"Character" In *Dawncar Investments Ltd v Plews* (1993) 25 HLR 639, [1994] 1 EGLR 141, CA the character of a district was held to be a relevant consideration for the purposes of the Rent Act 1977 Sch 15 Pt IV para 5(1)(a) as it is for para 5(1)(b).

PART V
PROVISIONS APPLYING TO CASES 11, 12 AND 20

III L&T [86]

1. In this Part of this Schedule—

"mortgage" includes a charge and "mortgagee" shall be construed accordingly;
"owner" means, in relation to Case 11, the owner-occupier; and
"successor in title" means any person deriving title from the owner, other than a purchaser for value or a person deriving title from a purchaser for value.

2. The conditions referred to in paragraph (c) in each of Cases 11 and 12 and in paragraph (e)(ii) of Case 20 are that—

(a) the dwelling-house is required as a residence for the owner or any member of his family who resided with the owner when he last occupied the dwelling-house as a residence;

(b) the owner has retired from regular employment and requires the dwelling-house as a residence;

(c) the owner has died and the dwelling-house is required as a residence for a member of his family who was residing with him at the time of his death;

(d) the owner has died and the dwelling-house is required by a successor in title as his residence or for the purpose of disposing of it with vacant possession;

(e) the dwelling-house is subject to a mortgage, made by deed and granted before the tenancy, and the mortgagee—

(i) is entitled to exercise a power of sale conferred on him by the mortgage or by section 101 of the Law of Property Act 1925; and

(ii) requires the dwelling-house for the purpose of disposing of it with vacant possession in exercise of that power; and

(f) the dwelling-house is not reasonably suitable to the needs of the owner, having regard to his place of work, and he requires it for the purpose of disposing of it with vacant possession and of using the proceeds of that disposal in acquiring, as his residence, a dwelling-house which is more suitable to those needs.

III L&T [86.1]

House required for disposal Rent Act 1977 Sch 15 Pt V para 2(f) may be satisfied where the owner has immediate plans for acquiring another house which is more suitable for his work needs, but not where such acquisition is merely a possibility for the indefinite future: *Bissessar v Ghosn* (1985) 18 HLR 486, CA.

SCHEDULE 16

FURTHER GROUNDS FOR POSSESSION OF DWELLING-HOUSES LET ON OR SUBJECT TO TENANCIES TO WHICH SECTION 99 APPLIES

Section 99

CASE I

ALTERNATIVE ACCOMMODATION NOT PROVIDED OR ARRANGED BY HOUSING AUTHORITY

III L&T [87]

1. The court is satisfied that suitable alternative accommodation is available for the tenant, or will be available for him when the order for possession takes effect.

2. Accommodation shall be deemed suitable in this Case if it consists of—

(a) premises which are to be let as a separate dwelling such that they will then be let on a protected tenancy, or

(b) premises which are to be let as a separate dwelling on terms which will, in the opinion of the court, afford to the tenant security of tenure reasonably equivalent to the security afforded by Part VII of this Act in the case of a protected tenancy,

and, in the opinion of the court, the accommodation fulfils the conditions in paragraph 3 below.

3.—(1) The accommodation must be reasonably suitable to the needs of the tenant and his family as regards proximity to place of work and either—

(a) similar as regards rental and extent to the accommodation afforded by dwelling-houses provided in the neighbourhood by the [local housing authority] concerned for persons whose needs as regards extent are similar to those of the tenant and his family, or

(b) reasonably suitable to the means of the tenant, and to the needs of the tenant and his family as regards extent and character.

(2) For the purposes of sub-paragraph (1)(a) above, a certificate of the local housing authority concerned stating—

(a) the extent of the accommodation afforded by dwelling-houses provided by the authority to meet the needs of tenants with families of such number as may be specified in the certificate, and

(b) the amount of the rent charged by the local housing authority concerned for dwelling-houses affording accommodation of that extent,

shall be conclusive evidence of the facts so stated.

(3) If any furniture was provided by the landlord for use under the tenancy, furniture must be provided for use in the alternative accommodation which is either similar, or is reasonably suitable to the needs of the tenant and his family.

4. Accommodation shall not be deemed to be suitable to the needs of the tenant and his family if the result of their occupation of the accommodation would be that it would be an overcrowded dwelling-house for the purposes of Part X of the Housing Act 1985.

5. Any document purporting to be a certificate of the local housing authority concerned issued for the purposes of this Case and to be signed by the proper officer of the authority shall be received in evidence and, unless the contrary is shown, shall be deemed to be such a certificate without further proof.

6. In this Case no account shall be taken of accommodation as respects which an offer has been made, or notice has been given, as mentioned in paragraph 1 of Case II below.

7. In this Case and in Case II below "the local housing authority" has the same meaning as in the Housing Act 1985.

CASE II

ALTERNATIVE ACCOMMODATION PROVIDED OR ARRANGED BY HOUSING AUTHORITY

1. The local housing authority concerned have made an offer in writing to the tenant of alternative accommodation which appears to them to be suitable, specifying the date when the accommodation will be available and the date (not being less than 14 days from the date of offer) by which the offer must be accepted.

or

The local housing authority concerned have given notice in writing to the tenant that they have received from a person specified in the notice an offer in writing to rehouse the tenant in alternative accommodation which appears to the housing authority concerned to be suitable, and the notice specifies both the date when the accommodation will be available and the date (not being less than 14 days from the date when the notice was given to the tenant) by which the offer must be accepted.

2. The landlord shows that the tenant accepted the offer (by the housing authority or other person) within the time duly specified in the offer.

or

The landlord shows that the tenant did not so accept the offer, and the tenant does not satisfy the court that he acted reasonably in failing to accept the offer.

3.—(1) The accommodation offered must in the opinion of the court fulfil the conditions of this paragraph.

(2) The accommodation must be reasonably suitable to the needs of the tenant and his family as regards proximity to place of work.

(3) The accommodation must be reasonably suitable to the means of the tenant, and to the needs of the tenant and his family as regards extent.

4. If the accommodation offered is available for a limited period only, the [local housing authority's offer] or notice under paragraph 1 of this Case must contain an assurance that other accommodation—

- (a) the availability of which is not so limited,
- (b) which appears to them to be suitable, and
- (c) which fulfils the conditions in paragraph 3 above,

will be offered to the tenant as soon as practicable.

III L&T [87.1]

Further grounds This schedule makes special provision for recovering possession from tenants who would have been protected occupants or statutory tenants under the Rent (Agriculture) Act 1976 were it not for the fact that they are protected under the Rent Act 1977.

PROTECTION FROM EVICTION ACT 1977

(c 43)

GENERAL NOTES ON PROTECTION FROM EVICTION ACT 1977

III L&T [88]

This Act, as amended by the Housing Acts 1980 and 1988 and the Local Government and Housing Act 1989, protects occupiers of residential premises against eviction without due process of law. It provides criminal sanctions for breach. Note, however, that the Act has been specified in the Regulatory Enforcement Act 2008 as an Act which local authorities may be allowed to enforce by imposing fixed financial penalties instead of criminal prosecution.

Breach of this Act does not give the tenant a cause of action for damages: see *McCall v Abelesz* [1976] QB 585, [1976] 1 All ER 727, CA. Moreover a breach of the covenant of quiet enjoyment which does not cause financial loss entitles the tenant to no more than nominal damages: *Kenny v Preen* [1963] 1 QB 499, [1962] 3 All ER 814, CA followed in *Branchett v Beaney* [1992] 3 All ER 910, CA.

However, the deficiencies of the common law have been mitigated by statute. The Housing Act 1988, in addition to amending the Protection from Eviction Act 1977, created a new statutory right to damages for unlawful eviction. The text of the relevant provisions ss 27 and 28 of that Act, is set out at paras **III L&T [232]–III L&T [233]**. More recently, harassment was made a tort by the Protection from Harassment Act 1977: see the title HARASSMENT at paras **III HAR [1]–III HAR [8]**.

III L&T [88A]

Precedents A precedent for particulars of claim for damages under ss 27 and 28 following harassment and wrongful eviction is given at **BCCP O[207]**. Such a claim which, irrespective of value, cannot be allocated to the small claims track (see CPR Pt 26 r 26.7(4) (para **CPR 26.7**)) should be brought by means of a Pt 7 claim form.

III L&T [89]

2. Restriction on re-entry without due process of law

Where any premises are let as a dwelling on a lease which is subject to a right of re-entry or forfeiture it shall not be lawful to enforce that right otherwise than by proceedings in the court while any person is lawfully residing in the premises or part of them.

III L&T [89.1]

Let as a dwelling See the notes to s 1 of the Rent Act 1977 (at para **III L&T [68]**). The word "let" has an extended meaning: see s 8(2), post. The phrase "let as a dwelling" means "let wholly or partly as a dwelling" and so applies to premises that are let for mixed residential and business purposes: *Patel v Pirabakaran* [2006] EWCA Civ 685, [2006] 4 All ER 506, [2006] All ER (D) 389 (May), (2006) Times 19 July.

III L&T [89.2]

The court See s 9 post.

III L&T [90]

3. Prohibition of eviction without due process of law

(1) Where any premises have been let as a dwelling under a tenancy which is neither a statutorily protected tenancy nor an excluded tenancy and—

(a) the tenancy (in this section referred to as the former tenancy) has come to an end, but

(b) the occupier continues to reside in the premises or part of them,

it shall not be lawful for the owner to enforce against the occupier, otherwise than by proceedings in the court, his right to recover possession of the premises.

(2) In this section "the occupier", in relation to any premises, means any person lawfully residing in the premises or part of them at the termination of the former tenancy.

(2A) Subsections (1) and (2) above apply in relation to any restricted contract (within the meaning of the Rent Act 1977) which—

(a) creates a licence; and

(b) is entered into after the commencement of section 69 of the Housing Act 1980;

as they apply in relation to a restricted contract which creates a tenancy.

(2B) Subsections (1) and (2) above apply in relation to any premises occupied as a dwelling under a licence, other than an excluded licence, as they apply in relation to premises let as a dwelling under a tenancy, and in those subsections the expressions "let" and "tenancy" shall be construed accordingly.

(2C) References in the preceding provisions of this section and section 4(2A) below to an excluded tenancy do not apply to—

(a) a tenancy entered into before the date on which the Housing Act 1988 came into force, or

(b) a tenancy entered into on or after that date but pursuant to a contract made before that date,

but, subject to that, "excluded tenancy" and "excluded licence" shall be construed in accordance with section 3A below.

(3) This section shall, with the necessary modifications, apply where the owner's right to recover possession arises on the death of the tenant under a statutory tenancy within the meaning of the Rent Act 1977 or the Rent (Agriculture) Act 1976.

III L&T [90.1]–III L&T [90.2]

The court See s 9.

III L&T [90.3]

Occupation A tenant continues to occupy and reside during short periods of absence: *Schon v Camden London Borough* (1986) 84 LGR 830, 53 P & CR 361, DC. In *Norton v Knowles* [1969] 1 QB 572, it was held that an occupier of a caravan was within the protection of the Act.

III L&T [90.4]

Due process of law The fact that an order for possession has been made and ignored does not justify an eviction except pursuant to a warrant: *Haniff v Robinson* [1993] QB 419, [1993] 1 All ER 185, CA.

III L&T [90.5]

Warrant to enforce possession order A warrant for possession issued pursuant to an order is effective against persons of whose existence the landlord was unaware: *R v Wandsworth County Court, ex p Wandsworth London Borough Council* [1975] 3 All ER 390, [1975] 1 WLR 1314. Similarly an order for possession against one member of a family justifies the eviction by warrant of all the members in occupation: *Thompson v Elmbridge Borough Council* [1987] 1 WLR 1425, CA.

III L&T [90.6]

Rental purchase By para 61 of Sch 25 to the Housing Act 1980, the Protection from Eviction Act 1977 applies to a person let into possession of a dwelling house under a rental purchase agreement (within the meaning of s 88 of the 1980 Act) as if it had been let to him as a dwelling under a tenancy which is not a statutorily protected tenancy and that tenancy had come to an end on the termination of the agreement or of his right to possession under it.

III L&T [90.7]

Bed and breakfast accommodation Section 3 does not cover homeless people for whom the council has arranged temporary accommodation in a private hotel: *Mohamed v Manek and Kensington and Chelsea Royal Borough* (1995) 27 HLR 439, (1995) Times, 28 April, CA. The same reasoning applies to exclude from protection any temporary accommodation provided under s 188(1) or 190(2)(a) of the Housing Act 1996: see the notes to those sections at **III L&T [303A.2]** and **L&T [303B.1]**. Note also that, although eviction without a court order could interfere with the occupier's right to respect for his home under art 8 of the Convention, such interference has been held to be necessary, within art 8.2: *Desnousse v Newham London Borough Council* [2006] EWCA Civ 547, [2006] 3 WLR 349, (2006) Times 28 June.

In *R (on the application of ZH and CN) v London Borough of Newham* [2014] UKSC 62, [2014] 3 WLR 1548, [2014] LGR 842 it was confirmed that the decisions in *Mohamed v Manek* and in *Desnousse v Newham London Borough Council* remain binding on the Court of Appeal.

III L&T [90.8]

Statutorily protected tenancy See s 8(1), post for the meaning of these words.

III L&T [90.9]

Owner This includes a mortgagee entitled to possession: s 8(3); however, s 3(1) does not prevent a mortgagee from enforcing his right to possession against a tenant of the mortgagor where that tenancy is not effective against the mortgagee: see *Bolton Building Society v Cobb* [1965] 3 All ER 814, [1966] 1 WLR 1.

III L&T [90.10]

Human rights A former joint tenant who remains in occupation after termination of the tenancy by the other has a Convention right under Art 8 to respect for his home. However, Art 8 cannot be relied on to defeat proprietary or contractual rights to possession. Accordingly, a public authority landlord was entitled to claim possession; but an unfair exercise of the right may be capable of challenge by judicial review; see the majority decision in *Harrow London Borough Council v Qazi* [2003] UKHL 43, [2004] 1 AC 983, [2003] 4 All ER 461. Note, however, the decision in *Kay v Lambeth London Borough Council* [2006] 2 AC 465, [2006] 2 WLR 570, [2006] 4 All ER 128 that, in so far as *Harrow London Borough Council v Qazi* decided that the enforcement of a right to possession in accordance with the domestic law of property could never be incompatible with the Art 8 of the Convention, that had to be modified in the light of *Connors v United Kingdom* (66746/01) [2005] 40 EHRR 9; moreover, that it was open to an occupier to raise an Art 8 defence to possession proceedings in the county court rather than by way of judicial review.

Section 3 has been held to be compatible with Art 8 as the section does nothing more than prohibit a property-owner from repossessing property without first seeking a possession order in court: see *R (on the application of Coombes) v Secretary of State for Communities and Local Government* [2010] EWHC 666 (Admin), [2010] 2 All ER 940, [2010] LGR 514 where the court also held that there was nothing in the wording of section 3 that makes it impossible for a county court to consider a defence based on Art 8 following the guidance of the House of Lords in *Kay v Lambeth London Borough Council* (above) and *Doherty v Birmingham City Council* [2009] 1 AC 367.

III L&T [90.11]

Flat over the shop The expression "let as a dwelling" includes premises which are let as a shop with living accommodation above. Possession may not therefore be retaken without a court order: *Patel v Pirabakaran* [2006] EWCA Civ 685, [2006] 4 All ER 506, [2006] All ER (D) 389 (May), (2006) Times 19 July.

III L&T [90.12]

Excluded tenancies and excluded licences The circumstances in which a tenancy or licence is excluded are listed in s 3A at **III L&T [91]**. It has been held that a licence to occupy without paying rent is not excluded where the licensee is obliged to keep the property repaired and insured, thereby providing "money's worth" for the purposes of s 3A (7)(b): *Polarpark Enterprises Inc v Allason* [2007] EWHC 1088 (Ch), (2007) Times 26 June, Briggs J. The court, for the purpose of s 3(1) is the county court (see s 9(1)(a)); accordingly, in *Polarpark Enterprises* the High Court had no jurisdiction to permit the property owner to issue a writ of possession, and the proceedings had to be transferred to the county court for the purposes of execution.

III L&T [91]

3A. Excluded tenancies and licences

(1) Any reference in this Act to an excluded tenancy or an excluded licence is a reference to a tenancy or licence which is excluded by virtue of any of the following provisions of this section.

(2) A tenancy or licence is excluded if—

- (a) under its terms the occupier shares any accommodation with the landlord or licensor; and
- (b) immediately before the tenancy or licence was granted and also at the time it comes to an end, the landlord or licensor occupied as his only or principal home premises of which the whole or part of the shared accommodation formed part.

(3) A tenancy or licence is also excluded if—

- (a) under its terms the occupier shares any accommodation with a member of the family of the landlord or licensor;
- (b) immediately before the tenancy or licence was granted and also at the time it comes to an end, the member of the family of the landlord or licensor occupied as his only or principal home premises of which the whole or part of the shared accommodation formed part; and
- (c) immediately before the tenancy or licence was granted and also at the time it comes to an end, the landlord or licensor occupied as his only or

principal home premises in the same building as the shared accommodation and that building is not a purpose-built block of flats.

(4) For the purposes of subsections (2) and (3) above, an occupier shares accommodation with another person if he has the use of it in common with that person (whether or not also in common with others) and any reference in those subsections to shared accommodation shall be construed accordingly, and if, in relation to any tenancy or licence, there is at any time more than one person who is the landlord or licensor, any reference in those subsections to the landlord or licensor shall be construed as a reference to any one of those persons.

(5) In subsections (2) to (4) above—

(a) "accommodation" includes neither an area used for storage nor a staircase, passage, corridor or other means of access;

(b) "occupier" means, in relation to a tenancy, the tenant and, in relation to a licence, the licensee; and

(c) "purpose-built block of flats" has the same meaning as in Part III of Schedule 1 to the Housing Act 1988;

and section 113 of the Housing Act 1985 shall apply to determine whether a person is for the purposes of subsection (3) above a member of another's family as it applies for the purposes of Part IV of that Act.

(6) A tenancy or licence is excluded if it was granted as a temporary expedient to a person who entered the premises in question or any other premises as a trespasser (whether or not, before the beginning of that tenancy or licence, another tenancy or licence to occupy the premises or any other premises had been granted to him).

(7) A tenancy or licence is excluded if—

(a) it confers on the tenant or licensee the right to occupy the premises for a holiday only; or

(b) it is granted otherwise than for money or money's worth.

(7A) A tenancy or licence is excluded if it is granted in order to provide accommodation under *section 4 or* Part VI of the Immigration and Asylum Act 1999

[(7B) Section 32 of the Nationality, Immigration and Asylum Act 2002 (accommodation centre: tenure) provides for a resident's licence to occupy an accommodation centre to be an excluded licence.]

(7C) A tenancy or licence is excluded if it is granted in order to provide accommodation under the Displaced Persons (Temporary Protection) Regulations 2005.

(7D) A tenancy or licence is excluded if—

(a) it is a residential tenancy agreement within the meaning of Chapter 1 of Part 3 of the Immigration Act 2014, and

(b) the condition in section 33D(2) of that Act is met in relation to that agreement.

(8) A licence is excluded if it confers rights of occupation in a hostel, within the meaning of the Housing Act 1985, which is provided by—

(a) the council of a county, county borough, district or London Borough, the Common Council of the City of London, the Council of the Isle of Scilly, the Inner London Education Authority, a fire and rescue authority created by an order under section 4A of the Fire and Rescue Services Act 2004, the London Fire Commissioner, a joint authority within the meaning of the Local Government Act 1985 or a residuary body within the meaning of that Act;

[(aa) an economic prosperity board established under section 88 of the Local Democracy, Economic Development and Construction Act 2009;

(ab) a combined authority established under section 103 of that Act;]

(b) a development corporation within the meaning of the New Towns Act 1981;

(c) the new towns residuary body;

(d) an urban development corporation established by an order under section 135 of the Local Government, Planning and Land Act 1980;

(da) a Mayoral development corporation;

(e) a housing action trust established under Part III of the Housing Act 1988;

(f) [. . .];

(g) the Regulator of Social Housing;

(ga) the Secretary of State under section 89 of the Housing Associations Act 1985;

(h) a housing trust (within the meaning of the Housing Associations Act 1985) which is a charity, a private registered provider of social housing or a registered social landlord (within the meaning of the Housing Act 1985); or

(i) any other person who is, or who belongs to a class of person which is, specified in an order made by the Secretary of State.

(8A) In subsection (8)(c) above "new towns residuary body" means—

(a) in relation to England, the Homes and Communities Agency so far as exercising functions in relation to anything transferred (or to be transferred) to it as mentioned in section 52(1)(a) to (d) of the Housing and Regeneration Act 2008 or the Greater London Authority so far as exercising its new towns and urban development functions; and

(b) in relation to Wales, means the Welsh Ministers so far as exercising functions in relation to anything transferred (or to be transferred) to them as mentioned in section 36(1)(a)(i) to (iii) of the New Towns Act 1981.

(9) The power to make an order under subsection (8)(i) above shall be exercisable by statutory instrument which shall be subject to annulment in pursuance of a resolution of either House of Parliament.

Amendment *In sub-s 7A text in italic is deleted by the Immigration Act 2016 with effect from a date to be appointed. Sub-section 7B is inserted by the Nationality, Immigration and Asylum Act 2002 with effect from a date to be appointed. Sub-section (8)(a) is amended, with effect from 3 April 2017 and 1 April 2018, by the Policing and Crime Act 2017.*

III L&T [91.1]

Generally This section was inserted by the Housing Act 1988 s 31, with effect from 15 January 1989. Part III of Sch 1 to that Act, which is referred to in sub-s (5)(c), is set out at para **III L&T [241]**. Section 113 of the Housing Act 1985, which is also referred to in sub-s (5), is set out at para **III L&T [119]**. Amendments to sub-s (8)(a) were made by the Local Government (Wales) Act 1994 and s 3A(8)(h) was substituted by the Housing Act (Consequential Provisions) Order 1996, SI 1996/2325. Sub-section (7A) has been inserted by Sch 14 of the Immigration and Asylum Act 1999. Subsections (f), (g) and (ga) are set out as repealed, amended and inserted by the Government of Wales Act 1998, Sch 16 and Sch 18, Pts IV and VI.

III L&T [91.2]

Order As to the powers in sub-s (8), see the Protection from Eviction (Excluded Licences) Order 1991, SI 1991/1943; see also the Protection from Eviction (Excluded Licences) (The Shaftesbury Society) Order 1999, SI 1999/1758, which specified the Shaftesbury Society for the purpose of s 3A(8)(i).

III L&T [91.3]

Secretary of State The functions of a minister of the Crown under this Act, so far as exercisable in relation to Wales, have been transferred to the National Assembly for Wales, by the National Assembly for Wales (Transfer of Functions) Order 1999, SI 1999/672, art 2, Sch 1.

III L&T [91.4]

Landlord's only or principal home In *Sumeghova v McMahon* (2002) Times, 6 November, CA the Court held that, in deciding whether premises were the landlord's only or principal home, the place where the landlord slept was of the utmost importance.

III L&T [91.5]

Hostel In *Rogerson v Wigan Metropolitan Borough Council* [2005] 2 All ER 1000 the court held that, where the claimant was compelled to share some facilities with someone he had not chosen, it was inappropriate to describe him as being in separate accommodation for the purposes of the Housing Act 1985 s 622. Enforced sharing meant that the premises in question were in a hostel; accordingly, by virtue of s 3A(8) the claimant was not entitled to the protection afforded by the 1977 Act.

III L&T [91.6]

Period of notice For obiter observations by the Court of Appeal as to the appropriate period of notice to terminate an excluded licence see *Gibson v Douglas* [2016] EWCA Civ 1266; the period is unlikely to be measured in minutes, hours or even days, but it might typically be a period measured in weeks rather than months or years.

III L&T [92]

4. Special provisions for agricultural employees

(1) This section shall apply where the tenant under the former tenancy (within the meaning of section 3 of this Act) occupied the premises under the terms of his employment as a person employed in agriculture, as defined in section 1 of the Rent (Agriculture) Act 1976, but is not a statutory tenant as defined in that Act.

(2) In this section "the occupier", in relation to any premises, means—

(a) the tenant under the former tenancy; or

(b) the surviving spouse or surviving civil partner of the tenant under the former tenancy residing with him at his death or, if the former tenant leaves no such surviving spouse or surviving civil partner, any member of his family residing with him at his death.

(2A) In accordance with section 3(2B) above, any reference in subsections (1) and (2) above to the tenant under the former tenancy includes a reference to the licensee under a licence (other than an excluded licence) which has come to an end (being a licence to occupy premises as a dwelling); and in the following provisions of this section the expressions "tenancy" and "rent" and any other expressions referable to a tenancy shall be construed accordingly.

(3) Without prejudice to any power of the court apart from this section to postpone the operation or suspend the execution of an order for possession, if in proceedings by the owner against the occupier the court makes an order for the possession of the premises the court may suspend the execution of the order on such terms and conditions, including conditions as to the payment by the occupier of arrears of rent, mesne profits and otherwise as the court thinks reasonable.

(4) Where the order for possession is made within the period of 6 months beginning with the date when the former tenancy came to an end, then, without prejudice to any powers of the court under the preceding provisions of this section or apart from this section to postpone the operation or suspend the execution of the order for a longer period, the court shall suspend the execution of the order for the remainder of the said period of 6 months unless the court—

(a) is satisfied either—

(i) that other suitable accommodation is, or will within that period be made, available to the occupier; or

(ii) that the efficient management of any agricultural land or the efficient carrying on of any agricultural operations would be seriously prejudiced unless the premises are available for occupation by a person employed or to be employed by the owner; or

(iii) that greater hardship (being hardship in respect of matters other than the carrying on of such a business as aforesaid) would be caused by the suspension of the order until the end of that period than by its execution within that period; or

(iv) that the occupier, or any person residing or lodging with the occupier, has been causing damage to the premises or has been guilty of conduct which is a nuisance or annoyance to persons occupying other premises; and

(b) considers that it would be reasonable not to suspend the execution of the order for the remainder of that period.

(5) Where the court suspends the execution of an order for possession under subsection (4) above it shall do so on such terms and conditions, including conditions as to the payment by the occupier of arrears of rent, mesne profits and otherwise as the court thinks reasonable.

(6) A decision of the court not to suspend the execution of the order under subsection (4) above shall not prejudice any other power of the court to postpone the operation or suspend the execution of the order for the whole or part of the period of 6 months mentioned in that subsection.

(7) Where the court has, under the preceding provisions of this section, suspended the execution of an order for possession, it may from time to time vary the period of suspension or terminate it and may vary any terms or conditions imposed by virtue of this section.

(8) In considering whether or how to exercise its powers under subsection (3) above, the court shall have regard to all the circumstances and, in particular, to—

(a) whether other suitable accommodation is or can be made available to the occupier;

(b) whether the efficient management of any agricultural land or the efficient carrying on of any agricultural operations would be seriously prejudiced unless the premises were available for occupation by a person employed or to be employed by the owner; and

(c) whether greater hardship would be caused by the suspension of the execution of the order than by its execution without suspension or further suspension.

(9) Where in proceedings for the recovery of possession of the premises the court makes an order for possession but suspends the execution of the order under this section, it shall make no order for costs, unless it appears to the court, having regard to the conduct of the owner or of the occupier, that there are special reasons for making such an order.

(10) Where, in the case of an order for possession of the premises to which subsection (4) above applies, the execution of the order is not suspended under that subsection or, the execution of the order having been so suspended, the suspension is terminated, then, if it is subsequently made to appear to the court that the failure to suspend the execution of the order or, as the case may be, the termination of the suspension was—

(a) attributable to the provisions of paragraph (a)(ii) of subsection (4), and

(b) due to misrepresentation or concealment of material facts by the owner of the premises,

the court may order the owner to pay to the occupier such sum as appears sufficient as compensation for damage or loss sustained by the occupier as a result of that failure or termination.

III L&T [92.1]–III L&T [92.2]

Member of his family The same expression is used in Sch 1 to the Rent Act 1977: see the notes thereto at **III L&T [81.3]**.

LANDLORD & TENANT AND HOUSING

III L&T [92.3]

Without prejudice to the power of the court The court has an inherent power to postpone the date for possession for a limited period when making an order for possession: see *Sheffield Corpn v Luxford* [1929] 2 KB 180, DC. This power is now limited by s 89 of the Housing Act 1980 (see para **III L&T [98]**).

III L&T [92.4]

Suspend the execution of the order See, for example, *Crane v Morris* [1965] 3 All ER 77, [1965] 1 WLR 1104, CA.

III L&T [92.5]

Special reasons for making such an order In *Wilson v Croft* [1971] 1 QB 241, [1970] 2 All ER 623, CA, it was held that the onus was on the owner asking for an order for costs to satisfy the court that special reasons existed; the owner's generous conduct in not claiming payment for a period of occupation by the defendant was a special reason. If the occupier took no steps to find alternative accommodation, that would be a special reason: *Wilson v Croft*, supra.

III L&T [93]

5. Validity of notices to quit

(1) Subject to subsection (1B) below no notice by a landlord or a tenant to quit any premises let (whether before or after the commencement of this Act) as a dwelling shall be valid unless—

(a) it is in writing and contains such information as may be prescribed, and

(b) it is given not less than 4 weeks before the date on which it is to take effect.

(1A) Subject to subsection (1B) below, no notice by a licensor or licensee to determine a periodic licence to occupy premises as a dwelling (whether the licence was granted before or after the passing of this Act) shall be valid unless—

(a) it is in writing and contains such information as may be prescribed, and

(b) it is given not less than 4 weeks before the date on which it is to take effect.

(1B) Nothing in subsection (1) or subsection (1A) above applies to—

(a) premises let on an excluded tenancy which is entered into on or after the date on which the Housing Act 1988 came into force unless it is entered into pursuant to a contract made before that date; or

(b) premises occupied under an excluded licence.

(2) In this section "prescribed" means prescribed by regulations made by the Secretary of State by statutory instrument, and a statutory instrument containing any such regulations shall be subject to annulment in pursuance of a resolution of either House of Parliament.

(3) Regulations under this section may make different provision in relation to different descriptions of lettings and different circumstances.

III L&T [93.1]

No notice... to quit This provision does not apply to a tenancy at will or a licence: *Crane v Morris* [1965] 3 All ER 77, [1965] 1 WLR 1104, CA. The requirement, in sub-s (1A), that a four-week notice in writing is needed to terminate a periodic licence, does not apply where an employee is licensed to occupy premises for the better performance of his duties. In such a case the licence ends with the employment: *Norris v Checksfield* [1991] 4 All ER 327, [1991] 1 WLR 1241, CA.

III L&T [93.2]

Expiry of fixed term After the expiry of a fixed 12 month term the tenancy becomes a monthly tenancy, terminable by the giving of a month's notice: *Adler v Blackman* [1953] 1 QB 146, [1952] 2 All ER 945, CA; *Kinnear v Whittaker* [2011] EWHC 1479 (QB), [2011] 2 P & CR D49.

III L&T [93.3]

Information prescribed The Notice to Quit (Prescribed Information) Regulations 1988, SI 1988/2201, prescribe the information to be contained in a notice to quit given by a landlord. But a notice in the old form is not necessarily invalid: see *Meretune Investments v Martin* [1984] CLY 1917. Note that the prescribing function of the Secretary of State, so far as exercisable in relation to Wales, has been transferred to the National Assembly for Wales, by the National Assembly for Wales (Transfer of Functions) Order 1999, SI 1999/672, art 2, Sch 1.

In *Thompson v Roberts* [2012] EWHC 2160 (QB) the landlord, by letter, gave notice pursuant to s 21 of the Housing Act 1988 that she required possession of the demised premises after two months and, in the same envelope, a separate notice containing the 'Prescribed Information' terminating the tenancy at the expiration of the period of the tenancy which would expire after the expiration of four weeks. On a finding that two months' notice was required contractually, and upon consideration of *Kinnear v Whittaker* [2011] EWHC 1479 (QB), [2011] 2 P & CR D49, it was held that the court could look at both documents together when deciding whether notice to quit had been validly given to satisfy the requirements of s 5.

III L&T [93.4]

Precedent See **BCCP O[48]** for a form of notice to quit, including prescribed information.

III L&T [93.5]

Not less than four weeks Notice given on a particular day of the week to expire on the same day four weeks hence is good: *Schnabel v Allard* [1967] 1 QB 627, [1966] 3 All ER 816, CA. However, a proper quitting date at common law must still be specified in the notice. A notice to quit business premises "within" the specified period has been construed as allowing the full period and was therefore held to be valid: *Manorlike Ltd v Le Vitas Travel Agency and Consultancy Services Ltd* [1986] 1 All ER 573, [1986] 1 EGLR 79, CA. However, where a month's notice in writing is required to terminate a monthly tenancy, the notice must be expressed to expire on the rent day, or the day before, even where the agreement provides that "no other formality will be required": *Harley v Calder* (1989) 21 HLR 214, CA. It is open to a tenant (though not one of two or more joint tenants, as to which see **III L&T [93.7]**) to waive the benefit of s 5(1) and to agree with the landlord that a notice to quit shall be effective notwithstanding that it gives less than the required four weeks' notice: see *Hackney London Borough Council v Snowden* (2000) 33 HLR 554, CA where three days' notice by the tenant was held to be effective.

III L&T [93.6]

Notice by one of two landlords A notice issued by one of two landlords is not invalid unless issued in breach of trust: *Leckhampton Dairies Ltd v Artus Whitfield Ltd* (1986) 130 Sol Jo 225.

III L&T [93.7]

Notice by one of two tenants One of two joint tenants may terminate a tenancy by giving notice, without the consent of the other: *Greenwich London Borough Council v McGrady* (1982) 81 LGR 288, CA; *Parsons v Parsons* [1983] 1 WLR 1390, CA; *Hammersmith and Fulham London Borough Council v Monk* [1992] 1 AC 478, [1992] 1 All ER 1, HL; see also *Newlon Housing Trust v Alsulaimen* [1999] 1 AC 313, [1998] 4 All ER 1, HL. But for these purposes the notice is not effective if it does not comply with s 5(1) by allowing at least four weeks: *Hounslow London Borough Council v Pilling* [1994] 1 All ER 432, [1993] 1 WLR 1242, CA. A notice given by a wife is not necessarily a breach of trust vis-à-vis the joint tenant husband from whom she wishes to be separated: *Crawley Borough Council v Ure* [1996] QB 13, [1996] 1 All ER 724, CA.

The giving of notice to quit by a joint tenant is not the exercise by a trustee of a power or duty or "function" within s 11. The provisions of that section regarding the consultation of beneficiaries do not apply: *Notting Hill Housing Trust v Brackley* [2001] EWCA Civ 601, [2001] 35 EG 106.

Where a tenancy in joint names is terminated by the departing wife leaving husband and child in occupation, the Council landlord is not contravening Art 8 by claiming possession: *Hounslow London Borough Council v Adjei* [2004] EWHC 207 (Ch), [2004] 2 All ER 636. See also *Sims v Dacorum Borough Council* [2014] UKSC 63, where the Supreme Court held that the rule in *Hammersmith and Fulham London Borough Council v Monk* is not incompatible with either Art 8 or Art 1 of the First Protocol.

III L&T [93.8]

Agricultural holding The requirement to serve a notice in a prescribed form does not apply where the occupant has an agricultural holding: *National Trust for Places of Historic Interest or Natural Beauty v Knipe* [1997] 4 All ER 627, [1998] 1 WLR 230, CA.

LANDLORD & TENANT AND HOUSING

III L&T [93.9]

Service on the Public Trustee By s 9 of the Administration of Estates Act 1925, as amended by s 14 of the Law of Property (Miscellaneous Provisions) Act 1994, the estate of a deceased person without personal representatives vests in the Public Trustee. Documents which need to be served on the deceased person should be served on the Public Trustee in accordance with s 18 of the 1994 Act. This has implications for the serving of a wide range of notices on deceased persons under the various Landlord and Tenant Acts and the Leasehold Reform Acts of 1967 and 1993. The Public Trustee's address to which notices should be sent is: PO Box 3010, London WC2 6JS. If the notice sent to the Public Trustee is not expressed to expire on a date that is consistent with the expiry date in the notice served at the premises it may be invalid for non-compliance with s 18: see *Hackney London Borough Council v Pavey*, reported in Legal Action (May 2018) at p 34.

III L&T [94]

8. Interpretation

(1) In this Act "statutorily protected tenancy" means—

(a) a protected tenancy within the meaning of the Rent Act 1977 or a tenancy to which Part I of the Landlord and Tenant Act 1954 applies;

(b) a protected occupancy or statutory tenancy as defined in the Rent (Agriculture) Act 1976;

(c) a tenancy to which Part II of the Landlord and Tenant Act 1954 applies;

(d) a tenancy of an agricultural holding within the meaning of the Agricultural Holdings Act 1986 which is a tenancy in relation to which that Act applies;

(e) an assured tenancy or assured agricultural occupancy under Part I of the Housing Act 1988;

(f) a tenancy to which Schedule 10 to the Local Government and Housing Act 1989 applies.

(g) a farm business tenancy within the meaning of the Agricultural Tenancies Act 1995.

(2) For the purposes of Part I of this Act a person who, under the terms of his employment, had exclusive possession of any premises other than as a tenant shall be deemed to have been a tenant and the expressions "let" and "tenancy" shall be construed accordingly.

(3) In Part I of this Act "the owner", in relation to any premises, means the person who, as against the occupier, is entitled to possession thereof.

(4) In this Act "excluded tenancy" and "excluded licence" have the meaning assigned by section 3A of this Act.

(5) If, on or after the date on which the Housing Act 1988 came into force, the terms of an excluded tenancy or excluded licence entered into before that date are varied, then—

(a) if the variation affects the amount of the rent which is payable under the tenancy or licence, the tenancy or licence shall be treated for the purposes of sections 3(2C) and 5(1B) above as a new tenancy or licence entered into at the time of the variation; and

(b) if the variation does not affect the amount of the rent which is so payable, nothing in this Act shall affect the determination of the question whether the variation is such as to give rise to a new tenancy or licence.

(6) Any reference in subsection (5) above to a variation affecting the amount of the rent which is payable under a tenancy or licence does not include a reference to—

(a) a reduction or increase effected under Part III or Part VI of the Rent Act 1977 (rents under regulated tenancies and housing association

(a) the order is made in an action by a mortgagee for possession; or
(b) the order is made in an action for forfeiture of a lease; or
(c) the court had power to make the order only if it considered it reasonable to make it; or
(d) the order relates to a dwelling-house which is the subject of a restricted contract (within the meaning of section 19 of the 1977 Act); or
(e) the order is made in proceedings brought as mentioned in section 88 (1) above.

III L&T [98.1]

The general rule In *Bain & Co v Church Comrs for England* [1989] 1 WLR 24 this section was held to apply to the county court, not the High Court. However, in *Hackney London Borough Council v Side by Side (Kids) Ltd* [2003] EWHC 1813 (QB), [2004] 2 All ER 373, (2003) Times, 5 August the court, declining to follow *Bain* as being 'plainly wrong', held that the section does apply to the High Court. It does not purport to confer jurisdiction on the court to allow time (whether by postponing, varying, suspending or staying the date when the order for possession is to take effect) but rather to restrict the exercise of the jurisdiction which already exists. It affects in particular the court's inherent power to postpone the date for possession when making an order against a former tenant or service occupant: see *Sheffield Corpn v Luxford* [1929] 2 KB 180 and the cases in the notes to the County Courts Act 1984, s 21 (see paras **II CCA [11.1]–II CCA [11.8]**); see also *Boyland & Son Ltd v Rand* [2006] EWCA Civ 1860, [2007] HLR 369. However, the restriction does not prevent an appeal court from postponing enforcement of a possession order so as to preserve the position until the appeal against the making of the possession order has been heard: *Admiral Taverns (Cygnet) Ltd v Daniel* [2008] EWHC 1688 (QB), [2008] All ER (D) 274 (Jul).

A general rule is now established for those possession cases where the court has a non-statutory discretion in fixing the date when possession is to be given. The rule is that the interval between the date of the order and the date for possession is not normally to exceed 14 days, but a longer period may be allowed, if exceptional hardship is shown. But six weeks in all is the absolute limit for any case to which the Housing Act 1980 s 89 (1) applies. In *Hackney London Borough Council v Side by Side (Kids) Ltd* (above) the court held, with some hesitation, that the section applies to consent orders.

In *R (on the application of JL) v Secretary of State for Defence* [2012] EWHC 2216 (Admin), [2012] All ER (D) 370 (Jul), the landlord had obtained a possession order in respect of residential premises. In subsequent proceedings for enforcement of the possession order, the court noted that s 89 made plain that, once a possession order was granted in a case that fell within s 89(1), it should be capable of being swiftly enforced. The court also held that, where appropriate (and particularly where no such review had been conducted at the possession order stage), an Article 8 proportionality review could be considered at the enforcement stage.

III L&T [98.1A]

Operation of s 89 in relation to assured shorthold tenancies Where postponement of possession is sought by a former assured shorthold tenant, on the ground of exceptional hardship under s 89, the judge may direct a hearing of that issue which (if directed) must be held before the date on which possession is to be given up. If, at such a hearing, the judge is satisfied that exceptional hardship would be caused by requiring possession to be given up by the date in the order for possession, he may vary the date on which possession must be given up: para **CPR 55.18**. The judge may postpone possession on the grounds of exceptional hardship without directing a hearing if he considers that possession should be given up six weeks after the date of the order or (if the defendant has requested postponement to an earlier date) on that date, and the claimant indicated on his claim form that he would be content for the court to make such an order without a hearing: see the Practice Direction to CPR Pt 55 paras 8.1 to 8.3 (para **CPR PD 55**).

III L&T [98.2]

Restricted contracts An exception is made, in the Housing Act 1980 s 89(2)(d), for any restricted contract to which the Rent Act 1977 s 19 applies. The repeal of that section by the Housing Act 1988 does not affect existing contracts: see the Rent Act 1977 s 106A (see para **III L&T [74]**), which enables the court to stay or suspend execution or postpone the date of possession for up to 3 months, in the case of a restricted contract.

III L&T [98.3]

Rental purchase The exception made by the Housing Act 1980 s 89(2)(e) is for "rental purchase" of a dwelling house, that is where the price is payable by three or more instalments and completion is deferred until the whole or a specified part is paid. If the buyer defaults in such a case and the seller takes proceedings for possession the Housing Act 1980 s 88 (see para **III L&T [97]**) enables the court to postpone, stay or suspend the giving of possession for such period or periods as the court thinks fit.

III L&T [98.4]

Trespassers on private land and human rights Section 89 has been held to be compatible with the Convention: see *Hounslow London Borough Council v Powell* [2011] UKSC 8, [2011] 2 AC 186, [2011] 2 All ER 129.

Article 8 may be engaged where trespassers have set up their home on private land and the court, as a public body, must apply proportionality when dealing with a claim for possession. But the exercise of discretion would seem to be subject to the provisions of s 89: see judgment of Sir Alan Ward in *Malik v Fassenfelt (since dec'd)* [2013] EWCA Civ 798, [2013] All ER (D) 44 (Jul), but note that both Toulson and Lloyd LLJ declined to hold that Article 8 was engaged as against a private landowner (the point not having been argued). The Court of Appeal has since reiterated that Article 8 considerations arise only in the case of public authority landlords: *McDonald (by her litigation friend) v McDonald (acting by the joint receivers)* [2014] EWCA Civ 1049, [2014] 2 P & CR 377, [2014] HLR 643. See also *McDonald v McDonald* [2016] UKSC 28, where the Supreme Court (upholding the decision of the Court of Appeal) held that, although there were some ECtHR authorities which supported the notion that Art 8 was engaged as against a private landlord, there was no support for the proposition that the judge could have been required to consider the proportionality of the order which he would have made under the 1980 and 1988 Housing Acts.

HOUSING ACT 1985

(c 68)

GENERAL NOTES ON HOUSING ACT 1985

III L&T [99]

Jurisdiction The High Court and the county court each have unlimited jurisdiction to determine questions concerning secure tenancies and the right to buy. But a person who starts proceedings in the High Court will not be entitled to costs: Housing Act 1985 ss 110, 181 (see paras **III L&T [116]**, **III L&T [127]**). Furthermore claims for possession of land can only be started in the High Court in exceptional circumstances. All possession claims must be started in the county court for the district in which the land is situated unless the claimant can certify (and verify with a statement of truth (see CPR PD 22 para 1.1(5) at para **CPR PD 22**)) that there are complicated disputes of fact or there are points of law of general importance. The value of the property and the amount of any financial claim may be relevant circumstances, but these factors alone will not normally justify starting the claim in the High Court: see para **CPR 55.3** and the Practice Direction to CPR Pt 55 paras 1.1 to 1.4 (para **CPR PD 55**).

III L&T [99A]

Changes made by the Localism Act 2011 The Localism Act 2011 inserted ss 107A to 107E on flexible tenancies and made changes to provisions in ss 83, 109, 86A, 87, 89, 90 and Sch 2 regarding security of tenure and succession. The changes were all brought fully into force on 1 April 2012 by the Localism Act (Commencement No 6 and Transitional, Transitory and Savings Provisions) Order 2012, SI 2012/1463.

III L&T [100]

Precedents and procedure The procedure set out in Section I of CPR Pt 55 must be used. Possession claims under the Housing Act 1985 must therefore be started by means of claim form N5. Particulars of claim must be filed and served with the claim form (see para **CPR 55.4**). The contents of the particulars of claim must comply with the requirements of CPR Pt 16 (see para **CPR 16**) and the Practice Direction to CPR Pt 55 para 2.1 (para **CPR PD 55**). Where the possession claim relates to residential property and includes a claim for non-payment of rent the particulars of claim must also comply with CPR Pt 55 Practice Direction para 2.3 (para **CPR PD 55**); the particulars of claim in Form N119 should therefore be used for such claims. Although an acknowledgment of service is not required, a defence should be filed. The defence to a general possession claim should be in Form N11 and the defence to a claim for possession for residential premises which includes a claim for non-payment of rent should be in Form N11R. If the defendant does not file a defence within 14 days of service of the particulars of claim, he may take part in the hearing but the court will take into account his failure when deciding costs: para **CPR 55.7**. A table of the appropriate forms for possession claims can be found at **BCCP O[12]**; the forms can also be found in the Forms supplement, the FORMS section of your CD-ROM and at **BCCP O[80]** onwards.

For examples of particulars of claim for use in claims under the Housing Act 1985, see **BCCP O[152]–BCCP O[154]**.

PART I
INTRODUCTORY PROVISIONS

LOCAL HOUSING AUTHORITIES

III L&T [101]

1. Local housing authorities

In this Act "local housing authority" means a district council, a London borough council, the Common Council of the City of London, a Welsh county council or county borough council or the Council of the Isles of Scilly.

OTHER AUTHORITIES AND BODIES

III L&T [102]

4. Other descriptions of authority

In this Act—

(a) "housing authority" means a local housing authority or a new town corporation;

(b) "new town corporation" means a development corporation or the new towns residuary body;

(c) "development corporation" means a development corporation established by an order made, or having effect as if made, under the New Towns Act 1981;

(d) "urban development corporation" means an urban development corporation established under Part XVI of the Local Government, Planning and Land Act 1980;

(e) "local authority" means a county, county borough, district or London borough council, the Common Council of the City of London or the Council of the Isles of Scilly, in sections 43, 44 and 232 includes the Broads Authority, in sections 438, 441, 442, 443 and 458 includes the Broads Authority, a joint authority established by Part 4 of the Local Government Act 1985, an economic prosperity board, a combined authority, a fire and rescue authority created by an order under section 4A of the Fire and Rescue Services Act 2004. . . and the London Fire Commissioner, and in sections 45(2)(b), 50(2), 51(6), 80(1), 157(1), 171(2), . . . 573(1), paragraph 2(1) of Schedule 1, grounds 7 and 12 in Schedule 2, ground 5 in Schedule 3, paragraph 7(1) of Schedule 4, paragraph 5(1)(b) of Schedule 5 and Schedule 16 includes . . . the Broads Authority, a police and crime commissioner . . ., a joint authority established by Part 4 of the Local Government Act 1985, an economic prosperity board, a combined authority, a fire and rescue authority created by an order under section 4A of the Fire and Rescue Services Act 2004 . . . and the London Fire Commissioner;

(f) "housing action trust" means a housing action trust established under Part III of the Housing Act 1988.

(g) "new towns residuary body" means—

- (i) in relation to England, the Homes and Communities Agency so far as exercising functions in relation to anything transferred (or to be transferred) to it as mentioned in section 52(1)(a) to (d) of the Housing and Regeneration Act 2008 or the Greater London Authority so far as exercising its new towns and urban development functions; and
- (ii) in relation to Wales, the Welsh Ministers so far as exercising functions in relation to anything transferred (or to be transferred) to them as mentioned in section 36(1)(a) (i) to (iii) of the New Towns Act 1981.

(2) In this section:

"combined authority" means a combined authority established under section 103 of the Local Democracy, Economic Development and Construction Act 2009;

"economic prosperity board" means an economic prosperity board established under section 88 of that Act;

. . .

LANDLORD & TENANT AND HOUSING

PART IV
SECURE TENANCIES AND RIGHTS OF SECURE TENANTS

SECURE TENANCIES

III L&T [103]

79. Secure tenancies

(1) A tenancy under which a dwelling-house is let as a separate dwelling is a secure tenancy at any time when the conditions described in sections 80 and 81 as the landlord condition and the tenant condition are satisfied.

(2) Subsection (1) has effect subject to

(a) the exceptions in Schedule 1 (tenancies which are not secure tenancies),

(b) sections 89 (3) and (4) and 90 (3) and (4) (tenancies ceasing to be secure after death of tenant), and

(c) sections 91 (2) and 93 (2) (tenancies ceasing to be secure in consequence of assignment or subletting).

(3) The provisions of this Part apply in relation to a licence to occupy a dwelling-house (whether or not granted for a consideration) as they apply in relation to a tenancy.

(4) Subsection (3) does not apply to a licence granted as a temporary expedient to a person who entered the dwelling house or any other land as a trespasser (whether or not, before the grant of that licence, another licence to occupy that or another dwelling-house had been granted to him).

III L&T [103.1]

Dwelling-house See the Housing Act 1985 s 112 (see para **III L&T [118]**) and the case law on the construction of the same word in the notes to the Rent Act 1977 s 1 (see para **III L&T [68]**).

III L&T [103.2]

Let as a separate dwelling Here again the same words appear in the Rent Act 1977 s 1 (see para **III L&T [68]**) and case law on their construction is noted there. A tenancy is not invalidated by the fact that the tenant is illegally present in the United Kingdom having overstayed the terms on which he was allowed in: *Akinbolu v Hackney London Borough Council* (1996) 29 HLR 259, [1996] NPC 60, CA.

III L&T [103.3]

"At any time" A subtenant of part of premises let to the mesne landlord by the local authority for business use may become a secure tenant of the authority on surrender of the lease: *Basingstoke and Deane Borough Council v Paice* (1995) 27 HLR 433, [1995] 2 EGLR 9, CA.

III L&T [103.3A]

Selection of tenants A local authority's duty to allocate residential accommodation in accordance with its statutory housing allocation scheme under Part VI of the Housing Act 1996 is distinct from its ability to dispose of accommodation by way of secure tenancies in accordance with its statutory powers; secure tenancies granted to tenants who had not been selected in accordance with the allocation scheme were valid: see *Birmingham City Council v Qasim* [2009] EWCA Civ 1080.

III L&T [103.4]

Licence to occupy Where a housing authority makes it clear in writing that it requires an occupant of premises to move out of possession it does not create a tenancy, or a licence within the Housing Act 1985 s 79(3) (see para **III L&T [103]**), by accepting payments described as damages for unlawful use and occupation or by granting a rent rebate: *Westminster City Council v Basson* (1990) 23 HLR 225, [1991] 1 EGLR 277, CA. A hostel occupant may have a licence to occupy a dwelling-house, within the Housing Act 1985 s 79 (3): but not if there is a sharing of facilities and services which is incompatible with its being a "separate" dwelling-house: *Central YMCA Housing Association Ltd v Saunders* (1990) 23 HLR 212, CA; *Central YMCA Housing Association Ltd at St Giles Hotel Ltd v Goodman* (1991) 24 HLR 109, CA. In *Westminster City Council v Clarke* [1992] 2 AC 288, [1992] 1 All ER 695, HL, the House of Lords held, reversing the Court of Appeal, that a hostel resident's licence to occupy gave him rights corresponding to those of a lodger, not the rights of security which would arise under the Housing Act 1985. This was followed in *Parkins v Westminster City Council* (1997) 30 HLR 894, [1998] 1 EGLR 22, where an occupant of a flat had exclusive occupation of a bedroom only and shared the rest. In *Tyler v Royal Borough of Kensington and Chelsea* (1990) 23 HLR 380, CA, it was held that a secure tenant who is given a licence to occupy different premises while repairs are carried out does not acquire a "secure" licence. Also, in *Shepherd's Bush Housing Association v HATS Co-operative* (1991) 24 HLR 176, CA, licensees of a fully mutual housing co-operative were held not to be licensees or tenants of the housing association of which the co-operative was licensee. A secure tenancy, for the purposes of s 79 is one in which there is a direct landlord and tenant relationship and where both the landlord condition in s 80 of the Act and the tenant condition in s 81 of the Act are satisfied. Accordingly, where a local authority passed premises to a housing trust and the trust granted sub-licences to homeless people, no secure tenancies arose, either on the grant of the sub-licence or on its termination, provided that the trust had granted the licences as principal, not as agent for the council: see *Kay v Lambeth London Borough Council* [2004] EWCA Civ 926, [2004] 3 WLR 1396, (2004) Times, 26 July; appeal dismissed by the House of Lords in *Kay v Lambeth London Borough Council* [2006] 2 AC 465, [2006] 2 WLR 570, [2006] 4 All ER 128.

LANDLORD & TENANT AND HOUSING

III L&T [103.4A]

Variation of the terms of the tenancy The landlord has the power to vary the terms of the tenancy by serving a notice in accordance with s 103 of the Housing Act 1985; but it has been doubted whether this power may be exercised to change terms other than the amount of the rent without the agreement of the tenant. A unilateral change, except as to rent, would appear to be invalidated by regulations 5 and 8 of the Unfair Terms in Consumer Contracts Regulations (SI 1999/2083): *Governors of the Peabody Trust v Reeve* [2008] EWHC 1432 (Ch), [2008] 43 EG 196, (2008) Times, 9 June, Ch D.

III L&T [103.5]

Agreement following possession order Where a local authority obtains a final order for possession and then enters into a fresh agreement which provides for the payment of the arrears the effect may be to create a new secure tenancy, but all the elements of a fresh contract must be present: *Southwark London Borough Council v Logan* (1995) 29 HLR 40, CA; *Greenwich London Borough Council v Regan* (1996) 28 HLR 469, CA; *Hackney London Borough Council v Porter* (1996) 29 HLR 401, CA.

In *Stirling v Leadenhall Residential 2 Ltd* [2001] EWCA Civ 1011, [2001] 3 All ER 645 (a case concerning a private sector letting), it was common ground that service of notice of increase in rent upon a person remaining in occupation following a possession order, paying rent arrears and mesne profits, created a new tenancy.

III L&T [103.6]

Human rights A former joint tenant who remains in occupation after termination of the tenancy by the other has a Convention right under Art 8 to respect for his home. However, Art 8 cannot be relied on to defeat proprietary or contractual rights to possession. Accordingly, a public authority landlord was entitled to claim possession; but an unfair exercise of the right may be capable of challenge by judicial review; see the majority decision in *Harrow London Borough Council v Qazi* [2003] UKHL 43, [2004] 1 AC 983, [2003] 4 All ER 461. Note, however, the decision of the House of Lords in *Kay v Lambeth London Borough Council* [2006] 2 AC 465, [2006] 2 WLR 570, [2006] 4 All ER 128 that, in so far as *Harrow London Borough Council v Qazi* decided that the enforcement of a right to possession in accordance with the domestic law of property could never be incompatible with the Art 8 of the Convention, that had to be modified in the light of *Connors v United Kingdom* (66746/01) [2005] 40 EHRR 9; moreover, that it was open to an occupier to raise an Art 8 defence to possession proceedings in the county court rather than by way of judicial review (a point subsequently emphasised in *Manchester City Council v Pinnock* [2010] 3 WLR 1441 (see below)).

Where a housing authority takes a series of decisions regarding the eviction of an unlawful occupier from his, or her, home, each decision has to be reasonable to satisfy the requirements of Article 8 and reasonableness connotes something wider than rationality. The authority should take account of the personal circumstances of the occupiers which are known since, although those circumstances could not make it unreasonable to decide to take possession proceedings they might be relevant to deciding whether and for how long to postpone execution of an order for possession: *Central Bedfordshire Council v Housing Action Zone Ltd* (2009) Times, 23 July, CA.

Judges faced with a defence under Article 8 to a claim by a housing authority for possession should proceed on the assumption that domestic law strikes a fair balance and is compatible with the Convention. If an argument is raised as to the law being incompatible and it is not possible to construe the law as compatible, that issue should be dealt with by the High Court.

If on the other hand an argument is raised that the decision to claim possession was, in the particular circumstances of the case, an improper, and therefore invalid, exercise of power, such a line of defence should be allowed to proceed in the county court: *Kay v Lambeth London Borough Council* (above).

There are two possible gateways for a defence to summary judgment for possession: (i) that a seriously arguable case is made under Article 8, but only where it is possible to adapt the domestic law to make it more Convention-compliant; and (ii) that a seriously arguable challenge is made on conventional judicial review grounds to the local authority's decision to recover possession: *Doherty v Birmingham City Council* [2006] EWCA Civ 1739, [2007] LGR 165, [2007] HLR 32.

In *Manchester City Council v Pinnock* [2010] UKSC 45, [2010] 3 WLR 1441, [2010] 44 LS Gaz R 16 the Supreme Court (applying *Kay v United Kingdom (Application No 37341/06)* [2010] NLJR 1346, (2010) Times, 18 October) identified clear ECHR jurisprudence to the effect that any person at risk of being dispossessed of his home at a local authority's suit should, in principle, have the right to question the measure's proportionality under Art 8, even if his right of occupation under domestic law had ended (though it would only be in exceptional cases that Art 8 proportionality would arguably give a right to continued possession where the applicant had no right to remain under domestic law). Where, therefore, a local authority applied to a court for an order for possession of a person's home, the court had power to assess the proportionality of making the order and, in making that assessment, to resolve any relevant factual dispute (not following *Qazi, Kay v Lambeth and Doherty v Birmingham City Council* on this point). A procedure limited to considering proportionality through traditional judicial review without the court making its own factual assessment in an appropriate case was inadequate. Moreover, it was unsafe only to consider proportionality in exceptional cases; the question was always whether the eviction was a proportionate means of achieving a legitimate aim. The Supreme Court also confirmed that s 7(1)(b) of the Human Rights Act 1998 conferred the necessary jurisdiction on county courts as well as the High Court. Tenants could therefore challenge possession proceedings in the proceedings themselves, even if they were in the county court.

III L&T [103.7]

Liability for mesne profits A former tenant who remains in possession after the end of the tenancy is liable for mesne profits but the liability ceases as soon as he goes out of possession even if he does not notify the landlord; *Jones v Merton London Borough Council v Jones* [2008] EWCA Civ 660, [2008] 4 All ER 287.

III L&T [104]

80. The landlord condition

(1) The landlord condition is that the interest of the landlord belongs to one of the following authorities or bodies—

a local authority,

a development corporation,

a housing action trust

a Mayoral development corporation,

an urban development corporation, in the case of a tenancy falling within subsections (2A) to (2E), the Homes and Communities Agency, the Greater London Authority or the Welsh Ministers (as the case may be),

. . .

the Relevant Authority

a housing trust which is a charity, or

a housing association to which this section applies by virtue of subsection (2) or housing co-operative to which this section applies.

(2) This section applies to—

(a) a housing association which—

(i) is a private registered provider of social housing or a registered social landlord, but

(ii) is not a co-operative housing association, and

(b) a co-operative housing association which is neither a private registered provider of social housing nor a registered social landlord.

(2A) A tenancy falls within this subsection if the interest of the landlord is transferred to—

(a) the Homes and Communities Agency as mentioned in section 52(1)(a) to (d) of the Housing and Regeneration Act 2008,

(aa) the Greater London Authority as mentioned in section 333ZI(2)(a) to (d) of the Greater London Authority Act 1999, or

(b) the Welsh Ministers as mentioned in section 36(1)(a)(i) to (iii) of the New Towns Act 1981.

(2B) A tenancy falls within this subsection if it is entered into pursuant to a contract under which the rights and liabilities of the prospective landlord are transferred to the Homes and Communities Agency, the Greater London Authority or the Welsh Ministers as mentioned in subsection (2A)(a), (aa) or (b) (as the case may be).

(2C) A tenancy falls within this subsection if it is granted by the Homes and Communities Agency, the Greater London Authority or the Welsh Ministers to a person (alone or jointly with others) who, immediately before it was entered into, was a secure tenant of the Homes and Communities Agency, the Greater London Authority or the Welsh Ministers (as the case may be).

(2D) A tenancy falls within this subsection if—

(a) it is granted by the Homes and Communities Agency, the Greater London Authority or the Welsh Ministers to a person (alone or jointly with others),

(b) before the grant of the tenancy, an order for possession of a dwelling-house let under a secure tenancy was made against the person (alone or jointly with others) and in favour of the Homes and Communities Agency, the Greater London Authority or the Welsh Ministers (as the case may be) on the court being satisfied as mentioned in section 84(2)(b) or (c), and

(c) the tenancy is of the premises which constitute the suitable accommodation as to which the court was so satisfied.

(2E) A tenancy falls within this subsection if it is granted by the Homes and Communities Agency, the Greater London Authority or the Welsh Ministers pursuant to an obligation under section 554(2A).

(3) If a co-operative housing association ceases to be a private registered provider of social housing or a registered social landlord, it shall, within the period of 21 days beginning with the date on which it ceases to be such a body, notify each of its tenants who thereby becomes a secure tenant, in writing, that he has become a secure tenant.

(4) This section applies to a housing co-operative within the meaning of section 27B (agreements under certain superseded provisions) where the dwelling-house is comprised in a housing co-operative agreement within the meaning of that section.

(5) In this Act and in any provision made under this Act, or made by or under any other enactment, a reference to—

(a) a person within section 80 or 80(1) of this Act, or

(b) a person who satisfies the landlord condition under this section,

includes a reference to the Homes and Communities Agency, the Greater London Authority or to the Welsh Ministers so far as acting in their capacity as landlord (or, in the case of disposals, former landlord) in respect of a tenancy which falls within subsections (2A) to (2E) above but, subject to this, does not include the Homes and Communities Agency, the Greater London Authority or the Welsh Ministers.

(6) Subsection (5)—

(a) applies whether the person is described as an authority, body or landlord or in any other way and whether the reference is otherwise expressed in a different way, and

(b) is subject to any provision to the contrary.

Amendments *Section 80 is set out subject to the amendments and repeals effected by Schedule 18 to the Housing Act 1988. Those amendments were not effective in relation to protected or statutory tenancies under the Rent Act 1977 which have become secure tenancies. Subject to savings and transitional provisions, from 1 April 2010 the Housing and Regeneration Act 2008 (Consequential Provisions) Order 2010 makes provision, in those excepted cases, for references to the Regulator of Social Housing and private registered providers of social housing to be inserted in substitution for the Housing Corporation and housing associations. Text is shown as amended, subject to savings, by the 2010 Order and by the Localism Act 2011.*

III L&T [104.1]

Joint landlords In *R v Council of the City of Plymouth and Cornwall County Council, ex p Freeman* (1987) 19 HLR 328, CA, the Court of Appeal held, reversing the decision of Hodgson J (1986) 18 HLR 243, that the landlord condition was *not* satisfied where the interest belonged to one of the relevant authorities jointly with a body which was outside the scope of the section.

III L&T [104.2]

Housing association In *Bhai v Black Roof Community Housing Association Ltd* [2001] 2 All ER 865, CA, the housing association landlord changed, during the course of the tenancy, from a fully mutual to a non-mutual association; the court held that, by virtue of the operation of Sch 18 para 4(c) of the Housing Act 1988, the landlord's condition was satisfied.

Where the interest of a housing authority is terminated by the council which owns the property the effect is to terminate the right of the association to take possession proceedings against its tenants, except where such a right is reserved by the lease: *Alamo Housing Association Co-operative Ltd v Meredith* [2003] EWCA Civ 495, [2003] HLR 947, (2003) Times, 21 April.

If the landlord condition is not satisfied the circumstances and terms of the grant may be such that the grant is for an uncertain term. In *Mexfield Housing Co-operative Ltd v Berrisford* [2011] UKSC 52, [2012] 1 AC 955, [2012] 1 All ER 1393 the Supreme Court held that the effect of s 149(6) of the Law of Property Act 1925 was that the agreement was to be treated as a tenancy for a term of 90 years, determinable on the tenant's death or in accordance with its express terms; and that, accordingly, the landlord was not entitled to possession. In *Southward Housing Co-operative v Walker* [2015] EWHC 1615, [2015] 2 P & CR 13 the court, considering *Mexfield*, held that to treat a tenancy granted by a fully mutual housing association as a 90-year tenancy under s 149(6) confounded the parties' intentions and fundamental aspects of their agreement; it was therefore treated as a contractual licence. The court declined to hold that the provision in the Housing Act 1985 excluding fully mutual housing co-operatives' tenancies from security of tenure was incompatible with ECHR Arts 8 and 14.

III L&T [104.3]

Tenancy promised by councillor on terms to be agreed In *Hackney London Borough Council v Amadi* [2001] EWCA Civ 850 it was held that a promise by a Labour Councillor, the leader of the Labour Group, to grant the defendant occupier a tenancy on terms to be agreed, was not a concluded contract and was not made as agent for the local authority.

III L&T [104.4]

Registration of title The transfer of an unregistered legal estate in land in circumstances where s 171A of the Housing Act 1985 applies (namely where a person ceases to be a secure tenant because a landlord disposes of its interest to a private sector landlord) is an is an event requiring compulsory registration: s 4(1)(b) of the Land Registration Act 2002.

III L&T [105]

81. The tenant condition

The tenant condition is that the tenant is an individual and occupies the dwelling-house as his only or principal home; or, where the tenancy is a joint tenancy, that each of the joint tenants is an individual and at least one of them occupies the dwelling-house as his only or principal home.

III L&T [105.1]

Home A tenant may have more than one home; and occupation, for the purposes of the Housing Act 1980 s 81 does not require actual physical presence so long as the tenant intends to live there and there are signs of occupation, such as his furniture, in the premises: *Crawley Borough Council v Sawyer* (1987) 20 HLR 98, CA. In deciding whether a tenant intends to live in a dwelling house, the court will focus not on fleeting changes of mind but on the enduring intention: *Hammersmith and Fulham London Borough Council v Clarke* (2000) 33 HLR 881, CA. In *Notting Hill Housing Trust v Etoria* [1989] CLY 1912, cc, the tenant condition was held to be satisfied although the tenant was serving a prison sentence: his brother was looking after the home as caretaker until his return. A tenancy which ceased to be secure when the tenant went out of occupation may become secure again on his return: *Hussey v Camden London Borough Council* (1994) 27 HLR 5, CA.

However, the fact that the tenant has returned to live by the date of the hearing is not conclusive proof that there always was an intention to return. The issue as to whether the premises were the tenant's principal home has to be ascertained at the date of the expiry of a notice to quit and is to be determined objectively not simply on the basis of the tenant's statements of intention: *Islington London Borough Council v Boyle and Collier* [2011] EWCA Civ 1450, [2012] PTSR 1093, [2012] 1 P & CR D35.

III L&T [105.2]

Letting to a company A purported letting of council property to a company cannot create a secure tenancy: *Camden London Borough Council v Shortlife Community Housing Ltd* (1992) 25 HLR 330.

III L&T [105.3]

Insolvency A tenant does not necessarily lose security by becoming insolvent. See the provisions of the Insolvency Act 1986 s 283 (3A), noted under the Rent Act 1977 s 2 (see para **III L&T [69.4]**).

III L&T [105.4]

Granting a tenancy to a minor A minor is prevented by s.1 (6) of the Law of Property Act 1925 from holding a legal estate in land. But a council may grant a tenancy to a minor which is effective in equity. Where, however, a council purports to grant a minor a legal estate as a tenant the effect is to create a trust whereby the council holds the tenancy on trust for the minor in accordance with paragraph 11(1) of Schedule 1 to the Trusts of Land and Appointment of Trustees Act 1996. For so long as the council holds the legal tenancy as trustee it cannot serve an effective notice to quit on the minor: *Birmingham City Council v Dixon* [2009] EWHC 761 (Admin), [2010] 1 WLR 32, 173 JP 233.

[GRANT OF NEW SECURE TENANCIES IN ENGLAND]

III L&T [105A]

[81A. New English secure tenancies to be between 2 and 10 years in general]

[(1) A person may grant a secure tenancy of a dwelling-house in England only if it is a tenancy for a fixed term that is—

(a) at least 2 years, and

(b) no longer than the permitted maximum length.

(2) The permitted maximum length is 10 years, unless subsection (3) applies.

(3) If the person granting the tenancy has been notified in writing that a child aged under 9 will live in the dwelling-house, the permitted maximum length is the period—

(a) beginning with the day on which the tenancy is granted, and

(b) ending with the day on which the child will reach the age of 19.

(4) If a person purports to grant a secure tenancy in breach of subsection (1), it takes effect as a tenancy for a fixed term of 5 years.

(5) In deciding what length of tenancy to grant in a case to which this section applies a person must have regard to any guidance given by the Secretary of State.

(6) This section does not apply to the grant of an old-style secure tenancy (as to which, see section 81B).]

Amendment *Section 81A is inserted, from a date to be appointed, by the Housing and Planning Act 2016.*

III L&T [105B]

[81B. Cases where old-style English secure tenancies may be granted]

[(1) A person may grant an old-style secure tenancy of a dwelling-house in England only—

(a) in circumstances specified in regulations made by the Secretary of State,

(b) in accordance with subsection (2)[, (2A) or (2B)], or

(c) if required to do so by section 158(9B) of the Localism Act 2011 (which relates to transfer requests made before section 121 of the Housing and Planning Act 2016 comes into force).

(2) A local housing authority that grants a secure tenancy of a dwelling-house in England must grant an old-style secure tenancy if—

(a) the tenancy is offered as a replacement for an old-style secure tenancy of some other dwelling-house, and

(b) the tenant has not made an application to move.

[(2A) A local housing authority that grants a secure tenancy of a dwelling-house in England must grant an old-style secure tenancy if—

(a) the tenancy is offered to a person who is or was a tenant of some other dwelling-house under a qualifying tenancy (whether as the sole tenant or as a joint tenant), and

(b) the authority is satisfied that—

(i) the person or a member of the person's household is or has been a victim of domestic abuse carried out by another person, and

(ii) the new tenancy is granted for reasons connected with that abuse.

(2B) A local housing authority that grants a secure tenancy of a dwelling-house in England must grant an old-style secure tenancy if—

(a) the tenancy is offered to a person who was a joint tenant of that dwelling-house under an old-style secure tenancy, and

(b) the authority is satisfied that—

(i) the person or a member of the person's household is or has been a victim of domestic abuse carried out by another person, and

(ii) the new tenancy is granted for reasons connected with that abuse.

(2C) In subsections (2A) and (2B)—

"abuse" means—

(a) violence,

(b) threatening, intimidating, coercive or controlling behaviour, or

(c) any other form of abuse, including emotional, financial, physical, psychological or sexual abuse;

"domestic abuse" is abuse where the victim is or has been—

(a) in the same family or household as the abuser, or

(b) in an intimate personal relationship with the abuser;

"qualifying tenancy" means a tenancy of a dwelling-house in England which is—

(a) an old-style secure tenancy, or

(b) an assured tenancy which is not an assured shorthold tenancy and which is granted by a private registered provider of social housing, by the Regulator of Social Housing or by a housing trust which is a charity.]

(3) Other provisions of this Part set out the consequences of a tenancy being an old-style secure tenancy.

(4) Regulations under subsection (1) may include transitional or saving provision.

(5) Regulations under subsection (1) are to be made by statutory instrument.

(6) A statutory instrument containing regulations under subsection (1) may not be made unless a draft of the instrument has been laid before and approved by a resolution of each House of Parliament.]

Amendment *Section 81B is inserted, from a date to be appointed, by s 118 of, and Schedule 7 to, the Housing and Planning Act 2016. Sub-section (1)(b) is amended and sub-ss (2A) to (2C) are inserted by the Secure Tenancies (Victims of Domestic Abuse) Act 2018 with effect from a date to be appointed.*

III L&T [105C]

[81C. Duty to offer new secure tenancy in limited circumstances]

[(1) This section applies where a change in circumstances means that a tenancy that is not a secure tenancy would become a secure tenancy but for the exception in paragraph 1ZA of Schedule 1.

(2) The landlord must, within the period of 28 days, make the tenant a written offer of a secure tenancy in return for the tenant surrendering the original tenancy.

(3) If the tenant accepts in writing within the period of 28 days beginning with the day on which the tenant receives the offer, the landlord must grant the secure tenancy on the tenant surrendering the original tenancy.]

Amendment *Section 81C is inserted, from a date to be appointed, by s 118 of, and Schedule 7 to, the Housing and Planning Act 2016.*

III L&T [105D]

[81D. Review of decisions about length of secure tenancies in England]

[(1) A person who is offered a secure tenancy of a dwelling-house in England (under section 81C or otherwise) may request a review under this section, unless the tenancy on offer is an old-style secure tenancy.

(2) The sole purpose of a review under this section is to consider whether the length of the tenancy is in accordance with any policy that the prospective landlord has about the length of secure tenancies it grants.

(3) The request must be made before the end of—

- (a) the period of 21 days beginning with the day on which the person making the request first receives the offer, or
- (b) such longer period as the prospective landlord may allow in writing.

(4) On receiving the request the prospective landlord must carry out the review.

(5) On completing the review the prospective landlord must—

- (a) notify the tenant in writing of the outcome,
- (b) revise its offer or confirm its original decision about the length of the tenancy, and
- (c) if it decides to confirm its original decision, give reasons.

(6) The Secretary of State may by regulations make provision about the procedure to be followed in connection with a review under this section.

(7) The regulations may, in particular—

- (a) require the review to be carried out by a person of appropriate seniority who was not involved in the original decision;
- (b) make provision as to the circumstances in which the person who requested the review is entitled to an oral hearing, and whether and by whom that person may be represented.

(8) Regulations under this section may include transitional or saving provision.

(9) Regulations under this section are to be made by statutory instrument which is subject to annulment in pursuance of a resolution of either House of Parliament.]

Amendment *Section 81D is inserted, from a date to be appointed, by s 118 of, and Schedule 7 to, the Housing and Planning Act 2016.*

III L&T [105D.1]

Phasing out lifetime tenancies Sections 81A to 81D, when in force, have the effect of phasing out lifetime tenancies. Secure tenancies will generally have to be for a fixed term and will not automatically be renewed. Local authorities may generally only grant secure tenancies for a fixed term of between 2 and 10 years or, where a child under 9 years lives in the property, until the child turns 19. Local authorities must have regard to any guidance issued by the Secretary of State when deciding what length of tenancy to grant and a tenant may request a review of the landlord's decision as to the length of the fixed term. If a landlord tries to grant a lifetime tenancy or a tenancy shorter than 2 years or longer than the maximum permitted period, the tenancy defaults to a 5 year fixed term. Existing lifetime tenants must be given a further lifetime tenancy if they are required to move by the landlord and the landlord has discretion to grant a lifetime tenancy in other circumstances to be set out in regulations.

III L&T [106]

82. Security of tenure

[(A1) A fixed-term secure tenancy of a dwelling-house in England that is granted on or after the day on which paragraph 4 of Schedule 7 to the Housing and Planning Act 2016 comes fully into force cannot be brought to an end by the landlord except by—

(a) obtaining—

(i) an order of the court for the possession of the dwelling-house, and

(ii) the execution of the order, or

(b) obtaining a demotion order under section 82A.

(A2) A secure tenancy can be brought to an end by the landlord as mentioned in subsection (A1)(a) whether or not the tenancy contains terms for it to be brought to an end.]

(1) A secure tenancy which is either

(a) a weekly or other periodic tenancy, or

(b) a tenancy for a term certain *but* [, other than one to which subsection (A1) applies, that is] subject to termination by the landlord,

cannot be brought to an end by the landlord except [as] [mentioned in subsection (1A).

(1A) The tenancy may be brought to an end by the landlord—

(a) obtaining-

(i) an order of the court for the possession of the dwelling-house, and

(ii) the execution of the order,

(b) obtaining an order under subsection (3), or

(c) obtaining a demotion order under section 82A.

(2) In the case mentioned in subsection [(A1)(a) or] (1A)(a), the tenancy ends when the order is executed.

(3) Where a secure tenancy is a tenancy for a term certain but with a provision for re-entry or forfeiture, the court shall not order possession of the dwelling-house in pursuance of that provision, but in a case where the court would have made such an order it shall instead make an order terminating the tenancy on a date specified in the order and *section 86 (periodic tenancy arising on termination of fixed terms) shall apply* [section 86 or 86D shall apply].

(4) Section 146 of the Law of Property Act 1925 (restriction on and relief against forfeiture), except subsection (4) (vesting in under-lessee), and any other enactment or rule of law relating to forfeiture, shall apply in relation to proceedings for an order under subsection (3) of this section as if they were proceedings to enforce a right of re-entry or forfeiture.

Amendment *From a date to be appointed, sub-sections (A1) and (A2) and text in square brackets in ss (1) and (2) inserted, and text in italics deleted, by s 119 of the Housing and Planning Act 2016. Text in italics deleted and text in square brackets inserted in s 83(3) by s 118 of, and Schedule 7 to, the Housing and Planning Act 2016.*

III L&T [106.A1]

A secure tenancy may now be brought to an end by a demotion order under s 82A (see para **III L&T [106A]**).

III L&T [106.1]

Date tenancy comes to an end Before the amendments effected to subsections (1) and (2) by Schedule 11 to the Housing and Regeneration Act 2008 came into force, where a landlord obtained an order for possession the tenancy ended on the date on which the tenant was to give up possession in pursuance of the order. Where, therefore, an order for possession was suspended on the making of certain payments and there was default in making those payments, the tenancy ended on the date of the default: *Thompson v Elmbridge Borough Council* [1987] 1 WLR 1425, CA. A tenant who remains in possession thereafter does so as a 'tolerated trespasser'.

Section 82, as amended, solves the problem of the tolerated trespasser prospectively with effect from 20 May 2009. However, as the Supreme Court made clear in *Austin v Southwark London Borough Council* [2010] UKSC 28, [2010] 4 All ER 16, [2010] 3 WLR 144, the law as settled in Thompson (and acted on in thousands of cases by local authority landlords) remains unchanged (see also *Knowsley Housing Trust v White* [2008] UKHL 70, [2009] 1 AC 636, [2009] 2 All ER 829). As regards existing tolerated trespassers with effect from 20th May 2009, see Part 2 of Schedule 11 to the Housing and Regeneration Act 2008 (para **III L&T [345]**).

Once the secure tenancy has come to an end by an order under the Housing Act 1985 s 82 (3), a periodic tenancy arises by virtue of the Housing Act 1985 s 86 (see para **III L&T [111]**) and possession may be ordered in separate proceedings under the Housing Act 1985 s 84 (see para **III L&T [109]**), after service of the notices required by the Housing Act 1985 s 83 (see para **III L&T [107]**). The form of notice is regulated by the Secure Tenancies (Notices) Regulations 1987, SI 1987/755 (as amended by SI 1997/71 and SI 1997/377). As to the validity of such regulations see *Wansbeck District Council v Charlton* (1981) 42 P & CR 162, CA. For the text of the prescribed notice, see **BCCP O[151]**.

III L&T [106.2]

"Any other enactment" See, in particular the County Courts Act 1984 s 138 (see para **II CCA [133]**).

III L&T [106.3]

Termination by the tenant A secure tenancy may be terminated by a notice given by the tenant or, in the case of a joint tenancy, by one of them: *Greenwich London Borough Council v McGrady* (1983) 46 P & CR 223, CA; *Parsons v Parsons* [1983] 1 WLR 1390; *Hammersmith and Fulham London Borough Council v Monk* [1992] 1 AC 478, [1992] 1 All ER 1, HL. On the other hand, a notice by one of two joint tenants which does not comply with the Protection from Eviction Act 1977 s 5 (1) is ineffective to terminate the tenancy of the other joint tenant: *London Borough Council of Hounslow v Pilling* [1994] 1 All ER 432, [1993] 1 WLR 1242, CA. In contrast, it is open to a sole secure tenant to waive the benefit of section 5(1) and to agree with the landlord that a notice to quit shall be effective notwithstanding that it gives less than the four weeks' notice required: see *Hackney London Borough Council v Snowden* (2000) 33 HLR 554, CA where three days' notice by the tenant was held to be effective. An authority which acts on a defective notice by one tenant may be liable in damages to the other: *Osei-Bonsu v Wandsworth London Borough Council* [1999] 1 All ER 265, [1999] 1 WLR 1011, CA. For an example of the court finding surrender by operation of law on the facts see *Ealing Family Housing Association v McKenzie* [2003] EWCA Civ 1602, [2004] 1 P & CR D39, (2003) Times, 30 October.

Where the husband is the sole tenant and terminates the tenancy by notice, the wife who remains in occupation may be ordered out without a breach of Convention rights under articles 8(2) or 14: *Royal Borough of Kensington and Chelsea v O'Sullivan* [2003] EWCA Civ 371, [2003] HLR 877, (2003) Times, 27 March, CA. Similarly, where a tenancy in joint names is terminated by the departing wife leaving husband and child in occupation, the Council landlord is not contravening Art 8 by claiming possession: *Hounslow London Borough Council v Adjei* [2004] EWHC 207 (Ch), [2004] 2 All ER 636. See also *Sims v Dacorum Borough Council* [2014] 3 WLR 1600, [2015] 1 All ER 834, where the Supreme Court upheld the decision of the Court of Appeal that the rule in *Hammersmith and Fulham London Borough Council v Monk* (a substantive rule of property and contract law) is not incompatible with either Art 8 or Art 1 of the First Protocol.

It is doubtful whether Parliament intended a tenancy at will to be a secure tenancy, even where the conditions in ss 80 and 81 are satisfied, and once a tenancy at will is terminated the occupier's status is that of a trespasser: *Banjo v Brent London Borough Council* [2005] EWCA Civ 292, [2005] 13 EG CS 134.

LANDLORD & TENANT AND HOUSING

Where one of two joint tenants gives a notice to quit, following representations by the landlord that its effect would be simply to release that joint tenant from further liability, it has been held that the notice is nevertheless effective to terminate the tenancy vis-à-vis both joint tenants: *Dyer v Potter* [2011] EWCA Civ 1417, [2011] All ER (D) 06 (Dec).

III L&T [106.3A]

Status of former tenant who stays on after termination by the other tenant A former joint tenant who remains in occupation after termination of the tenancy by the other has a Convention right under Art 8 to respect for his home. However, Art 8 cannot be relied on to defeat proprietary or contractual rights to possession. Accordingly, a public authority landlord was entitled to claim possession; but an unfair exercise of the right may be capable of challenge by judicial review; see the majority decision in *Harrow London Borough Council v Qazi* [2003] UKHL 43, [2003] 4 All ER 461, [2003] 3 WLR 792, Times, 1 August. For the case law on the status of a "tolerated trespasser" see **III L&T [103.5]**. Note, however, the decision in *Kay v Lambeth London Borough Council* [2006] 2 AC 465, [2006] 2 WLR 570, [2006] 4 All ER 128 that, in so far as *Harrow London Borough Council v Qazi* decided that the enforcement of a right to possession in accordance with the domestic law of property could never be incompatible with the Art 8 of the Convention, that had to be modified in the light of *Connors v United Kingdom* (66746/01) [2005] 40 EHRR 9; moreover, that it was open to an occupier to raise an Art 8 defence to possession proceedings in the county court rather than by way of judicial review (a point subsequently emphasised in *Manchester City Council v Pinnock* [2010] 3 WLR 1441 (see para **III L&T [103.6]**)).

Article 8 may be engaged where trespassers have set up their home on private land and the court, as a public body, must apply proportionality when dealing with a claim for possession. But the exercise of discretion would seem to be subject to the provisions of s 89 of the Housing Act 1980: see judgment of Sir Alan Ward in *Malik v Fassenfelt (since dec'd)* [2013] EWCA Civ 798, [2013] All ER (D) 44 (Jul), but note that both Toulson and Lloyd LLJ declined to hold that Article 8 was engaged as against a private landowner (the point not having been argued). The Court of Appeal has since reiterated that Article 8 considerations arise only in the case of public authority landlords: *McDonald (by her litigation friend) v McDonald (acting by the joint receivers)* [2014] EWCA Civ 1049, [2014] 2 P & CR 377, [2014] HLR 643. See also *McDonald v McDonald* [2016] UKSC 28, where the Supreme Court (upholding the decision of the Court of Appeal) held that, although there were some ECtHR authorities which supported the notion that Art 8 was engaged as against a private landlord, there was no support for the proposition that the judge could have been required to consider the proportionality of the order which he would have made under the 1980 and 1988 Housing Acts.

III L&T [106.4]

Husband and wife Where husband and wife are joint tenants, a notice to quit given by one is not a "disposition" which the other may have set aside under the Matrimonial Causes Act 1973 s 37: *Newton Housing Trust v Alsulaimen* [1999] 1 AC 313, [1998] 4 All ER 1, HL applied in *Bater v Bater* [1999] 4 All ER 944, CA where it was also held that a wife's notice was valid even though its effect was to deprive the landlord of the right to buy; the court observed that the husband might prevent the situation arising by applying for an injunction.

In *Harrow London Borough Council v Johnstone* [1997] 1 All ER 929, [1997] 1 WLR 459, HL the House of Lords, reversing the Court of Appeal, held a wife's notice to be valid, although given at a time when she was enjoined not to exclude her husband from the home.

Where a housing authority urges a wife who has left jointly tenanted property to give them a notice to quit for the purpose of enabling them to evict the husband, their action may be held to have interfered with the husband's Article 8 right to respect for his home and family life: *McCann v UK (Application No 19009/04)* (2008) Times, 23 May, ECtHR, [2008] All ER (D) 146 (May).

III L&T [106.5]

Release of joint interest A secure tenancy cannot be assigned: s 91(1) Housing Act 1985. In *Burton v Camden London Borough Council* [2000] 2 AC 399, [2000] 1 All ER 943, HL, one of two joint tenants (in an attempt to circumvent the effect of s 91(1)) executed a deed of release to the other of his joint interest. The House of Lords (reversing the Court of Appeal) held that the intention was to change the identity of the tenant, that the transaction entered into had to be regarded as an assignment and was thus prohibited.

III L&T [106.6]

Non-occupation A tenancy ceases to be a secure tenancy when the tenant goes out of occupation, because the tenant condition in the Housing Act 1985 s 81 is no longer satisfied: *R v Croydon London Borough Council, ex p Toth* (1986) 18 HLR 493. But a secure tenancy may be reinstated by return: *Hussey v Camden London Borough Council* (1994) 27 HLR 5, CA.

III L&T [106.7]

Surrender A secure tenancy may be surrendered by operation of law where the wife tenant, being out of possession, gives notice that she no longer wants it and the council is unwilling to recognise the husband as a new tenant: *Brent London Borough Council v Sharma* (1992) 25 HLR 257, [1992] NPC 102, CA. However, a husband who leaves and hands over the keys under a court order is not necessarily surrendering the tenancy: *Osie-Bonsu v Wandsworth London Borough Council* [1999] 1 All ER 265, [1999] 1 WLR 1011, CA. For a further example of surrender by operation of law by a departing spouse tenant see *Sanctuary Housing Association v Campbell* [1999] 3 All ER 460, [1999] 1 WLR 1279, CA. The posting of the keys to the landlord is not, in itself, a surrender. It is an offer of surrender by the tenant which is effective if, but only if, the landlord accepts: *Laine v Cadwallader* (2000) 80 P & CR D44, CA.

In *Ealing Family Housing Association v McKenzie* [2003] EWCA Civ 1602, [2004] 1 P & CR D39 it was held that a tenancy had been terminated by surrender when a departing tenant gave the landlord a notice to quit which was not legally valid but on which the landlord acted by transferring her rent account to new premises.

III L&T [106.8]

Right to buy: competing claims Where the tenant has a right to buy, but the local authority has brought possession proceedings under s 82, the court should decide between the competing claims by conducting a balancing exercise: *Basildon District Council v Wahlen* [2006] EWCA Civ 326, [2006] 1 WLR 2744, (2006) Times, 17 April.

ORDERS FOR POSSESSION AND EXPIRY OF TERM ETC

III L&T [106A]

82A. Demotion because of anti-social behaviour

(1) This section applies to a secure tenancy if the landlord is—

(a) a local housing authority;

(b) a housing action trust;

(ba) a private registered provider of social housing;

(c) a registered social landlord.

(2) The landlord may apply to the county court for a demotion order.

(3) A demotion order has the following effect—

(a) the secure tenancy is terminated with effect from the date specified in the order;

(b) if the tenant remains in occupation of the dwelling-house after that date a demoted tenancy is created with effect from that date;

(c) it is a term of the demoted tenancy that any arrears of rent payable at the termination of the secure tenancy become payable under the demoted tenancy;

(d) it is also a term of the demoted tenancy that any rent paid in advance or overpaid at the termination of the secure tenancy is credited to the tenant's liability to pay rent under the demoted tenancy.

(4) The court must not make a demotion order unless it is satisfied—

(a) that the tenant or a person residing in or visiting the dwelling-house has engaged or has threatened to engage in—

(i) conduct that is capable of causing nuisance or annoyance to some person (who need not be a particular identified person) and that directly or indirectly relates to or affects the landlord's housing management functions, or

(ii) conduct that consists of or involves using housing accommodation owned or managed by the landlord for an unlawful purpose, and

(b) that it is reasonable to make the order.

[(4A) The court may not make a demotion order in relation to a secure tenancy of a dwelling-house in England if—

(a) the landlord is a local housing authority or housing action trust, and

(b) the term has less than 1 year and 9 months left to run.

(4B) But subsection (4A) does not apply to a tenancy to which an exception in section 86A(2) or (3) applies.]

(5) Each of the following has effect in respect of a demoted tenancy at the time it is created by virtue of an order under this section as it has effect in relation to the secure tenancy at the time it is terminated by virtue of the order—

(a) the parties to the tenancy;

(b) *the period of the tenancy;* [the period or term of the tenancy (but see subsection (6));]

(c) the amount of the rent;

(d) the dates on which the rent is payable.

(6) *Subsection (5)(b) does not apply if the secure tenancy was for a fixed term and in such a case the demoted tenancy is a weekly periodic tenancy.* [Subsection (5)(b) does not apply if—

(a) the secure tenancy was for a fixed term and was an old-style secure tenancy or a flexible tenancy, or

(b) the secure tenancy was for a fixed term and was a tenancy of a dwelling-house in Wales,

and in such a case the demoted tenancy is a weekly periodic tenancy.]

(7) If the landlord of the demoted tenancy serves on the tenant a statement of any other express terms of the secure tenancy which are to apply to the demoted tenancy such terms are also terms of the demoted tenancy.

(7A) In subsection (4)(a)(ii) "housing accommodation" includes—

(a) flats, lodging-houses and hostels;

(b) any yard, garden, outhouses and appurtenances belonging to the accommodation or usually enjoyed with it;

(c) any common areas used in connection with the accommodation.

(8) For the purposes of this section a demoted tenancy is—

(a) a tenancy to which section 143A of the Housing Act 1996 applies if the landlord of the secure tenancy is a local housing authority or a housing action trust;

(b) a tenancy to which section 20B of the Housing Act 1988 applies if the landlord of the secure tenancy is a private registered provider of social housing or a registered social landlord.

Amendment *From a date to be appointed text in square brackets inserted, and text in italics deleted, by s 118 of, and Schedule 7 to, the Housing and Planning Act 2016.*

III L&T [106A.1]

Section 82A provides that a local authority, a housing action trust or a registered social landlord can apply for a 'demotion order' which will end the secure tenancy on a specified date. If the tenant remains in occupation, a new demoted tenancy will begin on the same date. The court may only make the order if the tenant or another resident of or a visitor to the tenant's home has behaved in a way which is capable of causing nuisance or annoyance, or if such person has used the premises for illegal purposes. The court must also be satisfied that it is reasonable to make the order.

Section 82A(8) defines what is meant by a demoted tenancy. Any rent owed or overpaid on the tenant's rent account under the secure tenancy will be transferred across to the demoted tenancy. Section 82A(5) deals with certain basic terms of the demoted tenancy at the point at which it is created.

CPR 65.11 to 65.20 (see para **CPR 65**) and CPR PD 65 paras 5.1 to 9.3 (see para **CPR PD 65**) apply. Claim form N6 and particulars of claim N122 must be used. For the prescribed contents of the particulars of claim, see CPR PD 65 para 7.1. The defence must be in form N11D. Where a demotion order is claimed in the alternative to a possession order, the claimant must use the Part 55 procedure (see CPR 65.12); Forms N5 and N119 have been updated to incorporate demotion claims.

III L&T [106A.2]

Demotion orders and hearsay evidence A demotion order has been held to be a reasonable way of balancing the parents' rights to a secure home with the public interest in preventing anti-social behaviour by their children: *Washington Housing Company Ltd v Morson* [2005] EWHC 3407 (Ch), 25 October 2005, Patten J. It was held in the same case that, although much of the evidence of anti-social behaviour was hearsay, the trial judge, when considering the factors in s 4(2) of the Civil Evidence Act 1995, at **CPR 33[2]**, was entitled to weigh up the case as a whole, including the admitted background and to accept the veracity of the hearsay.

III L&T [106A.3]

Human rights The Demoted Tenancies (Review of Decisions) (England) Regulations 2004, SI 2004/1679 have been held to comply with Article 6 of the Convention: *R (Gilboy) v Liverpool City Council* [2008] EWCA Civ 751, [2008] 4 All ER 127 in which the Court concluded that it was bound by the conclusions of the Court of Appeal in *R (on the application of McLellan) v Bracknell Forest District Council* [2002] QB 1129 when rejecting a similar challenge to the introductory tenancies scheme. See also *Manchester City Council v Pinnock* [2010] UKSC 45, [2010] 3 WLR 1441. In *Corby Borough Council v Scott; West Kent Housing Association Ltd v Haycraft* [2012] EWCA Civ 276, [2012] LGR 493, [2012] 21 Estates Gazette 100 the Court of Appeal held that the effect of the reasoning in *Pinnock* seemed to be that, at least in relation to demoted and introductory tenancies, it will only be in 'very highly exceptional cases' that it will be appropriate for the court to consider a proportionality argument, although exceptionality is an outcome and not a guide. While holding that it was not appropriate for the Court of Appeal to give firm guidance on the procedure to be adopted in possession cases where the tenant raises Article 8, the court felt it was right to emphasise the desirability of a judge considering at an early stage whether the tenant had an arguable case on Article 8 proportionality, before the issue was ordered to be heard. If it was a case that could not succeed, then it should not be allowed to take up further court time and to delay the landlord's right to possession.

III L&T [107]

83. Proceedings for possession or termination: [general] notice requirements

[(A1) This section applies in relation to proceedings for an order mentioned in section *82(1A)* [82(A1) or (1A)] other than—

(a) proceedings for possession of a dwelling-house under section 84A (absolute ground for possession for anti-social behaviour), including proceedings where possession is also sought on one or more of the grounds set out in Schedule 2, or

(b) *proceedings for possession of a dwelling-house under section 107D (recovery of possession on expiry of flexible tenancy).* [proceedings for possession of a dwelling-house under section 86E (recovery of possession on expiry of certain English secure tenancies)]

(1) The court shall not entertain proceedings to which this section applies unless

(a) the landlord has served a notice on the tenant complying with the provisions of this section, or

(b) the court considers it just and equitable to dispense with the requirement of such a notice.

(2) A notice under this section shall

(a) be in a form prescribed by regulations made by the Secretary of State,

(b) specify the ground on which the court will be asked to make the order] and

(c) give particulars of that ground.

(3) Where the tenancy is a periodic tenancy and the ground or one of the grounds specified in the notice is Ground 2 in Schedule 2 (nuisance or other anti-social behaviour), the notice

(a) shall also

(i) state that proceedings for the possession of the dwelling-house may be begun immediately, and

(ii) specify the date sought by the landlord as the date on which the tenant is to give up possession of the dwelling-house, and

(b) ceases to be in force twelve months after the date so specified.

(4) Where the tenancy is a periodic tenancy and Ground 2 in Schedule 2 is not specified in the notice, the notice

(a) shall also specify the date after which proceedings for the possession of the dwelling-house may be begun, and

(b) ceases to be in force twelve months after the date so specified.

(4A) If the proceedings are for a demotion order under section 82A the notice

(a) must specify the date after which the proceedings may be begun;

(b) ceases to be in force twelve months after the date so specified.

(5) The date specified in accordance with subsection (3), (4) or (4A) must not be earlier than the date on which the tenancy could, apart from this Part, be brought to an end by notice to quit given by the landlord on the same date as the notice under this section.

(6) Where a notice under this section is served with respect to a secure tenancy for a term certain, it has effect also with respect to any periodic tenancy arising on the termination of that tenancy by virtue of section 86; and subsections (3) and (4) of this section do not apply to the notice.

(7) Regulations under this section shall be made by statutory instrument and may make different provision with respect to different cases or descriptions of case, including different provision for different areas.

Amendment *From a date to be appointed text in square brackets in s 83(A1) is inserted, and text in italics deleted, by s 119 of the Housing and Planning Act 2016; new s 83(A1)(b) is inserted, from a date to be appointed, by s 118 of, and Schedule 7 to, the Housing and Planning Act 2016. Note that, by virtue of paragraph 33 of Schedule 7, the amendment to s 83 (replacing references to proceedings for possession under section 107D) does not apply in relation to a flexible tenancy the term of which ends within the period of 9 months beginning with the day on which paragraph 4 of Schedule 7 comes into force.*

III L&T [107.1]

Form of Notice The form of notice of proceedings under s 83 is prescribed by The Secure Tenancies (Notices) (Amendment) (England) Regulations 2004 SI 2004/1627.

III L&T [107A]

83ZA. Notice requirements in relation to proceedings for possession on absolute ground for anti-social behaviour

(1) This section applies in relation to proceedings for possession of a dwelling-house under section 84A (absolute ground for possession for anti-social behaviour), including proceedings where possession is also sought on one or more of the grounds set out in Schedule 2.

(2) The court must not entertain the proceedings unless the landlord has served on the tenant a notice under this section.

(3) The notice must—

(a) state that the court will be asked to make an order under section 84A for the possession of the dwelling-house,

(b) set out the reasons for the landlord's decision to apply for the order (including the condition or conditions in section 84A on which the landlord proposes to rely), and

(c) inform the tenant of any right that the tenant may have under section 85ZA to request a review of the landlord's decision and of the time within which the request must be made.

(4) In a case where possession is also sought on one or more of the grounds set out in Schedule 2, the notice must also—

(a) specify the ground on which the court will be asked to make the order, and

(b) give particulars of that ground.

(5) A notice which states that the landlord proposes to rely upon condition 1, 3 or 5 in section 84A—

(a) must also state the conviction on which the landlord proposes to rely, and

(b) must be served on the tenant within—

(i) the period of 12 months beginning with the day of the conviction, or

(ii) if there is an appeal against the conviction, the period of 12 months beginning with the day on which the appeal is finally determined or abandoned.

(6) A notice which states that the landlord proposes to rely upon condition 2 in section 84A—

(a) must also state the finding on which the landlord proposes to rely, and

(b) must be served on the tenant within—

(i) the period of 12 months beginning with the day on which the court has made the finding, or

(ii) if there is an appeal against the finding, the period of 12 months beginning with the day on which the appeal is finally determined, abandoned or withdrawn.

(7) A notice which states that the landlord proposes to rely upon condition 4 in section 84A—

(a) must also state the closure order concerned, and

(b) must be served on the tenant within—

(i) the period of 3 months beginning with the day on which the closure order was made, or

(ii) if there is an appeal against the making of the order, the period of 3 months beginning with the day on which the appeal is finally determined, abandoned or withdrawn.

(8) A notice under this section must also inform the tenant that, if the tenant needs help or advice about the notice and what to do about it, the tenant should take it immediately to a Citizens' Advice Bureau, a housing aid centre, a law centre or a solicitor.

(9) The notice—

(a) must also specify the date after which proceedings for the possession of the dwelling-house may be begun, and

(b) ceases to be in force 12 months after the date so specified.

(10) The date specified in accordance with subsection (9)(a) must not be earlier than—

(a) in the case of a periodic tenancy, the date on which the tenancy could, apart from this Part, be brought to an end by notice to quit given by the landlord on the same day as the notice under this section;

(b) in the case of a secure tenancy for a term certain, one month after the date of the service of the notice.

(11) Where a notice under this section is served with respect to a secure tenancy for a term certain, it has effect also with respect to any periodic tenancy arising on the termination of that tenancy by virtue of section 86; and subsection (10)(a) does not apply to the notice.

III L&T [108]

83A. Additional requirements in relation to certain proceedings for possession

(1) Where a notice under section 83 has been served on a tenant containing the information mentioned in subsection (3) (a) of that section, the court shall not entertain proceedings for the possession of the dwelling-house unless they are begun at a time when the notice is still in force.

LANDLORD & TENANT AND HOUSING

(2) Where

(a) a notice under section 83 or 83ZA has been served on a tenant, and

(b) a date after which proceedings may be begun has been specified in the notice in accordance with section 83(4)(a) or section 83ZA(9)(a),

the court shall not entertain proceedings for the possession of the dwelling-house unless they are begun after the date so specified and at a time when the notice is still in force.

(3) Where

(a) the ground or one of the grounds specified in a notice under section 83 or 83ZA is Ground 2A in Schedule 2 (domestic violence), and

(b) the partner who has left the dwelling-house as mentioned in that ground is not a tenant of the dwelling-house,

the court shall not entertain proceedings for the possession of the dwelling-house unless it is satisfied that the landlord has served a copy of the notice on the partner who has left or has taken all reasonable steps to serve a copy of the notice on that partner.

This subsection has effect subject to subsection (5).

(4) Where

(a) Ground 2A in Schedule 2 is added to a notice under section 83 or 83ZA with the leave of the court after proceedings for possession are begun, and

(b) the partner who has left the dwelling-house as mentioned in that ground is not a party to the proceedings,

the court shall not continue to entertain the proceedings unless it is satisfied that the landlord has served a notice under subsection (6) on the partner who has left or has taken all reasonable steps to serve a notice on that partner.

This subsection has effect subject to subsection (5).

(5) Where subsection (3) or (4) applies and Ground 2 in Schedule 2 (nuisance or other anti-social behaviour) is also specified in a notice under section 83 or a notice is served under section 83ZA, the court may dispense with the requirements as to service in relation to the partner who has left the dwelling-house if it considers it just and equitable to do so.

(6) A notice under this subsection shall

(a) state that proceedings for the possession of the dwelling-house have begun,

(b) specify the ground or grounds on which possession is being sought, and

(c) give particulars of the ground or grounds.

NOTES TO SECTIONS 83 AND 83A

III L&T [108.A1]

Changes effected by the Anti-Social Behaviour Act 2003 With effect from 30 June 2004, s 83 of the Housing Act 1985 was amended to ensure that landlords are required to serve notice on secure tenants before issuing demotion proceedings (as defined in s 82A(8)): see the Anti-social Behaviour Act 2003 (Commencement No 3 and Savings) Order 2004, SI 2004/1502. For the form and content of the notice for possession of demoted tenancies see the Secure Tenancies (Notices) (Amendment) (England) Regulations 2004 SI 2004/1627; see also the Demoted Tenancies (Review of Decisions) (England) Regulations 2004, SI 2004/1679. In Wales the form of notice is prescribed by SI 2005/1226 and the review procedure is prescribed by SI 2005/1228. The notice of proceedings required by s 6A of the Housing Act 1988 is not prescribed.

III L&T [108.1]

Service Service by any method which does not come to the knowledge of the person to be served (eg by leaving the notice at the last known address) is ineffective unless provided for in the agreement: *Wandsworth London Borough v Atwell* [1995] EGCS 68, CA. Service of a notice to quit at the last known address is not within the scope of Law of Property Act 1925 s 196, nor the Local Government Act 1972 s 233: *Enfield London Borough Council v Devonish* (1996) 74 P & CR 288, 29 HLR 691, CA. However, service at the last known address may be valid if provision for such service is made in the agreement: *Chesterfield Borough Council v Crossley* (24 April 1998, reported in *Legal Action* (1998) June at p 10). Where service at the last known address is provided for, service by posting the notice may be valid although the intended recipient does not know of it and the notice is returned to the sender undelivered: *Blunden v Frogmore Investments Ltd* [2002] EWCA Civ 573, [2003] 2 P & CR 84, [2002] 29 EG 153.

III L&T [108.2]

Regulations See the Secure Tenancies (Notices) Regulations 1987, SI 1987/755 (as amended by SI 1997/71 and SI 1997/377). The text of the prescribed form in which the notice must appear is set out at **BCCP O[151]** and it should be used for proceedings under the old Housing Act 1985 s 83.

III L&T [108.3]

Proceedings Possession claims must be started by means of claim form N5. Particulars of claim must be filed and served with the claim form (see para **CPR 55.4**). The contents of the particulars of claim must comply with the requirements of **CPR 16** and the Practice Direction to CPR Pt 55 para 2.1 (see para **CPR PD 55**). For particulars of claim in claims for possession under the Housing Act 1985, see **BCCP O[152]–BCCP O[154]**. Where the possession claim relates to residential property and includes a claim for non-payment of rent, the particulars of claim must also comply with CPR Pt 55 Practice Direction para 2.3 (para **CPR PD 55**); the particulars of claim in Form N119 should therefore be used on such claims. The defence to a general possession claim should be in Form N11 and the defence to a claim for possession for residential premises which includes a claim for non-payment of rent should be in Form N11R. If the defendant does not file a defence within 14 days of service of the particulars of claim, he may take part in the hearing but the court will take into account his failure when deciding costs: para **CPR 55.7**. A table of the appropriate forms in possession claims can be found at **BCCP O[12]**; the forms can also be found in the Forms supplement, the FORMS section of your CD-ROM and at **BCCP O[80]** onwards.

LANDLORD & TENANT AND HOUSING

With effect from 2 October 2006, a social landlord (such as a local authority, a Registered Social Landlord and a Housing Action Trust) which brings a residential possession claim based solely on claims for rent arrears should comply with the Pre-Action Protocol for Possession Claims Based on Rent Arrears. Courts will take into account whether the Protocol has been followed when considering what orders to make. The Protocol does not apply to claims in respect of long leases or to claims for possession where there is no security of tenure. If, after complying with the initial requirements of the Protocol, a social landlord decides to resort to court proceedings, it should take care to comply with paragraphs 12 and 13. If either the landlord or the tenant fails unreasonably to comply with the Protocol they may face sanctions (see paragraphs 14 and 15).

III L&T [108.4]

Particulars of the grounds A notice specifying arrears of rent as a ground will be invalid if it does not give particulars of the amount: *Torridge District Council v Jones* (1985) 18 HLR 107, [1985] 2 EGLR 54, CA. On the other hand a notice on the ground of arrears of rent meets the requirements of the Regulations and the Housing Act 1985 s 83 (2)(c) if it indicates the period of indebtedness and how the sum is to be calculated (*Marath v MacGillivray* (1996) 28 HLR 484, [1996] NPC 11, CA) or if it particularises the indebtedness, even though arrears of rent and rates are described comprehensively as "rent": *Dudley Metropolitan Borough Council v Bailey* (1990) 22 HLR 424, [1991] 1 EGLR 53, CA. The county court decision in *Waltham Forest London Borough Council v England*, that the general words "major refurbishment scheme" did not give adequate particulars for the purposes of Ground 10, is reported in *Legal Action* (1994) March at p 11.

III L&T [108.5]

Just and equitable to dispense The power, under s 83(1)(b), to dispense with the requirements is similar to that included in the Rent Act 1977, Sch 15, Case 11 (see para **III L&T [83]**) and in the Housing Act 1988 s 8 (see para **III L&T [217]**). The case law noted under those provisions may be relevant to the exercise of the power under the Housing Act 1985 s 83(1)(b).

III L&T [108.6]

Landlord's failure to provide address Landlords may not rely on arrears of rent where they have failed to provide an address in breach of the Landlord and Tenant Act 1987 s 48 (see para **III L&T [204]**). But they may rely on past arrears once the requirements of the section have been met; and a subsequent notice is not necessarily invalidated by referring to the past arrears as due at a time when the landlords were still in breach: *Lindsey Trading Properties Inc v Dallhold Estates (UK) Pty Ltd* (1993) 70 P & CR 332, CA.

III L&T [108.7]

Human rights In *R (on the application of Gilboy) v Liverpool CC* [2007] EWHC 2335 (Admin), [2007] LGR 837 it was held that there is no material distinction between the legislation relating to introductory tenancies (as to which, see para **III L&T [280.1A]** and see also *R (on the application of McLellan) v Bracknell Forest District Council* [2001] EWCA Civ 1510, [2002] QB 1129, [2002] 1 All ER 899) and the legislation relating to demoted tenancies. The Demoted Tenancies (Review of Decisions) (England) Regulations 2004, SI 2004/1679 were therefore held to be compatible with Article 6 of the Convention.

III L&T [109]

84. Grounds and orders for possession

(1) The court shall not make an order for the possession of a dwelling-house let under a secure tenancy except on one or more of the grounds set out in Schedule 2 or in accordance with section 84A (absolute ground for possession for anti-social behaviour) or *section 107D (recovery of possession on expiry of flexible tenancy)* [section 86E (recovery of possession on expiry of certain English secure tenancies)].

(2) The court shall not make an order for possession

(a) on the grounds set out in Part I of Schedule 2 (grounds 1 to 8), unless it considers it reasonable to make the order,

(b) on the grounds set out in Part II of that Schedule (grounds 9 to 11), unless it is satisfied that suitable accommodation will be available for the tenant when the order takes effect,

(c) on the grounds set out on Part III of that Schedule (grounds 12 to 16), unless it both considers it reasonable to make the order and is satisfied that suitable accommodation will be available for the tenant when the order takes effect;

and Part IV of that Schedule has effect for determining whether suitable accommodation will be available for a tenant.

(3) Where a notice under section 83 or 83ZA has been served on the tenant, the court shall not make an order on any of the grounds mentioned in subsection (2) unless the ground is specified in the notice; but the grounds so specified may be altered or added to with the leave of the court.

(4) Where a date is specified in a notice under section 83 in accordance with subsection (3) of that section, the court shall not make an order which requires the tenant to give up possession of the dwelling-house in question before the date so specified.

Amendment *Text in italics is deleted and text in square brackets is inserted in s 84(1), from a date to be appointed, by s 118 of, and Schedule 7 to, the Housing and Planning Act 2016. Note that, by virtue of paragraph 33 of Schedule 7, the amendment to s 84 (replacing references to proceedings for possession under section 107D) does not apply in relation to a flexible tenancy the term of which ends within the period of 9 months beginning with the day on which paragraph 4 of Schedule 7 comes into force.*

III L&T [109.1]

Consent order In order to justify an order being made without an investigation of the facts, there must be an express admission of facts which, if proved, would provide grounds for an order: *Wandsworth London Borough Council v Fadayomi* [1987] 3 All ER 474, [1987] 1 WLR 1473, CA. A similar point emerges in *Hounslow London Borough Council v McBride* (1998) 31 HLR 143. See too the notes to the Rent Act 1977 s 98 (see para **III L&T [71.5]**) and the notes to the Housing Act 1988 s 7 (see para **III L&T [216.2A]**). There may, however, be a sufficient investigation to justify an order by consent where the case is settled after the tenant has given evidence: *R v Worthing Borough Council, ex p Bruce* (1991) 24 HLR 261, [1992] COD 42; on appeal [1994] 1 EGLR 116, [1994] 24 EG 149, CA.

III L&T [109.1A]

Restrictions on right of appeal As regards a decision to make a possession order on grounds in Part I of Schedule 2, an appeal on a question of fact is barred by s 77(6)(e) of the County Courts Act 1984: see *London Borough of Croydon v Crawford* [2010] EWCA Civ 618 where a possession order on the ground of nuisance and annoyance was upheld although based on hearsay evidence.

III L&T [109.2]

The court considers it reasonable The same words are used in the Rent Act 1977 s 98(1) (see para **III L&T [71]**). In *Enfield Borough Council v French* (1984) 49 P & CR 223, CA, the Court of Appeal upheld a judge's finding that it was reasonable for a local authority to offer alternative accommodation to a tenant who was a bachelor where their policy was to offer two-bedroomed accommodation, such as his, to families with a child, even though certain of the tenant's needs (eg regarding a garden) would not be met. The test of reasonableness must be applied to the making of the proposed order for possession not aspects of the local authority's planning policy eg in relation to the parking of caravans: *Barking and Dagenham London Borough Council v Hyatt and Hyatt* (1991) 24 HLR 406, CA. It is only in a very special case that a court may properly refuse to order possession in a case where the tenant insists on breaking the conditions eg that dogs may not be kept: *Sheffield City Council v Jepson* (1993) 25 HLR 299, CA; *Green v Sheffield City Council* (1993) 26 HLR 349, CA. In a case of continuing nuisance, which may take the form of abusive language, it is unreasonable to refuse an order for possession: *Woking Borough Council v Bystram* [1993] EGCS 208, [1994] CLY 2297, CA. The unavailability of alternative accommodation is not a sufficient ground for refusing an order based on nuisance: *Darlington Borough Council v Sterling* (1997) 29 HLR 309, CA. Similarly, using the premises for illegal drug supply justifies an order for possession, regardless of whether the evicted person may be treated as intentionally homeless: *Bristol City Council v Mousah* (1996) 30 HLR 32, CA. Also where a tenancy has been obtained by fraud (Ground 5) the Court of Appeal will be slow to interfere with the trial judge's decision that it is reasonable to make the order: *Rushcliffe Borough Council v Watson* (1991) 24 HLR 124. But it may do so if the court has taken into account an irrelevant consideration, eg that the evicted tenant may be categorised as intentionally homeless: *Shrewsbury and Atcham Borough Council v Evans* (1997) 30 HLR 123, CA. Absence of personal fault on the part of the tenant may be a relevant consideration when the court considers whether it would be reasonable to make a possession order and whether to suspend the order: *Portsmouth City Council v Bryant* (2000) 32 HLR 906, CA. However, the fact that a tenant with a bad record of nuisance and annoyance moderated his behaviour after the start of proceedings does not make it unreasonable for possession to be ordered without a suspension: *Barnet London Borough Council v Lincoln* [2001] EWCA Civ 823. When deciding whether it is reasonable to order possession under Ground 2 (nuisance, annoyance or conviction of an offence), it is wrong for the court to consider the availability of other remedies such as an injunction to restrain anti-social behaviour; see *Newcastle City Council v Morrison* (2000) 32 HLR 891, CA.

Where the tenant is unable to control a young offender or to eject him from the family home the fact that that an anti-social behaviour order has been made against him does not prevent the court from making an outright order for possession on the ground of nuisance, although it may be appropriate, in the circumstances, to suspend the order for possession or to make enforcement subject to the grant, on notice of application, of permission to enforce: *Knowsley Housing Trust v McMullen* [2006] EWCA Civ 589, (2006) Times, 22 May, CA.

III L&T [109.2A]

Eviction of a disabled person In *Manchester City Council v Romano* [2004] EWCA Civ 834, [2004] 4 All ER 21 extensive guidance is given as to the approach the court should take when the defendant asserts that the eviction is unlawful because it discriminates on the ground of disability and where the claimants seek to justify the eviction on grounds within s 24(2) of the Disability Discrimination Act 1995. The issues are best considered in the context of whether it would be reasonable to make an order for possession. The court must weigh the disability discrimination against the countervailing interest of the social landlord in obtaining possession. For tenants to succeed they must show some considerable hardship which they cannot fairly be asked to bear. The question whether a defence of disability discrimination is seriously arguable can be decided summarily in accordance with CPR 55.8 without a full trial: *Akerman-Livingstone v Aster Communities Ltd (formerly Flourish Homes Ltd)* [2014] EWCA Civ 1081, [2014] 1 WLR 3980, [2014] HLR 659 (a decision on the applicability of s 15 of the Equality Act 2010).

A possession order may be unlawful on the ground that it discriminates against a person with a disability even where that person has no security of tenure (for example under s 93 of the Housing Act 1985 – sub-letting without consent) and the court would otherwise have no discretion but to make an order for possession: *Lewisham London Borough Council v Malcolm* [2007] EWCA Civ 763, (2007) Times 28 August, CA. However the House of Lords concluded that the possession order was because of a gross breach of the tenancy (subletting without consent and moving out) and that the making of the possession order was not for a reason which related to the tenant's disability: *Lewisham London Borough Council v Malcolm* [2008] UKHL 43, [2008] 1 AC 1399, [2008] 4 All ER 525.

III L&T [109.2B]

Duties of public authorities when carrying out their functions The terms of s 149 of the Equality Act 2010 apply to the carrying out of any functions of a public authority and impose upon the public authority the public sector equality duty ('PSED'). The section has been held to apply to a housing authority in connection with the taking of possession proceedings and also in the discharge of its duties to the disabled under Part 7 of the Housing Act 1996: *Barnsley Metropolitan Borough Council v Norton* (2011) Times, 8 September, CA.

However, in *Forward v Aldwyck Housing Group Ltd* [2019] EWHC 24 (QB) a possession order made in favour of a housing association on the basis of the tenant's anti-social behaviour was upheld on appeal where, although the trial judge had failed properly to consider matters under s 149 when making the order, she had been entitled to find that the order was a proportionate means of achieving a legitimate aim.

The Court of Appeal has indicated, in *Powell v Dacorum Borough Council* [2019] EWCA Civ 23 that previous judgments on the application and working of the PSED have to be taken in their context; that, while the PSED is of universal application to the functions of public authorities, its application will differ from case to case, depending on the function being exercised and the facts of the case.

III L&T [109.3]

Arrears of rent With effect from 2 October 2006, a social landlord which brings a residential possession claim based solely on claims for rent arrears should comply with the Pre-Action Protocol for Possession Claims Based on Rent Arrears. Courts will take into account whether the Protocol has been followed when considering what orders to make.

It may well be reasonable to refuse an order where the admitted arrears are being steadily reduced and the current rent paid, albeit by direct payments of social security to the landlord: *Woodspring District Council v Taylor* (1982) 4 HLR 95, 133 NLJ 556, CA. See too *Second WRVS Housing Society Ltd v Blair* (1986) 19 HLR 104, CA. Conversely, where the tenant has withheld rent over a long period and claimed damages for non-repair, but has failed in the claim for damages and made no proposals for paying off the arrears, an order for possession may well be reasonable: *Haringey London Borough Council v Stewart* (1991) 23 HLR 557, [1991] 2 EGLR 252, CA. Where a claim based on rent arrears is resisted on the ground that the tenant had been wrongfully denied housing benefit, the judge does not have jurisdiction to overrule or set aside a decision by the appropriate tribunal that the tenant was not entitled: *Waltham Forest London Borough Council v Roberts* [2004] EWCA Civ 940, (2004) 148 Sol Jo LB 910.

III L&T [109.4]

Ultra vires A tenant who disputes the arrears on the ground that increases were ultra vires may raise the issue as a defence to county court proceedings for possession and is not bound to raise it by proceedings in the High Court for judicial review: *Wandsworth London Borough Council v Winder* [1985] AC 461, [1984] 3 All ER 83, CA, distinguishing *O'Reilly v Mackman* [1983] 2 AC 237, [1982] 3 All ER 1124, HL. Indeed the issue may be raised as a defence in the county court where proceedings for judicial review are in prospect: *R v Crown Court at Oxford, ex p Smith* (1989) 154 JP 422, 154 LGR 458. On the other hand, the validity of a local authority's decision to take proceedings for possession may not be challenged in those proceedings, but only by application to the High Court for judicial review; and an adjournment for the purpose ought not necessarily to be granted: *Waverley Borough Council v Hilden* [1988] 1 All ER 807, [1988] 1 WLR 246; *Avon County Council v Buscott* [1988] QB 656, [1988] 1 All ER 841, CA. The Court of Appeal has upheld the dismissal of a housing authority's proceedings for possession where the decision not to offer the deceased husband's tenancy to the estranged widow was flawed: *Leicester City Council v Shearer* [2013] EWCA Civ 1467, [2014] HLR 100.

III L&T [109.5]

Alterations and additions The power to allow an alteration or addition to the grounds includes the power to allow an alteration or addition to the particulars: *Camden London Borough Council v Oppong* (1996) 28 HLR 701, Times, 13 March, CA.

III L&T [109.6]

Forms and precedents Possession claims must be started by means of claim form N5. Particulars of claim must be filed and served with the claim form (see para **CPR 55.4**). The contents of the particulars of claim must comply with the requirements of CPR Pt 16 (see para **CPR 16**) and CPR Pt 55 Practice Direction para 2.1 (para **CPR PD 55**). Precedents for particulars of claim claiming possession from a secure tenant are set out at **BCCP O[152]–BCCP O[154]**. Where the possession claim relates to residential property and includes a claim for non-payment of rent, the particulars of claim must also comply with CPR Pt 55 para 2.3 (para **CPR PD 55**); the particulars of claim in Form N119 should therefore be used on such claims. The defence to a general possession claim should be in Form N11 and the defence to a claim for possession for residential premises which includes a claim for non-payment of rent should be in Form N11R. If the defendant does not file a defence within 14 days of service of the particulars of claim, he may take part in the hearing but the court will take into account his failure when deciding costs: para **CPR 55.7**. A table of the appropriate forms for use in possession claims can be found at **BCCP O[12]**; the forms can also be found in the Forms supplement, the FORMS section of your CD-ROM and at **BCCP O[80]** onwards.

III L&T [109A]

84A. Absolute ground for possession for anti-social behaviour

(1) If the court is satisfied that any of the following conditions is met, it must make an order for the possession of a dwelling-house let under a secure tenancy. This is subject to subsection (2) (and to any available defence based on the tenant's Convention rights, within the meaning of the Human Rights Act 1998).

(2) Subsection (1) applies only where the landlord has complied with any obligations it has under section 85ZA (review of decision to seek possession).

(3) Condition 1 is that—

- (a) the tenant, or a person residing in or visiting the dwelling-house, has been convicted of a serious offence, and
- (b) the serious offence—
  - (i) was committed (wholly or partly) in, or in the locality of, the dwelling-house,
  - (ii) was committed elsewhere against a person with a right (of whatever description) to reside in, or occupy housing accommodation in the locality of, the dwelling-house, or
  - (iii) was committed elsewhere against the landlord of the dwelling-house, or a person employed (whether or not by the landlord) in connection with the exercise of the landlord's housing management functions, and directly or indirectly related to or affected those functions.

(4) Condition 2 is that a court has found in relevant proceedings that the tenant, or a person residing in or visiting the dwelling-house, has breached a provision of an injunction under section 1 of the Anti-social Behaviour, Crime and Policing Act 2014, other than a provision requiring a person to participate in a particular activity, and—

- (a) the breach occurred in, or in the locality of, the dwelling-house, or
- (b) the breach occurred elsewhere and the provision breached was a provision intended to prevent—
  - (i) conduct that is capable of causing nuisance or annoyance to a person with a right (of whatever description) to reside in, or occupy housing accommodation in the locality of, the dwelling-house, or
  - (ii) conduct that is capable of causing nuisance or annoyance to the landlord of the dwelling-house, or a person employed (whether or not by the landlord) in connection with the exercise of the landlord's housing management functions, and that is directly or indirectly related to or affects those functions.

(5) Condition 3 is that the tenant, or a person residing in or visiting the dwelling-house, has been convicted of an offence under section 30 of the Anti-social Behaviour, Crime and Policing Act 2014 consisting of a breach of a provision of a criminal behaviour order prohibiting a person from doing anything described in the order, and the offence involved—

(a) a breach that occurred in, or in the locality of, the dwelling-house, or
(b) a breach that occurred elsewhere of a provision intended to prevent—
(i) behaviour that causes or is likely to cause harassment, alarm or distress to a person with a right (of whatever description) to reside in, or occupy housing accommodation in the locality of, the dwelling-house, or
(ii) behaviour that causes or is likely to cause harassment, alarm or distress to the landlord of the dwelling-house, or a person employed (whether or not by the landlord) in connection with the exercise of the landlord's housing management functions, and that is directly or indirectly related to or affects those functions.

(6) Condition 4 is that—
(a) the dwelling-house is or has been subject to a closure order under section 80 of the Anti-social Behaviour, Crime and Policing Act 2014, and
(b) access to the dwelling-house has been prohibited (under the closure order or under a closure notice issued under section 76 of that Act) for a continuous period of more than 48 hours.

(7) Condition 5 is that—
(a) the tenant, or a person residing in or visiting the dwelling-house, has been convicted of an offence under—
(i) section 80(4) of the Environmental Protection Act 1990 (breach of abatement notice in relation to statutory nuisance), or
(ii) section 82(8) of that Act (breach of court order to abate statutory nuisance etc), and
(b) the nuisance concerned was noise emitted from the dwelling-house which was a statutory nuisance for the purposes of Part 3 of that Act by virtue of section 79(1)(g) of that Act (noise emitted from premises so as to be prejudicial to health or a nuisance).

(8) Condition 1, 2, 3, 4 or 5 is not met if—
(a) there is an appeal against the conviction, finding or order concerned which has not been finally determined, abandoned or withdrawn, or
(b) the final determination of the appeal results in the conviction, finding or order being overturned.

(9) In this section—
"relevant proceedings" means proceedings for contempt of court or proceedings under Schedule 2 to the Anti-social Behaviour, Crime and Policing Act 2014;
"serious offence" means an offence which—
(a) was committed on or after the day on which subsection (3) comes into force,
(b) is specified, or falls within a description specified, in Schedule 2A at the time the offence was committed and at the time the court is considering the matter, and
(c) is not an offence that is triable only summarily by virtue of section 22 of the Magistrates' Courts Act 1980 (either-way offences where value involved is small).

(10) The Secretary of State may by order amend Schedule 2A as it applies in relation to dwelling-houses in England by—
(a) adding an indictable offence;
(b) removing an offence.

(11) The Welsh Ministers may by order amend Schedule 2A as it applies in relation to dwelling-houses in Wales by—
(a) adding an indictable offence;
(b) removing an offence.

(12) An order under subsection (10) or (11)—

(a) is to be made by statutory instrument;

(b) may make different provision for different purposes;

(c) may include incidental, supplementary, consequential, transitional or saving provision.

(13) A statutory instrument containing an order under subsection (10) or (11) may not be made unless a draft of the instrument has been laid before and approved by a resolution of—

(a) each House of Parliament (in the case of an order of the Secretary of State), or

(b) the National Assembly for Wales (in the case of an order of the Welsh Ministers).

Amendment *Section 84A was inserted by s 94 of the Anti-social Behaviour, Crime and Policing Act 2014 with effect from 20 October 2014. Regulations prescribing the review procedure to be followed in respect of secure council tenants also came into force on 20 October 2014: see the Absolute Ground for Possession for Anti-social Behaviour (Review Procedure) (England) Regulations 2014 (SI 2014/2554).*

LANDLORD & TENANT AND HOUSING

III L&T [110]

85. Extended discretion of court in certain proceedings for possession

(1) Where proceedings are brought for possession of a dwelling-house let under a secure tenancy on any of the grounds set out in Part I or Part III of Schedule 2 (grounds 1 to 8 and 12 to 16: cases in which the court must be satisfied that it is reasonable to make a possession order), the court may adjourn the proceedings for such period or periods as it thinks fit.

(2) On the making of an order for possession of such a dwelling-house on any of those grounds, or at any time before the execution of the order, the court may

(a) stay or suspend the execution of the order, or

(b) postpone the date of possession,

for such period or periods as the court thinks fit.

(3) On such an adjournment, stay, suspension or postponement the court

(a) shall impose conditions with respect to the payment by the tenant of arrears of rent (if any) and rent . . . unless it considers that to do so would cause exceptional hardship to the tenant or would otherwise be unreasonable, and

(b) may impose such other conditions as it thinks fit.

(4) If the conditions are complied with, the court may, if it thinks fit, discharge or rescind the order for possession.

[(4) The court may discharge or rescind the order for possession if it thinks it appropriate to do so having had regard to—

(a) any conditions imposed under subsection (3), and

(b) the conduct of the tenant in connection with those conditions.]

(5) . . .

(5A) . . .

Amendment *Text in italic is repealed by Schedule 11 to the Housing and Regeneration Act 2008 which also inserts the text in square brackets. Most of these changes were brought into force on 19 May 2009, by SI 2009/1261, but not the new sub-section (4).*

III L&T [110.1]

Extended discretion This section corresponds to the Rent Act 1977 s 100 (see para **III L&T [73]** and the notes thereto).

A distinction is drawn, in sub-section (2), between staying or suspending the execution of a possession order and postponing the date of possession. If the date for possession is postponed then the tenancy continues during the period of postponement. If an order specifies a date for giving up possession, but provides that enforcement of the order is stayed for so long as specified conditions are met the effect of such an order has been held to be that the tenancy is brought to an end on the date specified for possession and does not continue during the period of the stay or suspension and the former tenant who complies with the specified conditions becomes a 'tolerated trespasser': see, for example, *Harlow District Council v Hall* [2006] EWCA Civ 156, [2006] 1 WLR 2116, [2006] HLR 27, (2006) Legal Action April 31. For further guidance on the approach to be taken to the exercise of discretion by the court when considering whether to make a suspended possession order see *City West Housing Trust v Massey* [2016] EWCA Civ 704.

The term 'tolerated trespasser' has been described in *Knowsley Housing Trust v White* [2008] UKHL 70, [2009] 1 AC 636, [2009] All ER 829 as "conceptually peculiar" and "oxymoronic" but as having become "too firmly embedded to be dislodged". The many problems created by the invention of the tolerated trespasser have, however, been addressed by the decision in *Knowsley Housing Trust* that an assured tenancy subject to a suspended possession order does not come to an end until possession is delivered up.

Note that, when brought into force, new sub-s 85(4) is intended to have the effect of ensuring that no tolerated trespassers are created in the future. For the treatment of "tolerated trespassers" arising by virtue of existing possession orders, see Part 2 of Schedule 11 to the Housing and Regeneration Act 2008 (see para **III L&T [345]**) in force (save for regulating powers which are already in force) from a date to be appointed.

Prior to the decision in *Knowsley Housing Trust* the Court of Appeal had approved the following wording where the intention of the court was that, so long as the conditions were met, the defendant should remain a tenant and not become a 'tolerated trespasser':

1 The defendant give the claimant possession of *[address of the property]* on or before *[date]* provided that the date for possession will be postponed and the defendant's tenancy of the premises will continue, so long as the defendant pays the claimant the current rent and in addition the rent arrears and costs by the instalments set out below.

see *Bristol City Council v Hassan* [2006] EWCA Civ 656, [2006] 4 All ER 420, [2006] 1 WLR 2582, where the Court further recommended the further form of wording and procedure for the kind of case where a defaulting tenant is to be allowed a chance of retaining the tenancy on terms:

1 The defendant is to give up possession of *[address]* to the claimant.

2 The date on which the defendant is to give up possession of the property to the claimant is postponed to a date to be fixed by the court on the application of the claimant.

3 The defendant must pay the claimant £ for rent arrears and £ for costs. The total judgment debt is £ to be paid by instalments as specified in paragraph 4 below.

4 The claimant shall not be entitled to make an application for a date to be fixed for the giving up of possession and the termination of the defendant's tenancy so long as the defendant pays the claimant the current rent together with instalments of £ per week towards the judgment debt.

5 The first payment of the current rent and the instalment must be made on or before *[date]*.

6 Any application to fix the date on which the defendant is to give up possession must be determined on the papers without a hearing (unless the district judge considers that such a hearing is appropriate) provided that

(a) the claimant has written to the defendant at least 14 days before making its application giving details of the current arrears and its intention to request that a date be fixed; and

(b) a copy of that letter (and the defendant's response, if any) together with the rent account showing any transactions since the date of this order are attached to the application.

7 This order shall cease to be enforceable *[on date]* *[*when the judgment debt is satisfied*]*.

8 All further proceedings pursuant to the present application are adjourned.

The Court further advised that it would be consistent with good practice if the landlord were to notify the tenant of the adverse consequences of the termination of his/her tenancy when embarking on the process that may lead to a possession order.

Reference should be made to paragraph 10 of **CPR PD 55** which provides a procedure, for and formalises the making of, postponed possession orders along the lines suggested in *Bristol CC v Hassan* (above). See also Form N28A Order for possession (rented premises) (postponed).

Note also the decision in *Knowsley Housing Trust v White* [2008] UKHL 70, [2009] All ER 829 where the House of Lords held that, on a fair reading of s 85, it is open to the court to include a proleptic discharge provision in a suspended order for possession; that the section should be construed, as far as permissible, to confer as much flexibility as possible on the court, and in such a way as to minimise future uncertainty and need for further applications.

III L&T [110.1A]

Suspension of possession The court may, having regard to the public interest, suspend an order for possession if immediate eviction would be likely to cause a former criminal to resume a life of crime: *Greenwich London Borough Council v Grogan* (2000) 33 HLR 140, CA. However, this consideration must be balanced against the needs of other tenants and of others on the housing list. Thus, in *Lambeth London Borough Council v Howard* [2001] EWCA Civ 468, (2001) 33 HLR 58, an immediate order for possession was held to be appropriate where there had been a course of harassment of a neighbour; the Court of Appeal rejecting the argument that an immediate order breached Art 8 of the European Convention on Human Rights and holding that the eviction (which must be effected in accordance with the law) had to be balanced against the neighbour's right to live in peace. In *Gallagher v Castle Vale Action Trust Ltd* [2001] EWCA Civ 944, (2001) 33 HLR 810, the trial judge made an outright possession order in a claim based upon Ground 2 of Schedule 2 (nuisance). On reducing the order to a suspended order, the Court of Appeal noted that Art 8 reinforced the importance of only making an order depriving a person of his home where a clear case for doing so had been made out and stressed the desirability of the court making clear its reasons for making an outright as opposed to a suspended order. Where a tenant was found to have created a serious nuisance, using premises for car repairs and being racially abusive, it was held that it was against the public interest in law and order to refuse a possession order: *West Kent Housing Association Ltd v Davies* (1998) 31 HLR 415, CA. Also, in *Canterbury City Council v Lowe* [2001] L & TR 14, CA, the court ordered immediate possession and did not regard the grant of an injunction as sufficient protection, on the facts of the case, to justify a suspension. "At any time before the execution of the order" does not extend to the period after a former tenant has voluntarily given up possession; in such circumstances, the court has no power to stay or postpone the date for possession under s. 85(2) because execution of the order is no longer required: *Dunn v Bradford Metropolitan District Council; Marston v Leeds City Council* [2002] EWCA Civ 1137, [2003] HLR 154, [2002] All ER (D) 479 (Jul).

In *Norwich City Council v Famuyiwa* [2004] EWCA Civ 1770, (2005) Times, 4 January, [2004] All ER (D) 332 (Dec), CA, the Court of Appeal held, in a case where possession was claimed on Grounds 1 and 2 in Sch 2, that it was wrong for the judge to refuse an order for possession and grant an injunction to restrain the behaviour complained of and that, at the stage of deciding whether it was reasonable to make a possession order, the court should consider whether it could meet the circumstances of the case by postponing the date for possession and imposing conditions.

There is no general rule that, following the making and breach of a postponed possession order, applications to fix a date for possession should be dealt with summarily. If there is an issue as to whether the terms of postponement have been broken, the issue needs to be determined at a hearing: *Wandsworth London Borough Council v Whibley* [2008] EWCA Civ 1259, (2008) Times 25 November.

Although, when considering whether to suspend an order for possession under s 85(2), the court might not be mandated to take account of the factors at s 85A(2) (see para **III L&T [110A]**), such factors are clearly highly relevant to the exercise of the judgment to be made in relation to the power to suspend: *Birmingham City Council v Ashton* [2012] EWCA Civ 1557, [2012] All ER (D) 353 (Nov).

III L&T [110.1B]

Discharge of possession order Where the terms of a suspended possession order were not initially complied with by the tenant but the tenant subsequently complied with a later agreement made with the landlord, the court was entitled to exercise its discretion to discharge the possession order under s 85(4): *Lambeth London Borough Council v Rogers* (1999) 32 HLR 361, [2000] 1 EGLR 28, CA (approved by the House of Lords in *Knowsley Housing Trust v White* [2008] UKHL 70, [2009] All ER 829 and previously followed in *Clements v Lambeth London Borough Council* [2000] LAG July 28 (county court), where one of the considerations taken into account was the obligation to respect the individual's home under Art 8 of the Convention (see para **III HUM [30]**)).

In *Knowsley Housing Trust v White* [2008] UKHL 70, [2009] 1 AC 636, [2009] All ER 829 the House of Lords held (overruling earlier decisions to the contrary in *Marshall v Bradford Metropolitan District Council* [2001] EWCA Civ 594, [2002] HLR 428 and *Swindon*

LANDLORD & TENANT AND HOUSING

Borough Council v Aston [2003] HLR 610) that a tenant can make an application under sub-s (2) for a postponement or under sub-s (4) for a discharge even where the terms of an earlier suspension have not been fully met: the court's powers include the power to vary those conditions on the application. A former secure tenant's right to apply under s 85 survives his death and may be exercised by the tenant's personal representative: see *Austin v Southwark London Borough Council* [2010] UKSC 28, [2010] 4 All ER 16, [2010] 3 WLR 144, overruling *Brent London Borough Council v Knightley* (1997) 2 FLR 1, CA.

III L&T [110.1C]

Stay of execution An executed warrant for possession may not be set aside except where the possession order itself is set aside or it is shown that the warrant was obtained by fraud and was executed oppressively or in abuse of process: *Hammersmith and Fulham London Borough Council v Hill* (1994) 27 HLR 368, [1994] 2 EGLR 51, CA; *Tower Hamlets London Borough Council v Azad* (1997) 30 HLR 241, CA. In *Lambeth London Borough Council v Hughes* (2000) 33 HLR 350, CA, where a secure tenant, against whom an order and warrant for possession had been obtained, was informed by his landlord that he must pay off all rent arrears in order to prevent eviction and was not informed of his right to apply for a stay or suspension under s 85, and the court office then mistakenly advised the tenant that there was no warrant for possession against him, it was held that there had been oppression and the tenant was entitled to apply for a stay. See also *Hammersmith and Fulham London Borough Council v Lemeh* (2000) 33 HLR 231, 80 P & CR D25, CA, where the Court held that misleading information from a court office, depriving a tenant of the opportunity to take steps to have execution of a warrant for possession stayed prior to execution, could amount to oppression thereby entitling the Court to set aside execution of the warrant. Compare, however, *Jephson Homes Housing Association v Moisejevs* [2001] 2 All ER 901, CA: a possession warrant obtained and executed against a secure tenant without fault on anyone's part was not to be set aside as oppressive or an abuse of process; nor was the eviction oppressive merely because the tenant did not appreciate until after the event that she might have applied for stay or suspension under s 85; nor was there any requirement that a tenant should be given notice of a request for the issue of a possession warrant in all cases. See also the notes on CCR Ord 26 rr 5 and 17 (see paras **CCR 26r5** and **CCR 26r17**). In *Sheffield City Council v Hopkins* [2001] EWCA Civ 1023, [2001] 27 LS Gaz R 38 the court held that, when hearing a tenant's application for suspension of a warrant of possession, it is not confined to matters relating to the original grounds for possession (eg rent arrears) but may take account of other matters such as acts of nuisance. The court also observed that Art 8 of the Convention needed to be borne in mind. Its significance was that a person should not be deprived of a home (by refusing a suspension) unless the court's decision was reasonable in the light of a serious breach of tenancy obligations leading to a possession order and, in the case of conditional suspension, the clear establishment of a breach of condition. The court stressed that all allegations made against a tenant should be notified to him.

III L&T [110.1D]

Immediate order where possession already postponed As long as the guidance laid down in *Sheffield City Council v Hopkins* [2001] EWCA Civ 1023, [2001] 27 LS Gaz R 38 (see para **III L&T [110.1C]**) is taken into account by the court on the application, the court is entitled to make an immediate possession order even though an existing postponed order has been complied with and has not expired: *Manchester City Council v Finn* [2002] EWCA Civ 1998, [2003] HLR 596, [2002] All ER (D) 299 (Dec).

III L&T [110.1E]

Tenant's application after execution of a possession order The powers of the court under s 85(2) may only be exercised before execution of the possession order. In *Hackney London Borough Council v Findlay* [2011] EWCA Civ 8 the tenant, who failed to attend the possession hearing, applied, after execution, to have the possession order which had been made against him in his absence set aside under **CPR 3.1**. The Court of Appeal held (distinguishing *Forcelux Ltd v Binnie* [2009] EWCA Civ 854) that a possession order, once made, forms a proper basis for execution unless the tenant has made an application under s 85(2) during the period provided for; that, in the absence of some unusual and highly compelling factor (such as existed in *Forcelux*), a court that was asked to set aside a possession order under **CPR 3.1** should, in general, apply the requirements of **CPR 39.3(5)**.

III L&T [110.2]

Orders under the Family Law Act 1996 See the title Family Proceedings at para **III FAM [86]**.

III L&T [110.3]

New agreement Where a possession order is stayed on terms relating to the payment of arrears and the tenant defaults any new arrangement that the council accepts is unlikely to create a new tenancy although it could do so if this was what the parties intended: *Greenwich London Borough Council v Regan* (1996) 72 P & CR 507, 28 HLR 469, CA.

III L&T [110.4]

Compliance with conditions of suspension In *Knowsley Housing Trust v White* [2008] UKHL 70, [2009] 1 AC 636, [2009] All ER 829 the House of Lords held (overruling earlier decisions to the contrary in *Marshall v Bradford Metropolitan District Council* [2002] HLR 22, CA and *Swindon Borough Council v Aston* [2003] HLR 610) that a tenant can make an application under sub-s (2) for a postponement or under sub-s (4) for a discharge even where the terms of an earlier suspension have not been fully met: the court's powers include the power to vary those conditions on the application.

Where a possession order allowed the tenant time to pay off the arrears of rent but the tenant failed to comply and stayed on, paying off the arrears over a longer period, it was held that the landlord was entitled to bring a second claim for possession, relying on the fact that the tenancy had been ended by the first order and no fresh tenancy had been granted: *London and Quadrant Housing Trust v Ansell* (2007) Times, 25 April, CA.

III L&T [110.5]

Human rights: respect for home The administrative act of issuing a warrant for possession does not by itself infringe rights under the Convention, given that reasonable grounds for making a possession order have to be established and the court has a discretion to suspend or stay the enforcement of the order or the warrant: *Southwark London Borough Council v St Brice (Lord Chancellor's Department Intervener)* [2001] EWCA Civ 1138, [2002] 1 WLR 1537.

Note also that CPR 83.2(3)(e) applies to a court order for possession that is suspended so long as the occupier complies with specified conditions. If the occupier fails to comply the claimant may not apply for a warrant of possession under CPR 83.26 without the permission of the court; and this must be applied for in accordance with CPR 83.2(4): *Cardiff County Council v Lee (Flowers)* [2016] EWCA Civ 1034. In that case, however, the Court of Appeal held that the issue of the warrant under CPR 83.26 was not void but was a procedural error which was capable of validation by the court in the exercise of its discretion under CPR 3.10.

In order to avoid the need for a separate application to the court for permission, Form N325A has been introduced for use where a warrant of possession is sought following the grant of a suspended order for possession. Form N445 (in its revised form) may be used where a reissue of a warrant of possession is sought.

III L&T [110.6]

Right of application A former secure tenant's right to apply under s 85 survives his death and may be exercised by the tenant's personal representative: see *Austin v Southwark London Borough Council* [2010] UKSC 28, [2010] 4 All ER 16, [2010] 3 WLR 144, overruling *Brent London Borough Council v Knightley* (1997) 2 FLR 1, CA.

III L&T [110A]

85A. Proceedings for possession on non-absolute grounds: anti-social behaviour

(1) This section applies if the court is considering under section 84(2)(a) whether it is reasonable to make an order for possession on ground 2 set out in Part 1 of Schedule 2 (conduct of tenant or other person).

(2) The court must consider, in particular—

(a) the effect that the nuisance or annoyance has had on persons other than the person against whom the order is sought;

(b) any continuing effect the nuisance or annoyance is likely to have on such persons;

(c) the effect that the nuisance or annoyance would be likely to have on such persons if the conduct is repeated.

III L&T [110A.1]

Effect on neighbours In *Manchester City Council v Higgins* [2005] EWCA Civ 1423 the trial judge made a suspended possession order where possession was claimed under ground 2. The Court of Appeal substituted an immediate possession order, holding that the judge had

LANDLORD & TENANT AND HOUSING

failed adequately to take into account the effect of anti-social behaviour on the tenant's neighbours as he was required to do by s 85A. The Court also considered that, in the absence of any remorse or well founded expectation of improvement, an immediate possession order was necessary and proportionate under Art 8 of the Convention in order to meet the need to protect the rights and freedoms of the neighbours. See also *Fletcher v Sheffield City Council* [2007] EWHC 419 (Ch), [2007] HLR 387 (Lewison J) Lawtel Doc No AC9100966. It has been held unreasonable to make an order of the ground of anti-social behaviour by the son where he was prosecuted but acquitted and had moved away from the area, to live with his father in a different borough: *Wandsworth London Borough Council v Webb* (2009) Times, 5 January, CA.

III L&T [110A.2]

Statutory factors The court must consider the statutory factors at (a), (b) and (c) before deciding whether it is reasonable to refuse an order: *Lincoln City Council v Bird* [2015] EWHC 843 (QB), 165 NLJ 7650, [2015] 2 P & CR D30, [2015] All ER (D) 109 (Apr).

III L&T [110B]

85ZA. Review of decision to seek possession on absolute ground for anti-social behaviour

(1) A tenant may request a review of a landlord's decision to seek an order for possession of a dwelling-house under section 84A if the interest of the landlord belongs to—

- (a) a local housing authority, or
- (b) a housing action trust.

(2) Such a request must be made in writing before the end of the period of 7 days beginning with the day on which the notice under section 83ZA is served.

(3) On a request being duly made to it, the landlord must review its decision.

(4) The landlord must notify the tenant in writing of the decision on the review.

(5) If the decision is to confirm the original decision, the landlord must also notify the tenant of the reasons for the decision.

(6) The review must be carried out, and the tenant notified, before the day specified in the notice under section 83ZA as the day after which proceedings for the possession of the dwelling-house may be begun.

(7) The Secretary of State may by regulations make provision about the procedure to be followed in connection with a review under this section that relates to an order for possession of a dwelling-house in England.

(8) The Welsh Ministers may by regulations make provision about the procedure to be followed in connection with a review under this section that relates to an order for possession of a dwelling-house in Wales.

(9) Regulations under subsections (7) and (8) may, in particular, make provision—

- (a) requiring the decision on review to be made by a person of appropriate seniority who was not involved in the original decision, and
- (b) as to the circumstances in which the person concerned is entitled to an oral hearing, and whether and by whom the person may be represented at such a hearing.

(10) Regulations under this section—

- (a) may contain transitional or saving provision;
- (b) are to be made by statutory instrument which—
  - (i) in the case of regulations made by the Secretary of State, is subject to annulment in pursuance of a resolution of either House of Parliament;
  - (ii) in the case of regulations made by the Welsh Ministers, is subject to annulment in pursuance of a resolution of the National Assembly for Wales.

III L&T [110B.1]

Procedure for review in Wales The procedure for applying in Wales for a review under s 85ZA is set out in the Secure Tenancies (Absolute Ground for Possession for Anti- Social Behaviour) (Review Procedure) (Wales) Regulations 2014, SI 2014/3278.

III L&T [110B.2]

The seven day period The authority has no duty, or power, to conduct a statutory review where the request in writing is made outside the seven day period: *Harris v Mayor and Burgesses of the London Borough of Hounslow* [2017] EWCA Civ 1476, [2017] All ER (D) 53 (Oct).

III L&T [111]

86. Periodic tenancy arising on termination of fixed terms

(1) Where a secure tenancy [to which this section applies] ("the first tenancy") is a tenancy for a term certain and comes to an end

(a) by effluxion of time, or

(b) by an order of the court under section 82 (3) (termination in pursuance of provision for re-entry or forfeiture),

a periodic tenancy of the same dwelling-house arises by virtue of this section, unless the tenant is granted another secure tenancy of the same dwelling-house (whether a tenancy for a term certain or a periodic tenancy) to begin on the coming to an end of the first tenancy.

[(1A) This section applies to a secure tenancy of a dwelling-house in Wales.

(1B) This section also applies to a secure tenancy of a dwelling-house in England that is—

(a) an old-style secure tenancy, or

(b) a flexible tenancy the term of which ends within the period of 9 months beginning with the day on which paragraph 4 of Schedule 7 to the Housing and Planning Act 2016 comes fully into force,

unless it is a tenancy excluded by subsection (1C).]

(1C) This section does not apply to a secure tenancy of a dwelling-house in England if—

(a) the original secure tenant has died,

(b) the tenancy has been vested in, or otherwise disposed of to, the current tenant in the course of the administration of the original tenant's estate, and

(c) the current tenant qualified to succeed the original tenant under section 86G(2) or (4).]

(2) Where a periodic tenancy arises by virtue of *this section* [subsection (1)]—

(a) the periods of the tenancy are the same as those for which rent was last payable under the first tenancy, and

(b) the parties and the terms of the tenancy are the same as those of the first tenancy at the end of it;

except that the terms are confined to those which are compatible with a periodic tenancy and do not include any provision for re-entry or forfeiture.

Amendment *Text in italics is deleted, and text in square brackets at (1A) and (1B) is inserted, from a date to be appointed, by s 118 of, and Schedule 7 to, the Housing and Planning Act 2016. Sub-section (1C) is inserted, from a date to be appointed, by s 120 of, and Schedule 8 to, the Housing and Planning Act 2016.*

III L&T [111.1]

No security for tenant at will A former tenant who remains in occupation without paying rent after the expiry of a fixed term of more than 21 years has no more than a tenancy at will, which is ended by the taking of proceedings for possession. The tenancy at will does not take effect as a secure tenancy: *Banjo v Brent London Borough Council* [2005] EWCA Civ 292, [2005] 13 EG CS 134.

[ENGLISH SECURE TENANCIES: REVIEW, RENEWAL AND POSSESSION]

III L&T [111A]

[86A. English tenancies: review to determine what to do at end of fixed term]

[(1) The landlord under a fixed term secure tenancy of a dwelling-house in England must carry out a review to decide what to do at the end of the term, unless one of the following exceptions applies.

(2) Exception 1 is where the tenancy is an old style secure tenancy.

(3) Exception 2 is where the tenancy is a flexible tenancy the term of which ends within the period of 9 months beginning with the day on which paragraph 4 of Schedule 7 to the Housing and Planning Act 2016 comes fully into force.

(4) A review under this section must be carried out while the term has 6 to 9 months left to run.

(5) On a review under this section the landlord must decide which of the following options to take.

Option 1: offer to grant a new secure tenancy of the dwelling-house at the end of the current tenancy.

Option 2: seek possession of the dwelling house at the end of the current tenancy but offer to grant a secure tenancy of another dwelling-house instead.

Option 3: seek possession of the dwelling-house at the end of the current tenancy without offering to grant a secure tenancy of another dwelling-house.

(6) The landlord must also—

(a) offer the tenant advice on buying a home if the landlord considers that to be a realistic option for the tenant, and

(b) in appropriate cases, offer the tenant advice on other housing options.]

Amendment *Section 86A is inserted (and former s 86A renumbered and amended as s 86G), from a date to be appointed, by ss 118 and 120 of, and Schedules 7 and 8 to, the Housing and Planning Act 2016.*

III L&T [111B]

[86B. Notification of outcome of review under section 86A]

[(1) On completing a review under section 86A the landlord must notify the tenant in writing of the outcome of the review.

(2) The notice must be given by no later than 6 months before the end of the term of the current tenancy.

(3) The notice must state which of the options mentioned in section 86A the landlord has decided to take.

(4) If the landlord has decided to seek possession of the dwelling-house at the end of the secure tenancy the notice must also—

(a) inform the tenant of the right under section 86C to request the landlord to reconsider, and

(b) specify the time limit for making a request under that section.

(5) If the notice states that the landlord has decided to offer a new tenancy and the tenant accepts in writing before the end of the current tenancy, the landlord must grant the new tenancy in accordance with the offer.]

Amendment *Section 86B is inserted from a date to be appointed, by ss 118 and 120 of, and Schedules 7 and 8 to, the Housing and Planning Act 2016.*

III L&T [111C]

[86C. Reconsideration of decision not to grant a tenancy]

[(1) Where a tenant is notified that the outcome of a review under section 86A is that the landlord has decided to seek possession of the dwelling-house at the end of the current tenancy, the tenant may request the landlord to reconsider its decision.

(2) The request must be made before the end of the period of 21 days beginning with the day on which tenant was notified of the decision.

(3) On receiving the request, the landlord must reconsider its decision.

(4) The landlord must, in particular, consider whether the original decision is in accordance with any policy that the landlord has about the circumstances in which it will grant a further tenancy on the coming to an end of an existing fixed term tenancy.

(5) Once the landlord has reconsidered the decision the landlord must—

- (a) notify the tenant in writing of the outcome,
- (b) revise or confirm its original decision, and
- (c) if it decides to confirm its original decision, give reasons.

(6) The Secretary of State may by regulations make provision about the procedure to be followed in connection with reconsidering a decision for the purposes of this section.

(7) The regulations may, in particular—

- (a) require the original decision to be reconsidered by a person of appropriate seniority who was not involved in the original decision, and
- (b) make provision as to the circumstances in which the person who requested the landlord to reconsider the original decision is entitled to an oral hearing, and whether and by whom that person may be represented.

(8) Regulations under this section may include transitional or saving provision.

(9) Regulations under this section are to be made by statutory instrument which is subject to annulment in pursuance of a resolution of either House of Parliament.]

LANDLORD & TENANT AND HOUSING

Amendment *Section 86C is inserted from a date to be appointed, by ss 118 and 120 of, and Schedules 7 and 8 to, the Housing and Planning Act 2016.*

III L&T [111D]

[86D. Fixed term tenancy arising on termination of previous fixed term]

[(1) This section applies to a secure tenancy of a dwelling-house in England other than—

- (a) an old-style secure tenancy, or
- (b) a flexible tenancy the term of which ends within the period of 9 months beginning with the day on which paragraph 4 of Schedule 7 to the Housing and Planning Act 2016 comes fully into force.

(2) If the tenancy comes to an end by virtue of the term expiring, or by virtue of an order under section 82(3), a new tenancy of the same dwelling-house arises by virtue of this subsection.

(3) Where the landlord has offered the tenant a new tenancy of the same dwelling-house following a review under section 86A but the tenant has failed to accept, the new tenancy that arises by virtue of subsection (2) is a fixed term tenancy of whatever length the landlord offered.

(4) In any other case, the new tenancy that arises by virtue of subsection (2) is a 5 year fixed term tenancy.

(5) The parties and other terms of a new tenancy that arises by virtue of subsection (2) are the same as those of the tenancy that it replaces, except that the terms are confined to those which are compatible with a tenancy of the length determined in accordance with subsection (3) or (4).

(6) A new tenancy does not arise by virtue of subsection (2) if the tenant has been granted another secure tenancy of the same dwelling-house to begin at the same time as the earlier tenancy ends.]

Amendment *Section 86D is inserted from a date to be appointed, by ss 118 and 120 of, and Schedules 7 and 8 to, the Housing and Planning Act 2016.*

III L&T [111E]

[86E. Recovery of possession of secure tenancies in England]

[(1) The landlord under a secure tenancy of a dwelling-house in England may bring proceedings for possession under this section if—

- (a) the landlord has decided on a review under section 86A to seek possession at the end of the tenancy, and
- (b) the landlord has not subsequently revised the decision under section 86C.

(2) If the landlord brings proceedings under this section the court must make an order for possession if satisfied that—

- (a) the landlord has complied with all of the requirements of sections 86A to 86C,
- (b) the tenancy that was the subject of the review section 86A has ended,
- (c) the proceedings were commenced before the end of the period of 3 months beginning with the day on which the tenancy ended, and
- (d) the only fixed term tenancy still in existence is a new secure tenancy arising by virtue of section 86D.

(3) But the court may refuse to grant an order for possession under this section if the court considers that a decision of the landlord under section 86A or 86C was wrong in law.

(4) Where a court makes an order for possession of a dwelling-house under this section, any fixed term tenancy arising by virtue of section 86D on the coming to an end of the tenancy that was the subject of the review under section 86A comes to an end (without further notice) in accordance with section 82(2).

(5) This section does not limit any right of the landlord under a secure tenancy to recover possession of the dwelling-house let on the tenancy in accordance with other provisions of this Part.]

Amendment *Section 86E is inserted from a date to be appointed, by ss 118 and 120 of, and Schedules 7 and 8 to, the Housing and Planning Act 2016.*

TERMINATION OF ENGLISH SECURE TENANCIES BY TENANT

III L&T [111F]

[86F. Termination of English secure tenancies by tenant]

[(1) It is a term of every secure tenancy of a dwelling-house in England, other than an old-style secure tenancy, that the tenant may terminate the tenancy in accordance with the following provisions of this section.

(2) The tenant must serve a notice in writing on the landlord stating that the tenancy will be terminated on the date specified in the notice.

(3) That date must be after the end of the period of four weeks beginning with the date on which the notice is served.

(4) The landlord may agree with the tenant to dispense with the requirement in subsection (2) or (3).

(5) The tenancy is terminated on the date specified in the notice or (as the case may be) determined in accordance with arrangements made under subsection (4) only if on that date—

- (a) no arrears of rent are payable under the tenancy, and
- (b) the tenant is not otherwise materially in breach of a term of the tenancy.]

Amendment *Section 86F is inserted from a date to be appointed, by ss 118 of, and Schedule 7 to, the Housing and Planning Act 2016.*

SUCCESSION ON DEATH OF TENANT

III L&T [111G]

[86G] *86A.* Persons qualified to succeed tenant: England

(1) A person ("P") is qualified to succeed the tenant under a secure tenancy of a dwelling-house in England if—

(a) P occupies the dwelling-house as P's only or principal home at the time of the tenant's death, and

(b) P is the tenant's spouse or civil partner.

(2) A person ("P") is qualified to succeed the tenant under a secure tenancy of a dwelling-house in England if—

(a) at the time of the tenant's death the dwelling-house is not occupied by a spouse or civil partner of the tenant as his or her only or principal home,

(b) an express term of the tenancy makes provision for a person other than such a spouse or civil partner of the tenant to succeed to the tenancy, and

(c) P's succession is in accordance with that term.

(3) Subsection (1) or (2) does not apply if the tenant was a successor as defined in section 88.

(4) In such a case, a person ("P") is qualified to succeed the tenant if—

(a) an express term of the tenancy makes provision for a person to succeed a successor to the tenancy, and

(b) P's succession is in accordance with that term.

(5) For the purposes of this section—

(a) a person who was living with the tenant as the tenant's wife or husband is to be treated as the tenant's spouse, and

(b) a person who was living with the tenant as if they were civil partners is to be treated as the tenant's civil partner.

(6) Subsection (7) applies if, on the death of the tenant, there is by virtue of subsection (5) more than one person who fulfils the condition in subsection (1)(b).

(7) Such one of those persons as may be agreed between them or as may, where there is no such agreement, be selected by the landlord is for the purpose of this section to be treated (according to whether that one of them is of the opposite sex to, or of the same sex as, the tenant) as the tenant's spouse or civil partner.

[(8) This section applies to a tenancy that was granted before 1 April 2012, or that arose by virtue of section 86 on the coming to the end of a secure tenancy granted before 1 April 2012, as it applies to a secure tenancy granted on or after that day.]

Amendment *Former s 86A is renumbered and amended as s 86G, from a date to be appointed, by ss 120 and 216(3) of, and Schedule 8 to, the Housing and Planning Act 2016.*

III L&T [111G.1]

Reviewing, renewing and terminating fixed term tenancies Sections 86A to 86F deal with the process for reviewing, renewing and terminating fixed term tenancies. A landlord must carry out a review between 6 and 9 months before the end of the fixed term to decide whether to grant a new tenancy in the same or a different dwelling house or to end the tenancy without offering another. Where appropriate, the local authority must provide advice on buying a home or other housing options. The landlord must notify the tenant of the outcome of the review and the tenant may ask the landlord to reconsider a decision to terminate the tenancy. If the landlord does not grant a new tenancy at the end of the old one, or seeks possession of the property, the default position is that a new 5 year tenancy arises automatically at the end of the tenancy. This does not prevent the landlord from recovering possession of the property but ensures that the tenancy does not become a lifetime tenancy at the end of the term.

Section 86E prescribes the process by which a landlord may recover possession of a property at the end of the fixed term.

III L&T [112]

87. Persons qualified to succeed tenant: Wales

A person is qualified to succeed the tenant under a secure tenancy of a dwelling house in Wales if he occupies the dwelling-house as his only or principal home at the time of the tenant's death and either

(a) he is the tenant's spouse or civil partner, or

(b) he is another member of the tenant's family and has resided with the tenant throughout the period of twelve months ending with the tenant's death;

unless, in either case, the tenant was himself a successor, as defined in section 88.

III L&T [112.1]

Secure tenancy A former secure tenant's right to apply under s 85 survives his death and may be exercised by the tenant's personal representative: see *Austin v Southwark London Borough Council* [2010] UKSC 28, [2010] 4 All ER 16, [2010] 3 WLR 144, overruling *Brent London Borough Council v Knightley* (1997) 2 FLR 1, CA.

III L&T [112.2]

Member of the tenant's family See the Housing Act 1985 s 113 and notes thereto (see para **III L&T [119]**). In Application 11716/85: *S v United Kingdom* (1986) 47 DR 274, EComHR the European Commission of Human Rights rejected complaints that the exclusion of a lesbian partner from the succession rights accorded to the tenant's family broke the terms of the Convention. In *Fitzpatrick v Sterling Housing Association Ltd* [2001] 1 AC 27, [1999] 4 All ER 705, HL (a case which concerned a claim to a statutory tenancy by succession under the Rent Act 1977) the House of Lords held that the surviving member of a stable and permanent homosexual relationship is a member of the deceased tenant's family. Note also the decision of the Court of Appeal in *Ghaidan v Godin-Mendoza* [2002] EWCA Civ 1533, [2003] Ch 380, [2002] 4 All ER 1162, (2002) Times, 14 November, referred to at para **III L&T [81.2]**. The House of Lords held, dismissing the appeal, that it was possible to interpret Sch 1 para 2 so that it was compliant with the Convention. The court was required to depart from the interpretation of para 2 in *Fitzpatrick v Sterling Housing Association* (above) and held that paragraph 2 should be read, and given effect, as if the survivor of a homosexual couple living together was the surviving spouse of the original tenant: *Ghaidan v Godin-Mendoza* [2004] UKHL 30, [2004] 2 AC 557, [2004] 3 All ER 411. Note that, in a decision as to whether the claimant was entitled to succeed to an assured tenancy under s 17 of the Housing Act 1988, the court held that, to be treated as the spouse when of the same gender as the deceased, the survivor would have to demonstrate a lifetime emotional commitment which was openly and unequivocally displayed to the whole world: *Southern Housing Group Ltd v Nutting* [2004] EWHC 2982 (Ch), [2004] All ER (D) 347 (Dec), (2005) Times, 5 January.

III L&T [112.3]

Minor child A minor may succeed to a secure tenancy, but only the equitable interest passes until he or she becomes 18: *Kingston upon Thames Borough Council v Prince* [1999] 1 FLR 593, [1999] Fam Law 84, CA.

III L&T [112.4]

Residing with A member of the family may be regarded as "residing with" the tenant although he, or she, has another residence elsewhere, but not if the intention is to return to that other residence eventually: *Swanbrae Ltd v Elliott* (1986) 131 Sol Jo 410, 19 HLR 86, CA; *Camden London Borough Council v Goldenborg* (1996) 73 P & CR 376, [1996] 3 FCR 9, CA. See also (applying the reasoning in *Swanbrae Ltd v Elliott) Freeman v Islington London Borough Council* [2009] EWCA Civ 536, [2009] 24 EG 85 (CS) where a successor's claim was rejected even though the successor was living in the same premises as the tenant seven days a week. The Court held that staying in the property was not enough: "residing with" involves some element of making a home together.

The requirement of 12 months' residence with the tenant does not require 12 months at the council premises in question. In *Waltham Forest London Borough Council v Thomas* [1992] 2 AC 198, [1992] 3 All ER 244, HL, the House of Lords overruled the Court of Appeal decision to the contrary in *South Northamptonshire District Council v Power* [1987] 3 All ER 831, [1987] 1 WLR 1433, CA. On the other hand a person who resided with the tenant for the 12 months and claims to succeed on the ground that the two of them were living together as husband and wife must show that they were living together in such a relationship for the full 12 months: *Westminster City Council v Peart* (1991) 24 HLR 389, CA. In *Sheffield City Council v Wall* [2006] EWCA Civ 495, a foster son had been absent for 2 weeks of the relevant 12 month period. He always intended to return. The trial judge nevertheless made an order for possession against him on the ground that he was not a successor. The Court of Appeal, on remitting the case for rehearing, held that, in deciding residence, it was necessary to consider the mental as well as the physical elements of residence.

The positions in England and Wales are different. For secure tenancies granted after 1 April 2012, the Localism Act 2011 amended the 1985 Act as regards secure tenancies in England so as to equate the positions of common law spouses and legal spouses (thus removing the effect of the 12-month condition in the case of common law spouses). The 12-month period still applies in Wales. However, in *Turley v Wandsworth London Borough Council* [2017] EWCA Civ 1476 the Court of Appeal (treating the positions of common law and legal spouses as analogous) held that the requirement, up until 1 April 2012, that the long-term partner of a secure tenant (and thus a member of his family: s 113) had to have resided with the secure tenant throughout the 12-month period, in order to succeed them, was not manifestly without reasonable foundation and was thus justified and proportionate for the purpose of ECHR art 8 and art 14.

III L&T [112.5]

Only one person can succeed The provisions contemplate one person only as a successor: the tenancy cannot pass to two, or more, jointly: *Newham London Borough Council v Phillips* [1998] 1 FLR 613, [1998] Fam Law 140, CA. The 'one succession rule' is not incompatible with Art 8 and 14 rights: *Haringey London Borough Council v Siwami* [2018] EWHC 2733 (QB).

III L&T [112.6]

Tenancy in joint names Where the survivor of joint tenants became the sole tenant before secure tenancies were introduced by the Housing Act 1980, the tenant is not to be regarded as a "successor" for the purposes of this section: *Birmingham City Council v Walker* [2007] 2 AC 262, [2007] 2 WLR 1057, [2007] 3 All ER 445.

Where a mother and father were joint tenants but the father had left home before the mother died, it was held that the resident daughter could not succeed to the tenancy on her mother's death This was because the common law rights of survivorship of a joint tenant were not displaced by the provisions of s 89; the joint tenancy had become the sole tenancy of the father and had ceased to be a secure tenancy because the tenant condition, in s 81, was not satisfied: *Solihull Metropolitan Borough Council v Hickin* [2012] UKSC 39, [2012] 1 WLR 2295, [2012] 4 All ER 867.

III L&T [112.7]

Human rights Where an occupier had no right of succession to the tenancy of his deceased grandmother the Court of Appeal held that the judge had erred in finding exceptional circumstances so as to justify dismissal of a local authority's claim for possession on human rights grounds. The threshold for a successful Article 8 defence is a high one and will only be met in a small proportion of cases: *Thurrock Borough Council v West* [2012] EWCA Civ 1435, [2012] All ER (D) 99 (Nov), following *Manchester City Council v Pinnock* [2010] UKSC 45, [2010] 3 WLR 1441.

Article 8 may be engaged where trespassers have set up their home on private land and the court, as a public body, must apply proportionality when dealing with a claim for possession. But the exercise of discretion would seem to be subject to the provisions of s 89 of the Housing Act 1980: see the judgment of Sir Alan Ward in *Malik v Fassenfelt (since dec'd)* [2013] EWCA Civ 798, [2013] All ER (D) 44 (Jul), but note that both Toulson and Lloyd LLJ declined to hold that Article 8 was engaged as against a private landowner (the point not having been argued). The Court of Appeal has since reiterated that Article 8 considerations arise only in the case of public authority landlords: *McDonald (by her litigation friend) v McDonald (acting by the joint receivers)* [2014] EWCA Civ 1049, [2014] 2 P & CR 377, [2014] HLR 643. In *R (on the application of Turley) v Wandsworth London Borough* [2014] EWHC 4040 (Admin) the condition in s 87 that the long-term partner of a secure tenant should have resided with him throughout the 12-month period preceding his death was held to be objectively and reasonably justified and proportionate.

III L&T [113]

88. Cases where the tenant is a successor

(1) The tenant is himself a successor if

(a) the tenancy vested in him by virtue of section 89 (succession to a periodic tenancy), or

(b) he was a joint tenant and has become the sole tenant, or

[(ba) the tenancy arose by virtue of section 89(2A) (fixed term tenancy arising in certain cases following succession to periodic tenancy), or]

(c) the tenancy arose by virtue of section 86 (periodic tenancy arising on ending the term certain) and the first tenancy there mentioned was granted to another person or jointly to him and another person, or

(d) he became the tenant on the tenancy being assigned to him (but subject to subsections (2) to (3)), or

(e) he became the tenant on the tenancy being vested in him on the death of the previous tenant, or

(f) the tenancy was previously an introductory tenancy and he was a successor to the introductory tenancy.

(2) A tenant to whom the tenancy was assigned in pursuance of an order under section 23A or 24 of the Matrimonial Causes Act 1973 (property adjustment orders in connection with matrimonial proceedings or section 17 (1) of the Matrimonial and Family Proceedings Act 1984 (property adjustment orders after overseas divorce, etc.)) is a successor only if the other party to the marriage was a successor.

(2A) A tenant to whom the tenancy was assigned in pursuance of an order under Part 2 of Schedule 5, or paragraph 9(2) or (3) of Schedule 7, to the Civil Partnership Act 2004 (property adjustment orders in connection with civil partnership proceedings or after overseas dissolution of civil partnership, etc.) is a successor only if the other civil partner was a successor.

(3) A tenant to whom the tenancy was assigned by virtue of section 92 (assignments by way of exchange) is a successor only if he was a successor in relation to the tenancy which he himself assigned by virtue of that section.

(4) Where within six months of the coming to an end of a secure tenancy which is a periodic tenancy ("the former tenancy") the tenant becomes a tenant under another secure tenancy which is a periodic tenancy, and

(a) the tenant was a successor in relation to the former tenancy, and

(b) under the other tenancy either the dwelling-house or the landlord, or both, are the same as under the former tenancy,

the tenant is also a successor in relation to the other tenancy unless the agreement creating that tenancy otherwise provides.

Amendment *From a date to be appointed, sub-section (1)(ba) is inserted by s 120 of, and Schedule 8 to, the Housing and Planning Act 2016.*

III L&T [113.1]

Joint tenancy In *Bassetlaw District Council v Renshaw* [1992] 1 All ER 925, CA, the Court of Appeal held that the wording of the Housing Act 1985 s 88(1)(b) did not apply in the case of a wife who had been a joint tenant but who had been given a sole tenancy when her husband terminated his interest by notice.

III L&T [113.2]

Introductory tenancy The Housing Act 1985 s 88(1)(f) was added by the Housing Act 1996 Sch 14. The scope and content of introductory tenancies are covered in the Housing Act 1996 ss 124–140 (see paras **III L&T [280]–III L&T [296]**) ss 141–143.

III L&T [114]

89. Succession to periodic tenancy

(1) This section applies where a secure tenant dies and the tenancy is a periodic tenancy.

(1A) Where there is a person qualified to succeed the tenant under section *86A* [86G], the tenancy vests by virtue of this section—

(a) in that person, or

(b) if there is more than one such person, in such one of them as may be agreed between them or as may, where there is no agreement, be selected by the landlord.

(2) Where there is a person qualified to succeed the tenant under section 87, the tenancy vests by virtue of this section in that person, or if there is more than one such person in the one to be preferred in accordance with the following rules—

(a) the tenant's spouse or civil partner is to be preferred to another member of the tenant's family;

(b) of two or more other members of the tenant's family such of them is to be preferred as may be agreed between them or as may, where there is no such agreement, be selected by the landlord.

[(2A) Where the tenancy vests in a person qualified to succeed the tenant under section 86G(2) or (4) and continues to be a secure tenancy—

(a) the periodic tenancy ("the old tenancy") comes to an end immediately after vesting, and

(b) a new tenancy of the same dwelling-house arises by virtue of this subsection for a fixed term of 5 years.

(2B) The parties and terms of a tenancy arising by virtue of subsection (2A) are the same as those of the tenancy that it replaces, except that the terms are confined to those which are compatible with a tenancy for a fixed term of 5 years.

(2C) Where a possession order was in force in relation to the old tenancy—

(a) the possession order is to be treated, so far as possible, as if it applied in relation to the new tenancy, and

(b) any other court orders made in connection with the possession order are also to be treated, so far as possible, as if they applied in relation to the new tenancy.

(2D) In subsection (2C) "possession order" means an order for possession of the dwelling house.]

(3) Where there is no person qualified to succeed the tenant, the tenancy ceases to be a secure tenancy

(a) when it is vested or otherwise disposed of in the course of the administration of the tenant's estate, unless the vesting or other disposal is in pursuance of an order made under

(i) section 23A or 24 of the Matrimonial Causes Act 1973 (property adjustment orders made in connection with matrimonial proceedings),

(ii) section 17 (1) of the Matrimonial and Family Proceedings Act 1984 (property adjustment orders after overseas divorce, &c.), or

(iii) paragraph 1 of Schedule 1 to the Children Act 1989 (orders for financial relief against parents); or

(iv) Part 2 of Schedule 5, or paragraph 9(2) or (3) of Schedule 7, to the Civil Partnership Act 2004 (property adjustment orders in connection with civil partnership proceedings or after overseas dissolution of civil partnership, etc.)

(b) when it is known that when the tenancy is so vested or disposed of it will not be in pursuance of such an order.

(4) A tenancy which ceases to be a secure tenancy by virtue of this section cannot subsequently become a secure tenancy.

Amendment *Text is shown as amended by section 160 of the Localism Act 2011; in force from 1 April 2012. Section 160(6) provides that the amendments do not apply in relation to a secure tenancy granted before the day on which s 160 comes into force, or came into being by virtue of section 86 of the Housing Act 1985 on the coming to an end of a secure tenancy within paragraph (a). Sub-sections (2A) to (2D) are inserted, from a date to be appointed, by s 120 of, and Schedule 8 to, the Housing and Planning Act 2016.*

III L&T [115]

90. Devolution of term certain

(1) This section applies where a secure tenant dies and the tenancy is a tenancy for a term certain.

(2) The tenancy remains a secure tenancy until

- (a) it is vested or otherwise disposed of in the course of the administration of the tenant's estate, as mentioned in subsection (3), or
- (b) it is known that when it is so vested or disposed of it will not be a secure tenancy.

(3) The tenancy ceases to be a secure tenancy on being vested or otherwise disposed of in the course of administration of the tenant's estate, unless

- (a) the vesting or other disposal is in pursuance of an order made under
  - (i) section 23A or 24 of the Matrimonial Causes Act 1973 (property adjustment orders in connection with matrimonial proceedings),
  - (ii) section 17 (1) of the Matrimonial and Family Proceedings Act 1984 (property adjustment orders after overseas divorce, &c.),
  - (iii) paragraph 1 of Schedule 1 to the Children Act 1989 (orders for financial relief against parents); or
  - (iv) Part 2 of Schedule 5, or paragraph 9(2) or (3) of Schedule 7, to the Civil Partnership Act 2004 (property adjustment orders in connection with civil partnership proceedings or after overseas dissolution of civil partnership, etc.)
- (b) the vesting or other disposal is to a person qualified to succeed the tenant.

(4) A tenancy which ceases to be a secure tenancy by virtue of this section cannot subsequently become a secure tenancy.

(5) The following provisions apply where a tenancy that was a secure tenancy of a dwelling-house in England

- (a) has been vested or otherwise disposed of in the course of the administration of the secure tenant's estate, and
- (b) has ceased to be a secure tenancy by virtue of this section.

(6) Subject as follows, the landlord may apply to the court for an order for possession of the dwelling-house let under the tenancy.

(7) The court may not entertain proceedings for an order for possession under this section unless—

- (a) the landlord has served notice in writing on the tenant—
  - (i) stating that the landlord requires possession of the dwelling-house, and
  - (ii) specifying a date after which proceedings for an order for possession may be begun, and
- (b) that date has passed without the tenant giving up possession of the dwelling-house.

(8) The date mentioned in subsection (7)(a)(ii) must fall after the end of the period of four weeks beginning with the date on which the notice is served on the tenant.

(9) On an application to the court for an order for possession under this section, the court must make such an order if it is satisfied that subsection (5) applies to the tenancy.

(10) The tenancy ends when the order is executed.

III L&T [115A]

107A. *Flexible tenancies*

(1) For the purposes of this Act, a flexible tenancy is a secure tenancy to which any of the following subsections applies.

(2) This subsection applies to a secure tenancy if—

(a) it is granted by a landlord in England for a term certain of not less than two years, and

(b) before it was granted the person who became the landlord under the tenancy served a written notice on the person who became the tenant under the tenancy stating that the tenancy would be a flexible tenancy.

(3) This subsection applies to a secure tenancy if—

(a) it becomes a secure tenancy by virtue of a notice under paragraph 4ZA(2) of Schedule 1 (family intervention tenancies becoming secure tenancies),

(b) the landlord under the family intervention tenancy in question was a local housing authority in England,

(c) the family intervention tenancy was granted to a person on the coming to an end of a flexible tenancy under which the person was a tenant,

(d) the notice states that the tenancy is to become a secure tenancy that is a flexible tenancy for a term certain of the length specified in the notice, and sets out the other express terms of the tenancy, and

(e) the length of the term specified in the notice is at least two years.

(4) The length of the term of a flexible tenancy that becomes such a tenancy by virtue of subsection (3) is that specified in the notice under paragraph 4ZA(2) of Schedule 1.

(5) The other express terms of the flexible tenancy are those set out in the notice, so far as those terms are compatible with the statutory provisions relating to flexible tenancies; and in this subsection "statutory provision" means any provision made by or under an Act.

(6) This subsection applies to a secure tenancy if—

(a) it is created by virtue of section 137A of the Housing Act 1996 (introductory tenancies becoming flexible tenancies), or

(b) it arises by virtue of section 143MA of that Act (demoted tenancies becoming flexible tenancies).

Amendment *Repealed with savings by s 118 of and Schedule 7 to, the Housing and Planning Act 2016, with effect from a day to be appointed.*

III L&T [115A.1]

Flexible tenancies Sections 107A to 107E were introduced by s 154 of the Localism Act 2011 with effect from 1 April 2012. Section 107A introduced the concept of the flexible tenancy, and provided for the circumstances in which such a tenancy might arise. It is a form of secure tenancy. Provided the conditions set out in s 107D are satisfied, on or after the coming to an end of a flexible tenancy the court must make an order for possession unless the review process provided for in ss 107D(6) and 107E is engaged. Sections 83 and 84 of the 1985 Act are amended so as to allow the procedure under s 107D to operate independently from the general requirements which apply to possession claims against secure tenants. Sections 137A and 143M of the Housing Act 1996 make provision respectively for introductory and demoted tenancies to become flexible tenancies; see **III L&T [293.1]** and **III L&T [296MA]**. Note that, by virtue of s 118 of, and Schedule 7 to, the Housing and Planning Act 2016, from a date to be appointed ss 107A to 107E are repealed and a flexible tenancy is redefined by s 115B (see **III L&T [119A]**). However, by virtue of paragraph 33 of Schedule 7 to the Housing and Planning Act 2016, despite the repeal of ss 107D and 107E of the Housing Act 1985, those sections will continue to apply in relation to a flexible tenancy the term of which ends within the period of 9 months beginning with the day on which paragraph 4 of Schedule 7 comes fully into force. Moreover, amendments made to ss 83 and 84 of the Housing Act 1985 (replacing references to proceedings for possession under section 107D) do not apply in relation to such a tenancy.

III L&T [115B]

107B. *Review of decisions relating to flexible tenancies*

(1) This section applies if a person ("the prospective landlord")—

(a) offers to grant a flexible tenancy (whether or not on the coming to an end of an existing tenancy of any kind), or

(b) serves a notice under section 137A of the Housing Act 1996 stating that, on the coming to an end of an introductory tenancy, it will become a flexible tenancy.

(2) A person to whom the offer is made or on whom the notice is served ("the person concerned") may request a review of the prospective landlord's decision about the length of the term of the tenancy.

(3) The review may only be requested on the basis that the length of the term does not accord with a policy of the prospective landlord as to the length of the terms of the flexible tenancies it grants.

(4) A request for a review must be made before the end of—

(a) the period of 21 days beginning with the day on which the person concerned first receives the offer or notice, or

(b) such longer period as the prospective landlord may in writing allow.

(5) On a request being duly made to it, the prospective landlord must review its decision.

(6) The Secretary of State may by regulations make provision about the procedure to be followed in connection with a review under this section.

(7) The regulations may, in particular, make provision—

(a) requiring the decision on the review to be made by a person of appropriate seniority who was not involved in the original decision, and

(b) as to the circumstances in which the person concerned is entitled to an oral hearing, and whether and by whom the person may be represented at such a hearing.

(8) The prospective landlord must notify the person concerned in writing of the decision on the review.

(9) If the decision is to confirm the original decision, the prospective landlord must also notify the person of the reasons for the decision.

(10) Regulations under this section—

(a) may contain transitional or saving provision;

(b) are to be made by statutory instrument which is subject to annulment in pursuance of a resolution of either House of Parliament.

Amendment *Repealed with savings by s 118 of and Schedule 7 to, the Housing and Planning Act 2016, with effect from a day to be appointed.*

III L&T [115B.1]

Regulations regarding review procedures The Secretary of State has made regulations in respect of review procedures with effect from 1 April 2012. See the Flexible Tenancies (Review Procedures) Regulations 2012, SI 2012/695.

III L&T [115C]

107C. *Termination of flexible tenancy by tenant*

(1) It is a term of every flexible tenancy that the tenant may terminate the tenancy in accordance with the following provisions of this section.

(2) The tenant must serve a notice in writing on the landlord stating that the tenancy will be terminated on the date specified in the notice.

(3) That date must be after the end of the period of four weeks beginning with the date on which the notice is served.

(4) The landlord may agree with the tenant to dispense with the requirement in subsection (2) or (3).

(5) The tenancy is terminated on the date specified in the notice or (as the case may be) determined in accordance with arrangements made under subsection (4) only if on that date—

- *(a) no arrears of rent are payable under the tenancy, and*
- *(b) the tenant is not otherwise materially in breach of a term of the tenancy.*

Amendment *Repealed with savings by s 118 of and Schedule 7 to, the Housing and Planning Act 2016, with effect from a day to be appointed.*

III L&T [115D]

107D. ***Recovery of possession on expiry of flexible tenancy***

(1) Subject as follows, on or after the coming to an end of a flexible tenancy a court must make an order for possession of the dwelling-house let on the tenancy if it is satisfied that the following conditions are met.

(2) Condition 1 is that the flexible tenancy has come to an end and no further secure tenancy (whether or not a flexible tenancy) is for the time being in existence, other than a secure tenancy that is a periodic tenancy (whether or not arising by virtue of section 86).

(3) Condition 2 is that the landlord has given the tenant not less than six months' notice in writing—

- *(a) stating that the landlord does not propose to grant another tenancy on the expiry of the flexible tenancy,*
- *(b) setting out the landlord's reasons for not proposing to grant another tenancy, and*
- *(c) informing the tenant of the tenant's right to request a review of the landlord's proposal and of the time within which such a request must be made.*

(4) Condition 3 is that the landlord has given the tenant not less than two months' notice in writing stating that the landlord requires possession of the dwelling-house.

(5) A notice under subsection (4) may be given before or on the day on which the tenancy comes to an end.

(6) The court may refuse to grant an order for possession under this section if—

- *(a) the tenant has in accordance with section 107E requested a review of the landlord's proposal not to grant another tenancy on the expiry of the flexible tenancy, and*
- *(b) the court is satisfied that the landlord has failed to carry out the review in accordance with provision made by or under that section or that the decision on the review is otherwise wrong in law.*

(7) If a court refuses to grant an order for possession by virtue of subsection (6) it may make such directions as to the holding of a review or further review under section 107E as it thinks fit.

(8) This section has effect notwithstanding that, on the coming to an end of the flexible tenancy, a periodic tenancy arises by virtue of section 86.

(9) Where a court makes an order for possession of a dwelling-house by virtue of this section, any periodic tenancy arising by virtue of section 86 on the coming to an end of the flexible tenancy comes to an end (without further notice and regardless of the period) in accordance with section 82(2).

(10) This section is without prejudice to any right of the landlord under a flexible tenancy to recover possession of the dwelling-house let on the tenancy in accordance with this Part.

Amendment *Repealed with savings by s 118 of and Schedule 7 to, the Housing and Planning Act 2016, with effect from a day to be appointed.*

III L&T [115E]

107E. *Review of decision to seek possession*

(1) A request for a review of a landlord's decision to seek an order for possession of a dwelling-house let under a flexible tenancy must be made before the end of the period of 21 days beginning with the day on which the notice under section 107D(3) is served.

(2) On a request being duly made to it, the landlord must review its decision.

(3) The review must, in particular, consider whether the decision is in accordance with any policy of the landlord as to the circumstances in which it will grant a further tenancy on the coming to an end of an existing flexible tenancy.

(4) The Secretary of State may by regulations make provision about the procedure to be followed in connection with a review under this section.

(5) The regulations may, in particular, make provision—

- *(a) requiring the decision on the review to be made by a person of appropriate seniority who was not involved in the original decision, and*
- *(b) as to the circumstances in which the person concerned is entitled to an oral hearing, and whether and by whom the person may be represented at such a hearing.*

(6) The landlord must notify the tenant in writing of the decision on the review.

(7) If the decision is to confirm the original decision, the landlord must also notify the tenant of the reasons for the decision.

(8) The review must be carried out, and the tenant notified, before the date specified in the notice of proceedings as the date after which proceedings for the possession of the dwelling-house may be begun.

(9) Regulations under this section—

- *(a) may contain transitional or saving provision;*
- *(b) are to be made by statutory instrument which is subject to annulment in pursuance of a resolution of either House of Parliament.*

Amendment *Repealed with savings by s 118 of and Schedule 7 to, the Housing and Planning Act 2016, with effect from a day to be appointed.*

III L&T [116]

110. Jurisdiction of county court

(1) The county court has jurisdiction to determine questions arising under this Part and to entertain proceedings brought under this Part and claims, for whatever amount, in connection with a secure tenancy.

(2) That jurisdiction includes jurisdiction to entertain proceedings on the following questions

- (a) whether a consent required by section 92 (assignment by way of exchange) was withheld otherwise than on one or more of the grounds set out in Schedule 3,
- (b) whether a consent required by section 93(1)(b) or 97(1) (landlord's consent to subletting of part of dwelling-house or to carrying out of improvements) was withheld or unreasonably withheld, or
- (c) whether a statement supplied in pursuance of section 104 (2) (b) (written statement of certain terms of tenancy) is accurate,

withstanding that no other relief is sought than a declaration.

If a person takes proceedings in the High Court which, by virtue of this ... he could have taken in the county court, he is not entitled to recover any

III [illegible]

"Any question arising" The appropriate procedure for having any question arising under Part IV [illegible] determined by the county court is, in summary, as follows: (1) claims for possession which include non-payment of rent must be by particulars of claim in Form [illegible]; (2) claims for possession on other grounds should be by particulars [illegible] form N5; (2) claims for [illegible] (see **CPR PD 55**), [illegible] in compliance with para 2.1 of the Practice Direction to CPR Pt 55 (see para **CPR 16**)) attached to claim form N5; (3) questions which are unlikely to involve a formal dispute of fact should be brought by Pt 8 claim form; (4) claims which, before 26 April [illegible] would have been brought by originating application should be brought by Pt 8 claim form [illegible] or misused its powers under this Part, the [illegible] housing authority appears to have exceeded [illegible] appropriate way of raising the question of legality may be by applying to the High Court for a judicial review of [illegible]

[illegible] *Rules and directions* [illegible] *Constitutional Reform Act 2005.*

question of legality may be by applying to the High Court for having any question determined [illegible] authority appears to have [illegible] appropriate way of raising the [illegible] judicial review under CPR Sch 1 RSC Ord 53 (see para **RSC 53**).

III L&T [117.2]

Rules and directions The Housing Act 1980 (Registrars' Jurisdiction) Direction 1985 directed that a district judge had jurisdiction to make an order under the Housing Act 1980 s 34 (now the Housing Act 1985 s 84 (see para **III L&T [109]**)) for the possession of a dwelling-house.

III L&T [118]

112. Meaning of "dwelling-house"

(1) For the purposes of this Part a dwelling-house may be a house or a part of a house.

(2) Land let together with a dwelling-house shall be treated for the purposes of this Part as part of the dwelling-house unless the land is agricultural land (as defined in section 26 (3)(a) of the General Rate Act 1967) exceeding two acres.

III L&T [119]

113. Members of a person's family

(1) A person is a member of another's family within the meaning of this Part if

- (a) he is the spouse or civil partner of that person, or he and that person live together as husband and wife or as if they were civil partners, or
- (b) he is the person's parent, grandparent, child, grandchild, brother, sister, uncle, aunt, nephew or niece.

(2) For the purpose of subsection (1) (b)

- (a) a relationship by marriage or civil partnership shall be treated as a relationship by blood,
- (b) a relationship of the half-blood shall be treated as a relationship of the whole blood,
- (c) the stepchild of a person shall be treated as his child, and
- (d) an illegitimate child shall be treated as the legitimate child of his mother and reputed father.

LANDLORD & TENANT AND HOUSING

III L&T [119.1]

Member of the family The provisions regarding the persons who may succeed to [illegible] tenancy by virtue of membership of the tenant's family are to be contrasted with the provisions of the Rent Act 1977 Sch 1 (see para **III L&T [81]**) and with the decisions [illegible] the Rent Act in, for example, *Carega Properties SA v Sharratt* [1979] 2 All ER 1084, [illegible] 1 WLR 928, HL, *Watson v Lucas* [1980] 3 All ER 647, [1980] 1 WLR 1493, CA and [illegible] *v Sterling Housing Association Ltd* [2001] 1 AC 27, [1999] 4 All ER 705, HL [illegible] decision of the House of Lords in *Ghaidan v Godin-Mendoza* [2004] UKHL [illegible] 557, [2004] 3 All ER 411 referred to at para **III L&T [81.2]**. In a decision [illegible] claimant was entitled to succeed to an assured tenancy under s 17 of the [illegible] the court held that, to be treated as the spouse when of the same [illegible] the survivor would have to demonstrate a lifetime emotional [illegible] and unequivocally displayed to the whole world: Souther[illegible] EWHC 2982 (Ch), [2004] All ER (D) 347 (Dec), (2005) [illegible] been held to include a foster child who is trea[illegible] foster parents; Re[illegible] Borough Council [illegible] the list of family [illegible] relatives is not [illegible] child is not [illegible] relationship [illegible] *v Personal Representatives of June Wall* [illegible]

[illegible] Borough Council [illegible] [2002] 4 All [illegible] is exhaustive and [illegible] s 113(1): children are members [illegible] legitimate or illegitimate, or the [illegible] incompatible with Arts 8 and 14 of the [illegible]

III L&T [119.2]

Succession by a minor A minor [illegible] minority, the legal interest should be vested in trustees [illegible] and Appointment of Trustees Act 1996 [illegible] Kingston [illegible] Royal London Borough v Prince [1999] 1 FLR 593, [1999] [illegible] Law 84, CA [illegible]

III L&T [119.3]

Living as husband and wife Persons of the same sex who live together are not living together "as husband and wife" for the purposes of the section: *Harrogate Borough Council v Simpson* [1985] RVR 10, CA. See also *Fitzpatrick v Sterling Housing Association Ltd* [2001] 1 AC 27, [1999] 4 All ER 705, HL. The Court of Appeal decided (in *Ghaidan v Godin-Mendoza* [2002] EWCA Civ 1533, [2003] Ch 380, [2002] 4 All ER 1162) that para 2(2) of Sch 1 to the Rent Act 1977, as construed in *Fitzpatrick*, violates the provisions of Art 14 of the Convention on Human Rights as being discriminatory. Accordingly, the words 'as his or her wife or husband' had to be read as meaning 'as if they were his or her wife or husband'. The House of Lords held, dismissing the appeal, that it was possible to interpret Sch 1 para.2 so that it was compliant with the Convention. The court was required to depart from the interpretation of para 2 in *Fitzpatrick v Sterling Housing Association* (supra) and held that para 2 should be read, and given effect, as if the survivor of a homosexual couple living together was the surviving spouse of the original tenant: *Ghaidan v Godin-Mendoza* [2004] UKHL 30, [2004] 2 AC 557, [2004] 3 All ER 411. A similar approach is likely to be taken to the construction of s 113(1)(a). In a decision as to whether the claimant was entitled to succeed to an assured tenancy under s 17 of the Housing Act 1988, the court held that, to be treated as the spouse when of the same gender as the deceased, the survivor would have to demonstrate a lifetime emotional commitment which was openly and unequivocally displayed to the whole world: *Southern Housing Group Ltd v Nutting* [2004] EWHC 2982 (Ch), [2004] All ER (D) 347 (Dec), (2005) Times, 5 January.

III L&T [119A]

114. Meaning of "landlord authority"

(1) In this Part "landlord authority" means—

a local housing authority,

a private registered provider of social housing other than a co-operative housing association,

a registered social landlord other than a co-operative housing association,

a housing trust which is a charity,

a development corporation,

a Mayoral development corporation,

a housing action trust, or

an urban development corporation, . . .

PART V
THE RIGHT TO BUY

GENERAL NOTES ON THE RIGHT TO BUY

III L&T [120]

Part V The Housing Act 1985 ss 118, 119–120, 121, 122–131, Schs 4, 5, are concerned with the right to buy and the Housing Act 1985 ss 143–149 provide in similar terms for acquisition on rent to mortgage terms. Proceedings may be taken in the county court or the High Court, but there is no entitlement to costs in the High Court: Housing Act 1985 s 181 (see para **III L&T [127]**). The sections most often litigated are those listed below: Housing Act 1985 ss 121, 136, 138, 139, 176 and 177 (see paras **III L&T [121]-III L&T [126]**). Practitioners should note the amendments effected to the right to buy scheme by the Housing Act 2004.

The Housing (Right to Buy) (Maximum Percentage Discount) (England) Order 2014, SI 2014/1915 provides the same discount for houses as for flats. A new Right to Buy Form, RTB1, has been prescribed by SI 2014/1797.

III L&T [121]

121. Circumstances in which the right to buy cannot be exercised

(1) The right to buy cannot be exercised if the tenant is subject to an order of the court for possession of the dwelling-house.

(2) The right to buy cannot be exercised if the person, or one of the persons, to whom the right to buy belongs

- (a) has a bankruptcy petition pending against him,
- (b) [. . .],
- (c) is an undischarged bankrupt, [...]
- (d) has made a composition or arrangement with his creditors the terms of which remain to be fulfilled, or
- (e) is a person in relation to whom a moratorium period under a debt relief order applies (under Part 7A of the Insolvency Act 1986).

(3) The right to buy cannot be exercised at any time during the suspension period under an order made under section 121A in respect of the secure tenancy.

III L&T [121.1]

Exercise of right to buy A tenant is treated as exercising his right to buy at every step up to and including completion of the purchase. Accordingly, if any circumstances within the Housing Act 1985 s 121, such as the making of an order for possession, arise between the date of the tenant's original notice of exercise of the right to buy and the date of completion the right to buy is excluded: *Enfield London Borough Council v McKeon* [1986] 2 All ER 730, [1986] 1 WLR 1007, CA. However, if a secure tenancy is revived as a result of the discharge of an order for possession under s.85(4), the tenant's right to buy is also revived together with any accrued steps in the right to buy procedure: *Honeygan-Green v Islington London Borough Council* [2008] EWCA Civ 363[2008] 1 WLR 1350, [2008] 4 All ER 459 (upheld by the House of Lords in *Knowsley Housing Trust v White, Honeygan-Green v Islington London Borough Council* [2008] UKHL 70, [2009] 1 AC 636, [2009] All ER 829). The right to buy is not affected by the fact that the tenant is in breach of covenant (*Bristol City Council v Lovell* (1996) 29 HLR 528; revsd [1998] 1 WLR 446, CA) or by proceedings for possession in which no order for possession has yet been made: *Dance v Welwyn Hatfield District Council* [1990] 3 All ER 572, [1990] 1 WLR 1097, CA. The right to buy may not be exercised by a former secure tenant who has lost security because of a change in his terms of employment: *Elvidge v Coventry City Council* [1994] QB 241, [1993] 4 All ER 903, CA. *In Bhai v Black Roof Community Housing Association Ltd* [2001] 2 All ER 865, CA, the housing association landlord changed, during the course of the tenancy, from a fully mutual to a non-mutual association; the court held that, by virtue of the operation of Sch 18 para 4(c) of the Housing Act 1988, the tenant was a secure tenant entitled to exercise the right to buy. Although s.121 extinguishes a secure tenant's right to buy the property in respect of which a possession order has been made, it does not extinguish a right to buy another property of which the tenant has become a secure tenant: *Manchester City Council v Benjamin* [2008] EWCA Civ 189, [2009] 1 All ER 798, [2009] 1 WLR 2202.

LANDLORD & TENANT AND HOUSING

Exercise of right to buy From 3 April 2007 the right to buy should be claimed by using the form RTB1 introduced by the Housing (Right to Buy)(Prescribed Forms)(Amendment) (England) Regulations 2007, SI 2007/784. For Wales see the Housing (Right to Buy) (Prescribed Forms) (Wales) Regulations 2015, SI 2015/1320 as amended by the Housing (Right to Buy) (Prescribed Forms) (Wales) (Amendment) Regulations 2015, SI 2015/1795; forms to be used as from 22 January 2015 and, as amended, from 19 October 2015.

III L&T [121.1A]

Dwelling house located within the green belt In *R (on the application of O'Byrne) v Secretary of State for the Environment, Transport and the Regions* [2001] EWCA Civ 499, [2002] HLR 567, it was held that there was no place within the mechanics of the right to buy legislation where the Green Belt legislation could properly be operated. The material provisions of the Housing Act 1985 were so inconsistent with or repugnant to the material provisions of the Green Belt (London and Home Counties) Act 1938 that the two could not stand together. The 1938 Act was pro tanto impliedly repealed by the 1985 Act. This decision has been upheld by the House of Lords ([2002] UKHL 45, [2003] 1 All ER 15, [2002] 1 WLR 3250) on the basis that the 1938 Act has no application to dispositions of Green Belt land otherwise within that Act where the disposition is brought about by the compulsory provisions of Part V of the Housing Act 1985.

III L&T [121.2]

Receiving order The Housing Act 1985 s 121 (2)(b), relating to receiving orders, was repealed, as from 29 December 1986, by the Insolvency Act 1985 s 235 (3), Sch 10, Part III. For transitional provisions and savings, see the Insolvency Act 1986 s 437, Sch 11, Pt. II.

III L&T [121.3]

Effect of insolvency See the provisions of the Insolvency Act 1986 s 283 (3A), noted under the Rent Act 1977 s 2 regarding the effect of insolvency (see para **III L&T [69.4]**).

III L&T [121A]

121A. Order suspending right to buy because of anti-social behaviour

(1) The court may, on the application of the landlord under a secure tenancy, make a suspension order in respect of the tenancy.

(2) A suspension order is an order providing that the right to buy may not be exercised in relation to the dwelling-house during such period as is specified in the order ("the suspension period").

(3) The court must not make a suspension order unless it is satisfied—

- (a) that the tenant, or a person residing in or visiting the dwelling-house, has engaged or threatened to engage in—
  - (i) conduct that is capable of causing nuisance or annoyance to some person (who need not be a particular identified person) and that directly or indirectly relates to or affects the landlord's housing management functions, or
  - (ii) conduct that consists of or involves using housing accommodation owned or managed by the landlord for an unlawful purpose, and
- (b) that it is reasonable to make the order.

(4) When deciding whether it is reasonable to make the order, the court must consider, in particular-

- (a) whether it is desirable for the dwelling-house to be managed by the landlord during the suspension period; and
- (b) where the conduct mentioned in subsection (3)(a) consists of conduct by a person which is capable of causing nuisance or annoyance, the effect that the conduct (or the threat of it) has had on other persons, or would have if repeated.

(5) Where a suspension order is made-

- (a) any existing claim to exercise the right to buy in relation to the dwelling-house ceases to be effective as from the beginning of the suspension period, and

(b) section 138(1) shall not apply to the landlord, in connection with such a claim, at any time after the beginning of that period, but

(c) the order does not affect the computation of any period in accordance with Schedule 4.

(6) The court may, on the application of the landlord, make (on one or more occasions) a further order which extends the suspension period under the suspension order by such period as is specified in the further order.

(7) The court must not make such a further order unless it is satisfied—

(a) that, since the making of the suspension order (or the last order under subsection (6)), the tenant, or a person residing in or visiting the dwelling-house, has engaged or threatened to engage in—

(i) conduct that is capable of causing nuisance or annoyance to some person (who need not be a particular identified person) and that directly or indirectly relates to or affects the landlord's housing management functions, or

(ii) conduct that consists of or involves using housing accommodation owned or managed by the landlord for an unlawful purpose, and

(b) that it is reasonable to make the further order.

(8) When deciding whether it is reasonable to make such a further order, the court must consider, in particular—

(a) whether it is desirable for the dwelling-house to be managed by the landlord during the further period of suspension; and

(b) where the conduct mentioned in subsection (7)(a) consists of conduct by a person which is capable of causing nuisance or annoyance, the effect that the conduct (or the threat of it) has had on other persons, or would have if repeated.

(9) In this section any reference to the tenant under a secure tenancy is, in relation to a joint tenancy, a reference to any of the joint tenants.

(10) In this section "housing accommodation" includes—

(a) flats, lodging-houses and hostels;

(b) any yard, garden, outhouses and appurtenances belonging to the accommodation or usually enjoyed with it;

(c) any common areas used in connection with the accommodation.

III L&T [121A.1]

Procedure Amendments have been made to **CPR 55** and **CPR 65** to take account of and make provision for applications for suspension orders under s 121A. Reference should be made to **CPR PD 65** paras 5 to 7 for details of the procedure and the prescribed contents for particulars of claim.

CHANGE OF TENANT OR LANDLORD AFTER SERVICE OF NOTICE CLAIMING RIGHT TO BUY

III L&T [122]

136. Change of secure tenant after notice claiming right to buy

(1) Where, after a secure tenant ("the former tenant") has given a notice claiming the right to buy, another person ("the new tenant")

(a) becomes the secure tenant under the same secure tenancy, otherwise than on an assignment made by virtue of section 92 (assignments by way of exchange), or

(b) becomes the secure tenant under a periodic tenancy arising by virtue of section 86 (periodic tenancy arising on termination of fixed term) on the coming to an end of the secure tenancy, the new tenant shall be in the same position as if the notice had been given by him and he had been the secure tenant at the time it was given.

(2) If a notice under section 125 (landlord's notice of purchase price and other matters) has been served on the former tenant, then, whether or not the former tenant has served a notice under subsection (1) of section 125D (tenant's notice of intention), the new tenant shall serve a notice under that subsection within the period of twelve weeks beginning with whichever of the following is the later—

(a) his becoming the secure tenant, . . .

(b) where the right to have the value of the dwelling-house determined or re-determined by the district valuer is or has been exercised by him or the former tenant, (or where the right to have the value of the dwelling-house re-determined by the district valuer is or has been exercised by the landlord), the relevant event.

(2A) In subsection (2)(b) "the relevant event" means—

(a) where a review notice was capable of being served under section 128A in relation to the determination or re-determination but no such notice was served during the period permitted by that section, the service of the notice under section 128(5) stating the effect of the determination or re-determination,

(b) where a review notice was served under section 128A in relation to the determination or re-determination and section 128B(3) applied, the service on the new tenant or (as the case may be) the former tenant of the notice under section 128B(3), and

(c) where a review notice was served under section 128A in relation to the determination or re-determination and section 128B(5) applied, the service of the notice under section 128B(7).

(6) The preceding provisions of this section do not confer any right on a person required in pursuance of section 123 (claim to share right to buy with members of family) to share the right to buy, unless he could have been validly so required had the notice claiming to exercise the right to buy been given by the new tenant.

(7) The preceding provisions of this section apply with the necessary modifications if there is a further change in the person who is the secure tenant.

III L&T [122.1]

Loss of security before completion A tenant who ceases to reside in the house which he has applied to buy thereby ceases to be a "secure" tenant and is no longer entitled to exercise his right to buy: *Sutton London Borough Council v Swann* (1985) 18 HLR 140, CA. The right was held to have been forfeited between contract and completion in *Muir Group Housing Association Ltd v Thornley* (1992) 91 LGR 1, 25 HLR 89, CA, because the tenant had moved out and sublet the whole house on an assured shorthold tenancy. Similarly where, before completion, the tenant moves out and sublets (*Jennings and Jennings v Epping Forest District Council* (1992) 25 HLR 241, CA) or dies without a successor (*Bradford Metropolitan City Council v McMahon* [1993] 4 All ER 237, [1994] 1 WLR 52, CA). On the other hand, where a secure tenant dies after giving a notice, the successor takes over the predecessor's rights including the discount to which he was entitled when he gave the notice: *McIntyre v Merthyr Tydfil Borough Council* (1989) 21 HLR 320, CA. The trustees of the estate may insist on completing the transaction: *Cooper v City of Edinburgh District Council* (1991) 23 HLR 349, HL. So may the statutory successor: *Harrow London Borough Council v Tonge* (1992) 91 LGR 81, 25 HLR 99, CA. However, where possession proceedings are pending, the tenant may not insist on having them adjourned in order for questions of a right to buy to be decided first. The court has a wide discretion, under CPR 3.1 (2)(b) (see para **CPR 3.1**), to grant or refuse an adjournment and an inherent discretion to hear cases in whatever order appears just and convenient: *Bristol City Council v Lovell* [1998] 1 All ER 775, [1998] 1 WLR 446, HL. See also *Kensington and Chelsea Royal London Borough Council v Hislop* [2004] EWHC 2944 (Ch), [2004] 1 All ER 1036.

Where the tenant has a right to buy but the local authority has brought possession proceedings on a ground in Schedule 2, the court should decide between the competing claims by conducting a balancing exercise: *Basildon District Council v Wahlen* [2006] EWCA Civ 326, [2007] 1 All ER 718, [2006] 1 WLR 2744, (2006) Times, 17 April.

III L&T [122.2]

Effect of an order for possession Where an order for possession has been made which brings the tenancy to an end but defers enforcement on conditions, the former tenant no longer has the right to buy: *Knowsley Housing Trust v White* [2007] EWCA Civ 404, [2007] 4 All ER 800. However, if a secure tenancy is revived as a result of the discharge of an order for possession under s.85(4), the tenant's right to buy is also revived together with any accrued steps in the right to buy procedure: *Honeygan-Green v Islington London Borough Council* [2008] EWCA Civ 363[2008] 1 WLR 1350, [2008] 4 All ER 459 (upheld by the House of Lords in *Knowsley Housing Trust v White, Honeygan-Green v Islington London Borough Council* [2008] UKHL 70, [2009] 1 AC 636, [2009] All ER 829).

COMPLETION OF PURCHASE IN PURSUANCE OF RIGHT TO BUY

III L&T [123]

138. Duty of landlord to convey freehold or grant lease

(1) Where a secure tenant has claimed to exercise the right to buy and that right has been established, then, as soon as all matters relating to the grant [. . .] have been agreed or determined, the landlord shall make to the tenant—

(a) if the dwelling-house is a house and the landlord owns the freehold, a grant of the dwelling-house for an estate in fee simple absolute, or

(b) if the landlord does not own the freehold or if the dwelling-house is a flat (whether or not the landlord owns the freehold), a grant of a lease of the dwelling-house,

in accordance with the following provisions of this Part.

(2) If the tenant has failed to pay the rent or any other payment due from him as a tenant for a period of four weeks after it has been lawfully demanded from him, the landlord is not bound to comply with subsection (1) while the whole or part of that payment remains outstanding.

(2A) Subsection (2B) applies if an application is pending before any court—

(a) for a demotion order, Ground 2 or 2ZA possession order or section 84A possession order to be made in respect of the tenant, or

(b) for a suspension order to be made in respect of the tenancy.

(2B) The landlord is not bound to comply with subsection (1) until such time (if any) as the application is determined without—

(a) a demotion order, an operative Ground 2 or 2ZA possession order or an operative section 84A possession order being made in respect of the tenant, or

(b) a suspension order being made in respect of the tenancy,

or the application is withdrawn.

(2C) For the purposes of subsection (2A) and (2B)—

"demotion order" means a demotion order under section 82A;

"Ground 2 or 2ZA possession order" means an order for possession under Ground 2 or Ground 2ZA in Schedule 2;

"operative Ground 2 or 2ZA possession order" means an order made under Ground 2 or Ground 2ZA in Schedule 2 which requires possession of the dwelling-house to be given up on a date specified in the order;

"operative section 84A possession order" means an order under section 84A which requires possession of the dwelling-house to be given up on a date specified in the order;

"section 84A possession order" means an order for possession under section 84A;

"suspension order" means a suspension order under section 121A.

(2D) Subsection (1) has effect subject to section 121A(5) (disapplication of subsection (1) where suspension order is made).

(2E) Subsection (1) also has effect subject to—

(a) section 138A(2) (operation of subsection (1) suspended while initial demolition notice is in force), and

(b) section 138B(2) (subsection (1) disapplied where final demolition notice is served).

(3) The duty imposed on the landlord by subsection (1) is enforceable by injunction.

III L&T [123.1]

"Agreed or determined" The county court has jurisdiction, under the Housing Act 1985 s 181 (see para **III L&T [127]**), to determine any question arising under Part I that cannot be resolved by agreement and the Secretary of State has power under the Housing Act 1985 s 170, to assist the claimant in such proceedings or in proceedings to enforce the landlord's duty under this section. A precedent for a Pt 8 claim form seeking a declaration of entitlement is given at **BCCP O[155]** and **BCCP O[156]** is an Acknowledgment of Service (reflecting Form N210) indicating denial of entitlement. In *Martin v Medina Housing Association Ltd* [2006] EWCA Civ 367, (2006) 15 EG 134 (CS), (2006) Times, April 20, it was held that oral expression of an intention not to proceed with the purchase, accompanied by lengthy inactivity, justified a finding that, although the right to buy had been established, the stage had not been reached where all matters relating to the grant had been agreed or determined within the meaning of s 138(1).

III L&T [123.2]

Duty under sub-section (1) enforceable by injunction If the landlord fails to make a grant, in breach of his duty under the Housing Act 1985 s 138(1), the tenant may proceed against him in the county court for an injunction enjoining him to execute the necessary deed. The effect of CPR Pt 4 and the Practice Direction thereto (see para **CPR 4** and para **CPR PD 4**) is that the application for the injunction should be by Form N16A. An order by the court, enjoining the defendant to make the grant, may be enforced by committal (CPR Sch 2 CCR Ord 29 r 1, see para **CCR 29r1**)). However, the court may instead make an order for the instrument to be executed by someone else, nominated for that purpose. The power of the High Court to make such an order derives from the Supreme Court Act 1981 s 39 (see para **II SCA [40]**) and the county court has equivalent power by virtue of the County Courts Act 1984 s 38 (see para **II CCA [21]**); *Danchevsky v Danchevsky* [1975] Fam 17, [1974] 3 All ER 934, CA. There is no discretion to refuse an injunction to enforce what is a statutory obligation: *Taylor v Newham London Borough Council* [1993] 2 All ER 649, [1993] 1 WLR 444, CA.

III L&T [123.3]

Loss of security before completion See note to the Housing Act 1985 s 136 at para **III L&T [122.1]**.

III L&T [123.4]

House in need of repair A tenant exercising a right to buy may not insist on the carrying out of repairs as part of the transaction since disrepair, or structural deficiency affecting the premises, are not matters "relating to the grant" which the authority is bound to make: *Ryan v Islington London Borough Council* [2009] EWCA Civ 578, (2009) Times, 29 July, CA.

III L&T [123A]

138A. Effect of initial demolition notice served before completion

(1) This section applies where—

(a) an initial demolition notice is served on a secure tenant under Schedule 5A, and

(b) the notice is served on the tenant before the landlord has made to him such a grant as is required by section 138(1) in respect of a claim by the tenant to exercise the right to buy.

(2) In such a case the landlord is not bound to comply with section 138(1), in connection with any such claim by the tenant, so long as the initial demolition notice remains in force under Schedule 5A.

(3) Section 138C provides a right to compensation in certain cases where this section applies.

III L&T [123B]

138B. Effect of final demolition notice served before completion

(1) This section applies where-

(a) a secure tenant has claimed to exercise the right to buy, but

(b) before the landlord has made to the tenant such a grant as is required by section 138(1) in respect of the claim, a final demolition notice is served on the tenant under paragraph 13 of Schedule 5.

(2) In such a case-

(a) the tenant's claim ceases to be effective as from the time when the final demolition notice comes into force under that paragraph, and

(b) section 138(1) accordingly does not apply to the landlord, in connection with the tenant's claim, at any time after the notice comes into force.

(3) Section 138C provides a right to compensation in certain cases where this section applies.

III L&T [123C]

138C. Compensation where demolition notice served

(1) This section applies where-

(a) a secure tenant has claimed to exercise the right to buy,

(b) before the landlord has made to the tenant such a grant as is required by section 138(1) in respect of the claim, either an initial demolition notice is served on the tenant under Schedule 5A or a final demolition notice is served on him under paragraph 13 of Schedule 5, and

(c) the tenant's claim is established before that notice comes into force under Schedule 5A or paragraph 13 of Schedule 5 (as the case may be).

(2) If, within the period of three months beginning with the date when the notice comes into force ("the operative date"), the tenant serves on the landlord a written notice claiming an amount of compensation under subsection (3), the landlord shall pay that amount to the tenant.

(3) Compensation under this subsection is compensation in respect of expenditure reasonably incurred by the tenant before the operative date in respect of legal and other fees, and other professional costs and expenses, payable in connection with the exercise by him of the right to buy.

(4) A notice under subsection (2) must be accompanied by receipts or other documents showing that the tenant incurred the expenditure in question.

III L&T [124]

139. Terms and effect of conveyance or grant and mortgage

(1) A conveyance of the freehold executed in pursuance of the right to buy shall conform with Parts I and II of Schedule 6; a grant of a lease so executed shall conform with Parts I and III of that Schedule; and Part IV of that Schedule has effect in relation to certain charges.

(2) The secure tenancy comes to an end on the grant to the tenant of an estate in fee simple, or of a lease, in pursuance of the provisions of this Part relating to the right to buy; and if there is then a subtenancy section 139 of the Law of Property Act 1925 (effect of extinguishment of reversion) applies as on a merger or surrender.

(3) [. . .]

III L&T [124.1]

Schedule 6 The Housing Act 1985 Sch 6 provides in detail for the conveyance of freeholds and the grant of leases, pursuant to the right to buy and is divided into four Parts:

(1) common provisions regarding such matters as rights of support and rights of way and the avoidance of any term which purports to enable the landlord to charge the tenant for, or in connection with, the giving of any consent or approval;

(2) provisions governing the conveyance of the freehold;

(3) provisions governing leases, including provisions for service charges and other contributions payable by the tenant and for the avoidance of restrictions on assignments and subletting; and

(4) charges, supplemented in this regard by the Housing (Right to Buy) (Service Charges) Order 1986, SI 1986/2195, and other matters eg the avoidance of provisions in a head lease or agreement which would otherwise prohibit or restrict the granting of a lease in pursuance of the right to buy.

Schedule 6 It was held in *Coventry City Council v Cole* [1994] 1 All ER 997, [1994] 1 WLR 398, CA, that although provisions creating variable service charges are invalid this does not affect fixed service charges which are subject to indexation.

The tenant is entitled to offset rent paid during a period of the landlord's delay against the price, as provided in ss 153A(5) and 153B. This has been held to include rent paid in the form of housing benefit: *Hanoman v Southwark London Borough Council (No 2)* [2008] EWCA Civ 624, [2009] 1 WLR 374, [2009] PTSR 69, confirmed by the House of Lords in *Hanoman v Southwark London Borough Council (No 2)* [2009] UKHL 29, [2009] 4 All ER 585, [2009] 1 WLR 1367.

III L&T [124.2]

Such covenants and conditions as are reasonable By the Housing Act 1985 Sch 6 para 5, the conveyance may, subject to Parts II and III of that schedule, include such covenants and conditions as are reasonable. However, the reasonableness cannot be questioned after execution of the conveyance: *Sheffield City Council v Jackson* [1998] 3 All ER 260, [1998] 1 WLR 1591, CA. The Secretary of State has power under s 170, to assist the would-be purchaser in such proceedings. In *R v Braintree District Council, ex p Halls* (2000) 80 P & CR 266, CA, the Court of Appeal, reversing the decision at first instance, held that a restrictive covenant, which prohibited the building of more than one dwelling-house on the property purchased by the tenant, was unlawful. The landlord's purpose in imposing the restrictive covenant was to realise any future development value in the property. This was held to be contrary to the policy of Part V of the 1985 Act which is to enable tenants to enjoy the fruits of home ownership which includes any rise in the value of the property. Contrast *Caradon District Council v Paton* (2000) 33 HLR 360, [2000] 3 EGLR 57, CA, where the court enforced, by means of an injunction, a restrictive covenant which prohibited use of the property otherwise than as a private dwelling and which had been breached by the grant of short holiday lets.

III L&T [124.3]

Registration of title By the Housing Act 1985 s 154, all conveyances and grants are to be registered under the Land Registration Act 1925 s 123 and, in the case of unregistered land, the landlord must give the tenant a certificate, in a form approved by the Chief Land Registrar, stating that he is entitled to convey or make the grant subject only to the incumbrances etc stated in the conveyance or grant or summarised in the certificate. See now s 4(1)(e) of the Land Registration Act 2002 which provides that the grant of a lease, in pursuance of the right to buy, out of an unregistered legal estate in land is an event requiring compulsory registration.

III L&T [125]

176. Notices

(1) The Secretary of State may by regulations prescribe the form of any notice under this Part and the particulars to be contained in the notice.

(2) Where the form of, and the particulars to be contained in, a notice under this Part are so prescribed, a tenant who proposes to claim, or has claimed, to exercise the right to buy may request the landlord to supply him with a form for use in giving such notice; and the landlord shall do so within seven days of the request.

(3) A notice under this Part may be served by sending it by post.

(4) Where the landlord is a housing association, a notice to be served by the tenant on the landlord under this Part may be served by leaving it at, or sending it to, the principal office of the association or the office of the association with which the tenant usually deals.

(5) Regulations under this section

(a) may make different provision with respect to different cases or descriptions of case, including different provision for different areas, and

(b) shall be made by statutory instrument.

III L&T [125.1]

Forms See the Housing (Right to Buy) (Prescribed Forms) Regulations 1986, SI 1986/2194) (as amended by SI 1989/239, SI 1992/1707, SI 1993/2246, SI 1996/2652, SI 2005/1736 and SI 2005/2876). The Housing (Right to Buy) (Prescribed Forms) (Welsh Forms) Regulations 1994, SI 1994/2932 prescribe Welsh versions of the forms of notice for use in connection with the right to buy under the Housing Act 1985 ss 122(1), 124(1). For the prescribed information to be given by the landlord to secure tenants in relation to the right to buy see the Housing (Right to Buy)(Information to Secure Tenants)(England) Order 2005, SI 2005/1735.

III L&T [125.2]

Service by post Service is deemed to have been effected at the time at which a properly addressed and stamped letter would be delivered in the ordinary course of post, unless the contrary is proved: Interpretation Act 1978 s 7.

III L&T [126]

177. Errors and omissions in notices

(1) A notice served by a tenant under this Part is not invalidated by an error in, or omission from, the particulars which are required by regulations under section 176 to be contained in the notice.

(2) Where as a result of such an error or omission

(a) the landlord has mistakenly admitted or denied the right to buy or the [right to acquire on rent to mortgage terms] in a notice under section 124 or 146, or

(b) the landlord . . . has formed a mistaken opinion as to any matter required to be stated in a notice by any of the provisions mentioned in subsection (3) and has stated that opinion in the notice,

the parties shall, as soon as practicable after they become aware of the mistake, take all such steps (whether by way of amending, withdrawing or re-serving any notice or extending any period or otherwise) as may be requisite for the purpose of securing that all parties are, as nearly as may be, in the same position as they would have been if the mistake had not been made.

(3) The provisions referred to in subsection (2) (b) are

section 125 (notice of purchase price, etc.),

[. . .]

[section 146 (landlord's notice admitting or denying right to acquire on rent to mortgage terms).]

[. . .]

(4) Subsection (2) does not apply where the tenant has exercised the right to which the notice relates before the parties become aware of the mistake.

III L&T [126.1]

It is immaterial that notices refer to the wrong statute if substantially the same as notices in proper form; and in any case the housing authority may waive an error on the tenant's part: *Milne-Berry v Tower Hamlets London Borough Council* (1995) 28 HLR 225, [1995] EGCS 86.

III L&T [127]

181. Jurisdiction of county court

(1) The county court has jurisdiction—

(a) to entertain any proceedings brought under this Part, and

(b) to determine any question arising under this Part or under a conveyance or grant executed in pursuance of the right to acquire on rent to mortgage terms;

but subject to sections 128, 128B, 155C and 158 < . . . > (which provide for matters of valuation to be determined by the district valuer).

(2) The jurisdiction conferred by this section includes jurisdiction to entertain proceedings on any such question as is mentioned in subsection (1)(b) notwithstanding that no other relief is sought than a declaration.

(3) If a person takes proceedings in the High Court which, by virtue of this section, he could have taken in the county court, he is not entitled to recover any costs.

(4) . . .

(5) . . .

Amendment *Text in italic is repealed by the Courts and Legal Services Act 1990, s 125(7), Sch 20, as from a day to be appointed.*

III L&T [127.1]

Determine any question arising The court's power under s 181 includes power to make a declaration as to the tenant's rights: *Francis v Southwark London Borough Council* [2011] EWCA Civ 1418, [2012] 01 LS Gaz R 15, [2011] All ER (D) 54 (Dec), where the court held that the landlord's only duty, when giving notice under s 124 in response to the tenant's notice exercising the right to buy, is to state its opinion as to whether the right to buy exists and that the 1985 Act has not created any remedy in damages.

PART VI
REPAIR NOTICES

REPAIR NOTICES

With effect from 6 April 2006, Part I of Housing Act 2004 introduced a new system for assessing the condition of residential premises and for the enforcement of housing standards in relation to such premises. Sections 189 to 208 of the 1985 Act were repealed, and enforcement and appeals under Part I of the 2004 Act are within the jurisdiction of the magistrate court and the appropriate tribunal.

PART IX
SLUM CLEARANCE

DEMOLITION OR CLOSING OF UNFIT PREMISES BEYOND REPAIR AT REASONABLE COST

III L&T [132]

With effect from 6 April 2006 appeals against demolition orders have been within the jurisdiction of the appropriate tribunal. The county court retains jurisdiction, under s 270(2), to make a possession order where a demolition order has operative and the consequent notice to quit has expired.

III L&T [133]

265. Demolition orders

(1) If-

(a) the local housing authority are satisfied that a category 1 hazard exists in a dwelling or HMO which is not a flat, and

(b) this subsection is not disapplied by subsection (5),

making a demolition order in respect of the dwelling or HMO is a course of action available to the authority in relation to the hazard for the purposes of section 5 of the Housing Act 2004 (category 1 hazards: general duty to take enforcement action).

(2) If, in the case of any building containing one or more flats-

(a) the local housing authority are satisfied that a category 1 hazard exists in one or more of the flats contained in the building or in any common parts of the building, and

(b) this subsection is not disapplied by subsection (5),

making a demolition order in respect of the building is a course of action available to the authority in relation to the hazard for the purposes of section 5 of the Housing Act 2004.

(3) The local housing authority may make a demolition order in respect of a dwelling or HMO which is not a flat if-

(a) they are satisfied that a category 2 hazard exists in the dwelling or HMO,

(b) this subsection is not disapplied by subsection (5), and

(c) the circumstances of the case are circumstances specified or described in an order made by the Secretary of State.

(4) The local housing authority may make a demolition order in respect of any building containing one or more flats if-

(a) they are satisfied that a category 2 hazard exists in one or more of the flats contained in the building or in any common parts of the building,

(b) this subsection is not disapplied by subsection (5), and

(c) the circumstances of the case are circumstances specified or described in an order made by the Secretary of State.

(5) None of subsections (1) to (4) applies if a management order under Chapter 1 or 2 of Part 4 is in force in relation to the premises concerned.

(6) This section also has effect subject to section 304(1) (no demolition order to be made in respect of listed building).

(7) In this section "HMO" means house in multiple occupation.

(8) An order made under subsection (3) or (4)-

(a) may make different provision for different cases or descriptions of case (including different provision for different areas);

(b) may contain such incidental, supplementary, consequential, transitory, transitional or saving provision as the Secretary of State considers appropriate; and

(c) shall be made by statutory instrument which shall be subject to annulment in pursuance of a resolution of either House of Parliament.

(9) Sections 584A and 584B provide for the payment of compensation where demolition orders are made under this section, and for the repayment of such compensation in certain circumstances.

III L&T [134]

267. Content of demolition . . .

(1) A demolition order is an order requiring that the premises

(a) be vacated within a specified period (of at least 28 days) from the date on which the order becomes operative, and

(b) be demolished within six weeks after the end of that period or, if it is not vacated before the end of that period, after the date on which it is vacated or, in either case, within such longer period as in the circumstances the local housing authority consider it reasonable to specify.

(2) . . .

(3) . . .

LANDLORD & TENANT AND HOUSING

III L&T [135]–III L&T [136]

268. Service of copies of demolition order

(1) A local housing authority who have made a demolition order must serve a copy of the order on every person who, to their knowledge, is-

- (a) an owner or occupier of the whole or part of the premises to which the order relates,
- (b) authorised to permit persons to occupy the whole or part of those premises, or
- (c) a mortgagee of the whole or part of the premises.

(2) The copies required to be served under subsection (1) shall be served within the period of seven days beginning with the day on which the order is made.

(3) A copy of the order is to be regarded as having been served on every occupier in accordance with subsections (1) and (2) if a copy of the order is fixed to some conspicuous part of the premises within the period of seven days mentioned in subsection (2).

(4) A demolition order against which no appeal is brought under section 269 becomes operative at the end of the period of 28 days beginning with the day on which the order is made and is final and conclusive as to matters which could be raised on an appeal.

(5) Section 246 of the Housing Act 2004 (service of notices)-

- (a) applies in relation to copies required to be served under this section (instead of section 617 below), and
- (b) so applies as it applies in relation to documents required to be served under any provision of Parts 1 to 4 of that Act.

III L&T [135.1]

Service of notices See Housing Act 1985 s 617 (see para **III L&T [153]**) and the notes to Housing Act 1985 ss 189, 190 (see para **III L&T [129.5]**).

DEMOLITION ORDERS

III L&T [137]–III L&T [151]

270. Demolition orders: recovery of possession of building to be demolished

(1) Where a demolition order has become operative with respect to any premises, the local housing authority shall serve on any occupier of the premises or any part of the premises a notice

- (a) stating the effect of the order,
- (b) specifying the date by which the order requires the premises to be vacated, and
- (c) requiring him to quit the premises before that date or before the expiration of 28 days from the service of the notice, whichever may be the later.

(2) If any person is in occupation of the premises, or any part of them, at any time after the date on which the notice requires the premises to be vacated, the local housing authority or an owner of the premises may apply to the county court which shall thereupon order vacant possession of the premises or part to be given to the applicant within such period, of not less than two or more than four weeks, as the court may determine.

(3) Nothing in the Rent Acts or Part I of the Housing Act 1988 affects the provisions of this section relating to the obtaining possession of any premises.

(4) Expenses incurred by the local housing authority under this section in obtaining possession of any premises, or part of any premises, may be recovered by them by action from the owner, or from any of the owners, of the premises.

III L&T [137.1]

Application to the county court An application under s 270(2) is a claim for possession of land and the procedure set out in CPR Pt 55 must be used.

The demolition order must be operative at the date of issue and the application should specify the notice relied on: *Beaney v Branchett* (1987) 19 HLR 471, [1987] 2 EGLR 115, CA. An order should not be made against an occupying tenant unless the tenancy has been terminated: *Aslan v Murphy* [1989] 3 All ER 130, [1990] 1 WLR 766, CA.

PART XVIII
MISCELLANEOUS AND GENERAL PROVISIONS

GENERAL PROVISIONS RELATING TO HOUSING CONDITIONS

III L&T [152]

610. Power of court to authorise conversion of house into flats

(1) The local housing authority or a person interested in any premises may apply to the county court where

(a) owing to changes in the character of the neighbourhood in which the premises are situated, they cannot readily be let as a single dwelling-house but could readily be let for occupation if converted into two or more dwelling-houses, or

(b) planning permission has been granted under Part III of the Town and Country Planning Act 1990 (general planning control) for the use of the premises as converted into two or more separate dwelling-houses instead of as a single dwelling-house,

and the conversion is prohibited or restricted by the provisions of the lease of the premises, or by restrictive covenant affecting the premises, or otherwise.

(2) The court may, after giving any person interested an opportunity of being heard, vary the terms of the lease or other instrument imposing the prohibition or restriction, subject to such conditions and upon such terms as the court may think just.

III L&T [152.1]

Local housing authority See the Housing Act 1985 ss 1 (see **III L&T [101]**), 2 (2).

III L&T [152.2]

"Apply to the county court" Where, before 26 April 1999, a claim would have been brought in the county court by originating application, section B of CPR PD 8B applies. CPR PD 8B para B.8 directs that, save where a particular form is prescribed by Table 2 of CPR 8B, a Pt 8 claim form must be used (see para **CPR PD 8B**).

III L&T [152.3]

Conversion This expression does not necessarily imply structural alteration and therefore the conversion of a house into single-room "flatlets" may be permitted under the section; the question whether the proposed conversion is in accordance with the general character of the neighbourhood is one for the county court judge: *Stack v Church Comrs for England* [1952] 1 All ER 1352, CA.

III L&T [152.4]

Town and Country Planning Act 1990 Under the Town and Country Planning Act 1990 s 57 permission is required in respect of any "development" of land, ie, the carrying out of building, engineering, mining or other operations in, on, over or under the land, or the making of any material change in the use of any buildings or other land (Town and Country Planning Act 1990 s 55(1)). It is expressly declared that the use as two or more separate dwelling-houses of any building used as a single dwelling-house involves a material change in the use of the building and of each part thereof which is so used (Town and Country Planning Act 1990 s 55(3)).

III L&T [152.5]

Separate dwelling-houses The Housing Act 1985 s 610(1)(b) applies only where the dwelling-houses into which a house is to be converted will be entirely contained in the house; the court cannot authorise the conversion of a house into flats which will be partly comprised in an adjoining house: *Josephine Trust Ltd v Champagne* [1963] 2 QB 160, [1962] 3 All ER 136, CA.

III L&T [152.6]

Discretion of the court The court is not bound to vary a lease because planning permission has been granted for the use of the premises as two or more separate dwelling-houses; the word "may" is not to be construed as "shall": *Sarum Trust v Duke of Westminster* (1953) 161 Estates Gazettes 104, CA. Furthermore, the court's task on an application under s 610(1)(b) is separate from the planning process and requires an independent exercise of judgment by the court. Any factual assessment which may have been made by the planning authority is not determinative and the court has to examine the facts for itself and carry out its own balancing exercise: *Lawntown Ltd v Camenzuli* [2007] EWCA Civ 949, [2008] 1 All ER 446.

III L&T [153]

617. Service of notices

(1) Where under any provision of this Act it is the duty of a local housing authority to serve a document on a person who is to the knowledge of the authority

(a) a person having control of premises, however defined, or

(b) a person managing premises, however defined, or

(c) a person having an estate or interest in premises, whether or not restricted to persons who are owners or lessees or mortgagees or to any other class of those having an estate or interest in premises,

the authority shall take reasonable steps to identify the person or persons coming within the description in that provision.

(2) A person having an estate or interest in premises may for the purposes of any provision to which subsection (1) applies give notice to the local housing authority of his interest in the premises and they shall enter the notice in their records.

(3) A document required or authorised by this Act to be served on a person as being a person having control of premises (however defined) may, if it is not practicable after reasonable enquiry to ascertain the name or address of that person, be served by

(a) addressing it to him by the description of "person having control of" the premises (naming them) to which it relates, and

(b) delivering it to some person on the premises or, if there is no person on the premises to whom it can be delivered, by affixing it, or a copy of it, to some conspicuous part of the premises.

(4) Where under any provision of this Act a document is to be served on

(a) the person having control of premises, however defined, or

(b) the person managing premises, however defined, or

(c) the owner of premises, however defined,

and more than one person comes within the description in the enactment, the document may be served on more than one of those persons.

III L&T [153.1]

Person having control etc See the Housing Act 1985 s 207 (see para **III L&T [131]**) and the notes at para **III L&T [131.1]**.

III L&T [154]

621. Meaning of "lease" and "tenancy" and related expressions

(1) In this Act "lease" and "tenancy" have the same meaning.

(2) Both expressions include

(a) a sub-lease or sub-tenancy, and

(b) an agreement for a lease or tenancy (or sub-lease or sub-tenancy).

(3) The expressions "lessor" and "lessee" and "landlord" and "tenant", and references to letting, to the grant of a lease or to covenants or terms, shall be construed accordingly.

III L&T [154.1]

The definition of "lease" and "tenancy" excludes a statutory tenancy arising under the Rent Acts: *Johnson v Felton* (1994) 27 HLR 265, [1994] EGCS 135, CA.

III L&T [155]

622. Minor definitions: general

(1) In this Act

"assured tenancy" has the same meaning as in Part I of the Housing Act 1988;

"assured agricultural occupancy" has the same meaning as in Part I of the Housing Act 1988;

"authorised deposit taker" means—

(a) a person who has permission under Part 4A of the Financial Services and Markets Act 2000 to accept deposits, or

(b) an EEA firm of the kind mentioned in paragraph 5(b) of Schedule 3 to that Act who has permission under paragraph 15 of that Schedule (as a result of qualifying for authorisation under paragraph 12 of that Schedule) to accept deposits;

"authorised insurer" means—

(a) a person who has permission under Part 4A of the Financial Services and Markets Act 2000 to effect or carry out contracts of insurance, or

(b) an EEA firm of the kind mentioned in paragraph 5(b) of Schedule 3 to that Act who has permission under paragraph 15 of that Schedule (as a result of qualifying for authorisation under paragraph 12 of that Schedule) to effect or carry out contracts of insurance;

"authorised mortgage lender" means—

(a) a person who has permission under Part 4A of the Financial Services and Markets Act 2000 to enter into a regulated mortgage contract as lender,

(b) an EEA firm of the kind mentioned in paragraph (5)(b) of Schedule 3 to that Act who has permission under paragraph 15 of that Schedule (as a result of qualifying for authorisation under paragraph 12 of that Schedule) to enter into a regulated mortgage contract as lender, or

(c) a Treaty firm within the meaning of Schedule 4 to that Act who has permission under paragraph 4 of that Schedule (as a result of qualifying for authorisation under paragraph 2 of that Schedule) to enter into a regulated mortgage contract as lender;

[. . .]

"building regulations" means

(a) building regulations made under Part I of the Building Act 1984,

(b) [. . .] or

(c) any provision of a local Act, or of a byelaw made under a local Act, dealing with the construction and drainage of new buildings and the laying out and construction of new streets;

[. . .]

"cemetery" has the same meaning as in section 214 of the Local Government Act 1972;

[...]

"district valuer", in relation to any land in the district of a local housing authority, means an officer of the Commissioners of Inland Revenue appointed by them for the purpose of exercising, in relation to that district, the functions of the district valuer under this Act;

"friendly society" means a friendly society, or a branch of a friendly society, registered under the Friendly Societies Act 1974 or earlier legislation;

"general rate fund" means

(a) in relation to the Council of the Isles of Scilly, the general fund of that council;

(b) in relation to the Common Council of the City of London, that council's general rate;

"hostel" means a building in which is provided, for persons generally or for a class or classes of persons

(a) residential accommodation otherwise than in separate and self-contained sets of premises, and

(b) either board or facilities for the preparation of food adequate to the needs of those persons, or both;

[. . .]

"protected occupancy" and "protected occupier" have the same meaning as in the Rent (Agriculture) Act 1976;

"protected tenancy" has the same meaning as in the Rent Act 1977;

"regular armed forces of the Crown" means the regular forces as defined by section 374 of the Armed Forces Act 2006;

"the Rent Acts" means the Rent Act 1977 and the Rent (Agriculture) Act 1976;

"restricted contract" has the same meaning as in the Rent Act 1977;

"shared ownership lease" means a lease

(a) granted on payment of a premium calculated by reference to a percentage of the value of the dwelling or of the cost of providing it, or

(b) under which the tenant (or his personal representatives) will or may be entitled to a sum calculated by reference, directly or indirectly, to the value of the dwelling;

[. . .]

"statutory tenancy" and "statutory tenant" mean a statutory tenancy or statutory tenant within the meaning of the Rent Act 1977 or the Rent (Agriculture) Act 1976;

"street" includes any court, alley, passage, square or row of houses, whether a thoroughfare or not;

"subsidiary" has the meaning given by section 1159 of the Companies Act 2006;

[. . .]

(2) The definitions of "authorised deposit taker", "authorised insurer" and "authorised mortgage lender" in subsection (1) must be read with—

(a) section 22 of the Financial Services and Markets Act 2000;

(b) any relevant order under that section; and

(c) Schedule 2 to that Act.

Schedules

SCHEDULE 1

TENANCIES WHICH ARE NOT SECURE TENANCIES

Section 79

III L&T [156]

Long leases

1. A tenancy is not a secure tenancy if it is a long tenancy.

Certain English tenancies that were not secure tenancies when originally granted

[1ZA. A tenancy of a dwelling-house in England cannot become a secure tenancy if—

(a) it was granted on or after the day on which paragraph 4 of Schedule 7 to the Housing and Planning Act 2016 came fully into force,

(b) it was not a secure tenancy or an introductory tenancy at the time it was granted, and

(c) it is a periodic tenancy or a tenancy for a fixed term of less than 2 years or more than 5 years.]

Introductory tenancies

1A. A tenancy is not a secure tenancy if it is an introductory tenancy or a tenancy which has ceased to be an introductory tenancy

(a) by virtue of section 133 (3) of the Housing Act 1996 (disposal on death to non-qualifying person), or

(b) by virtue of the tenant, or in the case of a joint tenancy every tenant, ceasing to occupy the dwelling-house as his only or principal home.

Premises occupied in connection with employment

2. (1) Subject to subparagraph (4B), a tenancy is not a secure tenancy if the tenant is an employee of the landlord or of

a local authority,
a development corporation,
a housing action trust,
a Mayoral development corporation,
an urban development corporation,
[. . .] or
the governors of an aided school,

and his contract of employment requires him to occupy the dwelling-house for the better performance of his duties.

(2) Subject to subparagraph (4B), a tenancy is not a secure tenancy if the tenant is a member of a police force and the dwelling-house is provided for him free of rent and rates in pursuance of regulations made under section 50 of the Police Act 1996 (general regulations as to government, administration and conditions of service of police forces).

(3) Subject to subparagraph (4B), a tenancy is not a secure tenancy if the tenant is an employee of a fire authority (within the meaning of the Fire Services Acts 1947 and 1959) and

(a) his contract of employment requires him to live in close proximity to a particular fire station, and

(b) the dwelling-house was let to him by the authority in consequence of that requirement.

(4) Subject to subparagraph (4A) and (4B), a tenancy is not a secure tenancy if

LANDLORD & TENANT AND HOUSING

(a) within the period of three years immediately preceding the grant the conditions mentioned in sub-paragraph (1), (2) or (3) have been satisfied with respect to a tenancy of the dwelling-house, and

(b) before the grant the landlord notified the tenant in writing of the circumstances in which this exception applies and that in its opinion the proposed tenancy would fall within this exception.

[. . .]

(4A) Except where the landlord is a local housing authority, a tenancy under sub-paragraph (4) shall become a secure tenancy when the periods during which the conditions mentioned in sub-paragraph (1), (2) or (3) are not satisfied with respect to the tenancy amount in aggregate to more than three years.

(4B) Where the landlord is a local housing authority, a tenancy under sub-paragraph (1), (2), (3) or (4) shall become a secure tenancy if the authority notify the tenant that the tenancy is to be regarded as a secure tenancy.

(5) In this paragraph "contract of employment" means a contract of service or apprenticeship, whether express or implied and (if express) whether oral or in writing.

Land acquired for development

3. (1) A tenancy is not a secure tenancy if the dwelling-house is on land which has been acquired for development and the dwelling-house is used by the landlord, pending development of the land, as temporary housing accommodation.

(2) In this paragraph "development" has the meaning given by section 55 of the Town and Country Planning Act 1990 (general definition of development for purposes of that Act).

Accommodation for homeless persons

4. A tenancy granted in pursuance of any function under Part VII of the Housing Act 1996 (homelessness) is not a secure tenancy unless the local housing authority concerned have notified the tenant that the tenancy is to be regarded as a secure tenancy.

Family intervention tenancies

4ZA (1) A tenancy is not a secure tenancy if it is a family intervention tenancy.

(2) But a tenancy mentioned in sub-paragraph (1) becomes a secure tenancy if the landlord notifies the tenant that it is to be regarded as a secure tenancy.

[(2A) A notice under sub-paragraph (2) that relates to a tenancy of a dwelling-house in England must—

(a) state that the tenancy is to become a secure tenancy for a fixed term of a length specified in the notice, and

(b) set out the other express terms of the tenancy.

(2B) The length of the term specified in a notice in accordance with sub-paragraph (2A) must not be—

(a) less than 2 years, or

(b) more than the permitted maximum length.

(2C) The permitted maximum length is 10 years, unless sub-paragraph (2D) applies.

(2D) If the landlord has been notified in writing that a child aged under 9 will live in the dwelling-house, the permitted maximum length is the period—

(a) beginning with the day on which the tenancy becomes a secure tenancy, and

(b) ending with the day on which the child will reach the age of 19.

(2E) In deciding what length to specify in a notice under sub-paragraph (2A)(a) the landlord must have regard to any guidance given by the Secretary of State.

(2F) Where a notice is given in accordance with sub-paragraph (2A) the length of the secure tenancy, and the other terms, are those set out in the notice.

(2G) Sub-paragraphs (2A) to (2F) do not apply to notices given before the day on which paragraph 4 of Schedule 7 to the Housing and Planning Act 2016 comes fully into force.]

(3) In this paragraph "a family intervention tenancy" means, subject to sub-paragraph (4), a tenancy granted by a local housing authority in respect of a dwelling-house—

(a) to a person ("the new tenant") against whom a relevant possession order in respect of another dwelling-house—

(i) has been made, in relation to a secure tenancy . . . ;

(ii) could, in the opinion of the authority, have been so made in relation to such a tenancy; or

(iii) could, in the opinion of the authority, have been so made if the person had had such a tenancy; and

(b) for the purposes of the provision of behaviour support services.

(4) A tenancy is not a family intervention tenancy for the purposes of this paragraph if the local housing authority has failed to serve a notice under sub-paragraph (5) on the new tenant before the new tenant entered into the tenancy.

(5) A notice under this sub-paragraph is a notice stating—

(a) the reasons for offering the tenancy to the new tenant;

(b) the dwelling-house in respect of which the tenancy is to be granted;

(c) the other main terms of the tenancy (including any requirements on the new tenant in respect of behaviour support services);

(d) the security of tenure available under the tenancy and any loss of security of tenure which is likely to result from the new tenant agreeing to enter into the tenancy;

(e) that the new tenant is not obliged to enter into the tenancy or (unless otherwise required to do so) to surrender any existing tenancy or possession of a dwelling-house;

(f) any likely action by the local housing authority if the new tenant does not enter into the tenancy or surrender any existing tenancy or possession of a dwelling-house.

(6) The appropriate national authority may by regulations made by statutory instrument amend sub-paragraph (5).

(7) A notice under sub-paragraph (5) must contain advice to the new tenant as to how the new tenant may be able to obtain assistance in relation to the notice.

(8) The appropriate national authority may by regulations made by statutory instrument make provision about the type of advice to be provided in such notices.

(9) Regulations under this paragraph may contain such transitional, transitory or saving provision as the appropriate national authority considers appropriate.

(10) A statutory instrument containing (whether alone or with other provision) regulations under this paragraph which amend or repeal any of paragraphs (a) to (f) of sub-paragraph (5) may not be made—

(a) by the Secretary of State unless a draft of the instrument has been laid before, and approved by a resolution of, each House of Parliament; and

(b) by the Welsh Ministers unless a draft of the instrument has been laid before, and approved by a resolution of, the National Assembly for Wales.

(11) Subject to this, a statutory instrument containing regulations made under this paragraph—

(a) by the Secretary of State is subject to annulment in pursuance of a resolution of either House of Parliament; and

(b) by the Welsh Ministers is subject to annulment in pursuance of a resolution of the National Assembly for Wales.

(12) In this paragraph—

- "appropriate national authority"—

(a) in relation to England, means the Secretary of State; and

LANDLORD & TENANT AND HOUSING

(b) in relation to Wales, means the Welsh Ministers;

- "behaviour support agreement" means an agreement in writing about behaviour and the provision of support services made between the new tenant and the local housing authority concerned (or between persons who include those persons);
- "behaviour support services" means relevant support services to be provided by any person to—
  (a) the new tenant; or
  (b) any person who is to reside with the new tenant;

for the purpose of addressing the kind of behaviour which led to the new tenant falling within sub-paragraph (3)(a);

- "family intervention tenancy" has the meaning given by sub-paragraph (3);
- "the new tenant" has the meaning given by sub-paragraph (3)(a);
- "relevant possession order" means—
  (a) a possession order under section 84 that is made on ground 2, 2ZA or 2A of Part 1 of Schedule 2, or
  (b) a possession order under section 84A;
- "relevant support services" means support services of a kind identified in a behaviour support agreement and designed to meet such needs of the recipient as are identified in the agreement.

Accommodation for asylum-seekers

4A. (1) A tenancy is not a secure tenancy if it is granted in order to provide accommodation under section 4 or Part VI of the Immigration and Asylum Act 1999

(2) A tenancy mentioned in sub-paragraph (1) becomes a secure tenancy if the landlord notifies the tenant that it is to be regarded as a secure tenancy.

Temporary accommodation for persons taking up employment

5. (1) Subject to sub-paragraphs (1A) and (1B), a tenancy is not a secure tenancy if

(a) the person to whom the tenancy was granted was not, immediately before the grant, resident in the district in which the dwelling-house is situated,

(b) before the grant of the tenancy, he obtained employment, or an offer of employment, in the district or its surrounding area,

(c) the tenancy was granted to him for the purpose of meeting his need for temporary accommodation in the district or its surrounding area in order to work there, and of enabling him to find permanent accommodation there, and

(d) the landlord notified him in writing of the circumstances in which this exception applies and that in its opinion the proposed tenancy would fall within this exception.

(1A) Except where the landlord is a local housing authority, a tenancy under sub-paragraph (1) shall become a secure tenancy on the expiry of one year from the grant or on earlier notification by the landlord to the tenant that the tenancy is to be regarded as a secure tenancy.

(1B) Where the landlord is a local housing authority, a tenancy under sub-paragraph (1) shall become a secure tenancy if at any time the authority notify the tenant that the tenancy is to be regarded as a secure tenancy.

(2) In this paragraph

"district" means district of a local housing authority; and

"surrounding area", in relation to a district, means the area consisting of each district that adjoins it.

Short-term arrangements

6. A tenancy is not a secure tenancy if

(a) the dwelling-house has been leased to the landlord with vacant possession for use as temporary housing accommodation,

(b) the terms on which it has been leased include provision for the lessor to obtain vacant possession from the landlord on the expiry of a specified period or when required by the lessor,

(c) the lessor is not a body which is capable of granting secure tenancies, and

(d) the landlord has no interest in the dwelling-house other than under the lease in question or as a mortgagee.

Temporary accommodation during works

7. A tenancy is not a secure tenancy if

(a) the dwelling-house has been made available for occupation by the tenant (or a predecessor in title of his) while works are carried out on the dwelling-house which he previously occupied as his home, and

(b) the tenant or predecessor was not a secure tenant of that other dwelling-house at the time when he ceased to occupy it as his home.

Agricultural holdings

8.(1) A tenancy is not a secure tenancy if

(a) the dwelling-house is comprised in an agricultural holding and is occupied by the person responsible for the control (whether as tenant or as servant or agent of the tenant) of the farming of the holding, or

(b) the dwelling-house is comprised in the holding held under a farm business tenancy and is occupied by the person responsible for the control (whether as tenant or as servant or agent of the tenant) of the management of the holding.

(2) In sub-paragraph (1) above

"agricultural holding" means any agricultural holding within the meaning of the Agricultural Holdings Act 1986 held under a tenancy in relation to which that Act applies, and

"farm business tenancy", and "holding" in relation to such a tenancy, have the same meaning as in the Agricultural Tenancies Act 1995.

Licensed premises

9. A tenancy is not a secure tenancy if the dwelling-house consists of or includes premises licensed for the sale of intoxicating liquor for consumption on the premises.

Student lettings

10.(1) Subject to sub-paragraphs (2A) and (2B), a tenancy of a dwelling-house is not a secure tenancy if

(a) it is granted for the purpose of enabling the tenant to attend a designated course at an educational establishment, and

(b) before the grant of the tenancy the landlord notified him in writing of the circumstances in which this exception applies and that in its opinion the proposed tenancy would fall within this exception.

[. . .]

(2) A landlord's notice under sub-paragraph (1) (b) shall specify the educational establishment which the person concerned proposes to attend.

(2A) Except where the landlord is a local housing authority, a tenancy under sub-paragraph (1) shall become a secure tenancy on the expiry of the period specified in sub-paragraph (3) or on earlier notification by the landlord to the tenant that the tenancy is to be regarded as a secure tenancy.

(2B) Where the landlord is a local housing authority, a tenancy under sub-paragraph (1) shall become a secure tenancy if at any time the authority notify the tenant that the tenancy is to be regarded as a secure tenancy.

(3) The period referred to in sub-paragraph (2A) is

(a) in a case where the tenant attends a designated course at the educational establishment specified in the landlord's notice, the period ending six months after the tenant ceases to attend that (or any other) designated course at that establishment;

(b) in any other case, the period ending six months after the grant of the tenancy.

(4) In this paragraph

"designated course" means a course of any kind designated by regulations made by the Secretary of State for the purposes of this paragraph;

"educational establishment" means a university or [institution which provides higher education or further education (or both); and for the purposes of this definition "higher education" and "further education" have the same meaning as in the Education Act 1996.

(5) Regulations under sub-paragraph (4) shall be made by statutory instrument and may make different provision with respect to different cases or descriptions of case, including different provision for different areas.

1954 Act tenancies

11. A tenancy is not a secure tenancy if it is one to which Part II of the Landlord and Tenant Act 1954 applies (tenancies of premises occupied for business purposes).

Almshouses

12. A licence to occupy a dwelling-house is not a secure tenancy if

(a) the dwelling-house is an almshouse, and

(b) the licence was granted by or on behalf of a charity which

(i) is authorised under its trusts to maintain the dwelling-house as an almshouse, and

(ii) has no power under its trusts to grant a tenancy of the dwelling-house;

and in this paragraph "almshouse" means any premises maintained as an almshouse, whether they are called an almshouse or not; and "trusts", in relation to a charity, means the provisions establishing it as a charity and regulating its purposes and administration, whether those provisions take effect by way of trust or not.

Amendment *Ground 1ZA and paragraphs (2A) to (2G) of ground 4ZA are introduced, from a date to be appointed, by s 118 of, and Schedule 7 to, the Housing and Planning Act 2016.*

III L&T [156.1]

Interpretation Certain expressions in this schedule are defined elsewhere as follows: "local authority" (Housing Act 1985 s 4 (see para **III L&T [102]**)), "new town corporation" (Housing Act 1985 s 4 (see para **III L&T [102]**)), "urban development corporation" (Housing Act 1985 s 4 (see para **III L&T [102]**)), "dwelling-house" (Housing Act 1985 s 112 (see **III L&T [118]**)), "long tenancy" (Housing Act 1985 s 115).

III L&T [156.2]

Occupation in connection with employment It is for the landlord to prove that the contract of employment requires occupation of the dwelling-house: *McEwan v Annandale and Eskdale District Council* 1989 SLT (Lands Tr) 95. But such a term does not have to be expressed; it may be implied: *South Glamorgan County Council v Griffiths* (1992) 24 HLR 334, CA. It was not implied, however, in the case of a headmaster in *Hughes v Greenwich London Borough Council* [1994] 1 AC 170, [1993] 4 All ER 577, HL. As for "occupy the dwelling-house for the better performance of his duties" in Housing Act 1985 Sch 1 para 2(1), the court may look beyond the written contract of employment to the factual background leading to the tenant's occupation, in determining whether the requirement is satisfied: *Campbell v City of Edinburgh District Council* 1987 SLT 51. Where there is an issue as to whether the contract of employment requires the employee to occupy the dwelling house for the better performance of his or her duties the court should ascertain what those duties are and then decide whether it is practicable to perform them without occupying the dwelling house: *Surrey County Council v Lamond* (1999) 31 HLR 1051, [1999] EGLR 32, CA. In *Barron v Borders Regional Council* 1987 SLT (Lands Tr) 36, the Lands Tribunal rejected the argument that a headmaster was prevented by equivalent provisions in Scottish legislation from purchasing the schoolhouse. It was held, in *Berkshire County Council v Greenfield* [1996] EGCS 38, CA, that a school caretaker who stayed on after employment ceased but who obtained a caretaker post with the same employer but for another school might be able to establish that the tenancy had become a secure one after the first job ended. The test is objective. The word "for" in para 2(1) should be read as "to enable", and the essential question is whether the required occupation of the property was intended to promote, and was reasonably capable of promoting, the better performance of the employee's duties: see *Wragg v Surrey County Council* [2008] EWCA Civ 19.

A tenancy may cease to be secure if an employee is required by a variation in the contract to occupy the premises for the better performance of his duties: *Elvidge v Coventry City Council* [1994] QB 241, [1993] 4 All ER 903, CA. See now Housing Act 1985 Sch 1 para 2 (4A), (4B), but the tenancy of a school caretaker does not become secure because he stays in occupation after retirement: *South Glamorgan County Council v Griffiths* (1992) 24 HLR 334, [1992] 2 EGLR 232, CA; *Brent London Borough Council v Charles* (1997) 29 HLR 876, CA.

A possession order may be made where the conditions in para 2(1) were not satisfied at the outset but only by a later variation in the terms of the employment: *Coleman v Ipswich Borough Council* [2001] EWCA Civ 852.

A policeman's accommodation is within para 2(2) even though he is liable to pay for the supply of water. The argument that the liability to suppliers following the abolition of water rates by the Water Industry Act 1991 was a form of "rates" was rejected in *Holmes v South Yorkshire Police Authority* [2008] EWCA Civ 51.

Schedule 1 para 2 is not incompatible with ECHR art 14, read with art 8. Service occupiers do not enjoy security of tenure because they are being accommodated as a condition of their employment. The exception is rational; if the employment ceases, the local authority employer is then able to house a replacement in the same accommodation: *Hertfordshire County Council v Davies* [2017] EWHC 1488.

III L&T [156.3]

Land acquired for development The Housing Act 1985 Sch 1 para 3(1) prevents a secure tenancy arising from temporary housing of persons "pending development of the land" even where the intended development differs from that for which the land was acquired: *Attley v Cherwell District Council* (1989) 21 HLR 613, CA. It is not necessary, for the purposes of this provision, that the acquisition (for development) should have been by the landlord: *Hyde Housing Association Ltd v Harrison* (1990) 23 HLR 57, [1991] 1 EGLR 51, CA. Development cannot be regarded as "pending" if the necessary planning permission has been refused: *Lillieshall Road Housing Co-operative Ltd v Brennan* (1991) 24 HLR 195, CA.

III L&T [156.4]

Accommodation for homeless persons Cases on Housing Act 1985 Sch 1 para 4, as enacted, establish that a person given exclusive possession of accommodation under the Housing (Homeless Persons) Act 1977 s 3(4) (Housing Act 1996 s 188) will be treated as being granted a tenancy rather than a licence, even though inquiries as to the existence of a priority need are still pending: such a tenancy becomes secure after 12 months from the (Housing Act 1985) s 64 notification: *Eastleigh Borough Council v Walsh* [1985] 2 All ER 112, [1985] 1 WLR 525, HL. On the other hand, in *Kensington and Chelsea Royal Borough Council v Hayden* (1984) 17 HLR 114, [1985] CLY 1643, CA and again in *Ogwr Borough Council v Dykes* [1989] 2 All ER 880, [1989] 1 WLR 295, CA the Court of Appeal upheld a possession order against a person who had been let into occupation under the Housing (Homeless Persons) Act 1977 s 4(3) (Housing Act 1985 s 65(3)), on the grounds that he had been granted a licence, not a tenancy, and that it had been terminated within 12 months. But in *Family Housing Association v Jones* [1990] 1 All ER 385, [1990] 1 WLR 779, CA, the Court of Appeal doubted whether temporary housing could be construed as creating a bare licence in the case of a self-contained flat with exclusive possession. On the other hand, the Housing Act 1985 Sch 1 para 4, which applies to tenancies granted to accommodate the homeless on or after 1 April 1997, is unlikely to give rise to such questions. If a case falls within paragraph 4 and paragraph 6 as well, possession may be granted as falling within paragraph 4 without the further ground being advanced: *City of Westminster v Boraliu* [2007] EWCA Civ 1339, [2008] 1 WLR 2408, [2008] HLR 42.

The notification requirement under Sch 1, para 4 requires the landlord to notify tenant that the tenancy was to be regarded as secure at the date of grant, and not merely at some unspecified date in the future. The signing by tenants of an introductory tenancy which included the words "the tenancy will become a secure tenancy at the end of the trial period" did not amount to notification by a local authority of a secure tenancy under para 4: see *Wandsworth London Borough Council v Tompkins* [2015] EWCA Civ 846, [2015] All ER (D) 26 (Aug).

III L&T [156.5]

Short-term arrangements The requirement in Housing Act 1985 Sch 1 para 6(a) that the dwelling-house should have been leased to the landlord is satisfied where the landlord holds under a licence: *Tower Hamlets London Borough Council v Miah* [1992] QB 622, [1992] 2 All ER 667, CA. The purpose of paragraph 6 is to encourage private landlords, who want to be able to get their properties back on short notice, to enter into temporary arrangements with local authorities to provide accommodation. But all four requirements have to be met. A head lease which provides that the premises will be yielded up with vacant possession at the end or sooner determination of the term, but which does not add "or when required by him" has been held not to satisfy the condition in sub-paragraph (b): *Haringey London Borough Council v Hickey* [2006] EWCA Civ 373, [2006] HLR 36, (2006) Times 5 June.

III L&T [156.5A]

Temporary accommodation during works Para 7 does not apply where the displaced tenant had a secure tenancy in the first place. If the tenant refuses to return when the works have been completed, possession of the temporary accommodation may be recovered instead under ground 8 of Sch 2: *Lambeth London Borough Council v Gent* [2001] Legal Action July 32, Lambeth Cty Ct.

III L&T [156.6]

"Designated course" The following courses are designated for the purposes of Housing Act 1985 Sch 1 para 10, by the Secure Tenancies (Designated Courses) Regulations 1980, SI 1980/1407

(a) any full-time course of which s 1 of the Education Act 1962 from time to time applies;
(b) any full-time post-graduate course, that is to say, a course to which only students who hold a first degree of a university or an equivalent qualification are admitted; and
(c) any other full-time course provided by an establishment of further education which is maintained or assisted by a local education authority or in respect of the maintenance of which grants are for the time being paid in pursuance of Regulations made under s 100 (1)(b) of the Education Act 1944.

Full-time courses at other establishments were designated by the Secure Tenancies (Designated Courses) (Amendment) Regulations 1993, SI 1993/931.

III L&T [156.7]

1954 Act tenancies A secure tenancy does not arise where the premises were formerly occupied for combined business and residential use: *Webb v Barnet London Borough Council* (1988) 21 HLR 228, [1989] 1 EGLR 49, CA.

III L&T [156.8]

Family intervention tenancies Paragraph 4ZA (family intervention tenancies) was inserted by s 297 of the Housing and Regeneration Act 2008 and brought into force by SI 2008/3068 on 1 January 2009, but not so as to affect tenancies granted before that date. Provisions regarding the termination of such tenancies are contained in section 298 of that Act, the text of which is set out at **III L&T [344]**. See also the Family Intervention Tenancies (Review of Local Authority Decisions) (England) Regulations 2008, SI 2008/3111.

SCHEDULE 2

GROUNDS FOR POSSESSION OF DWELLING-HOUSES LET UNDER SECURE TENANCIES

Section 84

PART I

GROUNDS ON WHICH COURT MAY ORDER POSSESSION IF IT CONSIDERS IT REASONABLE

GROUND 1

III L&T [157]

Rent lawfully due from the tenant has not been paid or an obligation of the tenancy has been broken or not performed.

GROUND 2

The tenant or a person residing in or visiting the dwelling-house

(a) has been guilty of conduct causing or likely to cause a nuisance or annoyance to a person residing, visiting or otherwise engaging in a lawful activity in the locality,

[(aa) has been guilty of conduct causing or likely to cause a nuisance or annoyance to the landlord of the dwelling-house, or a person employed (whether or not by the landlord) in connection with the exercise of the landlord's housing management functions, and that is directly or indirectly related to or affects those functions,], or

(b) has been convicted of

(i) using the dwelling-house or allowing it to be used for immoral or illegal purposes, or

(ii) an indictable offence committed in, or in the locality of, the dwelling-house.

GROUND 2ZA

The tenant or an adult residing in the dwelling-house has been convicted of an indictable offence which took place during, and at the scene of, a riot in the United Kingdom.

In this Ground—

"adult" means a person aged 18 or over;

"indictable offence" does not include an offence that is triable only summarily by virtue of section 22 of the Magistrates' Courts Act 1980 (either way offences where value involved is small);

"riot" is to be construed in accordance with section 1 of the Public Order Act 1986.

This Ground applies only in relation to dwelling-houses in England.

GROUND 2A

The dwelling-house was occupied (whether alone or with others) by a married couple, a couple who are civil partners of each other, a couple living together as husband and wife or a couple living together as if they were civil partners and

(a) one or both of the partners is a tenant of the dwelling-house,

(b) one partner has left because of violence or threats of violence by the other towards

(i) that partner, or

(ii) a member of the family of that partner who was residing with that partner immediately before the partner left, and

(c) the court is satisfied that the partner who has left is unlikely to return.

GROUND 3

The condition of the dwelling-house or of any of the common parts has deteriorated owing to acts of waste by, or the neglect or default of, the tenant or a person residing in the dwelling-house and, in the case of an act of waste by, or the neglect or default of, a person lodging with the tenant or a sub-tenant of his, the tenant has not taken such steps as he ought reasonably to have taken for the removal of the lodger or sub-tenant.

GROUND 4

The condition of furniture provided by the landlord for use under the tenancy, or for use in the common parts, has deteriorated owing to ill-treatment by the tenant or a person residing in the dwelling-house and, in the case of ill-treatment by a person lodging with the tenant or a sub-tenant of his, the tenant has not taken such steps as he ought reasonably to have taken for the removal of the lodger or sub-tenant.

GROUND 5

The tenant is the person, or one of the persons, to whom the tenancy was granted and the landlord was induced to grant the tenancy by a false statement made knowingly or recklessly [by

(a) tenant, or

(b) a person acting at the tenant's instigation.]

GROUND 6

The tenancy was assigned to the tenant, or to a predecessor in title of his who is a member of his family and is residing in the dwelling-house, by an assignment made by virtue of section 92 (assignments by way of exchange) and a premium was paid either in connection with that assignment or the assignment which the tenant or predecessor himself made by virtue of that section.

In this paragraph "premium" means any fine or other like sum and any other pecuniary consideration in addition to rent.

GROUND 7

The dwelling-house forms part of, or is within the curtilage of, a building which, or so much of it as is held by the landlord, is held mainly for purposes other than housing purposes and consists mainly of accommodation other than housing accommodation, and

(a) the dwelling-house was let to the tenant or a predecessor in title of his in consequence of the tenant or predecessor being in the employment of the landlord, or of

a local authority,

a development corporation,

a housing action trust,

a Mayoral development corporation,

an urban development corporation,

[. . .], or

the governors of an aided school,

and

(b) the tenant or a person residing in the dwelling-house has been guilty of conduct such that, having regard to the purpose for which the building is used, it would not be right for him to continue in occupation of the dwelling-house.

GROUND 8

The dwelling-house was made available for occupation by the tenant (or a predecessor in title of his) while works were carried out on the dwelling-house which he previously occupied as his only or principal home and

(a) the tenant (or predecessor) was a secure tenant of the other dwelling-house at the time when he ceased to occupy it as his home,

(b) the tenant (or predecessor) accepted the tenancy of the dwelling-house of which possession is sought on the understanding that he would give up occupation when, on completion of the works, the other dwelling-house was again available for occupation by him under a secure tenancy, and

(c) the works have been completed and the other dwelling-house is so available.

III L&T [157.1]

Interpretation See the Housing Act 1985 s 4 (see para **III L&T [102]**) for definition of the bodies specified in Housing Act 1985 Sch 2 Pt I Ground 7.

III L&T [157.2]

Grounds 1 to 4 These correspond, with certain alterations, to the Rent Act 1977, Sch 15 Cases 1–4 (see para **III L&T [82]**), except that Ground 2A which was added by the Housing Act 1996 s 145. The creation of a sub-tenancy may be a breach for the purposes of Ground 1 although the tenant's mind may have been confused and uncertain at the time: *Brent London Borough Council v Cronin* (1997) 30 HLR 43, CA.

III L&T [157.2A]

Ground 1 A social landlord which brings a residential possession claim based solely on claims for rent arrears should comply with the Pre-Action Protocol for Possession Claims Based on Rent Arrears. Courts will take into account whether the Protocol has been followed when considering what orders to make. The Protocol does not apply to claims in respect of long leases or to claims for possession where there is no security of tenure. If, after complying with the initial requirements of the Protocol, a social landlord decides to resort to court proceedings, it should take care to comply with paragraphs 12 and 13. If either the landlord or the tenant fails unreasonably to comply with the Protocol they may face sanctions (see paragraphs 14 and 15).

III L&T [157.2AA]

Ground 2 Where Ground 2 (nuisance, annoyance or conviction of an offence) has been established, it may be appropriate to make a suspended possession order on condition that the tenant commits no further breaches of his tenancy; see *Greenwich London Borough Council v Grogan* (2000) 33 HLR 140, CA. However, when deciding whether it is reasonable to order possession under Ground 2, it is wrong for the court to consider the availability of other remedies such as an injunction to restrain anti-social behaviour; see *Newcastle City Council v Morrison* (2000) 32 HLR 891, CA. In *Harlow District Council v Sewell* (1999) LAG February 2000, 25 the Court of Appeal held that it is a nuisance for the purpose of Ground 2 to keep an excessive number of cats if they roam on to neighbouring property, defecate and cause damage, even though the requirements of common law nuisance may not be satisfied.

A local authority was held to be entitled to an outright possession order against a tenant who had been convicted of being knowingly concerned in the cultivation of cannabis, since only in exceptional circumstances, where there was cogent evidence to demonstrate that the tenant's particular conduct had ceased, should an order be suspended: see *Sandwell Metropolitan Borough Council v Hensley* [2007] EWCA Civ 1425, 151 Sol Jo LB 1436.

In a case where atrocious and intimidating behaviour by a mother and a 13 year old son, who was subject to an anti-social behaviour order, made life intolerable for neighbours and where there was no expression of remorse or well founded expectation of improvement a suspended order should not have been made and an order for immediate possession was substituted by the Court of Appeal: *Manchester City Council v Higgins* [2005] EWCA Civ 1423, [2006] 1 All ER 841, (2005) Times, 14 December.

III L&T [157.2B]

Ground 2A In *Camden London Borough Council v Mallett* (2001) 33 HLR 204, CA, it was held that a landlord relying on Ground 2A had to show that the violence, or threat of violence, was the dominant cause of the partner leaving and not simply "a" cause of the partner leaving the dwelling-house.

III L&T [157.3]

Rent and water rates Where a local authority agrees with a water company and with its tenants that it will collect water rates on the company's behalf, a failure by the tenant to pay the water rates is a breach of obligation within the Housing Act 1985 Sch 2 Pt I Ground 1: *Lambeth London Borough Council v Thomas* (1997) 30 HLR 89, CA. A new tenant who promises to pay off the arrears of rent of the former tenant is not in breach under Ground 1 if he/she fails to keep the promise because the new tenant has not inherited the former tenant's obligation to discharge the arrears nor is the obligation a term of the new tenancy: *Notting Hill Housing Trust v Jones* (1999) 20 January, LAG March 1999 23, CA.

III L&T [157.4]

Nuisance caused by someone residing with the tenant A possession order may be made against the tenant because of the nuisance caused by the tenant's son even though the tenant may not be at fault: *Kensington and Chelsea Royal London Borough Council v Simmonds* [1996] 3 FCR 246, 29 HLR 507, CA (followed in *London Borough of Camden v Gilsenan* (1998) 31 HLR 81, CA) and see also *West Kent Housing Association v Davies* (1998) 31 HLR 415, CA. In *Portsmouth City Council v Bryant* (2000) 32 HLR 906, CA the court confirmed that no personal fault on the tenant's part is required to bring a case within Ground 2. See also *Greenwich London Borough Council v Tuitt* [2014] EWCA Civ 1669,

[2015] HLR 197 where the Court of Appeal approved an outright order for possession in a case where the tenant's young son, who was a member of a gang, was convicted of a serious assault, although the mother, who was the tenant, was not complicit in his violence and anti-social behaviour. However, the absence of personal fault would be a relevant consideration when the court considered whether it would be reasonable to make a possession order and whether to suspend the order (and may also raise issues under Art 8 of the Convention on Human Rights, per Sedley LJ). The acts of nuisance or annoyance may take place away from the dwelling-house so long as they affect persons in the neighbourhood: *Northampton Borough Council v Lovatt* (1997) 96 LGR 548, 30 HLR 182, CA.

III L&T [157.5]

Ground 5 The Housing Act 1985 Sch 2 Pt I Ground 5 is printed as amended by the Housing Act 1996 s 146 with effect from 4 February 1997, except where notice of proceedings had already been given under the old law. Where Housing Act 1985 Sch 2 Pt I Ground 5 is established the Court of Appeal will be slow to interfere with the trial judge's decision that it is reasonable to make the order: *Rushcliffe Borough Council v Watson* (1991) 24 HLR 124, CA. It is not a basis for evicting someone who concealed the fact that his right to be in the country had come to an end: *Akinbolu v Hackney London Borough Council* (1996) 29 HLR 259, [1996] NPC 60, CA. Where a tenancy has been obtained by deliberate lying the court's decision on whether it is reasonable to order possession should not anticipate a local authority decision that consequent homelessness must be treated as "intentional" but should weigh the nature and extent of the dishonesty along with other relevant circumstances: *Shrewsbury and Atcham Borough Council v Evans* (1997) 30 HLR 123, CA. See also *Lewisham London Borough Council v Akinsola* (2000) 32 HLR 414, CA.

False statements by the tenant, about the ownership of other property and income from it, have been held sufficient to make a case under Ground 5; *Waltham Forest London Borough Council v Roberts* [2004] EWCA Civ 940, [2005] HLR 2.

A possession order may be made against a fraudulent tenant, based on ground 5, but not against a lawful assignee of the tenancy, even where the assignee is a party to the original deception: *Islington London Borough Council v Uckac* [2006] EWCA Civ 340, [2006] 1 WLR 1303, (2006) Times, 19 April, CA.

III L&T [157.6]

Ground 7 Housing action trust employment has been added to Housing Act 1985 Sch 2 Pt I Ground 7 para (a) by the Housing Act 1988 s 83(6).

III L&T [157.7]

Curtilage In *Dyer v Dorset County Council* [1989] QB 346, [1988] 3 WLR 213, CA, a staff house in college grounds was held not to be within the curtilage of the college building: a curtilage is a small court or piece of ground attached to a dwelling-house and forming one enclosure with it. See, too, *Barwick v Kent County Council* (1992) 24 HLR 341, [1992] EGCS 12, CA. In *Skerritts of Nottingham v Secretary of State for the Environment, Transport and the Regions (No 2)* [2001] QB 59, [2000] 3 WLR 511, CA it was doubted whether a curtilage must necessarily be a small area.

III L&T [157.8]

Forms and Precedents For particulars of claim for possession under the Housing Act 1985, see **BCCP O[152]–BCCP O[154]**. All claims for recovery of possession of land must now be brought under CPR Pt 55 (see para **CPR 55**). The particulars of claim must be filed and served with the claim form (see para **CPR 55.4**) and the contents of the particulars of claim must comply with the requirements of CPR Pt 16 (see para **CPR 16**) and CPR PD 55 para 2.1 (see para **CPR PD 55**). Where the possession claim relates to residential property and includes a claim for non-payment of rent the particulars of claim must also comply with CPR PD 55 para 2.3 (see para **CPR PD 55**); the particulars of claim in Form N119 should therefore be used for such claims. The defence to a general possession claim should be in Form N11 and the defence to a claim for possession for residential premises which includes a claim for non-payment of rent should be in Form N11R. If the defendant does not file a defence within 14 days of service of the particulars of claim, he may take part in the hearing but the court will take into account his failure when deciding costs: para **CPR 55.7**. A table of the appropriate forms to be used in possession claims can be found at **BCCP O[12]**; the forms can also be found in the Forms supplement, the FORMS section of your CD-ROM and at **BCCP O[80]** onwards.

PART II

GROUNDS ON WHICH THE COURT MAY ORDER POSSESSION IF SUITABLE ALTERNATIVE ACCOMMODATION IS AVAILABLE

GROUND 9

III L&T [158]

The dwelling-house is overcrowded, within the meaning of Part X, in such circumstances as to render the occupier guilty of an offence.

GROUND 10

The landlord intends, within a reasonable time of obtaining possession of the dwelling-house

(a) to demolish or reconstruct the building or part of the building comprising the dwelling-house, or

(b) to carry out work on that building or on land let together with, and thus treated as part of, the dwelling-house,

and cannot reasonably do so without obtaining possession of the dwelling-house.

GROUND 10A

The dwelling-house is in an area which is the subject of a redevelopment scheme approved by the Secretary of State or the Regulator of Social Housing or Scottish Homes in accordance with Part V of this Schedule and the landlord intends within a reasonable time of obtaining possession to dispose of the dwelling-house in accordance with the scheme.

or

Part of the dwelling-house is in such an area and the landlord intends within a reasonable time of obtaining possession to dispose of that part in accordance with the scheme and for that purpose reasonably requires possession of the dwelling-house.

GROUND 11

The landlord is a charity and the tenant's continued occupation of the dwelling-house would conflict with the objects of the charity.

III L&T [158.1]

Ground 9 This corresponds to the Rent Act 1977 s 101.

III L&T [158.2]

Ground 10 This is similar to the Landlord and Tenant Act 1954 s 30 (1)(f) (see para **III L&T [22]**). In *Wansbeck District Council v Marley* (1987) 20 HLR 247, CA, the Court of Appeal held that the authority must show a *settled* intention to carry out work, although a formal resolution is not necessary; and must establish the impracticability of carrying out the work without first obtaining possession. As to the particulars required by Housing Act 1985 s 83 (2)(c) (see para **III L&T [107]**), see the notes to that section (see para **III L&T [108.4]**).

III L&T [158.3]

Charity "Charity" has the same meaning as in the Charities Act 1993; see Housing Act 1985 s 622 (see para **III L&T [155]**).

LANDLORD & TENANT AND HOUSING

PART III

GROUNDS ON WHICH THE COURT MAY ORDER POSSESSION IF IT CONSIDERS IT REASONABLE AND SUITABLE ALTERNATIVE ACCOMMODATION IS AVAILABLE

GROUND 12

III L&T [159]

The dwelling-house forms part of, or is within the curtilage of, a building which, or so much of it as is held by the landlord, is held mainly for purposes other than housing purposes and consists mainly of accommodation other than housing accommodation, or is situated in a cemetery, and

(a) the dwelling-house was let to the tenant or a predecessor in title of his in consequence of the tenant or predecessor being in the employment of the landlord or of

a local authority,

a development corporation,

a housing action trust,

[a Mayoral development corporation,]

an urban development corporation,

[. . .], or

the governors of an aided school,

and that employment has ceased, and

(b) the landlord reasonably requires the dwelling-house for occupation as a residence for some person either engaged in the employment of the landlord, or of such a body, or with whom a contract for such employment has been entered into conditional on housing being provided.

GROUND 13

The dwelling-house has features which are substantially different from those of ordinary dwelling-houses and which are designed to make it suitable for occupation by a physically disabled person who requires accommodation of a kind provided by the dwelling-house and

(a) there is no longer such a person residing in the dwelling-house, and

(b) the landlord requires it for occupation (whether alone or with members of his family) by such a person.

GROUND 14

The landlord is a housing association or housing trust which lets dwelling-houses only for occupation (whether alone or with others) by persons whose circumstances (other than merely financial circumstances) make it especially difficult for them to satisfy their needs for housing, and

(a) either there is no longer such a person residing in the dwelling-house or the tenant has received from a local housing authority an offer of accommodation in premises which are to be let as a separate dwelling under a secure tenancy, and

(b) the landlord requires the dwelling-house for occupation (whether alone or with members of his family) by such a person.

GROUND 15

The dwelling-house is one of a group of dwelling-houses which it is the practice of the landlord to let for occupation by persons with special needs and

(a) a social service or special facility is provided in close proximity to the group of dwelling-houses in order to assist persons with those special needs,

(b) there is no longer a person with those special needs residing in the dwelling-house, and

(c) the landlord requires the dwelling-house for occupation (whether alone or with members of his family) by a person who has those special needs.

GROUND 15A

The dwelling-house is in England, the accommodation afforded by it is more extensive than is reasonably required by the tenant and—

(a) the tenancy vested in the tenant by virtue of section 89 (succession to periodic tenancy) or 90 (devolution of term certain) in a case where the tenant was not the previous tenant's spouse or civil partner, and

(b) notice of the proceedings for possession was served under section 83 (or, where no such notice was served, the proceedings for possession were begun) more than six months but less than twelve months after the relevant date.

For this purpose "the relevant date" is—

(a) the date of the previous tenant's death, or

(b) if the court so directs, the date on which, in the opinion of the court, the landlord (or, in the case of joint landlords, any one of them) became aware of the previous tenant's death.

The matters to be taken into account by the court in determining whether it is reasonable to make an order on this ground include—

(a) the age of the tenant,

(b) the period (if any) during which the tenant has occupied the dwelling-house as the tenant's only or principal home, and

(c) any financial or other support given by the tenant to the previous tenant.

GROUND 16

The dwelling-house is in Wales and the accommodation afforded by it is more extensive than is reasonably required by the tenant and

(a) the tenancy vested in the tenant by virtue of section 89 (succession to periodic tenancy) [or 90 (devolution of term certain)], the tenant being qualified to succeed by virtue of section 87 (b) (members of family other than spouse), and

(b) notice of the proceedings for possession was served under section 83 (or, where no such notice was served, the proceedings for possession were begun) more than six months but less than twelve months the relevant date.

For this purpose "the relevant date" is—

(a) the date of the previous tenant's death, or

(b) if the court so directs, the date on which, in the opinion of the court, the landlord (or, in the case of joint landlords, any one of them) became aware of the previous tenant's death.

The matters to be taken into account by the court in determining whether it is reasonable to make an order on this ground include

(a) the age of the tenant,

(b) the period during which the tenant has occupied the dwelling-house as his only or principal home, and

(c) any financial or other support given by the tenant to the previous tenant.

III L&T [159.1]

Ground 15 In *Martin v Motherwell District Council* 1991 SLT (Lands Tr) 4 the Lands Tribunal held that 36 specially designed houses for the disabled were not a "group" because they were not physically close to each other or linked by a common call system or warden facility.

III L&T [159.1A]

Ground 15A Ground 15A inserted by s 162 of the Localism Act 2011; in force from 1 April 2012.

III L&T [159.2]

Ground 16 On the coming into force of s 162 of the Localism Act 2011 on 1 April 2012 Ground 16 was amended so as to apply only to dwellings in Wales. Three conditions have to be satisfied before an order for possession can be made under Ground 16: First, that the accommodation is more extensive than required by the tenant, secondly, that suitable alternative accommodation will be available and, thirdly, that it is reasonable to make the order. The findings in respect of all three conditions should be made in the light of the circumstances (for example as to the composition of the family of a tenant who has succeeded to a secure tenancy) at the date of the hearing: *Wandsworth London Borough Council v Randall* [2007] EWCA Civ 1126, [2007] All ER (D) 98 (Nov). In addition, if the proceedings are not started within a year of the death the conditions of Ground 16 are not fulfilled, even where the death has been deliberately concealed throughout the statutory period: *Newport City Council v Charles* (2008) Times, 11 August, CA. For a case where the first two requirements were satisfied but not the third see *Bracknell Forest Borough Council v Green* [2009] EWCA Civ 238, 153 Sol Jo (no 12) 28, [2009] 2 P&CR D10.

PART IV
SUITABILITY OF ACCOMMODATION

III L&T [160]

1. For the purposes of section 84 (2) (b) and (c) (case in which court is not to make an order for possession unless satisfied that suitable accommodation will be available) accommodation is suitable if it consists of premises
   - (a) which are to be let as a separate dwelling under a secure tenancy, or
   - (b) which are to be let as a separate dwelling under a protected tenancy, not being a tenancy under which the landlord might recover possession under one of the Cases in Part II of Schedule 15 to the Rent Act 1977 (cases where court must order possession), or
   - (c) which are to be let as a separate dwelling under an assured tenancy which is neither an assured shorthold tenancy, within the meaning of Part I of the Housing Act 1988, nor a tenancy under which the landlord might recover possession under any of Grounds 1 to 5 in Sch 2 to that Act,

and, in the opinion of the court, the accommodation is reasonably suitable to the needs of the tenant and his family.

2. In determining whether the accommodation is reasonably suitable to the needs of the tenant and his family, regard shall be had to
   - (a) the nature of the accommodation which it is the practice of the landlord to allocate to persons with similar needs;
   - (b) the distance of the accommodation available from the place of work or education of the tenant and of any members of his family;
   - (c) its distance from the home of any member of the tenant's family if proximity to it is essential to that member's or the tenant's well-being;
   - (d) the needs (as regards extent of accommodation) and means of the tenant and his family;
   - (e) the terms on which the accommodation is available and the terms of the secure tenancy;
   - (f) if furniture was provided by the landlord for use under the secure tenancy, whether furniture is to be provided for use in the other accommodation, and if so the nature of the furniture to be provided.

3. Where possession of a dwelling-house is sought on ground 9 (overcrowding such as to render occupier guilty of offence), other accommodation may be reasonably suitable to the needs of the tenant and his family notwithstanding that the permitted number of persons for that accommodation, as defined in

section 326 (3) (overcrowding: the space standard), is less than the number of persons living in the dwelling-house of which possession is sought.

4.(1) A certificate of the appropriate local housing authority that they will provide suitable accommodation for the tenant by a date specified in the certificate is conclusive evidence that suitable accommodation will be available for him by that date.

(2) The appropriate local housing authority is the authority for the district in which the dwelling-house of which possession is sought is situated.

(3) This paragraph does not apply where the landlord is a local housing authority.

III L&T [160.1]

Accommodation is suitable In the Rent Act 1977 Sch 15 Pt IV (see para **III L&T [85]**), accommodation is "deemed" to be suitable if certain conditions are satisfied. It is not clear whether the conditions specified are indicative or exhaustive of what is suitable for the purposes of that Act; see the notes thereto (see para **III L&T [85.2]**). The use of the word "is" here makes clear that Housing Act 1985 Sch 2 Pt IV para 1 is exhaustive and not merely indicative. In *R v Brent London Borough Council, ex p Omar* (1991) 23 HLR 446 (a decision on the duty to house the homeless in suitable accommodation) the Divisional Court held that housing on an estate which made the would-be tenant suicidal because of its resemblance to a prison might be regarded as unsuitable.

Where there was no alternative accommodation available at the time of the hearing, the court's decision that it would be available when the order took effect was upheld on appeal. The expression 'suitable alternative accommodation' in Part IV was broad enough to encompass accommodation identified by reference to its essential characteristics and did not require the identification of a specific property. The Court of Appeal further held that circumstances might sometimes justify a conditional order which would only be effective if suitable accommodation did indeed become available and gave guidance as to the content of such a conditional order: *Reading Borough Council v Holt* [2013] EWCA Civ 641, [2013] HLR 536, [2013] PLSCS 128.

III L&T [160.2]

Reasonably suitable to the needs of the tenant and his family It is necessary to provide for the needs of all the members of the tenant's family living in the family, including an estranged wife: *Wandsworth London Borough Council v Fadayomi* [1987] 3 All ER 474, [1987] 1 WLR 1473, CA. In addition to the matters found in Housing Act 1985 Sch 2 Pt IV para 2 (a) to (f) see also the notes to the Rent Act 1977 Sch 15 Pt IV (see para **III L&T [85.7]**). A tenant's need for a garden may be a need within Housing Act 1985 Sch 2 Pt IV para 1 if his hobbies include gardening, but the alternative accommodation may be reasonably suitable even though one particular need cannot be met: *Enfield Borough Council v French* (1984) 49 P & CR 223, 17 HLR 211, CA.

PART V
APPROVAL OF REDEVELOPMENT SCHEMES FOR PURPOSES OF GROUND 10A

III L&T [161]

1.(1) The Secretary of State may, on the application of the landlord, approve for the purposes of ground 10A in Part II of this Schedule a scheme for the disposal and redevelopment of an area of land consisting of or including the whole or part of one or more dwelling-houses.

(2) For this purpose

(a) "disposal" means a disposal of any interest in the land (including the grant of an option), and

(b) "redevelopment" means the demolition or reconstruction of buildings or the carrying out of other works to buildings or land;

and it is immaterial whether the disposal is to precede or follow the redevelopment.

(3) The Secretary of State may on the application of the landlord approve a variation of a scheme previously approved by him and may, in particular, approve a variation adding land to the area subject to the scheme.

2.(1) Where a landlord proposes to apply to the Secretary of State for the approval or variation of a scheme it shall serve a notice in writing on any secure tenant of a dwelling-house affected by the proposal stating

(a) the main features of the proposed scheme or, as the case may be, the scheme as proposed to be varied,

(b) that the landlord proposes to apply to the Secretary of State for approval of the scheme or variation, and

(c) the effect of such approval, by virtue of section 84 and ground 10A in Part II of this Schedule, in relation to proceedings for possession of the dwelling-house,

and informing the tenant that he may, within such period as the landlord may allow (which shall be at least 28 days from service of the notice), make representations to the landlord about the proposal.

(2) The landlord shall not apply to the Secretary of State until it has considered any representations made to it within that period.

(3) In the case of a landlord to which section 105 applies (consultation on matters of housing management) the provisions of this paragraph apply in place of the provisions of that section in relation to the approval or variation of a redevelopment scheme.

(1) In considering whether to give his approval to a scheme or variation the Secretary of State shall take into account, in particular

(a) the effect of the scheme on the extent and character of housing accommodation in the neighbourhood,

(b) over what period of time it is proposed that the disposal and redevelopment will take place in accordance with the scheme, and

(c) to what extent the scheme includes provision for housing provided under the scheme to be sold or let to existing tenants or persons nominated by the landlord;

and he shall take into account any representations made to him and, so far as they are brought to his notice, any representations made to the landlord.

(2) The landlord shall give to the Secretary of State such information as to the representations made to it, and other relevant matters, as the Secretary of State may require.

4. The Secretary of State shall not approve a scheme or variation so as to include in the area subject to the scheme

(a) part only of one or more dwelling-houses, or

(b) one or more dwelling-houses not themselves affected by the works involved in redevelopment but which are proposed to be disposed of along with other land which is so affected,

unless he is satisfied that the inclusion is justified in the circumstances.

5.(1) Approval may be given subject to conditions and may be expressed to expire after a specified period.

(2) The Secretary of State, on the application of the landlord or otherwise, may vary an approval so as to

(a) add, remove or vary conditions to which the approval is subject; or

(b) extend or restrict the period after which the approval is to expire.

(3) Where approval is given subject to conditions, the landlord may serve a notice under section 83 or 83ZA (notice of proceedings for possession) specifying ground 10A notwithstanding that the conditions are not yet fulfilled but the court shall not make an order for possession on that ground unless satisfied that they are or will be fulfilled.

6. Where the landlord is a private registered provider of social housing or a housing association registered in the register maintained by Scottish Homes under section 3 of the Housing Associations Act 1985, the Regulator of Social Housing,

or Scottish Homes, (and not the Secretary of State) has the functions conferred by this Part of this Schedule.

7. In this Part of this Schedule references to the landlord of a dwelling-house include any authority or body within section 80 (the landlord condition for secure tenancies) having an interest of any description in the dwelling-house.

SCHEDULE 2A

ABSOLUTE GROUND FOR POSSESSION FOR ANTI-SOCIAL BEHAVIOUR: SERIOUS OFFENCES

Section 84A(9)

VIOLENT OFFENCES

III L&T [161A]

1 Murder.

2 Manslaughter.

3 Kidnapping.

4 False imprisonment.

5 An offence under any of the following sections of the Offences against the Person Act 1861—

- (a) section 4 (soliciting murder),
- (b) section 16 (threats to kill),
- (c) section 18 (wounding with intent to cause grievous bodily harm),
- (d) section 20 (malicious wounding),
- (e) section 21 (attempting to choke, suffocate or strangle in order to commit or assist in committing an indictable offence),
- (f) section 22 (using chloroform etc to commit or assist in the committing of any indictable offence),
- (g) section 23 (maliciously administering poison etc so as to endanger life or inflict grievous bodily harm),
- (h) section 24 (maliciously administering poison etc with intent to injure, aggrieve or annoy any other person),
- (i) section 27 (abandoning or exposing children whereby life is endangered or health permanently injured),
- (j) section 28 (causing bodily injury by explosives),
- (k) section 29 (using explosives etc with intent to do grievous bodily harm),
- (l) section 30 (placing explosives with intent to do bodily injury),
- (m) section 31 (setting spring guns etc with intent to do grievous bodily harm),
- (n) section 38 (assault with intent to resist arrest),
- (o) section 47 (assault occasioning actual bodily harm).

6 An offence under any of the following sections of the Explosive Substances Act 1883—

- (a) section 2 (causing explosion likely to endanger life or property),
- (b) section 3 (attempt to cause explosion, or making or keeping explosive with intent to endanger life or property),
- (c) section 4 (making or possession of explosive under suspicious circumstances).

7 An offence under section 1 of the Infant Life (Preservation) Act 1929 (child destruction).

8 An offence under section 1 of the Children and Young Persons Act 1933 (cruelty to children).

9 An offence under section 1 of the Infanticide Act 1938 (infanticide).

10 An offence under any of the following sections of the Public Order Act 1986—

- (a) section 1 (riot),
- (b) section 2 (violent disorder),

(c) section 3 (affray).

11 An offence under either of the following sections of the Protection from Harassment Act 1997—

(a) section 4 (putting people in fear of violence),

(b) section 4A (stalking involving fear of violence or serious alarm or distress).

12 An offence under any of the following provisions of the Crime and Disorder Act 1998—

(a) section 29 (racially or religiously aggravated assaults),

(b) section 31(1)(a) or (b) (racially or religiously aggravated offences under section 4 or 4A of the Public Order Act 1986),

(c) section 32 (racially or religiously aggravated harassment etc).

13 An offence under either of the following sections of the Female Genital Mutilation Act 2003—

(a) section 1 (female genital mutilation),

(b) section 2 (assisting a girl to mutilate her own genitalia).

14 An offence under section 5 of the Domestic Violence, Crime and Victims Act 2004 (causing or allowing the death of a child or vulnerable adult).

SEXUAL OFFENCES

15 An offence under section 33A of the Sexual Offences Act 1956 (keeping a brothel used for prostitution).

16 An offence under section 1 of the Protection of Children Act 1978 (indecent photographs of children).

17 An offence under section 160 of the Criminal Justice Act 1988 (possession of indecent photograph of a child).

18 An indictable offence under Part 1 of the Sexual Offences Act 2003 (sexual offences).

OFFENSIVE WEAPONS

19 An offence under either of the following sections of the Prevention of Crime Act 1953—

(a) section 1 (prohibition of the carrying of offensive weapons without lawful authority or reasonable excuse),

(b) section 1A (threatening with offensive weapon in public).

20 An offence under any of the following provisions of the Firearms Act 1968—

(a) section 16 (possession of firearm with intent to endanger life),

(b) section 16A (possession of firearm with intent to cause fear of violence),

(c) section 17(1) (use of firearm to resist arrest),

(d) section 17(2) (possession of firearm at time of committing or being arrested for offence specified in Schedule 1 to the Act of 1968),

(e) section 18 (carrying a firearm with criminal intent),

(f) section 19 (carrying a firearm in a public place),

(g) section 20 (trespassing with firearm),

(h) section 21 (possession of firearms by persons previously convicted of crime).

21 An offence under either of the following sections of the Criminal Justice Act 1988—

(a) section 139 (having article with blade or point in public place),

(b) section 139AA (threatening with article with blade or point or offensive weapon).

OFFENCES AGAINST PROPERTY

22 An offence under any of the following sections of the Theft Act 1968—

(a) section 8 (robbery or assault with intent to rob),

(b) section 9 (burglary),

(c) section 10 (aggravated burglary).

23 An offence under section 1 of the Criminal Damage Act 1971 (destroying or damaging property).

24 An offence under section 30 of the Crime and Disorder Act 1998 (racially or religiously aggravated criminal damage).

ROAD TRAFFIC OFFENCES

25 An offence under section 35 of the Offences against the Person Act 1861 (injuring persons by furious driving).

26 An offence under section 12A of the Theft Act 1968 (aggravated vehicle-taking involving an accident which caused the death of any person).

27 An offence under any of the following sections of the Road Traffic Act 1988—

(a) section 1 (causing death by dangerous driving),

(b) section 1A (causing serious injury by dangerous driving),

(c) section 3A (causing death by careless driving when under influence of drink or drugs).

DRUG-RELATED OFFENCES

28 An offence under any of the following provisions of the Misuse of Drugs Act 1971—

(a) section 4 (restriction of production and supply of controlled drugs),

(b) section 5(3) (possession of controlled drugs with intent to supply),

(c) section 8(a) or (b) (occupiers etc of premises to be punishable for permitting unlawful production or supply etc of controlled drugs there).

29 An offence under section 6 of that Act (restrictions of cultivation of cannabis plant) where the cultivation is for profit and the whole or a substantial part of the dwelling-house concerned is used for the cultivation.

MODERN SLAVERY

29A An offence under either of the following sections of the Modern Slavery Act 2015—

(a) section 1 (slavery, servitude and forced or compulsory labour),

(b) section 2 (human trafficking).

INCHOATE OFFENCES

30

(1) An offence of attempting or conspiring the commission of an offence specified or described in this Schedule.

(2) An offence under Part 2 of the Serious Crime Act 2007 (encouraging or assisting) where the offence (or one of the offences) which the person in question intends or believes would be committed is an offence specified or described in this Schedule.

(3) An offence of aiding, abetting, counselling or procuring the commission of an offence specified or described in this Schedule.

SCOPE OF OFFENCES

31 Where this Schedule refers to offences which are offences under the law of England and Wales and another country or territory, the reference is to be read as limited to the offences so far as they are offences under the law of England and Wales.

III L&T [161A.1]

Paragraph 29A: inserted in relation to England by SI 2016/244 and, in relation to Wales, by SI 2016/173. Date in force (in relation to Wales) 16 February 2016; date in force (in relation to England): 17 March 2016.

LANDLORD AND TENANT ACT 1985

(c 70)

GENERAL NOTES ON LANDLORD AND TENANT ACT 1985

III L&T [162]

Jurisdiction The two main topics covered in the provisions set out below are (1) repairing obligations (Landlord and Tenant Act 1985 ss 11–17) (see paras **III L&T [164]–III L&T [170]**) and (2) service charges. The county court has jurisdiction to make a declaration as to the application of Landlord and Tenant Act 1985 s 11 to a lease (Landlord and Tenant Act 1985 s 15, see para **III L&T [168]**) unless excluded under an agreement authorised by the court (Landlord and Tenant Act 1985 s 12, see para **III L&T [165]**). Questions as to the reasonableness of a service charge are now primarily within the jurisdiction of a leasehold valuation tribunal (Landlord and Tenant Act 1985 s 19, see para **III L&T [172]**). The county court can also make an order requiring the landlord to nominate another insurer where the one specified by him under the tenancy is unsatisfactory (Landlord and Tenant Act 1985 Schedule, para 8 (as amended by the Housing Act 1996 s 83 and applied by s 30A of the Landlord and Tenant Act 1985 (**III L&T [176]**). The High Court has concurrent jurisdiction. However, claims under the Landlord and Tenant Act 1985 are landlord and tenant claims within the meaning of CPR Pt 56. They must therefore be started in the county court for the district in which the land is situated (see para **CPR 56.2**). Only in exceptional circumstances (where the claimant can certify that there are complicated disputes of fact or there are points of law of general importance) may a landlord and tenant claim be started in the High Court. The value of the property and the amount of any financial claim may be relevant circumstances, but these factors alone will not normally justify starting the claim in the High Court: CPR PD 56 paras 2.1 to 2.5 (para **CPR PD 56**). If the claim is brought in the High Court then, with effect from 2 December 2002, CPR PD 56 para 2.6 (para **CPR PD 56**) makes clear that the claim must be brought in the Chancery Division.

III L&T [163]

Precedents All claims under the Landlord and Tenant Act 1985 must be brought by means of the Pt 8 procedure, as modified by the Practice Direction to CPR Pt 56: CPR PD 56 para 2.1. The only modification relating to claims under the 1985 Act is found in CPR PD 56 para 6.1, which provides for the manner in which a claim is to be transferred to a leasehold valuation tribunal if the court has ordered a transfer under s 31C of the Act. For a precedent of a Pt 8 claim form seeking a variation of repair obligations under s 12(2) of the Landlord and Tenant Act 1985, see **BCCP O[55]**.

REPAIRING OBLIGATIONS

III L&T [164]

11. Repairing obligations in short leases

(1) In a lease to which this section applies (as to which see sections 13 and 14) there is implied a covenant by the lessor

(a) to keep in repair the structure and exterior of the dwelling-house (including drains, gutters and external pipes),

(b) to keep in repair and proper working order the installations in the dwelling-house for the supply of water, gas and electricity and for sanitation (including basins, sinks, baths and sanitary conveniences, but not other fixtures, fittings and appliances for making use of the supply of water, gas or electricity), and

(c) to keep in repair and proper working order the installations in the dwelling-house for space heating and heating water.

(1A) If a lease to which this section applies is a lease of a dwelling-house which forms part only of a building, then, subject to subsection (1B), the covenant implied by subsection (1) shall have effect as if

(a) the reference in paragraph (a) of that subsection to the dwelling-house included a reference to any part of the building in which the lessor has an estate or interest; and

(b) any reference in paragraphs (b) and (c) of that subsection to an installation in the dwelling-house included a reference to an installation which, directly or indirectly, serves the dwelling-house and which either

(i) forms part of any part of a building in which the lessor has an estate or interest; or

(ii) is owned by the lessor or under his control.

(1B) Nothing in subsection (1A) shall be construed as requiring the lessor to carry out any works or repairs unless the disrepair (or failure to maintain in working order) is such as to affect the lessee's enjoyment of the dwelling-house or of any common parts, as defined in section 60 (1) of the Landlord and Tenant Act 1987, which the lessee, as such, is entitled to use.]

(2) The covenant implied by subsection (1) ("the lessor's repairing covenant") shall not be construed as requiring the lessor

(a) to carry out works or repairs for which the lessee is liable by virtue of his duty to use the premises in a tenant-like manner, or would be so liable but for an express covenant on his part,

(b) to rebuild or reinstate the premises in the case of destruction or damage by fire, or by tempest, flood or other inevitable accident, or

(c) to keep in repair or maintain anything which the lessee is entitled to remove from the dwelling-house.

(3) In determining the standard of repair required by the lessor's repairing covenant, regard shall be had to the age, character and prospective life of the dwelling-house and the locality in which it is situated.

(3A) In any case where

(a) the lessor's repairing covenant has effect as mentioned in subsection (1A), and

(b) in order to comply with the covenant the lessor needs to carry out works or repairs otherwise than in, or to an installation in, the dwelling-house, and

(c) the lessor does not have a sufficient right in the part of the building or the installation concerned to enable him to carry out the required works or repairs,

then, in any proceedings relating to a failure to comply with the lessor's repairing covenant, so far at it requires the lessor to carry out the works or repairs in question, it shall be a defence for the lessor to prove that he used all reasonable endeavours to obtain, but was unable to obtain, such rights as would be adequate to enable him to carry out the works or repairs.

(4) A covenant by the lessee for the repair of the premises is of no effect so far as it relates to the matters mentioned in subsection (1) (a) to (c), except so far as it imposes on the lessee any of the requirements mentioned in subsection (2) (a) or (c).

(5) The reference in subsection (4) to a covenant by the lessee for the repair of the premises includes a covenant

(a) to put in repair or deliver up in repair,

(b) to paint, point, or render,

(c) to pay money in lieu of repairs by the lessee, or

(d) to pay money on account of repairs by the lessor.

(6) In a lease in which the lessor's repairing covenant is implied there is also implied a covenant by the lessee that the lessor, or any person authorised by him in writing, may at reasonable times of the day and on giving 24 hours' notice in writing to the occupier, enter the premises comprised in the lease for the purpose of viewing their condition and state of repair.

III L&T [164.1]

Covenant to keep in repair The obligation to keep the structure in repair may include renewing a damp course or foundations where defects have arisen: *Smedley v Chumley and Hawke Ltd* (1981) 44 P & CR 50, CA; *Elmcroft Developments Ltd v Tankersley-Sawyer* (1984) 15 HLR 63, [1984] 1 EGLR 47, CA; *Stent v Monmouth District Council* (1987) 54 P & CR 193, 19 HLR 269, CA, or renewing plaster which has perished as a result of saturation: *Staves v Leeds City Council* (1990) 23 HLR 107, [1992] 2 EGLR 37, CA (although as to internal plasterwork, see *Irvine v Moran* (1990) 24 HLR 1, [1991] 1 EGLR 261), or replacing external cladding, even though its defective condition is due to the original construction of the building: *Crédit Suisse v Beegas Nominees Ltd* [1994] 4 All ER 803, 69 P & CR 177. The mere existence of damp is not disrepair; but if there is damage or deterioration, such as defective plaster, then the covenantor is liable to remedy that damage, and that obligation might include installing a damp-proof course to prevent further damage: see *Uddin v Islington London Borough Council* [2015] EWCA Civ 369, [2015] HLR 584, [2015] PLSCS 128, applying *Elmcroft Developments Ltd*. But the obligation does not include renewing substantially the whole of the demised premises: *Ravenseft Properties Ltd v Davstone (Holdings) Ltd* [1980] QB 12, [1979] 1 All ER 929; *McDougall v Easington District Council* (1989) 21 HLR 310, CA; nor altering the design to include, for example, a damp course or different windows or additional insulation: *Wainwright v Leeds City Council* (1984) 13 HLR 117, CA; *Quick v Taff-Ely Borough Council* [1986] QB 809, [1985] 3 All ER 321, CA. See also *Eyre v McCracken* (2000) 80 P & CR 220, CA. In distinguishing between a "repair" and an "improvement" it is appropriate to consider specifically (a) the contractual relationship between the parties at the date of letting; (b) the substantiality of the work required; and (c) the probable cost of the work related to the capital value of the property: *Post Office v Aquarius Properties Ltd* [1985] 2 EGLR 105, 276 Estates Gazette 923. The decision, at first instance, that the work to remedy the defective structure was not within the repairing covenant, was upheld on appeal on the ground that the defect arose in the original construction of the building: *Post Office v Aquarius Properties Ltd* [1987] 1 All ER 1055, 54 P & CR 61, CA; but much depends on the actual words used: *Crédit Suisse v Beegas Nominees Ltd* [1994] 4 All ER 803, 69 P & CR 177. On the other hand the complete replacement of a pitched roof could be a "repair", according to *Murray v Birmingham City Council* (1987) 20 HLR 39, CA (and see *New England Properties v Portsmouth New Shops* (1993) 67 P & CR 141, [1993] 1 EGLR 84), although it was held not to be within a repairing covenant in *Elite Investments Ltd v T I Bainbridge Silencers Ltd* [1986] 2 EGLR 43, 280 Estates Gazette 1001. So, too, the conversion of a flat roof to a pitched roof constitutes "works of maintenance" for the purposes of the Local Authorities (Goods and Services) Act

1970 s 1 (4): *R v Hackney London Borough Council, ex p Secretary of State for Environment* (1989) 88 LGR 96. Where the terms of a tenancy required the landlord not only to maintain the dwelling in good repair but also in good condition, this was construed as requiring the landlord to insulate the building to prevent mould: *Welsh v Greenwich London Borough Council* (2000) 81 P & CR 144, 33 HLR 438, CA.

A former tenant whose status is that of a tolerated trespasser has no remedy for breach of a repairing covenant though a remedy may lie in the tort of nuisance: *Pemberton v Southwark London Borough Council* [2000] 3 All ER 924, [2000] 1 WLR 1672, CA.

Where, however, a tolerated trespasser obtains the discharge of a possession order under section 85 of the Housing Act 1985, the landlord's repairing obligations are retrospectively revived: *Lambeth London Borough Council v Rogers* (1999) 32 HLR 361, [2000] 1 EGLR 28, CA.

There is no implied covenant that premises which are let should be fit for human habitation and the obligation to keep in good repair is not to be construed as including an obligation on public housing authorities to see that premises are fit (eg by not being subject to damp and condensation): *Lee v Leeds City Council, Ratcliffe v Sandwell Metropolitan Borough Council* [2002] EWCA Civ 06, [2002] 1 WLR 1488.

III L&T [164.2]

Latent defects The repairing covenant does not normally impose any obligations in respect of latent defects until the landlord has notice of them: see *O'Brien v Robinson* [1973] AC 912, [1973] 1 All ER 583, HL; *Al Hassani v Merrigan* (1987) 20 HLR 238, [1988] 1 EGLR 93, CA. But if he has notice of them it does not matter whether it took the form of a formal complaint by the tenant: *Dinefwr Borough Council v Jones* (1987) 19 HLR 445, [1987] 2 EGLR 58, CA; *Hall v Howard* (1988) 20 HLR 566, [1988] 2 EGLR 75, CA (valuation report sent to landlord in unsuccessful negotiations for purchase of reversion by tenant). And a landlord may be in breach without notice as regards the duty to repair parts of the building excluded from the demise: *British Telecommunications plc v Sun Life Assurance Society plc* [1996] Ch 69, [1995] 4 All ER 44, CA.

In *Earle v Charalambous* [2006] EWCA Civ 1338,(2006) 42 EG 245 (CS), Times, 15 November, the Court of Appeal drew attention to the distinction, in the case of a standard lessor's repairing covenant, between disrepair in the demised premises, in respect of which there is no breach until the lessor has received notice of the defect and a reasonable time to carry out remedial works, and disrepair in other parts of the building within the lessor's control in respect of which the general rule (as stated in *British Telecommunications Plc v Sun Life Assurance Society Plc* (supra)) is that the lessor is in breach as soon as the disrepair arises.

As regards the safety of common parts of a building, the Supreme Court has held (reversing the decision of the Court of Appeal) that, since any want of repair would be known first to the tenant, the duty of the landlord to attend to any disrepair did not arise until the tenant had given notice of it: *Edwards v Kumarasamy* [2016] UKSC 40.

III L&T [164.2A]

Landlord's liability under the Defective Premises Act 1982 The landlord's responsibilities, under s 4 of the Defective Premises Act 1972 are not limited to defects which have been brought to his, or her, notice: *Sykes v Harry* [2001] EWCA Civ 167, [2001] QB 1014.

The repairing duty of a landlord under s 4 does not extend beyond the lessor's duty of maintenance and repair owed under the lease. Thus the danger from the use of annealed glass in a front door would not put the landlord in breach of s 4 if the door was not broken or otherwise in need of maintenance or repair: *Alker v Collingwood Housing Association* [2007] All ER (D) 98 (Feb), (2007) Times, 14 February, CA.

A defect in construction, such as the failure to provide a handrail in breach of building regulations, has been held to be outside the duty of 'repair' and therefore not a relevant defect for the purposes of the Defective Premises Act 1982: *Dodd v Raebarn Estates* [2016] EWHC 262 (QB), [2016] All ER (D) 212 (Feb).

III L&T [164.2B]

Landlord's liability for breach of covenant An award of damages under section 11 of the Act is for a breach of contract, not for a tort committed by the landlord. It is therefore logical for the calculation of the award for damages for stress and inconvenience to be related to the fact that the tenant is not getting proper value for the rent: *Shine v English Churches Housing Group* [2004] EWCA Civ 434, [2004] All ER (D) 125 (Apr), (2004) Times, 2 June, [2004] HLR 42. In fact, in that case the damages were reduced to a figure well below the rental value of the premises because (i) the judge should have started with the basic rule that damages for discomfort and inconvenience should not exceed the rental value and (ii) a substantial discount was required to reflect the tenant's repeated refusal to consider offers of alternative accommodation while the repairs were being done.

III L&T [164.3]

Structure and installations The structure of a house consists of those elements which give the premises their essential appearance, stability and shape: *Irvine v Moran* (1990) 24 HLR 1. It may include plaster forming part of or applied to walls and ceilings: *Grand v Gill* [2011] 1 WLR 2253; [2011] 3 All ER 1043, and the steps and path constituting the means of access to the premises: *Brown v Liverpool Corpn* [1969] 3 All ER 1345, CA, but not a yard at the rear of a house: *Hopwood v Cannock Chase District Council* [1975] 1 All ER 796, [1975] 1 WLR 373, CA. Where essential means of access to a building are retained by the landlord, there is an implied obligation to take reasonable care to keep those parts in reasonable repair, which can only be displaced by an express exclusion: *Liverpool City Council v Irwin* [1977] AC 239, [1976] 2 All ER 39, HL; *King v South Northamptonshire District Council* (1991) 64 P & CR 35, [1992] 1 EGLR 53, CA. Where the dwelling consists of a flat in a block of flats the structure and exterior is that of the particular flat and not that of the whole building: *Campden Hill Towers Ltd v Gardner* [1977] QB 823, [1977] 1 All ER 739, CA. However, the roof over the top floor flat may be part of its "structure and exterior" although not part of the premises demised: *Douglas-Scott v Scorgie* [1984] 1 All ER 1086, [1984] 1 WLR 716, CA and *Irvine v Moran* (1990) 24 HLR 1. See too *Straudley Investments Ltd v Barpress Ltd* [1987] 1 EGLR 69, 282 Estates Gazette 1124, CA. In *Ibrahim v Dovecorn Reversions Ltd* [2001] 30 EG 116, Ch D, the court held that a roof terrace was comprised within the "main structure" of a block of residential flats, such that responsibility for its repair and maintenance lay with the landlord and not with those tenants who had the exclusive use of it. See also *Petersson v Pitt Place (Epsom) Ltd* [2001] EWCA Civ 86, (2001) 82 P & CR 276, where, on similar facts, it was held that the courts will strive to avoid a conclusion that landlords and tenants have overlapping repair obligations. Failure to lag a pipe so that it burst when frozen is a breach of covenant, without the need for a report by the tenant: *Passley v Wandsworth London Borough Council* (1998) 30 HLR 165, CA.

Repair of the "main structures" has been held to include strengthening the floor joists: *Marlborough Park Services Ltd v Rowe* [2006] EWCA Civ 436, [2006] HLR 30.

III L&T [164.4]

Sound-proofing The landlord is not liable for breach of covenant of quiet enjoyment if the flats are not adequately sound-proofed: *Southwark London Borough Council v Mills* [2001] Ch 1, [1999] 2 WLR 409, CA. Nor are they liable in nuisance: *Baxter v Camden London Borough Council (No 2)* [2001] QB 1, sub nom *Baxter v Camden London Borough Council* [1999] 1 All ER 237, CA. Note that in *Southwark London Borough Council v Tanner* [2001] 1 AC 1, sub nom *Southwark London Borough Council v Mills* [1999] 4 All ER 449, HL; *Baxter v Camden London Borough Council (No 2)* [2001] 1 AC 1, sub nom *Baxter v Camden London Borough Council* [1999] 4 All ER 449, HL, the House of Lords dismissed the consolidated appeals by the tenants. See also *Hussain v Lancaster City Council* [2000] QB 1, [1999] 4 All ER 125, CA and *Lippiatt v South Gloucester Council* [2000] QB 51, [1999] 4 All ER 149, CA. In *Southwark London Borough Council v Long* [2002] EWCA Civ 403, [2002] HLR 983, Times, 16 April the court held that the covenant for quiet enjoyment was not a warranty as to fitness of the premises and that design defects in the refuse collection facilities at the flats did not entail any breach of the covenant for quiet enjoyment.

III L&T [164.5]

Lessee's liability Apart from express contract a weekly tenant's only duty is to use the premises in a tenant-like manner: *Warren v Keen* [1954] 1 QB 15, [1953] 2 All ER 1118, CA. For the meaning of this duty, see per Denning LJ. The question whether a tenant with unlagged pipes should drain the system for periods of absence depends on the severity of the weather and the length of contemplated absence: *Wycombe Health Authority v Barnett* (1982) 47 P & CR 394, CA.

III L&T [164.6]

Standard of repair The presence or absence of a hazard is not a criterion: *Windever v Liverpool City Council* [1994] CLY 2816 (cc). For cases on the application of Landlord and Tenant Act 1985 s 11 (3) see *Newham London Borough v Patel* (1978) 13 HLR 77, CA and *McClean v Liverpool City Council* (1987) 20 HLR 25, CA. If the standard of repair is sufficient having regard to the date of construction the landlord who lets an unfurnished dwelling is not liable at common law for damage caused by its unfitness for modern ways of living: *Rimmer v Liverpool City Council* [1985] QB 1, [1984] 1 All ER 930, CA; *McNerny v Lambeth London Borough Council* (1988) 21 HLR 188, CA, but if he is responsible for the design and construction of the dwelling, he is bound to take reasonable care that it is free from defects likely to cause injury to any person whom he ought reasonably to have in contemplation: *Targett v Torfaen Borough Council* [1992] 3 All ER 27, CA. See also *Adams v Rhymney Valley District Council* (2000) 33 HLR 446, [2000] 3 EGLR 25, CA where (in a case where the tenants were trapped in a fire) it was held that the landlord had not acted negligently in choosing and installing lockable windows and was under no duty to provide a smoke alarm. A landlord's duty to allow a tenant quiet possession was held not to involve a duty to install soundproofing in a council block: *Southwark London Borough Council v Mills* [2001] Ch 1, [1999] 2 WLR 409, CA (Gibson LJ dissenting). In view of Landlord and Tenant Act 1985 s 11 (3) it is sufficient for the landlord of a Grade 1 listed building to carry out running repairs to the roof although it has become so dilapidated through age that it really needs to be replaced: *Trustees of the Dame Margaret Hungerford Charity v Beazeley* (1993) 26 HLR 269, [1993] 2 EGLR 143, CA.

III L&T [164.6A]

Proper working order In so far as installations for the supply of water, gas and electricity are concerned, an installation is in proper working order if it is able to function under those conditions of supply which it is reasonable to anticipate: *O'Connor v Old Etonians Housing Association Ltd* [2002] EWCA Civ 150, [2002] Ch 295, [2002] 2 All ER 1015. The tenant of second floor flat has been held not liable to a sub-tenant for a failure in the water supply due to works done on a lower part of the building in which the tenant had no interest: *Niazi Services Ltd v Van der Loo* [2004] EWCA Civ 53, [2004] 1 WLR 1254.

III L&T [164.7]

Within a reasonable time Repairs must be effected within a reasonable time of receiving notice of the defect. A week may be an unreasonably short time: *Morris v Liverpool City Council* (1987) 20 HLR 498, [1988] 1 EGLR 47, CA.

III L&T [164.8]

Breach of lessor's covenant The measure of damages for breach of the lessor's covenant to repair is the difference in the value of the premises to the tenant from the date of his notice to repair down to the hearing of the claim. But general damages may be allowed for inconvenience and physical hardship. In *Taylor v Knowsley Borough Council* (1985) 17 HLR 376, CA, the Court of Appeal upheld an award of £159 for failure to supply hot water and mend a leak, but indicated that a higher award might have been appropriate if the tenant had had a young family. In *Chiodi's Personal Representatives v De Marney* (1988) 21 HLR 6, [1988] 2 EGLR 64, the Court of Appeal declined to interfere with an award of £5,460 for inconvenience and distress through damp and cold suffered for three-and-a-half years by a tenant who was in poor health and largely housebound, although the award was at the very top of the scale. The measure of damages for non-repair may be compensated by a sum representing the difference between the actual rent and the rent properly chargeable for unrepaired property and/or by general damages for discomfort and inconvenience. The award may be made up of either or, part one and part the other, but they should not be judged as two separate and cumulative heads of award: *Wallace v Manchester City Council* (1998) 30 HLR 1111, CA. See also *English Churches Housing Group v Shine* [2006] EWCA Civ 434, (2006) Times, 2 June. Note, however, that in *Earle v Charalambous* [2006] EWCA Civ 1090, 150 Sol Jo LB 1056, a case concerning a long lease, the Court of Appeal stated that distress and inconvenience caused by disrepair were not free-standing heads of claim, but were symptomatic of interference with the tenant's enjoyment his long lease, which was a valuable property asset. Accordingly, if the landlord's breach had the effect of depriving the tenant of that enjoyment for a significant period, an assessment of the resulting reduction in rental value was likely to be the most appropriate starting point for assessment of damages. See also *Moorjani v Durban Estates Ltd* [2015] EWCA Civ 1252, [2015] All ER (D) 83 (Dec) where the Court of Appeal confirmed that a residential lessee's loss lies in the impairment of the amenity value of his proprietary interest, of which discomfort, inconvenience and distress are only symptoms; accordingly, the fact that the lessee claimant had chosen to live elsewhere for reasons unconnected with the disrepair was not fatal to his claim.

General damages will not be reduced merely because the tenant has not accepted offers of alternative accommodation: *Lubren v London Borough of Lambeth* (1987) 20 HLR 165, CA. But a small reduction was made in *Minchburn Ltd v Peck* (1987) 20 HLR 392, [1988] 1 EGLR 53, CA, because the tenant delayed in giving notice of the defects. A landlord's breach does not entitle the tenant to bring the tenancy to an end, but if he moves because the premises are not reasonably habitable, he may be allowed as damages his removal expenses and the rent he has paid in the new premises: *Daejan Properties Ltd v Bauwens* (1964) cited in 109 Sol Jo at 362 (county court). If, because of the breach, the council serve a notice and carry out remedial work, the tenant may recover damages for inconvenience and the cost of finishing off the work or redecoration, without deducting anything for "betterment": *McGreal v Wake* (1983) 13 HLR 107, [1984] 1 EGLR 42, CA; *Bradley v Chorley Borough Council* [1985] 2 EGLR 49, CA. A tenant may obtain damages for breach of a covenant to repair notwithstanding the fact that a rent officer has fixed a fair rent taking into account the state of disrepair: *Sturolson & Co v Mauroux* (1988) 20 HLR 332, CA. It will not be reasonable to order possession on the ground of arrears of rent if the tenant has withheld his rent on account of a breach of the landlord's covenant for which damages in excess of the arrears are awarded on a counterclaim: *Televantos v McCulloch* (1990) 23 HLR 412, [1991] 1 EGLR 123, CA. In a case under Landlord and Tenant Act 1985 s 11 a qualifying fee for a surveyor should be allowed if it was reasonable to bring him to court to give evidence: *Leather v Liverpool City Council* [1994] CLY 2117 (cc).

III L&T [164.8A]

Relationship with covenant for quiet enjoyment A landlord, when complying with a repair covenant, is required to take all reasonable steps to avoid breaching the covenant for quiet enjoyment, not all possible steps: *Goldmile Properties Ltd v Lechouritis* [2003] EWCA Civ 49, [2003] 2 P & CR 1, [2003] All ER (D) 278 (Jan).

III L&T [164.9]

Liability for burglary due to insecure outer door In *Marshall v Rubypoint Ltd* (1997) 29 HLR 850, [1997] 1 EGLR 69, CA the lessor was held liable for a burglary of the lessee's premises, as a reasonably foreseeable consequence of failure to keep the outer door secure. The chain of causation was not broken by the burglar's forcing the lessee's inner door as well.

III L&T [164.10]

Set-off against rent A tenant who has spent money in carrying out repairs for which the landlord, after due notice, is responsible may recoup himself out of future rents and defend any action for payment: *Waters v Weigall* (1795) 2 Anst 575; *Lee-Parker v Izzet* [1971] 3 All ER 1099, [1971] 1 WLR 1688 and see *Televantos v McCulloch* (1990) 23 HLR 412, [1991] 1 EGLR 123, CA Similarly a tenant's claim for unliquidated damages for breach of the landlord's repairing obligations may be set off against a claim by the landlord for rent: *British Anzani (Felixstowe) Ltd v International Marine Management (UK) Ltd* [1980] QB 137, [1979] 2 All ER 1063, distinguishing *Hart v Rogers* [1916] 1 KB 646, because of its failure to take account of the Judicature Acts. The tenant was similarly successful in *Brent London Borough v Murphy* [1995] CLY 1575 (county court affirmed by CA). So leave to defend will be given to enable a set-off of either kind to be raised: *Asco Developments Ltd v Gordon* [1978] 2 EGLR 41, and it is also available against a claim by the landlord to levy distress: *Eller v Grovecrest Investments Ltd* [1995] QB 272, [1994] 4 All ER 845, CA. A provision in a lease that the rent shall be paid "without any deductions" is not sufficiently clear to exclude the tenant's equitable right to set off unliquidated claims for the landlord's breach of covenant against the rent due: *Connaught Restaurants Ltd v Indoor Leisure Ltd* [1994] 4 All ER 834, [1994] 1 WLR 501, CA, disapproving *Famous Army Stores v Meehan* [1993] 1 EGLR 73, [1993] 09 EG 111, where such a clause was held to prevent the tenant setting off building costs and other losses arising from the landlord's breach of duty to obtain a fire certificate. If, however, a clause of this kind appears in a lease, it will not be struck down by the Unfair Contract Terms Act 1977 s 3 (see para **III CON [58]**): *Electricity Supply Nominees Ltd v IAF Group plc* [1993] 3 All ER 372, [1993] 1 WLR 1059 followed in *Unchained Growth III plc v Granby Village (Manchester) Management Co Ltd* [2000] 1 WLR 739, [2000] L & TR 186, CA. Consider, however, the Unfair Terms in Consumer Contracts Regulations 1999, SI 1999/2083; see also the Office of Fair Trading's Guidance on Unfair Terms in Tenancy Agreements (November 2001) which identifies a "no set-off" clause as a term which may be considered unfair.

A tenant who has made an overpayment of rent may rely on it as an equitable, not legal, set-off; which must be taken into account by a landlord distraining for arrears: *Fuller v Happy Shopper Markets Ltd* [2001] 1 WLR 1681, following *Eller v Grovecrest Investments Ltd* [1995] QB 272, [1994] 4 All ER 845, CA.

A tenant with a claim against an assignor landlord for disrepair may set off the damages against the current landlord's claim for assigned rent arrears: *Muscat v Smith* [2003] EWCA Civ 962, [2003] 1 WLR 2853, (2003) Times, 12 August, CA applying *Hanak v Green* [1958] 2 QB 9, [1958] 2 All ER 141, CA and approving *Lotteryking Ltd v AMEC Properties Ltd* [1995] 2 EGLR 13.

Where the repairing obligation is expressed to be "subject to the receipt by the lessor of the maintenance contribution from the tenant" the landlord is not liable to a tenant who has evinced an intention not to pay service charges: *Bluestorm Ltd v Portvale Holdings Ltd* [2004] EWCA Civ 289, [2004] 22 EG 142.

As regards ss 3 and 23(1) of the Landlord and Tenant (Covenants) Act 1995, their combined effect is to make the benefit and burden of covenants pass with the estate for the future but to leave past rights and obligations with the lessor: *Edlington Properties Ltd v JH Fenner and Co Ltd* [2005] EWHC 2158 (QB), [2006] 1 All ER 98,(2005) Times, 4 November, Bean J, upheld on appeal [2006] EWCA Civ 403, [2006] 3 All ER 1200, (2006) Times, 12 May. Accordingly, the tenant in that case was not entitled to set off, against post-assignment rent due to the assignee of the freehold, a claim for damages against the original freeholder for defective construction of the building.

III L&T [164.11]

Assignment by lessee It was held in *City and Metropolitan Properties Ltd v Greycroft Ltd* [1987] 3 All ER 839, [1987] 1 WLR 1085 that the tenant's right to recover damages for disrepair from his former lessor was not affected by assignment of his lease.

III L&T [164.12]

Enforcement of undertaking to effect repairs: judicial notice When penalising a housing authority for breach of a court undertaking to effect certain repairs, the judge may properly take into account a record of broken undertakings in other proceedings. The county court is a local court and its judicial officers are expected to acquire and use local knowledge. Judicial notice may properly be taken of conduct which is notorious or which is, or can be, clearly established by reference to court records: *Mullen v Hackney London Borough Council* [1997] 2 All ER 906, [1997] 1 WLR 1103, CA, in which a fine of £5,000 was upheld.

III L&T [164.13]

Small claims arbitration Where a tenant had brought an action against his local authority landlord for breach of the implied covenant to repair, an application by the defendant for arbitration instead of trial was refused in view of the imbalance between the parties: *Higham and Higham v Liverpool City Council* [1993] CLY 2467 (county court). However the Court of Appeal has since held small claims arbitration to be appropriate if the damages at stake are within the limit, even though specific performance is claimed as well. See *Joyce v Liverpool City Council* [1996] QB 252, [1995] 3 All ER 110, CA. Note the statement of value which a tenant must now give under CPR Pt 16 r 16.3(4). If the cost of repairs is less than £1000 and the financial value of any claim for damages is less than £1000 the claim will be assigned to the small claims track: see CPR Part 26 r 26.6(1)(b).

III L&T [164.14]

Expert evidence Provided it can be demonstrated that the person in question has the relevant expertise and is aware of an expert's primary duty to the court, a person employed by a party to litigation may give expert evidence on the question of disrepair: see *Field v Leeds City Council* (1999) 32 HLR 618, CA. See also the cases referred to at para **CPR 35.1[3]** and the rules relating to expert evidence generally, paras **CPR 35** and **CPR PD 35**.

III L&T [164.15]

Housing disrepair protocol There is now a Pre-Action Protocol for housing disrepair cases which can be found at **PRO 9** in Vol 1 of the *Civil Court Practice*. Practitioners should note that, should a claim proceed to litigation, the court will expect all parties to have complied with the Protocol so far as possible. Failure to follow the Protocol may have adverse consequences in costs.

III L&T [164.16]

Energy performance certificates As from 1 October 2008 landlords are required, by the Energy Performance of Buildings (Certificates and Inspections) (England and Wales) Regulations 2007, SI 2007/991, to obtain an energy performance certificate, from an accredited energy assessor, and to give it to every new tenant of a self-contained dwelling. The certificate will contain recommendations to both parties to improve energy-efficiency. There is no compulsion to take the recommended steps (although they may attract a tax saving allowance) but a penalty may be imposed if the landlord fails to give the tenant the necessary certificate. Regulation 51 provides a right of appeal to the county court against the imposition of such a penalty.

III L&T [165]

12. Restriction on contracting out of section 11

(1) A covenant or agreement, whether contained in a lease to which section 11 applies or in an agreement collateral to such a lease, is void in so far as it purports

(a) to exclude or limit the obligations of the lessor or the immunities of the lessee under that section, or

(b) to authorise any forfeiture or impose on the lessee any penalty, disability or obligation in the event of his enforcing or relying upon those obligations or immunities,

unless the inclusion of the provision was authorised by the county court.

(2) The county court may, by order made with the consent of the parties, authorise the inclusion in a lease, or in an agreement collateral to a lease, of provisions excluding or modifying in relation to the lease, the provisions of section 11 with respect to the repairing obligations of the parties if it appears to the court that it is reasonable to do so, having regard to all the circumstances of the case, including the other terms and conditions of the lease.

III L&T [165.1]

Modifications of implied covenants An application to the county court for an order under s 12 must be made by using the Pt 8 procedure (see para **III L&T [163]**). The application may be made jointly by the parties to the proposed lease or it may be made by one of the parties and the other joined as a respondent. For a precedent, see **BCCP O[55]**.

III L&T [166]

13. Leases to which section 11 applies: general rule

(1) Section 11 (repairing obligations) applies to a lease of a dwelling-house granted on or after 24th October 1961 for a term of less than seven years.

(1A) Section 11 also applies to a lease of a dwelling-house in England granted on or after the day on which section 166 of the Localism Act 2011 came into force which is—

(a) a secure tenancy for a fixed term of seven years or more granted by a person within section 80(1) of the Housing Act 1985 (secure tenancies: the landlord condition), or

(b) an assured tenancy for a fixed term of seven years or more that—

(i) is not a shared ownership lease, and

(ii) is granted by a private registered provider of social housing.

[(1AB) Section 11 also applies to a lease of a dwelling-house in England which is an introductory tenancy for a fixed term of seven years or more granted on or after the day on which paragraph 4 of Schedule 7 to the Housing and Planning Act 2016 comes fully into force.]

(1B) *In subsection (1A)* [In this section]—

"assured tenancy" has the same meaning as in Part 1 of the Housing Act 1988;

["introductory tenancy" has the same meaning as in Chapter 1 of Part 5 of the Housing Act 2016;]

"secure tenancy" has the meaning given by section 79 of the Housing Act 1985; and

"shared ownership lease" means a lease—

(a) granted on payment of a premium calculated by reference to a percentage of the value of the dwelling-house or of the cost of providing it, or

(b) under which the lessee (or the lessee's personal representatives) will or may be entitled to a sum calculated by reference, directly or indirectly, to the value of the dwelling-house.

(2) In determining whether a lease is one to which section 11 applies

(a) any part of the term which falls before the grant shall be left out of account and the lease shall be treated as a lease for a term commencing with the grant,

(b) a lease which is determinable at the option of the lessor before the expiration of seven years from the commencement of the term shall be treated as a lease for a term of less than seven years, and

(c) a lease (other than a lease to which paragraph (b) applies) shall not be treated as a lease for a term of less than seven years if it confers on the lessee an option for renewal for a term which, together with the original term, amounts to seven years or more.

(3) This section has effect subject to
section 14 (leases to which section 11 applies: exceptions), and
section 32 (2) (provisions not applying to tenancies within Part II of the Landlord and Tenant Act 1954).

Amendment *Text in italic is deleted, and text in square brackets is inserted, from a date to be appointed, by s 118 of, and Schedule 7 to, the Housing and Planning Act 2016.*

III L&T [166.1]

"A lease for a term of less than seven years" An agreement for a seven-year lease is outside the section, because an agreement for a lease is as good as a lease, by virtue of Landlord and Tenant Act 1985 s 36(2)(b) (see para **III L&T [178]**); this is so even though the lease is not executed until some days after the date of agreement: *Brikom Investments Ltd v Seaford* [1981] 2 All ER 783, [1981] 1 WLR 863, CA. On the other hand the grantor of a seven year lease who seeks to recover the full registered rent which has been assessed on the basis of the lessor's being liable for such repairs may be estopped thereby from denying his liability for them: *Brikom Investments Ltd v Seaford* [1981] 2 All ER 783, [1981] 1 WLR 863, CA.

III L&T [167]

14. Leases to which section 11 applies: exceptions

(1) Section 11 (repairing obligations) does not apply to a new lease granted to an existing tenant, or to a former tenant still in possession, if the previous lease was not a lease to which section 11 applied (and, in the case of a lease granted before 24th October 1961, would not have been if it had been granted on or after that date).

(2) In subsection (1)

"existing tenant" means a person who is when, or immediately before the new lease is granted, the lessee under another lease of the dwelling-house;

"former tenant still in possession" means a person who

(a) was the lessee under another lease of the dwelling-house which terminated at some time before the new lease was granted, and

(b) between the termination of that other lease and the grant of the new lease was continuously in possession of the dwelling-house or of the rents and profits of the dwelling-house; and

"the previous lease" means the other lease referred to in the above definitions.

(3) Section 11 does not apply to a lease of a dwelling-house which is a tenancy of an agricultural holding within the meaning of the Agricultural Holdings Act 1986 and in relation to which that Act applies or to a farm business tenancy within the meaning of the Agricultural Tenancies Act 1995.

(4) Section 11 does not apply to a lease granted on or after 3rd October 1980 to
a local authority,
a National Park authority,
a new town corporation,
an urban development corporation,
a Mayoral development corporation,
the Development Board for Rural Wales,
a non-profit registered provider of social housing,
a registered social landlord,
a co-operative housing association, or
an educational institution or other body specified, or of a class specified by regulations under section 8 of the Rent Act 1977 or paragraph 8 of Schedule 1 to the Housing Act 1988 (bodies making student lettings), or
a housing trust established under Part III of the Housing Act 1988.

(5) Section 11 does not apply to a lease granted on or after 3rd October 1980 to

LANDLORD & TENANT AND HOUSING

(a) Her Majesty in right of the Crown (unless the lease is under the management of the Crown Estate Commissioners), or

(b) a government department or a person holding in trust for Her Majesty for the purposes of a government department.

III L&T [167.1]

Definitions For definitions of "co-operative housing association", "housing association", "local authority", "new town corporation", "registered social landlord" and "urban development corporation" see Landlord and Tenant Act 1985 s 38 (see para **III L&T [180]**).

III L&T [167.2]

Business tenancies A further exception is made, by Landlord and Tenant Act 1985 s 32 (2), a new lease to which the Landlord and Tenant Act 1954 Pt II applies and the previous tenancy was also such a lease or would be but for the Landlord and Tenant Act 1954 s 28 (see para **III L&T [20]**).

III L&T [167.3]

The Crown For the position of the Crown see *Department of Transport v Egoroff* (1986) 18 HLR 326, 278 Estates Gazette 1361, CA.

III L&T [168]

15. Jurisdiction of county court

The county court has jurisdiction to make a declaration that section 11 (repairing obligations) applies, or does not apply, to a lease

(a) whatever the net value of the property in question, and

(b) notwithstanding that no other relief is sought than a declaration.

III L&T [168.1]

Declaration An application to the county court for a declaration under this section should be made using the Pt 8 procedure (see para **III L&T [163]**).

III L&T [168.2]

Declaratory jurisdiction In its current form s 38 of the County Courts Act 1984 (see para **II CCA [21]**) enables the county courts to grant declarations as to the rights of the parties in situations not covered by s 15 of the Landlord and Tenant Act 1985: see *Calcott v JS Bloor (Measham) Ltd* [1998] 1 WLR 1490, CA; *Osei-Bonsu v Wandsworth London Borough Council* [1999] 1 All ER 265, [1999] 1 WLR 1011, CA.

III L&T [169]

16. Meaning of "lease" and related expressions

In sections 11 to 15 (repairing obligations in short leases)

(a) "lease" does not include a mortgage term;

(b) "lease of a dwelling-house" means a lease by which a building or part of a building is let wholly or mainly as a private residence, and "dwelling-house" means that building or part of a building;

(c) "lessee" and "lessor" mean, respectively, the person for the time being entitled to the term of a lease and to the reversion expectant on it.

III L&T [170]

17. Specific performance of landlord's repairing obligations

(1) In proceedings in which a tenant of dwelling-house alleges a breach on the part of his landlord of a repairing covenant relating to any part of the premises in which the dwelling is comprised, the court may order specific performance of the covenant whether or not the breach relates to a part of the premises let to the tenant and notwithstanding any equitable rule restricting the scope of the remedy, whether on the basis of a lack of mutuality or otherwise.

(2) In this section

(a) "tenant" includes a statutory tenant,

(b) in relation to a statutory tenant the reference to the premises let to him is to the premises of which he is a statutory tenant,

(c) "landlord", in relation to a tenant, includes any person against whom the tenant has a right to enforce a repairing covenant, and

(d) "repairing covenant" means a covenant to repair, maintain, renew, construct or replace any property.

III L&T [170.1]

Dwelling See Landlord and Tenant Act 1985 s 38 (see para **III L&T [180]**) for definition.

III L&T [170.2]

Breach of repairing covenant An application for specific performance under this section should be made by using the Pt 8 procedure: CPR PD 56 para 2.1 (para **CPR PD 56**). Specific performance may be ordered against a tenant to do repairs in the very rare case where it is appropriate. An example is where the landlord has no right to enter and do the repairs himself and where the carrying out of the repairs would not be oppressive, having regard to the tenant's protection under the Leasehold Property (Repairs) Act 1938: *Rainbow Estates Ltd v Tokenhold Ltd* [1999] Ch 64, [1998] 2 All ER 860.

III L&T [170.3]

Business tenancies Business tenancies are excepted from the scope of this section by Landlord and Tenant Act 1985 s 32 (1).

III L&T [170.4]

Statutory tenant See Landlord and Tenant Act 1985 s 37 (see para **III L&T [179]**) for definition.

III L&T [170.5]

Lack of mutuality Outside the provisions of this section lack of mutuality may be a ground for refusing specific performance of repairing covenants: *Hill v Barclay* (1810) 16 Ves 402. But the remedy may be granted in appropriate cases: *Jeune v Queens Cross Properties Ltd* [1974] Ch 97, [1973] 3 All ER 97; *Claridge and Meersewan v Swallow Securities* [1985] CLY 1866 (county court), *Parker v Camden London Borough Council* [1986] Ch 162, [1985] 2 All ER 141, CA and *Posner v Scott-Lewis* [1987] Ch 25, [1986] 3 All ER 513.

SERVICE CHARGES

III L&T [171]

18. Meaning of "service charge" and "relevant costs"

(1) In the following provisions of this Act "service charge" means an amount payable by a tenant of a dwelling as part of or in addition to the rent

(a) which is payable, directly or indirectly, for services, repairs, maintenance, improvements or insurance or the landlord's costs of management, and

(b) the whole or part of which varies or may vary according to the relevant costs.

(2) The relevant costs are the costs or estimated costs incurred or to be incurred by or on behalf of the landlord, or a superior landlord, in connection with the matters for which the service charge is payable.

(3) For this purpose

(a) "costs" includes overheads, and

(b) costs are relevant costs in relation to a service charge whether they are incurred, or to be incurred, in the period for which the service charge is payable or in an earlier or later period.

III L&T [171.1]

Landlord, tenant Landlord and Tenant Act 1985 s 30 provides that "landlord" includes any person who has a right to enforce a service charge, and "tenant" includes a statutory tenant and a sub-tenant. Thus, a management company which is entitled to enforce service charges under a lease is a landlord and its costs are relevant costs which may be challenged as being unreasonable: *Cinnamon Ltd v Morgan* [2001] EWCA Civ 1616, [2002f] 2 P & CR 139. Where a manager is appointed by a tribunal under Part II of the Landlord and Tenant Act 1987, the claims made by the manager regarding costs of repair and other services are not made as manager of the landlord. Leaseholders therefore have no right to set off claims against the landlord for breach of repairing obligations in reduction of their liability to the manager: *Maunder Taylor v Blaquiere* [2002] EWCA Civ 1633, [2003] 1 WLR 379, (2002) Times, 21 November.

The expression "tenant of a dwelling" in s 18 does not require that the tenant has to be in occupation of the dwelling; it could include a tenant who has sublet and lives elsewhere, and the subtenant had locus standi to apply for a determination by a leasehold valuation tribunal as to the amount of service charge payable, notwithstanding that the obligation to pay is with the tenant: *Ruddy v Oakfern Properties Ltd* [2006] EWCA Civ 1389, [2007] 1 All ER 337.

III L&T [171.2]

Invalid service charges In *Broadwater Court Management Co Ltd v Jackson-Mann* [1997] EGCS 145, CA, certain audit fees and registration fees were disallowed as falling outside the service charge agreement.

Although the lessee failed in her appeal over various charges and expenses to do with setting up and running the RTM company, the Upper Tribunal (George Bartlett QC) made it clear that the lessee's liability for service charges depended on the terms of the lease: *Wilson v Lesley Place (RTM) Co Ltd* [2010] UKUT 342 (LC). It is not impossible for some of the RTM expenses to be outside the terms of the service charge provision in which case they will be borne by the members of the company and not recovered from the lessee.

III L&T [171.3]

Exception These provisions are disapplied by Landlord and Tenant Act 1985 ss 26 and 27 in the case of tenancies with a registered rent or with certain public authorities or certain business tenancies.

III L&T [171.4]

Liability under company resolution Where a tenant is a member of the landlord company and that company passes a resolution that members should pay into a Recovery Fund members are liable to pay accordingly, even though the debt is not recoverable as a service charge: *Morshead Mansions Ltd v Leon di Marco* [2008] EWCA Civ 1371, (2009) Times, 25 February.

III L&T [171.5]

Fixed charges The definition requires that the charge for services must vary with the cost. Charges which are fixed, increasing by fixed proportions at specified times, fall outside the definition: *Arnold v Britton* [2013] EWCA Civ 902, [2013] All ER (D) 254 (Jul). See also *Arnold v Britton* [2015] UKSC 36 where, upholding the Court of Appeal, the Supreme Court held that there is no special rule of interpretation which requires service charge clauses to be construed restrictively, and decided that the natural meaning of a service charge clause in a long-lease of a holiday chalet was that the charge was £90 in the first year, rising by 10% per annum thereafter; the fact that, after a number of years, the charge would significantly exceed the cost of providing the services was no reason to depart from the natural meaning of the clause. Where an allowance for the lessor's management costs was calculated so as to be increased annually by reference to an external index and not by reference to the costs actually incurred or estimated that did not fall within the definition of 'service charge': see *Anchor Trust v Waby* [2018] UKUT 370 (LC).

III L&T [171.6]

Code of Management Practice A revised Code of Management Practice in respect of service charges for residential premises) was issued by the Royal Institution of Chartered Surveyors and received statutory approval in SI 2016/518.

III L&T [172]

19. Limitation of service charges: reasonableness

(1) Relevant costs shall be taken into account in determining the amount of a service charge payable for a period

(a) only to the extent that they are reasonably incurred, and

(b) where they are incurred on the provision of services or the carrying out of works, only if the services or works are of a reasonable standard;

and the amount payable shall be limited accordingly.

(2) Where a service charge is payable before the relevant costs are incurred, no greater amount than is reasonable is so payable, and after the relevant costs have been incurred any necessary adjustment shall be made by repayment, reduction or subsequent charges or otherwise.

(2A)-(4) . . .

(5) *If a person takes any proceedings in the High Court in pursuance of any of the provisions of this Act relating to service charges and he could have taken those proceedings in the county court, he shall not be entitled to recover any costs.*

Amendment *Sub-section (5) is repealed by the Courts and Legal Services Act 1990, with effect from a date to be appointed.*

III L&T [172.1]

Declarations and injunctions Where a tenant disputes the need for repairs, the appropriate remedy to seek in the county court is a declaration under County Court Act 1984 s 38 (see para **II CCA [21]**), not an injunction to stop the landlord carrying out the repairs in accordance with the covenant: *Hi-lift Elevator Services v Temple* (1994) 28 HLR 1, CA. *Hi-lift Elevator* was distinguished in *Bounds v London Borough of Camden* [1999] CLY 3728, Central London County Court, on the ground that it was decided before the enactment of s 19(2B). An injunction may be appropriate provided suitable cross undertakings are given.

Section 19(4), under which the county court was empowered to grant declaratory relief in relation to the cost of services, was repealed by s 227 of the Housing Act 1996. Since 1 September 1997, by virtue of ss 19(2A) and (2B), a tenant has had a right of recourse to a leasehold valuation tribunal in relation to the reasonableness of service charges. Provision is made by s 31C (see **III L&T [177]**) for existing proceedings in the county court, which fall within the jurisdiction of a leasehold valuation, to be transferred. Where, however, there is no cost benefit in transferring proceedings to a leasehold valuation tribunal and there are matters which are not suitable for determination by the tribunal, transfer is likely to be refused: *Aylesbond Estates Ltd v McMillan* (1998) 32 HLR 1, CA. Note also that the Housing Act 1996 s 84 (see para **III L&T [278]**) entitles a recognised tenant's association to appoint a surveyor to advise on matters relating to service charges with statutory rights of access to documents and premises.

Although leaseholders may in some circumstances use self-help to abate nuisances or fix necessary repairs (see *Granada Theatres v Freehold Investment (Leytonstone)* [1959] Ch 592) they may not bring in their own contractors after the landlord has awarded the contract to someone else in accordance with the s 20 procedure: *Metropolitan Properties Co Ltd v Wilson* [2002] EWHC 1853 (Ch).

III L&T [172.1A]

Liability of leaseholder to pay appropriate proportion Where the lease provides for each leaseholder to pay the "due proportion" of the service charges payable by all, the obligation is not void for uncertainty but is an obligation to pay a fair and reasonable proportion: *Hackney London Borough Council v Thompson* [2001] L & T R 7, CA.

III L&T [172.1B]

Relevant costs reasonably incurred Where the service charge comprises work carried out under a public procurement contract that was subject to competitive tendering the component elements may still be disallowed if unreasonable: *Rey-Ordieres v Lewisham London Borough Council* [2013] UKUT 14 (LC), 8 January 2013, in which certain management fees and 'on-costs' were disallowed. Where the cost of emergency repair work would have been much less if the remedial maintenance work had been carried earlier, the additional cost is nevertheless recoverable as reasonably incurred: *Continental Property Ventures Inc v White* [2006] 16 EG 148, [2006] 1 EGLR 85; *Daejan Properties Ltd v Griffin* [2014] UKUT 206 (LC), [2014] PLSCS 172.

Where, in the context of the Grenfell Tower fire and their obligations under the Regulatory Reform (Fire Safety) Order 2005, SI 2005/1541, the freeholders deployed a 'waking watch', as an interim safety measure, the cost was held to be reasonably incurred and recoverable: *E&J Ground Rents No 11 LLP v Various Leaseholders of Fresh Apartments, Salford* (2018) First Tier Tribunal (Property Chamber) Manchester, 24 January 2018.

III L&T [172.1C]

Cap on local authority service charges Service charges by local authority lessors are capped (in England) by the Social Landlords Mandatory Reduction of Service Charges (England) Directions 2014.

III L&T [172.2]

Precedents Precedents in respect of a claim for unpaid service charges and a defence to such a claim are set out at **BCCP O[59]** and **BCCP O[60]**. Any claim in relation to service charges brought under the Landlord and Tenant Act 1985 should be by Part 8 claim form using the Part 8 procedure: CPR PD 56 para 2.1 (para **CPR PD 56**).

III L&T [172.3]

Forfeiture Restrictions on forfeiture for non-payment of service charge are provided by the Housing Act 1996 ss 81, 82 (see paras **III L&T [276]** and **III L&T [277]**). For changes effected by s 167 of the Commonhold and Leasehold Reform Act 2002, see para **III L&T [2.4]** and para **III L&T [317]**.

III L&T [173]

20. Limitation of service charges: consultation requirements

(1) Where this section applies to any qualifying works or qualifying long term agreement, the relevant contributions of tenants are limited in accordance with subsection (6) or (7) (or both) unless the consultation requirements have been either—

(a) complied with in relation to the works or agreement, or

(b) dispensed with in relation to the works or agreement by (or on appeal from) the appropriate tribunal.

(2) In this section "relevant contribution", in relation to a tenant and any works or agreement, is the amount which he may be required under the terms of his lease to contribute (by the payment of service charges) to relevant costs incurred on carrying out the works or under the agreement.

(3) This section applies to qualifying works if relevant costs incurred on carrying out the works exceed an appropriate amount.

(4) The Secretary of State may by regulations provide that this section applies to a qualifying long term agreement—

(a) if relevant costs incurred under the agreement exceed an appropriate amount, or

(b) if relevant costs incurred under the agreement during a period prescribed by the regulations exceed an appropriate amount.

(5) An appropriate amount is an amount set by regulations made by the Secretary of State; and the regulations may make provision for either or both of the following to be an appropriate amount—

(a) an amount prescribed by, or determined in accordance with, the regulations, and

(b) an amount which results in the relevant contribution of any one or more tenants being an amount prescribed by, or determined in accordance with, the regulations.

(6) Where an appropriate amount is set by virtue of paragraph (a) of subsection (5), the amount of the relevant costs incurred on carrying out the works or under the agreement which may be taken into account in determining the relevant contributions of tenants is limited to the appropriate amount.

(7) Where an appropriate amount is set by virtue of paragraph (b) of that subsection, the amount of the relevant contribution of the tenant, or each of the tenants, whose relevant contribution would otherwise exceed the amount prescribed by, or determined in accordance with, the regulations is limited to the amount so prescribed or determined.

III L&T [173.1]

Services, repairs, maintenance "Repairs" have been held not to include improvements: *Mullaney v Maybourne Grange (Croydon) Management Co Ltd* [1986] 1 EGLR 70 and *Sutton (Hastoe) Housing Association v Williams* (1988) 20 HLR 321, CA; but it was decided in the latter case that a covenant to pay a service charge for an improvement, being outside the scope of the statutory restrictions, was enforceable at common law. Where external windows are not included in the demise, the replacement of defective frames may be covered by a landlord's covenant to do repairs for which the tenant is not responsible so as to enable him to recover the cost as a service charge: *Reston Ltd v Hudson* [1990] 2 EGLR 51, [1990] 37 EG 86. If the service charge is limited to sums "expended or incurred or payable by the landlord", it does not permit a charge for repairs etc to be made for sums not yet paid or payable by the landlord: *Capital and Counties Freehold Equity Trust Ltd v BL plc* [1987] 2 EGLR 49, 283 Estates Gazette 563. A provision for recovery of the costs of "beneficial services" does not cover internal decoration and repair of common parts or external repairs: *Lloyds Bank plc v Bowker Orford* [1992] 2 EGLR 44, [1992] 31 EG 68.

Work carried out by the landlord may be charged to the tenant only to the extent that it is of a standard for which the tenant can fairly be expected to pay having regard to the tenant's more limited interest. If the landlords insist on a more expensive programme of repairs because of their longer term interests, they may have to bear the excess: *Fluor Daniel Properties Ltd v Shortlands Investments Ltd* [2001] 2 EGLR 103.

In the case of improvements that are discretionary the lessor must take particular account of the interests of resident lessees and their views and the impact of them financially of an expensive scheme: *London Borough of Hounslow v Waaler* [2017] EWCA Civ 25, [2017] All ER (D) 32 (Feb).

III L&T [173.1A]

Lease of more than one dwelling A person may be "the tenant of a dwelling" even though his tenancy includes other property or more than one dwelling. Section 20 applies to the entire lease; accordingly where the s 20 consultation process had not been followed, the entire service charge was irrecoverable: *Heron Maple House Ltd v Central Estates Ltd* [2002] 13 EG 102, Central London County Court.

III L&T [173.2]

Interest Interest charges on the landlord's bank account relating to maintenance costs are recoverable if on its proper construction the lease so provides: *Skilleter v Charles* (1992) 24 HLR 421, [1992] 1 EGLR 73, CA, but in *Boldmark Ltd v Cohen* (1986) 19 HLR 136, [1986] 1 EGLR 47, CA, a service charge agreement for "yearly costs, expenses and outgoings" was construed as not covering the landlord's interest liability.

III L&T [173.3]

Legal and management costs A provision for the reimbursement of costs and expenses reasonably incurred may be interpreted as including legal costs: *Delahay v Maltlodge* [1987] CLY 2158 (county court), such as the costs of an application to determine the liability for particular repairs: *Reston Ltd v Hudson* [1990] 2 EGLR 51, [1990] 37 EG 86; but not so as to enable the landlord to recover from one tenant the costs of proceedings against other tenants: *Sella House Ltd v Mears* (1988) 21 HLR 147, [1989] 1 EGLR 65, CA, or to recover, from the tenants as a whole, costs incurred by the landlord in compromised proceedings brought by a majority of the tenants for such relief as the appointment of independent managing agents: *Morgan v Stainer* (1992) 25 HLR 467, [1993] 2 EGLR 73. Where a lease expressly permits the services of a managing agent, there is no reason why the landlord should not employ and charge for the services of a company owned by him, provided the arrangement is not a mere sham: *Skilleter v Charles* (1992) 24 HLR 421, [1992] 1 EGLR 73, CA. A provision for recovery of the costs of "beneficial services" covers the employment of managing agents and also the notional rent of the caretaker's flat: *Lloyds Bank plc v Bowker Orford* [1992] 2 EGLR 44, [1992] 31 EG 68. Provisions in a long lease entitling recovery of the costs of all other services which the landlord may provide and reasonable and proper fees for general management were held not to include the recovery of legal costs in *St Mary's Mansions Ltd v Limegate Investments Co Ltd* [2002] EWCA Civ 1491, [2003] HLR 319. In *Earl of Cadogan v 27/29 Sloane Gardens Ltd* [2006] 24 EG 178, Lands Tr, the tribunal held, construing the relevant leases as a whole, that "expenditure" included the notional market rental of accommodation for a caretaker which the lessor was required to provide rent free.

III L&T [173.3A]

Insurance discounts A local authority landlord was held liable to account to the leaseholders for discounts in the insurance premium but not liable to account for discounts in respect of services provided by the landlord to the insurers: *Williams v Southwark London Borough Council* [2000] LGR 646, 33 HLR 224, ChD.

III L&T [173.3B]

Porter In *Veena SA v Cheong* [2003] 1 EGLR 175, the Lands Tribunal upheld a decision that the cost of engaging a full-time porter was unreasonable: the cost of engaging one part-time was allowed.

III L&T [173.3C]

Consultation requirements The consultation requirements are found in the Service Charges (Consultation Requirements) (England) Regulations 2003, SI 2003/1987 as amended, with effect from 12 November 2004, by the Service Charges (Consultation Requirements) (Amendment) (No 2) (England) Regulations 2004, SI 2004/2939. For Wales, with effect from 31 March 2004, see the Service Charges (Consultation Requirements) (Wales) Regulations 2004, SI 2004/684 (W 72) as amended by SI 2005/1357.

Note the decision in *Daejan Investments v Benson* [2009] UKUT 233 (LC), [2010] 2 P & CR 116 that the lessor's failure to consult on estimates for doing £270,000 worth of repairs meant that the lessor could recover no more than £250 from each of the five lessees. The Supreme Court allowed the appeal by Daejan and held that the tribunal had power, when exercising its discretion to dispense with the consultation requirements to make the grant of dispensation subject to conditions, including where appropriate the reduction of the sum claimed to reflect the financial prejudice caused by lack of consultation: *Daejan Investments Ltd v Benson* [2013] UKSC 14, [2013] 2 All ER 375, [2013] 1 WLR 854.

The Court of Appeal upheld the Tribunal decision to enforce the limit on charges recoverable because of a failure to carry out the statutory consultation in *Daejan Investments Ltd v Benson* [2011] EWCA Civ 38, [2011] 2 P & CR 15, [2011] 05 EG 105 (CS). The Court ruled that prejudice to the leaseholders was an important consideration but that the financial impact on the service providers of refusing dispensation was not relevant. The sorts of cases where dispensation might be appropriate were (i) where emergency works are needed (ii) where there is only one specialist contractor who could, realistically, be awarded the contract and (iii) where there has been only a minor breach which caused no prejudice to the leaseholders. The provisions in s 20 limiting tenants' contributions to the cost of 'qualifying works' are not to be interpreted in such a way that the landlord was required to consult the tenants on any service charge items, however small, once the limit for contributions had been reached: *Phillips v Francis (Secretary of State for Communities and Local Government)* [2014] EWCA Civ 1395. See note at **III L&T [173.5]**.

Where there has been a minor breach of the consultation requirements it will be important to see whether lessees were prejudiced, but where there has been no consultation at all it may be reasonable to assume prejudice and, if no good reason is put forward on the lessor's behalf, to restrict the charge to the statutory maximum: *Stenau Properties Ltd v Leek* [2010] UKUT 478 (LC). On the other hand, the failure to serve the section 20 notice until after publication of the contract on the Official Journal has been held to be a minor error for which dispensation should be allowed: *Mayor and Burgesses of Newham London Borough Council v Hannan* [2011] UKUT 406 (LC).

The consultation requirements in respect of qualifying long term agreements do not apply to long-term agreements entered into in relation to buildings which have not yet been constructed or which are not let at the time of the agreement: *BDW Trading Ltd and Comet Square Phase 2 Block Management Co Ltd v South Anglia Housing Ltd* [2013] EWHC 2169 (Ch), [2013] All ER (D) 183 (Jul).

Where lessors decide, after consulting on one set of estimates, that further work should be included in the scheme, they are not necessarily bound to start fresh consultations if that would be unreasonable in the circumstances: *Reedbase Ltd v Fattal* [2018] EWCA Civ 840, [2018] 2 P & CR 14.

III L&T [173.3D]

Service charge information Note that the leaseholder is given further rights to service charge information by amendments to ss 21 onwards made by ss 152 onwards of the Commonhold and Leasehold Reform Act 2002 and by further amendments made by Sch 12 to the Housing and Regeneration Act 2008. Note also that the Secretary of State has given statutory approval (SI 2009/512) of the Service Charge Residential Management Code, published by RICS, in relation to the management of residential properties in England.

III L&T [173.4]

Price index Where an agreement linked increases in the service charge to the retail price index for so long as that index was published or available, it was held that the link remained effective even though the commodities and services on which the index was based had changed and the figures had been brought back to a base of 100: *Cumshaw Ltd v Bowen*

[1987] 1 EGLR 30, 281 Estates Gazette 68. An annual fixed charge subject to increases in a published index of building costs is not a service charge, as it does not vary according to the "relevant costs": *Coventry City Council v Cole* [1994] 1 All ER 997, [1994] 1 WLR 398, CA.

A fixed service charge which provided for annual increases of 10%, calculated on a compound basis, has been held recoverable although the impact on the leaseholders was alarmingly severe: *Arnold v Britton* [2015] UKSC 36, [2015] 2 WLR 1593, 165 NLJ 7657.

III L&T [173.5]

The specified limit The Service Charge (Estimates and Consultation) Order 1988, SI 1988/1285 prescribed £50 for Landlord and Tenant Act 1985 s 20(3)(a) and £1000 for Landlord and Tenant Act 1985 s 20(3)(b) as from 1 September 1988.

The appropriate amount for s 20(3) is now £250 (qualifying works) and £100 (qualifying long term agreement). In *Phillips v Francis (Secretary of State for Communities and Local Government)* [2014] EWCA Civ 1395 the Court of Appeal, rejecting "the aggregating approach" adopted below and adopting instead "the sets approach", held that a series of small one-off repairs should not be aggregated to determine whether the £250 limit has been exceeded and consultation is required; one should look instead to see whether a set of work will exceed the £250 limit. To apply the aggregation approach to every item of maintenance and repair, some of which might be of an emergency nature, would give rise to serious practical and administrative problems and could not have been intended by Parliament. The imposition of the specified limit does not apply to amounts required to be paid on account in advance of the execution of major works: *23 Dollis Avenue (1998) Ltd v Vejdani* [2016] UKUT 365 (LC).

III L&T [173.6]

Grant-aided works By the Landlord and Tenant Act 1985 s 20A (inserted by the Housing and Planning Act 1986 Sch 5 para 9) the amount of service charge payable is to be reduced by the amount of any grant under the Housing Act 1985 Pt XV.

III L&T [173.7]

Dispensing with requirements See the note on the exercise of the dispensing power, in similar terms, in connection with the Rent Act 1977 Sch 15 Pt II Case 11 (see para **III L&T [83]**) and see *Wilson v Stone* [1998] 2 EGLR 155, [1998] 26 EG 153, LT for a case where the requirements were dispensed with. Contrast *Martin v Maryland Estates Ltd* (1999) 32 HLR 116, [1999] 2 EGLR 53 where the Court of Appeal upheld the judge's refusal to dispense with the requirements in relation to substantial additional works and held that a common sense approach was required in separating one batch of works from another for the purpose of s 20(1). Where the lease itself requires a copy of the specification and estimates of major repairs to be submitted to the tenant before the works are carried out, the cost will not be recoverable unless the obligation is complied with, and in the absence of any specific provision in the lease there will be no dispensing power: *Northways Flats Management Co (Camden) Ltd v Wimpey Pension Trustees Ltd* [1992] 2 EGLR 42, [1992] 31 EG 65, CA.

III L&T [173.8]

Assignment of lease Notwithstanding an assignment of the lease, the original tenant remains liable for payment of a service charge under an express covenant, as indicated by the words "yielding and paying therefor": *Royton Industries Ltd v Lawrence* [1994] 1 EGLR 110, [1994] 20 EG 151.

III L&T [174]

20B. Limitation of service charges: time limit on making demands

(1) If any of the relevant costs taken into account in determining the amount of any service charge were incurred more than 18 months before a demand for payment of the service charge is served on the tenant, then (subject to subsection (2)), the tenant shall not be liable to pay so much of the service charge as reflects the costs so incurred.

(2) Subsection (1) shall not apply if, within the period of 18 months beginning with the date when the relevant costs in question were incurred, the tenant was notified in writing that those costs had been incurred and that he would subsequently be required under the terms of his lease to contribute to them by the payment of a service charge.

III L&T [174.1]

Estimated costs and payments on account Section 20B(1) does not apply unless the demand is in respect of costs that have actually been incurred; accordingly, a landlord's letter requiring payment of service charges based on the estimated cost of major works did not constitute a valid demand for the purposes of the lease, nor was it a valid demand or relevant notification for the purpose of s 20B: *Brent London Borough Council v Shulem B Association Ltd* [2011] EWHC 1663 (Ch), [2011] 4 All ER 778, [2011] 1 WLR 3014.

Where a leaseholder is required to make an advance payment 'on account' before the costs have been incurred, the 18 month limitation period does not start from the demand or the payment, but only when the costs have been incurred: *Gilje v Charlesgrove Investments Ltd* [2004] 1 All ER 91. Even then, it will not start to run in respect of the costs already covered by the payment in advance, but only as regards the excess. The decision in *Gilje* must now be read in the light of *Skelton v DBS Homes (Kings Hill) Ltd* [2017] EWCA Civ 1139, [2017] All ER (D) 196 (Jul), where the court held that the reference to the amounts of a service charge demand include those covered by an on-account demand for estimated costs, so the 18–month time limit operates between the incurring of the costs and the service of a demand for an advance payment on account. The point of difference is that in *Skelton* the court accepted that a demand for payment on account of estimated costs fell within the definition, in s 18, of a 'service charge' and therefore came within s 20B.

III L&T [174.2]

Date when charge is incurred It has been held that the date when the cost is incurred is not on the supply of the service but on the presentation of the invoice or other demand: *OM Property Management Ltd v Burr* [2013] EWCA Civ 479, [2013] 1 WLR 3071, [2013] 2 P & CR 215.

Where the cost of providing services is incurred by a superior landlord, and the charge is passed down a chain of intermediate leases before ultimately being paid by the occupational leaseholder, successive 18-month time limits apply to each demand made in the chain: *Westmark (Lettings) Ltd v Peddle* [2018] UKUT 449 (LC), [2018] HLR 10.

III L&T [175]

20C. Limitation of service charges: costs of proceedings

(1) A tenant may make an application for an order that all or any of the costs incurred, or to be incurred, by the landlord in connection with proceedings before a court, residential property tribunal or leasehold valuation tribunal or the First-tier Tribunal, or the Upper Tribunal, or in connection with arbitration proceedings, are not to be regarded as relevant costs to be taken into account in determining the amount of any service charge payable by the tenant or any other person or persons specified in the application.

(2) The application shall be made

- (a) in the case of court proceedings, to the court before which the proceedings are taking place or, if the application is made after the proceedings are concluded, to the county court;
- (aa) in the case of proceedings before a residential property tribunal, to a leasehold valuation tribunal;
- (b) in the case of proceedings before a leasehold valuation tribunal, to the tribunal before which the proceedings are taking place or, if the application is made after the proceedings are concluded, to any leasehold valuation tribunal;
- (ba) in the case of proceedings before the First-tier Tribunal, to the tribunal;
- (c) in the case of proceedings before the Upper Tribunal, to the tribunal;
- (d) in the case of arbitration proceedings, to the arbitral tribunal or, if the application is made after the proceedings are concluded, to a county court.

(3) The court or tribunal to which the application is made may make such order on the application as it considers just and equitable in the circumstances.

NOTES TO SECTIONS 20B AND 20C

III L&T [175.1]

Relevant costs Although the landlord's costs of forfeiture proceedings for breach of covenant by a tenant will normally be regarded as management costs and therefore recoverable as a service charge even if the tenant is ultimately granted relief, yet where the tenant had been successful in litigation and the landlord had been ordered to pay a proportion of his costs, the Court of Appeal upheld an order under s 20C that the landlord's costs be left out of account in calculating the service charge payable by the tenant: *Iperion Investments Corpn v Broadwalk House Residents Ltd* (1994) 27 HLR 196, [1995] 2 EGLR 47, CA. Provisions in a long lease entitling recovery of the costs of all other services which the landlord may provide and reasonable and proper fees for general management were held not to include the recovery of legal costs in *St Mary's Mansions Ltd v Limegate Investments Co Ltd* [2002] EWCA Civ 1491, [2003] HLR 319. For the approach on the recoverability of litigation costs under a service charge clause see *Union Pension Trustees Ltd v Slavin* [2015] UKUT 103 (LC) and *Sinclair Gardens Investments (Kensington) Ltd v Avon Estates (London) Ltd* [2016] UKUT 317 (LC).

It has been held that a provision in a lease whereby the lessee agreed to indemnify the lessor against costs, claims and demands did not allow the lessor to claim an administration fee for having to prompt the lessee to pay the ground rent. The Upper Tribunal held that 'indemnity' meant reimbursing for a liability incurred to an external party: *Fairhold Freeholds No 2 Ltd v Moody* [2016] UKUT 311 (LC).

III L&T [175.1A]

Just and equitable For a case where the discretion was exercised in favour of the landlord, see *Bretby Hall Management Co Ltd v Pratt* [2017] UKUT 0070 (LC).

III L&T [175.2]

County court jurisdiction An application under the Landlord and Tenant Act 1985 s 20C (2)(a) should be made by application in accordance with CPR 23 (see para **CPR 23**).

III L&T [175A]

21B. Notice to accompany demands for service charges

(1) A demand for the payment of a service charge must be accompanied by a summary of the rights and obligations of tenants of dwellings in relation to service charges.

(2) The Secretary of State may make regulations prescribing requirements as to the form and content of such summaries of rights and obligations.

(3) A tenant may withhold payment of a service charge which has been demanded from him if subsection (1) is not complied with in relation to the demand.

(4) Where a tenant withholds a service charge under this section, any provisions of the lease relating to non-payment or late payment of service charges do not have effect in relation to the period for which he so withholds it.

(5) Regulations under subsection (2) may make different provision for different purposes.

(6) Regulations under subsection (2) shall be made by statutory instrument which shall be subject to annulment in pursuance of a resolution of either House of Parliament.

III L&T [175A.1]

Commencement This section was brought fully into force in England by the Commonhold and Leasehold Reform Act 2002 (Commencement No 6) (England) Order 2007, SI 2007/1256, with effect from 1 October 2007. The notice is required in respect of demands made after 1 October 2007 although the work may have been carried out before: *Amourgam v Valepark Properties Ltd* [2011] UKUT 261 (LC). The section came into force in Wales with effect from 30 November 2007: see the Commonhold and Leasehold Reform Act 2002 (Commencement No 4) (Wales) Order 2007, SI 2007/3161.

III L&T [175A.2]

Regulations The Service Charges (Summary of Rights and Obligations, and Transitional Obligations) (England) Regulations 2007, SI 2007/1257 prescribe the form and contents of the summary of tenants' rights and obligations which must accompany any demand for the payment of a service charge served on or after 1 October 2007, subject to transitional provisions. The sanction for non-compliance is that the tenant is entitled to withhold payment.

III L&T [175A.3]

Obligation to produce accounts and offer inspection The obligations under ss 21 and 22 to produce accounts and grant document inspection may be enforced by injunction: *Morshead Mansions Ltd v Di Marco* [2013] EWHC 1068 (Ch), [2013] All ER (D) 14 (May).

INSURANCE

III L&T [176]–III L&T [177]

30A. Rights of tenants with respect to insurance

The Schedule of this Act (which confers on tenants certain rights with respect to the insurance of their dwellings) shall have effect.

III L&T [176.1]

The Schedule The Landlord and Tenant Act 1985 s 30A and the Schedule confer on tenants certain rights regarding insurance. These rights include the right to insist on information about insurance and to notify insurers of possible claims and the right, under the Landlord and Tenant Act 1985 Schedule para 8, to challenge the landlord's choice of insurers. However, the landlord is not obliged to shop around for the cheapest insurer; it is sufficient if the transaction between him and the chosen insurer is carried out in the normal course of business: *Havenridge Ltd v Boston Dyers Ltd* [1994] 2 EGLR 73, [1994] 49 EG 111, CA. Proceedings under Landlord and Tenant Act 1985 Schedule para 8 should be brought by Pt 8 claim form using the Pt 8 procedure: CPR PD para 2.1 (para **CPR PD 56**). The text of Landlord and Tenant Act 1985 Schedule para 8 is as follows:

RIGHT TO CHALLENGE LANDLORD'S CHOICE OF INSURERS

8.

(1) This paragraph applies where a tenancy of a dwelling requires the tenant to insure the dwelling with an insurer nominated or approved by the landlord.

(2) The tenant or landlord may apply to a county court or leasehold valuation tribunal for a determination whether—

- (a) the insurance which is available from the nominated or approved insurer for insuring the tenant's dwelling is unsatisfactory in any respect, or
- (b) the premiums payable in respect of any such insurance are excessive.

(3) No such application may be made in respect of a matter which—

- (a) has been agreed or admitted by the tenant,
- (b) under an arbitration agreement to which the tenant is a party is to be referred to arbitration, or
- (c) has been the subject of determination by a court or arbitral tribunal.

(4) On an application under this paragraph the court or tribunal may make—

- (a) an order requiring the landlord to nominate or approve such other insurer as is specified in the order, or
- (b) an order requiring him to nominate or approve another insurer who satisfies such requirements in relation to the insurance of the dwelling as are specified in the order.

(5) [. . .]

(6) An agreement by the tenant of a dwelling (other than an arbitration agreement) is void in so far as it purports to provide for a determination in a particular manner, or on particular evidence, of any question which may be the subject of an application under this paragraph.

III L&T [176.2]

Leaseholder's obligation to insure with an insurer nominated or approved by the landlord Note that a leaseholder now has the right, subject to certain conditions, to choose an insurer who has not been nominated or approved by the landlord. The right arises under s 164 of the Commonhold and Leasehold Reform Act 2002, but the leaseholder must meet the requirements of the Leasehold Houses (Notice of Insurance Cover) (England) Regulations 2004, SI 2004/3097, as amended by SI 2005/177 or, in Wales, the requirements laid down in SI 2005/1354.

III L&T [176.3]

Challenging block insurance under s 27A In *Cos Services Ltd v Nicholson* [2017] UKUT 382 (LC), a case decided under s 27A, premiums for block insurance were held to be unreasonable and the lessor was required to explain the process by which the insurer and premium had been selected with reference to the steps taken to assess the current market.

SUPPLEMENTARY PROVISIONS

LANDLORD & TENANT AND HOUSING

III L&T [178]

36. Meaning of "lease" and "tenancy" and related expressions

(1) In this Act "lease" and "tenancy" have the same meaning.

(2) Both expressions include

(a) a sub-lease or sub-tenancy, and

(b) an agreement for a lease or tenancy (or sub-lease or sub-tenancy).

(3) The expressions "lessor" and "lessee" and "landlord" and "tenant", and references to letting, to the grant of a lease or to covenants or terms, shall be construed accordingly.

III L&T [179]

37. Meaning of "statutory tenant" and related expressions

In this Act

(a) "statutory tenancy" and "statutory tenant" mean a statutory tenancy or statutory tenant within the meaning of the Rent Act 1977 or the Rent (Agriculture) Act 1976; and

(b) "landlord", in relation to a statutory tenant, means the person who, apart from the statutory tenancy, would be entitled to possession of the premises.

III L&T [180]

38. Minor definitions

In this Act

"address" means a person's place of abode or place of business or, in the case of a company, its registered office,

"appropriate tribunal" means—

(a) in relation to a dwelling in England the First-tier Tribunal or, where determined by or under Tribunal Procedure Rules, the Upper Tribunal; and

(b) in relation to a dwelling in England the First-tier Tribunal or, where determined by or under Tribunal Procedure Rules, the Upper Tribunal; and

"arbitration agreement", "arbitration proceedings" and "arbitral tribunal" have the same meaning as in Part I of the Arbitration Act 1996 and post-dispute arbitration agreement, in relation to any matter, means an arbitration agreement made after a dispute about the matter has arisen;

"co-operative housing association" has the same meaning as in the Housing Associations Act 1985;

"dwelling" means a building or part of a building occupied or intended to be occupied as a separate dwelling, together with any yard, garden, outhouses and appurtenances belonging to it or usually enjoyed with it;

"housing association" has the same meaning as in the Housing Associations Act 1985;

"local authority" means a district, county, county borough or London borough council, the Common Council of the City of London or the Council of the Isles of Scilly and in sections 14(4), 26(1) and 28(6) includes . . . the Broads Authority, a police and crime commissioner, the Mayor's Office for Policing and Crime . . . a joint authority established by Part IV of the Local Government Act 1985, an economic prosperity board established under section 88 of the Local Democracy, Economic Development and Construction Act 2009, a combined authority established under section 103 of that Act. . . *and the London Fire and Emergency Planning Authority* [and the London Fire Commissioner];

"local housing authority" has the meaning given by section 1 of the Housing Act 1985;

"new town corporation" means—

(a) a development corporation established by an order made, or treated as made, under the New Towns Act 1981,

(b) the Homes and Communities Agency so far as exercising functions in relation to anything transferred (or to be transferred) to it as mentioned in section 52(1)(a) to (d) of the Housing and Regeneration Act 2008, or

(ba) the Greater London Authority so far as exercising its new towns and urban development functions, or

(c) the Welsh Ministers so far as exercising functions in relation to anything transferred (or to be transferred) to them as mentioned in section 36(1)(a)(i) to (iii) of the New Towns Act 1981;

"protected tenancy" has the same meaning as in the Rent Act 1977;

"registered social landlord", has the same meaning as in the Housing Act 1985 (see section 5 (4) and (5) of that Act);

"registered contract" has the same meaning as in the Rent Act 1977;

"urban development corporation" has the same meaning as in Part XVI of the Local Government, Planning and Land Act 1980.

Amendment *Text in italic is deleted and text in square brackets is inserted by the Policing and Crime Act 2017, with effect from a date to be appointed.*

LANDLORD AND TENANT ACT 1987

(c 31)

GENERAL NOTES ON LANDLORD AND TENANT ACT 1987

III L&T [181]

Jurisdiction The Landlord and Tenant Act 1987 s 52 (see para **III L&T [205]**) confers jurisdiction on the county courts, concurrently with the High Court, to hear proceedings and to determine questions under Landlord and Tenant Act 1987 Pts I, III and IV, other than those reserved, by Landlord and Tenant Act 1987 s 52A (see para **III L&T [206]**) to leasehold valuation tribunals. Applications under Landlord and Tenant Act 1987 Pt II, for the appointment of a manager, should be made to the leasehold valuation tribunal (a point reinforced in *Stylli v Hamberton Property Inc* [2002] EWHC 394 (Ch), [2002] All ER (D) 28 (Mar), (2002) Independent, 15 April; see also the case on a successful application reported at *Queensbridge Investments Ltd v Lodge, Davda, Heskel and Arora* [2015] UKUT 635 (LC)). It should be noted, however, that claims brought in the court under the Landlord and Tenant Act 1987 are landlord and tenant claims within the meaning of CPR Pt 56 (see para **CPR 56**). They must therefore be started in the county court for the district in which the land is situated (see para **CPR 56.2**). Only in exceptional circumstances (where the claimant can certify that there are complicated disputes of fact or there are points of law of general importance) may a landlord and tenant claim be started in the High Court. The value of the property and the amount of any financial claim may be relevant circumstances, but these factors alone will not normally justify starting the claim in the High Court: (see CPR PD 56 paras 2.1 to 2.5 (para **CPR PD 56**)). If the claim is brought in the High Court then, with effect from 2 December 2002, CPR PD 56 para 2.6 (para **CPR PD 56**) makes clear that the claim must be brought in the Chancery Division.

III L&T [182]

Parts I, III and IV The broad aim of each of these Parts is to alter the balance of advantage of leaseholders in a block of flats against their landlord. Landlord and Tenant Act 1987 Pt I gives leaseholders a right of first refusal to stop the freehold being sold over their heads; Landlord and Tenant Act 1987 Pt III gives them a right to acquire the freehold where the landlord is in breach and likely to remain so; and Landlord and Tenant Act 1987 Pt IV enables leaseholders to have leases varied to remove anomalous provisions.

III L&T [183]

Landlord's duty to provide information In Landlord and Tenant Act 1987 ss 47 and 48 (see paras **III L&T [203]** and **III L&T [204]**) require landlords to provide information as to the name and address for paying rent and serving notices.

III L&T [184]

Procedure in relation to Parts I, III and IV The claimant in a claim under the Landlord and Tenant Act 1987 must use the Pt 8 procedure, as modified by CPR Pt 56 and CPR PD 56: CPR PD 56 para 2.1 (para **CPR PD 56**). The modifications to the procedure relating to claims under the 1987 Act are set out in CPR PD 56 paras 7.1 to 10.2, to which the practitioner should refer. A summary of the effect of these paras is found at para **CPR 56.1[1]**. A precedent for a claim for the acquisition of the freehold can be found at **BCCP O[401]** and a precedent for a claim for variation of a lease at **BCCP O[402]**.

PART I
TENANT'S RIGHTS OF FIRST REFUSAL

RIGHTS OF FIRST REFUSAL

III L&T [185]

5. Landlord required to serve offer notice on tenants

(1) Where the landlord proposes to make a relevant disposal affecting premises to which this Part applies, he shall serve a notice under this section (an "offer notice") on the qualifying tenants of the flats contained in the premises (the "constituent flats").

(2) An offer notice must comply with the requirements of whichever is applicable of the following sections

section 5A (requirements in a case of contract to be completed by conveyance, &c.),

section 5B (requirements in case of sale at auction),

section 5C (requirements in case of grant of option or right of pre-emption),

section 5D (requirements in case of conveyance not preceded by contract, &c.);

and in the case of a disposal to which section 5E applies (disposal for non-monetary consideration) shall also comply with the requirements of that section.

(3) Where a landlord proposes to effect a transaction involving the disposal of an estate or interest in more than one building (whether or not involving the same estate or interest), he shall, for the purpose of complying with this section, sever the transaction so as to deal with each building separately.

(4) If, as a result of the offer notice being served on different tenants on different dates, the period specified in the notice as the period for accepting the offer would end on different dates, the notice shall have effect in relation to all the qualifying tenants on whom it is served as if it provided for that period to end with the latest of those dates.

(5) A landlord who has not served an offer notice on all of the qualifying tenants on whom it was required to be served shall nevertheless be treated as having complied with this section

(a) if he has served an offer notice on not less than 90% of the qualifying tenants on whom such a notice was so required to be served, or

(b) where the qualifying tenants on whom it was required to be served number less than ten, if he has served such a notice on all but one of them.

III L&T [185.1]

More than one building Although s 5(3) requires that more than one building should not be treated together as a single building it has been held that this is allowable, as a matter of interpretation, in a case where the occupants of the qualifying flats in each of the buildings share the use of the same appurtenant premises: *Long Acre Securities Ltd v Karet* [2004] EWHC 442 (Ch), [2004] 3 WLR 866. See also the note on "building" at **III L&T [186.4]**.

III L&T [186]

5A. Offer notice: requirements in case of contract to be completed by conveyance, etc

(1) The following requirements must be met in relation to an offer notice where the disposal consists of entering into a contract to create or transfer an estate or interest in land.

(2) The notice must contain particulars of the principal terms of the disposal proposed by the landlord, including in particular

- (a) the property, and the estate or interest in that property, to which the contract relates,
- (b) the principal terms of the contract (including the deposit and consideration required).

(3) The notice must state that the notice constitutes an offer by the landlord to enter into a contract on those terms which may be accepted by the requisite majority of qualifying tenants of the constituent flats.

(4) The notice must specify a period within which that offer may be so accepted, being a period of not less than two months which is to begin with the date of service of the notice.

(5) The notice must specify a further period of not less than two months within which a person or persons may be nominated by the tenants under section 6.

(6) This section does not apply to the grant of an option or right of pre-emption (see section 5C).

NOTES TO SECTIONS 5 AND 5A

III L&T [186.1]

Relationship to the pre-existing law The Housing Act 1996 s 89 extended the scope of the Landlord and Tenant Act 1987 Pt I so that the right of first refusal became exercisable not only in relation to a disposal of an estate or interest in land but also in relation to a contract to create or transfer an estate or interest in land. The effect was to undo the decision in *Mainwaring v Trustees of Henry Smith's Charity* [1998] QB 1, [1996] 2 All ER 220, CA. Landlord and Tenant Act 1987 ss 5, 6–10 were therefore rewritten to cover different kinds of contracts (Landlord and Tenant Act 1987 ss 5A–5E covering respectively: contract to be completed by conveyance, sale by auction, creation of option or right of pre-emption, conveyance without contract, and disposal for non-monetary consideration) and to apply a new, simplified procedure throughout. Landlord and Tenant Act 1987 ss 5–17 as enacted were accordingly replaced by new provisions set out in the Housing Act 1996 Sch 6, with effect from 1 October 1996: Housing Act 1996 (Commencement No 2 and Savings) Order 1996, SI 1996/2212.

III L&T [186.2]

Rights of first refusal These sections require the landlord who proposes to dispose of his interest to give qualifying tenants of flats notice of his intention and the chance to nominate someone to buy that interest. It will normally be advisable for the tenants to form their own company for the purchase. Landlord and Tenant Act 1987 s 1(1) prohibits a landlord from disposing of his interest without giving a s 5 notice; but if he does so the tenants may exercise their rights under Landlord and Tenant Act 1987 ss 11 (see para **III L&T [187]**), 12–14 against the new landlord instead, or, if the new landlord has disposed of his interest to someone else, against that person, as provided in Landlord and Tenant Act 1987 s 16 (see para **III L&T [188]**). Breach of s 5 by a landlord will not support an action for conspiracy by unlawful means nor (it seems) for breach of statutory duty: *Michaels v Taylor Woodrow Developments Ltd* [2001] Ch 493, [2000] 4 All ER 645, ChD.

The court will have regard to the commercial realities. In *Kensington Heights Commercial Co Ltd v Campden Hill Developments Ltd* [2007] EWCA Civ 245, [2007] 2 All ER 751, [2007] 2 WLR 1040 the landlord entered into an agreement to surrender a headlease. This was a relevant disposal which triggered the landlord's obligation to give notice under s 5 (which the landlord did not do). However, the surrender was in return for the grant of a longer term; the landlord was therefore enlarging its head leasehold interest rather than disposing of it. The court accordingly declined to order a disposal to the qualifying tenants under s 12B.

III L&T [186.3]

Landlord, qualifying tenant By Landlord and Tenant Act 1987 s 2 (1) "landlord" means the immediate landlord and, where there is a statutory tenancy (under the Rent Act 1977 or the Rent (Agriculture) Act 1976), the person who would otherwise be entitled to possession. By Landlord and Tenant Act 1987 s 2 (2) "landlord" includes also the landlord's landlord (and so on) where each intermediate landlord has a lease for less than seven years or which is terminable by the landlord within the first seven years.

Any tenant (including a statutory tenant) of a flat, and by Landlord and Tenant Act 1987 s 20(3) a successor of such a tenant, is a qualifying tenant, according to Landlord and Tenant Act 1987 s 3(1), unless the tenancy is (a) a protected shorthold as defined by the Housing Act 1980 s 52 or (b) a business tenancy to which the Landlord and Tenant Act 1954 Pt II applies or (c) terminable on the cessation of his employment or (d) an assured tenancy or assured agricultural occupancy within the meaning of the Housing Act 1988 Pt I Landlord and Tenant Act 1987 s 3(2) also excludes a person who is, by virtue of one or more tenancies falling outside of Landlord and Tenant Act 1987 s 3(1)(a)–(d), the tenant not only of the flat in question but also of at least two other flats contained in the premises.

III L&T [186.4]

Premises to which Part I applies Landlord and Tenant Act 1987 s 1 (2) applies Part I to any building (whole or part) in which two or more flats are held by qualifying tenants and outnumber the flats not so held. But important exceptions are made for premises with either an "exempt landlord" or a "resident landlord" (explained in Landlord and Tenant Act 1987 s 58), and for premises partly occupied for non-residential purposes, if the internal floor area of the non-residential part is more than 50% of the whole, excluding common parts. Also premises are excluded by Landlord and Tenant Act 1987 s 18 where the prospective purchaser has served preliminary notices on the qualifying tenants but no more than 50% have availed themselves of the right of first refusal or would wish to do so. "Building" includes the gardens and other appurtenances of the flats which are expressly or impliedly included in the demises of the flats to the tenants but not garages which are held under separate leases: *Denetower Ltd v Toop* [1991] 3 All ER 661, [1991] 1 WLR 945, CA. The disposal of an interest in part of a property is a disposal affecting those premises within the meaning of the Act. However, depending on the circumstances, not everything within the curtilage of a building is properly to be regarded as part of the building for the purposes of the Act: *Dartmouth Court Blackheath Ltd v Berisworth Ltd* [2008] EWHC 350 (Ch), (2008) 9 EG 200 (CS).

III L&T [186.5]

Exempt landlord, resident landlord Landlord and Tenant Act 1987 s 58 exempts local authorities and other public bodies with responsibilities for housing. The Crown is also exempt, except that Landlord and Tenant Act 1987 s 56(1) applies the Act to a tenancy from the Crown if there has ceased to be a Crown interest in the land subject to it. Premises with a resident landlord are excluded provided that it is not a purpose-built block and he or she has his only or principal residence there for the last 12 months.

III L&T [186.6]

Relevant disposal Landlord and Tenant Act 1987 s 4(1) makes it a general rule that any disposal of the landlord's estate or interest (legal or equitable) is a relevant disposal, unless it takes the form of a grant of a tenancy of a single flat.

III L&T [186.7]

Offer subject to contract By Landlord and Tenant Act 1987 s 20 (2), any reference in this Part to an offer, counter-offer, acceptance etc is to be read as referring to an offer etc subject to contract.

III L&T [186.8]

Acceptance of landlord's offer, rejection, counter-offer and fresh offer Where the requisite majority of qualifying tenants serve a notice of acceptance in time, Landlord and Tenant Act 1987 s 6 provides that the landlord may not dispose of his interest to anyone but the nominee; but if there is no acceptance or no one is nominated in time he is permitted by Landlord and Tenant Act 1987 ss 6, 7 to dispose of it outside on the same terms, except that the price may be higher. If disposal to the nominee requires consent, which is withheld unreasonably, the landlord is required by Landlord and Tenant Act 1987 s 8E(1) to take proceedings for a declaration to this effect. It was held in *Mainwaring v Trustees of Henry Smith's Charity (No 2)* (1996) 29 HLR 572, [1997] 1 EGLR 93, CA that a tenant's acceptance may be withdrawn although expressed to be irrevocable.

III L&T [186.9]

Withdrawal and lapse Despite acceptance of his offer the landlord may decide not to dispose of his interest after all, or the premises may cease to be premises to which Landlord and Tenant Act 1987 Pt I applies, or the number of qualifying tenants wishing to proceed may fall below the requisite number. In any such case Landlord and Tenant Act 1987 ss 9A, 9B, 10 provide that the landlord, or as the case may be the tenants, may serve a notice of withdrawal, or lapse. Where a conveyance of freehold property prevented the purchaser from reselling the property without first offering to sell it back to the vendor and gave the vendor two months in which to accept, it was held that any such offer could be withdrawn before acceptance within the stipulated time: *Tuck v Baker* [1990] 2 EGLR 195, [1990] 32 EG 46, CA.

III L&T [186.10]

Enforcement of obligations under Part I See Landlord and Tenant Act 1987 ss 19, 52 and notes thereto (see paras **III L&T [189]** onwards and **III L&T [205]** onwards), regarding enforcement by proceedings in the county court.

III L&T [186.11]

Service of notices Regarding the form and content of notices and the manner of service, see Landlord and Tenant Act 1987 s 54 and the notes thereto (see para **III L&T [207]** onwards). See also CPR PD 56 para 10.2 (para **CPR PD 56**), which states that if a notice is to be served in or before a claim under the 1987 Act, it must be served in accordance with s 54, and, in the case of service on a landlord, at the address given under s 48(1). It should also be noted that all documents must be served by the parties: CPR PD 56 para 10.1 (para **CPR PD 56**).

Where the landlord proposes to dispose of an estate comprising more than one building, s 5(3) requires a separate notice for each building. But where a building includes several structures it is not necessary for there to be a separate notice for each structure: *Long Acre Securities Ltd v Karet* [2004] EWHC 442 (Ch)[2004] 3 WLR 866.

LANDLORD & TENANT AND HOUSING

ENFORCEMENT BY TENANTS OF RIGHTS AGAINST PURCHASERS

III L&T [187]

11. Circumstances in which tenants' rights enforceable against purchaser

(1) The following provisions of this Part apply where a landlord has made a relevant disposal affecting premises to which at the time of the disposal this Part applied ("the original disposal"), and either

(a) no notice was served by the landlord under section 5 with respect to that disposal, or

(b) the disposal was made in contravention of any provision of sections 6 to 10,

and the premises are still premises to which this Part applies.

(2) In those circumstances the requisite majority of the qualifying tenants of the flats contained in the premises affected by the relevant disposal (the "constituent flats") have the rights conferred by the following provisions

section 11A (right to information as to terms of disposal, &c.),

section 12A (right of qualifying tenants to take benefit of contract),

section 12B (right of qualifying tenants to compel sale, &c. by purchaser), and

section 12C (right of qualifying tenants to compel grant of new tenancy by superior landlord).

(3) In those sections the transferee under the original disposal (or, in the case of the surrender of a tenancy, the superior landlord) is referred to as "the purchaser". This shall not be read as restricting the operation of those provisions to disposals for consideration.

III L&T [187.1]

Relationship to pre-existing law The Housing Act 1996 s 92, Sch 6 substituted ss 11–14 in place of the originally enacted Landlord and Tenant Act 1987 ss 11–15. The changes were largely consequential on the enlargement of the right of first refusal to cover a "disposal" which takes the form of a contract to create or transfer an estate or interest in land: see the notes to Landlord and Tenant Act 1987 ss 5 and 5A (see para **III L&T [186.1]** onwards). In order to give teeth to the newly enlarged right it was necessary to expand the powers of enforcement (within Landlord and Tenant Act 1987 s 11) to cover a right to information (Landlord and Tenant Act 1987 s 11A), a right of qualifying tenants to take the benefit of the contract (Landlord and Tenant Act 1987 s 12A), a right to compel sale (Landlord and Tenant Act 1987 s 12B) and a right to compel grant of a new tenancy (Landlord and Tenant Act 1987 s 12C). Supplementary provisions were included to provide for nominated persons (Landlord and Tenant Act 1987 s 12D) and the powers of leasehold valuation tribunals to determine questions arising in connection with matters arising (Landlord and Tenant Act 1987 s 13). Section 14 of the 1987 Act makes provision for the withdrawal of a nominated person from exercising the right to compel a sale or grant of a new tenancy.

Where a landlord has entered into a contract to surrender a head lease without serving a notice on the qualifying tenants they are entitled to serve a notice under s 12C requiring him to grant a new lease to their nominee on the same terms as the surrendered lease: *Kensington Heights Commercial Co Ltd v Campden Hill Developments Ltd* (2007) Times, 20 April, CA.

III L&T [187.2]

Landlord, qualifying tenant, relevant disposal, premises to which Part I applies, service of notices As to these matters, see the notes at para **III L&T [186.2]** onwards.

III L&T [187.3]

Notice under section 3 of the 1985 Act The Landlord and Tenant Act 1985 s 3 requires notice to be given to the tenant of the landlord's assignment of his interest.

III L&T [187.4]

Response to tenants' notice If a landlord provides information on receipt of a tenants' notice but denies that he is doing so in compliance with it, it is not a compliant response and time for serving a purchase notice does not start to run: *Staszewski v Maribella Ltd* (1997) 30 HLR 213, [1998] 1 EGLR 34, CA.

III L&T [187.5]

Incumbrance In *Englefield Court Tenants v Skeels* [1990] 2 EGLR 230, [1990] 37 EG 91, a long lease of the roof space granted by the new landlord to her husband after the original disposal was held by the rent assessment committee to constitute an incumbrance for the purposes of Landlord and Tenant Act 1987 s 11(4)(b), as enacted. But it is otherwise where the lease itself qualifies as a relevant disposal or has been granted after a s 11 notice has been served in respect of the original disposal and the statutory procedures are being actively pursued: *Nolan v Eagle Wharf Developments Ltd* [1992] 2 EGLR 223, [1992] 46 EG 113 (rent assessment committee).

Where the new landlord lets a vacant flat he could be creating an incumbrance. But the grant of a reversionary lease was held not to create an incumbrance within Landlord and Tenant Act 1987 s 12(4), as enacted; it was an event which triggered the operation of s 16: *Belvedere Court Management Ltd v Frogmore Developments Ltd* [1997] QB 858, [1996] 1 All ER 312, CA.

III L&T [187.6]

Redemption of the new landlord's mortgage The Landlord and Tenant Act 1987 Sch 1 Pt I provides for the nominated person to redeem the new landlord's mortgage out of the purchase money which should, if difficulty arises, be paid into court.

III L&T [187.7]

Change in circumstances The fact that the new landlord had, by forfeiting the leases of two of the flats, obtained vacant possession of them was held not to be a change in circumstances justifying an increase in the consideration payable, as his title not having been registered at the relevant time it was doubtful whether the forfeiture was valid, and in any event the tenants' mortgagees had a subsisting claim to relief from forfeiture which they were likely to obtain: *Crumpton v Unifox Properties Ltd* (1992) 25 HLR 121, [1992] 2 EGLR 82, CA.

ENFORCEMENT BY TENANTS OF RIGHTS AGAINST SUBSEQUENT PURCHASERS

III L&T [188]

16. Rights of qualifying tenants against subsequent purchaser

(1) This section applies where, at the time when a notice is served on the purchaser under section 11A, 12A, 12B or 12C, he no longer holds the estate or interest that was the subject-matter of the original disposal.

(2) In the case of a notice under section 11A (right to information as to terms of disposal, &c.) the purchaser shall, within the period for complying with that notice

(a) serve notice on the person specified in the notice as the person to whom particulars are to be provided of the name and address of the person to whom he has disposed of that estate or interest ("the subsequent purchaser"), and

(b) serve on the subsequent purchaser a copy of the notice under section 11A and of the particulars given by him in response to it.

(3) In the case of a notice under section 12A, 12B or 12C the purchaser shall forthwith

(a) forward the notice to the subsequent purchaser, and

(b) serve on the nominated person notice of the name and address of the subsequent purchaser.

(4) Once the purchaser serves a notice in accordance with subsection (2) (a) or (3) (b), sections 12A to 14 shall, instead of applying to the purchaser, apply to the subsequent purchaser as if he were the transferee under the original disposal.

(5) Subsections (1) to (4) have effect, with any necessary modifications, in a case where, instead of disposing of the whole of the estate or interest referred to in subsection (1) to another person, the purchaser has disposed of it in part or in parts to one or more other persons.

In such a case, sections 12A to 14

(a) apply to the purchaser in relation to any part of that estate or interest retained by him, and

(b) in relation to any part of that estate or interest disposed of to any other person, apply to that other person instead as if he were (as respects that part) the transferee under the original disposal.

III L&T [188.1]

Defective notice In *E I Naschie v The Pitt Place (Epsom) Ltd* (1998) Times, 27 May, CA, a notice under the old Landlord and Tenant Act 1987 s 2 was held to be defective because given on behalf of tenants who had not given express authority or were not resident, or who had died or moved.

SUPPLEMENTARY

III L&T [189]

19. Enforcement of obligations under Part I

(1) The court may, on the application of any person interested, make an order requiring any person who has made default in complying with any duty imposed on him by any provision of this Part to make good the default within such time as is specified in the order.

(2) An application shall not be made under subsection (1) unless

(a) a notice has been previously served on the person in question requiring him to make good the default, and

(b) more than 14 days have elapsed since the date of service of that notice without his having done so.

(3) The restriction imposed by section 1 (1) may be enforced by an injunction granted by the court.

III L&T [189.1]

Court "Court" means the High Court or a county court: s 52 (see para **III L&T [205]**). Note, however, that, save in exceptional circumstances, a claim under s 19 should be started in the county court for the district in which the land is situated: see para **CPR 56.2** and the note at para **III L&T [181]**.

III L&T [189.2]

Application CPR PD 56 requires that an application under s 19 is made using the Pt 8 procedure. CPR PD 56 para 7.1 states that a copy of the notice served under s 19(2)(a) of the 1987 Act must accompany the claim form (see para **CPR PD 56**).

III L&T [189.3]

Service of notice See Landlord and Tenant Act 1987 s 54 and notes to that section (see para **III L&T [207]** onwards), regarding the manner of serving notices. See also CPR PD 56 para 10.2, which states that if a notice is to be served in or before a claim under the 1987 Act, it must be served in accordance with s 54, and, in the case of service on a landlord, at the address given under s 48(1). It should also be noted that all documents must be served by the parties: CPR PD 56 para 10.1 (see para **CPR PD 56**).

III L&T [189.4]

Order enforceable by injunction An order enjoining the landlord to sell or make a grant may be enforced by committal. However, the court may instead make an order for the instrument to be executed by someone else under powers conferred on the High Court by the Supreme Court Act 1981 s 39 (see para **II SCA [40]**) and in the county courts by the County Courts Act 1984 s 38 (see para **II CCA [21]**): *Danchevsky v Danchevsky* [1975] Fam 17, [1974] 3 All ER 934, CA.

III L&T [189.5]

Application should be made promptly The discretion may be exercised against making an order under s 19 if the claimant has not acted sufficiently promptly: see *Michaels v Harley House (Marylebone) Ltd* [2000] Ch 104, [1999] 1 All ER 356, CA.

III L&T [190]

25. Compulsory acquisition of landlord's interest by qualifying tenants

(1) This Part has effect for the purpose of enabling qualifying tenants of flats contained in any premises to which this Part applies to make an application to the court for an order providing for a person nominated by them to acquire their landlord's interest in the premises without his consent; and any such order is referred to in this Part as "an acquisition order".

(2) Subject to subsections (4) and (5), this Part applies to premises if

(a) they consist of the whole or part of a building; and

(b) they contain two or more flats held by tenants of the landlord who are qualifying tenants; and

(c) the total number of flats held by such tenants is not less than two-thirds of the total number of flats contained in the premises.

(3) [Repealed 1993]

(4) This Part does not apply to premises falling within subsection (2) if

(a) any part or parts of the premises is or are occupied or intended to be occupied otherwise than for residential purposes; and

(b) the internal floor area of that part or those parts (taken together) exceeds 50 per cent. of the internal floor area of the premises (taken as a whole);

and for the purposes of this subsection the internal floor area of any common parts shall be disregarded.

(5) This Part also does not apply to any such premises at a time when

(a) the interest of the landlord in the premises is held by an exempt landlord or a resident landlord, or

(b) the premises are included within the functional land of any charity.

(6) The Secretary of State may by order substitute for the percentage for the time being specified in subsection (4) (b) such other percentage as is specified in the order.

III L&T [190.1]

Generally Compulsory acquisition under Landlord and Tenant Act 1987 Pt III by long-leaseholders enables them, where a landlord is in serious breach of his obligations, to force him to sell them his interest, and so provides a fairer and cheaper method of giving them a greater stake in the property than the continuing expense of a court order for the appointment of a manager.

III L&T [190.2]

Qualifying tenants Only tenants with long leases, as defined in Landlord and Tenant Act 1987 s 59(3) (see para **III L&T [208]**), qualify as tenants for this purpose and some of these are excepted by Landlord and Tenant Act 1987 s 26(1) (see para **III L&T [191]**), which excludes business tenancies; others are excepted by Landlord and Tenant Act 1987 s 26 (2), (3).

III L&T [190.3]

Flat, common parts, functional land of any charity Provision is made in Landlord and Tenant Act 1987 ss 59 and 60(1) (see paras **III L&T [208]** and **III L&T [209]**) for the interpretation of "landlord" and "tenant", "common parts", "flat", "functional land" and "charity".

III L&T [191]

26. Qualifying tenants

(1) Subject to subsections (2) and (3), a person is a qualifying tenant of a flat for the purposes of this Part if he is the tenant of the flat under a long lease other than one constituting a tenancy to which Part II of the Landlord and Tenant Act 1954 applies.

(2) A person is not to be regarded as being a qualifying tenant of a flat contained in any particular premises consisting of the whole or part of a building if by virtue of one or more long leases none of which constitutes a tenancy to which Part II of the Landlord and Tenant Act 1954 applies, he is the tenant not only of the flat in question but also of at least two other flats contained in those premises.

(3) A tenant of a flat under a long lease whose landlord is a qualifying tenant of that flat is not to be regarded as being a qualifying tenant of that flat.

[(4) For the purposes of subsection (2) any tenant of a flat contained in the premises in question who is a body corporate shall be treated as the tenant of any other flat so contained and let to an associated company, as defined in section 20 (1).]

III L&T [192]

27. Preliminary notice by tenants

(1) Before an application for an acquisition order is made in respect of any premises to which this Part applies, a notice under this section must (subject to subsection (3)) be served on the landlord by qualifying tenants of the flats contained in the premises who, at the date when it is served, constitute the requisite majority of such tenants.

(2) A notice under this section must

(a) specify the names of the qualifying tenants by whom it is served, the addresses of their flats and the name and the address in England and

Wales of a person on whom the landlord may serve notices (including notices in proceedings) in connection with this Part instead of serving them on those tenants;

(b) state that those tenants intend to make an application for an acquisition order to be made by the court in respect of such premises to which this Part applies as are specified in the notice, but (if paragraph (d) is applicable) that they will not do so if the landlord complies with the requirement specified in pursuance of that paragraph;

(c) specify the grounds on which the court would be asked to make such an order and the matters that would be relied on by the tenants for the purpose of establishing those grounds;

(d) where those matters are capable of being remedied by the landlord, require the landlord, within such reasonable period as is specified in the notice, to take such steps for the purpose of remedying them as are so specified; and

(e) contain such information (if any) as the Secretary of State may by regulations prescribe.

(3) The court may by order dispense with the requirement to serve a notice under this section in a case where it is satisfied that it would not be reasonably practicable to serve such a notice on the landlord, but the court may, when doing so, direct that such other notices are served, or such other steps are taken, as it thinks fit.

(4) Any reference in this Part to the requisite majority of qualifying tenants of the flats contained in any premises is a reference to qualifying tenants of the flats so contained with not less than two-thirds of the available votes; and for the purposes of this subsection

(a) the total number of available votes shall correspond to the total number of those flats for the time being let to qualifying tenants; and

(b) there shall be one available vote in respect of each of the flats so let which shall be attributed to the qualifying tenant to whom it is let.

(5) Nothing in this Part shall be construed as requiring the persons constituting any such majority in any one context to be the same as the persons constituting any such majority in any other context.

III L&T [192.1]

Contents of a notice In *Wildsmith (Maxwell Brent) v Arrowgame Ltd* [2012] EWHC 3315 (Ch), [2012] All ER (D) 277 (Nov) the court analysed the meaning of 'grounds' and 'matters' in s 27(3) and their relationship with the conditions set out in s 29 and emphasised that a valid notice under s 27 had to spell out the reasons why the tenants thought it was appropriate for the court to exercise its discretion to make an acquisition order.

III L&T [193]

28. Applications for acquisition orders

(1) An application for an acquisition order in respect of any premises to which this Part applies must be made by qualifying tenants of the flats contained in the premises who, at the date when it is made, constitute the requisite majority of such tenants.

(2) No such application shall be made to the court unless

(a) in a case where a notice has been served under section 27, either

(i) the period specified in pursuance of paragraph (d) of subsection (2) of that section has expired without the landlord having taken the steps that he was required to take in pursuance of that provision, or

(ii) that paragraph was not applicable in the circumstances of the case; or

(b) in a case where the requirement to serve such a notice has been dispensed with by an order under subsection (3) of that section, either

(i) any notices required to be served, and any other steps required to be taken, by virtue of the order have been served or (as the case may be) taken, or

(ii) no direction was given by the court when making the order.

(3) An application for an acquisition order may, subject to the preceding provisions of this Part, be made in respect of two or more premises to which this Part applies.

(4) Rules of court shall make provision

(a) for requiring notice of an application for an acquisition order in respect of any premises to be served on such descriptions of persons as may be specified in the rules; and

(b) for enabling persons served with any such notice to be joined as parties to the proceedings.

(5) The Land Charges Act 1972 and the Land Registration Act 2002 shall apply in relation to an application for an acquisition order as they apply in relation to other pending land actions.

III L&T [194]

29. Conditions for making acquisition orders

(1) The court may, on an application for an acquisition order, make such an order in respect of any premises if

(a) the court is satisfied

(i) that those premises were, at the date of service on the landlord of the notice (if any) under section 27 and on the date when the application was made, premises to which this Part applies, and

(ii) that they have not ceased to be such premises since the date when the application was made, and

(b) either of the conditions specified in subsections (2) and (3) is fulfilled with respect to those premises, and

(c) the court considers it appropriate to make the order in the circumstances of the case.

(2) The first of the conditions referred to in subsection (1) (b) is that the court is satisfied

(a) that the landlord either is in breach of any obligation owed by him to the applicants under their leases and relating to the management of the premises in question, or any part of them, or (in the case of an obligation dependent on notice) would be in breach of any such obligation but for the fact that it has not been reasonably practicable for the tenant to give him the appropriate notice, and

(b) that the circumstances by virtue of which he is (or would be) in breach of any such obligation are likely to continue, [. . .]

(c) [. . .]

(2A) The reference in subsection (2) to the management of any premises includes a reference to the repair, maintenance, improvement or insurance of those premises.

(3) The second of those conditions is that, both at the date when the application was made and throughout the period of two years immediately preceding that date, there was in force an appointment under Part II of a person to act as manager in relation to the premises in question [which was made by reason of an act or omission on the part of the landlord].

(4) An acquisition order may, if the court thinks fit

(a) include any yard, garden, outhouse or appurtenance belonging to, or usually enjoyed with, the premises specified in the application on which the order is made;

(b) exclude any part of the premises so specified.

(5) Where

(a) the premises in respect of which an application for an acquisition order is made consist of part only of more extensive premises in which the landlord has an interest, and

(b) it appears to the court that the landlord's interest in the latter premises is not reasonably capable of being severed, either in the manner contemplated by the application or in any manner authorised by virtue of subsection (4) (b),

then, notwithstanding that paragraphs (a) and (b) of subsection (1) apply, the court shall not make an acquisition order on the application.

(6) In a case where an application for an acquisition order was preceded by the service of a notice under section 27, the court may, if it thinks fit, make such an order notwithstanding

(a) that any period specified in the notice in pursuance of subsection (2) (d) of that section was not a reasonable period, or

(b) that the notice failed in any other respect to comply with any requirement contained in subsection (2) of that section or in any regulations applying to the notice under section 54 (3).

(7) Where any premises are premises to which this Part applies at the time when an application for an acquisition order is made in respect of them, then, for the purposes of this section and the following provisions of this Part, they shall not cease to be such premises by reason only that

(a) the interest of the landlord in them subsequently becomes held by—

(i) an exempt landlord or a resident landlord, or

(ii) the Welsh Ministers in their new towns residuary capacity, or

(b) they subsequently become included within the functional land of any charity.

III L&T [194.1]

Service of notices Regarding the form and content of notices and the manner of service, see Landlord and Tenant Act 1987 s 54 and the notes to that section (see para **III L&T [207]** onwards). The service of a defective notice does not prevent the court from making an order under Landlord and Tenant Act 1987 s 28 (see para **III L&T [193]**) if it thinks fit: see Landlord and Tenant Act 1987 s 29 (6). See also CPR PD 56 para 10.2, which states that if a notice is to be served in or before a claim under the 1987 Act, it must be served in accordance with s 54, and, in the case of service on a landlord, at the address given under s 48(1). It should also be noted that all documents must be served by the parties: CPR PD 56 para 10.1 (para **CPR PD 56**).

III L&T [194.2]

Prescribed information The power under Landlord and Tenant Act 1987 s 27(2)(e) (see para **III L&T [192]**) to prescribe additional information has not been exercised at the date of going to press.

III L&T [194.3]

Application to the court A claim for an acquisition order under s 28 of the Landlord and Tenant Act 1987 must be brought using the Pt 8 procedure as modified by CPR PD 56. Detailed requirements are set out at CPR PD 56 paras 8.2 to 8.6 (para **CPR PD 56**). Para 8.2 sets out the required contents of the claim form. A copy of the notice served on the landlord under s 27 of the 1987 Act must accompany the claim form unless the court has dispensed with the requirement to serve a notice under s 27(3) of the 1987 Act (para 8.3). The landlord of the property (and the nominated person, if he is not a claimant) must be defendants (para 8.4). A copy of the claim form must be served on each of the persons named by the claimant under para 8.2(4)(b) together with a notice that he may apply to be made a party (para 8.5). If the nominated person pays money into court in accordance with an order under s 33(1) of the 1987 Act, he must file a copy of the certificate of the surveyor selected under s 33(2)(a) of that Act (para 8.6).

Where for 14 years there had been no active management by the freeholder, who was in substantial breach of his obligations under the leases, and a receiver appointed by the court for the last ten years had only been able to keep the problem in check and not to remedy the situation altogether, the court concluded that the appointment of a manager would not solve the problem and an acquisition order was granted, the claimant's costs of the application to be deducted from the consideration money: *Gray v Standard Home & Counties Properties Ltd* (1994) 26 HLR 565, [1994] 1 EGLR 119.

III L&T [194.4]

Precedents For a precedent of a Pt 8 claim for an acquisition order, see **BCCP O[401]**.

III L&T [194.5]

Rules of court The relevant rule is now CPR Pt 56 (see para **CPR 56**) and its Practice Direction (see para **CPR PD 56**).

III L&T [194.6]

Premises to which Part III applies The premises to which Landlord and Tenant Act 1987 Pt III applies are defined by Landlord and Tenant Act 1987 s 25(2)–(5) (see para **III L&T [190]**), and the fact that they cease for specified reasons to be within the definition during the course of the proceedings is immaterial: see Landlord and Tenant Act 1987 s 29(7).

LANDLORD & TENANT AND HOUSING

III L&T [195]

30. Content of acquisition orders

(1) Where an acquisition order is made by the court, the order shall (except in a case falling within section 33 (1)) provide for the nominated person to be entitled to acquire the landlord's interest in the premises specified in the order on such terms as may be determined

(a) by agreement between the landlord and the qualifying tenants in whose favour the order is made, or

(b) in default of agreement, by the appropriate tribunal under section 31.

(2) An acquisition order may be granted subject to such conditions as the court thinks fit, and in particular its operation may be suspended on terms fixed by the court.

(3) References in this Part, in relation to an acquisition order, to the nominated person are references to such person or persons as may be nominated for the purposes of this Part by the persons applying for the order.

(4) Those persons must secure that the nominated person is joined as a party to the application, and no further nomination of a person for the purposes of this Part shall be made by them after the order is made (whether in addition to, or in substitution for, the existing nominated person) except with the approval of the court.

(5) Where the landlord is, by virtue of any covenant, condition or other obligation, precluded from disposing of his interest in the premises in respect of which an acquisition order has been made unless the consent of some other person is obtained

(a) he shall use his best endeavours to secure that the consent of that person to that disposal is obtained and, if it appears to him that that person is obliged not to withhold his consent unreasonably but has nevertheless so withheld it, shall institute proceedings for a declaration to that effect; but

(b) if

(i) the landlord has discharged any duty imposed on him by paragraph (a), and

(ii) the consent of that person has been withheld, and

(iii) no such declaration has been made,

the order shall cease to have effect.

(6) The Land Charges Act 1972 and the Land Registration Act 2002 shall apply in relation to an acquisition order as they apply in relation to an order affecting land made by the court for the purpose of enforcing a judgment or recognisance.

(7) For the purposes of this Part, "appropriate tribunal" means—

(a) in relation to premises in England, the First-tier Tribunal or, where determined by or under Tribunal Procedure Rules, the Upper Tribunal; and

(b) in relation to premises in Wales, a leasehold valuation tribunal.

III L&T [195.1]

Determination of terms In default of agreement, the terms of acquisition must be determined by a rent assessment committee; see eg *139 Finborough Road Management Ltd v Mansoor* [1990] 2 EGLR 225, [1990] 32 EG 55. The county court has no jurisdiction; see Landlord and Tenant Act 1987 s 52(1) (see para **III L&T [205]**). However, the rent assessment committee's jurisdiction does not include making decisions as to the legal validity of notices (see para **III L&T [206.1]**). Also, in *Stapel v Bellshore Property Investments Ltd* [2000] CLY 3948 the Leasehold Valuation Tribunal (London) held that it had no power to give a final ruling on the meaning of the terms of the lease and in particular the words "the building".

III L&T [195.2]

Registration as a land charge An acquisition order should be registered under the Land Charges Act 1972 s 1(1)(c).

III L&T [196]

32. Discharge of existing mortgages

(1) Where the landlord's interest in any premises is acquired in pursuance of an acquisition order, the instrument by virtue of which it is so acquired shall (subject to subsection (2) and Part II of Schedule 1) operate to discharge the premises from any charge on that interest to secure the payment of money or the performance of any other obligation by the landlord or any other person.

(2) Subsection (1) does not apply to any such charge if

(a) it has been agreed between the landlord and either

(i) the qualifying tenants in whose favour the order was made, or

(ii) the nominated person,

that the landlord's interest should be acquired subject to the charge, or

(b) the court is satisfied, whether on the application for the order or on an application made by the person entitled to the benefit of the charge, that in the exceptional circumstances of the case it would be fair and reasonable that the landlord's interest should be so acquired, and orders accordingly.

(3) This section and Part II of Schedule 1 shall apply, with any necessary modifications, to mortgages and liens as they apply to charges; but nothing in those provisions shall apply to a rentcharge.

III L&T [197]

33. Acquisition order where landlord cannot be found

(1) Where an acquisition order is made by the court in a case where the landlord cannot be found, or his identity cannot be ascertained, the order shall provide for the landlord's interest in the premises specified in the order to vest in the nominated person on the following terms, namely

(a) such terms as to payment as are specified in subsection (2), and

(b) such other terms as the court thinks fit, being terms which, in the opinion of the court, correspond so far as possible to those on which the interest might be expected to be transferred if it were being transferred by the landlord.

(2) The terms as to payment referred to in subsection (1) (a) are terms requiring the payment into court of

(a) such amount as a surveyor selected by the Senior President of Tribunals may certify to be in his opinion the amount which the landlord's interest might be expected to realise if sold as mentioned in section 31 (2); and

(b) any amounts or estimated amounts remaining due to the landlord from any tenants of his of any premises comprised in the premises in respect of which the order is made, being amounts or estimated amounts determined by the court as being due from those persons under the terms of their leases.

(3) Where any amount or amounts required by virtue of subsection (2) to be paid into court are so paid, the landlord's interest shall, by virtue of this section, vest in the nominated person in accordance with the order.

III L&T [198]

34. Discharge of acquisition order and withdrawal by tenants

(1) If, on an application by a landlord in respect of whose interest an acquisition order has been made, the court is satisfied

(a) that the nominated person has had a reasonable time within which to effect the acquisition of that interest in pursuance of the order but has not done so, or

(b) that the number of qualifying tenants of flats contained in the premises in question who desire to proceed with the acquisition of the landlord's interest is less than the requisite majority of qualifying tenants of the flats contained in those premises, or

(c) that the premises in question have ceased to be premises to which this Part applies,

the court may discharge the order.

(2) Where

(a) a notice is served on the landlord by the qualifying tenants by whom a notice has been served under section 27 or (as the case may be) by whom an application has been made for an acquisition order, or by the person nominated for the purposes of this Part by any such tenants, and

(b) the notice indicates an intention no longer to proceed with the acquisition of the landlord's interest in the premises in question,

the landlord may (except in a case where subsection (4) applies) recover under this subsection any costs reasonably incurred by him in connection with the disposal by him of that interest down to the time when the notice is served; and, if the notice is served after the making of an acquisition order, that order shall cease to have effect.

(3) If (whether before or after the making of an acquisition order) the nominated person becomes aware

(a) that the number of qualifying tenants of flats contained in the premises in question who desire to proceed with the acquisition of the landlord's interest is less than the requisite majority of qualifying tenants of the flats contained in those premises, or

(b) that those premises have ceased to be premises to which this Part applies,

he shall forthwith serve on the landlord a notice indicating an intention no longer to proceed with the acquisition of that interest, and subsection (2) shall apply accordingly.

(4) If, at any time when any proceedings taken under or by virtue of this Part are pending before the court or the Upper Tribunal

- (a) such a notice as is mentioned in subsection (2) or (3) is served on the landlord, or
- (b) the nominated person indicates that he is no longer willing to act in the matter and nobody is nominated for the purposes of this Part in his place, or
- (c) the number of qualifying tenants of flats contained in the premises in question who desire to proceed with the acquisition of the landlord's interest falls below the requisite majority of qualifying tenants of the flats contained in those premises, or
- (d) those premises cease to be premises to which this Part applies,

or if the court discharges an acquisition order under subsection (1), the landlord may recover such costs incurred by him in connection with the disposal by him of his interest in those premises as the court or (as the case may be) the Tribunal may determine.

(5) The costs that may be recovered by the landlord under subsection (2) or (4) include costs incurred by him in connection with any proceedings under this Part (other than proceedings before the appropriate tribunal).

(6) Any liability for costs arising under this section shall be the joint and several liability of the following persons, namely

- (a) where the liability arises before the making of an application for an acquisition order, the tenants by whom a notice was served under section 27, or
- (b) where the liability arises after the making of such an application, the tenants by whom the application was made,

together with (in either case) any person nominated by those tenants for the purposes of this Part.

(7) In relation to any time when a tenant falling within paragraph (a) or (b) of subsection (6) has ceased to have vested in him the interest under his lease, that paragraph shall be construed as applying instead to the person who is for the time being the successor in title to that interest.

(8) Nothing in this section shall be construed as authorising the court to discharge an acquisition order where the landlord's interest has already been acquired in pursuance of the order.

(9) If

- (a) an acquisition order is discharged, or ceases to have effect, by virtue of any provision of this Part, and
- (b) the order has been protected by an entry registered under the Land Charges Act 1972 or the Land Registration Act 2002,

the court may by order direct that that entry shall be cancelled.

III L&T [198.1]

Requisite majority of qualifying tenants See Landlord and Tenant Act 1987 s 26 (qualifying tenants) (see para **III L&T [191]**) and, as regards the requisite majority, Landlord and Tenant Act 1987 s 27(4) (see para **III L&T [192]**).

III L&T [198.2]

Nominated person See Landlord and Tenant Act 1987 s 30(3) (see para **III L&T [195]**).

III L&T [198.3]

Service of notice As to the form and service of notices, see Landlord and Tenant Act 1987 s 54, and notes on that section (see para **III L&T [207]** onwards). See also CPR PD 56 para 10.2 (para **CPR PD 56**), which states that if a notice is to be served in or before a claim under the 1987 Act, it must be served in accordance with s 54, and, in the case of service on a landlord, at the address given under s 48(1). It should also be noted that all documents must be served by the parties: CPR PD 56 para 10.1 (para **CPR PD 56**).

PART IV
VARIATION OF LEASES

APPLICATIONS RELATING TO FLATS

III L&T [199]

35. Application by party to lease for variation of lease

(1) Any party to a long lease of a flat may make an application to the appropriate tribunal for an order varying the lease in such manner as is specified in the application.

(2) The grounds on which any such application may be made are that the lease fails to make satisfactory provision with respect to one or more of the following matters, namely

- (a) the repair or maintenance of
  - (i) the flat in question, or
  - (ii) the building containing the flat, or
  - (iii) any land or building which is let to the tenant under the lease or in respect of which rights are conferred on him under it;
- (b) the insurance of the building containing the flat or of any such land or building as is mentioned in paragraph (a)(iii);
- (c) the repair or maintenance of any installations (whether they are in the same building as the flat or not) which are reasonably necessary to ensure that occupiers of the flat enjoy a reasonable standard of accommodation;
- (d) the provision or maintenance of any services which are reasonably necessary to ensure that occupiers of the flat enjoy a reasonable standard of accommodation (whether they are services connected with any such installations or not, and whether they are services provided for the benefit of those occupiers or services provided for the benefit of the occupiers of a number of flats including that flat);
- (e) the recovery by one party to the lease from another party to it of expenditure incurred or to be incurred by him, or on his behalf, for the benefit of that other party or of a number of persons who include that other party;
- (f) the computation of a service charge payable under the lease;
- (g) such other matters as may be prescribed by regulations made by the Secretary of State.

(3) For the purposes of subsection (2) (c) and (d) the factors for determining, in relation to the occupiers of a flat, what is a reasonable standard of accommodation may include

- (a) factors relating to the safety and security of the flat and its occupiers and of any common parts of the building containing the flat; and
- (b) other factors relating to the condition of any such common parts.

(3A) For the purposes of subsection (2)(e) the factors for determining, in relation to a service charge payable under a lease, whether the lease makes satisfactory provision include whether it makes provision for an amount to be payable (by way of interest or otherwise) in respect of a failure to pay the service charge by the due date.

(4) For the purposes of subsection (2) (f) a lease fails to make satisfactory provision with respect to the computation of a service charge payable under it if

LANDLORD & TENANT AND HOUSING

(c) which, in a case where the lease requires the tenant to effect insurance with a specified insurer, requires the tenant to effect insurance otherwise than with another specified insurer.

(8) A tribunal may, instead of making an order varying a lease in such manner as is specified in the order, make an order directing the parties to the lease to vary it in such manner as is so specified; and accordingly any reference in this Part (however expressed) to an order which effects any variation of a lease or to any variation effected by an order shall include a reference to an order which directs the parties to a lease to effect a variation of it or (as the case may be) a reference to any variation effected in pursuance of such an order.

(9) A tribunal may by order direct that a memorandum of any variation of a lease effected by an order under this section shall be endorsed on such documents as are specified in the order.

(10) Where a tribunal makes an order under this section varying a lease the tribunal may, if it thinks fit, make an order providing for any party to the lease to pay, to any other party to the lease or to any other person, compensation in respect of any loss or disadvantage that the tribunal considers he is likely to suffer as a result of the variation.

III L&T [201]

39. Effect of orders varying leases: applications by third parties

(1) Any variation effected by an order under section 38 shall be binding not only on the parties to the lease for the time being but also on other persons (including any predecessors in title of those parties), whether or not they were parties to the proceedings in which the order was made or were served with a notice by virtue of section 35 (5).

(2) Without prejudice to the generality of subsection (1), any variation effected by any such order shall be binding on any surety who has guaranteed the performance of any obligation varied by the order; and the surety shall accordingly be taken to have guaranteed the performance of that obligation as so varied.

(3) Where any such order has been made and a person was, by virtue of section 35(5), required to be served with a notice relating to the proceedings in which it was made, but he was not so served, he may—

(a) bring an action for damages for breach of statutory duty against the person by whom any such notice was so required to be served in respect of that person's failure to serve it;

(b) apply to the appropriate tribunal for the cancellation or modification of the variation in question.

(4) A tribunal may, on an application under subsection (3)(b) with respect to any variation of a lease—

(a) by order cancel that variation or modify it in such manner as is specified in the order, or

(b) make such an order as is mentioned in section 38(10) in favour of the person making the application,

as it thinks fit.

(5) Where a variation is cancelled or modified under paragraph (a) of subsection (4)—

(a) the cancellation or modification shall take effect as from the date of the making of the order under that paragraph or as from such later date as may be specified in the order, and

(b) the tribunal may by order direct that a memorandum of the cancellation or modification shall be endorsed on such documents as are specified in the order;

and, in a case where a variation is so modified, subsections (1) and (2) above shall, as from the date when the modification takes effect, apply to the variation as modified.

III L&T [201.1]

Damages Damages under Landlord and Tenant Act 1987 s 39(3)(a) may be recovered in the county court without limit: para (l) of art 2(1) of the High Court and County Courts Jurisdiction Order 1991, SI 1991/724 (see para **II HCJ [3]**).

III L&T [201.2]

Directions A direction under Landlord and Tenant Act 1987 s 38(8) (see para **III L&T [200]**) to vary a lease, or under Landlord and Tenant Act 1987 ss 38(9) or 39(5)(b) to endorse a memorandum, may be enforced, where the party concerned refuses to execute the necessary instrument, by the court's appointing someone else to do it for him: *Danchevsky v Danchevsky* [1975] Fam 17, [1974] 3 All ER 934, CA. The county court's powers in this respect derive from the Supreme Court Act 1981 s 39 (see para **II SCA [40]**) and the County Courts Act 1984 s 38 (see para **II CCA [21]**).

APPLICATIONS RELATING TO DWELLINGS OTHER THAN FLATS

III L&T [202]

40. Application for variation of insurance provisions of lease of dwelling other than a flat

(1) Any party to a long lease of a dwelling may make an application to the appropriate tribunal for an order varying the lease, in such manner as is specified in the application, on the grounds that the lease fails to make satisfactory provision with respect to any matter relating to the insurance of the dwelling, including the recovery of the costs of such insurance.

(2) Sections 36 and 38 shall apply to an application under subsection (1) subject to the modifications specified in subsection (3).

(3) Those modifications are as follows

(a) in section 36

(i) in subsection (1), the reference to section 35 shall be read as a reference to subsection (1) above, and

(ii) in subsection (2), any reference to a flat shall be read as a reference to a dwelling; and

(b) in section 38

(i) any reference to an application under section 35 shall be read as a reference to an application under subsection (1) above, and

(ii) any reference to an application under section 36 shall be read as a reference to an application under section 36 as applied by subsection (2) above.

(4) For the purposes of this section, a long lease shall not be regarded as a long lease of a dwelling if

(a) the demised premises consist of three or more dwellings; or

(b) the lease constitutes a tenancy to which Part II of the Landlord and Tenant Act 1954 applies.

(4A) Without prejudice to subsection (4), an application under subsection (1) may not be made by a person who is a tenant under a long lease of a dwelling if, by virtue of that lease and one or more other long leases of dwellings, he is also a tenant from the same landlord of at least two other dwellings.

(4B) For the purposes of subsection (4A), any tenant of a dwelling who is a body corporate shall be treated as a tenant of any other dwelling held from the same landlord which is let under a long lease to an associated company as defined in section 20 (1).

(5) In this section "dwelling" means a dwelling other than a flat.

(6) For the purposes of subsection (1), "appropriate tribunal" means—

(a) if one or more of the dwellings concerned is in England, the First-tier Tribunal or, where determined by or under Tribunal Procedure Rules, the Upper Tribunal; and

(b) if one or more of the dwellings concerned is in Wales, a leasehold valuation tribunal.

III L&T [202.1]

Long lease of a dwelling other than a flat Landlord and Tenant Act 1987 s 59(3) (see para **III L&T [208]**), explains "long lease"; and "dwelling" and "flat" are defined in Landlord and Tenant Act 1987 s 60(1) (see para **III L&T [209]**). Note, however, that Landlord and Tenant Act 1987 s 40(5) restricts the scope of this section by giving "dwelling" a narrower meaning which excludes "flat".

III L&T [202.2]

Choice of insurer Apart from this section the landlord is entitled to arrange insurance in the normal course of business through insurers of his choice although the management company might have obtained lower rates elsewhere: *Berrycroft Management Co Ltd v Sinclair Gardens Investment (Kensington) Ltd* (1996) 29 HLR 444, [1997] 1 EGLR 47, CA.

III L&T [202.3]

Application to the court See notes at para **III L&T [199.3]**.

PART VI
INFORMATION TO BE FURNISHED TO TENANTS

III L&T [203]

47. Landlord's name and address to be contained in demands for rent etc

(1) Where any written demand is given to a tenant of premises to which this Part applies, the demand must contain the following information, namely—

(a) the name and address of the Landlord, and

(b) if that address is not in England and Wales, an address in England and Wales at which notices (including notices in proceedings) may be served on the landlord by the tenant.

(2) Where—

(a) a tenant of any such premises is given such a demand, but

(b) it does not contain any information required to be contained in it by virtue of subsection (1),

then (subject to subsection (3)) any part of the amount demanded which consists of a service charge or an administration charge ("the relevant amount") shall be treated for all purposes as not being due from the tenant to the landlord at any time before that information is furnished by the landlord by notice given to the tenant.

(3) The relevant amount shall not be so treated in relation to any time when, by virtue of an order of any court or tribunal, there is in force an appointment of a receiver or manager whose functions include the receiving of service charges or (as the case may be) administration charges from the tenant.

(4) In this section "demand" means a demand for rent or other sums payable to the landlord under the terms of the tenancy.

III L&T [203.1]

Failure to notify These sections apply to premises which consist of or include a dwelling and are not held under a tenancy to which the Landlord and Tenant Act 1954 Pt II, applies: Landlord and Tenant Act 1987 s 46(1). They therefore apply to an agricultural holding let with a dwelling house: *Lindsey Trading Properties Inc v Dallhold Estates (UK) Pty Ltd* (1993) 70 P & CR 332, *sub nom Dallhold Estates (UK) Pty Ltd v Lindsey Trading Properties Inc* [1994] 1 EGLR 93, CA. "Service charge" has the meaning given by the Landlord and Tenant Act 1985 s 18(1) (see para **III L&T [171]**): Landlord and Tenant Act 1987 s 46(2).

III L&T [203.2]

Retrospection Landlord and Tenant Act 1987 s 48 (see para **III L&T [204]**) applies to tenancies created and rent in arrear before 1 February 1988, the date when the section came into force: *Hussain v Singh* [1993] 2 EGLR 70, [1993] 31 EG 75, CA.

III L&T [203.3]

Landlord's address The notice must be in writing and not merely oral; but a separate notice is not required for the purposes of Landlord and Tenant Act 1987 s 48 (see para **III L&T [204]**) and therefore a statement in the lease of the landlord's address in England and Wales is sufficient, provided it is not qualified, eg as being for the payment of rent only: *Rogan v Woodfield Building Services Ltd* (1994) 27 HLR 78, [1995] 1 EGLR 72, CA. It has been held that where the landlord is a limited company, a letter specifying its registered office is not good enough, since it does not make it definitively clear to the tenant that this is the address at which notices may be served on the landlord: *Milestate v Clarke* [1994] CLY 2740 (county court). But the opposite view was taken in a subsequent county court decision: *Knolldowne Properties v Bromley & Cogger* [1995] CLY 3002, cc. As to the sufficiency of giving the name and address of the landlord's agent see *Marath v MacGillivray* (1996) 28 HLR 484, [1996] NPC 11, CA. See also *Beitov Properties Ltd v Martin* [2012] UKUT 133 (LC), [2012] 2 P & CR D31 where it was held that it is not sufficient to give the name of the landlord plus the address of the managing agents; the requirement is to give the address at which the landlord can be found. It has been held by the Upper Tribunal that where a landlord served a demand for service charges without giving the address, but subsequently served the same demand with the address included, this made the earlier demand good retrospectively: *Johnson v County Bideford Ltd* [2012] UKUT 457 (LC).

III L&T [203.4]

"For all purposes" These words in Landlord and Tenant Act 1987 s 48 (2) (see para **III L&T [204]**) mean, for example, that failure by the landlord to include the required information will disable him from forfeiting the lease on the ground of non-payment of the amount demanded: *Hussain v Singh* [1993] 2 EGLR 70, [1993] 31 EG 75, CA. But Landlord and Tenant Act 1987 s 48 does not destroy the landlord's right to claim rent before service of notice; once notice has been given, the statutory purpose is satisfied and all rent then accruing becomes due: *Lindsey Trading Property Inc v Dallhold Estates (UK) Pty Ltd* (1993) 70 P & CR 332, sub nom *Dallhold Estates (UK) Pty Ltd v Lindsey Trading Properties Inc* [1994] 1 EGLR 93, CA. If the failure to comply is purely formal, semble the court can, when the point is raised, allow a notice to be served followed by an amendment of the claim: *Rogan v Woodfield Building Services Ltd* (1994) 27 HLR 78, [1995] 1 EGLR 72, CA.

III L&T [204]

48. Notification by landlord of address for service of notices

(1) A landlord of premises to which this Part applies shall by notice furnish the tenant with an address in England and Wales at which notices (including notices in proceedings) may be served on him by the tenant.

(2) Where a landlord of any such premises fails to comply with subsection (1), any rent, service charge or administration charge otherwise due from the tenant to the landlord shall (subject to subsection (3)) be treated for all purposes as not being due from the tenant to the landlord at any time before the landlord does comply with that subsection.

(3) Any such rent, service charge or administration charge shall not be so treated in relation to any time when, by virtue of an order of any court or tribunal, there is in force an appointment of a receiver or manager whose functions include the receiving of rent, service charges or (as the case may be) administration charges from the tenant.

III L&T [204.1]

A notice served under the Housing Act 1988 s 21 which informed the tenant of the name and address of the landlord's agent without limitation or qualification was held to be a notice sufficient for the purpose of s 48(1): see *Drew-Morgan v Hamid-Zadeh* (1999) 32 HLR 316, [1999] 2 EGLR 13, CA.

PART VII
GENERAL

III L&T [205]–III L&T [206]

52. Jurisdiction of county courts

(1) The county court shall have jurisdiction to hear and determine any question arising under any provision to which this section applies (other than a question falling within the jurisdiction of the appropriate tribunal by virtue of section 13(1) or 31(1)).

(2) This section applies to

(a) any provision of Parts I and III;

(b) any provision of section 42; and

(c) any provision of sections 46 to 48.

(3) Where any proceedings under any provision to which this section applies are being taken in the county court, the county court shall have jurisdiction to hear and determine any other proceedings joined with those proceedings, notwithstanding that the other proceedings would, apart from this subsection, be outside the court's jurisdiction.

(4) *If a person takes any proceedings under any such provision in the High Court he shall not be entitled to recover any more costs of those proceedings than those to which he would have been entitled if the proceedings had been taken in [the county court]; and in any such case the taxing master shall have the same power of directing on what county court scale costs are to be allowed, and of allowing any item of costs, as the judge would have had if the proceedings had been taken in the county court.*

(5) *Subsection (4) shall not apply where the purpose of taking the proceedings in the High Court was to enable them to be joined with any proceedings already pending before that court (not being proceedings taken under any provision to which this section applies).*

Amendment *Text in italic is repealed by the Courts and Legal Services Act 1990, with effect from a date to be appointed.*

III L&T [205.1]

County court determination of questions Claims brought in the court under the Landlord and Tenant Act 1987 are landlord and tenant claims within the meaning of CPR 56. They must therefore be started in the county court for the district in which the land is situated (see para **CPR 56.2**). Only in exceptional circumstances (where the claimant can certify, and verify with a statement of truth (see CPR PD 22 para 1.1(5) at para **CPR PD 22**), that there are complicated disputes of fact or there are points of law of general importance) may a landlord and tenant claim be started in the High Court. If the claim is brought in the High Court then, with effect from 2 December 2002, CPR PD 56 para 2.6 (see para **CPR PD 56**) makes clear that the claim must be brought in the Chancery Division. Save where modified (as to which see, in particular paras **III L&T [194.3]** and **III L&T [199.3]**), the Pt 8 procedure must be used.

III L&T [205.2]

Section 42 Landlord and Tenant Act 1987 s 42 provides for service charge contributions to be paid into a trust fund and for the investment of the fund.

III L&T [207]

54. Notices

(1) Any notice required or authorised to be served under this Act—

(a) shall be in writing; and

(b) may be sent by post.

(2) Any notice purporting to be a notice served under any provision of Part I or III by the requisite majority of any qualifying tenants (as defined for the purposes of that provision) shall specify the names of all of the persons by whom it is served and the addresses of the flats of which they are qualifying tenants.

(3) The Secretary of State may by regulations prescribe—

(a) the form of any notices required or authorised to be served under or in pursuance of any provision of Parts I to III, and

(b) the particulars which any such notices must contain (whether in addition to, or in substitution for, any particulars required by virtue of the provision in question).

(4) Subsection (3)(b) shall not be construed as authorising the Secretary of State to make regulations under subsection (3) varying any of the periods specified in section 5A(4) or (5), 5B(5) or (6), 5C(4) or (5), 5D(4) or (5) or 5E(3) (which accordingly can only be varied by regulations under section 20(4)).

III L&T [207.1]

Service in court proceedings CPR PD 56 para 10.2 requires that if a notice is to be served in or before a claim under the 1987 Act, it must be served in accordance with s 54, and, in the case of service on a landlord, at the address given under s 48(1). All documents must be served by the parties: CPR PD 56 para 10.1 (para **CPR PD 56**).

III L&T [207.2]

Service by post The provisions of the Interpretation Act 1978 s 7 (references to service by post) apply.

III L&T [207.3]

Specifying the addresses A failure to specify the addresses of individual qualifying tenants does not invalidate the notice, when they are readily and indisputably ascertainable by the landlord: *M25 Group Ltd v Tudor* [2003] EWCA Civ 1760, [2004] 2 All ER 80, [2004] 06 EG 146.

III L&T [208]

59. Meaning of "lease", "long lease" and related expressions

(1) In the Act "lease" and "tenancy" have the same meaning; and both expressions include

(a) a sub-lease or sub-tenancy, and

(b) an agreement for a lease or tenancy (or for a sub-lease or sub-tenancy).

(2) The expressions "landlord" and "tenant", and references to letting, to the grant of a lease or to covenants or the terms of a lease shall be construed accordingly.

(3) In this Act "long lease" means

(a) a lease granted for a term certain exceeding 21 years, whether or not it is (or may become) terminable before the end of that term by notice given by the tenant or by re-entry or forfeiture;

(b) a lease for a term fixed by law under a grant with a covenant or obligation for perpetual renewal, other than a lease by sub-demise from one which is not a long lease; or

(c) a lease granted in pursuance of Part V of the Housing Act 1985 (the right to buy), including a lease granted in pursuance of that Part as it has effect by virtue of section 17 of the Housing Act 1996 (the right to acquire).

III L&T [209]

60. General interpretation

(1) In this Act

"the 1985 Act" means the Landlord and Tenant Act 1985;

... "charitable purposes", in relation to a charity, means charitable purposes whether of that charity or of that charity and other charities;

"common parts", in relation to any building or part of a building, includes the structure and exterior of that building or part and any common facilities within it;

"the court" means the High Court or the county court;

"dwelling" means a building or part of a building occupied or intended to be occupied as a separate dwelling, together with any yard, garden, outhouses and appurtenances belonging to it or usually enjoyed with it;

"exempt landlord" has the meaning given by section 58 (1);

"flat" means a separate set of premises, whether or not on the same floor, which

(a) forms part of a building, and

(b) is divided horizontally from some other part of that building, and

(c) is constructed or adapted for use for the purposes of a dwelling;

"functional land", in relation to a charity, means land occupied by the charity, or by trustees for it, and wholly or mainly used for charitable purposes;

"landlord" (except for the purposes of Part I) means the immediate landlord or, in relation to a statutory tenant, the person who, apart from the statutory tenancy, would be entitled to possession of the premises subject to the tenancy;

"lease" and related expressions shall be construed in accordance with section 59 (1) and (2);

"long lease" has the meaning given by section 59 (3);

"mortgage" includes any charge or lien, and references to a mortgagee shall be construed accordingly;

"notices in proceedings" means notices or other documents served in, or in connection with, any legal proceedings;

"resident landlord" shall be construed in accordance with section 58 (2);

"statutory tenancy" and "statutory tenant" means a statutory tenancy or statutory tenant within the meaning of the Rent Act 1977 or the Rent (Agriculture) Act 1976;

"tenancy" includes a statutory tenancy.

(1A) In this Act a reference to the Welsh Ministers in their new towns residuary capacity means the Welsh Ministers so far as exercising functions in relation to anything transferred (or to be transferred) to them as mentioned in section 36(1)(a)(i) to (iii) of the New Towns Act 1981.

(2) [. . .]

LANDLORD AND TENANT ACT 1988

(c 26)

GENERAL NOTE ON LANDLORD AND TENANT ACT 1988

III L&T [209A]

The Landlord and Tenant Act 1988 imposes statutory duties in connection with covenants to which the Landlord and Tenant Act 1927, s 19(1) applies (see **III L & T [7]**) . A landlord must give his reasons for refusing consent in writing and is confined to his written reasons: *Norwich Union Life Assurance v Shopmoor Ltd* [1998] 3 All ER 32, [1999] 1 WLR 531; *Footwear Corpn Ltd v Amplight Properties Ltd* [1998] 3 All ER 52, [1999] 1 WLR 551. The landlord should give reasons for refusing consent within a reasonable time of the application for it and should not be permitted to rely on other reasons at a later stage: *London & Argyll Developments Ltd v Mount Cook Land Ltd* [2002] All ER (D) 06 (Oct).

III L&T [209B]

1. Qualified duty to consent to assigning, underletting etc. of premises

(1) This section applies in any case where—

(a) a tenancy includes a covenant on the part of the tenant not to enter into one or more of the following transactions, that is—

(i) assigning,

(ii) underletting,

(iii) charging, or

(iv) parting with the possession of,

the premises comprised in the tenancy or any part of the premises without the consent of the landlord or some other person, but

(b) the covenant is subject to the qualification that the consent is not to be unreasonably withheld (whether or not it is also subject to any other qualification).

(2) In this section and section 2 of this Act—

(a) references to a proposed transaction are to any assignment, underletting, charging or parting with possession to which the covenant relates, and

(b) references to the person who may consent to such a transaction are to the person who under the covenant may consent to the tenant entering into the proposed transaction.

(3) Where there is served on the person who may consent to a proposed transaction a written application by the tenant for consent to the transaction, he owes a duty to the tenant within a reasonable time—

(a) to give consent, except in a case where it is reasonable not to give consent,

(b) to serve on the tenant written notice of his decision whether or not to give consent specifying in addition—

(i) if the consent is given subject to conditions, the conditions,

(ii) if the consent is withheld, the reasons for withholding it.

(4) Giving consent subject to any condition that is not a reasonable condition does not satisfy the duty under subsection (3)(a) above.

(5) For the purposes of this Act it is reasonable for a person not to give consent to a proposed transaction only in a case where, if he withheld consent and the tenant completed the transaction, the tenant would be in breach of a covenant.

(6) It is for the person who owed any duty under subsection (3) above—

(a) if he gave consent and the question arises whether he gave it within a reasonable time, to show that he did,

(b) if he gave consent subject to any condition and the question arises whether the condition was a reasonable condition, to show that it was,

(c) if he did not give consent and the question arises whether it was reasonable for him not to do so, to show that it was reasonable, and, if the question arises whether he served notice under that subsection within a reasonable time, to show that he did.

III L&T [209B.1]

Landlord's statutory duty Section 1 imposes on a landlord, who is asked to consent to a proposed assignment, underletting etc, an extensive statutory duty, the effect of which, in short, is that the landlord must either give consent or be prepared to justify refusal as being reasonable.

The section reverses the burden of proof at common law. It is for the landlord (a) if he gave consent and the question arises whether he gave it within a reasonable time, to show that he did; (b) if he gave consent subject to any condition and the question arises whether the condition was a reasonable condition, to show that it was; (c) if he did not give consent and the question arises whether it was reasonable for him not to do so, to show that it was not unreasonable; and, (d) if the question arises whether he served notice of his decision within a reasonable time, to show that he did. The landlord must give written notice of his decision.

The landlord is also confined to reasons given in his written notice: see *Footwear Corporation v Amplight Properties* [1999] 1 WLR 551 and *Go West v Spigarolo* [2003] 2 WLR 986, 1002, CA.

III L&T [209B.2]

More than one reason A landlord may seek to rely upon more than one reason for withholding consent to a proposed assignment etc. If the landlord has a good and a bad reason for withholding consent, consent may nevertheless have been reasonably withheld if the good reason is a sufficient reason and is not otherwise vitiated by the bad reason: *BRS v Templeheights* [1998] 2 EGLR 182. The approach in *BRS v Templeheights* was approved by the Court of Appeal in *No 1 West India Quay v (Residential) Ltd v East Tower Apartments Ltd* [2018] HLR 20: 'If the decision would have been the same without reliance on the bad reason, then the decision (looked at overall) is good. In that situation the bad reason will not have vitiated or infected the good one'. The question is 'whether the decision to refuse consent was reasonable; not whether all the reasons for the decision were reasonable'.

HOUSING ACT 1988

(c 50)

GENERAL NOTES ON HOUSING ACT 1988

III L&T [210]

Jurisdiction The Housing Act 1988 Pt I introduced a new species of "assured" tenancy to take the place of regulated tenancies, assured shorthold tenancies and assured agricultural occupancies. The Housing Act 1988 s 40 (see para **III L&T [237]**) has conferred substantially the same jurisdiction on the county courts in respect of the new arrangements as in the case of the old.

The High Court has jurisdiction too. However, claims for possession of land can only be started in the High Court in exceptional circumstances. All possession claims must be started in the county court for the district in which the land is situated unless the claimant can certify that there are complicated disputes of fact or there are points of law of general importance. The value of the property and the amount of any financial claim may be relevant circumstances, but these factors alone will not normally justify starting the claim in the High Court: see para **CPR 55.3** and CPR PD 55 paras 1.1 to 1.4 (para **CPR PD 55**).

Changes made by the Localism Act 2011 The Localism Act 2011 amended ss 216, 223, 228A, 228B, 228C and 229 with effect from 1 April 2012: see the No 6 Order 2012, SI 2012/1463.

III L&T [211]

Procedure The procedure set out in Section I of CPR Pt 55 must be used. Possession claims under the Housing Act 1988 must therefore be started by means of claim form N5. Particulars of claim must be filed and served with the claim form (see para **CPR 55.4**). The contents of the particulars of claim must comply with the requirements of CPR Pt 16 (see para **CPR 16**) and CPR PD 55 para 2.1 (see para **CPR PD 55**). Where the possession claim relates to residential property and includes a claim for non-payment of rent the particulars of claim must also comply with CPR PD 55 para 2.3; the particulars of claim in Form N119 should therefore be used on such claims. Although an acknowledgement of service is not required, a defence should be filed. The defence to a general possession claim should be in Form N11 and the defence to a claim for possession for residential premises which includes a claim for non-payment of rent should be in Form N11R. If the defendant does not file a defence within 14 days of service of the particulars of claim, he may take part in the hearing but the court will take into account his failure when deciding costs: para **CPR 55.7**. A table of the appropriate forms in possession claims can be found at **BCCP O[12]**; the forms can also be found in the Forms supplement, the FORMS section of your CD-ROM and at **BCCP O[80]** onwards.

Section II of CPR Pt 55 (see para **CPR 55**) and Section II of CPR PD 55 (see para **CPR PD 55**) set out detailed procedural requirements for accelerated possession claims of property let on an assured shorthold tenancy. Such claims can now only be brought under s 21 of the Act and where the conditions at para **CPR 55.12** are satisfied. A claim form N5B and a Form N11B defence, which must be filed within 14 days of service of the claim form, are prescribed. Specimens can be found at **BCCP O[82]** and **BCCP O[83]**. CPR 55.16–55.18 (paras **CPR 55 16–CPR 55.18**) and CPR PD 55 para 18 (para **CPR PD 55**) set out detailed provisions for the consideration of the papers by the judge and the making of an order for possession (with or without a hearing as appropriate) and postponement of possession on the ground of exceptional hardship (with or without a hearing as appropriate). For details of the s 21 accelerated procedure, see paras **III L&T [229.3]–III L&T [229.3A]**).

III L&T [211.A]

Possession claims online **CPR 55.10A** provides that a practice direction may make provision for a claimant to start certain types of possession claim in certain courts by requesting the issue of a claim form electronically. The practice direction is **CPR PD 55B**. It provides for a 'Possession Claims Online' scheme to operate in specified county courts. A claim may be started online if it is brought under Section I of **CPR 55**, it includes a possession claim for residential property by a landlord against a tenant, solely on the ground of arrears of rent (but not a claim for forfeiture of a lease) and does not include a claim for any other remedy except for payment of arrears of rent. interest and costs. Details of the procedure are found in paragraphs 6 to 14 of the **CPR PD 55B**. The facility is operated on http://www.possessionclaim.gov.uk.

III L&T [212]

Precedents For an example of particulars of claim in a claim for possession under the Housing Act 1988, see **BCCP O[202]**. Where non-payment of rent is relied on the claimant should use Form N5 and attach to it particulars of claim in Form N119: see the precedent at **BCCP O[204]**. Specimens of a claim form for accelerated possession and a defence to such a claim can be found at **BCCP O[82]** and **BCCP O[83]**.

PART I
RENTED ACCOMMODATION

CHAPTER I ASSURED TENANCIES

Meaning of assured tenancy etc.

III L&T [213]

1. Assured tenancies

(1) A tenancy under which a dwelling-house is let as a separate dwelling is for the purposes of this Act an assured tenancy if and so long as

(a) the tenant or, as the case may be, each of the joint tenants is an individual; and

(b) the tenant or, as the case may be, at least one of the joint tenants occupies the dwelling-house as his only or principal home; and

(c) the tenancy is not one which, by virtue of subsection (2) or subsection (6) below, cannot be an assured tenancy.

(1A) Subsection (1) has effect subject to section 15A (loss of assured tenancy status).

(2) Subject to subsection (3) below, if and so long as a tenancy falls within any paragraph in Part I of Schedule 1 to this Act, it cannot be an assured tenancy; and in that Schedule

(a) "tenancy" means a tenancy under which a dwelling-house is let as a separate dwelling;

(b) Part II has effect for determining the rateable value of a dwelling-house for the purposes of Part I; and

(c) Part III has effect for supplementing paragraph 10 in Part I.

(2A) The Secretary of State may by order replace any amount referred to in paragraphs 2 and 3A of Schedule 1 to this Act by such amount as is specified in the order; and such an order shall be made by statutory instrument which shall be subject to annulment in pursuance of a resolution of either House of Parliament.

(3) Except as provided in Chapter V below, at the commencement of this Act, a tenancy

(a) under which a dwelling-house was then let as a separate dwelling, and

(b) which immediately before that commencement was an assured tenancy for the purposes of sections 56 to 58 of the Housing Act 1980 (tenancies granted by approved bodies),

shall become an assured tenancy for the purposes of this Act.

(4) In relation to an assured tenancy falling within subsection (3) above

(a) Part I of Schedule 1 to this Act shall have effect, subject to subsection (5) below, as if it consisted only of paragraphs 11 and 12; and

(b) sections 56 to 58 of the Housing Act 1980 (and Schedule 5 to that Act) shall not apply after the commencement of this Act.

(5) In any case where

(a) immediately before the commencement of this Act the landlord under a tenancy is a fully mutual housing association, and

(b) at the commencement of this Act the tenancy becomes an assured tenancy by virtue of subsection (3) above,

then, so long as that association remains the landlord under that tenancy (and under any statutory periodic tenancy which arises on the coming to an end of that tenancy), paragraph 12 of Schedule 1 to this Act shall have effect in relation to that tenancy with the omission of sub-paragraph (1) (h).

(6), (7) [. . .]

III L&T [213.1]

Occupies Where a tenant sublets and ceases to live in the premises the onus is on him or her to show objective evidence of continuing occupation. Otherwise the court will treat the tenant as outside the scope of the Housing Act 1988 s 1(1) (see para **III L&T [213]**) and the security provided by the Act: *Ujima Housing Association v Ansah* (1997) 30 HLR 831, CA. See also *Fanning v Waltham Forest Housing Association* [2001] L & TR 41, QBD. Special provision is made by the Housing Act 1988 ss 3 and 4 for shared accommodation and lawful subletting.

III L&T [213.2]

Only or principal home See the Housing Act 1985 s 81, for notes on this expression (see para **III L&T [105]** onwards).

III L&T [213.3]

Dwelling-house let as a separate dwelling By the Housing Act 1988 s 45(1) (see para **III L&T [238]**) "dwelling-house" may be a house or part of a house. Cases on the interpretation of this word and of the words "let as a separate dwelling" which are noted under the Rent Act 1977 s 1 (see **III L&T [68]**), may be relevant to the interpretation of the same words in this Act. In *Chelsea Yacht & Boat Co Ltd v Pope* [2000] 1 WLR 1941, CA it was held, applying the considerations in *Elitestone Ltd v Morris* [1997] 2 All ER 513, [1997] 1 WLR 687, HL (see para **III L&T [68.5]**) that a moveable houseboat secured by an anchor and ropes was a chattel and had not become part of the land and was therefore not capable of being the subject of an assured tenancy. Similarly, it has been held that a houseboat resting on wooden platforms, supported by piles driven into a plot of land (the bed of a harbour), may not be treated as part of the plot. Such a construction is not affixed to the land and remains a chattel which, as designed, is moveable and may not be classed as a dwelling-house. The occupier is a licensee not a tenant: *Tristmire Ltd v Mew* [2011] EWCA Civ 912, [2011] All ER (D) 278 (Jul). In *Uratemp Ventures Ltd v Collins* [2001] UKHL 43, [2002] 1 AC 301, [2002] 1 All ER 46, it was held that a single hotel room was capable of constituting a "separate dwelling" and if the occupant had exclusive possession he occupied by virtue of an assured tenancy not a licence; the presence or absence of cooking facilities was irrelevant to the issue of exclusive occupation.

III L&T [213.3A]

More than a bare licence Where the tenants of a plot of land in a naturist resort turned a chalet on the plot into a dwelling-house by extensive building work, it was held that the chalet was attached to the land and that their tenancy of the plot was an assured tenancy which could not be terminated by a notice to quit; there was no basis for attributing to the parties the intention to create a scheme involving a gratuitous licence to occupy the chalet: *Spielplatz Ltd v Pearson* [2015] EWCA Civ 804, [2015] HLR 791, [2015] All ER (D) 40 (Aug). It was not material that both landlord and tenant believed that the chalet belonged to the tenants.

III L&T [213.4]

Almshouse It was held in *Gray v Taylor* [1998] 4 All ER 17, [1998] 1 WLR 1093, CA, that the occupation of an almshouse by the beneficiary of a charitable trust is a licence not a tenancy.

III L&T [213.5]

Tenant sharing accommodation with persons other than landlord Section 3 protects tenancies where accommodation is shared with persons other than the landlord. But if the landlord reserves the right to re-enter and share, so taking the tenancy outside the scope of s 3, the position should be made clear to the tenant: *Miller v Eyo* (1998) 31 HLR 306, [1998] NPC 95, CA.

III L&T [213.6]

Schedule 1 exclusions Housing Act 1988 Sch 1, para 1 (see para **III L&T [239]**) excludes any tenancy entered into, or pursuant to a contract made, before commencement on 15 January 1989, except in the case of old-style assured tenancies under the Housing Act 1980, ss 56–58. Provision is made in the Housing Act 1988 s 1(3), (4) (see para **III L&T [213]**) for converting these into new-style assured tenancies; further provision is made by the Housing Act 1988, s 37. In other respects the exclusions in the Housing Act 1988 Sch 1 follow the pattern of exclusions from Rent Act protection (business tenancies, holiday lets, resident landlords etc).

Also excluded (by paragraph 2(1)(b) of Sch 1) is a tenancy under which the rent payable for the time being is payable at a rate exceeding £25,000 a year. With effect from 10 October 2010, the ceiling of £25,000 has been raised to £100,000 by the Assured Tenancies (Amendment) England Order 2010, SI 2010/908.

III L&T [213.7]

Agreement following possession order An arrangement entered into after a possession order may create a new tenancy. Thus, in *Stirling v Leadenhall Residents 2 Ltd* [2001] EWCA Civ 1011, [2001] 3 All ER 645, it was common ground that service of notice of increase in rent upon a person remaining in occupation following a possession order, paying rent arrears and mesne profits, created a new tenancy. See also the cases noted at para **III L&T [103.5]** in relation to secure tenancies.

III L&T [214]

5. Security of tenure

(1) An assured tenancy cannot be brought to an end by the landlord except by—

(a) obtaining—

(i) an order of the court for possession of the dwelling-house under section 7 or 21, and

(ii) the execution of the order,

(b) obtaining an order of the court under section 6A (demotion order),

(c) in the case of a fixed term tenancy which contains power for the landlord to determine the tenancy in certain circumstances, by the exercise of that power, or

(d) in the case of an assured tenancy—

(i) which is a residential tenancy agreement within the meaning of Chapter 1 of Part 3 of the Immigration Act 2014, and

(ii) in relation to which the condition in section 33D(2) of that Act is met,

giving a notice in accordance with that section, [or

(e) in the case of an assured shorthold tenancy, serving a notice in accordance with section 57 of the Housing and Planning Act 2016.]

and, accordingly, the service by the landlord of a notice to quit is of no effect in relation to a periodic assured tenancy.

(1A) Where an order of the court for possession of the dwelling-house is obtained, the tenancy ends when the order is executed.

(2) If an assured tenancy which is a fixed term tenancy comes to an end otherwise than by virtue of

(a) an order of the court of the kind mentioned in subsection (1)(a) or (b) or any other order of the court, or

(b) a surrender or other action on the part of the tenant, or

(c) the giving of a notice under section 33D of the Immigration Act 2014,

then, subject to section 7 and Chapter II below, the tenant shall be entitled to remain in possession of the dwelling-house let under that tenancy and, subject to subsection (4) below, his right to possession shall depend upon a periodic tenancy arising by virtue of this section.

(3) The periodic tenancy referred to in subsection (2) above is one

(a) taking effect in possession immediately on the coming to an end of the fixed term tenancy;

(b) deemed to have been granted by the person who was the landlord under the fixed term tenancy immediately before it came to an end to the person who was then the tenant under that tenancy;

(c) under which the premises which are let are the same dwelling-house as was let under the fixed term tenancy;

(d) under which the periods of the tenancy are the same as those for which rent was last payable under the fixed term tenancy; and

(e) under which, subject to the following provisions of this Part of this Act, the other terms are the same as those of the fixed term tenancy immediately before it came to an end, except that any term which makes provision for determination by the landlord or the tenant shall not have effect while the tenancy remains an assured tenancy.

(4) The periodic tenancy referred to in subsection (2) above shall not arise if, on the coming to an end of the fixed term tenancy, the tenant is entitled, by virtue of the grant of another tenancy, to possession of the same or substantially the same dwelling-house as was let to him under the fixed term tenancy.

(5) If, on or before the date on which a tenancy is entered into or is deemed to have been granted as mentioned in subsection (3) (b) above, the person who is to be the tenant under that tenancy

(a) enters into an obligation to do any act which (apart from this subsection) will cause the tenancy to come to an end at a time when it is an assured tenancy, or

(b) executes, signs or gives any surrender, notice to quit or other document which (apart from this subsection) has the effect of bringing the tenancy to an end at a time when it is an assured tenancy, the obligation referred to in paragraph (a) above shall not be enforceable or, as the case may be, the surrender, notice to quit or other document referred to in paragraph (b) above shall be of no effect.

(5A) Nothing in subsection (5) affects any right of pre-emption

(a) which is exercisable by the landlord under a tenancy in circumstances where the tenant indicates his intention to dispose of the whole of his interest under the tenancy, and

(b) in pursuance of which the landlord would be required to pay, in respect of the acquisition of that interest, an amount representing its market value.

"Dispose" means dispose by assignment or surrender, and "acquisition" has a corresponding meaning.

(6) If, by virtue of any provision of this Part of this Act, Part I of Schedule 1 to this Act has effect in relation to a fixed term tenancy as if it consisted only of paragraphs 11 and 12, that Part shall have the like effect in relation to any periodic tenancy which arises by virtue of this section on the coming to an end of the fixed term tenancy.

(7) Any reference in this Part of this Act to a statutory periodic tenancy is a reference to a periodic tenancy arising by virtue of this section.

Amendment *This section is shown as amended by s 40 of the Immigration Act 2016 with effect from 1 December 2016 (SI 2016/1037).*

III L&T [214.1]

Fixed term tenancy This is defined, by the Housing Act 1988 s 45(1) (see para **III L&T [238]**), as any tenancy other than a periodic tenancy.

III L&T [214.2]

Order of the court See the notes to the Housing Act 1988 s 40, at paras **III L&T [237.1]–III L&T [237.3]**.

III L&T [214.2A]

Periods of the periodic tenancy On the expiry of a fixed term assured shorthold tenancy granted initially for a period of 2 years (and, upon renewal, for a term of one year less a day) at a rent expressed as a yearly figure payable quarterly in advance, the statutory periodic tenancy arising under s 5 is a quarterly one, not a yearly one: *Church Commissioners for England v Meya* [2006] EWCA Civ 821, (2006) 34 EG 90, Times 4 July; regard must be had to the word "last" in s 5(3)(d) and the court should then ascertain the period covered by the last payment.

III L&T [214.2B]

Abandoned premises Sections 57 to 62 of the Housing and Planning Act 2016 (at paras **III L&T [351]–III L&T [357]**) provide a procedure by which a landlord may recover possession of a property where it has been abandoned, without the need for a court order.

III L&T [214.3]

Absentee tenants A tenant may lose security by the unequivocal giving up of possession: *Love and Lugg v Herrity* (1990) 23 HLR 217, CA. Also a tenant who sublets and moves out of occupation loses the statutory protection which covers only tenants who meet the requirements of the Housing Act 1988 s 1(1) (see para **III L&T [213]**): *Ujima Housing Association v Ansah* (1997) 30 HLR 831, CA, followed in *Fanning v Waltham Forest Community Based Housing Association* [2001] L & TR 41.

III L&T [214.4]

Effect of insolvency See the provisions of the Insolvency Act 1986 s 283(3A) regarding the effect on the tenancy of insolvency. A commentary is provided under the Rent Act 1977 s 2 in connection with protected tenancies at para **III L&T [69.4]**.

III L&T [214.5]

Clause providing for excessive rent increase as a way of undermining security of tenure Where a tenancy agreement provides for an excessive rent increase as a means of coercing the tenant into terminating the tenancy it may be held to be invalid because of inconsistency with the security of tenure which the statute confers: *Bankway Properties Ltd v Dunsford* [2001] EWCA Civ 528, [2001] 1 WLR 1369.

III L&T [214.6]

Human rights A former joint tenant who remains in occupation after termination of the tenancy by the other has a Convention right under Article 8 to respect for his home. However, Art 8 cannot be relied on to defeat proprietary or contractual rights to possession. Accordingly, a public authority landlord was entitled to claim possession; but an unfair exercise of the right may be capable of challenge by judicial review; see the majority decision in *Harrow London Borough Council v Qazi* [2003] UKHL 43, [2004] 1 AC 983, [2003] 4 All ER 461. Note, however, the decision in *Lambeth London Borough Council v Kay* [2006] UKHL 10, [2006] 2 AC 465, [2006] 2 WLR 570, [2006] 4 All ER 128 that, in so far as *Harrow London Borough Council v Qazi* decided that the enforcement of a right to possession in accordance with the domestic law of property could never be incompatible with the Art 8 of the Convention, that had to be modified in the light of *Connors v United Kingdom* (66746/01) [2005] 40 EHRR 9; moreover, that it was open to an occupier to raise an Art 8 defence to possession proceedings in the county court rather than by way of judicial review (a point subsequently emphasised in *Manchester City Council v Pinnock* [2010] UKSC 45, [2010] 3 WLR 1441, [2010] 44 LS Gaz R 16 (see para **III L&T [103.6]**)). Article 8 may be engaged where trespassers have set up their home on private land and the court, as a public body, must apply proportionality when dealing with a claim for possession. But the exercise of discretion would seem to be subject to the provisions of s 89 of the Housing Act 1980: *Malik v Fassenfelt (since dec'd)* [2013] EWCA Civ 798, [2013] All ER (D) 44 (Jul). The Court of Appeal has also held that Article 8 considerations arise only in the case of public authority landlords: *McDonald (by her litigation friend) v McDonald (acting by the joint receivers)* [2014] EWCA Civ 1049, [2014] 2 P & CR 377, [2014] HLR 643; see also *McDonald v McDonald* [2016] UKSC 28, where the Supreme Court (upholding the decision of the Court of Appeal) held that, although there were some ECtHR authorities which supported the notion that Art 8 was engaged as against a private landlord, there was no support for the proposition that the judge could have been required to consider the proportionality of the order which he would have made under the 1980 and 1988 Housing Acts.

LANDLORD & TENANT AND HOUSING

III L&T [215]

6. Fixing of terms of statutory periodic tenancy

(1) In this section, in relation to a statutory periodic tenancy,

(a) "the former tenancy" means the fixed term tenancy on the coming to an end of which the statutory periodic tenancy arises; and

(b) "the implied terms" means the terms of the tenancy which have effect by virtue of section 5 (3) (e) above, other than terms as to the amount of the rent;

but nothing in the following provisions of this section applies to a statutory periodic tenancy at a time when, by virtue of paragraph 11 or paragraph 12 in Part I of Schedule 1 to this Act, it cannot be an assured tenancy.

(2) Not later than the first anniversary of the day on which the former tenancy came to an end, the landlord may serve on the tenant, or the tenant may serve on the landlord, a notice in the prescribed form proposing terms of the statutory periodic tenancy different from the implied terms and, if the landlord or the tenant considers it appropriate, proposing an adjustment of the amount of the rent to take account of the proposed terms.

(3) Where a notice has been served under subsection (2) above,

(a) within the period of three months beginning on the date on which the notice was served on him, the landlord or the tenant, as the case may be, may, by an application in the prescribed form, refer the notice to the appropriate tribunal under subsection (4) below; and

(b) if the notice is not so referred, then, with effect from such date, not falling within the period referred to in paragraph (a) above, as may be specified in the notice, the terms proposed in the notice shall become terms of the tenancy in substitution for any of the implied terms dealing with the same subject matter and the amount of the rent shall be varied in accordance with any adjustment so proposed.

(4) Where a notice under subsection (2) above is referred to the appropriate tribunal, the appropriate tribunal shall consider the terms proposed in the notice and shall determine whether those terms, or some other terms (dealing with the same subject matter as the proposed terms), are such as, in the appropriate tribunal's opinion, might reasonably be expected to be found in an assured periodic tenancy of the dwelling-house concerned, being a tenancy

(a) which begins on the coming to an end of the former tenancy; and

(b) which is granted by a willing landlord on terms which, except in so far as they relate to the subject matter of the proposed terms, are those of the statutory periodic tenancy at the time of the appropriate tribunal's consideration.

(5) Whether or not a notice under subsection (2) above proposes an adjustment of the amount of the rent under the statutory periodic tenancy, where the appropriate tribunal determine any terms under subsection (4) above, they shall, if they consider it appropriate, specify such an adjustment to take account of the terms so determined.

(6) In making a determination under subsection (4) above, or specifying an adjustment of an amount of rent under subsection (5) above, there shall be disregarded any effect on the terms or the amount of the rent attributable to the granting of a tenancy to a sitting tenant.

(7) Where a notice under subsection (2) above is referred to the appropriate tribunal, then, unless the landlord and the tenant otherwise agree, with effect from such date as the committee may direct

(a) the terms determined by the appropriate tribunal shall become terms of the statutory periodic tenancy in substitution for any of the implied terms dealing with the same subject matter; and

(b) the amount of the rent under the statutory periodic tenancy shall be altered to accord with any adjustment specified by the appropriate tribunal;

but for the purposes of paragraph (b) above the appropriate tribunal shall not direct a date earlier than the date specified, in accordance with subsection (3) (b) above, in the notice referred to them.

(8) Nothing in this section requires the appropriate tribunal to continue with a determination under subsection (4) above if the landlord and tenant give notice in writing that they no longer require such a determination or if the tenancy has come to an end.

III L&T [215.1]

Notice in the prescribed form See the Assured Tenancies and Agricultural Occupancies (Forms) (England) Regulations 2015 (SI 2015/620) as amended by SI 2015/1646, SI 2016/443 and SI 2016/1118.

III L&T [215.2]

Rent assessment committee The powers and procedures of rent assessment committees are as provided by the Rent Act 1977, as amended by this Act, and by regulations made under s 74 of that Act, as amended.

III L&T [215A]

6A. Demotion because of anti-social behaviour

(1) This section applies to an assured tenancy if

(a) the landlord is a non-profit registered provider of social housing,

(b) the landlord is a profit-making registered provider of social housing and the dwelling house let on the tenancy is social housing within the meaning of Part 2 of the Housing and Regeneration Act 2008, or

(c) the landlord is a registered social landlord.

(2) The landlord may apply to the county court for a demotion order.

(3) A demotion order has the following effect—

(a) the assured tenancy is terminated with effect from the date specified in the order;

(b) if the tenant remains in occupation of the dwelling-house after that date a demoted tenancy is created with effect from that date;

(c) it is a term of the demoted tenancy that any arrears of rent payable at the termination of the assured tenancy become payable under the demoted tenancy;

(d) it is also a term of the demoted tenancy that any rent paid in advance or overpaid at the termination of the assured tenancy is credited to the tenant's liability to pay rent under the demoted tenancy.

(4) The court must not make a demotion order unless it is satisfied—

(a) that the tenant or a person residing in or visiting the dwelling-house has engaged or has threatened to engage in—

(i) conduct that is capable of causing nuisance or annoyance to some person (who need not be a particular identified person) and that directly or indirectly relates to or affects the landlord's housing management functions, or

(ii) conduct that consists of or involves using housing accommodation owned or managed by the landlord for an unlawful purpose, and

(b) that it is reasonable to make the order.

(5) The court must not entertain proceedings for a demotion order unless—

(a) the landlord has served on the tenant a notice under subsection (6), or

(b) the court thinks it is just and equitable to dispense with the requirement of the notice.

(6) The notice must—

(a) give particulars of the conduct in respect of which the order is sought;

(b) state that the proceedings will not begin before the date specified in the notice;

(c) state that the proceedings will not begin after the end of the period of twelve months beginning with the date of service of the notice.

(7) The date specified for the purposes of subsection (6)(b) must not be before the end of the period of two weeks beginning with the date of service of the notice.

(8) Each of the following has effect in respect of a demoted tenancy at the time it is created by virtue of an order under this section as it has effect in relation to the assured tenancy at the time it is terminated by virtue of the order—

(a) the parties to the tenancy;

(b) the period of the tenancy;

(c) the amount of the rent;

(d) the dates on which the rent is payable.

(9) Subsection (8)(b) does not apply if the assured tenancy was for a fixed term and in such a case the demoted tenancy is a weekly periodic tenancy.

(10) If the landlord of the demoted tenancy serves on the tenant a statement of any other express terms of the assured tenancy which are to apply to the demoted tenancy such terms are also terms of the demoted tenancy.

[(10A) In subsection (4)(a) "housing-related anti-social conduct" has the same meaning as in section 153A of the Housing Act 1996.]

(10A) In subsection (4)(a)(ii) "housing accommodation" includes—

(a) flats, lodging-houses and hostels;

(b) any yard, garden, outhouses and appurtenances belonging to the accommodation or usually enjoyed with it;

(c) any common areas used in connection with the accommodation.

(11) For the purposes of this section a demoted tenancy is a tenancy to which section 20B of the Housing Act 1988 applies.

Amendment *First sub-section (10A) inserted by the Police and Justice Act 2006, with effect from a date to be appointed.*

III L&T [215A.1]

Section 6A deals with the demotion of assured tenants of registered social landlords. A demotion order will end the assured tenancy on a specified date. If the tenant remains in occupation, a new demoted assured shorthold tenancy will begin on the same date. The court may only make the order if the tenant, another resident of or visitor to the tenant's home has behaved in a way which is capable of causing nuisance or annoyance or if such a person has used the premises for illegal purposes. The court must also be satisfied that it is reasonable to make the order.

In England the notice of proceedings under section 83 of the Housing Act is now prescribed by SI 2004/1627 and the review procedure is prescribed by SI 2004/1679. In Wales the form of notice is prescribed by SI 2005/1226 and the review procedure is prescribed by SI 2005/1228. The notice of proceedings required by s 6A of the Housing Act 1988 is not prescribed.

CPR 65.11 to 65.20 (see para **CPR 65**) and CPR PD 65 paras 5.1 to 9.3 (see para **CPR PD 65**) apply. Claim form N6 and particulars of claim N122 must be used. For the prescribed contents of the particulars of claim, see CPR PD 65 para 7.1. The defence must be in form N11D. Where a demotion order is claimed in the alternative to a possession order, the claimant must use the Part 55 procedure (see CPR 65.12); Forms N5 and N119 have been updated to incorporate demotion claims.

III L&T [215A.2]

Demotion orders and hearsay evidence A demotion order has been held to be a reasonable way of balancing the parents' rights to a secure home with the public interest in preventing anti-social behaviour by their children: *Washington Housing Company Ltd v Morson* [2005] EWHC 3407 (Ch), 25 October 2005, Patten J. It was held in the same case that, although much of the evidence of anti-social behaviour was hearsay, the trial judge, when considering the factors in s 4(2) of the Civil Evidence Act 1995, at **CPR 33[2]**, was entitled to weigh up the case as a whole, including the admitted background and to accept the veracity of the hearsay.

III L&T [216]

7. Orders for possession

(1) The court shall not make an order for possession of a dwelling-house let on an assured tenancy except on one or more of the grounds set out in Schedule 2 to this Act; but nothing in this Part of this Act relates to proceedings for possession of such a dwelling-house which are brought by a mortgagee, within the meaning of the Law of Property Act 1925, who has lent money on the security of the assured tenancy.

(2) The following provisions of this section have effect, subject to section 8 below, in relation to proceedings for the recovery of possession of a dwelling-house let on an assured tenancy.

(3) If the court is satisfied that any of the grounds in Part I of Schedule 2 to this Act is established then, subject to subsections (5A) and (6) and section 10A below (and to any available defence based on the tenant's Convention rights, within the meaning of the Human Rights Act 1998), the court shall make an order for possession.

(4) If the court is satisfied that any of the grounds in Part II of Schedule 2 to this Act is established, then, subject to subsections (5A) and (6) below, the court may make an order for possession if it considers it reasonable to do so.

(5) Part III of Schedule 2 to this Act shall have effect for supplementing Ground 9 in that Schedule and Part IV of that Schedule shall have effect in relation to notices given as mentioned in Grounds 1 to 5 of that Schedule.

(5A) The court shall not make an order for possession of a dwelling-house let on an assured periodic tenancy arising under Schedule 10 to the Local Government and Housing Act 1989 on any of the following grounds; that is to say,

III L&T [217]

8. Notice of proceedings for possession

(1) The court shall not entertain proceedings for possession of a dwelling-house let on an assured tenancy unless

(a) the landlord or, in the case of joint landlords, at least one of them has served on the tenant a notice in accordance with this section and the proceedings are begun within the time limits stated in the notice in accordance with subsections (3A) to (4B) below; or

(b) the court considers it just and equitable to dispense with the requirement of such a notice.

(2) The court shall not make an order for possession on any of the grounds in Schedule 2 to this Act unless that ground and particulars of it are specified in the notice under this section; but the grounds specified in such a notice may be altered or added to with the leave of the court.

(3) A notice under this section is one in the prescribed form informing the tenant that

(a) the landlord intends to begin proceedings for possession of the dwelling-house on one or more of the grounds specified in the notice; and

(b) those proceedings will not begin earlier than a date specified in the notice in accordance with subsections (3A) to (4B) below; and

(c) those proceedings will not begin later than twelve months from the date of service of the notice.

(3A) If a notice under this section specifies in accordance with subsection (3)(a) Ground 7A in Schedule 2 to this Act (whether with or without other grounds), the date specified in the notice as mentioned in subsection (3)(b) is not to be earlier than—

(a) in the case of a periodic tenancy, the earliest date on which, apart from section 5(1), the tenancy could be brought to an end by a notice to quit given by the landlord on the same date as the date of service of the notice under this section;

(b) in the case of a fixed term tenancy, one month after the date on which the notice was served.

(4) If a notice under this section specifies in accordance with subsection (3) (a) above Ground 14 in Schedule 2 to this Act (whether without other grounds or with any ground other than Ground 7A), the date specified in the notice as mentioned in subsection (3) (b) above shall not be earlier than the date of the service of the notice.

(4A) If a notice under this section specifies in accordance with subsection (3) (a) above, any of Grounds 1, 2, 5 to 7, 9 and 16 in Schedule 2 to this Act (whether without other grounds or with any ground other than Ground 7A or 14), the date specified in the notice as mentioned in subsection (3) (b) above shall not be earlier than

(a) two months from the date of service of the notice; and

(b) if the tenancy is a periodic tenancy, the earliest date on which, apart from section 5 (1) above, the tenancy could be brought to an end by a notice to quit given by the landlord on the same date as the date of service of the notice under this section.

(4B) In any other case, the date specified in the notice as mentioned in subsection (3) (b) above shall not be earlier than the expiry of the period of two weeks from the date of the service of the notice.

LANDLORD & TENANT AND HOUSING

(4C) A notice under this section that specifies in accordance with subsection (3)(a) Ground 7A in Schedule 2 to this Act (whether with or without other grounds) must be served on the tenant within the time period specified in subsection (4D), (4E) or (4F).

(4D) Where the landlord proposes to rely on condition 1, 3 or 5 in Ground 7A, the notice must be served on the tenant within—

(a) the period of 12 months beginning with the day of the conviction, or

(b) if there is an appeal against the conviction, the period of 12 months beginning with the day on which the appeal is finally determined or abandoned.

(4E) Where the landlord proposes to rely on condition 2 in Ground 7A, the notice must be served on the tenant within—

(a) the period of 12 months beginning with the day on which the court has made the finding, or

(b) if there is an appeal against the finding, the period of 12 months beginning with the day on which the appeal is finally determined, abandoned or withdrawn.

(4F) Where the landlord proposes to rely on condition 4 in Ground 7A, the notice must be served on the tenant within—

(a) the period of 3 months beginning with the day on which the closure order was made, or

(b) if there is an appeal against the making of the order, the period of 3 months beginning with the day on which the appeal is finally determined, abandoned or withdrawn.

(5) The court may not exercise the power conferred by subsection (1) (b) above if the landlord seeks to recover possession on Ground 7A, 7B or 8 in Schedule 2 to this Act.

(6) Where a notice under this section

(a) is served at a time when the dwelling-house is let on a fixed term tenancy, or

(b) is served after a fixed term tenancy has come to an end but relates (in whole or in part) to events occurring during that tenancy,

the notice shall have effect notwithstanding that the tenant becomes or has become tenant under a statutory periodic tenancy arising on the coming to an end of the fixed term tenancy.

III L&T [217.1]

Generally This section is similar to the Housing Act 1985 s 83 and reference should be made to the notes to that section, at para **III L&T [108.1]**.

III L&T [217.2]

Joint landlords The general rule to which the Housing Act 1988 s 8(1)(a) provides an exception is that a reference to a landlord is to all persons who jointly constitute the landlord: see the Housing Act 1988 s 45(3) (see para **III L&T [238]**).

III L&T [217.3]

Notice in the prescribed form See the Assured Tenancies and Agricultural Occupancies (Forms) (England) Regulations 2015 (SI 2015/620) as amended by SI 2015/1646, SI 2016/443 and SI 2016/1118.

A notice of proceedings under the Housing Act 1988 Sch 2 Ground 8 (see para **III L&T [242]**) must specify the substance eg "at least three months' rent is in arrears" although the exact words of the statute need not be used; but the notice is defective if it omits the words "both at the date of service of the notice and at the date of the hearing" and the explanation that "rent" means rent lawfully due from the tenant: *Mountain v Hastings* (1993) 25 HLR 427, [1993] 2 EGLR 53, CA. The notice of grounds is valid if it clearly alleges three months' rent overdue and indicates how much or how the tenant can ascertain how much is due; it is not necessary to specify in terms the amount due: *Marath v MacGillivray* (1996) 28 HLR 484, [1996] NPC 11, CA. See also *Masih v Yousaf* [2014] HLR 27.

III L&T [217.4]

The court considers it just and equitable to dispense See the notes to the Rent Act 1977 Sch 15 Case 11, at para **III L&T [83]**, regarding the exercise of a discretion to dispense with the requirements of notice in proceedings for possession. See too *Kelsey Housing Association v King* (1995) 28 HLR 270, Times, 8 August, CA, regarding the proper exercise of the discretion. For a case where the landlord served a notice which gave less than the required period of notice but s 8(1)(b) was applied, see *North British Housing Association v Sheridan* (1999) 32 HLR 346, [1999] 2 EGLR 138, CA.

III L&T [217.5]

Service Service of the notice by delivering it to the tenant's address is not invalidated by the incapacity of the tenant: *Tadema Holdings Ltd v Ferguson* (1999) 32 HLR 866, CA.

III L&T [217.6]

Possession proceedings interrupted by a transfer of property to a registered social landlord Where a local authority, which has started possession proceedings against a secure tenant, then transfers the property to a registered social landlord, the tenant becomes an assured tenant against whom an order may not normally be made without the service of notice of proceedings under s 8 of the 1988 Act. However, the court may dispense with service of the notice, in the interests of saving time and costs, provided that there is no injustice to the defendants. The appropriate procedure is for the new landlord to apply to be substituted as claimant and for permission to make clear, by amendment, that the grounds relied on do not go outside the grounds available against a secure tenant: *Knowsley Housing Trust v Revell* [2003] EWCA Civ 496, [2003] HLR 958, (2003) Times, 17 April.

LANDLORD & TENANT AND HOUSING

III L&T [218]

8A. Additional notice requirements: ground of domestic violence

(1) Where the ground specified in a notice under section 8 (whether with or without other grounds) is Ground 14A in Schedule 2 to this Act and the partner who has left the dwelling-house as mentioned in that ground is not a tenant of the dwelling-house, the court shall not entertain proceedings for possession of the dwelling-house unless

(a) the landlord or, in the case of joint landlords, at least one of them has served on the partner who has left a copy of the notice or has taken all reasonable steps to serve a copy of the notice on that partner, or

(b) the court considers it just and equitable to dispense with such requirements as to service.

(2) Where Ground 14A in Schedule 2 to this Act is added to a notice under section 8 with the leave of the court after proceedings for possession are begun and the partner who has left the dwelling-house as mentioned in that ground is not a party to the proceedings, the court shall not continue to entertain the proceedings unless

(a) the landlord or in the case of joint landlords, at least one of them has served a notice under subsection (3) below on the partner who has left or has taken all reasonable steps to serve such a notice on that partner, or

(b) the court considers it just and equitable to dispense with the requirement of such a notice.

(3) A notice under this subsection shall

(a) state that proceedings for the possession of the dwelling-house have begun,

(b) specify the ground or grounds on which possession is being sought, and

(c) give particulars of the ground or grounds.

III L&T [219]

9. Extended discretion of court in possession claims

(1) Subject to subsection (6) below, the court may adjourn for such period or periods as it thinks fit proceedings for possession of a dwelling-house let on an assured tenancy.

(2) On the making of an order for possession of a dwelling-house let on an assured tenancy or at any time before the execution of such an order, the court, subject to subsection (6) below, may

(a) stay or suspend execution of the order, or

(b) postpone the date of possession,

for such period or periods as the court thinks just.

(3) On any such adjournment as is referred to in subsection (1) above or on any such stay, suspension or postponement as is referred to in subsection (2) above, the court, unless it considers that to do so would cause exceptional hardship to the tenant or would otherwise be unreasonable, shall impose conditions with regard to payment by the tenant of arrears of rent (if any) and rent and may impose such other conditions as it thinks fit.

(4) If any such conditions as are referred to in subsection (3) above are complied with, the court may, if it thinks fit, discharge or rescind any such order as is referred to in subsection (2) above.

[(4) The court may discharge or rescind any such order as is referred to in subsection (2) if it thinks it appropriate to do so having had regard to—

(a) any conditions imposed under subsection (3), and

(b) the conduct of the tenant in connection with those conditions.]

(5) . . .

(5A) . . .

(6) This section does not apply if the court is satisfied that the landlord is entitled to possession of the dwelling-house

(a) on any of the grounds in Part I of Schedule 2 to this Act; or

(b) by virtue of subsection (1) or subsection (4) of section 21 below.

Amendment *Text is as repealed or amended by Schedule 11 to the Housing and Regeneration Act 2008 with effect from 20 May 2009 by SI 2009/1261. Note, however, that the substitution of sub-section (4) is not yet in force.*

III L&T [219.1]

Extended discretion Reference may be made to the notes at paras **III L&T [110.1]–[110.1C]**. Where a possession order was made but it was unclear whether it was on a ground in Part I, the court may exercise its discretion to suspend on a subsequent application: *Capital Prime Plus v Wills* (1999) 31 HLR 926, CA. See also *Diab v Countrywide Rentals 1 plc* (2001) Independent, 5 November, ChD, where the court held that, if a possession order was made on one of the mandatory grounds, it was essential that that fact appeared on the face of the order; it was not proper for the court to revisit the possession order at a later date (eg at the hearing of an application to suspend the warrant) in order to determine upon what ground the possession order had been made. It is not legitimate, under s 9, for the court to order an adjournment for the purpose of enabling a tenant to reduce rent arrears below the threshold in Sch 2 Part I Ground 8 of the Act save in exceptional circumstances; the power to adjourn is not to be exercised so as to defeat the policy of the Act or the rights which it conferred on landlords: see *North British Housing Association Ltd v Matthews* [2005] 2 All ER 667, [2004] EWCA Civ 1736, [2004] All ER (D) 344 (Dec). In *New Charter Housing (North) Ltd v Ashcroft* [2004] EWCA Civ 310(2004) 148 Sol Jo LB 352, the Court of Appeal overturned a suspension in a nuisance case, stressing the importance of the interests of neighbours and the likelihood that anti-social behaviour would continue.

For further guidance on the approach to be taken to the exercise of discretion by the court when considering whether to make a suspended possession order see *City West Housing Trust v Massey* [2016] EWCA Civ 704.

III L&T [219.2]

Tolerated trespasser Note the effect of the decision of the House of Lords in *Knowsley Housing Trust v White* [2008] UKHL 70, [2009] All ER 829; see para **III L&T [110.1]**. In *Stirling* *v Leadenhall Residential 2 Ltd* [2001] EWCA Civ 1011, [2001] 3 All ER 645, it was common ground that service of notice of increase in rent upon a person remaining in occupation following a possession order, paying rent arrears and mesne profits, created a new tenancy.

III L&T [219.3]

Postponement and suspension It may be appropriate, in a case where it is reasonable to order possession on the ground of anti-social behaviour to suspend the order on terms that there should be no further breaches of the tenancy: *Moat Housing Group South Ltd v Harris* [2005] EWCA Civ 287, (2005) Times, 23 March. But to justify a suspension there must be a sound basis for the hope that the anti-social behaviour that has led to the making of the possession order will cease: see *Friendship Care and Housing Association v Begum* [2011] EWCA Civ 1807, [2011] All ER (D) 238 (Nov).

In addition to the power to suspend an order for possession the court has power, in an appropriate case, to order that the date for possession be postponed until after a further application to the court by the housing authority in the event of further breach: *Norwich City Council v Famuyiwa* [2004] EWCA Civ 1770, (2005) Times, 24 January.

For further observations on the use of postponed possession orders and possession orders with suspended execution, see the Court of Appeal judgments in *Harlow District Council v Hall* [2006] EWCA Civ 156, [2006] All ER (D) 393 (Feb). Refer also to the discussion at para **III L&T [110.1]**.

Where the court makes an order for possession to be given by a certain date, in Form N28, the tenancy ends on that date and if the former tenant remains in possession during a period when execution of the order for possession is suspended his, or her, status is that of a tolerated trespasser, without the contractual or statutory rights of an assured tenant: *Knowsley Housing Trust v White* [2007] EWCA Civ 404, [2007] All ER (D) 38 (May), (2007) Times, 15 May.

LANDLORD & TENANT AND HOUSING

III L&T [219A]

9A. Proceedings for possession [on non-absolute grounds]: anti-social behaviour

(1) This section applies if the court is considering under section 7(4) whether it is reasonable to make an order for possession on ground 14 set out in Part 2 of Schedule 2 (conduct of tenant or other person).

(2) The court must consider, in particular—

(a) the effect that the nuisance or annoyance has had on persons other than the person against whom the order is sought;

(b) any continuing effect the nuisance or annoyance is likely to have on such persons;

(c) the effect that the nuisance or annoyance would be likely to have on such persons if the conduct is repeated.

III L&T [219A.1]

The effect of s 9A is that, when a court is considering whether it is reasonable to grant a possession order against a secure or assured tenant under one of the nuisance grounds for possession, the court must give particular consideration to the actual or likely effect which the anti-social behaviour has had or could have on others. In striking the balance between the competing interests of the tenant and those of the neighbours there is a limit to which the court can tolerate anti-social behaviour against neighbours for the sake of the needs of the tenant and the tenant's children: *London Quadrant Housing Trust v Root* (2005) HLR 28, CA.

III L&T [220]

10. Special provisions applicable to shared accommodation

(1) This section applies in a case falling within subsection (1) of section 3 above and expressions used in this section have the same meaning as in that section.

(2) Without prejudice to the enforcement of any order made under subsection (3) below, while the tenant is in possession of the separate accommodation, no order shall be made for possession of any of the shared accommodation, whether on the application of the immediate landlord of the tenant or on the application of any person under whom that landlord derives title, unless a like order has been made, or is made at the same time, in respect of the separate accommodation; and the provisions of section 6 above shall have effect accordingly.

(3) On the application of the landlord, the court may make such order as it thinks just either

(a) terminating the right of the tenant to use the whole or any part of the shared accommodation other than living accommodation; or

(b) modifying his right to use the whole or any part of the shared accommodation, whether by varying the persons or increasing the number of persons entitled to the use of that accommodation or otherwise.

(4) No order shall be made under subsection (3) above so as to effect any termination or modification of the rights of the tenant which, apart from section 3 (3) above, could not be effected by or under the terms of the tenancy.

III L&T [220A]

10A. Power to order transfer of tenancy in certain cases

(1) This section applies on an application for an order for possession of a dwelling-house let on an assured tenancy if the court is satisfied that—

(a) Ground 7B in Schedule 2 is established,

(b) no other ground in that Schedule is established, or one or more grounds in Part 2 of that Schedule are established but it is not reasonable to make an order for possession on that ground or those grounds,

(c) the tenancy is a joint tenancy, and

(d) one or more of the tenants is a qualifying tenant.

(2) In subsection (1)(d) "qualifying tenant" means a person who (within the meaning of Ground 7B) is not disqualified as a result of the person's immigration status from occupying the dwelling-house under the tenancy.

(3) The court may, instead of making an order for possession, order that the tenant's interest under the tenancy is to be transferred so that it is held—

(a) if there is one qualifying tenant, by the qualifying tenant as sole tenant, or

(b) if there is more than one qualifying tenant, by all of them as joint tenants.

(4) The effect of an order under this section is that, from the time the order takes effect, the qualifying tenant or tenants—

(a) are entitled to performance of the landlord's covenants under the tenancy, and

(b) are liable to perform the tenant's covenants under the tenancy.

(5) The effect of an order under this section is that, from the time it takes effect, any other person who was a tenant under the tenancy before the order took effect—

(a) ceases to be entitled to performance of the landlord's covenants under the tenancy, or

(b) ceases to be liable to perform the tenant's covenants under the tenancy.

(6) Subsection (5) does not remove any right or liability of the person which accrued before the order took effect.

(7) An order under this section does not operate to create a new tenancy as between the landlord and the qualifying tenant or tenants.

(8) In particular, if the tenancy is a fixed term tenancy, the term comes to an end at the same time as if the order had not been made.

Amendment *Section 10A is inserted by s 41 of the Immigration Act 2016 with effect from 1 December 2016 (SI 2016/1037) and applies to tenancies entered into before that date.*

III L&T [221]

11. Payment of removal expenses in certain cases

(1) Where a court makes an order for possession of a dwelling-house let on an assured tenancy on Ground 6 or Ground 9 in Schedule 2 to this Act (but not on any other ground), the landlord shall pay to the tenant a sum equal to the reasonable expenses likely to be incurred by the tenant in removing from the dwelling-house.

(2) Any question as to the amount of the sum referred to in subsection (1) above shall be determined by agreement between the landlord and the tenant or, in default of agreement, by the court.

(3) Any sum payable to a tenant by virtue of this section shall be recoverable as a civil debt due from the landlord.

III L&T [221.1]

Determination by the court The court's determination should be sought by an application, after judgment, in the main proceedings in accordance with CPR Pt 23 (see para **CPR 23**).

III L&T [221.2]

Recoverable as a civil debt The Housing Act 1988 s 40 (see para **III L&T [237]**) enables the county court to determine the amount of the removal expenses at a sum beyond the court's ordinary jurisdiction and allows a claim for such a sum to be made in the county court, at least if joined in the same proceedings.

III L&T [222]

12. Compensation for misrepresentation or concealment

Where a landlord obtains an order for possession of a dwelling-house let on an assured tenancy on one or more of the grounds in Schedule 2 to this Act and it is subsequently made to appear to the court that the order was obtained by misrepresentation or concealment of material facts, the court may order the landlord to pay to the former tenant such sum as appears sufficient as compensation for damage or loss sustained by that tenant as a result of the order.

III L&T [222.1]

Generally This is in the same legal form as the Rent Act 1977 s 102, and the Landlord and Tenant Act 1954 s 55.

III L&T [222A]

13. Increases of rent under assured periodic tenancies

(1) This section applies to—

- (a) a statutory periodic tenancy other than one which, by virtue of paragraph 11 or paragraph 12 in Part I of Schedule 1 to this Act, cannot for the time being be an assured tenancy; and
- (b) any other periodic tenancy which is an assured tenancy, other than one in relation to which there is a provision, for the time being binding on the tenant, under which the rent for a particular period of the tenancy will or may be greater than the rent for an earlier period.

(2) For the purpose of securing an increase in the rent under a tenancy to which this section applies, the landlord may serve on the tenant a notice in the prescribed form proposing a new rent to take effect at the beginning of a new period of the tenancy specified in the notice, being a period beginning not earlier than—

- (a) the minimum period after the date of the service of the notice; and
- (b) except in the case of a statutory periodic tenancy—
  - (i) in the case of an assured agricultural occupancy, the first anniversary of the date on which the first period of the tenancy began;

(ii) in any other case, on the date that falls 52 weeks after the date on which the first period of the tenancy began; and

(c) if the rent under the tenancy has previously been increased by virtue of a notice under this subsection or a determination under section 14 below—

(i) in the case of an assured agricultural occupancy, the first anniversary of the date on which the increased rent took effect;

(ii) in any other case, the appropriate date.

(3) The minimum period referred to in subsection (2) above is—

(a) in the case of a yearly tenancy, six months;

(b) in the case of a tenancy where the period is less than a month, one month; and

(c) in any other case, a period equal to the period of the tenancy.

(3A) The appropriate date referred to in subsection (2)(c)(ii) above is—

(a) in a case to which subsection (3B) below applies, the date that falls 53 weeks after the date on which the increased rent took effect;

(b) in any other case, the date that falls 52 weeks after the date on which the increased rent took effect.

(3B) This subsection applies where -

(a) the rent under the tenancy has been increased by virtue of a notice under this section or a determination under section 14 below on at least one occasion after the coming into force of the Regulatory Reform (Assured Periodic Tenancies) (Rent Increases) Order 2003; and

(b) the fifty-third week after the date on which the last such increase took effect begins more than six days before the anniversary of the date on which the first such increase took effect

(4) Where a notice is served under subsection (2) above, a new rent specified in the notice shall take effect as mentioned in the notice unless, before the beginning of the new period specified in the notice,—

(a) the tenant by an application in the prescribed form refers the notice to the appropriate tribunal; or

(b) the landlord and the tenant agree on a variation of the rent which is different from that proposed in the notice or agree that the rent should not be varied.

(5) Nothing in this section (or in section 14 below) affects the right of the landlord and the tenant under an assured tenancy to vary by agreement any term of the tenancy (including a term relating to rent).

III L&T [222A.1]

Generally For "assured tenancy" see Housing Act 1988 s 1 (see para **III L&T [213]**) and for "statutory periodic tenancy" see Housing Act 1988 s 5(7) (see para **III L&T [214]**). An assured tenancy which provides expressly for the review and increase of rent is excluded from s 13 by the terms of sub s (1)(b): *Contour Homes Ltd v Rowen* [2007] EWCA Civ 842, [2007] 1 WLR 2982.

III L&T [222A.2]

Notice in the prescribed form For the form of notice for the purpose of s 13(2), see Form 4A prescribed by the Assured Tenancies and Agricultural Occupancies (Forms) (Amendment) (England) Regulations 2002, SI 2002/337. For the form of application for the purpose of s 13(4), see Form 5 prescribed by the Assured Tenancies and Agricultural Occupancies (Forms) Regulations 1997, SI 1997/ 194.

Regarding the forms of notice for increasing rent, note the changes made by the Assured Tenancies and Agricultural Occupancies (Forms) (England) Regulations 2015 SI 2015/620 with effect from 6 April 2015.

III L&T [222A.3]

Refers the notice "Refers" in s 13(4)(a) means "delivers to": *R (Lester) v London Rent Assessment Committee* [2003] EWCA Civ 319, [2003] 1 WLR 1449, (2003) Times, 25 March.

III L&T [222A.4]

Rent review clause in the contractual tenancy Upon the expiry of an assured tenancy it becomes a statutory periodic tenancy by virtue of s 5(2). A rent review clause in the original assured tenancy purporting to govern the position once it had been superseded by a statutory periodic tenancy is of no effect; section 13(1)(b), and the statutory scheme for rent increase, prevails: *London District Properties Management Ltd v Goolamy* [2009] EWHC 1367 (Admin), [2010] 1 P&CR 1, [2009] 38 EG 110.

III L&T [223]

17. Succession to assured tenancy

(1) Subject to subsection (1D), In any case where

(a) the sole tenant under an assured periodic tenancy dies, and

(b) immediately before the death, the tenant's spouse or civil partner was occupying the dwelling-house as his or her only or principal home.

(c) . . .

then, on the death, the tenancy vests by virtue of this section in the spouse or civil partner (and, accordingly, does not devolve under the tenant's will or intestacy).

(1A) Subject to subsection (1D), in any case where—

(a) there is an assured periodic tenancy of a dwelling-house in England under which—

(i) the landlord is a private registered provider of social housing, and

(ii) the tenant is a sole tenant,

(b) the tenant under the tenancy dies,

(c) immediately before the death, the dwelling-house was not occupied by a spouse or civil partner of the tenant as his or her only or principal home,

(d) an express term of the tenancy makes provision for a person other than such a spouse or civil partner of the tenant to succeed to the tenancy, and

(e) there is a person whose succession is in accordance with that term, then, on the death, the tenancy vests by virtue of this section in that person (and, accordingly, does not devolve under the tenant's will or intestacy).

(1B) Subject to subsection (1D), in any case where—

(a) there is an assured tenancy of a dwelling-house in England for a fixed term of not less than two years under which—

(i) the landlord is a private registered provider of social housing, and

(ii) the tenant is a sole tenant,

(b) the tenant under the tenancy dies, and

(c) immediately before the death, the tenant's spouse or civil partner was occupying the dwelling-house as his or her only or principal home,

then, on the death, the tenancy vests by virtue of this section in the spouse or civil partner (and, accordingly, does not devolve under the tenant's will or intestacy).

(1C) Subject to subsection (1D), in any case where—

(a) there is an assured tenancy of a dwelling-house in England for a fixed term of not less than two years under which—

(i) the landlord is a private registered provider of social housing, and

(ii) the tenant is a sole tenant,

(b) the tenant under the tenancy dies,

(c) immediately before the death, the dwelling-house was not occupied by a spouse or civil partner of the tenant as his or her only or principal home,

(d) an express term of the tenancy makes provision for a person other than such a spouse or civil partner of the tenant to succeed to the tenancy, and

(e) there is a person whose succession is in accordance with that term, then, on the death, the tenancy vests by virtue of this section in that person (and accordingly does not devolve under the tenant's will or intestacy).

(1D) Subsection (1), (1A), (1B) or (1C) does not apply if the tenant was himself a successor as defined in subsection (2) or subsection (3).

(1E) In such a case, on the death, the tenancy vests by virtue of this section in a person ("P") (and, accordingly, does not devolve under the tenant's will or intestacy) if, and only if—

(a) (in a case within subsection (1)) the tenancy is of a dwelling-house in England under which the landlord is a private registered provider of social housing,

(b) an express term of the tenancy makes provision for a person to succeed a successor to the tenancy, and

(c) P's succession is in accordance with that term.

(2) For the purposes of this section, a tenant is a successor in relation to a tenancy if

(a) the tenancy became vested in him either by virtue of this section or under the will or intestacy of a previous tenant; or

(b) at some time before the tenant's death the tenancy was a joint tenancy held by himself and one or more other persons and, prior to his death, he became the sole tenant by survivorship; or

(c) he became entitled to the tenancy as mentioned in section 39 (5) below.

(3) For the purposes of this section, a tenant is also a successor in relation to a tenancy (in this subsection referred to as "the new tenancy") which was granted to him (alone or jointly with others) if

(a) at some time before the grant of the new tenancy, he was, by virtue of subsection (2) above, a successor in relation to an earlier tenancy of the same or substantially the same dwelling-house as is let under the new tenancy; and

(b) at all times since he became such a successor he has been a tenant (alone or jointly with others) of the dwelling-house which is let under the new tenancy or of a dwelling-house which is substantially the same as that dwelling-house.

(4) For the purposes of this section-

(a) a person who was living with the tenant as his or her wife or husband shall be treated as the tenant's spouse, and

(b) a person who was living with the tenant as if they were civil partners shall be treated as the tenant's civil partner.

(5) If, on the death of the tenant, there is, by virtue of subsection (4) above, more than one person who fulfils the condition in subsection (1)(b) or (1B)(c) above, such one of them as may be decided by agreement or, in default of agreement, by the county court shall for the purposes of this section be treated as the tenant's spouse, or if that person is the same sex as the tenant, and falls within subsection (4)(b), as the tenant's civil partner.

(6) If, on the death of the tenant, there is more than one person in whom the tenancy would otherwise vest by virtue of subsection (1A), (1C) or (1E), the tenancy vests in such one of them as may be agreed between them or, in default of agreement, as is determined by the county court.

(7) This section does not apply to a fixed term assured tenancy that is a lease of a dwelling-house—

(a) granted on payment of a premium calculated by reference to a percentage of the value of the dwelling-house or of the cost of providing it, or

(b) under which the lessee (or the lessee's personal representatives) will or may be entitled to a sum calculated by reference, directly or indirectly, to the value of the dwelling-house.

III L&T [223.1]

Assured periodic tenancy This means an assured tenancy within the Housing Act 1988 s 1 (see para **III L&T [213]**), unless it is for a fixed term: Housing Act 1988 s 45(1) (see para **III L&T [238]**).

III L&T [223.2]

Decided by the county court If there is unlikely to be a substantial dispute of fact proceedings to obtain a decision should be by Pt 8 claim form in accordance with CPR Pt 8 (see **CPR 8**). The court has a very wide discretion: *Williams v Williams* [1970] 3 All ER 988, [1970] 1 WLR 1530, CA.

III L&T [223.3]

Living together as husband and wife The wording of the Housing Act 1988 s 17(4) is similar to the Housing Act 1985 s 113(1)(a) (see para **III L&T [119]**). In *Harrogate Borough Council v Simpson* [1985] RVR 10, CA, it was held that persons of the same sex who live together are not living together "as husband and wife" for the purposes of that provision of the Housing Act 1985. Contrast the position on succession to statutory tenancies (see para **III L&T [81.3]**). Also living together as husband and wife connotes a settled intention: *Westminster City Council v Peart* (1991) 24 HLR 389, CA.

In a decision as to whether the claimant was entitled to succeed to an assured tenancy under s 17, the court held that, to be treated as the spouse when of the same gender as the deceased, the survivor would have to demonstrate a lifetime emotional commitment which was openly and unequivocally displayed to the whole world: *Southern Housing Group Ltd v Nutting* [2004] EWHC (Ch), [2004] All ER (D) 347 (Dec), (2005) Times, 5 January, ChD. See also the notes at para **III L&T [81.2]**, **III L&T [112.2]**, and **III L&T [119.1]** and the decision of the House of Lords in *Ghaidan v Godin-Mendoza* [2004] UKHL 30, [2004] 2 AC 557, [2004] 3 All ER 411, HL. For a further consideration of the test, and application of it to the facts, see *Amicus Horizon Ltd v Mabott and Brand* [2012] EWCA Civ 895.

III L&T [224]

18. Provisions as to reversions on assured tenancies

(1) If at any time

(a) a dwelling-house is for the time being lawfully let on an assured tenancy, and

(b) the landlord under the assured tenancy is himself a tenant under a superior tenancy, and

(c) the superior tenancy comes to an end,

then, subject to subsection (2) below, the assured tenancy shall continue in existence as a tenancy held of the person whose interest would, apart from the continuance of the assured tenancy, entitle him to actual possession of the dwelling-house at that time.

(2) Subsection (1) above does not apply to an assured tenancy if the interest which, by virtue of that subsection, would become that of the landlord, is such that, by virtue of Schedule 1 to this Act, the tenancy could not be an assured tenancy.

(3) Where, by virtue of any provision of this Part of this Act, an assured tenancy which is a periodic tenancy (including a statutory periodic tenancy) continues beyond the beginning of a reversionary tenancy which was granted (whether before, on or after the commencement of this Act) so as to begin on or after

(a) the date on which the previous contractual assured tenancy came to an end, or

(b) a date on which, apart from any provision of this Part, the periodic tenancy could have been brought to an end by the landlord by notice to quit,

the reversionary tenancy shall have effect as if it had been granted subject to the periodic tenancy.

(4) The reference in subsection (3) above to the previous contractual assured tenancy applies only where the periodic tenancy referred to in that subsection is a statutory periodic tenancy and is a reference to the fixed-term tenancy which immediately preceded the statutory periodic tenancy.

III L&T [225]

19. ***Restriction on levy of distress for rent***

Repealed.

III L&T [225.1]

Generally See the notes to the Rent Act 1977 s 147, at para **III L&T [80.1]**, on which this section is modelled.

CHAPTER II ASSURED SHORTHOLD TENANCIES

III L&T [226]

19A. Assured shorthold tenancies: post-Housing Act 1996 tenancies

An assured tenancy which

(a) is entered into on or after the day on which section 96 of the Housing Act 1996 comes into force (otherwise than pursuant to a contract made before that day), or

(b) comes into being by virtue of section 5 above on the coming to an end of an assured tenancy within paragraph (a) above,

is an assured shorthold tenancy unless it falls within any paragraph in Schedule 2A to this Act.

III L&T [227]

20. Assured shorthold tenancies: pre-Housing Act 1996 tenancies

(1) Subject to subsection (3) below, an assured tenancy which is not one to which section 19A above applies is an assured shorthold tenancy if

(a) it is a fixed term tenancy granted for a term certain of not less than six months,

(b) there is no power for the landlord to determine the tenancy at any time earlier than six months from the beginning of the tenancy, and

(c) a notice in respect of it is served as mentioned in subsection (2) below.

(2) The notice referred to in subsection (1) (c) above is one which

(a) is in such form as may be prescribed;

(b) is served before the assured tenancy is entered into;

(c) is served by the person who is to be the landlord under the assured tenancy on the person who is to be the tenant under that tenancy; and

(d) states that the assured tenancy to which it relates is to be a shorthold tenancy.

(3) Notwithstanding anything in subsection (1) above, where

(a) immediately before a tenancy (in this subsection referred to as "the new tenancy") is granted, the person to whom it is granted or, as the case may be, at least one of the persons to whom it is granted was a tenant under an assured tenancy which was not a shorthold tenancy, and

(b) the new tenancy is granted by the person who, immediately before the beginning of the tenancy, was the landlord under the assured tenancy referred to in paragraph (a) above,

the new tenancy cannot be an assured shorthold tenancy.

(4) Subject to subsection (5) below, if, on the coming to an end of an assured shorthold tenancy (including a tenancy which was an assured shorthold but ceased to be assured before it came to an end), a new tenancy of the same or substantially the same premises comes into being under which the landlord and the tenant are the same as at the coming to an end of the earlier tenancy, then, if and so long as the new tenancy is an assured tenancy, it shall be an assured shorthold tenancy, whether or not it fulfils the conditions in paragraphs (a) to (c) of subsection (1) above.

(5) Subsection (4) above does not apply if, before the new tenancy is entered into (or, in the case of a statutory periodic tenancy, takes effect in possession), the landlord serves notice on the tenant that the new tenancy is not to be a shorthold tenancy.

(5A) Subsections (3) and (4) above do not apply where the new tenancy is one to which section 19A above applies.

(6) In the case of joint landlords

(a) the reference in subsection (2) (c) above to the person who is to be the landlord is a reference to at least one of the persons who are to be joint landlords; and

(b) the reference in subsection (5) above to the landlord is a reference to at least one of the joint landlords.

(7) [. . .]

III L&T [227.1]

Pre-Housing Act 1996 The date when the 1996 Act (and s 20A of the 1988 Act, see para **III L&T [228]**) came into force was 28 February 1997.

III L&T [227.1A]

Fixed term tenancy A tenancy of residential premises "for a term certain of one year and . . . thereafter from month to month" creates a fixed term and hence constitutes an assured shorthold tenancy: *Goodman v Evely* [2001] EWCA Civ 980, [2001] PLSCS 17.

III L&T [227.2]

Notice in a prescribed form The notice was Form 7, prescribed by the Assured Tenancies and Agricultural Occupancies (Forms) Regulations 1988, SI 1988/2203, as amended by SI 1989/146, SI 1990/1532 and SI 1993/654, and now revoked by the Assured Tenancies and Agricultural Occupancies (Forms) Regulations 1997, SI 1997/194.

A notice served under the Housing Act 1988 s 20 to create a shorthold must correctly state the commencement date and the term date in order to be valid although an evident clerical error may be disregarded, if it is one which the ordinary addressee would see through: *Panayi and Pyrkos v Roberts* (1993) 25 HLR 421, [1993] 2 EGLR 51, CA. In *Andrews v Brewer* (1997) 30 HLR 203, CA a notice was held valid despite an obvious error in the date and the omission of a note the absence of which did not work to the detriment of the tenant. In *York v Casey* (1998) 31 HLR 209, [1998] 2 EGLR 25, Gibson LJ applying the *Mannai* test (*Mannai Investment Co Ltd v Eagle Star Life Assurance Co Ltd* [1997] AC 749, [1997] 3 All ER 352, HL) stated "what the court must do is to see whether the error in the notice was obvious or evident and, secondly, whether notwithstanding that error the notice read in its context is sufficiently clear to leave a reasonable recipient in no reasonable doubt as to the terms of the notice". Note, however, that a notice given under s 20 which contains dates differing from those in the tenancy agreement cannot be saved if it is not obvious what the correct dates should have been: *Clickex Ltd v McCann* (1999) 32 HLR 324, [1999] 2 EGLR 63, CA.

A notice may be validly served on the same day as the tenancy starts, provided it is served before the tenancy's entered into: *Bedding v McCarthy* (1993) 27 HLR 103, [1994] 2 EGLR 40, CA.

Notice in a prescribed form A notice is invalid if it does not include the prescribed instructions and advice since it is not substantially to the same effect as a notice in the prescribed form: *Manel v Memon* (2000) 80 P & CR D22, CA, applying the tests in *Tegerdine v Brooks* (1977) 36 P & CR 261, 267.

In *Ravenseft Properties Ltd v Hall* [2001] EWCA Civ 2034, [2002] HLR 624 the court held that the question whether a notice was "substantially to the same effect" as the prescribed form was a matter of fact and degree in each case. The court identified (as the two guiding principles) the purposive approach adopted in *Manel v Memon* and the test applied by GIBSON LJ (quoted above) in *York v Casey*.

III L&T [227.2A]

Service of notice by or on agent A notice under s 20 is not required to be personally served upon the tenant but may validly be served upon his duly authorised agent: *Yenula Properties Ltd v Naidu* [2002] EWCA Civ 719, [2003] HLR 229, Times, 5 June. A notice completed by the landlord's agents, omitting particulars of the landlord, was held to be valid in *B Osborn & Co Ltd v Dior* [2003] EWCA Civ 281, [2003] HLR 649.

III L&T [227.3]

Operation of subsection (4) Housing Act 1988 s 20(4) can operate more than once: *Lower Street Properties Ltd v Jones* (1996) 28 HLR 877, [1996] NPC 29, CA.

III L&T [227.4]

Joint landlords The provisions of the Housing Act 1988 s 20(6) are exceptions to the general rule, in the Housing Act 1988 s 45(3) (see para **III L&T [238]**), that any reference to a landlord is to all persons who jointly constitute the landlord.

III L&T [227.5]

Re-entry and forfeiture The fact that a landlord has brought an assured shorthold tenancy to an end by forfeiture for arrears of rent or on some other ground does not entitle him to seek an order for possession under the Housing Act 1988 s 21 (see para **III L&T [229]**) (see Housing Act 1988 s 45(4), see para **III L&T [238]**); he must instead seek an order for possession under the Housing Act 1988 s 7(6) (see para **III L&T [216]**), after giving notice in accordance with the Housing Act 1988 s 8 (see para **III L&T [217]**). Form N119 (see **BCCP O[204]**) should be used where arrears of rent are relied on. If a valid order for possession is made, the court's power to grant relief under s 138 of the County Courts Act 1984 cannot be invoked: see *Artesian Residential Investments Ltd v Beck* [2000] QB 541, [1999] 3 All ER 113, CA.

III L&T [227.6]

Surrender A tenant who moves out of premises without informing the landlord does not thereby surrender the tenancy: there must be an acceptance by the landlord of the implied offer of surrender: *Belcourt Estates Ltd v Adesina* [2005] EWCA Civ 208, (2005) 149 Sol Jo LB 265. For case law to the same effect in the context of tenancies within the Housing Act 1985 see L&T [106.7].

III L&T [228]

20A. Post-Housing Act 1996 tenancies: duty of landlord to provide statement as to terms of tenancy

(1) Subject to subsection (3) below, a tenant under an assured shorthold tenancy to which section 19A above applies may, by notice in writing, require the landlord under that tenancy to provide him with a written statement of any term of the tenancy which

- (a) falls within subsection (2) below, and
- (b) is not evidenced in writing.

(2) The following terms of a tenancy fall within this subsection, namely

- (a) the date on which the tenancy began or, if it is a statutory periodic tenancy or a tenancy to which section 39 (7) below applies, the date on which the tenancy came into being,
- (b) the rent payable under the tenancy and the dates on which that rent is payable,
- (c) any term providing for a review of the rent payable under the tenancy, and

(d) in the case of a fixed term tenancy, the length of the fixed term.

(3) No notice may be given under subsection (1) above in relation to a term of the tenancy if

(a) the landlord under the tenancy has provided a statement of that term in response to an earlier notice under that subsection given by the tenant under the tenancy, and

(b) the term has not been varied since the provision of the statement referred to in paragraph (a) above.

(4) A landlord who fails, without reasonable excuse, to comply with a notice under subsection (1) above within the period of 28 days beginning with the date on which he received the notice is liable on summary conviction to a fine not exceeding level 4 on the standard scale.

(5) A statement provided for the purposes of subsection (1) above shall not be regarded as conclusive evidence of what was agreed by the parties to the tenancy in question.

(6) Where

(a) a term of a statutory periodic tenancy is one which has effect by virtue of section 5 (3) (e) above, or

(b) a term of a tenancy to which subsection (7) of section 39 below applies is one which has effect by virtue of subsection (6) (e) of that section,

subsection (1) above shall have effect in relation to it as if paragraph (b) related to the term of the tenancy from which it derives.

(7) In subsections (1) and (3) above

(a) references to the tenant under the tenancy shall, in the case of joint tenants, be taken to be references to any of the tenants, and

(b) references to the landlord under the tenancy shall, in the case of joint landlords, be taken to be references to any of the landlords.

III L&T [228A]

20B Demoted assured shorthold tenancies

(1) An assured tenancy is an assured shorthold tenancy to which this section applies (a demoted assured shorthold tenancy) if—

(a) the tenancy is created by virtue of an order of the court under section 82A of the Housing Act 1985 or section 6A of this Act (a demotion order), and

(b) the landlord is a private registered provider of social housing or a registered social landlord.

(2) At the end of the period of one year starting with the day when the demotion order takes effect a demoted assured shorthold tenancy ceases to be an assured shorthold tenancy unless subsection (3) applies, but see section 20C.

(3) This subsection applies if before the end of the period mentioned in subsection (2) the landlord gives notice of proceedings for possession of the dwelling house.

(4) If subsection (3) applies the tenancy continues to be a demoted assured shorthold tenancy until the end of the period mentioned in subsection (2) or (if later) until one of the following occurs—

(a) the notice of proceedings for possession is withdrawn;

(b) the proceedings are determined in favour of the tenant;

(c) the period of six months beginning with the date on which the notice is given ends and no proceedings for possession have been brought.

(5) Registered social landlord has the same meaning as in Part 1 of the Housing Act 1996.

III L&T [228A.1]

Generally Section 20B sets out the legal basis for the form of demoted tenancy that can be used by registered social landlords. A demoted assured shorthold tenancy is an assured shorthold tenancy during the demoted period but there is provision for the demoted assured shorthold tenancy automatically to turn into an assured tenancy after one year unless the landlord has (during that year) issued notice of proceedings for possession. If such a notice is issued, the tenancy will remain a demoted assured shorthold tenancy until the notice is withdrawn or six months have passed and no proceedings have been issued. If proceedings have been issued, the tenancy will remain a demoted assured shorthold tenancy until the proceedings are determined in favour of the tenant. A demoted assured shorthold tenancy will be terminable at any time during the demotion period. Unlike the position with non-demoted assured shorthold tenancies, a possession order granted on the basis that the landlord has given the required notice under s 21(4) of the 1988 Act can take effect within the first six months of the tenancy.

III L&T [228A.2]

Proceedings for possession A council's decision to take proceedings for possession in accordance with the Demoted Tenancies (Review of Decisions) (England) Regulations 2004, SI 2004/1679 may not be challenged for non-compliance with Article 6 of the Convention: *R (Gilboy) v Liverpool City Council* [2007] EWHC 2335 (Admin).

III L&T [228B]

20C. Assured shorthold tenancies following demoted tenancies

(1) Subsection (2) applies if—

(a) section 20B applies to an assured shorthold tenancy of a dwelling-house in England ("the demoted tenancy"),

(b) the landlord is a private registered provider of social housing,

(c) the demoted tenancy was created by an order under section 6A made after the coming into force of section 163(2) of the Localism Act 2011,

(d) the assured tenancy that was terminated by that order was an assured shorthold tenancy that, whether or not it was a fixed term tenancy when terminated by the order, was granted for a term certain of not less than two years,

(e) apart from subsection (2), the demoted tenancy would cease to be an assured shorthold tenancy by virtue of section 20B(2) or (4), and

(f) the landlord has served a notice within subsection (3) on the tenant before the demoted tenancy ceases to be an assured shorthold tenancy by virtue of section 20B(2) or (4).

(2) The demoted tenancy does not cease to be an assured shorthold tenancy by virtue of section 20B(2) or (4), and at the time when it would otherwise cease to be an assured shorthold tenancy by virtue of section 20B(2) to (4)—

(a) it becomes an assured shorthold tenancy which is a fixed term tenancy for a term certain, and

(b) section 20B ceases to apply to it.

(3) The notice must—

(a) state that, on ceasing to be a demoted assured shorthold tenancy, the tenancy will become an assured shorthold tenancy which is a fixed term tenancy for a term certain of the length specified in the notice,

(b) specify a period of at least two years as the length of the term of the tenancy, and

(c) set out the other express terms of the tenancy.

(4) Where an assured shorthold tenancy becomes a fixed term tenancy by virtue of subsection (2)—

(a) the length of its term is that specified in the notice under subsection (3), and

(b) its other express terms are those set out in the notice.

III L&T [228C]

20D. Assured shorthold tenancies following family intervention tenancies

(1) An assured tenancy that arises by virtue of a notice under paragraph 12ZA(2) of Schedule 1 in respect of a family intervention tenancy is an assured shorthold tenancy if—

- (a) the landlord under the assured tenancy is a private registered provider of social housing,
- (b) the dwelling-house is in England,
- (c) the family intervention tenancy was granted to a person on the coming to an end of an assured shorthold tenancy under which the person was a tenant, and
- (d) the notice states that the family intervention tenancy is to be regarded as an assured shorthold tenancy.

(2) This section does not apply if the family intervention tenancy was granted before the coming into force of section 163(3) of the Localism Act 2011.

III L&T [229]

21. Recovery of possession on expiry or termination of assured shorthold tenancy

(1) Without prejudice to any right of the landlord under an assured shorthold tenancy to recover possession of the dwelling-house let on the tenancy in accordance with Chapter I above, on or after the coming to an end of an assured shorthold tenancy which was a fixed term tenancy, a court shall make an order for possession of the dwelling-house if it is satisfied

- (a) that the assured shorthold tenancy has come to an end and no further assured tenancy (whether shorthold or not) is for the time being in existence, other than an assured shorthold periodic tenancy (whether statutory or not); and
- (b) the landlord or, in the case of joint landlords, at least one of them has given to the tenant not less than two months' notice in writing stating that he requires possession of the dwelling-house.

(1A) Subsection (1B) applies to an assured shorthold tenancy of a dwelling-house in England if—

- (a) it is a fixed term tenancy for a term certain of not less than two years, and
- (b) the landlord is a private registered provider of social housing.

(1B) The court may not make an order for possession of the dwelling-house let on the tenancy unless the landlord has given to the tenant not less than six months' notice in writing—

- (a) stating that the landlord does not propose to grant another tenancy on the expiry of the fixed term tenancy, and
- (b) informing the tenant of how to obtain help or advice about the notice and, in particular, of any obligation of the landlord to provide help or advice.

(2) A notice under paragraph (b) of subsection (1) above may be given before or on the day on which the tenancy comes to an end; and that subsection shall have effect notwithstanding that on the coming to an end of the fixed term tenancy a statutory periodic tenancy arises.

(3) Where a court makes an order for possession of a dwelling-house by virtue of subsection (1) above, any statutory periodic tenancy which has arisen on the coming to an end of the assured shorthold tenancy shall end (without further notice and regardless of the period) in accordance with section 5(1A).

(4) Without prejudice to any such right as is referred to in subsection (1) above, a court shall make an order for possession of a dwelling-house let on an assured shorthold tenancy which is a periodic tenancy if the court is satisfied

(a) that the landlord or, in the case of joint landlords, at least one of them has given to the tenant a notice in writing stating that, after a date specified in the notice, being the last day of a period of the tenancy and not earlier than two months after the date the notice was given, possession of the dwelling-house is required by virtue of this section; and

(b) that the date specified in the notice under paragraph (a) above is not earlier than the earliest day on which, apart from section 5 (1) above, the tenancy could be brought to an end by a notice to quit given by the landlord on the same date as the notice under paragraph (a) above.

(4ZA) In the case of a dwelling-house in England, subsection (4)(a) above has effect with the omission of the requirement for the date specified in the notice to be the last day of a period of the tenancy.

(4A) Where a court makes an order for possession of a dwelling-house by virtue of subsection (4) above, the assured shorthold tenancy shall end in accordance with section 5(1A).

(4B) A notice under subsection (1) or (4) may not be given in relation to an assured shorthold tenancy of a dwelling-house in England—

(a) in the case of a tenancy which is not a replacement tenancy, within the period of four months beginning with the day on which the tenancy began, and

(b) in the case of a replacement tenancy, within the period of four months beginning with the day on which the original tenancy began.

(4C) Subsection (4B) does not apply where the tenancy has arisen due to section 5(2).

(4D) Subject to subsection (4E), proceedings for an order for possession under this section in relation to a dwelling-house in England may not be begun after the end of the period of six months beginning with the date on which the notice was given under subsection (1) or (4).

(4E) Where—

(a) a notice under subsection (4) has been given in relation to a dwelling-house in England, and

(b) paragraph (b) of that subsection requires the date specified in the notice to be more than two months after the date the notice was given,

proceedings for an order for possession under this section may not be begun after the end of the period of four months beginning with the date specified in the notice.

(5) Where an order for possession under subsection (1) or (4) above is made in relation to a dwelling-house let on a tenancy to which section 19A above applies, the order may not be made so as to take effect earlier than

(a) in the case of a tenancy which is not a replacement tenancy, six months after the beginning of the tenancy, and

(b) in the case of a replacement tenancy, six months after the beginning of the original tenancy.

(6) In subsections (4B)(b) and (5)(b) above, the reference to the original tenancy is

(a) where the replacement tenancy came into being on the coming to an end of a tenancy which was not a replacement tenancy, to the immediately preceding tenancy, and

(b) where there have been successive replacement tenancies, to the tenancy immediately preceding the first in the succession of replacement tenancies.

(7) For the purposes of this section, a replacement tenancy is a tenancy

(a) which comes into being on the coming to an end of an assured shorthold tenancy, and

(b) under which, on its coming into being

(i) the landlord and tenant are the same as under the earlier tenancy as at its coming to an end, and

(ii) the premises let are the same or substantially the same as those let under the earlier tenancy as at that time.

(8) The Secretary of State may by regulations made by statutory instrument prescribe the form of a notice under subsection (1) or (4) given in relation to an assured shorthold tenancy of a dwelling-house in England.

(9) A statutory instrument containing regulations made under subsection (8) is subject to annulment in pursuance of a resolution of either House of Parliament.

Amendment *Sub-sections (1A) and (1B) are inserted by s 164 of the Localism Act 2011; in force from 1 April 2012. Section 164(2) of the Localism Act provides that the amendment does not apply in relation to an assured shorthold tenancy granted before the day on which the section comes into force, or which came into being by virtue of s 5 of the Housing Act 1988) on the coming to an end of an assured shorthold tenancy within sub-paragraph (a). As regards the insertion of sub-ss (4A) to (4E), the amendment of sub-s (6) and the addition of sub-ss (8) and (9), see the note at* **III L&T [229.7]**.

LANDLORD & TENANT AND HOUSING

III L&T [229.1]

Statutory periodic tenancy See the Housing Act 1988 s 5 (7), at para **III L&T [214]**.

III L&T [229.2]

The court See notes to the Housing Act 1988 s 40 (see para **III L&T [237]** onwards).

III L&T [229.2A]

Human rights: Housing Act 1988 s 21(4) Mandatory possession orders under Housing Act 1988 s 21(4) do not infringe Convention rights under Art 8. A procedure for the recovery of possession is necessary in a democratic society and the terms of s 21(4), expressing the will of Parliament, should be accepted as legitimate and proportionate: *Poplar Housing and Regeneration Community Association Ltd v Donoghue* [2001] EWCA Civ 595, [2002] QB 48, [2001] 4 All ER 604. An order giving a private landlord possession of a property held on an assured shorthold tenancy after serving a notice to quit under s 21(4)(b) does not breach Art 8: see *McDonald v McDonald* [2016] UKSC 28, where the Supreme Court held that, although there were some ECtHR authorities which supported the notion that Art 8 was engaged, there was no support for the proposition that the judge could have been required to consider the proportionality of the order which he would have made under the 1980 and 1988 Housing Acts.

III L&T [229.3]

Accelerated procedure for possession Section II of CPR Pt 55 (para **CPR 55**) and Section II of CPR PD 55 (para **CPR PD 55**) set out detailed procedural requirements for accelerated possession claims of property let on an assured shorthold tenancy. Such claims can now only be brought under s 21 of the Act and where the conditions in para **CPR 55.12** are satisfied. Claim form N5B and Form N11B defence, which must be filed within 14 days of service of the claim form, are prescribed. Specimens can be found at **BCCP O[82]** and **BCCP O[83]**.

CPR 55.16–55.18 (paras **CPR 55 16–CPR 55.18**) and CPR PD 55 paras 8.1 to 8.4 (para **CPR PD 55**) set out detailed provisions for the consideration of the papers by the judge and the making of an order for possession (with or without a hearing as appropriate). Where the judge is not satisfied (i) that the claim form was served and (ii) that the claimant has established that he is entitled to recover possession under s 21, he will direct that a date be fixed for a hearing and give any appropriate case management directions; or he may strike out the claim if the claim form discloses no reasonable grounds for bringing the claim. If, on the other hand, the judge is satisfied as to these matters he will make an order for possession without a hearing, see para **CPR 55.17** and CPR PD 55 para 8.1 (para **CPR PD 55**). In *Manel v Memon* (2000) 80 P & CR D22, CA, the Court of Appeal (in a decision on CCR Ord 49 r 6A, now revoked) considered the correct approach for the court in deciding whether it was "not satisfied" and stated that where, on its face, a reply raised an arguable defence, the judge could not be satisfied and had to fix a day for a hearing.

III L&T [229.3A]

Postponement of possession: exceptional hardship The procedure is set out at para **CPR 55.18** and in CPR PD 55 paras 8.2 to 8.4 (para **CPR PD 55**). If the defendant seeks postponement of possession on the ground of exceptional hardship under s 89 of Housing Act 1980, the judge has two options. He may postpone possession without directing a hearing but only if he considers that possession should be given up six weeks after the date of the order (or, if the defendant has requested postponement to an earlier date, on that date) and the claimant indicated on his claim form that he would be content for the court to make such an order without a hearing. In all other case the judge will direct a hearing of the issue of exceptional hardship. The hearing must be held before the date on which possession is to be given up. Where the judge is satisfied at the hearing that exceptional hardship would be caused by requiring possession to be given up by the date in the order of possession, he may vary the date on which possession must be given up, but the varied date may be no later than six weeks after the making of the order for possession.

III L&T [229.3B]

Notice under subsection (1) or (4) In *Spencer v Taylor* [2013] EWCA Civ 1600, [2014] HLR 113, [2013] All ER (D) 230 (Dec), Lewison LJ analysed s 21 in some detail. He addressed the view, held by some, that a section 21(1) notice is the appropriate notice where the contractual fixed term has not yet expired and that a section 21(4) notice is the appropriate notice after the contractual term has expired. This view is seemingly based on a reading of s 21(2) to the effect that a section 21(1) notice may only be served notice before or on the day on which the tenancy comes to an end. Lewison LJ points out that that is not what s 21(2) says. It seems, therefore, that a section 21(1) notice (which is not required to specify, or expire on, any particular date) is the appropriate notice both before and after expiry of a fixed term and that a section 21(4) notice may well be confined to cases where the periodic tenancy to which s 21(4) refers was a periodic tenancy from the outset.

Note that, as regards all ASTs created on or after 1 October 2015, the single prescribed Form 6A must in any event be used, whether possession is sought under s 21(1) or 21(4): see para **III L&T [229.7A]**.

III L&T [229.4]

Expiry of the notice The notice required by the Housing Act 1988 s 21(1)(b) must have expired before proceedings are started: *Lower Street Properties Ltd v Jones* (1996) 28 HLR 877, [1996] NPC 29, CA. In *Fernandez v McDonald* [2003] EWCA Civ 1219, [2003] 4 All ER 1033, (2003) Times, 9 October it was held that a notice which described the day following the last day of the shorthold periodic tenancy as the date for possession did not meet the requirements of s 21(4)(a) and was invalid. It should have identified the last date of the period. A notice expressed to expire "at the end of the period of your tenancy" has been held to be valid because it had the same meaning as "after the end of the period of your tenancy": *Notting Hill Housing Trust v Roomus* [2006] EWCA Civ 407, [2006] 1 WLR 1365. Although a notice that fails to specify a date that is the last day of a period of the tenancy is invalid (see *Fernandez v McDonald* above) a mistaken date did not invalidate a notice where the notice also contained the formula requiring possession "at the end of the period of your tenancy that will end after the expiry of two months from the service of this notice upon you": see *Spencer v Taylor* [2013] EWCA Civ 1600.

The requirement that the notice should expire on the last day of a period of the tenancy does not, however, apply to tenancies granted on or after 1 October 2015: see s 21(4ZA). From 1 October 2018 this subsection applies to all tenancies whenever they were created.

III L&T [229.4A]

The landlord The notice required by s 21(1)(b), in order to be effective, must come from the 'landlord' at the date that the notice was given. Where a mesne tenancy existed, the fact that it was to come to an end by the date specified in the notice would not render the head landlord a 'landlord' at the date of the notice: *Barrow v Kazim* [2018] EWCA Civ 2414.

III L&T [229.5]

Notices and break clauses A notice served under the Housing Act 1988 s 21(1)(b) may be sufficient to terminate a fixed term contract under a break clause: *Aylward v Fawaz* (1996) 29 HLR 408, Times, 15 July, CA. As regards tenancies granted on or after 1 October 2015 the notice may not be served within the first four months: see s 21(4B). From 1 October 2018 this subsection applies to all tenancies, whenever they were created.

III L&T [229.6]

Notice disallowed A landlord may be barred from serving a section 21 notice. Section 215 of the Housing Act 2004 precludes service of a section 21 notice where there is non-compliance with the tenancy deposit scheme: see **III L&T [324]**. Section 21B of the Housing Act 1988 (which was inserted by s 38 of the Deregulation Act 2015) precludes service of a section 21 notice if the landlord is in breach of a requirement imposed by regulations under sub-s 21B(1); note that this does not apply to tenancies granted before 1 October 2015 until October 2018.

Section 61 of the 2004 Act provides for the compulsory licensing of housing in multiple occupation and section 75 provides, as a sanction, that the landlord of an assured shorthold tenancy may not terminate it by a section 21 notice if the tenancy is located in an unlicensed house in multiple occupation (HMO). An HMO is defined by article 3 of the Licensing of Houses in Multiple Occupation (Prescribed Descriptions) (England) Order 2006, SI 2006/371 the basic conditions for an HMO being that (a) the HMO or any part of it comprises three storeys or more; (b) it is occupied by five or more persons; and (c) it is occupied by persons living in two or more single households. For additional conditions to be included in licences, see the Licensing of Houses in Multiple Occupation (Mandatory Conditions of Licences) (England) Regulations 2018, SI 2018/616.

III L&T [229.7]

The Deregulation Act amendments Sub-section (4ZA) was inserted by s 35 of the Deregulation Act 2015 and s 36 inserted sub-ss (4A), (4B), (4C), (4D) and (4E) and made a consequential amendment to sub-s (6). Subsections (8) and (9), which empower the Secretary of State prescribe the form of termination notices, were inserted by s 37 and came into force on 1 July 2015.

In addition, the Deregulation Act 2015 inserted ss 21A, 21B and 21C, which appear below, as provided by ss 38, 39 and 40.

All these amendments have effect in relation to assured shorthold tenancies granted on or after 1 October 2015, which is the commencement date set by SI 2015/994. However, it is provided, by s 41 of the Act that the new provisions to do not apply to tenancies already in existence on that date, until 1 October 2018. After 1 October the requirements to all tenancies, whenever they were granted.

III L&T [229.7A]

Prescribed form of notice In the case of a tenancy granted on or after 1 October 2015 the notice must be in the form prescribed by the Assured Shorthold Tenancy Notices and Prescribed Requirements Regulations 2015, SI 2015/1646, as amended by SI 2015/1725. In the explanatory memorandum to SI 2015/1646 it was noted that the lack of a standard form for a section 21 notice and lack of certainty over notice periods had led to a large number of notices being deemed to defective and treated as invalid by the courts. The notes to the new prescribed form (Form 6A) make clear that the form must be used for all ASTs created on or after 1 October 2015 (except for statutory periodic tenancies which came into being on or after 1 October 2015 at the end of fixed term ASTs created before 1 October 2015). The notes go on to say that, although there is no obligation to use Form N6 in relation to ASTs created prior to 1 October 2015, the form may nevertheless be used for all ASTs.

III L&T [229.8]

Retaliatory eviction Sections 33 and 34 of the Deregulation Act 2015 establish a new statutory regime for preventing retaliatory eviction. They were brought into force on 1 October 2015 by SI 2015/994 and apply to tenancies granted on or after that date but not to pre-existing tenancies until 1 October 2018. The provisions are as follows:

33. Preventing retaliatory eviction

(1) Where a relevant notice is served in relation to a dwelling-house in England, a section 21 notice may not be given in relation to an assured shorthold tenancy of the dwelling-house—

(a) within six months beginning with the day of service of the relevant notice, or

(b) where the operation of the relevant notice has been suspended, within six months beginning with the day on which the suspension ends.

(2) A section 21 notice given in relation to an assured shorthold tenancy of a dwelling-house in England is invalid where—

(a) before the section 21 notice was given, the tenant made a complaint in writing to the landlord regarding the condition of the dwelling-house at the time of the complaint,

(b) the landlord—

(i) did not provide a response to the complaint within 14 days beginning with the day on which the complaint was given,

(ii) provided a response to the complaint that was not an adequate response, or

(iii) gave a section 21 notice in relation to the dwelling-house following the complaint,

(c) the tenant then made a complaint to the relevant local housing authority about the same, or substantially the same, subject matter as the complaint to the landlord,

(d) the relevant local housing authority served a relevant notice in relation to the dwelling-house in response to the complaint, and

(e) if the section 21 notice was not given before the tenant's complaint to the local housing authority, it was given before the service of the relevant notice.

(3) The reference in subsection (2) to an adequate response by the landlord is to a response in writing which—

(a) provides a description of the action that the landlord proposes to take to address the complaint, and

(b) sets out a reasonable timescale within which that action will be taken.

(4) Subsection (2) applies despite the requirement in paragraph (a) for a complaint to be in writing not having been met where the tenant does not know the landlord's postal or e-mail address.

(5) Subsection (2) applies despite the requirements in paragraphs (a) and (b) not having been met where the tenant made reasonable efforts to contact the landlord to complain about the condition of the dwelling-house but was unable to do so.

(6) The court must strike out proceedings for an order for possession under section 21 of the Housing Act 1988 in relation to a dwelling-house in England if, before the order is made, the section 21 notice that would otherwise require the court to make an order for possession in relation to the dwelling-house has become invalid under subsection (2).

(7) An order for possession of a dwelling-house in England made under section 21 of the Housing Act 1988 must not be set aside on the ground that a relevant notice was served in relation to the dwelling-house after the order for possession was made.

(8) Subsection (1) does not apply where the section 21 notice is given after—

(a) the relevant notice has been wholly revoked under section 16 of the Housing Act 2004 as a result of the notice having been served in error,

(b) the relevant notice has been quashed under paragraph 15 of Schedule 1 to that Act,

(c) a decision of the relevant local housing authority to refuse to revoke the relevant notice has been reversed under paragraph 18 of Schedule 1 to that Act, or

(d) a decision of the relevant local housing authority to take the action to which the relevant notice relates has been reversed under section 45 of that Act.

(9) Subsection (2) does not apply where the operation of the relevant notice has been suspended.

(10) References in this section and section 34 to a relevant notice served, or complaint made, in relation to a dwelling-house include a relevant notice served, or complaint made, in relation to any common parts of the building of which the dwelling-house forms a part.

(11) But subsection (10) applies only if—

(a) the landlord has a controlling interest in the common parts in question, and

(b) the condition of those common parts is such as to affect the tenant's enjoyment of the dwelling-house or of any common parts which the tenant is entitled to use.

(12) In this section and section 34 a reference to a complaint to a landlord includes a complaint made to a person acting on behalf of the landlord in relation to the tenancy.

(13) In this section and section 34—

"assured shorthold tenancy" means a tenancy within section 19A or 20 of the Housing Act 1988;

"common parts", in relation to a building, includes—

(a) the structure and exterior of the building, and

(b) common facilities provided (whether or not in the building) for persons who include one or more of the occupiers of the building;

"controlling interest" means an interest which is such as to entitle the landlord to decide whether action is taken in relation to a complaint within this section or a relevant notice;

"dwelling-house" has the meaning given by section 45 of the Housing Act 1988;

"relevant local housing authority", in relation to a dwelling-house, means the local housing authority as defined in section 261(2) and (3) of the Housing Act 2004 within whose area the dwelling-house is located;

"relevant notice" means—

(a) a notice served under section 11 of the Housing Act 2004 (improvement notices relating to category 1 hazards),

(b) a notice served under section 12 of that Act (improvement notices relating to category 2 hazards), or

(c) a notice served under section 40(7) of that Act (emergency remedial action);

"section 21 notice" means a notice given under section 21(1)(b) or (4)(a) of the Housing Act 1988 (recovery of possession on termination of shorthold tenancy).

34. Further exemptions to section 33

(1) Subsections (1) and (2) of section 33 do not apply where the condition of the dwelling-house or common parts that gave rise to the service of the relevant notice is due to a breach by the tenant of—

(a) the duty to use the dwelling-house in a tenant-like manner, or

(b) an express term of the tenancy to the same effect.

(2) Subsections (1) and (2) of section 33 do not apply where at the time the section 21 notice is given the dwelling-house is genuinely on the market for sale.

(3) For the purposes of subsection (2), a dwelling-house is not genuinely on the market for sale if, in particular, the landlord intends to sell the landlord's interest in the dwelling-house to—

(a) a person associated with the landlord,

(b) a business partner of the landlord,

(c) a person associated with a business partner of the landlord, or

(d) a business partner of a person associated with the landlord.

(4) In subsection (3), references to a person who is associated with another person are to be read in accordance with section 178 of the Housing Act 1996.

(5) For the purposes of subsection (3), a business partner of a person ("P") is a person who is—

(a) a director, secretary or other officer of a company of which P is also a director, secretary or other officer,

(b) a director, secretary or other officer of a company in which P has a shareholding or other financial interest,

(c) a person who has a shareholding or other financial interest in a company of which P is a director, secretary or other officer,

(d) an employee of P,

(e) a person by whom P is employed, or

(f) a partner of a partnership of which P is also a partner.

(6) Subsections (1) and (2) of section 33 do not apply where the landlord is a private registered provider of social housing.

(7) Subsections (1) and (2) of section 33 do not apply where—

(a) the dwelling-house is subject to a mortgage granted before the beginning of the tenancy,

(b) the mortgagee is entitled to exercise a power of sale conferred on the mortgagee by the mortgage or by section 101 of the Law of Property Act 1925, and

(c) at the time the section 21 notice is given the mortgagee requires possession of the dwelling-house for the purpose of disposing of it with vacant possession in exercise of that power.

(8) In subsection (7)—

(a) "mortgage" includes a charge, and

(b) "mortgagee" includes a receiver appointed by the mortgagee under the terms of the mortgage or in accordance with the Law of Property Act 1925.

III L&T [229A]

[21A. Compliance with prescribed legal requirements]

[(1) A notice under subsection (1) or (4) of section 21 may not be given in relation to an assured shorthold tenancy of a dwelling-house in England at a time when the landlord is in breach of a prescribed requirement.

(2) The requirements that may be prescribed are requirements imposed on landlords by any enactment and which relate to—

(a) the condition of dwelling-houses or their common parts,

(b) the health and safety of occupiers of dwelling-houses, or

(c) the energy performance of dwelling-houses.

(3) In subsection (2) "enactment" includes an enactment contained in subordinate legislation within the meaning of the Interpretation Act 1978.

(4) For the purposes of subsection (2)(a) "common parts" has the same meaning as in Ground 13 in Part 2 of Schedule 2.

(5) A statutory instrument containing regulations made under this section is subject to annulment in pursuance of a resolution of either House of Parliament.]

III L&T [229A.1]

Tenancies not terminable while the landlord is in breach of statutory obligations This section was inserted by section 38 of the Deregulation Act 2015 but does not apply to tenancies granted before 1 October 2015, until 1 October 2018. The regulation-making powers became available from 1 July 2015. Certain requirements are also prescribed by the Assured Shorthold Tenancy Notices and Prescribed Requirements (England) Regulations 2015, SI 2015/1646, which require a landlord, in regard to a tenancy granted on or after 1 October 2015, to provide an energy performance certificate and a gas safety certificate and a copy of 'How to rent: the checklist for renting in England'.

III L&T [229A.2]

Gas Safety Certificate Regulation 36(6) of the Gas Safety (Installation and Use) Regulations 1998, SI 1998/2451 provides that a tenant must be provided with a copy of the gas safety certificate before going into occupation. It has been held that failure to do so invalidates a subsequent termination notice under s 21: *Assured Property Services Limited v Ooo* (2017) 30 June in the County Court at Edmonton, reported in Legal Action September 2017, at p 31. Note, however, that, in a further County Court decision, *Walcott v Jones* (2017)(Central London) (Judge Hand QC) 15 November, the court, in considering whether the additional obligations imposed by ss 21A and 21B invalidated a section 21 notice served in respect of an assured shorthold tenancy which had begun in 2007, held that, for the purpose of s 41 of the Deregulation Act 2015, the assured tenancy had been 'granted' in 2007 and not on any later extension or deemed re-letting.

III L&T [229B]

[21B. Requirement for landlord to provide prescribed information]

[(1) The Secretary of State may by regulations require information about the rights and responsibilities of a landlord and a tenant under an assured shorthold tenancy of a dwelling-house in England (or any related matters) to be given by a landlord under such a tenancy, or a person acting on behalf of such a landlord, to the tenant under such a tenancy.

(2) Regulations under subsection (1) may—

(a) require the information to be given in the form of a document produced by the Secretary of State or another person,

(b) provide that the document to be given is the version that has effect at the time the requirement applies, and

(c) specify cases where the requirement does not apply.

(3) A notice under subsection (1) or (4) of section 21 may not be given in relation to an assured shorthold tenancy of a dwelling-house in England at a time when the landlord is in breach of a requirement imposed by regulations under subsection (1).

(4) A statutory instrument containing regulations made under subsection (1) is subject to annulment in pursuance of a resolution of either House of Parliament.]

III L&T [229B.1]

Information and rights and obligations This section was inserted by section 39 of the Deregulation Act 2015 but does not apply to tenancies granted before 1 October 2015, until 1 October 2018. The regulation-making powers became available from 1 July 2015. The

Assured Shorthold Tenancy Notices and Prescribed Requirements (England) Regulations 2015, SI 2015/1646, require a landlord to provide certain information in regard to a tenancy granted on or after 1 October 2015, including a copy of 'How to rent: the checklist for renting in England'.

III L&T [229C]

[21C. Repayment of rent where tenancy ends before end of a period]

[(1) A tenant under an assured shorthold tenancy of a dwelling-house in England is entitled to a repayment of rent from the landlord where—

- (a) as a result of the service of a notice under section 21 the tenancy is brought to an end before the end of a period of the tenancy,
- (b) the tenant has paid rent in advance for that period, and
- (c) the tenant was not in occupation of the dwelling-house for one or more whole days of that period.

(2) The amount of repayment to which a tenant is entitled under subsection (1) is to be calculated in accordance with the following formula—

R x (D / P)

where—

R is the rent paid for the final period;

D is the number of whole days of the final period for which the tenant was not in occupation of the dwelling-house; and

P is the number of whole days in that period.

(3) If the repayment of rent described in subsections (1) and (2) has not been made when the court makes an order for possession under section 21, the court must order the landlord to repay the amount of rent to which the tenant is entitled.

(4) Nothing in this section affects any other right of the tenant to a repayment of rent from the landlord.]

III L&T [229C.1]

Repayment of rent in advance This section was inserted by section 39 of the Deregulation Act 2015 but does not apply to tenancies granted before 1 October 2015, until 1 October 2018. As for those to which the new section does not apply, the Apportionment Act 1870 may provide the solution.

CHAPTER III ASSURED AGRICULTURAL OCCUPANCIES

III L&T [230]

24. Assured agricultural occupancies

(1) A tenancy or licence of a dwelling-house is for the purposes of this Part of this Act an "assured agricultural occupancy" if

- (a) it is of a description specified in subsection (2) below; and
- (b) by virtue of any provision of Schedule 3 to this Act the agricultural worker condition is for the time being fulfilled with respect to the dwelling-house subject to the tenancy or licence.

(2) The following are the tenancies and licences referred to in subsection (1) (a) above

- (a) an assured tenancy which is not an assured shorthold tenancy;
- (b) a tenancy which does not fall within paragraph (a) above by reason only of paragraph 3, 3A, 3B or paragraph 7 of Schedule 1 to this Act (or of more than one of those paragraphs) and is not an excepted tenancy; and
- (c) a licence under which a person has the exclusive occupation of a dwelling-house as a separate dwelling and which, if it conferred a sufficient interest in land to be a tenancy, would be a tenancy falling within paragraph (a) or paragraph (b) above.

LANDLORD & TENANT AND HOUSING

(2A) For the purposes of subsection (2) (b) above, a tenancy is an excepted tenancy if it is

(a) a tenancy of an agricultural holding within the meaning of the Agricultural Holdings Act 1986 in relation to which that Act applies, or

(b) a farm business tenancy within the meaning of the Agricultural Tenancies Act 1995.

(3) For the purposes of Chapter I above and the following provisions of this Chapter, every assured agricultural occupancy which is not an assured tenancy shall be treated as if it were such a tenancy and any reference to a tenant, a landlord or any other expression appropriate to a tenancy shall be construed accordingly; but the provisions of Chapter I above shall have effect in relation to every assured agricultural occupancy subject to the provisions of this Chapter.

(4) Section 14 above shall apply in relation to an assured agricultural occupancy as if in subsection (1) of that section the reference to an assured tenancy were a reference to an assured agricultural occupancy.

III L&T [230.1]

Assured tenancy, assured shorthold tenancy See Housing Act 1988 ss 1, 20 (see paras **III L&T [213]**, **III L&T [227]**), respectively.

III L&T [230.2]

Schedule 1, paragraph 3 or 7 Housing Act 1988 Sch 1 paras 3, 3A, 3B, 3C (see para **III L&T [239]**) exclude tenancies at a low rent and para 7 excludes tenancies of agricultural holdings.

III L&T [230.3]

Proceedings for possession Proceedings for possession follow the same pattern as for proceedings in the county court generally for possession of land (see note at para **III L&T [211]**).

III L&T [230.4]

Forms See the Assured Tenancies and Agricultural Occupancies (Forms) (England) Regulations 2015, SI 2015/620, as amended by SI 2015/1646 and subsequently by SI 2016/443 and SI 2016/1118.

III L&T [231]

25. Security of tenure

(1) If a statutory periodic tenancy arises on the coming to an end of an assured agricultural occupancy

(a) it shall be an assured agricultural occupancy as long as, by virtue of any provision of Schedule 3 to this Act, the agricultural worker condition is for the time being fulfilled with respect to the dwelling-house in question; and

(b) if no rent was payable under the assured agricultural occupancy which constitutes the fixed term tenancy referred to in subsection (2) of section 5 above, subsection (3) (d) of that section shall apply as if for the words "the same as those for which rent was last payable under" there were substituted "monthly beginning on the day following the coming to an end of".

(2) In its application to an assured agricultural occupancy, Part II of Schedule 2 to this Act shall have effect with the omission of Ground 16.

(3) In its application to an assured agricultural occupancy, Part III of Schedule 2 to this Act shall have effect as if any reference in paragraph 2 to an assured tenancy included a reference to an assured agricultural occupancy.

(4) If the tenant under an assured agricultural occupancy gives notice to terminate his employment then, notwithstanding anything in any agreement or otherwise, that notice shall not constitute a notice to quit as respects the assured agricultural occupancy.
(5) Nothing in subsection (4) above affects the operation of an actual notice to quit given in respect of an assured agricultural occupancy.

III L&T [231.1]

Ground 16 Housing Act 1988 Sch 2 Pt II Ground 16 (see para **III L&T [243]**) is that the letting was in consequence of employment which has ceased.

CHAPTER IV PROTECTION FROM EVICTION

III L&T [232]

27. Damages for unlawful eviction

(1) This section applies if, at any time after 9 June 1988, a landlord (in this section referred to as "the landlord in default") or any person acting on behalf of the landlord in default unlawfully deprives the residential occupier of any premises of his occupation of the whole or part of the premises.

(2) This section also applies if, at any time after 9 June 1988, a landlord (in this section referred to as "the landlord in default") or any person acting on behalf of the landlord in default

- (a) attempts unlawfully to deprive the residential occupier of any premises of his occupation of the whole or part of the premises, or
- (b) knowing or having reasonable cause to believe that the conduct is likely to cause the residential occupier of any premises
  - (i) to give up his occupation of the premises or any part thereof, or
  - (ii) to refrain from exercising any right or pursuing any remedy in respect of the premises or any part thereof,

  does acts likely to interfere with the peace or comfort of the residential occupier or members of his household, or persistently withdraws or withholds services reasonably required for the occupation of the premises as a residence,

and, as a result, the residential occupier gives up his occupation of the premises as a residence.

(3) Subject to the following provisions of this section, where this section applies, the landlord in default shall, by virtue of this section, be liable to pay to the former residential occupier, in respect of his loss of the right to occupy the premises in question as his residence, damages assessed on the basis set out in section 28 below.

(4) Any liability arising by virtue of subsection (3) above

- (a) shall be in the nature of a liability in tort; and
- (b) subject to subsection (5) below, shall be in addition to any liability arising apart from this section (whether in tort, contract or otherwise).

(5) Nothing in this section affects the right of a residential occupier to enforce any liability which arises apart from this section in respect of his loss of the right to occupy premises as his residence; but damages shall not be awarded both in respect of such a liability and in respect of a liability arising by virtue of this section on account of the same loss.

(6) No liability shall arise by virtue of subsection (3) above if

- (a) before the date on which proceedings to enforce the liability are finally disposed of, the former residential occupier is reinstated in the premises in question in such circumstances that he becomes again the residential occupier of them; or

(b) at the request of the former residential occupier, a court makes an order (whether in the nature of an injunction or otherwise) as a result of which he is reinstated as mentioned in paragraph (a) above;

and, for the purposes of paragraph (a) above, proceedings to enforce a liability are finally disposed of on the earliest date by which the proceedings (including any proceedings on or in consequence of an appeal) have been determined and any time for appealing or further appealing has expired, except that if any appeal is abandoned, the proceedings shall be taken to be disposed of on the date of the abandonment.

(7) If, in proceedings to enforce a liability arising by virtue of subsection (3) above, it appears to the court

(a) that, prior to the event which gave rise to the liability, the conduct of the former residential occupier or any person living with him in the premises concerned was such that it is reasonable to mitigate the damages for which the landlord in default would otherwise be liable, or

(b) that, before the proceedings were begun, the landlord in default offered to reinstate the former residential occupier in the premises in question and either it was unreasonable of the former residential occupier to refuse that offer or, if he had obtained alternative accommodation before the offer was made, it would have been unreasonable of him to refuse that offer if he had not obtained that accommodation,

the court may reduce the amount of damages which would otherwise be payable to such amount as it thinks appropriate.

(8) In proceedings to enforce a liability arising by virtue of subsection (3) above, it shall be a defence for the defendant to prove that he believed, and had reasonable cause to believe

(a) that the residential occupier had ceased to reside in the premises in question at the time when he was deprived of occupation as mentioned in subsection (1) above or, as the case may be, when the attempt was made or the acts were done as a result of which he gave up his occupation of those premises; or

(b) that, where the liability would otherwise arise by virtue only of the doing of acts or the withdrawal or withholding of services, he had reasonable grounds for doing the acts or withdrawing or withholding the services in question.

(9) In this section

(a) "residential occupier", in relation to any premises, has the same meaning as in section 1 of the 1977 Act;

(b) "the right to occupy", in relation to a residential occupier, includes any restriction on the right of another person to recover possession of the premises in question;

(c) "landlord", in relation to a residential occupier, means the person who, but for the occupier's right to occupy, would be entitled to occupation of the premises and any superior landlord under whom that person derives title;

(d) "former residential occupier", in relation to any premises, means the person who was the residential occupier until he was deprived of or gave up his occupation as mentioned in subsection (1) or subsection (2) above (and, in relation to a former residential occupier, "the right to occupy" and "landlord" shall be construed accordingly).

III L&T [232.1]

Unlawfully deprives A landlord acting under a court order for possession is not acting unlawfully even though the order may later be set aside: *Hillgate House Ltd v Expert Clothing Service and Sales Ltd* [1987] 1 EGLR 65; *Brent London Borough Council v Botu* (2000) 33 HLR 151, CA. An eviction may be unlawful if carried out without a warrant even though a possession order may have been obtained: *Haniff v Robinson* [1993] QB 419, [1993] 1 All ER 185, CA. In *Murray v Aslam* (1994) 27 HLR 284, [1994] EGCS 160, CA, the court doubted whether changing the locks and putting the possessions outside fell within the Housing Act 1988 s 27 seeing that the tenant was readmitted two hours later. On the other hand, letting the premises while the tenant was on holiday and requiring him to share with the new occupants on his return was effectively driving him out by "acts likely to interfere with peace or comfort": *Abbott v Bayley* (1999) 32 HLR 72, 77 P & CR D44, CA.

III L&T [232.2]

Reinstatement The "provision" of a key is not by itself "reinstatement" or an "offer of reinstatement" where the front door lock is broken and the room in question has been wrecked: *Tagro v Cafane* [1991] 2 All ER 235, [1991] 1 WLR 378, CA. But a genuine offer to reinstate may be effective even if made after the commencement of proceedings for an injunction if made before the amendment of the claim to include damages under Housing Act 1988 s 27: *Tagro v Cafane* [1991] 2 All ER 235, [1991] 1 WLR 378, CA. An evicted tenant must choose between reinstatement and damages under s 27 (3), but need not do so until the hearing: *Osei-Bonsu v Wandsworth London Borough Council* [1999] 1 All ER 265, [1999] 1 WLR 1011, CA.

III L&T [232.3]

Residential occupier By the Protection from Eviction Act 1977 s 1, to which reference is made in the Housing Act 1988 s 27(9)(a), a residential occupier means "a person occupying the premises as a residence, whether under a contract or by virtue of any enactment or rule of law giving him the right to remain in occupation or restricting the right of any other person to recover possession of the premises". By the Housing Act 1980 Sch 25 para 61, the definition includes also a person let into possession of a dwelling-house under the terms of a rental purchase agreement. However, a "residential occupier", does not include a hotel guest paying a daily rate: *Brillouet v Landless* (1995) 28 HLR 836, CA.

III L&T [232.4]

Occupier's conduct The occupier's failure to pay rent is "conduct" within the Housing Act 1988 s 27(7)(a), which may provide a basis for reducing the amount of damages: *Regalgrand Ltd v Dickerson* (1996) 29 HLR 620, 74 P & CR 312, CA.

III L&T [232.5]

Landlord Purchasers of the property may be "landlords" within the Housing Act 1988 s 27 (9)(c) although only licensees vis-à-vis the vendors: *Jones and Lee v Miah and Miah* (1992) 24 HLR 578, [1992] 2 EGLR 50, CA. Also where there is a mortgage and the mortgagee takes possession and appoints a receiver who makes an unlawful eviction, it is the mortgagor, not the mortgagee, who is liable in damages: *Mehta v Royal Bank of Scotland plc* (1999) 32 HLR 45, [1999] 3 EGLR 153. The statute does not impose liability on persons responsible for an eviction who are not landlords: *Sampson v Wilson* [1996] Ch 39, [1995] 3 WLR 455, CA. Section 44 provides that this section and s 28 do not bind the Crown.

III L&T [232.6]

Liability apart from this section In *McCormack v Namjou* [1990] CLY 1725, cc, a tenant was reinstated seven days after a violent eviction and therefore outside the scope of the Housing Act 1988 s 27; but an award was made of £1260 general damages for the seven days out, £1500 by way of aggravated damages and £2000 by way of exemplary damages.

III L&T [232.7]

Set off of occupancy damages Where damages are awarded under the Housing Act 1988 s 27(3), the claimant is required by the Housing Act 1988 s 27(5) to treat that award as excluding further compensation at common law for the loss of the right to occupy the premises. In *Mason v Nwokorie* [1994] 1 EGLR 59, [1994] 05 EG 155, CA the Court of Appeal disallowed separate awards of aggravated damages and general damages on the ground that they were covered by the Housing Act 1988 s 27(5). Semble, separate awards for exemplary damages or for assault or damage to property would have been sustainable, if justified on the facts. Exemplary damages may be inappropriate, however, where the statutory compensation is significantly more than would be awarded at common law: *Francis v Brown* (1997) 30 HLR 143, [1997] CLY 3286, CA.

III L&T [232.8]

General damages for tortious acts preceding eviction General damages may be awarded in respect of wrongful acts of harassment which precede an unlawful eviction and such an award may be made in addition to the statutory award for the eviction: *Kaur v Gill* (1995) Times, 15 June, CA.

III L&T [232.9]

Statutory defence By s 27(8)(a) it is a defence for the landlord to prove that he believed, and had reasonable cause to believe, that, at the material time the residential occupier had ceased to reside on the premises. In *Osei-Bousa v Wandsworth London Borough Council* [1999] 1 All ER 265, [1999] 1 WLR 1011, CA where the landlord, acting on the defective notice to quit of one of two joint tenants, refused to allow the other tenant to return, it was held that the defence was not made out.

III L&T [232.10]

Precedent For a precedent for particulars of claim for statutory damages and also damages at common law, see **BCCP O[207]** which is suitable for inclusion in the claim form required by CPR 7 (see para **CPR 7**).

III L&T [233]

28. The measure of damages

(1) The basis for the assessment of damages referred to in section 27 (3) above is the difference in value, determined as at the time immediately before the residential occupier ceased to occupy the premises in question as his residence, between

(a) the value of the interest of the landlord in default determined on the assumption that the residential occupier continues to have the same right to occupy the premises as before that time; and

(b) the value of that interest determined on the assumption that the residential occupier has ceased to have that right.

(2) In relation to any premises, any reference in this section to the interest of the landlord in default is a reference to his interest in the building in which the premises in question are comprised (whether or not that building contains any other premises) together with its curtilage.

(3) For the purposes of the valuations referred to subsection (1) above, it shall be assumed

(a) that the landlord in default is selling his interest on the open market to a willing buyer;

(b) that neither the residential occupier nor any member of his family wishes to buy; and

(c) that it is unlawful to carry out any substantial development of any of the land in which the landlord's interest subsists or to demolish the whole or part of any building on that land.

(4) In this section "the landlord in default" has the same meaning as in section 27 above and subsection (9) of that section applies in relation to this section as it applies in relation to that.

(5) Section 113 of the Housing Act 1985 (meaning of "members of a person's family") applies for the purposes of subsection (3) (b) above.

(6) The reference in subsection (3) (c) above to substantial development of any of the land in which the landlord's interest subsists is a reference to any development other than

(a) development for which planning permission is granted by a general development order for the time being in force and which is carried out so as to comply with any condition or limitation subject to which planning permission is so granted; or

(b) a change of use resulting in the building referred to in subsection (2) above or any part of it being used as, or as part of, one or more dwelling-houses;

and in this subsection "general development order" has the same meaning as in section 56 (6) of the Town and Country Planning Act 1990 and other expressions have the same meaning as in that Act.

III L&T [233.1]

Awards of damages In *Tagro v Cafane* [1991] 2 All ER 235, [1991] 1 WLR 378, CA, the Court of Appeal upheld an award of £31,000, although on the high side, because the judge had applied the section correctly, adopting the claimant's expert's valuations. In *Farthing and Hughes v Colisanti* [1994] CLY 1769 (cc) the district judge assessed the damages for contravention of the statute at £9,000, which was to be divided equally between the two claimants, and awarded an additional £1,500 by way of exemplary damages.

In *Lambeth London Borough Council v Loveridge* [2014] UKSC 65 the Supreme Court has ruled on the proper approach to the calculation of damages under section 28.

III L&T [233.2]

Value of the interest determined The calculation of statutory compensation should be based on an evaluation of the rights of those involved: *Jones and Lee v Miah and Miah* (1992) 24 HLR 578, [1992] 2 EGLR 50, CA. In a case where the tenant has already given notice terminating his rights of occupancy from a certain date the court should have regard to the small remaining rights of occupancy when calculating the measure of damage: *King v Jackson* (1997) 30 HLR 541, [1998] 1 EGLR 30, CA.

III L&T [233.3]

Measurable gain for the landlord The measure of damages has to take account of the presence in the building of other tenants and licensees. If, as a result of their continuing presence, the eviction of the claimant causes no measurable gain for the landlord in the value of the property, the measure of damage is nil: *Melville v Bruton* (1996) 29 HLR 319, 140 Sol Jo LB 117, CA.

LANDLORD & TENANT AND HOUSING

CHAPTER V PHASING OUT OF RENT ACTS AND OTHER TRANSITIONAL PROVISIONS

III L&T [234]

34. New protected tenancies and agricultural occupancies restricted to special cases

(1) A tenancy which is entered into on or after the commencement of this Act cannot be a protected tenancy, unless

(a) it is entered into in pursuance of a contract made before the commencement of this Act; or

(b) it is granted to a person (alone or jointly with others) who, immediately before the tenancy was granted, was a protected or statutory tenant and is so granted by the person who at that time was the landlord (or one of the joint landlords) under the protected or statutory tenancy; or

(c) it is granted to a person (alone or jointly with others) in the following circumstances

(i) prior to the grant of the tenancy, an order for possession of a dwelling-house was made against him (alone or jointly with others) on the court being satisfied as mentioned in section 98 (1) (a) of, or Case 1 in Schedule 16 to, the Rent Act 1977 or Case 1 in Schedule 4 to the Rent (Agriculture) Act 1976 (suitable alternative accommodation available); and

(ii) the tenancy is of the premises which constitute the suitable alternative accommodation as to which the court was so satisfied; and

(iii) in the proceedings for possession the court considered that, in the circumstances, the grant of an assured tenancy would not afford the required security and, accordingly, directed that the tenancy would be a protected tenancy; or

(d) it is a tenancy under which the interest of the landlord was at the time the tenancy was granted held by the Commission for the New Towns or a development corporation, within the meaning of section 80 of the Housing Act 1985, and, before the date which has effect by virtue of paragraph (a) or paragraph (b) of subsection (4) of section 38 below, ceased to be so held by virtue of a disposal by the Commission for the New Towns made pursuant to a direction under section 37 of the New Towns Act 1981.

(2) In subsection (1) (b) above "protected tenant" and "statutory tenant" do not include

(a) a tenant under a protected shorthold tenancy;

(b) a protected or statutory tenant of a dwelling-house which was let under a protected shorthold tenancy which ended before the commencement of this Act and in respect of which at that commencement either there has been no grant of a further tenancy or any grant of a further tenancy has been to the person who, immediately before the grant, was in possession of the dwelling-house as a protected or statutory tenant;

and in this subsection "protected shorthold tenancy" includes a tenancy which, in proceedings for possession under Case 19 in Schedule 15 to the Rent Act 1977, is treated as a protected shorthold tenancy.

(3) In any case where

(a) by virtue of subsections (1) and (2) above, a tenancy entered into on or after the commencement of this Act is an assured tenancy, but

(b) apart from subsection (2) above, the effect of subsection (1) (b) above would be that the tenancy would be a protected tenancy, and

(c) the landlord and the tenant under the tenancy are the same as at the coming to an end of the protected or statutory tenancy which, apart from subsection (2) above, would fall within subsection (1) (b) above,

the tenancy shall be an assured shorthold tenancy (whether or not, in the case of a tenancy to which the provision applies, it fulfils the conditions in section 20 (1) above) unless, before the tenancy is entered into, the landlord serves notice on the tenant that it is not to be a shorthold tenancy.

(4) A licence or tenancy which is entered into on or after the commencement of this Act cannot be a relevant licence or relevant tenancy for the purposes of the Rent (Agriculture) Act 1976 (in this subsection referred to as "the 1976 Act") unless

(a) it is entered into in pursuance of a contract made before the commencement of this Act; or

(b) it is granted to a person (alone or jointly with others) who, immediately before the licence or tenancy was granted, was a protected occupier or statutory tenant, within the meaning of the 1976 Act, and is so granted by the person who at that time was the landlord or licensor (or one of the joint landlords or licensors) under the protected occupancy or statutory tenancy in question.

(5) Except as provided in subsection (4) above, expressions used in this section have the same meaning as in the Rent Act 1977.

III L&T [234.1]

Former shorthold The statutory tenancy arising on the expiry of a Rent Act protected shorthold does not fall within the scope of this section: *Ridehalgh v Horsefield* (1992) 24 HLR 453, [1992] NPC 46, CA.

III L&T [234.2]

New tenancy to which sub-s (1)(b) applies The tenancy need not be of the same premises and where the provisions of the Housing Act 1988 s 34(1)(b) apply they are mandatory: *Laimond Properties v Al-Shakarchi* (1998) 30 HLR 1099, [1998] NPC 19, CA.

The grant of a tenancy of more rooms than before does not necessarily involve a surrender of the former tenancy. The new tenancy is therefore protected: *Arogol Co Ltd v Rajah* [2001] EWCA Civ 454, [2002] HLR 422.

The new tenancy must, however, take effect immediately; there must be no gap between the surrender of the old tenancy and the start of the new: *Truro Diocesan Board of Finance Ltd v Foley* [2009] 1 All ER 814.

III L&T [234.3]

Required security in alternative accommodation The court should not make a direction under the Housing Act 1988 s 34(1)(c)(iii) if satisfied that an assured tenancy of suitable alternative accommodation would provide the required security: *Laimond Properties Ltd v Al-Shakarchi* (1998) 30 HLR 1099, [1998] NPC 19, CA.

III L&T [234.4]

Protection confined to those who were Rent Act protected on 15 January 1989 The status of being a protected tenant does not pass from the protected tenant to someone holding jointly with him or her if that person did not become a joint tenant until after 15 January 1989: *Secretarial Nominee Company Ltd v Thomas* [2005] EWCA Civ 1008, (2005) Times 20 September.

III L&T [235]

38. Transfer of existing tenancies from public to private sector

(1) The provisions of subsection (3) below apply in relation to a tenancy which was entered into before, or pursuant to a contract made before, the commencement of this Act if,

(a) at that commencement or, if it is later, at the time it is entered into, the interest of the landlord is held by a public body (within the meaning of subsection (5) below); and

(b) at some time after that commencement, the interest of the landlord ceases to be so held.

(2) The provisions of subsection (3) below also apply in relation to a tenancy which was entered into before, or pursuant to a contract made before, the commencement of this Act if,

(a) at the commencement of this Act or, if it is later, at the time it is entered into, it is a housing association tenancy; and

(b) at some time after that commencement, it ceases to be such a tenancy.

(3) Subject to subsections (4), (4ZA), (4A), (4BA) and (4B), below on and after the time referred to in subsection (1)(b) or, as the case may be, subsection (2)(b) above—

(a) the tenancy shall not be capable of being a protected tenancy, a protected occupancy or a housing association tenancy;

(b) the tenancy shall not be capable of being a secure tenancy unless (and only at a time when) the interest of the landlord under the tenancy is (or is again) held by a public body; and

(c) paragraph 1 of Schedule 1 to this Act shall not apply in relation to it, and the question whether at any time thereafter it becomes (or remains) an assured tenancy shall be determined accordingly.

(4) In relation to a tenancy under which, at the commencement of this Act or, if it is later, at the time the tenancy is entered into, the interest of the landlord is held by the Commission for the New Towns or a development corporation, within the meaning of section 80 of the Housing Act 1985 and which subsequently ceases to be so held by virtue of a disposal by the Commission for the New Towns made pursuant to a direction under section 37 of the New Towns Act 1981, subsections (1) and (3) above shall have effect as if any reference in subsection (1) above to the commencement of this Act were a reference to—

(a) the date on which expires the period of two years beginning on the day this Act is passed; or

(b) if the Secretary of State by order made by statutory instrument within that period so provides, such other date (whether earlier or later) as may be specified by the order for the purposes of this subsection.

LANDLORD & TENANT AND HOUSING

(4ZA) In relation to any time on or after the coming into force of this subsection, subsection (4) applies as if—

(a) the references to the Commission for the New Towns were references to the new towns residuary body;

(b) in the case of a disposal by the English new towns residuary body, the reference to section 37 of the New Towns Act 1981 were a reference to section 47 of the Housing and Regeneration Act 2008; and

(c) in the case of a disposal by the Welsh new towns residuary body, the words "made pursuant to a direction under section 37 of the New Towns Act 1981" were omitted.

(4A) Where, by virtue of a disposal falling within subsection (4) above and made before the date which has effect by virtue of paragraph (a) or paragraph (b) of that subsection, the interest of the landlord under a tenancy passes to a private registered provider of social housing or a registered social landlord (within the meaning of the Housing Act 1985 (see section 5 (4) and (5) of that Act)), then, notwithstanding anything in subsection (3) above, so long as the tenancy continues to be held by a body which would have been specified in subsection (1) of section 80 of the Housing Act 1985 if the repeal of provisions of that section effected by this Act had not been made, the tenancy shall continue to be a secure tenancy and to be capable of being a housing association tenancy.

(4BA) The references in subsections (4A) and (4B) to a body which would have been specified in subsection (1) of section 80 of the Housing Act 1985 if the repeal of provisions of that section effected by this Act had not been made includes a reference to the new towns residuary body.

(4B) Where, by virtue of a disposal by the Secretary of State made in the exercise by him of functions under Part III of the Housing Associations Act 1985, the interest of the landlord under a secure tenancy passes to a registered social landlord (within the meaning of the Housing Act 1985) then, notwithstanding anything in subsection (3) above, so long as the tenancy continues to be held by a body which would have been specified in subsection (1) of section 80 of the Housing Act 1985 if the repeal of provisions of that section effected by this Act had not been made, the tenancy shall continue to be a secure tenancy and to be capable of being a housing association tenancy.

(5) For the purposes of this section, the interest of a landlord under a tenancy is held by a public body at a time when

(a) it belongs to a local authority, a development corporation or an urban development corporation, all within the meaning of section 80 of the Housing Act 1985; or

(b) it belongs to a housing action trust established under Part III of this Act; or

(c) [. . .]; or

(d) it belongs to Her Majesty in right of the Crown or to a government department or is held in trust for Her Majesty for the purposes of a government department.

(5A) In this section "new towns residuary body" means—

(a) in relation to times before the coming into force of this subsection, the Commission for the New Towns; and

(b) in relation to other times—

(i) in relation to England, the Homes and Communities Agency so far as exercising functions in relation to anything transferred (or to be transferred) to it as mentioned in section 52(1)(a) to (d) of the Housing and Regeneration Act 2008 or the Greater London Authority so far as exercising its new towns and urban development functions (and any reference to the English new towns residuary body shall be construed accordingly); and

(ii) in relation to Wales, the Welsh Ministers so far as exercising functions in relation to anything transferred (or to be transferred) to them as mentioned in section 36(1)(a)(i) to (iii) of the New Towns Act 1981 (and any reference to the Welsh new towns residuary body shall be construed accordingly).

(6) In this section

(a) "housing association tenancy" means a tenancy to which Part VI of the Rent Act 1977 applies;

(b) "protected tenancy" has the same meaning as in that Act; and

(c) "protected occupancy" has the same meaning as in the Rent (Agriculture) Act 1976.

III L&T [235.1]

Public body Where the Crown Estate Commissioners sold the reversionary interest in residential properties to a housing association then, on application of sub-sections 38(3) and (5)(d), the occupying tenants became assured tenants rather than secure tenants: *Crown Estate Commissioners v Governors of the Peabody Trust* [2011] EWHC 1467 (Ch), [2011] NLJR 884, [2011] 24 EG 109 (CS).

III L&T [236]

39. Statutory tenants: succession

(1) [. . .]

(2) Where the person who is the original tenant, within the meaning of Part I of Schedule 1 to the Rent Act 1977, dies after the commencement of this Act, that Part shall have effect subject to the amendments in Part I of Schedule 4 to this Act.

(3) Where subsection (2) above does not apply but the person who is the first successor, within the meaning of Part I of Schedule 1 to the Rent Act 1977, dies after the commencement of this Act, that Part shall have effect subject to the amendments in paragraphs 5 to 9 of Part I of Schedule 4 to this Act.

(4) In any case where the original occupier, within the meaning of section 4 of the Rent (Agriculture) Act 1976 (statutory tenants and tenancies) dies after the commencement of this Act, that section shall have effect subject to the amendments in Part II of Schedule 4 to this Act.

(5) In any case where, by virtue of any provision of

(a) Part I of Schedule 1 to the Rent Act 1977, as amended in accordance with subsection (2) or subsection (3) above, or

(b) section 4 of the Rent (Agriculture) Act 1976, as amended in accordance with subsection (4) above,

a person (in the following provisions of this section referred to as "the successor") becomes entitled to an assured tenancy of a dwelling-house by succession, that tenancy shall be a periodic tenancy arising by virtue of this section.

(6) Where, by virtue of subsection (5) above, the successor becomes entitled to an assured periodic tenancy, that tenancy is one

(a) taking effect in possession immediately after the death of the protected or statutory tenant or protected occupier (in the following provisions of this section referred to as "the predecessor") on whose death the successor became so entitled;

(b) deemed to have been granted to the successor by the person who, immediately before the death of the predecessor, was the landlord of the predecessor under his tenancy;

(c) under which the premises which are let are the same dwelling-house as, immediately before his death, the predecessor occupied under his tenancy;

(d) under which the periods of the tenancy are the same as those for which rent was last payable by the predecessor under his tenancy;

LANDLORD & TENANT AND HOUSING

(e) under which, subject to sections 13 to 15 above, the other terms are the same as those on which, under his tenancy, the predecessor occupied the dwelling-house immediately before his death; and

(f) which, for the purposes of section 13 (2) above, is treated as a statutory periodic tenancy;

and in paragraphs (b) to (e) above "under his tenancy", in relation to the predecessor, means under his protected tenancy or protected occupancy or in his capacity as a statutory tenant.

(7) If, immediately before the death of the predecessor, the landlord might have recovered possession of the dwelling-house under Case 19 in Schedule 15 to the Rent Act 1977, the assured periodic tenancy to which the successor becomes entitled shall be an assured shorthold tenancy (whether or, not in the case of a tenancy to which the provision applies, it fulfils the conditions in section 20 (1) above).

(8) If, immediately before his death, the predecessor was a protected occupier or statutory tenant within the meaning of the Rent (Agriculture) Act 1976, the assured periodic tenancy to which the successor becomes entitled shall be an assured agricultural occupancy (whether or not it fulfils the conditions in section 24 (1) above).

(9) Where, immediately before his death, the predecessor was a tenant under a fixed term tenancy, section 6 above shall apply in relation to the assured periodic tenancy to which the successor becomes entitled on the predecessor's death subject to the following modifications

(a) for any reference to a statutory periodic tenancy there shall be substituted a reference to the assured periodic tenancy to which the successor becomes so entitled;

(b) in subsection (1) of that section, paragraph (a) shall be omitted and the reference in paragraph (b) to section 5 (3) (e) above shall be construed as a reference to subsection (6) (e) above; and

(c) for any reference to the coming to an end of the former tenancy there shall be substituted a reference to the date of the predecessor's death.

(10) If and so long as a dwelling-house is subject to an assured tenancy to which the successor has become entitled by succession, section 7 above and Schedule 2 to this Act shall have effect subject to the modifications in Part III of Schedule 4 to this Act; and in that Part "the predecessor" and "the successor" have the same meaning as in this section.

CHAPTER VI GENERAL PROVISIONS

III L&T [237]

40. Jurisdiction of county courts

(1) The county court shall have jurisdiction to hear and determine any question arising under any provision of

(a) Chapters I to III and V above, or

(b) sections 27 and 28 above,

other than a question falling within the jurisdiction of the appropriate tribunal by virtue of any such provision.

(2) [. . .]

(3) Where any proceedings under any provision mentioned in subsection (1) above are being taken in the county court, the court shall have jurisdiction to hear and determine any other proceedings joined with those proceedings, notwithstanding that, apart from this subsection, those other proceedings would be outside the court's jurisdiction.

(4) If any person takes any proceedings under any provision mentioned in subsection (1) above in the High Court, he shall not be entitled to recover any more costs of those proceedings than those to which he would have been entitled if the proceedings had been taken in the county court: and in such a case the taxing master shall have the same power of directing on what county court scale costs are to be allowed, and of allowing any item of costs, as the judge would have had if the proceedings had been taken in the county court.

(5) Subsection (4) above shall not apply where the purpose of taking the proceedings in the High Court was to enable them to be joined with any proceedings already pending before that court (not being proceedings taken under any provision mentioned in subsection (1) above).

Amendment *Sub-sections (4) and (5) are prospectively repealed by the Courts and Legal Services Act 1990, as from a day to be appointed.*

III L&T [237.1]

Questions for rent assessment committees The jurisdiction of rent assessment committees under this Act includes fixing the terms of a statutory periodic tenancy (Housing Act 1988 s 6, see para **III L&T [215]**) and determining rent (Housing Act 1988 ss 14 and 22).

III L&T [237.2]

Questions for county court The main questions which can arise for a county court under Chapters I to III and V are as follows: (a) claims for possession – the claimant must use particulars of claim attached to Form N5; (b) claims for possession where non-payment of rent is relied on – the Claimant must use particulars of claim in Form N119 attached to Form N5; (c) claims for possession under the accelerated procedure – Form N5B must be used; (d) claims for compensation for misrepresentation or concealment (s 12) or for unlawful eviction (s 27) – the claimant may use a Pt 7 or 8 claim form or an application notice under CPR Pt 23, as appropriate.

For details of the procedures, see paras **III L&T [211]**, **III L&T [216.1]**, **III L&T [216.1A]**, **III L&T [229.3]** and **III L&T [229.3A]**.

III L&T [237.3]

Costs The Housing Act 1988 s 40(4), (5) are prospectively repealed by the Courts and Legal Services Act 1990 Sch 20. The Courts and Legal Services Act 1990 s 4 makes fresh provision, by substituting a new Supreme Court Act 1981 s 51 (see para **II SCA [50]**), for penalising litigants who issue in the High Court when they ought reasonably to have issued in the county court.

III L&T [238]

45. Interpretation of Part I

(1) In this Part of this Act, except where the context otherwise requires,

"appropriate tribunal" means—

(a) in relation to a dwelling-house in England, the First-tier Tribunal or, where determined by or under Tribunal Procedure Rules, the Upper Tribunal;

(b) in relation to a dwelling-house in Wales, a rent assessment committee;

"dwelling-house" may be a house or part of a house;

"fixed term tenancy" means any tenancy other than a periodic tenancy;

"fully mutual housing association" has the same meaning as in Part I of the Housing Associations Act 1985;

"landlord" includes any person from time to time deriving title under the original landlord and also includes, in relation to a dwelling-house, any person other than a tenant who is, or but for the existence of an assured tenancy would be, entitled to possession of the dwelling-house;

"let" includes "sub-let";

"prescribed" means prescribed by regulations made by the Secretary of State by statutory instrument;

"rates" includes water rates and charges but does not include an owner's drainage rate, as defined in section 63 (2) (a) of the Land Drainage Act 1976;

"secure tenancy" has the meaning assigned by section 79 of the Housing Act 1985;

"statutory periodic tenancy" has the meaning assigned by section 5 (7) above;

"tenancy" includes a sub-tenancy and an agreement for a tenancy or sub-tenancy; and

"tenant" includes a sub-tenant and any person deriving title under the original tenant or sub-tenant.

(2) Subject to paragraph 11 of Schedule 2 to this Act, any reference in this Part of this Act to the beginning of a tenancy is a reference to the day on which the tenancy is entered into or, if it is later, the day on which, under the terms of any lease, agreement or other document, the tenant is entitled to possession under the tenancy.

(3) Where two or more persons jointly constitute either the landlord or the tenant in relation to a tenancy, then, except where this Part of this Act otherwise provides, any reference to the landlord or to the tenant is a reference to all the persons who jointly constitute the landlord or the tenant, as the case may require.

(4) For the avoidance of doubt, it is hereby declared that any reference in this Part of this Act (however expressed) to a power for a landlord to determine a tenancy does not include a reference to a power of re-entry or forfeiture for breach of any term or condition of the tenancy.

(5) Regulations under subsection (1) above may make different provision with respect to different cases or descriptions of case, including different provision for different areas.

Schedules

SCHEDULE 1
TENANCIES WHICH CANNOT BE ASSURED TENANCIES

Section 1

PART I
THE TENANCIES

TENANCIES ENTERED INTO BEFORE COMMENCEMENT

III L&T [239]

1 A tenancy which is entered into before, or pursuant to a contract made before, the commencement of this Act.

TENANCIES OF DWELLING-HOUSES WITH HIGH RATEABLE VALUES

2 (1) A tenancy—

(a) which is entered into on or after 1st April 1990 (otherwise than, where the dwelling-house had a rateable value on 31st March 1990, in pursuance of a contract made before 1st April 1990), and

(b) under which the rent payable for the time being is payable at a rate exceeding £25,000 a year.

(2) In sub-paragraph (1) "rent" does not include any sum payable by the tenant as is expressed (in whatever terms) to be payable in respect of rates [council tax], services, management, repairs, maintenance or insurance, unless it could not have been regarded by the parties to the tenancy as a sum so payable.

2A A tenancy—

(a) which was entered into before 1st April 1990, or on or after that date in pursuance of a contract made before that date, and

(b) under which the dwelling-house had a rateable value on 31st March 1990 which, if it is in Greater London, exceeded £1,500 and, if it is elsewhere, exceeded £750.

TENANCIES AT A LOW RENT

3 A tenancy under which for the time being no rent is payable.

3A A tenancy—

(a) which is entered into on or after 1st April 1990 (otherwise than, where the dwelling-house had a rateable value on 31st March 1990, in pursuance of a contract made before 1st April 1990), and

(b) under which the rent payable for the time being is payable at a rate of, if the dwelling-house is in Greater London, £1,000 or less a year and, if it is elsewhere, £250 or less a year.

3B A tenancy—

(a) which was entered into before 1st April 1990 or, where the dwelling-house had a rateable value on 31st March 1990, on or after 1st April 1990 in pursuance of a contract made before that date, and

(b) under which the rent for the time being payable is less than two-thirds of the rateable value of the dwelling-house on 31st March 1990.

3C Paragraph 2(2) above applies for the purposes of paragraphs 3, 3A and 3B as it applies for the purposes of paragraph 2(1).

BUSINESS TENANCIES

4 A tenancy to which Part II of the Landlord and Tenant Act 1954 applies (business tenancies).

LICENSED PREMISES

5 A tenancy under which the dwelling-house consists of or comprises premises licensed for the sale of intoxicating liquors for consumption on the premises.

TENANCIES OF AGRICULTURAL LAND

6 (1) A tenancy under which agricultural land, exceeding two acres, is let together with the dwelling-house.

(2) In this paragraph "agricultural land" has the meaning set out in section 26(3)(a) of the General Rate Act 1967 (exclusion of agricultural land and premises from liability for rating).

TENANCIES OF AGRICULTURAL HOLDINGS ETC

7 (1) A tenancy under which the dwelling-house—

(a) is comprised in an agricultural holding, and

(b) is occupied by the person responsible for the control (whether as tenant or as servant or agent of the tenant) of the farming of the holding.

(2) A tenancy under which the dwelling-house—

(a) is comprised in the holding held under a farm business tenancy, and

(b) is occupied by the person responsible for the control (whether as tenant or as servant or agent of the tenant) of the management of the holding.

(3) In this paragraph—

"agricultural holding" means any agricultural holding within the meaning of the Agricultural Holdings Act 1986 held under a tenancy in relation to which that Act applies, and "farm business tenancy" and "holding", in relation to such a tenancy, have the same meaning as in the Agricultural Tenancies Act 1995.

LETTINGS TO STUDENTS

8 (1) A tenancy which is granted to a person who is pursuing, or intends to pursue, a course of study provided by a specified educational institution and is so granted either by that institution or by another specified institution or body of persons.

(2) In sub-paragraph (1) above "specified" means specified, or of a class specified, for the purposes of this paragraph by regulations made by the Secretary of State by statutory instrument.

(3) A statutory instrument made in the exercise of the power conferred by sub-paragraph (2) above shall be subject to annulment in pursuance of a resolution of either House of Parliament.

HOLIDAY LETTINGS

9 A tenancy the purpose of which is to confer on the tenant the right to occupy the dwelling-house for a holiday.

RESIDENT LANDLORDS

10 (1) A tenancy in respect of which the following conditions are fulfilled—

(a) that the dwelling-house forms part only of a building and, except in a case where the dwelling-house also forms part of a flat, the building is not a purpose-built block of flats; and

(b) that, subject to Part III of this Schedule, the tenancy was granted by an individual who, at the time when the tenancy was granted, occupied as his only or principal home another dwelling-house which,—

(i) in the case mentioned in paragraph (a) above, also forms part of the flat; or

(ii) in any other case, also forms part of the building; and

(c) that, subject to Part III of this Schedule, at all times since the tenancy was granted the interest of the landlord under the tenancy has belonged to an individual who, at the time he owned that interest, occupied as his only or principal home another dwelling-house which,—

(i) in the case mentioned in paragraph (a) above, also formed part of the flat; or

(ii) in any other case, also formed part of the building; and

(d) that the tenancy is not one which is excluded from this sub-paragraph by sub-paragraph (3) below.

(2) If a tenancy was granted by two or more persons jointly, the reference in sub-paragraph (1)(b) above to an individual is a reference to any one of those persons and if the interest of the landlord is for the time being held by two or more persons jointly, the reference in sub-paragraph (1)(c) above to an individual is a reference to any one of those persons.

(3) A tenancy (in this sub-paragraph referred to as "the new tenancy") is excluded from sub-paragraph (1) above if—

(a) it is granted to a person (alone, or jointly with others) who, immediately before it was granted, was a tenant under an assured tenancy (in this sub-paragraph referred to as "the former tenancy") of the same dwelling-house or of another dwelling-house which forms part of the building in question; and

(b) the landlord under the new tenancy and under the former tenancy is the same person or, if either of those tenancies is or was granted by two or more persons jointly, the same person is the landlord or one of the landlords under each tenancy.

CROWN TENANCIES

11 (1) A tenancy under which the interest of the landlord belongs to Her Majesty in right of the Crown or to a government department or is held in trust for Her Majesty for the purposes of a government department.

(2) The reference in sub-paragraph (1) above to the case where the interest of the landlord belongs to Her Majesty in right of the Crown does not include the case ... that interest is under the management of the Crown Estate Commissioners

... by the Secretary of State as the result of the exercise by him of ... Part III of the Housing Associations Act 1985.

LOCAL AUTHORITY TENANCIES

12 (1) A tenancy ... the interest of the landlord belongs to—

(a) a local authority, ... in sub-paragraph (2) below;

(b) the Homes and Co... Agency but only if the tenancy falls within subsections (2A) to (2E) of ... 80 of the Housing Act 1985;

(ba) the Welsh Ministers but only if the tenancy falls within subsections (2A) to (2E) of section 80 of the Housing Act 1985;

(c) . . .

(d) an urban development corporation established by an order under section 135 of the Local Government, Planning and Land Act 1980;

(da) a Mayoral development corporation;

(e) a development corporation, within the meaning of the New Towns Act 1981;

(f) an authority established under section 10 of the Local Government Act 1985 (waste disposal authorities);

(fa) . . .

(g) a residuary body, within the meaning of the Local Government Act 1985;

(gg) The Residuary Body for Wales (Corff Gweddilliol Cymru);

(h) a fully mutual housing association, unless the tenancy is one which is ... from this sub-paragraph by sub-paragraph (3) below; or

... established under Part III of this Act.

... for the purposes of sub-paragraph (1)(a) ...

(a) the council of a county, county borough, district or London borough;

(b) the Common Council of the City of London;

(c) the Council of the Isles of Scilly;

(d) the Broads ...

(da) a National Park authority;

... Local Government Act 1985; ... section 88 of the Local ... section 103 of that Act; and ... Construction Act 2009; ... Wales;

... landlord belongs to a fully mutual housing ... paragraph (1) if all of the following ...

(c) the tenancy is granted on or after the date on which this sub-paragraph comes into force;

(d) the tenancy is in writing;

(e) before the tenancy is granted, the landlord has served on the person who is to be the tenant a notice stating that the tenancy is to be excluded from sub-paragraph (1);

(f) the tenancy states that it is excluded from sub-paragraph (1).

FAMILY INTERVENTION TENANCIES

12ZA (1) A family intervention tenancy.

(2) But a family intervention tenancy becomes an assured tenancy if the lan[illegible] notifies the tenant that it is to be regarded as an assured tenancy.

(3) In this paragraph "a family intervention tenancy" means [illegible] order under paragraph (4), a tenancy granted by a private registered prov[illegible] or a registered social landlord ("the landlord") in respe[illegible]

(a) to a person ("the new tenant") against [illegible]sured tenancy, on ground 7A of section 7 in respect of another dw[illegible] ground 14, 14ZA or 14A of Part 2 of

(i) has been made, in relati[illegible] Part 1 of Schedul[illegible] [illegible]ord, have been so made in relation Schedule 2 [illegible] the opinion of the la[illegible]

(ii) could [illegible] such a tenancy; [illegible] opinion of the landlord, have been so made if the

(iii) could, in the [illegible] person had had such a tenancy; and [illegible] provision of behaviour support services.

(b) for the purposes of the [illegible]

(4) A tenancy is not a family intervention tenancy for the purposes of this paragraph if the landlord has failed to serve a notice under sub-paragraph (5) on the new tenant before the new tenant entered into the tenancy.

(5) A notice under this sub-paragraph is a notice stating—

(a) the reasons for offering the tenancy to the new tenant;

(b) the dwelling-house in respect of which the tenancy is to b[illegible]

(c) the other main terms of the tenancy (including [illegible] new tenant agreeing new tenant in respect of behavio[illegible]

(d) the security of tenure [illegible] security of te[illegible] to enter into the tenancy; [illegible] not obliged to enter into the tenancy or (unless that the new tenant is not obliged to enter into the otherwise required to do so) to surrender any existing tenancy or possession of a dwelling-house;

(e) [illegible] any existing tenancy or possession of a dwelling-[illegible] any likely [illegible] house.

(f) [illegible] national authority may by regulation [illegible] the new tenant as to how [illegible] to obtain advice to the new tenant as to [illegible] relation to the notice.

(7) The appropriate national authority [illegible]

(8) [illegible] amend [illegible] instrument [illegible] sub-paragraph [illegible] any [illegible] statutory [illegible]

(9) Regulations [illegible] paragraph [illegible] saving provision [illegible] notices [illegible]

(10) A statutory [illegible] to ob[illegible] regulations under this [illegible] may be [illegible] Parliament.

of sub-paragraph (5) may [illegible]

(a) by the Secretary [illegible] before, and approved by [illegible] regarding the termination of such tenancies are contained in section 298 of that Act, the text of which is set out at **III L&T [344]**. See also the Family Intervention Tenancies (Review of Local Authority Decisions) (England) Regulations 2008, SI 2008/3111.

III L&T [239.6]

Exclusion of tenancies with a high rent With effect from 10 October 2010 the assured tenancy ceiling of £25,000 annual rent, in Sch 1, para 2(1)(b), has been raised to £100,000 by the Assured Tenancies (Amendment) (England) Order 2010, SI 2010/908. In Wales the same increase was effected, as from 1st December 2011, by the Assured Tenancies (Amendment of Rental Threshold) (Wales) Order 2011, SI 2011/1409 (W 169).

PART II
RATEABLE VALUES

III L&T [240]

14. (1) The rateable value of a dwelling-house at any time shall be ascertained for the purposes of Part I of this Schedule as follows

(a) if the dwelling-house is a hereditament for which a rateable value is then shown in the valuation list, it shall be that rateable value;

(b) if the dwelling-house forms part only of such a hereditament or consists of or forms part of more than one such hereditament, its rateable value shall be taken to be such value as is found by a proper apportionment or aggregation of the rateable value or values so shown.

(2) Any question arising under this Part of this Schedule as to the proper apportionment or aggregation of any value or values shall be determined by the county court and the decision of that court shall be final.

15. Where, after the time at which the rateable value of a dwelling-house is material for the purposes of any provision of Part I of this Schedule, the valuation list is altered so as to vary the rateable value of the hereditament of which the dwelling-house consists (in whole or in part) or forms part and the alteration has effect from that time or from an earlier time, the rateable value of the dwelling-house at the material time shall be ascertained as if the value shown in the valuation list at the material time had been the value shown in the list as altered.

16. Paragraphs 14 and 15 above apply in relation to any other land which, under section 2 of this Act, is treated as part of a dwelling-house as they apply in relation to the dwelling-house itself.

III L&T [240.1]

Certification of rateable value Provision is made in the Local Government Finance (Repeals, Savings and Consequential Amendments) Order 1990, SI 1990/776, art 4 for the certification of rateable values in respect of premises comprised in assured tenancies entered into before 1 April 1990 (when rates and rateable values were abolished) where either no rateable value had been assigned or proposed at that date, or no variation in the value had been made or proposed following structural alteration of the premises.

PART III
PROVISIONS FOR DETERMINING APPLICATION OF PARAGRAPH 10 (RESIDENT LANDLORDS)

III L&T [241]

17. (1) In determining whether the condition in paragraph 10(1)(c) above is at any time fulfilled with respect to a tenancy, there shall be disregarded

(a) any period of not more than twenty-eight days, beginning with the date on which the interest of the landlord under the tenancy becomes vested at law and in equity in an individual who, during that period, does not occupy as his only or principal home another dwelling-house which forms part of the building or, as the case may be, flat concerned;

(b) if, within a period falling within paragraph (a) above, the individual concerned notifies the tenant in writing of his intention to occupy as his only or principal home another dwelling-house in the building or, as the case may be, flat concerned, the period beginning with the date on which the interest of the landlord under the tenancy becomes vested in that individual as mentioned in that paragraph and ending

(i) at the expiry of the period of six months beginning on that date, or

(ii) on the date on which that interest ceases to be so vested, or

(iii) on the date on which that interest becomes again vested in such an individual as is mentioned in paragraph 10(1)(c) or the condition in that paragraph becomes deemed to be fulfilled by virtue of paragraph 18(1) or paragraph 20 below,

whichever is the earlier; and

(c) any period of not more than two years beginning with the date on which the interest of the landlord under the tenancy becomes, and during which it remains, vested

(i) in trustees as such; or

(ii) by virtue of section 9 of the Administration of Estates Act 1925, in the Probate Judge or the Public Trustee.

(2) Where the interest of the landlord under a tenancy becomes vested at law and in equity in two or more persons jointly, of whom at least one was an individual, sub-paragraph (1) above shall have effect subject to the following modifications

(a) in paragraph (a) for the words from "an individual" to "occupy" there shall be substituted "the joint landlords if, during that period none of them occupies"; and

(b) in paragraph (b) for the words "the individual concerned" there shall be substituted "any of the joint landlords who is an individual" and for the words "that individual" there shall be substituted "the joint landlords".

18. (1) During any period when

(a) the interest of the landlord under the tenancy referred to in paragraph 10 above is vested in trustees as such, and

(b) that interest is . . . held on trust for any person who or for two or more persons of whom at least one occupies as his only or principal home a dwelling-house which forms part of the building or, as the case may be, flat referred to in paragraph 10 (1) (a),

the condition in paragraph 10(1)(c) shall be deemed to be fulfilled and accordingly, no part of that period shall be disregarded by virtue of paragraph 17 above.

(2) If a period during which the condition in paragraph 10(1)(c) is deemed to be fulfilled by virtue of sub-paragraph (1) above comes to an end on the death of a person who was in occupation of a dwelling-house as mentioned in paragraph (b) of that sub-paragraph, then, in determining whether that condition is at any time thereafter fulfilled, there shall be disregarded any period

(a) which begins on the date of the death;

(b) during which the interest of the landlord remains vested as mentioned in sub-paragraph (1)(a) above; and

(c) which ends at the expiry of the period of two years beginning on the date of the death or on any earlier date on which the condition in paragraph 10(1)(c) becomes again deemed to be fulfilled by virtue of sub-paragraph (1) above.

19. In any case where

(a) immediately before a tenancy comes to an end the condition in paragraph 10(1)(c) is deemed to be fulfilled by virtue of paragraph 18(1) above, and

(b) on the coming to an end of that tenancy the trustees in whom the interest of the landlord is vested grant a new tenancy of the same or substantially the same dwelling-house to a person (alone or jointly with others) who was the tenant or one of the tenants under the previous tenancy,

the condition in paragraph 10(1)(b) above shall be deemed to be fulfilled with respect to the new tenancy.

20. (1) The tenancy referred to in paragraph 10 above falls within this paragraph if the interest of the landlord under the tenancy becomes vested in the personal representatives of a deceased person acting in that capacity.

(2) If the tenancy falls within this paragraph, the condition in paragraph 10 (1) (c) shall be deemed to be fulfilled for any period, beginning with the date on which the interest becomes vested in the personal representatives and not exceeding two years, during which the interest of the landlord remains so vested.

21. Throughout any period which, by virtue of paragraph 17 or paragraph 18(2) above, falls to be disregarded for the purpose of determining whether the condition in paragraph 10(1)(c) is fulfilled with respect to a tenancy, no order shall be made for possession of the dwelling-house subject to that tenancy, other than an order which might be made if that tenancy were or, as the case may be, had been an assured tenancy.

22. For the purposes of paragraph 10 above, a building is a purpose-built block of flats if as constructed it contained, and it contains, two or more flats; and for this purpose "flat" means a dwelling-house which

(a) forms part only of a building; and

(b) is separated horizontally from another dwelling-house which forms part of the same building.

SCHEDULE 2

GROUNDS FOR POSSESSION OF DWELLING-HOUSES LET ON ASSURED TENANCIES

Section 7

PART I

GROUNDS ON WHICH COURT MUST ORDER POSSESSION

GROUND 1

III L&T [242]

Not later than the beginning of the tenancy the landlord gave notice in writing to the tenant that possession might be recovered on this ground or the court is of the opinion that it is just and equitable to dispense with the requirement of notice and (in either case)

(a) at some time before the beginning of the tenancy, the landlord who is seeking possession or, in the case of joint landlords seeking possession, at least one of them occupied the dwelling-house as his only or principal home; or

(b) the landlord who is seeking possession or, in the case of joint landlords seeking possession, at least one of them requires the dwelling-house as his, his spouse's or his civil partner's only or principal home and neither the landlord (or, in the case of joint landlords, any one of them) nor any other person who, as landlord, derived title under the landlord who gave the notice mentioned above acquired the reversion on the tenancy for money or money's worth.

GROUND 2

The dwelling-house is subject to a mortgage granted before the beginning of the tenancy and

(a) the mortgagee is entitled to exercise a power of sale conferred on him by the mortgage or by section 101 of the Law of Property Act 1925; and
(b) the mortgagee requires possession of the dwelling-house for the purpose of disposing of it with vacant possession in exercise of that power; and
(c) either notice was given as mentioned in Ground 1 above or the court is satisfied that it is just and equitable to dispense with the requirement of notice;

and for the purposes of this ground "mortgage" includes a charge and "mortgagee" shall be construed accordingly.

Ground 3

The tenancy is a fixed term tenancy for a term not exceeding eight months and
(a) not later than the beginning of the tenancy the landlord gave notice in writing to the tenant that possession might be recovered on this ground; and
(b) at some time within the period of twelve months ending with the beginning of the tenancy, the dwelling-house was occupied under a right to occupy it for a holiday.

Ground 4

The tenancy is a fixed term tenancy for a term not exceeding twelve months and
(a) not later than the beginning of the tenancy the landlord gave notice in writing to the tenant that possession might be recovered on this ground; and
(b) at some time within the period of twelve months ending with the beginning of the tenancy, the dwelling-house was let on a tenancy falling within paragraph 8 of Schedule 1 to this Act.

Ground 5

The dwelling-house is held for the purpose of being available for occupation by a minister of religion as a residence from which to perform the duties of his office and
(a) not later than the beginning of the tenancy the landlord gave notice in writing to the tenant that possession might be recovered on this ground; and
(b) the court is satisfied that the dwelling-house is required for occupation by a minister of religion as such a residence.

Ground 6

The landlord who is seeking possession or, if that landlord is a non-profit registered provider of social housing, registered social landlord or charitable housing trust, or (where the dwelling-house is social housing within the meaning of Part 2 of the Housing and Regeneration Act 2008) a profit-making registered provider of social housing, a superior landlord intends to demolish or reconstruct the whole or a substantial part of the dwelling-house or to carry out substantial works on the dwelling-house or any part thereof or any building of which it forms part and the following conditions are fulfilled—
(a) the intended work cannot reasonably be carried out without the tenant giving up possession of the dwelling-house because—
(i) the tenant is not willing to agree to such a variation of the terms of the tenancy as would give such access and other facilities as would permit the intended work to be carried out, or
(ii) the nature of the intended work is such that no such variation is practicable, or

(iii) the tenant is not willing to accept an assured tenancy of such part only of the dwelling-house (in this sub-paragraph referred to as "the reduced part") as would leave in the possession of his landlord so much of the dwelling-house as would be reasonable to enable the intended work to be carried out and, where appropriate, as would give such access and other facilities over the reduced part as would permit the intended work to be carried out, or

(iv) the nature of the intended work is such that such a tenancy is not practicable; and

(b) either the landlord seeking possession acquired his interest in the dwelling-house before the grant of the tenancy or that interest was in existence at the time of that grant and neither that landlord (or, in the case of joint landlords, any of them) nor any other person who, alone or jointly with others, has acquired that interest since that time acquired it for money or money's worth; and

(c) the assured tenancy on which the dwelling-house is let did not come into being by virtue of any provision of Schedule 1 to the Rent Act 1977, as amended by Part I of Schedule 4 to this Act or, as the case may be, section 4 of the Rent (Agriculture) Act 1976, as amended by Part II of that Schedule.

For the purposes of this ground, if, immediately before the grant of the tenancy, the tenant to whom it was granted or, if it was granted to joint tenants, any of them was the tenant or one of the joint tenants of the dwelling-house concerned under an earlier assured tenancy [or, as the case may be, under a tenancy to which Schedule 10 to the Local Government and Housing Act 1989 applied], any reference in paragraph (b) above to the grant of the tenancy is a reference to the grant of that earlier assured tenancy or, as the case may be, to the grant of the tenancy to which the said Schedule 10 applied.

For the purposes of this ground "registered social landlord" has the same meaning as in the Housing Act 1985 (see section 5(4) and (5) of that Act)] and "charitable housing trust" means a housing trust, within the meaning of the Housing Associations Act 1985, which is a charity...

[. . .]

Ground 7

The tenancy is a periodic tenancy (including a statutory periodic tenancy) or a fixed term tenancy of a dwelling-house in England, which has devolved under the will or intestacy of the former tenant and the proceedings for the recovery of possession are begun not later than twelve months after the death of the former tenant or, if the court so directs, after the date on which, in the opinion of the court, the landlord or, in the case of joint landlords, any one of them became aware of the former tenant's death.

For the purposes of this ground, the acceptance by the landlord of rent from a new tenant after the death of the former tenant shall not be regarded as creating a new tenancy, unless the landlord agrees in writing to a change (as compared with the tenancy before the death) in the amount of the rent, the period [or length of term] of the tenancy, the premises which are let or any other term of the tenancy.

This ground does not apply to a fixed term tenancy that is a lease of a dwelling-house—

(a) granted on payment of a premium calculated by reference to a percentage of the value of the dwelling-house or of the cost of providing it, or

(b) under which the lessee (or the lessee's personal representatives) will or may be entitled to a sum calculated by reference, directly or indirectly, to the value of the dwelling-house.

GROUND 8

Both at the date of the service of the notice under section 8 of this Act relating to the proceedings for possession and at the date of the hearing

(a) if rent is payable weekly or fortnightly, at least eight weeks' rent is unpaid;

(b) if rent is payable monthly, at least two months' rent is unpaid;

(c) if rent is payable quarterly, at least one quarter's rent is more than three months in arrears; and

(d) if rent is payable yearly, at least three months' rent is more than three months in arrears;

and for the purpose of this ground "rent" means rent lawfully due from the tenant.

III L&T [242.1]

Rent Act cases The Housing Act 1988 Sch 2 Pt I Grounds 1, 3, 4 and 5 have some points of similarity with the Rent Act 1977 Sch 15 Cases 11, 13, 14 and 15 (see para **III L&T [83]**) respectively.

III L&T [242.2]

Just and equitable The discretion to grant possession under Housing Act 1988 Sch 2 Pt I Ground 1 (b), although the requirement as to notice was not satisfied, may be exercised where this would be just and equitable, without it being necessary to show exceptional circumstances: *Boyle v Verrall* (1996) 29 HLR 436, [1997] 1 EGLR 25, CA; *Mustafa v Ruddock* (1997) 30 HLR 495, CA.

III L&T [242.3]

Grounds 1, 3, 4 and 5 The accelerated procedure for obtaining possession under Grounds 1, 3, 4 or 5 is no longer available following the revocation, with effect from 2 October 2000, of CCR 49 r6.

III L&T [242.4]

Precedents for possession claims For a summary of the prescribed forms for possession claims, see paras **III L&T [211]** and **III L&T [237.2]** and **BCCP O[12]**. For precedents, see **BCCP O[201]–BCCP O[204]**.

III L&T [242.5]

Ground 6 Ground 6 has various features in common with the Landlord and Tenant Act 1954 s 30 (1)(f) (landlord's intention to demolish etc. as a ground for offering a new tenancy) (see para **III L&T [22]**): the notes on that provision may assist in the interpretation of Housing Act 1988 Sch 2 Ground 6. References to "registered social landlords" were included by the Housing Act 1996 (Consequential Provisions) Order 1996, SI 1996/2325. Further references to non-profit and profit-making providers of social housing included with effect, subject to savings and transitional provisions, from 1 April 2010: see the Housing and Regeneration Act 2008 (Consequential Provisions) Order 2010.

III L&T [242.5A]

Ground 7 Ground 7 shown as amended (by deletion of text in italics and insertion of text in square brackets) by s 162 of the Localism Act 2011 (section in force from 1 April 2012) and also by Part 23 of Sch 25 to the 2011 Act with effect from 3 August 2012. "Proceedings for the recovery of possession" (which must be brought within one of the specified 12-month periods) begin when the landlord commences court proceedings and not when he serves a s 8 notice; see *Shepping v Osada* (2000) 33 HLR 146, [2000] 2 EGLR 38, CA.

III L&T [242.6]

Ground 8 The Housing Act 1988 Sch 2 Ground 8 paras (a) and (b) are printed with the reduced periods of weeks and months substituted by the Housing Act 1996 s 101. The amendments took effect on 28 February 1997 except where Housing Act 1988 s 8 notices (see para **III L&T [217]**) had already been served or dispensed with: Housing Act 1996 (Commencement No 7 and Savings) Order 1997, SI 1997/225. Where possession is ordered on Ground 8 the order should say so, otherwise it may be inferred that is was ordered on Ground 10, thus permitting subsequent applications to suspend which would otherwise be excluded by s 9(6): see *Capital Prime Plus plc v Wills* (1998) 31 HLR 926, CA.

Where a cheque for the rent is offered and accepted before the hearing but not cleared until after the hearing during an adjournment period, the payment is effective from the time that it was delivered: *Day v Coltrane* [2003] EWCA Civ 342, [2003] 1 WLR 1379, (2003) Times,

14 April applying the principle established in *Marrecco v Richardson* [1908] 2 KB 584, CA. The position is unclear where the hearing is adjourned for other reasons, such as for the trial of the tenant's claim for damages for disrepair: *Mountain v Hastings* (1993) 25 HLR 427.

Where, at the date of the hearing, a sum ordered to be paid into court (under **CPR 3.1**) was available in court subject only to determination of a counterclaim, it was held that to ignore that sum, in assessing arrears for the purpose of Ground 8, would lead to an artificial and inequitable result: see *Etherington v Burt* [2004] EWHC 95 (QB). Note, however, that it is not legitimate for the court to order an adjournment for the purpose of enabling a tenant to reduce rent arrears below the threshold in Ground 8 save in exceptional circumstances; the power to adjourn is not to be exercised so as to defeat the policy of the Act or the rights which it conferred on landlords: see *North British Housing Association Ltd v Lorraine Matthews* [2004] EWCA Civ 1736, [2004] All ER (D) 344 (Dec).

III L&T [242.6A]

Effect of tenant's bankruptcy The making of a bankruptcy order or a debt relief order does not preclude the making of a possession order against an assured tenant on the ground of rent arrears. Where the arrears are provable in the tenant's bankruptcy or are subject to the debt relief order, no order for payment of arrears can be made: *Sharples v Places for People Homes Ltd* [2011] EWCA Civ 813, [2011] All ER (D) 170 (Jul).

III L&T [242.7]

Rent unpaid but tendered by a third party A landlord is entitled to rely on Housing Act 1988 Sch 2 Ground 8 and to reject payment in respect of arrears if the payment is tendered by a resident third party who is not a tenant, nor acting as authorised agent of the tenant: *Bessa Plus plc v Lancaster* (1997) 30 HLR 48, CA.

III L&T [242.8]

Beginning of the tenancy See Housing Act 1988 s 45(2) (see para **III L&T [238]**) and Sch 2 Ground 11 (see para **III L&T [245]**) for the meaning of "beginning of the tenancy".

III L&T [242.9]

Assured tenancy by succession It is provided by Housing Act 1988 s 39(10) (see para **III L&T [236]**), Sch 4 para 15(1) that, in the case of an assured tenancy by succession, any notice given to the predecessor for the purposes of the Rent Act 1977 Sch 15 Case 13, 14, or 15 (see para **III L&T [83]**), is to be treated as given for the purposes of the Housing Act 1988 Sch 2 Ground 3, 4 or, as the case may be.

III L&T [242.10]

Joint landlords The Housing Act 1988 Sch 2 Ground 7 (see para **III L&T [245]**) provides, as an exception to the general rule in the Housing Act 1988 s 45(3) (see para **III L&T [238]**), that the notice required to be given by the landlord, for Housing Act 1988 Sch 2 Grounds 1–5, may in the case of joint landlords be given by one of them.

PART II
GROUNDS ON WHICH COURT MAY ORDER POSSESSION

Ground 9

III L&T [243]

Suitable alternative accommodation is available for the tenant or will be available for him when the order for possession takes effect.

Ground 10

Some rent lawfully due from the tenant

(a) is unpaid on the date on which the proceedings for possession are begun; and

(b) except where subsection (1) (b) of section 8 of this Act applies, was in arrears at the date of the service of the notice under that section relating to those proceedings.

Ground 11

Whether or not any rent is in arrears on the date on which proceedings for possession are begun, the tenant has persistently delayed paying rent which has become lawfully due.

Ground 12

Any obligation of the tenancy (other than one related to the payment of rent) has been broken or not performed.

Ground 13

The condition of the dwelling-house or any of the common parts has deteriorated owing to acts of waste by, or the neglect or default of, the tenant or any other person residing in the dwelling-house and, in the case of an act of waste by, or the neglect or default of, a person lodging with the tenant or a sub-tenant of his, the tenant has not taken such steps as he ought reasonably to have taken for the removal of the lodger or sub-tenant.

For the purposes of this ground, "common parts" means any part of a building comprising the dwelling-house and any other premises which the tenant is entitled under the terms of the tenancy to use in common with the occupiers of other dwelling-houses in which the landlord has an estate or interest.

Ground 14

The tenant or a person residing in or visiting the dwelling house

(a) has been guilty of conduct causing or likely to cause a nuisance or annoyance to a person residing, visiting or otherwise engaging in a lawful activity in the locality,

[(aa) has been guilty of conduct causing or likely to cause a nuisance or annoyance to the landlord of the dwelling-house, or a person employed (whether or not by the landlord) in connection with the exercise of the landlord's housing management functions, and that is directly or indirectly related to or affects those functions,] or

(b) has been convicted of

(i) using the dwelling-house or allowing it to be used for immoral or illegal purposes, or

(ii) an indictable offence committed in, or in the locality of, the dwelling-house.

Ground 14ZA

The tenant or an adult residing in the dwelling-house has been convicted of an indictable offence which took place during, and at the scene of, a riot in the United Kingdom.

In this Ground—

"adult" means a person aged 18 or over;

"indictable offence" does not include an offence that is triable only summarily by virtue of section 22 of the Magistrates' Courts Act 1980 (either way offences where value involved is small);

"riot" is to be construed in accordance with section 1 of the Public Order Act 1986.

This Ground applies only in relation to dwelling-houses in England.

Ground 14A

The dwelling-house was occupied (whether alone or with others) by a married couple, a couple who are civil partners of each other, a couple living together as husband and wife or a couple living together as if they were civil partners and

(a) one or both of the partners is a tenant of the dwelling-house,

(b) the landlord who is seeking possession is a non-profit registered provider of social housing, a registered social landlord or a charitable housing trust or, where the dwelling-house is social housing within the meaning of Part 2 of the Housing and Regeneration Act 2008, a profit-making provider of social housing,

(c) one partner has left the dwelling-house because of violence or threats of violence by the other towards

(i) that partner, or

(ii) a member of the family of that partner who was residing with that partner immediately before the partner left, and

(d) the court is satisfied that the partner who has left is unlikely to return.

For the purposes of this ground "registered social landlord" and "member of the family" have the same meaning as in Part I of the Housing Act 1996 and "charitable housing trust" means a housing trust, within the meaning of the Housing Associations Act 1985, which is a charity...

GROUND 15

The condition of any furniture provided for use under the tenancy has, in the opinion of the court, deteriorated owing to ill-treatment by the tenant or any other person residing in the dwelling-house and, in the case of ill-treatment by a person lodging with the tenant or by a sub-tenant of his, the tenant has not taken such steps as he ought reasonably to have taken for the removal of the lodger or sub-tenant.

GROUND 16

The dwelling-house was let to the tenant in consequence of his employment by the landlord seeking possession or a previous landlord under the tenancy and the tenant has ceased to be in that employment.

For the purposes of this ground, at a time when the landlord is or was the Secretary of State, employment by a health service body, as defined in s 60(7) of the National Health Service and Community Care Act 1990, or by a Local Health Board, shall be regarded as employment by the Secretary of State.

GROUND 17

The tenant is the person, or one of the persons, to whom the tenancy was granted and the landlord was induced to grant the tenancy by a false statement made knowingly or recklessly by

(a) the tenant, or

(b) a person acting at the tenant's instigation.

PART III
SUITABLE ALTERNATIVE ACCOMMODATION

III L&T [244]

1. For the purposes of Ground 9 above, a certificate of the local housing authority for the district in which the dwelling-house in question is situated, certifying that the authority will provide suitable alternative accommodation for the tenant by a date specified in the certificate, shall be conclusive evidence that suitable alternative accommodation will be available for him by that date.

2. Where no such certificate as is mentioned in paragraph 1 above is produced to the court, accommodation shall be deemed to be suitable for the purposes of Ground 9 above if it consists of either

(a) premises which are to be let as a separate dwelling such that they will then be let on an assured tenancy, other than

(i) a tenancy in respect of which notice is given not later than the beginning of the tenancy that possession might be recovered on any of Grounds 1 to 5 above, or

(ii) an assured shorthold tenancy, within the meaning of Chapter II of Part I of this Act, or

(b) premises to be let as a separate dwelling on terms which will, in the opinion of the court, afford to the tenant security of tenure reasonably equivalent to the security afforded by Chapter I of Part I of this Act in the case of an assured tenancy of a kind mentioned in sub-paragraph (a) above,

and, in the opinion of the court, the accommodation fulfils the relevant conditions as defined in paragraph 3 below.

3. (1) For the purposes of paragraph 2 above, the relevant conditions are that the accommodation is reasonably suitable to the needs of the tenant and his family as regards proximity to place of work, and either

(a) similar as regards rental and extent to the accommodation afforded by dwelling-houses provided in the neighbourhood by any local housing authority for persons whose needs as regards extent are, in the opinion of the court, similar to those of the tenant and of his family; or

(b) reasonably suitable to the means of the tenant and to the needs of the tenant and his family as regards extent and character; and

that if any furniture was provided for use under the assured tenancy in question, furniture is provided for use in the accommodation which is either similar to that so provided or is reasonably suitable to the needs of the tenant and his family.

(2) For the purposes of sub-paragraph (1) (a) above, a certificate of a local housing authority stating

(a) the extent of the accommodation afforded by dwelling-houses provided by the authority to meet the needs of tenants with families of such number as may be specified in the certificate, and

(b) the amount of the rent charged by the authority for dwelling-houses affording accommodation of that extent,

shall be conclusive evidence of the facts so stated.

4. Accommodation shall not be deemed to be suitable to the needs of the tenant and his family if the result of their occupation of the accommodation would be that it would be an overcrowded dwelling-house for the purposes of Part X of the Housing Act 1985.

5. Any document purporting to be a certificate of a local housing authority named therein issued for the purposes of this Part of this Schedule and to be signed by the proper officer of that authority shall be received in evidence and, unless the contrary is shown, shall be deemed to be such a certificate without further proof.

6. In this Part of this Schedule "local housing authority" and "district", in relation to such an authority, have the same meaning as in the Housing Act 1985.

NOTES TO SCHEDULE 2, PARTS II AND III

III L&T [244.1]

Generally Housing Act Sch 2 Pt II Ground 9 (see para **III L&T [243]**) is precedented by the Rent Act 1977 s 98(1)(a) (see para **III L&T [71]**); Grounds 10, 11 and 12 (see para **III L&T [243]**) are variants on the Rent Act 1977 Sch 15 Case 1 (see para **III L&T [82]**). Housing Act Sch 2 Pt II Grounds 13, 14 and 15 (see **III L&T [243]**) correspond to the Rent Act 1977 Sch 15 Cases 3, 2 and 4 respectively (see para **III L&T [82]**); Ground 16 (see para **III L&T [243]**) is a modified version of the Rent Act 1977 Sch 15 Case 8 (see para **III L&T [82]**). The Housing Act 1988 Sch 2 Part III is in substantially the same terms as the Rent Act 1977 Sch 15 Pt IV. The notes on the Rent Act provisions include case law which is relevant to the interpretation of equivalent terms and provisions in the Housing Act 1988 Sch 2 Pts II and III. Housing Act 1988 Sch 2 Ground 14 (see para **III L&T [243]**) was expanded and Ground 14A (see para **III L&T [243]**) was added by the Housing Act 1996 s 148, and Ground 17 (see para **III L&T [243]**) was added by the Housing Act 1996 s 102. The Housing Act 1996 changes were brought into force, with savings, on 28 February 1997 by the Housing Act 1996 (Commencement No 7 and Savings) Order 1997, SI 1997/225.

III L&T [244.1A]

Restrictions on right of appeal As regards a decision to make a possession order on grounds in Part I of Schedule 2, an appeal on a question of fact is barred by s 77(6)(ee) of the County Courts Act 1984: see *London Borough of Croydon v Crawford* [2010] EWCA Civ 618 where a possession order on the ground of nuisance and annoyance was upheld although based on hearsay evidence.

III L&T [244.2]

Procedure Possession claims are governed by CPR Pt 55 (see para **CPR 55**). For details of the procedures, see paras **III L&T [211]**, **III L&T [216.1]**, **III L&T [216.1A]**, **III L&T [229.3]** and **III L&T [229.3A]**. For a summary of the prescribed forms for use in possession claims, see **BCCP O[12]**. For precedents, see **BCCP O[202]–BCCP O[204]**.

III L&T [244.2A]

Grounds 10 and 11 For the impact of the tenant's bankruptcy on a claim for possession based on rent arrears see **III L&T [242.6A]**.

III L&T [244.2AA]

Offence or nuisance by person residing with the tenant Although Ground 14 is drafted to cover the case of offence or nuisance by persons residing with the tenant, the lease itself may be drawn more narrowly so that the Ground may be invoked only on the ground of offence or nuisance by the tenant: *Pollards Hill Housing Association v Marsh* [2002] EWCA Civ 199, [2002] HLR 662.

III L&T [244.2B]

Conviction within Ground 14 Where a person is convicted of an arrestable offence committed before the grant of the tenancy it is, nevertheless, a ground for a possession order under ground 14(b)(ii): *Raglan Housing Association Ltd v Fairclough* [2007] EWCA Civ 1087, [2007] 45 EG 163 (CS).

III L&T [244.2BA]

Anonymous hearsay Anonymous hearsay evidence of antisocial behaviour may be admitted: *Boyd v Incommunities Ltd* [2013] EWCA Civ 756, [2013] All ER (D) 258 (Jun), where the court referred to the approval of such practice in *Moat Housing Group South Ltd v Harris* [2005] EWCA Civ 287, [2006] QB 606, [2005] 4 All ER 1051 and the guidance given in that case at paras 136 and 140.

III L&T [244.2C]

• **Domestic violence: Ground 14A** The violence for the purpose of Ground 14 does not have to have occurred while the couple are still living in the property as a couple: see *Metropolitan Housing Trust v Hadjazi* [2010] EWCA Civ 750, [2010] HLR 636, [2010] NLJR 975.

III L&T [244.3]

Ground 16 and the ending of employment The Housing Act 1988 Sch 2 Ground 16 para 2 (see para **III L&T [243]**) was added by the National Health Service and Community Care Act 1990 s 60, Sch 8 para 10 (removal of Crown immunities), with effect from 1 April 1991.

III L&T [244.4]

Tenant with a mental impairment The court should not make a possession order which evicted a disabled person (albeit that it was admitted that the disability in that case caused a nuisance or annoyance) unless the eviction could be justified under s 24 of the Disability Discrimination Act 1995 (such as on grounds of health and safety): *North Devon Homes Ltd v Brazier* [2003] EWHC 574 (QB), [2003] HLR 905. In *Knowsley Housing Trust v McMullen* [2006] EWCA Civ 539, (2006) Times 22 May, the tenant's son had a mental impairment which rendered him disabled within the meaning of the Disability Discrimination Act 1995. The tenant was unable to restrain her son from committing nuisance at the premises. The Court of Appeal considered that, in the circumstances of that case, a suspended possession order, with provision for the landlord to apply for permission to apply for a warrant of possession, was appropriate.

ASSURED AGRICULTURAL OCCUPANCIES

9. (1) An assured tenancy

(a) in the case of which the agricultural worker condition is, by virtue of any provision of Schedule 3 to this Act, for the time being fulfilled with respect to the dwelling-house subject to the tenancy, and

(b) which does not fall within sub-paragraph (2) or (4) below.

(2) An assured tenancy falls within this sub-paragraph if

(a) before it is entered into, a notice

(i) in such form as may be prescribed, and

(ii) stating that the tenancy is to be a shorthold tenancy,

is served by the person who is to be the landlord under the tenancy on the person who is to be the tenant under it, and

(b) it is not an excepted tenancy.

(3) For the purposes of sub-paragraph (2) (b) above, an assured tenancy is an excepted tenancy if

(a) the person to whom it is granted, or as the case may be, at least one of the persons to whom it is granted was, immediately before it is granted, a tenant or licensee under an assured agricultural occupancy, and

(b) the person by whom it is granted or, as the case may be, at least one of the persons by whom it is granted was, immediately before it is granted, a landlord or licensor under the assured agricultural occupancy referred to in paragraph (a) above.

(4) An assured tenancy falls within this sub-paragraph if it comes into being by virtue of section 5 above on the coming to an end of a tenancy falling within sub-paragraph (2) above.

III L&T [246.1]

Tenancies excluded by notice The words 'Assured Tenancy' on the cover of a rent book are not a notice complying with the requirements of Sch 2A para 1 or para 2: see *Andrews v Cunningham* [2007] EWCA Civ 762.

A letter from a landlord to its tenant stating that his probationary tenancy had been completed and that he was now an assured tenant was held to be a notice for the purpose of Sch 2A para 2 and could be relied upon by the tenant albeit that the landlord had previously indicated that it was seeking possession of the property: *Chadwick v Saxon Weald Homes Ltd* [2011] EWCA Civ 1202, [2012] P & CR D15, [2011] All ER (D) 231 (Oct).

III L&T [246.2]

Tenancies replacing non-shortholds The prescribed form of notice for the purpose of paragraph 7(2)(a) is Form 8 contained in the Assured Tenancies and Agricultural Occupancies (Forms) Regulations 1997, SI 1997/194. In *Kahlon v Isherwood* [2011] EWCA Civ 602, [2011] HLR 38 it was held that a schedule to a Tomlin order recording an agreement that the tenant would enter into an assured shorthold tenancy to replace an assured tenancy was not substantially to the same effect as the prescribed form and could not amount to notice given before a tenancy was entered into.

LEASEHOLD REFORM, HOUSING AND URBAN DEVELOPMENT ACT 1993

(c 28)

GENERAL NOTES ON LEASEHOLD REFORM, HOUSING AND URBAN DEVELOPMENT ACT 1993

III L&T [247]

Jurisdiction The Leasehold Reform, Housing and Urban Development Act 1993 Pt I conferred jurisdiction on the county courts in the matter of collective leasehold enfranchisement, lease renewal and management audit (of the lessor's management). The High Court has concurrent jurisdiction with the county court but only on matters joined with High Court proceedings, as provided in Leasehold Reform, Housing and Urban Development Act 1993 s 90(3) (see para **III L&T [268]**).

III L&T [248]

Regulations The provisions of the Leasehold Reform, Housing and Urban Development Act 1993 in respect of leasehold enfranchisement and lease renewal are supplemented by the Leasehold Reform (Collective Enfranchisement and Lease Renewal) Regulations 1993, SI 1993/2407, as amended by the Leasehold Reform (Collective Enfranchisement and Lease Renewal) (Amendment) (England) Regulations 2003, SI 2003/1990.

III L&T [248A]

Precedents Precedents for claims under the 1993 Act can be found at **BCCP O[1102]** and **BCCP O[1103]**.

PART I
LANDLORD AND TENANT

CHAPTER I COLLECTIVE ENFRANCHISEMENT IN CASE OF TENANTS OF FLATS

Preliminary

III L&T [249]

1. The right to collective enfranchisement

(1) This Chapter has effect for the purpose of conferring *on qualifying tenants of flats contained in premises to which this Chapter applies on the relevant date the right, exercisable subject to and in accordance with this Chapter, to have the freehold of those premises acquired on their behalf—*

(a) *by a person or persons appointed by them for the purpose, and*

(b) *at a price determined in accordance with this Chapter*; [the right to acquire the freehold of premises to which this Chapter applies on the relevant date, at a price determined in accordance with this Chapter, exercisable subject to and in accordance with this Chapter by a company (referred to in this Chapter as a RTE company) of which qualifying tenants of flats contained in the premises are members;]

and that right is referred to in this Chapter as "the right to collective enfranchisement".

(2) Where the right to collective enfranchisement is exercised in relation to any such premises ("the relevant premises")—

(a) *the qualifying tenants by whom the right is exercised shall be entitled, subject to and in accordance with this Chapter, to have acquired*, [the RTE company by which the right to collective enfranchisement is exercised is entitled, subject to and in accordance with this Chapter, to acquire,] in like manner, the freehold of any property which is not comprised in the relevant premises but to which this paragraph applies by virtue of subsection (3); and

(b) section 2 has effect with respect to the acquisition of leasehold interests to which paragraph (a) or (b) of subsection (1) of that section applies.

(3) Subsection (2)(a) applies to any property if < . . . > at the relevant date either—

(a) it is appurtenant property which is demised by the lease held by a qualifying tenant of a flat contained in the relevant premises; or

(b) it is property which any such tenant is entitled under the terms of the lease of his flat to use in common with the occupiers of other premises (whether those premises are contained in the relevant premises or not).

(4) The right of acquisition in respect of the freehold of any such property as is mentioned in subsection (3)(b) shall, however, be taken to be satisfied with respect to that property if, on the acquisition of the relevant premises in pursuance of this Chapter, either—

(a) there are granted by the [person who owns the freehold of that property]—

(i) over that property, or

(ii) over any other property,

such permanent rights as will ensure that thereafter the occupier of the flat referred to in that provision has as nearly as may be the same rights as those enjoyed in relation to that property on the relevant date by the qualifying tenant under the terms of his lease; or

(b) there is acquired from the [person who owns the freehold of that property] the freehold of any other property over which any such permanent rights may be granted.

(5) A claim by *qualifying tenants* [a RTE company] to exercise the right to collective enfranchisement may be made in relation to any premises to which this Chapter applies despite the fact that those premises are less extensive than the entirety of the premises in relation to which *those tenants are* [the RTE company is] entitled to exercise that right.

(6) Any right or obligation under this Chapter to acquire any interest in property shall not extend to underlying minerals in which that interest subsists if—

(a) the owner of the interest requires the minerals to be excepted, and

(b) proper provision is made for the support of the property as it is enjoyed on the relevant date.

(7) In this section—

"appurtenant property", in relation to a flat, means any garage, outhouse, garden, yard or appurtenances belonging to, or usually enjoyed with, the flat;

< . . . >

"the relevant premises" means any such premises as are referred to in subsection (2).

(8) In this Chapter "the relevant date", in relation to any claim to exercise the right to collective enfranchisement, means the date on which notice of the claim is given under section 13.

Amendments *Text in italic deleted and text in square brackets inserted by s 124 of and Schedule 8 to the Commonhold and Leasehold Reform Act 2002. Date in force to be appointed.*

III L&T [249.1]

Detailed provisions Succeeding sections identify premises to which the Chapter applies (Leasehold Reform, Housing and Urban Development Act 1993 ss 3, 4) and provide for qualifying tenants (Leasehold Reform, Housing and Urban Development Act 1993 s 5) to be resident (Leasehold Reform, Housing and Urban Development Act 1993 s 6) with long leases (Leasehold Reform, Housing and Urban Development Act 1993 s 7) at a low rent (Leasehold Reform, Housing and Urban Development Act 1993 s 8). The procedure for exercising the right is by notice (Leasehold Reform, Housing and Urban Development Act 1993 s 13) The court proceedings may follow under Leasehold Reform, Housing and Urban Development Act 1993 ss 22, 23, 24, 25, 26, 27 (see paras **III L&T [250]-III L&T [255]**).

The right to collective enfranchisement is excluded by s 5(2)(b) where the landlord is a charitable housing trust and the granting of leases is in pursuit of its charitable purposes. It has been held, however, that the exclusion does not apply unless the accommodation is provided as social housing: *Richmond Housing Partnership Ltd v Brick Farm Management Ltd* [2005] EWHC 1650 (QB), (2005) Times, 30 August, QB.

The obligation on a leaseholder to provide a Land Registry extract in response to a section 20 notice does not require the production of an office copy that is "up to date": *Raymere Ltd v Belle View Gardens Ltd* [2004] EWCA Civ 996, [2004] Ch 29.

Although s 10 exempts a resident freeholder from collective enfranchisement, the exemption applies only where that person has owned the same interest as a resident freeholder for the period back to before the conversion of the house in question into flats. The exemption does not apply where the interest was at one time an interest under a trust and at another time an interest as freeholder: *Slamon v Planchon* [2004] EWCA Civ 799, [2004] 4 All ER 407, (2004) Times, 28 July.

III L&T [249.2]

Forfeited leases A tenant whose lease has been forfeited by court order loses the right to serve a notice because of the restrictions imposed by the Leasehold Reform, Housing and Urban Development Act 1993 s 13(13) and Sch 3. But the notice may be served with the leave of the court. If notice is served without leave it is invalid and cannot be validated by leave granted subsequently: *Martin v Maryland Estates Ltd* (1998) 31 HLR 218, [1998] 25 EG 169, CA.

III L&T [249.3]

Amendments made by the Commonhold and Leasehold Reform Act 2002 Section 126 of the Commonhold and Leasehold Reform Act 2002 amended s 18(1) and Sch 6 to provide that, where qualifying tenants are buying the freehold, the price to be paid should reflect the value of the interests held by all the landlords in the property concerned at the date of the s 13 notice.

III L&T [249.4]

Validity of tenant's notice A s 13 notice was invalid where the notice did not identify all the qualifying tenants or state their addresses in the property. Those failures went to the very heart of the right to collective enfranchisement, since the information required by statute was intended to disclose, on the face of the notice, the number of qualifying tenants in the premises: *Natt v Osman* [2015] 1 WLR 1536.

Where tenants served a notice under s 13 of the 1993 Act for collective enfranchisement, and subsequently accepted that their notice was invalid, there was no statutory prohibition preventing the tenants from serving another notice under s 13: *Sinclair Gardens Investments (Kensington) Ltd v Poets Chase Freehold Co Ltd* [2007] EWHC 1776 (Ch), [2007] 49 EG 104.

A notice may relate to a self-contained flat which is capable of further sub-division: *Craftrule Ltd v 41-60 Albert Palace Mansions (Freehold) Ltd* [2010] EWHC 1230 (Ch), [2010] 3 All ER 952, [2010] 1 WLR 2046.

A s 13 notice is a document to which the Companies Act 1985, s 36A applies. A company signing such a notice must therefore do so either by its seal or by the signature of two directors or a director and the secretary: *Hilmi & Associates Ltd v 20 Pembridge Villas Freehold Ltd* [2010] EWCA Civ 314, [2010] 3 All ER 391, [2010] 1 WLR 2750.

Where the landlord responds to a notice by a counter-notice denying that the applicant is a qualifying tenant, the applicant should seek a ruling on that issue. If the applicant discontinues his application then, notwithstanding his statutory right to serve a further notice after the expiry of 12 months, such further notice, giving rise to the same issues, will be struck out as an abuse of process: *Westbrook Dolphin Square Ltd v Friends Provident Life and Pensions Ltd* [2011] EWHC 2302 (Ch), [2011] All ER (D) 70 (Sep), applying *Henderson v Henderson* (1843–60) All ER Rep 378. However, the Supreme Court ruled otherwise: **CPR 38.7** does not empower the court to refuse a second set of proceedings under s 22 of the Leasehold Reform etc Act 1993 since s 29 specifically entitles an applicant to withdraw a claim to enfranchisement and to reassert it after the lapse of 12 months: *Westbrook Dolphin Square Ltd v Friends Life Ltd* [2012] EWCA Civ 666, [2012] 4 All ER 148, [2012] 1 WLR 2752.

III L&T [250]

22. Proceedings relating to validity of initial notice

(1) Where—

(a) the reversioner in respect of the specified premises has given the *nominee purchaser* [RTE company] a counter-notice under section 21 which (whether it complies with the requirement set out in subsection (2)(b) or (c) of that section) contains such a statement as is mentioned in subsection (2)(b) of that section, but

(b) the court is satisfied, on an application made by the *nominee purchaser, that the participating tenants were* [RTE company, that it was] on the relevant date entitled to exercise the right to collective enfranchisement in relation to the specified premises,

the court shall by order make a declaration to that effect.

(2) Any application for an order under subsection (1) must be made not later than the end of the period of two months beginning with the date of the giving of the counter-notice to the *nominee purchaser* [RTE company].

(3) If on any such application the court makes an order under subsection (1), then (subject to subsection (4)) the court shall make an order—

(a) declaring that the reversioner's counter-notice shall be of no effect, and

(b) requiring the reversioner to give a further counter-notice to the *nominee purchaser* [RTE company] by such date as is specified in the order.

(4) Subsection (3) shall not apply if—

(a) the counter-notice complies with the requirement set out in section 21(2)(c), and

(b) either—

(i) an application for an order under section 23(1) is pending, or

(ii) the period specified in section 23(3) as the period for the making of such an application has not expired.

(5) Subsections (3) to (5) of section 21 shall apply to any further counter-notice required to be given by the reversioner under subsection (3) above as if it were a counter-notice under that section complying with the requirement set out in subsection (2)(a) of that section.

(6) If an application by the *nominee purchaser* [RTE company] for an order under subsection (1) is dismissed by the court, the initial notice shall cease to have effect at the time when the order dismissing the application becomes final.

Amendments *Text in italic deleted and text in square brackets inserted by s 124 of and Schedule 8 to the Commonhold and Leasehold Reform Act 2002. Date in force to be appointed.*

III L&T [250.1]

Applications to court The procedure for claims under the 1993 Act is now dealt with in CPR PD 56 paras 14.1 to 14.7 (para **CPR PD 56**) as prescribed by CPR 56.4 (see para **CPR 56.4**). Claims under ss 23, 26 and 50 must be made in accordance with the Part 8 procedure.

In *Westbrook Dolphin Square Ltd v Friends Life Ltd* [2012] EWCA Civ 666, [2012] 4 All ER 148, [2012] 1 WLR 2752 the court held that the 1993 Act contemplates that tenants can make successive applications to the court under s 22 and that s 29 deals expressly with the case where an application is discontinued. The provisions on discontinuance in CPR 38.7 do not apply in such circumstances, and a second or subsequent application under s 22 is not, without more, an abuse of process.

III L&T [250.2]

Section 21 counter-notice For the prescribed contents of the section 21 counter notice, see the Leasehold Reform (Collective Enfranchisement) (Counter-notices) (England) Regulations 2002, SI 2002/3208. In 7 *Strathray Gardens Ltd v Pointstar Shipping & Finance Ltd* [2004] EWCA Civ 1669, [2004] All ER (D) 240 (Dec), the Court of Appeal held that the requirement in these regulations for a negative statement, namely that the premises were not in the area of a scheme approved as an estate management scheme, was not mandatory.

It has been further held that the fact that a landlord's counter-notice makes an offer which is unrealistically high does not invalidate the notice provided the notice is given in good faith: *Nine Cornwall Crescent London Ltd v Kensington and Chelsea London Borough Council* [2005] 4 All ER 1207, (2005) Times, 29 March, CA. It was noted in that case that if the landlords had not made a valid counter-offer they would have been obliged to sell the freehold to the tenants on the tenants' terms, according to the decision in *Willingale v Globalrange Ltd* [2000] 2 EGLR 55.

On the other hand the requirement for the reversioner to set out additional leaseback proposals in the s 21 counter-notice means that they cannot be validly set out in any subsequent document: *Cawthorne v Hamdan* [2007] EWCA Civ 6, [2007] 2 All ER 116.

III L&T [251]

23. Tenants' claim liable to be defeated where landlord intends to redevelop

(1) Where the reversioner in respect of the specified premises has given a counter-notice under section 21 which complies with the requirement set out in subsection (2) (c) of that section, the court may, on the application of any appropriate landlord, by order declare that the right to collective enfranchisement shall not be exercisable in relation to those premises by reason of that landlord's intention to redevelop the whole or a substantial part of the premises.

(2) The court shall not make an order under subsection (1) unless it is satisfied

(a) that not less than two-thirds of all the long leases on which flats contained in the specified premises are held are due to terminate within the period of five years beginning with the relevant date; and

(b) that for the purposes of redevelopment the applicant intends, once the leases in question have so terminated

(i) to demolish or reconstruct, or

(ii) to carry out substantial works of construction on,

the whole or a substantial part of the specified premises; and

(c) that he could not reasonably do so without obtaining possession of the flats demised by those leases.

(3) Any application for an order under subsection (1) must be made within the period of two months beginning with the date of the giving of the counter-notice to the *nominee purchaser* [RTE company]; but, where the counter-notice is one falling within section 22 (1) (a), such an application shall not be proceeded with until such time (if any) as an order under section 22 (1) becomes final.

(4) Where an order under subsection (1) is made by the court, the initial notice shall cease to have effect on the order becoming final.

(5) Where an application for an order under subsection (1) is dismissed by the court, the court shall make an order

(a) declaring that the reversioner's counter-notice shall be of no effect, and

(b) requiring the reversioner to give a further counter-notice to the *nominee purchaser* [RTE company] by such date as is specified in the order.

(6) Where

(a) the reversioner has given such a counter-notice as is mentioned in subsection (1), but

(b) either

(i) no application for an order under that subsection is made within the period referred to in subsection (3), or

(ii) such an application is so made but is subsequently withdrawn,

then (subject to subsection (8)), the reversioner shall give a further counter-notice to the *nominee purchaser* [RTE company] within the period of two months beginning with the appropriate date.

(7) In subsection (6) "the appropriate date" means

(a) if subsection (6) (b) (i) applies, the date immediately following the end of the period referred to in subsection (3); and

(b) if subsection (6) (b) (ii) applies, the date of withdrawal of the application.

(8) Subsection (6) shall not apply if any application has been made by the *nominee purchaser* [RTE company] under section 22 (1).

(9) Subsections (3) to (5) of section 21 shall apply to any further counter-notice required to be given by the reversioner under subsection (5) or (6) above as if it were a counter-notice under that section complying with the requirement set out in subsection (2) (a) of that section.

(10) In this section "appropriate landlord", in relation to the specified premises, means

(a) the reversioner or any other relevant landlord; or

(b) any two or more persons falling within paragraph (a) who are acting together.

Amendments *Text in italic deleted and text in square brackets inserted by s 124 of and Schedule 8 to the Commonhold and Leasehold Reform Act 2002. Date in force to be appointed.*

III L&T [251.1]

Applications to court Particular provision is made in CPR PD 56 para 14.2 (para **CPR PD 56**) for an application to the county court under Leasehold Reform, Housing and Urban

III L&T [252.4]

Completion of acquisition The detailed procedure for completion of the acquisition is set out in the Leasehold Reform, Housing and Urban Development Act 1993 ss 34–37, and in Schs 7–10; also in the Leasehold Reform (Collective Enfranchisement and Lease Renewal) Regulations 1993, SI 1993/2407, as amended by the Leasehold Reform (Collective Enfranchisement and Lease Renewal) (Amendment) (England) Regulations 2003, SI 2003/1990.

III L&T [253]

25. Applications where reversioner fails to give counter-notice or further counter-notice

(1) Where the initial notice has been given in accordance with section 13 but—

(a) the reversioner has failed to give the *nominee purchaser* [RTE company] a counter-notice in accordance with section 21(1), or

(b) if required to give the *nominee purchaser* [RTE company] a further counter-notice by or by virtue of section 22(3) or section 23(5) or (6), the reversioner has failed to comply with that requirement,

the court may, on the application of the *nominee purchaser* [RTE company], make an order determining the terms on which *he* [RTE company] is to acquire, in accordance with the proposals contained in the initial notice, such interests and rights as are specified in it under section 13(3).

(2) The terms determined by the court under subsection (1) shall, if Part II of Schedule 9 is applicable, include terms which provide for the leasing back, in accordance with section 36 and that Part of that Schedule, of flats or other units contained in the specified premises.

(3) The court shall not make any order on an application made by virtue of paragraph (a) of subsection (1) unless it is satisfied—

(a) that the *participating tenants were* [RTE company was] on the relevant date entitled to exercise the right to collective enfranchisement in relation to the specified premises; and

(b) if applicable, that the requirements of Part II of Schedule 3 were complied with as respects the giving of copies of the initial notice.

(4) Any application for an order under subsection (1) must be made not later than the end of the period of six months beginning with the date by which the counter-notice or further counter-notice referred to in that subsection was to be given to the *nominee purchaser* [RTE company].

(5) Where—

(a) the terms of acquisition have been determined by an order of the court under subsection (1), but

(b) a binding contract incorporating those terms has not been entered into by the end of the appropriate period specified in subsection (8),

the court may, on the application of either the *nominee purchaser* [RTE company] or the reversioner, make such order under subsection (6) as it thinks fit.

(6) The court may under this subsection make an order—

(a) providing for the interests to be acquired by the *nominee purchaser* [RTE company] to be vested in *him* [it] on the terms referred to in subsection (5);

(b) providing for those interests to be vested in *him* [it] on those terms, but subject to such modifications as—

(i) may have been determined by the appropriate tribunal, on the application of either the *nominee purchaser* [RTE company] or the reversioner, to be required by reason of any change in circumstances since the time when the terms were determined as mentioned in that subsection, and

(ii) are specified in the order; or

LANDLORD & TENANT AND HOUSING

(c) providing for the initial notice to be deemed to have been withdrawn at the end of the appropriate-period specified in subsection (8);

and Schedule 5 shall have effect in relation to any such order as is mentioned in paragraph (a) or (b) above.

(7) Any application for an order under subsection (6) must be made not later than the end of the period of two months beginning immediately after the end of the appropriate period specified in subsection (8).

(8) For the purposes of this section the appropriate period is—

(a) the period of two months beginning with the date when the order of the court under subsection (1) becomes final, or

(b) such other period as may have been fixed by the court when making that order.

Amendments *Text in italic deleted and text in square brackets inserted by s 124 of and Schedule 8 to the Commonhold and Leasehold Reform Act 2002. Date in force to be appointed.*

III L&T [253.1]

The court "may" make an order This does not mean that the court has a general discretion. Where a nominee tenant has served a notice pursuant to s 13 but the reversioner has failed to serve a counter-notice, the court (if satisfied that other statutory provisions had been complied with) is obliged to make an order: *Willingale v Global Grange Ltd* (2000) 80 P & CR 448, CA. The principle in *Cadogan v Morris* (1998) 77 P & CR 336 (a decision concerning a tenant's notice under section 42) nevertheless applies – the proposals in the notice must be realistic.

III L&T [254]

26. Applications where relevant landlord cannot be found

(1) Where *not less than two-thirds of the qualifying tenants of flats contained in any premises to which this Chapter applies desire to make a claim to exercise the right to collective enfranchisement in relation to those premises* [a RTE company which satisfies the requirement in section 13(2)(b) wishes to make a claim to exercise the right to collective enfranchisement] but—

(a) (in a case to which section 9(1) applies) the person who owns the freehold of the premises cannot be found or his identity cannot be ascertained, or

(b) (in a case to which section 9(2) [or (2A)] applies) each of the relevant landlords is someone who cannot be found or whose identity cannot be ascertained,

the court may, on the application of the *qualifying tenants in question* [RTE company], make a vesting order under this subsection—

(i) with respect to any interests of that person (whether in those premises or in any other property) which are liable to acquisition *on behalf of those tenants* [by the RTE company] by virtue of section 1(1) or (2)(a) or section 2(1), or

(ii) with respect to any interests of those landlords which are so liable to acquisition by virtue of any of those provisions,

as the case may be.

(2) Where in a case to which section 9(2) applies—

(a) *not less than two-thirds of the qualifying tenants of flats contained in any premises to which this Chapter applies desire to make a claim to exercise the right to collective enfranchisement in relation to those premises* [a RTE company which satisfies the requirement in section 13(2)(b) wishes to make a claim to exercise the right to collective enfranchisement], and

(b) paragraph (b) of subsection (1) does not apply, but

(c) a notice of that claim or (as the case may be) a copy of such a notice cannot be given in accordance with section 13 or Part II of Schedule 3 to any person to whom it would otherwise be required to be so given because he cannot be found or his identity cannot be ascertained,

the court may, on the application of the *qualifying tenants in question* [RTE company], make an order dispensing with the need to give such a notice or (as the case may be) a copy of such a notice to that person.

(3) If[, in a case to which section 9(2) applies,] that person is the person who owns the freehold of the premises, then on the application of *those tenants* [the RTE company], the court may, in connection with an order under subsection (2), make an order appointing any other relevant landlord to be the reversioner in respect of the premises in place of that person; and if it does so references in this Chapter to the reversioner shall apply accordingly.

[(3A) Where in a case to which section 9(2A) applies—

(a) *not less than two-thirds of the qualifying tenants of flats contained in any premises to which this Chapter applies desire to make a claim to exercise the right to collective enfranchisement in relation to those premises* [a RTE company which satisfies the requirement in section 13(2)(b) wishes to make a claim to exercise the right to collective enfranchisement], and

(b) paragraph (b) of subsection (1) does not apply, but

(c) a copy of a notice of that claim cannot be given in accordance with Part II of Schedule 3 to any person to whom it would otherwise be required to be so given because he cannot be found or his identity cannot be ascertained,

the court may, on the application of the *qualifying tenants in question* [RTE company], make an order dispensing with the need to give a copy of such a notice to that person.]

(4) The court shall not make an order on any application under subsection (1)[, (2) or (3A)] unless it is satisfied—

(a) that on the date of the making of the application the premises to which the application relates were premises to which this Chapter applies; and

(b) that on that date the *applicants* [RTE company] would not have been precluded by any provision of this Chapter from giving a valid notice under section 13 with respect to those premises [and that the RTE company has given notice of the application to each person who is the qualifying tenant of a flat contained in those premises].

(5) Before making any such order the court may require the *applicants* [RTE company] to take such further steps by way of advertisement or otherwise as the court thinks proper for the purpose of tracing the person or persons in question; and if, after an application is made for a vesting order under subsection (1) and before any interest is vested in pursuance of the application, the person or (as the case may be) any of the persons referred to in paragraph (a) or (b) of that subsection is traced, then no further proceedings shall be taken with a view to any interest being so vested, but (subject to subsection (6))—

(a) the rights and obligations of all parties shall be determined as if the *applicants* [RTE company] had, at the date of the application, duly given notice under section 13 of *their* [its] claim to exercise the right to collective enfranchisement in relation to the premises to which the application relates; and

(b) the court may give such directions as the court thinks fit as to the steps to be taken for giving effect to those rights and obligations, including directions modifying or dispensing with any of the requirements of this Chapter or of regulations made under this Part.

(6) An application for a vesting order under subsection (1) may be withdrawn at any time before execution of a conveyance under section 27(3) and, after it is withdrawn, subsection (5)(a) above shall not apply; but where any step is taken (whether by the *applicants* [RTE company] or otherwise) for the purpose of giving effect to subsection (5)(a) in the case of any application, the application shall not afterwards be withdrawn except—

(a) with the consent of every person who is the owner of any interest the vesting of which is sought by the *applicants* [RTE company], or

(b) by leave of the court,

and the court shall not give leave unless it appears to the court just to do so by reason of matters coming to the knowledge of the *applicants* [RTE company] in consequence of the tracing of any such person.

(7) Where an order has been made under subsection (2) [or (3A)] dispensing with the need to give a notice under section 13, or a copy of such a notice, to a particular person with respect to any particular premises, then if—

(a) a notice is subsequently given under that section with respect to those premises, and

(b) in reliance on the order, the notice or a copy of the notice is not to be given to that person,

the notice must contain a statement of the effect of the order.

(8) Where a notice under section 13 contains such a statement in accordance with subsection (7) above, then in determining for the purposes of any provision of this Chapter whether the requirements of section 13 or Part II of Schedule 3 have been complied with in relation to the notice, those requirements shall be deemed to have been complied with so far as relating to the giving of the notice or a copy of it to the person referred to in subsection (7) above.

(9) Rules of court shall make provision—

(a) for requiring notice of any application under subsection (3) to be served by the *persons making the application on any person who the applicants know or have* [RTE company on any person who it knows or has] reason to believe is a relevant landlord; and

(b) for enabling persons served with any such notice to be joined as parties to the proceedings.

Amendments *Text in italic deleted and text in square brackets inserted by s 124 of and Schedule 8 to the Commonhold and Leasehold Reform Act 2002. Date in force to be appointed.*

III L&T [254.1]

Rules of court The relevant rules are now CPR PD 56 paras 14.3 and 14.4 (see para **CPR PD 56**).

An application under s 26(1) or (2) must be made by the issue of a claim form in accordance with the Pt 8 procedure, which need not be served on any other party. The court may grant or refuse the application or give directions for its future conduct, including the addition as defendants of such persons as appear to have an interest in it.

An application under s 26(3) must be made by the issue of a claim form in accordance with the Pt 8 procedure. The claimants must serve the claim form on any person who they know or have reason to believe is a relevant landlord, giving particulars of the claim and the hearing date and informing that person of his right to be joined as a party to the claim. A person so served must be joined as a defendant to the claim if he gives notice in writing to the court of his wish to be added as a party, and the court will notify all other parties of the addition. The landlord whom it is sought to appoint as the reversioner must, in any event, be a defendant and must file an acknowledgment of service.

III L&T [255]

27. Supplementary provisions relating to vesting orders under section 26 (1)

(1) A vesting order under section 26(1) is an order providing for the vesting of any such interests as are referred to in paragraph (i) or (ii) of that provision—

(a) in *such person or persons as may be appointed for the purpose by the applicants for the order* [the RTE company], and

(b) on such terms as may be determined by the appropriate tribunal to be appropriate with a view to the interests being vested in *that person or those persons* [the RTE company] in like manner (so far as the circumstances permit) as if the *applicants had* [RTE company had], at the date of *their* [its] application, given notice under section 13 of *their* [its] claim to exercise the right to collective enfranchisement in relation to the premises with respect to which the order is made.

(2) If the appropriate tribunal so determines in the case of a vesting order under section 26(1), the order shall have effect in relation to interests which are less extensive than those specified in the application on which the order was made.

(3) Where any interests are to be vested in *any person or persons* [the RTE company] by virtue of a vesting order under section 26(1), then on *his or their* [its] paying into court the appropriate sum in respect of each of those interests there shall be executed by such person as the court may designate a conveyance which—

(a) is in a form approved by the appropriate tribunal, and

(b) contains such provisions as may be so approved for the purpose of giving effect so far as possible to the requirements of section 34 and Schedule 7;

and that conveyance shall be effective to vest in the *person or persons to whom the conveyance is made* [RTE company] the interests expressed to be conveyed, subject to and in accordance with the terms of the conveyance.

(4) In connection with the determination by the appropriate tribunal of any question as to the interests to be conveyed by any such conveyance, or as to the rights with or subject to which they are to be conveyed, it shall be assumed (unless the contrary is shown) that any person whose interests are to be conveyed ("the transferor") has no interest in property other than those interests and, for the purpose of excepting them from the conveyance, any minerals underlying the property in question.

(5) The appropriate sum which in accordance with subsection (3) is to be paid into court in respect of any interest is the aggregate of—

(a) such amount as may be determined by the appropriate tribunal to be the price which would be payable in respect of that interest in accordance with Schedule 6 if the interest were being acquired in pursuance of such a notice as is mentioned in subsection (1)(b); and

(b) any amounts or estimated amounts determined by such a tribunal as being, at the time of execution of the conveyance, due to the transferor from any tenants of his of premises comprised in the premises in which that interest subsists (whether due under or in respect of their leases or under or in respect of agreements collateral thereto).

(6) Where any interest is vested in *any person or persons* [the RTE company] in accordance with this section, the payment into court of the appropriate sum in respect of that interest shall be taken to have satisfied any claims against the *applicants for the vesting order under section 26(1), their personal representatives or assigns* [RTE company] in respect of the price payable under this Chapter for the acquisition of that interest.

(7) Where any interest is so vested in *any person or persons* [the RTE company], section 32(5) shall apply in relation to *his or their acquisition of that interest as it applies in relation to the acquisition of any interest by a nominee purchaser* [its acquisition of that interest].

Amendments *Text in italic deleted and text in square brackets inserted by s 124 of and Schedule 8 to the Commonhold and Leasehold Reform Act 2002. Date in force to be appointed.*

III L&T [255.1]

Payment into court The procedure for paying money into court under s 27(3), and the appropriate court, is now regulated by CPR PD 56 para 14.5 (para **CPR PD 56**).

III L&T [255.2]

Designation of a conveyancer The power to designate a conveyancer is not limited to the conveyancers approved by the Lord Chancellor under the Supreme Court Act 1981 s 131.

Supplemental

III L&T [256]

38. Interpretation of Chapter I

(1) In this Chapter (unless the context otherwise requires)

"conveyance" includes assignment, transfer and surrender, and related expressions shall be construed accordingly;

"appropriate tribunal" means—

(a) in relation to premises in England, the First-tier Tribunal or, where determined by or under Tribunal Procedure Rules, the Upper Tribunal; and

(b) in relation to premises in Wales, a leasehold valuation tribunal;

"the initial notice" means the notice given under section 13;

"introductory tenancy" has the same meaning as in Chapter 1 of Part V of the Housing Act 1996;

["participating member" has the meaning given by section 4B;]

["the notice of invitation to participate" means the notice given under section 12A;]

"the nominee purchaser" shall be construed in accordance with section 15;

"the participating tenants" shall be construed in accordance with section 14;

"premises with a resident landlord" shall be construed in accordance with section 10;

"public sector landlord" means any of the persons listed in section 171 (2) of the Housing Act 1985;

"qualifying tenant" shall be construed in accordance with section 5;

"the relevant date" has the meaning given by section 1 (8);

"relevant landlord" and "the reversioner" shall be construed in accordance with section 9;

"the right to collective enfranchisement" means the right specified in section 1 (1);

["RTE company" shall be construed in accordance with sections 1(1) and 4A;]

"secure tenancy" has the meaning given by section 79 of the Housing Act 1985;

"the specified premises" shall be construed in accordance with section 13 (12);

"the terms of acquisition" has the meaning given by section 24 (8);

"unit" means

(a) a flat;

(b) any other separate set of premises which is constructed or adapted for use for the purposes of a dwelling; or

(c) a separate set of premises let, or intended for letting, on a business lease.

(2) Any reference in this Chapter (however expressed) to the acquisition or proposed acquisition by *the nominee purchaser* [a RTE company] is a reference to the acquisition or proposed acquisition by the *nominee purchaser, on behalf of the participating tenants*, [RTE company] of such freehold and other interests as fall to be so acquired under a contract entered into in pursuance of the initial notice.

(3) Any reference in this Chapter to the interest of a relevant landlord in the specified premises is a reference to the interest in those premises by virtue of which he is, in accordance with section 9(2)(b) [or (2A)(b)], a relevant landlord.

(4) Any reference in this Chapter to agreement in relation to all or any of the terms of acquisition is a reference to agreement subject to contract.

Amendments *Text in italic deleted and text in square brackets inserted by s 124 of and Schedule 8 to the Commonhold and Leasehold Reform Act 2002. Date in force to be appointed.*

CHAPTER II INDIVIDUAL RIGHT OF TENANT OF FLAT TO ACQUIRE NEW LEASE

Preliminary

III L&T [257]

39. Right of qualifying tenant of flat to acquire new lease

(1) This Chapter has effect for the purpose of conferring on a tenant of a flat, in the circumstances mentioned in subsection (2), the right, exercisable subject to and in accordance with this Chapter, to acquire a new lease of the flat on payment of a premium determined in accordance with this Chapter.

(2) Those circumstances are that on the relevant date for the purposes of this Chapter—

(a) the tenant has for the last two years been a qualifying tenant of the flat;

(b) . . .

(2A) . . .

(2B) . . .

(3) The following provisions, namely—

(a) section 5 (with the omission of subsections (5) and (6)),

(b) section 7, < . . . >

(c) . . .

(d) . . .

shall apply for the purposes of this Chapter as they apply for the purposes of Chapter I; and references in this Chapter to a qualifying tenant of a flat shall accordingly be construed by reference to those provisions.

(3A) On the death of a person who has for the two years before his death been a qualifying tenant of a flat, the right conferred by this Chapter is exercisable, subject to and in accordance with this Chapter, by his personal representatives; and, accordingly, in such a case references in this Chapter to the tenant shall, in so far as the context permits, be to the personal representatives.

(4) For the purposes of this Chapter a person can be (or be among those constituting) the qualifying tenant of each of two or more flats at the same time, whether he is tenant of those flats under one lease or under two or more separate leases.

(4A) . . .

(5) . . .

(6) . . .

(7) The right conferred by this Chapter on a tenant to acquire a new lease shall not extend to underlying minerals comprised in his existing lease if—

(a) the landlord requires the minerals to be excepted, and

(b) proper provision is made for the support of the premises demised by that existing lease as they are enjoyed on the relevant date.

(8) In this Chapter "the relevant date", in relation to a claim by a tenant under this Chapter, means the date on which notice of the claim is given to the landlord under section 42.

III L&T [257.1]

Application of sections 5, 7 and 8 The Leasehold Reform, Housing and Urban Development Act 1993 ss 5, 7, 8 define "qualifying tenants", "long lease" and "low rent". Note, however, that there is no disqualification in Part II, as there is in Part I, of a person who is the tenant of three or more flats in the same building; this is the effect of disapplying Leasehold Reform, Housing and Urban Development Act 1993 s 5(5), (6).

III L&T [257.2]

Flat See Leasehold Reform, Housing and Urban Development Act 1993 s 101(1) (see para **III L&T [273]**) for the definition of "flat" and Leasehold Reform, Housing and Urban Development Act 1993 s 62(2), (3) (see para **III L&T [265]**) regarding the inclusion of garages, gardens etc.

It is possible to be a qualifying tenant and therefore to acquire a new lease of the flat although the existing lease includes more than the flat itself: *Maurice v Hollow-Ware Products Ltd* [2005] EWHC 815 (Ch), (2005) Times, 31 March.

III L&T [257.3]

Grant of a new lease The scope of the obligation to grant a new lease is defined by Leasehold Reform, Housing and Urban Development Act 1993 s 56; provision is made in Leasehold Reform, Housing and Urban Development Act 1993 s 57 for the terms of the new lease and, in Leasehold Reform, Housing and Urban Development Act 1993 s 58, for the terms in a case where the interest of either the tenant or the landlord is subject to a mortgage.

III L&T [257.4]

Further renewal Leasehold Reform, Housing and Urban Development Act 1993 s 59 provides a right of further renewal but without security of tenure.

III L&T [257.5]

Costs Leasehold Reform, Housing and Urban Development Act 1993 s 60 provides for the costs incurred in connection with the lease renewal to be paid by the tenant.

III L&T [257.6]

Procedure The procedure for further steps in the renewal is regulated by the Leasehold Reform (Collective Enfranchisement and Lease Renewal) Regulations 1993, SI 1993/2407, Sch 2, as amended by the Leasehold Reform (Collective Enfranchisement and Lease Renewal) (Amendment) (England) Regulations 2003, SI 2003/1990. Provision is also made for preliminary inquiries (Leasehold Reform, Housing and Urban Development Act 1993 s 41), a tenant's notice (Leasehold Reform, Housing and Urban Development Act 1993 ss 42, 43), access by landlords for valuation purposes (Leasehold Reform, Housing and Urban Development Act 1993 s 44) and a landlord's counter-notice (Leasehold Reform, Housing and Urban Development Act 1993 s 45).

III L&T [257.7]

Validity of notices The premium proposed by the tenant in the tenant's notice under s 42 or by the landlord in the counter-notice under s 45 must be realistic, otherwise the notice is invalid: *Cadogan v Morris* (1998) 77 P & CR 336, 31 HLR 732, CA. A lessee's notice specifying a premium of £100,000 was held invalid in *Mount Cook Land Ltd v Rosen* [2003] 10 EG 165 on the ground that the figure was unrealistic, being only about 44% of what valuation evidence said the appropriate figure should be. A tenant's notice under s 42 which fails to specify a date, not less than two months after service, for service of the landlord's counter-notice is invalid; the notice cannot be saved under Sch 12 para 9 to the Act because the defect is not an "inaccuracy": see *Trustees of John Lyons Charity v Secchi* (1999) 32 HLR 820, [1999] 3 EGLR 49, CA where it was also held, on the facts, that the notice could not be saved either by the principles in *Mannai Investments Co Ltd v Eagle Star Life Assurance* [1997] AC 749, [1999] 3 All ER 352, HL. See also *Burman v Mount Cook Land Ltd* [2001] EWCA Civ 1712, [2002] 1 All ER 144, where the court held that the only question was whether the landlord's counter-notice complied with the requirements of the Act; a notice which failed to state whether the landlord admitted the tenant's right to acquire a new lease and, if so, which (if any) of the tenant's proposals for the new lease were acceptable, was therefore invalid.

The requirement for a valid counter-notice may however be waived: *Latifi v Colherne Court Freehold Ltd* [2002] EWHC 2873 (QB), [2003] 12 EG 130. A failure to serve third parties does not invalidate the notice except where the tenant has exercised the right to obtain information as to their identity: *Wellcome Trust Ltd v Bellhurst Ltd* [2002] EWCA Civ 790, [2003] HLR 102.

It was held, in *Lay v Ackerman* [2004] EWCA Civ 184, [2004] HLR 684, [2004] All ER (D) 109 (Mar), that a counter-notice served under s 45 which incorrectly identified the landlord was nevertheless valid because a reasonable person would have had no doubt that it was served by or behalf of the landlord.

A tenants' notice under s 42 is required to be signed by the tenants if the property is in Wales, but not if in England. This is provided by s 99(5)(a) of the Act, as amended by the Leasehold Reform (Amendment) Act 2014.

LANDLORD & TENANT AND HOUSING

III L&T [257.8]

Rights of head lessee A head-lessee has the right to an extension of the lease: *Howard de Walden Estates Ltd v Aggio* [2008] UKHL 44, [2009] 1 AC 39, [2008] 4 All ER 382, [2008] 3 WLR 244 (reversing *Aggio v Howard de Walden Estates Ltd* [2007] EWCA Civ 499, [2007] 3 All ER 910, [2007] 3 WLR 542).

III L&T [258]

46. Proceedings relating to validity of tenant's notice

(1) Where

(a) the landlord has given the tenant a counter-notice under section 45 which (whether it complies with the requirement set out in subsection (2) (b) or (c) of that section) contains such a statement as is mentioned in subsection (2) (b) of that section, and

(b) the court is satisfied, on an application made by the landlord, that on the relevant date the tenant had no right under this Chapter to acquire a new lease of his flat,

the court shall by order make a declaration to that effect.

(2) Any application for an order under subsection (1) must be made not later than the end of the period of two months beginning with the date of the giving of the counter-notice to the tenant; and if, in a case falling within paragraph (a) of that subsection, either

(a) no application for such an order is made by the landlord within that period, or

(b) such an application is so made but is subsequently withdrawn,

section 49 shall apply as if the landlord had not given the counter-notice.

(3) If on any such application the court makes such a declaration as is mentioned in subsection (1), the tenant's notice shall cease to have effect on the order becoming final.

(4) If, however, any such application is dismissed by the court, then (subject to subsection (5)) the court shall make an order

(a) declaring that the landlord's counter-notice shall be of no effect, and

(b) requiring the landlord to give a further counter-notice to the tenant by such date as is specified in the order.

(5) Subsection (4) shall not apply if

(a) the counter-notice complies with the requirement set out in section 45 (2) (c), and

(b) either

(i) an application for an order under section 47 (1) is pending, or

(ii) the period specified in section 47 (3) as the period for the making of such an application has not expired.

(6) Subsection (3) of section 45 shall apply to any further counter-notice required to be given by the landlord under subsection (4) above as if it were a counter-notice under that section complying with the requirement set out in subsection (2) (a) of that section.

III L&T [259]

47. Application to defeat tenant's claim where landlord intends to redevelop

(1) Where the landlord has given the tenant a counter-notice under section 45 which complies with the requirement set out in subsection (2) (c) of that section, the court may, on the application of the landlord, by order declare that the right to acquire a new lease shall not be exercisable by the tenant by reason of the landlord's intention to redevelop any premises in which the tenant's flat is contained; and on such an order becoming final the tenant's notice shall cease to have effect.

(2) The court shall not make an order under subsection (1) unless it is satisfied

(a) that the tenant's lease of his flat is due to terminate within the period of five years beginning with the relevant date; and

(b) that for the purposes of redevelopment the landlord intends, once the lease has so terminated

(i) to demolish or reconstruct, or

(ii) to carry out substantial works of construction on,

the whole or a substantial part of any premises in which the flat is contained; and

(c) that he could not reasonably do so without obtaining possession of the flat.

(3) Any application for an order under subsection (1) must be made within the period of two months beginning with the date of the giving of the counter-notice to the tenant; but, where the counter-notice is one falling within section 46 (1) (a), such an application shall not be proceeded with until such time (if any) as any order dismissing an application under section 46 (1) becomes final.

(4) Where an application for an order under subsection (1) is dismissed by the court, the court shall make an order

(a) declaring that the landlord's counter-notice shall be of no effect, and

(b) requiring the landlord to give a further counter-notice to the tenant by such date as is specified in the order.

(5) Where

(a) the landlord has given such a counter-notice as is mentioned in subsection (1), but

(b) either

(i) no application for an order under that subsection is made within the period referred to in subsection (3), or

(ii) such an application is so made but is subsequently withdrawn,

then (subject to subsection (7)), the landlord shall give a further counter-notice to the tenant within the period of two months beginning with the appropriate date.

(6) In subsection (5) "the appropriate date" means

(a) if subsection (5) (b) (i) applies, the date immediately following the end of the period referred to in subsection (3); and

(b) if subsection (5) (b) (ii) applies, the date of withdrawal of the application.

(7) Subsection (5) shall not apply if any application has been made by the landlord for an order under section 46 (1).

(8) Subsection (3) of section 45 shall apply to any further counter-notice required to be given by the landlord under subsection (4) or (5) above as if it were a counter-notice under that section complying with the requirement set out in subsection (2) (a) of that section.

III L&T [259.1]

Premises in which the flat is contained The House of Lords has held that "any premises in which the flat is contained" (s 47(2)(b)) has to be an objectively recognisable physical space, something which the landlord, the tenant and a visitor would recognise as "premises". While much will depend upon the physical facts on the ground, in the case of a single block of flats with several entrances leading to separate staircases, the whole block of flats was the premises: *Majorstake Ltd v Curtis* [2008] UKHL 10, overturning Court of Appeal decision that the words could apply to two adjacent flats (one on top of the other or side by side).

III L&T [260]

48. Applications where terms in dispute or failure to enter into new lease

(1) Where the landlord has given the tenant

(a) a counter-notice under section 45 which complies with the requirement set out in subsection (2) (a) of that section, or

(b) a further counter-notice required by or by virtue of section 46 (4) or section 47 (4) or (5),

but any of the terms of acquisition remain in dispute at the end of the period of two months beginning with the date when the counter-notice or further counter-notice was so given, the appropriate tribunal may, on the application of either the tenant or the landlord, determine the matters in dispute.

(2) Any application under subsection (1) must be made not later than the end of the period of six months beginning with the date on which the counter-notice or further counter-notice was given to the tenant.

(3) Where

(a) the landlord has given the tenant such a counter-notice or further counter-notice as is mentioned in subsection (1) (a) or (b), and

(b) all the terms of acquisition have been either agreed between those persons or determined by the appropriate tribunal under subsection (1),

but a new lease has not been entered into in pursuance of the tenant's notice by the end of the appropriate period specified in subsection (6), the court may, on the application of either the tenant or the landlord, make such order as it thinks fit with respect to the performance or discharge of any obligations arising out of that notice.

(4) Any such order may provide for the tenant's notice to be deemed to have been withdrawn at the end of the appropriate period specified in subsection (6).

(5) Any application for an order under subsection (3) must be made not later than the end of the period of two months beginning immediately after the end of the appropriate period specified in subsection (6).

(6) For the purposes of this section the appropriate period is

(a) where all of the terms of acquisition have been agreed between the tenant and the landlord, the period of two months beginning with the date when those terms were finally so agreed; or

(b) where all or any of those terms have been determined by the appropriate tribunal under subsection (1)

(i) the period of two months beginning with the date when the decision of the tribunal under subsection (1) becomes final, or

(ii) such other period as may have been fixed by the tribunal when making its determination.

(7) In this Chapter "the terms of acquisition", in relation to a claim by a tenant under this Chapter, means the terms on which the tenant is to acquire a new lease of his flat, whether they relate to the terms to be contained in the lease or to the premium or any other amount payable by virtue of Schedule 13 in connection with the grant of the lease, or otherwise.

III L&T [260.1]

Identifying the terms of acquisition In *Greenpine Investment Holding Ltd v Howard De Walden Estates Ltd* [2016] EWHC 1923 (Ch) the court examined the operation of the statutory scheme in the 1993 Act in order to determine when a "term of acquisition" had to be identified as being a matter in dispute between the parties for the purposes of s 48(1); the court concluded that such terms were the proposals contained in a tenant's notice and a landlord's counter-notice at the relevant time, which meant that the time limit for applying to enforce or discharge the statutory contract ran from the time, as defined in s 48(6), when the terms of acquisition – not other terms or requirements – had been agreed or determined by the tribunal.

III L&T [260.2]

Making the application Section 48(2) requires the application to be 'made' within six months of the service of the landlord's counter-notice. The word 'made' connotes a unilateral act by the applicant, who makes the application by starting the proceedings. The application could be started in only two ways: by 'sending' or 'delivering' a notice of application to the tribunal. Either sending or delivering the notice was effective to start the proceedings, and therefore the posting of a correctly addressed and sufficiently stamped notice of application to the tribunal was sufficient. The relevant date was thus the date of posting, not of receipt: *Mahtaban Salehabady v Trustees of The Eyre Estate* [2017] UKUT 60 (LC).

III L&T [261]

49. Applications where landlord fails to give counter-notice or further counter-notice

(1) Where the tenant's notice has been given in accordance with section 42 but

- (a) the landlord has failed to give the tenant a counter-notice in accordance with section 45 (1), or
- (b) if required to give a further counter-notice to the tenant by or by virtue of section 46 (4) or section 47 (4) or (5), the landlord has failed to comply with that requirement,

the court may, on the application of the tenant, make an order determining, in accordance with the proposals contained in the tenant's notice, the terms of acquisition.

(2) The court shall not make such an order on an application made by virtue of paragraph (a) of subsection (1) unless it is satisfied

- (a) that on the relevant date the tenant had the right to acquire a new lease of his flat; and
- (b) if applicable, that the requirements of Part I of Schedule 11 were complied with as respects the giving of copies of the tenant's notice.

(3) Any application for an order under subsection (1) must be made not later than the end of the period of six months beginning with the date by which the counter-notice or further counter-notice referred to in that subsection was required to be given.

(4) Where

- (a) the terms of acquisition have been determined by an order of the court under this section, but
- (b) a new lease has not been entered into in pursuance of the tenant's notice by the end of the appropriate period specified in subsection (7),

the court may, on the application of either the tenant or the landlord, make such order as it thinks fit with respect to the performance or discharge of any obligations arising out of that notice.

(5) Any such order may provide for the tenant's notice to be deemed to have been withdrawn at the end of the appropriate period specified in subsection (7).

(6) Any application for an order under subsection (4) must be made not later than the end of the period of two months beginning immediately after the end of the appropriate period specified in subsection (7).

(7) For the purposes of this section the appropriate period is

(a) the period of two months beginning with the date when the order of the court under subsection (1) becomes final, or

(b) such other period as may have been fixed by the court when making that order.

III L&T [262]

50. Applications where landlord cannot be found

(1) Where

(a) a qualifying tenant of a flat desired to make a claim to exercise the right to acquire a new lease of his flat, but

(b) the landlord cannot be found or his identity cannot be ascertained,

the court may, on the application of the tenant, make a vesting order under this subsection.

(2) Where

(a) a qualifying tenant of a flat desires to make such a claim as is mentioned in subsection (1), and

(b) paragraph (b) of that subsection does not apply, but

(c) a copy of a notice of that claim cannot be given in accordance with Part I of Schedule 11 to any person to whom it would otherwise be required to be so given because that person cannot be found or his identity cannot be ascertained,

the court may, on the application of the tenant, make an order dispensing with the need to give a copy of such a notice to that person.

(3) The court shall not make an order on any application under subsection (1) or (2) unless it is satisfied

(a) that on the date of the making of the application the tenant had the right to acquire a new lease of his flat; and

(b) that on that date he would not have been precluded by any provision of this Chapter from giving a valid notice under section 42 with respect to his flat.

(4) Before making any such order the court may require the tenant to take such further steps by way of advertisement or otherwise as the court thinks proper for the purpose of tracing the person in question; and if, after an application is made for a vesting order under subsection (1) and before any lease is executed in pursuance of the application, the landlord is traced, then no further proceedings shall be taken with a view to a lease being so executed, but (subject to subsection (5))

(a) the rights and obligations of all parties shall be determined as if the tenant had, at the date of the application, duly given notice under section 42 of his claim to exercise the right to acquire a new lease of his flat; and

(b) the court may give such directions as the court thinks fit as to the steps to be taken for giving effect to those rights and obligations, including directions modifying or dispensing with any of the requirements of this Chapter or of regulations made under this Part.

(5) An application for a vesting order under subsection (1) may be withdrawn at any time before execution of a lease under section 51 (3) and, after it is withdrawn, subsection (4) (a) above shall not apply; but where any step is taken

(whether by the landlord or the tenant) for the purpose of giving effect to subsection (4) (a) in the case of any application, the application shall not afterwards be withdrawn except

(a) with the consent of the landlord, or

(b) by leave of the court,

and the court shall not give leave unless it appears to the court just to do so by reason of matters coming to the knowledge of the tenant in consequence of the tracing of the landlord.

(6) Where an order has been made under subsection (2) dispensing with the need to give a copy of a notice under section 42 to a particular person with respect to any flat, then if

(a) a notice is subsequently given under that section with respect to that flat, and

(b) in reliance on the order, a copy of the notice is not to be given to that person,

the notice must contain a statement of the effect of the order.

(7) Where a notice under section 42 contains such a statement in accordance with subsection (6) above, then in determining for the purposes of any provision of this Chapter whether the requirements of Part I of Schedule 11 have been complied with in relation to the notice, those requirements shall be deemed to have been complied with so far as relating to the giving of a copy of the notice to the person referred to in subsection (6) above.

NOTES TO SECTIONS 46–50

III L&T [262A]

Premises in which the flat is contained The House of Lords, reversing the Court of Appeal decision at [2006] EWCA Civ 1171, [2006] 37 EG 194, [2006] 3 WLR 1114, held that "premises in which the flat is contained" had to be interpreted objectively: *Majorstake Ltd v Curtis* [2008] UKHL 10, [2008] 2 All ER 303, [2008] All ER (D) 70 (Feb), (2008) Times, 12 February. The result in the instant case, about development of two flats in a block, was that the block constituted the "premises", whereas the two flats together did not.

III L&T [262.1]

Application to the court An application under s 50(1) or (2) must be made by the issue of a claim form in accordance with the Pt 8 procedure, which need not be served on any other party. The court may grant or refuse the application or give directions for its future conduct, including the addition as defendants of such persons as appear to have an interest in it.

III L&T [262.2]

Validity of tenant's notice The court has jurisdiction to rule on the validity of a notice under Leasehold Reform, Housing and Urban Development Act 1993 s 42, and the price proposed by the tenant in the tenant's notice under s 42 or by the landlord in the counter-notice under s 45 must be a realistic figure otherwise the notice is invalid: *Cadogan v Morris* (1998) 77 P & CR 336, 31 HLR 732, CA. See also the note at para **III L&T [257.7]**.

III L&T [262.3]

The terms of acquisition Either party may apply, under Leasehold Reform, Housing and Urban Development Act 1993 s 48(1) (see para **III L&T [260]**), for matters remaining in dispute after two months to be determined by a leasehold valuation tribunal. A likely area for dispute is the premium payable for the renewal. In *Hordern v Viscount Chelsea* [1997] 1 EGLR 195, [1997] 07 EG 144, the Leasehold Valuation Tribunal took the value of a 90-year lease, added 1% for equivalent freehold interest and made a 25% deduction to reflect the risk of the tenant claiming security of tenure under the Landlord and Tenant Act 1954 Pt 1.

III L&T [263]

51. Supplementary provisions relating to vesting orders under section 50(1)

(1) A vesting order under section 50 (1) is an order providing for the surrender of the tenant's lease of his flat and for the granting to him of a new lease of it on such terms as may be determined by the appropriate tribunal to be appropriate with a view to the lease being granted to him in like manner (so far as the circumstances permit) as if he had, at the date of his application, given notice under section 42 of his claim to exercise the right to acquire a new lease of his flat.

(2) If the appropriate tribunal so determines in the case of a vesting order under section 50 (1), the order shall have effect in relation to property which is less extensive than that specified in the application on which the order was made.

(3) Where any lease is to be granted to a tenant by virtue of a vesting order under section 50 (1), then on his paying into court the appropriate sum there shall be executed by such person as the court may designate a lease which

- (a) is in a form approved by the appropriate tribunal, and
- (b) contains such provisions as may be so approved for the purpose of giving effect so far as possible to section 56 (1) and section 57 (as that section applies in accordance with subsections (7) and (8) below);

and that lease shall be effective to vest in the person to whom it is granted the property expressed to be demised by it, subject to and in accordance with the terms of the lease.

(4) In connection with the determination by the appropriate tribunal of any question as to the property to be demised by any such lease, or as to the rights with or subject to which it is to be demised, it shall be assumed (unless the contrary is shown) that the landlord has no interest in property other than the property to be demised and, for the purpose of excepting them from the lease, any minerals underlying that property.

(5) The appropriate sum to be paid into court in accordance with subsection (3) is the aggregate of

- (a) such amount as may be determined by the appropriate tribunal to be the premium which is payable under Schedule 13 in respect of the grant of the new lease;
- (b) such other amount or amounts (if any) as may be determined by such a tribunal to be payable by virtue of that Schedule in connection with the grant of that lease; and
- (c) any amounts or estimated amounts determined by such a tribunal as being, at the time of execution of that lease, due to the landlord from the tenant (whether due under or in respect of the tenant's lease of his flat or under or in respect of an agreement collateral thereto).

(6) Where any lease is granted to a person in accordance with this section, the payment into court of the appropriate sum shall be taken to have satisfied any claims against the tenant, his personal representatives or assigns in respect of the premium and any other amounts payable as mentioned in subsection (5) (a) and (b).

(7) Subject to subsection (8), the following provisions, namely

- (a) sections 57 to 59, and
- (b) section 61 and Schedule 14,

shall, so far as capable of applying to a lease granted in accordance with this section, apply to such a lease as they apply to a lease granted under section 56; and subsections (6) and (7) of that section shall apply in relation to a lease granted in accordance with this section as they apply in relation to a lease granted under that section.

(8) In its application to a lease granted in accordance with this section

- (a) section 57 shall have effect as if

(i) any reference to the relevant date were a reference to the date of the application under section 50 (1) in pursuance of which the vesting order under that provision was made, and

(ii) in subsection (5) the reference to section 56 (3) (a) were a reference to subsection (5) (c) above; and

(b) section 58 shall have effect as if

(i) in subsection (3) the second reference to the landlord were a reference to the person designated under subsection (3) above, and

(ii) subsections (6) (a) and (7) were omitted.

III L&T [263.1]

Payment into court The procedure for paying money into court under s 51(3), and the appropriate court, is now regulated by the Practice Direction to CPR Pt 56 para 14.5 (see para **CPR PD 56**).

Landlord's right to terminate new lease

III L&T [264]

61. Landlord's right to terminate new lease on grounds of redevelopment

(1) Where a lease of a flat ("the new lease") has been granted under section 56 but the court is satisfied, on an application made by the landlord

(a) that for the purposes of redevelopment the landlord intends

(i) to demolish or reconstruct, or

(ii) to carry out substantial works of construction on,

the whole or a substantial part of any premises in which the flat is contained, and

(b) that he could not reasonably do so without obtaining possession of the flat,

the court shall by order declare that the landlord is entitled as against the tenant to obtain possession of the flat and the tenant is entitled to be paid compensation by the landlord for the loss of the flat.

(2) An application for an order under this section may be made

(a) at any time during the period of 12 months ending with the term date of the lease in relation to which the right to acquire a new lease was exercised; and

(b) at any time during the period of five years ending with the term date of the new lease.

(3) Where the new lease is not the first lease to be granted under section 56 in respect of a flat, subsection (2) shall apply as if paragraph (b) included a reference to the term date of any previous lease granted under that section in respect of the flat, but paragraph (a) shall be taken to be referring to the term date of the lease in relation to which the right to acquire a new lease was first exercised.

(4) Where an order is made under this section, the new lease shall determine, and compensation shall become payable, in accordance with Schedule 14 to this Act; and the provisions of that Schedule shall have effect as regards the measure of compensation payable by virtue of any such order and the effects of any such order where there are sub-leases, and as regards other matters relating to orders and applications under this section.

(5) Except in subsection (1) (a) or (b), any reference in this section to the flat held by the tenant under the new lease includes any premises let with the flat under that lease.

III L&T [264.1]

Application to the court Although no specific procedure is prescribed in the Practice Direction to CPR Pt 56 (see para **CPR PD 56**) for applications under s 61, it is suggested, having regard to the general scheme of CPR PD 56 and also to the fact that applications of this nature would formerly have been by originating application, that the proceedings should be by Pt 8 claim form.

Supplemental

III L&T [265]

62. Interpretation of Chapter II

(1) In this Chapter

"appropriate tribunal" means—

(a) in relation to premises in England, the First-tier Tribunal or, where determined by or under Tribunal Procedure Rules, the Upper Tribunal; and

(b) in relation to premises in Wales, a leasehold valuation tribunal;

"the existing lease", in relation to a claim by a tenant under this Chapter, means the lease in relation to which the claim is made;

"the landlord", in relation to such a claim, has the meaning given by section 40 (1);

"mortgage" includes a charge or lien;

"qualifying tenant" shall be construed in accordance with section 39 (3);

"the relevant date" (unless the context otherwise requires) has the meaning given by section 39 (8);

"the tenant's notice" means the notice given under section 42;

"the terms of acquisition" shall be construed in accordance with section 48 (7);

"third party", in relation to a lease, means any person who is a party to the lease apart from the tenant under the lease and his immediate landlord.

(2) Subject to subsection (3), references in this Chapter to a flat, in relation to a claim by a tenant under this Chapter, include any garage, outhouse, garden, yard and appurtenances belonging to, or usually enjoyed with, the flat and let to the tenant with the flat on the relevant date (or, in a case where an application is made under section 50 (1), on the date of the making of the application).

(3) Subsection (2) does not apply

(a) to any reference to a flat in section 47 or 55 (1); or

(b) to any reference to a flat (not falling within paragraph (a) above) which occurs in the context of a reference to any premises containing the flat.

III L&T [265.1]

"Appurtenance" A separately let store-room may be an appurtenance even though situated several floors below the flat: *Viscount Chelsea v McGirk* (1996) 73 P & CR 483, 29 HLR 294, CA.

CHAPTER V TENANTS' RIGHT TO MANAGEMENT AUDIT

III L&T [266]

76. Right to audit management by landlord

(1) This Chapter has effect to confer on two or more qualifying tenants of dwellings held on leases from the same landlord the right, exercisable subject to and in accordance with this Chapter, to have an audit carried out on their behalf which relates to the management of the relevant premises and any appurtenant property by or on behalf of the landlord.

(2) That right shall be exercisable

(a) where the relevant premises consist of or include two dwellings let to qualifying tenants of the same landlord, by either or both of those tenants; and

(b) where the relevant premises consist of or include three or more dwellings let to qualifying tenants of the same landlord, by not less than two-thirds of those tenants;

and in this Chapter the dwellings let to those qualifying tenants are referred to as "the constituent dwellings".

(3) In relation to an audit on behalf of two or more qualifying tenants

(a) "the relevant premises" means so much of

(i) the building or buildings containing the dwellings let to those tenants, and

(ii) any other building or buildings,

as constitutes premises in relation to which management functions are discharged in respect of the costs of which common service charge contributions are payable under the leases of those qualifying tenants; and

(b) "appurtenant property" means so much of any property not contained in the relevant premises as constitutes property in relation to which any such management functions are discharged.

(4) This Chapter also has effect to confer on a single qualifying tenant of a dwelling the right, exercisable subject to and in accordance with this Chapter, to have an audit carried out on his behalf which relates to the management of the relevant premises and any appurtenant property by or on behalf of the landlord.

(5) That right shall be exercisable by a single qualifying tenant of a dwelling where the relevant premises contain no other dwelling let to a qualifying tenant apart from that let to him.

(6) In relation to an audit on behalf of a single qualifying tenant

(a) "the relevant premises" means so much of

(i) the building containing the dwelling let to him, and

(ii) any other building or buildings,

as constitutes premises in relation to which management functions are discharged in respect of the costs of which a service charge is payable under his lease (whether as a common service charge contribution or otherwise); and

(b) "appurtenant property" means so much of any property not contained in the relevant premises as constitutes property in relation to which any such management functions are discharged.

(7) The provisions of sections 78 to 83 shall, with any necessary modifications, have effect in relation to an audit on behalf of a single qualifying tenant as they have effect in relation to an audit on behalf of two or more qualifying tenants.

(8) For the purposes of this section common service charge contributions are payable by two or more persons under their leases if they may be required under the terms of those leases to contribute to the same costs by the payment of service charges.

III L&T [266.1]

Qualifying tenant This expression is defined in Leasehold Reform, Housing and Urban Development Act 1993 s 77.

III L&T [266.2]

Landlord This means the immediate landlord: Leasehold Reform, Housing and Urban Development Act 1993 s 84.

III L&T [266.3]

Management functions This includes functions with respect to the provision of services or the repair, maintenance or insurance of property: Leasehold Reform, Housing and Urban Development Act 1993 s 84.

III L&T [266.4]

Service charge This has the meaning given by the Landlord and Tenant Act 1985 s 18(1) (see para **III L&T [171]**).

III L&T [266.5]

Exercise of right to have a management audit This right is exercised by notice under Leasehold Reform, Housing and Urban Development Act 1993 s 80.

III L&T [267]

81. Procedure following giving of notice under section 80

(1) Where the landlord is given a notice under section 80, then within the period of one month beginning with the date of the giving of the notice, he shall—

- (a) comply with it so far as it relates to documents within section 79(2);
- (b) either—
  - (i) comply with it, or
  - (ii) give the auditor a notice stating that he objects to doing so for such reasons as are specified in the notice,

  so far as it relates to documents within section 79(2A); and
- (c) if a date is specified in the notice under subsection (3)(d) of that section, either approve the date or propose another date for the carrying out of an inspection under section 79(4).

(2) Any date proposed by the landlord under subsection (1)(c) must be a date falling not later than the end of the period of two months beginning with the date of the giving of the notice under section 80.

(3) Where a relevant person is given a notice under section 79, then within the period of one month beginning with the date of the giving of the notice, he shall either—

- (a) comply with it, or
- (b) give the auditor a notice stating that he objects to doing so for such reasons as are specified in the notice,

in the case of every document or description of document specified in the notice.

(4) If by the end of the period of two months beginning with—

- (a) the date of the giving of the notice under section 80, or
- (b) the date of the giving of such a notice under section 79 as is mentioned in subsection (3) above,

the landlord or (as the case may be) a relevant person has failed to comply with any requirement of the notice, the court may, on the application of the auditor, make an order requiring the landlord or (as the case may be) the relevant person to comply with that requirement within such period as is specified in the order.

(5) The court shall not make an order under subsection (4) in respect of any document or documents unless it is satisfied that the document or documents falls or fall within section 79(2) or (2A).

(6) If by the end of the period of two months specified in subsection (2) no inspection under section 79(4) has been carried out by the auditor, the court may, on the application of the auditor, make an order providing for such an inspection to be carried out on such date as is specified in the order.

(7) Any application for an order under subsection (4) or (6) must be made before the end of the period of four months beginning with—

- (a) in the case of an application made in connection with a notice given under section 80, the date of the giving of that notice; or

(b) in the case of an application made in connection with such a notice under section 79 as is mentioned in subsection (3) above, the date of the giving of that notice.

III L&T [267.1]

"Court" This means a county court; see the Leasehold Reform, Housing and Urban Development Act 1993 s 90 (see para **III L&T [268]**). Although no specific procedure is prescribed in the Practice Direction to CPR Pt 56 (see para **CPR PD 56**) for applications under s 81, it is suggested, having regard to the general scheme of CPR PD 56, that the application should be by Pt 8 claim form.

III L&T [267.2]

Supplementary provisions The Leasehold Reform, Housing and Urban Development Act 1993 s 83 makes provision for cases in which (a) a landlord disposes of the whole or part of his interest after receiving a notice under Leasehold Reform, Housing and Urban Development Act 1993 s 80, and (b) a person to whom notice has been given as a relevant person within the meaning of Leasehold Reform, Housing and Urban Development Act 1993 s 79(7), ceases to be such. It also prevents a further notice being given within 12 months after notice to the landlord or a relevant person.

III L&T [267.3]

Relief against forfeiture Where a tenant owes rent but has not admitted or agreed to owing service charges as well the landlord's right of re-entry is exercisable only in respect of the rent and the jurisdiction, under s 146 of the Law of Property Act 1925, to grant relief as regards unpaid service charges, is not available. However, for the purposes of s 138 of the County Courts Act 1984, the court's discretion to grant relief provides for the payment of "all the rent in arrear" and this might be interpreted as including service charges, if treated as rent by the terms of the lease: *Mohammadi v Anston Investments Ltd* [2003] EWCA Civ 981, [2004] HLR 88.

CHAPTER VII GENERAL

III L&T [268]

90. Jurisdiction of county courts

(1) Any jurisdiction expressed to be conferred on the court by this Part shall be exercised by the county court.

(2) There shall also be brought in the county court any proceedings for determining any question arising under or by virtue of any provision of Chapter I or II or this Chapter which is not a question falling within its jurisdiction by virtue of subsection (1) or one falling within the jurisdiction of the appropriate tribunal (within the meaning of section 91) by virtue of that section.

(3) Where, however, there are brought in the High Court any proceedings which, apart from this subsection, are proceedings within the jurisdiction of the High Court, the High Court shall have jurisdiction to hear and determine any proceedings joined with those proceedings which are proceedings within the jurisdiction of the county court by virtue of subsection (1) or (2).

(4) Where any proceedings are brought in the county court by virtue of subsection (1) or (2), the court shall have jurisdiction to hear and determine any other proceedings joined with those proceedings, despite the fact that, apart from this subsection, those other proceedings would be outside the court's jurisdiction.

III L&T [269]

91. Jurisdiction of [...] tribunals

(1) Any question arising in relation to any of the matters specified in subsection (2) shall, in default of agreement, be determined by the appropriate tribunal.

(2) Those matters are—

(a) the terms of acquisition relating to—

(i) any interest which is to be acquired by a *nominee purchaser* [RTE company] in pursuance of Chapter I, or

(ii) any new lease which is to be granted to a tenant in pursuance of Chapter II,

including in particular any matter which needs to be determined for the purposes of any provision of Schedule 6 or 13;

(b) the terms of any lease which is to be granted in accordance with section 36 and Schedule 9;

(c) the amount of any payment falling to be made by virtue of section 18(2);

(ca) the amount of any compensation payable under section 37A;

(cb) the amount of any compensation payable under section 61A;

(d) the amount of any costs payable by any person or persons by virtue of any provision of Chapter I or II and, in the case of costs to which section 33(1) or 60(1) applies, the liability of any person or persons by virtue of any such provision to pay any such costs; and

(e) the apportionment between two or more persons of any amount (whether of costs or otherwise) payable by virtue of any such provision.

(3)-(8) . . .

(9) The appropriate tribunal may, when determining the property in which any interest is to be acquired in pursuance of a notice under section 13 or 42, specify in its determination property which is less extensive than that specified in that notice.

(10) . . .

(11) In this section—

"the nominee purchaser" and "the participating tenants" have ["RTE company" has] the same meaning as in Chapter I;

"the terms of acquisition" shall be construed in accordance with section 24(8) or section 48(7), as appropriate;

(12) For the purposes of this section, "appropriate tribunal" means—

(a) in relation to property in England, the First-tier Tribunal or, where determined by or under Tribunal Procedure Rules, the Upper Tribunal; and

(a) in relation to property in Wales, a leasehold valuation tribunal.

Amendments *Text is as provided by the Commonhold and Leasehold Reform Act 2002 with effect from 30 September 2003: Commonhold and Leasehold Reform Act 2002 (Commencement No 2 and Savings) (England) Order 2003, SI 2003/1986. Date in force to be appointed in relation to deletion of text in italic and insertion of text in square brackets in sub-ss (2) and (11).*

III L&T [269.1]

Procedure for transfer from court to tribunal If an order is made transferring an application to a leasehold valuation tribunal under s 91(4), the court will send notice of the transfer to all parties to the application and send to the tribunal copies of the order of transfer and all documents filed in the proceedings: CPR PD 56 para 14.6 (para **CPR PD 56**).

III L&T [270]

92. Enforcement of obligations under Chapters I and II

(1) The court may, on the application of any person interested, make an order requiring any person who has failed to comply with any requirement imposed on him under or by virtue of any provision of Chapter I or II to make good the default within such time as is specified in the order.

(2) An application shall not be made under subsection (1) unless

(a) a notice has been previously given to the person in question requiring him to make good the default, and

(b) more than 14 days have elapsed since the date of the giving of that notice without his having done so.

III L&T [270.1]

Procedure for enforcement Non-compliance with a court order under the Leasehold Reform, Housing and Urban Development Act 1993, which includes a penal notice, is prima facie contempt of court. See CPR Sch 2 CCR Ord 29 r 1 (see para **CCR 29r1**), for the procedure for enforcement once an order of the court has been made, served and disobeyed.

III L&T [271]

93. Agreements excluding or modifying rights of tenant under Chapter I or II

(1) Except as provided by this section, any agreement relating to a lease (whether contained in the instrument creating the lease or not and whether made before the creation of the lease or not) shall be void in so far as it—

(a) purports to exclude or modify—

(i) any entitlement to *participate in the making of a claim to exercise* [be, or do any thing as, a member of a RTE company for the purpose of the exercise of] the right to collective enfranchisement under Chapter I,

(ii) any right to acquire a new lease under Chapter II, or

(iii) any right to compensation under section 61; or

(b) provides for the termination or surrender of the lease in the event of the tenant becoming *a participating tenant for the purposes of Chapter I or* [, or doing any thing as, a member of a RTE company (within the meaning of Chapter 1) or of such a RTE company doing any thing or in the event of a tenant] giving a notice under section 42; or

(c) provides for the imposition of any penalty or disability *on the tenant in that event* [in the event of a tenant becoming, or doing any thing as, a member of such a RTE company or of such a RTE company doing any thing].

(2) Subsection (1) shall not be taken to preclude a tenant from surrendering his lease, and shall not—

(a) invalidate any agreement for the acquisition on behalf of a tenant of an interest superior to his lease, or for the acquisition by a tenant of a new lease, on terms different from those provided by Chapters I and II; or

(b) where a tenant has *become a participating tenant for the purposes of Chapter I or has* given a notice under section 42, invalidate—

(i) any agreement that the notice given under *section 13 or (as the case may be)* section 42 shall cease to have effect, or

(ii) any provision of such an agreement excluding or restricting for a period not exceeding three years any such *entitlement or* right as is mentioned in subsection (1)(a)*(i) or* (ii); or

(c) where a tenant's right to compensation under section 61 has accrued, invalidate any agreement as to the amount of the compensation.

(3) Where—

(a) a tenant having the right to acquire a new lease under Chapter II—

(i) has entered into an agreement for the surrender of his lease without the prior approval of the court, or

(ii) has entered into an agreement for the grant of a new lease without any of the terms of acquisition (within the meaning of that Chapter) having been determined by the appropriate tribunal (within the meaning of that Chapter) under that Chapter, or

(b) a tenant has been granted a new lease under Chapter II or by virtue of subsection (4) below and, on his landlord claiming possession for the purposes of redevelopment, enters into an agreement without the prior approval of the court for the surrender of the lease,

then on the application of the tenant the county court, or any court in which proceedings are brought on the agreement, may, if in its opinion the tenant is not adequately recompensed under the agreement for his rights under Chapter II, set aside or vary the agreement and give such other relief as appears to it to be just having regard to the situation and conduct of the parties.

(4) Where a tenant has the right to acquire a new lease under Chapter II, there may with the approval of the court be granted to him in satisfaction of that right a new lease on such terms as may be approved by the court, which may include terms excluding or modifying—

(a) any entitlement to *participate in the making of a claim to exercise* [be, or do any thing as, a member of a RTE company for the purpose of the exercise of] the right to collective enfranchisement under Chapter I, or

(b) any right to acquire a further lease under Chapter II.

(5) Subject to the provisions specified in subsection (6) and to subsection (7), a lease may be granted by virtue of subsection (4), and shall if so granted be binding on persons entitled to any interest in or charge on the landlord's estate—

(a) despite the fact that, apart from this subsection, it would not be authorised against any such persons, and

(b) despite any statutory or other restrictions on the landlord's powers of leasing.

(6) The provisions referred to in subsection (5) are—

(a) sections 117 to 121 of the Charities Act 2011 (restrictions on disposition of charity land); and

(b) paragraph 8(2)(c) of Schedule 2 to this Act.

(7) Where the existing lease of the tenant is granted after the commencement of Chapter II and, the grant being subsequent to the creation of a charge on the landlord's estate, the existing lease is not binding on the persons interested in the charge, a lease granted by virtue of subsection (4) shall not be binding on those persons.

(8) Where a lease is granted by virtue of subsection (4), then except in so far as provision is made to the contrary by the terms of the lease, the following provisions shall apply in relation to the lease as they apply in relation to a lease granted under section 56, namely—

(a) section 58(3), (5) and (6);

(b) section 59(2) to (5); and

(c) section 61 and Schedule 14;

and subsections (5) to (7) of section 56 shall apply in relation to the lease as they apply in relation to a lease granted under that section.

Amendments *Text in italic deleted and text in square brackets inserted by s 124 of and Schedule 8 to the Commonhold and Leasehold Reform Act 2002. Date in force to be appointed.*

III L&T [272]

99. Notices

(1) Any notice required or authorised to be given under this Part

(a) shall be in writing; and

(b) may be sent by post.

(2) Where in accordance with Chapter I or II an address in England and Wales is specified as an address at which notices may be given to any person or persons under that Chapter

(a) any notice required or authorised to be given to that person or those persons under that Chapter may (without prejudice to the operation of subsection (3)) be given to him or them at the address so specified; but

(b) if a new address in England and Wales is so specified in substitution for that address by the giving of a notice to that effect, any notice so required or authorised to be given may be given to him or them at that new address instead.

(3) Where a tenant is required or authorised to give any notice under Chapter I or II to a person who

(a) is the tenant's immediate landlord, and

(b) is such a landlord in respect of premises to which Part VI of the Landlord and Tenant Act 1987 (information to be furnished to tenants) applies,

the tenant may, unless he has been subsequently notified by the landlord of a different address in England and Wales for the purposes of this section, give the notice to the landlord

(i) at the address last furnished to the tenant as the landlord's address for service in accordance with section 48 of that Act (notification of address for service of notices on landlord); or

(ii) if no such address has been furnished, at the address last furnished to the tenant as the landlord's address in accordance with section 47 of that Act (landlord's name and address to be contained in demands for rent).

(4) Subsections (2) and (3) apply to notices in proceedings under Chapter I or II as they apply to notices required or authorised to be given under that Chapter.

(5) Any notice which is given under Chapter I or II by any tenants or tenant must be signed by or on behalf of each of the tenants, or (as the case may be) by or on behalf of the tenant, by whom it is given.

(6) The Secretary of State may by regulations prescribe

(a) the form of any notice required or authorised to be given under this Part; and

(b) the particulars which any such notice must contain (whether in addition to, or in substitution for, any particulars required by virtue of any provision of this Part).

III L&T [272.1]

Signed by the tenant In *St Ermines Property Co Ltd v Tingay* [2002] EWHC 1673 (Ch), [2002] 40 EG 174, the Court held that a notice served under s 42 could only be signed by the tenant personally and was invalid if signed on the tenant's behalf by an attorney.

III L&T [273]

101. General interpretation of Part I

(1) In this Part

"business lease" means a tenancy to which Part II of the Landlord and Tenant Act 1954 applies;

"common parts", in relation to any building or part of a building, includes the structure and exterior of that building or part and any common facilities within it;

"the court" (unless the context otherwise requires) means, by virtue of section 90 (1), the county court;

"disposal" means a disposal whether by the creation or the transfer of an interest, and includes the surrender of a lease and the grant of an option or right of pre-emption, and "acquisition" shall be construed accordingly (as shall expressions related to either of these expressions);

"dwelling" means any building or part of a building occupied or intended to be occupied as a separate dwelling;

"flat" means a separate set of premises (whether or not on the same floor)

(a) which forms part of a building, and

(b) which is constructed or adapted for use for the purposes of a dwelling, and

(c) either the whole or a material part of which lies above or below some other part of the building;

"interest" includes estate;

"lease" and "tenancy", and related expressions, shall be construed in accordance with subsection (2);

"the term date", in relation to a lease granted for a term of years certain, means (subject to subsection (6)) the date of expiry of that term, and, in relation to a tenancy to which any of the provisions of section 102 applies, shall be construed in accordance with those provisions.

(2) In this Part "lease" and "tenancy" have the same meaning, and both expressions include (where the context so permits)

(a) a sub-lease or sub-tenancy, and

(b) an agreement for a lease or tenancy (or for a sub-lease or sub-tenancy),

but do not include a tenancy at will or at sufferance; and the expressions "landlord" and "tenant", and references to letting, to the grant of a lease or to covenants or the terms of a lease, shall be construed accordingly.

(3) In this Part any reference (however expressed) to the lease held by a qualifying tenant of a flat is a reference to a lease held by him under which the demised premises consist of or include the flat (whether with or without one or more other flats).

(4) Where two or more persons jointly constitute either the landlord or the tenant or qualifying tenant in relation to a lease of a flat, any reference in this Part to the landlord or to the tenant or qualifying tenant is (unless the context otherwise requires) a reference to both or all of the persons who jointly constitute the landlord or the tenant or qualifying tenant, as the case may require.

(5) Any reference in this Part to the date of the commencement of a lease is a reference to the date of the commencement of the term of the lease.

(6) In the case of a lease which derives (in accordance with section 7 (6)) from more than one separate lease, references in this Part to the date of the commencement of the lease or to the term date shall, if the terms of the separate leases commenced at different dates or those leases have different term dates, have effect as references to the date of the commencement, or (as the case may be) to the term date, of the lease comprising the flat in question (or the earliest date of commencement or earliest term date of the leases comprising it).

(7) For the purposes of this Part property is let with other property if the properties are let either under the same lease or under leases which, in accordance with section 7 (6), are treated as a single lease.

(8) For the purposes of this Part any lease which is reversionary on another lease shall be treated as if it were a concurrent lease intermediate between that other lease and any interest superior to that other lease.

(9) For the purposes of this Part an order of a court or a decision of a leasehold valuation tribunal the First-tier Tribunal or Upper Tribunal is to be treated as becoming final

(a) if not appealed against, on the expiry of the time for bringing an appeal; or

(b) if appealed against and not set aside in consequence of the appeal, at the time when the appeal and any further appeal is disposed of

(i) by the determination of it and the expiry of the time for bringing a further appeal (if any), or

LANDLORD & TENANT AND HOUSING

(ii) by its being abandoned or otherwise ceasing to have effect.

III L&T [273.1]

Common parts A caretaker's flat in a building was held to be included in the 'common parts' of the building, and was therefore liable to acquisition, as it amounted to a common facility for the benefit of the lessees. Access to the caretaker's flat was not necessary; it was sufficient that the lessees shared the benefit of it by enjoying the services for which it was provided: see *Earl Cadogan v Panagopoulos* [2010] EWCA Civ 1259.

III L&T [273.2]

Flat In *Aldford House Freehold Ltd v (1) Grosvenor (Mayfair) Estate* [2018] EWHC 3430, the court, applying *Boss Holdings Ltd v Grosvenor West End Properties Ltd* [2008] UKHL 5 and *Day v Hosebay Ltd* [2012] UKSC 41, held that the statutory definition of 'flat' was concerned with the purpose for which premises had been constructed or subsequently adapted. The question is whether they had been constructed or adapted for use for the purpose of a dwelling or for some other purpose. The test is not whether the premises had reached such an extent of fitting out, or remained in such good condition, that they could actually be used for living in on the relevant date.

HOUSING ACT 1996

(c 52)

GENERAL NOTES ON HOUSING ACT 1996

III L&T [274]

Jurisdiction The sections of the Housing Act 1996 set out below confer extensive jurisdiction on the county courts. The High Court has concurrent jurisdiction but without an entitlement to recover High Court costs (Housing Act 1996 s 138, see para **III L&T [294]**), except in the grant of injunctions against anti-social behaviour under Housing Act 1996 ss 152–158 (see paras **III L&T [297]–III L&T [303]**). Proceedings for possession under the 1996 Act are possession claims within the meaning of CPR Pt 55 (see para **CPR 55**). All possession claims must be started in the county court for the district in which the land is situated unless the claimant can certify (and verify with a statement of truth (see CPR PD 22 para 1.1(5) at para **CPR PD 22**)) that there are complicated disputes of fact or there are points of law of general importance. The value of the property and the amount of any financial claim may be relevant circumstances, but these factors alone will not normally justify starting the claim in the High Court: see paras **CPR 55.3** and CPR PD 55 paras 1.1 to 1.4 (para **CPR PD 55**).

III L&T [274A]

Homelessness Part VII (HOMELESSNESS) sets out the responsibilities of housing authorities to advise on homelessness and to provide accommodation The text starts at **III L&T [303A]** and provides for decisions to be reviewed and appealed, on a point of law, to the county court: s 204, at **III L&T [306]**. Amendments have been made by the Homelessness Reduction Act 2017 the relevant provisions of which came into force on 3 April 2018 by virtue of the Homelessness Reduction Act 2017 (Commencement and Transitional and Savings Provisions) Regulations 2018, SI 2018/167.

III L&T [275]

Precedents Precedents for a service charge forfeiture notice can be found at **BCCP O[50]**, for claiming possession from an introductory tenant at **BCCP O[1003]** and for an application for an injunction (anti-social behaviour) at **BCCP O[1001]**.

PART III
LANDLORD AND TENANT

CHAPTER I TENANTS' RIGHTS

III L&T [276]

81. Restriction on termination of tenancy for failure to pay service charge

(1) A landlord may not, in relation to premises let as a dwelling, exercise a right of re-entry or forfeiture for failure by a tenant to pay a service charge or administration charge unless—

(a) it is finally determined by (or on appeal from) the appropriate tribunal or by a court, or by an arbitral tribunal in proceedings pursuant to a post-dispute arbitration agreement, that the amount of the service charge or administration charge is payable by him, or

(b) the tenant has admitted that it is so payable.

(2) The landlord may not exercise a right of re-entry or forfeiture by virtue of subsection (1)(a) until after the end of the period of 14 days beginning with the day after that on which the final determination is made.

(3) For the purposes of this section it is finally determined that the amount of a service charge or administration charge is payable—

(a) if a decision that it is payable is not appealed against or otherwise challenged, at the end of the time for bringing an appeal or other challenge, or

(b) if such a decision is appealed against or otherwise challenged and not set aside in consequence of the appeal or other challenge, at the time specified in subsection (3A).

(3A) The time referred to in subsection (3)(b) is the time when the appeal or other challenge is disposed of—

(a) by the determination of the appeal or other challenge and the expiry of the time for bringing a subsequent appeal (if any), or

(b) by its being abandoned or otherwise ceasing to have effect.

(4) The reference in subsection (1) to premises let as a dwelling does not include premises let on—

(a) a tenancy to which Part II of the Landlord and Tenant Act 1954 applies (business tenancies),

(b) a tenancy of an agricultural holding within the meaning of the Agricultural Holdings Act 1986 in relation to which that Act applies, or

(c) a farm business tenancy within the meaning of the Agricultural Tenancies Act 1995.

(4A) References in this section to the exercise of a right of re-entry or forfeiture include the service of a notice under section 146(1) of the Law of Property Act 1925 (restriction on re-entry or forfeiture).

(5) In this section

(a) "administration charge" has the meaning given by Part 1 of Schedule 11 to the Commonhold and Leasehold Reform Act 2002,

(b) "arbitration agreement" and "arbitral tribunal" have the same meaning as in Part 1 of the Arbitration Act 1996 (c 23) and "post-dispute arbitration agreement", in relation to any matter, means an arbitration agreement made after a dispute about the matter has arisen,

(c) "dwelling" has the same meaning as in the Landlord and Tenant Act 1985 (c 70), and

(d) "service charge" means a service charge within the meaning of section 18(1) of the Landlord and Tenant Act 1985, other than one excluded from that section by section 27 of that Act (rent of dwelling registered and not entered as variable).

(5A) Any order of a court to give effect to a determination of the appropriate tribunal shall be treated as a determination by the court for the purposes of this section.

(6) Nothing in this section affects the exercise of a right of re-entry or forfeiture on other grounds.

(7) For the purposes of this section, "appropriate tribunal" means—

(a) in relation to premises in England, the First-tier Tribunal or, where determined by or under Tribunal Procedure Rules, the Upper Tribunal; and

(b) in relation to premises in Wales, a leasehold valuation tribunal.

LANDLORD & TENANT AND HOUSING

III L&T [276.1]

Determination by a court A judgment in default for service charges was held to be a determination by a court for the purpose of s 81(1)(b) (in its original unamended form): *Southwark London Borough Council v Tornaritis* [1999] CLY 3744, CC. Note, however, that in *Hillbrow (Richmond) v Alogaily* [2006] 2 CL 347, CC, the court held that a default judgment is not a final determination for the purposes of s 81 in its current form (ie as amended by the Commonhold and Leasehold Reform Act 2002). A purported re-entry without a determination or admission is ineffective as regards arrears of service charge, though it may be effective as regards non-payment of ground rent, in which case s 138 of the County Courts Act 1984 (**II CCA [133]**) comes into play: *Mohammadi v Anston Investments Ltd and Shellpoint Trustees Ltd* [2003] EWCA Civ 981, (2003) 147 Sol Jo LB 1024. It has been held, at county court level, that a default judgment for unpaid service charges qualifies as a final determination for the purposes of the amended s 81: *Church Commissioners for England v Royale Enterprises* [2012] Legal Action 20 (Jan), Central London County Court 22 September 2011.

III L&T [276.2]

Waiver It is possible for a landlord, during the period in which he is prevented from exercising his right of re-entry by s 81, to waive the right to forfeit a lease for non-payment of service charges: *Stemp v 6 Ladbroke Gardens Management Ltd* [2018] UKUT 375 (LC).

III L&T [277]

82. Notice under s 146 of the Law of Property Act 1925

(1) Nothing in section 81 (restriction on termination of tenancy for failure to pay service charge) affects the power of a landlord to serve a notice under section 146 (1) of the Law of Property Act 1925 (restrictions on and relief against forfeiture: notice of breach of covenant or condition).

(2) But such a notice in respect of premises let as a dwelling and failure to pay a service charge is ineffective unless it complies with the following requirements.

(3) It must state that section 81 applies and set out the effect of subsection (1) of that section.

The Secretary of State may by regulations prescribe a form of words to be used for that purpose.

(4) The information or words required must be in characters not less conspicuous than those used in the notice

(a) to indicate that the tenancy may be forfeited, or

(b) to specify the breach complained of,

whichever is the more conspicuous.

(5) In this section "premises let as a dwelling" and "service charge" have the same meaning as in section 81.

(6) Regulations under this section

(a) shall be made by statutory instrument, and

(b) may make different provision for different cases or classes of case including different areas.

Repeal of section *Whole section repealed by the Commonhold and Leasehold Reform Act 2002 with effect from 28 February 2005: see the Commonhold and Leasehold Reform Act 2002 (Commencement No 5 and Saving and Transitional Provision) Order 2004 SI 2004/3056.*

III L&T [278]

84. Right to appoint surveyor to advise on matters relating to service charges

(1) A recognised tenants' association may appoint a surveyor for the purposes of this section to advise on any matters relating to, or which may give rise to, service charges payable to a landlord by one or more members of the association.

The provisions of Schedule 4 have effect for conferring on a surveyor so appointed rights of access to documents and premises.

(2) A person shall not be so appointed unless he is a qualified surveyor.

For this purpose "qualified surveyor" has the same meaning as in section 78 (4) (a) of the Leasehold Reform, Housing and Urban Development Act 1993 (persons qualified for appointment to carry out management audit).

(3) The appointment shall take effect for the purposes of this section upon notice in writing being given to the landlord by the association stating the name and address of the surveyor, the duration of his appointment and the matters in respect of which he is appointed.

(4) An appointment shall cease to have effect for the purposes of this section if the association gives notice in writing to the landlord to that effect or if the association ceases to exist.

(5) A notice is duly given under this section to a landlord of any tenants if it is given to a person who receives on behalf of the landlord the rent payable by those tenants; and a person to whom such a notice is so given shall forward it as soon as may be to the landlord.

(6) In this section

"recognised tenants' association" has the same meaning as in the provisions of the Landlord and Tenant Act 1985 relating to service charges (see section 29 of that Act); and "service charge" means a service charge within the meaning of section 18 (1) of that Act, other than one excluded from that section by section 27 of that Act (rent of dwelling registered and not entered as variable).

III L&T [278.1]

Enforcement If rights conferred by these provisions are disputed or denied they may be enforced by court order, made on an originating application. Jurisdiction is conferred on the court by the Housing Act 1996 Sch 4 para 5 as follows:

ENFORCEMENT OF RIGHTS BY THE COURT

5. (1) If the landlord or other person to whom notice was given under paragraph 3 has not, by the end of the period of one month beginning with the date on which notice was given, complied with the notice, the court may, on the application of the surveyor, make an order requiring him to do so within such period as is specified in the order.

(2) If the landlord does not, within a reasonable period after the making of a request under paragraph 4, afford the surveyor reasonable access for the purposes of carrying out an inspection under that paragraph, the court may, on the application of the surveyor, make an order requiring the landlord to do so on such date as is specified in the order.

(3) An application for an order under this paragraph must be made before the end of the period of four months beginning with the date on which notice was given under paragraph 3 or the request was made under paragraph 4.

(4) An order under this paragraph may be made in general terms or may require the landlord or other person to do specific things, as the court thinks fit.

III L&T [278.2]

Precedent A precedent for an application to the court is provided in **BCCP O[1002]**. Proceedings should be by Pt 8 claim form: see CPR Pt 8 Practice Direction 8B (see para **CPR PD 8B**).

III L&T [279]

95. Jurisdiction of county courts

(1) Any jurisdiction expressed by a provision to which this section applies to be conferred on the court shall be exercised by the county court.

(2) There shall also be brought in the county court any proceedings for determining any question arising under or by virtue of any provision to which this section applies.

(3) Where, however, other proceedings are properly brought in the High Court, that court has jurisdiction to hear and determine proceedings to which subsection (1) or (2) applies which are joined with those proceedings.

(4) Where proceedings are brought in the county court by virtue of subsection (1) or (2), that court has jurisdiction to hear and determine other proceedings joined with those proceedings despite the fact that they would otherwise be outside its jurisdiction.

(5) The provisions to which this section applies are

(a) section 81 (restriction on termination of tenancy for failure to pay service charge), and

(b) section 84 (right to appoint surveyor to advise on matters relating to service charges) and Schedule 4 (rights exercisable by surveyor appointed by tenants' association).

III L&T [279.1]

Enforcing rights of surveyor to inspect A surveyor seeking an order requiring compliance should proceed in the county court by Pt 8 claim form. The court's powers, and the timetable, are set out in the Housing Act 1996 Sch 4 para 5, which is noted under Housing Act 1996 s 84 (see para **III L&T [278.1]**).

PART V
CONDUCT OF TENANTS

CHAPTER 1 INTRODUCTORY TENANCIES

General provisions

III L&T [280]

124. Introductory tenancies

(1) A local housing authority or a housing action trust may elect to operate an introductory tenancy regime.

[(1A) When such an election is in force, every fixed term tenancy of a dwelling-house in England entered into or adopted by the authority or trust shall, if it would otherwise be a secure tenancy, be an introductory tenancy, unless section 124A(7) applies or immediately before the tenancy was entered into or adopted the tenant or, in the case of joint tenants, one or more of them was—

(a) a secure tenant of the same or another dwelling-house, or

(b) a tenant under a relevant assured tenancy, other than an assured shorthold tenancy, of the same or another dwellinghouse.]

(2) When such an election is in force, every periodic tenancy of a dwelling-house [in Wales] entered into or adopted by the authority or trust, shall, if it would otherwise be a secure tenancy, be an introductory tenancy, unless immediately before the tenancy was entered into or adopted the tenant, or, in the case of joint tenants, one or more of them was

(a) a secure tenant of the same or another dwelling-house, or

(b) a tenant under a relevant assured tenancy, other than an assured shorthold tenancy, of the same or another dwelling-house.

(2A) In *subsection (2)(b)* [subsections (1A)(b) and (2)(b)] "relevant assured tenancy" means—

(a) an assured tenancy in respect of social housing under which the landlord is a private registered provider of social housing, or

(b) an assured tenancy under which the landlord is a registered social landlord;

and for these purposes "social housing" has the same meaning as in Part 2 of the Housing and Regeneration Act 2008.

(3) *Subsection (2) does* [Subsections (1A) and (2) do] not apply to a tenancy entered into or adopted in pursuance of a contract made before the election was made.

(4) For the purposes of this Chapter a periodic tenancy is adopted by a person if that person becomes the landlord under the tenancy, whether on a disposal or surrender of the interest of the former landlord.

(5) An election under this section may be revoked at any time, without prejudice to the making of a further election.

[(6) In relation to a tenancy entered into or adopted by a local housing authority or a housing action trust before the day on which paragraph 4 of Schedule 7 to the Housing and Planning Act 2016 comes fully into force, this section has effect—

(a) as if subsection (1A) were omitted, and

(b) as if, in subsection (2), the words "in Wales" were omitted.]

Amendment *Text in italic is deleted, and text in square brackets is inserted, from a date to be appointed, by s 118 of, and Schedule 7 to, the Housing and Planning Act 2016.*

III L&T [280.1]

Introductory tenancies and secure tenancies Introductory tenancies have some of the characteristics of secure tenancies within the Housing Act 1985 Pt IV, but without security. Notes on the comparable provisions in the Housing Act 1985 may assist in interpreting the provisions in this Chapter eg in relation to the application to licences (Housing Act 1985 s 79, see para **III L&T [103]**), rights of succession (Housing Act 1985 ss 87–89, 113, see paras **III L&T [112]–III L&T [114]**, **III L&T [119]**) and notice of proceedings for possession (Housing Act 1985 s 83, see para **III L&T [107]**). The Housing Act 1985 s 111A applies the provisions of Housing Act 1985 ss 102(1), (2),(3)(a), 103 and 108 (variation of terms) to introductory tenancies. The Housing Act 2004 inserts into the Housing Act 1996 (by ss 125A and 125B) provisions for the extension of the trial period under an introductory tenancy by six months and for review of a landlord's decision to extend the trial period; see paras **III L&T [281A]–III L&T [281AA]**.

III L&T [280.1A]

Human rights Introductory tenancies have been held to be compatible with Arts 6 and 8 of the European Convention on Human Rights: *R (on the application of McLellan) v Bracknell Forest District Council* [2001] EWCA Civ 1510, [2002] QB 1129, [2002] 1 All ER 899. Furthermore, Article 8 cannot be relied on to defeat proprietary or contractual rights to possession: *Harrow London Borough Council v Qazi* [2003] UKHL 43, [2004] 1 AC 983, [2003] 4 All ER 461. Note, however, the decision in *Kay v Lambeth London Borough Council* [2006] UKHL 10, [2006] 2 AC 465, [2006] 2 WLR 570, [2006] 4 All ER 128 that, in so far as *Harrow London Borough Council v Qazi* decided that the enforcement of a right to possession in accordance with the domestic law of property could never be incompatible with the Art 8 of the Convention, that had to be modified in the light of *Connors v United Kingdom* (66746/01) [2005] 40 EHRR 9; moreover, that it was open to an occupier to raise an Art 8 defence to possession proceedings in the county court rather than by way of judicial review. (a point subsequently emphasised in *Manchester City Council v Pinnock* [2010] UKSC 45, [2010] 3 WLR 1441, [2010] 44 LS Gaz R 16 (see para **III L&T [103.6]**)).

In *Corby Borough Council v Scott; West Kent Housing Association Ltd v Haycraft* [2012] EWCA Civ 276, [2012] LGR 493, [2012] 21 Estates Gazette 100 the Court of Appeal held that the effect of the reasoning in Pinnock seemed to be that, at least in relation to demoted and introductory tenancies, it will only be in 'very highly exceptional cases' that it will be appropriate for the court to consider a proportionality argument, although 'exceptionality is an outcome and not a guide. While holding that it was not appropriate for the Court of Appeal to give firm guidance on the procedure to be adopted in possession cases where the tenant raises Article 8, the court felt it was right to emphasise the desirability of a judge considering at an early stage whether the tenant had an arguable case on Article 8 proportionality, before the issue was ordered to be heard. If it was a case that could not succeed, then it should not be allowed to take up further court time and to delay the landlord's right to possession.

If, between the start of proceedings and the hearing, the introductory tenant's behaviour and attitude have changed for the better, a possession order may be refused as being disproportionate and unnecessary even though possession was properly sought on the basis of antisocial behaviour. The proportionality review should be conducted on the evidence available at the date of the hearing: *Southend-On-Sea Borough Council v Armour* [2014] EWCA Civ 231, [2014] All ER (D) 170 (Mar).

III L&T [280.2]

Jurisdiction of county court The county court has jurisdiction, under the Housing Act 1996 s 138, to determine questions and to entertain proceedings eg for possession (though all possession claims must be brought in accordance with CPR Pt 55 (para **CPR 55**)). Proceedings to determine questions arising under the Housing Act 1996 ss 136, 137 (see paras **III L&T [292]**, **III L&T [293]**) should be brought by claim form in accordance with CPR Pts 7 (see para **CPR 7**) or 8 (see para **CPR 8**).

III L&T [280A]

[124A. New introductory tenancies in England: overall length]

[(1) A local housing authority or a housing action trust may enter into an introductory tenancy of a dwelling-house in England only if it is a tenancy for a fixed term that is—

(a) at least 2 years, and
(b) no longer than the permitted maximum length.

(2) The permitted maximum length is 10 years, unless subsection (3) applies.

(3) If the person entering into the tenancy has been notified in writing that a child aged under 9 will live in the dwelling-house, the permitted maximum length is the period—

(a) beginning with the day on which the tenancy is entered into, and
(b) ending with the day on which the child will reach the age of 19.

(4) If a local housing authority or a housing action trust purports to enter into an introductory tenancy in breach of subsection (1), it takes effect as a tenancy for a fixed term of 5 years.

(5) In deciding what length of tenancy to enter into in a case to which subsection (1) applies, the local housing authority or housing action trust must have regard to any guidance given by the Secretary of State.

(6) Subsections (1) and (4) apply only to tenancies entered into on or after the day on which paragraph 4 of Schedule 7 to the Housing and Planning Act 2016 comes fully into force.

(7) A tenancy of a dwelling-house in England that is adopted by a local housing authority or a housing action trust does not become an introductory tenancy if—

- (a) it is adopted on or after the day on which paragraph 4 of Schedule 7 to the Housing and Planning Act 2016 came fully into force, and
- (b) the tenancy is a periodic tenancy or it is a tenancy for a fixed term of less than 2 years or more than 5 years.

(8) Subsections (9) and (10) apply where a tenancy that has been adopted by a local housing authority or a housing action trust is not an introductory tenancy but would (on adoption or at any later time) become a secure tenancy but for subsection (7).

(9) The local housing authority or housing action trust must, within the period of 28 days, make the tenant a written offer of an introductory tenancy in return for the tenant surrendering the original tenancy.

(10) If the tenant accepts in writing within the period of 28 days beginning with the day on which the tenant receives the offer, the local housing authority or housing action trust must grant an introductory tenancy on the tenant surrendering the original tenancy.]

Amendment *Section 124A is inserted, from a date to be appointed, by s 118 of, and Schedule 7 to, the Housing and Planning Act 2016.*

III L&T [280B]

[124B. Review of decisions about length of introductory tenancies in England]

[(1) A person who is offered an introductory tenancy of a dwelling-house in England may request a review under this section.

(2) The sole purpose of a review under this section is to consider whether the length of the tenancy is in accordance with any policy that the prospective landlord has about the length of introductory tenancies it grants.

(3) The request must be made before the end of—

- (a) the period of 21 days beginning with the day on which the person making the request first receives the offer, or
- (b) such longer period as the prospective landlord may allow in writing.

(4) On receiving the request the prospective landlord must carry out the review.

(5) On completing the review the prospective landlord must—

- (a) notify the tenant in writing of the outcome,
- (b) revise its offer or confirm its original decision about the length of the tenancy, and
- (c) if it decides to confirm its original decision, give reasons.

(6) The Secretary of State may by regulations make provision about the procedure to be followed in connection with a review under this section.

(7) The regulations may, in particular—

- (a) require the review to be carried out by a person of appropriate seniority who was not involved in the original decision;
- (b) make provision as to the circumstances in which the person who requested the review is entitled to an oral hearing, and whether and by whom that person may be represented.]

Amendment *Section 124B is inserted, from a date to be appointed, by s 118 of, and Schedule 7 to, the Housing and Planning Act 2016.*

III L&T [281]

125. Duration of introductory tenancy

(1) A tenancy remains an introductory tenancy until the end of the trial period, unless one of the events mentioned in subsection (5) occurs before the end of that period.

(2) The "trial period" is the period of one year beginning with

- (a) in the case of a tenancy which was entered into by a local housing authority or housing action trust
  - (i) the date on which the tenancy was entered into, or
  - (ii) if later, the date on which a tenant was first entitled to possession under the tenancy; or
- (b) in the case of a tenancy which was adopted by a local housing authority or housing action trust, the date of adoption;

but this is subject to subsections (3) and (4) and to section 125A (extension of trial period by 6 months.

(3) Where the tenant under an introductory tenancy was formerly a tenant under another introductory tenancy, or a relevant assured shorthold tenancy, any period or periods during which he was such a tenant shall count towards the trial period, provided

- (a) if there was such period, it ended immediately before the date specified in subsection (2), and
- (b) if there was more than one such period, the most recent period ended immediately before that date and each period succeeded the other without interruption.

(3A) In sub-section (3) "relevant assured shorthold tenancy" means –

- (a) an assured shorthold tenancy in respect of social housing under which the landlord is a private registered provider of social housing, or
- (b) an assured shorthold tenancy under which the landlord is a registered social landlord;

and for these purposes "social housing" has the same meaning as in Part 2 of the Housing and Regeneration Act 2008.

(4) Where there are joint tenants under an introductory tenancy, the reference in subsection (3) to the tenant shall be construed as referring to the joint tenant in whose case the application of that subsection produces the earliest starting date for the trial period.

(5) A tenancy ceases to be an introductory tenancy if, before the end of the trial period

- (a) the circumstances are such that the tenancy would not otherwise be a secure tenancy,
- (b) a person or body other than a local housing authority or housing action trust becomes the landlord under the tenancy,
- (c) the election in force when the tenancy was entered into or adopted is revoked, or
- (d) the tenancy ceases to be an introductory tenancy by virtue of section 133 (3) (succession).

(6) A tenancy does not come to an end merely because it ceases to be an introductory tenancy, but a tenancy which has once ceased to be an introductory tenancy cannot subsequently become an introductory tenancy.

(7) This section has effect subject to section 130 (effect of beginning proceedings for possession).

III L&T [281A]

125A. Extension of trial period by 6 months

(1) If *both* [each] of the following conditions are met in relation to an introductory tenancy, the trial period is extended by 6 months.

(2) The first condition is that the landlord has served a notice of extension on the tenant at least 8 weeks before the original expiry date.

(3) The second condition is that either-

(a) the tenant has not requested a review under section 125B in accordance with subsection (1) of that section, or

(b) if he has, the decision on the review was to confirm the landlord's decision to extend the trial period.

[(3A) The third condition must be met only if the introductory tenancy—

(a) is one to which section 124A(1) or (2) applies, or

(b) is adopted by a local housing authority or housing action trust on or after the day on which paragraph 4 of Schedule 7 came fully into force.

(3B) The third condition is that the new expiry date would be before the period mentioned in section 86A(3) of the Housing Act 1985 (review to determine what to do at end of fixed term secure tenancy); and for this purpose "the new expiry date" means the last day of the 6 month extension period mentioned in subsection (1).]

(4) A notice of extension is a notice—

(a) stating that the landlord has decided that the period for which the tenancy is to be an introductory tenancy should be extended by 6 months, and

(b) complying with subsection (5).

(5) A notice of extension must-

(a) set out the reasons for the landlord's decision, and

(b) inform the tenant of his right to request a review of the landlord's decision and of the time within which such a request must be made.

(6) In this section and section 125B "the original expiry date" means the last day of the period of one year that would apply as the trial period apart from this section.

Amendment *Text in italic is deleted, and text in square brackets is inserted, from a date to be appointed, by s 118 of, and Schedule 7 to, the Housing and Planning Act 2016.*

III L&T [281B]

125B. Review of decision to extend trial period

(1) A request for review of the landlord's decision that the trial period for an introductory tenancy should be extended under section 125A must be made before the end of the period of 14 days beginning with the day on which the notice of extension is served.

(2) On a request being duly made to it, the landlord shall review its decision.

(3) The Secretary of State may make provision by regulations as to the procedure to be followed in connection with a review under this section.

Nothing in the following provisions affects the generality of this power.

(4) Provision may be made by regulations-

(a) requiring the decision on review to be made by a person of appropriate seniority who was not involved in the original decision, and

(b) as to the circumstances in which the person concerned is entitled to an oral hearing, and whether and by whom he may be represented at such a hearing.

(5) The landlord shall notify the tenant of the decision on the review.

If the decision is to confirm the original decision, the landlord shall also notify him of the reasons for the decision.

(6) The review shall be carried out and the tenant notified before the original expiry date.

III L&T [281B.1]

Regulations as to procedure For the procedure on a review under s 125B, see the Introductory Tenancies (Review of Decisions to Extend a Trial Period) (England) Regulations 2006, SI 2006/1077.

III L&T [282]

126. Licences

(1) The provisions of this Chapter apply in relation to a licence to occupy a dwelling-house (whether or not granted for a consideration) as they apply in relation to a tenancy.

(2) Subsection (1) does not apply to a licence granted as a temporary expedient to a person who entered the dwelling-house or any other land as a trespasser (whether or not, before the grant of that licence, another licence to occupy that or another dwelling-house had been granted to him).

Proceedings for possession

III L&T [283]

127. Proceedings for possession

(1) The landlord may only bring an introductory tenancy to an end by obtaining:

(a) an order of the court for possession of the dwelling-house, and

(b) the execution of the order.

(1A) In such a case, the tenancy ends when the order is executed.

(2) The court shall make an order of the kind mentioned in subsection (1)(a) unless the provisions of section 128 apply.

(3) . . .

III L&T [283.1]

Precedent A precedent for particulars of claim for possession is set out at **BCCP O[1003]**. It is suitable for attachment to Form N5.

III L&T [283.2]

Mandatory obligation to grant possession Where a council has complied with the requirements of s 128 regarding notice, the county court has no discretion other than to make an order for possession though the court may allow an opportunity for judicial review of the council's decision to bring possession proceedings: *Manchester City Council v Cochrane* [1999] 1 WLR 809, CA. The court has a general duty in possession proceedings relating to an introductory tenancy to consider the procedure which has been followed by the local authority when conducting the s 129 review, and to have in mind both the statutory procedure (because of s 127(2)) and the Convention on Human Rights (because of the court's role as a public authority). If there has been a flaw in the local authority's procedure, the court should allow an opportunity for challenge by way of judicial review However, a possession action should not be adjourned (or a possession order set aside) for this purpose if the application for judicial review has no realistic prospect of success: *Merton London Borough Council v Williams* [2002] EWCA Civ 980, [2003] HLR 257.

If the landlord has complied with the requirements of s 128 (see **III L&T [284]**), the court has no discretion other than to make an order for possession. However, lawfulness is an inherent requirement of the procedure. Accordingly, it is open to the court to consider whether the procedure has been lawfully followed having regard to the tenant's article 8 Convention rights. The court may therefore deal with a defence which relies on an alleged breach of article 8 and the court's powers of review can, in an appropriate case, extend to reconsidering for itself the facts found by a local authority, or to considering facts which have arisen since the issue of

LANDLORD & TENANT AND HOUSING

proceedings, by hearing evidence and forming its own view: *Hounslow London Borough Council v Powell* [2011] 2 WLR 287, applying to possession proceedings in the case of an introductory tenancy the approach which had been adopted in relation to a demoted tenancy in *Manchester City Council v Pinnock* [2010] 3 WLR 1441.

III L&T [284]

128. Notice of proceedings for possession

(1) The court shall not entertain proceedings for the possession of a dwelling-house let under an introductory tenancy unless the landlord has served on the tenant a notice of proceedings complying with this section.

(2) The notice shall state that the court will be asked to make an order for the possession of the dwelling-house.

(3) The notice shall set out the reasons for the landlord's decision to apply for such an order.

(4) The notice shall specify a date after which proceedings for the possession of the dwelling-house may be begun.

The date so specified must not be earlier than the date on which the tenancy could, apart from this Chapter, be brought to an end by notice to quit given by the landlord on the same date as the notice of proceedings. [The date so specified—

- (a) in a case where the introductory tenancy is a periodic tenancy, must not be earlier than the date on which the tenancy could, apart from this Chapter, be brought to an end by notice to quit given by the landlord on the same date as the proceedings, and
- (b) in a case where the introductory tenancy is a fixed term tenancy, must not be earlier than the end of the period of 6 weeks beginning with the date on which the notice of proceedings is served.]

(5) The court shall not entertain any proceedings for possession of the dwelling-house unless they are begun after the date specified in the notice of proceedings.

(6) The notice shall inform the tenant of his right to request a review of the landlord's decision to seek an order for possession and of the time within which such a request must be made.

(7) The notice shall also inform the tenant that if he needs help or advice about the notice, and what to do about it, he should take it immediately to a Citizens' Advice Bureau, a housing aid centre, a law centre or a solicitor.

Amendment *Text in italic is deleted, and text in square brackets is inserted, from a date to be appointed, by s 118 of, and Schedule 7 to, the Housing and Planning Act 2016.*

III L&T [284.1]

Notice The situation may arise where a notice is served on the grounds of arrears and the tenant is informed, after a review, that possession proceedings will not be taken so long as the arrears are reduced on a regular basis. If, in such a case, the tenant fails to comply, the authority may take proceedings in reliance on the original notice without having to serve a second one: *Cardiff City Council v Stone* [2002] EWCA Civ 298, [2003] HLR 678, (2002) Times, 19 February.

Any notice which states that the court will be asked to make an order for possession must set out reasons. If it does not do so the court may not entertain proceedings on it: *Forbes v Lambeth London Borough Council* [2003] EWHC 222 (Admin)(2003) Times, 10 March. If additional reasons are to be relied on, the proper procedure is to serve a further s 128 notice. However, in *R (on the application of Laporte) v Newham London Borough Council* [2004] EWHC 227 (Admin), [2004] All ER (D) 309 (Jan) the Court declined to quash a review hearing where a further notice had not been served, because it was satisfied that the result would have been the same even if the additional grounds had been left out of account.

There is no prescribed form for a s 128 notice. The question, therefore, is whether the document or documents relied on can reasonably be described as a notice. A notice for the purposes of s 128 could be comprised in more than one document. There is no reason why an accompanying information leaflet should not be treated as part of the notice if the reasonable recipient would have understood that the documents were intended to be read together: *Islington London Borough Council v Dyer* [2017] EWCA Civ 150.

III L&T [285]

129. Review of decision to seek possession

(1) A request for a review of the landlord's decision to seek an order for possession of a dwelling-house let under an introductory tenancy must be made before the end of the period of 14 days beginning with the day on which the notice of proceedings is served.

(2) On a request being duly made to it, the landlord shall review its decision.

(3) The Secretary of State may make provision by regulations as to the procedure to be followed in connection with a review under this section.

Nothing in the following provisions affects the generality of this power.

(4) Provision may be made by regulations

(a) requiring the decision on review to be made by a person of appropriate seniority who was not involved in the original decision, and

(b) as to the circumstances in which the person concerned is entitled to an oral hearing, and whether and by whom he may be represented at such a hearing.

(5) The landlord shall notify the person concerned of the decision on the review.

If the decision is to confirm the original decision, the landlord shall also notify him of the reasons for the decision.

(6) The review shall be carried out and the tenant notified before the date specified in the notice of proceedings as the date after which proceedings for the possession of the dwelling-house may be begun.

III L&T [285.1]

Regulations See the Introductory Tenants (Review) Regulations 1997, SI 1997/72.

III L&T [285.2]

Late review A review may be valid although not carried out until after the date specified in the notice, as required by sub-s (6), and possession proceedings may proceed concurrently with the holding of the review: *R (on the application of McDonagh) v Salisbury District Council* [2001] EWHC Admin 567, [2001] All ER (D) 58 (Jul), (2001) Times, 15 August.

III L&T [285.3]

Judicial review of decision on review In *R (on the application of Johns and McLellan) v Bracknell Forest District Council* (2001) 33 HLR 495, the Administrative Court rejected claims that the decision on review contravened Arts 6 and 8 of the Convention. As to the need for a fair and impartial hearing, this was provided, as in planning cases, by the availability of judicial review. As regards the right to respect for the home, the decision to interfere with it was proportionate and corresponded with a pressing social need. See also the decision of the Court of Appeal to the same effect in *R (on the application of McLellan) v Bracknell Forest Borough Council* [2001] EWCA Civ 1510, [2002] QB 1129.

III L&T [285.4]

Additional grounds relied on for the purposes of the review If additional grounds are to be relied on at a review hearing the proper procedure is to serve a further s 128 notice. In *R (on the application of Laporte) v Newham London Borough Council* [2004] EWHC 227 (Admin), [2004] All ER (D) 309 (Jan) the Court declined to quash a review hearing where a further notice had not been served, because it was satisfied that the result would have been the same even if the additional grounds had been left out of account.

III L&T [285.5]

Where original decision is not confirmed on review In order for the court to have jurisdiction to make a possession order, a decision under s 129 reviewing a decision to apply for a possession order in respect of an introductory tenancy under s 128 has to confirm the s 128 decision: see *Camden London Borough Council v Stafford* [2012] EWCA Civ 839, [2012] 4 All ER 180, [2012] HLR 616.

III L&T [286]

130. Effect of beginning proceedings for possession

(1) This section applies where the landlord has begun proceedings for the possession of a dwelling-house let under an introductory tenancy and

(a) the trial period ends, or

(b) any of the events specified in section 125(5) occurs (events on which a tenancy ceases to be an introductory tenancy).

(2) Subject to the following provisions, the tenancy remains an introductory tenancy until

(a) the tenancy comes to an end in accordance with section 127(1A), or

(b) the proceedings are otherwise finally determined.

(3) If any of the events specified in section 125(5)(b) to (d) occurs, the tenancy shall thereupon cease to be an introductory tenancy but

(a) the landlord (or, as the case may be, the new landlord) may continue the proceedings, and

(b) if he does so, section 127(1A) and (2) (termination by landlord) apply as if the tenancy had remained an introductory tenancy.

(4) Where in accordance with subsection (3) a tenancy ceases to be an introductory tenancy and becomes a secure tenancy, the tenant is not entitled to exercise the right to buy under Part V of the Housing Act 1985 unless and until the proceedings are finally determined on terms such that he is not required to give up possession of the dwelling-house.

(5) For the purposes of this section proceedings shall be treated as finally determined if they are withdrawn or any appeal is abandoned or the time for appealing expires without an appeal being brought.

III L&T [286.1]

Beginning proceedings Proceedings are brought when the proceedings have been issued by the court rather than when the claim form has been lodged with the county court. Accordingly, where, between the date of lodging and issue, an introductory tenancy had become a secure tenancy after one year, the claim for possession failed. CPR PD 7 para 5.1, which states that, where a claim form has been received in the court office on a date earlier than the date on which it was issued by the court, the claim is "brought" for the purposes of the Limitation Act 1980 and any other relevant statute on that earlier date, was held not to apply: see *Salford City Council v Garner* (2004) Times, 10 March, CA.

Succession on death of tenant

III L&T [286A]

[130A. Persons qualified to succeed to introductory tenancy: England]

[(1) A person is qualified to succeed the tenant under an introductory tenancy of a dwelling-house in England if—

(a) the person occupies the dwelling-house as his or her only or principal home at the time of the tenant's death, and

(b) the person is the tenant's spouse or civil partner.

(2) A person is qualified to succeed the tenant under an introductory tenancy of a dwelling-house in England if—

(a) at the time of the tenant's death the dwelling-house is not occupied by a spouse or civil partner of the tenant as his or her only or principal home,

(b) an express term of the tenancy makes provision for a person other than such a spouse or civil partner of the tenant to succeed to the tenancy, and

(c) the person's succession is in accordance with that term.

(3) Subsection (1) or (2) does not apply if the tenant was a successor as defined in section 132.

(4) In such a case, a person is qualified to succeed the tenant if—

- (a) an express term of the tenancy makes provision for a person to succeed a successor to the tenancy, and
- (b) the person's succession is in accordance with that term.

(5) For the purposes of this section a person who was living with the tenant as the tenant's wife or husband is to be treated as the tenant's spouse.

(6) Subsection (7) applies if, on the death of the tenant, there is by virtue of subsection (5) more than one person who fulfils the condition in subsection (1)(b).

(7) Such one of those persons as may be agreed between them or as may, where there is no such agreement, be selected by the landlord is for the purpose of this section to be treated as the fulfilling that condition.]

Amendment *Section 130A is inserted, from a date to be appointed, by s 120 of, and Schedule 8 to, the Housing and Planning Act 2016. Note that, by virtue of para 16 of Schedule 8, the insertion of s 130A does not apply in relation to an introductory tenancy granted before the day on which Schedule 8 comes into force.*

LANDLORD & TENANT AND HOUSING

III L&T [287]

131. Persons qualified *to succeed tenant* [to introductory tenancy: Wales]

A person is qualified to succeed the tenant under an introductory tenancy [of a dwelling-house in Wales] if he occupies the dwelling-house as his only or principal home at the time of the tenant's death and either—

- (a) he is the tenant's spouse, or
- (b) he is another member of the tenant's family and has resided with the tenant throughout the period of twelve months ending with the tenant's death;

unless, in either case, the tenant was himself a successor, as defined in section 132.

Amendment *Text in italic is deleted and text in square brackets is inserted, from a date to be appointed, by s 120 of, and Schedule 8 to, the Housing and Planning Act 2016. Note that, by virtue of para 15 of Schedule 8, the amendments do not apply in relation to cases where the tenant under a secure tenancy dies before Schedule 8 comes into force. Moreover, by virtue of para 16 of Schedule 8, the amendment to s 131 do not apply in relation to an introductory tenancy granted before the day on which Schedule 8 comes into force.*

III L&T [288]

132. Cases where the tenant is a successor

(1) The tenant is himself a successor if

- (a) the tenancy vested in him by virtue of section 133 (succession to introductory tenancy),
- (b) he was a joint tenant and has become the sole tenant,
- (c) he became the tenant on the tenancy being assigned to him (but subject to subsections (2) and (3)), or
- (d) he became the tenant on the tenancy being vested in him on the death of the previous tenant.

(2) A tenant to whom the tenancy was assigned in pursuance of an order under section 24 of the Matrimonial Causes Act 1973 (property adjustment orders in connection with matrimonial proceedings) or section 17 (1) of the Matrimonial and Family Proceedings Act 1984 (property adjustment orders after overseas divorce, &c.) is a successor only if the other party to the marriage was a successor.

(2A) A tenant to whom the tenancy was assigned in pursuance of an order under Part 2 of Schedule 5, or paragraph 9(2) or (3) of Schedule 7, to the Civil Partnership Act 2004 (property adjustment orders in connection with civil partnership proceedings or after overseas dissolution of civil partnership, etc.) is a successor only if the other civil partner was a successor.

(3) Where within six months of the coming to an end of an introductory tenancy ("the former tenancy") the tenant becomes a tenant under another introductory tenancy, and

- (a) the tenant was a successor in relation to the former tenancy, and
- (b) under the other tenancy either the dwelling-house or the landlord, or both, are the same as under the former tenancy,

the tenant is also a successor in relation to the other tenancy unless the agreement creating that tenancy otherwise provides.

III L&T [289]

133. Succession to introductory tenancy

(1) This section applies where a tenant under an introductory tenancy dies.

[(1A) Where there is a person qualified to succeed the tenant under section 130A, the tenancy vests by virtue of this section—

- (a) in that person, or
- (b) if there is more than one such person, in such one of them as may be agreed between them or as may, where there is no agreement, be selected by the landlord.]

(2) Where there is a person qualified to succeed the tenant [under section 131], the tenancy vests by virtue of this section in that person, or if there is more than one such person in the one to be preferred in accordance with the following rules

- (a) the tenant's spouse or civil partner is to be preferred to another member of the tenant's family;
- (b) of two or more other members of the tenant's family such of them is to be preferred as may be agreed between them or as may, where there is no such agreement, be selected by the landlord.

(3) Where there is no person qualified to succeed the tenant, the tenancy ceases to be an introductory tenancy

- (a) when it is vested or otherwise disposed of in the course of the administration of the tenant's estate, unless the vesting or other disposal is in pursuance of an order made under
  - (i) section 24 of the Matrimonial Causes Act 1973 (property adjustment orders made in connection with matrimonial proceedings),
  - (ii) section 17 (1) of the Matrimonial and Family Proceedings Act 1984 (property adjustment orders after overseas divorce, &c.),
  - (iii) paragraph 1 of Schedule 1 to the Children Act 1989 (orders for financial relief against parents); or
  - (iv) Part 2 of Schedule 5, or paragraph 9(2) or (3) of Schedule 7, to the Civil Partnership Act 2004 (property adjustment orders in connection with civil partnership proceedings or after overseas dissolution of civil partnership, etc.)
- (b) when it is known that when the tenancy is so vested or disposed of it will not be in pursuance of such an order.

Amendment *Text in italic is deleted and text in square brackets is inserted, from a date to be appointed, by s 120 of, and Schedule 8 to, the Housing and Planning Act 2016. Note that, by virtue of para 15 of Schedule 8, the amendments do not apply in relation to cases where the tenant under a secure tenancy dies before Schedule 8 comes into force. Moreover, by virtue of para 16 of Schedule 8, the amendment to s 131 do not apply in relation to an introductory tenancy granted before the day on which Schedule 8 comes into force.*

Assignment

III L&T [290]

134. Assignment in general prohibited

(1) An introductory tenancy is not capable of being assigned except in the cases mentioned in subsection (2).

(2) The exceptions are

(a) an assignment in pursuance of an order made under

(i) section 24 of the Matrimonial Causes Act 1973 (property adjustment orders in connection with matrimonial proceedings),

(ii) section 17 (1) of the Matrimonial and Family Proceedings Act 1984 (property adjustment orders after overseas divorce, &c.),

(iii) paragraph 1 of Schedule 1 to the Children Act 1989 (orders for financial relief against parents), or

(iv) Part 2 of Schedule 5, or paragraph 9(2) or (3) of Schedule 7, to the Civil Partnership Act 2004 (property adjustment orders in connection with civil partnership proceedings or after overseas dissolution of civil partnership, etc.)

(b) an assignment to a person who would be qualified to succeed the tenant if the tenant died immediately before the assignment.

(3) Subsection (1) also applies to a tenancy which is not an introductory tenancy but would be if the tenant, or where the tenancy is a joint tenancy, at least one of the tenants, were occupying or continuing to occupy the dwelling-house as his only or principal home.

Repairs

III L&T [291]

135. Right to carry out repairs

The Secretary of State may by regulations made under section 96 of the Housing Act 1985 (secure tenants: right to carry out repairs) apply to introductory tenants any provision made under that section in relation to secure tenants.

III L&T [291.1]

Regulations The provision under the Housing Act 1985 s 96 has been applied by the Secure Tenants of Local Housing Authorities (Right to Repair) (Amendment) Regulations 1997, SI 1997/73 which made appropriate amendments to the Secure Tenants of Local Housing Authorities (Right to Repair) Regulations 1994, SI 1994/133.

Provision of information and consultation

III L&T [292]

136. Provision of information about tenancies

(1) Every local housing authority or housing action trust which lets dwelling-houses under introductory tenancies shall from time to time publish information about its introductory tenancies, in such form as it considers best suited to explain in simple terms, and, so far as it considers it appropriate, the effect of

(a) the express terms of its introductory tenancies,

(b) the provisions of this Chapter, and

(c) the provisions of sections 11 to 16 of the Landlord and Tenant Act 1985 (landlord's repairing obligations),

and shall ensure that so far as is reasonably practicable the information so published is kept up to date.

(2) The landlord under an introductory tenancy shall supply the tenant with

(a) a copy of the information for introductory tenants published by it under subsection (1), and

(b) a written statement of the terms of the tenancy, so far as they are neither expressed in the lease or written tenancy agreement (if any) nor implied by law;

and the statement required by paragraph (b) shall be supplied on the grant of the tenancy or as soon as practicable afterwards.

III L&T [293]

137. Consultation on matters of housing management

(1) This section applies in relation to every local housing authority and housing action trust which lets dwelling-houses under introductory tenancies and which is a landlord authority for the purposes of Part IV of the Housing Act 1985 (secure tenancies).

(2) The authority or trust shall maintain such arrangements as it considers appropriate to enable those of its introductory tenants who are likely to be substantially affected by a relevant matter of housing management

(a) to be informed of the proposals of the authority or trust in respect of the matter, and

(b) to make their views known to the authority or trust within a specified period;

and the authority or trust shall, before making a decision on the matter, consider any representations made to it in accordance with those arrangements.

(3) A matter is one of housing management if, in the opinion of the authority or trust concerned, it relates to

(a) the management, improvement, maintenance or demolition of dwelling-houses let by the authority or trust under introductory or secure tenancies, or

(b) the provision of services or amenities in connection with such dwelling-houses;

but not so far as it relates to the rent payable under an introductory or secure tenancy or to charges for services or facilities provided by the authority or trust.

(4) A matter is relevant if, in the opinion of the authority or trust concerned, it represents

(a) a new programme of maintenance, improvement or demolition, or

(b) a change in the practice or policy of the authority or trust,

and is likely substantially to affect either its introductory tenants as a whole or a group of them who form a distinct social group or occupy dwelling-houses which constitute a distinct class (whether by reference to the kind of dwelling-house, or the housing estate or other larger area in which they are situated).

(5) In the case of a local housing authority, the reference in subsection (3) to the provision of services or amenities is a reference only to the provision of services or amenities by the authority acting in its capacity as landlord of the dwelling-houses concerned.

(6) The authority or trust shall publish details of the arrangements which it makes under this section, and a copy of the documents published under this subsection shall

(a) be made available at its principal office for inspection at all reasonable hours, without charge, by members of the public, and

(b) be given, on payment of a reasonable fee, to any member of the public who asks for one.

(2) [illegible] *tenancy* [illegible] which paragraph [illegible] into force and, before [illegible] landlord under the tenancy [illegible] became the tenant under the tenancy [illegible]

(a) stating that, on ceasing to [illegible] would become a secure tenancy [illegible] term certain of the length specified in the [illegible] specifying a period of at least two years as the [illegible] tenancy, and

(b) setting out the other express terms of the tenancy.

[illegible] The length [illegible] express term of a flexible tenancy that becomes such a tenancy [illegible] in the notice under subsection (2). [illegible] those set out in the notice [illegible] compatible with the statutory provisions relating to flexible tenancies; and in this subsection "statutory provision" means any provision made by or under an Act.

Amendment Text in italic is deleted and text in square brackets is inserted, from a date to be appointed, by s 118 of, and Schedule 7 to, the Housing and Planning Act 2016.

III L&T [293A.1]

Flexible tenancies Section 137A (introduced by section 155 of the Localism Act 2011, in force from 1 April 2012) prescribes the circumstances in which an introductory tenancy may become a flexible tenancy. For flexible tenancies see also **III L&T [115.1]** to **III L&T [115.6]**.

Supplementary

III L&T [294]

138. Jurisdiction of county court

(1) The county court has jurisdiction to determine questions arising under this Chapter and to entertain proceedings brought under this Chapter and claims, for whatever amount, in connection with an introductory tenancy.

(2) That jurisdiction includes jurisdiction to entertain proceedings as to whether a statement supplied in pursuance of section 136 (2) (written statement of certain terms of tenancy) is accurate notwithstanding that no other relief is sought than a declaration.

(3) If a person takes proceedings in the [illegible] which, by virtue of this section, he could have taken in the county court, he is not entitled to recover any costs.

(4) The Lord Chancellor [illegible] directions as he thinks fit for the purpose [illegible] *of any jurisdiction* [illegible] *and* [illegible] *proceedings in private* [illegible] *exercisable by statutory instrument which shall be* [illegible] *of a resolution of either House of Parliament.*

(5) The rules and [illegible]

(a) fo[illegible]

III L&T [294.1]

Court proceedings The usual way of having a question determined by a county court is by claim form in accordance with CPR Pt 7 (see para **CPR 7**) or, if no substantial dispute of fact is likely to arise, CPR Pt 8 (see para **CPR 8**). Note, however, that if a claim under this Chapter involves a claim for possession, CPR 55.2 (see para **CPR 55.2**) directs that the procedure set out in Section I of CPR 55 must be used. An application to the High Court for judicial review should not be made if the issue can be raised under the Housing Act 1996 s 138 for the determination of a county court. However, the Court of Appeal held in *Manchester City Council v Cochrane* [1999] 1 WLR 809, CA, that a challenge to the decision to claim possession on the ground that the review under s 129 (see para **III L&T [285]**) was flawed could not be raised as a defence to the county court, but only by proceedings for judicial review.

III L&T [294.2]

Rules and directions No rules or directions had been made or given, at the time of going to print. For the general provisions as to a district judge's jurisdiction, see CPR PD 2B para 11.1 (para **CPR PD 2B**).

III L&T [295]

139. Meaning of "dwelling-house"

(1) For the purposes of this Chapter a dwelling-house may [illegible] part of a house.

(2) Land let together with a dwelling-ho[illegible] for the purposes of this Chapter as part of the dwelling [illegible] the land is agricultural land which would not be [illegible] section 112 (2) of that Act) of the Housing Act 1985 (see [illegible]

III L&T [296]

140. Members of a person's family: Chapter I

(1) A person is a member of another's family within the meaning of this Chapter if

(a) he is the spouse of [illegible] person, or he and that person live together as husband and wife, or

(b) he is that person's parent, grandparent, child, grandchild, brother, sister, uncle, aunt, nephew or [illegible].

(2) For the purpose of subsection (1) (b)

(a) a relationship by marriage shall be treated as a relationship by blood,

(b) a relationship of the half-blood shall be treated as a relationship of the whole blood, and

(c) the stepchild of a person shall be treated as his child.

CHAPTER 1A DEMOTED TENANCIES

[illegible] provisions

III L&T [2[illegible]]

143A. Demoted tenancies

(1) This section applies to a periodic [illegible] following conditions is satisfied.

(2) The first condition is that the landlord [illegible] housing action trust [illegible] of the

(3) The second condition is that the tenant [illegible] Housing Act 1985 is satisfied.

(4) The third condition is that the tenancy is created [illegible] order under section 82A of that Act.

(5) In this Chapter—

he must take the notice immediately to a Citizen's Advice Bureau, a housing aid centre, a law centre or a solicitor.

Amendment *Text in italic is deleted from a date to be appointed, by s 118 of, and Schedule 7 to, the Housing and Planning Act 2016.*

III L&T [296E.1]

Procedure Proceedings against a tenant of a demoted tenancy for possession must be brought under the procedure in CPR Part 55: see CPR PD 65 paragraph 11.1 (para **CPR PD 65**).

III L&T [296F]

143F. Review of decision to seek possession

(1) Before the end of the period of 14 days beginning with the date of service of a notice for possession of a dwelling-house let under a demoted tenancy the tenant may request the landlord to review its decision to seek an order for possession.

(2) If a request is made in accordance with subsection (1) the landlord must review the decision.

(3) The Secretary of State may by regulations make provision as to the procedure to be followed in connection with a review under this section.

(4) The regulations may include provision—

- (a) requiring the decision on review to be made by a person of appropriate seniority who was not involved in the original decision;
- (b) as to the circumstances in which the tenant is entitled to an oral hearing, and whether and by whom he may be represented at the hearing.

(5) The landlord must notify the tenant—

- (a) of the decision on the review;
- (b) of the reasons for the decision.

(6) The review must be carried out and notice given under subsection (5) before the date specified in the notice of proceedings as the date after which proceedings for possession of the dwelling-house may be begun.

III L&T [296F.1]

Demoted tenancies The review procedure is prescribed by the Demoted Tenancies (Review of Decisions)(England) Regulations 2004, SI 2004/1679. The Regulations have been held to comply with Article 6 of the Convention: *R (Gilboy) v Liverpool City Council* [2008] EWCA Civ 751 in which the Court concluded that it was bound by the conclusions of the Court of Appeal in *McLellan v Bracknell Forest Borough Council* [2001] EWCA Civ 1510, [2002] QB 1129 when rejecting a similar challenge to the introductory tenancies scheme. For the review procedure in Wales see the Demoted Tenancies (Review of Decisions)(Wales) Regulations 2005, SI 2005/1228.

III L&T [296G]

143G. Effect of proceedings for possession

(1) This section applies if the landlord has begun proceedings for the possession of a dwelling-house let under a demoted tenancy and—

- (a) the demotion period ends, or
- (b) any of paragraphs (a) to (c) of section 143B(2) applies (circumstances in which a tenancy ceases to be a demoted tenancy).

(2) If any of paragraphs (a) to (c) of section 143B(2) applies the tenancy ceases to be a demoted tenancy but the landlord (or the new landlord as the case may be) may continue the proceedings.

(3) Subsection (4) applies if in accordance with subsection (2) a tenancy ceases to be a demoted tenancy and becomes a secure tenancy.

(4) The tenant is not entitled to exercise the right to buy unless—

- (a) the proceedings are finally determined, and

LANDLORD & TENANT AND HOUSING

(b) he is not required to give up possession of the dwelling-house.

(5) The proceedings must be treated as finally determined if—

(a) they are withdrawn;

(b) any appeal is abandoned;

(c) the time for appealing expires without an appeal being brought.

Succession

III L&T [296GA]

[143GA. Persons qualified to succeed to demoted tenancy: England]

[(1) A person is qualified to succeed the tenant under a demoted tenancy of a dwelling-house in England if—

(a) the person occupies the dwelling-house as his or her only or principal home at the time of the tenant's death, and

(b) the person is the tenant's spouse or civil partner.

(2) A person is qualified to succeed the tenant under a demoted tenancy of a dwelling-house in England if—

(a) at the time of the tenant's death the dwelling-house is not occupied by a spouse or civil partner of the tenant as his or her only or principal home,

(b) an express term of the tenancy makes provision for a person other than such a spouse or civil partner of the tenant to succeed to the tenancy, and

(c) the person's succession is in accordance with that term.

(3) Subsection (1) or (2) does not apply if the tenant was a successor as defined in section 132.

(4) In such a case, a person is qualified to succeed the tenant if—

(a) an express term of the tenancy makes provision for a person to succeed a successor to the tenancy, and

(b) the person's succession is in accordance with that term.

(5) For the purposes of this section a person who was living with the tenant as the tenant's wife or husband is to be treated as the tenant's spouse.

(6) Subsection (7) applies if, on the death of the tenant, there is by virtue of subsection (5) more than one person who fulfils the condition in subsection (1)(b).

(7) Such one of those persons as may be agreed between them or as may, where there is no such agreement, be selected by the landlord is for the purpose of this section to be treated as fulfilling that condition.

(8) This section applies to a tenancy that became a demoted tenancy before or after Schedule 8 of the Housing Act 2015 comes into force.

Amendment *Section 143GA is inserted from a date to be appointed, by s 120 of, and Schedule 8 to, the Housing and Planning Act 2016. Note that, by virtue of para 17 of Schedule 8, the amendments do not apply in relation to cases where the tenant under a demoted tenancy dies before Schedule 8 comes into force.*

III L&T [296GB]

[143GB. Succession to demoted tenancy: England]

[(1) This section applies if the tenant under a demoted tenancy of a dwelling-house in England dies.

(2) Where there is a person qualified to succeed the tenant under section 143GA, the tenancy vests by virtue of this section—

(a) in that person, or

(b) if there is more than one such person, in such one of them as may be agreed between them or as may, where there is no agreement, be selected by the landlord.

(3) Where a periodic demoted tenancy vests in a person qualified to succeed the tenant under section 143GA(2) or (4) and continues to be a demoted tenancy—

(a) the tenancy comes to an end immediately after vesting, and

(b) a new tenancy of the same dwelling-house arises by virtue of this subsection for a fixed term of 5 years.

(4) The parties and terms of a tenancy arising by virtue of subsection (3) are the same as those of the tenancy that it replaces, except that the terms are confined to those which are compatible with a tenancy for a fixed term of 5 years.

(5) Where a demoted tenancy comes to an end and a new tenancy arises by virtue of subsection (3), as from that time the demotion order is to be treated for all purposes as it had been made in relation to the new tenancy (and the demotion period remains the same).]

Amendment *Section 143GB is inserted from a date to be appointed, by s 120 of, and Schedule 8 to, the Housing and Planning Act 2016. Note that, by virtue of para 17 of Schedule 8, the amendments do not apply in relation to cases where the tenant under a demoted tenancy dies before Schedule 8 comes into force.*

LANDLORD & TENANT AND HOUSING

III L&T [296H]

143H. Succession to demoted tenancy [: Wales]

(1) This section applies if the tenant [of a dwelling-house in Wales] under a demoted tenancy dies.

(2) If the tenant was a successor, the tenancy—

(a) ceases to be a demoted tenancy, but

(b) does not become a secure tenancy.

(3) In any other case a person is qualified to succeed the tenant if—

(a) he occupies the dwelling-house as his only or principal home at the time of the tenant's death,

(b) he is a member of the tenant's family, and

(c) he has resided with the tenant throughout the period of 12 months ending with the tenant's death.

(4) If only one person is qualified to succeed under subsection (3) the tenancy vests in him by virtue of this section.

(5) If there is more than one such person the tenancy vests by virtue of this section in the person preferred in accordance with the following rules—

(a) the tenant's spouse or civil partner or (if the tenant has neither spouse nor civil partner) the person mentioned in section 143P(1)(b) is to be preferred to another member of the tenant's family;

(b) if there are two or more other members of the tenant's family the person preferred may be agreed between them or (if there is no such agreement) selected by the landlord.

Amendment *Text in square brackets is inserted from a date to be appointed, by s 120 of, and Schedule 8 to, the Housing and Planning Act 2016. Note that, by virtue of para 17 of Schedule 8, the amendments do not apply in relation to cases where the tenant under a demoted tenancy dies before Schedule 8 comes into force.*

III L&T [296I]

143I. No successor tenant: termination

(1) This section applies if the demoted tenant dies and no person is qualified to succeed to the tenancy as mentioned in section [143GA or] 143H(3).

(2) The tenancy ceases to be a demoted tenancy if either subsection (3) or (4) applies.

(3) This subsection applies if the tenancy is vested or otherwise disposed of in the course of the administration of the tenant's estate unless the vesting or other disposal is in pursuance of an order under—

(a) section 23A or 24 of the Matrimonial Causes Act 1973 (property adjustment orders in connection with matrimonial proceedings);

(b) section 17(1) of the Matrimonial and Family Proceedings Act 1984 (property adjustment orders after overseas divorce, etc);

(c) paragraph 1 of Schedule 1 to the Children Act 1989 (orders for financial relief against parents).

(d) Part 2 of Schedule 5, or paragraph 9(2) or (3) of Schedule 7, to the Civil Partnership Act 2004 (property adjustment orders in connection with civil partnership proceedings or after overseas dissolution of civil partnership, etc.)

(4) This subsection applies if it is known that when the tenancy is vested or otherwise disposed of in the course of the administration of the tenant's estate it will not be in pursuance of an order mentioned in subsection (3).

(5) A tenancy which ceases to be a demoted tenancy by virtue of this section cannot subsequently become a secure tenancy.

Amendment *Text in square brackets is inserted from a date to be appointed, by s 120 of, and Schedule 8 to, the Housing and Planning Act 2016. Note that, by virtue of para 17 of Schedule 8, the amendments do not apply in relation to cases where the tenant under a demoted tenancy dies before Schedule 8 comes into force.*

III L&T [296J]

143J. Successor tenants

(1) This section applies for the purpose of sections 143H and 143I.

(2) A person is a successor to a secure tenancy which is terminated by a demotion order if any of subsections (3) to (6) applies to him.

(3) The tenancy vested in him—

(a) by virtue of section 89 of the Housing Act 1985 or section 133 of this Act;

(b) under the will or intestacy of the preceding tenant.

[(3A) The tenancy arose by virtue of section 89(2A) of the Housing Act 1985.]

(4) The tenancy arose by virtue of section 86 of the Housing Act 1985 and the original fixed term was granted—

(a) to another person, or

(b) to him jointly with another person.

(5) He became the tenant on the tenancy being assigned to him unless—

(a) the tenancy was assigned-

(i) in proceedings under section 24 of the Matrimonial Causes Act 1973 (property adjustment orders in connection with matrimonial proceedings) or section 17(1) of the Matrimonial and Family Proceedings Act 1984 (property adjustment orders after overseas divorce, etc.), or

(ii) in proceedings under Part 2 of Schedule 5, or paragraph 9(2) or (3) of Schedule 7, to the Civil Partnership Act 2004 (property adjustment orders in connection with civil partnership proceedings or after overseas dissolution of civil partnership, etc.),

(b) where the tenancy was assigned as mentioned in paragraph (a)(i), neither he nor the other party to the marriage was a successor, and

(c) where the tenancy was assigned as mentioned in paragraph (a)(ii), neither he nor the other civil partner was a successor.

(6) He became the tenant on assignment under section 92 of the Housing Act 1985 if he himself was a successor to the tenancy which he assigned in exchange.

(7) *A person is the successor to a demoted tenancy if the tenancy vested in him by virtue of section 143H(4) or (5).* [A person is the successor to a demoted tenancy if—

- (a) the tenancy vests in the person by virtue of section 143GB(2) or 143H(4) or (5), or
- (b) the tenancy arose by virtue of section 143GB(3).]

(8) A person is the successor to a joint tenancy if he has become the sole tenant.

Amendment *Text in italic is deleted and text in square brackets is inserted from a date to be appointed, by s 120 of, and Schedule 8 to, the Housing and Planning Act 2016. Note that, by virtue of para 17 of Schedule 8, the amendments do not apply in relation to cases where the tenant under a demoted tenancy dies before Schedule 8 comes into force.*

Assignment

III L&T [296K]

143K. Restriction on assignment

(1) A demoted tenancy is not capable of being assigned except as mentioned in subsection (2).

(2) The exceptions are assignment in pursuance of an order made under—

- (a) section 24 of the Matrimonial Causes Act 1973 (property adjustment orders in connection with matrimonial proceedings);
- (b) section 17(1) of the Matrimonial and Family Proceedings Act 1984 (property adjustment orders after overseas divorce, etc);
- (c) paragraph 1 of Schedule 1 to the Children Act 1989 (orders for financial relief against parents).
- (d) Part 2 of Schedule 5, or paragraph 9(2) or (3) of Schedule 7, to the Civil Partnership Act 2004 (property adjustment orders in connection with civil partnership proceedings or after overseas dissolution of civil partnership, etc.)

Repairs

III L&T [296L]

143L. Right to carry out repairs

The Secretary of State may by regulations under section 96 of the Housing Act 1985 (secure tenants: right to carry out repairs) apply to demoted tenants any provision made under that section in relation to secure tenants.

Provision of information

III L&T [296M]

143M. Provision of information

(1) This section applies to a local housing authority or a housing action trust if it is the landlord of a demoted tenancy.

(2) The landlord must from time to time publish information about the demoted tenancy in such form as it thinks best suited to explain in simple terms and so far as it considers appropriate the effect of—

- (a) the express terms of the demoted tenancy;
- (b) the provisions of this Chapter;
- (c) the provisions of sections 11 to 16 of the Landlord and Tenant Act 1985 (landlord's repairing obligations).

(3) The landlord must ensure that information published under subsection (2) is, so far as is reasonably practicable, kept up to date.

(4) The landlord must supply the tenant with—

(a) a copy of the information published under subsection (2);

(b) a written statement of the terms of the tenancy, so far as they are neither expressed in the lease or written tenancy agreement (if any) nor implied by law.

(5) The statement required by subsection (4)(b) must be supplied on the grant of the tenancy or as soon as practicable afterwards.

III L&T [296M.1]

Statement of terms Proceedings as to whether a statement supplied in pursuance to s 143M(4)(b) is accurate must be brought under the procedure in Part 8: see CPR PD 65 paragraph 11.1 (see para **CPR PD 65**).

III L&T [296MA]

143MA. Demoted tenancies that are to become flexible tenancies

(1) Subsection (2) applies to a demoted tenancy of a dwelling-house in England that—

(a) was created on the termination of a flexible tenancy within the meaning of *section 107A of the Housing Act 1985* [section 115B of the Housing Act 1985 (certain tenancies granted etc before the day on which paragraph 4 of Schedule 7 to the Housing and Planning Act 2016 came fully into force], and

(b) ceases to be a demoted tenancy and becomes a secure tenancy in accordance with this Chapter.

(2) If the landlord has served a notice within subsection (3) on the tenant before the end of the demoted tenancy then, on ceasing to be a demoted tenancy, the tenancy becomes a secure tenancy for a term certain that is a flexible tenancy.

(3) The notice must—

(a) state that, on ceasing to be a demoted tenancy, the tenancy will become a secure tenancy that is a flexible tenancy for a term certain of the length specified in the notice,

(b) specify a period of at least two years as the length of the term of the tenancy, and

(c) set out the other express terms of the tenancy.

[(3A) If the notice is given on or after the day on which paragraph 4 of Schedule 7 to the Housing and Planning Act 2016 comes fully into force, the period specified under subsection (3)(b) must be no longer than the permitted maximum length.

(3B) The permitted maximum length is 10 years, unless subsection (3C) applies.

(3C) If the landlord has been notified in writing that a child aged under 9 will live in the dwelling-house, the permitted maximum length is the period—

(a) beginning with the day on which the tenancy becomes a secure tenancy, and

(b) ending with the day on which the child will reach the age of 19.

(3D) In deciding what length to specify in a notice under paragraph (3)(b) the landlord must have regard to any guidance given by the Secretary of State.]

(4) The length of the term of a flexible tenancy that becomes such a tenancy by virtue of this section is that specified in the notice under subsection (3).

(5) The other express terms of the flexible tenancy are those set out in the notice, so far as those terms are compatible with the statutory provisions relating to flexible tenancies; and in this subsection "statutory provision" means any provision made by or under an Act.

Amendment *Text in italic is deleted and text in square brackets is inserted from a date to be appointed, by s 120 of, and Schedule 8 to, the Housing and Planning Act 2016. Note that, by virtue of para 17 of Schedule 8, the amendments do not apply in relation to cases where the tenant under a demoted tenancy dies before Schedule 8 comes into force.*

III L&T [296MA.1]

Flexible tenancies Section 143MA (introduced by s 155 of the Localism Act 2011, in force from 1 April 2012) prescribes the circumstances in which a demoted tenancy may become a flexible tenancy. For flexible tenancies see also **III L&T [115.1]** to **III L&T [115.6]**.

III L&T [296MB]

[143MB. Default flexible tenancies when no notice given under section 143MA]

[(1) This section applies where—

(a) a landlord has the power to serve a notice under section 143MA on the tenant under a demoted tenancy but fails to do so, and

(b) the tenancy comes to an end on or after the day on which paragraph 4 of Schedule 7 to the Housing and Planning Act 2016 comes fully into force.

(2) On ceasing to be a demoted tenancy, the tenancy becomes a secure tenancy for a fixed term of 5 years that is a flexible tenancy.

(3) The terms of the new tenancy are the same as those of the tenancy that it replaces, so far as those terms are compatible with—

(a) a tenancy for a fixed term of 5 years, and

(b) the statutory provisions relating to flexible tenancies (within the meaning given by section 143MA(5).]

Amendment *Section 143MB is inserted from a date to be appointed, by s 118 of, and Schedule 7 to, the Housing and Planning Act 2016.*

III L&T [296MA.1]

Flexible tenancies Section 143MA (introduced by s 155 of the Localism Act 2011, in force from 1 April 2012) prescribes the circumstances in which a demoted tenancy may become a flexible tenancy. For flexible tenancies see also **III L&T [115.1]** to **III L&T [115.6]**.

Supplementary

III L&T [296N]

143N. Jurisdiction of county court

(1) The county court has jurisdiction—

(a) to determine questions arising under this Chapter;

(b) to entertain proceedings brought under this Chapter;

(c) to determine claims (for whatever amount) in connection with a demoted tenancy.

(2) The jurisdiction includes jurisdiction to entertain proceedings as to whether a statement supplied in pursuance of section 143M(4)(b) (written statement of certain terms of tenancy) is accurate.

(3) For the purposes of subsection (2) it is immaterial that no relief other than a declaration is sought.

(4) If a person takes proceedings in the High Court which, by virtue of this section, he could have taken in the county court he is not entitled to recover any costs.

(5) ...

(6) ...

(7) ...

III L&T [296O]

143O. Meaning of dwelling house

(1) For the purposes of this Chapter a dwelling-house may be a house or a part of a house.

(2) Land let together with a dwelling-house must be treated for the purposes of this Chapter as part of the dwelling-house unless the land is agricultural land which would not be treated as part of a dwelling-house for the purposes of Part 4 of the Housing Act 1985.

III L&T [296P]

143P. Members of a person's family

(1) For the purposes of this Chapter a person is a member of another's family if—

(a) he is the spouse or civil partner of that person;

(b) he and that person live together as a couple in an enduring family relationship, but he does not fall within paragraph (c);

(c) he is that person's parent, grandparent, child, grandchild, brother, sister, uncle, aunt, nephew or niece.

(2) For the purposes of subsection (1)(b) it is immaterial that two persons living together in an enduring family relationship are of the same sex.

(3) For the purposes of subsection (1)(c)—

(a) a relationship by marriage or civil partnership must be treated as a relationship by blood;

(b) a relationship of the half-blood must be treated as a relationship of the whole blood;

(c) a stepchild of a person must be treated as his child."

CHAPTER III INJUNCTIONS AGAINST ANTI-SOCIAL BEHAVIOUR

III L&T [297]–III L&T [303]

Repeals effected by the Anti-social Behaviour, Crime and Policing Act 2014 Sections 153A to 158 of the Housing Act 1996 were repealed with effect from 23 March 2015.

Anti-social Behaviour Injunctions are replaced by injunctions to prevent anti-social behaviour (defined in section 2 of the Anti-social Behaviour, Crime and Policing Act 2014 Act). Part I of the 2014 Act (set out at **III ANSB [52]**) enables local authorities and housing providers to apply for injunctions where conduct is capable of causing a nuisance or annoyance to a person in relation to that person's occupation of residential premises or where the conduct is capable of causing a housing related nuisance or annoyance to any person.

PART VII
HOMELESSNESS

Interim duty to accommodate

III L&T [303A]

188. Interim duty to accommodate in case of apparent priority need

(1) If the local housing authority have reason to believe that an applicant may be homeless, eligible for assistance and have a priority need, they must secure that accommodation is available for the applicant's occupation.

(1ZA) In a case in which the local housing authority conclude their inquiries under section 184 and decide that the applicant does not have a priority need—

(a) where the authority decide that they do not owe the applicant a duty under section 189B(2), the duty under subsection (1) comes to an end when the authority notify the applicant of that decision, or

(b) otherwise, the duty under subsection (1) comes to an end upon the authority notifying the applicant of their decision that, upon the duty under section 189B(2) coming to an end, they do not owe the applicant any duty under section 190 or 193.

(1ZB) In any other case, the duty under subsection (1) comes to an end upon the later of—

(a) the duty owed to the applicant under section 189B(2) coming to an end or the authority notifying the applicant that they have decided that they do not owe the applicant a duty under that section, and

(b) the authority notifying the applicant of their decision as to what other duty (if any) they owe to the applicant under the following provisions of this Part upon the duty under section 189B(2) coming to an end.

(1A) But if the local housing authority have reason to believe that the duty under section 193(2) may apply in relation to an applicant in the circumstances referred to in section 195A(1), they shall secure that accommodation is available for the applicant's occupation until the later of paragraph (a) or (b) of subsection (1ZB) regardless of whether the applicant has a priority need.

(2) The duty under this section arises irrespective of any possibility of the referral of the applicant's case to another local housing authority (see sections 198 to 200).

(2A) For the purposes of this section, where the applicant requests a review under section 202(1)(h) of the authority's decision as to the suitability of accommodation offered to the applicant by way of a final accommodation offer or a final Part 6 offer (within the meaning of section 193A), the authority's duty to the applicant under section 189B(2) is not to be taken to have come to an end under section 193A(2) until the decision on the review has been notified to the applicant.

(3) Otherwise, the duty under this section comes to an end in accordance with subsections (1ZA) to (1A), regardless of any review requested by the applicant under section 202.

But the authority may secure that accommodation is available for the applicant's occupation pending a decision on review.

LANDLORD & TENANT AND HOUSING

III L&T [303A.1]

Eligibility The eligibility of persons from abroad for accommodation or assistance is restricted by the Allocation of Housing and Homelessness (Eligibility) (England) Regulations 2006, SI 2006/1294, as amended by SI 2006/2527. Note also the changes made by the Allocation of Housing and Homelessness (Eligibility) (England) (Amendment) Regulations 2009, SI 2009/358 for Zimbabweans and the amendments in SI 2006/2007 for Montserratians. The 2006 Regulations were further amended by the Allocation of Housing and Homelessness (Eligibility) (England) Regulations 2016, SI 2016/965 and the Allocation of Housing and Homelessness (Eligibility) (England) (No 2) Regulations 2018, SI 2016/1056.

A Dutch citizen who had only been employed as a steward at a tennis tournament in the United Kingdom for two weeks within a six month period qualified as a "worker" under the Immigration (European Economic Area) Regulations 2006, reg 6(2)(b)(ii) and was therefore eligible for housing assistance pursuant to reg 6(2)(a): *Mohammed Barry v Southwark London Borough Council* [2008] EWCA Civ 1440.

III L&T [303A.2]

Eviction from accommodation provided under this section Where a local housing authority terminates a licence to occupy accommodation which it granted under this section, the occupier may be evicted without a court order. This is because the premises are not "occupied as a dwelling under a licence" for the purposes of s 3(2B) of the Protection from Eviction Act 1997 (at **III L&T [90]**), and, although eviction without a court order could interfere with the occupier's right to respect for his home under Art 8 of the Convention, such interference has been held to be necessary, within Art 8.2: *Desnousse v Newham London Borough Council* [2006] EWCA Civ 547, (2006) Times, 28 June, applying *Mohamed v Manek and Kensington and Chelsea Royal Borough* (1995) 27 HLR 439. In *R (on the application of CN) v Lewisham London Borough Council* [2013] HLR 46 it was confirmed that the decisions in *Mohamed v Manek* and in *Desnousse v Newham London Borough Council* remain binding on the Court of Appeal.

III L&T [303A.3]

Decision on application for accommodation pending review Where there has been an adverse decision on homelessness followed by an application for a review and also an application for interim accommodation pending the review, the latter application may be decided by the same officer as the one who made the original adverse decision: *R (Abdi) v Lambeth London Borough Council* [2007] EWHC 1565 (Admin), (2007) Times, 11 July. Once a housing authority has offered, or secured an offer of, suitable temporary accommodation, ordinarily it will have performed its statutory duty under s 188 notwithstanding an applicant's refusal of the offer: *R (on the application of Brooks) v Islington London Borough Council* [2015] EWHC 2657 (Admin), 165 NLJ 7670, [2015] All ER (D) 103 (Sep).

III L&T [303A.4]

Homeless A person is not homeless if there is accommodation available, not necessarily in this country, which it would be reasonable to occupy for a continuing period: see s 175(3) as interpreted in *Waltham Forest London Borough Council v Maloba* [2007] EWCA Civ 1281, (2008) Times, 16 January, also reported as *Waltham Forest London Borough Council v Maloba* [2008] 2 All ER 701.

III L&T [303A.5]

Homeless teenage children Once it appears to the housing department of a local authority that a 16 or 17 year old may be homeless, that authority should accommodate him/her under s 188 pending clarification of whether the local children's services authority owes a duty to provide accommodation under s 20 of the Children Act 1989: *R (on the application of M) v Hammersmith and Fulham London Borough Council* [2008] UKHL 14, [2008] 1 WLR 535, [2008] 4 All ER 271. See also *R (MM) v Lewisham London Borough Council* [2009] EWHC 416 (Admin), 6 March 2009 to the same effect.

The Homelessness (Priority Need for Accommodation) (England) Order 2002 (SI 2002/2051) assumes that there will be some homeless teenagers, for example from a foreign country, who are not owed a duty under s 20 of the Children Act 1989. However, where the criteria are satisfied the authority must meet its obligations under s 20 and cannot side-step that duty by arranging accommodation under the homelessness provisions in the Housing Act 1996: see *R (on the application of G) v Southwark London Borough Council* [2009] UKHL 26, [2009] 3 All ER 189, [2009] 1WLR 1299.

In assessing whether a young person is a child or an adult the court should make a decision on the balance of probabilities: it is not that either side has a burden of proving status: *R (on the application of CJ) v Cardiff City Council* [2011] EWCA Civ 1590, [2012] 2 All ER 836, [2012] LGR 157.

III L&T [303A.6]

Applicant lacking capacity An application for accommodation or assistance cannot be entertained if made by a person who lacks capacity: *WB v W District Council* [2018] EWCA Civ 928.

III L&T [303A.7]

Remedy for breach Where a housing authority fails in its interim duty to provide accommodation it may be liable in damages for breach of Article 8 of the Convention. But there is no civil remedy for breach of statutory duty or in the tort of negligence: *R (on the application of McDonagh) v Enfield London Borough Council* [2018] EWHC 1287 (Admin).

III L&T [303AA]

189. Priority need for accommodation

(1) The following have a priority need for accommodation-

(a) a pregnant woman or a person with whom she resides or might reasonably be expected to reside;

(b) a person with whom dependent children reside or might reasonably be expected to reside;

(c) a person who is vulnerable as a result of old age, mental illness or handicap or physical disability or other special reason, or with whom such a person resides or might reasonably be expected to reside;

(d) a person who is homeless or threatened with homelessness as a result of an emergency such as flood, fire or other disaster.

(2) The Secretary of State may by order-

(a) specify further descriptions of persons as having a priority need for accommodation, and

(b) amend or repeal any part of subsection (1).

(3) Before making such an order the Secretary of State shall consult such associations representing relevant authorities, and such other persons, as he considers appropriate.

(4) No such order shall be made unless a draft of it has been approved by resolution of each House of Parliament.

III L&T [303AA.1]

Regulations under section 189(2) Pursuant to the power under sub-s (2), the Secretary of State has made the Homelessness (Priority Need for Accommodation) (England) Order 2002, SI 2002/2051. As a result, the additional persons having priority need for accommodation are as follows: (1) A person aged sixteen or seventeen who is not a relevant child for the purposes of s 23A of the Children Act 1989 and to whom a local authority does not otherwise owe a duty to provide accommodation under section 20 of that Act. (2) A person (other than a relevant student) who (a) is under twenty-one; and (b) at any time after reaching the age of sixteen, but while still under eighteen, was, but is no longer, looked after, accommodated or fostered. (3) The following persons who are vulnerable as a result of an institutional background: (a) A person (other than a relevant student) who has reached the age of twenty-one and who is vulnerable as a result of having been looked after, accommodated or fostered; (b) A person who is vulnerable as a result of having been a member of Her Majesty's regular naval, military or air forces; (c) A person who is vulnerable as a result of (i) having served a custodial sentence (within the meaning of s 76 of the Powers of Criminal Courts (Sentencing) Act 2000), (ii) having been committed for contempt of court or any other kindred offence or (iii) having been remanded in custody (within the meaning of paragraph (b), (c) or (d) of s 88(1) of that Act). (4) A person who is vulnerable as a result of ceasing to occupy accommodation by reason of violence from another person or threats of violence from another person which are likely to be carried out.

Note the conditions imposed on migrant nationals of the ten additional countries by the Allocation of Housing and Homelessness (Amendment) (England) Regulations 2004 SI 2004/1235

LANDLORD & TENANT AND HOUSING

III L&T [303AA.2]

Homelessness as a result of an emergency. The sudden and unexplained removal of a caravan in which the applicant had been living could fall within s 189(1)(d), but not if the occupier had nowhere to locate it as a residence since he was already homeless by virtue of s 175(2)(b). The occupant's status as a homeless person prior to the removal of the caravan made it impossible to contend that the homelessness was caused by its removal: *Higgs v Brighton and Hove City Council* [2003] EWCA Civ 895, [2003] 3 All ER 753, [2003] 1 WLR 2241.

III L&T [303AA.3]

Vulnerability The test of vulnerability is whether a person's "ability to fend for himself when homeless will result in injury or detriment to him which would not be suffered by an ordinary homeless person who was able to cope": see *R v Camden London Borough Council, ex p Pereira* (1998) 31 HLR 317, 330, per Hobhouse LJ. This test should be applied in preference to the less stringent test of "would be likely to suffer injury or detriment" propounded in The Homelessness Code of Guidance for Local Authorities issued by the Secretary of State under s 182: *Griffin v Westminster City Council* [2004] EWCA Civ 108, (2004) Times 4 February. However, the "Pereira test" is a judicial guide to interpretation and application of s 189(1)(c) and should not be applied as if it was a statutory formulation and, for the purpose of applying the vulnerability test, a local housing authority should assess it on the assumption that an applicant had become or would become street homeless, not on his ability to fend for himself while he was still housed: see *Naser Osmani v Camden London Borough Council* [2004] EWCA Civ 1706, (2004) 149 Sol Jo LB 61. In a case of depressive illness, *Hall v Wandsworth London Borough Council* [2004] EWCA Civ 110, Mance LJ said the question was "whether the medical evidence justified a conclusion that the applicant could not cope as an ordinary person, so that injury or detriment would result, when a less vulnerable person would be able to cope without injury or detriment". Drug addiction, and the need for accommodation to achieve stabilisation during treatment, may not be enough to establish vulnerability: *Simms v Islington London Borough Council* [2008] EWCA Civ 1083, [2008] All ER (D) 146 (Oct), (2008) Times, 3 December.

The assessment of entitlement to disability benefit is a wholly different exercise to the assessment of vulnerability: see *Mangion v London Borough of Lewisham* (2008) Lawtel 11 December, where the court held that a review officer had reached the correct conclusion when ruling that a homeless person, who suffered from back and alcohol problems, was not in priority need of housing. Vulnerability may be outweighed by the presence of family support: *Kanu v The London Borough of Southwark* [2014] EWCA Civ 1085, [2014] LGR 785, [2014] PTSR 1197.

See also notes at para **III L&T [306.4A]**.

In one important respect the *Pereira* test has been modified by the Supreme Court in *Hotak v Southwark London Borough Council; Kanu v Southwark London Borough Council; Johnson v Solihull Metropolitan Borough Council* [2015] UKSC 30, [2015] 3 All ER 1053, [2015] 2 WLR 1341, [2015] HLR 460. The rules laid down in *Hotak* is that the authority or reviewing officer, when assessing vulnerability, should compare the assessment subject with an ordinary person if made homeless not an ordinary actual homeless person. See also *Hackney London Borough Council v Mohammed Abdul Haque* [2017] EWCA Civ 4 where, applying *Hotak*, the Court of Appeal considered the impact of the public sector equality duty on a local authority's assessment of the suitability of accommodation provided to a disabled homeless man, and held that the decision-maker was not required to spell out whether the applicant had a protected characteristic.

III L&T [303AA.4]

Parent with a dependent child Section 185(4), before it was amended, was declared to be incompatible with the ban on discrimination in article 14 of the Convention on Human Rights: see *R (Morris) v Westminster City Council* [2004] EWHC 2191 (Admin), (2004) Times, 20 October. The offending provision in s 185(4) was put right, from 2 March 2009, by amendments made by the Housing and Regeneration Act 2008, s 314 and Sch 15 which introduced the concept of a 'restricted person' (see para **III L&T [303E.8A]**. In *Lepko-Bozua v Hackney London Borough Council* [2010] EWCA Civ 909, [2010] All ER (D) 298 (Jul) the applicant's dependent French niece (who had not acquired a right of residence in the United Kingdom) lived with her. She applied to the local authority for accommodation as a homeless person. The court held that the local authority was entitled to conclude that the applicant was not in priority need. The French niece was a restricted person; the local authority's duty was therefore the limited duty under s 193(7AA).

In *Holmes-Moorhouse v Richmond-Upon-Thames London Borough Council* [2009] UKHL 7, [2009] 3 All ER 277, [2009] 1 WLR 413 the House of Lords has given guidance as to the approach to be followed by local housing authorities, under s 189(1)(b), when determining whether an applicant for assistance, who had been granted a shared residence order, was a person with whom dependent children 'might reasonably be expected to reside'. The House of Lords observed in *Holmes-Moorhouse* that it would only be in very exceptional circumstances that it would be reasonable to expect a child who had a home with one parent to be provided under Part VII of the 1996 Act with another so that he could reside with the other parent as well. Nevertheless, in *Said El Goure v Royal Borough of Kensington and Chelsea* [2012] EWCA Civ 670, [2012] HLR 577 the court reiterated that the statutory test was as set out in s 189(1)(b) and stated that the reference to 'exceptional' in *Holmes-Moorhouse* was not as a substitute test or as a gloss on the statutory provision; it was simply an observation on the probable outcome or result of applying the statutory test. Applying the principles in *Holmes-Moorhouse*, it has been held that a husband, separated from his wife and disabled son, ought reasonably to have accepted an offer of a one-bedroom flat; the court rejecting the argument that because his son stayed with him at weekends he needed more extensive accommodation: *Dixon v Haringey London Borough Council* [2013] EWCA Civ 1050.

A period of residence by the applicant's children in s 188 temporary accommodation provided to the applicant should be taken into account for the purpose of determining questions of the applicant's priority need under s 189(1)(b): *Bull v Oxford City Council* [2011] EWCA Civ 609, [2011] 22 LS Gaz R 19, [2011] All ER (D) 189 (May).

III L&T [303AA.5]

Persons from abroad Section 185 excludes persons from abroad. They are not eligible for protection when homeless, except that the exclusion does not apply to EU workers and their families who have a right to reside. See, for example, *R (on the application of Mohamed) v Harrow London Borough Council* [2005] EWHC 3194 (Admin), [2005] All ER (D) 180 (Dec) 13 December.

Duty to assess every eligible applicant's case and agree a plan

III L&T [303AB]

189A. Assessments and personalised plan

(1) If the local housing authority are satisfied that an applicant is —

(a) homeless or threatened with homelessness, and
(b) eligible for assistance,

the authority must make an assessment of the applicant's case.

(2) The authority's assessment of the applicant's case must include an assessment of—

(a) the circumstances that caused the applicant to become homeless or threatened with homelessness,
(b) the housing needs of the applicant including, in particular, what accommodation would be suitable for the applicant and any persons with whom the applicant resides or might reasonably be expected to reside ("other relevant persons"), and
(c) what support would be necessary for the applicant and any other relevant persons to be able to have and retain suitable accommodation.

(3) The authority must notify the applicant, in writing, of the assessment that the authority make.

(4) After the assessment has been made, the authority must try to agree with the applicant—

(a) any steps the applicant is to be required to take for the purposes of securing that the applicant and any other relevant persons have and are able to retain suitable accommodation, and
(b) the steps the authority are to take under this Part for those purposes.

(5) If the authority and the applicant reach an agreement, the authority must record it in writing.

(6) If the authority and the applicant cannot reach an agreement, the authority must record in writing—

(a) why they could not agree,
(b) any steps the authority consider it would be reasonable to require the applicant to take for the purposes mentioned in subsection (4)(a), and
(c) the steps the authority are to take under this Part for those purposes.

(7) The authority may include in a written record produced under subsection (5) or (6) any advice for the applicant that the authority consider appropriate (including any steps the authority consider it would be a good idea for the applicant to take but which the applicant should not be required to take).

(8) The authority must give to the applicant a copy of any written record produced under subsection (5) or (6).

(9) Until such time as the authority consider that they owe the applicant no duty under any of the following sections of this Part, the authority must keep under review—

(a) their assessment of the applicant's case, and
(b) the appropriateness of any agreement reached under subsection (4) or steps recorded under subsection (6)(b) or (c).

(10) If—

(a) the authority's assessment of any of the matters mentioned in subsection (2) changes, or
(b) the authority's assessment of the applicant's case otherwise changes such that the authority consider it appropriate to do so,

the authority must notify the applicant, in writing, of how their assessment of the applicant's case has changed (whether by providing the applicant with a revised written assessment or otherwise).

(11) If the authority consider that any agreement reached under subsection (4) or any step recorded under subsection (6)(b) or (c) is no longer appropriate—

(a) the authority must notify the applicant, in writing, that they consider the agreement or step is no longer appropriate,

(b) any failure, after the notification is given, to take a step that was agreed to in the agreement or recorded under subsection (6)(b) or (c) is to be disregarded for the purposes of this Part, and

(c) subsections (4) to (8) apply as they applied after the assessment was made.

(12) A notification under this section or a copy of any written record produced under subsection (5) or (6), if not received by the applicant, is to be treated as having been given to the applicant if it is made available at the authority's office for a reasonable period for collection by or on behalf of the applicant.

Duties to persons found to be homeless or threatened with homelessness

III L&T [303AC]

189B. Initial duty owed to all eligible persons who are homeless

(1) This section applies where the local housing authority are satisfied that an applicant is—

(a) homeless, and

(b) eligible for assistance.

(2) Unless the authority refer the application to another local housing authority in England (see section 198(A1)), the authority must take reasonable steps to help the applicant to secure that suitable accommodation becomes available for the applicant's occupation for at least—

(a) 6 months, or

(b) such longer period not exceeding 12 months as may be prescribed.

(3) In deciding what steps they are to take, the authority must have regard to their assessment of the applicant's case under section 189A.

(4) Where the authority—

(a) are satisfied that the applicant has a priority need, and

(b) are not satisfied that the applicant became homeless intentionally,

the duty under subsection (2) comes to an end at the end of the period of 56 days beginning with the day the authority are first satisfied as mentioned in subsection (1).

(5) If any of the circumstances mentioned in subsection (7) apply, the authority may give notice to the applicant bringing the duty under subsection (2) to an end.

(6) The notice must—

(a) specify which of the circumstances apply, and

(b) inform the applicant that the applicant has a right to request a review of the authority's decision to bring the duty under subsection (2) to an end and of the time within which such a request must be made.

(7) The circumstances are that the authority are satisfied that—

(a) the applicant has—

(i) suitable accommodation available for occupation, and

(ii) a reasonable prospect of having suitable accommodation available for occupation for at least 6 months, or such longer period not exceeding 12 months as may be prescribed, from the date of the notice,

(b) the authority have complied with the duty under subsection (2) and the period of 56 days beginning with the day that the authority are first satisfied as mentioned in subsection (1) has ended (whether or not the applicant has secured accommodation),

(c) the applicant has refused an offer of suitable accommodation and, on the date of refusal, there was a reasonable prospect that suitable accommodation would be available for occupation by the applicant for at least 6 months or such longer period not exceeding 12 months as may be prescribed,

(d) the applicant has become homeless intentionally from any accommodation that has been made available to the applicant as a result of the authority's exercise of their functions under subsection (2),

(e) the applicant is no longer eligible for assistance, or

(f) the applicant has withdrawn the application mentioned in section 183(1).

(8) A notice under this section must be given in writing and, if not received by the applicant, is to be treated as having been given to the applicant if it is made available at the authority's office for a reasonable period for collection by or on behalf of the applicant.

(9) The duty under subsection (2) can also be brought to an end under—

(a) section 193A (consequences of refusal of final accommodation offer or final Part 6 offer at the initial relief stage), or

(b) sections 193B and 193C (notices in cases of applicant's deliberate and unreasonable refusal to co-operate).

III L&T [303B]

190. Duties to persons becoming homeless intentionally

(1) This section applies where—

(a) the local housing authority are satisfied that an applicant—

(i) is homeless and eligible for assistance, but

(ii) became homeless intentionally,

(b) the authority are also satisfied that the applicant has a priority need, and

(c) the authority's duty to the applicant under section 189B(2) has come to an end.

(2) The authority must—

(a) secure that accommodation is available for his occupation for such period as they consider will give him a reasonable opportunity of securing accommodation for his occupation, and

(b) provide him with [(or secure that he is provided with) advice and assistance] in any attempts he may make to secure that accommodation becomes available for his occupation.

(3) ...

(4) In deciding what advice and assistance is to be provided under this section, the authority must have regard to their assessment of the applicant's case under section 189A.

(5) The advice and assistance provided under subsection (2)(b) or (3) must include information about the likely availability in the authority's district of types of accommodation appropriate to the applicant's housing needs (including, in particular, the location and sources of such types of accommodation).

III L&T [303B.1]

Eviction from accommodation provided under this section Where a local housing authority terminates a licence to occupy accommodation which it granted under this section, the occupier may be evicted without a court order. This is because the premises are not "occupied as a dwelling under a licence" for the purposes of s 3(2B) of the Protection from Eviction Act 1997 (at **III L&T [90]**), and, although eviction without a court order could interfere with the occupier's right to respect for his home under Art 8 of the Convention, such interference has been held to be necessary, within Art 8.2: *Desnousse v Newham London Borough Council* [2006] EWCA Civ 547, [2006] 3 WLR 349, (2006) Times 28 June, applying

Mohamed v Manek and Kensington and Chelsea Royal Borough (1995) 27 HLR 439. In *R (on the application of CN) v Lewisham London Borough Council* [2013] HLR 46 it was confirmed that the decisions in *Mohamed v Manek* and in *Desnousse v Newham London Borough Council* remain binding on the Court of Appeal.

III L&T [303B.2]

Reasonable opportunity of securing accommodation In deciding what amounts to a "reasonable opportunity" the authority may not have regard to considerations peculiar to it, such as the extent of its resources and other demands upon it. It Is the opportunity given to the applicant that has to be reasonable, and not what may be reasonable from the authority's standpoint. *R (on the application of Conville) v Richmond upon Thames London Borough Council* [2006] EWCA Civ 718, [2006] 4 All ER 917, (2006) Times 3 July. "Accommodation" for the purposes of s 190(2) does not mean accommodation that an individual thinks is suitable or desirable: *Nipyo v Croydon London Borough Council* [2008] EWHC 847 (Admin), [2008] HLR 37.

III L&T [303B.3]

Discretion In *Lee-Lawrence v Penwith District Council* [2006] EWCA Civ 1672, the Court of Appeal held that it was Parliament's intention that a local authority had the discretion to make decisions on homelessness and, in so holding, applied *R v Hillingdon London Borough Council, ex p Pulhofer* [1986] AC 484. In the latter case, the House of Lords had observed that it is the duty of the court to leave decisions to the public body to whom Parliament has entrusted the decision-making power, save where it is obvious that the public body, consciously or unconsciously, has acted perversely.

III L&T [303B.4]

Homelessness of disabled person On an application to be accepted as a homeless because of the inadequacy of the accommodation occupied, the housing authority's decision under s 184 of the Housing Act 1996 is require by s 149(3)(b) and (4) to focus on the particular needs of that person not the generalised needs of others on the housing list: *Lomax v Gosport Borough Council* [2018] EWCA Civ 1846.

III L&T [303C]

191. Becoming homeless intentionally

(1) A person becomes homeless intentionally if he deliberately does or fails to do anything in consequence of which he ceases to occupy accommodation which is available for his occupation and which it would have been reasonable for him to continue to occupy.

(2) For the purposes of subsection (1) an act or omission in good faith on the part of a person who was unaware of any relevant fact shall not be treated as deliberate.

(3) A person shall be treated as becoming homeless intentionally if—

- (a) he enters into an arrangement under which he is required to cease to occupy accommodation which it would have been reasonable for him to continue to occupy, and
- (b) the purpose of the arrangement is to enable him to become entitled to assistance under this Part,

and there is no other good reason why he is homeless.

(4) < . . . >

III L&T [303C.1]

Intentionally homeless The Homelessness (Suitability of Accommodation) Order 1996 specifies various matters which must be taken into account in assessing whether it would have been reasonable for a person to continue to occupy particular accommodation. The Homelessness Code of Guidance for Local Authorities issued in 2006 also addresses various aspects of the statutory scheme. In *Birmingham City Council v Balog* [2013] EWCA Civ 1582, [2013] All ER (D) 129 (Dec) the Court of Appeal, in upholding the decision of the original review officer, applied the guidance in *Holmes-Moorhouse v Richmond-upon-Thames London Borough Council* [2009] UKHL 7, [2009] 3 All ER 277, [2009] 1 WLR 413 to the effect that the court should not adopt a nit-picking approach, when confronted with an appeal against a review decision and should be realistic and practical in its approach.

A person who loses accommodation as a result of receiving a prison sentence for various criminal offences may properly be regarded as intentionally homeless: see *Minchin v Sheffield City Council* (2000) Times, 26 April, CA, where the court rejected the contention that the offences had to be committed while the claimant was occupying the accommodation in question. See also *Stewart v Lambeth London Borough Council* [2002] EWCA Civ 753, [2002] HLR 747, (2002) Times, 28 May, where the Court held that imprisonment could not be described as settled accommodation so as to throw off the status of homelessness. A woman who leaves her partner because of his violence, taking the children with her, is not to be treated as intentionally homeless merely because she could have remained and sought an injunction and ouster order: *Bond v Leicester City Council* [2001] EWCA Civ 1544, [2002] 1 FCR 566. In *Bratton v Croydon London Borough Council* [2002] EWCA Civ 1494, [2002] All ER (D) 404 (Jul) it was held that a local authority is required, when considering whether a person has become intentionally homeless, to ascertain whether there is a causal link between the actions of the person and the loss of their home; this means that there must be not only a factual link between the conduct of the tenant and the loss of the home, but also some real and sensible connection between those two events which would naturally and reasonably lead to that happening. Thus, a tenant whose tenancy was not renewed because she used the rent money to pay for the repair of her washing machine was held to be intentionally homeless: *Najim v Enfield London Borough Council* [2015] EWCA Civ 319, [2015] HLR 337.

For the obligation of the review officer, when conducting a s 202 review, to consider the issue of good faith under s 191(2) (even if that issue has not been raised by the tenant), see *O'Connor v Kensington and Chelsea London Borough Council* [2004] EWCA Civ 394, [2004] All ER (D) 552 (Mar). When considering whether "it would have been reasonable for him to continue to occupy" accommodation under s 191(1), the local housing authority has to disregard the conduct or course of conduct of a homeless person that had led him to leave that home: *Denton v Southwark London Borough Council* [2007] EWCA Civ 623, [2007] All ER (D) 56 (Jul).

Where a tenant is dispossessed on the ground of nuisance or annoyance on the part of others residing in the tenant's dwelling-house, it does not follow necessarily that the dispossessed tenant is homeless intentionally. Where that person has not personally committed a nuisance or annoyance and has tried to restrain the other residents from doing so the finding that the homelessness is intentional is not justified: *Griffiths v St Helens Metropolitan Borough Council*, a decision of His Honour Judge Mackay in the St Helens County Court on 28 July 2004, reported briefly in (2005) Legal Action January at p 29.

In *Osei v Southwark London Borough Council* [2007] EWCA Civ 787, [2007] All ER (D) 383 (Jul) the court held that a local authority was entitled to conclude that a Spanish citizen, who had surrendered his tenancy of a property in Spain and brought his family to the UK (where he was working), was intentionally homeless.

In a case where a tenant with a history of rent arrears exercised her right to buy her home and took on mortgage repayments which were higher than the rent the court held that the subsequent repossession by the mortgagees made her intentionally homeless: *Watchman v Ipswich Borough Council* [2007] EWCA Civ 348, [2007] HLR 33.

Where a possession order was made against a tenant on the ground of breach of the terms of the tenancy by refusing to allow gas safety checks it was held that the reviewing officer was entitled to base a finding of intentionally homeless on the decision in the possession proceedings and was not required to go behind its terms: *Sheppard v Richmond-upon-Thames London Borough Council* [2012] EWCA Civ 302.

Where an order for possession is made because the tenant has failed to provide information needed for an award of housing benefit, and has failed to pay even the expected shortfall, that person is intentionally homeless and the situation is not affected by a backdated award of housing benefit obtained later: *Oduneye v Brent London Borough Council* [2018] EWCA Civ 1595, [2018] HLR 45.

III L&T [303C.2]

Acts or omissions in good faith in ignorance of a relevant fact Sub-sections (1) and (2) should be addressed separately. The first question is whether a deliberate act or omission has resulted in the loss of accommodation and the next question is whether the apparently deliberate act or omission should not be regarded as deliberate because it was done in good faith in ignorance of a relevant fact: *O'Connor v Kensington and Chelsea Royal London Borough Council* [2004] EWCA Civ 394, [2004] HLR 37. See also *Ugiagbe v Southwark London Borough Council* [2009] EWCA Civ 31: although ceasing to occupy accommodation on the landlord's demand was a deliberate act under s 191(1), the giving up of accommodation could not be treated as deliberate pursuant to s 191(2) since the tenant was unaware of a relevant fact, namely that she had security of tenure, and her act of giving up accommodation had been done in good faith.

Ignorance of the true prospect for future employment, at a new location, may constitute a "relevant fact" provided it is sufficiently specific (ie related to specific employment) and is based on some genuine investigation and not mere "aspiration": *Aw-Aden v Birmingham*

City Council [2005] EWCA Civ 1834 in which it was held that the appellant's prospects, when leaving Belgium to seek work in Birmingham, did not meet that threshold and rested on little more than a wing and a prayer; the necessary specificity was missing. See also *F v Birmingham City Council* [2006] EWCA Civ 1427, 150 Sol Jo LB 1466 where a council tenant had given up her tenancy and taken privately rented accommodation ignoring advice that, in doing so, she risked being intentionally homeless and without considering whether she would be able to afford to pay the rent. The Court of Appeal held that she was intentionally homeless.

In *Alfonso-da-Trindade v Hackney London Borough Council* [2017] EWCA Civ 942, the applicant had deliberately left her home on the island of Sao Tome in order to come to the UK to seek medical treatment for her daughter. She stayed with her sister in London who was then evicted. The applicant contended that, when leaving her home in Sao Tome, she had not known that her sister would be evicted and was thus unaware of a relevant fact. The Court of Appeal, applying *Najim v Enfield London Borough Council* [2015] EWCA Civ 319, [2015] HLR 337, held that an applicant seeking to bring herself within s 191(2) had to show that, at the time of her s 191(1) action or omission, she had an active belief that a specific state of affairs would arise or continue in the future, based on a genuine investigation about her prospects, not on mere aspiration. Her belief about her current prospects regarding the future could then properly be regarded as belief about a current relevant fact, such that if that belief could be seen to be unjustified by what a fully informed appreciation of her prospects at the time would have revealed, her mistake would qualify as unawareness of a relevant fact within s 191(2). The local authority had been entitled to decide that the appellant had not made a proper investigation of her prospects of UK accommodation at the time she left Sao Tome. Therefore, her case did not fall within s 191(2).

A period of intentional homelessness may be brought to an end by a supervening event that makes the applicant unintentionally homeless at the time of the decision on review: *Haile v Waltham Forest London Borough* [2015] UKSC 34, [2015] 2 WLR 1441, [2015] HLR 492.

In a case where an intentionally homeless person was allowed to occupy the room of a family member for £500 a month during the time that that person was away at university it was held that the accommodation was not 'settled' but merely a precarious licence which did not break the intentionally homeless chain of causation: *Doka v Southwark London Borough Council* [2017] EWCA Civ 1532.

III L&T [303C.3]

Accommodation that is available It has been held that a women's refuge is no more than a staging post, so that victims of domestic violence do not cease to be homeless when given shelter by a women's refuge: *Manchester City Council v Moran* [2009] UKHL 36, [2009] 4 All ER 161, [2009] 1 WLR 1506.

III L&T [303C.4]

Children's welfare In *Huzrat v Hounslow London Borough Council* [2013] All ER (D) 242 (Nov), the Court of Appeal held that the duty under the Children Act 2004, s 11 to safeguard and promote the welfare of children did not affect decisions taken under s 191. The Court of Appeal has further held that s 11 does not create a free-standing duty to safeguard children in the context of homelessness, such as would require an additional assessment on top of the statutory requirements of the Housing Act 1996: *Mohamoud v Royal Borough of Kensington and Chelsea* [2015] EWCA Civ 780, [2015] HLR 762, [2015] All ER (D) 243 (Jul). Both the local authority and the court did, however, have to act compatibly with ECHR Art 8, and the best interests of any children might be relevant to the proportionality of any interference with the rights guaranteed by that Article.

III L&T [303D]

192. *Duty to persons not in priority need who are not homeless intentionally*
Repealed.

III L&T [303E]

193. Duty to persons with priority need who are not homeless intentionally

(1) This section applies where—

(a) the local housing authority—

(i) are satisfied that an applicant is homeless and eligible for assistance, and

(ii) are not satisfied that the applicant became homeless intentionally,

(b) the authority are also satisfied that the applicant has a priority need, and

(c) the authority's duty to the applicant under section 189B(2) has come to an end.

. . .

(1A) But this section does not apply if—

(a) section 193A(3) disapplies this section, or

(b) the authority have given notice to the applicant under section 193B(2).

(2) Unless the authority refer the application to another local housing authority (see section 198), they shall secure that accommodation is available for occupation by the applicant.

(3) The authority are subject to the duty under this section until it ceases by virtue of any of the following provisions of this section.

...

(3B) In this section "a restricted case" means a case where the local housing authority would not be satisfied as mentioned in subsection (1) without having had regard to a restricted person.

(5) The local housing authority shall cease to be subject to the duty under this section if—

(a) the applicant, having been informed by the authority of the possible consequence of refusal or acceptance and of the right to request a review of the suitability of the accommodation, refuses an offer of accommodation which the authority are satisfied is suitable for the applicant,

(b) that offer of accommodation is not an offer of accommodation under Part 6 or a private rented sector offer, and

(c) the authority notify the applicant that they regard themselves as ceasing to be subject to the duty under this section.

(6) The local housing authority shall cease to be subject to the duty under this section if the applicant—

(a) ceases to be eligible for assistance,

(b) becomes homeless intentionally from the accommodation made available for his occupation,

(c) accepts an offer of accommodation under Part VI (allocation of housing), or

(cc) accepts an offer of an assured tenancy (other than an assured shorthold tenancy) from a private landlord,

(d) otherwise voluntarily ceases to occupy as his only or principal home the accommodation made available for his occupation.

(7) The local housing authority shall also cease to be subject to the duty under this section if the applicant, having been informed of the possible consequence of refusal or acceptance and of his right to request a review of the suitability of the accommodation, refuses a final offer of accommodation under Part 6.

(7A) An offer of accommodation under Part 6 is a final offer for the purposes of subsection (7) if it is made in writing and states that it is a final offer for the purposes of subsection (7).

(7AA) The authority shall also cease to be subject to the duty under this section if the applicant, having been informed in writing of the matters mentioned in subsection (7AB)—

(a) accepts a private rented sector offer, or

(b) refuses such an offer.

(7AB) The matters are—

(a) the possible consequence of refusal or acceptance of the offer, and

(b) that the applicant has the right to request a review of the suitability of the accommodation, and

(c) in a case which is not a restricted case, the effect under section 195A of a further application to a local housing authority within two years of acceptance of the offer.

(7AC) For the purposes of this section an offer is a private rented sector offer if—

(a) it is an offer of an assured shorthold tenancy made by a private landlord to the applicant in relation to any accommodation which is, or may become, available for the applicant's occupation,

(b) it is made, with the approval of the authority, in pursuance of arrangements made by the authority with the landlord with a view to bringing the authority's duty under this section to an end, and

(c) the tenancy being offered is a fixed term tenancy (within the meaning of Part 1 of the Housing Act 1988) for a period of at least 12 months.

(7AD) In a restricted case the authority shall, so far as reasonably practicable, bring their duty under this section to an end as mentioned in subsection (7AA).

...

(7F) The local housing authority shall not—

(a) make a final offer of accommodation under Part 6 for the purposes of subsection (7); or

(ab) approve a private rented sector offer; or

...

unless they are satisfied that the accommodation is suitable for the applicant and that subsection (8) does not apply to the applicant.

(8) This subsection applies to an applicant if—

(a) the applicant is under contractual or other obligations in respect of the applicant's existing accommodation, and

(b) the applicant is not able to bring those obligations to an end before being required to take up the offer.

(9) A person who ceases to be owed the duty under this section may make a fresh application to the authority for accommodation or assistance in obtaining accommodation.

(10) The appropriate authority may provide by regulations that subsection (7AC)(c) is to have effect as if it referred to a period of the length specified in the regulations.

(11) Regulations under subsection (10)—

(a) may not specify a period of less than 12 months, and

(b) may not apply to restricted cases.

(12) In subsection (10) "the appropriate authority"—

(a) in relation to local housing authorities in England, means the Secretary of State;

(b) in relation to local housing authorities in Wales, means the Welsh Ministers.

III L&T [303E.1]

Suitability See the Homelessness (Suitability of Accommodation) (England) Order 2003, SI 2003/3326, made under ss 210 and 215 which states what should be taken into account and specifies circumstances which make accommodation unsuitable.

III L&T [303E.1A]

Factors to be considered For guidance on the factors which a local housing authority might properly take into account when carrying out its duties under s 193(2) see *Nzolameso v Westminster City Council* [2015] UKSC 22, [2015] 2 All ER 942, [2015] LGR 215. Before determining to offer accommodation in another district the authority should address the issues mentioned in s 208 and in the Homelessness Code of Guidance for Local Authorities 2006, the Homelessness (Suitability of Accommodation) (England) Order 2012, SI

2012/2601 and the Supplementary Guidance on the homelessness changes in the Localism Act 2011 and on the Homelessness (Suitability of Accommodation) (England) Order 2012. In all cases authorities should also have regard to their duty under s 11 of the Children Act 2004 to safeguard children and promote their welfare.

In determining whether accommodation is suitable the local authority is required by s 210(1) to have regard to Parts 1 to 4 of the Housing Act 2004 (removal of hazards in categories 1 and 2). However, the authority is not required, whenever an applicant complains about the condition of accommodation offered under s 193(2), to conduct a full hazard inspection and assessment before a decision on suitability could be made: see *Firoozmand v London Borough of Lambeth* [2015] EWCA Civ 952, [2015] All ER (D) 20 (Sep), where the court observed that local authorities operate on tight budgets and have to exercise judgment when deciding whether to conduct a full scale inspection and assessment.

III L&T [303E.1B]

Duty to accommodate family member normally residing with the applicant It has been held that, having regard to the wording of s 176(a), the duty to accommodate a homeless applicant in priority need extends to any family member who normally resides with the applicant: *R (Ogbeni) v Tower Hamlets London Borough Council* [2008] EWHC 2444 (Admin), [2008] All ER (D) 67 (Aug). Furthermore, the obligation to accommodate the claimant 'together with' other household members cannot lawfully be performed by the provision of two separate self-contained units: *Sharif v Camden London Borough Council* [2011] EWCA Civ 463.

But the Supreme Court favoured a broader interpretation of 'living together' that could be satisfied by two units of accommodation if so close that they enabled the family to live 'together' in practical terms: *Sharif v Camden London Borough Council* [2013] UKSC 10, [2013] 2 All ER 309, [2013] LGR 556.

III L&T [303E.2]

Rescission of decision made by mistake A housing authority is entitled to revisit and rescind a decision that it had an obligation to house an applicant under s 193 where the decision had resulted from a fundamental mistake of fact: *Porteous v West Dorset District Council* [2004] EWCA Civ 244, [2004] LGR 577.

III L&T [303E.3]

Making a fresh application Where a further application is nothing more than a re-run on the same facts as a previous application that has been rejected, the council is entitled to refuse to entertain it: *Minhas v Wandsworth London Borough Council* [2004] EWCA Civ 856. However, this applies only where the application is based on exactly the same facts as the earlier application: the general rule is that the authority has an obligation to consider a second homelessness application: *R (Griffin) v Southwark London Borough Council* (2005) Times, 3 January, QBD, following the decision in *R v Harrow London Borough Council, ex p Fahia* [1998] 4 All ER 137, [1998] 1 WLR 1396, HL. On receiving a subsequent application the local authority should compare the circumstances with those known to the authority at the time of the earlier decision. It is for the applicant to identify new facts which are not trivial or fanciful and which make the subsequent application different from the previous one. Then the authority must treat the subsequent application as valid: *Tower Hamlets London Borough Council v Begum (Rikha)* [2005] EWCA Civ 340, [2005] 1 WLR 2103. See also *R (on the application of Hindis Abdulrahman) v Hillingdon London Borough Council* [2016] EWHC 2647 (Admin) where the court held that, in refusing to accept an application for assistance under s 183, a local authority had acted irrationally in concluding that it was based upon exactly the same facts as in a previous application by the same applicant where her husband had left and three of her children were no longer dependent on her.

III L&T [303E.4]

Cultural aversion to conventional housing In *Codona v Mid-Bedfordshire District Council* [2004] EWCA Civ 925, [2005] HLR 1, (2004) 148 Sol Jo LB 910, Times, 21 July, the Court of Appeal held that, by offering conventional temporary accommodation to a homeless Romany gypsy family, a local authority had discharged its statutory duty to secure accommodation for them under s 193 (and also ss 176 and 206), and had not violated the family's human rights, despite their cultural aversion to bricks and mortar. The ECtHR declared Ms Codona's complaint that the United Kingdom had infringed her rights under Arts 8 and 14 to be inadmissible, but might have reached a different conclusion if the authority had at its disposal accommodation which was suitable for her cultural needs (ie a caravan rather than bricks and mortar): *Codona v United Kingdom*, Application No 485/05 7 February 2006, ECtHR. See also *Slattery v Basildon Borough Council* [2014] EWCA Civ 30 where the Court of Appeal explained *Codona* and reconciled it with, and followed, *Sheridan v Basildon Borough Council* [2012] EWCA Civ 335, [2012] HLR 29 in which it was held that a local authority was not disabled from relying on the absence of caravan site accommodation by its alleged failure to exercise its powers under s 24 of the Caravan Sites and Control of Development Act 1960. Where there is such cultural aversion the housing authority, noting the position, may discharge its duty by offering conventional housing if there is no practical alternative: *Lee v Rhondda Cynon Taf CBC* [2008] EWCA Civ 1013.

III L&T [303E.5]

Accommodation offered unseen In *R (on the application of Khatun) v Newham London Borough* [2004] EWCA Civ 55, [2004] 3 WLR 417, the Court of Appeal held that the authority's policy of requiring homeless persons to accept or decline accommodation offered under s 193(2) without a prior view was not unlawful.

III L&T [303E.5A]

Auto-bidding procedure In *R (on the application of Tout A Tout) v Haringey London Borough Council* [2012] EWHC 873 (Admin), [2012] All ER (D) 16 (Apr) the court held that, on the facts of that case, an 'auto-bidding' procedure operated by a local authority was a lawful scheme for allocating housing to those in temporary accommodation.

III L&T [303E.6]

Offer of an assured shorthold tenancy The refusal of an offer of an assured shorthold tenancy does not normally bring the main housing duty to an end. But if the offer is made on the basis that the main housing duty will continue if and when the assured shorthold tenancy ends, then the refusal of such an offer would discharge the authority from further performance of its main duty. Because of the importance of this distinction the authority should include a statement in the offer acknowledging the continuation of the main housing duty: *Griffiths v St Helens Metropolitan Borough Council* [2006] EWCA Civ 160, (2006) Times, 24 April, (2006) Legal Action April 33.

Under s 193(5) a local authority has to be satisfied that the accommodation offered is suitable but it is not required to be satisfied that, in addition, it would be reasonable for the applicant to accept the offer as is the case under s 193(7). An authority making an offer of accommodation should, therefore, always make clear whether the offer is being made under s 193(5) for temporary accommodation or s 193(7) for permanent accommodation: *Ravichandran v Lewisham London Borough Council* [2010] EWCA Civ 755, (2010) Times 19 July, CA. However, a superfluous reference to reasonableness in the context of a letter sent to a homeless person in accordance with s 193(5) did not vitiate a local authority's decision that suitable accommodation, which was refused, had been provided: *Vilvarasa v Harrow London Borough Council* [2010] EWCA Civ 1278.

In *Maswaku v Westminster City Council* [2012] EWCA Civ 669, [2012] HLR 589 the court held that the statutory obligation on the local authority, under s 193(5) (in its un-amended form), was to inform the applicant of the 'possible consequence of refusal'. It was not required to spell out the possibilities of eviction, her right to make a fresh application or the loss of priority on the waiting list. In *R (on the application of Faizi) v London Borough of Brent* [2015] EWHC 2449 (Admin) the court held that s 193(5) makes clear that, from the moment a person has refused an offer of suitable accommodation, the duty on the local housing authority to provide accommodation ceases; there is no duty, to provide accommodation pending a review or appeal against that decision.

III L&T [303E.6A]

Duty to accommodate during period before eviction Where a court orders possession of accommodation the occupant is thereby threatened with homelessness for the purposes of s 184 and, on receiving an application for accommodation, the local authority must make immediate inquiries and must secure accommodation under s 195 if satisfied as to eligibility for assistance and priority need. The Act does not permit the authority to do nothing until eviction. Collins J allowed an application for judicial review on these grounds in *R v Newham London Borough Council, ex p Khan* (2000) Times, 9 May, DC. He also held, on the same application, that the authority's refusal to house the family together was irrational in the *Wednesbury* sense.

III L&T [303E.6B]

Relief of overcrowding Where the premises are statutorily overcrowded, applying the "space" standard under s 326 Table II of the Housing Act 1985, and the home is so overcrowded that it is no longer reasonable to occupy, as provided in s 175(3), the occupants should be treated as homeless: *Elrify v Westminster City Council* (2007) Times, 23 March, CA. On the other hand the fact that premises are statutorily overcrowded does not necessarily preclude a finding that, having regard to local conditions, it would be reasonable for the claimant to continue to occupy them: *Harouki v Kensington and Chelsea London Borough Council* [2007] EWCA Civ 1000, (2007) Times 12 November. Where premises are overcrowded it is a question of fact whether the accommodation is suitable for occupation in the short term. It is unlawful to leave families in overcrowded accommodation indefinitely: *Ali v Birmingham City Council* [2009] UKHL 36, [2009] 4 All ER 161, [2009] 1 WLR 1506; *R (Aweys) v Birmingham City Council* [2009] UKHL 36, (2009) Times, 7 July.

III L&T [303E.6C]

Occupants outgrowing existing accommodation A housing authority's duty under s 193 was held to have been discharged where its offer of alternative accommodation to a family, which had outgrown its existing accommodation, was declined. The authority was not required to give the family a choice of accepting the alternative accommodation or remaining in the existing accommodation: *Muhubo Mohammed Muse v Brent London Borough Council* [2008] EWCA Civ 1447.

III L&T [303E.6D]

Refuge for victims of violence It has been held that victims of domestic violence do not cease to be homeless when given shelter by a women's refuge, since this is no more than a staging post: *Manchester City Council v Moran* [2009] UKHL 36, [2009] 4 All ER 161, [2009] 1 WLR 1506.

III L&T [303E.7]

Suitable and reasonable to accept To discharge its duty, in accordance with sub-s (7F), the authority must be satisfied not only that the accommodation was suitable but also that it was reasonable to accept the offer. The needs of the applicant to be protected from domestic violence and to be located near to support networks should be considered as material not only as to suitability but also as to whether the offer ought reasonably to be accepted. The authority must address, and be satisfied on, both issues: *Slater v Lewisham London Borough Council* [2006] EWCA Civ 394, [2006] FCR 90, (2006) Times, 3 May, CA.

Where accommodation is offered and rejected the council should make clear the consequences of rejecting a final offer but need not refer expressly to sub-s 193(7): *Omar v Birmingham City Council* [2007] EWCA Civ 610, [2007] HLR 43, (2007) Times, 12 June.

It is possible and desirable for both suitability and reasonableness to be reviewed at the same time and that should be made clear to the applicant: *Ravichandran v Lewisham London Borough Council* [2010] EWCA Civ 755, (2010) Times 19 July. As to a superfluous reference to reasonableness see *Vilvarasa v Harrow London Borough Council* [2010] EWCA Civ 1278 noted at para **III L&T [303E.6]**. It has been held that a husband, separated from his wife and disabled son, ought reasonably to have accepted an offer of a one-bedroom flat. The Court rejected the argument that, because his son stayed with him at weekends, he needed more extensive accommodation: *Dixon v Haringey LBC* [2013] EWCA Civ 1050, applying the principles in *Holmes-Moorhouse v Richmond-upon-Thames London Borough Council* [2009] UKHL 7, [2009] 3 All ER 277, [2009] 1 WLR 413.

There is no obligation on an authority to support an offer with reasons why the accommodation was suitable and acceptable: *Akhtar v Birmingham City Council* [2011] EWCA Civ 383, [2011] NLJR 597, [2011] HLR 28; followed in *Solihull MPC v Khan* [2014] EWCA Civ 41 which explained that the absence of a duty to give reasons in an offer enabled local authorities to act more expeditiously, as they could make their final offers in a standard format rather than in individually-crafted letters.

In *Alibkhiet v Brent London Borough Council* [2018] EWCA Civ 2742 the Court of Appeal, in the light of the evidence as to the resources available to the local authority, and its housing policy (which should be made publicly available), and avoiding a 'nit-picking' approach in its approach to a review decision (following *Holmes-Moorhouse*), held that the authority had lawfully discharged its duty under s 193 by offering to accommodate a homeless person outside its district.

III L&T [303E.7A]

Terms of final offer Where an offer letter clearly stated that it was a final offer, and the consequences of refusal, the local authority had discharged its duty under the Housing Act 1996 s 193 even though the letter did not say that it was it is a final offer for the purposes of sub-s 193(7); slavish repetition of the exact words of the subsection was not required where all matters of substance required by statute were expressly contained in the letter: *Omar v Birmingham City Council* [2007] EWCA Civ 610, [2007] HLR 43, (2007) Times, June 12.

III L&T [303E.8]

Accommodation for asylum seekers, Accession State nationals and those subject to immigration control Section 11(3) of the Asylum and Immigration (Treatment of Claimants, etc) Act 2004 disapplies s 193 where the person was provided with accommodation in Scotland, otherwise than in an accommodation centre, but has no local connection with any district in England and Wales or in Scotland.

An EEA (European Economic Area) national who does not have the right to reside in the United Kingdom (although not requiring leave to enter) is a person subject to immigration control for the purposes of Homelessness (England) Regulations 2000, reg 3(1)(i) with the result that he may not be excluded from applying for housing assistance: *Barnet London Borough Council v Ismail* [2006] EWCA Civ 383, (2006) Times 25 April. See now the Allocation of Housing and Homelessness (Eligibility) (England) Regulations 2006, SI 2006/1294, as amended by SI 2006/2007 (which offer special treatment to persons who left the territory of Montserrat after 1 November 1995 because of the effect on that territory of a volcanic eruption and to those who left Lebanon on or after 12 July 2006 because of the armed conflict there). Further amendments were made by the Allocation of Housing and Homelessness (Eligibility) (England) (Amendment) Regulations 2009, SI 2009/358, to cover the homeless from Zimbabwe.

See also *Putans v Tower Hamlets London Borough Council* [2006] EWHC 1634 (Ch) where it was held that a citizen from an Accession State who had been employed but had lost his job was not eligible for housing assistance.

III L&T [303E.8A]

Restricted cases and restricted persons "A restricted person" means a person (a) who is not eligible for assistance under the Act, (b) who is subject to immigration control within the meaning of the Asylum and Immigration Act 1996 and (c) either (i) who does not have leave to enter or remain in the United Kingdom or (ii) whose leave to enter or remain in the United Kingdom is subject to a condition to maintain and accommodate himself, and any dependants, without recourse to public funds: section 184(7) so provides.

In *Lepko-Bozua v Hackney London Borough Council* [2010] EWCA Civ 909, [2010] All ER (D) 298 (Jul) the applicant's dependent French niece (who had not acquired a right of residence in the United Kingdom) lived with her. She applied to the local authority for accommodation as a homeless person. The court held that the local authority was entitled to conclude that the applicant was not in priority need. The French niece was a restricted person; the local authority's duty was therefore the limited duty under s 193(7AA).

III L&T [303E.9]

Suitability: proposed alterations In *Basra Boreh v Ealing London Borough Council* [2008] EWCA Civ 1176 the court held that the suitability of accommodation offered by a housing authority to a homeless disabled person is not to be judged exclusively by reference to the condition of the accommodation at the time of the offer; there should also be taken into account any adaptations or alterations that are proposed at the time of the offer. However, any such proposals have to be the subject of assurances that an applicant could fairly regard as certain, binding and enforceable.

III L&T [303E.9A]

Suitability of accommodation for the disabled In the case of a homeless applicant who is vulnerable by reason of disabilities, the authority must be satisfied that he, or she, has a protected characteristic within s 6 of the Equality Act 2010 and should then focus of the consequences of the impairments and the suitability of the accommodation in the context of the needs arising from them: *London Borough of Hackney v Haque* [2017] EWCA Civ 4, [2017] HLR 233, [2017] All ER (D) 68 (Jan).

III L&T [303E.10]

Accommodation for homeless teenage children A local authority, when meeting its statutory obligation to provide housing to a minor, should expressly recognise in any agreement entered into that, because the applicant was a minor, the authority was not granting a legal estate, but was ensuring that accommodation was available by granting something other than a legal estate: see *Hammersmith and Fulham London Borough Council v Alexander-David* [2009] EWCA Civ 259, [2009] 3 All ER 1098, [2009] 2 FLR 329 where, on the facts, the local authority was held to have been both (i) lessor and (ii) trustee for the minor beneficiary and to have acted in breach of trust (and ineffectively) by serving a notice to quit on the minor.

III L&T [303E.11]

Human rights A local authority's decision under s 193(5) that it had discharged its duty to secure that accommodation was available for occupation by a homeless applicant was not a determination of that person's 'civil rights' within the meaning of Art 6(1): see *Ali v Birmingham City Council* [2010] UKSC 8. In *Poshteh v Kensington & Chelsea London Borough Council* [2017] UKSC 36, the Supreme Court declined to depart from its decision in Ali. The decision of the ECHR to the opposite effect in *Ali v United Kingdom (40378/10)* (2016) 63 EHRR 20 did not persuade the Supreme Court to change its view.

In *Brian Holmes v Westminster City Council* [2011] EWHC 2857 (QB), [2011] All ER (D) 21 (Nov) the court, applying *Hounslow London Borough Council v Powell* [2011] 2 WLR 287 and *Manchester City Council v Pinnock* [2010] 3 WLR 1441 (see **III L&T [283.2]**) held that a judge was entitled to grant, on a summary basis, a local authority's claim for possession against a non-secure tenant who had not shown substantial grounds to establish the need for a hearing to find the facts that the local authority alleged had taken place.

In *Akerman-Livingstone v Aster Communities Ltd (formerly Flourish Homes Ltd)* [2015] UKSC 15, [2015] AC 1399, [2015] 3 All ER 725 the local authority discharged its s 193 duty by securing temporary accommodation for the applicant with a social landlord. The applicant having then refused all offers of suitable permanent accommodation, the local authority declared its s 193 duty discharged and the social landlord brought possession proceedings. The applicant argued that the proceedings amounted to disability discrimination within the meaning of ss 15 and 35(1)(b) of the Equality Act 2010, and that they violated his rights under ECHR Art 8. The Supreme Court held that the protection afforded by s 35(1)(b) was stronger than that afforded by Art 8 and that the court could not therefore take the summary approach which is permitted where an Art 8 defence is raised.

III L&T [303E.12]

Deferral In *R (on the application of Cranfield-Adams) v Richmond Upon Thames London Borough Council* [2012] EWHC 3334 (Admin), [2012] All ER (D) 114 (Jun) it was held to be lawful for an authority, and in accordance with its duty under s 193, to defer a homeless person's application for housing for two years where he had previously refused a suitable offer of accommodation.

III L&T [303F]

198. Referral of case to another local housing authority

(A1) If the local housing authority would be subject to the duty under section 189B (initial duty owed to all eligible persons who are homeless) but consider that the conditions are met for referral of the case to another local housing authority in England, they may notify that other authority of their opinion.

(1) If the local housing authority would be subject to the duty under section 193 (accommodation for those with priority need who are not homeless intentionally) but consider that the conditions are met for referral of the case to another local housing authority, they may notify that other authority of their opinion.

(2) The conditions for referral of the case to another authority are met if-

- (a) neither the applicant nor any person who might reasonably be expected to reside with him has a local connection with the district of the authority to whom his application was made,
- (b) the applicant or a person who might reasonably be expected to reside with him has a local connection with the district of that other authority, and
- (c) neither the applicant nor any person who might reasonably be expected to reside with him will run the risk of domestic violence in that other district.

(2ZA) The conditions for referral of the case to another authority are also met if—

- (a) the application is made within the period of two years beginning with the date on which the applicant accepted an offer from the other authority under section 193(7AA) (private rented sector offer), and
- (b) neither the applicant nor any person who might reasonably be expected to reside with the applicant will run the risk of domestic violence in the district of the other authority.

(2A) But the conditions for referral mentioned in subsection (2) or (2ZA) are not met if-

- (a) the applicant or any person who might reasonably be expected to reside with him has suffered violence (other than domestic violence) in the district of the other authority; and

(b) it is probable that the return to that district of the victim will lead to further violence of a similar kind against him.

(3) For the purposes of subsections (2), (2ZA) and (2A) "violence" means-

(a) violence from another person; or

(b) threats of violence from another person which are likely to be carried out;

and violence is "domestic violence" if it is from a person who is associated with the victim.

(4) The conditions for referral of the case to another authority are also met if-

(a) the applicant was on a previous application made to that other authority placed(in pursuance of their functions under this Part) in accommodation in the district of the authority to whom his application is now made, and

(b) the previous application was within such period as may be prescribed of the present application.

(5) The question whether the conditions for referral of a case are satisfied shall be decided by agreement between the notifying authority and the notified authority or, in default of agreement, in accordance with such arrangements as the Secretary of State may direct by order.

(6) An order may direct that the arrangements shall be-

(a) those agreed by any relevant authorities or associations of relevant authorities, or

(b) in default of such agreement, such arrangements as appear to the Secretary of State to be suitable, after consultation with such associations representing relevant authorities, and such other persons, as he thinks appropriate.

(7) No such order shall be made unless a draft of the order has been approved by a resolution of each House of Parliament.

III L&T [303F.1]

Prescribed period for referral The prescribed period for sub-s (4)(b) is 5 years plus the period between the previous application and placement: Allocation of Housing and Homelessness (Miscellaneous Provisions) (England) Regulations 2006, SI 2006/2527.

III L&T [303F.1A]

Conditions for referral Before determining to offer accommodation in another district the authority should address the issues mentioned in s 208 and in the Homelessness Code of Guidance for Local Authorities 2006, the Homelessness (Suitability of Accommodation) (England) Order 2012, SI 2012/2601 and the Supplementary Guidance on the homelessness changes in the Localism Act 2011 and on the Homelessness (Suitability of Accommodation) (England) Order 2012. In all cases the authority should also have regard to their duty under s 11 of the Children Act 2004 to safeguard children and promote their welfare: *Nzolameso v Westminster City Council* [2015] UKSC 22, [2015] 2 All ER 942, [2015] LGR 215.

III L&T [303F.2]

Violence 'Violence' is not limited to physical violence but may also include threatening or intimidating behaviour and any other form of abuse which, directly or indirectly, might give rise to the risk of harm: *Yemshaw v Hounslow London Borough Council* [2011] 1 WLR 433, [2011] 1 All ER 912, over-ruling *Danesh v Kensington and Chelsea Royal London Borough Council* [2007] 1 WLR 69, CA. A person who is at risk of domestic violence or other violence is automatically homeless, as provided in s 177(1), and may not be treated as intentionally homeless on leaving the accommodation in question.

III L&T [303G]

199. Local connection

(1) A person has a local connection with the district of a local housing authority if he has a connection with it-

(a) because he is, or in the past was, normally resident there, and that residence is or was of his own choice,

(b) because he is employed there,

(c) because of family associations, or

(d) because of special circumstances.

(2) . . .

(3) Residence in a district is not of a person's own choice if-

(a) . . .

(b) he, or a person who might reasonably be expected to reside with him, becomes resident there because he is detained under the authority of an Act of Parliament.

(4) . . .

(5) The Secretary of State may by order specify circumstances in which-

(a) a person is not to be treated as employed in a district, or

(b) residence in a district is not to be treated as of a person's own choice.

(6) A person has a local connection with the district of a local housing authority if he was (at any time) provided with accommodation in that district under section 95 of the Immigration and Asylum Act 1999 (support for asylum seekers).

(7) But subsection (6) does not apply-

(a) to the provision of accommodation for a person in a district of a local housing authority if he was subsequently provided with accommodation in the district of another local housing authority under section 95 of that Act, or

(b) to the provision of accommodation in an accommodation centre by virtue of section 22 of the Nationality, Immigration and Asylum Act 2002 (c. 41) (use of accommodation centres for section 95 support).

(8) While a local authority in England have a duty towards a person under section 23C of the Children Act 1989 (continuing functions in respect of former relevant children)—

(a) if the local authority is a local housing authority, the person has a local connection with their district, and

(b) otherwise, the person has a local connection with every district of a local housing authority that falls within the area of the local authority.

(9) In subsection (8), "local authority" has the same meaning as in the Children Act 1989 (see section 105 of that Act).

(10) Where, by virtue of being provided with accommodation under section 22A of the Children Act 1989 (provision of accommodation for children in care), a person is normally resident in the district of a local housing authority in England for a continuous period of at least two years, some or all of which falls before the person attains the age of 16, the person has a local connection with that district.

(11) A person ceases to have a local connection with a district under subsection (10) upon attaining the age of 21 (but this does not affect whether the person has a local connection with that district under any other provision of this section).

III L&T [303G.1]

Residence to be one of choice In *Al-Ameri v Royal Borough of Kensington and Chelsea* [2003] EWCA Civ 235, [2003] 2 All ER 1, [2003] 1 WLR 1289 it was held that residence by an applicant asylum seeker in National Asylum Support Service accommodation could not be regarded as residence of the applicant's own choice and accordingly did not constitute normal residence of choice giving rise to a local connection within the meaning of s 199(1)(a). This decision was upheld by the House of Lords: *Al-Ameri v Kensington and Chelsea Royal London Borough Council* [2004] UKHL 4, [2004] 2 AC 159, [2004] 1 All ER 1104, (2004) Times 6 February. Note, however, that the decision is reversed by legislative amendments made by the Asylum and Immigration (Treatment of Claimants etc) Act 2004. The reasoning in *Al-Ameri* in relation to the phrase 'of his own choice' remains binding: see *NJ v Wandsworth London Borough Council* [2013] EWCA Civ 1373, [2013] All ER (D) 91 (Nov), where the court

LANDLORD & TENANT AND HOUSING

held that a victim of domestic violence who had resided in a refuge had done so of her own choice; she could have applied to any other local authority for accommodation, but had voluntarily chosen to seek help from the charity which found the refuge for her.

III L&T [303G.2]

Guidelines for establishing a local connection Guidelines for determining whether the conditions for referral are met are provided in Annex II of the Homelessness Code of Guidance for Local Authorities (issued July 2002, revised 5 January 2005). However an authority is entitled to find that an applicant has a local connection because of "family associations" although there are no near relatives in the district or where the relatives have not been living there for a five year period: see *Ozbek v Ipswich Borough Council* [2006] EWCA Civ 534, (2006) Times 7 June, where the court observed that it was desirable, if the statutory referral scheme was to work smoothly, that both the referring authority and the authority to which the application was referred applied the guidelines generally to all applications which came before them so that both could speedily agree on the issues of local connection.

Right to request review of decision

III L&T [304]

202. Right to request review of decision

(1) An applicant has the right to request a review of—

(a) any decision of a local housing authority as to his eligibility for assistance,

(b) any decision of a local housing authority as to what duty (if any) is owed to him under sections 189B to 193C and 195 (duties to persons found to be homeless or threatened with homelessness),

(ba) any decision of a local housing authority—

(i) as to the steps they are to take under subsection (2) of section 189B, or

(ii) to give notice under subsection (5) of that section bringing to an end their duty to the applicant under subsection (2) of that section,

(bb) any decision of a local housing authority to give notice to the applicant under section 193B(2) (notice given to those who deliberately and unreasonably refuse to co-operate),

(bc) any decision of a local housing authority—

(i) as to the steps they are to take under subsection (2) of section 195, or

(ii) to give notice under subsection (5) of that section bringing to an end their duty to the applicant under subsection (2) of that section,

(c) any decision of a local housing authority to notify another authority under section 198(1) (referral of cases),

(d) any decision under section 198(5) whether the conditions are met for the referral of his case,

(e) any decision under section 200(3) or (4) (decision as to duty owed to applicant whose case is considered for referral or referred), . . .

(f) any decision of a local housing authority as to the suitability of accommodation offered to him in discharge of their duty under any of the provisions mentioned in paragraph (b) or (e) or as to the suitability of accommodation offered to him as mentioned in section 193(7),

(g) any decision of a local housing authority as to the suitability of accommodation offered to him by way of a private rented sector offer (within the meaning of section 193); or

(h) any decision of a local housing authority as to the suitability of accommodation offered to the applicant by way of a final accommodation offer or a final Part 6 offer (within the meaning of section 193A or 193C).

(1A) An applicant who is offered accommodation as mentioned in section 193(5), (7) or (7AA) may under subsection (1)(f) or (as the case may be) (g) request a review of the suitability of the accommodation offered to him whether or not he has accepted the offer.

(1B) An applicant may, under subsection (1)(h), request a review of the suitability of the accommodation offered whether or not the applicant has accepted the offer.

(2) There is no right to request a review of the decision reached on an earlier review.

(3) A request for review must be made before the end of the period of 21 days beginning with the day on which he is notified of the authority's decision or such longer period as the authority may in writing allow.

(4) On a request being duly made to them, the authority or authorities concerned shall review their decision.

III L&T [304.1]

Conditions for referral One of the conditions for referral to another district, under the Housing Act 1996 s 198, is that the applicant has a local connection with another district which may arise by reason of "family associations", as provided in s 199(1)(c). It was held in *Munting v Hammersmith and Fulham London Borough Council* [1998] CLY 3017, cc, that regularly staying with the mother's boyfriend in another district could be construed as a family association.

III L&T [304.2]

Review The review is the final administrative stage in determining the application and, given the importance of the decision, the authority conducting a review under s 202 is obliged to consider all the facts afresh: *R v Ealing London Borough Council, ex p Surdonja* [2001] QB 97, sub nom *Surdonja v Ealing London Borough Council* [2000] 2 All ER 597, CA. *Mohamed v Hammersmith and Fulham London Borough Council* [2001] UKHL 57, [2002] 1 AC 547 confirms that the review should take account of fresh facts predating the decision and also subsequent developments. It also established that interim residence provided by the reviewing authority should be regarded as normal residence for the purposes of establishing a local connection. If the review is likely to involve resolving material disputes on primary facts the local authority would be well-advised to contract out the review to an independent and impartial tribunal pursuant to its powers under the Local Authorities (Contracting out of Allocation of Housing and Homelessness Functions) Order 1996, SI 1996/3205; otherwise the review is likely to involve an infringement of Art 6(1) of the European Convention on Human Rights: *Adan v Newham London Borough Council* [2001] EWCA Civ 931, [2002] 1 All ER 931, CA. See also *Heald v Brent London Borough Council* [2009] EWCA Civ 930, [2009] LGR 937 where the Court of Appeal confirmed that the relevant legislative provisions permit a local housing authority to contract out to a third party the carrying out of a s 202 review and held that, in the circumstances of that case, the third party did not lack sufficient independence and impartiality.

In *Runa Begum v Tower Hamlets London Borough Council* [2003] UKHL 5, [2003] 2 AC 430, [2003] 1 All ER 731, the House of Lords affirmed the Court of Appeal's decision that the statutory scheme of a s 202 review and a s 204 appeal is sufficient to comply with the requirements of Art 6(1) of the Convention. Where a decision is amenable to review under s 202 it is not appropriate to seek judicial review: *R v London Borough of Merton, ex p Sembi* (1999) Times, 9 June, DC.

It was decided in *Hackney London Borough Council v Sareen* [2003] EWCA Civ 351, [2003] HLR 800, (2003) Times, 9 April that there is no right of review, or appeal as regards a successful application which gives the applicant what he or she asked for.

A housing authority is entitled to revisit and rescind a decision that it had an obligation to house an applicant under s 193 where the decision had resulted from a fundamental mistake of fact: *Porteous v West Dorset District Council* [2004] EWCA Civ 244, [2004] LGR 277.

Where a housing authority's decision has been appealed successfully to the county court and the authority has embarked on an appeal to the Court of Appeal, it is verging on abuse of process for the authority to carry out a further review of the challenged decision, without disclosing this to the court. The more appropriate course would be for the parties to agree that the performance of the duty under s 202(4) should await the outcome of the appeal or, failing that, for the authority to invite the court, on the application for permission, to stay the effect of the order quashing the first review decision until after the determination of the appeal: *William v Wandsworth London Borough Council; Bellamy v Hounslow London Borough Council* [2006] EWCA Civ 535, (2006) Times 6 June.

A reviewing officer can make a decision which is less favourable to the applicant than the original decision, as in *Temur v Hackney London Borough Council* [2014] EWCA Civ 877, [2014] LGR 689, [2015] PTSR 1.

III L&T [304.2A]

Review and acceptance It was held by the Court of Appeal (in a decision made before the Homelessness Act 2002 came into force) that if an offer of housing is accepted it is not open to the person housed to insist on a review at the same time: *Alghile v Westminster City Council* [2001] EWCA Civ 363, (2001) 33 HLR 627, doubting the contrary decision in *R v Kensington and Chelsea Royal London Borough Council v Byfield* (1997) 31 HLR 913. Subsection 202(1A) of the Housing Act 1996, which came into force on the date of enactment of the Homelessness Act 2002 on 26 February 2002 (see s 8 of the 2002 Act), appears to have reversed the effect of *Alghile*.

The homeless person does not have the right to view the accommodation offered and the authority is not bound to take account of the applicant's views as to adequacy: *R (on the application of Khatun) v Newham London Borough Council* [2004] EWCA Civ 55, [2004] 3 WLR 417.

III L&T [304.2B]

Late request for a review The authority has a wide discretion to extend time under s 202(3) upon application, but the statute contemplates only one application. If the discretion has been exercised in a principled way the decision can only be impugned on traditional administrative law grounds: *R (on the application of C) v Lewisham London Borough Council* [2003] EWCA Civ 927, [2003] 3 All ER 1277.

III L&T [304.3]

Decision as to duty owed under s 202(1)(b) In *Warsame v Hounslow London Borough Council* [2000] 1 WLR 696, 32 HLR 335, CA, the court held that s 202(1)(b) applies not only to a decision that a duty is no longer owed but also to the decision that the duty had been discharged by the offer of alternative accommodation.

III L&T [304.4]

Where a court orders possession of accommodation the occupant is thereby threatened with homelessness for the purposes of s 184 and, on receiving an application for accommodation, the local authority must make immediate inquiries and must secure accommodation under s 195 if satisfied as to eligibility for assistance and priority need. The Act does not permit the authority to do nothing until eviction. Collins J allowed an application for judicial review on these grounds in *R v Newham London Borough Council, ex p Khan* (2000) Times, 9 May, DC. He also held, on the same application, that the authority's refusal to house the family together was irrational in the *Wednesbury* sense.

III L&T [304.5]

Effect of breach of duty Breach by a housing authority of the duty to provide accommodation for a homeless family does not give rise to a remedy in damages: *R (on the application of Morris) v Newham London Borough Council* [2002] EWHC 1262 (Admin), [2002] All ER (D) 402 (May), where it was also held that that there had not been a breach of Convention rights under Art 8 since that Article did not confer a right to a home.

III L&T [304.6]

Disability Discrimination Act 1995 The duty in s 49A(1) of the Disability Discrimination Act 1995 Act applies to local authorities in carrying out all of their functions under Pt VII of the Housing Act 1996. So, in making determinations under Part VII (whether at the initial stage or on review under s 202), where a person's disability could be of relevance, a local authority has to have due regard to the need to take steps to take account of the disabilities: *Pieretti v London Borough of Enfield* [2010] EWCA Civ 1104, [2010] NLJR 1458, applied in *Birmingham City Council v Wilson* [2016] EWCA Civ 1137 in relation to duties of a local authority arising under s 149 of the Equality Act 2010.

III L&T [305]

203. Procedure on a review

(1) The Secretary of State may make provision by regulations as to the procedure to be followed in connection with a review under section 202.

Nothing in the following provisions affects the generality of this power.

(2) Provision may be made by regulations

(a) requiring the decision on review to be made by a person of appropriate seniority who was not involved in the original decision, and

(b) as to the circumstances in which the applicant is entitled to an oral hearing, and whether and by whom he may be represented at such a hearing.

(3) The authority, or as the case may be either of the authorities, concerned shall notify the applicant of the decision on the review.

(4) If the decision is

(a) to confirm the original decision on any issue against the interests of the applicant, or

(b) to confirm a previous decision

(i) to notify another authority under section 198 (referral of cases), or

(ii) that the conditions are met for the referral of his case,

they shall also notify him of the reasons for the decision.

(5) In any case they shall inform the applicant of his right to appeal to the county court on a point of law, and of the period within which such an appeal must be made (see section 204).

(6) Notice of the decision shall not be treated as given unless and until subsection (5), and where applicable subsection (4), is complied with.

(7) Provision may be made by regulations as to the period within which the review must be carried out and notice given of the decision.

(8) Notice required to be given to a person under this section shall be given in writing and, if not received by him, shall be treated as having been given if it is made available at the authority's office for a reasonable period for collection by him or on his behalf.

III L&T [305.1]

An officer conducting a review under s 202 has to consider all the up-to-date facts afresh: *R v Ealing London Borough Council, ex p Surdonja* [2001] QB 97, sub nom *Surdonja v Ealing London Borough Council* [2000] 2 All ER 597, CA, which also held that the date of the review is the relevant date for determining whether the applicant has a local connection. See also the notes at para **III L&T [304.2]**. In *Runa Begum v Tower Hamlets London Borough Council* [2003] UKHL 5, [2003] 2 AC 430, [2003] 1 All ER 731 (referred to at para **III L&T [304.2]**), the House of Lords held that an officer conducting a s 202 review is manifestly not an independent tribunal for the purposes of Art 6(1) of the Convention. The review can be contracted out to a third party unless the third party lacks the necessary independence and impartiality or the appearance of such: *Heald v Brent London Borough Council* [2009] EWCA Civ 930, [2009] LGR 937.

Where a review results in a fresh decision, this may be the subject of a further review which may be undertaken by the same officer. However, the second decision may be set aside on appeal if there has been actual bias or unfairness or if a fair-minded and informed observer would have been likely to conclude that there was a real possibility of bias: see *Feld v Barnet London Borough Council* [2004] EWCA Civ 1307, (2004) Times, 26 October applying the test for apparent bias laid down in *Porter v Magill* [2001] UKHL 67, [2002] 2 AC 257.

Where the council has taken a view that it has offered suitable property and in that process has discharged its duty to accommodate, the question for the reviewer is whether the council was right at the date of the decision on the facts as at that date: *Omar v Westminster City Council* [2008] EWCA Civ 421, [2008] HLR 36, (2008) Times, 25 March, CA, applying *Mohammed v Hammersmith and Fulham London Borough Council* [2002] 1 AC 547, as explained in *Osselly v Westminster City Council* [2007] EWCA Civ 1108.

III L&T [305.1A]

The offer of accommodation in the district of another housing authority Before determining to offer accommodation in another district the authority should address the issues mentioned in s 208 and in the Homelessness Code of Guidance for Local Authorities 2006, the Homelessness (Suitability of Accommodation) (England) Order 2012, SI 2012/2601 and the Supplementary Guidance on the homelessness changes in the Localism Act 2011 and on the Homelessness (Suitability of Accommodation) (England) Order 2012. In all cases the authority should also have regard to their duty under s 11 of the Children Act 2004 to safeguard children and promote their welfare: *Nzolameso v Westminster City Council* [2015] UKSC 22, [2015] 2 All ER 942, [2015] LGR 215.

III L&T [305.2]

Regulations See now the Homelessness (Review Procedure etc) Regulations 2018, SI 2018/223, in force except Part 4 on 3 April 2018, and Part 4 on 1 October 2018.

III L&T [305.3]

Where the reviewer considers that there is a deficiency or irregularity in the original decision Regulation 8(2) of the Allocation of Housing and Homelessness (Review procedures) regulations 1999, SI 1999/71 provides that "If the reviewer considers that there is a deficiency or irregularity in the original decision or in the manner in which it was made but is minded nevertheless to make a decision which is against the interests of the applicant on one or more issues the reviewer shall notify the applicant: (a) that the reviewer is so minded and the reasons why; and (b) that the applicant . . . may make representations to the reviewer orally or in writing . . . " The authority is not required to interview the applicant in every case, nor to notify in advance every applicant whose application is to be rejected: see *Tetteh v Kingston upon Thames Royal London Borough Council* [2004] EWCA Civ 1775, [2004] HLR 21. The Secretary of State's Homelessness Code of Guidance for Local Authorities (2002) suggests that the typical judicial review grounds would constitute "deficiency or irregularity". But the reviewer ought also to act on a "deficiency" where, looked at broadly, an important aspect of the case had not been dealt with adequately by the original decision-maker: *Hall v Wandsworth London Borough Council* [2004] EWCA Civ 1740, [2005] 2 All ER 192, [2004] All ER (D) 293 (Dec), (2005) Times, 7 January. Regulation 8(2) imposes a dual obligation which is mandatory: the review officer has no discretion to dispense with the performance of either obligation: *Johnston v Lambeth London Borough Council* (2008) Times, 30 June, CA.

Regulation 8(2) is engaged where, although the local authority's original decision could not itself be faulted, there has been a change in the factual position by the time the review decision is made such as to render the original decision deficient: *Banks v Kingston-Upon-Thames RBC* [2008] EWCA Civ 1443. In *Mohamoud v Birmingham City Council* [2014] EWCA Civ 227, [2015] PTSR 17, [2014] HLR 345 the court held that regulation 8(2) must be given a purposive interpretation.

III L&T [305.4]

Request for sight of documentary material before making representations Where a reasonable request is made for copies of documents on the homelessness file (and the interview notes) in order that effective representations may be made, the review decision should not be made without complying with the request: *Aw-Aden v Birmingham City Council* [2005] EWCA Civ 1834, per Brooke LJ.

III L&T [305.5]

Right to demand oral hearing It has been held that regulation 8(2) of the Allocation of Housing and Homelessness (Review Procedures) Regulations 1999, SI 1999/71 confer on the applicant the right to demand an oral hearing in the form of a face to face meeting with the reviewing officers: *Makisi v Birmingham City Council* [2011] EWCA Civ 355, [2011] 05 LS Gaz R 20, (2011) Times 3 May.

III L&T [305.6]

Duty to state reasons There is no duty to give reasons for a decision in the applicant's favour: *Akhtar v Birmingham City Council* [2011] EWCA Civ 383, [2011] NLJR 597, (2011) Times, 22 April; followed in *Solihull MPC v Khan* [2014] EWCA Civ 41 which explained that the absence of a duty to give reasons in an offer enabled local authorities to act more expeditiously, as they could make their final offers in a standard format rather than in individually-crafted letters.

III L&T [306]

204. Right of appeal to county court on point of law

(1) If an applicant who has requested a review under section 202—

(a) is dissatisfied with the decision on the review, or

(b) is not notified of the decision on the review within the time prescribed under section 203,

he may appeal to the county court on any point of law arising from the decision or, as the case may be, the original decision.

(2) An appeal must be brought within 21 days of his being notified of the decision or, as the case may be, of the date on which he should have been notified of a decision on review.

(2A) The court may give permission for an appeal to be brought after the end of the period allowed by subsection (2), but only if it is satisfied—

(a) where permission is sought before the end of that period, that there is a good reason for the applicant to be unable to bring the appeal in time; or

(b) where permission is sought after that time, that there was a good reason for the applicant's failure to bring the appeal in time and for any delay in applying for permission.

(3) On appeal the court may make such order confirming, quashing or varying the decision as it thinks fit.

(4) Where the authority were under a duty under section 188, 190, 199A or 200 to secure that accommodation is available for the applicant's occupation, they may secure that accommodation is so available—

(a) during the period for appealing under this section against the authority's decision, and

(b) if an appeal is brought, until the appeal (and any further appeal) is finally determined.

III L&T [306.1]

Review procedures See now the Homelessness (Review Procedure etc) Regulations 2018, SI 2018/223, in force except Part 4 on 3 April 2018, and Part 4 on 1 October 2018.

III L&T [306.2]

Appeal to the county court It was held in *R v London Borough of Merton, ex p Sembi* (1999) Times, 9 June, QBD that a person dissatisfied with a review under s 202 should proceed by way of appeal under s 204 and not by way of judicial review. In *Nipa Begum v Tower Hamlets London Borough Council* [2000] 1 WLR 306, CA the court held that the court's jurisdiction under s 204 is akin to that of judicial review in the High Court. See also *Crawley Borough Council v B* (2000) Times, 28 March, CA – the jurisdiction is essentially a public law jurisdiction (note however CPR 52.11(1) (para **CPR 52.11**). See also *O'Connor v Kensington and Chelsea Royal London Borough Council* [2004] EWCA Civ 394, [2004] All ER (D) 552 (Mar) where the Court of Appeal considered the extent to which, having regard to s 204(3), the county court judge may substitute his own decision for that of the authority. The judge has no power under s 204 to direct that a further review be conducted by an independent and impartial tribunal; that is tantamount to mandamus which, by virtue of s 38(3)(a) of the County Courts Act 1984, is beyond the powers of the county court: *Adan v Newham London Borough Council* [2001] EWCA Civ 1916, [2002] 1 All ER 931. In *Runa Begum v Tower Hamlets London Borough Council* [2003] UKHL 5, [2003] 2 AC 430, [2003] 1 All ER 731, the House of Lords held that the statutory scheme imposed by Part VII of the Housing Act 1996 and the fact that the review process under s 202 was conducted at a senior administrative level and subject to detailed statutory rules to ensure fair decision-making, meant that a full fact finding jurisdiction in the appellate court was not required and that the county court's appellate jurisdiction under s 204, exercising the normal judicial review jurisdiction of the High Court, was sufficient to satisfy the requirements of Art 6(1) of the Convention. See also *Ali v Birmingham City Council* [2010] UKSC 8.

A review under s 202 may exceptionally be challenged by judicial review if the 21 days for appealing have expired: see *R v Lambeth London Borough Council, ex p Alleyne* (11 May 1999, unreported) (but see now the court's power to extend the time for appealing under s 204(2A)).

III L&T [306.2A]

Procedure on appeal to the county court Appeals to the county court are governed by CPR Pt 52 and CPR PD 52 (see paras **CPR 52** and **CPR PD 52**). For a detailed explanation of the operation of CPR PD 52 following changes effective from 30 June 2004, see *Scribes West Ltd v Relsa Anstalt (No 1)* [2004] EWCA Civ 835, (2004) Times, 8 July. The appeal should be made by means of the prescribed Appellant's Notice (Form N161); a precedent for an appeal to the county court under s 204 is provided at **BCCP F[301]**. An appeal under s 204 is a "statutory appeal" as defined by CPR PD 52 para 17.1(1). CPR PD 52 para 17.2 states that, subject to the amendments in CPR PD 52 paras 17.3 – 17.6, CPR Pt 52 applies to statutory appeals. However, that is subject to any provision in any enactment (see CPR PD 52 para 17.1(2) and also CPR Pt 52.1(4)). It would seem, therefore, that the 21-day period referred to in s 204(2) will prevail over the 28-day period referred to in CPR PD 52 para. 17.3. The 21-day period for appealing runs from the date of the original review under s 202(1) and is not displaced by any reconsideration of that review: see *Demetri v Westminster City Council* [2000] 1 WLR 772, CA where the court indicated that the only situation in which time would run from the later review would be where the authority made clear that it was carrying out a new review and was treating the original review as no longer valid. For the meaning of "filing" see CPR 2.3 (at para **CPR 2.3**). In a decision based on CPR Sch 2, CCR Ord 2 r 4 (now revoked) it was held that an appellant was in time where he received the decision on 4 July and could not file it on 25 July (a Saturday) because the office was closed and so filed it on the following Monday: *Aadan v Brent London Borough Council* (1999) 32 HLR 848, CA. See also *Van Aken v Camden London Borough Council* [2002] EWCA Civ 1724, [2002] All ER (D) 170 (Oct), (2002) Times, 28 October, where the court held an appeal notice put through the letter box of the court after office hours on the last day of the prescribed period was "filed" for the purpose of CPR 2.3 and was thus within the prescribed period. Note, however, that since 30 September 2002 the court has had power to extend the 21-day period (see s 204(2A) and see also para **III L&T [306.2AA]**). The application of CPR 52 to statutory appeals by para 17.2 does not impose a requirement for permission to appeal where otherwise the right to appeal is unrestricted: *Colley v Council for Licensed Conveyancers* [2001] EWCA Civ 1137, [2001] 4 All ER 998.

The court may admit evidence, on hearing the appeal, to elucidate, correct or add to the reasons contained in the decision letter under appeal, but should be very cautious about doing so: *Hijazi v Royal Borough of Kensington and Chelsea* [2003] EWCA Civ 692, [2003] HLR 1113. Evidential material over and above the contents of the housing file and the reviewing officer's decision is limited to that which is necessary to illuminate the points of law that are to be relied upon in the appeal or the issue of what, if any, relief ought to be granted: *Cramp v Hastings Borough Council; Phillips v Camden London Borough Council* [2005] EWCA Civ 1005.

An appellant should include appeals under s 204 and s 204A in one appellant's notice. If it is not possible to do so (for example because an urgent application under s 204A is required), the appeals may be included in separate appellant's notices (CPR PD 52 para 24.2 (see para **CPR PD 52**)).

A district judge may not hear appeals under this section: CPR PD 2B para 9 (see para **CPR PD 2B**).

III L&T [306.2AA]

Power to extend time for appealing Sub-section 204(2A) of the 1996 Act provides that the court may give permission for an appeal to be brought after the end of the 21-day period allowed by sub-s (2) if the conditions of sub-s (2A) are satisfied. If the court is not satisfied of good reasons for a failure to bring an appeal in time, it cannot go on to consider the merits. The word "only" in s 204(2A) provides a threshold that has to be passed before the merits can be considered. The court may not have regard to the criteria in CPR r 3.9, or any other criteria, other than those specified in s 204(2A): see *Short v Birmingham City Council* [2004] EWHC 2112 (QB), [2004] All ER (D) 67 (Sep). In *Peake v Hackney London Borough Council* [2013] EWHC 2528 (QB), [2013] All ER (D) 197 (Jul), the court held that the requirement in sub-s (2A) that there be good reasons for delay in bringing an appeal was compatible with Article 6 of the European Convention on Human Rights.

III L&T [306.2AB]

Power of the court to substitute its own decision The court's jurisdiction under s 204 is akin to that of judicial review in the High Court. CPR 54.19(3) is therefore relevant; where the court considers that there is no purpose to be served in remitting the matter to the decision maker it may take the decision itself. In *O'Connor v Kensington & Chelsea Royal London Borough Council* [2004] EWCA Civ 394, [2004] HLR 37 the Court of Appeal considered the extent to which, having regard to s 204(3), the county court judge may substitute his own decision for that of the authority. The test appears to be that the court conducting the judicial review may give the decision which a properly directed tribunal would have made if it is inevitable that that is what they would have decided: see also *Ali & Nessa v Newham London Borough Council* [2001] EWCA Civ 73 and *Ekwuru v Westminster City Council* [2003] EWCA

Civ 1293, [2004] HLR 14. In *Wandsworth London Borough Council v Phillip Allison* [2008] EWCA Civ 354 the court held that a judge had no power under s 204 to quash a housing authority's decision that an applicant was not in priority need for housing within the Housing Act 1996, s 189(1)(c) unless the authority's decision was *Wednesbury* unreasonable.

In *Bubb v Wandsworth London Borough Council* [2011] EWCA Civ 1285 the local authority, having sent a letter (receipt of which was disputed) offering permanent accommodation to a homeless person in temporary accommodation, decided that it had discharged its duty under s 193(7). The court held that, when considering an appeal under s 204, the exercise carried out by the county court was substantially the same as that of the High Court in a judicial review application and it was not for the judge to make his own findings of fact. The decision of the local authority that the letter had been received could not be impugned. In *Richmond Upon Thames London Borough Council v Kubicek* [2012] EWHC 3292 (QB), [2012] All ER (D) 321 (Nov) the court held, applying *Bubb*, that the county court has no jurisdiction under s 204 to find relevant facts, the responsibility for ascertaining the facts being vested, under Part VII of the 1996 Act, in the local housing authority.

Further authority is to be found in *Crossley v City of Westminster* [2006] EWCA Civ 140, judgment of Sedley LJ.

III L&T [306.2B]

Appeal from the county court An appeal against a decision of the county court made under s 204 is to the Court of Appeal: see Access to Justice Act 1999 (Destination of Appeals) Order 2000, SI 2000/1071, art 5 and see also *Azimi v Newham London Borough Council* (26 July 2000, unreported) CA. The more restrictive test for permission applies (see para **CPR 52.13**).

III L&T [306.3]

Departmental guidance Local authorities should have regard to the Departmental *Codes of Guidance on the Housing Act 1996 Part VII (Allocations of Housing Accommodation and Homelessness Allocations)*: *R v Newham London Borough Council, ex p Ojuri (No 2)* (1998) Times, 29 August.

Currently Departmental Guidance to Local Authorities is to be found in a publication by the Department of the Communities and Local Government *Homelessness: Code of Guidance for Local Authorities* (July 2006).

III L&T [306.4]

Point of law Points of law on which an appeal will lie include not only matters of legal interpretation but also (applying the reasoning of Lord Bridge in *Chief Adjudication Officer v Foster* [1993] AC 754, [1993] 1 All ER 705, HL) a full range of issues which would otherwise be raised by an application to the Divisional Court for judicial review, such as procedural error and questions of vires. Although applications for judicial review may still exceptionally be made, the courts will not normally grant leave for judicial review where there is another avenue of appeal: *R v Epping and Harlow General Comrs, ex p Goldstraw* [1983] 3 All ER 257, CA per Lord Donaldson MR; *R v Chief Constable of Merseyside Police, ex p Calveley* [1986] QB 424, [1986] 1 All ER 257, CA. See now *R v London Borough of Merton, ex p Sembi* (1999) Times, 9 June, DC (see para **III L&T [306.2]**).

County court judges may take into account factual matters not known to the decision maker if proved by "fresh evidence". In *E v Secretary of State for the Home Office* [2004] EWCA Civ 49, [2004] QB 1044 the court held that

- an appeal on a point of law may be made on the basis of unfairness resulting from "misunderstanding or ignorance of an established and relevant fact";
- fresh evidence may be admitted on such an appeal in order to establish the true facts; and
- the discretion to admit such evidence is subject to *Ladd v Marshall* principles, but they may be departed from in exceptional circumstances, where the interests of justice require.

Since the appeal right is based on a point of law and differs from the appeal right under s 204A, which is in the nature of judicial review, it follows that legal aid is not available under the "judicial review" rubric in LASPO 2012, Sch 1, Part I, paragraph 19(10): *Bhatia Best Ltd v Lord Chancellor* [2014] EWHC 746 (QB), [2014] 3 All ER 573, [2014] 1 WLR 3487.

III L&T [306.4A]

Vulnerability The correct approach to the issue of vulnerability, as an element of "priority need" was considered in *R v Camden London Borough, ex p Pereira* (1998) 31 HLR 317, CA. See also the Homelessness (Priority Need for Accommodation) (England) Order 2002, SI 2002/2051.

Vulnerability The test of vulnerability is that the person's "ability to fend for himself when homeless will result in injury or detriment to him which would not be suffered by an ordinary homeless person who was able to cope": *R v Camden London Borough Council, ex p Pereira* (1998) 31 HLR 317, 330, Hobhouse LJ. This test should be applied in preference to the less stringent test of "would be likely to suffer injury or detriment" propounded in *The Homelessness Code of Guidance for Local Authorities* issued by the Secretary of State under s 182: *Griffin v Westminster City Council* [2004] EWCA Civ 108, [2004] All ER (D) 262 (Jan). However, the "Pereira test" is a judicial guide to interpretation and application of s 189(1)(c) and should not be applied as if it was a statutory formulation and, for the purpose of applying the vulnerability test, a local housing authority should assess it on the assumption that an applicant had become or would become street homeless, not on his ability to fend for himself while he was still housed: see *Osmani v Camden London Borough Council* [2004] EWCA Civ 1706, (2004) 149 Sol Jo LB 61.

In a case of depressive illness, *Hall v Wandsworth London Borough Council* [2004] EWCA Civ 110, Mance LJ said the question was "whether the medical evidence justified a conclusion that the applicant could not cope as an ordinary person, so that injury or detriment would result, when a less vulnerable person would be able to cope without injury or detriment".

Drug addiction, and the need for accommodation to achieve stabilisation during treatment, may not be enough to establish vulnerability: *Simms v Islington London Borough Council* [2008] EWCA Civ 1083, [2008] All ER (D) 146 (Oct), (2008) Times, 3 December.

See also notes at para **III L&T [303AA.3]**.

III L&T [306.4B]

Offer must mention the possibility of review A take it or leave it offer is unlawful if it does not mention the possibility of review: *R v Kensington and Chelsea Royal London Borough Council, ex p Byfield* (1997) 31 HLR 913.

III L&T [306.4C]

Intentionally homeless A person who lost accommodation as a result of receiving a prison sentence for various criminal offences may properly be regarded as intentionally homeless: see *Minchin v Sheffield City Council* (2000) Times, 26 April, CA, where the court rejected the contention that the offences had to be committed while the claimant was occupying the accommodation in question; and see also *Stewart v Lambeth London Borough Council* [2002] EWCA Civ 753, [2002] All ER (D) 260 (Apr), (2002) Times, 28 May, where the Court held that imprisonment could not be described as settled accommodation so as to throw off the status of homelessness. A woman who leaves her partner because of his violence, taking the children with her, is not to be treated as intentionally homeless merely because she could have remained and sought an injunction and ouster order: *Bond v Leicester City Council* [2001] EWCA Civ 1544, [2002] 1 FCR 566, [2002] HLR 5. In *Bratton v Croydon London Borough Council* [2002] EWCA Civ 1494, [2002] All ER (D) 404 (Jul) it was held that a local authority is required, when considering whether a person has become intentionally homeless, to ascertain whether there is a causal link between the actions of the person and the loss of their home; this means that there must be not only a factual link between the conduct of the tenant and the loss of the home, but also some real and sensible connection between those two events which would naturally and reasonably lead to that happening. Thus, a tenant whose tenancy was not renewed because she used the rent money to pay for the repair of her washing machine was held to be intentionally homeless: *Najim v Enfield London Borough Council* [2015] EWCA Civ 319, [2015] HLR 337. Where a person has been intentionally homeless, but subsequently finds and loses a new home, the question for the authority, and the court, is whether the tenancy of the new home constitutes settled accommodation for the purpose of breaking the chain of causation from past intentional homelessness: see *Din v Wandsworth London Borough Council* [1983] 1 AC 657, HL and *R v Brent London Borough Council, ex p Awua* [1996] AC 55. See also *Haile v London Borough of Waltham Forest* [2014] EWCA Civ 792, [2014] PTSR 1376, [2014] HLR 550: the relevant question is whether the homelessness was intentional at the date when the applicant quit the accommodation, not at the date of the local authority's decision. In *Knight v Vale Royal Borough Council* (2003) Times, 4 September, CA it was held that accommodation let on a six month assured shorthold tenancy was capable of being, and likely to be, settled accommodation. See also *Huda v Redbridge London Borough Council* [2016] EWCA Civ 709 where the court held that, in determining whether accommodation provided by the local authority under s 190 could be regarded as "settled", all relevant facts had to be considered; that no distinction could be drawn between factors evident from the occupation agreement and factors that arose outside the agreement. For the obligation of the review officer, when conducting a s 202 review, to consider the issue of good faith under s 191(2) (even if that issue has not been raised by the tenant), see *O'Connor v Kensington and Chelsea Royal London Borough Council* [2004] EWCA Civ 394, [2004] All ER (D) 552 (Mar).

III L&T [306.4D]

Local authority's duty to family threatened with homelessness When a possession order has been made against a person, that person is threatened with homelessness for the purposes of the Housing Act 1996. A local authority did not comply with its statutory obligations under s 184 by advising such a person to stay in the property in question until evicted, thereby postponing its duty to inquire as to whether it owed a housing duty to that person. Furthermore, the local authority's decision to split a single family unit was irrational in the Wednesbury sense: see *R v Newham London Borough Council, ex p Khan and Hussain* (2000) 33 HLR 269, Times, 9 May, QBD; see also *R (Sacupima) v Newham London Borough Council* [2001] 1 WLR 563, (2000) Times, 1 December, CA.

III L&T [306.4E]

Dependant child A 17-year-old wife in full-time education may be a dependant child vis-à-vis her parents but not vis-à-vis her husband for the purposes of s 189(1)(b): *Ekinci v Hackney London Borough Council* [2001] EWCA Civ 776, [2002] HLR 12. If a child is in priority need, the imminence of the 18th birthday cannot justify a decision to the contrary nor can the defect by cured on review by the coming of age before completion of the review. Nor is it proper to deprive a child of a right by postponing a decision until after the 18th birthday, whether by persuading the parents into mediation or otherwise: *Robinson v Hammersmith and Fulham London Borough Council* [2006] EWCA Civ 1122, [2006] 1 WLR 3295, (2006) Times 5 September.

III L&T [306.5]

Interim housing pending appeal The authority has a discretion under the Housing Act 1996 s 204 (4) to provide interim housing pending appeal. Where it decided not to do so, it was held the county court could not order it to do so pending the appeal: *Ali v Westminster City Council* [1999] 1 All ER 450, [1999] 1 WLR 384, CA. This decision is effectively reversed (with effect from 30 September 2002) by the court's power under s 204A(4)(a) (see para **III L&T [306A.1]**). The authority's decision may exceptionally be challenged by judicial review, but only where they have acted as though they had no discretion at all: *R v Brighton and Hove Council, ex p Nacion* (1999) 31 HLR 1095, CA. In *ex p Nacion* the application for leave to apply for judicial review was dismissed and the court indicated that such applications should be strongly discouraged. The court referred to the guidance as to the exercise of its discretion under s 204(2) given in *R v Camden London Borough Council, ex p Mohammed* (1997) 30 HLR 315. In the circumstances, it may be that the appropriate course is for the appellant to request the county court to fix an early return day so that the appeal may be heard within the breathing space which the authority should allow in accordance with *R v Newham London Borough Council, ex p Ojuri (No 5)* (1998) 31 HLR 631.

An authority, when considering an application for interim accommodation pending an appeal against a review decision, is obliged to consider the grounds for appeal in relation to the review decision appealed: *Lewis v Havering London Borough Council* [2006] EWCA Civ 1793, [2007] HLR 20. The application for temporary accommodation pending review does not have to be determined by a senior officer not involved in the original decision under s 184; it may be determined by the original decision-maker: *R (Abdi) v Lambeth London Borough Council* [2007] EWHC 1565 (Admin), (2007) Times 11 July, QBD.

III L&T [306A]

204A. Section 204(4): appeals

(1) This section applies where an applicant has the right to appeal to the county court against a local housing authority's decision on a review.

(2) If the applicant is dissatisfied with a decision by the authority—

- (a) not to exercise their power under section 204(4) ("the section 204(4) power") in his case;
- (b) to exercise that power for a limited period ending before the final determination by the county court of his appeal under section 204(1) ("the main appeal"); or
- (c) to cease exercising that power before that time,

he may appeal to the county court against the decision.

(3) An appeal under this section may not be brought after the final determination by the county court of the main appeal.

(4) On an appeal under this section the court—

LANDLORD & TENANT AND HOUSING

(a) may order the authority to secure that accommodation is available for the applicant's occupation until the determination of the appeal (or such earlier time as the court may specify); and

(b) shall confirm or quash the decision appealed against,

and in considering whether to confirm or quash the decision the court shall apply the principles applied by the High Court on an application for judicial review.

(5) If the court quashes the decision it may order the authority to exercise the section 204(4) power in the applicant's case for such period as may be specified in the order.

(6) An order under subsection (5)—

(a) may only be made if the court is satisfied that failure to exercise the section 204(4) power in accordance with the order would substantially prejudice the applicant's ability to pursue the main appeal;

(b) may not specify any period ending after the final determination by the county court of the main appeal.

III L&T [306A.1]

Extended powers on appeals Under s 204A, where a person has a right of appeal to the county court against an authority's review under s 204(1) and is dissatisfied with a decision by the authority (a) not to exercise its power to secure continued accommodation for him under s 204(4)(a) or (b) to exercise that power for a limited period ending before the final determination by the county court of his appeal under s 204(1) ("the main appeal") or (c) to cease exercising that power before that time, he may appeal to the county court against that decision. The appeal may not be brought after the final determination by the county court of the main appeal.

On an appeal under s 204A, the court may, by s 204A(4)(a), order the authority to secure that accommodation is available for the applicant's occupation until the determination of the appeal (or such earlier time as the court may specify), and shall confirm or quash the decision appealed against. In considering whether to confirm or quash the decision the court shall apply the principles applied by the High Court on an application for judicial review. If the court quashes the decision it may, under sub-s 204A(5), order the authority to exercise the s 204(4) power in the applicant's case for such period as may be specified in the order.

It was held in *Francis v Royal Borough of Kensington and Chelsea* [2003] EWCA Civ 443, [2003] 2 All ER 1052, [2003] 1 WLR 2248 that the appeal against a refusal of interim housing is not to be regarded as akin to an application for interim relief. The county court should instead apply the decision-making approach laid down by Latham J in *R v Camden London Borough Council, ex p Mohammed* (1997) 30 HLR 315 and approved *in R v Brighton and Hove Council, ex p Nacion* (1999) 31 HLR 1095, CA. This means deciding first whether there are grounds for quashing the decision: otherwise there can be no basis for considering whether to order the provision of interim accommodation.

The Court of Appeal has no jurisdiction to entertain an application for temporary accommodation pending an application for permission to appeal against the county court's decision in the main appeal under s 204(1): *Johnson v Lord Mayor and Citizens of Westminster* [2013] EWCA Civ 773, [2013] NLJR 19, [2013] HLR 45. The refusal of temporary accommodation may, in such circumstances, be challenged by an application for judicial review.

III L&T [306A.2]

Procedure on interim housing appeal An appellant should include appeals under s 204 and s 204A in one appellant's notice. If it is not possible to do so (for example because an urgent application under s 204A is required), the appeals may be included in separate appellant's notices (CPR PD 52 para 24.2 (see para **CPR PD 52**)). An appeal under s 204A may include an application for an order under s 204A(4)(a) requiring the authority to secure that accommodation is available for the applicant's occupation. If, exceptionally, the court makes an order under s 204A(4)(a) without notice, the appellant's notice must be served on the authority together with the order. Such an order will normally require the authority to secure that accommodation is available until a hearing date when the authority can make representations as to whether the order under s 204A(4)(a) should be continued.

A district judge may not hear appeals under either ss 204 or 204A (see para **CPR PD 2B**).

Schedule

SCHEDULE 15

ARREST FOR ANTI-SOCIAL BEHAVIOUR: POWERS OF HIGH COURT AND COUNTY COURT TO REMAND

Section 155 (6)

INTRODUCTORY

III L&T [307]

1. (1) The provisions of this Schedule apply where the court has power to remand a person under section 155 (2) or (5) (arrest for breach of injunction, &c.).

(2) In this Schedule "the court" means the High Court or the county court and includes

(a) in relation to the High Court, a judge of that court, and

(b) in relation to the county court, a judge or district judge of that court.

REMAND IN CUSTODY OR ON BAIL

2. (1) The court may

(a) remand him in custody, that is, commit him to custody to be brought before the court at the end of the period of remand or at such earlier time as the court may require, or

(b) remand him on bail, in accordance with the following provisions.

(2) The court may remand him on bail

(a) by taking from him a recognizance, with or without sureties, conditioned as provided in paragraph 3, or

(b) by fixing the amount of the recognizances with a view to their being taken subsequently, and in the meantime committing him to custody as mentioned in sub-paragraph (1) (a).

(3) Where a person is brought before the court after remand, the court may further remand him.

3. (1) Where a person is remanded on bail, the court may direct that his recognizance be conditioned for his appearance

(a) before that court at the end of the period of remand, or

(b) at every time and place to which during the course of the proceedings the hearing may from time to time be adjourned.

(2) Where a recognizance is conditioned for a person's appearance as mentioned in sub-paragraph (1) (b), the fixing of any time for him next to appear shall be deemed to be a remand.

(3) Nothing in this paragraph affects the power of the court at any subsequent hearing to remand him afresh.

4. (1) The court shall not remand a person for a period exceeding 8 clear days, except that

(a) if the court remands him on bail, it may remand him for a longer period if he and the other party consent, and

(b) if the court adjourns a case under section 156 (1) (remand for medical examination and report), the court may remand him for the period of the adjournment.

(2) Where the court has power to remand a person in custody it may, if the remand is for a period not exceeding 3 clear days, commit him to the custody of a constable.

FURTHER REMAND

5. (1) If the court is satisfied that a person who has been remanded is unable by reason of illness or accident to appear or be brought before the court at the expiration of the period for which he was remanded, the court may, in his absence, remand him for a further time.

This power may, in the case of a person who was remanded on bail, be exercised by enlarging his recognizance and those of any sureties for him to a later time.

(2) Where a person remanded on bail is bound to appear before the court at any time and the court has no power to remand him under sub-paragraph (1), the court may in his absence enlarge his recognizance and those of any sureties for him to a later time.

The enlargement of his recognizance shall be deemed to be a further remand.

(3) Paragraph 4 (1) (limit of period of remand) does not apply to the exercise of the powers conferred by this paragraph.

POSTPONEMENT OF TAKING OF RECOGNIZANCE

6. Where under paragraph 2 (2) (b) the court fixes the amount in which the principal and his sureties, if any, are to be bound, the recognizance may afterwards be taken by such person as may be prescribed by rules of court, with the same consequences as if it had been entered into before the court.

III L&T [307.1]

Schedule 15 came into force by virtue of the Housing Act 1996 (Commencement No 13) Order 2001, SI 2001/3164. See also the notes at para **III L&T [300.2]**.

HOUSING GRANTS, CONSTRUCTION AND REGENERATION ACT 1996

(c 53)

GENERAL NOTES ON HOUSING GRANTS, CONSTRUCTION AND REGENERATION ACT 1996

III L&T [308]

Jurisdiction of county court The county courts are empowered to hear appeals against deferred action notices and decisions to renew such notices. The jurisdiction is similar to that conferred by Housing Act 1985 ss 189–191 in respect of local housing authority notices: see notes at paras **III L&T [129.1]** and **III L&T [130.1]**.

III L&T [308A]

Sections 108–114 of the Act provide for disputes in certain construction contracts to be referred for adjudication in accordance with the Scheme for Construction Contracts (England and Wales) Regulations 1998, SI 1998/694. The recovery of money due under the decision is governed by s 42 of the Arbitration Act 1996(see **III ARB [12]**), and may be the subject of a court decision. In one such case the Court of Appeal held that the arbitrator was not entitled to fees for arriving at a decision in breach of the rules of natural justice: *Systech International Ltd v PC Harrington Contractors Ltd* [2012] EWCA Civ 1371, [2013] 2 All ER 69, [2013] 1 All ER (Comm) 1074.

III L&T [309]

Precedents As from 2 May 2000, all appeals must be brought by means of the prescribed Appellant's Notice (**FORM N161**).

PART I

CHAPTER IV DEFERRED ACTION NOTICES &C

Deferred action notices

III L&T [310]

81. *Deferred action notices*

(1) If the local housing authority are satisfied that a dwelling-house or house in multiple occupation is unfit for human habitation, but are satisfied that serving a deferred action notice is the most satisfactory course of action, they shall serve such a notice.

(2) A deferred action notice is a notice

(a) stating that the premises are unfit for human habitation,

(b) specifying the works which, in the opinion of the authority, are required to make the premises fit for human habitation, and

(c) stating the other courses of action which are available to the authority if the premises remain unfit for human habitation.

(3) The notice becomes operative, if no appeal is brought, on the expiry of 21 days from the date of the service of the notice and is final and conclusive as to matters which could have been raised on an appeal.

(4) A deferred action notice which has become operative is a local land charge so long as it remains operative.

(5) The fact that a deferred action notice has been served does not prevent the local housing authority from taking any other course of action in relation to the premises at any time.

Repeal *Repealed by the Housing Act 2004.*

III L&T [310.1]

Charges The authority is empowered by the Housing Grants, Construction and Regeneration Act 1996 s 87 to make a reasonable charge (maximum £300: Housing (Maximum Charge for Enforcement Action) Order 1996, SI 1996/2886) for the expense of the enforcement action, which is recoverable under the Housing Grants, Construction and Regeneration Act 1996 s 88.

III L&T [311]

82. *Service of deferred action notices*

(1) The local housing authority shall serve a deferred action notice

(a) in the case of a notice relating to a dwelling-house, on the person having control of the dwelling-house as defined in section 207 of the Housing Act 1985;

(b) in the case of a notice relating to a house in multiple occupation, on the person having control of the house as defined in section 398 of that Act.

(2) Where the authority are satisfied that a dwelling house which is a flat, or a flat in multiple occupation, is unfit for human habitation by virtue of section 604 (2) of the Housing Act 1985, they shall also serve the notice on the person having control (as defined in section 207 of that Act) of the building or part of the building in question.

(3) In the case of a house in multiple occupation, the authority may serve the notice on the person managing the house instead of the person having control of the house.

(4) Where the authority serve a notice under subsection (1), (2) or (3)

- *(a) they shall also serve a copy of the notice on any other person having an interest in the premises concerned, whether as freeholder, mortgagee or lessee (within the meaning of Part VI of the Housing Act 1985), and*
- *(b) they may serve a copy of the notice on any person having a licence to occupy the premises.*

(5) Section 617 of the Housing Act 1985 (service of notices) applies for the purpose of this section as it applies for the purpose of that Act.

Repeal *Repealed by the Housing Act 2004.*

III L&T [312]

83. *Appeals against deferred action notices*

(1) A person aggrieved by a deferred action notice may within 21 days after the service of the notice appeal to the county court.

(2) Without prejudice to the generality of subsection (1), it is a ground of appeal that serving a notice under section 189 of the Housing Act 1985, or making a closing order under section 264 of that Act or a demolition order under section 265 of that Act, is a more satisfactory course of action.

(3) Where the grounds on which an appeal is brought are or include that specified in subsection (2), the court, on the hearing of the appeal, shall have regard to any guidance given to the local housing authority under section 604A of the Housing Act 1985 or section 85 of this Act.

(4) On an appeal the court may make such order either confirming, quashing or varying the notice as it thinks fit.

(5) Where the appeal is allowed and the reason or one of the reasons for allowing the appeal is that serving a notice under section 189 of that Act or making a closing order under section 264 of that Act or a demolition order under section 265 of that Act is a more satisfactory course of action, the judge shall, if requested to do so by the appellant or the local housing authority, include in his judgment a finding to that effect.

(6) If an appeal is brought, the deferred action notice does not become operative until—

- *(a) a decision on the appeal confirming the notice (with or without variation) is given and the period within which an appeal to the Court of Appeal may be brought expires without any such appeal having been brought, or*
- *(b) if a further appeal to the Court of Appeal is brought, a decision on that appeal is given confirming the notice (with or without variation);*

and for this purpose the withdrawal of an appeal has the same effect as a decision confirming the notice or decision appealed against.

Repeal *Repealed by the Housing Act 2004.*

III L&T [312.1]

Appeal to the county court Appeals to the county court initiated after 2 May 2000 are governed by CPR Pt 52 and CPR PD 52 (see paras **CPR 52** and **CPR PD 52**). An appeal under s 83(1) is a "statutory appeal" as defined by CPR PD 52 para 17.1(1). CPR PD 52 para 17.2 states that, subject to the amendments in CPR PD 52 paras 17.3 – 17.6, CPR Pt 52 applies to statutory appeals. However, that is subject to any provision in any enactment (see CPR PD 52 para 17.1(2) and also CPR Pt 52.1(4)). It would seem, therefore, that the 21-day period referred to in s 83(1) will prevail over the 28 day period referred to in CPR PD 52 para. 17.3. Under s 83(4) the court may make such order either confirming, quashing or varying the notice as it thinks fit (note however CPR 52.11(1) (at para **CPR 52.11**). All appeals must now be brought by means of the prescribed Appellant's Notice (**FORM N161**).

III L&T [312.2]

Make such order See the note to Housing Act 1985 s 191, at para **III L&T [130.2]**, and the provisions in the Housing Grants, Construction and Regeneration Act 1996 s 83(2) and (5) regarding the contention that a notice under the Housing Act 1985 would have been a more satisfactory course of action. Where the authority has made a charge and the appeal is allowed, the court may reduce or quash the charge under the Housing Grants, Construction and Regeneration Act 1996 s 87(6) or order repayment.

III L&T [312.3]

Review of deferred action notice A notice may be reviewed under the Housing Grants, Construction and Regeneration Act 1996 s 84 (see para **III L&T [313]**), with the same right of appeal as in the case of the initial notice.

III L&T [313]

84. *Review of deferred action notices*

(1) The local housing authority may at any time review any deferred action notice served by them, and they shall do so not later than two years after the notice becomes operative and at intervals of not more than two years thereafter.

The Secretary of State may by order amend this subsection so as to specify such other period or periods as he considers appropriate.

(2) The authority shall for the purposes of any such review inspect the premises concerned.

For this purpose sections 197 (powers of entry) and 198 (penalty for obstruction) of the Housing Act 1985 apply as they apply for the purposes of Part VI of that Act.

(3) If the authority are satisfied that the deferred action notice remains the most satisfactory course of action, they shall renew the notice and serve notice of their decision.

(4) The provisions of section 82 (service of deferred action notice) and section 83 (1) to (5) (appeals against deferred action notices) apply in relation to the authority's decision to renew a deferred action notice as in relation to the original notice.

(5) If an appeal is brought against the decision to renew a deferred action notice, the notice remains operative until any decision on the appeal, or any further appeal, quashing or varying the notice.

(6) If the authority take action in relation to the premises under any of the provisions listed in section 604A (1) of the Housing Act 1985, the deferred action notice shall cease to be operative on the relevant notice, order or declaration becoming operative.

Repeal *Repealed by the Housing Act 2004.*

LANDLORD & TENANT AND HOUSING

COMMONHOLD AND LEASEHOLD REFORM ACT 2002

(c 15)

GENERAL NOTES ON COMMONHOLD AND LEASEHOLD REFORM ACT 2002

III L&T [314]

Part I of the Commonhold and Leasehold Reform Act 2002, which introduces the concept of commonhold, contains a number of provisions concerning applications to the court. The relevant provisions, some of which depend on related regulations, are set out in this section.

Part II of the Commonhold and Leasehold Reform Act 2002 effected substantial changes to the Leasehold Reform Act 1967, the Landlord and Tenant Act 1985, the Landlord and Tenant Act 1987, the Leasehold Reform, Housing and Urban Development Act 1993 and the Housing Act 1996. Those changes, and relevant commencement dates, are found in the relevant parts of this volume. In addition, ss 71 to 73, 75 to 77, 79, 81 to 83, 85 to 91, 93 to 103, 105 to 109, 111 to 113, 159, 163, 173, of and Schs 6 and 7 to the Commonhold and Leasehold Reform Act 2002 give substantial effect to the new 'right to manage', namely the acquisition and exercise of rights in relation to the management of qualifying premises by a company known as a RTM company. Under s 107 of the Act, the county court may, on the application of any person interested, make orders to ensure compliance with, and making good of default in relation to, the requirements imposed by Act. Section 107 is set out below. Reference should also be made to the Right to Manage (Prescribed Particulars and Forms) (England) Regulations 2010, SI 2010/825 which replaced the 2003 Regulations of the same name as from 19 April 2010.

PART I
COMMONHOLD

REGISTRATION

III L&T [314A]

2. Application

(1) The Registrar shall register a freehold estate in land as a freehold estate in commonhold land if—

- (a) the registered freeholder of the land makes an application under this section, and
- (b) no part of the land is already commonhold land.

(2) An application under this section must be accompanied by the documents listed in Schedule 1.

(3) A person is the registered freeholder of land for the purposes of this Part if—

- (a) he is registered as the proprietor of a freehold estate in the land with absolute title, or
- (b) he has applied, and the Registrar is satisfied that he is entitled, to be registered as mentioned in paragraph (a).

III L&T [314B]

3. Consent

(1) An application under section 2 may not be made in respect of a freehold estate in land without the consent of anyone who—

- (a) is the registered proprietor of the freehold estate in the whole or part of the land,
- (b) is the registered proprietor of a leasehold estate in the whole or part of the land granted for a term of more than than 21 years,
- (c) is the registered proprietor of a charge over the whole or part of the land, or
- (d) falls within any other class of person which may be prescribed.

(2) Regulations shall make provision about consent for the purposes of this section; in particular, the regulations may make provision—

- (a) prescribing the form of consent;
- (b) about the effect and duration of consent (including provision for consent to bind successors);
- (c) about withdrawal of consent (including provision preventing withdrawal in specified circumstances);
- (d) for consent given for the purpose of one application under section 2 to have effect for the purpose of another application;
- (e) for consent to be deemed to have been given in specified circumstances;
- (f) enabling a court to dispense with a requirement for consent in specified circumstances.

(3) An order under subsection (2)(f) dispensing with a requirement for consent—

- (a) may be absolute or conditional, and
- (b) may make such other provision as the court thinks appropriate.

III L&T [314B.1]

Regulations The regulations made under s 3 are the Commonhold Regulations 2004, SI 2004/1829.

COMMONHOLD UNIT

III L&T [314C]

17 Leasing: residential

(1) It shall not be possible to create a term of years absolute in a residential commonhold unit unless the term satisfies prescribed conditions.

(2) The conditions may relate to—

- (a) length;
- (b) the circumstances in which the term is granted;
- (c) any other matter.

(3) Subject to subsection (4), an instrument or agreement shall be of no effect to the extent that it purports to create a term of years in contravention of subsection (1).

(4) Where an instrument or agreement purports to create a term of years in contravention of subsection (1) a party to the instrument or agreement may apply to the court for an order—

- (a) providing for the instrument or agreement to have effect as if it provided for the creation of a term of years of a specified kind;
- (b) providing for the return or payment of money;
- (c) making such other provision as the court thinks appropriate.

(5) A commonhold unit is residential if provision made in the commonhold community statement by virtue of section 14(1) requires it to be used only—

(a) for residential purposes, or
(b) for residential and other incidental purposes.

III L&T [314D]

23. Changing size

(1) An amendment of a commonhold community statement which redefines the extent of a commonhold unit may not be made unless the unit-holder consents—

(a) in writing, and
(b) before the amendment is made.

(2) But regulations may enable a court to dispense with the requirement for consent on the application of a commonhold association in prescribed circumstances.

III L&T [314E]

24. Changing size: charged unit

(1) This section applies to an amendment of a commonhold community statement which redefines the extent of a commonhold unit over which there is a registered charge.

(2) The amendment may not be made unless the registered proprietor of the charge consents—

(a) in writing, and
(b) before the amendment is made.

(3) But regulations may enable a court to dispense with the requirement for consent on the application of a commonhold association in prescribed circumstances.

(4) If the amendment removes land from the commonhold unit, the charge shall by virtue of this subsection be extinguished to the extent that it relates to the land which is removed.

(5) If the amendment adds land to the unit, the charge shall by virtue of this subsection be extended so as to relate to the land which is added.

(6) Regulations may make provision—

(a) requiring notice to be given to the Registrar in circumstances to which this section applies;
(b) requiring the Registrar to alter the register to reflect the application of subsection (4) or (5).

III L&T [314.E1]

Regulations The regulations made under s 24(6) are the Commonhold Regulations 2004, SI 2004/1829.

OPERATION OF COMMONHOLD

III L&T [314F]

40. Rectification of documents

(1) A unit-holder may apply to the court for a declaration that—

(a) the articles of association of the relevant commonhold association do not comply with regulations under paragraph 2(1) of Schedule 3;
(b) the relevant commonhold community statement does not comply with a requirement imposed by or by virtue of this Part.

(2) On granting a declaration under this section the court may make any order which appears to it to be appropriate.

(3) An order under subsection (2) may, in particular—

(a) require a director or other specified officer of a commonhold association to take steps to alter or amend a document;

(b) require a director or other specified officer of a commonhold association to take specified steps;

(c) make an award of compensation (whether or not contingent upon the occurrence or non-occurrence of a specified event) to be paid by the commonhold association to a specified person;

(d) make provision for land to cease to be commonhold land.

(4) An application under subsection (1) must be made—

(a) within the period of three months beginning with the day on which the applicant became a unit-holder,

(b) within three months of the commencement of the alleged failure to comply, or

(c) with the permission of the court.

PART II
LEASEHOLD REFORM

SUPPLEMENTARY

III L&T [315]

107. Enforcement of obligations

(1) The county court may, on the application of any person interested, make an order requiring a person who has failed to comply with a requirement imposed on him by, under or by virtue of any provision of this Chapter to make good the default within such time as is specified in the order.

(2) An application shall not be made under subsection (1) unless—

(a) a notice has been previously given to the person in question requiring him to make good the default, and

(b) more than 14 days have elapsed since the date of the giving of that notice without his having done so.

III L&T [315.1]

Failure to comply with procedural requirements An RTM, set up by qualifying tenants, may acquire the right to manage by serving notices in accordance with ss 78 and 79. A non-compliant notice is invalid: *Natt v Osman* [2014] EWCA Civ 1520, [2015] 1 WLR 1536, [2015] 1 P & CR 201. However, it has been held that a failure to offer inspection at the weekend was a trivial breach of s 78(5)(b) by which landlords were not adversely affected and that a failure to serve a copy on one of the intermediate landlords, as required by s 79(6)(a), was of no significance since that landlord had no management responsibilities. In the circumstances the service of the notices was held to be valid: *Elim Court RTM Co Ltd v Avon Freeholds Ltd* [2017] EWCA Civ 89, [2017] 2 P & CR 130, [2017] HLR 299.

INSURANCE

III L&T [315A]

164. Insurance otherwise than with landlord's insurer

(1) This section applies where a long lease of a house requires the tenant to insure the house with an insurer nominated or approved by the landlord ("the landlord's insurer").

(2) The tenant is not required to effect the insurance with the landlord's insurer if—

(a) the house is insured under a policy of insurance issued by an authorised insurer,

(b) the policy covers the interests of both the landlord and the tenant,

(c) the policy covers all the risks which the lease requires be covered by insurance provided by the landlord's insurer,

(d) the amount of the cover is not less than that which the lease requires to be provided by such insurance, and

(e) the tenant satisfies subsection (3).

(3) To satisfy this subsection the tenant—

(a) must have given a notice of cover to the landlord before the end of the period of fourteen days beginning with the relevant date, and

(b) if (after that date) he has been requested to do so by a new landlord, must have given a notice of cover to him within the period of fourteen days beginning with the day on which the request was given.

(4) For the purposes of subsection (3)—

(a) if the policy has not been renewed the relevant date is the day on which it took effect and if it has been renewed it is the day from which it was last renewed, and

(b) a person is a new landlord on any day if he acquired the interest of the previous landlord under the lease on a disposal made by him during the period of one month ending with that day.

(5) A notice of cover is a notice specifying—

(a) the name of the insurer,

(b) the risks covered by the policy,

(c) the amount and period of the cover, and

(d) such further information as may be prescribed.

(6) A notice of cover—

(a) must be in the prescribed form, and

(b) may be sent by post.

(7) If a notice of cover is sent by post, it may be addressed to the landlord at the address specified in subsection (8).

(8) That address is—

(a) the address last furnished to the tenant as the landlord's address for service in accordance with section 48 of the 1987 Act (notification of address for service of notices on landlord), or

(b) if no such address has been so furnished, the address last furnished to the tenant as the landlord's address in accordance with section 47 of the 1987 Act (landlord's name and address to be contained in demands for rent).

(9) But the tenant may not give a notice of cover to the landlord at the address specified in subsection (8) if he has been notified by the landlord of a different address in England and Wales at which he wishes to be given any such notice.

(10) In this section-

"authorised insurer", in relation to a policy of insurance, means a person who may carry on in the United Kingdom the business of effecting or carrying out contracts of insurance of the sort provided under the policy without contravening the prohibition imposed by section 19 of the Financial Services and Markets Act 2000 (c. 8),

"house" has the same meaning as for the purposes of Part 1 of the 1967 Act,

"landlord" and "tenant" have the same meanings as in Chapter 1 of this Part,

"long lease" has the meaning given by sections 76 and 77 of this Act, and

"prescribed" means prescribed by regulations made by the appropriate national authority.

III L&T [315A.1]

Form of Notice For the prescribed form of notice in England, with effect from 28 February 2005, see the Leasehold Houses (Notice of Insurance Cover) (England) Regulations 2004, SI 2004/3097 as amended by the Leasehold Houses (Notice of Insurance Cover) (England) (Amendment) Regulations 2005, SI 2005/177.

For Wales, with effect from 31 May 2005, see the Leasehold Houses (Notice of Insurance Cover) (Wales) Regulations 2005 SI 2005/1354.

GROUND RENT

III L&T [316]

166. Requirement to notify long leaseholders that rent is due

(1) A tenant under a long lease of a dwelling is not liable to make a payment of rent under the lease unless the landlord has given him a notice relating to the payment; and the date on which he is liable to make the payment is that specified in the notice.

(2) The notice must specify—

(a) the amount of the payment,

(b) the date on which the tenant is liable to make it, and

(c) if different from that date, the date on which he would have been liable to make it in accordance with the lease,

and shall contain any such further information as may be prescribed.

(3) The date on which the tenant is liable to make the payment must not be—

(a) either less than 30 days or more than 60 days after the day on which the notice is given, or

(b) before that on which he would have been liable to make it in accordance with the lease.

(4) If the date on which the tenant is liable to make the payment is after that on which he would have been liable to make it in accordance with the lease, any provisions of the lease relating to non-payment or late payment of rent have effect accordingly.

(5) The notice—

(a) must be in the prescribed form, and

(b) may be sent by post.

(6) If the notice is sent by post, it must be addressed to a tenant at the dwelling unless he has notified the landlord in writing of a different address in England and Wales at which he wishes to be given notices under this section (in which case it must be addressed to him there).

(7) In this section "rent" does not include—

(a) a service charge (within the meaning of section 18(1) of the 1985 Act), or

(b) an administration charge (within the meaning of Part 1 of Schedule 11 to this Act).

(8) In this section "long lease of a dwelling" does not include—

(a) a tenancy to which Part 2 of the Landlord and Tenant Act 1954 (c. 56) (business tenancies) applies,

(b) a tenancy of an agricultural holding within the meaning of the Agricultural Holdings Act 1986 (c. 5) in relation to which that Act applies, or

(c) a farm business tenancy within the meaning of the Agricultural Tenancies Act 1995 (c. 8).

(9) In this section—

"dwelling" has the same meaning as in the 1985 Act,

"landlord" and "tenant" have the same meanings as in Chapter 1 of this Part,

"long lease" has the meaning given by sections 76 and 77 of this Act, and
"prescribed" means prescribed by regulations made by the appropriate national authority.

III L&T [316.1]

A notice under s 166(1) must contain (in addition to the information specified in s 166(2)(a) and (b) and, if applicable, (c)) the information prescribed in the Landlord and Tenant (Notice of Rent) (England) Regulations 2004, SI 2004/3096. The notice must also be in the form set out in the Schedule to those regulations as corrected in April 2011 and as amended by the Transfer of Tribunal (Functions) Order 2013, SI 2013/1036. For Wales, see the Landlord and Tenant (Notice of Rent) (Wales) Regulations 2005, SI 2005/1355.

A minor discrepancy between the notice served by the landlord and the prescribed form of the notice was insufficient to invalidate the notice: *Cheerupmate2 Ltd v Calce* [2018] EWCA Civ 2230.

Compliance by the landlord with section 166 Is a condition precedent to the tenant's liability for ground rent under a long lease: *Chasewood Park Residents Ltd v Kim* [2010] EWHC 579 (Ch).

FORFEITURE OF LEASES OF DWELLINGS

III L&T [317]

167. Failure to pay small amount for short period

(1) A landlord under a long lease of a dwelling may not exercise a right of re-entry or forfeiture for failure by a tenant to pay an amount consisting of rent, service charges or administration charges (or a combination of them) ("the unpaid amount") unless the unpaid amount—

(a) exceeds the prescribed sum, or

(b) consists of or includes an amount which has been payable for more than a prescribed period.

(2) The sum prescribed under subsection (1)(a) must not exceed £500.

(3) If the unpaid amount includes a default charge, it is to be treated for the purposes of subsection (1)(a) as reduced by the amount of the charge; and for this purpose "default charge" means an administration charge payable in respect of the tenant's failure to pay any part of the unpaid amount.

(4) In this section "long lease of a dwelling" does not include—

(a) a tenancy to which Part 2 of the Landlord and Tenant Act 1954 (c. 56) (business tenancies) applies,

(b) a tenancy of an agricultural holding within the meaning of the Agricultural Holdings Act 1986 (c. 5) in relation to which that Act applies, or

(c) a farm business tenancy within the meaning of the Agricultural Tenancies Act 1995 (c. 8).

(5) In this section—

"administration charge" has the same meaning as in Part 1 of Schedule 11,

"dwelling" has the same meaning as in the 1985 Act,

"landlord" and "tenant" have the same meaning as in Chapter 1 of this Part,

"long lease" has the meaning given by sections 76 and 77 of this Act, except that a shared ownership lease is a long lease whatever the tenant's total share,

"prescribed" means prescribed by regulations made by the appropriate national authority, and

"service charge" has the meaning given by section 18(1) of the 1985 Act.

III L&T [317.1]

Prescribed sum and period The prescribed sum is £350 in England (see the Rights of Re-entry and Forfeiture (Prescribed Sum and Period) (England) Regulations 2004, SI 2004/3086) and also in Wales (see the Rights of Re-entry and Forfeiture (Prescribed Sum and Period) (Wales) Regulations 2005, SI 2005/1352). The prescribed period is 3 years. For the purpose of calculating the 3 year period, the rent becomes payable on the date of payment set out in the s 166 notice: *Cheerupmate2 Ltd v Calce* [2017] UKUT 377 (TCC).

III L&T [318]

168. No forfeiture notice before determination of breach

(1) A landlord under a long lease of a dwelling may not serve a notice under section 146(1) of the Law of Property Act 1925 (c. 20) (restriction on forfeiture) in respect of a breach by a tenant of a covenant or condition in the lease unless subsection (2) is satisfied.

(2) This subsection is satisfied if—

- (a) it has been finally determined on an application under subsection (4) that the breach has occurred,
- (b) the tenant has admitted the breach, or
- (c) a court in any proceedings, or an arbitral tribunal in proceedings pursuant to a post-dispute arbitration agreement, has finally determined that the breach has occurred.

(3) But a notice may not be served by virtue of subsection (2)(a) or (c) until after the end of the period of 14 days beginning with the day after that on which the final determination is made.

(4) A landlord under a long lease of a dwelling may make an application to the appropriate tribunal for a determination that a breach of a covenant or condition in the lease has occurred.

(5) But a landlord may not make an application under subsection (4) in respect of a matter which—

- (a) has been, or is to be, referred to arbitration pursuant to a post-dispute arbitration agreement to which the tenant is a party,
- (b) has been the subject of determination by a court, or
- (c) has been the subject of determination by an arbitral tribunal pursuant to a post-dispute arbitration agreement.

(6) For the purposes of subsection (4), "appropriate tribunal" means—

- (a) in relation to a dwelling in England, the First-tier Tribunal or, where determined by or under Tribunal Procedure Rules, the Upper Tribunal; and
- (b) in relation to a dwelling in Wales, a leasehold valuation tribunal.

III L&T [318.1]

Jurisdiction of the county court Although the county court does not have jurisdiction to make a determination under s. 168(4), it nevertheless has a general jurisdiction to make a declaration as to breach of covenant under s 15 of the County Courts Act 1984 and such a declaration is effective for the purpose of s 168: see *Cussens v Realreed Ltd* [2013] EWHC 1229 (QB), [2013] 2 P & CR D27.

III L&T [319]

169. Section 168: supplementary

(1) An agreement by a tenant under a long lease of a dwelling (other than a post-dispute arbitration agreement) is void in so far as it purports to provide for a determination—

- (a) in a particular manner, or
- (b) on particular evidence,

of any question which may be the subject of an application under section 168(4).

(2) For the purposes of section 168 it is finally determined that a breach of a covenant or condition in a lease has occurred—

LANDLORD & TENANT AND HOUSING

(a) if a decision that it has occurred is not appealed against or otherwise challenged, at the end of the period for bringing an appeal or other challenge, or

(b) if such a decision is appealed against or otherwise challenged and not set aside in consequence of the appeal or other challenge, at the time specified in subsection (3).

(3) The time referred to in subsection (2)(b) is the time when the appeal or other challenge is disposed of—

(a) by the determination of the appeal or other challenge and the expiry of the time for bringing a subsequent appeal (if any), or

(b) by its being abandoned or otherwise ceasing to have effect.

(4) In section 168 and this section "long lease of a dwelling" does not include—

(a) a tenancy to which Part 2 of the Landlord and Tenant Act 1954 (c. 56) (business tenancies) applies,

(b) a tenancy of an agricultural holding within the meaning of the Agricultural Holdings Act 1986 (c. 5) in relation to which that Act applies, or

(c) a farm business tenancy within the meaning of the Agricultural Tenancies Act 1995 (c. 8).

(5) In section 168 and this section—

"arbitration agreement" and "arbitral tribunal" have the same meaning as in Part 1 of the Arbitration Act 1996 (c. 23) and "post-dispute arbitration agreement", in relation to any breach (or alleged breach), means an arbitration agreement made after the breach has occurred (or is alleged to have occurred),

"dwelling" has the same meaning as in the 1985 Act,

"landlord" and "tenant" have the same meaning as in Chapter 1 of this Part, and

"long lease" has the meaning given by sections 76 and 77 of this Act, except that a shared ownership lease is a long lease whatever the tenant's total share.

(6) Section 146(7) of the Law of Property Act 1925 (c. 20) applies for the purposes of section 168 and this section.

(7) Nothing in section 168 affects the service of a notice under section 146(1) of the Law of Property Act 1925 in respect of a failure to pay—

(a) a service charge (within the meaning of section 18(1) of the 1985 Act), or

(b) an administration charge (within the meaning of Part 1 of Schedule 11 to this Act).

HOUSING ACT 2004

(c 34)

GENERAL NOTES ON HOUSING ACT 2004

III L&T [320]

Sections 212 to 215 of the Housing Act 2004 deal with tenancy deposit schemes (and, in particular, the jurisdiction of the county court to make orders under s 214) and are set out in this part of Volume 2.

The general effect of Parts 1 to 4 of the Housing Act 2004 was to introduce controls over unfit housing (in place of the controls provided by the Housing Act 1985) and to replace the old right of appeal to the county court with a new right of appeal to the Residential Property Tribunal, subject to the payment of fees under SI 2006/830 and in accordance with procedure laid down in SI 2006/831.

Section 61 of the 2004 Act provides for the compulsory licensing of housing in multiple occupation and s 75 provides, as a sanction, that the landlord of an assured shorthold tenancy may not terminate it by a notice under s 21 of the Housing Act 1988 if it is located in an unlicensed house in multiple occupation (HMO). An HMO is defined by art 3 of the Licensing of Houses in Multiple Occupation (Prescribed descriptions) (England) Order 2006, SI 2006/371, the basic conditions for an HMO being that (a) the HMO or any part of it comprises three storeys or more; (b) it is occupied by five or more persons; and (c) it is occupied by persons living in two or more single households.

Landlords should take particular note of Part 6, Chapter 4 of the 2004 Act which contains ss 212 to 215 set out below. These sections, which came into force on 6 April 2007, were significantly amended by section 184 of the Localism Act 2011. All of the Localism Act amendments were brought into force on 6 April 2012 by the Localism Act 2011 (Commencement No 4 and Transitional, Transitory and Saving Provisions Order (LA (Commencement No 4) Order) 2012, SI 2012/628. Article 16 of that order provides that existing unprotected deposits must be protected by 6 May 2012.

Amendments made by sections 31 and 32 of the Deregulation Act 2015 establish a separate regime for the protection and recovery of deposits taken before 6 April 2007. This has been achieved by the insertion of sections 215A, 215B and 215C, with effect from 26 March 2015, the day when the Deregulation Act 2015 was passed. Section 212A was subsequently inserted by the Housing and Planning Act 2016, s 128(3), with effect from 6 April 2017.

LANDLORD & TENANT AND HOUSING

CHAPTER 4

TENANCY DEPOSIT SCHEMES

III L&T [321]

212. Tenancy deposit schemes

(1) The appropriate national authority must make arrangements for securing that one or more tenancy deposit schemes are available for the purpose of safeguarding tenancy deposits paid in connection with shorthold tenancies.

(2) For the purposes of this Chapter a "tenancy deposit scheme" is a scheme which—

(a) is made for the purpose of safeguarding tenancy deposits paid in connection with shorthold tenancies and facilitating the resolution of disputes arising in connection with such deposits, and

(b) complies with the requirements of Schedule 10.

(3) Arrangements under subsection (1) must be arrangements made with any body or person under which the body or person ("the scheme administrator") undertakes to establish and maintain a tenancy deposit scheme of a description specified in the arrangements.

(4) The appropriate national authority may—

(a) give financial assistance to the scheme administrator;

(b) make payments to the scheme administrator (otherwise than as financial assistance) in pursuance of arrangements under subsection (1).

(5) The appropriate national authority may, in such manner and on such terms as it thinks fit, guarantee the discharge of any financial obligation incurred by the scheme administrator in connection with arrangements under subsection (1).

(6) Arrangements under subsection (1) must require the scheme administrator to give the appropriate national authority, in such manner and at such times as it may specify, such information and facilities for obtaining information as it may specify.

(6A) For further provision about what must be included in the arrangements, see section 212A.

(7) The appropriate national authority may make regulations conferring or imposing—

(a) on scheme administrators, or

(b) on scheme administrators of any description specified in the regulations,

such powers or duties in connection with arrangements under subsection (1) as are so specified.

(8) In this Chapter—

"authorised", in relation to a tenancy deposit scheme, means that the scheme is in force in accordance with arrangements under subsection (1);

"custodial scheme" and "insurance scheme" have the meaning given by paragraph 1(2) and (3) of Schedule 10);

"money" means money in the form of cash or otherwise;

"shorthold tenancy" means an assured shorthold tenancy within the meaning of Chapter 2 of Part 1 of the Housing Act 1988 (c. 50);

"tenancy deposit", in relation to a shorthold tenancy, means any money intended to be held (by the landlord or otherwise) as security for—

(a) the performance of any obligations of the tenant, or

(b) the discharge of any liability of his,

arising under or in connection with the tenancy.

(9) In this Chapter—

(a) references to a landlord or landlords in relation to any shorthold tenancy or tenancies include references to a person or persons acting on his or their behalf in relation to the tenancy or tenancies, and

(b) references to a tenancy deposit being held in accordance with a scheme include, in the case of a custodial scheme, references to an amount representing the deposit being held in accordance with the scheme.

III L&T [321.1]

Shorthold tenancy Where there is a resident landlord, the tenancy is excluded from being an assured shorthold by paragraph 10 of Sch 2 to the Housing Act 1988, so the tenancy deposit schemes have no application: *Garcia v Choudhury* [2012] EWCA Civ 731.

III L&T [321.2]

Definition of a tenancy deposit A tenancy deposit is money held or intended to be held as security for performance by the tenant or the discharge of obligation. Where a payment of rent in advance is required this is not be treated as a deposit unless the wording of the tenancy makes it clear that it is being held as security for the performance or discharge of obligations: *Johnson v Old* [2013] EWCA Civ 415, [2013] 2 P & CR D15, [2013] HLR 344.

III L&T [321A]

212A. Provision of information to local authorities

(1) Arrangements under section 212(1) made by the Secretary of State must require the scheme administrator—

(a) to give a local housing authority in England any specified information that they request, or

(b) to provide facilities for the sharing of specified information with a local housing authority in England.

(2) In subsection (1) "specified information" means information, of a description specified in the arrangements, that relates to a tenancy of premises In the local housing authority's area.

(3) Arrangements made by virtue of this section may make the requirement to provide information or facilities to a local housing authority conditional on the payment of a fee.

(4) Arrangements made by virtue of this section may include supplementary provision, for example about—

(a) the form or manner in which any information is to be provided,

(b) the time or times at which it is to be provided, and

(c) the notification of anyone to whom the information relates.

(5) Information obtained by a local housing authority by virtue of this section may be used only—

(a) for a purpose connected with the exercise of the authority's functions under any of Parts 1 to 4 in relation to any premises, or

(b) for the purpose of investigating whether an offence has been committed under any of those Parts in relation to any premises.

(6) Information obtained by a local housing authority by virtue of this section may be supplied to a person providing services to the authority for a purpose listed in subsection (5).

(7) The Secretary of State may by regulations amend the list of purposes in subsection (5).

III L&T [322]

213. Requirements relating to tenancy deposits

(1) Any tenancy deposit paid to a person in connection with a shorthold tenancy must, as from the time when it is received, be dealt with in accordance with an authorised scheme.

(2) No person may require the payment of a tenancy deposit in connection with a shorthold tenancy which is not to be subject to the requirement in subsection (1).

(3) Where a landlord receives a tenancy deposit in connection with a shorthold tenancy, the initial requirements of an authorised scheme must be complied with by the landlord in relation to the deposit within the period of 30 days beginning with the date on which it is received.

(4) For the purposes of this section "the initial requirements" of an authorised scheme are such requirements imposed by the scheme as fall to be complied with by a landlord on receiving such a tenancy deposit.

(5) A landlord who has received such a tenancy deposit must give the tenant and any relevant person such information relating to—

(a) the authorised scheme applying to the deposit,

(b) compliance by the landlord with the initial requirements of the scheme in relation to the deposit, and

(c) the operation of provisions of this Chapter in relation to the deposit,

as may be prescribed.

(6) The information required by subsection (5) must be given to the tenant and any relevant person—

(a) in the prescribed form or in a form substantially to the same effect, and

(b) within the period of 30 days beginning with the date on which the deposit is received by the landlord.

(7) No person may, in connection with a shorthold tenancy, require a deposit which consists of property other than money.

(8) In subsection (7) "deposit" means a transfer of property intended to be held (by the landlord or otherwise) as security for—

(a) the performance of any obligations of the tenant, or

(b) the discharge of any liability of his,

arising under or in connection with the tenancy.

(9) The provisions of this section apply despite any agreement to the contrary.

(10) In this section—

"prescribed" means prescribed by an order made by the appropriate national authority;

"property" means moveable property;

"relevant person" means any person who, in accordance with arrangements made with the tenant, paid the deposit on behalf of the tenant.

III L&T [322.1]

Prescribed information For the prescribed information for the purposes of s 213(5) see the Housing (Tenancy Deposits) (Prescribed Information) Order, SI 2007/797.

III L&T [322.2]

Failure to comply The information prescribed by the 2007 Order is of real importance to a tenant and is not to be regarded as a mere matter of procedure or of subsidiary importance: see *Ayannuga v Swindells* [2012] EWCA Civ 1789, [2013] All ER (D) 78 (Jan), where the court held that there had been no substantial compliance with the statutory requirements, declared that the tenant was entitled to repayment of the deposit within 14 days and also ordered the landlord to pay the tenant an amount equal to three times the amount of the deposit.

Although a deposit did not have to be protected if taken in respect of a fixed term granted before 6 April 2007, the requirements for protection came into play in respect of the subsequent periodic tenancy: *Superstrike Ltd v Rodrigues* [2013] EWCA Civ 669, [2013] 1 WLR 3848, [2013] 2 P & CR D52, in which it was further held that non-compliance barred the landlord from giving a s 21 notice (see s 215 at **III L&T [324]**). See also *Charalambous v NG* [2014] EWCA Civ 1604, 165 NLJ 7636, where the court held that a landlord was precluded from serving a s 21 notice where the tenant's deposit had not been paid into an authorised scheme as required by s 213, notwithstanding the fact that, when the deposit was originally paid, there had been no obligation to do so. Note, however, that ss 215A to 215C (see **III L&T [324A]**) have the effect of reversing the decision in *Superstrike Ltd v Rodrigues*.

III L&T [323]

214. Proceedings relating to tenancy deposits

(1) Where a tenancy deposit has been paid in connection with a shorthold tenancy on or after 6 April 2007, the tenant or any relevant person (as defined by section 213(10)) may make an application to the county court on the grounds—

(a) that section 213(3) or (6) has not been complied with in relation to the deposit, or

(b) that he has been notified by the landlord that a particular authorised scheme applies to the deposit but has been unable to obtain confirmation from the scheme administrator that the deposit is being held in accordance with the scheme.

(1A) Subsection (1) also applies in a case where the tenancy has ended, and in such a case the reference in subsection (1) to the tenant is to a person who was a tenant under the tenancy.

(2) Subsections (3) and (4) apply in the case of an application under subsection (1) if the tenancy has not ended and the court—

(a) is satisfied that section 213(3) or (6) has not been complied with in relation to the deposit, or

(b) is not satisfied that the deposit is being held in accordance with an authorised scheme,

as the case may be.

(2A) Subsections (3A) and (4) apply in the case of an application under subsection (1) if the tenancy has ended (whether before or after the making of the application) and the court—

- (a) is satisfied that section 213(3) or (6) has not been complied with in relation to the deposit, or
- (b) is not satisfied that the deposit is being held in accordance with an authorised scheme,

as the case may be.

(3) The court must, as it thinks fit, either—

- (a) order the person who appears to the court to be holding the deposit to repay it to the applicant, or
- (b) order that person to pay the deposit into the designated account held by the scheme administrator under an authorised custodial scheme,

within the period of 14 days beginning with the date of the making of the order.

(3A) The court may order the person who appears to the court to be holding the deposit to repay all or part of it to the applicant within the period of 14 days beginning with the date of the making of the order.

(4) The court must also order the landlord to pay to the applicant a sum of money not less than the amount of the deposit and not more than three times the amount of the deposit within the period of 14 days beginning with the date of the making of the order.

(5) Where any deposit given in connection with a shorthold tenancy could not be lawfully required as a result of section 213(7), the property in question is recoverable from the person holding it by the person by whom it was given as a deposit.

(6) In subsection (5) "deposit" has the meaning given by section 213(8).

III L&T [323.1]

Procedure An application under s 214 is a "landlord and tenant claim" for the purpose of CPR 56 (see para **CPR 56.1**).

III L&T [323.2]

Rights arising on non-compliance The amendments effected to ss 213 to 215 by section 184 of the Localism Act 2011 have made significant changes. The time limits within which the landlord must comply with the requirement to protect a deposit taken in accordance with the rules of a tenancy deposit scheme and within which the landlord must provide prescribed information to the tenant have been extended from 14 to 30 days. Penalties for non-compliance apply when the landlord has not complied within those time limits, and the penalties also apply when the tenancy has ended. Section 214(4) of the Housing Act 2004 is amended to give the court a discretion as to the level of the penalty that may be imposed.

Practitioners should therefore note that the decisions in the following case commentary relate to ss 213 and 214 in their unamended form.

It has been held in the county court that where the landlord satisfies the initial requirements of the scheme and subsequently provides the prescribed information to the tenant but does so more than 14 days after receipt of the deposit, this does not entitle the tenant to an award under s 214(4). The court accepted the submission in that case that the landlord had discharged his duty under s 213(6)(a) by providing the information and that the failure to do so within 14 days, as required by s 213(6)(b), was irrelevant: *Harvey v Bamforth* a decision of HHJ Bullimore in the Sheffield County Court on 8 August 2008, [2008] 46 EG 119, also reported in Legal Action (2008) November p 18. See also *Draycott v Hannell Lettings Ltd* [2010] EWHC 217 (QB): where a landlord receives a deposit for an assured shorthold tenancy and protects it before the start of proceedings, but not within 14 days of receipt, then although there is a breach of s 213 there is no breach of the 'initial requirements of the scheme'; the landlord is therefore not subject to the penalty provision in s 214(4). Also the reference to the liability of the landlord is to be construed, in accordance with s 212(9), as including that of the landlord's agent.

In *Vision Enterprises Ltd (t/a Universal Estates) v Tiensia* [2010] EWCA Civ 1224, [2010] NLJR 1614 the Court of Appeal, approving the decision in *Draycott*, held that late compliance by a landlord with his obligations under s 213 gave him a complete defence to any claim by a tenant under s 214. The relevant date by which the landlord has to comply with the initial requirements and notification requirements is the date of the hearing of the tenant's s 214 application. Where a tenant makes a claim alleging breach of the statutory provisions, the landlord has until the date of the hearing to comply with his dual obligations of safeguarding the tenant's deposit and providing the requisite information in the prescribed form. The dual obligations are continuing obligations once a deposit has been paid. The obligation to give the prescribed information therefore continues, irrespective of whether the deposit had been returned before the date of the hearing: *Suurpere v Nice* [2011] EWHC 2003 (QB), [2011] All ER (D) 36 (Aug).

III L&T [323.3]

After the tenancy has ended In a case concerning s 214 (it its unamended form) the court held that an application could be made after the lease had ended: *Gladehurst Properties Ltd v Hashemi* [2011] EWCA Civ 604, [2011] All ER (D) 180 (May), followed in *Suurpere v Nice* [2011] EWHC 2003 (QB), [2011] All ER (D) 36 (Aug), although with a different result on the facts. Note, however, the change effected by s 214(1A).

III L&T [324]

215. Sanctions for non-compliance

(1) Subject to subsection (2A), if (whether before, on or after 6 April 2007) a tenancy deposit has been paid in connection with a shorthold tenancy, no section 21 notice may be given in relation to the tenancy at a time when the deposit is not being held in accordance with an authorised scheme.

(1A) Subject to subsection (2A), if a tenancy deposit has been paid in connection with a shorthold tenancy on or after 6 April 2007, no section 21 notice may be given in relation to the tenancy at a time when section 213(3) has not been complied with in relation to the deposit.

(2) Subject to subsection (2A), if section 213(6) is not complied with in relation to a deposit given in connection with a shorthold tenancy, no section 21 notice may be given in relation to the tenancy until such time as section 213(6)(a) is complied with.

(2A) Subsections (1), (1A) and (2) do not apply in a case where—

(a) the deposit has been returned to the tenant in full or with such deductions as are agreed between the landlord and tenant, or

(b) an application to the county court has been made under section 214(1) and has been determined by the court, withdrawn or settled by agreement between the parties.

(3) If any deposit given in connection with a shorthold tenancy could not be lawfully required as a result of section 213(7), no section 21 notice may be given in relation to the tenancy until such time as the property in question is returned to the person by whom it was given as a deposit.

(4) In subsection (3) "deposit" has the meaning given by section 213(8).

(5) In this section a "section 21 notice" means a notice under section 21(1)(b) or (4)(a) of the Housing Act 1988 (recovery of possession on termination of shorthold tenancy).

III L&T [324.1]

General note on tenancy deposit schemes A landlord who takes a deposit at the start of a tenancy, as a security against default, must handle the deposit in accordance with an "authorised scheme". A landlord who fails to comply faces severe sanctions: (i) the tenant may obtain an order for compliance in which case the court must, in addition, order the landlord to pay the tenant a sum three times the size of the deposit (see s 214(4) at **III L&T [323]**) and (ii) a non-compliant landlord cannot serve notice under s 21 of the Housing Act 1988 (recovery of possession on expiry of the assured shorthold tenancy) (**III L&T [229]**) until he, or she, has complied.

For details of the requirements of the scheme see Sch 10 of the 2004 Act as amended by the Housing (Tenancy Deposit Schemes) Order SI 2007/796.

Where, under arrangements made under s 212, a custodial scheme is in operation, at the end of a tenancy a deposit that has been secured in the custodial scheme must be paid in accordance with para 4 of the Sch 10. Where the scheme provides for any amount so paid to

(b) proceedings under either of those sections in respect of a tenancy which have been finally determined before the commencement date.

(3) Subsection (5) applies in respect of a tenancy if—

(a) proceedings under section 214 in respect of the tenancy have been instituted before the commencement date but have not been settled or finally determined before that date, and

(b) because of section 215A(4) or 215B(2), the court decides—

(i) not to make an order under section 214(4) in respect of the tenancy, or

(ii) to allow an appeal by the landlord against such an order.

(4) Subsection (5) also applies in respect of a tenancy if—

(a) proceedings for possession under section 21 of the Housing Act 1988 in respect of the tenancy have been instituted before the commencement date but have not been settled or finally determined before that date, and

(b) because of section 215A(4) or 215B(2), the court decides—

(i) to make an order for possession under that section in respect of the tenancy, or

(ii) to allow an appeal by the landlord against a refusal to make such an order.

(5) Where this subsection applies, the court must not order the tenant or any relevant person (as defined by section 213(10)) to pay the landlord's costs, to the extent that the court reasonably considers those costs are attributable to the proceedings under section 214 of this Act or (as the case may be) section 21 of the Housing Act 1988.

(6) Proceedings have been "finally determined" for the purposes of this section if—

(a) they have been determined by a court, and

(b) there is no further right to appeal against the determination.

(7) There is no further right to appeal against a court determination if there is no right to appeal against the determination, or there is such a right but—

(a) the time limit for making an appeal has expired without an appeal being brought, or

(b) an appeal brought within that time limit has been withdrawn.

(8) In this section "the commencement date" means the date on which the Deregulation Act 2015 is passed.

TRIBUNALS, COURTS AND ENFORCEMENT ACT 2007

(c 15)

III L&T [325]

General note on the Tribunals, Courts and Enforcement Act 2007 Distress for rent is an ancient common law remedy which enables landlords to recover rent arrears, without going to court, by taking goods from demised premises and either holding those goods until the rent arrears have been paid or selling the goods. Part 3 Chapter 2 (ss 71 to 87) of the Tribunals, Courts and Enforcement Act 2007 (in force from 6 April 2014) abolishes the common law right to distrain for arrears of rent and introduces a modified regime for recovering rent arrears in the commercial property sector.

Section 72 of the Act creates a statutory right for a landlord of commercial premises to recover rent arrears by using the procedure in Sch 12 for taking control of the tenant's goods. The statutory right of commercial rent arrears recovery (known as CRAR) is available only to landlords of commercial premises.

Section 78 of the Act sets out the powers of the court to intervene in the exercise of CRAR. The following conditions must be satisfied: (i) notice of enforcement has been served on the tenant; (ii) the tenant has made an application to the court to intervene; (iii) the court is satisfied that the circumstances meet the prescribed grounds for intervening.

The court may make an order to set aside the notice of enforcement, which effectively cancels the notice and prevents the landlord from taking any further steps under CRAR in relation to that notice. Alternatively, the court may suspend the use of CRAR, by making an order that no further steps may be taken in exercise of CRAR without further order by the court.

These provisions came into effect on 6 April 2014 which was the date set for the coming into force of the Taking Control of Goods Regulations 2013, SI 2013/1894 and the Taking Control of Goods (Fees) Regulations 2014, SI 2014/1.

CHAPTER 2

RENT ARREARS RECOVERY

III L&T [326]

71. Abolition of common law right

The common law right to distrain for arrears of rent is abolished.

III L&T [327]

72. Commercial rent arrears recovery (CRAR)

(1) A landlord under a lease of commercial premises may use the procedure in Schedule 12 (taking control of goods) to recover from the tenant rent payable under the lease.

(2) A landlord's power under subsection (1) is referred to as CRAR (commercial rent arrears recovery).

III L&T [328]

73. Landlord

(1) In this Chapter "landlord", in relation to a lease, means the person for the time being entitled to the immediate reversion in the property comprised in the lease.

(2) That is subject to the following.

(3) In the case of a tenancy by estoppel, a person is "entitled to the immediate reversion" if he is entitled to it as between himself and the tenant.

(4) If there are joint tenants of the immediate reversion, or if a number of persons are entitled to the immediate reversion as between themselves and the tenant-

(a) "landlord" means any one of them;

(b) CRAR may be exercised to recover rent due to all of them.

(5) If the immediate reversion is mortgaged, "landlord" means-

(a) the mortgagee, if he has given notice of his intention to take possession or enter into receipt of rents and profits;

(b) otherwise, the mortgagor.

(6) Subsection (5) applies whether the lease is made before or after the mortgage is created, but CRAR is not exercisable by a mortgagee in relation to a lease that does not bind him.

(7) Where a receiver is appointed by a court in relation to the immediate reversion, CRAR is exercisable by the receiver in the name of the landlord.

(8) Any authorisation of a person to exercise CRAR on another's behalf must be in writing and must comply with any prescribed requirements.

(9) This Chapter applies to any other person entitled to exercise CRAR as it applies to a landlord.

III L&T [329]

74. Lease

(1) "Lease" means a tenancy in law or in equity, including a tenancy at will, but not including a tenancy at sufferance.

(2) A lease must be evidenced in writing.

(3) References to a lease are to a lease as varied from time to time (whether or not the variation is in writing).

(4) This section applies for the purposes of this Chapter.

III L&T [330]

75. Commercial premises

(1) A lease (A) is of commercial premises if none of the demised premises is-

(a) let under lease A as a dwelling,

(b) let under an inferior lease (B) as a dwelling, or

(c) occupied as a dwelling.

(2) The "demised premises" in this section include anything on them.

(3) "Let as a dwelling" means let on terms permitting only occupation as a dwelling or other use combined with occupation as a dwelling.

(4) Premises are not within subsection (1)(b) if letting them as a dwelling is a breach of a lease superior to lease B.

(5) Premises are not within subsection (1)(c) if occupying them as a dwelling is a breach of lease A or a lease superior to lease A.

(6) This section applies for the purposes of this Chapter.

III L&T [331]

76. Rent

(1) "Rent" means the amount payable under a lease (in advance or in arrear) for possession and use of the demised premises, together with-

(a) any interest payable on that amount under the lease, and

(b) any value added tax chargeable on that amount or interest.

(2) "Rent" does not include any sum in respect of rates, council tax, services, repairs, maintenance, insurance or other ancillary matters (whether or not called "rent" in the lease).

(3) The amount payable for possession and use of the demised premises, where it is not otherwise identifiable, is to be taken to be so much of the total amount payable under the lease as is reasonably attributable to possession and use.

(4) Where a rent is payable under or by virtue of Part 2 of the Landlord and Tenant Act 1954 (c. 56), the amount payable under the lease for possession and use of those premises is to be taken to be that rent.

(5) This section applies for the purposes of this Chapter except sections 71 and 85.

III L&T [332]

77. The rent recoverable

(1) CRAR is not exercisable except to recover rent that meets each of these conditions-

(a) it has become due and payable before notice of enforcement is given;

(b) it is certain, or capable of being calculated with certainty.

(2) The amount of any rent recoverable by CRAR is reduced by any permitted deduction.

(3) CRAR is exercisable only if the net unpaid rent is at least the minimum amount immediately before each of these-

(a) the time when notice of enforcement is given;

(b) the first time that goods are taken control of after that notice.

(4) The minimum amount is to be calculated in accordance with regulations.

(5) The net unpaid rent is the amount of rent that meets the conditions in subsection (1), less-

(a) any interest or value added tax included in that amount under section 76(1)(a) or (b), and

(b) any permitted deductions.

(6) Regulations may provide for subsection (5)(a) not to apply in specified cases.

(7) Permitted deductions, against any rent, are any deduction, recoupment or set-off that the tenant would be entitled to claim (in law or equity) in an action by the landlord for that rent.

III L&T [333]

78. Intervention of the court

(1) If notice of enforcement is given in exercise (or purported exercise) of CRAR the court may make either or both of these orders on the application of the tenant-

(a) an order setting aside the notice;

(b) an order that no further step may be taken under CRAR, without further order, in relation to the rent claimed.

(2) Regulations may make provision about-

(a) the further orders that may be made for the purposes of subsection (1)(b);

(b) grounds of which the court must be satisfied before making an order or further order.

(3) In this section "the court" means the High Court or the county court], as rules of court may provide.

III L&T [334]

79. Use of CRAR after end of lease

(1) When the lease ends, CRAR ceases to be exercisable, with these exceptions.

(2) CRAR continues to be exercisable in relation to goods taken control of under it-

(a) before the lease ended, or

(b) under subsection (3).

(3) CRAR continues to be exercisable in relation to rent due and payable before the lease ended, if the conditions in subsection (4) are met.

(4) These are the conditions-

(a) the lease did not end by forfeiture;

(b) not more than 6 months has passed since the day when it ended;

(c) the rent was due from the person who was the tenant at the end of the lease;

(d) that person remains in possession of any part of the demised premises;

(e) any new lease under which that person remains in possession is a lease of commercial premises;

(f) the person who was the landlord at the end of the lease remains entitled to the immediate reversion.

(5) In deciding whether a person remains in possession under a new lease, section 74(2) (lease to be evidenced in writing) does not apply.

(6) In the case of a tenancy by estoppel, the person who was the landlord remains "entitled to the immediate reversion" if the estoppel with regard to the tenancy continues.

(7) A lease ends when the tenant ceases to be entitled to possession of the demised premises under the lease together with any continuation of it by operation of an enactment or of a rule of law.

III L&T [335]

80. Agricultural holdings

(1) This section applies to the exercise of CRAR where the premises concerned are an agricultural holding.

(2) CRAR is not exercisable to recover rent that became due more than a year before notice of enforcement is given.

(3) For the purposes of subsection (2), deferred rent becomes due at the time to which payment is deferred.

(4) "Deferred rent" means rent the payment of which has been deferred, according to the ordinary course of dealing between the landlord and the tenant, to the end of a quarter or half-year after it legally became due.

(5) The permitted deductions under section 77(7) at any time include any compensation due to the tenant in respect of the holding, under the 1986 Act or under custom or agreement, that has been ascertained at that time.

(6) In this section-

the "1986 Act" means the Agricultural Holdings Act 1986 (c. 5);

"agricultural holding" has the meaning given by section 1 of the 1986 Act.

III L&T [336]

81. Right to rent from sub-tenant

(1) This section applies where CRAR is exercisable by a landlord to recover rent due and payable from a tenant (the immediate tenant).

(2) The landlord may serve a notice on any sub-tenant.

(3) The notice must state the amount of rent that the landlord has the right to recover from the immediate tenant by CRAR (the "notified amount").

(4) When it takes effect the notice transfers to the landlord the right to recover, receive and give a discharge for any rent payable by the sub-tenant under the sub-lease, until-

(a) the notified amount has been paid (by payments under the notice or otherwise), or

(b) the notice is replaced or withdrawn.

(5) A notice under this section takes effect at the end of a period to be determined by regulations.

(6) Regulations may state-

(a) the form of a notice under this section;

(b) what it must contain;

(c) how it must be served;

(d) what must be done to withdraw it.

(7) In determining for the purposes of this section whether CRAR is exercisable, section 77 applies with these modifications-

(a) if notice of enforcement has not been given, references to that notice are to be read as references to the notice under this section;

(b) if goods have not been taken control of, section 77(3)(b) does not apply.

(8) In this section and sections 82 to 84-

(a) "sub-tenant" means a tenant (below the immediate tenant) of any of the premises comprised in the headlease (and "sub-lease" is to be read accordingly);

(b) "headlease" means the lease between the landlord and the immediate tenant.

III L&T [337]

82. Off-setting payments under a notice

(1) For any amount that a sub-tenant pays under a notice under section 81, he may deduct an equal amount from the rent that would be due to his immediate landlord under the sub-lease.

(2) If an amount is deducted under subsection (1) or this subsection from rent due to a superior sub-tenant, that sub-tenant may deduct an equal amount from any rent due from him under his sub-lease.

(3) Subsection (1) applies even if the sub-tenant's payment or part of it is not due under the notice, if it is not due because-

(a) the notified amount has already been paid (wholly or partly otherwise than under the notice), or

(b) the notice has been replaced by a notice served on another sub-tenant.

(4) That is subject to the following.

(5) Subsection (1) does not apply if the landlord withdraws the notice before the payment is made.

(6) Where the notified amount has already been paid (or will be exceeded by the payment), subsection (1) does not apply (or does not apply to the excess) if the sub-tenant has notice of that when making the payment.

(7) Subsection (1) does not apply if, before the payment is made, payments under the notice at least equal the notified amount.

(8) Subsection (1) does not apply to a part of the payment if, with the rest of the payment, payments under the notice at least equal the notified amount.

(9) Where the notice has been replaced by one served on another sub-tenant, subsection (1) does not apply if the sub-tenant has notice of that when making the payment.

III L&T [338]

83. Withdrawal and replacement of notices

(1) A notice under section 81 is replaced if the landlord serves another notice on the same sub-tenant for a notified amount covering the same rent or part of that rent.

(2) A notice under section 81 served on one sub-tenant is also replaced if-

(a) the landlord serves a notice on another sub-tenant for a notified amount covering the same rent or part of that rent, and

(b) in relation to any of the premises comprised in the first sub-tenant's sub-lease, the second sub-tenant is an inferior or superior sub-tenant.

(3) The landlord must withdraw a notice under section 81 if any of these happens-

(a) the notice is replaced;

(b) the notified amount is paid, unless it is paid wholly by the sub-tenant.

III L&T [339]

84. Recovery of sums due and overpayments

(1) For the purposes of the recovery of sums payable by a sub-tenant under a notice under section 81 (including recovery by CRAR), the sub-tenant is to be treated as the immediate tenant of the landlord, and the sums are to be treated as rent accordingly.

(2) But those sums (as opposed to rent due from the immediate tenant) are not recoverable by notice under section 81 served on an inferior sub-tenant.

(3) Any payment received by the landlord that the sub-tenant purports to make under a notice under section 81, and that is not due under the notice for any reason, is to be treated as a payment of rent by the immediate tenant, for the purposes of the retention of the payment by the landlord and (if no rent is due) for the purposes of any claim by the immediate tenant to recover the payment.

(4) But subsection (3) does not affect any claim by the sub-tenant against the immediate tenant.

III L&T [340]

85. Contracts for similar rights to be void

(1) A provision of a contract is void to the extent that it would do any of these-

(a) confer a right to seize or otherwise take control of goods to recover amounts within subsection (2);

(b) confer a right to sell goods to recover amounts within subsection (2);

(c) modify the effect of section 72(1), except in accordance with subsection (3).

(2) The amounts are any amounts payable-

(a) as rent;

(b) under a lease (other than as rent);

(c) under an agreement collateral to a lease;

(d) under an instrument creating a rentcharge;

(e) in respect of breach of a covenant or condition in a lease, in an agreement collateral to a lease or in an instrument creating a rentcharge;

(f) under an indemnity in respect of a payment within paragraphs (a) to (e).

(3) A provision of a contract is not void under subsection (1)(c) to the extent that it prevents or restricts the exercise of CRAR.

(4) In this section-

"lease" also includes a licence to occupy land;

"rent" and "rentcharge" have the meaning given by section 205(1) of the Law of Property Act 1925 (c. 20).

III L&T [341]

86. Amendments

Schedule 14 makes minor and consequential amendments (including repeals of powers to distrain for rentcharges and other amounts within section 85(2)).

III L&T [342]

87. Interpretation of Chapter

In this Chapter-

"landlord" has the meaning given by section 73;

"lease" has the meaning given by section 74 (subject to section 85(4));

"notice of enforcement" means notice under paragraph 7 of Schedule 12;

"rent" (except in sections 71 and 85) has the meaning given by section 76;

"tenant", in relation to a lease, means the tenant for the time being under the lease.

HOUSING AND REGENERATION ACT 2008

(c 17)

GENERAL NOTES ON HOUSING AND REGENERATION ACT 2008

III L&T [343]

Sections 294 to 319 of this Act and Schedules 11, 12 and 15 amend the rights and remedies of landlords and tenants in the areas of possession orders (and "tolerated trespassers"), service charges, the right to buy, leasehold enfranchisement and homelessness. Many of these provisions make changes to the civil jurisdiction of the county court, mainly by amending existing legislation, in particular the Leasehold Reform Act 1967, the Landlord and tenant Act 1985 and the Housing Acts 1985, 1988 and 1996. The amendments have therefore been incorporated into the text of those statutes where they appear, with notes as to their commencement and effect.

There are, in addition, two sets of provisions which do not amend the existing legislation but are free-standing. Firstly, s 298 which deals with the termination of family intervention tenancies; secondly, Part 2 of Schedule 11 which provides for the impact of the new regime for "tolerated trespassers" on cases where possession orders have already been made when the substance of Schedule 11 (as opposed to the regulation-making power) is brought into force. These provisions are set out below. Section 298 (termination of family intervention tenancies) was brought fully into force on 1 January 2009 by SI 2008/3068.

III L&T [344]

298. Certain family intervention tenancies: termination

(1) A local housing authority must not serve a notice to quit on the tenant of a family intervention tenancy unless—

- (a) the authority has served a notice under subsection (2) on the tenant, and
- (b) either—
  - (i) the tenant has not requested a review of the kind mentioned in subsection (2)(e) within the period of 14 days beginning with the service of the notice,
  - (ii) any such request has been withdrawn, or
  - (iii) the authority has served a notice on the tenant under subsection (4)(b).

(2) A notice under this subsection is a notice in writing stating—

- (a) that the authority has decided to serve a notice to quit on the tenant,
- (b) the effect of serving a notice to quit,
- (c) the reasons for the authority's decision,
- (d) when the authority is intending to serve the notice to quit, and
- (e) that the tenant has the right to request, within the period of 14 days beginning with the service of the notice under this subsection, a review of the authority's decision.

(3) Subsection (4) applies if the tenant requests a review of the kind mentioned in subsection (2)(e) within the period of 14 days beginning with the service of the notice under subsection (2) and the request is not withdrawn.

(4) The local housing authority must—

- (a) review its decision to serve a notice to quit on the tenant, and
- (b) serve a notice on the tenant informing the tenant of the decision of the authority on the review and the reasons for it.

(5) The appropriate national authority may by regulations make provision about the procedure to be followed in connection with such a review.

(6) Regulations under subsection (5) may, in particular—

- (a) specify the description of person who is to make the decision on a review,
- (b) specify the circumstances in which the tenant is entitled to an oral hearing on a review,
- (c) specify whether, and by whom, the tenant is entitled to be represented at such a hearing.

(7) A notice under subsection (2), and a notice to quit, served by a local housing authority in respect of a family intervention tenancy must contain advice to the tenant as to how the tenant may be able to obtain assistance in relation to the notice.

(8) The appropriate national authority may by regulations make provision about the type of advice to be provided in such notices.

(9) In this section—

"appropriate national authority" means—

- (a) in relation to England, the Secretary of State, and
- (b) in relation to Wales, the Welsh Ministers,

"family intervention tenancy" has the same meaning as in paragraph 4ZA of Schedule 1 to the Housing Act 1985 (c. 68),

and other expressions used in this section and in paragraph 4ZA of that Schedule have the same meaning as in that paragraph.

(10) This section does not apply to any tenancy granted before the coming into force of this section.

LANDLORD & TENANT AND HOUSING

III L&T [344.1]

Procedure for review of Family Intervention Tenancy decisions Procedure for the review of Family Intervention tenancy decisions is to be found in the Family Intervention Tenancies (Review of Local Authority Decisions) (England) Regulations 2008, SI 2008/3111.

SCHEDULE 11
POSSESSION ORDERS RELATING TO CERTAIN TENANCIES

PART 2
REPLACEMENT OF CERTAIN TERMINATED TENANCIES

CIRCUMSTANCES IN WHICH REPLACEMENT TENANCIES ARISE

III L&T [345]

15 In this Part of this Schedule "an original tenancy" means any secure tenancy, assured tenancy, introductory tenancy or demoted tenancy—

- (a) in respect of which a possession order was made before the commencement date, and
- (b) which ended before that date pursuant to the order but not on the execution of the order.

16 (1) A new tenancy of the dwelling-house which was let under the original tenancy is treated as arising on the commencement date between the ex-landlord and the ex-tenant if—

- (a) on that date—
  - (i) the home condition is met, and
  - (ii) the ex-landlord is entitled to let the dwelling-house, and
- (b) the ex-landlord and the ex-tenant have not entered into another tenancy after the date on which the original tenancy ended but before the commencement date.

(2) The home condition is that the dwelling-house which was let under the original tenancy—

- (a) is, on the commencement date, the only or principal home of the ex-tenant, and
- (b) has been the only or principal home of the ex-tenant throughout the termination period.

(3) In this Part of this Schedule "the termination period" means the period—

- (a) beginning with the end of the original tenancy, and
- (b) ending with the commencement date.

(4) For the purposes of sub-paragraph (2)(a) the dwelling-house is the only or principal home of the ex-tenant on the commencement date even though the ex-tenant is then absent from the dwelling-house as a result of having been evicted in pursuance of a warrant if the warrant is subsequently set aside but the possession order under which it was granted remains in force.

(5) In that case, the new tenancy is treated as arising on the first day (if any) on which the ex-tenant resumes occupation of the dwelling-house as that person's only or principal home.

(6) For the purposes of sub-paragraph (2)(b) any period of time within the termination period is to be ignored if—

- (a) it is a period in which the ex-tenant was absent from the dwelling-house as a result of having been evicted in pursuance of a warrant which was then set aside although the possession order under which it was granted remained in force, and
- (b) the ex-tenant subsequently resumes occupation of the dwelling-house as the ex-tenant's only or principal home.

(7) The appropriate national authority may by order provide for particular cases or descriptions of case, or particular circumstances, where the home condition is met where it would not otherwise be met.

NATURE OF REPLACEMENT TENANCIES

17 The new tenancy is to be—

(a) a secure tenancy if—

(i) the original tenancy was a secure tenancy, or

(ii) the original tenancy was an introductory tenancy but no election by the ex-landlord under section 124 of the Housing Act 1996 (c. 52) is in force on the day on which the new tenancy arises,

(b) an assured shorthold tenancy if the original tenancy was an assured shorthold tenancy,

(c) an assured tenancy which is not an assured shorthold tenancy if the original tenancy was a tenancy of that kind,

(d) an introductory tenancy if the original tenancy was an introductory tenancy and an election by the ex-landlord under section 124 of the Housing Act 1996 is in force on the day on which the new tenancy arises,

(e) a demoted tenancy to which section 20B of the Housing Act 1988 (c. 50) applies if the original tenancy was a demoted tenancy of that kind, and

(f) a demoted tenancy to which section 143A of the Housing Act 1996 applies if the original tenancy was a demoted tenancy of that kind.

18 (1) The new tenancy is, subject as follows, to have effect on the same terms and conditions as those applicable to the original tenancy immediately before it ended.

(2) The terms and conditions of the new tenancy are to be treated as modified so as to reflect, so far as applicable, any changes made during the termination period to the level of payments for the ex-tenant's occupation of the dwelling-house or to the other terms and conditions of the occupation.

(3) The terms and conditions of the new tenancy are to be treated as modified so that any outstanding liabilities owed by the ex-tenant to the ex-landlord in respect of payments for the ex-tenant's occupation of the dwelling-house during the termination period are liabilities in respect of rent under the new tenancy.

(4) The appropriate national authority may by order provide for other modifications of the terms and conditions of the new tenancy.

(5) Nothing in sub-paragraphs (2) to (4) is to be read as permitting modifications of the new tenancy which would not have been possible if the original tenancy had remained a tenancy throughout the termination period.

(6) The terms and conditions of a new secure tenancy which arises by virtue of paragraph 17(a)(ii) are to be treated as modified so far as necessary to reflect the fact that the new tenancy is a secure tenancy and not an introductory tenancy.

19 (1) Any provision which is made by or under an enactment and relates to a secure tenancy, assured tenancy, introductory tenancy or demoted tenancy applies, subject as follows, to a new tenancy of a corresponding kind.

(2) Any such provision which relates to an introductory tenancy applies to a new tenancy which is an introductory tenancy as if the trial period mentioned in section 125(2) of the Housing Act 1996 (c. 52) were the period of one year beginning with the day on which the new tenancy arises.

(3) Any such provision which relates to a demoted tenancy applies to a new tenancy which is a demoted tenancy as if the demotion period mentioned in section 20B(2) of the Housing Act 1988 (c. 50) or section 143B(1) of the Housing Act 1996 were the period of one year beginning with the day on which the new tenancy arises.

(4) The appropriate national authority may by order modify any provision made by or under an enactment in its application to a new tenancy.

STATUS OF POSSESSION ORDER AND OTHER COURT ORDERS

20 (1) The possession order in pursuance of which the original tenancy ended is to be treated, so far as practicable, as if it applies to the new tenancy.

(2) Any court orders made before the commencement date which—

- (a) are in force on that date,
- (b) relate to the occupation of the dwelling-house, and
- (c) were made in contemplation of, in consequence of or otherwise in connection with the possession order,

are to be treated, so far as practicable, as if they apply to the new tenancy.

CONTINUITY OF TENANCIES

21 (1) The new tenancy and the original tenancy are to be treated for the relevant purposes as—

- (a) the same tenancy, and
- (b) a tenancy which continued uninterrupted throughout the termination period.

(2) The relevant purposes are—

- (a) determining whether the ex-tenant is a successor in relation to the new tenancy,
- (b) calculating on or after the commencement date the period qualifying, or the aggregate of such periods, under Schedule 4 to the Housing Act 1985 (c. 68) (qualifying period for right to buy and discount),
- (c) determining on or after the commencement date whether the condition set out in paragraph (b) of Ground 8 of Schedule 2 to that Act is met, and
- (d) any other purposes specified by the appropriate national authority by order.

(3) In proceedings on a relevant claim the court concerned may order that the new tenancy and the original tenancy are to be treated for the purposes of the claim as—

- (a) the same tenancy, and
- (b) a tenancy which continued uninterrupted throughout the termination period.

(4) The following are relevant claims—

- (a) a claim by the ex-tenant or the ex-landlord against the other for breach of a term or condition of the original tenancy—
  - (i) in respect of which proceedings are brought on or after the commencement date, or
  - (ii) in respect of which proceedings were brought, but were not finally determined, before that date,
- (b) a claim by the ex-tenant against the ex-landlord for breach of statutory duty in respect of which proceedings are or were brought as mentioned in paragraph (a)(i) or (ii), and
- (c) any other claim of a description specified by the appropriate national authority by order.

(5) For the purposes of sub-paragraph (4)(a) proceedings must be treated as finally determined if—

- (a) they are withdrawn,
- (b) any appeal is abandoned, or
- (c) the time for appealing has expired without an appeal being brought.

COMPLIANCE WITH CONSULTATION REQUIREMENTS

22 (1) The fact that—

(a) the views of the ex-tenant during the termination period were not sought or taken into account when they should have been sought or taken into account, or

(b) the views of the ex-tenant during that period were sought or taken into account when they should not have been sought or taken into account,

is not to be taken to mean that the consultation requirements were not complied with.

(2) The consultation requirements are—

(a) the requirements under—

(i) section 105(1) of the Housing Act 1985 (c. 68),

(ii) paragraphs 3 and 4 of Schedule 3A to that Act,

(iii) regulations made under section 27AB of that Act which relate to arranging for ballots or polls with respect to a proposal to enter into a management agreement, and

(iv) section 137(2) of the Housing Act 1996 (c. 52), and

(b) any other requirements specified by the appropriate national authority by order.

JOINT TENANCIES

23 (1) In the application of this Part of this Schedule in relation to an original tenancy which was a joint tenancy, a reference to the dwelling-house being the only or principal home of the ex-tenant is to be treated as a reference to the dwelling-house being the only or principal home of at least one of the ex-tenants of the joint tenancy.

(2) The appropriate national authority may by order provide for this Part of this Schedule to apply in relation to an original tenancy which was a joint tenancy subject to such additional modifications as may be specified in the order.

SUCCESSOR LANDLORDS

24 (1) The appropriate national authority may by order provide for this Part of this Schedule to apply, subject to such modifications as may be specified in the order, to successor landlord cases.

(2) For the purposes of sub-paragraph (1) a successor landlord case is a case, in relation to an original tenancy, where the interest of the ex-landlord in the dwelling-house—

(a) has been transferred to another person after the end of the original tenancy and before the commencement date, and

(b) on the commencement date, belongs to the person to whom it has been transferred or a subsequent transferee.

SUPPLEMENTARY

25 In determining for the purposes of this Part of this Schedule whether a tenancy has ended, any ending which was temporary because the tenancy was restored in consequence of a court order is to be ignored.

26 (1) In this Part of this Schedule—

"appropriate national authority" means—

(a) in relation to a dwelling-house in England, the Secretary of State, and

(b) in relation to a dwelling-house in Wales, the Welsh Ministers,

"assured shorthold tenancy" and "assured tenancy" have the same meanings as in Part 1 of the Housing Act 1988 (c. 50) but do not include a demoted tenancy to which section 20B of that Act applies, "the commencement date" means the day on which section 299 comes into force for purposes other than the purposes of the Secretary of State or the Welsh Ministers making orders under this Part of this Schedule,

"demoted tenancy" means a tenancy to which section 20B of the Act of 1988 or section 143A of the Housing Act 1996 (c. 52) applies,

"dwelling-house"—

(a) in relation to an assured tenancy, or a tenancy to which section 20B of the Act of 1988 applies, has the same meaning as in Part 1 of that Act,

(b) in relation to a tenancy to which section 143A of the Act of 1996 applies, has the same meaning as in Chapter 1A of Part 5 of that Act,

(c) in relation to an introductory tenancy, has the meaning given by section 139 of the Act of 1996, and

(d) in relation to a secure tenancy, has the meaning given by section 112 of the Housing Act 1985 (c. 68),

"ex-landlord" means the person who was the landlord under an original tenancy,

"ex-tenant" means the person who was the tenant under an original tenancy,

"introductory tenancy" has the same meaning as in Chapter 1 of Part 5 of the Act of 1996,

"modification" includes omission,

"new tenancy" means a tenancy which is treated as arising by virtue of paragraph 16,

"original tenancy" has the meaning given by paragraph 15,

"possession order", in relation to a tenancy, means a court order for the possession of the dwelling-house,

"secure tenancy" has the same meaning as in Part 4 of the Act of 1985,

"successor"—

(a) in relation to a new tenancy which is an assured tenancy or which is a demoted tenancy to which section 20B of the Act of 1988 applies, has the same meaning as in section 17 of that Act,

(b) in relation to a new tenancy which is a demoted tenancy to which section 143A of the Act of 1996 applies, has the meaning given by section 143J of that Act,

(c) in relation to a new tenancy which is an introductory tenancy, has the same meaning as in section 132 of the Act of 1996, and

(d) in relation to a new tenancy which is a secure tenancy, has the same meaning as in section 88 of the Act of 1985.

"termination period" has the meaning given by paragraph 16(3).

(2) For the purposes of the definition of "appropriate national authority" in sub-paragraph (1) a dwelling-house which is partly in England and partly in Wales is to be treated—

(a) as being in England if it is treated as situated in the area of a billing authority in England by virtue of regulations under section 1(3) of the Local Government Finance Act 1992 (c. 14) (council tax in respect of dwellings), and

(b) as being in Wales if it is treated as situated in the area of a billing authority in Wales by virtue of regulations under that section.

Commencement *The whole of Schedule 11, with the exception of paragraphs 3(3), 8(3) and 14(3) (which relate to the court's discretionary powers under section 85(4) of the Housing Act 1985 and section 9(4) of the Housing Act 1988), in force from 20 May 2009: Housing and Regeneration Act 2008 (Commencement No.5) Order 2009, SI2009/1261.*

Part 2 of Schedule 11 also applies, subject to specified modifications, to successor landlord cases: Housing (Replacement of Terminated Tenancies) (Successor Landlords) (England) Order 2009, SI2009/1262. For Wales see SI2009/1260.

III L&T [345.1]

A replacement tenancy arises The general effect of Part 2 of Sch 11 is, subject to prescribed conditions, to restore tolerated trespassers to their former status as tenants by means of a replacement tenancy. Where, before 20 May 2009, a secure or introductory or demoted tenancy had been brought to an end pursuant to a possession order, but the order had not been executed, a replacement tenancy is treated as having arisen between the ex-landlord and the ex-tenant on that date. The conditions are (i) that the dwelling-house under the original tenancy must have been the only or principal home of the ex-tenant throughout the period from the end of the original tenancy up to and including 20 May 2009, (ii) that on 20 May 2009 the ex-landlord must have been entitled to let the dwelling-house and (iii) that the ex-landlord and the ex-tenant must not have entered into another tenancy between the end of the original tenancy and 20 May 2009.

LOCALISM ACT 2011

(c 20)

GENERAL NOTES ON LOCALISM ACT 2011

III L&T [346]

The Localism Act 2011 has introduced the concept of the flexible tenancy. The Housing Act 1985 is amended by the addition of ss 107A to 107E with consequential amendments to ss 83 and 84; see **III L&T [115.1]** to **III L&T [115.6]**. Provision is also made, by the introduction of ss 137A and 143MA of the Housing Act 1996, for introductory and demoted tenancies to become flexible tenancies: see **III L&T [293.1]** and **III L&T [296MA]**.

The 2011 Act also, by introducing ss 20C and 20D of the Housing Act 1988 (see **III L&T [228B]** to **III L&T [228C]**) prescribes the circumstances in which assured shorthold tenancies may follow on from demoted tenancies and family intervention tenancies. Amendments to s 17 of the 1988 Act introduce additional succession rights to assured tenancies: see **III L&T [223]**.

Amendments are also made to ss 213 to 215 of the Housing Act 2004 in relation to tenancy deposits: see **III L&T [322]** to **III L&T [324]**.

All amendments have been inserted in the relevant Housing Acts. In addition, ss 158 and 159 have a free-standing impact and are set out here. Those sections, together with Schedule 14, provide that, subject to certain conditions, existing secure and assured tenants are able to retain a similar level of security on exchanging their property with a social tenant with a less secure tenancy. These provisions, on transfer of secure and assured tenancies, were brought into force on 1 April 2012: SI 2012/628.

III L&T [347]

158. Secure and assured tenancies: transfer of tenancy

(1) This section applies if the tenants ("the relevant tenants") under two or more tenancies of dwelling-houses in England ("the existing tenancies") make a request in writing to the landlord under each existing tenancy asking the landlord to—

(a) permit the relevant tenant or tenants under the existing tenancy to surrender it, and

(b) grant a new tenancy of the dwelling-house let under the tenancy to another relevant tenant or other relevant tenants.

(2) The landlord must comply with the request if the following conditions are met.

(3) The first condition is that at least one of the existing tenancies is—

(a) a secure tenancy that is not *a flexible tenancy* [an old-style secure tenancy], or

(b) an assured tenancy—

(i) which is not an assured shorthold tenancy, and

(ii) under which the landlord is the Regulator of Social Housing, a private registered provider of social housing or a housing trust which is a charity.

(4) The second condition is that at least one of the existing tenancies is—

(a) a secure tenancy that *is a flexible tenancy* [is not an old-style secure tenancy], or

(b) an assured shorthold tenancy under which the landlord is the Regulator of Social Housing, a private registered provider of social housing or a housing trust which is a charity.

(5) The third condition is that the remaining existing tenancies (if any) fall within subsection (3) or (4).

(6) *The fourth condition is that at least one of the existing tenancies to which subsection (3) applies was granted before the day on which this section came into force.*

(7) The *fifth* [fourth] condition is that none of the landlords under the existing tenancies has refused to comply with the request (and see further section 159).

(8) *Subsection (9) applies where a relevant tenant's existing tenancy is—* [The new tenancy is to be granted on whatever terms the landlord determines.]

(a) *a secure tenancy that is not a flexible tenancy, or*

(b) *an assured tenancy that is not an assured shorthold tenancy.*

(9) *The new tenancy granted to the relevant tenant pursuant to this section must be—* [A landlord must, on request by a relevant tenant, inform the tenant of the terms on which a new tenancy will be granted to that tenant.]

(a) *a secure tenancy that is not a flexible tenancy, or*

(b) *an assured tenancy that is not an assured shorthold tenancy, according to the landlord's capacity to grant a tenancy of either kind.*

[(9A) Subsection (9B) applies in a case where—

(a) the request was made before section 121 of the Housing and Planning Act 2016 came into force, and

(b) one or more of the landlords had not yet complied with the request when that section came into force.

(9B) In that case any new tenancy granted in pursuance of this section to a relevant tenant whose existing tenancy is an old-style secure tenancy, or an assured tenancy that is not an assured shorthold tenancy, must be—

(a) an old-style secure tenancy, or

(b) an assured tenancy that is not an assured shorthold tenancy,

according to the landlord's capacity to grant a tenancy of either kind.]

(10) The Secretary of State may by regulations provide that this section does not apply in relation to an assured shorthold tenancy of a kind specified in the regulations.

Amendment *Text in italic is deleted and text in square brackets is inserted by the Housing and Planning Act 2016, with effect from a date to be appointed.*

III L&T [348]–III L&T [350]

159. Further provisions about transfer of tenancy under section 158

(1) A landlord may refuse to comply with a request under section 158 only on one or more of the grounds set out in Schedule 14 (and in that Schedule references to the new tenancy are to the tenancy that the landlord has been requested to grant under that section).

(2) If the landlord refuses to comply with the request otherwise than on one of those grounds, the landlord is treated for the purposes of section 158 as not having refused to comply with the request.

(3) A landlord may not rely on any of the grounds set out in Schedule 14 unless the landlord has, within the period of 42 days beginning with receipt of the relevant tenants' request, given each of the tenants a notice specifying the ground and giving particulars of it.

(4) The duty imposed on a landlord by section 158 is enforceable by injunction.

(5) The county court has jurisdiction to entertain any proceedings brought pursuant to subsection (4).

(6) In section 158, this section and Schedule 14—

(a) "secure tenancy" has the meaning given by section 79 of the Housing Act 1985,

(b) *"flexible tenancy" has the meaning given by section 107A [115B] of that Act,*

(c) "assured tenancy" and "assured shorthold tenancy" have the same meaning as in Part 1 of the Housing Act 1988, and

(d) other expressions defined in the Housing Act 1985 or the Housing Act 1988 have the same meaning as in that Act (and, if they are defined in both Acts, have the same meaning as in the Housing Act 1985).

(7) In section 160(1) of the Housing Act 1996 (cases where provisions about allocations do not apply), for the "or" at the end of paragraph (d) substitute—

"(da) is granted in response to a request under section 158 of the Localism Act 2011 (transfer of tenancy), or".

Amendment *Text in italic is deleted and text in square brackets is inserted in sub-s (6)(b), from a date to be appointed, by s 118 of, and Schedule 7 to, the Housing and Planning Act 2016.*

Sub-section (6), para (b) is repealed by the Housing and Planning Act 2016, with effect from a date to be appointed.

III L&T [348.1]

Enforcement of landlord's duty The landlord's duty to comply with the relevant tenants' request for surrender and grant of a new tenancy (provided the prescribed conditions are met) is enforceable by injunction in the county court: ss 159(4) and (5).

LANDLORD & TENANT AND HOUSING

HOUSING AND PLANNING ACT 2016

(c 22)

GENERAL NOTES ON HOUSING AND PLANNING ACT 2016

III L&T [351]

Sections 57 to 62 of the Housing and Planning Act 2016 (in force from a date to be appointed) provide a procedure by which a landlord, without the need for a court order, may recover possession of abandoned premises. Section 57 provides that, if the tenancy relates to premises in England, a private landlord may give a tenant notice which brings the tenancy to an end on the day on which the notice was given, provided certain conditions are met. Those conditions are that a prescribed amount of rent is unpaid (the 'unpaid rent condition' set out in s 58), that the landlord has given a series of warning notices as required by s 59 and that neither the tenant nor a named occupier nor deposit payer has responded in writing to those warning notices before the date specified in the notices. The methods for giving notices under ss 57 and 59 are prescribed in s 61. By s 60, a tenant whose tenancy has been brought to an end by a s 57 notice, but who had a good reason for failing to respond to the warning notices may apply to the county court, within 6 months of the notice bringing the tenancy to an end, for an order reinstating the tenancy, and the county court, if satisfied that the tenant had a good reason for not responding, may make any order it thinks fit for the purpose of reinstating the tenancy.

III L&T [352]

57. Recovering abandoned premises

A private landlord may give a tenant a notice bringing an assured shorthold tenancy to an end on the day on which the notice is given if—

(a) the tenancy relates to premises in England,
(b) the unpaid rent condition is met (see section 58),
(c) the landlord has given the warning notices required by section 59, and
(d) no tenant, named occupier or deposit payer has responded in writing to any of those

notices before the date specified in the warning notices.

III L&T [353]

58. The unpaid rent condition

(1) The unpaid rent condition is met if—

(a) rent is payable weekly or fortnightly and at least eight consecutive weeks' rent is unpaid,
(b) rent is payable monthly and at least two consecutive months' rent is unpaid,
(c) rent is payable quarterly and at least one quarter's rent is more than three months in arrears, or
(d) rent is payable yearly and at least three months' rent is more than three months in arrears.

(2) If the unpaid rent condition has been met and a new payment of rent is made before the notice under section 57 is given, the unpaid rent condition ceases to be met (irrespective of the period to which the new payment of rent relates).

(3) In this section "rent" means rent lawfully due from the tenant.

III L&T [354]

59. Warning notices

(1) Before bringing a tenancy to an end under section 57 the landlord must give three warning notices, at different times, in accordance with this section.

(2) The first two warning notices must be given to the following using one of the methods in section 61(2) or (3)—

(a) the tenant,
(b) any named occupiers, and
(c) any deposit payers.

(3) The third warning notice must be given by fixing it to some conspicuous part of the premises to which the tenancy relates.

(4) Each warning notice must explain—

(a) that the landlord believes the premises to have been abandoned,
(b) that the tenant, a named occupier or a deposit payer must respond in writing before a specified date if the premises have not been abandoned, and
(c) that the landlord proposes to bring the tenancy to an end if no tenant, named occupier or deposit payer responds in writing before that date.

(5) The date specified under subsection (4)(b) must be after the end of the period of 8 weeks beginning with the day on which the first warning notice is given to the tenant.

(6) The first warning notice may be given even if the unpaid rent condition is not yet met.

(7) The second warning notice may be given only once the unpaid rent condition has been met.

(8) The second warning notice must be given at least two weeks, and no more than 4 weeks, after the first warning notice.

(9) The third warning notice must be given before the period of 5 days ending with the date specified in the warning notices under subsection (4)(b).

(10) The Secretary of State may make regulations setting out the form that the third warning notice must take.

(11) In this Part—

"deposit payer" means a person who the landlord knows paid a tenancy deposit in relation to the tenancy on behalf of the tenant;

"named occupier" means a person named in the tenancy as a person who may live at the premises to which the tenancy relates.

III L&T [355]

60. Reinstatement

(1) Where a tenancy is brought to an end by a notice under section 57 the tenant may apply to the county court for an order reinstating the tenancy if the tenant has a good reason for having failed to respond to the warning notices.

(2) If the county court finds that the tenant had a good reason for failing to respond to the warning notices it may make any order it thinks fit for the purpose of reinstating the tenancy.

(3) An application under this section may not be made after the end of the period of 6 months beginning with the day on which the notice under section 57 is given.

III L&T [356]

61. Methods for giving notices under sections 57 and 59

(1) This section sets out the methods for giving—

(a) a notice under section 57;

(b) the first or second warning notice under section 59.

(2) The notice may given by delivering it to the tenant, named occupier or deposit payer in person.

(3) If the notice is not delivered to the tenant, named occupier or deposit payer in person it must be given by—

(a) leaving it at, or sending it to, the premises to which the tenancy relates,

(b) leaving it at, or sending it to, every other postal address in the United Kingdom that the tenant, named occupier or deposit payer has given the landlord as a contact address for giving notices,

(c) sending it to every email address that the tenant, named occupier or deposit payer has given the landlord as a contact address for giving notices, and

(d) in the case of a tenant, leaving it at or sending it to every postal address in the United Kingdom of every guarantor, marked for the attention of the tenant.

(4) In subsection (3) "guarantor", in relation to a tenant, means a person who has agreed with the landlord to guarantee the performance by the tenant of any of the tenant's obligations under the tenancy.

III L&T [357]

62. Interpretation of Part

In this Part—

"assured shorthold tenancy" has the same meaning as in Part 1 of the Housing Act 1988;

"named occupier" has the meaning given by section 59;

"private landlord" means a landlord who is not within section 80(1) of the Housing Act 1985 (the landlord condition for secure tenancies);

"tenancy deposit" , in relation to a tenancy, means any money intended to be held (by the landlord or otherwise) as security for—

(a) the performance of any obligations of the tenant arising under or in connection with the tenancy, or

(b) the discharge of any liability of the tenant arising under or in connection with the tenancy;

"warning notice" means a notice under section 59.

HOMES (FITNESS FOR HUMAN HABITATION) ACT 2018

(c 34)

GENERAL NOTE ON HOMES (FITNESS FOR HUMAN HABITATION) ACT 2018

III L&T [358]

The Homes (Fitness for Human Habitation) Act 2018 comes into force on 20 March 2019. It introduces a requirement of fitness for human habitation into residential lease and tenancies granted after that date. It achieves its purpose by insertions in the Landlord and Tenant Act 1985.

III L&T [359]

1. Fitness for human habitation

(1) The Landlord and Tenant Act 1985 is amended in accordance with subsections (2) to (5).

(2) In section 8 (implied terms as to fitness for human habitation)—

(a) in the heading, after "habitation" insert ": Wales";

(b) in subsection (1), after "house", in the first place it occurs, insert "in Wales".

(3) After section 9 (application of section 8 to certain houses occupied by agricultural workers) insert—

"9A Fitness for human habitation of dwellings in England

(1) In a lease to which this section applies of a dwelling in England (see section 9B), there is implied a covenant by the lessor that the dwelling—

(a) is fit for human habitation at the time the lease is granted or otherwise created or, if later, at the beginning of the term of the lease, and

(b) will remain fit for human habitation during the term of the lease.

(2) The implied covenant is not to be taken as requiring the lessor—

(a) to carry out works or repairs for which the lessee is liable by virtue of—

(i) the duty of the lessee to use the premises in a tenant-like manner, or

(ii) an express covenant of the lessee of substantially the same effect as that duty;

(b) to rebuild or reinstate the dwelling in the case of destruction or damage by fire, storm, flood or other inevitable accident;

(c) to keep in repair or maintain anything which the lessee is entitled to remove from the dwelling;

(d) to carry out works or repairs which, if carried out, would put the lessor in breach of any obligation imposed by any enactment (whenever passed or made);

(e) to carry out works or repairs requiring the consent of a superior landlord or other third party in circumstances where consent has not been obtained following reasonable endeavours to obtain it.

(3) The implied covenant is also not to be taken as imposing on the lessor any liability in respect of the dwelling being unfit for human habitation if the unfitness is wholly or mainly attributable to—

(a) the lessee's own breach of covenant, or

(b) disrepair which the lessor is not obliged to make good because of an exclusion or modification under section 12 (power of county court to authorise exclusions or modifications in leases in respect of repairing obligations under section 11).

(4) Any provision of a lease or of any agreement relating to a lease (whether made before or after the grant or creation of the lease) is void to the extent that it purports—

(a) to exclude or limit the obligations of the lessor under the implied covenant, or

(b) to authorise any forfeiture or impose on the lessee any penalty, disability or obligation in the event of the lessee enforcing or relying upon those obligations.

(5) Where in any proceedings before a court it is alleged that a lessor is in breach of an obligation under the implied covenant, the court may order specific performance of the obligation (regardless of any equitable rule restricting the scope of that remedy).

(6) Where a lease to which this section applies of a dwelling in England forms part only of a building, the implied covenant has effect as if the reference to the dwelling in subsection (1) included a reference to any common parts of the building in which the lessor has an estate or interest.

(7) In a lease to which this section applies of a dwelling in England, there is also implied a covenant by the lessee that the lessor, or a person authorised in writing by the lessor, may enter the dwelling for the purpose of viewing its condition and state of repair.

(8) The covenant implied by subsection (7) requires entry to the dwelling to be permitted—

(a) only at reasonable times of the day, and

(b) only if at least 24 hours' notice in writing has been given to the occupier of the dwelling.

(9) In this section—

"common parts" has the meaning given by section 60(1) of the Landlord and Tenant Act 1987;

"lease" does not include a mortgage term;

"lessee" means the person for the time being entitled to the term of a lease;

"lessor" means the person for the time being entitled to the reversion expectant on a lease.

9B Leases to which section 9A applies

(1) Section 9A applies to a lease under which a dwelling is let wholly or mainly for human habitation if either of the following applies—

- (a) the lease is for a term of less than 7 years, or
- (b) the lease is of a kind mentioned in subsection (1A) or (1AB) of section 13 (leases to which section 11 applies: secure, assured or introductory tenancies for fixed term of 7 years or more).

This is subject as follows.

(2) Section 9A does not apply to any lease of a kind mentioned in section 14 (exceptions for leases to which section 11 applies).

(3) Except as mentioned in subsections (4), (5) and (6), section 9A does not apply to a lease granted—

- (a) before the commencement date, or
- (b) on or after that date in pursuance of an agreement entered into, or an order of a court made, before the commencement date.

(4) Section 9A applies to a periodic or secure tenancy that is in existence on the commencement date, but in the case of any such tenancy the covenant implied by that section has effect in the following way—

- (a) subsection (1)(a) of that section has effect as if the reference to the later of the times there mentioned were a reference to the time that begins at the end of the period of 12 months beginning with the commencement date, and
- (b) subsection (1)(b) of that section has effect only in respect of times falling after the end of that 12 month period.

(5) Section 9A applies to a periodic or secure tenancy that comes into existence after the commencement date on expiry of a term of a lease granted before that date.

(6) Section 9A applies to a lease for a fixed term which—

- (a) is granted or renewed before the commencement date, and
- (b) is renewed for a further fixed term on or after that date,

and for this purpose the renewal on or after the commencement date is to be treated as a grant of the lease on or after that date.

(7) For the purposes of subsection (1) it is immaterial—

- (a) whether the dwelling is to be occupied under the lease or under an inferior lease derived out of it, or
- (b) that the lease also demises other property (which may consist of or include one or more other dwellings).

(8) In determining for the purposes of subsection (1)(a) whether a lease is for a term of less than 7 years—

- (a) any part of the term falling before the grant or creation is to be ignored and the lease is to be treated as a lease for a term commencing with the grant or creation;
- (b) a lease which is determinable at the option of the lessor before the expiry of 7 years from the commencement of the term is to be treated as a lease for a term of less than 7 years;
- (c) a lease (other than one to which paragraph (b) applies) is not to be treated as a lease for a term of less than 7 years if it confers on the lessee an option for renewal for a term which, together with the original term, amounts to 7 years or more.

(9) In this section—

"the commencement date" means the date on which the Homes (Fitness for Human Habitation) Act 2018 comes into force;

"lease", "lessee" and "lessor" have the same meanings as in section 9A;

"secure tenancy" has the meaning given by section 79 of the Housing Act 1985.

9C Application of section 9A to certain dwellings occupied by agricultural workers

(1) This section applies where under a contract of employment of a worker employed in agriculture—

(a) the provision of a dwelling for the worker's occupation forms part of the worker's remuneration, and

(b) the provisions of section 9A (implied term as to fitness for human habitation of dwellings in England) are inapplicable by reason only of the dwelling not being let to the worker.

(2) There is implied as part of the contract of employment (in spite of any stipulation to the contrary) a term having the same effect as the covenant that would be implied by section 9A if the dwelling were let by a lease to which that section applies.

(3) The provisions of section 9A apply accordingly—

(a) with the substitution of "employer" and "employee" for "lessor" and "lessee", and

(b) with such other modifications as may be necessary.

(4) This section does not affect—

(a) any obligation of a person other than the employer to repair a dwelling to which the covenant implied by section 9A applies by virtue of this section, or

(b) any remedy for enforcing such an obligation."

(4) In section 10 (fitncss for human habitation)—

(a) the existing text becomes subsection (1);

(b) in that subsection—

(i) after "house", in both places where it occurs, insert "or dwelling";

(ii) after "facilities for preparation and cooking of food and for the disposal of waste water;" insert—

"in relation to a dwelling in England, any prescribed hazard;";

(c) after that subsection insert—

"(2) In subsection (1) "prescribed hazard" means any matter or circumstance amounting to a hazard for the time being prescribed in regulations made by the Secretary of State under section 2 of the Housing Act 2004.

(3) The definition of "hazard" in section 2(1) of the Housing Act 2004 applies for the purposes of subsection (2) as though the reference to a potential occupier were omitted."

(5) In section 39 (index of defined expressions), after the entry in the list for "lease, lessee and lessor (generally)" insert—

"(in the provisions relating to fitness for human habitation of dwellings in England)	section 9A(9)".

(6) In section 302 of the Housing Act 1985 (management and repair of houses acquired under section 300 or retained under section 301), in paragraph (c)—

(a) for "section 8" substitute "sections 8 and 9A", and

(b) for "does" substitute "do".

LANDLORD & TENANT AND HOUSING

III L&T [360]

2. Extent, commencement and short title

(1) This Act extends to England and Wales.

(2) This Act comes into force at the end of the period of three months beginning with the day on which it is passed.

(3) This Act may be cited as the Homes (Fitness for Human Habitation) Act 2018.

LIMITATION

TABLE OF CONTENTS

LIMITATION ACT 1980

(c 58)

GENERAL NOTES ON LIMITATION ACT 1980

III LIM [1]

The full text of the 1980 Act has been included in this section save for the following:

- Section 27A Actions for recovery of property obtained through unlawful conduct etc.
- Section 27B Actions for recovery of property for purposes of an external order.
- Section 27C Actions for exploitation proceeds orders.
- Section 34 which was repealed by the Arbitration Act 1996 s 107(2), Sch 4.
- Section 37 Application to the Crown and the Duke of Cornwall
- Section 40 Transitional provisions, amendments and repeals
- Section 41 Short title, commencement and extent
- Sch 2 Transitional provisions

Sections 96–98 and Sch 6 to the Land Registration Act 2002 (at paras **III LIM [49]–III LIM [52]**) provide a new adverse possession regime for registered land from the date of their coming into force in October 2003.

For the substantive law see 28 *Halsbury's Laws* (4th edn reissue) title LIMITATION OF ACTIONS, para 801.

III LIM [1A]

The function of limitation statutes Limitation statutes seek to regulate the balance between interests which compete and sometimes conflict *viz* the interest of the claimant in having the most extensive opportunity to pursue claims for legal redress and the interest of the defendant in not having to defend stale proceedings because it is unfair for the "sword of Damocles" to hang over him indefinitely and the passage of time causes memories to fade and evidence to be lost. As Briggs LJ put it in *Hawkes v County Leasing Asset Management Ltd* [2015] EWCA Civ 1251, [2015] All ER (D) 73 (Dec) (at [28]):

> 'The limitation regime exists mainly to serve the public interest in the prohibition of stale claims. It confers a statutory defence to such claims by reference to an essentially mechanical computation of time, without regard to the merits of the claim, to any question whether the defendant deserves protection (otherwise than by reference to the elapse of time) and applies regardless of the reasons for a claim not having been brought earlier, such as the impecuniosity of the claimant or, in the case of a corporate claimant, negligence, laziness, or even disloyalty on the part of those fiduciaries or stakeholders responsible for its affairs.'

There are a number of limited exceptions to this rigid and blind application of the statutory limitation periods as set out below.

III LIM [1B]

The scope of the Act The Limitation Act 1980 sets out the time limits within which a claimant is entitled to "bring actions". The term "actions" includes "any proceeding in a court of law, including an ecclesiastical court" (see s 38(1) of the Limitation Act 1980). The Foreign Limitation Periods Act 1984 applies the limitation rules of any foreign law which is applicable to proceedings in England and Wales. The Act applies to arbitral proceedings as it applies to legal proceedings (see s 13 of the Arbitration Act 1996).

It has been said (see *Chagos Islanders v A-G* [2004] EWCA Civ 997, (2004) Times, 21 September) that the 1980 Act is intended to be a complete code (although it is a consolidating rather than codifying statute) and is accordingly to be taken (subject to the defences which are peculiar to equity) exhaustively to provide for the circumstances in which limitation defences may or may not be taken but this is subject to the important qualification that s 39 provides a saving for "other limitation enactments", that is other statutes which apply specific time limits for the bringing of certain claims whether created by those statutes or to which a time limit under the Limitation Act 1980 would otherwise apply. Amongst the many examples of such time limits are those applicable to the carriage of goods and persons by sea, road, rail and air; director's disqualification proceedings (s 6 of the Company Directors Disqualification Act 1986); employment claims in the employment tribunal principally relating to dismissal and discrimination; but note that even common law claims for breach of contract and wrongful dismissal which would be subject to 6-year time limits if brought in the ordinary courts are subject to much shorter time limits in the employment tribunal; Inheritance (Provision for Family and Dependents) Act 1975, s 4; Taxes Management Act 1970, ss 34, 36 and 43.

It is, however, open to a defendant

- to contract not to take; or
- to waive or to be estopped from invoking

a limitation defence but the requirements for establishing such a waiver or estoppel are stringent and thus rarely fulfilled: see the helpful summary in *Fortisbank SA v Trenwick International Ltd* [2005] EWHC 399 (Comm), [2005] Lloyd's Rep IR 464 at para 30 and also *Ace Insurance v Surendranath Seechurn* [2002] EWCA Civ 67, [2002] 2 Lloyds Rep 390 at para 26.

The claimant needs to show:

(a) That there is a clear, unequivocal, unambiguous and unconditional promise by the defendant that it will not raise the defence that the action is statute [or otherwise time-] barred.

(b) That the conduct relied upon is not capable of more than one explanation and, therefore, equivocal: *Allied Marine Transport Ltd v Vale do Rio Doce Navegacao SA, The Leonidas D* [1985] 2 All ER 796, [1985] 2 Lloyds Rep 18 — silence or inaction will almost always be equivocal and thus insufficient. For a (rare) case in which there was a duty to take a limitation point and thus inaction was enough see *MIOM 1 Ltd v Sea Echo ENE* [2011] EWHC 2715 (Admlty), [2012] 1 Lloyd's Rep 140 (in the context of the 2-year limitation period under s 190 of the Merchant Shipping Act 1995).

(c) That, objectively construed, the representation or promise in question was that a limitation defence would not be raised.

LIMITATION

(d) That a sufficiently unequivocal representation has been relied upon by the claimant in altering its position to its detriment or so that it would otherwise be inequitable or unconscionable for the defendant not to be held to the representation.

(e) Any such reliance must be positive in the sense that the representee must show that it attached significance to the representation alleged and acted on it. *HIH Casualty and General Insurance Limited v AXA Corporate Solutions* [2003] 1 Lloyds Rep IR 1 at [29]. If the limitation period has already expired then the claimant has lost nothing.

The mere fact of negotiations before and/or after the expiry of the limitation period cannot constitute a waiver or an estoppel: *Super Chem Products Ltd v American Life and General Insurance Co Ltd* [2004] UKPC 2, [2004] 2 All ER 358, [2004] 1 All ER (Comm) 713 and *Hillingdon London Borough Council v ARC Ltd* [2000] 3 EGLR 97, [2000] RVR 283, CA. For a rare case in which such an estoppel was established see *Saunders v Caerphilly County Borough Council* [2015] EWHC 1632 (Ch), [2015] 2 P & CR 418, [2015] All ER (D) 155 (Jun).

Parties to a contract may agree to a longer or shorter limitation period than would otherwise apply – subject to the provisions of the Unfair Contract Terms Act 1977 (see eg *Granville Oil and Chemicals Ltd v Davis Turner & Co Ltd* [2003] EWCA Civ 570, [2003] 1 All ER (Comm) 819, [2003] 2 Lloyd's Rep 356) and it is not uncommon in professional negligence litigation for the parties to agree to suspend the running of time during the currency of a "Standstill agreement" to that effect.

The court also has a limited discretion to disapply the limitation period applicable to certain specific claims: see s 32A (defamation) and s 33 (personal injury) of the Limitation Act 1980

In the case of fraud, deliberate concealment or mistake, the running of the limitation period is suspended until the claimant discovered or could with reasonable diligence have discovered the fraud, deliberate concealment or mistake: see s 32 at **III LIM [36]** below.

III LIM [1C]

Unjust enrichment The Limitation Act 1980 pre-dates the modern conception of the law of unjust enrichment and makes almost no provision for the claims which fall within its ambit. (The Law Commission's proposals for reform would have remedied this lacuna but no such reform can be expected in the foreseeable future – see **III LIM [1H]** below). There are some exceptions and so s 22(a) (**III LIM [27]**) regulates personal and proprietary claims to a share of the estate of a deceased. Restitutionary claims in respect of breach of trust or trust property are subject to s 21 (**III LIM [26]**). Contribution claims pursuant to the Civil Liability (Contribution) Act 1978 are subject to s 10 of the Act (**III LIM [12]**) and restitutionary claims pursuant to the Law Reform (Frustrated Contracts) Act 1943 fall under s 9 (sums recoverable by virtue of any enactment) (**III LIM [11]**). As for the rest, the courts have largely been resistant to the conclusion that only the equitable doctrine of laches applies and have therefore invoked s 5 (simple contract – **III LIM [7]**) more (or less) comfortably to fill the gap. In this connection see 'Restitution: overpayment' at **III LIM [7.1C]** and *Aspect Contracts (Asbestos) Ltd v Higgins Construction plc* [2015] UKSC 38.

III LIM [1D]

Burden of proof Once a limitation defence is pleaded, it is for the claimant to demonstrate that the cause of action accrued within the limitation period and once that is established, the (evidential) burden passes to the defendant to show that this is not the case; *Cartledge v E Jopling & Sons Ltd* [1963] AC 758 at 784, [1963] 1 All ER 341, HL.

III LIM [1E]

The effect of the expiry of the limitation period With three exceptions, the effect of the expiry of any limitation period under the Act is merely to bar the claimant's remedy rather than to extinguish the claim. It therefore does not of itself deprive the court of jurisdiction and must be pleaded by the defendant if it wishes to rely on it by way of defence (CPR PD 16, para 13.1). Once pleaded and, if valid, it is however a complete defence to the claim to which it applies.

In the following cases the expiry of the limitation period *does* extinguish the cause of action/title of the claimant:

- conversion (other than certain instances of theft) – s 3(2);
- defective products – s 11A(3);
- land – s 17.

III LIM [1F]

The running of time Time begins to run from the date on which the cause of action accrues. This is a matter of substantive rather than procedural law and depends upon the precise legal ingredients of the claim in question. In *Letang v Cooper* [1965] 1 QB 232 (at 242–243) Lord Diplock said that:

"A cause of action is simply a factual situation the existence of which entitles one person to obtain from the court a remedy against another person."

A cause of action comprises:

"every fact which it would be necessary for the plaintiff to prove if traversed, in order to support his right to the judgment of the court":

(see *Read v Brown* (1888) 22 QBD 128 affirmed in *Coburn v Colledge* [1897] 1 QB 702). Query (as Longmore LJ rhetorically wondered in *Aspect Contracts (Asbestos) Ltd v Higgins Construction plc* [2013] EWCA Civ 1541, [2013] 49 EG 77 (CS) whether a claim for a negative declaration (ie of non-liability) is subject to the Limitation Act and therefore capable of being statute barred since a cause of action conventionally involves an assertion of entitlement.

Generally, time stops running when the claim is "brought". This is not the issue of the claim form (which is the start of the proceedings for most purposes) but instead when the claim form is received by the court for the purposes of such issue: *Barnes v St Helens Metropolitan Borough Council* [2006] EWCA Civ 1372, [2007] 3 All ER 525, [2007] PIQR P118.

Time starts to run from the day after the day on which the cause of action arose (since parts of days are ignored): *Marren v Dawson Bentley and Co Ltd* [1961] 2 QB 135, [1961] 2 All ER 270.

The claim form must be despatched to the defendant within its validity period CPR PD 7, paras 5.1 and 5.2 - four months for service within the jurisdiction and six months if serving outside the jurisdiction (see CPR 7.5) although these periods are capable (in limited circumstances) of extension by the court (see CPR 7.6).

It is common for claimants who are not yet ready to serve proceedings and/or plead a detailed claim to issue "protective" proceedings in reliance upon the time allowed for service in order to preserve the limitation position. But note that in any case in which the claim form has been issued but not yet served it is open to the defendant to serve a notice on the claimant requiring its service in not less than 14 days. The exercise of this right is very rarely encountered and obviously depends, amongst other things, on the defendant knowing that a claim form has been issued (see CPR 7.7).

Where the claim form, request for issue and the correct fee are shown to have been lodged with the court office within time, the claim is not statute barred even though the papers are mislaid within the office and a second set has to be submitted for issue at a time when the limitation period has run out: *Page v Hewetts Solicitors* [2012] EWCA Civ 805.

Where the local limitation period is suspended as regards proceedings in the country where the cause of action arose, because of a local ban on such proceedings, the suspension cannot be invoked to stop time running for the purposes of proceedings in the United Kingdom since the local ban has no application to such proceedings: *Ministry of Defence v Iraqi Civilians* [2016] UKSC 25, [2016] All ER (D) 88 (May).

III LIM [1G]

The effect of the commencement of insolvency proceedings In general, limitation periods cease to run at the commencement of the winding up (or, as the case may be, bankruptcy) so long as they had not already expired by that date: *Re General Rolling Stock Co* (1872) 7 Ch App 646 and *Financial Services Compensation Scheme Ltd v Larnell (Insurances) Ltd* [2005] EWCA Civ 1408, [2006] QB 808, [2006] 2 WLR 751. This principle does not apply to companies in administrative receivership.

For the post-dissolution position see ss 1029–1032 of the Companies Act 2006 in Companies at **III COM [1022]–[1029]**. Section 1032 provides, so far as immediately relevant, as follows:

'(1) The general effect of an order by the court for restoration to the register is that the company is deemed to have continued in existence as if it had not been dissolved or struck off the register.

...

(3) The court may give such directions and make such provision as seems just for placing the company and all other persons in the same position (as nearly as may be) as if the company had not been dissolved or struck off the register.'

Typically, the exercise of the discretion to give directions pursuant to s 1032(3) involves disapplying the limitation period between dissolution/striking off and restoration for the benefit of creditors (see *Davy v Pickering* [2015] EWHC 380 (Ch), [2015] 2 BCLC 116, [2015] All ER (D) 238 (Feb) for a recent example of additional directions which may be 'just' in such a case). However, as the sub-section contemplates, a similar direction may be made in favour of the company but only, it seems, in exceptional circumstances given that its effect is completely to override the statutory limitation regime. Thus, fairness will generally require that the company, like any other claimant faced with a limitation defence, should be left to attempt to meet that defence by recourse to the statutory regime in the 1980 Act: see *Regent Leisuretime v Natwest Finance Ltd* [2003] EWCA Civ 391 and *Hawkes v County Leasing Asset Management Ltd* [2015] EWCA Civ 1251, [2015] All ER (D) 73 (Dec).

The making of a bankruptcy order does not stop time running in respect of debts which are not included in the bankruptcy: *Anglo-Manx Group Ltd v Aitken* [2002] BPIR 215.

III LIM [1H]

Proposals for reform In 2002 the Law Commission's Report on Limitation of Actions (Law Commission Report 270) proposed the enactment of a standard limitation period of three years which would run from the date the claimant knows, or ought reasonably to have known, the facts which give rise to the cause of action, the identity of the defendant and, if the claimant has suffered injury, loss or damage or the defendant has received a benefit, that the injury, loss, damage or benefit was significant. Defendants to all but personal injury claims would be protected by a "long stop" preventing claims from being brought more than ten years after the relevant events took place. Although these recommendations received broad acceptance by the then government, reform has been slow to materialise. In December 2008 the Leader of the House of Commons announced the Government's intention to publish a draft Civil Law Reform Bill in 2009 which would include proposed changes to the law of limitation but the published bill did not do so and the then Government indicated in November 2009 that in the light of the remedy by intervening judicial decisions of the most pressing problems identified by the Law Commission and the high cost of reform it had decided against legislation. The Government has since changed but there is no indication of any alteration in this attitude.

III LIM [2]

1. Time limits under Part I subject to extension or exclusion under Part II

(1) This Part of this Act gives the ordinary time limits for bringing actions of the various classes mentioned in the following provisions of this Part.

(2) The ordinary time limits given in this Part of this Act are subject to extension or exclusion in accordance with the provisions of Part II of this Act.

III LIM [3]

2. Time limit for actions founded on tort

An action founded on tort shall not be brought after the expiration of six years from the date on which the cause of action accrued.

III LIM [3.1]

Personal Injury See s 11 below at para **III LIM [13]**.

III LIM [3.2]

Founded on tort A tort consists in "a breach of duty which gives a private law right to the party injured to recover compensatory damages at common law from the party causing the injury": *Banque Bruxelles Lambert SA v Eagle Star Insurance Co Ltd* [1997] AC 191, HL. Section 2 of the Limitation Act 1980 is drawn in broad terms and was intended to contemplate new rights. Claims for damages in respect of breaches of European Community law by the UK government by its enactment of the Merchant Shipping Act 1988 were claims in tort within s 2 rather than s 9 of the Limitation Act 1980: *R v Secretary of State for Transport, ex p Factortame Ltd (No 7)* [2001] 1 WLR 942.

No period of limitation applies to the power of the Office of Fair Trading to impose fines pursuant to s 36 of the Competition Act 1998 for infringements of the Chapter 1 prohibition in that Act. The word 'action' in neither s 2 nor s 9 of the Limitation Act applies to the inception of administrative investigations and so does not apply to the issue of either a statement of objections or a penalty notice by the OFT: *Quarmby Construction Company Ltd v Office of Fair Trading* [2011] CAT 11.

A claim for a declaration that someone had not committed a tort does not fall within s 2 whether directly or by analogy. (The position is the same in relation to non-liability for breach of contract and s 5 of the Act): see *Aspect Contracts (Asbestos) Ltd v Higgins Construction plc* [2015] UKSC 38, [2015] 4 All ER 482, [2015] 1 WLR 2961.

III LIM [3.2A]

Deliberate assault Claims for injuries arising from deliberate assaults fall within the meaning of "negligence, nuisance or breach of duty" in section 11(1) and are thus subject to the special three-year limitation period applicable to such claims (and also therefore to the discretion under section 33 to disapply the limitation period) rather than the fixed six-year limitation period under section 2. So held the House of Lords in *A v Hoare* [2008] UKHL 6, [2008] 1 AC 844, [2008] 2 WLR 311, [2008] 2 All ER 1, [2008] 1 FLR thereby overruling (in accordance with *Practice Statement (Judicial Precedent)* [1966] 1 WLR 1234) its earlier decision in *Stubbings v Webb* [1993] AC 498, [1993] 1 All ER 322, HL. In *Letang v Cooper* [1964] 2 All ER 929 the Court of Appeal had held that trespass to the person amounted to "breach of duty" within the meaning of what was then the proviso to s 2(1) of the Limitation Act 1939. The Court of Appeal did so in reliance upon the dictum of Adam J in *Kruber v Grzesiak* [1963] VR 621 that

> "I would see no sufficient reason for excluding an action for trespass to the person] from the description of an action for damages for breach of duty, especially when it is provided that the duty may be one existing independently of any contract or any provision made by or under a statute. After all, do not all torts arise from breach of duty – the tort of trespass to the person arising from the breach of a general duty not to inflict direct and immediate injury to the person of another either intentionally or negligently in the absence of lawful excuse?"

In preserving the words "negligence, nuisance or breach of duty" when it came to enact the Limitation Act 1975, the House of Lords in *A v Hoare* concluded that parliament must have intended them to bear the meaning which they had previously been given in the courts of England and Australia.

The decision in *A v Hoare* brings to an ultimately satisfactory conclusion the unfortunate and unjust *cul-de-sac* into which English jurisprudence had ventured in respect of the limitation period applicable to deliberate assaults. In this regard see *Stubbings v Webb* [1993] AC 498, [1993] 1 All ER 322, HL itself (which was referred, without success for the plaintiff, to the European Court of Human Rights in *Stubbings v United Kingdom* (1996) 23 EHRR 213, [1997] 3 FCR 157, [1997] 1 FLR 105, EHCR.

The problem was brought into rather sharper focus in *S v W* [1995] 1 FLR 862; [1995] PIQR P470, sub nom *Seymour v Williams* [1995] PIQR P470, CA, where the plaintiff brought proceedings against her father for alleged physical and sexual abuse and against her mother for breaching her parental duty by permitting the abuse to occur. Applying *Stubbings*, the claim against the father was held to be statute barred under s 2 of the Act but the claim against the mother was held to be subject to section 11 and thus capable of an extension to the applicable 3-year limitation period under s 33.

The courts repeatedly recognised that a state of affairs in which a claim in respect of the *less* culpable conduct enjoys a more flexible limitation period represented a serious anomaly in the law. The Law Commission recommended that claims for intentionally and negligently caused personal injury should be subject to the same limitation rules, namely a 3 year limitation period which the court would have a discretionary power to disapply. (See Limitation of Actions (Law Com No 270), paras 1.5, 3.156, 3.162, 3.169 and Appendix A, Draft Bill, clauses 1, 2, 12 and 38.) But despite the Government's acceptance of this report no parliamentary time has been found for the necessary legislation. In *A v Hoare* [2005] EWHC 2161 (QB) *Stubbings* was therefore applied in another hard case. The claimant was the victim of an attempted rape by a serial sexual offender. He was sentenced to life imprisonment for that and a number of other sexual offences. The primary limitation period expired in February 1994 and any civil claim during that period would have been futile since he had no money. In 2004, however, he won £7 million on the National Lottery. A issued proceedings against him in December 2004. The claimant failed in the High Court (Times, 27 October 2005) and Court of Appeal ([2006] 1 WLR 2320, [2006] 2 FLR 727, Times, April 28, 2006 where it was conjoined with *H v Suffolk County Council & Secretary of State for Constitutional Affairs, X v Wandsworth London Borough Council*) on the basis that *Stubbings* was binding upon them. Moreover, since the 6-year limitation period under s 2 had expired before the Human Rights Act 1998 had come into force, s 3(1) of that Act could not be used to construe s 11 of the Limitation Act differently from the House of Lords in *Stubbings*.

The decision in *A v Hoare* also removed the need for claimants to deploy the rather artificial claim of "systemic negligence" against employers/supervisors of the tortfeasor in order to evade the consequences of the expiry of the limitation period under s 2. See **III LIM [13.1]** for cases in which an institution is sued for the indecent acts of its employees towards those in its care.

LIMITATION

III LIM [3.3]

"Shall not be brought" The date of bringing proceedings for the purposes of the Limitation Act 1980 is not necessarily the same date as the start of the proceedings under the CPR. Under the Rules, proceedings are started when the court issues a claim form at the request of the claimant and a claim form is issued on the date entered on the form by the court: see CPR 7.2(1), (2). This date will be relevant for the purposes of, for example, costs and Part 36 payments. However, proceedings are "brought" for the purposes of the Limitation Act 1980 and any other relevant statute when the claim form is received in the court office: see the Practice Direction to CPR Part 7, para 5.1 (see **CPR PD 7**). Note that although the court itself will record the date on which the claim form was received by the court (para 5.2), it is recommended that where the expiry of the limitation period is approaching, the parties themselves should make arrangements to record the date (para 5.4).

In *St Helens Metropolitan Borough Council v Barnes* [2006] EWCA Civ 1372, [2007] 1 WLR 879 (considered and explained by the Court of Appeal in *Page v Hewetts Solicitors* [2012] EWCA Civ 805, [2012] All ER (D) 78 (Jun)) it was held that the question when an action is 'brought' is a matter of construction of the Limitation Act not of the CPR or its Practice Directions. The ratio of *St Helens v Barnes* is that once the claimant has delivered his request for the issue of a claim form (accompanied by the claim form and fee) to the court office he has 'brought' his action. The policy underlying this construction of the Act is that the claimant has then done all that is required of him and he should not be responsible for any subsequent shortcomings of the court; as Lewison LJ put it (at para [25] of *Page v Hewetts*) 'It is, alas, not unknown for the court to fail to follow the systems that should have been followed; and to mislay important documents'. The fee which accompanies the claim form must be the correct fee, if it is not then the claimant has not done all that is required of it and the action is not brought – see *Page v Hewetts Solicitors* [2013] EWHC 2845 (Ch), [2013] All ER (D) 189 (Sep) where it was held on the hearing of a preliminary issue directed by the Court of Appeal that the fee of £990 which had been lodged with the claim form by the claimant's solicitors was incorrect and thus insufficient since this was the issue fee required for a money claim whereas the claim form also sought an account of profits which attracted an additional fee of £400. The claim had not, therefore, been brought in time.

The effect of the expiry of the limitation period is generally that the remedy, but not the right, is barred (see *C & M Matthews Ltd v Marsden Building Society* [1951] Ch 758 for the source of this proposition in respect of claims in tort). There are exceptions: see, in particular, ss 3 and 4 (conversion/theft), s 17 (title to land), s 11A(3) (consumer protection against defective products) and s 14B(2) (the long-stop in cases of latent damage) where the cause of action is extinguished. Where, however, the remedy only is barred, the limitation defence must be specifically pleaded by the defendant. If it is not, then the court may proceed to decide upon the merits of the claim notwithstanding the existence of a clear limitation defence.

III LIM [3.4]

"Six years from" The day on which the cause of action accrued is excluded from the computation of the period within which the action should be brought: see *Marren v Dawson Bentley & Co Ltd* [1961] 2 QB 135, [1961] 2 All ER 270. If the court office is closed all day on the last day of the period, the period would be extended until the next day on which the court offices were open: see *Pritam Kaur v S Russell & Sons Ltd* [1973] QB 336, [1973] 1 All ER 617.

However, no extra days will be added where the court is open but entry is refused: *Croke v Secretary of State for Communities and Local Government* [2016] EWHC 2484 (Admin).

The exclusion of the day in which the cause of action accrued does not apply if it accrued on the first stroke of midnight: *Matthew v Sedman* [2017] EWHC 3527 (Ch).

III LIM [3.5]

The date on which the cause of action accrued Where the tort is actionable *per se* (intentional trespass) time runs from the date of its commission; where there is a continuing tort, such as a continuing nuisance, so long as it continues it gives rise to a fresh cause of action, but damages can only be recovered in respect of that part of the wrong which occurred within the period of limitation prior to the commencement of proceedings: *Cartwright v GKN Sankey Ltd* [1972] 2 Lloyd's Rep 242.

Where the tort is actionable only on proof of damage time runs from the date of the damage: *Pirelli General Cable Works Ltd v Oscar Faber & Partners* [1983] 2 AC 1, [1983]1 All ER 65, HL. This is so even where the victim is wholly ignorant of its occurrence (see, however, the decision of the Privy Council in *Invercargill City Council v Hamlin* [1996] AC 624, [1996] 1 All ER 756 for a different approach (albeit in New Zealand law) based on the nature of the damage). In *Abbott v Will Gannon & Smith Ltd* [2005] EWCA Civ 198, [2005] BLR 195, [2005] PNLR 30, (2005) Times, April 28 the Court of Appeal held that *Pirelli* had not been expressly or implied overruled by the decision of the House of Lords in *Murphy v Brentwood District Council* [1991] 1 AC 398, [1990] 3 WLR 414, [1990] 2 All ER 908. The harshness of this rule has been ameliorated in part by the date of knowledge provisions in respect of personal injury in ss 11,12 and 14 (see **III LIM [13]**, **III LIM [15]** and **III LIM [17]**); defective products in s 11A (see **III LIM [14]**) and negligence (other than personal injury) in s 14A (see **III LIM [18]**).

In withdrawal of support cases a new cause of action accrues with each subsidence even though each subsidence results from the same excavation: see *Darley Main Colliery Co v Mitchell* (1886) 11 App Cas 127. In *Phonographic Performance Ltd v Department of Trade and Industry* [2004] EWHC 1795 (Ch), [2004] 1 WLR 2893, [2005] 1 All ER 369, [2005] RPC 8, (2004) Times, 27 August, it was held (applying *Darley*) that a claim that the defendant department had failed properly to implement Council Directive 92/100 related to a continuing breach in respect of which a new cause action accrued every time damage was suffered therefrom.

In a case where the Law Society relied on negligent reports by a firm of accountants that a fraudulent solicitor's accounts were in order and was subsequently called on to indemnify the clients who had been defrauded, it was held that the Law Society's cause of action against the accountants accrued when the client made a claim, not at the much earlier date when a *purely* contingent liability to the client arose out of the solicitor's fraud: *Law Society v Sephton & Co (A Firm)* [2006] UKHL 22, [2006] 2 AC 543, [2006] 3 All ER 401, (2006) Times, 11 May. The mere possibility of a claim on the fund did not constitute actual damage so as to complete and cause the accrual of the cause of action. See the fuller discussion below at **III LIM [3.6]**.

In claims against the government for *Francovich* damages for its failure properly to implement EU law, a cause of action accrued to claimants who had suffered personal injury at the time of the occurrence of those injuries in circumstances where, but for that default in implementation, the claims for personal injury would have been more valuable: *Spencer v Secretary of Work and Pensions; Moore v Secretary of State for Transport* [2008] EWCA Civ 750, [2008] 3 CMLR 429, [2008] ICR 1359, [2008] IRLR 911, [2008] Times, 24 July.

Section 2(2) of the Torts (Interference with Goods) Act 1977 provides that an action lies in conversion for loss or destruction of goods and corresponds with the prior common law tort of detinue in respect of which it was held in *Clayton v Le Roy* [1911] 2 KB 1031, [1911–13] All ER Rep 284, CA that the accrual of the cause of action requires a demand for the goods to be returned *and* an unequivocal refusal to return them. It has been held that *Clayton* applies to the successor statutory tort (see *Schwarzschild v Harrods Ltd* [2008] EWHC 521 (QB), [2008] All ER (D) 299 (Mar)) and is to be preferred (save in an exceptional factual case) to other authorities which seem to suggest that mere neglect or failure to comply with a demand can qualify as refusal.

III LIM [3.6]

Professional negligence Where a person assumes responsibility to perform professional services for someone who relies on those services, a duty in the tort of negligence to exercise reasonable skill and care arises even if the services are performed under a contract between those parties: see *Henderson v Merrett Syndicates* [1995] 2 AC 145, [1994] 3 All ER 506, HL. The limitation period for both contract and tort claims is six years; but time in contract runs from the date of breach, while in negligence it runs from the occurrence of damage. Damage may occur later than the breach which causes it, in which case claims in the tort of negligence may provide a more generous time limit even without the benefit of the latent damage provisions, which apply in tort but not contract (see **III LIM [18]** below).

However, in *Nykredit Mortgage Bank plc v Edward Erdman Group Ltd (No 2)* [1998] 1 All ER 305 Lord Nicholls said that:

> within the bounds of sense and reasonableness the policy of the law should be to advance, rather than retard, the accrual of a cause of action. This is especially so if the law provides parallel causes of action in contract and in tort in respect of the same conduct. The disparity between the time when these parallel causes of action arise should be smaller, rather than greater.

In *Forster v Outred & Co* [1982] 2 All ER 753, [1982] 1 WLR 86, the plaintiff had signed a mortgage on her farm which secured a third party's business loan to her son. That business was a failure and the plaintiff was required to pay a substantial sum to the lender. She brought a claim against her solicitors alleging that they had negligently failed to explain the transaction to her. The question arose whether she suffered damage when she executed the mortgage (more than six years before the claim was brought) or when she was called upon to pay. The Court of Appeal adopted [at pages 94 and 98] the following proposition as correctly stating the law as to the meaning of "actual damage"

> any detriment, liability or loss capable of assessment in money terms and it includes liabilities which may arise on a contingency, particularly a contingency over which the

LIMITATION

> plaintiff has no control; things like loss of earning capacity, loss of a chance or bargain, loss of profit, losses incurred from onerous provisions or covenants in leases . . .

The Court of Appeal concluded that the plaintiff had suffered loss on execution of the mortgage because (as Dunn LJ put it at 100)

> as soon as she executed the mortgage the plaintiff not only became liable under its express terms but also – and more importantly – the value of the equity of redemption of her property was reduced. Before she executed the mortgage deed she owned the property free from incumbrances; thereafter she became the owner of a property subject to a mortgage. That, in my view, was a quantifiable loss and as from that date her cause of action against her solicitor was complete . . .

Although the court's judgment was given *extempore* on an interlocutory application the decision in *Forster v Outred* has assumed the status of *locus classicus* and its statement of principle has been variously followed and applied and was approved by the House of Lords in *Nykredit Mortgage Bank plc v Edward Erdman Group Ltd (No 2)* [1998] 1 All ER 305, [1997] 1 WLR 1627, HL. Whether the damage in a professional negligence case occurs at the time of the claimant's reliance on the defendant's advice or at some later date is a question of fact in each case. Immediate damage was held to have been suffered in *Knapp v Ecclesiastical Insurance Group plc* [1998] PNLR 172, CA, where the plaintiff paid a premium for a fire insurance policy which was voidable because of his broker's negligent failure to disclose material facts. The loss was immediate because from the outset he did not have a policy which was binding on the insurer. (See also the reinsurance case of *Iron Trade Mutual Insurance Co Ltd v J K Buckenham Ltd* [1990] 1 All ER 808.)

Similarly, in *D W Moore & Co Ltd v Ferrier* [1988] 1 WLR 267 a solicitor was instructed to prepare contracts for a new director of an insurance business but negligently failed to draft effective post-termination restrictive covenants. The Court of Appeal held that the contracts were immediately less valuable than they would have been with effective covenants and that actual damage was therefore suffered on execution rather than years later when their enforcement was attempted. (See also the often-cited case of *Bell v Peter Browne & Co* [1990] 2 QB 495.) The essential feature of these "transaction" cases where damage is suffered in reliance on the professional's advice is that the claimant has paid money, transferred property, incurred liabilities or suffered diminution in the value of an asset and in return obtained less than he should have got even if there may be further (and greater) loss which is contingent such (in *Forster*) as the failure of the son's business and the enforcement of the security, the occurrence (in *Knapp*) of the putatively insured fire and the making of a claim on the policy and (in *Moore*) the departure of the director for a competing business. In each case the claimant was financially worse at the outset in a way which was measurable even if only with difficulty. Thus in the important decision of the High Court of Australia in *Wardley Australia Ltd v State of Western Australia* (1992) 175 CLR 514, 109 ALR 247 Brennan J said (175 CLR 514 at 536) that

> A plaintiff may suffer economic loss or damage in a number of ways: by payment of money, by transfer of property, by diminution in the value of an asset or by the incurring of a liability. Whether loss or damage is actually suffered when any of these events occurs depends on the value of the benefit, if any, acquired by the plaintiff by paying the money, transferring the property, having the value of the asset diminished or incurring the liability. If the plaintiff acquires no benefit, the loss or damage is suffered when the event occurs. At that time, the plaintiff's net worth is reduced. And that is so even if the quantification of that loss or damage is not then ascertainable.

However, the position may be otherwise where the transaction in question imposes benefits and burdens. As Brennan J went on to say

> But if a benefit is acquired by the plaintiff, it may not be possible to ascertain whether loss or damage has been suffered at the time when the burden is borne – that is, at the time of the payment, the transfer, the diminution in value of the asset or the incurring of the liability. A transaction in which there are benefits and burdens results in loss or damage only if an adverse balance is struck.

This "adverse balance" approach is illustrated by the decision of the House of Lords in *Nykredit Mortgage Bank plc v Edward Erdman Group Ltd (No 2)* [1998] 1 All ER 305, [1997] 1 WLR 1627, HL where, by reason of a surveyor's negligent valuation the plaintiff lender had acquired what proved to be inadequate security for his loan. It was held that damage did not occur immediately but instead when the amount owed to the lender exceeded the value of its rights under the transaction (ie the value of the borrower's covenant plus security). Reference should be made to the speech of Lord Nicholls for the application of the "basic comparison" in cases where, but for the negligence in question, the lender would have made no loan at all. See also *First National Commercial Bank plc v Humberts (a firm)* [1995] 2 All ER 673, CA and also *Arrowhead Capital Finance Ltd (In liq) v KPMG LLP* [2012] EWHC 1801 (Comm), [2012] STC 2503, [2012] PNLR 30.

An analogous situation can arise in cases where solicitors conduct litigation negligently. There it has been said that the claimant's claim is a chose in action which is effectively entrusted to the solicitor to bring it to maturity. Time will begin to run in a claim in respect of the negligence of the solicitor in question when the value of the chose in action is substantially diminished (*Khan v R M Falvey & Co (a firm)* [2002] EWCA Civ 400, [2002] PNLR 28, (2002) Times, 12 April applying *Nykredit*) or extinguished by permitting it to become statute-barred or to be struck out (*Hopkins v Mackenzie* (1994) 138 Sol Jo LB 222, 23 BMLR 132, CA – although, to the extent that *Hopkins* held that time did not start to run until the claim is struck out, *Khan* held it to have been wrongly decided) or "doomed to failure" because there was no arguable defence to an application to strike the claim out (see *Hatton v Chafes* [2003] PNLR 489 at paras 23 and 82.) See also *Cohen v Kingsley Napley (A Firm)* [2005] EWHC 899 (QB), (2005) PNLR 37.

Since the cause of action in such a case can accrue when there is at least a significant risk of an adverse event occurring rather than when it in fact occurs, the effect of *Khan v Falvey* clearly extends beyond the limited scenario of striking-out by reason of delay. In *Polley v Warner Goodman & Street Solicitors (A Firm)* [2003] PNLR 784, CA, the claimant's solicitors failed to serve a County Court summons within the four-month period of its validity but they obtained an extension of time to do so *ex parte*. The defendant subsequently applied to set-this order for an extension aside. It was held that since there was no good reason for an extension and thus no defence to the application to set-aside, the cause of action accrued at the time by which the solicitors should reasonably have served the summons ie the last day of its original period of validity. In *Berney v Saul (Thomas) (t/a Thomas Saul & Co Solicitors)* [2013] EWCA Civ 640, [2013] PNLR 26, the Court of Appeal took the view that it was unnecessary to try to reconcile the arguable inconsistency between Hopkins, Khan and Hatton since the question of accrual is essentially a factual question in the particular case. In *Berney*, the claimant was considered to have had an unanswerable claim for personal injury which she alleged that she had been forced to settle for less than it was worth by reason of the defendant solicitor's negligence. In a claim in respect of the negligent conduct of litigation it does not necessarily follow that actionable damage occurs only on settlement and the Court in *Berney* took differing views about whether this was so (and which repay study). They were all agreed, however, that no actionable loss had occurred more than 6 years before the professional negligence claim was brought.

In *Law Society v Sephton & Co (A Firm)* [2006] UKHL 22, [2006] 2 AC 543, [2006] 3 All ER 401 the question arose whether purely contingent damage was actual damage for the purposes of the tort of negligence. The defendant accountants had negligently approved the accounts of a solicitor who was in fact misappropriating large amounts of money from client accounts. As a consequence of those appropriations various clients made claims for payments from the Solicitors Compensation Fund which the claimant administered. It sought damages in respect of the compensation payments which it had then made. The question arose whether the claimant suffered damage when each appropriation occurred or when each claim for compensation was made (or indeed when it resolved to meet a particular claim.) It was clear that the making of an appropriation gave rise only to the possibility of the society receiving and having to pay a claim: was this possibility damage? Their Lordships considered that the claimant's loss was purely contingent until a claim was made and that there was no case – apart perhaps from the decision of the Court of Appeal in *Gordon v JB Wheatley & Co* [2000] Lloyd's Rep PN 605, (2000) Times, 6 June, the correctness of which they doubted – in which the incurring of a contingent liability was held to be actual damage. Indeed they were influenced by the view taken by the High Court of Australia in *Wardley* (supra) that there was no such English authority:

> It has been contended that the principle underlying the English decisions extends to the point that a plaintiff sustains loss on entry into an agreement notwithstanding that the loss to which the plaintiff is subjected by the agreement is a loss upon a contingency. For our part, we doubt that the decisions travel so far. Rather, it seems to us, the decisions in cases which involve contingent loss were decisions which turned on the plaintiff sustaining measurable loss at an earlier time, quite apart from the contingent loss which threatened at a later date . . . If . . . the English decisions properly understood support the proposition that where, as a result of the defendant's negligent misrepresentation, the plaintiff enters into a contract which exposes him or her to a contingent loss or liability, the plaintiff first suffers loss or damage on entry into the contract, we do not agree with them. In our opinion, in such a case, the plaintiff sustains no actual damage until the contingency is fulfilled and the loss becomes actual; until that happens the loss is prospective and may never be incurred. (175 CLR 514 at 531)

The High Court of Australia had already explained that despite the inclusion of "liabilities which may arise on a contingency" in the definition of actual damage given by the Court of Appeal in *Forster*, the decision in that case could be explained "by reference to the immediate effect of the execution of the mortgage on the value of the plaintiff's equity of redemption". Lords Hoffmann and Scott considered that the High Court's analysis provided the answer to the appeal in *Law Society v Sephton* and the House decided that since the possibility of having to pay money in the future was not damage until that contingency crystallised, time only began to run against the claimant when a claim for compensation was made. The treatment of *Law Society v Sephton* in subsequent cases indicates that it is to be understood as turning on its very special facts if, which is also open to question, it was rightly decided at all.

In *Axa Insurance Ltd v Akther & Darby Solicitors* [2009] EWCA Civ 1166, [2010] 1 WLR 1662, [2010] PNLR 10 the claimant insurer had written "after the event" (ATE) legal expenses insurance policies. A panel of solicitors took on personal injury claims for claimants each of which had to have at least a 51% chance of success and a quantum of more than £1,000 for the relevant ATE policies to be issued. The claimant made serious losses from the policies and claimed that the defendant solicitors had (1) negligently assessed claims as having the requisite chances of success and (2) subsequently failed to conduct the claims competently and failed to notify the claimant when a claim's prospects of success fell below 51%. The question arose whether the claimant had suffered actual damage in respect of the negligent vetting and conduct of claims only when a claim came to be made on the relevant ATE policy or at an earlier stage. By a majority (Arden and Longmore LJJ) the Court of Appeal (distinguishing *Law Society v Sephton & Co*) characterised the case as comprising a flawed bilateral transaction rather than a merely contingent liability because

- there was measurable loss at the inception of the policies in that they were worth less than they would have been had there been proper vetting by the defendant solicitor;
- the premiums, which were for reserve and investment against future claims, had been harmed or undermined by the negligence of the solicitors;
- from inception, the greater risk of a claim meant that the premiums were not as great as they should have been and, correspondingly, there was a greater risk of a claim than there should have been.

While rejecting any rigid categorisation of cases, the Court identified *Axa* as a case involving a transaction which had been entered into in reliance upon the professional defendant's advice. This made it easier to conclude that time began to run from the time of entry into the transaction because, on the various analyses of the majority, the claimant had received "a less valuable bundle of rights" by reason of the negligence. It followed that the cause of action in respect of the "vetting claims" had accrued at the time of the issue of the ATE policies and, in respect of the "conduct claims" which alleged a failure to notify, at the time when notification should have taken place.

The length and complexity of the judgments indicates that *Sephton* is not necessarily easy to apply. Arden LJ noted the apparently inexplicable difference in the *limitation* treatment of a claimant who gives security for what would otherwise be a contingent liability and a claimant who does not (and which was said in both *Wardley* and *Sephton* to explain the result in *Forster*). The absence of anything resembling a security in *Axa* influenced Lloyd LJ in his dissenting conclusion (which for this reason applied rather than distinguished *Sephton*) that damage was indeed contingent until the claimant first came under an actual liability to make a payment under the relevant ATE policy.

Longmore LJ said (at para 83 of *Axa*, echoing what Lord Nicholls had said in *Nykredit)*

> "In a case where, on any view, the natural cause of action is for breach of contract, the courts should not favour a much later date of accrual for the co-existing action in tort unless they are compelled to do so."

This could be said to be a necessary *quid pro quo* for the recognition in *Henderson v Merrett* of a parallel duty in tort in the first place but the distinction currently made between secured and unsecured cases seems to lack principled justification and for that reason to justify the consideration of the Supreme Court.

In *Pegasus Management Holdings SCA v Ernst & Young (a firm)* [2010] EWCA Civ 181, [2010] 3 All ER 297, [2010] 2 All ER (Comm) 191 the question of actual or contingent damage arose once again. The facts were complicated but, in essence, the claimant sued the defendant tax advisers and accountants alleging that but for their negligence a substantial charge to capital gains tax would have been avoided. On a preliminary issue as to limitation, it was argued that no financial loss (and thus no actual damage) was suffered until the CGT charge became unavoidable on the happening of a number of foreseeable but uncertain future events and that this was later than the date on which the main transaction – subscribing to $150m of shares – had occurred. After an extensive review of the relevant authorities, the Court of

Appeal held that the case fell into the "wrong transaction" category *ie but for* the alleged negligence of the defendants, the claimant would still have entered into a similar transaction. The key question was then whether the claimant had obtained what he should have obtained from entering into the actual transaction.

In a wrong transaction case this was not to be answered by a purely financial analysis *ie* at what point was the claimant financially worse off, but could take into account the fact that the transaction which did take place did not provide the claimant with all that it should have received (see *Baker v Ollard and Bentley (a firm)* (1982) 126 Sol Jo 593, CA and the cases which follow it):

> "If a professional defendant is instructed by his client to achieve result X and he negligently achieves result Y that is equally valuable in monetary terms but does not give the client what he ought to have received, it would be surprising if he could answer the client's claim by saying he had suffered no financial loss."

Per Rimer LJ in *Pegasus* at para 82.

The connection between the missing feature of the transaction and the suffering of damage is not automatic but will usually be a matter of ready inference and then, if it is the case that greater or more obviously *financial* loss depend on the occurrence of possible but not certain future events, this goes to the assessment of quantum rather than to the existence of liability.

In *Pegasus* the result of the transaction was that without the corporate structure which the defendants should have advised, the claimant lacked the flexibility he would have had and this was irremediable even though some, but not necessarily all, of the CGT liability might still have been avoidable. The claimant was therefore immediately in a materially worse commercial position than he ought to have been.

Unlike *Axa Insurance Ltd*, the Court in *Pegasus* embraced rather than rejected the classification of the cases into categories at least as a helpful tool for analysing and applying the authorities. It is possible, tentatively, to present these categories as follows

- 'no transaction' cases – where the claimant asserts that, but for the negligence, he would not have entered into the transaction at all;
- 'wrong transaction' cases - where the claimant would have entered into a transaction similar to the one into which he entered by reason of the negligence;
- cases which fall into neither category (and involve entering into no transaction). *Law Society v Sephton* falls into this category as do many of the cases involving the negligent conduct of litigation.

In a "wrong transaction" case, actual damage will usually occur upon entry into the transaction when (and if) the claimant does not receive what he ought to have received from the transaction. This does not depend on his necessarily being financially worse off at that stage but merely that the transaction failed to include a particular (and material) aspect which the claimant did or was entitled to expect. (On this point see also the decision of the Court of Appeal in *Watkins v Jones Maidment Wilson (a firm)* [2008] EWCA Civ 134, 118 ConLR 1, 10 EG 166 (CS).)

The occurrence of damage is of course a question of fact in each case but, save in exceptional cases, the answer is likely to be found in the existing law which sets a low threshold for the suffering of damage and as Pegasus makes clear, actual damage in "wrong" or "flawed" transaction cases can include a thwarted expectation rather than merely financial loss. *Law Society v Sephton* is frequently invoked by claimants seeking to retard the accrual of causes of action but remote possibilities do not necessarily make damage merely contingent; as Stephen Males QC put it in *Arrowhead Capital Finance Ltd (In Liquidation) v KPMG LLP* [2012] EWHC 1801 (Comm), [2012] PNLR 30 (at para [86]):

> 'It is always possible that the effect of a defendant's negligence may go unnoticed. For example, a purchaser who buys a house with a defective title as a result of his solicitor's negligence may be lucky when he comes to sell the house because his own purchaser's solicitor fails to spot the defect. But that does not mean that he has not suffered actual measurable damage.'

Where it is self-evident that actual damage has been suffered on entry into a transaction then it will often be appropriate to determine such limitation questions summarily on an application to strike out. Where, however, evidence of eg diminution in value is necessary but more appropriately a matter for trial then summary disposal may not be suitable – see eg *Venulum Property Investments Ltd v Space Architects Ltd* [2013] EWHC 3948 (TCC), [2014] All ER (D) 43 (Jan) where the court was just persuaded to take the latter course in a claim against architects where the limitation question depended on whether the cause of action accrued on the claimant's entry into a contract conditional on the grant of planning permission or on the later grant of that planning permission.

Daniels v Thompson [2004] EWCA Civ 307, [2004] PNLR 33, (2003) Times, 23 March was another difficult case in which the Court of Appeal held that a cause of action against a solicitor's firm in respect of negligent advice on the operation of an inheritance tax avoidance scheme began to run from the date on which the client relied upon the advice in question rather than the date of her death.

It was held in *Byrne v Hall Pain & Foster (a firm)* [1999] 2 All ER 400, [1999] 1 WLR 1849, CA that in the simple case of a property purchased as a result of a negligent valuation, a claim by the purchaser accrues on the date of exchange rather than completion of contract and this is so even though the buyer may also have a right to rescind the contract on the grounds of the seller's misrepresentation and could therefore be said to be only conditionally bound before completion: *Green v Eadie* (18 November 2011, unreported) Chancery Division.

Where professional negligence is alleged in the distribution of an estate without regard to a notified third party claim, the cause of action dates from the distribution not the subsequent establishment of that third party claim: *Lane v Cullen Solicitors* [2011] EWCA Civ 547, (2011) Times, 16 May.

III LIM [3.6A]

Professional negligence and immunity Where a proposed defendant is immune from suit and the immunity is subsequently removed, the date of the cause of action is not deferred, for limitation purposes, to the date of the removal: *Awoyami v Radford* [2007] EWHC 1671 (Admin), [2007] NLJR 1046, (2007) Times, 23 July, *per* Lloyd Jones J. This case concerned an 11-year old claim in professional negligence and the effect of the decision of the House of Lords in *Arthur J S Hall & Co (a firm) v Simons* [2002] 1 AC 615, [2000] 3 All ER 673 that the common law principle of advocate immunity could no longer be justified and that the change applied retrospectively.

III LIM [3.7]

Defective premises Any cause of action for breach of the duty under s 1 of the Defective Premises Act 1972 is deemed by sub-section (5) to have accrued at the time when the dwelling was completed, except that where work is done afterwards to rectify the earlier work the cause of action accrues when that work is finished. The latter provision was held to apply in *Alderson v Beetham Organisation Ltd* [2003] EWCA Civ 408, [2003] 1 WLR 1686, (2003) Times, 19 April in a case where the later work to rectify a problem with damp was not directed at the original damp proofing which was defective.

III LIM [3.8]

Misrepresentation Act 1967 The precise juridical status of (and thus the primary limitation period applicable to) section 2(1) of the Misrepresentation Act 1967 was left open by the Court of Appeal in *Law v Society of Lloyd's* [2003] EWCA Civ 1887, (2004) Times, 23 January, where Waller LJ giving the judgment of the Court said that its 'present view is that it is an action founded on a tort, albeit a statutory tort, and thus within s 2'. This view that claims under s 2(1) of the 1967 Act are subject to a 6-year period of limitation – whether by dint of s 2 or s 9 of the 1980 Act – was followed in *Green v Eadie* Ch D (18 November 2011, unreported) Chancery Division, where the judge expressed a preference for the view that such a claim was 'founded on tort' within the meaning of s 2 on the basis that s 2(1) of the 1967 Act created a 'statutory extension of the law of deceit'.

Section 2(1) of the 1967 Act provides that 'Where a person has entered into a contract after a misrepresentation has been made to him by another party thereto and as a result thereof he has suffered loss . . . ' and the cause of action is therefore complete (as with the tort of negligence) on the occurrence of damage. However, despite the common use of the shorthand 'negligent misrepresentation', claims under s 2(1) are not based on negligence since lack of reasonable care is part of the statutory defence to the claim but not of the cause of action itself. The latent damage provisions of s 14A of the 1980 Act do not therefore apply to it – see *Law v Society of Lloyd's* [2003] EWCA Civ 1887, (2004) Times, 23 January.

III LIM [4]

3. Time limit in case of successive conversions and extinction of title of owner of converted goods

(1) Where any cause of action in respect of the conversion of a chattel has accrued to any person and, before he recovers possession of the chattel, a further conversion takes place, no action shall be brought in respect of the further conversion after the expiration of six years from the accrual of the cause of action in respect of the original conversion.

(2) Where any such cause of action has accrued to any person and the period prescribed for bringing that action has expired and he has not during that period recovered possession of the chattel, the title of that person to the chattel shall be extinguished.

III LIM [4.1]

Accrual of cause of action in respect of the original conversion Time runs from the date of the first conversion even if it was committed by a thief unknown to the claimant: see *R B Policies at Lloyd's v Butler* [1950] 1 KB 76, [1949] 2 All ER 226. However, see s 4 below in respect of theft, as opposed to an honest conversion.

Section 3(2) provides an exception to the general rule that the expiry of the limitation period bars only the remedy in relation to a cause of action.

III LIM [4.2]

No action shall be brought See the note in s 2 at para **III LIM [3.3]** as to when an action is brought for the purposes of the Limitation Act 1980.

III LIM [5]

4. Special time limit in case of theft

(1) The right of any person from whom a chattel is stolen to bring an action in respect of the theft shall not be subject to the time limits under sections 2 and 3 (1) of this Act, but if his title to the chattel is extinguished under section 3 (2) of this Act he may not bring an action in respect of a theft preceding the loss of his title, unless the theft in question preceded the conversion from which time began to run for the purposes of section 3 (2).

(2) Subsection (1) above shall apply to any conversion related to the theft of a chattel as it applies to the theft of a chattel; and, except as provided below, every conversion following the theft of a chattel before the person from whom it is stolen recovers possession of it shall be regarded for the purposes of this section as related to the theft.

If anyone purchases the stolen chattel in good faith neither the purchase nor any conversion following it shall be regarded as related to the theft.

(3) Any cause of action accruing in respect of the theft or any conversion related to the theft of a chattel to any person from whom the chattel is stolen shall be disregarded for the purpose of applying section 3 (1) or (2) of this Act to his case.

(4) Where in any action brought in respect of the conversion of a chattel it is proved that the chattel was stolen from the plaintiff or anyone through whom he claims it shall be presumed that any conversion following the theft is related to the theft unless the contrary is shown.

(5) In this section "theft" includes—

- (a) any conduct outside England and Wales which would be theft if committed in England and Wales; and
- (b) obtaining any chattel (in England and Wales or elsewhere) by—
  - (i) blackmail (within the meaning of section 21 of the Theft Act 1968), or
  - (ii) fraud (within the meaning of the Fraud Act 2006);

and references in this section to a chattel being "stolen" shall be construed accordingly.

III LIM [5.1]

May not bring an action See the note in s 2 at para **III LIM [3.3]** as to when an action is brought for the purposes of the Limitation Act 1980.

III LIM [5.2]

The purpose of this somewhat convoluted section is to prevent periods operating to the advantage of the thief or anyone taking the goods from the thief. However, once a purchaser obtains the goods in good faith from either the thief or from someone who has received the

LIMITATION

goods as a result of a conversion related to the theft, then the limitation period begins to run to extinguish the title to the goods, ie six years from the date of the bona fide purchase. The following summary may assist in understanding the section:

(a) If B steals goods from A, the limitation periods provided by ss 2 or 3(1) of the Act do not apply to prevent A bringing an action in respect of the theft against B at any time.

(b) If B then sells the goods to C who knows of the theft, or if the goods are given to C who does not know of the theft, conversion is related to the theft and so A can bring an action against B and C in conversion at any time. The same will apply to all subsequent conversions unless there is a purchase in good faith.

(c) If B or C sell the goods to D who purchases them in good faith, A will not be able to bring an action against D six years after the sale as the limitation period under s 3(1) will apply. However, even when the title to the goods has been extinguished by the operation of s 3(2) six years after the purchase in good faith, A will still be able to bring an action for damages against the original thief and anyone involved in a theft-related conversion prior to the purchase in good faith.

(d) If there is an honest conversion by E and the goods are subsequently stolen from E by F, then any action by A is barred against either E or F six years following the original honest conversion.

In *Nicole De Preval v Adrian Alan Ltd* (24 January 1997, unreported) QBD, the claimant brought an action for the recovery of two candelabra stolen in 1986. It was held that the onus was on the defendant to show that he had purchased the stolen goods in good faith for the purpose of s 4. In this instance, the defendant failed to discharge the onus with the result that his limitation defence failed. See also *Gotha City and Germany v Sotheby's & Cobert Finance SA* (1998) Times, 8 October, in which the court considered the relationship between the public policy in English law that time does not run in favour of a thief nor any transferee who is not a purchaser in good faith and the relevant limitation period under German federal law.

III LIM [6]

4A. Time limit for actions for defamation or malicious falsehood

The time limit under section 2 of this Act shall not apply to an action for—

(a) libel or slander, or

(b) slander of title, slander of goods or other malicious falsehood,

but no such action shall be brought after the expiration of one year from the date on which the cause of action accrued.

III LIM [6.1]

This section was substituted by s 5 of the Defamation Act 1996 in relation to causes of action arising on or after 4 September 1996. Section 4A disapplies s 2 of the Limitation Act 1980 and therefore the 6-year limitation period which would otherwise apply.

The limitation period for claims for:

(a) libel;
(b) slander;
(c) slander of title;
(d) slander of goods; or
(e) other malicious falsehood

is one year subject to the discretionary – but rarely exercised – power of the court to disapply this limitation period – see s 32A below (at para **III LIM [37]**.

III LIM [6.2]

No such action shall be brought See the note in s 2 at para **III LIM [3.3]** as to when an action is brought for the purposes of the Limitation Act 1980.

III LIM [6.3]

Archive material on the Internet Where material from earlier publications is continuously accessible on the publisher's website it is continuously being re-published. The limitation period does not start to run from the date when it was first made accessible. This interpretation of s 4A does not infringe Art 10 of the Convention on Human Rights (see para **III HUM [32]**), since the restriction on freedom of expression is not disproportionate: *Loutchansky v Times Newspapers Ltd (No 2)* [2001] EWCA Civ 1805, [2002] QB 783, [2002] 1 All ER 652. See also the (rather extreme) case of *Duke of Brunswick v Harmer* (1849) 14 QB 185.

III LIM [6.4]

Time starts to run on publication although the identity of the tortfeasor is unknown It has been held that time starts to run on publication of the libel, even though the identity of the tortfeasor may be unknown, and that where the identity becomes known outside the limitation period an application may be made to extend time under s 32A: *Edwards v Golding* (2007) Times, 22 May, CA.

The common law rule that the cause of action accrues on publication is not affected by s 1(1) of the Defamation Act 2013: *Lachaux v Independent Press Ltd* (2017) Times, 10 October, CA.

III LIM [6.5]

Malicious falsehood In claims for malicious falsehood, including slander of title or goods, it is necessary for the claimant to prove not only that the words were false but also:

(a) that they were published maliciously; and
(b) that they caused special damage unless the circumstances of the case bring it within the statutory exceptions in s 3(1) of the Defamation Act 1952 *viz* if the words:
  (i) are calculated to cause pecuniary damage to the claimant and are published in writing or other permanent form; or
  (ii) are calculated to cause pecuniary damage to the claimant in respect of any office, profession, calling, trade or business held or carried on by him at the time of publication.

See *Joyce v Sengupta* [1993] 1 All ER 897, [1993] 1 WLR 337, CA.

III LIM [7]

5. Time limit for actions founded on simple contract

An action founded on simple contract shall not be brought after the expiration of six years from the date on which the cause of action accrued.

III LIM [7.1]

Accrual of cause of action The cause of action accrues upon occurrence of the relevant breach and not the time of damage: see *Gibbs v Guild* (1881) 8 QBD 296. Where the parties remain in a contractual relationship and the breach consists of a failure to perform a contractual undertaking, time may not run until the date when the relevant obligation becomes impossible to perform: see *Midland Bank Trust Co Ltd v Hett, Stubbs and Kemp* [1979] Ch 384, [1978] 3 All ER 571 (cf the different result in *Bell v Peter Browne & Co* [1990] 2 QB 495, [1990] 3 All ER 124, CA.)

In the case of a final agreement on the amount to be paid, following a judgment or award as to liability, time runs from the date of the conclusion of the agreement, not from the earlier judgment or award. On the other hand the running of time is not postponed until the liability in respect of costs has been finalised: *R G Carter Building Ltd v Kier Business Services Ltd* [2018] EWHC 729 (TCC).

III LIM [7.1A]

Anticipatory breach Where a party to a contract indicates by words or conduct that it cannot/does not intend to perform its obligations then the other may choose between:

(a) accepting the repudiatory breach and claiming damages immediately; or
(b) waiting until the contractually agreed time for performance arrives.

Where the anticipatory breach is accepted by the innocent party, then time will run from the date of such acceptance (*Hochster v de la Tour* (1853) 2 E & B 678) but where the innocent party elects to wait for the time of performance then – so long as he remains ready, willing and able to perform his obligations under the contract – then time will run from the time when the other party's performance was due, but was not provided, under the contract.

III LIM [7.1B]

Founded on simple contract Simple contract includes all contracts which are not contracts of record or contracts under seal. The words are sufficiently broad to cover an action for money had and received: see *Westdeutsche Landesbank Girozentrale v Islington London Borough Council* [1994] 4 All ER 890 at 942–3, [1994] 1 WLR 938, CA.

A claim against solicitors for compensation for breach of fiduciary duty in their conduct of a conveyancing transaction is akin to a claim for damages in contract and, accordingly, the limitation period under s 5 of the Limitation Act 1980 is applicable: *Leeds and Holbeck Building Society v Arthur & Co* [2001] All ER (D) 66 (May).

LIMITATION

However, s 5 does not apply (whether directly or by analogy) to a claim for specific performance of a contract: see *P&O Nedlloyd BV v Arab Metals Co* [2006] EWCA Civ 1717, [2007] 2 All ER (Comm) 401, [2007] 1 WLR 2288. (See **III LIM [40.2]** below.)

A claim for a declaration that someone has not committed a breach of contract does not fall within s 5 whether directly or by analogy. (The position is the same in relation to non-liability for a tort and s 2 of the Act): see *Aspect Contracts (Asbestos) Ltd v Higgins Construction plc* [2015] UKSC 38, [2015] 4 All ER 482, [2015] 1 WLR 2961.

III LIM [7.1C]

Restitution: overpayment Restitution in the context of overpayment (in relation to an adjudication, but it is submitted that its principles are of general application) was considered by the Supreme Court in *Aspect Contracts (Asbestos) Ltd v Higgins Construction plc* [2015] UKSC 38, in which it was held that:

(1) A paying party had a directly enforceable right to recover any overpayment to which the adjudicator's decision could be shown to have led, once there had been a final determination of the dispute. On whatever basis the right had arisen, the same restitutionary considerations underlay it. If and to the extent that the basis on which the payment had been made fell away as a result of the court's determination, an overpayment was, retrospectively, established. Either by contractual implication or, if not, then by virtue of an independent restitutionary obligation, repayment had to that extent been required. Since the claimant's cause of action had arisen from payment and was only for repayment, it was, whether analysed in implied contractual or restitutionary terms, a cause of action which could be brought at any time within six years after the date of payment to the defendant.

(2) For that purpose an independent restitutionary claim fell to be regarded as 'founded on simple contract' within s 5 of the 1980 Act. Whether by way of further implication or to give effect to an additional restitutionary right existing independently as a matter of law, the court had the power to order the payee to pay appropriate interest in respect of the overpayment. (See paras [23]–[34] of the judgment)

III LIM [7.2]

Mortgage debt In the case of a residual mortgage debt after the recovery of possession and sale, it was held in *Bristol and West plc v Bartlett; Paragon Finance plc v Banks; Halifax plc v Grant* [2002] EWCA Civ 1181, [2002] 4 All ER 544, [2002] 2 All ER (Comm) 1105 that s 20 (and not ss 5 or 8) of the Act applies to such a claim. Neither the sale of the relevant property nor s 35 of the Land Registration Act 2002 discharge the mortgagor's obligation under the covenant to pay contained in the mortgage deed. Accordingly, on the date of accrual of the mortgagee's cause of action it has 12 years in which to sue to recover outstanding principal and six years in respect of outstanding interest.

In the absence of any express provision, there is an implied obligation upon the mortgagor to repay the balance of the mortgage debt upon default in the payment of instalments and it is at this point that the mortgagee's cause of action accrues, see *Wilkinson v West Bromwich Building Society* [2004] EWCA Civ 1063, 148 Sol Jo LB 975.

III LIM [7.2A]

Construction adjudication Where one party pays money to the other in compliance with a decision of an adjudicator under s 108(3) of the Housing Grants, Construction and Regeneration Act 1996 (and Sch 1 of the Scheme for Construction Contracts (England and Wales) Regulations 1998) there is to be implied a term that that party is entitled to have the dispute finally determined by legal proceedings. The limitation period under s 5 of the Limitation Act in respect of that right to a final termination runs from the date of such payment: see *Jim Ennis Construction Ltd v Premier Asphalt Ltd* [2009] EWHC 1906 (TCC), 125 Con LR 141, [2009] 41 EG 116 and *Aspect Contracts (Asbestos) Ltd v Higgins Construction plc* [2015] UKSC 38, [2015] 4 All ER 482, [2015] 1 WLR 2961.

III LIM [7.3]

Shall not be brought See the note in s 2 at para **III LIM [3.3]** as to when an action is brought for the purposes of the Limitation Act 1980.

See also *Royal Norwegian Government v Constant & Constant* [1960] 2 Lloyd's Rep 431 for the application in contract of the principle that the remedy, but not the right, is barred upon the expiry of the limitation period.

III LIM [7.4]

Under a "superseded policies" clause, the indemnity applied to loss caused by an act committed during the currency of the old policy provided that it was discovered not later than 24 months after the end of the old policy; the trigger for the accrual of the insured's cause of action is the occurrence of loss and not its subsequent discovery: *Universities Superannuation Scheme Ltd v Royal Insurance (UK) Ltd* [2000] 1 All ER (Comm) 266, [2000] Lloyd's Rep IR 524.

III LIM [7.5]

Other limitation statutes Section 39 of the Act provides a saving for other limitation statutes. In a contractual context note in particular the following special (shorter) limitation periods applying to claims arising from contracts of international transit:

(a) Carriage by sea:
  (i) Carriage of Goods by Sea Act 1971 (cargo claims) – 1 year;
  (ii) Athens Convention 1974 (claims for death or personal injury to passengers or damage to luggage) – 2 years.
(b) Carriage by Air Act 1961 (persons, baggage & cargo) - 2 years.
(c) Carriage by Rail – the International Transport Conventions Act 1983 – 3 years for injury or death or 1 year for other claims.
(d) Carriage of Goods by Road Act 1965 – 1 year (ordinarily).

III LIM [7A]

5A. Additional time limit for actions for damages for late payment of insurance claims

(1) An action in respect of breach of the term implied into a contract of insurance by section 13A of the Insurance Act 2015 (late payment of claims) may not be brought after the expiration of one year from the date on which the insurer has paid all the sums referred to in subsection (1) of that section.

(2) Any payment which extinguishes an insurer's liability to pay a sum referred to in section 13A of the Insurance Act 2015 is to be treated for the purposes of this section as payment of that sum.

III LIM [8]

6. Special time limit for actions in respect of certain loans

(1) Subject to subsection (3) below, section 5 of this Act shall not bar the right of action on a contract of loan to which this section applies.

(2) This section applies to any contract of loan which—

  (a) does not provide for repayment of the debt on or before a fixed or determinable date; and
  (b) does not effectively (whether or not it purports to do so) make the obligation to repay the debt conditional on a demand for repayment made by or on behalf of the creditor or on any other matter;

except where in connection with taking the loan the debtor enters into any collateral obligation to pay the amount of the debt or any part of it (as, for example, by delivering a promissory note as security for the debt) on terms which would exclude the application of this section to the contract of loan if they applied directly to repayment of the debt.

(3) Where a demand in writing for repayment of the debt under a contract of loan to which this section applies is made by or on behalf of the creditor (or, where there are joint creditors, by or on behalf of any one of them) section 5 of this Act shall thereupon apply as if the cause of action to recover the debt had accrued on the date on which the demand was made.

(4) In this section "promissory note" has the same meaning as in the Bills of Exchange Act 1882.

III LIM [8.1]

Effect of a fresh demand A creditor may not start time running afresh simply by making a fresh demand. But if an earlier demand is withdrawn, the making of a subsequent demand may be effective to start time running: *Mahomed v Bank of Baroda* [1998] 47 LS Gaz R 29, sub nom *Bank of Baroda v Mahomed* [1999] 1 Lloyd's Rep Bank 14, CA.

III LIM [9]

7. Time limit for actions to enforce certain awards

An action to enforce an award, where the submission is not by an instrument under seal, shall not be brought after the expiration of six years from the date on which the cause of action accrued.

III LIM [9.1]

Shall not be brought See the note in s 2 at para **III LIM [3.3]** as to when an action is brought for the purposes of the Limitation Act 1980.

III LIM [9.2]

Generally, time will run under s 7 *not* from the date upon which the award is made or published, but from the date when the paying party is in breach of its implied obligation to pay the award: see eg *Agromet Motoimport Ltd v Maulden Engineering Co (Beds) Ltd* [1985] 2 All ER 436, [1985] 1 WLR 762.

Section 7 of the Limitation Act 1980, applies to applications under s 26 of the Arbitration Act 1950 and to the (materially identical) provisions of s 66 of the Arbitration Act 1996: see *National Ability SA v Tinna Oils & Chemicals Ltd* [2009] EWCA Civ 1330, (2009) Times, 24 December.

III LIM [10]

8. Time limit for actions on a specialty

(1) An action upon a specialty shall not be brought after the expiration of twelve years from the date on which the cause of action accrued.

(2) Subsection (1) above shall not affect any action for which a shorter period of limitation is prescribed by any other provision of this Act.

III LIM [10.1]

Specialty The word "specialty" usually denotes a contract under seal but it extends also to obligations imposed by statute: see *Collin v Duke of Westminster* [1985] QB 581, [1985] 1 All ER 463, CA; *Aiken v Stewart Wrightson Members' Agency Ltd* [1995] 3 All ER 449, [1995] 1 WLR 1281. Other examples of specialties include a foreign contract under seal, a bond, a deed, and a covenant. Note, however, that a shorter period of limitation is prescribed by s 9 below for the recovery of sums recoverable by virtue of any enactment: see *Central Electricity Generating Board v Halifax Corpn* [1963] AC 785, [1962] 3 All ER 915, HL; followed in *Rowan Companies Inc v Lambert Eggink Offshore Transport Consultants VOF* [1999] 2 Lloyd's Rep 443.

Actions on a specialty are not confined to claims for liquidated sums: see eg *Aiken v Stewart Wrightson Member's Agency Ltd* [1995] 1 WLR 1281.

A borrower's application to reopen a secured loan agreement as an extortionate credit bargain under s 139 of the Consumer Credit Act 1974 comes within s 8 and not s 9, the 12-year limitation period running from the date of the agreement: *Rahman v Sterling Credit Ltd* [2001] 1 WLR 496, 33 HLR 708, CA. See also *Nolan v Wright* [2009] EWHC 305 (Ch), [2009] 3 All ER 828, [2009] 2 All ER (Comm) 503.

Where a mortgage deed expressly provided that a shortfall remaining after the realisation of the security was to be treated as a loan outstanding by the borrower to the lender, it was held that a claim for the remaining debt was a claim upon a specialty under s 8: *Global Financial Recoveries Ltd v Jones* [2000] 02 LS Gaz R 30, 144 Sol Jo LB 32, distinguishing *Hopkinson v Tupper* [2000] CLY 4656, CA (Transcript 9212392, 30 January 1997). See now, however, *Bristol and West plc v Bartlett; Paragon Finance plc v Banks; Halifax plc v Grant* [2002] EWCA Civ 1181, [2002] 4 All ER 544, (2002) Times, 9 September, in which it was held that a claim by a mortgagee against its mortgagor in respect of any shortfall after a sale by the mortgagee of the mortgaged property falls under s 20 of the Limitation Act 1980. Accordingly, on the date of accrual of the mortgagee's cause of action, it had 12 years in which to sue to recover outstanding principal and six years in respect of outstanding interest. In the absence of any express provision, there is an implied obligation upon the mortgagor to repay the balance of the mortgage debt upon default in the payment of instalments and it is at this point that the mortgagee's cause of action accrues, see the decision of the House of Lords in *Wilkinson v West Bromwich Building Society* [2005] 1 WLR 2303, [2005] 4 All ER 97.

III LIM [10.2]

The duty of a mortgagee on the sale of the mortgaged property arises in equity and not in contract. Accordingly, an action for breach of that duty is not an action on a specialty within s 8. Rather the claim corresponds with the remedy available for negligence at common law and, by operation of s 36 of the 1980 Act, the court applies the limitation period of six years provided by s 2: *Raja v Lloyds TSB Bank plc* [2001] Lloyd's Rep Bank 113, CA.

III LIM [10.3]

Shall not be brought See the note in s 2 at para **III LIM [3.3]** as to when an action is brought for the purposes of the Limitation Act 1980.

III LIM [11]

9. Time limit for actions for sums recoverable by statute

(1) An action to recover any sum recoverable by virtue of any enactment shall not be brought after the expiration of six years from the date on which the cause of action accrued.

(2) Subsection (1) above shall not affect any action to which section 10 [or 10A] of this Act applies.

Amendment *Text in square brackets is inserted by the Automated and Electric Vehicles Act 2018 with effect from a date to be appointed.*

III LIM [11.1]

Sum recoverable by virtue of any enactment Section 10 necessarily applies to a wide variety of statutory rights of recovery and, in the normal way, does not specify when the cause of action accrues. Rather, as a matter of general principle, the cause of action under the relevant statutory provision will be complete when all of its ingredients exist or have occurred – see *Coburn v Colledge* [1897] 1 QB 702 at **III LIM [1E]** above.

The necessary legal ingredients of the cause of action do not include merely procedural steps which are not conditions precedent to the existence of a right of recovery. Thus

(a) in *Coburn v Colledge* itself, the solicitor's right to recover fees for work done accrued on the completion of that work rather than on the expiration of one month from the delivery of the bill of costs pursuant to what was then s 37 of the Solicitors Act, 1843;

(b) in *Hillingdon London Borough Council v ARC Ltd* [1999] Ch 139, CA it was held that s 9 applies to a claim for compensation for compulsory purchase resulting from the entry of the Council under s 11 of the Compulsory Purchase Act 1965 and that the cause of action accrued at the date of entry even though the sum recoverable remained to be quantified by a tribunal other than a court of law;

(c) in *Legal Services Commission v Rasool* [2008] EWCA Civ 154, [2008] 3 All ER 381, [2008] 1 WLR 2711, it was held that where a legal aid certificate was revoked for non-disclosure the Legal Aid Board's right of recovery of its expenditure from the legally aided person under reg 86 of the Civil Legal Aid (General) Regulations 1989 arose on revocation of the certificate not on the subsequent payment of the solicitor's taxed costs.

Section 9 of the 1980 Act applies to a claim for compensation under s 28 of the Highways Act 1980: *Rotherwick's Executors v Oxfordshire County Council* [2000] 2 EGLR 84, [2000] 28 EG 144.

Section 9 also applies to restitutionary claims under the Law Reform (Frustrated Contracts) Act 1943, the cause of action presumably accruing as at the date of frustration.

Section 9 does not apply to a liability to pay council tax under the Local Government Act 1992 and reg 34(3) of the Council Tax (Administration and Enforcement) Regulations 1992. It follows that s 9 does not apply to the presentation of a winding-up petition in relation to sums due under liability orders for unpaid council tax: see *Bolsover District Council v Ashfield Nominees Ltd* [2010] EWCA Civ 1129, [2010] RA 523, [2010] NLJR 1490.

Note that some statutes declare sums to be specialty debts and which thus fall within s 8 above. Since the repeal of s 14(2) of the Companies Act 1985 on 1 October 2009, sums due from shareholders to companies under their memorandum or articles are subject to the 6-year time limit under s 5 of the 1980 Act – see s 33(2) of the Companies Act 2006.

LIMITATION

The word 'sum' in s 9(1) is not restricted to claims for liquidated sums of money: *Rowan Companies Inc v Lambert Eggink Offshore Transport Consultants VOF* [1999] 2 Lloyd's Rep 443 (an unliquidated claim under the Dutch Commercial Code); *Re Farmizer Products Ltd* (a claim under s 214 of the Insolvency Act 1986) [1997] BCC 655 and *Green v Eadie* Ch D 18 November 2011 (a claim under s 2(1) of the Misrepresentation Act 1967).

A claim against an insurer under s 151 of the Road Traffic Act 1988 would appear to be a claim 'by virtue of an enactment' not a claim on a simple contract, applying the reasoning of the Privy Council in *Maharaj v Motor One Insurance Co Ltd* (2018) Times, 8 May, PC.

III LIM [11.2]

Shall not be brought See the note in s 2 at para **III LIM [3.3]** as to when an action is brought for the purposes of the Limitation Act 1980.

III LIM [12]

10. Special time limit for claiming contribution

(1) Where under section 1 of the Civil Liability (Contribution) Act 1978 any person becomes entitled to a right to recover contribution in respect of any damage from any other person, no action to recover contribution by virtue of that right shall be brought after the expiration of two years from the date on which that right accrued.

(2) For the purposes of this section the date on which a right to recover contribution in respect of any damage accrues to any person (referred to below in this section as "the relevant date") shall be ascertained as provided in subsections (3) and (4) below.

(3) If the person in question is held liable in respect of that damage—

(a) by a judgment given in any civil proceedings; or

(b) by an award made on any arbitration;

the relevant date shall be the date on which the judgment is given, or the date of the award (as the case may be).

For the purposes of this subsection no account shall be taken of any judgment or award given or made on appeal in so far as it varies the amount of damages awarded against the person in question.

(4) If, in any case not within subsection (3) above, the person in question makes or agrees to make any payment to one or more persons in compensation for that damage (whether he admits any liability in respect of the damage or not), the relevant date shall be the earliest date on which the amount to be paid by him is agreed between him (or his representative) and the person (or each of the persons, as the case may be) to whom the payment is to be made.

(5) An action to recover contribution shall be one to which sections 28, 32, 33A and 35 of this Act apply, but otherwise Parts II and III of this Act (except sections 34, 37 and 38) shall not apply for the purposes of this section.

III LIM [12.1]

Contribution The right to recover contribution from another person in respect of the same wrong arises under the Civil Liability (Contribution) Act 1978. If the limitation period which bars the claimant's remedy against the person claiming the contribution has expired, the latter can still bring contribution proceedings against a third party. However, if the claimant's right has been extinguished the right to contribution ceases: s 1(3) of the Civil Liability (Contribution) Act 1978; for example, the 12-year period in respect of actions for recovery for land (s 15 see para **III LIM [20]**) extinguishes the right rather than bars the remedy.

Section 10(1) of the Limitation Act 1980 provides that contribution claims are subject to a limitation period of two years which runs from the date on which the right to contribution accrues. That date is ascertained by reference to sub-s 10(3) and 10(4). Given that s 10(4) specifically contemplates a situation in which the person 'makes or agrees to make any payment', the literal meaning of the words 'the earliest date on which the amount to be paid by him is agreed' would seem to be that in either case it is the date of agreement rather than payment which sets the clock running. This is presumably directed at the (usual) situation in which payment follows agreement with the intention that it is from that earlier agreement – rather than after any delay *before* payment actually occurs – that time begins to run; the touchstone being the ascertainment of quantum.

Section 1(4) of the Civil Liability (Contribution) Act 1978 provides that

> '(4) A person who has made or agreed to make any payment in bona fide settlement or compromise of any claim made against him in respect of any damage (including a payment into court which has been accepted) shall be entitled to recover contribution in accordance with this section without regard to whether or not he himself is or ever was liable in respect of the damage, provided, however, that he would have been liable assuming that the factual basis of the claim against him could be established.'

This appears to mean that a person is 'entitled to recover contribution' when *either* he has 'made or agreed to make any payment in bona fide settlement or compromise of any claim' – in other words it is at the occurrence of either that the statutory cause of action accrues. Generally speaking, the Limitation Act, as a procedural statute, specifies the time limits that apply to various causes of action but does not interfere with the question when such cause of action accrues since that is a matter of separate, substantive law. There is, however, no reason in principle why the 1980 Act could not provide that time should run from a point which is not necessarily the accrual of the claim. (Cf *Baker & Davies plc v Leslie Wilks Associates (a firm)* [2005] 3 All ER 603 where it was said that '[s]ection 10 of the 1980 Act, albeit that it arises out of an enactment of the 1978 Act, is directed to time limitation and not to narrowing the nature of the right to contribution'. [*per* HHJ Havery at para 15]). Section 10(4) could have said that time runs from the earliest of either such payment or settlement but did not do so. Save in the case, say, of an interim payment, the circumstances in which payment of a sum in settlement takes place before an agreement as to the amount of any settlement must be relatively rare. In *Baker & Davies plc v Leslie Wilks Associates (a firm)* [2005] 3 All ER 603 earlier remedial works – and which were held to be the equivalent of a payment in compensation within the meaning of s 10(4) – did not set the limitation clock running; instead this was held to have occurred some years later when an agreement was made in full and final settlement and which amongst other things accepted the adequacy of the earlier remedial works. Moreover, in *Aer Lingus v Gildacroft* [2006] EWCA Civ 4, [2006] 2 All ER 290, [2006] 1 WLR 1173 – which concerned the adjudication of liability under s 10(3) – Rix LJ said that 'Section 10(4) therefore suggests that the critical matter is the ascertainment by agreement of the settlement sum.' Any apparent inconsistency between s 10(4) of the 1980 Act and s 1(4) of the 1978 Act disappears once it is appreciated that a payment cannot really be made 'in bona fide settlement or compromise' without some agreement or understanding to that effect.

III LIM [12.2]

No action... shall be brought See the note in s 2 at para **III LIM [3.3]** as to when an action is brought for the purposes of the Limitation Act 1980.

III LIM [12.2A]

The meaning of Judgment or Award The judgment or award referred to in section 10(3) is a judgment or award which ascertains the quantum, and not merely the existence, of the liability of the tortfeasor seeking contribution under the 1978 Act. *Aer Lingus v Gildacroft Ltd* [2006] 2 All ER 290, [2006] 1 WLR 1173.

III LIM [12.2B]

Judgment or agreement: ss (3) and (4), when time starts to run The wording of ss (3) is resonant of a judgment which imposes liability without the consent of the party in question. Where, however, an agreement to make a payment is subsequently embodied in a consent order it is a question of fact whether the pre-existing agreement falls, without more, within the terms of ss (4) so as to start time running thereunder. It may not do so where the agreement calls for such an order to be made but the decisive question will usually be whether the agreement itself gives rise to an enforceable liability to pay. See *Knight v Rochdale Healthcare NHS Trust* [2003] EWHC 1831, [2003] 4 All ER 416, 74 BMLR 204.

Where a claim is settled by the acceptance of a CPR Part 36 offer, there will not usually be a judgment determining that the defendant is liable. In the usual Part 36 case s 10(3) will therefore be irrelevant and s 10(4) is instead engaged. Section 10(4) focuses on the sum which the defendant agrees to pay for the actual damage caused and not on any ancillary liability to pay legal costs and this is what the word 'damage' means throughout s 10. It follows that, so long as there is an agreement to pay a sum of money for damage (in that sense), time to bring a contribution claim runs from that agreement and not from any later agreement or judicial assessment of costs. See *Chief Constable of Hampshire v Southampton City Council* [2014] EWCA Civ 1541 where time under s 10 was held to run from the defendant's acceptance of the claimant's Part 36 offer.

III LIM [12.3]

Application of section 35 The same rules as to third party proceedings, set-offs and counterclaims provided in s 35 apply to a claim for contribution (see para **III LIM [39]**).

III LIM [12.4]

Contribution claims outside section 1 of the 1978 Act Rights of contribution in respect of debt, as between joint guarantors of a loan, are not claims "in respect of any damage" and are therefore not subject to the special limitation period in s 10(1): *Hampton v Minns* [2002] 1 All ER (Comm) 481, [2002] 1 WLR 1.

III LIM [12A]

[10A. Special time limit for actions by insurers etc in respect of automated vehicles]

[(1) Where by virtue of section 5 of the Automated and Electric Vehicles Act 2018 an insurer or vehicle owner becomes entitled to bring an action against any person, the action shall not be brought after the expiration of two years from the date on which the right of action accrued (under subsection (5) of that section).

(2) An action referred to in subsection (1) shall be one to which sections 32, 33A and 35 of this Act apply, but otherwise Parts 2 and 3 of this Act (except sections 37 and 38) shall not apply for the purposes of this section.]

Amendment *Section 10A is inserted by the Automated and Electric Vehicles Act 2018 with effect from a date to be appointed.*

III LIM [13]

11. Special time limit for actions in respect of personal injuries

(1) This section applies to any action for damages for negligence, nuisance or breach of duty (whether the duty exists by virtue of a contract or of provision made by or under a statute or independently of any contract or any such provision) where the damages claimed by the plaintiff for the negligence, nuisance or breach of duty consist of or include damages in respect of personal injuries to the plaintiff or any other person.

(1A) This section does not apply to any action brought for damages under section 3 of the Protection from Harassment Act 1997.

(2) None of the time limits given in the preceding provisions of this Act shall apply to an action to which this section applies.

(3) An action to which this section applies shall not be brought after the expiration of the period applicable in accordance with subsection (4) or (5) below.

(4) Except where subsection (5) below applies, the period applicable is three years from—

(a) the date on which the cause of action accrued; or

(b) the date of knowledge (if later) of the person injured.

(5) If the person injured dies before the expiration of the period mentioned in subsection (4) above, the period applicable as respects the cause of action surviving for the benefit of his estate by virtue of section 1 of the Law Reform (Miscellaneous Provisions) Act 1934 shall be three years from—

(a) the date of death; or

(b) the date of the personal representative's knowledge;

whichever is the later.

(6) For the purposes of this section "personal representative" includes any person who is or has been a personal representative of the deceased, including an executor who has not proved the will (whether or not he has renounced probate) but not anyone appointed only as a special personal representative in relation to settled land; and regard shall be had to any knowledge acquired by any such person while a personal representative or previously.

(7) If there is more than one personal representative, and their dates of knowledge are different, subsection (5)(b) above shall be read as referring to the earliest of those dates.

III LIM [13.1]

Deliberate assault and "breach of duty" Claims for injuries arising from deliberate assaults fall within the meaning of "negligence, nuisance or breach of duty" in section 11(1) and are thus subject to the special three-year limitation period applicable to such claims (and also therefore to the discretion under section 33 to disapply the limitation period) rather than the fixed six-year limitation period under section 2. So held the House of Lords in *A v Hoare* [2008] UKHL 6, [2008] 1 AC 844, [2008] 2 WLR 311, [2008] 2 All ER 1, [2008] 1 FLR, thereby overruling (in accordance with *Practice Statement (Judicial Precedent)* [1966] 1 WLR 1234) its earlier decision in *Stubbings v Webb* [1993] AC 498, [1993] 1 All ER 322, HL. In *Letang v Cooper* [1964] 2 All ER 929 the Court of Appeal had held that trespass to the person amounted to "breach of duty" within the meaning of what was then the proviso to s 2(1) of the Limitation Act 1939. The Court of Appeal did so in reliance upon the dictum of Adam J in *Kruber v Grzesiak* [1963] VR 621 that

> "I would see no sufficient reason for excluding an action for trespass to the person] from the description of an action for damages for breach of duty, especially when it is provided that the duty may be one existing independently of any contract or any provision made by or under a statute. After all, do not all torts arise from breach of duty – the tort of trespass to the person arising from the breach of a general duty not to inflict direct and immediate injury to the person of another either intentionally or negligently in the absence of lawful excuse?"

In preserving the words "negligence, nuisance or breach of duty" when it came to enact the Limitation Act 1975, the House of Lords in *A v Hoare* concluded that parliament must have intended them to bear the meaning which they had previously been given in the courts of England and Australia.

The decision in *A v Hoare* brought to an ultimately satisfactory conclusion the unfortunate *cul-de-sac* into which English jurisprudence had ventured in respect of the limitation period applicable to deliberate assaults. In this regard see *Stubbings v Webb* [1993] AC 498, [1993] 1 All ER 322, HL itself (which was referred, without success for the plaintiff, to the European Court of Human Rights in *Stubbings v United Kingdom* (1996) 23 EHRR 213, [1997] 3 FCR 157, [1997] 1 FLR 105, EHCR).

The problem was brought into rather sharper focus in *S v W* [1995] 1 FLR 862, [1995] PIQR P470, sub nom *Seymour v Williams* [1995] PIQR P470, CA, where the plaintiff brought proceedings against her father for alleged physical and sexual abuse and against her mother for breaching her parental duty by permitting the abuse to occur. Applying *Stubbings*, the claim against the father was held to be statute barred under s 2 of the Act but the claim against the mother was held to be subject to s 11 and thus capable of an extension to the applicable 3-year limitation period under s 33.

The courts repeatedly recognised that a state of affairs in which a claim in respect of the *less* culpable conduct enjoys a more flexible limitation period represented a serious anomaly in the law. The Law Commission recommended that claims for intentionally and negligently caused personal injury should be subject to the same limitation rules, namely a 3 year limitation period which the court would have a discretionary power to disapply. (See Limitation of Actions (Law Com No 270), paras 1.5, 3.156, 3.162, 3.169 and Appendix A, Draft Bill, clauses 1, 2, 12 and 38.) But despite the Government's acceptance of this report no parliamentary time has yet been found for the necessary legislation. In *A v Hoare* [2005] EWHC 2161 (QB) *Stubbings* was therefore applied in another hard case. The claimant was the victim of an attempted rape by a serial sexual offender. He was sentenced to life imprisonment for that and a number of other sexual offences. The primary limitation period expired in February 1994 and any civil claim during that period would have been futile since he had no money. In 2004, however, he won £7 million on the National Lottery. *A* issued proceedings against him in December 2004. The claimant failed in the High Court (Times, 27 October 2005) and Court of Appeal ([2006] 1 WLR 2320; [2006] 2 FLR 727; Times, April 28, 2006 where it was conjoined with *H v Suffolk County Council & Secretary of State for Constitutional Affairs, X v Wandsworth London Borough Council*) on the basis that *Stubbings* was binding upon them. Moreover, since the 6-year limitation period under s 2 had expired before the Human Rights Act 1998 had come into force, s 3(1) of that Act could not be used to construe s 11 of the Limitation Act differently from the House of Lords in *Stubbings*.

The decision in *A v Hoare* also removes the need for claimants to deploy the rather artificial claim of "systemic negligence" against employers/supervisors of the tortfeasor in order to evade the consequences of the expiry of the limitation period under section 2. For example, in *KR v Bryn Alyn Community (Holdings) Ltd (in Liquidation)* [2003] EWCA Civ 85, [2003] QB

1441, [2003] 1 FLR 1203, (2003) Times, 17 February past residents of a number of children's homes brought claims against their owner in respect of deliberate abuse inflicted by some of its employees. The owner was vicariously liable for those actions (by reason of the decision in of the House of Lords in *Lister v Hesley Hall Ltd* [2002] 1 AC 215 that sexual abuse is not necessarily outside the scope of an employment) but (following *Stubbings*) since they were deliberate the claims in respect of them did not fall within s 11 (but rather within s 2) and were therefore statute-barred. Alternative allegations of systemic negligence against the owners of that home in respect of those deliberate actions were held to be within s 11. Two other claims in vicarious liability and systemic negligence subsequently followed the decision in *KR v Bryn Alyn viz H v Suffolk County Council and X and Y v Wandsworth London Borough Council* [2006] 1 WLR 2320, [2006] 2 FLR 727, (2006) Times, 28 April, CA. The appeals in these cases were allowed by the House of Lords on the s 2 / s 11 point in *A v Hoare* [2008] UKHL 6, [2008] 1 AC 844, [2008] 2 WLR 311, [2008] 2 All ER 1, [2008] 1 FLR.

(Note that *KR v Bryn Alyn* was disapproved in *A v Hoare* in relation to s 14(2) – see **III LIM [17.2]**.)

A claim brought against a public authority pursuant to the Human Rights Act 1998 to which a one-year time limit applies, subject to a discretion to extend time where it is equitable to do so having regard to all the circumstances: pursuant to the Human Rights Act 1998, s 7(5)(a),(b). For guidance on the approach the Court should take when exercising its discretion under s 7(5)(b), see *Dunn v Parole Board* [2009] 1 WLR 728 and *Rabone v Pennine Care NHS Foundation Trust* [2012] UKSC 2. For an example of a subsequent (unsuccessful) application to extend time under s 7(5)(b), see *AP v Tameside Metropolitan Borough Council* [2017] EWHC 65 (QB) where King J also rejected the argument that s 7(5) should be read as creating a rebuttable presumption in favour of the grant of an extension of time for claimants lacking capacity.

III LIM [13.2]

Damages in respect of personal injuries Where as the result of a breach of contract the claimant had lost the right to recover compensation for personal injuries the claim does not come within this section: see *Ackbar v C F Green & Co Ltd* [1975] QB 582, [1975] 2 All ER 65.

An employee's claim against an employer for failing to advise him as to the benefits he was entitled to on suffering personal injury in the course of his employment was a claim for negligent advice and not a claim in respect of damages for personal injury under s 11: *Gaud v Leeds Health Authority* (1999) 49 BMLR 105, CA.

It is not necessary that the breach of duty physically caused the personal injury; the words of s 11 required only that the damages claimed for the breach of duty consisted of or included personal injury. Accordingly, where the action was against a car owner for allowing the driver to drive uninsured and the claim was for damages in respect of the loss of the opportunity to be paid by insurers, the three year limitation period applied: *Norman v Ali* [2000] Lloyd's Rep IR 395, CA.

A claim arising from a council's failure to diagnose dyslexia while at school is a claim for personal injuries: *Adams v Bracknell Forest Borough Council* [2005] 1 AC 76, [2004] WLR 89, [2004] 3 All ER 897, [2005] PIQR P2 approving the decision of the Court of Appeal in *Robinson v St Helens Metropolitan Borough Council* [2003] PIQR P9. See also *Phelps v Hillingdon London Borough Council* [2001] 2 AC 619, [2000] 4 All ER 504, HL where it was held that failure to mitigate a congenital condition such as dyslexia could amount to personal injury.

In *Dryden v Johnson Matthey plc* [2018] UKSC 18 the Supreme Court explored the ambit of 'personal injury' in the context of a claim for damages for sensitisation to platinum salt as a result of improper exposure to platinum salts at work. It was held that the concept of actionable personal injury was broad enough to include such sensitisation, although asymptomatic, because it constituted a change to the claimants' physiological make-up which had impaired their bodily capacity for work in that further exposure carried with it a risk of an allergic reaction; for that reason the claimants were no longer able to work in any environment where further exposure might occur. Once the sensitisation was identified as an actionable personal injury, the employer's argument that the claims for loss of earnings were in reality for pure economic loss fell away.

Fear, whether caused by negligence or trespass, does not amount to personal injury: *Kimanthi v Foreign and Commonwealth Office* [2018] EWHC 1305 (QB).

III LIM [13.3]

Financial losses A claim came within the section where the only loss caused by the defendant's breach of duty was financial loss of profit resulting from the claimant's injury: see *Howe v David Brown Tractors (Retail) Ltd* [1991] 4 All ER 30, CA.

A claim for the cost of bringing up a child conceived after an unsuccessful sterilisation is a claim which includes personal injuries within the meaning of s 11(1): *Walkin v South Manchester Health Authority* [1995] 4 All ER 132, [1995] 1 WLR 1543, CA.

III LIM [13.4]

Action against solicitor Where a claimant has a claim in negligence against his solicitor for allowing a personal injury claim to be struck out, the six-year limitation period applies, ie it is not a claim for "damages in respect of personal injury". The limitation period begins, however, from the date on which the value of the claimant's cause of action is substantially diminished (in accordance with the reasoning in *Nykredit Mortgage Bank plc v Edward Erdman Group Ltd (No 2)* [1997] 1 WLR 1627): see *Khan v RM Farley & Co (a firm)* [2002] EWHC Civ 400, [2002] PNLR 28, (2002) Times, 12 April. To the extent that *Hopkins v MacKenzie* (1994) 138 Sol Jo LB 222, 23 BMLR 132, CA decided that damage does not occur before the date upon which the claim is struck out, it was wrong.

III LIM [13.5]

Sub-section (1A) This sub-section was inserted by the Protection from Harassment Act 1997 s 6.

III LIM [13.6]

Shall not be brought See the note in s 2 at para **III LIM [3.3]** as to when an action is brought for the purposes of the Limitation Act 1980.

III LIM [13.7]

Date on which cause of action accrued The date of the accident is excluded, so proceedings may be started on the third anniversary (*Marren v Dawson Bentley & Co Ltd* [1961] 2 QB 135, [1961] 2 All ER 270) or, if the courts are then closed, on the day that they re-open: *Pritam Kaur v S Russell & Sons Ltd* [1973] QB 336, [1973] 1 All ER 617, CA.

However, no extra days will be added where the court is open but entry is refused: *Croke v Secretary of State for Communities and Local Government* [2016] EWHC 2484 (Admin).

III LIM [13.8]

Date of knowledge See s 14 of the Limitation Act 1980 at para **III LIM [17]**.

III LIM [13.9]

Limitation defences under preceding limitation acts In *McDonnell v Congregation of the Christian Brothers Trustees* [2003] EWCA Civ 2095, [2001] All ER (D) 488 (Oct), the claimant brought proceedings 53 years after the last incident of alleged assault could have occurred. He claimed that until 1997 he lacked the knowledge required by ss 11 and 14 of the Limitation Act 1980 or alternatively that the discretion to disapply the limitation period ought to be exercised. It was held that the claimant's claim was statute barred under the Limitation Act 1939, which prescribed a six-year period of limitation. Section 1 of the Law Reform (Limitation of Actions) Act 1954 had replaced the six-year period under the 1939 Act with a period of three years but had preserved the six-year period for claims in which the cause of action had already accrued before the 1954 Act came into force. The claimant's cause of action had so accrued and s 1(3) of the Limitation Act 1963 applied only to a case in which the limitation period was three years. The claimant could not therefore avail himself of the provisions of the 1963 Act or the successor 1980 Act. On appeal the House of Lords affirmed the Court of Appeal's decision at [2003] UKHL 63, [2004] 1 AC 1101, [2004] 1 All ER 641, [2003] 3 WLR 1627 despite entertaining a degree of doubt whether its previous decision in *Arnold v Central Electricity Generating Board* [1988] AC 228, [1987] 3 All ER 694 as to the effect of the Limitation Act 1975 was correct.

III LIM [13.10]

Limitation defences under other limitation provisions: international or domestic carriage by sea A claim for personal injury or death to a passenger in the course of international or domestic carriage by sea, to which a two-year limitation period applies from the date of actual or intended disembarkation (or two years from the date of death, if later), subject to a three-year longstop from the date of actual or intended disembarkation pursuant to the Athens Convention 1974, as modified by domestic legislation: Athens Convention Relating to the Carriage of Passengers and their Luggage by Sea, 1974, Art 16. (The Athens Convention was originally enacted into UK law by s 14 of the Merchant Shipping Act 1979, but is now incorporated into UK law by s 183 of the Merchant Shipping Act 1995.)

Importantly, this three-year long stop is absolute and there is no discretionary power of the court to disapply it under s 33 of the Limitation Act 1980 or otherwise *Higham v Stena Sealink Ltd* [1996] 1 WLR 1107, CA. The words in Art 16(3) of the Athens Convention that the law seized of the matter shall govern 'the grounds of suspension and interruption of limitation

LIMITATION

periods' are wide enough to cover domestic rules which postpone the start of a limitation period (for example in the case of a minor) as well as those which stop the clock after the limitation period had begun: *Warner v Scapa Flow Charters* [2018] UKSC 52.

The time limit provisions of the Athens Convention do not apply to contribution proceedings against a carrier brought under the Civil Liability (Contribution) Act 1978 in respect of an employer's liability for personal injury to its employee. Such an action is not an action for damages for personal injury to a passenger brought against a carrier within the meaning of the Convention. A claim for a contribution is autonomous and derives from the English domestic statutory entitlement to contribution: *The South West Strategic Health Authority v Bay Island Voyages* [2016] 2 WLR 649, [2016] 4 All ER 107.

III LIM [14]

11A. Actions in respect of defective products

(1) This section shall apply to an action for damages by virtue of any provision of Part I of the Consumer Protection Act 1987.

(2) None of the time limits given in the preceding provisions of this Act shall apply to an action to which this section applies.

(3) An action to which this section applies shall not be brought after the expiration of the period of ten years from the relevant time, within the meaning of section 4 of the said Act of 1987; and this subsection shall operate to extinguish a right of action and shall do so whether or not that right of action had accrued, or time under the following provisions of this Act had begun to run, at the end of the said period of ten years.

(4) Subject to subsection (5) below, an action to which this section applies in which the damages claimed by the plaintiff consist of or include damages in respect of personal injuries to the plaintiff or any other person or loss of or damage to any property, shall not be brought after the expiration of the period of three years from whichever is the later of—

(a) the date on which the cause of action accrued; and

(b) the date of knowledge of the injured person or, in the case of loss of or damage to property, the date of knowledge of the plaintiff or (if earlier) of any person in whom his cause of action was previously vested.

(5) If in a case where the damages claimed by the plaintiff consist of or include damages in respect of personal injuries to the plaintiff or any other person the injured person died before the expiration of the period mentioned in subsection (4) above, that subsection shall have effect as respects the cause of action surviving for the benefit of his estate by virtue of section 1 of the Law Reform (Miscellaneous Provisions) Act 1934 as if for the reference to that period there were substituted a reference to the period of three years from whichever is the later of—

(a) the date of death; and

(b) the date of the personal representative's knowledge.

(6) For the purposes of this section "personal representative" includes any person who is or has been a personal representative of the deceased, including an executor who has not proved the will (whether or not he has renounced probate) but not anyone appointed only as a special personal representative in relation to settled land; and regard shall be had to any knowledge acquired by any such person while a personal representative or previously.

(7) If there is more than one personal representative and their dates of knowledge are different, subsection (5)(b) above shall be read as referring to the earliest of those dates.

(8) Expressions used in this section or section 14 of this Act and in Part I of the Consumer Protection Act 1987 have the same meanings in this section or that section as in that Part; and section 1 (1) of that Act (Part I to be construed as enacted for the purpose of complying with the product liability Directive) shall apply for the purpose of construing this section and the following provisions of this Act so far as they relate to an action by virtue of any provision of that Part as it applies for the purpose of construing that Part.

III LIM [14.1]

This section was inserted by the Consumer Protection Act 1987 s 6(6), Sch 1, para 1.

III LIM [14.2]

Shall not be brought See the note in s 2 at para **III LIM [3.3]** as to when an action is brought for the purposes of the Limitation Act 1980.

III LIM [14.2A]

Relevant time By s 4(2) (and 2(2)) of the 1987 Act the "the relevant time"

(a) in relation to electricity, means the time at which it was generated, being a time before it was transmitted or distributed;

(b) in relation to any other product, means

 (i) in the case of a defendant who is under s 2(2)

 – the producer of the product;

 – a person who, by putting his name on the product or using a trade mark or other distinguishing mark in relation to the product, has held himself out to be the producer of the product; or

 – a person who has imported the product into a member State from a place outside the member States in order, in the course of any business of his, to supply it to another.

 the time when he supplied the product to another

 (ii) in the case of a defendant who falls into none of these s 2(2) categories then the relevant time is the time when the product was last supplied by a person to whom that subsection does apply in relation to the product.

III LIM [14.3]

The ten-year long-stop The ten-year long-stop in s 11A(3), upon the expiry of which the cause of action is extinguished (and which gives effect to Art 11 of the Directive), is "a period of limitation under . . . the Limitation Act 1980" for the purposes of CPR 19.5(1). The court could therefore exercise its discretion to substitute a defendant under s 35 of the Limitation Act 1980 and CPR 19.5 after the expiry of that ten-year period: *Horne-Roberts (a Child) v Merck & Co Inc* [2001] All ER (D) 320 (Feb), QBD. This decision was affirmed by the Court of Appeal: [2001] EWCA Civ 2006, [2002] 1 WLR 1662, (2002) Times, 10 January and was applied in a situation where the mistake was discovered by the claimant before the expiry of the 10-year period but the application to substitute was only made after expiry: see *O'Byrne v Aventis Pasteur MSD Ltd* [2006] EWHC 2562 (QB), [2007] 1 WLR 757, 92 BMLR 130; affd sub nom *O'Byrne v Aventis Pasteur SA* [2007] EWCA Civ 939, [2008] 1 WLR 1188, [2008] Bus LR 993 but the House of Lords in *O'Byrne* (at [2008] UKHL 34, [2008] 4 All ER 881, [2008] CMLR 10) subsequently decided that it was not clear whether if a claimant had instituted proceedings against someone whom he described as the producer, but had mistakenly named someone who was not the producer, it was consistent with Art 11 of the Product Liability Directive for the court to have the power to rule that the proceedings should qualify as having been instituted against the real producer and amended accordingly. It therefore referred the matter to the ECJ which gave judgment its judgment in *Aventis Pasteur SA v OB; sub nom O'Byrne v Aventis Pasteur SA* C-358/08 (2009) Times, 9 December, ECJ and which is explained at **III LIM [39.9A]** below.

LIMITATION

III LIM [14A]

[11B. Actions against insurers etc of automated vehicles]

[(1) None of the time limits given in the preceding provisions of this Act shall apply to an action for damages under section 2 of the Automated and Electric Vehicles Act 2018 (liability of insurer etc where accident caused by automated vehicle).

But this subsection does not affect the application of section 5A of this Act.

(2) An action for damages against an insurer under subsection (1) of section 2 of the Automated and Electric Vehicles Act 2018 (including an action by an insured person under a contract of insurance in respect of the insurer's obligations under that section) shall not be brought after the expiration of the period of three years from—

 (a) the date of the accident referred to in that subsection; or

 (b) where subsection (3) below applies, the date of knowledge of the person injured (if later).

(3) This subsection applies where the damages claimed consist of or include damages in respect of personal injuries (to the claimant or any other person).

(4) An action for damages against the owner of a vehicle under subsection (2) of that section shall not be brought after the expiration of the period of three years from—

(a) the date of the accident referred to in that subsection; or

(b) where subsection (3) above applies, the date of knowledge of the person injured (if later).

(5) If a person injured in the accident dies before the expiration of the period mentioned in subsection (2) or (4) above, the period applicable as respects the cause of action surviving for the benefit of the person's estate by virtue of section 1 of the Law Reform (Miscellaneous Provisions) Act 1934 shall be three years from—

(a) the date of death; or

(b) where subsection (3) above applies, the date of the personal representative's knowledge (if later).

(6) If there is more than one personal representative, and their dates of knowledge are different, subsection (5)(b) above shall be read as referring to the earliest of those dates.

(7) In this section "personal representative" has the same meaning as in section 11 of this Act.]

Amendment *Section 11B is inserted by the Automated and Electric Vehicles Act 2018 with effect from a date to be appointed.*

III LIM [15]

12. Special time limit for actions under Fatal Accidents legislation

(1) An action under the Fatal Accidents Act 1976 shall not be brought if the death occurred when the person injured could no longer maintain an action and recover damages in respect of the injury (whether because of a time limit in this Act or in any other Act, or for any other reason).

Where any such action by the injured person would have been barred by the time limit in section 11 *or 11A* [11A or 11B] of this Act, no account shall be taken of the possibility of that time limit being overridden under section 33 of this Act.

(2) None of the time limits given in the preceding provisions of this Act shall apply to an action under the Fatal Accidents Act 1976, but no such action shall be brought after the expiration of three years from—

(a) the date of death; or

(b) the date of knowledge of the person for whose benefit the action is brought;

whichever is the later.

(3) An action under the Fatal Accidents Act 1976 shall be one to which sections 28, 33, 33A, 33B and 35 of this Act apply, and the application to any such action of the time limit under subsection (2) above shall be subject to section 39; but otherwise Parts II and III of this Act shall not apply to any such action.

Amendment *Text in italic is deleted and text in square brackets is inserted by the Automated and Electric Vehicles Act 2018 with effect from a date to be appointed.*

III LIM [15.1]

Shall not be brought See the note in s 2 at para **III LIM [3.3]** as to when an action is brought for the purposes of the Limitation Act 1980.

III LIM [15.2]

Date of knowledge See s 14 of the Limitation Act 1980 at para **III LIM [17]**. Where there is more than one person for whose benefit an action is brought: see s 13 of the Limitation Act 1980 at para **III LIM [16]**.

III LIM [15.3]

Barring of deceased's claim If the deceased's claim was barred by the provisions of s 11, the court may nevertheless exercise its discretion under s 33 to allow the dependant's claims to proceed. But there is no such power where the deceased's claim has been made and struck out for want of prosecution: *Chappell v Cooper* [1980] 2 All ER 463, [1980] 1 WLR 958, CA. See s 33(2) of the Limitation Act 1980 at para **III LIM [38]**. In *Skitt v Khan* [1997] 8 Med LR 105, CA an extension in favour of a widow was set aside on the ground that the deceased could, although with difficulty, have obtained a medical report to support proceedings but had decided not to do so over three years before his death.

III LIM [16]

13. Operation of time limit under section 12 in relation to different dependants

(1) Where there is more than one person for whose benefit an action under the Fatal Accidents Act 1976 is brought, section 12 (2)(b) of this Act shall be applied separately to each of them.

(2) Subject to subsection (3) below, if by virtue of subsection (1) above the action would be outside the time limit given by section 12 (2) as regards one or more, but not all, of the persons for whose benefit it is brought, the court shall direct that any person as regards whom the action would be outside that limit shall be excluded from those for whom the action is brought.

(3) The court shall not give such a direction if it is shown that if the action were brought exclusively for the benefit of the person in question it would not be defeated by a defence of limitation (whether in consequence of section 28 of this Act or an agreement between the parties not to raise the defence, or otherwise).

III LIM [16.1]

An action... is brought See the note in s 2 at para **III LIM [3.3]** as to when an action is brought for the purposes of the Limitation Act 1980.

III LIM [17]

14. Definition of date of knowledge for purposes of *sections 11 and 12* [sections 11 to 12]

(1) Subject to *subsection (1A)* [subsections (1A) and (1B)] below, in sections 11 and 12 of this Act references to a person's date of knowledge are references to the date on which he first had knowledge of the following facts—

- (a) that the injury in question was significant; and
- (b) that the injury was attributable in whole or in part to the act or omission which is alleged to constitute negligence, nuisance or breach of duty; and
- (c) the identity of the defendant; and
- (d) if it is alleged that the act or omission was that of a person other than the defendant, the identity of that person and the additional facts supporting the bringing of an action against the defendant;

and knowledge that any acts or omissions did or did not, as a matter of law, involve negligence, nuisance or breach of duty is irrelevant.

(1A) In section 11A of this Act and in section 12 of this Act so far as that section applies to an action by virtue of section 6 (1)(a) of the Consumer Protection Act 1987 (death caused by defective product) references to a person's date of knowledge are references to the date on which he first had knowledge of the following facts—

- (a) such facts about the damage caused by the defect as would lead a reasonable person who had suffered such damage to consider it sufficiently serious to justify his instituting proceedings for damages against a defendant who did not dispute liability and was able to satisfy a judgment; and

LIMITATION

(b) that the damage was wholly or partly attributable to the facts and circumstances alleged to constitute the defect; and

(c) the identity of the defendant;

but, in determining the date on which a person first had such knowledge there shall be disregarded both the extent (if any) of that person's knowledge on any date of whether particular facts or circumstances would or would not, as a matter of law, constitute a defect and, in a case relating to loss of or damage to property, any knowledge which that person had on a date on which he had no right of action by virtue of Part I of that Act in respect of the loss or damage.

[(1B) In section 11B of this Act and in section 12 of this Act so far as that section applies to an action by virtue of section 6(1)(a) of the Automated and Electric Vehicles Act 2018 ("the 2018 Act") (death caused by automated vehicle) references to a person's date of knowledge are references to the date on which he first had knowledge of the following facts—

(a) that the injury in question was significant; and

(b) that the injury was attributable in whole or in part to an accident caused by an automated vehicle when driving itself; and

(c) the identity of the insurer of the vehicle (in the case of an action under section 2(1) of the 2018 Act) or the owner of the vehicle (in the case of an action under section 2(2) of that Act).

Expressions used in this subsection that are defined for the purposes of Part 1 of the 2018 Act have the same meaning in this subsection as in that Part.]

(2) For the purposes of this section an injury is significant if the person whose date of knowledge is in question would reasonably have considered it sufficiently serious to justify his instituting proceedings for damages against a defendant who did not dispute liability and was able to satisfy a judgment.

(3) For the purposes of this section a person's knowledge includes knowledge which he might reasonably have been expected to acquire—

(a) from facts observable or ascertainable by him; or

(b) from facts ascertainable by him with the help of medical or other appropriate expert advice which it is reasonable for him to seek;

but a person shall not be fixed under this subsection with knowledge of a fact ascertainable only with the help of expert advice so long as he has taken all reasonable steps to obtain (and, where appropriate, to act on) that advice.

Amendment *Text in italic is deleted and text in square brackets is inserted by the Automated and Electric Vehicles Act 2018 with effect from a date to be appointed.*

III LIM [17.1]

Date of knowledge For a full consideration as to what constitutes 'knowledge' and as to the date on which knowledge arises see *Nash v Eli Lily & Co* [1993] 4 All ER 383, [1993] 1 WLR 782, CA.

III LIM [17.1A]

S 14(1)(b) knowledge 'that the injury was attributable...' Once a claimant is shown to have knowledge that his injury is attributable to the act or omission of the defendant, the subsequent obtaining of expert advice for the purpose of legal proceedings which is to the effect that the injury is not so attributable does not retrospectively cause him never to have had such knowledge: see *Nash* at 795. The Court of Appeal in *Young v Western Power Distribution (South West) plc* [2003] EWCA Civ 1034, [2003] 1 WLR 2868, (2003) Times, 19 August considered this to be unsatisfactory but nonetheless a correct statement of the law based upon the words of the statute.

In *AB v Ministry of Defence* [2012] UKSC 9, [2012] 3 All ER 673, [2012] 2 WLR 643 the Supreme Court held that by the time that proceedings are brought, a claimant necessarily has knowledge that his injuries are attributable to the defendant's negligence, nuisance, or breach of duty and indeed declares as much by his statement of truth. It is legally impossible for the claimant to lack knowledge of attributability until some time afterwards. A claimant is likely to have that knowledge of attributability when he first reasonably believes the relevant facts – see *Halford v Brookes* [1991] 3 All ER 559, [1991] 1 WLR 428 – with sufficient confidence to justify embarking on the preliminaries to the issue of proceedings.

III LIM [17.2]

Knowledge of significant injury: Objective v subjective The test for 'significant injury' in s 14(2) is subjective only to the extent that it requires the court to consider what the claimant actually knew of his injury rather than the injury as it actually was (if different). This knowledge might in a particular case have to be supplemented by the knowledge which may be imputed under s 14(3). However, the test to be applied under s 14(2) is objective ie would a reasonable person with the claimant's knowledge (actual and imputed) have considered the injury sufficiently serious to justify proceedings. See the decision of the House of Lords in *A v Hoare* [2008] UKHL 6, [2008] 1 AC 844, [2008] 2 WLR 311, [2008] 2 All ER 1, [2008] 1 FLR and in particular that part which deals with the appeal in *Young v Catholic Care (Diocese of Leeds) and the Home Office* in which this question arose. Their Lordships particularly deprecated the tendency in some of the cases of attributing to the *reasonable* claimant such factors as the intelligence of the *actual* claimant. It follows that the mixed, subjective/objective analysis, of the Court of Appeal in *McCafferty v Metropolitan Police District Receiver* [1977] 2 All ER 756, [1977] 1 WLR 1073, CA is finally laid to rest.

According to Lord Hoffman in *A v Hoare* (at para 43), s 14(2) assumes "a practical and relatively unsophisticated approach to the question of knowledge" and he distinguished between the different effects of the use of the word "reasonably" in sub-ss 14(2) and 14(3):

> . . . *Adams* [see below at **III LIM [17.4A]**] was dealing with section 14(3), which is very different in its purpose from section 14(2). The test for imputing knowledge in section 14(3) is by reference to what the claimant ought reasonably to have *done*. It asks whether he ought reasonably to have acquired certain knowledge from observable or ascertainable facts or to have obtained expert advice. But section 14(2) is simply a standard of seriousness applied to what the claimant knew or must be treated as having known. It involves no inquiry into what the claimant ought to have done.
>
> The difference between section 14(2) and 14(3) emerges very clearly if one considers the relevance in each case of the claimant's injury. Because section 14(3) turns on what the claimant ought reasonably to have done, one must take into account the injury which the claimant has suffered. You do not assume that a person who has been blinded could reasonably have acquired knowledge by seeing things. In section 14(2), on the other hand, the test is external to the claimant and involves no inquiry into what he ought reasonably to have done. It is applied to what the claimant knew or was deemed to have known but the standard itself is impersonal. The effect of the claimant's injuries upon what he could reasonably have been expected to do is therefore irrelevant.

It is clear then that the decision of the House of Lords on s 14(3) must be confined to its subject matter rather than *Adams v Bracknell Forest Borough Council* [2004] UKHL 29, [2004] 3 All ER 897, [2004] 3 WLR 89, (2004) Times, 24 June. (See below at note 17.4A.)

A v Hoare represents the latest and, perhaps, final word on the vexed question of the meaning of section 14(2) in which the cases, generally speaking, have gradually evolved a more objective construction of the test. Hitherto the most recent appellate salvo had been *McCoubrey v Ministry of Defence* [2007] EWCA Civ 17, [2007] All ER (D) 185 (Jan), (2007) Times, 26 January – though not mentioned by the House in Hoare. There, the Court of Appeal decided that the proper approach to section 14(2) was to consider the reaction to the injury (as opposed to its possible consequences) of a reasonable person in the objective circumstances of the actual claimant, while disregarding his actual personal attributes such as intelligence, aspirations aggressiveness etc. On the facts of *McCoubrey* it was held that this permitted the assumption to be made that the claimant was a serving soldier who was aged 18 at the time of the injury but in the light of Lord Hoffmann's statement in *Hoare* (at para 35) that:

> "[o]nce you have ascertained what the claimant knew and what he should be treated as having known, the actual claimant drops out of the picture"

it may be doubted whether even this was relevant to s 14(2).

Their Lordships in *Hoare* emphasised, however, that the law did not treat as irrelevant the question whether the actual claimant, taking into account his psychological state in consequence of the injury, could reasonably have been expected to institute proceedings but that this arose not under s 14(2) but rather under s 33, sub-s (3)(a) of which specifically provides that one of the matters to be taken into account in the exercise of the discretion is "the reasons for . . . the delay on the part of the plaintiff".

The decision in *A v Hoare* put beyond any doubt the irrelevance to s 14(2) of a particular claimant's willingness to resort to litigation: see *Collins v Tesco* (24 July 2003, unreported), CA.

Knowledge of significant injury: Objective v subjective A claimant may have sufficient knowledge of the existence of a significant injury even if this is contrary to expert advice received by him. The provisions of s 33 are still available where this would result in injustice: *Joseph Sniezek v Bundy (Letchworth) Ltd* [2000] PIQR P213, CA.

In a medical negligence action for mis-prescription of drugs the claimant argued that he was unaware he had suffered significant injury attributable to the defendants until he knew that the therapeutic effects of the drug were outweighed by undesirable side effects. It was held that this benefit-deficit equation was not relevant in determining whether the claimant is aware that he himself is suffering from "significant injury": *Briggs v Pitt-Payne & Lias* [1999] Lloyd's Rep Med 1, CA.

A patient, whose condition deteriorated following an operation, inferred that the operation had not been a success but had nothing to alert him to the fact that he had been injured during the operation; it was held that in those circumstances he could not be said to be fixed with relevant knowledge for the purposes of s 14(1)(a): *James v East Dorset Health Authority* (1999) 59 BMLR 196, (1999) Times, 7 December.

Where the claim made is in relation to the exacerbation of an existing condition, the knowledge required is that the exacerbation is significant: *Colin McManus v Mannings Marine Ltd* [2001] EWCA Civ 1668, [2001] All ER (D) 426 (Oct).

For a case on industrial deafness which the claimant thought at the time was due to wax and/or infection, see *Field v British Coal Corpn* [2008] EWCA Civ 912, [2008] All ER (D) 417 (Jul), in which the date of knowledge was taken to be the later date when a consultant confirmed an industrial cause since the claimant ought not reasonably to have reached this state of knowledge at any earlier date.

III LIM [17.3]

Knowledge that injury attributable to acts or omissions Time starts to run against a claimant for the purpose of this section when he knew that the injury on which he founded his claim was capable of being attributed to an act or omission of the defendant irrespective of whether, at that point, he knew that the act or omission was actionable or tortious: see *Dobbie v Medway Health Authority* [1994] 4 All ER 450, [1994] 1 WLR 1234, CA; *Broadley v Guy Clapham & Co* [1994] 4 All ER 439, CA.

In *Spargo v North Essex District Health Authority* [1997] PIQR P235, CA, the court distilled a number of principles from the authorities: (1) the knowledge required is broad knowledge of the essence of the causally relevant act or omission to which the injury is attributable; (2) "attributable" means "capable of being attributed to" in the sense of being a real possibility; (3) a claimant will have the requisite knowledge when he or she knows enough to make it reasonable to begin to investigate whether there is a case against the defendant. Such knowledge would be constituted by a sufficiently firm belief to consult a solicitor to seek advice about making a claim; (4) the requisite knowledge will not exist if the claimant is "barking up the wrong tree" in his or her identification of the acts or omissions *or* has only vague knowledge *or* believes that the injury is capable of being attributed to the act or omission but is not sure without consulting an expert before he or she could properly be said to know what "it" was. See also *Hayward v Sharrard* (2000) 56 BMLR 155, CA. In *Harrison v Isle of Wight NHS Primary Care Trust* [2013] EWHC 442 (QB), [2013] Med LR 334, the Claimant was held to have acquired the requisite knowledge when she discovered, after a second operation in 2009, the true cause of the shoulder pain which she had suffered constantly since an operation 4 years earlier. Time therefore began to run only then and not when she had previously instructed solicitors and they had written to the defendant in 2008 alleging that her pain had been caused by a different act of negligence.

The limitation period starts to run from when the claimant had knowledge that the lesser part of her injury was attributable to an act or omission of the defendant and not when she knew that the greater part of her injury was so attributable: *Roberts v Winbow* (1998) 49 BMLR 134.

On the other hand, it was held in *Rowbottom v Royal Masonic Hospital* [2002] EWCA Civ 87, [2003] PIQR P1, CA that time did not start to run with knowledge of the injury to health following a hip replacement operation, but only after evidence had been obtained regarding the failure to administer antibiotics. The claimant had previously had no knowledge of this failure.

In *AB v Ministry of Defence* [2010] EWCA Civ 1317, [2010] NLJR 1686 over a thousand former servicemen claimed that their exposure to radiation in nuclear tests in the 1950s had caused them injury. On a preliminary issue as to limitation, the Court of Appeal held that all but one of the lead claims before them had been brought more than three years after the claimant's date of knowledge stating (at para 85) that

> "[i]t is clear from the principles set out in *Spargo* that it is the knowledge of possibilities that matters; a claimant needs only enough knowledge for it to be reasonable to expect

him to set about investigation. He can have knowledge even though there is no helpful evidence yet available to him."

The Court of Appeal went on to agree with the judge that the wealth of extant documentation meant that a fair trial was still possible but decided that the claimants' evidential difficulties on the question of causation made it inappropriate to exercise the s 33 discretion in their favour.

III LIM [17.4]

Knowledge of identity of defendant or other person It is not sufficient that the claimant knows that the defendant company is part of a group of companies; he must find out its separate identity: *Simpson v Norwest Holst Southern Ltd* [1980] 2 All ER 471, [1980] 1 WLR 968, CA. But he must make reasonable enquiries: see *Common v Croft* [1980] LS Gaz R 358, in which the defendant was known to have been prosecuted, and the terms of sub-s (3). See also *Henderson v Temple Pier Co Ltd* [1998] 3 All ER 324, [1998] 1 WLR 1540, CA.

In *Brian Cressey v E Timm & Son Ltd* [2005] EWCA Civ 763, [2005] 1 WLR 3926, (2005) Times, 25 July the Court of Appeal held that where the identity of the claimant's employer was uncertain or had been wrongly communicated to the employee, the occurrence of the date of knowledge could be postponed for as long as it would reasonably take for the necessary inquiries into the question to be made.

III LIM [17.4A]

Section 14(3) – constructive knowledge generally The test of constructive knowledge in section 14(3) is an objective one but this supposedly straightforward proposition is not always easy to apply. The difficulty arises because the reasonable person by reference to whom the matter is to be judged must obviously be placed in the position of the claimant. In *Nash v Eli Lilly & Co* [1993] 1 WLR 782 Purchas LJ had said that "In considering whether or not the inquiry [that is, of an expert] is, or is not, reasonable, the situation, character and intelligence of the plaintiff must be relevant". In *Forbes v Wandsworth Health Authority* [1997] QB 402, [1996] 4 All ER 881, the Court of Appeal sought to qualify this apparent intrusion into the test of a subjective element. In particular Stuart-Smith said (at page 414) that

> "It does not seem to me that the fact that a plaintiff is more trusting, incurious, indolent, resigned or uncomplaining by nature can be a relevant characteristic, since this too undermines any objective approach."

and Evans LJ indicated (at 422) that

> "'I doubt, however, whether it is appropriate to regard this issue in terms of a decision made consciously or unconsciously by the deceased whether to accept his lot or consider making a claim. If the question is whether, objectively and reasonably, he could be expected to have obtained further advice, then I do not see that his actual mental processes are relevant at all."

and (at 423) that

> "As to situation, there is no difficulty. The reasonable man must be placed in the situation that the plaintiff was. The reference to character and intelligence, however, suggest that regard should be had to personal characteristics of the plaintiff, and this I find difficult to square with the application of an objective and, therefore, equal standard."

However he went on to say that

> "It may also be possible to give the references to character and intelligence a limited meaning, for there could be circumstances where the nature of the alleged negligence was such that those attributes of the 'reasonable man' might be relevant in applying the objective test."

Each case turns on its own facts and Evans LJ indicated that it would be wrong to introduce categories or general rules about reasonableness in the application of the statutory test.

The Court of Appeal in *Smith* referred to these *dicta* with approval but even this distinction between situation and personal attributes may be an uncertain one on the facts of a particular case. In *Adams v Bracknell Forest Borough Council* [2004] UKHL 29, [2004] 3 All ER 897, [2004] 3 WLR 89, (2004) Times, 24 June, the claimant brought proceedings against a local authority in respect of its allegedly negligent failure to diagnose his dyslexia while he was a pupil from 1977 to 1988 at schools for which it was responsible. It was held in *Robinson v St Helens Metropolitan Borough Council* that such a claim is a claim for personal injuries and thus subject to the 3-year time limit under s 11. The claimant in *Adams* only acquired actual knowledge in 1999 as a result of a chance conversation at a party. It

LIMITATION

was held at first instance that he was not to be fixed with constructive knowledge before that date since although he was aware that he suffered from serious difficulties in reading and writing he had found ways of coping with the problem and was embarrassed to discuss it and this decision was affirmed by the Court of Appeal on the basis that an aspect of the condition was inhibition in revealing and discussing it and which it was permissible to take into account. (Cf *Rowe v Kingston Upon Hull City Council* (25 July 2003, unreported), CA, where the dyslexic claimant had *actual* knowledge of his condition and that he could have been helped). The House of Lords allowed the defendant's appeal in *Adams* holding that in deciding what knowledge a claimant might reasonably be expected to acquire the claimant is to be assumed to be a person who has suffered the injury in question, but in all other respects he is to be treated as a reasonable person. The court therefore has to consider what a reasonable person in the claimant's position would have done and aspects of character (shyness, embarrassment, etc) or intelligence which are peculiar to the claimant are to be disregarded. If, however, the injury affects the claimant's ability to acquire knowledge or to seek expert advice, then these are matters that can be taken into account. There is, however, a normal expectation that a person suffering from a significant injury would be inquisitive of its cause and that this was also the expectation of dyslexics. Were it otherwise, the limitation period would run indefinitely. On the facts, there was no special inhibiting factor of which the court could take account and the claimant therefore had constructive knowledge significantly more than three years before the issue of proceedings. Their lordships declined to exercise the discretion under s 33 of the Limitation Act. See also *Smith v Hampshire County Council* [2007] EWCA Civ 246, [2007] ELR 321. The presumption that a person who has suffered a significant injury will be sufficiently curious about its cause to seek expert advice is not irrebuttable; it is capable of being displaced where, exceptionally, a reasonable person in the position of the claimant would not have sought such advice: *Johnson v Ministry of Defence* [2012] EWCA Civ 1505, [2012] All ER (D) 254 (Nov).

Knowledge that an injury is 'significant' does not of itself constitute constructive knowledge. Rather this question is to be decided by reference to the knowledge which a person might reasonably be expected to acquire in all the circumstances of the case: *Whiston v London Strategic Health Authority* [2010] EWCA Civ 195, [2010] 3 All ER 452, [2010] 1 WLR 1582, 113 BMLR 110. As Cox J put it in *Khairule v North West Strategic Health Authority* [2008] EWHC 1537 (QB) (at [60]):

> 'When assessing the extent to which someone is reasonably to be expected to be curious as to the cause of his particular disability, there is in my view a distinction to be drawn between someone who has lived with a disability and its effects from birth and someone who suffers injury following an adverse incident which happens in later years. This claimant's cerebral palsy was, I agree, part of him and part of his life and he had lived with it for as long as he could remember.'

III LIM [17.4B]

Knowledge which he might reasonably have been expected to acquire Where the claimant was injured in 1960 but did not acquire actual knowledge of all the relevant facts until 1994, it was held that the claim was statute barred. Some degree of objectivity must be required in determining when it is reasonable for someone to seek advice; the claimant should have sought medical advice on her injury long before she did: *Fenech v East London and City Health Authority* [2000] Lloyd's Rep Med 35, CA.

III LIM [17.5]

Knowledge from facts observable or ascertainable For the purposes of s 14 "knowledge" is the state of mind which actually exists or might have existed if the claimant, acting reasonably, acquired knowledge from the facts ascertainable by him or which he could have acquired with the help of medical or other expert advice which it was reasonable for him to obtain: *Nash v Eli Lilly & Co* [1993] 4 All ER 383, [1993] 1 WLR 782, CA; *Forbes v Wandsworth Health Authority* [1997] QB 402, [1996] 4 All ER 881, CA. But knowledge of an injury will not start time running if the claimant, even if he is aware of the injury, reasonably considered it insufficiently serious to justify proceedings against an acquiescent and creditworthy defendant: *Dobbie v Medway Health Authority* [1994] 4 All ER 450, [1994] 1 WLR 1234, CA. On the other hand, time starts running once the claimant makes a connection between the injury and an admittedly mistaken diagnosis, even though expert advice to support legal proceedings is not obtained until later: *Spargo v North Essex Health Authority* [1997] PIQR P235, [1997] 8 Med LR 125, CA. A similar conclusion was reached in *Saxby v Morgan* [1997] 8 Med LR 293, CA.

In a claim for medical negligence, where the claimant had suffered hypoxic brain damage at birth, commenced over 25 years after the birth, it was held that there was no reason to interpret s 14 and s 14(3) as imputing actual knowledge of the parent to the child when it reached 18; nor would it have been reasonable for the claimant to have pursued with his mother what had happened at his birth, particularly as she would not have said anything about it until the birth of her grandson: *Appleby v Walsall Health Authority* [1999] Lloyd's Rep Med 154. See also *Parry v Clwyd Health Authority* [1998] 8 Med LR 243, [1997] PIQR P1.

III LIM [17.6]

Knowledge from facts ascertainable with the help of expert advice The claimant is fixed with expert knowledge which it would be reasonable for him, in his state of health, to obtain: *Newton v Cammell Laird & Co (Shipbuilders and Engineers) Ltd* [1969] 1 All ER 708, [1969] 1 WLR 415, CA. He may have sufficient knowledge although an expert's report has still to be made: *Wilkinson v Ancliff (BLT) Ltd* [1986] 3 All ER 427, [1986] 1 WLR 1352, CA. In *Halford v Brookes* [1991] 3 All ER 559, [1991] 1 WLR 428, CA, the claimant was held to have knowledge for the purposes of s 14 at the time of the criminal trial of the defendant, not at the later date when she first received legal advice about the possibility of a civil remedy.

Where the claimant's knowledge as to whether an injury was attributable to an employer's negligence could only be obtained with the help of expert medical advice, and all reasonable steps had been taken to obtain that advice once he was alerted to the possibility, he should not be fixed with the requisite knowledge under this section until the expert medical advice had been obtained in accordance with the proviso in s 14(3): *Ali v Courtaulds Textiles Ltd* (1999) 52 BMLR 129, CA.

See also the discussion at **III LIM [17.4A]** above.

III LIM [18]

14A. Special time limit for negligence actions where facts relevant to cause of action are not known at date of accrual

(1) This section applies to any action for damages for negligence, other than one to which section 11 of this Act applies, where the starting date for reckoning the period of limitation under subsection (4)(b) below falls after the date on which the cause of action accrued.

(2) Section 2 of this Act shall not apply to an action to which this section applies.

(3) An action to which this section applies shall not be brought after the expiration of the period applicable in accordance with subsection (4) below.

(4) That period is either—

(a) six years from the date on which the cause of action accrued; or

(b) three years from the starting date as defined by subsection (5) below, if that period expires later than the period mentioned in paragraph (a) above.

(5) For the purposes of this section, the starting date for reckoning the period of limitation under subsection (4)(b) above is the earliest date on which the plaintiff or any person in whom the cause of action was vested before him first had both the knowledge required for bringing an action for damages in respect of the relevant damage and a right to bring such an action.

(6) In subsection (5) above "the knowledge required for bringing an action for damages in respect of the relevant damage" means knowledge both—

(a) of the material facts about the damage in respect of which damages are claimed; and

(b) of the other facts relevant to the current action mentioned in subsection (8) below.

(7) For the purposes of subsection (6)(a) above, the material facts about the damage are such facts about the damage as would lead a reasonable person who had suffered such damage to consider it sufficiently serious to justify his instituting proceedings for damages against a defendant who did not dispute liability and was able to satisfy a judgment.

(8) The other facts referred to in subsection (6)(b) above are—

(a) that the damage was attributable in whole or in part to the act or omission which is alleged to constitute negligence; and

(b) the identity of the defendant; and

(c) if it is alleged that the act or omission was that of a person other than the defendant, the identity of that person and the additional facts supporting the bringing of an action against the defendant.

(9) Knowledge that any acts or omissions did or did not, as a matter of law, involve negligence is irrelevant for the purposes of subsection (5) above.

(10) For the purposes of this section a person's knowledge includes knowledge which he might reasonably have been expected to acquire—

(a) from facts observable or ascertainable by him; or

(b) from facts ascertainable by him with the help of appropriate expert advice which it is reasonable for him to seek;

but a person shall not be taken by virtue of this subsection to have knowledge of a fact ascertainable only with the help of expert advice so long as he has taken all reasonable steps to obtain (and, where appropriate, to act on) that advice.

III LIM [18.1]

Insolvency The general rule (see **III LIM [2.1]**) that limitation periods cease to run at the commencement of the winding up (or, as the case maybe, bankruptcy) so long as they had not already expired by that date applies also to s 14A and indeed s 14B. See *Financial Services Compensation Scheme Ltd v Larnell (Insurances) Ltd* [2006] EWCA Civ 1408, [2006] QB 808.

III LIM [18.1A]

Personal injury not included Section 14A does not apply to personal injury litigation: see s 11 of the 1980 Act.

III LIM [18.2]

Contract The section does not extend to an action for breach of a contractual duty to take care: see *Iron Trade Mutual Insurance Co Ltd v J K Buckenham Ltd* [1990] 1 All ER 808, [1989] 2 Lloyd's Rep 85 approved in *Société Commerciale de Réassurance v ERAS (International) Ltd* [1992] 2 All ER 82n, CA in which Mustill LJ held that the words "[t]his section applies to any action for damages for negligence"

> . . . denote in our minds an action asserting that the defendant has committed the tort of negligence.

Misrepresentation It was for this reason that the Court of Appeal in *Laws v Society of Lloyd's* decided that s 14A does not apply to the statutory cause of action created by s 2(1) of the Misrepresentation Act 1967 since the section does not require the claimant to show that the defendant has been negligent. Instead, what might informally be called negligence becomes relevant only to the defendant's statutory defence that he did believe and had reasonable grounds for believing that the representation was true.

III LIM [18.2A]

Financial Services Section 14A does not apply to a claim under s 62 of the Financial Services Act 1986: see *Martin v Britannia Life* [2000] Lloyd's Rep PN 412, at 9.2.

III LIM [18.3]

"Shall not be brought" See the note in s 2 at para **III LIM [3.3]** as to when an action is brought for the purposes of the Limitation Act 1980.

III LIM [18.4]

Date of accrual of cause of action The cause of actions accrues when the damage occurs: see *Pirelli General Cable Works Ltd v Oscar Faber & Partners* [1983] 2 AC 1, [1983] 1 All ER 65, HL.

III LIM [18.4A]

The knowledge to be attributed to a corporate claimant. In *Meridian Global Funds Management Asia Ltd v Securities Commission* [1995] 2 AC 500 (*not* a limitation case) it was held by the House of Lords that the knowledge (and acts) of natural persons are usually to be attributed to companies by

(a) "primary rules of attribution" derived from their memorandum and articles; and

(b) "general rules of attribution" derived from company law and the general law of eg agency, vicarious liability *&c*.

Exceptionally these general rules may not be consistent with the purpose of a particular provision and in such a case a special rule might have to be formulated. It follows that the "directing mind and will" of the company (see *Lennard's Carrying Co Ltd v Asiatic Petroleum Co Ltd* [1915] AC 705) may not have to be identified in every case.

In *3M United Kingdom plc v Linklaters & Paines* [2005] EWHC 1382 (Ch), [2005] PNLR 46 (affirmed by the Court of Appeal on other grounds at [2006] PNLR 3) (which was a limitation case) Hart J said that

> . . . it was quite consistent with the content and purpose of s 14A for there to be attribution to a corporate claimant of two separate pieces of individual knowledge if, in the particular context, it is reasonable to suppose that the relevant information would in fact have been aggregated within the organisation. That is to say no more than what is already spelled out in s 14A(10)(a).

III LIM [18.4B]

14A(5) the knowledge which the claimant is deemed to have In *Graham v Entec Europe Ltd* [2003] 4 All ER 1345, (2003) Times, 10 September, CA, it was held that:

(a) the knowledge of a loss adjuster investigating and advising on a claim on behalf of insurers for the purpose of pursuing a subrogated claim by those insurers, is to be treated as the knowledge of the insurers for the purposes of s 14A(5);

(b) words "the plaintiff" in s 14A(5) should be construed as meaning/extending to a plaintiff whether suing in his own name or the name of another by way of subrogation.

Generally it is for the claimant to plead and to prove that it acquired the requisite knowledge not more than 3 years before the action is brought: *Nash v Eli Lilly & Co* [1993] 4 All ER 383, [1993] 1 WLR 782, CA and *Haward v Fawcetts (a firm)* [2006] UKHL 9, [2006] 3 All ER 497, [2006] 1 WLR 682.

III LIM [18.5]

"as would lead a reasonable person who had suffered such damage to consider it sufficiently serious" Section 14A(7) establishes a wholly objective test and the consequence is that the qualifying threshold of damage is low. In the case of a negligent survey, for example, it has been held that there is only one cause of action, namely the negligent making of the report. In *Horbury v Craig Hall & Rutley* (20 February 1989, unreported), CA, the claimant bought a house in 1980. In 1982 she discovered a defect in the chimney breast which would cost £132 to remedy. In 1985 she discovered dry rot which would cost some £50,000 to remedy. It was held that by the time the writ was issued in 1988 the alternative three-year period had already expired since it had begun in 1982 and not 1985. See also *Hamlin v Edwin Evans* [1996] 2 EGLR 106, [1996] PNLR 398.

In the surveyor cases the negligent making of a report has been held to involve one duty, the breach of which gives rise to one cause of action. In other cases this may not always be so. In the solicitors' case of *Birmingham Midshires Building Society v JD Wretham* [1999] Lloyd's Rep PN 133, [1999] 07 EG 138, the claimant mortgagee brought proceedings in negligence against solicitors acting for the purchaser and the mortgagee. The principal allegation was that the defendants failed to inform the claimant of material respects within their knowledge in which the borrower's involvement with and purchase of the property differed, to the substantial detriment of the security, from the information given in the mortgage application. It was not until September 1995 that the claimant had the requisite knowledge of that failure. In 1991 the claimant had known that the defendant had failed to report the existence of demolition order in respect of the property, but the claimant took no action in this respect. At the hearing of a preliminary issue, the defendants argued that where the claimant had not sued upon a potential claim of which it had earlier knowledge, it was debarred from pursuing the claim on which it does sue, and of which it admittedly did not have the requisite knowledge until well within the relevant limitation period under s 14A. This argument was rejected by the court, which held that on the facts there were two separate duties breached with the effect that the running of time in respect of the first had no effect on the second.

In *Capita ATL Pension Trustees Ltd v Sedgwick Financial Services Ltd* [2016] EHWC 214 (Ch), Proudman J noted the terms of s 14A(10), but pointed out that they only apply where the relevant fact, namely the potential liability of the defendant, was ascertainable only with the help of expert advice. Where, as in that case, the claimant, realising that there might be a cause of action against the defendant, entered into a standstill agreement with it, the fact that it had taken all reasonable steps to obtain the expert advice was immaterial.

III LIM [18.6]

Causally relevant knowledge required In *Hallam-Eames v Merrett Syndicates Ltd* [1995] 7 Med LR 122, it was held that the knowledge required was "that which is causally relevant for the purposes of an allegation of negligence". In *Dobbie v Medway Health Authority* [1994]

LIMITATION

4 All ER 450, [1994] 1 WLR 1234, CA, Hoffmann LJ said that it was necessary to "look at the way the claimant puts his case, distil what he is complaining about and ask whether he had in broad terms knowledge of the facts on which that complaint is based".

In *Gold v Mincoff Science and Gold* [2001] 03 LS Gaz R 44, ChD, Neuberger J said: "... what a claimant has to know before time starts running against him is those facts which, if pleaded, would be sufficient to constitute a valid claim, not liable to be struck out for want of some essential allegation, against the defendants in negligence".

III LIM [18.7]

Knowledge of negligence is irrelevant In *HF Pensions Trustees Ltd v Ellison* [1999] Lloyd's Rep PN 489, the claimant transferred surplus pension funds in reliance on allegedly negligent advice. It was held by Jonathan Parker LJ that for the purposes of s 14A time starts to run from the date of knowledge of all the material facts, and not from the time when the claimant knew that those facts gave rise to a claim in negligence (see s 14A(9) at para **III LIM [18]** and *Bradstock Trustee Services Ltd v Nabarro Nathanson* [1995] 4 All ER 888, [1995] 1 WLR 1405.). Accordingly, the start date was when the transfer had been effected and not when another court had ruled that the transfer was unlawful; the claim was therefore statute barred (*cf. Perry v Moysey* [1998] PNLR 657). See also *Fennon v Hodari & Co (a firm)* [2001] Lloyds Rep PN 183 and *Bowie v Southorns (a firm)* [2002] EWHC 1389 (QB), [2002] All ER (D) 119 (Jul).

In *Haward v Fawcetts* [2004] EWCA Civ 240, [2004] PNLR 34, the claimants had made investments in a company from 1995 to 1997 in reliance upon the advice of the defendant accountants. The company did not flourish and in 1999 the claimants received advice which suggested that the defendants might have been negligent. Proceedings were commenced in 2001 and the defendants pleaded a limitation defence. At first instance it was held (in reliance upon *Bradstock Trustee Services*)

(a) that the making of each payment constituted damage;
(b) that the claimants had known all that they needed to know when they made each payment and, in particular, that they knew that they were relying on the defendants' advice in making the investments and thus that loss and advice (or lack thereof) were causally connected.

On appeal, Jonathan Parker LJ revisited *HF Pension Trustees Ltd* and said of s 14A(9) that

> It is clear from the words of the section itself (looking no further for the moment) that it is concerned with knowledge of facts, as opposed to knowledge of matters of law. In particular, subsection (9) specifically excludes knowledge that the defendant acted negligently.

He went on to hold that the concept of "attributability" in s 14A(8)(a) is similar but not identical to causation. Instead, the defining factor is causal relevance. Where damage has only one possible cause then the question of the causal relevance of that cause to the (factual) allegations of negligence "answer[s] itself" (per Jonathan Parker LJ) It is otherwise where there is more than one possible cause. *Haward* was just such a case in that there was more than one possible reason why the company had made losses and failed. As in *Hallam-Eames*, more was required for the necessary connection to be made and this was supplied by the advice received by the claimants in 1999. *Bradstock Trustees* and *HF Pension Trustees* were distinguished as cases in which there was a single possible cause ie the advice which had led to the making of the payments which were later held to have been unlawful.

In the House of Lords in *Haward v Fawcetts (a firm)* [2006] UKHL 9, [2006] 3 All ER 497, this aspect of Jonathan Parker LJ's reasoning (and thus his conclusion) was subject to some criticism. In the first place, it was said to be enough that the claimants knew that the defendant's acts or omissions were a contributory cause of the losses. Once they knew that the fact that there may have been possible other causes would then be irrelevant. Their lordships also considered that the Court of Appeal's analysis had focused on the wrong event. The "damage" allegedly caused by the defendant's negligence was not the failure of the Company – for which the defendant could not be made liable – but instead the making of loss-making investments. The claimants were seeking to make the defendant responsible for their losses consequent upon the making of the investments and they therefore needed to know only of the losses and that the defendant's acts or omissions were causative of the making of the investments which led to them. They obviously had the latter knowledge at the time of the investments and all that it was then necessary for them to discover was that the investments were lost which had soon become apparent. The only knowledge which they did not at that stage have was that the defendant's advice (or the lack of it) had been negligent but this, by reason of s 14A(9), is irrelevant.

This analysis also made it unnecessary - so far as the knowledge required for the start date to occur – for the claimants in *Haward* to know not only that the investments had merely been lost but that they had been intrinsically unsound at the outset which knowledge the Court of Appeal had also treated as necessary. Their Lordships thought this was a detail too far and indeed that it was just the sort of matter for which the 3-year period allowed by s 14A is intended to provide time to investigate. See too *Shore v Sedgwick Financial Services Ltd* [2008] EWCA Civ 863, [2008] All ER (D) 304 (Jul).

Also relevant in the special context of negligent legal advice is the decision of Hart J in *3M United Kingdom plc v Linklaters & Paines* [2005] EWHC 1382 (Ch), [2005] PNLR 46 (affirmed by the Court of Appeal on other grounds at [2006] PNLR 3) in which he expressed the obiter view "apart from authority" that a damage-causing legal consequence of other facts was potentially as much a fact for the purposes of s 14A as, for example, a damage-causing physical consequence and went on to cast some upon doubt Jonathan Parker LJ's interpretation of s 14A(9) in *HF Pension Trustees Ltd* and *Haward v Fawcetts* suggesting that there was no rational basis for treating cases of negligent legal advice any differently. As Hart J put it:

> . . . where the negligence consists in the very failure by the professional defendant to advise the lay claimant of that [legal] consequence, the proposition that the claimant should nonetheless be treated as having knowledge of that consequence for limitation purposes (when his very complaint is that he should have been but was not told it by the defendant) is almost absurd. It is certainly counter-intuitive and unattractive.

Finally, in this difficult area it is worth returning to what Hoffman LJ said in *Hallam-Eames v Merrett Syndicates Ltd* [1996] 7 Med LR 122:

> The plaintiff does not have to know that he has a cause of action or that the defendant's acts can be characterised in law as negligent or as falling short of some standard of professional or other behaviour. But, as Hoffmann LJ said in *Broadley*, the words "which is alleged to constitute negligence" serve to identify the facts of which the plaintiff must have knowledge. He must have known the facts which can fairly be described as constituting the negligence of which he complains. It may be that knowledge of such facts will also serve to bring home to him the fact that the defendant has been negligent or at fault. But that is not in itself a reason for saying that he need not have known them.

These criticisms of the decision in HF Pension Trustees have now been vindicated by the decision of the House of Lords in *Haward v Fawcetts* ([2006] UKHL 9, [2006] 3 All ER 497) albeit in what seem to be *obiter dicta*. Lord Nicholls (at para 13) began on a salutary note:

> A linguistic point which can give rise to confusion, should be noted here. Sometimes the essence of a claimant's case may lie in an alleged act or omission by the defendant which cannot easily be described, at least in general terms, without recourse to language suggestive of fault: for instance, that 'something had gone wrong' in the conduct of the claimant's medical operation, or that the accountant's advice was 'flawed'. Use of such language does not mean the facts thus compendiously described have necessarily stepped outside the scope of section 14A(8)(a). In this context there can be no objection to the use of language of this character so long as this does not lead to any blurring of the boundary between the essential and the irrelevant.

Lord Walker, referring to *HF Pension Trustees* said [at para 61] that

> [u]ntil [HF Pension Trustees] knew that they had received seriously incorrect advice which overlooked the need for propriety in exercising fiduciary powers, they did not know that the interests of their beneficiaries, the scheme members, were being prejudiced. This lack of knowledge did not mean merely that they were ignorant of having a cause of action in negligence against the solicitors; more fundamentally and more relevantly, they did not know that they (on behalf of the beneficiaries) had suffered any damage at all . . . In short, they knew the bare facts, but they were ignorant of their real significance. Their ignorance was at a different and more basic level than that addressed by section 14A(9).

Lord Mance thought that the notion that the trustees did not know that they had suffered any damage was a possible analysis but himself considered (at para 117) that the unlawfulness of the Trustees' transfers

> . . . should, in context, have been regarded as an (unknown) fact - an aspect of the acts or omissions alleged to constitute negligence . . .

but that

> [i]n either case, it should not have been until the impermissibility was known to the claimants that time started running against them.

This all seems ineluctably to suggest a less mechanistic application of s 14A(9) and a rather more clear-sighted appreciation of the very reason for the enactment of these latent damage provisions. A little earlier at (para 115) Lord Mance had said that

Hart & Honoré, in Causation in the Law (2nd Ed.) p. 38, demonstrate that the concepts of causation (dependent on knowing what is factually usual) and reprehensibility (central to the concept of breach of duty) are conceptually distinct, although on the particular facts coincident.

In other words, one needs to know the former not the latter, even if by knowing the former one might also know the latter.

III LIM [18.8]

Constructive knowledge Where it was alleged that the defendant solicitor negligently facilitated a mortgage fraud, it was held that the claimant was not entitled to rely on s 14A and the claim was statute barred; at an early stage it had sufficient information to investigate such a case where serious losses had been incurred in circumstances suggesting a subsale at an inflated price. Moreover, it was immaterial that pertinent information might not have come to the notice of each responsible department, as an organisation like the claimant could reasonably be expected to have put into place a system for its dissemination. It was therefore fixed with knowledge that it should reasonably have acquired: *Abbey National plc v Sayer Moore (a firm)* [1999] EGCS 114. See also *Skipton Building Society v Sorsky* [2003] EWHC 930 (QB).

In *Mortgage Corpn v Lambert & Co* [2000] Lloyd's Rep Bank 207, [2000] PNLR 820, CA, on the other hand, it was held that the claim was not statute barred under s 14A in a claim concerning a negligent mortgage valuation. The claimant had received estimated values of the property prior to the three years before the issue of the writ. Although the reports contained estimates by unqualified persons and were obtained for purposes other than valuation, it was held on appeal that they "might well" have caused a reasonable lender to question the original valuation. It was also held, however, that a reasonable lender put on inquiry as to the validity of the original valuation might not obtain such a retrospective valuation with the result that the claimant was not to be fixed with constructive knowledge.

See also *Caroline Rose Webster v Cooper & Burnett (a firm)* [2000] PNLR 240, CA; *Lloyds Bank plc v Burd Pearse* [1999] EGCS 99; on appeal [2001] EGCS 39, CA; *Finance for Mortgages Ltd v Farley & Co* [1998] PNLR 145; and *Halford v Brookes* [1991] 1 WLR 428.

In *Henderson v Temple Pier Co Ltd* it was held, on the equivalent wording of s 14(3) of the Limitation Act, that establishing the name of a ship was not something which required legal expertise. The incompetent failure of the claimant's solicitor to do so therefore did not prevent the claimant from being fixed with the knowledge which the solicitor ought reasonably to have acquired. There seems to be no reason for not giving the same effect to s 14A(5) the wording of which is materially the same.

In *Gravgaard v Aldridge & Brownlee (a firm)* [2004] EWCA Civ 1529, [2004] All ER (D) 134 (Dec) it was held that the claimant could be fixed with knowledge which she would have acquired if, as would have been reasonable, she had sought advice earlier about a separate, though related, cause of action against another party

> . . . the fact that [the claimant] is wrong in thinking that she has a good defence does not resolve the question whether she should have taken advice which would have caused the potential claim against the respondents to be exposed. *Per* Arden LJ.

Section 14A(1), requires the court to have regard to a *reasonable* person in the position of the claimant.

If a claimant takes reasonable steps to obtain and to act on the advice of an expert then the claimant is to be treated as knowing only what that expert in fact advised rather than what the expert should have advised (but did not): see *Lenderink-Woods v Zurich Assurance Ltd* [2015] EWHC 3634 (Ch), [2015] All ER (D) 131 (Dec) at [31].

III LIM [19]

14B. Overriding time limit for negligence actions not involving personal injuries

(1) An action for damages for negligence, other than one to which section 11 of this Act applies, shall not be brought after the expiration of fifteen years from the date (or, if more than one, from the last of the dates) on which there occurred any act or omission—

(a) which is alleged to constitute negligence; and

(b) to which the damage in respect of which damages are claimed is alleged to be attributable (in whole or in part).

(2) This section bars the right of action in a case to which subsection (1) above applies notwithstanding that—

(a) the cause of action has not yet accrued; or

(b) where section 14A of this Act applies to the action, the date which is for the purposes of that section the starting date for reckoning the period mentioned in subsection (4)(b) of that section has not yet occurred;

before the end of the period of limitation prescribed by this section.

III LIM [19.1]

"Shall not be brought" See the note in s 2 at para **III LIM [3.3]** as to when an action is brought for the purposes of the Limitation Act 1980.

III LIM [19.2]

"bars the right of action" In *Financial Services Compensation Scheme Ltd v Larnell (Insurances) Ltd* [2005] EWCA Civ 1408, [2006] 2 WLR 751, [2006] BCC 690, [2006] PNLR 13 the Court of Appeal held that section 14B does not operate to extinguish the cause of action; both because much more explicit language would be required for it to have this exceptional effect and because there was no obvious reason of policy why it should do so.

In *Financial Services Compensation Scheme Ltd v Larnell (Insurances) Ltd* itself the effect of this was that a claim in negligence was not statute-barred where it was brought against an insolvent financial adviser with a view to invoking the claimant's rights under the Third Party (Rights Against Insurers) Act 1930. The 15 year period under s 14B had elapsed *after* the defendant's winding up commenced (when time under any then unexpired period of limitation would have stopped running pursuant to the insolvency "exception" see **III LIM 2.1**) but *prior* to the commencement of proceedings against the defendant.

III LIM [20]

15. Time limit for actions to recover land

(1) No action shall be brought by any person to recover any land after the expiration of twelve years from the date on which the right of action accrued to him or, if it first accrued to some person through whom he claims, to that person.

(2) Subject to the following provisions of this section, where—

(a) the estate or interest claimed was an estate or interest in reversion or remainder or any other future estate or interest and the right of action to recover the land accrued on the date on which the estate or interest fell into possession by the determination of the preceding estate or interest; and

(b) the person entitled to the preceding estate or interest (not being a term of years absolute) was not in possession of the land on that date;

no action shall be brought by the person entitled to the succeeding estate or interest after the expiration of twelve years from the date on which the right of action accrued to the person entitled to the preceding estate or interest or six years from the date on which the right of action accrued to the person entitled to the succeeding estate or interest, whichever period last expires.

(3) Subsection (2) above shall not apply to any estate or interest which falls into possession on the determination of an entailed interest and which might have been barred by the person entitled to the entailed interest.

(4) No person shall bring an action to recover any estate or interest in land under an assurance taking effect after the right of action to recover the land had accrued to the person by whom the assurance was made or some person through whom he claimed or some person entitled to a preceding estate or interest, unless the action is brought within the period during which the person by whom the assurance was made could have brought such an action.

(5) Where any person is entitled to any estate or interest in land in possession and, while so entitled, is also entitled to any future estate or interest in that land, and his right to recover the estate or interest in possession is barred under this Act, no action shall be brought by that person, or by any person claiming through him, in respect of the future estate or interest, unless in the meantime possession of the land has been recovered by a person entitled to an intermediate estate or interest.

(6) Part I of Schedule 1 to this Act contains provisions for determining the date of accrual of rights of action to recover land in the cases there mentioned.

(7) Part II of that Schedule contains provisions modifying the provisions of this section in their application to actions brought by, or by a person claiming through, the Crown or any spiritual or eleemosynary corporation sole.

III LIM [20.1]

Changes in relation to registered land On 13 October 2003, ss 15–17 and Sch 1 to the Limitation Act 1980 ceased to apply to registered estates in land or rentcharges. Instead, the regime set out in ss 96–98 and Sch 6 to the Land Registration Act 2002 (see paras **III LIM [49]–III LIM [52]**) applies to adverse possession cases in relation to land which is registered at the time when the squatter applies for registration in his name even if the land has not been registered for the whole of the requisite ten-year period under the 2002 Act.

Since the coming into force of these provisions, there have accordingly been two adverse possession regimes: one for registered and one for unregistered land. The juridical rationale for the distinction (and for the change) is that, in the case of registered land, title is principally based on registration whereas title to unregistered land is based on possession. At another level, there had been growing concern at the relative ease with which adverse possession can be established under the 1980 Act, namely the mere effluxion of time. The Law Commission (see Law Com 271 "Land Registration for the 21st Century – A Conveyancing Revolution") considered this to be unjustified in relation to registered land where certainty of title presents no difficulty of investigation.

It should however be noted that by para 18(1) of Schedule 2 (Transition) of the Land Registration Act 2002, the pre-Act régime continues to apply to registered land in respect of which the squatter has already extinguished the owner's title by adverse possession as at 13 October 2003.

III LIM [20.1A]

No action... shall be brought See the note in s 2 at para **III LIM [3.3]** as to when an action is brought for the purposes of the Limitation Act 1980. The issue of a claim does not stop time running except for the purpose of those proceedings. The defendant to a second set of proceedings may rely on periods of adverse possession during the first set of proceedings, which had been struck out. *Markfield Investments Ltd v Evans* [2001] 2 All ER 238, [2001] 1 WLR 1321, CA.

III LIM [20.1B]

"land" See s 38(1) for the definition of land.

III LIM [20.1C]

"right of action" See s 38(7) for the definition of right of action.

III LIM [20.1D]

Mortgages Time starts to run for the purposes of s 15(1) on the date on which the mortgagee becomes entitled to possession. In order for time to run it is not necessary for the mortgagor to be in possession without the consent of the mortgagee: *Ashe v National Westminster Bank Plc* [2007] EWHC 494 (Ch), (2007) 12 EG 155 (CS), [2007] NPC 36.

Ashe was upheld on appeal (at [2008] EWCA Civ 55, [2008] BPIR 1) but does not apply to charging orders because the holder of a charging order does not have a right to possession such that time can run against it under s 15: *Yorkshire Bank Finance Ltd v Mulhall* [2008] EWCA Civ 1156, [2009] 2 All ER (Comm) 164, [2009] 1 P & CR 345.

III LIM [20.2]

Application to Land Registry Neither an application to the Land Registry to warn off cautions nor the issue of an originating summons seeking removal of the cautions constituted an "action . . . brought . . . to recover any land" within the meaning of s 15(1). Accordingly, time only stopped running when the claimants issued their action for the possession of the disputed land: *JA Pye (Oxford) Ltd v Graham* [2000] Ch 676, [2000] 3 WLR 242.

III LIM [20.3]

Equity Where a brother claimed to establish title by adverse possession as against his siblings under s 15(1), it was held that he held the property on constructive trust. Accordingly, the action was not statute barred by virtue of s 21 of the Limitation Act 1980, which provides that no limitation period applies to an action for the recovery of trust property from a trustee: *James v Williams* [2000] Ch 1, [1999] 3 All ER 309, CA. In *Earnshaw v*

Hartley [2000] Ch 155, [1999] 3 WLR 709, CA, it was held that time did not run for the purposes of s 15(1) where the beneficial interests of the claimants in the unadministered estate was a sufficient interest for the purposes of paragraph 9 of Sch 1 of the Limitation Act 1980.

Where there had been a representation by silence that a property was unoccupied (community charge registration forms were not completed), the occupier was not estopped from claiming adverse possession because (1) the representation was not believed, (2) the failure to complete the registration form had not caused the loss claimed, (3) the detriment was not material: *Ellis v London Borough of Lambeth* (1999) 32 HLR 596, [1999] EGCS 101.

III LIM [20.4]

Adverse possession Paragraph 8(1) of Sch 1 to the Act (which deals with the "Accrual of Rights of Action to Recover Land") defines adverse possession merely as a situation in which "the land is in the possession of some person in whose favour the period of limitation can run".

The period of limitation cannot run in favour of someone with registered title to the land. Thus where, in error, the same land is concurrently registered in two different titles the actual possessor cannot establish adverse possession because until rectification of the register to show the true position such possession is not unlawful. It follows that until such rectification the true owner could not seek recovery of possession from the actual possessor because it has no better title, rather they both have the same title: see *Parshall v Hackney* [2013] EWCA Civ 240, [2013] Ch 568, [2013] 3 All ER 224. The 1980 Act does not apply to the statutory right to apply to rectify the land register.

Possession may still qualify as adverse possession despite the fact that the possession (or part of it) amounts to a criminal offence within the meaning of s 144 of the Legal Aid, Sentencing and Punishment of Offenders Act 2012 which came into force in September 2012 and which criminalises trespass involving 'living in' a residential building: see *R (on the application of Best) v Chief Land Registrar (Secretary of State for Justice, interested party)* [2014] EWHC 1370 (Admin), [2014] 3 All ER 637, [2014] PLSCS 141, a case of registered land under the Land Registration Act 2002.

Comprehensive definition must therefore be sought in the case law. Five requirements have been posited: (1) the squatter must have been in actual possession of the land; (2) possession must have been exclusive; (3) the paper owner of the land must have discontinued possession or have been dispossessed; (4) the squatter must have intended to possess the land (ie had the requisite *animus possidendi* according to the traditional formulation); and (5) the possession must have been adverse in the statutory sense – the "right of action" must have accrued: see *Prudential Assurance Co Ltd v Waterloo Real Estate Inc* [1999] 2 EGLR 85. See also *Powell v McFarlane* (1979) 38 P & CR 452; *Buckinghamshire County Council v Moran* [1990] Ch 623. Possession fulfilling these conditions must also be continuous for the 12-year period. In *Buckinghamshire County Council v Moran* [1990] Ch 623, Slade J said:

> 'Factual possession signifies an appropriate degree of physical control. It must be a single and [exclusive] possession, though there can be a single possession exercised by or on behalf of several persons jointly. Thus an owner of land and a person intruding on that land without his consent cannot both be in possession of the land at the same time. The question what acts constitute a sufficient degree of exclusive physical control must depend on the circumstances, in particular the nature of the land and the manner in which land of that nature is commonly used or enjoyed. . . . Everything must depend on the particular circumstances, but broadly, I think what must be shown as constituting factual possession is that the alleged possessor has been dealing with the land in question as an occupying owner might have been expected to deal with it and that no-one else has done so.'

This passage was cited with approval by the House of Lords in *J A Pye (Oxford) Ltd v Graham* [2002] UKHL 30, [2003] 1 AC 419, [2002] 3 All ER 865.

A squatter seeking to defeat an owner's claim for possession needed only to have a manifested intention to possess "for the time being": *Powell v McFarlane* (1977) 38 P & CR 452. The fact that he intended or expected to leave the property at some time in the future is not inconsistent with having that intention. It followed that so long as he remained in actual possession for the requisite 12 years with that intention, he could fulfil the requirements of s 15. It is also possible for an occupier to be in actual possession even where he wrongly believes that he has a tenancy; it is not necessary for him to show that he had an intention to exclude the paper owner but merely to possess the land: *Ofulue v Bossert* [2008] EWCA Civ 7, [2008] HRLR 20, [2008] UKHRR 447, (2008) Times, 11 February. See also *Alston & Sons Ltd v BOCM Pauls Ltd* [2008] EWHC 3310 (Ch), [2008] All ER (D) 312 (Nov) where the squatter's recognition that he might have to leave did not make his intention to possess insufficient.

Where actual possession is established there is little scope for a distinction between occupation which amounts only to trespass and occupation which amounts to adverse possession: *Lambeth London Borough Council v Blackburn* [2001] EWCA Civ 912, (2001) 82 P & CR 494 (see also *Topplan Estates v Townley* [2004] EWCA Civ 1369, (2004) Times, 15 November). In *J A Pye (Oxford) Ltd v Graham* [2002] UKHL 30, [2003] 1 AC 419, [2002] 3 All ER 865 the House of Lords held that the sufficiency of possession is not diminished or qualified by willingness on the part of the squatter to pay the owner for the occupation (following *Ocean Estates Ltd v Pinder* [1969] 2 AC 19, PC) and did not depend on the intention of the true owner in relation to the land – especially where such intention is unknown to the squatter (finally disapproving the "heresy" in *Leigh v Jack* (1879) 5 Ex D 264). Lord Browne-Wilkinson indicated that "much confusion and complication would be avoided if reference to adverse possession were to be avoided so far as possible and effect instead given to the clear words of the Acts. The question is simply whether the defendant squatter has dispossessed the paper owner by going into ordinary possession of the land for the requisite period without the consent of the owner." See also "*Adverse Possession: The Abolition of Heresies*" [2002] 66 Conv 480. The majority of the cases relate to the status of squatters and the word "dispossession" will therefore be an apt description of the requirements in such a case but it must not be considered to imply any limitation on the circumstances in which time can run. The term "adverse possession" refers to the capacity of the person in possession rather than the nature of that possession and means only ordinary possession by a person in whose favour the limitation period could run.

Thus mortgagors in ordinary possession of the property after the grant of a legal charge are in possession which is capable of being "adverse" to any accrued right to possession which the mortgagee may have either because of some default by the mortgagor or because the particular form of charge gives an immediate right to possession after execution. The mortgagors' possession is based upon their registered legal title rather than the mortgagee's interest and they therefore do not need the permission of the mortgagee and where this is neither sought nor given (and the mere failure to enforce an accrued right to possession does not amount to granting implied permission) then the failure by a mortgagor in possession to make any payment to the mortgagee for more than 12 years entitled the mortgagors to a declaration that the legal charge had been extinguished by s 17 of the Act. See *Ashe v National Westminster Bank plc* [2008] EWCA Civ 55, [2008] 1 WLR 710, [2008] All ER (D) 128 (Feb), (2008) 7 EG 143 (CS).

The question of sufficient possession depends, in every case, on the facts including the nature of the land in question. In *Inglewood Investments Co Ltd v Baker* [2002] EWCA Civ 1733, [2003] 2 P & CR 319 even the erection of a fence was insufficient since its purpose was to keep sheep in rather than the rest of the world out.

In *Smith v Waterman & Bostock* [2003] EWHC 1266 (Ch), [2003] All ER (D) 72 (Jun) it was said that the mere going on to the land by the owner or his agents did not interrupt the continuity of possession for the purposes of the Limitation Act where the squatter was otherwise in factual possession. Factual possession does not depend upon continuous physical occupation and intermittent use may suffice – see *Havering London Borough Council v Chambers* [2011] EWCA Civ 1576, [2012] 1 P & CR 373, [2012] P & CR D39.

In *Lambeth London Borough Council v Archangel* [2002] 1 P & CR 230, 33 HLR 490, CA, the squatter sought to resist the council's claim for possession on the basis of his rent-free occupation since 1985. His claim failed because of a letter which he had written in 1993 which mentioned the need to refurbish "Lambeth's property". He was held to have acknowledged the council's title. See also *Bigden v London Borough of Lambeth* [2000] EGCS 147, where a petition which acknowledged the council's right to sell the properties constituted sufficient acknowledgment of better title to defeat the claim for adverse possession. For acknowledgement generally see s 29 below at **III LIM [33]**.

It does not appear to be possible to establish adverse possession of any part of the highway, see *R (on the application of Smith) v Land Registry (Cambridgeshire County Council, interested party)* [2010] EWCA Civ 200, [2011] QB 413, [2010] 3 All ER 113. This principle has subsequently been applied by analogy to a claim for adverse possession of the riverbed where title to it was vested by statute in the Port of London Authority for the purposes of regulating the public right of navigation of the river. See *Couper v Albion Properties Ltd* [2013] EWHC 2993 (Ch), [2013] All ER (D) 113 (Oct).

Implied consent may be sufficient to negative adverse possession but for this to be implied from the circumstances of the case there must be some overt act by the landowner or some demonstrable circumstance from which the consent can be implied: see *Lambeth London Borough Council v Rumbelow* (25 January 2001, unreported), Ch D. It does not matter whether the user was aware of the overt act or demonstrable circumstance so long as a reasonable person would have appreciated that the use was with the permission of the owner.

Where an occupier of land is negotiating with its owner for the grant of some interest in that land, it may be a natural inference from the circumstances that the owner permits the occupier to occupy the land pending the result of those negotiations: see *Colin Dawson Windows Ltd v King's Lynn & West Norfolk Borough Council* [2005] EWCA Civ 9, [2005] 2 P & CR 19 and *Bath & North East Somerset District Council v Nicholson* [2002] 10 EGCS 156.

III LIM [20.4A]

Vessels on the foreshore or riverbed The mooring of a vessel on a river or foreshore may amount to adverse possession of the bed below, though only resting on it at low tide: *Port of London Authority v Ashmore* [2009] EWHC 954 (Ch), [2009] 4 All ER 665. Cf *Couper v Albion Properties Ltd* [2013] EWHC 2993 (Ch), [2013] All ER (D) 113 (Oct).

The act of mooring a boat on a tidal river gives no insight into a boat owner's intentions and was as equivocal an act of possession as could be imagined: see *Port of London Authority v Mendoza* [2017] UKUT 146 (TCC). Installing a septic tank with associated pipe work on the disputed land was equally referable to an intention to acquire an easement: *Howell v Shoreham Port Authority* (2015) Ref/2014/0056/0582. It was held that the first instance decision in *Port of London Authority v Ashmore* [2009] EWHC 954 (Ch) was not to be regarded as authority to the contrary. There is no absolute rule that adverse possession is impossible wherever there are public rights of navigation. No analogy can be drawn between highways and rivers: see *Port of London Authority v Mendoza* [2017] UKUT 146 (TCC), where the Upper Tribunal refused to follow obiter remarks to the contrary in *Couper v Albion Properties Ltd* [2013] EWHC 2993 (Ch).

III LIM [20.5]

The human rights dimension In 2005, a Chamber of the European Court of Human Rights held that the relevant provisions of the Land Registration Act 1925 and the Limitation Act 1980 contravene Article 1, Protocol 1 of the European Convention because they deprive persons of their land in circumstances which are disproportionate and without compensation: see *JA Pye v United Kingdom (Application No 44302/02)* [2005] 49 EG 50, a decision prefigured by the first instance decision of Nicholas Strauss QC in *Beaulane Properties Ltd v Palmer* [2005] EWHC 1071 (Ch), [2005] 14 EG 129 (CS).

The UK Government requested that the case be referred to the Grand Chamber of the ECHR in accordance with Art 43 of the Convention. In its decision on 30 August 2007 (see (2008) 46 EHRR 45, 23 BHRC 405, [2007] RVR 302, (2007) Times, 1 October, [2007] 41 EG 200 (CS)) the Grand Chamber (by ten votes to seven) differed from the Chamber and held that there had been no violation on the grounds that:

(a) Article 1 Protocol 1 was engaged but by reason of "control of use" rather than a "deprivation of possessions".

(b) A 12-year limitation period for the bringing of claims for the recovery of land pursued a legitimate aim in the general interest and, in the context of the margin of appreciation allowed to states in implementing social and economic policies, the extinguishment of title upon the expiry of that period could not be said to be manifestly without foundation. Indeed, the extinguishment of title could be seen as little more than the regularising of the respective positions of previous owner and adverse possessor.

(c) So far as the question of "fair balance" was concerned this was not upset bearing in mind once again the state's margin of appreciation. As a "control of use" the jurisprudence on compensation for deprivation was not directly applicable but in any event the Court accepted the UK's submission that the notion of compensation would not be consistent with the purpose of limitation periods. It was also the case that the Applicant could with relative ease have stopped the limitation period from running eg by asking for rent or bringing possession proceedings. Moreover the substantial loss suffered by the applicant in this case (which appeared to lie between £2.5m and £10m) could not ultimately be relevant where the fulfilment of the aims of limitation laws depended on their applicability regardless of the size of the claim.

The dissenting judgments provide some intellectual and moral succour to those – including some distinguished members of the English judiciary – who have considered the effect of ss 15-17 to be disproportionate but with the coming into force of the Land Registration Act 2002 the debate has lost at least some of its practical importance.

The adverse possession provisions of the Limitation Act 1980 are therefore compatible with the European Convention and it is not open to a court to hold otherwise in a particular case merely because it seems distinguishable on its facts. The Court could only do so where, in a specific case, the application of the 1980 Act produced such an anomalous result that it was possible to say that the margin of appreciation allowed by the Strasbourg court had been exceeded: *Ofulue v Bossert* [2008] EWCA Civ 7, [2008] HRLR 20, [2008] UKHRR 447, (2008) Times, 11 February.

III LIM [21]

16. Time limit for redemption actions

When a mortgagee of land has been in possession of any of the mortgaged land for a period of twelve years, no action to redeem the land of which the mortgagee has been so in possession shall be brought after the end of that period by the mortgagor or any person claiming through him.

III LIM [21.1]

No action... shall be brought See the note in s 2 at para **III LIM [3.3]** as to when an action is brought for the purposes of the Limitation Act 1980.

III LIM [22]

17. Extinction of title to land after expiration of time limit

Subject to—

(a) section 18 of this Act . . .

(b) . . .

at the expiration of the period prescribed by this Act for any person to bring an action to recover land (including a redemption action) the title of that person to the land shall be extinguished.

III LIM [22.1]

Party walls Note, among other things, the decision in *Prudential Assurance Co Ltd v Waterloo Real Estate Inc* [1999] 3 EGLR 85, [1999] 17 EG 131, CA, that ownership of a party wall can be acquired by the adverse possession of one of the two owners.

III LIM [22.2]

Acquisition of a leasehold not defeated by surrender It was decided in *Central London Commercial Estates Ltd v Kato Kagako Ltd* [1998] 4 All ER 948 that a squatter's 12 years of adverse possession against a leaseholder of registered land entitled the squatter to registration under the Land Registration Act 1925 s 75 and that this right could not be defeated by surrender of the lease.

III LIM [22.3]

Bring an action See the note in s 2 at para **III LIM [3.3]** as to when an action is brought for the purposes of the Limitation Act 1980.

III LIM [23]

18. Settled land and land held on trust

(1) Subject to section 21 (1) and (2) of this Act, the provisions of this Act shall apply to equitable interests in land [. . .] as they apply to legal estates.

Accordingly a right of action to recover the land shall, for the purposes of this Act but not otherwise, be treated as accruing to a person entitled in possession to such an equitable interest in the like manner and circumstances, and on the same date, as it would accrue if his interest were a legal estate in the land (and any relevant provision of Part I of Schedule 1 to this Act shall apply in any such case accordingly).

(2) Where the period prescribed by this Act has expired for the bringing of an action to recover land by a tenant for life or a statutory owner of settled land—

(a) his legal estate shall not be extinguished if and so long as the right of action to recover the land of any person entitled to a beneficial interest in the land either has not accrued or has not been barred by this Act; and

(b) the legal estate shall accordingly remain vested in the tenant for life or statutory owner and shall devolve in accordance with the Settled Land Act 1925;

but if and when every such right of action has been barred by this Act, his legal estate shall be extinguished.

(3) Where any land is held upon trust [. . .] and the period prescribed by this Act has expired for the bringing of an action to recover the land by the trustees, the estate of the trustees shall not be extinguished if and so long as the right of action to recover the land of any person entitled to a beneficial interest in the land [. . .] either has not accrued or has not been barred by this Act; but if and when every such right of action has been so barred the estate of the trustees shall be extinguished.

(4) Where—

(a) any settled land is vested in a statutory owner; or

(b) any land is held upon trust [. . .];

an action to recover the land may be brought by the statutory owner or trustees on behalf of any person entitled to a beneficial interest in possession in the land [. . .] whose right of action has not been barred by this Act, notwithstanding that the right of action of the statutory owner or trustees would apart from this provision have been barred by this Act.

III LIM [23.1]

Bringing of an action See the note in s 2 at para **III LIM [3.3]** as to when an action is brought for the purposes of the Limitation Act 1980.

III LIM [24]

19. Time limit for actions to recover rent

No action shall be brought, and the power conferred by section 72(1) of the Tribunals, Courts and Enforcement Act 2007 shall not be exercisable, to recover arrears of rent, or damages in respect of arrears of rent, after the expiration of six years from the date on which the arrears became due.

III LIM [24.1]

No action shall be brought See the note in s 2 at para **III LIM [3.3]** as to when an action is brought for the purposes of the Limitation Act 1980.

III LIM [25]

20. Time limit for actions to recover money secured by a mortgage or charge or to recover proceeds of the sale of land

(1) No action shall be brought to recover—

(a) any principal sum of money secured by a mortgage or other charge on property (whether real or personal); or

(b) proceeds of the sale of land;

after the expiration of twelve years from the date on which the right to receive the money accrued.

(2) No foreclosure action in respect of mortgaged personal property shall be brought after the expiration of twelve years from the date on which the right to foreclose accrued.

But if the mortgagee was in possession of the mortgaged property after that date, the right to foreclose on the property which was in his possession shall not be treated as having accrued for the purposes of this subsection until the date on which his possession discontinued.

(3) The right to receive any principal sum of money secured by a mortgage or other charge and the right to foreclose on the property subject to the mortgage or charge shall not be treated as accruing so long as that property comprises any future interest or any life insurance policy which has not matured or been determined.

LIMITATION

(4) Nothing in this section shall apply to a foreclosure action in respect of mortgaged land, but the provisions of this Act relating to actions to recover land shall apply to such an action.

(5) Subject to subsections (6) and (7) below, no action to recover arrears of interest payable in respect of any sum of money secured by a mortgage or other charge or payable in respect of proceeds of the sale of land, or to recover damages in respect of such arrears shall be brought after the expiration of six years from the date on which the interest became due.

(6) Where—

(a) a prior mortgagee or other incumbrancer has been in possession of the property charged; and

(b) an action is brought within one year of the discontinuance of that possession by the subsequent incumbrancer;

the subsequent incumbrancer may recover by that action all the arrears of interest which fell due during the period of possession by the prior incumbrancer or damages in respect of those arrears, notwithstanding that the period exceeded six years.

(7) Where—

(a) the property subject to the mortgage or charge comprises any future interest or life insurance policy; and

(b) it is a term of the mortgage or charge that arrears of interest shall be treated as part of the principal sum of money secured by the mortgage or charge;

interest shall not be treated as becoming due before the right to recover the principal sum of money has accrued or is treated as having accrued.

III LIM [25.1]

No action shall be brought See the note in s 2 at para **III LIM [3.3]** as to when an action is brought for the purposes of the Limitation Act 1980.

III LIM [25.2]

It has been held (applying *Ezekiel v Orakpo* [1997] 1 WLR 340 – see **III LIM [25.3]**) that neither s 20(1) nor 24(1) (nor indeed any other provision of the 1980 Act) applies to the enforcement of a charging order: *Yorkshire Bank Finance Ltd v Mulhall* [2008] EWCA Civ 1156, [2008] 43 EG 195 (CS), [2008] All ER (D) 241 (Oct).

III LIM [25.3]

Date when the right accrued The "right to receive the money" must be a present rather than deferred right. A charging order made under s 313 of the Insolvency Act 1986 secures a future obligation which only becomes present when an order for sale is made by the Court and it is only then that time can start to run: *Gotham v Doodes* [2006] EWCA Civ 1080, 2006] NLJR 1325. The Court of Appeal, unlike the judge, did not feel itself constrained to follow *Hornsey Local Board v Monarch Investment Building Society* (1890) LR 24 QBD 1.

In the absence of any express provision, there is an implied obligation upon the mortgagor to repay the balance of the mortgage debt upon default in the payment of instalments and it is at this point that the mortgagee's cause of action under ss (1) accrues, seethe decision of the House of Lords in *Wilkinson v West Bromwich Building Society* [2005] 1 WLR 2303, [2005] 4 All ER 97.

The six-year period under ss (5) runs from the date when the lender could first have brought an action to recover the interest, not from the date when, under the loan agreement, the interest was due to be paid: *Barclays Bank plc v Walters* (1988) Times, 20 October, CA.

III LIM [25.4]

Interest recoverable on enforcing a charging order by sale Sub-section (5) does not limit the recovery of interest to a six-year period upon an application to enforce a charging order by sale: *Ezekiel v Orakpo* [1997] 1 WLR 340, CA, not following *Poole Corpn v Moody* [1945] KB 350, sub nom *Moody v Poole Corpn* [1945] 1 All ER 536, CA. But see "*Ezekiel v Orakpo* [1997] 1 WLR 340: *wrongly decided?*" Conveyancer and Property Lawyer (Conv (2007) September/October Pages 407-416). It has since been held that the reasoning in *Ezekiel v Orakpo* [1997] 1 WLR 340 applies equally to s 20(1).

III LIM [25.5]

Mortgagee's claim for shortfall on sale A claim by a mortgagee against its mortgagor in respect of any shortfall after a sale by the mortgagee of the mortgaged property falls under s 20 of the Limitation Act 1980 rather than under s 5 or even s 8. Neither the sale of the relevant property nor s 35 of the Land Registration Act 2002 discharged the mortgagor's obligation under the covenant to pay contained in the mortgage deed. Accordingly, on the date of accrual of the mortgagee's cause of action, it had 12 years in which to sue to recover outstanding principal and six years in respect of outstanding interest. See: *Bristol and West plc v Bartlett; Paragon Finance plc v Banks; Halifax plc v Grant* [2002] EWCA Civ 1181, [2002] 4 All ER 544, (2002) Times, 9 September. In *Scottish Equitable plc v Thompson* [2003] EWCA Civ 225, [2003] HLR 690 the Court of Appeal held that the reasoning in *Bartlett* applied to a claim brought by a second mortgagee where the relevant loan was secured both at the date of advance and the date of accrual of the right of recovery and was thus unaffected by the fact that the property was subsequently repossessed and sold by the first mortgagee.

III LIM [26]

21. Time limit for actions in respect of trust property

(1) No period of limitation prescribed by this Act shall apply to an action by a beneficiary under a trust, being an action—

(a) in respect of any fraud or fraudulent breach of trust to which the trustee was a party or privy; or

(b) to recover from the trustee trust property or the proceeds of trust property in the possession of the trustee, or previously received by the trustee and converted to his use.

(2) Where a trustee who is also a beneficiary under the trust receives or retains trust property or its proceeds as his share on a distribution of trust property under the trust, his liability in any action brought by virtue of subsection (1)(b) above to recover that property or its proceeds after the expiration of the period of limitation prescribed by this Act for bringing an action to recover trust property shall be limited to the excess over his proper share.

This subsection only applies if the trustee acted honestly and reasonably in making the distribution.

(3) Subject to the preceding provisions of this section, an action by a beneficiary to recover trust property or in respect of any breach of trust, not being an action for which a period of limitation is prescribed by any other provision of this Act, shall not be brought after the expiration of six years from the date on which the right of action accrued.

For the purposes of this subsection, the right of action shall not be treated as having accrued to any beneficiary entitled to a future interest in the trust property until the interest fell into possession.

(4) No beneficiary as against whom there would be a good defence under this Act shall derive any greater or other benefit from a judgment or order obtained by any other beneficiary than he could have obtained if he had brought the action and this Act had been pleaded in defence.

III LIM [26.1]

Bringing an action See the note in s 2 at para **III LIM [3.3]** as to when an action is brought for the purposes of the Limitation Act 1980.

III LIM [26.1A]

Meaning of "trust" and "trustee" These extend to both implied and constructive trusts. See s 38(1) (**III LIM [41]**) which applies s 68 of the Trustee Act 1925. Query whether s 21 applies to resulting trustees.

It has been held that a director is a trustee of the property of the company, within the extended definition of "trustee" contained in s 38(1), and is therefore a trustee for the purposes of ss 21(1) and 21(3). Where the breaches of fiduciary duty by a director are found to be fraudulent s 21(1)(a) prevents time running and the defence under sub-s (3) is not available: *First Subsea Ltd (formerly BSW Ltd) v Balltec Ltd* [2017] EWCA Civ 186, (2017) Times, 12 May, [2017] All ER (D) 219 (Mar).

III LIM [26.1B]

Fraud and fraudulent breach of trust In *Armitage v Nurse* [1998] Ch 241 (at 251D, 260G) Millett LJ held that a breach of trust is fraudulent, if it is dishonest. Dishonest:

> '... connotes at the minimum an intention on the part of the trustee to pursue a particular course of action, either knowing that it is contrary to the interests of the company or being recklessly indifferent whether it is contrary to their interests or not.'

He went on to say that:

> 'It is the duty of a trustee to manage the trust property and deal with it in the interests of the beneficiaries. If he acts in a way which he does not honestly believe is in the interests of the beneficiaries then he is acting dishonestly.' (p 251D–F)

Subsequently, in *Twinsectra v Yardley* [2002] UKHL 12, [2002] 2 AC 164. Lord Hutton (at paras 27 and 38) explained the requirement of the objective and subjective limbs of the "combined test" for dishonesty in that:

> '... it must be established that the defendant's conduct was dishonest by the ordinary standards of reasonable and honest people and that he himself realised that by those standards his conduct was dishonest.'

III LIM [26.2]

S 21(1) and constructive trustees In *Paragon Finance plc v DB Thakerar & Co* [1999] 1 All ER 400, CA Millett LJ identified two types of "constructive" trustee. The first, "Class 1" (and sometimes called "institutional") encompasses those who, though not expressly appointed as trustees, have assumed the duties of a trustee as a consequence of a lawful transaction which is independent of and took place prior to the breach of trust and which is not itself impugned by the claimant. In the case of "Class 2" (sometimes called "remedial") constructive trusts on the other hand the trust obligation arises directly from the unlawful transaction which is impugned by the claimant. A Class 1 trustee is a true trustee whereas a Class 2 trustee is not and it might therefore be thought to follow that both s 21(1)(a) (fraudulent breach of trust) and s 21(1)(b) (recovery of trust property) would apply to Class 1 trusts/trustees only. This was certainly what Millett LJ thought (but did not decide) in *Paragon:*

> 'There is a case for treating fraudulent breach of trust differently from other frauds, but only if what is involved really is a breach of trust. There is no case for distinguishing between an action for damages for fraud at common law and its counterpart in equity based on the same facts merely because equity employs the formula of constructive trust to justify the exercise of the equitable jurisdiction.'

In *DEG-Deutsche Investitions and Entwicklungsgesellschaft GmbH v Koshy (No 2) (Gwembe Valley Development Co Ltd v Koshy)* [2004] 1 BCLC 131, (2003) Times, 9 September) the Court of Appeal held (differing from the trial judge) that s 21(1)(b) did not apply to a claim against a company director for an account of secret profits arising out of the misapplication of company assets. Rather, his personal liability to account was a 'Class 2' trust within the classification in *Paragon Finance plc v DB Thakerar & Co* [1999] 1 All ER 400, CA and there was thus no claim to recover trust property within s 21(1)(b). This was so even though the director was in a pre-existing fiduciary relationship with the company. However, since the judge had found that the director's breach of fiduciary duty had been dishonest it was held that s 21(1)(a) applied with the result that there was no period of limitation and accordingly none of the accounts sought by the claimant was statute-barred. This conclusion did not seem to be consistent with earlier paragraphs in the Court's judgment and which said (at paras 90-1) that s 21 (s 21(1)) does not apply to class 2 trusts/fiduciary duties. The finding that the defendant was a class 2 trustee should therefore have excluded him from 21(1)(a) since dishonesty is, on this view, an additional not alternative requirement for its application.

In *Halton International Inc v Guernroy Ltd* [2006] EWCA Civ 801, [2006] All ER (D) 302 (Jun) Carnwath LJ, a member of the Court in *Gwembe*, recognised that *Gwembe* 'proceeded on the premise that fraud was sufficient to bring the case within s 21(1)(a)' but suggested that its decision 'may be better explained by reference to the alternative ground of fraudulent concealment: s 32'. In *J D Wetherspoon plc v Van de Berg & Co* [2007] EWHC 1044 (Ch), [2007] PNLR 28 Lewison J considered that he was bound by *Gwembe* but in *Kleanthous v Paphitis* [2011] EWHC 2287 (Ch) Newey J has recently expressed the view that 'a higher Court would be very likely to hold that section 21(1)(a) of the Limitation Act 1980, like section 21(1)(b), does not apply to class 2 constructive trusts' and only this interpretation seems to be consistent with the rationale give for the absence of any limitation period in s 21(1) viz that the section:

> '. . . is about deemed possession: the fiction that the possession of a property by a trustee is treated from the outset as that of the beneficiary. In the words of Millett LJ [in

Paragon], the possession of the trustee is "taken from the first for and on behalf of the beneficiaries" and is "consequently treated as the possession of the beneficiaries". An action by the beneficiary to recover that property is not time-barred, because in legal theory it has been in his possession throughout.'

S 21(1) and constructive trustees *Per* Carnwath LJ in *Halton International Inc.*

It is therefore open to a Class 2 trustee to plead a limitation defence (see *Dubai Aluminium co Ltd v Salaam* [2003] 2 AC 366 on this point and below at **III LIM [26.2A]** and **III LIM [43]**) subject, of course, to the extent that the claim against it is based on fraud and therefore engages s 32(1)(a), see **III LIM [36]** below.

Section 21(1)(a) does not apply to an action against someone who dishonestly assists a breach of trust (or knowingly receives the proceeds of such a breach of trust); see *Central Bank of Nigeria v Williams* [2014] AC 1189, [2014] 2 WLR 355, [2014] 2 All ER 489. Section 21(1)(a) only applies to Class 1 (ie true) trustees (within the *Paragon Finance* classification – see above) and not to those who are merely subject to an ancillary liability as if they were trustees. Similarly, s 21(3) – an action 'in respect of' any fraud or fraudulent breach of trust to which the trustee was a party or privy – only applies to claims against Class 1 (true) trustees. See also *Cattley v Pollard* [2006] EWHC 3130 (Ch), [2007] 2 All ER 1086, [2007] 3 WLR 317.

III LIM [26.2A]

Scope of s 21(1)(b) For the operation of s 21(1)(b) in the context of an adverse possession claim see *James v Williams* [2000] Ch 1, [1999] 3 All ER 309, CA, at **III LIM [20.3]** above.

Section 21(1)(b) may be used by a liquidator to recover money misapplied by an employee of the company in liquidation in the purchase of property: *Bank of Credit and Commerce International (Overseas) Ltd v Jan* (1999) 17 November, Trans Ref CH 1998 B 1572.

The distinction between true (or institutional) constructive trusts and remedial constructive trusts survived the passing of the Limitation Act 1939: *Paragon Finance plc v DB Thakerar & Co* [1999] 1 All ER 400, CA. A "remedial constructive trust" (Class 2 trust), which is merely the creation by the court by way of a suitable remedy to meet the wrongdoing alleged, needs to be distinguished from the constructive trust (Class 1 trust) whereby the trustee receives the trust property as the result of a transaction by which both parties intend to create a trust from the outset. In the latter case no limitation period applies under s 21 whereas the constructive trustee under a remedial constructive trust is able to rely on the limitation defence by analogy (see s 36 at para **III LIM [40]**): *Coulthard v Disco Mix Club Ltd* [1999] 2 All ER 457, [2000] 1 WLR 707.

In *Clarke (Executor of the Will of Francis Bacon) v Marlborough Fine Art (London) Ltd* [2002] 1 WLR 1731, (2001) Times, 5 July, the court rejected the argument that a claim of undue influence should be subject to a six-year time period by analogy with the statute. No case could be cited in which a Court of Equity had ever done so. Instead any such defence would be limited to laches or acquiescence, see *Coulthard v Disco Mix Club Ltd* [1999] 2 All ER 457, [2000] 1 WLR 707; *Allcard v Skinner* (1887) 36 Ch D 145. See also below at **III LIM [40.4]**.

Directors who had transferred company property to themselves in breach of fiduciary duty were to be treated as having committed a breach of trust. A claim against them to recover that property or the proceeds of that property was a claim within s 21(1)(b) of the Act because they owed pre-existing fiduciary duties in respect of company property and were therefore Class 1 trustees: *JJ Harrison (Properties) Ltd v Harrison* [2001] EWCA Civ 1467, [2002] 1 BCLC 162. (See also *DEG-Deutsche Investitions and Entwicklungsgesellschaft GmbH v Koshy (No 2) (Gwembe Valley Development Co Ltd v Koshy)* [2002] 1 BCLC 478, (2001) Times, 10 December where the director's liability to account did not depend on his pre-existing fiduciary or trust-like responsibility for company property and was not therefore subject to s 21(1)(b) – see **III LIM [26.1]** above.) The position is similar where the fiduciary uses the property of his principal to confer a benefit on a company which he controls or causes his principal to incur a liability for the benefit of a company which he controls: see *Re Pantone 485 Ltd* [2002] 1 BCLC 266 and *Wilson v Masters International Ltd* [2010] BCC 834.

A bribe or other secret profit obtained by an agent (or other fiduciary) is held on trust for the principal by that agent and the principal therefore has a proprietary claim to it which, for limitation purposes, falls within s 21(1)(b) of the 1980 Act and is not subject to a statutory limitation period: see *FHR European Ventures LLP v Mankarious* [2014] UKSC 45, [2014] 4 All ER 79, [2014] 3 WLR 535. (The Supreme Court in *FHR* thereby overruled, amongst others, the decision of the Court of Appeal in *Sinclair Investments (UK) Ltd v Versailles Trade Finance Ltd (in admin)* [2011] EWCA Civ 347, [2012] Ch 453, [2011] 4 All ER 335. *Page v Hewetts Solicitors* [2011] EWHC 2449 (Ch), [2012] 1 P & CR D7 was therefore wrongly decided on the question of limitation.

The defences of laches and acquiescence are available to claims which fall under under s 21(1)(b): *Green v Gaul* [2006] EWCA Civ 1124, [2006] 4 All ER 1110.

Directors of limited companies are sometimes said to be trustees. This is partly attributable to the historical origins of the office of director. Companies were often constituted in earlier times under deeds of settlement of which those who directed the company's affairs were appointed as trustees. Certainly, directors are fiduciaries and owe some of the duties of trustees, but they are trustees only in respect of property actually coming into their hands. In *Re Lands Allotment Co* [1894] 1 Ch 616, CA a defendant director was held entitled to rely upon a limitation defence when he was sued for misfeasance. The wrongful act concerned was the making on behalf of the company of an unauthorised investment of the company's funds, but the application of the assets was honest. On the other hand, it has been held by the Court of Appeal that a company director who profited by deliberate and thus dishonest breach of the equitable rules against dealing with a company's property, without making proper disclosure, was liable as a fiduciary without the benefit of a limitation period *Gwembe Valley Development Co Ltd v Koshy* [2003] EWCA Civ 1478, [2004] 1 BCLC 131. It has also been held by Ferris J, giving summary judgment to the claimant liquidator in *Re Westminster Property Management Ltd* [2002] All ER (D) 432 (Mar), that unauthorised and improper drawings by directors was a form of misfeasance in respect of which no limitation defence was applicable. It constituted the misapplication of trust property taken by the directors. Accordingly, s 21(1)(b) of the Act applied (if the drawings were not simply to be treated as illegal loans to directors which were expressly forbidden by s 330 of the Companies Act 1985).

The application of s 21(1)(b) and relevant authorities, in relation to company directors and generally, was considered in *Vivendi SA v Richards* [2013] EWHC 3006 (Ch), [2013] Bus LR D63, [2013] All ER (D) 112 (Oct), where Newey J held that s 21 of the Limitation Act 1980 applies in relation to company directors as well as true trustees: see *Gwembe Valley Development Co Ltd v Koshy* [2003] EWCA Civ 1048, [2004] 1 BCLC 131, at [111]–[112]. In consequence, a claim against a director will become statute-barred after six years unless s 21(1) of the 1980 Act is in point.

For s 21(1)(a) to be applicable to a claim against a director, the director must have been implicated in dishonest conduct. In *Armitage v Nurse* [1998] Ch 241, the Court of Appeal concluded (at 260) that s 21(1)(a) is 'limited to cases of fraud or fraudulent breach of trust properly so called, that is to say to cases involving dishonesty'. A trustee will, Millett LJ explained (at 251), be acting dishonestly if he 'acts in a way which he does not believe is in . . . interests [of the beneficiaries]'.

Where a director has been guilty of dishonest conduct, s 21(1)(a) may preclude the normal six-year limitation period from operating, not only as regards the director himself, but also in relation to anyone who dishonestly assisted him in his breach of duty. The decision of the Court of Appeal in *Williams v Central Bank of Nigeria* [2012] EWCA Civ 415, [2013] QB 499 is authority for the proposition that:

> '... an action by a beneficiary under a trust may be brought in respect of any fraud or fraudulent breach of trust to which the trustee was party or privy against both that trustee and any other person who dishonestly assisted him in such fraud or fraudulent breach of trust, in either case, after the expiration of the period for which section 21(3) provides.'

Section 21(1)(b) applies to claims 'to recover from the trustee trust property or the proceeds of trust property in the possession of the trustee, or previously received by the trustee and converted to his use'. A director need not necessarily still have the relevant property; the provision extends to claims to recover property 'previously received by the trustee and converted to his use': see eg *JJ Harrison (Properties) Ltd v Harrison* [2001] EWCA Civ 1467, [2002] BCC 729, at [39]–[40].

And see the decision of Mr Richard Field QC, sitting as a deputy High Court judge, in *Re Pantone 485 Ltd* [2002] 1 BCLC 266 which indicates that s 21(1)(b) can apply where property has been transferred to a company controlled by a director rather than to the director himself.

In *Burnden Holdings (UK) Ltd v Fielding* (2018) Times, 19 March, SC, a profitable company (by a non-fraudulent but unlawful distribution) was separated from its parent company by means of a series of corporate transactions, with the parent company then going into liquidation. It was held that there was no limitation period for the liquidator to start proceedings to recover the value of the misappropriated property from the directors involved. The fact that the misappropriated property had remained legally and beneficially owned by corporate vehicles throughout, rather than becoming vested in law or in equity in the defaulting directors, did not affect the statutory disapplication of the limitation period. In the context of company property, directors were to be treated as being in possession of the trust property from the outset. It was a conversion of the shareholding to their own use because of the economic benefit which they stood to derive from being the majority shareholders in the company to which the distribution was made. By the time of that conversion the defendants had previously received the property because, as directors of the claimant company, they had been its fiduciary stewards from the outset.

III LIM [26.3]

Claims by beneficiaries Section 21(3) bars claims by beneficiaries as well as claims by trustees: *Davies v Sharples* [2006] EWHC 362, [2006] WTLR 839, Patten J. But s 21(1)(b) applics to claims by beneficiaries to recover trust property from personal representatives: *Green v Gaul* [2006] EWCA Civ 1124, [2006] 4 All ER 1110 – laches and acquiescence are therefore available defences to such claims.

The reference in s 21(3) of the 1980 Act to an action by beneficiaries includes, at least by analogy, claims brought exclusively on their behalf by trustees who have no personal interest in the outcome. See *Cattley v Pollard* [2006] EWHC 3130 (Ch), [2007] 2 All ER 1086, [2007] 3 WLR 317. A discretionary beneficiary has no beneficial interest in trust property and is therefore excluded from the limitation imposed by sub s(3): *Armitage v Nurse* [1998] Ch 241, [1997] 3 WLR 1046, CA.

III LIM [26.4]

Fiduciaries The word "fiduciary" is nowhere mentioned in the Limitation Act. Fiduciary relationships can arise in a number of different situations but a six year limitation period will apply either directly or by analogy under the Act to claims in respect of breaches of fiduciary duty unless the case falls within the express exclusions (dealing with trustees &c) or the ambit of some exclusionary authority. Ordinarily, personal claims against fiduciaries will be subject to a six year period by analogy with claims in tort or contract under sections 2 and 5 respectively. By contrast, claims for equitable remedies (such as an account) for breach of fiduciary duty will usually fall within one of the subsections of s 21 depending on the precise characteristics of the fiduciary and his conduct. Even then, a six year time limit will normally apply under section 21(3) unless the case can be brought within the exceptions under ss 21(1)(a) (for fraud) or (b) (for Class 1 trust as explained in *Paragon Finance v DB Thakerar & Co* [1999] 1 All ER 400, CA see **III LIM [26.2]** and **III LIM [40.3]** below),

A director has responsibilities akin to those of a trustee in the management of the property of the company and applying it on behalf of the company in its interests and those of all of its members. A claim for an account against a director for the breach of such duties will therefore be subject to s 21. See: *DEG-Deutsche Investitions and Entwicklungsgesellschaft GmbH v Koshy (No 2)* (*Gwembe Valley Development Co Ltd v Koshy* [2004] 1 BCLC 131; Times, September 9, 2003).

Where a director used company money to confer a benefit on another company controlled by him, that amounted to a conversion of trust property. Therefore a claim against the director for equitable compensation for breach of fiduciary duty in that regard fell within the scope of the Limitation Act 1980, s 21(1)(b) and was not subject to a six-year limitation period (*Burnden Holdings (UK) Ltd v Fielding* [2016] EWCA Civ 557 followed). The claim for equitable compensation for breach of fiduciary duty was not statute-barred (see *Bhullar* v *Bhullar* [2017] EWHC 407 (Ch), para 127, Davies J).

III LIM [27]

22. Time limit for actions claiming personal estate of a deceased person

Subject to section 21 (1) and (2) of this Act—

(a) no action in respect of any claim to the personal estate of a deceased person or to any share or interest in any such estate (whether under a will or on intestacy) shall be brought after the expiration of twelve years from the date on which the right to receive the share or interest accrued; and

(b) no action to recover arrears of interest in respect of any legacy, or damages in respect of such arrears, shall be brought after the expiration of six years from the date on which the interest became due.

III LIM [27.1]

No action... shall be brought See the note in s 2 at para **III LIM [3.3]** as to when an action is brought for the purposes of the Limitation Act 1980.

III LIM [27.2]

The ambit of 22(a) Section 22(a) does not apply to proceedings to remove a personal representative.

LIMITATION

Section 22(a) applies to restitutionary claims brought by beneficiaries against the recipients of property which should not have been distributed to them under a will or intestacy, but has no application in the case of trusts created by a will once the administration of the estate has been completed: *Davies v Sharples* [2006] EWHC 362, [2006] WTLR 839, Patten J.

III LIM [27.3]

The date on which the right to receive the share or interest accrued "[T]he better view" is that the period under s 22(a) does not begin to run until the administrator has paid the costs, funeral and testamentary and administration expenses, debts and other liabilities properly payable out of the assets in his hands, and provided for the payment of any pecuniary legacies. *Green v Gaul* [2006] EWCA Civ 1124, [2006] 4 All ER 1110.

III LIM [28]

23. Time limit in respect of actions for an account

An action for an account shall not be brought after the expiration of any time limit under this Act which is applicable to the claim which is the basis of the duty to account.

III LIM [28.1]

No action... shall be brought See the note in s 2 at para **III LIM [3.3]** as to when an action is brought for the purposes of the Limitation Act 1980.

III LIM [28.2]

Duty to account Breach of a duty to account, even when owed by a person in a fiduciary position, gave rise only to a contractual claim and so subject to s 5 of the 1980 Act: *Coulthard v Disco Mix Club Ltd* [1999] 2 All ER 457, [2000] 1 WLR 707.

III LIM [29]

24. Time limit for actions to enforce judgments

(1) An action shall not be brought upon any judgment after the expiration of six years from the date on which the judgment became enforceable.

(2) No arrears of interest in respect of any judgment debt shall be recovered after the expiration of six years from the date on which the interest became due.

III LIM [29.1]

An action shall not be brought See the note in s 2 at para **III LIM [3.3]** as to when an action is brought for the purposes of the Limitation Act 1980.

III LIM [29.2]

Enforcement of judgments but not by actions Sub-section (1) does not bar the enforcement of a judgment by execution or other methods short of "action": *National Westminster Bank plc v Powney* [1991] Ch 339, [1990] 2 All ER 416, CA; *Lowsley v Forbes (t/a LE Design Services)* [1999] 1 AC 329, [1998] 3 All ER 897, HL.

In *Bank of Scotland v Bennett* [2004] EWCA Civ 988, (2004) Times, 4 August, CA the Court decided not to strike out a second action where enforcement of the original judgment might be barred by s 24(1) and the judgment creditor wished to preserve its right to proceed in bankruptcy against the judgment debtor.

In the case of a judgment obtained in England and Wales, a second claim based on the judgment in the first might be struck out as an abuse of process: *E D & F Man (Sugar) Ltd v Haryanto (No 3)* (1996) Times, 9 August, CA. But the second claim might be justified by special circumstances, such as that the judgment was founded on the defendant's fraud and that the defendant was avoiding or contesting reasonably timely efforts to enforce and that the six year time limit on enforcement would run out before satisfaction of the judgment had been obtained: *Kuwait Oil Tankers Co SAK v Al Bader* [2008] EWHC 2432 (Comm), [2008] All ER (D) 165 (Oct).

III LIM [29.3]

Enforcement of right to interest on judgment Following the reasoning in *National Westminster Bank plc v Powney* [1991] Ch 339, [1990] 2 All ER 416, CA, interest may be recovered by the enforcement process outside the six year period. The word "action" in s 24(1) does not include processes of execution, which may take place outside the six-year period; but s 24(2) limits the recoverable arrears of interest to six years: *Lowsley v Forbes* [1999] 1 AC 329, [1998] 3 All ER 897, HL.

III LIM [29.4]

Statutory demands and winding-up petitions In *Re a Debtor (No 50A-SD-1995)* [1997] Ch 310, [1997] 2 All ER 789 it was held that a statutory demand is an "action" for the purposes of s 24 and so may not be issued in a respect of a judgment which was given more than six years previously (this decision was followed in *Re a Debtor (No 647-SD-1999)* (2000) Times, 10 April, where the Revenue sought to rely on the provisions of s 37(2) of the 1980 Act) However, in *Ridgeway Motors Ltd v Altis Ltd* [2004] EWHC 1535 (Ch), [2004] All ER (D) 320 (May) the court declined to follow *Re a Debtor* on the basis of its inconsistency with the decision of the House of Lords in *Lowsley v Forbes* [1999] 1 AC 329, [1998] 3 All ER 897, HL that the word "action" in s 24 means a fresh action and does not include proceedings by way of execution. See also the Report of the Law Reform Committee on Limitation of Actions 1977 (Cmnd. 6923)

On the other hand a winding-up petition has been held not to be an action for the purposes of the section, so is not barred after six years from the judgment: *Ridgeway Motors (Isleworth) Ltd v ALTS Ltd* [2005] EWCA Civ 92, (2005) Times, 24 February.

III LIM [29.5]

Judgment for costs In the case of a judgment or order for the payment of costs, the limitation period for enforcement does not start to run until the amount of the debt has been quantified: *Times Newspapers Ltd v Jaghit Singh Chohan* [2001] EWCA Civ 964, [2001] 1 WLR 1859.

III LIM [30]

26. Administration to date back to death

For the purposes of the provisions of this Act relating to actions for the recovery of land and advowsons an administrator of the estate of a deceased person shall be [illegible] as if there had been no interval of time between the death of the [illegible] administration.

III LIM [31]

28. Extension of limitation period in case of disability

(1) Subject to the following provisions of this section, if on the date when any right of action accrued for which a period of limitation is prescribed by this Act, the person to whom it accrued was under a disability, the action may be brought at any time before the expiration of six years from the date when he ceased to be under a disability or died (whichever first occurred) notwithstanding that the period of limitation has expired.

(2) This section shall not affect any case where the right of action first accrued to some person (not under a disability) through whom the person under a disability claims.

(3) When a right of action which has accrued to a person under a disability accrues, on the death of that person while still under a disability, to another person under a disability, no further extension of time shall be allowed by reason of the disability of the second person.

(4) No action to recover land or money charged on land shall be brought by virtue of this section by any person after the expiration of thirty years from the date on which the right of action accrued to that person or some person through whom he claims.

(4A) If the action is one to which section 4A of this Act applies, subsection (1) above shall have effect—

(a) in the case of an action for libel or slander, as if for the words from "at any time" to "occurred)" there were substituted the words "by him at any time before the expiration of one year from the date on which he ceased to be under a disability"; and

LIMITATION

> (b) in the case of an action for slander of title, slander of goods or other malicious falsehood, as if for the words "six years" there were substituted the words "one year".
>
> (5) If the action is one to which section 10 of this Act applies, subsection (1) above shall have effect as if for the words "six years" there were substituted the words "two years".
>
> (6) If the action is one to which section 11 [, 11B] or 12 (2) of this Act applies, subsection (1) above shall have effect as if for the words "six years" there were substituted the words "three years".
>
> (7) If the action is one to which section 11A of this Act applies or one by virtue of section 6 (1)(a) of the Consumer Protection Act 1987 (death caused by defective product), subsection (1) above—
>
> (a) shall not apply to the time limit prescribed by subsection (3) of the said section 11A or to that time limit as applied by virtue of section 12 (1) of this Act; and
>
> (b) in relation to any other time limit prescribed by this Act shall have effect as if for the words "six years" there were substituted the words "three years".

Amendment *Text in square brackets is inserted by the Automated and Electric Vehicles Act 2018 with effect from a date to be appointed.*

III LIM [31.1]

The action may be brought See the note in s 2 at para **III LIM [3.3]** as to when an action is brought for the purposes of the Limitation Act 1980.

In *Evans v Secretary of State for the Environment, Transport and the Regions (C-63/01)* (2005) All ER (EC) 763 ECJ (5th Chamber) the European Court of Justice ruled that in order to comply with Council Directive 84/5/EEC (OJ 1984 L8/17) in relation to damage caused by uninsured drivers the protection provided by the national scheme had to be equivalent to and as effective as the protection afforded by the same state to victims of insured drivers. Since the three year time limit for bringing a claim against the Motor Insurers' [illegible] Untraced Drivers [illegible] of the Limitation Act 1980 the law has [illegible] Directive 84/5 to give disadvantaged minors a claim for Francovich damages against the Secretary of State: *Byrne v Motor Insurers' Bureau* [2008] EWCA Civ 574, [2009] QB 66, [2008] 4 All ER 476.

III LIM [31.2]

Disability For the purposes of the Limitation Act 1980 a person is deemed to be under a disability while an infant (under 18) or 'lacks mental capacity': see s 38(2) of the Act at **III LIM [41.1]** below for the definition of that term.

The definition of the relevant mental impairment has changed over the life of the Act. The current definition in s 38(2) refers to the Mental Capacity Act 2005 and has applied since 1 October 2007. However, the previous definition will still apply in some cases because it has been held that in a case where there is a statutory change in the definition of what qualifies as a (mental) disability during the course of a mental impairment, the law which should be applied to decide that question is the law when the cause of action accrued, not the law when the claim is brought: see *Seaton v Seddon* [2012] EWHC 735 (Ch), [2013] 1 All ER 29, [2012] 1 WLR 3636 departing from the contrary decision in *Maga v Archbishop of Birmingham* [2009] EWHC 780 (QB).

Where the cause of action accrued at a time when the previous law applied – viz s 38(2) unamended and the now repealed s 38(3)-(4) – then those provided as follows:

> '(2) For the purposes of this Act a person shall be treated as under a disability while he is an infant, or of unsound mind.
>
> (3) For the purposes of subsection (2) above a person is of unsound mind if he is a person who by reason of mental disorder within the meaning of the Mental Health Act 1983, is incapable of managing or administering his property and affairs.
>
> (4) Without prejudice to the generality of subsection (3) above, a person shall be conclusively presumed for the purposes of subsection (2) above to be of unsound mind -
>
> (a) while he is liable to be detained or subject to guardianship under the Mental Health Act 1983 (otherwise than by virtue of section 35 or 89); and

It seems that the debtor must not only acknowledge the amount but also the basis of its recovery if there is or may be more than one. Thus it has been held to be possible, in principle, for s 29 to apply to a restitutionary claim for repayment of tax paid under a mistake of law but that the part-payment by the Revenue on which the claimants relied had been made in respect of a right to repayment under section 80 of VATA 1980 and not in respect of the non-statutory common law restitutionary right to compound interest on which the claimants were relying in the current proceedings – *FJ Chalke Ltd v Revenue and Customs Comrs* [2009] EWHC 952 (Ch), [2009] 3 CMLR 479, [2009] STC 2027, [2009] SWTI 1694; affd [2010] EWCA Civ 313, [2010] STC 1640, 154 Sol Jo (no 13) 30.

In *Lambeth London Borough Council v Archangel* [2002] 1 P & CR 230, 33 HLR 490, CA, the squatter sought to resist the council's claim for possession on the basis of his rent-free occupation since 1985. His claim failed because of a letter which he had written in 1993 which mentioned the need to refurbish "Lambeth's property". He was held to have acknowledged the council's title. See also *Bigden v London Borough of Lambeth* [2001] 33 HLR 43, [2000] EGCS 147, where a petition which acknowledged the council's right to sell the properties constituted sufficient acknowledgment of better title to defeat the claim for adverse possession. Simon Brown LJ indicated (at para 60) that there is no reason for a court to strain against finding that there has been an acknowledgment.

Although s 29 refers to an acknowledgement of "title" it does not necessarily follow that a squatter's acceptance of the paper owner's title paramount also amounts to an acknowledgement of his right to possession. An effective acknowledgement must be focused on the right which is in dispute – see eg *Surrendra Overseas Ltd v Sri Lanka (The Apj Akash)* [1977] 1 WLR 565 at 575 and *Flynn (Deceased, Re) (No 2)* [1969] 2 Ch 403, [1969] 2 WLR 1148.

The acknowledgment of the paper title is not effective unless made by or on behalf of the person in possession of the land: *Tower Hamlets London Borough Council v Barrett* [2005] EWCA Civ 923, [2006] 1 P&CR 9, CA and this is so even though the owner does not have to know who is in possession, and the person acknowledging does not have to know who is the owner: *Allen v Matthews* [2007] EWCA Civ 216, [2007] BPIR 281, [2007] NPC 30.

III LIM [33.2]

Appropriation of payment on account At common law a creditor who receives a payment generally on account may appropriate it in his discretion to whichever account he chooses and may apply it to the payment of interest rather than capital: *The Mecca* [1897] AC 286, HL. There are, however, statutory restrictions eg Consumer Credit Act 1974 s 81.

III LIM [33.3]

Acknowledgment of debt or liquidated pecuniary claim An acknowledgment requires an unqualified admission that an existing debt is owed but it need not specify the amount so long as that is capable of proof by extrinsic evidence without any further agreement between the parties: see in particular *Dungate v Dungate* [1965] 3 All ER 393 and also *Good v Parry* [1963] 2 QB 418, CA and *Ross v McGrath* [2004] EWCA Civ 1054, [2004] All ER (D) 238 (Jul).

The words "any debt" in s 29(5)(a) includes a judgment debt; see *Van Heeran v Cooper* (Ch D, 8 December 2012).

A "liquidated pecuniary claim" does not include a claim for damages in tort for s 29(5)(a) contemplates "a claim made under a contract or else a claim of a similar nature" (*per* Jackson J in *Dwr Cymru v Carmarthenshire County Council* [2004] EWHC 2991 (TCC), [2004] All ER (D) 307 (Oct)). However, in *Amantilla Ltd v Telefusion plc* (1987) 9 Con LR 139, s 29(5)(a) was applied to a quantum meruit claim for the reasonable value of building works provided under a contract which failed on the ground that there had been no agreement as to price. *Amantilla* was endorsed by the Court of Appeal in *Phillips & Co v Bath Housing Co-operative Ltd* [2012] EWCA Civ 1591, [2012] All ER (D) 92 (Dec) where a solicitor's claim against a client on a bill of costs which, though claimed in a specific amount, is treated as unascertained until assessed was nonetheless considered to be capable of acknowledgement. This involved interpreting the word 'liquidated' in s 29(5)(a) as requiring less 'precision and certainty' than it does in the context of a bankruptcy petition or summary judgment. As Lloyd LJ put it (at para [42]):

> 'A claim, after all, is unilateral, and something which is to be relied on as an acknowledgment is likely to come into being relatively early on. It would be understandable if things occurring at that stage could be looked at in a more general way than is appropriate or necessary once one comes to a judicial determination of rights, or, as in the case of bankruptcy, the assertion of remedies against the proved or alleged debtor.'

The decision in *Amantilla* was extended to apply to the more purely restitutionary claim for interest on money mistakenly paid as unlawfully exacted VAT in *FJ Chalke Ltd v Revenue and Customs Comrs* [2009] EWHC 952 (Ch), [2009] 3 CMLR 479, [2009] STC 2027 approved, obiter, on appeal at [2010] EWCA Civ 313, [2010] STC 1640.

III LIM [33.4]

Acknowledgments and without prejudice communications Admission of a sum due in truly 'without prejudice' negotiations or communications, or in a statement which is privileged from disclosure, will not be admissible in evidence and therefore will not constitute an acknowledgment of a debt owed by the debtor. The rule is 'founded on the public policy of encouraging litigants to settle their differences rather than litigate them to a finish' (*per* Lord Griffiths in *Rush & Tomkins v Greater London Council* [1989] AC 1280 at 1299, [1988] 3 All ER 737, HL) but also upon 'the express or implied agreement of the parties themselves that communications in the course of their negotiations should not be admissible in evidence' *(per Robert Walker LJ in Unilever plc v The Procter & Gamble Co* [2001] 1 All ER 783 at 789–790, [2000] 1 WLR 2436 at 2442).

The principal exceptions to the rule preventing without prejudice communications from being referred to in court are:

(a) where, but then only to the extent that, the parties have otherwise agreed such as in communications 'without prejudice, save as to costs';
(b) communications which are said to have concluded in a contract or an estoppel or where they contain a misrepresentation;
(c) communications which are alleged to comprise or include unambiguous impropriety or provide an explanation for delay;
(d) where an independent fact in no way connected with the merits of the cause is admissible even if made in the course of negotiations for a settlement.

In *Bradford & Bingley plc v Mohammed Rashid* [2006] UKHL 37, [2006] 1 WLR 2066, [2006] 4 All ER 705 Lord Hoffmann (alone) considered that the without prejudice rule, to the extent that it is based upon public policy rather than the agreement of the parties, does not apply at all to the use of a statement as an acknowledgement for the purposes of section 29(5). He thought that the rule is not concerned with the admissibility of statements which are relevant otherwise than as admissions, ie independently of the truth of the facts alleged to have been admitted. However, in *Ofulue v Bossert* [2009] UKHL 16, [2009] 1 AC 990, [2009] 3 All ER 93 the House of Lords subsequently rejected this distinction between acknowledgements and admissions as too subtle to apply in practice and inconsistent with the generous ambit of the rule as it had developed in this jurisdiction. Instead, Lord Neuberger endorsed the following dictum from the decision of the Court of Appeal in *Unilever plc v The Procter & Gamble Co* [2000] 1 WLR 2436 that:

> "the protection of admissions against interest is the most important practical effect of the rule. But to dissect out identifiable admissions and withhold protection from the rest of without prejudice communications (except for a special reason) would not only create huge practical difficulties but would be contrary to the underlying objective of giving protection to the parties, in the words of Lord Griffiths in the Rush & Tompkins case [1989] AC 1280, 1300: to speak freely about all issues in the litigation both factual and legal when seeking compromise and, for the purpose of establishing a basis of compromise, admitting certain facts. Parties cannot speak freely at a without prejudice meeting if they must constantly monitor every sentence, with lawyers or patent agents sitting at their shoulders as minders." (*per* Robert Walker LJ at 2448-2449),

In *Rashid* itself it was held that correspondence from a debtor which put forward apparently without prejudice proposals to the creditor for payment of "the outstanding balance" were not protected by privilege because they could not relate to the settlement of a dispute since the debt was admitted. It thus amounted to an acknowledgement of the debt in question. On the other hand a without prejudice communication which contained a statement which, but for the privilege attaching to it, would otherwise amount to an acknowledgement might retain that privileged character when subsequently supplied to the creditor for another purpose: *Lia Oil SA v Erg Petroli Spa* [2007] EWHC 505 (Comm), [2007] 2 Lloyd's Rep 509.

III LIM [33.5]

An action... may be brought See the note in s 2 at para **III LIM [3.3]** as to when an action is brought for the purposes of the Limitation Act 1980.

III LIM [34]

30. Formal provisions as to acknowledgments and part payments

(1) To be effective for the purposes of section 29 of this Act, an acknowledgment must be in writing and signed by the person making it.

(2) For the purposes of section 29, any acknowledgment or payment—

(a) may be made by the agent of the person by whom it is required to be made under that section; and

(b) shall be made to the person, or to an agent of the person, whose title or claim is being acknowledged or, as the case may be, in respect of whose claim the payment is being made.

III LIM [34.1]

Although part payment can "intelligibly" be seen as a sub-category of acknowledgement, the Act deals with it separately and equally; it is thus a freestanding mechanism for the computation of time into which is neither necessary (nor proper) to import the extra requirements to which the law of acknowledgement has historically become subject – see *Bradford & Bingley plc v Ashcroft* [2010] EWCA Civ 223, [2010] P & CR 193.

III LIM [34.1A]

"signed by the person making it" In *Good Challenger Navegante S A v MetalExportImport SA* [2003] EWCA Civ 1668, [2004] 1 Lloyd's Rep 67, (2003) Times, 27 November the question for the first time arose whether a purported acknowledgement could be "signed by the person making it" where the name of the acknowledging party had been typed. The document in question was a telex which by its very nature could not be signed in the strict sense of the maker's name or characteristic mark being inscribed in his own hand. The Court of Appeal (agreeing with the Judge) held that the word "signed" should be construed as meaning that the maker has by his name or mark signified his approval of the contents of the document. (See *Schneider v Norris* (1814) 2 M & S 286, per Lord Ellenborough CJ and *Decouvreur v Jordan* (1987) Times, 25 May, per Nourse LJ at para 20 both decided under s 4 of the Statute of Frauds 1677. See also *The Anemone* [1987] 1 Lloyd's Rep 546.) Whether and how this is achieved will depend upon the nature and format of the document in question. In the case of a formal written contract the insertion by a party (or his agent) of his name would be required but in the case of a telex or similar document a typed signature would suffice so long as there was no difficulty as to authenticity or authority.

III LIM [34.2]

Made to a creditor or his agent In *Re Compania de Electricidad* [1980] Ch 146 Slade J said (at 193F) in relation to the similarly worded provisions in s 24 of the Limitation Act 1939, that:

> In my judgment, though no authority has been cited to me which either confirms or rejects such proposition, a written acknowledgement cannot be said to be "made to" a creditor or his agent, within the meaning of section 24(2) unless either (a) it is delivered to the creditor or his agent by or with the authority of the debtor or (b) it is expressly or implicitly addressed to and is actually received by the creditor or his agent.
>
> In my judgment, in case (a) it would not matter that the acknowledgement was not, according to its terms, expressly or implicitly addressed to the recipient. In case (b) it would not matter that the acknowledgement reached the hands of the creditor otherwise than by or with the authority of the debtor. In either case, however, it would be necessary that the creditor should actually receive the acknowledgment before he could rely on it.

Thus in *Rehman v Benfield* [2006] EWCA Civ 1392, [2006] All ER (D) 319 (Oct) the occupant's signature of the counterpart of a sham lease was sufficient to amount to her acknowledgement of the owner's title when it was sent to solicitors apparently acting for him even though the signature could not give rise to a valid lease.

In order to constitute valid acknowledgement, the agent's receipt must be in its capacity as agent. In *Emile Elias & Co Ltd v A-G* [2011] UKPC 19, [2012] 2 LRC 354 the person to whom the alleged acknowledgement was made was the managing director of a creditor but it was shown to him in confidence in his capacity as a member of a government committee charged with reviewing sums owed by the government to various contractors and not to him (and certainly not addressed to him) as an agent of the creditor. It could not therefore be an acknowledgement.

III LIM [34.3]

Statements in pleadings A statement in a pleading or statement of case, or in any other court document, is capable of amounting to an acknowledgment for the purposes of s 29 but its effect is confined to the date upon which it is provided to the person to whom the acknowledgment is made rather than continuing from day to day for the duration of the proceedings in question. The affirmation of a previous acknowledgement in a pleading would normally require a fresh written and signed document (including an amended defence) or, possibly, an act such as re-service of the original defence. Merely taking steps in the action would not qualify. See *Ofulue v Bossert* [2009] UKHL 16, [2009] 1 AC 990, [2009] 3 All ER 93 and *Horner v Cartwright* (unreported) 11 July 1989, CA.

III LIM [34.4]

Agents On normal principles, an acknowledgment by an agent must be within the agent's actual or apparent authority. Thus, in *Re Transplanters (Holding Co) Ltd* [1958] 1 WLR 822, it was held that the signature of an auditor on a company balance sheet did not amount to an acknowledgment of a debt as the auditor had no authority to give any acknowledgment. Winn-Parry J pointed out that in signing a balance sheet the auditor's duty is to make a report to the company and the signature is to warrant that he has properly performed his statutory duty. See also *Re Compania de Electricidad* [1980] Ch 146 but compare, however, the different result reached in *Jones v Bellgrove Properties Ltd* [1949] 2 KB 700, [1949] 2 All ER 198, CA and *Ledingham v Bemejo Estancia Co Ltd* [1949] 2 KB 417, [1949] 1 All ER 749, CA. Payments in respect of mortgage interest made direct to the mortgagee by the Benefits Agency have been held to have been made on behalf of the mortgagor so as to amount to part payments: *Bradford & Bingley Plc v Cutler* [2008] EWCA Civ 74.

In *Wright v Pepin* [1954] 1 WLR 635 a solicitor had authority to write letters putting his client's affairs in order but no specific authority to acknowledge a debt. A letter from the solicitor was held to be an acknowledgment of the debt where he had authority to write a letter in which an acknowledgment was to be found:

> "It seems clear that it is not necessary that the agent should have authority to acknowledge, for instance . . . the existence of the mortgage. It seems to be enough that the agent should have authority to write the letter which she does in fact write, and that what is said in the letter is within the scope of the agent's authority." ([1954] 1 WLR 635 at 639, per HARMAN J.)

In *Re Lord Clifden Annaly v Agar-Ellis* [1900] 1 Ch 774 it was held that the realisation of a security by the mortgagee, without any involvement of the mortgagor or his agent, is not a payment by a person liable for the debt or by the agent of such a person and was thus not capable of amounting to a part payment. See also *UCB Corporate Services Ltd v Kohli* [2004] EWHC 1126 (Ch), [2004] 2 All ER (Comm) 422.

In *Harlock v Ashberry* (1882) 19 Ch D 539 a payment of rent made by a tenant of the mortgaged property to the mortgagee in response to a notice by the mortgagee requiring the rent to be paid to him was held not to be a part payment within the meaning of the limitation statutes.

III LIM [35]

31. Effect of acknowledgment or part payment on persons other than the maker or recipient

(1) An acknowledgment of the title to any land, benefice, or mortgaged personalty by any person in possession of it shall bind all other persons in possession during the ensuing period of limitation.

(2) A payment in respect of a mortgage debt by the mortgagor or any other person liable for the debt, or by any person in possession of the mortgaged property, shall, so far as any right of the mortgagee to foreclose or otherwise to recover the property is concerned, bind all other persons in possession of the mortgaged property during the ensuing period of limitation.

(3) Where two or more mortgagees are by virtue of the mortgage in possession of the mortgaged land, an acknowledgment of the mortgagor's title or of his equity of redemption by one of the mortgagees shall only bind him and his successors and shall not bind any other mortgagee or his successors.

(4) Where in a case within subsection (3) above the mortgagee by whom the acknowledgment is given is entitled to a part of the mortgaged land and not to any ascertained part of the mortgage debt the mortgagor shall be entitled to redeem

that part of the land on payment, with interest, of the part of the mortgage debt which bears the same proportion to the whole of the debt as the value of the part of the land bears to the whole of the mortgaged land.

(5) Where there are two or more mortgagors, and the title or equity of redemption of one of the mortgagors is acknowledged as mentioned above in this section, the acknowledgment shall be treated as having been made to all the mortgagors.

(6) An acknowledgment of any debt or other liquidated pecuniary claim shall bind the acknowledgor and his successors but not any other person.

(7) A payment made in respect of any debt or other liquidated pecuniary claim shall bind all persons liable in respect of the debt or claim.

(8) An acknowledgment by one of several personal representatives of any claim to the personal estate of a deceased person or to any share or interest in any such estate, or a payment by one of several personal representatives in respect of any such claim, shall bind the estate of the deceased person.

(9) In this section "successor", in relation to any mortgagee or person liable in respect of any debt or claim, means his personal representatives and any other person on whom the rights under the mortgage or, as the case may be, the liability in respect of the debt or claim devolve (whether on death or bankruptcy or the disposition of property or the determination of a limited estate or interest in settled property or otherwise).

III LIM [36]

32. Postponement of limitation period in case of fraud, concealment or mistake

(1) Subject to subsections (3) *and (4A)* [, (4A) and (4B)] below, where in the case of any action for which a period of limitation is prescribed by this Act, either—

(a) the action is based upon the fraud of the defendant; or

(b) any fact relevant to the plaintiff's right of action has been deliberately concealed from him by the defendant; or

(c) the action is for relief from the consequences of a mistake;

the period of limitation shall not begin to run until the plaintiff has discovered the fraud, concealment or mistake (as the case may be) or could with reasonable diligence have discovered it.

References in this subsection to the defendant include references to the defendant's agent and to any person through whom the defendant claims and his agent.

(2) For the purposes of subsection (1) above, deliberate commission of a breach of duty in circumstances in which it is unlikely to be discovered for some time amounts to deliberate concealment of the facts involved in that breach of duty.

(3) Nothing in this section shall enable any action—

(a) to recover, or recover the value of, any property; or

(b) to enforce any charge against, or set aside any transaction affecting, any property;

to be brought against the purchaser of the property or any person claiming through him in any case where the property has been purchased for valuable consideration by an innocent third party since the fraud or concealment or (as the case may be) the transaction in which the mistake was made took place.

(4) A purchaser is an innocent third party for the purposes of this section—

(a) in the case of fraud or concealment of any fact relevant to the plaintiff's right of action, if he was not a party to the fraud or (as the case may be) to the concealment of that fact and did not at the time of the purchase know or have reason to believe that the fraud or concealment had taken place; and

LIMITATION

(b) in the case of mistake, if he did not at the time of the purchase know or have reason to believe that the mistake had been made.

(4A) Subsection (1) above shall not apply in relation to the time limit prescribed by section 11A (3) of this Act or in relation to that time limit as applied by virtue of section 12(1) of this Act.

[(4B) Subsection (1) above shall not apply in relation to the time limit prescribed by section 11B(2) or (4) of this Act or in relation to that time limit as applied by virtue of section 12(1) of this Act.]

(5) Sections 14A and 14B of this Act shall not apply to any action to which subsection (1)(b) above applies (and accordingly the period of limitation referred to in that subsection, in any case to which either of those sections would otherwise apply, is the period applicable under section 2 of this Act).

Amendment *Text in italic is deleted and text in square brackets is inserted by the Automated and Electric Vehicles Act 2018 with effect from a date to be appointed.*

III LIM [36.1]

Bringing of an action See the note in s 2 at para **III LIM [3.3]** as to when an action is brought for the purposes of the Limitation Act 1980.

III LIM [36.1A]

Generally Section 32 does not apply to the time limit prescribed by s 24(2) of the Limitation Act 1980 since the recovery of interest by way of execution on a judgment is not a "right of action" within the meaning of s 32: *Lowsley v Forbes (t/a LE Design Services)* [1999] 1 AC 329, [1998] 3 All ER 897, HL. Only s 32(1)(b) (deliberate concealment) arose in *Lowsley* but both s 32(1)(a) and 32(1)(c) also apply only to "actions".

It has been said that the mischief at which s 32(1)(b) is aimed is "to ensure that the Act does not operate to bar the claim of a plaintiff whose ignorance of the relevant facts is due to the improper actions of the defendant" (*per* Lord Browne-Wilkinson in *Sheldon v RHM Outhwaite (Underwriting Agencies) Ltd* [1996] AC 102 at 142F, HL.) On the other hand section 32(1)(b) should be construed relatively narrowly: *Johnson v Chief Constable of Surrey* (1992) Times, 23 November, CA. "[R]ight of action" includes and will usually mean no more than "cause of action" (*C v Mirror Group Newspapers* [1996] 4 All ER 511 at 516) and therefore consists in "[e]very fact which it would be necessary for the plaintiff to prove, if traversed, in order to support his right to the judgment of the court" (*Coburn v Colledge* [1897] 1 QB 702, CA).

III LIM [36.1B]

"could with reasonable diligence" In *Paragon Finance plc v DB Thakerar & Co* [1999] 1 All ER 400, CA, it was held on appeal that the judge should not have been satisfied on the material before him that the claimants could not with reasonable diligence have discovered the fraud before the relevant date. The burden of proof is on the claimant, and it must establish that it could not have discovered the fraud without exceptional measures which they could not reasonably have been expected to take. See also *Clef Aquitaine SARL v Laporte Materials (Barrow) Ltd* [2001] QB 488, [2000] 3 All ER 493, CA, where "reasonable diligence" was distinguished from "exceptional measures". In *UCB Home Loans Corpn Ltd v Carr* [2000] 1 Lloyd's Rep PN 754, however, Crane J expressed the view that Millett LJ's use of the word "exceptional" imposed too high a standard and ought to be omitted. The Court of Appeal in *Biggs v Sotnicks (a firm)* [2002] EWCA Civ 272, [2002] Lloyd's Rep PN 221, CA has now reasserted the relative rigour of the *Paragon Finance* formulation and disapproved of the contrary dicta in *UCB Home Loans*. In *Law Society v Sephton* the Court of Appeal held that Millett LJ's formulation in *Paragon* involved an assumption that the claimant wished to discover whether there had been a fraud, deliberate concealment or mistake: "reasonable diligence pre-supposes a desire to investigate." In *A-G of Zambia (for and on behalf of the Republic of Zambia) v Meer Care & Desai (a firm)* [2007] EWHC 952 (Ch), [2007] All ER (D) 97 (May) Peter Smith J explained these authorities in the following way (at para 410)

> "If exceptional measures show that the misconduct on the part of the Defendant could have been discovered that will count against the Claimant unless the Claimant shows it would be unreasonable for him to take such steps. In other words the exceptional measures need not be taken if it is reasonable for him so to act. If it is unreasonable for him so to act then the exceptional measures and the fruits of such exceptional measures must be taken into account."

In *Peconic Industrial Development Ltd v Lau Kwok Fai* [2009] HKFCA 16 (CA (HK) the question of reasonable diligence arose in the context of the materially identical wording of s 26 of the Hong Kong Limitation Ordinance, Cap 347. The main judgment of the Hong Kong Court of

Final Appeal was given by Lord Hoffman who (at para 29) said that the purpose of the Act is "to avoid the investigation of whether the defendant was fraudulent after a lapse of time which could prejudice his ability to rebut the charge" and that "(t)he question of what the plaintiff could with reasonable diligence have discovered must be answered dispassionately and without regard to what may be perceived as the merits." As to the application of the test he said (at para 30):

> What does "the plaintiff . . . could with reasonable diligence have discovered [the fraud]" mean? The word "reasonable" denotes an objective standard. But that is not the end of the matter. It is the plaintiff who is supposed to have shown reasonable diligence. This leaves open to argument the extent to which the personal characteristics of the plaintiff are to be taken into account in deciding what diligence he could reasonably have been expected to have shown. It does not follow that because an objective standard is applied, he must be assumed to have been someone else. The extent to which the characteristics of the actual plaintiff are ignored depends upon the reason for invoking an objective standard. (Some of these questions are discussed in the context of the postponement of the running of the limitation period in personal injury cases in *Adams v Bracknell Forest Borough Council* [2005] 1 AC 76 and *A v Hoare* [2008] 1 AC 844).

He went on to say that the question what the claimant could have done assumes that the claimant has suffered the loss which he claims to have suffered and displays "some curiosity" about what caused it.

III LIM [36.1C]

Fraud Section 32(1)(a) of the 1980 Act contemplates that the limitation period will run from the time when the claimant first acquires knowledge of the fraud ie knowledge that the alleged deceit has been perpetrated. It is the fraud, not the damage or other consequences which flow from it, of which the claimant must hitherto have been ignorant: *RB Policies at Lloyd's v Butler* [1950] 1 KB 76, [1949] 2 All ER 226.

In the case of fraudulent misrepresentation this means that (subject to the provisions as to reasonable discoverability – see **III LIM [36.1B]** below) the claimant must know not only that the representation was not true but that it had been made without belief in its truth. See, for example, *Barnstaple Boat Co Ltd v Jones* [2007] EWCA Civ 727, [2008] 1 All ER 1124, 151 Sol Jo LB 987 which is also authority for the proposition that the required knowledge is of the precise fraud which is pleaded rather than fraud in some more general sense, although the latter may make the pleaded fraud reasonably discoverable at an earlier stage than it was in fact discovered.

Claims for dishonest assistance do not fall within s 21(1)(a) of the 1980 Act but instead s 21(3). In *Cattley v Pollard* [2006] EWHC 3130 (Ch), [2007] 2 All ER 1086, [2007] 3 WLR 317 the claimants successfully relied on s 32(1))(a) to bring their dishonest assistance claims within the limitation period the relevant question in such cases being when the Defendant's alleged assistance or receipt (in knowing receipt) were discovered (or could with reasonable diligence have been discovered) rather than the original wrongdoer's breach of trust or fiduciary duty.

III LIM [36.2]

Deliberately concealed The running of time will be postponed where there has been a deliberate concealment of facts relevant to the cause of action until the concealment is or should have been reasonably discovered irrespective of whether such concealment is contemporaneous with or subsequent to the accrual of the cause of action: see *Sheldon v RHM Outhwaite (Underwriting Agencies) Ltd* [1996] AC 102, [1995] 2 All ER 558, HL.

Interpretation of section 32(1)(b):

- Section 32(1)(b) is a provision whose apparently broad terms are to be construed narrowly. See *Johnson v Chief Constable of Surrey* (CA, unreported, 23 November 1992) and *C v Mirror Group Newspapers Ltd* [1997] 1 WLR 131 (CA).
- There is a distinction between facts which found the cause of action and facts which improve the prospect of succeeding in the claim or are broadly relevant to a claimant's case. Section 32(1)(b) is concerned only with the former and therefore relates to the concealment of 'any fact which the [claimant] has to prove to establish a prima facie case'. See *Johnson, C v MGN and AIC Ltd v ITS Testing Services (UK) Ltd, The 'Kriti Palm'* [2006] EWCA Civ 1601.
- Successful reliance on s 32(1)(b) depends on satisfying 'a statement of claim test' ie. the concealed facts must be those which are essential for a claimant to plead and prove in order to establish a prima facie case, see *Johnson, C v MGN*. In *The 'Kriti Palm'* Buxton LJ at [453] said that:

LIMITATION

> '... what must be concealed is something essential to complete the cause of action. It is not enough that evidence that might enhance the claim is concealed, provided that the claim can be properly pleaded without it.'

The allegedly concealed facts must therefore be compared to the statement of claim. See also *Arcadia Group Brands Ltd v Visa Inc* [2015] EWCA Civ 883, [2015] 5 CMLR 846, [2015] All ER (D) 43 (Aug) for the application of the statement of claim test in a competition claim (as to which it was held that no special limitation considerations arise.)

- Thus s 32(1)(b) does not apply to:
  - new facts which might make a claimant's case stronger: *Johnson*;
  - newly discovered evidence, even if it significantly assists the claimant's case: *The 'Kriti Palm'*; nor to
  - facts relevant to the claimant's ability to defeat a possible defence: *C v MGN*.
- in *Gold v Mincoff, Science & Gold* [2001] Lloyd's Rep PN 423 (a case on s 14A but in which both *Johnson* and *C v MGN* were referred to) Neuberger J said that what a claimant has to know before time starts running against him under s 32(1)(b) are those facts which, if pleaded, would be sufficient to constitute a valid claim, not liable to be struck out for want of some essential allegation.

Where deliberate breach of duty was alleged, s 32(2) (following *Cave*) required deliberate wrongdoing by the defendants; where the claimant had not pleaded that the alleged breaches of duty had been committed with knowledge that they were wrongful, the claim would have been struck out but for an alternative allegation raised in response to a request for further information: *Trilogy Management Ltd v Harcus Sinclair (A Firm)* [2016] EWHC 170 (Ch), The Chancellor, Sir Terence Etherton.

In *Williams v Fanshaw Porter & Hazelhurst (a firm)* [2004] EWCA Civ 157, [2004] 2 All ER 616, [2004] PNLR 29, (2004) Times, 27 February, the defendant solicitors were conducting clinical negligence litigation on behalf of the claimant. Proceedings were brought in May 1994. In August 1994, the defendants compromised the claim without the instructions of the claimant and without telling her that they had done so. In December 1994, they made an unsuccessful application to remedy the situation. Again they did not tell the claimant. It was only in July 1995 that they explained to her what had happened but they did not advise her to seek independent legal advice until June 1996 after fresh proceedings had been commenced and struck out and an appeal against that striking out had failed. The claimant finally brought proceedings against the defendants in December 2000. They alleged that since it was more than six years since the compromise of the original proceedings the claimant was out of time. The claimant relied upon s 32(1)(b) or, alternatively, s 32(2). It was held at first instance that the defendant has not known at the time of the consent order or the failed attempt to rejoin the defendant to the original proceedings that he had been negligent and that he had not deliberately concealed any relevant matter from the claimant.

On appeal, Park J made 4 observations about the effect of s 32(1)(b):

- it is not necessary that the existence of a right of action be concealed but merely *a* fact which is relevant to it;
- the fact has to be one which the defendant knows since one cannot conceal what one does not know. It is not, however, necessary for the defendant to know that the fact is relevant to the right of action although this will usually be the case;
- the section does not require *all* facts relevant to the cause of action to have been concealed. Instead. it is sufficient for *any* such fact to have been concealed.
- the concept of "deliberate" concealment requires conscious concealment

> ". . . the defendant must have considered whether to inform the claimant of the fact and decided not to. I would go further and accept that the fact which he decides not to disclose either must be one which it was his duty to disclose, or must at least be one which he would ordinarily have disclosed in the normal course of his relationship with the claimant, but in the case of which he consciously decided to depart from what he would normally have done and to keep quiet about it."
>
> (*per* Park J, at para 14(iv)).

It was held that the defendants had deliberately concealed their agreement to a consent order and that it had been made and that these were facts which were plainly relevant to the right of action against them. Neither was discovered by the claimant until July 1995 or June 1996 because the defendants had not told her about them although they had considered doing so. They had been under a clear professional duty to inform the claimant but had failed to do so and it made no difference that their motive had been to avoid embarrassment rather than to conceal the existence of a potential cause of action against them nor that they had honestly (albeit misguidedly) believed that the problems were remediable by further procedural action. In his judgment, Mance LJ expressed his doubt whether in the absence of a duty to speak mere non-disclosure would qualify as deliberate concealment. This view is to contrasted with *Cave v Robinson Jarvis & Rolf (a firm)* [2002] UKHL 18, [2002] 2 All ER 641, [2002] 2 WLR 1107 (see below) where Lord Scott (at para 60) said (obiter in this regard) that deliberate concealment involved either "a positive act of concealment or . . . a withholding of relevant information, but, in either case, with the intention of concealing the fact or facts in question".

The recovery of interest by way of execution on a judgment is not a "right of action" within the meaning of s 32(1)(b) and so the commencement of the six year period imposed by s 24(2) could not be deferred by virtue of s 32(1)(b); even if it were, it is doubtful whether the defendant's concealment of himself or his assets would be the concealment of a fact relevant to such a right of action: *Lowsley v Forbes (t/a LE Design Services)* [1999] 1 AC 329, [1998] 3 All ER 897, HL.

For the purpose of s 32(1)(b) the facts relevant to a claimant's cause of action were those which were sufficient to constitute or complete a cause of action, not all those facts which might be evidentially material to proving a claim; also "fraud" for the purposes of s 32(1)(a) meant those facts which a claimant relied on to justify an allegation of fraud, not the label of fraud which was attached to or could be inferred from those facts: *Cia de Seguros Imperio v Heath (REBX) Ltd* [1999] 1 All ER (Comm) 750. The claimant does not need to know *why* the other party has breached the contract or failed to comply with its duty. In a professional negligence context, the cause of action is complete on the occurrence of breach (contract) or actionable damage (negligence), the defendant's reason or motive for its act or omission is therefore irrelevant and thus not a matter which it is necessary for the claimant to be able to plead: *Warring-Davies (Kenneth) v Ford & Warren* [2012] EWHC 3523 (QB), [2012] All ER (D) 98 (Dec).

In *Brocklesby v Armitage & Guest* [2001] 1 All ER 172, [2000] PNLR 33, CA the Court of Appeal held that "deliberate" meant no more than intentional (in the sense of non-accidental) and that, contrary to previous assumption and authority (see in particular the, possibly, obiter remarks of Lord Browne-Wilkinson in *Sheldon v RHM Outhwaite (Underwriting Agencies) Ltd* [1996] AC 102, [1995] 2 All ER 558, HL), deliberate concealment did not require unconscionable behaviour or knowledge of any legal consequence (see para **III LIM [36.5]** and the other cases there cited). The most striking effect of this *Brocklesby* re-interpretation was in the application of the deeming provision in s 32(2) in professional negligence cases.

In *Cave v Robinson Jarvis & Rolf (a firm)* [2002] UKHL 18, [2002] 2 All ER 641, [2002] 2 WLR 1107, however, the House of Lords overruled *Brocklesby*'s re-interpretation of the word "deliberate". According to Lord Millett:

> 'section 32 deprives a defendant of a limitation defence in two situations: (i) where he takes active steps to conceal his own breach of duty after he has become aware of it; and (ii) where he is guilty of deliberate wrongdoing and conceals or fails to disclose it in circumstances where it is unlikely to be discovered for some time. But it does not deprive a defendant of a limitation defence where he is charged with negligence if, being unaware of his error or that he has failed to take proper care, there has been nothing for him to disclose."'

The status quo ante has effectively been restored, save that Lord Scott expressly disavowed the suggestion that to fall within s 32(1)(b) (or s 32(2)) the actions of the defendant had to be "unconscionable". These words are not found in the section and there is no warrant for their importation. In practice this makes little or no difference since it is hard indeed to envisage a situation in which deliberate concealment of wrongdoing or deliberate wrongdoing could occur without unconscionability on the part of the actor.

A deliberate concealment may be effective to postpone the start of the limitation period although the cause of action had accrued beforehand. This was the conclusion in *Williams v Fanshaw Porter and Hazelhurst (a firm)* [2004] EWCA Civ 157, [2004] 2 All ER 616 in which solicitors concealed from their client that they had agreed on her behalf to a consent order for the dismissal of her claim for medical negligence.

In *Williams v Lishman, Sidwell, Campbell & Price Ltd* [2010] EWCA Civ 418, [2010] PNLR 25 it was suggested *obiter* that it is in principle possible for an initial loss which would otherwise complete a claimant's cause of action in negligence but which was deliberately concealed by the defendant to remain a "fact relevant to the plaintiff's right of action" (within the meaning of s 32(1)(b)) even after the occurrence of a later loss arising from *the same breach* and which the defendant has not deliberately concealed.

In *Skerratt v Linfax Ltd (t/a Go Karting for Fun)* [2003] EWCA Civ 695, [2003] All ER (D) 49 (May) the claimant alleged that the effect of a disclaimer which he signed before being injured on a go-karting track operated by the defendants was that it was being represented that he would have no cause of action in such an eventuality and that this amounted to deliberate concealment. The claimant lost on the facts but in *obiter dicta* the Court of Appeal observed that it was difficult to conceive of a situation in which s 32(1)(b) could apply to concealment which was alleged to have taken place *before* the accrual of a cause of action (see also

LIMITATION

Sheldon v RHM Outhwaite (Underwriting Agencies) Ltd [1996] AC 102, [1995] 2 All ER 558, HL) The Court also doubted whether the very existence of a cause of action was itself a fact relevant to the right of action and thus capable of deliberate concealment within the section.

A deliberate concealment, for example of the results of tests carried out in a professional capacity, may give rise to a separate cause of action: *AIC Ltd v ITS Testing Services (UK) Ltd (The Kriti Palm)* [2006] EWCA Civ 1601, [2007] 1 All ER (Comm) 667.

III LIM [36.3]

Amending out of time to allege concealment A claimant may arguably be able to amend to include a fresh cause of action outside the limitation period where it is alleged that there has been a deliberate concealment of a breach of duty and the deliberateness of the breach was an essential element of the new cause of action and pleaded as such. However, leave to amend should be refused where the court could not safely conclude that the success of the new claims as pleaded would of necessity also determine whether the breaches so established were "deliberate commissions of breach of duty" in the sense of s 32 of the 1980 Act so that no limitation defence could have succeeded: *Mortgage Corpn v Alexander Johnson (a firm)* (1999) Times, 22 September. This question arose in relation to proposed new allegations of breach of fiduciary duty in *Mortgage Express v Abensons* [2012] EWHC 1000 (Ch), [2012] 27 Estates Gazette 90, [2012] 18 EG 103 (CS). There it was held that the element of deliberateness required by s 32(2) is not necessarily provided by proof of breach of fiduciary duty; it depends on the particular duty alleged. In *Bristol & West Building Society v Mothew (t/a Stapley & Co)* [1998] Ch 1, [1996] 4 All ER 698, CA, Millett LJ identified two particular rules:

- the 'duty of good faith': in a situation where the fiduciary acts for two principals with potentially conflicting interests he must serve each as faithfully and loyally as the other. Millett LJ explained that 'conduct which is in breach of this duty need not be dishonest but it must be intentional'. Unconscious omission is insufficient and thus proof of breach of this duty does arguably satisfy the requirements of s 32(2);
- on the other hand, the 'actual conflict rule' requires the fiduciary 'to take care not to find himself in a position where there is an actual conflict of duty so that he cannot fulfil his obligations to one principal without failing in his obligations to the other'. It has not been decided (and it is thus unclear) that breach of this duty requires an awareness of the conflict in question.

Unless the claimant can show that the defendant has no arguable limitation defence then the proper practice is for permission to amend to be refused and for the claimant to make the claim in question in new proceedings to be heard together or to be consolidated with the existing claim. This is because by the doctrine of 'relation back' new claims are deemed to have been made when the claim was first brought rather than when the amendment was allowed, with the effect that the defendant is deprived of any limitation defence – see *Welsh Development Agency v Redpath Dorman Long* [1994] 1 WLR 1409. There is no arguable (or relevant) limitation defence where the very ingredients of the new claim (if made out) also fulfil the requirements of eg s 32(2) but where it cannot be said that the mental elements are clearly the same or equivalent – as in the case of breach of fiduciary duty – then permission to amend ought to be refused.

III LIM [36.4]

Section 32(2) - Deliberate commission of a breach of duty In *Brocklesby v Armitage & Guest* [2001] 1 All ER 172, [2000] PNLR 33, CA, a claim against solicitors for negligence, it was held that the claimant could rely on the extended limitation period under s 32(1)(b) as expanded by sub-s (2) since it was sufficient that the solicitor intentionally committed the act complained of, and that the act or omission did involve a breach of duty whether or not the actor appreciated its legal consequences. This case was expressly followed in *Liverpool Roman Catholic Archdiocese Trustees Inc v Goldberg* [2001] 1 All ER 182, where Laddie J held that '"any intentional act which amounts to a breach of duty amounts to a deliberate commission of a breach of duty and triggers section 32(2)"'.

The House of Lords has now overruled both of these cases on this point (see para **III LIM [36.2]**) and, to the extent that other cases have been decided in reliance upon them, those cases have suffered the same fate. In *Cave v Robinson Jarvis and Rolf (a firm)* [2002] UKHL 18, [2003] 1 AC 384, [2002] 2 All ER 641 Lord Scott analysed the effect of s 32(2) in this way:

> "Subsection (2), however, provides an alternative route. The claimant need not concentrate on the allegedly concealed facts but can instead concentrate on the commission of the breach of duty. If the claimant can show that the defendant knew he was committing a breach of duty, or intended to commit the breach of duty – I can discern no difference between the two formulations; each would constitute, in my opinion, a deliberate commission of the breach – then, if the circumstances are such that the claimant is unlikely to discover for some time that the breach of duty has been committed, the facts

involved in the breach are taken to have been deliberately concealed for subsection (1)(b) purposes. I do not agree with Mr Doctor that the sub-section, thus construed, adds nothing. It provides an alternative, and in some cases what may well be an easier, means of establishing the facts necessary to bring the case within section 32(1)(b)."

In *Tucker v Allen* [2001] PNLR 884, [2001] 26 EG 161 (CS) it was held that deliberate concealment was established where a solicitor had failed, in breach of the Law Society Code of Conduct, to inform the claimant that she should seek independent advice. It is not clear to what extent the *Tucker's* reliance on *Brocklesby* undermines its authority but in any event it is not obvious that a failure to advise a client to seek independent advice will *per se* amount to the deliberate concealment of a fact relevant to the right of action. Instead it may depend upon what else the client does not know and/or the solicitor has not disclosed. In *Williams v Fanshaw Porter & Hazelhurst (a firm)* [2004] EWCA Civ 157, [2004] 2 All ER 616, [2004] PNLR 29, (2004) Times, 27 February, the defendant had compromised part of the claimant's clinical negligence claim without telling her. He also failed to inform her of a further failed application to re-join the doctor in question. It was held that facts relevant to the claimant's right of action had been concealed. Mance LJ said (at para 29) that

> there is no doubt that a solicitor owes a duty to keep his client informed about the general conduct of a matter he is handling as well as about any error in the handling of the client's affairs which may give the client cause for complaint against the solicitor.

However, in *Gold v Mincoff Science & Gold (a firm)* [2001] Lloyd's Rep PN 423 Neuberger J said

> 'Mr Davidson [for the defendants] rightly warns against the court being too easily persuaded by the claimant that he has a fresh cause of action against his solicitor on the basis that the solicitor failed to advise, at some point after his initial negligence, that he had been negligent. If such an argument were too readily accepted, it would have two unsatisfactory consequences. First, it would enable the provisions of the 1980 Act to be evaded in many cases in an artificial way. Secondly, it would effectively impose on a solicitor some sort of implied general retainer. Accordingly, I would accept that it would be a relatively exceptional case where the court would be prepared to hold that a solicitor's negligence claim that was otherwise statute-barred could, albeit in a slightly different guise, be resurrected on the basis that, at a time within the limitation period and less than six years before the issue of proceedings, the solicitor failed to advise that he had been negligent. Only if the facts clearly warrant such a conclusion should the court adopt it, in my view.'

The Court of Appeal approved of this passage in *Ezekiel v Lehrer* [2002] EWCA Civ 16, [2002] Lloyd's Rep PN 260. Compliance with the terms of solicitors' professional indemnity policies will, in any event, usually preclude the making of any admission of negligence/liability.

In *Giles v Rhind* [2008] EWCA Civ 118, [2008] 3 All ER 697, [2008] 3 WLR 1233, [2008] 2 BCLC 1 the Court of Appeal rejected a construction of 32(2) which would limit it to breaches of contractual or tortious duties or of equitable or fiduciary duties since both the natural meaning of the word "duty", *viz* obligation or constraint, and the mischief to which s 32 is directed favoured a broader construction. It therefore held that s 32(2) was capable of applying to s 423 of the Insolvency Act 1986 (transactions at an undervalue). Arden LJ observed (at para 42) that:

> [f]or s 32(2) to apply, (1) there must be the deliberate commission of an act; (2) that act must amount to a "breach of duty"; and (3) that breach of duty must occur in circumstances in which it is unlikely to be discovered for some time. If those ingredients are satisfied, then the next step (where the claimant relies on s 32(1)(b)) is to go back to s 32(1)(b) and to identify the facts that are involved in the relevant breach of duty. After that, those facts can be tested against the right of action relied on in the proceedings. There is no need, as I see it, on an ordinary reading of s 32(1) (b) to show that the right of action was for a breach of duty. All that it is necessary to show is that the relevant facts involved a breach of duty.

III LIM [36.5]

"the action is for relief from the consequences of a mistake" In *Phillips-Higgins v Harper* [1954] 1 QB 411, [1954] 1 All ER 116, it was held that the sub-section only applied where the mistake is an essential ingredient of the cause of action pleaded but some have doubted whether this view is correct: see *Denys v Shuckburgh* (1840) 4 Y & C Ex 42, 160 ER 912; *Baker v Courage & Co* [1910] 1 KB 56 and Edelman: *Limitation Periods and the Theory of*

LIMITATION

Unjust Enrichment [2005] MLR 848. However, in *Test Claimants in the FII Group Litigation v Revenue and Customs Comrs* [2010] EWCA Civ 103, [2010] STI 562 the Court of Appeal decided that mistake does have to be an essential ingredient of the cause of action for s 32(1)(c) because:

– that is the thrust of previous authority;
– the words 'relief from the consequences of a mistake' themselves suggest a narrow interpretation of the scope of the sub-section;
– the wider interpretation of the sub-section would lead:

'to undesirable uncertainty as to its scope, whereas if it has the meaning ascribed to it in *Phillips-Higgins v Harper*, its ambit is clear. Moreover, extending the scope of liabilities of indefinite duration, the existence of which after the expiration of the normal limitation period may be unknown to the obligor, is not obviously desirable.'

See also *FJ Chalke Ltd v Revenue & Customs Comrs* [2010] EWCA Civ 313, [2010] STC 1640.

III LIM [36.6]

Mistake of law The House of Lords held in *Kleinwort Benson Ltd v Lincoln City Council* [1999] 2 AC 349, [1998] 4 All ER 513, HL (an action for the recovery on the ground of mistake of money paid under interest swap agreements subsequently held to have been void as *ultra vires* the local authorities in question), that s 32(1)(c) applies also to a mistake of law as well as to a mistake of fact. Such mistakes include not only mistakes as to the effect of the currently declared or understood state of the law but also to subsequent changes in the law. Lord Goff put it thus:

"To me, it is plain that the money was indeed paid over under a mistake, the mistake being a mistake of law. The payer believed, when he paid the money, that he was bound in law to pay it. He is now told that, on the law as held to be applicable at the date of the payment, he was not bound to pay it. Plainly, therefore, he paid the money under a mistake of law, and, accordingly, subject to any applicable defences, he is entitled to recover it."

Lord Goff expressly recognised that the consequence of this was that the cause of action in such a case may be extended for an indefinite period of time but he considered that this was a matter which required consideration by the legislature rather than their Lordships. There is helpful comment on the state of mind of the putatively mistaken payer in the speech of Lord Hope who also refers to the judgment of Mason CJ said in *David Securities Pty Ltd v Commonwealth Bank of Australia* (1992) 175 CLR 353.

This decision was applied in *Deutsche Morgan Grenfell Group plc v IRC* [2003] EWHC 1779, [2003] 4 All ER 645, (2003) Times, 30 July. In this complicated case the claimant in a test case under a group litigation order sought to recover Advance Corporation Tax from the Revenue in respect of payments which it had made to foreign holding companies. At the time at which the payments were made such payments could not benefit from "group income" elections. This restriction was held by the European Court of Justice to be contrary to Article 52 of the EC Treaty in *Metallgesellschaft Ltd v IRC and A-G* and *Hoechst v IRC and A-G*: C-397, 410/98 [2001] STC 452. Its judgment was given in March 2001 and the claimant brought its proceedings within 6 years. It was held that the claimant only discovered its mistake when the ECJ's judgment was given.

Section 320 of the Finance Act 2004 (see *Europcar UK Ltd v Revenue & Customs Commissioners* [2008] EWHC 1363 (Ch)[2008] STC 2751) in effect reverses the effect of this decision for the future. In the present cases the Revenue appealed to the Court of Appeal which held ([2006] Ch 243, [2005] 3 All ER 1025, [2006] 2 WLR 103, [2005] STC 329), primarily on the basis of Lord Goff's speeches in the *Woolwich* and *Kleinwort Benson* cases, that a claimant who makes a payment to the Revenue under a mistake of law is not entitled to a restitutionary remedy in respect of that payment otherwise than under the *Woolwich* principle (where the demand is unlawful) or under the relevant statutory regime (where the demand is lawful). The Court of Appeal held that they represent distinct, mutually exclusive and exhaustive régimes but the House of Lords has subsequently taken a different view: see [2006] UKHL 49, [2006] 3 WLR 781, (2006) Times, 26 October.

Their Lordships could see no good reason why the right to restitution of payments made under a mistake of law which had been recognised in the *Kleinwort Benson* case should not apply to mistaken payments of tax and they specifically disagreed that Lord Goff had been saying so in his speech in that case. They also found themselves unable to infer that Parliament had intended to exclude a common law remedy in all cases of mistake (whether of fact or law) in which the Revenue was unjustly enriched but which did not fall within s 33 of the 1980 Act. They decided by a majority that the claim could properly be described as being for relief from the consequences of a mistake within the meaning of s 32(1)(c). Lord Scott dissented on the issue of mistake which issue is variously explored in their Lordships' opinions and repays close reading as a matter of general principle. The majority held that since the claimant had not discovered this mistake until the ECJ pronounced its judgment, only then did time start to run.

In *Test Claimants in the FII Group Litigation v Revenue and Customs Comrs* [2012] 2 WLR 1149, [2012] Bus LR 1033, [2012] 3 All ER 909, [2012] STC 1362, [2012] BTC 312, [2012] STI 1707, [2012] 2 AC 337 the Supreme Court has referred the question of the compatibility of s 320 with EU law to the ECJ.

III LIM [37]

32A. Discretionary exclusion of time limit for actions for defamation or malicious falsehood

(1) If it appears to the court that it would be equitable to allow an action to proceed having regard to the degree to which—

- (a) the operation of section 4A of this Act prejudices the plaintiff or any person whom he represents, and
- (b) any decision of the court under this subsection would prejudice the defendant or any person whom he represents,

the court may direct that that section shall not apply to the action or shall not apply to any specified cause of action to which the action relates.

(2) In acting under this section the court shall have regard to all the circumstances of the case and in particular to—

- (a) the length of, and the reasons for, the delay on the part of the plaintiff;
- (b) where the reason or one of the reasons for the delay was that all or any of the facts relevant to the cause of action did not become known to the plaintiff until after the end of the period mentioned in section 4A—
  - (i) the date on which any such facts did become known to him, and
  - (ii) the extent to which he acted promptly and reasonably once he knew whether or not the facts in question might be capable of giving rise to an action; and
- (c) the extent to which, having regard to the delay, relevant evidence is likely—
  - (i) to be unavailable, or
  - (ii) to be less cogent than if the action had been brought within the period mentioned in section 4A.

(3) In the case of an action for slander of title, slander of goods or other malicious falsehood brought by a personal representative—

- (a) the references in subsection (2) above to the plaintiff shall be construed as including the deceased person to whom the cause of action accrued and any previous personal representative of that person; and
- (b) nothing in section 28(3) of this Act shall be construed as affecting the court's discretion under this section.

(4) In this section "the court" means the court in which the action has been brought.

III LIM [37.1]

This section was substituted by s 5 of the Defamation Act 1996 in relation to causes of action arising on or after 4 September 1996.

III LIM [37.2]

The exercise of the discretion Although the discretion under s 32A is unfettered, the policy is that defamation claims should be brought quickly and pursued vigorously: *Steedman v BBC* [2001] EWCA Civ 1534, 145 Sol Jo LB 259, [2001] 47 LS Gaz R 27; *Buckley v Dalziel* [2007] EWHC 1025 (QB), [2007] 1 WLR 2933, (2007) Times, 7 June; *Adelson v Associated Newspapers Ltd* [2007] EWHC 3028 (QB), [2007] All ER (D) 305 (Dec); and *Brady v Norman* [2010] EWHC 1215 (QB), [2010] All ER (D) 269 (May).

LIMITATION

A claimant is expected to pursue his complaint promptly irrespective of the limitation period and whether he knew about it because, not to do so, is inconsistent with a genuine wish to pursue vindication of his character promptly and vigorously: see *Bewry v Reed Elsevier* [2014] EWCA Civ 1411.

The effect of any delay on the ability of the defendant to defend a defamation action is an important but by no means decisive factor (except, perhaps, where any delay was very short) in the assessment of the equitability of disapplying the limitation period. The availability to the claimant of a claim against its solicitors is a legitimate factor to be taken into consideration: *Steedman v BBC* [2001] EWCA Civ 1534, [2001] 47 LS Gaz R 27 The approach taken to the exercise of discretion in personal injury cases is of limited value in cases of time-barred defamation where the circumstances are likely to be different: *Brady v Norman* [2011] EWCA Civ 107, [2011] CP Rep 23, [2011] EMLR 16.

When assessing the overall circumstances for the purposes of the s 32A discretion it is relevant to take into account the extent to which the claimant will obtain any 'sufficient tangible or legitimate advantage' from the disapplication of the one-year limitation period and in particular the existence of 'any real need for vindication': *Khalil v North Bristol NHS Trust* [2013] EWHC 85 (QB).

The extent of the delay since the expiry of the limitation period should be viewed in the context of the shortness of the one-year period allowed under s 4A. Accordingly, delay which may seem relatively small in the context of a three or six-year limitation period may be rather more significant in the context of the one- year period: *Cornwall Gardens Pte Ltd v Ro Garrard & Co Ltd* (9 May 2001, unreported), CA; *cf Muter v Newcastle upon Tyne Aero Club* [2001] All ER (D) 237 (Dec), QBD where the delay in question amounted to a few days only. There is a potential tension between the desirability of negotiations and the shortness of the limitation period see: *Bewry v Reed Elsevier UK Ltd (t/a LexisNexis)* [2013] EWHC 3182 (QB) where the claimant's attempts to negotiate before commencing proceedings were considered to be reasonable.

The court also needs to balance the relevant rights under the European Convention on Human Rights 1950 including the fact that being sued is of itself a serious interference with the right of freedom of expression: see *Jameel v Dow Jones & Co Inc* [2005] EWCA Civ 75, [2005] QB 946, [2005] 2 WLR 1614; *Lonzim plc v Sprague* [2009] EWHC 2838 (QB), [2009] All ER (D) 132 (Nov) and *Brady v Norman* [2010] EWHC 1215 (QB), [2010] All ER (D) 269 (May).

Time starts to run on publication of the libel even though the identity of the tortfeasor may be unknown. Where identity is discovered outside the limitation period an application may be made to extend time under s 32A: *Edwards v Golding* (2007) Times, 22 May, CA.

In *Maccaba v Litchenstein* [2003] EWHC 1325 (QB), [2003] All ER (D) 266 (Apr) there were nine claims of slander all but two of which were in time. These were permitted to proceed because they were comparable to the slander claims which were within time and involved the same facts as a harassment claim which was not statute barred.

The Neill Committee (The Working Group of the Supreme Court Procedure Committee under the Chairmanship of Lord Justice Neill (July 1991)) suggested that reasons which might lead to the exercise of the discretion could include the existence of intervening professional disciplinary or criminal proceedings prompted by the libel (provided that prompt complaint had been made about the libel) or even (possibly) difficulty in obtaining funding to commence proceedings:

(a) in *Khilili v Bennett* [2000] EMLR 996, CA a libel action issued in time but which the claimant had delayed pursuing pending the outcome of other proceedings was reinstated; and
(b) in *Hinks v Channel 4 Television Corpn* (2000) LTL 3/3/2000 (where there was an outstanding complaint to regulators) it was held that in such cases libel proceedings should be issued, and then stayed.

'the facts relevant to the cause of action' The relevant facts are those which the claimant has to prove to establish a prima facie case, not facts relevant to rebutting a possible defence. In *C v Mirror Group Newspapers* [1996] 4 All ER 511, [1997] 1 WLR 131 the claimant knew that the words complained of had been spoken but was under the misapprehension that they had been said in court and were thus privileged. It was held that when she knew that they had been said she knew all of the relevant facts.

III LIM [38]

33. Discretionary exclusion of time limit for actions in respect of personal injuries or death

(1) If it appears to the court that it would be equitable to allow an action to proceed having regard to the degree to which—

(a) the provisions of section 11 *or 11A* [, 11A, 11B] or 12 of this Act prejudice the plaintiff or any person whom he represents; and

(b) any decision of the court under this subsection would prejudice the defendant or any person whom he represents;

the court may direct that those provisions shall not apply to the action, or shall not apply to any specified cause of action to which the action relates.

(1A) The court shall not under this section disapply—

(a) subsection (3) of section 11A; or

(b) where the damages claimed by the plaintiff are confined to damages for loss of or damage to any property, any other provision in its application to an action by virtue of Part I of the Consumer Protection Act 1987.

[(1B) Where the damages claimed are confined to damages for loss of or damage to any property, the court shall not under this section disapply any provision in its application to an action under section 2 of the Automated and Electric Vehicles Act 2018.]

(2) The court shall not under this section disapply section 12(1) except where the reason why the person injured could no longer maintain an action was because of the time limit in section 11 *or subsection (4) of section 11A* [, 11A(4) or 11B(2) or (4)]..

If, for example, the person injured could at his death no longer maintain an action under the Fatal Accidents Act 1976 because of the time limit in Article 29 in Schedule 1 to the Carriage by Air Act 1961, the court has no power to direct that section 12 (1) shall not apply.

(3) In acting under this section the court shall have regard to all the circumstances of the case and in particular to—

(a) the length of, and the reasons for, the delay on the part of the plaintiff;

(b) the extent to which, having regard to the delay, the evidence adduced or likely to be adduced by the plaintiff or the defendant is or is likely to be less cogent than if the action had been brought within the time allowed by section 11, by section 11A [, by section 11B] or (as the case may be) by section 12;

(c) the conduct of the defendant after the cause of action arose, including the extent (if any) to which he responded to requests reasonably made by the plaintiff for information or inspection for the purpose of ascertaining facts which were or might be relevant to the plaintiff's cause of action against the defendant;

(d) the duration of any disability of the plaintiff arising after the date of the accrual of the cause of action;

(e) the extent to which the plaintiff acted promptly and reasonably once he knew whether or not the act or omission of the defendant, to which the injury was attributable, might be capable at that time of giving rise to an action for damages;

(f) the steps, if any, taken by the plaintiff to obtain medical, legal or other expert advice and the nature of any such advice he may have received.

(4) In a case where the person injured died when, because of section 11 *or subsection (4) of section 11A* [, 11A(4) or 11B(2) or (4)], he could no longer maintain an action and recover damages in respect of the injury, the court shall have regard in particular to the length of, and the reasons for, the delay on the part of the deceased.

(5) In a case under subsection (4) above, or any other case where the time limit, or one of the time limits, depends on the date of knowledge of a person other than the plaintiff, subsection (3) above shall have effect with appropriate modifications,

and shall have effect in particular as if references to the plaintiff included references to any person whose date of knowledge is or was relevant in determining a time limit.

(6) A direction by the court disapplying the provisions of section 12 (1) shall operate to disapply the provisions to the same effect in section 1 (1) of the Fatal Accidents Act 1976.

(7) In this section "the court" means the court in which the action has been brought.

(8) References in this section to section 11 *or 11A* [, 11A or 11B] include references to that section as extended by any of the provisions of this Part of this Act other than this section or by any provision of Part III of this Act.

Amendment *Text in italic is deleted and text in square brackets is inserted by the Automated and Electric Vehicles Act 2018 with effect from a date to be appointed.*

III LIM [38.1]

Personal injuries or death Claims for injuries arising from deliberate assaults fall within the meaning of 'negligence, nuisance or breach of duty' in s 11(1) rather than the fixed six-year limitation period under s 2 and are thus subject to the special three-year limitation period applicable to such claims and also therefore to the discretion under s 33 to disapply that limitation period. So held the House of Lords in *A v Hoare* [2008] UKHL 6, [2008] 1 AC 844, [2008] 2 WLR 311, [2008] 2 All ER 1, [2008] 1 FLR overruling its previous decision in *Stubbings v Webb* [1993] AC 498, [1993] 1 All ER 322, HL. (For ss 11 and 13 see para **III LIM [13]** and para **III LIM [16]**).

III LIM [38.2]

If it appears equitable the court may direct This section gives wide powers to override limitation periods under the Act (but not under the Athens Convention: *Higham v Stena Sealink Ltd* [1996] 3 All ER 660, [1996] 1 WLR 1107, CA) in personal injury litigation. The House of Lords in *Horton v Sadler* [2006] UKHL 27, [2006] 3 All ER 1177, [2006] 2 WLR 1346 and in *A v Hoare* [2008] UKHL 6, [2008] 1 AC 844, [2008] 2 WLR 311, [2008] 2 All ER 1, [2008] 1 FLR has held that the discretion is not one which is confined to "residual cases" but is broad and unfettered. Indeed, the stricter interpretations of s 14(2) (in *A v Hoare*) and of s 14(3) (in *Adams v Bracknell Forest Borough Council* [2004] UKHL 29, [2004] 3 All ER 897) were consciously influenced by the consideration that a broad discretion to do justice between the parties under s 33 militated against permitting too much latitude to claimants under s 14. The theme, then, is that where the question at issue is the claimant's ability to proceed with his or her claim as of right under s 14 (rather than as a matter of discretion under s 33) then greater account should be taken of the injustice to the defendant.

The burden lies on the claimant in an application under s 33 but (at least in abstract) it is not helpful to characterise it as heavy (or light); it all depends on the facts: *Sayers v Lord Chelwood* [2012] EWCA Civ 1715, [2013] 2 All ER 232, 157 Sol Jo (no 1) 31. See also *Roberts v Comr of Police of the Metropolis* [2012] EWCA Civ 799, [2012] All ER (D) 159 (Jun) where (even on the particular facts) the Court of Appeal considered that the judge had erred by treating the seriousness of the allegation as increasing the burden on the claimant.

An application for a direction may be initiated by the claimant as an application in the proceedings or in response to a defendant's application to strike out. A direction disapplying the Act is a final order: *Dale v British Coal Corpn* [1993] 1 All ER 317, [1992] 1 WLR 964, CA. The court may postpone a decision on the application until the trial. The same principles should be applied to a late claim where a group action is already on foot as where one is not: *Nash v Eli Lilly & Co* [1993] 4 All ER 383, [1993] 1 WLR 782, CA. In a case where a direction has been made in favour of one party it was held inequitable to refuse it to another: *Feveyear v Cole* [1993] PIQR P42, [1993] CLY 2606, CA. Also a direction was made in *Ward v Foss* (1993) Times, 29 November, CA to facilitate a claim for 'lost years' which would otherwise have failed because of a change in the law. It would not be equitable for an action by the claimant to proceed where the claimant had failed to give a truthful and accurate history to the doctors and the court: *Long v Tolchard & Sons Ltd* (2000) Times, 5 January, CA.

The term 'all the circumstances of the case' includes a 'broad merits test' in accordance with which it would be inappropriate for the court to disapply the limitation period if the claimants' prospects of success are slight: *B v Ministry of Defence* [2010] EWCA Civ 1317, (2011) 117 BMLR 101. See also *Mutua v Foreign and Commonwealth Office* [2012] EWHC 2678 (QB), [2012] NLJR 1291 where novel allegations of vicarious liability were considered to be sufficiently arguable in a continuously developing area of the law but in *AB v Ministry of*

Defence [2010] EWCA Civ 1317, 117 BMLR 101, [2010] NLJR 1686; affd [2012] UKSC 9, [2012] 3 All ER 673, [2012] 2 WLR 643 the Supreme Court endorsed the refusal of the Court of Appeal to extend time where the claims had no realistic prospect of success on causation.

In *JL v Bowen* [2017] EWCA Civ 82 the Court of Appeal held that the judge had erred in his approach to s 33, when exercising his discretion to disapply the limitation period in relation to a claim for alleged historical child sex abuse, because he had failed to have regard to the factual findings he had made in relation to the underlying claim at a trial where the substance of the claim and the limitation issue were heard at the same time. The findings and conclusions arising from the judge's rejection of the bulk of the claim and, more generally the adverse findings he made against the claimant, were important in determining the length of delay in bringing the claim, the reasons for delay and the extent of prejudice suffered by the defendants in defending the claim. Taking into account the adverse findings and conclusions reached by the judge, the Court of Appeal held that the prejudice to the defendants in disapplying the limitation period significantly outweighed any prejudice to the claimant in not doing so, and reversed the judge's decision to allow the claim to proceed.

III LIM [38.2A]

On restoration of a company to the register – ss 1029-1032 of the Companies Act 2006 (see Companies III COM [1022]) On an application to restore a dissolved (or struck-off) company to the register under s 1029 of the Companies Act 2006 the court may, in addition to granting the application, direct under s 1032(3) that the period between the dissolution (or striking off) of the company and the making of the order restoring it is not to count for the purposes of any relevant limitation statute. See *Re Philip Powis Ltd* [1998] 1 BCLC 440, CA on the predecessor provision in s 651 of the Companies Act 1985.

However, the effect of such a direction is equivalent to the granting of an application under s 33 of the Limitation Act 1980 and, accordingly, no such direction should normally be given unless: (1) everyone who could be expected to oppose it (including the insurers of the company) have been given notice of it; (2) that the court has before it all the evidence which the parties would wish to adduce on an application under s 33; and (3) that an application under s 33 would be bound to succeed. Where these conditions are not satisfied then the prospective claimant should be left to make an application under s 33: *Smith v White Knight Laundry Ltd* [2001] EWCA Civ 660, [2001] 3 All ER 862, [2001] 2 BCLC 206. See also *Re Workvale* [1992] 1 WLR 416 and the observations of the Court of Appeal in *Regent Leisuretime Ltd v NatWest Finance Ltd (Formerly County Natwest Ltd)* [2003] EWCA Civ 391, a non-PI case.

On the facts it may be appropriate to disapply the limitation period for a time which is shorter than the period of the company's dissolution: see the Scottish case of *Whitbread (Hotels) Ltd & Whitbread (GC) Ltd v Walkmore (95) Ltd* (2002) Times, 18 January, Court of Session (Outer House).

III LIM [38.3]

Prejudice The jurisprudence on the exercise of the s 33 discretion and, in particular, what counts as relevant prejudice to each of the claimant and the defendant has been significantly refined over the last few years.

In *Cain v Francis* [2008] EWCA Civ 1451, [2009] 2 All ER 579, [2009] 3 WLR 551 the Court of Appeal heard conjoined appeals in cases where liability had been admitted in pre-action correspondence but, through the fault of solicitors, proceedings had been issued outside the limitation period. The extension of time was therefore sought under s 33. The principal issue was whether the loss of a limitation defence should be regarded as relevant prejudice to the defendant. The Court of Appeal emphasised the need for consistency on such a fundamental issue while recognising that the existing authorities hardly spoke with one voice. The Court gave the following guidance:

(a) whether it was equitable (meaning fair and just) to allow an action to proceed was at the heart of the s 33 discretion;
(b) a defendant should only be spared having to defend proceedings if the passage of time had significantly diminished its ability to do so whether in respect of liability or quantum;
(c) a literal interpretation did appear to suggest that the defendant's liability to pay damages if the time limit were disapplied amounted to relevant prejudice but this is wrong. The loss of such a "windfall" limitation defence is not a relevant factor.
(d) the fact that the claimant had a good claim against a solicitor was only relevant if there was substantive prejudice to the defendant's ability to defend itself;
(e) the mere length of the delay was not, of itself, a deciding factor since the question was what prejudice had been caused by the actual delay;
(f) the reason for the delay could still be a relevant factor;

LIMITATION

(g) it was also relevant to consider whether the defendant knew that there was to be a claim and had (even if it did not take) the opportunity to investigate within the limitation period.

Where the delay was due to the misleading advice of counsel and solicitors, and there was no doubt that there would be prejudice to the claimant if the claim was struck out and she was left with a claim that had to be somewhat speculative against solicitors and counsel, it would be equitable to allow the action to proceed under s 33: *Pratima Rani Das v Dr Durga Ganju* [1999] Lloyd's Rep Med 198, CA.

The financial value of the claim (compared to the cost and trouble to the Defendant) may also be a relevant factor in the exercise of the discretion: *Kew v Bettamix* [2006] EWCA Civ 1535, 150 Sol Jo LB 1534.

Prejudice to the defendant can include prejudice not only in defending the claimant's claim (but, in the light of *Cain v Francis* this must be forensic prejudice) but also in seeking contribution from another person, see *Buckler v Sheffield City Council* [2004] EWCA Civ 920, [2005] PIQR P3. The court may take into account any prejudice to the defendant's insurers since they are, for these purposes a composite unit: *Kelly v Bastible* (1997) 36 BMLR 51, [1997] 8 Med LR 15, CA.

In a claim for medical negligence, where the claimant suffered hypoxic brain damage at birth, commenced over 25 years after the birth, the defendant's argument under s 33 was rejected; the claimant would be just as affected by the absence of live witnesses who could give evidence or whom he could cross-examine, as the defendants would be in rebutting the case. Accordingly, the prejudice to the defendants was not such as to prevent a fair and equitable trial on the evidence which existed: *Appleby v Walsall Health Authority* [1999] Lloyd's Rep Med 154.

A fair trial may be possible even where most of the potential oral witnesses are dead if questions of fact can be satisfactorily resolved by reference to documentary evidence: see *Mutua v Foreign and Commonwealth Office* [2012] EWHC 2678 (QB), [2012] NLJR 1291 where the claims arose out of allegations of torture in Kenya in the 1950s.

An extension of time was refused in a case where the defendant NHS Hospital Trust would not, due to passage of time, be in a position to defend the claimant's personal injury claim: *Pennine Acute Hospitals NHS Trust v De Meza* [2017] EWCA Civ 1711, [2017] All ER (D) 92 (Nov).

More generally, Etherton MR has provided a useful summary of relevant considerations in the context of an application under s 33 in *Carroll v Chief Constable of Greater Manchester Police* [2017] EWCA Civ 1992, [2017] All ER (D) 48 (Dec).

III LIM [38.4]

Settlement of similar claims The fact that insurers have settled previous claims of a similar nature does not mean there was no prejudice caused by the delay in the case in question: *Price v United Engineering Steels Ltd* [1998] PIQR P407, CA.

III LIM [38.4A]

Delay The relevant period is from the expiry of the limitation period up to the time of issue of proceedings: *Thompson v Brown Construction (Ebbw Vale) Ltd* [1981] 2 All ER 296, [1981] 1 WLR 744; *Pratima Rani Das v Dr Durga Ganju* [1999] Lloyd's Rep Med 198, 48 BMLR 83, CA. However, the entire period since the accrual of the cause of action can be considered as ' all part of the circumstances of the case': *Smith v Leicestershire Health Authority* [1998] Lloyd's Rep Med 77 at 91.

There is little authority on the effect of the time which has passed before the commencement of the limitation period. This question arises where pursuant to the date of knowledge provisions in s 11(4) and s 14 of the 1980 Act (see **III LIM [13]** and **III LIM [17]** above) there is a substantial period of time between the accrual of the cause of action (viz the suffering of damage) and the claimant's date of knowledge of it. That pre-commencement period cannot be relevant under s 33(3)(b) because the 'delay' to which it refers is delay after the commencement of the limitation period.

In *Collins v Secretary of State for Business Innovation & Skills* [2014] EWCA Civ 717, [2014] PIQR P19, [2014] Med LR 291 the Claimant had been exposed to asbestos between 1947 and 1967 and subsequently developed lung cancer. At first instance he was held to have had constructive knowledge in 2003 (but actual knowledge in 2009) that the cancer was capable of being attributed to that asbestos exposure. Proceedings were brought against the defendants only in 2012 and, on a preliminary issue as to limitation, the judge refused to disapply the limitation period. On appeal, Jackson LJ said this about the relevance of the passage of time before the commencement of the limitation period:

(i) 'The period of time which elapses between a tortfeasor's breach of duty and the commencement of the limitation period must be part of "the circumstances of the case" within the meaning of section 33(3).

(ii) The primary factors to which the court must have regard are those set out in section 33(3)(a) to (f). Parliament has singled those factors out for special mention.

(iii) Therefore, although the court will have regard to time elapsed before the claimant's date of knowledge, the court will accord less weight to this factor. It will treat pre-limitation period effluxion of time as merely one of the relevant factors to take into account.'

As the judge went on to observe, such pre-commencement delay may be invoked by either party: by the claimant to say that recent delay has had little or no further impact on the cogency of the evidence and by the defendant to say that the pre-commencement delay has already caused such serious obstacles to defending the claim that more recent delay should be treated as seriously prejudicial. It will all depend on the facts.

III LIM [38.5]

Length of and reasons for delay For cases where the court exercised discretion in favour of claimants who delayed claiming while continuing to work, see *Buck v English Electric Co Ltd* [1978] 1 All ER 271, [1977] 1 WLR 806 and *McCafferty v Metropolitan Police District Receiver* [1977] 2 All ER 756, [1977] 1 WLR 1073, CA. However the Court of Appeal departed from *Buck v English Electric* in the later case of *Barrand v British Cellophane plc* (1995) Times, 16 February, CA, and emphasised that the question whether to grant leave was not to be decided on the same principles as whether to strike out. In particular, the claimant had the burden of proof on questions of delay and prejudice when applying for leave, whereas the defendant had the burden when applying to strike out. Also there was a statutory checklist in sub-s (3) for the applications for leave. It was held equitable to override the limitation period where the delay was short and liability not in dispute in *Hartley v Birmingham City District Council* [1992] 2 All ER 213, [1992] 1 WLR 968, CA; *Ramsden v Lee* [1992] 2 All ER 204, CA. Note, however, that in considering the length of the delay and the reasons for it, as required by paragraph (3)(a) the court should not bring in criteria of reasonableness: *Coad v Cornwall and Isles of Scilly Health Authority* [1997] 1 WLR 189, [1997] PIQR P92, CA. In a class action against tobacco companies it was held that the limitation period should not be extended under s 33 where the claimant, having acquired the relevant knowledge, did nothing until a situation arose which enabled him to embark upon litigation which he was previously unable or unwilling to bring for whatever reason. Furthermore the claims possessed a limited financial value compared with their potentially vast cost, and could also be described as speculative: *Hodgson v Imperial Tobacco Ltd* [1998] 2 All ER 673, [1998] 1 WLR 1056, CA.

In the context of a mesothelioma claim, the shock of an unexpected diagnosis of mesothelioma, the adverse effects of chemotherapy treatment, a period of unexpected remission during which the deceased endeavoured to keep life as normal for his wife and children as possible and a desire not to saddle his family with debt where it was considered that any evidential prejudice caused to the defendant by the ten-week delay was not such that it outweighed the factors in favour of disapplying the limitation period: *Sanderson v City of Bradford Metropolitan Borough Council* [2016] EWHC 527 (QB).

In *Corbin v Penfold Metallising Co Ltd* (2000) Times, 2 May, CA, the court emphasised that there is no principle of law that delay by solicitors is to be attributed to the claimant where the claimant has acted reasonably and promptly. See also *Steeds v Peverel Management Services Ltd* (2001) Times, 16 May.

In the unusual circumstances of *Daley v Bakiyev* [2016] EWHC 1972 (QB) (in which the claimant sought damages for an attempted murder he alleged had been organised by the defendant), Supperstone J commented (obiter) that, had he considered the claimant to be in a position to make out his claim on the facts, he would have exercised the s 33 discretion and allowed the claim to proceed notwithstanding that it had been issued more than eight years after the attack.

In a claim arising out of alleged sexual assaults committed by a local priest against two brothers between 1979 and 1983 in the case of the younger brother and from around 1983 to 1986 in the case of the older brother. Proceedings were not commenced until June 2012, more than 20 years after expiry of the limitation period (on the claimants' respective 21st birthdays). The judge dismissed the claims on the basis that the evidence was not sufficiently reliable or accurate for the claimants to discharge the burden of proof. He also confirmed that, if he was wrong in that conclusion, he would have refused the s 33 application. No particular reason had been advanced why either claimant should have delayed as long as each did after both were prepared openly to acknowledge what had happened. The delay in bringing proceedings had also had a significant effect on the cogency of the evidence, and in particular the psychiatric experts' task of establishing the causal relevance of the alleged abuse, as distinct from other potentially relevant life events, to the claimants' psychiatric conditions had been made more difficult by the passage of time. Overall, the judge did not consider that a fair trial was any longer possible: *F&S v TH* [2016] EWHC 1605 (QB), Langstaff J.

CD v Catholic Child Welfare Society [2016] EWHC 3335 (QB), HHJ Gosnell, was a leading case in group litigation arising out of allegations of historical physical and sexual abuse against members of staff at a reformatory school. The claimant was aged 36 at the date of trial and his claim, including an allegation of rape, related to events which allegedly took place when he was aged 12. There had been a delay of almost seven years in issuing proceedings. The judge accepted as genuine the claimant's explanation for not bringing a claim sooner, namely that he had felt too embarrassed and ashamed to report the abuse and had wished to repress his painful memories of his experiences. The judge acknowledged that the delay would have had some effect on the cogency of the witness evidence but the rape allegation was unlikely to be affected by the passage of time in terms of cogency given that it was not something that either participant should have forgotten. Missing documentation was very limited and of only peripheral relevance. Overall, the judge held that it would be harsh to hold the delay against the claimant, a fair trial could still take place and it would be equitable to allow the claim to proceed. (See also the same judge's s 33 decisions in the related cases of *EF v Catholic Child Welfare Society* [2016] EWHC 3336 (QB) and *GH v Catholic Child Welfare Society* [2016] EWHC 3337 (QB).)

III LIM [38.6]

Cogency of evidence and of case generally The court is required by sub-s (3)(b) to have regard to the effect of the passage of time on the cogency of evidence; and it was said in *Buck v English Electric Co Ltd* [1978] 1 All ER 271, [1977] 1 WLR 806 that evidence may be presumed to be less cogent after five years. However, in *Halford v Brookes* [1991] 3 All ER 559, [1991] 1 WLR 428, CA, the Court of Appeal allowed the claimant to proceed with a claim against two defendants for killing her daughter, although the claim was six years out of time: the outcome would not depend on the recollection of witnesses but on a decision as to which of the defendants was telling the truth. The fact that the defendants might not be able to satisfy a judgment was not a relevant circumstance. On the other hand, where particulars of the claim are given so late that it is virtually impossible for the defendant to investigate, the prejudice to the defendant is such that it would require exceptional circumstances for the court to disapply s 11: *Dale v British Coal Corpn (No 2)* (1992) 136 Sol Jo LB 199, CA.

But the fact that a fair trial is still possible may be trumped by other considerations. In *AB v Ministry of Defence* [2010] EWCA Civ 1317, [2010] NLJR 1686 over a thousand former servicemen claimed that their exposure to radiation in nuclear tests in the 1950s had caused them injury. On a preliminary issue as to limitation, the Court of Appeal held that all but one of the lead claims before them had been brought more than three years after the claimant's date of knowledge. When it came to the question whether the s 33 discretion should be exercised in their favour, the Court of Appeal decided that the claimants' evidential difficulties in proving causation were simply too great to justify the time and expense of their being allowed to proceed to trial.

Previous authorities indicate that a judge ought to decide how to exercise the discretion under s 33 before reaching conclusions on liability. This is because the discretion is to be exercised not on the basis that the abuse (or other injury) had or had not occurred, but on an overall assessment of the relevant factors and which will include the cogency of the evidence and the effect which the delay has had on it. These authorities do not however prescribe a rigid formula and so long as the judge exercised the discretion on the basis of an analysis of the relevant considerations the fact that her judgment happened to deal first with the question whether the abuse had in fact occurred did not vitiate her (subsequent) exercise of the s 33 discretion: *Raggett v Society of Jesus Trust of 1929 for Roman Catholic Purposes* [2010] EWCA Civ 1002, 154 Sol Jo (no 34) 30, [2010] NLJR 1228.

In *De Meza v Pennine Acute Hospitals NHS Trust* [2017] EWCA Civ 1711, the Court of Appeal held that the first instance judge had been wrong to assume that the claim had merit and should have taken into account that the claim was weak when deciding the s 33 issue.

III LIM [38.6A]

Particular considerations in sexual abuse cases In *A v Hoare* [2008] UKHL 6, [2008] 1 AC 844, [2008] 2 WLR 311, [2008] 2 All ER 1, [2008] 1 FLR, the House of Lords held that claims for personal injury occasioned by deliberate assaults were claims within s 11 (see **III LIM [13.1]**) and, therefore, subject to ss 14 and 33. Anticipating that the effect of this ruling (and their construction of s 14(2)) would be that a considerable number of historic claims in respect of sexual abuse might now be brought, Lord Brown made three observations:

(1) Future claims may be expected to be brought against employers (or others allegedly responsible for abusers) on the basis of vicarious liability for sexual assaults rather than for "systemic negligence" in failing to prevent them. It is likely that they will involve significantly narrower factual disputes than hitherto and this "is likely to bear significantly upon the possibility of having a fair trial." [Para 85]

(2) A greater number of claims are now likely to be made many years after the abuse complained of. Whether or not it will be possible for defendants to investigate these sufficiently for there to be a reasonable prospect of a fair trial will depend upon a

number of factors, not least when the complaint was first made and with what effect. On one side there will be cases where a complaint has been made and recorded, especially if the accused has been convicted in respect of the conduct in question. On the other side, will be the cases where the complaint comes out of the blue with no apparent support for it except, possibly, that the defendant has been accused or convicted of similar abuse of others. Not everyone bringing even a genuine claim for damages for sexual abuse which has taken place long in the past can expect the court to exercise the discretion in his favour; a fair trial, including a fair opportunity for the defendant to investigate the allegations, may be rendered quite impossible after a long delay even where the nature of the claimant's situation is capable of providing a reasonable explanation for the delay. [Paras 86-87]

(3) The definition of "significant injury" in s 14(2) refers to the justifiability of bringing proceedings against a defendant "able to satisfy a judgment". This is not surprising since it would not ordinarily be sensible to sue an indigent defendant. It would be most unfortunate if people felt obliged (often at public expense) to bring proceedings for sexual abuse against indigent defendants simply with a view to their possible future enforcement.

In *AB v Nugent Care Society; R v Wirral Metropolitan Borough Council* [2009] EWCA Civ 827, [2009] Fam Law 1045, 153 Sol Jo (no 30) 28 the Court of Appeal made further observations about cases of alleged child abuse:

(a) for a claimant to succeed there has to be proof:
   (i) that the alleged abuse occurred;
   (ii) that the defendant is vicariously liable for the abuse;
   (iii) that the abuse caused psychiatric/psychological damage; and
   (iv) quantum;
(b) s 14 was now to be construed more narrowly and based on an objective standard. The effect of the decision in *A v Hoare* is to transfer from s 14 to s 33 the consideration of issues based on the subjective knowledge of the individual claimant;
(c) the changes will make it easier for claimants to succeed in that:
   (i) there is no need to establish systemic negligence; and
   (ii) the evidence that a claimant was inhibited by the abuse is now relevant to the exercise of discretion;
(d) the focus is on the broad nature of the discretion and not solely on the prejudice to the defendant;
(e) a judge must consider all the circumstances, including the prejudice to the defendant. This includes considering what evidence might have been available to the defendant if the trial had occurred earlier.

III LIM [38.7]

Disability of the claimant For the purposes of sub-s (3)(d), the "disability of the claimant" means a mental disorder within the Mental Health Act 1983, as defined in s 38(2) of the Limitation Act 1980. However, lesser forms of disability, such as memory loss following the accident, may be relevant circumstances which would justify a disapplication of the limitation period: *Thomas v Plaistow* [1997] 17 LS Gaz R 25, [1997] PIQR P 540, CA. See also *Davis v Jacobs and Camden and Islington Health Authority and Novartis Pharmaceuticals (UK) Ltd* [1999] Lloyd's Rep Med 72. It was decided in *Donovan v Gwentoys Ltd* [1990] 1 All ER 1018, [1990] 1 WLR 472, HL that it would not be equitable to allow the claimant's claim to proceed having regard to the long period during which the claimant was a minor and the fact that the defendants had no notice of the claim. See also *Doughty v North Staffordshire Health Authority* [1992] 3 Med LR 81, [1992] CLY 2821 and *Headford v Bristol and District Health Authority* [1995] 6 Med LR 1, 24 BMLR 20, CA.

III LIM [38.8]

Second action out of time In *Walkley v Precision Forgings Ltd* [1979] 2 All ER 548, [1979] 1 WLR 606, HL it was held that it is only in the most exceptional circumstances that a second action may be allowed to proceed out of time under section 33. The principle is to be found in Lord Wilberforce's speech in *Walkley* [1979] 1 WLR 606 at 609:

> "The provisions of section 2A [now section 11] are those which require an action for personal injuries to be brought within three years. So subsection (1)(a) [now section 33] must be contemplating a case in which, because the three years have expired without an action being brought, section 2A applies to the prejudice of the plaintiff. But if the plaintiff has brought his action within the three years, how has he been prejudiced by section 2A? This I fail to understand. If this argument is sound, the respondent's case fails in limine. He brought his first action within the normal limitation period, and if he has suffered any prejudice, it is by his own inaction and not by the operation of the Act."

This passage was subsequently elaborated in *Deerness v John R Keeble & Son (Brantham) Ltd* [1983] 2 Lloyd's Rep 260, HL the effect of which was that as a matter of construction *Walkley* either applied or it did not and there was therefore no question of exceptional circumstances permitting reliance on s 33 in a *Walkley* case unless, perhaps, the defendant was guilty of some unconscionable or other conduct amounting to an estoppel. Nonetheless, the perceived injustice produced by the *Walkley* construction led a generation of judges to distinguish *Walkley* from the cases before them. This was done with the best of intentions but often the most slender and even doubtful of grounds. This did no service to the principled application and development of the law.

In *Horton v Sadler* [2006] UKHL 27, [2006] 3 All ER 1177, [2006] 2 WLR 1346 the House of Lords decided to depart from its decision in *Walkley*. It did so on the basis that the reasoning in *Walkley* was unsound and that its effect was to deprive litigants of a right which the legislature had intended them to have. In so doing, their Lordships not only took the rare step of departing from their own previous decision but (as Lord Hoffman put it) had to overcome "a reluctance verging on disbelief" to conclude that the opinions of Lords Wilberforce and Diplock in *Walkley* were "quite wrong".

The question whether the resources of the Court have been misused may be an appropriate matter for consideration in relation to "all the circumstances of the case": *Leeson v Marsden* [2008] EWHC 1011 (QB), 103 BMLR 49.

The fact that there has been a negligent failure to serve a claim form within the time permitted by CPR 7.5 or CPR 7.6 is not of itself an abuse of process and it followed that a second claim brought after the expiry of the limitation period and which thus sought the exercise of the s 33 discretion in its favour was not liable to be struck out by reason only of the failure to serve the first proceedings in time. See *Aktas v Adepta* [2010] EWCA Civ 1170.

III LIM [38.9]

Powers of appellate court The power to disapply the limitation period under s 33 is discretionary. It follows that, in the normal way, an appellate court can interfere with the exercise of that discretion only if the judge had made an error of law, or had wrongly taken something into account or wrongly failed to take something into account, or had exercised the discretion in a way that was plainly wrong: *Sophia Hayward v Professor W J W Sharrard* (2000) 56 BMLR 155, CA.

III LIM [38A]

33A. Extension of time limits because of mediation in certain cross-border disputes

(1) In this section—

(a) "Mediation Directive" means Directive 2008/52/EC of the European Parliament and of the Council of 21 May 2008 on certain aspects of mediation in civil and commercial matters,

(b) "mediation" has the meaning given by article 3(a) of the Mediation Directive,

(c) "mediator" has the meaning given by article 3(b) of the Mediation Directive, and

(d) "relevant dispute" means a dispute to which article 8(1) of the Mediation Directive applies (certain cross-border disputes).

(2) Subsection (3) applies where—

(a) a time limit under this Act relates to the subject of the whole or part of a relevant dispute,

(b) a mediation in relation to the relevant dispute starts before the time limit expires, and

(c) if not extended by this section, the time limit would expire before the mediation ends or less than eight weeks after it ends.

(3) For the purposes of initiating judicial proceedings or arbitration, the time limit expires instead at the end of eight weeks after the mediation ends (subject to subsection (4)).

(4) If a time limit has been extended by this section, subsections (2) and (3) apply to the extended time limit as they apply to a time limit mentioned in subsection (2)(a).

(5) Where more than one time limit applies in relation to a relevant dispute, the extension by subsection (3) of one of those time limits does not affect the others.

(6) For the purposes of this section, a mediation starts on the date of the agreement to mediate that is entered into by the parties and the mediator.

(7) For the purposes of this section, a mediation ends on the date of the first of these to occur—

- (a) the parties reach an agreement in resolution of the relevant dispute,
- (b) a party completes the notification of the other parties that it has withdrawn from the mediation,
- (c) a party to whom a qualifying request is made fails to give a response reaching the other parties within 14 days of the request,
- (d) after the parties are notified that the mediator's appointment has ended (by death, resignation or otherwise), they fail to agree within 14 days to seek to appoint a replacement mediator,
- (e) the mediation otherwise comes to an end pursuant to the terms of the agreement to mediate.

(8) For the purpose of subsection (7), a qualifying request is a request by a party that another (A) confirm to all parties that A is continuing with the mediation.

(9) In the case of any relevant dispute, references in this section to a mediation are references to the mediation so far as it relates to that dispute, and references to a party are to be read accordingly.

III LIM [38A.1]

This section was inserted by the Cross-Border Mediation (EU Directive) Regulations 2011.

III LIM [38B]

33B. Extension of time limits because of alternative dispute resolution in certain cross border or domestic contractual disputes.

(1) In this section—

- (a) "ADR Directive" means Directive 2013/11/EU of the European Parliament and of the Council of 21 May 2013 on alternative dispute resolution for consumer disputes and amending Regulation (EC) No 2006/2004 and Directive 2009/22/EC;
- (b) "ADR entity" has the meaning given by article 4(1)(h) of the ADR Directive;
- (c) . . .
- (d) "ADR procedure" has the meaning given by article 4(1)(g) of the ADR Directive;
- (e) "non-binding ADR procedure" means an ADR procedure the outcome of which is not binding on the parties;
- (f) "relevant dispute" means a dispute to which Article 12(1) of the ADR Directive applies (certain cross-border or domestic contractual disputes brought by a consumer against a trader).

(2) Subsection (3) applies where—

- (a) a time limit under this Act relates to the subject of the whole or part of a relevant dispute;
- (b) a non-binding ADR procedure in relation to the relevant dispute starts before the time limit expires; and
- (c) if not extended by this section, the time limit would expire before the non-binding ADR procedure ends or less than eight weeks after it ends.

(3) For the purposes of initiating judicial proceedings, the time limit expires instead at the end of eight weeks after the non-binding ADR procedure ends (subject to subsection (4)).

LIMITATION

(4) If a time limit has been extended by this section, subsections (2) and (3) apply to the extended time limit as they apply to a time limit mentioned in subsection (2)(a).

(5) Where more than one time limit applies in relation to a relevant dispute, the extension by subsection (3) of one of those time limits does not affect the others.

(6) For the purposes of this section, a non-binding ADR procedure starts in relation to a relevant dispute on the date when the dispute is first sent or otherwise communicated to the ADR entity in accordance with the entity's rules regarding the submission of complaints.

(7) For the purposes of this section, the non-binding ADR procedure ends on the date of the first of these to occur—

- (a) the parties reach an agreement in resolution of the relevant dispute;
- (b) a party completes the notification of the other parties that it has withdrawn from the non-binding ADR procedure;
- (c) a party to whom a qualifying request is made fails to give a response reaching the other parties within 14 days of the request;
- (d) the ADR entity notifies the party that submitted the relevant dispute to the ADR entity that, in accordance with its policy, the ADR entity refuses to deal with the relevant dispute;
- (e) after the parties are notified that the ADR entity can no longer act in relation to the relevant dispute (for whatever reason), the parties fail to agree within 14 days to submit the dispute to an alternative ADR entity;
- (f) the non-binding ADR procedure otherwise comes to an end pursuant to the rules of the ADR entity.

(8) For the purpose of subsection (7), a qualifying request is a request by a party that another (A) confirm to all parties that A is continuing with the non-binding ADR procedure.

(9) In the case of any relevant dispute, references in this section to a non-binding ADR procedure are references to the non-binding ADR procedure so far as it relates to that dispute, and references to a party are to be read accordingly.

III LIM [38B.1]

This section was inserted by the Alternative Dispute Resolution for Consumer Disputes (Amendment) Regulations 2015, reg 4. It came into force on 9 July 2015.

III LIM [39]

35. New claims in pending actions: rules of court

(1) For the purposes of this Act, any new claim made in the course of any action shall be deemed to be a separate action and to have been commenced—

- (a) in the case of a new claim made in or by way of third party proceedings, on the date on which those proceedings were commenced; and
- (b) in the case of any other new claim, on the same date as the original action.

(2) In this section a new claim means any claim by way of set-off or counterclaim, and any claim involving either—

- (a) the addition or substitution of a new cause of action; or
- (b) the addition or substitution of a new party;

and "third party proceedings" means any proceedings brought in the course of any action by any party to the action against a person not previously a party to the action, other than proceedings brought by joining any such person as defendant to any claim already made in the original action by the party bringing the proceedings.

(3) Except as provided by section 33 of this Act or by rules of court, neither the High Court nor the county court shall allow a new claim within subsection (1)(b) above, other than an original set-off or counterclaim, to be made in the course of any action after the expiry of any time limit under this Act which would affect a new action to enforce that claim.

For the purposes of this subsection, a claim is an original set-off or an original counterclaim if it is a claim made by way of set-off or (as the case may be) by way of counterclaim by a party who has not previously made any claim in the action.

(4) Rules of court may provide for allowing a new claim to which subsection (3) above applies to be made as there mentioned, but only if the conditions specified in subsection (5) below are satisfied, and subject to any further restrictions the rules may impose.

(5) The conditions referred to in subsection (4) above are the following—

(a) in the case of a claim involving a new cause of action, if the new cause of action arises out of the same facts or substantially the same facts as are already in issue on any claim previously made in the original action; and

(b) in the case of a claim involving a new party, if the addition or substitution of the new party is necessary for the determination of the original action.

(6) The addition or substitution of a new party shall not be regarded for the purposes of subsection (5)(b) above as necessary for the determination of the original action unless either—

(a) the new party is substituted for a party whose name was given in any claim made in the original action in mistake for the new party's name; or

(b) any claim already made in the original action cannot be maintained by or against an existing party unless the new party is joined or substituted as plaintiff or defendant in that action.

(7) Subject to subsection (4) above, rules of court may provide for allowing a party to any action to claim relief in a new capacity in respect of a new cause of action notwithstanding that he had no title to make that claim at the date of the commencement of the action.

This subsection shall not be taken as prejudicing the power of rules of court to provide for allowing a party to claim relief in a new capacity without adding or substituting a new cause of action.

(8) Subsections (3) to (7) above shall apply in relation to a new claim made in the course of third party proceedings as if those proceedings were the original action, and subject to such other modifications as may be prescribed by rules of court in any case or class of case.

(9) [. . .]

III LIM [39.1]

General This section deals with limitation in the context of the addition of new claims or parties in actions which have already commenced. It is a convoluted piece of drafting. The general principles, laid down by the section, may be summarised as follows:

(a) a new claim for the purposes of the Act means: any claim by way of set-off, a counterclaim, the addition of a new cause of action and the addition or substitution of a new party (s 35(2));

(b) a set-off, counterclaim and third party proceedings are deemed to be separate actions (s 35(1));

(c) third party proceedings in the context of this section mean proceedings by which a person not previously a party to the action is added; they do not include the addition of a party as a defendant to any claim already made in the action (s 35(3));

(d) a new claim by way of third party proceedings is deemed to have been commenced on the date when the third party proceedings were in fact commenced (s 35(1)(a));

LIMITATION

(e) a new claim consisting of a set-off, counterclaim, the addition of a new cause of action or the addition or substitution of a new party is deemed to have been commenced on the same date as the original action commenced (s 35(1)(b));

(f) a party to the action (who has not previously made a set-off or counterclaim in the action) may be permitted to make a set-off or counterclaim after the expiry of a limitation period (s 35(3)); apart from that exception or s 33 of the Act or any exception provided by the rules: the court shall not allow the making of any new claim after the expiry of any time limit under the Act (s 35(3));

(g) the Rules and the Act (combined) permit the addition of a new cause of action outside of a limitation period if the new cause of action arises out of the same or substantially the same facts as are already in issue on any claim previously made in the original action (s 35(5)(a));

(h) the Rules and the Act (combined) permit the addition of a claim involving a new party, if the addition or substitution of the new party is necessary (as defined in s 35(6)) for the determination of the original action.

The above principles apply to new claims made in third party proceedings; for that purpose the third party proceedings are to be treated as "original" proceedings (s 35(8)).

III LIM [39.2]

Rules of court The relevant rules of court are CPR 17.4 and 19.4 (see para **CPR 17.4** and **CPR 19.4**). Decisions under the corresponding pre-CPR rules (viz RSC Ord 15 r 6, RSC Ord 20 r 5, and CCR Ord 15 r 1) remain relevant.

III LIM [39.3]

Third party proceedings The relevant rules of court are CPR Pt 20 see para **CPR 20**.

III LIM [39.4]

New claim On its true construction the definition of "new claim" in s 35(2) of the Limitation Act 1980 does not include the substitution of a party who had succeeded to a claim already represented in existing proceedings and which does not involve a new cause of action. Accordingly, a substitution under RSC Ord 15 r 7 did not fall within either limb of s 35(2)(a) or (b): see *Yorkshire Regional Health Authority v Fairclough Building Ltd* [1996] 1 All ER 519, [1996] 1 WLR 210, CA. The case provides a useful analysis of what constitutes a new claim for the purpose of sub-s (2).

Where the defendant shows that it has a prima facie defence of limitation, the burden is then on the claimant to show that the defence is not reasonably arguable (see *Mercer Ltd v Ballinger* [2014] EWCA Civ 996, [2014] 1 WLR 3597). If it fails to do so then the Court has two options:

- to refuse the claimant's application, leaving it to issue separate proceedings in respect of the new claim, in which the defendant could plead its limitation defence and that claim be heard together or to be consolidated with the existing claim; or
- to order that the limitation issue be determined as a preliminary issue.

This is because by the doctrine of 'relation back' new claims are deemed to have been made when the claim was first brought rather than when the amendment was allowed, with the effect that the defendant is deprived of any limitation defence: see *Welsh Development Agency v Redpath Dorman Long Ltd* [1994] 4 All ER 10, [1994] 1 WLR 1409, CA and *Chandra v Brooke North (A Firm)* [2013] EWCA Civ 1559, (2013) 151 Con LR 113.

Section 35 of the Limitation Act 1980 and RSC Ord 20 r 5 (now CPR 17.3 and CPR 17.4 at para **CPR 17.3** and para **CPR 17.4**) whereby an action could be deemed to have commenced against a substituted party on the same date as the original action, did not apply where a contractual or substantive time limit, such as that in the Hague Rules, had expired and the cause of action is extinguished: see *Payabi v Armstel Shipping Corpn* [1992] QB 907, [1992] 3 All ER 329.

In *Oates v Harte Reade & Co* [1999] 1 FLR 1221 the claimant brought proceedings alleging professional negligence and breach of contract against her former solicitors and claimed damages for financial loss and for stress and anxiety. The Master agreed with the defendant's contention that the action included a claim for damages in respect of personal injuries and was therefore statute barred. However, he allowed the claimant to amend her statement of claim by deleting the personal injury claim, treating the application as a substitution of a new cause of action under s 35. On appeal it was held that s 35 did not apply as the deletion of one variety of damages claimed did not amount to a new nor to a substituted cause of action.

A claim made under the law of one state is a different cause of action to a claim made under the law of a different state: *Latreefers Inc v Hobson* [2002] EWHC 1586 (Ch), [2002] All ER (D) 375 (Jul).

III LIM [39.5]

Set-off and counterclaim A set-off or counterclaim in an existing action is a separate action and is deemed to have been started on the same date as the original action in which the set-off or counterclaim is made (s 35(1)(b)). It is not clear whether the date for the commencement of the original action for the purposes of s 35(1)(b) is the date when the claim form was issued or the date when it was lodged with the court (CPR r 7.2(1), (2) and the Practice Direction to Part 7, paras 5.1 to 5.4). Where the set-off or counterclaim is raised in third party proceedings commenced (the combined effect of s 35(8) and s 35(1)(b)). "Third party proceedings" fall within the concept of Part 20 claims; a Part 20 claim is made when the Part 20 claim form is issued (CPR r 20.7) but, for the purposes of the Limitation Act 1980 and any other relevant statute, the proceedings are brought when the Part 20 claim form is lodged with the court (Practice Direction to Part 7, paras 5.1 to 5.4). A party may make a set-off or counterclaim outside the limitation period provided that he has not already made a set-off or counterclaim in the action (s 35(3)). In other words, any party may – outside the limitation period – make a set-off or counterclaim once. This entitlement is, however, always subject to the court's case management powers under the CPR Part 3 and the overriding objective in Part 1.

An "original counterclaim" means only a cause of action which might be asserted by an existing defendant against a claimant. The nature of the cause of action on which the counterclaim is founded is not integral to the concept of counterclaim so long as the party asserting that cause of action is on one side of the record and at least one of the parties against whom it is asserted is on the other: *Law Society of England and Wales v Wemyss* [2008] EWHC 2515 (Ch), [2009] 1 All ER 752.

III LIM [39.6]

Sub-section (3) The relevant date for expiry was the date at which the amendment was actually made, which by definition could be no earlier than the date at which leave was granted to make the amendment. Accordingly, unless a case came within one of the exceptions, leave could not be given after the time limit had expired and that applied even if the limitation period had not expired when the application for leave to amend was made: *Welsh Development Agency v Redpath Dorman Long Ltd*, [1994] 4 All ER 10, [1994] 1 WLR 1409, CA, overruling *Kennett v Brown* [1988] 2 All ER 600, [1998] 1 WLR 582, CA.

CPR 40.7 at **CPR 40** had introduced a notable change to the dating of orders; the discretion was now confined to dating an order to a later date. In any event the critical date is not the date of the application or even the date of any order for joinder. It is the date upon which service is effected and that must be within the limitation period: *Rowan Companies Inc v Lambert Eggink Offshore Transport Consultants VOF* [1999] 2 Lloyd's Rep 443.

III LIM [39.6A]

Change in capacity: sub-s (7) The rule referred to in section 35(7) is now CPR 17.4(4). The change in capacity which is contemplated by s 35(7) is an alteration from a representative capacity, or personal capacity to another representative capacity, or (in the case of a representative claim) to a personal capacity. Where, therefore, a claimant brought proceedings in respect of which the cause of action was, by reason of her antecedent bankruptcy, vested in her trustee in bankruptcy, the subsequent assignment of that cause of action to her involved no change in capacity. She had brought the claim personally and sought to continue the claim personally. Section 35(7) did not apply to such a case and the amendment to plead and rely upon the assignment was out of time and should not be allowed: *Haq v Singh* [2001] EWCA Civ 957, [2001] 1 WLR 1594.

III LIM [39.7]

Section 33 Where it was sought to add an additional party to the proceedings in circumstances where formerly RSC Ord 15 r 6(5)(a) applied, it was necessary for an application to be made under s 33 before or at the same time as the application to amend the writ was made: see *Howe v David Brown Tractors (Retail) Ltd* [1991] 4 All ER 30, CA.

III LIM [39.8]

New cause of action In order to determine whether a proposed amendment involves the addition of a new cause of action, the court compares the essential factual elements in the cause of action already pleaded with the essential factual elements in the cause of action proposed: *Revenue and Customs Comrs v Begum (Noorasa)* [2010] EWHC 1799 (Ch), [2011] BPIR 59 and *Steamship Mutual Underwriting Association Ltd v Trollope & Colls (City) Ltd* (1986) 6 Con LR 11, 33 BLR 77, CA. See also *Savings and Investment Bank Ltd v Fincken* [2001] EWCA Civ 1639, [2002] 48 LS Gaz R 29, (2001) Times, 15 November.

This involves comparing the existing particulars of claim (not Claim Form) with the proposed Amended Particulars of Claim: *Chandra v Brooke North (A Firm)* [2013] EWCA Civ 1559, [2013] All ER (D) 88 (Dec).

LIMITATION

The policy of the Act is that where particular facts are already in issue between the parties and must for that reason be determined in any event, then new causes of action which substantially arise from those facts may be introduced outside the relevant limitation period. It has been said that the question whether a new cause of action arises out of the same facts as those already pleaded is substantially a matter of impression: *Welsh Development Agency v Redpath Dorman Long Ltd* [1994] 4 All ER 10, [1994] 1 WLR 1409, CA but in *Paragon Finance Plc v DB Thakerar & Co* [1999] 1 All ER 400 at 418, Millett LJ suggested that 'impression' was an approach which might be appropriate in borderline cases but that the question generally required analysis. The 'impression' approach has generally prevailed in subsequent authorities.

The words 'the same facts or substantially the same facts' in s 35(5)(a) are not synonymous with 'similar' even if the latter might sometimes be a convenient shorthand. Save where the facts engaged by the proposed amendment are precisely the same as those which are already in issue, it will usually be necessary for the Court to consider to what extent the amendment would require the investigation of new facts. See *Mercer Ltd v Ballinger* [2014] EWCA Civ 996, [2014] 1 WLR 3597 on all of these points.

A new allegation of fraudulent misrepresentation will not usually arise from the same or substantially the same facts as an existing allegation of negligent misrepresentation because of the need in the case of fraud to allege knowledge that the representation was false and an intention that the recipient of the statement should understand it in the sense that it was false: see *McEneaney v Ulster Bank Ireland Ltd* [2015] EWHC 3173 (Comm), [2015] All ER (D) 149 (Dec).

A breach of a duty which has not previously been pleaded will usually be a new claim. Whether a different breach of a duty which has already been pleaded amounts to a new claim is a question of fact and degree. In a construction claim an amendment to allege that the breach of a previously pleaded duty caused damage to a different (ie unpleaded) part of the building will generally amount to a new claim: *Secretary of State for Transport v Pell Frischmann Consultants Ltd* [2006] EWHC 2909 (TCC), [2007] BLR 46.

In *Goode v Martin* [2001] EWCA Civ 1899, [2002] 1 All ER 620; [2002] 1 WLR 1828, the claimant sought to amend her particulars of claim outside the limitation period to rely upon facts first pleaded by the defendant in his defence as a further allegation of negligence. The Court of Appeal held that the reference in s 35(5) to "the same facts as are already in issue on any claim" includes facts contained in the defence and that CPR 17.4(2) should be interpreted accordingly. Such an interpretation was permissible under the Human Rights Act 1998 since the claimant would otherwise be unjustifiably impeded from access to the court. See also *Hemmingway v Roddam* (18 September 2003, unreported), CA.

Where there are several defendants the court may allow a claimant to plead a new cause of action based upon substantially the same facts as have been put in issue by the defence of any defendant. Facts pleaded in the defence of one defendant may therefore be adopted as the basis of a new claim against another defendant after the expiry of the limitation period: see *Charles Church Developments Ltd v Stent Foundations Ltd* [2006] EWHC 3158 (TCC), [2007] 1 WLR 1203, [2007] BLR 81.

In *Paragon Finance plc v DB Thakerar & Co (a firm)* [1999] 1 All ER 400, CA, the claimant commenced proceedings alleging breach of contract, negligence, and breach of fiduciary duty. After the expiry of the limitation period the claimant sought to amend the pleadings to allege fraud, conspiracy to defraud, fraudulent breach of trust and intentional breach of fiduciary duty. It was held that the new allegation of wrongdoing where previously no intentional wrongdoing had been alleged constitutes the introduction of a new cause of action. However, a claim based on allegations of fraud and dishonesty did not involve substantially the same facts as a claim based on allegations of negligence, and so leave to amend would be refused. See also *Coulthard v Disco Mix Club Ltd* [1999] 2 All ER 457, [2000] 1 WLR 707; *Cia de Seguros Imperio v Heath (REBX) Ltd* [1999] 1 All ER (Comm) 750.

In a case of breach of warranty and misrepresentation, the addition of a further instance of such breach did not constitute a new cause of action: *Savings & Investment Bank Ltd v Fincken* (2001) Times, 15 November, CA.

An amendment which had the effect of alleging that money was held on implied rather than constructive trust did not involve the pleading of a new cause of action: *Abbey National plc v John Perry & Co* [2001] EWCA Civ 1630, [2001] All ER (D) 348 (Oct).

III LIM [39.9]

Amendments which relate back The court has a discretion to allow amendments out of time which correct the name of a party, in the circumstances mentioned in s 35(6) of the Limitation Act 1980, or which add a time-barred cause of action, provided that the substantive proceedings were started within the limitation period: see *Hancock Shipping Co Ltd v Kawasaki Heavy Industries Ltd, The Caspar Trader* [1992] 3 All ER 132, [1992] 1 WLR 1025, CA. In *Evans Construction Co Ltd v Charrington & Co Ltd* [1983] QB 810, [1983] 1 All ER 310, CA, the correction of the name of the landlord was allowed outside the timetable laid down by Part II of the Landlord and Tenant Act 1954; it was held that RSC Ord 20 r 5 could not be applied to correct a mistake as to the actual identity of a party sought to be sued but it could be applied to correct a mistake make in describing or naming a party providing the identity of the party was known to the person making the mistake and the mistake was not misleading. See also *Signet Group plc v Hammerson UK Properties Ltd* [1998] 03 LS Gaz R 25, 142 Sol Jo LB 70, CA, where leave was given under RSC Ord 20 r 5 for an amendment to correct the name of a party to proceedings, which would have the effect of substituting a new party even though the amendment was made outside the statutory time limit for commencing proceedings; the correction related back to the commencement of proceedings. Accordingly, the Limitation Act 1980 cannot be pleaded as a defence. A precedent form of application is provided in **BCCP C[56]**.

Where only one of the original joint owners of property (to whom the duty in question had been jointly owed) brought a claim for the whole of the loss alleged to have been sustained rather than the half to which the one joint owner was entitled, the court could in its discretion permit the joinder of the other joint owner as being necessary for the determination of that action since it was, in fact, a joint claim: *Merrett v Babb* [2001] EWCA 214, [2001] QB 1174, [2001] 3 WLR 1.

III LIM [39.9A]

Substitution and addition of parties See *Parsons v George* [2004] EWCA Civ 912, [2004] 3 All ER 633, [2004] 1 WLR 3264 for an analysis of the effect of CPR 19.5(1) and in particular the scope of 19.5(1)(c) which is concerned with changes of parties under "any other enactment which allows such change, or under which a change is allowed". See also the notes to CPR 19.5 in Volume 1 at para **CPR 19.5**.

There seems to be no reason of principle why the court may not grant permission both to substitute a claimant under CPR 19.5 and to add new claims that fall within CPR 17.4(3) but the new claims cannot be deployed to show that the claim has been brought in the name of the incorrect party. (See also **III LIM [39.9B]** below: the assertion of a new claim does not make substitution "necessary" within. the meaning of s 35(5)(b).)

It has been held to be clear from the language of CPR 19.5(3)(a) that the person who made the mistake in naming the party must be the person who was responsible, whether directly or through an agent, for the issue of the claim form. As a matter of causation that person must also show that, but for the mistake, the proposed new party would have been named at the outset: *Adelson (Sheldon) v Associated Newspapers Ltd* [2007] EWCA Civ 701, [2007] 4 All ER 330, (2007) Times, 18 July, CA. The Court also indicated, *obiter*, that in principle, an amendment to join additional claimants might qualify as a substitution of parties, even though this would result (on the facts) in 3 corporate claims for libel being made instead of the one which had originally been pleaded.

The definition of mistake in the context of s 35(6)(a) (and **CPR 19.5(3)**) is not limited to situations in which the claimant had always intended to sue one party but had mistakenly brought proceedings against another. Accordingly, where it was always intended to sue the manufacturer of a particular vaccine but a mistake was made as to the identity of the manufacturer the court could order the substitution of the actual manufacturer: *Horne-Roberts v Merck & Co Inc* [2001] All ER (D) 320 (Feb), QBD. This decision was affirmed by the Court of Appeal: [2001] EWCA Civ 2006, [2002] 1 WLR 1662, 65 BMLR 79 which adopted a test posited by Lloyd LJ in *The Sardinia Sulcis v Al Tawwab* [1991] 1 Lloyd's LR 201 at 207, CA in respect of 'the person intended to be sued':

> "In one sense a plaintiff always intends to sue the person who is liable for the wrong which he has suffered. But the test cannot be as wide as that. Otherwise there could never be any doubt as to the person intended to be sued, and leave to amend would always be given. So there must be some narrower test. In *Mitchell v. Harris Engineering* the identity of the person intended to be sued was the plaintiff's employers. In *Evans v Charrington* it was the current landlord. In *Thistle Hotels v McAlpine* the identity of the person intending to sue was the proprietor of the hotel. In *The Joanna Borchard* it was the cargo-owner or consignee. In all these cases it was possible to identify the intending plaintiff or intended defendant by reference to a description which was more or less specific to the particular case. Thus if, in the case of an intended defendant, the plaintiff gets the right description but the wrong name, there is unlikely to be any doubt as to the identity of the person intended to be sued. But if he gets the wrong description, it will be otherwise."

This identity/name dichotomy was subsequently applied by the Court of Appeal in *Kesslar v Moore & Tibbits* [2004] EWCA Civ 1551, [2005] PLNR 17, where the claimant had always intended to sue a particular solicitor whose alleged negligence had occurred at a now dissolved firm. The substitution of the individual for a wrongly named successor firm was therefore permitted. The Court of Appeal in *Sheldon Adelson v Associated Newspapers Ltd* [2007] 4 All ER 330, [2008] 1 WLR 585 held that, although pre-CPR authority, the Sardinia Sulcis remains good law since it and RSC Order 20 rule 5 were concerned with (and indeed made under the authority of) the same statutory provision as CPR 19.5. However, unlike Order 20 Rule 5(3), CPR 19.5 contains no requirement that the mistake was 'not misleading or such as to cause any reasonable doubt as to the identity of the person... intended to be sued' and to that extent relaxes the requirements to be satisfied. (Compare CPR 17.4(3) which does contain such a requirement, but which applies to amendments made after the end of the limitation period to correct the name of a party where this does not involve the addition or substitution of a new party.)

In principle *The Sardinia Sulcis* test is therefore capable of being satisfied where the proper defendant is unaware of the claim until after the expiry of the limitation period but most of the cases involve:

(a) some connection between the named and correct parties and
(b) the proposed new defendant or its agent having some awareness of the existing proceedings.

Where this is not so, the court is less likely to exercise its discretion to permit amendment: *Horne-Roberts v Merck & Co Inc* [2001] EWCA Civ 2006, [2002] 1 WLR 1662, 65 BMLR 79 (where substitution was permitted even though the new defendant did not become aware of the claim until after the expiry of the limitation period).

In any event, the question of awareness of error etc is to be judged objectively: *Lockheed Martin Corporation v Willis Group Ltd* [2010] EWCA Civ 927, (2010) Times, 5 October, [2010] PNLR 34 inter alia explaining dicta of Lord Phillips in *Adelson v Associated Newspapers Ltd* [2007] EWCA Civ 701, [2007] 4 All ER 330, [2008] 1 WLR 585.

In *Insight Group Ltd v Kingston Smith (a firm)* [2012] EWHC 3644 (QB), [2012] All ER (D) 191 (Dec) Leggatt J, in a useful discussion of the cases, questioned the utility of the *Sardinia Sulcis* test at the same time as affirming its present applicability. He said that 'the only way in which the *Sardinia Sulcis* test is workable at all is to identify the relevant description of the intended claimant or defendant by reference to what description is material from a legal point of view to the claim made' (at [52]) and (at [53]) explained this as follows:

> 'A person who is an employer or a landlord or who owns property or cargo carried on board a ship acquires by virtue of that role a set of legal rights and obligations which will generally be material to the claim made in the action. Thus, where for example the defendant is sued for breach of a duty owed by reason of being the claimant's employer, or landlord, then that will be the relevant description of the intended defendant, and if the claimant turns out to have been mistaken in thinking that the person sued fitted that description because the actual employer or landlord was someone else, the mistake can be characterised as one as to name.'

See also the distinction drawn in *American Leisure Group v Olswang LLP* [2015] EWHC 629 (Ch), [2015] All ER (D) 135 (Mar) between (1) the claimant suing an LLP in the mistaken belief that it, rather than a former partnership, provided the services and (2) the claimant knowing that the services were provided by the former partnership but mistakenly believing that the LLP is legally liable for the negligence of the earlier firm. Relief is available in the first but not the second case.

In *O'Byrne v Aventis Pasteur MSD Ltd* [2006] EWHC 2562 (QB), [2007] 1 WLR 757; affd sub nom *O'Byrne v Aventis Pasteur SA* [2007] EWCA Civ 966, 98 BMLR 160 the claimant had brought proceedings against a defendant in the mistaken belief that it was the producer of the relevant vaccine but had discovered that it was only the supplier before the limitation period had expired. By the time that he applied to substitute the correct defendant the 10-year period for bringing a claim which is prescribed by Directive 85/374 on liability for defective products (and enacted in s 11A(3) of the Limitation Act 1980) had expired. The concept of 'mistake' in s 35(6)(a) was held by the Court of Appeal to be wide enough to permit substitution in these circumstances but the House of Lords (at [2008] UKHL 34, [2008] 4 All ER 881) subsequently referred to the ECJ the question whether it was consistent with the Product Liability Directive 85/374 for the laws of a member state to allow substitution of a new defendant in a claim brought under that Directive after the 10-year period for enforcing rights under Art 11 of the Directive had expired in circumstances where the only person named as a defendant in proceedings instituted during the 10-year period was someone who did not fall within Art 3 of the Directive. In its judgment in *Aventis Pasteur SA v OB, sub nom O'Byrne v Aventis Pasteur SA* C-358/08, [2009] All ER (D) 228 (Dec) the ECJ ruled that:

(a) Art 11 does preclude national legislation which allows the substitution of one defendant for another in legal proceedings, from being applied in a way which permitted a 'producer', within the meaning of Art 3 of the Directive, to be sued, after the expiry of the period prescribed by that article, as defendant in proceedings brought within that period against another person;
(b) but Art 11 had to be interpreted as not precluding a national court from holding that, in the proceedings instituted within the period prescribed by that article against the wholly-owned subsidiary of the 'producer' (within the meaning of Art 3(1) of the

Directive), that producer could be substituted for that subsidiary if that court found that the putting into circulation of the product in question was, in fact, determined by that producer.

(c) Art 3(3) of the Directive had to be interpreted as meaning that, where the person injured by an allegedly defective product was not reasonably able to identify the producer of that product before exercising his rights against the supplier of that product, that supplier had to be treated as a 'producer' for the purposes, in particular, of the application of Art 11 of the Directive, if it did not inform the injured person, on its own initiative and promptly, of the identity of the producer or its own supplier.

The ingenious substitution allowed by the Court of Appeal was eventually rejected by the Supreme Court on the ground that the facts did not permit a substitution within the parameters set by the ECJ because the putting into circulation of the product had not been determined by the manufacturer but by its wholly owned subsidiary: *O'Byrne v Aventis Pasteur SA* [2010] UKSC 23, [2010] 4 All ER 1, [2010] 1 WLR 1412.

In *Weston v Gribben* [2006] EWCA Civ 1425, 150 Sol Jo LB 1463 the Court of Appeal suggested that a useful test for the permissibility of adding a party was to ask whether the identity of the claimant (or the defendant) could be changed without significantly changing the claim but to the extent that this test is wider than that posited in the *Sardinia Sulcis* it has now been disapproved: see *Sheldon Adelson v Associated Newspapers Ltd* [2007] 4 All ER 330, (2007) Times, 18 July, CA.

Where a new claimant is substituted on the ground that the cause of action has been assigned after issue the conditions of sub-s (5) are satisfied: *Finlan v Eyton Morris Winfield (a firm)* [2007] EWHC 914 (Ch), [2007] 4 All ER 128.

III LIM [39.9B]

Whether the substitution is 'necessary' The provisions for substitution or addition of parties after the expiration of the limitation period are directed at errors in the constitution or formality of the action in relation to the parties joined to it, or the capacity in which they are sued, and which in either case make the existing action unsustainable: thus the addition or substitution of parties has to be necessary to cure some defect. The relevant question is whether the substitution is necessary for the maintenance and determination of the original proceedings not the assertion of a new claim: see *Roberts v Gill & Co* [2010] UKSC 22, [2011] 1 AC 240, [2010] 4 All ER 367 and *Nemeti v Sabre Insurance Co Ltd* [2013] EWCA Civ 1555, [2013] All ER (D) 16 (Dec).

Where a new party is to be substituted for a party whose name was given in the original claim in mistake for the new party's name, substitution is 'necessary' for the determination of the original action, for the purposes of s 35(6)(b): *O'Byrne v Aventis Pasteur MSD Ltd* [2006] EWHC 2562 (QB), [2006] 92 BMLR 130, QBD, Teare J, affirmed by the Court of Appeal at [2007] EWCA CIV 966, [2007] 98 BMLR 160 where it was said (at para 59) that "[t]he natural meaning of that language seems to us to be that, if there is either a mistake of a kind sufficient to satisfy (a) or the kind of necessity identified in (b), then the test of necessity in subsection (5) is satisfied, but not otherwise".

In *Parkinson Engineering Services plc (in liq) v Swan* [2009] EWCA Civ 1366, [2010] 1 BCLC 163, (2010) Times, 13 January a company brought proceedings against administrators and the company was subsequently ordered to be wound up. The liquidator obtained permission to be substituted for the company as claimant in the proceedings after the expiry of the limitation period on the ground that the substitution of the liquidator was 'necessary' for the purposes of CPR 19.5 (3)(b) as well as s 35(5)(b) of the Limitation Act 1980:

III LIM [39.9C]

Parties necessary to the original claim In a claim against solicitors for the negligent preparation of a will it is not possible, after the expiry of the limitation period, to add the administrators of the estate as defendants, with a view to making a derivative claim on behalf of the estate because the administrators would not be necessary parties to the original claim: *Roberts v Gill & Co* [2010] UKSC 22, [2010] 4 All ER 367, [2010] 2 WLR 1227.

III LIM [39.10]

Foreign Limitation Periods In this paragraph "any relevant period of limitation" includes a time limit which applies to the proceedings in question by virtue of the Foreign Limitation Periods Act 1984.

III LIM [39.11]

Amending defence to add a counterclaim In *JFS (UK) Ltd v DWRr Cymru CYF* [1999] 1 WLR 231, CA, it was held that a defendant is not prevented by s 35(3) from amending a defence to include a counterclaim out of time where the defence, although not making positive averments, does not make a claim in the form of a set-off. Counterclaim or other claim for relief.

LIMITATION

III LIM [40]

36. Equitable jurisdiction and remedies

(1) The following time limits under this Act, that is to say—

(a) the time limit under section 2 for actions founded on tort;

(aa) the time limit under section 4A for actions for libel or slander, or for slander of title, slander of goods or other malicious falsehood;

(b) the time limit under section 5 for actions founded on simple contract;

(c) the time limit under section 7 for actions to enforce awards where the submission is not by an instrument under seal;

(d) the time limit under section 8 for actions on a specialty;

(e) the time limit under section 9 for actions to recover a sum recoverable by virtue of any enactment; and

(f) the time limit under section 24 for actions to enforce a judgment;

shall not apply to any claim for specific performance of a contract or for an injunction or for other equitable relief, except in so far as any such time limit may be applied by the court by analogy in like manner as the corresponding time limit under any enactment repealed by the Limitation Act 1939 was applied before 1st July 1940.

(2) Nothing in this Act shall affect any equitable jurisdiction to refuse relief on the ground of acquiescence or otherwise.

III LIM [40.1]

Breach of fiduciary duty The word "fiduciary" is nowhere mentioned in the Limitation Act. Fiduciary relationships can arise in a number of different situations but a six year limitation period will apply either directly or by analogy under the Act to claims in respect of breaches of fiduciary duty unless the case falls within the express exclusions (dealing with trustees &c) or the ambit of some exclusionary authority. Ordinarily, personal claims against fiduciaries will be subject to a six year period by analogy with claims in tort or contract under ss 2 and 5 respectively. By contrast, claims for equitable remedies (such as an account) for breach of fiduciary duty will usually fall within one of the subsections of s 21 depending on the precise characteristics of the fiduciary and his conduct. Even then, a six year time limit will normally apply under section 21(3) unless the case can be brought within the exceptions under ss 21(1)(a) (for fraud) or (b) (for Class 1 trust as explained in *Paragon Finance v DB Thakerar & Co* [1999] 1 All ER 400, CA see **III LIM [26.2]** and **III LIM [40.3]** below).

A director has responsibilities akin to those of a trustee in the management of the property of the company and applying it on behalf of the company in its interests and those of all of its members. A claim for an account against a director for the breach of such duties will therefore be subject to section 21. See: *DEG-Deutsche Investitions and Entwicklungsgesellschaft GmbH v Koshy (No 2)* (*Gwembe Valley Development Co Ltd v Thomas Koshy* [2004] 1 BCLC 131, (2003) Times, 9 September).

Where the claimant sought to rely on s 36 in order to defeat a limitation defence by claiming damages for alleged breaches of fiduciary duty in respect of under-accounting, it was held that no distinction in point of limitation could be made between an action for damages for fraud at common law and its counterpart in equity on the same facts: *Coulthard v Disco Mix Club Ltd* [1999] 2 All ER 457, [2000] 1 WLR 707. This decision was applied in *Cia de Seguros Imperio v Heath (REBX) Ltd* [1999] 1 All ER (Comm) 750, a decision upheld by the Court of Appeal: [2000] 2 All ER (Comm) 787, [2001] 1 WLR 112, where common law claims for breach of contract and breach of duty were held to be based on precisely the same factual allegations as a concurrent claim for dishonest breach of fiduciary duty albeit that the latter additionally involved an allegation of intention.

III LIM [40.2]

Breach of contract – specific performance The application of section 36(1)(b) will in some cases require historical inquiry. Before 1st July 1940 the corresponding time limit applicable to claims based on simple contract was contained in the Limitation Act 1623 (which introduced the 6-year time limit) and section 3 of the Civil Procedure Act 1833. In *P&O Nedlloyd BV v Arab Metals Co* [2006] EWCA Civ 1717 the parties were unable to produce any authority prior to 1st July 1940 (or indeed thereafter) which provided an answer to the question whether the 6-year time limit applicable to simple contract claims would have been applied to a claim for specific performance of a contract. The Court in *P&O Nedlloyd*, after considering certain *dicta* in *Knox v Gye* (1872) LR 5 HL 656 and *Paragon Finance plc v DB Thakerar & Co* [1999] 1 All ER 400 said that

> . . . if a statutory limitation provision, properly interpreted, applies to the claim under consideration, equity will apply it in obedience to the statute, as indeed it must. However, even if the limitation period does not apply because the claim is for an exclusively equitable remedy, the court will nonetheless apply it by analogy if the remedy in equity is "correspondent to the remedy at law". In other words, where the suit in equity corresponds with an action at law a court of equity adopts the statutory rule as its own rule of procedure. (*Per* Moore-Bick LJ)

The Court distinguished *Coulthard v Disco Mix Club Ltd* [1999] 2 All ER 457, [2000] 1 WLR 707 and *Cia de Seguros Imperio v Heath (REBX) Ltd* [2000] 2 All ER (Comm) 787, [2001] 1 WLR 112 as cases in which the same facts give rise to a claim, whether at law or in equity and where the same kind of relief was obtainable. It held that specific performance was different because:

– comparable relief was not available from the common law courts and
– the facts needed to support a claim for specific performance are not in all respects the same as those necessary to support a claim for breach of contract. Indeed, as *Hasham v Zenab* [1960] AC 316 (PC) showed, specific performance might be decreed even where no claim for breach of contract had yet arisen.

This absence of correspondence between remedies and between the necessary supporting facts was regarded as fatal to the application of s 5 by analogy but, as Moore-Bick LJ pointed out, this was not a licence to claimants to delay in the bringing of their claims for specific performance since there were many authorities in which such claims were denied on the grounds of laches long before 6 years had elapsed.

III LIM [40.3]

Constructive trusts The distinction between true (or institutional) constructive trusts and remedial constructive trusts survived the passing of the Limitation Act 1939 and the latter do not therefore fall within s 21 of the 1980 Act (which concerns time limits for claims in respect of trust property): *Paragon Finance plc v DB Thakerar & Co* [1999] 1 All ER 400, CA. Millett LJ also said that:

> The law on this subject has been settled for more than a hundred years. An action for an account brought by a principal against his agent is barred by the statutes of limitation unless the agent is more than a mere agent but is a trustee of the money which he received: see *Burdick v Garrick* (1870) LR 5 Ch App 233, Knox v Gye (1872) LR 5 HL 656 and *Re Sharpe, Re Bennett, Masonic and General Life Assurance Co v Sharpe* [1892] 1 Ch 154. A claim for an account in equity, absent any trust, has no equitable element; it is based on legal, not equitable rights: see *How v Earl Winterton* [1896] 2 Ch 626 at 639 per Lindley LJ. Where the agent's liability to account was contractual equity acted in obedience to the statute: see *Hovenden v Lord Annesley* (1806) 2 Sch & Lef 607 at 631 per Lord Redesdale. Where, as in *Knox v Gye*, there was no contractual relationship between the parties, so that the liability was exclusively equitable, the court acted by analogy with the statute. Its power to do so is implicitly preserved by s 36 of the 1980 Act.

III LIM [40.4]

Undue Influence In *Clarke v Marlborough Fine Art (London) Ltd* [2002] 1 WLR 1731, (2001) Times, 5 July, ChD, the court rejected the argument that a claim of undue influence should be subject to a six-year time period by analogy with the statute. No case could be cited in which a Court of Equity had ever done so. Instead any such defence would be limited to laches or acquiescence, see *Coulthard v Disco Mix Club Ltd* [1999] 2 All ER 457, [2000] 1 WLR 707; *Allcard v Skinner* (1887) 36 Ch D 145.

III LIM [40.5]

Duty of care Where the claim involved a breach of a duty of care in equity which corresponded with the remedy available for negligence at common law, by operation of s 36 of the 1980 Act, the court had to apply the limitation period of six years provided for by s 2: *Raja v Lloyds TSB Bank plc* [2001] Lloyd's Rep Bank 113, CA.

> " . . . it is important to note the different senses in which the word 'laches' is used. Sometimes it is used as a synonym for 'delay': . . . Sometimes it is used to describe the lapse of a sufficient period of time to draw the inference that the plaintiff had previously approved of the status quo which, by his suit, he wishes to disturb . . . More often, it is used not only in the second sense just mentioned but also to comprehend that degree of delay which when coupled with prejudice to the defendant or third parties, will operate as a defence in equity."

LIMITATION

See Meagher, Gummow and Lehane's *Equity, Doctrines and Remedies*, 4th edn (2002) at para 36-050. This note of caution was adopted by Moore-Bick LJ in *P&O Nedlloyd BV v Arab Metals Co* [2006] EWCA Civ 1717 but he indicated that despite the lack of consistency with which the term laches is used in the cases, delay was an essential feature. Delay was held not to defeat the claimant's claim to the proceeds of sale of a house which had been vested in joint names, the other owner having subsequently sold her beneficial interest to the claimant for a sum which had been paid. If the house had not been sold the claimant would have been entitled to specific performance even after six years: *Frawley v Neill* (1999) 143 Sol Jo LB 98, CA. In that case the court held that the defence of laches was to be applied to deprive someone of a beneficial right or interest only where in would be unconscionable to give it effect. For instances of unconscionability see *Taylor Fashions Ltd v Liverpool Victoria Trustees Co Ltd* [1982] QB 133n, [1981] 1 All ER 897, CA and *Habib Bank Ltd v Habib Bank AG Zurich* [1981] 2 All ER 650, [1981] 1 WLR 1265 and for the general approach see *Williams v Greatrex* [1956] 3 All ER 705, [1957] 1 WLR 31, CA. In *Jones v Stones* [1999] 1 WLR 739, CA, the court allowed an appeal against a finding of acquiescence based on delay alone. The court of trial should instead have addressed three other questions: (1) whether the claimants had, by action or inaction, encouraged the defendant to believe that he was entitled to act as he did, (2) whether any such encouragement had caused the defendant any detriment, and (3) whether it would, in all the circumstances, be unconscionable for the claimants to assert their legal right.

A delay of 40 years in asserting a share of the copyright in a musical work has been held not to be barred by laches in a case where the defendants were unable to demonstrate that they had suffered any prejudice from the delay: *Fisher v Brooker* [2009] UKHL 41, [2009] 4 All ER 789, [2009] 1 WLR 1764.

III LIM [41]

38. Interpretation

(1) In this Act, unless the context otherwise requires—

"action" includes any proceeding in a court of law, including an ecclesiastical court (and see subsection (11) below);

"land" includes corporeal hereditaments, tithes and . . . any legal or equitable estate or interest therein . . . but except as provided above in this definition does not include any incorporeal hereditament;

"personal estate" and "personal property" do not include chattels real;

"personal injuries" includes any disease and any impairment of a person's physical or mental condition, and "injury" and cognate expressions shall be construed accordingly;

"rent" includes a rentcharge and a rentservice; "rentcharge" means any annuity or periodical sum of money charged upon or payable out of land, except a rent service or interest on a mortgage on land;

"settled land", "statutory owner" and "tenant for life" have the same meanings respectively as in the Settled Land Act 1925;

"trust" and "trustee" have the same meanings respectively as in the Trustee Act 1925; and

. . .

(2) For the purposes of this Act a person shall be treated as under a disability while he is an infant, or lacks capacity (within the meaning of the Mental Capacity Act 2005) to conduct legal proceedings).

(3) . . .

(4) . . .

(5) Subject to subsection (6) below, a person shall be treated as claiming through another person if he became entitled by, through, under, or by the act of that other person to the right claimed, and any person whose estate or interest might have been barred by a person entitled to an entailed interest in possession shall be treated as claiming through the person so entitled.

(6) A person becoming entitled to any estate or interest by virtue of a special power of appointment shall not be treated as claiming through the appointor.

(7) References in this Act to a right of action to recover land shall include references to a right to enter into possession of the land or, in the case of tithes, to distrain for arrears of tithe, and references to the bringing of such an action shall include references to the making of such an entry or distress.

(8) References in this Act to the possession of land shall, in the case of tithes and rentcharges, be construed as references to the receipt of the tithe or rent, and references to the date of dispossession or discontinuance of possession of land shall, in the case of rent charges, be construed as references to the date of the last receipt of rent.

(9) References in Part II of this Act to a right of action shall include references to—

- (a) a cause of action;
- (b) a right to receive money secured by a mortgage or charge on any property;
- (c) a right to recover proceeds of the sale of land; and
- (d) a right to receive a share or interest in the personal estate of a deceased person.

(10) References in Part II to the date of the accrual of a right of action shall be construed—

- (a) in the case of an action upon a judgment, as references to the date on which the judgment became enforceable; and
- (b) in the case of an action to recover arrears of rent or interest, or damages in respect of arrears of rent or interest, as references to the date on which the rent or interest became due.

Amendment *Text in italic is deleted and text in square brackets is inserted by the Tribunals, Courts and Enforcement Act 2007, with effect from a date to be appointed.*

III LIM [41.1]

With effect from 1 October 2007 sub-ss 38(3)-(4) were repealed and sub-section 38(2) was amended to read as follows:

> 'For the purposes of this Act a person shall be treated as under a disability while he is an infant, or lacks capacity (within the meaning of the Mental Capacity Act 2005) to conduct legal proceedings.'

LIMITATION

Sections 1-3 of the Mental Capacity Act 2005 provide, so far as relevant, as follows:

1. The principles

(1) The following principles apply for the purposes of this Act.

(2) A person must be assumed to have capacity unless it is established that he lacks capacity.

(3) A person is not to be treated as unable to make a decision unless all practicable steps to help him to do so have been taken without success.

(4) A person is not to be treated as unable to make a decision merely because he makes an unwise decision.

...

2. People who lack capacity

(1) For the purposes of this Act, a person lacks capacity in relation to a matter if at the material time he is unable to make a decision for himself in relation to the matter because of an impairment of, or a disturbance in the functioning of, the mind or brain.

(2) It does not matter whether the impairment or disturbance is permanent or temporary.

(3) A lack of capacity cannot be established merely by reference to

(a) a person's age or appearance, or

(b) a condition of his, or an aspect of his behaviour, which might lead others to make unjustified assumptions about his capacity.

(4) In proceedings under this Act or any other enactment, any question whether a person lacks capacity within the meaning of this Act must be decided on the balance of probabilities.

...

3. Inability to make decisions

(1) For the purposes of section 2, a person is unable to make a decision for himself if he is unable—

(a) to understand the information relevant to the decision,
(b) to retain that information,
(c) to use or weigh that information as part of the process of making the decision, or
(d) to communicate his decision (whether by talking, using sign language or any other means).

(2) A person is not to be regarded as unable to understand the information relevant to a decision if he is able to understand an explanation of it given to him in a way that is appropriate to his circumstances (using simple language, visual aids or any other means).

(3) The fact that a person is able to retain the information relevant to a decision for a short period only does not prevent him from being regarded as able to make the decision.

(4) The information relevant to a decision includes information about the reasonably foreseeable consequences of—

(a) deciding one way or another, or
(b) failing to make the decision.'

Section 42 of the 2005 Act provides for the issue of codes of practice by the Lord Chancellor for the purpose, *inter alia*, of assessing whether a person has capacity in relation to any matter: s 42(5) provides that:

'If it appears to a court or tribunal conducting any . . . civil proceedings that—

(a) a provision of a code,...

is relevant to a question arising in the proceedings, the provision . . . must be taken into account in deciding the question.'

Thus, under the 2005 Act:

- There is a rebuttable presumption that a person has mental capacity.
- The matters relevant to whether a person in fact lacks mental capacity are wider than under the previous law.
- A person is not to be held to lack capacity merely because of age, appearance, medical condition or an aspect of behaviour.
- There is no longer any conclusive presumption in particular circumstances.

The general policy of the 2005 Act is that because of the drastic implications of a finding that a person lacks mental capacity, it should not readily be made. As under the previous law, however, the question is 'issue-specific' (see *Seaton v Seddon* [2012] EWHC 735 (Ch), [2013] 1 All ER 29, [2012] 1 WLR 3636).

III LIM [41A]

39. Saving for other limitation enactments

This Act shall not apply to any action or arbitration for which a period of limitation is prescribed by or under any other enactment (whether passed before or after the passing of this Act) or to any action or arbitration to which the Crown is a party and for which, if it were between subjects, a period of limitation would be prescribed by or under any such other enactment.

SCHEDULE 1
PROVISIONS WITH RESPECT TO ACTIONS TO RECOVER LAND

PART I
ACCRUAL OF RIGHTS OF ACTION TO RECOVER LAND

III LIM [42]

1 Accrual of right of action in case of present interests in land

Where the person bringing an action to recover land, or some person through whom he claims, has been in possession of the land, and has while entitled to the land been dispossessed or discontinued his possession, the right of action shall be treated as having accrued on the date of the dispossession or discontinuance.

III LIM [42.1]

"right of action" For the definition of this pivotal phrase, see s 38(7) (para **III LIM [41]**).

Dispossession comes about when a squatter drives the owner from possession of the land whereas *discontinuance* occurs when the owner goes out of possession and a squatter afterwards takes possession. Either is sufficient for adverse possession: *Buckinghamshire County Council v Moran* [1990] Ch 623.

The rule in para 1 is subject to the exceptions in paras 2 and 3.

2 Where any person brings an action to recover any land of a deceased person (whether under a will or on intestacy) and the deceased person—

(a) was on the date of his death in possession of the land or, in the case of a rentcharge created by will or taking effect upon his death, in possession of the land charged; and

(b) was the last person entitled to the land to be in possession of it;

the right of action shall be treated as having accrued on the date of his death.

III LIM [42.2]

"right of action" For the definition of this pivotal phrase, see s 38(7) (para **III LIM [41]**).

3 Where any person brings an action to recover land, being an estate or interest in possession assured otherwise than by will to him, or to some person through whom he claims, and—

(a) the person making the assurance was on the date when the assurance took effect in possession of the land or, in the case of a rentcharge created by the assurance, in possession of the land charged; and

(b) no person has been in possession of the land by virtue of the assurance;

the right of action shall be treated as having accrued on the date when the assurance took effect.

III LIM [42.3]

"right of action" For the definition of this pivotal phrase, see s 38(7) (para **III LIM [41]**).

III LIM [42.4]

Assurance The word assurance is not defined by the Act but normally denotes something which operates to transfer land. In *Hughes v Griffin* [1968] 1 All ER 460, [1969] 1 WLR 23, CA, the assurance was a deed.

4 Accrual of right of action in case of future interests

The right of action to recover any land shall, in a case where—

(a) the estate or interest claimed was an estate or interest in reversion or remainder or any other future estate or interest; and

(b) no person has taken possession of the land by virtue of the estate or interest claimed;

LIMITATION

be treated as having accrued on the date on which the estate or interest fell into possession by the determination of the preceding estate or interest.

III LIM [42.5]

"right of action" For the definition of this pivotal phrase, see s 38(7) (para **III LIM [41]**).

If adverse possession is taken prior to the falling in of the interest in reversion or remainder, the right of action only accrues to the reversioner or remainderman when the interest does fall in. Two alternative limitation periods are then available: twelve years from dispossession *or* six years from the falling in of the interest.

5 (1) Subject to sub-paragraph (2) below, a tenancy from year to year or other period, without a lease in writing, shall for the purposes of this Act be treated as being determined at the expiration of the first year or other period; and accordingly the right of action of the person entitled to the land subject to the tenancy shall be treated as having accrued at the date on which in accordance with this sub-paragraph the tenancy is determined.

(2) Where any rent has subsequently been received in respect of the tenancy, the right of action shall be treated as having accrued on the date of the last receipt of rent.

III LIM [42.6]

"right of action" For the definition of this pivotal phrase, see s 38(7) (para **III LIM [41]**).

A document cannot be a "lease in writing" within the meaning of paragraph 5 of Schedule 1 unless it is dispositive and creates an estate in land in accordance with the Law of Property Act 1925. See *Long v Tower Hamlets London Borough Council* [1998] Ch 197, [1996] 2 All ER 683.

As soon as a tenancy is determined in accordance with paragraph 5 of the Act, continued possession of the former tenant becomes adverse for the purposes of limitation; see *Williams v Jones* [2002] EWCA Civ 1097, [2002] 3 EGLR 69, [2002] 40 EG 169.

So long as the original lease has expired and there is no subsequent payment of rent, para 5(2) was held to apply even where the possessor believed that he was a tenant: *Lodge v Wakefield Metropolitan District Council* [1995] 2 EGLR 124, [1995] 38 EG 136.

6 (1) Where—

(a) any person is in possession of land by virtue of a lease in writing by which a rent of not less than ten pounds a year is reserved; and

(b) the rent is received by some person wrongfully claiming to be entitled to the land in reversion immediately expectant on the determination of the lease; and

(c) no rent is subsequently received by the person rightfully so entitled;

the right of action to recover the land of the person rightfully so entitled shall be treated as having accrued on the date when the rent was first received by the person wrongfully claiming to be so entitled and not on the date of the determination of the lease.

(2) Sub-paragraph (1) above shall not apply to any lease granted by the Crown.

III LIM [42.7]

"right of action" For the definition of this pivotal phrase, see s 38(7) (para **III LIM [41]**).

III LIM [42.8]

"lease in writing" The writing must itself create a lease, ie it must be dispositive. Writing which is only evidence of a lease is outside the concept. See, eg *Long v Tower Hamlets London Borough Council* [1998] Ch 197, [1996] 2 All ER 683; *Moses v Lovegrove* [1952] 2 QB 533, CA; *Doe d Landsell v Gower* (1851) 17 QB 589.

7 Accrual of right of action in case of forfeiture or breach of condition

(1) Subject to sub-paragraph (2) below, a right of action to recover land by virtue of a forfeiture or breach of condition shall be treated as having accrued on the date on which the forfeiture was incurred or the condition broken.

(2) If any such right has accrued to a person entitled to an estate or interest in reversion or remainder and the land was not recovered by virtue of that right, the right of action to recover the land shall not be treated as having accrued to that person until his estate or interest fell into possession, as if no such forfeiture or breach of condition had occurred.

III LIM [42.9]

"right of action" For the definition of this pivotal phrase, see s 38(7) (para **III LIM [41]**).

III LIM [42.9A]

Relief from forfeiture The corollary to forfeiture is relief therefrom, which was historically, and remains essentially, equitable. The Limitation Act does not provide any limitation period for such an application. Notwithstanding this, there are limitation constraints affecting the commencement of proceedings for relief. These fall into two categories, depending on whether the forfeiture results from a court order in proceedings within the scope of the Common Law Procedure Act 1852, or has been effected by peaceable re-entry.

Until the Landlord and Tenant Act 1730, the jurisdiction to grant relief was entirely equitable. That Act concerned proceedings for forfeiture where the ground was that there were six months of arrears of rent. It provided that in such a case an application for relief had to be made within a period of six months after execution of the order for possession.

The provision was re-enacted in s 210 of the Common Law Procedure Act 1852, which is still in force. This restriction differs in nature from the general right to commence proceedings within the time limits provided by the Limitation Act in that it operates as a cap on the time for an application, because in the exercise of its equitable jurisdiction, the grant of for relief might be refused on the ground of a delay of less than six months, depending on the circumstances. Section 210 of the 1852 Act has no application to the other category of forfeiture, peaceable re-entry, or to forfeiture proceedings where the Act does not apply, such as for breaches of other covenants or arrears of rent of less than six months.

In the second category, the issue of whether the application for relief has been brought in time is not a strict limitation issue, but a factor, often the main factor, in the exercise of the court's equitable jurisdiction. The court has to weigh the reasons for the delay against the prejudice to the landlord of granting relief. The greater the delay, the greater the likelihood that the landlord has been prejudiced by incurring expense and by altering his position in other ways. The court will look at the six-month restriction under the 1852 Act as an analogy, but will not be bound by it. In a case concerning an application for relief from forfeiture made some 14 months after the landlord had peaceably re-entered, the court, having considered all the circumstances, particularly the reasons for the delay, granted relief on the basis that the tenant paid the cost and expenses of the landlord resulting from the re-entry, together with the arrears of rent: *Pineport Ltd v Grangeglen Ltd* [2016] EWHC 1318 (Ch).

LIMITATION

8 Right of action not to accrue or continue unless there is adverse possession

(1) No right of action to recover land shall be treated as accruing unless the land is in the possession of some person in whose favour the period of limitation can run (referred to below in this paragraph as "adverse possession"); and where under the preceding provisions of this Schedule any such right of action is treated as accruing on a certain date and no person is in adverse possession on that date, the right of action shall not be treated as accruing unless and until adverse possession is taken of the land.

(2) Where a right of action to recover land has accrued and after its accrual, before the right is barred, the land ceases to be in adverse possession, the right of action shall no longer be treated as having accrued and no fresh right of action shall be treated as accruing unless and until the land is again taken into adverse possession.

(3) For the purposes of this paragraph—

(a) possession of any land subject to a rentcharge by a person (other than the person entitled to the rentcharge) who does not pay the rent shall be treated as adverse possession of the rentcharge; and

(b) receipt of rent under a lease by a person wrongfully claiming to be entitled to the land in reversion immediately expectant on the determination of the lease shall be treated as adverse possession of the land.

(4) For the purpose of determining whether a person occupying any land is in adverse possession of the land it shall not be assumed by implication of law that his occupation is by permission of the person entitled to the land merely by virtue of the fact that his occupation is not inconsistent with the latter's present or future enjoyment of the land.

This provision shall not be taken as prejudicing a finding to the effect that a person's occupation of any land is by implied permission of the person entitled to the land in any case where such a finding is justified on the actual facts of the case.

III LIM [42.10]

"right of action" For the definition of this pivotal phrase, see s 38(7) (para **III LIM [41]**).

III LIM [42.11]

Adverse possession The Act's definition of the concept of adverse possession is limited to "the land is in the possession of some person in whose favour the period of limitation can run". Comprehensive definition must instead be sought in the cases. Five requirements have been posited: (1) the squatter must have been in actual possession of the land; (2) that possession must have been exclusive; (3) the paper owner of the land must have discontinued possession or have been dispossessed; (4) the squatter must have intended to possess the land (ie had the requisite *animus possidendi* according to the traditional formulation); and (5) the possession must have been adverse in the statutory sense – the "right of action" must have accrued: *Prudential Assurance Co Ltd v Waterloo Real Estate Inc* [1999] 2 EGLR 85. See also *Powell v McFarlane* (1979) 38 P & CR 452; *Buckinghamshire County Council v Moran* [1990] Ch 623. Possession fulfilling these conditions must also be continuous for the 12-year period. Possession may still qualify as adverse possession despite the fact that the possession (or part of it) amounts to a criminal offence within the meaning of s 144 of the Legal Aid, Sentencing and Punishment of Offenders Act 2012 which came into force in September 2012 and which criminalises trespass involving 'living in' a residential building: see *R (on the application of Best) v Chief Land Registrar (Secretary of State for Justice, interested party)* [2014] EWHC 1370 (Admin), [2014] 3 All ER 637, [2014] PLSCS 141, a case of registered land under the Land Registration Act 2002.

The period of limitation cannot run in favour of someone with registered title to the land. Thus where, in error, the same land is concurrently registered in two different titles the actual possessor cannot establish adverse possession because until rectification of the register to show the true position such possession is not unlawful. It follows that until such rectification the true owner could not seek recovery of possession from the actual possessor because it has no better title, rather they both have the same title: see *Parshall v Hackney* [2013] EWCA Civ 240, [2013] Ch 568, [2013] 3 All ER 224. The 1980 Act does not apply to the statutory right to apply to rectify the land register.

The existence of actual possession is an objective question (*West Bank Estates Ltd v Arthur* [1967] 1 AC 665) whereas the intention to possess is of course subjective. No intention to obtain ownership is required: *Buckinghamshire County Council v Moran* [1990] Ch 623. On the other hand, a squatter who believed that he was the owner has been held to have had the requisition intention to possess: *Hughes v Cook* (1994) Independent, 21 March.

A squatter seeking to defeat an owner's claim for possession needed only to have a manifested intention to possess "for the time being": *Powell v McFarlane* (1977) 38 P & CR 452. The fact that he intended or expected to leave the property at some time in the future is not inconsistent with having that intention. It followed that so long as he remained in actual possession for the requisite 12 years with that intention, he could fulfil the requirements of s 15. Where actual possession is established there is little scope for a distinction between occupation which amounts only to trespass and occupation which amounts to adverse possession: *London Borough of Lambeth v Blackburn* [2001] EWCA Civ 912, (2001) 82 P & CR 494, 33 HLR 847, CA.

In *Archangel v London Borough of Lambeth* [2000] EGCS 148, CA, the squatter sought to resist the council's claim for possession on the basis of his rent-free occupation since 1985. His claim failed because of a letter which he had written in 1993 which mentioned the need to refurbish "Lambeth's property". He was held to have acknowledged the council's title. See also *Bigden v London Borough of Lambeth* [2000] EGCS 147, where a petition which acknowledged the council's right to sell the properties constituted sufficient acknowledgment of better title to defeat the claim for adverse possession.

Paragraph 8 of Schedule 1 to the Limitation Act 1980 applies to all actions to recover land, including cases falling within paragraph 3. It therefore includes claims by legal mortgagees against mortgagors in possession. The term "adverse possession" refers to the capacity of the person in possession rather than the nature of that possession and means only ordinary possession by a person in whose favour the limitation period could run.

Mortgagors in ordinary possession of the property after the grant of a legal charge are in possession which is capable of being adverse to any accrued right to possession which the mortgagee may have either because of some default by the mortgagor or by reason of the precise form of the charge which may give an immediate right to possession upon execution. The mortgagors' possession is based upon their registered legal title rather than the mortgagee's interest and they therefore do not need the permission of the mortgagee and where this is neither sought nor given (and the mere failure to enforce an accrued right to possession does not amount to granting implied permission) then the failure by a mortgagor in possession to make any payment to the mortgagee for more than 12 years entitled the mortgagors to a declaration that the legal charge had been extinguished by s 17 of the Act. See *Ashe v National Westminster Bank plc* [2008] EWCA Civ 55, [2008] 1 WLR 710, [2008] All ER (D) 128 (Feb), (2008) 7 EG 143 (CS).

It does not appear to be possible to establish adverse possession of any part of the highway, see *R (on the application of Smith) v Land Registry (Cambridgeshire County Council, interested party)* [2010] EWCA Civ 200, [2011] QB 413, [2010] 3 All ER 113, [2010] 3 WLR 1223, [2010] 2 P & CR 00. This principle has subsequently been applied by analogy to a claim for adverse possession of the riverbed where title to it was vested by statute in the Port of London Authority for the purposes of regulating the public right of navigation of the river: see *Couper v Albion Properties Ltd* [2013] EWHC 2993 (Ch), [2013] All ER (D) 113 (Oct).

Consent can be implied from the circumstances of the case but this requires some overt act by the landowner or some demonstrable circumstance from which the consent can be implied: see *Lambeth London Borough Council v Rumbelow* (25 January 2001, unreported), Ch D. It does not matter whether the user was aware of the overt act or demonstrable circumstance so long as a reasonable person would have appreciated that the use was with the permission of the owner.

Where an occupier of land is negotiating with its owner for the grant of some interest in that land it may be a natural inference from the circumstances that the owner permits the occupier to occupy the land pending the result of those negotiations: see *Colin Dawson Windows Ltd v King's Lynn & West Norfolk Borough Council* [2005] EWCA Civ 9, [2005] 2 P & CR 19 and *Bath & North Somerset District Council v Nicholson* [2002] 10 EGCS 156.

III LIM [42.12]

The human rights dimension In 2005, a Chamber of the European Court of Human Rights held that the relevant provisions of the Land Registration Act 1925 and the Limitation Act 1980 contravene Article 1, Protocol 1 of the European Convention because they deprive persons of their land in circumstances which are disproportionate and without compensation: see *JA Pye v United Kingdom (Application No 44302/02)* [2005] 49 EG 50, a decision prefigured by the first instance decision of Nicholas Strauss QC in *Beaulane Properties Ltd v Palmer* [2005] EWHC 1071 (Ch), [2005] 14 EG 129 (CS). The UK Government requested that the case be referred to the Grand Chamber of the ECHR in accordance with Article 43 of the Convention. In its decision on 30 August 2007 (see (2008) 46 EHRR 45, 23 BHRC 405, [2007] RVR 302, Times, October 1, 2007, [2007] 41 EG 200 (CS)) the Grand Chamber (by ten votes to seven) differed from the Chamber's decision and held that there had been no violation on the grounds that:

(a) Article 1 Protocol 1 was engaged but by reason of "control of use" rather than a "deprivation of possessions".

(b) A 12-year limitation period for the bringing of claims for the recovery of land pursued a legitimate aim in the general interest and, in the context of the margin of appreciation allowed to states in implementing social and economic policies, the extinguishment of title upon the expiry of that period could not be said to be manifestly without foundation. Indeed, the extinguishment of title could be seen as little more than the regularising of the respective positions of previous owner and adverse possessor.

(c) So far as the question of "fair balance" was concerned this was not upset bearing in mind once again the state's margin of appreciation. As a "control of use" the jurisprudence on compensation for deprivation was not directly applicable but in any event the Court accepted the UK's submission that the notion of compensation would not be consistent with the purpose of limitation periods. It was also the case that the Applicant could with relative ease have stopped the limitation period from running eg by asking for rent or bringing possession proceedings. Moreover the substantial loss suffered by the applicant in this case (which appeared to lie between £2.5m and £10m) could not ultimately be relevant where the fulfilment of the aims of limitation laws depended on their applicability regardless of the size of the claim.

LIMITATION

The dissenting judgments provide some intellectual and moral succour to those – including some distinguished members of the English judiciary – who have considered the effect of ss 15-17 to be disproportionate but with the coming into force of the Land Registration Act 2002 the debate has lost some of its practical importance.

The adverse possession provisions of the Limitation Act 1980 are therefore compatible with the European Convention and it is not open to a court to hold otherwise in a particular case merely because it seems distinguishable on its facts. The Court could only do so where, in a specific case, the application of the 1980 Act produced such an anomalous result that it was possible to say that the margin of appreciation allowed by the Strasbourg court had been exceeded: *Ofulue v Bossert* [2008] EWCA Civ 7, [2008] HRLR 20, [2008] UKHRR 447, (2008) Times, 11 February.

III LIM [42.13]

Interruption of adverse possession: para 8(2) Where adverse possession is interrupted before the effluxion of the 12-year period under s 15(1), the fresh right of action which accrues in the event of subsequent adverse possession starts the 12-year period running all over again. However, the identity of the squatter need not remain the same throughout the 12-year period. So long as continuity of adverse possession remains, a successor squatter can rely upon the period of adverse possession under his predecessor: *Mount Carmel Investments Ltd v Peter Thurlow Ltd* [1988] 3 All ER 129, [1988] 1 WLR 1078, CA.

9 Possession of beneficiary not adverse to others interested in settled land or land held on trust for sale

Where any settled land or any land [subject to a trust of land] is in the possession of a person entitled to a beneficial interest in the land . . . (not being a person solely or absolutely entitled to the land . . .), no right of action to recover the land shall be treated for the purposes of this Act as accruing during that possession to any person in whom the land is vested as tenant for life, statutory owner or trustee, or to any other person entitled to a beneficial interest in the land . . .

III LIM [42.14]

"right of action" For the definition of this pivotal phrase, see s 38(7) (para **III LIM [41]**).

Time does not run in favour of the beneficiary in possession in the circumstances contemplated by para 9.

The words "subject to a trust of land" were substituted for the previous wording by the Trusts of Land and Appointment of Trustees Act 1996 s 25(1), (2), Sch 3, para 18, Sch 4.

PART II
MODIFICATIONS OF SECTION 15 WHERE CROWN OR CERTAIN CORPORATIONS SOLE ARE INVOLVED

III LIM [43]

10 Subject to paragraph 11 below, section 15(1) of this Act shall apply to the bringing of an action to recover any land by the Crown or by any spiritual or eleemosynary corporation sole with the substitution for the reference to twelve years of a reference to thirty years.

11 (1) An action to recover foreshore may be brought by the Crown at any time before the expiration of sixty years from the date mentioned in section 15(1) of this Act.

(2) Where any right of action to recover land which has ceased to be foreshore but remains in the ownership of the Crown accrued when the land was foreshore, the action may be brought at any time before the expiration of—

(a) sixty years from the date of accrual of the right of action; or

(b) thirty years from the date when the land ceased to be foreshore;

whichever period first expires.

(3) In this paragraph "foreshore" means the shore and bed of the sea and of any tidal water, below the line of the medium high tide between the spring tides and the neap tides.

12 Notwithstanding section 15(1) of this Act, where in the case of any action brought by a person other than the Crown or a spiritual or eleemosynary corporation sole the right of action first accrued to the Crown or any such corporation sole through whom the person in question claims, the action may be brought at any time before the expiration of—

(a) the period during which the action could have been brought by the Crown or the corporation sole; or

(b) twelve years from the date on which the right of action accrued to some person other than the Crown or the corporation sole;

whichever period first expires.

13 Section 15(2) of this Act shall apply in any case where the Crown or a spiritual or eleemosynary corporation sole is entitled to the succeeding estate or interest with the substitution—

(a) for the reference to twelve years of a reference to thirty years; and

(b) for the reference to six years of a reference to twelve years.

III LIM [43.1]

The Crown The special periods in Part II apply to actions brought by but not against the Crown or the other specified bodies. Thus, in the latter case, where the Crown or any of these bodies is the squatter, the limitation period is 12 years in the normal way.

There is no principle which precludes the Crown from claiming adverse possession where its original entry on to the land was unlawful: *Roberts v Crown Estate Comrs* [2008] EWCA Civ 98, [2008] Ch 439, [2008] 2 WLR 1111.

Where the Crown acquires land which is adversely possessed by others, the Crown has 30 years from when the adverse possession started in which to assert title. A successor in title to the Crown has the same period (or 12 years from acquiring title if this is shorter): *Hill v Transport for London* [2005] EWHC 856 (Ch), [2005] 3 All ER 677, (2005) Times, 30 May, Rimer J.

LIMITATION

LATENT DAMAGE ACT 1986

(c 37)

III LIM [44]

1. Time limits for negligence actions in respect of latent damage not involving personal injuries

[. . .]

III LIM [44.1]

Amendment This section inserts ss 14A and 14B of the Limitation Act 1980 (see paras **III LIM [18]** and **III LIM [19]** respectively).

III LIM [45]

2. Provisions consequential on section 1

[. . .]

III LIM [45.1]

Amendment This section inserts ss 28A and 32(5) of the Limitation Act 1980 (see paras **III LIM [32]** and **III LIM [36]** respectively).

III LIM [46]

3. Accrual of cause of action to successive owners in respect of latent damage to property

(1) Subject to the following provisions of this section, where—

(a) a cause of action ("the original cause of action") has accrued to any person in respect of any negligence to which damage to any property in which he has an interest is attributable (in whole or in part); and

(b) another person acquires an interest in that property after the date on which the original cause of action accrued but before the material facts about the damage have become known to any person who, at the time when he first has knowledge of those facts, has any interest in the property;

a fresh cause of action in respect of that negligence shall accrue to that other person on the date on which he acquires his interest in the property.

(2) A cause of action accruing to any person by virtue of subsection (1) above—

(a) shall be treated as if based on breach of a duty of care at common law owed to the person to whom it accrues; and

(b) shall be treated for the purposes of section 14A of the 1980 Act (special time limit for negligence actions where facts relevant to cause of action are not known at date of accrual) as having accrued on the date on which the original cause of action accrued.

(3) Section 28 of the 1980 Act (extension of limitation period in case of disability) shall not apply in relation to any such cause of action.

(4) Subsection (1) above shall not apply in any case where the person acquiring an interest in the damaged property is either—

(a) a person in whom the original cause of action vests by operation of law; or

(b) a person in whom the interest in that property vests by virtue of any order made by a court under section 538 of the Companies Act 1985 (vesting of company property in liquidator).

(5) For the purposes of subsection (1)(*b*) above, the material facts about the damage are such facts about the damage as would lead a reasonable person who has an interest in the damaged property at the time when those facts become known to him to consider it sufficiently serious to justify his instituting proceedings for damages against a defendant who did not dispute liability and was able to satisfy a judgment.

(6) For the purposes of this section a person's knowledge includes knowledge which he might reasonably have been expected to acquire—

(a) from facts observable or ascertainable by him; or

(b) from facts ascertainable by him with the help of appropriate expert advice which it is reasonable for him to seek;

but a person shall not be taken by virtue of this subsection to have knowledge of a fact ascertainable by him only with the help of expert advice so long as he has taken all reasonable steps to obtain (and, where appropriate, to act on) that advice.

(7) This section shall bind the Crown, but as regards the Crown's liability in tort shall not bind the Crown further than the Crown is made liable in tort by the Crown Proceedings Act 1947.

III LIM [46.1]

The effect of s 3(1) A fresh cause of action in respect of the negligence thus accrues to the "other person" on the date of the acquisition of his interest resulting in a (potential) extension to the limitation period of three years from the starting date (date of discoverability) under s 14A(4)(b) of the Act. This is so even if the primary six-year limitation period (based on accrual) has already expired. The fresh cause of action can only accrue to the successor where no predecessor with an interest in the property has had the requisite knowledge at the time when he had that interest.

III LIM [46.2]

"shall be treated": s 3(2) This fresh cause of action is treated, by legal fiction, as if it arose from a breach owed to the "other person" and it does not change the date of accrual which is thus treated as the date of original accrual, ie the suffering of the damage.

III LIM [46.3]

"the material facts" The "material facts" in s 3(1)(b) are defined (in s 3(5)) *mutatis mutandis* in the same way as in s 14A(7) (ie the objective test involving the same hypothetical defendant), except that awareness of these facts only becomes material when it coincides with the possession of an interest in the property.

"Knowledge" includes constructive knowledge defined (by s 3(6)) in the same way as in s 14A(10). Knowledge acquired *after* the interest has ended is irrelevant for the purposes of the starting date of the special three-year period. Knowledge acquired, however, *before* acquiring an interest in the property is relevant since upon acquisition the necessary coincidence of knowledge and ownership will exist.

III LIM [46.4]

Interest, not ownership, required Section 3 requires an interest in, and thus not necessarily ownership of, the property in question. Thus a leasehold or reversionary interest would be within the ambit of this definition.

Furthermore, the section does not require that the person first interested in the property has divested himself of that interest before a fresh cause of action can accrue to another person acquiring "an" interest.

III LIM [46.5]

"property" This is not defined and thus seems to apply to personal as well as to real property. See *Homburg Houtimport v Agrosin Private Ltd, The Starsin* [2000] 1 Lloyd's Rep 85, in which this proposition seems to have been assumed to be correct.

III LIM [46.6]

Disability: s 3(3) Section 28 of the 1980 Act does not apply to the fresh cause of action created by s 3(1). Instead, s 28A applies, so that where at the time of the starting date under s 14A(5) (which under s 3 will only occur where there is also possession of an interest in the relevant property) the claimant is under a disability, the claim may be brought at any time within three years from the claimant's cessation of disability or death, subject (under s 28A(2)) to the long-stop provisions of s 14B.

III LIM [47]

4. Transitional provisions

(1) Nothing in section 1 or 2 of this Act shall—

(a) enable any action to be brought which was barred by the 1980 Act or (as the case may be) by the Limitation Act 1939 before this Act comes into force; or

(b) affect any action commenced before this Act comes into force.

(2) Subject to subsection (1) above, sections 1 and 2 of this Act shall have effect in relation to causes of action accruing before, as well as in relation to causes of action accruing after, this Act comes into force.

(3) Section 3 of this Act shall only apply in cases where an interest in damaged property is acquired after this Act comes into force but shall so apply, subject to subsection (4) below, irrespective of whether the original cause of action accrued before or after this Act comes into force.

(4) Where—

(a) a person acquires an interest in damaged property in circumstances to which section 3 would apart from this subsection apply; but

(b) the original cause of action accrued more than six years before this Act comes into force;

a cause of action shall not accrue to that person by virtue of subsection (1) of that section unless section 32(1)(*b*) of the 1980 Act (postponement of limitation period in case of deliberate concealment of relevant facts) would apply to any action founded on the original cause of action.

III LIM [47.1]

Limited application of s 3 Section 3(3) is qualified by s 4(4). It follows that s 3, like s 14A, does not revive a cause of action already barred by the effluxion of time by the time the Latent Damage Act 1986 came into force on 18 September 1986.

III LIM [48]

5. Citation, interpretation, commencement and extent

(1) This Act may be cited as the Latent Damage Act 1986.

(2) In this Act—

"the 1980 Act" has the meaning given by section 1; and

"action" includes any proceeding in a court of law, an arbitration and any new claim within the meaning of section 35 of the 1980 Act (new claims in pending actions).

(3) This Act shall come into force at the end of the period of two months beginning with the date on which it is passed.

(4) This Act extends to England and Wales only.

LAND REGISTRATION ACT 2002

(c 9)

PART 9
ADVERSE POSSESSION

III LIM [49]

96. Disapplication of periods of limitation

(1) No period of limitation under section 15 of the Limitation Act 1980 (c 58) (time limits in relation to recovery of land) shall run against any person, other than a chargee, in relation to an estate in land or rentcharge the title to which is registered.

(2) No period of limitation under section 16 of that Act (time limits in relation to redemption of land) shall run against any person in relation to such an estate in land or rentcharge.

(3) Accordingly, section 17 of that Act (extinction of title on expiry of time limit) does not operate to extinguish the title of any person where, by virtue of this section, a period of limitation does not run against him.

III LIM [49.1]

Commencement Sections 96–98 came into force on 13 October 2003.

Section 96(1)

III LIM [49.2]

The effect of section 96 Where the title to an "estate in land" (defined by s 1(1) of the Law of Property Act 1925) or rentcharge is registered, the limitation periods in respect of actions to recover land are disapplied. Time continues to run under the 1980 Act against a chargee. The 1980 Act will also continue to apply to the following situations:

(a) claims by tenants of leases for 21 years or less which were granted before the Land Registration Act came into force;
(b) claims by a licensee or tenant at will;
(c) where a lease becomes capable of forfeiture or a right of re-entry arises in relation to a fee simple;
(d) where a squatter wishes to recover possession from a subsequent squatter.

The 1980 Act also continues to apply to registered land in respect of which the squatter has already extinguished the owner's title by adverse possession as at 13 October 2003 see para 18(1) of Schedule 2 (Transition) of the Land Registration Act 2002,

Section 96(2) Where s 96 applies, a mortgagor will no longer lose his right to redeem the mortgage after the mortgagor has been in possession for 12 years. Since a mortgagee will never be in "adverse possession" (see Sch 6, para 1 to the 2002 Act) it will not be able to apply to be registered as the proprietor of the estate on the expiry of ten years in possession.

From the coming into force of these provisions, there have accordingly been two adverse possession regimes: one for registered and one for unregistered land. The juridical rationale for the distinction (and for the change) is that, in the case of registered land, title is based on registration whereas unregistered land title is based on possession. At another level, there had been growing concern at the relative ease with which adverse possession can be established under the 1980 Act, namely the mere effluxion of time. The Law Commission (see Law Com No 271) considered this to be unjustified in relation to registered land where certainty of title presents no difficulty of investigation.

III LIM [50]

97. Registration of adverse possessor

Schedule 6 (which makes provision about the registration of an adverse possessor of an estate in land or rentcharge) has effect.

III LIM [50.A1]

Counter-notice Any of those notified can serve a counter-notice on the Registrar within a required period of time requiring him to deal with the applications pursuant to Sch 6, para 5: Land Registration Act 2002, Sch 6, para 3. The time for serving a counter-notice is 12 noon on the 65th business day after the date of issue of the Registrar's notice (Land Registration Rules 2003, r 189). The counter-notice must be in prescribed form NAP (Land Registration Rules 2003, r 190(1)(a)). The owner should tick the second box in panel 5 requiring the application to be dealt with under the Land Registration Act 2002, Sch 6, para 5: see *Hopkins v Beacon* [2011] EWHC 2899 (Ch). If the box in panel 5 has not been ticked, it is too late to take the point requiring the Registrar to deal with the application pursuant to Sch 6, para 5 for the first time in the owner's statement case in proceedings before the First-tier Tribunal: *King v Suffolk County Council* (2017) REF/2015/0687.) Any of those notified can (if appropriate), alternatively or additionally, object on the basis that the squatter has not been in adverse possession for the necessary period. (The objection can be made by ticking the third box in panel 5 and filling in panel 6 of prescribed form NAP.)

In order to prevent the possession being adverse the owner may give permission unilaterally: it is not necessary that the permission be acknowledged by the squatter: *BP Properties Ltd v Buckler* (1988) 55 P & CR 337, CA, approved and applied by the Privy Council in *Smith v Molyneux* [2016] UKPC 35, [28].

III LIM [50.1]

Schedule 6 Schedule 6 contains the details of the new adverse possession regime.

III LIM [51]

98. Defences

(1) A person has a defence to an action for possession of land if—

(a) on the day immediately preceding that on which the action was brought he was entitled to make an application under paragraph 1 of Schedule 6 to be registered as the proprietor of an estate in the land, and

(b) had he made such an application on that day, the condition in paragraph 5(4) of that Schedule would have been satisfied.

(2) A judgment for possession of land ceases to be enforceable at the end of the period of two years beginning with the date of the judgment if the proceedings in which the judgment is given were commenced against a person who was at that time entitled to make an application under paragraph 1 of Schedule 6.

(3) A person has a defence to an action for possession of land if on the day immediately preceding that on which the action was brought he was entitled to make an application under paragraph 6 of Schedule 6 to be registered as the proprietor of an estate in the land.

(4) A judgment for possession of land ceases to be enforceable at the end of the period of two years beginning with the date of the judgment if, at the end of that period, the person against whom the judgment was given is entitled to make an application under paragraph 6 of Schedule 6 to be registered as the proprietor of an estate in the land.

(5) Where in any proceedings a court determines that—

(a) a person is entitled to a defence under this section, or

(b) a judgment for possession has ceased to be enforceable against a person by virtue of subsection (4),

the court must order the registrar to register him as the proprietor of the estate in relation to which he is entitled to make an application under Schedule 6.

(6) The defences under this section are additional to any other defences a person may have.

(7) Rules may make provision to prohibit the recovery of rent due under a rentcharge from a person who has been in adverse possession of the rentcharge.

III LIM [51.1]

The effect of section 98 The clear intention of this section is that a squatter who is the defendant to a claim for the possession of land is to be in a position analogous to that under Sch 6 even though he may have made no or no successful application under s 96 and Sch 6 to be registered as proprietor of the relevant land. The new regime is thus intended to be comprehensive.

Section 98(1) A squatter has a defence to a possession claim where he has been in adverse possession of land adjacent to his under the reasonable (but mistaken) belief that he was the owner and fulfils the other conditions contained in Sch6, para 5(4).

Section 98(2) A judgment for possession obtained against a relevant squatter will cease to be enforceable after only two rather than the usual six years.

Section 98(3) Under Sch 6, para 6 to the Land Registration Act 2002, where a squatter's application for registration is rejected, he may make a further application to be registered if he is in adverse possession of the estate from the date of the first application until two years from the date of its rejection. Thus, if nothing was done by the registered proprietor to obtain possession during that period, or judgment was obtained but was not enforced within two years or possession proceedings were brought but were dismissed or struck out, then the squatter has a defence to a (further) claim.

Section 98(4) A judgment for possession of land will cease to be enforceable where:

(a) the squatter has been in adverse possession for over ten years;
(b) an application for registration under Sch 1, para 1 has been rejected;
(c) within two years of that rejection the judgment for possession was obtained;

(d) no step is taken to enforce the judgment within two years of its being obtained.

Section 98(5) Where the court is satisfied that a squatter has a defence under s 98 or a judgment for possession is no longer enforceable against the squatter pursuant to s 98(4) it must order the registration of the squatter as proprietor.

Section 98(6) Section 98 does not exclude defences which are otherwise available to the squatter such as an independent right to possession or a proprietary estoppel.

SCHEDULE 6

REGISTRATION OF ADVERSE POSSESSOR

Section 97

III LIM [52]

1 Right to apply for registration

(1) Subject to paragraph 16, a person may apply to the registrar to be registered as the proprietor of a registered estate in land if he has been in adverse possession of the estate for the period of ten years ending on the date of the application.

(2) Subject to paragraph 16, a person may also apply to the registrar to be registered as the proprietor of a registered estate in land if—

- (a) he has in the period of six months ending on the date of the application ceased to be in adverse possession of the estate because of eviction by the registered proprietor, or a person claiming under the registered proprietor,
- (b) on the day before his eviction he was entitled to make an application under sub-paragraph (1), and
- (c) the eviction was not pursuant to a judgment for possession.

(3) However, a person may not make an application under this paragraph if—

- (a) he is a defendant in proceedings which involve asserting a right to possession of the land, or
- (b) judgment for possession of the land has been given against him in the last two years.

(4) For the purposes of sub-paragraph (1), the estate need not have been registered throughout the period of adverse possession.

III LIM [52.1]

"Adverse possession" The effect of para 15 of Sch 6 is that the phrase "adverse possession" in the Land Registration Act 2002 has the same meaning as under the Limitation Act 1980: see therefore paras **III LIM [20]** and **III LIM [42]** above.

The requisite period of adverse possession under the new regime will be ten years rather than the 12-year period under the Limitation Act 1980.

The new regime applies to land which is registered at the date of application. However, the land need not have been registered for the whole of the period of adverse possession or, indeed, for any particular length of time. See, however, the exception in para 5(4) below, which requires that the land must have been registered for more than one year before application for registration.

III LIM [52.2]

Paragraph 1(2) The effect of para 1(2) is that there is no advantage to the owner in obtaining possession by re-entry. Thus, even though the squatter may be deprived of the protection which s 98 would have afforded were proceedings to have been brought against him, he may nonetheless apply to be registered as proprietor.

2 Notification of application

(1) The registrar must give notice of an application under paragraph 1 to—

- (a) the proprietor of the estate to which the application relates,
- (b) the proprietor of any registered charge on the estate,

LIMITATION

(c) where the estate is leasehold, the proprietor of any superior registered estate,
(d) any person who is registered in accordance with rules as a person to be notified under this paragraph, and
(e) such other persons as rules may provide.

(2) Notice under this paragraph shall include notice of the effect of paragraph 4.

III LIM [52.3]

Paragraph 2(1)d The Law Commission (see Law Com 271 "Land Registration for the 21st Century – A Conveyancing Revolution") gave the examples of an equitable chargee or the beneficiary of a rentcharge as persons likely to fall into this category. Rule 194 of the Land Registration Rules (SI 2003/1417) specifies the procedure to be followed by those who can satisfy the registrar that they have "an interest in a registered estate in land or a registered rentcharge which would be prejudiced by the registration of any other person as proprietor".

III LIM [52.4]

Paragraph 2(1)e Similarly, the Charity Commission or a trustee in bankruptcy might be examples of bodies or persons falling within this category.

3 Treatment of application

(1) A person given notice under paragraph 2 may require that the application to which the notice relates be dealt with under paragraph 5.

(2) The right under this paragraph is exercisable by notice to the registrar given before the end of such period as rules may provide.

4 If an application under paragraph 1 is not required to be dealt with under paragraph 5, the applicant is entitled to be entered in the register as the new proprietor of the estate.

5 (1) If an application under paragraph 1 is required to be dealt with under this paragraph, the applicant is only entitled to be registered as the new proprietor of the estate if any of the following conditions is met.

(2) The first condition is that—
(a) it would be unconscionable because of an equity by estoppel for the registered proprietor to seek to dispossess the applicant, and
(b) the circumstances are such that the applicant ought to be registered as the proprietor.

(3) The second condition is that the applicant is for some other reason entitled to be registered as the proprietor of the estate.

(4) The third condition is that—
(a) the land to which the application relates is adjacent to land belonging to the applicant,
(b) the exact line of the boundary between the two has not been determined under rules under section 60,
(c) for at least ten years of the period of adverse possession ending on the date of the application, the applicant (or any predecessor in title) reasonably believed that the land to which the application relates belonged to him, and
(d) the estate to which the application relates was registered more than one year prior to the date of the application.

(5) In relation to an application under paragraph 1(2), this paragraph has effect as if the reference in sub-paragraph (4)(c) to the date of the application were to the day before the date of the applicant's eviction.

III LIM [52.4A]

Rule 189 of the Land Registration Rules (SI 2003/1417) provides that the period under s 3(2) is the period ending at 12 noon on the sixty-fifth business day after the date of issue of the notice.

In order to invoke the jurisdiction of an adjudicator the recipient of an adverse possession notice must indicate not only an objection to the registration but also a wish to apply for the issues to be dealt with under paragraph 5. A failure to tick the boxes is not necessarily fatal to the application but it cannot proceed unless the intention to invoke paragraph 5 is made clear: *Hopkins v Beacon* [2011] EWHC 2899 (Ch).

III LIM [52.5]

Squatter's proof of entitlement to registration Upon the service of a counter-notice, it is for the squatter to show that he fulfils one of the three prescribed conditions. If, as seems likely given that the service of a counter-notice involves an objection to the squatter's application, there is a dispute as to entitlement then this is to be resolved by the Adjudicator to the Land Registry (see ss 107–114 and Sch 9 to the Land Registration Act 2002). In order to defeat a claim to title to land by adverse possession on the basis of an interruption which stopped time running the paper title owner must show possession to the exclusion of the person claiming adverse possession: *Zarb v Parry* [2011] EWCA Civ 1306, [2012] 2 All ER 320, [2012] 1 WLR 1240.

Para 5(2) refers to the equitable doctrine of proprietary estoppel. Section 110(4) provides that where the Adjudicator is not satisfied that the equity established by the applicant justifies his registration as proprietor, the Adjudicator may nonetheless give effect to it in any way which would be available to the High Court in the exercise of its equitable jurisdiction. For a helpful discussion of the effect of this provision see Nield *Adverse possession and estoppel* 68 Conv 123.

III LIM [52.6]

Paragraph 5(3) The Law Commission gave two examples of the sorts of case which would fall under para 5(3) (see Law Com 271 "Land Registration for the 21st Century – A Conveyancing Revolution"):

(a) if the applicant's entitlement to the land arises under the will or in the intestacy of the deceased proprietor but no assent was executed in favour of the applicant;

(b) if the applicant contracted to buy the land and paid the purchase price but the legal estate was not transferred.

III LIM [52.7]

Paragraph 5(4) If the boundary has been determined under the rules made under s 60 then this will be shown on the register.

It is anticipated that para 5(4) will not be brought into force until one year after the rest of Schedule 6.

III LIM [52.8]

Paragraph 5(5) The period of adverse possession in such a case thus runs from the day before eviction rather than application.

6 Right to make further application for registration

(1) Where a person's application under paragraph 1 is rejected, he may make a further application to be registered as the proprietor of the estate if he is in adverse possession of the estate from the date of the application until the last day of the period of two years beginning with the date of its rejection.

(1A) Sub-paragraph (1) is subject to paragraph 16.

(2) However, a person may not make an application under this paragraph if—

(a) he is a defendant in proceedings which involve asserting a right to possession of the land,

(b) judgment for possession of the land has been given against him in the last two years, or

(c) he has been evicted from the land pursuant to a judgment for possession.

7 If a person makes an application under paragraph 6, he is entitled to be entered in the register as the new proprietor of the estate.

8 Restriction on applications

(1) No one may apply under this Schedule to be registered as the proprietor of an estate in land during, or before the end of twelve months after the end of, any

LIMITATION

period in which the existing registered proprietor is for the purposes of the Limitation (Enemies and War Prisoners) Act 1945 (8 & 9 Geo 6 c 16)—

(a) an enemy, or

(b) detained in enemy territory.

(2) No-one may apply under this Schedule to be registered as the proprietor of an estate in land during any period in which the existing registered proprietor is—

(a) unable because of mental disability to make decisions about issues of the kind to which such an application would give rise, or

(b) unable to communicate such decisions because of mental disability or physical impairment.

(3) For the purposes of sub-paragraph (2), "mental disability" means a disability or disorder of the mind or brain, whether permanent or temporary, which results in an impairment or disturbance of mental functioning.

(4) Where it appears to the registrar that sub-paragraph (1) or (2) applies in relation to an estate in land, he may include a note to that effect in the register.

III LIM [52.9]

Paragraph 8(2) Unlike s 28(1) of the Limitation Act 1980, which requires that the disability existed on accrual of the cause of action, para 8(2) of Sch 6 protects the proprietor where the disability exists at the date of application for registration. Paragraph 8(2)(b) protects those suffering from a relevant *physical* as well as mental disability.

9 Effect of registration

(1) Where a person is registered as the proprietor of an estate in land in pursuance of an application under this Schedule, the title by virtue of adverse possession which he had at the time of the application is extinguished.

(2) Subject to sub-paragraph (3), the registration of a person under this Schedule as the proprietor of an estate in land does not affect the priority of any interest affecting the estate.

(3) Subject to sub-paragraph (4), where a person is registered under this Schedule as the proprietor of an estate, the estate is vested in him free of any registered charge affecting the estate immediately before his registration.

(4) Sub-paragraph (3) does not apply where registration as proprietor is in pursuance of an application determined by reference to whether any of the conditions in paragraph 5 applies.

III LIM [52.10]

Paragraph 9(3) and (4) Where the chargee had the chance to object by counter-notice to the application but did not do so, the application will take the estate free of the charge.

10 Apportionment and discharge of charges

(1) Where—

(a) a registered estate continues to be subject to a charge notwithstanding the registration of a person under this Schedule as the proprietor, and

(b) the charge affects property other than the estate,

the proprietor of the estate may require the chargee to apportion the amount secured by the charge at that time between the estate and the other property on the basis of their respective values.

(2) The person requiring the apportionment is entitled to a discharge of his estate from the charge on payment of—

(a) the amount apportioned to the estate, and

(b) the costs incurred by the chargee as a result of the apportionment.

(3) On a discharge under this paragraph, the liability of the chargor to the chargee is reduced by the amount apportioned to the estate.

(4) Rules may make provision about apportionment under this paragraph, in particular, provision about—

(a) procedure,

(b) valuation,

(c) calculation of costs payable under sub-paragraph (2)(b), and
(d) payment of the costs of the chargor.

III LIM [52.11]

The effect of this paragraph is that the rule in *Caroll v Manek* (1999) 79 P & CR 173 (namely that the squatter must pay the whole amount due under the charge in order to redeem) will not apply to cases to which Schedule 6 applies.

11 Meaning of "adverse possession"

(1) A person is in adverse possession of an estate in land for the purposes of this Schedule if, but for section 96, a period of limitation under section 15 of the Limitation Act 1980 (c 58) would run in his favour in relation to the estate.

(2) A person is also to be regarded for those purposes as having been in adverse possession of an estate in land—

(a) where he is the successor in title to an estate in the land, during any period of adverse possession by a predecessor in title to that estate, or
(b) during any period of adverse possession by another person which comes between, and is continuous with, periods of adverse possession of his own.

(3) In determining whether for the purposes of this paragraph a period of limitation would run under section 15 of the Limitation Act 1980, there are to be disregarded—

(a) the commencement of any legal proceedings, and
(b) paragraph 6 of Schedule 1 to that Act.

III LIM [52.12]

The general effect of para 11(1) is that "adverse possession" under the Land Registration Act 2002 has the same meaning as it does under s 15 of the Limitation Act 1980: see paras **III LIM [20]** and **III LIM [42]**.

Para 11(2) provides for two situations in which a squatter may qualify without personally having been in possession for the whole of the ten-year period.

III LIM [52.13]

Paragraph 11(3)(a) In *Markfield Investments Ltd v Evans* [2001] 2 All ER 238, [2001] 1 WLR 1321, CA it was held that the issue of a claim does not stop time running except for the purpose of those proceedings. Paragraph 11(3)(a) disapplies this principle.

III LIM [52.14]

Paragraph 11(3)(b) Paragraph 6 of Schedule 1 relates to adverse possession of reversions.

12 Trusts

A person is not to be regarded as being in adverse possession of an estate for the purposes of this Schedule at any time when the estate is subject to a trust, unless the interest of each of the beneficiaries in the estate is an interest in possession.

III LIM [52.15]

Beneficiaries under trusts of land The effect of para 12 is that a squatter will not be in adverse possession of land held under a trust unless the last of any successive interests thereunder has fallen into possession.

13 Crown foreshore

(1) Where—

(a) a person is in adverse possession of an estate in land,
(b) the estate belongs to Her Majesty in right of the Crown or the Duchy of Lancaster or to the Duchy of Cornwall, and
(c) the land consists of foreshore,

paragraph 1(1) is to have effect as if the reference to ten years were to sixty years.

(2) For the purposes of sub-paragraph (1), land is to be treated as foreshore if it has been foreshore at any time in the previous ten years.

(3) In this paragraph, "foreshore" means the shore and bed of the sea and of any tidal water, below the line of the medium high tide between the spring and neap tides.

14 Rentcharges

Rules must make provision to apply the preceding provisions of this Schedule to registered rentcharges, subject to such modifications and exceptions as the rules may provide.

III LIM [52.16]

Special rules in respect of rentcharges Schedule 8 to the Land Registration Rules (SI 2003/1417) contains the modified version of Sch 6 to the Act which is applicable to rentcharges. See also rules 191–193.

The rules are necessary since para 1 only permits application for registration to be made in respect of estates in land. A rentcharge is not an estate in land.

15 Procedure

Rules may make provision about the procedure to be followed pursuant to an application under this Schedule.

III LIM [52.17]

See the Land Registration Rules (SI 2003/1417) and in particular rules 187–194.

16 Extension of time limits because of mediation in certain cross-border disputes

(1) In this paragraph—

(a) "Mediation Directive" means Directive 2008/52/EC of the European Parliament and of the Council of 21 May 2008 on certain aspects of mediation in civil and commercial matters,

(b) "mediation" has the meaning given by article 3(a) of the Mediation Directive,

(c) "mediator" has the meaning given by article 3(b) of the Mediation Directive, and

(d) "relevant dispute" means a dispute to which article 8(1) of the Mediation Directive applies (certain cross-border disputes).

(2) Sub-paragraph (3) applies where—

(a) a period of time is prescribed by paragraph 1(1), 1(2)(a) or 6(1) in relation to the whole or part of a relevant dispute,

(b) a mediation in relation to the relevant dispute starts before the period expires, and

(c) if not extended by this paragraph, the period would expire before the mediation ends or less than eight weeks after it ends.

(3) The period expires instead at the end of eight weeks after the mediation ends (subject to sub-paragraph (4)).

(4) If a period has been extended by this paragraph, sub-paragraphs (2) and (3) apply to the extended period as they apply to a period mentioned in sub-paragraph (2)(a).

(5) Where more than one period applies in relation to a relevant dispute, the extension by sub-paragraph (3) of one of those periods does not affect the others.

(6) For the purposes of this paragraph, a mediation starts on the date of the agreement to mediate that is entered into by the parties and the mediator.

(7) For the purposes of this paragraph, a mediation ends on date of the first of these to occur—

(a) the parties reach an agreement in resolution of the relevant dispute,

(b) a party completes the notification of the other parties that it has withdrawn from the mediation,

(c) a party to whom a qualifying request is made fails to give a response reaching the other parties within 14 days of the request,

(d) the parties, after being notified that the mediator's appointment has ended (by death, resignation or otherwise), fail to agree within 14 days to seek to appoint a replacement mediator,

(e) the mediation otherwise comes to an end pursuant to the terms of the agreement to mediate.

(8) For the purpose of sub-paragraph (7), a qualifying request is a request by a party that another (A) confirm to all parties that A is continuing with the mediation.

(9) In the case of any relevant dispute, references in this paragraph to a mediation are references to the mediation so far as it relates to that dispute, and references to a party are to be read accordingly.

MENTAL CAPACITY AND MENTAL HEALTH

TABLE OF CONTENTS

INTRODUCTION

III MEN [1]

Legislation in 2005 (Mental Capacity Act 2005) and in 2007 (Mental Health Act 2007) introduced radical changes in approach and practice in relation to mental health. With the creation of a new Court of Protection, and the separation of the registration and supervisory roles to a newly formed Office of Public Guardian, Parliament heralded a sea change with regard to the issue of mental capacity. The 2007 legislation revised and updated procedures with regard to mental health, but also introduced into the Court of Protection jurisdiction to deal with issues of deprivation of liberty. This latter jurisdiction with its important human rights concerns is developing rapidly as the nominated judges of the Court of Protection interpret and apply the Act having regard to the jurisprudence of the European Court of Human Rights.

The adjustments to the respective legislation and key features are dealt with at the commencement of each jurisdiction and are highlighted in the General Notes.

GENERAL NOTES ON MENTAL CAPACITY

III MEN [2]

Jurisdiction On 1 October 2007 the Mental Capacity Act 2005 came into force, and at that stage Part VII of the Mental Health Act 1983 was repealed. By virtue of s 45 of the Mental Capacity Act 2005 a new superior court of record was established, known as the Court of Protection, which could sit at any place in England and Wales on any day and at any time. Provision was made for the Lord Chancellor to appoint a central office and registry and by s 45(6) of the Mental Capacity Act 2005 the office of the Supreme Court (now the Senior Courts) called the Court of Protection ceased to exist. Pursuant to s 46 of the Mental Capacity Act 2005, the President of the Family Division has been nominated President of the Court of Protection, and only judges nominated by the President may exercise the jurisdiction of the court.

Introduced with the Mental Capacity Act 2005 were the original Court of Protection Rules 2007, SI 2007/1744, together with Practice Directions. However, they were replaced by the Court of Protection Rules 2017 (SI 2017/1035) and a whole new set of Practice Directions, which came into force on 1 December 2017 and which apply to all proceedings before the court, along with statutory in 'The Code of Practice'. Section 42(4) of the Mental Capacity Act 2005 imposes a duty on certain people to 'have regard to any relevant code' if acting in relation to a person who lacks capacity.

On 1 April 2009, the Mental Health Act 2007 introduced significant amendments to the Mental Capacity Act 2005 primarily relating to issues of deprivation of liberty. Amendments to the Court of Protection Rules 2007 led to a specific Practice Direction supplementing Part 10A of the Rules, setting out the procedure to be followed in deprivation of liberty applications, relating to Standard and Urgent authorisations. A supplement to the main Mental Capacity Act 2005 Code of Practice (Deprivation of Liberty Safeguards Code of Practice) was published, to which regard must similarly be made. On 17 November 2014 a further Practice Direction 10AA was made updating the supplemental Practice Direction and introducing a streamlined procedure relating to applications made under s 4A(3) and (4) of the Mental Capacity Act 2005, where authorisation is sought pursuant to s 16(2)(a) of the

MENTAL CAPACITY AND MENTAL HEALTH

Mental Capacity Act 2005 to sanction arrangements for where an individual who lacks capacity should live and where restrictions involve a deprivation of liberty. These are now all consolidated into Part 11 of the 2017 Rules and Practice Direction 11A.

The Mental Capacity Act 2005 also introduced a new regime for Lasting Powers of Attorney to replace Enduring Powers of Attorney, which had been made possible by the Enduring Powers of Attorney Act 1985. Schedules 4 and 5 to the Mental Capacity Act 2005, and regs 23 to 29 of the Lasting Powers of Attorney, Enduring Powers of Attorney and Public Guardian Regulations 2007, SI 2007/1253 now govern the practice regarding registration and challenging the validity of these instruments.

It is to be noted that the Mental Capacity Act 2005 enabled the Lord Chancellor to appoint a Public Guardian, and it falls as part of the function of the office of the Public Guardian to establish and maintain registers of enduring powers of attorney, lasting powers of attorney, orders appointing deputies and the supervision of deputies. By reg 43 of the Lasting Powers of Attorney, Enduring Powers of Attorney and Public Guardian Regulations 2007, the Public Guardian may make application to the Court of Protection in connection with those functions under the Mental Capacity Act 2005.

III MEN [3]

The general powers of the Court of Protection The court has in connection with its jurisdiction the same powers, rights, privileges and authority as the High Court. The powers of the court extend from the personal health and welfare of an individual who lacks mental capacity, to their property and affairs. The court may make declarations as to whether a person has or lacks capacity to make a decision or decisions on matters specified or described in the declaration, together with the lawfulness of any act done or yet to be done in relation to that person, including any omission or course of conduct. The court may make a decision or decisions on 'P's' behalf ('P' being the incapacitated person) in relation to any matter or matters concerning personal welfare or property and affairs including deciding whether it is in 'P's' best interests to appoint a deputy to make such decisions, and thereafter having conferred such powers, their subsequent variation, discharge or revocation of appointment. The court's jurisdiction extends to the determination of validity, meaning and effect of enduring or lasting powers of attorney, including the authorisation of certain actions of the attorneys, and their removal if so appropriate.

The court has jurisdiction over serious medical issues and the validity and applicability of 'Advance Decisions' to refuse treatment.

By virtue of s 4A of the Mental Capacity Act 2005, the Court of Protection has the power to authorise P's deprivation of liberty. The framework of the amendments made by the Mental Health Act 2007 also provide a procedure for appeals to be made to the Court of Protection against urgent and standard authorisations made by managing authorities of hospitals and registered care homes.

In the event of a breach of the Article 5 rights of 'P', the court may award damages.

III MEN [4]

The principles and best interests The Mental Capacity Act 2005 establishes that certain principles shall apply with the assumption that a person has capacity unless established that they lack capacity. Individuals are not to be treated as unable to make a decision unless all practicable steps have been taken to help that person to do so without success, nor merely because they make an unwise decision. Any act done or decision made under the Act for or on behalf of a person who lacks capacity must be done, or made, in that person's best interests and before the act is done, or the decision is made, regard must be had as to whether the purpose for which it is needed can be as effectively achieved in a way that is less restrictive of the person's rights and freedom of action.

For the purposes of the Act, a person lacks capacity in relation to a matter if at the material time he or she is unable to make a decision for themselves in relation to the matter because of an impairment of, or a disturbance in the functioning of, the mind or brain, irrespective of whether the impairment is permanent or temporary.

In determining what is in a person's best interests, the person making the determination must not make it merely on the basis of the person's age or appearance, or a condition of, or an aspect of his or her behaviour which might lead others to make unjustified assumptions about what might be in that person's best interests. The person making the determination is required to consider all the relevant circumstances and in particular take certain steps pursuant to s 4(3)–(7) of the Mental Capacity Act 2005, where relevant circumstances are those of which the person making the determination is aware and which it would be reasonable to regard as relevant.

III MEN [5]

Procedures Sections 9–14 of the Mental Capacity Act 2005 establish the nature of lasting powers of attorney, the appointment of donees, restrictions, scope of authority including gifts, revocation and certain statutory protections for donees. Schedule 1 of the Mental Capacity Act 2005 Parts 1–4 set out the requirements as to the instrument, its registration, cancellation of registration and notification of severance and the recording of alterations to registered powers. Part 2 of the Lasting Powers of Attorney, Enduring Powers of Attorney and Public Guardian Regulations 2007, SI 2007/1253 applies to the procedures for registering lasting powers of attorney, the giving of notice of application to register, and the giving of notice of any objection to registration to the Public Guardian. Regulation 15 deals with any objection to the registration of an instrument as a lasting power of attorney made to the Court of Protection, with reg 15(2) setting out the grounds for such application. The powers of the Court of Protection in relation to both validity and operation of lasting powers of attorney are provided for by ss 22–23 of the Mental Capacity Act 2005.

By s 66 and Sch 7 of the Mental Capacity Act 2005, the Enduring Powers of Attorney Act 1985 was repealed, and Schedule 4 of the Mental Capacity Act 2005 has effect in place of the 1985 Act in relation to those enduring powers of attorney created before the commencement of the Mental Capacity Act 2005. Part 3 of the Lasting Powers of Attorney, Enduring Powers of Attorney and Public Guardian Regulations 2007, SI 2007/1253 applies to notices of intention to apply for registration, the registration and objection to the registration of such instruments.

Parts 6 and 7 of the Court of Protection Rules 2017, SI 2017/1035 encompass the procedures for service and for notifying 'P' (the person lacking capacity) of applications made to the court, and Part 8 deals with Permission. Parts 9 and 10 relate to the starting of proceedings and applications within proceedings. Part 4 and Practice Direction 4A provides important procedural guidance for preparation for hearings before the court, including the imposition of reporting restrictions. Part 19 sets out the distinct rules with regards to costs, which apply to Court of Protection applications, with Practice Directions making provision for fixed costs in certain circumstances. Part 20 deals with Appeals from decisions of the Court, but regard should also be made to the ability to apply for reconsideration of court orders pursuant to r 13.4 of the Court of Protection Rules 2017. Transitory and transitional provisions are set out at Part 24. Throughout, the rules are supplemented by Practice Directions.

There exist additionally two distinct separate procedures relating to matters concerning deprivation of liberty.

The first applies to the court's oversight of the statutory procedure, applying to those over 18 years living within hospitals and care homes. Distinct special Deprivation of Liberty (DoL) Court forms apply to these applications made under s 21A of the Mental Capacity Act 2005. The procedure relates to a standard or urgent authorisation under Schedule A1 of the Mental Capacity Act 2005 and where issues arise concerning depriving a person of his or her liberty; or the process connected with or consequent upon such application. Part 11 of the Rules and Part 1 of Practice Direction 11A must be followed in respect of those applications.

There is also a streamlined procedure relating solely to applications made under section 4A(3) and (4) of the Mental Capacity Act 2005, where authorisation is sought pursuant to section 16(2)(a) of the Mental Capacity Act 2005 was introduced to authorise arrangements as to where an individual lacking capacity should live and where restrictions involve a deprivation of liberty. This is dealt with in Part 2 of Practice Direction 11A. A stand-alone application form (COPDOL10) is mandatory for such an application and certain of the Rules and procedures relating to permission, service and notification have been modified.

Rule 1.2 of the Court of Protection Rules 2017 provides that in each case the court must consider having regard to certain criteria (r 1.2(1)(a)–(d)) whether it should direct that 'P' should be joined as a party (r 1.2(2)(a)) whether 'P's' participation should be secured by the appointment of an accredited legal representative (r 1.2(2)(b)), whether 'P's' participation should be secured by appointment of a representative whose function shall be to provide the court with information relating to section 4(6) matters (r 1.2(2)(c)) whether P should have the opportunity to address (directly or indirectly) the judge (r 1.2(2)(d)) or whether 'P's' interests and position can be properly secured without such direction (r 1.2(2)(e)). The appointment of litigation friends, accredited legal representatives and representatives under r 1.2(2)(c) are dealt with in Part 17 of the Court of Protection Rules 2017 and Practice Directions 17A and 17B and see also Practice Direction 1A (see **III MEN [498]** and **III MEN [680]** et seq).

In 2016, two 'pilot' schemes were introduced. The purpose of the Transparency Pilot was to enable the public to attend Court of Protection hearings, whilst not compromising the privacy of the parties concerned. This is now enshrined in Practice Direction 4C. Additionally, practitioners should note the changes being introduced into the practice and procedure of the Court of Protection during 2016 by way of Pilot Schemes. The Court in pursuing a policy of regionalisation and transparency utilises nominated judges sitting throughout England and Wales by referring case to the regional hubs, and introduced new Case Management Procedures to enable more focused hearings. On 29 January 2016 Practice Direction – Transparency Pilot was commenced. This Direction relates to those matters described in para 1.3 of the Practice Direction and requires the Court to sit in public subject to reporting restrictions leading to orders requiring confidentiality and anonymity (see **III MEN [6]**). In such cases the rule which will apply to 'attended hearings' defined by para 2.2 will be for a public hearing. The court will retain discretion to exclude the public from all or part of a hearing, but must give reasons for so doing. The Transparency Pilot has been extended until 31 August 2017.

The Case Management Pilot was introduced to tackle the perceived delay and cost of proceedings, particularly in the welfare jurisdiction: see *Re A and B (Court of Protection: Delay and Costs)* [2014] EWCOP 48 (Mr Justice Peter Jackson). The pilot scheme, applying to all proceedings which were started on or after 1 September 2016 operated to create pathways for the management of welfare and property and affairs matters and. The Case Management Pilot is now subsumed into the rules. The pathways are now part of Practice Direction 3B.

The Case Management Pilot further introduced amendments to the Rules relating to expert evidence now enshrined in Part 15 and Practice Direction 15 and Section 49 Reports in rr 14.24–14.25 and Practice Direction 14E. Practice Direction 14E revises the structure of such reports and as to the steps of preparing to seek such a report, commissioning the report and the content of the report. Practice Direction 14E includes a revised draft order as an Annex.

The role of the Official Solicitor in proceedings before the Court of Protection is often pivotal, and because of the demands upon his office, the President of the Court of Protection has issued guidance in respect of the role of the Official Solicitor in particular relating to welfare cases, including medical cases. See: *Practice Guidance: Official Solicitor acting as Guardian ad Litem or Litigation Friend* [2011] 1 FLR 944 issued in December 2010. The Guidance is a strong reminder to practitioners that, before agreeing to act for a protected person, the Official Solicitor will need to be satisfied (a) that there is satisfactory evidence of incapacity (b) that there is security for the costs of legal representation and (c) that there is no other person who is suitable and willing to act as litigation friend. The decision of *AB (by his litigation friend NW) v A local authority* [2011] EWHC 3151 (COP), [2011] NLJR 1744 addressed the use of the Relevant Person's Representative as Litigation Friend clarified further in *RD (Duties and Powers of Relevant Person's Representatives and Section 39D* [2016] EWCOP 49 in which Baker J provides clear guidance on the distinct roles of 'RPR's' and IMCA's appointed under section 39D. The decision in *B v B* [2010] EWHC 543 (Fam) confirms the approach of authorising costs of the Official Solicitor on an indemnity basis.

Practitioners intending to issue cases which might involve serious medical issues or welfare cases should note carefully the approach adopted by the Official Solicitor in accepting cases and will need to ensure that the maximum relevant information is available at the earliest stage. As to the recoverability by the Official Solicitor of one half of his costs, see *The NHS Trust v D (by his litigation friend, the Official Solicitor)* [2012] EWHC 886 (COP), [2012] NLJR 1421 (**III MEN [707.1]**) and further the judgment of Keehan J in *NHS Trust and Others (Rev1)* [2014] EWCOP 30 where in a comprehensive Annex he set out guidance for processing applications where hospitals are planning the arrangements to support the labour of a pregnant individual who may be subject to both Mental Health Act 1983 and Mental Capacity Act 2005 jurisdictions.

III MEN [6]

Jurisdiction to restrict publication Proceedings in the Court of Protection as a general rule are to be held in private in accordance with r 4.1 of the Court of Protection Rules 2017, and Practice Direction 4A and 4C relating to the Court of Protection Reporting Restrictions. However proceedings may be held in public if 'good reason' is established (r 4.4(a)). The existence of good reason does not automatically lift the requirement of privacy, but Article 8 (respect for family and private life) and Article 10 (freedom of expression) are then engaged and a balance must be struck: *Independent News and Media Ltd v A* (2009) Times, 17 November, in which Hedley J decided, on balance that the media should be allowed to attend on the grounds that (1) issues concerning the particular individual were already in the public domain, (2) the court retained power to preserve privacy while addressing the issues, and (3) it was in the public interest that the general public should understand the jurisdiction and how it was exercised in such cases.

The Court of Appeal upheld the decision in the *Independent News and Media Ltd v A* [2010] EWCA Civ 343, [2010] 3 All ER 32, [2010] 2 FCR 187, differing only as to the point when Article 10 was engaged, which the Court of Appeal decided was as soon as the application under r 93(1)(a) was made.

Even if held in private, the court may authorise the publication of such information relating to the proceedings as it may specify, or the text or a summary of the whole or part of a judgment or order made by the court, including removing the anonymity of any party, *Hillingdon London Borough Council v Neary* [2011] EWHC 413 (COP), [2011] Fam Law 476, [2011] NLJR 404. In *Aidiniantz v Aidiniantz* [2015] EWCOP 65, 165 NLJ 7673, [2015] All ER (D) 103 (Oct) the court removed the anonymity of parties where it was concluded that the parties had engaged in acrimonious litigation and that their conduct was such that it was not in the public interest to suppress the relevant information.

In *W (by her Litigation Friend, B) v M (An Adult Patient, by her Litigation Friend, The Official Solicitor), S, A NHS Primary Care Trust, Times Newspapers Limited* [2011] EWHC 1197 (COP), Mr Justice Baker with the approval of the President set out guidelines for the structure of Reporting Restriction Orders and other injunctions arising from the exercise of the Court of Protection's jurisdiction, this procedure being examined and applied in *Re P* [2015] EWCOP 15, [2015] All ER (D) 196 (Mar) where Newton J noted the importance of procedural fairness and the importance of openness in the process of the court to ensure its integrity

The issue of publicity and committal proceedings has now been addressed and clear mandatory guidance provided which apply to the Court of Protection. The procedure for all committal proceedings must now follow not only the relevant rules but also the Practice Direction: Committal for Contempt of Court – Open Court issued by the Lord Chief Justice on 26 March 2015 and the Practice Guidance: Committal for Contempt of Court – Open Court dated 24 June 2015. This Practice Direction and Guidance supersede all previous Practice Directions and Guidance. The Practice Direction addresses issues of public and private hearings, the engagement of the Press and the issue of judgments. In a clear indication of the importance of Open Justice strict procedures are applied for the publicity of the hearing, the notification of press, the publication of the outcome and the limiting of matters in private. The Guidance addresses questions which arose surrounding press notification, and judgments. See Court of Protection Rules 2017, Part 21 and Practice Direction 21A at **III MEN [734]** et seq and see also CPR 81.28.

In *Re V (Out of Hours: Reporting Order)* [2015] EWCOP 83 the court dealing with an out of hours request to continue anonymity of 'P' by extending a Reporting Restriction Order following her death followed the judgment of Peter Jackson J in *The Press Association v Newcastle Upon Tyne Hospitals Foundation Trust* [2014] EWCOP 6 in determining that the court had such jurisdiction and in particular that it was appropriate to so grant pending a full determination at a fully constituted hearing. In *V v Associated Newspapers Ltd* [2016] EWCOP 21 Mr Justice Charles addressed the issue of the jurisdiction of the Court of Protection to rule and order following 'P's' death in extending a reporting restrictions order, finding he that considered that the Court had such jurisdiction. And in *M v Press Association* [2016] EWCOP 34 and *University College London Hospitals NHS Foundation Trust* [2016] EWCOP 28 both Hayden J and Peter Jackson J applied the principles set down by Charles J in addressing similar such orders. However clear guidance was given that each case is determined upon the merits and circumstances of the individual, and a warning given against transporting comments from one case to another.

In *Practice Guidance (Transparency in the Court of Protection)* [2014] EWCOP B2 the President set out requirements for the publication of judgments of the Court of Protection. A Pilot Scheme was introduced on 29 January 2016 and now extended until 31 August 2017, and in so far as the Pilot affects a case, the rule will be for a public hearing subject to a restrictive order, with the Court retaining power to exclude the public for all or part of the proceedings subject to providing reasons.

See also s 12(1)(b) of the Administration of Justice Act 1960, at **III COT [8]**.

III MEN [7]

Declarations regarding medical treatment Section 5 of the Mental Capacity Act 2005 makes provision whereby carers, and health and social care professionals are permitted to carry out certain acts in connection with the personal care, health care and treatment of a person notwithstanding that person lacking capacity to consent to the act or acts. The Code of Practice at para 6.5 identifies a range of actions which might be covered by s 5 of the 2005 Act. However paragraph 6.18 of the Code recognises that some treatment and some decisions are so serious that there must be referral to the court to authorise the treatment and make such decisions. It had been accepted that where a person is in a vegetative state (or persistent vegetative state – PVS) an application has to be made to the Court in order to authorise the withdrawal of treatment (usually in the form of clinically assisted nutrition and hydration ('CANH')) (see the previous Practice Direction 9E). However, this is now in doubt. Following comments by Peter Jackson J in *M (by her litigation friend, B) v A Hospital* [2017] EWCOP 19, [2018] 1 WLR 465, [2017] Fam Law 1296 doubting the need for the order of the Court in such circumstances, an application was made to the High Court for a declaration to that effect. In *NHS Trust v Mr Y (by his litigation friend, the Official Solicitor) and Mrs Y* [2017] EWHC 2866, O'Farrell J declared there was no requirement for an order of the Court where there was agreement between those who made the decision-clinicians/carers and family members. The Supreme Court has now upheld the outcome of the High Court. In *An NHS Trust v Y* [2018] UKSC 46 the Court decided there was no common law requirement for an application to be made in every case where it was proposed CANH was to be withdrawn. Adequate protections were given by the MCA, the Code of Practice and the relevant GMC Guidance. Provided there was agreement between the treating doctors and P's family, and the MCA was followed, there was no need (and nothing) for the Court to adjudicate. However, an application was inevitable where there was disagreement. See also

MENTAL CAPACITY AND MENTAL HEALTH

University College London Hospitals NHS Foundation Trust v KG [2018] EWCOP 29 which advocates a cautious approach when deciding whether to make an application to the Court, albeit in this case where experimental treatment was proposed.

The authority of the Court of Protection is confirmed by s 15 of the Mental Capacity Act 2005, to make declarations as to the lawfulness of treatment of an incapacitated adult. In *DH NHS Foundation Trust v PS* [2010] EWHC 1217 (Fam) the President authorised treatment for cancer to an individual lacking capacity, notwithstanding that individual's phobia of needles and reluctance for such treatment, in finding that it was in P's best interests to be sedated and to undergo the operation, the President further considered that any post-operative detention in hospital was for the best interests of P and that it was not necessary to invoke the deprivation of liberty provisions of Schedule A1 of the 2005 Act. This decision was followed in *An NHS trust v K (by her litigation friend, the Official Solicitor)* [2012] EWHC 2922 (COP), [2012] All ER (D) 129 (Oct), where Holman J relying upon the earlier authority approved a plan which included provision for covert sedation to be given, to facilitate discussion with P as to the plans for surgery, and prior to anaesthesia.

Except in accordance with circumstances set out in the Mental Capacity Act 2005 and the Court of Protection Rules 2017, permission will be required to make an application in respect of welfare and health matters. In addition, where the application relates to serious medical treatment then Practice Direction 10B (Urgent and Interim Applications) may have to be addressed. If the Official Solicitor is likely to be engaged, then see **III MEN [5]** above. See also Part 3 and Practice Direction 3A. In particular, para 2(a) viz 'where an application is made to the court in relation to an ethical dilemma in an untested area, the proceedings must be conducted by a Tier 3 judge'. Where a declaration of incompatibility is sought, the President, Chancellor or a High Court Judge (see para (2)(b)).

This is now subject to Practice Direction 4C (supplementing r 4.3) which varies the rules for a public hearing subject to a restrictive order (see **III MEN [525]**).

Issues which previously fell within the inherent jurisdiction of the High Court and now fall to be dealt with by the Court of Protection would be such as in the case of sterilisation: *Re F (mental patient: sterilisation)* [1990] 2 AC 1, sub nom *F v West Berkshire Health Authority (Mental Health Act Commission intervening)* [1989] 2 All ER 545, HL (now see *A Local Authority v K (by the Official Solicitor)* [2013] EWHC 242 (COP), 130 BMLR 195), or where the patient is in a persistent vegetative state: *Airedale National Health Service Trust v Bland* [1993] 1 All ER 821, HL. In *W Healthcare NHS Trust v KH* [2004] EWCA Civ 1324, [2005] All ER (D) 94 (Jan), (2004) Times, 9 December, the Court of Appeal upheld the decision at first instance that nutrition should not be withdrawn from a severely disabled patient who was not in a permanent vegetative state, despite the unanimous view of the family that this should happen. In *Re S (adult patient: sterilisation)* [2001] Fam 15, sub nom *Re SL (adult patient) (medical treatment)* [2000] 3 WLR 1288, CA it was held that sterilisation requiring invasive surgery was not in the best interests of the patient in question. It was further held that, for the purposes of the declaration of lawfulness, the choice between different options for treatment should be made by the court, not the doctors and the principle in *Bolam v Friern Hospital Management Committee* [1957] 2 All ER 118, [1957] 1 WLR 582, did not apply, except to limit the kinds of treatment that may be regarded as in the best interests of the patient: *Simms v Simms* [2002] EWHC 2734 (Fam), [2003] Fam 83, [2003] 1 All ER 669. In *A NHS Trust v DE (appearing by his litigation friend the Official Solicitor)* [2013] EWHC 2562 (Fam), [2013] 3 FCR 343, 133 BMLR 123, the court addressed the issue of authorising and declaring that it was in P's best interests to undergo a vasectomy, and lawful for the appropriate medical steps to be undertaken.

Although pre the commencement of the Mental Capacity Act 2005, it is prudent to have regard to the *Practice Note (Official Solicitor: Declaratory Proceedings: Medical and Welfare Decisions for Adults Who Lack capacity)* [2006] 2 FLR 373, and where there may be an issue concerning whether an individual has or has not capacity to make a decision, there may be occasions when the nominated judge may sit such that he or she may exercise both inherent jurisdiction of the Family Division, and that under the Mental Capacity Act 2005 (see *A Local Authority v DL (vulnerable adults: non molestation injunction)* [2010] EWHC 2675 (Fam), [2011] Fam 189, [2011] 3 WLR 445).

Useful examples of the Court of Protection addressing these issues, and applying the statutory principles of the Act and the Code can be seen at *W (by her Litigation Friend B) and M (by her Litigation Friend the Official Solicitor) v S and A NHS Primary Care Trust* [2011] EWHC 2433 (Fam), where Baker J declined to extend the approach adopted in *Bland* (*Airedale NHS Trust v Bland* [1993] AC 789, [1993] 1 All ER 821, HL) to a case involving an individual in a minimally conscious state, and drew attention to the provisions of paragraphs 5.31 and 5.38 of the Code of Practice. Again in *Re D (withdrawal of treatment)* [2012] EWHC 885 (COP), [2012] All ER (D) 163 (Oct), and in *A Local Authority v E (by her Litigation Friend, the Official Solicitor)* [2012] EWHC 1639 (COP), [2012] 2 FCR 523, 127 BMLR 133 Peter Jackson J approached the issues of withdrawal of life sustaining treatment and expressions of wishes of P which fell short of Advance Directives under s 25 of the Mental Capacity Act 2005. In *Gloucestershire Clinical Commissioning Group v AB (by his litigation friend the Official Solicitor, and CD* [2014] (unreported) Baker J addressed the assessment procedure for those in a vegetative state and the assessment tool 'Sensory Modality Assessment and Rehabilitation Technique' and accepted that assessment in finding under ss 2 and 3 of the Act that P lacked capacity to make a decision relating to his continued receipt of artificial nutrition and hydration. See also *Hertfordshire County Council v AB* [2018] EWHC 3103 (Fam), where Mrs Justice Gwynneth Knowles used the inherent jurisdiction to authorise the continued deprivation of liberty of a conditionally discharged patient whose status was unlawful following *Secretary of State for Justice v MM* [2017] EWCA Civ 194 (upheld by the Supreme Court at [2018] UKSC 60).

In the event that proceedings are required beyond the authority of the Court of Protection, then the following direction of the President of the Family Division applies, namely that proceedings for a declaration should be heard in the Family Division and permanent vegetative state cases should be issued in the Principal Registry: *Practice Direction (Declaratory Proceedings: Incapacitated Adults)* [2002] 1 WLR 325, with the proceedings being commenced under the alternative procedure for claims in Part 8 even where there is a substantial dispute of fact: *M v B* [2005] EWHC 1681 (Fam), Sumner J.

Note, however, that if the task of the court is to review the decision of a public authority taken in the exercise of some statutory power, the proceedings should be by application for judicial review under **CPR 54**: *A (A Patient) v A Health Authority* (2002) Times, 12 March. See Article 5 of the Convention on Human Rights and *R (on the application of H) v Secretary of State for Health* [2004] EWCA Civ 1609, (2004) Times, 8 December.

In relation to treatment of a seriously disabled child, where hospital doctors believed that the best interests of the child required treatment to which the child's mother is resolutely opposed their administration of the treatment without obtaining a court order has been held to contravene the rights of the child to respect for his private life: *Glass v United Kingdom (Application 61827/00)* [2004] 1 FCR 553, [2004] 1 FLR 1019, ECtHR.

In *A Local Authority v FG and Others (No 1)* [2011] EWHC 3932 (COP), Hedley J reminded parties and advisers that it was the role of the court to approach issues of welfare and capacity by ascertaining the facts, applying the statutory principles and reaching a conclusion, recognising that each case should be decided upon its own facts. He found it inappropriate therefore for there to be cited a multiplicity of first instance judgments.

Where there is doubt whether treatment under s 63 of the Mental Health Act 1983 would be within the definition of 'medical treatment' in s 145 of that Act, the appropriate course is to apply to the court for the treatment to be approved: *A NHS Trust v Dr A* [2013] EWHC 2442 (COP), [2013] All ER (D) 07 (Sep).

III MEN [8]

Interim powers of the Court, and the call for reports The interim jurisdiction of the court is set out at s 48 of the Mental Capacity Act 2005, and the engagement of the court's powers arises, if there is sufficient evidence to justify a reasonable belief that 'P' may lack capacity (see *Re F* [2009] EWHC B30 (Fam), HHJ Marshall QC). But see *Wandsworth London Borough Council v AMcC* [2017] EWHC 2435 (Fam) Hayden J, where the Court emphasised the need for cogent evidence to support the interim finding (see para [65]). Of note is the caution against lengthy fact finding interim hearings given by Cobb J in *LBX v TT and Others* [2014] EWCOP 24.

In furtherance of its role, the Court, whose procedure is inquisitorial as opposed to adversarial, may by applying s 49 of the Mental Capacity Act 2005, call for reports from the Public Guardian, a Court of Protection Visitor, a Local Authority or NHS body. The Court of Protection Visitors' panel is maintained by the Public Guardian, and by s 61 of the Mental Capacity Act 2005, such a visitor can be either a 'General Visitor', or a 'Special Visitor'. Circumstance may arise when the Court will invite the Official Solicitor to represent the interests of the incapacitated person; however awareness should be made of the President's guidance on the engagement of the Official Solicitor (*President's Guidance* December 2010) see **III MEN [5]**. See also Practice Directions 14E – Section 49 Reports

III MEN [9]

Deprivation of Liberty The Mental Capacity Act 2005, s 4A(5) and Schedule A1, following the amendments pursuant to the Mental Health Act 2007, now provides a statutory framework for the authorisation, and consideration of issues relating to the deprivation of liberty of individuals who through lack of mental capacity cannot consent to such deprivation when it is in their best interests for their care or treatment.

The jurisdiction is distinct and separate to that which continues to apply under the Mental Health Act 1983 as amended, primarily relating to medical treatment for those suffering from mental disorder, and their accommodation and care within a hospital environment. However in *Munjaz v United Kingdom* [2012] ECHR 1704 it was held that notwithstanding detention under Mental Health Act 1983, the principles of deprivation of liberty were still applicable and it would be dependent on the specific circumstances as to whether the restrictions amounted to such a deprivation.

The amendments to the legislation stemmed from a decision of the European Court of Human Rights in *HL v United Kingdom (Application 45508/99)* (2004) 40 EHRR 761, (2005) 81 BMLR 131 which reversed a decision of the House of Lords which had relied upon the common law doctrine of necessity as a justification, where appropriate, for restraining or detaining an incapacitated person for his or her own interest.

The court must now consider whether an individual lacking capacity has been, or may be deprived of their liberty contrary to Article 5(1) of the European Convention of Human Rights, and whether the detention was arbitrary and not in accordance with a procedure prescribed by law. Further the court will review whether the procedures established, satisfy Article 5(4) enabling a prompt review of such deprivation.

Regard should be made at all stages to the guidance in the Deprivation of Liberty Safeguards Code of Practice that came into effect on 1 April 2009. Further in *P v M* [2011] COPLR Con Vol 947 Hedley J drew attention that when dealing with individuals lacking capacity, it was important for the court to balance the competing emotional and relational factors with the cautious protective approach of institutions.

Case law that has arisen since the commencement of the Court's powers on 1st April 2009, has concentrated on two strands:

First, the powers of the court derived from the Mental Capacity Act 2005 with regard to standard and urgent authorisations, and the interplay between mental capacity and mental health legislation (see *W Primary Care Trust v TB* [2009] EWHC 1737 (Fam), [2010] 2 All ER 331, [2010] 1 WLR 2662 and *A County Council v MB (by Official Solicitor as her Litigation Friend), JB, and A Residential Home* [2010] EWHC 2508 (COP)).

Second, what constitutes 'deprivation of liberty' and the procedures to be adopted for control and review? In a landmark judgment the Supreme Court provided guidance on the proper approach to determining the issue of care arrangements which fell outside the standard and urgent authorisation procedure and applied only to registered care homes and hospitals. In the matter of *P (by his litigation friend the Official Solicitor) v Cheshire West and Chester Council and another; P and Q (by their litigation friend the Official Solicitor) v Surrey County Council* [2014] UKSC 19 Baroness Hale provided further guidance on issues that should be considered in determining whether in fact deprivation of liberty was occurring in any factual circumstance. Referring to European case law at paragraph 37 of her judgment she identified three common grounds, namely (i) the objective component of confinement in a particular restricted place for a not negligible length of time; (ii) the subjective component of lack of valid consent; and (iii) the attribution of responsibility.

In direct response to that judgment following guidance given by the President in two judgments *Re X (Deprivation of Liberty)* [2014] EWCOP 25, 141 BMLR 212, and *Re X (Deprivation of Liberty (No 2)* [2014] EWCOP 37, 141 BMLR 225 a streamlined procedure was introduced on 17 November 2014 pursuant to a further Practice Direction 10AA (now Practice Direction 11A to the 2017 Rules) relating to applications made under s 4A(3) and (4) of the Mental Capacity Act 2005, where authorisation is sought pursuant to s 16(2)(a) of the Mental Capacity Act 2005 to sanction arrangements for where an individual who lacks capacity should live and where restrictions involve a deprivation of liberty (see **III MEN [619]**). In *Re X (Court of Protection Practice)* [2015] EWCA Civ 599, 165 NLJ 7659, [2015] All ER (D) 188 (Jun) the Court of Appeal in finding no jurisdiction to consider an appeal as against the procedural directions of the President in obiter were critical of the streamlined process and the absence of 'P' being a party to such applications, however in *Re NRA* [2015] EWCOP 59, 165 NLJ 7671, [2015] All ER (D) 122 (Sep) Charles J as Vice President of the Court of Protection in addressing the obiter of the Court of Appeal gave judgment distinguishing the procedure of the Court of Protection and re-affirming the streamlined procedure subject to modification.

In *Secretary for State for Justice v Staffordshire County Council* [2016] EWCA Civ 1317 the Court of Appeal upholding a decision of the Vice President of the Court of Protection found that where 'P' lacked capacity to conduct proceedings, make decisions as to where he should live and what care and treatment he needed, and where restrictions were in place pursuant to a care plan which constituted a deprivation of liberty and for the purposes of the Act, then notwithstanding that such care and support was given entirely by private sector providers in private accommodation an application to the Court of Protection for a welfare order was required that it was in 'P's' best interests so to live within his domestic property and to receive such care and support pursuant to his Care Plan and to the extent that those arrangements were a deprivation of liberty to make a declaration that such deprivation of his liberty was in his best interests. The order made provision for a system of review by the court.

See also *R (on the application of Ferreira) v Senior Coroner for Inner South London & Kings College Hospital* [2017] EWCA Civ 31 where P was found not to have been deprived of her liberty – in a ICU setting – at the time of her death because 'she was being treated for a physical illness and her treatment was that which it appeared to all intents would have been administered to a person who did not have her mental impairment' (per Arden LJ at [10]).

A high security hospital's policy on secluding patients in certain circumstances is not in breach of the Convention so long as the policy aims to strike an acceptable balance between (a) recognising the status of mental patients as particularly vulnerable detainees and (b) deferring to the advice of expert mental health practitioners: *R (on the application of Munjaz) v Mersey Care NHS Trust* [2005] UKHL 58, [2006] 2 AC 148, [2006] 4 All ER 736; *Munjaz v United Kingdom (Application No 2913/06)* [2012] ECHR 1704, (2012) Times, 09 October.

III MEN [10]

Declarations regarding accommodation and care Prior to the commencement of the Mental Capacity Act 2005, the Court of Appeal exercising the High Court's inherent jurisdiction, determined in *Re F (Adult Patient)* [2000] 3 FCR 30, [2000] 2 FLR 512, CA, that it had power to grant declarations, as a matter of necessity, as to how an incapacitated adult should be accommodated and cared for. Sedley LJ added that 'the court had jurisdiction to declare what was in the patient's best interests as regards care and restrictions necessary for the patient's safety and that this was not in conflict with Convention rights'. However now see ss 2–6 of the Mental Capacity Act 2005, and any such application should be commenced under the Act, having regard to both s 16 and s 17 of the Mental Capacity Act 2005, and the deprivation of liberty provisions. A significant decision of the Supreme Court in the matter of *P (by his litigation friend the Official Solicitor) v Cheshire West and Chester Council and another; P and Q (by their litigation friend the Official Solicitor) v Surrey County Council* [2014] UKSC 19 addressed the test to be adopted in such matters. Baroness Hale held that 'it was axiomatic that people with disabilities, both mental and physical, have the same human rights as the rest of the human race . . . what it means to be deprived of liberty must be the same for everyone, whether or not they have physical or mental disabilities'. In addressing the question as to whether there is an 'acid test' for deprivation of liberty, her Ladyship stated' that whilst no guidance could be given, 'the answer . . . lies in those features which have consistently been regarded as "key" in the jurisprudence which started with *HL v United Kingdom* 40 EHRR 761 that the person concerned "was under continuous supervision and control and was not free to leave"'. Further her Ladyship found that certain factors were not relevant to any determination of deprivation of liberty, namely (i) whether a person was compliant or lacked objection, (ii) the relative normality of the placement (whatever the comparison made), and (iii) the reason or purpose behind a particular placement'.

The President through directions given in a number of conjoined cases has provided guidance for determining specific applications addressing living arrangements and potential situations of deprivation of liberty following the Supreme Court's judgment. In *Re X (Deprivation of Liberty)* [2014] EWCOP 25, 141 BMLR 212, and *Re X (Deprivation of Liberty (No 2)* [2014] EWCOP 37, 141 BMLR 225 the President addressed and highlighted the appropriate approach to be adopted leading to a streamlined procedure under Practice Direction 10AA (now Practice Direction 11A to the 2017 Rules). Such applications will initially be processed separate from other welfare issues and will focus upon the Care Plan (now described as a 'Support Plan') of an individual who lacks capacity and in so far as their living arrangement incorporates a deprivation of liberty, the authorisation of that Plan (see **III MEN [619]**).

The consideration of issues of deprivation of liberty and Article 5 will be a feature of the development of this jurisprudence and practitioners will need to be aware of the close proximity of decisions for vulnerable adults and children. The decision of the Court of Appeal in *RK (by her Litigation Friend, the Official Solicitor) v BCC* [2011] EWCA Civ 1305, [2011] All ER (D) 28 (Dec) demonstrates the contrasting approach of the court when considering the accommodation of a child under s 20 of the Children Act 1989 and the issue of deprivation of liberty under Article 5 ECHR. But this decision which predates the Supreme Court in *P (by his litigation friend the Official Solicitor) v Cheshire West and Chester Council and another; P and Q (by their litigation friend the Official Solicitor) v Surrey County Council* [2014] UKSC 19 will now have to be applied in the context and in the light of that decision. (See the joint guidance of 12 February 2014 given by the President and the National Director, Social Care, Ofsted 'Deprivation of Liberty – Guidance for providers of children's homes and residential special schools', now the subject of a note by the President not to be followed) and the decisions of Holman J in *Liverpool City Council v SG (by her litigation friends and parents, J, S and G)* [2014] EWCOP 10, [2014] PTSR D20, [2014] All ER (D) 32 (Jul) and *Barnsley Metropolitan Borough Council v GS* [2014] EWCOP 46, [2014] All ER (D) 214 (Nov) where he concluded the court did have jurisdiction to determine the issue of deprivation of liberty in respect of an adult residing within a children's home. In *D (A Child; deprivation of liberty)* [2015] EWHC 922 Keehan J considered the care arrangements of a 15 year old and in declaring that such arrangements amounted to a deprivation of liberty found that the parents within the parameters of their parental responsibility could consent to such arrangements, such decision falling within the 'zone of parental responsibility'. Returning to this issue in *Birmingham City Council v D* [2016] EWCOP 8 Keehan J considered the position of 16 and 17 year olds and found that (i) a parent could not consent to the confinement of a child who has attained the age of 16 years, and (ii) that he could not accept that the accommodation of a young person pursuant to s 20 of the Children Act 1989 could never amount to a deprivation of liberty. Now, following *D (a child)* [2017] EWCA Civ 1695, any person under 18 maybe deprived of their liberty if they lack capacity/are not *Gillick* competent and their parent consents to the deprivation, provided it is within the zone of parental responsibility (at the time of writing, the Supreme Court's decision on this was awaited).

III MEN [10A]

Property and affairs and the role of deputy and attorney under the Mental Capacity Act 2005 As the Mental Capacity Act 2005 becomes more extensively applied and the Public Guardian registers more powers of attorney and supervises more deputies appointed under the Mental Capacity Act 2005, the Court of Protection has commenced to provide guidance on specific issues arising in respect of the administration of the property and affairs of those whose management and control lies in the hands of either attorneys or deputies, and where the individual ceases to have mental capacity to make such decisions.

In *Re AS, SH v LC* [2013] COPLR 29 the court addressed the issue of competing candidates for appointment of a deputy for property and affairs. Senior Judge Lush referring to certain pre-Mental Capacity Act 2005 authorities indicated that the discretion to appoint was a judicial decision exercised in 'P's best interests (sub-ss 16(2) and 16(4) considered). That in the absence of satisfactory reasons to appoint a third party, then generally it will be in P's best interests to appoint a family member or close friend as a deputy in preference to a stranger. A panel deputy was considered as an appointment of last resort. Whilst identifying the historic approach of preference of appointment, the Senior Judge keenly stressed that at all stages an appointment was fact specific and dependent on P's' best interests. *Re P (vulnerable adult) (capacity: appointment of deputies)* [2010] EWHC 1592 (Fam), [2010] 2 FLR 1712, [2010] Fam Law 1073 applied. The fact specific nature of the Court's jurisdiction was demonstrated in *Re FH* [2016] EWCOP 14 where the Senior Judge addressed the issue of the functional illiteracy of the proposed deputy.

In *Re M, N v O and P* [2013] COPLR 91 the Senior Judge again in dealing with competing applications for the appointment of a deputy for property and affairs, applied the relevant principles under s 16(2) and (4) and the s 1 principles before applying the s 4 best interests balance sheet approach. Specifically the court relied upon an earlier decision of *Re W (Enduring Power of Attorney)* [2000] Ch 343, [2000] 1 All ER 175 in addressing issues of conflict of family members and impact of suitability for appointment. Such an approach was clearly shown in the judgment in *Re PMB* [2014] EWCOP 42 where the Senior Judge provided a demonstration of the structure for exercising judicial discretion in sibling rivalry over the appointment of a deputy.

In *Re RP* [2016] EWCOP 1 the Senior Judge drew attention of the importance of a deputy not appearing to act with bias, reflecting the decision in *Porter v Magill* [2002] 2 AC 357 at 103, and in *EG v RS* [2010] EWCOP 3073.

In *Re Harcourt, The Public Guardian v A* [2013] COPLR 69 the court contrasted its role in respect of attorneys appointed under Enduring Powers of Attorney with those appointed under Lasting Powers of Attorney. In applying the relevant s 22(4) of the Mental Capacity Act 2005, the Senior Judge found P lacked capacity to revoke the instrument, but that it was in P's best interests for revocation. However such revocation affecting as it did P's Article 8 ECHR rights was a breach of such rights, but was justified as necessary and proportionate. *K v A Local Authority and LBX* [2012] EWCA Civ 79, [2012] 1 FCR 441 applied.

In *Re Various Incapacitated Persons (Appointment of Trust Corporations as Deputies)* [2018] EWCOP 3, the Senior Judge (HHJ Hilder) considered the principles to be applied when considering whether to appoint trust corporations as deputies.

The decision in *Re Harcourt* above was followed in *Re Buckley, The Public Guardian v C* [2013] COPLR 39, when the Senior Judge again addressed the duties and responsibilities of an attorney in keeping records, presenting accounts and proper management and control of a donor's estate. The guidance in that decision reflected not just upon issues of prudent investment policy, but also addressed the issue gifts and the need to apply to the court for prior authority. Attorneys were expected to have full regard to the Codes of Practice

Re GM [2013] COPLR 290 addressed the scope and power of deputies to make gifts from P's estate as authorised under their order of appointment. In considering the scope of powers granted to attorneys appointed under enduring powers of attorney and lasting powers of attorney, the Senior Judge reflecting on his judgment in *Re Buckley* drew attention when discharging two deputies for property and affairs and refusing to grant retrospective approval of gifts amounting to £204,459.74 to the limited powers of deputies to make gifts without express prior authority of the court and the importance of having regard to the assistance of the Code of Practice in considering and deciding the appropriateness and level of making of gifts.

In *Re AFR* [2016] EWCOP 73 the Senior Judge highlighted the importance of deputies having regard to the Code of Practice paras 8.56 and 8.58 to understand the importance of their fiduciary duties, drawing attention in *Re JW* [2016] EWCOP 82 to the potential for conflicts of interests, to which para 8.59 of the Code is pertinent.

In decisions of the Vice President of the Court, Mr Justice Charles addressed in *PJV v The Assistant Director Adult Social Care Newcastle City Council* [2016] EWCOP 7 the issue of deputies being authorised to apply to the Criminal Injuries Compensation Authority on behalf of an individual lacking mental capacity to so apply, and the structure of any Trust arising from any such award made concluding his determinations made in *PJV v The Assistant Director Adult Social Care Newcastle City Council* [2015] EWCOP 87.

In *Watt v ABC* [2016] EWCOP 2532 the Vice President correcting what he saw as a misinterpretation of *SM v HM* [2012] COPLR 187 addressed the correct procedure to be adopted when courts including the Queen's Bench Division were considering at the point of determining a claim on behalf of a person lacking mental capacity to direct future management of damages the relative merits of appointing a deputy or establishing a settlement with control divested to Trustees.

In a Court of Appeal decision addressing acts undertaken by an attorney under an enduring power of attorney in a period predating the implementation of the Mental Capacity Act 2005 the court distinguished the regulation of the donor's affairs which fell within the scope of s 7(1) of the Enduring Power of Attorney Act 1985 (now repealed) and those acts which arose from other subsisting relationships existing between the donor and attorney. However what was clear was the expectation that there existed after registration of an enduring power of attorney a general bar on an attorney acting upon a donor's instructions or consent to do something which is not authorised by the registered instrument unless authorisation of the court is obtained: *Day v Harris* [2013] EWCA Civ 191, [2013] 3 WLR 1560, 16 ITELR 111.

Frequently applications are made under s 18(1)(i) of the Mental Capacity Act 2005 for authority to be granted to a deputy to execute a statutory will. The decision of HHJ Behrens in *NT v FS (by his litigation friend, the Official Solicitor)* [2013] EWHC 684 (COP), [2013] All ER (D) 292 (Mar) provides a composite guide of the relevant authorities which must be addressed in determining such applications, and the power of the court to authorise gifts beyond the scope of a deputy's appointment (s 18(1)(b)). In *Re D* [2016] EWCOP 35 the Senior Judge addressed the issue of giving notice under the rules and the exercise of the court's powers under r 38 to dispense with service.

GENERAL NOTES ON MENTAL HEALTH

III MEN [11]

Jurisdiction of the civil courts In 2007 the Mental Health Act 2007 received Royal Assent, and introduced amendments to the Mental Health Act 1983. As from 1st April 2009, when the deprivation of liberty provisions incorporated within the Mental Health Act 2007 came into effect, the statutory jurisdiction of the civil courts is now to be found in only two pieces of legislation: the heavily revised Mental Health Act 1983 and the Mental Capacity Act 2005.

Practitioners should be aware of the provisions of the Civil Procedure Rules 1998 Part 21 and in particular CPR 21.1 and CPR 21.2 in respect of those who may lack capacity to litigate. See **CPR 21.2[1]** for further discussion, but it is important to record the mandatory requirement of CPR 21.2(1) for the appointment of a litigation friend to conduct proceedings on behalf of a 'protected party' as defined by CPR 21.1(2)(d), confirmed in *Ganley v Jones* [2011] EWCA Civ 75, [2011] All ER (D) 58 (Jul).

In *Dunhill (a protected party by her litigation friend Tasker) v Burgin* [2014] UKSC 18 the Supreme Court confirmed that the appropriate approach under CPR 21 was whether the individual had the necessary mental capacity to commence and conduct the proceedings, namely to litigate, rather than a narrow interpretation limited to any one aspect within litigation.

III MEN [12]

Non-statutory jurisdiction The court's powers in relation to incapacitated persons and their property and affairs are not limited to the powers conferred by statute. There are, in addition, the inherent powers of the court to act, where serious justiciable issues arise which require resolution in the best interests of the incapacitated patient. It has been held that the court's inherent jurisdiction may be exercised by a High Court Judge for the protection of incapacitated persons and also, in some circumstances, for the protection of vulnerable people who have legal capacity: *A Local Authority v DL, RL and ML (vulnerable adults: non molestation injunction)* [2010] EWHC 2675 (Fam), [2011] Fam 189, [2011] 3 WLR 445, Wall P; affirmed on appeal in *A Local Authority v DL* [2012] EWCA Civ 253, [2012] 3 All ER 1064, [2012] 3 WLR 1439.

Importantly however in decisions of Baker J in *Re DB* [2016] EWCOP 30 and Peter Jackson J in *Re Clarke* [2016] EWCOP 46 both judges noted the importance for the court first needing to ascertain the 'habitual residence' of 'P' before proceeding either confirming jurisdiction or determining that the judge might have to proceed by the inherent jurisdiction of the High Court. The court proceeded by adopting the definition of 'habitual residence' as determined by Moylan J in *An English Authority v SW* [2014] EWCOP 43 namely that within the Mental Capacity Act 2005, the definition used within family law statutes and instruments in particular Council Regulation (EC) 2201/2003 ('Brussels IIA') should be adopted. See also *Hertfordshire County Council v AB* [2018] EWHC 3103 (Fam) (per Gwynneth Knowles, J) in which the inherent jurisdiction was used to regularise the arrangements of a conditionally discharged patient, living in the community under conditions that amounted to a deprivation of his liberty, and were therefore unlawful. It is not known whether this decision is subject to an appeal.

III MEN [13]

Jurisdiction to restrict publication The High Court has a long established jurisdiction to grant injunctions restricting the publication of reports affecting the interests of vulnerable adults. But it should balance the competing rights under Article 8 (respect for family and private life) and Article 10 (freedom of expression) before doing so: *Local Authority v Health Authority (disclosure: restriction on publication)* [2003] EWHC 2746 (Fam), [2004] Fam 96, [2004] 1 All ER 480. A judgment of Munby LJ, *RB (Adult); A London Borough v RB (Adult) (No 4)* [2011] EWHC 3017 (Fam) sets out guidance in respect of the publication of judgments in cases heard under the inherent jurisdiction of the Family Division of the High Court, and in the absence of any relevant statutory restriction, it would necessitate the party seeking anonymity or a restriction on publication to apply for such an order.

That former guidance has been now amended by the implementation of a Practice Guidance issued on 16 January 2014 which is effective from 3 February 2014. As part of the process of development of the Family Court and the transparency of court proceedings, the President Sir James Munby as both President of the Family Division and of the Court of Protection, has provided guidance applicable to various aspects of the work of the courts, and paragraph 14(ii) applies to all judgments delivered by High Court judges (and persons sitting as judges of the High Court) exercising the inherent jurisdiction to make orders in respect of children and incapacitated or vulnerable adults. The Guidance distinguishes between judgments delivered which must ordinarily be allowed to be published and those which may be published (paras 15–18). At para 17 a comprehensive Schedule (Schedule 2) provides guidance on the sphere of the work of the court in respect of which judgments must ordinarily be allowed to be published. The Guidance gives direction to parties in respect of anonymising and costs of transcript (paras 20–23).

See also s 12(1)(b) of the Administration of Justice Act 1960, at **III COT [8]**.

On 29 January 2016 pursuant to r 9A of the 2007 Rules there was introduced into the Court of Protection a pilot for hearings which fall within the scope of para 1.3 of the Transparency Pilot Practice Direction. Such cases are to be held in public subject to a restriction order dealing with confidentiality and anonymity. The Pilot was extended until 1 August 2017. Save for that Pilot Scheme regard must be had to the restrictions on the reporting of proceedings within the Court of Protection: see **III MEN [6]** and see rr 90 to 93 of the Court of Protection Rules 2007, SI 2007/1744 and the Practice Direction 13A Court of Protection Reporting Restrictions. In *P (by his litigation friend the Official Solicitor) v Independent Print Ltd* [2011] EWCA Civ 756, [2012] 2 FCR 503, [2012] 1 FLR 212 the Court of Appeal reaffirmed its approach in *Independent News & Media Ltd v A (by his litigation friend the Official Solicitor)* [2010] EWCA Civ 343, [2010] 3 All ER 32, [2010] 1 WLR 2262 and found that although the best interests of P was a material factor, it could not dictate the decision which effectively was concerned with the administration of the court's process. In *W (by her litigation friend B) v M (by her litigation friend, the Official Solicitor)* [2011] EWHC 1197(COP), [2011] NLJR 811 Baker J. provided guidance on the making of a reporting restriction order and as to the formatting of such orders for cases arising in the Court of Protection.

In *V v Associated Newspapers Ltd* [2016] EWCOP 21 it was found that reporting restrictions may, in an appropriate case be extended beyond the death of 'P' and include, the reporting of the inquest.

However in tandem with the Publication of Guidance for the Family Court, guidance has now been given by the President in *Practice Guidance (Transparency in the Court of Protection)* [2014] EWCOP B implementing a separate Practice Guidance effective from 3 February 2014. As part of the process of development of the Court of Protection and the transparency of court proceedings, the President Sir James Munby as President of the Court of Protection has provided guidance applicable to various aspects of the work of the court. Paragraph 14 provides that the Guidance applies to all judgments delivered by the Senior Judge, nominated Circuit Judges and High Court Judges. The Guidance distinguishes the approach to be adopted for publication of judgments delivered between those which must ordinarily be allowed to be published and those which may be published (paras 15–18). At paragraph 17 a comprehensive Schedule provides guidance on the sphere of the work of the court in respect of which the starting point is that permission should be granted for judgments to be published unless there are compelling reasons why the judgment should not be published. The Guidance gives direction to parties in respect of anonymising and costs of transcript (paras 20–23).

In respect of committal proceedings before the Court of Protection and the issue of publicity, the procedure for all committal proceedings must now follow not only the relevant rules but also the Practice Direction: Committal for Contempt of Court – Open Court issued by the Lord Chief Justice on 26 March 2015 and the Practice Guidance: Committal for Contempt of Court – Open Court dated 24 June 2015. This Practice Direction and Guidance supersede all previous Practice directions and Guidance. The Practice Direction addresses issues of public and private hearings, the engagement of the Press and the issue of judgments. In a clear indication of the importance of Open Justice strict procedures are applied for the publicity of the hearing, the notification of press, the publication of the outcome and the limiting of matters in private. The Guidance addresses questions which arose surrounding press notification, and judgment (see Court of Protection Rules 2007, r 188 and see also CPR 81.28).

III MEN [14]

Inherent jurisdiction: Declarations regarding accommodation, care and validity of certain acts The High Court's inherent jurisdiction, was in *Re F (Adult Patient)* [2000] 3 FCR 30, [2000] 2 FLR 512, CA, confirmed when the Court of Appeal determined that it had power to grant declarations, as a matter of necessity, as to how an incapacitated adult should be accommodated and cared for: However now see **III MEN [9]** and **III MEN [10]** above. In *A Local Authority v SY (by her litigation friend, the Official Solicitor)* [2013] EWHC 3485 (COP), [2013] All ER (D) 119 (Nov) Keehan J found that notwithstanding the commencement of the Mental Capacity Act 2005, the High Court once seized of a matter could still exercise its inherent jurisdiction following Parker J in *XCC v AA* [2013] EWHC 2183 (COP) by declaring a ceremony undertaken by P who lacked capacity at the relevant time a non-marriage such a decision being outside the scope of the Mental Capacity Act 2005.

Reflecting upon the interrelationship of the Mental Health Act 1983 and the Mental Capacity Act 2005, the powers and limitations of the court within those jurisdictions and the question of whether the court was able to direct or authorise the force feeding of an individual who was found to lack capacity to decide whether to accept nutrition and hydration against the risk of starvation to death whilst resident at an NHS Trust hospital, Baker J in *A NHS Trust v Dr A* [2013] EWHC 2442 (COP), [2013] All ER (D) 07 (Sep) ultimately turned to the inherent jurisdiction of the High Court in making appropriate declarations including a provision for deprivation of liberty subject to compliance with Article 5 ECHR.

See also *Hertfordshire County Council v AB* [2018] EWHC 3103 (Fam) (per Gwynneth Knowles, J).

III MEN [15]

Judicial review Duties are imposed by the Act on health authorities and local authorities whose decisions may be challenged by claims for judicial review in accordance with CPR Part 54. More recently it was held that local authorities had to provide (and pay for) aftercare services for persons detained under s 3 and discharged and that they could not require the individual to pay for them even where damages had been awarded for future care: *R (Tinsley) v Manchester City Council* (2018) Times 16 January, CA. See, for example, *R v Ealing District Health Authority, ex p Fox* [1993] 3 All ER 170, [1993] 1 WLR 373 in which it was held that s 117 imposed duties on health authorities but that they were not absolute. See also *R v Richmond London Borough Council, ex p Watson* [2001] 1 All ER 436, [2000] 3 WLR 1127, CA in which it was held that the local authority could not exercise powers under National Assistance Act 1948 s 21 to make charges for residential accommodation provided under s 117 and *DM v Doncaster Metropolitan Borough Council* [2011] EWHC 3652 (Admin), where it was held that the Act did not impose duties to accommodate by any express words, nor by way of necessary implication, and confirmed *GJ v Foundation Trust PCT and the Secretary of State for Health* [2009] EWHC 2972 (Fam), [2010] Fam 70, [2010] 3 WLR 840 that the Mental Health Act 1983 had primacy over the Mental Capacity Act 2005 if the individual the subject of the proceedings fell within the former jurisdiction.

For the substantive law see 30 *Halsbury's Laws* (4th edn, reissue) title MENTAL HEALTH, para 1201.

MENTAL HEALTH ACT 1983

(c 20)

III MEN [16]

1. Application of Act: 'mental disorder'

(1) The provisions of this Act shall have effect with respect to the reception, care and treatment of mentally disordered patients, the management of their property and other related matters.

(2) In this Act—

'mental disorder' means any disorder or disability of the mind; and 'mentally disordered' shall be construed accordingly;

and other expressions shall have the meanings assigned to them in section 145 below.

(2A) But a person with learning disability shall not be considered by reason of that disability to be—

(a) suffering from mental disorder for the purposes of the provisions mentioned in subsection (2B) below; or

(b) requiring treatment in hospital for mental disorder for the purposes of sections 17E and 50 to 53 below,

unless that disability is associated with abnormally aggressive or seriously irresponsible conduct on his part.

(2B) The provisions are—

(a) sections 3, 7, 17A, 20 and 20A below;

(b) sections 35 to 38, 45A, 47, 48 and 51 below; and

(c) section 72(1)(b) and (c) and (4) below.

(3) Dependence on alcohol or drugs is not considered to be a disorder or disability of the mind for the purposes of subsection (2) above.

(4) In subsection (2A) above, 'learning disability' means a state of arrested or incomplete development of the mind which includes significant impairment of intelligence and social functioning.

III MEN [16.1]

Application of the Code of Practice Guiding principles have been issued to which regard should be given by all those undertaking functions under the Mental Health Act 1983. Those principles are set out in the revised Code of Practice Mental Health Act 1983 published in 2015 pursuant to s 118 of the 1983 Act.

GENERAL NOTES ON PARTS II–VI

III MEN [17]

Statutory powers in relation to patients Part II of the Act (ss 2–31) empowers a patient's nearest relative, or an approved social worker, to apply for a patient to be admitted to hospital for assessment or treatment or to be appointed guardian. In *R (Von Brandenburg) v East London and City Mental Health NHS Trust* [2001] EWCA Civ 239, [2002] QB 235, [2001] 3 WLR 588, it was held that it would be unlawful for a social worker to make an application for readmission under s 3 immediately upon discharge ordered by a Tribunal. The House of Lords reached the same conclusion, ruling that an approved social worker who knew of the discharge ordered by the mental health tribunal could not lawfully apply for the patient's re-admission except on the basis of fresh information which put a significantly differently complexion on the case: *R (on the application of Von Brandenburg) v East London and City Mental Health NHS Trust* [2003] UKHL 58, [2004] 2 AC 280, [2004] 1 All ER 400. Paragraphs 14.26 to 14.29 of the Code of Practice Mental Health Act 1983 address and provide guidance on the use of ss 2 and 3.

The court in *R v Pathfinder NHS Trust, ex p W* (2000) 3 CCL Rep 271 followed the *Von Brandenburg* decision regarding a purported over-riding of a Tribunal decision on a patient's mental state. On the other hand an application for re-admission does not need to be supported by evidence of 'change of circumstance' so long as the s 3 criteria are satisfied. Note also the decision in *St George's Healthcare NHS Trust v S* [1999] Fam 26, [1998] 3 All ER 673, CA regarding the kind of treatment that is covered by the Act and procedures to be followed in regard to other kinds of treatment such as childbirth. Section 23 gives managers a general discretion to discharge. They are not restricted to considering the criteria in s 3 alone and are not bound to accept the conclusion of the patient's responsible medical officer: *R v Riverside Mental Health Trust, ex p Huzzey* (1998) 43 BMLR 167, Times, 18 May, Latham J. In *South Staffordshire and Shropshire HealthCare NHS Foundation Trust v The Hospital Managers of St George' Hospital* [2016] EWHC 1196 (Admin) Cranston J recalled that the powers of the Managers Panel equated to that of a Tribunal exercising its powers under s 72 of the Act. This also means that the responsible clinician may bring judicial review proceedings against the managers of his own hospital, even though that maybe seen as the hospital judicially reviewing itself.

Where deferred conditional discharge has been granted to a restricted patient the Secretary of State should exercise his powers under s 17 rather than those under s 42 when giving or refusing consent to leave of absence from hospital: *R (A) v Secretary of State for the Home Department* (2002) Times, 5 September.

Part III (ss 36–55) deals with criminal proceedings and sentencing and Part IV (ss 56–64) sets out protective provisions on treatment without consent, which may not be adequate in all cases to secure the patient's Convention rights: *R (Wilkinson) v Broadmoor Special Hospital Authority* [2001] EWCA Civ 1545, [2002] 1 WLR 419. Part V (ss 65–79) is concerned with Mental Health Review Tribunals and s 78(8) provides for a Mental Health Review Tribunal to state a case on a point of law. However, a more appropriate way of raising a point of law before the High Court is to apply for judicial review and, where the case is strong, for a stay of the implementation of the decision: *R (H) v Ashworth Hospital Authority* [2002] EWCA Civ 923, [2003] 1 WLR 127, (2002) Times, 10 July.

In *R (on the application of B) v Ashworth Hospital Authority* [2005] UKHL 20, [2005] 2 All ER 289 the decision of the CA was reversed. It was held that a patient who was detained under statutory powers could be treated compulsorily under s 63 not only for the condition specified in the order for detention but also for any other kind of disorder or disability of mind from which he was suffering.

Of note was the confirmation in *C (By his litigation friend, the Official Solicitor) v A Borough Council* [2011] EWHC 3321 (COP), [2011] All ER (D) 203 (Dec) by Peter Jackson J of the decision of Charles J in *GJ v Foundation Trust PCT and the Secretary of State for Health* [2009] EWHC 2972 (Fam), [2010] Fam 70, [2010] 3 WLR 840 that in general the Mental Health Act 1983 where it applies, has primacy over the Mental Capacity Act 2005. Such an approach was confirmed by the Divisional Court in *R (on the application of Sawida Sessay) v South London & Maudsley NHS Foundation Trust* [2011] EWHC 2617 (QB), [2012] QB 760, [2012] 2 WLR 1071, where it was firmly stated, that Part II of the Mental Health Act 1983 provides a comprehensive code for compulsory admission to hospital for non-compliant incapacitated patients, and the common law principle of necessity could not apply (in that case admission under s 4 being an alternative route for admission). However Charles J in *AM v South London & Maudsley NHS Foundation Trust and Secretary of State for Health* [2013] UKUT 365 (AAC) highlighted that when dealing with a compliant mentally incapacitated patient requiring detention, decision makers had to consider the alternative of whether such assessment or treatment should be within the structure of the Mental Capacity Act 2005 deprivation of liberty safeguarding structure. He expressed concern that his earlier judgment which was case and fact specific may have led to a presumption of primacy of the Mental Health Act 1983, stating 'that general propositions in respect of issues that arise concerning the interrelationship between the two Acts are dangerous'.

A violation of Article 5 (4) of the European Convention of Human Rights was found to occur where there was failure to provide a method for a challenge to be made in respect of detention by a mentally incapacitated patient: *MH v United Kingdom (Application No 11577/06)* (2013) 58 EHRR 965, 136 BMLR 17, ECtHR.

Where there is doubt whether treatment under s 63 of the Mental Health Act 1983 would be within the definition of 'medical treatment' in s 145, the appropriate course is to apply to the court for the treatment to be approved: *A NHS Trust v Dr A* [2013] EWHC 2442 (COP), [2013] All ER (D) 07 (Sep).

III MEN [17A]

Developing jurisprudence on deprivation of liberty The First-Tier Tribunal (England) or Mental Health Review Tribunal for Wales (in Wales) have limited jurisdiction under statute. The tribunal reviews the criteria under which orders continue under s 72 of the Mental Health Act 1983 – for example detention under ss 2, 3 or 37, or a community treatment order (CTO) under ss 17A–17F, or guardianship under ss 7 and 8. With restricted cases, the tribunal will also consider the possible conditions to be imposed on conditional discharges. The tribunal does not have a general fact finding jurisdiction. To what extent is the tribunal to consider whether Articles of the European Convention are engaged in cases brought before it? It is established law that the conditions imposed on a conditional discharge may not lawfully amount to a deprivation of the patient's liberty (see *Secretary of State for Justice v MM* [2018] UKSC 60) so a tribunal must consider the facts giving rise to a deprivation of liberty (applying *Cheshire West & Chester Council v P* [2014] UKSC 19). Equally, the conditions attached to a community treatment order (CTO). may also not amount to a deprivation of the patient's liberty (see *Welsh Ministers v PJ* [2018] UKSC 66). That being said, although the tribunal should be alive to whether conditions amount to a deprivation of liberty, its jurisdiction is limited by s 72 of the Mental Health Act, and does not include the varying or striking out of conditions. The proper route for such a challenge is that of judicial review. see also *Djaba v West London Mental Health Trust and Secretary of State for Justice* [2017] EWCA Civ 436.

III MEN [18]

Changes made by the Mental Health Act 2007 The Mental Health Act 2007 has amended every part of the Mental Health Act 1983. The main focus of the amending legislation is the detention of persons with mental disorders without their consent: and the need for procedural and other safeguards to preserve their human rights and to protect them from exploitation. The amendments are mainly in the following subject areas:

- definition of mental disorder (see s 1, above)
- criteria for detention
- professional roles of, amongst others, approved social workers (see s 10, below)
- nearest relative (see ss 26–30, below)
- supervised community treatment
- Mental Health Review Tribunals
- Advocacy
- Electro-convulsive therapy.

III MEN [19]

10. Transfer of guardianship in case of death, incapacity etc., of guardian

(1) If any person (other than a local social services authority) who is the guardian of a patient received into guardianship under this Part of this Act—

(a) dies; or

(b) gives notice in writing to the local social services authority that he desires to relinquish the functions of guardian,

the guardianship of the patient shall thereupon vest in the local social services authority, but without prejudice to any power to transfer the patient into the guardianship of another person in pursuance of regulations under section 19 below.

(2) If any such person, not having given notice under subsection (1)(b) above, is incapacitated by illness or any other cause from performing the functions of guardian of the patient, those functions may, during his incapacity, be performed on his behalf by the local social services authority or by any other person approved for the purposes by that authority.

(3) If it appears to the county court, upon application made by an approved mental health professional acting on behalf of the local social services authority that any person other than a local social services authority having the guardianship of a patient received into guardianship under this Part of this Act has performed his functions negligently or in a manner contrary to the interests of the welfare of the patient, the court may order that the guardianship of the patient be transferred to the local social services authority or to any other person approved for the purpose by that authority.

(4) Where the guardianship of a patient is transferred to a local social services authority or other person by or under this section, subsection (2)(c) of section 19 below shall apply as if the patient had been transferred into the guardianship of that authority or person in pursuance of regulations under that section.

(5) In this section 'the local social services authority', in relation to a person (other than a local social services authority) who is the guardian of a patient, means the local social services authority for the area in which that person resides (or resided immediately before his death).

III MEN [19.1]

Application to the County Court The application to the County Court must be made by Part 8 claim form, using Form N208 and must follow the other requirements of paragraph 18 of the Practice Direction supplementing Part 8, in volume 1, at para **CPR PD 8A.18**. Once issued, the application will be heard at a county court hearing centre (Crime and Courts Act 2013, s 17).

The provisions of the Mental Health (Hospital, Guardianship and Treatment) (England) Regulations 2008, SI 2008/1184, reg 26(1)(k) and for proceedings before the Civil Courts sitting in Wales, the provisions of Mental Health (Hospital, Guardianship, Community Treatment and Consent to Treatment) (Wales) Regulations 2008, SI 2008/2439, reg 31 apply in respect of informing the patients nearest relative of the transfer of guardianship.

III MEN [20]

26. Definition of 'relative' and 'nearest relative'

(1) In this Part of this Act 'relative' means any of the following persons:—

- (a) husband or wife or civil partner;
- (b) son or daughter;
- (c) father or mother;
- (d) brother or sister;
- (e) grandparent;
- (f) grandchild;
- (g) uncle or aunt;
- (h) nephew or niece.

(2) In deducing relationships for the purposes of this section, any relationship of the half-blood shall be treated as a relationship of the whole blood, and an illegitimate person shall be treated as the legitimate child of

- (a) his mother, and
- (b) if his father has parental responsibility for him within the meaning of section 3 of the Children Act 1989, his father.

(3) In this Part of this Act, subject to the provisions of this section and to the following provisions of this Part of this Act, the 'nearest relative' means the person first described in subsection (1) above who is for the time being surviving, relatives of the whole blood being preferred to relatives of the same description of the half-blood and the elder or eldest of two or more relatives described in any paragraph of that subsection being preferred to the other or others of those relatives, regardless of sex.

(4) Subject to the provisions of this section and to the following provisions of this Part of this Act, where the patient ordinarily resides with or is cared for by one or more of his relatives (or, if he is for the time being an in-patient in a hospital, he last ordinarily resided with or was cared for by one or more of his relatives) his nearest relative shall be determined—

- (a) by giving preference to that relative or those relatives over the other or others; and
- (b) as between two or more such relatives, in accordance with subsection (3) above.

(5) Where the person who, under subsection (3) or (4) above, would be the nearest relative of a patient—

(a) in the case of a patient ordinarily resident in the United Kingdom, the Channel Islands or the Isle of Man, is not so resident; or

(b) is the husband or wife or civil partner of the patient, but is permanently separated from the patient, either by agreement or under an order of a court, or has deserted or has been deserted by the patient for a period which has come to an end; or

(c) is a person other than the husband, wife, civil partner, father or mother of the patient, and is for the time being under 18 years of age; . . .

(d) [. . .]

the nearest relative of the patient shall be ascertained as if that person were dead.

(6) In this section 'husband', 'wife' and 'civil partner' include a person who is living with the patient as the patient's husband or wife or as if they were civil partners, as the case may be (or, if the patient is for the time being an in-patient in a hospital, was so living until the patient was admitted), and has been or had been so living for a period of not less than six months; but a person shall not be treated by virtue of this subsection as the nearest relative of a married patient or a patient in a civil partnership unless the husband, wife or civil partner of the patient is disregarded by virtue of paragraph (b) of subsection (5) above.

(7) A person, other than a relative, with whom the patient ordinarily resides (or, if the patient is for the time being an in-patient in a hospital, last ordinarily resided before he was admitted), and with whom he has or had been ordinarily residing for a period of not less than five years, shall be treated for the purposes of this Part of this Act as if he were a relative but—

(a) shall be treated for the purposes of subsection (3) above as if mentioned last in subsection (1) above; and

(b) shall not be treated by virtue of this subsection as the nearest relative of a married patient or a patient in a civil partnership unless the husband, wife or civil partner of the patient is disregarded by virtue of paragraph (b) of subsection (5) above.

III MEN [20.1]

Appointment of nearest relative under s 26 In *JT v United Kingdom* (Application 26494/95) [2000] 1 FLR 909, ECtHR, the claimant asserted that her inability to change an unacceptable 'nearest relative' infringed her Convention rights (Art 8) and the UK Government agreed and undertook to bring forward amending legislation.

The word 'ordinarily' in s 26(4) qualifies the verb 'resided with' not the verb 'cared for by'. So long as the relative provides more than minimal care the social worker is entitled to decide that such a relative meets the 'nearest' without making inquiries into the possibility of competing claims: *Re D (Mental Patient: Habeas corpus)* [2000] 2 FLR 848, CA. The Court of Appeal in *R (on the application of Cornwall Council) v Secretary of State for Health* [2014] EWCA Civ 12, [2014] 3 All ER 603, [2014] 1 WLR 3408 held that the approach of the court in determining 'the place of ordinary residence' was a question of fact, and the words must be given their 'ordinary and natural meaning'. Upon appeal the Supreme Court found that the 'meaning of the term may be strongly influenced by its statutory context'; was the 'period of actual residence' 'sufficiently settled'. See *R (on the application of Cornwall County Council) v Secretary of State for Health* [2015] UKSC 46, [2015] 3 WLR 213, [2015] All ER (D) 91 (Jul).

In *MA v Secretary of State for Health* [2012] UKUT 474 (AAC) it was held that the 'bundle of rights conferred upon the nearest relative by the 1983 Act in particular the right to discharge are civil rights for the purposes of Article 6 ECHR.

III MEN [20.2]

Guidance on the identification, appointment and displacement of the nearest relative The revised Code of Practice Mental Health Act 1983 Chapter 5 provides guidance in respect of the nearest relative.

III MEN [21]

27. Children and young persons in care

Where—

(a) a patient who is a child or young person is in the care of a local authority by virtue of a care order within the meaning of the Children Act 1989; or

(b) the rights and powers of a parent of a patient who is a child or young person are vested in a local authority by virtue of section 16 of the Social Work (Scotland) Act 1968,

the authority shall be deemed to be the nearest relative of the patient in preference to any person except the patient's husband or wife or civil partner (if any).

III MEN [21.1]

Guidance on children and young people under the age of 18 The revised Code of Practice Mental Health Act 1983 Chapter 19 provides guidance in respect of children and young people under the age of 18.

III MEN [22]

28. Nearest relative of minor under guardianship

(1) Where—

(a) a guardian has been appointed for a person who has not attained the age of eighteen years; or

(b) a person is named in a child arrangements order (as defined by section 8 of the Children Act 1989) as a person with whom a person who has not attained the age of eighteen years is to live,

the guardian (or guardians, where there is more than one) or the person so named (or the persons so named, where there is more than one) shall, to the exclusion of any other person, be deemed to be his nearest relative.

(2) Subsection (5) of section 26 above shall apply in relation to a person who is, or who is one of the persons, deemed to be the nearest relative of a patient by virtue of this section as it applies in relation to a person who would be the nearest relative under subsection (3) of that section.

(3) In this section 'guardian' includes a special guardian (within the meaning of the Children Act 1989), but does not include a guardian under this Part of this Act.

(4) In this section 'court' includes a court in Scotland or Northern Ireland, and 'enactment' includes an enactment of the Parliament of Northern Ireland, a Measure of the Northern Ireland Assembly and an Order in Council under Schedule 1 of the Northern Ireland Act 1974.

III MEN [23]

29. Appointment by court of acting nearest relative

(1) The county court may, upon application made in accordance with the provisions of this section in respect of a patient, by order direct that the functions of the nearest relative of the patient under this Part of this Act and sections 66 and 69 below shall, during the continuance in force of the order, be exercisable by the person specified in the order.

(1A) If the court decides to make an order on an application under subsection (1) above, the following rules have effect for the purposes of specifying a person in the order—

(a) if a person is nominated in the application to act as the patient's nearest relative and that person is, in the opinion of the court, a suitable person to act as such and is willing to do so, the court shall specify that person (or, if there are two or more such persons, such one of them as the court thinks fit);

(b) otherwise, the court shall specify such person as is, in its opinion, a suitable person to act as the patient's nearest relative and is willing to do so.

(2) An order under this section may be made on the application of—

(za) the patient;

(a) any relative of the patient;

(b) any other person with whom the patient is residing (or, if the patient is then an in-patient in a hospital, was last residing before he was admitted); or

(c) an approved mental health professional.

(3) An application for an order under this section may be made upon any of the following grounds, that is to say—

(a) that the patient has no nearest relative within the meaning of this Act, or that it is not reasonably practicable to ascertain whether he has such a relative, or who that relative is;

(b) that the nearest relative of the patient is incapable of acting as such by reason of mental disorder or other illness;

(c) that the nearest relative of the patient unreasonably objects to the making of an application for admission for treatment or a guardianship application in respect of the patient;

(d) that the nearest relative of the patient has exercised without due regard to the welfare of the patient or the interests of the public his power to discharge the patient under this Part of this Act, or is likely to do so; or

(e) that the nearest relative of the patient is otherwise not a suitable person to act as such.

(4) If, immediately before the expiration of the period for which a patient is liable to be detained by virtue of an application for admission for assessment, an application under this section, which is an application made on the ground specified in subsection (3)(c) or (d) above, is pending in respect of the patient, that period shall be extended—

(a) in any case, until the application under this section has been finally disposed of; and

(b) if an order is made in pursuance of the application under this section, for a further period of seven days;

and for the purposes of this subsection an application under this section shall be deemed to have been finally disposed of at the expiration of the time allowed for appealing from the decision of the court or, if notice of appeal has been given within that time, when the appeal has been heard or withdrawn, and 'pending' shall be construed accordingly.

(5) An order made on the ground specified in subsection (3)(a), (b) or (e) above may specify a period for which it is to continue in force unless previously discharged under section 30 below.

(6) While an order made under this section is in force, the provisions of this Part of this Act (other than this section and section 30 below) and sections 66, 69, 132(4) and 133 below shall apply in relation to the patient as if for any reference to the nearest relative of the patient there were substituted a reference to the person having the functions of that relative and (without prejudice to section 30 below) shall so apply notwithstanding that the person who was the patient's nearest relative when the order was made is no longer his nearest relative; but this subsection shall not apply to section 66 below in the case mentioned in paragraph (h) of subsection (1) of that section.

III MEN [23.1]

Application to the County Court The application to the County Court must be made by CPR Part 8 claim form. Using Form N208 and must follow the requirements of paragraph 18 of the Practice Direction supplementing Part 8, in Volume 1, at para **CPR PD 8A.18**. In *Barnet London Borough Council v Robin* (1999) 2 CCL Rep 454, the Court of Appeal upheld a county court order based on the likelihood of the nearest relative's discharging the patient without due regard to the patient's welfare.

In particular, the application should be heard in the court for the district in which the patient's place of residence is situated or in the court which made the order appointing the acting nearest relative. It may be made by the patient himself, any relative of the patient, any other person with whom the patient is residing (or if the patient is then an in-patient in a hospital, was last residing before hc was admitted, or an approved mental health professional.

Addressing the approach of the court in determining the issue of 'unreasonably objects' under s 29(3)(c) it has been held that this must subsist both at the date of the application and of the hearing see *Lewis v Gibson* [2005] EWCA Civ 587, [2005] 2 FCR 241, 87 BMLR 93 and that the county court should when determining the issue apply an objective test of a what a reasonable person placed in the same circumstances would determine and not whether the nearest relative was from their own subjective viewpoint acting reasonably *W v L* [1974] QB 711, [1973] 3 All ER 884, CA.

In *C (By his litigation friend, the Official Solicitor) v A Borough Council* [2011] EWHC 3321 (COP), [2011] All ER (D) 203 (Dec) Peter Jackson J explored the interrelationship between Guardianship under Mental Health Act 1983, and issues of deprivation of liberty and welfare arising under the Mental Capacity Act 2005. Finding that the powers of a guardian pursuant to s 8 to compel a person to reside in a particular place to the exclusion of others including the Court of Protection left the court without jurisdiction under the Mental Capacity Act 2005, he invited the relinquishment of the guardianship contending that substantial issues of this nature should be determined by the Court of Protection utilising its powers under s 16 of the Mental Capacity Act 2005.

The Code of Practice Mental Health Act 1983 at Chapter 5 provides guidance in respect of the displacing of the nearest relative and the supporting of the Patient.

III MEN [23.2]

Points of practice Section 29(3) orders may be made without notice, on an interim basis, in exercise of the general jurisdiction conferred by s 38 of the County Courts Act 1984, but applicants ought not, as a matter of practice, to act on authority conferred on them by an interim order to have the patient admitted under s 3. The better course would be to obtain a final ruling first (extending the detention under s 29(4) if necessary to allow the time): *R v Central London County Court, ex p London* [1999] QB 1260, [1999] 3 All ER 991, CA, considered in *R (on the application of M) v Homerton University Hospital* [2008] EWCA Civ 197.

III MEN [23.3]

Disclosure of reports The court may receive reports from a medical practitioner, probation officer or local authority provided that the substance is disclosed to the nearest relative: CCR Order 49 r 12(4). But the nearest relative is not entitled to have such reports disclosed ahead of proceedings and it is not a breach Convention rights under Art 6 for such reports to be withheld at that stage: *R (on the application of S) v City of Plymouth* [2001] All ER (D) 09 (Sept), Kay J.

III MEN [23.4]

Period of extended detention Section 29(4) has been held to be incompatible with Art 5(4) of the Convention in that it does not provide for the reference to the court of the case of a patient detained under s 2 whose detention has been extended by the operation of s 29(4): *R (on the application of H) v Secretary of State for Health* [2004] EWCA Civ 1609, [2005] 3 All ER 468, (2004) 148 Sol Jo LB 1437, (2004) Times, 8 December. But the House of Lords reversed the decision of the Court of Appeal in *R (MH) v Secretary of State for Health* [2005] UKHL 60, (2005) Times, 25 October. They concluded, as regards s 29(4), that there was only a problem if the county court proceedings were slow, in which case the Secretary of State's discretionary powers under s 67 should be invoked so as to avoid a breach of Article 5.4. This decision was upheld in the subsequent appeal heard by the European Court of Human Rights: *MH v United Kingdom (Application No 11577/06)* (2013) 58 EHRR 965, 136 BMLR 17, ECtHR.

In *MA v Secretary of State for Health* [2012] UKUT 474 (AAC) it was held that the 'bundle of rights conferred upon the nearest relative by the 1983 Act in particular the right to discharge are civil rights for the purposes of Article 6 ECHR Further that the fact that a patient's nearest relative did not have a right to apply to a tribunal on behalf of a person who was detained for assessment and whose detention had been extended as a result of s 29(4) did not constitute a breach of the Convention as an application for judicial review was an available and adequate remedy.

MENTAL CAPACITY AND MENTAL HEALTH

III MEN [24]

30. Discharge and variation of orders under s 29

(1) An order made under section 29 above in respect of a patient may be discharged by the county court upon application made—

(a) in any case, by the patient or the person having the functions of the nearest relative of the patient by virtue of the order;

(b) where the order was made on the ground specified in paragraph (a), (b) or (e) of section 29(3) above, or where the person who was the nearest relative of the patient when the order was made has ceased to be his nearest relative, on the application of the nearest relative of the patient.

(1A) But, in the case of an order made on the ground specified in paragraph (e) of section 29(3) above, an application may not be made under subsection (1)(b) above by the person who was the nearest relative of the patient when the order was made except with leave of the county court.

(2) An order made under section 29 above in respect of a patient may be varied by the county court, on the application of the patient or of the person having the functions of the nearest relative by virtue of the order or on the application of an approved mental health professional, by substituting another person for the person having those functions.

(2A) If the court decides to vary an order on an application under subsection (2) above, the following rules have effect for the purposes of substituting another person—

(a) if a person is nominated in the application to act as the patient's nearest relative and that person is, in the opinion of the court, a suitable person to act as such and is willing to do so, the court shall specify that person (or, if there are two or more such persons, such one of them as the court thinks fit);

(b) otherwise, the court shall specify such person as is, in its opinion, a suitable person to act as the patient's nearest relative and is willing to do so.

(3) If the person having the functions of the nearest relative of a patient by virtue of an order under section 29 above dies—

(a) subsections (1) and (2) above shall apply as if for any reference to that person there were substituted a reference to any relative of the patient, and

(b) until the order is discharged or varied under those provisions the functions of the nearest relative under this Part of this Act and sections 66 and 69 below shall not be exercisable by any person.

(4) An order made on the ground specified in paragraph (c) or (d) of section 29(3) above shall, unless previously discharged under subsection (1) above, cease to have effect as follows—

(a) if—

(i) on the date of the order the patient was liable to be detained or subject to guardianship by virtue of a relevant application, order or direction; or

(ii) he becomes so liable or subject within the period of three months beginning with that date; or

(iii) he was a community patient on the date of the order,

it shall cease to have effect when he is discharged under section 23 above or 72 below or the relevant application, order or direction otherwise ceases to have effect (except as a result of his being transferred in pursuance of regulations under section 19 above);

(b) otherwise, it shall cease to have effect at the end of the period of three months beginning with the date of the order.

(4A) In subsection (4) above, reference to a relevant application, order or direction is to any of the following—

(a) an application for admission for treatment;

(b) a guardianship application;

(c) an order or direction under Part 3 of this Act (other than under section 35, 36 or 38).

(4B) An order made on the ground specified in paragraph (a), (b) or (e) of section 29(3) above shall—

(a) if a period was specified under section 29(5) above, cease to have effect on expiry of that period, unless previously discharged under subsection (1) above;

(b) if no such period was specified, remain in force until it is discharged under subsection (1) above.

(5) The discharge or variation under this section of an order made under section 29 above shall not affect the validity of anything previously done in pursuance of the order.

III MEN [24.1]

Procedure The application may be made by claim form in accordance with CPR Part 8 (at para **CPR 8**). Arguably, as an alternative, it may be made by a CPR Part 23 (see para **CPR 23**) application in the proceedings in which the order was made.

PART VII
MANAGEMENT OF PROPERTY AND AFFAIRS OF PATIENTS

Part VII (ss 93-105) was repealed by s 67(2) of the Mental Capacity Act 2005 with effect from 1 October 2007, but subject to the savings and transitional provisions in Schedule 5 to the Mental Capacity Act 2007, at **III MEN [142]**. A new Court of Protection takes its place, constituted by ss 45 to 56 of that Act, which are set out at **III MEN [83]**–**III MEN [94]** below.

PART X
MISCELLANEOUS

III MEN [25]

131. Informal admission of patients

(1) Nothing in this Act shall be construed as preventing a patient who requires treatment for mental disorder from being admitted to any hospital registered establishment in pursuance of arrangements made in that behalf and without any application, order or direction rendering him liable to be detained under this Act, or from remaining in any hospital or registered establishment in pursuance of such arrangements after he has ceased to be so liable to be detained.

(2) Subsections (3) and (4) below apply in the case of a patient aged 16 or 17 years who has capacity to consent to the making of such arrangements as are mentioned in subsection (1) above.

(3) If the patient consents to the making of the arrangements, they may be made, carried out and determined on the basis of that consent even though there are one or more persons who have parental responsibility for him.

(4) If the patient does not consent to the making of the arrangements, they may not be made, carried out or determined on the basis of the consent of a person who has parental responsibility for him.

(5) In this section—

(a) the reference to a patient who has capacity is to be read in accordance with the Mental Capacity Act 2005; and

(b) 'parental responsibility' has the same meaning as in the Children Act 1989.

III MEN [25.1]

Informal admission where patient unable to consent A patient may be readmitted informally, in accordance with s 131, although unable to consent for lack of capacity: *R v Bournewood Community and Mental Health NHS Trust, ex p L* [1999] 1 AC 458, [1998] 3 All ER 289, HL. But detention in such circumstances will be contrary to Arts 5(1) and 5(4) unless there are procedural safeguards to protect the patient against an assumption by the authority of full control over his liberty and treatment: *HL v United Kingdom (Application 45508/99)* (2004) 40 EHRR 761, 81 BMLR 131. In *AM v South London & Maudsley NHS Foundation Trust* [2013] UKUT 0365 (AAC). Mr Justice Charles considered the inter-relationship of the Mental Health jurisdiction and that of the Mental Capacity Act 2005 in respect of a compliant incapacitated person and the appropriateness of applying the DOLS safeguarding procedure (see also *GJ v Foundation Trust etc* [2009] EWHC 2972 (Fam). See Chapter 14 of the Code of Practice Mental Health Act 1983 and in particular paragraph 14.16 regarding fluctuating capacity. Chapter 19 addresses issues regarding children under 16 years of age and *Gillick* competency (paragraph 19.65). See further deprivation of liberty under Mental Capacity Act 2005 as amended **III MEN [9]** above.

III MEN [26]

134. Correspondence of patients

(1) A postal packet addressed to any person by a patient detained in a hospital under this Act and delivered by the patient for dispatch may be withheld from the postal operator concerned—

- (a) if that person has requested that communications addressed to him by the patient should be withheld; or
- (b) subject to subsection (3) below, if the hospital is one at which high security psychiatric services are provided and the managers of the hospital consider that the postal packet is likely—
  - (i) to cause distress to the person to whom it is addressed or to any other person (not being a person on the staff of the hospital); or
  - (ii) to cause danger to any person;

and any request for the purposes of paragraph (a) above shall be made by a notice in writing given to the managers of the hospital, or the approved clinician with overall responsibility for the patient's case [...].

(2) Subject to subsection (3) below, a postal packet addressed to a patient detained under this Act in a hospital at which high security psychiatric services are provided may be withheld from the patient if, in the opinion of the managers of the hospital, it is necessary to do so in the interests of the safety of the patient or for the protection of other persons.

(3) Subsections (1)(b) and (2) above do not apply to any postal packet addressed by a patient to, or sent to a patient by or on behalf of—

- (a) any Minister of the Crown or the Scottish Ministers or Member of either House of Parliament or member of the Scottish Parliament or of the Northern Ireland Assembly;
- (aa) any of the Welsh Ministers, the Counsel General to the Welsh Assembly Government or a member of the National Assembly for Wales;
- (b) any judge or officer of the Court of Protection, any of the Court of Protection Visitors or any person asked by that Court for a report under section 49 of the Mental Capacity Act 2005 concerning the patient;
- (c) the Parliamentary Commissioner for Administration, the Scottish Public Services Ombudsman, the Public Services Ombudsman for Wales, the Health Service Commissioner for England or a Local Commissioner within the meaning of Part III of the Local Government Act 1974;
- (ca) the Care Quality Commission;
- (d) the First-tier Tribunal or the Mental Health Review Tribunal for Wales;
- (e) the National Health Service Commissioning Board, a clinical commissioning group, a Local Health Board or Special Health

Authority, a local social services authority, a Community Health Council, a local probation board established under section 4 of the Criminal Justice and Court Services Act 2000 or a provider of probation services;

(ea) a provider of a patient advocacy and liaison service for the assistance of patients at the hospital and their families and carers;

(eb) a provider of independent advocacy services for the patient;

(f) the managers of the hospital in which the patient is detained;

(g) any legally qualified person instructed by the patient to act as his legal adviser; or

(h) the European Commission of Human Rights or the European Court of Human Rights

and for the purposes of paragraph (d) above the reference to the First-tier Tribunal is a reference to that tribunal so far as it is acting for the purposes of any proceedings under this Act or paragraph 5(2) of the Schedule to the Repatriation of Prisoners Act 1984.

(3A) In subsection (3) above—

(a) 'patient advocacy and liaison service' means a service of a description prescribed by regulations made by the Secretary of State, and

(b) 'independent advocacy services' means services provided under—

(i) arrangements under section 130A or section 130E above;

(ii) arrangements under section 223A of the Local Government and Public Involvement in Health Act 2007 or section 187 of the National Health Service (Wales) Act 2006; or

(iii) arrangements of a description prescribed as mentioned in paragraph (a) above.

(4) The managers of a hospital may inspect and open any postal packet for the purposes of determining—

(a) whether it is one to which subsection (1) or (2) applies, and

(b) in the case of a postal packet to which subsection (1) or (2) above applies, whether or not it should be withheld under that subsection;

and the power to withhold a postal packet under either of those subsections includes power to withhold anything contained in it.

(5) Where a postal packet or anything contained in it is withheld under subsection (1) or (2) above the managers of the hospital shall record that fact in writing.

(6) Where a postal packet or anything contained in it is withheld under subsection (1)(b) or (2) above the managers of the hospital shall within seven days give notice of that fact to the patient and, in the case of a packet withheld under subsection (2) above, to the person (if known) by whom the postal packet was sent; and any such notice shall be given in writing and shall contain a statement of the effect of section 134A(1) to (4).

(7) The functions of the managers of a hospital under this section shall be discharged on their behalf by a person on the staff of the hospital appointed by them for that purpose and different persons may be appointed to discharge different functions.

(8) The Secretary of State may make regulations with respect to the exercise of the powers conferred by this section.

(9) In this section and section 134A 'hospital' has the same meaning as in Part II of this Act and 'postal operator' and 'postal packet' have the same meaning as in the Postal Services Act 2000< . . . >.

III MEN [26.1]

Regulations under this section See the Mental Health (Hospital, Guardianship and Treatment) (England) Regulations 2008, SI 2008/1184, rr 29–31. Note for proceedings before the Civil Courts sitting in Wales, the provisions of Mental Health (Hospital, Guardianship, Community Treatment and Consent to Treatment) (Wales) Regulations 2008, SI 2008/2439 may apply.

III MEN [26.2]

Injunction to prevent correspondence In *Broadmoor Hospital Authority v R* [2000] 2 All ER 727, 52 BMLR 137, CA, the court held that, although it could grant an injunction to assist in the performance of its statutory responsibilities, it was limited to protecting interests internal to the hospital. An injunction which effectively prevented the patient's agents from dealing with his book was disallowed.

III MEN [27]

139. Protection for acts done in pursuance of this Act

(1) No person shall be liable, whether on the ground of want of jurisdiction or on any other ground, to any civil or criminal proceedings to which he would have been liable apart from this section in respect of any act purporting to be done in pursuance of this Act or any regulations or rules made under this Act, unless the act was done in bad faith or without reasonable care.

(2) No civil proceedings shall be brought against any person in any court in respect of any such act without the leave of the High Court; and no criminal proceedings shall be brought against any person in any court in respect of any such act except by or with the consent of the Director of Public Prosecutions.

(3) This section does not apply to proceedings for an offence under this Act, being proceedings which, under any other provision of this Act, can be instituted only by or with the consent of the Director of Public Prosecutions.

(4) This section does not apply to proceedings against the Secretary of State or against the National Health Service Commissioning Board, a clinical commissioning group, a Local Health Board or Special Health Authority or against a National Health Service trust established under the National Health Service (Wales) Act 2006 or NHS foundation trust or against the Department of Justice in Northern Ireland or against a person who has functions under this Act by virtue of section 12ZA in so far as the proceedings relate to the exercise of those functions.

(5) In relation to Northern Ireland the reference in this section to the Director of Public Prosecutions shall be construed as a reference to the Director of Public Prosecutions for Northern Ireland.

III MEN [27.1]

Leave of the High Court The court's permission to start proceedings may be sought by application in accordance with CPR Part 23 (see para **CPR 23** in Volume 1). The application should be made to a judge, because Masters and district judges are denied the power to make orders under this section by para 3.1(g) of the Practice Direction 2B–Allocation of cases to Levels of Judiciary: **CPR PD 2B**.

Proceedings started without such permission are a nullity: *Pountney v Griffiths* [1976] AC 314, [1975] 2 All ER 881, HL; *Seal v Chief Constable of South Wales Police* [2005] EWCA Civ 586, (2005) Times, 31 May, [2007] UKHL 31, [2007] 4 All ER 177, (2007) Times, 5 July.

The order of a judge refusing leave under s 139(2), is an interim and not a final order, and as such leave to appeal of that judge, or, of the Court of Appeal is required: *Moore v Metropolitan Police Comr* [1968] 1 QB 26, [1967] 2 All ER 827, CA.

In *David Johnston v Chief Constable of Merseyside* [2009] EWHC 2969 (QB) the Court of Appeal held, that in considering an application under s 139(2) the court had to apply the test in *Winch v Hayward* [1986] QB 296, [1985] 3 All ER 97, CA and also must consider whether the proposed claim had a real prospect of success. Applying this test and proceeding to evaluate the claim and the considering an argument relating to compatibility of s 139(2) with Article 14 of the ECHR Bean J in *Enfield London Borough Council (Secretary of State for Health intervening)* [2013] EWHC 1180 (QB), 132 BMLR 227 found that the earlier finding in *Seal v Chief Constable of South Wales Police* [2007] UKHL 31, [2007] 4 All ER 177, [2007] 1 WLR 1910 that 'the protection of those responsible for the care of mental patients from being harassed by litigation has been accepted as a legitimate objective' was a conclusive answer to the Article 14 claim, and found no merit in the arguments proposed concerning s 11(4) of the 1983 Act.

In *M (by his litigation friend TM) v Hackney London Borough Council* [2011] EWCA Civ 4, [2011] 3 All ER 529, [2011] 1 WLR 2873 the Court of Appeal asserted, that in appropriate cases, the effect of the provision of s 139(1) was to limit the civil liability of an Approved Mental Health Practitioner (AMHP), and a local authority (where relevant) for the AHMP's unlawful act to cases where the act was done in bad faith or without reasonable care. That restriction however is subject to the provisions of the Human Rights Act. For an example of this see *DD v Durham County Council* [2012] EWHC 1053 (QB), [2012] PTSR D35, Where Eady J applied the principles set out by Collins J, at first instance in *M* (above) (paragraph 21) as to the application of s 139(2), and reiterated the relatively low threshold test for granting leave as confirmed in Seal and Winch above, namely whether there is 'a real prospect of success'.

III MEN [27.2]

Contravention of human rights It has been held that s 139(1)'s restricted provision for civil liability should be read subject to s 3 of the Human Rights Act 1998 so as to allow compensation to be claimed for unlawful detention based on an invalid application for admission as a patient: *M v Hackney London Borough Council* (2011) Times, 17 February, [2011] 3 All ER 529.

ENDURING POWERS OF ATTORNEY ACT 1985

(c 29)

GENERAL NOTES ON THE ENDURING POWERS OF ATTORNEY ACT 1985

III MEN [28]

Repeal of the Act as from 1 October 2007 The Enduring Powers of Attorney Act 1985 created a new power of attorney which differed from the ordinary power of attorney in that it survived the onset of the donor's incapacity. The Act provided formalities for the execution of such a power and for its registration upon the onset of incapacity. However, the Act was repealed by s 67(2) of the Mental Capacity Act 2005 with effect from 1 October 2007 when the provisions of that Act on lasting powers of attorney were brought into force. But a legal framework for enduring powers of attorney which had already been granted was retained in revised form: see s 66(3) and Schedule 4, at **III MEN [104]** and **III MEN [134]**, and the repeal of the Act is subject to the transitional provisions in Part 2 of Schedule 5 to the Mental Capacity Act 2005, at **III MEN [143]**.

III MEN [29]

Registration of enduring powers of attorney created before 1 October 2007 Regulations 23 to 29 of the Lasting Powers of Attorney, Enduring Powers of Attorney and Public Guardian Regulations 2007, SI 2007/1253 lay down the procedure for activating existing enduring powers of attorney which were unregistered at 1 October 2007. Two new forms are prescribed by regs 23 and 24, one for giving notice of intention to apply for registration and the other for the application itself to the Public Guardian; and regs 25 onwards deal with the problems which can arise in the case of objections, revocation of the power and loss or destruction of the instrument, see **III MEN [433]** below.

MENTAL CAPACITY ACT 2005

(c 9)

MENTAL CAPACITY AND MENTAL HEALTH

GENERAL NOTES ON THE MENTAL CAPACITY ACT 2005

III MEN [30]

The Mental Capacity Act 2005 is divided into Part 1 Persons who lack capacity, Part 2 The Court of Protection and the Public Guardian and Part 3 Miscellaneous and general.

The main purposes of Part 1 are to reform and clarify the law relating to mental capacity for the benefit of those who lack it. Sections 1 to 4 establish the 5 principles to be applied for the purposes of the Act, the defining of capacity, the inability to make decisions and 'best interests'. Sections 4A and 4B give guidance on restrictions on deprivation of liberty, and authority for such deprivation if necessary for life sustaining treatment etc. Sections 5 to 8 set out the rights and obligations which arise whenever anyone treats or acts for a person who lacks capacity without being authorised to do so by the court or under a power of attorney. Sections 9 to 14 give legal effect to lasting powers of attorney, which replace enduring powers of attorney and include within their scope the making of decisions as to personal welfare. The provisions of ss 15 to 20 empower the court to make declarations and decisions regarding those who lack capacity and the application of Part 1 generally, including the appointment of deputies to manage the property and affairs and make welfare decisions, for and on behalf of persons who lack capacity. Section 21 regulates the transfer of proceedings relating to people under the age of 18, and s 21A establishes the powers of the court on issues of deprivation of liberty in relation to standard and urgent authorisations

MENTAL CAPACITY AND MENTAL HEALTH

made under Schedule A1. Sections 22 and 23 set out the powers of the court in respect of the validity and operation of lasting powers of attorney. Sections 24 to 26 give validity to advance decisions to refuse treatment; and ss 27 to 29 exclude certain decision-making (as to family relationships, Mental Health Act matters and voting rights) from the scope of the Act. Part 1 further includes provisions regulating the carrying out of research on persons who lack capacity (ss 30 to 34), the establishment of an independent mental capacity advocate service (ss 35, 36, and 41), the publication of Codes of Practice (ss 42 and 43) and the creation of an offence of ill-treatment, or wilful neglect, of a person who lacks capacity (s 44).

Sections 37 to 39 deal with provisions relating to serious medical treatment by an NHS body, the provision of accommodation by such a body, or by a local authority, and important provisions (ss 39A, 39B, 39C, 39D, and 39E) were incorporated arising from the Mental Health Act 2007 amendments relating specifically to deprivation of liberty issues and the procedures where a person becomes subject to Schedule A1 of the Act.

Part 2 of the Act, creates the new Court of Protection, identifying its judges, and providing supplementary powers. Sections 50 to 53 establish the court's practice and procedure and by ss 54 to 56 the provisions and powers in respect of fees and costs. Sections 57 to 60 establish the role of the Public Guardian the extent of the functions of that officer, the establishment of the Public Guardian Board (now abolished) and the provision of annual reports. Section 61 defines the status of Court of Protection Visitors.

The text of the Act as amended is set out below, together with the first five Schedules including Schedules A1 and 1A.

The key provisions of the Act (including those introducing lasting powers of attorney, a new Court of Protection and the office of Public Guardian), were all brought into force by the Mental Capacity Act 2005 (Commencement No 2) Order 2007, SI 2007/1897, with effect from 1 October 2007. Deprivation of Liberty safeguards were added to the Act, because of the requirements of Article 5 of the Convention on Human Rights and decided cases noted at **III MEN [9]**, above. The safeguards are now provided in new ss 4A, 4B, 16A and Schedules A1 and 1A which were inserted by s 50 of the Mental Health Act 2007 and brought fully into force on 1 April 2009 by the Mental Health Act 2007 (Commencement No 10 and Transitional Provisions) Order 2009, SI 2009/139. The Deprivation of Liberty Safeguards Code of Practice, which was issued on 26 August 2008, also came into force on 1 April 2009.

PART 1
PERSONS WHO LACK CAPACITY
THE PRINCIPLES

III MEN [31]

1. The principles

(1) The following principles apply for the purposes of this Act.

(2) A person must be assumed to have capacity unless it is established that he lacks capacity.

(3) A person is not to be treated as unable to make a decision unless all practicable steps to help him to do so have been taken without success.

(4) A person is not to be treated as unable to make a decision merely because he makes an unwise decision.

(5) An act done, or decision made, under this Act for or on behalf of a person who lacks capacity must be done, or made, in his best interests.

(6) Before the act is done, or the decision is made, regard must be had to whether the purpose for which it is needed can be as effectively achieved in a way that is less restrictive of the person's rights and freedom of action.

III MEN [31.1]

The Principles This section establishes the central principles to the Mental Capacity Act 2005 and in all determinations regard must be given to both the principles (s 1) and best interests (s 4). There is the presumption of capacity and regard must be given to the provisions of s 2 and s 3 which provide guidance as to identifying whether an individual lacks capacity and the basis for determining that an individual is unable to make a decision.

The emphasis of the provisions of the Act is the enabling of individuals to reach their own decisions and the Code of Practice provides useful guidance on the range of practicable steps that may be taken to assist an individual in reaching his or her decision (Chapter 3). In *D Borough Council v AB* [2011] EWHC 101 (COP) Mostyn J, explored this issue of s 1(3) 'practicable steps' in relation to ability to consent to sexual relations and provided interim orders to enable opportunity for a Local Authority to take further steps 'of a sex-educative nature' to attempt to increase the individual's 'requisite level of capacity so that the present regime of deprivation of liberty could be lifted'. This decision was followed by Baker J in *A Local Authority v TZ (by his litigation friend, the Official Solicitor)* [2013] EWHC 2322 (COP), [2013] All ER (D) 144 (Oct), where it was determined that P had capacity to consent to and engage in sexual relations and where the court opposed the imposition of a higher standard for capacity in reaching decisions when addressing the third limb of s 3 of the Act (s 3(1)(c)), and reminding itself of the provisions of s 1(4) of the Act and that a person was not to be treated as unable to make a decision merely because it was unwise.

See also *CH (by his litigation friend, the Official Solicitor) v A Metropolitan Council* [2017] EWCOP 12, Sir Mark Hedley, where approval was granted to the settlement of a claim for damages for breach of P's Article 8 rights, where education that ought to have been made available for P to enable him to regain capacity to consent to sexual relations was delayed by the local authority. He had been prohibited from having sex with his wife for a prolonged period of time as a result. His wife also settled her Human Rights Act claim.

Declaring that P lacked capacity to marry, Bodey J in *A LA v AK* [2013] COPLR 163 stressed the importance of a the court having regard to the entirety of the evidence both expert and lay witness, when applying the principles of the Act and considering the issue of capacity. He cautions of the need to guard against an over paternalistic approach.

In *ZH (A Protected Party by GH, his Litigation Friend) v Metropolitan Police Comr* [2012] EWHC 604 (QB) Sir Robert Nelson in examining the conduct of police officers and the availability of the provision of s 5 and s 6 of the Act to meet their conduct, stresses the necessity at all relevant stages of considering whether there might be a less restrictive way of dealing with the matter under s 1(6) of the Act. This decision was upheld on appeal in *ZH (by his litigation friend) v Metropolitan Police Comr* [2013] EWCA Civ 69, [2013] 3 All ER 113, [2013] 1 WLR 3021.

III MEN [31.2]

The Codes of Practice and the Principles Chapter 2 of the Mental Capacity Act 2005 Code of Practice provides guidance on the statutory principles and how they should be applied. Chapter 3 of the Mental Capacity Act 2005 Code of Practice provides guidance and examples of how people may be assisted to reach their own decisions.

PRELIMINARY

III MEN [32]

2. People who lack capacity

(1) For the purposes of this Act, a person lacks capacity in relation to a matter if at the material time he is unable to make a decision for himself in relation to the matter because of an impairment of, or a disturbance in the functioning of, the mind or brain.

(2) It does not matter whether the impairment or disturbance is permanent or temporary.

(3) A lack of capacity cannot be established merely by reference to—

- (a) a person's age or appearance, or
- (b) a condition of his, or an aspect of his behaviour, which might lead others to make unjustified assumptions about his capacity.

(4) In proceedings under this Act or any other enactment, any question whether a person lacks capacity within the meaning of this Act must be decided on the balance of probabilities.

(5) No power which a person ('D') may exercise under this Act—

- (a) in relation to a person who lacks capacity, or
- (b) where D reasonably thinks that a person lacks capacity,

is exercisable in relation to a person under 16.

(6) Subsection (5) is subject to section 18(3).

III MEN [32.1]

Mental capacity and litigation If the litigant lacks mental capacity, because, for example, he or she is unable to use or weigh information as part of the process of making a decision, a litigation friend must be appointed in the litigation, as required by CPR 21.1 and CPR 21.2: *Ganley v Jones* [2011] EWCA Civ 75, [2011] All ER (D) 58 (Jul).

As an example of the utilisation of the Act and the correct application of the relevant tests of capacity in ensuring that any decision is time and fact specific, in *A B and C v X and Z* [2012] EWHC 2400 (COP) Hedley J upon the evidence and expert opinion before him was able to declare that applying the test in *Masterman-Lister v Brutton & Co* [2002] EWCA Civ 1889, [2003] 3 All ER 162, [2003] 1 WLR 1511, P lacked capacity to litigate, lacked capacity to manage his own property and affairs, but applying *Banks v Goodfellow* (1870) LR 5 QB 549 did have capacity to make a will, and applying the test in *Re E (An alleged Patient), Sheffield City Council v E and S* [2004] EWHC 2008 (Fam) the Applicants had not discharged the burden of showing that P lacked capacity to marry.

Exploring further the intention of the Mental Capacity Act 2005, in *Re P (Abortion)* [2013] EWHC 50 (COP) Hedley J in considering inter alia whether P had capacity to litigate and to make decisions to undergo a termination stated 'the intention of the Act is not to dress a person lacking in capacity in forensic cotton wool but to allow them as far as possible to make the same mistakes that all other human beings are at liberty to make and not infrequently do'.

Where an issue arises as to whether an individual may lack capacity for the purposes of CPR 21(1)(ii)(c), the court has held that the provisions of ss 1 and 2 of the Mental Capacity Act 2005 must be applied and in particular the assumption that a person has capacity unless it was established to the contrary. Medical evidence it was held would ordinarily be required: *Baker Tilly (A Firm) v Makar* [2013] EWHC 759 (QB).

In *Blankley v Central Manchester and Manchester Children's University Hospitals NHS Trust* [2014] EWHC 168 (QB), [2014] 2 All ER 1104, [2014] 1 WLR 2683 the court in a costs assessment addressed the issue of fluctuating capacity and its impact upon a solicitor's retainer under a Conditional Fee Agreement.

III MEN [33]

3. Inability to make decisions

(1) For the purposes of section 2, a person is unable to make a decision for himself if he is unable—

- (a) to understand the information relevant to the decision,
- (b) to retain that information,
- (c) to use or weigh that information as part of the process of making the decision, or
- (d) to communicate his decision (whether by talking, using sign language or any other means).

(2) A person is not to be regarded as unable to understand the information relevant to a decision if he is able to understand an explanation of it given to him in a way that is appropriate to his circumstances (using simple language, visual aids or any other means).

(3) The fact that a person is able to retain the information relevant to a decision for a short period only does not prevent him from being regarded as able to make the decision.

(4) The information relevant to a decision includes information about the reasonably foreseeable consequences of—

- (a) deciding one way or another, or
- (b) failing to make the decision.

III MEN [33.1]

Inability to make decisions These principles have application in all cases regarding the decision whether or not an individual has or has not capacity to make a decision or undertake an act.

In *Re LT (vulnerable adult) (decision making capacity)* [2010] EWHC 1910 (Fam), [2011] 1 FLR 594, [2010] Fam Law 1283, the President recorded that the role of the court was to apply the plain language of the 2005 Act to the relevant specific facts, and that it was generally inappropriate or unnecessary to consider case law pre-dating the statute save in exceptional cases. In interpreting s 3(1)(c) of the 2005 Act, the individual incapacities were not to be treated as cumulative, and that an individual lacked capacity if any one of the sub-ss (a) to (d) applied. In furtherance of this guidance, Hedley J in *A Local Authority v FG and Others (No 1)* [2011] EWHC 3932 (COP) cautioned against the citation of first instance judgments when addressing the issue of capacity enabling the court to focus on its role of fact finding, applying the statutory principles, and reaching its conclusion.

In *LBL v RYJ and VJ* [2010] EWHC 2665 (COP)[2011] 1 FLR 1279 the court re-iterated that s 2(1) must be read as meaning that capacity was to be assessed in relation to the particular type of decision at the time the decision needed to be made, not the person's ability to make decisions generally or in abstract. The fact of inconsistency was not necessarily a sign of confusion; equally confusion was not necessarily an indication of incapacity. Having regard to s 3, it was only necessary for the individual under review to comprehend and weigh the salient details relevant to the decision to be made, rather than being able to give weight to every consideration that would otherwise be utilised in formulating a decision 'objectively in that person's best interests.

In *Re MM* [2011] 1 FLR 712 it was held, that if an issue as to capacity arose, then it was incumbent upon those involved to act with all expediency in securing determination of that capacity. In that respect the President in *A v A local authority, A Care Home Manager and S* [2011] EWHC 727 (COP), [2011] 2 FLR 459, [2011] Fam Law 590 used the court's powers to commission a report from a Court of Protection Special Visitor under s 49 as to both capacity and best interests (see **III MEN [87]**).

In engaging an expert to provide a report as to P's capacity Baker J in *SC v BS and A Local Authority* [2012] COPLR 567 warned that 'provisional views' as to capacity should not be given until the full history of P had been considered.

Understanding of information on which to base a decision, for example about avoiding pregnancy by adopting contraceptive procedures, does not necessarily mean that the person concerned has capacity to adopt or reject it. Another important element is the ability to use or weigh the information, in accordance with sub-s (1)(c), as part of the process of making the decision. For example, a woman whose free will is overborne by domestic violence may understand the information about contraception but lack the capacity to make a decision about it: *A Local Authority v Mrs A (by the Official Solicitor)* [2010] EWHC 1549 (Fam), [2010] Fam Law 928.

It was for the court to assess and evaluate the relevant evidence relating to capacity, and in *PH v A Local Authority* [2011] EWHC 1704 (Fam) Peter Jackson J held that in determining issues of capacity there was no requirement to introduce a threshold condition and for such evidence to be 'compelling' before a finding could be made. Similarly, it was not necessary for the statutory test to be construed narrowly. Professionals working with individuals were further cautioned to avoid adopting a protective approach in assessments of capacity which should provide for objectivity and detachment. This was demonstrated in *Heart of England NHS Foundation Trust v JB (by her litigation friend, the Official Solicitor)* [2014] EWHC 342 (COP), 137 BMLR 232 where the same judge found that a whilst P had a disturbance in the functioning of her mind in the form of paranoid schizophrenia, it had not been established that she lacked capacity to make a decision about surgery for herself.

Some decisions as to capacity may be status or act specific whereas others may be person specific, a distinction that is apparently drawn in s 27 and in s 17. The issue is, in any case, the same, namely, whether the person is able to make a decision for himself, or herself, 'in relation to a matter': *PC (by her litigation friend the Official Solicitor) v A Local Authority* [2013] EWCA Civ 478, [2014] 2 WLR 1, [2013] NLJR 17 in which the court stressed that there was no justification for the plain words of the section to be embellished.

In *CS (Termination of Pregnancy)* [2016] EWCOP 10, Baker J provided a summary of the relevant law and guidance for the approach to be adopted by a court where it was found that P lacked capacity in respect of her decision to undergo a termination of pregnancy and was expressing fluctuating wishes. The decision addresses this interrelationship of ss 2 and 3 and the consequential best interests decision under s 4.

Further, it has been held that every single issue of capacity that falls to be determined under Part 1 has to be evaluated by applying s 3(1) of the Act in full and considering each of the four elements of the decision-making process, and where the issue was capacity to consent to sexual relationships the test was general and issue specific, rather than person or event specific: *IM v LM (by her litigation friend, the Official Solicitor) (capacity to consent to sexual relations)* [2014] EWCA Civ 37, [2014] 3 All ER 491, [2014] 3 WLR 409. This decision was followed and applied in *A Local Authority v TZ* [2014] EWHC 973 (COP) where Baker J preferred the approach of the court continuing to make certain welfare decisions as opposed to the appointment of a welfare deputy (see Code of Practice, paras 5.8, 8.31–8.39).

In *Kings College Hospital NHS Foundation Trust v C* [2015] EWCOP 80, [2015] All ER (D) 09 (Dec) MacDonald J in addressing the issue of whether a Trust had established on the balance of probability that an individual lacked capacity to decide whether or not to accept treatment by way of analysis, provided an extensive resume of the relevant law to be applied by any decision maker. Followed and adopted by Cobb J in *Re Z* [2016] EWCOP 4 the court cautioned itself firstly to avoid considering outcome when determining 'P's' functional ability, and further that the test is 'P's' functionality at the time of hearing which is relevant, with P not being required to use or weigh every detail of the respective option available, merely salient points: *CC v KK and STCC* [2012] EWHC 2136 applied.

III MEN [33.2]

The Code of Practice and assisting 'P' in reaching decisions The Mental Capacity Act 2005 Code of Practice provides important guidance as to steps to be taken in determining capacity and to assist individuals to reach their own decision: see Chapters 3 and 4.

III MEN [33.3]

Consent to sexual intercourse An issue may arise as to whether a person has capacity to consent to sexual intercourse. In order to possess capacity to consent to sexual relations, a person clearly has to have a basic understanding of the mechanics of the physical act and of the risk of pregnancy and avoidable ill-health. Moral and emotional components were not to be incorporated into the legal test beyond the requirement that a person understands the issue of choice and can refuse sexual relations: *A Local Authority v H* [2012] EWHC 49 (COP), [2012] 1 FCR 590, 124 BMLR 98 and *A Local Authority v TZ (by his litigation friend, the Official Solicitor)* [2013] EWHC 2322 (COP), [2013] All ER (D) 144 (Oct). See also s 27(1) (b) at **III MEN [61]**. In *IM v LM (by her litigation friend, the Official Solicitor) (capacity to consent to sexual relations)* [2014] EWCA Civ 37, [2014] 3 All ER 491, [2014] 3 WLR 409 the Court of Appeal stated that the test for capacity to consent to sexual relationships was general and issue specific rather than person or event specific.

In *Re DD (No 4) (Sterilisation)* [2015] EWCOP 4, [2015] All ER (D) 96 (Feb) Cobb J addressed the issue of capacity to make decisions in relation to contraception and sterilisation and analysed by reference to s 3(1)(a) ('ability to understand'), s 3(1)(c) ('ability to use or weigh'), s 1(3) ('all practical steps been taken') and s 4(3) ('likelihood of regaining capacity') the capacity of the individual to make the relevant decisions.

In *London Borough of Southwark v KA (Capacity to Marry)* [2016] EWCOP 20 Mrs Justice Parker at para 32 of her judgment provides a schedule of relevant authorities put to her in respect of the issue before her and reflecting upon the decision of Hedley J in *A Local Authority v H* [2012] EWHC 49 (COP) confirmed that it would be 'invidious to be asked to disagree with decisions of Judges with concurrent or higher jurisdiction, but that the decision had to be taken on the basis of the statute'.

See also *CH v A Metropolitan Council* [2017] EWCOP 12 where damages were approved for a man and his wife who were prevented from engaging in sexual relations because the local authority assessed him as lacking capacity to consent. Damages were awarded for breach of Art 8 because the authority delayed in providing the man with education that would have enabled him to consent.

As capacity is issue specific, there can be a tension between the outcomes of assessments, for instance where P does not lack capacity to consent to sexual relations, but does lack the capacity to choose with whom to have contact. This can give rise to difficult questions when balancing best interests in areas in which P has capacity as a result of needing make decisions in areas where they do not have capacity. In one case the Judge suggested that all such cases should be heard by High Court judges: see *Manchester City Council v LC and KR* [2018] EWCOP 30 (Mr Justice Hayden at para [24]).

III MEN [33.4]

Gifts and wills As regards the capacity to make a gift, it has been held at first instance that the common law test in *Re Beaney* [1978] 2 All 595, [1978] 1 WLR 770 should be applied in preference to the test in s 3(1): *Re Estate of Joyce Smith (deceased); Kicks v Leigh* [2014] EWHC 3926 (Ch), [2015] WTLR 579, [2014] All ER (D) 295 (Nov). As regards the capacity to make a will, it has been held that the propositions in ss 1(2) and 3(1) are inconsistent with the common law as stated in *Banks v Goodfellow* (1870) LR 5 QB 549, [1861–73] All ER Rep 47 and that the common law test is to be preferred: unreported decision in *Walker v Badmin* [2014] Lexis Citation 237, [2014] All ER (D) 258 (Nov).

In *McCabe v McCabe* [2015] EWHC 1591 (Ch) the presence of Alzheimer's disease was found not necessarily to negate testamentary capacity. See also *Lloyd v Jones* [2016] EWHC 1308 (Ch), [2016] All ER (D) 39 (Jun) where a will was upheld in a case where the Testator had dementia.

III MEN [34]

4. Best interests

(1) In determining for the purposes of this Act what is in a person's best interests, the person making the determination must not make it merely on the basis of—

(a) the person's age or appearance, or
(b) a condition of his, or an aspect of his behaviour, which might lead others to make unjustified assumptions about what might be in his best interests.

(2) The person making the determination must consider all the relevant circumstances and, in particular, take the following steps.

(3) He must consider—
(a) whether it is likely that the person will at some time have capacity in relation to the matter in question, and
(b) if it appears likely that he will, when that is likely to be.

(4) He must, so far as reasonably practicable, permit and encourage the person to participate, or to improve his ability to participate, as fully as possible in any act done for him and any decision affecting him.

(5) Where the determination relates to life-sustaining treatment he must not, in considering whether the treatment is in the best interests of the person concerned, be motivated by a desire to bring about his death.

(6) He must consider, so far as is reasonably ascertainable—
(a) the person's past and present wishes and feelings (and, in particular, any relevant written statement made by him when he had capacity),
(b) the beliefs and values that would be likely to influence his decision if he had capacity, and
(c) the other factors that he would be likely to consider if he were able to do so.

(7) He must take into account, if it is practicable and appropriate to consult them, the views of—
(a) anyone named by the person as someone to be consulted on the matter in question or on matters of that kind,
(b) anyone engaged in caring for the person or interested in his welfare,
(c) any donee of a lasting power of attorney granted by the person, and
(d) any deputy appointed for the person by the court,

as to what would be in the person's best interests and, in particular, as to the matters mentioned in subsection (6).

(8) The duties imposed by subsections (1) to (7) also apply in relation to the exercise of any powers which—
(a) are exercisable under a lasting power of attorney, or
(b) are exercisable by a person under this Act where he reasonably believes that another person lacks capacity.

(9) In the case of an act done, or a decision made, by a person other than the court, there is sufficient compliance with this section if (having complied with the requirements of subsections (1) to (7)) he reasonably believes that what he does or decides is in the best interests of the person concerned.

(10) 'Life-sustaining treatment' means treatment which in the view of a person providing health care for the person concerned is necessary to sustain life.

(11) 'Relevant circumstances' are those—
(a) of which the person making the determination is aware, and
(b) which it would be reasonable to regard as relevant.

III MEN [34.1]

The duty to act in the best interests of 'P' The decision maker, including where that is the Court, may only take a decision for P that P would be able to taken himself if he had capacity: see *N v A CCG* [2017] UKSC 22. The extent to which options maybe explored by the Court was a matter of case management and not of jurisdiction.

Issues concerning medical treatment in the best interests of the patient were previously decided according to common law and relevant decisions are noted at **III MEN [7]**, above. However, the Act provides a new approach to weighing the best interests, importantly the taking account of the wishes of the incapacitated person. In *Re S and S (Protected Persons), C v V* [2009] WTLR 315, [2008] EWHC B16 (Fam), the weight to be attached to P's wishes and feelings in the context of the 2005 Act was considered, and the new approach that should be adopted was further considered in an application for authority to make a statutory will: *Re P* [2009] EWHC 163 (Ch), [2009] 2 All ER 1198. The decision-maker has to adopt a structured decision-making process, weighing the various factors and then arrive at a value judgment as to what the decision should be 'in the P's best interests': *Re M (vulnerable adult) (testamentary capacity)* [2009] EWHC 2525 (Fam), [2010] 3 All ER 682, [2011] 1 WLR 344. In *Re M (vulnerable adult) (testamentary capacity)* Munby J (as he then was) set out comprehensively the approach on the 'question of weight to be afforded to P's incapacitous wishes and feelings. Firstly such wishes and feelings will always be a significant factor to which the court will place close regard. Secondly the weight attached to such wishes and feelings will always be case-specific and fact-specific. Thirdly in considering the weight and importance to be attached to such wishes and feelings the court is required by s 4(2) to have regard to all the relevant circumstances, including (a) the degree of P's incapacity, (b) the strength and consistency of P's views, (c) the impact on P of knowledge that her wishes and feelings are not being given effect to, (d) the extent to which P's wishes and feelings are, or are not rational, sensible, responsible and pragmatically capable of sensible implementation in the particular circumstances. And (e) crucially the extent to which P's wishes and feelings if given effect to can properly be accommodated within the court's overall assessment of what is in her best interest. In *Re DT* [2015] EWCOP 10, [2015] All ER (D) 48 (Mar) Senior Judge Lush in dismissing an application of the Public Guardian to revoke and cancel the registration of an Enduring Power of Attorney applied para 58 of the judgment of HHJ Hazel Marshall QC in *Re S and S (Protected Persons), C v V* [2009] WTLR 315, [2008] EWHC B16 (Fam) in assessing the present wishes of the Donor in continuing the appointment of her sons to act as her attorneys.

See *A NHS Trust v DE (by litigation friend the Official Solicitor) and FG and JK, C Local Authority, and B Partnership Trust* [2013] EWHC 2562 (Fam) for application of the issue of best interests in relation to a decision to authorise a vasectomy.

For an issue of P's life time maintenance payments to family members being determined in her best interests, see *In the matter of G (TJ)* [2010] EWHC 3005 (COP), and in *Re X, Y and Z (Minors)* [2014] EWHC 872 (COP) the court addressed the issue of authorising payments for foster care determining that it was in P's best interests. In *A NHS Trust, B PCT v DU, AO, EB, AU* [2009] EWHC 3504 (Fam) Hedley J explored the issue of P's best interests in both the context of medical treatment and a return by P to her native Nigeria.

In *K v A Local Authority* [2012] EWCA Civ 79, [2012] 1 FCR 441 the Court of Appeal rejected the attempt to introduce authorities stemming from wardship and the case law pertaining to the previous exercise of the High Court's inherent jurisdiction when considering best interests. It was confirmed that the framework of s 4, the checklist, and application of the s 1 principles was to be applied in determining issues under the Act.

The Supreme Court in its first consideration of the Act in relation to medical treatment and the withdrawal of life-sustaining treatment held that the starting point is a strong presumption that it is in a person's best interest to stay alive. Nevertheless that is not absolute: *Aintree University Hospitals NHS Foundation Trust v James* [2013] UKSC 67, [2013] 3 WLR 1299, (2013) Times, 19 November. For an earlier decision applying the best interest test, and in the face of the adamantine approach of the patient that she did not wish to be kept alive, the court declaring that it was not in P's interest to forcibly provide nutrition or hydration see *The NHS Trust v L* [2012] EWHC 2741 (COP). In another case where it was obvious that an incapacitous patient would, had they had capacity, refuse life-sustaining retreatment the court took the wishes into account and decided against declaring it legal to administer such treatment: *Sheffield Teaching Hospitals NHS Foundation Trust v TH* [2014] EWCOP 4, 164 NLJ 7609, [2014] All ER (D) 209 (May).

The 'best interests' approach was applied in circumstances where the issue involved the withdrawal of CANH: see *M v N* [2015] EWCOP 76, [2015] All ER (D) 198 (Nov).

In *Cambridge University Hospital NHS Foundation Trust v BF* [2016] EWCOP 26 MacDonald J following the Supreme Court guidance addressed the issue of treatment of 'P's' ovarian cancer and the resultant risks of being deprived permanently of her ability to have children.

In *An NHS Trust v Mrs H and KH* [2013] COPLR 12 the court in exercising its jurisdiction and applying s 4(6) of the Act declined to provide a blanket declaration in respect of medical treatment and refused to endorse an advanced care plan, but preferred to provide individual declarations as to the best interests of P in relation to specific treatment issues, and as was confirmed in *Re M (Best Interests: Deprivation of Liberty)* [2013] EWHC 3456 (COP) the court would in evaluating best interests seek to create and apply a balance sheet approach in reaching its determination. Finding that it was not in P's best interests to undergo a sterilisation procedure, Cobb J in *A Local Authority v K (by the Official Solicitor)* [2013] EWHC 242 (COP), 130 BMLR 195 determined that any non-therapeutic sterilisation was to be brought back to the court, confirming that it was in her best interests that the court should bring as much clarity as possible to medical treatment issues at the time the matter was before it, recognising that the process of assessments was intrusive and unsettling. Two judgments which demonstrate the importance of the court applying the principles of the Act and examining the best interests of each individual led in one such case to the authorising of the amputation of a limb (*Surrey and Sussex Healthcare NHS Trust v MSAB* [2015] EWCOP 50, [2015] All ER (D) 92 (Aug)) and in *Wye Valley NHS Trust v B* [2015] EWCOP 60, [2015] All ER (D) 04 (Oct) to a decision not to so authorise. In applying the same relevant law, the court demonstrated the importance of each case being fact specific.

The decision of Hayden J in *An NHS Foundation Trust v A and M and P and a Local Authority* [2014] EWHC 920 (COP) provides a useful and clear demonstration of the balance sheet approach to be adopted in determining best interests when considering the issue of insertion of an NJ tube and the appropriate feeding regimes in respect of an anorexic 16 year old, and in *Re P* [2015] EWCOP 42, [2015] All ER (D) 292 (Jun) the court stressed the importance in having regard to the Code of Practice in considering decisions about life-sustaining treatment (see Chapter 5 paras 5.31 to 5.33). See also *Secretary of State for the Home Department v Skripal* [2018] EWCOP 6, Williams J); it was in the best interests of P for blood samples to be taken to test for the presence and provenance of a chemical agent that had rendered them dangerously ill, and incapacitous.

III MEN [34.2]

The Code of Practice and best interests Regard should be made to the Mental Capacity Act 2005 Code of Practice, Chapter 5.

III MEN [35]

4A. Restriction on deprivation of liberty

(1) This Act does not authorise any person ('D') to deprive any other person ('P') of his liberty.

(2) But that is subject to—

(a) the following provisions of this section, and

(b) section 4B.

(3) D may deprive P of his liberty if, by doing so, D is giving effect to a relevant decision of the court.

(4) A relevant decision of the court is a decision made by an order under section 16(2)(a) in relation to a matter concerning P's personal welfare.

(5) D may deprive P of his liberty if the deprivation is authorised by Schedule A1 (hospital and care home residents: deprivation of liberty).

III MEN [35.1]

Restrictions on deprivation of liberty In early case law *G v E, A Local Authority and F* [2010] EWHC 621 (Fam); *A County Council v MB (by the Official Solicitor as her Litigation Friend) and JB and A Residential Home* [2010] EWHC 2508 (COP); and *Surrey County Council and CA and LA v MIG (Incapacitated Adult) & MEG (Incapacitated Minor)* [2010] EWHC 785 (Fam), the High Court sought to establish principles and consistency of interpretation as to that which would amount to deprivation of liberty having regard to the decisions established in Strasbourg case law, decisions on restrictions of liberty affirmed by the House of Lords, and the specific circumstances of the individuals lacking capacity, their needs and best interests. In *P (MIG) and Q (MEG) v Surrey County Council* [2011] EWCA Civ 190, [2011] 1 FCR 559, [2011] 2 FLR 583 the Court of Appeal set out specific factors which they considered the court should have regard when addressing the issue of whether a particular arrangement amounted to a deprivation of liberty, and which they revisited in *Cheshire West and Chester Council v P* [2011] EWCA Civ 1257. (See notes above at **III MEN [9]** and **III MEN [10]**). However, in a landmark decision the Supreme Court overturned these decisions in the matter of *P (by his litigation friend the Official Solicitor) v Cheshire West and Chester Council and another; P and Q (by their litigation friend the Official Solicitor) v Surrey County Council* [2014] UKSC 19. In a majority decision, the Court addressed the test to be adopted in such matters.

Baroness Hale in the lead judgment held that 'it was axiomatic that people with disabilities, both mental and physical, have the same human rights as the rest of the human race' . . . 'what it means to be deprived of liberty must be the same for everyone, whether or not they have physical or mental disabilities'. In addressing the question as to whether there is an 'acid test' for deprivation of liberty, her Ladyship stated' that whilst no guidance could be given, 'the answer . . . lies in those features which have consistently been regarded as "key" in the jurisprudence which started with *HL v United Kingdom* 40 EHRR 761 that the person concerned "was under continuous supervision and control and was not free to leave"

'. Further her Ladyship found that certain factors were not relevant to any determination of deprivation of liberty, namely (i) whether a person was compliant or lacked objection, (ii) the relative normality of the placement (whatever the comparison made), and (iii) the reason or purpose behind a particular placement'.

Applying relevant Strasbourg jurisprudence, Baroness Hale provided further guidance on issues that should be considered in determining whether in fact deprivation of liberty was occurring in any factual circumstance. Referring to European case law at paragraph 37 of her judgment she identified three common grounds, namely (i) the objective component of confinement in a particular restricted place for a not negligible length of time; (ii) the subjective component of lack of valid consent; and (iii) the attribution of responsibility.

The *Cheshire West* test has been found not to apply in some cases where P is receiving physical treatment intensive care: see *R (on the application of Ferreira) v HM Senior Coroner for Inner South London* [2017] EWCA Civ 31.

In subsequent decisions the Court has examined the relationship of the judgment of the Supreme Court to adolescents approaching their majority. Mr Justice Keehan in *D (A Child; deprivation of liberty)* [2015] EWHC 922 (Fam) concluded that the arrangements presented to him amounted to a deprivation of liberty, and parents of a 15 year old were able to consent to the arrangements such a decision falling within the 'zone of parental responsibility'. Returning to this issue in *Birmingham City Council v D* [2016] EWCOP 8 Keehan J held that a parent could not consent to the confinement of a child who has attained the age of 16 years. That, however, was reversed by the Court of Appeal in *Re D (Residence Order: Deprivation of Liberty)* [2017] EWCA Civ 1695, and the decision of the Supreme Court is now awaited to settle this issue.

In direct response to the judgment of the Supreme Court and following guidance given by the President in two judgments *Re X (Deprivation of Liberty)* [2014] EWCOP 25, 141 BMLR 212, and *Re X (Deprivation of Liberty (No 2)* [2014] EWCOP 37, 141 BMLR 225 a streamlined procedure was introduced on 17 November 2014 pursuant to a further Practice Direction 10AA relating to applications made under s 4A(3) and (4) of the Mental Capacity Act 2005, where authorisation is sought pursuant to s 16(2)(a) of the Mental Capacity Act 2005 to sanction arrangements for where an individual who lacks capacity should live and where restrictions involve a deprivation of liberty. In *Re X (Court of Protection Practice)* [2015] EWCA Civ 599 the Court of Appeal in finding no jurisdiction to consider an appeal as against the procedural directions of the President in obiter were critical of the streamlined process and the absence of 'P' being a party to such applications, however in *Re NRA* [2015] EWCOP 59 Charles J as Vice President of the Court of Protection in addressing the obiter of the Court of Appeal gave judgment distinguishing the procedure of the Court of Protection and re-affirming the streamlined procedure subject to modification.

The decision in *W Primary Care Trust v TB* [2009] EWHC 1737 (Fam), [2010] 1 FLR 682 provides a useful analysis of the principles under s 4A, s 16(2)(a) and Schedule A1 and the need to clarify both the establishment in which P resides or may reside subsequently, and the inter relationship of the Mental Capacity Act 2005, the Mental Health Act 1983, and the powers of the Court of Protection.

In *Re GJ, NJ and BJ (Incapacitated Adults)* [2008] EWHC 1097 (Fam), [2008] 2 FLR 1295 and in *Re BJ (Incapacitated Adult)* [2009] EWHC 3310 (Fam), [2010] 1 FLR 1373, [2010] Fam Law 242 Munby LJ identified the nature, level and procedure of reviews that should be established and returned to the court where orders are made depriving an individual of their liberty.

In *A Local Authority v PB and P (By his Litigation Friend the Official Solicitor* [2011] EWHC 2657 (COP), Charles J provided a reminder, that where the question of deprivation of liberty arose, the most important issue was whether the care regime was in P's best interests. In borderline cases or where there was a potential deprivation of liberty, then contingency plans must be implemented to ensure no breach of Article 5 together with reviews. If applicable the Dols regime under Schedule A1 should be used in preference to authorisation and review by the court (see **III MEN [108]**).

In *Secretary for State for Justice v Staffordshire County Council* [2016] EWCA Civ 1317 the Court of Appeal upholding a decision of the Vice President of the Court of Protection found that where 'P' lacked capacity to conduct proceedings, make decisions as to where he should live and what care and treatment he needed, and where restrictions were in place pursuant to a care plan which constituted a deprivation of liberty and for the purposes of the Act, then notwithstanding that such care and support was given entirely by private sector providers in private accommodation an application to the Court of Protection for a welfare order was required that it was in 'P's' best interests so to live within his domestic property and to receive such care and support pursuant to his Care Plan and to the extent that those arrangements were a deprivation of liberty to make a declaration that such deprivation of his liberty was in his best interests. The order made provision for a system of review by the court.

In *Re AJ (Deprivation of Liberty Safeguards)* [2015] EWCOP 5, [2015] 3 WLR 683, [2015] All ER (D) 217 (Feb) Baker J reflecting on the decision of Peter Jackson J in *Hillingdon London Borough Council v Neary* [2011] EWHC 1377 (COP), [2011] 4 All ER 584, [2011] 3 FCR 448 stressed the obligation on the State to ensure a person deprived of their liberty was not merely 'entitled but enabled to have their lawfulness of his detention reviewed speedily by a court', and drew attention to the importance in the selection of a 'relevant person's representative' under para 139(1) of Part 10 of Schedule A1 and of an IMCA under s 39D of the Act. At paras 133–140 of his judgment guidance was given to professionals, local authorities and those family and friends engaged in DOLS applications in an 8 point structured approach.

In *Y County Council v ZZ* [2013] COPLR 463 Moor J whilst recognising that the court did not have jurisdiction to make decisions regarding P's place of residence because of the existence of a guardianship order under s 8 of the Mental Health Act 1983 considered that the court retained jurisdiction to declare whether such placement constituted a deprivation of liberty, and whether it was lawful. In confirming the primacy of the Mental Health Act over the Mental Capacity Act he referred to and followed the judgment of Peter Jackson J in *C (by his litigation friend, the Official Solicitor) v A Borough Council* [2011] EWHC 3321 (COP), [2011] All ER (D) 203 (Dec).

The issue of the tension between the Mental Health Act 1983 and Mental Capacity Act 2005 was returned to by Charles J in *AM v South London & Maudsley NHS Foundation Trust and Secretary of State for Health* [2013] UKUT 365 (AAC) when he revisited an earlier decision in *GJ v Foundation Trust* [2009] EWHC 2972 (Fam), [2010] Fam 70, [2010] 3 WLR 840 and references to primacy were fact specific to issues before any court and the determination of relevant provisions of both Acts relating to those specific issues.

III MEN [35.2]

The Deprivation of Liberty Safeguards – Code of Practice 'Deprivation of liberty safeguards', The Code of Practice supplemental to the Mental Capacity Act 2005 Code of Practice came into force on 1 April 2009. The Code provides important guidance and assistance in considering issues in respect of deprivation of liberty and the appropriateness of applications.

Chapters 1 and 2 provide an overview of the safeguards and as to the identification of potential deprivation of liberty.

Chapters 3 and 4 provide guidance on the manner and timing of applications for authorisation of deprivation of liberty, including the process for standard authorisation.

Chapter 5 provides guidance on the procedure following the assessment process.

Chapter 6 considers issues surrounding urgent authorisation of deprivation of liberty.

Chapter 7 concerns the role of the relevant person's representative, and the instruction of IMCA.

Chapters 8 and 9 give guidance on issues as to review and ending of authorisations, and the action to take if deprivation of liberty is thought to be occurring.

Chapter 10 provides guidance on the role of the Court of Protection, and the timing of applications to the court.

Chapter 11 provides information on the monitoring of safeguards.

There are 4 annexes to the Code providing specific information on the overview of the deprivation liberty process (Annex 1). The approach to be adopted by managing authorities and supervisory bodies in respect of deprivation of liberty authorisations (Annex 2 and Annex 3) and Annex 4 which provides for guidance on the standard authorisation review process.

III MEN [36]

4B. Deprivation of liberty necessary for life-sustaining treatment etc.

(1) If the following conditions are met, D is authorised to deprive P of his liberty while a decision as respects any relevant issue is sought from the court.

(2) The first condition is that there is a question about whether D is authorised to deprive P of his liberty under section 4A.

(3) The second condition is that the deprivation of liberty—

- (a) is wholly or partly for the purpose of—
  - (i) giving P life-sustaining treatment, or
  - (ii) doing any vital act, or
- (b) consists wholly or partly of—
  - (i) giving P life-sustaining treatment, or

(ii) doing any vital act.

(4) The third condition is that the deprivation of liberty is necessary in order to—

(a) give the life-sustaining treatment, or

(b) do the vital act.

(5) A vital act is any act which the person doing it reasonably believes to be necessary to prevent a serious deterioration in P's condition.

III MEN [37]

5. Acts in connection with care or treatment

(1) If a person ('D') does an act in connection with the care or treatment of another person ('P'), the act is one to which this section applies if—

(a) before doing the act, D takes reasonable steps to establish whether P lacks capacity in relation to the matter in question, and

(b) when doing the act, D reasonably believes—

(i) that P lacks capacity in relation to the matter, and

(ii) that it will be in P's best interests for the act to be done.

(2) D does not incur any liability in relation to the act that he would not have incurred if P—

(a) had had capacity to consent in relation to the matter, and

(b) had consented to D's doing the act.

(3) Nothing in this section excludes a person's civil liability for loss or damage, or his criminal liability, resulting from his negligence in doing the act.

(4) Nothing in this section affects the operation of sections 24 to 26 (advance decisions to refuse treatment).

III MEN [38]

6. Section 5 acts: limitations

(1) If D does an act that is intended to restrain P, it is not an act to which section 5 applies unless two further conditions are satisfied.

(2) The first condition is that D reasonably believes that it is necessary to do the act in order to prevent harm to P.

(3) The second is that the act is a proportionate response to—

(a) the likelihood of P's suffering harm, and

(b) the seriousness of that harm.

(4) For the purposes of this section D restrains P if he—

(a) uses, or threatens to use, force to secure the doing of an act which P resists, or

(b) restricts P's liberty of movement, whether or not P resists.

(5) . . .

(6) Section 5 does not authorise a person to do an act which conflicts with a decision made, within the scope of his authority and in accordance with this Part, by—

(a) a donee of a lasting power of attorney granted by P, or

(b) a deputy appointed for P by the court.

(7) But nothing in subsection (6) stops a person—

(a) providing life-sustaining treatment, or

(b) doing any act which he reasonably believes to be necessary to prevent a serious deterioration in P's condition,

while a decision as respects any relevant issue is sought from the court.

III MEN [38.1]

The doctrine of necessity For a discussion of the common law doctrine of necessity in relation to detention and treatment of the incapacitated see **III MEN [9]**.

In *ZH (A Protected Party by GH, his Litigation Friend) v The Commissioner of Police for the Metropolis* [2012] EWHC 604 (QB) (affirmed by the Court of Appeal at [2013] EWCA Civ 69) Sir Robert Nelson held that once force was used it was for those using the force to demonstrate that they had complied with the provisions of the Act, a mere honest belief or acting in good faith was not sufficient. Where the provisions of the Act applied, the common law defence of necessity has no application.

III MEN [38.2]

The powers of the police — admission under the Mental Health Act 1983 and ss 5 and 6 of the Act In *R (on the application of Sessay) v South London & Maudsley NHS Foundation Trust* [2011] EWHC 2617 (QB), [2011] All ER (D) 159 (Oct) the Divisional Court examined the interplay of ss 5 and 6 of Mental Capacity Act 2005, the appropriate procedures for admission under the MHA 1983 and breaches of Articles 5 and 8 ECHR, finding that ss 135 and 138 were the exclusive powers available to police officers to remove persons who appear to be mentally disordered to a place of safety, and that ss 5 and 6 conferred no such authority of removal for the purposes of s 135 MHA 1983.

III MEN [38.3]

Guidance on the 2005 Code of Practice Chapter 6 of the Mental Capacity Act 2005 Code of Practice provides guidance on the protection offered by the Act to those providing care or treatment. It is important to have regard to the Code and guidance, and within any subsequent application to the court, whether civil or criminal, consideration will be given to provisions of the Code, and failure to comply with the code must be taken into account in deciding any relevant question (s 42(5) of the Mental Capacity Act 2005): **III MEN [80]**.

III MEN [38.4]

Best interests and human rights It has been held that the forcible restraint, with handcuffs and leg restraints of a vulnerable teenage boy who was autistic, epileptic and lacked understanding, was in the particular circumstances of the case a breach of Articles 3 and 5 and not in his best interests. An award of £28,250 for false imprisonment was upheld by the Court of Appeal: *ZH (by his litigation friend) v Metropolitan Police Comr* [2013] EWCA Civ 69, [2013] 3 All ER 113, [2013] 1 WLR 3021.

Where a patient, whether mentally incapacitated or not, is in intensive care and heavily sedated this is for pressing medical reasons not a matter of State detention or deprivation of liberty: *R (LF) v HM Senior Coroner for Inner South London* (2016) Times 16 January, Div Ct.

III MEN [39]

7. Payment for necessary goods and services

(1) If necessary goods or services are supplied to a person who lacks capacity to contract for the supply, he must pay a reasonable price for them.

(2) 'Necessary' means suitable to a person's condition in life and to his actual requirements at the time when the goods or services are supplied.

III MEN [39.1]

Common law right to payment The creditor's right to be paid a reasonable price for the delivery of necessary goods or services was a recognised head of quasi-contract at common law which was acknowledged in s 2 of the Sale of Goods Act 1893 and s 3 of the Sale of Goods Act 1979.

III MEN [39.2]

Necessary services and tenancy payments In *Wychavon District Council v EM* [2012] UKUT 12 (AAC) the Upper Tribunal, departing from its earlier decision in [2011] UKUT 144 (AAC) held that an individual was liable to make payments in accordance with a tenancy agreement because the accommodation was necessary to P and the obligation arose either by implication at common law or under s 7 of the Act.

In *Aster Healthcare Ltd v Estate of Mr Shafi* [2014] EWHC 77 (QB), [2014] 3 All ER 283, [2014] PTSR 888 it was held that this section did not apply where the services were provided pursuant to an arrangement between a service provider and a local authority providing accommodation in accordance with its statutory obligations under Part III of the National Assistance Act 1948. On appeal the Court of Appeal in *Aster Healthcare Ltd v Estate of Shafi* [2014] EWCA Civ 1350, [2014] PTSR 1507, 164 NLJ 7631 found that whether a claimant could avail themselves of s 7 was fact specific 'would they have provided the services to 'P' on terms that he would not pay for them'

III MEN [40]

8. Expenditure

(1) If an act to which section 5 applies involves expenditure, it is lawful for D—

(a) to pledge P's credit for the purpose of the expenditure, and

(b) to apply money in P's possession for meeting the expenditure.

(2) If the expenditure is borne for P by D, it is lawful for D—

(a) to reimburse himself out of money in P's possession, or

(b) to be otherwise indemnified by P.

(3) Subsections (1) and (2) do not affect any power under which (apart from those subsections) a person—

(a) has lawful control of P's money or other property, and

(b) has power to spend money for P's benefit.

LASTING POWERS OF ATTORNEY

III MEN [41]

9. Lasting powers of attorney

(1) A lasting power of attorney is a power of attorney under which the donor ('P') confers on the donee (or donees) authority to make decisions about all or any of the following—

(a) P's personal welfare or specified matters concerning P's personal welfare, and

(b) P's property and affairs or specified matters concerning P's property and affairs,

and which includes authority to make such decisions in circumstances where P no longer has capacity.

(2) A lasting power of attorney is not created unless—

(a) section 10 is complied with,

(b) an instrument conferring authority of the kind mentioned in subsection (1) is made and registered in accordance with Schedule 1, and

(c) at the time when P executes the instrument, P has reached 18 and has capacity to execute it.

(3) An instrument which—

(a) purports to create a lasting power of attorney, but

(b) does not comply with this section, section 10 or Schedule 1,

confers no authority.

(4) The authority conferred by a lasting power of attorney is subject to—

(a) the provisions of this Act and, in particular, sections 1 (the principles) and 4 (best interests), and

(b) any conditions or restrictions specified in the instrument.

III MEN [41.1]

Lasting Powers of 'Attorney and the Code of Practice Chapter 7 of the Mental Capacity Act 2005 Code of Practice provides guidance and examples of scenarios relating to Lasting Powers of Attorney.

III MEN [41.2]

An instrument made and registered in accordance with Schedule 1 Schedule 1 requires the instrument to be made in a prescribed form and registered in accordance with regulations: see the Lasting Powers of Attorney, Enduring Powers of Attorney and Public Guardian Regulations 2007, SI 2007/1253, regs 1–22.

The separation of the roles of the Office of Public Guardian and the Court of Protection since 1 October 2007 still leads to problems, difficulties and delay. The responsibility for registration is firmly under the management control of the Public Guardian, and the Court's engagement is solely in respect of issues requiring judicial determination.

III MEN [41.2]

Capacity to execute the instrument The question whether the donor has capacity to execute the instrument should be determined by the application of the principles in s 1. It was decided, in a case under the Enduring Powers of Attorney Act 1985, that a donor may have sufficient understanding to have capacity to execute a document, although not capable of managing his or her property and affairs: *Re K, Re F (enduring powers of attorney)* [1988] Ch 310, [1988] 1 All ER 358. A presumption in favour of the donor having capacity at the date of executing the instrument was applied (see *Re W* [2001] Ch 609, [2001] 4 All ER 88, CA).

III MEN [42]

10. Appointment of donees

(1) A donee of a lasting power of attorney must be—

(a) an individual who has reached 18, or

(b) if the power relates only to P's property and affairs, either such an individual or a trust corporation.

(2) An individual who is bankrupt or is a person in relation to whom a debt relief order is made may not be appointed as donee of a lasting power of attorney in relation to P's property and affairs.

(3) Subsections (4) to (7) apply in relation to an instrument under which two or more persons are to act as donees of a lasting power of attorney.

(4) The instrument may appoint them to act—

(a) jointly,

(b) jointly and severally, or

(c) jointly in respect of some matters and jointly and severally in respect of others.

(5) To the extent to which it does not specify whether they are to act jointly or jointly and severally, the instrument is to be assumed to appoint them to act jointly.

(6) If they are to act jointly, a failure, as respects one of them, to comply with the requirements of subsection (1) or (2) or Part 1 or 2 of Schedule 1 prevents a lasting power of attorney from being created.

(7) If they are to act jointly and severally, a failure, as respects one of them, to comply with the requirements of subsection (1) or (2) or Part 1 or 2 of Schedule 1—

(a) prevents the appointment taking effect in his case, but

(b) does not prevent a lasting power of attorney from being created in the case of the other or others.

(8) An instrument used to create a lasting power of attorney—

(a) cannot give the donee (or, if more than one, any of them) power to appoint a substitute or successor, but

(b) may itself appoint a person to replace the donee (or, if more than one, any of them) on the occurrence of an event mentioned in section 13(6)(a) to (d) which has the effect of terminating the donee's appointment.

III MEN [42.1]

The appointment of a replacement attorney to succeed another replacement attorney In *The Public Guardian v Boff* [2013] COPLR 653 Senior Judge Lush approached the construction of s 10 (8) and found that a donor could not under the provisions of s 10(8) be able to appoint successive replacement attorneys Referring to the ambiguities arising from pre-legislative history, the learned judge held 'I find that a replacement attorney can only replace an original attorney and cannot replace a replacement attorney'. In *Re Miles* [2014] EWCOP 40, [2015] WTLR 287, [2014] All ER (D) 87 (Nov) the Senior Judge addressing the question of whether it was permissible for a donor of an LPA to appoint more than one attorney to act jointly with survivorship by expressly re-appointing the continuing attorney or attorneys, found that the fact that the Forms are prescribed, and that authority for such a step could not be found within the structure of the Act precluded such an act being permissible, and accordingly severed the relevant provision. However this decision was overturned upon appeal before Nugee J in *Miles v Public Guardian and Beattie v Public Guardian* [2015] EWHC 2960 (Ch) finding that 'a purposive and beneficial interpretation of the Act ought to be applied'.

III MEN [43]

11. Lasting powers of attorney: restrictions

(1) A lasting power of attorney does not authorise the donee (or, if more than one, any of them) to do an act that is intended to restrain P, unless three conditions are satisfied.

(2) The first condition is that P lacks, or the donee reasonably believes that P lacks, capacity in relation to the matter in question.

(3) The second is that the donee reasonably believes that it is necessary to do the act in order to prevent harm to P.

(4) The third is that the act is a proportionate response to—

- (a) the likelihood of P's suffering harm, and
- (b) the seriousness of that harm.

(5) For the purposes of this section, the donee restrains P if he—

- (a) uses, or threatens to use, force to secure the doing of an act which P resists, or
- (b) restricts P's liberty of movement, whether or not P resists,

or if he authorises another person to do any of those things.

. . .

(7) Where a lasting power of attorney authorises the donee (or, if more than one, any of them) to make decisions about P's personal welfare, the authority—

- (a) does not extend to making such decisions in circumstances other than those where P lacks, or the donee reasonably believes that P lacks, capacity,
- (b) is subject to sections 24 to 26 (advance decisions to refuse treatment), and
- (c) extends to giving or refusing consent to the carrying out or continuation of a treatment by a person providing health care for P.

(8) But subsection (7)(c)—

- (a) does not authorise the giving or refusing of consent to the carrying out or continuation of life-sustaining treatment, unless the instrument contains express provision to that effect, and
- (b) is subject to any conditions or restrictions in the instrument.

III MEN [44]

12. Scope of lasting powers of attorney: gifts

(1) Where a lasting power of attorney confers authority to make decisions about P's property and affairs, it does not authorise a donee (or, if more than one, any of them) to dispose of the donor's property by making gifts except to the extent permitted by subsection (2).

(2) The donee may make gifts—

- (a) on customary occasions to persons (including himself) who are related to or connected with the donor, or
- (b) to any charity to whom the donor made or might have been expected to make gifts,

if the value of each such gift is not unreasonable having regard to all the circumstances and, in particular, the size of the donor's estate.

(3) 'Customary occasion' means—

(a) the occasion or anniversary of a birth, a marriage or the formation of a civil partnership, or

(b) any other occasion on which presents are customarily given within families or among friends or associates.

(4) Subsection (2) is subject to any conditions or restrictions in the instrument.

III MEN [44.1]

Restrictions upon the authority of a Donee to make gifts A Donee of a registered lasting power of attorney who contemplates the making of a gift beyond the scope of this section should have regard to Practice Direction 9D (see **III MEN [603]**) and in particular paras 5 and 6 which identify applications which may or may not be suitable to the procedure. Paragraph 8 provides guidance on the process of such an application and relevant forms. Regard should be given to Part 9 which apply to the making of application to the Court of Protection. See **III MEN [584]** to **III MEN [599]**. By virtue of The Tribunals, Courts and Enforcement Act 2007 (Consequential Amendments) Order 2012 (SI 2012/2404) amendments were introduced to the Mental Capacity Act 2005 whereby provision was made to reflect the introduction of debt relief orders and debt relief restriction orders (see Schedule 2 paragraph 53 of the 2012 Order).

The decisions of Senior Judge Lush in *Re Buckley, The Public Guardian v C* [2013] COPLR 39 and in *Re Harcourt, The Public Guardian v A* [2013] COPLR 69 provide clear demonstration of the importance seen by the court of the role of an attorney in properly safeguarding and managing the affairs of a donor. See **III MEN [10A]**; and in *Re AH* [2016] EWCOP 9 the Senior Judge drew attention to the provisions of para 7.51 of the Code of Practice and the fiduciary duties and responsibilities of the Attorney.

In *Re VH (Revocation of Lasting Power of Attorney)* [2014] EWCOP 15 the Senior Judge on an application for revocation of a power of attorney by the Public Guardian applied the principles set down by Nource QC (now Nource LJ) sitting as a deputy judge of the High Court in *Re Beaney, deceased* [1978] 2 All ER 595 as to the test to be applied when considering capacity to make a gift.

III MEN [45]

13. Revocation of lasting powers of attorney etc.

(1) This section applies if—

(a) P has executed an instrument with a view to creating a lasting power of attorney, or

(b) a lasting power of attorney is registered as having been conferred by P,

and in this section references to revoking the power include revoking the instrument.

(2) P may, at any time when he has capacity to do so, revoke the power.

(3) P's bankruptcy, or the making of a debt relief order (under Part 7A of the Insolvency Act 1986) in respect of P, revokes the power so far as it relates to P's property and affairs.

(4) But where P is bankrupt merely because an interim bankruptcy restrictions order has effect in respect of him, or where P is subject to an interim debt relief restriction order (under Schedule 4ZB of the Insolvency Act 1986) the power is suspended, so far as it relates to P's property and affairs, for so long as the order has effect.

(5) The occurrence in relation to a donee of an event mentioned in subsection (6)—

(a) terminates his appointment, and

(b) except in the cases given in subsection (7), revokes the power.

(6) The events are—

(a) the disclaimer of the appointment by the donee in accordance with such requirements as may be prescribed for the purposes of this section in regulations made by the Lord Chancellor,

(b) subject to subsections (8) and (9), the death or bankruptcy of the donee or, the making of a debt relief order (under Part 7 of the Insolvency Act

1986) in respect of the donee, or if the donee is a trust corporation, its winding-up or dissolution,

(c) subject to subsection (11), the dissolution or annulment of a marriage or civil partnership between the donor and the donee,

(d) the lack of capacity of the donee.

(7) The cases are—

(a) the donee is replaced under the terms of the instrument,

(b) he is one of two or more persons appointed to act as donees jointly and severally in respect of any matter and, after the event, there is at least one remaining donee.

(8) The bankruptcy of a donee or the making of a debt relief order (under Part 7A of the Insolvency Act 1986) in respect of the donee does not terminate his appointment, or revoke the power, in so far as his authority relates to P's personal welfare.

(9) Where the donee is bankrupt merely because an interim bankruptcy restrictions order has effect in respect of him, or where the donee is subject to an interim debt relief restrictions order (under Schedule 4ZB of the Insolvency Act 1986) his appointment and the power are suspended, so far as they relate to P's property and affairs, for so long as the order has effect.

(10) Where the donee is one of two or more appointed to act jointly and severally under the power in respect of any matter, the reference in subsection (9) to the suspension of the power is to its suspension in so far as it relates to that donee.

(11) The dissolution or annulment of a marriage or civil partnership does not terminate the appointment of a donee, or revoke the power, if the instrument provided that it was not to do so.

III MEN [46]

14. Protection of donee and others if no power created or power revoked

(1) Subsections (2) and (3) apply if—

(a) an instrument has been registered under Schedule 1 as a lasting power of attorney, but

(b) a lasting power of attorney was not created,

whether or not the registration has been cancelled at the time of the act or transaction in question.

(2) A donee who acts in purported exercise of the power does not incur any liability (to P or any other person) because of the non-existence of the power unless at the time of acting he—

(a) knows that a lasting power of attorney was not created, or

(b) is aware of circumstances which, if a lasting power of attorney had been created, would have terminated his authority to act as a donee.

(3) Any transaction between the donee and another person is, in favour of that person, as valid as if the power had been in existence, unless at the time of the transaction that person has knowledge of a matter referred to in subsection (2).

(4) If the interest of a purchaser depends on whether a transaction between the donee and the other person was valid by virtue of subsection (3), it is conclusively presumed in favour of the purchaser that the transaction was valid if—

(a) the transaction was completed within 12 months of the date on which the instrument was registered, or

(b) the other person makes a statutory declaration, before or within 3 months after the completion of the purchase, that he had no reason at the time of the transaction to doubt that the donee had authority to dispose of the property which was the subject of the transaction.

(5) In its application to a lasting power of attorney which relates to matters in addition to P's property and affairs, section 5 of the Powers of Attorney Act 1971 (c 27) (protection where power is revoked) has effect as if references to revocation included the cessation of the power in relation to P's property and affairs.

(6) Where two or more donees are appointed under a lasting power of attorney, this section applies as if references to the donee were to all or any of them.

GENERAL POWERS OF THE COURT AND APPOINTMENT OF DEPUTIES

III MEN [47]

15. Power to make declarations

(1) The court may make declarations as to—

(a) whether a person has or lacks capacity to make a decision specified in the declaration;

(b) whether a person has or lacks capacity to make decisions on such matters as are described in the declaration;

(c) the lawfulness or otherwise of any act done, or yet to be done, in relation to that person.

(2) 'Act' includes an omission and a course of conduct.

III MEN [47.1]

Declarations and applying to the court Applications for declarations should be made using the relevant Court of Protection forms and procedure. Part 9 of the Court of Protection Rules 2017 sets out the manner of starting proceedings and if permission is required then regard must be given to Part 8 (see **III MEN [577]** and **III MEN [582]**. If the applications seek a declaration concerning serious medical treatment, then Practice Direction 9E must be followed: **III MEN [604]**.

In *LG v DK* [2011] EWHC 2453 (COP), [2012] 2 All ER 115, [2012] 1 FCR 476 the President explored the inter relationship of the powers of the Court of Protection to make declarations and the distinct jurisdiction provided to the Family law courts (now the Family Court) under s 21(4) Family Law Reform Act 1969. The decision demonstrates the constructive approach of the senior judiciary to promote the welfare of an individual lacking capacity if the decision is in that person's best interest.

A declaration regarding best interests or lawfulness is not enforceable by proceedings for contempt. In this respect it differs from an order made under s 16: *MASM v MMAM* [2015] EWCOP 3, 165 NLJ 7640, [2015] All ER (D) 238 (Jan). In *Re MN (Adult)* [2015] EWCA Civ 411, [2015] All ER (D) 69 (May) the President drew attention to the very distinct wording of s 15(1)(c) which he held did not confer any general power to the Court to make bare declarations as to best interests, but rather he identified the preference for orders being framed in terms of relief under s 16 as opposed to s 15 unless the desired order clearly falls within the ambit of the latter section.

In the case of an application to authorise a deprivation of liberty in order to implement a care package on which a welfare order is based it is not necessary for the patient to be a party: *Re NRA* [2015] EWCOP 59, [2015] All ER (D) 122 (Sep).

III MEN [47.2]

Declarations as to lawfulness In a case where an incapacitated person was kept at a secret location his mother was held to be entitled to a declaration by the Court of Protection that her rights under Art 8 of the Convention were infringed: *YA (F) v A Local Authority* [2010] EWHC 2770 (Fam).

III MEN [47.3]

Declarations and the limit of the Court of Protection's jurisdiction In *XCC v AA, BB, CC, and DD* [2012] EWHC 2183 (COP), [2012] All ER (D) 38 (Aug) Parker J found that the Court of Protection's jurisdiction to make declarations did not extend to make a non-recognition declaration in respect of a marriage, determining that that in itself was not a personal welfare decision. This should be contrasted with the Court's willingness to use the jurisdiction to make a declaration in appropriate circumstances that it would be unlawful for a person to be married within the court's jurisdiction.

The issue of the scope of the jurisdiction of the Court of Protection was the subject of clear guidance by the President of the Court of Protection sitting in *MN (Adult)* [2015] EWCA Civ 411 where the Court of Appeal identified that proceedings before the Court of Protection must be proportionate and not seek to trammel on possible 'public law issues'. At para 80 the President states clearly that ' the function of the court is to take on behalf of adults who lack capacity the decisions which if they had capacity they would take themselves', and at para 82 cautioned upon factual enquiries designed as a springboard for proceedings before the Administrative Court. This was followed in *North Yorkshire County Council v MAG* [2016] EWCOP 5 where Cobb J applying the Court of Appeal decision referred to the importance of the court 'making decisions in the light of circumstances as they are or may reasonable be expected to be', with the court 'having no power to conjure resources'.

III MEN [47.4]

Declarations regarding medical treatment and best interests of 'P' The Supreme Court in its first consideration of the Act in relation to medical treatment and the withdrawal of life-sustaining treatment held that the starting point is a strong presumption that it is in a person's best interest to stay alive. Nevertheless that is not absolute, see *Aintree University Hospitals NHS Foundation Trust v James* [2013] UKSC 67, [2013] 3 WLR 1299, (2013) Times, 19 November. In this decision the Supreme Court stressed the importance of considering the relevant provisions of paras 5.31 to 5.33 of the Mental Capacity Act 2005 Code of Practice as a whole and whilst confirming that it gives useful guidance derived from earlier case law as to when life-sustaining treatment may not be in P's best interests, it was clearly stated that the Code is not a statute and should not be so construed. In *Re N* [2015] EWCOP 76 followed in *Re O (Withdrawal of Medical Treatment)* [2016] EWCOP 24 Hayden J provided practical utilisation of the Act, Code and the Supreme Court decision applying the principles to whether it was in the best interests of P to receive life sustaining treatment by means of Clinically Assisted Nutrition and Hydration (CANH) provided through a percutaneous endoscopic gastronomy (PEG) tube.

In *Sheffield Teaching Hospitals NHS Foundation Trust v TH* [2014] EWCOP 4 Hayden J applied the principles drawn from the Aintree decision to grant declarations in respect of an individual said to be in the lower spectrum of a minimally conscious state, where the individual had made a valid advance decision. Similarly in *County Durham & Darlington NHS Foundation Trust v PP* [2014] EWCOP 9 Cobb J applied the principle whilst 'the starting point is a strong presumption that it is in a person's best interests to stay alive . . . this is not absolute', and clearly identifying that the decision is on based upon the best interests principle and not by 'substituted judgment'. See also *Briggs v Briggs (No 2)* [2016] EWCOP 53.

III MEN [47.5]

Power to authorise deprivation of liberty in a Children's home. In *Liverpool City Council v SG (by her litigation friends and parents, J,S and G)* [2014] EWCOP 10, [2014] PTSR D20 (per Holman J) the authority of the Court to authorise a person who is not a child to be deprived of his liberty in a children's home and subject to the Children's Homes Regulations 2001 (as amended) was confirmed. This decision was followed by Holman J in what he described as a 'sequel to his earlier judgment in "the Liverpool case"'. Considering the Regulations, the Guidance of the President and National Director, Social Care, Ofsted of 12 February 2014 and s 22 of the Care Standards Act 2000, he found that the court still retained jurisdiction to authorise any deprivation of liberty in these circumstances: *Barnsley Metropolitan Borough Council v GS* [2014] EWCOP 46. In *Birmingham City Council v D* [2016] EWCOP 8 following from his earlier decision in *D (A Child; deprivation of liberty)* [2015] EWHC 922 Keehan J considered the above issues and found in the light of the Strasbourg jurisprudence that he could not accept that the accommodation of a young person pursuant to s 20 of the Children Act 1989 could never amount to a deprivation of liberty.

III MEN [47.6]

Declarations as to care provision Where the parents wish to challenge the care arrangements made for an incapacitated adult the Court's powers are limited to declaring whether the arrangements are lawful. There is no power to order different arrangements or to entertain arguments on 'best interests': *N v A Clinical Commissioning Group* [2017] UKSC 22, [2017] 2 WLR 1011, 155 BMLR 1.

III MEN [48]

16. Powers to make decisions and appoint deputies: general

(1) This section applies if a person ('P') lacks capacity in relation to a matter or matters concerning—

(a) P's personal welfare, or
(b) P's property and affairs.

(2) The court may—

(a) by making an order, make the decision or decisions on P's behalf in relation to the matter or matters, or

(b) appoint a person (a 'deputy') to make decisions on P's behalf in relation to the matter or matters.

(3) The powers of the court under this section are subject to the provisions of this Act and, in particular, to sections 1 (the principles) and 4 (best interests).

(4) When deciding whether it is in P's best interests to appoint a deputy, the court must have regard (in addition to the matters mentioned in section 4) to the principles that—

(a) a decision by the court is to be preferred to the appointment of a deputy to make a decision, and

(b) the powers conferred on a deputy should be as limited in scope and duration as is reasonably practicable in the circumstances.

(5) The court may make such further orders or give such directions, and confer on a deputy such powers or impose on him such duties, as it thinks necessary or expedient for giving effect to, or otherwise in connection with, an order or appointment made by it under subsection (2).

(6) Without prejudice to section 4, the court may make the order, give the directions or make the appointment on such terms as it considers are in P's best interests, even though no application is before the court for an order, directions or an appointment on those terms.

(7) An order of the court may be varied or discharged by a subsequent order.

(8) The court may, in particular, revoke the appointment of a deputy or vary the powers conferred on him if it is satisfied that the deputy—

(a) has behaved, or is behaving, in a way that contravenes the authority conferred on him by the court or is not in P's best interests, or

(b) proposes to behave in a way that would contravene that authority or would not be in P's best interests.

III MEN [48.1]

The appointment of a deputy and s 16(4) The principles regarding applications to appoint a deputy in relation to welfare decisions, and s 16(4), have been considered and in *LB of Havering v LD, KD* [2010] EWHC 3876 (COP) HHJ Turner QC highlighted the need to incorporate consideration of Chapter 6 of the Code of Practice when having regard to such an application.

In *Re A* [2016] EWCOP 3 HC the Senior Judge addressed the principles to be adopted if faced with choosing between potential deputies, and in *Re RP* [2016] EWCOP 1 dealt with the issue of a professional deputy who it was said was aligning with one party in preference to another. Finally in *Re FH* [2016] EWCOP14 the Senior Judge addressed the issue where a potential deputy themselves was said to have 'functional illiteracy'.

III MEN [48.2]

The revocation of appointment of a deputy and s 16(8) The decision of Senior Judge Lush in *Re GM* [2013] COPLR 290 provides useful guidance on the role of deputies, and the expectation of the court in protecting and properly managing the assets of P. In a series of cases the Senior Judge demonstrated the balance sheet approach of deciding between competing family members (*Re DG* [2014] EWCOP 31). In *Re PMB* [2014] EWCOP 42 the Senior Judge demonstrated the practical approach of dealing with sibling rivalry and the protection of P's affairs by appointing joint deputies, and in *Re BM* [2014] EWCOP B20 the Senior Judge provided guidance on the approach to be applied in determining suitability of competing family members and the appointment of an independent professional deputy. In situations where family members applying for deputyship fail to notify relevant family members and issues subsequently arise as to their suitability to act, such conduct may lead to a departure from the general rule as to costs (see r 159) (*Re BIM, DM and AM* [2014] EWCOP 39).

In *Re Joan Treadwell (dec'd)* [2013] EWHC 2409 (COP) the Senior Judge following the death of P within proceedings before him for consideration of approval of gifts which exceeded the authority of a deputy, proceeded to permit the Public Guardian to apply to call in the security bond and forewarned those appointed as a deputy that proposed gifts must comply with existing guidance or prior authority must be obtained. Failure to do so could lead if it was in P's best interests to the removal of a deputy, or the calling in of the security.

In *Haringey v CM* [2014] EWCOP B23, [2014] WTLR 1689 the Senior Judge addressed the issue of undue influence on the part of an individual acting on behalf of P, and referred to Article 12 of the Convention on the Rights of Persons with Disabilities that requires 'States Parties . . . shall ensure that measures relating to the exercise of legal capacity respect the rights, will and preferences of the person, [and] are free of conflict of interest and undue influence'. This approach was further adopted in *Re JW* [2015] EWCOP 82, [2015] All ER (D) 46 (Dec) where the Senior Judge demonstrated the approach of other Commonwealth countries in addressing issues of fiduciary duty and potential conflict of interest and the importance of paragraph 8.58 of the Code of Practice. This issue of conflict of personal interests was again revisited in *Re AFR* [2015] EWCOP 73, [2015] All ER (D) 109 (Nov) with the Senior Judge stressed the necessity of deputies having regard and awareness of their duties under the Code of Practice 8.56–8.58. See Chapter 8 of the Code of Practice and also **III MEN [10A]**.

III MEN [48.3]

Applications The Court of Protection Rules 2017 provide guidance and framework for applications made under this section and the relevant provisions of Part 9 and 10 apply, depending upon whether it is the start of proceedings (rr 9.1–9.16) (**III MEN [584]** to **III MEN [599]**) or an application within existing proceedings (rr 10.1–10.9) (**III MEN [607]** to **III MEN [615]**). Rule 10.5 provides guidance where applications are made without notice (**III MEN [611]**) and r 10.10 deals with the powers to grant interim remedies (**III MEN [616]**). Practice Directions 9A–G (**III MEN [600]** to **III MEN [606]**) and 10A and B (**III MEN [617]** to **III MEN [618]**) should be considered, and Practitioners must ensure that if the application relates to an issue of Deprivation of Liberty, that regard is made to the correctly identified s 21A procedure under Practice Direction 11A (**III MEN [620]**) or to the s 4A(3) and s 16(2)(a) procedure under the same.

III MEN [48.4]

The Code of Practice guidance on the role of the court and court appointed deputies Chapter 8 of the Mental Capacity Act 2005 Code of Practice provides guidance on the role of the Court of Protection and of court appointed deputies.

III MEN [48.5]

Blood tests Should a paternity issue arise in proceedings before the Court of Protection, the court has jurisdiction under s 21(4) of the Family Law Act 1969 to give the consent of an incapacitated adult to the taking of blood or other bodily sample for the purpose of resolving the issue: *LG v DK* [2011] EWHC 2453 (COP), [2012] 2 All ER 115, [2012] 1 FCR 476.

III MEN [48.6]

Powers of the Court of Protection In *N v A CCG* [2017] UKSC 22 the Supreme Court considered the scope of the Court of Protection's powers to make declarations under ss 15 and 16 of the Mental Capacity Act. Where a dispute arose over the care of a person lacking capacity to make relevant decisions, the Court could use its powers under s 15 to declare the lawfulness, or otherwise, of the options, depending on whether it was in the person's best interests. However, the Court has no greater powers to oblige others to what was best for the person than the person would himself if he had the capacity to make a choice. The Court may investigate options but, using its case management powers, it may decline to do so where it would serve no purpose to do so because the option was not available.

See also Charles J in *A Local Authority v PB* [2011] EWHC 502 (COP) when it was held that where a court was exercising a welfare or best interests jurisdiction it was choosing between available options This decision of Charles J had been followed in *RA Local Authority v PB* [2011] EWHC 2675 (COP), [2011] All ER (D) 242 (Oct) when again Charles J noting the unwillingness of a local authority to offer supported placement, found that the court's role was not to review the rights or wrongs of past disputes, but that the primary driver was 'the degree and nature of the support P now requires and will do so for the remainder of life'. Drawing upon these authorities and the decision of Bodey J in *Re SK* [2013] EWHC (COP) where he had arising from personal injury proceedings in the Queen's Bench Division held that the court's role was to address the present best interests of P choosing between current foreseeable or reasonably available options, Eleanor King J clearly accepted the authority restated by Baroness Hale in *Aintree University Hospitals NHS Foundation Trust v James* [2013] UKSC 67, [2013] 3 WLR 1299, (2013) Times, 19 November that the 'court has no greater powers than the patient would have if he were of full capacity'.

III MEN [49]

16A. Section 16 powers: Mental Health Act patients etc.

(1) If a person is ineligible to be deprived of liberty by this Act, the court may not include in a welfare order provision which authorises the person to be deprived of his liberty.

(2) If—

(a) a welfare order includes provision which authorises a person to be deprived of his liberty, and

(b) that person becomes ineligible to be deprived of liberty by this Act,

the provision ceases to have effect for as long as the person remains ineligible.

(3) Nothing in subsection (2) affects the power of the court under section 16(7) to vary or discharge the welfare order.

(4) For the purposes of this section—

(a) Schedule 1A applies for determining whether or not P is ineligible to be deprived of liberty by this Act;

(b) 'welfare order' means an order under section 16(2)(a).

III MEN [49.1]

Identifying the powers of the court In *Re M* [2011] EWHC 3590 (COP) Mostyn J distinguished orders made under the provisions of paragraph 19 of Schedule 3 of the Act with welfare orders made under s 16A of and Schedule 1A to the Act. See **III MEN [131]**.

In *Great Western Hospitals NHS Foundation Trust v AA* [2014] EWHC 132 (Fam), [2014] Fam Law 412 Hayden J found in a matter involving a 25 year old with bipolar disorder and a decision to proceed with an elective Caesarean pursuant to his powers under the Mental Capacity Act 2005 that such powers were compromised (see *A NHS Trust v Dr A* [2013] EWHC 2442 (COP)) and applied the inherent jurisdiction of the court in making declarations and authorising steps to be taken by the treating hospital, where the measures involved both serious medical treatment and deprivation of liberty. In *Northamptonshire Healthcare NHS Foundation Trust v MML (Rev 1)* [2014] EWCOP 2 Hayden J encountering the difficulties of reaching a decision in the best interests of P by virtue of the interplay of the Mental Health Act regime and the potential lacunae under the Mental Capacity Act 2005 and inherent jurisdiction, and recognising the possible impact of actions by a nearest relative invited the President of the First Tier Mental Health Tribunal to allocate a judge for the purposes of judicial continuity.

III MEN [49.2]

Applications under section 16(2)(a) for an order authorising a deprivation of liberty under section 4A(3) and (4) – the streamlined procedure In the wake of the decision of the Supreme Court in the matter of *P (by his litigation friend the Official Solicitor) v Cheshire West and Chester Council and another; P and Q (by their litigation friend the Official Solicitor) v Surrey County Council* [2014] UKSC 19 guidance was given by the President in two judgments *Re X (Deprivation of Liberty)* [2014] EWCOP 25, and *Re X (Deprivation of Liberty (No 2)* [2014] EWCOP 37 and a streamlined procedure was introduced on 17 November 2014 pursuant to a further Practice Direction 10AA relating to applications made under s 4A(3) and (4) of the Mental Capacity Act 2005, where authorisation is sought pursuant to s 16(2)(a) of the Mental Capacity Act 2005 to sanction arrangements for where an individual who lacks capacity should live and where restrictions involve a deprivation of liberty (Practice Direction 11A). In essence the court is being asked to approve a Care Plan (now referred to as a 'Support Plan'), and to authorise restrictions that amount to a deprivation of liberty contained in that Plan. This procedure does not apply to hospitals or Care homes where standard or urgent authorisations exist and apply, or a challenge is required under s 21A of the Act. The procedure is set out in Part 1 of Practice Direction 11A, and Form COPDOL10 is mandatory. The application form has annexes and attachments which provide essential information to the court to enable determination on paper, and a draft order must be submitted. The maximum duration of any order made is 12 months, and the court will give direction s to renewal and review. The annexes deal with the procedure for prior notification and consultation with both P and other persons, and the substantive rules regarding permission and notification are amended and where appropriate disapplied.

Whilst in *Re X (Court of Protection Practice)* [2015] EWCA Civ 599, 165 NLJ 7659, [2015] All ER (D) 188 (Jun) the Court of Appeal in obiter took issue with the President as to absence of 'P' being a party to the streamlined procedure, Charles J the Vice President in *Re*

NRA [2015] EWCOP 59, 165 NLJ 7671, [2015] All ER (D) 122 (Sep) distinguished the role of the Court of Protection in its application of the streamlined procedure which would continue subject to modifications.

III MEN [50]

17. Section 16 powers: personal welfare

(1) The powers under section 16 as respects P's personal welfare extend in particular to—

(a) deciding where P is to live;

(b) deciding what contact, if any, P is to have with any specified persons;

(c) making an order prohibiting a named person from having contact with P;

(d) giving or refusing consent to the carrying out or continuation of a treatment by a person providing health care for P;

(e) giving a direction that a person responsible for P's health care allow a different person to take over that responsibility.

(2) Subsection (1) is subject to section 20 (restrictions on deputies).

III MEN [50.1]

Personal welfare applications the importance of identifying issues Applications regarding personal welfare and the appointment of a deputy have given rise to difficulties with the Senior Judge identifying that many applications fail at the permission stage through a lack of relevant information being provided. Applications fail to provide adequate sufficient evidence supportive of the court exercising its discretion and often the forms require careful completion and detail. Judicial comment has been made as to the appropriateness of appointment of a deputy to take personal welfare decisions in the light of s 16(4), and regard should be given to those decisions before making application. See *London Borough of Havering v LD and KD* [2010] EWHC 3876 (COP). In *Donna v Martin* [2015] EWCOP 23 Senior Judge Lush in addressing the issue of reconsideration of decision not to appoint family members as deputies highlighted the inappropriateness of such appointment where there was hostility within the family and also towards Care staff supporting 'P'.

As an example of the fact specific nature of the decisions of the Court, in *Derbyshire County Council v AC* [2014] EWCOP 38 Cobb J found that the individual before him lacked capacity to make decisions as to her care, and contact with others, but did have capacity to make decisions relating to sexual relations and residence.

In *NCC v PB (by her litigation friend the Official Solicitor)* [2014] EWCOP 14 Parker J warned of the risks of undue influence and the overbearing will of those engaged in supporting individuals who lack capacity and the impact of such conduct on the ability of that individual to use and weigh information and make decisions.

In *Staffordshire County Council v SSRK* [2016] EWCOP 27 the Vice President found that where an individual lacked capacity to make decisions on the regime of care, treatment and support that he should receive, and where applying *Surrey County Council v P and others; Cheshire West and Chester Council v P* [2014] UKSC 14 'P's' care regime created on an objective assessment a deprivation of liberty, then application should be made to the court for a welfare order whereby the court could if appropriate authorise the deprivation of liberty within the care regime, providing scope for review by the court. This decision was in *Secretary for State for Justice v Staffordshire County Council* [2016] EWCA Civ 1317 upheld by the Court of Appeal.

III MEN [51]

18. Section 16 powers: property and affairs

(1) The powers under section 16 as respects P's property and affairs extend in particular to—

(a) the control and management of P's property;

(b) the sale, exchange, charging, gift or other disposition of P's property;

(c) the acquisition of property in P's name or on P's behalf;

(d) the carrying on, on P's behalf, of any profession, trade or business;

(e) the taking of a decision which will have the effect of dissolving a partnership of which P is a member;

(f) the carrying out of any contract entered into by P;

(g) the discharge of P's debts and of any of P's obligations, whether legally enforceable or not;

(h) the settlement of any of P's property, whether for P's benefit or for the benefit of others;

(i) the execution for P of a will;

(j) the exercise of any power (including a power to consent) vested in P whether beneficially or as trustee or otherwise;

(k) the conduct of legal proceedings in P's name or on P's behalf.

(2) No will may be made under subsection (1)(i) at a time when P has not reached 18.

(3) The powers under section 16 as respects any other matter relating to P's property and affairs may be exercised even though P has not reached 16, if the court considers it likely that P will still lack capacity to make decisions in respect of that matter when he reaches 18.

(4) Schedule 2 supplements the provisions of this section.

(5) Section 16(7) (variation and discharge of court orders) is subject to paragraph 6 of Schedule 2.

(6) Subsection (1) is subject to section 20 (restrictions on deputies).

III MEN [51.1]

Statutory wills The court is authorised by s 18(1)(i) to exercise powers in relation to the execution of a will. A deputy is prevented, by s 20(3)(b), from executing a will on behalf of an individual lacking capacity. It is not within the deputy's normal range of powers but the deputy may properly execute a will (a statutory will) if the court so orders: *Re D (statutory will)* [2010] EWHC 2159 (Ch), [2010] NLJR 1190 (Aug) (applying *In the Matter of P* [2009] EWHC 163 (Ch)) in which it was decided that the execution of a statutory will which reflected the individual's reasonable instructions when he had capacity was in that person's best interests. He would then be remembered for having done 'the right thing' whereas the alternative would be to bequeath a contentious probate dispute over the validity of a subsequent instrument.

In *Re JC; D v JC, JG, A, B, C* [2012] COPLR 540 Senior Judge Lush provided a useful demonstration of the procedure the court would follow, in applying a the checklist of factors under s 4 of the Act, the application of the 'balance sheet approach', the identification of 'factors' of magnetic importance, and the jurisprudence surrounding acts done in a person's best interests such that they would be remembered for "doing the right thing" by their will.

The decision of HHJ Behrens in *NT (the Deputy of the First Respondent) v FS (by his litigation friend the Official Solicitor)* [2013] EWHC 684 (COP) draws together the 4 key authorities to be applied by the court in determining such an application *Re P* [2009] EWHC 163 (Ch), [2010] Ch 33, [2009] 2 All ER 1198; *Re M* [2011] 1 WLR 344; *Re G (TJ)* [2011] WTLR 231 and *Re JC* [2012] COPLR 540 (see above) and applies these principles to the determination of the best interests of P when authorising a statutory will.

In *Re D* [2016] EWCOP 35 the Senior Judge addressed the importance of compliance with the rules in giving notice in respect of potential respondents to proceedings relating to statutory will applications. The judgment is equally applicable to all matters before the Court.

III MEN [51.2]

Applications Applications to start proceedings should be made in accordance with Part 9 of the Court of Protection Rules 2017 and regard had to the provisions of Practice Directions 9A–F. In addition to the form COP1 and its annexes, specific information is required pursuant to paragraph 6(a)–(p). Paragraph sets out requirements as to who must be served or notified. The Practice Direction relates similarly to codicils, settlements and other dealings with P's property.

III MEN [51.3]

Guidance in respect of declarations regarding personal injury trusts HHJ Marshall QC in *SM v HM (by the Official Solicitor as her Litigation Friend* [2012] COPLR 187 considered the circumstances when it is appropriate to authorise the creation of a trust (in particular a personal injury trust) under s 18(1)(h), as a means of administering P's assets, however in *Watt v ABC* [2016] EWCOP 2532 Charles J as Vice President of the Court found that the decision of HHJ Marshall QC was mistakenly being applied, and should not be seen as suggesting a presumption or default result. What was required was a detailed weighing exercise in each case. Giving guidance his lordship referred to the importance of (a) considering the management regime of a substantial award of damages at the earliest practicable point in time, (b) an analysis of what 'P' has and has not the capacity to do and of his or her likely future capacity or vulnerability. (c) early identification of competing factors relevant to 'P's' circumstances to then balance the factors favouring the use of the statutory scheme relating to deputies against the relevant competing factors in the case, (d) identification of the terms, effects (including taxation and the costs of rival possibilities, and (e) the appropriate listing of the issues. Regard should be made to this decision if such an application is considered appropriate.

III MEN [51.4]

Statutory wills and disputes regarding existing wills In *Re D (Statutory Will)* [2010] EWHC 2159 (Ch), [2010] NLJR 1190, [2010] All ER (D) 102 (Aug) HHJ Hodge QC determined that the provisions of the Mental Capacity Act 2005 enabled the court to determine issues concerning the validity of wills and that the role of the Court of Protection was not limited solely to authorising the creation of statutory wills or amending wills where there had been a material change of circumstances. See Schedule 2 of the Act for supplementary provisions **III MEN [127]**.

III MEN [51.5]

Declarations as to capacity to conduct proceedings and annulment of marriage In *Tower Hamlets London Borough Council v BB, AM, SB and EL Trust* [2011] EWHC 2853 (Fam), [2012] 1 FLR 1080, [2012] Fam Law 143 Ryder J used the provisions of s 16 and s 18(k) of the Act when declaring that P lacked capacity to conduct proceedings, and then that it was in P's best interests to give directions regarding an application under the Matrimonial Causes Act 1973 for the annulment of P's marriage.

III MEN [51.6]

Authorising a loan or gift In *Re AK (gift application)* [2014] EWHC B11 (COP) Senior Judge Lush addressed the principles to be applied when decisions arose where P had lacked capacity from birth, and in distinguishing his earlier decision in *Re JDS* (*KGS v JDS (by his litigation friend, the Official Solicitor)* [2012] EWHC 302 (COP), [2012] NLJR 1536) he authorised an interest free loan to family members as opposed to an outright gift. These decisions were applied by the Senior Judge in *Re A* [2015] EWCOP 46 when the Court authorised the application of a part of P's damages towards the educational fees of her sibling.

In two judgments which provide guidance to those parents who provide gratuitous care for their incapacitated dependants, the Senior Judge in *Re HC* [2015] EWCOP 29, [2015] All ER (D) 165 (Apr) identified the relevant law as to payments for gratuitous care and the manner in which the court would apply those principles, and this was confirmed and applied in *Re HNL* [2015] EWCOP 77, [2015] All ER (D) 199 (Nov).

III MEN [51.7]

Guidance on the role of the Court in applications to the Criminal Injuries Compensation Authority In two judgments addressing s 18(1)(h) the Vice President provided guidance to practitioners on the approach of the court where the Criminal Injuries Compensation Authority requires a trust to be created to exclude the possibility that an assailant may benefit from a compensation award proposed in respect of an individual who lacks capacity to so execute. The judgments in *PJV v The Assistant Director Adult Social Care Newcastle City Council* [2015] EWCOP 87 and *PJV v The Assistant Director Adult Social Care Newcastle City Council* [2016] EWCOP 7 identify the relevant law, the powers of the Court and the procedure to be adopted, including suggested specimen clauses for deputyship orders and Declaration of Trust.

III MEN [52]

19. Appointment of deputies

(1) A deputy appointed by the court must be—

(a) an individual who has reached 18, or

(b) as respects powers in relation to property and affairs, an individual who has reached 18 or a trust corporation.

(2) The court may appoint an individual by appointing the holder for the time being of a specified office or position.

(3) A person may not be appointed as a deputy without his consent.

(4) The court may appoint two or more deputies to act—

(a) jointly,

(b) jointly and severally, or

(c) jointly in respect of some matters and jointly and severally in respect of others.

(5) When appointing a deputy or deputies, the court may at the same time appoint one or more other persons to succeed the existing deputy or those deputies—

(a) in such circumstances, or on the happening of such events, as may be specified by the court;

(b) for such period as may be so specified.

(6) A deputy is to be treated as P's agent in relation to anything done or decided by him within the scope of his appointment and in accordance with this Part.

(7) The deputy is entitled—

(a) to be reimbursed out of P's property for his reasonable expenses in discharging his functions, and

(b) if the court so directs when appointing him, to remuneration out of P's property for discharging them.

(8) The court may confer on a deputy powers to—

(a) take possession or control of all or any specified part of P's property;

(b) exercise all or any specified powers in respect of it, including such powers of investment as the court may determine.

(9) The court may require a deputy—

(a) to give to the Public Guardian such security as the court thinks fit for the due discharge of his functions, and

(b) to submit to the Public Guardian such reports at such times or at such intervals as the court may direct.

III MEN [52.1]

The test for appointing deputies In *SBC v PBA* [2011] EWHC 2580 (Fam) Roderic Wood J held that the test for appointing a deputy (whether to manage property and affairs, or to take decisions regarding personal health or welfare) was to be derived from the unvarnished words of the Act, and the guidance under the Code of Practice (Provisions 8.25, 8.31, 835, and 8.38)) did not impose an additional requirement.

In *Re AS, SH v LC* [2013] COPLR 29 Senior Judge Lush addressed the issue of competing applicants seeking to be considered for appointment as a deputy for property and affairs. Guidance was given as to the approach to be adopted taking into account certain pre-Mental Capacity Act 2005 authorities and the preference for appointment from within the family if in P' best interests so to do, over the appointment of a stranger. However what was clear is that the court would proceed by approaching all applications through s 16(2) and s 16(4) and then apply both the s 1 (principles) and s 4 (best interests) test in exercising its discretion. Further in referring to preference of appointment within the family, the learned Judge was clear that this should not be viewed as a list of priority, and each and every matter is determined upon its merits and distinct factual basis. This approach was addressed further in *Re BM* [2014] EWCOP B20 and in *Re AW* [2015] EWCOP 16, [2015] All ER (D) 242 (Mar) where in the latter case the Senior Judge Lush drew upon the fact that P had appointed one of the competing parties her executor; applying *Re Joan Treadwell, dec'd* [2013] COPLR 587 See further **III MEN [10A]**.

In *Re PL* [2015] EWCOP 14, [2015] All ER (D) 176 (Mar) Senior Judge Lush stressed the expectation that deputies should have a clear awareness of their fiduciary responsibilities and practical responsibilities and of the roles of the Curt of Protection and Office of Public Guardian, and in consequence of a wilful refusal to comply with those duties a deputy will be removed; see *Re CJ* [2015] EWCOP 21, [2015] All ER (D) 322 (Mar) and *Re AFR* [2015] EWCOP 73, [2015] All ER (D) 109 (Nov).

In *Re ES* [2014] EWHC B6 Senior Judge Lush drawing upon the principles he had adopted in *Re M: N v O and P* [2013] COPLR 91 emphasises the broad discretion given to the court in appointing a deputy for property and affairs. In *Suffolk County Council v JU* [2014] EWCOP 21 this was demonstrated where in applying the best interest test, and recognising the wishes and feelings of P as a 'magnetic factor', the Judge appointed a Local Authority as a deputy over a family member who was estranged from P. In *Re GMP* [2015] EWCOP 67, [2015] All ER (D) 171 (Oct) Senior Judge Lush reflected upon the issue of the cost of the administration of a deputyship drawing attention to his comments in *Re DT* [2015] EWCOP 10, [2015] All ER (D) 48 (Mar) where he had considered the potential costs of a Panel Deputy.

III MEN [52.2]

The test for calling in a security bond In *Re Gladys Meek* [2014] EWCOP 1, [2014] WTLR 1155 HHJ Hodge QC addressed the issues which should be considered when calling in a bond in the absence of statutory guidance.

III MEN [52.3]

The appointment of successive deputies In *Re H* [2015] EWCOP 52, [2015] All ER (D) 57 (Aug) Senior Judge Lush gave guidance as to the approach of the court when invited to appoint successive deputies under s 19(5) above.

III MEN [53]

20. Restrictions on deputies

(1) A deputy does not have power to make a decision on behalf of P in relation to a matter if he knows or has reasonable grounds for believing that P has capacity in relation to the matter.

(2) Nothing in section 16(5) or 17 permits a deputy to be given power—

(a) to prohibit a named person from having contact with P;

(b) to direct a person responsible for P's health care to allow a different person to take over that responsibility.

(3) A deputy may not be given powers with respect to—

(a) the settlement of any of P's property, whether for P's benefit or for the benefit of others,

(b) the execution for P of a will, or

(c) the exercise of any power (including a power to consent) vested in P whether beneficially or as trustee or otherwise.

(4) A deputy may not be given power to make a decision on behalf of P which is inconsistent with a decision made, within the scope of his authority and in accordance with this Act, by the donee of a lasting power of attorney granted by P (or, if there is more than one donee, by any of them).

(5) A deputy may not refuse consent to the carrying out or continuation of life-sustaining treatment in relation to P.

(6) The authority conferred on a deputy is subject to the provisions of this Act and, in particular, sections 1 (the principles) and 4 (best interests).

(7) A deputy may not do an act that is intended to restrain P unless four conditions are satisfied.

(8) The first condition is that, in doing the act, the deputy is acting within the scope of an authority expressly conferred on him by the court.

(9) The second is that P lacks, or the deputy reasonably believes that P lacks, capacity in relation to the matter in question.

(10) The third is that the deputy reasonably believes that it is necessary to do the act in order to prevent harm to P.

(11) The fourth is that the act is a proportionate response to—

(a) the likelihood of P's suffering harm, and

(b) the seriousness of that harm.

(12) For the purposes of this section, a deputy restrains P if he—

(a) uses, or threatens to use, force to secure the doing of an act which P resists, or

(b) restricts P's liberty of movement, whether or not P resists,

or if he authorises another person to do any of those things.

(13) . . .

III MEN [54]

21. Transfer of proceedings relating to people under 18

(1) The Lord Chief Justice, with the concurrence of the Lord Chancellor, may by order make provision as to the transfer of proceedings relating to a person under 18, in such circumstances as are specified in the order—

(a) from the Court of Protection to a court having jurisdiction under the Children Act 1989 (c 41), or

(b) from a court having jurisdiction under that Act to the Court of Protection.

(2) The Lord Chief Justice may nominate any of the following to exercise his functions under this section—

(a) the President of the Court of Protection;

(b) a judicial office holder (as defined in section 109(4) of the Constitutional Reform Act 2005).

III MEN [54.1]

Transfer of proceedings The Mental Capacity Act 2005 (Transfer of Proceedings) Order 2007, SI 2007/1899 provides for the transfer of proceedings between the Court of Protection and a court having jurisdiction under the Children Act 1989.

Powers of the court in relation to Schedule A1

III MEN [55]

21A. Powers of court in relation to Schedule A1

(1) This section applies if either of the following has been given under Schedule A1—

(a) a standard authorisation;

(b) an urgent authorisation.

(2) Where a standard authorisation has been given, the court may determine any question relating to any of the following matters—

(a) whether the relevant person meets one or more of the qualifying requirements;

(b) the period during which the standard authorisation is to be in force;

(c) the purpose for which the standard authorisation is given;

(d) the conditions subject to which the standard authorisation is given.

(3) If the court determines any question under subsection (2), the court may make an order—

(a) varying or terminating the standard authorisation, or

(b) directing the supervisory body to vary or terminate the standard authorisation.

(4) Where an urgent authorisation has been given, the court may determine any question relating to any of the following matters—

(a) whether the urgent authorisation should have been given;

(b) the period during which the urgent authorisation is to be in force;

(c) the purpose for which the urgent authorisation is given.

(5) Where the court determines any question under subsection (4), the court may make an order—

(a) varying or terminating the urgent authorisation, or

(b) directing the managing authority of the relevant hospital or care home to vary or terminate the urgent authorisation.

(6) Where the court makes an order under subsection (3) or (5), the court may make an order about a person's liability for any act done in connection with the standard or urgent authorisation before its variation or termination.

(7) An order under subsection (6) may, in particular, exclude a person from liability.

III MEN [55.1]

Applications This section enables the Court of Protection to vary or discharge an urgent or standard authorisation. It also entitles the applicant to benefit from non-means tested legal aid, which is not the case where the challenge to deprivation of liberty is not under s 21A: Civil Legal Aid (Financial Resources and Payment for Services) Regulations 2013 (SI 2013/480), reg 5(1)(g). In *Director of Legal Aid Casework v Briggs* [2017] EWCA Civ 1169 the Court of Appeal held that the subject matter of a s 21A challenge had to relate to deprivation of liberty and not, as in that case, only to serious medical treatment where the patient's deprivation of liberty was not an issue. Practice Direction 11A must now be complied with. In *G v E* [2010] EWCA Civ 822 the Court of Appeal determined that the provisions of the Act as amended was Article 5 compliant. In *RB (by his litigation friend) v Brighton & Hove City Council* [2014] EWCA Civ 561, (2014) Times, 12 June the Court of Appeal stressed the importance of parties recognising that proceedings should focus on the fact specific nature of circumstances relating to P avoiding the temptation to draw upon previous decided cases addressing issues of 'capacity'.

Regard should be made to the guidance in the Deprivation of Liberty Code of Practice 2007.

In *Re HA* [2012] EWHC 1068 (COP) Charles J gave guidance as to the correct approach where a standard authorisation might cease during the continuance of proceedings under s 21A, holding that it should be for the court to make interim orders authorising deprivation of liberty. Further he held that if the proceedings concluded determining that P should remain in a care home or hospital, it was preferable for the Statutory scheme under Schedule A1 with its checks and balances to apply rather than reviews by the court.

Baker J in *A Primary Care Trust LDV* [2013] EWHC 272 (Fam) approached the position where a trust was seeking a declaration as to whether P's circumstances amounted to a deprivation of liberty and in assessing P's capacity to consent, what information was relevant to that decision, In declaring that the arrangements for P's care and treatment objectively constituted a deprivation of liberty and providing clarification of the information required when considering the issue of consent, the judge followed the decision of the Court of Appeal in *Cheshire West and Chester Council v P* [2011] EWCA 1257 finding objectively such deprivation of liberty was on the facts established. In his judgment he drew attention to the guidance given in Chapter 2 of the Deprivation of liberty safeguards Code of Practice, and in particular paragraph 2.5. However in reversing the decision of the Court of Appeal in *Cheshire West*, regard must now be made to the Supreme Court's ruling on deprivation of liberty in *P (by his litigation friend the Official Solicitor) v Cheshire West and Chester Council and another; P and Q (by their litigation friend the Official Solicitor) v Surrey County Council* [2014] UKSC 19 where Baroness Hale provided guidance on issues that should be considered in determining whether in fact deprivation of liberty was occurring in any factual circumstance. Referring to European case law at paragraph 37 of her judgment she identified 3 common grounds, namely (i) the objective component of confinement in a particular restricted place for a not negligible length of time; (ii) the subjective component of lack of valid consent; and (iii) the attribution of responsibility.

In direct response to that judgment following guidance given by the President in two judgments: *Re X (Deprivation of Liberty)* [2014] EWCOP 25, 141 BMLR 212, and *Re X (Deprivation of Liberty (No 2)* [2014] EWCOP 37, 141 BMLR 225 a streamlined procedure was introduced on 17 November 2014 pursuant to a further Practice Direction 10AA relating to applications made under s 4A(3) and (4) of the Mental Capacity Act 2005, where authorisation is sought pursuant to s 16(2)(a) of the Mental Capacity Act 2005 to sanction arrangements for where an individual who lacks capacity should live and where restrictions involve a deprivation of liberty.

In *UF v X County Council (No 2)* [2014] EWCOP 18 Cobb J in a detailed judgment addressed the issue of the decision between two options, residential care and care at home with a package of support, and in an examination of the evidence and of P's best interests, it was recognised that whilst the court would seek to implement the least restrictive option, that such a consideration might have to 'yield to a wider best interests principle' (*London Borough of Havering v LD & KD* [2010] EWHC 3876 (COP) at [9]).

III MEN [55.2]

Detention of alcoholic for medical purposes Detention was ordered in the best interests of an alcoholic with a brain injury who was not at the time capable of independent living outside an institutional setting: *RB (by his litigation friend) v Brighton & Hove City Council* [2014] EWCA Civ 561, (2014) Times, 12 June.

POWERS OF THE COURT IN RELATION TO LASTING POWERS OF ATTORNEY

III MEN [56]

22. Powers of court in relation to validity of lasting powers of attorney

(1) This section and section 23 apply if—

(a) a person ('P') has executed or purported to execute an instrument with a view to creating a lasting power of attorney, or

(b) an instrument has been registered as a lasting power of attorney conferred by P.

(2) The court may determine any question relating to—

(a) whether one or more of the requirements for the creation of a lasting power of attorney have been met;

(b) whether the power has been revoked or has otherwise come to an end.

(3) Subsection (4) applies if the court is satisfied—

(a) that fraud or undue pressure was used to induce P—

(i) to execute an instrument for the purpose of creating a lasting power of attorney, or

(ii) to create a lasting power of attorney, or

(b) that the donee (or, if more than one, any of them) of a lasting power of attorney—

(i) has behaved, or is behaving, in a way that contravenes his authority or is not in P's best interests, or

(ii) proposes to behave in a way that would contravene his authority or would not be in P's best interests.

(4) The court may—

(a) direct that an instrument purporting to create the lasting power of attorney is not to be registered, or

(b) if P lacks capacity to do so, revoke the instrument or the lasting power of attorney.

(5) If there is more than one donee, the court may under subsection (4)(b) revoke the instrument or the lasting power of attorney so far as it relates to any of them.

(6) 'Donee' includes an intended donee.

III MEN [56.1]

Applications and the Court of Protection Rules Applications to the Court of Protection should be made by reference to the Court of Protection Rules 2017 and in particular Part 9. Rule 9.7 provides specific guidance as to service in respect of applications under both ss 22, and 23 (below): see **III MEN [590]**.

III MEN [56.2]

The test to apply if revoking an instrument In *Re J* [2011] COPLR Con Vol 716 HHJ Marshall QC in interpreting s 22(3)(b) considered that a two stage approach should be adopted. First, identifying the allegedly offending behaviour or prospective behaviour, and then second, looking at all the circumstances and context before deciding whether, taking everything into account, it really did amount to behaviour which it is not in P's best interests, or can fairly be characterised as such. Finally the court would then determine whether taking everything into account including the fact that it is behaviour in some other capacity, it also gives good reason to take the very serious step of revoking the LPA. In *Re ARL* [2015] EWCOP 55 Senior Judge Lush in applying the guidance of *Re J* found against one of two attorneys, such that in revoking the instrument, he was able to proceed to appoint the attorney not found to have acted inappropriately as a joint deputy with another. In *Re ID (Revocation of LPA)* [2015] EWCOP 19, [2015] All ER (D) 225 (Mar) Senior Judge applying the *Re J* principles was able to find that there was a joint liability of attorneys in failing to pay care fees and personal allowances on behalf of the Donor and in *Re MC* [2015] EWCOP 32, [2015] All ER (D) 78 (May) distinguish the acts of the two attorneys.

Senior Judge Lush addressed issues concerning the use or misuse of funds held by an attorney in a fiduciary capacity and in *Re Buckley, The Public Guardian v C* [2013] COPLR 39 he provided guidance on the responsibilities of an attorney for investment of a donor's estate and further that attorneys must not only be deemed to know the law, but be fully aware of their responsibilities including familiarisation with the Code of Practice. In particular he drew attention to para 7.60 thereof. This was followed in *The Public Guardian v ICL* [2015] EWCOP 55, [2015] WTLR 1489, [2015] All ER (D) 98 (Aug) and in *Re DWA* [2015] EWCOP 72, [2015] All ER (D) 82 (Nov) where the Senior Judge Lush stressed the importance of attorneys having regard to paras 7.60 to 7.68 of the Code of Practice. See Chapter 7 of the Code of Practice and further **III MEN [10A]**. The Senior Judge revisited the importance of the Code of Practice and in particular para 7.51 in his decision in *Re AH* [2016] EWCOP 9 where it is clearly stated that an attorney must meet certain standards, and if failing to do so, may be removed.

Where a family member acted in bad faith in commencing proceedings to remove an attorney acting under a Lasting Power of Attorney, Senior Judge Lush exercised his discretion under r 159 in *Re BN* [2015] EWCOP 11 to make an adverse costs order.

In *Re DP (Revocation of Lasting Power of Attorney)* [2014] EWCOP B4 the Senior Judge clarified the important investigative role of the Public Guardian and the function of the General Visitor and in *Re CT* [2014] EWCOP 51, [2015] WTLR 1441, [2014] All ER (D) 26 (Dec) the Senior Judge exercised his discretion to depart from the general rule of costs in making no order for costs where a respondent had unjustifiably attacked the independence of the Special Visitor and their non-cooperation with the investigation of the Public Guardian and the work of the Visitor. In *Re PST* [2014] EWCOP 52, [2014] All ER (D) 123 (Dec) the Senior Judge severed a provision in an LPA which sought to restrict 'a public authority from obtaining any information about the donor's property and financial affairs at any time' asserting that such provision was contrary to public policy.

In *London Borough of Redbridge v G* [2014] EWCOP 17 Ms Justice Russell DBE in concluding a fact finding investigation of P's best interests and future accommodation found that in the light of her decision, that the existing LPA for health and welfare should be revoked relying upon the use of undue pressure by the donee.

III MEN [56.3]

Revocation by the court under section 22(4)(b) The court may revoke a lasting power where the donor lacks capacity. Where, however, it is unclear whether the donor has capacity to revoke, an assessment by a Court of Protection special visitor is required. In a case where this situation arose the court ordered that, pending the advice of the special visitor, the authority under the existing lasting power should be suspended and that a member of the donor's family should be appointed as an interim deputy: *Re YW* [2016] EWCOP 18, [2016] All ER (D) 45 (Apr).

III MEN [57]

23. Powers of court in relation to operation of lasting powers of attorney

(1) The court may determine any question as to the meaning or effect of a lasting power of attorney or an instrument purporting to create one.

(2) The court may—

- (a) give directions with respect to decisions—
  - (i) which the donee of a lasting power of attorney has authority to make, and
  - (ii) which P lacks capacity to make;
- (b) give any consent or authorisation to act which the donee would have to obtain from P if P had capacity to give it.

(3) The court may, if P lacks capacity to do so—

- (a) give directions to the donee with respect to the rendering by him of reports or accounts and the production of records kept by him for that purpose;
- (b) require the donee to supply information or produce documents or things in his possession as donee;
- (c) give directions with respect to the remuneration or expenses of the donee;
- (d) relieve the donee wholly or partly from any liability which he has or may have incurred on account of a breach of his duties as donee.

(4) The court may authorise the making of gifts which are not within section 12(2) (permitted gifts).

(5) Where two or more donees are appointed under a lasting power of attorney, this section applies as if references to the donee were to all or any of them.

III MEN [57.1]

Procedure For procedure see **III MEN [56.1]** above and **III MEN [590]** below.

III MEN [57.2]

Guidance on fiduciary responsibilities of an attorney and procedure for removal Senior Judge Lush in a series of cases commenced by the Public Guardian has given both guidance and warning to attorneys of the need to familiarise themselves with their powers both at law and as recommended by the Code of Practice. He has drawn attention to the care which must be adopted in investment, separation of funds and adopting strict records of movement of funds. He has provided a clear reminder of the limitations on gifts being made without prior authority, and the starting position in respect of level of gifting see *Re Harcourt, The Public Guardian v A* [2013] COPLR 69 and *Re Buckley, The Public Guardian v C* [2013] COPLR 39. In *The Public Guardian v W* [2014] EWCOP B24 the Senior Judge in revoking an LPA stressed the importance of maintaining accounts, paying care home fees and providing to the Public Guardian a full account if so required. In *Public Guardian v AW (Application to revoke Lasting Power of Attorney)* [2014] EWCOP 28, [2014] WTLR 1705 the Senior Judge recorded that it was in the interest of those attorneys who found a potential conflict of interest in the application of the Donor's funds to apply to the Court for authority under s 23(2)(b) of the Act. Similarly in *The Public Guardian v DH* [2014] EWCOP 15, *Re PST* [2014] EWCOP 52, [2014] All ER (D) 123 (Dec) and in *The Public Guardian v AC* [2014] EWCOP 41 the Court demonstrated that lasting powers of attorneys would be revoked if financial abuse occurred. See also **III MEN [10A]**.

In *Re AH* [2016] EWCOP 9 the Senior Judge at paras 26 and 27 of his judgment identified all of the relevant duties of an Attorney by reference to the Code of Practice, indicating clearly that an Attorney falling short of meeting those standards could be faced with removal.

In *Re AMH* [2015] EWCOP 70, [2015] All ER (D) 21 (Nov) Senior Judge Lush highlighted the United Nations Convention on the Rights of Persons with Disabilities ratified in the United Kingdom in 2009, and of Article 12.4 as to the importance of measures to respect that the 'rights will and preferences of the person are free from conflict of interest and undue influence', and that the safeguards are 'proportionate to the degree to which such measures affect the person's rights and interests.

III MEN [57.3]

Guidance on costs and effect of disclaimer on living will In *N v E* [2014] EWCOP 27 Senior Judge Lush addressed the rules relating to costs and in particular referred to the decision of *Re Cathcart* [1892] 1 Ch 549 and the principle that the court should have regard to the respective means of the parties when exercising its discretion as to costs. Further, where an individual had made an advance decision ('her living will') the court could make a declaration under s 26(4) of the Act if this prevented such an advance decision failing in the event of the revocation of a lasting power of attorney.

III MEN [57.4]

Revocation of a digital lasting power of attorney In *JL (Revocation of Lasting Power of Attorney* [2014] EWCOP 36 the Senior Judge in removing an attorney for financial abuse raised the issue of undue pressure and the vulnerability of the Donor. He stressed the importance of those using the digital system of ensuring that the documents were clearly read and understood as to their obligations and fiduciary responsibilities, in particular to the seriousness and consequences of signing the declaration.

III MEN [57.5]

Guidance on responsibilities of an attorney under a health and welfare LPA and procedure for removal In *The Public Guardian v Marvin* [2014] EWCOP 47 the Senior Judge in upholding the continued role of the attorney identified the importance of any attorney working with relevant social services in the best interests of a Donor and the consequences of a conflict arising between an attorney and statutory care providers

III MEN [58]

24. Advance decisions to refuse treatment: general

(1) 'Advance decision' means a decision made by a person ('P'), after he has reached 18 and when he has capacity to do so, that if—

(a) at a later time and in such circumstances as he may specify, a specified treatment is proposed to be carried out or continued by a person providing health care for him, and

(b) at that time he lacks capacity to consent to the carrying out or continuation of the treatment,

the specified treatment is not to be carried out or continued.

(2) For the purposes of subsection (1)(a), a decision may be regarded as specifying a treatment or circumstances even though expressed in layman's terms.

(3) P may withdraw or alter an advance decision at any time when he has capacity to do so.

(4) A withdrawal (including a partial withdrawal) need not be in writing.

(5) An alteration of an advance decision need not be in writing (unless section 25(5) applies in relation to the decision resulting from the alteration).

III MEN [58.1]

The Code of Practice and advance decisions Chapter 9 of the Mental Capacity Act 2005 Code of Practice provides guidance on the issues concerning advance decisions to refuse treatment. It is important to have regard to the Code and guidance, and within any subsequent application to the court, whether civil or criminal, consideration will be given to provisions of the Code, and failure to comply with the code must be taken into account in deciding any relevant question (s 42(5) of the Mental Capacity Act 2005): see **III MEN [80]**.

III MEN [58.2]

Need to specify treatment and circumstances See the 'balance sheet' approach and the importance to be attached to the preservation of life: *Re M* [2011] EWHC 2443 (Fam), [2011] All ER (D) 142 (Sep), (2011) Times, 1 December per Baker J. There was no advance decision within s 24 in that case but such a decision would be binding only if it specified the treatment and circumstances in issue.

III MEN [59]

25. Validity and applicability of advance decisions

(1) An advance decision does not affect the liability which a person may incur for carrying out or continuing a treatment in relation to P unless the decision is at the material time—

(a) valid, and

(b) applicable to the treatment.

(2) An advance decision is not valid if P—

(a) has withdrawn the decision at a time when he had capacity to do so,

(b) has, under a lasting power of attorney created after the advance decision was made, conferred authority on the donee (or, if more than one, any of them) to give or refuse consent to the treatment to which the advance decision relates, or

(c) has done anything else clearly inconsistent with the advance decision remaining his fixed decision.

(3) An advance decision is not applicable to the treatment in question if at the material time P has capacity to give or refuse consent to it.

(4) An advance decision is not applicable to the treatment in question if—

(a) that treatment is not the treatment specified in the advance decision,

(b) any circumstances specified in the advance decision are absent, or

(c) there are reasonable grounds for believing that circumstances exist which P did not anticipate at the time of the advance decision and which would have affected his decision had he anticipated them.

(5) An advance decision is not applicable to life-sustaining treatment unless—

(a) the decision is verified by a statement by P to the effect that it is to apply to that treatment even if life is at risk, and

(b) the decision and statement comply with subsection (6).

(6) A decision or statement complies with this subsection only if—

(a) it is in writing,

(b) it is signed by P or by another person in P's presence and by P's direction,

(c) the signature is made or acknowledged by P in the presence of a witness, and

(d) the witness signs it, or acknowledges his signature, in P's presence.

(7) The existence of any lasting power of attorney other than one of a description mentioned in subsection (2)(b) does not prevent the advance decision from being regarded as valid and applicable.

III MEN [60]

26. Effect of advance decisions

(1) If P has made an advance decision which is—

(a) valid, and

(b) applicable to a treatment,

the decision has effect as if he had made it, and had had capacity to make it, at the time when the question arises whether the treatment should be carried out or continued.

(2) A person does not incur liability for carrying out or continuing the treatment unless, at the time, he is satisfied that an advance decision exists which is valid and applicable to the treatment.

(3) A person does not incur liability for the consequences of withholding or withdrawing a treatment from P if, at the time, he reasonably believes that an advance decision exists which is valid and applicable to the treatment.

(4) The court may make a declaration as to whether an advance decision—

(a) exists;

(b) is valid;

(c) is applicable to a treatment.

(5) Nothing in an apparent advance decision stops a person—

(a) providing life-sustaining treatment, or

(b) doing any act he reasonably believes to be necessary to prevent a serious deterioration in P's condition,

while a decision as respects any relevant issue is sought from the court.

III MEN [60.1]

Declarations and applications regarding advance decisions An application for a declaration would require compliance with Court of Protection Rules 2017, Part 9. Rules 9.1–9.4 provide guidance on the submission of relevant Forms and information, and rr 9.5–9.6 provide guidance for the progress of the application, including service, notification if necessary and responding to the application. See **III MEN [584]** to **III MEN [589]**.

In *X Primary Care Trust v XB* [2012] EWHC 1390 (Fam), 127 BMLR 122 Theis J highlighted the importance of ensuring that if an issue arose regarding the validity of an advance decision, it must be investigated by the relevant authorities as a matter of urgency. In particular regard should be made to the guidance in paragraphs 9.10–9.24, and 9.28 of the Code of Practice.

In *A Local Authority v E (by her litigation friend, the Official Solicitor)* [2012] EWHC 1639 (COP), [2012] 2 FCR 523, 127 BMLR 133 Peter Jackson J stressed the importance of Paragraph 9.67 of the Code of Practice, and the bringing before the court any doubt or disagreement as to the validity of an advance decision.

The case of *Re D (withdrawal of treatment)* [2012] EWHC 885 (COP), [2012] All ER (D) 163 (Oct) highlights the need to ensure that any Advance Directive complies with the strict requirements of s 25 of the Act. In that case Peter Jackson J used the letters of P which fell short of formal advance decisions to assist in evaluating P's best interests in determining the issue of withdrawal of life sustaining treatment. In that respect the decision of Holman J in *An NHS Trust v K (by her litigation friend, the Official Solicitor)* [2012] EWHC 2922 (COP), [2012] All ER (D) 129 (Oct) demonstrates the use of the balance sheet in weighing the benefits and burden of surgery.

In a case concerning a 23 year old who had made an advanced decision not to consent to blood transfusions, the court in *Nottingham Healthcare NHS Trust v J* [2014] EWHC 1136 (COP) recognised the difficulties and dilemmas faced by treating physicians, but would still uphold the importance of individuals being able to make and rely upon advance decisions in the event that subsequently they lacked mental capacity.

In *Sheffield Teaching Hospitals NHS Foundation Trust v TH* [2014] EWCOP 4 Hayden J applied the principles drawn from the decision in *Aintree University Hospitals NHS Foundation Trust v James* [2013] UKSC 67, [2014] AC 591, [2014] 1 All ER 573 to grant declarations in respect of an individual said to be in the lower spectrum of a minimally conscious state, where the individual had made a valid advance decision.

III MEN [61]

27. Family relationships etc.

(1) Nothing in this Act permits a decision on any of the following matters to be made on behalf of a person—

- (a) consenting to marriage or a civil partnership,
- (b) consenting to have sexual relations,
- (c) consenting to a decree of divorce being granted on the basis of two years' separation,
- (d) consenting to a dissolution order being made in relation to a civil partnership on the basis of two years' separation,
- (e) consenting to a child's being placed for adoption by an adoption agency,
- (f) consenting to the making of an adoption order,
- (g) discharging parental responsibilities in matters not relating to a child's property,
- (h) giving a consent under the Human Fertilisation and Embryology Act 1990 (c. 37).

(2) 'Adoption order' means—

- (a) an adoption order within the meaning of the Adoption and Children Act 2002 (c. 38) (including a future adoption order), and
- (b) an order under section 84 of that Act (parental responsibility prior to adoption abroad).

III MEN [62]

28. Mental Health Act matters

(1) Nothing in this Act authorises anyone—

- (a) to give a patient medical treatment for mental disorder, or
- (b) to consent to a patient's being given medical treatment for mental disorder,

if, at the time when it is proposed to treat the patient, his treatment is regulated by Part 4 of the Mental Health Act.

(2) 'Medical treatment', 'mental disorder' and 'patient' have the same meaning as in that Act.

III MEN [63]

29. Voting rights

(1) Nothing in this Act permits a decision on voting at an election for any public office, or at a referendum, to be made on behalf of a person.

(2) 'Referendum' has the same meaning as in section 101 of the Political Parties, Elections and Referendums Act 2000 (c. 41).

III MEN [64]

30. Research

(1) Intrusive research carried out on, or in relation to, a person who lacks capacity to consent to it is unlawful unless it is carried out—

(a) as part of a research project which is for the time being approved by the appropriate body for the purposes of this Act in accordance with section 31, and

(b) in accordance with sections 32 and 33.

(2) Research is intrusive if it is of a kind that would be unlawful if it was carried out—

(a) on or in relation to a person who had capacity to consent to it, but

(b) without his consent.

(3) A clinical trial which is subject to the provisions of clinical trials regulations is not to be treated as research for the purposes of this section.

(4) 'Appropriate body', in relation to a research project, means the person, committee or other body specified in regulations made by the appropriate authority as the appropriate body in relation to a project of the kind in question.

(5) 'Clinical trials regulations' means—

(a) the Medicines for Human Use (Clinical Trials) Regulations 2004 (S.I.2004/1031) and any other regulations replacing those regulations or amending them, and

(b) any other regulations relating to clinical trials and designated by the Secretary of State as clinical trials regulations for the purposes of this section.

(6) In this section, section 32 and section 34, 'appropriate authority' means—

(a) in relation to the carrying out of research in England, the Secretary of State, and

(b) in relation to the carrying out of research in Wales, the National Assembly for Wales.

III MEN [64.1]

The Code of Practice and guidance Chapter 11 of the Mental Capacity Act 2005 Code of Practice provides guidance on how the Mental Capacity Act 2005 affects research projects involving a person who lacks capacity. It is important to have regard to the Code and guidance, and within any subsequent application to the court, whether civil or criminal, consideration will be given to provisions of the Code, and failure to comply with the code must be taken into account in deciding any relevant question (s 42(5) of the Mental Capacity Act 2005): see **III MEN [80]**.

III MEN [65]

31. Requirements for approval

(1) The appropriate body may not approve a research project for the purposes of this Act unless satisfied that the following requirements will be met in relation to research carried out as part of the project on, or in relation to, a person who lacks capacity to consent to taking part in the project ('P').

(2) The research must be connected with—

(a) an impairing condition affecting P, or

(b) its treatment.

(3) 'Impairing condition' means a condition which is (or may be) attributable to, or which causes or contributes to (or may cause or contribute to), the impairment of, or disturbance in the functioning of, the mind or brain.

(4) There must be reasonable grounds for believing that research of comparable effectiveness cannot be carried out if the project has to be confined to, or relate only to, persons who have capacity to consent to taking part in it.

(5) The research must—

(a) have the potential to benefit P without imposing on P a burden that is disproportionate to the potential benefit to P, or

(b) be intended to provide knowledge of the causes or treatment of, or of the care of persons affected by, the same or a similar condition.

(6) If the research falls within paragraph (b) of subsection (5) but not within paragraph (a), there must be reasonable grounds for believing—

(a) that the risk to P from taking part in the project is likely to be negligible, and

(b) that anything done to, or in relation to, P will not—

(i) interfere with P's freedom of action or privacy in a significant way, or

(ii) be unduly invasive or restrictive.

(7) There must be reasonable arrangements in place for ensuring that the requirements of sections 32 and 33 will be met.

III MEN [66]

32. Consulting carers etc.

(1) This section applies if a person ('R')—

(a) is conducting an approved research project, and

(b) wishes to carry out research, as part of the project, on or in relation to a person ('P') who lacks capacity to consent to taking part in the project.

(2) R must take reasonable steps to identify a person who—

(a) otherwise than in a professional capacity or for remuneration, is engaged in caring for P or is interested in P's welfare, and

(b) is prepared to be consulted by R under this section.

(3) If R is unable to identify such a person he must, in accordance with guidance issued by the appropriate authority, nominate a person who—

(a) is prepared to be consulted by R under this section, but

(b) has no connection with the project.

(4) R must provide the person identified under subsection (2), or nominated under subsection (3), with information about the project and ask him—

(a) for advice as to whether P should take part in the project, and

(b) what, in his opinion, P's wishes and feelings about taking part in the project would be likely to be if P had capacity in relation to the matter.

(5) If, at any time, the person consulted advises R that in his opinion P's wishes and feelings would be likely to lead him to decline to take part in the project (or to wish to withdraw from it) if he had capacity in relation to the matter, R must ensure—

(a) if P is not already taking part in the project, that he does not take part in it;

(b) if P is taking part in the project, that he is withdrawn from it.

(6) But subsection (5)(b) does not require treatment that P has been receiving as part of the project to be discontinued if R has reasonable grounds for believing that there would be a significant risk to P's health if it were discontinued.

(7) The fact that a person is the donee of a lasting power of attorney given by P, or is P's deputy, does not prevent him from being the person consulted under this section.

(8) Subsection (9) applies if treatment is being, or is about to be, provided for P as a matter of urgency and R considers that, having regard to the nature of the research and of the particular circumstances of the case—

(a) it is also necessary to take action for the purposes of the research as a matter of urgency, but

(b) it is not reasonably practicable to consult under the previous provisions of this section.

(9) R may take the action if—

(a) he has the agreement of a registered medical practitioner who is not involved in the organisation or conduct of the research project, or

(b) where it is not reasonably practicable in the time available to obtain that agreement, he acts in accordance with a procedure approved by the appropriate body at the time when the research project was approved under section 31.

(10) But R may not continue to act in reliance on subsection (9) if he has reasonable grounds for believing that it is no longer necessary to take the action as a matter of urgency.

III MEN [67]

33. Additional safeguards

(1) This section applies in relation to a person who is taking part in an approved research project even though he lacks capacity to consent to taking part.

(2) Nothing may be done to, or in relation to, him in the course of the research—

(a) to which he appears to object (whether by showing signs of resistance or otherwise) except where what is being done is intended to protect him from harm or to reduce or prevent pain or discomfort, or

(b) which would be contrary to—

(i) an advance decision of his which has effect, or

(ii) any other form of statement made by him and not subsequently withdrawn, of which R is aware.

(3) The interests of the person must be assumed to outweigh those of science and society.

(4) If he indicates (in any way) that he wishes to be withdrawn from the project he must be withdrawn without delay.

(5) P must be withdrawn from the project, without delay, if at any time the person conducting the research has reasonable grounds for believing that one or more of the requirements set out in section 31(2) to (7) is no longer met in relation to research being carried out on, or in relation to, P.

(6) But neither subsection (4) nor subsection (5) requires treatment that P has been receiving as part of the project to be discontinued if R has reasonable grounds for believing that there would be a significant risk to P's health if it were discontinued.

III MEN [68]

34. Loss of capacity during research project

(1) This section applies where a person ('P')—

(a) has consented to take part in a research project begun before the commencement of section 30, but

(b) before the conclusion of the project, loses capacity to consent to continue to take part in it.

(2) The appropriate authority may by regulations provide that, despite P's loss of capacity, research of a prescribed kind may be carried out on, or in relation to, P if—

(a) the project satisfies prescribed requirements,

(b) any information or material relating to P which is used in the research is of a prescribed description and was obtained before P's loss of capacity, and

(c) the person conducting the project takes in relation to P such steps as may be prescribed for the purpose of protecting him.

(3) The regulations may, in particular,—
- (a) make provision about when, for the purposes of the regulations, a project is to be treated as having begun;
- (b) include provision similar to any made by section 31, 32 or 33.

III MEN [69]

35. Appointment of independent mental capacity advocates

(1) The responsible authority must make such arrangements as it considers reasonable to enable persons ('independent mental capacity advocates') to be available to represent and support persons to whom acts or decisions proposed under sections 37, 38 and 39 relate.

(2) The appropriate authority may make regulations as to the appointment of independent mental capacity advocates.

(3) The regulations may, in particular, provide—
- (a) that a person may act as an independent mental capacity advocate only in such circumstances, or only subject to such conditions, as may be prescribed;
- (b) for the appointment of a person as an independent mental capacity advocate to be subject to approval in accordance with the regulations.

(4) In making arrangements under subsection (1), the responsible authority must have regard to the principle that a person to whom a proposed act or decision relates should, so far as practicable, be represented and supported by a person who is independent of any person who will be responsible for the act or decision.

(5) The arrangements may include provision for payments to be made to, or in relation to, persons carrying out functions in accordance with the arrangements.

(6) For the purpose of enabling him to carry out his functions, an independent mental capacity advocate—
- (a) may interview in private the person whom he has been instructed to represent, and
- (b) may, at all reasonable times, examine and take copies of—
  - (i) any health record,
  - (ii) any record of, or held by, a local authority and compiled in connection with a social services function, and
  - (iii) any record held by a person registered under Part 2 of the Care Standards Act 2000 (c 14), Chapter 2 of Part 1 of the Health and Social Care Act 2008 or Part 1 of the Regulation and Inspection of Social Care (Wales) Act 2016 (anaw 2),

  which the person holding the record considers may be relevant to the independent mental capacity advocate's investigation.

(6A) In subsections (1) and (4), "the responsible authority" means—
- (a) in relation to the provision of the services of independent mental capacity advocates in the area of a local authority in England, that local authority, and
- (b) in relation to the provision of the services of independent mental capacity advocates in Wales, the Welsh Ministers.

(6B) In subsection (6A)(a), "local authority" has the meaning given in section 64(1) except that it does not include the council of a county or county borough in Wales.

(7) In this section, section 36 and section 37, 'the appropriate authority' means—
- (a) in relation to the provision of the services of independent mental capacity advocates in England, the Secretary of State, and
- (b) in relation to the provision of the services of independent mental capacity advocates in Wales, the National Assembly for Wales.

III MEN [69.1]

The appointment of an IMCA and the need for promptness In *The London Borough of Hillingdon v Steven Neary and Mark Neary and The Equality and Human Rights Commission* [2011] EWHC 1377 (COP), Jackson J was critical of the delay caused by the local authority in referring the matter to the court, but in particular the tardiness in taking steps to appoint an IMCA.

III MEN [69.2]

The Codes of Practice and the appointment of an IMCA Chapter 10 of the Mental Capacity Act 2005 Code of Practice provides guidance on the role of the IMCA service. The Code of Practice – Deprivation of Liberty Safeguards at Chapters 3.22–3.28, and 7.34–7.41 provide important guidance on the appointment of an IMCA.

It is important to have regard to the Code and guidance, and within any subsequent application to the court, whether civil or criminal, consideration will be given to provisions of the Code, and failure to comply with the code must be taken into account in deciding any relevant question (s 42(5) of the Mental Capacity Act 2005): see **III MEN [80]**.

III MEN [70]

36. Functions of independent mental capacity advocates

(1) The appropriate authority may make regulations as to the functions of independent mental capacity advocates.

(2) The regulations may, in particular, make provision requiring an advocate to take such steps as may be prescribed for the purpose of—

- (a) providing support to the person whom he has been instructed to represent ('P') so that P may participate as fully as possible in any relevant decision;
- (b) obtaining and evaluating relevant information;
- (c) ascertaining what P's wishes and feelings would be likely to be, and the beliefs and values that would be likely to influence P, if he had capacity;
- (d) ascertaining what alternative courses of action are available in relation to P;
- (e) obtaining a further medical opinion where treatment is proposed and the advocate thinks that one should be obtained.

(3) The regulations may also make provision as to circumstances in which the advocate may challenge, or provide assistance for the purpose of challenging, any relevant decision.

III MEN [71]

37. Provision of serious medical treatment by NHS body

(1) This section applies if an NHS body—

- (a) is proposing to provide, or secure the provision of, serious medical treatment for a person ('P') who lacks capacity to consent to the treatment, and
- (b) is satisfied that there is no person, other than one engaged in providing care or treatment for P in a professional capacity or for remuneration, whom it would be appropriate to consult in determining what would be in P's best interests.

(2) But this section does not apply if P's treatment is regulated by Part 4 of the Mental Health Act.

(3) Before the treatment is provided, the NHS body must instruct an independent mental capacity advocate to represent P.

(4) If the treatment needs to be provided as a matter of urgency, it may be provided even though the NHS body has not been able to comply with subsection (3).

(5) The NHS body must, in providing or securing the provision of treatment for P, take into account any information given, or submissions made, by the independent mental capacity advocate.

(6) 'Serious medical treatment' means treatment which involves providing, withholding or withdrawing treatment of a kind prescribed by regulations made by the appropriate authority.

(7) 'NHS body' has such meaning as may be prescribed by regulations made for the purposes of this section by—

(a) the Secretary of State, in relation to bodies in England, or

(b) the National Assembly for Wales, in relation to bodies in Wales.

III MEN [72]

38. Provision of accommodation by NHS body

(1) This section applies if an NHS body proposes to make arrangements—

(a) for the provision of accommodation in a hospital or care home for a person ('P') who lacks capacity to agree to the arrangements, or

(b) for a change in P's accommodation to another hospital or care home, and is satisfied that there is no person, other than one engaged in providing care or treatment for P in a professional capacity or for remuneration, whom it would be appropriate for it to consult in determining what would be in P's best interests.

(2) But this section does not apply if P is accommodated as a result of an obligation imposed on him under the Mental Health Act.

(2A) And this section does not apply if—

(a) an independent mental capacity advocate must be appointed under section 39A or 39C (whether or not by the NHS body) to represent P, and

(b) the hospital or care home in which P is to be accommodated under the arrangements referred to in this section is the relevant hospital or care home under the authorisation referred to in that section.

(3) Before making the arrangements, the NHS body must instruct an independent mental capacity advocate to represent P unless it is satisfied that—

(a) the accommodation is likely to be provided for a continuous period which is less than the applicable period, or

(b) the arrangements need to be made as a matter of urgency.

(4) If the NHS body—

(a) did not instruct an independent mental capacity advocate to represent P before making the arrangements because it was satisfied that subsection (3)(a) or (b) applied, but

(b) subsequently has reason to believe that the accommodation is likely to be provided for a continuous period—

(i) beginning with the day on which accommodation was first provided in accordance with the arrangements, and

(ii) ending on or after the expiry of the applicable period,

it must instruct an independent mental capacity advocate to represent P.

(5) The NHS body must, in deciding what arrangements to make for P, take into account any information given, or submissions made, by the independent mental capacity advocate.

(6) "Care home" means—

(a) a care home in England within the meaning given in section 3 of the Care Standards Act 2000 (c 14), and

(b) a place in Wales at which a care home service within the meaning of Part 1 of the Regulation and Inspection of Social Care (Wales) Act 2016 is provided wholly or mainly to persons aged 18 or over.

(7) 'Hospital' means—

(a) in relation to England, a hospital as defined by section 275 of the National Health Service Act 2006; and

(b) in relation to Wales, a health service hospital as defined by section 206 of the National Health Service (Wales) Act 2006 or an independent hospital as defined by section 2 of the Care Standards Act 2000.

(8) 'NHS body' has such meaning as may be prescribed by regulations made for the purposes of this section by—

(a) the Secretary of State, in relation to bodies in England, or

(b) the National Assembly for Wales, in relation to bodies in Wales.

(9) 'Applicable period' means—

(a) in relation to accommodation in a hospital, 28 days, and

(b) in relation to accommodation in a care home, 8 weeks.

(10) For the purposes of subsection (1), a person appointed under Part 10 of Schedule A1 to be P's representative is not, by virtue of that appointment, engaged in providing care or treatment for P in a professional capacity or for remuneration.

III MEN [72.1]

Appointing an IMCA and avoiding delay The decision of Jackson J in *The London Borough of Hillingdon v Steven Neary and Mark Neary* [2011] EWHC 413 (COP) stresses the importance of avoiding delay in the appointment of an IMCA.

III MEN [73]

39A. Person becomes subject to Schedule A1

(1) This section applies if—

(a) a person ('P') becomes subject to Schedule A1, and

(b) the managing authority of the relevant hospital or care home are satisfied that there is no person, other than one engaged in providing care or treatment for P in a professional capacity or for remuneration, whom it would be appropriate to consult in determining what would be in P's best interests.

(2) The managing authority must notify the supervisory body that this section applies.

(3) The supervisory body must instruct an independent mental capacity advocate to represent P.

(4) Schedule A1 makes provision about the role of an independent mental capacity advocate appointed under this section.

(5) This section is subject to paragraph 161 of Schedule A1.

(6) For the purposes of subsection (1), a person appointed under Part 10 of Schedule A1 to be P's representative is not, by virtue of that appointment, engaged in providing care or treatment for P in a professional capacity or for remuneration.

III MEN [73.1]

Progressing applications promptly In *The London Borough of Hillingdon v Steven Neary and Mark Neary* [2011] EWHC 413 (COP) criticism was made of a local authority for delaying the appointment of an IMCA, and the subsequent delay in commencing proceedings. The importance of the authority acting purposively and timely and the care to be adopted when selecting a relevant person's representative was stressed in *AJ (Deprivation of Liberty Safeguards)* [2015] EWCOP 5. For application to the court, see Practice Direction 11A (**III MEN [620]**).

III MEN [73.2]

The Deprivation of liberty safeguarding Code of Practice Regard should be given to the guidance given in the Deprivation of Liberty Safeguards Code of Practice as to the role and engagement of the IMCA. See chapters 3 and 7.

III MEN [74]

39B. Section 39A: supplementary provision

(1) This section applies for the purposes of section 39A.

(2) P becomes subject to Schedule A1 in any of the following cases.

(3) The first case is where an urgent authorisation is given in relation to P under paragraph 76(2) of Schedule A1 (urgent authorisation given before request made for standard authorisation).

(4) The second case is where the following conditions are met.

(5) The first condition is that a request is made under Schedule A1 for a standard authorisation to be given in relation to P ('the requested authorisation').

(6) The second condition is that no urgent authorisation was given under paragraph 76(2) of Schedule A1 before that request was made.

(7) The third condition is that the requested authorisation will not be in force on or before, or immediately after, the expiry of an existing standard authorisation.

(8) The expiry of a standard authorisation is the date when the authorisation is expected to cease to be in force.

(9) The third case is where, under paragraph 69 of Schedule A1, the supervisory body select a person to carry out an assessment of whether or not the relevant person is a detained resident.

III MEN [75]

39C. Person unrepresented whilst subject to Schedule A1

(1) This section applies if—

- (a) an authorisation under Schedule A1 is in force in relation to a person ('P'),
- (b) the appointment of a person as P's representative ends in accordance with regulations made under Part 10 of Schedule A1, and
- (c) the managing authority of the relevant hospital or care home are satisfied that there is no person, other than one engaged in providing care or treatment for P in a professional capacity or for remuneration, whom it would be appropriate to consult in determining what would be in P's best interests.

(2) The managing authority must notify the supervisory body that this section applies.

(3) The supervisory body must instruct an independent mental capacity advocate to represent P.

(4) Paragraph 159 of Schedule A1 makes provision about the role of an independent mental capacity advocate appointed under this section.

(5) The appointment of an independent mental capacity advocate under this section ends when a new appointment of a person as P's representative is made in accordance with Part 10 of Schedule A1.

(6) For the purposes of subsection (1), a person appointed under Part 10 of Schedule A1 to be P's representative is not, by virtue of that appointment, engaged in providing care or treatment for P in a professional capacity or for remuneration.

III MEN [76]

39D. Person subject to Schedule A1 without paid representative

(1) This section applies if—

(a) an authorisation under Schedule A1 is in force in relation to a person ('P'),

(b) P has a representative ('R') appointed under Part 10 of Schedule A1, and

(c) R is not being paid under regulations under Part 10 of Schedule A1 for acting as P's representative.

(2) The supervisory body must instruct an independent mental capacity advocate to represent P in any of the following cases.

(3) The first case is where P makes a request to the supervisory body to instruct an advocate.

(4) The second case is where R makes a request to the supervisory body to instruct an advocate.

(5) The third case is where the supervisory body have reason to believe one or more of the following—

(a) that, without the help of an advocate, P and R would be unable to exercise one or both of the relevant rights;

(b) that P and R have each failed to exercise a relevant right when it would have been reasonable to exercise it;

(c) that P and R are each unlikely to exercise a relevant right when it would be reasonable to exercise it.

(6) The duty in subsection (2) is subject to section 39E.

(7) If an advocate is appointed under this section, the advocate is, in particular, to take such steps as are practicable to help P and R to understand the following matters—

(a) the effect of the authorisation;

(b) the purpose of the authorisation;

(c) the duration of the authorisation;

(d) any conditions to which the authorisation is subject;

(e) the reasons why each assessor who carried out an assessment in connection with the request for the authorisation, or in connection with a review of the authorisation, decided that P met the qualifying requirement in question;

(f) the relevant rights;

(g) how to exercise the relevant rights.

(8) The advocate is, in particular, to take such steps as are practicable to help P or R—

(a) to exercise the right to apply to court, if it appears to the advocate that P or R wishes to exercise that right, or

(b) to exercise the right of review, if it appears to the advocate that P or R wishes to exercise that right.

(9) If the advocate helps P or R to exercise the right of review—

(a) the advocate may make submissions to the supervisory body on the question of whether a qualifying requirement is reviewable;

(b) the advocate may give information, or make submissions, to any assessor carrying out a review assessment.

(10) In this section—

'relevant rights' means—

(a) the right to apply to court, and

(b) the right of review;

'right to apply to court' means the right to make an application to the court to exercise its jurisdiction under section 21A;

'right of review' means the right under Part 8 of Schedule A1 to request a review.

III MEN [76.1]

Applications and procedure Delay in commencing appropriate referral to the court has been the subject of judicial comment in *The London Borough of Hillingdon v Steven Neary and Mark Neary* [2011] EWHC 413 (COP). Followed and highlighted in *Re AJ (Deprivation of Liberty Safeguards)* [2015] EWCOP 5, [2015] 3 WLR 683, [2015] All ER (D) 217 (Feb). Applications should be made by referral to Practice Direction 11A. See **III MEN [619]** to **III MEN [620]**.

In *RD v Others (Duties and Powers of the Relevant Person's Representative and Section 39D IMCAS* [2016] EWCOP 49 Baker J revisiting his earlier decision in *Re AJ (Deprivation of Liberty Safeguards)* [2015] EWCOP 5 addressed the role of the IMCA and their duties and the appropriate approach to taking decisions as to making an application to the Court of Protection under s 21A of the Act to challenge a standard authorisation under Schedule A1. Distinguishing the different roles of the IMCA and the relevant person's representative, the more restricted role of the IMCA was noted (paras 83–86).

III MEN [77]

39E. Limitation on duty to instruct advocate under section 39D

(1) This section applies if an advocate is already representing P in accordance with an instruction under section 39D.

(2) Section 39D(2) does not require another advocate to be instructed, unless the following conditions are met.

(3) The first condition is that the existing advocate was instructed—

- (a) because of a request by R, or
- (b) because the supervisory body had reason to believe one or more of the things in section 39D(5).

(4) The second condition is that the other advocate would be instructed because of a request by P.

III MEN [78]

40. Exceptions

(1) The duty imposed by section 37(3), 38(3) or (4), 39(4) or (5), 39A(3), 39C(3) or 39D(2) does not apply where there is—

- (a) a person nominated by P (in whatever manner) as a person to be consulted on matters to which that duty relates,
- (b) a donee of a lasting power of attorney created by P who is authorised to make decisions in relation to those matters, or
- (c) a deputy appointed by the court for P with power to make decisions in relation to those matters.

(2) A person appointed under Part 10 of Schedule A1 to be P's representative is not by virtue of that appointment, a person nominated by P as a person to be consulted in matters to which a duty mentioned in subsection (1) relates.

III MEN [79]

41. Power to adjust role of independent mental capacity advocate

(1) The appropriate authority may make regulations—

- (a) expanding the role of independent mental capacity advocates in relation to persons who lack capacity, and
- (b) adjusting the obligation to make arrangements imposed by section 35.

(2) The regulations may, in particular—

- (a) prescribe circumstances (different to those set out in sections 37, 38 and 39) in which an independent mental capacity advocate must, or circumstances in which one may, be instructed by a person of a prescribed description to represent a person who lacks capacity, and
- (b) include provision similar to any made by section 37, 38, 39 or 40.

(3) 'Appropriate authority' has the same meaning as in section 35.

III MEN [80]

42. Codes of practice

(1) The Lord Chancellor must prepare and issue one or more codes of practice—

(a) for the guidance of persons assessing whether a person has capacity in relation to any matter,

(b) for the guidance of persons acting in connection with the care or treatment of another person (see section 5),

(c) for the guidance of donees of lasting powers of attorney,

(d) for the guidance of deputies appointed by the court,

(e) for the guidance of persons carrying out research in reliance on any provision made by or under this Act (and otherwise with respect to sections 30 to 34),

(f) for the guidance of independent mental capacity advocates,

(g) with respect to the provisions of sections 24 to 26 (advance decisions and apparent advance decisions), and

(h) with respect to such other matters concerned with this Act as he thinks fit.

(2) The Lord Chancellor may from time to time revise a code.

(3) The Lord Chancellor may delegate the preparation or revision of the whole or any part of a code so far as he considers expedient.

(4) It is the duty of a person to have regard to any relevant code if he is acting in relation to a person who lacks capacity and is doing so in one or more of the following ways—

(a) as the donee of a lasting power of attorney,

(b) as a deputy appointed by the court,

(c) as a person carrying out research in reliance on any provision made by or under this Act (see sections 30 to 34),

(d) as an independent mental capacity advocate,

(e) in a professional capacity,

(f) for remuneration.

(5) If it appears to a court or tribunal conducting any criminal or civil proceedings that—

(a) a provision of a code, or

(b) a failure to comply with a code,

is relevant to a question arising in the proceedings, the provision or failure must be taken into account in deciding the question.

(6) A code under subsection (1)(d) may contain separate guidance for deputies appointed by virtue of paragraph 1(2) of Schedule 5 (functions of deputy conferred on receiver appointed under the Mental Health Act).

(7) In this section and in section 43, 'code' means a code prepared or revised under this section.

III MEN [80.1]

The Codes of Practice See Mental Capacity Act 2005 Code of Practice and the Deprivation of Liberty Safeguards Code of Practice. Criticism has been made of parties who fail to have regard to the Codes, and the courts are obliged to have regard to the guidance given in the Codes when considering any matter. See *R (on the application of C) v A Local Authority* [2011] EWHC 1539 (Admin), [2011] All ER (D) 171 (Jun), where Ryder J at paras 62-65 highlights the importance of regard to the Codes. In fact, the DOLS Code of Practice is of limited value in identifying deprivation of liberty, since the *Cheshire West* case.

III MEN [81]

43. Codes of practice: procedure

(1) Before preparing or revising a code, the Lord Chancellor must consult—

(a) the National Assembly for Wales, and
(b) such other persons as he considers appropriate.

(2) The Lord Chancellor may not issue a code unless—
(a) a draft of the code has been laid by him before both Houses of Parliament, and
(b) the 40 day period has elapsed without either House resolving not to approve the draft.

(3) The Lord Chancellor must arrange for any code that he has issued to be published in such a way as he considers appropriate for bringing it to the attention of persons likely to be concerned with its provisions.

(4) '40 day period', in relation to the draft of a proposed code, means—
(a) if the draft is laid before one House on a day later than the day on which it is laid before the other House, the period of 40 days beginning with the later of the two days;
(b) in any other case, the period of 40 days beginning with the day on which it is laid before each House.

(5) In calculating the period of 40 days, no account is to be taken of any period during which Parliament is dissolved or prorogued or during which both Houses are adjourned for more than 4 days.

III MEN [81.1]

Applying the Code of Practice In *Mental Health and Acute Trust and the Council v DD* [2014] EWCOP 11 Mr Justice Cobb in a structured application of the principles and best interest to issues concerning a Caesarean birth, the delivery and any deprivation of liberty, discussed the issue of future guidance on contraception. In considering the provisions of ss 42(4) and 42(5) of the Act, he agreed with Roderic Wood J in *SBC v PBA* [2011] EWHC 2580 (Fam) that the section did not impose a 'duty' to have regard to the relevant Code which was a 'guidance'.

III MEN [82]

44. Ill-treatment or neglect

(1) Subsection (2) applies if a person ('D')—
(a) has the care of a person ('P') who lacks, or whom D reasonably believes to lack, capacity,
(b) is the donee of a lasting power of attorney, or an enduring power of attorney (within the meaning of Schedule 4), created by P, or
(c) is a deputy appointed by the court for P.

(2) D is guilty of an offence if he ill-treats or wilfully neglects P.

(3) A person guilty of an offence under this section is liable—
(a) on summary conviction, to imprisonment for a term not exceeding 12 months or a fine not exceeding the statutory maximum or both;
(b) on conviction on indictment, to imprisonment for a term not exceeding 5 years or a fine or both.

III MEN [82.1]

Criminal proceedings and applying the Act In *R v Dunn* [2010] EWCA Crim 2395 and *R v Hopkins; R v Priest* [2011] EWCA 1513 the Court of Criminal Appeal provided clarification as to the constituent elements of the offence of wilful neglect and gave guidance as to the issues to be considered by any jury.

These judgments were revisited in *R v Ligaya Nursing* [2012] EWCA Crim 2521, [2012] All ER (D) 04 (Dec) when the Lord Chief Justice recognised the difficulty of the legislation but confirmed that the purpose of the section is clear. The question as to whether P had been so neglected was to be examined against the context of the statutory provisions which should seek to respect P's autonomy. Section 44 was not an absolute offence. Actions and omissions or both which reflect or are believed to reflect the protected autonomy of the individual needing care do not constitute wilful neglect. Accordingly within those clear principles the issue in an individual prosecution should be fact specific.

In *R v Patel* [2013] EWCA Crim 965 the consideration of directions to the jury in respect of the meaning of 'neglect' and 'wilful' was considered. The Court of Appeal held that 'the actus reus of the offence is complete if a nurse or medical practitioner neglects to do that which should be done in the treatment of the patient and that neglect is wilful if a nurse or medical practitioner knows that it is necessary to administer a piece of treatment and deliberately decides not to carry out the treatment which is within their power but which they cannot face performing . . . if the appellant was acting at a time of stress that would be a matter which the judge could take into account at time of sentence'.

PART 2
THE COURT OF PROTECTION AND THE PUBLIC GUARDIAN
THE COURT OF PROTECTION

III MEN [83]

45. The Court of Protection

(1) There is to be a superior court of record known as the Court of Protection.

(2) The court is to have an official seal.

(3) The court may sit at any place in England and Wales, on any day and at any time.

(4) The court is to have a central office and registry at a place appointed by the Lord Chancellor, after consulting the Lord Chief Justice.

(5) The Lord Chancellor may, after consulting the Lord Chief Justice, designate as additional registries of the court any district registry of the High Court and any county court office.

(5A) The Lord Chief Justice may nominate any of the following to exercise his functions under this section—

- (a) the President of the Court of Protection;
- (b) a judicial office holder (as defined in section 109(4) of the Constitutional Reform Act 2005).

(6) The office of the Supreme Court called the Court of Protection ceases to exist.

III MEN [83.1]

As from 9 December 2013 the Court of Protection has relocated and the new address is First Avenue House, 42–49 High Holborn, London, WC1A 9JA. (Postal address: The Court of Protection, PO Box No 70185 London WC1A 9JA). DX 160013 KINGSWAY 7. Tel No. 0300 456 4600.

In *R (on the application of ZYN) v Walsall Metropolitan Borough Council* [2014] EWHC 1918 (Admin), [2015] 1 All ER 165, [2014] PTSR 1356 Mr Justice Leggatt found that whilst statute had created a new Court of Protection; that for the purposes of paragraph 44 of Schedule 10 of the Income Support Regulations, notwithstanding the effect of s 45(6) of the Mental Capacity Act 2005, Parliament had intended the provisions of the Regulations to apply to the new Court, and powers derived therefrom.

III MEN [84]

46. The judges of the Court of Protection

(1) Subject to Court of Protection Rules under section 51(2)(d), the jurisdiction of the court is exercisable by a judge nominated for that purpose by—

- (a) the Lord Chief Justice, or
- (b) where nominated by the Lord Chief Justice to act on his behalf under this subsection—
  - (i) the President of the Court of Protection; or
  - (ii) a judicial office holder (as defined in section 109(4) of the Constitutional Reform Act 2005).

(2) To be nominated, a judge must be—

- (a) the President of the Family Division,
- (b) the Chancellor of the High Court,

(c) a puisne judge of the High Court,
(d) a circuit judge,
(e) a district judge,
(f) a District Judge (Magistrates' Courts),
(g) a judge of the First-tier Tribunal, or of the Upper Tribunal, by virtue of appointment under paragraph 1(1) of Schedule 2 or 3 to the Tribunals, Courts and Enforcement Act 2007,
(h) a transferred-in judge of the First-tier Tribunal or of the Upper Tribunal (see section 31(2) of that Act),
(i) a deputy judge of the Upper Tribunal (whether under paragraph 7 of Schedule 3 to, or section 31(2) of, that Act),
(j) the Chamber President, or Deputy Chamber President, of a chamber of the First-tier Tribunal or of a chamber of the Upper Tribunal,
(k) the Judge Advocate General,
(l) a Recorder,
(m) the holder of an office listed in the first column of the table in section 89(3C) of the Senior Courts Act 1981 (senior High Court Masters etc),
(n) a holder of an office listed in column 1 of Part 2 of Schedule 2 to that Act (High Court Masters etc),
(o) a deputy district judge appointed under section 102 of that Act or under section 8 of the County Courts Act 1984,
(p) a member of a panel of Employment Judges established for England and Wales or for Scotland,
(q) a person appointed under section 30(1)(a) or (b) of the Courts-Martial (Appeals) Act 1951 (assistants to the Judge Advocate General),
(r) a deputy judge of the High Court,
(s) the Senior President of Tribunals,
(t) an ordinary judge of the Court of Appeal (including the vice-president, if any, of either division of that court),
(u) the President of the Queen's Bench Division,
(v) the Master of the Rolls, or
(w) the Lord Chief Justice.

(3) The Lord Chief Justice, after consulting the Lord Chancellor, must—
(a) appoint one of the judges nominated by virtue of subsection (2)(a) to (c) to be President of the Court of Protection, and
(b) appoint another of those judges to be Vice-President of the Court of Protection.

(4) The Lord Chief Justice, after consulting the Lord Chancellor, must appoint one of the judges nominated by virtue of subsection (2)(d) to (q) to be Senior Judge of the Court of Protection, having such administrative functions in relation to the court as the Lord Chancellor, after consulting the Lord Chief Justice, may direct.

III MEN [84.1]

Nominations and appointments on coming into force By article 4 of the Mental Capacity Act 2005 (Transitional and Consequential Provisions) Order 2007, SI 2007/1898, the Master of the old Court of Protection is to be treated as being a circuit judge nominated under s 46(1) and also as having been appointed the Senior Judge of the Court of Protection under s 46(4).

III MEN [84.2]

Urgent out of hours business Nominations have now been made by the President to appoint all High Court Judges of the Family and Chancery Divisions as nominated judges and all Queen's Bench Division judges to hear urgent out of hours' applications where a Family Division judge is not available.

SUPPLEMENTARY POWERS

III MEN [85]

47. General powers and effect of orders etc.

(1) The court has in connection with its jurisdiction the same powers, rights, privileges and authority as the High Court.

(2) Section 204 of the Law of Property Act 1925 (c 20) (orders of High Court conclusive in favour of purchasers) applies in relation to orders and directions of the court as it applies to orders of the High Court.

(3) Office copies of orders made, directions given or other instruments issued by the court and sealed with its official seal are admissible in all legal proceedings as evidence of the originals without any further proof.

III MEN [85.1]

Power to award damages for infringement of the Convention on Human Rights In a case where an incapacitated person was kept at a secret location his mother was held to be entitled to an award of damages in the Court of Protection for unlawful interference with her right to family life: *YA (F) v A Local Authority* [2010] EWHC 2770 (Fam)[2011] 1 WLR 1505.

III MEN [86]

48. Interim orders and directions

The court may, pending the determination of an application to it in relation to a person ('P'), make an order or give directions in respect of any matter if—

(a) there is reason to believe that P lacks capacity in relation to the matter,

(b) the matter is one to which its powers under this Act extend, and

(c) it is in P's best interests to make the order, or give the directions, without delay.

III MEN [86.1]

Interim orders In a case considering the manner in which s.48 was engaged, it was held that the test was primarily a two stage process. Was there evidence giving good cause for concern that P may lack capacity in some regard, and if that is raised as a serious possibility, then the court would consider at the second stage, what action, if any, it is in P's best interests to take before a final determination of his capacity can be made: *Re F (Mental Capacity: Interim Jurisdiction)* [2009] EWHC B30 (FAM)[2010] 2FLR 28. This was applied and followed in SMBC v WMP, RG and GG and others [2011] EWHC B13 (COP).

In *LBX v TT* [2014] ECOP 24 Cobb J provided strong guidance upon the approach that should be adopted when considering the appropriateness of a fact finding exercise at an interim stage, when the court was exercising its jurisdiction under s 48 of the Act. In particular he stressed the role of the court in active case management under r 5(2) to decide matters promptly.

III MEN [86.2]

Applications for urgent and interim orders Applications for urgent and interim orders other than those raising issues as to deprivation of liberty (see Practice Direction 11A at **III MEN [620]**) should be made using the procedure and guidance under Practice Direction 10B. See **III MEN [618]**.

III MEN [87]

49. Power to call for reports

(1) This section applies where, in proceedings brought in respect of a person ('P') under Part 1, the court is considering a question relating to P.

(2) The court may require a report to be made to it by the Public Guardian or by a Court of Protection Visitor.

(3) The court may require a local authority, or an NHS body, to arrange for a report to be made—

(a) by one of its officers or employees, or

(b) by such other person (other than the Public Guardian or a Court of Protection Visitor) as the authority, or the NHS body, considers appropriate.

(4) The report must deal with such matters relating to P as the court may direct.

(5) Court of Protection Rules may specify matters which, unless the court directs otherwise, must also be dealt with in the report.

(6) The report may be made in writing or orally, as the court may direct.

(7) In complying with a requirement, the Public Guardian or a Court of Protection Visitor may, at all reasonable times, examine and take copies of—

(a) any health record,

(b) any record of, or held by, a local authority and compiled in connection with a social services function, and

(c) any record held by a person registered under Part 2 of the Care Standards Act 2000 (c 14), Chapter 2 of Part 1 of the Health and Social Care Act 2008 or Part 1 of the Regulation and Inspection of Social Care (Wales) Act 2016,

so far as the record relates to P.

(8) If the Public Guardian or a Court of Protection Visitor is making a visit in the course of complying with a requirement, he may interview P in private.

(9) If a Court of Protection Visitor who is a Special Visitor is making a visit in the course of complying with a requirement, he may if the court so directs carry out in private a medical, psychiatric or psychological examination of P's capacity and condition.

(10) 'NHS body' has the meaning given in section 148 of the Health and Social Care (Community Health and Standards) Act 2003 (c 43).

(11) 'Requirement' means a requirement imposed under subsection (2) or (3).

III MEN [87.1]

Ability to require reports These principles were applied in *A v A Local Authority, A Care Home Manager, and S* [2011] EWHC 727 (COP) where the President in considering issues of deprivation of liberty authorised the commissioning of a report by a Court of Protection Special Visitor to investigate issues of both capacity and bests interests, at the behest of the Official Solicitor prior to making a final order.

III MEN [87.2]

Guidance on obtaining reports and court control of questions to experts Court of Protection Rules 2017, rr 3.7, 14.25 and 14.25, together with Practice Direction 14E, give guidance when reports are directed by the court, and the power of the court to limit questions to such an expert. See **III MEN [657]**.

PRACTICE AND PROCEDURE

III MEN [88]

50. Applications to the Court of Protection

(1) No permission is required for an application to the court for the exercise of any of its powers under this Act—

(a) by a person who lacks, or is alleged to lack, capacity,

(b) if such a person has not reached 18, by anyone with parental responsibility for him,

(c) by the donor or a donee of a lasting power of attorney to which the application relates,

(d) by a deputy appointed by the court for a person to whom the application relates, or

(e) by a person named in an existing order of the court, if the application relates to the order.

(1A) Nor is permission required for an application to the court under section 21A by the relevant person's representative.

(2) But, subject to Court of Protection Rules and to paragraph 20(2) of Schedule 3 (declarations relating to private international law), permission is required for any other application to the court.

(3) In deciding whether to grant permission the court must, in particular, have regard to—

- (a) the applicant's connection with the person to whom the application relates,
- (b) the reasons for the application,
- (c) the benefit to the person to whom the application relates of a proposed order or directions, and
- (d) whether the benefit can be achieved in any other way.

(4) 'Parental responsibility' has the same meaning as in the Children Act 1989 (c 41).

III MEN [88.1]

Guidance on seeking permission and relevant rules Part 8 of the Court of Protection Rules 2017 provides guidance as to where permission is not required (r 8.2). Rule 8.4 sets out the procedure for application and the information and evidence required (with reference to r 3.6(3) an how the Court will deal with such an application). See **III MEN [580]**. However regard should be made to Practice Direction 11A and para 44 regarding the procedure for permission in applications relating to the streamlined procedure under s 16(2)(a) for an order authorising deprivation of liberty under s 4A(3) and (4) of the Act (see **III MEN [619]**).

III MEN [88.2]

The seeking of permission and the Code of Practice Chapter 15 of the Mental Capacity Act 2005 Code of Practice provides guidance as to appropriate measures to be implemented in attempts to resolve disagreements and disputes regarding issues covered by the Mental Capacity Act 2005. It is important to have regard to the Code and guidance, and within any subsequent application to the court, whether civil or criminal, consideration will be given to provisions of the Code, and failure to comply with the code must be taken into account in deciding any relevant question (s 42(5) of the Mental Capacity Act 2005): see **III MEN [80]**.

III MEN [89]

51. Court of Protection Rules

(1) Rules of court with respect to the practice and procedure of the court (to be called 'Court of Protection Rules') may be made in accordance with Part 1 of Schedule 1 to the Constitutional Reform Act 2005.

(2) Court of Protection Rules may, in particular, make provision—

- (a) as to the manner and form in which proceedings are to be commenced;
- (b) as to the persons entitled to be notified of, and be made parties to, the proceedings;
- (c) for the allocation, in such circumstances as may be specified, of any specified description of proceedings to a specified judge or to specified descriptions of judges;
- (d) for the exercise of the jurisdiction of the court, in such circumstances as may be specified, by its officers or other staff;
- (e) for enabling the court to appoint a suitable person (who may, with his consent, be the Official Solicitor) to act in the name of, or on behalf of, or to represent the person to whom the proceedings relate;
- (f) for enabling an application to the court to be disposed of without a hearing;
- (g) for enabling the court to proceed with, or with any part of, a hearing in the absence of the person to whom the proceedings relate;
- (h) for enabling or requiring the proceedings or any part of them to be conducted in private and for enabling the court to determine who is to

be admitted when the court sits in private and to exclude specified persons when it sits in public;

(i) as to what may be received as evidence (whether or not admissible apart from the rules) and the manner in which it is to be presented;

(j) for the enforcement of orders made and directions given in the proceedings.

(3) Court of Protection Rules may, instead of providing for any matter, refer to provision made or to be made about that matter by directions.

(4) Court of Protection Rules may make different provision for different areas.

III MEN [89.1]

The Court of Protection Rules The original Court of Protection Rules 2007, SI 2007/1744 were duly made to come into force on 1 October 2007. They were revoked by the Court of Protection Rules 2017, SI 2017/1035. See **III MEN [144]**.

III MEN [89.2]

Privacy On 29 January 2016 pursuant to the then r 9A there was introduced into the Court of Protection a pilot for hearings which fall within the scope of para 1.3 of the Transparency Pilot Practice Direction. This procedure is now incorporated into Part 4 of the Rules. Such cases are to be held in public subject to a restriction order dealing with confidentiality and anonymity. However, they may be held in public if 'good reason' is established. The existence of good reason does not automatically lift the requirement of privacy, but Arts 10 and 8 are then engaged and a balance must be struck: *Independent News and Media Ltd v A* (20 09) Times, 17 November, in which Hedley J decided, on balance that the media should be allowed to attend on the grounds that (1) issues concerning the particular individual were already in the public domain; (2) the court retained power to preserve privacy while addressing the issues; and (3) it was in the public interest that the general public should understand the jurisdiction and how it was exercised in such cases. This decision was confirmed in *Independent News and Media Ltd v A* [2010] EWCA Civ 343, [2010] 3 All ER 32, [2010] 2 FCR 187 and followed in *London Borough of Hillingdon v Steven Neary and Mark Neary* [2011] EWHC 413 (COP).

See now the decision in *DH NHS Foundation Trust v PS (by her litigation friend the Official Solicitor)* [2010] EWHC 1217 (Fam), [2010] 2 FLR 1236, [2010] Fam Law 927 to the effect that judgments of the Court of Protection should be given in open court, suitably anonymised to protect the parties. Such judgments ought to be in the public domain and might be of assistance to others faced with a similar dilemma (in the instant case whether necessary surgery could lawfully proceed without the consent of the patient).

In *W (by her litigation friend B) v M (an Adult patient, by her litigation friend, the Official Solicitor), S, A NHS PCT and Times Newspapers Ltd* [2011] EWHC 1197(COP) Baker J provided guidance on the making of a reporting restriction order and as to the formatting of such orders for cases arising in the Court of Protection.

See further the Guidance of the President given on 16 January 2014 setting out the procedure for publication of the judgments of the court as from 3 February 2014. See **III MEN [13]**.

III MEN [90]

52. Practice directions

(1) Directions as to the practice and procedure of the court may be given in accordance with Part 1 of Schedule 2 to the Constitutional Reform Act 2005.

(2) Practice directions given otherwise than under subsection (1) may not be given without the approval of—

(a) the Lord Chancellor, and

(b) the Lord Chief Justice.

(3) The Lord Chief Justice may nominate any of the following to exercise his functions under this section—

(a) the President of the Court of Protection;

(b) a judicial office holder (as defined in section 109(4) of the Constitutional Reform Act 2005).

III MEN [90.1]

The practice directions summarised and in force Practice Directions have now been given pursuant to Court of Protection Rules 2017, with previous Practice Directions having been revoked upon the commencement of the new Rules on 1 December 2017:

Practice Direction 1A – Participation of P: see **III MEN [498]**.

Practice Direction 2A – levels of judiciary: see **III MEN [505]**.

Practice Direction 2B – authorised Court officers: see **III MEN [506]**.

Practice Direction 2C – the application of the Civil Procedure Rules 1998 and the Family Procedure Rules 2010: see **III MEN [507]**.

Practice Direction 3A – the Court's jurisdiction to be exercised by certain judges: see **III MEN [517]**.

Practice Direction 3B – case pathways: see **III MEN [518]**.

Practice Direction 4A – hearings (including reporting restrictions): see **III MEN [423]**.

Practice Direction 4B – Court Bundle: see **III MEN [424]**.

Practice Direction 4C – Transparency: see **III MEN [425]**.

Practice Direction 5A – Court Documents: see **III MEN [542]**.

Practice Direction 5B – Statements of Truth: see **III MEN [543]**.

Practice Direction 6A – Service of Documents: see **III MEN [563]**.

Practice Direction 6B – Service Out of the Jurisdiction: see **III MEN [564]**.

Practice Direction 7A – Notifying P: see **III MEN [576]**.

Practice Direction 8A – Permission: see **III MEN [583]**.

Practice Direction 9A – The Application Form: see **III MEN [600]**.

Practice Direction 9B – Notification of other persons that an application form has been issued: see **III MEN [601]**.

Practice Direction 9C – Responding to an application: see **III MEN [602]**.

Practice Direction 9D – Applications by Currently Appointed Deputies, Attorneys and Donees in Relation to P's Property and Affairs: see **III MEN [603]**.

Practice Direction 9E – Applications Relating to Statutory Wills, Codicils, Settlements and Other Dealings With P's Property: see **III MEN [604]**.

Practice Direction 9F – Applications to Appoint or Discharge a Trustee: see **III MEN [605]**.

Practice Direction 9G – Applications Relating to the Registration of Enduring Powers of Attorney : see **III MEN [606]**.

Practice Direction 10A – Applications within proceedings: see **III MEN [617]**.

Practice Direction 10B – Urgent and Interim Applications: see **III MEN [618]**.

Practice Direction 11A – Deprivation of Liberty Applications: see **III MEN [620]**.

Practice Direction 12A – Human Rights Act 1998: see **III MEN [622]**.

Practice Direction 13A – Procedure for disputing the court's jurisdiction: see **III MEN [627]**.

Practice Direction 14A – Written Evidence: see **III MEN [653]**.

Practice Direction 14B – Depositions: see **III MEN [654]**.

Practice Direction 14C – Fees for examiners of the Court: see **III MEN [655]**.

Practice Direction 14D – Witness summons: see **III MEN [656]**.

Practice Direction 14E – Section 49 Reports: see **III MEN [657]**.

Practice Direction 15A – Expert evidence: see **III MEN [671]**.

Practice Direction 17A – Litigation Friend: see **III MEN [694]**.

Practice Direction 17B – Rule 1.2 Representatives: see **III MEN [695]**.

Practice Direction 18A – Change of Solicitor: see **III MEN [701]**.

Practice Direction 19A – Costs: see **III MEN [716]**.

Practice Direction 19B – Fixed costs in the Court of Protection: see **III MEN [717]**.

Practice Direction 20A – Appeals: see **III MEN [732]**.

Practice Direction 20B – Allocation of Appeals: see **III MEN [733]**.

Practice Direction 21A – Contempt of Court: see **III MEN [766]**.

Practice Direction 22A – Civil Restraint Orders: see **III MEN [768]**.

Practice Direction 23A – International Protection of Adults: see **III MEN [775]**.

Practice Direction 24A – Request for directions where notice of objection prevents the Public Guardian from registering an Enduring Power of Attorney: see **III MEN [782]**.

Practice Direction 24B – Where P ceases to lack capacity or dies: see **III MEN [783]**.

Practice Direction 24C – Transitional provisions: see **III MEN [784]**.

III MEN [91]

53. Rights of appeal

(1) Subject to the provisions of this section, an appeal lies to the Court of Appeal from any decision of the court.

(2) Court of Protection Rules may provide that, where a decision of the court is made by a specified description of person, an appeal from the decision lies to a specified description of judge of the court and not to the Court of Appeal.

(3) [...]

(4) Court of Protection Rules may make provision—

(a) that, in such cases as may be specified, an appeal from a decision of the court may not be made without permission;

(b) as to the person or persons entitled to grant permission to appeal;

(c) as to any requirements to be satisfied before permission is granted;

(d) that where a ... judge of the court makes a decision on an appeal, no appeal may be made to the Court of Appeal from that decision unless the Court of Appeal considers that—

(i) the appeal would raise an important point of principle or practice, or

(ii) there is some other compelling reason for the Court of Appeal to hear it;

(e) as to any considerations to be taken into account in relation to granting or refusing permission to appeal.

III MEN [91.1]

Relevant rules relating to appeals See Court of Protection Rules 2017, Part 20 in particular rr 20.5, 20.6 and 20.8 and the Practice Direction 20A: see **III MEN [718]** to **III MEN [732]**. See also *A (a patient) (Court of Protection: Appeal)* [2013] EWCA Civ 1661, [2014] 1 WLR 3773 on second appeals and the application of the rule in *Lane v Esdaille* [1891] AC 210 HL(E).

III MEN [91.2]

Appealable decisions The right of appeal exists only in respect of decisions taken in relation to the litigation before the court and not in respect of other cases that may come before the court in the future: *Re X (Court of Protection: Deprivation of Liberty) (Nos 1 and 2)* [2015] EWCA Civ 599, (2015) Times, 10 July.

FEES AND COSTS

III MEN [92]

54. Fees

(1) The Lord Chancellor may with the consent of the Treasury by order prescribe fees payable in respect of anything dealt with by the court.

(2) An order under this section may in particular contain provision as to—

(a) scales or rates of fees;

(b) exemptions from and reductions in fees;

(c) remission of fees in whole or in part.

(3) Before making an order under this section, the Lord Chancellor must consult—

(a) the President of the Court of Protection,

(b) the Vice-President of the Court of Protection, and

(c) the Senior Judge of the Court of Protection.

(4) The Lord Chancellor must take such steps as are reasonably practicable to bring information about fees to the attention of persons likely to have to pay them.

(5) Fees payable under this section are recoverable summarily as a civil debt.

III MEN [92.1]

The relevant rules relating to costs in matters before the Court of Protection See Court of Protection Rules 2017 Part 19 and the relevant general rr 19.2–19.5 together with Practice Directions 19A and 19B: see **III MEN [702]** to **III MEN [717]**.

III MEN [93]

55. Costs

(1) Subject to Court of Protection Rules, the costs of and incidental to all proceedings in the court are in its discretion.

(2) The rules may in particular make provision for regulating matters relating to the costs of those proceedings, including prescribing scales of costs to be paid to legal or other representatives.

(3) The court has full power to determine by whom and to what extent the costs are to be paid.

(4) The court may, in any proceedings—

(a) disallow, or

(b) order the legal or other representatives concerned to meet,

the whole of any wasted costs or such part of them as may be determined in accordance with the rules.

(5) 'Legal or other representative', in relation to a party to proceedings, means any person exercising a right of audience or right to conduct litigation on his behalf.

(6) 'Wasted costs' means any costs incurred by a party—

(a) as a result of any improper, unreasonable or negligent act or omission on the part of any legal or other representative or any employee of such a representative, or

(b) which, in the light of any such act or omission occurring after they were incurred, the court considers it is unreasonable to expect that party to pay.

III MEN [93.1]

Costs decisions In a case considering the rules relating to costs and the manner in which such issues should be determined, Baker J conceded that there was relatively little reported authority on how the Court of Protection should exercise its powers: *Cheshire West and Chester Council v P (by his litigation friend the Official Solicitor) & M* [2011] EWHC 1330 (COP). In that case the court addressed the issue of costs within the framework of deprivation of liberty proceedings and the welfare jurisdiction of the court. In *EG v RS, JS v BEN PCT* [2010] EWHC 3073 (COP) the court considered the issue and principles of conduct within the framework of the Court of Protection costs rules, and in *RC, (deceased)* [2011] 1 FLR 1447 the Senior Judge gave guidance on the issue of costs arising from contested Lasting Powers of Attorney for personal welfare, and in *Re CT* [2014] EWCOP 51, [2015] WTLR 1441, [2014] All ER (D) 26 (Dec) the Senior Judge disapplied the general rule as to costs when finding that an attorney had failed to cooperate with the Public Guardian and obstructed a Court of Protection Special Visitor.

In *Court of Protection: Delay and Costs; Cases A and B* [2014] EWCOP 48, [2014] All ER (D) 02 (Dec) Peter Jackson J expressed concern at the failure of case management and the issues of delay which impacted upon the overriding objective and the effect of excessive costs and the need for practitioners to exercise professional cooperation and the duty of parties to ensure that costs are reasonable.

In *Ragny Sharma and Paul Judkins v Hunters* [2011] EWHC 2546 (COP) Henderson J. gave guidance on the issue concerning wasted costs and applications to show cause as applied to Court of Protection proceedings.

In *Cheshire West and Chester Council v P* [2011] EWCA Civ 1333 the Court of Appeal confirmed that in respect of appeals from the Court of Protection the ordinary costs rules in CPR 44.3 shall apply. See para **CPR 44.3** in Volume 1.

In *Blankley v Central Manchester and Manchester Children's University Hospital NHS Trust* [2015] EWCA Civ 18, [2015] All ER (D) 207 (Jan) the Court of Appeal found that the intervening incapacity of a claimant did not frustrate the continuance of a Conditional Fee Agreement.

III MEN [94]

56. Fees and costs: supplementary

(1) Court of Protection Rules may make provision—

(a) as to the way in which, and funds from which, fees and costs are to be paid;

(b) for charging fees and costs upon the estate of the person to whom the proceedings relate;

(c) for the payment of fees and costs within a specified time of the death of the person to whom the proceedings relate or the conclusion of the proceedings.

(2) A charge on the estate of a person created by virtue of subsection (1)(b) does not cause any interest of the person in any property to fail or determine or to be prevented from recommencing.

III MEN [94.1]

Relevant rules relating to fixed costs See Court of Protection Rules Part 19 and Practice Directions 19A and 19B: **III MEN [702]** to **III MEN [717]**

THE PUBLIC GUARDIAN

III MEN [95]

57. The Public Guardian

(1) For the purposes of this Act, there is to be an officer, to be known as the Public Guardian.

(2) The Public Guardian is to be appointed by the Lord Chancellor.

(3) There is to be paid to the Public Guardian out of money provided by Parliament such salary as the Lord Chancellor may determine.

(4) The Lord Chancellor may, after consulting the Public Guardian—

(a) provide him with such officers and staff, or

(b) enter into such contracts with other persons for the provision (by them or their sub-contractors) of officers, staff or services,

as the Lord Chancellor thinks necessary for the proper discharge of the Public Guardian's functions.

(5) Any functions of the Public Guardian may, to the extent authorised by him, be performed by any of his officers.

III MEN [96]

58. Functions of the Public Guardian

(1) The Public Guardian has the following functions—

(a) establishing and maintaining a register of lasting powers of attorney,

(b) establishing and maintaining a register of orders appointing deputies,

(c) supervising deputies appointed by the court,

(d) directing a Court of Protection Visitor to visit—

(i) a donee of a lasting power of attorney,

(ii) a deputy appointed by the court, or

(iii) the person granting the power of attorney or for whom the deputy is appointed ('P'),

and to make a report to the Public Guardian on such matters as he may direct,

(e) receiving security which the court requires a person to give for the discharge of his functions,

(f) receiving reports from donees of lasting powers of attorney and deputies appointed by the court,

(g) reporting to the court on such matters relating to proceedings under this Act as the court requires,

(h) dealing with representations (including complaints) about the way in which a donee of a lasting power of attorney or a deputy appointed by the court is exercising his powers,

(i) publishing, in any manner the Public Guardian thinks appropriate, any information he thinks appropriate about the discharge of his functions.

(2) The functions conferred by subsection (1)(c) and (h) may be discharged in co-operation with any other person who has functions in relation to the care or treatment of P.

(2A) The Public Guardian also has the following functions—

(a) establishing and maintaining a register of guardianship orders,

(b) supervising guardians,

(c) receiving security which the court requires a guardian to give for the exercise of the guardian's functions,

(d) receiving reports from guardians,

(e) reporting to the court on such matters relating to proceedings under the Guardianship (Missing Persons) Act 2017 as the court requires,

(f) dealing with representations (including complaints) about the way in which a guardian is exercising the guardian's functions, and

(g) publishing, in any manner the Public Guardian thinks appropriate, information about the exercise of his or her functions in connection with guardians and guardianship orders.

(3) The Lord Chancellor may by regulations make provision—

(a) conferring on the Public Guardian other functions in connection with this Act or the Guardianship (Missing Persons) Act 2017;

(b) in connection with the discharge by the Public Guardian of his functions.

(4) Regulations made under subsection (3)(b) may in particular make provision as to—

(a) the giving of security by deputies appointed by the court or guardians and the enforcement and discharge of security so given;

(b) the fees which may be charged by the Public Guardian;

(c) the way in which, and funds from which, such fees are to be paid;

(d) exemptions from and reductions in such fees;

(e) remission of such fees in whole or in part;

(f) the making of reports to the Public Guardian by deputies appointed by the court and others who are directed by the court to carry out any transaction for a person who lacks capacity;

(g) the making of reports to the Public Guardian by guardians.

(5) For the purpose of enabling him to carry out his functions in relation to lasting powers of attorney or deputies, the Public Guardian may, at all reasonable times, examine and take copies of—

(a) any health record,

(b) any record of, or held by, a local authority and compiled in connection with a social services function, and

(c) any record held by a person registered under Part 2 of the Care Standards Act 2000 (c 14), Chapter 2 of Part 1 of the Health and Social Care Act 2008 or Part 1 of the Regulation and Inspection of Social Care (Wales) Act 2016,

so far as the record relates to P.

(6) The Public Guardian may also for that purpose interview P in private.

(7) In this section "guardian" and "guardianship order" have the same meaning as in the Guardianship (Missing Persons) Act 2017.

III MEN [96.1]

Regulations See the Lasting Powers of Attorney, Enduring Powers of Attorney and Public Guardian Regulations 2007, SI 2007/1253, regs 30 to 48.

III MEN [96.2]

Relevant rules relating to applications of the Public Guardian Court of Protection Rules 2017, r 24.4 and Practice Direction 24A provide guidance on applications by the Public Guardian to the Court of Protection. See **III MEN [779]** and **III MEN [782]**.

III MEN [96.3]

The Code of Practice and the Public Guardian Chapter 14 of the Mental Capacity Act 2005 Code of Practice provides guidance as to the role of the Public Guardian, and to the measures of protection available for people who lack capacity to make decisions for themselves.

III MEN [97]

59. ***Public Guardian Board***

Repealed.

III MEN [98]

60. Annual report

(1) The Public Guardian must make an annual report to the Lord Chancellor about the discharge of his functions.

(2) The Lord Chancellor must, within one month of receiving the report, lay a copy of it before Parliament.

COURT OF PROTECTION VISITORS

III MEN [99]

61. Court of Protection Visitors

(1) A Court of Protection Visitor is a person who is appointed by the Lord Chancellor to—

(a) a panel of Special Visitors, or

(b) a panel of General Visitors.

(2) A person is not qualified to be a Special Visitor unless he—

(a) is a registered medical practitioner or appears to the Lord Chancellor to have other suitable qualifications or training, and

(b) appears to the Lord Chancellor to have special knowledge of and experience in cases of impairment of or disturbance in the functioning of the mind or brain.

(3) A General Visitor need not have a medical qualification.

(4) A Court of Protection Visitor—

(a) may be appointed for such term and subject to such conditions, and

(b) may be paid such remuneration and allowances,

as the Lord Chancellor may determine.

(5) For the purpose of carrying out his functions under this Act in relation to a person who lacks capacity ('P'), a Court of Protection Visitor may, at all reasonable times, examine and take copies of—

(a) any health record,

(b) any record of, or held by, a local authority and compiled in connection with a social services function, and

(c) any record held by a person registered under Part 2 of the Care Standards Act 2000 (c 14), Chapter 2 of Part 1 of the Health and Social Care Act 2008 or Part 1 of the Regulation and Inspection of Social Care (Wales) Act 2016,

so far as the record relates to P.

(6) A Court of Protection Visitor may also for that purpose interview P in private.

III MEN [99.1]

Rules and Practice Direction relevant to the reports of a Visitor Court of Protection Rules 2017, rr 3.7(2), 14.24 and 14.25, together with Practice Direction 14E give guidance when reports are directed by the court, and the power of the court to limit questions to such an expert. See **III MEN [657]**.

PART 3
MISCELLANEOUS AND GENERAL

DECLARATORY PROVISION

III MEN [100]

62. Scope of the Act

For the avoidance of doubt, it is hereby declared that nothing in this Act is to be taken to affect the law relating to murder or manslaughter or the operation of section 2 of the Suicide Act 1961 (c 60) (assisting suicide).

PRIVATE INTERNATIONAL LAW

III MEN [101]

63. International protection of adults

Schedule 3—

(a) gives effect in England and Wales to the Convention on the International Protection of Adults signed at the Hague on 13th January 2000 (Cm 5881) (in so far as this Act does not otherwise do so), and

(b) makes related provision as to the private international law of England and Wales.

III MEN [101.1]

Issues concerning ratification In *Re MN* [2010] EWHC 1926 (Fam) Hedley J recorded that, as at July 2010, the UK had not ratified the Hague Convention on the International Protection of Adults in respect of England and Wales, and that as such the provisions of the Convention could not apply, but the case itself was governed by s 63 of and Sch 3 to the Act. See **III MEN [128]**.

In *PO v JO and GO, RO, MP and Inverclyde Council* [2013] EWHC 3932 (COP) the President confirmed the approach of Hedley J, in addressing the issues of 'habitual residence' of 'P'.

In *The Health Service Executive of Ireland v PA* [20151] EWCOP 38, [2015] All ER (D) 139 (Jun) and in *Re PD* [2015] EWCOP 48, [2015] All ER (D) 225 (Jul) Mr Justice Baker declined to give guidelines in respect of what was said to be similar fact cases finding that the court would apply the provisions of the Act and in particular Schedule 3 to each factual matrix, and that the purpose of Schedule 3 was to facilitate the recognition and enforcement of protective measures for the benefit of vulnerable adults.

GENERAL

III MEN [102]

64. Interpretation

(1) In this Act—

'the 1985 Act' means the Enduring Powers of Attorney Act 1985 (c 29),

'advance decision' has the meaning given in section 24(1),

'authorisation under Schedule A1' means either—

(a) a standard authorisation under that Schedule, or

(b) an urgent authorisation under that Schedule;

'the court' means the Court of Protection established by section 45,

'Court of Protection Rules' has the meaning given in section 51(1),

'Court of Protection Visitor' has the meaning given in section 61,

'deputy' has the meaning given in section 16(2)(b),

'enactment' includes a provision of subordinate legislation (within the meaning of the Interpretation Act 1978 (c 30)),

"health record" has the same meaning as in the Data Protection Act 2018 (see section 205 of that Act);

'the Human Rights Convention' has the same meaning as 'the Convention' in the Human Rights Act 1998 (c 42),

'independent mental capacity advocate' has the meaning given in section 35(1),

'lasting power of attorney' has the meaning given in section 9,

'life-sustaining treatment' has the meaning given in section 4(10),

'local authority', except in Schedule A1 means—

(a) the council of a county in England in which there are no district councils,

(b) the council of a district in England,

(c) the council of a county or county borough in Wales,

(d) the council of a London borough,

(e) the Common Council of the City of London, or

(f) the Council of the Isles of Scilly,

'Mental Health Act' means the Mental Health Act 1983 (c 20),

'prescribed', in relation to regulations made under this Act, means prescribed by those regulations,

'property' includes any thing in action and any interest in real or personal property,

'public authority' has the same meaning as in the Human Rights Act 1998,

'Public Guardian' has the meaning given in section 57,

'purchaser' and 'purchase' have the meaning given in section 205(1) of the Law of Property Act 1925 (c 20),

'social services function' has the meaning given in section 1A of the Local Authority Social Services Act 1970 (c 42),

'treatment' includes a diagnostic or other procedure,

'trust corporation' has the meaning given in section 68(1) of the Trustee Act 1925 (c19), and

'will' includes codicil.

(2) In this Act, references to making decisions, in relation to a donee of a lasting power of attorney or a deputy appointed by the court, include, where appropriate, acting on decisions made.

(3) In this Act, references to the bankruptcy of an individual include a case where a bankruptcy restrictions order under the Insolvency Act 1986 (c 45) has effect in respect of him.

(3A) In this Act references to a debt relief order (under Part 7A of the Insolvency Act 1986) being made in relation to an individual include a case where a debt relief restrictions order under the Insolvency Act 1986 has effect in respect of him.

(4) 'Bankruptcy restrictions order' includes an interim bankruptcy restrictions order.

(4A) 'Debt relief restrictions order' includes an interim debt relief restrictions order.

(5) In this Act, references to deprivation of a person's liberty have the same meaning as in Article 5(1) of the Human Rights Convention.

(6) For the purposes of such references, it does not matter whether a person is deprived of his liberty by a public authority or not.

III MEN [103]

65. Rules, regulations and orders

(1) Any power to make rules, regulations or orders under this Act, other than the power in section 21—

- (a) is exercisable by statutory instrument;
- (b) includes power to make supplementary, incidental, consequential, transitional or saving provision;
- (c) includes power to make different provision for different cases.

(2) Any statutory instrument containing rules, regulations or orders made by the Lord Chancellor or the Secretary of State under this Act, other than—

- (a) regulations under section 34 (loss of capacity during research project),
- (b) regulations under section 41 (adjusting role of independent mental capacity advocacy service),
- (c) regulations under paragraph 32(1)(b) of Schedule 3 (private international law relating to the protection of adults),
- (d) an order of the kind mentioned in section 67(6) (consequential amendments of primary legislation), or
- (e) an order under section 68 (commencement),

is subject to annulment in pursuance of a resolution of either House of Parliament.

(3) A statutory instrument containing an Order in Council under paragraph 31 of Schedule 3 (provision to give further effect to Hague Convention) is subject to annulment in pursuance of a resolution of either House of Parliament.

(4) A statutory instrument containing regulations made by the Secretary of State under section 34 or 41 or by the Lord Chancellor under paragraph 32(1)(b) of Schedule 3 may not be made unless a draft has been laid before and approved by resolution of each House of Parliament.

(4A) Subsection (2) does not apply to a statutory instrument containing regulations made by the Secretary of State under Schedule A1.

(4B) If such a statutory instrument contains regulations under paragraph 42(2)(b), 129, 162 or 164 of Schedule A1 (whether or not it also contains other regulations), the instrument may not be made unless a draft has been laid before and approved by resolution of each House of Parliament.

(4C) Subject to that, such a statutory instrument is subject to annulment in pursuance of a resolution of either House of Parliament.

(5) An order under section 21—

(a) may include supplementary, incidental, consequential, transitional or saving provision;
(b) may make different provision for different cases;
(c) is to be made in the form of a statutory instrument to which the Statutory Instruments Act 1946 applies as if the order were made by a Minister of the Crown; and
(d) is subject to annulment in pursuance of a resolution of either House of Parliament.

III MEN [104]

66. Existing receivers and enduring powers of attorney etc.

(1) The following provisions cease to have effect—
(a) Part 7 of the Mental Health Act,
(b) the Enduring Powers of Attorney Act 1985 (c 29).

(2) No enduring power of attorney within the meaning of the 1985 Act is to be created after the commencement of subsection (1)(b).

(3) Schedule 4 has effect in place of the 1985 Act in relation to any enduring power of attorney created before the commencement of subsection (1)(b).

(4) Schedule 5 contains transitional provisions and savings in relation to Part 7 of the Mental Health Act and the 1985 Act.

III MEN [105]

67. Minor and consequential amendments and repeals

(1) Schedule 6 contains minor and consequential amendments.

(2) Schedule 7 contains repeals.

(3) The Lord Chancellor may by order make supplementary, incidental, consequential, transitional or saving provision for the purposes of, in consequence of, or for giving full effect to a provision of this Act.

(4) An order under subsection (3) may, in particular—
(a) provide for a provision of this Act which comes into force before another provision of this Act has come into force to have effect, until the other provision has come into force, with specified modifications;
(b) amend, repeal or revoke an enactment, other than one contained in an Act or Measure passed in a Session after the one in which this Act is passed.

(5) The amendments that may be made under subsection (4)(b) are in addition to those made by or under any other provision of this Act.

(6) An order under subsection (3) which amends or repeals a provision of an Act or Measure may not be made unless a draft has been laid before and approved by resolution of each House of Parliament.

III MEN [106]

68. Commencement and extent

(1) This Act, other than sections 30 to 41, comes into force in accordance with provision made by order by the Lord Chancellor.

(2) Sections 30 to 41 come into force in accordance with provision made by order by—
(a) the Secretary of State, in relation to England, and
(b) the National Assembly for Wales, in relation to Wales.

(3) An order under this section may appoint different days for different provisions and different purposes.

(4) Subject to subsections (5) and (6), this Act extends to England and Wales only.

(5) The following provisions extend to the United Kingdom—

(a) paragraph 16(1) of Schedule 1 (evidence of instruments and of registration of lasting powers of attorney),

(b) paragraph 15(3) of Schedule 4 (evidence of instruments and of registration of enduring powers of attorney).

(6) Subject to any provision made in Schedule 6, the amendments and repeals made by Schedules 6 and 7 have the same extent as the enactments to which they relate.

III MEN [106.1]

Relevant commencement orders There have been a number of commencement orders: Mental Capacity Act 2005 (Commencement No 1) Order 2006, SI 2006/2814; Mental Capacity Act 2005 (Commencement No 1) (Amendment) Order 2006, SI 2006/3473; Mental Capacity Act 2005 (Commencement No 1) (England and Wales) Order 2007, SI 2007/563; Mental Capacity Act 2005 (Commencement No 2) Order 2007, SI 2007/1897.

III MEN [107]

69. Short title

This Act may be cited as the Mental Capacity Act 2005.

SCHEDULE A1
HOSPITAL AND CARE HOME RESIDENTS: DEPRIVATION OF LIBERTY

PART 1
AUTHORISATION TO DEPRIVE RESIDENTS OF LIBERTY ETC.

APPLICATION OF PART

III MEN [108]

1 (1) This Part applies if the following conditions are met.

(2) The first condition is that a person ("P") is detained in a hospital or care home—for the purpose of being given care or treatment—in circumstances which amount to deprivation of the person's liberty.

(3) The second condition is that a standard or urgent authorisation is in force.

(4) The third condition is that the standard or urgent authorisation relates—

(a) to P, and

(b) to the hospital or care home in which P is detained.

AUTHORISATION TO DEPRIVE P OF LIBERTY

2 The managing authority of the hospital or care home may deprive P of his liberty by detaining him as mentioned in paragraph 1(2).

NO LIABILITY FOR ACTS DONE FOR PURPOSE OF DEPRIVING P OF LIBERTY

3 (1) This paragraph applies to any act which a person ("D") does for the purpose of detaining P as mentioned in paragraph 1(2).

(2) D does not incur any liability in relation to the act that he would not have incurred if P—

(a) had had capacity to consent in relation to D's doing the act, and

(b) had consented to D's doing the act.

No protection for negligent acts etc.

4 (1) Paragraphs 2 and 3 do not exclude a person's civil liability for loss or damage, or his criminal liability, resulting from his negligence in doing any thing.
(2) Paragraphs 2 and 3 do not authorise a person to do anything otherwise than for the purpose of the standard or urgent authorisation that is in force.
(3) In a case where a standard authorisation is in force, paragraphs 2 and 3 do not authorise a person to do anything which does not comply with the conditions (if any) included in the authorisation.

PART 2
INTERPRETATION: MAIN TERMS

Introduction

III MEN [109]

5 This Part applies for the purposes of this Schedule.

Detained resident

6 "Detained resident" means a person detained in a hospital or care home—for the purpose of being given care or treatment—in circumstances which amount to deprivation of the person's liberty.

Relevant person etc.

7 In relation to a person who is, or is to be, a detained resident—
"relevant person" means the person in question;
"relevant hospital or care home" means the hospital or care home in question;
"relevant care or treatment" means the care or treatment in question.

Authorisations

8 "Standard authorisation" means an authorisation given under Part 4.

9 "Urgent authorisation" means an authorisation given under Part 5.

10 "Authorisation under this Schedule" means either of the following—
(a) a standard authorisation;
(b) an urgent authorisation.

11 (1) The purpose of a standard authorisation is the purpose which is stated in the authorisation in accordance with paragraph 55(1)(d).
(2) The purpose of an urgent authorisation is the purpose which is stated in the authorisation in accordance with paragraph 80(d).

PART 3
THE QUALIFYING REQUIREMENTS

The qualifying requirements

III MEN [110]

12 (1) These are the qualifying requirements referred to in this Schedule—
(a) the age requirement;

(b) the mental health requirement;
(c) the mental capacity requirement;
(d) the best interests requirement;
(e) the eligibility requirement;
(f) the no refusals requirement.

(2) Any question of whether a person who is, or is to be, a detained resident meets the qualifying requirements is to be determined in accordance with this Part.

(3) In a case where—

(a) the question of whether a person meets a particular qualifying requirement arises in relation to the giving of a standard authorisation, and
(b) any circumstances relevant to determining that question are expected to change between the time when the determination is made and the time when the authorisation is expected to come into force,

those circumstances are to be taken into account as they are expected to be at the later time.

THE AGE REQUIREMENT

13 The relevant person meets the age requirement if he has reached 18.

THE MENTAL HEALTH REQUIREMENT

14 (1) The relevant person meets the mental health requirement if he is suffering from mental disorder (within the meaning of the Mental Health Act, but disregarding any exclusion for persons with learning disability).

(2) An exclusion for persons with learning disability is any provision of the Mental Health Act which provides for a person with learning disability not to be regarded as suffering from mental disorder for one or more purposes of that Act.

THE MENTAL CAPACITY REQUIREMENT

15 The relevant person meets the mental capacity requirement if he lacks capacity in relation to the question whether or not he should be accommodated in the relevant hospital or care home for the purpose of being given the relevant care or treatment.

THE BEST INTERESTS REQUIREMENT

16 (1) The relevant person meets the best interests requirement if all of the following conditions are met.

(2) The first condition is that the relevant person is, or is to be, a detained resident.

(3) The second condition is that it is in the best interests of the relevant person for him to be a detained resident.

(4) The third condition is that, in order to prevent harm to the relevant person, it is necessary for him to be a detained resident.

(5) The fourth condition is that it is a proportionate response to—

(a) the likelihood of the relevant person suffering harm, and
(b) the seriousness of that harm,

for him to be a detained resident.

THE ELIGIBILITY REQUIREMENT

17 (1) The relevant person meets the eligibility requirement unless he is ineligible to be deprived of liberty by this Act.

(2) Schedule 1A applies for the purpose of determining whether or not P is ineligible to be deprived of liberty by this Act.

THE NO REFUSALS REQUIREMENT

18 The relevant person meets the no refusals requirement unless there is a refusal within the meaning of paragraph 19 or 20.

19 (1) There is a refusal if these conditions are met—

(a) the relevant person has made an advance decision;

(b) the advance decision is valid;

(c) the advance decision is applicable to some or all of the relevant treatment.

(2) Expressions used in this paragraph and any of sections 24, 25 or 26 have the same meaning in this paragraph as in that section.

20 (1) There is a refusal if it would be in conflict with a valid decision of a donee or deputy for the relevant person to be accommodated in the relevant hospital or care home for the purpose of receiving some or all of the relevant care or treatment—

(a) in circumstances which amount to deprivation of the person's liberty, or

(b) at all.

(2) A donee is a donee of a lasting power of attorney granted by the relevant person.

(3) A decision of a donee or deputy is valid if it is made—

(a) within the scope of his authority as donee or deputy, and

(b) in accordance with Part 1 of this Act.

PART 4

STANDARD AUTHORISATIONS

SUPERVISORY BODY TO GIVE AUTHORISATION

III MEN [111]

21 Only the supervisory body may give a standard authorisation.

22 The supervisory body may not give a standard authorisation unless—

(a) the managing authority of the relevant hospital or care home have requested it, or

(b) paragraph 71 applies (right of third party to require consideration of whether authorisation needed).

23 The managing authority may not make a request for a standard authorisation unless—

(a) they are required to do so by paragraph 24 (as read with paragraphs 27 to 29),

(b) they are required to do so by paragraph 25 (as read with paragraph 28), or

(c) they are permitted to do so by paragraph 30.

DUTY TO REQUEST AUTHORISATION: BASIC CASES

24 (1) The managing authority must request a standard authorisation in any of the following cases.

(2) The first case is where it appears to the managing authority that the relevant person—

(a) is not yet accommodated in the relevant hospital or care home,

(b) is likely—at some time within the next 28 days—to be a detained resident in the relevant hospital or care home, and
(c) is likely—
(i) at that time, or
(ii) at some later time within the next 28 days,
to meet all of the qualifying requirements.

(3) The second case is where it appears to the managing authority that the relevant person—
(a) is already accommodated in the relevant hospital or care home,
(b) is likely—at some time within the next 28 days—to be a detained resident in the relevant hospital or care home, and
(c) is likely—
(i) at that time, or
(ii) at some later time within the next 28 days,
to meet all of the qualifying requirements.

(4) The third case is where it appears to the managing authority that the relevant person—
(a) is a detained resident in the relevant hospital or care home, and
(b) meets all of the qualifying requirements, or is likely to do so at some time within the next 28 days.

(5) This paragraph is subject to paragraphs 27 to 29.

Duty to request authorisation: change in place of detention

25 (1) The relevant managing authority must request a standard authorisation if it appears to them that these conditions are met.
(2) The first condition is that a standard authorisation—
(a) has been given, and
(b) has not ceased to be in force.
(3) The second condition is that there is, or is to be, a change in the place of detention.
(4) This paragraph is subject to paragraph 28.

26 (1) This paragraph applies for the purposes of paragraph 25.
(2) There is a change in the place of detention if the relevant person—
(a) ceases to be a detained resident in the stated hospital or care home, and
(b) becomes a detained resident in a different hospital or care home ("the new hospital or care home").
(3) The stated hospital or care home is the hospital or care home to which the standard authorisation relates.
(4) The relevant managing authority are the managing authority of the new hospital or care home.

Other authority for detention: request for authorisation

27 (1) This paragraph applies if, by virtue of section 4A(3), a decision of the court authorises the relevant person to be a detained resident.
(2) Paragraph 24 does not require a request for a standard authorisation to be made in relation to that detention unless these conditions are met.
(3) The first condition is that the standard authorisation would be in force at a time immediately after the expiry of the other authority.
(4) The second condition is that the standard authorisation would not be in force at any time on or before the expiry of the other authority.
(5) The third condition is that it would, in the managing authority's view, be unreasonable to delay making the request until a time nearer the expiry of the other authority.

(6) In this paragraph—

(a) the other authority is—

(i) the decision mentioned in sub-paragraph (1), or

(ii) any further decision of the court which, by virtue of section 4A(3), authorises, or is expected to authorise, the relevant person to be a detained resident;

(b) the expiry of the other authority is the time when the other authority is expected to cease to authorise the relevant person to be a detained resident.

REQUEST REFUSED: NO FURTHER REQUEST UNLESS CHANGE OF CIRCUMSTANCES

28 (1) This paragraph applies if—

(a) a managing authority request a standard authorisation under paragraph 24 or 25, and

(b) the supervisory body are prohibited by paragraph 50(2) from giving the authorisation.

(2) Paragraph 24 or 25 does not require that managing authority to make a new request for a standard authorisation unless it appears to the managing authority that—

(a) there has been a change in the relevant person's case, and

(b) because of that change, the supervisory body are likely to give a standard authorisation if requested.

AUTHORISATION GIVEN: REQUEST FOR FURTHER AUTHORISATION

29 (1) This paragraph applies if a standard authorisation—

(a) has been given in relation to the detention of the relevant person, and

(b) that authorisation ("the existing authorisation") has not ceased to be in force.

(2) Paragraph 24 does not require a new request for a standard authorisation ("the new authorisation") to be made unless these conditions are met.

(3) The first condition is that the new authorisation would be in force at a time immediately after the expiry of the existing authorisation.

(4) The second condition is that the new authorisation would not be in force at any time on or before the expiry of the existing authorisation.

(5) The third condition is that it would, in the managing authority's view, be unreasonable to delay making the request until a time nearer the expiry of the existing authorisation.

(6) The expiry of the existing authorisation is the time when it is expected to cease to be in force.

POWER TO REQUEST AUTHORISATION

30 (1) This paragraph applies if—

(a) a standard authorisation has been given in relation to the detention of the relevant person,

(b) that authorisation ("the existing authorisation") has not ceased to be in force,

(c) the requirement under paragraph 24 to make a request for a new standard authorisation does not apply, because of paragraph 29, and

(d) a review of the existing authorisation has been requested, or is being carried out, in accordance with Part 8.

(2) The managing authority may request a new standard authorisation which would be in force on or before the expiry of the existing authorisation; but only if it would also be in force immediately after that expiry.

(3) The expiry of the existing authorisation is the time when it is expected to cease to be in force.
(4) Further provision relating to cases where a request is made under this paragraph can be found in—
- (a) paragraph 62 (effect of decision about request), and
- (b) paragraph 124 (effect of request on Part 8 review).

Information included in request

31 A request for a standard authorisation must include the information (if any) required by regulations.

Records of requests

32 (1) The managing authority of a hospital or care home must keep a written record of—
- (a) each request that they make for a standard authorisation, and
- (b) the reasons for making each request.

(2) A supervisory body must keep a written record of each request for a standard authorisation that is made to them.

Relevant person must be assessed

33 (1) This paragraph applies if the supervisory body are requested to give a standard authorisation.
(2) The supervisory body must secure that all of these assessments are carried out in relation to the relevant person—
- (a) an age assessment;
- (b) a mental health assessment;
- (c) a mental capacity assessment;
- (d) a best interests assessment;
- (e) an eligibility assessment;
- (f) a no refusals assessment.

(3) The person who carries out any such assessment is referred to as the assessor.
(4) Regulations may be made about the period (or periods) within which assessors must carry out assessments.
(5) This paragraph is subject to paragraphs 49 and 133.

Age assessment

34 An age assessment is an assessment of whether the relevant person meets the age requirement.

Mental health assessment

35 A mental health assessment is an assessment of whether the relevant person meets the mental health requirement.

36 When carrying out a mental health assessment, the assessor must also—
- (a) consider how (if at all) the relevant person's mental health is likely to be affected by his being a detained resident, and
- (b) notify the best interests assessor of his conclusions.

MENTAL CAPACITY ASSESSMENT

37 A mental capacity assessment is an assessment of whether the relevant person meets the mental capacity requirement.

BEST INTERESTS ASSESSMENT

38 A best interests assessment is an assessment of whether the relevant person meets the best interests requirement.

39 (1) In carrying out a best interests assessment, the assessor must comply with the duties in sub-paragraphs (2) and (3).

(2) The assessor must consult the managing authority of the relevant hospital or care home.

(3) The assessor must have regard to all of the following—

- (a) the conclusions which the mental health assessor has notified to the best interests assessor in accordance with paragraph 36(b);
- (b) any relevant needs assessment;
- (c) any relevant care plan.

(4) A relevant needs assessment is an assessment of the relevant person's needs which—

- (a) was carried out in connection with the relevant person being accommodated in the relevant hospital or care home, and
- (b) was carried out by or on behalf of—
  - (i) the managing authority of the relevant hospital or care home, or
  - (ii) the supervisory body.

(5) A relevant care plan is a care plan which—

- (a) sets out how the relevant person's needs are to be met whilst he is accommodated in the relevant hospital or care home, and
- (b) was drawn up by or on behalf of—
  - (i) the managing authority of the relevant hospital or care home, or
  - (ii) the supervisory body.

(6) The managing authority must give the assessor a copy of—

- (a) any relevant needs assessment carried out by them or on their behalf, or
- (b) any relevant care plan drawn up by them or on their behalf.

(7) The supervisory body must give the assessor a copy of—

- (a) any relevant needs assessment carried out by them or on their behalf, or
- (b) any relevant care plan drawn up by them or on their behalf.

(8) The duties in sub-paragraphs (2) and (3) do not affect any other duty to consult or to take the views of others into account.

40 (1) This paragraph applies whatever conclusion the best interests assessment comes to.

(2) The assessor must state in the best interests assessment the name and address of every interested person whom he has consulted in carrying out the assessment.

41 Paragraphs 42 and 43 apply if the best interests assessment comes to the conclusion that the relevant person meets the best interests requirement.

42 (1) The assessor must state in the assessment the maximum authorisation period.

(2) The maximum authorisation period is the shorter of these periods—

(a) the period which, in the assessor's opinion, would be the appropriate maximum period for the relevant person to be a detained resident under the standard authorisation that has been requested;

(b) 1 year, or such shorter period as may be prescribed in regulations.

(3) Regulations under sub-paragraph (2)(b)—

(a) need not provide for a shorter period to apply in relation to all standard authorisations;

(b) may provide for different periods to apply in relation to different kinds of standard authorisations.

(4) Before making regulations under sub-paragraph (2)(b) the Secretary of State must consult all of the following—

(a) each body required by regulations under paragraph 162 to monitor and report on the operation of this Schedule in relation to England;

(b) such other persons as the Secretary of State considers it appropriate to consult.

(5) Before making regulations under sub-paragraph (2)(b) the National Assembly for Wales must consult all of the following—

(a) each person or body directed under paragraph 163(2) to carry out any function of the Assembly of monitoring and reporting on the operation of this Schedule in relation to Wales;

(b) such other persons as the Assembly considers it appropriate to consult.

43 The assessor may include in the assessment recommendations about conditions to which the standard authorisation is, or is not, to be subject in accordance with paragraph 53.

44 (1) This paragraph applies if the best interests assessment comes to the conclusion that the relevant person does not meet the best interests requirement.

(2) If, on the basis of the information taken into account in carrying out the assessment, it appears to the assessor that there is an unauthorised deprivation of liberty, he must include a statement to that effect in the assessment.

(3) There is an unauthorised deprivation of liberty if the managing authority of the relevant hospital or care home are already depriving the relevant person of his liberty without authority of the kind mentioned in section 4A.

45 The duties with which the best interests assessor must comply are subject to the provision included in appointment regulations under Part 10 (in particular, provision made under paragraph 146).

Eligibility assessment

46 An eligibility assessment is an assessment of whether the relevant person meets the eligibility requirement.

47 (1) Regulations may—

(a) require an eligibility assessor to request a best interests assessor to provide relevant eligibility information, and

(b) require the best interests assessor, if such a request is made, to provide such relevant eligibility information as he may have.

(2) In this paragraph—

"best interests assessor" means any person who is carrying out, or has carried out, a best interests assessment in relation to the relevant person;

"eligibility assessor" means a person carrying out an eligibility assessment in relation to the relevant person;

"relevant eligibility information" is information relevant to assessing whether or not the relevant person is ineligible by virtue of paragraph 5 of Schedule 1A.

MENTAL CAPACITY AND MENTAL HEALTH

No refusals assessment

48 A no refusals assessment is an assessment of whether the relevant person meets the no refusals requirement.

Equivalent assessment already carried out

49 (1) The supervisory body are not required by paragraph 33 to secure that a particular kind of assessment ("the required assessment") is carried out in relation to the relevant person if the following conditions are met.

(2) The first condition is that the supervisory body have a written copy of an assessment of the relevant person ("the existing assessment") that has already been carried out.

(3) The second condition is that the existing assessment complies with all requirements under this Schedule with which the required assessment would have to comply (if it were carried out).

(4) The third condition is that the existing assessment was carried out within the previous 12 months; but this condition need not be met if the required assessment is an age assessment.

(5) The fourth condition is that the supervisory body are satisfied that there is no reason why the existing assessment may no longer be accurate.

(6) If the required assessment is a best interests assessment, in satisfying themselves as mentioned in sub-paragraph (5), the supervisory body must take into account any information given, or submissions made, by—

(a) the relevant person's representative,

(b) any section 39C IMCA, or

(c) any section 39D IMCA.

(7) It does not matter whether the existing assessment was carried out in connection with a request for a standard authorisation or for some other purpose.

(8) If, because of this paragraph, the supervisory body are not required by paragraph 33 to secure that the required assessment is carried out, the existing assessment is to be treated for the purposes of this Schedule—

(a) as an assessment of the same kind as the required assessment, and

(b) as having been carried out under paragraph 33 in connection with the request for the standard authorisation.

Duty to give authorisation

50 (1) The supervisory body must give a standard authorisation if—

(a) all assessments are positive, and

(b) the supervisory body have written copies of all those assessments.

(2) The supervisory body must not give a standard authorisation except in accordance with sub-paragraph (1).

(3) All assessments are positive if each assessment carried out under paragraph 33 has come to the conclusion that the relevant person meets the qualifying requirement to which the assessment relates.

Terms of authorisation

51 (1) If the supervisory body are required to give a standard authorisation, they must decide the period during which the authorisation is to be in force.

(2) That period must not exceed the maximum authorisation period stated in the best interests assessment.

52 A standard authorisation may provide for the authorisation to come into force at a time after it is given.

53 (1) A standard authorisation may be given subject to conditions.

(2) Before deciding whether to give the authorisation subject to conditions, the supervisory body must have regard to any recommendations in the best interests assessment about such conditions.

(3) The managing authority of the relevant hospital or care home must ensure that any conditions are complied with.

FORM OF AUTHORISATION

54 A standard authorisation must be in writing.

55 (1) A standard authorisation must state the following things—

(a) the name of the relevant person;
(b) the name of the relevant hospital or care home;
(c) the period during which the authorisation is to be in force;
(d) the purpose for which the authorisation is given;
(e) any conditions subject to which the authorisation is given;
(f) the reason why each qualifying requirement is met.

(2) The statement of the reason why the eligibility requirement is met must be framed by reference to the cases in the table in paragraph 2 of Schedule 1A.

56 (1) If the name of the relevant hospital or care home changes, the standard authorisation is to be read as if it stated the current name of the hospital or care home.

(2) But sub-paragraph (1) is subject to any provision relating to the change of name which is made in any enactment or in any instrument made under an enactment.

DUTY TO GIVE INFORMATION ABOUT DECISION

57 (1) This paragraph applies if—

(a) a request is made for a standard authorisation, and
(b) the supervisory body are required by paragraph 50(1) to give the standard authorisation.

(2) The supervisory body must give a copy of the authorisation to each of the following—

(a) the relevant person's representative;
(b) the managing authority of the relevant hospital or care home;
(c) the relevant person;
(d) any section 39A IMCA;
(e) every interested person consulted by the best interests assessor.

(3) The supervisory body must comply with this paragraph as soon as practicable after they give the standard authorisation.

58 (1) This paragraph applies if—

(a) a request is made for a standard authorisation, and
(b) the supervisory body are prohibited by paragraph 50(2) from giving the standard authorisation.

(2) The supervisory body must give notice, stating that they are prohibited from giving the authorisation, to each of the following—

(a) the managing authority of the relevant hospital or care home;
(b) the relevant person;
(c) any section 39A IMCA;
(d) every interested person consulted by the best interests assessor.

(3) The supervisory body must comply with this paragraph as soon as practicable after it becomes apparent to them that they are prohibited from giving the authorisation.

Duty to give information about effect of authorisation

59 (1) This paragraph applies if a standard authorisation is given.

(2) The managing authority of the relevant hospital or care home must take such steps as are practicable to ensure that the relevant person understands all of the following—

- (a) the effect of the authorisation;
- (b) the right to make an application to the court to exercise its jurisdiction under section 21A;
- (c) the right under Part 8 to request a review;
- (d) the right to have a section 39D IMCA appointed;
- (e) how to have a section 39D IMCA appointed.

(3) Those steps must be taken as soon as is practicable after the authorisation is given.

(4) Those steps must include the giving of appropriate information both orally and in writing.

(5) Any written information given to the relevant person must also be given by the managing authority to the relevant person's representative.

(6) They must give the information to the representative as soon as is practicable after it is given to the relevant person.

(7) Sub-paragraph (8) applies if the managing authority is notified that a section 39D IMCA has been appointed.

(8) As soon as is practicable after being notified, the managing authority must give the section 39D IMCA a copy of the written information given in accordance with sub-paragraph (4).

Records of authorisations

60 A supervisory body must keep a written record of all of the following information—

- (a) the standard authorisations that they have given;
- (b) the requests for standard authorisations in response to which they have not given an authorisation;
- (c) in relation to each standard authorisation given: the matters stated in the authorisation in accordance with paragraph 55.

Variation of an authorisation

61 (1) A standard authorisation may not be varied except in accordance with Part 7 or 8.

(2) This paragraph does not affect the powers of the Court of Protection or of any other court.

Effect of decision about request made under paragraph 25 or 30

62 (1) This paragraph applies where the managing authority request a new standard authorisation under either of the following—

- (a) paragraph 25 (change in place of detention);
- (b) paragraph 30 (existing authorisation subject to review).

(2) If the supervisory body are required by paragraph 50(1) to give the new authorisation, the existing authorisation terminates at the time when the new authorisation comes into force.

(3) If the supervisory body are prohibited by paragraph 50(2) from giving the new authorisation, there is no effect on the existing authorisation's continuation in force.

WHEN AN AUTHORISATION IS IN FORCE

63 (1) A standard authorisation comes into force when it is given.

(2) But if the authorisation provides for it to come into force at a later time, it comes into force at that time.

64 (1) A standard authorisation ceases to be in force at the end of the period stated in the authorisation in accordance with paragraph 55(1)(c).

(2) But if the authorisation terminates before then in accordance with paragraph 62(2) or any other provision of this Schedule, it ceases to be in force when the termination takes effect.

(3) This paragraph does not affect the powers of the Court of Protection or of any other court.

65 (1) This paragraph applies if a standard authorisation ceases to be in force.

(2) The supervisory body must give notice that the authorisation has ceased to be in force.

(3) The supervisory body must give that notice to all of the following—

(a) the managing authority of the relevant hospital or care home;

(b) the relevant person;

(c) the relevant person's representative;

(d) every interested person consulted by the best interests assessor.

(4) The supervisory body must give that notice as soon as practicable after the authorisation ceases to be in force.

WHEN A REQUEST FOR A STANDARD AUTHORISATION IS "DISPOSED OF"

66 A request for a standard authorisation is to be regarded for the purposes of this Schedule as disposed of if the supervisory body have given—

(a) a copy of the authorisation in accordance with paragraph 57, or

(b) notice in accordance with paragraph 58.

RIGHT OF THIRD PARTY TO REQUIRE CONSIDERATION OF WHETHER AUTHORISATION NEEDED

67 For the purposes of paragraphs 68 to 73 there is an unauthorised deprivation of liberty if—

(a) a person is already a detained resident in a hospital or care home, and

(b) the detention of the person is not authorised as mentioned in section 4A.

68 (1) If the following conditions are met, an eligible person may request the supervisory body to decide whether or not there is an unauthorised deprivation of liberty.

(2) The first condition is that the eligible person has notified the managing authority of the relevant hospital or care home that it appears to the eligible person that there is an unauthorised deprivation of liberty.

(3) The second condition is that the eligible person has asked the managing authority to request a standard authorisation in relation to the detention of the relevant person.

(4) The third condition is that the managing authority has not requested a standard authorisation within a reasonable period after the eligible person asks it to do so.

(5) In this paragraph "eligible person" means any person other than the managing authority of the relevant hospital or care home.

69 (1) This paragraph applies if an eligible person requests the supervisory body to decide whether or not there is an unauthorised deprivation of liberty.

(2) The supervisory body must select and appoint a person to carry out an assessment of whether or not the relevant person is a detained resident.

(3) But the supervisory body need not select and appoint a person to carry out such an assessment in either of these cases.

(4) The first case is where it appears to the supervisory body that the request by the eligible person is frivolous or vexatious.

(5) The second case is where it appears to the supervisory body that—

- (a) the question of whether or not there is an unauthorised deprivation of liberty has already been decided, and
- (b) since that decision, there has been no change of circumstances which would merit the question being decided again.

(6) The supervisory body must not select and appoint a person to carry out an assessment under this paragraph unless it appears to the supervisory body that the person would be—

- (a) suitable to carry out a best interests assessment (if one were obtained in connection with a request for a standard authorisation relating to the relevant person), and
- (b) eligible to carry out such a best interests assessment.

(7) The supervisory body must notify the persons specified in sub-paragraph (8)—

- (a) that the supervisory body have been requested to decide whether or not there is an unauthorised deprivation of liberty;
- (b) of their decision whether or not to select and appoint a person to carry out an assessment under this paragraph;
- (c) if their decision is to select and appoint a person, of the person appointed.

(8) The persons referred to in sub-paragraph (7) are—

- (a) the eligible person who made the request under paragraph 68;
- (b) the person to whom the request relates;
- (c) the managing authority of the relevant hospital or care home;
- (d) any section 39A IMCA.

70 (1) Regulations may be made about the period within which an assessment under paragraph 69 must be carried out.

(2) Regulations made under paragraph 129(3) apply in relation to the selection and appointment of a person under paragraph 69 as they apply to the selection of a person under paragraph 129 to carry out a best interests assessment.

(3) The following provisions apply to an assessment under paragraph 69 as they apply to an assessment carried out in connection with a request for a standard authorisation—

- (a) paragraph 131 (examination and copying of records);
- (b) paragraph 132 (representations);
- (c) paragraphs 134 and 135(1) and (2) (duty to keep records and give copies).

(4) The copies of the assessment which the supervisory body are required to give under paragraph 135(2) must be given as soon as practicable after the supervisory body are themselves given a copy of the assessment.

71 (1) This paragraph applies if—

- (a) the supervisory body obtain an assessment under paragraph 69,
- (b) the assessment comes to the conclusion that the relevant person is a detained resident, and
- (c) it appears to the supervisory body that the detention of the person is not authorised as mentioned in section 4A.

(2) This Schedule (including Part 5) applies as if the managing authority of the relevant hospital or care home had, in accordance with Part 4, requested the

supervisory body to give a standard authorisation in relation to the relevant person.

(3) The managing authority of the relevant hospital or care home must supply the supervisory body with the information (if any) which the managing authority would, by virtue of paragraph 31, have had to include in a request for a standard authorisation.

(4) The supervisory body must notify the persons specified in paragraph 69(8)—

(a) of the outcome of the assessment obtained under paragraph 69, and

(b) that this Schedule applies as mentioned in sub-paragraph (2).

72 (1) This paragraph applies if—

(a) the supervisory body obtain an assessment under paragraph 69, and

(b) the assessment comes to the conclusion that the relevant person is not a detained resident.

(2) The supervisory body must notify the persons specified in paragraph 69(8) of the outcome of the assessment.

73 (1) This paragraph applies if—

(a) the supervisory body obtain an assessment under paragraph 69,

(b) the assessment comes to the conclusion that the relevant person is a detained resident, and

(c) it appears to the supervisory body that the detention of the person is authorised as mentioned in section 4A.

(2) The supervisory body must notify the persons specified in paragraph 69(8)—

(a) of the outcome of the assessment, and

(b) that it appears to the supervisory body that the detention is authorised.

PART 5
URGENT AUTHORISATIONS

MANAGING AUTHORITY TO GIVE AUTHORISATION

III MEN [112]

74 Only the managing authority of the relevant hospital or care home may give an urgent authorisation.

75 The managing authority may give an urgent authorisation only if they are required to do so by paragraph 76 (as read with paragraph 77).

DUTY TO GIVE AUTHORISATION

76 (1) The managing authority must give an urgent authorisation in either of the following cases.

(2) The first case is where—

(a) the managing authority are required to make a request under paragraph 24 or 25 for a standard authorisation, and

(b) they believe that the need for the relevant person to be a detained resident is so urgent that it is appropriate for the detention to begin before they make the request.

(3) The second case is where—

(a) the managing authority have made a request under paragraph 24 or 25 for a standard authorisation, and

(b) they believe that the need for the relevant person to be a detained resident is so urgent that it is appropriate for the detention to begin before the request is disposed of.

(4) References in this paragraph to the detention of the relevant person are references to the detention to which paragraph 24 or 25 relates.

(5) This paragraph is subject to paragraph 77.

77 (1) This paragraph applies where the managing authority have given an urgent authorisation ("the original authorisation") in connection with a case where a person is, or is to be, a detained resident ("the existing detention").
(2) No new urgent authorisation is to be given under paragraph 76 in connection with the existing detention.
(3) But the managing authority may request the supervisory body to extend the duration of the original authorisation.
(4) Only one request under sub-paragraph (3) may be made in relation to the original authorisation.
(5) Paragraphs 84 to 86 apply to any request made under sub-paragraph (3).

TERMS OF AUTHORISATION

78 (1) If the managing authority decide to give an urgent authorisation, they must decide the period during which the authorisation is to be in force.
(2) That period must not exceed 7 days.

FORM OF AUTHORISATION

79 An urgent authorisation must be in writing.

80 An urgent authorisation must state the following things—
(a) the name of the relevant person;
(b) the name of the relevant hospital or care home;
(c) the period during which the authorisation is to be in force;
(d) the purpose for which the authorisation is given.

81 (1) If the name of the relevant hospital or care home changes, the urgent authorisation is to be read as if it stated the current name of the hospital or care home.
(2) But sub-paragraph (1) is subject to any provision relating to the change of name which is made in any enactment or in any instrument made under an enactment.

DUTY TO KEEP RECORDS AND GIVE COPIES

82 (1) This paragraph applies if an urgent authorisation is given.
(2) The managing authority must keep a written record of why they have given the urgent authorisation.
(3) As soon as practicable after giving the authorisation, the managing authority must give a copy of the authorisation to all of the following—
(a) the relevant person;
(b) any section 39A IMCA.

DUTY TO GIVE INFORMATION ABOUT AUTHORISATION

83 (1) This paragraph applies if an urgent authorisation is given.
(2) The managing authority of the relevant hospital or care home must take such steps as are practicable to ensure that the relevant person understands all of the following—
(a) the effect of the authorisation;
(b) the right to make an application to the court to exercise its jurisdiction under section 21A.
(3) Those steps must be taken as soon as is practicable after the authorisation is given.

(4) Those steps must include the giving of appropriate information both orally and in writing.

REQUEST FOR EXTENSION OF DURATION

84 (1) This paragraph applies if the managing authority make a request under paragraph 77 for the supervisory body to extend the duration of the original authorisation.

(2) The managing authority must keep a written record of why they have made the request.

(3) The managing authority must give the relevant person notice that they have made the request.

(4) The supervisory body may extend the duration of the original authorisation if it appears to them that—

(a) the managing authority have made the required request for a standard authorisation,

(b) there are exceptional reasons why it has not yet been possible for that request to be disposed of, and

(c) it is essential for the existing detention to continue until the request is disposed of.

(5) The supervisory body must keep a written record that the request has been made to them.

(6) In this paragraph and paragraphs 85 and 86—

(a) "original authorisation" and "existing detention" have the same meaning as in paragraph 77;

(b) the required request for a standard authorisation is the request that is referred to in paragraph 76(2) or (3).

85 (1) This paragraph applies if, under paragraph 84, the supervisory body decide to extend the duration of the original authorisation.

(2) The supervisory body must decide the period of the extension.

(3) That period must not exceed 7 days.

(4) The supervisory body must give the managing authority notice stating the period of the extension.

(5) The managing authority must then vary the original authorisation so that it states the extended duration.

(6) Paragraphs 82(3) and 83 apply (with the necessary modifications) to the variation of the original authorisation as they apply to the giving of an urgent authorisation.

(7) The supervisory body must keep a written record of—

(a) the outcome of the request, and

(b) the period of the extension.

86 (1) This paragraph applies if, under paragraph 84, the supervisory body decide not to extend the duration of the original authorisation.

(2) The supervisory body must give the managing authority notice stating—

(a) the decision, and

(b) their reasons for making it.

(3) The managing authority must give a copy of that notice to all of the following—

(a) the relevant person;

(b) any section 39A IMCA.

(4) The supervisory body must keep a written record of the outcome of the request.

NO VARIATION

87 (1) An urgent authorisation may not be varied except in accordance with paragraph 85.
(2) This paragraph does not affect the powers of the Court of Protection or of any other court.

WHEN AN AUTHORISATION IS IN FORCE

88 An urgent authorisation comes into force when it is given.

89 (1) An urgent authorisation ceases to be in force at the end of the period stated in the authorisation in accordance with paragraph 80(c) (subject to any variation in accordance with paragraph 85).
(2) But if the required request is disposed of before the end of that period, the urgent authorisation ceases to be in force as follows.
(3) If the supervisory body are required by paragraph 50(1) to give the requested authorisation, the urgent authorisation ceases to be in force when the requested authorisation comes into force.
(4) If the supervisory body are prohibited by paragraph 50(2) from giving the requested authorisation, the urgent authorisation ceases to be in force when the managing authority receive notice under paragraph 58.
(5) In this paragraph—
"required request" means the request referred to in paragraph 76(2) or (3);
"requested authorisation" means the standard authorisation to which the required request relates.
(6) This paragraph does not affect the powers of the Court of Protection or of any other court.

90 (1) This paragraph applies if an urgent authorisation ceases to be in force.
(2) The supervisory body must give notice that the authorisation has ceased to be in force.
(3) The supervisory body must give that notice to all of the following—
(a) the relevant person;
(b) any section 39A IMCA.
(4) The supervisory body must give that notice as soon as practicable after the authorisation ceases to be in force.

PART 6
ELIGIBILITY REQUIREMENT NOT MET: SUSPENSION OF STANDARD AUTHORISATION

III MEN [113]

91 (1) This Part applies if the following conditions are met.
(2) The first condition is that a standard authorisation—
(a) has been given, and
(b) has not ceased to be in force.
(3) The second condition is that the managing authority of the relevant hospital or care home are satisfied that the relevant person has ceased to meet the eligibility requirement.
(4) But this Part does not apply if the relevant person is ineligible by virtue of paragraph 5 of Schedule 1A (in which case see Part 8).

92 The managing authority of the relevant hospital or care home must give the supervisory body notice that the relevant person has ceased to meet the eligibility requirement.

93 (1) This paragraph applies if the managing authority give the supervisory body notice under paragraph 92.

(2) The standard authorisation is suspended from the time when the notice is given.

(3) The supervisory body must give notice that the standard authorisation has been suspended to the following persons—

(a) the relevant person;

(b) the relevant person's representative;

(c) the managing authority of the relevant hospital or care home.

94 (1) This paragraph applies if, whilst the standard authorisation is suspended, the managing authority are satisfied that the relevant person meets the eligibility requirement again.

(2) The managing authority must give the supervisory body notice that the relevant person meets the eligibility requirement again.

95 (1) This paragraph applies if the managing authority give the supervisory body notice under paragraph 94.

(2) The standard authorisation ceases to be suspended from the time when the notice is given.

(3) The supervisory body must give notice that the standard authorisation has ceased to be suspended to the following persons—

(a) the relevant person;

(b) the relevant person's representative;

(c) any section 39D IMCA;

(d) the managing authority of the relevant hospital or care home.

(4) The supervisory body must give notice under this paragraph as soon as practicable after they are given notice under paragraph 94.

96 (1) This paragraph applies if no notice is given under paragraph 94 before the end of the relevant 28 day period.

(2) The standard authorisation ceases to have effect at the end of the relevant 28 day period.

(3) The relevant 28 day period is the period of 28 days beginning with the day on which the standard authorisation is suspended under paragraph 93.

97 The effect of suspending the standard authorisation is that Part 1 ceases to apply for as long as the authorisation is suspended.

PART 7
STANDARD AUTHORISATIONS: CHANGE IN SUPERVISORY RESPONSIBILITY

Application of this Part

III MEN [114]

98 (1) This Part applies if these conditions are met.

(2) The first condition is that a standard authorisation—

(a) has been given, and

(b) has not ceased to be in force.

(3) The second condition is that there is a change in supervisory responsibility.

(4) The third condition is that there is not a change in the place of detention (within the meaning of paragraph 25).

99 For the purposes of this Part there is a change in supervisory responsibility if—

(a) one body ("the old supervisory body") have ceased to be supervisory body in relation to the standard authorisation, and

(b) a different body ("the new supervisory body") have become supervisory body in relation to the standard authorisation.

EFFECT OF CHANGE IN SUPERVISORY RESPONSIBILITY

100 (1) The new supervisory body becomes the supervisory body in relation to the authorisation.

(2) Anything done by or in relation to the old supervisory body in connection with the authorisation has effect, so far as is necessary for continuing its effect after the change, as if done by or in relation to the new supervisory body.

(3) Anything which relates to the authorisation and which is in the process of being done by or in relation to the old supervisory body at the time of the change may be continued by or in relation to the new supervisory body.

(4) But—

(a) the old supervisory body do not, by virtue of this paragraph, cease to be liable for anything done by them in connection with the authorisation before the change; and

(b) the new supervisory body do not, by virtue of this paragraph, become liable for any such thing.

PART 8
STANDARD AUTHORISATIONS: REVIEW

APPLICATION OF THIS PART

III MEN [115]

101 (1) This Part applies if a standard authorisation—

(a) has been given, and

(b) has not ceased to be in force.

(2) Paragraphs 102 to 122 are subject to paragraphs 123 to 125.

REVIEW BY SUPERVISORY BODY

102 (1) The supervisory body may at any time carry out a review of the standard authorisation in accordance with this Part.

(2) The supervisory body must carry out such a review if they are requested to do so by an eligible person.

(3) Each of the following is an eligible person—

(a) the relevant person;

(b) the relevant person's representative;

(c) the managing authority of the relevant hospital or care home.

REQUEST FOR REVIEW

103 (1) An eligible person may, at any time, request the supervisory body to carry out a review of the standard authorisation in accordance with this Part.

(2) The managing authority of the relevant hospital or care home must make such a request if one or more of the qualifying requirements appear to them to be reviewable.

GROUNDS FOR REVIEW

104 (1) Paragraphs 105 to 107 set out the grounds on which the qualifying requirements are reviewable.

(2) A qualifying requirement is not reviewable on any other ground.

Non-qualification ground

105 (1) Any of the following qualifying requirements is reviewable on the ground that the relevant person does not meet the requirement—

(a) the age requirement;
(b) the mental health requirement;
(c) the mental capacity requirement;
(d) the best interests requirement;
(e) the no refusals requirement.

(2) The eligibility requirement is reviewable on the ground that the relevant person is ineligible by virtue of paragraph 5 of Schedule 1A.

(3) The ground in sub-paragraph (1) and the ground in sub-paragraph (2) are referred to as the non-qualification ground.

Change of reason ground

106 (1) Any of the following qualifying requirements is reviewable on the ground set out in sub-paragraph (2)—

(a) the mental health requirement;
(b) the mental capacity requirement;
(c) the best interests requirement;
(d) the eligibility requirement;
(e) the no refusals requirement.

(2) The ground is that the reason why the relevant person meets the requirement is not the reason stated in the standard authorisation.

(3) This ground is referred to as the change of reason ground.

Variation of conditions ground

107 (1) The best interests requirement is reviewable on the ground that—

(a) there has been a change in the relevant person's case, and
(b) because of that change, it would be appropriate to vary the conditions to which the standard authorisation is subject.

(2) This ground is referred to as the variation of conditions ground.

(3) A reference to varying the conditions to which the standard authorisation is subject is a reference to—

(a) amendment of an existing condition,
(b) omission of an existing condition, or
(c) inclusion of a new condition (whether or not there are already any existing conditions).

Notice that review to be carried out

108 (1) If the supervisory body are to carry out a review of the standard authorisation, they must give notice of the review to the following persons—

(a) the relevant person;
(b) the relevant person's representative;
(c) the managing authority of the relevant hospital or care home.

(2) The supervisory body must give the notice—

(a) before they begin the review, or
(b) if that is not practicable, as soon as practicable after they have begun it.

(3) This paragraph does not require the supervisory body to give notice to any person who has requested the review.

MENTAL CAPACITY AND MENTAL HEALTH

Starting a review

109 To start a review of the standard authorisation, the supervisory body must decide which, if any, of the qualifying requirements appear to be reviewable.

No reviewable qualifying requirements

110 (1) This paragraph applies if no qualifying requirements appear to be reviewable.
(2) This Part does not require the supervisory body to take any action in respect of the standard authorisation.

One or more reviewable qualifying requirements

111 (1) This paragraph applies if one or more qualifying requirements appear to be reviewable.
(2) The supervisory body must secure that a separate review assessment is carried out in relation to each qualifying requirement which appears to be reviewable.
(3) But sub-paragraph (2) does not require the supervisory body to secure that a best interests review assessment is carried out in a case where the best interests requirement appears to the supervisory body to be non-assessable.
(4) The best interests requirement is non-assessable if—
(a) the requirement is reviewable only on the variation of conditions ground, and
(b) the change in the relevant person's case is not significant.
(5) In making any decision whether the change in the relevant person's case is significant, regard must be had to—
(a) the nature of the change, and
(b) the period that the change is likely to last for.

Review assessments

112 (1) A review assessment is an assessment of whether the relevant person meets a qualifying requirement.
(2) In relation to a review assessment—
(a) a negative conclusion is a conclusion that the relevant person does not meet the qualifying requirement to which the assessment relates;
(b) a positive conclusion is a conclusion that the relevant person meets the qualifying requirement to which the assessment relates.
(3) An age review assessment is a review assessment carried out in relation to the age requirement.
(4) A mental health review assessment is a review assessment carried out in relation to the mental health requirement.
(5) A mental capacity review assessment is a review assessment carried out in relation to the mental capacity requirement.
(6) A best interests review assessment is a review assessment carried out in relation to the best interests requirement.
(7) An eligibility review assessment is a review assessment carried out in relation to the eligibility requirement.
(8) A no refusals review assessment is a review assessment carried out in relation to the no refusals requirement.

113 (1) In carrying out a review assessment, the assessor must comply with any duties which would be imposed upon him under Part 4 if the assessment were being carried out in connection with a request for a standard authorisation.
(2) But in the case of a best interests review assessment, paragraphs 43 and 44 do not apply.

(3) Instead of what is required by paragraph 43, the best interests review assessment must include recommendations about whether—and, if so, how—it would be appropriate to vary the conditions to which the standard authorisation is subject.

BEST INTERESTS REQUIREMENT REVIEWABLE BUT NON-ASSESSABLE

114 (1) This paragraph applies in a case where—
(a) the best interests requirement appears to be reviewable, but
(b) in accordance with paragraph 111(3), the supervisory body are not required to secure that a best interests review assessment is carried out.
(2) The supervisory body may vary the conditions to which the standard authorisation is subject in such ways (if any) as the supervisory body think are appropriate in the circumstances.

BEST INTERESTS REVIEW ASSESSMENT POSITIVE

115 (1) This paragraph applies in a case where—
(a) a best interests review assessment is carried out, and
(b) the assessment comes to a positive conclusion.
(2) The supervisory body must decide the following questions—
(a) whether or not the best interests requirement is reviewable on the change of reason ground;
(b) whether or not the best interests requirement is reviewable on the variation of conditions ground;
(c) if so, whether or not the change in the person's case is significant.
(3) If the supervisory body decide that the best interests requirement is reviewable on the change of reason ground, they must vary the standard authorisation so that it states the reason why the relevant person now meets that requirement.
(4) If the supervisory body decide that—
(a) the best interests requirement is reviewable on the variation of conditions ground, and
(b) the change in the relevant person's case is not significant,
they may vary the conditions to which the standard authorisation is subject in such ways (if any) as they think are appropriate in the circumstances.
(5) If the supervisory body decide that—
(a) the best interests requirement is reviewable on the variation of conditions ground, and
(b) the change in the relevant person's case is significant,
they must vary the conditions to which the standard authorisation is subject in such ways as they think are appropriate in the circumstances.
(6) If the supervisory body decide that the best interests requirement is not reviewable on—
(a) the change of reason ground, or
(b) the variation of conditions ground,
this Part does not require the supervisory body to take any action in respect of the standard authorisation so far as the best interests requirement relates to it.

MENTAL HEALTH, MENTAL CAPACITY, ELIGIBILITY OR NO REFUSALS REVIEW ASSESSMENT POSITIVE

116 (1) This paragraph applies if the following conditions are met.
(2) The first condition is that one or more of the following are carried out—
(a) a mental health review assessment;
(b) a mental capacity review assessment;

(c) an eligibility review assessment;
(d) a no refusals review assessment.

(3) The second condition is that each assessment carried out comes to a positive conclusion.

(4) The supervisory body must decide whether or not each of the assessed qualifying requirements is reviewable on the change of reason ground.

(5) If the supervisory body decide that any of the assessed qualifying requirements is reviewable on the change of reason ground, they must vary the standard authorisation so that it states the reason why the relevant person now meets the requirement or requirements in question.

(6) If the supervisory body decide that none of the assessed qualifying requirements are reviewable on the change of reason ground, this Part does not require the supervisory body to take any action in respect of the standard authorisation so far as those requirements relate to it.

(7) An assessed qualifying requirement is a qualifying requirement in relation to which a review assessment is carried out.

One or more review assessments negative

117 (1) This paragraph applies if one or more of the review assessments carried out comes to a negative conclusion.

(2) The supervisory body must terminate the standard authorisation with immediate effect.

Completion of a review

118 (1) The review of the standard authorisation is complete in any of the following cases.

(2) The first case is where paragraph 110 applies.

(3) The second case is where—
(a) paragraph 111 applies, and
(b) paragraph 117 requires the supervisory body to terminate the standard authorisation.

(4) In such a case, the supervisory body need not comply with any of the other provisions of paragraphs 114 to 116 which would be applicable to the review (were it not for this sub-paragraph).

(5) The third case is where—
(a) paragraph 111 applies,
(b) paragraph 117 does not require the supervisory body to terminate the standard authorisation, and
(c) the supervisory body comply with all of the provisions of paragraphs 114 to 116 (so far as they are applicable to the review).

Variations under this Part

119 Any variation of the standard authorisation made under this Part must be in writing.

Notice of outcome of review

120 (1) When the review of the standard authorisation is complete, the supervisory body must give notice to all of the following—
(a) the managing authority of the relevant hospital or care home;
(b) the relevant person;
(c) the relevant person's representative;
(d) any section 39D IMCA.

(2) That notice must state—

(a) the outcome of the review, and

(b) what variation (if any) has been made to the authorisation under this Part.

III MEN [115.1]

Issues concerning actions of IMCA and RPR upon receipt of notification of outcome In *RD & Others (Duties and Powers of Relevant Person's Representatives and Section 39D IMCAs)* [2016] EWCOP 49 Baker J set out clear guidance to RPRs and IMCAs as to their responsibilities under the Act, when determining whether an application should be made on behalf of P to the court under s 21A in respect of a standard authorisation made under Schedule A1.

RECORDS

121 A supervisory body must keep a written record of the following information—

(a) each request for a review that is made to them;

(b) the outcome of each request;

(c) each review which they carry out;

(d) the outcome of each review which they carry out;

(e) any variation of an authorisation made in consequence of a review.

RELATIONSHIP BETWEEN REVIEW AND SUSPENSION UNDER PART 6

122 (1) This paragraph applies if a standard authorisation is suspended in accordance with Part 6.

(2) No review may be requested under this Part whilst the standard authorisation is suspended.

(3) If a review has already been requested, or is being carried out, when the standard authorisation is suspended, no steps are to be taken in connection with that review whilst the authorisation is suspended.

RELATIONSHIP BETWEEN REVIEW AND REQUEST FOR NEW AUTHORISATION

123 (1) This paragraph applies if, in accordance with paragraph 24 (as read with paragraph 29), the managing authority of the relevant hospital or care home make a request for a new standard authorisation which would be in force after the expiry of the existing authorisation.

(2) No review may be requested under this Part until the request for the new standard authorisation has been disposed of.

(3) If a review has already been requested, or is being carried out, when the new standard authorisation is requested, no steps are to be taken in connection with that review until the request for the new standard authorisation has been disposed of.

124 (1) This paragraph applies if—

(a) a review under this Part has been requested, or is being carried out, and

(b) the managing authority of the relevant hospital or care home make a request under paragraph 30 for a new standard authorisation which would be in force on or before, and after, the expiry of the existing authorisation.

(2) No steps are to be taken in connection with the review under this Part until the request for the new standard authorisation has been disposed of.

125 In paragraphs 123 and 124—

(a) the existing authorisation is the authorisation referred to in paragraph 101;

(b) the expiry of the existing authorisation is the time when it is expected to cease to be in force.

PART 9
ASSESSMENTS UNDER THIS SCHEDULE

Introduction

III MEN [116]

126 This Part contains provision about assessments under this Schedule.

127 An assessment under this Schedule is either of the following—
(a) an assessment carried out in connection with a request for a standard authorisation under Part 4;
(b) a review assessment carried out in connection with a review of a standard authorisation under Part 8.

128 In this Part, in relation to an assessment under this Schedule—
"assessor" means the person carrying out the assessment;
"relevant procedure" means—
(a) the request for the standard authorisation, or
(b) the review of the standard authorisation;
"supervisory body" means the supervisory body responsible for securing that the assessment is carried out.

Supervisory body to select assessor

129 (1) It is for the supervisory body to select a person to carry out an assessment under this Schedule.
(2) The supervisory body must not select a person to carry out an assessment unless the person—
(a) appears to the supervisory body to be suitable to carry out the assessment (having regard, in particular, to the type of assessment and the person to be assessed), and
(b) is eligible to carry out the assessment.
(3) Regulations may make provision about the selection, and eligibility, of persons to carry out assessments under this Schedule.
(4) Sub-paragraphs (5) and (6) apply if two or more assessments are to be obtained for the purposes of the relevant procedure.
(5) In a case where the assessments to be obtained include a mental health assessment and a best interests assessment, the supervisory body must not select the same person to carry out both assessments.
(6) Except as prohibited by sub-paragraph (5), the supervisory body may select the same person to carry out any number of the assessments which the person appears to be suitable, and is eligible, to carry out.

130 (1) This paragraph applies to regulations under paragraph 129(3).
(2) The regulations may make provision relating to a person's—
(a) qualifications,
(b) skills,
(c) training,
(d) experience,
(e) relationship to, or connection with, the relevant person or any other person,
(f) involvement in the care or treatment of the relevant person,
(g) connection with the supervisory body, or
(h) connection with the relevant hospital or care home, or with any other establishment or undertaking.

(2A)

(a) the provision that the regulations may make in relation to a person's training in connection with best interests assessments includes provision for particular training to be specified by Social Work England or the Secretary of State otherwise than in the regulations;

(b) the provision that the regulations may make in relation to a person's training in connection with other assessments includes provision for particular training to be specified by the Secretary of State otherwise than in the regulations.

(2B) The regulations may give Social Work England power to charge fees for specifying any training as mentioned in sub-paragraph (2A)(a).

(2C) If the regulations give Social Work England power to charge fees, section 50(2) to (7) of the Children and Social Work Act 2017 apply for the purposes of sub-paragraph (2B) as they apply for the purposes of that section.

(3) In relation to Wales the provision that the regulations may make in relation to a person's training may provide for particular training to be specified by the Welsh Ministers otherwise than in the regulations.

(4) ...

(5) The regulations may make provision requiring a person to be insured in respect of liabilities that may arise in connection with the carrying out of an assessment.

(6) In relation to cases where two or more assessments are to be obtained for the purposes of the relevant procedure, the regulations may limit the number, kind or combination of assessments which a particular person is eligible to carry out.

(7) Sub-paragraphs (2) to (6) do not limit the generality of the provision that may be made in the regulations.

EXAMINATION AND COPYING OF RECORDS

131 An assessor may, at all reasonable times, examine and take copies of—

(a) any health record,

(b) any record of, or held by, a local authority and compiled in accordance with a social services function, and

(c) any record held by a person registered under Part 2 of the Care Standards Act 2000 or Chapter 2 of Part 1 of the Health and Social Care Act 2008,

which the assessor considers may be relevant to the assessment which is being carried out.

REPRESENTATIONS

132 In carrying out an assessment under this Schedule, the assessor must take into account any information given, or submissions made, by any of the following—

(a) the relevant person's representative;

(b) any section 39A IMCA;

(c) any section 39C IMCA;

(d) any section 39D IMCA.

ASSESSMENTS TO STOP IF ANY COMES TO NEGATIVE CONCLUSION

133 (1) This paragraph applies if an assessment under this Schedule comes to the conclusion that the relevant person does not meet one of the qualifying requirements.

(2) This Schedule does not require the supervisory body to secure that any other assessments under this Schedule are carried out in relation to the relevant procedure.

(3) The supervisory body must give notice to any assessor who is carrying out another assessment in connection with the relevant procedure that they are to cease carrying out that assessment.

(4) If an assessor receives such notice, this Schedule does not require the assessor to continue carrying out that assessment.

DUTY TO KEEP RECORDS AND GIVE COPIES

134 (1) This paragraph applies if an assessor has carried out an assessment under this Schedule (whatever conclusions the assessment has come to).

(2) The assessor must keep a written record of the assessment.

(3) As soon as practicable after carrying out the assessment, the assessor must give copies of the assessment to the supervisory body.

135 (1) This paragraph applies to the supervisory body if they are given a copy of an assessment under this Schedule.

(2) The supervisory body must give copies of the assessment to all of the following—

(a) the managing authority of the relevant hospital or care home;

(b) the relevant person;

(c) any section 39A IMCA;

(d) the relevant person's representative.

(3) If—

(a) the assessment is obtained in relation to a request for a standard authorisation, and

(b) the supervisory body are required by paragraph 50(1) to give the standard authorisation,

the supervisory body must give the copies of the assessment when they give copies of the authorisation in accordance with paragraph 57.

(4) If—

(a) the assessment is obtained in relation to a request for a standard authorisation, and

(b) the supervisory body are prohibited by paragraph 50(2) from giving the standard authorisation,

the supervisory body must give the copies of the assessment when they give notice in accordance with paragraph 58.

(5) If the assessment is obtained in connection with the review of a standard authorisation, the supervisory body must give the copies of the assessment when they give notice in accordance with paragraph 120.

136 (1) This paragraph applies to the supervisory body if—

(a) they are given a copy of a best interests assessment, and

(b) the assessment includes, in accordance with paragraph 44(2), a statement that it appears to the assessor that there is an unauthorised deprivation of liberty.

(2) The supervisory body must notify all of the persons listed in sub-paragraph (3) that the assessment includes such a statement.

(3) Those persons are—

(a) the managing authority of the relevant hospital or care home;

(b) the relevant person;

(c) any section 39A IMCA;

(d) any interested person consulted by the best interests assessor.

(4) The supervisory body must comply with this paragraph when (or at some time before) they comply with paragraph 135.

PART 10
RELEVANT PERSON'S REPRESENTATIVE

THE REPRESENTATIVE

III MEN [117]

137 In this Schedule the relevant person's representative is the person appointed as such in accordance with this Part.

138 (1) Regulations may make provision about the selection and appointment of representatives.
(2) In this Part such regulations are referred to as "appointment regulations".

SUPERVISORY BODY TO APPOINT REPRESENTATIVE

139 (1) The supervisory body must appoint a person to be the relevant person's representative as soon as practicable after a standard authorisation is given.
(2) The supervisory body must appoint a person to be the relevant person's representative if a vacancy arises whilst a standard authorisation is in force.
(3) Where a vacancy arises, the appointment under sub-paragraph (2) is to be made as soon as practicable after the supervisory body becomes aware of the vacancy.

140 (1) The selection of a person for appointment under paragraph 139 must not be made unless it appears to the person making the selection that the prospective representative would, if appointed—
(a) maintain contact with the relevant person,
(b) represent the relevant person in matters relating to or connected with this Schedule, and
(c) support the relevant person in matters relating to or connected with this Schedule.

141 (1) Any appointment of a representative for a relevant person is in addition to, and does not affect, any appointment of a donee or deputy.
(2) The functions of any representative are in addition to, and do not affect—
(a) the authority of any donee,
(b) the powers of any deputy, or
(c) any powers of the court.

APPOINTMENT REGULATIONS

142 Appointment regulations may provide that the procedure for appointing a representative may begin at any time after a request for a standard authorisation is made (including a time before the request has been disposed of).

143 (1) Appointment regulations may make provision about who is to select a person for appointment as a representative.
(2) But regulations under this paragraph may only provide for the following to make a selection—
(a) the relevant person, if he has capacity in relation to the question of which person should be his representative;
(b) a donee of a lasting power of attorney granted by the relevant person, if it is within the scope of his authority to select a person;
(c) a deputy, if it is within the scope of his authority to select a person;
(d) a best interests assessor;
(e) the supervisory body.

(3) Regulations under this paragraph may provide that a selection by the relevant person, a donee or a deputy is subject to approval by a best interests assessor or the supervisory body.

(4) Regulations under this paragraph may provide that, if more than one selection is necessary in connection with the appointment of a particular representative—

(a) the same person may make more than one selection;

(b) different persons may make different selections.

(5) For the purposes of this paragraph a best interests assessor is a person carrying out a best interests assessment in connection with the standard authorisation in question (including the giving of that authorisation).

144 (1) Appointment regulations may make provision about who may, or may not, be—

(a) selected for appointment as a representative, or

(b) appointed as a representative.

(2) Regulations under this paragraph may relate to any of the following matters—

(a) a person's age;

(b) a person's suitability;

(c) a person's independence;

(d) a person's willingness;

(e) a person's qualifications.

145 Appointment regulations may make provision about the formalities of appointing a person as a representative.

146 In a case where a best interests assessor is to select a person to be appointed as a representative, appointment regulations may provide for the variation of the assessor's duties in relation to the assessment which he is carrying out.

Monitoring of representatives

147 Regulations may make provision requiring the managing authority of the relevant hospital or care home to—

(a) monitor, and

(b) report to the supervisory body on,

the extent to which a representative is maintaining contact with the relevant person.

Termination

148 Regulations may make provision about the circumstances in which the appointment of a person as the relevant person's representative ends or may be ended.

149 Regulations may make provision about the formalities of ending the appointment of a person as a representative.

Suspension of representative's functions

150 (1) Regulations may make provision about the circumstances in which functions exercisable by, or in relation to, the relevant person's representative (whether under this Schedule or not) may be—

(a) suspended, and

(b) if suspended, revived.

(2) The regulations may make provision about the formalities for giving effect to the suspension or revival of a function.

(3) The regulations may make provision about the effect of the suspension or revival of a function.

PAYMENT OF REPRESENTATIVE

151 Regulations may make provision for payments to be made to, or in relation to, persons exercising functions as the relevant person's representative.

REGULATIONS UNDER THIS PART

152 The provisions of this Part which specify provision that may be made in regulations under this Part do not affect the generality of the power to make such regulations.

EFFECT OF APPOINTMENT OF SECTION 39C IMCA

153 Paragraphs 159 and 160 make provision about the exercise of functions by, or towards, the relevant person's representative during periods when—
- (a) no person is appointed as the relevant person's representative, but
- (b) a person is appointed as a section 39C IMCA.

PART 11
IMCAS

APPLICATION OF PART

III MEN [118]

154 This Part applies for the purposes of this Schedule.

THE IMCAS

155 A section 39A IMCA is an independent mental capacity advocate appointed under section 39A.

156 A section 39C IMCA is an independent mental capacity advocate appointed under section 39C

157 A section 39D IMCA is an independent mental capacity advocate appointed under section 39D.

158 An IMCA is a section 39A IMCA or a section 39C IMCA or a section 39D IMCA.

SECTION 39C IMCA: FUNCTIONS

159 (1) This paragraph applies if, and for as long as, there is a section 39C IMCA.
(2) In the application of the relevant provisions, references to the relevant person's representative are to be read as references to the section 39C IMCA.
(3) But sub-paragraph (2) does not apply to any function under the relevant provisions for as long as the function is suspended in accordance with provision made under Part 10.
(4) In this paragraph and paragraph 160 the relevant provisions are—
- (a) paragraph 102(3)(b) (request for review under Part 8);
- (b) paragraph 108(1)(b) (notice of review under Part 8);
- (c) paragraph 120(1)(c) (notice of outcome of review under Part 8).

160 (1) This paragraph applies if—
- (a) a person is appointed as the relevant person's representative, and

MENTAL CAPACITY AND MENTAL HEALTH

(b) a person accordingly ceases to hold an appointment as a section 39C IMCA.

(2) Where a function under a relevant provision has been exercised by, or towards, the section 39C IMCA, there is no requirement for that function to be exercised again by, or towards, the relevant person's representative.

SECTION 39A IMCA: RESTRICTION OF FUNCTIONS

161 (1) This paragraph applies if—

(a) there is a section 39A IMCA, and

(b) a person is appointed under Part 10 to be the relevant person's representative (whether or not that person, or any person subsequently appointed, is currently the relevant person's representative).

(2) The duties imposed on, and the powers exercisable by, the section 39A IMCA do not apply.

(3) The duties imposed on, and the powers exercisable by, any other person do not apply, so far as they fall to be performed or exercised towards the section 39A IMCA.

(4) But sub-paragraph (2) does not apply to any power of challenge exercisable by the section 39A IMCA.

(5) And sub-paragraph (3) does not apply to any duty or power of any other person so far as it relates to any power of challenge exercisable by the section 39A IMCA.

(6) Before exercising any power of challenge, the section 39A IMCA must take the views of the relevant person's representative into account.

(7) A power of challenge is a power to make an application to the court to exercise its jurisdiction under section 21A in connection with the giving of the standard authorisation.

PART 12

MISCELLANEOUS

MONITORING OF OPERATION OF SCHEDULE

III MEN [119]

162 (1) Regulations may make provision for, and in connection with, requiring one or more prescribed bodies to monitor, and report on, the operation of this Schedule in relation to England.

(2) The regulations may, in particular, give a prescribed body authority to do one or more of the following things—

(a) to visit hospitals and care homes;

(b) to visit and interview persons accommodated in hospitals and care homes;

(c) to require the production of, and to inspect, records relating to the care or treatment of persons.

(3) "Prescribed" means prescribed in regulations under this paragraph.

163 (1) Regulations may make provision for, and in connection with, enabling the National Assembly for Wales to monitor, and report on, the operation of this Schedule in relation to Wales.

(2) The National Assembly may direct one or more persons or bodies to carry out the Assembly's functions under regulations under this paragraph.

DISCLOSURE OF INFORMATION

164 (1) Regulations may require either or both of the following to disclose prescribed information to prescribed bodies—

(a) supervisory bodies;

(b) managing authorities of hospitals or care homes.

(2) "Prescribed" means prescribed in regulations under this paragraph.

(3) Regulations under this paragraph may only prescribe information relating to matters with which this Schedule is concerned.

DIRECTIONS BY NATIONAL ASSEMBLY IN RELATION TO SUPERVISORY FUNCTIONS

165 (1) The National Assembly for Wales may direct a Local Health Board to exercise in relation to its area any supervisory functions which are specified in the direction.

(2) Directions under this paragraph must not preclude the National Assembly from exercising the functions specified in the directions.

(3) In this paragraph "supervisory functions" means functions which the National Assembly have as supervisory body, so far as they are exercisable in relation to hospitals (whether NHS or independent hospitals, and whether in Wales or England).

166 (1) This paragraph applies where, under paragraph 165, a Local Health Board ("the specified LHB") is directed to exercise supervisory functions ("delegated functions").

(2) The National Assembly for Wales may give directions to the specified LHB about the Board's exercise of delegated functions.

(3) The National Assembly may give directions for any delegated functions to be exercised, on behalf of the specified LHB, by a committee, sub-committee or officer of that Board.

(4) The National Assembly may give directions providing for any delegated functions to be exercised by the specified LHB jointly with one or more other Local Health Boards.

(5) Where, under sub-paragraph (4), delegated functions are exercisable jointly, the National Assembly may give directions providing for the functions to be exercised, on behalf of the Local Health Boards in question, by a joint committee or joint sub-committee.

167 (1) Directions under paragraph 165 must be given in regulations.

(2) Directions under paragraph 166 may be given—

(a) in regulations, or

(b) by instrument in writing.

168 The power under paragraph 165 or paragraph 166 to give directions includes power to vary or revoke directions given under that paragraph.

NOTICES

169 Any notice under this Schedule must be in writing.

REGULATIONS

170 (1) This paragraph applies to all regulations under this Schedule, except regulations under paragraph 162, 163, 167 or 183.

(2) It is for the Secretary of State to make such regulations in relation to authorisations under this Schedule which relate to hospitals and care homes situated in England.

(3) It is for the National Assembly for Wales to make such regulations in relation to authorisations under this Schedule which relate to hospitals and care homes situated in Wales.

171 It is for the Secretary of State to make regulations under paragraph 162.

172 It is for the National Assembly for Wales to make regulations under paragraph 163 or 167.

173 (1) This paragraph applies to regulations under paragraph 183.

(2) It is for the Secretary of State to make such regulations in relation to cases where a question as to the ordinary residence of a person is to be determined by the Secretary of State.

(3) It is for the National Assembly for Wales to make such regulations in relation to cases where a question as to the ordinary residence of a person is to be determined by the National Assembly.

PART 13
INTERPRETATION

INTRODUCTION

III MEN [120]

174 This Part applies for the purposes of this Schedule.

HOSPITALS AND THEIR MANAGING AUTHORITIES

175 (1) "Hospital" means—

(a) an NHS hospital, or

(b) an independent hospital.

(2) "NHS hospital" means—

(a) a health service hospital as defined by section 275 of the National Health Service Act 2006 or section 206 of the National Health Service (Wales) Act 2006, or

(b) a hospital as defined by section 206 of the National Health Service (Wales) Act 2006 vested in a Local Health Board.

(3) Independent hospital"—

(a) in relation to England, means a hospital as defined by section 275 of the National Health Service Act 2006 that is not an NHS hospital; and

(b) in relation to Wales, means a hospital as defined by section 2 of the Care Standards Act 2000 that is not an NHS hospital.

176 (1) "Managing authority", in relation to an NHS hospital, means—

(a) if the hospital—

(i) is vested in the appropriate national authority for the purposes of its functions under the National Health Service Act 2006 or of the National Health Service (Wales) Act 2006, or

(ii) consists of any accommodation provided by a local authority and used as a hospital by or on behalf of the appropriate national authority under either of those Acts,

the Local Health Board or Special Health Authority responsible for the administration of the hospital;

(aa) in relation to England, if the hospital falls within paragraph (a)(i) or (ii) and no Special Health Authority has responsibility for its administration, the Secretary of State;

(b) if the hospital is vested in a National Health Service trust or NHS foundation trust, that trust;

(c) if the hospital is vested in a Local Health Board, that Board.

(2) For this purpose the appropriate national authority is—

(a) in relation to England: the Secretary of State;

(b) in relation to Wales: the National Assembly for Wales;

(c) in relation to England and Wales: the Secretary of State and the National Assembly acting jointly.

177 "Managing authority", in relation to an independent hospital, means—

(a) in relation to England, the person registered, or required to be registered, under Chapter 2 of Part 1 of the Health and Social Care Act 2008 in respect of regulated activities (within the meaning of that Part) carried on in the hospital, and

(b) in relation to Wales, the person registered, or required to be registered, under Part 2 of the Care Standards Act 2000 in respect of the hospital.

CARE HOMES AND THEIR MANAGING AUTHORITIES

178 "Care home" means—

(a) a care home in England within the meaning given by section 3 of the Care Standards Act 2000, and

(b) a place in Wales at which a care home service within the meaning of Part 1 of the Regulation and Inspection of Social Care (Wales) Act 2016 is provided wholly or mainly to persons aged 18 or over.

179 "Managing authority", in relation to a care home, means—

(a) in relation to England, the person registered, or required to be registered, under Chapter 2 of Part 1 of the Health and Social Care Act 2008 in respect of the provision of residential accommodation, together with nursing or personal care, in the care home, and

(b) in relation to Wales, the person registered, or required to be registered, under Part 1 of the Regulation and Inspection of Social Care (Wales) Act 2016 in respect of the care home.

SUPERVISORY BODIES: HOSPITALS

180 (1) The identity of the supervisory body is determined under this paragraph in cases where the relevant hospital is situated in England.

(2) If the relevant person is ordinarily resident in the area of a local authority in England, the supervisory body are that local authority.

(3) If the relevant person is not ordinarily resident in England and the National Assembly for Wales or a Local Health Board commission the relevant care or treatment, the National Assembly are the supervisory body.

(4) In any other case, the supervisory body are the local authority for the area in which the relevant hospital is situated.

(4A) Local authority" means—

(a) the council of a county;

(b) the council of a district for which there is no county council;

(c) the council of a London borough;

(d) the Common Council of the City of London;

(e) the Council of the Isles of Scilly.

(5) If a hospital is situated in the areas of two (or more) local authorities, it is to be regarded for the purposes of sub-paragraph (4) as situated in whichever of the areas the greater (or greatest) part of the hospital is situated.

181 (1) The identity of the supervisory body is determined under this paragraph in cases where the relevant hospital is situated in Wales.

(2) The National Assembly for Wales are the supervisory body.

MENTAL CAPACITY AND MENTAL HEALTH

(3) But if the relevant person is ordinarily resident in the area of a local authority in England, the supervisory body are that local authority.

(4A) Local authority" means—

(a) the council of a county;
(b) the council of a district for which there is no county council;
(c) the council of a London borough;
(d) the Common Council of the City of London;
(e) the Council of the Isles of Scilly.

Supervisory bodies: care homes

182 (1) The identity of the supervisory body is determined under this paragraph in cases where the relevant care home is situated in England or in Wales.

(2) The supervisory body are the local authority for the area in which the relevant person is ordinarily resident.

(3) But if the relevant person is not ordinarily resident in the area of a local authority, the supervisory body are the local authority for the area in which the care home is situated.

(4) In relation to England "local authority" means—

(a) the council of a county;
(b) the council of a district for which there is no county council;
(c) the council of a London borough;
(d) the Common Council of the City of London;
(e) the Council of the Isles of Scilly.

(5) In relation to Wales "local authority" means the council of a county or county borough.

(6) If a care home is situated in the areas of two (or more) local authorities, it is to be regarded for the purposes of sub-paragraph (3) as situated in whichever of the areas the greater (or greatest) part of the care home is situated.

Supervisory bodies: determination of place of ordinary residence

183 (1) Subsections (5) and (6) of section 24 of the National Assistance Act 1948 (deemed place of ordinary residence) apply to any determination of where a person is ordinarily resident for the purposes of paragraphs 180, 181 and 182 as those subsections apply to such a determination for the purposes specified in those subsections.

(2) In the application of section 24(6) of the 1948 Act by virtue of subsection (1) to any determination of where a person is ordinarily resident for the purposes of paragraph 182, section 24(6) is to be read as if it referred to a hospital vested in a Local Health Board as well as to hospitals vested in the Secretary of State and the other bodies mentioned in section 24(6).

(2A) Section 39(1), (2) and (4) to (6) of the Care Act 2014 and paragraphs 1(1), 2(1) and 8 of Schedule 1 to that Act apply to any determination of where a person is ordinarily resident for the purposes of paragraphs 180, 181 and 182 as they apply for the purposes of Part 1 of that Act.

(3) Any question arising as to the ordinary residence of a person is to be determined by the Secretary of State or by the National Assembly for Wales.

(4) The Secretary of State and the National Assembly must make and publish arrangements for determining which cases are to be dealt with by the Secretary of State and which are to be dealt with by the National Assembly.

(5) Those arrangements may include provision for the Secretary of State and the National Assembly to agree, in relation to any question that has arisen, which of them is to deal with the case.

(6) Regulations may make provision about arrangements that are to have effect before, upon, or after the determination of any question as to the ordinary residence of a person.

(7) The regulations may, in particular, authorise or require a local authority to do any or all of the following things—

- (a) to act as supervisory body even though it may wish to dispute that it is the supervisory body;
- (b) to become the supervisory body in place of another local authority;
- (c) to recover from another local authority expenditure incurred in exercising functions as the supervisory body.

SAME BODY MANAGING AUTHORITY AND SUPERVISORY BODY

184 (1) This paragraph applies if, in connection with a particular person's detention as a resident in a hospital or care home, the same body are both—

- (a) the managing authority of the relevant hospital or care home, and
- (b) the supervisory body.

(2) The fact that a single body are acting in both capacities does not prevent the body from carrying out functions under this Schedule in each capacity.

(3) But, in such a case, this Schedule has effect subject to any modifications contained in regulations that may be made for this purpose.

INTERESTED PERSONS

185 Each of the following is an interested person—

- (a) the relevant person's spouse or civil partner;
- (b) where the relevant person and another person are not married to each other, nor in a civil partnership with each other, but are living together as if they were a married couple: that other person;
- (d) the relevant person's children and step-children;
- (e) the relevant person's parents and step-parents;
- (f) the relevant person's brothers and sisters, half-brothers and half-sisters, and stepbrothers and stepsisters;
- (g) the relevant person's grandparents;
- (h) a deputy appointed for the relevant person by the court;
- (i) a donee of a lasting power of attorney granted by the relevant person.

186 (1) An interested person consulted by the best interests assessor is any person whose name is stated in the relevant best interests assessment in accordance with paragraph 40 (interested persons whom the assessor consulted in carrying out the assessment).

(2) The relevant best interests assessment is the most recent best interests assessment carried out in connection with the standard authorisation in question (whether the assessment was carried out under Part 4 or Part 8).

187 Where this Schedule imposes on a person a duty towards an interested person, the duty does not apply if the person on whom the duty is imposed—

- (a) is not aware of the interested person's identity or of a way of contacting him, and
- (b) cannot reasonably ascertain it.

188 The following table contains an index of provisions defining or otherwise explaining expressions used in this Schedule—

age assessment	paragraph 34
age requirement	paragraph 13

age review assessment	paragraph 112(3)
appointment regulations	paragraph 138
assessment under this Schedule	paragraph 127
assessor (except in Part 8)	paragraph 33
assessor (in Part 8)	paragraphs 33 and 128
authorisation under this Schedule	paragraph 10
best interests (determination of)	section 4
best interests assessment	paragraph 38
best interests requirement	paragraph 16
best interests review assessment	paragraph 112(6)
care home	paragraph 178
change of reason ground	paragraph 106
complete (in relation to a review of a standard authorisation)	paragraph 118
deprivation of a person's liberty	section 64(5) and (6)
Deputy	section 16(2)(b)
detained resident	paragraph 6
disposed of (in relation to a request for a standard authorisation)	paragraph 66
eligibility assessment	paragraph 46
eligibility requirement	paragraph 17
eligibility review assessment	paragraph 112(7)
eligible person (in relation to paragraphs 68 to 73)	paragraph 68
eligible person (in relation to Part 8)	paragraph 102(3)
expiry (in relation to an existing authorisation)	paragraph 125(b)
existing authorisation (in Part 8)	paragraph 125(a)
Hospital	paragraph 175
IMCA	paragraph 158
in force (in relation to a standard authorisation)	paragraphs 63 and 64
in force (in relation to an urgent authorisation)	paragraphs 88 and 89
ineligible (in relation to the eligibility requirement)	Schedule 1A
interested person	paragraph 185
interested person consulted by the best interests assessor	paragraph 186
lack of capacity	section 2
lasting power of attorney	section 9
managing authority (in relation to a care home)	paragraph 179
managing authority (in relation to a hospital)	paragraph 176 or 177
maximum authorisation period	paragraph 42
mental capacity assessment	paragraph 37
mental capacity requirement	paragraph 15
mental capacity review assessment	paragraph 112(5)

mental health assessment	paragraph 35
mental health requirement	paragraph 14
mental health review assessment	paragraph 112(4)
negative conclusion	paragraph 112(2)(a)
new supervisory body	paragraph 99(b)
no refusals assessment	paragraph 48
no refusals requirement	paragraph 18
no refusals review assessment	paragraph 112(8)
non-qualification ground	paragraph 105
old supervisory body	paragraph 99(a)
positive conclusion	paragraph 112(2)(b)
purpose of a standard authorisation	paragraph 11(1)
purpose of an urgent authorisation	paragraph 11(2)
qualifying requirements	paragraph 12
refusal (for the purposes of the no refusals requirement)	paragraphs 19 and 20
relevant care or treatment	paragraph 7
relevant hospital or care home	paragraph 7
relevant managing authority	paragraph 26(4)
relevant person	paragraph 7
relevant person's representative	paragraph 137
relevant procedure	paragraph 128
review assessment	paragraph 112(1)
Reviewable	paragraph 104
section 39A IMCA	paragraph 155
section 39C IMCA	paragraph 156
section 39D IMCA	paragraph 157
standard authorisation	paragraph 8
supervisory body (except in Part 8)	paragraph 180, 181 or 182
supervisory body (in Part 8)	paragraph 128 and paragraph 180, 181 or 182
unauthorised deprivation of liberty (in relation to paragraphs 68 to 73)	paragraph 67
urgent authorisation	paragraph 9
variation of conditions ground	paragraph 107

SCHEDULE 1
LASTING POWERS OF ATTORNEY: FORMALITIES

PART 1
MAKING INSTRUMENTS

GENERAL REQUIREMENTS AS TO MAKING INSTRUMENTS

III MEN [121]

1 (1) An instrument is not made in accordance with this Schedule unless—
  (a) it is in the prescribed form,
  (b) it complies with paragraph 2, and

(c) any prescribed requirements in connection with its execution are satisfied.

(2) Regulations may make different provision according to whether—

(a) the instrument relates to personal welfare or to property and affairs (or to both);

(b) only one or more than one donee is to be appointed (and if more than one, whether jointly or jointly and severally).

(3) In this Schedule—

(a) 'prescribed' means prescribed by regulations, and

(b) 'regulations' means regulations made for the purposes of this Schedule by the Lord Chancellor.

REQUIREMENTS AS TO CONTENT OF INSTRUMENTS

2 (1) The instrument must include—

(a) the prescribed information about the purpose of the instrument and the effect of a lasting power of attorney,

(b) a statement by the donor to the effect that he—

(i) has read the prescribed information or a prescribed part of it (or has had it read to him), and

(ii) intends the authority conferred under the instrument to include authority to make decisions on his behalf in circumstances where he no longer has capacity,

(c) a statement by the donor—

(i) naming a person or persons whom the donor wishes to be notified of any application for the registration of the instrument, or

(ii) stating that there are no persons whom he wishes to be notified of any such application,

(d) a statement by the donee (or, if more than one, each of them) to the effect that he—

(i) has read the prescribed information or a prescribed part of it (or has had it read to him), and

(ii) understands the duties imposed on a donee of a lasting power of attorney under sections 1 (the principles) and 4 (best interests), and

(e) a certificate by a person of a prescribed description that, in his opinion, at the time when the donor executes the instrument—

(i) the donor understands the purpose of the instrument and the scope of the authority conferred under it,

(ii) no fraud or undue pressure is being used to induce the donor to create a lasting power of attorney, and

(iii) there is nothing else which would prevent a lasting power of attorney from being created by the instrument.

(2) Regulations may—

(a) prescribe a maximum number of named persons;

(b) provide that, where the instrument includes a statement under sub-paragraph (1)(c)(ii), two persons of a prescribed description must each give a certificate under sub-paragraph (1)(e).

(3) The persons who may be named persons do not include a person who is appointed as donee under the instrument.

(4) In this Schedule, 'named person' means a person named under sub-paragraph (1)(c).

(5) A certificate under sub-paragraph (1)(e)—

(a) must be made in the prescribed form, and

(b) must include any prescribed information.

(6) The certificate may not be given by a person appointed as donee under the instrument.

FAILURE TO COMPLY WITH PRESCRIBED FORM

3 (1) If an instrument differs in an immaterial respect in form or mode of expression from the prescribed form, it is to be treated by the Public Guardian as sufficient in point of form and expression.

(2) The court may declare that an instrument which is not in the prescribed form is to be treated as if it were, if it is satisfied that the persons executing the instrument intended it to create a lasting power of attorney.

III MEN [121.1]

Prescribed forms See the Lasting Powers of Attorney, Enduring Powers of Attorney and Public Guardian Regulations 2007, SI 2007/1253, regs 5–9, the Lasting Powers of Attorney, Enduring Powers of Attorney and Public Guardian (Amendment) Regulations 2009, SI 2009/1884, the Lasting Powers of Attorney, Enduring Powers of Attorney and Public Guardian Regulations 2011, SI 2011/2189, the Lasting Powers of Attorney, Enduring Powers of Attorney and Public Guardian Regulations 2013, SI 2013/506 and the Lasting Powers of Attorney, Enduring Powers of Attorney and Public Guardian Regulations 2015, SI 2015/899. Separate forms are to be used for financial property and affairs on the one hand and for personal welfare on the other.

The Mental Capacity Act 2005 Code of Practice provides guidance on Lasting Powers of Attorney at Chapter 7.

Applications for a declaration to the court should be commenced under Court of Protection Rules 2017, Part 9, noting the provisions of r 9.7 which relate separately to issues of validity and operation of an LPA under ss 22 and 23 of MCA 2005. See **III MEN [590]**.

PART 2

REGISTRATION

APPLICATIONS AND PROCEDURE FOR REGISTRATION

III MEN [122]

4 (1) An application to the Public Guardian for the registration of an instrument intended to create a lasting power of attorney—

- (a) must be made in the prescribed form, and
- (b) must include any prescribed information.

(2) The application may be made—

- (a) by the donor,
- (b) by the donee or donees, or
- (c) if the instrument appoints two or more donees to act jointly and severally in respect of any matter, by any of the donees.

(3) The application must be accompanied by—

- (a) the instrument, and
- (b) any fee provided for under section 58(4)(b).

(4) A person who, in an application for registration, makes a statement which he knows to be false in a material particular is guilty of an offence and is liable—

- (a) on summary conviction, to imprisonment for a term not exceeding 12 months or a fine not exceeding the statutory maximum or both;
- (b) on conviction on indictment, to imprisonment for a term not exceeding 2 years or a fine or both.

5 Subject to paragraphs 11 to 14, the Public Guardian must register the instrument as a lasting power of attorney at the end of the prescribed period.

III MEN [122.1]

The Regulations and the prescribed period The Lasting Powers of Attorney, Enduring Powers of Attorney and Public Guardian Regulations 2007, SI 2007/1253 provided that the prescribed form is LPA001. Up until 1 April 2013 the prescribed period was of 6 weeks commencing with the date on which the Public Guardian gives the last notice pursuant to paras 7 or 8 below. Lasting Powers of Attorney, Enduring Powers of Attorney and Public Guardian Regulations 2007, SI 2007/1253, reg 12 applied. However from 1 April 2013 the time limits were amended, and the statutory waiting period is now 4 weeks not 6 weeks, and the related objection period is now 3 weeks instead of 5 weeks: Lasting Powers of Attorney and Public Guardian (Amendment) Regulations 2013, SI 2013/0506. Now see the Lasting Powers of Attorney, Enduring Powers of Attorney and Public Guardian (Amendment) Regulations 2015, SI 2015/899 in respect of the current Forms.

NOTIFICATION REQUIREMENTS

6 (1) A donor about to make an application under paragraph 4(2)(a) must notify any named persons that he is about to do so.

(2) The donee (or donees) about to make an application under paragraph 4(2)(b) or (c) must notify any named persons that he is (or they are) about to do so.

7 As soon as is practicable after receiving an application by the donor under paragraph 4(2)(a), the Public Guardian must notify the donee (or donees) that the application has been received.

8 (1) As soon as is practicable after receiving an application by a donee (or donees) under paragraph 4(2)(b), the Public Guardian must notify the donor that the application has been received.

(2) As soon as is practicable after receiving an application by a donee under paragraph 4(2)(c), the Public Guardian must notify—

(a) the donor, and

(b) the donee or donees who did not join in making the application,

that the application has been received.

9 (1) A notice under paragraph 6 must be made in the prescribed form.

(2) A notice under paragraph 6, 7 or 8 must include such information, if any, as may be prescribed.

III MEN [122.2]

Notifications and objection periods The Public Guardian gives notice by post in Form LPA003A. See Schedule 4 to Lasting Powers of Attorney, Enduring Powers of Attorney and Public Guardian Regulations 2007, SI 2007/1253. And see now the Lasting Powers of Attorney and Public Guardian (Amendment) Regulations 2013, SI 2013/0506 and the Lasting Powers of Attorney, Enduring Powers of Attorney and Public Guardian (Amendment) Regulations 2015, SI 2015/899.

POWER TO DISPENSE WITH NOTIFICATION REQUIREMENTS

10 The court may—

(a) on the application of the donor, dispense with the requirement to notify under paragraph 6(1), or

(b) on the application of the donee or donees concerned, dispense with the requirement to notify under paragraph 6(2),

if satisfied that no useful purpose would be served by giving the notice.

III MEN [122.3]

Applications to the court Applications to the court should be commenced under Court of Protection Rules 2017, Part 9, noting the provisions of r 9.7 which relate separately to issues of validity and operation of an LPA under ss 22 and 23 of MCA 2005. See **III MEN [590]**.

INSTRUMENT NOT MADE PROPERLY OR CONTAINING INEFFECTIVE PROVISION

11 (1) If it appears to the Public Guardian that an instrument accompanying an application under paragraph 4 is not made in accordance with this Schedule, he must not register the instrument unless the court directs him to do so.

(2) Sub-paragraph (3) applies if it appears to the Public Guardian that the instrument contains a provision which—

- (a) would be ineffective as part of a lasting power of attorney, or
- (b) would prevent the instrument from operating as a valid lasting power of attorney.

(3) The Public Guardian—

- (a) must apply to the court for it to determine the matter under section 23(1), and
- (b) pending the determination by the court, must not register the instrument.

(4) Sub-paragraph (5) applies if the court determines under section 23(1) (whether or not on an application by the Public Guardian) that the instrument contains a provision which—

- (a) would be ineffective as part of a lasting power of attorney, or
- (b) would prevent the instrument from operating as a valid lasting power of attorney.

(5) The court must—

- (a) notify the Public Guardian that it has severed the provision, or
- (b) direct him not to register the instrument.

(6) Where the court notifies the Public Guardian that it has severed a provision, he must register the instrument with a note to that effect attached to it.

III MEN [122.4]

Applications to the court concerning ineffective provisions of an instrument Applications for a determination by the court should be commenced under Court of Protection Rules 2017, Part 9, noting the provisions of r 9.7 which relate separately to issues of validity and operation of an LPA under ss 22 and 23 of MCA 2005. See **III MEN [590]**.

DEPUTY ALREADY APPOINTED

12 (1) Sub-paragraph (2) applies if it appears to the Public Guardian that—

- (a) there is a deputy appointed by the court for the donor, and
- (b) the powers conferred on the deputy would, if the instrument were registered, to any extent conflict with the powers conferred on the attorney.

(2) The Public Guardian must not register the instrument unless the court directs him to do so.

III MEN [122.5]

Applications to the court for directions Applications for a direction by the court should be commenced under Court of Protection Rules 2017, Part 9, noting the provisions of r 9.7 which relate separately to issues of validity and operation of an LPA under ss 22 and 23 of MCA 2005. See **III MEN [590]**.

OBJECTION BY DONEE OR NAMED PERSON

13 (1) Sub-paragraph (2) applies if a donee or a named person—

- (a) receives a notice under paragraph 6, 7 or 8 of an application for the registration of an instrument, and
- (b) before the end of the prescribed period, gives notice to the Public Guardian of an objection to the registration on the ground that an event

mentioned in section 13(3) or (6)(a) to (d) has occurred which has revoked the instrument.

(2) If the Public Guardian is satisfied that the ground for making the objection is established, he must not register the instrument unless the court, on the application of the person applying for the registration—

(a) is satisfied that the ground is not established, and

(b) directs the Public Guardian to register the instrument.

(3) Sub-paragraph (4) applies if a donee or a named person—

(a) receives a notice under paragraph 6, 7 or 8 of an application for the registration of an instrument, and

(b) before the end of the prescribed period—

(i) makes an application to the court objecting to the registration on a prescribed ground, and

(ii) notifies the Public Guardian of the application.

(4) The Public Guardian must not register the instrument unless the court directs him to do so.

III MEN [122.6]

Applying to the court to object The provisions of r 9.7(2) of the Court of Protection Rules 2017 dis-apply the provisions of rr 9.6 and 9.10 in certain circumstances, and the provisions of rr 9.7(3)–9.7(5) apply. See **III MEN [590]**. The appropriate notice to the Public Guardian under para 13(1)(b) is in Form LPA007. The application to the court is in form COP7.

OBJECTION BY DONOR

14 (1) This paragraph applies if the donor—

(a) receives a notice under paragraph 8 of an application for the registration of an instrument, and

(b) before the end of the prescribed period, gives notice to the Public Guardian of an objection to the registration.

(2) The Public Guardian must not register the instrument unless the court, on the application of the donee or, if more than one, any of them—

(a) is satisfied that the donor lacks capacity to object to the registration, and

(b) directs the Public Guardian to register the instrument.

III MEN [122.7]

Procedure for a donor to apply to the court The donor gives notice in Form LPA006. The provisions of rr 9.7(2)–9.7(5) apply to any application made to the court by a donee. See **III MEN [590]**.

NOTIFICATION OF REGISTRATION

15 Where an instrument is registered under this Schedule, the Public Guardian must give notice of the fact in the prescribed form to—

(a) the donor, and

(b) the donee or, if more than one, each of them.

III MEN [122.8]

Relevant forms for notification Schedule 5 of Lasting Powers of Attorney, Enduring Powers of Attorney and Public Guardian Regulations 2007, SI 2007/1253 provides that notice is given in Form LPA004 and see now theLasting Powers of Attorney, Enduring Powers of Attorney and Public Guardian (Amendment) Regulations 2015, SI 2015/899.

EVIDENCE OF REGISTRATION

16 (1) A document purporting to be an office copy of an instrument registered under this Schedule is, in any part of the United Kingdom, evidence of—
(a) the contents of the instrument, and
(b) the fact that it has been registered.
(2) Sub-paragraph (1) is without prejudice to—
(a) section 3 of the Powers of Attorney Act 1971 (c 27) (proof by certified copy), and
(b) any other method of proof authorised by law.

III MEN [122.9]

Regulations See the Lasting Powers of Attorney, Enduring Powers of Attorney and Public Guardian Regulations 2007, SI 2007/1253, regs 10–17 and the Lasting Powers of Attorney, Enduring Powers of Attorney and Public Guardian (Amendment) Regulations 2015, SI 2015/899.

PART 3
CANCELLATION OF REGISTRATION AND NOTIFICATION OF SEVERANCE

III MEN [123]

17 (1) The Public Guardian must cancel the registration of an instrument as a lasting power of attorney on being satisfied that the power has been revoked—
(a) as a result of the donor's bankruptcy, or a debt relief order (under Part 7A of the Insolvency Act 1986) having been made in respect of the donor, or
(b) on the occurrence of an event mentioned in section 13(6)(a) to (d).
(2) If the Public Guardian cancels the registration of an instrument he must notify—
(a) the donor, and
(b) the donee or, if more than one, each of them.

18 The court must direct the Public Guardian to cancel the registration of an instrument as a lasting power of attorney if it—
(a) determines under section 22(2)(a) that a requirement for creating the power was not met,
(b) determines under section 22(2)(b) that the power has been revoked or has otherwise come to an end, or
(c) revokes the power under section 22(4)(b) (fraud etc.).

19 (1) Sub-paragraph (2) applies if the court determines under section 23(1) that a lasting power of attorney contains a provision which—
(a) is ineffective as part of a lasting power of attorney, or
(b) prevents the instrument from operating as a valid lasting power of attorney.
(2) The court must—
(a) notify the Public Guardian that it has severed the provision, or
(b) direct him to cancel the registration of the instrument as a lasting power of attorney.

20 On the cancellation of the registration of an instrument, the instrument and any office copies of it must be delivered up to the Public Guardian to be cancelled.

III MEN [123.1]

• **Regulations** See the Lasting Powers of Attorney, Enduring Powers of Attorney and Public Guardian Regulations 2007, SI 2007/1253, as amended by SI 2007/2161, particularly regs 18-22 regarding steps to be taken if an instrument is changed, revoked, lost or destroyed.

In *The Public Guardian v Miles* [2014] EWCOP 40 the Senior Judge found that provisions in an LPA which sought to re-appoint an original attorney to act alone before any substitute attorney acts where a joint appointment has failed was an ineffective provision and was required to be severed before registration. However this decision was overturned upon appeal before Nugee J in *Miles v Public Guardian and Beattie v Public Guardian* [2015] EWHC 2960 (Ch) finding that 'a purposive and beneficial interpretation of the Act ought to be applied'.

PART 4

RECORDS OF ALTERATIONS IN REGISTERED POWERS

PARTIAL REVOCATION OR SUSPENSION OF POWER AS A RESULT OF BANKRUPTCY

III MEN [124]

21 If in the case of a registered instrument it appears to the Public Guardian that under section 13 a lasting power of attorney is revoked, or suspended, in relation to the donor's property and affairs (but not in relation to other matters), the Public Guardian must attach to the instrument a note to that effect.

TERMINATION OF APPOINTMENT OF DONEE WHICH DOES NOT REVOKE POWER

22 If in the case of a registered instrument it appears to the Public Guardian that an event has occurred—

(a) which has terminated the appointment of the donee, but
(b) which has not revoked the instrument,

the Public Guardian must attach to the instrument a note to that effect.

REPLACEMENT OF DONEE

23 If in the case of a registered instrument it appears to the Public Guardian that the donee has been replaced under the terms of the instrument the Public Guardian must attach to the instrument a note to that effect.

SEVERANCE OF INEFFECTIVE PROVISIONS

24 If in the case of a registered instrument the court notifies the Public Guardian under paragraph 19(2)(a) that it has severed a provision of the instrument, the Public Guardian must attach to it a note to that effect.

NOTIFICATION OF ALTERATIONS

25 If the Public Guardian attaches a note to an instrument under paragraph 21, 22, 23 or 24 he must give notice of the note to the donee or donees of the power (or, as the case may be, to the other donee or donees of the power).

SCHEDULE 1A

PERSONS INELIGIBLE TO BE DEPRIVED OF LIBERTY BY THIS ACT

PART 1
INELIGIBLE PERSONS
APPLICATION

III MEN [125]

1 This Schedule applies for the purposes of—
(a) section 16A, and
(b) paragraph 17 of Schedule A1.

DETERMINING INELIGIBILITY

2 A person ('P') is ineligible to be deprived of liberty by this Act ('ineligible') if—
(a) P falls within one of the cases set out in the second column of the following table, and
(b) the corresponding entry in the third column of the table—or the provision, or one of the provisions, referred to in that entry—provides that he is ineligible.

	Status of P	*Determination of ineligibility*
Case A	P is— (a) subject to the hospital treatment regime, and (b) detained in a hospital under that regime.	P is ineligible.
Case B	P is— (a) subject to the hospital treatment regime, but (b) not detained in a hospital under that regime.	See paragraphs 3 and 4.
Case C	P is subject to the community treatment regime.	See paragraphs 3 and 4.
Case D	P is subject to the guardianship regime.	See paragraphs 3 and 5.
Case E	P is— (a) within the scope of the Mental Health Act, but (b) not subject to any of the mental health regimes.	See paragraph 5.

AUTHORISED COURSE OF ACTION NOT IN ACCORDANCE WITH REGIME

3 (1) This paragraph applies in cases B, C and D in the table in paragraph 2.

MENTAL CAPACITY AND MENTAL HEALTH

(2) P is ineligible if the authorised course of action is not in accordance with a requirement which the relevant regime imposes.
(3) That includes any requirement as to where P is, or is not, to reside.
(4) The relevant regime is the mental health regime to which P is subject.

TREATMENT FOR MENTAL DISORDER IN A HOSPITAL

4 (1) This paragraph applies in cases B and C in the table in paragraph 2.
(2) P is ineligible if the relevant care or treatment consists in whole or in part of medical treatment for mental disorder in a hospital.

P OBJECTS TO BEING A MENTAL HEALTH PATIENT ETC.

5 (1) This paragraph applies in cases D and E in the table in paragraph 2.
(2) P is ineligible if the following conditions are met.
(3) The first condition is that the relevant instrument authorises P to be a mental health patient.
(4) The second condition is that P objects—
(a) to being a mental health patient, or
(b) to being given some or all of the mental health treatment.
(5) The third condition is that a donee or deputy has not made a valid decision to consent to each matter to which P objects.
(6) In determining whether or not P objects to something, regard must be had to all the circumstances (so far as they are reasonably ascertainable), including the following—
(a) P's behaviour;
(b) P's wishes and feelings;
(c) P's views, beliefs and values.
(7) But regard is to be had to circumstances from the past only so far as it is still appropriate to have regard to them.

PART 2
INTERPRETATION

APPLICATION

III MEN [126]

6 This Part applies for the purposes of this Schedule.

MENTAL HEALTH REGIMES

7 The mental health regimes are—
(a) the hospital treatment regime,
(b) the community treatment regime, and
(c) the guardianship regime.

HOSPITAL TREATMENT REGIME

8 (1) P is subject to the hospital treatment regime if he is subject to—
(a) a hospital treatment obligation under the relevant enactment, or
(b) an obligation under another England and Wales enactment which has the same effect as a hospital treatment obligation.

(2) But where P is subject to any such obligation, he is to be regarded as not subject to the hospital treatment regime during any period when he is subject to the community treatment regime.
(3) A hospital treatment obligation is an application, order or direction of a kind listed in the first column of the following table.
(4) In relation to a hospital treatment obligation, the relevant enactment is the enactment in the Mental Health Act which is referred to in the corresponding entry in the second column of the following table.

Hospital treatment obligation	*Relevant enactment*
Application for admission for assessment	Section 2
Application for admission for assessment	Section 4
Application for admission for treatment	Section 3
Order for remand to hospital	Section 35
Order for remand to hospital	Section 36
Hospital order	Section 37
Interim hospital order	Section 38
Order for detention in hospital	Section 44
Hospital direction	Section 45A
Transfer direction	Section 47
Transfer direction	Section 48
Hospital order	Section 51

COMMUNITY TREATMENT REGIME

9 P is subject to the community treatment regime if he is subject to—
(a) a community treatment order under section 17A of the Mental Health Act, or
(b) an obligation under another England and Wales enactment which has the same effect as a community treatment order.

GUARDIANSHIP REGIME

10 P is subject to the guardianship regime if he is subject to—
(a) a guardianship application under section 7 of the Mental Health Act,
(b) a guardianship order under section 37 of the Mental Health Act, or
(c) an obligation under another England and Wales enactment which has the same effect as a guardianship application or guardianship order.

ENGLAND AND WALES ENACTMENTS

11 (1) An England and Wales enactment is an enactment which extends to England and Wales (whether or not it also extends elsewhere).
(2) It does not matter if the enactment is in the Mental Health Act or not.

P WITHIN SCOPE OF MENTAL HEALTH ACT

12 (1) P is within the scope of the Mental Health Act if—

(a) an application in respect of P could be made under section 2 or 3 of the Mental Health Act, and

(b) P could be detained in a hospital in pursuance of such an application, were one made.

(2) The following provisions of this paragraph apply when determining whether an application in respect of P could be made under section 2 or 3 of the Mental Health Act.

(3) If the grounds in section 2(2) of the Mental Health Act are met in P's case, it is to be assumed that the recommendations referred to in section 2(3) of that Act have been given.

(4) If the grounds in section 3(2) of the Mental Health Act are met in P's case, it is to be assumed that the recommendations referred to in section 3(3) of that Act have been given.

(5) In determining whether the ground in section 3(2)(c) of the Mental Health Act is met in P's case, it is to be assumed that the treatment referred to in section 3(2)(c) cannot be provided under this Act.

AUTHORISED COURSE OF ACTION, RELEVANT CARE OR TREATMENT & RELEVANT INSTRUMENT

13 In a case where this Schedule applies for the purposes of section 16A—

'authorised course of action' means any course of action amounting to deprivation of liberty which the order under section 16(2)(a) authorises;

'relevant care or treatment' means any care or treatment which—

(a) comprises, or forms part of, the authorised course of action, or

(b) is to be given in connection with the authorised course of action;

'relevant instrument' means the order under section 16(2)(a).

14 In a case where this Schedule applies for the purposes of paragraph 17 of Schedule A1—

'authorised course of action' means the accommodation of the relevant person in the relevant hospital or care home for the purpose of being given the relevant care or treatment;

'relevant care or treatment' has the same meaning as in Schedule A1;

'relevant instrument' means the standard authorisation under Schedule A1.

15 (1) This paragraph applies where the question whether a person is ineligible to be deprived of liberty by this Act is relevant to either of these decisions—

(a) whether or not to include particular provision ('the proposed provision') in an order under section 16(2)(a);

(b) whether or not to give a standard authorisation under Schedule A1.

(2) A reference in this Schedule to the authorised course of action or the relevant care or treatment is to be read as a reference to that thing as it would be if—

(a) the proposed provision were included in the order, or

(b) the standard authorisation were given.

(3) A reference in this Schedule to the relevant instrument is to be read as follows—

(a) where the relevant instrument is an order under section 16(2)(a): as a reference to the order as it would be if the proposed provision were included in it;

(b) where the relevant instrument is a standard authorisation: as a reference to the standard authorisation as it would be if it were given.

EXPRESSIONS USED IN PARAGRAPH 5

16 (1) These expressions have the meanings given—

'donee' means a donee of a lasting power of attorney granted by P;

'mental health patient' means a person accommodated in a hospital for the purpose of being given medical treatment for mental disorder;

'mental health treatment' means the medical treatment for mental disorder referred to in the definition of 'mental health patient'.

(2) A decision of a donee or deputy is valid if it is made—

(a) within the scope of his authority as donee or deputy, and

(b) in accordance with Part 1 of this Act.

EXPRESSIONS WITH SAME MEANING AS IN MENTAL HEALTH ACT

17 (1) 'Hospital' has the same meaning as in Part 2 of the Mental Health Act.

(2) 'Medical treatment' has the same meaning as in the Mental Health Act.

(3) 'Mental disorder' has the same meaning as in Schedule A1 (see paragraph 14).

SCHEDULE 2

PROPERTY AND AFFAIRS: SUPPLEMENTARY PROVISIONS

WILLS: GENERAL

III MEN [127]

1 Paragraphs 2 to 4 apply in relation to the execution of a will, by virtue of section 18, on behalf of P.

PROVISION THAT MAY BE MADE IN WILL

2 The will may make any provision (whether by disposing of property or exercising a power or otherwise) which could be made by a will executed by P if he had capacity to make it.

WILLS: REQUIREMENTS RELATING TO EXECUTION

3 (1) Sub-paragraph (2) applies if under section 16 the court makes an order or gives directions requiring or authorising a person ('the authorised person') to execute a will on behalf of P.

(2) Any will executed in pursuance of the order or direction—

(a) must state that it is signed by P acting by the authorised person,

(b) must be signed by the authorised person with the name of P and his own name, in the presence of two or more witnesses present at the same time,

(c) must be attested and subscribed by those witnesses in the presence of the authorised person, and

(d) must be sealed with the official seal of the court.

WILLS: EFFECT OF EXECUTION

4 (1) This paragraph applies where a will is executed in accordance with paragraph 3.

(2) The Wills Act 1837 (c 26) has effect in relation to the will as if it were signed by P by his own hand, except that—

(a) section 9 of the 1837 Act (requirements as to signing and attestation) does not apply, and

(b) in the subsequent provisions of the 1837 Act any reference to execution in the manner required by the previous provisions is to be read as a reference to execution in accordance with paragraph 3.

(3) The will has the same effect for all purposes as if—

(a) P had had the capacity to make a valid will, and

(b) the will had been executed by him in the manner required by the 1837 Act.

(4) But sub-paragraph (3) does not have effect in relation to the will—

(a) in so far as it disposes of immovable property outside England and Wales, or

(b) in so far as it relates to any other property or matter if, when the will is executed—

(i) P is domiciled outside England and Wales, and

(ii) the condition in sub-paragraph (5) is met.

(5) The condition is that, under the law of P's domicile, any question of his testamentary capacity would fall to be determined in accordance with the law of a place outside England and Wales.

III MEN [127.1]

Applications for statutory wills and the validity of current wills In *Re D (Statutory Will)* [2010] EWHC 2159 (Ch), [2010] NLJR 1190, [2010] All ER (D) 102 (Aug) HHJ Hodge QC determined that the provisions of the Mental Capacity Act 2005 enabled the court to determine issues concerning the validity of wills and that the role of the Court of Protection was not limited solely to authorising the creation of statutory wills or amending wills where there had been a material change of circumstances. See **III MEN [51]** above. See also *ADS v DSM and JKS (by the Official Solicitor)* [2017] EWCOP 8.

VESTING ORDERS ANCILLARY TO SETTLEMENT ETC.

5 (1) If provision is made by virtue of section 18 for—

(a) the settlement of any property of P, or

(b) the exercise of a power vested in him of appointing trustees or retiring from a trust,

the court may also make as respects the property settled or the trust property such consequential vesting or other orders as the case may require.

(2) The power under sub-paragraph (1) includes, in the case of the exercise of such a power, any order which could have been made in such a case under Part 4 of the Trustee Act 1925 (c 19).

VARIATION OF SETTLEMENTS

6 (1) If a settlement has been made by virtue of section 18, the court may by order vary or revoke the settlement if—

(a) the settlement makes provision for its variation or revocation,

(b) the court is satisfied that a material fact was not disclosed when the settlement was made, or

(c) the court is satisfied that there has been a substantial change of circumstances.

(2) Any such order may give such consequential directions as the court thinks fit.

III MEN [127.2]

Applications to the court in respect of personal injury trusts See **III MEN [51]** and note the decision of HHJ Marshall QC in *The Matter of HM; SM v HM (by the Official Solicitor as*

Litigation Friend) [2012] COPLR 187 which considered the circumstances when it is appropriate to authorise the creation of a trust, in particular a personal injury trust under s 18(1)(h). However in *Watt v ABC* [2016] EWCOP 2532 Charles J as Vice President of the Court found that the decision of HHJ Marshall QC was mistakenly being applied, and should not be seen as suggesting a presumption or default result. What was required was a detailed weighing exercise in each case. Giving guidance his lordship referred to the importance of (a) considering the management regime of a substantial award of damages at the earliest practicable point in time, (b) an analysis of what 'P' has and has not the capacity to do and of his or her likely future capacity or vulnerability. (c) early identification of competing factors relevant to 'P's' circumstances to then balance the factors favouring the use of the statutory scheme relating to deputies against the relevant competing factors in the case, (d) identification of the terms, effects (including taxation and the costs of rival possibilities, and (e) the appropriate listing of the issues. Regard should be made to this decision if such an application is considered appropriate.

VESTING OF STOCK IN CURATOR APPOINTED OUTSIDE ENGLAND AND WALES

7 (1) Sub-paragraph (2) applies if the court is satisfied—

(a) that under the law prevailing in a place outside England and Wales a person ('M') has been appointed to exercise powers in respect of the property or affairs of P on the ground (however formulated) that P lacks capacity to make decisions with respect to the management and administration of his property and affairs, and

(b) that, having regard to the nature of the appointment and to the circumstances of the case, it is expedient that the court should exercise its powers under this paragraph.

(2) The court may direct—

(a) any stocks standing in the name of P, or

(b) the right to receive dividends from the stocks,

to be transferred into M's name or otherwise dealt with as required by M, and may give such directions as the court thinks fit for dealing with accrued dividends from the stocks.

(3) 'Stocks' includes—

(a) shares, and

(b) any funds, annuity or security transferable in the books kept by any body corporate or unincorporated company or society or by an instrument of transfer either alone or accompanied by other formalities,

and 'dividends' is to be construed accordingly.

PRESERVATION OF INTERESTS IN PROPERTY DISPOSED OF ON BEHALF OF PERSON LACKING CAPACITY

8 (1) Sub-paragraphs (2) and (3) apply if—

(a) P's property has been disposed of by virtue of section 18,

(b) under P's will or intestacy, or by a gift perfected or nomination taking effect on his death, any other person would have taken an interest in the property but for the disposal, and

(c) on P's death, any property belonging to P's estate represents the property disposed of.

(2) The person takes the same interest, if and so far as circumstances allow, in the property representing the property disposed of.

(3) If the property disposed of was real property, any property representing it is to be treated, so long as it remains part of P's estate, as if it were real property.

(4) The court may direct that, on a disposal of P's property—

(a) which is made by virtue of section 18, and

(b) which would apart from this paragraph result in the conversion of personal property into real property,

property representing the property disposed of is to be treated, so long as it remains P's property or forms part of P's estate, as if it were personal property.

(5) References in sub-paragraphs (1) to (4) to the disposal of property are to—

(a) the sale, exchange, charging of or other dealing (otherwise than by will) with property other than money;

(b) the removal of property from one place to another;

(c) the application of money in acquiring property;

(d) the transfer of money from one account to another;

and references to property representing property disposed of are to be construed accordingly and as including the result of successive disposals.

(6) The court may give such directions as appear to it necessary or expedient for the purpose of facilitating the operation of sub-paragraphs (1) to (3), including the carrying of money to a separate account and the transfer of property other than money.

9 (1) Sub-paragraph (2) applies if the court has ordered or directed the expenditure of money—

(a) for carrying out permanent improvements on any of P's property, or

(b) otherwise for the permanent benefit of any of P's property.

(2) The court may order that—

(a) the whole of the money expended or to be expended, or

(b) any part of it,

is to be a charge on the property either without interest or with interest at a specified rate.

(3) An order under sub-paragraph (2) may provide for excluding or restricting the operation of paragraph 8(1) to (3).

(4) A charge under sub-paragraph (2) may be made in favour of such person as may be just and, in particular, where the money charged is paid out of P's general estate, may be made in favour of a person as trustee for P.

(5) No charge under sub-paragraph (2) may confer any right of sale or foreclosure during P's lifetime.

POWERS AS PATRON OF BENEFICE

10 (1) Any functions which P has as patron of a benefice may be discharged only by a person ('R') appointed by the court.

(2) R must be an individual capable of appointment under section 8(1)(b) of the 1986 Measure (which provides for an individual able to make a declaration of communicant status, a clerk in Holy Orders, etc. to be appointed to discharge a registered patron's functions).

(3) The 1986 Measure applies to R as it applies to an individual appointed by the registered patron of the benefice under section 8(1)(b) or (3) of that Measure to discharge his functions as patron.

(4) 'The 1986 Measure' means the Patronage (Benefices) Measure 1986 (No 3).

SCHEDULE 3
INTERNATIONAL PROTECTION OF ADULTS

PART 1
PRELIMINARY
INTRODUCTION

III MEN [128]

1 This Part applies for the purposes of this Schedule.

THE CONVENTION

2 (1) 'Convention' means the Convention referred to in section 63.
(2) 'Convention country' means a country in which the Convention is in force.
(3) A reference to an Article or Chapter is to an Article or Chapter of the Convention.
(4) An expression which appears in this Schedule and in the Convention is to be construed in accordance with the Convention.

COUNTRIES, TERRITORIES AND NATIONALS

3 (1) 'Country' includes a territory which has its own system of law.
(2) Where a country has more than one territory with its own system of law, a reference to the country, in relation to one of its nationals, is to the territory with which the national has the closer, or the closest, connection.

ADULTS WITH INCAPACITY

4 (1) 'Adult' means (subject to sub-paragraph (2)) a person who—
(a) as a result of an impairment or insufficiency of his personal faculties, cannot protect his interests, and
(b) has reached 16.
(2) But 'adult' does not include a child to whom either of the following applies:
(a) the Convention on Jurisdiction, Applicable Law, Recognition, Enforcement and Co-operation in Respect of Parental Responsibility and Measures for the Protection of Children that was signed at the Hague on 19th October 1996;
(b) Council Regulation (EC) No. 2201/2003 concerning jurisdiction and the recognition and enforcement of judgments in matrimonial matters and the matters of parental responsibility.

PROTECTIVE MEASURES

5 (1) 'Protective measure' means a measure directed to the protection of the person or property of an adult; and it may deal in particular with any of the following—
(a) the determination of incapacity and the institution of a protective regime,
(b) placing the adult under the protection of an appropriate authority,
(c) guardianship, curatorship or any corresponding system,
(d) the designation and functions of a person having charge of the adult's person or property, or representing or otherwise helping him,

(e) placing the adult in a place where protection can be provided,
(f) administering, conserving or disposing of the adult's property,
(g) authorising a specific intervention for the protection of the person or property of the adult.

(2) Where a measure of like effect to a protective measure has been taken in relation to a person before he reaches 16, this Schedule applies to the measure in so far as it has effect in relation to him once he has reached 16.

CENTRAL AUTHORITY

6 (1) Any function under the Convention of a Central Authority is exercisable in England and Wales by the Lord Chancellor.

(2) A communication may be sent to the Central Authority in relation to England and Wales by sending it to the Lord Chancellor.

PART 2
JURISDICTION OF COMPETENT AUTHORITY

SCOPE OF JURISDICTION

III MEN [129]

7 (1) The court may exercise its functions under this Act (in so far as it cannot otherwise do so) in relation to—
(a) an adult habitually resident in England and Wales,
(b) an adult's property in England and Wales,
(c) an adult present in England and Wales or who has property there, if the matter is urgent, or
(d) an adult present in England and Wales, if a protective measure which is temporary and limited in its effect to England and Wales is proposed in relation to him.

(2) An adult present in England and Wales is to be treated for the purposes of this paragraph as habitually resident there if—
(a) his habitual residence cannot be ascertained,
(b) he is a refugee, or
(c) he has been displaced as a result of disturbance in the country of his habitual residence.

8 (1) The court may also exercise its functions under this Act (in so far as it cannot otherwise do so) in relation to an adult if sub-paragraph (2) or (3) applies in relation to him.

(2) This sub-paragraph applies in relation to an adult if—
(a) he is a British citizen,
(b) he has a closer connection with England and Wales than with Scotland or Northern Ireland, and
(c) Article 7 has, in relation to the matter concerned, been complied with.

(3) This sub-paragraph applies in relation to an adult if the Lord Chancellor, having consulted such persons as he considers appropriate, agrees to a request under Article 8 in relation to the adult.

EXERCISE OF JURISDICTION

9 (1) This paragraph applies where jurisdiction is exercisable under this Schedule in connection with a matter which involves a Convention country other than England and Wales.

(2) Any Article on which the jurisdiction is based applies in relation to the matter in so far as it involves the other country (and the court must, accordingly, comply with any duty conferred on it as a result).

(3) Article 12 also applies, so far as its provisions allow, in relation to the matter in so far as it involves the other country.

10 A reference in this Schedule to the exercise of jurisdiction under this Schedule is to the exercise of functions under this Act as a result of this Part of this Schedule.

PART 3
APPLICABLE LAW

APPLICABLE LAW

III MEN [130]

11 In exercising jurisdiction under this Schedule, the court may, if it thinks that the matter has a substantial connection with a country other than England and Wales, apply the law of that other country.

12 Where a protective measure is taken in one country but implemented in another, the conditions of implementation are governed by the law of the other country.

LASTING POWERS OF ATTORNEY, ETC.

13 (1) If the donor of a lasting power is habitually resident in England and Wales at the time of granting the power, the law applicable to the existence, extent, modification or extinction of the power is—

- (a) the law of England and Wales, or
- (b) if he specifies in writing the law of a connected country for the purpose, that law.

(2) If he is habitually resident in another country at that time, but England and Wales is a connected country, the law applicable in that respect is—

- (a) the law of the other country, or
- (b) if he specifies in writing the law of England and Wales for the purpose, that law.

(3) A country is connected, in relation to the donor, if it is a country—

- (a) of which he is a national,
- (b) in which he was habitually resident, or
- (c) in which he has property.

(4) Where this paragraph applies as a result of sub-paragraph (3)(c), it applies only in relation to the property which the donor has in the connected country.

(5) The law applicable to the manner of the exercise of a lasting power is the law of the country where it is exercised.

(6) In this Part of this Schedule, 'lasting power' means—

- (a) a lasting power of attorney (see section 9),
- (b) an enduring power of attorney within the meaning of Schedule 4, or
- (c) any other power of like effect.

14 (1) Where a lasting power is not exercised in a manner sufficient to guarantee the protection of the person or property of the donor, the court, in exercising jurisdiction under this Schedule, may disapply or modify the power.

(2) Where, in accordance with this Part of this Schedule, the law applicable to the power is, in one or more respects, that of a country other than England and Wales, the court must, so far as possible, have regard to the law of the other country in that respect (or those respects).

15 Regulations may provide for Schedule 1 (lasting powers of attorney: formalities) to apply with modifications in relation to a lasting power which comes within paragraph 13(6)(c) above.

PROTECTION OF THIRD PARTIES

16 (1) This paragraph applies where a person (a 'representative') in purported exercise of an authority to act on behalf of an adult enters into a transaction with a third party.

(2) The validity of the transaction may not be questioned in proceedings, nor may the third party be held liable, merely because—

(a) where the representative and third party are in England and Wales when entering into the transaction, sub-paragraph (3) applies;

(b) where they are in another country at that time, sub-paragraph (4) applies.

(3) This sub-paragraph applies if—

(a) the law applicable to the authority in one or more respects is, as a result of this Schedule, the law of a country other than England and Wales, and

(b) the representative is not entitled to exercise the authority in that respect (or those respects) under the law of that other country.

(4) This sub-paragraph applies if—

(a) the law applicable to the authority in one or more respects is, as a result of this Part of this Schedule, the law of England and Wales, and

(b) the representative is not entitled to exercise the authority in that respect (or those respects) under that law.

(5) This paragraph does not apply if the third party knew or ought to have known that the applicable law was—

(a) in a case within sub-paragraph (3), the law of the other country;

(b) in a case within sub-paragraph (4), the law of England and Wales.

MANDATORY RULES

17 Where the court is entitled to exercise jurisdiction under this Schedule, the mandatory provisions of the law of England and Wales apply, regardless of any system of law which would otherwise apply in relation to the matter.

PUBLIC POLICY

18 Nothing in this Part of this Schedule requires or enables the application in England and Wales of a provision of the law of another country if its application would be manifestly contrary to public policy.

PART 4

RECOGNITION AND ENFORCEMENT

RECOGNITION

III MEN [131]

19 (1) A protective measure taken in relation to an adult under the law of a country other than England and Wales is to be recognised in England and Wales if it was taken on the ground that the adult is habitually resident in the other country.

(2) A protective measure taken in relation to an adult under the law of a Convention country other than England and Wales is to be recognised in England and Wales if it was taken on a ground mentioned in Chapter 2 (jurisdiction).

(3) But the court may disapply this paragraph in relation to a measure if it thinks that—

- (a) the case in which the measure was taken was not urgent,
- (b) the adult was not given an opportunity to be heard, and
- (c) that omission amounted to a breach of natural justice.

(4) It may also disapply this paragraph in relation to a measure if it thinks that—

- (a) recognition of the measure would be manifestly contrary to public policy,
- (b) the measure would be inconsistent with a mandatory provision of the law of England and Wales, or
- (c) the measure is inconsistent with one subsequently taken, or recognised, in England and Wales in relation to the adult.

(5) And the court may disapply this paragraph in relation to a measure taken under the law of a Convention country in a matter to which Article 33 applies, if the court thinks that that Article has not been complied with in connection with that matter.

20 (1) An interested person may apply to the court for a declaration as to whether a protective measure taken under the law of a country other than England and Wales is to be recognised in England and Wales.

(2) No permission is required for an application to the court under this paragraph.

21 For the purposes of paragraphs 19 and 20, any finding of fact relied on when the measure was taken is conclusive.

ENFORCEMENT

22 (1) An interested person may apply to the court for a declaration as to whether a protective measure taken under the law of, and enforceable in, a country other than England and Wales is enforceable, or to be registered, in England and Wales in accordance with Court of Protection Rules.

(2) The court must make the declaration if—

- (a) the measure comes within sub-paragraph (1) or (2) of paragraph 19, and
- (b) the paragraph is not disapplied in relation to it as a result of sub-paragraph (3), (4) or (5).

(3) A measure to which a declaration under this paragraph relates is enforceable in England and Wales as if it were a measure of like effect taken by the court.

MEASURES TAKEN IN RELATION TO THOSE AGED UNDER 16

23 (1) This paragraph applies where—

- (a) provision giving effect to, or otherwise deriving from, the Convention in a country other than England and Wales applies in relation to a person who has not reached 16, and
- (b) a measure is taken in relation to that person in reliance on that provision.

(2) This Part of this Schedule applies in relation to that measure as it applies in relation to a protective measure taken in relation to an adult under the law of a Convention country other than England and Wales.

SUPPLEMENTARY

24 The court may not review the merits of a measure taken outside England and Wales except to establish whether the measure complies with this Schedule in so far as it is, as a result of this Schedule, required to do so.

25 Court of Protection Rules may make provision about an application under paragraph 20 or 22.

PART 5
CO-OPERATION

PROPOSAL FOR CROSS-BORDER PLACEMENT

III MEN [132]

26 (1) This paragraph applies where a public authority proposes to place an adult in an establishment in a Convention country other than England and Wales.
(2) The public authority must consult an appropriate authority in that other country about the proposed placement and, for that purpose, must send it—
(a) a report on the adult, and
(b) a statement of its reasons for the proposed placement.
(3) If the appropriate authority in the other country opposes the proposed placement within a reasonable time, the public authority may not proceed with it.

27 A proposal received by a public authority under Article 33 in relation to an adult is to proceed unless the authority opposes it within a reasonable time.

ADULT IN DANGER ETC.

28 (1) This paragraph applies if a public authority is told that an adult—
(a) who is in serious danger, and
(b) in relation to whom the public authority has taken, or is considering taking, protective measures,
is, or has become resident, in a Convention country other than England and Wales.
(2) The public authority must tell an appropriate authority in that other country about—
(a) the danger, and
(b) the measures taken or under consideration.

29 A public authority may not request from, or send to, an appropriate authority in a Convention country information in accordance with Chapter 5 (co-operation) in relation to an adult if it thinks that doing so—
(a) would be likely to endanger the adult or his property, or
(b) would amount to a serious threat to the liberty or life of a member of the adult's family.

PART 6
GENERAL

CERTIFICATES

III MEN [133]

30 A certificate given under Article 38 by an authority in a Convention country other than England and Wales is, unless the contrary is shown, proof of the matters contained in it.

POWERS TO MAKE FURTHER PROVISION AS TO PRIVATE INTERNATIONAL LAW

31 Her Majesty may by Order in Council confer on the Lord Chancellor, the court or another public authority functions for enabling the Convention to be given effect in England and Wales.

32 (1) Regulations may make provision—
(a) giving further effect to the Convention, or
(b) otherwise about the private international law of England and Wales in relation to the protection of adults.

(2) The regulations may—
(a) confer functions on the court or another public authority;
(b) amend this Schedule;
(c) provide for this Schedule to apply with specified modifications;
(d) make provision about countries other than Convention countries.

EXCEPTIONS

33 Nothing in this Schedule applies, and no provision made under paragraph 32 is to apply, to any matter to which the Convention, as a result of Article 4, does not apply.

REGULATIONS AND ORDERS

34 A reference in this Schedule to regulations or an order (other than an Order in Council) is to regulations or an order made for the purposes of this Schedule by the Lord Chancellor.

COMMENCEMENT

35 The following provisions of this Schedule have effect only if the Convention is in force in accordance with Article 57—
(a) paragraph 8,
(b) paragraph 9,
(c) paragraph 19(2) and (5),
(d) Part 5,
(e) paragraph 30

III MEN [133.1]

The application of Schedule 3 and the issue of jurisdiction These principles were considered by Hedley J *In Re MN* [2010] EWHC 1926 (Fam) in respect of questions concerning the recognition and enforcement of an order of a court of competent jurisdiction in California. It was recorded at that stage that due to absence of ratification, the provisions of The Hague Convention on the International Protection of Adults did not apply, but that s 63 and Schedule 3 of the Act governed the proceedings.

In *Re M* [2012] EWHC 3590 (COP) Mostyn J found that an order made in Eire could be determined as a protective measure for the purposes of paragraph 19(1) of Schedule 3 and that recognition was mandatory subject to limitations provided under paras 19(3) and (4) of the Schedule.

As a result of ratification made on 27 July 2012, the Hague Convention of 1996 on Jurisdiction, Applicable Law, Recognition, Enforcement and Co-operation in Respect of Parental Responsibility and Measures for the Protection of Children came into force for the United Kingdom on 1 November 2012. See Regulation 17, and para 10 of The Parental Responsibility and Measures for the Protection of Children (International Obligations) (England and Wales and Northern Ireland) Regulations 2010 (SI 2010/1898). It is argued that this ratification however is not such as to formally ratify in full the Convention of the International Protection of Adults and this was so held in *In the matter of PO, JO v GO, RO, MP and Inver Clyde Council* [2013] EWHC 3932 (COP), [2013] All ER (D) 151 (Dec) where the

President LJ Munby in considering the jurisdiction of the Court of Protection in relation to a person moved between England and Scotland indicated that the court must turn to the Mental Capacity Act 2005 as opposed to the Convention.

III MEN [133.2]

Habitual residence and the application of Schedule 3 In *In the matter of PO, JO v GO, RO, MP and Inver Clyde Council* [2013] EWHC 3932 (COP), [2013] All ER (D) 151 (Dec) the President, addressing the interpretation of paragraph 7 of Schedule 3 and the meaning of 'habitual residence', noted that neither the Mental Capacity Act 2005 or Hague Convention provided no definition, but he drew upon the Hague convention Explanatory Report of Paul Lagarde dated 5th January 2000, and the decision of Hedley J in *Re MN* [2010] EWHC 1926 (Fam) see above. The President confirmed that the issue of 'habitual residence' was a question of fact to be determined as at the date of the hearing and not at the date of any application. Further that habitual residence can in principle be lost and another habitual residence acquired on the same day. Further that in determining such a fact, the provision of s 1(5) whereby a decision made had to be made in P's best interests was not determinative when addressing the issue of forum.

In *DB* [2016] EWCOP 30 Mr Justice Baker applied these principles in considering the competing arguments over jurisdiction between England and Scotland.

In *The Health Service Executive of Ireland v PA* [20151] EWCOP 38, [2015] All ER (D) 139 (Jun) and in *Re PD* [2015] EWCOP 48, [2015] All ER (D) 225 (Jul) Mr Justice Baker declined to give guidelines in respect of what was said to be similar fact cases finding that the court would apply the provisions of the Act and in particular Schedule 3 to each factual matrix, and that the purpose of Schedule 3 was to facilitate the recognition and enforcement of protective measures for the benefit of vulnerable adults.

SCHEDULE 4
PROVISIONS APPLYING TO EXISTING ENDURING POWERS OF ATTORNEY

PART 1
ENDURING POWERS OF ATTORNEY

ENDURING POWER OF ATTORNEY TO SURVIVE MENTAL INCAPACITY OF DONOR

III MEN [134]

1 (1) Where an individual has created a power of attorney which is an enduring power within the meaning of this Schedule—

(a) the power is not revoked by any subsequent mental incapacity of his,

(b) upon such incapacity supervening, the donee of the power may not do anything under the authority of the power except as provided by sub-paragraph (2) unless or until the instrument creating the power is registered under paragraph 13, and

(c) if and so long as paragraph (b) operates to suspend the donee's authority to act under the power, section 5 of the Powers of Attorney Act 1971 (c 27) (protection of donee and third persons), so far as applicable, applies as if the power had been revoked by the donor's mental incapacity,

and, accordingly, section 1 of this Act does not apply.

(2) Despite sub-paragraph (1)(b), where the attorney has made an application for registration of the instrument then, until it is registered, the attorney may take action under the power—

(a) to maintain the donor or prevent loss to his estate, or

(b) to maintain himself or other persons in so far as paragraph 3(2) permits him to do so.

(3) Where the attorney purports to act as provided by sub-paragraph (2) then, in favour of a person who deals with him without knowledge that the attorney is acting

otherwise than in accordance with sub-paragraph (2)(a) or (b), the transaction between them is as valid as if the attorney were acting in accordance with sub-paragraph (2)(a) or (b).

III MEN [134.1]

Relevant date for execution of an enduring power of attorney instrument For the purposes of the Act, the enduring power of attorney must have been executed prior to 1 October 2007 and be in accordance with para 2 of Sch 4.

CHARACTERISTICS OF AN ENDURING POWER OF ATTORNEY

2 (1) Subject to sub-paragraphs (5) and (6) and paragraph 20, a power of attorney is an enduring power within the meaning of this Schedule if the instrument which creates the power—

(a) is in the prescribed form,
(b) was executed in the prescribed manner by the donor and the attorney, and
(c) incorporated at the time of execution by the donor the prescribed explanatory information.

(2) In this paragraph, 'prescribed' means prescribed by such of the following regulations as applied when the instrument was executed—

(a) the Enduring Powers of Attorney (Prescribed Form) Regulations 1986 (SI 1986/126),
(b) the Enduring Powers of Attorney (Prescribed Form) Regulations 1987 (SI 1987/1612),
(c) the Enduring Powers of Attorney (Prescribed Form) Regulations 1990 (SI 1990/1376),
(d) the Enduring Powers of Attorney (Welsh Language Prescribed Form) Regulations 2000 (SI 2000/289).

(3) An instrument in the prescribed form purporting to have been executed in the prescribed manner is to be taken, in the absence of evidence to the contrary, to be a document which incorporated at the time of execution by the donor the prescribed explanatory information.

(4) If an instrument differs in an immaterial respect in form or mode of expression from the prescribed form it is to be treated as sufficient in point of form and expression.

(5) A power of attorney cannot be an enduring power unless, when he executes the instrument creating it, the attorney is—

(a) an individual who has reached 18 and is not bankrupt or is not subject to a debt relief order (under Part 7A of the Insolvency Act 1986), or
(b) a trust corporation.

(6) A power of attorney which gives the attorney a right to appoint a substitute or successor cannot be an enduring power.

(7) An enduring power is revoked by the bankruptcy of the donor or attorney or the making of a debt relief order (under Part 7A of the Insolvency Act 1986) in respect of the donor or attorney.

(8) But where the donor or attorney is bankrupt merely because an interim bankruptcy restrictions order has effect in respect of him or where the donor or attorney is subject to an interim debt relief restrictions order, the power is suspended for so long as the order has effect.

(9) An enduring power is revoked if the court—

(a) exercises a power under sections 16 to 20 in relation to the donor, and
(b) directs that the enduring power is to be revoked.

(10) No disclaimer of an enduring power, whether by deed or otherwise, is valid unless and until the attorney gives notice of it to the donor or, where paragraph 4(6) or 15(1) applies, to the Public Guardian.

III MEN [134.2]

Applications to the court and appointment of a deputy Sections 16–20 enable the court to make decisions and declarations in respect of an individual who lacks capacity, and to appoint a deputy for property and affairs. An application to the court should have regard to Part 9 of the Court of Protection Rules 2017 and in particular r 9.8. See **III MEN [591]**.

SCOPE OF AUTHORITY ETC. OF ATTORNEY UNDER ENDURING POWER

3 (1) If the instrument which creates an enduring power of attorney is expressed to confer general authority on the attorney, the instrument operates to confer, subject to—

(a) the restriction imposed by sub-paragraph (3), and
(b) any conditions or restrictions contained in the instrument,

authority to do on behalf of the donor anything which the donor could lawfully do by an attorney at the time when the donor executed the instrument.

(2) Subject to any conditions or restrictions contained in the instrument, an attorney under an enduring power, whether general or limited, may (without obtaining any consent) act under the power so as to benefit himself or other persons than the donor to the following extent but no further—

(a) he may so act in relation to himself or in relation to any other person if the donor might be expected to provide for his or that person's needs respectively, and
(b) he may do whatever the donor might be expected to do to meet those needs.

(3) Without prejudice to sub-paragraph (2) but subject to any conditions or restrictions contained in the instrument, an attorney under an enduring power, whether general or limited, may (without obtaining any consent) dispose of the property of the donor by way of gift to the following extent but no further—

(a) he may make gifts of a seasonal nature or at a time, or on an anniversary, of a birth, a marriage or the formation of a civil partnership, to persons (including himself) who are related to or connected with the donor, and
(b) he may make gifts to any charity to whom the donor made or might be expected to make gifts,

provided that the value of each such gift is not unreasonable having regard to all the circumstances and in particular the size of the donor's estate.

III MEN [134.3]

Applications to the court for authority Applications to the court for authority to carry out certain acts in relation to P's property, should be made under Court of Protection Rules 2017 Part 9 (**III MEN [584]**), regard should be had to Practice Direction 9D and Practice Direction 9F. See **III MEN [603]** and **III MEN [605]**.

PART 2
ACTION ON ACTUAL OR IMPENDING INCAPACITY OF DONOR

DUTIES OF ATTORNEY IN EVENT OF ACTUAL OR IMPENDING INCAPACITY OF DONOR

III MEN [135]

4 (1) Sub-paragraphs (2) to (6) apply if the attorney under an enduring power has reason to believe that the donor is or is becoming mentally incapable.

(2) The attorney must, as soon as practicable, make an application to the Public Guardian for the registration of the instrument creating the power.

(3) Before making an application for registration the attorney must comply with the provisions as to notice set out in Part 3 of this Schedule.

(4) An application for registration—
  (a) must be made in the prescribed form, and
  (b) must contain such statements as may be prescribed.
(5) The attorney—
  (a) may, before making an application for the registration of the instrument, refer to the court for its determination any question as to the validity of the power, and
  (b) must comply with any direction given to him by the court on that determination.
(6) No disclaimer of the power is valid unless and until the attorney gives notice of it to the Public Guardian; and the Public Guardian must notify the donor if he receives a notice under this sub-paragraph.
(7) A person who, in an application for registration, makes a statement which he knows to be false in a material particular is guilty of an offence and is liable—
  (a) on summary conviction, to imprisonment for a term not exceeding 12 months or a fine not exceeding the statutory maximum or both;
  (b) on conviction on indictment, to imprisonment for a term not exceeding 2 years or a fine or both.
(8) In this paragraph, 'prescribed' means prescribed by regulations made for the purposes of this Schedule by the Lord Chancellor.

III MEN [135.1]

Applications to the Public Guardian For applications to the Public Guardian regard should be made to Schedule 8 of Lasting Powers of Attorney, Enduring Powers of Attorney and Public Guardian Regulations 2007, SI 2007/1253. Subsequent amendments have occurred pursuant to the Public Guardian (Fees, etc) Regulations 2007 SI 2007/2051, the Lasting Powers of Attorney, Enduring Powers of Attorney and Public Guardian (Amendment) Regulations 2007, SI 2007/2161 and the Lasting Powers of Attorney, Enduring Powers of Attorney and Public Guardian Regulations 2009, SI 2009/1884.

III MEN [135.2]

Applications to the court For applications to the court under para 4(5) the application should be under the Court of Protection Rules 2017, Part 9 with particular regard to r 9.8. See **III MEN [591]**.

PART 3
NOTIFICATION PRIOR TO REGISTRATION

DUTY TO GIVE NOTICE TO RELATIVES

III MEN [136]

5 Subject to paragraph 7, before making an application for registration the attorney must give notice of his intention to do so to all those persons (if any) who are entitled to receive notice by virtue of paragraph 6.

6 (1) Subject to sub-paragraphs (2) to (4), persons of the following classes ('relatives') are entitled to receive notice under paragraph 5—
  (a) the donor's spouse or civil partner,
  (b) the donor's children,
  (c) the donor's parents,
  (d) the donor's brothers and sisters, whether of the whole or half blood,
  (e) the widow, widower or surviving civil partner of a child of the donor,
  (f) the donor's grandchildren,
  (g) the children of the donor's brothers and sisters of the whole blood,
  (h) the children of the donor's brothers and sisters of the half blood,
  (i) the donor's uncles and aunts of the whole blood,
  (j) the children of the donor's uncles and aunts of the whole blood.
(2) A person is not entitled to receive notice under paragraph 5 if—

(a) his name or address is not known to the attorney and cannot be reasonably ascertained by him, or

(b) the attorney has reason to believe that he has not reached 18 or is mentally incapable.

(3) Except where sub-paragraph (4) applies—

(a) no more than 3 persons are entitled to receive notice under paragraph 5, and

(b) in determining the persons who are so entitled, persons falling within the class in sub-paragraph (1)(a) are to be preferred to persons falling within the class in sub-paragraph (1)(b), those falling within the class in sub-paragraph (1)(b) are to be preferred to those falling within the class in sub-paragraph (1)(c), and so on.

(4) Despite the limit of 3 specified in sub-paragraph (3), where—

(a) there is more than one person falling within any of classes (a) to (j) of sub-paragraph (1), and

(b) at least one of those persons would be entitled to receive notice under paragraph 5,

then, subject to sub-paragraph (2), all the persons falling within that class are entitled to receive notice under paragraph 5.

7 (1) An attorney is not required to give notice under paragraph 5—

(a) to himself, or

(b) to any other attorney under the power who is joining in making the application,

even though he or, as the case may be, the other attorney is entitled to receive notice by virtue of paragraph 6.

(2) In the case of any person who is entitled to receive notice by virtue of paragraph 6, the attorney, before applying for registration, may make an application to the court to be dispensed from the requirement to give him notice; and the court must grant the application if it is satisfied—

(a) that it would be undesirable or impracticable for the attorney to give him notice, or

(b) that no useful purpose is likely to be served by giving him notice.

III MEN [136.1]

Applications to the court For applications to the court under para 7(2) the application should be under the Court of Protection Rules 2017, Part 9 with particular regard to r 9.8. See **III MEN [591]**.

DUTY TO GIVE NOTICE TO DONOR

8 (1) Subject to sub-paragraph (2), before making an application for registration the attorney must give notice of his intention to do so to the donor.

(2) Paragraph 7(2) applies in relation to the donor as it applies in relation to a person who is entitled to receive notice under paragraph 5.

CONTENTS OF NOTICES

9 A notice to relatives under this Part of this Schedule must—

(a) be in the prescribed form,

(b) state that the attorney proposes to make an application to the Public Guardian for the registration of the instrument creating the enduring power in question,

(c) inform the person to whom it is given of his right to object to the registration under paragraph 13(4), and

(d) specify, as the grounds on which an objection to registration may be made, the grounds set out in paragraph 13(9).

10 A notice to the donor under this Part of this Schedule—

(a) must be in the prescribed form,

(b) must contain the statement mentioned in paragraph 9(b), and

(c) must inform the donor that, while the instrument remains registered, any revocation of the power by him will be ineffective unless and until the revocation is confirmed by the court.

III MEN [136.2]

Applications to the court and procedure Schedule 7 of Lasting Powers of Attorney, Enduring Powers of Attorney and Public Guardian Regulations 2007, SI 2007/1253 as amended by Public Guardian (Fees, etc.) Regulations 2007 SI 2007/2051 applies to paras 9 and 10 above.

For applications to the court under para 10(c) the application should be under the Court of Protection Rules 2017, Part 9 with particular regard to r 9.8. See **III MEN [591]**.

DUTY TO GIVE NOTICE TO OTHER ATTORNEYS

11 (1) Subject to sub-paragraph (2), before making an application for registration an attorney under a joint and several power must give notice of his intention to do so to any other attorney under the power who is not joining in making the application; and paragraphs 7(2) and 9 apply in relation to attorneys entitled to receive notice by virtue of this paragraph as they apply in relation to persons entitled to receive notice by virtue of paragraph 6.

(2) An attorney is not entitled to receive notice by virtue of this paragraph if—

(a) his address is not known to the applying attorney and cannot reasonably be ascertained by him, or

(b) the applying attorney has reason to believe that he has not reached 18 or is mentally incapable.

SUPPLEMENTARY

12 Despite section 7 of the Interpretation Act 1978 (c 30) (construction of references to service by post), for the purposes of this Part of this Schedule a notice given by post is to be regarded as given on the date on which it was posted.

III MEN [136.3]

Regulations Lasting Powers of Attorney, Enduring Powers of Attorney and Public Guardian Regulations 2007, SI 2007/1253, as amended by SI 2007/2161, regs 23–29 regarding the new procedures for giving notice of intention to register.

PART 4
REGISTRATION

REGISTRATION OF INSTRUMENT CREATING POWER

III MEN [137]

13 (1) If an application is made in accordance with paragraph 4(3) and (4) the Public Guardian must, subject to the provisions of this paragraph, register the instrument to which the application relates.

(2) If it appears to the Public Guardian that—

(a) there is a deputy appointed for the donor of the power created by the instrument, and

MENTAL CAPACITY AND MENTAL HEALTH

(b) the powers conferred on the deputy would, if the instrument were registered, to any extent conflict with the powers conferred on the attorney,

the Public Guardian must not register the instrument except in accordance with the court's directions.

(3) The court may, on the application of the attorney, direct the Public Guardian to register an instrument even though notice has not been given as required by paragraph 4(3) and Part 3 of this Schedule to a person entitled to receive it, if the court is satisfied—

(a) that it was undesirable or impracticable for the attorney to give notice to that person, or

(b) that no useful purpose is likely to be served by giving him notice.

(4) Sub-paragraph (5) applies if, before the end of the period of 5 weeks beginning with the date (or the latest date) on which the attorney gave notice under paragraph 5 of an application for registration, the Public Guardian receives a valid notice of objection to the registration from a person entitled to notice of the application.

(5) The Public Guardian must not register the instrument except in accordance with the court's directions.

(6) Sub-paragraph (7) applies if, in the case of an application for registration—

(a) it appears from the application that there is no one to whom notice has been given under paragraph 5, or

(b) the Public Guardian has reason to believe that appropriate inquiries might bring to light evidence on which he could be satisfied that one of the grounds of objection set out in sub-paragraph (9) was established.

(7) The Public Guardian—

(a) must not register the instrument, and

(b) must undertake such inquiries as he thinks appropriate in all the circumstances.

(8) If, having complied with sub-paragraph (7)(b), the Public Guardian is satisfied that one of the grounds of objection set out in sub-paragraph (9) is established—

(a) the attorney may apply to the court for directions, and

(b) the Public Guardian must not register the instrument except in accordance with the court's directions.

(9) A notice of objection under this paragraph is valid if made on one or more of the following grounds—

(a) that the power purported to have been created by the instrument was not valid as an enduring power of attorney,

(b) that the power created by the instrument no longer subsists,

(c) that the application is premature because the donor is not yet becoming mentally incapable,

(d) that fraud or undue pressure was used to induce the donor to create the power,

(e) that, having regard to all the circumstances and in particular the attorney's relationship to or connection with the donor, the attorney is unsuitable to be the donor's attorney.

(10) If any of those grounds is established to the satisfaction of the court it must direct the Public Guardian not to register the instrument, but if not so satisfied it must direct its registration.

(11) If the court directs the Public Guardian not to register an instrument because it is satisfied that the ground in sub-paragraph (9)(d) or (e) is established, it must by order revoke the power created by the instrument.

(12) If the court directs the Public Guardian not to register an instrument because it is satisfied that any ground in sub-paragraph (9) except that in paragraph (c) is established, the instrument must be delivered up to be cancelled unless the court otherwise directs.

III MEN [137.1]

Applications to the court For applications to the court under paragraph 13 the application should be made under the Court of Protection Rules 2017, Part 9 with particular regard to r 9.8. See **III MEN [591]**.

REGISTER OF ENDURING POWERS

14 The Public Guardian has the function of establishing and maintaining a register of enduring powers for the purposes of this Schedule.

PART 5

LEGAL POSITION AFTER REGISTRATION

EFFECT AND PROOF OF REGISTRATION

III MEN [138]

15 (1) The effect of the registration of an instrument under paragraph 13 is that—

(a) no revocation of the power by the donor is valid unless and until the court confirms the revocation under paragraph 16(3);

(b) no disclaimer of the power is valid unless and until the attorney gives notice of it to the Public Guardian;

(c) the donor may not extend or restrict the scope of the authority conferred by the instrument and no instruction or consent given by him after registration, in the case of a consent, confers any right and, in the case of an instruction, imposes or confers any obligation or right on or creates any liability of the attorney or other persons having notice of the instruction or consent.

(2) Sub-paragraph (1) applies for so long as the instrument is registered under paragraph 13 whether or not the donor is for the time being mentally incapable.

(3) A document purporting to be an office copy of an instrument registered under this Schedule is, in any part of the United Kingdom, evidence of—

(a) the contents of the instrument, and

(b) the fact that it has been so registered.

(4) Sub-paragraph (3) is without prejudice to section 3 of the Powers of Attorney Act 1971 (c 27) (proof by certified copies) and to any other method of proof authorised by law.

FUNCTIONS OF COURT WITH REGARD TO REGISTERED POWER

16 (1) Where an instrument has been registered under paragraph 13, the court has the following functions with respect to the power and the donor of and the attorney appointed to act under the power.

(2) The court may—

(a) determine any question as to the meaning or effect of the instrument;

(b) give directions with respect to—

(i) the management or disposal by the attorney of the property and affairs of the donor;

(ii) the rendering of accounts by the attorney and the production of the records kept by him for the purpose;

(iii) the remuneration or expenses of the attorney whether or not in default of or in accordance with any provision made by the instrument, including directions for the repayment of excessive or the payment of additional remuneration;

(c) require the attorney to supply information or produce documents or things in his possession as attorney;

(d) give any consent or authorisation to act which the attorney would have to obtain from a mentally capable donor;

(e) authorise the attorney to act so as to benefit himself or other persons than the donor otherwise than in accordance with paragraph 3(2) and (3) (but subject to any conditions or restrictions contained in the instrument);

(f) relieve the attorney wholly or partly from any liability which he has or may have incurred on account of a breach of his duties as attorney.

(3) On application made for the purpose by or on behalf of the donor, the court must confirm the revocation of the power if satisfied that the donor—

(a) has done whatever is necessary in law to effect an express revocation of the power, and

(b) was mentally capable of revoking a power of attorney when he did so (whether or not he is so when the court considers the application).

(4) The court must direct the Public Guardian to cancel the registration of an instrument registered under paragraph 13 in any of the following circumstances—

(a) on confirming the revocation of the power under sub-paragraph (3),

(b) on directing under paragraph 2(9)(b) that the power is to be revoked,

(c) on being satisfied that the donor is and is likely to remain mentally capable,

(d) on being satisfied that the power has expired or has been revoked by the mental incapacity of the attorney,

(e) on being satisfied that the power was not a valid and subsisting enduring power when registration was effected,

(f) on being satisfied that fraud or undue pressure was used to induce the donor to create the power,

(g) on being satisfied that, having regard to all the circumstances and in particular the attorney's relationship to or connection with the donor, the attorney is unsuitable to be the donor's attorney.

(5) If the court directs the Public Guardian to cancel the registration of an instrument on being satisfied of the matters specified in sub-paragraph (4)(f) or (g) it must by order revoke the power created by the instrument.

(6) If the court directs the cancellation of the registration of an instrument under sub-paragraph (4) except paragraph (c) the instrument must be delivered up to the Public Guardian to be cancelled, unless the court otherwise directs.

III MEN [138.1]

Applications to the court For applications to the court under paragraphs 16(2), (3), (4) and (6) the application should be under the Court of Protection Rules 2017, Part 9 with particular regard to r 9.8. See **III MEN [591]**.

In *AB (Revocation of Enduring Power of Attorney* [2014] EWCOP 12, followed in *Re G* [2015] EWCOP 66, [2015] All ER (D) 143 (Oct), Senior Judge Lush reviewed the history of the approach of the former Court of Protection in considering the 'unsuitability' of an attorney. In distinguishing the criteria for revoking an LPA, he stressed the fact specific nature of each case when applying the relevant provisions and principles of the Mental Capacity Act 2005. This approach was further demonstrated in *Re RG* [2015] EWCOP 2 where the Senior Judge distinguished the acts of the joint and several attorneys and referring to the importance of respecting the rights of RG in accordance with Article 12.4 of the United Nations Convention on the Rights of Persons with Disabilities, and of complying with resolution 1859 of the Parliamentary Assembly of the Council of Europe(passed on 25 January 2012), he found on the facts that limiting the instrument to a sole attorney had regard to this being the least restrictive alternative to appointing a deputy for property and affairs.

In *Re SF* [2015] EWCOP 68, [2015] All ER (D) 236 (Oct) Senior Judge Lush highlighted the fiduciary duty of attorneys and drew attention to Chapter 7 of the Code of Practice, in particular 7.79, recording that 'all attorneys must comply with the duties described in paras 7.58–7.68 of the Code'. In *Re P* [2015] EWCOP 37, [2015] All ER (D) 117 (Jun) the Senior Judge had reviewed the differential in the criteria for removing attorneys under a Lasting Power of Attorney with those applicable to an Enduring Power of Attorney, but also the distinct financial duties (paras 28–35).

In a decision of the Senior Judge in *Re DT* [2015] EWCOP 10, [2015] All ER (D) 48 (Mar) the court in dismissing an application to revoke an Enduring Power of Attorney referred to the judgment of HHJ Hazel Marshall QC in *Re S and S (Protected Persons)* [2008] COPLR Con Vol 1074 determining that the wishes of the donor were neither irrational, impracticable or irresponsible in seeking the continuance of her sons to continue to act as her attorneys.

The court in *Re ED* [2015] EWCOP 26, [2015] All ER (D) 147 (Apr) drew attention to the criminal sanctions contained in para 4(7) of Schedule 4 (see **III MEN [135]**) in revoking an Enduring Power of Attorney where one of the Attorneys had made a false statement when completing from EP2PG for the purposes of registering the Instrument with the Office of Public Guardian.

CANCELLATION OF REGISTRATION BY PUBLIC GUARDIAN

17 The Public Guardian must cancel the registration of an instrument creating an enduring power of attorney—

(a) on receipt of a disclaimer signed by the attorney;

(b) if satisfied that the power has been revoked by the death or bankruptcy of the donor or attorney or the making of a debt relief order (under Part 7A of the Insolvency Act 1986) in respect of the donor or attorney or, if the attorney is a body corporate, by its winding up or dissolution;

(c) on receipt of notification from the court that the court has revoked the power;

(d) on confirmation from the court that the donor has revoked the power.

PART 6
PROTECTION OF ATTORNEY AND THIRD PARTIES

PROTECTION OF ATTORNEY AND THIRD PERSONS WHERE POWER IS INVALID OR REVOKED

III MEN [139]

18 (1) Sub-paragraphs (2) and (3) apply where an instrument which did not create a valid power of attorney has been registered under paragraph 13 (whether or not the registration has been cancelled at the time of the act or transaction in question).

(2) An attorney who acts in pursuance of the power does not incur any liability (either to the donor or to any other person) because of the non-existence of the power unless at the time of acting he knows—

(a) that the instrument did not create a valid enduring power,

(b) that an event has occurred which, if the instrument had created a valid enduring power, would have had the effect of revoking the power, or

(c) that, if the instrument had created a valid enduring power, the power would have expired before that time.

(3) Any transaction between the attorney and another person is, in favour of that person, as valid as if the power had then been in existence, unless at the time of the transaction that person has knowledge of any of the matters mentioned in sub-paragraph (2).

(4) If the interest of a purchaser depends on whether a transaction between the attorney and another person was valid by virtue of sub-paragraph (3), it is conclusively presumed in favour of the purchaser that the transaction was valid if—

(a) the transaction between that person and the attorney was completed within 12 months of the date on which the instrument was registered, or

(b) that person makes a statutory declaration, before or within 3 months after the completion of the purchase, that he had no reason at the time of the transaction to doubt that the attorney had authority to dispose of the property which was the subject of the transaction.

(5) For the purposes of section 5 of the Powers of Attorney Act 1971 (c 27) (protection where power is revoked) in its application to an enduring power the

revocation of which by the donor is by virtue of paragraph 15 invalid unless and until confirmed by the court under paragraph 16—

(a) knowledge of the confirmation of the revocation is knowledge of the revocation of the power, but

(b) knowledge of the unconfirmed revocation is not.

FURTHER PROTECTION OF ATTORNEY AND THIRD PERSONS

19 (1) If—

(a) an instrument framed in a form prescribed as mentioned in paragraph 2(2) creates a power which is not a valid enduring power, and

(b) the power is revoked by the mental incapacity of the donor,

sub-paragraphs (2) and (3) apply, whether or not the instrument has been registered.

(2) An attorney who acts in pursuance of the power does not, by reason of the revocation, incur any liability (either to the donor or to any other person) unless at the time of acting he knows—

(a) that the instrument did not create a valid enduring power, and

(b) that the donor has become mentally incapable.

(3) Any transaction between the attorney and another person is, in favour of that person, as valid as if the power had then been in existence, unless at the time of the transaction that person knows—

(a) that the instrument did not create a valid enduring power, and

(b) that the donor has become mentally incapable.

(4) Paragraph 18(4) applies for the purpose of determining whether a transaction was valid by virtue of sub-paragraph (3) as it applies for the purpose or determining whether a transaction was valid by virtue of paragraph 18(3).

PART 7

JOINT AND JOINT AND SEVERAL ATTORNEYS

APPLICATION TO APPOINT JOINT AND JOINT AND SEVERAL ATTORNEYS

III MEN [140]

20 (1) An instrument which appoints more than one person to be an attorney cannot create an enduring power unless the attorneys are appointed to act—

(a) jointly, or

(b) jointly and severally.

(2) This Schedule, in its application to joint attorneys, applies to them collectively as it applies to a single attorney but subject to the modifications specified in paragraph 21.

(3) This Schedule, in its application to joint and several attorneys, applies with the modifications specified in sub-paragraphs (4) to (7) and in paragraph 22.

(4) A failure, as respects any one attorney, to comply with the requirements for the creation of enduring powers—

(a) prevents the instrument from creating such a power in his case, but

(b) does not affect its efficacy for that purpose as respects the other or others or its efficacy in his case for the purpose of creating a power of attorney which is not an enduring power.

(5) If one or more but not both or all the attorneys makes or joins in making an application for registration of the instrument—

(a) an attorney who is not an applicant as well as one who is may act pending the registration of the instrument as provided in paragraph 1(2),

(b) notice of the application must also be given under Part 3 of this Schedule to the other attorney or attorneys, and

(c) objection may validly be taken to the registration on a ground relating to an attorney or to the power of an attorney who is not an applicant as well as to one or the power of one who is an applicant.

(6) The Public Guardian is not precluded by paragraph 13(5) or (8) from registering an instrument and the court must not direct him not to do so under paragraph 13(10) if an enduring power subsists as respects some attorney who is not affected by the ground or grounds of the objection in question; and where the Public Guardian registers an instrument in that case, he must make against the registration an entry in the prescribed form.

(7) Sub-paragraph (6) does not preclude the court from revoking a power in so far as it confers a power on any other attorney in respect of whom the ground in paragraph 13(9)(d) or (e) is established; and where any ground in paragraph 13(9) affecting any other attorney is established the court must direct the Public Guardian to make against the registration an entry in the prescribed form.

(8) In sub-paragraph (4), 'the requirements for the creation of enduring powers' means the provisions of—

(a) paragraph 2 other than sub-paragraphs (8) and (9), and

(b) the regulations mentioned in paragraph 2.

JOINT ATTORNEYS

21 (1) In paragraph 2(5), the reference to the time when the attorney executes the instrument is to be read as a reference to the time when the second or last attorney executes the instrument.

(2) In paragraph 2(6) to (8), the reference to the attorney is to be read as a reference to any attorney under the power.

(3) Paragraph 13 has effect as if the ground of objection to the registration of the instrument specified in sub-paragraph (9)(e) applied to any attorney under the power.

(4) In paragraph 16(2), references to the attorney are to be read as including references to any attorney under the power.

(5) In paragraph 16(4), references to the attorney are to be read as including references to any attorney under the power.

(6) In paragraph 17, references to the attorney are to be read as including references to any attorney under the power.

JOINT AND SEVERAL ATTORNEYS

22 (1) In paragraph 2(7), the reference to the bankruptcy of the attorney is to be read as a reference to the bankruptcy of the last remaining attorney under the power; and the bankruptcy of any other attorney under the power causes that person to cease to be an attorney under the power.

(1A) In paragraph 2(7), the reference to the making of a debt relief order (under Part 7A of the Insolvency Act 1986) in respect of the attorney is to be read as a reference to the making of a debt relief order in respect of the last remaining attorney under the power; and the making of a debt relief order in respect of any other attorney under the power causes that person to cease to be an attorney under the power.

(2) In paragraph 2(8), the reference to the suspension of the power is to be read as a reference to its suspension in so far as it relates to the attorney in respect of whom the interim bankruptcy restrictions order has effect.

(2A) In paragraph 2(8) the reference to the suspension of the power is to be read as a reference to its suspension in so far as it relates to the attorney in respect of whom the interim debt relief restrictions order has effect.

(3) The restriction upon disclaimer imposed by paragraph 4(6) applies only to those attorneys who have reason to believe that the donor is or is becoming mentally incapable.

III MEN [140.1]

Ability to appoint successive attorneyships In *The Matter of J (Enduring Power of Attorney)* [2009] EWHC 436 (Ch) Lewison J held that the provisions of paragraph 20(1) of the Schedule should be construed as permitting a donor to appoint successive attorneyships by a single document.

PART 8
INTERPRETATION

III MEN [141]

23 (1) In this Schedule—

'enduring power' is to be construed in accordance with paragraph 2,

'mentally incapable' or 'mental incapacity', except where it refers to revocation at common law, means in relation to any person, that he is incapable by reason of mental disorder of managing and administering his property and affairs and 'mentally capable' and 'mental capacity' are to be construed accordingly,

'notice' means notice in writing, and

'prescribed', except for the purposes of paragraph 2, means prescribed by regulations made for the purposes of this Schedule by the Lord Chancellor.

(1A) In sub-paragraph (1), 'mental disorder' has the same meaning as in the Mental Health Act but disregarding the amendments made to that Act by the Mental Health Act 2007.

(2) Any question arising under or for the purposes of this Schedule as to what the donor of the power might at any time be expected to do is to be determined by assuming that he had full mental capacity at the time but otherwise by reference to the circumstances existing at that time.

III MEN [141.1]

Relevant applicable regulations Lasting Powers of Attorney, Enduring Powers of Attorney and Public Guardian Regulations 2007, SI 2007/1253 as amended by Public Guardian (Fees, etc.) Regulations 2007, SI 2007/2051, the Lasting Powers of Attorney, Enduring Powers of Attorney and Public Guardian (Amendment) Regulations 2007, SI 2007/2161, the Lasting Powers of Attorney, Enduring Powers of Attorney and Public Guardian (Amendment) Regulations 2009, SI 2009/1884, the Lasting Powers of Attorney, Enduring Powers of Attorney and Public Guardian (Amendment) Regulations 2010, SI 2010/1063, the Public Guardian Fees etc) (Amendment) Regulations 2011, SI 2011/2189, the Lasting Powers of Attorney, Enduring Powers of Attorney and Public Guardian (Amendment) Regulations 2013, SI 2013/506, and now see the Lasting Powers of Attorney, Enduring Powers of Attorney and Public Guardian (Amendment) Regulations 2015, SI 2015/899.

SCHEDULE 5
TRANSITIONAL PROVISIONS AND SAVINGS

PART 1
REPEAL OF PART 7 OF THE MENTAL HEALTH ACT 1983

EXISTING RECEIVERS

III MEN [142]

1 (1) This paragraph applies where, immediately before the commencement day, there is a receiver ('R') for a person ('P') appointed under section 99 of the Mental Health Act.

(2) On and after that day—

(a) this Act applies as if R were a deputy appointed for P by the court, but with the functions that R had as receiver immediately before that day, and

(b) a reference in any other enactment to a deputy appointed by the court includes a person appointed as a deputy as a result of paragraph (a).

(3) On any application to it by R, the court may end R's appointment as P's deputy.

(4) Where, as a result of section 20(1), R may not make a decision on behalf of P in relation to a relevant matter, R must apply to the court.

(5) If, on the application, the court is satisfied that P is capable of managing his property and affairs in relation to the relevant matter—

(a) it must make an order ending R's appointment as P's deputy in relation to that matter, but

(b) it may, in relation to any other matter, exercise in relation to P any of the powers which it has under sections 15 to 19.

(6) If it is not satisfied, the court may exercise in relation to P any of the powers which it has under sections 15 to 19.

(7) R's appointment as P's deputy ceases to have effect if P dies.

(8) 'Relevant matter' means a matter in relation to which, immediately before the commencement day, R was authorised to act as P's receiver.

(9) In sub-paragraph (1), the reference to a receiver appointed under section 99 of the Mental Health Act includes a reference to a person who by virtue of Schedule 5 to that Act was deemed to be a receiver appointed under that section.

ORDERS, APPOINTMENTS ETC.

2 (1) Any order or appointment made, direction or authority given or other thing done which has, or by virtue of Schedule 5 to the Mental Health Act was deemed to have, effect under Part 7 of the Act immediately before the commencement day is to continue to have effect despite the repeal of Part 7.

(2) In so far as any such order, appointment, direction, authority or thing could have been made, given or done under sections 15 to 20 if those sections had then been in force—

(a) it is to be treated as made, given or done under those sections, and

(b) the powers of variation and discharge conferred by section 16(7) apply accordingly.

(3) Sub-paragraph (1)—

(a) does not apply to nominations under section 93(1) or (4) of the Mental Health Act, and

(b) as respects receivers, has effect subject to paragraph 1.

(4) This Act does not affect the operation of section 109 of the Mental Health Act (effect and proof of orders etc.) in relation to orders made and directions given under Part 7 of that Act.

(5) This paragraph is without prejudice to section 16 of the Interpretation Act 1978 (c 30) (general savings on repeal).

PENDING PROCEEDINGS

3 (1) Any application for the exercise of a power under Part 7 of the Mental Health Act which is pending immediately before the commencement day is to be treated, in so far as a corresponding power is exercisable under sections 16 to 20, as an application for the exercise of that power.

(2) For the purposes of sub-paragraph (1) an application for the appointment of a receiver is to be treated as an application for the appointment of a deputy.

APPEALS

4 (1) Part 7 of the Mental Health Act and the rules made under it are to continue to apply to any appeal brought by virtue of section 105 of that Act which has not been determined before the commencement day.

(2) If in the case of an appeal brought by virtue of section 105(1) (appeal to nominated judge) the judge nominated under section 93 of the Mental Health Act has begun to hear the appeal, he is to continue to do so but otherwise it is to be heard by a puisne judge of the High Court nominated under section 46.

FEES

5 All fees and other payments which, having become due, have not been paid to the former Court of Protection before the commencement day, are to be paid to the new Court of Protection.

COURT RECORDS

6 (1) The records of the former Court of Protection are to be treated, on and after the commencement day, as records of the new Court of Protection and are to be dealt with accordingly under the Public Records Act 1958 (c 51).

(2) On and after the commencement day, the Public Guardian is, for the purpose of exercising any of his functions, to be given such access as he may require to such of the records mentioned in sub-paragraph (1) as relate to the appointment of receivers under section 99 of the Mental Health Act.

EXISTING CHARGES

7 This Act does not affect the operation in relation to a charge created before the commencement day of—

(a) so much of section 101(6) of the Mental Health Act as precludes a charge created under section 101(5) from conferring a right of sale or foreclosure during the lifetime of the patient, or

(b) section 106(6) of the Mental Health Act (charge created by virtue of section 106(5) not to cause interest to fail etc.).

PRESERVATION OF INTERESTS ON DISPOSAL OF PROPERTY

8 Paragraph 8(1) of Schedule 2 applies in relation to any disposal of property (within the meaning of that provision) by a person living on 1st November 1960, being a disposal effected under the Lunacy Act 1890 (c 5) as it applies in relation to the disposal of property effected under sections 16 to 20.

ACCOUNTS

9 Court of Protection Rules may provide that, in a case where paragraph 1 applies, R is to have a duty to render accounts—

(a) while he is receiver;

(b) after he is discharged.

INTERPRETATION

10 In this Part of this Schedule—

(a) 'the commencement day' means the day on which section 66(1)(a) (repeal of Part 7 of the Mental Health Act) comes into force,
(b) 'the former Court of Protection' means the office abolished by section 45, and
(c) 'the new Court of Protection' means the court established by that section.

PART 2
REPEAL OF THE ENDURING POWERS OF ATTORNEY ACT 1985

ORDERS, DETERMINATIONS, ETC.

III MEN [143]–III MEN [429]

11 (1) Any order or determination made, or other thing done, under the 1985 Act which has effect immediately before the commencement day continues to have effect despite the repeal of that Act.
(2) In so far as any such order, determination or thing could have been made or done under Schedule 4 if it had then been in force—
(a) it is to be treated as made or done under that Schedule, and
(b) the powers of variation and discharge exercisable by the court apply accordingly.
(3) Any instrument registered under the 1985 Act is to be treated as having been registered by the Public Guardian under Schedule 4.
(4) This paragraph is without prejudice to section 16 of the Interpretation Act 1978 (c 30) (general savings on repeal).

PENDING PROCEEDINGS

12 (1) An application for the exercise of a power under the 1985 Act which is pending immediately before the commencement day is to be treated, in so far as a corresponding power is exercisable under Schedule 4, as an application for the exercise of that power.
(2) For the purposes of sub-paragraph (1)—
(a) a pending application under section 4(2) of the 1985 Act for the registration of an instrument is to be treated as an application to the Public Guardian under paragraph 4 of Schedule 4 and any notice given in connection with that application under Schedule 1 to the 1985 Act is to be treated as given under Part 3 of Schedule 4,
(b) a notice of objection to the registration of an instrument is to be treated as a notice of objection under paragraph 13 of Schedule 4, and
(c) pending proceedings under section 5 of the 1985 Act are to be treated as proceedings on an application for the exercise by the court of a power which would become exercisable in relation to an instrument under paragraph 16(2) of Schedule 4 on its registration.

APPEALS

13 (1) The 1985 Act and, so far as relevant, the provisions of Part 7 of the Mental Health Act and the rules made under it as applied by section 10 of the 1985 Act are to continue to have effect in relation to any appeal brought by virtue of section 10(1)(c) of the 1985 Act which has not been determined before the commencement day.
(2) If, in the case of an appeal brought by virtue of section 105(1) of the Mental Health Act as applied by section 10(1)(c) of the 1985 Act (appeal to nominated

judge), the judge nominated under section 93 of the Mental Health Act has begun to hear the appeal, he is to continue to do so but otherwise the appeal is to be heard by a puisne judge of the High Court nominated under section 46.

EXERCISE OF POWERS OF DONOR AS TRUSTEE

14 (1) Section 2(8) of the 1985 Act (which prevents a power of attorney under section 25 of the Trustee Act 1925 (c 19) as enacted from being an enduring power) is to continue to apply to any enduring power—

(a) created before 1st March 2000, and

(b) having effect immediately before the commencement day.

(2) Section 3(3) of the 1985 Act (which entitles the donee of an enduring power to exercise the donor's powers as trustee) is to continue to apply to any enduring power to which, as a result of the provision mentioned in sub-paragraph (3), it applies immediately before the commencement day.

(3) The provision is section 4(3)(a) of the Trustee Delegation Act 1999 (c 15) (which provides for section 3(3) of the 1985 Act to cease to apply to an enduring power when its registration is cancelled, if it was registered in response to an application made before 1st March 2001).

(4) Even though section 4 of the 1999 Act is repealed by this Act, that section is to continue to apply in relation to an enduring power—

(a) to which section 3(3) of the 1985 Act applies as a result of sub-paragraph (2), or

(b) to which, immediately before the repeal of section 4 of the 1999 Act, section 1 of that Act applies as a result of section 4 of it.

(5) The reference in section 1(9) of the 1999 Act to section 4(6) of that Act is to be read with sub-paragraphs (2) to (4).

INTERPRETATION

15 In this Part of this Schedule, 'the commencement day' means the day on which section 66(1)(b) (repeal of the 1985 Act) comes into force.

MENTAL CAPACITY ACT 2005: CODE OF PRACTICE

GENERAL NOTES ON THE MENTAL CAPACITY ACT 2005: CODE OF PRACTICE

III MEN [430]

The Mental Capacity Act 2005, covering England and Wales, provides a statutory framework for people who lack capacity to make decisions for themselves, or who have capacity and want to make preparations for a time when they may lack capacity in the future. It sets out who can take decisions, in which situations, and how they should go about this. The Act received Royal Assent on 7 April 2005 and will come into force during 2007.

The legal framework provided by the Mental Capacity Act 2005 is supported by the Code of Practice, which provides guidance and information about how the Act works in practice. Section 42 of the Act requires the Lord Chancellor to produce a Code of Practice for the guidance of a range of people with different duties and functions under the Act.

The Code has statutory force, which means that certain categories of people have a legal duty to have regard to it when working with or caring for adults who may lack capacity to make decisions for themselves. These categories of people are listed in the Code.

The Mental Capacity Act 2005: Code of Practice can be found online, on the GOV.UK website, at: www.gov.uk/government/uploads/system/uploads/attachment_data/file/497253/Mental-capacity-act-code-of-practice.pdf.

LASTING POWERS OF ATTORNEY, ENDURING POWERS OF ATTORNEY AND PUBLIC GUARDIAN REGULATIONS 2007

2007 No 1253

MENTAL CAPACITY AND MENTAL HEALTH

GENERAL NOTES ON THE LASTING POWERS OF ATTORNEY, ENDURING POWERS OF ATTORNEY AND PUBLIC GUARDIAN REGULATIONS

III MEN [431]

Commencement and scope of the Regulations The Lasting Powers of Attorney, Enduring Powers of Attorney and Public Guardian Regulations 2007, SI 2007/1253 were made on 16 April 2007 to come into force on 1 October 2007. They provide for changes under three main headings: Lasting Powers of Attorney, Enduring Powers of Attorney and the functions of the Public Guardian. Note the procedural changes made by the amending regulations in SI 2013/506.

III MEN [432]

Lasting powers of attorney Sections 5 to 22 of the Mental Capacity Act 2005 provide for the creation, registration and revocation of lasting powers of attorney. Like enduring powers of attorney, they enable the attorney to take decisions on behalf of the donor of the power which the donor no longer has the legal capacity to take. But there are significant differences. A lasting power is not created unless it has been made in the prescribed form and registered in accordance with the Act. Different forms are to be used according to whether the instrument is intended to confer authority to make decisions about the donor's personal welfare or about the donor's property and affairs. Regulations 18 to 22 specify steps to be taken if an instrument is changed, revoked, lost or destroyed.

III MEN [433]

Enduring powers of attorney Although no new enduring powers of attorney may be created, there are many already in existence which may be exercised on behalf of living donors. Regulations 23 to 29 lay down the new procedures for giving notice of intention to register them.

III MEN [434]

The Public Guardian Regulations 30 to 48 make further provision for the functions of the Public Guardian, a new office created by s 57 of the Mental Capacity Act 2005, with effect from 1 October 2007. The main statutory functions are set out in s 58, at **III MEN [96]**.

PART 1
PRELIMINARY

III MEN [435]

1 Citation and commencement

(1) These Regulations may be cited as the Lasting Powers of Attorney, Enduring Powers of Attorney and Public Guardian Regulations 2007.

(2) These Regulations shall come into force on 1 October 2007.

III MEN [436]

2 Interpretation

(1) In these Regulations—

"the Act" means the Mental Capacity Act 2005;

"court" means the Court of Protection;

"LPA certificate", in relation to an instrument made with a view to creating a lasting power of attorney, means the certificate which is required to be included in the instrument by virtue of paragraph 2(1)(e) of Schedule 1 to the Act;

"person to notify", in relation to an instrument made with a view to creating a lasting power of attorney, means a person who, under Schedule 1, paragraph 2(1)(c)(i) of the Act, is named in the instrument as being a person to be notified of any application for the registration of the instrument;

MENTAL CAPACITY AND MENTAL HEALTH

"prescribed information", in relation to any instrument intended to create a lasting power of attorney, means the information contained in the form used for the instrument which appears under the heading "Section 8—Your legal rights and responsibilities".

III MEN [437]

3 Minimal differences from forms prescribed in these Regulations

(1) In these Regulations, any reference to a form—

(a) in the case of a form set out in Schedules 1 to 7 to these Regulations, is to be regarded as including a Welsh version of that form; and

(b) in the case of a form set out in Schedules 2 to 7 to these Regulations, is to be regarded as also including—

(i) a form to the same effect but which differs in an immaterial respect in form or mode of expression;

(ii) a form to the same effect but with such variations as the circumstances may require or the court or the Public Guardian may approve; or

(iii) a Welsh version of a form within (i) or (ii).

III MEN [438]

4 Computation of time

(1) This regulation shows how to calculate any period of time which is specified in these Regulations.

(2) A period of time expressed as a number of days must be computed as clear days.

(3) Where the specified period is 7 days or less, and would include a day which is not a business day, that day does not count.

(4) When the specified period for doing any act at the office of the Public Guardian ends on a day on which the office is closed, that act will be done in time if done on the next day on which the office is open.

(5) In this regulation—

"business day" means a day other than—

(a) a Saturday, Sunday, Christmas Day or Good Friday; or

(b) a bank holiday under the Banking and Financial Dealings Act 1971, in England and Wales; and

"clear days" means that in computing the number of days—

(a) the day on which the period begins, and

(b) if the end of the period is defined by reference to an event, the day on which that event occurs,

are not included.

PART 2
LASTING POWERS OF ATTORNEY

INSTRUMENTS INTENDED TO CREATE A LASTING POWER OF ATTORNEY

III MEN [439]

5 Forms for lasting powers of attorney

The forms set out in Parts 1 and 2 of Schedule 1 to these Regulations are the forms which, in the circumstances to which they apply, are to be used for instruments intended to create a lasting power of attorney.

III MEN [440]

6 Maximum number of [people to notify]

The maximum number of people to notify that the donor of a lasting power of attorney may specify in the instrument intended to create the power is 5.

III MEN [441]

7 . . .

Revoked.

III MEN [442]

8 Persons who may provide an LPA certificate

(1) Subject to paragraph (3), the following persons may give an LPA certificate—

(a) a person chosen by the donor as being someone who has known him personally for the period of at least two years which ends immediately before the date on which that person signs the LPA certificate;

(b) a person chosen by the donor who, on account of his professional skills and expertise, reasonably considers that he is competent to make the judgments necessary to certify the matters set out in paragraph (2)(1)(e) of Schedule 1 to the Act.

(2) The following are examples of persons within paragraph (1)(b)—

(a) a registered health care professional;

(b) a barrister, solicitor or advocate called or admitted in any part of the United Kingdom;

(c) a registered social worker; or

(d) an independent mental capacity advocate.

(3) A person is disqualified from giving an LPA certificate in respect of any instrument intended to create a lasting power of attorney if that person is—

(a) a family member of the donor;

(b) a donee of that power;

(c) a donee of—

(i) any other lasting power of attorney, or

(ii) an enduring power of attorney,

which has been executed by the donor (whether or not it has been revoked);

(d) a family member of a donee within sub-paragraph (b);

(e) a director or employee of a trust corporation acting as a donee within sub-paragraph (b);

(f) a business partner or employee of—

(i) the donor, or

(ii) a donee within sub-paragraph (b);

(g) an owner, director, manager or employee of any care home in which the donor is living when the instrument is executed; or

(h) a family member of a person within sub-paragraph (g).

(4) In this regulation—

"care home" means—

(a) a care home in England within the meaning given by section 3 of the Care Standards Act 2000, and

(b) a place in Wales at which a care home service, within the meaning of Part 1 of the Regulation and Inspection of Social Care (Wales) Act 2016, is provided wholly or mainly to persons aged 18 or over;

"registered health care professional" means a person who is a member of a profession regulated by a body mentioned in section 25(3) of the National Health Service Reform and Health Care Professions Act 2002; and

"registered social worker" means a person registered as a social worker in a register maintained by—

- (a) the Health and Care Professions Council;
- (b) Social Care Wales;
- (c) the Scottish Social Services Council; or
- (d) the Northern Ireland Social Care Council.

III MEN [443]

9 Execution of instrument

(1) An instrument intended to create a lasting power of attorney must be executed in accordance with this regulation.

(2) The donor must read (or have read to him) all the prescribed information.

(3) As soon as reasonably practicable after the steps required by paragraph (2) have been taken, the donor must—

- (a) complete the provisions of Sections 1 to 7 of the instrument that apply to him (or direct another person to do so); and
- (b) subject to paragraph (7), in the presence of a witness—
  - (i) sign Section 9 of the instrument if the instrument is intended to create a lasting power of attorney for property and financial affairs (Form LP1F); or
  - (ii) sign Sections 5 and 9 of the instrument if the instrument is intended to create a lasting power of attorney for health and welfare (Form LP1H).

(4) As soon as reasonably practicable after the steps required by paragraph (3) have been taken—

- (a) the person giving an LPA certificate. . .
- (b) . . .

must complete the LPA certificate at Section 10 of the instrument and sign it.

(5) As soon as reasonably practicable after the steps required by paragraph (4) have been taken—

- (a) the donee, or
- (b) if more than one, each of the donees,

must read (or have read to him) all the prescribed information.

(6) As soon as reasonably practicable after the steps required by paragraph (5) have been taken, the donee or, if more than one, each of them—

- (a) must complete the provisions of Section 11 of the instrument that apply to him (or direct another person to do so); and
- (b) subject to paragraph (7), must sign Section 11 of the instrument in the presence of a witness.

(7) If the instrument is to be signed by any person at the direction of the donor, or at the direction of any donee, the signature must be done in the presence of two witnesses.

(8) For the purposes of this regulation—

- (a) the donor may not witness any signature required for the power;
- (b) a donee may not witness any signature required for the power apart from that of another donee.

(9) A person witnessing a signature must—

- (a) sign the instrument; and
- (b) give his full name and address.

(10) Any reference in this regulation to a person signing an instrument (however expressed) includes his signing it by means of a mark made on the instrument at the appropriate place.

REGISTERING THE INSTRUMENT

III MEN [444]

10 Notice to be given by a person about to apply for registration of lasting power of attorney

Schedule 2 to these Regulations sets out the form of notice (Form LPA3) which must be given by a donor or donee who is about to make an application for the registration of an instrument intended to create a lasting power of attorney.

III MEN [445]

11 Application for registration

(1) An application to the Public Guardian for the registration of an instrument intended to create a lasting power of attorney that is in Form LP1F or LP1H must be made by completion of Sections 12 and 13, the relevant parts of Section 14 and Section 15 of that Form.

(2) An application to the Public Guardian for the registration of an instrument intended to create a lasting power of attorney that is in a pre-July 2015 form must be made by using Form LP2 set out in Schedule 3 to these Regulations.

(3) An application to the Public Guardian for the registration of an instrument intended to create a lasting power of attorney where the application is a repeat application ("a reduced fee repeat application") may only be made if—

- (a) the initial application for the registration of a lasting power of attorney is made on or after 1st October 2011;
- (b) the initial application was returned to the applicant as invalid;
- (c) the reduced fee repeat application is submitted for registration within three months of the date on which the initial application was returned to the applicant as invalid; and
- (d) the reduced fee for such applications applies.

(4) Where the initial application for the registration of the lasting power of attorney was made in accordance with paragraph (1) using Form LP1F or LP1H, a reduced fee repeat application must also be made by the completion of Form LP1F or LP1H as appropriate, including completion of the repeat application option in Section 14 of that Form.

(5) Where the initial application for the registration of the lasting power of attorney was made in accordance with paragraph (2) using a pre-July 2015 form, a reduced fee repeat application must be made by the completion of Form LP1F or LP1H as appropriate, including completion of the repeat application option in Section 14 of that Form.

(6) Where the instrument to be registered which is sent with the application is neither—

- (a) the original instrument intended to create the power; nor
- (b) a certified copy of it,

the Public Guardian must not register the instrument unless the court directs the Public Guardian to do so.

(7) In this regulation—

- (a) "pre-July 2015 form" means a valid instrument intended to create a lasting power of attorney that is not in Form LP1F or LP1H but that complies with these Regulations as they were in force immediately before 1st July 2015; and

(b) "certified copy" means a photographic or other facsimile copy which is certified as an accurate copy by—
  (i) the donor; or
  (ii) a solicitor or notary.

III MEN [446]

12 Period to elapse before registration in cases not involving objection or defect

The period at the end of which the Public Guardian must register an instrument in accordance with paragraph 5 of Schedule 1 to the Act is the period of 4 weeks beginning with—

(a) the date on which the Public Guardian gave the notice or notices under paragraph 7 or 8 of Schedule 1 to the Act of receipt of an application for registration; or
(b) if notices were given on more than one date, the latest of those dates.

III MEN [447]

13 Notice of receipt of application for registration

(1) Part 1 of Schedule 4 to these Regulations sets out the form of notice ("LPA 003A") which the Public Guardian must give to the donee (or donees) when the Public Guardian receives an application for the registration of a lasting power of attorney.

(2) Part 2 of Schedule 4 sets out the form of notice ("LPA 003B") which the Public Guardian must give to the donor when the Public Guardian receives such an application.

(3) Where it appears to the Public Guardian that there is good reason to do so, the Public Guardian must also provide (or arrange for the provision of) an explanation to the donor of—

(a) the notice referred to in paragraph (2) and what the effect of it is; and
(b) why it is being brought to his attention.

(4) Any information provided under paragraph (3) must be provided—

(a) to the donor personally; and
(b) in a way that is appropriate to the donor's circumstances (for example using simple language, visual aids or other appropriate means).

III MEN [448]

14 Objection to registration: notice to Public Guardian to be given by the donee of the power or a named person

(1) This regulation deals with any objection to the registration of an instrument as a lasting power of attorney which is to be made to the Public Guardian by the donee of the power or a person to notify.

(2) Where the donee of the power or a person to notify—

(a) is entitled to receive notice under paragraph 6, 7 or 8 of Schedule 1 to the Act of an application for the registration of the instrument, and
(b) wishes to object to registration on a ground set out in paragraph 13(1) of Schedule 1 to the Act,

he must do so before the end of the period of 3 weeks beginning with the date on which the notice is given.

(3) A notice of objection must be given in writing, setting out—

(a) the name and address of the objector;
(b) . . . the name and address of the donor of the power;
(c) if known, the name and address of the donee (or donees); and
(d) the ground for making the objection.

(4) The Public Guardian must notify the objector as to whether he is satisfied that the ground of the objection is established.

(5) At any time after receiving the notice of objection and before giving the notice required by paragraph (4), the Public Guardian may require the objector to provide such further information, or produce such documents, as the Public Guardian reasonably considers necessary to enable him to determine whether the ground for making the objection is established.

(6) Where—

(a) the Public Guardian is satisfied that the ground of the objection is established, but

(b) by virtue of section 13(7) of the Act, the instrument is not revoked,

the notice under paragraph (4) must contain a statement to that effect.

(7) Nothing in this regulation prevents an objector from making a further objection under paragraph 13 of Schedule 1 to the Act where—

(a) the notice under paragraph (4) indicates that the Public Guardian is not satisfied that the particular ground of objection to which that notice relates is established; and

(b) the period specified in paragraph (2) has not expired.

III MEN [449]

14A Objection to registration: notice to Public Guardian to be given by the donor

(1) This regulation deals with any objection to the registration of an instrument as a lasting power of attorney which is to be made to the Public Guardian by the donor of the power.

(2) Where the donor of the power—

(a) is entitled to receive notice under paragraph 8 of Schedule 1 to the Act of an application for the registration of the instrument, and

(b) wishes to object to the registration,

he must do so before the end of the period of 3 weeks beginning with the date on which the notice is given.

(3) The donor of the power must give notice of his objection in writing to the Public Guardian, setting out—

(a) the name and address of the donor of the power;

(b) if known, the name and address of the donee (or donees); and

(c) the ground for making the objection.

III MEN [450]

15 Objection to registration: application to the court

(1) This regulation deals with any objection to the registration of an instrument as a lasting power of attorney which is to be made to the court.

(2) The grounds for making an application to the court are—

(a) that one or more of the requirements for the creation of a lasting power of attorney have not been met;

(b) that the power has been revoked, or has otherwise come to an end, on a ground other than the grounds set out in paragraph 13(1) of Schedule 1 to the Act;

(c) any of the grounds set out in paragraph (a) or (b) of section 22(3) of the Act.

(3) Where any person—

(a) is entitled to receive notice under paragraph 6, 7 or 8 of Schedule 1 to the Act of an application for the registration of the instrument, and

(b) wishes to object to registration on one or more of the grounds set out in paragraph (2), he must make an application to the court before the end of the period of 3 weeks beginning with the date on which the notice is given.

(4) The notice of an application to the court, which a person making an objection to the court is required to give to the Public Guardian under paragraph 13(3)(b)(ii) of Schedule 1 to the Act, must be in writing.

III MEN [451]

16 Notifying applicants of non-registration of lasting power of attorney

Where the Public Guardian is prevented from registering an instrument as a lasting power of attorney by virtue of—

(a) paragraph 11(1) of Schedule 1 to the Act (instrument not made in accordance with Schedule),
(b) paragraph 12(2) of that Schedule (deputy already appointed),
(c) paragraph 13(2) of that Schedule (objection by donee or named person on grounds of bankruptcy, disclaimer, death etc),
(d) paragraph 14(2) of that Schedule (objection by donor), or
(e) regulation 11(2) of these Regulations (application for registration not accompanied by original instrument or certified copy),

he must notify the person (or persons) who applied for registration of that fact.

III MEN [452]

17 Notice to be given on registration of lasting power of attorney

(1) Where the Public Guardian registers an instrument as a lasting power of attorney, he must—

(a) retain a copy of the instrument; and
(b) return to the person (or persons) who applied for registration the original instrument, or the certified copy of it, which accompanied the application for registration.

(2) Schedule 5 to these Regulations sets out the form of notice ("LPA 004") which the Public Guardian must give to the donor and donee (or donees) when the Public Guardian registers an instrument.

(3) Where it appears to the Public Guardian that there is good reason to do so, the Public Guardian must also provide (or arrange for the provision of) an explanation to the donor of—

(a) the notice referred to in paragraph (2) and what the effect of it is; and
(b) why it is being brought to his attention.

(4) Any information provided under paragraph (3) must be provided—

(a) to the donor personally; and
(b) in a way that is appropriate to the donor's circumstances (for example using simple language, visual aids or other appropriate means).

(5) "Certified copy" is to be construed in accordance with regulation 11(3).

POST-REGISTRATION

III MEN [453]

18 Changes to instrument registered as lasting power of attorney

(1) This regulation applies in any case where any of paragraphs 21 to 24 of Schedule 1 to the Act requires the Public Guardian to attach a note to an instrument registered as a lasting power of attorney.

(2) The Public Guardian must give a notice to the donor and the donee (or, if more than one, each of them) requiring him to deliver to the Public Guardian—

(a) the original instrument which was sent to the Public Guardian for registration;

(b) any office copy of that registered instrument; and

(c) any certified copy of that registered instrument.

(3) On receipt of the document, the Public Guardian must—

(a) attach the required note; and

(b) return the document to the person from whom it was obtained.

III MEN [454]

19 Loss or destruction of instrument registered as lasting power of attorney

(1) This regulation applies where—

(a) a person is required by or under the Act to deliver up to the Public Guardian any of the following documents—

(i) an instrument registered as a lasting power of attorney;

(ii) an office copy of that registered instrument;

(iii) a certified copy of that registered instrument; and

(b) the document has been lost or destroyed.

(2) The person required to deliver up the document must provide to the Public Guardian in writing—

(a) if known, the date of the loss or destruction and the circumstances in which it occurred;

(b) otherwise, a statement of when he last had the document in his possession.

III MEN [455]

20 Disclaimer of appointment by a donee of lasting power of attorney

(1) Schedule 6 to these Regulations sets out the form ("LPA 005") which a donee of an instrument registered as a lasting power of attorney must use to disclaim his appointment as donee.

(2) The donee must send—

(a) the completed form to the donor; and

(b) a copy of it to—

(i) the Public Guardian; and

(ii) any other donee who, for the time being, is appointed under the power.

III MEN [456]

21 Revocation by donor of lasting power of attorney

(1) A donor who revokes a lasting power to attorney must—

(a) notify the Public Guardian that he has done so; and

(b) notify the donee (or, if more than one, each of them) of the revocation.

(2) Where the Public Guardian receives a notice under paragraph (1)(a), he must cancel the registration of the instrument creating the power if he is satisfied that the donor has taken such steps as are necessary in law to revoke it.

(3) The Public Guardian may require the donor to provide such further information, or produce such documents, as the Public Guardian reasonably considers necessary to enable him to determine whether the steps necessary for revocation have been taken.

(4) Where the Public Guardian cancels the registration of the instrument he must notify—

(a) the donor; and

(b) the donee or, if more than one, each of them.

III MEN [457]

22 Revocation of a lasting power of attorney on death of donor

(1) The Public Guardian must cancel the registration of an instrument as a lasting power of attorney if he is satisfied that the power has been revoked as a result of the donor's death.

(2) Where the Public Guardian cancels the registration of an instrument he must notify the donee or, if more than one, each of them.

PART 3
ENDURING POWERS OF ATTORNEY

III MEN [458]

23 Notice of intention to apply for registration of enduring power of attorney

(1) Schedule 7 to these Regulations sets out the form of notice ("EP1PG") which an attorney (or attorneys) under an enduring power of attorney must give of his intention to make an application for the registration of the instrument creating the power.

(2) In the case of the notice to be given to the donor, the attorney must also provide (or arrange for the provision of) an explanation to the donor of—

(a) the notice and what the effect of it is; and

(b) why it is being brought to his attention.

(3) The information provided under paragraph (2) must be provided—

(a) to the donor personally; and

(b) in a way that is appropriate to the donor's circumstances (for example using simple language, visual aids or other appropriate means).

III MEN [459]

24 Application for registration

(1) Schedule 8 to these Regulations sets out the form ("EP2PG") which must be used for making an application to the Public Guardian for the registration of an instrument creating an enduring power of attorney.

(1A) The Public Guardian must not register an instrument where only a certified copy of the instrument is sent with the application, unless the applicant verifies that he cannot produce the original instrument because it has been lost or, as the case may be, destroyed.

(2) Where the instrument to be registered which is sent with the application is neither—

(a) the original instrument creating the power, nor

(b) a certified copy of it in relation to which paragraph (1A) has been complied with,

the Public Guardian must not register the instrument unless the court directs him to do so.

(3) "Certified copy", in relation to an enduring power of attorney, means a copy certified in accordance with section 3 of the Powers of Attorney Act 1971.

III MEN [460]

25 Notice of objection to registration

(1) This regulation deals with any objection to the registration of an instrument creating an enduring power of attorney which is to be made to the Public Guardian under paragraph 13(4) of Schedule 4 to the Act.

(2) A notice of objection must be given in writing, setting out—

(a) the name and address of the objector;

(b) if different, the name and address of the donor of the power;
(c) if known, the name and address of the attorney (or attorneys); and
(d) the ground for making the objection.

III MEN [461]

26 Notifying applicants of non-registration of enduring power of attorney

Where the Public Guardian is prevented from registering an instrument creating an enduring power of attorney by virtue of—

(a) paragraph 13(2) of Schedule 4 to the Act (deputy already appointed),
(b) paragraph 13(5) of that Schedule (receipt by Public Guardian of valid notice of objection from person entitled to notice of application to register),
(c) paragraph 13(7) of that Schedule (Public Guardian required to undertake appropriate enquiries in certain circumstances), or
(d) regulation 24(2) of these Regulations (application for registration not accompanied by original instrument or certified copy),

he must notify the person (or persons) who applied for registration of that fact.

III MEN [462]

27 Registration of instrument creating an enduring power of attorney

(1) Where the Public Guardian registers an instrument creating an enduring power of attorney, he must—

(a) retain a copy of the instrument; and
(b) return to the person (or persons) who applied for registration the original instrument, or the certified copy of it, which accompanied the application.

(2) "Certified copy" has the same meaning as in regulation 24(3).

III MEN [463]

28 Objection or revocation not applying to all joint and several attorneys

In a case within paragraph 20(6) or (7) of Schedule 4 to the Act, the form of the entry to be made in the register in respect of an instrument creating the enduring power of attorney is a stamp bearing the following words (inserting the information indicated, as appropriate)—

"THE REGISTRATION OF THIS ENDURING POWER OF ATTORNEY IS QUALIFIED AND EXTENDS TO THE APPOINTMENT OF .... (insert name of attorney(s) not affected by ground(s) of objection or revocation) ONLY AS THE ATTORNEY(S) OF .... (insert name of donor)".

III MEN [464]

29 Loss or destruction of instrument registered as enduring power of attorney

(1) This regulation applies where—

(a) a person is required by or under the Act to deliver up to the Public Guardian any of the following documents—
   (i) an instrument registered as an enduring power of attorney;
   (ii) an office copy of that registered instrument; or
   (iii) a certified copy of that registered instrument; and
(b) the document has been lost or destroyed.

(2) The person who is required to deliver up the document must provide to the Public Guardian in writing—

(a) if known, the date of the loss or destruction and the circumstances in which it occurred;

(b) otherwise, a statement of when he last had the document in his possession.

PART 4
FUNCTIONS OF THE PUBLIC GUARDIAN

THE REGISTERS

III MEN [465]

30 Establishing and maintaining the registers

(1) In this Part "the registers" means—

(a) the register of lasting powers of attorney,

(b) the register of enduring powers of attorney, and

(c) the register of court orders appointing deputies,

which the Public Guardian must establish and maintain.

(2) On each register the Public Guardian may include—

(a) such descriptions of information about a registered instrument or a registered order as the Public Guardian considers appropriate; and

(b) entries which relate to an instrument or order for which registration has been cancelled.

III MEN [466]

31 Disclosure of information on a register: search by the Public Guardian

(1) Any person may, by an application made under paragraph (2), request the Public Guardian to carry out a search of one or more of the registers.

(2) An application must—

(a) state—

(i) the register or registers to be searched;

(ii) the name of the person to whom the application relates; and

(iii) such other details about that person as the Public Guardian may require for the purpose of carrying out the search; and

(b) be accompanied by any fee provided for under section 58(4)(b) of the Act.

(3) The Public Guardian may require the applicant to provide such further information, or produce such documents, as the Public Guardian reasonably considers necessary to enable him to carry out the search.

(4) As soon as reasonably practicable after receiving the application—

(a) the Public Guardian must notify the applicant of the result of the search; and

(b) in the event that it reveals one or more entries on the register, the Public Guardian must disclose to the applicant all the information appearing on the register in respect of each entry.

III MEN [467]

32 Disclosure of additional information held by the Public Guardian

(1) This regulation applies in any case where, as a result of a search made under regulation 31, a person has obtained information relating to a registered instrument or a registered order which confers authority to make decisions about matters concerning a person ("P").

(2) On receipt of an application made in accordance with paragraph (4), the Public Guardian may, if he considers that there is good reason to do so, disclose to the applicant such additional information as he considers appropriate.

(3) "Additional information" means any information relating to P—

(a) which the Public Guardian has obtained in exercising the functions conferred on him under the Act; but

(b) which does not appear on the register.

(4) An application must state—

(a) the name of P;

(b) the reasons for making the application; and

(c) what steps, if any, the applicant has taken to obtain the information from P.

(5) The Public Guardian may require the applicant to provide such further information, or produce such documents, as the Public Guardian reasonably considers necessary to enable him to determine the application.

(6) In determining whether to disclose any additional information relating to P, the Public Guardian must, in particular, have regard to—

(a) the connection between P and the applicant;

(b) the reasons for requesting the information (in particular, why the information cannot or should not be obtained directly from P);

(c) the benefit to P, or any detriment he may suffer, if a disclosure is made; and

(d) any detriment that another person may suffer if a disclosure is made.

Security for discharge of functions

III MEN [468]

33 Persons required to give security for the discharge of their functions

(1) This regulation applies in any case where the court orders a person ("S") to give to the Public Guardian security for the discharge of his functions.

(2) The security must be given by S—

(a) by means of a bond which is entered into in accordance with regulation 34; or

(b) in such other manner as the court may direct.

(3) For the purposes of paragraph (2)(a), S complies with the requirement to give the security only if—

(a) the endorsement required by regulation 34(2) has been provided; and

(b) the person who provided it has notified the Public Guardian of that fact.

(4) For the purposes of paragraph (2)(b), S complies with the requirement to give the security—

(a) in any case where the court directs that any other endorsement must be provided, only if—

(i) that endorsement has been provided; and

(ii) the person who provided it has notified the Public Guardian of that fact;

(b) in any case where the court directs that any other requirements must be met in relation to the giving of the security, only if the Public Guardian is satisfied that those other requirements have been met.

III MEN [469]

34 Security given under regulation 33(2)(a): requirement for endorsement

(1) This regulation has effect for the purposes of regulation 33(2)(a).

(2) A bond is entered into in accordance with this regulation only if it is endorsed by—

(a) an authorised insurance company; or

(b) an authorised deposit-taker.

(3) A person may enter into the bond under—

(a) arrangements made by the Public Guardian; or

(b) other arrangements which are made by the person entering into the bond or on his behalf.

(4) The Public Guardian may make arrangements with any person specified in paragraph (2) with a view to facilitating the provision by them of bonds which persons required to give security to the Public Guardian may enter into.

(5) In this regulation—

"authorised insurance company" means—

(a) a person who has permission under Part 4 of the Financial Services and Markets Act 2000 to effect or carry out contracts of insurance;

(b) *an EEA firm of the kind mentioned in paragraph 5(d) of Schedule 3 to that Act, which has permission under paragraph 15 of that Schedule to effect or carry out contracts of insurance;*

(c) a person who carries on insurance market activity (within the meaning given in section 316(3) of that Act); and

"authorised deposit-taker" means—

(a) a person who has permission under Part 4 of the Financial Services and Markets Act 2000 to accept deposits;

(b) *an EEA firm of the kind mentioned in paragraph 5(d) of Schedule 3 to that Act, which has permission under paragraph 15 of that Schedule to accept deposits.*

(6) The definitions of "authorised insurance company" and "authorised deposit-taker" must be read with—

(a) section 22 of the Financial Services and Markets Act 2000;

(b) any relevant order under that section; and

(c) Schedule 2 to that Act.

Amendment *Test in italic is revoked with effect from exit day (as defined in the European Union (Withdrawal) Act 2018, s 20(1)–(5)): see SI 2018/1149, reg 1(3).*

III MEN [470]

35 Security given under regulation 33(2)(a): maintenance or replacement

(1) This regulation applies to any security given under regulation 33(2)(a).

(2) At such times or at such intervals as the Public Guardian may direct by notice in writing, any person ("S") who has given the security must satisfy the Public Guardian that any premiums payable in respect of it have been paid.

(3) Where S proposes to replace a security already given by him, the new security is not to be regarded as having been given until the Public Guardian is satisfied that—

(a) the requirements set out in sub-paragraphs (a) and (b) of regulation 33(3) have been met in relation to it; and

(b) no payment is due from S in connection with the discharge of his functions.

(4) The Public Guardian must, if satisfied as to the matters in paragraph (3), provide written notice of that fact to S within 2 weeks of being given notification in accordance with regulation 33(3)(b) in relation to the new security.

III MEN [471]

36 Enforcement following court order of any endorsed security

(1) This regulation applies to any security given to the Public Guardian in respect of which an endorsement has been provided.

(2) Where the court orders the enforcement of the security, the Public Guardian must—

(a) notify any person who endorsed the security of the contents of the order; and

(b) notify the court when payment has been made of the amount secured.

III MEN [472]

37 Discharge of any endorsed security

(1) This regulation applies to any security given by a person ("S") to the Public Guardian in respect of which an endorsement has been provided.

(2) The security may be discharged if the court makes an order discharging it.

(3) Otherwise the security may not be discharged—

(a) if the person on whose behalf S was appointed to act dies, until the end of the period of 2 years beginning on the date of his death; or

(b) in any other case, until the end of the period of 7 years beginning on whichever of the following dates first occurs—

(i) if S dies, the date of his death;

(ii) if the court makes an order which discharges S but which does not also discharge the security under paragraph (2), the date of the order;

(iii) the date when S otherwise ceases to be under a duty to discharge the functions in respect of which he was ordered to give security.

(3A) Where S has replaced a security ("the original security") previously given by S and the Public Guardian has provided notice in accordance with regulation 35(4), the original security shall stand discharged 2 years from the date on which that notice was issued unless discharged by earlier order of the court upon application under paragraph (2).

(4) For the purposes of paragraph (3), if a person takes any step with a view to discharging the security before the end of the period specified in that paragraph, the security is to be treated for all purposes as if it were still in place.

(5) For the purposes of paragraph (3A), if a person takes any step otherwise than under paragraph (2) with a view to discharging the original security before the end of the period specified paragraph (3A), the security is to be treated for all purposes as if it were still in place.

DEPUTIES

III MEN [473]

38 Application for additional time to submit a report

(1) This regulation applies where the court requires a deputy to submit a report to the Public Guardian and specifies a time or interval for it to be submitted.

(2) A deputy may apply to the Public Guardian requesting more time for submitting a particular report.

(3) An application must—

(a) state the reason for requesting more time; and

(b) contain or be accompanied by such information as the Public Guardian may reasonably require to determine the application.

(4) In response to an application, the Public Guardian may, if he considers it appropriate to do so, undertake that he will not take steps to secure performance of the deputy's duty to submit the report at the relevant time on the condition that the report is submitted on or before such later date as he may specify.

III MEN [474]

39 Content of reports

(1) Any report which the court requires a deputy to submit to the Public Guardian must include such material as the court may direct.

(2) The report must also contain or be accompanied by—

- (a) specified information or information of a specified description; or
- (b) specified documents or documents of a specified description.

(3) But paragraph (2)—

- (a) extends only to information or documents which are reasonably required in connection with the exercise by the Public Guardian of functions conferred on him under the Act; and
- (b) is subject to paragraph (1) and to any other directions given by the court.

(4) Where powers as respects a person's property and affairs are conferred on a deputy under section 16 of the Act, the information specified by the Public Guardian under paragraph (2) may include accounts which—

- (a) deal with specified matters; and
- (b) are provided in a specified form.

(5) The Public Guardian may require—

- (a) any information provided to be verified in such manner, or
- (b) any document produced to be authenticated in such manner,

as he may reasonably require.

(6) "Specified" means specified in a notice in writing given to the deputy by the Public Guardian.

III MEN [475]

40 Power to require final report on termination of appointment

(1) This regulation applies where—

- (a) the person on whose behalf a deputy was appointed to act has died;
- (b) the deputy has died;
- (c) the court has made an order discharging the deputy; or
- (d) the deputy otherwise ceases to be under a duty to discharge the functions to which his appointment relates.

(2) The Public Guardian may require the deputy (or, in the case of the deputy's death, his personal representatives) to submit a final report on the discharge of his functions.

(3) A final report must be submitted—

- (a) before the end of such reasonable period as may be specified; and
- (b) at such place as may be specified.

(4) The Public Guardian must consider the final report, together with any other information that he may have relating to the discharge by the deputy of his functions.

(5) Where the Public Guardian is dissatisfied with any aspect of the final report he may apply to the court for an appropriate remedy (including enforcement of security given by the deputy).

(6) "Specified" means specified in a notice in writing given to the deputy or his personal representatives by the Public Guardian.

III MEN [476]

41 Power to require information from deputies

(1) This regulation applies in any case where—

(a) the Public Guardian has received representations (including complaints) about—
   (i) the way in which a deputy is exercising his powers; or
   (ii) any failure to exercise them; or
(b) it appears to the Public Guardian that there are other circumstances which—
   (i) give rise to concerns about, or dissatisfaction with, the conduct of the deputy (including any failure to act); or
   (ii) otherwise constitute good reason to seek information about the deputy's discharge of his functions.

(2) The Public Guardian may require the deputy—
(a) to provide specified information or information of a specified description; or
(b) to produce specified documents or documents of a specified description.

(3) The information or documents must be provided or produced—
(a) before the end of such reasonable period as may be specified; and
(b) at such place as may be specified.

(4) The Public Guardian may require—
(a) any information provided to be verified in such manner, or
(b) any document produced to be authenticated in such manner,

as he may reasonably require.

(5) "Specified" means specified in a notice in writing given to the deputy by the Public Guardian.

III MEN [477]

42 Right of deputy to require review of decisions made by the Public Guardian

(1) A deputy may require the Public Guardian to reconsider any decision he has made in relation to the deputy.

(2) The right under paragraph (1) is exercisable by giving notice of exercise of the right to the Public Guardian before the end of the period of 14 days beginning with the date on which notice of the decision is given to the deputy.

(3) The notice of exercise of the right must—
(a) state the grounds on which reconsideration is required; and
(b) contain or be accompanied by any relevant information or documents.

(4) At any time after receiving the notice and before reconsidering the decision to which it relates, the Public Guardian may require the deputy to provide him with such further information, or to produce such documents, as he reasonably considers necessary to enable him to reconsider the matter.

(5) The Public Guardian must give to the deputy—
(a) written notice of his decision on reconsideration, and
(b) if he upholds the previous decision, a statement of his reasons.

MISCELLANEOUS FUNCTIONS

III MEN [478]

43 Applications to the Court of Protection

The Public Guardian has the function of making applications to the court in connection with his functions under the Act in such circumstances as he considers it necessary or appropriate to do so.

III MEN [479]

44 Visits by the Public Guardian or by Court of Protection Visitors at his direction

(1) This regulation applies where the Public Guardian visits, or directs a Court of Protection Visitor to visit, any person under any provision of the Act or these Regulations.

(2) The Public Guardian must notify (or make arrangements to notify) the person to be visited of—

(a) the date or dates on which it is proposed that the visit will take place;

(b) to the extent that it is practicable to do so, any specific matters likely to be covered in the course of the visit; and

(c) any proposal to inform any other person that the visit is to take place.

(3) Where the visit is to be carried out by a Court of Protection Visitor—

(a) the Public Guardian may—

(i) give such directions to the Visitor, and

(ii) provide him with such information concerning the person to be visited,

as the Public Guardian considers necessary for the purposes of enabling the visit to take place and the Visitor to prepare any report the Public Guardian may require; and

(b) the Visitor must seek to carry out the visit and take all reasonable steps to obtain such other information as he considers necessary for the purpose of preparing a report.

(4) A Court of Protection Visitor must submit any report requested by the Public Guardian in accordance with any timetable specified by the Public Guardian.

(5) If he considers it appropriate to do so, the Public Guardian may, in relation to any person interviewed in the course of preparing a report—

(a) disclose the report to him; and

(b) invite him to comment on it.

III MEN [480]

45 Functions in relation to persons carrying out specific transactions

(1) This regulation applies where, in accordance with an order made under section 16(2)(a) of the Act, a person ("T") has been authorised to carry out any transaction for a person who lacks capacity.

(2) The Public Guardian has the functions of—

(a) receiving any reports from T which the court may require;

(b) dealing with representations (including complaints) about—

(i) the way in which the transaction has been or is being carried out; or

(ii) any failure to carry it out.

(3) Regulations 38 to 41 have effect in relation to T as they have effect in relation a deputy.

III MEN [481]

46 Power to require information from donees of lasting power of attorney

(1) This regulation applies where it appears to the Public Guardian that there are circumstances suggesting that the donee of a lasting power of attorney may—

(a) have behaved, or may be behaving, in a way that contravenes his authority or is not in the best interests of the donor of the power,

(b) be proposing to behave in a way that would contravene that authority or would not be in the donor's best interests, or

(c) have failed to comply with the requirements of an order made, or directions given, by the court.

(2) The Public Guardian may require the donee—

(a) to provide specified information or information of a specified description; or

(b) to produce specified documents or documents of a specified description.

(3) The information or documents must be provided or produced—

(a) before the end of such reasonable period as may be specified; and

(b) at such place as may be specified.

(4) The Public Guardian may require—

(a) any information provided to be verified in such manner, or

(b) any document produced to be authenticated in such manner,

as he may reasonably require.

(5) "Specified" means specified in a notice in writing given to the donee by the Public Guardian.

III MEN [482]

47 Power to require information from attorneys under enduring power of attorney

(1) This regulation applies where it appears to the Public Guardian that there are circumstances suggesting that, having regard to all the circumstances (and in particular the attorney's relationship to or connection with the donor) the attorney under a registered enduring power of attorney may be unsuitable to be the donor's attorney.

(2) The Public Guardian may require the attorney—

(a) to provide specified information or information of a specified description; or

(b) to produce specified documents or documents of a specified description.

(3) The information or documents must be provided or produced—

(a) before the end of such reasonable period as may be specified; and

(b) at such place as may be specified.

(4) The Public Guardian may require—

(a) any information provided to be verified in such manner, or

(b) any document produced to be authenticated in such manner,

as he may reasonably require.

(5) "Specified" means specified in a notice in writing given to the attorney by the Public Guardian.

III MEN [483]–III MEN [490]

48 Other functions in relation to enduring powers of attorney

(1) The Public Guardian has the following functions—

(a) directing a Court of Protection Visitor—

(i) to visit an attorney under a registered enduring power of attorney, or

(ii) to visit the donor of a registered enduring power of attorney,

and to make a report to the Public Guardian on such matters as he may direct;

(b) dealing with representations (including complaints) about the way in which an attorney under a registered enduring power of attorney is exercising his powers.

(2) The functions conferred by paragraph (1) may be discharged in co-operation with any other person who has functions in relation to the care or treatment of P.

Editorial note *The Schedules to the Lasting Powers of Attorney, Enduring Powers of Attorney and Public Guardian Regulations 2007 contain forms for making and registering a lasting power of attorney. These forms are not reproduced here but are available from the Office of the Public Guardian (see www.gov.uk/government/organisations/office-of-the-public-guardian).*

COURT OF PROTECTION RULES 2017

2017 No 1035

GENERAL NOTES ON THE COURT OF PROTECTION RULES 2017

III MEN [491]

Following concerns about unfocused and wasteful procedures in the Court of Protection (see *A & B (Court of Protection: Delay and Costs)* [2014] EWCOP 48, Peter Jackson J) and work by the Rules Committee, a number of Pilots, in particular concerning Case Management were introduced in 2016. Finally, on 1 December 2017, the new Court of Protections Rules 2017, SI 2017/1035 came into force, along with relevant Practice Directions. These Rules replace the 2007 Rules in their entirety. The Rules supplement the Mental Capacity Act 2005 and establish the practice and procedure to be adopted in respect of applications and issues arising before the Court of Protection. The 2017 Rules, unlike their predecessor, are set out in very much the same way as the Civil Procedure Rules. They incorporate the principles of the overriding objective and reinforce the need for appropriate and efficient case management. There are distinct differences between the two sets of rules, however. At the core of the Mental Capacity Act 2005 is the individual 'P' who lacks mental capacity and in particular the need to ensure that acts done, and decisions made reflect that person's best interests. Similarly within the Court of Protection Rules, at r 1.1(3)(b), in dealing with cases justly, so far as is practicable, one must ensure that 'P's' interests and position are properly considered.

The Rules are divided into 24 Parts, and the Practice Directions expand and amplify certain parts of the Rules, and introduce the relevant Forms and Procedural documentation which is specific to the Court of Protection and its work. As well as its welfare and property and affairs jurisdictions, the Court of Protection has a specific role in reviewing the legality of deprivation liberty, particularly, where there is a challenge to an urgent or standard authorisation. This is dealt with in Part 11 the practice direction and forms, which must be complied with and used where applications are made within the framework of such issues.

The Rules are arranged as follows.

Part 1 contains the Overriding Objective, and the duties to further it – including specifying the duties of the parties, legal representatives and litigants in person. It also concerns as the Participation of P.

Part 2 contains Interpretation and General Provisions- including definitions, the tiers of judiciary, computation of time, and the application of the Civil Procedure Rules and Family Procedure Rules, the Court may apply.

Part 3 concerns allocation of cases to certain specific judges or classes of judges; the Court's powers of case management, including allocations to pathways (Personal Welfare, Property and Affairs or Mixed Welfare and Property pathways).

Part 4 relates to hearings; this mainly covers whether the hearing shall be in public of private and the publication of information.

Parts 5 and 6 concern Court the documents required for court and their service.

Part 7 outlines the circumstances in which P is and is not required to be notified. Part 8 deals with permission to start proceedings.

How to start proceedings and the parties to the proceedings is the subject of Part 9. Applications within proceedings is the subject matter of Part 10.

Part 11 is concerned with Deprivation of Liberty. Part 12 covers Human Rights.

In Part 13, Jurisdiction, withdrawal of Proceedings, Participation in Hearings and Reconsideration of decisions are dealt with. Admissions, Evidence and Depositions as well as Section 49 Reports are the subject of Part 14. Part 15 deals with experts, including the crucial function of restricting expert evidence to that which is 'necessary to assist the court to resolve the issues in the proceedings' (r 15.3(1)). Part 16 concerns Disclosure.

Litigation Friends and Rule 1.2 Representatives are the concern of Part 17. Change of Solicitor is regulated by Part 18.

The issue of costs is covered in Part 19, the general rules in property and affairs and health and welfare remaining the same, as well as the principles concerning the departure from those principles. Part 20 concerns Appeals.

Part 21 deals with applications and proceedings in relation to contempt of Court and Part 22 with civil restraint orders.

Part 23 is concerned with the international protection of adults.

Miscellaneous in Part 24 concerns enforcement methods, security for discharge of functions under the Mental Capacity Act, directions when there is an objection to the registration of an enduring power of attorney.

PART 1
THE OVERRIDING OBJECTIVE

III MEN [492]

1.1 Overriding objective

(1) These Rules have the overriding objective of enabling the court to deal with a case justly and at proportionate cost, having regard to the principles contained in the Act.

(2) The court will seek to give effect to the overriding objective when it—

(a) exercises any power under the Rules; or

(b) interprets any rule or practice direction.

(3) Dealing with a case justly and at proportionate cost includes, so far as is practicable—

(a) ensuring that it is dealt with expeditiously and fairly;

(b) ensuring that P's interests and position are properly considered;

(c) dealing with the case in ways which are proportionate to the nature, importance and complexity of the issues;

(d) ensuring that the parties are on an equal footing;

(e) saving expense;

(f) allotting to it an appropriate share of the court's resources, while taking account of the need to allot resources to other cases; and

(g) enforcing compliance with rules, practice directions and orders.

III MEN [492.1]

Contrasting the overriding objective of the Court of Protection and that relating to the civil courts Whilst the overriding objective bears similarity to the overriding objective of the CPR, r 1.1(3)(b) ensures that P's interests and position are specifically considered in every determination.

In *A Local Authority v PB and P* [2011] EWHC 502 (COP) Charles J set out guidelines for good practice in welfare proceedings, the provision of position statements and for early defining of issues.

III MEN [493]

1.2 Participation of P

(1) The court must in each case, on its own initiative or on the application of any person, consider whether it should make one or more of the directions in paragraph (2), having regard to—

(a) the nature and extent of the information before the court;

(b) the issues raised in the case;

(c) whether a matter is contentious; and

(d) whether P has been notified in accordance with the provisions of Part 7 and what, if anything, P has said or done in response to such notification.

(2) The directions are that—

(a) P should be joined as a party;

(b) P's participation should be secured by the appointment of an accredited legal representative to represent P in the proceedings and to discharge such other functions as the court may direct;

(c) P's participation should be secured by the appointment of a representative whose function shall be to provide the court with information as to the matters set out in section 4(6) of the Act and to discharge such other functions as the court may direct;

(d) P should have the opportunity to address (directly or indirectly) the judge determining the application and, if so directed, the circumstances in which that should occur;

(e) P's interests and position can properly be secured without any direction under sub-paragraphs (a) to (d) being made or by the making of an alternative direction meeting the overriding objective.

(3) Any appointment or directions made pursuant to paragraph (2)(b) to (e) may be made for such period or periods as the court thinks fit.

(4) Unless P has capacity to conduct the proceedings, an order joining P as a party shall only take effect—

(a) on the appointment of a litigation friend on P's behalf; or

(b) if the court so directs, on or after the appointment of an accredited legal representative.

(5) If the court has directed that P should be joined as a party but such joinder does not occur because no litigation friend or accredited legal representative is appointed, the court shall record in a judgment or order—

(a) the fact that no such appointment was made; and

(b) the reasons given for that appointment not being made.

(6) A practice direction may make additional or supplementary provision in respect of any of the matters set out in this rule.

(The appointment of litigation friends, accredited legal representatives and representatives under paragraph (2)(c) is dealt with under Part 17.)

("Accredited legal representative" is defined in rule 2.1.)

III MEN [493.1]

Accredited legal representative There is a positive duty on the court to consider the extent of 'P's' participation in proceedings and direct. As is observed the Rules make provision for a rule 1.2 representative (previously known as a rule 3A representative)), addressed by Charles J in his judgment in *Re NRA* [2015] EWCOP 59, 165 NLJ 7671, [2015] All ER (D) 122 (Sep). See now Practice Direction 2A (**III MEN [505]**).

DUTIES TO FURTHER THE OVERRIDING OBJECTIVE

III MEN [494]

1.3 Court's duty to manage cases

(1) The court must further the overriding objective by actively managing cases.

(2) The court must manage a case at all times and in particular—

(a) when a case is referred to a judge;

(b) at every hearing, whether listed by the court on its own initiative or on application by a party;

(c) at all stages of a final hearing; and

(d) when considering enforcement measures including committal.

(3) Active case management includes—

(a) considering the appropriate case pathway for the case;

(b) ensuring—

(i) that the appropriate judge is allocated to the case;

(ii) judicial continuity, so far as practicable;

(c) avoiding delay and keeping costs down;

(d) encouraging the parties to co-operate with each other in the conduct of the proceedings;

(e) identifying at an early stage—

(i) the issues; and

(ii) who should be a party to the proceedings;

(f) deciding promptly—

(i) which issues need a full investigation and hearing and which do not; and

(ii) the procedure to be followed in the case;

(g) deciding the order in which issues are to be resolved;
(h) encouraging the parties to use an alternative dispute resolution procedure if the court considers that appropriate;
(i) fixing timetables or otherwise controlling the progress of the case;
(j) considering whether the likely benefits of taking a particular step justify the cost of taking it;
(k) dealing with as many aspects of the case as the court can on the same occasion;
(l) dealing with the case without the parties needing to attend at court;
(m) making use of technology;
(n) giving directions to ensure that the case proceeds quickly and efficiently;
(o) considering whether any hearing should be heard in public; and
(p) considering whether any document relating to proceedings should be a public document and, if so, whether and to what extent it should be redacted.

(Rules 4.2 to 4.4 make provision about the court's powers to authorise publication of information about proceedings and to order that a hearing be held in public.)

III MEN [494.1]

The importance of active case management Active case management is an integral aspect of the role of any judge and parties must be prepared to assist the court at the conclusion of any hearing to progress the application by way of directions. In *Re AVS v A NHS Foundation Trust* [2010] EWHC 2746 (COP) the President indicated that he considered that direction appointments were of the utmost importance in proceedings of any kind. Such directions included the appointment of litigation friends, and the control of evidence under r 14.2(a) (**III MEN [629]**).

III MEN [495]

1.4 The duty of the parties

(1) The parties are required to help the court to further the overriding objective.

(2) Without prejudice to the generality of paragraph (1), each party is required to—

(a) ask the court to take steps to manage the case if—
(i) an order or direction of the court appears not to deal with an issue; or
(ii) if a matter including any new circumstances, issue or dispute arises of which the court is unaware;
(b) identify before issue if the case is within the scope of one of the case pathways and comply with the requirements of the applicable case pathway;
(c) co-operate with the other parties and with the court in identifying and narrowing the issues that need to be determined by the court, and the timetable for that determination;
(d) adhere to the timetable set by these Rules and by the court;
(e) comply with all directions and orders of the court;
(f) be full and frank in the disclosure of information and evidence to the court (including any disclosure ordered under Part 16);
(g) co-operate with the other parties in all aspects of the conduct of the proceedings, including in the preparation of bundles.

(3) If the court determines that any party has failed without reasonable excuse to satisfy the requirements of this rule, it may under rule 19.5 depart from the general rules about costs in so far as they apply to that party.

(Rule 16.2(2) deals with the requirements of general disclosure.)

III MEN [496]

1.5 The duty of legal representatives

(1) Legal representatives of parties are required to help the court to further the overriding objective.

(2) Without prejudice to the generality of paragraph (1), a legal representative of a party must—

(a) comply with any applicable rules, practice directions or orders of the court;

(b) follow (where appropriate) the applicable case pathway; and

(c) address whether the case can be swiftly resolved.

III MEN [497]

1.6 The duty of unrepresented litigants

(1) Without prejudice to the generality of rule 1.4, unrepresented litigants are required to help the court to further the overriding objective.

(2) This includes—

(a) engaging with the process applicable in the case and co-operating with the court and the other parties;

(b) seeking the court's direction if an issue or dispute arises in the case;

(c) presenting their case fairly; and

(d) seeking early resolution of any dispute where practicable.

PRACTICE DIRECTION 1A — PARTICIPATION OF P

III MEN [498]

This Practice Direction supplements Part 1 of the Court of Protection Rules 2017

1 Developments in the case law both of the European Court of Human Rights and domestic courts have highlighted the importance of ensuring that P takes an appropriate part in the proceedings and the court is properly informed about P; and the difficulties of securing this in a way which is proportionate to the issues involved and the nature of the decisions which need to be taken and avoids excessive delay and cost.

2 To this end, rule 1.2 makes provision to—

(a) ensure that in every case the question of what is required to ensure that P's "voice" is properly before the court is addressed; and

(b) provide flexibility allowing for a range of different methods to achieve this,

with the purpose of ensuring that the court is in a position to make a properly informed decision at all relevant stages of a case.

3 The great majority of cases in terms of numbers before the Court of Protection relate to non-contentious matters concerning property and affairs, where there is a need to preserve P's resources and experience has shown that they can be dealt with on paper and without joining P as a party or appointing anyone to represent P. This is covered by rule 1.2(2)(e) which provides that none of the listed directions need be made.

4 Other cases, involving a range of issues relating to both property and affairs and personal welfare do or may call for a higher level of participation by or on behalf of P at one or more stages of the case.

5 Rule 1.2 accordingly requires the court in every case to consider whether it should make one, or more, of a number of possible directions for securing P's participation. These directions cover a range from the joining of P as a party securing P's participation by the appointment of an accredited legal representative; securing P's participation by the appointment of a representative; securing P's participation by giving P the opportunity to address the judge directly or indirectly; and securing P's participation in some other way which meets the overriding objective.

6 In considering whether it should make any of these directions, and if so which of them, the court is required to have regard to a range of factors to determine the participation and representation needed. In this way the court is both required and enabled to tailor the provision it directs for P's participation and representation to the circumstances of the individual case.

7 If the court concludes that P lacks capacity to conduct the proceedings and the circumstances require that P should be joined as a party, the order joining P as a party shall only take effect on the appointment of a litigation friend or, if the court so directs, on or after the appointment of an accredited legal representative. This enables steps to be taken and orders to be made before P becomes a party. During that period P's participation can be secured and the court can seek relevant information in any of the ways set out in rule 1.2(2)(b) to (e).

8 Provisions relating to the appointment of a litigation friend and rule 1.2 representatives (namely an accredited legal representative appointed pursuant to rule 1.2(2)(b) and a representative appointed pursuant to rule 1.2(2)(c)) are contained in Part 17. Rule 1.2 representatives can only be appointed with their consent.

9 An accredited legal representative is defined in rule 2.1. When such representatives exist one can be appointed whether or not P is joined as a party and this may be of assistance if urgent orders are needed, particularly if they are likely to have an impact on the final orders (e.g. an urgent order relating to residence).

10 When P lacks capacity to conduct the proceedings and is made a party an accredited legal representative is not intended as a substitute for a litigation friend, but as an alternative in a suitable case (or in the early stages of the case).

11 When P lacks capacity to conduct the proceedings and an order that he or she is to be a party is made factors relevant to the choice between appointing a litigation friend and an accredited legal representative to represent him or her as a party will include—

- Whether there will be a need for expert or other evidence to be obtained and filed, or other material gathered, on P's behalf;
- The nature and complexity of the case;
- The likely range of issues.

12 In other cases their nature and complexity, the issues raised or likely to be raised in them and the stage they have reached could mean that the assistance of an accredited legal representative is not required or is inappropriate and that P's participation is best secured and the court will be properly informed by the appointment of a representative under rule 1.2(2)(c) (who could be a friend, an IMCA, an advocate appointed under the Care Act 2014, a family member or anyone with relevant knowledge) or by directions being made under rule 1.2(2)(d) or (e).

13 A rule 1.2 representative must be able to discharge his or her functions fairly and competently. It is possible that a rule 1.2 representative may be in, or find himself or herself in, a personal or professional position in which he or she cannot properly represent P, provide the court with information about P or carry out other functions directed by the court. In such a case, Section 2 of Part 17 allows for the court to vary the terms of the appointment with a view to resolving the difficulty, or to discharge the appointment altogether (in which case the court will consider afresh whether it should make one or more of the directions in paragraph (2) of rule 1.2).

III MEN [498.1]

Accredited legal representative This scheme is now in existence: see www.lawsociety.org.uk/support-services/advice/practice-notes/accredited-legal-representatives-in-the-court-of-protection/.

PART 2
INTERPRETATION AND GENERAL PROVISIONS

III MEN [499]

2.1 Interpretation

In these Rules—

"the Act" means the Mental Capacity Act 2005;

"accredited legal representative" means a legal representative authorised pursuant to a scheme of accreditation approved by the President to represent persons meeting the definition of "P" in this rule in proceedings before the court;

"applicant" means a person who makes, or who seeks permission to make, an application to the court;

"application form" means the document that is to be used to begin proceedings in accordance with Part 9 of these Rules or any other provision of these Rules or the practice directions which requires the use of an application form;

"application notice" means the document that is to be used to make an application in accordance with Part 10 of these Rules or any other provision of these Rules or the practice directions which requires the use of an application notice;

"attorney" means the person appointed as such by an enduring power of attorney created, or purporting to have been created, in accordance with the regulations mentioned in paragraph 2 of Schedule 4 to the Act;

"business day" means a day other than—

(a) a Saturday, Sunday, Christmas Day or Good Friday; or

(b) a bank holiday in England and Wales, under the Banking and Financial Dealings Act 1971;

"child" means a person under 18;

"civil restraint order" means an order restraining a party—

(a) from making any further applications in current proceedings (a limited civil restraint order);

(b) from making certain applications in the Court of Protection (an extended civil restraint order); or

(c) from making any application in the Court of Protection (a general civil restraint order);

"court" means the Court of Protection;

"deputy" means a deputy appointed under the Act;

"donee" means the donee of a lasting power of attorney;

"donor" means the donor of a lasting power of attorney, except where the expression is used in rule 9.8 or 24.4(5) (where it means the donor of an enduring power of attorney);

"enduring power of attorney" means an instrument created in accordance with such of the regulations mentioned in paragraph 2 of Schedule 4 to the Act as applied when it was executed;

"filing" in relation to a document means delivering it, by post or otherwise, to the court office;

"hearing" includes a hearing conducted by telephone, video link, or any other method permitted or directed by the court;

"judge" means a judge nominated to be a judge of the court under the Act;

"lasting power of attorney" has the meaning given in section 9 of the Act;

"legal representative" means a—

(a) barrister;

(b) solicitor;

(c) solicitor's employee;

(d) manager of a body recognised under section 9 of the Administration of Justice Act 1985; or

(e) person who, for the purposes of the Legal Services Act 2007, is an authorised person in relation to an activity which constitutes the conduct of litigation (within the meaning of that Act),

who has been instructed to act for a party in relation to any application;

"legally aided person" means a person to whom civil legal services (within the meaning of the Legal Aid, Sentencing and Punishment of Offenders Act 2012) have been made available under arrangements made for the purposes of Part 1 of that Act;

"order" includes a declaration made by the court;

"P" means—

(a) any person (other than a protected party) who lacks or, so far as consistent with the context, is alleged to lack capacity to make a decision or decisions in relation to any matter that is the subject of an application to the court; and

(b) a relevant person as defined by paragraph 7 of Schedule A1 to the Act,

and references to a person who lacks capacity are to be construed in accordance with the Act;

"party" is to be construed in accordance with rule 9.13;

"personal welfare" is to be construed in accordance with section 17 of the Act;

"President" and "Vice-President" refer to those judges appointed as such under section 46(3)(a) and (b) of the Act;

"property and affairs" is to be construed in accordance with section 18 of the Act;

"protected party" means a party or an intended party (other than P or a child) who lacks capacity to conduct the proceedings;

"representative" means a person appointed under rule 1.2(2)(c), except where the context otherwise requires;

"respondent" means a person who is named as a respondent in the application form or notice, as the case may be;

"rule 1.2 representative" means a representative or an accredited legal representative;

"Senior Judge" means the judge who has been nominated to be Senior Judge under section 46(4) of the Act, and references in these Rules to a circuit judge include the Senior Judge;

"Tier 1 Judge" means any judge nominated to act as a judge of the Court of Protection under section 46 of the Act who is neither a Tier 2 Judge nor a Tier 3 Judge;

"Tier 2 Judge" means—

(a) the Senior Judge; and

(b) such other judges nominated to act as a judge of the Court of Protection under section 46 of the Act as may be set out in the relevant practice direction;

"Tier 3 Judge" means—

(a) the President;

(b) the Vice-President; and

(c) such other judges nominated to act as a judge of the Court of Protection under section 46 of the Act as may be set out in the relevant practice direction;

"Visitor" means a person appointed as such by the Lord Chancellor under section 61 of the Act.

III MEN [500]

2.2 Court officers

(1) Where these Rules permit or require the court to perform an act of a purely formal or administrative character, that act may be performed by a court officer.

(2) A requirement that a court officer carry out any act at the request of any person is subject to the payment of any fee required by a fees order for the carrying out of that act.

III MEN [501]

2.3 Court officers—authorisation

(1) The Senior Judge or the President or the Vice-President may authorise a court officer to exercise the jurisdiction of the court in such circumstances as may be set out in the relevant practice direction.

(2) A court officer who has been authorised under paragraph (1)—

(a) must refer to a judge any application, proceedings or any question arising in any application or proceedings which ought, in the officer's opinion, to be considered by a judge;

(b) may not deal with any application or proceedings or any question arising in any application or proceedings by way of a hearing; and

(c) may not deal with an application for the reconsideration of an order made by that court officer or another court officer.

III MEN [502]

2.4 Computation of time

(1) This rule shows how to calculate any period of time which is specified—

(a) by these Rules;

(b) by a practice direction; or

(c) in an order or direction of the court.

(2) A period of time expressed as a number of days must be computed as clear days.

(3) In this rule, "clear days" means that in computing the number of days—

(a) the day on which the period begins; and

(b) if the end of the period is defined by reference to an event, the day on which that event occurs,

are not included.

(4) Where the specified period is 7 days or less, and would include a day which is not a business day, that day does not count.

(5) When the specified period for doing any act at the court office ends on a day on which the office is closed, that act will be done in time if done on the next day on which the court office is open.

III MEN [503]

2.5 Application of the Civil Procedure Rules and Family Procedure Rules

(1) In any case not expressly provided for by these Rules or the practice directions made under them, the court may apply either the Civil Procedure Rules 1998 or the Family Procedure Rules 2010 (including in either case the practice directions made under them) with any necessary modifications, in so far as is necessary to further the overriding objective.

(2) A reference in these Rules to the Civil Procedure Rules 1998 or to the Family Procedure Rules 2010 is to the version of those rules in force at the date specified for the purpose of that reference in the relevant practice direction.

III MEN [504]

2.6 Pilot schemes

(1) Practice directions may make provision for the operation of pilot schemes for assessing the use of new practices and procedures in connection with proceedings—

(a) for specified periods; and

(b) in relation to proceedings—

(i) in specified parts of the country; or

(ii) relating to specified types of application.

(2) Practice directions may modify or disapply any provision of these Rules during the operation of such pilot schemes.

PRACTICE DIRECTION 2A — LEVELS OF JUDICIARY

III MEN [505]

This Practice Direction supplements Part 2 of the Court of Protection Rules 2017

GENERAL

1.1 Rule 2.1 makes provision for a practice direction to set out which of the judges who have been nominated to act as a judge of the Court of Protection under section 46 of the Act are to be Tier 2 Judges and Tier 3 Judges.

1.2 A judge who has been nominated to act as a judge of the Court of Protection under section 46 of the Act and who is neither a Tier 2 Judge nor a Tier 3 Judge is a Tier 1 Judge.

1.3 Rule 13.4 makes provision as to which judges of the Court of Protection may reconsider decisions made by Tier 1 Judges, Tier 2 Judges and Tier 3 Judges.

1.4 Part 20 makes provision as to the destination of appeals from Tier 1 Judges, Tier 2 Judges and Tier 3 Judges.

TIER 2 JUDGES

2 The following judges are Tier 2 Judges for the purposes of the Court of Protection Rules 2017:

(a) The Senior Judge

(b) a judge who has been nominated to act as a judge of the Court of Protection under section 46 of the Act by virtue of holding one of the following offices:

(i) a circuit judge;
(ii) a recorder;
(iii) a judge of the Upper Tribunal, by virtue of appointment under paragraph 1(1) of Schedule 3 to the Tribunals, Courts and Enforcement Act 2007,
(iv) a transferred-in judge of the Upper Tribunal (see section 31(2) of the Tribunals, Courts and Enforcement Act 2007),
(v) a deputy judge of the Upper Tribunal (whether under paragraph 7 of Schedule 3 to, or section 31(2) of, the Tribunals, Courts and Enforcement Act 2007),
(vi) the Judge Advocate General,
(vii) a person appointed under section 30(1)(a) or (b) of the Courts-Martial (Appeals) Act 1951 (assistants to the Judge Advocate General),
(viii) the Chamber President, or Deputy Chamber President, of a chamber of the First-tier Tribunal or of a chamber of the Upper Tribunal.

TIER 3 JUDGES

3. The following judges are Tier 3 Judges for the purposes of the Court of Protection Rules 2017:

(a) The President;
(b) The Vice-President;
(c) a judge who has been nominated to act as a judge of the Court of Protection under section 46 of the Act by virtue of holding one of the following offices:
  (i) The President of the Family Division
  (ii) The Chancellor
  (iii) The President of the Queen's Bench Division
  (iv) The Master of the Rolls
  (v) The Lord Chief Justice
  (vi) The Senior President of Tribunals
  (vii) a puisne judge of the High Court
  (viii) a deputy judge of the High Court
  (ix) an ordinary judge of the Court of Appeal (including the vice-president, if any, of either division of that court).

PRACTICE DIRECTION 2B — AUTHORISED COURT OFFICERS

III MEN [506]

This practice direction supplements Part 2 of the Court of Protection Rules 2017

GENERAL

1.1 Rule 2.3 enables a practice direction to specify the circumstances in which an authorised court officer is able to exercise the jurisdiction of the court.

1.2 A court officer is so authorised by the Senior Judge or the President pursuant to rule 2.3(1).

APPLICATIONS THAT MAY BE DEALT WITH BY AUTHORISED COURT OFFICERS

2.1 Subject to paragraphs 2.2, 3 and 4.2 an authorised court officer may deal with any of the following applications:

(a) applications to appoint a deputy for property and affairs;
(b) applications to vary the powers of a deputy appointed for property and affairs under an existing order;
(c) applications to discharge a deputy for property and affairs and appoint a replacement deputy;
(d) applications to appoint and discharge a trustee;
(e) applications to sell or purchase real property on behalf of P;
(f) applications to vary the security in relation to a deputy for property and affairs;
(g) applications to discharge the security when the appointment of a deputy for property and affairs comes to an end;
(h) applications for the release of funds for the maintenance of P, or P's property, or to discharge any debts incurred by P;
(i) applications to sell or otherwise deal with P's investments;
(j) applications for authority to apply for a grant of probate or representation for the use and benefit of P;
(k) applications to let and manage property belonging to P;
(l) applications for a detailed assessment of costs;
(m) applications to obtain a copy of P's will;
(n) applications to inspect or obtain copy documents from the records of the court; and
(o) applications which relate to one or more of the preceding paragraphs and which a judge has directed should be dealt with by an authorised court officer.

2.2 An authorised court officer may not conduct a hearing and must refer to a judge any application or any question arising in any application which is contentious or which, in the opinion of the officer:

(a) is complex;
(b) requires a hearing; or
(c) for any other reason ought to be considered by a judge.

CASE MANAGEMENT POWERS OF AUTHORISED COURT OFFICERS

3. Authorised court officers may only exercise the following case management powers when dealing with any of the applications listed at paragraph 2.1:

(a) extend or shorten the time for compliance with any rule, practice direction, or court order or direction pursuant to rule 3.1(2)(a) (even if an application for extension is made after the time for compliance has expired);
(b) take any step or give any direction for the purpose of managing the case and furthering the overriding objective pursuant to rule 3.1(2)(n);
(c) make any order they consider appropriate pursuant to rule 3.1(5) even if a party has not sought that order; and
(d) vary or revoke an order pursuant to rule 3.1(6).

RECONSIDERATION OF DECISIONS OF AUTHORISED COURT OFFICERS

4.1 P, any party to the proceedings or any other person affected by an order made by an authorised court officer may apply to the court, pursuant to rule 13.4, to have the order reconsidered by a judge.

4.2 An authorised court officer may not in any circumstances deal with an application for reconsideration of an order made by him or made by another authorised court officer.

APPEALS AGAINST DECISIONS OF AUTHORISED COURT OFFICERS

5.1 No appeal lies against a decision of an authorised court officer. If P, any party, or any other person affected by an order of an authorised court officer is dissatisfied with a decision made by that officer they should apply for it to be reconsidered by a judge pursuant to rule 13.4 and to paragraph 4 of this Practice Direction.

PRACTICE DIRECTION 2C — APPLICATION OF THE CIVIL PROCEDURE RULES 1998 AND THE FAMILY PROCEDURE RULES 2010

III MEN [507]

This Practice Direction supplements Part 2 of the Court of Protection Rules 2017

1 Rule 2.5(2) allows a practice direction to specify the date at which the relevant versions of the Civil Procedure Rules 1998 and the Family Procedure Rules 2010 were in force for the purposes of references to either body of those Rules in the Court of Protection Rules 2017.

2 A reference in these Rules to the Civil Procedure Rules 1998 is to that version of those Rules in force on the 6th April 2017.

3. A reference in these Rules to the Family Procedure Rules 2010 is to that version of those Rules in force on the 6th April 2017.

PART 3
MANAGING THE CASE

III MEN [508]

3.1 The court's general powers of case management

(1) The list of powers in this rule is in addition to any powers given to the court by any other rule or practice direction or by any other enactment or any powers it may otherwise have.

(2) The court may—

- (a) extend or shorten the time for compliance with any rule, practice direction, or court order or direction (even if an application for extension is made after the time for compliance has expired);
- (b) adjourn or bring forward a hearing;
- (c) require P, a party, a party's legal representative or litigation friend, or P's rule 1.2 representative, to attend court;
- (d) hold a hearing and receive evidence by telephone or any other method of direct oral communication;
- (e) stay the whole or part of any proceedings or judgment either generally or until a specified date or event;
- (f) consolidate proceedings;
- (g) hear two or more applications on the same occasion;
- (h) direct a separate hearing of any issue;
- (i) decide the order in which issues are to be heard;
- (j) exclude an issue from consideration;

(k) dismiss or give judgment on an application after a decision is made on a preliminary basis;

(l) direct any party to file and serve an estimate of costs;

(m) direct or limit the means of communication to be used by the parties; and

(n) take any step or give any direction for the purpose of managing the case and furthering the overriding objective.

(3) A judge to whom a matter is allocated may, if the judge considers that the matter is one which ought properly to be dealt with by another judge, transfer the matter to such a judge.

(4) Where the court gives directions it may take into account whether or not a party has complied with any rule or practice direction.

(5) The court may make any order it considers appropriate even if a party has not sought that order.

(6) A power of the court under these Rules to make an order includes a power to vary or revoke the order.

(Rules 1.3 to 1.6 concern the duty of the court to further the overriding objective by actively managing cases, and the duty of parties, legal representatives and unrepresented litigants to assist the court in furthering the overriding objective.)

III MEN [509]

3.2 Case management—unrepresented parties

(1) This rule applies in any proceedings where at least one party is unrepresented.

(2) When the court is exercising any powers of case management, it must have regard to the fact that at least one party is unrepresented.

(3) The court must adopt such procedure at any hearing as it considers appropriate to further the overriding objective.

(4) At any hearing when the court is taking evidence, this may include—

(a) ascertaining from an unrepresented party the matters about which the witness may be able to give evidence or on which the witness ought to be cross-examined; and

(b) putting or causing to be put to the witness such questions as may appear to the court to be proper.

III MEN [510]

3.3 Court's power to dispense with requirement of any rule

In addition to its general powers and the powers listed in rule 3.1, the court may dispense with the requirements of any rule.

III MEN [511]

3.4 Exercise of powers on the court's own initiative

(1) Except where these Rules or another enactment make different provision, the court may exercise its powers on its own initiative.

(2) The court may make an order on its own initiative without hearing the parties or giving them the opportunity to make representations.

(3) Where the court proposes to make an order on its own initiative it may give the parties and any other person it thinks fit an opportunity to make representations and, where it does so, must specify the time by which, and the manner in which, the representations must be made.

(4) Where the court proposes—

(a) to make an order on its own initiative; and

(b) to hold a hearing to decide whether to make the order,

it must give the parties and may give any person it thinks likely to be affected by the order at least 3 days' notice of the hearing.

III MEN [512]

3.5 General power of the court to rectify matters where there has been an error of procedure

Where there has been an error of procedure, such as a failure to comply with a rule or practice direction—

(a) the error does not invalidate any step taken in the proceedings unless the court so orders; and

(b) the court may waive the error or require it to be remedied or may make such other order as appears to the court to be just.

III MEN [513]

3.6 Dealing with the application

(1) This rule and rule 3.7 are subject to any provision made by a practice direction in respect of the case pathway to which the case is allocated.

(2) As soon as practicable after any application has been issued the court shall consider how to deal with it.

(3) Where permission to start proceedings is required, and whether or not it has been applied for, the court's consideration under paragraph (2) shall include whether to grant or refuse permission without a hearing, or to direct a hearing to consider whether permission should be granted.

(4) The court may deal with an application or any part of an application at a hearing or without a hearing.

(5) In considering whether it is necessary to hold a hearing, the court shall, as appropriate, have regard to—

(a) the nature of the proceedings and the orders sought;

(b) whether the application is opposed by a person who appears to the court to have an interest in matters relating to P's best interests;

(c) whether the application involves a substantial dispute of fact;

(d) the complexity of the facts and the law;

(e) any wider public interest in the proceedings;

(f) the circumstances of P and of any party, in particular as to whether their rights would be adequately protected if a hearing were not held;

(g) whether the parties agree that the court should dispose of the application without a hearing; and

(h) any other matter specified in the relevant practice direction.

(6) Where the court considers that a hearing is necessary it shall—

(a) give notice of the hearing date to the parties and to any other person it directs;

(b) state what is to be dealt with at the hearing, including whether the matter is to be disposed of at that hearing; and

(c) consider whether it is appropriate—

(i) for the hearing or any part of it to be in public; and

(ii) to make any order under rule 4.1, 4.2 or 4.3.

(Rule 3.9 and Practice Direction 3B make provision about the case pathways.)

III MEN [514]

3.7 Directions

(1) The court may—

(a) give directions in writing; or

(b) set a date for a directions hearing; and

(c) do anything else that may be set out in a practice direction.

(2) When giving directions, the court may do any of the following—

(a) require a report under section 49 of the Act and give directions as to any such report;

(b) give directions as to any requirements contained in these Rules or a practice direction for the giving of notification to any person or for that person to do anything in response to a notification;

(c) if the court considers that any other person or persons should be a party to the proceedings, give directions joining them as a party;

(d) if the court considers that any party to the proceedings should not be a party, give directions for that person's removal as a party;

(e) give directions for the management of the case and set a timetable for the steps to be taken between the giving of directions and the hearing;

(f) subject to rule 3.8, give directions as to the type of judge who is to hear the case;

(g) give directions as to whether the proceedings or any part of them are to be heard in public, or as to whether any particular person should be permitted to attend the hearing, or as to whether any publication of the proceedings is to be permitted;

(h) give directions as to the disclosure of documents, service of witness statements and any expert evidence;

(i) give directions as to the attendance of witnesses and as to whether, and the extent to which, cross-examination will be permitted at any hearing; and

(j) give such other directions as the court may think fit.

(3) The court may give directions at any time—

(a) on its own initiative; or

(b) on the application of a party.

(4) Subject to paragraphs (5) and (6) and unless these Rules or a practice direction provide otherwise or the court directs otherwise, the time specified by a rule or by the court for a person to do any act may be varied by the written agreement of the parties.

(5) A party must apply to the court if that party wishes to vary—

(a) the date the court has fixed for the final hearing; or

(b) the period within which the final hearing is to take place.

(6) The time specified by a rule or practice direction or by the court may not be varied by the parties if the variation would make it necessary to vary the date the court has fixed for any hearing or the period within which the final hearing is to take place.

(Participation of P in proceedings is addressed in rule 1.2 (participation of P) and Part 17 (litigation friends and rule 1.2 representatives).)

III MEN [514.1]

Applications to the court and procedural guidance For s 49 reports see **III MEN [87]**, and Practice Direction 14E which provides supplemental directions: **III MEN [657]**.

If an issue involves Serious Medical Treatment then regard should be made to Practice Direction 3A: **III MEN [517]**.

For appointment of litigation friend see Part 17 and Practice Direction 17A: **III MEN [694]**. If the Official Solicitor is being considered, see *Practice Guidance: Official Solicitor acting as Guardian ad Litem or Litigation Friend* [2011] 1 FLR 944.

III MEN [514.2]

Where the Case Management Pilot applies see rules 3.7 and 3.9 of the Pilot Rules (**III MEN [504]**).

ALLOCATION OF PROCEEDINGS

III MEN [515]

3.8 Court's jurisdiction in certain kinds of cases to be exercised by certain judges

(1) A practice direction made under this rule may specify certain categories of case to be dealt with by a specific judge or a specific class of judges.

(2) Applications in any matter other than those specified in the practice direction referred to in paragraph (1) may be dealt with by any judge.

III MEN [516]

3.9 Allocation of cases to case pathways

(1) This rule provides for the allocation of cases to case pathways.

(2) There are three case pathways—

- (a) the Personal Welfare Pathway;
- (b) the Property and Affairs Pathway;
- (c) the Mixed Welfare and Property Pathway.

(3) Each case shall on issue be allocated to one of the three case pathways unless (subject to paragraph (5)) it is in an excepted class of case.

(4) Excepted classes of case may be specified in a practice direction.

(5) The court may direct that a case shall be allocated to a case pathway notwithstanding that it is in an excepted class of cases.

(6) A practice direction may make provision for—

- (a) the scope of each case pathway; and
- (b) how cases in each case pathway are to be managed.

(Practice Direction 3B makes provision in relation to the case pathways and excepted classes of case.)

PRACTICE DIRECTION 3A – COURT'S JURISDICTION TO BE EXERCISED BY CERTAIN JUDGES

III MEN [517]

This practice direction supplements Part 3 of the Court of Protection Rules 2017

GENERAL

1 Rule 3.8 allows a practice direction to specify that certain categories of case must be dealt with by a specific judge or a specific class of judges.

CASES CONCERNING AN ETHICAL DILEMMA IN AN UNTESTED AREA OR DECLARATIONS OF INCOMPATIBILITY PURSUANT TO SECTION 4 OF THE HUMAN RIGHTS ACT 1998

(a) Where an application is made to the court in relation to an ethical dilemma in an untested area, the proceedings must be conducted by a Tier 3 judge;

(b) Where an application is made to the court pursuant to rule 12.1, in which a declaration of incompatibility pursuant to section 4 of the Human Rights Act

1998 is sought, the proceedings (including permission, the giving of any directions, and any hearing) must be conducted by a judge of the court who has been nominated as such by virtue of section 46(2)(a) to (c) of the Act (i.e. the President of the Family Division, the Chancellor or a puisne judge of the High Court).

COURT'S GENERAL DISCRETION AS TO ALLOCATION

3 The Senior Judge or a Tier 3 Judge may determine whether a matter is one that is to be allocated pursuant to this practice direction.

4 The judge to whom a matter is allocated in accordance with this practice direction may determine that the matter or parts of it may properly be heard by a judge of the court other than a Tier 3 Judge or one nominated by virtue of section 46(2)(a) to (c) of the Act; and may reallocate the matter or part of it accordingly.

PRACTICE DIRECTION 3B – CASE PATHWAYS

III MEN [518]

This practice direction supplements Part 3 of the Court of Protection Rules 2017

NOTE: Rule 9.12(5) and (7) do not apply where a case is allocated to a case pathway.

In applying this practice direction, the parties must have regard to any guidance issued in relation to allocation of Court of Protection cases to Tier 3 Judges.

PART 1 – SCOPE OF THE CASE MANAGEMENT PATHWAYS

1.1 Rule 3.9 provides for each case which is started in the CoP to be allocated to one of three case management pathways on issue, unless the case falls within an excepted class of cases specified in a practice direction. The excepted classes of case which are specified for this purpose are –

(a) uncontested applications;
(b) applications for statutory wills and gifts;
(c) applications made by the Public Guardian;
(d) applications in Form COPDOL11;
(e) applications in Form DLA; and
(f) Schedule 3 applications (under Part 23 of the Rules).

1.2 The scope of the pathways is as follows –

The personal welfare pathway (Part 2 of this practice direction)

This will be the normal pathway for a case in which an application is made to the court to make or authorise one or more decisions and/or actions and/or declarations relating to P's personal welfare only.

The property and affairs pathway (Part 3 of this practice direction)

This will be the normal pathway for a case in which an application is made to the Court to make or authorise one or more decisions and/or actions and/or declarations relating to P's property and financial affairs only.

The mixed welfare and property pathway (Part 4 of this practice direction)

This will be the normal pathway for a case in which the court is to be asked to make or authorise one or more decisions and/or actions and/or declarations relating not only to P's property and financial affairs but also P's personal welfare.

PART 2 – THE PERSONAL WELFARE PATHWAY

2.1 The Personal Welfare Pathway comprises six stages –

(a) The pre-issue stage (see paragraph 2.2);
(b) The point of issue of the application (see paragraph 2.3);
(c) Case management on issue (see paragraph 2.4);
(d) The Case Management Conference (see paragraph 2.5);
(e) The Final Management Hearing (see paragraph 2.6);
(f) The Final Hearing (see paragraph 2.7).

2.2 **The pre-issue stage**

(1) In all cases

The applicant must take all necessary steps to –

(a) identify all potential respondents to the proceedings which the applicant proposes to start, and any other interested parties;
(b) notify P (where possible) and the potential respondents and other interested parties identified in accordance with sub-paragraph (a) of the applicant's intention to start the proceedings unless the matters which the court would be asked to determine can be resolved without the need for proceedings;
(c) explain to those notified in accordance with sub-paragraph (b) the nature of the proceedings which the applicant proposes to start, and the matters which the court would be asked to determine in those proceedings;
(d) set out the applicant's proposals for resolving those matters without the need for proceedings;
(e) engage with those notified in accordance with sub-paragraph (b) to resolve those matters as far as possible;
(f) ensure, where it is not possible to resolve those matters without starting proceedings, that all the documents and information required by paragraph 2.3 will be ready to be included with the application.

(2) Additionally, in urgent cases

Where the applicant intends to make an urgent or interim application, the applicant must consider –

(a) why the case is urgent and what the consequences will be if the case is not treated as urgent;
(b) if any of the steps in paragraph 2.2(1) cannot be taken, why this is the case and what the consequences would be if those steps were taken;
(c) whether there is any specific deadline, and what that deadline is;
(d) whether there are issues which are not urgent and how those could be separated from those which are urgent.

2.3 **The point of issue of the application**

(1) In all cases

The applicant must include in the application, or refer in the application to and file with it, the following documents or information –

(a) a draft final order or explanation of the order that is sought;
(b) a clear explanation of why an order, and the specific order sought, is required;
(c) an explanation of the nature of the dispute;
(d) a statement of what is expected of P's family and/or other connected individuals;
(e) the names of the key people involved in the case, and the nature of their involvement;

MENTAL CAPACITY AND MENTAL HEALTH

(f) a list of the options for P;
(g) a needs assessment, including where appropriate a risk assessment;
(h) a support plan for P, with a time line, including where appropriate a transfer plan;
(i) evidence that the key individuals and agencies have been consulted;
(j) confirmation that a best interests meeting has taken place, and a copy of the minutes of that meeting;
(k) any relevant medical evidence;
(l) except in applications under section 21A of the Act, a report from a medical practitioner or other appropriately qualified professional on P's litigation capacity and capacity to make decisions on the issues in the case;
(m) an explanation of how P can be supported to maximise any decision-making capacity which P has (if possible);
(n) an indication of whether there is likely to be a public law challenge in the case, and if so, the nature of the challenge which is anticipated;
(o) a statement of how it is proposed that P will be involved in the case.

(2) Additionally, in urgent cases

Where the application is urgent, the applicant must include in the application, or refer in the application to and file with it, the following information or documents in addition to those in paragraph 2.3(1) –

(a) why the case is urgent and what the consequences will be if the case is not treated as urgent;
(b) if any of the steps in paragraph 2.2(1) cannot be taken, why this is the case and what the consequences would be if those steps were taken;
(c) confirmation of any specific deadline;
(d) information identifying and separating the issues which are urgent from those which are not urgent.

2.4 **Case management on issue**

(1) In all cases

Upon issue of the application, the papers will be placed before a judge for gatekeeping and initial case management directions. These will include –

(a) gatekeeping: allocating the case to the correct level of judge, having regard to any guidance issued in relation to allocation of Court of Protection cases to Tier 3 Judges;
(b) listing for a Case Management Conference within 28 days (unless the matter is urgent, in which case paragraph 2.4(2) applies);
(c) directions to ensure the Case Management Conference is utilised properly;
(d) considering whether it is necessary for P to be joined as a party, and whether any other persons should be invited to attend the Case Management Conference so that they may apply to be joined (but not making any order for any person other than P to be joined at this stage);
(e) directing the parties to consider who can act as litigation friend or rule 1.2 representative for P if necessary;
(f) considering what details of P's estate should be provided for the purposes of securing litigation funding or otherwise;
(g) considering whether an advocates' meeting should take place before the case management conference, and ordering such a meeting if appropriate;
(h) ordering the preparation of a core bundle (which must not exceed 150 pages, unless the court directs otherwise) for the Case Management Conference.

(2) Additionally, in urgent cases

Where the application is urgent –

(a) if the case is within a category which must be heard by a Tier 3 Judge in accordance with any guidance issued in relation to allocation of Court of Protection cases to Tier 3 Judges, it must be transferred to a Tier 3 Judge;
(b) the case will be listed urgently in accordance with the judge's directions.

2.5 **The case management conference**

At the Case Management Conference, the court will –

(a) record the issues in dispute;
(b) record what has been agreed between the parties;
(c) record which issues are not to be the subject of adjudication in the case;
(d) consider the appropriate judge for the case;
(e) allocate a judge to the case;
(f) actively consider and decide, having regard to rule 1.2, how P is to be involved in the case;
(g) consider whether a litigation friend is required for P, and if so, who is to be the litigation friend, and if the Official Solicitor is to be the litigation friend, declare that the appointment of the Official Solicitor is a last resort;
(h) determine who should be a party;
(i) set a timetable for the proceedings;
(j) fix a date for the Final Management Hearing, and set a target date for the Final Hearing or fix a trial window as appropriate;
(k) consider whether a further best interests meeting is required, and if so, give directions for that meeting;
(l) give directions for evidence, including disclosure and expert reports (if appropriate having regard to sub-paragraph (m));
(m) actively consider whether a section 49 report or the use of a rule 1.2 representative could achieve a better result than the use of an expert;
(n) consider whether there should be a public hearing;
(o) give any other directions as appropriate to further the overriding objective.

2.6 **The final management hearing**

(1) A Final Management Hearing will be listed to enable the court to determine whether the case can be resolved, and if not, to ensure that the trial is properly prepared, giving directions as necessary for that purpose.

(2) A meeting should take place at least five days before the Final Management Hearing between advocates and, so far as practicable, any unrepresented parties, with the purpose of resolving or narrowing the issues to be determined at the Final Management Hearing, addressing each of the matters required by Practice Direction 4B and preparing a draft order.

(3) The applicant (or, if the applicant is not represented but the respondent is represented, the respondent) must, not later than 3 days before the Final Management Hearing, file a core bundle, which must comply with the requirements of Practice Direction 4B and in particular include the documents specified in paragraphs 4.2 and 4.3 of that Practice Direction.

(4) If sub-paragraph (3) has not been complied with, or any other directions have not been complied with, the court will consider whether to adjourn the hearing, and if it does so, will consider making an order as to costs.

2.7 **The final hearing**

(1) Unless otherwise directed by the court, a meeting should take place at least five days before the Final Hearing between advocates and, so far as practicable, any unrepresented parties, with the purpose of resolving or narrowing the issues to be determined at the Final Hearing.

(2) The applicant (or, if the applicant is not represented but the respondent is represented, the respondent) must, not later than 3 days before the Final Hearing, file a bundle, which must –

(a) comply with the requirements of Practice Direction 4B, with particular reference to paragraphs 4.6 and 4.7 of that Practice Direction; and
(b) not generally exceed 350 pages and in any event not contain more than one copy of the same document.

(3) If sub-paragraph (2) has not been complied with, or any other directions have not been complied with, the court will consider whether to adjourn the hearing, and if it does so, will consider making an order as to costs.

PART 3 – THE PROPERTY AND AFFAIRS PATHWAY

(1) The Property and Affairs Pathway commences at a later stage than the Personal Welfare Pathway. It is recognised that contentious property and affairs applications tend to arise when a routine application is made, for example for the appointment of a deputy, and that application is opposed. The vast majority of applications, however, remain unopposed, and there is not the need for a pre-issue stage which there is in personal welfare cases.

(2) The Property and Affairs Pathway comprises four stages –

(a) *When the application becomes contested* (see paragraph 3.2);
(b) *Case management on allocation to pathway* (see paragraph 3.3);
(c) *The Dispute Resolution Hearing* (see paragraph 3.4);
(d) *The Final Hearing* (see paragraph 3.5).

(3) *Urgent applications* are less likely in property and affairs cases; but paragraph 3.6 contains provision for their management.

3.2 **When the application becomes contested**

(1) When the court is notified in Form COP5 that a property and affairs application is opposed, or that the respondent wishes to seek a different order from that applied for, the case must be allocated to the Property and Affairs Pathway.

(2) A copy of the notification in Form COP5 must be served by the court on the applicant together with the order allocating the case to the Property and Affairs Pathway (see paragraph 3.3; and see also the opening paragraph of this practice direction which disapplies rule 9.12(5) and (7)).

3.3 **Case management on allocation to pathway**

(1) Following notification in Form COP5 that the case is contested, the papers will be placed before a judge who will allocate the case to the Property and Affairs Pathway and either –

- list the case for a Dispute Resolution Hearing; or
- transfer the case to the most appropriate regional court outside the Central Office and Registry for listing of the Dispute Resolution Hearing and future case management.

(2) The judge will also order the respondent to file a summary of the reasons for opposing the application or for seeking a different order, if the reasons are not clear from Form COP5 submitted by the respondent.

3.4 **The dispute resolution hearing**

(1) All parties must attend the Dispute Resolution Hearing, unless the court directs otherwise; but the Dispute Resolution Hearing is not an attended hearing for the purposes of Practice Direction 4C.

(2) The Dispute Resolution Hearing will normally take place before a District Judge.

(3) The purpose of the Dispute Resolution Hearing is to enable the court to determine whether the case can be resolved and avoid unnecessary litigation, and so –

(a) in order for the Dispute Resolution Hearing to be effective, parties must approach it openly and without reserve; and
(b) the content of the hearing is not to be disclosed and evidence of anything said or of any admission made in the course of the hearing will not be admissible in evidence, except at the trial of a person for an offence committed at the hearing.

(4) The court will give its view on the likely outcome of the proceedings.

(5) If the parties reach agreement to settle the case, the court will make a final order if it considers it in P's best interests.

(6) If the parties do not reach agreement, the court will give directions for the management of the case and for a Final Hearing, having regard to the list of matters in paragraph 2.5, and the requirements of Practice Direction 4B in relation to the preparation of a bundle.

(7) The Final Hearing must be listed before a different judge, and the judge will mark the order accordingly.

3.5 **The final hearing**

The final hearing will take place in accordance with the directions given at or following the Dispute Resolution Hearing.

3.6 **Urgent applications**

(1) Where a property and affairs application is urgent, the applicant should bear in mind the obligation on parties to co-operate in rule 1.4(2)(c).

(2) The applicant must include in the application, or refer in the application to and file with it, the following information or documents –

(a) an explanation of why the case is urgent and what the consequences will be if the case is not treated as urgent;
(b) if the application is made without notice, an explanation why it was not possible to make the application on notice, and what the consequences would be if the application were to proceed on notice and the order or an interim order were not made immediately;
(c) confirmation of any specific deadline;
(d) information identifying and separating the issues which are urgent from those which are not urgent.

(3) On issue, the case will be listed urgently in accordance with the judge's directions after considering the papers, which may, if the matter appears or is confirmed to be contentious, be that –

(a) the case will proceed to a Dispute Resolution Hearing but listed urgently; or
(b) the case may be listed for an interim hearing to decide the urgent matter or matters in the case, and the court can decide at that hearing whether any further hearing is necessary and if so, whether that further hearing should include a Dispute Resolution Hearing or not.

PART 4 – THE MIXED WELFARE AND PROPERTY PATHWAY

(1) Where a case contains both personal welfare and property and affairs elements, the court has the power to use whichever of the personal welfare or the property and affairs pathway it considers most suitable, or to direct the use of elements of both those pathways if it considers that appropriate.

(2) The Mixed Welfare and Property Pathway, therefore, comprises two stages before the court makes a decision about which pathway, or a mixture of elements of both pathways, is most appropriate –

- The *pre-issue* stage, during which the prospective parties are expected to identify which pathway is most appropriate to the case and to comply with the requirements of that pathway and seek to resolve issues as far as possible;
- The *point of issue of the application*, for which the parties must file a list of issues to allow the court to identify which pathway, or mixture of elements, is most appropriate.

(3) *Case management*: On issue of the application, the papers will be placed before a judge who will either –

(a) order the case to be allocated to a pathway and give directions accordingly; or

MENTAL CAPACITY AND MENTAL HEALTH

(b) give directions as to the elements of each pathway which are to apply and the procedure the case will follow.

PART 4
HEARINGS

PRIVATE HEARINGS

III MEN [519]

4.1 General rule—hearing to be held in private

(1) The general rule is that a hearing is to be held in private.

(2) A private hearing is a hearing which only the following persons are entitled to attend—

(a) the parties;

(b) P (whether or not a party);

(c) any person acting in the proceedings as a litigation friend or rule 1.2 representative;

(d) any legal representative of a person specified in any of sub-paragraphs (a) or (b); and

(e) any court officer.

(3) In relation to a private hearing, the court may make an order—

(a) authorising any person, or class of persons, to attend the hearing or a part of it; or

(b) excluding any person, or class of persons, from attending the hearing or a part of it.

(4) The general rule in paragraph (1) does not apply to a hearing for a committal order or writ of sequestration (in respect of which rule 21.27 makes provision).

III MEN [519.1]

Applications to the court and procedural guidance On 29 January 2016, pursuant to rule 9A, a Pilot Scheme was introduced until 31 August 2017 which materially affects the holding of proceedings in private in respect of cases to which the Practice Direction –Transparency Pilot applies (see **III MEN [525]**). Practitioners must have regard to rr 90 to 93, the Practice Direction and draft order; for Pilot Schemes, see **III MEN [504]**.

For discussion on issues arising from the general rule and for details of cases in which the Court including the Court of Appeal have given guidance on the interpretation thereof: see **III MEN [6]**.

Application to the court should be made under Part 10 and be commenced on form COP9. See **III MEN [607]**.

III MEN [519.2]

Where the Case Management Pilot applies see Pilot Part 4 and rules 4.1 to 4.4 (rule 90 is now rule 4.1) of the Pilot Rules (**III MEN [504]**).

III MEN [520]

4.2 Court's general power to authorise publication of information about proceedings

(1) For the purposes of the law relating to contempt of court, information relating to proceedings held in private (whether or not contained in a document filed with the court) may be communicated in accordance with paragraph (2) or (3).

(2) The court may make an order authorising—

(a) the publication or communication of such information or material relating to the proceedings as it may specify; or

(b) the publication of the text or a summary of the whole or part of a judgment or order made by the court.

(3) Subject to any direction of the court, information referred to in paragraph (1) may be communicated in accordance with Practice Direction 4A.

(4) Where the court makes an order under paragraph (2) it may do so on such terms as it thinks fit, and in particular may—

(a) impose restrictions on the publication of the identity of—

(i) any party;

(ii) P (whether or not a party);

(iii) any witness; or

(iv) any other person;

(b) prohibit the publication of any information that may lead to any such person being identified;

(c) prohibit the further publication of any information relating to the proceedings from such date as the court may specify; or

(d) impose such other restrictions on the publication of information relating to the proceedings as the court may specify.

(5) The court may on its own initiative or upon request authorise communication—

(a) for the purposes set out in Practice Direction 4A; or

(b) for such other purposes as it considers appropriate,

of information held by it.

III MEN [520.1]

Guidance on issues of publication and anonymity For cases in which judicial comment was made on the issue of anonymity, and guidance on the prohibition of publication and ordering of restrictions, see *London Borough of Hillingdon v Steven Neary and Mark Neary* [2011] EWHC 413 (COP), and *W (By her Litigation Friend, B) v M (An Adult Patient, By her litigation friend, the Official Solicitor), S, A NHS Primary Care Trust, Times Newspapers Limited* [2011] EWHC 1197 (COP) (**III MEN [6]**).

See now the Practice Guidance issued by the President of the Court of Protection providing guidelines on the approach to publication of judgments of the court as from 3 February 2014: *Practice Guidance (Transparency in the Court of Protection)* [2014] EWHC B2 (COP) (see **III MEN [13]**).

The procedure for all committal proceedings must now follow not only the relevant rules but also the Practice Direction: Committal for Contempt of Court – Open Court issued by the Lord Chief Justice on 26 March 2015 and the Practice Guidance: Committal for Contempt of Court – Open Court dated 24 June 2015. This Practice Direction and Guidance supersede all previous Practice directions and Guidance. The Practice Direction addresses issues of public and private hearings, the engagement of the Press and the issue of judgments. In a clear indication of the importance of Open Justice strict procedures are applied for the publicity of the hearing, the notification of press, the publication of the outcome and the limiting of matters in private. The Guidance addresses questions which had arisen surrounding press notification, and judgments. See Court of Protection Rules 2017, rule 21.28 at **III MEN [761]** and see also CPR 81.28.

In *Public Guardian v JM* [2014] WTLR 979, [2014] All ER (D), 103 (Feb)LRC 428, [2014] All ER (D) 185 (Mar) the President whilst recording the Article 8 rights of an attorney, permitted his name to be published balancing his rights as against the issues of misconduct found and the importance of the transparency of the Court's proceedings.

III MEN [520.2]

Where the Case Management Pilot applies see rule 4.2 of the Pilot Rules (**III MEN [504]**).

Power to order a public hearing

III MEN [521]

4.3 Court's power to order that a hearing be held in public

(1) The court may make an order—

(a) for a hearing to be held in public;

(b) for a part of a hearing to be held in public; or

(c) excluding any person, or class of persons, from attending a public hearing or a part of it.

(2) Where the court makes an order under paragraph (1), it may in the same order or by a subsequent order—

(a) impose restrictions on the publication of the identity of—

(i) any party;

(ii) P (whether or not a party);

(iii) any witness; or

(iv) any other person;

(b) prohibit the publication of any information that may lead to any such person being identified;

(c) prohibit the further publication of any information relating to the proceedings from such date as the court may specify; or

(d) impose such other restrictions on the publication of information relating to the proceedings as the court may specify.

(3) A practice direction may provide for circumstances in which the court will ordinarily make an order under paragraph (1), and for the terms of the order under paragraph (2) which the court will ordinarily make in such circumstances.

III MEN [521.1]

Guidance on issues relating to reporting restrictions In the decision of *W (By her Litigation Friend, B) v M (An Adult Patient, By her Litigation Friend, The Official Solicitor), S, A NHS Primary Care Trust, Times Newspapers Limited* [2011] EWHC 1197 (COP), Mr Justice Baker with the approval of the President set out guidelines for the structure of Reporting Restriction Orders and other injunctions arising from the exercise of the Court of Protection's jurisdiction. See **III MEN [6]**.

The decision of Mr Peter Jackson in *Newcastle upon Tyne Hospitals Foundation Trust v LM* [2014] EWHC 454 (COP), 137 BMLR 226 a case concerning a declaration not to give blood products to a Jehovah's Witness provides a good demonstration of the structure and format of a Reporting Restrictions order. In *Re V (Out of Hours: Reporting Order)* [2015] EWCOP 83 the court dealing with an out of hours request to continue anonymity of 'P' by extending a Reporting Restriction Order following her death followed the judgment of Peter Jackson J in *Press Association v Newcastle Upon Tyne Hospitals Foundation Trust* [2014] EWCOP 6, [2014] All ER (D) 166 (Jun) in determining that the court had such jurisdiction and in particular that it was appropriate to so grant pending a full determination at a fully constituted hearing.

III MEN [521.2]

Where the Case Management Pilot applies see rule 4.3 of the Pilot Rules (**III MEN [504]**).

Supplementary

III MEN [522]

4.4 Supplementary provisions relating to public or private hearings

(1) Subject to provision in a practice direction made under rule 4.3(3), an order under rule 4.1, 4.2 or 4.3 may be made—

(a) only where it appears to the court that there is good reason for making the order;

(b) at any time; and

(c) either on the court's own initiative or on an application made by any person in accordance with Part 10.

(2) A practice direction may make further provision in connection with—

(a) private hearings;

(b) public hearings; or

(c) the publication of information about any proceedings.

III MEN [522.1]

Guidance on applications to the court and issues of publicity For consideration of the issue of good reason, see *Independent News and Media Ltd v A* [2010] EWCA Civ 343, [2010] 3 All ER 32, [2010] 2 FCR 187, and the discussion at **III MEN [6]** above. In *P (by his litigation friend the Official Solicitor) v Independent Print Ltd* [2011] EWCA Civ 756, [2012] 2 FCR 503, [2012] 1 FLR 212 the court in emphasising the proper approach of the 2 stage test, confirmed that whilst the best interests of P was a material factor, it did not dictate the decision which was a case management decision having regard to the correct application of the rules to the particular circumstances before the court.

Practice Direction 13A provides guidance on the powers of the court to impose reporting restrictions, the giving of notification and notices, the hearing and scope of order. The Annex provides an example of a reporting restriction order (**III MEN [523]**). See further *W (by her Litigation Friend, B) v M (An Adult Patient, By her Litigation Friend, The Official Solicitor), S, A NHS Primary Care Trust, Times Newspapers Limited* [2011] EWHC 1197 (COP). Mr Justice Baker with the approval of the President set out guidelines for the structure of Reporting Restriction Orders and other injunctions arising from the exercise of the Court of Protection's jurisdiction. For an example of the court exercising this power see *An NHS Trust v The Patient* [2014] EWCOP 54, [2015] All ER (D) 58 (Jan), where Holman J imposed reporting restrictions and subsequently reported the successful outcome of the operation on P.

In *Re V (Out of Hours: Reporting Order)* [2015] EWCOP 83 the court dealing with an out of hours request to continue anonymity of 'P' by extending a Reporting Restriction Order following her death followed the judgment of Peter Jackson J in *Press Association v Newcastle Upon Tyne Hospitals Foundation Trust* [2014] EWCOP 6, [2014] All ER (D) 166 (Jun) in determining that the court had such jurisdiction and in particular that it was appropriate to so grant pending a full determination at a fully constituted hearing.

See further **III MEN [13]** for the Guidance of the President dated 16 January 2014 in respect of publication of judgments as from 3 February 2014.

III MEN [522.2]

Where the Case Management Pilot applies see rule 4.4 of the Pilot Rules (**III MEN [504]**).

PRACTICE DIRECTION 4A – HEARINGS (INCLUDING REPORTING RESTRICTIONS)

III MEN [523]

This practice direction supplements Part 4 of the Court of Protection Rules 2007

GENERAL

1 Under rules 4.1 to 4.3, the default position is that hearings before the court will be in private but the court may order that the whole or part of any hearing is to be held in public. Practice Direction 4C sets out the circumstances in which the court will ordinarily make such an order, and the terms of the order it will ordinarily make. The court also has power to –

(a) authorise the publication of information about a private hearing;
(b) authorise persons to attend a private hearing;
(c) exclude persons from attending either a private or public hearing; or
(d) restrict or prohibit the publication of information about a private or public hearing.

2 Part 1 of this practice direction applies to any application for an order under rules 4.1 to 4.3, but not to any case where the court makes an order pursuant to Practice Direction 4C.

MENTAL CAPACITY AND MENTAL HEALTH

3 Part 2 of this practice direction makes additional provision in relation to orders founded on Convention rights which would restrict the publication of information. Part 2 does not apply where the court makes an order pursuant to Practice Direction 4C, but will apply if different or additional restrictions on the publication of information relating to the proceedings are imposed in a subsequent order.

(Section 1 of the Human Rights Act 1998 defines "the Convention rights".)

PART 1
APPLICATIONS UNDER RULES 4.1 TO 4.3

4 An application for an order under rule 4.1, 4.2 or 4.3 must be commenced by filing an application notice form using COP9 in accordance with Part 10.

5 For the purposes of rules 4.1 to 4.3, a statement of truth in an application notice may be made by a person who is not a party.

6 For an application commenced under rule 4.1, 4.2 or 4.3, the court should consider whether to direct that the application should be dealt with as a discrete issue.

PART 2
POWERS OF THE COURT TO IMPOSE REPORTING RESTRICTIONS

Court sitting in private

7 Section 12(1) of the Administration of Justice Act 1960 provides that, in any proceedings brought under the Mental Capacity Act 2005 before a court which is sitting in private, publication of information about the proceedings will generally be contempt of court. However, rule 4.2(1) makes it clear that there will be no contempt where the court has authorised the publication of the information under rule 4.2 or the publication is authorised in accordance with Part 3 of this Practice Direction. Where the court makes an order authorising publication, it may (at the same time or subsequently) restrict or prohibit the publication of information relating to a person's identity. Such restrictions may be imposed either on an application made by any person (usually a party to the proceedings) or of the court's own initiative.

8 The general rule is that hearings will be in private and that there can be no lawful publication of information unless the court has authorised it or the publication is authorised in accordance with Part 3 of this Practice Direction. Where reporting restrictions are imposed as part of the order authorising publication, they will simply set out what can be published and there will be no need to comply with the requirements as to notice which are set out in Part 2 of this practice direction. But if the restrictions are subsequent to the order authorising publication, then the requirements of Part 2 should be complied with.

Court sitting in public

9 Where a hearing is to be held in public as a result of a court order under rule 4.3, the court may restrict or prohibit the publication of information about the proceedings. Such restrictions may be imposed either on an application made by any person (usually a party to the proceedings) or of the court's own initiative.

NOTIFICATION IN RELATION TO REPORTING RESTRICTIONS

10 In connection with the imposition of reporting restrictions, attention is drawn to section 12(2) of the Human Rights Act 1998. This means that where an application has been made for an order restricting the exercise of the right to freedom of expression, the order must not be made where the person against whom the application is made is neither present nor represented unless the court is satisfied –

(a) that the applicant has taken all practicable steps to notify the respondent; or
(b) that there are compelling reasons why the respondent should not be notified.

11 The need to ensure that P's Convention rights are protected may be at issue when the court is considering whether to make an order that a public hearing should be held. Part 2 of this practice direction should therefore be complied with where the court is considering making an order under rule 4.3(2) of its own initiative.

12 In summary, the requirements to notify in accordance with the requirements of Part 2 of this practice direction will apply in any case where –

(a) the court has made an order for the publication of information about proceedings which are conducted in private and, after the order has been made:
   (i) an application founded on P's Convention rights is made to the court for an order under rule 4.2(4) which would impose restrictions (or further restrictions) on the information that may be published, or
   (ii) of its own initiative, the court is considering whether to impose such restrictions on the basis of P's Convention rights; or
(b) the court has already made an order for a hearing to be held in public and:
   (i) an application founded on Convention rights is made to the court for an order under rule 4.3(2) which would impose restrictions (or further restrictions) on the information that may be published, or
   (ii) of its own initiative, the court is considering whether to vary or impose further such restrictions.

NOTICE OF REPORTING RESTRICTIONS TO BE GIVEN TO NATIONAL NEWS MEDIA

13 Notice of the possibility that reporting restrictions may be imposed can be effected via the Press Association's CopyDirect service, to which national newspapers and broadcasters subscribe as a means of receiving notice of such applications. Such service should be the norm. The court retains the power to make orders without notice (whether in response to an application or of its own initiative) but such cases will be exceptional.

14 CopyDirect will be responsible for notifying the individual media organisations. Where the order would affect the world at large this is sufficient service for the purposes of advance notice. The website: www.medialawyer.press.net/courtapplications gives details of the organisations represented and instructions for service of the application.

NOTICE OF AN APPLICATION TO BE GIVEN BY APPLICANT

15 A person who has made an application founded on Convention rights should give advance notice of the application to the national media via the Press Association's CopyDirect service. He or she should first telephone CopyDirect (tel. no 0870 837 6429). Unless an order pursuant to rule 5.11 has been made, a copy of the following documents should be sent either by fax (fax no 0870 830 6949) or to the e-mail address provided by CopyDirect –

(a) the application form or application notice seeking the restriction order;
(b) the witness statement filed in support;
(c) any legal submissions in support; and
(d) an explanatory note setting out the nature of the proceedings.

16 It is helpful if applications are accompanied by an explanatory note from which persons served can readily understand the nature of the case (though care should be taken that the information does not breach any rule or order of the court in relation to the use or publication of information).

17 Unless there is a particular reason not to do so, copies of all the documents referred to above should be served. If there is a reason for not serving some or all of the documents (or parts of them), the applicant should ensure sufficient detail is given to enable the media to make an informed decision as to whether it wishes to attend a hearing or be legally represented.

18 The CopyDirect service does not extend to local or regional media or magazines. If service of the application on any specific organisation or person not covered is required, it should be effected directly.

19 The court may dispense with any of the requirements set out in paragraphs 15 to 18.

NOTICE OF OWN-INITIATIVE ORDER TO BE GIVEN BY COURT

20 In any case where the court gives advance notice of an own-initiative order to the national media, it will send such of the information listed in paragraph 15 as it considers necessary.

RESPONDING TO A NOTICE

21 Where a media organisation or any other person has been notified of an application or own-initiative order, they may decide that they wish to participate in any hearing to determine whether reporting restrictions should be imposed. In order to take part, the organisation or person must file an acknowledgment of service ('the acknowledgment') using form COP5 within 14 days beginning with the date on which the notice of the reporting restrictions was given to them by Copy-Direct.

22 The acknowledgment must be filed in accordance with rule 9.15.

23 A person who has filed an acknowledgment will not become a party to the substantive proceedings (i.e. the proceedings in relation to which an application form was filed) except to such extent (if any) as the court may direct.

THE HEARING

24 Any application or own-initiative order which invokes Convention rights will involve a balancing of rights under Article 8 (right to respect for private and family life) and Article 10 (freedom of expression). There is no automatic precedence as between these Articles, and both are subject to qualification where (among other considerations) the rights of others are engaged.

25 In the case of an application, section 12(4) of the Human Rights Act 1998 requires the court to have particular regard to the importance of freedom of expression. It must also have regard to the extent to which material has or is about to become available to the public, the extent of the public interest in such material being published and the terms of any relevant privacy code.

26 The same approach will be taken where the court is considering an own-initiative order imposing reporting restrictions.

SCOPE OF ORDER

Persons protected

27 The aim should be to protect P rather than to confer anonymity on other individuals or organisations. However, the order may include restrictions on identifying or approaching specified family members, carers, doctors or organisations or other persons as the court directs in cases where the absence of such restriction is likely to prejudice their ability to care for P, or where identification of such persons might lead to identification of P and defeat the purpose of the order. In cases where the court receives expert evidence the identity of the experts (as opposed to treating clinicians) is not normally subject to restriction, unless evidence in support is provided for such a restriction.

Information already in the public domain

28 Orders will not usually be made prohibiting publication of material which is already in the public domain, other than in exceptional cases.

Duration of order

29 Orders should last for no longer than is necessary to achieve the purpose for which they are made. The order may need to last until P's death. In some cases a later date may be necessary, for example to maintain the anonymity of doctors or carers after the death of a patient.

PART 3
COMMUNICATION OF INFORMATION RELATING TO PROCEEDINGS HELD IN PRIVATE

Introduction

30. Rule 4.2 deals with the communication of information (whether or not contained in a document filed with the court) relating to proceedings in the Court of Protection which are held in private. Rule 4.3 permits the court to impose restrictions on the publication of information where proceedings are heard in public.

31. Subject to any direction of the court, information may be communicated for the purposes of the law relating to contempt in accordance with paragraphs 33 to 37.

32. Nothing in this Part of this Practice Direction permits the communication to the public at large or any section of the public of any information relating to the proceedings.

Communication of information – general

33. Information may be communicated where the communication is to—

(a) a party;
(b) the legal representative of a party;
(c) an accredited legal representative or a representative within the meaning of rule 1.2;
(d) a professional legal adviser;
(e) the Director of Legal Aid Casework;
(f) an expert whose instruction by a party has been authorised by the court for the purposes of the proceedings;
(g) any person instructed to make a report under section 49 of the Mental Capacity Act 2005;
(h) the Official Solicitor (prior to the Official Solicitor becoming a litigation friend);
(i) the Public Guardian;
(j) a Court of Protection Visitor appointed under section 61(4) of the Mental Capacity Act 2005.

Communication of information for purposes connected with the proceedings

34. (1) A party or the legal representative of a party, on behalf of and upon the instructions of that party, may communicate information relating to the proceedings to any person where necessary to enable that party –

(a) by confidential discussion, to obtain support, advice or assistance in the conduct of the proceedings;
(b) to engage in mediation or other forms of non-court dispute resolution;
(c) to make and pursue a complaint against a person or body concerned in the proceedings; or
(d) to make and pursue a complaint regarding the law, policy or procedure relating to proceedings in the Court of Protection.

(2) Where information is communicated to any person in accordance with subparagraph (1)(a), no further communication by that person is permitted.

MENTAL CAPACITY AND MENTAL HEALTH

(3) When information relating to the proceedings is communicated to any person in accordance with sub-paragraphs (1)(b),(c) or (d)—

(a) the recipient may communicate that information to a further recipient, provided that –
   (i) the party who initially communicated the information consents to that further communication; and
   (ii) the further communication is made only for the purpose or purposes for which the party made the initial communication; and

(b) the information may be successively communicated to and by further recipients on as many occasions as may be necessary to fulfil the purpose for which the information was initially communicated, provided that on each such occasion the conditions in sub-paragraph (a) are met.

Communication of information by a party etc. for other purposes

35. A person specified in the first column of the following table may communicate to a person listed in the second column such information as is specified in the third column for the purpose or purposes specified in the fourth column –

A party	A lay adviser, a McKenzie Friend, or a person arranging or providing pro bono legal services	Any information relating to the proceedings	To enable the party to obtain advice or assistance in relation to the proceedings
A party	A health care professional or a person or body providing counselling services for persons lacking capacity or their families	Any information relating to the proceedings	To enable the party or a member of the party's family to obtain health care or counselling
A party	The European Court of Human Rights	Any information relating to the proceedings	For the purpose of making an application to the European Court of Human Rights
A party, any person lawfully in receipt of information or a court officer	A person or body conducting an approved research project	Any information relating to the proceedings	For the purpose of an approved research project
A legal representative or a professional legal adviser, and the Public Guardian	A person or body responsible for investigating or determining complaints in relation to legal representatives or professional legal advisers	Any information relating to the proceedings	For the purposes of the investigation or determination of a complaint in relation to a legal representative or a professional legal adviser
A legal representative or a professional legal adviser	A person or body assessing quality assurance systems	Any information relating to the proceedings	To enable the legal representative or professional legal adviser to obtain a quality assurance assessment

A legal representative or a professional legal adviser	A professional indemnity insurer	Any information relating to the proceedings	To enable the professional indemnity insurer to be notified of a claim or complaint, or potential claim or complaint, in relation to the legal representative or professional legal adviser, and the legal representative or professional legal adviser to obtain advice in respect of that claim or complaint
A party, or the Public Guardian	A police officer	Any information relating to the proceedings	For the purpose of a criminal investigation
A party or any person lawfully in receipt of information	A member of the Crown Prosecution Service	Any information relating to the proceedings	To enable the Crown Prosecution Service to discharge its functions under any enactment
A party or any person lawfully in receipt of information	(a) an Independent Mental Capacity Advocate acting pursuant to section 35 of and Schedule A1 to the Mental Capacity Act 2005; (b) a relevant person's representative appointed in accordance with Part 10 of Schedule A1 to the Mental Capacity Act 2005; (c) an independent advocate acting pursuant to section 67(2) of the Care Act 2014 or a person exercising equivalent functions under the Social Services and Well-being (Wales) Act 2014; (d) a professional acting in furtherance of adult safeguarding or the	Any information relating to the proceedings	To enable the recipient to discharge their functions under any enactment

MENTAL CAPACITY AND MENTAL HEALTH

	protection of children		
A legal representative or a professional legal adviser	An accreditation body	Any information relating to the proceedings providing that it does not, or is not likely to, identify any person involved in the proceedings	To enable the legal representative or professional legal adviser to obtain accreditation

Communication to and by Ministers of the Crown and Welsh Ministers

36. A person specified in the first column of the following table may communicate to a person listed in the second column such information as is specified in the third column for the purpose or purposes specified in the fourth column

A party or any person lawfully in receipt of information relating to the proceedings	A Minister of the Crown with responsibility for a government department engaged, or potentially engaged, in an application before the European Court of Human Rights relating to the proceedings	Any information relating to the proceedings of which he or she is in lawful possession	To provide the department with information relevant, or potentially relevant, to the proceedings before the European Court of Human Rights
A Minister of the Crown	The European Court of Human Rights	Any information relating to the proceedings of which he or she is in lawful possession	For the purpose of engagement in an application before the European Court of Human Rights relating to the proceedings
A Minister of the Crown	Lawyers advising or representing the United Kingdom in an application before the European Court of Human Rights relating to the proceedings	Any information relating to the proceedings of which he or she is in lawful possession	For the purpose of receiving advice or for effective representation in relation to the application before the European Court of Human Rights
A Minister of the Crown or a Welsh Minister	Another Minister, or Ministers, of the Crown or a Welsh Minister	Any information relating to the proceedings of which he or she is in lawful possession	For the purpose of notification, discussion and the giving or receiving of advice regarding issues raised by the information in which the relevant departments have, or may have, an interest

37. (1) This paragraph applies to communications made in accordance with paragraphs 35 and 36 and the reference in this paragraph to 'the table' means the table in the relevant paragraph.

(2) A person in the second column of the table may only communicate information relating to the proceedings received from a person in the first column for the purpose or purposes –

(a) for which he or she received that information;
(b) of professional development or training, providing that any communication does not, or is not likely to, identify any person involved in the proceedings without that person's consent; or
(c) of fulfilling a statutory process.

38. In this Practice Direction –

'accreditation body' means –

(a) The Law Society, or
(b) the Lord Chancellor in exercise of the Lord Chancellor's functions in relation to legal aid;

'approved research project' means a project of research –

(a) approved in writing by a Secretary of State after consultation with the President of the Court of Protection, or
(b) approved in writing by the President of the Court of Protection.

'body assessing quality assurance systems' includes –

(a) The Law Society,
(b) the Lord Chancellor in exercise of the Lord Chancellor's functions in relation to legal aid, or
(c) The General Council of the Bar;

'body or person responsible for investigating or determining complaints in relation to legal representatives or professional legal advisers' means –

(a) The Law Society,
(b) The General Council of the Bar,
(c) The Institute of Legal Executives,
(d) The Legal Services Ombudsman; or
(e) The Office of Legal Complaints.

'criminal investigation' means an investigation conducted by police officers with a view to it being ascertained –

(a) whether a person should be charged with an offence, or
(b) whether a person charged with an offence is guilty of it;

'health care professional' means –

(a) a registered medical practitioner,
(b) a registered nurse or midwife, or
(c) a clinical psychologist.

'lay adviser' means a non-professional person who gives lay advice on behalf of an organisation in the lay advice sector;

'McKenzie Friend' means any person permitted by the court to sit beside an unrepresented litigant in court to assist that litigant by prompting, taking notes and giving advice.

'professional acting in furtherance of adult safeguarding or the protection of children' includes –

(a) a social worker or any other officer of a local authority exercising adult safeguarding or child protection functions;

MENTAL CAPACITY AND MENTAL HEALTH

(b) a police officer who is –
  (i) exercising powers under section 46 of the Children Act 1989; or
  (ii) serving in a child protection unit or a paedophile unit of a police force;
(c) an officer of the National Society for the Prevention of Cruelty to Children; or
(d) a member or employee of the Disclosure and Barring Service, being the body established under section 87(1) of the Protection of Freedoms Act 2012.

III MEN [523.1]

Principles applied when considering applications to publicise proceedings In the case of *A (by his litigation friend the Official Solicitor) v Independent News & Media Ltd* [2010] EWHC 2858 (Fam) the Court of Appeal re-affirmed the principles to be adopted when considering any request to report or publicise proceedings of the Court of Protection. In a subsequent decision Baker J with the approval of the President of the Court of Protection provided guidance on procedural issues concerning the making of injunctions in conjunction with reporting restrictions: See *W (by her litigation friend, B) and M, (an Adult Patient by her litigation friend the Official Solicitor) v S, A NHS PCT & Times Newspapers Ltd* [2011] EWHC 1197 (COP).

In *Press Association v Newcastle upon Tyne Hospitals Foundation Trust* [2014] EWCOP 6 the issue of the duration of orders for anonymity afforded parties to proceedings where the person lacking capacity had died, was considered both as to jurisdiction and the balance of interests.

Further now see **III MEN [13]** above and the Guidance of the President in respect of publication of the judgments of the Court of Protection as from 3 February 2014. Additional guidance was provided by the President for the purposes of citation and posting of judgments ('EWCOP' replacing 'EWHC . . . (COP)' from 22 April 2014).

PRACTICE DIRECTION 4B – COURT BUNDLES

III MEN [524]

This practice direction supplements Part 4 of the Court of Protection Rules 2017

INTRODUCTION

1 This practice direction is issued to achieve consistency in the preparation of court bundles in the Court of Protection.

APPLICATION OF THE PRACTICE DIRECTION

2.1 Except as specified in paragraph 2.4, and subject to a direction under paragraph 2.5 or specific directions given in any particular case, this practice direction applies to all hearings in the Court of Protection –

(a) before the President of the Family Division, the Chancellor or a puisne judge of the High Court;
(b) relating in whole or in part to personal welfare, health or deprivation of liberty that are listed for a hearing of one hour or more before a judge other than a judge specified at sub-paragraph (a);
(c) relating solely to property and affairs that are listed before a judge other than a judge specified at sub-paragraph (a) for –
  (i) a final hearing; or
  (ii) an interim hearing of one hour or more.

2.2 'Hearings' includes all appearances before a judge whether with or without notice to other parties and whether for directions or for substantive relief.

2.3 This practice direction applies whether a bundle is being lodged for the first time or is being re-lodged for a further hearing.

2.4 This practice direction does not apply to the hearing of any urgent application if and to the extent that it is impractical to comply with it.

2.5 The President may, after such consultation as is appropriate, direct that this practice direction will apply to such other hearings as he may specify irrespective of the length of hearing.

RESPONSIBILITY FOR THE PREPARATION OF THE BUNDLE

3.1 A bundle for the use of the court at the hearing must be provided by the party in the position of applicant at the hearing (or, if there are cross-applications, by the party whose application was first in time) or, if that person is a litigant in person, then (and subject to any direction by the court) by the first listed respondent who is not a litigant in person or P.

3.2 Where the first named respondent is P and he or she is represented by the Official Solicitor, the responsibility for preparing the bundle will fall to the next named respondent who is represented.

3.3 The party preparing the bundle must paginate it. If possible the contents of the bundle must be agreed by all parties.

CONTENTS OF THE BUNDLE

4.1 The bundle must contain copies of all documents relevant to the hearing, in chronological order from the front of the bundle, paginated (either in separate sections or sequentially), indexed and divided into separate sections as follows –

(a) preliminary documents (see paragraphs 4.2 to 4.7);
(b) any other case management documents required by any other practice direction;
(c) a time estimate (see paragraph 10.1);
(d) applications and orders including all Court of Protection forms filed with the application;
(e) any registered enduring or lasting power of attorney;
(f) any urgent or standard authorisation given under Schedule A1 of the Mental Capacity Act 2005;
(g) statements and affidavits (which must state on the top right corner of the front page the date when it was signed or sworn);
(h) care plans (where appropriate);
(i) experts' reports and other reports; and
(j) other documents, divided into further sections as may be appropriate.

PRELIMINARY DOCUMENTS FOR DIRECTIONS AND INTERIM HEARINGS

4.2 At the start of the bundle there must be inserted a document or documents prepared by each party ("the preliminary documents for a directions or interim hearing") which should set out (either within the preliminary documents themselves or by cross-reference to what is set out in another document that is in, or is to be put in the bundle) –

(a) a case summary;
(b) a chronology of relevant events;
(c) the issues for determination at the hearing;
(d) an outline of the likely factual and legal issues at the trial of the case;
(e) the relief sought at the hearing; and
(f) a list of essential reading.

4.3 Where appropriate, the preliminary documents for a directions or interim hearing should include –

(a) a description of relevant family members and other persons who may be affected by or interested in the relief sought;
(b) a particularised account of the issues in the case;
(c) the legal propositions relied on, and in particular whether it is asserted that any issue is not governed by the Mental Capacity Act 2005;
(d) any directions sought concerning the identification and determination of the facts that are agreed, the facts the court will be invited to find and the factors it will be invited to take into account based on such agreed facts or findings of facts;
(e) any directions sought concerning the alternatives the court will be invited to consider in determining what is in P's best interests;
(f) any directions sought relating to expert evidence;
(g) any other directions sought; and
(h) a skeleton argument.

PRELIMINARY DOCUMENTS FOR FACT FINDING HEARINGS

4.4 At the start of the bundle there must be inserted a document or documents prepared by each party ("the preliminary documents for a fact finding hearing") which should set out (either within the preliminary documents themselves, or by cross-reference to what is set out in another document that is in, or is to be put in the bundle) –

(a) the findings of fact that the court is being asked to make; and
(b) cross references to the evidence relied on to found those findings.

4.5 Where appropriate, the preliminary documents for a fact finding hearing should include –

(a) a chronology;
(b) a skeleton argument; and
(c) a description of relevant family members and other persons who may be affected by or interested in the relief sought.

PRELIMINARY DOCUMENTS FOR FINAL HEARINGS

4.6 At the start of the bundle there must be inserted a document or documents prepared by each party ("the preliminary documents for a final hearing") which should set out (either within the preliminary documents themselves, or by cross-reference to what is set out in another document that is in, or is to be put in the bundle) –

(a) the relief sought;
(b) a skeleton argument.

4.7 Where appropriate, the preliminary documents for a final hearing should include –

(a) a chronology;
(b) the findings of fact that the court is being invited to make and the factors based on such findings or agreed facts that the court is being invited to take into account;
(c) an appropriately particularised description of the alternatives the court is being invited to consider; and
(d) a description of relevant family members and other persons who may be affected by or interested in the relief sought.

4.8 Each of the preliminary documents must state on the front page immediately below the heading the date when it was prepared and the date of the hearing for which it was prepared.

4.9 All case summaries, chronologies and skeleton arguments contained in the preliminary documents must be cross-referenced to the relevant pages of the bundle.

4.10 Where the nature of the hearing is such that a complete bundle of all documents is unnecessary, the bundle (which need not be repaginated) may comprise only those documents necessary for the hearing, but –

(a) the preliminary documents must state that the bundle is limited or incomplete; and
(b) the bundle must if reasonably practicable be in a form agreed by all parties.

4.11 Where the bundle is re-lodged in accordance with paragraph 9.2, before it is re-lodged –

(a) the bundle must be updated as appropriate; and
(b) all superseded documents must be removed from the bundle.

FORMAT OF THE BUNDLE

5.1 The bundle must be contained in one or more A4 size ring binders or lever arch files (each lever arch file being limited to 350 pages).

5.2 All ring binders and lever arch files must have clearly marked on the front and the spine –

(a) the title and number of the case;
(b) the court where the case has been listed;
(c) the hearing date and time;
(d) if known, the name of the judge hearing the case; and (e) where there is more than one ring binder or lever arch file, a distinguishing letter (A, B, C etc.) or number and confirmation of the total number of binders or files (1 of 3 etc.).

TIMETABLE FOR PREPARING AND LODGING THE BUNDLE

6.1 The party preparing the bundle must, whether or not the bundle has been agreed, provide a paginated index and, when practicable, paginated copies of updating material to all other parties not less than 5 working days before the hearing.

6.2 Where counsel is to be instructed at any hearing, a paginated bundle must (if not already in counsel's possession) be delivered to counsel by the person instructing that counsel not less than 4 working days before the hearing.

6.3 The bundle (with the exception of the preliminary documents, if and insofar as they are not then available) must be lodged with the court not less than 3 working days before the hearing, or at such other time as may be specified by the judge.

6.4 The preliminary documents (and where appropriate any documents referred to therein that are not in the bundle) must be lodged with the court no later than 11 am on the day before the hearing and, where the hearing is before a judge of the High Court and the name of the judge is known, must at the same time be sent by e-mail to the judge's clerk.

LODGING THE BUNDLE

7.1 The bundle must be lodged at the appropriate office as detailed at paragraph 7.2. If the bundle is lodged in the wrong place the judge may –

(a) treat the bundle as having not been lodged; and
(b) take the steps referred to in paragraph 12.

7.2 Unless the judge has given some other direction as to where the bundle in any particular case is to be lodged (for example a direction that the bundle is to be lodged with the judge's clerk) the bundle must be lodged –

(a) for hearings before a judge of the Family Division, in the office of the Clerk of the Rules, 1st Mezzanine, Queen's Building, Royal Courts of Justice, Strand, London WC2A 2LL (DX 44450 Strand);

MENTAL CAPACITY AND MENTAL HEALTH

(b) for hearings before a judge of the Chancery Division, in the office of the Chancery Judges' Listing Officer, 7 Rolls Building, Fetter Lane, London EC4 1NL (DX 160040 Strand 7);
(c) for hearings at the central registry of the Court of Protection in the office of the Listing & Appeals team, Court of Protection, PO Box 70185, First Avenue House, 42- 49 High Holborn, London WC1A 9JA (DX 160013 Kingsway 7);
(d) for hearings in the Central Family Court at First Avenue House, at the List Office counter, 3rd floor, First Avenue House, 42-49 High Holborn, London, WC1V 6NP (DX 160010 Kingsway 7); and
(e) for hearings at any other court, including regional courts where a Court of Protection judge is sitting, at such place as may be designated and in default of any such designation, at the court office or Court of Protection section of the court where the hearing is to take place.

7.3 Any bundle sent to the court by post, DX or courier must be clearly addressed to the appropriate office and must show the date and place of the hearing on the outside of any packaging as well as on the bundle itself. It must in particular expressly and prominently state that it relates to Court of Protection business.

LODGING THE BUNDLE – ADDITIONAL REQUIREMENTS FOR CASES BEING HEARD AT THE CENTRAL FAMILY COURT OR BEFORE A TIER 3 JUDGE AT THE RCJ

8.1 In the case of hearings at the Central Family Court or before a Tier 3 Judge at the RCJ, parties must –

(a) if the bundle or preliminary and other documents are delivered personally, ensure that they obtain a receipt from the clerk accepting it or them; and
(b) if the bundle or preliminary and other documents are sent by post or DX, ensure that they obtain proof of posting or despatch.

8.2 The receipt (or proof of posting or despatch, as the case may be) must be brought to court on the day of the hearing and must be produced to the court if requested. If the receipt (or proof of posting or despatch) cannot be produced to the court the judge may –

(a) treat the bundle as having not been lodged; and
(b) take the steps referred to in paragraph 12.

8.3 For hearings at the RCJ before a Tier 3 Judge –

(a) bundles or preliminary and other documents delivered after 11 am on the day before the hearing will not be accepted by the Clerk of the Rules or Chancery Judges' Listing Officer and must be delivered directly to the clerk of the judge hearing the case;
(b) upon learning before which judge a hearing is to take place, the clerk to counsel, or other advocate, representing the party responsible for the bundle must, no later than 3 pm the day before the hearing, telephone the clerk of the judge hearing the case to ascertain whether the judge has received the bundle (including the preliminary and other documents), and, if not, must organise prompt delivery.

REMOVING AND RE-LODGING THE BUNDLE

9.1 Following completion of the hearing the party responsible for the bundle must retrieve it from the court immediately or, if that is not practicable, must collect it from the court within five working days. Bundles which are not collected within the stipulated time may be destroyed.

9.2 The bundle must be re-lodged for the next (and for any further hearings of whatever type) in accordance with the provisions of this practice direction and in a form, which complies with paragraphs 5.1 and 5.2.

TIME ESTIMATES

10.1 In every case a time estimate for the hearing must be prepared which must so far as practicable be agreed by all parties and must –

(a) specify separately:
  (i) the time estimated to be required for judicial pre-reading;
  (ii) the time required for hearing all evidence and submissions; and
  (iii) the time estimated to be required for preparing and delivering judgment; and
(b) be prepared on the basis that before they give evidence all witnesses will have read all relevant filed statements and reports.

10.2 Once a case has been listed, any change in time estimates must be notified immediately by telephone (and then immediately confirmed in writing) –

(a) in the case of hearings in the RCJ, to the Clerk of the Rules or the Chancery Judges' Listing Officer as appropriate;
(b) in the case of hearings in the central Registry of the Court of Protection, to the Diary Manager in the Listing & Appeals team at the Court of Protection;
(c) in the case of hearings in the Central Family Court at First Avenue House, to the List Officer at First Avenue House; and
(d) in the case of hearings elsewhere, to the relevant listing officer.

TAKING CASES OUT OF THE LIST

11 As soon as it becomes known that a hearing will no longer be effective, whether as a result of the parties reaching agreement or for any other reason, the parties or their representatives must immediately notify the court by telephone and by letter. The letter, which must wherever possible be a joint letter sent on behalf of all parties with their signatures applied or appended, must include –

(a) a short background summary of the case;
(b) the written consent of each party who consents and, where a party does not consent, details of the steps which have been taken to obtain that party's consent and, where known, an explanation of why that consent has not been given;
(c) a draft of the order being sought; and
(d) enough information to enable the court to decide –
  (i) whether to take the case out of the list; and
  (ii) whether to make the proposed order.

PENALTIES FOR FAILURE TO COMPLY WITH THIS PRACTICE DIRECTION

12 Failure to comply with any part of this practice direction may result in the judge removing the case from the list or putting the case further back in the list and may also result in a 'wasted costs' order in accordance with CPR Part 46.8 or some other adverse costs order.

PRACTICE DIRECTION 4C — TRANSPARENCY

III MEN [525]

This practice direction supplements Part 4 of the Court of Protection Rules 2017

1.1 This practice direction is made under rule 4.3. It provides for the circumstances in which the court will ordinarily make an order under rule 4.3(1) and for the terms of the order under rule 4.3(2) which the court will ordinarily make in such circumstances.

1.2 This practice direction applies to hearings in all proceedings except applications for a committal order (for which rule 21.27 makes specific provision).

2.1 The court will ordinarily (and so without any application being made) –

(a) make an order under rule 4.3(1)(a) that any attended hearing shall be in public; and
(b) in the same order, impose restrictions under rule 4.3(2) in relation to the publication of information about the proceedings.

2.2 An 'attended hearing', except where a practice direction provides otherwise, means a hearing where one or more of the parties to the proceedings have been invited to attend the court for the determination of the application. A Dispute Resolution Hearing is not an attended hearing for this purpose.

2.3 An order pursuant to paragraph 2.1 will ordinarily be in the terms of the standard order approved by the President of the Court of Protection and published on the judicial website at www.judiciary.gov.uk/publication-court/court-of-protection /.

2.4 The court may decide not to make an order pursuant to paragraph 2.1 if it appears to the court that there is good reason for not making the order, but will consider whether it would be appropriate instead to make an order (under rule 4.3(1)(b) or (c)) –

(a) for a part only of the hearing to be held in public; or
(b) excluding any persons, or class of persons from the hearing, or from such part of the hearing as is held in public.

2.5 (1) In deciding whether there is good reason not to make an order pursuant to paragraph 2.1 and whether to make an order pursuant to paragraph 2.4 instead, the court will have regard in particular to –

(a) the need to protect P or another person involved in the proceedings;
(b) the nature of the evidence in the proceedings;
(c) whether earlier hearings in the proceedings have taken place in private;
(d) whether the court location where the hearing will be held has facilities appropriate to allowing general public access to the hearing, and whether it would be practicable or proportionate to move to another location or hearing room;
(e) whether there is any risk of disruption to the hearing if there is general public access to it;
(f) whether, if there is good reason for not allowing general public access, there also exists good reason to deny access to duly accredited representatives of news gathering and reporting organisations.

(2) In sub-paragraph (1)(f), 'duly accredited' refers to accreditation in accordance with any administrative scheme for the time being approved for the purposes of this practice direction by the Lord Chancellor.

2.6 Where the court makes an order pursuant to paragraph 2.1 or 2.4 that an attended hearing or part of it is to be in public, the court will grant, to any person who would have been entitled under the Legal Services Act 2007 to exercise rights of audience at that hearing if such an order had not been made and the hearing was held in private (and who is not otherwise entitled to exercise such rights), the equivalent rights of audience at that attended hearing and any further attended hearing, unless the court is satisfied that there is good reason not to do so.

PART 5
COURT DOCUMENTS

III MEN [526]

5.1 Documents used in court proceedings

(1) The court will seal or otherwise authenticate with the stamp of the court the following documents on issue—

- (a) an application form;
- (b) an application notice;
- (c) an order; and
- (d) any other document which a rule or practice direction requires to be sealed or stamped.

(2) Where the Rules or any practice direction require a document to be signed, that requirement is satisfied if the signature is printed by computer or other mechanical means.

(3) A practice direction may make provision for documents to be filed or sent to the court by—

- (a) facsimile; or
- (b) other means.

III MEN [527]

5.2 Documents required to be verified by a statement of truth

(1) The following documents must be verified by a statement of truth—

- (a) an application form, an application notice, an appellant's notice or a respondent's notice, where the applicant (or appellant or respondent as the case may be) seeks to rely upon matters set out in the document as evidence;
- (b) a witness statement;
- (c) a certificate of—
  - (i) service or non-service; or
  - (ii) notification or non-notification;
- (d) a deputy's declaration; and
- (e) any other document required by a rule or practice direction to be so verified.

(2) Subject to paragraph (3), a statement of truth is a statement that—

- (a) the party putting forward the document;
- (b) in the case of a witness statement, the maker of the witness statement; or
- (c) in the case of a certificate referred to in paragraph (1)(c), the person who signs the certificate,

believes that the facts stated in the document being verified are true.

(3) If a party is conducting proceedings with a litigation friend, the statement of truth in—

- (a) an application form;
- (b) an application notice; or
- (c) an appellant's notice or a respondent's notice,

is a statement that the litigation friend believes that the facts stated in the document being verified are true.

(4) The statement of truth must be signed—

- (a) in the case of an application form, an application notice, an appellant's notice or a respondent's notice—
  - (i) by the party or litigation friend; or

(ii) by the legal representative on behalf of the party or litigation friend; and

(b) in the case of a witness statement, by the maker of the statement.

(5) A statement of truth which is not contained in the document which it verifies must clearly identify that document.

(6) A statement of truth in an application form, an application notice, an appellant's notice or a respondent's notice may be made by—

(a) a person who is not a party; or

(b) two or three parties jointly,

where this is permitted by a relevant practice direction.

III MEN [528]

5.3 Position statement not required to be verified by statement of truth
Nothing in these Rules requires a position statement to be verified by a statement of truth.

III MEN [529]

5.4 Failure to verify a document
If an application form, an application notice, an appellant's notice or a respondent's notice is not verified by a statement of truth, the applicant (or appellant or respondent as the case may be) may not rely upon the document as evidence of any of the matters set out in it unless the court permits.

III MEN [530]

5.5 Failure to verify a witness statement
If a witness statement is not verified by a statement of truth, it shall not be admissible in evidence unless the court permits.

III MEN [531]

5.6 False statements
(1) Proceedings for contempt of court may be brought against a person if that person makes, or causes to be made, a false statement in a document verified by a statement of truth without an honest belief in its truth.

(2) Proceedings under this rule may be brought only—

(i) by the Attorney General; or

(ii) with the permission of the court.

III MEN [532]

5.7 Personal details
(1) Where a party does not wish to reveal—

(a) his or her home address or telephone number;

(b) P's home address or telephone number;

(c) the name of the person with whom P is living (if that person is not the applicant); or

(d) the address or telephone number of his or her place of business, or the place of business of any of the persons mentioned in sub-paragraphs (b) or (c),

that party must provide those particulars to the court.

(2) Where paragraph (1) applies, the particulars given must not be given to any person unless the court so directs.

(3) Where a party changes home address during the course of the proceedings, that party must give notice in writing of the change to the court.

(4) Where a party does not reveal his or her home address, that party must nonetheless provide an address for service which must be within the jurisdiction of the court.

III MEN [533]

5.8 Supply of documents to a party from court records

Unless the court orders otherwise, a party to proceedings may inspect or obtain from the records of the court a copy of—

(a) any document filed by a party to the proceedings; or

(b) any communication in the proceedings between the court and—

(i) a party to the proceedings; or

(ii) another person.

III MEN [534]

5.9 Supply of documents to a non-party from court records

(1) Subject to rules 5.12 and 4.3(2), a person who is not a party to proceedings may inspect or obtain from the court records a copy of any judgment or order given or made in public.

(2) The court may, on an application made to it, authorise a person who is not a party to proceedings to—

(a) inspect any other documents in the court records; or

(b) obtain a copy of any such documents, or extracts from such documents.

(3) A person making an application for an authorisation under paragraph (2) must do so in accordance with Part 10.

(4) Before giving an authorisation under paragraph (2), the court will consider whether any document is to be provided on an edited basis.

III MEN [535]

5.10 Subsequent use of court documents

(1) Where a document has been filed or disclosed, a party to whom it was provided may use the document only for the purpose of the proceedings in which it was filed or disclosed, except where—

(a) the document has been read to or by the court or referred to at a public hearing; or

(b) the court otherwise permits.

(2) Paragraph (1)(a) is subject to any order of the court made under rule 4.3(2).

III MEN [536]

5.11 Editing information in court documents

(1) A party may apply to the court for an order that a specified part of a document is to be edited prior to the document's service or disclosure.

(2) An order under paragraph (1) may be made at any time.

(3) Where the court makes an order under this rule any subsequent use of that document in the proceedings shall be of the document as edited, unless the court directs otherwise.

(4) An application under this rule must be made in accordance with Part 10.

III MEN [537]

5.12 Public Guardian to be supplied with court documents relevant to supervision of deputies

(1) This rule applies in any case where the court makes an order—

(a) appointing a person to act as a deputy; or

(b) varying an order under which a deputy has been appointed.

(2) Subject to paragraphs (3) and (6), the Public Guardian is entitled to be supplied with a copy of qualifying documents if the Public Guardian reasonably considers that it is necessary to have regard to them in connection with the discharge of the Public Guardian's functions under section 58 of the Act in relation to supervision of deputies.

(3) The court may direct that the right to be supplied with documents under paragraph (2) does not apply in relation to such one or more documents, or descriptions of documents, as the court may specify.

(4) A direction under paragraph (3) or (6) may be given—

(a) either on the court's own initiative or on an application made to it; and

(b) either—

(i) at the same time as the court makes the order which appoints the deputy, or which varies it; or

(ii) subsequently.

(5) "Qualifying documents" means documents which—

(a) are filed in court in connection with the proceedings in which the court makes the order referred to in paragraph (1); and

(b) are relevant to—

(i) the decision to appoint the deputy;

(ii) any powers conferred on the deputy;

(iii) any duties imposed on the deputy; or

(iv) any other terms applying to those powers and duties which are contained in the order.

(6) The court may direct that any document is to be provided to the Public Guardian on an edited basis.

III MEN [538]

5.13 Provision of court order to Public Guardian

Any order of the court requiring the Public Guardian to do something, or not to do something, must be served on the Public Guardian as soon as practicable and in any event not later than 7 days after the order was made.

III MEN [539]

5.14 Amendment of application

(1) The court may allow or direct an applicant, at any stage of the proceedings, to amend the application form or notice.

(2) The amendment may be effected by making in writing the necessary alterations to the application form or notice, but if the amendments are so numerous or of such a nature or length that written alteration would make it difficult or inconvenient to read, a fresh document amended as allowed or directed may be required.

III MEN [540]

5.15 Clerical mistakes or slips

The court may at any time correct any clerical mistakes in an order or direction or any error arising in an order or direction from any accidental slip or omission.

III MEN [541]

5.16 Endorsement of amendment

Where an application form or notice, order or direction has been amended under this Part, a note shall be placed on it showing the date on which it was amended, and the alteration shall be sealed.

PRACTICE DIRECTION 5A – COURT DOCUMENTS

III MEN [542]

This practice direction supplements Part 5 of the Court of Protection Rules 2017

SIGNATURE OF DOCUMENTS BY MECHANICAL MEANS

1. Where, under rule 5.1(2), a replica signature is printed electronically or by other mechanical means on any document, the name of the person whose signature is printed must also be printed so that the person may be identified.

FORM OF DOCUMENTS

2. Documents drafted by a legal representative should bear his signature and if they are drafted by a legal representative as a member or employee of a firm, they should state the capacity in which he is signing, and the name of the firm by which he is employed.

3. Every document prepared by a party for filing or use at the court must:

(a) unless the nature of the document renders it impracticable, be on A4 paper of durable quality having a margin not less than 3.5 centimetres wide;
(b) be fully legible and should normally be typed;
(c) where possible be bound securely in a manner which would not hamper filing;
(d) have the pages numbered consecutively;
(e) be divided into numbered paragraphs; and
(f) have all numbers, including dates, expressed as figures.

4. A document which is a copy produced by a colour photostat machine or other similar device may be filed at the court office provided that the coloured date seal of the court is not reproduced on the copy.

DOCUMENTS FOR FILING AT COURT

5. The date on which a document was filed at court must be recorded on the document. This may be done with a seal or a receipt stamp.

6. Particulars of the date of delivery at a court office of any document for filing and the title of the proceedings in which the document is filed shall be entered in court records, on the court file, or on a computer kept in the court office for that purpose. Except where a document has been delivered at the court office through the post, the time of delivery should also be recorded.

FILING BY FACSIMILE

7. In relation to the filing of documents by facsimile ('fax'):

(a) subject to subparagraphs (h) and (i), a party may file a document at court by sending it by fax;
(b) where a party files a document by fax, he must not send a hard copy in addition;
(c) a party filing a document by fax should be aware that the document is not filed at court until it is delivered by the court's fax machine, regardless of the time that is shown to have been transmitted from the party's machine;

(d) the time of delivery of the faxed document will be recorded on it in accordance with paragraph 6;

(e) it remains the responsibility of the party to ensure that the document is delivered to the court in time;

(f) if a fax is delivered after 4pm, it will be treated as filed on the next day the court office is open;

(g) if a fax relates to a hearing, the date and time of the hearing should be prominently displayed;

(h) fax should not be used to send letters or documents of a routine or non-urgent nature;

(i) fax should not be used, except in an unavoidable emergency, to deliver:
   (i) a document which attracts a fee;
   (ii) a document relating to a hearing less than 2 hours ahead of that hearing; or
   (iii) skeleton arguments;

(j) where paragraph 7(i)(i) applies, the fax should give an explanation for the emergency and include an undertaking that the fee or money has been dispatched that day by post or will be paid at the court office counter the following business day; and

(k) where the court has several fax machines, each allocated to an individual section, fax messages should only be sent to the machine of the section for which the message is intended.

EDITING INFORMATION FROM COURT DOCUMENTS

8. An application made pursuant to rule 5.11 for an order that a specified part of a document is to be edited must be made in accordance with the Part 10 procedure, using a COP9 application notice.

9. The person making the application must provide the court with a draft copy of the document which is sought to be edited, with the part or parts which are sought to be deleted clearly marked.

COPIES

10. Unless:

(a) a rule or practice direction provides otherwise; or

(b) the court directs otherwise,

when a document is to be filed at the court, the person filing the document must provide the original and one copy of the document.

III MEN [542.1]

Statement of truth Rule 5.2(3) provides that where a party is conducting proceedings with a litigation friend, a statement of truth in an application form, application notice or respondent's notice is a statement that the litigation friend believes the facts stated in the document being verified are true.

PRACTICE DIRECTION 5B – STATEMENTS OF TRUTH

III MEN [543]

This practice direction supplements Part 5 of the Court of Protection Rules 2017

GENERAL

1. Rule 5.2 makes provision for certain documents to be verified by a statement of truth. These documents are specified in rule 5.2(1).

FORM OF THE STATEMENT OF TRUTH

2. The form of the statement of truth verifying an application form is as follows:

'[I believe] [The applicant believes] that the facts stated in this application form and its annex(es) are true.'

Rule 5.2(3) provides that where a party is conducting proceedings with a litigation friend, a statement of truth in an application form, application notice or respondent's notice is a statement that the litigation friend believes the facts stated in the document being verified are true.

3. The form of the statement of truth verifying a document for court proceedings is as follows:

'[I believe] [The (applicant or as may be) believes] that the facts stated in this [name of document being verified] [and attachments] are true.'

4. The form of the statement of truth verifying a witness statement is as follows:

'I believe that the facts stated in this witness statement are true.'

5. The form of the statement of truth verifying an expert's report or a report prepared pursuant to section 49 of the Act is as follows:

'I confirm that insofar as the facts stated in my report are within my own knowledge I have made clear which they are and I believe them to be true and that the opinions expressed represent my true and complete professional opinion.'

6. Where the statement of truth is contained in a separate document, the document being verified should be identified in the statement of truth by including in the statement of truth:

(a) the name of the person to whom the proceedings relate (P) (unless an order to the contrary pursuant to rule 5.11 has been made);
(b) the case number as entered on the application form, if available;
(c) the date the application form was issued, if available; and
(d) the title of the document being verified.

WHO MAY SIGN THE STATEMENT OF TRUTH

7. A statement of truth verifying a witness statement must be signed by the witness.

8. A statement of truth verifying an expert's report must be signed by the expert.

9. A statement of truth verifying a report prepared pursuant to section 49 of the Act must be signed by the person who prepared the report.

10. The individual who signs a statement of truth must print his name clearly beneath his signature.

11. Where a document is to be verified on behalf of a company or other corporation the statement of truth must be signed by a person holding a senior position in the company or corporation. That person must state the office or position he holds.

12. For the purposes of paragraph 11, each of the following persons is a person holding a senior position:

(a) in respect of a registered company or corporation, a director, the treasurer, secretary, chief executive, manager or other officer of the company or corporation; and
(b) in respect of a corporation which is not registered, in addition to those persons set out in (a), the mayor, chairman, president, town clerk or similar officer of the corporation.

13. Where the document is to be verified on behalf of a partnership, those who may sign the statement of truth are:

(a) any of the partners; and
(b) a person having the control or management of the partnership business.

14. Where a party is legally represented, the legal representative may sign the statement of truth on behalf of the client. The statement signed by the legal representative will refer to the client's belief, not the belief of the legal representative. In signing he must state the capacity in which he signs and the name of his firm where appropriate.

15. A legal representative who signs a statement of truth must sign in his own name and not that of his firm or employer.

16. Where a legal representative has signed a statement of truth, his signature will be taken by the court as his statement:

(a) that the client on whose behalf he has signed had authorised him to do so;
(b) that before signing he had explained to the client that in signing the statement of truth he would be confirming the client's belief that the facts stated in the document were true; and
(c) that before signing he had informed the client of the possible consequences to the client if it should subsequently appear that the client did not have an honest belief in the truth of those facts.

(Rule 5.6 sets out the consequences of verifying a document containing a false statement without an honest belief in its truth.)

PERSONS UNABLE TO READ OR SIGN DOCUMENTS TO BE VERIFIED BY A STATEMENT OF TRUTH

17. Where a document containing a statement of truth is to be signed by a person who is unable to read or sign the document, it must contain a certificate made by an authorised person.

18. An authorised person is a person able to administer oaths and take affidavits but need not be independent of the parties or their representatives.

19. The authorised person must certify:

(a) that the document has been read to the person signing it;
(b) that the person appeared to understand it and approved its content as accurate;
(c) that the declaration of truth has been read to that person;
(d) that the person appeared to understand the declaration and the consequences of making a false declaration (see rule 5.6); and
(e) that the person signed or made his mark in the presence of the authorised person.

FORM OF CERTIFICATE OF AUTHORISED PERSON

20. 'I certify that I [name and address of authorised person] have read over the contents of this document and the declaration of truth to the person signing the document [if there are exhibits, add 'and explained the nature and effect of the exhibits referred to in it'] who appeared to understand (a) the document and approved its content as accurate and (b) the declaration of truth and the consequences of making a false declaration, and made [his] [her] mark in my

presence.'

PART 6
SERVICE OF DOCUMENTS

Service generally

III MEN [544]

6.1 Scope

(1) Subject to paragraph (2), the Rules in this Part apply to—

(a) the service of documents; and

(b) the requirements under rule 9.10 for a person to be notified of the issue of an application form,

and references to "serve", "service", "notice" and "notify", and kindred expressions, shall be construed accordingly.

(2) The rules in this Part do not apply where—

(a) any other enactment, a rule in another Part or a practice direction makes different provision; or

(b) the court directs otherwise.

III MEN [545]

6.2 Who is to serve

(1) The general rule is that the following documents are to be served by the court—

(a) an order or judgment of the court;

(b) an acknowledgment of service or notification; and

(c) except where the application is for an order for committal, a notice of hearing.

(2) Any other document is to be served by the party seeking to rely upon it, except where—

(a) a rule or practice direction provides otherwise; or

(b) the court directs otherwise.

(3) Where the court is to serve a document—

(a) it is for the court to decide which of the methods of service specified in rule 6.3 is to be used; and

(b) if the document is being served on behalf of a party, that party must provide sufficient copies.

III MEN [546]

6.3 Methods of service

(1) A document may be served by any of the methods specified in this rule.

(2) Where it is not known whether a solicitor is acting on behalf of a person, the document may be served by—

(a) delivering it to the person personally;

(b) delivering it to the person's home address or last known home address; or

(c) sending it to that address, or last known address, by first class post (or by an alternative method of service which provides for delivery on the next working day).

(3) Where a solicitor—

(a) is authorised to accept service on behalf of a person; and

(b) has informed the person serving the document in writing that the solicitor is so authorised,

the document must be served on the solicitor unless personal service is required by an enactment, rule, practice direction or court order.

(4) Where it appears to the court that there is a good reason to authorise service by a method other than those specified in paragraphs (2) and (3), the court may direct that service is to be effected by that method.

(5) A direction that service is to be effected by an alternative method must specify—

(a) the method of service; and

(b) the date on which the document will be deemed to be served.

(6) A practice direction may set out how documents are to be served by document exchange, electronic communication or other means.

III MEN [547]

6.4 Service of documents on children and protected parties

(1) The following table shows the person on whom a document must be served if it is a document which would otherwise be served on—

(a) a child; or

(b) a protected party.

Type of document	*Nature of party*	*Person to be served*
Application form	Child	—A person who has parental responsibility for the child within the meaning of the Children Act 1989; or —if there is no such person, a person with whom the child resides or in whose care the child is.
Application form	Protected party	—The person who is authorised to conduct the proceedings in the protected party's name or on the protected party's behalf; or —a person who is a duly appointed attorney, donee or deputy of the protected party; or —if there is no such person, a person with whom the protected party lives or in whose care the protected party is.
Application for an order appointing a litigation friend, where a child or protected party has no litigation friend	Child or protected party	—See rule 17.6 (appointment of litigation friend by court order—supplementary).
Any other document	Child or protected party	—The litigation friend or other duly authorised person who is conducting the proceedings on

	behalf of the child or protected party.

(2) The court may make an order for service on a child or a protected party by permitting the document to be served on some person other than the person specified in the table in paragraph (1) (which may include service on the child or the protected party).

(3) An application for an order under paragraph (2) may be made without notice.

(4) The court may order that, although a document has been served on someone other than the person specified in the table in paragraph (1), the document is to be treated as if it had been properly served.

(5) This rule does not apply in relation to the service of documents on a child in any case where the court has made an order under rule 17.2(4) permitting the child to conduct proceedings without a litigation friend.

III MEN [548]

6.5 Service of documents on P if P becomes a party

(1) If P becomes a party to the proceedings, all documents to be served on P must be served on P's litigation friend or as directed by the court on P's behalf.

(2) The court may make an order for service on P by permitting the document to be served on some person other than the person specified in paragraph (1) (which may include service on P).

(3) An application for an order under paragraph (2) may be made without notice.

(4) The court may order that, although a document has been served on someone other than a person specified in paragraph (1), the document is to be treated as if it had been properly served.

(5) This rule does not apply in relation to the service of documents on P in any case where the court has made an order under rule 17.5(1)(b) (power of court to bring to an end the appointment of a litigation friend).

(Rule 7.3 requires P to be notified where a direction has been made under rule 1.2, and of the appointment of a litigation friend, accredited legal representative or representative.)

III MEN [549]

6.6 Substituted service

Where it appears to the court that it is impracticable for any reason to serve a document in accordance with any of the methods provided under rule 6.3, the court may make an order for substituted service of the document by taking such steps as the court may direct to bring it to the notice of the person to be served.

III MEN [550]

6.7 Deemed service

(1) A document which is served in accordance with these Rules or any relevant practice direction shall be deemed to be served on the day shown in the following table.

Method of service	*Deemed day of service*
First class post (or other service for next-day delivery)	The second day after it was posted.

MENTAL CAPACITY AND MENTAL HEALTH

Document exchange	The second day after it was left at the document exchange.
Delivering the document to a permitted address	The day after it was delivered to that address.
Fax	If it is transmitted on a business day before 4 pm, on that day; or in any other case, on the business day after the day on which it is transmitted.
Other electronic means	The second day after the day on which it is transmitted.

(2) If a document is served personally—

(a) after 5 pm on a business day; or

(b) at any time on a Saturday, Sunday or a Bank Holiday,

it will be treated as being served on the next business day.

III MEN [551]

6.8 Certificate of service

(1) Where a rule, practice direction or court order requires a certificate of service for the document, the certificate must state the details set out in the following table.

Method of service	*Details to be certified*
First class post (or any other service for next-day delivery)	Date of posting.
Personal service	Date of personal service.
Document exchange	Date when the document was left at the document exchange.
Delivery of the document to a permitted address	Date when the document was delivered to that address.
Fax	Date of transmission.
Other electronic means	Date of transmission and the means used.
Alternative method permitted by the court	As required by the court.

(2) The certificate must be filed within 7 days after service of the document to which it relates.

III MEN [552]

6.9 Certificate of non-service

(1) Where an applicant or other person is unable to serve any document under these Rules or as directed by the court, that person must file a certificate of non-service stating the reasons why service has not been effected.

(2) The certificate of non-service must be filed within 7 days of the latest date on which service should have been effected.

III MEN [553]

6.10 Power of court to dispense with service

(1) The court may dispense with any requirement to serve a document.

(2) An application for an order to dispense with service may be made without notice.

Service out of the jurisdiction

III MEN [554]

6.11 Scope and interpretation

(1) This rule and rules 6.12 to 6.19 make provision about—

(a) service of application forms and other documents out of the jurisdiction; and

(b) the procedure for service.

(2) In this rule and rules 6.12 to 6.19—

"application form" includes an application notice;

"Commonwealth State" means a State listed in Schedule 3 to the British Nationality Act 1981;

"jurisdiction" means, unless the context otherwise requires, England and Wales and any part of the territorial waters of the United Kingdom adjoining England and Wales;

"Member State" means a Member State of the European Union;

"the Service Convention" means the Convention on the service abroad of judicial and extra-judicial documents in civil or commercial matters signed at the Hague on November 15, 1965;

"Service Convention country" means a country, not being a Member State, which is a party to the Service Convention; and

"the Service Regulation" means Regulation (EC) No 1393/2007 of the European Parliament and of the Council of 13 November 2007 on the service in the Member States of judicial and extra-judicial documents in civil and commercial matters (service of documents) and repealing Council Regulation (EC) No 1348/2000.

(3) In rules 6.12 to 6.19, a reference to service by a party includes service by a person who is not a party where service by such a person is required under these Rules.

III MEN [555]

6.12 Service of application form and other documents out of the jurisdiction

(1) Subject to paragraph (2), any document to be served for the purposes of these Rules may be served out of the jurisdiction without the permission of the court.

(2) An application form may not be served out of the jurisdiction unless the court has power to determine the application to which it relates under the Act.

III MEN [556]

6.13 Period for acknowledging service or responding to application where application is served out of the jurisdiction

(1) This rule applies where, under these Rules, a party is required to file—

(a) an acknowledgment of service; or

(b) an answer to an application,

and sets out the time period for doing so where the application is served out of the jurisdiction.

(2) Where the applicant serves an application on a respondent in—

(a) Scotland or Northern Ireland; or
(b) a Member State or Service Convention country within Europe,

the period for filing an acknowledgment of service or an answer to an application is 21 days after service of the application.

(3) Where the applicant serves an application on a respondent in a Service Convention country outside Europe, the period for filing an acknowledgment of service or an answer to an application is 31 days after service of the application.

(4) Where the applicant serves an application on a respondent in a country not referred to in paragraphs (2) and (3), the period for filing an acknowledgment of service or an answer to an application is set out in Practice Direction 6B.

III MEN [557]

6.14 Method of service—general provisions

(1) This rule contains general provisions about the method of service of an application form or other document on a party out of the jurisdiction.

Where service is to be effected on a party in Scotland or Northern Ireland

(2) Where a party serves an application form or other document on a party in Scotland or Northern Ireland, it must be served by a method permitted by this Part.

Where service is to be effected out of the United Kingdom

(3) Where an application form or other document is to be served on a person out of the United Kingdom, it may be served by any method—

(a) provided for by—
  (i) rule 6.15 (service in accordance with the Service Regulation); or
  (ii) rule 6.16 (service through foreign governments, judicial authorities and British Consular authorities); or
(b) permitted by the law of the country in which it is to be served.

(4) Nothing in paragraph (3) or in any court order authorises or requires any person to do anything which is contrary to the law of the country where the application form or other document is to be served.

III MEN [558]

6.15 Service in accordance with the Service Regulation

(1) This rule applies where an application form or other document is to be served on a person out of the United Kingdom in accordance with the Service Regulation.

(2) The person wishing to serve must file—

(a) the application form or other document;
(b) any translation; and
(c) any other documents required by the Service Regulation.

(3) When the person wishing to serve files the documents referred to in paragraph (2), the court officer must—

(a) seal, or otherwise authenticate with the stamp of the court, the copy of the application form; and
(b) forward the documents to the Senior Master of the Queen's Bench Division.

(4) In addition to the documents referred to in paragraph (2), the person wishing to serve may, if of the view that this would assist in ensuring effective service, file a photograph of the person to be served.

(The Service Regulation can be found at the web address given in Practice Direction 6B.)

(Rule 6.16 makes provision for service on a person in a Service Convention country.)

III MEN [559]

6.16 Service through foreign governments, judicial authorities and British Consular authorities

(1) Where an application form or other document is to be served on a person in a Service Convention country, it may be served—

- (a) through the authority designated under the Service Convention in respect of that country; or
- (b) if the law of that country permits, through—
  - (i) the judicial authorities of that country; or
  - (ii) a British Consular authority in that country.

(2) Where an application form or other document is to be served on a person in a country which is not a Service Convention country, it may be served, if the law of that country so permits, through—

- (a) the government of that country, where that government is willing to serve it; or
- (b) a British Consular authority in that country.

(3) Where an application form or other document is to be served in—

- (a) any Commonwealth State which is not a Service Convention country;
- (b) the Isle of Man or the Channel Islands; or
- (c) any British Overseas Territory,

the methods of service permitted by paragraphs (1)(b) and (2) are not available and the person wishing to serve, or that person's agent, must effect service direct unless Practice Direction 6B provides otherwise.

(4) This rule does not apply where service is to be effected in accordance with the Service Regulation.

(Rule 6.15 makes provision for service on a party in a Member State in accordance with the Service Regulation.)

(A list of British Overseas Territories is reproduced in Practice Direction 6B.)

III MEN [560]

6.17 Procedure where service is to be through foreign governments, judicial authorities and British Consular authorities

(1) This rule applies where an application form or other document is to be served under rule 6.16(1) or (2).

(2) Where this rule applies, the person wishing to serve must file—

- (a) a request for service of the application form or other document, by specifying one or more of the methods in rule 6.16(1) or (2);
- (b) a copy of the application form or other document;
- (c) any other documents or copies of documents required by Practice Direction 6B; and
- (d) any translation required under rule 6.18.

(3) When the person wishing to serve files the documents specified in paragraph (2), the court officer must—

- (a) seal, or otherwise authenticate with the stamp of the court, the copy of the application form; and
- (b) forward the documents to the Senior Master of the Queen's Bench Division.

(4) The Senior Master shall send documents forwarded under this rule—

- (a) where the application form or other document is being served through the authority designated under the Service Convention, to that authority; or

(b) in any other case, to the Foreign and Commonwealth Office with a request that it arranges for the application form or other document to be served.

(5) An official certificate which—

(a) states that the method requested under paragraph (2)(a) has been performed and the date of such performance;

(b) states, where more than one method is requested under paragraph (2)(a), which method was used; and

(c) is made by—

(i) a British Consular authority in the country where the method requested under paragraph (2)(a) was performed;

(ii) the government or judicial authorities in that country; or

(iii) the authority designated in respect of that country under the Service Convention,

is evidence of the facts stated in the certificate.

(6) A document purporting to be an official certificate under paragraph (5) is to be treated as such a certificate unless it is proved not to be.

III MEN [561]

6.18 Translation of application form or other document

(1) Except where paragraphs (4) and (5) apply, every copy of the application form or other document filed under rule 6.16 (service through foreign governments, judicial authorities and British Consular authorities) must be accompanied by a translation of the application form or other document.

(2) The translation must be—

(a) in the official language of the country in which it is to be served; or

(b) if there is more than one official language of that country, in any official language which is appropriate to the place in the country where the application form or other document is to be served.

(3) Every translation filed under this rule must be accompanied by a statement by the person making it that it is a correct translation, and the statement must include that person's name, address and qualifications for making the translation.

(4) The applicant is not required to file a translation of the application form or other document filed under rule 6.16 where it is to be served in a country of which English is an official language.

(5) The applicant is not required to file a translation of the application form or other document filed under rule 6.16 where—

(a) the person on whom the document is to be served is able to read and understand English; and

(b) service of the document is to be effected directly on that person.

(This rule does not apply to service in accordance with the Service Regulation, which contains its own provisions about the translation of documents.)

III MEN [562]

6.19 Undertaking to be responsible for expenses of the Foreign and Commonwealth Office

Every request for service under rule 6.17 (procedure where service is to be through foreign governments, judicial authorities, etc) must contain an undertaking by the person making the request—

(a) to be responsible for all expenses incurred by the Foreign and Commonwealth Office or foreign judicial authority; and

(b) to pay those expenses to the Foreign and Commonwealth Office or foreign judicial authority on being informed of the amount.

PRACTICE DIRECTION 6A – SERVICE OF DOCUMENTS

III MEN [563]

This practice direction supplements Part 6 of the Court of Protection Rules 2017

SERVICE BY DOCUMENT EXCHANGE

1. Rule 6.3(6) allows documents to be served by document exchange in accordance with a practice direction.

2. Service by document exchange (DX) may take place only where –

(a) the party's address for service includes a numbered box at a DX; or
(b) the writing paper of the party who is to be served or of his legal representative sets out the DX box number; and
(c) the party or his legal representative has not indicated in writing that he is unwilling to accept service by DX.

3. Service by DX is effected by leaving the document addressed to the numbered box –

(a) at the DX of the party who is to be served; or
(b) at a DX which sends documents to the party's DX every business day.

SERVICE BY ELECTRONIC MEANS

4. Rule 6.3(6) allows documents to be served by electronic means in accordance with a practice direction.

5. Subject to the provisions of paragraph 7 below, where a document is to be served by electronic means –

(a) the party who is to be served or his legal representative must have previously expressly indicated in writing to the party serving –
 (i) that he is willing to accept service by electronic means, and
 (ii) the fax number, e-mail address, or electronic identification to which it should be sent; and
(b) the following shall be taken as sufficient written identification for the purposes of the preceding paragraph:
 (i) a fax number set out on the writing paper of the legal representative of the party who is to be served, or
 (ii) a fax number, e-mail address or electronic identification set out on an application form or a response to an application filed with the court.

6. Where a party seeks to serve a document by electronic means he should first seek to clarify with the party who is to be served whether there are any limitations to the recipient's agreement to accept service by such means, including in relation to the format in which documents are to be sent and the maximum size of attachments that may be received.

7. An address for service given by a party must be within the jurisdiction and any fax number must be at the address for service. Where an email address or electronic identification is given in conjunction with an address for service, the email address or electronic identification will be deemed to be at the address for service.

8. Where a document is served by electronic means, the party serving the document need not in addition send a hard copy by post or document exchange.

SERVICE ON BUSINESS PARTNERS

9. A document which is served by leaving it with a person at the principal or last known place of business of the partnership, must at the same time have served with it a notice as to whether the person is being served –

(a) as a partner;
(b) as a person having control or management of the partnership business; or
(c) as both.

SERVICE ON A COMPANY OR OTHER CORPORATION

10. Personal service on a registered company or corporation in accordance with rule 6.3 is effected by leaving a document with a person holding a senior position in the company or corporation.

11. Each of the following persons is a person holding a senior position –
(a) in respect of a registered company or corporation, a director, the treasurer, secretary, chief executive, manager or other officer of the company or corporation; and
(b) in respect of a corporation which is not registered, in addition to those persons set out in (a), the mayor, chairman, president, town clerk or similar officer of the corporation.

CHANGE OF ADDRESS

12. A party or his legal representative who changes his address for service shall give notice in writing of the change as soon as it has taken place to the court and every other party.

SERVICE BY THE COURT

13. Where the court effects service of a document, the method will normally be by first class post.

14. Where the court effects service of an acknowledgment of service, the court will also serve or deliver a copy of any notice of funding that has been filed provided –

(a) it was filed at the same time as the acknowledgment of service; and
(b) copies were provided for service.

APPLICATIONS FOR SERVICE BY AN ALTERNATIVE METHOD

15. An application for an order for service by an alternative method pursuant to rule 31(4) must be made by filing a COP9 application notice in accordance with Part 10, and supported by a witness statement containing evidence which states –
(a) the reason an order for an alternative method of service is sought;
(b) what steps have been taken to serve by other permitted means; and
(c) the alternative method of service that is proposed, and the reason/s why it is believed that service by such a method will come to the notice of the person to be served.

CERTIFICATE OF SERVICE OR NON-SERVICE

16. Where a certificate of service or non-service is required to be filed, forms COP20A and COP20B should be used.

APPLICATION TO DISPENSE WITH SERVICE

17. An application for an order to dispense with service pursuant to rule 6.10 should be made by filing a COP9 application notice in accordance with Part 10.

PRACTICE DIRECTION 6B – SERVICE OUT OF THE JURISDICTION

III MEN [564]

This practice direction supplements Part 6 of the Court of Protection Rules 2017

SCOPE OF THIS PRACTICE DIRECTION

1.1 This Practice Direction supplements rules 6.11 to 6.19 (service out of the jurisdiction) of Part 6.

DOCUMENTS TO BE FILED UNDER RULE 6.17(2)(C)

2.1 A party must provide the following documents for each party to be served out of the jurisdiction –

(1) a copy of the application form and any other relevant documents;
(2) a duplicate of the application form, copies of any documents accompanying the application and copies of any other relevant documents;
(3) forms for responding to the application; and
(4) any translation required under rule 6.18 in duplicate.

2.2 Some countries require legalisation of the document to be served and some require a formal letter of request which must be signed by the Senior Master. Any queries on this should be addressed to the Foreign Process Section (Room E16) at the Royal Courts of Justice.

SERVICE IN A COMMONWEALTH STATE OR BRITISH OVERSEAS TERRITORY

3.1 The judicial authorities of certain Commonwealth States which are not a party to the Hague Convention require service to be in accordance with rule 6.16(1)(b)(i) and not 6.16(3). A list of such countries can be obtained from the Foreign Process Section (Room E02) at the Royal Courts of Justice.

3.2 The list of British overseas territories is contained in Schedule 6 to the British Nationality Act 1981. For ease of reference, these are –

(a) Anguilla;
(b) Bermuda;
(c) British Antarctic Territory;
(d) British Indian Ocean Territory;
(e) British Virgin Islands;
(f) Cayman Islands;
(g) Falkland Islands;
(h) Gibraltar;
(i) Montserrat;
(j) Pitcairn, Henderson, Ducie and Oeno;
(k) St. Helena and Dependencies;
(l) South Georgia and the South Sandwich Islands;
(m) Sovereign Base Areas of Akrotiri and Dhekelia; and
(n) Turks and Caicos Islands.

PERIOD FOR RESPONDING TO AN APPLICATION

4.1 Where rule 6.13(4) applies, the periods within which the respondent must file an acknowledgment of service or an answer to the application is the number of days listed in the Table after service of the application.

4.2 Where an application is served out of the jurisdiction any statement as to the period for responding to the application contained in any of the forms required by the Court of Protection Rules to accompany the application must specify the period prescribed under rule 6.13.

PERIOD FOR RESPONDING TO A DOCUMENT OTHER THAN AN APPLICATION

5.1 Where a document other than an application is served out of the jurisdiction, the period for responding is 7 days less than the number of days listed in the Table.

FURTHER INFORMATION

5.2 Further information concerning service out of the jurisdiction can be obtained from the Foreign Process Section, Room E16, Royal Courts of Justice, Strand, London WC2A 2LL (telephone 020 7947 6691).

Table

Place or country	Number of days
Afghanistan	23
Albania	25
Algeria	22
Andorra	21
Angola	22
Anguilla	31
Antigua and Barbuda	23
Antilles (Netherlands)	31
Argentina	22
Armenia	21
Ascension Island	31
Australia	25
Austria	21
Azerbaijan	22
Azores	23
Bahamas	22
Bahrain	22
Balearic Islands	21
Bangladesh	23
Barbados	23
Belarus	21
Belgium	21
Belize	23
Benin	25
Bermuda	31
Bhutan	28
Bolivia	23
Bosnia and Herzegovina	21
Botswana	23
Brazil	22
British Virgin Islands	31

Place or country	**Number of days**
Brunei	25
Bulgaria	23
Burkina Faso	23
Burma	23
Burundi	22
Cambodia	28
Cameroon	22
Canada	22
Canary Islands	22
Cape Verde	25
Caroline Islands	31
Cayman Islands	31
Central African Republic	25
Chad	25
Chile	22
China	24
China (Hong Kong)	31
China (Macau)	31
China (Taiwan)	23
China (Tibet)	34
Christmas Island	27
Cocos (Keeling) Islands	41
Colombia	22
Comoros	23
Congo (formerly Congo Brazzaville or French Congo)	25
Congo (Democratic Republic)	25
Corsica	21
Costa Rica	23
Croatia	21
Cuba	24
Cyprus	31
Czech Republic	21
Denmark	21
Djibouti	22
Dominica	23
Dominican Republic	23
East Timor	25
Ecuador	22
Egypt	22
El Salvador	25
Equatorial Guinea	23
Eritrea	22
Estonia	21
Ethiopia	22
Falkland Islands and Dependencies	31

Place or country	Number of days
Faroe Islands	31
Fiji	23
Finland	24
France	21
French Guyana	31
French Polynesia	31
French West Indies	31
Gabon	25
Gambia	22
Georgia	21
Germany	21
Ghana	22
Gibraltar	31
Greece	21
Greenland	31
Grenada	24
Guatemala	24
Guernsey	21
Guinea	22
Guinea-Bissau	22
Guyana	22
Haiti	23
Holland (Netherlands)	21
Honduras	24
Hungary	22
Iceland	22
India	23
Indonesia	22
Iran	22
Iraq	22
Ireland (Republic of)	21
Ireland (Northern)	21
Isle of Man	21
Israel	22
Italy	21
Ivory Coast	22
Jamaica	22
Japan	23
Jersey	21
Jordan	23
Kazakhstan	21
Kenya	22
Kiribati	23
Korea (North)	28
Korea (South)	24
Kosovo	21

Place or country	Number of days
Kuwait	22
Kyrgyzstan	21
Laos	30
Latvia	21
Lebanon	22
Lesotho	23
Liberia	22
Libya	21
Liechtenstein	21
Lithuania	21
Luxembourg	21
Macedonia	21
Madagascar	23
Madeira	31
Malawi	23
Malaysia	24
Maldives	26
Mali	25
Malta	21
Mariana Islands	26
Marshall Islands	32
Mauritania	23
Mauritius	22
Mexico	23
Micronesia	23
Moldova	21
Monaco	21
Mongolia	24
Montenegro	21
Montserrat	31
Morocco	22
Mozambique	23
Namibia	23
Nauru	36
Nepal	23
Netherlands	21
Nevis	24
New Caledonia	31
New Zealand	26
New Zealand Island Territories	50
Nicaragua	24
Niger (Republic of)	25
Nigeria	22
Norfolk Island	31
Norway	21
Oman (Sultanate of)	22

Place or country	Number of days
Pakistan	23
Palau	23
Panama	26
Papua New Guinea	26
Paraguay	22
Peru	22
Philippines	23
Pitcairn, Henderson, Ducie and Oeno Islands	31
Poland	21
Portugal	21
Portuguese Timor	31
Puerto Rico	23
Qatar	23
Reunion	31
Romania	22
Russia	21
Rwanda	23
Sabah	23
St. Helena	31
St. Kitts and Nevis	24
St. Lucia	24
St. Pierre and Miquelon	31
St. Vincent and the Grenadines	24
Samoa (U.S.A. Territory) (See also Western Samoa)	30
San Marino	21
Sao Tome and Principe	25
Sarawak	28
Saudi Arabia	24
Scotland	21
Senegal	22
Serbia	21
Seychelles	22
Sierra Leone	22
Singapore	22
Slovakia	21
Slovenia	21
Society Islands (French Polynesia)	31
Solomon Islands	29
Somalia	22
South Africa	22
South Georgia (Falkland Island Dependencies)	31
South Orkneys	21
South Shetlands	21
Spain	21

Place or country	Number of days
Spanish Territories of North Africa	31
Sri Lanka	23
Sudan	22
Surinam	22
Swaziland	22
Sweden	21
Switzerland	21
Syria	23
Tajikistan	21
Tanzania	22
Thailand	23
Togo	22
Tonga	30
Trinidad and Tobago	23
Tristan Da Cunha	31
Tunisia	22
Turkey	21
Turkmenistan	21
Turks & Caicos Islands	31
Tuvalu	23
Uganda	22
Ukraine	21
United Arab Emirates	22
United States of America	22
Uruguay	22
Uzbekistan	21
Vanuatu	29
Vatican City State	21
Venezuela	22
Vietnam	28
Virgin Islands – U.S.A	24
Wake Island	25
Western Samoa	34
Yemen (Republic of)	30
Zaire	25
Zambia	23
Zimbabwe	22

The Service Regulation

The Service Regulation can be found on the Eur-Lex website at –

eur-lex.europa.eu/eli/reg/2007/1393/oj

PART 7
NOTIFYING P

GENERAL REQUIREMENT TO NOTIFY P

III MEN [565]

7.1 General

(1) Subject to paragraphs (2) and (3), the rules in this Part apply where P is to be given notice of any matter or document, or is to be provided with any document, either under the Rules or in accordance with an order or direction of the court.

(2) Subject to rule 7.3, if P becomes a party, the rules in this Part do not apply and service is to be effected in accordance with Part 6 or as directed by the court.

(3) In any case the court may, either on its own initiative or on application, direct that P must not be notified of any matter or document, or provided with any document, whether in accordance with this Part or at all.

(4) Subject to paragraph (5), where P is a child—

(a) if the person to be notified under this rule is a person with parental responsibility for the child within the meaning of the Children Act 1989 or, if there is no such person, a person with whom the child resides or in whose care the child is;

(b) all references to "P" in this Part, except that in paragraph (2), are to be read as referring to the person notified in accordance with sub-paragraph (a).

(5) Paragraph (4) does not apply, and there is no requirement to notify P, where the person referred to in paragraph (4)(a) has already been served or notified of the relevant matter in accordance with another rule or practice direction.

III MEN [566]

7.2 Who is to notify P

(1) Where P is to be notified under this Part, notification must be effected by—

(a) the applicant;

(b) the appellant (where the matter relates to an appeal);

(c) an agent duly appointed by the applicant or the appellant; or

(d) such other person as the court may direct.

(2) The person within paragraph (1) is referred to in this Part as "the person effecting notification".

III MEN [567]

7.3 Notifying P of appointment of a litigation friend, etc

P must be notified—

(a) where a direction has been made under rule 1.2; and

(b) of the appointment of a litigation friend, accredited legal representative or representative on P's behalf.

CIRCUMSTANCES IN WHICH P MUST BE NOTIFIED

III MEN [568]

7.4 Application form

(1) P must be notified—

(a) that an application form has been issued by the court;

(b) that an application form has been withdrawn; and

(c) of the date on which a hearing is to be held in relation to the matter, where that hearing is for disposing of the application.

(2) Where P is to be notified that an application form has been issued, the person effecting notification must explain to P—

(a) who the applicant is;

(b) that the application raises the question of whether P lacks capacity in relation to a matter or matters, and what that means;

(c) what will happen if the court makes the order or direction that has been applied for; and

(d) where the application contains a proposal for the appointment of a person to make decisions on P's behalf in relation to the matter to which the application relates, details of who that person is.

(3) Where P is to be notified that an application form has been withdrawn, the person effecting notification must explain to P—

(a) that the application form has been withdrawn; and

(b) the consequences of that withdrawal.

(4) The person effecting notification must also inform P that P may seek advice and assistance in relation to any matter of which P is notified.

III MEN [569]

7.5 Appeals

(1) P must be notified—

(a) that an appellant's notice has been issued by the court;

(b) that an appellant's notice has been withdrawn; and

(c) of the date on which a hearing is to be held in relation to the matter, where that hearing is for disposing of the appellant's notice.

(2) Where P is to be notified that an appellant's notice has been issued, the person effecting notification must explain to P—

(a) who the appellant is;

(b) the issues raised by the appeal; and

(c) what will happen if the court makes the order or direction that has been applied for.

(3) Where P is to be notified that an appellant's notice has been withdrawn, the person effecting notification must explain to P—

(a) that the appellant's notice has been withdrawn; and

(b) the consequences of that withdrawal.

(4) The person effecting notification must also inform P that P may seek advice and assistance in relation to any matter of which P is notified.

III MEN [570]

7.6 Decisions and orders of the court

(1) P must be notified of any decision of the court relating to P except for a case management decision.

(2) Where P is notified in accordance with this rule, the person effecting notification must explain to P the effect of the decision.

(3) The person effecting notification must also inform P that P may seek advice and assistance in relation to any matter of which P is notified.

(4) The person effecting notification must also provide P with a copy of any order relating to a decision of which P must be notified in accordance with paragraph (1).

III MEN [571]

7.7 Other matters

(1) This rule applies where the court directs that P is to be notified of any other matter.

(2) The person effecting notification must explain to P such matters as may be directed by the court.

(3) The person effecting notification must also inform P that P may seek advice and assistance in relation to any matter of which P is notified.

Manner of notification and accompanying documents

III MEN [572]

7.8 Manner of notification

(1) Where P is to be notified under this Part, the person effecting notification must provide P with, or arrange for P to be provided with, the information specified in rules 7.3 to 7.7 in a way that is appropriate to P's circumstances (for example, using simple language, visual aids or any other appropriate means).

(2) The information referred to in paragraph (1) must be provided to P personally.

(3) P must be provided with the information mentioned in paragraph (1) as soon as practicable and in any event within 14 days of the date on which—

- (a) the application form or appellant's notice was issued or withdrawn;
- (b) the decision was made;
- (c) the person effecting notification received the notice of hearing from the court and in any event no later than 14 days before the date specified in the notice of the hearing; and
- (d) the order referred to in rule 7.6(4) was served upon the person who is required to effect notification of P under that rule,

as the case may be.

(4) Where the provisions of rule 7.1(4) apply, paragraphs (1) and (2) of this rule do not apply and the person effecting notification may provide information and documents of which P must be notified to the person to be notified under rule 7.1(4), by any method by which service of documents would be permitted under rule 6.3.

III MEN [573]

7.9 Acknowledgment of notification

Where P is notified that an application form or an appellant's notice has been issued, P must also be provided with a form for acknowledging notification.

III MEN [574]

7.10 Certificate of notification

(1) The person effecting notification must, within 7 days beginning with the date on which notification in accordance with this Part was given, file a certificate of notification which certifies—

- (a) the date on which, and how, P was notified; and
- (b) that P was notified in accordance with this Part.

(2) Subject to paragraph (3), the person effecting notification in accordance with this Part must in the certificate required by paragraph (1) describe the steps taken to enable P to understand, and the extent to which P appears to have understood, the information.

(3) Where the provisions of rule 7.1(4) apply, paragraph (2) does not apply.

III MEN [575]

7.11 Dispensing with requirement to notify, etc

(1) The applicant, the appellant or other person directed by the court to effect notification may apply to the court seeking an order—

(a) dispensing with the requirement to comply with the provisions in this Part; or

(b) requiring some other person to comply with the provisions in this Part.

(2) An application under this rule must be made in accordance with Part 10.

PRACTICE DIRECTION 7A – NOTIFYING P

III MEN [576]

This practice direction supplements Part 7 of the Court of Protection Rules 2017

GENERAL

1 Part 7 sets out the procedure to be followed where P is to be given notice of any matter or document, or provided with any document. Where P becomes a party, Part 7 does not apply (except for rule 7.3) and service is to be effected in accordance with Part 6 or as directed by the court.

WHEN P MUST BE NOTIFIED

2 P must be notified of the things specified in rules 7.3 to 7.7, unless the court directs otherwise. P must, therefore, be notified –

(a) that an application form has been issued by the court or withdrawn;

(b) that an appellant's notice has been issued by the court or withdrawn;

(c) that the court has made a decision relating to him or her (other than a case management decision);

(d) of a direction under rule 1.2 and of the appointment of a litigation friend, accredited legal representative, or representative on his or her behalf; and

(e) of any other matter as the court may direct.

WHEN P MAY BE NOTIFIED OF AN APPLICATION NOTICE

3 The applicant is not required to, but may notify P of an application notice that is issued in accordance with Part 10. This should be done if the applicant considers it appropriate to do so, and must be done if the court makes a direction to that effect.

4 Where P is to be notified of an application notice, unless the court directs otherwise, the person notifying P must explain to P –

(a) who the applicant is;

(b) what the application is about;

(c) what will happen if the court makes the order or direction that has been applied for; and

(d) that P may seek advice and assistance in relation to any matter of which he is notified.

5 The person effecting notification must provide P with the information referred to in paragraph 4 in the manner set out in rule 7.8, and must comply with rules 7.9 and 7.10.

MENTAL CAPACITY AND MENTAL HEALTH

HOW AND OF WHAT P IS TO BE NOTIFIED

6 Rule 7.8 sets out the manner in which P is to be notified, and rules 7.3 to 7.7 set out the matters of which P is to be notified. Rule 7.9 provides that P must be provided with a COP5 form for acknowledging notification. P must also be provided with a COP14 form which explains the matter for which notification is being provided.

CERTIFICATES OF NOTIFICATION AND NON-NOTIFICATION

7 Rule 7.10 requires the person notifying P to file a certificate within 7 days of providing notification. Where a person fails to notify P (or is unable to do so), the person must file a certificate of non-notification. Certificates of notification, or non-notification (as appropriate), must be filed using forms COP20A and COP20B.

DISPENSING WITH NOTIFICATION

8 The person required to notify P may apply to the court for an order either –

(a) dispensing with the requirement to notify P; or
(b) requiring some other person to effect the notification,

using a COP9 application notice in accordance with Part 10.

9 Such an application would be appropriate where, for example, P is in a permanent vegetative state or a minimally conscious state; or where notification by the applicant is likely to cause significant and disproportionate distress to P.

PART 8
PERMISSION

III MEN [577]

8.1 General

Subject to these Rules and to section 50(1) of, and paragraph 20 of Schedule 3 to, the Act, the applicant must apply for permission to start proceedings under the Act.

(Section 50(1) of the Act specifies the persons who do not need to apply for permission. Paragraph 20 of Schedule 3 to the Act specifies an application for which permission is not needed.)

III MEN [577.1]

Guidance on the issue of permission The provisions of Part 8 should be read in conjunction with ss 50 and 50(1) of the Mental Capacity Act 2005 (see **III MEN [88]** to **III MEN [89]**). Practice Direction 8A identifies the procedure when seeking permission (para 1) and the documents that must be filed at court in notification (**III MEN [583]**).

The Act at s 50 provides when permission is required, and the provisions of s 50(1) identifies at s 50(1)(a)–(e) the individuals who need not seek permission to bring an application: the person who lacks capacity, a person who has parental responsibility for a person who lacks capacity who is under 18 years, the donor of a lasting power of attorney to which the application relates, a deputy appointed by the court for a person to whom the application relates, or a person named in an existing order of the court if the application relates to that order.

The subsequent rules 8.2 to 8.4, provide further provision for where the court's permission is not required (rule 8.2), where part of the application concerns matters for which permission is required and part for which permission is not required (rule 8.3) and the procedure if permission is required (rule 8.4) and see rule 3.6(3) (**III MEN [513]**).

In *NK v (1) VW (by her litigation friend the Official Solicitor) (2) LCC (3) JW (4) WW* [2012] COPLR105, Macur J argued that by utilisation of the court management powers under Rule 3, the court was required in determining permission to prevent not only frivolous and abusive applications but also those which had no realistic prospect of success.

III MEN [578]

8.2 Where the court's permission is not required

The permission of the court is not required—

(a) where an application is made by—
 (i) the Official Solicitor; or
 (ii) the Public Guardian;
(b) where the application concerns—
 (i) P's property and affairs;
 (ii) a lasting power of attorney which is, or purports to be, created under the Act; or
 (iii) an instrument which is, or purports to be, an enduring power of attorney;
(c) where an application is made under section 21A of the Act;
(d) where an application is made for an order under section 16(2)(a) of the Act, which is to be relied on to authorise the deprivation of P's liberty pursuant to section 4A(3) of the Act;
(e) where an application is made in accordance with Part 10;
(f) where a person files an acknowledgment of service or notification in accordance with this Part or Part 9, for any order proposed that is different from that sought by the applicant; or
(g) in any other case specified for this purpose in a practice direction.

III MEN [578.1]

Permission and the relevant person's representative In *AB (by a litigation friend NW) v A Local authority* [2011] EWHC 3151 (COP), [2011] NLJR 1744, [2011] All ER (D) 37 (Dec) Mostyn J addressed the issues of appointment of a relevant person's representative, the engagement of the Official Solicitor, and considered this in conjunction with Part 17 appointment of litigation friend (**III MEN [680]**), Schedule A1, Part 10 paras 137–153 dealing with the relevant person's representative (**III MEN [117]**), and s 50 of the Mental Capacity Act 2005 (**III MEN [88]**).

III MEN [579]

8.3 Permission—supplementary

Where part of the application concerns a matter which requires permission, and part of it does not, permission need only be sought for that part of it which requires permission.

III MEN [580]

8.4 Application for permission

Where permission is required, the applicant must apply for permission when making an application.

(Rule 3.6(3) explains how the court will deal with an application for permission.)

III MEN [580.1]

Applications to the court Separate application Forms are now not required. The application should be made in accordance with the Form relevant to the application and the appropriate information provided. See **III MEN [583]**.

III MEN [581]

8.5 Service of an order giving or refusing permission

The court must serve—

(a) the order granting or refusing permission;
(b) if refusing permission without a hearing, the reasons for its decision in summary form; and
(c) any directions,

on the applicant and on any other person served with or notified of the application form.

III MEN [582]

8.6 Appeal against a permission decision following a hearing

Where the court grants or refuses permission following a hearing, any appeal against the permission decision shall be dealt with in accordance with Part 20 (appeals).

(Rule 13.4 deals with reconsideration of orders and decisions made without a hearing or without notice to any person who is affected by such order or decision.)

III MEN [582.1]

For procedure under Part 20 see **III MEN [718]** and Practice Direction 20A (**III MEN [732]**). If the decision is made without a hearing then application may be made under rule 13.4 for reconsideration (see **III MEN [626]**).

PRACTICE DIRECTION 8A – PERMISSION

III MEN [583]

This practice direction supplements Part 8 of the Court of Protection Rules 2017

WHERE PERMISSION IS REQUIRED

1 An applicant must apply for permission in the application form to start proceedings under the Act, unless either section 50 of, paragraph 20(2) of Schedule 3 to, the Act or rule 8.2 applies. The applicant must apply for permission when making the application, in accordance with rule 8.4.

2 If part of the application is a matter for which permission is required and part of it is not, permission must be sought for the part that requires it.

3 In such circumstances, the applicant may file a single application form seeking both orders.

NOTICE OF HEARING

4 Where the court decides to hold a hearing in order to make a decision as to permission, it will notify the parties and such other persons it requires to be notified under rule 3.6(6)(a).

PART 9

HOW TO START AND RESPOND TO PROCEEDINGS, AND PARTIES TO PROCEEDINGS

INITIAL STEPS

III MEN [584]

9.1 General

(1) Applications to the court to start proceedings must be made in accordance with this Part and, as applicable, Part 8 and the relevant practice directions.

(2) The appropriate forms must be used in the cases to which they apply, with such variations as the case requires, but not so as to omit any information or guidance which any form gives to the intended recipient.

III MEN [584.1]

Applications to the court and the issue of permission Part 8 relates to the issue of permission (see **III MEN [577]** above).

In all proceedings before the Court of Protection, the appropriate forms must be used. The following forms are the most commonly required.

If the application relates to a deprivation of liberty issue, then regard should be had to Practice Direction 11A and the forms set out therein must be used. See **III MEN [620]**.

If the application relates to the streamlined procedure under section 16(2)(a) for an order authorising deprivation of liberty under section 4A(3) and (4) of the Act then the procedure is set out in Practice Direction 11A, and Form COPDOL10 is mandatory. The application form has annexes and attachments which provide essential information to the court to enable determination on paper, and a draft order must be submitted. The substantive rules regarding permission and notification are amended and where appropriate disapplied. See **III MEN [619]**.

Under Part 9, Form COP1 is the general application form and in the event that the application relates to property and affairs issues, then COP1A should be filed. This form will provide comprehensive information regarding P's income, capital assets and other relevant details.

If the matter relates to welfare or health issues, then form COP1B should be filed with COP1. Care may need to be given at this stage as to whether the application requires permission See Part 8 above (**III MEN [577]**).

Form COP3 is the relevant form providing medical evidence assessing capacity. In health and welfare applications, the court may accept a detailed medical report provided the report incorporates the information required within COP3 (see Practice Direction 9A, para 12; **III MEN [600]**).

Form COP4 must be completed by the individual who seeks appointment as a deputy. See Practice Direction 9A, para 12; **III MEN [600]**.

Form COP5 is a form for the purposes of Acknowledgment of service/notification. It should be completed and filed in the following circumstances:

- if served with COP1, COP7 or COP8, and a person wishes to take part in the proceedings: **III MEN [595]**, **III MEN [602]** and **III MEN [606]**.
- a COP14 notice about proceedings in the Court of Protection about you has been received and you wish to be joined as a party.
- a COP15 notice that an application has been issued by the court and the person wishes to be joined as a party.

Where an issue arises relating to the registration of a lasting power of attorney or to an enduring power of attorney and the application is to the court as opposed to the Public Guardian, then COP7 must be used in respect of objection to registration of an LPA and Form COP8 if the objection relates to the registration of an EPA. See Practice Direction 9G at **III MEN [606]**

Form COP9 is the relevant application form to be used in applications made within proceedings or under Part 10 (see **III MEN [607]**).

Form COP10 relates to where a person wishes to be joined as a party to oppose an application. See Practice Direction 9C para 5: **III MEN [602]**.

Form COP12 is a form of special undertaking to be used in applications to which Practice Direction 9F relates (see **III MEN [605]**).

COP14 is the Notice of proceedings served upon the incapacitated person 'P' notifying that person of proceedings about them (see **III MEN [576]**).

Form COP15 is to be used for notification. See Practice Direction 9B, para 12 (**III MEN [601]**)

Form COP17 is the request form used by the Public Guardian to seek directions where objection has been raised to an enduring power of attorney. See r 24.4 and Practice Direction 24A para 4: **III MEN [779]**.

Form COP20A and Form COP20B are the appropriate certificates for service/ non-service, and notification and non-notification (see **III MEN [551.1]**).

Form COP22 is the form of suitability of litigation friend: **III MEN [694]**.

COP23 is the form of Certificate for refusal of witness to attend before an examiner: **III MEN [646]**.

Form COP24 is the form of Witness statement. See Practice Direction 14A for more detailed requirements: **III MEN [653]**.

Form COP25 is the form of affidavit. See Practice Direction 14A for more detailed requirements: **III MEN [653]**.

Form COP28 is a general notice of hearing form.

Form COP29 is a notice of Committal hearing. See Part 21 and Practice Direction 21A for more detailed requirements: **III MEN [734]** to **III MEN [766]**.

Form COP30 is the Notice of Change of solicitor. See **III MEN [701]**.

Form COP31 is notice of intention to file evidence by deposition: see **III MEN [647]**.

Form COP35 is the Appellant's Notice and Form COP36 the Respondent's Notice. Form COP37 is the form for skeleton argument. Regard should be had to Part 20 and Practice Direction 20A and to the more detailed requirements; see **III MEN [732]**.

Practice Directions PD9A–H supplement Part 9 applications

Practice Direction 9A concerns the application form its contents, statement of truth, the documents to be filed with the application, and starting proceedings (see **III MEN [600]**).

Practice Direction 9B concerns those who should be notified of the issue of an application and method of notification (see **III MEN [601]**).

Practice Direction 9C concerns responding to an application, signing the acknowledgment, providing an address for service and consequential corrections and amendments to the acknowledgment (see **III MEN [602]**).

Practice Direction 9D concerns applications by currently appointed deputies, attorneys and donees in relation to P's property and affairs. The Practice Direction gives guidance to applications that may or may not be suitable for the procedure set out in that practice direction, and on rights of reconsideration (see **III MEN [603]**).

Practice Direction 9E concerns applications relating to statutory wills, codicils, settlements and other dealings with P's property. The practice direction identifies the information to be submitted, the individuals to be notified and procedure on execution of a will. The annex provides an example of a statutory will. See **III MEN [604]**.

Practice Direction 9F concerns applications to appoint or discharge a trustee, identifying the type of proceedings to which it applies, the requirements of information and the additional information to be provided where the application relates to real property, See **III MEN [605]**.

Practice Direction 9G concerns applications relating to the registration of enduring powers of attorney. See **III MEN [606]**.

Guidance has been given by the Court in relation to specific applications, predominantly from Local Authority deputies relating to tenancy agreements. In the event that an individual lacks mental capacity to sign a tenancy agreement or terminate such an agreement, then anyone intending to sign on that person's behalf can only do so if authorised by the Court of Protection. The court is willing to consider a single bulk application provided that the application does not include further direction or authority, and may be made by COP 1 supported by a COP 3 assessment for each individual and a statement setting out the circumstances in COP 24. The provisions as to notice under COP 14 apply with certification of notification by COP 20A. If the circumstances are found to be satisfied the court will issue a single order dealing with all of those encompassed within the application (Guidance issued February 2012). The court will however have to be satisfied that relevant issues as to potential deprivation of liberty have been considered, and if necessary application will have to be made under the streamlined procedure.

III MEN [585]

9.2 When proceedings are started

(1) The general rule is that proceedings are started when the court issues an application form at the request of the applicant.

(2) An application form is issued on the date entered on the application form by the court.

III MEN [586]

9.3 Contents of the application form

The application form must—

(a) state the matter which the applicant wants the court to decide;

(b) state the order which the applicant is seeking;

(c) name—

(i) the applicant;

(ii) P;

(iii) as a respondent, any person (other than P) whom the applicant reasonably believes to have an interest which means that that person ought to be heard in relation to the application (as opposed to being notified of it in accordance with rule 9.10);

(iv) any person whom the applicant intends to notify in accordance with rule 9.10; and

(d) if the applicant is applying in a representative capacity, state what that capacity is.

III MEN [586.1]

Applications to the court and procedure Practice Direction 9A, paras 2–5 supplement this rule as to the relevant requirements to be incorporated in the application form. Paragraphs 6–8 deal with issues concerning the statement of truth. See **III MEN [600]**.

III MEN [587]

9.4 Documents to be filed with the application form

Where an applicant files the application form with the court, the applicant must also file—

(a) in accordance with the relevant practice direction, any evidence on which the applicant intends to rely;

(b) an assessment of capacity form, where this is required by the relevant practice direction;

(c) any other documents referred to in the application form; and

(d) such other information and material as may be set out in a practice direction.

III MEN [587.1]

Guidance on filing of documents and time frames Practice Direction 9A, paras 9–14 provide supplemental guidance and requirements as to the documents to be filed and the timing of such filing. See **III MEN [600]**.

III MEN [588]

9.5 What the court will do when an application form is filed

As soon as practicable after an application form is filed the court must issue it and do anything else that may be set out in a practice direction.

STEPS FOLLOWING ISSUE OF APPLICATION FORM

III MEN [589]

9.6 Applicant to serve the application form on named respondents

(1) As soon as practicable and in any event within 14 days of the date on which the application form was issued, the applicant must serve a copy of the application form on any person who is named as a respondent in the application form, together with copies of any documents filed in accordance with rule 9.4 and a form for acknowledging service.

(2) The applicant must file a certificate of service within 7 days beginning with the date on which the documents were served.

III MEN [589.1]

Applications to the court and procedure Regard should be made to Practice Direction 9A, paras 9–14 as to the documents that were required to be filed. Form COP20B is the relevant form for certifying service (see **III MEN [551.1]**).

III MEN [590]

9.7 Applications relating to lasting powers of attorney

(1) Where the application concerns the powers of the court under section 22 or 23 of the Act (powers of the court in relation to the validity and operation of lasting powers of attorney) the applicant must serve a copy of the application form, together with copies of any documents filed in accordance with rule 9.4 and a form for acknowledging service—

- (a) unless the applicant is the donor or donee of the lasting power of attorney ("the power"), on the donor and every donee of the power;
- (b) if the applicant is the donor, on every donee of the power; or
- (c) if the applicant is a donee, on the donor and any other donee of the power,

but only if the persons mentioned in sub-paragraphs (a) to (c) have not been served or notified under any other rule.

(2) Where the application is solely in respect of an objection to the registration of the power, the requirements of rules 9.6 and 9.10 do not apply to an application made under this rule by—

- (a) a donee of the power; or
- (b) a person named in a statement made by the donor of the power in accordance with paragraph 2(1)(c)(i) of Schedule 1 to the Act.

(3) The applicant must comply with paragraph (1) as soon as practicable and in any event within 14 days of the date on which the application form was issued.

(4) The applicant must file a certificate of service with 7 days beginning with the date on which the documents were served.

(5) Where the applicant knows or has reasonable grounds to believe that the donor of the power lacks capacity to make a decision in relation to any matter that is the subject of the application, the applicant must notify the donor in accordance with Part 7.

III MEN [590.1]

Applications to the court and lasting powers of attorney This rule should be considered in conjunction with ss 22 and 23 of the Mental Capacity Act 2005 and the consideration by the court of issues concerning the validity and operation of lasting powers of attorney (see **III MEN [56]** to **III MEN [57]**). Forms COP20A and COP20B are the relevant forms for certifying service (see **III MEN [551.1]**).

III MEN [591]

9.8 Applications relating to enduring powers of attorney

(1) Where the application concerns the powers of the court under paragraphs 2(9), 4(5)(a) and (b), 7(2), 10(c), 13, or 16(2), (3), (4) and (6) of Schedule 4 to the Act, the applicant must serve a copy of the application form, together with copies of any documents filed in accordance with rule 9.4 and a form for acknowledging service—

- (a) unless the applicant is the donor or attorney under the enduring power of attorney ("the power"), on the donor and every attorney under the power;
- (b) if the applicant is the donor, on every attorney under the power; or
- (c) if the applicant is an attorney, on the donor and any other attorney under the power,

but only if the persons mentioned in sub-paragraphs (a) to (c) have not been served or notified under any other rule.

(2) Where the application is solely in respect of an objection to the registration of the power, the requirements of rules 9.6 and 9.10 do not apply to an application made under this rule by—

- (a) an attorney under the power; or

(b) a person listed in paragraph 6(1) of Schedule 4 to the Act.

(3) The applicant must comply with paragraph (1) as soon as practicable and in any event within 14 days of the date on which the application form was issued.

(4) The applicant must file a certificate of service within 7 days beginning with the date on which the documents were served.

(5) Where the applicant knows or has reasonable grounds to believe that the donor of the power lacks capacity to make a decision in relation to any matter that is the subject of the application, the applicant must notify the donor in accordance with Part 7.

III MEN [591.1]

Applications to the court and enduring powers of attorney Regard should be made to Sch 4 of the Mental Capacity Act 2005 (see **III MEN [134]**) above.

The specific applications are: the revocation of an enduring power of attorney (para 2(9)), referral to the court on an issue of validity (para 4(5)(a) and (b)), application to dispense with notice of registration (para 7(2)), issues relating to notice to donor of registration (para 10(c)), issues concerning registration by the Public Guardian (para 13) and applications regarding the determination of issues relating to the enduring power of attorney and the cancellation of registration (paras 16(2),(3),(4) and (6)).

III MEN [592]

9.9 Applicant to notify P of an application

P must be notified in accordance with Part 7 that an application form has been issued, unless the requirement to do so has been dispensed with under rule 7.11.

III MEN [593]

9.10 Applicant to notify other persons of an application

(1) As soon as practicable and in any event within 14 days of the date on which the application form was issued, the applicant must notify the persons specified in the relevant practice direction—

(a) that an application has been issued;

(b) whether it relates to the exercise of the court's jurisdiction in relation to P's property and affairs, or P's personal welfare, or to both; and

(c) of the order or orders sought.

(2) Notification of the issue of the application form must be accompanied by a form for acknowledging notification.

(3) The applicant must file a certificate of notification within 7 days beginning with the date on which notification was given.

III MEN [593.1]

Procedural guidance on notification Practice Direction 9B provides supplemental direction with regard to notification to be provided. See **III MEN [601]**. Practice Direction 9E, para 9 (**III MEN [604]**) sets out important guidance as to those who should be respondents and given notice of an application in relation to statutory will, codicils, settlements and other dealings with P's property.

III MEN [594]

9.11 Requirements for certain applications

A practice direction may make additional or different provision in relation to specified applications.

III MEN [594.1]

Guidance on applications to the court in respect of deprivation of liberty issues See Practice Directions PD9D–G (**III MEN [600]**) and Practice Direction 11A in respect of deprivation of liberty applications (**III MEN [6223]**).

III MEN [594.2]

Guidance on applications to the court in respect of tenancy agreements See Court of Protection Guidance 2012 on tenancy agreements, the requirements of which are set out above at **III MEN [584.1]**.

The guidance relates specifically to the single issue of signing and terminating tenancy agreements either for an individual or group of individuals where there is no other authority sought, and those persons lack capacity to so act. To specifically answer points raised on this issue, the court has issued guidance on the circumstances when this procedure is appropriate. (Applications to the Court of Protection in relation to tenancy agreements: http://hmctsformfinder.justice.gov.uk).

Responding to an application

III MEN [595]

9.12 Responding to an application

(1) A person who is served with or notified of an application form and who wishes to take part in proceedings must file an acknowledgment of service or notification in accordance with this rule.

(2) The acknowledgment of service or notification must be filed not more than 14 days after the application form was served or notification of the application was given.

(3) The court must serve the acknowledgment of service or notification on the applicant and on any other person who has filed such an acknowledgment.

(4) The acknowledgment of service or notification must—

- (a) state whether the person acknowledging service or notification consents to the application;
- (b) state whether that person opposes the application and, if so, set out the grounds for doing so;
- (c) state whether that person seeks a different order from that set out in the application form and, if so, set out what that order is;
- (d) provide an address for service, which must be within the jurisdiction of the court;; and
- (e) be signed by that person or that person's legal representative.

(5) Subject to rules 15.2 and 15.5 (restriction on filing an expert's report and court's power to restrict expert evidence), unless the court directs otherwise, where a person who has been served in accordance with rule 9.6, 9.7 or 9.8 opposes the application or seeks a different order, that person must within 28 days of such service file a witness statement containing any evidence upon which that person intends to rely.

(6) In addition to complying with the other requirements of this rule, an acknowledgment of notification filed by a person notified of the application in accordance with rule 9.7(5), 9.8(5), 9.9 or 9.10 must—

- (a) indicate whether the person wishes to be joined as a party to the proceedings; and
- (b) state the person's interest in the proceedings.

(7) Subject to rules 15.2 and 15.5 (restriction on filing an expert's report and court's power to restrict expert evidence), unless the court directs otherwise, where a person has been notified in accordance with rule 9.7(5), 9.8(5), 9.9 or 9.10, that person must within 28 days of such notification file a witness statement containing any evidence of that person's interest in the proceedings and, if that person opposes the application or seeks a different order, any evidence upon which that person intends to rely.

(8) The court must consider whether to join a person mentioned in paragraph (6) as a party to the proceedings and, if it decides to do so, must make an order to that effect.

(9) Where a person who is notified in accordance with rule 9.7(5), 9.8(5), 9.9 or 9.10 complies with the requirements of this rule, that person need not comply with the requirements of rule 9.15 (application to be joined as a party).

(10) A practice direction may make provision about responding to applications.

III MEN [595.1]

Responding to applications to the court Practice Direction 9C relates to responding to an application (see **III MEN [603]**). Form COP5 must be used if a person wishes to be a party to the proceedings, paras 3 and 4 set out the position of those who are either served or notified. Paragraph 5 records that a person neither served nor notified but wishing to become a party must apply in Form COP10 to be joined (rule 9.15). See **III MEN [598]**.

THE PARTIES TO THE PROCEEDINGS

III MEN [596]

9.13 Parties to the proceedings

(1) Unless the court directs otherwise, the parties to any proceedings are—

- (a) the applicant; and
- (b) any person who is named as a respondent in the application form and who files an acknowledgment of service in respect of the application form.

(2) The court may order a person to be joined as a party if it considers that it is desirable to do so for the purpose of dealing with the application.

(3) The court may at any time direct that any person who is a party to the proceedings is to be removed as a party.

(4) Unless the court orders otherwise, P shall not be named as a respondent to any proceedings.

(5) A party to the proceedings is bound by any order or direction of the court made in the course of those proceedings.

III MEN [596.1]

Applications to the court and the joining of parties The court itself will consider at upon issue, the participation of 'P' and regard should be made to rule 1.2 see (**III MEN [493]**) and Practice Direction 2A (**III MEN [505]**).

III MEN [596.2]

The issue of joining of parties and 'sufficient interest' In *Re SK* [2012] EWHC 1990 (COP), Bodey J considered the interrelationship of parties in Queen's Bench personal injury proceedings and welfare proceedings before the Court of Protection. He held that rule 9.13 and rule 9.15 (see below) should be considered together, and that it should be interpreted to mean 'a sufficient interest' in the proceedings.

In *Re G (Adult)* [2014] EWCOP 1361 (COP), [2014] All ER (D) 27 (May) the President, applying the provisions of rules 73 and 75, considered the application of a newspaper publishing group to be joined as a party. In an analysis of the relevant provisions of Article 8 and Article 10 of the European Convention on Human Rights, the President found that the engagement of the applicant's Article 10 rights did not give them 'sufficient interest' to be joined.

III MEN [597]

9.14 Persons to be bound as if parties

(1) The persons mentioned in paragraph (2) shall be bound by any order made or directions given by the court in the same way that a party to the proceedings is so bound.

(2) The persons referred to in paragraph (1) are—

- (a) P; and
- (b) any person who has been served with or notified of an application form in accordance with these Rules.

III MEN [598]

9.15 Application to be joined as a party

(1) Any person with sufficient interest may apply to the court to be joined as a party to the proceedings.

(2) An application to be joined as a party must be made by filing an application notice in accordance with Part 10, which must—

- (a) state the full name and address of the person seeking to be joined as a party to the proceedings;
- (b) state that person's interest in the proceedings;
- (c) state whether that person consents to the application;
- (d) state whether that person opposes the application and, if so, set out the grounds for doing so;
- (e) state whether that person proposes that an order different from that set out in the application form should be made and, if so, set out what that order is;
- (f) provide an address for service, which must be within the jurisdiction of the court; and
- (g) be signed by that person or that person's legal representative.

(3) Subject to rules 15.2 and 15.5 (restriction on filing an expert's report and court's power to restrict expert evidence), a person's application to be joined must be accompanied by—

- (a) a witness statement containing evidence of that person's interest in the proceedings and, if that person proposes that an order different from that set out in the application form should be made, the evidence on which that person intends to rely; and
- (b) a sufficient number of copies of the application notice to enable service of the application on every other party to the proceedings.

(4) The court must serve the application notice and any accompanying documents on all parties to the proceedings.

(5) The court must consider whether to join a person applying under this rule as a party to the proceedings and, if it decides to do so, must make an order to that effect.

III MEN [598.1]

Procedure to join existing proceedings See para 5 of Practice Direction 9C. Form COP10 is to be used **III MEN [602]**.

III MEN [599]

9.16 Application for removal as a party to proceedings

A person who wishes to be removed as a party to the proceedings must apply to the court for an order to that effect in accordance with Part 10.

III MEN [599.1]

Applications to the court For applications under Part 10 see **III MEN [607]** below

PRACTICE DIRECTION 9A – THE APPLICATION FORM

III MEN [600]

This practice direction supplements Part 9 of the Court of Protection Rules 2017

THE APPLICATION FORM

1 To begin proceedings, the applicant must file an application form using form COP1.

2 The application form must –

(a) state the matter which the applicant wants the court to decide;
(b) state the order which the applicant is seeking;
(c) name (unless an order to the contrary pursuant to rule 5.11 has been made) –
  (i) the applicant,
  (ii) P,
  (iii) as a respondent, any person (other than P) whom the applicant reasonably believes to have an interest which means that he ought to be heard in relation to the application (as opposed to being notified of it), and
  (iv) any person whom the applicant intends to notify in accordance with rule 9.10; and
(d) if the applicant is applying in a representative capacity, state what that capacity is.

3 The application form must include (unless an order to the contrary pursuant to rule 5.11 has been made):

(a) an address at which the applicant resides or carries on business;
(b) an address at which P resides or carries on business;
(c) an address at which each person named as a respondent to the proceedings resides or carries on business, and details of how each respondent is connected to P; and
(d) an address at which any person (other than P) whom the applicant intends to notify of the application resides or carries on business, and details of how each person is connected to P.

4 Paragraph 3 applies even though a solicitor or litigation friend has agreed, as the case may be, to accept service.

5 The application form must be headed with the name of the person to whom the application relates (unless an order to the contrary pursuant to rule 5.11 has been made).

STATEMENT OF TRUTH

6 Rule 5.2 requires an application form to be verified by a statement of truth where the applicant seeks to rely on matters set out in it as evidence.

7 The form of the statement of truth is as follows –

'[I believe] [The applicant believes] that the facts stated in this application form and its annex(es) are true.'

8 Attention is drawn to rule 5.6 which sets out the consequences of verifying an application form containing a false statement without an honest belief in its truth.

(Practice direction B accompanying Part 5 sets out more detailed requirements for statements of truth.)

DOCUMENTS TO BE FILED WITH THE APPLICATION FORM

9 The application form must be supported by evidence set out in either –

(a) a witness statement; or
(b) the application form provided it is verified by a statement of truth.

10 A witness statement must be verified by a statement of truth in the following terms –

'I believe that the facts stated in this witness statement are true.'

11 The evidence must set out the facts on which the applicant relies, and all material facts known to the applicant of which the court should be made aware.

12 The documents or instruments, as the case may be, specified in the table below must be filed with the court along with the application form, unless this is impractical or the court has directed otherwise.

Type of document or instrument	***When document is to be filed***
Assessment of capacity form (COP3)	All applications except those concerning the court's powers under section 22 or 23 of, Schedule 4 of the Act, or applications made under practice direction 9D.
Annex A: Supporting information for property and affairs applications (COP1A)	Where an order relating to P's property and affairs is sought.
Annex B: Supporting information for personal welfare applications (COP1B)	Where an order relating to P's personal welfare is sought.
Deputy's declaration (COP4)	Where the application is for the appointment of a deputy.
Annex C supporting information for statutory will, codicil, gift(s), deed of variation or settlement of property (COP1C)	Where an order relating to a statutory will, codicil, gift(s), deed of variation or settlement of property is sought
Annex D Supporting information for applications to appoint or discharge a trustee (COP1D)	Where an order relating to the appointment or discharge of a trustee is sought.
Annex E Supporting information for an application by an existing deputy or attorney (COP1E)	Where the application is made by a person appointed deputy, an attorney under a registered enduring power of attorney or a donee of a registered lasting power of attorney; and the application relates to the applicant's powers and duties as deputy, attorney or donee in connection with P's property and affairs.
Annex F Supporting information relating to the validity or operation of an enduring power of attorney or lasting power of attorney (COP1F)	Where an order relating to the validity or operation of an enduring power of attorney or lasting power of attorney order is sought.
Lasting power of attorney or enduring power of attorney	Where the application concerns the court's power under section 22 or 23 of, or Schedule 4 to, the Act (where available).
Order appointing a deputy	Where the application relates to or is made by a deputy.
Order appointing a litigation friend	Where the application is made by, or where the application relates to the appointment of, a litigation friend.
Order of the Court of Protection	Where the application relates to the order.
Order of another court (and where the judgment is not in English, a translation of it into English:	Where the application relates to an order made by another court.

Type of document or instrument	*When document is to be filed*
(i) certified by a notary public or other qualified person; or (ii) accompanied by written evidence confirming that the translation is accurate).	

13 Rule 5.1 and practice direction A accompanying Part 5 set out how documents are to be filed at court.

14 If the applicant is unable to complete an assessment of capacity form (as may be the case, for example, where P does not reside with the applicant and the applicant is unable to take P to a doctor, or where P refuses to undergo the assessment), the applicant should file a witness statement with the application form explaining –

(a) why he has not been able to obtain an assessment of capacity;
(b) what attempts (if any) he has made to obtain an assessment of capacity; and
(c) why he knows or believes that P lacks capacity to make a decision or decisions in relation to any matter that is subject of the proposed application.

START OF PROCEEDINGS

15 The date on which the application form was received by the court will be recorded by a date stamp either on the application form held on the court file or on the letter that accompanied the application form when it was received by the court.

16 Any enquiry as to the date on which the court received an application form should be directed to a court officer.

III MEN [600.1]

Applications to the court and permission Regard must be given at all stages prior to issue as to whether permission is required (see Part 8 above **III MEN [577]**). The appropriate forms must be used, and if the application relates to an issue of deprivation of liberty then Practice Direction 11A must be considered and if applicable either the DOLs forms must be used or the COPDOL 10 form if the procedure relates to an application under sections 4A(3) and 16(2)(a) of the Act (see **III MEN [619]** to **III MEN [620]**).

PRACTICE DIRECTION 9B – NOTIFICATION OF OTHER PERSONS THAT AN APPLICATION FORM HAS BEEN ISSUED

III MEN [601]

This practice direction supplements Part 9 of the Court of Protection Rules 2017

GENERAL

1 Rule 9.10 requires the applicant to notify certain persons of the application in accordance with the relevant practice direction.

WHO IS TO BE NOTIFIED

2 The persons who should be notified will vary according to the nature of the application.

3 A person who has been named as respondent in the application form should not also be notified. Any reference in this practice direction to a person to be notified does not apply where the person has already been named as a respondent.

4 The applicant must seek to identify at least three persons who are likely to have an interest in being notified that an application form has been issued. The applicant should notify them –

(a) that an application form has been issued;
(b) whether it relates to the exercise of the court's jurisdiction in relation to P's property and affairs, or his personal welfare, or both; and
(c) of the order or orders sought.

5 Members of P's close family are, by virtue of their relationship to P, likely to have an interest in being notified that an application has been made to the court concerning P. It should be presumed, for example that a spouse or civil partner, any other partner, parents and children are likely to have an interest in the application.

6 This presumption may be displaced where the applicant is aware of circumstances which reasonably indicate that P's family should not be notified, but that others should be notified instead. For example, where the applicant knows that the relative in question has had little or no involvement in P's life and has shown no inclination to do so, the applicant may reasonably conclude that that relative need not be notified. In some cases, P may be closer to persons who are not relatives and if so, it will be appropriate to notify them instead of family members.

7 The following list of people is ordered according to the presumed closeness in terms of relationship to P. They should be notified in descending order (as appropriate to P's circumstances) –

(a) spouse or civil partner;
(b) person who is not a spouse or a civil partner but who has been living with P as if they were;
(c) parent or guardian;
(d) child;
(e) brother or sister;
(f) grandparent or grandchild;
(g) aunt or uncle;
(h) child of a person falling within subparagraph (e);
(i) step-parent; and
(j) half-brother or half-sister.

(If any of the people to be notified are children or protected parties, see rule 6.4.)

8 Where the applicant decides that a person listed in one of the categories in paragraph 7 ought to be notified, and there are other persons in that category (e.g. P has four siblings), the applicant should notify all persons falling within that category unless there is a good reason not to do so. For example, it may be a good reason not to notify every person in the category if one or more of them has had little or no involvement in P's life and has shown no inclination to do so.

9 Where the applicant chooses not to notify a person listed in paragraph 7 because the presumption has been displaced (see paragraphs 6 and 8 above) the evidence in support of the application form must also set out why that person was not notified.

10 In addition to the list in paragraph 7, the following persons must be notified where appropriate –

(a) where P is under 18, any person with parental responsibility for P within the meaning of the Children Act 1989;
(b) any legal or natural person who is likely to be affected by the outcome of any application. For example, where there is an organisation (including an NHS

body) responsible for P's care (and the application is made by another person) the organisation should be notified where the application relates to the provision to, or withdrawal from, P of medical or other treatment or accommodation;

(c) any deputy appointed by the court, an attorney appointed under an enduring power of attorney or a donee of a lasting power of attorney (where that person has power to make decisions on behalf of P in regard to a matter to which the application relates). For example, where the application relates to P's property, and a deputy has been appointed to make decisions in relation to P's property, the deputy should be notified; and

(d) any other person not already mentioned whom the applicant reasonably considers has an interest in being notified that an application form has been issued. For example, P may have a close friend with an interest in being notified because he provides care to P on an informal basis.

11 Where the applicant chooses not to notify a person listed in paragraph 10 the evidence in support of the application form must also set out why that person was not notified.

METHOD OF NOTIFICATION

12 Notification must be provided using a COP15 form.

13 The provisions of Part 6 and Practice Direction A accompanying Part 6 apply similarly to notification as they do to service.

III MEN [601.1]

Procedure for notification The provisions of rule 9.7(5) (see **III MEN [590]**) relating to lasting powers of attorney and rule 9.8(5) (see **III MEN [591]**) relating to enduring powers of attorney make alternative direction regarding the notification to be given for such applications.

PRACTICE DIRECTION 9C – RESPONDING TO AN APPLICATION

III MEN [602]

This practice direction supplements Part 9 of the Court of Protection Rules 2017

GENERAL

1 Rule 9.12(10) enables a practice direction to make provision about responding to applications. Rule 9.12 sets out the procedure to be followed where a person who has been served with or notified of an application form wishes to become, or apply to become, a party to proceedings.

2 Rule 9.15 sets out the procedure to be followed where a person who has not been served with or notified of an application form in accordance with rules 9.6 to 9.10 wishes to apply to become a party to proceedings.

RESPONDING TO THE APPLICATION

Persons served with an application

3 Where a person is served with an application form pursuant to rule 9.6, 9.7 or 9.8 that person must, if he or she wishes to be a party to the proceedings, file an acknowledgment of service using Form COP5 in accordance with rule 9.12. By doing this, the person becomes a party.

Persons notified of an application

4 Where a person has been notified of an application pursuant to rule 9.7(5), 9.8(5), 9.9 or 9.10, that person must, if he or she wishes to be a party to the proceedings, apply to the court to be joined as a party by filing an acknowledgment of notification using Form COP5 in accordance with rule 9.12.

Persons not served with or notified of an application

5 Where a person was not served with or notified of an application form, that person must, if he or she wishes to be a party to the proceedings, apply to the court to be joined as a party, by filing an application to be joined using Form COP10 in accordance with rule 9.15.

Signing the acknowledgment

6 An acknowledgment must be signed by the person acknowledging service or notification, or by his legal representative or litigation friend.

7 Where the respondent is a company or other corporation, a person holding a senior position in the company or corporation may sign the acknowledgment on the respondent's behalf, but must state the position he holds.

8 Each of the following persons is a person holding a senior position –

(a) in respect of a registered company or corporation, a director, the treasurer, secretary, chief executive, manager or other officer of the company or corporation; and

(b) in respect of a corporation which is not a registered company, in addition to those persons set out at (a), the mayor, chairman, president, town clerk or similar officer of the corporation.

9 Where the respondent is a partnership, the acknowledgment may be signed by –

(a) any of the partners; or

(b) a person having the control or management of the partnership business.

10 The name of the person acknowledging service or notification should be set out in full on the acknowledgment.

11 If two or more persons acknowledge service or notification of an application through the same legal representative at the same time, only one acknowledgment of service need be used.

ADDRESS FOR SERVICE

12 The acknowledgment must include an address for the service of documents, which must be within the jurisdiction of the court.

13 When the person acknowledging service or notification is represented by a legal representative, and the legal representative has signed the acknowledgment, the address must be the legal representative's business address.

CORRECTIONS AND AMENDMENTS TO THE ACKNOWLEDGMENT

14 Where the name of the person acknowledging service or notification has been set out incorrectly on the application form, it should be correctly set out in the acknowledgment followed by the words 'described as' and the incorrect name.

15 An acknowledgment of service or notification may be amended only with the permission of the court.

16 An application under paragraph 15 must be made by filing a COP9 application notice in accordance with Part 10 and supported by evidence.

PRACTICE DIRECTION 9D – APPLICATIONS BY CURRENTLY APPOINTED DEPUTIES, ATTORNEYS AND DONEES IN RELATION TO P'S PROPERTY AND AFFAIRS

III MEN [603]

This practice direction supplements Part 9 of the Court of Protection Rules 2017

GENERAL

1 Rule 9.11 enables a practice direction to make additional or different provision in relation to specified applications.

APPLICATIONS TO WHICH THIS PRACTICE DIRECTION APPLIES

2 This practice direction applies to applications –

(a) which are made by a person who is appointed to act as a deputy for P, or by an attorney under a registered enduring power of attorney or a donee of a registered lasting power of attorney;
(b) which relate to the applicant's powers and duties as a deputy, attorney or donee, in connection with making decisions as to P's property and affairs;
(c) where the applicant reasonably considers that the order sought is not likely to be significant to P's estate or to any other of P's interests; and
(d) where the applicant knows, or reasonably believes, that there are unlikely to be any objections to the application he proposes to make.

3 Applications may only be made using the procedure in this practice direction if the deputy, attorney or donee does not have the authority to make the decision or decisions in question.

APPLICATIONS BY DEPUTIES WHICH MAY BE SUITABLE FOR THE PROCEDURE SET OUT IN THIS PRACTICE DIRECTION

4 Examples of applications by deputies that may be suitable for the procedure in this practice direction include, but are not limited to –

(a) applications for regular payments from P's assets to the deputy in respect of remuneration;
(b) applications seeking minor variations only as to the expenses that can be paid from P's estate;
(c) applications to change an accounting period;
(d) applications to set or change the time by which an annual account may be submitted;
(e) applications in relation to the sale of property owned by P, where the sale is non-contentious;
(f) applications for authority to disclose information as to P's assets, state of health or other circumstances;

MENTAL CAPACITY AND MENTAL HEALTH

(g) applications to make a gift or loan from P's assets, provided that the sum in question is not disproportionately large when compared to the size of P's estate as a whole;

(h) applications to sell or otherwise deal with P's investments, provided that the sum in question is not disproportionately large when compared to the size of P's estate as a whole;

(i) applications for the receipt or discharge of a sum due to or by P;

(j) applications for authority to apply for a grant of probate or representation, where P would be the person entitled to the grant but for his lack of capacity;

(k) applications relating to the lease or grant of a tenancy in relation to property owned by P;

(l) applications for release of funds to repair or improve P's property;

(m) applications to sell P's furniture or effects;

(n) applications for release of capital to meet expenses required for the care of P;

(o) applications to arrange an overdraft or bank loan on P's behalf;

(p) applications to open a bank account on behalf of P or for the purpose of the deputyship at a private bank, a bank that is not located in England and Wales, or at a bank which has unusual conditions attached to the operation of the account; and

(q) applications for the variation of an order for security made pursuant to rule 24.3.

APPLICATIONS BY ATTORNEYS OR DONEES WHICH MAY BE SUITABLE FOR THE PROCEDURE SET OUT IN THIS PRACTICE DIRECTION

5 Examples of applications by attorneys or donees that may be suitable for the procedure in this practice direction include, but are not limited to –

(a) applications for regular payments from P's assets to the attorney or donee in respect of remuneration;

(b) applications to make a gift from P's assets, provided that the sum in question is not disproportionately large when compared to the size of P's estate as a whole;

(c) applications to authorise a sale of P's property to the attorney or donee, or a family member of P, the attorney or donee, at proper market value, and provided that the market value of the property in question is not disproportionately large when compared to the size of P's estate as a whole;

(d) applications for authority to obtain a copy of P's will;

(e) applications for the approval of equity releases; and

(f) applications for orders for sale pursuant to paragraphs 8 and 9 of Schedule 2 to the Act.

APPLICATIONS WHICH ARE NOT SUITABLE FOR THE PROCEDURE SET OUT IN THIS PRACTICE DIRECTION

6 Examples of applications which are not suitable for the procedure in this practice direction include, but are not limited to –

(a) applications for the removal of a deputy;

(b) applications seeking authorisation to commence, continue or defend litigation on behalf of P;

(c) applications for the settlement of P's property, whether for P's benefit or for the benefit of others;

(d) applications to vary the terms of a trust or estate in which P has an interest;

(e) applications for a statutory will or codicil; and

(f) applications to operate or cease to operate a business belonging to P, or to dissolve a partnership of which P is a member.

7 An application which is likely to be contested, or which involves large sums of money (when compared to the size of P's estate as a whole) is not suitable for the procedure set out in this practice direction.

PROCEDURE FOR APPLICATIONS TO WHICH THIS PRACTICE DIRECTION APPLIES

8 Applications must be made by filing a COP1 application form, together with any evidence in support of the application. However, Annexes A and B to the application form (COP1A and COP1B) are not required to be filed, nor is an assessment of capacity form.

9 Notwithstanding rules 9.6 to 9.10, applications to which this Practice Direction applies may be made, in the first instance, without serving the application form on anyone and without notifying anyone that the application has been made.

10 The court may decide, upon considering the application, that other persons ought to be notified of the application and given the opportunity to respond. In such a case, the court will give directions as to who should be served with or notified of the application and the manner in which they are to be served or notified, as the case may be.

11 The court may deal with the application without a hearing and will give directions as to who should be served with any order that it makes.

RIGHT OF RECONSIDERATION

12 Where the application is determined without notice having been given to any person or without a hearing, P, any party or any person affected by the order may apply to the court, within 21 days of having been served with the court's order, to have the order reconsidered. An application to have an order reconsidered must be made by filing a COP9 application notice in accordance with Part 10.

III MEN [603.1]

Applications to the court for reconsideration The right to apply for consideration arises from rule 13.4; see **III MEN [626]**.

The previous Practice Direction 9E, concerning Serious Medical Treatment cases had not been replaced at the time of writing.

III MEN [603.2]

Guidance on applications to the court in respect of serious medical treatment For further guidance on cases concerning serious medical treatment see **III MEN [7]** above.

Practice Direction 9B provides guidance on notification to be given of the application, see **III MEN [601]**.

For allocation of judiciary under s 46(2)(a)–(c) of the Mental Capacity Act 2005 see **III MEN [84]** above.

Urgent applications should be made with regard to Practice Direction 10B (**III MEN [618]**) and if an issue involves deprivation of liberty, regard should be made to Practice Direction 11A (**III MEN [620]**).

Regard should be made to the Code of Practice, paragraph 5.29 to 5.36, but whilst not receiving detailed submissions on the accuracy of paragraph 5.33 Baker J, clearly stated, that in so far as issues concerned 'Artificial Nutrition and Hydration' ('ANH'), the legal position has been clear since Bland (*Airedale NHS Trust v Bland* [1993] AC 789, [1993] 1 All ER 821, HL). Until recently, and as was set out in the Court of Protection Rules 2007 Practice Direction 9E paragraph 5, all decisions about the proposed withholding or withdrawal of ANH from a person in a permanent vegetative state ('PVS') or minimally conscious state ('MCS') should always be brought to the court. However, in *NHS Trust v. Mr Y (by his litigation friend, the Official Solicitor) & Mrs Y* [2017] EWHC 2866 (QB), O'Farrell J made a declaration that it was not mandatory to bring an application before the Court concerning the withdrawal of clinically assisted nutrition and hydration (CANH) where the clinicians have followed the Mental Capacity Act and good medical practice and there is no dispute with the family of the person concerned (or others interested in his welfare)and there are no other doubts or concerns. The decision has leapfrogged the Court of Appeal and is due to be heard by the Supreme Court in the Spring of 2018.

III MEN [603.3]

Good Practice in applying out of hours In *Sandwell and West Birmingham Hospitals NHS Trust v CD* [2014] EWCOP 23, 178 CL&J 530 Mrs Justice Theis in reviewing an out of hours application relating to significant medical health issues gave at paragraph 39 of her judgment five clear procedural steps that should be followed (i) appropriate measures for family to participate, (ii) early engagement of the Official Solicitor ,(iii) proper use of the Urgent Applications Judge and Clerk of the Rules, (iv) provision of a word version of a draft order, and (v) appropriate information relating to the history of P's quality of life.

PRACTICE DIRECTION 9E – APPLICATIONS RELATING TO STATUTORY WILLS, CODICILS, SETTLEMENTS AND OTHER DEALINGS WITH P'S PROPERTY

III MEN [604]

This practice direction supplements Part 9 of the Court of Protection Rules 2017

GENERAL

1 Rule 9.11 enables a practice direction to make additional or different provision in relation to specified applications.

APPLICATIONS TO WHICH THIS PRACTICE DIRECTION APPLIES

2 This practice direction makes provision for applications that relate to –

(a) the execution of a will or codicil of P;
(b) the settlement of any of P's property; and
(c) the sale, exchange, charging, gift or other disposition of P's property.

3 A deputy may not be given powers with respect to –

(a) the settlement of any of P's property;
(b) the execution of a will of P; or
(c) the exercise of any power (including a power to consent) vested in P whether beneficially or as a trustee or otherwise.

4 Hence, an application must be made to the court for a decision in relation to such matters. This practice direction is concerned with matters mentioned at paragraphs 3(a) and (b) above. Practice direction G accompanying Part 9 contains provisions as to applications falling with paragraph 3(c).

PERMISSION TO MAKE APPLICATIONS TO THE COURT

5 Section 50(1) of, paragraph 20(2) to Schedule 3 to, the Act and rule 8.2 set out the circumstances in which permission is or is not required to make an application to the court for the exercise of any of its powers under the Act.

INFORMATION TO BE PROVIDED WITH APPLICATION FORM

6 In addition to the application form COP1 (and its annexes) and any information or documents required to be provided by the Rules or another practice direction, the following information must be provided (in the form of a witness statement, attaching documents as exhibits where necessary) for any application to which this practice direction applies –

(a) where the application is for the execution of a statutory will or codicil, a copy of the draft will or codicil, plus one copy;
(b) a copy of any existing will or codicil;
(c) any consents to act by proposed executors;
(d) details of P's family, preferably in the form of a family tree, including details of the full name and date of birth of each person included in the family tree;
(e) a schedule showing details of P's current assets, with up to date valuations;
(f) a schedule showing the estimated net yearly income and spending of P;
(g) a statement showing P's needs, both current and future estimates, and his general circumstances;
(h) if P is living in National Health Service accommodation, information on whether he may be discharged to local authority accommodation, to other fee-paying accommodation or to his own home;
(i) if the applicant considers it relevant, full details of the resources of any proposed beneficiary, and details of any likely changes if the application is successful;
(j) details of any capital gains tax, inheritance tax or income tax which may be chargeable in respect of the subject matter of the application;
(k) an explanation of the effect, if any, that the proposed changes will have on P's circumstances, preferably in the form of a 'before and after' schedule of assets and income;
(l) if appropriate, a statement of whether any land would be affected by the proposed will or settlement and if so, details of its location and title number, if applicable;
(m) where the application is for a settlement of property or for the variation of an existing settlement or trust, a draft of the proposed deed, plus one copy;
(n) a copy of any registered enduring power of attorney or lasting power of attorney;
(o) confirmation that P is a resident of England or Wales; and
(p) an up to date report of P's present medical condition, life expectancy, likelihood of requiring increased expenditure in the foreseeable future, and testamentary capacity.

7 The court may direct that other material is to be filed by the applicant, and if it does, the information will be set out in the form of a witness statement.

8 If any of the information mentioned above has been provided already (e.g. by way of inclusion in an annex to the application form) it need not be provided again.

RESPONDENTS AND PERSONS WHO MUST BE NOTIFIED OF AN APPLICATION

9 The applicant must name as a respondent –

(a) any beneficiary under an existing will or codicil who is likely to be materially or adversely affected by the application;
(b) any beneficiary under a proposed will or codicil who is likely to be materially or adversely affected by the application; and
(c) any prospective beneficiary under P's intestacy where P has no existing will.

(Practice direction B accompanying Part 9 sets out the procedure for notifying others of an application.)

10 The court will consider at the earliest opportunity whether P should be joined as a party to the proceedings and, if he is so joined, the court will consider whether the Official Solicitor should be invited to act as a litigation friend, or whether some other person should be appointed as a litigation friend.

PROCEDURE ON EXECUTION OF A WILL

11 Once a will of P has been executed, the applicant must send the original and two copies of the will to the court for sealing.

12 The court shall seal the original and the copy and return both documents to the applicant.

(Paragraph 3(2) of Schedule 2 to the Mental Capacity Act 2005 sets out the requirements for execution of a will on behalf of P, where the will is executed pursuant to an order or direction of the court.)

ANNEX — EXAMPLE FORM OF STATUTORY WILL

(This only shows the manner in which the authorised person makes the will and executes the same.)

This is the last will of me AB [the person who lacks capacity] of ____________ acting by CD the person authorised in that behalf by an order dated the ____________ day of ____________ 20____________ made under the Mental Capacity Act 2005.

I revoke all my former wills and codicils and declare this to be my last will.

1. I appoint EF and GH to be executors and trustees of this my will.
2. I give ____

In witness of which this will is signed by me AB acting by CD under the order mentioned above on (date).

SIGNED by the said AB [the person who lacks capacity]

by the said CD [authorised person]

and by the said CD with his (or her) own AB [person who lacks capacity

name pursuant to the said order in our CD [authorised person]

presence and attested by us in the

presence of the said CD.

[Name and addresses of witness]

Sealed with the official seal of the Court of Protection the ____________ day of ____________ 20____________

III MEN [604.1]

Guidance on applications to the court in respect of statutory wills See s 18(1)(i) of the Mental Capacity Act 2005 and the notes thereto at **III MEN [51]** above. In having regard to the wishes of P and the application of the principles and best interests determination, consideration should be given to the guidance provided in the judgments in *Re S and S (Protected Persons), C v V* [2009] WTLR 315; *Re P (Statutory Will)* [2010] Ch 33; and *Re M* [2010] 3All ER 682.

PRACTICE DIRECTION 9F — APPLICATIONS TO APPOINT OR DISCHARGE A TRUSTEE

III MEN [605]

This practice direction supplements Part 9 of the Court of Protection Rules 2017

GENERAL

1 Rule 9.11 enables a practice direction to make additional or different provision in relation to specified applications.

APPLICATIONS TO WHICH THIS PRACTICE DIRECTION APPLIES

2 This practice direction makes provision for applications –

(a) for the exercise of any power (including a power to consent) vested in P whether as a trustee or otherwise (section 18(1)(j) of the Act);
(b) under section 36(9) of the Trustee Act 1925 for leave to appoint a new trustee in place of P;
(c) under section 54 of the Trustee Act 1925 as to the court's jurisdiction;
(d) under section 20 of the Trusts of Land and Appointment of Trustees Act 1996; or
(e) for the court's approval of the appointment of a trustee in accordance with the terms of a trust.

3 A deputy may not be appointed to exercise any power vested in P, whether as a trustee or otherwise. Hence, an application must be made to the court for the court to make such a decision.

PERMISSION TO MAKE APPLICATIONS TO THE COURT

4 Section 50(1) of, paragraph 20(2) to Schedule 3 to, the Act and rule 8.21 set out the circumstances in which permission is or is not required to make an application to the court for the exercise of any of its powers under the Act.

INFORMATION TO BE PROVIDED WITH THE APPLICATION FORM

5 In addition to the application form COP1 (and its annexes) and any information or documents required to be provided by the Rules or another practice direction, the following information must be provided (in the form of a witness statement, attaching documents as exhibits where necessary) for any application to which this Practice Direction applies–

(a) a copy of the existing trust document;
(b) where relevant, a copy of any original conveyance, transfer, lease, assignment, settlement trust or will trust;
(c) the names and addresses of any present trustees and details of any beneficial interest they have in the trust property. If the present trustees are not the original trustees, an explanation should be provided as to how they became trustees and copies of any deeds of appointment and retirement should be provided;
(d) the full name, address and date of birth of any person proposed to replace P as a trustee, and details of his relationship to P;
(e) confirmation that the trust is not under an order for administration in the Chancery Division;
(f) if there is only one continuing trustee, the applicant must confirm that both the trustee and the proposed new trustee have not made an enduring power of attorney or a lasting power of attorney in favour of the other party;
(g) if an enduring power of attorney or a lasting power of attorney has been executed by a continuing trustee, a certified copy of that document must be provided. If the power has not been registered, the applicant must confirm that the trustee is still capable of carrying out his duties as a trustee;
(h) the full name and address of any person who has an interest in any trust property as the beneficiary of a will, and whether any of them are children or persons who lack capacity;
(i) if the proposed new trustee is not a solicitor or a trust corporation (for example, a bank) and has not been appointed as a deputy for the trustee lacking capacity, the applicant must provide a witness statement from a person independent of the applicant, who has no interest in the trust property, attesting to the applicant's fitness to be appointed as trustee;

(j) if the application relates to a transfer of assets in a will trust or similar settlement into the names of new trustees, accurate details of the trust assets must be provided (including full details of any stocks and shares held);
(k) a copy of any notice of severance and evidence of service;
(l) a copy of the will and grant of probate to the deceased's estate (where relevant);
(m) confirmation of all relevant consents; and
(n) a copy of a signed trustee's special undertaking.

6 The court may direct that other material is to be filed by the applicant, and if it does, the information will be set out in the form of a witness statement.

7 If any of the information mentioned above has been provided already (e.g. by way of inclusion in an annex to the application form) it need not be provided again.

ADDITIONAL INFORMATION TO BE PROVIDED WHERE THE APPLICATION RELATES TO REAL PROPERTY

8 In addition to the information specified in paragraph 5 above, where the application relates to real property, the information specified in paragraph 9 below must be provided. The information will be set out in the form of a witness statement.

9 The information which must be provided is –

(a) the address of the property concerned, and whether it is freehold or leasehold;
(b) the title number of the property and a copy of its entry in the Land Registry (if registered land). If the land is unregistered, the applicant should inform the court accordingly; and
(c) if the property is leasehold the applicant should advise the court as to whether he has a licence or consent to the assignment, and provide a copy of the same (or advise if a licence or consent is not necessary and the reason why it is not needed).

10 If any of the information mentioned above has been provided already (e.g. by way of inclusion in an annex to the application form) it need not be provided again.

PRACTICE DIRECTION 9G – APPLICATIONS RELATING TO THE REGISTRATION OF ENDURING POWERS OF ATTORNEY

III MEN [606]

This practice direction supplements Part 9 of the Court of Protection Rules 2017

GENERAL

1. Rule 9.11 enables a practice direction to make additional or different provision in relation to specified applications.

Applications to which this practice direction applies

2. This practice direction applies where –

(a) an application has been made to the Public Guardian to register an instrument creating an enduring power of attorney; and

(b) the Public Guardian has received a notice of objection to registration which prevents him from registering the instrument except in accordance with the court's directions.

OBJECTIONS TO REGISTRATION

3. A notice of objection will prevent the Public Guardian from registering the instrument if the objection is made on one of the following grounds –

(a) that the power purported to have been created by the instrument was not valid as an enduring power of attorney;
(b) that the power created by the instrument no longer subsists;
(c) that the application is premature because the donor is not yet becoming mentally incapable;
(d) that fraud or undue pressure was used to induce the donor to create the power; or
(e) that, having regard to all the circumstances and in particular the attorney's relationship to or connection with the donor, the attorney is unsuitable to be the donor's attorney.

4. This practice direction sets out the procedure to be followed by a person entitled to be given notice of the application to register the instrument who wishes to apply to the court for –

(a) directions that the instrument should be registered; or
(b) directions that the instrument should not be registered.

5. The persons who are entitled to receive notice of an application are the donor, certain of his relatives and any attorneys under the enduring power who are not making the application for registration.

PROCEDURE FOR APPLICATIONS TO WHICH THIS PRACTICE DIRECTION APPLIES

6. An application must be made using form COP8.

(Practice direction B accompanying Part 5 sets out more detailed requirements for statements of truth.)

7. The application form must state –

(a) what directions the applicant is seeking; and
(b) if the applicant objects to registration, the grounds on which he does so; or
(c) if the applicant is seeking registration, his reasons for doing so.

8. The application form must be supported by evidence set out in either –

(a) a witness statement; or
(b) if it is verified by a statement of truth, the application form.

9. As soon as practicable and in any event within 14 days of the application form being issued, the applicant must serve a copy of the application form, together with an acknowledgment of service using form COP5 –

(a) unless the applicant is the donor or an attorney, on the donor of the power and every attorney under the power;
(b) if he is the donor, on every attorney under the power; or
(c) if he is an attorney, on the donor and any other attorney under the power.

10. Where the applicant knows or has reasonable grounds to believe that the donor of the power lacks capacity to make a decision in relation to any matter that is the subject of the application, he must notify the donor of the application in accordance with Part 7.

III MEN [606.1]

Applications to the court — guidance and procedure See Sch 4 of the Mental Capacity Act 2005 (**III MEN [134]**). The Schedule provides guidance as to those to whom notice should be given (paras 5 to 11).

Form COP8 must be used (para 6) and Practice Direction 5B provides guidance on the requirements for the statement of truth (see **III MEN [543]**). Acknowledgment form COP5 must be used.

PART 10
APPLICATIONS WITHIN PROCEEDINGS

III MEN [607]

10.1 Types of applications for which the Part 10 procedure may be used

(1) The Part 10 procedure is the procedure set out in this Part.

(2) The Part 10 procedure may be used if the application is made by any person—

(a) in the course of existing proceedings; or

(b) as provided for in a rule or practice direction.

(3) The court may grant an interim remedy before an application form has been issued only if—

(a) the matter is urgent; or

(b) it is otherwise necessary to do so in the interests of justice.

(4) An application made during the course of existing proceedings includes an application made during appeal proceedings.

(5) Where the application seeks solely to withdraw an existing application—

(a) the applicant must file a written request for permission setting out succinctly the reasons for the request;

(b) the request must be in an application notice;

(c) the court may permit an application to be made orally at a hearing or in such alternative written form as it thinks fit.

(6) Where the court deals with a written request under paragraph (5) without a hearing, rule 13.4 applies to any order so made.

(Rule 13.2 requires the court's permission to withdraw proceedings.)

III MEN [607.1]

Applications to the court practice and procedure Practice Direction 10A provides supplemental directions regarding applications within proceedings. Paragraph 2 requires the application to be made by filing form COP9: **III MEN [617]**. Paragraphs 1–16 deal with provisions for issue, the supporting documents, service and notification, and procedure to listing. Paragraph 17 deals with matters that may be raised in the application. Paragraphs 18–20 and para 21 provide guidance upon telephone hearings and video conference. Paragraphs 22–23 provide guidance on consent orders: **III MEN [617]**.

Practice Direction 10B provides guidance on urgent applications and applications made without notice: **III MEN [618]**.

Practice Direction 11A provides mandatory guidance in the event that an application concerns a deprivation of liberty. In such a case practitioners must with care ensure whether their application relates to an application in respect of a standard or urgent authorisation when the procedure provides for the use of separate distinct forms (DOL Forms A–E), or where the application relates to approval of a Care plan ('Support Plan') which may involve deprivation of liberty. In that event, a form COPDOL10 must be completed and the streamlined procedure followed pursuant to the judgments *Re X (Deprivation of Liberty)* [2014] EWCOP 25, and *Re X (Deprivation of Liberty (No 2)* [2014] EWCOP 37. The streamlined procedure was introduced on 17 November 2014 pursuant to a further Practice Direction 10AA (now Practice Direction 11A) relating to applications made under section 4A(3) and (4) of the Mental Capacity Act 2005, where authorisation is sought pursuant to section 16(2)(a) of the Mental Capacity Act 2005 to sanction arrangements for where an individual who lacks capacity should live and where restrictions involve a deprivation of liberty (see **III MEN [620]**).

Form DLA is the general application form

Form DLB is the request for urgent consideration

Form DLC the former permission form is no longer required

Form DLD is the Certificate of service/non-service, notification/non-notification form

Form DLE is the form of Acknowledgment of service/notification. See Practice Direction 11A, para 3.1.

Form COPDOL10 and the Annex A B C are the mandatory forms for the streamlined procedure: **III MEN [620]**.

III MEN [608]

10.2 Application notice to be filed

(1) Subject to paragraph (5), the applicant must file an application notice to make an application under this Part.

(2) The applicant must, when filing the application notice, file the evidence on which the applicant relies (unless such evidence has already been filed).

(3) The court must issue the application notice and, if there is to be a hearing, give notice of the date on which the matter is to be heard by the court.

(4) Notice under paragraph (3) must be given to—

(a) the applicant;

(b) anyone who is named as a respondent in the application notice (if not otherwise a party to the proceedings);

(c) every party to the proceedings; and

(d) any other person, as the court may direct.

(5) An applicant may make an application under this Part without filing an application notice if—

(a) this is permitted by any rule or practice direction; or

(b) the court dispenses with the requirement for an application notice.

(6) If the applicant makes an application without giving notice, the evidence in support of the application notice must state why notice has not been given.

III MEN [608.1]

Applications to the court and procedure Form COP9 is the form to be used. See Practice Direction 10A, para 2: **III MEN [617]**. Form COP24 is the relevant form for a witness statement.

III MEN [609]

10.3 What an application notice must include

An application notice must state—

(a) what order or direction the applicant is seeking;

(b) briefly, the grounds on which the applicant is seeking the order or direction; and

(c) such other information as may be required by any rule or practice direction.

III MEN [609.1]

Applications to the court and procedure Practice Direction 10A, paras 3–4 set out details of other information that is required to be provided: **III MEN [617]**.

III MEN [610]

10.4 Service of an application notice

(1) Subject to paragraphs (4) and (5), the applicant must serve a copy of the application notice on—

(a) anyone who is named as a respondent in the application notice (if not otherwise a party to the proceedings);

(b) every party to the proceedings; and

(c) any other person, as the court may direct,

as soon as possible and in any event within 14 days of the date on which it was issued.

(2) The application notice must be accompanied by a copy of the evidence filed in support.

(3) The applicant must file a certificate of service within 7 days beginning with the date on which the documents were served.

(4) This rule does not require a copy of evidence to be served on a person on whom it has already been served, but the applicant must in such a case give to that person notice of the evidence on which the applicant intends to rely.

(5) An application may be made without serving a copy of the application notice if this is permitted by—

(a) a rule;

(b) a practice direction; or

(c) the court.

III MEN [610.1]

Applications to the court and the filing of supporting evidence Supporting evidence should be in form COP24 (see **III MEN [617]**). Practice Direction 10A at paras 8–11 provides further guidance as to service, and applications to the court to determine issues as to service. Evidence should be filed setting out why service has not been effected (para 11): **III MEN [617]**. Practice Direction 4B provides guidance as to the construction of bundles for hearings (see **III MEN [524]**).

III MEN [611]

10.5 Applications without notice

(1) This rule applies where the court has dealt with an application which was made without notice having been given to any person.

(2) Where the court makes an order, whether granting or dismissing the application, the applicant must, as soon as practicable or within such period as the court may direct, serve the documents mentioned in paragraph (3) on—

(a) anyone named as a respondent in the application notice (if not otherwise a party to the proceedings);

(b) every party to the proceedings; and

(c) any other person, as the court may direct.

(3) The documents referred to in paragraph (2) are—

(a) a copy of the application notice;

(b) the court's order; and

(c) any evidence filed in support of the application.

(Rule 13.4 provides for reconsideration of orders made without a hearing or without notice to a person.)

III MEN [239.1]

Applications to the court and relevant procedure See Practice Direction 10A, paras 12 and 13 for procedural steps on the issue of an application and the notice to usually be given: **III MEN [617]**.

For procedure under rule 13.4 see **III MEN [626]**.

III MEN [612]

10.6 Security for costs

(1) A respondent to any application may apply for security for the respondent's costs of the proceedings.

(2) An application for security for costs must be supported by written evidence.

(3) Where the court makes an order for security for costs, it must—

(a) determine the amount of security; and

(b) direct—

(i) the manner in which; and
(ii) the time within which,

the security must be given.

III MEN [613]

10.7 Conditions to be satisfied

(1) The court may make an order for security for costs under rule 10.6—
(a) if it is satisfied, having regard to all the circumstances of the case, that it is just to make such an order; and
(b) if—
(i) one or more of the conditions in paragraph (2) applies; or
(ii) an enactment permits the court to require security for costs.

(2) The conditions are—
(a) the applicant is—
(i) resident out of the jurisdiction; but
(ii) not resident in a Brussels Contracting State, a State bound by the Lugano Convention or a Regulation State, as defined in section 1(3) of the Civil Jurisdiction and Judgments Act 1982;
(b) the applicant is a company or other body (whether incorporated inside or outside Great Britain) and there is reason to believe that it will be unable to pay the respondent's costs if ordered to do so;
(c) the applicant has changed address since proceedings were commenced with a view to avoiding the consequences of the litigation;
(d) the applicant failed to give an address, or gave an incorrect address, in the application form commencing the proceedings;
(e) the applicant is acting as a nominal applicant and there is reason to believe that the applicant will be unable to pay the respondent's costs if ordered to do so;
(f) the applicant has taken steps in relation to the applicant's assets that would make it difficult to enforce an order for costs against the applicant.

III MEN [614]

10.8 Security for costs other than from the applicant

(1) The respondent may seek an order against a person other than the applicant, and the court may make an order for security for costs against that person, if—
(a) it is satisfied, having regard to all the circumstances of the case, that it is just to make such an order; and
(b) one or more of the conditions in paragraph (2) applies.

(2) The conditions are that the person—
(a) has assigned the right to the substantive matter to the applicant with a view to avoiding the possibility of a costs order being made against the person; or
(b) has contributed or agreed to contribute to the applicant's costs in return for a share of any money or property which the applicant may recover or be awarded in the proceedings; and

is a person against whom a costs order may be made.

(Rule 19.12 makes provision about costs orders against non-parties.)

III MEN [615]

10.9 Security for costs of an appeal

(1) The court may order security for costs of an appeal against—
(a) an appellant;

(b) a respondent who also appeals,

on the same grounds as it may order security for costs against an applicant under rule 10.6.

(2) The court may also make an order under paragraph (1) where the appellant or the respondent who also appeals is a limited company and there is reason to believe it will be unable to pay the costs of the other parties to the appeal should its appeal be unsuccessful.

INTERIM REMEDIES

III MEN [616]

10.10 Orders for interim remedies

(1) The court may grant the following interim remedies—

(a) an interim injunction;

(b) an interim declaration; or

(c) any other interim order it considers appropriate.

(2) Unless the court orders otherwise, a person on whom an application form is served under Part 9, or who is given notice of such an application, may not apply for an interim remedy before filing an acknowledgment of service or notification in accordance with Part 9.

(3) This rule does not limit any other power of the court to grant interim relief.

III MEN [616.1]

Procedure for urgent applications to the court Practice Direction 10B provides supplemental directions in matters requiring urgent and interim applications: **III MEN [618]**.

PRACTICE DIRECTION 10A – APPLICATIONS WITHIN PROCEEDINGS

III MEN [617]

This practice direction supplements Part 10 of the Court of Protection Rules 2017

APPLICATION NOTICE

1 Rule 10.1 provides that an applicant may use the Part 10 procedure if the application is made:

(a) in the course of existing proceedings; or
(b) as provided for in a rule or relevant practice direction.

2 An application under Part 10 must be made by filing an application notice using form COP9.

3 An application notice must, in addition to the matters set out in rule 10.3, be signed and include (unless an order to the contrary pursuant to rule 5.11 has been made) –

(a) the name of the person to whom the application relates (P);
(b) the case number (if available);
(c) the full name of the applicant;
(d) where the applicant is not already a party, his address; and
(e) a draft of the order sought.

4 If the order sought is unusually long or complex, a disk containing the draft order sought should be made available to the court in a format compatible with the word processing software used by the court. (Queries in relation to software should be directed to a court officer.)

5 The application notice must be supported by evidence set out in either –

(a) a witness statement; or
(b) the application notice provided that it is verified by a statement of truth.

6 For the purposes of rules 4.1 to 4.3, a statement of truth in an application notice may be made by a person who is not a party.

7 The evidence must set out the facts on which the applicant relies for the application, and all material facts known to the applicant of which the court should be made aware.

8 A copy of the application notice and evidence in support must be served by the person making the application as soon as practicable and in any event within 14 days of the application notice being issued.

9 An application may be made without service of an application notice only –

(a) where there is exceptional urgency;
(b) where the overriding objective is best furthered by doing so;
(c) by consent of all parties;
(d) with the permission of the court; or
(e) where a rule or other practice direction permits.

(Practice direction B accompanying Part 10 sets out more detailed requirements for urgent applications.)

10 Where an application is made without service on the respondent, the evidence in support of the application must also set out why service was not effected.

11 The court may decide, upon considering the application, that other persons ought to be served with or notified of it and have the opportunity of responding. In such a case, the court will give directions as to who should be served with or notified of the application.

12 On receipt of an application notice, the court will issue the application notice and, if there is to be a hearing, give notice of the date on which the matter is to be heard by the court.

13 Notice will be given to –

(a) the applicant;
(b) anyone who is named as a respondent in the application notice (if not otherwise a party to the proceedings);
(c) every other party to the proceedings; and
(d) any other person, as the court may direct.

14 Any directions given by the court may specify the form that the evidence is to take and when it is to be served.

15 Applications should wherever possible be made so that they can be considered at a directions hearing or other hearing for which a date has already been fixed or for which a date is about to be fixed.

16 Where a date for a hearing has been fixed and a party wishes to make an application at that hearing but does not have sufficient time to file an application notice, he should inform the court (if possible in writing) and, if possible, the other parties as soon as he can of the nature of the application and the reason for it. He should then make the application orally at the hearing.

TYPE OF CASE MAY BE INDICATED IN THE APPLICATION NOTICE

17 The applicant may indicated in the application notice that the application –

(a) is urgent;
(b) should be dealt with by a particular judge or level of judge within the court;
(c) requires a hearing; or
(d) any combination of the above.

TELEPHONE HEARINGS

18 The court may direct that an application or part of an application will be dealt with by a telephone hearing.

19 The applicant should indicate in his application notice if he seeks a direction pursuant to paragraph 17. Where he has not done so but nevertheless wishes to seek such a direction the request should be made as early as possible.

20 A direction under paragraph 17 will not normally be given unless every party entitled to be given notice of the application and to be heard at the hearing has consented to the direction.

VIDEO CONFERENCING

21 Where the parties to a matter wish to use video conferencing facilities, and those facilities are available, they should apply to the court for such a direction.

(Practice direction A accompanying Part 14 contains guidance on the use of video conferencing.)

CONSENT ORDERS

22 The parties to an application for a consent order must ensure that they provide the court with any material it needs to be satisfied that it is appropriate to make the order. Subject to any rule or practice direction, a letter signed by all parties will generally be acceptable for this purpose.

23 Where an order has been agreed in relation to an application for which a hearing date has been fixed, the parties must inform the court immediately.

PRACTICE DIRECTION 10B – URGENT AND INTERIM APPLICATIONS

III MEN [618]

This practice direction supplements Part 10 of the Court of Protection Rules 2017

URGENT APPLICATIONS AND APPLICATIONS WITHOUT NOTICE

1 These fall into two categories –

(a) applications where an application form has already been issued; and
(b) applications where an application form has not yet been issued,

and, in both cases, where notice of the application has not been given to the respondent(s).

2 Wherever possible, urgent applications should be made within court hours. These applications will normally be dealt with at court but cases of extreme urgency may be dealt with by telephone. Telephone contact may be made with the court during business hours on 0300 456 4600.

3 When it is not possible to apply within court hours, contact should be made with the security office at the Royal Courts of Justice on 020 7947 6260. The security officer should be informed of the nature of the case.

4 In some cases, urgent applications arise because applications to the court have not been pursued sufficiently promptly. This is undesirable, and should be avoided. A judge who has concerns that the facility for urgent applications may have been abused may require the applicant or the applicant's representative to attend at a subsequent hearing to provide an explanation for the delay.

APPLICATIONS WITHOUT NOTICE

5 The applicant should take steps to advise the respondent(s) by telephone or in writing of the application, unless justice would be defeated if notice were given.

6 If an order is made without notice to any other party, the order will ordinarily contain –

(a) an undertaking by the applicant to the court to serve the application notice, evidence in support and any order made on the respondent and any other person the court may direct as soon as practicable or as ordered by the court; and

(b) a return date for a further hearing at which the other parties can be present.

APPLICATIONS WHERE AN APPLICATION FORM HAS ALREADY BEEN ISSUED

7 An application notice using form COP9, evidence in support and a draft order should be filed with the court in advance of the hearing wherever possible. If the order sought is unusually long or complex, a disk containing the draft order sought should be made available to the court in a format compatible with the word processing software used by the court. (Queries in relation to software should be directed to a court officer.)

(Practice direction A accompanying Part 10 sets out more detailed requirements in relation to an application notice.)

8 If an application is made before the application notice has been filed, a draft order should be provided at the hearing, and the application notice and evidence in support must be filed with the court on the next working day or as ordered by the court.

APPLICATIONS MADE BEFORE THE ISSUE OF AN APPLICATION FORM

9 Where the exceptional urgency of the matter requires, an application may be started without filing an application form if the court allows it (but where time permits an application should be made in writing). In such a case, an application may be made to the court orally. The court will require an undertaking that the application form in the terms of the oral application be filed on the next working day, or as required by the court.

10 An order made before the issue of the application form should state in the title after the names of the applicant and the respondent, "the Applicant and Respondent in an Intended Application".

APPLICATIONS MADE BY TELEPHONE

11 Where it is not possible to file an application form or notice, applications can be made by telephone in accordance with the contact details set out in paragraphs 2 and 3 of this practice direction.

HEARINGS CONDUCTED BY TELEPHONE

12 When a hearing is to take place by telephone, if practical it should be conducted by tape-recorded conference call, and arranged (and paid for in the first instance) by the applicant. All parties and the judge should be informed that the call is being recorded by the service provider. The applicant should order a transcript of the hearing from the service provider.

TYPE OF CASE MAY BE INDICATED IN THE APPLICATION NOTICE

13 The applicant may indicate in the application notice that the application –

(a) is urgent;
(b) should be dealt with by a particular judge or level of judge within the court;
(c) requires a hearing; or
(d) any combination of the above.

INTERIM INJUNCTION APPLICATIONS

14 Rule 10.10 enables the court to grant an interim injunction.

15 Any judge of the court may vary or discharge an interim injunction granted by any judge of the court.

16 Any order for an interim injunction must set out clearly what the respondent or any other person must or must not do. The order may contain an undertaking by the applicant to pay any damages which the respondent(s) sustains which the court considers the applicant should pay.

PART 11
DEPRIVATION OF LIBERTY

III MEN [619]

11.1 Deprivation of liberty

The practice direction to this Part sets out procedure governing—

(a) applications to the court for orders relating to the deprivation, or proposed deprivation, of liberty of P; and
(b) proceedings (for example, relating to costs or appeals) connected with or consequent on such applications.

III MEN [619.1]

Guidance on applications to the court in respect of deprivation of liberty issues The provisions of Practice Direction 11A must be followed in all applications engaging s 21A of the Mental Capacity Act 2005 (see **III MEN [55]**) relating to a standard or urgent authorisation under Schedule A1 of the Mental Capacity Act 2005 to deprive a person of his or her liberty (see **III MEN [108]**). The DOL Forms must also be used as provided by para 2(a) (see **III MEN [620]**).

A streamlined procedure was introduced on 17 November 2014 relating to applications made under section 4A(3) and (4) of the Mental Capacity Act 2005, where authorisation is sought pursuant to section 16(2)(a) of the Mental Capacity Act 2005 to sanction arrangements for where an individual who lacks capacity should live and where restrictions involve a deprivation of liberty.

For discussion on the issue of deprivation of liberty see **III MEN [9]** and **III MEN [10]** above. Regard should be made to the provisions of the 'Deprivation of Liberty Safeguards Code of Practice' and in particular Chapter 10.

PRACTICE DIRECTION 11A – DEPRIVATION OF LIBERTY APPLICATIONS

III MEN [620]

This practice direction supplements Part 11 of the Court of Protection Rules 2017

INTRODUCTION

1 This Practice Direction is in three parts. Part 1 addresses the procedure to be followed in applications to the court for orders under section 21A of the Mental Capacity Act 2005 relating to a standard or urgent authorisation under Schedule A1 of that Act to deprive a person of his or her liberty; or proceedings (for example, relating to costs or appeals) connected with or consequent upon such applications. Part 2 addresses the procedure to be followed in applications under s 16(2)(a) of that Act to authorise deprivation of liberty under section 4A(3) and (4) pursuant to a streamlined procedure. Part 3 makes provision common to applications under both Parts 1 and 2.

PART 1 – APPLICATIONS UNDER SECTION 21A RELATING TO A STANDARD OR URGENT AUTHORISATION UNDER SCHEDULE A1

2 This Part sets out the procedure to be followed in applications to the court for orders under section 21A of the Mental Capacity Act 2005 relating to a standard or urgent authorisation under Schedule A1 of that Act to deprive a person of his or her liberty. By their nature, such applications are of special urgency and therefore will be dealt with by the court according to the special procedure described here. Other applications may, while not being DoL applications within the meaning of the term explained above, raise issues relating to deprivation of liberty and require similarly urgent attention; and while the special DoL procedure will not apply to such applications, they should be raised with the DoL team at the earliest possible stage so that they can be handled appropriately. The key features of the special DoL procedure are –

(a) special DoL court forms ensure that DoL court papers stand out as such and receive special handling by the court office;
(b) the application is placed before a judge of the court as soon as possible – if necessary, before issue of the application – for judicial directions to be given as to the steps to be taken in the application, and who is to take each step and by when;
(c) the usual Court of Protection Rules (for example, as to method and timing of service of the application) will apply only so far as consistent with the judicial directions given for the particular case;
(d) a dedicated team in the court office ("the DoL team") will deal with DoL applications at all stages, including liaison with would-be applicants/other parties;
(e) the progress of each DoL case will be monitored by a judge assigned to that case, assisted by the DoL team.

Urgent applications

4 In extremely urgent cases, the DoL team can arrange for a telephone application to be made to the judge for directions and/or an interim order even before the application has been issued. In such cases the applicant must contact the DoL team and provide the following information –

(a) the parties' details

MENTAL CAPACITY AND MENTAL HEALTH

(b) where the parties live
(c) the issue to be decided
(d) the date of urgent or standard authorisation
(e) the date of effective detention
(f) the parties' legal representatives
(g) any family members or others who are involved
(h) whether there have been any other court proceedings involving the parties and if so, where.

5 Contact details for the DoLS team may be found on www.gov.uk as part of the information for the Court of Protection and for Deprivation of Liberty.

6 The public counter is open between 9.30 am to 4.30 am on working days. The DoL team can receive telephone calls and faxes between 9.00 am and 5.00 pm. Faxes transmitted after 4.30 pm will be dealt with the next working day.

7 When in an emergency it is necessary to make a telephone application to a judge outside normal court hours, the security office at the Royal Courts of Justice should be contacted on 020 7947 6260. The security officer should be informed of the nature of the case. In the Family Division, the out-of-hours application procedure involves the judge being contacted through a Family Division duty officer, and the RCJ security officer will need to contact the duty officer and not the judge's clerk or the judge.

8 Intending applicants/other parties may find it helpful to refer to –

(a) the Code of Practice Deprivation of Liberty Safeguards (June 2008), ISBN 978-0113228157, supplementing the main Mental Capacity Act 2005 Code of Practice: in particular Chapter 10, What is the Court of Protection and who can apply to it?; and
(b) the judgment of Mr Justice Munby in *Salford City Council v GJ, NJ and BJ (Incapacitated Adults)* [2008] EWHC 1097 (Fam); [2008] 2 FLR 1295. Although this case was decided before the coming into force of the DoL amendments to the Mental Capacity Act 2005, it sets out helpful guidance on the appropriate court procedures for cases relating to the deprivation of liberty of adults.

9 The DoL team will be pleased to explain the court's procedures for handling DoL cases. Please note that the team (as with all court staff) is not permitted to give advice on matters of law. Please do not contact the DoL team unless your inquiry concerns a deprivation of liberty question (whether relating to a potential application, or a case which is already lodged with the Court).

DoL court forms

10 The special DoL court forms are as follows:

(a) **DLA: Deprivation of Liberty Application Form:** to be used for all DoL applications;
(b) **DLB: Deprivation of Liberty Request for Urgent Consideration:** this short form allows applicants to set out the reasons why the case is urgent, the timetable they wish the case to follow, and any interim relief sought. A draft of any order sought should be attached. Ideally, the DLB (plus any draft order) should be placed at the top of the draft application and both issued and served together;
(c) **DLD: Deprivation of Liberty Certificate of Service/non-service and Certificate of notification/non-notification;**
(d) **DLE: Deprivation of Liberty Acknowledgement of service/notification.**

These forms can be obtained from the Court of Protection office or downloaded from the court's website http://hmctsformfinder.justice.gov.uk/HMCTS/GetForms.do?court_forms_category=court_of_protection..

11 To ensure that papers relating to DoL applications are promptly directed to the DoL team at the court, it is essential that the appropriate DoL court forms are used.

12 The DoL court forms should be used for, and only for, DoL applications. If in such a case it is anticipated that other issues may arise, the DoL forms should identify and describe briefly those issues and any relief which may be sought in respect of them: sections 3.5 and 5 of form DLA, the Deprivation of Liberty Application Form, offer an opportunity to do this. "Other issues" are perhaps most likely to arise in the event that the court decides the DoL application in the applicant's favour. In such a case, if the applicant has already identified the "other issues" in his/her form DLA, the court will be able to address these, either by dealing with them immediately or by giving directions for their future handling.

13 Accordingly, unless the court expressly directs, applicants should not issue a second and separate application (using the standard court forms) relating to any "other issues".

14 Where an application seeks relief concerning a deprivation of P's liberty other than under section 21A in respect of a standard or urgent authorisation (for example, where the application is for an order under section 16(2)(a)), the dedicated DoL court forms should not be used. Rather the standard court forms should be used for such an application, but it should be made clear on them that relief relating to a deprivation of P's liberty is being sought, and the proposed applicant should contact the DoL team to discuss handling at the earliest possible stage before issuing the application.

How to issue a DoL application

15 To issue a DoL application, the following forms should be filed at court –

(a) Form DLA;
(b) Form DLB (plus draft order);
(c) the appropriate court fee.

Where a draft order is lodged with the court, it would be helpful – although not compulsory — if an electronic version of the order could also be lodged on disc, if possible.

16 In cases of extreme emergency or where it is not possible to attend at the court office, for example during weekends, the court will expect an applicant to undertake to file form DLA and to pay the court fee unless an exemption applies.

Inviting the court to make judicial directions for the handling of the application

17 The following is a sample list of possible issues which the court is likely to wish to consider in judicial directions in a DoL case. It is intended as a prompt, not as a definitive list of the issues that may need to be covered –

(a) upon whom, by when and how service of the application should be effected;
(b) dispensing with acknowledgement of service of the application or allowing a short period of time for so doing, which in some cases may amount to a few hours only;
(c) whether further lay or expert evidence should be obtained;
(d) whether P/the detained person should be a party and represented by the Official Solicitor and whether any other person should be a party;
(e) whether any family members should be formally notified of the application and of any hearing and joined as parties;
(f) fixing a date for a First Hearing and giving a time estimate;
(g) fixing a trial window for any final hearing and giving a time estimate;
(h) the level of judge appropriate to hear the case;
(i) whether the case is such that it should be immediately transferred to the High Court for a Tier 3 Judge to give directions;
(j) provision for a bundle for the judge at the First Hearing.

18 If you are an applicant without legal representation, and you are not sure exactly what directions you should ask for, you may prefer simply to invite the judge to make appropriate directions in light of the nature and urgency of the case as you

have explained it on the DLB form. In exceptionally urgent cases, there may not be time to formulate draft directions: the court will understand if applicants in such cases (whether or not legally represented) simply ask the judge for appropriate directions.

After issue of the application

19 The DoL team will immediately take steps to ensure that the application is placed before a judge nominated to hear Court of Protection cases and DoL applications. Out of hours, at weekends and on public holidays, the application will be placed before the judge who is most immediately available.

20 As soon as the court office is put on notice of a DoL application, the DoL team will notify a judge to put the judge on stand-by to deal with the application. The judge will consider the application on the papers and make a first order.

Steps after the judge's first order

21 The DoL team will –

(a) action every point in the judge's note or instruction;
(b) refer any query that arises to the judge immediately or, if not available, to another judge;
(c) make all arrangements for any transfer of the case to another court and/or for a hearing.

22 The applicant or his/her legal representative should follow all steps in the judge's order and –

(a) form DLD should be filed with the court if appropriate; and
(b) form DLE should be included in any documents served unless ordered otherwise.

The First Hearing

23 The First Hearing will be listed for the court to fix a date for any subsequent hearing(s), give directions and/or to make an interim or final order if appropriate. The court will make such orders and give such directions as are appropriate in the case.

24 The court will aim to have the First Hearing before a judge of every DoL application within 5 working days of the date of issue of the application.

25 Applicants can indicate on the DLB form if they think that the application needs to be considered within a shorter timetable, and set out proposals for such a timetable. On the first paper consideration the court will consider when the First Hearing should be listed.

26 If time allows and no specific direction has been made by the court, an indexed and paginated bundle should be prepared for the judge and any skeleton arguments and draft orders given to the court as soon as they are available. A copy of the index should be provided to all parties and, where another party appears in person, a copy of the bundle should be provided.

PART 2 – APPLICATIONS UNDER SECTION 16(2)(A) FOR AN ORDER AUTHORISING DEPRIVATION OF LIBERTY UNDER SECTION 4A(3) AND (4) PURSUANT TO A STREAMLINED PROCEDURE

27 This Part sets out the procedure to be followed in applications to the court under section 16(2)(a) to authorise deprivation of liberty under section 4A(3) of the Act pursuant to a streamlined procedure and applies only to such applications.

Reference should be made generally to the decision of the Supreme Court in *P (by his litigation friend the Official Solicitor) v Cheshire West and Chester Council and another; P and Q (by their litigation friend the Official Solicitor) v Surrey County Council* [2014] UKSC 19, and in relation to the procedure in these cases, to the judgments of the President of the Court of Protection in *Re X and others (Deprivation of Liberty)* [2014] EWCOP 25 and in *Re X and others (Deprivation of Liberty) (Number 2)* [2014] EWCOP 37.

Making the application

28 To bring proceedings, the applicant must file an application using form COPDOL10, verified by a statement of truth and accompanied by all attachments and evidence required by that form and its annexes.

29 The application form and accompanying annexes and attachments are specifically designed to ensure that the applicant provides the court with essential information and evidence as to the proposed measures, on the basis of which the court may adjudicate as to the appropriateness of authorising a deprivation of liberty, and in particular to identify whether a case is suitable for consideration without an oral hearing. The use of the form and its annexes is mandatory and they must be provided fully completed and verified by the required statements of truth.

30 The applicant must ensure that the evidence in the application form, accompanying annexes and attachments is succinct and focussed.

31 A separate application must be made for every individual for whom the applicant requests an authorisation of deprivation of liberty. However, where there are matters in relation to which the facts are identical for a number of individuals, such as common care arrangements, the applicant may, in addition to addressing the specific issues relating to each individual, attach a generic statement dealing with the common care arrangements or other matters common to those individuals.

Deponent

32 The applicant must consider carefully who should complete the form and each annex with regard to the nature of the evidence required by each. There is no requirement that the same individual should complete and verify by statement of truth the form and each annex and indeed it might be inappropriate for this to be the case, where different people are best placed to provide evidence on different matters.

Applicant's duty of full and frank disclosure

33 The applicant has a duty of full and frank disclosure to the court of all facts and matters that may have an impact on the court's decision whether to authorise the deprivation of liberty. The applicant should therefore scrutinise the circumstances of the case and clearly identify in the evidence in support (in Annex A to Form COPDOL 11) factors –

(a) needing particular judicial scrutiny;
(b) suggesting that the arrangements in relation to which authorisation is sought may not in fact be in the best interests of the person the application is about, or the least restrictive option; or
(c) otherwise tending to indicate that the order should not be made.

Pursuant to this duty, the applicant should also identify those persons, not consulted by the applicant, who are in the same category under paragraph 39 as persons with whom the applicant has consulted. Those persons must be listed in Annex B to form COPDOL 10 together with an explanation in that Annex of why they have not been consulted.

Draft order

34 The application must be accompanied by a draft of the order which the applicant seeks, including the duration of the authorisation sought, appropriate directions for review, and liberty to apply for its reconsideration.

Consultation with the person the application is about

35 Consultation with the person the application is about must take place before the application form is lodged with the court. The applicant must arrange for that person to be informed of the following matters –

(a) that the applicant is making an application to court;
(b) that the application is to consider whether the person lacks capacity to make decisions in relation to his or her residence and care, and whether to authorise a deprivation of their liberty in connection with the arrangements set out in the care plan;
(c) what the proposed arrangements under the order sought are;
(d) that the person is entitled to express his or her views, wishes and feelings in relation to the proposed arrangements and the application, and that the person undertaking the consultation will ensure that these are communicated to the court;
(e) that the person is entitled to seek to take part in the proceedings by being joined as a party or otherwise, what that means, and that the person undertaking the consultation will ensure that any such request is communicated to the court;
(f) that the person undertaking the consultation can help him or her to obtain advice and assistance if he or she does not agree with the proposed arrangements in the application.

36 The person undertaking the consultation must complete Annex C to form COPDOL 10.

37 The applicant must confirm that the person the application is about has been supported and assisted to express his or her views, wishes and feelings in relation to the application and the arrangements proposed in it, and encouraged to take part in the proceedings to the extent that he or she wishes, in accordance with section 4(4) of the Act.

Consultation with other persons regarding the making of the application

38 The consultation required by paragraph 39 below must take place before the application is lodged with the court.

39 The applicant must ensure that the following people are consulted about the intention to make the application –

(a) any donee of a lasting power of attorney granted by the person;
(b) any deputy appointed for the person by the court;

together with, if possible, at least three people in the following categories –

(c) anyone named by the person the application is about as someone to be consulted on the matters raised by the application; and
(d) anyone engaged in caring for the person or interested in his or her welfare.

40 When consulting such people, the applicant must inform them of the following matters –

(a) that the applicant is making an application to court;
(b) that the application is to consider whether the person the application is about lacks capacity to make decisions in relation to his or her residence and care and whether he or she should be deprived of liberty in connection with the arrangements set out in the care plan;
(c) what the proposed arrangements under the order are; and
(d) that the applicant is under an obligation to inform the person the application is about of the matters listed in paragraph 35 above, unless in the circumstances it is inappropriate for the applicant to give that person such information.

Dispensing with notification or service of the application form

41 Provided that the court is satisfied as to the adequacy of consultation with the person the application is about in accordance with paragraphs 35 to 37, and with other persons with whom consultation should take place in accordance with paragraphs 38 to 40, the court may dispense with notification of the issue of the application under rules 7.4, 9.9 and 9.10.

Court fees

42 An application fee is payable for all applications, and if the court decides to hold a hearing before making a decision, a hearing fee will be payable.

43 If an application is received without a fee it will be treated as incomplete and returned.

Applications suitable for the streamlined procedure

44 As soon as practicable after receipt the court officers will consider the suitability of the application to be the subject of paper determination, or to be considered at an oral hearing.

45 All applications considered suitable for the streamlined procedure will be referred to a judge for consideration without an oral hearing, as soon as practicable after receipt.

Applications not suitable for the streamlined procedure

46 If the judge considers that the application is not suitable for the streamlined process, case management directions shall be given.

Applicant to supply a copy of the order to each person consulted procedure

47 The applicant must provide all persons consulted, including the person the application is about, with a copy of the order made pursuant to the streamlined procedure granting or refusing the authorisation of the deprivation of liberty.

Review of the authorisation

48 An application for a review of the authorisation of the deprivation of liberty must be made in accordance with the terms of the order.

PART 3 – PROVISIONS COMMON TO APPLICATIONS UNDER PART 1 AND PART 2

Hearing in private

49 Part 4 of the Court of Protection Rules 2017 provides at rule 4.1, as supplemented by Practice Direction A to Part 4, that the general rule is that a hearing is held in private. Rule 4.3 allows the court to order that a hearing be in public if the criteria in rule 4.4 apply.

Costs

50 The general rule, in rule 19.3 of the Court of Protection Rules 2017, is that in a personal welfare case there will be no order as to costs of the proceedings. The general rule applies to DoL applications.

Appeals

51 Part 20 of the Court of Protection Rules 2017 applies to appeals. Permission is required to appeal (rules 20.5 and 20.6) and this will only be granted where the court considers that the appeal would have a real prospect of success or there is some other compelling reason why the appeal should be heard (rule 20.8).

III MEN [620.1]

Guidance on applications to the court in respect of deprivation of liberty The Practice Direction which came into force on 17 November 2014 introduces two distinct procedures relating to issues of deprivation of liberty. Part 1 relates to the established procedure where the issue relates to a standard or urgent authorisation under DOLs safeguarding procedure. Part 2 is a direct result of the decision of the Supreme Court in the matter of *P (by his litigation friend the Official Solicitor) v Cheshire West and Chester Council and another; P and Q (by their litigation friend the Official Solicitor) v Surrey County Council* [2014] UKSC 19 the mandatory procedure is designed to provide a streamlined determination of the appropriateness of the Care Plan ('Support Plan') of an individual who would be the subject of an application for a declaration under section 4A(3) and section 16(2)(a) of the Mental Capacity Act 2005, and where that Plan has restrictions in place which are a deprivation of liberty.

For Part 2, the procedure is mandatory and the Form and Annexes must be accurately completed. Regard should be given to the giving of notice and service and notification upon P and others (para 41). Based upon the application, the court will on paper approve the Plan and make an order to that effect providing authority for a maximum of 12 months and giving directions for review and reconsideration, or reject the application. If the application is capable of proceeding but an aspect of the application requires clarification, the court can direct for further evidence. Annex A seeks evidence in support of the application, Annex B ascertains the process of consultation with people who have an interest in P's personal welfare and Annex C clarifies the consultation with P and the support provided to P to both be involved in the proceedings, and to express wishes, feelings, beliefs and values that the court should take into account before authorising a deprivation of liberty. In addition to the fee of £400 (para 42), the applicant must file a draft order (para 34) and medical evidence (assessing capacity, and unsoundness of mind (paras 1 and 2 of Annex A)). The report in respect of the medical diagnosis of P's unsoundness of mind must be that of a registered medical practitioner.

III MEN [620.2]

Guidance on applications to the court in respect of deprivation of liberty issues and privacy, publicity and costs For consideration of the issues of publicity and the holding of the hearing in private see **III MEN [6]** above, and Part 13 and Practice Direction 13A: **III MEN [623]** to **III MEN [627]**. In *W (by her litigation friend B) v M (by her litigation friend, the Official Solicitor)* [2011] EWHC 1197(COP), [2011] NLJR 811 Baker J reminded applicants that application notices and submissions in support should clearly outline the orders sought and identify the categories of persons whose identity would be kept confidential under the proposed order.

For consideration of the Participation of 'P' see rule 1.2 (then rule 3A (**III MEN [493]**)) and Practice Direction 1A (**III MEN [498]**) in *Re NRA* [2015] EWCOP 59, 165 NLJ 7671, [2015] All ER (D) 122 (Sep) Mr Justice Charles provided guidance for applicants in identifying those who may be considered to act as rule 1.2(2)(c) representatives, and exploring the availability of litigation friends.

For consideration of the costs rules see Part 19 (see **III MEN [702]**), but note the decision of the Court of Appeal in confirming that the Civil Procedure Rules apply to proceedings before the Court of Appeal *Cheshire West and Chester Council v P* [2011] EWCA Civ 1333.

Practice Direction 4B makes provision for the preparation and consistency of court bundles, and save in emergency, should be followed. See **III MEN [524]**.

PART 12
HUMAN RIGHTS

III MEN [621]

12.1 General

(1) A party who seeks to rely upon any provision of or right arising under the Human Rights Act 1998 ("the 1998 Act") or who seeks a remedy available under that Act must inform the court in the manner set out in the relevant practice direction specifying—

(a) the Convention right (within the meaning of the 1998 Act) which it is alleged has been infringed and details of the alleged infringement; and

(b) the remedy sought and whether this includes a declaration of incompatibility under section 4 of the 1998 Act.

(2) The court may not make a declaration of incompatibility unless 21 days' notice, or such other period of notice as the court directs, has been given to the Crown.

(3) Where notice has been given to the Crown, a Minister or other person permitted by the 1998 Act shall be joined as a party on filing an application in accordance with rule 9.15 (application to be joined as a party).

III MEN [621.1]

Applications to the court Practice Direction 12A (**III MEN [622]**) provides guidance as to the forms to be used to either commence an application (COP1) or make an application within existing proceedings (COP9). Form COP5 is used in the event of the claim arising following service or notification of an application, and either Form COP35 or COP36 if arising from notice of appellant or Respondent (see Part 20 and Practice Direction 20A: **III MEN [718]**).

III MEN [621.2]

Guidance on applications to the court in respect of human rights issues Part 12 and Practice Direction 12A provides guidance on dealing with an application under rule 12.1 in which a declaration of incompatibility pursuant to s 4 of the Human Rights Act 1988 is sought (para 3(a): see **III MEN [621]**).

PRACTICE DIRECTION 12A – HUMAN RIGHTS ACT 1998

III MEN [622]

This practice direction supplements Part 12 of the Court of Protection Rules 2017

PROCEDURE FOR MAKING CLAIM

1 A claim made pursuant to rule 12.1 in relation to the Human Rights Act 1998 ('the 1998 Act') should be included in the application form using Form COP1. If the claim forms part of a response by a person served with or notified of the application, it should be included in the acknowledgment of service using Form COP5.

2 If the claim in relation to the 1998 Act is made during the course of proceedings, it should be made by filing an application notice using Form COP9.

3 If the claim is raised in an appeal, the claim should be filed with the appellant's or the respondent's notice as appropriate, using Form COP35 or COP36.

NOTICE TO THE CROWN

4 Where notice is served on the Crown in accordance with rule 12.1(2), notice of the claim must be served by the person making the claim on the person named in the list published under section 17 of the Crown Proceedings Act 1947.

5 The notice must be in the form directed by the court and will normally include the directions given by the court. The notice must also be served by the person making the claim on all the parties. The applicant must provide the Crown with a copy of the document in which the claim in relation to the 1998 Act is raised (for example, the application form).

6 The court may ask the parties to assist in the preparation of the notice.

JOINING OF THE CROWN

7 Unless the court orders otherwise, the Minister or other person permitted by the 1998 Act to be joined as a party must, if he or she wishes to be joined, file an application to be joined using Form COP10. (Section 5(2) of the 1998 Act entitles the Crown to be joined to proceedings where the court is considering whether to make a declaration of incompatibility, provided notice is given in accordance with rules of court. The Minister or other person will be regarded as having sufficient interest for the purpose of rule 9.15(1).)

8 Where the Minister has nominated a person to be joined as a party (as permitted by section 5(2) (a) of the 1998 Act) that person must (unless the court orders otherwise) file an application to be joined using Form COP10, which must also be accompanied by the Minister's written nomination.

(Paragraph 3(b) of Practice Direction 3A deals with allocation of an application for a declaration of incompatibility under section 4 of the Human Rights Act 1998.)

PART 13
JURISDICTION, WITHDRAWAL OF PROCEEDINGS, PARTICIPATION AND RECONSIDERATION

DISPUTING THE JURISDICTION OF THE COURT

III MEN [623]

13.1 Procedure for disputing the court's jurisdiction

(1) A person who wishes to—

(a) dispute the court's jurisdiction to hear an application; or

(b) argue that the court should not exercise its jurisdiction,

may apply to the court at any time for an order declaring that it has no such jurisdiction or should not exercise any jurisdiction that it may have.

(2) An application under this rule must be—

(a) made by using the form specified in the relevant practice direction; and

(b) supported by evidence.

(3) An order containing a declaration that the court has no jurisdiction or will not exercise its jurisdiction may also make further provision, including—

(a) setting aside the application;

(b) discharging any order made;

(c) staying the proceedings;

(d) discharging any litigation friend or rule 1.2 representative.

III MEN [623.1]

Contested issues of jurisdiction and the application of 'best interests' In *PO, In the matter of, JO v GO, RO, MP and Inver Clyde Council* [2013] EWHC 3932 (COP), [2013] All ER (D) 151

(Dec) the President held that in exercising his discretion under Rule 87(1)(b) that a decision to recognise or enforce an order was not a decision for and on behalf of 'P', and followed the decision of Hedley J in *Re MN* [2010] EWHC 1926 (Fam). The President held that such determination looked at the factual matrix as at the date of the decision and not the date of application, and consequently delay in proceedings may have a material impact upon the determination.

WITHDRAWAL OF PROCEEDINGS

III MEN [624]

13.2 Permission required to withdraw proceedings

(1) Proceedings may only be withdrawn with the permission of the court.

(2) An application to withdraw proceedings must be made in accordance with Part 10.

PARTICIPATION IN HEARINGS

III MEN [625]

13.3 Participation in hearings

(1) The court may hear P on the question of whether or not an order should be made, whether or not P is a party to the proceedings.

(2) The court may proceed with a hearing in the absence of P if it considers that it would be appropriate to do so.

(3) A person other than P who is served with or notified of the application may only take part in a hearing if—

(a) that person files an acknowledgment in accordance with these Rules and is made a party to the proceedings; or

(b) the court permits.

(Rule 1.2 deals with participation of P.)

RECONSIDERATION OF COURT ORDERS

III MEN [626]

13.4 Orders made without a hearing or without notice to any person

(1) This rule applies where the court makes an order—

(a) without a hearing; or

(b) without notice to any person who is affected by it.

(2) Where this rule applies—

(a) P;

(b) any party to the proceedings; or

(c) any other person affected by the order,

may apply to the court for reconsideration of the order made.

(3) An application under paragraph (2) must be made—

(a) within 21 days of the order being served or such other period as the court may direct; and

(b) in accordance with Part 10.

(4) The court shall—

(a) reconsider the order without directing a hearing; or

(b) fix a date for the matter to be heard and notify all parties to the proceedings, and such other persons as the court may direct, of that date.

(5) Where an application is made in accordance with this rule, the court may affirm, set aside or vary any order made.

(6) An order made by a court officer authorised under rule 2.3 may be reconsidered by any judge.

(7) An order made by a Tier 1 Judge may be reconsidered by any judge.

(8) An order made by a Tier 2 Judge may be reconsidered by any Tier 2 Judge or by a Tier 3 Judge.

(9) An order made by a Tier 3 Judge may be reconsidered by any Tier 3 Judge.

(10) In any case to which paragraphs (7) to (9) apply the reconsideration may be carried out by the judge who made the order being reconsidered.

(11) No application may be made seeking a reconsideration of—

(a) an order that has been made under paragraph (5); or

(b) an order granting or refusing permission to appeal.

(12) An appeal against an order made under paragraph (5) may be made in accordance with Part 20 (appeals).

(13) Any order made without a hearing or without notice to any person, other than one made under paragraph (5) or one granting or refusing permission to appeal, must contain a statement of the right to apply for a reconsideration of the decision in accordance with this rule.

(14) An application made under this rule may include a request that the court reconsider the matter at a hearing.

(Rule 2.3(2)(c) provides that a court officer authorised under that rule may not deal with an application for the reconsideration of an order made by that court officer or another court officer.)

III MEN [252.1]

Applications to the court for reconsideration; the status of the hearing In *Re S and S (Protected Persons)* [2009] WTLR 315 it was held that at the hearing of an application for reconsideration, it was in effect a hearing de novo. The application must be made in accordance with Part 10 procedure, and COP9 is the relevant application form: **III MEN [607]**.

III MEN [252.2]

Application for reconsideration of an order made under streamlined procedure – Part 2 of Practice Direction 11A Where an order is made under the streamlined procedure under Practice Direction 11A (Part 2), the Practice Direction makes specific provision for the review of such authorisation and the procedure pursuant to that order should be followed (para 49) (see **III MEN [620]**).

PRACTICE DIRECTION 13A – PROCEDURE FOR DISPUTING THE COURT'S JURISDICTION

III MEN [627]

This practice direction supplements Part 13 of the Court of Protection Rules 2017

DISPUTING THE JURISDICTION OF THE COURT – GENERALLY

1 A person who wishes to –

(a) dispute the court's jurisdiction to hear an application; or

(b) argue that the court should not exercise such jurisdiction as it may have,

may apply to the court for an order to that effect.

2 Where a person who has been served with or notified of an application form wishes to dispute the court's jurisdiction, that person must state this in the acknowledgment of service or notification (as the case may be), using Form COP5 filed in accordance with rule 9.12.

3 In any other case (with the exception of those cases provided for in paragraphs 4 to 6), a person who wishes to dispute the court's jurisdiction must do so by filing an application notice using Form COP9 in accordance with Part 10.

DISPUTING THE JURISDICTION OF THE COURT – WHERE P HAS OR REGAINS CAPACITY

4 Where P ceases to lack capacity in relation to the matter or matters to which the application relates, an application may be made to the court for the proceedings to come to an end.

5 Applications in such circumstances may only be made by the following persons –

(a) P;
(b) his litigation friend; or
(c) any other person who is a party to the proceedings.

6 The application must be made by filing an application notice using Form COP9 in accordance with Part 10. The application must be served on all other parties to the proceedings.

PART 14
ADMISSIONS, EVIDENCE AND DEPOSITIONS

ADMISSIONS

III MEN [628]

14.1 Making an admission

(1) Without prejudice to the ability to make an admission in any other way, a party may admit the truth of the whole or part of another party's case by giving notice in writing.

(2) The court may allow a party to amend or withdraw an admission

EVIDENCE

III MEN [629]

14.2 Power of court to [illegible]

[illegible] ires to decide those issues;
[illegible] to be placed before the court;
[illegible] lude evidence that would otherwise
[illegible] written or oral, as it thinks fit; and
[illegible] such information, whether oral or written,
[illegible] arty or any person who lacks competence to
[illegible] as th[illegible] urt considers sufficient, although not given on

MENTAL CAPACITY AND MENTAL HEALTH

oath and whether or not it would be admissible in a court of law apart from this rule.

III MEN [629.1]

Power of the court to control evidence In the case of *Enfield London Borough Council v SA (by her Litigation Friend, the Official Solicitor) FA and KA* [2010] EWHC 196 (Admin), [2010] 1 FLR 1836 it was held that r 95(d) empowered the court to admit hearsay evidence from a person who was not a competent witness, and which would otherwise be inadmissible under s 5 of the Civil Evidence Act 1995. The decision also provided guidance on the issues of "achieving best evidence", and the need to ensure application is made for authority from the court wherever possible.

In *AVS v NHS Foundation Trust* [2010] EWHC 2746 (COP), [2011] 1 FLR 967 the President exercised his case management powers under rule 95(a)–(c) in controlling the extent of evidence required in dealing with issues concerning urgent medical treatment.

In *A Local Authority v DS* [2012] EWHC 1442 (Fam), [2012] 1 WLR 3098, [2012] Fam Law 1078 the President reflecting upon the issue of appointment of experts set out good practice for applications for prior authority, the marshalling of papers to be submitted to the court and the framework for letters of instruction and court orders which may need to express reasons where public funding was in question. Whilst the President was sitting in the Family Division, given the clear overlap with welfare issues before the Court of Protection, the guidance is persuasive.

In *RC v CC* [2014] EWHC 131 (COP), [2014] 1 WLR 2731, [2015] 1 FCR 135 the President adopting the long established principles of open justice held that non-disclosure should be the exception and not the rule and that a court should be rigorous in its examination of the risk and gravity of the feared harm and should only order non-disclosure when the case for doing so is compelling. It is a test of 'strict necessity' what is 'strictly necessary'. And that the balance may need to be struck between limited or restricted disclosure of redacted material.

In *A Local Authority v M* [2014] EWCOP 33 Mr Justice Baker set out a paragraphs 83 to 90 [illegible] his judgment eight principles to be applied in a fact finding exercise including (i) burden and (ii) standard of proof, (iii) evidence and (iv) overview of evidence, (v) the use of expert evidence in context of all other evidence,(vi) ensuring experts keep within the bounds of expertise, (vii) assessments of credibility and reliability, and (viii) the treatment of lies and false untrue evidence [illegible] and the application of the decision in *R v Lucas* [1981] QB 720, [1981] 2 All ER 1008.

III MEN [630]

14.3 Evidence of witnesses—general rule

(1) The general rule is that any fact which needs to be proved by evidence of a witness is to be proved—

(a) where there is a final hearing, by the witness's oral evidence; or

(b) at any other hearing, [illegible] hearing, by the witness's evidence [illegible]

(2) Where a [illegible] witness [illegible] is ca[illegible] the court [illegible] statement of [illegible] oral evidence under paragraph (1)(a), the [illegible]

(3) A wi[illegible] another witne[illegible]

(a) give[illegible]

(b) witness [illegible] hence a[illegible] new [illegible] and [illegible] which [illegible]

(4) The court may [illegible] witness statement [illegible] confine the evidence of [illegible] there is good reason [illegible] of the witness statement.

(5) This rule is subject to [illegible]

(a) any provision to [illegible] orders that [illegible]

(b) any order or direction [illegible] elsewhere or

III MEN [631]

14.4 Written evidence—general rule

A party may not rely on written evidence [illegible]

(a) it has been filed in accordance with these Rules or a practice direction;
(b) it is expressly permitted by these Rules or a practice direction; or
(c) the court gives permission.

III MEN [632]

14.5 Evidence by video link or other means

The court may allow a witness to give evidence through a video link or by other communication technology.

III MEN [632.1]

Guidance on use of video conferencing Practice Direction 14A Annex 2 provides guidance on the use of video conferencing: **III MEN [653]**.

III MEN [633]

14.6 Service of witness statements for use at final hearing

(1) A witness statement is a written statement by a person which contains the evidence which that person would be allowed to give orally.

(2) The court will give directions about the service of any witness statement upon which a party intends to rely at the final hearing.

(3) The court may give directions as to the order in which witness statements are to be served.

(Rules 5.2 and 14.7 require witness statements to be verified by a statement of truth.)

III MEN [266.1]

Guidance on the format and content of witness statements Practice Direction 14A, paras 33- 50 provide guidance as to the format and content of witness statements and the requirement of the court. Form COP 24 is the applicable form. See **III MEN [653]**.

III MEN [634]

14.7 Form of witness statement

A witness statement must contain a statement of truth and comply with the requirements set out in the relevant practice direction.

III MEN [634.1]

The verification of witness statements Practice Direction 14A, paras 44-45 (see **III MEN [653]**) give guidance and example of the requirement for verification of truth, drawing attention to rule 5.6, and the consequences of verifying a false statement: **III MEN [531]**. Form COP24 is the applicable form.

III MEN [635]

14.8 Witness summaries

(1) A party who wishes to file a witness statement for use at the final hearing, but is unable to do so, may apply without notice to be permitted to file a witness summary instead.

(2) A witness summary is a summary of—

(a) the evidence, if known, which would otherwise be included in a witness statement; or
(b) if the evidence is not known, the matters about which the party filing the witness summary proposes to question the witness.

(3) Unless the court directs otherwise, a witness summary must include the name and address of the intended witness.

(4) Unless the court directs otherwise, a witness summary must be filed within the period in which a witness statement would have had to be filed.

(5) Where a party files a witness summary, so far as practicable, rules 14.3(3)(a) (amplifying witness statements) and 14.6 (service of witness statements for use at final hearing) shall apply to the summary.

III MEN [636]

14.9 Affidavit evidence

Evidence must be given by affidavit instead of or in addition to a witness statement if this is required by the court, a provision contained in any rule, a practice direction or any other enactment.

III MEN [636.1]

Procedures in respect of the format and use of affidavits Practice Direction 14A, paras 1–19 provides guidance on the format, content and requirements of the court in respect of an affidavit, See **III MEN [653]**. The applicable form is COP25.

III MEN [637]

14.10 Form of affidavit

An affidavit must comply with the requirements set out in the relevant practice direction.

III MEN [638]

14.11 Affidavit made outside the jurisdiction

A person may make an affidavit outside the jurisdiction in accordance with—

(a) this Part; or

(b) the law of the place where that person makes the affidavit.

III MEN [639]

14.12 Notarial acts and instruments

A notarial act or instrument may, without further proof, be received in evidence as duly authenticated in accordance with the requirements of law unless the contrary is proved.

III MEN [640]

14.13 Summoning of witnesses

(1) The court may allow or direct any party to issue a witness summons requiring the person named in it to attend before the court and give oral evidence or produce any document to the court.

(2) An application by a party for the issue of a witness summons may be made by filing an application notice with includes—

(a) the name and address of the applicant and the applicant's solicitor, if any;

(b) the name, address and occupation of the proposed witness;

(c) particulars of any document which the proposed witness is to be required to produce; and

(d) the grounds on which the application is made.

(3) The general rule is that a witness summons is binding if it is served at least 7 days before the date on which the witness is required to attend before the court, and the requirements of paragraph (6) have been complied with.

(4) The court may direct that a witness summons shall be binding although it will be served less than 7 days before the date on which the witness is required to attend before the court.

(5) Unless the court directs otherwise, a witness summons is to be served by the person making the application.

(6) At the time of service the witness must be offered or paid—

(a) a sum reasonably sufficient to cover the witness's expenses in travelling to and from the court; and

(b) such sum by way of compensation for loss of time as may be specified in the relevant practice direction.

(7) The court may order that the witness is to be paid such general costs as it considers appropriate.

III MEN [640.1]

Applications to the court for issuing witness summonses Practice Direction 14D provides guidance on the issuing of a witness summons (see **III MEN [656]**). Paragraph 3 identifies that Part 10 procedure applies and form COP9 should be used. See **III MEN [607]**.

III MEN [641]

14.14 Power of court to direct a party to provide information

(1) Where a party has access to information which is not reasonably available to the other party, the court may direct that party to prepare and file a document recording that information.

(2) The court shall give directions about serving a copy of that document on the other parties.

Depositions

III MEN [642]

14.15 Evidence by deposition

(1) A party may apply for an order for a person to be examined before the hearing takes place.

(2) A person from whom evidence is to be obtained following an order under this rule is referred to as a "deponent" and the evidence is referred to as a "deposition".

(3) An order under this rule shall be for a deponent to be examined on oath before—

(a) a circuit judge or a district judge, whether or not nominated as a judge of the court;

(b) an examiner of the court; or

(c) such other person as the court appoints.

(4) The order may require the production of any document which the court considers is necessary for the purposes of the examination.

(5) The order will state the date, time and place of the examination.

(6) At the time of service of the order, the deponent must be offered or paid—

(a) a sum reasonably sufficient to cover the deponent's expenses in travelling to and from the place of examination; and

(b) such sum by way of compensation for loss of time as may be specified in the relevant practice direction.

(7) Where the court makes an order for a deposition to be taken, it may also order the party who obtained the order to file a witness statement or witness summary in relation to the evidence to be given by the person to be examined.

III MEN [642.1]

Applications to the court and procedures for the taking of depositions Practice Direction 14B gives guidance in respect of depositions, in particular directions if the deposition is to be taken in England and Wales (paras 1–15), abroad where the Taking of Evidence Regulations do not apply (paras 16–22) or taking evidence between EU Member States (paras 23–33). Annex A provides a draft letter for matters under paras 16–22. Annex B a website link for Council Regulation (EC) No 1206/2001. See **III MEN [654]**.

III MEN [643]

14.16 Conduct of examination

(1) Subject to any directions contained in the order for examination, the examination must be conducted in the same way as if the witness were giving evidence at a final hearing.

(2) If all the parties are present, the examiner may conduct the examination of a person not named in the order for examination if all the parties and the person to be examined consent.

(3) The examiner must ensure that the evidence given by the witness is recorded in full.

(4) The examiner must send a copy of the deposition—

(a) to the person who obtained the order for the examination of the witness; and

(b) to the court.

(5) The court shall give directions as to the service of a copy of the deposition on the other parties.

III MEN [644]

14.17 Fees and expenses of examiners of the court

(1) An examiner of the court may charge a fee for the examination and need not send the deposition to the court until the fee is paid, unless the court directs otherwise.

(2) The examiner's fees and expenses must be paid by the party who obtained the order for examination.

(3) If the fees and expenses due to an examiner are not paid within a reasonable time, the examiner may report that fact to the court.

(4) The court may order the party who obtained the order for examination to deposit in the court office a specified sum in respect of the examiner's fees and, where it does so, the examiner shall not be asked to act until the sum has been deposited.

(5) An order under this rule does not affect any decision as to the person who is ultimately to bear the costs of the examination.

III MEN [644.1]

Guidance on fees in respect of an examination Practice Direction 14C provides supplemental guidance in respect of fees applicable and the calculation thereof: **III MEN [655]**.

III MEN [645]

14.18 Examiners of the court

(1) The Lord Chancellor shall appoint persons to be examiners of the court.

(2) The persons appointed shall be barristers or solicitor-advocates who have been practising for a period of not less than 3 years.

(3) The Lord Chancellor may revoke an appointment at any time.

(4) In addition to persons appointed in accordance with this rule, examiners appointed under rule 34.15 of the Civil Procedure Rules 1998 may act as examiners in the court.

III MEN [646]

14.19 Enforcing attendance of a witness

(1) If a person served with an order to attend before an examiner—

(a) fails to attend; or

(b) refuses to be sworn for the purpose of the examination or to answer any lawful question or produce any document at the examination,

a certificate of that person's failure or refusal, signed by the examiner, must be filed by the party requiring the deposition.

(2) On the certificate being filed, the party requiring the deposition may apply to the court for an order requiring that person to attend or to be sworn or to answer any question or produce any document, as the case may be.

(3) An application for an order under this rule may be made without notice.

(4) The court may order the person against whom an order is sought or made under this rule to pay any costs resulting from that person's failure or refusal.

III MEN [646.1]

Applications to the court and procedure Part 10 and Practice Direction 10A would apply. See **III MEN [607]**. Form COP9 would be required.

III MEN [647]

14.20 Use of deposition at a hearing

(1) A deposition ordered under rule 14.15, 14.22 or 14.23 may be put in evidence at a hearing unless the court orders otherwise.

(2) A party intending to put a deposition in evidence at a hearing must file notice of intention to do so on the court and serve the notice on every other party.

(3) Unless the court directs otherwise, that party must file the notice at least 14 days before the day fixed for the hearing.

(4) The court may require a deponent to attend the hearing and give evidence orally.

Taking evidence outside the jurisdiction

III MEN [648]

14.21 Interpretation

In this rule and rules 14.22 and 14.23—

(a) "Regulation State" has the same meaning as "Member State" in the Taking of Evidence Regulation, that is, all Member States except Denmark; and

(b) "the Taking of Evidence Regulation" means Council Regulation (EC) No 1206/2001 of 28 May 2001 on co-operation between the courts of Member States in the taking of evidence in civil and commercial matters.

III MEN [649]

14.22 Where a person to be examined is in another Regulation State

(1) This rule applies where a party wishes to take a deposition from a person who is—

(a) outside the jurisdiction; and

(b) in a Regulation State.

(2) The court may order the issue of the request to a designated court ("the requested court") in the Regulation State in which the proposed deponent is.

(3) If the court makes an order for the issue of a request, the party who sought the order must file—

(a) a draft Form A, as set out in the Annex to the Taking of Evidence Regulation (request for the taking of evidence);

(b) except where paragraph (4) applies, a translation of the form;

MENTAL CAPACITY AND MENTAL HEALTH

(c) an undertaking to be responsible for the costs sought by the requested court in relation to—
   (i) fees paid to experts and interpreters; and
   (ii) where requested by that party, the use of special procedure or communications technology; and
(d) an undertaking to be responsible for the court's expenses.

(4) There is no need to file a translation if—
(a) English is one of the official languages of the Regulation State where the examination is to take place; or
(b) the Regulation State has indicated, in accordance with the Taking of Evidence Regulation, that English is a language which it will accept.

(5) Where article 17 of the Taking of Evidence Regulation (direct taking of evidence by the requested court) allows evidence to be taken directly in another Regulation State, the court may make an order for the submission of a request in accordance with that article.

(6) If the court makes an order for the submission of a request under paragraph (5), the party who sought the order must file—
(a) a draft Form I as set out in the Annex to the Taking of Evidence Regulation (request for direct taking of evidence);
(b) except where paragraph (4) applies, a translation of the form; and
(c) an undertaking to be responsible for the requested court's expenses.

III MEN [649.1]

Applications to the court and procedure Practice Direction 14B, paras 9–10 is applicable. Form COP9 should be used: **III MEN [654]**.

III MEN [650]

14.23 Where a person to be examined is out of the jurisdiction—letter of request

(1) This rule applies where a party wishes to take a deposition from a person who is—
(a) out of the jurisdiction; and
(b) not in a Regulation State within the meaning of rule 14.21.

(2) The court may order the issue of a letter of request to the judicial authorities of the country in which the proposed deponent is.

(3) A letter of request is a request to a judicial authority to take the evidence of that person, or arrange for it to be taken.

(4) If the government of a country permits a person appointed by the court to examine a person in that country, the court may make an order appointing a special examiner for that purpose.

(5) A person may be examined under this rule on oath or affirmation in accordance with any procedure permitted in the country in which the examination is to take place.

(6) If the court makes an order for the issue of a letter of request, the party who sought the order must file—
(a) the following documents and, except where paragraph (7) applies, a translation of them—
   (i) a draft letter of request;
   (ii) a statement of the issues relevant to the proceedings; and
   (iii) a list of questions or the subject matter of questions to be put to the person to be examined; and
(b) an undertaking to be responsible for the Secretary of State's expenses.

(7) There is no need to file a translation if—
(a) English is one of the official languages of the country where the examination is to take place; or

(b) a practice direction has specified that country as a country where no translation is necessary.

III MEN [650.1]

Procedural guidance Practice Direction 14B, paras 16–22 and Annex A provide guidance: **III MEN [654]**.

SECTION 49 REPORTS

III MEN [651]

14.24 Reports under section 49 of the Act

(1) This rule applies where the court requires a report to be made to it under section 49 of the Act.

(2) It is the duty of the person who is required to make the report to help the court on the matters within that person's expertise.

(3) Unless the court directs otherwise, the person making the report must—

- (a) contact or seek to interview such persons as the person making the report thinks appropriate or as the court directs;
- (b) to the extent that it is practicable and appropriate to do so, ascertain what P's wishes and feelings are, and the beliefs and values that would be likely to influence P if P had the capacity to make a decision in relation to the matters to which the application relates;
- (c) describe P's circumstances; and
- (d) address such other matters as are required in a practice direction or as the court may direct.

(4) The court will send a copy of the report to the parties and to such persons as the court may direct.

(5) Subject to paragraphs (6) and (7), the person who is required to make the report may examine and take copies of any documents in the court records.

(6) The court may direct that the right to inspect documents under this rule does not apply in relation to such documents, or descriptions of documents, as the court may specify.

(7) The court may direct that any information is to be provided to the maker of the report on an edited basis.

III MEN [651.1]

The procedures in respect of reports and applications to the court Section 49 of the Mental Capacity Act 2005 enables the court to obtain reports dealing with such matters relating to P as the court may direct (**III MEN [87]**). Practice Direction 14E provides supplemental guidance as to the requirements of a s 49 report, and the Annex provides a specimen order (**III MEN [657]**).

Section 49(2) authorises the court to commission a report from the Public Guardian or from a Court of Protection Visitor (see s 61 in respect of Special and General Visitors, (**III MEN [99]**), and require reports to be commissioned from a local authority or NHS body (s 49(3), see **III MEN [87]**).

III MEN [652]

14.25 Written questions to person making a report under section 49

(1) Where a report is made under section 49 the court may, on the application of any party, permit written questions relevant to the issues before the court to be put to the person by whom the report was made.

(2) The questions sought to be put to the maker of the report shall be submitted to the court, and the court may put them to the maker of the report with such amendments (if any) as it thinks fit and the maker of the report shall give replies in writing to the questions so put.

(3) The court shall send a copy of the replies given by the maker of the report under this rule to the parties and to such other persons as the court may direct.

III MEN [652.1]

The control by the court of questioning of report providers An important feature of r 14.25 is the control of the Court as to questions to be put to the maker of the report.

PRACTICE DIRECTION 14A – WRITTEN EVIDENCE

III MEN [653]

This practice direction supplements Part 14 of the Court of Protection Rules 2017

WRITTEN EVIDENCE

Affidavits

Deponent

1 A deponent is a person who gives evidence by affidavit or affirmation.

Heading

2 The affidavit should be headed with the title of the proceedings, including the case number (if known) and the full name of the person to whom the proceedings relate (unless an order to the contrary pursuant to rule 5.11 has been made).

3 At the top right hand corner of the first page (and on the back-sheet) there should be clearly written –

(a) the party on whose behalf it is made (unless an order to the contrary pursuant to rule 5.11 has been made);
(b) the initials and surname of the deponent;
(c) the number of the affidavit in relation to that deponent; and
(d) the date sworn.

Body of affidavit

4 The affidavit must, if practicable, be in the deponent's own words. It should be expressed in the first person, and the deponent should –

(a) commence 'I (full name) of (address) state on oath . . . ';
(b) if giving evidence in his professional, business or other occupational capacity, give the address at which he works in (a) above, the position he holds and the name of his firm or employer;
(c) give his occupation or, if he has none, his description; and
(d) state if he is a party to the proceedings or employed by a party to the proceedings.

5 An affidavit must indicate –

(a) which of the statements in it are made from the deponent's own knowledge and which are matters of information or belief; and
(b) the source for any matters of information or belief.

6 Where a deponent –

(a) refers to an exhibit or exhibits, he should state 'there is now produced and shown to me marked " . . . " the (description of exhibit)'; and

(b) makes more than one affidavit (to which there are exhibits) in the same proceedings, the numbering of the exhibits should run consecutively throughout and not start again with each affidavit.

Jurat

7 The jurat of an affidavit is a statement set out at the end of the document which authenticates the affidavit.

8 It must –

(a) be signed by all deponents;
(b) be completed and signed by the person before whom the affidavit was sworn whose name and qualifications must be printed beneath his signature;
(c) contain the full address of the person before whom the affidavit was sworn; and
(d) follow immediately on from the text and not be put on a separate page.

Format of affidavits

9 An affidavit should:

(a) be produced on durable quality A4 paper with a 3.5 centimetre margin;
(b) be fully legible and should normally be typed on one side of the paper only;
(c) where possible, be bound securely in a manner which would not hamper filing;
(d) have the pages numbered consecutively as a separate document;
(e) be divided into numbered paragraphs; and
(f) have all numbers, including dates, expressed in figures.

10 It is usually convenient for an affidavit to follow the chronological sequence of events or matters dealt with. Each paragraph of an affidavit should as far as possible be confined to a distinct portion of the subject.

11 An affidavit must be included in, or attached to, a COP25 form.

Inability of deponent to read or sign affidavit

12 Where an affidavit is sworn by a person who is unable to read or sign it, the person before whom the affidavit is sworn must certify in the jurat that –

(a) he read the affidavit to the deponent;
(b) the deponent appeared to understand it; and
(c) the deponent signed, or made his mark, in his presence.

13 If that certificate is not included in the jurat, the affidavit may not be used in evidence unless the court is satisfied that it was read to the deponent and that he appeared to understand it. Two versions of the form of the jurat with the certificate are set out in Annex 1 to this practice direction.

Alterations to affidavits

14 Any alteration to an affidavit must be initialled by both the deponent and the person before whom the affidavit was sworn.

15 An affidavit which contains an alteration that has not been initialled may be filed or used in evidence only with the permission of the court.

Who may administer oaths

16 Only the following may administer oaths –

(a) Commissioners for Oaths;
(b) practising solicitors;
(c) other persons specified by statute;

(d) certain officials of the Senior Courts;
(e) a circuit judge or district judge;
(f) any justice of the peace; and
(g) certain officials of the County Court appointed for the purpose.

17 An affidavit must be sworn before a person independent of the parties or their representatives.

Filing of affidavits

18 If the court directs that an affidavit is to be filed, it must be filed in the court office.

19 Where an affidavit is in a foreign language –

(a) the party wishing to rely on it –
   (i) must have it translated, and
   (ii) must file the foreign language affidavit with the court; and
(b) the translator must make and file with the court an affidavit verifying the translation and exhibiting both the translation and a copy of the foreign language affidavit.

Exhibits

Manner of exhibiting documents

20 A document used in conjunction with an affidavit should be –

(a) produced to and verified by the deponent, and remain separate from the affidavit; and
(b) identified by a declaration of the person before whom the affidavit was sworn.

21 The declaration should be headed with the name of the proceedings in the same way as the affidavit.

22 The first page of each exhibit should be marked –

(a) as in paragraph 3 above; and
(b) with the exhibit mark referred to in the affidavit.

Letters

23 Copies of individual letters should be collected together and exhibited in a bundle or bundles. The letters should be arranged in chronological order with the earliest at the top, and firmly secured.

24 When a bundle of correspondence is exhibited it should be arranged and secured as above and numbered consecutively.

Other documents

25 Photocopies instead of original documents may be exhibited provided the originals are made available for inspection by other parties before the hearing and by the judge at the hearing.

26 Court documents must not be exhibited (official copies of such documents prove themselves).

Exhibits other than documents

27 Items other than documents should be clearly marked with an exhibit number or letter in such a manner that the mark cannot become detached from the exhibit.

28 Small items may be placed in a container and the container appropriately marked.

General provisions

29 Where an exhibit contains more than one document –

(a) the bundle should not be stapled but should be securely fastened in a way that does not hinder the reading of the documents; and

(b) the pages should be numbered consecutively at the bottom centre.

30 Every page of an exhibit should be clearly legible. Typed copies of illegible documents should be included, paginated with "a" etc. numbers.

31 Where on account of their bulk the service of copies of exhibits on the other parties would be difficult or impracticable, the directions of the court should be sought as to the arrangements for bringing the exhibits to the attention of the other parties and as to their custody pending the final hearing.

Affirmations

32 All provisions in this or any other practice direction relating to affidavits apply to affirmations with the following exceptions:

(a) the deponent should commence 'I (*name*) of (*address*) do solemnly and sincerely affirm . . .'; and

(b) in the jurat the word 'sworn' is replaced by the word 'affirmed'.

Witness statements

Heading

33 The witness statements should be headed with the title of the proceedings; including the case number (if known) and the full name of the person to whom the proceedings relate (unless an order to the contrary pursuant to rule 5.11 has been made).

34 At the top right hand corner of the first page there should be clearly written –

(a) the party on whose behalf it is made (unless an order to the contrary pursuant to rule 5.11 has been made);

(b) the initials and surname of the witness;

(c) the number of the statement in relation to that witness; and

(d) the date the statement was made.

Body of witness statement

35 The witness statement must, if practicable, be in the intended witness's own words. The statement should be expressed in the first person and should also state –

(a) his place of residence or, if he is making the statement in his professional, business or other occupational capacity, the address at which he works, the position he holds and the name of his firm or employer;

(b) his occupation, or if he has none, his description; and

(c) if he is a party to the proceedings or employed by a party to the proceedings.

36 A witness statement must indicate –

(a) which of the statements in it are made from the witness's own knowledge and which are matters of information or belief; and

(b) the source for any matters of information or belief.

37 An exhibit used in conjunction with a witness statement should be verified and identified by the witness and remain separate from the witness statement.

38 Where a witness refers to an exhibit or exhibits, he should state: 'I refer to the (*description of exhibit*) marked " . . . "'.

39 The provisions of paragraphs 22 to 31 apply similarly to witness statements as they do to affidavits, where appropriate.

40 Where a witness makes more than one witness statement to which there are exhibits, the numbering of the exhibits should run consecutively throughout and not start again with each witness statement.

Format of witness statement

41 A witness statement should adhere to the format specified in paragraph 9 for affidavits.

42 It is usually convenient for a witness statement to follow the chronological sequence of the events or matters dealt with and each paragraph of a witness statement should, as far as possible, be confined to a distinct portion of the subject.

43 A witness statement must be included in, or attached to, Form COP24.

Statement of truth

44 A witness statement is the equivalent of oral evidence which the witness would, if called, give in evidence. It must be verified by a statement of truth in the following terms –

'I believe that the facts stated in this witness statement are true.'

(Practice direction B accompanying Part 5 sets out more detailed requirements for statements of truth.)

45 Attention is drawn to rule 5.6 which sets out the consequences of verifying a witness statement containing a false statement without an honest belief in its truth.

Alterations to witness statements

46 Any alteration to a witness statement must be initialled by the person making the statement or by the authorised person where appropriate.

47 A witness statement which contains an alteration that has not been initialled may only be used in evidence with the permission of the court.

Filing of witness statements

48 Where a witness statement is in a foreign language –

(a) the party wishing to rely on it must –
  (i) have it translated, and
  (ii) file the foreign language witness statement with the court; and
(b) the translator must make and file with the court an affidavit verifying the translation and exhibiting both the translation and a copy of the foreign language witness statement.

Defects in affidavits, witness statements and exhibits

49 Where –

(a) an affidavit;
(b) a witness statement; or
(c) an exhibit to either an affidavit or a witness statement,

does not comply with Part 14 or this practice direction in relation to its form, the court may refuse to admit it as evidence and may refuse to allow the costs arising from its preparation.

50 However, the court may allow a person to file a defective affidavit or witness statement or to use a defective exhibit.

Agreed bundles for hearings

51 The court may give directions requiring the parties to use their best endeavours to agree a bundle or bundles of documents for use at any hearing.

52 All documents contained in bundles which have been agreed for use at a hearing shall be admissible at that hearing as evidence of their contents, unless –

(a) the court orders otherwise; or
(b) a party gives written notice of objection to the admissibility of particular documents.

Note that Practice Direction 4B now provides the requirements for the preparation of bundles for hearing (see **III MEN [524]**).

Evidence by video link

53 Guidance on the use of video conferencing is set out at Annex 2 to this practice direction.

Information

54 The court may direct a party with access to information which is not reasonably available to another party to serve on that other party a document which records the information. The document served must include sufficient details of all the facts, tests, experiments and assumptions which underlie any part of the information to enable the party on whom it is served to make, or to obtain, a proper interpretation of the information and an assessment of its significance.

Annex 1
Certificate to be used where a deponent to an affidavit is unable to read or sign it

Sworn at . . . this . . . day of . . . Before me, I having first read over the contents of this affidavit to the deponent [if there are exhibits, add "and explained the nature and effect of the exhibits referred to in it"] who appeared to understand it and approved its contents as accurate, and made his mark on the affidavit in my presence.

Or (after, *Before me*) the witness to the mark of the deponent having first sworn that he had read over etc. (*as above*) and that he saw him make his mark on the affidavit. (*Witness must sign*).

Certificate to be used where a deponent to an affirmation is unable to read or sign it

Affirmed at . . . this . . . day of . . . Before me, I having first read over the contents of this affirmation to the deponent [if there are exhibits, add "and explained the nature and effect of the exhibits referred to in it"] who appeared to understand it and approved its content as accurate, and made his mark on the affirmation in my presence.

Or (after, *Before me*) the witness to the mark of the deponent having been first sworn that he had read over etc. (*as above*) and that he saw him make his mark on the affirmation. (*Witness must sign*).

Annex 2
Guidance on the use of video conferencing

1 This guidance is for the use of video conferencing (VC) to provide evidence in the Court of Protection. It is in part based upon the VC guidance contained in the practice direction that supplements Part 32 of the Civil Procedure Rules.

2 Rule 14.5 of the Court of Protection Rules 2017 provides that the court may allow a witness to give evidence through a video link or by other means. It is, however, inevitably not as ideal as having the witness physically present in court. Its convenience should not therefore be allowed to dictate its use. Consideration should be given in each case as to whether its use is likely to be beneficial to the efficient, fair and economic disposal of the proceedings.

3 For VC purposes, the location at which the judge sits is referred to as the 'local site'. The local site may be either a courtroom with VC equipment either permanently or temporarily installed, or another venue such as a studio or conference room set-up for VC. The other site or sites to and from which transmission is made are referred to as 'the remote site'.

Preliminary arrangements

4 The court's permission is required for any part of any proceedings to be dealt with by means of VC. Before seeking a direction, the applicant should notify the appropriate court officer of the intention to seek it, and should enquire as to the availability of the court's VC equipment for the duration of the proposed VC. The application for a direction should be made to the court by filing a COP9 application notice in accordance with the Part 10 procedure.

5 If a witness at a remote site is to give evidence by an interpreter, consideration should be given at this stage as to whether the interpreter should be at the local site or the remote site.

6 Where the VC process is to be used to take evidence from a person in a foreign jurisdiction, the parties should consider whether that is permissible under local law.

7 If a VC direction is given, arrangements for the transmission will then need to be made. The court will ordinarily direct that the party seeking permission to use VC is to be responsible for this. That party is hereafter referred to as 'the VC arranging party'.

VC arranging party's responsibilities

8 The VC arranging party must contact the appropriate court officer and make arrangements for the VC transmission.

9 The court has established procedures with Her Majesty's Court and Tribunal Service that enables the witness's nearest local court with VC facilities to be used as the remote site. The VC arranging party must advise the court whether the party wishes to make use of local court facilities for the remote site.

10 If the party is unable to make use of local court VC facilities, then the VC arranging party is responsible for arranging an alternative remote site. This may consist of a solicitor's office or a commercial VC facility, and in some circumstances may require portable VC equipment to be brought to the witness. Details of the remote site, and of the equipment to be used, together with all necessary contact names and telephone numbers, will have to be provided to the court.

11 The VC arranging party must arrange for recording equipment to be provided by the court so that the evidence can be recorded. A court officer will normally be present to operate the recording equipment when the local site is a courtroom. The equipment should be set up and tested before the VC transmission.

12 In rare instances, it may be necessary for the local site to be somewhere other than the courtroom (or other VC facility onsite at the court). If this is the case, the VC arranging party should ensure –

(a) that arrangements are made, if practicable, for the royal coat of arms to be placed above the judge's seat at the alternate venue;
(b) that the number of microphones is adequate for the speakers;
(c) that the panning of the camera for the practitioners' table encompasses all legal representatives so that the viewer can see everyone seated there; and

(d) that a court officer is present to operate the recording equipment.

Court of Protection responsibilities

13 If the VC arranging party has advised that the party wishes to utilise local court facilities for the remote site, a court officer will contact the nearest local court (with VC facilities) to the witness and –

(a) agree and book a mutually convenient date and time for the attendance;
(b) advise the local court as to the number and details of those parties attending to give evidence by VC;
(c) confirm with the local court the reporting arrangements for the parties attending to give their evidence; and
(d) advise the parties by letter of the date, time and arrangements for attending the designated local court to give their evidence by VC.

Provided the local site is to be the courtroom (or other VC facility on-site at the court), a court officer will also –

(a) set-up the courtroom for the VC;
(b) establish the VC link with the remote site at the date and time that has been booked; and
(c) be available in order to deal with any technical problems during the transmission should they develop.

Local court responsibilities

15 The local court will advise the court staff (London or regional court as applicable) of the number to be called to establish the VC link with the remote site. Where the local court is utilising a third party networked VC service (such as the Martin Dawes service utilised by the closed nation-wide prison network), it will be responsible for arranging a bridging link for the date and time agreed.

16 The local court will make arrangements to meet the witness on their arrival at the court, escort them to the room where they are to give evidence by VC, switch on the VC equipment and ensure a link is established with the local site.

The hearing

17 Those involved with VC need to be aware that due to varying technology standards, there may be delays between the receipt of the picture and that of the accompanying sound. If due allowance is not made for this, there may be a tendency to 'speak over' the witness, whose voice will continue to be heard for a short period after he or she appears on the screen to have finished speaking.

18 Picture quality may also vary, and is generally enhanced if those appearing on VC monitors keep their movements to a minimum.

19 It is recommended that the practitioners and witness should arrive at their respective VC sites about 20 minutes prior to the scheduled commencement of the transmission.

20 Consideration will need to be given in advance to any documents to which the witness is likely to be referred. The parties should endeavour to agree on this. It will usually be most convenient for a bundle of the copy documents to be prepared in advance, which the VC arranging party should then send to the remote site.

21 Additional documents are sometimes quite properly introduced during the course of a witness's evidence. To cater for this, the VC arranging party should ensure that equipment is available to enable documents to be transmitted between sites during the course of the VC transmission. The procedure for conducting the transmission will be determined by the judge. The judge will also determine who is to control the cameras.

22 At the beginning of the transmission, the judge may wish to give directions as to the seating arrangements at the remote site so that those present are visible at the local site during the taking of the evidence.

23 The examination of the witness at the remote site should then follow as closely as possible the practice adopted when a witness is in the courtroom. During examination, cross-examination and re-examination, the witness must be able to see the legal representative asking the question and also any other person (whether another legal representative or the judge) making any statements in regard to the witness's evidence. It will in practice be most convenient if everyone remains seated throughout the transmission.

PRACTICE DIRECTION 14B – DEPOSITIONS

III MEN [654]

This practice direction supplements Part 14 of the Court of Protection Rules 2017

DEPOSITIONS TO BE TAKEN IN ENGLAND AND WALES

1 A party may apply for an order for a person to be examined on oath before –

(a) a judge;
(b) an examiner of the court; or
(c) such other person as the court may appoint.

2 The party who obtains an order for the examination of a deponent before an examiner of the court must –

(a) apply to the court for the allocation of an examiner;
(b) when allocated, provide the examiner with copies of all documents in the proceedings necessary to inform the examiner of the issues; and
(c) pay the deponent a sum to cover his travelling expenses to and from the examination and compensation for his loss of time.

3 In ensuring that the deponent's evidence is recorded in full, the court or the examiner may permit it to be recorded in full on audiotape or videotape, but the deposition must always be recorded in writing by the examiner or by a competent shorthand writer or stenographer.

4 If the deposition is not recorded word for word, it must contain, as nearly as may be, the statement of the deponent. The examiner may record word for word any particular questions or answers which appear to him to have special importance.

5 If a deponent objects to answering any question or where any objection is taken to any question, the examiner must –

(a) record in the deposition or a document attached to it:
 (i) the question,
 (ii) the nature of and grounds for the objection, and
 (iii) any answer given; and
(b) give his opinion as to the validity of the objection and must record it in the deposition or a document attached to it.

6 Documents and exhibits must –

(a) have an identifying number or letter marked on them by the examiner; and
(b) be preserved by the party or his legal representative who obtained the order for the examination, or as the court or the examiner may direct.

7 The examiner may put any question to the deponent as to –

(a) the meaning of any of his answers; or
(b) any matter arising in the course of the examination.

8 Where a deponent –

(a) fails to attend the examination; or
(b) refuses to:
 (i) be sworn, or
 (ii) answer any lawful question, or
 (iii) produce any document,

the examiner will sign a certificate of such failure or refusal and may include in his certificate any comment as to the conduct of the deponent or of any person attending the examination.

9 The party who obtained the order for the examination must file the certificate with the court and may apply for an order that the deponent attend for examination or such other order as he considers appropriate. The application must be made by filing a COP9 application notice, and may be made without notice.

10 The court will make such order on the application as it thinks fit including an order for the deponent to pay any costs resulting from his failure or refusal.

11 A deponent who wilfully refuses to obey an order made against him under Part 14 may be proceeded against for contempt of court.

12 A deposition must –

(a) be signed by the examiner;
(b) have any amendments to it initialled by the examiner and the deponent; and
(c) be endorsed by the examiner with:
 (i) a statement of the time occupied by the examination, and
 (ii) a record of any refusal by the deponent to sign the deposition and of his reasons for not doing so, and
 (iii) be sent by the examiner to the court where the proceedings are taking place for filing on the court file.

13 Rule 14.17 deals with the fees and expenses of the examiner.

DEPOSITIONS TO BE TAKEN IN ENGLAND AND WALES

Travelling expenses and compensation for loss of time

14 When a deponent is served with an order for examination he must be offered a sum to cover his travelling expenses to and from the examination and compensation for his loss of time.

15 The sum referred to in paragraph 14 is to be based on the sums payable to witnesses attending the Crown Court.

DEPOSITIONS TO BE TAKEN ABROAD FOR USE AS EVIDENCE IN PROCEEDINGS BEFORE COURTS IN ENGLAND AND WALES (WHERE THE TAKING OF EVIDENCE REGULATION DOES NOT APPLY)

16 Where a party wishes to take a deposition from a person outside the jurisdiction, the court may order the issue of a letter of request to the judicial authorities of the country in which the proposed deponent is.

17 An application for an order referred to in paragraph 16 should be made by filing a COP9 application notice in accordance with Part 10. The documents which a party applying for an order for the issue of a letter of request must file with his application notice are set out in rule 14.23.

18 In addition, the party applying for the order must file a draft order.

19 The application will be dealt with by the Senior Judge or his nominee who will, if appropriate, sign the letter of request.

20 If parties are in doubt as to whether a translation under rule 14.23(7) is required, they should seek guidance from the court office.

21 A special examiner appointed under rule 14.23(4) may be the British Consul or the Consul-General or his deputy in the country where the evidence is to be taken –

(a) if there is in respect of that country a Civil Procedure Convention providing for the taking of evidence in that country for the assistance of proceedings in the High Court or other court in this country; or
(b) with the consent of the Secretary of State.

22 The provisions of paragraphs 1 to 12 above apply to the depositions referred to in paragraphs 16 to 22.

TAKING OF EVIDENCE BETWEEN EU MEMBER STATES

Taking of Evidence Regulation

23 Where evidence is to be taken –

(a) from a person in another Member State of the European Union for use as evidence in proceedings before courts in England and Wales; or
(b) from a person in England and Wales for use as evidence in proceedings before a court in another Member State,

Council Regulation (EC) No 1206/2001 of 28 May 2001 on co-operation between the courts of the Member States in the taking of evidence in civil or commercial matters ('the Taking of Evidence Regulation') applies.

24 The website link to the Taking of Evidence Regulation is annexed to this practice direction as Annex B.

25 The Taking of Evidence Regulation does not apply to Denmark. In relation to Denmark, therefore, rule 14.23 will continue to apply.

(Article 21(1) of the Taking of Evidence Regulation provides that the Regulation prevails over other provisions contained in bilateral or multilateral agreements or arrangements concluded by the Member States and in particular the Hague Convention of 1 March 1954 on Civil Procedure and the Hague Convention of 18 March 1970 on the Taking of Evidence Abroad in Civil or Commercial Matters.)

MEANING OF 'DESIGNATED COURT'

26 In accordance with the Taking of Evidence Regulation, each Regulation State has prepared a list of courts competent to take evidence in accordance with the Regulation indicating the territorial and, where appropriate, special jurisdiction of those courts.

27 Where rule 14.22 refers to a 'designated court' in relation to another Regulation State, the reference is to the court, referred to in the list of competent courts of that State, which is appropriate to the application in hand.

EVIDENCE TO BE TAKEN IN ANOTHER REGULATION STATE FOR USE IN ENGLAND AND WALES

28 Where a person wishes to take a deposition from a person in another Regulation State, the court where the proceedings are taking place may order the issue of a request as is prescribed as Form A in the Taking of Evidence Regulation.

29 An application to the court for an order under rule 14.22 should be made by filing a COP9 application notice in accordance with Part 10.

30 Rule 14.22 provides that the party applying for the order must file a draft form of request in the prescribed form. Where completion of the form requires attachments or documents to accompany the form, these must also be filed.

31 If the court grants an order under rule 14.22, it will send the form of request directly to the designated court.

32 Where the taking of evidence requires the use of an expert, the designated court may require a deposit in advance towards the costs of that expert. Subject to any final order in relation to costs, the party who obtained the order is responsible for the payment of any such deposit which should be deposited with the court for onward transmission. Under the provisions of the Taking of Evidence Regulation, the designated court is not required to execute the request until such payment is received.

33 Article 17 permits the court where proceedings are taking place to take evidence directly from a deponent in another Regulation State if the conditions of the article are satisfied. Direct taking of evidence can only take place if evidence is given voluntarily without the need for coercive measures. Rule 14.22 provides for the court to make an order for the submission of a request to take evidence directly. The form of request is Form I annexed to the Taking of Evidence Regulation and rule 14.22 makes provision for a draft of this form to be filed by the party seeking the order.

An application for an order under rule 14.22 should be by filing a COP9 application notice in accordance with Part 10.

ANNEX A
DRAFT LETTER OF REQUEST (WHERE THE TAKING OF EVIDENCE REGULATION DOES NOT APPLY)

To the Competent Judicial Authority of in the of

I [name] Senior Judge of the Court of Protection of England and Wales respectfully request the assistance of your court with regard to the following matters.

1. An application is now pending in the Court of Protection in England and Wales entitled as follows [*set out full title and case number*] in which [*name*] of [*address*] is the applicant and [*name*] of [*address*] is the respondent.

2. The names and addresses of the representatives or agents of [set out names and addresses of representatives of the parties].

3. The application by the applicant is for:

[*set out the nature of the application*]

[*the order sought, and*]

[*a summary of the facts*.]

4. It is necessary for the purposes of justice and for the due determination of the matter in dispute between the parties that you cause the following witnesses, who are resident within your jurisdiction, to be examined. The names and addresses of the witnesses are as follows: [*set out names and addresses of witnesses*]

5. The witnesses should be examined on oath or if that is not possible within your laws or is impossible of performance by reason of the internal practice and procedure of your court or by reason of practical difficulties, they should be examined in accordance with whatever procedure your laws provide for in these matters.

6. Either

The witness should be examined in accordance with the list of questions annexed hereto.

Or

The witness should be examined regarding [*set out full details of evidence sought*].

N.B. Where the witness is required to produce documents, these should be clearly identified.

7. I would ask that you cause me, or the agents of the parties (if appointed), to be informed of the date and place where the examination is to take place.

8. Finally, I request that you will cause the evidence of the said witness to be reduced into writing and all documents produced on such examinations to be duly marked for identification and that you will further be pleased to authenticate such examinations by the seal of your court or in such other way as is in accordance with your procedure and return the written evidence and documents produced to me addressed as follows:

The Senior Judge

Court of Protection
First Avenue House
42–49 High Holborn
London WC1V 6NP
(DX 160013 Kingsway)

ANNEX B
COUNCIL REGULATION (EC) NO 1206/2001

This regulation can be found on the EU legislation website at //eur-lex.europa.eu.

PRACTICE DIRECTION 14C – FEES FOR EXAMINERS OF THE COURT

III MEN [655]

This practice direction supplements Part 14 of the Court of Protection Rules 2017

GENERAL

1 This practice direction sets out –

(a) how to calculate the fees an examiner of the court ('an examiner') may charge; and

(b) the expenses he may recover.

(Rule 14.15 provides that the court may make an order for evidence to be obtained by the examination of a witness before an examiner.)

2 Subject to any final order or direction of the court in relation to costs, the party who obtained the order for the examination must pay the fees and expenses of the examiner.

(Rule 14.17 permits an examiner to charge a fee for the examination and contains other provisions about his fees and expenses, and rule 14.18 provides who may be appointed as an examiner.)

THE EXAMINATION FEE

3 An examiner may charge an hourly rate for each hour (or part of an hour) that he is engaged in examining the witness.

4 The hourly rate is to be calculated by reference to the formula set out in paragraph 6.

5 The examination fee will be the hourly rate multiplied by the number of hours the examination has taken. That is:

Examination fee = hourly rate x number of hours.

HOW TO CALCULATE THE HOURLY RATE – THE FORMULA

6 Divide the amount of the minimum annual salary of a post within Group 7 of the judicial salary structure as designated by the Review Body on Senior Salaries, by 220 to give 'x'; and then divide 'x' by 6 to give the hourly rate.

That is:

$$\frac{\text{Minimum annual salary}}{220} = x$$

$$\frac{x}{6} = \text{hourly rate}$$

SINGLE FEE CHARGEABLE ON MAKING THE APPOINTMENT FOR EXAMINATION

7 An examiner is also entitled to charge a single fee of twice the hourly rate (calculated in accordance with paragraph 6 above) as "the appointment fee" when the appointment for the examination is made.

8 The examiner is entitled to retain the appointment fee where the witness fails to attend on the date and time arranged.

9 Where the examiner fails to attend on the date and time arranged he may not charge a further appointment fee for arranging a subsequent appointment.

(The examiner need not send the deposition to the court until his fees are paid, unless the court directs otherwise – see rule 14.17(1).)

Examiner's expenses

10 An examiner is also entitled to recover the following expenses –

(a) all reasonable travelling expenses;
(b) any other expenses reasonably incurred; and
(c) subject to paragraph 11, any reasonable charge for the room where the examination takes place.

11 No expenses may be recovered under sub-paragraph 10(c) if the examination takes place at the examiner's usual business address.

(If the examiner's fees and expenses are not paid within a reasonable time he may report the fact to the court - see rule 14.17(3).)

PRACTICE DIRECTION 14D – WITNESS SUMMONS

III MEN [656]

This practice direction supplements Part 14 of the Court of Protection Rules 2017

ISSUE OF A WITNESS SUMMONS

1 Rule 14.13 makes provision as to the taking out of a witness summons.

2 A witness summons may require a witness to –

(a) attend court to give evidence;
(b) produce documents to the court; or
(c) both (a) and (b),

on either a date fixed for a hearing or such date as the court may direct.

3 An application for a witness summons should be made by filing a COP9 application notice in accordance with the Part 10 procedure.

4 In the event the court grants the application, the witness summons will be prepared by the court.

5 A mistake in the name or address of a person named in the witness summons may be corrected if the summons has not been served.

6 If the mistake is a result of an error in the original application notice, an application to correct the mistake should be made by filing a further COP9 application notice in accordance with the Part 10 procedure. The application notice should set out the corrections that need to be made to the witness summons.

7 If the mistake is a result of a clerical mistake, the person taking out the summons should write to the court advising them of the mistake and seeking an amendment under rule 5.15 (clerical mistakes or slips).

8 The corrected summons must be re-sealed by the court and marked 'Amended and Re-sealed'.

TRAVELLING EXPENSES AND COMPENSATION FOR LOSS OF TIME

9 When a witness is served with a witness summons he must be offered a sum to cover his travelling expenses to and from the court and compensation for his loss of time.

10 The sum referred to in paragraph 9 is to be based on the sums payable to witnesses attending the Crown Court.

11 In addition, the witness must be paid such general or other costs as the court may allow.

PRACTICE DIRECTION 14E – SECTION 49 REPORTS

III MEN [657]

This practice direction supplements Part 14 of the Court of Protection Rules 2017

GENERAL

1 Attention is drawn to –

(a) section 49 of the Act – which makes provision for the court to require a report dealing with such matters relating to P as the court may direct;

(b) rule 3.7(2)(a) – which provides that the court, when giving directions, may require a section 49 report and give directions about any such report;
(c) rule 14.24 – which sets out the duties of a person required to prepare a section 49 report and specifies to whom the report may be sent; and
(d) rule 14.25 – which makes provision for the court to permit written questions to be put to a person who has made a section 49 report.

THE COURT'S DIRECTION FOR A REPORT

2 The Annex to this Practice Direction contains the form of an order requiring a report under section 49 of the Act and the forms of directions relating to the report. When requiring a section 49 report, the court will as far as possible base its order and directions on those forms.

3 The following are common factors which the court may consider when deciding whether to order a section 49 report –

(a) where P objects to the substantive application or wishes to be heard by the court and does not qualify for legal aid;
(b) where it has not been possible to appoint a litigation friend or rule 1.2 representative, including where the court has made a direction under rule 1.2(5);
(c) where a party is a litigant in person and does not qualify for legal aid;
(d) where the public body has recent knowledge of P; or it is reasonably expected that they have recent knowledge of P; or should have knowledge due to their statutory responsibilities under housing, social and/or health care legislation;
(e) the role of the public body is likely to be relevant to the decisions which the court will be asked to make;
(f) the application relates to an attorney or deputy and involves the exercise of the functions of the Public Guardian;
(g) evidence before the court does not adequately confirm the position regarding P's capacity or where it is borderline; or if information is required to inform any best interests decision to be made in relation to P by the court.

REPORTS BY PUBLIC GUARDIAN OR A COURT OF PROTECTION VISITOR

4 Where a report is to be prepared by either the Public Guardian or a Court of Protection Visitor , a copy of the approved order, the directions and the information described in paragraph 14 below will be sent by the Court to the Public Guardian.

5 In the case of a report which is to be made by a Court of Protection Visitor, the Public Guardian must ensure that a person is nominated from the panel of the General Visitors or the panel of Special Visitors, as appropriate.

6 The nomination of a Court of Protection Visitor should be made before the end of the period of 7 days beginning with the date on which the Public Guardian received a copy of the order.

REPORTS UNDER ARRANGEMENTS MADE BY A LOCAL AUTHORITY OR AN NHS BODY

7 Wherever practicable, before making an application for an order requiring a report under section 49, a party to proceedings should use their best endeavours to:

(a) make contact with an appropriate person within the relevant local authority or NHS body so they are made aware that an application is to be made; its purpose; and the issues or questions which are hoped to be addressed within the report;
(b) identify a named person or by reference to their office ('the senior officer') within the relevant local authority or NHS body who will be able to receive the court order on its behalf; and

MENTAL CAPACITY AND MENTAL HEALTH

(c) enquire as to the reasonableness and time scales for providing the report should the court order it.

8 The party making the application must submit a draft letter of instructions for the purpose of accompanying the order.

9 The court will make enquiry of the party making the application as to what efforts have been made to comply with paragraph 7 above, and the response of the relevant local authority or NHS body, and will take this into consideration before making an order.

10 Where a report is to be prepared under arrangements made by a local authority or an NHS body , a copy of the approved order (which is binding, notwithstanding that it may not yet be sealed), the information described in paragraph 14 below and the accompanying letter of instruction will be served by either (i) the party who made the application for a section 49 report or (ii) in the event that no party made the application, by the party determined by the court to be the most appropriate party to arrange service on the senior officer as soon as is reasonably practicable but in any event within 48 hours of the making of the order.

11 Upon receipt of the order the senior officer must ensure that –

(a) a person with appropriate expertise/knowledge is nominated to make the report; and
(b) the parties are notified of the name and contact details of the nominated person as soon as practicable.

12 The nomination should be made before the end of the period of 7 days beginning with the date on which the senior officer received a copy of the order.

13 The order must follow the format as set out in the Annex to this Practice Direction and specify the matters required to be addressed in paragraphs 9 and 10 therein.

ACCESS TO INFORMATION AND INTERVIEW P

14 The court will generally provide, or give permission to the party applying for the section 49 order to provide, to the person who is to produce a report –

(a) a copy of the application form, its annexes and any supporting evidence as may be redacted by direction of the court;
(b) the name and contact details of P;
(c) the name and contact details of the parties; and
(d) the name and contact details of any legal representative of a person specified in (b) or (c); and
(e) name and contact details of such other persons who are reasonably likely to be able to provide assistance to the nominated person for the completion of the report.

15 The court order requiring the report, the directions relating to it and the information described in paragraph 14 will generally be sent when the order is served by the party who is required to do so, by first class mail, electronic mail or by facsimile. If the circumstances warrant a different form of communication, the documents and information will also be sent by first class mail, electronic mail or by facsimile at the first available opportunity.

16 Section 49(7) of the Act sets out other documents relating to P which the Public Guardian or a Court of Protection Visitor may examine or take copies of for the purpose of making the report. Where appropriate, the order may also allow the same documents to be examined and copied by the nominated person who is to prepare the section 49 report under arrangements made by the relevant local authority or NHS body.

17 Sections 49(8) and (9) of the Act sets out that the Public Guardian or a Court of Protection Visitor may interview P in private. Where appropriate, the order may also allow P to be interviewed in private by the nominated person who is to prepare the section 49 report under arrangements made by the relevant local authority or NHS body.

THE CONTENTS OF THE REPORT

18 The person required to prepare a section 49 report must –

(a) prepare it having regard to the provisions of rule 14.24;
(b) produce it in the manner specified in this Practice Direction (subject to any directions given by the court); and
(c) produce it in accordance with the timetable set out in the court's directions.

19 The report should contain four main sections. These are –

(a) the details of the person who prepared the report;
(b) the details of P;
(c) the matters and material considered in preparing the report; and
(d) the conclusions reached.

20 In the first section (details of the person who prepared the report), the report should –

(a) state the full name of the person who prepared the report;
(b) state whether he was appointed under section 49(2) or (3) of the Act;
(c) state whether he is –
 (i) the Public Guardian,
 (ii) a General Visitor,
 (iii) a Special Visitor,
 (iv) an officer, employee or other person nominated by a local authority, or
 (v) an officer, employee or other person nominated by an NHS body;
(d) state his occupation or employment (for example, social worker employed by a local authority or general practitioner in private practice); and
(e) list his qualifications and experience.

21 In the second section (P's details), the report should (unless an order to the contrary pursuant to rule 5.11 has been made) –

(a) state P's full name, date of birth and present place of residence;
(b) state P's nationality, racial origin, cultural background and religious persuasion (if appropriate);
(c) identify P's immediate family (specifying their relationship to P and contact details);
(d) identify any other person who has a significant role in P's life (for example, a close friend or a carer) specifying their role and contact details; and
(e) give a summary of P's medical history.

22 In the third section (matters and material considered), the report should –

(a) list any interview conducted with P (specifying time and place);
(b) list any interview conducted with one or more persons other than P (specifying time and place);
(c) state –
 (i) whether any examination of P was conducted by a Special Visitor under section 49(9) of the Act, and
 (ii) the name and qualifications of any person who assisted with any such examination;
(d) give a summary of any key events in P's life which appear to have a direct bearing on the matters to be dealt with in the report;
(e) set out the details of any of the following material which was relied on in the preparation of the report –
 (i) any literature or other material,
 (ii) any records obtained under section 49(7) of the Act;
(f) set out the details of facts and opinions relied on in the preparation of the report (ensuring that there is a clear distinction between the two);
(g) where there is a range of opinion on an issue addressed in the report –
 (i) summarise the range of opinion,
 (ii) state the views held by the person who prepared the report and give reasons for them, and
 (iii) if those views are qualified in any way, state the nature of the qualification; and

MENTAL CAPACITY AND MENTAL HEALTH

(h) indicate which of the facts are within the knowledge of the person who prepared the report.

23 In the fourth section (conclusions), the report should –

(a) identify any issues or questions which were specified in the directions given by the court as being matters in which the court had a particular interest;
(b) address clearly such issues or questions;
(c) state clearly all conclusions reached by the person who prepared the report;
(d) state clearly the recommendations made by the person who prepared the report; and
(e) contain a statement of truth in the following terms:

'I confirm that insofar as the facts stated in my report are within my own knowledge I have made clear which they are, and I believe them to be true, and that the opinions I have expressed represent my true and complete professional opinion.'

ANNEX
ORDER FOR SECTION 49 REPORT

Requirement for section 49 report

1 A report is required pursuant to section 49 of the Mental Capacity Act 2005 in relation to [*insert name of P*], under Court of Protection case number [*insert case number*].

Person required to prepare the report

2 The report must be prepared by [the Public Guardian] [a Court of Protection Visitor who is a General Visitor] [a Court of Protection Visitor who is a Special Visitor] [a person nominated by the local authority] [XX, a person nominated by the local authority and considered by them to have the appropriate expertise/knowledge to provide the report] [a person nominated by the NHS body] [YY, a person nominated by the NHS body and considered by them to have the appropriate expertise/knowledge to provide the report].

3 [In the case of a report to be prepared by [a Special Visitor, the Visitor] [a medically qualified practitioner, the practitioner] may carry out in private a [medical] [psychiatric] [psychological] examination of P's capacity or condition].

Producing the report

4 [The report must be made to the court in writing]. [The report must be made orally to the court].

5 The report must be produced on or before [*insert date*].

6 [Where the report is made in writing, it must be delivered to the court by [first class post] [electronic mail] [facsimile].

Context of report

7 The court has received an application for the following [order/direction/declaration]:

[insert brief details of application, for example,

(a) XY be [appointed] [removed] as the [deputy] [attorney] for property and affairs/personal welfare for [*insert the name of P*];

(b) [*insert the name of P*] lacks mental capacity to [*insert decision, for example conduct the proceedings/ objects to . . . ../ decide where to reside*];
(c) it is in the best interests of [*insert the name of P*] that [*insert issue*];
(d) it is lawful in respect of [*insert name of P*] that [*insert issue*].

8 [*insert case summary*].

Content of report

9 Subject to any directions given under paragraph 11, the report must contain all the material required by relevant practice direction and be prepared in the form there specified.

10 The court is particularly interested in the following issues or questions and these must also be addressed in the report:

[*for example*

(a) whether [*insert the name of P*] has capacity in accordance with sections 2 and 3 of the Mental Capacity Act 2005, to [*insert issue, for example, object to/conduct proceedings/decide where to live*];
(b) if [he/she] lacks capacity, ascertain to the extent it is practicable and appropriate [his/her] present wishes and feelings and the beliefs and values that would be likely to influence [him/her] with regard to [insert the matter to which the application relates];
(c) if [he/she] lacks capacity, ascertain [his/her] present wishes and feelings as to how [his /her] participation could be secured by the appointment of a representative pursuant to Rule 1.2 of the Court of Protection Rules 2017;
(d) whether [he/she] should have the opportunity to address (directly or indirectly) the judge determining the application and the circumstances in which that should occur;
(e) describe [*insert the name of P*]'s circumstances;
(f) services and support would be provided to [*insert the name of P*]/funded for [*insert the name of P*] by [*insert the name of the public body*];
(g) whether what is sought by the application could be effectively achieved in a way which is less restrictive of [*insert name of P*]'s rights and freedom;
(h) the Public Guardian's views as to . . . .].

11 The report need not address the following:

(a) . . . .
(b) . . . .

Persons to whom report is likely to be disclosed

12 The report is to be prepared on the assumption that the court will pursuant to rule 14.24(4) of the Court of Protection Rules 2017 send a copy of it to the parties and such other persons as the court may direct. The court further directs that the report be sent to [*insert the name of P*] [*members of P's family*] [*XX County Council/ NHS Hospital Trust/ Clinical Commissioning Group/Local Health Board*] [*the parties only*] [*the parties and their legal representatives*] [*such other persons as the court may direct*]]

Persons to contact

13 The author of the report is authorised to contact and seek to interview the following person(s) for the purpose of preparing the report, with their contact details provided with this order:

(a) [*insert the name of P*] [in private] [in the presence of XX];
(b) [the parties];
(c) [their legal representatives];

(d) [*Others which may include for example, family, care and health providers*].

14 The author of the report [may interview [*insert the name of P*] in private] [may not interview [*insert the name of P*]].

Access to records

15 For the purpose of enabling the author to prepare the report, [he/she] is authorised to examine and have a copy of the following, which relate to [*insert the name of P*] and are relevant to the application:

[for example,

(a) a copy of the application form, its annexes and any supporting evidence [such papers may be redacted as required by the court];
(b) any health record;
(c) any record of, or held by, a local authority and compiled in connection with a social services function, and
(d) any record held by a person registered under Part 2 of the Care Standards Act 2000 or Chapter 2 of Part 1 of the Health and Social Care Act 2008.]

Where a report is made under arrangements by a local authority or NHS Body

16 [The party who made the application for a section 49 report] [the party the court decides is the most appropriate] shall serve a copy of the order on [the senior officer who will accept this order on behalf of the [*insert name of public body*] and who will inform the court of the name of the person who will prepare the report] [XX being the person identified as having the appropriate expertise/knowledge to provide the report] within 7 days of service of this order, notwithstanding that in the event the order has not been sealed by the court, it shall be binding.

Record of lack of representation

17 Pursuant to rule 1.2(5) of the Court of Protection Rules 2017, the Court records that [*insert name of P*] has been directed to be joined as a party but such joinder has not occurred because no litigation friend or accredited legal representative has been appointed because [*insert reasons*].

Other directions

(a) This order having been made without a hearing or without notice to any person affected by it; P, any party to the proceedings and any person affected by this order may apply to the court within 21 days of the order being served for reconsideration of this order pursuant to rule 13.4 of the Court of Protection Rules 2017 by filing an application notice (Form COP9) in accordance with Part 10 of those Rules]

[*or*]

(a) This order having been made [at an attended hearing] *(or if urgent)* [at an urgent hearing] leave to any person adversely affected by this order to apply to the court within 7 days of the order being served, to set aside, vary or stay the relevant disputed provision of this order by filing an application notice (Form COP9) in accordance with Part 10 of the Court of Protection Rules 2017];
(b) . . . .

PART 15
EXPERTS

III MEN [658]

15.1 References to expert

A reference to an expert in this Part—

(a) is to an expert who has been instructed to give or prepare evidence for the purpose of court proceedings; but

(b) does not include any person instructed to make a report under section 49 of the Act.

III MEN [658.1]

Practice Direction 15A provides guidance as to the general requirements of expert evidence, the form and content of the report, and as to the submission of questions (**III MEN [671]**). Practice Direction 14E should be followed if the report is ordered pursuant to s 49 of the Mental Capacity Act 2005 (**III MEN [657]**). The comments of Baker J in the cases of *SC v BS and A Local authority* [2012] COPLR 567; *PH v A Local Authority* [2011] EWHC 1704 (Fam), provide useful benchmarks for the selection of experts and the approach to undertaking the task of an assessment.

III MEN [659]

15.2 Restriction on filing an expert's report

(1) No person may file expert evidence unless the court or a practice direction permits, or if it is filed with the application form and is evidence—

(a) that P is a person who lacks capacity to make a decision or decisions in relation to the matter or matters to which the application relates;

(b) as to P's best interests; or

(c) that is required by any rule or practice direction to be filed with the application form.

(2) An applicant may only rely on any expert evidence so filed in support of the application form to the extent and for the purposes that the court allows.

(Rule 9.4(a) requires the applicant to file any evidence upon which the applicant wishes to rely with the application form.)

III MEN [659.1]

Guidance on the control by the court of use of expert evidence An important element of judicial case management is the control and authorisation of the use of expert evidence. Practice Direction 15A, para 1 reasserts that after an application form is issued, no person may file expert evidence other that by authority of the court or if a practice direction permits (**III MEN [671]**).

III MEN [660]

15.3 Duty to restrict expert evidence

(1) Expert evidence shall be restricted to that which is necessary to assist the court to resolve the issues in the proceedings.

(2) The court may give permission to file or adduce expert evidence as mentioned in rule 15.2(1) and 15.5(1) only if satisfied that the evidence—

(a) is necessary to assist the court to resolve the issues in the proceedings; and

(b) cannot otherwise be provided either—

(i) by a rule 1.2 representative; or

(ii) in a report under section 49 of the Act.

III MEN [661]

15.4 Experts—overriding duty to the court

(1) It is the duty of the expert to help the court on the matters within the expert's expertise.

(2) This duty overrides any obligation to the person from whom the expert has received instructions or by whom the expert is paid.

III MEN [662]

15.5 Court's power to restrict expert evidence

(1) Subject to rule 15.2, no party may file or adduce expert evidence unless the court or a practice direction permits.

(2) When a party applies for a direction under this rule, that party must—

- (a) identify the field in respect of which that party wishes to rely upon expert evidence, and the issues to which the expert evidence is to relate;
- (b) where practicable, identify the expert in that field upon whose evidence the party wishes to rely;
- (c) provide any other material information about the expert;
- (d) state whether the expert evidence could be obtained from a single joint expert;
- (e) provide any other information or documents required by a practice direction; and
- (f) provide a draft letter of instruction to the expert.

(3) When deciding whether to give permission as mentioned in paragraph (1), the court is to have regard in particular to—

- (a) the issues to which the expert evidence would relate;
- (b) the questions which the expert would answer;
- (c) the impact which giving permission would be likely to have on the timetable, duration and conduct of the proceedings;
- (d) any failure to comply with any direction of the court about expert evidence; and
- (e) the cost of the expert evidence.

(4) Where a direction is given under this rule, the court shall specify—

- (a) the field or fields in respect of which the expert evidence is to be provided;
- (b) the questions which the expert is required to answer; and
- (c) the date by which the expert is to provide the evidence.

(5) The court may specify the person who is to provide the evidence referred to in paragraph (3).

(6) Where a direction is given under this rule for a party to call an expert or put in evidence an expert's report, the court shall give directions for the service of the report on the parties and on such other persons as the court may direct.

(7) The court may limit the amount of the expert's fees and expenses that the party who wishes to rely upon the expert may recover from any other party.

III MEN [663]

15.6 General requirement for expert evidence to be given in a written report

Expert evidence is to be given in a written report unless the court directs otherwise.

III MEN [664]

15.7 Written questions to experts

(1) A party may put written questions to—

- (a) an expert instructed by another party; or

(b) a single joint expert appointed under rule 15.12,

about a report prepared by such a person.

(2) Written questions under paragraph (1)—

(a) may be put once only;

(b) must be put within 28 days beginning with the date on which the expert's report was served;

(c) must be for the purpose only of clarification of the report; and

(d) must be copied and sent to the other parties at the same time as they are sent to the expert.

(3) Paragraph (2) does not apply in any case where—

(a) the court permits it to be done on a further occasion;

(b) the other party or parties agree; or

(c) any practice direction provides otherwise.

(4) An expert's answers to questions put in accordance with paragraph (1) shall be treated as part of the expert's report.

(5) Paragraph (6) applies where—

(a) a party has put a written question to an expert instructed by another party in accordance with this rule; and

(b) the expert does not answer that question.

(6) The court may make one or both of the following orders in relation to the party who instructed the expert—

(a) that the party may not rely upon the evidence of that expert; or

(b) that the party may not recover the fees and expenses of that expert, or part of them, from any other party.

(7) Unless the court directs otherwise, and subject to any final costs order that may be made, the instructing party is responsible for the payment of the expert's fees and expenses, including the expert's costs of answering questions put by any other party.

III MEN [664.1]

Guidance on questions to experts Practice Direction 15A, paras 13–14 give guidance on questions to experts (**III MEN [671]**).

III MEN [665]

15.8 Contents of expert's report

(1) The court may give directions as to the matters to be covered in an expert's report.

(2) An expert's report must comply with the requirements set out in the relevant practice direction.

(3) At the end of an expert's report there must be a statement that the expert—

(a) understands his or her duty to the court; and

(b) has complied with that duty.

(4) The expert's report must state the substance of all material instructions, whether written or oral, on the basis of which the report was written.

(5) The instructions to the expert shall not be privileged against disclosure.

III MEN [665.1]

Guidance on the content of an expert report Practice Direction 15A, paras 8–12 provides guidance on the content of the report of an expert, (**III MEN [671]**). Paragraph 11 sets out the form of the statement of truth and Practice Direction 4B sets out more detailed requirements (**III MEN [524]**). The practice direction draws attention to rule 5.6, the verification of documents by statement of truth and consequences of verifying a false statement (**III MEN [531]**).

III MEN [666]

15.9 Use by one party of expert's report disclosed by another

Where a party has disclosed an expert's report, any party may use that expert's report as evidence at any hearing in the proceedings.

III MEN [667]

15.10 Discussions between experts

(1) The court may, at any stage, direct a discussion between experts for the purpose of requiring the experts to—

(a) identify and discuss the expert issues in the proceedings; and

(b) where possible, reach an agreed opinion on those issues.

(2) The court may specify the issues which the experts must discuss.

(3) The court may direct that following a discussion between the experts they must prepare a statement for the court showing—

(a) those issues on which they agree; and

(b) those issues on which they disagree and a summary of their reasons for disagreeing.

(4) Unless the court directs otherwise, the content of the discussions between experts may be referred to at any hearing or at any stage in the proceedings.

III MEN [667.1]

Narrowing issues through discussion In *Mental Health and Acute Trust v DD* [2014] EWCOP 8 Mrs Justice Pauffley commended the procedure for experts of differing disciplines to discuss the expert issues, seek to reach agreement, narrow the same and preparing a final statement summarising the areas of agreement and disagreement.

III MEN [668]

15.11 Expert's right to ask court for directions

(1) An expert may file a written request for directions to assist in carrying out the expert's functions as an expert.

(2) An expert must, unless the court directs otherwise, provide a copy of any proposed request for directions under paragraph (1)—

(a) to the party instructing the expert, at least 7 days before filing the request; and

(b) to all other parties, at least 4 days before filing it.

(3) The court, when it gives directions, may also direct that a party be served with a copy of the directions.

III MEN [668.1]

Applications to the court by an expert to clarify instructions In *SMBC v WMP, RG and GG (by their litigation friend, the Official Solicitor), HSG, SK, and SKG* [2011] EWHC B13 (COP) HHJ Cardinal concluded that where an expert discovered a lacuna in the information before him, good practice should have led to a question being raised under what is now rule 15.11 before completing the report.

III MEN [669]

15.12 Court's power to direct that evidence is to be given by a single joint expert

(1) Where two or more parties wish to submit expert evidence on a particular issue, the court may direct that the evidence on that issue is to be given by one expert only.

(2) The parties wishing to submit the expert evidence are called "the instructing parties".

(3) Where the instructing parties cannot agree who should be the expert, the court may—

(a) select the expert from a list prepared or identified by the instructing parties; or

(b) direct the manner by which the expert is to be selected.

III MEN [670]

15.13 Instructions to a single joint expert

(1) Where the court gives a direction under rule 15.12 for a single joint expert to be used, the instructions are to be contained in a jointly agreed letter unless the court directs otherwise.

(2) Where the instructions are to be contained in a jointly agreed letter, in default of agreement the instructions may be determined by the court on the written request of any instructing party copied to the other instructing parties.

(3) Where the court permits the instructing parties to give separate instructions to a single joint expert, unless the court directs otherwise, when an instructing party gives instructions to the expert, that party must at the same time send a copy of the instructions to the other instructing party or parties.

(4) The court may give directions about—

(a) the payment of the expert's fees and expenses; and

(b) any inspection, examination or experiments which the expert wishes to carry out.

(5) The court may, before an expert is instructed, limit the amount that can be paid by way of fees and expense to the expert.

(6) Unless the court directs otherwise, and subject to any final costs order that may be made, the instructing parties are jointly and severally liable for the payment of the expert's fees and expenses.

PRACTICE DIRECTION 15A – EXPERTS

III MEN [671]

This practice direction supplements Part 15 of the Court of Protection Rules 2017

GENERAL

1 Part 15 is intended to limit the use of expert evidence to that which is necessary to assist the court to resolve the issues in the proceedings. After an application form is issued, no person may file expert evidence unless the court or a practice direction permits.

EXPERT EVIDENCE – GENERAL REQUIREMENTS

2 It is the duty of an expert to help the court on matters within his own expertise.

3 Expert evidence should be the independent product of the expert uninfluenced by the pressures of the proceedings.

4 An expert should assist the court by providing objective, unbiased opinion on matters within his expertise, and should not assume the role of an advocate.

5 An expert should consider all material facts, including those which might detract from his opinion.

6 An expert should make it clear –

(a) when a question or issue falls outside his expertise; and
(b) when he is not able to reach a definite opinion, for example because he has insufficient information.

7 If, after producing a report, an expert changes his view on any material matter, such change of view should be communicated to all the parties without delay, and when appropriate to the court.

FORM AND CONTENT OF EXPERT'S REPORT

8 An expert's report should be addressed to the court and not to the party from whom the expert has received his instructions.

9 An expert's report must –

(a) give details of the expert's qualifications;
(b) give details of any literature or other material which the expert has relied on in making the report;
(c) contain a statement setting out the substance of all facts and instructions given to the expert which are material to the opinions expressed in the report or upon which those opinions are based (or annex the instructions insofar as they are in writing);
(d) make clear which of the facts stated in the report are within the expert's own knowledge;
(e) say who carried out any examination, measurement, test or experiment which the expert has used for the report, give the qualifications of that person, and say whether or not the test or experiment has been carried out under the expert's supervision;
(f) where there is a range of opinion on the matters dealt with in the report –
    (i) summarise the range of opinion, and
    (ii) give reasons for his own opinion;
(g) contain a summary of the conclusions reached;
(h) if the expert is not able to give his opinion without qualification, state the qualification; and
(i) contain a statement that the expert understands his duty to the court, and has complied and will continue to comply with that duty.

10 An expert's report must be verified by a statement of truth as well as containing the statements required in paragraph 9(h) and (i) above.

11 The form of the statement of truth is as follows:

> 'I confirm that insofar as the facts stated in my report are within my own knowledge I have made clear which they are and I believe them to be true and that the opinions I have expressed represent my true and complete professional opinion.'

12 Attention is drawn to rule 5.6 which sets out the consequences of verifying a document containing a false statement without an honest belief in its truth.

(Practice direction B accompanying Part 5 sets out more detailed requirements for statements of truth.)

QUESTIONS TO EXPERTS

13 Questions asked for the purpose of clarifying the expert's report should be put, in writing, to the expert not later than 28 days after service of the expert's report.

14 Where a party sends a written question or questions direct to an expert, a copy of the questions should, at the same time, be sent to the other party or parties.

ORDERS

15 Where an order requires an act to be done by an expert, or otherwise affects an expert, the party instructing that expert must serve a copy of the order on the expert instructed by him. In the case of a jointly instructed expert, the applicant

must serve the order.

PART 16
DISCLOSURE

III MEN [672]

16.1 Meaning of disclosure

A party discloses a document by stating that the document exists or has existed.

III MEN [673]

16.2 General or specific disclosure

(1) The court may either on its own initiative or on the application of a party make an order to give general or specific disclosure.

(2) General disclosure requires a party to disclose—

- (a) the documents on which that party relies; and
- (b) the documents which—
  - (i) adversely affect that party's own case;
  - (ii) adversely affect another party's case; or
  - (iii) support another party's case.

(3) An order for specific disclosure is an order that a party must do one or more of the following things—

- (a) disclose documents or classes of documents specified in the order;
- (b) carry out a search to the extent stated in the order; or
- (c) disclose any document located as a result of that search.

(4) A party's duty to disclose documents is limited to documents which are or have been in that party's control.

(5) For the purposes of paragraph (4) a party has or has had a document in that party's control if—

- (a) it is or was in that party's physical possession;
- (b) that party has or has had possession of it; or
- (c) that party has or has had a right to inspect or take copies of it.

III MEN [673.1]

General and specific disclosure In the case of *Enfield LBC v SA (by her litigation friend, the Official Solicitor) FA and KA* [2010] EWHC 196 (Admin), [2010] 1 FLR 1836, the court considered the issues of disclosure contrasting the obligation for full and frank disclosure within the Family Courts, and the obligations under the Court of Protection Rules. The court considered that making a specific disclosure order under r 16.2(3) would be justified in requiring such disclosure in fact finding cases. See now the duty of the parties under rule 1.4(2)(d) to be 'full and frank in the disclosure of information and evidence to the court (including any disclosure ordered under Part 16) (**III MEN [495]**).

III MEN [674]

16.3 Procedure for general or specific disclosure

(1) This rule applies where the court makes an order under rule 16.2 to give general or specific disclosure.

(2) Each party must make, and serve on every other party, a list of documents to be disclosed.

(3) A copy of each list must be filed within 7 days of the date on which it is served.

(4) The list must identify the documents in a convenient order and manner and as concisely as possible.

(5) The list must indicate—

(a) the documents in respect of which the party claims a right or duty to withhold inspection (see rule 16.7); and
(b) the documents that are no longer in the party's control, stating what has happened to them.

III MEN [675]

16.4 Ongoing duty of disclosure

(1) Where the court makes an order to give general or specific disclosure under rule 16.2, any party to whom the order applies is under a continuing duty to provide such disclosure as is required by the order until the proceedings are concluded.

(2) If a document to which the duty of disclosure imposed by paragraph (1) extends comes to a party's notice at any time during the proceedings, that party must immediately notify every other party.

III MEN [676]

16.5 Right to inspect documents

(1) A party to whom a document has been disclosed has a right to inspect any document disclosed to that party except where—
(a) the document is no longer in the control of the party who disclosed it; or
(b) the party disclosing the document has a right or duty to withhold inspection of it.

(2) The right to inspect disclosed documents extends to any document mentioned in—
(a) a document filed or served in the course of the proceedings by any other party; or
(b) correspondence sent by any other party.

III MEN [677]

16.6 Inspection and copying of documents

(1) Where a party has a right to inspect a document, that party—
(a) must give the party who disclosed the document written notice of the wish to inspect it; and
(b) may request a copy of the document.

(2) Not more than 14 days after the date on which the party who disclosed the document received the notice under paragraph (1)(a), that party must permit inspection of the document at a convenient place and time.

(3) Where a party has requested a copy of the document, the party who disclosed the document must supply the requesting party with a copy not more than 14 days after the date on which the request was received.

(4) For the purposes of paragraph (2), the party who disclosed the document must give reasonable notice of the time and place for inspection.

(5) For the purposes of paragraph (3), the party requesting a copy of the document is responsible for the payment of reasonable copying costs, subject to any final costs order that may be made.

III MEN [678]

16.7 Claim to withhold inspection or disclosure of documents

(1) A party who wishes to claim a right or duty to withhold inspection of a document, or part of a document, must state in writing—
(a) that that party has such a right or duty; and
(b) the grounds on which that party claims that right or duty.

(2) The statement must be made in the list in which the document is disclosed (see rule 16.3(2)).

(3) A party may, by filing an application notice in accordance with Part 10, apply to the court to decide whether the claim made under paragraph (1) should be upheld.

III MEN [678.1]

Disclosure and redaction the powers of the court In *RC v CC* [2014] EWCOP 131 the President considered in detail the historic approach to open justice and that 'non-disclosure should be the exception and not the rule'. The President examined the concept of 'strict necessity', and accepted that the burden falling on those seeking non-disclosure was 'a heavy one', with the rule and case law pointing to a presumption in favour of disclosure. The court reminded itself of its powers to disclose redacted material as a method of achieving the presumption.

III MEN [679]

16.8 Consequence of failure to disclose documents or permit inspection

A party may not rely upon any document which that party fails to disclose or in respect of which that party fails to permit inspection, unless the court permits.

PART 17
LITIGATION FRIENDS AND RULE 1.2 REPRESENTATIVES

SECTION 1—LITIGATION FRIENDS

III MEN [680]

17.1 Who may act as a litigation friend

(1) A person may act as a litigation friend on behalf of a person mentioned in paragraph (2) if that person—

- (a) can fairly and competently conduct proceedings on behalf of that person; and
- (b) has no interests adverse to those of that person.

(2) The persons for whom a litigation friend may act are—

- (a) P;
- (b) a child;
- (c) a protected party.

III MEN [680.1]

Guidance on appointments of a litigation friend Practice Direction 17A provides supplemental guidance to the appointment of a litigation friend. Provision is made for appointment without a court order (paras 4–11), appointment by court order (paras 12–14), the changing of a litigation friend (paras 15–17), and the procedure where the need for a litigation friend comes to an end (para 18) (**III MEN [694]**).

III MEN [681]

17.2 Requirement for a litigation friend

(1) This rule does not apply to P (whether P is an adult or a child).

(2) A protected party (if a party to the proceedings) must have a litigation friend.

(3) A child (if a party to the proceedings) must have a litigation friend to conduct those proceedings on that child's behalf unless the court makes an order under paragraph (4).

(4) The court may make an order permitting a child to conduct proceedings without a litigation friend.

(5) An application for an order under paragraph (4)—

(a) may be made by the child;

(b) if the child already has a litigation friend, must be made on notice to the litigation friend; and

(c) if the child has no litigation friend, may be made without notice.

(6) Where—

(a) the court has made an order under paragraph (4); and

(b) it subsequently appears to the court that it is desirable for a litigation friend to conduct the proceedings on behalf of the child,

the court may appoint a person to be the child's litigation friend.

III MEN [314.1]

Appointing the relevant person's representative as litigation friend In *AB (by a litigation friend NW) v A Local authority* [2011] EWHC 3151 (COP), [2011] NLJR 1744, [2011] All ER (D) 37 (Dec) Mostyn J examined the application of the principles established in Part 17, and the appropriateness of appointing a relevant person's representative (see Sch A1 of the Mental Capacity Act 2005 and Part 10 (**III MEN [108]**), as opposed to the Official Solicitor as litigation friend. See also *Re NRA* [2015] EWCOP 59, 165 NLJ 7671, [2015] All ER (D) 122 (Sep) and the discussion on the role of litigation friend in streamlined procedures for deprivation of liberty (**III MEN [243]** above).

III MEN [682]

17.3 Litigation friend without a court order

(1) This rule does not apply—

(a) in relation to P;

(b) where the court has appointed a person under rule 17.4 or 17.5; or

(c) where the Official Solicitor is to act as a litigation friend.

(2) A deputy with the power to conduct legal proceedings in the name of a protected party or on the protected party's behalf is entitled to be a litigation friend of the protected party in any proceedings to which the deputy's power relates.

(3) If no-one has been appointed by the court or, in the case of a protected party, there is no deputy with the power to conduct proceedings, a person who wishes to act as a litigation friend must—

(a) file a certificate of suitability stating that they satisfy the conditions in rule 17.1(1); and

(b) serve the certificate of suitability on—

(i) the person on whom an application form is to be served in accordance with rule 6.4 (service on children and protected parties); and

(ii) every other person who is a party to the proceedings.

(4) If the person referred to in paragraph (2) wishes to act as a litigation friend for the protected party, that person must file and serve on the persons mentioned in paragraph (3)(b) a copy of the court order which appointed that person.

III MEN [682.1]

Procedure and guidance Practice Direction 17A provides guidance at paras 4–11 (**III MEN [694]**).

Form COP22 is the relevant form of certificate of suitability of a litigation friend.

III MEN [683]

17.4 Litigation friend by court order

(1) The court may make an order appointing—

(a) the Official Solicitor; or

(b) some other person,

to act as a litigation friend for a protected party, a child or P.

(2) The court may make an order under paragraph (1)—

(a) either on its own initiative or on the application of any person; but

(b) only with the consent of the person to be appointed.

(3) An application for an order under paragraph (1) must be supported by evidence.

(4) The court may not appoint a litigation friend under this rule unless it is satisfied that the person to be appointed satisfies the conditions in rule 17.1(1).

(5) The court may at any stage of the proceedings give directions as to the appointment of a litigation friend.

(Rule 1.2 requires the court to consider how P should participate in the proceedings, which may be by way of being made a party and the appointment of a litigation friend under this Part.)

III MEN [316.1]

Practice and guidance Practice Direction 17A provides guidance at paras 12–14 (**III MEN [694]**).

For consideration of the appointment of the Official Solicitor as litigation friend, see *AB (by a litigation friend NW) v A Local authority* [2011] EWHC 3151 (COP), [2011] NLJR 1744, [2011] All ER (D) 37 (Dec) and in respect of welfare cases, *Practice Guidance: Official Solicitor acting as Guardian ad Litem or Litigation Friend* [2011] 1 FLR 944 (**III MEN [5]**). See also *Re NRA* [2015] EWCOP 59, 165 NLJ 7671, [2015] All ER (D) 122 (Sep) and the discussion on the role of litigation friend in streamlined procedures for deprivation of liberty (**III MEN [619]** above).

III MEN [684]

17.5 Court's power to prevent a person from acting as a litigation friend or to bring an end to an appointment of a person as a litigation friend or to appoint another one

(1) The court may either on its own initiative or on the application of any person—

(a) direct that a person may not act as a litigation friend;

(b) bring to an end a litigation friend's appointment; or

(c) appoint a new litigation friend in place of an existing one.

(2) If an application for an order under paragraph (1) is based on the conduct of the litigation friend, it must be supported by evidence.

(3) The court may not appoint a litigation friend under this rule unless it is satisfied that the person to be appointed satisfies the conditions in rule 17.1(1).

(4) The appointment of a litigation friend continues until brought to an end by court order.

(Rule 13.1 (procedure for disputing the court's jurisdiction) applies if P has capacity in relation to the matter or matters to which the application relates.)

III MEN [684.1]

Procedural guidance Practice Direction 17A provides guidance at paras 15–17 (**III MEN [694]**).

III MEN [685]

17.6 Appointment of litigation friend by court order—supplementary

The applicant must serve a copy of an application for an order under rule 17.4 or 17.5 on—

(a) the person on whom an application form is to be served in accordance with rule 6.4 (service on children and protected parties);

(b) every other person who is a party to the proceedings;

(c) any person who is the litigation friend, or who is purporting to act as the litigation friend, when the application is made; and

(d) unless that person is the applicant, the person who it is proposed should be the litigation friend,

as soon as practicable and in any event within 14 days of the date on which the application was issued.

III MEN [686]

17.7 Procedure where appointment of a litigation friend comes to an end for a child

When a child reaches 18, provided the child is neither—

(a) P; nor

(b) a protected party,

the litigation friend's appointment ends and the child must serve notice on every other party—

(i) stating that the child has reached full age;

(ii) stating that the appointment of the litigation friend has ended; and

(iii) providing an address for service.

III MEN [687]

17.8 Practice direction in relation to litigation friends

A practice direction may make additional or supplementary provision in relation to litigation friends.

III MEN [687.1]

Applications to the court Practice Direction 17A provides guidance at para 18 (**III MEN [694]**).

SECTION 2—RULE 1.2 REPRESENTATIVES

III MEN [688]

17.9 Who may act as a rule 1.2 representative for P

A person may act as an accredited legal representative, or a representative, for P, if that person can fairly and competently discharge his or her functions on behalf of P.

III MEN [689]

17.10 Rule 1.2 representative by court order

(1) The court may make an order appointing a person to act as a representative, or an accredited legal representative, for P.

(2) The court may make an order under paragraph (1)—

(a) either of its own initiative or on the application of any person; but

(b) only with the consent of the person to be appointed.

(3) The court may not appoint a representative or an accredited legal representative under this rule unless it is satisfied that the person to be appointed satisfies the conditions in rule 17.9.

(4) The court may at any stage of the proceedings give directions as to the terms of appointment of a representative or an accredited legal representative.

(Rule 1.2 requires the court to consider how P should participate in the proceedings, which may be by way of the appointment of a representative or accredited legal representative under this Part.)

III MEN [690]

17.11 Application by rule 1.2 representative or by P for directions

A representative, an accredited legal representative or P may, at any time and without giving notice to the other parties, apply to the court for directions relating to the performance, terms of appointment or continuation of the appointment of the representative or accredited legal representative.

III MEN [691]

17.12 Court's power to prevent a person from acting as a rule 1.2 representative or to bring an end to an appointment of a person as a rule 1.2 representative or to appoint another one

(1) The court may, either of its own initiative or on the application of any person—

- (a) direct that a person may not act as a representative or accredited legal representative;
- (b) bring to an end a representative's or accredited legal representative's appointment;
- (c) appoint a new representative or accredited legal representative in place of an existing one; or
- (d) vary the terms of a representative's or accredited legal representative's appointment.

(2) If an application for an order under paragraph (1) is based on the conduct of the representative or accredited legal representative, it must be supported by evidence.

(3) The court may not appoint a representative or accredited legal representative under this rule unless it is satisfied that the person to be appointed satisfies the conditions in rule 17.9.

(4) The appointment of a representative or accredited legal representative continues until brought to an end by court order.

(5) The court must bring to an end the appointment of a representative or an accredited legal representative if P has capacity to appoint such a representative and does not wish the appointment by the court to continue.

III MEN [692]

17.13 Appointment of rule 1.2 representative by court order—supplementary

The applicant must serve a copy of an application for an order under rule 17.10 or rule 17.12 on—

- (a) the person on whom an application form is to be served in accordance with rule 6.4 (service on children and protected parties);
- (b) every other person who is a party to the proceedings;
- (c) any person who is the representative, or accredited legal representative, or who is purporting to act as such representative, when the application is made; and
- (d) unless that person is the applicant, the person who it is proposed should be the representative or accredited legal representative,

as soon as practicable and in any event within 14 days of the date on which the application was issued.

III MEN [693]

17.14 Practice direction in relation to rule 1.2 representatives

A practice direction may make additional or supplementary provision in relation to representatives or accredited legal representatives.

III MEN [693.1]

Rule 1.2 representatives Practice Direction 17B provides guidance and supplements Part 17 (**III MEN [695]**).

PRACTICE DIRECTION 17A – LITIGATION FRIEND

III MEN [694]

This practice direction supplements Part 17 of the Court of Protection Rules 2017

GENERAL

1 Section 1 of Part 17 contains rules about the appointment of a litigation friend to conduct proceedings on behalf of P, a child, or a protected party . This practice direction is made under rule 17.8 and provides guidance in relation to the appointment and removal of a litigation friend pursuant to Part 17.

2 Rule 17.1 provides that a litigation friend may be appointed for –

(a) P;
(b) a child; or
(c) a protected party.

3 Where –

(a) P has a litigation friend, P should be referred to in the proceedings as 'P (by A.B., his litigation friend)';
(b) the protected party has a litigation friend, he should be referred to in the proceedings as 'E.F. (by A.B., his litigation friend)';
(c) a child has a litigation friend, the child should be referred to in the proceedings as 'C.D. (a child by A.B., his litigation friend)'; and
(d) a child is conducting proceedings on his own behalf, the child should be referred to in the proceedings as 'A.B. (a child)'.

LITIGATION FRIEND WITHOUT A COURT ORDER

4 Rule 17.3 makes provision for the appointment of a litigation friend without a court order. The rule does not apply –

(a) in relation to P;
(b) where the court has appointed a litigation friend; or
(c) where the Official Solicitor is to act as litigation friend.

DEPUTY AS A LITIGATION FRIEND

5 Rule 17.3(2) provides that where there is a deputy appointed with power to conduct legal proceedings in the name of the protected party or on the protected party's behalf, that deputy is entitled to be a litigation friend of the protected party in any proceedings to which the deputy's power relates. To be a litigation friend the deputy must file and serve a copy of the court order which appointed him or her on –

(a) every person on whom an application form in relation to a protected party must be served in accordance with rule 6.4; and
(b) every other person who is a party to the proceedings.

LITIGATION FRIEND WHERE THERE IS NO DEPUTY

6 A person who wishes to become a litigation friend without a court order pursuant to rule 17.3 must file a certificate of suitability using Form COP22.

7 In addition to the matters listed in rule 17.1(1), the certificate of suitability referred to in rule 17.3(3) which the litigation friend files must also –

(a) state that he consents to act;
(b) state that he or she knows or believes that the child or the protected party lacks capacity to conduct the proceedings himself or herself; and
(c) state the grounds of his or her belief and, if that belief is based upon medical opinion, or the opinion of another suitably qualified expert, attach any relevant document to the certificate.

8 The certificate of suitability must contain a statement of truth.

9 The litigation friend must serve the certificate of suitability on –

(a) every person on whom an application form must be served in accordance with rule 6.4; and
(b) every other person who is a party to the proceedings.

10 The litigation friend is not required to serve the document referred to in paragraph 7(c) when the litigation friend serves a certificate of suitability under paragraph 9 (unless the court directs otherwise).

11 The litigation friend must file the certificate of suitability together with a certificate of service of it when he first takes a step in the proceedings.

LITIGATION FRIEND BY COURT ORDER

12 Rule 17.4 sets out when and how the court may appoint a litigation friend, either on application or on its own initiative.

13 An application for an order appointing a litigation friend must be made by filing a COP9 application notice in accordance with the Part 10 procedure. The application must be supported by evidence, as required by rule 17.4(3).

14 The evidence in support must satisfy the court that the proposed litigation friend –

(a) consents to act;
(b) can fairly and competently conduct proceedings on behalf of P, the child, or the protected party; and
(c) has no interest adverse to that of P, the child, or the protected party.

CHANGE OF LITIGATION FRIEND AND PREVENTION OF PERSON ACTING AS LITIGATION FRIEND

15 Rule 17.5(1) provides that the court may, on application or on its own initiative –

(a) direct that a person may not act as a litigation friend;
(b) bring to an end a litigation friend's appointment; or
(c) appoint a new litigation friend in place of an existing one.

16 An application made pursuant to rule 17.5 should be made by filing a COP9 application notice in accordance with the Part 10 procedure.

PROCEDURE WHERE THE NEED FOR A LITIGATION FRIEND HAS COME TO AN END

17 Rule 17.7 makes provision for where the need for a litigation friend comes to an end during proceedings, for a child who is not P nor a protected party.

18 Where a child having reached full age files a notice under rule 17.7 and the notice states that the child intends to carry on with or continue to participate in the proceedings the child shall subsequently be described in the proceedings as:

'A.B. (formerly a child but now of full age).'

PRACTICE DIRECTION 17B – RULE 1.2 REPRESENTATIVES

III MEN [695]

This practice direction supplements Part 17 of the Court of Protection Rules 2017

1 Section 2 of Part 17 contains rules about the appointment of an accredited legal representative or a representative for P. This Practice Direction is made under rule 17.14 and provides guidance on the appointment and removal of an accredited legal representative or a representative pursuant to Part 17.

2 Rule 17.10 provides that an accredited legal representative or representative may be appointed for P.

3 An application for –

(a) the appointment of an accredited legal representative, or a representative pursuant to rule 17.10;
(b) directions pursuant to rule 17.11; or
(c) for an order under rule 17.12

should be made by filing an application in Form COP 9 under the procedure in Part 10.

4 In respect of an application pursuant to rule 17.10 or for the substitution of an accredited legal representative or a representative in place of an existing one pursuant to rule 17.12, the evidence in support must satisfy the court that the conditions in rule 17.9 are met.

PART 18
CHANGE OF SOLICITOR

III MEN [696]

18.1 Change of solicitor

(1) This rule applies where a party to proceedings—

(a) for whom a solicitor is acting wants to change solicitor or act in person; or
(b) after having conducted the proceedings in person, appoints a solicitor to act on his or her behalf (except where the solicitor is appointed only to act as an advocate for a hearing).

(2) The party proposing the change must—

(a) file a notice of the change with the court; and
(b) serve the notice of the change on every other party to the proceedings and, if there is one, on the solicitor who will cease to act.

(3) The notice must state the party's address for service.

(4) The notice filed at court must state that it has been served as required by paragraph (2)(b).

(5) Where there is a solicitor who will cease to act, that solicitor will continue to be considered the party's solicitor unless and until—

(a) the notice is filed and served in accordance with paragraphs (2), (3) and (4); or

(b) the court makes an order under rule 18.3 and the order is served in accordance with that rule.

III MEN [696.1]

Procedural guidance Practice Direction 18A provides guidance. If the change arises from the provisions of rule 18.1(1)(a) or (b), then form COP30 is the applicable form (Practice Direction 18A, para 2: **III MEN [701]**).

III MEN [697]

18.2 Legally aided persons

(1) Where the certificate of any person ("A") who is a legally aided person is revoked or withdrawn—

(a) the solicitor who acted for A will cease to be the solicitor acting in the case as soon as the solicitor's retainer is determined under regulation 24 or 41 of the Civil Legal Aid (Procedure) Regulations 2012; and

(b) if A wishes to continue and appoints a solicitor to act on his or her behalf, rule 18.1(2), (3) and (4) will apply as if A had previously conducted the proceedings in person.

(2) In this rule, "certificate" means a certificate issued under the Civil Legal Aid (Procedure) Regulations 2012.

III MEN [698]

18.3 Order that a solicitor has ceased to act

(1) A solicitor may apply for an order declaring that he or she has ceased to be the solicitor acting for a party.

(2) Where an application is made under this rule—

(a) the solicitor must serve the application notice on the party for whom the solicitor is acting, unless the court directs otherwise; and

(b) the application must be supported by evidence.

(3) Where the court makes an order that a solicitor has ceased to act, the solicitor must—

(a) serve a copy of the order on every other party to the proceedings; and

(b) file a certificate of service.

III MEN [698.1]

Applications to the court Practice Direction 18A, para 3 applies and the application is by way of form COP9, with form COP20 being the relevant certificate of service to be filed: **III MEN [701]**. But now see **III MEN [551.1]**

III MEN [699]

18.4 Removal of solicitor who has ceased to act on application of another party

(1) Where—

(a) a solicitor who has acted for a party—

(i) has died;

(ii) has become bankrupt;

(iii) has ceased to practice; or

(iv) cannot be found; and

(b) the party has not served a notice of change of solicitor or notice of intention to act in person as required by rule 18.1,

any other party may apply for an order declaring that the solicitor has ceased to be the solicitor acting for the other party in the case.

(2) Where an application is made under this rule, the applicant must serve the application on the party to whose solicitor the application relates, unless the court directs otherwise.

(3) Where the court makes an order under this rule—

(a) the court shall give directions about serving a copy of the order on every other party to the proceedings; and

(b) where the order is served by a party, that party must file a certificate of service.

III MEN [699.1]

Applications to the court and guidance Practice Direction 18A, para 3 is applicable and the application is made using form COP9 with COP20 being the applicable form for filing a certificate of service: **III MEN [701]**. See now **III MEN [551.1]**

III MEN [700]

18.5 Practice direction relating to change of solicitor

A practice direction may make additional or different provision in relation to change of solicitor.

PRACTICE DIRECTION 18A – CHANGE OF SOLICITOR

III MEN [701]

This practice direction supplements Part 18 of the Court of Protection Rules 2017

GENERAL

1 Part 18 contains rules about a change of solicitor. This practice direction is made under rule 18.5 and specifies the forms and procedures to be used in relation to a change of solicitor in specified circumstances.

WHERE FORM COP30 SHOULD BE USED

2 Form COP30 should be used where a party to proceedings –

(a) for whom a solicitor is acting, wishes to change his solicitor, or intends to act in person; or

(b) having conducted the proceedings in person, appoints a solicitor to act on his behalf (this requirement does not apply where a solicitor is appointed only to act as an advocate for a hearing).

WHERE FORM COP9 SHOULD BE USED

3 Form COP9 should be used where –

(a) a solicitor applies for an order declaring that he has ceased to be the solicitor acting for a party; or

(b) another party applies for an order declaring that the solicitor has ceased to be the solicitor acting for another party in the proceedings.

PART 19
COSTS

III MEN [702]

19.1 Interpretation

(1) In this Part—

"authorised court officer" means any officer of the Senior Courts Costs Office whom the Lord Chancellor has authorised to assess costs;

"costs" include fees, charges, disbursements, expenses, remuneration and any reimbursement allowed to a litigant in person;

"costs judge" means a taxing Master of the Senior Courts;

"costs officer" means a costs judge or an authorised court officer;

"detailed assessment" means the procedure by which the amount of costs or remuneration is decided by a costs officer in accordance with Part 47 of the Civil Procedure Rules 1998 (which are applied to proceedings under these Rules, with modifications, by rule 19.6);

"fixed costs" are to be construed in accordance with the relevant practice direction;

"fund" includes any estate or property held for the benefit of any person or class of persons, and any fund to which a trustee or personal representative is entitled in that capacity;

"paying party" means a party liable to pay costs;

"pro bono representation" means representation provided free of charge;

"receiving party" means a party entitled to be paid costs;

"summary assessment" means the procedure by which the court, when making an order about costs, orders payment of a sum of money instead of fixed costs or detailed assessment.

(2) The costs to which rules in this Part apply include—

(a) where the costs may be assessed by the court, costs payable by a client to his or her legal representative; and

(b) costs which are payable by one party to another party under the terms of a contract, where the court makes an order for an assessment of those costs.

(3) Where advocacy or litigation services are provided to a client under a conditional fee agreement, costs are recoverable under this Part notwithstanding that the client is liable to pay his or her legal representative's fees and expenses only to the extent that sums are recovered in respect of the proceedings, whether by way of costs or otherwise.

(4) In paragraph (3), the reference to a conditional fee agreement means an agreement enforceable under section 58 of the Courts and Legal Services Act 1990.

III MEN [703]

19.2 Property and affairs—the general rule

Where the proceedings concern P's property and affairs the general rule is that the costs of the proceedings, or of that part of the proceedings that concerns P's property and affairs, shall be paid by P or charged to P's estate.

III MEN [704]

19.3 Personal welfare—the general rule

Where the proceedings concern P's personal welfare the general rule is that there will be no order as to the costs of the proceedings, or of that part of the proceedings that concerns P's personal welfare.

III MEN [705]

19.4 Apportioning costs—the general rule

Where the proceedings concern both property and affairs and personal welfare the court, in so far as practicable, shall apportion the costs as between the respective issues.

III MEN [706]

19.5 Departing from the general rule

(1) The court may depart from rules 19.2 to 19.4 if the circumstances so justify, and in deciding whether departure is justified the court will have regard to all the circumstances including—

- (a) the conduct of the parties;
- (b) whether a party has succeeded on part of that party's case, even if not wholly successful; and
- (c) the role of any public body involved in the proceedings.

(2) The conduct of the parties includes—

- (a) conduct before, as well as during, the proceedings;
- (b) whether it was reasonable for a party to raise, pursue or contest a particular matter;
- (c) the manner in which a party has made or responded to an application or a particular issue;
- (d) whether a party who has succeeded in that party's application or response to an application, in whole or in part, exaggerated any matter contained in the application or response; and
- (e) any failure by a party to comply with a rule, practice direction or court order.

(3) Without prejudice to rules 19.2 to 19.4 and the foregoing provisions of this rule, the court may permit a party to recover their fixed costs in accordance with the relevant practice direction.

III MEN [707]

19.6 Rules about costs in the Civil Procedure Rules to apply

(1) Subject to the provisions of these Rules, Parts 44, 46 and 47 of the Civil Procedure Rules 1998 ("the 1998 Rules") apply with the modifications in this rule and such other modifications as may be appropriate, to costs incurred in relation to proceedings under these Rules as they apply to costs incurred in relation to proceedings in the High Court.

(2) Rules 3.12 to 3.18 of the 1998 Rules and Practice Direction 3E supporting those Rules do not apply in relation to proceedings under these Rules.

(3) The provisions of Part 47 of the 1998 Rules apply with the modifications in this rule and such other modifications as may be appropriate, to a detailed assessment of the remuneration of a deputy under these Rules as they apply to a detailed assessment of costs in proceedings to which the 1998 Rules apply.

(4) Where the definitions in Part 44 (referred to in Parts 44, 46 and 47) of the 1998 Rules are different from the definitions in rule 19.1 of these Rules, the latter definitions prevail.

(5) Rules 44.2(1) to (5), 44.4(3)(h), 44.5, 44.6, 44.9 and 44.13 to 44.18 of the 1998 Rules do not apply.

(6) For rule 46.1(1) of the 1998 Rules there is substituted—

"(1) This paragraph applies where a person applies for an order for specific disclosure before the commencement of proceedings.".

(7) Rules 46.2, 46.5 and 46.10 to 46.19 of the 1998 Rules do not apply.

(8) In rule 47.3(1)(c) of the 1998 Rules, the words "unless the costs are being assessed under rule 46.4 (costs where money is payable to a child or protected party)" are omitted.

(9) In rule 47.3(2) of the 1998 Rules, the words "or a District Judge" are omitted.

(10) Rule 47.4(3) and (4) of the 1998 Rules do not apply.

(11) Rules 47.9(4), 47.10 and 47.11 of the 1998 Rules do not apply where the costs are to be paid by P or charged to P's estate.

III MEN [707.1]

Costs arising in deprivation of liberty, welfare and medical treatment proceedings, and the costs of the Official Solicitor The court would exercise its jurisdiction and make awards within deprivation of liberty proceedings against a party on an indemnity basis where it was found that there had been misconduct within rule 19.5, see: *G v E (Costs)* [2010] EWHC 3385 (Fam), [2011] 1 FLR 1566. The decision of Baker J was affirmed in *Manchester City Council v GE (by his litigation friend, the Official Solicitor)* [2011] EWCA Civ 939, [2011] 2 FLR 1297, [2011] Fam Law 1196, followed in *Somerset County Council v MK* [2015] EWCOP B1.

In *Re AH (Costs) v AH v Hertfordshire Partnership NHS Foundation Trust* [2011] EWHC 3524 (COP), Peter Jackson J drawing upon the fact that the Court of Appeal had not sought to give guidance over and above the words of the Court of Protection Rules 2007 (which are identically worded to the 2017 rules), found that it was not necessary nor appropriate to be cited earlier Court of Protection decisions, holding that for the purposes of determining costs, each application must be considered upon its own merits or lack of merit. In *Re BN* [2015] EWCOP 11, [2015] All ER (D) 50 (Mar) the Senior Judge finding that a party acted in bad faith and had been motivated by spite exercised discretion under rule 159 to depart from the general rule.

In *NHS Trust v D (by his litigation friend, the Official Solicitor)* [2012] EWHC 886 (COP), [2012] NLJR 1421, Peter Jackson J at the conclusion of a medical treatment case followed the pre-Mental Capacity Act 2005 dispensation in respect of the costs of the Official Solicitor recognising their distinct public role in assisting the court in the most difficult of cases. Following the President's decision in *A Hospital v SW and a PCT* [2007] EWHC 425 (Fam), he held that the long standing practice of awarding the Official Solicitor one half his costs in such cases had not been varied by the introduction of the Rules, and on a pragmatic basis should be continued thereby providing certainty for those public bodies engaged in these issues.

III MEN [707.2]

Departing from the no order principle in welfare matters In *EG v RS, JS and BEN PCT* [2010] EWHC 3073 (COP) HHJ Cardinal considered the interrelationship of rules 157 and 159, in departing from the general rule of no order as to costs in welfare cases, **III MEN [704]**, **III MEN [706]**.

III MEN [707.3]

Application of wasted costs principles in the Court of Protection In *Ragny Sharma, Paul Judkins v Hunters* [2011] EWHC 2546 (COP) Henderson J provided guidance as to the appropriate approach of applying established case law principle to issues of wasted costs arising within the jurisdiction of the Court of Protection

III MEN [707.4]

Application of rule 19.3 and proceedings relating to lasting powers of attorney In *RC Deceased, SC v London Borough of Hackney* [2010] EWHC B29 (COP), Senior Judge Lush considered the applicability of rule 157 to contested proceedings relating to lasting powers of attorney: **III MEN [704]**.

III MEN [707.5]

Departing from the general rule in rule 19.5 and considering the conduct of parties In *JS v KB* [2014] EWHC 483 (COP), [2014] WTLR 991 Cobb J. identified the essential features of the Court's costs discretion under sections 55(1), 55(2) and 55(4) of the Mental Capacity Act 2005 and the approach in departing from the general rule in property and affairs matters due to the conduct of parties in acting without authority where informal family arrangements had been adopted. In *The Public Guardian v CT* [2014] EWCOP 51 Senior Judge Lush determined that an unjustified obstruction of the work of the Court of Protection Special Visitor warranted a departure from the general rule in respect of an attorney and make no order for costs.

Where a family member acted in bad faith in commencing proceedings to remove an attorney acting under a Lasting Power of Attorney, Senior Judge Lush exercised his discretion under rule 19.5 in *Re BN* [2015] EWCOP 11, [2015] All ER (D) 50 (Mar) to make an adverse costs order.

III MEN [707.6]

Appeals and the appropriate cost provisions In *Cheshire West and Chester Council v P* [2011] EWCA Civ 1333 the Court of Appeal held that if an appeal lay from the Court of Protection, the costs issues would be determined in accordance with CPR 44.3 (the unsuccessful party being liable to pay the costs, subject where relevant to any protection provided by s 11 of the Access to Justice Act 1999 (see **CPR 44.3** in Volume 1)), and the general rule under rule 19.3 in respect of welfare matters did not apply.

III MEN [707.7]

The relationship of CPR Rules and the COP Rules In *Re G (Adult)* [2014] EWCOP 5 the President in a resume of the costs rules found that the provisions of the COP rules were to be applied in determining costs as opposed to the CPR rules 44.3(2), (4), and (5), distinguishing between the regimes upon the basis that the key word of rules 19.2–19.4 were 'proceedings' and that accordingly that was the test to apply namely the identifying the nature of the 'proceedings' rather than the nature of the application within proceedings.

III MEN [708]

19.7 Detailed assessment of costs

(1) Where the court orders costs to be assessed by way of detailed assessment, the detailed assessment proceedings shall take place in the High Court.

(2) A fee is payable in respect of the detailed assessment of costs and on an appeal against a decision made in a detailed assessment of costs.

(3) Where a detailed assessment of costs has taken place, the amount payable by P is the amount which the court certifies as payable.

III MEN [709]

19.8 Employment of a solicitor by two or more persons

Where two or more persons having the same interest in relation to a matter act in relation to the proceedings by separate legal representatives, they shall not be permitted more than one set of costs of the representation unless and to the extent that the court certifies that the circumstances justify separate representation.

III MEN [710]

19.9 Costs of the Official Solicitor

Any costs incurred by the Official Solicitor in relation to proceedings under these Rules or in carrying out any directions given by the court and not provided for by remuneration under rule 19.13 shall be paid by such persons or out of such funds as the court may direct.

III MEN [710.1]

Costs ordered in favour of the Official Solicitor arising from conduct of a party In *North Somerset Council v LW* [2014] EWCOP 3 Keehan J provided a comprehensive summary of the costs regime of the Court and of its powers and on findings of failures by a trust made various stepped orders in respect of the costs to be paid applying the relevant principles.

III MEN [711]

19.10 Procedure for assessing costs

Where the court orders a party, or P, to pay costs to another party it may either—

(a) make a summary assessment of the costs; or

(b) order a detailed assessment of the costs by a costs officer;

unless any rule, practice direction or other enactment provides otherwise.

III MEN [712]

19.11 Costs following P's death

An order or direction that costs incurred during P's lifetime be paid out of or charged on P's estate may be made within 6 years after P's death.

III MEN [713]

19.12 Costs orders in favour of or against non-parties

(1) Where the court is considering whether to make a costs order in favour of or against a person who is not a party to proceedings, that person must be—

- (a) added as a party to the proceedings for the purposes of costs only;
- (b) served with such documents as the court may direct; and
- (c) given a reasonable opportunity to attend any hearing at which the court will consider the matter further.

(2) This rule does not apply where the court is considering whether to make an order against the Lord Chancellor in proceedings in which the Lord Chancellor has provided legal aid to a party to the proceedings.

III MEN [714]

19.13 Remuneration of a deputy, donee or attorney

(1) Where the court orders that a deputy, donee or attorney is entitled to remuneration out of P's estate for discharging functions as such, the court may make such order as it thinks fit including an order that—

- (a) the deputy, donee or attorney be paid a fixed amount;
- (b) the deputy, donee or attorney be paid at a specified rate; or
- (c) the amount of the remuneration shall be determined in accordance with the schedule of fees set out in the relevant practice direction.

(2) Any amount permitted by the court under paragraph (1) shall constitute a debt due from P's estate.

(3) The court may order a detailed assessment of the remuneration by a costs officer in accordance with rule 19.10(b).

III MEN [715]

19.14 Practice direction as to costs

A practice direction may make further provision in respect of costs in proceedings.

III MEN [715.1]

Guidance on fixed costs and the Court of Protection Practice Direction 19B provides guidance on the issue of fixed costs: see **III MEN [717]**.

On 1st May 2009, a Practice Direction was issued coming into effect from that date, and has been subsequently superseded by a further Practice Direction as from 1st February 2011. Claims for work undertaken prior to 1st May 2009, and prior to 1st February 2011, should be made applying the relevant rates for the given periods.

PRACTICE DIRECTION 19A – COSTS

III MEN [716]

This practice direction supplements Part 19 of the Court of Protection Rules 2017

MODIFICATIONS TO THE CIVIL PROCEDURE RULES 1998

1 The Practice Directions which supplement Parts 44 to 48 of the Civil Procedure Rules 1998 ("the CPR Practice Directions 44 to 48") apply, insofar as those Parts apply to proceedings in the Court of Protection, with such modifications as are appropriate together with the modifications specified in this practice direction.

Provisions which do not apply

2 The following provisions of CPR Practice Directions 44 to 48 do not apply—

(a) in CPR Practice Direction 44: paragraphs 3.1–3.7, 4.1, 7.1–7.3, 9.2(a), 9.3, 9.4, 9.9, 9.10 and 12.1–12.7;
(b) the whole of CPR Practice Direction 45;
(c) in CPR Practice Direction 46: paragraphs 1.1–2.1, 7.1–9.12 and 10.1–10.2;
(d) in CPR Practice Direction 47: paragraphs 4.1–4.3;
(e) in CPR Practice Direction 48: paragraphs 2.1–4.2.

Modifications of provisions which do apply

3 In paragraph 9.5(4) of CPR Practice Direction 44, the words 'any party against whom an order for payment of those costs is intended to be sought' are replaced with 'all parties to the proceedings and any other person that the court may direct.'

4 In paragraphs 5.4 and 5.9 of CPR Practice Direction 46 and paragraphs 3.3, 9.2, 13.7, 13.8(3), 15, 16.6, 17.4 and 18.8 of CPR Practice Direction 47, the words 'Part 23' are removed and replaced with 'Part 10 (Applications within proceedings)'.

5 In paragraph 1.2 of CPR Practice Direction 47, the words 'or the parties may agree in writing' are removed.

6 Paragraphs 1.3, 1.4, 3.2, 3.3, 10.5(a) 11.1, 11.3, 16.11(a), 20.4 and 20.6 of CPR Practice Direction 47 are to be read as if the references in those paragraphs to a district judge were removed.

7 In paragraph 6.1 of CPR Practice Direction 47, the words '(rule 2.11)' and '(rule 3.1(2)(a))' are omitted.

8 Paragraph 8.1 of CPR Practice Direction 47 is replaced with the following: 'A party may apply to the appropriate officer for an order to shorten or extend the time for service of points of dispute'.

9 In paragraph 10.3 of CPR Practice Direction 47, the words 'Rules 40.3' to 'default costs certificate' are replaced with the words 'rule 6.2 of the Court of Protection Rules 2017, which applies to the service of court orders'.

10 In paragraph 11.1 of CPR Practice Direction 47, the words 'A court officer' are replaced with 'An authorised court officer'.

11 In rule 11.3 of CPR Practice Direction 47, the following words are removed: 'rule 3.1(3) (which enables the court when making an order to make it subject to conditions) and to'.

12 References in CPR Practice Directions 44 to 48 to 'claimant' and 'defendant' shall be read, in proceedings to which this Practice Direction applies, as references to 'applicant' and 'respondent' respectively.

OTHER PROVISIONS

13 The Senior Courts Costs Office Guide of October 2013 gives practical information and guidance on dealing with costs, and contains, in Section 23 of the Guide, provision relating specifically to Court of Protection cases. Regard should accordingly be had to Section 23 and to those matters of good practice, guidance and procedure referred to in the Guide as are directly applicable to costs arising under Court of Protection Rules.

14 Section 23.1(a) of the Guide shall be read as if a reference to the Court of Protection Rules 2017 were substituted for the reference to the Court of Protection Rules 2007, and a reference to Practice Direction 19B read as a reference to the amended Practice Direction 19B supporting Part 19 of the Court of Protection Rules 2017.

15 The appropriate venue for detailed assessment of costs proceedings is the Senior Court Costs Office, Thomas More Building, Royal Courts of Justice, Strand, London WC2A 2LL (DX 44454 (Strand)). Details of how to contact the Senior Courts Costs Office are provided in Section 1 (Introduction) of the Senior Courts Costs Office Guide of October 2013.

PRACTICE DIRECTION 19B – FIXED COSTS IN THE COURT OF PROTECTION

III MEN [717]

This practice direction supplements Part 19 of the Court of Protection Rules 2017

GENERAL

1. This practice direction sets out the fixed costs that may be claimed by solicitors and public authorities acting in Court of Protection proceedings and the fixed amounts of remuneration that may be claimed by solicitors and office holders in public authorities appointed to act as a deputy for P. Rule 19.13 enables a practice direction to set out a schedule of fees to determine the amount of remuneration payable to deputies. Rule 19.14 enables a practice direction to make provision in respect of costs in proceedings.

2. The practice direction applies principally to solicitors or office holders in public authorities appointed to act as deputy. However, the court may direct that its provisions shall also apply to other professionals acting as deputy including accountants, case managers and not-for-profit organisations.

3. This practice direction applies where the period covered by the category of fixed costs or remuneration ends on or after 1 April 2017 relating to fixed costs issued by the Court of Protection. However solicitors and office holders in public authorities should continue to claim the rates applicable in the previous Practice Directions and Practice Notes, where the period covered by the category of fixed costs or remuneration ended before 1 April 2017.

WHEN DOES THIS PRACTICE DIRECTION APPLY?

4. Rule 19.2 provides that, where the proceedings concern P's property and affairs, the general rule is that costs of the proceedings shall be paid by P or charged to P's estate. The provisions of this practice direction apply where the professional or deputy is entitled to be paid costs out of P's estate. They do not apply where the court order provides for one party to receive costs from another.

CLAIMS GENERALLY

5. The court order or direction will state whether fixed costs or remuneration applies, or whether there is to be a detailed assessment by a costs officer. Where a court order or direction provides for a detailed assessment of costs, professionals may elect to take fixed costs or remuneration in lieu of a detailed assessment.

MENTAL CAPACITY AND MENTAL HEALTH

PAYMENTS ON ACCOUNT

6. Where professional deputies elect for detailed assessment of annual management charges, they may take payments on account for the first three quarters of the year, which are proportionate and reasonable taking into account the size of the estate and the functions they have performed. Interim quarterly bills must not exceed 25% of the estimated annual management charges - that is up to 75% for the whole year.

Interim bills of account must not be submitted to the Senior Courts Costs Office (SCCO). At the end of the annual management year, the deputy must submit their annual bill to the SCCO for detailed assessment and adjust the final total due to reflect payments on account already received.

THE OFFICE OF THE PUBLIC GUARDIAN

7. As part of its supervisory procedure, the Office of the Public Guardian (OPG) will ask professional deputies to estimate the amount of activity they anticipate being required on a case in the coming period, and the costs attendant on that. The professional deputy will share this estimate with the SCCO at the same time as they submit their costs for assessment.

SOLICITORS' COSTS IN COURT PROCEEDINGS

8. The fixed costs are as follows:

Category I. Work up to and including the date upon which the court makes an order appointing a deputy for property and affairs.

An amount not exceeding £950 (plus VAT)

Category II. Applications under sections 36(9) or 54 of the Trustee Act 1925 or section 20 of the Trusts of Land and Appointment of Trustees Act 1996 for the appointment of a new trustee in the place of 'P' and applications under section 18(1)(j) of the Mental Capacity Act 2005 for authority to exercise any power vested in P, whether beneficially, or as trustee, or otherwise

An amount not exceeding £500 (plus VAT)

9. The categories of fixed costs, above will apply as follows:

Category I to all orders appointing a deputy for property and affairs made on or after 1 April 2017.

Category II to all applications for the appointment of a new trustee made on or after 1 April 2017.

REMUNERATION OF SOLICITORS APPOINTED AS DEPUTY FOR P

10. The following fixed rates of remuneration will apply where the court appoints a solicitor to act as deputy (but not where an office holder of a public authority is appointed and employs a solicitor, or a solicitor employed by a public authority is appointed as an office holder of a public authority):

Category III. Annual management fee where the court appoints a professional deputy for property and affairs, payable on the anniversary of the court order.

An amount not exceeding

(a) for the first year: £1,670 (plus VAT)
(b) for the second and subsequent years: £1,320 (plus VAT)

Where the net assets of P are below £16,000, the professional deputy for property and affairs may take an annual management fee not exceeding 4.5% of P's net assets on the anniversary of the court order appointing the professional as deputy.

Category IV. Where the court appoints a professional deputy for health and welfare, the deputy may take an annual management fee not exceeding 2.5% of P's net assets on the anniversary of the court order appointing the professional as deputy for health and welfare up to a maximum of £555.

Category V. Preparation and lodgement of a report or an account to the Public Guardian

An amount not exceeding £265 (plus VAT)

Category VI.

(a) Preparation of a Basic HMRC income tax return (bank or NS&I interest and taxable benefits, discretionary trust or estate income) on behalf of P. An amount not exceeding £250 (plus VAT)

(b) Preparation of a Complex HMRC income tax return (bank or NS&I interest, multiple investment portfolios, taxable benefits, one or more rental properties) on behalf of P. An amount not exceeding £600 (plus VAT)

11. The categories of remuneration, above will apply as follows:

Category III and IV to all annual management fees for anniversaries falling on or after 1 January 2017

Category V to reports or accounts lodged on or after 1 April 2017

Category VI to all HMRC returns made on or after 1 April 2017

12. In cases where fixed costs are not appropriate, professionals may, if preferred, apply to the SCCO for a detailed assessment of costs. However, this does not apply if P's net assets are below £16,000 where the option for detailed assessment will only arise if the court makes a specific order for detailed assessment in relation to an estate with net assets of a value of less than £16,000.

13. Where the period for which an annual management fee claimed is less than one year, for example where the deputyship comes to an end before the anniversary of appointment, then the amount claimed must be the same proportion of the applicable fee as the period bears to one year.

CONVEYANCING COSTS

14. Where a deputy or other person authorised by the court is selling or purchasing a property on behalf of P, the following fixed rates will apply except where the sale or purchase is by trustees in which case, the costs should be agreed with the trustees:

Category VII. A value element of 0.15% of the consideration with a minimum sum of £400 and a maximum sum of £1,670, plus disbursements.

15. Category VII applies to any conveyancing transaction where contracts are exchanged on or after 1 April 2017.

REMUNERATION OF PUBLIC AUTHORITY DEPUTIES

16. The following fixed rates of remuneration will apply where the court appoints a holder of an office in a public authority to act as deputy:

Category I. Work up to and including the date upon which the court makes an order appointing a deputy for property and affairs.

An amount not exceeding £745

Category II. Annual management fee where the court appoints a local authority deputy for property and affairs, payable on the anniversary of the court order. Management costs are assumed to cover any incidental costs incurred in management of P's affairs with the exception of those mentioned under paragraph 20 below:

(a) For the first year: An amount not exceeding £775
(b) For the second and subsequent years: An amount not exceeding £650
(c) Where the net assets of P are below £16,000, the local authority deputy for property and affairs may take an annual management fee not exceeding 3.5% of P's net assets on the anniversary of the court order appointing the local authority as deputy
(d) Where the court appoints a local authority deputy for health and welfare, the local authority may take an annual management fee not exceeding 2.5% of P's net assets on the anniversary of the court order appointing the local authority as deputy for health and welfare up to a maximum of £555

Category III. Annual property management fee to include work involved in preparing property for sale, instructing agents, conveyancers, etc. or the ongoing maintenance of property including management and letting of a rental property or properties where P is a tenant.

An amount not exceeding £300

Category IV. Preparation and lodgement of an annual report or account to the Public Guardian

An amount not exceeding £216

Category V. Preparation of a Basic HMRC income tax return (bank or NS&I interest and taxable benefits) on behalf of P

An amount not exceeding £70

Preparation of a Complex HMRC income tax return (bank or NS&I interest, taxable benefits, small investment portfolio) on behalf of P

An amount not exceeding £140

17. The categories of remuneration, above will apply as follows:

Category I to all orders appointing a deputy for property and affairs made on or after 1 April 2017.

Category II to all annual management fees for anniversaries falling on or after 1 April 2017.

Category III on the anniversary of appointment as deputy where the anniversary falls on or after or upon completion of the sale of a property, where the transaction was concluded on or after 1 April 2017.

Category V to reports or accounts lodged on or after 1 April 2017.

18. Where the period for which the annual management fee ends before an anniversary, for example where the deputyship comes to an end before the anniversary of appointment, then the amount claimed must be the same proportion of the applicable fee as the period bears to one year.

OUTSOURCING OF WORK BY PUBLIC AUTHORITIES

19. Where public authorities outsource deputyship work, it is expected that the rates charged will be no more than that which would have been charged to the client if the public authority had remained as deputy.

DISBURSEMENTS

20. Public Authorities are allowed to use P's funds to pay for specialist services that P would have normally be expected to pay if P had retained capacity such as conveyancing, obtaining expert valuations and obtaining investment advice.

TRAVEL RATES

21. Public authority and other third sector deputies are allowed the fixed rate of

£40 per hour for travel costs.

PART 20
APPEALS

III MEN [718]

20.1 Scope of this Part

This Part applies to an appeal against any decision of the court.

III MEN [718.1]

Procedure and guidance Practice Direction 20A (**III MEN [732]**) provides supplemental directions on the making of appeals. In particular the following aspects are considered:

Permission (paras 2–3).

Appellant:

Appellant's Notice (paras 4–7). Extension of time for filing Appellant's Notice (paras 8–10). Documents to be filed and served with Appellant's Notice (paras 11–15). Skeleton Arguments (paras 16–21). Suitable record of judgment (paras 22–25). Transcripts or notes of evidence (paras 26–29).

Respondent:

Respondent (paras 20–32). Respondent's Notice (paras 33–39). Documents to be filed and served with Respondent's Notice (paras 40–43). Skeleton Argument (paras 44–49).

Appeal hearing (para 50).

Practice Direction 20A provides for the following forms to be used

Appellant's Notice – Form COP35. Respondent's Notice – Form COP36. Skeleton Argument – Form COP37.

Applications for reconsideration of decisions made without a hearing or without notice should be made under r 13.4 (see **III MEN [626]** above). Applications for reconsideration or appeal against a decision of an authorised officer should be made in accordance with para 4.1 of Practice Direction 2B (**III MEN [506]**) and r 13.4.

III MEN [718.2]

Guidance on the right to appeal Section 53 of the Mental Capacity Act 2005 establishes the rights to appeal; see **III MEN [91]** above

III MEN [719]

20.2 Interpretation

(1) In the following provisions of this Part—

- (a) "appeal judge" means a judge of the court to whom an appeal is made;
- (b) "first instance judge" means the judge of the court from whose decision an appeal is brought;
- (c) "appellant" means the person who brings or seeks to bring an appeal;
- (d) "respondent" means—
  - (i) a person other than the appellant who was a party to the proceedings before the first instance judge and who is affected by the appeal; or
  - (ii) a person who is permitted or directed by the first instance judge or the appeal judge to be party to the appeal; and
- (e) "a second appeal" means an appeal from a decision of a judge of the court which was itself made on appeal from a judge of the court.

(2) In this Part, where the expression "permission" is used it means "permission to appeal" unless otherwise stated.

III MEN [720]

20.3 Dealing with appeals

(1) The court may deal with an appeal or any part of an appeal at a hearing or without a hearing.

(2) In considering whether it is necessary to hold a hearing, the court shall have regard to the matters set out in rule 3.6(5).

(3) Any person bound by an order of the court by virtue of rule 9.14 (persons to be bound as if parties) may seek permission under this Part.

(4) All parties to an appeal must comply with any relevant practice direction.

(5) Where permission is required, it is to be granted or refused in accordance with this Part.

(Rule 13.4 provides for reconsideration of orders made without a hearing or without notice to a person.)

III MEN [720.1]

Applications to the court for reconsideration only For applications for reconsideration under rule 13.4 see **III MEN [626]** above

III MEN [721]

20.4 Destination of appeals

(1) An appeal from a decision of a judge of the court shall lie to the Court of Appeal in the following cases—

(a) where it is an appeal from a decision of a Tier 3 Judge; or

(b) where it is a second appeal.

(2) Subject to paragraph (1) and to any alternative provision made by the relevant practice direction—

(a) where the first instance judge was a Tier 1 Judge, any appeal shall be heard by a Tier 2 Judge;

(b) where the first instance judge was a Tier 2 Judge, any appeal shall be heard by a Tier 3 Judge.

(3) No appeal may be made against a decision of a court officer authorised under rule 2.3.

(A decision of a court officer authorised under rule 2.3 can be reconsidered by a judge under rule 13.4.)

III MEN [722]

20.5 Permission to appeal—appeals to the Court of Appeal

(1) Subject to rule 20.7, an appeal to the Court of Appeal against a decision of a judge of the court may not be made without permission.

(2) Where an appeal to the Court of Appeal is made from a decision of a Tier 3 Judge, permission may be granted by the first instance judge or by the Court of Appeal, unless the appeal is a second appeal.

(3) Where an appeal to the Court of Appeal is a second appeal, permission may only be granted by the Court of Appeal.

(4) No appeal shall lie against—

(a) the granting or refusal of permission under this rule; or

(b) an order allowing an extension of time for appealing from an order.

(The procedure for an appeal from a decision of a judge of the court to the Court of Appeal, including requirements for permission, is governed by the Civil Procedure Rules 1998.)

III MEN [723]

20.6 Permission to appeal—other cases

(1) Subject to rules 20.5 and 20.7, an appeal against a decision of the court may not be made without permission.

(2) An application for permission to appeal may be made to—

- (a) the first instance judge; or
- (b) another judge who satisfies the relevant condition in paragraph (4) or (5).

(3) Where an application for permission is refused by the first instance judge, a further application for permission may be made to a judge who satisfies the relevant condition in paragraph (4) or (5).

(4) Where the decision sought to be appealed is a decision of a Tier 1 Judge, permission may also be granted or refused by—

- (a) a Tier 2 Judge; or
- (b) a Tier 3 Judge.

(5) Where the decision sought to be appealed is a decision of a Tier 2 Judge, permission may also be granted or refused by a Tier 3 Judge.

(6) Subject to paragraph (7) and except where another rule or a practice direction provides otherwise, where a judge who satisfies the relevant condition in paragraph (4) or (5), without a hearing, refuses permission to appeal against the decision of the first instance judge, the person seeking permission may request the decision to be reconsidered at a hearing.

(7) Where a Tier 3 Judge or the Senior Judge refuses permission to appeal without a hearing and considers that the application is totally without merit, that judge may order that the person seeking permission may not request the decision to be reconsidered at a hearing.

(8) Subject to paragraph (6), no appeal shall lie against—

- (a) the granting or refusal of permission under this rule; or
- (b) an order allowing an extension of time for appealing from an order.

III MEN [723.1]

Applications to the court for committal For consideration of the requirements of an application for committal, and of an appeal against an order for committal see Part 21, rr 21.15–21.17 (**III MEN [748]** to **III MEN [750]**) and Practice Direction 21A (**III MEN [766]**).

III MEN [724]

20.7 Appeal against an order for committal to prison

Permission is not required to appeal against an order for committal to prison.

III MEN [725]

20.8 Matters to be taken into account when considering an application for permission

(1) Permission to appeal shall be granted only where—

- (a) the court considers that the appeal would have a real prospect of success; or
- (b) there is some other compelling reason why the appeal should be heard.

(2) An order giving permission may—

- (a) limit the issues to be heard; and
- (b) be made subject to conditions.

(3) Paragraphs (1) and (2) do not apply to second appeals.

III MEN [725.1]

Applications to the court for permission In *RC Deceased, SC v London Borough of Hackney* [2010] EWHC B29 (COP), Senior Judge Lush considered that permission should be granted where several procedural points required investigation and where it was appropriate for the court to give judgment clarifying the applicability of the general rule as to costs in personal welfare proceedings (r 19.3) (**III MEN [704]**) to proceedings relating to the cancellation of registration of an LPA for health and welfare.

III MEN [725.2]

Procedural guidance on applications to the court Practice Direction 20A makes provision as to whom the application for permission may be made (paras 2–3) (**III MEN [732]**).

III MEN [726]

20.9 Power to treat application for permission to appeal as application for reconsideration under rule 13.4

(1) Where a person seeking permission to appeal a decision would be entitled to seek reconsideration of that decision under rule 13.4 (or would have been so entitled had the application been made within 21 days of the date of that decision)—

(a) a practice direction may provide; or

(b) the court may direct,

that an application for permission shall be treated as an application for reconsideration under rule 13.4.

(2) In any case where paragraph (1) applies, the decision in question shall be reconsidered in accordance with the provisions of rule 13.4.

III MEN [726.1]

Procedures on appeal See Practice Direction 20A and the relevant COP Forms: **III MEN [732]**.

III MEN [727]

20.10 Appellant's notice

(1) Where the appellant seeks permission from a judge other than the first instance judge, it must be requested in the appellant's notice.

(2) The appellant must file an appellant's notice at the court within—

(a) such period as may be directed or specified in the order of the first instance judge; or

(b) where that judge makes no such direction or order, 21 days after the date of the decision being appealed.

(3) The court shall issue the appellant's notice and unless it orders otherwise, the appellant must serve the appellant's notice on each respondent and on such other persons as the court may direct, as soon as practicable and in any event within 21 days of the date on which it was issued.

(4) The appellant must file a certificate of service within 7 days beginning with the date on which the appellant served the appellant's notice.

III MEN [727.1]

Appeals and procedural guidance Form COP35 is the applicable Notice Form. Practice Direction 20A, paras 4–7 provide further directions as to the time limits for filing and serving the Appellants Notice and identifying the 3 separate procedures and timings, depending on whether permission was given, not given, or not required (**III MEN [732]**).

Practice Direction 20A, paras 11–15 provide information as to the documents to be filed and served with the appellant's notice (**III MEN [732]**).

Practice Direction 20A, paras 16–21 provide information and guidance as to the Appellant's skeleton argument, and form COP37 is the applicable form (**III MEN [732]**).

Practice Direction 20A, paras 22–29 provide guidance as to the procedures to be followed relating to records of judgment, and transcripts or notes of evidence (**III MEN [732]**).

Form COP20 is the relevant form of Certificate of Service, but now see **III MEN [551.1]**.

III MEN [728]

20.11 Respondent's notice

(1) A respondent who—

(a) is seeking permission from a judge other than the first instance judge; or

(b) wishes to ask the appeal judge to uphold the order of the first instance judge for reasons different from or additional to those given by the first instance judge,

must file a respondent's notice.

(2) Where the respondent seeks permission from a judge other than the first instance judge, permission must be requested in the respondent's notice.

(3) A respondent's notice must be filed within—

(a) such period as may be directed by the first instance judge; or

(b) where the first instance judge makes no such direction, 21 days beginning with the date referred to in paragraph (4).

(4) The date is the soonest of—

(a) the date on which the respondent is served with the appellant's notice where—

(i) permission was given by the first instance judge; or

(ii) permission is not required;

(b) the date on which the respondent is served with notification that a judge other than the first instance judge has given the appellant permission; or

(c) the date on which the respondent is served with the notification that the application for permission and the appeal itself are to be heard together.

(5) The court shall issue a respondent's notice, and unless it orders otherwise, the respondent must serve the respondent's notice on the appellant, any other respondent and on such other persons as the court may direct, as soon as practicable and in any event within 21 days of the date on which it was issued.

(6) The respondent must file a certificate of service within 7 days beginning with the date on which the copy of the respondent's notice was served.

III MEN [728.1]

Guidance for Respondents Practice Direction 20A, paras 30–32 provide guidance as to when a respondent requires permission and the timing of action to be taken by the respondent (**III MEN [732]**).

Practice Direction 20A, paras 33–39 (**III MEN [732]**), provide directions relating to the respondent's notice. Form COP36 is the relevant form.

Practice Direction 20A, paras 40–43 provide information as to the documents to be filed and served with the respondent's notice (**III MEN [732]**).

Practice Direction 20A, paras 44–49 provide information and guidance as to the Respondent's skeleton argument, and form COP37 is the applicable form (**III MEN [732]**).

Form COP20 is the relevant form of Certificate of Service, but now see **III MEN [551.1]**.

III MEN [729]

20.12 Variation of time

The parties may not agree to extend any date or time limit for or in respect of an appeal set by—

(a) these Rules;

(b) the relevant practice direction; or

(c) an order of the appeal judge or the first instance judge.

III MEN [729.1]

Guidance on applications to the court for an extension of time Practice Direction 20A, paras 8–10 provide guidance as to the procedure to apply where the appellant seeks an extension of time for filing an appellant's notice (**III MEN [732]**). By para 39, the provisions of paras 8–10 are made equally applicable to a respondent (**III MEN [732]**).

III MEN [730]

20.13 Power of appeal judge on appeal

(1) In relation to an appeal, an appeal judge has all the powers of the first instance judge whose decision is being appealed.

(2) In particular, the appeal judge has the power to—

(a) affirm, set aside or vary any order made by the first instance judge;

(b) refer any claim or issue to that judge for determination;

(c) order a new hearing;

(d) make a costs order.

(3) The appeal judge's powers may be exercised in relation to the whole or part of an order made by the first instance judge.

III MEN [731]

20.14 Determination of appeals

(1) An appeal shall be limited to a review of the decision of the first instance judge unless—

(a) a practice direction makes different provision for a particular category of appeal; or

(b) the appeal judge considers that in the circumstances of the appeal it would be in the interests of justice to hold a re-hearing.

(2) Unless the appeal judge orders otherwise, the appeal judge shall not receive—

(a) oral evidence; or

(b) evidence that was not before the first instance judge.

(3) The appeal judge shall allow an appeal where the decision of the first instance judge was—

(a) wrong; or

(b) unjust, because of a serious procedural or other irregularity in the proceedings before the first instance judge.

(4) The appeal judge may draw any inference of fact that the appeal judge considers justified on the evidence.

(5) At the hearing of the appeal, a party may not rely on a matter not contained in the appellant's or respondent's notice unless the appeal judge gives permission.

III MEN [731.1]

Application by the court of relevant principles In *EG v RS, JS and BEN PCT* [2010] EWHC 3073 (COP) para 22, HHJ Cardinal considered the application of these principles.

In *Re KJP* [2016] EWCOP 6 the Senior Judge in applying rules 173(1) and 179(3) found no merit in an application for permission to appeal, drawing attention to the importance of avoiding protracted litigation contrary to the best interests of P.

III MEN [731.2]

Procedure for appeals to the Court of Appeal For procedure for appeals to the Court of Appeal, the relevant procedure is in accordance with the provisions of the Civil Procedure Rules 1998. See **CPR 52** in Volume 1 and the special provisions relating to the Court of Appeal: **CPR 52.13**.

PRACTICE DIRECTION 20A – APPEALS

III MEN [732]

This practice direction supplements Part 20 of the Court of Protection Rules 2017

1 This practice direction applies to appeal proceedings within the Court of Protection pursuant to Part 20 (except where Part 22 makes different provision). Where an appeal lies to the Court of Appeal, the Civil Procedure Rules 1998 apply to such an appeal.

PERMISSION

2 Rules 20.5, 20.6 and 20.8 set out the procedure for seeking the court's permission to appeal.

3 Unless the appeal is against an order of committal to prison, the court's permission is required to appeal. An application for permission may be made either to the judge at the hearing at which the decision being appealed was made (the first instance judge), or to an appeal judge.

APPELLANT

Appellant's Notice

4 Rule 20.10 sets out the procedure and time limits for filing and serving an appellant's notice. This is summarised in the following table:

Permission given by the first instance judge	*Permission not given by a first instance judge*	*Permission not needed*
Appellant's notice to be filed within the time directed by the first instance judge; OR Where no time directed, within 21 days of the decision being appealed/ permission decision.	Appellant's notice including application for permission to be filed within 21 days of the decision being appealed.	Appellant's notice to be filed within 21 days of the decision being appealed.
Appellant's notice to be served on all respondents as soon as practicable, and no later than 21 days after it is issued.	Appellant's notice to be served on all respondents as soon as practicable, and no later than 21 days after it is issued.	Appellant's notice to be served on all respondents as soon as practicable, and no later than 21 days after it is issued.

5 Where the first instance judge announces his or her decision and reserves the reasons for judgment until a later date, the judge should, in the exercise of the powers under rule 20.10(2)(a), fix a period for filing the appellant's notice that takes this into account.

6 Except where the appeal judge orders otherwise, a sealed copy of the appellant's notice must be served on all respondents in accordance with the time limits prescribed by rule 20.10(3). At this time the appellant should also serve a skeleton argument on all respondents if permission was granted by the first instance judge.

7 The appellant must, within 7 days beginning on the date on which the copy of the appellant's notice was served, file a certificate of service in relation to service of the appellant's notice.

(Part 6 sets out the rules relating to service and Part 7 sets out the rules relating to notification of P, including the requirement to notify P that an appellant's notice has been issued by the court.)

Extension of time for filing appellant's notice

8 Where the time for filing an appellant's notice has expired, the appellant must –

(a) file an appellant's notice; and
(b) include in that appellant's notice an application for an extension of time.

9 The appellant's notice should state the reason(s) for the delay and the steps taken prior to the application being made.

10 Where the appellant's notice includes an application for an extension of time and permission to appeal has been given or is not required, the respondent has the right to be heard on that application.

Documents to be filed and served with appellant's notice

11 The appellant must file the following documents with his appellant's notice –

(a) one additional copy of the appellant's notice for the court;
(b) one copy of his skeleton argument;
(c) a sealed copy of the order being appealed;
(d) a copy of any order giving or refusing permission to appeal, together with a copy of the judge's reasons for allowing or refusing permission to appeal;
(e) any witness statements or affidavits in support of any application included in the appellant's notice;
(f) the application form and any application notice or response (where relevant to the subject of the appeal);
(g) any other documents which the appellant reasonably considers necessary to enable the court to reach its decision on the hearing of the application or appeal;
(h) a suitable record of the judgment of the first instance judge; and
(i) such other documents as the court may direct.

12 Where it is not possible to file all of the above documents with the appellant's notice, the appellant must indicate which documents have not yet been filed and the reasons why they are not currently available. The appellant must then provide a reasonable estimate of when the missing document or documents can be filed and file and serve them as soon as reasonably practicable.

13 Notice of an application to be made to the court for a remedy incidental to the appeal (e.g. an interim remedy under rule 10.10) may be included in the appellant's notice, or in an application notice using Form COP9 (which is to be attached to the appellant's notice).

14 The appellant should consider what other information the court will need. This may include a list of persons who feature in the case or glossaries of technical terms. A chronology of relevant events will be necessary in most appeals.

15 The information set out in paragraph 11 must be served on each respondent when the appellant's notice is served.

Skeleton arguments

16 The appellant's notice must, subject to paragraph 17, be accompanied by a skeleton argument using, or attached to, a skeleton argument in Form COP37.

17 Where the appellant is unable to provide a skeleton argument to accompany the appellant's notice it must be filed and served on all respondents within 21 days of filing the notice.

18 A skeleton argument must contain a numbered list of the points which the party wishes to make. These should both define and confine the areas of controversy. Each point should be stated as concisely as the nature of the case allows.

19 A numbered point must be followed by a referencc to any document on which the appellant wishes to rely.

20 A skeleton argument must state, in respect of each authority cited –

(a) the proposition of law that the authority demonstrates; and
(b) the parts of the authority (identified by page or paragraph references) that support the proposition.

21 If more than one authority is cited in support of a given proposition, the skeleton argument must briefly state the reason for taking that course. This statement should not materially add to the length of the skeleton argument but should be sufficient to demonstrate, in the context of the argument –

(a) the relevance of the authority or authorities to that argument; and
(b) that the citation is necessary for a proper presentation of that argument.

Suitable record of the judgment

22 Where the judgment to be appealed has been officially recorded by the court, an approved transcript of that record should accompany the appellant's notice. Photocopies will not be accepted for this purpose. However, where there is no officially recorded judgment, the forms of record of the judgment set out in paragraphs 23 to 25 will be acceptable.

Written judgments

23 Where the judgment was given in writing, a copy of that judgment endorsed with the judge's signature.

Note of judgment

24 When the judgment was not officially recorded or given in writing, a note of the judgment (agreed between the appellant's and respondent's advocates) should be submitted for approval to the first instance judge. If the parties cannot agree on a single note of the judgment, both versions should be provided to that judge with an explanatory letter. For the purpose of an application for permission to appeal the note need not be approved by the respondent or the first instance judge.

Advocates' notes of judgments where appellant is unrepresented

25 When the appellant was unrepresented before the first instance judge it is the duty of any advocate for the respondent to make his note of the judgment promptly available, free of charge, to the appellant where there is no officially recorded judgment or if the court so directs. Where the appellant was represented before the first instance judge, it is the duty of his own former advocate to make his note available in these circumstances. The appellant should submit the note of the judgment to the appeal judge.

Transcripts or notes of evidence

26 When the evidence is relevant to the appeal an official transcript of the relevant evidence must be obtained. Transcripts or notes of evidence are generally not needed for the purpose of determining an application for permission to appeal.

27 If evidence relevant to the appeal was not officially recorded, a typed version of the judge's notes of evidence must be obtained.

28 Where the first instance judge or the appeal judge is satisfied that –

(a) an unrepresented appellant; or

(b) an appellant whose legal representation is provided free of charge to the appellant and who is not in receipt of civil Legal Aid,

is in such poor financial circumstances that the cost of a transcript would be an excessive burden the court may certify that the cost of obtaining one official transcript should be borne at public expense.

29 In the case of a request for an official transcript of evidence or proceedings to be paid for at public expense, the court must also be satisfied that there are reasonable grounds for appeal. Whenever possible a request for a transcript at public expense should be made to the first instance judge when asking for permission to appeal.

RESPONDENT

30 A person who has been named as a respondent in appeal proceedings and who wishes only to request that the appeal judge upholds the judgment or order of the first instance judge, whether for the reasons given by the first instance judge or otherwise, does not make an appeal and does not therefore require permission to appeal in accordance with rules 20.5 and 20.6.

31 A person who has been named as a respondent in appeal proceedings, and who also wishes to seek permission to appeal must do so in accordance with rules 20.5 and 20.6.

32 Unless the court otherwise directs, a respondent need not take any action when served with an appellant's notice until such time as notification is given to the respondent that permission to appeal has been granted (unless paragraph 31 applies).

Respondent's notice

33 A respondent who wishes to appeal or who wishes to ask the appeal judge to uphold the order of the first instance judge for reasons different from or additional to those given by the first instance judge must file a respondent's notice.

34 If the respondent does not file a respondent's notice, he will not be entitled, except with the permission of the court, to rely on any reasons for upholding the decision which are different from or additional to those relied on by the first instance judge.

35 Rule 20.11 sets out the procedure and time limits for filing and serving a respondent's notice.

36 Where the first instance judge announces his or her decision and reserves the reasons for judgment until a later date, the judge should, in the exercise of the powers under rule 20.11(3)(a), fix a period for filing the respondent's notice that takes this into account.

37 Except where the appeal judge orders otherwise, a sealed copy of the respondent's notice must be served on all parties to the appeal proceedings in accordance with the time limits prescribed by rule 20.11(5), along with any other material required to be served in accordance with paragraphs 40 to 43 below.

38 The respondent must, within 7 days beginning with the date on which the copy of the respondent's notice was served, file a certificate of service in relation to service of the respondent's notice.

(Part 6 sets out the rules relating to service.)

39 Paragraphs 8 to 10 apply in respect of a respondent's notice as they apply to an appellant's notice.

Documents to be filed and served with respondent's notice

40 The respondent must file the following documents with his respondent's notice –

(a) one additional copy of the respondent's notice for the court;
(b) one copy of his skeleton argument;
(c) a sealed copy of the order being appealed;
(d) a copy of any order giving or refusing permission to appeal, together with a copy of the judge's reasons for allowing or refusing permission to appeal; and
(e) any witness statements or affidavits in support of any application included in the respondent's notice.
(f) any other documents which the respondent reasonably considers necessary to enable the court to reach its decision on the hearing of the application or appeal; and
(g) such other documents as the court may direct.

41 A respondent may include an application for a remedy incidental to the appeal as set out in paragraph 13.

42 The respondent should consider what other information the appeal judge will need. This may include a list of persons who feature in the case or glossaries of technical terms. A chronology of relevant events will be necessary in most appeals.

43 The information set out in paragraph 40 must be served on the appellant and any other respondent when the respondent's notice is served.

Skeleton argument

44 The respondent must file and serve a skeleton argument in all cases where he proposes to address arguments to the court.

45 The respondent's notice must, subject to paragraph 46, be accompanied by a skeleton argument using, or attached to, a skeleton argument in Form COP37.

46 Where the respondent is unable to provide a skeleton argument to accompany the respondent's notice it must be filed and served on all respondents within 21 days of filing the notice.

47 A respondent who does not file a respondent's notice but who files a skeleton argument must file and serve that skeleton argument at least 7 days before the appeal hearing.

48 A respondent's skeleton argument must conform to the requirements at paragraphs 18 to 21 with any necessary modifications. It should, where appropriate, answer the arguments set out in the appellant's skeleton argument.

49 Where a respondent's skeleton argument is not served with the respondent's notice, the respondent must serve his skeleton argument on all parties to the proceedings at the same time as he files it at the court, and must file a certificate of service.

APPEAL HEARING

50 The court will send the parties notification of the date of the hearing of the appeal, together with any other directions given by the court.

PRACTICE DIRECTION 20B – ALLOCATION OF APPEALS

III MEN [733]

This practice direction supplements Part 20 of the Court of Protection Rules 2017

GENERAL

1.1 Rule 20.4 provides for a practice direction to set out the destination of appeals from decisions of judges of the Court of Protection.

1.2 Rule 2.1 and Practice Direction 2A set out which judges of the Court of Protection are Tier 1 Judges, Tier 2 Judges and Tier 3 Judges

APPEALS TO THE COURT OF APPEAL

2.1 Rule 20.4(1) provides that an appeal from a judge of the Court of Protection lies to the Court of Appeal where –

(1) the appeal is from a decision of a Tier 3 Judge; or
(2) where the appeal is from a decision which was itself made on appeal ('a second appeal').

OTHER APPEALS

3.1 Rule 20.4(2) provides that the general rule in relation to other appeals is that –

(1) an appeal from a decision of a Tier 1 Judge lies to a Tier 2 Judge; and
(2) an appeal from a decision of a Tier 2 Judge lies to a Tier 3 Judge.

3.2 Notwithstanding rule 20.4(2), an appeal from a Tier 1 Judge may be heard by a Tier 3 Judge where –

(1) the Tier 1 Judge whose decision is being appealed; or
(2) a Tier 2 Judge; or
(3) a Tier 3 Judge

has directed that the appeal should be heard by a Tier 3 Judge. The judge making a direction under this paragraph need not be:

(a) the same judge who grants permission to appeal; or
(b) the judge who hears the appeal.

3.3 A direction under paragraph 3.2 may only be made if:

(1) the appeal would raise an important point of principle or practice; or
(2) there is some other compelling reason for a Tier 3 Judge to hear the appeal.

3.4 No appeal shall lie against a refusal by a judge to make a direction under paragraph 3.2.

TABLES

4.1 The following tables set out the destination of appeals from decisions of judges of the Court of Protection

Table 1 Appeals from a decision of a Tier 1 Judge

Appeal lies to	***In the following circumstances***	***Permission to appeal may be granted by***
Tier 2 Judge	This is the usual destination for appeals from a Tier 1 Judge	(1) The Tier 1 Judge whose decision is being appealed (2) A Tier 2 Judge (3) A Tier 3 Judge
Tier 3 Judge	It is certified by a judge listed in column 3 that (a) the appeal would raise an important point of principle or practice; or (b) there is some other compelling reason for a Tier 3 Judge to hear the appeal	(1) The Tier 1 Judge whose decision is being appealed (2) A Tier 2 Judge (3) A Tier 3 Judge

Table 2 Appeals from a decision of a Tier 2 Judge

Appeal lies to	***In the following circumstances***	***Permission to appeal may be granted by***
Tier 3 Judge	This is the usual destination for appeals from a Tier 2 Judge (other than second appeals)	(1) The Tier 2 Judge whose decision is being appealed (2) A Tier 3 Judge
Court of Appeal	The appeal is a second appeal.	The Court of Appeal

Table 3 Appeals from a decision of a Tier 3 Judge

Appeal lies to	***In the following circumstances***	***Permission to appeal may be granted by***
Court of Appeal	This is the usual destination for appeals from a Tier 3 Judge (other than second appeals)	(1) The Tier 3 Judge whose decision is being appealed (2) The Court of Appeal
Court of Appeal	The appeal is a second appeal.	The Court of Appeal

PART 21
APPLICATIONS AND PROCEEDINGS IN RELATION TO CONTEMPT OF COURT

SECTION 1—SCOPE AND INTERPRETATION

III MEN [734]

21.1 Scope

(1) This Part sets out the procedure in respect of—

- (a) committal for any breach of a judgment, order or undertaking to do or abstain from doing an act;
- (b) contempt in the face of the court;
- (c) committal for interference with the due administration of justice;
- (d) committal for making a false statement of truth; and
- (e) sequestration to enforce a judgment, order or undertaking.

(2) So far as applicable, and with the necessary modifications, this Part applies in relation to an order requiring a person—

- (a) guilty of contempt of court; or
- (b) punishable by virtue of any enactment as if that person had been guilty of contempt of the High Court,

to pay a fine or to give security for good behaviour, as it applies in relation to an order of committal.

III MEN [735]

21.2 Saving for other powers

(1) This Part is concerned only with procedure and does not itself confer upon the court the power to make an order for—

- (a) committal;
- (b) sequestration; or
- (c) the imposition of a fine in respect of contempt.

(2) Nothing in this Part affects the power of the court to make an order requiring a person—

- (a) guilty of contempt of court; or
- (b) punishable by virtue of any enactment as if that person had been guilty of contempt of the High Court,

to pay a fine or to give security for good behaviour.

(3) Nothing in this Part affects any statutory or inherent power of the court to make a committal order on its own initiative against a person guilty of contempt of court.

III MEN [736]

21.3 Interpretation

In this Part—

- (a) "applicant" means a person making—
  - (i) an application for permission to make a committal application;
  - (ii) a committal application; or
  - (iii) an application for a writ of sequestration;
- (b) "committal application" means any application for an order committing a person to prison;
- (c) "respondent" means a person—
  - (i) against whom a committal application is made or is intended to be made; or

(ii) against whose property it is sought to issue a writ of sequestration; and

(d) "undertaking" means an undertaking to the court.

SECTION 2—COMMITTAL FOR BREACH OF A JUDGMENT, ORDER OR UNDERTAKING TO DO OR ABSTAIN FROM DOING AN ACT

III MEN [737]

21.4 Enforcement of judgment, order or undertaking to do or abstain from doing an act

(1) If a person—

(a) required by a judgment or order of the court to do an act does not do it within the time fixed by the judgment or order; or

(b) disobeys a judgment or order not to do an act,

then, subject to the Debtors Acts 1869 and 1878 and to the provisions of these Rules, the judgment or order may be enforced by an order for committal.

(2) If the time fixed by the judgment or order for doing an act has been varied by a subsequent order, or agreement of the parties under rule 3.7(4), then references in paragraph (1)(a) to the time fixed are references to the time fixed by that subsequent order or agreement.

(3) If the person referred to in paragraph (1) is a company or other corporation, the committal order may be made against any director or other officer of that company or corporation.

(4) So far as applicable, and with the necessary modification, this Section applies to undertakings given by a party as it applies to judgments or orders.

III MEN [738]

21.5 Requirement for service of a copy judgment or order and time for service

(1) Unless the court dispenses with service under rule 21.8 a judgment or order may not be enforced under rule 21.4 unless a copy of it has been served on the person required to do or not to do the act in question, and in the case of a judgment or order requiring a person to do an act—

(a) the copy has been served before the end of the time fixed for doing the act, together with a copy of any order fixing that time;

(b) where the time has been varied by a subsequent order or agreement, a copy of that subsequent order or agreement has also been served; and

(c) where the judgment or order was made pursuant to an earlier judgment or order requiring the act to be done, a copy of the earlier judgment or order has also been served.

(2) Where the person referred to in paragraph (1) is a company or other corporation, a copy of the judgment or order must also be served on a director or officer of the company or corporation before the end of the time fixed for doing the act.

(3) Copies of the judgment or order and any orders or agreements fixing or varying the time for doing an act must be served in accordance with rule 21.6 or 21.7, or in accordance with an order for alternative service made under rule 21.8(2)(b).

III MEN [739]

21.6 Method of service—copies of judgments or orders

Subject to rules 21.7 and 21.8, copies of judgments or orders and any orders or agreements fixing or varying the time for doing an act must be served personally.

III MEN [740]

21.7 Method of service—copies of undertakings

(1) Subject to paragraph (2) and rule 21.8, a copy of any document recording an undertaking will be delivered by the court to the person who gave the undertaking by—

(a) handing to that person a copy of the document before that person leaves the court building;

(b) posting a copy to that person at the residence or place of business of that person where this is known; or

(c) posting a copy to that person's solicitor.

(2) If delivery cannot be effected in accordance with paragraph (1), the court officer must deliver a copy of the document to the party for whose benefit the undertaking was given and that party must serve it personally on the person who gave the undertaking as soon as practicable.

(3) Where the person referred to in paragraph (1) is a company or other corporation, a copy of the document must also be served on a director or officer of the company or corporation.

III MEN [741]

21.8 Dispensation with personal service

(1) In the case of a judgment or order requiring a person not to do an act, the court may dispense with service of a copy of the judgment or order in accordance with rules 21.5 to 21.7 if it is satisfied that the person has had notice of it by—

(a) being present when the judgment or order was given or made; or

(b) being in attendance at court where notice of the order or judgment was displayed; or

(c) being notified of its terms by telephone, email or otherwise.

(2) In the case of any judgment or order the court may—

(a) dispense with service under rules 21.5 to 21.7 if the court thinks it just to do so; or

(b) make an order in respect of service by an alternative method or at an alternative place.

III MEN [742]

21.9 Requirement for a penal notice on judgments and orders

(1) Subject to paragraph (2), a judgment or order to do or not to do an act may not be enforced under rule 21.4 unless there is prominently displayed, on the front of the copy of the judgment or order served in accordance with this Section, a warning to the person required to do or not to do the act in question that disobedience to the order would be a contempt of court punishable by imprisonment, a fine or sequestration of assets.

(2) An undertaking to do or not to do an act which is contained in a judgment or order may be enforced under rule 21.4 notwithstanding that the judgment or order does not contain the warning described in paragraph (1).

(Paragraphs 2.1 to 2.3 of Practice Direction 21A contain provision about penal notices and warnings in relation to undertakings.)

III MEN [743]

21.10 How to make the committal application

(1) A committal application is made by an application notice under Part 10 in the proceedings in which the judgment or order was made or the undertaking was given.

(2) Where the committal application is made against a person who is not an existing party to the proceedings, it is made against that person by an application notice under Part 10.

(3) The application notice must—

(a) set out in full the grounds on which the committal application is made and must identify, separately and numerically, each alleged act of contempt including, if known, the date of each of the alleged acts; and

(b) be supported by one or more affidavits containing all the evidence relied upon.

(4) Subject to paragraph (5), the application notice and the evidence in support must be served personally on the respondent.

(5) The court may—

(a) dispense with service under paragraph (4) if it considers it just to do so; or

(b) make an order in respect of service by an alternative method or at an alternative place.

III MEN [744]

21.11 Committal for breach of a solicitor's undertaking

(1) This rule applies where an order for committal is sought in respect of a breach by a solicitor of an undertaking given by the solicitor to the court in connection with proceedings before the court.

(2) The applicant must obtain permission from the court before making a committal application under this rule.

(3) The application for permission must be made by filing an application notice under Part 10.

(4) The application for permission must be supported by an affidavit setting out—

(a) the name, description and address of the respondent; and

(b) the grounds on which the committal order is sought.

(5) The application for permission may be made without notice.

(6) Rules 10.5 and 13.4 do not apply.

(7) Unless the applicant makes the committal application within 14 days after permission has been granted under this rule, the permission will lapse.

SECTION 3—CONTEMPT IN THE FACE OF THE COURT

III MEN [745]

21.12 Contempt in the face of the court

Where contempt has occurred in the face of the court, the court may deal with the matter on its own initiative and give such directions as it thinks fit for the disposal of the matter.

SECTION 4—COMMITTAL FOR INTERFERENCE WITH THE DUE ADMINISTRATION OF JUSTICE

III MEN [746]

21.13 Scope

(1) This Section regulates committal applications in relation to interference with the due administration of justice in connection with proceedings in the Court of Protection, except where the contempt is committed in the face of the court or consists of disobedience to an order of the court or a breach of an undertaking to the court.

(2) A committal application under this Section may not be made without the permission of the court.

(The procedure for applying for permission to make a committal application is set out in rule 21.15.)

(Rules 21.16(3) and (4) make provision for cases in which both this Section and Section 5 (Committal for making a false statement of truth) may be relevant.)

III MEN [747]

21.14 Court to which application for permission under this Section is to be made

(1) Where contempt of court is committed in connection with any proceedings in the Court of Protection, the application for permission may only be made to a Tier 3 Judge.

(2) Where contempt of court is committed otherwise than in connection with any proceedings, Part 81 of the Civil Procedure Rules 1998 applies.

III MEN [748]

21.15 Application for permission

(1) The application for permission to make a committal application must be made by an application notice under Part 10, and the application notice must include or be accompanied by—

- (a) a detailed statement of the applicant's grounds for making the committal application; and
- (b) an affidavit setting out the facts and exhibiting all documents relied upon.

(2) The application notice and the documents referred to in paragraph (1) must be served personally on the respondent unless the court otherwise directs.

(3) Within 14 days of service on the respondent of the application notice, the respondent—

- (a) must file and serve an acknowledgment of service; and
- (b) may file and serve evidence.

(4) The court will consider the application for permission at an oral hearing, unless it considers that such a hearing is not appropriate.

(5) If the respondent intends to appear at the oral hearing referred to in paragraph (4), the respondent must give 7 days' notice in writing of such intention to the court and any other party and at the same time provide a written summary of the submissions which the respondent proposes to make.

(6) Where permission to proceed is given, the court may give such directions as it thinks fit.

SECTION 5—COMMITTAL FOR MAKING A FALSE STATEMENT OF TRUTH

III MEN [749]

21.16 Scope and interaction with other Sections of this Part

(1) This Section contains rules about committal applications in relation to making, or causing to be made, a false statement in a document verified by a statement of truth, without an honest belief in its truth.

(2) Where the committal relates only to a false statement of truth, this Section applies.

(3) Where the committal application relates to both—

(a) a false statement of truth; and

(b) breach of a judgment, order or undertaking to do or abstain from doing an act,

then Section 2 (Committal for breach of a judgment, order or undertaking to do or abstain from doing an act) applies, but subject to paragraph (4).

(4) To the extent that a committal application referred to in paragraph (3) relates to a false statement of truth—

(a) the applicant must obtain the permission of the court in accordance with rule 21.17; or

(b) the court may direct that the matter be referred to the Attorney General with a request that the Attorney General consider whether to bring proceedings for contempt of court.

III MEN [750]

21.17 Committal application in relation to a false statement of truth

(1) A committal application in relation to a false statement of truth in connection with proceedings in the Court of Protection may be made only—

(a) with the permission of a Tier 3 Judge; or

(b) by the Attorney General.

(2) Where permission is required under paragraph (1)(a), rule 21.15 applies.

(3) The court may direct that the matter be referred to the Attorney General with a request that the Attorney General consider whether to bring proceedings for contempt of court.

SECTION 6—WRIT OF SEQUESTRATION TO ENFORCE A JUDGMENT, ORDER OR UNDERTAKING

III MEN [751]

21.18 Scope

This Section contains rules about applications for a writ of sequestration to enforce a judgment, order or undertaking.

III MEN [752]

21.19 Writ of sequestration to enforce a judgment, order or undertaking

(1) If—

(a) a person required by a judgment or order to do an act does not do it within the time fixed by the judgment or order; or

(b) a person disobeys a judgment or order not to do an act,

then, subject to the provisions of these Rules and if the court permits, the judgment or order may be enforced by a writ of sequestration against the property of that person.

(2) If the time fixed by the judgment or order for doing an act has been varied by a subsequent order, or agreement of the parties under rule 3.7(4), references in paragraph (1)(a) to the time fixed are references to the time fixed by that subsequent order or agreement.

(3) If the person referred to in paragraph (1) is a company or other corporation, the writ of sequestration may in addition be issued against the property of any director or other officer of that company or corporation.

(4) So far as applicable, and with the necessary modifications, this Section applies to undertakings given by a party as it applies to judgments or orders.

III MEN [753]

21.20 Requirement for service of a copy of the judgment or order and time for service

(1) Unless the court dispenses with service under rule 21.23, a judgment or order may not be enforced by writ of sequestration unless a copy of it has been served on the person required to do or not to do the act in question, and in the case of a judgment or order requiring a person to act—

- (a) the copy has been served before the end of the time fixed for doing the act, together with a copy of any order fixing that time;
- (b) where the time for doing the act has been varied by a subsequent order or agreement, a copy of that order or agreement has also been served; and
- (c) where the judgment or order was made pursuant to an earlier judgment or order requiring the act to be done, a copy of the earlier judgment or order has also been served.

(2) Where the person referred to in paragraph (1) is a company or other corporation, a copy of the judgment or order must also be served on a director or other officer of the company or corporation before the end of the time fixed for doing the act.

(3) Copies of the judgment or order and any orders or agreements fixing or varying the time for doing an act must be served in accordance with rule 21.21 or 21.22, or in accordance with an order for alternative service made under rule 21.23(2)(b).

III MEN [754]

21.21 Method of service—copies of judgments or orders

Subject to rules 21.22 and 21.23, copies of judgments or orders and any orders or agreements fixing or varying the time for doing an act must be served personally.

III MEN [755]

21.22 Method of service—copies of undertakings

(1) Subject to paragraph (2) and rule 21.23, a copy of any document recording an undertaking will be delivered by the court to the person who gave the undertaking by—

- (a) handing to that person a copy of the document before that person leaves the court building;
- (b) posting a copy to that person at the residence or place of business of that person where this is known; or
- (c) posting a copy to that person's address.

(2) If delivery cannot be effected in accordance with paragraph (1), the court officer must deliver a copy of the document to the party for whose benefit the undertaking was given, and that party must serve it personally on the person who gave the undertaking as soon as practicable.

(3) Where the person referred to in paragraph (1) is a company or other corporation, a copy of the judgment or order must also be served on a director or officer of the company or corporation.

III MEN [756]

21.23 Dispensation with personal service

(1) In the case of a judgment or order requiring a person to do or not to do an act, the court may dispense with service of a copy of the judgment or order in accordance with rules 21.20 to 21.22 if it is satisfied that the person has had notice of it by—

(a) being present when the judgment or order was made;

(b) being in attendance at court where notice of the order or judgment was displayed; or

(c) being notified of its terms by telephone, email or otherwise.

(2) In the case of any judgment or order the court may—

(a) dispense with service under rules 21.20 to 21.22 if the court thinks it just to do so; or

(b) make an order in respect of service by an alternative method or at an alternative place.

III MEN [757]

21.24 Requirement for a penal notice on judgments and orders

(1) Subject to paragraph (2), a judgment or order to do or not to do an act may not be enforced by a writ of sequestration unless there is prominently displayed, on the front of the copy of the judgment or order served in accordance with this Section, a warning to the person required to do or not to do the act in question that disobedience to the order would be a contempt of court punishable by imprisonment, a fine or sequestration of assets.

(2) An undertaking to do or not to do an act which is contained in a judgment or order may be enforced by a writ of sequestration notwithstanding that the judgment or order does not contain the warning described in paragraph (1).

(Paragraphs 2.1 to 2.3 of Practice Direction 21A contain provision about penal notices and warnings in relation to undertakings.)

III MEN [758]

21.25 How to make an application for permission to issue a writ of sequestration

(1) An application for permission to issue a writ of sequestration must be made to a Tier 3 Judge.

(2) An application for permission to issue a writ of sequestration must be made by filing an application notice under Part 10.

(3) The application notice must—

(a) set out in full the grounds on which the committal application is made and must identify, separately and numerically, each alleged act of contempt including, if known, the date of each of the alleged acts; and

(b) be supported by one or more affidavits containing all the evidence relied upon.

(4) Subject to paragraph (5), the application notice and the evidence in support must be served personally on the respondent.

(5) The court may—

(a) dispense with service under paragraph (4) if it considers it just to do so; or

(b) make an order in respect of service by an alternative method or at an alternative place.

III MEN [759]

21.26 Form of writ of sequestration

A writ of sequestration must be in Form No 67 as set out in either Practice Direction 5A supporting the Family Procedure Rules 2010 or Practice Direction 4 supporting the Civil Procedure Rules 1998 (or in a form containing corresponding provision).

SECTION 7—GENERAL RULES ABOUT COMMITTAL APPLICATIONS, ORDERS FOR COMMITTAL AND WRITS OF SEQUESTRATION

III MEN [760]

21.27 Hearing for committal order or writ of sequestration to be in public

(1) Notwithstanding rule 4.1 (general rule—hearing to be in private), when determining an application for committal or application for sequestration the court will hold the hearing in public unless it directs otherwise.

(2) If the court hearing an application in private decides to make a committal order against the respondent, it must in public state—

(a) the name of the respondent;

(b) in general terms, the nature of the contempt of court in respect of which the committal order is being made; and

(c) the length of the period of the committal order.

(3) Where a committal order is made in the absence of the respondent, the court may on its own initiative fix a date and time when the respondent is to be brought before the court.

III MEN [760.1]

Guidance on applications to the court in respect of contempt and committal For guidance and notes on the sanctions and sentences available for contempt, and the issue of release, see the General Notes to Committal in Volume 1 at paras **RSC 52 [1] – RSC 52 [4A]**. For consideration of the appropriate approach for dealing with committal concerning those under a disability see **RSC 52 [9]**. The relevant standard of proof is the criminal standard, see **RSC 52 [10]**.

III MEN [760.2]

Publicity and committals The procedure for all committal proceedings must now follow not only the relevant rules but also the Practice Direction: Committal for Contempt of Court – Open Court issued by the Lord Chief Justice on 26 March 2015 and the Practice Guidance: Committal for Contempt of Court – Open Court dated 24 June 2015. This Practice Direction and Guidance supersede all previous Practice Directions and Guidance. The Practice Direction addresses issues of public and private hearings, the engagement of the Press and the issue of judgments. In a clear indication of the importance of Open Justice strict procedures are applied for the publicity of the hearing, the notification of press, the publication of the outcome and the limiting of matters in private. The Guidance addresses questions which had arisen surrounding press notification, and judgments. See CPR 81.28.

In *A Local Authority v B, F & G* [2014] EWCOP B18 HHJ Cardinal applied the principles of *Hadkinson v Hadkinson* in considering an application by an individual who remained in contempt.

III MEN [761]

21.28 The hearing

(1) Unless the court hearing the committal application or application for sequestration otherwise permits, the applicant may not rely on—

(a) any grounds other than—

(i) those set out in the application notice; or

(ii) in relation to committal applications under Section 4, the statement of grounds required by rule 21.15(1)(a) (where not included in the application notice);

(b) any evidence unless it has been served in accordance with the relevant Section of this Part or a practice direction supplementing this Part.

(2) At the hearing, the respondent is entitled—

(a) to give oral evidence, whether or not the respondent has filed or served written evidence, and, if doing so, may be cross-examined; and

(b) with the permission of the court, to call a witness to give evidence whether or not the witness has made an affidavit or witness statement.

(3) The court may require or permit any party or other person (other than the respondent) to give oral evidence at the hearing.

(4) The court may give directions requiring the attendance for cross-examination of a witness who has given written evidence.

III MEN [762]

21.29 Power to suspend execution of a committal order

(1) The court making the committal order may also order that the execution of the order will be suspended for such period or on such terms and conditions as the court may specify.

(2) Unless the court otherwise directs, the applicant must serve on the respondent a copy of any order made under paragraph (1).

III MEN [763]

21.30 Warrant of committal

(1) If a committal order is made, the order will be for the issue of a warrant of committal.

(2) Unless the court orders otherwise—

(a) a copy of the committal order must be served on the respondent either before or at the time of the execution of the warrant of committal; or

(b) where the warrant of committal has been signed by the judge, the committal order may be served on the respondent at any time within 36 hours after the execution of the warrant.

(3) Without further order of the court, a warrant of committal must not be enforced more than 2 years after the date on which the warrant is issued.

III MEN [764]

21.31 Discharge of a person in custody

(1) A person committed to prison for contempt of court may apply to the court to be discharged.

(2) The application must—

(a) be in writing and attested by the governor of the prison (or any other officer of the prison not below the rank of principal officer);

(b) show that the person committed to prison for contempt has purged, or wishes to purge, the contempt; and

(c) be served on the person (if any) at whose instance the warrant of committal was issued at least one day before the application is made.

(3) Paragraph (2) does not apply to an application made by the Official Solicitor acting with official authority for the discharge of a person in custody.

III MEN [765]

21.32 Discharge of a person in custody where a writ of sequestration has been issued

Where—

(a) a writ of sequestration has been issued to enforce a judgment or order;

(b) the property is in the custody or power of the respondent;

(c) the respondent has been committed for failing to deliver up any property or deposit it in court or elsewhere; and

(d) the commissioners appointed by the writ of sequestration take possession of the property as if it belonged to the respondent,

then, without prejudice to rule 21.31(1) (discharge of a person in custody), the court may discharge the respondent and give such directions for dealing with the property taken by the commissioners as it thinks fit.

PRACTICE DIRECTION 21A – CONTEMPT OF COURT

III MEN [766]

This practice direction supplements Part 21 of the Court of Protection Rules 2017

SECTION 2 OF PART 21 – COMMITTAL FOR BREACH OF A JUDGMENT, ORDER OR UNDERTAKING TO DO OR ABSTAIN FROM DOING AN ACT

Requirement for a penal notice on judgments and orders – form of penal notice (Rule 21.9)

1. A judgment or order which restrains a party from doing an act or requires an act to be done must, if disobedience is to be dealt with by proceedings for contempt of court, have a penal notice endorsed on it as follows (or in words to substantially the same effect) –

> 'If you the within-named [. . .] do not comply with this order you may be held to be in contempt of court and imprisoned or fined, or your assets may be seized.'

Requirement for a penal notice on judgments and orders – undertakings (Rule 21.9)

2.1 Subject to rule 21.9(2) (which covers the case where the undertaking is contained in an order or judgment), the form of an undertaking to do or abstain from doing any act must be endorsed with a notice setting out the consequences of disobedience as follows (or in words to substantially the same effect) –

> 'You may be held to be in contempt of court and imprisoned or fined, or your assets may be seized, if you break the promises you have given to the court.'

2.2 The court may decline to –

(a) accept an undertaking; or

(b) deal with disobedience in respect of an undertaking by contempt of court proceedings.

unless the party giving the undertaking has made a signed statement to the effect that the party understands the terms of the undertaking and the consequences of failure to comply with it, as follows (or in words to substantially the same effect) –

> 'I understand the undertaking that I have given and that if I break any of my promises to the court I may be sent to prison, or fined, or my assets may be seized, for contempt of court.'

2.3 The statement need not be made before the court in person. It may be endorsed on the court copy of the undertaking or may be filed in a separate document such as a letter.

SECTION 3 OF PART 21 – CONTEMPT IN THE FACE OF THE COURT

Committal for contempt in the face of the court (Rule 21.12)

3.1 Where the committal proceedings relate to a contempt in the face of the court the matters referred to in paragraph 3.3 should be given particular attention. Normally it will be appropriate to defer consideration of the respondent's actions and behaviour to allow the respondent time to reflect on what has occurred. The time needed for the following procedures should allow such a period of reflection.

3.2 The use of the Part 10 procedure is not required for contempt in the face of the court, but other provisions of this practice direction should be applied, as necessary, or adapted to the circumstances.

3.3 The judge should –

(a) tell the respondent of the possible penalty that the respondent faces;
(b) inform the respondent in detail, and preferably in writing, of the actions and behaviour of the respondent which have given rise to the committal application;
(c) if the judge considers that an apology would remove the need for the committal application, tell the respondent;
(d) have regard to the need for the respondent to be –
  (i) allowed a reasonable time for responding to the committal application, including, if necessary, preparing a defence;
  (ii) made aware of the possible availability of criminal legal aid and how to contact the Legal Aid Agency;
  (iii) given the opportunity, if unrepresented, to obtain legal advice;
  (iv) if unable to understand English, allowed to make arrangements, seeking the court's assistance if necessary, for an interpreter to attend the hearing; and
  (v) brought back before the court for the committal application to be heard within a reasonable time;
(e) allow the respondent an opportunity to –
have regard to the need for the respondent to be –
  (i) apologise to the court;
  (ii) explain the respondent's actions and behaviour; and
  (iii) if the contempt is proved, to address the court on the penalty to be imposed on the respondent; and
(f) where appropriate, nominate a suitable person to give the respondent the information. (It is likely to be appropriate to nominate a person where the effective communication of information by the judge to the respondent was not possible when the incident occurred.)

3.4 If there is a risk of the appearance of bias, the judge should ask another judge to hear the committal application.

3.5 Where the committal application is to be heard by another judge, a written statement by the judge before whom the actions and behaviour of the respondent which have given rise to the committal application took place may be admitted as evidence of those actions and behaviour.

SECTION 5 OF PART 21 – COMMITTAL FOR MAKING A FALSE STATEMENT OF TRUTH

Committal application in relation to a false statement of truth (Rule 21.17)

4.1 Rule 21.17(1)(b) provides that a committal application may be made by the Attorney General. However the Attorney General prefers a request that comes from the court to one made direct by a party to the proceedings in which the alleged contempt occurred without prior consideration by the court. A request to the Attorney General is not a way of appealing against, or reviewing, the decision of the judge.

4.2 Where the permission of the court is sought under rule 21.17(1)(a), the affidavit evidence in support of the application must –

(a) identify the statement said to be false;
(b) explain –
  (i) why it is false; and
  (ii) why the maker knew the statement to be false at the time it was made; and
(c) explain why contempt proceedings would be appropriate in the light of the overriding objective in Part 1 of the Rules.

4.3 The court may –

(a) exercise any of its powers under the Rules (including the power to give directions under rule 21.15(6));
(b) initiate steps to consider if there is a contempt of court and, where there is, to punish it; or
(c) as provided by rule 21.17(3), direct that the matter be referred to the Attorney General with a request to consider whether to bring proceedings for contempt of court.

4.4 A request to the Attorney General to consider whether to bring proceedings for contempt of court must be made in writing and sent to the Attorney General's Office at 5–8 The Sanctuary, London SW1P 3JS.

4.5 A request to the Attorney General must be accompanied by a copy of any order directing that the matter be referred to the Attorney General and must –

(a) identify the statement said to be false;
(b) explain –
  (i) why it is false; and
  (ii) why the maker knew the statement to be false at the time it was made; and
(c) explain why contempt proceedings would be appropriate in the light of the overriding objective in Part 1 of the Rules.

4.6 Once the applicant receives the result of the request to the Attorney General, the applicant must send a copy of it to the court that will deal with the committal application, and the court will give such directions as it sees fit.

4.7 The rules do not change the law of contempt or introduce new categories of contempt. A person applying to commence such proceedings should consider whether the incident complained of does amount to contempt of court and whether such proceedings would further the overriding objective in Part 1 of the Rules.

SECTION 6 OF PART 21 – WRIT OF SEQUESTRATION TO ENFORCE A JUDGMENT, ORDER OR UNDERTAKING

Requirement for a penal notice on judgments and orders (Rule 21.24)

5 Paragraphs 1 and 2.1 to 2.3 apply to judgments or orders to be enforced by a writ of sequestration (subject in the case of undertakings to rule 21.24(2), which covers the case where the undertaking is contained in an order or judgment).

Levying execution on certain days

6 Unless the court orders otherwise, a writ of sequestration to enforce a judgment, order or undertaking must not be executed on a Sunday, Good Friday or Christmas Day.

SECTION 7 OF PART 21 – GENERAL RULES ABOUT COMMITTAL APPLICATIONS, ORDERS FOR COMMITTAL AND WRITS OF SEQUESTRATION

Human rights

7 In all cases the Convention rights of those involved should particularly be borne in mind. It should be noted that the standard of proof, having regard to the possibility that a person may be sent to prison, is that allegation be proved beyond reasonable doubt.

(Section 1 of the Human Rights Act 1998 defines 'the Convention rights'.)

Applications for committal after permission granted or where permission not needed

8.1 An application for an order of committal must be commenced by filing a COP9 application notice in accordance with Part 21.

8.2 The applicant must file the original and one copy of the application notice, together with the original and one copy of the affidavit that is required by rule 21.10.

8.3 The affidavit must contain –

(a) the name and description of the person making the application;
(b) the name, address and description of the person sought to be committed;
(c) the grounds on which committal is sought;
(d) a description of each alleged act of contempt, identifying:
 (i) each act separately and numerically, and
 (ii) if known, the date of each act; and
(e) any additional information required by paragraphs 8.4 and 8.5.

8.4 Where the allegation of contempt relates to prior proceedings before the court, the affidavit must also state:

(a) the case number of those prior proceedings;
(b) the date of the proceedings; and
(c) the name of P.

8.5 The affidavit must also set out in full any order, judgment or undertaking which it is alleged has been disobeyed or broken by the person sought to be committed. This will apply where the allegation of contempt is made on the grounds that –

(a) a person is required by a judgment or order to do an act, and has refused or neglected to do it within the time fixed by the judgment or order or any subsequent order;
(b) a person has disobeyed a judgment or order requiring that person to abstain from doing an act; or
(c) a person has breached the terms of an undertaking which that person gave to the court.

(Practice Direction A accompanying Part 14 sets out further details in relation to affidavits.)

Evidence

9.1 Written evidence in support of or in opposition to a committal application must be given by affidavit.

9.2 Written evidence served in support of or in opposition to a committal application must, unless the court directs otherwise, be filed.

9.3 The following rules do not apply to committal applications –

(a) rule 15.12 (Court's power to direct that evidence is to be given by a single joint expert); and

(b) rule 15.13 (Instructions to single joint expert).

Hearing of application (Rule 21.28)

10.1 When filing the application notice, the applicant must obtain from the court a date for the hearing of the committal application.

10.2 Unless the court otherwise directs, the hearing date of a committal application must not be less than 14 days after service of the application notice on the respondent. The hearing date must be specified in the application notice or in a Notice of Hearing attached to and served with the application notice.

10.3 The court may at any time give case management directions (including directions for the service of evidence by the person sought to be committed and evidence in reply by the applicant) or may hold a directions hearing.

10.4 The court may on the hearing date –

(a) give case management directions with a view to a hearing of the committal application on a future date; or

(b) if the committal application is ready to be heard, proceed forthwith to hear it.

10.5 Where the person sought to be committed gives oral evidence at the hearing (in accordance with rule 21.28(2)), he or she may be cross-examined.

10.6 In dealing with any committal application, the court will have regard to the need for the respondent to have details of the alleged acts of contempt and the opportunity to respond to the committal application.

10.7 The court will also have regard to the need for the respondent to be –

(a) allowed a reasonable time for responding to the committal application including, if necessary, preparing a defence;

(b) made aware of the possible availability of criminal legal aid and how to contact the Legal Aid Agency;

(c) given the opportunity, if unrepresented, to obtain legal advice; and

(d) if unable to understand English, allowed to make arrangements, seeking the assistance of the court if necessary, for an interpreter to attend the hearing.

Striking out, procedural defects and discontinuance

11.1 On application by the respondent or on its own initiative, the court may strike out a committal application if it appears to the court –

(a) that the application and the evidence served in support of it disclose no reasonable ground for alleging that the respondent is guilty of a contempt of court;

(b) that the application is an abuse of the court's process or, if made in existing proceedings, is otherwise likely to obstruct the just disposal of those proceedings; or

(c) that there has been a failure to comply with a rule, practice direction or court order.

11.2 The court may waive any procedural defect in the commencement or conduct of a committal application if satisfied that no injustice has been caused to the respondent by the defect.

11.3 A committal application may not be discontinued without the permission of the court.

Hearing of application

(a)
(b)

10. Where the person sought to be committed gives oral evidence at the hearing (in accordance with rule 187), he may be cross-examined.

PART 22
CIVIL RESTRAINT ORDERS

III MEN [767]

22.1 Powers of the court to make civil restraint orders

(1) If the court, whether or not on its own initiative, dismisses an application (including an application for permission) and considers that the application is totally without merit—

(a) the court's order must record that fact; and
(b) the court must at the same time consider whether it is appropriate to make a civil restraint order.

(2) Practice Direction 22A sets out—

(a) the circumstances in which the court has the power to make a civil restraint order against a party to proceedings;
(b) the procedure where a party applies for a civil restraint order against another party; and
(c) the consequences of the court making a civil restraint order.

PRACTICE DIRECTION 22A – CIVIL RESTRAINT ORDERS

III MEN [768]

This practice direction supplements Part 22 of the Court of Protection Rules 2017

INTRODUCTION

1. This practice direction applies where the court is considering whether to make –

(a) a limited civil restraint order;
(b) an extended civil restraint order; or
(c) a general civil restraint order,

against a party who has made applications which are totally without merit.

2. Rule 3.1 (General case management powers), rule 3.6(2)–(5) (Dealing with the application), rule 14.2 (Power of the court to control evidence), and rule 15.5 (Power of the court to restrict expert evidence) provide powers to the court to case manage and control the preparation, presentation and the conduct of any case before the court.

MENTAL CAPACITY AND MENTAL HEALTH

3. Rule 22.1 provides that where an application (including an application for permission) is dismissed, whether or not on the court's own initiative, and is totally without merit, the court order must specify that fact and the court must consider whether to make a civil restraint order.

LIMITED CIVIL RESTRAINT ORDERS

4. A limited civil restraint order may be made where a party has made 2 or more applications which are totally without merit.

5. Where the court makes a limited civil restraint order, the party against whom the order is made –

(a) will be restrained from making any further applications in the proceedings in which the order is made without first obtaining the permission of a judge identified in the order;
(b) may apply for amendment or discharge of the order, but only with the permission of a judge identified in the order; and
(c) may apply for permission to appeal the order and if permission is granted, may appeal the order.

6. Where a party who is subject to a limited civil restraint order –

(a) makes a further application in the proceedings in which the order is made without first obtaining the permission of a judge identified in the order, such application will automatically be dismissed –
    (i) without the judge having to make any further order; and
    (ii) without the need for the other party to respond to it; and
(b) repeatedly makes applications for permission pursuant to that order which are totally without merit, the court may direct that if the party makes any further application for permission which is totally without merit, the decision to dismiss the application will be final and there will be no right of appeal, unless the judge who refused permission grants permission to appeal.

7. A party who is subject to a limited civil restraint order may not make an application for permission under paragraphs 5(a) or (b) without first serving notice of the application on the other party in accordance with paragraph 8.

8. A notice under paragraph 7 must –

(a) set out the nature and grounds of the application; and
(b) provide the other party with at least 7 days within which to respond.

9. An application for permission under paragraphs 5(a) or (b) –

(a) must be made in writing;
(b) must include the other party's written response, if any, to the notice served under paragraph 7; and
(c) will be determined without a hearing.

10. Where a party makes an application for permission under paragraphs 5(a) or (b) and permission is refused, any application for permission to appeal –

(a) must be made in writing; and
(b) will be determined without a hearing.

11. A limited civil restraint order –

(a) is limited to the particular proceedings in which it is made;
(b) will remain in effect for the duration of the proceedings in which it is made, unless the court orders otherwise; and
(c) must identify the judge or judges to whom an application for permission under paragraphs 5(a), 5(b) or 10 should be made.

EXTENDED CIVIL RESTRAINT ORDERS

12. An extended civil restraint order may be made where a party has persistently made applications which are totally without merit.

13. Unless the court orders otherwise, where the court makes an extended civil restraint order, the party against whom the order is made –

(a) will be restrained from making applications in the Court of Protection concerning any matter involving or relating to or touching upon or leading to the proceedings in which the order is made without first obtaining the permission of a judge identified in the order;
(b) may apply for amendment or discharge of the order, but only with the permission of a judge identified in the order; and
(c) may apply for permission to appeal the order and if permission is granted, may appeal the order.

14. Where a party who is subject to an extended civil restraint order –

(a) makes an application in the Court of Protection concerning any matter involving or relating to or touching upon or leading to the proceedings in which the order is made without first obtaining the permission of a judge identified in the order, the application will automatically be struck out or dismissed –
    (i) without the judge having to make any further order; and
    (ii) without the need for the other party to respond to it; and
(b) repeatedly makes applications for permission pursuant to that order which are totally without merit, the court may direct that if the party makes any further application for permission which is totally without merit, the decision to dismiss the application will be final and there will be no right of appeal, unless the judge who refused permission grants permission to appeal.

15. A party who is subject to an extended civil restraint order may not make an application for permission under paragraphs 13(a) or (b) without first serving notice of the application on the other party in accordance with paragraph 16.

16. A notice under paragraph 15 must –

(a) set out the nature and grounds of the application; and
(b) provide the other party with at least 7 days within which to respond.

17. An application for permission under paragraphs 13(a) or (b) –

(a) must be made in writing;
(b) must include the other party's written response, if any, to the notice served under paragraph 15; and
(c) will be determined without a hearing.

18. Where a party makes an application for permission under paragraphs 13(a) or (b) and permission is refused, any application for permission to appeal –

(a) must be made in writing; and
(b) will be determined without a hearing.

19. An extended civil restraint order –

(a) will be made for a specified period not exceeding 2 years; and
(b) must identify the judge or judges to whom an application for permission under paragraphs 13(a), 13(b) or 18 should be made.

20. The court may extend the duration of an extended civil restraint order, if it considers it appropriate to do so, but the duration of the order must not be extended for a period greater than 2 years on any given occasion.

GENERAL CIVIL RESTRAINT ORDERS

21. A general civil restraint order may be made where the party against whom the order is made persists in making applications which are totally without merit, in circumstances where an extended civil restraint order would not be sufficient or appropriate.

22. Unless the court otherwise orders, where the court makes a general civil restraint order, the party against whom the order is made –

(a) will be restrained from making any application in the Court of Protection without first obtaining the permission of a judge identified in the order;
(b) may apply for amendment or discharge of the order, but only with the permission of a judge identified in the order; and
(c) may apply for permission to appeal the order and if permission is granted, may appeal the order.

23. Where a party who is subject to a general civil restraint order –

(a) makes an application in the Court of Protection without first obtaining the permission of a judge identified in the order, the application will automatically be struck out or dismissed –
 (i) without the judge having to make any further order; and
 (ii) without the need for the other party to respond to it; and
(b) repeatedly makes applications for permission pursuant to that order which are totally without merit, the court may direct that if the party makes any further application for permission which is totally without merit, the decision to dismiss that application will be final and there will be no right of appeal, unless the judge who refused permission grants permission to appeal.

24. A party who is subject to a general civil restraint order may not make an application for permission under paragraphs 22(a) or (b) without first serving notice of the application on the other party in accordance with paragraph 25.

25. A notice under paragraph 24 must –

(a) set out the nature and grounds of the application; and
(b) provide the other party with at least 7 days within which to respond.

26. An application for permission under paragraphs 22 (a) or (b) –

(a) must be made in writing;
(b) must include the other party's written response, if any, to the notice served under paragraph 24; and
(c) will be determined without a hearing.

27. Where a party makes an application for permission under paragraphs 22(a) or (b) and permission is refused, any application for permission to appeal –

(a) must be made in writing; and
(b) will be determined without a hearing.

28. A general civil restraint order –

(a) will be made for a specified period not exceeding 2 years; and
(b) must identify the judge or judges to whom an application for permission under paragraphs 22(a), 22(b) or 27 should be made.

29. The court may extend the duration of a general civil restraint order, if it considers it appropriate to do so, but the duration of the order must not be extended for a period greater than 2 years on any given occasion.

GENERAL

30. The other party or parties to the proceedings may apply for any civil restraint order.

31. An application under paragraph 30 must be made using the procedure in Part 9 unless the court otherwise directs and the application must specify which type of civil restraint order is sought.

PART 23
INTERNATIONAL PROTECTION OF ADULTS

III MEN [769]

23.1 Applications in connection with Schedule 3 to the Act—general

(1) This Part applies to applications made in connection with Schedule 3 to the Act.

(2) A practice direction may make additional or supplementary provision in respect of any of the matters in this Part.

III MEN [770]

23.2 Interpretation

(1) Unless otherwise provided in a practice direction made under rule 23.1(2), and subject to paragraph (2), an expression which appears both in this Part and in Schedule 3 to the Act is to be construed in accordance with Schedule 3 to the Act, including, where required by paragraph 2(4) of Schedule 3, construing it in accordance with the Convention.

(2) Notwithstanding the provisions of paragraph 13(6) of Schedule 3 to the Act, "lasting power" does not include—

(a) a lasting power of attorney within the meaning of section 9 of the Act; or

(b) an enduring power of attorney within the meaning of Schedule 4 to the Act.

(3) In this Part, "Schedule 3 application" means an application made under this Part (whether or not additional declarations or orders under sections 15 and 16 of the Act are sought as part of such application).

III MEN [771]

23.3 Application of these Rules in relation to Schedule 3 applications

(1) These Rules and accompanying practice directions apply in relation to Schedule 3 applications as if for "P" there were substituted "the adult".

(2) For the purposes of rule 1.2(4) and Part 17, the question of whether the adult has capacity to conduct proceedings in relation to a Schedule 3 application is to be determined in accordance with Part 1 of the Act.

(3) The permission of the court is not required for a Schedule 3 application.

III MEN [772]

23.4 Applications for recognition and enforcement

(1) An application for a declaration under paragraph 20 (recognition) or paragraph 22 (enforcement) of Schedule 3 to the Act is to be made in accordance with Part 9 and any practice direction made under rule 23.1(2).

(2) Without prejudice to its powers under Parts 6 (service) and 7 (notice), the court may dispense with service and notice where it thinks just to do so, having regard in particular to—

(a) whether the adult or (as the case may be) any respondent to the application is within the jurisdiction; and

(b) the need for applications for declarations of enforceability to be determined rapidly.

III MEN [773]

23.5 Applications in relation to lasting powers—disapplication or modification
An application under paragraph 14(1) of Schedule 3 to the Act for the court to disapply or modify a lasting power is to be made in accordance with Part 9 and any practice direction made under rule 23.1(2).

III MEN [774]

23.6 Applications in relation to lasting powers—declaration as to authority of donee of lasting power
An application for a declaration under section 15(1)(c) of the Act that a donee of a lasting power is acting lawfully when exercising authority under that lasting power is to be made in accordance with Part 9 and any practice direction made under rule 23.1(2).

PRACTICE DIRECTION 23A – INTERNATIONAL PROTECTION OF ADULTS

III MEN [775]

This practice direction supplements Part 23 of the Court of Protection Rules 2017

GENERAL

1. This practice direction is made under rule 23.1(2) (which enables a practice direction to make additional or supplementary provision in respect of any of the matters set out in Part 23), and makes provision in relation to Schedule 3 applications.

THE CONVENTION

2. Schedule 3 of the Act makes reference to 'the Convention'. This is defined by paragraph 2 of Schedule 3 and section 63 of the Act as the Convention on the International Protection of Adults signed at the Hague on 13 January 2000. The Convention was ratified by the United Kingdom on 5th November 2003, but only for Scotland: the Convention has not been ratified for England and Wales. Paragraphs 8, 9, 19(2) and (5), Part 5, and paragraph 30 of Schedule 3 to the Act have effect only if the Convention is in force in accordance with Article 57 and it has been held that it is not: those provisions are accordingly treated as having no effect.

DEFINITIONS

3. Subject to paragraphs 4 to 6, words that are defined in the Act or the Rules have the same meaning in this practice direction.

4. '*Country*': Paragraph 3(1) of Schedule 3 to the Act defines 'country' as including a territory which has its own system of law. For the purposes of the Act, the Rules and this practice direction, Scotland and Northern Ireland are considered to be foreign countries, as are (amongst others) British Overseas Territories and Crown Dependencies.

5. '*Lasting power*': Paragraph 13(6) of Schedule 3 to the Act defines 'lasting power' as –

(a) a lasting power of attorney within the meaning of section 9 of the Act
(b) an enduring power of attorney within the meaning of Schedule 4, or
(c) any other power of like effect.

6. For the purposes of Part 23 a power which would be a lasting power under paragraph 13(6) of Schedule 3 is excluded from the definition of 'lasting power' if (a) it is a lasting power of attorney within the meaning of section 9 of the Act, or (b) it is an enduring power of attorney within the meaning of Schedule 4 of the Act (Rule 23.2(2) provides for the exclusion of such lasting powers from the scope of Part 23). In this practice direction 'lasting power' has the same meaning as in Part 23.

PROCEDURE FOR MAKING A SCHEDULE 3 APPLICATION

7. A Schedule 3 application is to be made in accordance with Part 9 of the Rules subject to the modifications set out in this practice direction.

8. A Schedule 3 application is made by filing a COP 1 application form. The form shall be completed on the footing that the adult to whom the application relates is 'P' for the purposes of the form. (Rule 23.3(1) provides for the provisions of the Rules to apply to Schedule 3 applications as if references therein to 'P' were references to 'the adult').

9. Notwithstanding the terms of Practice Direction 9A, an applicant making a Schedule 3 application is not required to file –

(1) a COP 3 assessment of capacity form
(2) any of the annexes listed in Practice Direction 9A

unless the applicant is also asking the Court to make additional declarations and / or orders under sections 15 and / or 16 of the Act, in which case the applicant should also file a COP 3 assessment of capacity form and such annexes as the applicant would have been required to file had he or she been seeking only those declarations and / or orders under sections 15 and / or 16 of the Act.

10. An applicant making a Schedule 3 application should identify whether any person other than the adult has an interest in the application such that they should be named as a respondent to it. For example where a Schedule 3 application is being made in relation to a lasting power it will usually be appropriate to name the donees of the power as respondent (unless they are themselves the applicants).

11. Rule 9.10 and Practice Direction 9B (requirement to notify other individuals) shall not apply to a Schedule 3 application unless the applicant is also asking the Court to make additional declarations and/or orders under sections 15 and/or 16 of the Act, in which case the applicant should also notify such persons as the applicant would have been required to notify had he or she been seeking only those declarations and/or orders under sections 15 and/or 16 of the Act.

12. A Schedule 3 application should be accompanied by a COP 24 witness statement by or on behalf of the applicant. The evidence filed in support of the application should include –

(1) Where the application is made under rule 23.4 for recognition and / or enforcement of a protective measure under paragraph 20 or 22 of Schedule 3 to the Act:
(a) Evidence to demonstrate the basis upon which it is said that the person to whom the application relates is an adult for the purposes of Schedule 3 of the Act;
(b) An officially authenticated copy (and where necessary a certified translation) of the relevant court order or other document embodying the protective measure in respect of which recognition and/or enforcement is sought;
(c) Confirmation that the protective measure was taken on the basis that the adult was habitually resident in the other jurisdiction;
(d) Evidence to enable the Court to be satisfied –

MENTAL CAPACITY AND MENTAL HEALTH

(i) that the case in which the measure was taken was urgent; alternatively

(ii) that the adult to whom the protective measure related was given an opportunity to be heard by the foreign court or other body that took the protective measure.

(e) Evidence to enable the court to be satisfied that the steps leading to the protective measure being made complied with any relevant provisions of the European Convention on Human Rights.

(f) Details of any previous measures relating to the adult which have been the subject of a previous Schedule 3 application (whether or not such application was successful)

(g) Where enforcement is sought of a protective measure that has already been recognised by the Court, a copy of the order giving effect to that recognition.

(2) Where the application is made under rule 23.5 to disapply or modify a lasting power under Schedule 3 of the Act or under rule 23.6 for declarations as to the authority of the donee of a lasting power, a certified copy of the lasting power (and where necessary a certified translation thereof).

PROCEDURE AFTER ISSUE

13. A Schedule 3 application is an excepted application for purposes of Practice Direction 3B (Case Pathways – see Part 1, paragraph 1.1 of that practice direction).

14. When a Schedule 3 application is issued the application will be put before a judge to give directions. The judge will case manage the application and decide whether to allocate it to a pathway. Specifically the judge will consider whether to make one or more of the directions set out in rule 1.2(2) to enable the adult to whom it relates to participate in the application or to secure the adult's interests and position.

15. Where the judge considers that the adult should be joined as party to the proceedings the judge will direct the filing of a COP 3 Assessment of Capacity form or other expert evidence directed at the issue of the adult's capacity to conduct the proceedings before the Court. (Rule 23.3(2) provides for the issue of the adult's capacity to conduct the proceedings before the Court to be determined by reference to Part 1 of the Act).

16. An application under rule 23.4 for recognition and / or enforcement of a protective measure should be dealt with rapidly, and in reviewing the papers the Court will consider whether the order sought can be made without holding a hearing.

17. A Schedule 3 application under rule 23.4 for recognition and / or enforcement of a protective measure which –

(1) purports to authorise a deprivation of liberty of the adult to which it relates (other than a temporary or transient deprivation of liberty associated with the transfer of the adult to or from a specified place); or

(2) purports to authorise medical treatment

will usually –

(1) be determined after holding a hearing; and

(2) be allocated to the Senior Judge or a Tier 3 Judge.

APPLICATIONS INVOLVING ISSUES OF HABITUAL RESIDENCE

18. An application in which the Court is being asked to make a declaration that a person is habitually resident in England and Wales for the purposes of exercising its jurisdiction under sections 15 and / or 16 of the Act is not a Schedule 3 application for the purposes of the Rules or this practice direction unless an order under rules 23.4 to 23.6 is being sought within the application.

19. No determination as to a person's habitual residence is required in order for the court to hear an application under section 21A of the Act, although a determination may be required if the court is then invited to exercise its jurisdiction under sections 15 and / or 16 of the Act.

20. Where an application (whether or not a Schedule 3 application) seeks declarations as to a person's habitual residence the Court will in case managing the application have regard to ensure that the application is allocated to an appropriate level of judge.

PART 24
MISCELLANEOUS

III MEN [776]

24.1 Enforcement methods—general

(1) The relevant practice direction may set out methods of enforcing judgments or orders.

(2) An application for an order for enforcement may be made on application by any person in accordance with Part 10.

III MEN [776.1]

Guidance on applications to the court for committal Practice Direction 21A provides supplemental directions in particular in respect of applications for committal and the hearing of such application: **III MEN [766]**.

III MEN [777]

24.2 Enforcement methods—application of the Civil Procedure Rules 1998

The following provisions of the Civil Procedure Rules 1998 apply, as far as they are relevant and with such modifications as may be necessary, to the enforcement of orders made in proceedings under these Rules—

(a) Part 70 (General Rules about Enforcement of Judgments and Orders);
(b) Part 71 (Orders to Obtain Information from Judgment Debtors);
(c) Part 72 (Third Party Debt Orders);
(d) Part 73 (Charging Orders, Stop Orders and Stop Notices);
(e) Part 83 (Writs and Warrants—General Provisions); and
(f) Part 84 (Enforcement by Taking Control of Goods).

III MEN [777.1]

Applications to the court for enforcement of judgments For guidance and procedure concerning the general rules applicable to Enforcement of Judgments and orders see CPR Part 70 in Volume 1 at para **CPR 70 [1.1]**.

For procedure concerning the orders for obtaining information from judgment debtors see CPR Part 71 in Volume 1 at para **CPR 71 [1]**.

For procedure concerning Third Party Debt orders see CPR Part 72 in Volume 1 at para **CPR 72 [1]**.

For procedures concerning Charging orders, Stop orders and Stop notices see CPR Part 73 in Volume 1 at para **CPR 73 [2]**.

For guidance and procedure concerning the procedures of enforcement of Writs and Warrants – General Provisions and Enforcement by Taking Control of Goods see CPR Parts 83 and 84 in Volume 1 at para **CPR 83 [1]** and **CPR 84 [1]**.

III MEN [778]

24.3 Order or directions requiring a person to give security for discharge of functions

(1) This rule applies where the court makes an order or gives a direction—

(a) conferring functions on any person (whether as deputy or otherwise); and

(b) requiring that person to give security for the discharge of those functions.

(2) The person on whom functions are conferred must give the security before undertaking to discharge those functions, unless the court permits the security to be given subsequently.

(3) Paragraphs (4) to (6) apply where the security is required to be given before any action can be taken.

(4) Subject to paragraph (5), the security must be given in accordance with the requirements of regulation 33(2)(a) of the Public Guardian Regulations (which makes provision about the giving of security by means of a bond that is endorsed by an authorised insurance company or an authorised deposit-taker).

(5) The court may impose such other requirements in relation to the giving of the security as it considers appropriate (whether in addition to, or instead of, those specified in paragraph (4)).

(6) In specifying the date from which the order or directions referred to in paragraph (1) are to take effect, the court will have regard to the need to postpone that date for such reasonable period as would enable the Public Guardian to be satisfied that—

(a) if paragraph (4) applies, the requirements of regulation 34 of the Public Guardian Regulations have been met in relation to the security; and

(b) any other requirements imposed by the court under paragraph (5) have been met.

(7) "The Public Guardian Regulations" means the Lasting Power of Attorney, Enduring Powers of Attorney and Public Guardian Regulations 2007.

III MEN [778.1]

Guidance on the assessment of security bond levels In *Baker v H* [2010] 1 WLR 1103 HHJ Marshall QC gave guidance as to the approach to be adopted in establishing the appropriate level of security.

III MEN [779]

24.4 Objections to registration of an enduring power of attorney—request for directions

(1) This rule applies in any case where—

(a) the Public Guardian (having received a notice of objection to the registration of an instrument creating an enduring power of attorney) is prevented by paragraph 13(5) of Schedule 4 to the Act from registering the instrument except in accordance with the court's directions; and

(b) on or before the relevant day, no application for the court to give such directions has been made under Part 9 (how to start proceedings).

(2) In paragraph (1)(b) the relevant day is the later of—

(a) the final day of the period specified in paragraph 13(4) of Schedule 4 to the Act; or

(b) the final day of the period of 14 days beginning with the date on which the Public Guardian receives the notice of objection.

(3) The Public Guardian may seek the court's directions about registering the instrument, by filing a request in accordance with the relevant practice direction.

(4) As soon as practicable and in any event within 21 days of the date on which the request was made, the court shall notify—

(a) the person (or persons) who gave the notice of objection; and

(b) the attorney or, if more than one, each of them.

(5) As soon as practicable and in any event within 21 days of the date on which the request is filed, the Public Guardian must notify the donor of the power that the request has been so filed.

(6) The notice under paragraph (4) must—

(a) state that the Public Guardian has requested the court's directions about registration;

(b) state that the court will give directions in response to the request unless an application under Part 9 is made to it before the end of the period of 21 days commencing with the date on which the notice is issued; and

(c) set out the steps required to make such an application.

(7) "Notice of objection" means a notice of objection which is made in accordance with paragraph 13(4) of Schedule 4 to the Act.

III MEN [779.1]

Applications to the court by the Public Guardian Practice Direction 24A provides supplemental directions and guidance as to the procedure applicable: **III MEN [782]**. The Public Guardian must use form COP17 and notification is in accordance with Part 7. The applicable form to be used by a person wishing to participate in the proceedings is form COP8 (**III MEN [565]**).

This procedure should be distinguished from the applications made by any other person seeking direction of the court concerning registration. Practice Direction 9G and Part 9 (**III MEN [606]**) is the applicable procedure.

III MEN [780]

24.5 Disposal of property where P ceases to lack capacity

(1) This rule applies where P ceases to lack capacity.

(2) In this rule, "relevant property" means any property belonging to P and forming part of P's estate, and which—

(a) remains under the control of anyone appointed by order of the court; or

(b) is held under the direction of the court.

(3) The court may at any time make an order for any relevant property to be transferred to P, or at P's direction, provided that it is satisfied that P has the capacity to make decisions in relation to that property.

(4) An application for an order under this rule is to be made in accordance with Part 10.

III MEN [780.1]

Applications to the court and procedural guidance Practice Direction 24B provides guidance as to procedure: **III MEN [783]**. Paragraphs 1–4 provide directions for applications to end proceedings made by using Part 10 procedure and form COP9, see **III MEN [607]** above. Paragraphs 5–6 relate to applications where proceedings have concluded: **III MEN [783]**. Paragraphs 7–11 provide directions and information as to the procedure to be followed if P dies and for personal representatives and administrators on the issues of costs and funds held by the Court Funds Office (**III MEN [783]**).

III MEN [781]

24.6 Citation and commencement, revocations and transitional provision

(1) These Rules may be cited as the Court of Protection Rules 2017 and shall come into force on 1st December 2017.

(2) The rules in the Schedule are revoked as set out in the Schedule.

(3) A practice direction may make provision for the extent to which and manner in which these Rules shall apply to proceedings started before the day on which they come into force.

PRACTICE DIRECTION 24A – REQUEST FOR DIRECTIONS WHERE NOTICE OF OBJECTION PREVENTS PUBLIC GUARDIAN FROM REGISTERING ENDURING POWER OF ATTORNEY

III MEN [782]

This practice direction supplements Part 24 of the Court of Protection Rules 2017

1 Rule 24.4 provides for the Public Guardian to request the court's directions where a notice of objection prevents the registering of an instrument creating an enduring power of attorney. This practice direction makes provision about such requests.

(Practice Direction 9G deals with applications made by persons other than the Public Guardian who are seeking the court's directions about registration.)

2 Time limits apply before the Public Guardian can request directions. These are measured from the date (or the latest date) on which the attorney gave notice to the donor's relatives of the attorney's intention to make an application for the registration of the instrument creating the enduring power. The Public Guardian cannot request directions until 5 weeks have expired beginning with the date of notification.

3 However, this period is extended if it would otherwise expire less than 14 days after the Public Guardian receives the notice of objection which prevents the registering of the instrument. In this case, the Public Guardian may not request directions from the court until the end of the 14 day period which begins with the date on which the notice of objection was received.

4 The request for directions must be made using Form COP17. The Public Guardian must file the form and any document considered to assist the court to give directions about the registration of the instrument.

5 The Public Guardian will notify the donor in accordance with Part 7 that the Public Guardian has made a request within 21 days of the date on which the Public Guardian makes it. However, the Public Guardian is not required to serve the request on any other person or otherwise to notify them that a request has been made. The Public Guardian will participate in the proceedings only if the court so requests.

6 As soon as practicable after a request has been filed, notice of that fact will be given by a court officer to –

(a) the person (or persons) who gave the notice of objection; and
(b) the attorney under the enduring power or, if more than one, each of them.

7 Any person wishing to participate in the proceedings then has 21 days to file an application using Form COP8. The application must be made in accordance with the detailed requirements for applications relating to the registration of enduring powers of attorney, which are set out in Practice Direction 9G. If no such application is received, the court will proceed to consider the matter in response to the Public Guardian's request and will give directions to the Public Guardian.

PRACTICE DIRECTION 24B – WHERE P CEASES TO LACK CAPACITY OR DIES

III MEN [783]

This practice direction supplements Part 24 of the Court of Protection Rules 2017

GENERAL

1 An order of the Court of Protection will continue until it is discharged or, if made for a specified period, will cease to have effect when that period comes to an end.

2 Where P ceases to lack capacity or dies, steps may need to be taken to finalise the court's involvement in P's affairs.

Application to end proceedings

3 Where P ceases to lack capacity in relation to the matter or matters to which the proceedings relate, an application may be made by any of the following people to the court to end the proceedings and discharge any orders made in respect of that person –

(a) P;
(b) his litigation friend; or
(c) any other person who is a party to the proceedings.

4 An application under rule 24.5 should be made by filing a COP9 application notice in accordance with the Part 10 procedure, together with any evidence in support of the application. The application should in particular be supported by evidence that P no longer lacks capacity to make decisions in relation to the matter or matters to which the proceedings relate.

APPLICATIONS WHERE PROCEEDINGS HAVE CONCLUDED

5 Where P ceases to lack capacity after proceedings have concluded, an application may be made to the court to discharge any orders made (including an order appointing a deputy or an order in relation to a security bond) by filing a COP9 application notice in accordance with the Part 10 procedure, together with any evidence in support of the application. The application notice should set out details of the order or orders the applicant seeks to have discharged, and should in particular be supported by evidence that P no longer lacks capacity to make decisions in relation to the matter or matters to which the proceedings relate.

6 If the Court Funds Office is holding funds or assets on behalf of P, it will require an order of the court to the effect that P no longer lacks capacity to make decisions with regard to the use and disposition of those funds or assets before any funds or assets can be transferred to him.

PROCEDURE TO BE FOLLOWED WHEN P DIES

7 An application for any final directions needed following P's death (including to discharge an order appointing a deputy or to discharge a security bond) should be made by filing a COP9 application notice in accordance with the Part 10 procedure. An application should attach the original or a certified copy of P's death certificate.

8 Any security bond taken out by the deputy will remain in force until the end of the period of 2 years commencing with the date of P's death, or until it is discharged by the court.

9 The Public Guardian may require a deputy to submit a final report upon P's death. Before it will discharge a security bond, the court must be satisfied that the Public Guardian either –

(a) does not require a final report; or
(b) is satisfied with the final report provided by the deputy.

Personal representatives and administrators

10 Where there are solicitor's costs outstanding which would be due from P's estate, the personal representative or administrator may agree any of these costs without an order from the court. If these costs cannot be agreed, the personal representative, administrator or the solicitor may apply to the court for costs to be assessed, using a COP9 application notice in accordance with the Part 10 procedure.

11 If there are funds or other assets held in the Court Funds Office on behalf of P, P's personal representative or administrator will need to contact the Court Funds Office directly regarding those funds.

PRACTICE DIRECTION 24C – TRANSITIONAL PROVISIONS

III MEN [784]

This practice direction supplements Part 24 of the Court of Protection Rules 2017

INTRODUCTORY

1 In this practice direction –

(a) 'the Rules' means the Court of Protection Rules 2017;
(b) 'commencement' means 1 December 2017;
(c) 'the Previous Rules' means the Court of Protection Rules 2007, as in force immediately before commencement; and
(d) 'the pilot Practice Directions' means –
  (i) Practice Direction – Transparency;
  (ii) Practice Direction – Case Management Pilot; and
  (iii) Practice Direction – Section 49 Reports Pilot,

as those practice directions were in force immediately before commencement.

APPLICATIONS RECEIVED AFTER COMMENCEMENT

2 If an application under the Previous Rules or the pilot Practice Directions is received at the court on or after commencement, it will be returned.

3 However, an application made under the Rules using the version of the relevant form which was current immediately before commencement will be accepted until close of business on 12 January 2018, or such later date as the Senior Judge may direct.

APPLICATIONS RECEIVED BEFORE COMMENCEMENT

4 The general presumption will be that any step in proceedings which were started (in accordance with rule 62 of the Previous Rules) before commencement which is to be taken on or after commencement is to be taken under the Rules.

(Rule 62 of the Previous Rules provides that proceedings are started when the court issues an application form at the request of the applicant.)

5 However, the general presumption is subject to any directions given by the court, which may at any time direct how the Rules are to apply to the proceedings.

6 Any step already taken in the proceedings before commencement in accordance with the Previous Rules or the pilot Practice Directions will remain valid on or after commencement.

ORDERS MADE BEFORE COMMENCEMENT

7 Where a court order has been made before commencement under the Previous Rules or the pilot Practice Directions, the order must still be complied with on or after commencement.

MOBILE HOMES

TABLE OF CONTENTS

GENERAL NOTES ON MOBILE HOMES

III MOB [1]

Jurisdiction The jurisdiction conferred on county courts by these two Acts is limited. The Caravan Sites Act 1968 provides some protection against summary eviction but only where the caravan is stationed on a protected site with the agreement of the owner. A "protected site" is land in respect of which a site licence is required, or would be required if the owner were not the local authority. However it is not protected if the site licence is expressed to be granted for holiday use only or is otherwise subject to such conditions that there are times of the year when no caravan may be stationed on it. A residential occupier of a caravan stationed on a protected site is protected, by s 3 of the 1968 Act, against eviction and harassment and is entitled, by s 2, to at least 4 weeks' notice to determine the contract. Any eviction process which is not based on a court order is made unlawful by s 3(1) so the site owner who wishes to evict a caravan-dweller who entered lawfully on a protected site must take possession proceedings in accordance with **CPR 55**. The court has a discretion, in such proceedings, to suspend eviction orders in accordance with s 4 which is set out at **III MOB [4]**, except where there is no site licence in force. As regards a caravan brought on to a protected site without agreement, the general law relating to the eviction of trespassers applies. The same applies to the eviction of caravan-dwellers who have entered land which is not a protected site under a licence which has been terminated.

The Mobile Homes Act 1983, as enacted, conferred exclusive jurisdiction on the county courts to determine all issues arising under the Act including issues about the contractual arrangements between caravan-dweller and site-owner. However major changes were made, with effect from 30 April 2011 by the Mobile Homes Act 1983 (Jurisdiction of Residential Property Tribunals) (England) Order 2011, SI 2011/1005. This substituted a new s 4 which divided the jurisdiction into two (1) residential property tribunals had almost all the old county court jurisdiction transferred to them and (2) the county courts were left with the 'termination by owner' issues. These issues are most likely to arise in proceedings by the site owner for possession.

The Mobile Homes Act 2013 and the Mobile Homes (Wales) Act 2013 made extensive changes to the licensing of parks for mobile homes and created new offences. It also introduced 'site rules' and conferred on home owners fresh rights to sell or give away their mobile homes. However the Act made no significant changes to the jurisdiction of the county courts regarding the termination of agreements and claims for possession.

III MOB [2]

Caravans and mobile homes defined The 1968 Act is about caravans and the 1983 is about mobile homes, but they are one and the same. Section 16 of the former defines a "caravan" as having the same meaning as in Part I of the Caravan Sites and Control of Development Act 1960. "Mobile home" is defined by Mobile Homes Act 1983 s 5(1) (see para **III MOB [10]**) in exactly the same way. The definition of "caravan" in Part I of the 1960 Act, (s 29) is as follows:

"any structure designed or adapted for human habitation which is capable of being moved from one place to another (whether by being towed, or being transported on a motor vehicle or trailer) and any motor vehicle so designed or adapted, but does not include—

(a) any railway rolling stock which is for the time being on rails forming part of a railway system, or
(b) any tent."

Twin-unit caravans above a certain size are excepted from this definition by s 13(2), as amended, of the Caravan Sites Act 1968.

A movable chalet has been held to be within the definition: *Wyre Forest District Council v Secretary of State for the Environment* [1990] 2 AC 357, [1990] 1 All ER 780, HL. But a home is not within the definition if it has to be dismantled before it can be moved: *Carter v Secretary of State for the Environment and Carrick District Council* (28 April 1995, unreported), CA. Other homes which have been held to be outside the definition are a moored houseboat: *Roy Crimble Ltd v Edgecombe* (1981) 131 NLJ 928, CA and a van which could be lived in but which was not designed or adapted for the purpose: *Backer v Secretary of State for the Environment* [1983] 2 All ER 1021, [1983] 1 WLR 1485. A mobile home does not lose its status merely by the bolting on of a porch extension: *Howard v Charlton* (2002) Times, 19 August, CA.

III MOB [3]

Local authority caravan site for gypsies As enacted, both Acts defined 'protected site' as excluding local authority caravan sites that provided accommodation for gypsies. The effect was to allow caravan-dwellers on such sites to be evicted without a court order. This was held to be unlawful since it infringed the Convention rights of the caravan dwellers: *Connors v United Kingdom (Application 66746/01)* (2004) 40 EHRR 189, [2004] HLR 991, ECtHR. Section 318 of the Housing and Regeneration Act 2008 was passed to amend the definition by removing the exclusion with effect from 30 April 2011. At the same time an order was made, under s 2A of the Mobile Homes Act 1983, to amend the implied terms in Schedule 1 and to make consequential amendments: the Mobile Homes Act 1983 (Amendment of Schedule 1 and Consequential Amendments) (England) Order 2011, SI 2011/1003. By this order Part 1 of Schedule 1 (terms implied into agreements to which the Act applies) was divided into 4 chapters. Jurisdiction was conferred on the county court to rule on 'termination by owner' issues arising under Chapter 2 (Agreements relating to pitches other than pitches on gypsy and traveller sites) and Chapter 4 (Agreements relating to permanent pitches on gypsy and traveller sites). In contrast, all issues arising under Chapter 3 (implied terms in agreements relating to transit pitches on gypsy and traveller sites) are now for the residential property tribunals to determine. A 'transit pitch' means a pitch on which a person is entitled to station a mobile home under the terms of the agreement for a fixed period of up to 3 months: see Chapter 1 of Part 1 of Schedule 1.

III MOB [3A]

Mobile homes in Wales Authorities in Wales have power under s 56 of the Mobile Homes (Wales) Act 2013 to provide sites for mobile homes. Part 3 of the Housing (Wales) Act 2013 requires the authority to exercise that power when the housing authority's approved assessment certifies needs within the authority's area with respect to the provision of sites on which mobile homes may be stationed, but not to provide for the carrying on of activities normally carried out by Gypsies and Travellers.

CARAVAN SITES ACT 1968

(c 52)

III MOB [4]

4. Provision for suspension of eviction orders

(1) If in proceedings by the owner of a protected site the court makes an order for enforcing in relation thereto any such right as is mentioned in paragraph (b) of subsection (1) of section 3 of this Act, the court may (without prejudice to any power apart from this section to postpone the operation or suspend the execution of an order, and subject to the following provisions of this section) suspend the enforcement of the order for such period not exceeding twelve months from the date of the order as the court thinks reasonable.

(2) Where the court by virtue of this section suspends the enforcement of an order, it may impose such terms and conditions, including conditions as to the payment of rent or other periodical payments or of arrears of such rent or payments, as the court thinks reasonable.

(3) The court may from time to time, on the application of either party, extend, reduce or terminate the period of suspension ordered by virtue of this section, or vary any terms or conditions imposed thereunder, but shall not extend the period of suspension for more than twelve months at a time.

(4) In considering whether or how to exercise its powers under this section, the court shall have regard to all the circumstances, and in particular to the questions—

(a) whether the occupier of the caravan has failed, whether before or after the expiration or determination of the relevant residential contract, to observe any terms or conditions of that contract, any conditions of the site licence, or any reasonable rules made by the owner for the management and conduct of the site or the maintenance of caravans thereon;

(b) whether the occupier has unreasonably refused an offer by the owner to renew the residential contract or make another such contract for a reasonable period and on reasonable terms;

(c) whether the occupier has failed to make reasonable efforts to obtain elsewhere other suitable accommodation for his caravan (or, as the case may be, another suitable caravan and accommodation for it).

(5) Where the court makes such an order as is mentioned in subsection (1) of this section but suspends the enforcement of that order by virtue of this section, the court shall make no order for costs unless it appears to the court, having regard to the conduct of the owner or of the occupier, that there are special reasons for making such an order.

(6) The court shall not suspend the enforcement of an order by virtue of this section if—

(a) no site licence under Part I of the Caravan Sites and Control of Development Act 1960 is in force in respect of the site, and

(b) paragraph 11 or 11A of that Act does not apply

and where a site licence in respect of the site is expressed to expire at the end of a specified period, the period for which enforcement may be suspended by virtue of this section shall not extend beyond the expiration of the licence.

III MOB [4.1]

Protected site For the purposes of the 1968 Act and, with qualification, for the 1983 Act, "protected site" is defined by Caravan Sites Act 1968 s 1(2) as:

"any land in respect of which a site licence is required under Part I of the Caravan Sites and Control of Development Act 1960 or would be so required if paragraph 11 of Schedule 1 to that Act (exemption of land occupied by local authorities) were omitted, not being land in respect of which the relevant planning permission or site licence—

(a) is expressed to be granted for holiday use only; or

(b) is otherwise so expressed or subject to such conditions that there are times of the year when no caravan may be stationed on the land for human habitation."

Note, however, that the definition was amended, as from 18 January 2005, by s 209 of the Housing Act 2004. The effect of the amendment is to delete the words "paragraph 11 of Schedule 1 to that Act (exemption of land occupied by local authorities)" and to insert in their place the following words: "paragraph 11 or 11A of Schedule 1 to that Act (exemption of gypsy and other local authority sites)". Whereas the section as enacted empowered authorities to evict gypsies without a court order and thereby infringed their Article 8 rights, the effect of the amendments has been to bring the eviction process under court control, including a discretion to suspend. This makes it difficult to conceive of a case in which a public law defence would succeed: *Smith (on behalf of the Gypsy Council) v Buckland* [2007] EWCA Civ 1318.

A site does not fall within the definition of land in respect of which a site licence is required until planning permission necessary for the grant of a licence has been granted: *Balthasar v Mullane* (1985) 84 LGR 55, 17 HLR 561, CA; *Adams v Watkins* [1990] 2 EGLR 185, [1990] 30 EG 89, CA.

In a case where the grant of planning permission permitted the use of the site for both residential and holiday use and gave the site owner complete freedom to determine which pitches were to be used for which purpose, it was held that the site as a whole was a protected site: *John Romans Park Homes Ltd v Hancock, Newey and Hall* [2018] UKUT 249 (LC), 27 July 2018.

III MOB [4.2]

Protection from eviction and harassment Where a person is entitled, by licence or contract, to station a caravan on a protected site, s 2 of the Act requires any notice of termination of the contract or licence to be given "not less than four weeks before the date on which it is to take effect." Otherwise it is of no effect. Further protection is provided by s 3, as amended by the Housing Act 2004, s 210, which imposes criminal sanction in respect of unlawful eviction and harassment.

III MOB [5]

5. Supplementary

(1) In this Part of this Act "the court" means the county court.

(2) The power of the court under section 4 of this Act to suspend the enforcement of an order shall extend to any order made but not executed before the commencement of this Part of this Act.

(3) Nothing in this Part of this Act shall affect the operation of section 13 of the Compulsory Purchase Act 1965.

(4) Subsection (1) of section 12 of the Caravan Sites and Control of Development Act 1960 (power of site occupier to take possession and terminate a licence or tenancy in cases of contravention of section 1 of that Act) shall have effect subject to the foregoing provisions of this Part of this Act.

(5) The Protection from Eviction Act 1977 (protection against harassment and eviction without due process of law) shall not apply to any premises being a caravan stationed on a protected site.

MOBILE HOMES ACT 1983

(c 34)

III MOB [6]

1. Particulars of agreements

(1) This Act applies to any agreement under which a person ("the occupier") is entitled—

(a) to station a mobile home on land forming part of a protected site; and

(b) to occupy the mobile home as his only or main residence.

(2) Before making of an agreement to which this Act applies, the owner of the protected site ("the owner") shall give to the proposed occupier under the agreement a written statement which—

(a) specifies the names and addresses of the parties;

(b) includes particulars of the land on which the proposed occupier is to be entitled to station the mobile home that are sufficient to identify that land;

(c) sets out the express terms to be contained in the agreement (including any site rules (see section 2C));

(d) sets out the terms implied by section 2 (1) below; and

(e) complies with such other requirements as may be prescribed by regulations made by the Secretary of State.

(3) The written statement required by subsection (2) above must be given—

(a) not later than 28 days before the date on which any agreement for the sale of the mobile home to the proposed occupier is made, or

(b) (if no such agreement is made before the making of the agreement to which this Act applies) not later than 28 days before the date on which the agreement to which this Act applies is made.

(4) But if the proposed occupier consents in writing to that statement being given to him by a date ("the chosen date") which is less than 28 days before the date mentioned in subsection (3)(a) or (b) above, the statement must be given to him not later than the chosen date.

(5) If any express term other than a site rule (see section 2C)—

(a) is contained in an agreement to which this Act applies, but

(b) was not set out in a written statement given to the proposed occupier in accordance with subsections (2) to (4) above,

the term is unenforceable by the owner or any person within section 3(1) below. This is subject to any order made by the appropriate judicial body under section 2(3) below.

(6) If the owner has failed to give the occupier a written statement in accordance with subsections (2) to (4) above, the occupier may, at any time after the making of the agreement, apply to the appropriate judicial body for an order requiring the owner—

(a) to give him a written statement which complies with paragraphs (a) to (e) of subsection (2) (read with any modifications necessary to reflect the fact that the agreement has been made), and

(b) to do so not later than such date as is specified in the order.

(7) A statement required to be given to a person under this section may be either delivered to him personally or sent to him by post.

(8) Any reference in this section to the making of an agreement to which this Act applies includes a reference to any variation of an agreement by virtue of which the agreement becomes one to which this Act applies.

(8A) Subsections (3), (4) and (6) do not apply in relation to a person occupying or proposing to occupy a transit pitch on a local authority gypsy and traveller site or a county council gypsy and traveller site and in such cases, the reference in subsection (5) to subsections (2) to (4) is to be treated as a reference to subsection (2).

(8B) In subsection (8A) "county council gypsy and traveller site", "local authority gypsy and traveller site" and "transit pitch" all have the same meanings as in paragraph 1(4) of Chapter 1 of Part 1 of Schedule 1 to this Act.

(9) Regulations under this section—

(a) shall be made by statutory instrument;

(b) shall be subject to annulment in pursuance of a resolution of either House of Parliament; and

(c) may make different provision with respect to different cases or descriptions of case, including different provision for different areas.

III MOB [6.1]

Mobile home, protected site For definitions see para **III MOB [10]** and notes at para **III MOB [4.1]**.

III MOB [6.2]

Agreement under which a person is entitled It was held in *Ford v Morrison* [1997] CLY 4245, cc, that an employee who was allowed to station his own mobile home on site for the better performance of his duties was not entitled to protection since the occupation was that of the employer. In *Balthasar v Mullane* (1985) 84 LGR 55, 51 P & CR 107, CA, the Court of Appeal took the view than an "agreement" did not include a wholly gratuitous permission. On the other hand travelling showmen who took a one year lease of the showground which they had occupied as tenants for 50 years were held entitled to the protection of the Act: *West Lothian District Council v Morrison* 1987 SLT 361.

III MOB [6.3]

Regulations See the Mobile Homes Act 1983 (Written Statements) (England) Regulations 2011, SI 2011/1006, the Mobile Homes (Selling)(and Gifting)(England) Regulations 2013, SI 2013/981 and the Mobile Homes (Site Rules)(England) Regulations 2014, SI 2014/5. The last instrument amends the other two and makes provision for the making, variation and deletion of site rules.

III MOB [6.4]

The appropriate national authority Section 5 of the Act was amended by s 206(3) of the Housing Act 2004 to define the appropriate national authority as the Secretary of State in relation to England and the National Assembly of Wales in relation to Wales.

III MOB [6.5]

Variation of agreement It has been held that an agreement cannot be brought within the Act by subsequent variation on the grant of planning permission which makes it a 'protected site': sub-section (8) does not apply to an agreement if the site is not protected from the beginning or if it includes land which takes it outside the definition of a 'pitch': *Murphy v Wyatt* [2011] EWCA Civ 408, [2011] 1 WLR 2129, [2011] 2 P & CR 81.

III MOB [7]

2. Terms of agreements

(1) In any agreement to which this Act applies there shall be implied the applicable terms set out in Part I of Schedule 1 to this Act; and this subsection shall have effect notwithstanding any express term of the agreement.

(2) The appropriate judicial body may, on the application of either party made within the relevant period, order that there shall be implied in the agreement terms concerning the matters mentioned in Part II of Schedule 1 to this Act.

(3) The appropriate judicial body may, on the application of either party made within the relevant period, make an order—

(a) varying or deleting any express term of the agreement other than a site rule (see section 2C);

(b) in the case of any express term to which section 1(6) above applies other than a site rule (see section 2C), provide for the term to have full effect or to have such effect subject to any variation specified in the order.

(3A) In subsections (2) and (3) above "the relevant period" means the period beginning with the date on which the agreement is made and ending—

(a) six months after that date, or

(b) where a written statement relating to the agreement is given to the occupier after that date (whether or not in compliance with an order under section 1(6) above) other than a site rule (see section 2C), six months after the date on which the statement is given;

and section 1(8) above applies for the purposes of this subsection as it applies for the purposes of section 1.

(4) On an application under this section, the appropriate judicial body shall make such provision as the court considers just and equitable in the circumstances.

(5) The supplementary provisions in Part 3 to Schedule 1 to this Act have effect for the purposes of paragraphs 8 and 9 of Chapter 2 of Part 1 of that Schedule.

(6) Subsections (2) to (4) do not apply in relation to a person occupying or proposing to occupy a transit pitch on a local authority gypsy and traveller site or a county council gypsy and traveller site.

(7) In subsection (6) "county council gypsy and traveller site", "local authority gypsy and traveller site" and "transit pitch" all have the same meanings as in paragraph 1(4) of Chapter 1 of Part 1 of Schedule 1 to this Act.

III MOB [7.1]

The court may on application For procedure and venue see the note at **III MOB [3]**.The jurisdiction under sub-s (2) may be exercised although the agreement was delivered outside the three month period: *Barton v Care* (1992) 24 HLR 684, [1992] 2 EGLR 174, CA. In *Stroud v Weir Associates Ltd* (1985) 135 NLJ 791, the county court judge allowed an occupier who had made an application under s 1(5) (see para **III MOB [6]**) to apply instead for an order under s 2(3).

The court's jurisdiction is confined by s 4 to 'termination by owner' issues arising under Chapters 2 or 4 of Part 1 to Schedule 1 to the Act.

III MOB [7A]

2A. Power to amend implied terms

(1) The Secretary of State may by order make such amendments of Part 1 or 2 of Schedule 1 to this Act as the Secretary of State considers appropriate.

(2) An order under this section—

- (a) shall be made by statutory instrument;
- (b) may make different provision with respect to different cases or descriptions of case, including different provision for different areas;
- (c) may contain such incidental, supplementary, consequential, transitional or saving provisions as the authority making the order considers appropriate.

(3) Without prejudice to the generality of subsections (1) and (2), an order under this section may—

- (a) make provision for or in connection with the determination by the court or a tribunal of such questions, or the making by the court or a tribunal of such orders, as are specified in the order;
- (b) make such amendments of any provision of this Act as the authority making the order considers appropriate in consequence of any amendment made by the order in Part 1 or 2 of Schedule 1.

(4) The first order made under this section in relation to England or Wales respectively may provide for all or any of its provisions to apply in relation to agreements to which this Act applies that were made at any time before the day on which the order comes into force (as well as in relation to such agreements made on or after that day).

(5) No order may be made under this section unless the Secretary of State has consulted—

- (a) such organisations as appear to the Secretary of State to be representative of interests substantially affected by the order; and
- (b) such other persons as the Secretary of State considers appropriate.

(6) No order may be made under this section unless a draft of the order has been laid before, and approved by a resolution of, each House of Parliament.

III MOB [7A.1]

The appropriate national authority Section 5 of the Act was amended by s 206(3) of the Housing Act 2004 to define the appropriate national authority as the Secretary of State in relation to England and the National Assembly of Wales in relation to Wales.

III MOB [8]

3. Successors in title

(1) An agreement to which this Act applies shall be binding on and endure for the benefit of any successor in title of the owner and any person claiming through or under the owner or any such successor.

(2) Where an agreement to which this Act applies is lawfully assigned to any person, the agreement shall enure for the benefit of and be binding on that person.

(3) Where a person entitled to the benefit of and bound by an agreement to which this Act applies dies at a time when he is occupying the mobile home as his only or main residence, the agreement shall enure for the benefit of and be binding on—

- (a) any person residing with that person ("the deceased") at that time being—
  - (i) the widow, widower or surviving civil partner of the deceased; or
  - (ii) in default of a widow, widower or surviving civil partner so residing, any member of the deceased's family; or
- (b) in default of any such person so residing, the person entitled to the mobile home by virtue of the deceased's will or under the law relating to intestacy but subject to subsection (4) below.

(4) An agreement to which this Act applies shall not enure for the benefit of or be binding on a person by virtue of subsection 3(b) above in so far as—

- (a) it would, but for this subsection, enable or require that person to occupy the mobile home; or
- (b) it includes terms implied by virtue of paragraph 5, 8A, 8B or 9 of Chapter 2, or paragraph 5 of Chapter 4, of Part I of Schedule 1 to this Act;
- (c) [...]

III MOB [8.1]

Successor in title of the occupier Section 3(3)(b) was interpreted in *Berkeley Leisure Group v Scott and the Spastics' Society* [1993] CLY 4135 as passing the benefit of the occupier's agreement to the Spastics Society to whom he had left his whole estate by will.

III MOB [9]

4. Jurisdiction of a tribunal or the court

(1) In relation to a protected site, a tribunal has jurisdiction—

- (a) to determine any question arising under this Act or any agreement to which it applies; and
- (b) to entertain any proceedings brought under this Act or any such agreement,

subject to subsections (2) to (6).

(2) Subsection (1) applies in relation to a question irrespective of anything contained in an arbitration agreement which has been entered into before that question arose.

(3) In relation to a protected site, the court has jurisdiction—

- (a) to determine any question arising by virtue of paragraph 4, 5 or 5A(2)(b) of Chapter 2, or paragraph 4, 5 or 6(1)(b) of Chapter 4, of Part 1 of Schedule 1 (termination by owner) under this Act or any agreement to which it applies; and
- (b) to entertain any proceedings so arising brought under this Act or any such agreement,

subject to subsections (4) to (6).

(4) Subsection (5) applies if the owner and occupier have entered into an arbitration agreement before the question mentioned in subsection (3)(a) arises and the agreement applies to that question.

(5) A tribunal has jurisdiction to determine the question and entertain any proceedings arising instead of the court.

(6) Subsection (5) applies irrespective of anything contained in the arbitration agreement mentioned in subsection (4).

(7) [...]

III MOB [9.1]

Jurisdiction A major shift in jurisdiction was effected by the insertion of the new s 4 by the Mobile Homes Act 1983 (Jurisdiction of Residential Property Tribunals) (England) Order 2011, SI 2011/1005. In England the courts still have jurisdiction to decide questions arising under the 'termination by owner' provisions in paragraph 4, 5 or 5A(2)(b) of Chapter 2 of Part 1 of Schedule 1 and in paragraphs 4, 5 or 6(1)(b) of Chapter 4. All other issues and questions are for determination by residential property tribunals. The issues that are still within the jurisdiction of the county courts are most likely to arise in the context of a claim by the site-owner for possession. In Wales the exclusive jurisdiction of the county courts is preserved by sub-section (7). However, this was changed, as from 21 March 2012 by the Mobile Homes 1983 (Jurisdiction of Residential Property Tribunals) (Wales) Order 2012, SI 2012/899. The jurisdictional split between court and tribunal is now the same in Wales as in England.

III MOB [10]

5. Interpretation

(1) In this Act, unless the context otherwise requires—

"the appropriate judicial body" means whichever of the court or a tribunal has jurisdiction under section 4;

"arbitration agreement" means an agreement in writing to submit to arbitration any question arising under this Act or any agreement to which it applies;

"the court" means—

(a) in relation to England, the county court or, where the parties have entered into an arbitration agreement that applies to the question to be determined, the arbitrator;

(b) in relation to Scotland, the sheriff having jurisdiction where the protected site is situated or, where the parties have so agreed, the arbiter;

"local authority" has the same meaning as in Part I of the Caravan Sites and Control of Development Act 1960;

"mobile home" has the same meaning as "caravan" has in that Part of that Act;

"owner", in relation to a protected site, means the person who, by virtue of an estate or interest held by him, is entitled to possession of the site or would be so entitled but for the rights of any persons to station mobile homes on land forming part of the site;

"planning permission" means permission under Part III of the Town and Country Planning Act 1990 or Part III of the Town and Country Planning (Scotland) Act 1997;

"protected site" has the same meaning as in Part I of the Caravan Sites Act 1968.

["a tribunal" means, where the parties have entered into an arbitration agreement that applies to the question to be determined and that question arose before the agreement was made, the arbitrator; or, in other cases—

(a) in relation to England, the First-tier Tribunal or, where determined by or under Tribunal Procedure Rules, the Upper; and

(b) in relation to Wales, a residential property tribunal.

(2) In relation to an agreement to which this Act applies—

(a) any reference in this Act to the owner includes a reference to any person who is bound by and entitled to the benefit of the agreement by virtue of subsection (1) of section 3 above; and

(b) subject to subsection (4) of that section, any reference in this Act to the occupier includes a reference to any person who is entitled to the benefit of and bound by the agreement by virtue of subsection (2) or (3) of that section.

(3) A person is a member of another's family within the meaning of this Act if he is his spouse, civil partner, parent, grandparent, child, grandchild, brother, sister, uncle, aunt, nephew or niece; treating—

(a) any relationship by marriage or civil partnership as a relationship by blood, any relationship of the half blood as a relationship of the whole blood and the stepchild of any person as his child; and

(b) an illegitimate person as the legitimate child of his mother and reputed father;

or if they live together as husband and wife or as if they were civil partners.

III MOB [10.1]

Land occupied by a local authority The exclusion from the definition of "protected site" of land occupied by a local authority as a caravan site providing accommodation for gypsies leaves gypsy occupiers vulnerable to summary eviction for reasons which they cannot challenge. It was held in *Connors v United Kingdom (Application 66746/01)* (2004) 40 EHRR 189, [2004] HLR 991, ECtHR that such an interference with family life could not be justified within the appropriate margin of appreciation and that Convention rights under article 8 had been violated. The words excluding local authority caravan sites from the definition of "protected site" have been removed by s 318 of the Housing and Regeneration Act 2008.

SCHEDULE 1

AGREEMENTS UNDER ACT

III MOB [11]

PART I

TERMS IMPLIED BY ACT

CHAPTER 1 APPLICATION AND INTERPRETATION

1 (1) The implied terms set out in Chapter 2 apply to all agreements which relate to a pitch except an agreement which relates to a pitch on a local authority gypsy and traveller site or a county council gypsy and traveller site.

(2) The implied terms set out in Chapter 3 apply to an agreement which relates to a transit pitch on a local authority gypsy and traveller site or a county council gypsy and traveller site.

(3) The implied terms set out in Chapter 4 apply to an agreement which relates to a permanent pitch on a local authority gypsy and traveller site or a county council gypsy and traveller site.

(4) In this Part of this Schedule—

"caravan site" has the same meaning as in Part 1 of the Caravan Sites and Control of Development Act 1960,

"county council gypsy and traveller site" means any land which—

(a) is occupied by a county council as a caravan site providing accommodation for gypsies and travellers, and

(b) is a protected site,

"gypsies and travellers" means persons of nomadic habit of life, whatever their race or origin, but does not include members of an organised group of travelling showpeople, or persons engaged in travelling circuses, travelling together as such,

"local authority gypsy and traveller site" means any land which—

(a) is occupied by a local authority as a caravan site providing accommodation for gypsies and travellers, and

(b) is a protected site,

"permanent pitch" means a pitch which is not a transit pitch,

"pitch" means the land, forming part of a protected site and including any garden area, on which an occupier is entitled to station a mobile home under the terms of the agreement, and

"transit pitch" means a pitch on which a person is entitled to station a mobile home under the terms of the agreement for a fixed period of up to 3 months.

CHAPTER 2 AGREEMENTS RELATING TO PITCHES EXCEPT PITCHES ON LOCAL AUTHORITY GYPSY AND TRAVELLER SITES AND COUNTY COUNCIL GYPSY AND TRAVELLER SITES

DURATION OF AGREEMENT

1 Subject to paragraph 2 below, the right to station the mobile home on land forming part of the protected site shall subsist until the agreement is determined under paragraph 3, 4, 5 or 5A below.

1A (1) The right to station the mobile home under in paragraph 1 is not affected by—

(a) the expiry of a Part 1A site licence in accordance with section 32J(1)(b)(ii) of the 1960 Act,

(b) the refusal to issue or renew a Part 1A site licence under section 32D of the 1960 Act,

(c) the revocation of a Part 1A site licence under section 32L of the 1960 Act, or

(d) the expiry of a site licence in accordance with section 83(2) of the Housing (Scotland) Act 2014 (asp 14).

(2) Sub-paragraph (1) applies in relation to agreements that were made at any time before the day on which that sub-paragraph comes into force (as well as in relation to agreements made on or after that day).

(3) In this paragraph—

"the 1960 Act" means the Caravan Sites and Control of Development Act 1960 (c 62), and

"Part 1A site licence" has the same meaning as in section 32Z6 of the 1960 Act.

2 (1) If the owner's estate or interest is insufficient to enable him to grant the right for an indefinite period, the period for which the right subsists shall not extend beyond the date when the owner's estate or interest determines.

(2) If planning permission for the use of the protected site as a site for mobile homes has been granted in terms such that it will expire at the end of a specified period, the period for which the right subsists shall not extend beyond the date when the planning permission expires.

(3) If before the end of a period determined by this paragraph there is a change in circumstances which allows a longer period, account shall be taken of that change.

TERMINATION BY OCCUPIER

3 The occupier shall be entitled to terminate the agreement by notice in writing given to the owner not less than four weeks before the date on which it is to take effect.

4 The owner shall be entitled to terminate the agreement at a date to be determined by the court if, on the application of the owner, the appropriate judicial body—

(a) is satisfied that the occupier has breached a term of the agreement and, after service of a notice to remedy the breach, has not complied with the notice within a reasonable time; and

(b) considers it reasonable for the agreement to be terminated.

5 The owner shall be entitled to terminate the agreement at a date to be determined by the court if, on the application of the owner, the appropriate judicial body—

(a) is satisfied that the occupier is not occupying the mobile home as his only or main residence; and

(b) considers it reasonable for the agreement to be terminated.

5A (1) [...]

(2) The owner is entitled to terminate the agreement forthwith if—

(a) on the application of the owner, a tribunal has determined that, having regard to its condition, the mobile home is having a detrimental effect on the amenity of the site; and

(b) then, on the application of the owner, the appropriate judicial body, having regard to the tribunal's determination and to any other circumstances, considers it reasonable for the agreement to be terminated.

(3) Sub-paragraphs (4) and (5) apply if, on an application to the tribunal under sub-paragraph (2)(a)—

(a) the tribunal considers that, having regard to the present condition of the mobile home, it is having a detrimental effect on the amenity of the site, but

(b) it also considers that it would be reasonably practicable for particular repairs to be carried out on the mobile home that would result in the mobile home not having that detrimental effect, and

(c) the occupier indicates to the tribunal that the occupier intends to carry out those repairs.

(4) In such a case, the tribunal may make an interim order—

(a) specifying the repairs that must be carried out and the time within which they must be carried out; and

(b) adjourning the proceedings on the application for such period specified in the interim order as the tribunal considers reasonable to enable the repairs to be carried out.

(5) If the tribunal makes an interim order under sub-paragraph (4), it must not make a determination under sub-paragraph (2)(a) unless it is satisfied that the specified period has expired without the repairs having been carried out.

6 (A1) This paragraph applies in relation to a protected site in Wales.

(1) The owner shall be entitled to terminate the agreement forthwith if, on the application of the owner, the court is satisfied that, having regard to its condition, the mobile home—

(a) is having a detrimental effect on the amenity of the site; and

(b) the court considers it reasonable for the agreement to be terminated.

(2) . . .

(3) Sub-paragraphs (4) and (5) below apply if, on an application under sub-paragraph (1) above—

(a) the court considers that, having regard to the present condition of the mobile home, paragraph (a) of that sub-paragraph applies to it, but

(b) it also considers that it would be reasonably practicable for particular repairs to be carried out on the mobile home that would result in sub-paragraph (1)(a) not applying to it, and

(c) the occupier indicates that he intends to carry out those repairs.

(4) In such a case the court may make an order adjourning proceedings on the application for such period specified in the order as the court considers reasonable to allow the repairs to be carried out.

The repairs must be set out in the order.

(5) If the court makes such an order, the application shall not be further proceeded with unless the court is satisfied that the specified period has expired without the repairs having been carried out.]

REPAYMENT OF SUMS PAID BY OCCUPIER ON TERMINATION OF AGREEMENT

7 Where the agreement is terminated as mentioned in paragraph 3, 4, 5 or 6, the owner must, within 2 months of the date of the termination, repay to the occupier so much of any payment made by the occupier in pursuance of the agreement as is attributable to a period beginning after the date of termination.

SALE OF MOBILE HOME

7A (1) [...]

(2) Where the agreement is a new agreement, the occupier is entitled to sell the mobile home and to assign the agreement to the person to whom the mobile home is sold (referred to in this paragraph as the "new occupier") without the approval of the owner.

(3) In this paragraph and paragraph 7B, "new agreement" means an agreement—

(a) which was made after the commencement of this paragraph, or

(b) which was made before, but which has been assigned after, that commencement.

(4) The new occupier must, as soon as reasonably practicable, notify the owner of the completion of the sale and assignment of the agreement.

(5) The new occupier is required to pay the owner a commission on the sale of the mobile home at a rate not exceeding such rate as may be prescribed by regulations made by the Secretary of State.

(6) Except to the extent mentioned in sub-paragraph (5), the owner may not require any payment to be made (whether to the owner or otherwise) in connection with the sale of the mobile home and the assignment of the agreement to the new occupier.

(7) The Secretary of State may by regulations prescribe procedural requirements to be complied with by the owner, the occupier or the new occupier in connection with—

(a) the sale of the mobile home and assignment of the agreement;

(b) the payment of commission by virtue of sub-paragraph (5).

7B (1) Where the agreement is not a new agreement, the occupier is entitled to sell the mobile home and assign the agreement without the approval of the owner if—

(a) the occupier serves on the owner a notice (a "notice of proposed sale") that the occupier proposes to sell the mobile home, and assign the agreement, to the person named in the notice (the "proposed occupier"), and

(b) the first or second condition is satisfied.

(2) The first condition is that, within the period of 21 days beginning with the date on which the owner received the notice of proposed sale ("the 21-day period"), the occupier does not receive a notice from the owner that the owner has applied to a

tribunal for an order preventing the occupier from selling the mobile home, and assigning the agreement, to the proposed occupier (a "refusal order").

(3) The second condition is that—

(a) within the 21-day period—

(i) the owner applies to a tribunal for a refusal order, and

(ii) the occupier receives a notice of the application from the owner, and

(b) the tribunal rejects the application.

(4) If the owner applies to a tribunal for a refusal order within the 21-day period but the occupier does not receive notice of the application from the owner within that period—

(a) the application is to be treated as not having been made, and

(b) the first condition is accordingly to be treated as satisfied.

(5) A notice of proposed sale must include such information as may be prescribed in regulations made by the Secretary of State.

(6) A notice of proposed sale or notice of an application for a refusal order—

(a) must be in writing, and

(b) may be served by post.

(7) An application for a refusal order may be made only on one or more of the grounds prescribed in regulations made by the Secretary of State; and a notice of an application for a refusal order must specify the ground or grounds on which the application is made.

(8) The person to whom the mobile home is sold ("the new occupier") is required to pay the owner a commission on the sale of the mobile home at a rate not exceeding such rate as may be prescribed by regulations made by the Secretary of State.

(9) Except to the extent mentioned in sub-paragraph (8), the owner may not require any payment to be made (whether to the owner or otherwise) in connection with the sale of the mobile home and the assignment of the agreement.

(10) The Secretary of State may by regulations prescribe procedural requirements to be complied with by the owner, the occupier, a proposed occupier or the new occupier in connection with—

(a) the sale of the mobile home and assignment of the agreement;

(b) the payment of commission by virtue of sub-paragraph (8).

7C (1) Regulations under paragraph 7A or 7B must be made by statutory instrument and may—

(a) make different provision for different cases or descriptions of case, including different provision for different areas or for sales at different prices;

(b) contain incidental, supplementary, transitional or saving provisions.

(2) Regulations under paragraph 7A or 7B are subject to annulment in pursuance of a resolution of either House of Parliament.

8 *Repealed by the Mobile Homes (Wales) Act 2013.*

GIFT OF MOBILE HOME

8A (1) [...]

(2) Where the agreement is a new agreement (as defined by paragraph 7A(3)), provided that the occupier has supplied the owner with the relevant evidence, the occupier is entitled to give the mobile home, and to assign the agreement, to a member of the occupier's family (referred to in this paragraph as the "new occupier") without the approval of the owner.

(3) The relevant evidence is—

(a) evidence, or evidence of a description, prescribed in regulations made by the Secretary of State that the person to whom the occupier proposes to give the mobile home, and to assign the agreement, is a member of the occupier's family, or

(b) any other satisfactory evidence that the person concerned is a member of the occupier's family.

(4) The new occupier must, as soon as reasonably practicable, notify the owner of the receipt of the mobile home and assignment of the agreement.

(5) The owner may not require any payment to be made (whether to the owner or otherwise) in connection with the gift of the mobile home, and the assignment of the agreement, as mentioned in sub-paragraph (2).

(6) The Secretary of State may by regulations prescribe procedural requirements to be complied with by the owner, the occupier or the new occupier in connection with the gift of the mobile home, and assignment of the agreement, as mentioned in sub-paragraph (2).

8B (1) Where the agreement is not a new agreement (as defined by paragraph 7A(3)), the occupier is entitled to give the mobile home, and assign the agreement, to a member of the occupier's family (referred to in this paragraph as the "proposed occupier") without the approval of the owner if—

(a) the occupier serves on the owner a notice (a "notice of proposed gift") that the occupier proposes to give the mobile home to the proposed occupier, and

(b) the first or second condition is satisfied.

(2) The first condition is that, within the period of 21 days beginning with the date on which the owner received the notice of proposed gift ("the 21-day period"), the occupier does not receive a notice from the owner that the owner has applied to a tribunal for an order preventing the occupier from giving the mobile home, and assigning the agreement, to the proposed occupier (a "refusal order").

(3) The second condition is that—

(a) within the 21-day period—

(i) the owner applies to a tribunal for a refusal order, and

(ii) the occupier receives a notice of the application from the owner, and

(b) the tribunal rejects the application.

(4) If the owner applies to a tribunal for a refusal order within the 21-day period but the occupier does not receive notice of the application from the owner within that period—

(a) the application is to be treated as not having been made, and

(b) the first condition is accordingly to be treated as satisfied.

(5) A notice of proposed sale must include—

(a) the relevant evidence (as defined by paragraph 8A(3)), and

(b) such other information as may be prescribed in regulations made by the Secretary of State.

(6) A notice of proposed gift or notice of an application for a refusal order—

(a) must be in writing, and

(b) may be served by post.

(7) An application for a refusal order may be made only on one or more of the grounds prescribed in regulations made by the Secretary of State; and a notice of an application for a refusal order must specify the ground or grounds on which the application is made.

(8) The owner may not require any payment to be made (whether to the owner or otherwise) in connection with the gift of the mobile home, and the assignment of the agreement, as mentioned in sub-paragraph (1).

(9) The Secretary of State may by regulations prescribe procedural requirements to be complied with by the owner, the occupier, a proposed occupier or the person to whom the mobile home is given in connection with the gift of the mobile home, and assignment of the agreement, as mentioned in sub-paragraph (1).

8C (1) Regulations under paragraph 8A or 8B must be made by statutory instrument and may—

(a) make different provision for different cases or descriptions of case, including different provision for different areas;

(b) contain incidental, supplementary, transitional or saving provisions.

(2) Regulations under paragraph 8A or 8B are subject to annulment in pursuance of a resolution of either House of Parliament.

9 (1) This paragraph applies to an agreement which relates to a pitch other than a pitch on—

(a) a local authority gypsy and traveller site; or

(b) a registered social landlord gypsy and traveller site.

(2) Subject to sub-paragraph (5), the occupier is entitled to gift the mobile home, and to assign the agreement, to a member of the occupier's family (the "new occupier") without the approval of the owner.

(3) The occupier must, if requested by the owner, give the owner such evidence as the owner, acting reasonably, may require to confirm that the new occupier is a member of the occupier's family.

(4) The new occupier must, as soon as practicable, notify the owner of the new occupier's acceptance of the gift of the mobile home and assignation of the agreement.

(5) Neither the gift nor the assignation are to have any effect until the owner has received the evidence mentioned in sub-paragraph (3) and the notification required in sub-paragraph (4).

(6) The owner may not require any payment to be made (whether to the owner or otherwise) in connection with the gift of the mobile home, and the assignation of the agreement.

Re-siting of mobile home

10 (1) The owner shall be entitled to require that the occupier's right to station the mobile home is exercisable for any period in relation to another pitch forming part of the protected site ("the other pitch") if (and only if)—

(a) on the application of the owner, the appropriate judicial body is satisfied that the other pitch is broadly comparable to the occupier's original pitch and that it is reasonable for the mobile home to be stationed on the other pitch for that period; or

(b) the owner needs to carry out essential repair or emergency works that can only be carried out if the mobile home is moved to the other pitch for that period, and the other pitch is broadly comparable to the occupier's original pitch.

(2) If the owner requires the occupier to station the mobile home on the other pitch so that he can replace, or carry out repairs to, the base on which the mobile home is stationed, he must if the occupier so requires, or the appropriate judicial body on the application of the occupier so orders, secure that the mobile home is returned to the original pitch on the completion of the replacement or repairs.

(3) The owner shall pay all the costs and expenses incurred by the occupier in connection with his mobile home being moved to and from the other pitch.

(4) In this paragraph and in paragraph 13 below, "essential repair or emergency works" means—

(a) repairs to the base on which the mobile home is stationed;

(b) works or repairs needed to comply with any relevant legal requirements; or

(c) works or repairs in connection with restoration following flood, landslide or other natural disaster.

Quiet enjoyment of the mobile home

11 The occupier shall be entitled to quiet enjoyment of the mobile home together with the pitch during the continuance of the agreement, subject to paragraphs 10, 12, 13 and 14.

Owner's right of entry to the pitch

12 The owner may enter the pitch without prior notice between the hours of 9 am and 6 pm

(a) to deliver written communications, including post and notices, to the occupier; and

(b) to read any meter for gas, electricity, water, sewerage or other services supplied by the owner.

13 The owner may enter the pitch to carry out essential repair or emergency works on giving as much notice to the occupier (whether in writing or otherwise) as is reasonably practicable in the circumstances.

14 Unless the occupier has agreed otherwise, the owner may enter the pitch for a reason other than one specified in paragraph 12 or 13 only if he has given the occupier at least 14 clear days' written notice of the date, time and reason for his visit.

15 The rights conferred by paragraphs 12 to 14 above do not extend to the mobile home.

The pitch fee

16 The pitch fee can only be changed in accordance with paragraph 17, either—

(a) with the agreement of the occupier, or

(b) if the appropriate judicial body, on the application of the owner or the occupier, considers it reasonable for the pitch fee to be changed and makes an order determining the amount of the new pitch fee.

17 (1) The pitch fee shall be reviewed annually as at the review date.

(2) At least 28 clear days before the review date the owner shall serve on the occupier a written notice setting out his proposals in respect of the new pitch fee.

(2A) A notice under sub-paragraph (2) which proposes an increase in the pitch fee is of no effect unless it is accompanied by a document which complies with paragraph 25A.

(3) If the occupier agrees to the proposed new pitch fee, it shall be payable as from the review date.

(4) If the occupier does not agree to the proposed new pitch fee—

(a) the owner may apply to the appropriate judicial body for an order under paragraph 16(b) determining the amount of the new pitch fee;

(b) the occupier shall continue to pay the current pitch fee to the owner until such time as the new pitch fee is agreed by the occupier or an order determining the amount of the new pitch fee is made by the appropriate judicial body under paragraph 16(b); and

(c) the new pitch fee shall be payable as from the review date but the occupier shall not be treated as being in arrears until the 28th day after the date on which the new pitch fee is agreed or, as the case may be, the 28th day after the date of the appropriate judicial body order determining the amount of the new pitch fee.

(5) An application under sub-paragraph (4)(a) may be made at any time after the end of the period of 28 days beginning with the review date.

(6) Sub-paragraphs (7) to (10) apply if the owner—

(a) has not served the notice required by sub-paragraph (2) by the time by which it was required to be served, but

(b) at any time thereafter serves on the occupier a written notice setting out his proposals in respect of a new pitch fee.

(6A) A notice under sub-paragraph (6)(b) which proposes an increase in the pitch fee is of no effect unless it is accompanied by a document which complies with paragraph 25A.

(7) If (at any time) the occupier agrees to the proposed pitch fee, it shall be payable as from the 28th day after the date on which the owner serves the notice under sub-paragraph (6)(b).

(8) If the occupier has not agreed to the proposed pitch fee—

(a) the owner may apply to the appropriate judicial body for an order under paragraph 16(b) determining the amount of the new pitch fee;

(b) the occupier shall continue to pay the current pitch fee to the owner until such time as the new pitch fee is agreed by the occupier or an order determining the amount of the new pitch fee is made by the appropriate judicial body under paragraph 16(b); and

(c) if the appropriate judicial body makes such an order, the new pitch fee shall be payable as from the 28th day after the date on which the owner serves the notice under sub-paragraph (6)(b).

(9) An application under sub-paragraph (8) may be made at any time after the end of the period of 56 days beginning with date on which the owner serves the notice under sub-paragraph (6)(b).

(9A) A tribunal may permit an application under sub-paragraph (4)(a) or (8)(a) to be made to it outside the time limit specified in sub-paragraph (5) (in the case of an application under sub-paragraph (4)(a)) or in sub-paragraph (9) (in the case of an application under sub-paragraph (8)(a)) if it is satisfied that, in all the circumstances, there are good reasons for the failure to apply within the applicable time limit and for any delay since then in applying for permission to make the application out of time.

(10) The occupier shall not be treated as being in arrears—

(a) where sub-paragraph (7) applies, until the 28th day after the date on which the new pitch fee is agreed; or

(b) where sub-paragraph (8)(b) applies, until the 28th day after the date on which the new pitch fee is agreed or, as the case may be, the 28th day after the date of the appropriate judicial body order determining the amount of the new pitch fee.

(11) Sub-paragraph (12) applies if a tribunal, on the application of the occupier of a pitch, is satisfied that—

(a) a notice under sub-paragraph (2) or (6)(b) was of no effect as a result of sub-paragraph (2A) or (6A), but

(b) the occupier nonetheless paid the owner the pitch fee proposed in the notice.

(12) The tribunal may order the owner to pay the occupier, within the period of 21 days beginning with the date of the order, the difference between—

(a) the amount which the occupier was required to pay the owner for the period in question, and

(b) the amount which the occupier has paid the owner for that period.

18 (1) When determining the amount of the new pitch fee particular regard shall be had to—

(a) any sums expended by the owner since the last review date on improvements—

(i) which are for the benefit of the occupiers of mobile homes on the protected site;

(ii) which were the subject of consultation in accordance with paragraph 22(e) and (f) below; and

(iii) to which a majority of the occupiers have not disagreed in writing or which, in the case of such disagreement, the appropriate judicial body, on the application of the owner, has ordered should be taken into account when determining the amount of the new pitch fee;

(aa) any deterioration in the condition, and any decrease in the amenity, of the site or any adjoining land which is occupied or controlled by the owner since the date on which this paragraph came into force (in so far as regard has not previously been had to that deterioration or decrease for the purposes of this sub-paragraph);

(ab) any reduction in the services that the owner supplies to the site, pitch or mobile home, and any deterioration in the quality of those services, since the date on which this paragraph came into force (in so far as regard has not previously been had to that reduction or deterioration for the purposes of this sub-paragraph);

(b) any decrease in the amenity of the protected site since the last review date;

(ba) any direct effect on the costs payable by the owner in relation to the maintenance or management of the site of an enactment which has come into force since the last review date; and

(c) [...]

(1A) But no regard shall be had, when determining the amount of the new pitch fee, to any costs incurred by the owner since the last review date for the purpose of compliance with the amendments made to this Act by the Mobile Homes Act 2013.

(2) When calculating what constitutes a majority of the occupiers for the purposes of sub-paragraph (1)(b)(iii) each mobile home is to be taken to have only one occupier and, in the event of there being more than one occupier of a mobile home, its occupier is to be taken to be the occupier whose name first appears on the agreement.

(3) In a case where the pitch fee has not been previously reviewed, references in this paragraph to the last review date are to be read as references to the date when the agreement commenced.

19 (1) When determining the amount of the new pitch fee, any costs incurred by the owner in connection with expanding the protected site shall not be taken into account.

(2) When determining the amount of the new pitch fee, no regard may be had to any costs incurred by the owner in relation to the conduct of proceedings under this Act or the agreement.

(3) When determining the amount of the new pitch fee, no regard may be had to any fee required to be paid by the owner by virtue of—

(a) section 8(1B) of the Caravan Sites and Control of Development Act 1960 (fee for application for site licence conditions to be altered);

(b) section 10(1A) of that Act (fee for application for consent to transfer site licence).

(4) When determining the amount of the new pitch fee, no regard may be had to any costs incurred by the owner in connection with—

(a) any action taken by a local authority under sections 9A to 9I of the Caravan Sites and Control of Development Act 1960 (breach of licence condition, emergency action etc);

(b) the owner being convicted of an offence under section 9B of that Act (failure to comply with compliance notice).

20 (A1) Unless this would be unreasonable having regard to paragraph 18(1), there is a presumption that the pitch fee shall increase or decrease by a percentage which is no more than any percentage increase or decrease in the retail prices index calculated by reference only to—

(a) the latest index, and

(b) the index published for the month which was 12 months before that to which the latest index relates.

(A2) In sub-paragraph (A1), "the latest index"—

(a) in a case where the owner serves a notice under paragraph 17(2), means the last index published before the day on which that notice is served;

(b) in a case where the owner serves a notice under paragraph 17(6), means the last index published before the day by which the owner was required to serve a notice under paragraph 17(2).

(1), (2) [...]

Occupier's obligations

21 The occupier shall—

(a) pay the pitch fee to the owner;

(b) pay to the owner all sums due under the agreement in respect of gas, electricity, water, sewerage or other services supplied by the owner;

(c) keep the mobile home in a sound state of repair;

(d) maintain—

(i) the outside of the mobile home, and

(ii) the pitch, including all fences and outbuildings belonging to, or enjoyed with, it and the mobile home,

in a clean and tidy condition; and

(e) if requested by the owner, provide him with documentary evidence of any costs or expenses in respect of which the occupier seeks reimbursement.

Owner's obligations

22 The owner shall—

(a) if requested by the occupier, and on payment by the occupier of a charge of not more than £30, provide accurate written details of—

(i) the size of the pitch and the base on which the mobile home is stationed; and

(ii) the location of the pitch and the base within the protected site;

and such details must include measurements between identifiable fixed points on the protected site and the pitch and the base;

(b) if requested by the occupier, provide (free of charge) documentary evidence in support and explanation of—

(i) any new pitch fee;

(ii) any charges for gas, electricity, water, sewerage or other services payable by the occupier to the owner under the agreement; and

(iii) any other charges, costs or expenses payable by the occupier to the owner under the agreement;

(c) be responsible for repairing the base on which the mobile home is stationed and for maintaining any gas, electricity, water, sewerage or other services supplied by the owner to the pitch or to the mobile home;

(d) maintain in a clean and tidy condition those parts of the protected site, including access ways, site boundary fences and trees, which are not the responsibility of any occupier of a mobile home stationed on the protected site;

(e) consult the occupier about improvements to the protected site in general, and in particular about those which the owner wishes to be taken into account when determining the amount of any new pitch fee; and

(d) subject to paragraph (c) above, membership is open to all occupiers who own a mobile home on that site;

(e) it maintains a list of members which is open to public inspection together with the rules and constitution of the residents' association;

(f) it has a chairman, secretary and treasurer who are elected by and from among the members;

(g) with the exception of administrative decisions taken by the chairman, secretary and treasurer acting in their official capacities, decisions are taken by voting and there is only one vote for each mobile home; and

(h) the owner has acknowledged in writing to the secretary that the association is a qualifying residents' association, or, in default of this, the appropriate judicial body has so ordered.

(2) When calculating the percentage of occupiers for the purpose of sub-paragraph (1)(b) above, each mobile home shall be taken to have only one occupier and, in the event of there being more than one occupier of a mobile home, its occupier is to be taken to be the occupier whose name first appears on the agreement.

Interpretation

29 In this Chapter—

"pitch fee" means the amount which the occupier is required by the agreement to pay to the owner for the right to station the mobile home on the pitch and for use of the common areas of the protected site and their maintenance, but does not include amounts due in respect of gas, electricity, water and sewerage or other services, unless the agreement expressly provides that the pitch fee includes such amounts;

"retail prices index" means the general index (for all items) published by the Statistics Board or, if that index is not published for a relevant month, any substituted index or index figures published by that Board;

"review date" means the date specified in the written statement as the date on which the pitch fee will be reviewed in each year, or if no such date is specified, each anniversary of the date the agreement commenced; and

"written statement" means the written statement that the owner of the protected site is required to give to the occupier by section 1(2) of this Act.

CHAPTER 3 AGREEMENTS RELATING TO TRANSIT PITCHES ON A LOCAL AUTHORITY GYPSY AND TRAVELLER SITE OR A COUNTY COUNCIL GYPSY AND TRAVELLER SITE

Duration of agreement

1 Subject to paragraph 2, the right to station the mobile home on the transit pitch subsists until the fixed period set out in the agreement expires or termination of the agreement under paragraph 3 or 4, whichever is sooner.

2 (1) If the owner's estate or interest is insufficient to enable the owner to grant the right for the fixed period set out in the agreement, the period for which the right subsists does not extend beyond the date when the owner's estate or interest determines.

(2) If planning permission for the use of the protected site as a site for mobile homes has been granted in such terms that it will expire at the end of a specified period, the period for which the right subsists does not extend beyond the date when the planning permission expires.

(3) If planning permission for the use of the protected site as a site for mobile homes has been granted in terms such that it requires the owner to limit the

duration of stay for mobile homes on the site, the period for which the right subsists does not extend beyond that duration.

EARLY TERMINATION BY OCCUPIER

3 The occupier may terminate the agreement before the expiry of the fixed period set out in the agreement by giving written notice to the owner.

EARLY TERMINATION BY OWNER

4 The owner may terminate the agreement before the expiry of the fixed period set out in the agreement—

(a) without being required to show any reason, by giving written notice not less than four weeks before the date on which that notice is to take effect, or

(b) forthwith, where—

(i) the occupier has breached a term of the agreement and, after service of a notice to remedy the breach, has not complied with the notice within a reasonable time, and

(ii) the owner considers it reasonable for the agreement to be terminated.

RECOVERY OF OVERPAYMENTS BY OCCUPIER

5 Where the agreement is terminated as mentioned in paragraph 3 or 4, the occupier is entitled to recover from the owner so much of any payment made by the occupier in pursuance of the agreement as is attributable to a period beginning after the termination.

QUIET ENJOYMENT OF THE MOBILE HOME

6 The occupier is entitled to quiet enjoyment of the mobile home together with the pitch during the continuance of the agreement, subject to paragraphs 7, 8 and 9.

OWNER'S RIGHT OF ENTRY TO THE PITCH

7 The owner may enter the pitch without prior notice between the hours of 9am and 6pm—

(a) to deliver written communications, including post and notices, to the occupier; and

(b) to read any meter for gas, electricity, water, sewerage or other services supplied by the owner.

8 (1) The owner may enter the pitch to carry out essential repair or emergency works on giving as much notice to the occupier (whether in writing or otherwise) as is reasonably practicable in the circumstances.

(2) In this paragraph, "essential repair or emergency works" means—

(a) repairs to the base on which the mobile home is stationed;

(b) repairs to any outhouses and facilities provided by the owner on the pitch and to any gas, electricity, water, sewerage or other services or other amenities provided by the owner in such outhouses;

(c) works or repairs needed to comply with any relevant legal requirements; or

(d) works or repairs in connection with restoration following flood, landslide or other natural disaster.

9 Unless the occupier has agreed otherwise, the owner may enter the pitch for a reason other than one specified in paragraph 7 or 8 only if the owner has given the occupier at least 14 clear days' written notice of the date, time and reason for the owner's visit.

10 The rights conferred by paragraphs 7 to 9 do not extend to the mobile home.

OWNER'S NAME AND ADDRESS

11 (1) The owner must by notice inform the occupier of the address in England or Wales at which notices (including notices of proceedings) may be served on the owner by the occupier.

(2) If the owner fails to comply with sub-paragraph (1), then any amount otherwise due from the occupier to the owner in respect of the pitch fee is to be treated for all purposes as not being due from the occupier to the owner at any time before the owner does so comply.

(3) Where in accordance with the agreement the owner gives any written notice to the occupier the notice must contain the name and address of the owner.

(4) Where—

(a) the occupier receives such a notice, but

(b) it does not contain the information required to be contained in it by virtue of sub-paragraph (3),

the notice is to be treated as not having been given until such time as the owner gives the information to the occupier in respect of the notice.

(5) Nothing in sub-paragraphs (3) and (4) applies to any notice containing a demand to which paragraph 12(1) applies.

12 (1) Where the owner makes any demand for payment by the occupier of the pitch fee, or in respect of services supplied or other charges, the demand must contain the name and address of the owner.

(2) Where—

(a) the occupier receives such a demand, but

(b) it does not contain the information required to be contained in it by virtue of sub-paragraph (1),

the amount demanded is to be treated for all purposes as not being due from the occupier to the owner at any time before the owner gives that information to the occupier in respect of the demand.

INTERPRETATION

13 In this Chapter, "pitch fee" means the amount which the occupier is required by the agreement to pay to the owner for the right to station the mobile home on the pitch and for use of the common areas of the protected site and their maintenance, but does not include amounts due in respect of gas, electricity, water, sewerage or other services, unless the agreement expressly provides that the pitch fee includes such amounts.

CHAPTER 4 AGREEMENTS RELATING TO PERMANENT PITCHES ON A LOCAL AUTHORITY GYPSY AND TRAVELLER SITE OR A COUNTY COUNCIL GYPSY AND TRAVELLER SITE

DURATION OF AGREEMENT

1 Subject to paragraph 2, the right to station the mobile home on land forming part of the protected site subsists until the agreement is determined under paragraph 3, 4, 5 or 6.

2 (1) If the owner's estate or interest is insufficient to enable the owner to grant the right for an indefinite period, the period for which the right subsists does not extend beyond the date when the owner's estate or interest determines.

(2) If planning permission for the use of the protected site as a site for mobile homes has been granted in terms such that it will expire at the end of a specified period, the period for which the right subsists does not extend beyond the date when the planning permission expires.

(3) If before the end of a period determined by this paragraph there is a change in circumstances which allows a longer period, account is to be taken of that change.

TERMINATION BY OCCUPIER

3 The occupier is entitled to terminate the agreement by notice in writing given to the owner not less than four weeks before the date on which it is to take effect.

TERMINATION BY OWNER

4 The owner is entitled to terminate the agreement forthwith if, on the application of the owner, the appropriate judicial body—

(a) is satisfied that the occupier has breached a term of the agreement and, after service of a notice to remedy the breach, has not complied with the notice within a reasonable time; and

(b) considers it reasonable for the agreement to be terminated.

5 The owner is entitled to terminate the agreement forthwith if, on the application of the owner, the appropriate judicial body—

(a) is satisfied that the occupier is not occupying the mobile home as the occupier's only or main residence; and

(b) considers it reasonable for the agreement to be terminated.

6 (1) The owner is entitled to terminate the agreement forthwith if—

(a) on the application of the owner, a tribunal has determined that, having regard to its condition, the mobile home is having a detrimental effect on the amenity of the site, and

(b) then, on the application of the owner, the appropriate judicial body, having regard to the tribunal's determination and to any other circumstances, considers it reasonable for the agreement to be terminated.

(2) Sub-paragraphs (3) and (4) apply if, on an application to the tribunal under sub-paragraph (1)(a)—

(a) the tribunal considers that, having regard to the present condition of the mobile home, it is having a detrimental effect on the amenity of the site, but

(b) it also considers that it would be reasonably practicable for particular repairs to be carried out on the mobile home that would result in the mobile home not having that detrimental effect, and

(c) the occupier indicates to the tribunal that the occupier intends to carry out those repairs.

(3) In such a case the tribunal may make an interim order—

(a) specifying the repairs that must be carried out and the time within which they must be carried out, and

(b) adjourning the proceedings on the application for such period specified in the interim order as the tribunal considers reasonable to enable the repairs to be carried out.

(4) If the tribunal makes an interim order under sub-paragraph (3), it must not make a determination under sub-paragraph (1)(a) unless it is satisfied that the specified period has expired without the repairs having been carried out.

RECOVERY OF OVERPAYMENTS BY OCCUPIER

7 Where the agreement is terminated as mentioned in paragraph 3, 4, 5 or 6, the occupier is entitled to recover from the owner so much of any payment made by the occupier in pursuance of the agreement as is attributable to a period beginning after the termination.

RE-SITING OF MOBILE HOME

8 (1) The owner is entitled to require that the occupier's right to station the mobile home is exercisable for any period in relation to another pitch forming part of the protected site or a pitch forming part of another protected site ("the other pitch") if (and only if)—

(a) on the application of the owner, a tribunal is satisfied that the other pitch is broadly comparable to the occupier's original pitch and that it is reasonable for the mobile home to be stationed on the other pitch for that period; or

(b) the owner needs to carry out essential repair or emergency works that can only be carried out if the mobile home is moved to the other pitch for that period, and the other pitch is broadly comparable to the occupier's original pitch.

(2) If the owner requires the occupier to station the mobile home on the other pitch so that the owner can replace, or carry out repairs to, the base on which the mobile home is stationed, the owner must if the occupier so requires, or a tribunal on the application of the occupier so orders, secure that the mobile home is returned to the original pitch on the completion of the replacement or repairs.

(3) The owner must pay all the costs and expenses incurred by the occupier in connection with the mobile home being moved to and from the other pitch.

(4) In this paragraph and in paragraph 11, "essential repair or emergency works" means—

(a) repairs to the base on which the mobile home is stationed;

(b) repairs to any outhouses and facilities provided by the owner on the pitch and to any gas, electricity, water, sewerage or other services or other amenities provided by the owner in such outhouses;

(c) works or repairs needed to comply with any relevant legal requirements; or

(d) works or repairs in connection with restoration following flood, landslide or other natural disaster.

QUIET ENJOYMENT OF THE MOBILE HOME

9 The occupier is entitled to quiet enjoyment of the mobile home together with the pitch during the continuance of the agreement, subject to paragraphs 8, 10, 11 and 12.

OWNER'S RIGHT OF ENTRY TO THE PITCH

10 The owner may enter the pitch without prior notice between the hours of 9am and 6pm—

(a) to deliver written communications, including post and notices, to the occupier; and

(b) to read any meter for gas, electricity, water, sewerage or other services supplied by the owner.

11 The owner may enter the pitch to carry out essential repair or emergency works on giving as much notice to the occupier (whether in writing or otherwise) as is reasonably practicable in the circumstances.

12 Unless the occupier has agreed otherwise, the owner may enter the pitch for a reason other than one specified in paragraph 10 or 11 only if the owner has given the occupier at least 14 clear days' written notice of the date, time and reason for the owner's visit.

13 The rights conferred by paragraphs 10 to 12 do not extend to the mobile home.

THE PITCH FEE

14 The pitch fee can only be changed in accordance with paragraph 15, either—

(a) with the agreement of the occupier, or

(b) if a tribunal, on the application of the owner or the occupier, considers it reasonable for the pitch fee to be changed and makes an order determining the amount of the new pitch fee.

15 (1) The pitch fee will be reviewed annually as at the review date.

(2) At least 28 clear days before the review date the owner must serve on the occupier a written notice setting out the owner's proposals in respect of the new pitch fee.

(3) If the occupier agrees to the proposed new pitch fee, it is payable as from the review date.

(4) If the occupier does not agree to the proposed new pitch fee—

(a) the owner may apply to a tribunal for an order under paragraph 14(b) determining the amount of the new pitch fee;

(b) the occupier must continue to pay the current pitch fee to the owner until such time as the new pitch fee is agreed by the occupier or an order determining the amount of the new pitch fee is made by a tribunal under paragraph 14(b); and

(c) the new pitch fee is payable as from the review date but the occupier is not to be treated as being in arrears until the 28th day after the date on which the new pitch fee is agreed or, as the case may be, the 28th day after the date of a tribunal order determining the amount of the new pitch fee.

(5) An application under sub-paragraph (4)(a) may be made at any time after the end of the period of 28 days beginning with the review date but no later than three months after the review date.

(6) Sub-paragraphs (7) to (11) apply if the owner—

(a) has not served the notice required by sub-paragraph (2) by the time by which it was required to be served, but

(b) at any time thereafter serves on the occupier a written notice setting out the owner's proposals in respect of a new pitch fee.

(7) If (at any time) the occupier agrees to the proposed pitch fee, it is payable as from the 28th day after the date on which the owner serves the notice under sub-paragraph (6)(b).

(8) If the occupier has not agreed to the proposed pitch fee—

(a) the owner may apply to a tribunal for an order under paragraph 14(b) determining the amount of the new pitch fee;

(b) the occupier must continue to pay the current pitch fee to the owner until such time as the new pitch fee is agreed by the occupier or an order determining the amount of the new pitch fee is made by a tribunal under paragraph 14(b); and

(c) if a tribunal makes such an order, the new pitch fee is payable as from the 28th day after the date on which the owner serves the notice under sub-paragraph (6)(b).

(9) An application under sub-paragraph (8) may be made at any time after the end of the period of 56 days beginning with the date on which the owner serves the

notice under sub-paragraph (6)(b) but no later than four months after the date on which the owner serves that notice.

(10) A tribunal may permit an application under sub-paragraph (4)(a) or (8)(a) to be made to it outside the time limit specified in sub-paragraph (5) (in the case of an application under sub-paragraph (4)(a)) or in sub-paragraph (9) (in the case of an application under sub-paragraph (8)(a)) if it is satisfied that, in all the circumstances, there are good reasons for the failure to apply within the applicable time limit and for any delay since then in applying for permission to make the application out of time.

(11) The occupier is not to be treated as being in arrears—

(a) where sub-paragraph (7) applies, until the 28th day after the date on which the new pitch fee is agreed; or

(b) where sub-paragraph (8)(b) applies, until the 28th day after the date on which the new pitch fee is agreed or, as the case may be, the 28th day after the date of a tribunal order determining the amount of the new pitch fee.

16 (1) When determining the amount of the new pitch fee particular regard must be had to—

(a) any sums expended by the owner since the last review date on improvements—

(i) which are for the benefit of the occupiers of mobile homes on the protected site;

(ii) which were the subject of consultation in accordance with paragraph 20(f) and (g); and

(iii) to which a majority of the occupiers have not disagreed in writing or which, in the case of such disagreement, a tribunal, on the application of the owner, has ordered should be taken into account when determining the amount of the new pitch fee;

(b) any decrease in the amenity of the protected site since the last review date; and

(c) the effect of any enactment which has come into force since the last review date.

(2) When calculating what constitutes a majority of the occupiers for the purposes of sub-paragraph (1)(a)(iii) each mobile home is to be taken to have only one occupier and, in the event of there being more than one occupier of a mobile home, its occupier is to be taken to be the occupier whose name first appears on the agreement.

(3) In a case where the pitch fee has not been previously reviewed, references in this paragraph to the last review date are to be read as references to the date when the agreement commenced.

17 When determining the amount of the new pitch fee no regard may be had to—

(a) any costs incurred by the owner in connection with expanding the protected site, or

(b) any costs incurred by the owner in relation to the conduct of proceedings under this Act or the agreement.

18 (1) There is a presumption that the pitch fee will increase or decrease by a percentage which is no more than any percentage increase or decrease in the retail prices index since the last review date, unless this would be unreasonable having regard to paragraph 16(1).

(2) Paragraph 16(3) applies for the purposes of this paragraph as it applies for the purposes of paragraph 16.

OCCUPIER'S OBLIGATIONS

19 The occupier must—
(a) pay the pitch fee to the owner;
(b) pay to the owner all sums due under the agreement in respect of gas, electricity, water, sewerage or other services supplied by the owner;
(c) keep the mobile home in a sound state of repair;
(d) maintain—
(i) the outside of the mobile home, and
(ii) the pitch, including all fences and outbuildings belonging to, or enjoyed with, it and the mobile home,

in a clean and tidy condition; and
(e) if requested by the owner, provide the owner with documentary evidence of any costs or expenses in respect of which the occupier seeks reimbursement.

OWNER'S OBLIGATIONS

20 The owner must—
(a) if requested by the occupier, and on payment by the occupier of a charge of not more than £30, provide accurate written details of—
(i) the size of the pitch and the base on which the mobile home is stationed; and
(ii) the location of the pitch and the base within the protected site;

and such details must include measurements between identifiable fixed points on the protected site and the pitch and the base;
(b) if requested by the occupier, provide (free of charge) documentary evidence in support and explanation of—
(i) any new pitch fee;
(ii) any charges for gas, electricity, water, sewerage or other services payable by the occupier to the owner under the agreement; and
(iii) any other charges, costs or expenses payable by the occupier to the owner under the agreement;
(c) be responsible for repairing the base on which the mobile home is stationed and for maintaining any gas, electricity, water, sewerage or other services supplied by the owner to the pitch or to the mobile home;
(d) be responsible for repairing other amenities provided by the owner on the pitch including any outhouses and facilities provided;
(e) maintain in a clean and tidy condition those parts of the protected site, including access ways, site boundary fences and trees, which are not the responsibility of any occupier of a mobile home stationed on the protected site;
(f) consult the occupier about improvements to the protected site in general, and in particular about those which the owner wishes to be taken into account when determining the amount of any new pitch fee; and
(g) consult a qualifying residents' association, if there is one, about all matters which relate to the operation and management of, or improvements to, the protected site and may affect the occupiers either directly or indirectly.

21 The owner must not do or cause to be done anything which may adversely affect the ability of the occupier to perform the occupier's obligations under paragraph 19(c) and (d).

22 For the purposes of paragraph 20(f), to "consult" the occupier means—

(a) to give the occupier at least 28 clear days' notice in writing of the proposed improvements which—
  (i) describes the proposed improvements and how they will benefit the occupier in the long and short term;
  (ii) details how the pitch fee may be affected when it is next reviewed; and
  (iii) states when and where the occupier can make representations about the proposed improvements; and
(b) to take into account any representations made by the occupier about the proposed improvements, in accordance with paragraph (a)(iii), before undertaking them.

23 For the purposes of paragraph 20(g), to "consult" a qualifying residents' association means—
(a) to give the association at least 28 clear days' notice in writing of the matters referred to in paragraph 20(g) which—
  (i) describes the matters and how they may affect the occupiers either directly or indirectly in the long and short term; and
  (ii) states when and where the association can make representations about the matters;
(aa) no regard may be had to any costs paid, or to be paid, by the owner in connection with expenses recovered by a local authority under—
  (i) section 32Z2(2) of the Caravan Sites and Control of Development Act 1960;
  (ii) subsection (1)(a) or (c) of section 32Z3 of that Act; or
  (iii) section 32Z4 of that Act;
(ab) no regard may be had to any costs paid, or to be paid, by the owner in connection with the owner being convicted of an offence under Part 1A of the Caravan Sites and Control of Development Act 1960; and
(b) to take into account any representations made by the association, in accordance with paragraph (a)(ii), before proceeding with the matters.

OWNER'S NAME AND ADDRESS

24 (1) The owner must by notice inform the occupier and any qualifying residents' association of the address in England or Wales at which notices (including notices of proceedings) may be served on the owner by the occupier or a qualifying residents' association.
(2) If the owner fails to comply with sub-paragraph (1), then any amount otherwise due from the occupier to the owner in respect of the pitch fee is to be treated for all purposes as not being due from the occupier to the owner at any time before the owner does so comply.
(3) Where in accordance with the agreement the owner gives any written notice to the occupier or (as the case may be) a qualifying residents' association, the notice must contain the name and address of the owner.
(4) Where—
(a) the occupier or a qualifying residents' association receives such a notice, but
(b) it does not contain the information required to be contained in it by virtue of sub-paragraph (3),

the notice is to be treated as not having been given until such time as the owner gives the information to the occupier or (as the case may be) the association in respect of the notice.
(5) Nothing in sub-paragraphs (3) and (4) applies to any notice containing a demand to which paragraph 25(1) applies.

25 (1) Where the owner makes any demand for payment by the occupier of the pitch fee, or in respect of services supplied or other charges, the demand must contain the name and address of the owner.

(2) Where—

(a) the occupier receives such a demand, but

(b) it does not contain the information required to be contained in it by virtue of sub-paragraph (1),

the amount demanded is to be treated for all purposes as not being due from the occupier to the owner at any time before the owner gives that information to the occupier in respect of the demand.

Qualifying residents' association

26 (1) A residents' association is a qualifying residents' association in relation to a protected site if—

(a) it is an association representing the occupiers of mobile homes on that site;

(b) at least 50 per cent of the occupiers of the mobile homes on that site are members of the association;

(c) it is independent from the owner, who together with any agent or employee of the owner is excluded from membership;

(d) subject to paragraph (c), membership is open to all occupiers who own a mobile home on that site;

(e) it maintains a list of members which is open to public inspection together with the rules and constitution of the residents' association;

(f) it has a chair, secretary and treasurer who are elected by and from among the members;

(g) with the exception of administrative decisions taken by the chair, secretary and treasurer acting in their official capacities, decisions are taken by voting and there is only one vote for each mobile home; and

(h) the owner has acknowledged in writing to the secretary that the association is a qualifying residents' association, or, in default of this, a tribunal has so ordered.

(2) When calculating the percentage of occupiers for the purpose of sub-paragraph (1)(b), each mobile home is to be taken to have only one occupier and, in the event of there being more than one occupier of a mobile home, its occupier is to be taken to be the occupier whose name first appears on the agreement.

Interpretation

27 In this Chapter—

"pitch fee" means the amount which the occupier is required by the agreement to pay to the owner for the right to station the mobile home on the pitch and for use of the common areas of the protected site and their maintenance, but does not include amounts due in respect of gas, electricity, water, sewerage or other services, unless the agreement expressly provides that the pitch fee includes such amounts;

"retail prices index" means the general index (for all items) published by the Statistics Board or, if that index is not published for a relevant month, any substituted index or index figures published by the Board;

"review date" means the date specified in the written statement as the date on which the pitch fee will be reviewed in each year, or if no such date is specified, each anniversary of the date the agreement commenced; and

"written statement" means the written statement that the owner of the protected site is required to give to the occupier by section 1(2) of this Act.

PART 2
MATTERS CONCERNING WHICH TERMS MAY BE IMPLIED BY APPROPRIATE JUDICIAL BODY

1 . . .

2 The sums payable by the occupier in pursuance of the agreement and the times at which they are to be paid.

3 The review at yearly intervals of the sums so payable.

4 The provision or improvement of services available on the protected site, and the use by the occupier of such services.

5 The preservation of the amenity of the protected site.

6 . . .

7 . . .

PART 3
SUPPLEMENTARY PROVISIONS

REPEALED

Part 3 is repealed by the Mobile Homes (Wales) Act 2013 with effect from 5 November 2013.

III MOB [11.1]

Termination under paragraph 4 The owner may terminate under para 4 of Chapter 2 or Chapter 4 of Part 1 to Schedule 1, if there has been a breach. In a case where the breach was in unreasonably refusing to move to a broadly comparable site to allow the carrying out of essential repairs to the seawall it was held that the motives of the owner in identifying the need for repairs as essential was irrelevant providing that he can show that the works are essential: *Tapsell v Cemery* (1995) 27 HLR 114, CA, per Butler-Sloss LJ at p 117.

The onus is on the owner to prove that the conditions have been satisfied and he may rely on the defendant's admission in this regard. But where the admission is inconsistent with the known facts the court should not disregard the pleaded admission and dismiss the claim. Instead the court should invite the defendant to apply for permission to amend the defence in order to put the previously admitted facts in issue and then hear and resolve argument as whether such permission should be granted: *Loveridge & Loveridge v Healey* [2004] EWCA Civ 173, (2004) Times, 27 February, 148 Sol Jo LB 264.

Where an occupier breaks the terms of the licence by antisocial behaviour but then desists for a reasonable time, the breach may not be relied on as grounds for a court order terminating the agreement. The word 'within' should be read as meaning 'for' a reasonable time: *Wickland (Holdings) Ltd v Telchadder* (2014) Times, 19 November, Sup Ct.

III MOB [11.2]

Termination under paragraph 5 To succeed under para 5 of Chapter 2 or Chapter 4 of Part 1 to Schedule 1 the owner must satisfy the court that that the grounds (non-occupation as sole or main residence) exist at the date of the hearing: *Omar Parks Ltd v Elkington; Ron Grundy (Melbourne) Ltd v Boneheyo* [1993] 1 All ER 282, [1992] 1 WLR 1270, CA. In a case where the occupier had, with the agreement of the owner, bolted a porch extension on to her caravan it was held that the owner could not terminate on the ground that the caravan which she continued to occupy had ceased to be a mobile home: *Charlton v Howard* [2002] EWCA Civ 1086, [2003] 1 P & CR 343, [2002] 3 EGLR 65.

Note that the inclusion of additional land other than a garden is outside the definition of a 'pitch' and that an agreement which includes extra land is not within the scope of the Act: *Murphy v Wyatt* [2011] EWCA Civ 408, [2011] All ER (D) 112 (Apr).

III MOB [11.3]

Pitch fee The pitch fee may include charges for the supply of gas, electricity and other services if there is provision for it in the agreement. In a decided case on the interpretation of a standard form agreement it was held that the agreement covered reimbursement of expenditure on services but not a service charge for the owner's time and administrative costs in this regard: *PR Hardman & Partners v Greenwood* [2017] EWCA Civ 52, [2017] 4 WLR 59, [2017] HLR 287.

III MOB [11.4]

Re-siting of mobile home The site-owner is entitled to require the occupier to re-site the mobile home in the circumstances provided in para 10 of Chapter 2 and para 8 of Chapter 4 of Part 1 to Schedule 1.

One of the grounds is that essential repairs need to be carried out, although not necessarily as a matter of urgency, which can only be done if the mobile home is moved. It has been held (a) that what is 'essential' is not limited to what is essential for the management of the site, (b) that it is not necessary that the owner should be the person who carries them out and (c) that the motivation of the owner in identifying the need for essential repairs is not relevant, providing that he can show that the works are essential: *Tapsell v Cemery* (1995) 27 HLR 114, CA.

PATENTS AND OTHER INTELLECTUAL PROPERTY

TABLE OF CONTENTS

PATENTS

GENERAL NOTES ON PATENTS AND OTHER INTELLECTUAL PROPERTY

III PAT [1]

Intellectual property rights Some intellectual property rights, patents in particular, are subject to a statutory regime of registration with statutory powers of enforcement and rights of redress, including appeals to the court from decisions of the body granting the patent (called the Comptroller-General of Patents, Designs and Trade Marks, or the Comptroller for short). The main purpose of this title is to identify the jurisdiction conferred on the High Court, the Intellectual Property Enterprise Court (now part of the High Court but whose jurisdiction was formerly dealt with by the patents county court) and the ordinary county courts by the statutes in the table of contents. But there are, in addition, rights and remedies affecting intellectual property rights which derive from the ordinary law of contract and tort and equitable remedies. There are, for example, claims in respect of passing off of imitation products and breach of confidence as regards trade secrets and other information imparted or acquired in a confidential context. For the statutory jurisdiction in relation to personal data, see the title DATA PROTECTION. Readers were, in the previous edition, warned about the imminence of the Unified Patents Court which will be a single patents court, established under European Union law, conferring non-exclusive (for a lengthy transitional period) European wide jurisdiction over European wide patents. As far as the United Kingdom is concerned, the position is on hold pending the complications of Brexit.

III PAT [2]

General jurisdiction The grant of appropriate remedies in support of common law rights is part of the inherent jurisdiction of the High Court and concurrent jurisdiction is enjoyed by the ordinary county courts as well: see Senior Courts Act 1981 s 19(2)(b) (see para **II SCA [17]**), county courts Act 1984, ss 15 and 38 (see paras **II CCA [7]** and **II CCA [21]**) and the High Court and county courts Jurisdiction Order 1991, SI 1991/724, art 2(1)(l) (see para **II HCJ [3]**), though the county courts have no jurisdiction to decide patent matters or order delivery up or destruction of certain articles infringing trade marks. Infringements of community wide intellectual property rights (at present Trade Marks and Registered Designs) are justiciable in the High Court, and certain county courts of major cities in England and Wales. For an illustration of an injunction being granted to restrain passing off, as well as infringement of Trade Marks Act 1994 s 10(3) see *British Telecommunications plc v One in a Million Ltd* [1999] FSR 1, CA, in which the injunction was granted to restrain registration, for improper purposes, of well-known business names as domain names on the Internet.

III PAT [3]

Special jurisdiction Jurisdiction is conferred on the High Court to decide questions arising under the Patents Act 1977, the Copyright, Designs and Patents Act 1988 and the Trade Marks Act 1994. The High Court also has jurisdiction to grant relief and remedies where foreign patent, copyright, design and trade mark rights have been infringed: *Lucasfilm Ltd v Ainsworth* [2011] UKSC 39, [2011] All ER (D) 257 (Jul), (2011) Times, 3 August, Supreme Court.

Jurisdiction is conferred on the ordinary county courts by the High Court and county courts Jurisdiction Order 1991, SI 1991/724, art 2(1)(b) and (n) (see para **II HCJ [3]**) to make orders for the disposal of infringing copyright, design, illicit recordings etc under various provisions of the Copyright, Designs and Patents Act 1988. The Order, as amended in 2005, confers a broader jurisdiction under the Trade Marks Act 1994 on listed county courts which chancery expertise. In addition the listed county courts have been appointed Community trade mark courts from 1 April 2005, by the Community Trade Mark (Designation of Community Trade Mark Courts) Regulations 2005, SI 2005/440. Note, however, that the special jurisdiction of the Intellectual Property Enterprise Court has since been confined to claims with a value of no more than £500,000. Further, costs are limited to £50,000 recoverable by any receiving party, though this amount is allocated to different preparatory acts such as pleadings, witness statements, appearances and so on – see Part 45 rules 45.30–45.32 (paras **CPR 45.30–CPR 45.32**) and PD 45 Section 3 (see para **CPR PD 45.3**).

The right of the Intellectual Property Enterprise Court to hear any patent or design infringement action or matter includes the right to deal with any claims or matters ancillary thereto or arising therefrom, but not appeals from the Comptroller. An action for copyright infringement may be litigated in the Intellectual Property Enterprise Court provided that the infringement relates to designs recorded in design documents, even if so recorded before the commencement of the Act: *PSM International plc v Specialised Fastener Products (Southern) Ltd* [1993] FSR 113, Patents Co Ct. Further, a claim for copyright infringement might be included as "ancillary" to a patent claim; the court should adopt a purposive approach to the question whether an additional claim was sensibly treated as ancillary: *McDonald v Graham* [1994] RPC 407, CA.

III PAT [4]

Procedural rules Intellectual property claims are now subject to specialist procedures in CPR Part 63. Claims in respect of patents or registered designs must be made in the Patents Court or the Intellectual Property Enterprise Court and are subject to the procedures set out in **CPR 63.3–CPR 63.12**. Appeals from the Comptroller are subject to **CPR 63.17**. Claims under the Trade Marks Act 1994 are required by **CPR 63.13** to be brought in the Chancery Division of the High Court and are subject to the procedures in **CPR 63.13–CPR 63.15**. Following administrative changes the Chancery Division is now known as the Business and Property Court and the list in that court relating to Intellectual property is called the Intellectual Property List (ChD). Claims in the Chancery Division Patents Court are to remain in the Patents Court and those in the Intellectual Property Enterprise Court (which is part of the Chancery Division) likewise. The effect of this is that court headings are now expressed in terms of the level of court (The High Court of Justice), the division (The Business and Property Court), the list (Intellectual Property List (ChD)), the specialist court (the Patents Court or the Intellectual Property Enterprise Court as the case may be) and, finally, the district registry if outside London (such as Manchester, Birmingham, Bristol, Leeds or Cardiff District Registry).

III PAT [5]

Views of the European Patent Office Boards of Appeal The Court of Appeal is free to depart from its own previous decision where it is satisfied that the European Patent Office Boards of Appeal (an appeal board of a Centralised European patent granting authority) have formed a settled view of European patent law which is inconsistent with the Court of Appeal's earlier decision: *Actavis UK Ltd v Merck & Co Inc* [2008] EWCA Civ 444, [2009] 1 All ER 196, [2009] 1 WLR 1186.

III PAT [6]

Practice Direction: Patents and other intellectual property claims CPR Part 63 is supplemented by a Practice Direction at **CPR PD 63**. Paragraphs 2 to 17 of the Practice Direction cover the procedure for claims in the Patents Court or the Intellectual Property Enterprise Court and designate these courts as Community Design Courts under art 80(5) of Council Regulation (EC) 6/2002. Paragraph 3.1 of the Practice Direction provides that all claims under the Patents Act 1977 or in respect of registered designs, Community registered designs or semiconductor topography rights must be brought in the Patents Court or the Intellectual Property Enterprise Court. They must be marked "Patents Court" or "Intellectual Property Enterprise Court" in the top right-hand corner, below the title of the court in which they are issued. The Practice Direction also makes specific directions on case management (para 5) and disclosure (para 6) and on the procedure to be adopted for certain kinds of claims and situations. These include communication of information to the European Patents Office (para 13) and the Office for Harmonisation in the Internal Market (para 15). Paragraphs 18 to the end cover claims in respect of registered trade marks, European Community trade marks and other intellectual property rights. On 4 July 2017 specialist jurisdictions across England and Wales, including the Companies Court and the Commercial Court, were brought together under a single umbrella: the Business and Property Courts of England and Wales (B&PCs). In London the courts exercising the specialist jurisdictions continue to function in the Rolls Building in Fetter Lane. Outside London there are courts exercising the specialist jurisdictions in Birmingham, Bristol, Cardiff, Leeds and Manchester. In the five regional centres the cases are heard in what is now known as the Business and Property Courts List. It is emphasised that this is a question of listing nomenclature and is not an allocation question as such. The divisions and divisional courts (and their nomenclature) of the High Court (Chancery, Queen's Bench or Family) remain as before.

III PAT [6A]

Validity of compromise Where there has been a genuine dispute which has been settled by an agreement, the court will presume that the restraints agreed on were reasonable and should be enforced: *WWF – World Wide Fund for Nature (formerly World Wildlife Fund) v World Wrestling Federation Entertainment Inc* [2001] EWCA Civ 196, [2002] ETMR 564, [2002] FSR 530.

III PAT [6B]

Mediation Entitlement disputes inevitably give rise to many issues of fact and can become overheated and prolix, particularly where the parties' relationship has not been reduced to writing. The comptroller's jurisdiction should be reserved for relatively straightforward cases, complex cases being referred at an early stage to the High Court or the county court. It might make sense for a claimant to initiate proceedings simultaneously before the court and the comptroller with a view to making an immediate application to the comptroller for transfer. Alternatively early mediation might be appropriate, or MedArb, where a trusted mediator is authorised by both sides to decide the terms of a binding settlement. These general observations on the dispute resolution of disputes over patent entitlement were made by the Court of Appeal in *IDA Ltd v Southampton University* [2006] EWCA Civ 145, (2006) Times, 31 March, CA.

III PAT [7]

Allocation of business in patent proceedings Every patent claim must be litigated in the Patents Court (in the Chancery Division) or the Intellectual Property Enterprise Court (also in the Chancery Division). Patent actions are allocated to a specialist list with no track allocation (see CPR 26.2(2) (at para **CPR 26.2**) and **CPR 63.4**).

For the substantive law see 35 *Halsbury's Laws* (4th edn, reissue) title PATENTS AND REGISTERED DESIGNS, para 301; 9(2) *Halsbury's Laws* (4th edn, reissue) title COPYRIGHT, DESIGN RIGHTS AND RELATED RIGHTS, para 1; 48 *Halsbury's Laws* (4th edn, reissue) title TRADE MARKS AND TRADE NAMES, para 1 and 8(1) *Halsbury's Laws* (4th edn, reissue) title CONFIDENCE AND DATA PROTECTION, para 401.

PATENTS

PATENTS ACT 1977

(c 37)

GENERAL NOTES ON REFERENCES TO THE COURT BY THE COMPTROLLER

III PAT [8]

References by the Comptroller References to the High Court may be made by the Comptroller under ss 8(7), 12(2), 37(8) and 61(5) (see para **III PAT [13]**) as well as s 40 (see para **III PAT [10]–[11]**), known as declining to deal and which arises usually where it is more appropriate for the question in issue to be determined by the Court. For the procedure for such references see the Practice Direction at **CPR PD 63**.

III PAT [9]

34. Rectification of register

(1) The court may, on the application of any person aggrieved, order the register to be rectified by the making, or the variation or deletion, of any entry in it.

(2) In proceedings under this section the court may determine any question which it may be necessary or expedient to decide in connection with the rectification of the register.

(3) Rules of court may provide for the notification of any application under this section to the comptroller and for his appearance on the application and for giving effect to any order of the court on the application.

III PAT [9.1]

Procedure An application for rectification must be made by the issue of a CPR Part 7 claim form or, in existing proceedings, under CPR Part 20. Subsequent steps must comply with para 4 onwards of the Practice Direction at **CPR PD 63**. Note that a copy of any claim for rectification of the register of patents is required to be served on the Comptroller, together with copies of documents accompanying the claim. Paragraph 14 provides that any court order affecting the validity of an entry in the register must be served on the Comptroller by the party obtaining the order. Section 34 of the Act provides for instances where the comptroller has wrongfully entered a transaction on the register or has refused to enter such a transaction on the register (where, for instance, he has decided that the instrument ought to have been stamped when, in fact there is no requirement of it so be stamped). Disputes relating to inventorship or entitlement are dealt with elsewhere in the Act (see ss 8, 9, 13 and 37). The class of persons entitled to apply under this section is wide in that it is described as any person aggrieved, being persons both directly and indirectly affected by the entry (or lack thereof) on the register. Sub-section 2 provides that other questions may be decided at the same time, though this is no more than a statement of the inherent position of the court with respect to the regulation of its own procedure.

III PAT [10]–III PAT [11]

40. Compensation of employees for certain inventions

(1) Where it appears to the court or the comptroller on an application made by an employee within the prescribed period that—

(a) the employee has made an invention belonging to the employer for which a patent has been granted,

(b) having regard among other things to the size and nature of the employer's undertaking, the invention or the patent for it (or the combination of both) is of outstanding benefit to the employer, and

(c) by reason of those facts it is just that the employee should be awarded compensation to be paid by the employer,

the court or the comptroller may award him such compensation of an amount determined under section 41 below.

(2) Where it appears to the court or the comptroller on an application made by an employee within the prescribed period that—

(a) a patent has been granted for an invention made by and belonging to the employee;

(b) his rights in the invention, or in any patent or application for a patent for the invention, have since the appointed day been assigned to the employer or an exclusive licence under the patent or application has since the appointed day been granted to the employer;

(c) the benefit derived by the employee from the contract of assignment, assignation or grant or any ancillary contract ("the relevant contract") is inadequate in relation to the benefit derived by the employer from the *patent* [the invention or the patent for it (or both)]; and

(d) by reason of those facts it is just that the employee should be awarded compensation to be paid by the employer in addition to the benefit derived from the relevant contract;

the court or the comptroller may award him such compensation of an amount determined under section 41 below.

(3) Subsections (1) and (2) above shall not apply to the invention of an employee where a relevant collective agreement provides for the payment of compensation in respect of inventions of the same description as that invention to employees of the same description as that employee.

(4) Subsection (2) above shall have effect notwithstanding anything in the relevant contract or any agreement applicable to the invention (other than any such collective agreement).

(5) If it appears to the comptroller on an application under this section that the application involves matters which would more properly be determined by the court, he may decline to deal with it.

(6) In this section—

"the prescribed period", in relation to proceedings before the court, means the period prescribed by rules of court, and

"relevant collective agreement" means a collective agreement within the meaning of the Trade Union and Labour Relations (Consolidation) Act 1992, made by or on behalf of a trade union to which the employee belongs, and by the employer or an employers' association to which the employer belongs which is in force at the time of the making of the invention.

(7) References in this section to an invention belonging to an employer or employee are references to it so belonging as between the employer and the employee.

III PAT [11.1]

Inventions belonging to employers Where an employee is under a general duty to innovate new products for his employer, has the time to do so and did so in the employer's time, and the circumstances were such that an invention might reasonably be expected to result from carrying out his duties, the employer is entitled to claim ownership of those inventions: *Liffe Administration and Management v Pinkava* [2007] EWCA Civ 217, [2007] Bus LR 1369, [2007] 4 All ER 981, [2007] ICR 1489, [2007] RPC 667, [2007] All ER (D) 258 (Mar).

The existing sub-ss (1) and (2) are replaced or amended by the sub-ss in square brackets by the operation of s 10 of the Patents Act 2004.

Where the employer's title derives from the general rule in s 39 the employee may not claim beneficial ownership in equity on the ground that the employer's title is subject to a constructive or resulting trust: *Christopher S French v Paul J Mason* (1999] FSR 597. Proceedings for compensation must be brought by the issue of a CPR Part 7 claim form, marked "Patents Court", and must be issued within the period prescribed by paras (2) and (3) of **CPR 63.12**, which is broadly one year after the patent has ceased to have effect. Subsequent steps must comply with para 4 onwards of the Practice Direction at **CPR PD 63**. Note that the court is required Practice Direction to give directions as to: (1) the manner in which evidence is to be given, including any accounts or expenditure and receipts; and (2) the provision of reasonable facilities for inspecting and taking extracts from such accounts.

Under the old s 40 it had to be shown that the benefit must have resulted form the process of obtaining a patent (*Memco-Med Ltd's Patent* [1992] RPC 403) as opposed to any underlying intrinsic value in the invention itself. The new law requires the invention in question to be patented but the benefit can now flow form the intrinsic merit of the underlying invention. The compensation in question is determined by the operation of s 41 (fair share of the benefit or expected benefit of the invention, the patent for the invention or any assignment (but not licence) of the invention patent or application for a patent to a person connected with the employer) but under the new law any benefit which arises after the patent has expired, been surrendered or has been revoked will not be taken into account. The new law does not apply to existing patents.

See *Kelly v GE Healthcare Ltd* [2009] EWHC 181 (Pat), [2009] RPC 363, [2009] IP & T 927, Floyd J. It is a case where employees were successful in claiming compensation.

III PAT [11.2]

Inventions developed by former employee A former employee who develops a product using the former employer's trade secrets is not liable for breach of confidence if he or she was unaware of the secrets and of their being used in the development: *Vestergaard Frandsen A/S v Bestnet Europe Ltd* [2013] UKSC 31, [2013] 4 All ER 781, [2013] 1 WLR 1556.

III PAT [12]

58. References of disputes as to Crown use

(1) Any dispute as to—

(a) the exercise by a government department, or a person authorised by a government department, of the powers conferred by section 55 above,

(b) terms for the use of an invention for the services of the Crown under that section,

(c) the right of any person to receive any part of a payment made in pursuance of subsection (4) of that section, or

(d) the right of any person to receive a payment under section 57A,

may be referred to the court by either party to the dispute after a patent has been granted for the invention.

(2) If in such proceedings any question arises whether an invention has been recorded or tried as mentioned in section 55 above, and the disclosure of any document recording the invention, or of any evidence of the trial thereof, would in the opinion of the department be prejudicial to the public interest, the disclosure may be made confidentially to the other party's legal representative or to an independent expert mutually agreed upon.

(3) In determining under this section any dispute between a government department and any person as to the terms for the use of an invention for the services of the Crown, the court shall have regard—

(a) to any benefit or compensation which that person or any person from whom he derives title may have received or may be entitled to receive directly or indirectly from any government department in respect of the invention in question;

(b) to whether that person or any person from whom he derives title has in the court's opinion without reasonable cause failed to comply with a request of the department to use the invention for the services of the Crown on reasonable terms.

(4) In determining whether or not to grant any relief under subsection (1)(a), (b) or (c) above and the nature and extent of the relief granted the court shall, subject to the following provisions of this section, apply the principles applied by the court immediately before the appointed day to the granting of relief under section 48 of the 1949 Act.

(5) On a reference under this section the court may refuse to grant relief by way of compensation in respect of the use of an invention for the services of the Crown during any further period specified under section 25(4) above, but before the payment of the renewal fee and any additional fee prescribed for the purposes of that section.

(6) Where an amendment of the specification of a patent has been allowed under any of the provisions of this Act, [or, in the case of a European patent (UK), has been allowed under any of the provisions in the Agreement on a Unified

Patent Court,] the court shall not grant relief by way of compensation under this section in respect of any such use before the decision to allow the amendment unless the court is satisfied that—

(a) the specification of the patent as published was framed in good faith and with reasonable skill and knowledge and

(b) the relief is sought in good faith.

(7) If the validity of a patent is put in issue in proceedings under this section and it is found that the patent is only partially valid, the court may, subject to subsection (8) below, grant relief to the proprietor of the patent in respect of that part of the patent which is found to be valid and to have been used for the services of the Crown.

(8) Where in any such proceedings it is found that a patent is only partially valid, the court shall not grant relief by way of compensation, costs or expenses except where the proprietor of the patent proves that—

(a) the specification of the patent was framed in good faith and with reasonable skill and knowledge, and

(b) the relief is sought in good faith, and

in that event the court may grant relief in respect of that part of the patent which is valid and has been so used, subject to the discretion of the court as to costs and expenses and as to the date from which compensation should be awarded.

(9) As a condition of any such relief the court may direct that the specification of the patent shall be amended to its satisfaction upon an application made for that purpose under section 75 below, and an application may be so made accordingly, whether or not all other issues in the proceedings have been determined.

(9A) The court may also grant such relief in the case of a European patent (UK) on condition that the claims of the patent are limited to its satisfaction by the European Patent Office at the request of the proprietor.

(10) In considering the amount of any compensation for the use of an invention for the services of the Crown after publication of an application for a patent for the invention and before such a patent is granted, the court shall consider whether or not it would have been reasonable to expect, from a consideration of the application as published under section 16 above, that a patent would be granted conferring on the proprietor of the patent protection for an act of the same description as that found to constitute that use, and if the court finds that it would not have been reasonable, it shall reduce the compensation to such amount as it thinks just.

(11) Where by virtue of a transaction, instrument or event to which section 33 above applies a person becomes the proprietor or one of the proprietors or an exclusive licensee of a patent (the new proprietor or licensee) and a government department or a person authorised by a government department subsequently makes use under section 55 above of the patented invention, the new proprietor or licensee shall not be entitled to any compensation under section 55(4) above (as it stands or as modified by section 57(3) above), or to any compensation under section 57A above, in respect of a subsequent use of the invention before the transaction, instrument or event is registered unless—

(a) the transaction, instrument or event is registered within the period of six months beginning with its date; or

(b) the court is satisfied that it was not practicable to register the transaction, instrument or event before the end of that period and that it was registered as soon as practicable thereafter.

(12) In any proceedings under this section the court may at any time order the whole proceedings or any question or issue of fact arising in them to be referred, on such terms as the court may direct, to a Circuit judge discharging the functions

PATENTS

of an official referee or an arbitrator in England and Wales or Northern Ireland, or to an arbiter in Scotland; and references to the court in the foregoing provisions of this section shall be construed accordingly.

(13) One of two or more joint proprietors of a patent or application for a patent may without the concurrence of the others refer a dispute to the court under this section, but shall not do so unless the others are made parties to the proceedings; but any of the others made a defendant or defender shall not be liable for any costs or expenses unless he enters an appearance and takes part in the proceedings.

Amendment *Text in square brackets in sub-s (6) is inserted by the Patents (European Patent with Unitary Effect and Unified Patent Court) Order 2016, SI 2016/388 with effect from a date to be appointed.*

III PAT [12.1]

Crown use and compensation Circumstances may arise where there is a dispute as to whether a use is a Crown use within the meaning of ss 55(1) and 56(2)–(4) or whether the person making such use is afforded the partial protection of s 55(1). Further where there is a Crown user then the proprietor of the patent is entitled in certain circumstances to be compensated for such use and the court will consider the use made of the invention and the terms of such use by the Crown. The effect of this section is that the court may make an award of compensation or may determine entitlement to compensation under s 57(3) or 57A of the Patents Act 1977. This section is necessary because the Crown (being historically the body which granted the patent) was incapable of infringing rights conferred by patent, though it is probable that if this were ever a prerogative of the Crown it now exists solely on a legislative footing. There is nothing which prevents the Crown in proceedings under s 58 from putting the validity of the patent in issue. The provisions of s 55 provide that where, in essence, the Crown has recorded the invention as claimed in the patent or has tried to work such a patent before the priority date of the patent then no compensation is payable (though this record or working might not be novelty destroying, it defeats the right to compensation, giving, as it were, a kind of novelty destroying defence, special to the Crown) and s 58 allows the proprietor to ask the court to test whether such a record or use took place before the priority date of the patent.

III PAT [12.2]

Amendments by Patents Act 2004 Sub-sections (6), (8) and (9A) were amended by the operation of ss 2(2) and 3(2) of the Patents Act 2004, with effect from 13 December 2007. The amendments are intended to deal with the position where a patent proprietor is seeking a determination by the court of compensation for crown use (under s 55). Where the patent is partially valid (and therefore partially amended) then no compensation will be awarded where the proprietor has knowledge that the infringed claim was only partially valid. Where he has no such knowledge then he is entitled to damages in respect of the partially valid patent but not the invalid parts.

III PAT [13]

61. Proceedings for infringement of patent

(1) Subject to the following provisions of this Part of this Act, civil proceedings may be brought in the court by the proprietor of a patent in respect of any act alleged to infringe the patent and (without prejudice to any other jurisdiction of the court) in those proceedings a claim may be made—

- (a) for an injunction or interdict restraining the defendant or defender from any apprehended act of infringement;
- (b) for an order for him to deliver up or destroy any patented product in relation to which the patent is infringed or any article in which that product is inextricably comprised;
- (c) for damages in respect of the infringement;
- (d) for an account of the profits derived by him from the infringement;
- (e) for a declaration or declarator that the patent is valid and has been infringed by him.

(2) The court shall not, in respect of the same infringement, both award the proprietor of a patent damages and order that he shall be given an account of the profits.

(3) The proprietor of a patent and any other person may by agreement with each other refer to the comptroller the question whether that other person has infringed the patent and on the reference the proprietor of the patent may make any claim mentioned in subsection (1)(c) or (e) above.

(4) Except so far as the context requires, in the following provisions of this Act—

(a) any reference to proceedings for infringement and the bringing of such proceedings includes a reference to a reference under subsection (3) above and the making of such a reference;

(b) any reference to a claimant or pursuer includes a reference to the proprietor of the patent; and

(c) any reference to a defendant or defender includes a reference to any other party to the reference.

(5) If it appears to the comptroller on a reference under subsection (3) above that the question referred to him would more properly be determined by the court, he may decline to deal with it and the court shall have jurisdiction to determine the question as if the reference were proceedings brought in the court.

(6) Subject to the following provisions of this Part of this Act, in determining whether or not to grant any kind of relief claimed under this section and the extent of the relief granted the court or the comptroller shall apply the principles applied by the court in relation to that kind of relief immediately before the appointed day.

(7) If the comptroller awards any sum by way of damages on a reference under subsection (3) above, then—

(a) in England and Wales, the sum shall be recoverable, if the county court so orders, under section 85 of the County Courts Act 1984 or otherwise as if it were payable under an order of that court;

(b) in Scotland, payment of the sum may be enforced in like manner as an extract registered decree arbitral bearing a warrant for execution issued by the sheriff court of any sheriffdom in Scotland;

(c) in Northern Ireland, payment of the sum may be enforced as if it were a money judgment.

PATENTS

III PAT [13.1]

Remedies for infringement Sub-sections (4)(b) and (7) are amended or inserted by the operation of ss 14 and 11 respectively of the Patents Act 2004.

Section 61 provides for the type of relief which the claimant may seek from the court by way of injunction, delivery up, damages or an account of profits and declaration. The court can also make an award of costs either to be assessed or on a lump sum basis. The court is not entitled to order both an account and damages in respect of the same infringement but that does not mean that the court cannot (in appropriate circumstances) make differing orders in relation to different infringements forming part of the same overall cause of action. The parties may by agreement refer the question of infringement to the Comptroller who can decide the question or can decline to decide the question and cede jurisdiction to the court, though it is for the parties to make such reference to the court itself, the procedure is not automatic. Where the claimant is successful in his allegation of infringement and he has claimed both damages and an account of profits in the alternative then he will be put on his election, though he is entitled to disclosure from the defendant to enable his election to be informed: *Island Records Ltd v Tring International plc* [1995] FSR 560. The court will order an account of profits to be given as part of its equitable jurisdiction and as a result can take account of delay in appropriate circumstances and refuse to order under this head of relief (*Beloit Canada v Valmet (Canada)* [1997] EIPR D-236). Section 61 operates hand in hand with ss 62–69 all of which limit or qualify the entitlement of the proprietor to relief for infringement. Proceedings for infringement must be brought by the issue of a CPR Pt 7 claim, marked 'Patents Court' or 'Intellectual Property Enterprise Court', and subsequent steps must comply with para 4 onwards of the Practice Direction at **CPR PD 63**. Note that the claim form is required by para 11.1 to show which of the claims in the specification of the patent are alleged to be infringed and to give at least one example of each type of infringement. Also a copy of each document referred to in the claim form, and where necessary a translation of it, must be served with the claim form. Recent practice in the Patents Court suggests that in appropriate circumstances of utility the court can make a declaration (known as an *Arrow* declaration) that an activity of a would-be infringer constitutes or would constitute if carried out an obvious (ie a non-inventive) difference from or would be no different from technologies which existed before the filing or effective filing date for the relevant patent application and thus is non-infringing. The defence is effective on the basis that if the would-be infringing activity is indeed infringing then the patent is claiming something which is not inventive or not novel and the invention is thus not patentable: *Fujifilm Kyowa Kirin Biologics Co, Ltd v AbbVie Biotechnology Ltd (No 4)* [2017] EWHC 395 (Pat), [2018] RPC 1, Henry Carr J, approved in *Glaxo Group Ltd v Vectura Ltd* [2018] EWCA Civ 1496, (2018) Times, 21 August emphasising that the need for a declaration had to carry a degree of necessity or realty before am Arrow declaration would be granted.

The new sub-s (7) enables an award by the comptroller of damages for infringement to be recovered through the enforcement mechanism of the county court in England and Wales. No fresh proceedings are needed to enforce the award.

III PAT [13.1A]

Account of profits In principle an account of profits may be claimed in relation to activities which occurred prior to grant but, in bringing proceedings for infringement, it is necessary for the patentee and the exclusive licensee to both make the same manner of election. Further, when an account was ordered then, so far as that infringement is concerned, only one account would be ordered against the party who had infringed. The court so held in *Spring Form Inc v Toy Brokers Ltd* [2002] FSR 276, Pumfrey J, and further held that any election extended to all defendants and that it was not appropriate on the facts of that case to make an order for payment until a claimant had undertaken not to make a claim against any other defendant.

III PAT [13.2]

Injunction The standard form of injunction restraining the defendant from infringing the patent is widely drawn because of the ingenuity of the infringers: *Spectravest Inc v Aperknit Ltd* [1988] FSR 161, 174. In *Coflexip SA v Stolt Comex Seaway MS Ltd* [2001] 1 All ER 952 (Note), [2001] RPC 182, the Court of Appeal affirmed (on appeal from [1999] 2 All ER 593) that the correct practice of granting injunctions by reference to the rights of the claimant (as opposed to the acts of the defendant actually proved) should remain, otherwise considerable difficulties might be encountered in policing the effect of the injunction. See also *Microsoft Corpn v Plato Technology Ltd* [1999] FSR 834 where a very limited injunction was granted against an otherwise innocent trade mark and copyright infringer.

An injunction may be granted to prevent infringement for a period after the expiry of the patent if this is necessary to put the patent holder and the infringer on an equal footing: *Dyson Appliances Ltd v Hoover Ltd (No 2)* [2001] RPC 544.

III PAT [13.2A]

Publication of Judgment Article 15 of Directive 2004/48/EC of the European Parliament and of the Council of 29 April 2004 on the enforcement of intellectual property rights states that a winning claimant may also claim a right to have a favourable judgment published at the expense of the losing defendant:

> 'Member States shall ensure that, in legal proceedings instituted for infringement of an intellectual property right, the judicial authorities may order, at the request of the applicant and at the expense of the infringer, appropriate measures for the dissemination of the information concerning the decision, including displaying the decision and publishing it in full or in part. Member States may provide for other additional publicity measures which are appropriate to the particular circumstances, including prominent advertising.'

In *Samsung Electronics (UK) Ltd v Apple Inc* [2012] EWCA Civ 1430, [2013] EMLR 243, [2012] Info TLR 208, [2013] FSR 166 the Court of Appeal upheld an order for publication of the existence of a judgment in a prominent place in a newspaper without being interspersed with comment or other added matter if it was misleading but only because it was satisfied that there was uncertainty in the marketplace it being held (strictly obiter) that where there was not uncertainty then the court would not direct publication. However any other truthful comment would be permitted as a matter of free speech.

III PAT [13.2B]

Joinder There are cases where two or more defendants carry out an act of infringement. In such cases both defendants are jointly liable, provided that is can be shown that there was a combination (or procuration by one defendant) pursuant to the furtherance of a common design to carry out the acts of infringement. It is not necessary to show that the design was to carry out a deliberate act of infringement: See *Unilever plc v Gillette (UK) Ltd* [1989] RPC 583, CA.

III PAT [13.3]

Precedents See **BCCP L[1601]** onwards.

GENERAL NOTES ON SECTIONS 62–69

III PAT [14]

Section 62 provides for a partial defence to damages or an account if the defendant can show that at the date of the infringement he had no reasonable grounds for supposing that the patent existed and that the application of words such as "patent" or "patented" shall not be taken into account. The usual way that the proprietor is able to avoid the consequences of this section (in part at least) is to put the intended defendant on notice by bringing the defendant's attention to the patent, though the proprietor may be at risk of an allegation of making unjustified (described in statutory language as groundless) threats unless he words his notice carefully. The scope of things which the court is entitled to take into account when making an award of damages has been widened by reg 3 of the Intellectual Property (Enforcement etc.) Regulations 2006 (SI 2006/1028) which require the court to take into account "all appropriate aspects" relating to the actual prejudice caused to the claimant. Those aspects include "the negative economic consequences, including any lost profits, which the claimant has suffered, and any unfair profits made by the defendant" including "any moral prejudice caused by the defendant". It is unclear whether as a result of this there is now scope for the damages/account of profits divide.

Section 63 provides for the proprietor who has partially survived an attack on his patent and enables the court to grant relief in respect of that part which survives. Costs may not be awarded in the proprietor's favour in relation to that part of the patent which does not survive if the proprietor is unable to show that the invalid part of the patent was framed in good faith and with reasonable skill and knowledge and that the patent was knowingly infringed. The proprietor will not be entitled to partial relief unless the court directs that the patent be amended to exclude the invalid parts. Where a European Patent Office patent is in issue then damages may be granted if that patent is partially valid but on condition that a satisfactory application to amend is made to the European Patent Office.

Section 64 entitles an otherwise potential defendant who has worked an invention which otherwise falls within the claims of a patent and has done so before the priority date of the patent (even if such working is not novelty destroying) to continue working the invention notwithstanding the grant of a patent in respect of the invention. This immunity from suit also extends to situations where the defendant has made serious and effective preparations to work the invention without actually having done so. The section limits the activities of such a person to the acts carried out by him and not to his licensee, though he may authorise his partners. The rights relating to products so produced in accordance with this section are exhausted in relation to subsequent dealing.

Section 65 provides that where a patent (or part thereof) has survived an attack on its validity then the court can issue a certificate of contested validity which enables the proprietor to claim indemnity costs in relation to any subsequent attack on the patent (on the same grounds).

Section 66 provides for the position of co-proprietors. A single co-proprietor may bring proceedings for infringement and the other co-proprietors must be joined (either as claimants or as co-defendants, though if they are co-defendants and they do not participate then they are not to be liable for costs). A co-proprietor is entitled to do certain acts himself though (in the absence of any agreement to the contrary) a licence to work the invention, the subject of a patent, must be obtained from all of the proprietors subject to the defence that the person otherwise infringing the patent can claim that he was no more than an agent working for one or more of the proprietors pursuant to s 36(2)(a). Section 60 sets out what amounts to infringement, being a list of acts which are carried out without the consent of the proprietor. The question is, where there are two or more proprietors how that consent is to be given and s 66(1) provides for the mechanism. Consent can only be given by all proprietors unless there is agreement to the contrary.

Section 67 provides that after the date of a licence, the exclusive licensee's position must be taken into account when assessing or awarding damages or ordering an account of profits for infringement, that he has a like right of suit (provided that the proprietor is joined as a party as claimant or as co-defendant, though if as a co-defendant and he does not participate then he is not to be liable for costs).

Section 68 essentially provides the penalty for the non-registration of transactions (such as assignments and exclusive licences). Where the transaction is not registered then there is no right to costs (though damages are awardable) prior to the date of registration unless the registration was made within the period of six months from execution or so as is reasonably practicable thereafter if it was not reasonably practicable to register the transaction within the six-month period.

Section 69 allows the proprietor or the exclusive licensee to sue in respect of pre-grant infringements taking place after publication, though the proprietor or exclusive licensee may only enter suit after grant.

PATENTS

III PAT [15]

70. Threats of infringement proceedings

(1) A communication contains a "threat of infringement proceedings" if a reasonable person in the position of a recipient would understand from the communication that—

(a) a patent exists, and

(b) a person intends to bring proceedings (whether in a court in the United Kingdom or elsewhere) against another person for infringement of the patent by—

(i) an act done in the United Kingdom, or

(ii) an act which, if done, would be done in the United Kingdom.

(2) References in this section and in section 70C to a "recipient" include, in the case of a communication directed to the public or a section of the public, references to a person to whom the communication is directed.

III PAT [15.1]

Threats: general It is trite law that a person who makes threats of proceedings (other than mere notification of the existence of the patent) to another is liable to the other or a person aggrieved (such as the supplier of that other) in respect of those threats. Threats are only actionable however if made against so called secondary infringers (that is those who do not manufacture or import for disposal or use a process). The supposed rationale behind this rule is that secondary infringers are more likely to desist if threats are made against them. The threatening party can claim that its threats are justified, in that if proceedings for infringement had been mounted pursuant to the threat then a finding of infringement of a valid patent would follow, though it is always open to the threatened party to show that the patent is invalid. The threat, so far as an action for damages is concerned, must be the damage causing act, though an injunction to restrain repetition may still lie. In *Carflow Product (UK) Ltd v Linwood Securities Birmingham Ltd* [1998] FSR 691 (a case relating to threat for infringement of design right) it was accepted as law by the parties (and the judge) that the loss claimed by the threats had to flow from that threat and not by the issue of a subsequent claim. In *Alpi Pietro Le Figlio & Co v John Wright & Sons (Veneers)* [1972] RPC 125 Whitford J stated that in relation to the commencement of proceedings, the claimant was immune from an allegation of unjustified threats even if his allegations of infringement turned out to be bad. The court, on finding that an unjustified threat has been made may grant an injunction to restrain the continuance of the threat (though the threatening party would presumably be at liberty to renew his threat if new circumstances arose), a declaration that the threats were unjustified and damages. Proceedings are commenced in the usual way by way of claim form (whether CPR Part 7 or CPR Part 8) naming the threatening party as the defendant.

The new law (which came into force on 1 October 2017 – the Intellectual Property (Unjustified Threats) Act 2017)) also provides an additional defence to a proprietor making a threat to a secondary infringer where endeavours have been made to ascertain the identity of the primary infringer without success. If attempts have been made to trace the primary infringer and the proprietor notifies the secondary infringer of that fact then threats may be made with impunity against the secondary infringer in order to resolve the infringement dispute. Further changes to the law of threats are envisaged. The new s 70C of the Patents Act 1977 relates to threats made on or after 1 October 2017. Threats made prior to 1 October 2017 must be determined under the old s 70 – reg 3 of the Intellectual Property (Unjustified Threats) Act 2017 (Commencement and Transitional Provisions) Regulations 2017 (SI 2017/771). In the law of threats the (would be) primary infringer is the maker or the importer (who has invested much and is unlikely to back down in the face of a threat) whereas the (would be) secondary infringer is, euphemistically, the shop keeper who is keen to do anything to avoid costs and expense and will thus stop supplying articles to which the threats relate on a nuisance basis. In very general terms the secondary infringer is the person who is protected.

III PAT [15.2]

Threats and the Civil Procedure Rules Proceedings for relief against threats of infringement proceedings must be brought by the issue of a CPR Part 7 claim, marked 'Patents Court' or 'Intellectual Property Enterprise Court', and subsequent steps must comply with para 4 onwards of the Practice Direction at **CPR PD 63**. The overriding objective (see para **CPR 1.1**) and the general purpose of the Civil Procedure Rules means that the courts are likely to be more protective in relation to statements made in without-prejudice discussions even if those statements amount to threats to sue for patent infringement (which would be otherwise actionable) since not to do so would deprive the proprietor of the patent of the right to assert his true position and thereby disable the parties of the ability to negotiate with their eyes wide open. In *Unilever plc v Procter & Gamble Co* [2001] 1 All ER 783, [2001] 1 WLR 2436, the Court of Appeal concluded (and agreed with the judge at first instance [1999] FSR 849) that to say otherwise would be to undermine the public policy rationale for a rule of privilege, which protected disclosure of such discussions to the court and was currently stronger than ever before, that the parties should be encouraged to resolve disputes without litigation.

III PAT [15.3]

Threats: Construction of allegedly threatening letter Considerable care should be exercised in writing to a potential infringer since the test appears to be whether the overall message contains a threat. Thus in *L'Oreal (UK) Ltd v Johnson & Johnson* [2000] ETMR 691, [2000] FSR 686, even the most veiled threat was held to be arguably within the meaning of the expression "threat". Lightman J said at pp 694, 695:

> 'The [threatening] letter is the work of a master of Delphic utterances who uses all his skills to say everything and nothing and to convey an enigmatic message which has the same effect on the recipient as a threat or adverse claim whilst disclaiming to be either. He goes beyond merely reserving his clients' rights: he makes clear that no decision has yet been made to sue, but likewise makes clear that others who used the words on their packaging after pressure from the defendants succumbed to that pressure and desisted; that the defendants thought that the claimants had unfairly sought to benefit from the defendants' goodwill; that the defendants had six years to commence legal proceedings; and that the defendants would afford no comfort in respect of the possibility of such proceedings.'

PATENTS

III PAT [15A]

70A. Actionable threats

(1) Subject to subsections (2) to (5), a threat of infringement proceedings made by any person is actionable by any person aggrieved by the threat.

(2) A threat of infringement proceedings is not actionable if the infringement is alleged to consist of—

- (a) where the invention is a product, making a product for disposal or importing a product for disposal, or
- (b) where the invention is a process, using a process.

(3) A threat of infringement proceedings is not actionable if the infringement is alleged to consist of an act which, if done, would constitute an infringement of a kind mentioned in subsection (2)(a) or (b).

(4) A threat of infringement proceedings is not actionable if the threat—

- (a) is made to a person who has done, or intends to do, an act mentioned in subsection (2)(a) or (b) in relation to a product or process, and
- (b) is a threat of proceedings for an infringement alleged to consist of doing anything else in relation to that product or process.

(5) A threat of infringement proceedings which is not an express threat is not actionable if it is contained in a permitted communication.

(6) In sections 70C and 70D "an actionable threat" means a threat of infringement proceedings that is actionable in accordance with this section.

III PAT [15B]

70B. Permitted communications

(1) For the purposes of section 70A(5), a communication containing a threat of infringement proceedings is a "permitted communication" if—

- (a) the communication, so far as it contains information that relates to the threat, is made for a permitted purpose;
- (b) all of the information that relates to the threat is information that—
  - (i) is necessary for that purpose (see subsection (5)(a) to (c) for some examples of necessary information), and
  - (ii) the person making the communication reasonably believes is true.

(2) Each of the following is a "permitted purpose"—

- (a) giving notice that a patent exists;
- (b) discovering whether, or by whom, a patent has been infringed by an act mentioned in section 70A(2)(a) or (b);
- (c) giving notice that a person has a right in or under a patent, where another person's awareness of the right is relevant to any proceedings that may be brought in respect of the patent.

(3) The court may, having regard to the nature of the purposes listed in subsection (2)(a) to (c), treat any other purpose as a "permitted purpose" if it considers that it is in the interests of justice to do so.

(4) But the following may not be treated as a "permitted purpose"—

- (a) requesting a person to cease doing, for commercial purposes, anything in relation to a product or process,
- (b) requesting a person to deliver up or destroy a product, or
- (c) requesting a person to give an undertaking relating to a product or process.

(5) If any of the following information is included in a communication made for a permitted purpose, it is information that is "necessary for that purpose" (see subsection (1)(b)(i))—

- (a) a statement that a patent exists and is in force or that an application for a patent has been made;
- (b) details of the patent, or of a right in or under the patent, which—
  - (i) are accurate in all material respects, and
  - (ii) are not misleading in any material respect; and
- (c) information enabling the identification of the products or processes in respect of which it is alleged that acts infringing the patent have been carried out.

III PAT [15C]

70C. Remedies and defences

(1) Proceedings in respect of an actionable threat may be brought against the person who made the threat for—

- (a) a declaration that the threat is unjustified;
- (b) an injunction against the continuance of the threat;
- (c) damages in respect of any loss sustained by the aggrieved person by reason of the threat.

(2) In the application of subsection (1) to Scotland—

- (a) "declaration" means "declarator", and
- (b) "injunction" means "interdict".

(3) It is a defence for the person who made the threat to show that the act in respect of which proceedings were threatened constitutes (or if done would constitute) an infringement of the patent.

(4) It is a defence for the person who made the threat to show—

- (a) that, despite having taken reasonable steps, the person has not identified anyone who has done an act mentioned in section 70A(2)(a) or (b) in relation to the product or the use of a process which is the subject of the threat, and
- (b) that the person notified the recipient, before or at the time of making the threat, of the steps taken.

III PAT [15D]

70D. Professional advisers

(1) Proceedings in respect of an actionable threat may not be brought against a professional adviser (or any person vicariously liable for the actions of that professional adviser) if the conditions in subsection (3) are met.

(2) In this section "professional adviser" means a person who, in relation to the making of the communication containing the threat—

- (a) is acting in a professional capacity in providing legal services or the services of a trade mark attorney or a patent attorney, and
- (b) is regulated in the provision of legal services, or the services of a trade mark attorney or a patent attorney, by one or more regulatory bodies (whether through membership of a regulatory body, the issue of a licence to practise or any other means).

(3) The conditions are that—

- (a) in making the communication the professional adviser is acting on the instructions of another person, and
- (b) when the communication is made the professional adviser identifies the person on whose instructions the adviser is acting.

(4) This section does not affect any liability of the person on whose instructions the professional adviser is acting.

(5) It is for a person asserting that subsection (1) applies to prove (if required) that at the material time—

- (a) the person concerned was acting as a professional adviser, and
- (b) the conditions in subsection (3) were met.

III PAT [15E]

70E. Supplementary: pending registration

(1) In sections 70 and 70B references to a patent include references to an application for a patent that has been published under section 16.

(2) Where the threat of infringement proceedings is made after an application has been published (but before grant) the reference in section 70C(3) to "the patent" is to be treated as a reference to the patent as granted in pursuance of that application.

III PAT [15F]

70F. Supplementary: proceedings for delivery up etc

In section 70(1)(b) the reference to proceedings for infringement of a patent includes a reference to proceedings for an order under section 61(1)(b) (order to deliver up or destroy patented products etc) [and proceedings in the Unified Patent Court for an order for delivery up made in accordance with articles 32(1)(c) and 62(3) of the Agreement on a Unified Patent Court].

Amendment *Text in square brackets is inserted by the Intellectual Property (Unjustified Threats) Act 2017, with effect from a date to be appointed.*

III PAT [16]

71. Declaration or declarator as to non-infringement

(1) Without prejudice to the court's jurisdiction to make a declaration or declarator apart from this section, a declaration or declarator that an act does not, or a proposed act would not, constitute an infringement of a patent may be made by the court or the comptroller in proceedings between the person doing or proposing to do the act and the proprietor of the patent, notwithstanding that no assertion to the contrary has been made by the proprietor, if it is shown—

PATENTS

(a) that that person has applied in writing to the proprietor for a written acknowledgment to the effect of the declaration or declarator claimed, and has furnished him with full particulars in writing of the act in question; and

(b) that the proprietor has refused or failed to give any such acknowledgment.

(2) Subject to section 72 (5) below, a declaration made by the comptroller under this section shall have the same effect as a declaration or declarator by the court.

III PAT [16.1]

Section 71 letters In some cases a person who thinks that they are a potential defendant may seek comfort from the proprietor that his proposed acts or indeed the acts he is currently carrying out are non infringing. This is done by means of a s 71 letter in which the potential defendant sets out what he is doing in sufficient detail to enable the proprietor to determine whether what is stated in the s 71 letter is infringing or not. In s 71 cases the court may grant a declaration of non-infringement if, after the proprietor refusing to confirm non-infringement, the potential defendant applies for a suitable declaration. However it is important to set out with the requisite degree of clarity and particularity the nature of the acts carried out and care should be exercised in the preparation of a s 71 letter. Any doubts appearing in the s 71 letter must necessarily be resolved in favour of the proprietor (*Mallory Metallurgical Products Ltd v Black Sivals and Bryson Inc* [1977] RPC 321), though the most practicable course (in relation to product patents) is to provide an embodiment of the product for inspection but this must presuppose that it is possible to tell from the embodiment provided that it is or is not infringing. Likewise drawings may be provided (*MMD Design and Consultancy Ltd's Patent* [1989] RPC 131). The procedure to be followed is by the lodgment of claim form as against the proprietor. It will usually be the case that a CPR Pt 7 claim form is appropriate since questions under s 71 of the Patents Act 1977 are almost entirely fact driven and usually by reference to what the notional recipient of the s 71 letter would understand it to mean.

III PAT [17]

72. Power to revoke patents on application

(1) Subject to the following provisions of this Act, the court or the comptroller may by order revoke a patent for an invention on the application of any person (including the proprietor of the patent) on (but only on) any of the following grounds, that is to say—

(a) the invention is not a patentable invention;

(b) that the patent was granted to a person who was not entitled to be granted that patent;

(c) the specification of the patent does not disclose the invention clearly enough and completely enough for it to be performed by a person skilled in the art;

(d) the matter disclosed in the specification of the patent extends beyond that disclosed in the application for the patent, as filed, or, if the patent was granted on a new application filed under section 8(3), 12 or 37(4) above or as mentioned in section 15(9) above, in the earlier application, as filed;

(e) the protection conferred by the patent has been extended by an amendment which should not have been allowed.

(2) An application for the revocation of a patent on the ground mentioned in subsection (1)(b) above—

(a) may only be made by a person found by the court in an action for a declaration or declarator, or found by the court or the comptroller on a reference under section 37 above, to be entitled to be granted that patent or to be granted a patent for part of the matter comprised in the specification of the patent sought to be revoked; and

(b) may not be made if that action was commenced or that reference was made after the second anniversary of the date of the grant of the patent sought to be revoked, unless it is shown that any person registered as a proprietor of the patent knew at the time of the grant or of the transfer of the patent to him that he was not entitled to the patent.

(3) . . .

(4) An order under this section may be an order for the unconditional revocation of the patent or, where the court or the comptroller determines that one of the grounds mentioned in subsection (1) above has been established, but only so as to invalidate the patent to a limited extent, an order that the patent should be revoked unless within a specified time the specification is amended to the satisfaction of the court or the comptroller, as the case may be.

(4A) The reference in subsection (4) above to the specification being amended is to its being amended under section 75 below and also, in the case of a European patent (UK), to its being amended under any provision of the European Patent Convention under which the claims of the patent may be limited by amendment at the request of the proprietor.

(5) A decision of the comptroller or on appeal from the comptroller shall not estop any party to civil proceedings in which infringement of a patent is in issue from alleging invalidity of the patent on any of the grounds referred to in subsection (1) above, whether or not any of the issues involved were decided in the said decision.

(6) Where the comptroller refuses to grant an application made to him by any person under this section, no application (otherwise than by way of appeal or by way of putting validity in issue in proceedings for infringement) may be made to the court by that person under this section in relation to the patent concerned, without the leave of the court.

(7) Where the comptroller has not disposed of an application made to him under this section, the applicant may not apply to the court under this section in respect of the patent concerned unless either—

- (a) the proprietor of the patent agrees that the applicant may so apply, or
- (b) the comptroller certifies in writing that it appears to him that the question whether the patent should be revoked is one which would more properly be determined by the court.

III PAT [17.1]

Revocation proceedings Sub-section (4A) is due to be inserted by the operation of s 4 of the Patents Act 2004.

A person who comes to the view that a patent is invalid does not have to wait until he is sued for patent infringement before he can test the validity of the patent. He may apply to the court by the issue of a CPR Pt 7 claim for revocation of the patent (or part thereof). There are five grounds upon which validity may be put in issue being (1) that the invention is not patentable (that is it is not new, inventive, has no industrial utility or is excluded), (2) that the patentee was not qualified to be the applicant (or his predecessor in title in the case of assigned rights), (3) that the patent is not clear or complete such that it can be performed by the skilled addressee, (4) that the protection attained by the patent goes further than that disclosed in the application and (5) that the application was amended and that the amendment ought not to have been allowed. Any of the objections under the 5 grounds can have the effect of invalidating the entire patent or may have the effect of invalidating part of the patent, however, where the objection is in relation to entitlement then that objection can only be made by the person seeking to be affirmed as the person truly entitled. If the person truly entitled is successful in his application to revoke then the patent does not die but a right is vested in the applicant for revocation to file a new patent with a filing date being the same date as the original patent (see s 37(4)).

Questions of validity usually revolve around patentability and the reader is referred to the specialist texts for further information. In appropriate cases the court may allow the proprietor to amend his patent to escape invalidity and may set a time limit for the making of an application to amend the patent.

Unusually a party who initiates proceedings relating to validity before the comptroller and has a finding made against him may raise the issue again (subject to the perils associated with a certificate of contested validity where indemnity costs may be payable in future actions involving the same issues of validity) in infringement proceedings. However, if pure validity proceedings have been determined against the claimant he cannot issue proceedings afresh in the court, though he may appeal or raise the issue afresh in infringement proceedings. If, before a finding has been made by the comptroller, the parties agree that the court ought to determine the issue or if the comptroller so thinks then the matter may be raised afresh before the court and in accordance with Practice Direction 63.

In all cases where it is sought to raise the question of validity *ab initio* and not following the institution of infringement proceedings, the former route of petitioning the court to revoke is simply replaced by the claim form route where the party seeking to impugn the validity of the patent concerned issues a claim form seeking relief that the patent do stand revoked and costs. In such cases the need to serve particulars of validity is not absolved. An application for revocation should be made by the issue of a CPR Pt 7 claim, marked "Patents Court", and subsequent steps must comply with para 4 onwards of the Practice Direction at **CPR PD 63**. Note in particular the provisions in para 4 regarding the presentation of a claim that a patent or registered design is invalid.

Under the new law where a European Patent Office patent is in issue then damages may be granted if that patent is partially valid but n condition that a satisfactory application to amend is made to the European Patent Office.

III PAT [17.2]

Judicial approach to the issue of obviousness In determining whether a patent should be revoked for invalidity by reason of obviousness, the judge is not bound to follow the structured approach laid down in *Windsurfing International Inc v Tabur Marine (GB) Ltd* [1985] RPC 59, CA. The judge may instead go straight to the question of obviousness, provided that he or she adopts the mantle of the skilled person and addresses the right question: *David J Instance Ltd v Denny Bros Printing Ltd* [2002] EWCA Civ 939, [2002] RPC 321.

In relation to patents it is often the case that the facts of the case can be sufficiently complex that sight is lost of the purpose of the Court of Appeal as a review tribunal (as opposed to a re-hearing tribunal, which is only permissible if it is in the interests of justice to hold a re-hearing see para **CPR 52.11**). The Court of Appeal has made it clear in *Teva Pharmaceutical Industries Ltd v Instituto Gentill SpA* [2003] EWCA Civ 1545; (2003) Times, 16 December, CA that appeals against the essentially factual issues of novelty or obviousness will not be entertained unless the trial judge erred in principle. If that contention is to be made then a clear statement to that effect ought to be made in the skeleton arguments with a succinct statement of the principle involved and, unless the matter is self evident, the authority for that principle. The Court of Appeal will always be slow to interfere where inferences are drawn from primary facts: *Assicurazioni Generali SpA v Arab Insurance Group (BSC)* [2003] EWCA Civ 1642, [2003] 1 All ER (Comm) 140, 1 WLR 577 and the authorities cited therein.

III PAT [17.2A]

Revocation on the ground of insufficiency Where a patent claim relates to a product, rather than a method, the patent is not liable to revocation on the ground of insufficiency under s 72(1)(c) if the only inventive step involved in the product consists in the method by which it is made available and if its description and specification disclose only that inventive method and superior methods are found by others which owe nothing to that method: *Generics (UK) Ltd v H Lundbeck A/S* [2009] UKHL 12, [2009] 2 All ER 955, [2009] IP & T 496.

III PAT [17.3]

Withdrawal of revocation proceedings If revocation proceedings in court are withdrawn the court may not continue with them, having regard to **CPR 38**. However, the Comptroller has jurisdiction to continue with his examination of the validity of the patent: *R (on the application of Ash and Lacy Building Products Ltd) v Comptroller General of Patents, Designs and Trade Marks* [2002] EWHC 541 (Admin), [2002] All ER (D) 23 (Feb), (2002) Times, 12 March.

III PAT [17.4]

European revocation Where a European patent (UK) is revoked in accordance with the European Patent Convention, s 77(4A) provides that the patent is to be treated as having been revoked under the Patents Act 1977 from the outset. It is not permissible to stay a case where, during the proceedings, a final unappealable decision had been made in another valid forum (the European Patent Office) that the patent in issue was invalid even though a reference had been made to the European Court of Human Rights since the European Court of Human Rights had no power to reverse the decision of the European Patent Office: *ITP SA v Coflexip Stena Offshore Ltd* 2004 SLT 1285, (2004) Times, 29 November, Ct of Sess (Inner House).

In a case where the English courts held a patent to be valid but the Technical Board of Appeal of the European Patent Office subsequently amended it, it was held by the Supreme Court that the retrospective effect of the amendment invalidated infringement claims based the unamended grant: *Virgin Atlantic Airways Ltd v Zodiac Seats UK Ltd (formerly Contour*

Aerospace Ltd) [2013] UKSC 46, [2013] 4 All ER 715, [2013] 3 WLR 299. The Court rejected the contrary argument, based on res judicata, which had been accepted most recently in *Unilin Beheer BV v Berry Floor NV* [2007] EWCA Civ 364, [2008] 1 All ER 156, [2007] Bus LR 1140.

III PAT [18]

74. Proceedings in which validity of patent may be put in issue

(1) Subject to the following provisions of this section, the validity of a patent may be put in issue—

- (a) by way of defence, in proceedings for infringement of the patent under section 61 above or proceedings under section 69 above for infringement of rights conferred by the publication of an application;
- (b) in proceedings in respect of an actionable threat under section 70A above;
- (c) in proceedings in which a declaration in relation to the patent is sought under section 71 above;
- (d) in proceedings before the court or the comptroller under section 72 above for the revocation of the patent;
- (e) in proceedings under section 58 above.

(2) The validity of a patent may not be put in issue in any other proceedings and, in particular, no proceedings may be instituted (whether under this Act or otherwise) seeking only a declaration as to the validity or invalidity of a patent.

(3) The only grounds on which the validity of a patent may be put in issue (whether in proceedings for revocation under section 72 above or otherwise) are the grounds on which the patent may be revoked under that section.

(4) No determination shall be made in any proceedings mentioned in subsection (1) above on the validity of a patent which any person puts in issue on the ground mentioned in section 72 (1)(b) above unless—

- (a) it has been determined in entitlement proceedings commenced by that person or in the proceedings in which the validity of the patent is in issue that the patent should have been granted to him and not some other person; and
- (b) except where it has been so determined in entitlement proceedings, the proceedings in which the validity of the patent is in issue are commenced on or before the second anniversary of the date of the grant of the patent or it is shown that any person registered as a proprietor of the patent knew at the time of the grant or of the transfer of the patent to him that he was not entitled to the patent.

(5) Where the validity of a patent is put in issue by way of defence or counterclaim the court or the comptroller shall, if it or he thinks it just to do so, give the defendant an opportunity to comply with the condition in subsection (4)(a) above.

(6) In subsection (4) above "entitlement proceedings", in relation to a patent, means a reference under section 37(1) above on the ground that the patent was granted to a person not entitled to it or proceedings for a declaration or declarator that it was so granted.

(7) Where proceedings with respect to a patent are pending in the court under any provision of this Act mentioned in subsection (1) above, no proceedings may be instituted without the leave of the court before the comptroller with respect to that patent under section 61 (3), 69, 71 or 72 above.

(8) It is hereby declared that for the purposes of this Act the validity of a patent is not put in issue merely because—

- (a) the comptroller is considering its validity in order to decide whether to revoke it under section 73 above or

(b) its validity is being considered in connection with an opinion under section 74A below or a review of such an opinion.

III PAT [18.1]

Classes of proceedings There are five classes of proceedings where the breadth, validity or construction of the claims of a patent may be put in issue in court proceedings being (1) as a defence to an allegation of infringement, (2) threats proceedings, (3) s 71 letters, (4) proceedings pursuant to s 72 or (5) (see para **III PAT [17]**) Crown use disputes. Further, no person may put validity in issue and merely seek a declaration of invalidity or validity, he must seek more, though how much more is uncertain. Validity means validity in accordance with s 72 and no more, so for instance a fair basis objection (under s 14) would not found an objection to validity. Like s 72 the validity question has echoes in part at least in relation to entitlement, where a person cannot raise the question of validity unless he has won entitlement proceedings or has been declared as entitled and the issue of entitlement under this section is commenced within two years (unless the proprietor knows that he is not entitled). It is unlikely that in proceedings before the comptroller where entitlement is in issue there will not be an order for revocation followed by giving the person entitled the appropriate filing date under s 37. However, it may be that the person otherwise entitled cares not as to his entitlement but would rather see the person currently entitled divested of the patent. However, it is difficult to see what s 74(4)(a) adds to the current entitlement framework since if there have been prior entitlement proceedings or proceedings where entitlement is in issue between the person claiming entitlement (and/or claiming that the patent is invalid on that ground) and the extant proprietor, then the court or comptroller would have made the requisite entitlement order. Section 74 does provide for the situation where if entitlement proceedings are brought before the court the court is bound to give the applicant to opportunity to raise his entitlement in proceedings before the Comptroller. Entitlement proceedings may only be brought within a 2 year time limit from grant (unless the person registered as entitled knew that he ought not to have been) and amending an entitlement case out of time is not allowed (see *Phone-Poulence Rorer International Holdings Inc v Yeda Research and Development Co Ltd* [2006] EWCA Civ 1094, (2006) Times, 5 September).

III PAT [18.2]

Pleading requirements The requirements for pleading the question of validity (whether arising by way of claim, defence or Part 20 claim) are dealt with in the Practice Direction at **CPR PD 63**.

III PAT [18A]

74A. Opinions on matters prescribed in the rules

(1) The proprietor of a patent or any other person may request the comptroller to issue an opinion on a prescribed matter in relation to the patent.

(2) Subsection (1) above applies even if the patent has expired or has been surrendered.

(3) The comptroller shall issue an opinion if requested to do so under subsection (1) above, but shall not do so—

(a) in such circumstances as may be prescribed, or

(b) if for any reason he considers it inappropriate in all the circumstances to do so.

(4) An opinion under this section shall not be binding for any purposes.

(5) An opinion under this section shall be prepared by an examiner.

(6) In relation to a decision of the comptroller whether to issue an opinion under this section—

(a) for the purposes of section 101 below, only the person making the request under subsection (1) above shall be regarded as a party to a proceeding before the comptroller; and

(b) no appeal shall lie at the instance of any other person.

III PAT [18A.1]

In patent litigation technical issues may arise where it is helpful to get a quick view from a technical expert who is neutral and who is a civil servant at the patent office (an examiner) on matters of validity and infringement. The comptroller can decline to give an opinion if thought inappropriate to do so but the person making the request may be heard in the event of such a refusal and can appeal. The opinion is not binding.

III PAT [18B]

74B. Reviews of opinions under section 74A

(1) Rules may make provision for a review before the comptroller, on an application by the proprietor or an exclusive licensee of the patent in question, of an opinion under section 74A above.

(2) The rules may, in particular—

(a) prescribe the circumstances in which, and the period within which, an application may be made;

(b) provide that, in prescribed circumstances, proceedings for a review may not be brought or continued where other proceedings have been brought;

(c) . . .

(d) provide for there to be a right of appeal against a decision made on a review only in prescribed cases.

III PAT [18B.1]

Right of appeal Upon the true construction of this section and rule 77K of the 1995 Rules, an appeal should lie as of right where it relates to part of an opinion that has not been set aside on review: *Re DLP Ltd's Patent* [2007] EWHC 2669 (Pat), [2008] 1 All ER 839.

III PAT [19]

75. Amendment of patent in infringement or revocation proceedings

(1) In any proceedings before the court or the comptroller in which the validity of a patent may be put in issue the court or, as the case may be, the comptroller may, subject to section 76 below, allow the proprietor of the patent to amend the specification of the patent in such manner, and subject to such terms as to advertising the proposed amendment and as to costs, expenses or otherwise, as the court or comptroller thinks fit.

(2) A person may give notice to the court or the comptroller of his opposition to an amendment proposed by the proprietor of the patent under this section, and if he does so the court or the comptroller shall notify the proprietor and consider the opposition in deciding whether the amendment or any amendment should be allowed.

(3) An amendment of a specification of a patent under this section shall have effect and be deemed always to have had effect from the grant of the patent.

(4) Where an application for an order under this section is made to the court, the applicant shall notify the comptroller, who shall be entitled to appear and be heard and shall appear if so directed by the court.

(5) In considering whether or not to allow an amendment proposed under this section, the court or the comptroller shall have regard to any relevant principles applicable under the European Patent Convention.

III PAT [19.1]

General Amendment is the key remedy available to the proprietor in cases where he wishes to avoid revocation of his entire patent and where his patent or relevant claims are only partially valid. Section 76 provides that amendment shall not be allowed if the effect of the amendment is to widen the scope of the patent or claims thereof. It has long been recognised that an opportunity should be given to amend in order to cure such invalidity: *May and Baker Ltd v Boots Pure Drug Co Ltd* (1950) 67 RPC 23, at 40, HL. Obviously where the proposed amendment still leaves the patent invalid then the amendment will still not be allowed: *Minister of Agriculture's Patent* [1990] RPC 61. Amendment (by way of deletion) will almost always (subject to discretion) be allowed but any amendments which result in giving a second chance to the proprietor will not be allowed: *Van der Lely NV v Bamfords Ltd* [1964] RPC 54, 76. Prompt amendment is vital (*Smith Kline & French Laboratories Ltd v Evans Medical Ltd* [1989] FSR 561) and the breadth of the original claim is not usually a factor unless it can be shown that it was unduly wide and known to be so (*American Cyanamid's Patent* [1977] RPC 349). The Court of Appeal has suggested that if an application to amend is going to be made then it ought to be made clear that this is a case

PATENTS

which the proprietor intends to adopt at the earliest possible stage: *Procter & Gamble Co v Peaudouce (UK) Ltd* [1989] FSR 180, CA. Amendment ought to be raised before trial even though the issue cannot be determined until after trial.

III PAT [19.2]

Procedure Applications to amend patents (other than ones to amend obvious mistakes) may only arise in court during or after proceedings and, therefore, the correct procedure is to make an application before trial or during the course of trial or after judgment when it becomes clear that the patent is only partially valid, though as much notice as possible should be given. In other cases the application to amend must be made to the Comptroller at the Patent Office. Otherwise it is not possible to amend a patent on it own. The application notice must comply with the requirements of **CPR 63.10**, one of which is that it should be served on the Comptroller electronically whenever this is reasonably possible. The Comptroller is required to advertise the application forthwith in the Journal. Paragraph 10 of the Practice Direction at **CPR PD 63** requires any party or person seeking directions to file a document that states the directions sought and to do so not later than two days before the first hearing date. The same paragraph also requires electronic service on the Comptroller to comply with any requirements for the sending of electronic communications to the Comptroller.

III PAT [19.3]

Disclosure A patentee who is seeking to amend under s 75 is not obliged to disclose relevant documents to his opponent which are documents covered by legal professional privilege: *Oxford Gene Technology Ltd v Affymetrix Inc* [2001] FSR 136, (2000) Times, 5 December, CA.

Where the application is unopposed it is not necessary to disclose evidence beyond that already disclosed in the statement of reasons: *Swintex Ltd v Melba Products Ltd* [2001] FSR 4.

III PAT [19.4]

The discretion to allow amendment Generally speaking the court will usually allow amendment in the exercise of its discretion unless it is established that the amendment widens the protection (see s 76(3)(b)) that the original application for a patent was made in bad faith: *Matho Ltd v Michigan (Great Britain) Ltd* [1973] RPC 823 or there has been prejudicial delay in making the application. There is little jurisprudence on the question of discretion. In *Chiron Corpn v Organon Teknika Ltd (No 7)* and *Chiron Corpn v Murex Diagnostics Ltd (No 7)* [1994] FSR, 458 Aldous J held that s 63(2) disentitles the claimant to protection unless the claimant proves that he framed the original patent specification in good faith and with reasonable skill and knowledge. In that case only that part of the invention is protected but it may be a condition of granting that relief that the invalid portions are amended out. In *Chiron* Aldous J said that one must take account of material facts. Further a refusal to exercise a discretion to allow an amendment (and thus throwing the whole patent away) would be harsh and therefore such refusal should be entertained in very exceptional circumstances. There is also a material difference by mere deletion and validation by reformulation. Obviously the court will be more willing to allow the former than it will the latter. In *Chiron* Aldous J (after reviewing the authorities) said:

> 'In cases of deletion, a patentee will not be deprived of the fruits of his invention unless there are very compelling reasons to do so.'

In the case of *Hadley Industries plc v Metal Sections Ltd* [1999] All ER (D) 1144, Neuberger J held that there was in fact no discretion to refuse to allow an amendment since there was no corresponding discretion in the European Patent Office. However, the Court of Appeal in *Kimberly-Clarke Worldwide Inc v Procter & Gamble Ltd* [2000] FSR 235, [2000] RPC 422, CA pointed out that there was nothing in the Patents Act 1977 which required European Patent Office practice to be observed or followed and that if Parliament had intended such then it would have said so (as it had in relation to other parts of the Patents Act 1977). The implication here is, whatever the practice of the European Patent Office, the Patents Court retains a wide discretion to consider all matters which go to whether the applicant for a patent has made a covetous or over-wide claim, and may thus be regarded as having cynically exploited the patent system.

Under s 36 (as amended by s 9 of the Patents Act 2005) it is now expressly provided that no application may be made to amend, in relation to jointly owned patents, by a single owner. All of the other owners must consent.

III PAT [20]

97. Appeals from the Comptroller

(1) Except as provided by subsection (4) below, an appeal shall lie to the Patents Court from any decision of the comptroller under this Act or rules except any of the following decisions, that is to say—

(a) a decision falling within section 14 (7) above;

(b) a decision under section 16 (2) above to omit matter from a specification;

(c) a decision to give directions under subsection (1) or (2) of section 22 above;

(d) a decision under rules which is excepted by rules from the right of appeal conferred by this section.

(2) For the purpose of hearing appeals under this section the Patents Court may consist of one or more judges of that court in accordance with directions given by the Lord Chief Justice of England and Wales after consulting the Lord Chancellor; < . . . >

(3) An appeal shall not lie to the Court of Appeal from a decision of the Patents Court on appeal from a decision of the comptroller under this Act or rules—

(a) except where the comptroller's decision was given under section 8, 12, 18, 20, 27, 37, 40, 61, 72, 73 or 75 above; or

(b) except where the ground of appeal is that the decision of the Patents Court is wrong in law;

but an appeal shall only lie to the Court of Appeal under this section if leave to appeal is given by the Patents Court or the Court of Appeal.

(4) < . . . >

(4) The Lord Chief Justice may nominate a judicial office holder (as defined in section 109(4) of the Constitutional Reform Act 2005) to exercise his functions under subsection (2).

(5) [. . .]

III PAT [20.1]

Appeals from the Comptroller: Jurisdiction In some cases where the Comptroller is given original jurisdiction (and where he does not decline to deal, in which case either of the parties may re-refer the matter to the court on application) an appeal lies from him in all cases save where it results from a decision to reframe an abstract (s 14(7)), omission of matter which would generally be expected to encourage offensive, immoral or anti-social behaviour from an application (s 16(2)), directions relating to publication of inventions of importance in a national security context (s 22(1)), directions relating to publication of inventions of importance in public safety context (s 22(2)).

III PAT [20.2]

Appeals from the Comptroller: Procedure **CPR 63.16** provides that CPR Part 52 applies to appeals from the Comptroller, that patent appeals are to be made to the Patents Court and other appeals to the Chancery Division and that documents required by CPR Part 52 to be served must be served on the Comptroller or registrar as well. Note that where the Comptroller refers the whole proceedings or a question or issue to the court under s 251(1) of the Copyright, Designs and Patents Act 1988 the reference must be brought within 14 days of the reference.

III PAT [20.3]

Appeals from the Comptroller: Basis of appeal Although there is little doubt that in general terms the basis upon which appeals are determined from inferior tribunals in the area of patents and trade marks is by way of review (and not re-hearing), the court's approach is generally flexible. In *South Cone Inc v Bessant (t/a REEF)* [2001] 38 LS Gaz R 39, Pumfrey J said:

> "Findings of primary fact will not be disturbed unless the hearing officer made an error or (*sic*) principle or was plainly wrong on the evidence. His inferences from the primary facts may be reconsidered, but weight will be given to his experience. No question of the

PATENTS

exercise of a discretion arises. In this way, error will be corrected, but a different appreciation will not be substituted for that of the hearing officer if he has arrived at his conclusion without error."

III PAT [21]

99. General powers of the court

The court may, for the purpose of determining any question in the exercise of its original or appellate jurisdiction under this Act or any treaty or international convention to which the United Kingdom is a party, make any order or exercise any other power which the comptroller could have made or exercised for the purpose of determining that question.

III PAT [22]

99A. Power of Patents Court to order report

(1) Rules of court shall make provision empowering the Patents Court in any proceedings before it under this Act, on or without the application of any party, to order the Patent Office to inquire into and report on any question of fact or opinion.

(2) Where the court makes such an order on the application of a party, the fee payable to the Patent Office shall be at such rate as may be determined in accordance with rules of court and shall be costs of the proceedings unless otherwise ordered by the court.

(3) Where the court makes such an order of its own motion, the fee payable to the Patent Office shall be at such rate as may be determined by the Lord Chancellor with the approval of the Treasury and shall be paid out of money provided by Parliament.

COPYRIGHT, DESIGNS AND PATENTS ACT 1988

(c 48)

III PAT [23]

99. Order for delivery up

(1) Where a person—

(a) has an infringing copy of a work in his possession, custody or control in the course of a business, or

(b) has in his possession, custody or control an article specifically designed or adapted for making copies of a particular copyright work, knowing or having reason to believe that it has been or is to be used to make infringing copies,

the owner of the copyright in the work may apply to the court for an order that the infringing copy or article be delivered up to him or to such other person as the court may direct.

(2) An application shall not be made after the end of the period specified in section 113 (period after which remedy of delivery up not available); and no order shall be made unless the court also makes, or it appears to the court that there are grounds for making, an order under section 114 (order as to disposal of infringing copy or other article).

(3) A person to whom an infringing copy or other article is delivered up in pursuance of an order under this section shall, if an order under section 114 is not made, retain it pending the making of an order, or the decision not to make an order, under that section.

(4) Nothing in this section affects any other power of the court.

III PAT [23.1]

This section provides for the original and ancillary jurisdiction relating to the delivery up of infringing articles. The original jurisdiction exists where there is really no argument as to infringement at all (that is because the issue has been determined by the court and the goods in question have fallen into somebody else's hands or because the articles are clear infringements). Section 99 operates in tandem with s 114 (see para **III PAT [25]**) where the court has to consider whether to order destruction and no s 99 order will be made unless there are grounds for making an order under s 114. Where a s 114 determination has not be made then the person to whom the goods or articles in question have been delivered must hold them until a s 114 determination is made. Where a claimant applies for delivery up under this section of infringing copies or articles, para 23 of the Practice Direction at **CPR PD 63** requires that the claim for, or application notice, must be served on all identifiable persons who have an interest in them.

III PAT [23.2]

Precedents For precedents see **BCCP L[401], BCCP L[402]**.

III PAT [24]

102. Exercise of concurrent rights

(1) Where an action for infringement of copyright brought by the copyright owner or an exclusive licensee relates (wholly or partly) to an infringement in respect of which they have concurrent rights of action, the copyright owner or, as the case may be, the exclusive licensee may not, without the leave of the court, proceed with the action unless the other is either joined as a plaintiff or added as a defendant.

(2) A copyright owner or exclusive licensee who is added as a defendant in pursuance of subsection (1) is not liable for any costs in the action unless he takes part in the proceedings.

(3) The above provisions do not affect the granting of interlocutory relief on an application by a copyright owner or exclusive licensee alone.

(4) Where an action for infringement of copyright is brought which relates (wholly or partly) to an infringement in respect of which the copyright owner and an exclusive licensee have or had concurrent rights of action—

(a) the court shall in assessing damages take into account—

(i) the terms of the licence, and

(ii) any pecuniary remedy already awarded or available to either of them in respect of the infringement;

(b) no account of profits shall be directed if an award of damages has been made, or an account of profits has been directed, in favour of the other of them in respect of the infringement; and

(c) the court shall if an account of profits is directed apportion the profits between them as the court considers just, subject to any agreement between them;

and these provisions apply whether or not the copyright owner and the exclusive licensee are both parties to the action.

(5) The copyright owner shall notify any exclusive licensee having concurrent rights before applying for an order under section 99 (order for delivery up) or exercising the right conferred by section 100 (right of seizure); and the court may on the application of the licensee make such order under section 99 or, as the case may be, prohibiting or permitting the exercise by the copyright owner of the right conferred by section 100, as it thinks fit having regard to the terms of the licence.

III PAT [24.1]

This section provides for the position of exclusive licensees and copyright owners. Where the owner and the exclusive licensee have right of suit in respect of the same infringement then in order to avoid double recovery both are required to be joined (as co-claimant or one as claimant and the other as non-participating, non-cost paying co-defendant), though this is something which will need to be perfected by way of joinder if there is no joinder upon issue. The claimant may seek interlocutory relief in the meantime before he regularises his position and if the claimant is successful at trial then the court will have to take account of the concurrency in determining damages.

III PAT [25]

114. Order as to disposal of infringing copy or other article

(1) An application may be made to the court for an order that an infringing copy or other article delivered up in pursuance of an order under section 99 or 108, or seized and detained in pursuance of the right conferred by section 100, shall be—

(a) forfeited to the copyright owner, or

(b) destroyed or otherwise dealt with as the court may think fit,

or for a decision that no such order should be made.

(2) In considering what order (if any) should be made, the court shall consider whether other remedies available in an action for infringement of copyright would be adequate to compensate the copyright owner and to protect his interests.

(3) Provision shall be made by rules of court as to the service of notice on persons having an interest in the copy or other articles, and any such person is entitled—

(a) to appear in proceedings for an order under this section, whether or not he was served with notice, and

(b) to appeal against any order made, whether or not he appeared;

and an order shall not take effect until the end of the period within which notice of an appeal may be given or, if before the end of that period notice of appeal is duly given, until the final determination or abandonment of the proceedings on the appeal.

(4) Where there is more than one person interested in a copy or other article, the court shall make such order as it thinks just and may (in particular) direct that the article be sold, or otherwise dealt with, and the proceeds divided.

(5) If the court decides that no order should be made under this section, the person in whose possession, custody or control the copy or other article was before being delivered up or seized is entitled to its return.

(6) References in this section to a person having an interest in a copy or other article include any person in whose favour an order could be made in respect of it—

(a) under this section or under section 204 or 231 of this Act;

(b) under section 24D of the Registered Designs Act 1949;

(c) under section 19 of Trade Marks Act 1994 (including that section as applied by regulation 4 of the Community Trade Mark Regulations 2006 (SI 2006/1027)); or

(d) under regulation 1C of the Community Design Regulations 2005 (SI 2005/2339).

III PAT [25.1]

Procedure Proceedings under this section may be brought by the issue of a claim form or application notice, in the Chancery Division of the High Court, or in the Patents county court or in a county court where there is also a Chancery district registry, as provided in **CPR 63.13**. The claim form or notice is required, by para 23 of the Practice Direction at **CPR PD 63**, to be served on all identifiable persons who have an interest in the goods, material or articles.

This section operates in tandem with s 99 (see para **III PAT [23]**) in that it gives jurisdiction to the court to decide whether goods delivered up should be destroyed, otherwise dealt with or delivered up to the copyright owner. In some cases the defendant may say that the goods are not infringing goods and if there is a factual issue to be tried then the court may make appropriate orders preserving evidence, though these orders, being interlocutory and injunctive in nature will be governed by the usual rules relating to interlocutory injunctions.

III PAT [26]

115. Jurisdiction of county court and sheriff court

(1) In England and Wales the county court and in Northern Ireland a county court may entertain proceedings under—

section 99 (order for delivery up of infringing copy or other article),

section 101 (5) (order as to exercise of rights by copyright owner where exclusive licensee has concurrent rights), or

section 114 (order as to disposal of infringing copy or other article),

save that, in Northern Ireland, a county court may entertain such proceedings only where the value of the infringing copies and other articles in question does not exceed the county court limit for actions in tort.

(2) In Scotland proceedings for an order under any of those provisions may be brought in the sheriff court.

(3) Nothing in this section shall be construed as affecting the jurisdiction of the High Court or, in Scotland, the Court of Session.

III PAT [26.1]

The county courts (subject to its parochial jurisdiction) also have jurisdiction in relation to s 99 (see para **III PAT [23]**) and s 114 (see para **III PAT [25]**) as well as s 102(5) (see para **III PAT [24]**) in relation to the apportionment of damages for claimants who have concurrent rights.

III PAT [26A]

152. Appeal to the court on a point of law

(1) An appeal lies on any point of law arising from a decision of the Copyright Tribunal to the High Court or, in the case of proceedings of the Tribunal in Scotland, to the Court of Session.

(2) Provision shall be made by rules under section 150 limiting the time within which an appeal may be brought.

(3) Provision may be made by rules under that section—

(a) for suspending, or authorising or requiring the Tribunal to suspend, the operation of orders of the Tribunal in cases where its decision is appealed against;

(b) for modifying in relation to an order of the Tribunal whose operation is suspended the operation of any provision of this Act as to the effect of the order;

PATENTS

(c) for the publication of notices or the taking of other steps for securing that persons affected by the suspension of an order of the Tribunal will be informed of its suspension.

III PAT [26A.1]

Errors of fact The High Court only has jurisdiction in relation to appeals from the Copyright Tribunal. For an explanation of the functions and activities of the Copyright Tribunal see Freegard and Black *The Decisions of the UK Performing Right and Copyright Tribunal* (1st edn, 1997). Although s 152(1) confines appeals to points of law, a point of law may arise where the fact gathering exercise is so flawed as to amount to a miscarriage of justice (see: *Phonographic Performance Ltd v Candy Rock Recording Ltd* [1999] EMLR 806, Sir Richard Scott V-C).

III PAT [26A.2]

Additional evidence Often a question will arise on appeal from the copyright tribunal as to whether further evidence should be admitted on appeal. Given that appeals are only allowed in relation to matters of law it is unlikely that further evidence will be allowed on appeal. However, it is submitted that, if such evidence is to be adduced then its reception will be governed by the same rules that govern the reception of further evidence in the court of appeal (see: *Ladd v Marshall* [1954] 1 WLR 1489).

III PAT [26A.3]

Procedure An appeal from the copyright tribunal must be made within 28 days of the date of the decision to be appeal against (see r 42(1) of the Copyright Tribunal Rules 1989, SI 1989/1129). In other respects CPR Pt 52 applies.

III PAT [27]

195. Order for delivery up

(1) Where a person has in his possession, custody or control in the course of a business an illicit recording of a performance, a person having performer's rights or recording rights in relation to the performance under this Chapter may apply to the court for an order that the recording be delivered up to him or to such other person as the court may direct.

(2) An application shall not be made after the end of the period specified in section 203; and no order shall be made unless the court also makes, or it appears to the court that there are grounds for making, an order under section 204 (order as to disposal of illicit recording).

(3) A person to whom a recording is delivered up in pursuance of an order under this section shall, if an order under section 204 is not made, retain it pending the making of an order, or the decision not to make an order, under that section.

(4) Nothing in this section affects any other power of the court.

III PAT [27.1]

See para **III PAT [23.1]**.

III PAT [28]

204. Order as to disposal of illicit recording

(1) An application may be made to the court for an order that an illicit recording of a performance delivered up in pursuance of an order under section 195 or 199, or seized and detained in pursuance of the right conferred by section 196, shall be—

(a) forfeited to such person having performer's rights or recording rights in relation to the performance as the court may direct, or

(b) destroyed or otherwise dealt with as the court may think fit,

or for a decision that no such order should be made.

(2) In considering what order (if any) should be made, the court shall consider whether other remedies available in an action for infringement of the rights conferred by this Chapter would be adequate to compensate the person or persons entitled to the rights and to protect their interests.

(3) Provision shall be made by rules of court as to the service of notice on persons having an interest in the recording, and any such person is entitled—

- (a) to appear in proceedings for an order under this section, whether or not he was served with notice, and
- (b) to appeal against any order made, whether or not he appeared;

and an order shall not take effect until the end of the period within which notice of an appeal may be given or, if before the end of that period notice of appeal is duly given, until the final determination or abandonment of the proceedings on the appeal.

(4) Where there is more than one person interested in a recording, the court shall make such order as it thinks just and may (in particular) direct that the recording be sold, or otherwise dealt with, and the proceeds divided.

(5) If the court decides that no order should be made under this section, the person in whose possession, custody or control the recording was before being delivered up or seized is entitled to its return.

(6) References in this section to a person having an interest in a recording include any person in whose favour an order could be made in respect of the recording—

- (a) under this section or under section 114 or 231 of this Act;
- (b) under section 24D of the Registered Designs Act 1949;
- (c) under section 19 of Trade Marks Act 1994 (including that section as applied by regulation 4 of the Community Trade Mark Regulations 2006 (SI 2006/1027)); or
- (d) under regulation 1C of the Community Design Regulations 2005 (SI 2005/2339).

III PAT [28.1]

Procedure The procedure for proceeding under this section is the same as for s114, noted at para **III PAT [25.1]**.

III PAT [29]

230. Order for delivery up

(1) Where a person—

- (a) has in his possession, custody or control for commercial purposes an infringing article, or
- (b) has in his possession, custody or control anything specifically designed or adapted for making articles to a particular design, knowing or having reason to believe that it has been or is to be used to make an infringing article,

the owner of the design right in the design in question may apply to the court for an order that the infringing article or other thing be delivered up to him or to such other person as the court may direct.

(2) An application shall not be made after the end of the period specified in the following provisions of this section; and no order shall be made unless the court also makes, or it appears to the court that there are grounds for making, an order under section 231 (order as to disposal of infringing article, &c).

(3) An application for an order under this section may not be made after the end of the period of six years from the date on which the article or thing in question was made, subject to subsection (4).

(4) If during the whole or any part of that period the design right owner—

- (a) is under a disability, or

(b) is prevented by fraud or concealment from discovering the facts entitling him to apply for an order,

an application may be made at any time before the end of the period of six years from the date on which he ceased to be under a disability or, as the case may be, could with reasonable diligence have discovered those facts.

(5) In subsection (4) "disability"—

(a) in England and Wales, has the same meaning as in the Limitation Act 1980;

(b) in Scotland, means legal disability within the meaning of the Prescription and Limitation (Scotland) Act 1973;

(c) in Northern Ireland, has the same meaning as in the Statute of Limitations (Northern Ireland) 1958.

(6) A person to whom an infringing article or other thing is delivered up in pursuance of an order under this section shall, if an order under section 231 is not made, retain it pending the making of an order, or the decision not to make an order, under that section.

Nothing in this section affects any other power of the court.

III PAT [29.1]

Design right Design right, within the meaning of s 213(2) of the Act, may exist in the shape or configuration of the individual parts as well as in the whole: *Farmers Build Ltd v Carier Bulk Materials Handling Ltd* [1999] RPC 461, CA. It was also held that designs were "original" if they were not copies and that they were not "commonplace" merely because they improved existing articles.

III PAT [30]

231. Order as to disposal of infringing articles etc

(1) An application may be made to the court for an order that an infringing article or other thing delivered up in pursuance of an order under section 230 shall be—

(a) forfeited to the design right owner, or

(b) destroyed or otherwise dealt with as the court may think fit,

or for a decision that no such order should be made.

(2) In considering what order (if any) should be made, the court shall consider whether other remedies available in an action for infringement of design right would be adequate to compensate the design right owner and to protect his interests.

(3) Provision shall be made by rules of court as to the service of notice on persons having an interest in the article or other thing, and any such person is entitled—

(a) to appear in proceedings for an order under this section, whether or not he was served with notice, and

(b) to appeal against any order made, whether or not he appeared;

and an order shall not take effect until the end of the period within which notice of an appeal may be given or, if before the end of that period notice of appeal is duly given, until the final determination or abandonment of the proceedings on the appeal.

(4) Where there is more than one person interested in an article or other thing, the court shall make such order as it thinks just and may (in particular) direct that the thing be sold, or otherwise dealt with, and the proceeds divided.

(5) If the court decides that no order should be made under this section, the person in whose possession, custody or control the article or other thing was before being delivered up is entitled to its return.

(6) References in this section to a person having an interest in an article or other thing include any person in whose favour an order could be made in respect of it—

(a) under this section or under section 114 or 204 of this Act;
(b) under section 24D of the Registered Designs Act 1949;
(c) under section 19 of Trade Marks Act 1994 (including that section as applied by regulation 4 of the Community Trade Mark Regulations 2006 (SI 2006/1027)); or
(d) under regulation 1C of the Community Design Regulations 2005 (SI 2005/2339).

III PAT [30.1]

Procedure The procedure for proceeding under this section is the same as for s **114**, noted at para **III PAT [25.1]**.

III PAT [31]

235. Exercise of concurrent rights

(1) Where an action for infringement of design right brought by the design right owner or an exclusive licensee relates (wholly or partly) to an infringement in respect of which they have concurrent rights of action, the design right owner or, as the case may be, the exclusive licensee may not, without the leave of the court, proceed with the action unless the other is either joined as a plaintiff or added as a defendant.

(2) A design right owner or exclusive licensee who is added as a defendant in pursuance of subsection (1) is not liable for any costs in the action unless he takes part in the proceedings.

(3) The above provisions do not affect the granting of interlocutory relief on the application of the design right owner or an exclusive licensee.

(4) Where an action for infringement of design right is brought which relates (wholly or partly) to an infringement in respect of which the design right owner and an exclusive licensee have concurrent rights of action—

(a) the court shall, in assessing damages, take into account—
 (i) the terms of the licence, and
 (ii) any pecuniary remedy already awarded or available to either of them in respect of the infringement;
(b) no account of profits shall be directed if an award of damages has been made, or an account of profits has been directed, in favour of the other of them in respect of the infringement; and
(c) the court shall if an account of profits is directed apportion the profits between them as the court considers just, subject to any agreement between them;

and these provisions apply whether or not the design right owner and the exclusive licensee are both parties to the action.

(5) The design right owner shall notify any exclusive licensee having concurrent rights before applying for an order under section 230 (order for delivery up of infringing article, &c); and the court may on the application of the licensee make such order under that section as it thinks fit having regard to the terms of the licence.

III PAT [31.1]

See para **III PAT [24.1]**.

III PAT [32]

287. Patents county courts: special jurisdiction

Repealed.

III PAT [32.1]

The Intellectual Property Enterprise Court has the same jurisdiction as the Patents Court in relation to patents (save for appeals from the Comptroller) and designs and ancillary matters. Following *McDonald v Graham* [1994] RPC 407, CA, the jurisdiction is to be construed in a purposive sense so that pure copyright disputes which relate to designs can be heard in the Intellectual Property Enterprise Court.

Note that provisions has been made by the insertion of CPR 63.27 and CPR 63.28 for cases with a value of no more than £5,000 to be heard on the Small Claims Track in certain circumstances.

III PAT [33]–III PAT [36]

289. Transfer of proceedings between High Court and Intellectual Property Enterprise Court

Repealed.

III PAT [36.1]

Proceedings may be transferred as between the Intellectual Property Enterprise Court and the Patents Court upon application to the Intellectual Property Enterprise Court or the Patents Court in relation to proceeding on foot there. An application to transfer is made by way of an application notice in existing proceedings. Upon hearing an application for transfer, the court should consider the circumstances of each case and the state of the lists, as well as the financial position of the parties, the complexity and importance of the proceedings and their probable length: *Wesley Jessen Corpn v Coopervision Ltd* (2001) Times, 31 July.

Paragraph 9 of Practice Direction 30, at **CPR PD 30.9**, requires the court to consider whether a party can only afford to bring or defend the claim in the Intellectual Property Enterprise Court and the value of the claim, the complexity of the issues and the estimated length of trial. After taking all these considerations into account, the predecessor to the Intellectual Property Enterprise Court Judge (HHJ Birss QC) directed that there be a transfer to the Patents Court in *Alk-Bello Ltd v Meridian Technical Technologies* [2010] EWPCC 014 where he said that:

> 'The Decisive factor is that the [Intellectual Property Enterprise] Court was set up to ensure that small and medium sized enterprises and private individuals were not deterred from innovation by the potential cost of litigation to safeguard their rights.'

However the Patents Court determined that whilst this was an enormously important factor it was not decisive: *Environmental Recycling Technologies plc v Stillwell* [2012] EWHC 2097 (Pat), July 13, 2012 where the judge rejected an argument that because costs are capped in the Intellectual Property Enterprise Court a transfer down would be a denial of justice.

III PAT [36.2]

Patent attorneys have rights of audience in the Intellectual Property Enterprise Court in the same way that solicitors do and are to be treated as if they were solicitors (save that a patent attorney is not entitled to prepare a deed).

TRADE MARKS ACT 1994

(c 26)

PATENTS

GENERAL NOTES ON THE TRADE MARKS ACT 1994

III PAT [37]

The High Court and the county courts have concurrent jurisdiction in relation to certain aspects of the Trade Marks Act 1994. The expression "the court", for the purposes of the Trade Marks Act 1994, is deemed to be the High Court and only the High Court has jurisdiction in relation to most matters arising under that Act (compare the position in relation to copyright where there is apparent concurrent jurisdiction). The expressed concurrent jurisdiction of the county courts (which is probably *ultra vires*) is so limited as to be non-existent since by art 2(1)(b) of the High Court and county courts Jurisdiction Order 1991, SI 1991/724 (see para **II HCJ [3]**) the county courts have jurisdiction in relation to matters arising under s 19 of the Trade Marks Act 1994 (see para **III PAT [44]**), which is a provision relating to delivery up.

As far as the High Court is concerned the jurisdiction is two fold being firstly to decide questions of infringement and, upon such a finding, to make orders to restrain infringing activities, order delivery up, destruction or obliteration damages and/or accounts. The right to sue for infringement is actionable at the suit of the trade mark proprietor, (in certain circumstances) his licensee or (in certain circumstances) his exclusive licensee. The second aspect of the court's jurisdiction is to regulate the proprietor's monopoly in cases where the proprietor has either, by his subsequent acts or omissions (subsequent, that is, to registration) disentitled himself to his monopoly (in which cases the monopoly is said to be revocable and can be avoided as at the date that such disentitlement came about) or has wrongfully obtained his monopoly (in which cases the monopoly is said to be invalid and can be avoided ab initio). This second jurisdiction (which is by no means secondary) also relates to the position where the High Court is acting in its appellate capacity from decisions as to entitlement or registerability (though the procedure in respect of this is slightly different to CPR Part 7 (see para **CPR 7**) claims). The scope of things which the court is entitled to take into account when making an award of damages has been widened by reg 3 of the Intellectual Property (Enforcement etc.) Regulations 2006 (SI 2006/1028) which require the court to take into account "all appropriate aspects" relating to the actual prejudice caused to the claimant. Those aspects include "the negative economic consequences, including any lost profits, which the claimant has suffered, and any unfair profits made by the defendant" including "any moral prejudice caused by the defendant". It is unclear whether as a result of this there is now scope for the damages/account of profits divide.

Proceedings are brought by way of a claim in the usual way under CPR 7.2 (see para **CPR 7.2**).

III PAT [38]

Jurisdiction Part I of the Trade Marks Act 1994 (ss 1–50) implements Council Directive 89/104/EEC and represents the new substantive law of registered trade marks which is harmonised throughout the Community. The sections in Part I identified below and ss 64 and 76 (see paras **III PAT [49]** and **III PAT [50]**) in Part III confer jurisdiction on the High Court (s 75); and extensive jurisdiction under the Trade Marks Act 1994 was conferred on the county courts listed in para (7B) by the High Court and County Courts Jurisdiction (Amendment) Order 2005, SI 2005/587, with effect from 1 April 2005. Although s 75 of the Trade Marks Act 1994, as enacted, conferred jurisdiction on the High Court alone, the section was amended by s 1 of the Courts and Legal Services Act 1990 to enable the Lord Chancellor to designate business to county courts.

III PAT [38A]

European Community trade marks The Chancery Division of the High Court is the principal designated European Union Trade Mark Court under art 95(1) of Council Regulation (EC) 207/2009. Its role and its duties *vis-à-vis* the Office of Harmonisation in the Internal Market are set out in para 21 of the Practice Direction at **CPR PD 63**. In addition, changes made by the Community Trade Mark (Designation of Community Trade Mark Courts) Regulations 2005, SI 2005/440 have designated the patents county court and certain county courts with chancery expertise as Community trade mark courts with effect from 1 April 2005. The patents county court is, of course now defunct.

III PAT [39]

Procedure Claims under the 1994 Act are required, by **CPR 63.13**, to be brought in the Chancery Division. The claim form is required, by para 17.1 of the Practice Direction at **CPR PD 63**, to be marked "Intellectual Property" in the top right-hand corner, below the title of the court in which it is issued. It is provided in **CPR 63.14** that the claim form or application notice must be served on the registrar where the relief sought would, if granted, affect an entry in the United Kingdom register. See paras 14 and 18 to 20 of the Practice Direction at **CPR PD 63** regarding the role of the registrar when served.

III PAT [40]

1. Trade marks

(1) In this Act "trade mark" means any sign which is capable—

(a) of being represented in the register in a manner which enables the registrar and other competent authorities and the public to determine the clear and precise subject matter of the protection afforded to the proprietor, and

(b) of distinguishing goods or services of one undertaking from those of other undertakings.

A trade mark may, in particular, consist of words (including personal names), designs, letters, numerals, colours, sounds or the shape of goods or their packaging.

(2) References in this Act to a trade mark include, unless the context otherwise requires, references to a collective mark (see section 49) or certification mark (see section 50).

III PAT [40.1]

Capable of distinguishing goods or services of one undertaking So long as the mark has a distinctive character, which is distinctive of the proprietor, it need not be a unique identifier: *(1) Associated Newspapers Ltd and (2) Daily Mail and General Trust plc v Express Newspapers (An Unlimited Company, Incorrectly Sued as Express Newspapers Ltd)* [2003] EWHC 1322 (Ch), [2003] FSR 51, [2003] 31 LS Gaz R 32, Times, 17 June, Laddie J.

III PAT [41]

14. Action for infringement

(1) An infringement of a registered trade mark is actionable by the proprietor of the trade mark.

(2) In an action for infringement all such relief by way of damages, injunctions, accounts or otherwise is available to him as is available in respect of the infringement of any other property right.

III PAT [41.1]

Procedure An action relating to trade mark infringement is made by the usual claim form route. The defendant may challenge the validity of the registered trade mark in his defence and apply, by CPR Part 20 claim, for revocation of the registration, a declaration that it is invalid or rectification of the register. Where a defendant applies, by CPR Part 20 claim, for a declaration, the grant of which may affect an entry in the United Kingdom register, he must serve a copy of his Part 20 claim form on the registrar. Note also the provisions of paras 14 and 18 to 20 of the Practice Direction at **CPR PD 63** regarding the role of the registrar.

It has been held that a defendant who has opposed the registration unsuccessfully before the registrar is not estopped from challenging the validity of the trade mark on the same grounds in defence of infringement proceedings: *Special Effects Ltd v L'Oreal* [2007] EWCA Civ 1, (2007) Times, 24 January, [2007] Bus LR 759.

III PAT [41.2]

Infringement Infringement on its own comprises using another's registered trade mark (as a trade mark: see *R v Johnstone* [2003] UKHL 28, [2003] 3 All ER 884, [2003] 1 WLR 1736, though this question is by no means settled, also see: Case C-206/01: *Arsenal Football Club plc v Reed* [2003] Ch 454, [2003] All ER (EC) 1, ECJ) without consent so that the use is identical to the registered mark or that the use is not identical, but is so similar as to cause confusion. The meaning and scope of the expression "confusion" (said to include a likelihood of association) is a matter of developing law, as was explained by L ADDIE J in *Wagamama Ltd v City Centre Restaurants Ltd* [1995] FSR 713. The law of registered trade marks as set out in the Trade Marks Act 1994 allows some exceptions to infringement (see generally, *British Airways plc v Ryanair Ltd* [2001] FSR 541):

(1) where honest comparisons are being made to a competitor's product (see *Emaco Ltd v Dyson Appliances Ltd* [1999] ETMR 903) even where an exact reproduction of the trade mark is used, provided that there is no confusion (*0 $_2$ (UK) Ltd v Hutchinson 3G UK Ltd* [2008] WLR (D) 193;

(2) where the use of another's trade mark is in respect of goods for which that trade mark is not registered. The use should not take unfair advantage of the distinctive character or repute of the registration and must be with due cause. It is no defence to say that the use complained of was innocent (see: *Premier Brands UK Ltd v Typhoon Europe Ltd* [2000] FSR 767); and

(3) where the use is descriptive of something but provided that such use must always by honest as looked at in industrial or commercial matters. The list of permissible activities (subject to the proviso) is exhaustive and is set out in s 11 of the Trade Marks Act 1994. The burden of proving that such use does not satisfy the proviso is upon the person alleging infringement (see: *Barclays Bank plc v RBS Advanta* [1996] RPC 307).

For a claim for trade mark infringement under s 10(3) to succeed, the claimant has to provide evidence that the association between the mark and the defendant's sign is such that either the defendant gains an unfair advantage from association with the mark or that the association has damaged the reputation of that mark: *DaimlerChrysler AG v Javid Alavi (t/a Merc)* [2001] RPC 813. Also notwithstanding that s 10(3)(b), by its express words, only cedes protection in circumstances where the registered trade mark has repute (or, now, significant repute, see: Case C-375/97: *General Motors Corpn v Yplon SA* [1999] All ER (EC) 865, [1999] ECR I-5421, ECJ) and the defendant's activities are in relation to goods or services which are not similar to those for which the registered trade mark is registered, the position now appears to be that s 10(3)(b) must now be ignored, see: Case C-408/01: *Adidas-Salomon AG v Fitnessworld Trading Ltd* (2003) Times, 31 October, ECJ. As to whether ignoring a part of a domestic statute is permissible (which it is if it in conflict with European law) see: Case 269/80: *R v Tymen* [1981] ECR 3079, [1982] 2 CMLR 111, ECJ.

A trade mark owner cannot stop a rival from using an identical or similar sign in a comparative advertisement where the use is not likely to confuse the public, for example in comparative advertisements: *0 $_2$ Holdings Ltd v Hutchison 3G UK Ltd: C-533/06* [2008] 3 CMLR 397, [2008] RPC 905, ECJ.

III PAT [41.2A]

Passing Off The law relating to passing off is preserved by s 2(2) of the Act and the right to bring proceedings for passing off is not affected by the making of an application by another to register a trade mark which is the same as or similar to the trade dress forming the subject matter of the passing off action, see: *Inter Lotto (UK) Ltd v Camelot Group plc* [2003] EWHC 1256, [2003] 3 All ER 191, L ADDIE J affirmed on appeal [2003] EWCA Civ 1132, [2003] 4 All ER 575, Times, 20 August. This will lead to the situation where a person having a goodwill associated with a form of trade dress is able to sue a registered trade mark proprietor, notwithstanding the fact that the proprietor has rights ceded by the Act. Is seems therefore that if there is a valid cause of action in passing off, this overrides any rights given by the Act. Although this conflict was noted by the Court of Appeal, it said that s 2(2) of the Act was clear and that registered trade mark rights therefore had to be subservient to rights to protect goodwill.

III PAT [41.3]

Interim injunctions It is usually the case that in trade mark cases interim injunctions will be granted on the same grounds and upon the same basis as in other interim injunction cases.

However, where non-identical trade marks are in issue then absence of evidence of confusion is usually a significant factor against (but not fatal to) the grant of an interim injunction (see: *Baywatch Production Co Inc v Home Video Channel* [1997] FSR 22).

III PAT [42]

15. Order for erasure etc of offending sign

(1) Where a person is found to have infringed a registered trade mark, the court may make an order requiring him—

(a) to cause the offending sign to be erased, removed or obliterated from any infringing goods, material or articles in his possession, custody or control, or

(b) if it is not reasonably practicable for the offending sign to be erased, removed or obliterated, to secure the destruction of the infringing goods, material or articles in question.

(2) If an order under subsection (1) is not complied with, or it appears to the court likely that such an order would not be complied with, the court may order that the infringing goods, material or articles be delivered to such person as the court may direct for erasure, removal or obliteration of the sign, or for destruction, as the case may be.

III PAT [42.1]

Like the provisions relating to delivery up in relation to copyright and rights in performances (ss 99, 114, 195, 204, 235 and 287 of the Copyright, Designs and Patents Act 1988 (see paras **III PAT [23]**, **III PAT [25]**, **III PAT [27]**, **III PAT [28]**, **III PAT [31]** and **III PAT [32]**)) there is also original and ancillary jurisdiction to order erasure, destruction and delivery up of infringing goods (which are goods which have been marked with the registered trade mark in question), materials (which are not in themselves infringing goods as such but are used for labelling or packaging goods, or are business papers or advertising materials), or articles (which are things specifically designed or adapted for making copies of the registered trade mark in infringement thereof and the person who possesses it knows that fact).

III PAT [42.2]

Specific jurisdiction This provides the basis whereby the court can order erasure of a mark from goods or marks from other materials or articles which they adorn. The ancillary jurisdiction is probably inherent but depends for its efficacy on there being a finding of infringement. However, where there is such a finding (which implies that this jurisdiction is ancillary only and not original, this is not conclusive since it could be employed where one is attempting to deal with goods which have been found to be infringing, which did not form the subject matter of any infringement proceedings and which are, subsequently, found to be in the hands of others) then the court can order obliteration or destruction, and if the order for obliteration is not complied with, the court has jurisdiction to order that another person be given the goods, material or articles for the purposes of obliteration or destruction.

III PAT [42.3]

Company name Although the court may order a company to cease using an infringing name it may not order the registrar to change the name without a special resolution of the company: *Halifax plc v Halifax Repossessions Ltd* [2004] EWCA Civ 331, [2004] 1 BCLC 455, [2004] All ER (D) 07 (Feb). There is now in existence a company names tribunal (see s 69 of the Companies Act 2006) which seeks to resolve company name conflicts, though the jurisdiction of the tribunal does not have any interim powers and does not supplant any jurisdiction which the civil courts have to restrain name usage.

III PAT [43]

16. Order for delivery up of infringing goods, material or articles

(1) The proprietor of a registered trade mark may apply to the court for an order for the delivery up to him, or such other person as the court may direct, of any infringing goods, material or articles which a person has in his possession, custody or control in the course of a business.

(2) An application shall not be made after the end of the period specified in section 18 (period after which remedy of delivery up not available); and no order shall be made unless the court also makes, or it appears to the court that there are grounds for making, an order under section 19 (order as to disposal of infringing goods, &c).

(3) A person to whom any infringing goods, material or articles are delivered up in pursuance of an order under this section shall, if an order under section 19 is not made, retain them pending the making of an order, or the decision not to make an order, under that section.

(4) Nothing in this section affects any other power of the court.

III PAT [43.1]

It is apparent that this section does not depend for its efficacy on there being a finding of infringement, hence the jurisdiction is both original and ancillary. However, the fact that the goods, material or articles are infringing should not be in dispute for this section to work as part of the court's original jurisdiction. The court's power under this section is confined to delivery up only and the court may not make an order for delivery up if the infringing goods were marked more than six years past, if the material was marked more than six years past or if the articles were made more than six years past. The six year period is suspended if the relevant facts are concealed from the proprietor or if he is under a disability (which has the same meaning as disability within the meaning of the Limitation Act 1980 (see para **III LIM [1]**)).

III PAT [44]

19. Order as to disposal of infringing goods, material or articles – county court has power

(1) Where infringing goods, material or articles have been delivered up in pursuance of an order under section 16, an application may be made to the court—

(a) for an order that they be destroyed or forfeited to such person as the court may think fit, or

(b) for a decision that no such order should be made.

(2) In considering what order (if any) should be made, the court shall consider whether other remedies available in an action for infringement of the registered trade mark would be adequate to compensate the proprietor and any licensee and protect their interests.

(3) Provision shall be made by rules of court as to the service of notice on persons having an interest in the goods, material or articles, and any such person is entitled—

(a) to appear in proceedings for an order under this section, whether or not he was served with notice, and

(b) to appeal against any order made, whether or not he appeared;

and an order shall not take effect until the end of the period within which notice of an appeal may be given or, if before the end of that period notice of appeal is duly given, until the final determination or abandonment of the proceedings on the appeal.

(4) Where there is more than one person interested in the goods, material or articles, the court shall make such order as it thinks just.

(5) If the court decides that no order should be made under this section, the person in whose possession, custody or control the goods, material or articles were before being delivered up is entitled to their return.

(6) References in this section to a person having an interest in goods, material or articles include any person in whose favour an order could be made—

(a) under this section (including that section as applied by regulation 4 of the Community Trade Mark Regulations 2006 (SI 2006/1027));

(b) under section 24D of the Registered Designs Act 1949;

PATENTS

(c) under section 114, 204 or 231 of the Copyright, Designs and Patents Act 1988; or

(d) under regulation 1C of the Community Design Regulations 2005 (SI 2005/2339).

III PAT [44.1]

This section is designed to ensure that, insofar as is possible, the court does not order forfeiture if some other remedy will suffice (such as obliteration or export to a neutral market). Paragraph 23 of the Practice Direction at **CPR PD 63** provides that the applicant for an order must serve the claim form or application notice on all identifiable persons having an interest in the goods, material or articles.

III PAT [45]

21. Threats of infringement proceedings

(1) A communication contains a "threat of infringement proceedings" if a reasonable person in the position of a recipient would understand from the communication that—

(a) a registered trade mark exists, and

(b) a person intends to bring proceedings (whether in a court in the United Kingdom or elsewhere) against another person for infringement of the registered trade mark by—

(i) an act done in the United Kingdom, or

(ii) an act which, if done, would be done in the United Kingdom.

(2) References in this section and in section 21C to a "recipient" include, in the case of a communication directed to the public or a section of the public, references to a person to whom the communication is directed.

III PAT [45.1]

Threats: trade marks The rules governing threats made in relation to trade marks are similar in scope, effect and purpose to those relating to patents (see paras **III PAT [15.1]**–**III PAT [15.2]**) since the policy considerations governing them are the same. See also *L'Oreal (UK) Ltd v Johnson & Johnson* [2000] ETMR 691, [2000] FSR 686. Proceedings under the new s 21C of the Trade Marks Act 1994 (which came into force on and relates to threats made on or after 1 October 2017) must be determined under the old s 21.

It has been held that the exceptions (a) to (c) in subsection 21 (1) should not be construed widely but according to their ordinary meaning. Thus s 21(1)(a) should be limited to the physical act of affixing or applying a mark; and the use of the mark for advertising services should not be treated as coming within "the supply of services under the mark": *Best Buy Co Inc v Worldwide Sales Corpn Espana SL* [2011] EWCA Civ 618, [2011] Bus LR 1166, [2011] FSR 742.

The new law (which came into force on 1 October 2017 – the Intellectual Property (Unjustified Threats) Act 2017) also provides an additional defence to a proprietor making a threat to a secondary infringer where endeavours have been made to ascertain the identity of the primary infringer without success. If attempts have been made to trace the primary infringer and the proprietor notifies the secondary infringer of that fact then threats may be made with impunity against the secondary infringer in order to resolve the infringement dispute. Further changes to the law of threats are envisaged. The new s 21C of the Trade Marks Act 1994 relates to threats made on or after 1 October 2017. Threats made prior to 1 October 2017 must be determined under the old s 70 – reg 3 of the Intellectual Property (Unjustified Threats) Act 2017 (Commencement and Transitional Provisions) Regulations 2017 (SI 2017/771). In the law of threats the (would be) primary infringer is the maker or the importer (who has invested much and is unlikely to back down in the face of a threat) whereas the (would be) secondary infringer is, euphemistically, the shop keeper who is keen to do anything to avoid costs and expense and will thus stop supplying articles to which the threats relate on a nuisance basis. In very general terms the secondary infringer is the person who is protected.

III PAT [45A]

21A. Actionable threats

(1) Subject to subsections (2) to (6), a threat of infringement proceedings made by any person is actionable by any person aggrieved by the threat.

... of infringement proceedings is not actionable if the infringement is ... to consist of—

(a) applying, or causing another person to apply, a sign to goods or their packaging,

(b) importing, for disposal, goods to which, or to the packaging of which, a sign has been applied, or

(c) supplying services under a sign.

(3) A threat of infringement proceedings is not actionable if the infringement is alleged to consist of an act which, if done, would constitute an infringement of a kind mentioned in subsection (2)(a), (b) or (c).

(4) A threat of infringement proceedings is not actionable if the threat—

(a) is made to a person who has done, or intends to do, an act mentioned in subsection (2)(a) or (b) in relation to goods or their packaging, and

(b) is a threat of proceedings for an infringement alleged to consist of doing anything else in relation to those goods or their packaging.

(5) A threat of infringement proceedings is not actionable if the threat—

(a) is made to a person who has done, or intends to do, an act mentioned in subsection (2)(c) in relation to services, and

(b) is a threat of proceedings for an infringement alleged to consist of doing anything else in relation to those services.

(6) A threat of infringement proceedings which is not an express threat is not actionable if it is contained in a permitted communication.

(7) In sections 21C and 21D "an actionable threat" means a threat of infringement proceedings that is actionable in accordance with this section.

PATENTS

III PAT [45B]

21B. Permitted communications

(1) For the purposes of section 21A(6), a communication containing a threat of infringement proceedings is a "permitted communication" if—

(a) the communication, so far as it contains information that relates to the threat, is made for a permitted purpose;

(b) all of the information that relates to the threat is information that—

(i) is necessary for that purpose (see subsection (5)(a) to (c) for some examples of necessary information), and

(ii) the person making the communication reasonably believes is true.

(2) Each of the following is a "permitted purpose"—

(a) giving notice that a registered trade mark exists;

(b) discovering whether, or by whom, a registered trade mark has been infringed by an act mentioned in section 21A(2)(a), (b) or (c);

(c) giving notice that a person has a right in or under a registered trade mark, where another person's awareness of the right is relevant to any proceedings that may be brought in respect of the registered trade mark.

(3) The court may, having regard to the nature of the purposes listed in subsection (2)(a) to (c), treat any other purpose as a "permitted purpose" if it considers that it is in the interests of justice to do so.

(4) But the following may not be treated as a "permitted purpose"—

(a) requesting a person to cease using, in the course of trade, a sign in relation to goods or services,

(b) requesting a person to deliver up or destroy goods, or

(c) requesting a person to give an undertaking relating to the use of a sign in relation to goods or services.

(5) If any of the following information is included in a communication made for a permitted purpose, it is information that is "necessary for that purpose" (see subsection (1)(b)(i))—

- (a) a statement that a registered trade mark exists and is in force or that an application for the registration of a trade mark has been made;
- (b) details of the registered trade mark, or of a right in or under the registered trade mark, which—
  - (i) are accurate in all material respects, and
  - (ii) are not misleading in any material respect; and
- (c) information enabling the identification of the goods or their packaging, or the services, in relation to which it is alleged that the use of a sign constitutes an infringement of the registered trade mark.

III PAT [45C]

21C. Remedies and defences

(1) Proceedings in respect of an actionable threat may be brought against the person who made the threat for—

- (a) a declaration that the threat is unjustified;
- (b) an injunction against the continuance of the threat;
- (c) damages in respect of any loss sustained by the aggrieved person by reason of the threat.

(2) It is a defence for the person who made the threat to show that the act in respect of which proceedings were threatened constitutes (or if done would constitute) an infringement of the registered trade mark.

(3) It is a defence for the person who made the threat to show—

- (a) that, despite having taken reasonable steps, the person has not identified anyone who has done an act mentioned in section 21A(2)(a), (b) or (c) in relation to the goods or their packaging or the services which are the subject of the threat, and
- (b) that the person notified the recipient, before or at the time of making the threat, of the steps taken.

III PAT [45D]

21D. Professional advisers

(1) Proceedings in respect of an actionable threat may not be brought against a professional adviser (or any person vicariously liable for the actions of that professional adviser) if the conditions in subsection (3) are met.

(2) In this section "professional adviser" means a person who, in relation to the making of the communication containing the threat—

- (a) is acting in a professional capacity in providing legal services or the services of a trade mark attorney or a patent attorney, and
- (b) is regulated in the provision of legal services, or the services of a trade mark attorney or a patent attorney, by one or more regulatory bodies (whether through membership of a regulatory body, the issue of a licence to practise or any other means).

(3) The conditions are that—

- (a) in making the communication the professional adviser is acting on the instructions of another person, and
- (b) when the communication is made the professional adviser identifies the person on whose instructions the adviser is acting.

(4) This section does not affect any liability of the person on whose instructions the professional adviser is acting.

(5) It is for a person asserting that subsection (1) applies to prove (if required) that at the material time—

(a) the person concerned was acting as a professional adviser, and

(b) the conditions in subsection (3) were met.

III PAT [45E]

21E. Supplementary: pending registration

(1) In sections 21 and 21B references to a registered trade mark include references to a trade mark in respect of which an application for registration has been published under section 38.

(2) Where the threat of infringement proceedings is made after an application for registration has been published (but before registration) the reference in section 21C(2) to "the registered trade mark" is to be treated as a reference to the trade mark registered in pursuance of that application.

III PAT [45F]

21F. Supplementary: proceedings for delivery up etc

In section 21(1)(b) the reference to proceedings for infringement of a registered trade mark includes a reference to—

(a) proceedings for an order under section 16 (order for delivery up of infringing goods, material or articles), and

(b) proceedings for an order under section 19 (order as to disposal of infringing goods, material or articles).

III PAT [45G]

28. Licensing of registered trade mark

(1) A licence to use a registered trade mark may be general or limited.

A limited licence may, in particular, apply—

(a) in relation to some but not all of the goods or services for which the trade mark is registered, or

(b) in relation to use of the trade mark in a particular manner or a particular locality.

(2) A licence is not effective unless it is in writing signed by or on behalf of the grantor.

Except in Scotland, this requirement may be satisfied in a case where the grantor is a body corporate by the affixing of its seal.

(3) Unless the licence provides otherwise, it is binding on a successor in title to the grantor's interest.

References in this Act to doing anything with, or without, the consent of the proprietor of a registered trade mark shall be construed accordingly.

(4) Where the licence so provides, a sub-licence may be granted by the licensee; and references in this Act to a licence or licensee include a sub-licence or sub-licensee.

(5) The proprietor of a registered trade mark may invoke the rights conferred by that trade mark against a licensee who contravenes any provision in the licence with regard to—

(a) its duration,

(b) the form covered by the registration in which the trade mark may be used,

(c) the scope of the goods or services for which the licence is granted,

(d) the territory in which the trade mark may be affixed, or

(e) the quality of the goods manufactured or of the services provided by the licensee.

III PAT [45H]

29. Exclusive licences

(1) In this Act an "exclusive licence" means a licence (whether general or limited) authorizing the licensee to the exclusion of all other persons, including the person granting the licence, to use a registered trade mark in the manner authorised by the licence.

The expression "exclusive licensee" shall be construed accordingly.

(2) An exclusive licensee has the same rights against a successor in title who is bound by the licence as he has against the person granting the licence.

III PAT [45I]

30. General provisions as to rights of licensees in case of infringement

(1) This section has effect with respect to the rights of a licensee in relation to infringement of a registered trade mark.

The provisions of this section do not apply where or to the extent that, by virtue of section 31(1) below (exclusive licensee having rights and remedies of assignee), the licensee has a right to bring proceedings in his own name.

(1A) Except so far as the licence provides otherwise a licensee may only bring proceedings for infringement of the registered trade mark with the consent of the proprietor (but see subsections (2) and (3)).

(2) An exclusive licensee may call on the proprietor of the registered trade mark to take infringement proceedings in respect of any matter which affects his interests.

(3) If the proprietor mentioned in subsection (2)—

(a) refuses to do so, or

(b) fails to do so within two months after being called upon,

the exclusive licensee may bring the proceedings in his own name as if he were the proprietor.

(4) Where infringement proceedings are brought by a licensee by virtue of this section or with the consent of the proprietor or pursuant to the licence, the licensee may not, without the leave of the court, proceed with the action unless the proprietor is either joined as a plaintiff or added as a defendant.

This does not affect the granting of interlocutory relief on an application by a licensee alone.

(5) A proprietor who is added as a defendant as mentioned in subsection (4) shall not be made liable for any costs in the action unless he takes part in the proceedings.

(6) In infringement proceedings brought by the proprietor of a registered trade mark any loss suffered or likely to be suffered by licensees shall be taken into account; and the court may give such directions as it thinks fit as to the extent to which the plaintiff is to hold the proceeds of any pecuniary remedy on behalf of licensees.

(6A) Where the proprietor of a registered trade mark brings infringement proceedings, a licensee who has suffered loss is entitled to intervene in the proceedings for the purpose of obtaining compensation for that loss.

(7) The provisions of this section apply in relation to an exclusive licensee if or to the extent that he has, by virtue of section 31(1), the rights and remedies of an assignee as if he were the proprietor of the registered trade mark.

III PAT [45J]

31. Exclusive licensee having rights and remedies of assignee

(1) An exclusive licence may provide that the licensee shall have, to such extent as may he provided by the licence, the same rights and remedies in respect of matters occurring after the grant of the licence as if the licence had been an assignment.

Where or to the extent that such provision is made, the licensee is entitled, subject to the provisions of the licence and to the following provisions of this section, to bring infringement proceedings, against any person other than the proprietor, in his own name.

(2) Any such rights and remedies of an exclusive licensee are concurrent with those of the proprietor of the registered trade mark; and references to the proprietor of a registered trade mark in the provisions of this Act relating to infringement shall he construed accordingly.

(3) In an action brought by an exclusive licensee by virtue of this section a defendant may avail himself of any defence which would have been available to him if the action had been brought by the proprietor of the registered trade mark.

(4) Where proceedings for infringement of a registered trade mark brought by the proprietor or an exclusive licensee relate wholly or partly to an infringement in respect of which they have concurrent rights of action, the proprietor or, as the case may he, the exclusive licensee may not, without the leave of the court, proceed with the action unless the other is either joined as a plaintiff or added as a defendant.

This does not affect the granting of interlocutory relief on an application by a proprietor or exclusive licensee alone.

(5) A person who is added as a defendant as mentioned in subsection (4) shall not be made liable for any costs in the action unless he takes part in the proceedings.

(6) Where an action for infringement of a registered trade mark is brought which relates wholly or partly to an infringement in respect of which the proprietor and an exclusive licensee have or had concurrent rights of action–

- (a) the court shall in assessing damages take into account—
  - (i) the terms of the licence, and
  - (ii) any pecuniary remedy already awarded or available to either of them in respect of the infringement;
- (b) no account of profits shall he directed if an award of damages has been made, or an account of profits has been directed, in favour of the other of them in respect of the infringement; and
- (c) the court shall if an account of profits is directed apportion the profits between them as the court considers just, subject to any agreement between them.

The provisions of this subsection apply whether or not the proprietor and the exclusive licensee are both parties to the action; and if they are not both parties the court may give such directions as it thinks fit as to the extent to which the party to the proceedings is to hold the proceeds of any pecuniary remedy on behalf of the other.

(7) The proprietor of a registered trade mark shall notify any exclusive licensee who has a concurrent right of action before applying for an order under section 16 (order for delivery up); and the court may on the application of the licensee make such order under that section as it thinks fit having regard to the terms of the licence.

(8) The provisions of subsections (4) to (7) above have effect subject to any agreement to the contrary between the exclusive licensee and the proprietor.

GENERAL NOTES ON SECTIONS 29–31

III PAT [46]

Trade marks: Licensees These are deeming provisions which define what is an exclusive licence and who is a licensee. The licence (in order to be effective as a licence) has to be in writing though it does not have to be contractual. Further, if it is not contractual then there is no ability on the part of the exclusive licensee to stop the proprietor from interfering with the exclusivity, (though, depending upon the circumstances he might be estopped from doing so), thus it would appear that there is an implied requirement that there be some enforceable right in the exclusive licensee to prevent the proprietor from carrying out acts which would interfere with the exclusivity of the licence. It is unclear whether a consent to use a trade mark which forms the basis for an action for infringement (use without the consent of the proprietor) needs to be a licence. Traditionally there is no distinction between the two. There is certainly a confusion in the language used but nobody has yet suggested in proceedings that there needs to be any formality.

Trade marks: Ambit of licence and right to sue A licensee may sue in respect of rights which are infringed and form the basis of any granted licence although it is clear that where parliament provided for the rights granted by way of licence to be enforceable within the statutory framework as opposed to an interference with economic rights then actionability under such torts is proscribed (see, by analogy: *Oren v Red Box Toy Factory Ltd* [1999] FSR 785). Again, the licence needs to be in writing though it does not need to be contractual. The licensee is entitled to ask the proprietor to sue on behalf of the licensee and if the proprietor does not do so then the licensee may do so in his own name as if he were the proprietor. It is uncertain whether, in such circumstances, the licensee is entitled to bring proceedings in respect only of acts which affect his interests or in relation to the totality of the proprietor's interests, though where there are concurrent rights of action then the court is bound to take account of that fact as it is in relation to the position where the proprietor sues in respect of rights held by the licensees.

Trade marks: Parties In cases where the exclusive licensee sues then he may either join the proprietor as co-claimant (with the attendant liability as to costs) or as a non-participating co-defendant (with no liability as to costs). If the proprietor takes part in the proceedings then he can be liable for costs.

Trade marks: Entitlement of exclusive licensee to sue on its own In some cases the exclusive licence (whether contractual or otherwise) may itself provide for the position as between the proprietor and the licensee in the event that litigation becomes necessary for the exclusive licensee to sue as if he were the proprietor. This does not diminish the defences available to the defendant. In cases where applications for interlocutory relief are made (where time is usually of the essence) the exclusive licensee or the proprietor may act alone.

III PAT [47]

46. Revocation of registration

(1) The registration of a trade mark may be revoked on any of the following grounds—

(a) that within the period of five years following the date of completion of the registration procedure it has not been put to genuine use in the United Kingdom, by the proprietor or with his consent, in relation to the goods or services for which it is registered, and there are no proper reasons for non-use;

(b) that such use has been suspended for an uninterrupted period of five years, and there are no proper reasons for non-use;

(c) that, in consequence of acts or inactivity of the proprietor, it has become the common name in the trade for a product or service for which it is registered;

(d) that in consequence of the use made of it by the proprietor or with his consent in relation to the goods or services for which it is registered, it is liable to mislead the public, particularly as to the nature, quality or geographical origin of those goods or services.

(2) For the purposes of subsection (1) use of a trade mark includes use in a form (the "variant form") differing in elements which do not alter the distinctive character of the mark in the form in which it was registered (regardless of whether

or not the trade mark in the variant form is also registered in the name of the proprietor), and use in the United Kingdom includes affixing the trade mark to goods or to the packaging of goods in the United Kingdom solely for export purposes.

(3) The registration of a trade mark shall not be revoked on the ground mentioned in subsection (1)(a) or (b) if such use as is referred to in that paragraph is commenced or resumed after the expiry of the five year period and before the application for revocation is made:

Provided that, any such commencement or resumption of use after the expiry of the five year period but within the period of three months before the making of the application shall be disregarded unless preparations for the commencement or resumption began before the proprietor became aware that the application might be made.

(4) An application for revocation may be made by any person, and may be made either to the registrar or to the court, except that—

(a) if proceedings concerning the trade mark in question are pending in the court, the application must be made to the court; and

(b) if in any other case the application is made to the registrar, he may at any stage of the proceedings refer the application to the court.

(5) Where grounds for revocation exist in respect of only some of the goods or services for which the trade mark is registered, revocation shall relate to those goods or services only.

(6) Where the registration of a trade mark is revoked to any extent, the rights of the proprietor shall be deemed to have ceased to that extent as from—

(a) the date of the application for revocation, or

(b) if the registrar or court is satisfied that the grounds for revocation existed at an earlier date, that date

III PAT [47.1]

Procedure for raising questions of revocation The first aspect of the regulatory jurisdiction of the High Court (that is the jurisdiction to declare the rights obtained as revocable) may be raised either on its own, by way of counterclaim or by way of appeal from a determination of the registrar who has decided the issue already. The jurisdiction to revoke a United Kingdom registered trade mark essentially is in place to ensure that those who apply for and get registrations use them. Thus a person who does not use his trade mark (which is the subject of the registration) for five years from the time that the registration process has come to an end (although when could be a matter of controversy) or any uninterrupted five-year period (without proper excuse) is liable to have his registration revoked, which will take effect from the end of that five-year period, subject to the three-month proviso at the end of s 47(3). In some cases the proprietor may have lost control of his trade mark and it consequently has become a generic expression (eg "hoover" or "yo yo") or its continued use is misleading because of the use already made of it. In each case the court has the power to revoke the registration from a certain date. There will be nothing to stop recovery (by way of damage or account) in respect of acts constituting infringement occurring before that date, though whether the court will make such an order is a moot point and is, as yet, undecided under the new law.

It is apparent from s 46(1) of the Trade Marks Act 1994 that there is a discretionary jurisdiction as to whether to revoke a trade mark registration. In fact, current case law suggests that there is no discretion and if the conditions necessary for revocation or invalidity are established, then revocation or declarations of invalidity must follow as of course (see *Premier Brands UK Ltd v Typhoon Europe Ltd* [2000] FSR 767). In fact, the parent Directive (First Council Directive of 21 December 1988 to approximate the laws of the Member States relating to trade marks (89/104/EEC)) which gave birth to the Trade Marks Act 1994 is not so clear in its effect.

For the jurisdiction of the court to order part revocation in instances where only part of the registration is bad (eg where an over wide scope is claimed but there has only been limited use), see *Mercury Communications Ltd v Mercury Interactive (UK) Ltd* [1995] FSR 850.

Further, it might be that notwithstanding the expiry of the five-year periods referred to in s 46(1)(a), (b), there are "proper reasons" for non use. No guidance is given in the parent Directive as to what constitute proper reasons but it has been held that difficulties in setting up a production line can constitute proper reasons: *Magic Ball Trade Mark* [2000] ETMR 226.

In cases where the trade mark is under attack by reason of its non use, it is for the proprietor of the registered trade mark to show that it has been used: s 100 of the Trade Marks Act 1994.

The procedure for claiming revocation as part of a defence is explained at para **III PAT [41.1]**. Note that where proceedings or orders may affect the validity of entries in the register the provisions of paras 14 and 15 of the Practice Direction at **CPR PD 63** are applied by paras 20 and 21.

III PAT [48]

47. Grounds for invalidity of registration

(1) The registration of a trade mark may be declared invalid on he ground that the trade mark was registered in breach of section 3 or any of the provisions referred to in that section (absolute grounds for refusal of registration).

Where the trade mark was registered in breach of subsection (1)(b), (c) or (d) of that section, it shall not be declared invalid if, in consequence of the use which has been made of it, it has after registration acquired a distinctive character in relation to the goods or services for which it is registered.

(2) Subject to subsections (2A) and (2G), the registration of a trade mark may be declared invalid on the ground—

(a) that there is an earlier trade mark in relation to which the conditions set out in section 5(1), (2) or (3) obtain, or

(b) that there is an earlier right in relation to which the condition set out in section 5(4) is satisfied,

unless the proprietor of that earlier trade mark or other earlier right has consented to the registration.

(2ZA) The registration of a trade mark may be declared invalid on the ground that the trade mark was registered in breach of section 5(6).

(2A) The registration of a trade mark may not be declared invalid on the ground that there is an earlier trade mark unless—

(a) the registration procedure for the earlier trade mark was completed within the period of five years ending with the date of the application for the declaration,

(b) the registration procedure for the earlier trade mark was not completed before that date, or

(c) the use conditions are met.

(2B) The use conditions are met if—

(a) the earlier trade mark has been put to genuine use in the United Kingdom by the proprietor or with their consent in relation to the goods or services for which it is registered—

(i) within the period of 5 years ending with the date of application for the declaration, and

(ii) within the period of 5 years ending with the date of filing of the application for registration of the later trade mark or (where applicable) the date of the priority claimed in respect of that application where, at that date, the five year period within which the earlier trade mark should have been put to genuine use as provided in section 46(1)(a) has expired, or

(b) it has not been so used, but there are proper reasons for non-use.

(2C) For these purposes—

(a) use of a trade mark includes use in a form (the "variant form") differing in elements which do not alter the distinctive character of the mark in the form in which it was registered (regardless of whether or not the trade mark in the variant form is also registered in the name of the proprietor), and

(b) use in the United Kingdom includes affixing the trade mark to goods or to the packaging of goods in the United Kingdom solely for export purposes.

(2D) In relation to a European Union trade mark or international trade mark (EC), any reference in subsection (2B) or (2C) to the United Kingdom shall be construed as a reference to the European Union.

(2DA) In relation to an international trade mark (EC), the reference in subsection (2A)(a) to the completion of the registration procedure is to be construed as a reference to the publication by the European Union Intellectual Property Office of the matters referred to in Article 190(2) of the European Union Trade Mark Regulation.

(2E) Where an earlier trade mark satisfies the use conditions in respect of some only of the goods or services for which it is registered, it shall be treated for the purposes of this section as if it were registered only in respect of those goods or services.

(2F) Subsection (2A) does not apply where the earlier trade mark is a trade mark within section 6(1)(c).

(2G) An application for a declaration of invalidity on the basis of an earlier trade mark must be refused if it would have been refused, for any of the reasons set out in subsection (2H), had the application for the declaration been made on the date of filing of the application for registration of the later trade mark or (where applicable) the date of the priority claimed in respect of that application.

(2H) The reasons referred to in subsection (2G) are—

(a) that on the date in question the earlier trade mark was liable to be declared invalid by virtue of section 3(1)(b), (c) or (d), (and had not yet acquired a distinctive character as mentioned in the words after paragraph (d) in section 3(1));

(b) that the application for a declaration of invalidity is based on section 5(2) and the earlier trade mark had not yet become sufficiently distinctive to support a finding of likelihood of confusion within the meaning of section 5(2);

(c) that the application for a declaration of invalidity is based on section 5(3)(a) and the earlier trade mark had not yet acquired a reputation within the meaning of section 5(3).

(3) An application for a declaration of invalidity may be made by any person, and may be made either to the registrar or to the court, except that—

(a) if proceedings concerning the trade mark in question are pending in the court, the application must be made to the court; and

(b) if in any other case the application is made to the registrar, he may at any stage of the proceedings refer the application to the court.

(4) In the case of bad faith in the registration of a trade mark, the registrar himself may apply to the court for a declaration of the invalidity of the registration.

(5) Where the grounds of invalidity exist in respect of only some of the goods or services for which the trade mark is registered, the trade mark shall be declared invalid as regards those goods or services only.

(5A) An application for a declaration of invalidity may be filed on the basis of one or more earlier trade marks or other earlier rights provided they all belong to the same proprietor.

(6) Where the registration of a trade mark is declared invalid to any extent, the registration shall to that extent be deemed never to have been made:

Provided that this shall not affect transactions past and closed.

III PAT [48.1]

Procedure for raising questions of invalidity or revocation As with revocation, the first aspect of the regulatory jurisdiction of the High Court (that is the jurisdiction to declare the rights obtained as invalid) may be raised either on its own or by way of counterclaim or by way of appeal from a determination of the registrar who has decided the issue already. The jurisdiction to declare invalid a United Kingdom registered trade mark essentially is in place to ensure that those who apply for and get registrations do so in respect of valid marks which comply with the rules, as occasionally marks do slip through the net.

It is apparent from s 47(1) of the Trade Marks Act 1994 that there is a discretionary jurisdiction to have a trade mark declared invalid. In fact, current case law suggests that there is no discretion and if the conditions necessary for a declaration of invalidity are established then a declaration of invalidity must follow as of course (see *Premier Brands UK Ltd v Typhoon Europe Ltd* [2000] FSR 767). The parent Directive (First Council Directive of 21 December 1988 to approximate the laws of the Member States relating to trade marks (89/104/EEC)) which gave birth to the Trade Marks Act 1994 is not so clear in its effect.

In cases where the trade mark is under attack by reason of its non use, it is for the proprietor of the registered trade mark to show that it has been used (s 100 of the Trade Marks Act 1994). In some cases, however, the person impugning the registration of the trade mark may allege that the trade mark is not distinctive enough to qualify for protection. In this vein it is permissible for the proprietor to argue that notwithstanding that his registration was invalid, the position as it has now become is that the mark is sufficiently distinctive through use (see: *Midland Wheel Supplies Ltd's Application for Revocation* [2000] ETMR 256).

In some cases the applicant for registration (and thereafter proprietor or the relevant successor in title) will have obtained a registration for something which is either not a trade mark at all or amounts to an attempt to monopolise the English language (at least in so far as traders would wish to use it). In many cases the proprietor may be able to say that because of the use that he has made of that mark (notwithstanding its inherent unregistrability) the public associates him with that mark and so it is in fact a trade mark. Though the court would have to be persuaded that this were so for a substantial cross section of the public, see *British Sugar plc v James Robertson & Sons Ltd* [1996] RPC 281.

In other cases the proprietor will have applied for a trade mark in bad faith (eg because he applied merely defensively to keep others away from the sanctity of his core trading area).

In all of those circumstances provided that the proprietor cannot show by reason of subsequent use that the trade mark has in fact become distinctive he is liable to have his trade mark declared invalid and removed from the register as if the registration had never been granted at all.

The procedure for claiming revocation as part of a defence is explained at para **III PAT [41.1]**. Note that where proceedings or orders may affect the validity of entries in the register the provisions of paras 14 and 15 of the Practice Direction at **CPR PD 63** are applied by paras 20 and 21. Further, decisions made in proceedings in the Trade Mark Registry against one party do not give rise to an issue estoppel or a plea of *res judicata* in subsequent proceedings in the High Court since the decisions of the Registry are not final against the party who lost in those proceedings. Therefore, it is not an abuse of process for the party who loses in the Registry to raise similar issues in subsequent High Court proceedings between the same parties: *Special Effects Ltd v L'Oreal SA* [2007] EWCA Civ 1, [2007] Bus LR 759, [2007] ETMR 815, [2007] RPC 381, (2007) 151 Sol Jo LB 126, Times, January 24, 2007, [2007] All ER (D) 29 (Jan).

III PAT [49]

64. Rectification or correction of the register

(1) Any person having a sufficient interest may apply for the rectification of an error or omission in the register:

Provided that an application for rectification may not be made in respect of a matter affecting the validity of the registration of a trade mark.

(2) An application for rectification may be made either to the registrar or to the court, except that—

- (a) if proceedings concerning the trade mark in question are pending in the court, the application must be made to the court; and
- (b) if in any other case the application is made to the registrar, he may at any stage of the proceedings refer the application to the court.

(3) Except where the registrar or the court directs otherwise the effect of rectification of the register is that the error or omission in question shall be deemed never to have been made.

(4) The registrar may, on request made in the prescribed manner by the proprietor of a registered trade mark, or a licensee, enter any change in his name or address as recorded in the register.

(5) The registrar may remove from the register matter appearing to him to have ceased to have effect.

III PAT [49.1]

An application for rectification of correction is unlikely to be factually complex and it is even less likely that any facts will be in dispute. Accordingly, the most appropriate procedure is via a CPR Part 8 claim form (see para **CPR 8**).

III PAT [50]–III PAT [53]

76. Appeals from the registrar

(1) An appeal lies from any decision of the registrar under this Act, except as otherwise expressly provided by rules.

For this purpose "decision" includes any act of the registrar in exercise of a discretion vested in him by or under this Act.

(2) Any such appeal may be brought either to an appointed person or to the court.

(3) Where an appeal is made to an appointed person, he may refer the appeal to the court if—

(a) it appears to him that a point of general legal importance is involved,

(b) the registrar requests that it be so referred, or

(c) such a request is made by any party to the proceedings before the registrar in which the decision appealed against was made.

Before doing so the appointed person shall give the appellant and any other party to the appeal an opportunity to make representations as to whether the appeal should be referred to the court.

(4) Where an appeal is made to an appointed person and he does not refer it to the court, he shall hear and determine the appeal and his decision shall be final.

(5) The provisions of sections 68 and 69 (costs and security for costs; evidence) apply in relation to proceedings before an appointed person as in relation to proceedings before the registrar.

(6) In the application of this section to England and Wales, "the court" means the High Court.

III PAT [50]–III PAT [53.1]

Appeals to the court In other cases a party may wish to appeal from a decision of the registrar (the issue of revocability of invalidity being determined by him at first instance, being under his jurisdiction) and this is by way of appeal. Following on from the judgment of Sir Richard Scott VC in *Re Club Europe* [2000] RPC 329, evidence in such appeals may be augmented. The restrictive approach adopted by the Court of Appeal in *Ladd v Marshall* [1954] 3 All ER 745, [1954] 1 WLR 1489, CA was held to be inapplicable (or, more properly, not wholly applicable) in cases where public monopolies were in issue. Appeals are governed by CPR Part 52. Paragraph 25 of the Practice Direction at **CPR PD 63** provides that where an appeal is referred to the court under s 76(3) the appeal or reference must be brought within 14 days of the reference.

Since appeals to the court are governed by CPR Part 52 it follows that they will normally take the form of a review but that in rare case a re-hearing may be necessary in order to allow justice to be done: *Dyson Ltd v Registrar of Trademarks* [2003] EWHC 1062, [2003] 1 WLR 2406, Times, 23 May.

III PAT [50]–III PAT [53.2]

Appeals to the appointed person Section 76 enables parties to appeal to a person appointed by the Lord Chancellor for the purposes of hearing appeals from the registrar. The appointed person (referred to in the Trade Marks Act 1994 as the appointed person, and in delegated legislation as the person appointed) is usually a trade mark practitioner. Appeals to him are final, though he may refer the matter to the court if the registrar so requests, if the parties so request before the matter is decided by the registrar or if there is a sufficiently

PATENTS

important issue of law involved. David Kitchen QC as the appointed person in *Elizabeth Emanual Trade Mark* [2004] RPC 293 in deciding whether to refer said that "(a) the Appointed Person has a discretion whether or not to refer an appeal to the court; he has that discretion even if it appears to him that a point of general legal importance is involved; (b) the power to refer appeals to the court should be used sparingly, otherwise the clear object of the legislation to provide a relatively inexpensive, quick and final resolution of appeals by a specialist tribunal would be defeated; (c) it will be very rare to make a reference in circumstances where a point of general legal importance cannot be identified; (d) the cost and expense to the party not seeking to refer should be taken into account; this is a matter which may be of particular significance in a case where the party in question is an individual or small company or partnership; (e) regard must be had to the public interest generally. There is a public interest in having any uncertainty as to the state of the register resolved as soon as possible. On the other hand there is a public interest in having important points of law decided by the higher courts; (f) the attitude of the registrar is important but not decisive.

Appeals to the person appointed are beyond the scope of this text and guidance on appeals via that route are to be found in the Trade Marks Act 1994 itself: see the Trade Marks Rules 2000, SI 2000/136, in particular rr 63–65 thereof and Morcom, Roughton and Graham *The Modern Law of Trade Marks* (1st edn, 2000). In cases where the person appointed declines to deal with the matter (as he has the right to do) then the route by which the matter may be brought before the court is the same as for situations where the registrar declines to deal with it.

III PAT [50]–III PAT [53.3]

Appeals generally In cases of appeals to the appointed person or to the court, the appellate tribunal will wish to ensure that the trade marks registry has only acted on relevant issues and facts and that the party against whom an adverse holding or finding has been made has had an opportunity to address them. See *Xe Trade Mark* [2000] RPC 405.

GENERAL NOTE ON OLYMPIC SYMBOLS

III PAT [54]

Olympic symbols As far as Olympic symbols are concerned protection is given to the use of the 5 interlocking symbols, the motto of the International Olympic Committee (*Citius, altius, fortius*) and the words Olympiad, Olympiads, Olympian, Olympians, Olympic and Olympics. Although use of the Olympic trade marks is dealt with in much the same way as registered trade marks, the jurisdiction to sue for Olympic symbol right infringement stems from the Olympic Symbol etc (Protection) Act 1995. Infringement is any act of affixation to goods or the packaging thereof, incorporation in a flag or banner, offering or exposing for sale, putting on the market or stocking for those purposes goods which bear the protected symbol or words or whose packaging bears it, importation or exportation of goods which bear the symbol or words or whose packaging bears it, offering or supplying services under a sign which consists of or contains the symbol or protected words and use of the symbol or words on business papers or in advertising. The prohibited acts are only prohibited if carried out without the consent of the appointed proprietor (being the British Olympic Association whose registered offices are at 1 Wandsworth Plain, Wandsworth, London SW18 1EH: see art 2 Olympics Association Right (Appointment of Proprietor) Order 1995, SI 1995/2473) and a person is not liable for infringement if he uses the symbol or protected words as a result of a registered design right or a registered trade mark right. Neither is it an infringement to use the symbol or protected words if such use is part of a literary work, a dramatic work, a musical work, an artistic work, a sound recording, a film, a broadcast or a cable programme, within the meaning of Part I of the Copyright, Designs and Patents Act 1988 provided that such use is not intended to infringe or is not in relation to goods and services and is in accordance with honest practices in industrial or commercial matters. Further use is disregarded where the work is about the Olympic games or the Olympic movement and (where the use is in relation to goods) there is no intent to cause loss or benefit from gain. Finally if no association is created with the Olympic games or movement or the quality ordinarily associated with the games or the movement then there is no infringement. The usual rules relating to European (but not international) exhaustion of rights applies. Various other exceptions are set out in the controlling statute, such as prior use and so on.

The remedies are the usual ones being injunctions, delivery up and damages; and the Olympic rights are enforceable by way of criminal sanction as well as civil sanction. A claim in respect of Olympic symbols is required, by para 24 of the Practice Direction at **CPR PD 63**, to be brought in the Chancery Division or a county court where there is also a Chancery district registry. The claim form is required, by para 17, to be marked "Intellectual Property" in the top right-hand corner below the title of the court in which it is issued. Where an application is made under reg 5 of the Olympic Symbols Regulations the applicant must serve the claim form or application notice on all identifiable persons having an interest in the goods, materials or articles: see para 23 of the Practice Direction to CPR Part 63.

GENERAL NOTE ON THE ARTIST'S RESALE RIGHT REGULATIONS 2006, SI 2006/346

III PAT [55]

These Regulations (made to implement the Resale Rights Directive, 2001/84/EC) give artists and their successors certain royalty rights on a sliding scale, subject to a maximum amount of €12,500 and upon the resale of their creations where the piece is sold for more than €1,000. They do not confer any special jurisdiction on the civil courts but reg 15 gives the artist, or successor the right to obtain information about the terms of the resale within three years of the sale to which it relates and may apply to the county court for an order for that information to be supplied.

PERSONAL INJURY AND DEATH

TABLE OF CONTENTS

GENERAL NOTES ON PERSONAL INJURY LITIGATION

III PID [1]

Claim for personal injuries It is provided in **CPR 2.3** that 'claim for personal injuries' is to be interpreted in the Rules as 'proceedings in which there is a claim for damages in respect of personal injuries to the claimant or any other person or in respect of a person's death', and the term 'personal injuries' includes any disease and any impairment of a person's physical or mental condition.

III PID [2]

Pre-action practice in relation to claims for personal injury The introduction in 1998 of the Civil Procedure Rules was accompanied by the issue of a series of pre-action protocols, which were intended to guide the parties through an orderly exchange of information before the issue of proceedings, so as to narrow the issues and either to promote an early settlement or at least to help the efficient management of the case after issue. The court is reminded, in CPR 44.2(5)(a), of its power to take into account the conduct of the parties before and during the proceedings when exercising its discretion as to costs and, in particular the extent to which the parties have followed the Practice Direction (Pre-Action Conduct) at **PRO 1** in Volume 1 and any relevant pre-action protocol. Claimants who start proceedings which could have been avoided by following the protocols may as result be ordered to bear their own costs and to pay the other side's: *Burrows v Vauxhall Motors Ltd* [1997] 47 LS Gaz R 31, [1997] NLJR 1723, CA. In *Straker v Tudor Rose (a firm)* [2007] EWCA Civ 368, 151 Sol Jo LB 571, [2008] 2 Costs LR 205 the trial judge only awarded limited costs to the successful claimant despite the damages award exceeding the defendant's Part 36 payment. One of the reasons he gave was the claimant's failure to comply with para 1.4 of the Practice Direction (Pre-Action Conduct) as the claimant should have been more willing to negotiate a settlement. This was rejected on appeal, where it was held that the trial judge had started from the wrong place: as the claimant had beaten the defendant's Part 36 payment, the starting point was that he was entitled to his costs under the Part 36 provisions. The Court of Appeal held that it was mere speculation by the trial judge that the case would have settled had the claimant been more willing to negotiate. Furthermore, the defendant could have protected itself better by making a higher or further Part 36 payment which would have placed the claimant at risk of adverse cost consequences. See also the terms of CPR 36.17(2): '"more advantageous" means better in money terms by any amount'.

The relevant pre-action protocols for claims for personal injuries, clinical negligence and injuries causing death are:

- Pre-action Protocol for Personal Injury Claims at **III PID [42]** (including at para **III PID [42.4]** the Rehabilitation Code 2007);
- Pre-action Protocol for the Resolution of Clinical Disputes at **III PID [43]** (including at **III PID [43.2]** the protocol for obtaining hospital records);
- Pre-action Protocol for Disease and Illness Claims at **III PID [44]**;
- Pre-action Protocol for Low Value Personal Injury Claims in Road Traffic Accidents at **III PID [45]**;
- Pre-action Protocol for Low Value Personal Injury (Employers' Liability and Public Liability) Claims at **III PID [46]**.

The two Low Value protocols provide not only for certain procedural steps to be taken but also for fixed costs to apply in respect of claims that conclude either within the protocol process or after falling out of the protocol. See the Protocols below and CPR 45. However, claims which fall out of the protocol process and are subsequently allocated to the multi-track are no longer restricted to the fixed costs regime: *Qader v Esure Services Ltd* [2016] EWCA Civ 1109.

By the 75th Update to the CPR the Road Traffic Accident Pre-Action Protocol was amended in various respects for the purpose of ensuring that in personal injury claims to which the Protocol applied which were defined as 'soft tissue injury claims', the use and cost of medical reports were controlled, that in most cases only one medical report would be obtained, such a medical expert would be independent of any medical treatment provided to a claimant and offers were only made after a fixed cost medical report was obtained and disclosed. The introduction of this regime has involved the amendment of several CPR rules and practice directions. The new regime applies to claims in which the claim notification form was sent on or after 6 April 2015. These changes are mostly likely to affect whiplash type cases as well as other injuries which are medically defined as 'soft tissue' which fall within the Protocol. Another advantage of these changes is that they prevent insurers making low pre-medical evidence offers which would potentially result in under-settlement of claims.

III PID [2A]

Disclosure and inspection before the issue of the claim Sections 33 and 35 of the Senior Courts Act 1981, at **II SCA [33]** and **II SCA [35]**, empower the High Court to make orders on the application of a would-be claimant for the inspection, photographing and preservation of property, the taking of samples and the disclosure and production of documents. The county court has the same powers under sections 52 and 54 of the County Courts Act 1984, at **II CCA [31]** and **II CCA [33]**. An application for pre-action inspection etc of property should be made by application notice, in Form N244 and supported by evidence in accordance with **CPR 25.4** and **CPR 25.5**. An application for the pre-action disclosure and production of documents must comply with CPR 31.16 as well. A would-be claimant may also exercise his or her rights of access to personal data, conferred by s 7 of the Data Protection Act 1998, at **III DAT [17]**, and enforceable by the Information Commissioner or, under s 15, by the courts: see **III DAT [25]**. Pre-action access to medical notes and records is frequently obtained by this route. In cases where the would-be claimant is incapacitated or has died, rights of access may be exercised under s 3 of the Access to Health Records Act 1990. CPR Part 31 deals comprehensively with disclosure and inspection of documents (see **CPR 31.1** in Volume 1).

In *Personal Management Solutions Ltd v Gee 7 Group Ltd* [2015] EWHC 3859 (Ch) it was found that where an application for pre-action disclosure was only considered after a claim form had been issued, the court had no jurisdiction to allow such an application.

Although this was not the case on the facts, this may leave claimants facing an impending limitation bar with difficulties when applying for pre-action disclosure and then issuing a protective claim form.

One possible way around this problem is to issue a concurrent application under **CPR 31.12** with suitable evidence in support. However, although the Court would have jurisdiction to hear an application for specific disclosure it does not follow the Court will necessarily conclude any order for specific disclosure should be made before standard disclosure.

Particular rules apply to costs in applications for pre-action disclosure. See **CPR 46.1** and commentary thereon. Where the claim was commenced, but did not continue, under one of the Low Value Pre-Action Protocols, the fixed costs regime applies to the application: *Sharp v Leeds City Council* [2017] EWCA Civ 33.

III PID [2B]

Third party disclosure and inspection Sections 34 and 35 of the Senior Courts Act 1981, at **II SCA [34]** and **II SCA [35]**, and ss 53 and 54 of the County Courts Act 1984, at **II CCA [32]** and **II CCA [33]**, empower the High Court and the county courts to order the inspection, photographing and preservation of property in the hands of third parties and to order the disclosure of documents by third parties. These particular provisions are exercisable only in the case of claims for personal injury. An application notice is required, in Form N244, and evidence in support: see **CPR 25.4** and **CPR 25.5** and the provisions relating to access to documents in **CPR 31.17**.

III PID [2C]

Settlement offers before the issue of the claim Part 36 of the Rules makes special provision for offers to settle, which may be made pre-action or during proceedings. It enables, and in some cases requires, the court to impose particular financial sanctions in those circumstances where a Part 36 offer has been made, within the Rules, but not accepted. Part 36 was amended by The Civil Procedure (Amendment No 8) Rules 2014, which came into force on 6 April 2015, and the numbering of rules has therefore changed. The regime is applied, by CPR 36.7(1) to Part 36 offers made before the issue of proceedings and there are special rules for offers made under either of the Low Value Pre-Action Protocols: see **CPR 36.24**. As to contents, a Part 36 offer must make clear that it is made pursuant to Part 36 and must state whether it relates to the whole of the claim or just a specified part and whether it takes into account any counterclaim. It must also specify a period of not less than 21 days within which the defendant will be liable for the claimant's costs in accordance with rule **CPR 36.13** if the offer is accepted. A Part 36 offer may be withdrawn if not accepted within the specified period (21 days), but may be accepted later if not withdrawn: *Gibbon v Manchester City Council; LG Blower Specialist Bricklayer Ltd v Reeves* [2010] EWCA Civ 726, [2011] 2 All ER 258, [2010] 1 WLR 2081. Before 6 April 2015, if the offer stated that it would lapse if not accepted within the 21 day period it would not be considered to be a Part 36 offer and the consequences in **CPR 36.17** would not follow: *C v D* [2011] EWCA Civ 646; but for offers made on or after 6 April 2015, CPR 36.9 now permits an offer to be automatically withdrawn after the expiry of the relevant period in accordance with its terms. However, an unaccepted offer outside the scope of Part 36 still has some significance: it is taken into account under CPR 44.3 in the court's exercise of discretion as to awards of costs.

An offer to pay or accept a sum of money must be treated as inclusive of all interest down to the end of the relevant period. CPR 36.5(4) says:

'A Part 36 offer which offers to pay or offers to accept a sum of money will be treated as inclusive of all interest until:

(a) the date on which the period specified under rule 36.5(1)(c) expires; or
(b) if rule 36.5(2) applies, a date 21 days after the date the offer was made.'

On acceptance of a pre-action offer the liability for the costs of proceedings is to be treated as including such pre-action costs as would be allowed on a formal assessment: *Solomon v Cromwell Group plc* [2011] EWCA Civ 1584. A Part 36 offer may be made on Form N242A and will be treated as being made 'without prejudice except as to costs' under **CPR 36.16**. It is prudent to include these words at the top of any letter containing a Part 36 offer, so as to avoid the letter's accidental inclusion in the bundle of correspondence for the court. The consequences of failing to beat a Part 36 offer are found in **CPR 36.17**. The consequence to the defendant of not accepting a claimant's Part 36 offer where the claimant goes on to obtain judgment which is at least as advantageous as the offer should normally be an award of costs to the claimant on the indemnity basis from the expiry of the 21 days, together with interest on both those costs and any damages at a rate of up to 10% higher than base rate for the period after the 21 days, and an additional lump sum equal to 10% of the damages awarded up to damages of £500,000 and 5% of damages above £500,000 (subject to a maximum limit of £75,000). The consequence to the claimant of failing to obtain a judgment more advantageous than a defendant's Part 36 offer are that the defendant is entitled to its costs from the expiry of the 21 days together with interest (ie reversing the usual costs rule, against the otherwise successful claimant). For interest awards in respect of damages for personal injuries and fatal accidents in cases not covered by **CPR 36.17** see **CPR 16.4 [1.12]**.

The Civil Liability Act 2018 introduces a prohibition on the making of offers to settle certain personal injuries claims prior to the obtaining of medical evidence: see s 6. The Government's stated intention is that this legislation is to come into force with the rest of Part 1 of the Act in April 2020.

III PID [2D]

Admissions It is not unusual for a defendant, or a defendant's insurers, to make an admission of liability but to dispute the damages claimed. Sometimes defendants or insurers wish to withdraw an admission. The relevant rules are in CPR 14 and in the Practice Direction at **CPR PD 14**. The making and withdrawal of an admission before the start of proceedings is generally outside the rules: *Sowerby v Charlton* [2005] EWCA Civ 1610, [2006] 1 WLR 568, (2006) Times, 5 January, though such admission may be used in support of an application for summary judgment under **CPR 24**. However the position has been altered for personal injuries and clinical negligence cases by **CPR 14.1A** and **CPR 14.1B**, which now restrict a party's entitlement to withdraw certain pre-action admissions without the other party's consent or the court's permission, and entitle a party to seek judgment on the admission. For

PERSONAL INJURY AND DEATH

guidance on the exercise of the court's discretion to permit withdrawal, see para 7 of the Practice Direction at **CPR PD 14** and *Woodland (by her litigation friend) v Stopford* [2011] EWCA Civ 266, [2011] All ER (D) 185 (Mar); *Cavell v Transport for London* [2015] EWHC 2283 (QB), [2015] All ER (D) 36 (Aug); and *Wood v Days Healthcare UK Ltd* [2017] EWCA Civ 2097.

See the recent case of *Adriana Chimel v Damian Chibwana and Lloyd Williams* (2016) CC (Brighton) Judge Simpkiss 25/10/2016 regarding the status of admissions within the RTA Protocol. A defendant who had admitted liability within the portal for the RTA Protocol, albeit through the agency of his insurer, could not then bring a claim against the portal claimant which was inconsistent with that admission. However, an admission could not have any binding effect in regards to a subsequent claim between the portal defendant and a third party.

III PID [3]

Claim for personal injuries: the statement of case In order to assist in identifying the right track for a claim for personal injuries, the claimant is required, by **CPR 16.3**, to state the claim's value. All claimants must state that he/she expects to recover (i) not more than £10,000, (ii) more than £10,000 but not more than £25,000; (iii) more than £25,000; or (iv) that the claimant cannot say how much it likely to be recovered. In addition, in personal injuries claims the claimant must state whether he/she expects to recover not more than £1,000, or more than £1,000, in respect of damages for pain, suffering and loss of amenity. If the claim form is to be issued in the High Court, it must state that the claimant expects to recover more than £50,000 (CPR 16.3(5)(c)).

As regards the contents of the particulars of claim, note in particular the obligation to set out any claim for provisional damages and the grounds and also to include any claim for interest (**CPR 16.4**). Further provisions regarding personal injury claims and claims under the Fatal Accidents Act 1976 are set out in paragraphs 4 and 5 of the Practice Direction at **CPR PD 16**. Note, in particular, the requirements to state the claimant's date of birth and to attach a schedule of past and future expenses and losses. Where the claimant relies on the evidence of a medical practitioner a medical report must be attached to the particulars of claim.

There are two kinds of personal injury claim for which special procedures are provided. One is for mesothelioma cases, which are almost always based on the inhalation of asbestos dust at work. A detailed framework is provided for such litigation in Practice Direction 3D – Mesothelioma Claims at **CPR PD 3D**. The other is the Stage 3 procedure for low value personal injury claims in road traffic cases and also low value employers' and public liability cases where liability has been admitted. The assumption is that the Pre-action Protocol for such claims has been followed (**PRO 1** in Volume 1) but it has not been possible to agree the damages, or the agreement needs the court's approval because the claimant is a minor, or compliance with the protocol is not possible within the limitation period. For the purpose of Stage 3, the claim is presented to the court using the Part 8 procedure; and Practice Direction 8B, at **CPR PD 8B** must be observed

The RTA low value protocol applies from 30 April 2013 to claims up to £10,000 with substantially reduced fixed costs and from 31 July 2013 to claims up to £25,000.

III PID [3A]

Vicarious liability Vicarious liability has its origins in the law of 'master' and 'servant'. 'Every act which is done by a servant in the course of his duty is regarded as done by his master's orders and consequently is the same as if it were the master's own act': *Bartonshill Coal Co v McGuire* (1858) 3 Macq 300, at p 306, per Lord Chelmsford LC. This simple policy statement is carried through to today with two boundary lines drawn around vicarious liability: (1) the liability depends on the control exercisable by the employer or someone like an employer over the tortious offender and does not normally extend to the acts of independent contractors; and (2) even where the tort is committed by an employee it has to be in the course of employment. 'If he [the employee] was going on a frolic of his own, without being at all on his master's business, the master will not be liable': *Joel v Morrison* (1834) 6 C & P 501 at p 503. In the 21st century, however, the tendency has been to push vicarious liability out beyond its historic limits, in order, for example, to make churches and other institutions liable for acts of child abuse which were plainly contrary to the role for which the perpetrators, whether wardens or priests, were engaged: *Lister v Hesley Hall* [2002] 1 AC 215, [2011] 2 All ER 769; *Maga v Roman Catholic Archdiocese of Birmingham* [2010] EWCA Civ 256, [2010] PTSR 1618, (2010) Times, 25 March; *JGE v Trustees of the Portsmouth Roman Catholic Diocesan* [2012] EWCA Civ 938, [2012] IRLR 846, [2012] 30 LS Gaz R 20. See also *Catholic Child Welfare Society v Various Claimants* [2012] UKSC 56. In *XVW & YZA v Gravesend Grammar School for Girls and Adventure Life Signs Ltd* [2012] EWHC 575 (QB), [2012] All ER (D) 105 (Mar) three girls had been raped in Belize on a school trip by a third party assisting with the expedition, and their school and a specialist company which assisted in organising the expedition were not held variously liable. In *EL v Children's Society* [2012] EWHC 365 (QB), [2012] All ER (D) 08 (Mar) vicarious liability was not found in circumstances where sexual abuse was perpetrated into the 1950s by the houseparents' son. In *Weddall v*

Barchester Healthcare Ltd [2012] EWCA Civ 25, [2012] IRLR 307 the issue addressed was the liability of an employer for the intentional misconduct of an employee. Liability has been imposed upon trustees of a society for Jehovah's Witnesses for sexual assaults carried out by a ministerial servant and for the failure of the elders to take reasonable steps to protect the victim once they learnt of the abuse of another child (*A v The Trustees of the Watchtower Bible and Tract Society* [2015] EWHC 1722 (QB), 165 NLJ 7660, [2015] All ER (D) 249 (Jun)). In *Cox v Ministry of Justice* [2016] UKSC 10 the Supreme Court held that the prison authorities were vicariously liable for the negligent acts of a prisoner who was undertaking paid kitchen work at the time of acts. The court deemed the relationship between the prison and the prisoner to be 'akin to employment', thereby significantly extending the law on vicarious liability. In *Clive Bellman (A Protected Party by his litigation friend Nick Bellman) v Northampton Recruitment Ltd* [2018] EWCA Civ 2214 a company was held vicariously liable for an assault committed by its director and employee after a work Christmas party because there was sufficient connection between the assault and the position in which the director was employed to render the company liable under the principle of social justice. In a case arising out of an assault by an employee on a customer, the Supreme Court held the supermarket defendant liable and approved the 'close connection' test: *Mohamud v WM Morrison Supermarket plc* [2016] UKSC 11, [2016] All ER (D) 19 (Mar). Consideration was given to imposing vicarious liability on a bank for the sexual assaults of a doctor in the course of an examination on behalf of the bank in *Various Claimants v Barclays Bank plc* [2017] EWHC 1929. In *Armes v Nottinghamshire County Council* [2017] UKSC 60 the Supreme Court held that a local authority was vicariously liable for abuse perpetrated by foster parents with whom it had placed children in its care, applying the principles the court had recently identified in *Cox*. In *Razumas v Ministry of Justice* [2018] EWHC 215 (QB), however, the High Court found that the MOJ was not vicariously liable for negligent medical care carried out by healthcare services. That tort was not committed as a result of activity being taken by the healthcare providers on behalf of the MOJ, but on behalf of their contracting counterpart, the primary care trusts.

Vicarious liability for a third party's acts is distinct from a duty to take care to protect against the acts of a third party; see the consideration of such a duty in eg *Everett v Comojo (UK) Ltd (t/a The Metropolitan)* [2011] EWCA Civ 13, [2011] 4 All ER 315, [2012] 1 WLR 150.

Also distinct is the liability for the acts of a third party on the basis of a non-delegable duty of care. In the case of *Woodland v Essex County Council* [2013] UKSC 66, [2014] AC 537, [2014] 1 All ER 482, the Supreme Court summarised the factors that would give rise to the existence of a non-delegable duty of care. The local authority was found to have assumed a duty to ensure that the child claimant's swimming lessons were carefully conducted and supervised, by whomever it might get to perform those functions. The claimant was entrusted to the school for certain essential purposes, which included teaching and supervision. The swimming lessons were an integral part of the school's teaching function. They did not occur on school premises, but they occurred in school hours in a place where the school chose to carry out that part of its functions. The teaching and the supervisory functions of the school, and the control of the child that went with them, were delegated by the school to third parties, to the extent necessary to enable them to give swimming lessons. The alleged negligence occurred in the course of the very functions which the school assumed an obligation to perform and delegated to its contractors. It had to follow that if the latter were negligent in performing those functions and the claimant was injured as a result, the local authority was in breach of duty.

By contrast, in *Armes v Nottinghamshire County Council* [2017] UKSC 60, the Supreme Court held that the local authority did not owe a non-delegable duty to children in its care such as to render it liable for the abuse of foster parents with whom they had been placed by the local authority. The court held that the critical question, in deciding whether the local authority were in breach of a non-delegable duty in the present case, is whether the function of providing the child with day-to-day care, in the course of which the abuse occurred, was one which the local authority were themselves under a duty to perform with care for the safety of the child, or was one which they were merely bound to arrange to have performed, subject to a duty to take care in making and supervising those arrangements. As noted above, the court nonetheless held the local authority liable on the alternative basis of vicarious liability.

III PID [3B]

Time for issue and service Limitation periods are frequently relevant to the conduct of personal injury litigation and there is a large body of case law on the interpretation of the provisions of the Limitation Act 1980 and on the exercise of the discretionary powers conferred. These issues are considered fully in the title LIMITATION OF ACTIONS in Part III where the Limitation Act 1980 is set out and examined in detail (see para **III LIM [1]**). Note the three year time limit for personal injury claims, provided by s 11 of the Limitation Act 1980 at **III LIM [13]**. In the case of a living claimant the limitation period runs from the date on which the cause of action accrued or the date of knowledge, if later, and in the case of a claimant who has died before the expiry of the limitation period, it starts running again from the date of death or the date of the personal representative's knowledge, if later. Similar provision is made by s 12(2) for claims under the Fatal Accidents Act 1976 except that such a claim is barred by s 12(1) if barred by limitation during the claimant's lifetime. Similar provision is made, by s 11A, for product liability claims, with the addition of a 'long stop' which extinguishes any cause of action 10 years after 'the relevant time', as defined in s 4 of the Consumer Protection Act 1987. The date of knowledge is defined in s 14 of the Limitation Act 1980 and s 33 enables the court, in its discretion, to override the time bars in ss 11 and 11A and, in limited circumstances, 12. There is much case law on the interpretation and application of these provisions and it is summarised in notes to those sections at **III LIM [13]**, **III LIM [14]** and **III LIM [15]**.

Claims for personal injuries are often issued close to the expiry of the limitation period and so long as the claim forms (and particulars of claim) are properly served within the time allowed by **CPR 7.5**, the action can proceed. But problems will arise if, at the time the limitation period runs out, the appropriate defendants are no longer available for service or if the purported service turns out to be invalid. The court may, as a matter of discretion, extend the time for service under **CPR 7.6** and may, in exceptional circumstances, dispense with service altogether under **CPR 6.16**. But the court will need persuading, by cogent evidence that the claimant's solicitors did all they reasonably could to serve in time. Here again there is much case law on the exercise of discretion and it is covered in Volume 1 in notes to **CPR 6.16** and **CPR 7.6**.

III PID [3C]

Allocation to track The financial limit for the Small Claims Track is usually £10,000, but in the case of personal injury claims, in addition the value of the claim for damages for pain, suffering and loss of amenity should not be more than £1,000: **CPR 26.6**. The government has however indicated an intention to increase this limit, in particular, that the small claims limit will increase to £5,000 for RTA claims (excluding vulnerable road users) and to £2,000 for all other personal injury claims. It is possible but not guaranteed that the changes will come into effect in April 2020, which is the government's stated date for implementation of Part 1 of the Civil Liability Act 2018. Claims with a higher value are normally put on the Fast Track unless the value exceeds £25,000, in which case the matter will be allocated to the Multi-track. The court has a discretion to allocate to a track that is higher or lower than normal, having regard to the characteristics of the particular case identified in **CPR 26.8** and the pre-existing restriction on allocating down without consent has been removed.

III PID [3D]

Expert evidence The rules on expert evidence are set out in **CPR 35** and supported by the Practice Direction at **CPR PD 35**. Note also the Protocol for the Instruction of Experts, at **CPR 35 PRO**. Paragraph 13.5 of the protocol requires the expert to assert, in his or her report that he, or she, understands the duty to the court and requirements of the rules in Part 35. The special statement of truth that should come at the end of the report is mandatory. The court has the duty and power to restrict expert evidence, including the power to direct that evidence be given by a single joint expert: **CPR 35**, **CPR 35.4** and **CPR 35.7**. Restrictions and conditions are frequently imposed when a party wishes to withdraw the report of one expert in favour of a more favourable report by another. Relevant case law is summarised in the notes to **CPR 35.4**.

III PID [4]

Assessment of damages for personal injury In order to put a value on a claim for personal injuries it is usual to distinguish between two different heads of claim: (a) general damages, principally those for pain and suffering and loss of amenity; and (b) special damages and future financial losses, such as claims for loss of earnings, care and assistance and medical treatment. In relation to (b), one must consider monies recoverable to reimburse the state for benefits received as a result of the accident: see the Social Security (Recovery of Benefits) Act 1997 at **III PID [27]**. If the claimant has had the benefit of treatment under the National Health Service the defendant may have to pay NHS charges in accordance with ss 150–169 of the Health and Social Care (Community Health and Standards) Act 2003 but this payment does not come off the damages. Interest will be awarded in respect of all past losses.

Guidelines for general damages for pain, suffering and loss of amenity are set out in the Judicial College Guidelines for Assessment of Damages for Personal Injury, currently in its 14th edition. An increase in general damages for pain, suffering and loss of amenity of 10% falls to be applied unless the claimant entered into a conditional fee agreement before 1 April 2013: *Simmons v Castle (No 2)* [2012] EWCA Civ 1288, [2013] 1 All ER 334, [2013] 1 WLR 1239. The Guidelines provide figures with and without this uplift. The uplift is not discretionary and it must be applied to all awards of general damages even where the claimant is legally aided: *Summers v Bundy* [2016] EWCA Civ 126. The Civil Liability Act 2018 introduces fixed tariffs for compensation in 'whiplash' claims: see s 3. The government's stated intention is the changes shall come into force in April 2020 before which date the precise tariff will need to be fixed.

As regards the cost of future care there are likely to be great uncertainties which may make the award of a final lump sum less appropriate than either a provisional award (**III PID [5]**) or periodical payments (**III PID [5A]**). In respect of future losses generally, where a single lump sum is chosen as the best way of providing compensation, the Ogden tables provide multipliers that take account of mortality rates and other contingencies where appropriate. In 2001, the Lord Chancellor set the assumed discount rate to apply when selecting a multiplier at 2.5% by the Damages (Personal Injury) Order 2001, SI 2001/2301 under s 1 of the Damages Act 1996. By the Damages (Personal Injury) Order 2017, SI 2017/206 the discount rate was lowered by the Lord Chancellor to minus 0.75%, as from 20 March 2017. The Civil Liability Act 2018 introduces new provisions as to the determination of the discount rate. A first review must commence within 90 days of Royal Assent, ie on or before 19 March 2019. The review will be conducted by reference to the new process detailed in the Act. The first review must be completed and the Lord Chancellor must determine the new rate within 140 days of the review commencing, ie on or before 6 August 2019. The Lord Chancellor has the power to make an order which will prescribe different rates of return for different classes of case. See further comment on the Ogden tables at **III PID [13.7]** and on the assumed rate of interest at **III PID [24.1]**.

III PID [4A]

Assessment of damages where the tortious event occurs abroad Under Part III of the Private International Law (Miscellaneous Provisions) Act 1995, the general rule in respect of choice of law for personal injuries cases was that the applicable law is the law of the country where the injury was sustained, though this general rule could be displaced. However, the assessment of damages was treated as a matter of procedure, which was governed by the law of the forum (see s 14(3) of the 1995 Act, as interpreted in *Harding v Wealands* [2006] UKHL 32, [2007] 2 AC 1, [2006] 4 All ER 1). See also *Cox v Ergo Versicherung AG (formerly known as Victoria)* [2014] UKSC 22, [2014] AC 1379, [2014] 2 WLR 948. The power of the court under the Senior Courts Act 1981, s 35A to award interest on damages was to be characterised as a remedy and was governed by the law of the forum: *Maher v Groupama Grand Est* [2009] EWCA Civ 1191, [2009] All ER (D) 143 (Nov).

However, Regulation (EC) 864/2007, known as 'Rome II', supersedes the 1995 Act (see s 15A of the Act). This applies to accidents occurring after 11 January 2009: *Homawoo v GMF Assurances SA (C-412/10)* (ECJ). Rome II applies regardless of whether the accident takes place in an EU member state or outside the EU (Art 3). Under Rome II, the law in respect of the assessment of damages has been changed, contrary to the position in *Harding*, as Art 15 provides: 'The law applicable to non-contractual obligations under this Regulation shall govern in particular: . . . (c) the existence, the nature and the assessment of damage or the remedy claimed'. Article 4 of Rome II provides the general rule as to applicable law: 'Unless otherwise provided for in this Regulation, the law applicable to a non-contractual obligation arising out of a tort/delict shall be the law of the country in which the damage occurs irrespective of the country in which the event giving rise to the damage occurred and irrespective of the country or countries in which the indirect consequences of that event occur.' It provides exceptions where both parties have their habitual residence in the same country, 'where it is clear from all the circumstances of the case that the tort/delict is manifestly more closely connected with a [different] country', or where the parties reach an agreement as to choice of law. On the application of the exceptions, see, for instance, *Winrow v Hemphill* [2014] EWHC 3164 (QB). Rome II also has specific provisions relating to product liability.

Accordingly, now the general rule is that the assessment of damages is governed by the law of the country where the accident occurred. However the burden of pleading and proving that foreign law in fact differs from English law falls on the party seeking to rely on the foreign law.

While Rome II applies to the nature and assessment of damages, it does not apply to matters of 'evidence or procedure' (Art 1(3)). These are to be governed by the law of the forum. Accordingly, in an English case about a motorcyclist injured in France, French procedure in respect of expert evidence, in which the court appointed a single expert whose report should include the views of other experts and who there was only a limited opportunity to cross-examine, was not to be adopted; the English court is not seeking to achieve exactly the same award of damages as would have be made had the claim been tried by a French judge: *Wall v Mutuelle de Poitiers Assurances* [2014] EWCA Civ 138, [2014] 3 All ER 340, [2014] 1 WLR 4263. The law on the assessment of damages includes practice, conventions and guidelines (such as in England and Wales the 'Judicial College Guidelines for the Assessment of General Damages in Personal Injury Cases'), rather than these being matters of 'evidence or procedure': *Syred v Powszecnny Zaklad Ubezpieczen (PZU) SA* [2016] EWHC 254 (QB). The application of a particular discount rate when calculating future loss is a matter of the assessment of damages rather than evidence or procedure: *Stylianou v Toyoshima* [2013] EWHC 2188 (QB). On the approach to awarding interest, see *AS Latvijas Krajbanka (in liq) v Antonov* [2016] EWHC 1679 (Comm).

Where a claim is brought in England and Wales by a UK resident against the UK Motor Insurers' Bureau in respect of an accident that occurred in another member state, the compensation due should be assessed by reference to the law of that state and not by reference to English law: *Moreno v Motor Insurers' Bureau* [2016] UKSC 52, [2016] 1 WLR 3194, [2016] RTR 26, [2017] 4 All ER 28.

It remains to be seen what effect the United Kingdom's exit from the EU (pending at time of writing) will have on these matters.

However, even in cases governed by the Private International Law (Miscellaneous Provisions) Act 1995, rather than Rome II, the law of the forum does not necessarily determine the amount of the award. Where a widow's claim under the Fatal Accidents Act 1976 is based on a fatal accident in another country, the law of that country must be applied in the assessment if the substantive remedy is different from the remedy in England and Wales: *Cox v Ergo Versicherung AG* [2012] EWCA Civ 854, [2012] All ER (D) 168 (Jun), Smith LJ dissenting.

III PID [4B]

Assessment of damages on death Where the would-be claimant dies, the cause of action in respect of pain and suffering and loss of amenity survives, but only as regards the period of shortened life: there is no right to compensation for loss of future happiness or earnings: see s 1 of the Law Reform (Miscellaneous Provisions) Act 1934 at **III PID [8]**. If the death was caused by the tortious act, the personal representatives of the estate may claim on behalf of the dependants for their loss of dependency (the financial support the claimant would have provided) and funeral expenses. In assessing the damages for loss of dependency the Ogden tables may assist in determining the multiplier; and the assumed rate of interest will normally be as provided under the Damages Act 1976, as with non-fatal personal injuries claims: see **III PID [4]**.

In addition, the surviving spouse, or civil partner, is entitled to a fixed sum, currently £12,980 for bereavement; and, on the death of an unmarried minor, the bereavement money is payable to the parents or, if the child is born outside wedlock, to the mother. All this is considered in detail at **III PID [10]** to **III PID [15]** in ss 1 to 5 of the Fatal Accidents Act 1976 and the notes to those sections.

III PID [5]

Provisional damages Section 32A of the Senior Courts Act 1981 empowers the High Court to award provisional damages: see **II SCA [32]** and **II CCA [30]** for the equivalent provision in s 51 of the County Courts Act 1984. The purpose is to provide for the situation where, at the date of assessment, there is proved or admitted to be a chance that the claimant may later develop some serious disease or deterioration. In order to invoke this jurisdiction, the claimant must comply with the rules at **CPR 41.1** to **CPR 41.3A** and Practice Direction 41A – Provisional Damages. The particulars of claim must include a claim for provisional damages and the claimant must satisfy the court that the statutory conditions for a provisional award have been met. The court should then make an order in the form annexed to the Practice Direction with two main parts (1) an award of damages made on the assumption that the claimant will not develop a specified disease or type of deterioration and (2) the right to apply, within a specified period, for additional damages if the assumption proves false and the claimant develops the specified disease or type of deterioration.

III PID [5A]

Periodical payments Traditionally the courts have compensated injured claimants by the award of a single lump sum, based on conclusions about his or her probable life span and the shortening of it by the tortious act. There is clearly room for error in reaching these conclusions but no mechanism for correcting the error in the light of subsequent events, so long as the court was correct in its approach. This problem was addressed in the Damages Act 1996, s 2 of which empowers the courts to compensate future pecuniary loss by including an order for periodical payments in the award. This section, at **III PID [25]**, has been supplemented by the addition of s 2A and 2B and the making of an order to allow for the variation of the periodical payments in certain circumstances: see the Damages (Variation of Periodical Payments) Order 2005, SI 2005/84. The procedural requirements governing the making and variation of orders for periodical payments are set out in rules at **CPR 41.4** to **CPR 41.10** and in Practice Direction 41B – Periodical Payments under the Damages Act 1996, which is set out at **CPR PD 41B**.

III PID [5B]

Offers to settle Settlement offers within Part 36 may be made before the start of proceedings and the legal implications of such offers are considered at **III PID [2C]** and much of the commentary there applies equally to offers made once proceedings have begun. Points of particular importance are:

- Part 36 of the Rules makes special provision for formal offers which comply with the Rules: it enables, and in some cases requires, the court to impose particular sanctions in terms of interest and costs in those circumstances where a Part 36 offer has been made, within the Rules, but not accepted.
- As to contents, a Part 36 offer must make clear that it is made pursuant to Part 36 and must state whether it relates to the whole of the claim or just a specified part and whether it takes into account any counterclaim. It must also specify a period of not less than 21 days within which the defendant will be liable for the claimant's costs in accordance with rule **CPR 36.13** if the offer is accepted.
- Part 36 offers may be made in respect of intimated claims before proceedings are begun. However, once proceedings have begun, a Part 36 offer did not apply to a claim advanced in draft amended pleadings: *Hertel v Saunders* [2018] EWCA Civ 1831.
- In relation to an offer made prior to 6 April 2015, if the offer states that it will lapse if not accepted within the 21 day period it will not be a Part 36 offer and the associated consequences will not follow: *C v D* [2010] EWHC 2940 (Ch), [2011] 2 All ER 404, [2011] 1 WLR 331. However, an unaccepted offer outside the scope of Part 36 will still have some significance: it will be taken into account under CPR 44.3 in the court's exercise of discretion as to awards of costs.
- A Part 36 offer may be withdrawn if not accepted within the specified period (21 days), but may be accepted later if not withdrawn: *Gibbon v Manchester City Council; LG Blower Specialist Bricklayer Ltd v Reeves* [2010] EWCA Civ 726, [2011] 2 All ER 258, [2010] 1 WLR 2081. A court can give permission for an offer to be withdrawn after it has been accepted but would only do so in rare cases where the offeror can establish that circumstances have arisen that are so different from those contemplated when the offer was made that it would be appropriate to permit him to withdraw it: *Paul Ernest Milton v Schlegel Ltd* [2015] unreported.
- An offer to pay or accept a sum of money must be treated as inclusive of all interest down to the end of the relevant period: CPR 36.5(4).
- A Part 36 offer may be made on Form N242A and will be treated as being made WITHOUT PREJUDICE SAVE AS TO COSTS, under **CPR 36.16**. It is prudent to include these words at the top of any letter containing a Part 36 offer, so as to avoid the letter's accidental inclusion in the bundle of correspondence for the court.
- The consequences of failing to beat a Part 36 offer are found in **CPR 36.17**. The consequence to the defendant of not accepting a claimant's Part 36 offer where the claimant goes on to obtain judgment which is at least as advantageous as the offer should normally be an award of costs to the claimant on the indemnity basis from the expiry of the 21 days, together with interest on both those costs and any damages at a rate of up to 10% higher than base rate for the period after the 21 days, and an additional lump sum equal to 10% of the damages awarded up to damages of £500,000 and 5% of damages above £500,000 (subject to a maximum limit of £75,000). The normal consequences to the claimant of failing to obtain a judgment more advantageous than a defendant's Part 36 offer are that the defendant is entitled to its costs from the expiry of the 21 days together with interest (ie reversing the usual costs rule, against the otherwise successful claimant). The court considered when it might be appropriate to depart from the normal consequences in *Alan Yentob v MGN Ltd* [2015] EWCA Civ 1292. In *Briggs v CEF Holdings Ltd* 13 June 2017, unreported, the claimant accepted an earlier offer following an improvement in the prognosis of his injuries. The Court allowed the defendant's appeal, because the claimant had failed to show that the usual costs order was unjust. The Court stated that cases were fact specific, but the improved prognosis was part of the usual risks of litigation. In *Thakkar v Patel* [2017] EWCA Civ 117, the defendants were ordered to pay 75% of the claimant's costs despite the defendant's having made and withdrawn a higher Part 36 offer on the basis: (a) the offer was withdrawn before disclosure and exchange of statements so that the claimants had not been properly able to assess the overall value of the claim; and (b) while not amounting to an outright refusal to mediate, a real prospect of settlement was lost by the defendant's conduct in 'dragging their feet'. For interest awards in respect of damages for personal injuries and fatal accidents in cases not covered by **CPR 36.17** see CPR **16.4 [1.12]**. More generally, in *Marathon Asset Management LLP v Seddon* [2017] EWHC 479 (Comm), the Court stated that interest on costs are not to be awarded in excess of a normal commercial rate. However in *OMV Petrom SA v Glencore International AG* [2017] EWCA Civ 195 it was held that Part 36 consequences are not merely compensatory, and on the facts of the case the trial judge's award to the claimant of enhanced interest at less than 10% was overturned and increased to 10%. In *Webb v Liverpool Women's NHS Foundation Trust* [2016] EWCA Civ 365, the Court of Appeal overturned an order depriving a claimant of part of her costs where she had beaten her own Part 36 offer; it was held that an effective Part 36 offer curtails the court's discretion to deprive the successful claimant of part of its costs to reflect a lack of success on one or more issues, contrary to previous authority.

The provisions of Part 36 were amended by the Civil Procedure (Amendment No 8) Rules 2014. The revised Part 36 applies to offers made on or after 6 April 2015. Important amendments are:

- Time limited Part 36 offers that are automatically withdrawn after the expiry of the relevant period are permissible under rule CPR 36.9(4)(b).
- Under CPR 36.16, a judge may be told of the existence, but not the terms, of a Part 36 offer after judgment has been given on a preliminary issue. This assists a judge to make a determination about the costs relating to the preliminary issue.
- CPR 36.17(5)(e) requires that when the court is considering whether it would be unjust to order the usual Part 36 cost consequences, the court must take into account whether the offer was a genuine attempt to settle the proceedings. This is intended to apply in cases where the claimant has made a very high offer to settle, indicating an unwillingness to compromise, but has obtained judgment for a slightly higher sum. Prior to this amendment, this situation had been considered in *AB v CD* [2011] EWHC 602 (Ch), [2011] IP & T 504, [2011] All ER (D) 25 (Apr), where the High Court held that a claimant's Part 36 offer had to contain some genuine element of concession that was of significant value in the context of the litigation. In *Huck v Robson* [2002] EWCA Civ 398, [2003] 1 WLR 1340, [2002] All ER (D) 316 (Mar) a claimant's offer for 95% of the value of the claim had been considered valid. Following the amendment, it is not apparent that a very different approach has been taken. In *Jockey Club Racecourse Ltd v Willmott Dixon Construction Ltd* [2016] EWHC 167 (TCC), a 95% offer was effective in an open-and-shut case. See also *JMX (a child by his mother and litigation friend, FMX) v Norfolk and Norwich Hospitals NHS Foundation Trust* [2018] EWHC 185 (QB).
- CPR 36.2(3) states expressly that a Part 36 offer may be made in respect of a counterclaim or other additional claim and CPR 36.4 clarifies how Part 36 applies to appeals. There had previously been some confusion as to how the rules should apply in these situations.
- CPR 36.9(5) states that where an offeror changes the terms of an offer to make it more advantageous to the offeree, it is treated as a new offer rather than the withdrawal of the original offer.
- CPR 36.13(5) requires courts to make the usual costs order where a Part 36 offer is accepted late unless it would be unjust to do so. This wording has slightly changed from the earlier version, but this brings the CPR in line with the position that had developed in the case law and it has been confirmed that the proper approach to be taken has not changed (*Lumb v Hampsey* [2011] EWHC 2808 (QB), [2012] All ER (D) 18 (Feb); *RXDX (proceeding by his mother and litigation friend DXSX) v Northampton Borough Council* [2015] EWHC 1677 (QB), 165 NLJ 7658, [2015] All ER (D) 167 (Jun); *Purser (Gemma) v Hibbs (Robert)* [2015] EWHC 1792 (QB)).

III PID [5C]

Interim payments Provision is made for the ordering of interim payments under s 32 of the Senior Courts Act 1981 at **II SCA [31]** and s 51 of the County Courts Act 1984 at **II CCA [29]** and the rules in Volume 1 at **CPR 25.6** – **CPR 25.9**. A checklist for applying for an interim payment in a personal injury case is provided in the Practice Direction 25B – Interim Payments at **CPR PD 25B.1** onwards. Evidence must be filed dealing with:

- the sum of money sought by way of interim payment;
- the items or matters in respect of which the interim payment is sought;
- the sum of money for which final judgment is likely to be given;
- the reasons for believing that the conditions set out rule 25.7 are satisfied (the main conditions are that liability is admitted or the subject of a judgment or that the claimant would obtain judgment for a substantial amount of damages if the claim went to trial);
- any other relevant matters (such as contributory negligence and the exhibiting of medical reports);
- details of special damages and past and future loss; and
- in a claim under the Fatal Accidents Act 1976 details of the persons on whose behalf the claim is made and the nature of the claim.

Note also the requirement to file a copy of any Compensation Recovery Payment certificate in accordance with **CPR PD 25B.4** and that the court must not order an interim payment of more than a reasonable proportion of the likely amount of the final judgment: **CPR 25.7**. *FP v Taunton & Somerset NHS Trust* [2012] EWHC 3380 (QB) addresses the issue as to how to calculate an interim payment in a major claim where there is likely to be a periodical payments order. A more recent example is the case of *Sellar-Elliott v Howling* [2016] EWHC 443 (QB) where permission to appeal against an interim payment order of £100,000 was refused in a clinical negligence case where causation was in dispute.

Two recent examples of cases where significant interim payments have been ordered in personal injury cases in which claimants required money in order to move into specialist accommodation are: *Flanagan v Battie* [2017] EWHC 3044 (QB) and *Porter v Barts Health NHS Trust* [2017] EWHC 3205 (QB).

III PID [5D]

Success fees The statutory foundation for including success fees in conditional fee arrangements and making them recoverable from the unsuccessful defendant was in ss 58 and 58A of the Courts and Legal Services Act 1990, as inserted by s 27 of the Access to Justice Act 1999. For the text and commentary see **III FUND [26]** and the notes at **III FUND [26.1]** to **III FUND [26.7]**. However this has changed since the coming into force, on 1 April 2013, of ss 44 to 48 of the Legal Aid, Sentencing and Punishment of Offenders Act 2012. The text of these sections is set out at **III FUND [161]—III FUND [165]**, making success fees recoverable from the client instead of from the unsuccessful defendant (subject to a cap in personal injuries cases of 25% of the claimant's past loss and general damages). In cases where the claimant's right of recovery from the defendant is removed by the legislative change the claimant will have the benefit of the 10% uplift under *Simmons v Castle* [2012] EWCA Civ 1039, [2012] All ER (D) 335 (Jul). The uplift will not affect those cases where the claimant's success fees are recoverable under the old law: *Simmons v Castle (No 2)* [2012] EWCA Civ 1288, [2013] 1 All ER 334, [2013] 1 WLR 1239. CPR 21.12, which relates to the payment of success fees from damages awarded to claimants lacking capacity, was amended by the Civil Procedure (Amendment No 8) Rules 2014 with effect from 6 April 2015.

In *Budana v Leeds Teaching Hospitals NHS Trust* [2017] EWCA Civ 1980 the Court of Appeal considered the purported transfer of a conditional fee agreement between two firms of solicitors in respect of a personal injury claim. It held that the transfer had resulted in a novated contract rather than an assignment, but, for the purposes of the transitional provisions of the Legal Aid, Sentencing and Punishment of Offenders Act 2012, s 44(6), the success fee payable to the new firm of solicitors was payable under the conditional fee agreement by the defendants. Where there were assignments of a CFA to successive legal entities due to organisational changes within the firm: see *Plevin v Paragon Personal Finance Ltd* [2017] UKSC 23.

In *Coventry v Lawrence* [2015] UKSC 50, 165 NLJ 7663, [2015] All ER (D) 234 (Jul), a majority of the Supreme Court ruled that a successful claimant's right, under the regime existing before 1 April 2013, to recover from the defendant any success fee agreed pursuant to a conditional fee agreement entered and any premium paid for an after-the-event insurance policy does not breach the right to a fair trial under Article 6 of the European Convention on Human Rights.

In *BNM v MGN Ltd* [2017] EWCA Civ 1767, the Court of Appeal held that the new proportionality rules contained in the CPR 44.3(2) and CPR 44.3(5) did not apply on a standard basis of assessment to a 'pre-commencement funding arrangement' as defined in CPR 48.1. Instead, the former proportionality test contained in the old CPR 44.4(2) applied. Costs orders could therefore include provision for payment of success fees payable under conditional fee agreements and premiums payable under after-the-event insurance policies.

For a post-2013 case where the court reduced the solicitors' success fee payable by the client, see *Herbert v HH Law Ltd* [2018] EWHC 580 (QB) (note: appeal to the Court of Appeal pending).

III PID [5E]

Referral fees Sections 56–60 of the Legal Aid, Sentencing and Punishment of Offenders Act 2012, at **III FUND [173]—III FUND [176]**, have paved the way for rules and regulations to make contracts for the payment of referral fees unenforceable. The policy is to 'ban' the making of agreements for fees to be paid by regulated persons, typically personal injury practitioners, to agencies such as claims management businesses in return for the referral of clients with a claim. These sections contemplate the making of regulations by the Treasury to empower the Financial Services Authority to monitor and enforce compliance and rules, to the same end, by the General Council of the Bar, the Law Society and the Claims Management Regulator. See now the Legal Aid, Sentencing and Punishment of Offenders Act 2012 (Referral Fees) Regulations 2013.

Section 58 of the Criminal Justice and Courts Act 2015 prohibits regulated persons from offering inducements in relation to personal injury claims.

III PID [6]

Compensation Act 2006 The provisions of the Compensation Act 2006 have particular relevance to personal injury litigation. Section 1 requires a court, when determining whether the defendant should have taken certain steps to meet a standard of care in a case of negligence or breach of statutory duty, to have regard also to whether such steps might prevent or discourage a desirable activity. Section 2 provides that an apology or offer of treatment or redress is not, without more, to amount to an admission of liability. Section 3 provides for mesothelioma cases where it is unclear to what extent the disease was caused or aggravated by more than one negligent party. The section fixes them all with joint and several liability. The remaining sections of the Act tackle the perceived problem of claims management businesses which offer damages recovery services on exploitative terms. The Act makes such businesses unlawful unless authorised and regulated.

III PID [7]

Costs protection for claimants As part of the package of reforms in which recovery of success fees from defendants was removed, claimants were given some protection against adverse costs orders in personal injuries cases. The regime is called Qualified One Way Costs Shifting and the relevant rules, and commentary thereon, are found at CPR 44.13–CPR 44.17. This protection does not apply where the claimant has entered into a conditional fee agreement prior to 1 April 2013 (for consideration of the transitional provisions, see *Catalano v Espley-Tyas Development Group* [2017] EWCA Civ 1132). Various exceptions apply, as set out in the rules, such as where the claim is fundamentally dishonest (on which see *Howlett v Davies* [2017] EWCA Civ 1696). On whether a claim against the Motor Insurers Bureau falls within this regime, see *Howe v MIB* [2017] EWCA Civ 932.

III PID [7A]

Precedents There is a whole range of precedents for personal injury claims in **BCCP Division M**, covering a wide variety of situations as well as precedents for defences and a variety of interlocutory applications. Precedents for clinical negligence litigation are set out separately in **BCCP Division N**.

LAW REFORM (MISCELLANEOUS PROVISIONS) ACT 1934

(c 41)

III PID [8]

1. Effect of death on certain causes of action

(1) Subject to the provisions of this section, on the death of any person after the commencement of this Act all causes of action subsisting against or vested in him shall survive against, or, as the case may be, for the benefit of, his estate. Provided that this subsection shall not apply to causes of action for defamation.

(1A) The right of a person to claim under section 1A of the Fatal Accidents Act 1976 (bereavement) shall not survive for the benefit of his estate on his death.

(2) Where a cause of action survives as aforesaid for the benefit of the estate of a deceased person, the damages recoverable for the benefit of the estate of that person—

(a) shall not include—

(i) any exemplary damages;

(ii) any damages for loss of income in respect of any period after that person's death;

(b) [. . .]

(c) where the death of that person has been caused by the act or omission which gives rise to the cause of action, shall be calculated without reference to any loss or gain to his estate consequent on his death, except that a sum in respect of funeral expenses may be included.

(3) [. . .]

(4) Where damage has been suffered by reason of any act or omission in respect of which a cause of action would have subsisted against any person if that person had not died before or at the same time as the damage was suffered, there shall be

deemed, for the purposes of this Act, to have been subsisting against him before his death such cause of action in respect of that act or omission as would have subsisted if he had died after the damage was suffered.

(5) The rights conferred by this Act for the benefit of the estates of deceased persons shall be in addition to and not in derogation of any rights conferred on the dependants of deceased persons by the Fatal Accidents Acts 1976 to 1988 and so much of this Act as relates to causes of action against the estates of deceased persons shall apply in relation to causes of action under the said Acts as it applies in relation to other causes of action not expressly excepted from the operation of subsection (1) of this section.

(6) In the event of the insolvency of an estate against which proceedings are maintainable by virtue of this section, any liability in respect of the cause of action in respect of which the proceedings are maintainable shall be deemed to be a debt provable in the administration of the estate, notwithstanding that it is a demand in the nature of unliquidated damages arising otherwise than by a contract, promise or breach of trust.

(7) [. . .]

III PID [8.1]

Damages for pain between injury and death Although damages for pain generally survive for the benefit of the estate, courts have previously been reluctant to award damages for a period of suffering which is so short that it should be regarded as part of the death itself: see for example *Hicks v Chief Constable of South Yorkshire Police* [1992] 2 All ER 65, HL. However, the position at present appears to be that courts are able to make a general damages award for 'Injuries Resulting in Death' in circumstances where death results through immediate unconsciousness to full consciousness using the Judicial College Guidelines. This is arguably in tension with *Hicks* when it comes to making awards for death arising within a short period of time after injury.

In *Shaw v Kovac* [2017] EWCA Civ 1028, a claim for clinical negligence, the Court of Appeal observed that if a patient's suffering was increased by the knowledge that his personal autonomy had been invaded through want of informed consent, it could be reflected in the award of general damages for pain, suffering and loss of amenity.

III PID [8.2]

Future loss of earnings The Administration of Justice Act 1982 s 4(2) inserted the provision in s 1(2)(a)(ii) which prevents future loss of earnings surviving for the benefit of the estate. It applies to causes of action accruing on or after 1 January 1983; s 73(4) of the Administration of Justice Act 1982 so provides. As regards causes of action accruing before that date claims for future loss of earnings may still survive in accordance with *Gammell v Wilson* [1982] AC 27, [1981] 1 All ER 578, HL. In calculating the sum to be deducted for living expenses, when calculating loss of earnings, the court should assess the proportion of net earnings the earner would have spent on maintaining himself: *Harris v Empress Motors Ltd* [1983] 3 All ER 561, [1984] 1 WLR 212, CA; *Phipps v Brooks Dry Cleaning Services Ltd* (1996) 140 Sol Jo LB 173, CA.

III PID [8.3]

Unborn claimant Pre-birth injuries may provide the basis for a claim in accordance with the Congenital Disabilities (Civil Liability) Act 1976. They may also be actionable at common law: *Burton v Islington Health Authority*: *de Martell v Merton and Sutton Health Authority* [1993] QB 204, [1992] 3 All ER 833, CA. The claim is, in either case, conditional upon the claimant being born alive. However, a child has no cause of action for pain and suffering consequent upon being born disabled on account of any negligent failure to abort the foetus before birth: *McKay v Essex AHA* [1983] QB 1166.

III PID [8.4]

Death of claimant after start of proceedings On the death of the claimant an application should be made for the executors or administrators to continue the action on behalf of the estate. However, since the cause of action survives, steps taken between the death and the obtaining of the order are not invalid: *Fielding v Rigby* [1993] 4 All ER 294, [1993] 1 WLR 1355, CA (decided under the pre-CPR rules).

PERSONAL INJURY AND DEATH

LAW REFORM (CONTRIBUTORY NEGLIGENCE) ACT 1945

(c 28)

III PID [9]

1. Apportionment of liability in case of contributory negligence

(1) Where any person suffers damage as the result partly of his own fault and partly of the fault of any other person or persons, a claim in respect of that damage shall not be defeated by reason of the fault of the person suffering the damage, but the damages recoverable in respect thereof shall be reduced to such extent as the court thinks just and equitable having regard to the claimant's share in the responsibility for the damage:

Provided that—

(a) this subsection shall not operate to defeat any defence arising under a contract;

(b) where any contract or enactment providing for the limitation of liability is applicable to the claim, the amount of damages recoverable by the claimant by virtue of this subsection shall not exceed the maximum limit so applicable.

(2) Where damages are recoverable by any person by virtue of the foregoing subsection subject to such reduction as is therein mentioned, the court shall find and record the total damages which would have been recoverable if the claimant had not been at fault.

(3), (4) [. . .]

(5) Where, in any case to which subsection (1) of this section applies, one of the persons at fault avoids liability to any other such person or his personal representative by pleading the Limitation Act 1939, or any other enactment limiting the time within which proceedings may be taken, he shall not be entitled to recover any damages from that other person or representative by virtue of the said subsection.

(6) Where any case to which subsection (1) of this section applies is tried with a jury, the jury shall determine the total damages which would have been recoverable if the claimant had not been at fault and the extent to which those damages are to be reduced.

(7) [. . .]

III PID [9.1]

Damage Section 4 provides that 'damage' includes loss of life and personal injury. There can be no doubt that damage to property is included as well.

III PID [9.1A]

Contributory negligence should be pleaded As a matter of simple justice, and like any litigant in civil proceedings, a claimant is entitled to know of any misconduct, including negligence, alleged against him and to be provided with a proper opportunity to enable him to deal directly with and answer the allegation. Accordingly a failure to plead an allegation risks a judge being precluded from reducing an award on the ground of contributory negligence: *Dziennik v CTO Gesellschaft Fur Containertransport MBH* [2006] EWCA Civ 1456, [2006] All ER (D) 157 (Nov).

III PID [9.2]

Fault Section 4 provides that 'fault' means 'negligence, breach of statutory duty or other act or omission which gives rise to a liability in tort or would, apart from this Act, give rise to the defence of contributory negligence'.

III PID [9.2A]

Contributory negligence in relation to breach of statutory duty Where liability for breach of statutory duty is established it would be very unusual for a finding of contributory negligence to be as high as 75%: *Toole v Bolton Metropolitan Borough Council* [2002] EWCA Civ 588, [2002] All ER (D) 133 (Apr). There can be no finding of 100% contributory negligence. Either the claimant is wholly to blame for his injuries and there is no liability on the defendant or the defendant is to blame subject to a degree of contributory negligence on behalf of the claimant: see *Anderson v Newham College of Further Education* [2002] EWCA Civ 505.

III PID [9.2B]

Suicide Where the defendant's tortious act causes a depressive illness leading to suicide, the financial loss flowing from the death may be recoverable under the Fatal Accidents Act 1976, subject to a deduction for contributory negligence: *Corr v IBC Vehicles Ltd* [2008] UKHL 13, [2008] All ER (D) 386 (Feb), (2008) Times, 28 February.

III PID [9.2C]

Contributory negligence in relation to assault and battery The purpose of the Act is to relieve claimants whose actions would otherwise fail by instead reducing the damages awarded to them. Accordingly, contributory negligence is not available to reduce damages for assault and battery: *Co-operative group (CSW) Ltd v Pritchard* [2011] EWCA Civ 329, [2011] NLJR 510.

III PID [9.3]

Fault on the part of the claimant Two issues arise: is there any contributory negligence on the part of the claimant, and if so, what is the extent of the deduction that should be made.

As to the first question: A passenger is not required to question a driver as to how much alcohol he has consumed: *Booth v White* [2003] EWCA Civ 1708, (2003) 147 Sol Jo LB 1367. It has been held that a pedal cyclist whose head injuries were caused wholly or partly by the failure to wear a helmet could have the damages reduced on the ground of contributory negligence: *Smith v Finch* [2009] EWCH 53 (QB), [2009] All ER (D) 158 (Jan), in which there was no reduction because the defendant failed to prove a causal link between the injuries and the absence of helmet. There was found to be no contributory negligence where a bus mounted a pavement and collided with a pedestrian standing on a designated pavement area waiting to cross the road: *Osei-Antwi v South East London and Kent Bus Co Ltd* [2010] EWCA Civ 132, [2010] All ER (D) 207 (Jan).

As to the second question, when considering the apportionment between claimant and defendant, it is well-established that application of the s 1(1) test involves comparing the relative blameworthiness and causative potency of each party's actions. Beyond this, in most cases, the amount of the deduction for contributory negligence is very fact-specific and there are a large number of reported cases. Below are set out some examples only.

In *Brannan v Airtours plc* (1999) Times, 1 February, CA, the court reduced the claimant's contributory negligence from 75% to 50%. Where the Ministry of Defence failed sufficiently to look after a drunken naval airman, the damages were reduced by two thirds for contributory negligence: *Barrett v Ministry of Defence* [1995] 3 All ER 87, [1995] 1 WLR 1217, CA. The claimant motorcyclist's failure to fasten his crash-helmet was held to be contributory negligence (of 10%) in *Capps v Miller* [1989] 2 All ER 333, [1989] 1 WLR 839, CA. Where a defendant does a U-turn but fails to see the claimant coming and the claimant fails to see the U-turn until it is too late to avoid a collision, the blame falls equally on both: *Jenkins v Holt* [1999] RTR 411, CA. Damages were reduced by one half where a prisoner of sound mind committed suicide, it being the duty of the police to prevent him from harming himself: *Reeves v Metropolitan Police Comr* [2000] 1 AC 360, [1999] 3 All ER 897, HL. For apportionment of liability between a car driver and a pedestrian who ran across a highway in front of an oncoming vehicle, see *Belka v Prosperini* [2011] EWCA Civ 623; and where a motor coach eased into a major road through a gap in the traffic left by a tractor, which was being overtaken by a motor cyclist at the relevant time, see *Woodham v JM Turner (t/a Turners of Great Barton)* [2011] EWHC 1588 (QB), [2011] All ER (D) 133 (Jun).

It should be rare for a pedestrian to be found more responsible than the driver for injuries arising from a road traffic accident unless the pedestrian had suddenly moved into the path of the oncoming vehicle: *Lunt v Khelifa* [2002] EWCA Civ 801, [2002] All ER (D) 352 (May); *Eagle v Chambers* [2003] EWCA Civ 1107, [2004] RTR 115, (2003) Times, 1 September. The Court in *Lunt* observed that a high burden rested on drivers of motor vehicles to reflect the fact that a car was a potentially dangerous weapon. In *Eagle*, the Court noted that the

1945 Act refers to 'responsibility for the damage' (rather than the accident) and 'the potential destructive disparity between the parties can readily be taken into account as an aspect of blameworthiness'. The Court of Appeal further considered how liability should be apportioned in road traffic accidents between vehicles and pedestrians in *Sabir (suing by her Litigation Friend, the Official Solicitor) v Nana Osei-Kwabena* [2015] EWCA Civ 1213, [2015] All ER (D) 220 (Nov). The Court again emphasised the need to consider the relative causative potency and blameworthiness of the parties and noted that a motorist usually has a relatively high causative potency and blameworthiness because of the destructive potential of a car compared to a pedestrian.

Guidance was given on the amount of the deduction in cases of a failure to wear a seat-belt in *Froom v Butcher* [1976] QB 286, [1975] 3 All ER 520, CA. Where the seat-belt would have protected the passenger from injury entirely, the reduction is generally 25%, whereas if the failure would only have significantly reduced the severity of the injuries, a 15% reduction was suggested. In *Stanton v Collinson* [2010] EWCA Civ 81, [2010] RTR 284, Hughes LJ stated that 'There may, I accept, be unusual cases in which the two brackets of finding contemplated by *Froom v Butcher* are neither appropriate. But the Act requires that the reduction for contributory negligence shall be such as appears to the court to be just and equitable. It therefore permits an approach such as adopted in *Froom v Butcher* based upon two broad categories of typical case and the general proposition that, absent something exceptional, there should be no reduction in a case where the injury would not have been reduced "to a considerable extent" by the seat belt'. The *Froom* principles were applied in a case where a mother had failed to secure her daughter in an appropriate booster seat: *Williams v Estate of Williams (dec'd)* [2013] EWCA Civ 455, [2013] All ER (D) 245 (Apr). On the other hand, the duty of care to ambulance passengers, as regards the wearing of seat-belts, may be discharged by an obvious notice in the ambulance advising that the seat-belts provided should be used: *Eastman v South Thames Regional Health Authority* [1991] 2 Med LR 297, [1991] RTR 389, CA.

It is wrong in principle to make a finding of 100% contributory negligence as this would be tantamount to a finding of no fault on the part of the defendant: the Act is concerned with apportioning fault where there is fault on both sides: *Brumder v Motornet Service and Repairs Ltd* [2013] EWCA Civ 195, [2013] 3 All ER 412, [2013] 1 WLR 2783.

In *Jackson v Murray* [2015] UKSC 5, the Supreme Court addressed the circumstances in which appellate courts could permit an appeal concerning the appropriate apportionment of liability. It was held that apportionment is inevitably a somewhat rough and ready exercise and the test to be applied by the appellate court is whether the court below had gone wrong. In the absence of an identifiable error, such as an error of law, or the taking into account of an irrelevant matter, or the failure to take account of a relevant matter, it was only a difference of view as to the apportionment of responsibility which exceeded the ambit of reasonable disagreement that would warrant a conclusion that the court below had gone wrong.

III PID [9.3A]

Smoking and drug addiction An award in respect of death caused by lung cancer may be reduced because of contributory negligence on the part of the deceased. In a case where the deceased's lung cancer was caused partly by exposure to asbestos, for which the defendants were liable, and partly by smoking cigarettes, it was held that the failure to give up smoking after the risk of injury to health was made clear to him constituted contributory negligence: *Badger v Ministry of Defence* [2005] EWHC 2941 (QB), [2006] 3 All ER 173, per Stanley Burnton J. See also *Blackmore v Department for Communities and Local Government* [2018] QB 471.

On the other hand when a 29-year-old drug addict had a seizure and was injured falling from an upper bunk in a prison cell, it was held that becoming addicted to drugs was a 'fault', but since it dated from his mid-teenage years it was too remote to be brought into account in a successful claim arising out of the negligence of the prison staff: *St George v Home Office* [2008] EWCA Civ 1068, [2008] 4 All ER 1039.

In *Blackmore (Executrix of the Estate of Cyril Leonard Hollow) v Department for Communities & Local Government* [2017] EWCA Civ 1136, the Court of Appeal held that when apportioning responsibility for the purposes of s 1 of the Act in a fatal accident claim based on the exposure to asbestos of an employee who was a long-term smoker, a judge was entitled to differentiate between the blameworthiness of the employer and the employee, and to find that the employer should bear the greater responsibility given the breach of its strict statutory duty.

III PID [9.4]

Fault on the part of the defendant There are dicta in support of the application of the 1945 Act where the defendant is in breach of a contractual duty of care: *De Meza and Stuart v Apple* [1974] 1 Lloyd's Rep 508; *Quinn v Burch Bros (Builders) Ltd* [1966] 2 QB 370;

Artingstoll v Hewen's Garages Ltd [1973] RTR 197. But the 1945 Act does not apply where the defendant's liability arises from breach of a strict contractual duty: *Barclays Bank plc v Fairclough Buildings Ltd* [1995] QB 214, [1995] 1 All ER 289, CA.

III PID [9.4A]

Illegal acts by the claimant Where the claimant has acted illegally and the illegality is bound up within the claim although not included in the statement of case, the court may dismiss the claim on this ground (the defence of *ex turpi causa*). This was the outcome in *Cross v Kirkby* (2000) Times, 5 April, CA in which the defendant was defending himself against a hunt saboteur. The leading case is *Clunis v Camden and Islington Health Authority* [1998] QB 978, [1998] 3 All ER 180, CA. In *Henderson v Dorset Healthcare University NHS Foundation Trust* [2016] EWHC 3275 (QB) the court was bound by *Clunis and Gray v Thames Trains Ltd* [2009] UKHL 33 to reject, on public policy grounds, a damages claim brought by an individual who had pleaded guilty to manslaughter by reason of diminished responsibility when, owing to the defendant's negligence, she suffered a psychotic episode and killed her mother.

The House of Lords followed *Clunis* in *Gray v Thames Trains Ltd* [2009] UKHL 33, [2009] 4 All ER 81, [2009] 3 WLR 167 where it was held that loss flowing from a sentence of the court could not be recovered. In that case the claimant had committed manslaughter as a result of PTSD caused by the negligent train operators in the Ladbroke Grove rail crash. The claimant was precluded from recovering from the train operator, general damages and loss of earnings flowing from that crime. *Gray* was discussed further by the Supreme Court in *Patel v Mirza* [2017] AC 467.

In a case where one thief injured another by dangerous driving of the get-away vehicle, the claim by the injured thief was rejected because the injuries were a foreseeable risk of the illegal joint enterprise; however, it was suggested the doctrine should be applied flexibly and might not apply to a minor motoring offence: see *Joyce v O'Brien* [2013] EWCA Civ 546, [2013] 1 WLR 70, [2013] Lloyd's Rep IR 523. Where the criminal conduct was only one cause of the accident, that did not preclude recovery but the Court must also consider to what extent the claimant's criminal conduct directly caused the injury suffered, and should apportion liability accordingly (*McCracken (a protected party by his mother and litigation friend Deborah Norris) v Smith* [2015] EWCA Civ 380). See further *Clark (a protected party suing by his Mother and litigation friend Nicola Woods) v Farley* [2018] EWHC 1007 (QB) and *Wallett (on her own behalf and on behalf of the dependants of Ian Hill (deceased)) v Vickers* [2018] EWHC 3088 (QB).

Note that giving support to a dishonest claim by someone else, arising out of the same event, does not necessarily disqualify a claimant from proceeding with a well-founded claim: *Ul-Haq v Shah* [2009] EWCA Civ 542, [2010] 1 All ER 73, [2009] RTR 352; nor does a claimant who lies about the extent of his injuries lose the right to compensation for those which he in fact sustained save in exceptional cases: *Fairclough Homes Ltd v Summers* [2012] UKSC 26, [2012] 4 All ER 317, [2012] 1 WLR 2004. Since 13 April 2015 the courts have been empowered, by s 57 of the Criminal Justice and Courts Act 2015, to strike out a claim that would otherwise have succeeded if there has been fundamental dishonesty.

One could have a situation where the involvement of the claimant passenger in the criminal acts of the tortfeasor driver is not sufficiently proximate to deprive the claimant of a remedy against the tortfeasor but where the claimant is nevertheless unable to recover from the MIB: *Delaney v Pickett* [2011] EWCA Civ 1532, [2012] 1 WLR 2149, [2012] RTR 187 (the exclusion of the MIB's liability in these circumstances has been held to be a serious breach of the UK's obligations under Directive 72/166, Directive 84/5 and Directive 90/232: *Delaney v Secretary of State for Transport* [2015] EWCA Civ 172, [2015] 3 All ER 329).

A claim by passengers injured when trying to 'jump a taxi' was dismissed because their crime was not merely collateral to the injurious event, although the driver had been at fault: *Beaumont v Ferrer* [2016] EWCA Civ 768.

III PID [9.5]

Fatal Accidents Acts The contributory negligence of a dependent claimant may be taken into account in reduction of his own claim, and the contributory negligence of the deceased may also be taken into account if the death is on or after 1 January 1983: see the Fatal Accidents Act 1976 s 5 at para **III PID [15]**.

III PID [9.6]

Precedents For examples of defences pleading contributory negligence and volenti see **BCCP M[472]**, **BCCP M[473]**, **BCCP M[1289]**, **BCCP M[1311]**, **BCCP M[1317]**, **BCCP M[1882]**, **BCCP M[2459]**, **BCCP M[2460]**, **BCCP M[2485]–BCCP M[2487]**, **BCCP M[3056]**, **BCCP M[3482]** and **BCCP M[4108]**.

LAW REFORM (PERSONAL INJURIES) ACT 1948

(c 41)

III PID [9A]

1. Common employment

(1) It shall not be a defence to an employer who is sued in respect of personal injuries caused by the negligence of a person employed by him, that that person was at the time the injuries were caused in common employment with the person injured.

(2) Accordingly the Employers' Liability Act 1880 shall cease to have effect, and is hereby repealed.

(3) Any provision contained in a contract of service or apprenticeship, or in an agreement collateral thereto, (including a contract or agreement entered into before the commencement of this Act) shall be void in so far as it would have the effect of excluding or limiting any liability of the employer in respect of personal injuries caused to the person employed or apprenticed by the negligence of persons in common employment with him.

III PID [9B]

2. Measure of damages

(1)-(3) ...

(4) In an action for damages for personal injuries (including any such action arising out of a contract), there shall be disregarded, in determining the reasonableness of any expenses, the possibility of avoiding those expenses or part of them by taking advantage of facilities available under the National Health Service Act 2006 or the National Health Service (Wales) Act 2006 or the National Health Service (Scotland) Act 1947 or of any corresponding facilities in Northern Ireland.

(5)-(6) ...

III PID [9C]

3. Definition of "personal injury"

In this Act the expression "personal injury" includes any disease and any impairment of a person's physical or mental condition, and the expression "injured" shall be construed accordingly.

III PID [9D]

4. Application to Crown

This Act shall bind the Crown.

III PID [9E]

6. Short title and commencement

(1) This Act may be cited as the Law Reform (Personal Injuries) Act 1948.

(2) Section one and subsection (1) of section two of this Act shall apply only where the cause of action accrues on or after the day appointed for the National Insurance (Industrial Injuries) Act 1946 to take effect, but subsections (4) and (5) of the said section two shall apply whether the cause of action accrued or the action was commenced before or after the commencement of this Act.

FATAL ACCIDENTS ACT 1976

(c 30)

III PID [10]

1. Right of action for wrongful act causing death

(1) If death is caused by any wrongful act, neglect or default which is such as would (if death had not ensued) have entitled the person injured to maintain an action and recover damages in respect thereof, the person who would have been liable if death had not ensued shall be liable to an action for damages, notwithstanding the death of the person injured.

(2) Subject to section 1A (2) below, every such action shall be for the benefit of the dependants of the person ("the deceased") whose death has been so caused.

(3) In this Act "dependant" means—

(a) the wife or husband or former wife or husband of the deceased;

(aa) the civil partner or former civil partner of the deceased;

(b) any person who—

(i) was living with the deceased in the same household immediately before the date of the death; and

(ii) had been living with the deceased in the same household for at least two years before that date; and

(iii) was living during the whole of that period as the husband or wife or civil partner of the deceased;

(c) any parent or other ascendant of the deceased;

(d) any person who was treated by the deceased as his parent;

(e) any child or other descendant of the deceased;

(f) any person (not being a child of the deceased) who, in the case of any marriage to which the deceased was at any time a party, was treated by the deceased as a child of the family in relation to that marriage;

(fa) any person (not being a child of the deceased) who, in the case of any civil partnership to which the deceased was at any time a civil partner, was treated by the deceased as a child of the family in relation to that partnership;

(g) any person who is, or is the issue of, a brother, sister, uncle or aunt of the deceased.

(4) The reference to the former wife or husband of the deceased in subsection (3)(a) above includes a reference to a person whose marriage to the deceased has been annulled or declared void as well as a person whose marriage to the deceased has been dissolved.

(4A) The reference to the former civil partner of the deceased in subsection (3)(aa) above includes a reference to a person whose civil partnership with the deceased has been annulled as well as a person whose civil partnership with the deceased has been dissolved.

(5) In deducing any relationship for the purposes of subsection (3) above—

(a) any relationship by marriage or civil partnership shall be treated as a relationship by consanguinity, any relationship of the half blood as a relationship of the whole blood, and the stepchild of any person as his child, and

(b) an illegitimate person shall be treated as—

(i) the legitimate child of his mother and reputed father, or

(ii) in the case of a person who has a female parent by virtue of section 43 of the Human Fertilisation and Embryology Act 2008, the legitimate child of his mother and that female parent.

(6) Any reference in this Act to injury includes any disease and any impairment of a person's physical or mental condition

III PID [10.1]

Liability to the deceased A dependent has no claim under the FAA if the deceased, during his own lifetime, settled his own claim with the defendant: *Read v Great Eastern Railway* (1868) LR 3 QB 555, 18 LT 822. Thus a settlement, even at an obvious undervalue, during the lifetime of the claimant against a doctor barred her dependents from proceedings under the FAA 1976 after her death (the doctor having wrongly diagnosed a cancerous tumour as benign): *Thompson v Arnold* [2007] EWHC 1875 (QB), [1997] All ER (D) 38 (Aug). In contrast, a claim under the FAA was not barred where, following the death of a father in a road traffic accident (RTA), his solicitors negligently discontinued his action for personal injuries against a driver whose negligence had caused the accident: *Reader v Molesworths Bright Clegg (a Firm)* [2007] EWCA Civ 169, [2007] 3 All ER 107.

III PID [10.1A]

Wrongful act causing death Where the defendant's tortious act causes a depressive illness leading to suicide, the financial loss flowing from the death may be recoverable under the Fatal Accidents Act 1976, subject to a deduction for contributory negligence: *Corr v IBC Vehicles Ltd* [2008] UKHL 13, [2008] All ER (D) 386 (Feb),(2008) Times, 28 February.

III PID [10.2]

Former wife The words "former wife" include a woman who remarries after a divorce but who leaves the second husband and returns to the first. But to be entitled to claim she must establish a "dependency" as well as coming within one of the statutory categories: *Shepherd v Post Office* (1995) Times, 15 June, CA.

III PID [10.3]

Living with the deceased for at least two years The two-year period required by s 1(3)(b) is not broken by brief periods of absence: *Pounder v London Underground Ltd* [1995] PIQR P217.

The judge must be satisfied that a joint household has been established. The fact that a couple intend or plan to live in the same household is not enough; they must actually start doing so: *Kotke v Saffarini* [2005] EWCA Civ 221, [2005] 1 FCR 642, [2005] PIQR P26.

The two year cohabitation filter for living with a partner as husband and wife is Human Rights Act compliant: *Swift v Secretary of State for Justice* [2012] EWHC 2000 (QB), [2012] All ER (D) 225 (Jul).

III PID [10.4]

Adoption The claimant's adoption, following the death of the parents, must be taken into account in reducing the value of the dependency: *Watson v Willmott* [1991] 1 QB 140, [1991] 1 All ER 473.

III PID [10.4A]

Child's claim for loss of a mother's care Where a voluntary carer looks after a child on the death of the mother, the child may claim as damages the cost of the carer's services provided that such damages would be received in trust for the carer: *H v S* [2002] EWCA Civ 792, [2003] QB 965, sub nom *ATH v MS* [2002] NLJR 969, (2002) Times, 3 July, applying the principles in *Hunt v Severs* [1994] 2 AC 350, [1994] 2 All ER 385, HL.

III PID [10.5]

Pleading a claim under the Act For model particulars of claim see **BCCP M[4102], BCCP M[4103], BCCP M[4104], BCCP M[4106]**. These are suitable for inclusion in a claim form completed to meet the requirements of CPR Part 7 (see para **CPR 7**).

III PID [10.6]

Assessment of damages for accidents abroad See **III PID [4A]** for a summary of the case law on the application of the Private International Law (Miscellaneous Provisions) Act 1995 and of Rome II, to the assessment of damages for fatal accidents abroad. A claim under the Fatal Accidents Act 1976 is a claim based on English law, so is not available where the applicable law is foreign: *Brownlie v Four Seasons Holdings Inc* [2017] UKSC 80.

III PID [11]

1A. Bereavement

(1) An action under this Act may consist of or include a claim for damages for bereavement.

(2) A claim for damages for bereavement shall only be for the benefit—

(a) of the wife or husband or civil partner of the deceased; and

(b) where the deceased was a minor who was never married or a civil partner—

(i) of his parents, if he was legitimate; and

(ii) of his mother, if he was illegitimate.

(3) Subject to subsection (5) below, the sum to be awarded as damages under this section shall be £12,980.

(4) Where there is a claim for damages under this section for the benefit of both the parents of the deceased, the sum awarded shall be divided equally between them (subject to any deduction falling to be made in respect of costs not recovered from the defendant).

(5) The Lord Chancellor may by order made by statutory instrument, subject to annulment in pursuance of a resolution of either House of Parliament, amend this section by varying the sum for the time being specified in subsection (3) above.

III PID [11.1]

Claims under the section This section creates a new cause of action in respect of bereavement on or after 1 January 1983. Parents are not entitled to damages for the death of a child who is 18 or over, although he was a minor when he sustained the relevant injury: *Doleman v Deakin* [1990] 13 LS Gaz R 43, CA.

The level of award for bereavement damages was increased from £10,000 to £11,800 for cases where the cause of action arose after 1 January 2008: SI 2007/3489. It was further increased to £12,980 for cases where the cause of action arose after 1 April 2013: SI 2013/510.

Section 1A has been deemed incompatible with ECHR art 14, read in conjunction with art 8, to the extent that it excludes cohabitees of over two years from its scheme for bereavement damages: *Smith (suing in her own right and as the surviving partner of Bulloch, deceased) v Lancashire Teaching Hospitals NHS Foundation Trust* [2017] EWCA Civ 1916, (2018) Times, 08 January, [2017] All ER (D) 11 (Dec). In *Smith*, the court considered the correct test for determining whether the scheme was within the ambit of art 8, so as to engage art 14.

III PID [11.2]

Claims at common law Claims for nervous shock can lie outside the ambit of the Fatal Accidents Act 1976 where the death has led to actionable psychiatric injury. See **BPILS I [98.4]** onwards.

III PID [12]

2. Persons entitled to bring the action

(1) The action shall be brought by and in the name of the executor or administrator of the deceased.

(2) If—

(a) there is no executor or administrator of the deceased, or

(b) no action is brought within six months after the death by and in the name of an executor or administrator of the deceased,

the action may be brought by and in the name of all or any of the persons for whose benefit an executor or administrator could have brought it.

(3) Not more than one action shall lie for and in respect of the same subject matter of complaint.

(4) The plaintiff in the action shall be required to deliver to the defendant or his solicitor full particulars of the persons for whom and on whose behalf the action is brought and of the nature of the claim in respect of which damages are sought to be recovered.

III PID [12.1]

Fatal accident claim: viability of later children's claim after non-service of adult claim The Court of Appeal held that a second action is permissible where the first was not served, since "action" is to be interpreted as meaning a served process, and the first writ was not served: *Cachia v Faluyi* [2001] EWCA Civ 998, [2002] 1 All ER 192, [2001] 1 WLR 1966. To rule otherwise would bar access to the Court under art 6 of the European Convention on Human Rights.

III PID [13]

3. Assessment of damages

(1) In the action such damages, other than damages for bereavement, may be awarded as are proportioned to the injury resulting from the death to the dependants respectively.

(2) After deducting the costs not recovered from the defendant any amount recovered otherwise than as damages for bereavement shall be divided among the dependants in such shares as may be directed.

(3) In an action under this Act where there fall to be assessed damages payable to a widow in respect of the death of her husband there shall not be taken account the re-marriage of the widow or her prospects of remarriage.

(4) In an action under this Act where there fall to be assessed damages payable to a person who is a dependant by virtue of section 1 (3)(b) above in respect of the death of the person with whom the dependant was living as husband or wife or civil partner there shall be taken into account (together with any other matter that appears to the court to be relevant to the action) the fact that the dependant had no enforceable right to financial support by the deceased as a result of their living together.

(5) If the dependants have incurred funeral expenses in respect of the deceased, damages may be awarded in respect of those expenses.

(6) Money paid into court in satisfaction of a cause of action under this Act may be in one sum without specifying any person's share.

III PID [13.1]

Loss of employee's retirement pension Where a husband was in receipt of a retirement pension from his former employer's pension fund which constituted the whole or part of his income, the widow on his death suffers a loss of dependency and thus an 'injury' under s 3(1) of the Act for which she is entitled to damages; and the allowances paid to her after her husband's death can be disregarded, since these are benefits which accrued to her as a result of his death under s 4 of the Act: see *Pidduck v Eastern Scottish Omnibuses Ltd* [1990] 1 All ER 69, [1990] 1 WLR 993, CA.

III PID [13.1A]

Change in family circumstances See also *Welsh Ambulance Services NHS Trust v Williams* [2008] EWCA Civ 81, [2008] All ER (D) 221 (Feb) where the financial benefit that two children brought to the family subsequently to their father's death was irrelevant to the assessment of the dependency claim under s 3 of the Act. A dependant could not by his or her conduct after the death affect the value of the dependency.

For a more detailed consideration, please refer to **BPILS Division II**.

III PID [13.2]

Delay Normally delay is taken into account only in respect of interest: *Spittle v Bunney* [1988] 3 All ER 1031, [1988] 1 WLR 847. But in *Corbett v Barking, Havering and Brentford Health Authority* [1991] 2 QB 408, [1991] 1 All ER 498, CA, the Court of Appeal held (Ralph Gibson LJ dissenting) that the known fact of the dependant's survival over a long period up to the date of trial should be taken into account and that the multiplier should be increased accordingly.

III PID [13.3]

Remarriage of widow The marriage prospects of a widow may need to be taken into account in assessing the dependency of the children: *Goodburn v Thomas Cotton Ltd* [1968] 1 QB 845, [1968] 1 All ER 518, CA. Subsection (3) prevents the court from taking account of the widow's prospects of remarriage when assessing the value of her dependency. But the possibility of her marriage to the deceased being dissolved if he had lived is a relevant consideration: *Martin v Owen* (1992) Times, 21 May, CA.

III PID [13.4]

Value of dependency The modern practice is to value the dependencies on the deceased bread-winner by reference to his net income, after deducting money spent on himself: *Harris v Empress Motors Ltd* [1983] 3 All ER 561, [1984] 1 WLR 212, CA, but see also *Owen v Martin* [1992] PIQR Q15. But a parent may not claim for prospective dependency on a young child: *Croke v Wiseman* [1981] 3 All ER 852, [1982] 1 WLR 71, CA. In assessing damages under the Fatal Accidents Act 1976 the critical issue was the loss suffered by the claimant as a result of the deceased's death. The multiplier/multiplicand approach may be inappropriate for assessing the value of housekeeping assistance provided by a wife in declining health: *Thomas v Kwik Save Stores Ltd* (2000) Times, 27 June, CA in which the Court of Appeal stressed that only monetary loss could be compensated and reduced an award of £50,000 to £20,000.

III PID [13.5]

Dishonest income In *Hunter v Butler* [1996] RTR 396, (1995) Times, 28 December, CA, the court rejected a widow's claim for loss of dependency in respect of the deceased's "moonlighting"; that is, his income from part-time working combined with supplementary benefit to which he was not entitled. See also *Burns v Edman* [1970] 2 QB 541, [1970] 1 All ER 886.

III PID [13.6]

Choice of multiplier The multiplier is to be assessed by reference to a discount rate: *Wells v Wells* [1999] 1 AC 345, [1998] 3 All ER 481, HL. As from 20 March 2017 the discount rate has been set at minus 0.75%. The Government however published a consultation on the basis of formulating the discount rate and it is likely that there will be further change to the rate, likely to be upwards from the present rate. The Civil Liability Act 2018 has now been passed, under which the discount rate will further be considered. The correct date at which to assess the multiplier is the date of trial rather than the date of death: *Knauer v Ministry of Justice* [2016] UKSC 9, (2016) Times, 9 March.

III PID [13.7]

Actuarial evidence As regards actuarial evidence, the Law Commission's Report on Structured Settlements and Interim and Provisional Damages has recommended that the Actuarial Tables published by the Government Actuary's Department as *Actuarial Tables with explanatory notes for use in Personal Injury and Fatal Accident cases* (also known as the Ogden Tables) should be admitted in evidence in assessing damages, although technically hearsay. The recommendation has not yet been implemented. The Ogden Tables now include numerous tables for arriving at a multiplier after making allowance for population mortality (and certain other contingencies) and postulating a range of interest rates of up to 5%. Until such time as the Civil Evidence Act 1995, s 10 is brought into force the tables and the report will technically need to be proved in evidence by an actuary or other expert, but in practice this data is agreed. When determining a multiplier based on the life expectancy of a claimant in a personal injury action, the court should use as a starting point Tables 11–20 of the Ogden Tables published by the Government Actuary's Department. In *Biersheuval v Birrell* [1999] PIQR Q40 Eady J enhanced the multiplier to take into account the unusual and exceptional burden of Netherlands taxation. The claimant's advisers adopted a computer model, which the court accepted, generating life and earnings multipliers respectively of 31.14 and 30.37 generating a total award of about £9m.

Since 2007 the Ogden Tables have provided 'reduction factors' with which to modify the base multiplier in order to take account of risks other than mortality, including disability, educational attainment and employment status. However, the reduction for 'disability' is hard to apply because it provides a single figure for a very broad range of disabilities. In this respect departure from the Ogden formula may be justified in order to do justice in the particular circumstance of the case. In the Court of Appeal's decision in *Billett v Ministry of Defence* [2015] EWCA Civ 773, [2016] PIQR Q1, [2015] All ER (D) 256 (Jul), the Court gave useful guidance on the analysis of disability and when it will be more appropriate for a *Smith v Manchester* award to be granted rather than a multiplier/multiplicand approach to loss of earnings which relies on the reduction facts in Tables A–D.

Note that the Governments Actuary's Department has revised the Ogden Tables and that the revised version is available on it's website at http://www.gad.gov.uk under 'Other Services'.

III PID [13.8]

General damages for psychological effect of death In *Watson v Willmott* [1991] 1 QB 140, [1991] 1 All ER 473 the claimant dependant received no injuries in the traffic accident which killed his mother and seriously injured his father. However the psychological effect on the claimant was taken into account and £5,000 was awarded in this respect. See notes on s 1A (bereavement) see para **III PID [11.2]**.

III PID [13.9]

Funeral expenses To be recoverable under sub-s (5) funeral expenses must be reasonable, taking account of the deceased's station in life, creed and racial origin (*Gammell v Wilson* [1982] AC 27, [1980] 1 All ER 578, HL) and may include travel expenses: *Schneider v Eisovitch* [1960] 2 QB 430, [1960] 1 All ER 169. It is recognised that the occasion may involve hospitality on an appropriate scale: *Sally Ann Smith v Marchioness and Bowbelle* [1993] NLJR 813, [1993] 27 LS Gaz R 36. The claim for funeral expenses in personal injury cases must arise either: (1) where the expenses are incurred by the dependants of the deceased and s 3(5) of the Fatal Accidents Act 1976 applies; or (2) where the expenses are incurred by the deceased's estate and s 1(2)(c) of the Law Reform (Miscellaneous Provisions) Act 1934 applies. A living claimant cannot claim for anticipated funeral expenses based on a reduced life expectancy: see *Watson v Cakebread Robey Ltd* [2009] EWHC 1695 (QB), [2009] All ER (D) 124 (Jul). In *Brown v Hamind* [2013] EWHC 4067 (QB), the Defendant was found to have accelerated the Claimant's pre-existing symptoms and death. The judge found that the period of acceleration was around 12 months. The judge noted that recovery of funeral expenses 'may be recovered' and indeed usually are recovered under s 3(5) of the 1976 Act. However, this case involved the acceleration of the symptoms associated with a pre-existing condition by a relatively short period of time. The judge therefore refused to make such an award. In *Bateman v Hydro Agri (UK) Ltd* (September 15, 1995) a High Court Judge held that funeral expenses were a valid claim. In this case, the claimant was suffering from mesothelioma and was likely to die within three months of the date of the trial.

(This is a particularly complicated field of law. For further discussion please refer to **BPILS II[273.2]** onwards.)

III PID [13.10]

State benefits Where the deceased's family receives income-related benefits (income support, housing benefit, council tax benefit) before and after the death, the survivors cannot rely upon the drop in income as a loss of dependency. Nor can the recipient of invalid care allowance claim a loss on the tortious death of the invalid. But, where the deceased received severe disablement allowance and disability living allowance and thereby added to the family income, the survivors may claim the loss of the former and of the mobility and care components in the latter as a loss of dependency: *Cox v Hockenhull* [1999] 3 All ER 577, CA.

III PID [13.11]

Extra-marital affair Where the deceased had had an extra-marital affair for several years to the ignorance of his wife, the multiplier was reduced from 20 to 11 to take account of the insecurity of the marriage: *Dalziel v Donald* (20 October 2000, unreported), QBD.

III PID [13.12]

Apportioning the award Where a single sum has been awarded or agreed in respect of claims under the Fatal Accidents Act 1976 and the Law Reform (Miscellaneous Provisions) Act 1934, the court should apportion the money between those entitled to it, if not agreed by the parties. Where one of those entitled lacks legal capacity the court may make the apportionment when giving directions under CPR 21.11. See **CPR 41.3A**.

III PID [14]

4. Assessment of damages: disregard of benefits

In assessing damages in respect of a person's death in an action under this Act, benefits which have accrued or will or may accrue to any person from his estate or otherwise as a result of his death shall be disregarded.

III PID [14.1]

This section was substituted by s 3(1) of the Administration of Justice Act 1982. Benefits required by this section to be disregarded include an allowance paid to a widow by a former employer, based on the deceased's pension: *Pidduck v Eastern Scottish Omnibus Ltd* [1990] 2 All ER 69, [1990] 1 WLR 993, CA. Non-pecuniary benefits are to be disregarded as well as pecuniary: *Stanley v Saddique* [1992] QB 1, [1991] 1 All ER 529, which is authority for the following: (i) the word 'benefit' was not restricted to direct pecuniary benefit but included the benefit accruing to a claimant as a result of his absorption into a new family unit consisting of his father, stepmother and siblings; and that (ii) such benefit resulted from the death and thus by s 4 of the FAA was to be wholly disregarded for the purpose of assessing damages for loss of dependency. Each case turns on its own facts. Thus in *Hayden v Hayden* [1992] 4 All ER 681, [1992] 1 WLR 986, CA, services provided to a minor by the surviving father in place of those provided by the deceased mother were held not to be benefits accruing as a result of the death and thus not to be taken into account, where prior to the mother's death the father had not provided any support at all. It may be tentatively suggested that more recent cases tend to adopt the approach in *Stanley v Saddique* rather than *Hayden v Hayden*. Thus a payment from a provident fund scheme on the early retirement of an injured man should be disregarded in circumstances where the injury prevented him from working to normal retirement age and recovering larger payment: *McIntyre v Harland & Wolff plc* [2006] EWCA Civ 287, [2006] 1 WLR 2577; the loss of the latter payment was held recoverable under the Act from the employers who caused the injury, without deducting the early retirement payment since the latter was a benefit which accrued to the widow from the estate.

Money paid to a widow under death in service benefit scheme is excluded by s 4 and the issue of causation is not a matter of great importance: *Arnup v M W White Ltd* [2008] EWCA Civ 447, [2008] All ER (D) 73 (May), (2008) Times, 25 June. Since the statutory disregard provisions cover all benefits which accrue as the result of the death, it no longer matters whether a benefit accrues as a result of the death; it cannot be deducted in any event.

III PID [15]

5. Contributory negligence

Where any person dies as the result partly of his own fault and partly of the fault of any other person or persons, and accordingly if an action were brought for the benefit of the estate under the Law Reform (Miscellaneous Provisions) Act 1934 the damages recoverable would be reduced under section 1 (1) of the Law Reform (Contributory Negligence) Act 1945, any damages recoverable in an action under this Act shall be reduced to a proportionate extent.

III PID [15.1]

This section is printed as amended by s 3(2) of the Administration of Justice Act 1982 s 73(1) of which provides that its provisions do not apply to causes of action accruing before 1 January 1983: such cases are governed by the pre-existing law. As regards contributory negligence on the part of a dependant see *Dodds v Dodds* [1978] QB 543, [1978] 2 All ER 539.

PERSONAL INJURY AND DEATH

CIVIL LIABILITY (CONTRIBUTION) ACT 1978

(c 47)

III PID [16]

1. Entitlement to contribution

(1) Subject to the following provisions of this section, any person liable in respect of any damage suffered by another person may recover contribution from any other person liable in respect of the same damage (whether jointly with him or otherwise).

(2) A person shall be entitled to recover contribution by virtue of subsection (1) above notwithstanding that he has ceased to be liable in respect of the damage in question since the time when the damage occurred, provided that he was so liable immediately before he made or was ordered or agreed to make the payment in respect of which the contribution is sought.

(3) A person shall be liable to make contribution by virtue of subsection (1) above notwithstanding that he has ceased to be liable in respect of the damage in question since the time when the damage occurred, unless he ceased to be liable by virtue of the expiry of a period of limitation or prescription which extinguished the right on which the claim against him in respect of the damage was based.

(4) A person who has made or agreed to make any payment in bona fide settlement or compromise of any claim made against him in respect of any damage (including a payment into court which has been accepted) shall be entitled to recover contribution in accordance with this section without regard to whether or not he himself is or ever was liable in respect of the damage, provided, however, that he would have been liable assuming that the factual basis of the claim against him could be established.

(5) A judgment given in any action brought in any part of the United Kingdom by or on behalf of the person who suffered the damage in question against any person from whom contribution is sought under this section shall be conclusive in the proceedings for contribution as to any issue determined by that judgment in favour of the person from whom the contribution is sought.

(6) References in this section to a person's liability in respect of any damage are references to any such liability which has been or could be established in an action brought against him in England and Wales by or on behalf of the person who suffered the damage; but it is immaterial whether any issue arising in any such action was or would be determined (in accordance with the rules of private international law) by reference to the law of a country outside England and Wales.

III PID [16.1]

Person liable The meaning of "person liable" is explained in s 6(1) (see para **III PID [18]**) and "liability" is given an extended meaning, by sub-ss (2), (3) and (6), to cover, among other things, the potential liability of a foreign defendant against whom the proceedings have been brought, but stayed: *R A Lister & Co Ltd v EG Thomson (Shipping) Ltd (No 2)* [1987] 3 All ER 1032, [1987] 1 WLR 1614. Also a third party who has ceased to be liable to the claimant by reason of an agreed settlement of the claimant's claim may nevertheless be required to pay a contribution to the defendant: *Logan v Uttlesford District Council* (1984) 134 NLJ 500. But see *O'Boyle v Leiper* (1990) 134 Sol Jo 316 to the contrary effect. Where an undertaking is transferred under the Transfer of Undertakings (Protection of Employment) Regulations (SI

1981/1794) rights and duties of the employer pass. Regulation 5(2)(a), as amended, provides that "all the transferor's rights, powers, duties and liabilities under or in connection with any contract of employment shall be transferred by virtue of this regulation to the transferees." It was held in *Bernadone v Pall Mall Services Group Ltd* [1999] IRLR 617 by B LOFELD J that the transfer included the transferor's liability in tort to the injured claimant and the right to be indemnified under a contract of insurance.

III PID [16.1A]

Effect of compromise with one defendant A defendant sued by dependants may not claim a contribution from a person with whom the deceased made a settlement during his lifetime: *Jameson v Central Electricity Generating Board* [2000] 1 AC 455, [1999] 1 All ER 193, HL. It was also held in that case that the deceased's settlement with one defendant discharged the other from liability to the dependants. However, in *Heaton v Axa Equity and Law Life Assurance Society plc* [2002] UKHL 15, [2002] 2 AC 329, [2002] 2 All ER 961, the House of Lords held that the claimant's remedy against one defendant was not barred by a compromise with another. Also, it was held in the Court of Appeal, in *Minton v Kenburgh Investments (Northern) Ltd* (2000) Times, 11 July, that a compromise by a company liquidator of claims against directors did not bar the liquidator from proceeding against a firm of solicitors for negligence even though that opened up the possibility of the solicitors seeking an indemnity from the directors. If the second contributor is to escape, the crucial requirement seems to be that the first settlement should represent the full measure of the claimant's loss: *Heaton v Axa Equity and Law Life Assurance Society plc* [2002] UKHL 15, [2002] 2 AC 329, [2002] 2 All ER 961. See also *Cape & Dalgleish v Fitzgerald* [2002] UKHL 16, [2002] All ER (D) 231 (Apr). In *Anthony McGill v Sports & Entertainment Media Group* [2016] EWCA Civ 1063, the Court of Appeal held that a claimant's previous settlement with a contract breaker did not discharge his claims against the present defendants for inducing the breach of contract. The case provides helpful guidance on when a settlement with one defendant will also discharge claims against other defendants. It suggests that, where the causes of action against the different defendants are separate (ie where there is no joint liability), a court will not lightly conclude that settlement with one will discharge the others, unless it is clear that the effect of the first settlement was to extinguish the claimant's loss. *McGill* can be compared to *Vanden Recycling Ltd v Bevin Tumulty* [2017] EWCA Civ 354, where the Court of Appeal held that a consent order by which a tortfeasor agreed to pay a specified sum in damages to the claimant in full and final settlement of the claims against it was, in substance and effect, the same as an order made following a judgment. It was therefore a judgment by consent and its satisfaction would bar claims against tortfeasors liable for the same damage.

III PID [16.2]

Liability for the same damage A contribution may not be claimed between persons who are liable to the same claimant but for different amounts arising out of different causes of action: *Birse Construction Ltd v Haiste Ltd* [1996] 2 All ER 1, [1996] 1 WLR 675, CA. For a more recent decision to the same effect as *Birse Construction*, see *Hawkins & Harrison (A Firm) v Tyler* [2001] Lloyd's Rep PN 1, (2000) Times, 8 August, CA in which a building society suffered a substantial loss on the resale of mortgaged property which had been over-valued. The valuers settled the building society's claim against them for negligence by paying £400,000 but it was held that they could not recover a contribution from the mortgagors since their payment had not reduced the liability of the debtors. The House of Lords arrived at a similar conclusion in *Royal Brompton Hospital NHS Trust v Hammond (No 3)* [2002] UKHL 14, [2002] 2 All ER 801, (2002) Times, 26 April. In that case it was held that architects who were sued by the building owners could not claim a contribution from building contractors with whom the owners had settled out of court. The reasoning was that the architects and the builders were not liable for the same damage for the purposes of s 1(1).

On the other hand, in *Eastgate Group Ltd v Lindsey Morden Group Inc* [2001] EWCA Civ 1446, [2001] 2 All ER (Comm) 1050, the Court of Appeal allowed a contribution claim between the seller of a business with inaccurate accounts and the investigative accountants engaged by the purchaser. It was held that the two parties were liable for the same damage although the starting point for measuring the loss was different. See also *Hurstwood Developments Ltd v Motor & General and Andersley & Co Insurance Services Ltd* [2001] EWCA Civ 1785, [2002] PNLR 10.

III PID [16.2A]

Parent's failure to apply seat belt to child In a case where a child passenger was injured in a head-on collision, the negligent driver of the other car was awarded a 25% contribution from the child's parent for her failure to apply the seat belt properly: *Jones v Wilkins* [2001] 07 LS Gaz R 41, (2001) Times, 6 February, CA, following the reasoning in *Froom v Butcher* [1976] QB 286, [1975] 3 All ER 520, CA. More recently in the case of *Williams v Estate of Williams (dec'd)* [2013] EWCA Civ 455, [2013] All ER (D) 245 (Apr), the Court of Appeal found contributory negligence of 25% on the part of the mother of a child injured in a road traffic accident. The mother had failed to comply with the manufacturer's instructions when using a booster seat which was not appropriate to secure the child adequately.

III PID [16.3]

Limitation periods A person may be liable for the purposes of contribution proceedings although the claimant's remedy may have been statute-barred, unless the effect of the statute is also to extinguish the right, as in the case of s 11A of the Limitation Act 1980 in relation to proceedings under Part I of the Consumer Protection Act 1987 (see para **III LIM [14]**). The time limit for bringing contribution proceedings is fixed by the Limitation Act 1980 s 10 (see para **III LIM [12]**), at two years from the date of the finding, or acceptance, of liability. But where liability is decided, or admitted, ahead of the assessment of damages, the time does not start to run until the conclusion of the assessment: *Aer Lingus v Gildacroft Ltd* [2006] EWCA Civ 4, (2006) Times, 23 January. As to when time starts running where a binding settlement is reached, see *RG Carter Building Ltd v Kier Business Services Ltd (formerly Mouchel Business Services Ltd)* [2018] 4 All ER 456.

Rights of contribution in respect of debt, as between joint guarantors of a loan, are not claims "in respect of any damage" and are therefore not subject to the special limitation period in s 10(1): *Hampton v Minns* [2002] 1 WLR 1, (2001) Times, 27 March. The guarantee was to pay a sum of money to the bank when demand was made, and that was to be construed as one of debt and not of damages. The relevant limitation period was one of six years, pursuant to s 5 of the Limitation Act 1980. A contribution claim against a wrongdoer is not allowed by s 1(3) where the claimant's remedy against that person has been extinguished, but it is allowed where the time limit operates as a procedural bar only: *South West Strategic Health Authority v Bay Island Voyages* [2015] EWCA Civ 708, 165 NLJ 7663, [2015] All ER (D) 165 (Jul).

III PID [16.4]

Bona fide compromise Subsection (4) allows the claim to a contribution to be based on a bona fide settlement without the claimant having to prove his own liability. In *Arab Monetary Fund v Hashim (No 9)* (1993) Times, 17 June, Chadwick J held that the foreign law by which liability was to be determined was not part of the "factual basis" and that the proviso in sub-s (4) could not be interpreted as if it included a further assumption that the defendant would fail to establish the factual basis of any collateral defence. In *Arab Monetary Fund v Hashim (No 9)* (1999) Times, 11 October, the same judge held the Act to be applicable even though the proper law governing the contribution claim might be a foreign law. However, in *WH Newson v IMI* [2016] EWCA Civ 773, the Court of Appeal considered the earlier decision of *Arab Monetary Fund v Hashim* and held it had been wrong decided. Here, a Part 20 claimant had settled with the claimant in the main proceeding and then sought a contribution from the second Part 20 defendants. The proviso in s 1(4) does not permit an investigation as to whether the collateral defence would have succeeded. The Court of Appeal found that the section 'has provided expressly that there is to be no inquiry as to whether D1 was or was not actually liable to C'. All that is required is proof by D1 that the factual basis of the claim against him disclosed a reasonable cause of action. Accordingly, D1 satisfied the requirements of the proviso, and could therefore seek a contribution from D2.

In *Parkman Consulting Engineers v Cumbrian Industrials Ltd* [2001] EWCA Civ 1621, [2001] All ER (D) 436 (Oct) the claimants recovered a contribution (50%) towards their liability under a compromise made with landowners who had suffered damage from toxic waste which the claimants had been engaged by the defendants to advise on. It was held that the claim was well-founded since both parties were liable for the same damage and it was further held that the claimant could recover in respect of their liability for the injured party's costs.

III PID [16.4A]

A person who has made or agreed to make any payment in settlement A defendant who has settled a construction claim by carrying out remedial work may treat the value of the work as a "payment" for the purposes of sub-section (4), so as to found a claim for a contribution or indemnity from the consulting structural engineers: *Baker and Davies plc v Leslie Wilks Associates (a Firm)* [2005] EWHC 1179 (TCC), [2005] 3 All ER 603, (2005) Times, 16 August, CA.

III PID [16.5]

Judgment in the main proceedings Decisions on issues in the main proceedings brought by the claimant are binding, by sub-s (5), on the parties to the contribution proceedings, but not decisions to strike out for want of prosecution (*Hart v Hall and Pickles Ltd* [1969] 1 QB 405, [1968] 3 All ER 291, CA) or, seemingly, decisions that remedies are statute-barred. The word "judgment" should be construed as final judgment after any appeals have been determined: *Moy v Pettman Smith (a Firm)* (2005) Times, 4 February, HL.

In *Talbot v Berkshire County Council* [1994] QB 290, [1993] 4 All ER 9, CA it was held that a defendant who makes a contribution claim against a third party must raise in those proceedings any additional claim, arising out of the same facts, which he may have on his own behalf; subsequent proceedings may be struck out.

The costs of a successful personal injury claim may be passed on or shared in contribution proceedings, but where the claimant fails, the defendant is liable for the costs of the third party but cannot recover any costs from the claimant. This is because the QOCS rules in CPR 44.13–44.17 protect the injured claimant but not the successful defendant: *Wagenaar v Weekend Travel Ltd t/a Ski Weekend* [2014] EWCA Civ 1105, [2015] 1 WLR 1968, [2014] All ER (D) 24 (Aug).

III PID [17]

2. Assessment of contribution

(1) Subject to subsection (3) below, in any proceedings for contribution under section 1 above the amount of the contribution recoverable from any person shall be such as may be found by the court to be just and equitable having regard to the extent of that person's responsibility for the damage in question.

(2) Subject to subsection (3) below, the court shall have power in any such proceedings to exempt any person from liability to make contribution, or to direct the contribution to be recovered from any person shall amount to a complete indemnity.

(3) Where the amount of the damages which have or might have been awarded in respect of the damage in question in any action brought in England and Wales by or on behalf of the person who suffered it against the person from whom the contribution is sought was or would have been subject to—

- (a) any limit imposed by or under any enactment or by any agreement made before the damage occurred;
- (b) any reduction by virtue of section 1 of the Law Reform (Contributory Negligence) Act 1945 or section 5 of the Fatal Accidents Act 1976; or
- (c) any corresponding limit or reduction under the law of a country outside England and Wales;

the person from whom the contribution is sought shall not by virtue of any contribution awarded under section 1 above be required to pay in respect of the damage a greater amount than the amount of those damages as so limited or reduced.

III PID [17.1]

Previous apportionment In *Wall v Radford* [1991] 2 All ER 741, POPPLEWELL J held that tortfeasors might not seek a different apportionment in an action between them from that made in previous proceedings brought by a passenger.

III PID [17.1A]

Just and equitable apportionment Where two insurance companies are liable, by statute, to an injured third party, but would each be entitled to repudiate liability vis-à-vis the insured they should be ordered to share the liability equally: *Eagle Star Insurance Co Ltd v Provincial Insurance plc* [1994] 1 AC 130, [1993] 3 All ER 1, PC.

Where the claim in the main proceedings has been compromised without any finding of liability it may be difficult to apportion responsibility in the Part 20 proceedings on any basis other than equal shares. In *Abbey National Bank plc v Matthews & Son* (2003) Times, 31 March, mortgagees compromised a claim against their solicitors for loss and took an assignment of their rights over against a firm of surveyors. The court dismissed the contribution claim against the surveyors on the ground that it was not possible in the circumstances to determine a just and equitable contribution.

Although "responsibility" is not concerned exclusively with causative responsibility, there needs to be some sufficient relationship between the responsibility and the damage in question in order for it to be just and equitable to order a contribution: *Brian Warwicker Partnership v HOK International Ltd* [2005] EWCA Civ 962, (2005) Times 19 September.

III PID [17.2]

Disclosure In *Gnitrow Ltd v Cape plc* [2000] 3 All ER 763, CA a shipyard operator, claiming a contribution from another shipyard operator in respect of asbestosis claims by employees was ordered to disclose correspondence with a third operator regarding a possible agreement to make a contribution. The purpose of the disclosure was to assist the defendant in making a sensible Part 36 offer, but the documents were not to be shown to the judge until after decisions had been made on apportionment.

III PID [17.3]

Dividing the damages The Act is concerned with the sharing of liability between two or more wrong-doers, without limiting the liability of each in full to the claimant: *Sivanandan v Hackney London Borough Council* [2013] EWCA Civ 22, [2013] 2 All ER 940, [2013] ICR 672.

III PID [18]

6. Interpretation

(1) A person is liable in respect of any damage for the purposes of this Act if the person who suffered it (or anyone representing his estate or dependants) is entitled to recover compensation from him in respect of that damage (whatever the legal basis of his liability, whether tort, breach of contract, breach of trust or otherwise).

(2) References in this Act to an action brought by or on behalf of the person who suffered any damage include references to an action brought for the benefit of his estate or dependants.

(3) In this Act "dependants" has the same meaning as in the Fatal Accidents Act 1976.

(4) In this Act, except in section 1 (5) above, "action" means an action brought in England and Wales.

ADMINISTRATION OF JUSTICE ACT 1982

(c 53)

GENERAL NOTES ON SECTIONS 1 AND 5

III PID [19]–III PID [21]

The broad effect of section 1 The broad effect of this section is to abolish "loss of future happiness" as a head of claim where life has been shortened by the tortious act (*Rose v Ford* [1937] AC 826, [1937] 3 All ER 359, HL) but not to affect the right of the living claimant to compensation for pain and suffering and loss of future earnings. The section applies to cases where the cause of action accrued after 28 October 1982 or the claimant died after 1 January 1983: see s 73(1) and (3).

In respect of loss of future earnings for lost years, see the Law Reform (Miscellaneous Provisions) Act 1934 above.

III PID [22]–III PID [23A]

Hospital care at public expense Pursuant to the Administration of Justice Act 1982 s 5 (as from 1 January 1983), there shall be set off against any income lost by the claimant as a result of his injuries, any saving which is attributable to his maintenance wholly or partly at the public expense in a hospital, nursing home or other institution. The saving is not to be credited against anything but loss of earnings. In *Goldfinch v Scannell* [1993] PIQR Q143, CA Mr D Latham QC sitting as a judge of the High Court deducted from the loss of earnings claim, a sum for board/lodging which the claimant had obtained free of charge from the health service until the final discharge home. Deductions under this section are not to be confused with those allowable under the Social Security (Recovery of Benefits) Act 1997, s 8.

ROAD TRAFFIC ACT 1988

(c 52)

III PID [23B]

143. Users of motor vehicles to be insured or secured against third-party risks

(1) Subject to the provisions of this Part of this Act—

(a) a person must not use a motor vehicle on a road or other public place unless there is in force in relation to the use of the vehicle by that person such a policy of insurance or such a security in respect of third party risks as complies with the requirements of this Part of this Act, and

(b) a person must not cause or permit any other person to use a motor vehicle on a road or other public place unless there is in force in relation to the use of the vehicle by that other person such a policy of insurance or such a security in respect of third party risks as complies with the requirements of this Part of this Act.

[(1A) In the application of this Part to automated vehicles—

(a) subsection (1) above has effect with the omission of the words "or such a security in respect of third party risks" in paragraphs (a) and (b);

(b) this Part has effect with the omission of sections 146 and 147(2);

(c) any other references to a security or certificate of security in this Act are to be ignored.]

(2) If a person acts in contravention of subsection (1) above he is guilty of an offence.

(3) A person charged with using a motor vehicle in contravention of this section shall not be convicted if he proves—

(a) that the vehicle did not belong to him and was not in his possession under a contract of hiring or of loan,

(b) that he was using the vehicle in the course of his employment, and

(c) that he neither knew nor had reason to believe that there was not in force in relation to the vehicle such a policy of insurance or security as is mentioned in subsection (1) above.

(4) This Part of this Act does not apply to invalid carriages.

Amendment *Sub-section (1A) is inserted by the Automated and Electric Vehicles Act 2018 with effect from a date to be appointed.*

PERSONAL INJURY AND DEATH

III PID [23B.1]

In certain circumstances the injured claimant has the right to assert a claim against the defendant's insurer under the Third Party (Rights against Insurers) Act 1930. Also, as regard defendant drivers who have failed to maintain third party insurance as required by s 143 of the Road Traffic Act 1988, a claim may be made against the Motor Insurers Bureau under the Uninsured Drivers Agreement 1999. As drafted the Agreement is confined to accidents on roads in public places but this restriction was successfully challenged in the European Court of Justice in *Damijan Vnuk v Zavarovalnica Triglav d.d.* [2014] CJEU Case C-162/13. It was held in that case that the First European Directive on Motor Insurance Council Directive 72/166/EEC was not confined to road accidents in public places but extended to accidents involving the normal use of motor vehicles anywhere on land. See further *Lewis (by his litigation friend) v Tindale* [2018] EWHC 2376 (QB).

III PID [23B.2]

Third Parties (Rights against Insurers) Act 2010 The coming into force on 1 August 2016 of the Third Parties (Rights against Insurers) Act 2010 enables claimants to claim directly against the insurers of a driver who is insolvent.

It has been held that the rights under the 2010 Act may not be invoked retrospectively in respect of accidents occurring before 1 August 2016. See Schedule 3 and *Redman v Zurich Insurance plc and EJS1 Ltd* [2017] EWHC 1919 (QB), [2017] All ER (D) 07 (Aug).

III PID [23C]

145. Requirements in respect of policies of insurance

(1) In order to comply with the requirements of this Part of this Act, a policy of insurance must satisfy the following conditions.

(2) The policy must be issued by an authorised insurer.

(3) Subject to subsection (4) below, the policy—

(a) must insure such person, persons or classes of persons as may be specified in the policy in respect of any liability which may be incurred by him or them in respect of the death of or bodily injury to any person or damage to property caused by, or arising out of, the use of the vehicle on a road or other public place in Great Britain, and

(aa) must, in the case of a vehicle normally based in the territory of another member State, insure him or them in respect of any civil liability which may be incurred by him or them as a result of an event related to the use of the vehicle in Great Britain if,—

(i) according to the law of that territory, he or they would be required to be insured in respect of a civil liability which would arise under that law as a result of that event if the place where the vehicle was used when the event occurred were in that territory, and

(ii) the cover required by that law would be higher than that required by paragraph (a) above, and

(b) must, in the case of a vehicle normally based in Great Britain, insure him or them in respect of any liability which may be incurred by him or them in respect of the use of the vehicle and of any trailer, whether or not coupled, in the territory other than Great Britain and Gibraltar of each of the member States of the European Union according to

(i) the law on compulsory insurance against civil liability in respect of the use of vehicles of the State in whose territory the event giving rise to the liability occurred; or

(ii) if it would give higher cover, the law which would be applicable under this Part of this Act if the place where the vehicle was used when that event occurred were in Great Britain; and

(c) must also insure him or them in respect of any liability which may be incurred by him or them under the provisions of this Part of this Act relating to payment for emergency treatment.

[(3A) In the case of an automated vehicle, the policy must also provide for the insurer's obligations to an insured person under section 2(1) of the Automated and Electric Vehicles Act 2018 (liability of insurers etc where accident caused by automated vehicle) to be obligations under the policy. In this subsection "insured person" means a person who is covered under the policy for using the vehicle on a road or public place in Great Britain.]

(4) The policy shall not, by virtue of subsection (3)(a) above, be required—

(a) to cover liability in respect of the death, arising out of and in the course of his employment, of a person in the employment of a person insured by the policy or of bodily injury sustained by such a person arising out of and in the course of his employment, or

(b) to provide insurance of more than £1,200,000 in respect of all such liabilities as may be insured in respect of damage to property caused by, or arising out of, any one accident involving the vehicle, or

(c) to cover liability in respect of damage to the vehicle, or

(d) to cover liability in respect of damage to goods carried for hire or reward in or on the vehicle or in or on any trailer (whether or not coupled) drawn by the vehicle, or

(e) to cover any liability of a person in respect of damage to property in his custody or under his control, or

(f) to cover any contractual liability.

[Paragraph (a) does not apply where the vehicle in question is an automated vehicle.]

(4A) In the case of a person—

(a) carried in or upon a vehicle, or

(b) entering or getting on to, or alighting from, a vehicle,

the provisions of paragraph (a) of subsection (4) above do not apply unless cover in respect of the liability referred to in that paragraph is in fact provided pursuant to a requirement of the Employers' Liability (Compulsory Insurance) Act 1969.

(5) "Authorised insurer" has the same meaning as in section 95.

(6) If any person or body of persons ceases to be a member of the Motor Insurers' Bureau, that person or body shall not by virtue of that cease to be treated as an authorised insurer for the purposes of this Part of this Act —

(a) in relation to any policy issued by the insurer before ceasing to be such a member, or

(b) in relation to any obligation (whether arising before or after the insurer ceased to be such a member) which the insurer may be called upon to meet under or in consequence of any such policy or under section 157 of this Act by virtue of making a payment in pursuance of such an obligation.

Amendment *Text in square brackets is inserted by the Automated and Electric Vehicles Act 2018 with effect from a date to be appointed.*

III PID [23C.1]

Section 145 sets out the requirements for all Road Traffic Act policies which must include cover for any liabilities which may be incurred in respect of death of or bodily injury to any person or damage to property caused by, or arising out of, the use of the vehicle on a road in Great Britain. Additionally, the policy must be issued by an authorised insurer and must cover driving in all of Europe and must also insure against the cost of emergency treatment.

In *Roadpeace v Secretary of State for Transport and Motor Insurer's Bureau* [2017] EWHC 2725 (Admin), the High Court held that ss 143, 145 and 151 of the Act were compatible with the UK's obligations under Directive 2009/103 to ensure that vehicles would be covered by compulsory insurance, even though the Act allowed a number of exclusions to cover, such as deliberate damage and road rage. However, following the European Court of Justice's decision in *Vnuk v Zavarovalnica Triglav dd (C-162/13)* EU:C:2014:2146, it was held that compulsory insurance should be extended beyond vehicles used on roads. (See further *Lewis (by his litigation friend) v Tindale* [2018] EWHC 2376 (QB).)

PERSONAL INJURY AND DEATH

III PID [23C.2]

Sub-section 145(3) refers to the term 'use' of vehicles. Clearly driving a car is using it. Walking across the road to get petrol for a car when it had run out of petrol is also using the car: see *Dunthorne v Bentley* [1996] PIQR P323, CA. The term 'road' was dealt with by the House of Lords in the conjoined appeals of *Cutter v Eagle Star Insurance Co Ltd; Clarke v Kato* [1998] 4 All ER 417, [1998] 1 WLR 1647. The case concerned whether two different car parks fell within the definition 'road' as defined by s 192(1) of the Road Traffic Act 1988. The House of Lords held that the question 'is a place a road?' was one of fact to be determined after consideration of the physical character and the function which the place existed to serve. Having considered this in the respective cases, it was held that neither car park was a 'road'. This resulted in the implementation of the Motor Vehicles (Compulsory Insurance) Regulations 2000 which inserted the words 'or other public place' after the word 'road'. Unfortunately, the added terms are not defined in the Road Traffic Act 1988, which often leads to courts exercising their discretion and common sense on a case by case basis.

III PID [23C.3]

Sub-section 145(4) specifically excludes property damage over £1,000,000, comprehensive cover, hire goods, personal property, death or injury to persons arising in the course of their employment and any contractual liabilities.

III PID [23D]

146. Requirements in respect of securities

(1) In order to comply with the requirements of this Part of this Act, a security must satisfy the following conditions.

(2) The security must be given either by an authorised insurer or by some body of persons which carries on in the United Kingdom the business of giving securities of a like kind and has deposited and keeps deposited with the Accountant General of the Senior Courts the sum of £15,000 in respect of that business.

(3) Subject to subsection (4) below, the security must consist of an undertaking by the giver of the security to make good, subject to any conditions specified in it, any failure by the owner of the vehicle or such other persons or classes of persons as may be specified in the security duly to discharge any liability which may be incurred by him or them, being a liability required under section 145 of this Act to be covered by a policy of insurance.

(4) In the case of liabilities arising out of the use of a motor vehicle on a road or other public place in Great Britain the amount secured need not exceed—

- (a) in the case of an undertaking relating to the use of public service vehicles (within the meaning of the Public Passenger Vehicles Act 1981), £25,000,
- (b) in any other case, £5,000.

III PID [23E]

147. Issue of certificates of insurance and of security

(1) An insurer issuing a policy of insurance for the purposes of this Part of this Act must deliver to the person by whom the policy is effected a certificate (in this Part of this Act referred to as a "certificate of insurance") in the prescribed form and containing such particulars of any conditions subject to which the policy is issued and of any other matters as may be prescribed.

(1A) A certificate of insurance is to be treated for the purposes of subsection (1) as having been delivered to the person by whom the policy is effected if—

- (a) it is transmitted electronically by the insurer to the person in accordance with subsection (1B) below, or
- (b) it is made available by the insurer to the person on a website in accordance with subsection (1C) below.

(1B) A certificate is transmitted electronically by an insurer to a person in accordance with this subsection if—

(a) on effecting the policy to which the certificate relates, the person agreed to its electronic transmission for the purposes of subsection (1) above, and

(b) the certificate is transmitted by the insurer to an electronic address specified by the person for this purpose.

(1C) A certificate is made available by an insurer to a person on a website in accordance with this subsection if—

(a) on effecting the policy to which the certificate relates, the person agreed to its being made available on a website for the purposes of subsection (1) above,

(b) the insurer makes the certificate available to the person by placing an electronic copy of it on a website, and

(c) the person is notified by the insurer, in a manner agreed by the person, of—

(i) the certificate's presence on the website,

(ii) the address of the website,

(iii) the place on the website where he may access the certificate, and

(iv) how he may access the certificate.

(1D) Where a certificate made available on a website is treated by virtue of subsection (1A)(b) above as having been delivered by an insurer to a person, the insurer must ensure that the certificate remains continuously accessible to the person on the website until the expiry of the last day on which the policy to which it relates has effect.

(1E) For the purposes of subsection (1D) above, a certificate is to be treated as remaining continuously accessible to a person on a website, despite its being temporarily inaccessible to him on the website, if the insurer has taken all reasonable steps to make it continuously accessible to him on the website (including steps to remedy any temporary inaccessibility).

(2) A person giving a security for the purposes of this Part of this Act must deliver to the person to whom it is given a certificate (in this Part of this Act referred to as a "certificate of security") in the prescribed form and containing such particulars of any conditions subject to which the security is issued and of any other matters as may be prescribed.

(3) Different forms and different particulars may be prescribed for the purposes of subsection (1) or (2) above in relation to different cases or circumstances.

(4)–(5) . . .

III PID [23F]

148. Avoidance of certain exceptions to policies or securities

(1) Where a policy or security is issued or given for the purposes of this Part of this Act, so much of the policy or security as purports to restrict—

(a) the insurance of the persons insured by the policy, or

(b) the operation of the security,

(as the case may be) by reference to any of the matters mentioned in subsection (2) below shall, as respects such liabilities as are required to be covered by a policy under section 145 of this Act, be of no effect.

(2) Those matters are—

(a) the age or physical or mental condition of persons driving the vehicle,

(b) the condition of the vehicle,

(c) the number of persons that the vehicle carries,

(d) the weight or physical characteristics of the goods that the vehicle carries,

(e) the time at which or the areas within which the vehicle is used,

(f) the horsepower or cylinder capacity or value of the vehicle,

(g) the carrying on the vehicle of any particular apparatus, or

(h) the carrying on the vehicle of any particular means of identification other than any means of identification required to be carried by or under the Vehicle Excise and Registration Act 1994.

(3) Nothing in subsection (1) above requires an insurer or the giver of a security to pay any sum in respect of the liability of any person otherwise than in or towards the discharge of that liability.

(4) Any sum paid by an insurer or the giver of a security in or towards the discharge of any liability of any person which is covered by the policy or security by virtue only of subsection (1) above is recoverable by the insurer or giver of the security from that person.

(5) A condition in a policy or security issued or given for the purposes of this Part of this Act providing—

(a) that no liability shall arise under the policy or security, or

(b) that any liability so arising shall cease,

in the event of some specified thing being done or omitted to be done after the happening of the event giving rise to a claim under the policy or security, shall be of no effect in connection with such liabilities as are required to be covered by a policy under section 145 of this Act.

(6) Nothing in subsection (5) above shall be taken to render void any provision in a policy or security requiring the person insured or secured to pay to the insurer or the giver of the security any sums which the latter may have become liable to pay under the policy or security and which have been applied to the satisfaction of the claims of third parties.

(7) Notwithstanding anything in any enactment, a person issuing a policy of insurance under section 145 of this Act shall be liable to indemnify the persons or classes of persons specified in the policy in respect of any liability which the policy purports to cover in the case of those persons or classes of persons.

III PID [23G]

149. Avoidance of certain agreements as to liability towards passengers

(1) This section applies where a person uses a motor vehicle in circumstances such that under section 143 of this Act there is required to be in force in relation to his use of it such a policy of insurance or such a security in respect of third-party risks as complies with the requirements of this Part of this Act.

(2) If any other person is carried in or upon the vehicle while the user is so using it, any antecedent agreement or understanding between them (whether intended to be legally binding or not) shall be of no effect so far as it purports or might be held—

(a) to negative or restrict any such liability of the user in respect of persons carried in or upon the vehicle as is required by section 145 of this Act to be covered by a policy of insurance, or

(b) to impose any conditions with respect to the enforcement of any such liability of the user.

(3) The fact that a person so carried has willingly accepted as his the risk of negligence on the part of the user shall not be treated as negativing any such liability of the user.

(4) For the purposes of this section—

(a) references to a person being carried in or upon a vehicle include references to a person entering or getting on to, or alighting from, the vehicle, and

(b) the reference to an antecedent agreement is to one made at any time before the liability arose.

III PID [23H]

151. Duty of insurers or persons giving security to satisfy judgment against persons insured or secured against third-party risks

(1) This section applies where, after a policy or security is issued or given for the purposes of this Part of the Act, a judgment to which this subsection applies is obtained.

(2) Subsection (1) above applies to judgments relating to a liability with respect to any matter where liability with respect to that matter is required to be covered by a policy of insurance under section 145 of this Act and either—

- (a) it is a liability covered by the terms of the policy or security, and the judgment is obtained against any person who is insured by the policy or whose liability is covered by the security, as the case may be, or
- (b) it is a liability, other than an excluded liability, which would be so covered if the policy insured all persons or, as the case may be, the security covered the liability of all persons, and the judgment is obtained against any person other than one who is insured by the policy or, as the case may be, whose liability is covered by the security.

(3) In deciding for the purposes of subsection (2) above whether a liability is or would be covered by the terms of a policy or security, so much of the policy or security as purports to restrict, as the case may be, the insurance of the persons insured by the policy or the operation of the security by reference to the holding by the driver of the vehicle of a licence authorising him to drive it shall be treated as of no effect.

(4) In subsection (2)(b) above "excluded liability" means a liability in respect of the death of, or bodily injury to, or damage to the property of any person who, at the time of the use which gave rise to the liability, was allowing himself to be carried in or upon the vehicle and knew or had reason to believe that the vehicle had been stolen or unlawfully taken, not being a person who—

- (a) did not know and had no reason to believe that the vehicle had been stolen or unlawfully taken until after the commencement of his journey, and
- (b) could not reasonably have been expected to have alighted from the vehicle.

In this subsection the reference to a person being carried in or upon a vehicle includes a reference to a person entering or getting on to, or alighting from, the vehicle.

(5) Notwithstanding that the insurer may be entitled to avoid or cancel, or may have avoided or cancelled, the policy or security, he must, subject to the provisions of this section, pay to the persons entitled to the benefit of the judgment—

- (a) as regards liability in respect of death or bodily injury, any sum payable under the judgment in respect of the liability, together with any sum which, by virtue of any enactment relating to interest on judgments, is payable in respect of interest on that sum,
- (b) as regards liability in respect of damage to property, any sum required to be paid under subsection (6) below, and
- (c) any amount payable in respect of costs.

(6) This subsection requires—

- (a) where the total of any amount paid, payable or likely to be payable under the policy or security in respect of damage to property caused by, or arising out of, the accident in question does not exceed £1,000,000, the payment of any sum payable under the judgment in respect of the liability, together with any sum which, by virtue of any enactment relating to interest on judgments, is payable in respect of interest on that sum,

PERSONAL INJURY AND DEATH

(b) where that total exceeds £1,200,000, the payment of either—

(i) such proportion of any sum payable under the judgment in respect of the liability as £1,200,000 bears to that total, together with the same proportion of any sum which, by virtue of any enactment relating to interest on judgments, is payable in respect of interest on that sum, or

(ii) the difference between the total of any amounts already paid under the policy or security in respect of such damage and £1,200,000, together with such proportion of any sum which, by virtue of any enactment relating to interest on judgments, is payable in respect of interest on any sum payable under the judgment in respect of the liability as the difference bears to that sum,

whichever is the less, unless not less than £1,200,000 has already been paid under the policy or security in respect of such damage (in which case nothing is payable).

(7) Where an insurer becomes liable under this section to pay an amount in respect of a liability of a person who is insured by a policy or whose liability is covered by a security, he is entitled to recover from that person—

(a) that amount, in a case where he became liable to pay it by virtue only of subsection (3) above, or

(b) in a case where that amount exceeds the amount for which he would, apart from the provisions of this section, be liable under the policy or security in respect of that liability, the excess.

(8) Where an insurer becomes liable under this section to pay an amount in respect of a liability of a person who is not insured by a policy or whose liability is not covered by a security, he is entitled to recover the amount from that person or from any person who—

(a) is insured by the policy, or whose liability is covered by the security, by the terms of which the liability would be covered if the policy insured all persons or, as the case may be, the security covered the liability of all persons, and

(b) caused or permitted the use of the vehicle which gave rise to the liability.

(9) In this section—

(a) "insurer" includes a person giving a security,

(b) ...

(c) "liability covered by the terms of the policy or security" means a liability which is covered by the policy or security or which would be so covered but for the fact that the insurer is entitled to avoid or cancel, or has avoided or cancelled, the policy or security.

(10) In the application of this section to Scotland, the words "by virtue of any enactment relating to interest on judgments" in subsections (5) and (6) (in each place where they appear) shall be omitted.

III PID [23H.1]

A claimant who sues an insured defendant can usually gain no better rights against the defendant's insurer than the defendant himself had. Where a claimant sues and obtains judgment against the insured defendant, but the latter has breached a condition of his contract of insurance, then the insurer can refuse indemnity to compensate the claimant. Under s 151, however, upon judgment being obtained against the insured defendant by the claimant, the insurer is bound to compensate the claimant for the judgment sum notwithstanding the fact that the insurer refuses to indemnify its insured, subject to s 152 below. Section 151 thus restricts the circumstances in which an insurer can avoid liability to a claimant victim. Further, even if the driver was not insured under the policy covering the vehicle, so long as the vehicle was covered by a contract for insurance, the claimant can enforce the judgment against the insurer.

In *Cameron v Hussain* [2017] EWCA Civ 366 it was held that, in view of the statutory purpose of s 151, it was not necessary to name an identifiable driver as the defendant in the claim.

A complex and difficult situation arises from the provision of s 151(8) which provides that where an insurer becomes liable under this section to pay an amount in respect of a liability of a person not injured by the policy, the insurer is entitled to recover the amount paid from that person or from any person who is insured by the policy. This means that where the owner of a vehicle permits an uninsured or unlicensed driver to drive his/her vehicle which is subsequently involved in an accident, they can be held liable to repay the insurer for sums paid to an injured claimant (whether it is the owner or another). In the case of an injured owner/claimant this could well have the effect of wiping out his/her damages: see the case of *Churchill Insurance Co Ltd v Wilkinson; Evans v Equity Claims Ltd* [2012] EWCA Civ 1166, [2013] 1 All ER 1146, [2013] 1 WLR 1776.

III PID [23I]

152. Exceptions to section 151

(1) No sum is payable by an insurer under section 151 of this Act—

- (a) in respect of any judgment unless, before or within seven days after the commencement of the proceedings in which the judgment was given, the insurer had notice of the bringing of the proceedings, or
- (b) in respect of any judgment so long as execution on the judgment is stayed pending an appeal, or
- (c) in connection with any liability if, before the happening of the event which was the cause of the death or bodily injury or damage to property giving rise to the liability, the policy or security was cancelled by mutual consent or by virtue of any provision contained in it.

(2) Subject to subsection (3) below, no sum is payable by an insurer under section 151 of this Act if, in an action commenced before, or within three months after, the commencement of the proceedings in which the judgment was given, he has obtained a declaration—

- (a) that, apart from any provision contained in the policy or security, he is entitled to avoid the policy under either of the relevant insurance enactments, or the security on the ground that it was obtained—
  - (i) by the non-disclosure of a material fact, or
  - (ii) by a representation of fact which was false in some material particular, or
- (b) if he has avoided the policy under either of the relevant insurance enactments, or the security on that ground, that he was entitled so to do apart from any provision contained in the policy or security

and, for the purposes of this section, "material" means of such a nature as to influence the judgment of a prudent insurer in determining whether he will take the risk and, if so, at what premium and on what conditions.

(3) An insurer who has obtained such a declaration as is mentioned in subsection (2) above in an action does not by reason of that become entitled to the benefit of that subsection as respects any judgment obtained in proceedings commenced before the commencement of that action unless before, or within seven days after, the commencement of that action he has given notice of it to the person who is the plaintiff (or in Scotland pursuer) in those proceedings specifying the relevant insurance enactment or, in the case of a security, the non-disclosure or false representation on which he proposes to rely.

(4) A person to whom notice of such an action is so given is entitled, if he thinks fit, to be made a party to it.

(5) In this section, "relevant insurance enactment" means the Consumer Insurance (Disclosure and Representations) Act 2012 or Part 2 of the Insurance Act 2015.

III PID [23I.1]

To enforce a judgment gained obtained against an insured defendant, against an insurer, the latter must be given notice of the bringing of proceedings, either before or within 7 days of commencement of proceedings. This provision does not apply to the Uninsured Drivers Agreement 1999. According to s 152(2), the insurer can avoid payment where the insurer has obtained a declaration due to non-disclosure by its insured. In order to do so, the insurer must give notice to the claimant of the declaration proceedings. However, it has been held that this subsection is incompatible with EU law (*R (on the application of RoadPeace Ltd) v Secretary of State for Transport* [2018] 1 WLR 129).

III PID [23J]

157. Payment for hospital treatment of traffic casualties

(1) Subject to subsection (2) below, where—

(a) a payment, other than a payment under section 158 of this Act, is made (whether or not with an admission of liability) in respect of the death of, or bodily injury to, any person arising out of the use of a motor vehicle on a road or in some other public place, and

(b) the payment is made—

(i) by an authorised insurer, the payment being made under or in consequence of a policy issued under section 145 of this Act, or

(ii) by the owner of a vehicle in relation to the use of which a security under this Part of this Act is in force, or

(iii) by the owner of a vehicle who has made a deposit under this Part of this Act, and

(c) the person who has so died or been bodily injured has to the knowledge of the insurer or owner, as the case may be, received treatment at a hospital, whether as an in-patient or as an out-patient, in respect of the injury so arising,

the insurer or owner must pay the expenses reasonably incurred by the hospital in affording the treatment, after deducting from the expenses any moneys actually received in payment of a specific charge for the treatment, not being moneys received under any contributory scheme.

(2) The amount to be paid shall not exceed £2,949.00 for each person treated as an in-patient or £295.00 for each person treated as an out-patient.

(3) For the purposes of this section "expenses reasonably incurred" means—

(a) in relation to a person who receives treatment at a hospital as an in-patient, an amount for each day he is maintained in the hospital representing the average daily cost, for each in-patient, of the maintenance of the hospital and the staff of the hospital and the maintenance and treatment of the in-patients in the hospital, and

(b) in relation to a person who receives treatment at a hospital as an out-patient, reasonable expenses actually incurred.

III PID [23K]

158. Payment for emergency treatment of traffic casualties

(1) Subsection (2) below applies where—

(a) medical or surgical treatment or examination is immediately required as a result of bodily injury (including fatal injury) to a person caused by, or arising out of, the use of a motor vehicle on a road or in some other public place, and

(b) the treatment or examination so required (in this Part of this Act referred to as "emergency treatment") is effected by a legally qualified medical practitioner.

(2) The person who was using the vehicle at the time of the event out of which the bodily injury arose must, on a claim being made in accordance with the provisions of section 159 of this Act, pay to the practitioner (or, where emergency treatment is effected by more than one practitioner, to the practitioner by whom it is first effected)—

(a) a fee of £21.30 in respect of each person in whose case the emergency treatment is effected by him, and

(b) a sum, in respect of any distance in excess of two miles which he must cover in order—

(i) to proceed from the place from which he is summoned to the place where the emergency treatment is carried out by him, and

(ii) to return to the first mentioned place,

equal to 41 pence for every complete mile and additional part of a mile of that distance.

(3) Where emergency treatment is first effected in a hospital, the provisions of subsections (1) and (2) above with respect to payment of a fee shall, so far as applicable, but subject (as regards the recipient of a payment) to the provisions of section 159 of this Act, have effect with the substitution of references to the hospital for references to a legally qualified medical practitioner.

(4) Liability incurred under this section by the person using a vehicle shall, where the event out of which it arose was caused by the wrongful act of another person, be treated for the purposes of any claim to recover damage by reason of that wrongful act as damage sustained by the person using the vehicle.

ACCESS TO HEALTH RECORDS ACT 1990

(c 23)

III PID [23L]

1. "Health record" and related expressions

(1) In this Act "health record" means a record which—

(a) consists of information relating to the physical or mental health of an individual who can be identified from that information, or from that and other information in the possession of the holder of the record; and

(b) has been made by or on behalf of a health professional in connection with the care of that individual.

(2) In this Act "holder", in relation to a health record, means—

(a) in the case of a record made by a health professional performing primary medical services under a general medical services contract made with the National Health Service Commissioning Board or a

Local Health Board, the person or body who entered into the contract with the... Board (or, in a case where more than one person so entered into the contract, any such person);

(aa) in the case of a record made by a health professional performing such services in accordance with arrangements under section 92 or 107 of the National Health Service Act 2006, or section 50 or 64 of the National Health Service (Wales) Act 2006, with [the National Health Service Commissioning Board or a Local Health Board, the person or body which made the arrangements with the... Board (or, in a case where more than one person so made the arrangements, any such person);

(b) in the case of a record made by a health professional for purposes connected with the provision of health services by a health service body (and not falling within paragraph (aa) above), the health service body by which or on whose behalf the record is held;

(c) in any other case, the health professional by whom or on whose behalf the record is held.

(3) In this Act "patient", in relation to a health record, means the individual in connection with whose care the record has been made.

III PID [23M]

2. Health Professionals

In this Act, "health professional" has the same meaning as in the Data Protection Act 2018 (see section 204 of that Act).

III PID [23N]

3. Right of access to health records

(1) An application for access to a health record, or to any part of a health record, may be made to the holder of the record by any of the following, namely—

(a) ...

(b) ...

(cc) ...

(e) ...

(ee) where the record is held in Scotland and the patient is incapable, within the meaning of the Adults with Incapacity (Scotland) Act 2000 (asp 4) in relation to making or authorising the application, any person entitled to act on behalf of the patient under that Act;

(f) where the patient has died, the patient's personal representative and any person who may have a claim arising out of the patient's death;

[(g) where the patient has died, a medical examiner exercising functions by virtue of section 20 of the Coroners and Justice Act 2009 in relation to the death.]

(2) Subject to section 4 below, where an application is made under subsection (1) above the holder shall, within the requisite period, give access to the record, or the part of a record, to which the application relates—

(a) in the case of a record, by allowing the applicant to inspect the record or, where section 5 below applies, an extract setting out so much of the record as is not excluded by that section;

(b) in the case of a part of a record, by allowing the applicant to inspect an extract setting out that part or, where that section applies, so much of that part as is not so excluded; or

(c) in either case, if the applicant so requires, by supplying him with a copy of the record or extract.

(3) Where any information contained in a record or extract which is so allowed to be inspected, or a copy of which is so supplied, is expressed in terms which are not intelligible without explanation, an explanation of those terms shall be provided with the record or extract, or supplied with the copy.

(4) No fee shall be required for giving access under subsection (2) above . . .

[Paragraphs (a) and (b) above do not apply in the case of access for which an application is made under subsection (1)(g) above.]

(5) For the purposes of subsection (2) above the requisite period is—

- (a) where the application relates to a record, or part of a record, none of which was made before the beginning of the period of 40 days immediately preceding the date of the application, the period of 21 days beginning with that date;
- (b) in any other case, the period of 40 days beginning with that date.

(6) Where—

- (a) an application under subsection (1) above does not contain sufficient information to enable the holder of the record to identify the patient or,... to satisfy himself that the applicant is entitled to make the application; and
- (b) within the period of 14 days beginning with the date of the application, the holder of the record requests the applicant to furnish him with such further information as he may reasonably require for that purpose,

subsection (5) above shall have effect as if for any reference to that date there were substituted a reference to the date on which that further information is so furnished.

Amendment *Text in square brackets is inserted by the Coroners and Justice Act 2009 with effect from a date to be appointed.*

PERSONAL INJURY AND DEATH

III PID [23O]

4. Cases where right of access may be wholly excluded

(1) ...

(2) ...

(3) Where an application is made under subsection (1)(f) of section 3 above, access shall not be given under subsection (2) of that section if the record includes a note, made at the patient's request, that he did not wish access to be given on such an application.

III PID [23P]

5. Cases where right of access may be partially excluded

(1) Access shall not be given under section 3(2) above to any part of a health record—

- (a) which, in the opinion of the holder of the record, would disclose—
  - (i) information likely to cause serious harm to the physical or mental health... of any... individual; or
  - (ii) information relating to or provided by an individual, other than the patient, who could be identified from that information; or
- (b) which was made before the commencement of this Act.

(2) Subsection (1)(a)(ii) above shall not apply—

- (a) where the individual concerned has consented to the application; or
- (b) where that individual is a health professional who has been involved in the care of the patient;

and subsection (1)(b) above shall not apply where and to the extent that, in the opinion of the holder of the record, the giving of access is necessary in order to make intelligible any part of the record to which access is required to be given under section 3(2) above.

(3) Access shall not be given under section 3(2) to any part of a health record which, in the opinion of the holder of the record, would disclose—

(a) information provided by the patient in the expectation that it would not be disclosed to the applicant; or

(b) information obtained as a result of any examination or investigation to which the patient consented in the expectation that the information would not be so disclosed.

(4) Where an application is made under subsection (1)(f) of section 3 above, access shall not be given under subsection (2) of that section to any part of the record which, in the opinion of the holder of the record, would disclose information which is not relevant to any claim which may arise out of the patient's death.

(5) The Secretary of State may by regulations provide that, in such circumstances as may be prescribed by the regulations, access shall not be given under section 3(2) above to any part of a health record which satisfies such conditions as may be so prescribed.

III PID [23Q]

6. Correction of inaccurate health records

(1) Where a person considers that any information contained in a health record, or any part of a health record, to which he has been given access under section 3(2) above is inaccurate, he may apply to the holder of the record for the necessary correction to be made.

(2) On an application under subsection (1) above, the holder of the record shall—

(a) if he is satisfied that the information is inaccurate, make the necessary correction;

(b) if he is not so satisfied, make in the part of the record in which the information is contained a note of the matters in respect of which the information is considered by the applicant to be inaccurate; and

(c) in either case, without requiring any fee, supply the applicant with a copy of the correction or note.

(3) In this section "inaccurate" means incorrect, misleading or incomplete.

III PID [23R]

8. Applications to the court

(1) Subject to subsection (2) below, where the court is satisfied, on an application made by the person concerned within such period as may be prescribed by rules of court, that the holder of a health record has failed to comply with any requirement of this Act, the court may order the holder to comply with that requirement.

(2) The court shall not entertain an application under subsection (1) above unless it is satisfied that the applicant has taken all such steps to secure compliance with the requirement as may be prescribed by regulations made by the Secretary of State.

(3) For the purposes of subsection (2) above, the Secretary of State may by regulations require the holders of health records to make such arrangements for dealing with complaints that they have failed to comply with any requirements of this Act as may be prescribed by the regulations.

(4) For the purposes of determining any question whether an applicant is entitled to be given access under section 3(2) above to any health record, or any part of a health record, the court—

(a) may require the record or part to be made available for its own inspection; but

(b) shall not, pending determination of that question in the applicant's favour, require the record or part to be disclosed to him or his representatives whether by discovery (or, in Scotland, recovery) or otherwise.

(5) The jurisdiction conferred by this section shall be exercisable by the High Court or the county court or, in Scotland, by the Court of Session or the sheriff.

III PID [23R.1]

This section has been amended by the Crime and Courts Act 2013, Sch 9, para 52. For savings and transitional provisions see Sch 8 to the Act and Article 3 of SI 2014/954.

III PID [23S]

11. Interpretation

In this Act—

"application" means an application in writing and "apply" shall be construed accordingly;

"care" includes examination, investigation, diagnosis and treatment;

"general medical services contract" means a contract under section 84 of the National Health Service Act 2006 or section 42 of the National Health Service (Wales) Act 2006;

"Health Board" has the same meaning as in the National Health Service (Scotland) Act 1978;

"health service body" means—

(a) a... Health Authority, Special Health Authority or Local Health Board;

(b) a Health Board;

(c) ...

(d) a National Health Service trust first established under section 5 of the National Health Service and Community Care Act 1990, *section 25 of the National Health Service Act 2006, or* section 18 of the National Health Service (Wales) Act 2006 or section 12A of the National Health Service (Scotland) Act 1978;

(e) an NHS foundation trust;

(f) the Health and Social Care Information Centre;

"information", in relation to a health record, includes any expression of opinion about the patient;

"Local Health Board" means a Local Health Board established under section 11 of the National Health Service (Wales) Act 2006;

"make", in relation to such a record, includes compile

"Special Health Authority" means a Special Health Authority established under section 28 of the National Health Service Act 2006 or section 22 of the National Health Service (Wales) Act 2006;

Amendment *In definition "health service body" in para (d) words in italic repealed by the Health and Social Care Act 2012 with effect from a date to be appointed.*

III PID [23S.1]

This Act came into force on 1 November 1991. Its practical application, following the modifications introduced by the Data Protection Act 1998, is to enable the obtaining of the health records of persons who lack capacity, and more generally in relation to the medical records of deceased persons. However, in certain circumstances set out in the Act, disclosure can be refused — for example where the medical practitioner believes that disclosure is likely to have an adverse effect on the patient's health, or which may identify a third party.

It is important also to consider the provisions of the Access to Medical Records Act 1988 which deals with medical reports prepared for insurers/employers. Section 1 provides: 'It shall be the right of an individual to have access, in accordance with the provisions of this Act, to any medical report relating to the individual which is to be, or has been, supplied by a medical practitioner for employment purposes or insurance purposes.' Thus the Act allows patients to obtain access to reports for insurers or employers and provides for the patient to ask for amendments. The patient can require that his or her own comments are appended if the report is not corrected. The Act also requires that the patient's consent is obtained before any information is released to a third party in the context of reports requested by insurers or employers. The patient must be provided with the report before it is sent if the patient so wishes and the patient also has a right to refuse consent for the provisions of a report.

DAMAGES ACT 1996

(c 48)

III PID [23T]

A1. Assumed rate of return on investment of damages: England and Wales

(1) In determining the return to be expected from the investment of a sum awarded as damages for future pecuniary loss in an action for personal injury the court must, subject to and in accordance with rules of court made for the purposes of this section, take into account such rate of return (if any) as may from time to time be prescribed by an order made by the Lord Chancellor.

(2) Subsection (1) does not however prevent the court taking a different rate of return into account if any party to the proceedings shows that it is more appropriate in the case in question.

(3) An order under subsection (1) may prescribe different rates of return for different classes of case.

(4) An order under subsection (1) may in particular distinguish between classes of case by reference to—

- (a) the description of future pecuniary loss involved;
- (b) the length of the period during which future pecuniary loss is expected to occur;
- (c) the time when future pecuniary loss is expected to occur.

(5) Schedule A1 (which makes provision about determining the rate of return to be prescribed by an order under subsection (1)) has effect.

(6) An order under this section is to be made by statutory instrument subject to annulment in pursuance of a resolution of either House of Parliament.

III PID [23T.1]

Section A1 was inserted by the Civil Liability Act 2018 with effect from 20 December 2018.

III PID [24]

1. ***Assumed rate of return on investment of damages***

(1) In determining the return to be expected from the investment of a sum awarded as damages for future pecuniary loss in an action for personal injury the court shall, subject to and in accordance with rules of court made for the purposes of this section, take into account such rate of return (if any) as may from time to time be prescribed by an order made by the Lord Chancellor.

(2) Subsection (1) above shall not however prevent the court taking a different rate of return into account if any party to the proceedings shows that it is more appropriate in the case in question.

(3) An order under subsection (1) above may prescribe different rates of return for different classes of case.

(4) Before making an order under subsection (1) above the Lord Chancellor shall consult the Government Actuary and the Treasury; and any order under that subsection shall be made by statutory instrument subject to annulment in pursuance of a resolution of either House of Parliament.

(5) In the application of this section to Scotland—

(a) for the reference to the Lord Chancellor in subsections (1) and (4) there is substituted a reference to the Scottish Ministers; and

(b) in subsection (4)—

(i) "and the Treasury" is omitted; and

(ii) for "either House of Parliament" there is substituted "the Scottish Parliament".

(6) In the application of this section to Northern Ireland—

(a) for the reference to the Lord Chancellor in subsections (1) and (4) there is substituted a reference to the Department of Justice in Northern Ireland; and

(b) in subsection (4)—

(i) for the reference to the Treasury there is substituted a reference to the Department of Finance and Personnel in Northern Ireland; and

(ii) for "by statutory instrument" to "Parliament" there is substituted "by statutory rule for the purposes of the Statutory Rules (Northern Ireland) Order 1979, and is subject to negative resolution within the meaning of section 41(6) of the Interpretation Act (Northern Ireland) 1954".

Amendment *Section 1 is revoked by the Civil Liability Act 2018 with effect from 20 December 2018.*

III PID [24.1]

Order The purpose of the section is to enable the Lord Chancellor to make an order setting the rate of interest to be used in calculating the lump sum required to compensate for future financial losses in a personal injuries claim. It is currently set at minus 0.75%.

On 25 June 2001, the Lord Chancellor made the Damages (Personal Injury) Order 2001 (SI 2001/2301), setting for the foreseeable future a discount rate of 2.5%. That figure was subsequently reviewed by the Lord Chancellor because of certain limited inaccuracies in the information underlying the average yield figure on which he had based his reasoning in making the order. Such review did not lead to a change in the 2.5% figure. The rate has been and remains a highly contentious issue. Government consultations concerning the calculation of the discount rate were carried out in 2012 and 2013 and in 2014 the Lord Chancellor sought to appoint a panel of experts to provide advice. It was established in a Guernsey case, which went to the Privy Council on appeal, that the current rate of return on index-linked Government Stocks had fallen to well below 2.5% and close to zero: *Simon v Helmot* [2012] UKPC 5, 126 BMLR 73. This supported the contention that adopting the statutory rate of 2.5% led to significant under-compensation. No result of any review by the Lord Chancellor had been announced by the summer of 2016, and the Association of Personal Injury Lawyers threatened her with judicial review. A judicial review claim by the Association of British Insurers against the Lord Chancellor's decision to complete the review of the discount rate failed in January 2017: *R (on the application of ABI) v Lord Chancellor* [2017] EWHC 106 (Admin). The rate was ultimately lowered, from 20 March 2017, to minus 0.75%: Damages (Personal Injury) Order 2017, SI 2017/206. That reduction in rate led to far higher awards of damages in cases with substantial future losses. The Civil Liability Act 2018 introduces new provisions as to the determination of the discount rate. A first review must commence within 90 days of Royal Assent, ie on or before 19 March 2019. The review will be conducted by reference to the new process detailed in the Act. The first review must be completed and the Lord Chancellor must determine the new rate within 140 days of the review commencing, ie on or before 6 August 2019.

The adoption of a negative rate calls into question the approach taken to claims for the cost of alternative accommodation: *JR (a protected party) v Sheffield Teaching Hospitals NHS Foundation Trust* [2017] EWHC 1245 (QB); *Porter (a child) v Barts Health NHS Trust* [2017] EWHC 3205 (QB). It is anticipated, however, that the rate will change to positive in 2019 once the statutory review has been completed.

A rate different from that set by the Lord Chancellor as the assumed rate of return is appropriate only where either the case comes within a category which the Lord Chancellor has not considered and/or has special features which the Lord Chancellor has not taken into account: *Warriner v Warriner* [2002] EWCA Civ 81, [2003] 3 All ER 447, [2002] 1 WLR 1703, (2002) Times, 28 March. The Court may not subvert or undermine the discount rate to take account of the probability that medical costs will go up faster than the general rate of inflation: *Cooke v United Bristol Healthcare NHS Trust* [2003] EWCA Civ 1370, [2004] 1All ER 797, (2003) Times, 24 October.

For similar reasons it has been held that a court may not award as damages the predicted cost of investment advice and fund management charges, since these were taken into account in setting the rate: *Page v Plymouth Hospitals NHS Trust* [2004] EWHC 1154 (QB), [2004] 3 All ER 367. Nor may a court award as damages the fees likely to be charged by Court of Protection panel brokers for advice and dealing relating to the investment of the damages fund: *Eagle v Chambers (No 2)* [2004] EWCA Civ 1033, (2004) Times, 30 August, CA.

III PID [24.2]

Personal injury Section 7(1) provides, as regards the whole of the United Kingdom except Scotland, that personal injury "includes any disease and any impairment of a person's physical or mental condition and references to a claim or action for personal injury include references to such a claim or action brought by virtue of the Law Reform (Miscellaneous Provisions) Act 1934 and to a claim or action brought by virtue of the Fatal Accidents Act 1976". Provision is made in sub-s (3) for modifications in the application of s 7(1) to Northern Ireland.

III PID [25]

2. Periodical payments

(A1) In cases where Regulation (EC) No 1371/2007 of the European Parliament and of the Council of 23rd October 2007 on rail passengers' rights and obligations applies, this section needs to be read in the light of Article 30 of the Uniform Rules concerning the contract for the international carriage of passengers and luggage by rail (damages to be awarded as annuity on request), as set out in Annex I to that Regulation.

(1) A court awarding damages for future pecuniary loss in respect of personal injury—

- (a) may order that the damages are wholly or partly to take the form of periodical payments, and
- (b) shall consider whether to make that order.

(2) A court awarding other damages in respect of personal injury may, if the parties consent, order that the damages are wholly or partly to take the form of periodical payments.

(3) A court may not make an order for periodical payments unless satisfied that the continuity of payment under the order is reasonably secure.

(4) For the purpose of subsection (3) the continuity of payment under an order is reasonably secure if—

- (a) it is protected by a guarantee given under section 6 of or Schedule 1 to this Act,

(b) it is protected by a scheme under section 213 of the Financial Services and Markets Act 2000 (compensation) (whether or not as modified by section 4 of this Act), or

(c) the source of payment is a government or health service body.

(5) An order for periodical payments may include provision—

(a) requiring the party responsible for the payments to use a method (selected or to be selected by him) under which the continuity of payment is reasonably secure by virtue of subsection (4);

(b) about how the payments are to be made, if not by a method under which the continuity of payment is reasonably secure by virtue of subsection (4);

(c) requiring the party responsible for the payments to take specified action to secure continuity of payment, where continuity is not reasonably secure by virtue of subsection (4);

(d) enabling a party to apply for a variation of provision included under paragraph (a), (b) or (c).

(6) Where a person has a right to receive payments under an order for periodical payments, or where an arrangement is entered into in satisfaction of an order which gives a person a right to receive periodical payments, that person's right under the order or arrangement may not be assigned or charged without the approval of the court which made the order; and—

(a) a court shall not approve an assignment or charge unless satisfied that special circumstances make it necessary, and

(b) a purported assignment or charge, or agreement to assign or charge, is void unless approved by the court.

(7) Where an order is made for periodical payments, an alteration of the method by which the payments are made shall be treated as a breach of the order (whether or not the method was specified under subsection (5)(b)) unless—

(a) the court which made the order declares its satisfaction that the continuity of payment under the new method is reasonably secure,

(b) the new method is protected by a guarantee given under section 6 of or Schedule 1 to this Act,

(c) the new method is protected by a scheme under section 213 of the Financial Services and Markets Act 2000 (compensation) (whether or not as modified by section 4 of this Act), or

(d) the source of payment under the new method is a government or health service body.

(8) An order for periodical payments shall be treated as providing for the amount of payments to vary by reference to the retail prices index (within the meaning of section 833(2) of the Income and Corporation Taxes Act 1988) at such times, and in such a manner, as may be determined by or in accordance with Civil Procedure Rules.

(9) But an order for periodical payments may include provision—

(a) disapplying subsection (8), or

(b) modifying the effect of subsection (8).

III PID [25.1]

The new law on periodical payments Section 2, as originally enacted, made awards of periodical payments conditional on the consent of the parties. This section was replaced on 1 April 2005 by three new sections (2, 2A and 2B); and sections 4 and 5 were replaced at the same time by the new section 4 printed below. The broad effect of the new regime is to enable the court to order periodical payments for future pecuniary loss in respect of personal injury, without requiring the consent of the parties. The provisions on structured settlements, in sections 4 and 5 as originally enacted, were replaced by a new section 4 which now provides enhanced protection for periodical payments.

III PID [25.2]

Applicable rules of court The Civil Procedure Rules contain detailed provisions regarding claims in which an award of periodical payments may be appropriate. Section II of CPR Part 41 and Practice Direction 41B permit the parties to relevant litigation to set out in their statements of case whether and why an award of periodical payments would be more, or less, appropriate than a lump sum; the court is required to indicate which form of order is likely to be more appropriate; the court's order for periodical payments must include certain specified matters. CPR Part 36 contains requirements concerning periodical payments in respect of offers to settle claims that include future pecuniary loss: **CPR 36.18**. CPR PD 21 requires the court to be satisfied, when hearing an application to approve a settlement for a child or protected party, that the parties have considered whether damages should wholly or partly take the form of periodical payments, and further imposes certain requirements for such applications in respect of settlements which include provision for periodical payments. For pleadings and precedents see **BCCP M[62]** onwards.

III PID [25.2A]

Where an interim payment is sought under CPR 25.6 and a periodical payments order might be made at trial, the interim award should not normally exceed a reasonable proportion of the part of the predicted final award not potentially covered by the periodical payments order, that is to say a reasonable proportion of the predicted award for pain, suffering, loss of amenities, past losses, interest and, normally, accommodation; a larger interim payment can only be justified if the judge at the interim payment stage is satisfied there is a real need for the interim payment requested and can confidently predict that the trial judge will capitalise additional elements of future loss so as to produce a greater lump sum award: *Eeles v Cobham Hire Services* [2009] EWCA Civ 204. As to the quantum of an interim payment when the issue of future accommodation is not resolved in a catastrophic head injury claim in the context of an anticipated order for periodical payments, see *Brown v Emery* [2010] EWHC 388 (QB), [2010] All ER (D) 39 (Mar).

If the assessment of damages involves establishing where the injured claimant will be cared for and the charges which the local authority may make in this regard, it is desirable that the local authority should be added as a party: *Bottomley (by her litigation friend Helen Ryan) v East Midlands Strategic Health Authority* [2010] EWCA Civ 756, [2010] All ER (D) 23 (Jul).

III PID [25.3]

Government or health service body Section 2A(2) provides for the designation of government or health service bodies by Order of the Lord Chancellor, which was done by the Damages (Government and Health Service Bodies) Order 2005, SI 2005/474.

III PID [25.3A]

Reasonably secure As to the security of a periodical payments order within the meaning of the Damages Act 1996, see *YM (a child) v Gloucestershire NHS Foundation Trust* [2006] PIQR P432.

III PID [25.4]

Variation by reference to the retail prices index If a periodical payments order does not identify on its face the manner in which the amount of the payments is to vary, to maintain their real value, the retail price index applies, as provided in sub-s (8). However, the court has power, under sub-s (9), to disapply or modify the effect of sub-s (8) in relation to the retail price index; and the exercise of this power is not limited to exceptional circumstances: *Flora v Wakom (Heathrow) Ltd* [2006] EWCA Civ 1103, [2006] All ER (D) 426 (Jul).

In an early case following Flora, the court decided to make a lump sum order where there was evidence that increases in the wages of care workers would result in under-provision for a claimant requiring long term care, if variation by reference to the retail prices index were applied: *A v B Hospitals NHS Trust* [2006] EWHC 2833 (QB), [2006] All ER (D) 131 (Nov).

However in subsequent cases the court exercised its power under s 2(9) to amend the rate at which the payments would vary. In *Lee Thompstone v Tameside & Glossop Acute Services NHS Trust* [2006] EWHC 2904 (QB), [2006] All ER (D) 333 (Nov) Swift J made an order for periodical payments for care and case management which were to vary by reference to the index of occupational earnings for care assistants and home carers in the Annual Survey of Hours and Earnings Group 6115 (ASHE 6115) rather than the retail prices index. That decision was followed in a number of other first instance decisions. In *Sarwar v Ali* [2007] LS Law Med 375 the court similarly decided that an order for periodical payments in respect of future wage losses should vary in accordance with a wage-related measure rather than the retail prices index.

III PID [25B.2]

The Order The Damages (Variation of Periodical Payments) Order 2005, SI 2005/841, came into force on 1 April 2005. The text of its 14 articles is as follows:

THE DAMAGES (VARIATION OF PERIODICAL PAYMENTS) ORDER 2005, SI 2005/841

1 Citation, commencement, interpretation and extent

(1) This Order may be cited as the Damages (Variation of Periodical Payments) Order 2005 and shall come into force on the fourteenth day after the day on which it is made.

(2) In this Order—

(a) "the Act" means the Damages Act 1996;

(b) "agreement" means an agreement by parties to a claim or action for damages which settles the claim or action and which provides for periodical payments;

(c) "damages" means damages for future pecuniary loss in respect of personal injury;

(d) "defence society" means the Medical Defence Union or the Medical Protection Society;

(e) "variable agreement" means an agreement which contains a provision referred to in Article 9(1);

(f) "variable order" means an order for periodical payments which contains a provision referred to in Article 2.

(3) In the application of this Order to Northern Ireland —

(a) "claimant" means plaintiff;

(b) "permission" means leave;

(c) "statements of case" means, in the High Court, the writ and pleadings and, in the county court, the civil bill and any notice of intention to defend, defence, notice for particulars, replies and counterclaim.

(4) This Order extends to England and Wales and Northern Ireland.

(5) This Order applies to proceedings begun on or after the date on which it comes into force.

2 Power to make variable orders

If there is proved or admitted to be a chance that at some definite or indefinite time in the future the claimant will—

(a) as a result of the act or omission which gave rise to the cause of action, develop some serious disease or suffer some serious deterioration, or

(b) enjoy some significant improvement, in his physical or mental condition, where that condition had been adversely affected as a result of that act or omission,

the court may, on the application of a party, with the agreement of all the parties, or of its own initiative, provide in an order for periodical payments that it may be varied.

3 Defendant's financial resources

Unless—

(a) the defendant is insured in respect of the claim,

(b) the source of payment under the order for periodical payments is a government or health service body within the meaning of section 2A(2) of the Act,

(c) the payment is guaranteed under section 6 of or the Schedule to the Act, or

(d) (d) the order is made by consent and the claimant is neither a child, nor a person who lacks capacity within the meaning of the Mental Capacity Act 2005 (c 9) to administer and manage his property and affairs nor a patient within the meaning of Part VII of the Mental Health (Northern Ireland) Order 1986,

the court will take into account the defendant's likely future financial resources in considering whether to make a variable order.

4 Award of provisional damages

The court may make a variable order in addition to an order for an award of provisional damages made by virtue of section 32A of the Senior Courts Act 1981 or section 51 of the county courts Act 1984 or, in relation to Northern Ireland, paragraph 10(2)(a) of Schedule 6 to the Administration of Justice Act 1982.

5 Contents of variable order

Where the court makes a variable order—

(a) the damages must be assessed or agreed on the assumption that the disease, deterioration or improvement will not occur;

(b) the order must specify the disease or type of deterioration or improvement;

(c) the order may specify a period within which an application for it to be varied may be made;

(d) the order may specify more than one disease or type of deterioration or improvement and may, in respect of each, specify a different period within which an application for it to be varied may be made;

(e) the order must provide that a party must obtain the court's permission to apply for it to be varied, unless the court otherwise orders.

6 Applications to extend period for applying for permission to vary

Where a period is specified under Article 5(c) or (d)—

(a) a party may make more than one application to extend the period, and such an application is not to be treated as an application to vary a variable order for the purposes of Article 7;

(b) a party may not make an application for the variable order to be varied after the end of the period specified or such period as extended by the court.

7 Limit on number of applications to vary

A party may make only one application to vary a variable order in respect of each specified disease or type of deterioration or improvement.

8 Case file

(1) Where the court makes a variable order, the case file documents must be preserved by the court until the end of the period or periods specified under Article 5(c) or (d) or of any extension of them or, if no such period was specified, until the death of the claimant.

(2) The case file documents are, unless the court otherwise orders—

(a) the judgment as entered;

(b) the statements of case;

(c) the schedule of expenses and losses;

(d) a transcript of the judge's oral judgment;

(e) all medical reports relied on;

(f) a transcript of any parts of the claimant's own evidence which the judge considers necessary;

(g) any subsequent orders.

(3) A court officer must ensure that the case file documents are provided by the parties where necessary and filed on the court file.

(4) Where a variable order has been made, the legal representatives of the parties and, if the parties are insured, their insurers, must also preserve their own case file until the end of the period or periods specified under Article 5(c) or (d) or of any extension of them or, if no such period was specified, until the death of the claimant.

9 Variable agreements

(1) If there is agreed to be a chance that at some definite or indefinite time in the future the claimant will—

(a) as a result of the act or omission which gave rise to the cause of action, develop some serious disease or suffer some serious deterioration, or

(b) enjoy some significant improvement, in his physical or mental condition, where that condition had been adversely affected as a result of that act or omission,

the parties to an agreement may agree that a party to it may apply to the court subsequently for its terms to be varied.

(2) Where the parties agree to permit an application to vary the terms of an agreement, the agreement—

(a) must expressly state that a party to it may apply to the court for its terms to be varied;

(b) must specify the disease or type of deterioration or improvement;

(c) may specify a period within which an application for it to be varied may be made;

(d) may specify more than one disease or type of deterioration or improvement and may, in respect of each, specify a different period within which an application for it to be varied may be made.

(3) A party who is permitted by an agreement to apply for its terms to be varied must obtain the court's permission to apply for it to be varied.

10 Application for permission

(1) An application for permission to apply for a variable order or a variable agreement to be varied must be accompanied by evidence—

- (a) that the disease, deterioration or improvement specified in the order or agreement has occurred, and
- (b) that it has caused or is likely to cause an increase or decrease in the pecuniary loss suffered by the claimant.

(2) Where the applicant is the claimant and he knows that the defendant is insured in respect of the claim and the identity of the defendant's insurers, he must serve the application notice on the insurers as well as on the defendant.

(3) Where the applicant is the claimant and he knows that the defendant is a member of a defence society and the identity of the defence society, he must serve the application notice on the defence society as well as on the defendant.

(4) The respondent to the application may, within 28 days after service of the application, serve written representations on the applicant and, if he does, must file them with the court.

(5) The court will deal with the application without a hearing.

11 Refusal of permission

(1) Where permission is refused, the applicant may, within 14 days after service of the order, request the decision to be reconsidered at a hearing.

(2) No appeal lies from an order refusing permission after reconsideration.

12 Grant of permission

(1) Where permission is granted, the court will also give directions as to the application for the variation of the variable order or the variable agreement.

(2) Directions must include directions as to—

- (a) the date by which the application for variation must be served and filed;
- (b) the service and filing of evidence.

(3) No appeal lies from an order granting permission.

13 Order for variation

(1) On an application for the variation of a variable order or a variable agreement, if the court is satisfied—

- (a) that the disease, deterioration or improvement specified in the order or agreement has occurred, and
- (b) that it has caused or is likely to cause an increase or decrease in the pecuniary loss suffered by the claimant,

it may order—

- (i) the amount of annual payments to be varied, either from the date of the application for permission or from the date of the application to vary if the order did not require the permission of the court for an application to vary, or from such later date as it may specify in the order;
- (ii) how each payment is to be made during the year and at what intervals;
- (iii) a lump sum to be paid in addition to the existing periodical payments.

(2) Section 2(3) to (9) of the Act applies to orders under this Order as it applies to orders for periodical payments.

14 Application of rules of court

In England and Wales, the Civil Procedure Rules 1998 and in Northern Ireland, rules of court apply to applications under this Order, except where this Order makes provision inconsistent with Civil Procedure Rules or rules of court.

III PID [26]

3. Provisional damages and fatal accident claims

(1) This section applies where a person—

- (a) is awarded provisional damages; and
- (b) subsequently dies as a result of the act or omission which gave rise to the cause of action for which the damages were awarded.

PERSONAL INJURY AND DEATH

(2) The award of the provisional damages shall not operate as a bar to an action in respect of that person's death under the Fatal Accidents Act 1976.

(3) Such part (if any) of—

(a) the provisional damages; and

(b) any further damages awarded to the person in question before his death,

as was intended to compensate him for pecuniary loss in a period which in the event falls after his death shall be taken into account in assessing the amount of any loss of support suffered by the person or persons for whose benefit the action under the Fatal Accidents Act 1976 is brought.

(4) No award of further damages made in respect of that person after his death shall include any amount for loss of income in respect of any period after his death.

(5) In this section "provisional damages" means damages awarded by virtue of subsection (2)(a) of section 32A of the Senior Courts Act 1981 or section 51 of the county courts Act 1984 and "further damages" means damages awarded by virtue of subsection (2)(b) of either of those sections.

(6) Subsection (2) above applies whether the award of provisional damages was before or after the coming into force of that subsection; and subsections (3) and (4) apply to any award of damages under the 1976 Act or, as the case may be, further damages after the coming into force of those subsections.

(7) In the application of this section to Northern Ireland—

(a) for references to the Fatal Accidents Act 1976 there shall be substituted references to the Fatal Accidents (Northern Ireland) Order 1977;

(b) for the reference to subsection (2) (a) and (b) of section 32A of the Senior Courts Act 1981 and section 51 of the county courts Act 1984 there shall be substituted a reference to paragraph 10 (2) (a) and (b) of Schedule 6 to the Administration of Justice Act 1982.

III PID [26.1]

Orders for provisional damages The powers of the county court to order provisional damages are set out in the County Courts Act 1984 s 51 (see para **II CCA [30]**). The procedure for obtaining such orders is set out in CPR 41 (see para **CPR 41**) and PD 41A (see para **CPR PD 41A**).

III PID [26.2]

Removal of the bar It had been held in *Middleton v Elliott Turbo-machinery Ltd* (1990) Times, 29 October, CA that where a claimant obtained provisional damages for injuries from which he later died, his dependants were barred by the earlier decision from making claims under the Fatal Accidents Act 1976. The effect of s 3 is to remove the bar for the future, even as regards cases where the award of provisional damages was made before the coming into force of the section: see sub-s (6). Subject to the operation of the Limitation Act 1980, a claim may now be made under the Fatal Accidents Act 1976, notwithstanding an award of provisional damages, even where the death occurred before the coming into force of the section.

III PID [26A]

4. Enhanced protection for periodical payments

(1) Subsection (2) applies where—

(a) a person has a right to receive periodical payments, and

(b) his right is protected by a scheme under section 213 of the Financial Services and Markets Act 2000 (compensation), but only as to part of the payments.

(2) The protection provided by the scheme shall extend by virtue of this section to the whole of the payments.

(3) Subsection (4) applies where—

(a) one person ("the claimant") has a right to receive periodical payments from another person ("the defendant"),

(b) a third person ("the insurer") is required by or in pursuance of an arrangement entered into with the defendant (whether or not together with other persons and whether before or after the creation of the claimant's right) to make payments in satisfaction of the claimant's right or for the purpose of enabling it to be satisfied, and

(c) the claimant's right to receive the payments would be wholly or partly protected by a scheme under section 213 of the Financial Services and Markets Act 2000 if it arose from an arrangement of the same kind as that mentioned in paragraph (b) but made between the claimant and the insurer.

(4) For the purposes of the scheme under section 213 of that Act—

(a) the claimant shall be treated as having a right to receive the payments from the insurer under an arrangement of the same kind as that mentioned in subsection (3)(b),

(b) the protection under the scheme in respect of those payments shall extend by virtue of this section to the whole of the payments, and

(c) no person other than the claimant shall be entitled to protection under the scheme in respect of the payments.

(5) In this section "periodical payments" means periodical payments made pursuant to—

(a) an order of a court in so far as it is made in reliance on section 2 above (including an order as varied), or

(b) an agreement in so far as it settles a claim or action for damages in respect of personal injury (including an agreement as varied).

(6) In subsection (5)(b) the reference to an agreement in so far as it settles a claim or action for damages in respect of personal injury includes a reference to an undertaking given by the Motor Insurers' Bureau (being the company of that name incorporated on 14th June 1946 under the Companies Act 1929), or an Article 75 insurer under the Bureau's Articles of Association, in relation to a claim or action in respect of personal injury.

III PID [26A.1]

Changes made by the Courts Act 2003 Sections 4 and 5, as enacted, provided for structured settlements. Section 101 of the Courts Act 2005, which was brought into force on 1 April 2005, made substantial amendments to s 4 and repealed s 5. The amended text of s 4, printed above, now provides enhanced protection for periodical payments and has no application to structured settlements.

SOCIAL SECURITY (RECOVERY OF BENEFITS) ACT 1997

(c 27)

GENERAL NOTES ON SOCIAL SECURITY (RECOVERY OF BENEFITS) ACT 1997

III PID [27]

The Social Security (Recovery of Benefits) Act 1997 came into force on 6 October 1997 and applies to compensation payments made on or after that date, unless agreed or ordered before. It replaces Part IV of the Social Security Administration Act 1992 (ss 81–104). The obligation on the compensator is to reimburse the Secretary of State for all the social security benefits in any event, with currently no exemption for small payments. On the other hand the right of deduction vis-à-vis the claimant is less general than under the previous law; particular benefits can only be set against particular heads of compensation, as set out in Sch 2. Broadly the intention is to protect the pain and suffering element in the compensation from deduction.

III PID [28]

Compensation payments to which the Act applies The Act applies to all payments in respect of any person in consequence of any accident, injury or disease (s 1) except for payments mentioned in Part I of Sch 1 or in the Social Security (Recovery of Benefits) Regulations 1997, SI 1997/2205. Those exempted payments include payments under the Fatal Accidents Act 1976, compensation for sensorineural hearing loss where the loss is less than 50DB in one or both ears, and compensation paid under the Pneumoconiosis etc (Workers' Compensation) Act 1979 (which must be deducted in full from the damages: *Ballantine v Newalls Insulation Co Ltd* [2001] ICR 125, CA applying the principles in *Hodgson v Trapp* [1989] AC 807.

III PID [29]

Duty to provide information As with the earlier legislation duties are imposed on any person claiming compensation or in receipt of such a claim to provide information to the Department of Work and Pensions' Compensation Recovery Unit (contact details at www.gov.uk/government/collections/cru). Employers are similarly liable. The duties derive from s 23 of the Act and from the Social Security (Recovery of Benefits) Regulations 1997, SI 1997/2205 regs 3–6.

III PID [30]

Certificate of recoverable benefit Before making a compensation payment to which the Act applies, the compensator must apply, under s 4, for the Compensation Recovery Unit to provide a certificate of recoverable benefits, that is, accident- or disease-related benefits which are listed in Sch 2 column (2), below.

III PID [31]

Liability of compensator to pay the total recoverable benefit The compensator is liable, under s 6, to pay the Compensation Recovery Unit the full amount of the recoverable benefit immediately before paying the compensation, though no amount is payable until 14 days thereafter. Some of it may be deductible from the compensation but probably not all, see the following note.

III PID [32]

Reduction of compensation payment The compensator may make a deduction in respect of the benefit payment when paying the compensation, but only to the extent that the head of benefit reads across into a head of compensation, as provided in the columns of Sch 2, below. There may, therefore, be some recoverable benefit which cannot be deducted, eg where there is no award for anything but pain and suffering. There may also be situations in which the recoverable benefit exceeds the compensation awarded under that head. If the compensation is exceeded by the amount of recoverable benefit, the liability to pay compensation is discharged by a statement that the compensation due after making the deduction is nil (s 8). But the compensator's obligation to pay the total recoverable benefit to the Compensation Recovery Unit is unaffected. The compensator is required, in any case, to inform the recipient that the amount of the payment has been arrived at after making reductions, calculated by reference to a stated date (s 9).

Where an employer gave to a claimant a sum of £15,000 including £11,889 to which there was no contractual entitlement, and which was "to be treated as an advance against damages that may be awarded", such sum was to be taken into account and deducted from the damages award. The payment was expressly referable to any future award of damages and was not a mere benevolent payment: *Williams v BOC Gases Ltd* (2000) Times, 5 April, CA. *McCamley v Cammell Laird Shipbuilders* [1990] 1 All ER 854, [1990] 1 WLR 963 was to be confined to its own facts.

III PID [33]

Appeal against the certificate Provision is made in ss 10 to 14 for appeals against certificates and for their review, along the same lines as the pre-existing law.

III PID [34]

Complex cases Provision is made for complex cases in ss 18 and 19 and in the Social Security (Recovery of Benefits) Regulations 1997, SI 1997/2205 reg 9 (reduction of compensation: complex cases), reg 10 (structured settlements) and reg 11 (adjustments).

III PID [35]

Transitional provisions Regulation 12 of the same regulations provides for the old law to apply in certain transitional situations.

III PID [36]

Guidance The practicalities are explained at www.gov.uk/government/collections/cru.

III PID [37]

15. Court orders

(1) This section applies where a court makes an order for a compensation payment to be made in any case, unless the order is made with the consent of the injured person and the person by whom the payment is to be made.

(2) The court must, in the case of each head of compensation listed in column 1 of Schedule 2 to which any of the compensation payment is attributable, specify in the order the amount of the compensation payment which is attributable to that head.

III PID [37.1]

Heads of compensation See the three heads identified in Sch 2 at para **III PID [40]**, and the notes on applying the schedule. Note, however, that the damages are to be assessed without regard to the possibility of benefit deduction (s 17). Interest is awarded on the full amount of the damages, without regard to the prospect that the compensator may deduct benefits under the Act: *Wadey v Surrey County Council* [2000] 2 All ER 545, HL. However that award of interest on damages for past loss of earnings may be subject to the deduction in respect of benefit for loss of earnings: *Griffiths v British Coal Corpn* [2001] EWCA Civ 336, [2001] 1 WLR 1493.

III PID [37.2]

Relevant period The heads of compensation are expressed in terms of compensation for loss during the relevant period, that is, over the period down to payment or the first five years, whichever is the shorter (s 3).

The relevant period is explained in s 3 as follows:

3.

(1) In relation to a person ("the claimant") who has suffered any accident or injury or disease, "the relevant period" has the meaning given by the following subsections.

(2) Subject to sub-s (4), if it is a case of accident or injury, the relevant period is the period of five years immediately following the day on which the accident or injury in question occurred.

(3) Subject to sub-s (4), if it is a case of disease, the relevant period is the period of five years beginning with the date on which the claimant first claims a listed benefit in consequence of the disease.

(4) If at any time before the end of the period referred in sub-s (2) or (3)—

(a) a person makes a compensation payment in final discharge of any claim made by or in respect of the claimant and arising out of the accident, injury or disease, or

(b) an agreement is made under which an earlier compensation payment is treated as having been made in final discharge of any such claim,

the relevant period ends at that time.

PERSONAL INJURY AND DEATH

III PID [37.3]

Claim for loss of non-recoupable benefit A claimant may be entitled to claim as special damages the amount of any benefit which he was receiving before the accident and which, but for the accident, he would have continued to receive on a non-recoupable basis: *Neal v Bingle* [1998] QB 466, [1998] 2 All ER 58, CA, following *Hassall v Secretary of State for Social Security* [1995] 3 All ER 909, [1995] 1 WLR 812, CA.

III PID [37.4]

Payment for pain and suffering only Where parties wish to compromise on the basis that a payment is for pain and suffering only and not for loss of earnings (so as effectively to preclude liability to the DWP) see: *Black v Doncaster Metropolitan Borough Council* (1998) Times, 14 July, CA.

III PID [38]

16. Payments into court

(1) Regulations may make provision (including provision modifying this Act) for any case in which a payment into court is made.

(2) The regulations may (among other things) provide—

- (a) for the making of a payment into court to be treated in prescribed circumstances as the making of a compensation payment,
- (b) for application for, and issue of, certificates of recoverable benefits, and
- (c) for the relevant period to be treated as ending on a date determined in accordance with the regulations.

(3) Rules of court may make provision governing practice and procedure in such cases.

(4) This section does not extend to Scotland.

III PID [38.1]

Regulations Detailed provision for payments into court is made by the Social Security (Recovery of Benefits) Regulations 1997, SI 1997/2205, reg 8 as follows:

8. Payments into court

(1) Subject to the provisions of this regulation, where a party to an action makes a payment into court which, had it been paid directly to another party to the action ("the relevant party"), would have constituted a compensation payment—

- (a) the making of that payment shall be treated for the purposes of the 1997 Act as the making of a compensation payment;
- (b) a current certificate of recoverable benefits shall be lodged with the payment; and
- (c) where the payment is calculated under section 8, the compensator must give the relevant party the information specified in section 9 (1), instead of the person to whom the payment is made.

(2) The liability under section 6 (1) to pay an amount equal to the total amount of the recoverable benefits shall not arise until the person making the payment into court has been notified that the whole or any part of the payment into court has been paid out of court to or for the relevant party.

(3) Where a payment into court in satisfaction of his claim is accepted by the relevant party in the initial period, then as respects the compensator in question, the relevant period shall be taken to have ended, if it has not done so already, on the day on which the payment into court (or if there were two or more such payments, the last of them) was made.

(4) Where, after the expiry of the initial period, the payment into court is accepted in satisfaction of the relevant party's claim by consent between the parties, the relevant period shall end, if it has not done so already, on the date on which application to the court for the payment is made.

(5) Where, after the expiry of the initial period, payment out of court is made wholly or partly to or for the relevant party in accordance with an order of the court and in satisfaction of his claim, the relevant period shall end, if it has not done so already, on the date of that order.

(6) In paragraphs (3), (4) and (5), "the initial period" means the period of 21 days after the receipt by the relevant party to the action of notice of the payment into court having been made.

(7) Where a payment into court is paid out wholly to or for the party who made the payment (otherwise than to or for the relevant party to the action) the making of the payment into court shall cease to be regarded as the making of a compensation payment.

(8) A current certificate of recoverable benefits in paragraph (1) means one that is in force as described in section 4 (4).

III PID [38.2]

Certificate to be lodged with payment The compensator is required to lodge a current certificate of recoverable benefit whenever he makes a payment into court.

III PID [38.3]

Information about the amount deducted Where any amount of recoverable benefit has been deducted from the compensation paid into court, the compensator must inform the claimant that reductions that have been made. The compensator must also inform the claimant of the date by reference to which the calculation has been made, that is, the date of payment in. These requirements derive from ss 8 and 9 of the Act as applied to payments into court by the Social Security (Recovery of Benefits) Regulations 1997, SI 1997/2205, reg 8.

III PID [38.4]

Nil statements Where the benefit deduction under each head equals or exceeds the compensation due under each head, the compensator's liability under each head is discharged by deducting the sum and paying the Compensation Recovery Unit, and giving the claimant a statement saying so: s 8.

III PID [38.5]

The relevant period The 'relevant period' referred to in paras (3), (4)–(5) is the period following the accident during which listed benefits are recoverable; see s 3 of the Act.

III PID [38.6]

Beating the payment in The claimant is entitled to the full value of his or her general damages claim for pain, suffering and loss of amenity (as intended by Parliament). It is not appropriate for the claimant to make up any shortfall in damages by appealing the CRU certificate. CPR 36.22(6)(b) requires the payment into court notice to state 'the name and amount of any deductible amounts by which the gross amount is reduced', ie the amount by which the gross sum is reduced must be no more than the amount appropriate for the head of damages against which the benefits can be offset. Therefore unless the defendant makes a proper assessment of the award for general damages and makes it clear how the gross amount has been reduced in accordance with section 8, the notice will arguably not be proper and effective (unless suitable clarification has been obtained pursuant to a request under CPR 36.8).

III PID [39]

17. Benefits irrelevant in assessing damages

In assessing damages in respect of any accident, injury or disease, the amount of any listed benefits paid or likely to be paid is to be disregarded.

III PID [39.1]

Assessment of damages This section makes clear that damages are to be assessed in the normal way without taking account of deductions and it has been held that the same applies to awards of interest on the damages: *Wadey v Surrey County Council* [2000] 2 All ER 545, HL.

III PID [39.2]

Loss of non-recoupable benefits It was held in *Neal v Bingle* [1998] QB 466, [1998] 2 All ER 58, CA that a similarly worded provision in the 1992 Act did not prevent the claimant from claiming the loss of non-recoupable benefit as a head of special damage.

SCHEDULE 2
CALCULATION OF COMPENSATION PAYMENT

Section 8

III PID [40]

(1) *Head of compensation*		(2) *Benefit*
1.	Compensation for earnings lost during the relevant period	Universal credit [. . .] Disablement pension payable under section 103 of the 1992 Act Employment and support allowance Incapacity benefit *Income support* Invalidity pension and allowance Jobseeker's allowance Reduced earnings allowance Severe disablement allowance Sickness benefit Statutory sick pay Unemployability supplement Unemployment benefit
2.	Compensation for costs of care incurred during the relevant period	Attendance allowance Daily living component of personal independence payment *Care component of disability living allowance* Disablement pension increase payable under section 104 or 105 of the 1992 Act
3.	Compensation for loss of mobility during the relevant period	Mobility allowance Mobility component of personal independence payment *Mobility component of disability living allowance*

1. (1) References to incapacity benefit, invalidity pension and allowance, severe disablement allowance, sickness benefit and unemployment benefit also include any income support paid with each of those benefits on the same instrument of payment or paid concurrently with each of those benefits by means of an instrument for benefit payment.

(2) For the purpose of this Note, income support includes personal expenses addition, special transitional additions and transitional addition as defined in the Income Support (Transitional) Regulations 1987, SI 1997/1969.

2. Any reference to statutory sick pay—

(a) includes only 80 per cent of payments made between 6th April 1991 and 5th April 1994, and

(b) does not include payments made on or after 6th April 1994.

3. In this Schedule "the 1992 Act" means the Social Security Contributions and Benefits Act 1992.

III PID [40.1]

Compensation for loss of earnings An award of interest on damages for past loss of earnings is within the Sch 2 head of 'compensation for earnings lost' *Griffiths v British Coal Corpn* [2001] EWCA Civ 336, [2001] 1 WLR 1493. On unusual facts, in the case of a self-employed insurance broker 'compensation for earnings lost' has been held to apply to the gross fees lost and not the net profit: *Lowther v Chatwin* [2003] EWCA Civ 729, [2003] All ER (D) 294 (May), (2003) Times, 4 August.

III PID [40.2]

Compensation for loss of mobility The third head of compensation (loss of mobility) has been interpreted as not including pain, suffering or loss of amenity but only financial loss, eg taxi fares occasioned by the loss of mobility: *Mitchell v Laing* 1998 SC 342, Ct of Sess, Inner House.

COMPENSATION ACT 2006

(c 29)

III PID [40A]

1. Deterrent effect of potential liability

A court considering a claim in negligence or breach of statutory duty may, in determining whether the defendant should have taken particular steps to meet a standard of care (whether by taking precautions against a risk or otherwise), have regard to whether a requirement to take those steps might—

(a) prevent a desirable activity from being undertaken at all, to a particular extent or in a particular way, or

(b) discourage persons from undertaking functions in connection with a desirable activity.

III PID [40A.1]

Sections 1–3 of this Act came into force when the Act gained Royal Assent on 25 July 2006, though s 16(3) provides that s 3 of the Act shall be taken to have always had effect.

III PID [40A.2]

This section seeks to clarify the law relating to what constitutes a breach of duty of care and addresses the issue of what amounts to 'reasonable care' when a court is deciding whether that standard has been met. See *Hopps v Mott MacDonald and Ministry of Defence* [2009] EWHC 1881 (QB), [2009] All ER (D) 259 (Jul).

The Social Action, Responsibility and Heroism Act 2015 may also be of relevance. This Act requires that when courts are considering negligence or breach of statutory duty, they must have regard to whether a person was acting for the benefit of society, demonstrated a responsible approach towards protecting the safety or interests of others, or was acting heroically by intervening in an emergency to assist an individual in danger.

III PID [40B]

2. Apologies, offers of treatment or other redress
An apology, an offer of treatment or other redress, shall not of itself amount to an admission of negligence or breach of statutory duty.

III PID [40C]

3. Mesothelioma: damages

(1) This section applies where—

(a) a person ("the responsible person") has negligently or in breach of statutory duty caused or permitted another person ("the victim") to be exposed to asbestos,

(b) the victim has contracted mesothelioma as a result of exposure to asbestos,

(c) because of the nature of mesothelioma and the state of medical science, it is not possible to determine with certainty whether it was the exposure mentioned in paragraph (a) or another exposure which caused the victim to become ill, and

(d) the responsible person is liable in tort, by virtue of the exposure mentioned in paragraph (a), in connection with damage caused to the victim by the disease (whether by reason of having materially increased a risk or for any other reason).

(2) The responsible person shall be liable—

(a) in respect of the whole of the damage caused to the victim by the disease (irrespective of whether the victim was also exposed to asbestos—

(i) other than by the responsible person, whether or not in circumstances in which another person has liability in tort, or

(ii) by the responsible person in circumstances in which he has no liability in tort), and

(b) jointly and severally with any other responsible person.

(3) Subsection (2) does not prevent—

(a) one responsible person from claiming a contribution from another, or

(b) a finding of contributory negligence.

(4) In determining the extent of contributions of different responsible persons in accordance with subsection (3)(a), a court shall have regard to the relative lengths of the periods of exposure for which each was responsible; but this subsection shall not apply—

(a) if or to the extent that responsible persons agree to apportion responsibility amongst themselves on some other basis, or

(b) if or to the extent that the court thinks that another basis for determining contributions is more appropriate in the circumstances of a particular case.

(5) In subsection (1) the reference to causing or permitting a person to be exposed to asbestos includes a reference to failing to protect a person from exposure to asbestos.

(6) In the application of this section to Scotland—

(a) a reference to tort shall be taken as a reference to delict, and

(b) a reference to a court shall be taken to include a reference to a jury.

(7) The Treasury may make regulations about the provision of compensation to a responsible person where—

(a) he claims, or would claim, a contribution from another responsible person in accordance with subsection (3)(a), but

(b) he is unable or likely to be unable to obtain the contribution, because an insurer of the other responsible person is unable or likely to be unable to satisfy the claim for a contribution.

(8) The regulations may, in particular—

(a) ...

(b) replicate or apply (with or without modification) a transitional compensation provision;

(c) provide for a specified person to assess and pay compensation;

(d) provide for expenses incurred (including the payment of compensation) to be met out of levies collected in accordance with section 213(3)(b) of the Financial Services and Markets Act 2000 (c 8) (the Financial Services Compensation Scheme);

(e) modify the effect of a transitional compensation provision;

(f) enable the Financial Conduct Authority or the Prudential Regulation Authority to amend the Financial Services Compensation Scheme;

(g) modify the Financial Services and Markets Act 2000 in its application to an amendment pursuant to paragraph (f);

(h) make, or require the making of, provision for the making of a claim by a responsible person for compensation whether or not he has already satisfied claims in tort against him;

(i) make, or require the making of, provision which has effect in relation to claims for contributions made on or after the date on which this Act is passed.

(9) ...

(10) In subsections (7) and (8)—

(a) a reference to a responsible person includes a reference to an insurer of a responsible person, and

(b) "transitional compensation provision" means a provision of an enactment which is made under the Financial Services and Markets Act 2000 and—

(i) preserves the effect of the Policyholders Protection Act 1975 (c 75), or

(ii) applies the Financial Services Compensation Scheme in relation to matters arising before its establishment.

(11) Regulations under subsection (7)—

(a) may include consequential or incidental provision,

(b) may make provision which has effect generally or only in relation to specified cases or circumstances,

(c) may make different provision for different cases or circumstances,

(d) shall be made by statutory instrument, and

(e) may not be made unless a draft has been laid before and approved by resolution of each House of Parliament.

III PID [40C.1]

See also Compensation Act 2006 (Contribution for Mesothelioma Claims) Regulations 2006 (SI 2006/3259).

III PID [40C.2]

The principle aim of s 3 of the Act is to reverse, in respect of mesothelioma claims, the House of Lords decision in *Barker v Corus UK Ltd* [2006] UKHL 20, [2006] 2 AC 572, [2006] 3 All ER 785, where it was held that damages were to be apportioned according to the relative degree of contribution by the liable parties to the risk that the person would contract the disease. Section 3 permits a claimant to recover full compensation from any liable person, who in turn may seek a contribution from other liable persons. There is also provision (s 3(4)) for a finding of contribution on the part of the claimant where it is alleged that he/she negligently exposed themselves to asbestos. In *Sienkiewicz v Greif (UK) Ltd* [2011] UKSC 10,

[2011] 2 AC 229, [2011] 2 All ER 857, it was held that in a mesothelioma case, it was not open to a defendant to put a claimant to proof of causation by reference to a twofold increase in risk. The correct test on causation was said to be whether or not the tortious exposure had materially increased the risk.

CRIMINAL JUSTICE AND COURTS ACT 2015

(c 2)

s 57 Personal injury claims: cases of fundamental dishonesty . . . . III PID [41]

III PID [41]

57. Personal injury claims: cases of fundamental dishonesty

(1) This section applies where, in proceedings on a claim for damages in respect of personal injury ("the primary claim")—

(a) the court finds that the claimant is entitled to damages in respect of the claim, but

(b) on an application by the defendant for the dismissal of the claim under this section, the court is satisfied on the balance of probabilities that the claimant has been fundamentally dishonest in relation to the primary claim or a related claim.

(2) The court must dismiss the primary claim, unless it is satisfied that the claimant would suffer substantial injustice if the claim were dismissed.

(3) The duty under subsection (2) includes the dismissal of any element of the primary claim in respect of which the claimant has not been dishonest.

(4) The court's order dismissing the claim must record the amount of damages that the court would have awarded to the claimant in respect of the primary claim but for the dismissal of the claim.

(5) When assessing costs in the proceedings, a court which dismisses a claim under this section must deduct the amount recorded in accordance with subsection (4) from the amount which it would otherwise order the claimant to pay in respect of costs incurred by the defendant.

(6) If a claim is dismissed under this section, subsection (7) applies to—

(a) any subsequent criminal proceedings against the claimant in respect of the fundamental dishonesty mentioned in subsection (1)(b), and

(b) any subsequent proceedings for contempt of court against the claimant in respect of that dishonesty.

(7) If the court in those proceedings finds the claimant guilty of an offence or of contempt of court, it must have regard to the dismissal of the primary claim under this section when sentencing the claimant or otherwise disposing of the proceedings.

(8) In this section—

"claim" includes a counter-claim and, accordingly, "claimant" includes a counter-claimant and "defendant" includes a defendant to a counter-claim;

"personal injury" includes any disease and any other impairment of a person's physical or mental condition;

"related claim" means a claim for damages in respect of personal injury which is made—

(a) in connection with the same incident or series of incidents in connection with which the primary claim is made, and

(b) by a person other than the person who made the primary claim.

(9) This section does not apply to proceedings started by the issue of a claim form before the day on which this section comes into force.

III PID [41.1]

In *Summers v Fairclough Homes* [2012] UKSC 26 the Supreme Court gave guidance on the limited circumstances in which a claim by a dishonest claimant, who nonetheless had a partially valid claim, should be struck out. Section 57 was subsequently enacted and gives the court a broader power than that previously available in personal injuries claims. The section was considered in detail in *Sinfield v London Organising Committee* [2018] EWHC 51 (QB). *Sinfield* has in turn been applied in *Pinkus v Direct Line* [2018] EWHC 1671 (QB).

CIVIL LIABILITY ACT 2018

c 29

GENERAL NOTES ON PART 1 OF THE CIVIL LIABILITY ACT 2018

III PID [41A]

Part 1 of the Act institutes reform to 'whiplash' claims. The government's stated intention is that Part 1 of the Act will come into force in April 2020. However, the date is not yet known. When implemented, damages for whiplash injuries lasting up to two years will be set by reference to a tariff to be set by the Lord Chancellor following consultation with the Lord Chief Justice. A 'whiplash injury' is defined by the Act as 'an injury of soft tissue in the neck, back or shoulder that is . . . a sprain, strain, tear, rupture or lesser damage of a muscle, tendon or ligament in the neck, back or shoulder, or an injury of soft tissue associated with a muscle, tendon or ligament in the neck, back or shoulder'. The definition does not include 'an injury of soft tissue which is a part of or connected to another injury and the other injury is not an injury of soft tissue in the neck back or shoulder'. The Lord Chancellor has the power to review and amend the definition of 'whiplash' but cannot do so until 3 years have elapsed from this reform coming into force. The tariff will include cases where there is also a minor psychological injury (not defined). The tariff will not apply to claims by motorcyclists or their passengers, cyclists, pedestrians or other road users who are not using a motor vehicle. The regulations setting the tariff are to be kept under review. The first review must be completed within 3 years of the regulations first coming into force and thereafter within 3 years of the previous review date. The regulations may provide for the court to apply an uplift to the tariff in exceptional circumstances. The uplift is expected to be a maximum of 20% but this will be set by regulations. The Act contains provisions banning the settlement of whiplash claims before a medical report has been obtained. A portal system is being created to handle whiplash claims. The system will be designed for use by Litigants in Person and will be simple and user friendly. Large scale testing of the portal is currently due to commence in October 2019.

PART 1
WHIPLASH

DAMAGES

III PID [41B]

1 "Whiplash injury" etc

(1) In this Part "whiplash injury" means an injury of soft tissue in the neck, back or shoulder that is of a description falling within subsection (2), but not including an injury excepted by subsection (3).

(2) An injury falls within this subsection if it is—

(a) a sprain, strain, tear, rupture or lesser damage of a muscle, tendon or ligament in the neck, back or shoulder, or

(b) an injury of soft tissue associated with a muscle, tendon or ligament in the neck, back or shoulder.

(3) An injury is excepted by this subsection if—

(a) it is an injury of soft tissue which is a part of or connected to another injury, and

(b) the other injury is not an injury of soft tissue in the neck, back or shoulder of a description falling within subsection (2).

(4) For the purposes of this Part a person suffers a whiplash injury because of driver negligence if—

(a) when the person suffers the injury, the person—

(i) is using a motor vehicle other than a motor cycle on a road or other public place in England or Wales, or

(ii) is being carried in or on a motor vehicle other than a motor cycle while another uses the vehicle on a road or other public place in England or Wales,

(b) the injury is caused—

(i) by the negligence of one or more other persons, or

(ii) partly by the negligence of one or more other persons and partly by the negligence of the person who suffers the injury, and

(c) the negligence of the other person or persons consists in an act or acts done by the person or persons while using a motor vehicle on a road or other public place in England or Wales.

(5) The fact that the act or acts constituting the negligence of the other person or persons is or are also sufficient to establish another cause of action does not prevent subsection (4)(b) being satisfied.

(6) For the purposes of this section references to a person being carried in or on a vehicle include references to a person entering or getting on to, or alighting from, the vehicle.

(7) In this section—

"act" includes omission;

"motor cycle" has the meaning given by section 185(1) of the Road Traffic Act 1988;

"motor vehicle" means a mechanically propelled vehicle intended or adapted for use on roads;

"road" means a highway or other road to which the public has access, and includes bridges over which a road passes.

III PID [41C]

3 Damages for whiplash injuries

(1) This section applies in relation to the determination by a court of damages for pain, suffering and loss of amenity in a case where—

(a) a person ("the claimant") suffers a whiplash injury because of driver negligence, and

(b) the duration of the whiplash injury or any of the whiplash injuries suffered on that occasion—

(i) does not exceed, or is not likely to exceed, two years, or

(ii) would not have exceeded, or would not be likely to exceed, two years but for the claimant's failure to take reasonable steps to mitigate its effect.

(2) The amount of damages for pain, suffering and loss of amenity payable in respect of the whiplash injury or injuries, taken together, is to be an amount specified in regulations made by the Lord Chancellor.

(3) If the claimant suffers one or more minor psychological injuries on the same occasion as the whiplash injury or injuries, the amount of damages for pain, suffering and loss of amenity payable in respect of the minor psychological injury or the minor psychological injuries, taken together, is to be an amount specified in regulations made by the Lord Chancellor.

(4) If regulations made by the Lord Chancellor so provide, the amount of damages for pain, suffering and loss of amenity payable in respect of—

(a) the whiplash injury or injuries, and

(b) a minor psychological injury or injuries suffered by the claimant on the same occasion as the whiplash injury or injuries,

taken together, is to be an amount specified in regulations made by the Lord Chancellor (notwithstanding subsections (2) and (3)).

(5) Regulations under this section may in particular—

(a) specify different amounts in respect of different durations of injury;

(b) specify amounts in respect of minor psychological injuries by reference to the duration of the related whiplash injury or injuries.

(6) Regulations under this section may provide for a person to be treated as if the person had taken reasonable steps to mitigate the effect of the person's whiplash injury or minor psychological injury.

(7) Regulations under this section amending or replacing earlier regulations may increase or reduce amounts payable in respect of injuries.

(8) Nothing in this section prevents a court, in a case where a person suffers an injury or injuries in addition to an injury or injuries to which regulations under this section apply, awarding an amount of damages for pain, suffering and loss of amenity that reflects the combined effect of the person's injuries (subject to the limits imposed by regulations under this section).

(9) Nothing in this section prevents the amount of damages payable being reduced by virtue of section 1 of the Law Reform (Contributory Negligence) Act 1945.

(10) This section does not apply in relation to damages payable by a person because of the person's breach of the duty under section 143(1)(b) of the Road Traffic Act 1988 (duty not to cause or permit any other person to drive without insurance or security in respect of third party risks).

(11) The Lord Chancellor must consult the Lord Chief Justice before making regulations under this section.

(12) A statutory instrument containing regulations under this section is subject to affirmative resolution procedure.

III PID [41D]

4 Review of regulations under section 3

(1) The Lord Chancellor must carry out reviews of regulations made under section 3.

(2) The first review must be completed before the end of the period of three years beginning with the day on which the first regulations under section 3 come into force.

(3) Subsequent reviews must be completed before the end of the period of three years beginning with the day on which the previous review was completed.

(4) The Lord Chancellor must prepare and publish a report of each review.

(5) The Lord Chancellor must lay a copy of each report before Parliament.

III PID [41E]

5 Uplift in exceptional circumstances

(1) Regulations made by the Lord Chancellor may provide for a court—

- (a) to determine that the amount of damages payable for pain, suffering and loss of amenity in respect of one or more whiplash injuries is an amount greater than the tariff amount relating to that injury or those injuries;
- (b) to determine that the amount of damages payable for pain, suffering and loss of amenity in respect of one or more whiplash injuries and one or more minor psychological injuries, taken together, is an amount greater than the tariff amount relating to those injuries;
- (c) in a case where the court considers the combined effect of—
  - (i) an injury or injuries in respect of which a tariff amount is specified by regulations under section 3(2) or (4), and
  - (ii) one or more other injuries,

to determine that an amount greater than the tariff amount is to be taken into account when deciding the amount of damages payable for pain, suffering and loss of amenity in respect of the injuries mentioned in sub-paragraphs (i) and (ii).

(2) The regulations may require a court to be satisfied, before making the determination mentioned in subsection (1)(a), (b) or (c), that—

- (a) the degree of pain, suffering or loss of amenity caused by the whiplash injury or injuries in question makes it appropriate to use the greater amount, and
- (b) it is the case that—
  - (i) the whiplash injury is, or one or more of the whiplash injuries are, exceptionally severe, or
  - (ii) where the person's circumstances increase the pain, suffering or loss of amenity caused by the injury or injuries, those circumstances are exceptional.

(3) The regulations must specify the maximum percentage by which the greater amount mentioned in subsection (1)(a), (b) or (c) may exceed the relevant tariff amount.

(4) Regulations under this section amending or replacing earlier regulations may increase or reduce the maximum percentage.

(5) The Lord Chancellor must consult the Lord Chief Justice before making regulations under this section.

(6) A statutory instrument containing regulations under this section is subject to affirmative resolution procedure.

(7) In this section "tariff amount" means—

- (a) in relation to one or more whiplash injuries, the amount specified in respect of the injury or injuries by regulations under section 3(2);
- (b) in relation to one or more whiplash injuries and one or more minor psychological injuries, the amount specified in respect of the injuries by regulations under section 3(4).

Settlement of whiplash claims

III PID [41F]

6 Rules against settlement before medical report

(1) A regulated person is in breach of this section if—

(a) the regulated person knows or has reason to suspect that a whiplash claim is being made,

(b) the regulated person does, or arranges or advises the doing of, an act mentioned in subsection (2), without first seeing appropriate evidence of the whiplash injury or injuries, and

(c) the regulated person is acting as such when the regulated person does, or arranges or advises the doing of, that act.

(2) The acts referred to in subsection (1) are—

(a) inviting a person to offer a payment in settlement of the claim;

(b) offering a payment in settlement of the claim;

(c) making a payment in settlement of the claim;

(d) accepting a payment in settlement of the claim.

(3) The Lord Chancellor may by regulations make provision about what constitutes appropriate evidence of an injury for the purposes of this section.

(4) The regulations may in particular—

(a) specify the form of any evidence of an injury;

(b) specify the descriptions of persons who may provide evidence of an injury;

(c) require persons to be accredited for the purpose of providing evidence of an injury;

(d) make provision about accrediting persons, including provision for a person to be accredited by a body specified in the regulations.

(5) A statutory instrument containing regulations under this section is subject to affirmative resolution procedure.

(6) In this section "whiplash claim" means a claim that consists only of, or so much of a claim as consists of, a claim for damages for pain, suffering and loss of amenity caused by—

(a) one or more whiplash injuries suffered by a person on a particular occasion because of driver negligence and in relation to which section 3 applies, or

(b) a whiplash injury or injuries within paragraph (a) suffered by a person on a particular occasion and one or more minor psychological injuries suffered by the person on the same occasion as the whiplash injury or injuries.

PERSONAL INJURY AND DEATH

III PID [41G]

7 Effect of rules against settlement before medical report

(1) The relevant regulator must ensure that it has appropriate arrangements for monitoring and enforcing compliance with the restrictions imposed on regulated persons by section 6.

(2) The relevant regulator may make rules for the purposes of subsection (1).

(3) The rules may in particular provide that, in relation to anything done in breach of section 6, the relevant regulator may exercise any powers that the regulator would have in relation to anything done by the regulated person in breach of another restriction (subject to subsections (5) and (6)).

(4) Where the relevant regulator is the Financial Conduct Authority, section 8 applies instead of subsections (1) to (3).

(5) A breach of section 6—

(a) does not make a person guilty of an offence, and

(b) does not give rise to a right of action for breach of statutory duty.

(6) A breach of section 6 does not make an agreement to settle the whiplash claim in question void or unenforceable.

III PID [41H]

8 Regulation by the Financial Conduct Authority

(1) The Treasury may make regulations to enable the Financial Conduct Authority, where it is the relevant regulator, to take action for monitoring and enforcing compliance with the restrictions imposed on regulated persons by section 6.

(2) The regulations may apply, or make provision corresponding to, any of the provisions of the Financial Services and Markets Act 2000 with or without modification.

(3) Those provisions include in particular—

(a) provisions as to investigations, including powers of entry and search and criminal offences;

(b) provisions for the grant of an injunction in relation to a contravention or anticipated contravention;

(c) provisions giving Ministers or the Financial Conduct Authority powers to make subordinate legislation;

(d) provisions for the Financial Conduct Authority to charge fees.

(4) The power to make regulations under this section may not be used to make provision inconsistent with section 7(5) and (6).

(5) A statutory instrument containing regulations under this section is subject to affirmative resolution procedure.

PART 2
PERSONAL INJURY DISCOUNT RATE

GENERAL NOTES ON PART 2 OF THE CIVIL LIABILITY ACT 2018

III PID [41I]

The provision in Part 2 for the review of the discount rate commence upon Royal Assent, which occurred on 20 December 2018. The first review must commence within 90 days of Royal Assent, ie on or before 19 March 2019. The review will be conducted by reference to the new process detailed in the Act. The first review must be completed and the Lord Chancellor must determine the new rate within 140 days of the review commencing, ie on or before 6 August 2019. Following the completion of the review, the Lord Chancellor will publish an Order setting the new rate. The Lord Chancellor has the power to make an Order which will prescribe different rates of return for different classes of case. As now, the rate in the Order does not prevent the court taking a different rate of return into account if any party to the proceedings shows that it is more appropriate in the case in question.

It is not known precisely when the review will commence and be completed – although Parliament has stressed the need for the review to be swift. Neither is the new level of Discount Rate yet known. Current predictions are in the region of 1% to 1.5%. It is also unknown whether the Lord Chancellor will exercise his power to prescribe different rates for different classes of case (although this is not expected in the first review). Finally it is not yet known in what circumstances a court may apply a different rate of return.

III PID [41J]

10 Assumed rate of return on investment of damages

(1) Before section 1 of the Damages Act 1996 (assumed rate of return on investment of damages) insert—

"A1 Assumed rate of return on investment of damages: England and Wales

(1) In determining the return to be expected from the investment of a sum awarded as damages for future pecuniary loss in an action for personal injury the court must, subject to and in accordance with rules of court made for the purposes of this section, take into account such rate of return (if any) as may from time to time be prescribed by an order made by the Lord Chancellor.

(2) Subsection (1) does not however prevent the court taking a different rate of return into account if any party to the proceedings shows that it is more appropriate in the case in question.

(3) An order under subsection (1) may prescribe different rates of return for different classes of case.

(4) An order under subsection (1) may in particular distinguish between classes of case by reference to—

(a) the description of future pecuniary loss involved;

(b) the length of the period during which future pecuniary loss is expected to occur;

(c) the time when future pecuniary loss is expected to occur.

(5) Schedule A1 (which makes provision about determining the rate of return to be prescribed by an order under subsection (1)) has effect.

(6) An order under this section is to be made by statutory instrument subject to annulment in pursuance of a resolution of either House of Parliament."

(2) Before the Schedule to the Damages Act 1996 insert—

"SCHEDULE 1

ASSUMED RATE OF RETURN ON INVESTMENT OF DAMAGES: ENGLAND AND WALES

Periodic reviews of the rate of return

1 (1) The Lord Chancellor must review the rate of return periodically in accordance with this paragraph.

(2) The first review of the rate of return must be started within the 90 day period following commencement.

(3) Each subsequent review of the rate of return must be started within the 5 year period following the last review.

(4) It is for the Lord Chancellor to decide—

(a) when, within the 90 day period following commencement, a review under sub-paragraph (2) is to be started;

(b) when, within the 5 year period following the last review, a review under sub-paragraph (3) is to be started.

(5) In this paragraph—

"90 day period following commencement" means the period of 90 days beginning with the day on which this paragraph comes into force;

"5 year period following the last review" means the period of five years beginning with the day on which the last review under this paragraph (whether under sub-paragraph (2) or (3)) is concluded.

(6) For the purposes of this paragraph a review is concluded on the day when the Lord Chancellor makes a determination under paragraph 2 or 3 (as the case may be) as a result of the review.

Conducting the first review

2 (1) This paragraph applies when the Lord Chancellor is required by paragraph 1(2) to conduct a review of the rate of return.

(2) The Lord Chancellor must review the rate of return and determine whether it should be—

(a) changed to a different rate, or

(b) kept unchanged.

PERSONAL INJURY AND DEATH

(3) The Lord Chancellor must conduct that review and make that determination within the 140 day review period.

(4) In conducting the review, the Lord Chancellor must consult—

(a) the Government Actuary, and

(b) the Treasury.

(5) The consultation of the Government Actuary must start within the period of 20 days beginning with the day on which the 140 day review period starts.

(6) The Government Actuary must respond to the consultation within the period of 80 days beginning with the day on which the Government Actuary's response to the consultation is requested.

(7) The exercise of the power of the Lord Chancellor under this paragraph to determine whether the rate of return should be changed or kept unchanged is subject to paragraph 4.

(8) When deciding what response to give to the Lord Chancellor under this paragraph, the Government Actuary and the Treasury must take into account the duties imposed on the Lord Chancellor by paragraph 4.

(9) During any period when the office of Government Actuary is vacant, a reference in this paragraph to the Government Actuary is to be read as a reference to the Deputy Government Actuary.

(10) In this paragraph "140 day review period" means the period of 140 days beginning with the day which the Lord Chancellor decides (under paragraph 1) should be the day on which the review is to start.

Conducting later reviews

3 (1) This paragraph applies whenever the Lord Chancellor is required by paragraph 1(3) to conduct a review of the rate of return.

(2) The Lord Chancellor must review the rate of return and determine whether it should be—

(a) changed to a different rate, or

(b) kept unchanged.

(3) The Lord Chancellor must conduct that review and make that determination within the 180 day review period.

(4) In conducting the review, the Lord Chancellor must consult—

(a) the expert panel established for the review, and

(b) the Treasury.

(5) The expert panel must respond to the consultation within the period of 90 days beginning with the day on which its response to the consultation is requested.

(6) The exercise of the power of the Lord Chancellor under this paragraph to determine whether the rate of return should be changed or kept unchanged is subject to paragraph 4.

(7) When deciding what response to give to the Lord Chancellor under this paragraph, the expert panel and the Treasury must take into account the duties imposed on the Lord Chancellor by paragraph 4.

(8) In this paragraph "180 day review period" means the period of 180 days beginning with the day which the Lord Chancellor decides (under paragraph 1) should be the day on which the review is to start.

Determining the rate of return

4 (1) The Lord Chancellor must comply with this paragraph when determining under paragraph 2 or 3 whether the rate of return should be changed or kept unchanged ("the rate determination").

(2) The Lord Chancellor must make the rate determination on the basis that the rate of return should be the rate that, in the opinion of the Lord Chancellor, a recipient of relevant damages could reasonably be expected to achieve if the recipient invested the relevant damages for the purpose of securing that—

(a) the relevant damages would meet the losses and costs for which they are awarded;

(b) the relevant damages would meet those losses and costs at the time or times when they fall to be met by the relevant damages; and

(c) the relevant damages would be exhausted at the end of the period for which they are awarded.

(3) In making the rate determination as required by sub-paragraph (2), the Lord Chancellor must make the following assumptions—

(a) the assumption that the relevant damages are payable in a lump sum (rather than under an order for periodical payments);

(b) the assumption that the recipient of the relevant damages is properly advised on the investment of the relevant damages;

(c) the assumption that the recipient of the relevant damages invests the relevant damages in a diversified portfolio of investments;

(d) the assumption that the relevant damages are invested using an approach that involves—

(i) more risk than a very low level of risk, but

(ii) less risk than would ordinarily be accepted by a prudent and properly advised individual investor who has different financial aims.

(4) That does not limit the assumptions which the Lord Chancellor may make.

(5) In making the rate determination as required by sub-paragraph (2), the Lord Chancellor must—

(a) have regard to the actual returns that are available to investors;

(b) have regard to the actual investments made by investors of relevant damages; and

(c) make such allowances for taxation, inflation and investment management costs as the Lord Chancellor thinks appropriate.

(6) That does not limit the factors which may inform the Lord Chancellor when making the rate determination.

(7) In this paragraph "relevant damages" means a sum awarded as damages for future pecuniary loss in an action for personal injury.

Determination

5 When the Lord Chancellor makes a rate determination, the Lord Chancellor must—

(a) give reasons for the rate determination made, and

(b) publish such information as the Lord Chancellor thinks appropriate about—

(i) the response of the expert panel established for the review, or

(ii) in the case of a review required by paragraph 1(2), the response of the Government Actuary or the Deputy Government Actuary (as the case may be).

Expert panel

6 (1) For each review of a rate of return required by paragraph 1(3), the Lord Chancellor is to establish a panel (referred to in this Schedule as an "expert panel") consisting of—

(a) the Government Actuary, who is to chair the panel; and

(b) four other members appointed by the Lord Chancellor.

(2) The Lord Chancellor must exercise the power to appoint the appointed members to secure that—

(a) one appointed member has experience as an actuary;

(b) one appointed member has experience of managing investments;

(c) one appointed member has experience as an economist;
(d) one appointed member has experience in consumer matters as relating to investments.

(3) An expert panel established for a review of a rate of return ceases to exist once it has responded to the consultation relating to the review.

(4) A person may be a member of more than one expert panel at any one time.

(5) A person may not become an appointed member if the person is ineligible for membership.

(6) A person who is an appointed member ceases to be a member if the person becomes ineligible for membership.

(7) The Lord Chancellor may end an appointed member's membership of the panel if the Lord Chancellor is satisfied that—

(a) the person is unable or unwilling to take part in the panel's activities on a review conducted under paragraph 1;
(b) it is no longer appropriate for the person to be a member of the panel because of gross misconduct or impropriety;
(c) the person has become bankrupt, a debt relief order (under Part 7A of the Insolvency Act 1986) has been made in respect of the person, the person's estate has been sequestrated or the person has made an arrangement with or granted a trust deed for creditors.

(8) During any period when the office of Government Actuary is vacant the Deputy Government Actuary is to be a member of the panel and is to chair it.

(9) A person is "ineligible for membership" of an expert panel if the person is—

(a) a Minister of the Crown, or
(b) a person serving in a government department in employment in respect of which remuneration is payable out of money provided by Parliament.

(10) In this paragraph "appointed member" means a person appointed by the Lord Chancellor to be a member of an expert panel.

Proceedings, powers and funding of an expert panel

7 (1) The quorum of an expert panel is four members, one of whom must be the Government Actuary (or the Deputy Government Actuary when the office of Government Actuary is vacant).

(2) In the event of a tied vote on any decision, the person chairing the panel is to have a second casting vote.

(3) The panel may—

(a) invite other persons to attend, or to attend and speak at, any meeting of the panel;
(b) when exercising any function, take into account information submitted by, or obtained from, any other person (whether or not the production of the information has been commissioned by the panel).

(4) The Lord Chancellor must make arrangements for an expert panel to be provided with the resources which the Lord Chancellor considers to be appropriate for the panel to exercise its functions.

(5) The Government Actuary's Department, or any other government department, may enter into arrangements made by the Lord Chancellor under sub-paragraph (4).

(6) The Lord Chancellor must make arrangements for the appointed members of an expert panel to be paid any remuneration and expenses which the Lord Chancellor considers to be appropriate.

Application of this Schedule where there are several rates of return

8 (1) This paragraph applies if two or more rates of return are prescribed under section A1.

(2) The requirements—

(a) under paragraph 1 for a review to be conducted, and

(b) under paragraph 2 or 3 relating to how a review is conducted,

apply separately in relation to each rate of return.

(3) As respects a review relating to a particular rate of return, a reference in this Schedule to the last review conducted under a particular provision is to be read as a reference to the last review relating to that rate of return.

Interpretation

9 (1) In this Schedule—

"expert panel" means a panel established in accordance with paragraph 6;

"rate determination" has the meaning given by paragraph 4;

"rate of return" means a rate of return for the purposes of section A1.

(2) A provision of this Schedule that refers to the rate of return being changed is to be read as also referring to—

(a) the existing rate of return being replaced with no rate;

(b) a rate of return being introduced where there is no existing rate;

(c) the existing rate of return for a particular class of case being replaced with no rate;

(d) a rate of return being introduced for a particular class of case for which there is no existing rate.

(3) A provision of this Schedule that refers to the rate of return being kept unchanged is to be read as also referring to—

(a) the position that there is no rate of return being kept unchanged;

(b) the position that there is no rate of return for a particular class of case being kept unchanged.

(4) A provision of this Schedule that refers to a review of the rate of return is to be read as also referring to—

(a) a review of the position that no rate of return is prescribed;

(b) a review of the position that no rate of return is prescribed for a particular class of case."

(3) Any order made by the Lord Chancellor under section 1(1) of the Damages Act 1996 which relates to England and Wales and is in force immediately before the time when subsection (1) comes into force is to be treated after that time as if made by the Lord Chancellor under section A1(1) of that Act.

(4) In consequence of the amendments made by subsections (1) and (2), the Damages Act 1996 is amended as follows—

(a) section 1 is omitted;

(b) in section 2(4)(a), for "the Schedule" substitute "Schedule 1";

(c) in section 2(7)(b), for "the Schedule" substitute "Schedule 1";

(d) in section 6(9), for "The Schedule" substitute "Schedule 1";

(e) the existing Schedule becomes Schedule 1 (and, accordingly, for the heading "Schedule" substitute the heading "Schedule 1").

1. PRE-ACTION PROTOCOL FOR PERSONAL INJURY CLAIMS

1 INTRODUCTION

III PID [42]

1.1

1.1.1 This Protocol is primarily designed for personal injury claims which are likely to be allocated to the fast track and to the entirety of those claims: not only to the personal injury element of a claim which also includes, for instance, property damage. It is not intended to apply to claims which proceed under—

(a) the Pre-Action Protocol for Low Value Personal Injury Claims in Road Traffic Accidents from 31 July 2013;
(b) the Pre-Action Protocol for Low Value Personal Injury (Employers' Liability and Public Liability) Claims;
(c) the Pre-Action Protocol for the Resolution of Clinical Disputes; and
(d) the Pre-Action Protocol for Disease and Illness Claims.

1.1.2 If at any stage the claimant values the claim at more than the upper limit of the fast track, the claimant should notify the defendant as soon as possible. However, the "cards on the table" approach advocated by this Protocol is equally appropriate to higher value claims. The spirit, if not the letter of the Protocol, should still be followed for claims which could potentially be allocated multi-track.

1.2 Claims which exit either of the low value pre-action protocols listed at paragraph 1.1.1(a) and (b) ("the low value protocols") prior to Stage 2 will proceed under this Protocol from the point specified in those protocols, and as set out in paragraph 1.3.

1.3

1.3.1 Where a claim exits a low value protocol because the defendant considers that there is inadequate mandatory information in the Claim Notification Form ("CNF"), the claim will proceed under this Protocol from paragraph 5.1.

1.3.2 Where a defendant—

(a) alleges contributory negligence;
(b) does not complete and send the CNF Response; or
(c) does not admit liability,

the claim will proceed under this Protocol from paragraph 5.5.

1.4

1.4.1 This Protocol sets out conduct that the court would normally expect prospective parties to follow prior to the commencement of proceedings. It establishes a reasonable process and timetable for the exchange of information relevant to a dispute, sets standards for the content and quality of letters of claim, and in particular, the conduct of pre-action negotiations. In particular, the parts of this Protocol that are concerned with rehabilitation are likely to be of application in all claims.

1.4.2 The timetable and the arrangements for disclosing documents and obtaining expert evidence may need to be varied to suit the circumstances of the case. Where one or both parties consider the detail of the Protocol is not appropriate to the case, and proceedings are subsequently issued, the court will expect an explanation as to why the Protocol has not been followed, or has been varied.

1.5 Where either party fails to comply with this Protocol, the court may impose sanctions. When deciding whether to do so, the court will look at whether the parties have complied in substance with the relevant principles and requirements.

It will also consider the effect any non-compliance has had on another party. It is not likely to be concerned with minor or technical shortcomings (see paragraphs 13 to 15 of the Practice Direction on Pre-Action Conduct and Protocols).

Early Issue

1.6 The Protocol recommends that a defendant be given three months to investigate and respond to a claim before proceedings are issued. This may not always be possible, particularly where a claimant only consults a legal representative close to the end of any relevant limitation period. In these circumstances, the claimant's solicitor should give as much notice of the intention to issue proceedings as is practicable and the parties should consider whether the court might be invited to extend time for service of the claimant's supporting documents and for service of any defence, or alternatively, to stay the proceedings while the recommended steps in the Protocol are followed.

Litigants in Person

1.7 If a party to the claim does not have a legal representative they should still, in so far as reasonably possible, fully comply with this Protocol. Any reference to a claimant in this Protocol will also mean the claimant's legal representative.

2 OVERVIEW OF PROTOCOL – GENERAL AIM

2.1 The Protocol's objectives are to—

(a) encourage the exchange of early and full information about the dispute;
(b) encourage better and earlier pre-action investigation by all parties;
(c) enable the parties to avoid litigation by agreeing a settlement of the dispute before proceedings are commenced;
(d) support the just, proportionate and efficient management of proceedings where litigation cannot be avoided; and
(e) promote the provision of medical or rehabilitation treatment (not just in high value cases) to address the needs of the Claimant at the earliest possible opportunity.

3 THE PROTOCOL

An illustrative flow chart is attached at Annexe A which shows each of the steps that the parties are expected to take before the commencement of proceedings.

Letter of Notification

3.1 The claimant or his legal representative may wish to notify a defendant and/or the insurer as soon as they know a claim is likely to be made, but before they are able to send a detailed Letter of Claim, particularly, for instance, when the defendant has no or limited knowledge of the incident giving rise to the claim, or where the claimant is incurring significant expenditure as a result of the accident which he hopes the defendant might pay for, in whole or in part.

3.2 The Letter of Notification should advise the defendant and/or the insurer of any relevant information that is available to assist with determining issues of liability / suitability of the claim for an interim payment and/or early rehabilitation.

3.3 If the claimant or his legal representative gives notification before sending a Letter of Claim, it will not start the timetable for the Letter of Response. However the Letter of Notification should be acknowledged within 14 days of receipt.

4 REHABILITATION

4.1 The parties should consider as early as possible whether the claimant has reasonable needs that could be met by medical treatment or other rehabilitative measures. They should discuss how these needs might be addressed.

4.2 The Rehabilitation Code (which can be found at: www.iua.co.uk/IUA_Member/Publications) is likely to be helpful in considering how to identify the claimant's needs and how to address the cost of providing for those needs.

4.3 The time limit set out in paragraph 6.3 of this Protocol shall not be shortened, except by consent to allow these issues to be addressed.

4.4 Any immediate needs assessment report or documents associated with it that are obtained for the purposes of rehabilitation shall not be used in the litigation except by consent and shall in any event be exempt from the provisions of paragraphs 7.2 to 7.11 of this Protocol. Similarly, persons conducting the immediate needs assessment shall not be a compellable witness at court.

4.5 Consideration of rehabilitation options, by all parties, should be an on going process throughout the entire Protocol period.

5 LETTER OF CLAIM

5.1 Subject to paragraph 5.3 the claimant should send to the proposed defendant two copies of the Letter of Claim. One copy of the letter is for the defendant, the second for passing on to the insurers, as soon as possible, and, in any event, within 7 days of the day upon which the defendant received it.

5.2 The Letter of Claim should include the information described on the template at Annexe B1. The level of detail will need to be varied to suit the particular circumstances. In all cases there should be sufficient information for the defendant to assess liability and to enable the defendant to estimate the likely size and heads of the claim without necessarily addressing quantum in detail.

5.3 The letter should contain **a clear summary of the facts** on which the claim is based together with an indication of the **nature of any injuries** suffered, and the way in which these impact on the claimant's day to day functioning and prognosis. Any financial loss incurred by the claimant should be outlined with an indication of the heads of damage to be claimed and the amount of that loss, unless this is impracticable.

5.4 Details of the claimant's National Insurance number and date of birth should be supplied to the defendant's insurer once the defendant has responded to the Letter of Claim and confirmed the identity of the insurer. This information should not be supplied in the Letter of Claim.

5.5 Where a claim no longer continues under either low value protocol, the CNF completed by the claimant under those protocols can be used as the Letter of Claim under this Protocol unless the defendant has notified the claimant that there is inadequate information in the CNF.

5.6 Once the claimant has sent the Letter of Claim no further investigation on liability should normally be carried out within the Protocol period until a response is received from the defendant indicating whether liability is disputed.

Status of Letters of Claim and Response

5.7 Letters of Claim and Response are not intended to have the same formal status as a statement of case in proceedings. It would not be consistent with the spirit of the Protocol for a party to 'take a point' on this in the proceedings, provided that there was no obvious intention by the party who changed their position to mislead the other party.

6 THE RESPONSE

6.1 Attached at Annexe B2 is a template for the suggested contents of the Letter of Response: the level of detail will need to be varied to suit the particular circumstances.

6.2 The **defendant must reply within 21 calendar days** of the date of posting of the letter identifying the insurer (if any). If the insurer is aware of any significant omissions from the letter of claim they should identify them specifically. Similarly, if they are aware that another defendant has also been identified whom they believe would not be a correct defendant in any proceedings, they should notify the claimant without delay, with reasons, and in any event by the end of the Response period. Where there has been no reply by the defendant or insurer within 21 days, the claimant will be entitled to issue proceedings. Compliance with this paragraph will be taken into account on the question of any assessment of the defendant's costs.

6.3 The **defendant** (insurer) will have a **maximum of three months** from the date of acknowledgment of the Letter of Claim (or of the CNF where the claim commenced in a portal) **to investigate**. No later than the end of that period, The defendant (insurer) should reply by no later than the end of that period, stating if liability is admitted by admitting that the accident occurred, that the accident was caused by the defendant's breach of duty, and the claimant suffered loss and there is no defence under the Limitation Act 1980.

6.4 Where the accident occurred outside England and Wales and/or where the defendant is outside the jurisdiction, the time periods of 21 days and three months should normally be extended up to 42 days and six months.

6.5 If a **defendant denies liability** and/or causation, their version of events should be supplied. The defendant should also enclose with the response, **documents** in their possession which are **material to the issues** between the parties, and which would be likely to be ordered to be disclosed by the court, either on an application for pre-action disclosure, or on disclosure during proceedings. No charge will be made for providing copy documents under the Protocol.

6.6 An admission made by any party under this Protocol may well be binding on that party in the litigation. Further information about admissions made under this Protocol is to be found in Civil Procedure Rules ("CPR") rule 14.1A.

6.7 Following receipt of the Letter of Response, if the claimant is aware that there may be a delay of six months or more before the claimant decides if, when and how to proceed, the claimant should keep the defendant generally informed.

7 DISCLOSURE

Documents

7.1

7.1.1 The aim of early disclosure of documents by the defendant is not to encourage 'fishing expeditions' by the claimant, but to promote an early exchange of relevant information to help in clarifying or resolving issues in dispute. The claimant's solicitor can assist by identifying in the Letter of Claim or in a subsequent letter the particular categories of documents which they consider are relevant and why, with a brief explanation of their purported relevance if necessary.

7.1.2 Attached at Annexe C are **specimen**, but non-exhaustive, **lists** of documents likely to be material in different types of claim.

7.1.3 Pre-action disclosure will generally be limited to the documents required to be enclosed with the Letter of Claim and the Response. In cases where liability is admitted in full, disclosure will be limited to the documents relevant to quantum, the parties can agree that further disclosure may be given. If either or both of the parties consider that further disclosure should be given but there is disagreement about some aspect of that process, they may be able to make an application to the court for pre-action disclosure under Part 31 of the CPR. Parties should assist each other and avoid the necessity for such an application.

7.1.4 The protocol should also contain a requirement that the defendant is under a duty to preserve the disclosure documents and other evidence (CCTV for example). If the documents are destroyed, this could be an abuse of the court process.

Experts

7.2 Save for cases likely to be allocated to the multi-track, the Protocol encourages joint selection of, and access to, quantum experts, and, on occasion liability experts e.g. engineers. The expert report produced is not a joint report for the purposes of CPR Part 35. The Protocol promotes the practice of the claimant obtaining a medical report, disclosing it to the defendant who then asks questions and/or agrees it and does not obtain their own report. The Protocol provides for nomination of the expert by the claimant in personal injury claims.

7.3 Before any party instructs an expert, they should give the other party a list of the **name**(s) of **one or more experts** in the relevant speciality whom they consider are suitable to instruct.

7.4 Some solicitors choose to obtain medical reports through medical agencies, rather than directly from a specific doctor or hospital. The defendant's prior consent to this should be sought and, if the defendant so requests, the agency should be asked to provide in advance the names of the doctor(s) whom they are considering instructing.

7.5 Where a medical expert is to be instructed, the claimant's solicitor will organise access to relevant medical records – see specimen letter of instruction at Annexe D.

7.6 **Within 14 days of providing a list of experts** the other party may indicate an objection to one or more of the named experts. The first party should then instruct a mutually acceptable expert assuming there is one (this is not the same as a joint expert). It must be emphasised that when the claimant nominates an expert in the original Letter of Claim, the defendant has a further 14 days to object to one or more of the named experts after expiration of the 21 day period within which they have to reply to the Letter of Claim, as set out in paragraph 6.2.

7.7 If the defendant objects to all the listed experts, the parties may then instruct **experts of their own choice**. It will be for the court to decide, subsequently and if proceedings are issued, whether either party had acted unreasonably.

7.8 If the defendant does not object to an expert nominated by the claimant, they shall not be entitled to rely on their own expert evidence within that expert's area of expertise unless—

(a) the claimant agrees;
(b) the court so directs; or
(c) the claimant's expert report has been amended and the claimant is not prepared to disclose the original report.

7.9 **Any party may send to an agreed expert written questions** on the report, via the first party's solicitors. Such questions must be put within 28 days of service of the expert's report and must only be for the purpose of clarification of the report. The expert should send answers to the questions simultaneously to each party.

7.10 The cost of a report from an agreed expert will usually be paid by the instructing first party: the costs of the expert replying to questions will usually be borne by the party which asks the questions.

7.11 If necessary, after proceedings have commenced and with the permission of the court, the parties may obtain further expert reports. It would be for the court to decide whether the costs of more than one expert's report should be recoverable.

8 NEGOTIATIONS FOLLOWING AN ADMISSION

8.1

8.1.1 Where a defendant admits liability which has caused some damage, before proceedings are issued, the claimant should send to that defendant—

(a) any medical reports obtained under this Protocol on which the claimant relies; and

(b) a schedule of any past and future expenses and losses which are claimed, even if the schedule is necessarily provisional. The schedule should contain as much detail as reasonably practicable and should identify those losses that are ongoing. If the schedule is likely to be updated before the case is concluded, it should say so.

8.1.2 The claimant should delay issuing proceedings for 21 days from disclosure of (a) and (b) above (unless such delay would cause his claim to become time-barred), to enable the parties to consider whether the claim is capable of settlement.

8.2 CPR Part 36 permits claimants and defendants to make offers to settle pre-proceedings. Parties should always consider if it is appropriate to make a Part 36 Offer before issuing. If such an offer is made, the party making the offer must always try to supply sufficient evidence and/or information to enable the offer to be properly considered.

The level of detail will depend on the value of the claim. Medical reports may not be necessary where there is no significant continuing injury and a detailed schedule may not be necessary in a low value case.

9 ALTERNATIVE DISPUTE RESOLUTION

9.1

9.1.1 Litigation should be a last resort. As part of this Protocol, the parties should consider whether negotiation or some other form of Alternative Dispute Resolution ("ADR") might enable them to resolve their dispute without commencing proceedings.

9.1.2 Some of the options for resolving disputes without commencing proceedings are—

(a) discussions and negotiation (which may or may not include making Part 36 Offers or providing an explanation and/or apology);
(b) mediation, a third party facilitating a resolution;
(c) arbitration, a third party deciding the dispute; and
(d) early neutral evaluation, a third party giving an informed opinion on the dispute.

9.1.3 If proceedings are issued, the parties may be required by the court to provide evidence that ADR has been considered. It is expressly recognised that no party can or should be forced to mediate or enter into any form of ADR but unreasonable refusal to consider ADR will be taken into account by the court when deciding who bears the costs of the proceedings

9.2 Information on mediation and other forms of ADR is available in the *Jackson ADR Handbook* (available from Oxford University Press) or at—

- www.civilmediation.justice.gov.uk/
- www.adviceguide.org.uk/england/law_e/law_legal_system_e/law_taking_ l egal_action_e/alternatives_to_court.htm

10. QUANTIFICATION OF LOSS – SPECIAL DAMAGES

10.1 In all cases, if the defendant admits liability, the claimant will send to the defendant as soon as reasonably practicable a schedule of any past and future expenses and losses which he claims, even if the schedule is necessarily provisional. The schedule should contain as much detail as reasonably practicable and should identify those losses that are ongoing. If the schedule is likely to be updated before the case is concluded, it should say so. The claimant should keep the defendant informed as to the rate at which his financial loss is progressing throughout the entire Protocol period.

11 STOCKTAKE

11.1 Where the procedure set out in this Protocol has not resolved the dispute between the parties, each party should undertake a review of its own positions and the strengths and weaknesses of its case. The parties should then together consider the evidence and the arguments in order to see whether litigation can be avoided or, if that is not possible, for the issues between the parties to be narrowed before proceedings are issued. Where the defendant is insured and the pre-action steps have been taken by the insurer, the insurer would normally be expected to nominate solicitors to act in the proceedings and to accept service of the claim form and other documents on behalf of the defendant. The claimant or their solicitor is recommended to invite the insurer to nominate the insurer to nominate solicitors to act in the proceedings and do so 7 to 14 days before the intended issue date.

ANNEXE A
ILLUSTRATIVE FLOWCHART

III PID [42.1]

ANNEXE A - ILLUSTRATIVE FLOWCHART OF LIKELY PROGRESSION OF THE CLAIM UNDER THIS PROTOCOL

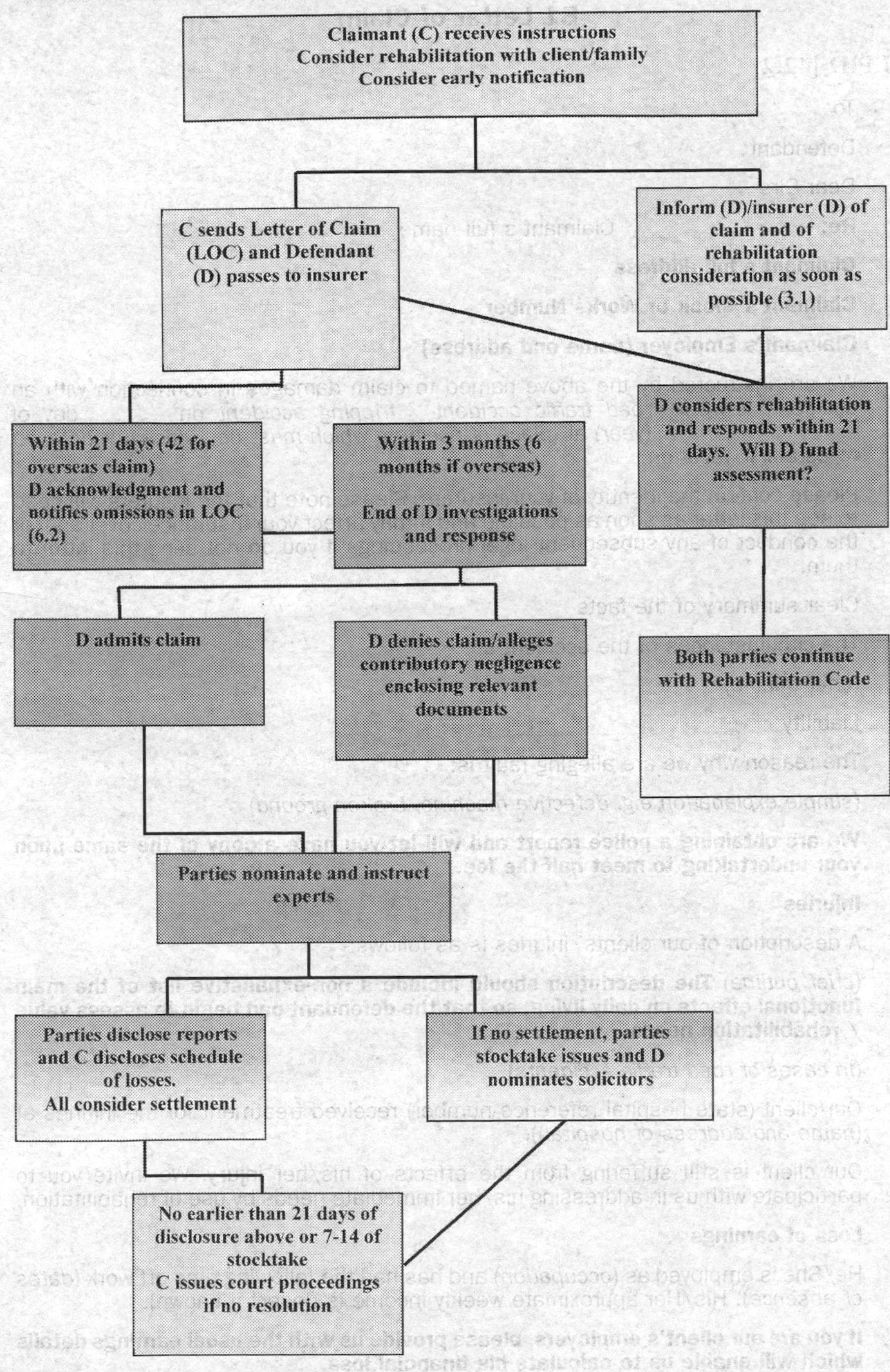

PERSONAL INJURY AND DEATH

ANNEXE B
TEMPLATES FOR LETTERS OF CLAIM AND RESPONSE

B1 Letter of Claim

III PID [42.2]

To

Defendant

Dear Sirs

Re: Claimant's full name

Claimant's full address

Claimant's Clock or Works Number

Claimant's Employer (name and address)

We are instructed by the above named to claim damages in connection with an *accident at work/ road traffic accident / tripping accident* on day of (*year*) at (*place of accident which must be sufficiently detailed to establish location*)

Please confirm the identity of your insurers. Please note that the insurers will need to see this letter as soon as possible and it may affect your insurance cover and/or the conduct of any subsequent legal proceedings if you do not send this letter to them.

Clear summary of the facts

The circumstances of the accident are:-

(*brief outline*)

Liability

The reason why we are alleging fault is:

(*simple explanation e.g. defective machine, broken ground*)

We are obtaining a police report and will let you have a copy of the same upon your undertaking to meet half the fee.

Injuries

A description of our clients' injuries is as follows:-

(*brief outline*) **The description should include a non-exhaustive list of the main functional effects on daily living, so that the defendant can begin to assess value / rehabilitation needs.**

(*In cases of road traffic accidents*)

Our client (state hospital reference number) received treatment for the injuries at (*name and address of hospital*)).

Our client is still suffering from the effects of his/her injury. We invite you to participate with us in addressing his/her immediate needs by use of rehabilitation.

Loss of earnings

He/She is employed as (*occupation*) and has had the following time off work (*dates of absence*). His/Her approximate weekly income is (insert if known).

If you are our client's employers, please provide us with the usual earnings details which will enable us to calculate his financial loss.

Other Financial Losses

We are also aware of the following (likely) financial losses:-

Details of the insurer

We have also sent a letter of claim to (*name and address*) and a copy of that letter is attached. We understand their insurers are (*name, address and claims number if known*).

At this stage of our enquiries we would expect the documents contained in parts (*insert appropriate parts of standard disclosure list*) to be relevant to this action.

A copy of this letter is attached for you to send to your insurers. Finally we expect an acknowledgment of this letter within 21 days by yourselves or your insurers.

Yours faithfully

B2 Letter of Response

To Claimant's legal representative

Dear Sirs

Letter of Response

[Claimant's name] v [Defendant's name]

Parties

We have been instructed to act on behalf of [defendant] in relation to your client's accident on [ ]. We note that you have also written to [defendant] in connection with this claim. We [do/do not] believe they are a relevant party because [ ]. [In addition we believe your claim should be directed against [defendant] for the following reasons:-

Liability

In respect of our client's liability for this accident we

admit the accident occurred and that our client is liable for loss and damage to the claimant the extent of which will require quantification.

Or

admit the accident occurred but deny that our client is responsible for any loss or damage alleged to have been caused for the following reasons:-

Or

do not admit the accident occurred either in the manner described in your letter of claim [or at all] because:-

Limitation

[We do not intend to raise any limitation defence]

Documents

We attach copies of the following documents in support of our client's position:-

You have requested copies of the following documents which we are not enclosing as we do not believe they are relevant for the following reasons:-

[It would assist our investigations if you could supply us with copies of the following documents]

Next Steps

In admitted cases

Please advise us which medical experts you are proposing to instruct.

PERSONAL INJURY AND DEATH

Please also supply us with your client's schedule of past and future expenses [if any] which are claimed, even if this can only be supplied on a provisional basis at present to assist us with making an appropriate reserve.

If you have identified that the claimant has any immediate need for additional medical treatment or other early rehabilitation intervention so that we can take instructions pursuant to the Rehabilitation Code.

In non-admitted cases

Please confirm we may now close our file. Alternatively, if you intend to proceed please advise which experts you are proposing to instruct.

Alternative Dispute Resolution

Include details of any options that may be considered whether on a without prejudice basis or otherwise

Yours faithfully

ANNEXE C
PRE-ACTION PERSONAL INJURY PROTOCOL STANDARD DISCLOSURE LISTS

RTA Cases

Section A

III PID [42.3]

In all cases where liability is at issue –

(i) documents identifying nature, extent and location of damage to defendant's vehicle where there is any dispute about point of impact;
(ii) MOT certificate where relevant;
(iii) maintenance records where vehicle defect is alleged or it is alleged by defendant that there was an unforeseen defect which caused or contributed to the accident.

Section B

Accident involving commercial vehicle as defendant –

(i) tachograph charts or entry from individual control book;
(ii) maintenance and repair records required for operators' licence where vehicle defect is alleged or it is alleged by defendant that there was an unforeseen defect which caused or contributed to the accident.

Section C

Cases against local authorities where highway design defect is alleged.

(i) documents produced to comply with Section 39 of the Road Traffic Act 1988 in respect of the duty designed to promote road safety to include studies into road accidents in the relevant area and documents relating to measures recommended to prevent accidents in the relevant area;
(ii) any Rule 43 reports produced at the request of a coroner pursuant to Schedule 5 of the Coroners & Justice Act 2009, for accidents occurring in the same locus as one covered by an earlier report.

Highway tripping claims

Documents from Highway Authority for a period of 12 months prior to the accident–

(i) records of inspection for the relevant stretch of highway;

(ii) maintenance records including records of independent contractors working in relevant area;
(iii) records of the minutes of Highway Authority meetings where maintenance or repair policy has been discussed or decided;
(iv) records of complaints about the state of highways;
(v) records of other accidents which have occurred on the relevant stretch of highway.

Workplace claims

General documents

(i) accident book entry;
(ii) other entries in the book or other accident books, relating to accidents or injuries similar to those suffered by our client (and if it is contended there are no such entries please confirm we may have facilities to inspect all accident books);
(iii) first aider report;
(iv) surgery record;
(v) foreman/supervisor accident report;
(vi) safety representative's accident report;
(vii) RIDDOR (Reporting of Injuries, Diseases and Dangerous Occurrences Regulations) report to HSE or relevant investigatory agency;
(viii) back to work interview notes and report;
(ix) all personnel/occupational health records relating to our client;
(x) other communications between defendants and HSE or other relevant investigatory agency;
(xi) minutes of Health and Safety Committee meeting(s) where accident/matter considered;
(xii) copies of all relevant CCTV footage and any other relevant photographs, videos and/or DVDs;
(xiii) copies of all electronic communications/documentation relating to the accident;
(xiv) earnings information where defendant is employer;
(xv) reports to DWP;
(xvi) manufacturer's or dealers instructions or recommendations concerning use of the work equipment;
(xvii) service or maintenance records of the work equipment;
(xviii) all documents recording arrangements for detecting, removing or cleaning up any articles or substances on the floor of the premises likely to cause a trip or slip;
(xix) work sheets and all other documents completed by or on behalf of those responsible for implementing the cleaning policy and recording work done;
(xx) all invoices, receipts and other documents relating to the purchase of relevant safety equipment to prevent a repetition of the accident;
(xxi) all correspondence, memoranda or other documentation received or brought into being concerning the condition or repair of the work equipment/the premises;
(xxii) all correspondence, instructions, estimates, invoices and other documentation submitted or received concerning repairs, remedial works or other works to the work equipment/the premises since the date of that accident;
(xxiii) work sheets and all other documents recording work done completed by those responsible for maintaining the work equipment/premises;
(xxiv) all relevant risk assessments;
(xxv) all reports, conclusions or recommendations following any enquiry or investigation into the accident;
(xxvi) the record kept of complaints made by employees together with all other documents recording in any way such complaints or actions taken thereon;
(xxvii) all other correspondence sent, or received, relating to our client's injury prior to receipt of this letter of claim;

(xxviii) documents listed above relating to any previous/similar accident/matter identified by the claimant and relied upon as proof of negligence including accident book entries;

Workplace claims – Disclosure where specific regulations apply

Section A – Management of Health and Safety at Work Regulations 1999

Documents including –

(i) Pre-accident Risk Assessment required by Regulation 3(1);
(ii) Post-accident Re-Assessment required by Regulation 3(2);
(iii) Accident Investigation Report prepared in implementing the requirements of Regulations 4 and 5;
(iv) Health Surveillance Records in appropriate cases required by Regulation 6;
(v) documents relating to the appointment of competent persons to assist required by Regulation 7;
(vi) documents relating to the employees health and safety training required by Regulation 8;
(vii) documents relating to necessary contacts with external services required by Regulation 9;
(viii) information provided to employees under Regulation 10.

Section B – Workplace (Health Safety and Welfare) Regulations 1992

Documents including –

(i) repair and maintenance records required by Regulation 5;
(ii) housekeeping records to comply with the requirements of Regulation 9;
(iii) hazard warning signs or notices to comply with Regulation 17 (Traffic Routes).

Section C – Provision and Use of work Equipment Regulations 1998

Documents including –

(i) manufacturers' specifications and instructions in respect of relevant work equipment establishing its suitability to comply with Regulation 4;
(ii) maintenance log/maintenance records required to comply with Regulation 5;
(iii) documents providing information and instructions to employees to comply with Regulation 8;
(iv) documents provided to the employee in respect of training for use to comply with Regulation 9;
(v) risk assessments/documents required to comply with Regulation 12;
(vi) any notice, sign or document relied upon as a defence to alleged breaches of Regulations 14 to 18 dealing with controls and control systems;
(vii) instruction/training documents issued to comply with the requirements of Regulation 22 insofar as it deals with maintenance operations where the machinery is not shut down;
(viii) copies of markings required to comply with Regulation 23;
(ix) copies of warnings required to comply with Regulation 24.

Section D – Personal Protective Equipment at Work Regulations 1992

Documents including –

(i) documents relating to the assessment of the Personal Protective Equipment to comply with Regulation 6;

(ii) documents relating to the maintenance and replacement of Personal Protective Equipment to comply with Regulation 7;
(iii) record of maintenance procedures for Personal Protective Equipment to comply with Regulation 7;
(iv) records of tests and examinations of Personal Protective Equipment to comply with Regulation 7;
(v) documents providing information, instruction and training in relation to the Personal Protective Equipment to comply with Regulation 9;
(vi) instructions for use of Personal Protective Equipment to include the manufacturers' instructions to comply with Regulation 10.

Section E – Manual Handling Operations Regulations 1992

Documents including –

(i) Manual Handling Risk Assessment carried out to comply with the requirements of Regulation 4(1)(b)(i);
(ii) re-assessment carried out post-accident to comply with requirements of Regulation 4(1)(b)(i);
(iii) documents showing the information provided to the employee to give general indications related to the load and precise indications on the weight of the load and the heaviest side of the load if the centre of gravity was not positioned centrally to comply with Regulation 4(1)(b)(iii);
(iv) documents relating to training in respect of manual handling operations and training records.

Section F – Health and Safety (Display Screen Equipment) Regulations 1992

Documents including –

(i) analysis of work stations to assess and reduce risks carried out to comply with the requirements of Regulation 2;
(ii) re-assessment of analysis of work stations to assess and reduce risks following development of symptoms by the claimant;
(iii) documents detailing the provision of training including training records to comply with the requirements of Regulation 6;
(iv) documents providing information to employees to comply with the requirements of Regulation 7.

Section G – Control of Substances Hazardous to Health Regulations 2002

Documents including –

(i) risk assessment carried out to comply with the requirements of Regulation 6;
(ii) reviewed risk assessment carried out to comply with the requirements of Regulation 6;
(iii) documents recording any changes to the risk assessment required to comply with Regulation 6 and steps taken to meet the requirements of Regulation 7;
(iv) copy labels from containers used for storage handling and disposal of carcinogenics to comply with the requirements of Regulation 7(2A)(h);
(v) warning signs identifying designation of areas and installations which may be contaminated by carcinogenics to comply with the requirements of Regulation 7(2A)(h);
(vi) documents relating to the assessment of the Personal Protective Equipment to comply with Regulation 7(3A);
(vii) documents relating to the maintenance and replacement of Personal Protective Equipment to comply with Regulation 7(3A);
(viii) record of maintenance procedures for Personal Protective Equipment to comply with Regulation 7(3A);
(ix) records of tests and examinations of Personal Protective Equipment to comply with Regulation 7(3A);

(x) documents providing information, instruction and training in relation to the Personal Protective Equipment to comply with Regulation 7(3A);
(xi) instructions for use of Personal Protective Equipment to include the manufacturers' instructions to comply with Regulation 7(3A);
(xii) air monitoring records for substances assigned a maximum exposure limit or occupational exposure standard to comply with the requirements of Regulation 7;
(xiii) maintenance examination and test of control measures records to comply with Regulation 9;
(xiv) monitoring records to comply with the requirements of Regulation 10;
(xv) health surveillance records to comply with the requirements of Regulation 11;
(xvi) documents detailing information, instruction and training including training records for employees to comply with the requirements of Regulation 12;
(xvii) all documents relating to arrangements and procedures to deal with accidents, incidents and emergencies required to comply with Regulation 13;
(xviii) labels and Health and Safety data sheets supplied to the employers to comply with the CHIP Regulations.

Section H – Construction (Design and Management) Regulations 2007

Documents including –

(i) notification of a project form (HSE F10) to comply with the requirements of Regulation 7;
(ii) Health and Safety Plan to comply with requirements of Regulation 15;
(iii) Health and Safety file to comply with the requirements of Regulations 12 and 14;
(iv) information and training records provided to comply with the requirements of Regulation 17;
(v) records of advice from and views of persons at work to comply with the requirements of Regulation 18;
(vi) reports of inspections made in accordance with Regulation 33;
(vii) records of checks for the purposes of Regulation 34;
(viii) emergency procedures for the purposes of Regulation 39.

Section I – Construction (Health, Safety & Welfare) Regulations 1996

Documents including –

(i) documents produced to comply with requirements of the Regulations.

Section J – Work at Height Regulations 2005

Documents including –

(i) documents relating to planning, supervision and safety carried out for Regulation 4;
(ii) documents relating to training for the purposes of Regulation 5;
(iii) documents relating to the risk assessment carried out for Regulation 6;
(iv) documents relating to the selection of work equipment for the purposes of Regulation 7;
(v) notices or other means in writing warning of fragile surfaces for the purposes of Regulation 9;
(vi) documents relating to any inspection carried out for Regulation 12;
(vii) documents relating to any inspection carried out for Regulation 13;
(viii) reports made for the purposes of Regulation 14;
(ix) any certificate issued for the purposes of Regulation 15.

Section K – Pressure Systems and Transportable Gas Containers Regulations 1989

(i) information and specimen markings provided to comply with the requirements of Regulation 5;
(ii) written statements specifying the safe operating limits of a system to comply with the requirements of Regulation 7;
(iii) copy of the written scheme of examination required to comply with the requirements of Regulation 8;
(iv) examination records required to comply with the requirements of Regulation 9;
(v) instructions provided for the use of operator to comply with Regulation 11;
(vi) records kept to comply with the requirements of Regulation 13;
(vii) records kept to comply with the requirements of Regulation 22.

Section L – Lifting Operations and Lifting Equipment Regulations 1998

Documents including –

(i) records kept to comply with the requirements of the Regulations including the records kept to comply with Regulation 6.

Section M – The Noise at Work Regulations 1989

Documents including –

(i) any risk assessment records required to comply with the requirements of Regulations 4 and 5;
(ii) manufacturers' literature in respect of all ear protection made available to claimant to comply with the requirements of Regulation 8;
(iii) all documents provided to the employee for the provision of information to comply with Regulation 11.

Section N – Control of Noise at Work Regulations 1989

Documents including –

(i) documents relating to the assessment of the level of noise to which employees are exposed to comply with Regulation 5;
(ii) documents relating to health surveillance of employees to comply with Regulation 9;
(iii) instruction and training records provided to employees to comply with Regulation 10.

Section O – Construction (Head Protection) Regulations 1989

Documents including –

(i) pre-accident assessment of head protection required to comply with Regulation 3(4);
(ii) post-accident re-assessment required to comply with Regulation 3(5).

Section P – The Construction (General Provisions) Regulations 1961

Documents including –

(i) report prepared following inspections and examinations of excavations etc. to comply with the requirements of Regulation 9.

Section Q – Gas Containers Regulations 1989

Documents including –

(i) information and specimen markings provided to comply with the requirements of Regulation 5;
(ii) written statements specifying the safe operating limits of a system to comply with the requirements of Regulation 7;
(iii) copy of the written scheme of examination required to comply with the requirements of Regulation 8;
(iv) examination records required to comply with the requirements of Regulation 9;
(v) instructions provided for the use of operator to comply with Regulation 11.

Section R – Control of Noise at Work Regulations 2005

Documents including –

(i) risk assessment records required to comply with the requirements of Regulations 4 and 5;
(ii) all documents relating to steps taken to comply with regulation 6;
(iii) all documents relating to and/or arising out of actions taken to comply including providing consideration of alternative work that the claimant could have engaged to comply with Regulation 7.

Section S – Mine and Quarries Act 1954

Documents including –

(i) documents produced to comply with requirements of the Act.

Section T – Control of Vibrations at Work Regulations 2005

Documents including –

(i) risk assessments and documents produced to comply with requirements of Regulations 6 and 8;
(ii) occupational health surveillance records produced to comply with Regulation 7.

ANNEXE D
LETTER OF INSTRUCTION TO MEDICAL EXPERT

III PID [42.4]

Dear Sir,

Re: (***Name and Address***)

D.O.B. –

Telephone No. –

Date of Accident –

We are acting for the above named in connection with injuries received in an accident which occurred on the above date. A summary of the main facts of the accident circumstances is provided below.

The main injuries appear to have been (*describe main injuries and functional impact on day to day living as in Letter of Claim*).

In order to assist with the preparation of your report we have enclosed the following documents:

Enclosures

1. Hospital Records

2. GP records

3. Statement of Events

We have not obtained [ ] records yet but will use our best endeavours to obtain these without delay if you request them.

We should be obliged if you would examine our Client and let us have a full and detailed report dealing with any relevant pre-accident medical history, the injuries sustained, treatment received and present condition, dealing in particular with the capacity for work and giving a prognosis.

It is central to our assessment of the extent of our Client's injuries to establish the extent and duration of any continuing disability. Accordingly, in the prognosis section we would ask you to specifically comment on any areas of continuing complaint or disability or impact on daily living. If there is such continuing disability you should comment upon the level of suffering or inconvenience caused and, if you are able, give your view as to when or if the complaint or disability is likely to resolve.

If our client requires further treatment, please can you advise of the cost on a private patient basis.

Please send our Client an appointment direct for this purpose. Should you be able to offer a cancellation appointment please contact our Client direct. We confirm we will be responsible for your reasonable fees.

We are obtaining the notes and records from our Client's GP and Hospitals attended and will forward them to you when they are to hand/or please request the GP and Hospital records direct and advise that any invoice for the provision of these records should be forwarded to us.

In order to comply with Court Rules we would be grateful if you would insert above your signature, the following statement: "I confirm that I have made clear which facts and matters referred to in this report are within my own knowledge and which are not. Those that are within my own knowledge I confirm to be true. The opinions I have expressed represent my true and complete professional opinions on the matters to which they refer".

In order to avoid further correspondence we can confirm that on the evidence we have there is no reason to suspect we may be pursuing a claim against the hospital or its staff.

We look forward to receiving your report within ____________ weeks. If you will not be able to prepare your report within this period please telephone us upon receipt of these instructions.

When acknowledging these instructions it would assist if you could give an estimate as to the likely time scale for the provision of your report and also an indication as to your fee.

Yours faithfully

2. PRE-ACTION PROTOCOL FOR THE RESOLUTION OF CLINICAL DISPUTES

1 INTRODUCTION

III PID [43]

1.1 This Protocol is intended to apply to all claims against hospitals, GPs, dentists and other healthcare providers (both NHS and private) which involve an injury that is alleged to be the result of clinical negligence. It is not intended to apply to claims covered by—

(a) the Pre-Action Protocol for Disease and Illness Claims;
(b) the Pre-Action Protocol for Personal Injury Claims;
(c) the Pre-Action Protocol for Low Value Personal Injury Claims in Road Traffic Accidents;
(d) the Pre-Action Protocol for Low Value Personal Injury (Employers' Liability and Public Liability) Claims; or
(e) Practice Direction 3D – Mesothelioma Claims.

1.2 This Protocol is intended to be sufficiently broad-based and flexible to apply to all sectors of healthcare, both public and private. It also recognises that a claimant and a defendant, as patient and healthcare provider, may have an ongoing relationship.

1.3 It is important that each party to a clinical dispute has sufficient information and understanding of the other's perspective and case to be able to investigate a claim efficiently and, where appropriate, to resolve it. This Protocol encourages a cards-on-the-table approach when something has gone wrong with a claimant's treatment or the claimant is dissatisfied with that treatment and/or the outcome.

1.4 This Protocol is now regarded by the courts as setting the standard of normal reasonable pre-action conduct for the resolution of clinical disputes.

1.5

1.5.1 This Protocol sets out the conduct that prospective parties would normally be expected to follow prior to the commencement of any proceedings. It establishes a reasonable process and timetable for the exchange of information relevant to a dispute, sets out the standards for the content and quality of letters of claim and sets standards for the conduct of pre-action negotiations.

1.5.2 The timetable and the arrangements for disclosing documents and obtaining expert evidence may need to be varied to suit the circumstances of the case. Where one or more parties consider the detail of the Protocol is not appropriate to the case, and proceedings are subsequently issued, the court will expect an explanation as to why the Protocol has not been followed, or has been varied.

Early Issue

1.6

1.6.1 The Protocol provides for a defendant to be given four months to investigate and respond to a Letter of Claim before proceedings are served. If this is not possible, the claimant's solicitor should give as much notice of the intention to issue proceedings as is practicable. This Protocol does not alter the statutory time limits for starting court proceedings. If a claim is issued after the relevant statutory limitation period has expired, the defendant will be entitled to use that as a defence to the claim. If proceedings are started to comply with the statutory time limit before the parties have followed the procedures in this Protocol, the parties should apply to the court for a stay of the proceedings while they so comply.

1.6.2 The parties should also consider whether there is likely to be a dispute as to limitation should a claim be pursued.

Enforcement of the Protocol and sanctions

1.7 Where either party fails to comply with this Protocol, the court may impose sanctions. When deciding whether to do so, the court will look at whether the parties have complied in substance with the Protocol's relevant principles and requirements. It will also consider the effect any non-compliance has had on any other party. It is not likely to be concerned with minor or technical shortcomings (see paragraph 4.3 to 4.5 of the Practice Direction on Pre-Action Conduct and Protocols).

Litigants in Person

1.8 If a party to a claim does not seek professional advice from a solicitor they should still, in so far as is reasonably possible, comply with the terms of this Protocol. In this Protocol "solicitor" is intended to encompass reference to any suitably legally qualified person.

If a party to a claim becomes aware that another party is a litigant in person, they should send a copy of this Protocol to the litigant in person at the earliest opportunity.

2 THE AIMS OF THE PROTOCOL

2.1 The **general** aims of the Protocol are –

(a) to maintain and/or restore the patient/healthcare provider relationship in an open and transparent way;

(b) to reduce delay and ensure that costs are proportionate; and

(c) to resolve as many disputes as possible without litigation.

2.2 The **specific** objectives are–

(a) to encourage openness, transparency and early communication of the perceived problem between patients and healthcare providers;

(b) to provide an opportunity for healthcare providers to identify whether notification of a notifiable safety incident has been, or should be, sent to the claimant in accordance with the duty of candour imposed by section 20 of the Health and Social Care Act 2008 (Regulated Activities) Regulations 2014;

(c) to ensure that sufficient medical and other information is disclosed promptly by both parties to enable each to understand the other's perspective and case, and to encourage early resolution or a narrowing of the issues in dispute;

(d) to provide an early opportunity for healthcare providers to identify cases where an investigation is required and to carry out that investigation promptly;

(e) to encourage healthcare providers to involve the *National Health Service Litigation Authority* (NHSLA) or their defence organisations or insurers at an early stage;

(f) to enable the parties to avoid litigation by agreeing a resolution of the dispute;

(g) to enable the parties to explore the use of mediation or to narrow the issues in dispute before proceedings are commenced;

(h) to enable parties to identify any issues that may require a separate or preliminary hearing, such as a dispute as to limitation;

(i) to support the efficient management of proceedings where litigation cannot be avoided;

(j) to discourage the prolonged pursuit of unmeritorious claims and the prolonged defence of meritorious claims;

PERSONAL INJURY AND DEATH

(k) to promote the provision of medical or rehabilitation treatment to address the needs of the claimant at the earliest opportunity; and

(l) to encourage the defendant to make an early apology to the claimant if appropriate.

2.3 This Protocol does not—

(a) provide any detailed guidance to healthcare providers on clinical risk management or the adoption of risk management systems and procedures;

(b) provide any detailed guidance on which adverse outcomes should trigger an investigation; or

(c) recommend changes to the codes of conduct of professionals in healthcare.

3 THE PROTOCOL

3.1 An illustrative flowchart is attached at Annex A which shows each of the stages that the parties are expected to take before the commencement of proceedings.

Obtaining health records

3.2 Any request for records by the **claimant** should–

(a) **provide sufficient information** to alert the defendant where an adverse outcome has been serious or has had serious consequences or may constitute a notifiable safety incident;

(b) be as **specific as possible** about the records which are required for an initial investigation of the claim (including, for example, a continuous copy of the CTG trace in birth injury cases); and

(c) include a request for any relevant guidelines, analyses, protocols or policies and any documents created in relation to an adverse incident, notifiable safety incident or complaint.

3.3 Requests for copies of the claimant's clinical records should be made using the Law Society and Department of Health approved **standard forms** (enclosed at Annex B), adapted as necessary.

3.4

3.4.1 The copy records should be provided **within 40 days** of the request and for a cost not exceeding the charges permissible under the Access to Health Records Act 1990 and/or the Data Protection Act 1998. Payment may be required in advance by the healthcare provider.

3.4.2 The claimant may also make a request under the Freedom of Information Act 2000.

3.5 At the earliest opportunity, legible copies of the claimant's medical and other records should be placed in an indexed and paginated bundle by the claimant. This bundle should be kept up to date.

3.6 In the rare circumstances that the defendant is in difficulty in complying with the request within 40 days, the **problem should be explained** quickly and details given of what is being done to resolve it.

3.7 If the defendant fails to provide the health records or an explanation for any delay within 40 days, the claimant or their adviser can then apply to the court under rule 31.16 of the Civil Procedure Rules 1998 ('CPR') for an **order for pre-action disclosure**. The court has the power to impose costs sanctions for unreasonable delay in providing records.

3.8 If either the claimant or the defendant considers **additional health records are required from a third party**, in the first instance these should be requested by or through the claimant. Third party healthcare providers are expected to co-operate. Rule 31.17 of the CPR sets out the procedure for applying to the court for pre-action disclosure by third parties.

Rehabilitation

3.9 The claimant and the defendant shall both consider as early as possible whether the claimant has reasonable needs that could be met by rehabilitation treatment or other measures. They should also discuss how these needs might be addressed. An immediate needs assessment report prepared for the purposes of rehabilitation should not be used in the litigation except by consent.

(A copy of the Rehabilitation Code can be found at: www.iua.co.uk/IUA_Member/Publications)

Letter of Notification

3.10 Annex C1 to this Protocol provides a **template for the recommended contents of a Letter of Notification**; the level of detail will need to be varied to suit the particular circumstances.

3.11

3.11.1 Following receipt and analysis of the records and, if appropriate, receipt of an initial supportive expert opinion, the claimant may wish to send a Letter of Notification to the defendant as soon as practicable.

3.11.2 The Letter of Notification should advise the defendant that this is a claim where a Letter of Claim is likely to be sent because a case as to breach of duty and/or causation has been identified. A copy of the Letter of Notification should also be sent to the NHSLA or, where known, other relevant medical defence organisation or indemnity provider.

3.12

3.12.1 On receipt of a Letter of Notification a defendant should—

(a) acknowledge the letter within 14 days of receipt;
(b) identify who will be dealing with the matter and to whom any Letter of Claim should be sent;
(c) consider whether to commence investigations and/or to obtain factual and expert evidence;
(d) consider whether any information could be passed to the claimant which might narrow the issues in dispute or lead to an early resolution of the claim; and
(e) forward a copy of the Letter of Notification to the NHSLA or other relevant medical defence organisation/indemnity provider.

3.12.2 The court may question any requests by the defendant for extension of time limits if a Letter of Notification was sent but did not prompt an initial investigation.

Letter of Claim

3.13 Annex C2 to this Protocol provides a **template for the recommended contents of a Letter of Claim**: the level of detail will need to be varied to suit the particular circumstances.

3.14 If, following the receipt and analysis of the records, and the receipt of any further advice (including from experts if necessary – see Section 4), the claimant decides that there are grounds for a claim, a letter of claim should be sent to the defendant as soon as practicable. Any letter of claim sent to an NHS Trust should be copied to the National Health Service Litigation Authority.

3.16 This letter should contain—

(a) a **clear summary of the facts** on which the claim is based, including the alleged adverse outcome, and the **main allegations of negligence**;
(b) a description of the **claimant's injuries**, and present condition and prognosis;

PERSONAL INJURY AND DEATH

(c) an outline of the **financial loss** incurred by the claimant, with an indication of the heads of damage to be claimed and the scale of the loss, unless this is impracticable;
(d) confirmation of the method of funding and whether any funding arrangement was entered into before or after April 2013; and
(e) the discipline of any expert from whom evidence has already been obtained.

3.17 The Letter of Claim should **refer to any relevant documents**, including health records, and if possible enclose copies of any of those which will not already be in the potential defendant's possession, e.g. any relevant general practitioner records if the claimant's claim is against a hospital.

3.18 **Sufficient information** must be given to enable the defendant to **focus investigations** and to put an initial valuation on the claim.

3.19 Letters of Claim are **not** intended to have the same formal status as Particulars of Claim, nor should any sanctions necessarily apply if the Letter of Claim and any subsequent Particulars of Claim in the proceedings differ.

3.20 **Proceedings should not be issued until after four months from the letter of claim.**

In certain instances it may not be possible for the claimant to serve a Letter of Claim more than four months before the expiry of the limitation period. If, for any reason, proceedings are started before the parties have complied, they should seek to agree to apply to the court for an order to stay the proceedings whilst the parties take steps to comply.

3.21 The claimant may want to make an **offer to settle** the claim at this early stage by putting forward an offer in respect of liability and/or an amount of compensation in accordance with the legal and procedural requirements of CPR Part 36 (possibly including any costs incurred to date). If an offer to settle is made, generally this should be supported by a medical report which deals with the injuries, condition and prognosis, and by a schedule of loss and supporting documentation. The level of detail necessary will depend on the value of the claim. Medical reports may not be necessary where there is no significant continuing injury and a detailed schedule may not be necessary in a low value case.

Letter of Response

3.22 Attached at Annex C3 is a template for the suggested contents of the **Letter of Response**: the level of detail will need to be varied to suit the particular circumstances.

3.23 The defendant should **acknowledge** the Letter of Claim **within 14 days of receipt** and should identify who will be dealing with the matter.

3.24 The defendant should, **within four months** of the Letter of Claim, provide a **reasoned answer** in the form of a **Letter of Response** in which the defendant should—

(a) if the **claim is admitted**, say so in clear terms;
(b) if only **part of the claim is admitted**, make clear which issues of breach of duty and/or causation are admitted and which are denied and why;
(c) state whether it is intended that any **admissions will be binding**;
(d) if the **claim is denied**, include specific comments on the allegations of negligence and, if a synopsis or chronology of relevant events has been provided and is disputed, the defendant's version of those events;
(e) if supportive expert evidence has been obtained, identify which disciplines of expert evidence have been relied upon and whether they relate to breach of duty and/or causation;
(f) if known, state whether the defendant requires copies of any relevant medical records obtained by the claimant (to be supplied for a reasonable copying charge);
(g) provide copies of any additional documents relied upon, e.g. an internal protocol;

(h) if not indemnified by the NHS, supply details of the relevant indemnity insurer; and
(i) inform the claimant of any other potential defendants to the claim.

3.25

3.25.1 If the defendant requires an extension of time for service of the Letter of Response, a request should be made as soon as the defendant becomes aware that it will be required and, in any event, within four months of the letter of claim.

3.25.2 The defendant should explain why any extension of time is necessary.

3.25.3 The claimant should adopt a reasonable approach to any request for an extension of time for provision of the reasoned answer.

3.26 If the claimant has made an offer to settle, the defendant should respond to that offer in the Letter of Response, preferably with reasons. The defendant may also make an offer to settle at this stage. Any offer made by the defendant should be made in accordance with the legal and procedural requirements of CPR Part 36 (possibly including any costs incurred to date). If an offer to settle is made, the defendant should provide sufficient medical or other evidence to allow the claimant to properly consider the offer. The level of detail necessary will depend on the value of the claim.

3.27 If the parties reach agreement on liability, or wish to explore the possibility of resolution with no admissions as to liability, but time is needed to resolve the value of the claim, they should aim to agree a reasonable period.

3.28 If the parties do not reach agreement on liability, they should discuss whether the claimant should start proceedings and whether the court might be invited to direct an early trial of a preliminary issue or of breach of duty and/or causation.

3.29 Following receipt of the Letter of Response, if the claimant is aware that there may be a delay of six months or more before the claimant decides if, when and how to proceed, the claimant should keep the defendant generally informed.

4 EXPERTS

4.1 In clinical negligence disputes separate **expert opinions** may be needed—

- on breach of duty;
- on causation;
- on the patient's condition and prognosis;
- to assist in valuing aspects of the claim.

4.2 It is recognised that in clinical negligence disputes, the parties and their advisers will require flexibility in their approach to expert evidence. The parties should co-operate when making decisions on appropriate medical specialisms, whether experts might be instructed jointly and whether any reports obtained pre-action might be shared.

4.3 Obtaining expert evidence will often be an expensive step and may take time, especially in specialised areas of medicine where there are limited numbers of suitable experts.

4.4 When considering what expert evidence may be required during the Protocol period, parties should be aware that the use of any expert reports obtained pre-action will only be permitted in proceedings with the express permission of the court.

5 ALTERNATIVE DISPUTE RESOLUTION

5.1 Litigation should be a last resort. As part of this Protocol, the parties should consider whether negotiation or some other form of alternative dispute resolution ('ADR') might enable them to resolve their dispute without commencing proceedings.

5.2 Some of the options for resolving disputes without commencing proceedings are—

(a) discussion and negotiation (which may or may not include making Part 36 Offers or providing an explanation and/or apology);
(b) mediation, a third party facilitating a resolution;
(c) arbitration, a third party deciding the dispute;
(d) early neutral evaluation, a third party giving an informed opinion on the dispute; and
(e) Ombudsmen schemes.

5.3 Information on mediation and other forms of ADR is available in the *Jackson ADR Handbook* (available from Oxford University Press) or at—

- www.civilmediation.justice.gov.uk/
- www.adviceguide.org.uk/england/law_e/law_legal_system_e/law_taking_legal_action_e/alternatives_to_court.htm

5.4 If proceedings are issued, the parties may be required by the court to provide evidence that ADR has been considered. It is expressly recognised that no party can or should be forced to mediate or enter into any form of ADR, but a party's silence in response to an invitation to participate in ADR might be considered unreasonable by the court and could lead to the court ordering that party to pay additional court costs.

6 STOCKTAKE

6.1

6.1.1 Where a dispute has not been resolved after the parties have followed the procedure set out in this Protocol, the parties should review their positions before the claimant issues court proceedings.

6.1.2 If proceedings cannot be avoided, the parties should continue to co-operate and should seek to prepare a chronology of events which identifies the facts or issues that are agreed and those that remain in dispute. The parties should also seek to agree the necessary procedural directions for efficient case management during the proceedings.

ANNEXE A
ILLUSTRATIVE FLOWCHART

III PID [43.1]

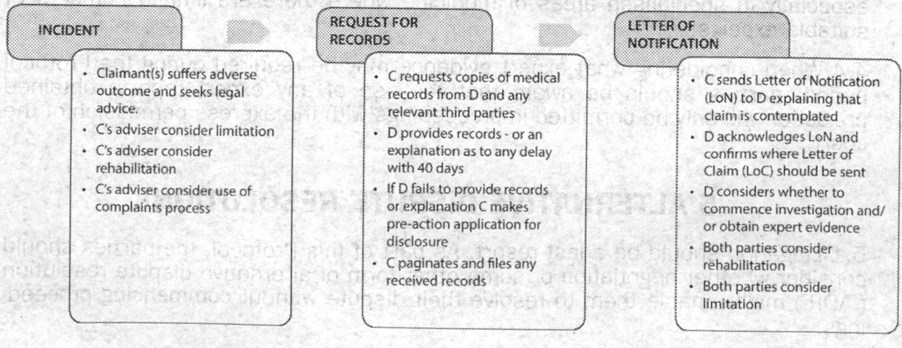

LETTER OF CLAIM

- C sends LoC to D and D's insurer detailing allegations as to breach of duty and causation
- C provides D with copies of relevant records and/ or a list of all records obtained
- C sets out chronology of events
- C provides evidence as to condition, prognosis and alleged quantum losses
- Both parties consider rehabilitation

LETTER OF RESPONSE

- D provides C with detailed Letter of Response (LoR) within 4 months
- LoR will set out any admissions or denials as to breach of duty and/or causation
- D identifies relevant medical records not referred to in LoC
- D agree C's chronology or provides alternative chronology
- Both parties consider rehabililtation

ADR

- Parties consider whether matter can be resolved without further recourse to the court
- Parties consider non-financial resolution (eg. face-to-face explanation, further treatment and/or apology)
- Parties consider financial settlement (without without admission of liability)
- Parties consider rehabilitation

STOCKTAKE

- Parties seektonarrow issues to dispute
- Parties seek to agree chronology and key facts
- Parties seek to identify any matters that could be dealt with as prelimiary issues (eg limitation)
- Parties consider rehabilitation
- Parties consider what further expert evidence will be issued
- Parties consider whether Protocol has been complied with

ANNEXE B
FORM FOR REQUESTING HEALTH RECORDS

III PID [43.2]

The form for obtaining health records is currently unavailable.

ANNEX C
TEMPLATES FOR LETTERS OF NOTIFICATION, CLAIM AND RESPONSE

Annex C1 Letter of Notification

III PID [43.3]

1 **To**

Defendant

Dear Sirs

Letter of Notification

Re: [Claimant's Name, Address, DoB and NHS Number]

We have been instructed to act on behalf of [Claimant's name] in relation to treatment carried out/care provided at [name of hospital or treatment centre] by [name of clinician(s) if known] on [insert date(s)].

The purpose of this letter is to notify you that, although we are not yet in a position to serve a formal Letter of Claim, our initial investigations indicate that a case as to breach of duty and/or causation has been identified. We therefore invite you to commence your own investigation and draw your attention to the fact that failure to do may be taken into account when considering the reasonableness of any subsequent application for an extension of time for the Letter of Response.

Defendant

We understand that you are the correct defendant in respect of treatment provided by [name of clinician] at [hospital/surgery/treatment centre] on [date(s)]. If you do not agree, please provide us with any information you have that may assist us to identify the correct defendant. Failure to do so may result in costs sanctions should proceedings be issued.

Summary of Facts and Alleged Adverse Outcome

[Outline what is alleged to have happened and provide a chronology of events with details of relevant known treatment/care.]

PERSONAL INJURY AND DEATH

Medical Records

[Provide index of records obtained and request for further records/information if required.]

Allegations of Negligence

[Brief outline of any alleged breach of duty and causal link with any damage suffered.]

Expert Evidence

[State whether expert evidence has been obtained or is awaited and, if so, the relevant discipline.]

Damage

[Brief outline of any injuries attributed to the alleged negligence and their functional impact.]

Funding

[If known, state method of funding and whether arrangement was entered into before or after April 2013.]

Rehabilitation

As a result of the allegedly negligent treatment, our client has injuries/needs that could be met by rehabilitation. We invite you to consider how this could be achieved.

Limitation

For the purposes of limitation, we calculate that any proceedings will need to be issued on or before [date].

Please acknowledge this letter by [insert date 14 days after deemed receipt] and confirm to whom any Letter of Claim should be sent. We enclose a duplicate of the letter for your insurer.

Recoverable Benefits

The claimant's National Insurance Number will be sent to you in a separate envelope.

We look forward to hearing from you.

Yours faithfully,

Annex C2 Letter of Claim

1 **To**

Defendant

Dear Sirs

Letter of Claim

[Claimant's name] –v– [Defendant's Name]

We have been instructed to act on behalf of [Claimant's name] in relation to treatment carried out/care provided at [name of hospital or treatment centre] by [name of clinician(s) if known] on [insert date(s)]. Please let us know if you do not believe that you are the appropriate defendant or if you are aware of any other potential defendants.

Claimant's details

Full name, DoB, address, NHS Number.

Dates of allegedly negligent treatment

- include chronology based on medical records.

Events giving rise to the claim:

- an outline of what happened, including details of other relevant treatments to the client by other healthcare providers.

Allegation of negligence and causal link with injuries:

- an outline of the allegations or a more detailed list in a complex case;
- an outline of the causal link between allegations and the injuries complained of;
- a copy of any supportive expert evidence (optional).

The Client's injuries, condition and future prognosis

- A copy of any supportive expert report (optional);
- Suggestions for rehabilitation;
- The discipline of any expert evidence obtained or proposed.

Clinical records (if not previously provided)

We enclose an index of all the relevant records that we hold. We shall be happy to provide copies of these on payment of our photocopying charges.

We enclose a request for copies of the following records which we believe that you hold. We confirm that we shall be responsible for your reasonable copying charges. Failure to provide these records may result in costs sanctions if proceedings are issued.

The likely value of the claim

- an outline of the main heads of damage, or, in straightforward cases, the details of loss;
- Part 36 settlement offer (optional);
- suggestions for ADR.

Funding

[State method of funding and whether arrangement was entered into before or after April 2013.]

We enclose a further copy of this letter for you to pass to your insurer. We look forward to receiving an acknowledgment of this letter within 14 days and your Letter of Response within 4 months of the date on which this letter was received. We calculate the date for receipt of your Letter of Response to be [date].

Recoverable Benefits

The claimant's National Insurance Number will be sent to you in a separate envelope.

We look forward to hearing from you.

Yours faithfully,

Annex C3 Letter of Response

1 **To**

Claimant

Dear Sirs

Letter of Response

[Claimant's name] –v– [Defendant's Name]

We have been instructed to act on behalf of [defendant] in relation to treatment carried out/care provided to [claimant] at [name of hospital or treatment centre] by [name of clinician(s) if known] on [insert date(s)].

The defendant [conveys sympathy for the adverse outcome/would like to offer an apology/denies that there was an adverse outcome].

Parties

It is accepted that [defendant] had a duty of care towards [claimant] in respect of [details if required] treatment/care provided to [claimant] at [location] on [date(s)].

However, [defendant] is not responsible for [details] care/treatment provided to [claimant] at [location] on [date(s)] by [name of clinician if known].

Records

We hold the following records . . .

We require copies of the following records . . .

Failure to provide these records may result in costs sanctions if proceedings are issued.

Comments on events and/or chronology:

We [agree the chronology enclosed with the Letter of Claim] [enclose a revised chronology of events].

We enclose copies of relevant [records/Protocols/internal investigations] in respect of the treatment/care that [claimant] received.

Liability

In respect of the specific allegations raised by the claimant, the defendant [has obtained an expert opinion and] responds as follows:-

[each allegation should be addressed separately. The defendant should explain which (if any) of the allegations of breach of duty and/or causation are admitted and why. The defendant should also make clear which allegations are denied and why].

Next Steps

The defendant suggests . . .

[e.g. no prospect of success for the claimant, resolution without admissions of liability, ADR, settlement offer, rehabilitation].

Yours faithfully,

PRE-ACTION PROTOCOL FOR DISEASE AND ILLNESS CLAIMS

1 INTRODUCTION

III PID [44]

1.1 Lord Woolf in his final Access to Justice Report of July 1996 recommended the development of protocols: 'To build on and increase the benefits of early but well informed settlements which genuinely satisfy both parties to a dispute.'

1.2 The aims of these protocols are:

- more contact between the parties
- better and earlier exchange of information
- better investigation by both sides
- to put the parties in a position where they may be able to settle cases fairly and early without litigation

- to enable proceedings to run to the court's timetable and efficiently, if litigation does become necessary.

1.3 The concept of protocols is relevant to a range of initiatives for good claims practice, especially:

- predictability in the time needed for steps to be taken
- standardisation of relevant information, including documents to be disclosed.

1.4 The Courts will be able to treat the standards set in protocols as the normal reasonable approach. If proceedings are issued, it will be for the court to decide whether non-compliance with a protocol should merit adverse consequences. Guidance on the court's likely approach will be given from time to time in practice directions.

1.5 If the court has to consider the question of compliance after proceedings have begun, it will not be concerned with minor infringements, e.g. failure by a short period to provide relevant information. One minor breach will not exempt the 'innocent' party from following the protocol. The court will look at the effect of non-compliance on the other party when deciding whether to impose sanctions.

2 NOTES OF GUIDANCE

Scope of the protocol

2.1 This protocol is intended to apply to all personal injury claims where the injury is not as the result of an accident but takes the form of an illness or disease.

2.2 This protocol covers disease claims which are likely to be complex and frequently not suitable for fast-track procedures even though they may fall within fast track limits. Disease for the purpose of this protocol primarily covers any illness physical or psychological, any disorder, ailment, affliction, complaint, malady, or derangement other than a physical or psychological injury solely caused by an accident or other similar single event.

2.3 In appropriate cases it may be agreed between the parties that this protocol can be applied rather than the Pre-Action Protocol for Personal Injury Claims where a single event occurs but causes a disease or illness.

2.4 This protocol is not limited to diseases occurring in the workplace but will embrace diseases occurring in other situations for example through occupation of premises or the use of products. It is not intended to cover those cases, which are dealt with as a 'group' or 'class' action.

2.5 The 'cards on the table' approach advocated by the Pre-Action Protocol for Personal Injury claims is equally appropriate to disease claims. The spirit of that protocol, and of the clinical negligence protocol is followed here, in accordance with the sense of the civil justice reforms.

2.6 The timetable and the arrangements for disclosing documents and obtaining expert evidence may need to be varied to suit the circumstances of the case. If a party considers the detail of the protocol to be inappropriate they should communicate their reasons to all of the parties at that stage. If proceedings are subsequently issued, the court will expect an explanation as to why the protocol has not been followed, or has been varied.

2.7 In a terminal disease claim with short life expectancy, for instance where a claimant has a disease such as mesothelioma, the time scale of the protocol is likely to be too long. In such a claim, the claimant may not be able to follow the protocol and the defendant would be expected to treat the claim with urgency including any request for an interim payment.

2.8 In a claim for mesothelioma, additional provisions apply, which are set out in Annex C of this protocol.

2A ALTERNATIVE DISPUTE RESOLUTION

2A.1 The parties should consider whether some form of alternative dispute resolution procedure would be more suitable than litigation, and if so, endeavour to agree which form to adopt. Both the Claimant and Defendant may be required by the Court to provide evidence that alternative means of resolving their dispute were considered. The Courts take the view that litigation should be a last resort, and that claims should not be issued prematurely when a settlement is still actively being explored. Parties are warned that if the protocol is not followed (including this paragraph) then the Court must have regard to such conduct when determining costs.

2A.2 It is not practicable in this protocol to address in detail how the parties might decide which method to adopt to resolve their particular dispute. However, summarised below are some of the options for resolving disputes without litigation:

- Discussion and negotiation.
- Early neutral evaluation by an independent third party (for example, a lawyer experienced in the field of disease or illness, or an individual experienced in the subject matter of the claim).
- Mediation - a form of facilitated negotiation assisted by an independent neutral party.
- Arbitration (where an independent person or body makes a binding decision.

2A.3 The Legal Services Commission has published a booklet on "Alternatives to Court", CLS Direct Information Leaflet 23 (http://www.communitylegaladvice.org.uk/media/808/FD/leaflet23e.pdf), which lists a number of organisations that provide alternative dispute resolution services.

2A.4 It is expressly recognised that no party can or should be forced to mediate or enter into any form of ADR, but the parties should continue to consider the possibility of reaching a settlement at all times.

3 THE AIMS OF THE PROTOCOL

3.1 The general aims of the protocol are –

- to resolve as many disputes as possible without litigation;
- where a claim cannot be resolved to identify the relevant issues which remain in dispute.

3.2 The specific objectives are –

OPENNESS

- to encourage early communication of the perceived problem between the parties or their insurers;
- to encourage employees to voice any concerns or worries about possible work related illness as soon as practicable;
- to encourage employers to develop systems of early reporting and investigation of suspected occupational health problems and to provide full and prompt explanations to concerned employees or former employees;
- to apply such principles to perceived problems outside the employer/employee relationship, for example occupiers of premises or land and producers of products;
- to ensure that sufficient information is disclosed by both parties to enable each to understand the other's perspective and case, and to encourage early resolution;

TIMELINESS

- to provide an early opportunity for employers (past or present) or their insurers to identify cases where an investigation is required and to carry out that investigation promptly;
- to encourage employers (past or present) or other defendants to involve and identify their insurers at an early stage;
- to ensure that all relevant records including health and personnel records are provided to employees (past or present) or their appointed representatives promptly on request, by any employer (past or present) or their insurers. This should be complied with to a realistic timetable;

- to ensure that relevant records which are in the claimant's possession including where appropriate GP and hospital records are made available to the defendant or to the nominated insurance manager or solicitor representing the defendant by claimants or their advisers at an appropriate stage;
- to proceed on a reasonable timetable where a resolution is not achievable to lay the ground to enable litigation to proceed at a reasonable and proportionate cost, and to limit the matters in contention;
- to communicate promptly where any of the requested information is not available or does not exist;
- to discourage the prolonged pursuit of unmeritorious claims and the prolonged defence of meritorious claims;
- to encourage all parties, at the earliest possible stage, to disclose voluntarily any additional documents which will assist in resolving any issue;
- to promote the provision of medical or rehabilitation treatment in appropriate cases to address the needs of the claimant.

4 THE PROTOCOL

This protocol is not a comprehensive code governing all the steps in disease claims. Rather it attempts to set out a code of good practice which parties should follow.

This protocol must be read in conjunction with the Practice Direction on Pre-Action Conduct.

Obtaining occupational records including health records

4.1 In appropriate cases, a potential claimant may request Occupational Records including Health Records and Personnel Records before sending a Letter of Claim.

4.2 Any request for records by the potential claimant or his adviser should provide sufficient information to alert the potential defendant or his insurer where a possible disease claim is being investigated; Annex A1 provides a suggested form for this purpose for use in cases arising from employment. Similar forms can be prepared and used in other situations.

4.3 The copy records should be provided within a maximum of 40 days of the request at no cost. Although these will primarily be occupational records, it will be good practice for a potential defendant to disclose product data documents identified by a potential claimant at this stage which may resolve a causation issue.

4.4 Where the **potential defendant** or his insurer has difficulty in providing information quickly (in particular where the information is, or may be, held by someone else such as the Health and Safety Executive) details should be provided of steps being taken to resolve this problem together with a reasonable time estimate for doing so.

4.5 If the potential defendant or his insurer fails to provide the records including health records within 40 days and fails to comply with paragraph 4.4 above, the potential claimant or his adviser may then apply to the court for an order for pre-action disclosure. The Civil Procedure Rules make pre-action applications to the court easier. The court also has the power to impose costs sanctions for unreasonable delay in providing records.

5 COMMUNICATION

5.1 If either the potential claimant or his adviser considers additional records are required from a third party, such as records from previous employers or GP and hospital records, in the first instance these should be requested by the potential claimant or their advisers. Third party record holders would be expected to co-operate. The Civil Procedure Rules enable parties to apply to the court for pre-action disclosure by third parties.

PERSONAL INJURY AND DEATH

5.2 As soon as the records have been received and analysed, the potential claimant or his adviser should consider whether a claim should be made. GP and hospital records will normally be obtained before a decision is reached.

5.3 If a decision is made not to proceed further at this stage against a party identified as a potential defendant, the potential claimant or his adviser should notify that potential defendant in writing as soon as practicable.

6 LETTER OF CLAIM

6.1 Where a decision is made to make a claim, the claimant shall send to the proposed defendant two copies of a letter of claim, as soon as sufficient information is available to substantiate a realistic claim and before issues of quantum are addressed in detail. One copy is for the defendants, the second for passing on to his insurers.

6.2 This letter shall contain a clear summary of the facts on which the claim is based, including details of the illness or disease alleged, and the main allegations of fault. It shall also give details of present condition and prognosis. The financial loss incurred by the claimant should be outlined. Where the case is funded by a conditional fee agreement, notification should be given of the existence of the agreement and where appropriate, that there is a success fee and insurance premium, although not the level of the success fee or premium.

6.3 Where the funding arrangement is an insurance policy the party must state—

(1) the name and address of the insurer;
(2) the policy number;
(3) the date of the policy;
(4) the claim or claims to which it relates (including Part 20 claims if any);
(5) the level of cover; and
(6) whether the premiums are staged and if so the points at which the increased premiums are payable.

6.4 Solicitors are recommended to use a standard format for such a letter – an example is at Annex B: this can be amended to suit the particular case, for example, if the client has rehabilitation needs these can also be detailed in the letter.

6.5 A chronology of the relevant events (e.g. dates or periods of exposure) should be provided. In the case of alleged occupational disease an appropriate employment history should also be provided (with a work history from HM Revenue and Customs), particularly if the claimant has been employed by a number of different employers and the illness in question has a long latency period. Where there is more than one employer the chronology should state if there was any relevant exposure during each of those different periods of employment. Details should also be given about any periods of self-employment during which there was any relevant exposure and whether any claims have been made and payments received under the Pneumoconiosis etc (Workers' Compensation) Act 1979.

6.6 The letter of claim should identify any relevant documents, including health records not already in the defendant's possession e.g. any relevant GP and hospital records. These will need to be disclosed in confidence to the nominated insurance manager or solicitor representing the defendant following receipt of their letter of acknowledgement. Where the action is brought under the Law Reform Act 1934 or the Fatal Accidents Act 1976 then relevant documents will normally include copies of the death certificate, the post mortem report, the inquest depositions and if obtained by that date the grant of probate or letters of administration.

6.7 The letter of claim should indicate whether a claim is also being made against any other potential defendant and identify any known insurer involved. Copies of any relevant result from the Association of British Insurers Employers' Liability Tracing Service, both positive and negative, should be attached to the letter of claim. If the claimant receives any insurance database results after sending the letter of claim those results should be forwarded to the defendant as soon as is reasonably practicable.

6.8 Sufficient information should be given to enable the defendant's insurer/solicitor to commence investigations and at least to put a broad valuation on the 'risk'.

6.9 It is not a requirement for the claimant to provide medical evidence with the letter of claim, but the claimant may choose to do so in very many cases.

6.10 Letters of claim and response are not intended to have the same status as a statement of case in proceedings. Matters may come to light as a result of investigation after the letter of claim has been sent, or after the defendant has responded, particularly if disclosure of documents takes place outside the recommended 90 day period. These circumstances could mean that the 'pleaded' case of one or both parties is presented slightly differently than in the letter of claim or response. It would not be consistent with the spirit of the protocol for a party to 'take a point' on this in the proceedings, provided that there was no obvious intention by the party who changed their position to mislead the other party.

6.10A Where a claim no longer continues under the Pre-Action Protocol for Low Value Personal Injury (Employers' Liability and Public Liability) Claims, the Claim Notification Form ('CNF') completed by the claimant under that Protocol can be used as the letter of claim under this protocol unless the defendant has notified the claimant that there is inadequate information in the CNF.

6.11 Proceedings should not be issued until after 90 days from the date of acknowledgement (see paragraph 7), unless there is a limitation problem and/or the claimant's position needs to be protected by early issue. (See paragraphs 2.6 and 2.7)

7 THE RESPONSE

7.1 The defendant should send an acknowledgement within 21 days of the date of posting of the letter of claim, identifying the liability insurer (if any) who will be dealing with the matter and, if necessary, identifying specifically any significant omissions from the Letter of Claim. If there has been no acknowledgement by the defendant or insurer within 21 days, the claimant will be entitled to issue proceedings.

7.2 The identity of all relevant insurers, if more than one, should be notified to the claimant by the insurer identified in the acknowledgement letter, within 30 days of the date of that acknowledgement. For claims with a long latency period it is recognised that it may not be possible to identify the full insurance history within 30 days. In these circumstances the insurer or defendant should notify the claimant in writing as soon as possible. In any event, within 30 days the insurer or the defendant should state which other insurers have been identified. Where insurers have not been identified the defendant or insurer should state what steps have been taken to determine this information.

7.3 The defendant or his representative should, within 90 days of the date of the acknowledgement letter, provide a reasoned answer: –

- if the claim is admitted, they should say so in clear terms;
- if only part of the claim is admitted they should make clear which issues of fault and/or causation and/or limitation are admitted and which remain in issue and why;
- if the claim is not admitted in full, they should explain why and should, for example, include comments on the employment status of the claimant, (including job description(s) and details of the department(s) where the claimant worked), the allegations of fault, causation and of limitation, and if a synopsis or chronology of relevant events has been provided and is disputed, their version of those events;
- if the claim is not admitted in full, the defendant should enclose with his letter of reply documents in his possession which are material to the issues between the parties and which would be likely to be ordered to be disclosed by the court, either on an application for pre-action disclosure, or on disclosure during proceedings. Reference can be made to the documents annexed to the personal injury protocol.

PERSONAL INJURY AND DEATH

- where more than one defendant receives a letter of claim, the timetable will be activated for each defendant by the date on the letter of claim addressed to them. If any defendant wishes to extend the timetable because the number of defendants will cause complications, they should seek agreement to a different timetable as soon as possible.

7.4 If the parties reach agreement on liability and/or causation, but time is needed to resolve other issues including the value of the claim, they should aim to agree a reasonable period.

7.5 Where it is not practicable for the defendant to complete his investigations within 90 days, the defendant should indicate the difficulties and outline the further time needed. Any request for an extension of time should be made, with reasons, as soon as the defendant becomes aware that an extension is needed and normally before the 90 day period has expired. Such an extension of time should be agreed in circumstances where reasonable justification has been shown. Lapse of many years since the circumstances giving rise to the claim does not, by itself, constitute reasonable justification for further time.

7.6 Where the relevant negligence occurred outside England and Wales and/or where the defendant is outside the jurisdiction, the time periods of 21 days and 90 days should normally be extended up to 42 days and 180 days.

8 SPECIAL DAMAGES

8.1 The claimant will send to the defendant as soon as practicable a Schedule of Special Damages with supporting documents, particularly where the defendant has admitted liability.

9 EXPERTS

9.1 In disease claims expert opinions may be needed on one or more of the following: –

- knowledge, fault, causation and apportionment;
- condition and prognosis;
- valuing aspects of the claim.

9.2 The civil justice reforms and the Civil Procedure Rules encourage economy in the use of experts and a less adversarial expert culture. It is recognised that in disease claims, the parties and their advisers will require flexibility in their approach to expert evidence. Decisions on whether experts might be instructed jointly, and on whether reports might be disclosed sequentially or by exchange, should rest with the parties and their advisers. Sharing expert evidence may be appropriate on various issues including those relating to the value of the claim. However, this protocol does not attempt to be prescriptive on issues in relation to expert evidence.

9.3 Obtaining expert evidence will often be an expensive step and may take time, especially in specialised areas where there are limited numbers of suitable experts. Claimants, defendants and their advisers, will therefore need to consider carefully how best to obtain any necessary expert help quickly and cost-effectively.

9.4 The protocol recognises that a flexible approach must be adopted in the obtaining of medical reports in claims of this type. There will be very many occasions where the claimant will need to obtain a medical report before writing the letter of claim. In such cases the defendant will be entitled to obtain their own medical report. In some other instances it may be more appropriate to send the letter of claim before the medical report is obtained. Defendants will usually need to see a medical report before they can reach a view on causation.

9.5 Where the parties agree the nomination of a single expert is appropriate, before any party instructs an expert he should give the other party a list of the name(s) of one or more experts in the relevant speciality whom he considers are suitable to instruct. The parties are encouraged to agree the instruction of a single expert to deal with discrete areas such as cost of care.

9.6 Within 14 days the other party may indicate an objection to one or more of the named experts. The first party should then instruct a mutually acceptable expert. If the Claimant nominates an expert in the original letter of claim, the 14 days is in addition to the 21 days in paragraph 7.1.

9.7 If the second party objects to all the listed experts, the parties may then instruct experts of their own choice. It would be for the court to decide subsequently, if proceedings are issued, whether either party had acted unreasonably.

9.8 If the second party does not object to an expert nominated, he shall not be entitled to rely on his own expert evidence within that particular speciality unless:

(a) the first party agrees,
(b) the court so directs, or
(c) the first party's expert report has been amended and the first party is not prepared to disclose the original report.

9.9 Either party may send to an agreed expert written questions on the report, relevant to the issues, via the first party's solicitors. The expert should send answers to the questions separately and directly to each party.

9.10 The cost of a report from an agreed expert will usually be paid by the instructing first party: the costs of the expert replying to questions will usually be borne by the party which asks the questions.

9.11 Where the defendant admits liability in whole or in part, before proceedings are issued, any medical report obtained under this protocol which the claimant relies upon, should be disclosed to the other party.

9.12 Where the defendant obtains a medical report on which he seeks to rely this should be disclosed to the claimant.

9.13 For further guidance see Part 35 of the CPR, Practice Direction 35 and the Protocol for the Instruction of Experts to give Evidence in Civil Claims which is annexed to that Practice Direction.

10 RESOLUTION OF ISSUES

10.1 The Civil Procedure Rules Part 36 enable claimants and defendants to make formal offers to settle before proceedings are started. Parties should consider making such an offer, since to do so often leads to settlement. If such an offer is made, the party making the offer must always supply sufficient evidence and/or information to enable the offer to be properly considered.

10.2 Where a claim is not resolved when the protocol has been followed, the parties might wish to carry out a 'stocktake' of the issues in dispute, and the evidence that the court is likely to need to decide those issues, before proceedings are started.

10.3 Prior to proceedings it will be usual for all parties to disclose those expert reports relating to liability and causation upon which they propose to rely.

10.4 The claimant should delay issuing proceedings for 21 days from disclosure of reports to enable the parties to consider whether the claim is capable of settlement.

10.5 Where the defendant is insured and the pre-action steps have been conducted by the insurer, the insurer would normally be expected to nominate solicitors to accept service of proceedings and the claimant's solicitor is recommended to invite the insurer to nominate solicitors to accept service of proceedings and to do so 7-14 days before the intended issue date.

11 LIMITATION

11.1 If by reason of complying with any part of this protocol a claimant's claim may be time-barred under any provision of the Limitation Act 1980, or any other legislation which imposes a time limit for bringing an action, the claimant may commence proceedings without complying with this protocol. In such circumstances, a claimant who commences proceedings without complying with all, or any part, of this protocol may apply to the court on notice for directions as to the timetable and form of procedure to be adopted, at the same time as he requests the court to issue proceedings. The court will consider whether to order a stay of the whole or part of the proceedings pending compliance with this protocol.

ANNEX A
LETTER REQUESTING OCCUPATIONAL RECORDS INCLUDING HEALTH RECORDS

III PID [44.1]

Dear Sirs,

We are acting on behalf of the above-named who has developed the following ***(insert disease***). We are investigating whether this disease may have been caused:

- ***during the course of his employment with you/name of employer if different***
- ***whilst at your premises at (address)***
- ***as a result of your product (name)***

We are writing this in accordance with the Protocol for Disease and Illness Claims.

We seek the following records:

(insert details, eg personnel/occupational health)

Please note your insurers may require you to advice them of this request.

We enclose a request form and expect to receive the records within 40 days. If you are not able to comply with this request within this time, please advise us of the reason.

Yours faithfully

ANNEX A1
APPLICATION ON BEHALF OF A POTENTIAL CLAIMANT FOR USE WHERE A DISEASE CLAIM IS BEING INVESTIGATED

Application on behalf of a potential claimant for use where a disease claim is being investigated

III PID [44.2]

This should be completed as fully as possible

Company

Name

And

Address

1a)	Full name of claimant (including previous surnames)	
b)	Address now	

c)	Address at date of termination of employment, if different	
d)	Date of birth (and death, if applicable)	
e)	National Insurance number, if available	
2	Department(s) where claimant worked	
3	This application is made because the claimant is considering	
a)	a claim against you as detailed in para 4	YES/NO
b)	Pursuing an action against someone else	YES/NO
4	If the answer to Q3(a) is 'Yes' details of	
	a) the likely nature of the claim, eg dermatitis	
	b) grounds for the claim, eg exposure to chemical	
	c) approximate dates of the events involved	
5	If the answer to Q3(b) is 'Yes' insert	
	a) the names of the proposed defendants	
	b) have legal proceedings been started?	YES/NO
	c) if appropriate, details of the claim and action number	
6	Any other relevant information or documents requested	

Signature of Solicitor

Name

Address

Ref.

Telephone Number

Fax number

I authorise you to disclose all of your records relating to me/the claimant to my solicitor and to your legal and insurance representatives.

Signature of Claimant

Signature of personal representative where claimant has died

PERSONAL INJURY AND DEATH

ANNEX B
TEMPLATE FOR LETTER OF CLAIM

III PID [44.3]

TEMPLATE FOR LETTER OF CLAIM

To: Defendant

Dear Sirs

Re: Claimant's full name

Claimant's full address

Claimant's National Insurance Number

Claimant's Date of Birth

Claimant's Clock or Works Number

Claimant's Employer (***name and address)***

We are instructed by the above named to claim damages in connection with a claim for: -

Specify occupational disease

We are writing this letter in accordance with the pre-action protocol for disease and illness claims.

Please confirm the identity of your insurers. Please note that your insurers will need to see this letter as soon as possible and it may affect your insurance cover if you do not send this to them.

The Claimant was employed by you ***(if the claim arises out of public or occupiers' liability give appropriate details)*** as ***job description*** from ***date*** to ***date***. During the relevant period of his employment he worked: -

description of precisely where the Claimant worked and what he did to include a description of any machines used and details of any exposure to noise or substances

The circumstances leading to the development of this condition are as follows: -

Give chronology of events (and in appropriate cases attach a work history from HM Revenue and Customs)

The reason why we are alleging fault is: -

Details should be given of contemporary and comparable employees who have suffered from similar problems if known; any protective equipment provided; complaints; the supervisors concerned, if known.

Our client's employment history is attached.

We have also made a claim against: -

Insert details

Their insurers' details are: -

Insert if known

We have the following documents in support of our client's claim and will disclose these in confidence to your nominated insurance manager or solicitor when we receive their acknowledgement letter.

e.g. Occupational health notes; GP notes

We have obtained a medical report from (name) and will disclose this when we receive your acknowledgement of this letter.

(This is optional at this stage)

From the information we presently have: -

(i) the Claimant first became aware of symptoms on ***(insert approximate date)***
(ii) the Claimant first received medical advice about those symptoms on ***(insert date) (give details of advice given if appropriate)***
(iii) the Claimant first believed that those symptoms might be due to exposure leading to this claim on ***(insert approximate date)***

A description of our client's condition is as follows: -

This should be sufficiently detailed to allow the Defendant to put a broad value on the claim

(For appropriate cases)

Our client is still suffering from the effect of his/her condition. We invite you to participate with us in addressing his/her immediate needs by use of rehabilitation.

He has the following time off work: -

Insert dates

He is presently employed as a ***job description*** and his average net weekly income is ***£***

If you are our client's employers, please provide us with the usual earnings details, which will enable us to calculate his financial loss.

Please note that we have entered into a conditional fee agreement with our client dated in relation to this claim which provides for a success fee within the meaning of section 58(2) of the Courts and Legal Services Act 1990. Our client has taken out an insurance policy dated with (name and address of insurance company) to which section 29 of the Access to Justice Act 1999 applies in respect of this claim. The policy number is [insert], the policy is dated [insert] and the level of cover is [insert]. The premiums payable under the insurance policy [are not] [are] staged [and the points at which the increase premiums are payable are as follows:].

A copy of this letter is attached for you to send to your insurers. Finally we expect an acknowledgement of this letter within 21 days by yourselves or your insurers.

Yours faithfully

ANNEX C
GUIDANCE FOR CASES INVOLVING MESOTHELIOMA – EARLY NOTIFICATION LETTER

Purpose

III PID [44.4]

1. The purpose of the early notification letter is twofold. First, the intention is to give defendants and their insurers as much advance warning as possible about the possibility of a claim so that they can begin to investigate the matter. This is particularly so where relevant information may be decades old and may take time to locate and retrieve. Second, where the claimant has severely limited life expectancy it gives advance warning to defendants of the need for urgency in locating relevant information.

2. It is intended that the early notification letter will be sent before the letter of claim and will not start the timetable for response as set out in paragraph 7 of this protocol.

3. As soon as sufficient information is available to identify a proposed defendant, the claimant should send to the proposed defendant two copies of the early notification letter. One copy is for the defendant, the second for passing on to the defendant's insurers. The claimant should also send a further copy of the same letter directly to the defendant's insurer, where known. In the case of a defunct company the further copy of the letter should be sent to the relevant insurer or handler of that defunct company.

Content of Early Notification Letter

4. All copies of the early notification letter should be clearly marked 'MESOTHELIOMA CLAIM'.

5. The early notification letter should contain basic information sufficient to identify the claimant, the periods of relevant exposure and the potential defendants. As a minimum, the early notification letter should contain the following information:

PERSONAL INJURY AND DEATH

(a) name and address of the claimant/deceased;
(b) national insurance number of the claimant/deceased (if known);
(c) claimant/deceased's date of birth;
(e) employers, where known, of relevant employment and or exposure;
(f) occupiers of premises, where known, of relevant employment and/or exposure;
(g) date or approximate dates, where known, of relevant employment and or exposure;
(h) direct contact details, including e-mail address, for the claimant's legal representative;
(i) marital status;
(j) details of dependents; and
(k) date of diagnosis.

6. Solicitors are recommended to use a standard format for the early notification letter. An example is set out in Annex D. This can be amended to suit the particular case.

7. The early notification letter should indicate whether a claim is also being made against any other potential defendant and identify any known insurer involved.

8. The early notification letter is not intended to have the same status as a statement of case in proceedings. Matters may come to light as a result of investigation after the letter of claim has been sent.

Employment and Exposure History

9. In view of the joint and several liability provided for in the Compensation Act 2006 in mesothelioma cases the information set out in paragraph 6.5 of this protocol is particularly relevant.

Defendant's response

10. The defendant should respond within 14 days of the date of the letter confirming that the matter is receiving urgent attention.

Compliance with this protocol

11. Attention is drawn to paragraph 9.1 of Practice Direction 3D (Mesothelioma Claims) which provides that in Living Mesothelioma Claims (normally where the claimant has severely limited life expectancy) strict adherence to this protocol may not be required. The issue of compliance with this protocol in relation to certain mesothelioma claims is also recognised at paragraph 2.7 of this protocol.

ANNEX D
EARLY NOTIFICATION LETTER FOR USE IN CASES INVOLVING MESOTHELIOMA

III PID [44.5]

URGENT – MESOTHELIOMA CLAIM

YOU MUST DEAL WITH THIS LETTER IMMEDIATELY

Dear Sirs,

We are acting on behalf of the above-named who has developed mesothelioma. We are investigating whether this disease may have been caused:

during the course of his employment with you/name of employer if different whilst at your premises at (*address*)

between the approximate dates of: (insert relevant dates of employment/at the premises)

as a result of your product (*name*)

Please note your insurers will require you to advise them of this letter. You must pass a copy of this letter to your insurer immediately.

We are writing this letter in accordance with the Pre-Action Protocol for Disease and Illness Claims.

Our client's details are as follows:

Name:

Address:

National Insurance Number (if known)

Date of Birth:

Marital status:

Details of dependents:

Date of diagnosis.

We require a response from you confirming this matter is receiving urgent attention within 14 days of the date of this letter.

The direct e-mail address, which you may use for urgent communications and which should be followed up with paper copies, is: (*insert e-mail address*)

Yours faithfully

PRE-ACTION PROTOCOL FOR LOW VALUE PERSONAL INJURY CLAIMS IN ROAD TRAFFIC ACCIDENTS

SECTION I INTRODUCTION

1 Definitions

III PID [45]

1.1 In this Protocol—

(A1) 'accredited medical expert' means a medical expert who—

(a) prepares a fixed cost medical report pursuant to paragraph 7.8A(1) before 6 April 2016 and, on the date that they are instructed, the expert is registered with MedCo as a provider of reports for soft tissue injury claims; or

(b) prepares a fixed cost medical report pursuant to paragraph 7.8A(1) on or after 6 April 2016 and, on the date that they are instructed, the expert is accredited by MedCo to provide reports for soft tissue injury claims;

(1) 'admission of liability' means the defendant admits that—

(a) the accident occurred;

(b) the accident was caused by the defendant's breach of duty;

(c) the defendant caused some loss to the claimant, the nature and extent of which is not admitted; and

(d) the defendant has no accrued defence to the claim under the Limitation Act 1980;

(1A) 'associate' means, in respect of a medical expert, a colleague, partner, director, employer or employee in the same practice and 'associated with' has the equivalent meaning;

(2) 'bank holiday' means a bank holiday under the Banking and Financial Dealings Act 1971;

(3) 'business day' means any day except Saturday, Sunday, a bank holiday, Good Friday or Christmas Day;

(4) 'certificate of recoverable benefits' has the same meaning as in rule 36.22(1)(e)(i) of the Civil Procedure Rules 1998.

(5) 'child' means a person under 18;

(6) 'claim' means a claim, prior to the start of proceedings, for payment of damages under the process set out in this Protocol;

(7) 'claimant' means a person starting a claim under this Protocol unless the context indicates that it means the claimant's legal representative;

(8) 'CNF' means a Claim Notification Form;

(9) 'deductible amount' has the same meaning as in rule 36.22(1)(d) of the Civil Procedure Rules 1998;

(10) 'defendant' means the insurer of the person who is subject to the claim under this Protocol, unless the context indicates that it means—

(a) the person who is subject to the claim;
(b) the defendant's legal representative;
(c) the Motor Insurers' Bureau ('MIB'); or
(d) a person falling within the exceptions in section 144 of the Road Traffic Act 1988 (a "self-insurer");

(10A) 'fixed cost medical report' means a report in a soft tissue injury claim which is from a medical expert who, save in exceptional circumstances —

(a) has not provided treatment to the claimant;
(b) is not associated with any person who has provided treatment; and
(c) does not propose or recommend treatment that they or an associate then provide;

(11) 'legal representative' has the same meaning as in rule 2.3(1) of the Civil Procedure Rules 1998;

(12) 'medical expert' means a person who is—

(a) registered with the General Medical Council;
(b) registered with the General Dental Council; or
(c) a Psychologist or Physiotherapist registered with the Health Professions Council;

(12A) 'MedCo' means MedCo Registration Solutions;

(13) 'motor vehicle' means a mechanically propelled vehicle intended for use on roads;

(14) 'pecuniary losses' means past and future expenses and losses;

(15) 'road' means any highway and any other road to which the public has access and includes bridges over which a road passes;

(16) 'road traffic accident' means an accident resulting in bodily injury to any person caused by, or arising out of, the use of a motor vehicle on a road or other public place in England and Wales unless the injury was caused wholly or in part by a breach by the defendant of one or more of the relevant statutory provisions[1] as defined by section 53 of the Health and Safety at Work etc Act 1974;

(16A) 'soft tissue injury claim' means a claim brought by an occupant of a motor vehicle where the significant physical injury caused is a soft tissue injury and includes claims where there is a minor psychological injury secondary in significance to the physical injury;

(17) 'Type C fixed costs' has the same meaning as in rule 45.18(2) of the Civil Procedure Rules 1998; and

(18) 'vehicle related damages' means damages for—

(a) the pre-accident value of the vehicle;
(b) vehicle repair;
(c) vehicle insurance excess; and
(d) vehicle hire;

1.2

(1) The 'Protocol upper limit' is—
(a) £25,000 where the accident occurred on or after 31 July 2013; or
(b) £10,000 where the accident occurred on or after 30 April 2010 and before 31 July 2013,

on a full liability basis including pecuniary losses but excluding interest.

(2) Any reference in this Protocol to a claim which is, or damages which are, valued at no more than the Protocol upper limit, or between £1,000 and the Protocol upper limit, is to be read in accordance with subparagraph (1).

1.3 A reference to a rule or practice direction, unless otherwise defined, is a reference to a rule in the Civil Procedure Rules 1998 ('CPR') or a practice direction supplementing them.

1.4 Subject to paragraph 1.5 the standard forms used in the process set out in this Protocol are available from Her Majesty's Courts and Tribunals Service ('HMCTS') website at www.justice.gov.uk/forms/hmcts—

(1) Claim Notification Form ('Form RTA 1'– referred to in this Protocol as 'the CNF');
(2) Defendant Only Claim Notification Form ('Form RTA 2');
(3) Medical Report Form ('Form RTA 3');
(4) Interim Settlement Pack Form ('Form RTA 4');
(5) Stage 2 Settlement Pack Form ('Form RTA 5');
(6) Court Proceedings Pack (Part A) Form ('Form RTA 6'); and
(7) Court Proceedings Pack (Part B) Form ('Form RTA 7').

1.5 The information required in Form RTA 3 may be provided in a different format to that set out in that Form.

---

1 See—

Control of Substances Hazardous to Health Regulations 2002 (SI 2002/2677)

Lifting Operations and Lifting Equipment Regulations 1998 (SI 1998/2307)

Management of Health and Safety at Work Regulations 1999 (SI 1999/3242)

Manual Handling Operations Regulations 1992 (SI 1992/2793)

Personal Protective Equipment at Work Regulations 1992 (SI 1992/2966)

Provision and Use of Work Equipment Regulations 1998 (SI 1998/2306)

Work at Height Regulations 2005 (SI 2005/735)

Workplace (Health, Safety and Welfare) Regulations 1992 (SI 1992/3004)

Construction (Design and Management) Regulations 2007 (SI 2007/320)

---

2 Preamble

2.1 This Protocol describes the behaviour the court expects of the parties prior to the start of proceedings where a claimant claims damages valued at no more than the Protocol upper limit as a result of a personal injury sustained by that person in a road traffic accident. The Civil Procedure Rules 1998 enable the court to impose costs sanctions where it is not followed.

3 Aims

3.1 The aim of this Protocol is to ensure that—

(1) the defendant pays damages and costs using the process set out in the Protocol without the need for the claimant to start proceedings;
(2) damages are paid within a reasonable time; and
(3) the claimant's legal representative receives the fixed costs at each appropriate stage.

3.2 In soft tissue injury claims, the additional aim of this Protocol is to ensure that—

(1) the use and cost of medical reports is controlled;
(2) in most cases only one medical report is obtained;
(3) the medical expert is normally independent of any medical treatment; and
(4) offers are made only after a fixed cost medical report has been obtained and disclosed.

4 Scope

4.1 This Protocol applies where—

(1) a claim for damages arises from a road traffic accident where the CNF is submitted on or after 31st July 2013;
(2) the claim includes damages in respect of personal injury;
(3) the claimant values the claim at no more than the Protocol upper limit; and
(4) if proceedings were started the small claims track would not be the normal track for that claim.

(Paragraphs 1.1(18) and 4.4 state the damages that are excluded for the purposes of valuing the claim under paragraph 4.1.)

(Rule 26.6 provides that the small claims track is not the normal track where the value of any claim for damages for personal injuries (defined as compensation for pain, suffering and loss of amenity) is more than £1,000.)

4.2 The Pre-Action Protocol for Low Value Personal Injury Claims in Road Traffic Accidents which commenced on 30th April 2010 will continue to apply (as it stood immediately before 31 July 2013) to all claims where the CNF was submitted before 31 July 2013.

4.3 This Protocol ceases to apply to a claim where, at any stage, the claimant notifies the defendant that the claim has now been revalued at more than the Protocol upper limit.

4.4 A claim may include vehicle related damages but these are excluded for the purposes of valuing the claim under paragraph 4.1.

4.5 This Protocol does not apply to a claim—

(1) in respect of a breach of duty owed to a road user by a person who is not a road user;
(2) made to the MIB pursuant to the Untraced Drivers' Agreement 2003 or any subsequent or supplementary Untraced Drivers' Agreements;
(3) where the claimant or defendant acts as personal representative of a deceased person;
(4) where the claimant or defendant is a protected party as defined in rule 21.1(2);
(5) where the claimant is bankrupt; or
(6) where the defendant's vehicle is registered outside the United Kingdom.

4.6 The fixed costs in rule 45.18 apply in relation to a claimant only where a claimant has a legal representative.

4.7

(1) Subject to subparagraph (2), provisions for soft tissue injury claims, and in particular the requirement that the first report from a medical expert must be a fixed cost medical report, apply to any such claim for damages which arises from a road traffic accident where the CNF is submitted on or after 1 October 2014.

(2) The provisions, in respect of soft tissue injury claims, for accredited medical experts and the MedCo Portal, and the provisions, in respect of all claims, for searches of ask.CUEPI.com, identified in the first column (and specified in the corresponding second column) below, apply to claims for damages which arise from a road traffic accident where the CNF is submitted on or after the corresponding date specified in the third column—

Column 1	Column 2	Column 3
Accredited medical experts	Paragraph 1.1(A1)	6 April 2015
In a soft tissue injury claim, the requirement that the first medical report must be a fixed cost medical report from an accredited medical expert selected via the MedCo Portal	Paragraphs 1.1(12A), 7.8A(1), 7.8B(3) and 7.32A	6 April 2015
Searches of askCUEPI.com	Paragraphs 5.10(3), 5.10A, 6.3A 6.8(2) and 6.9	1 June 2015

(3) In a soft tissue injury claim, where a medical expert is instructed to provide the first fixed cost medical report before 6 April 2015, but the CNF is submitted on or after that date, that report shall be treated as a fixed cost medical report obtained from an accredited medical expert selected via the MedCo Portal.

SECTION II GENERAL PROVISIONS

Communication between the parties

5.1 Subject to paragraph 6.1(2), where the Protocol requires information to be sent to a party it must be sent via www.claimsportal.org.uk (or any other Portal address that may be prescribed from time to time). The claimant will give an e-mail address for contact in the Claim Notification Form ('CNF'). All written communications not re quired by the Protocol must be sent by e-mail.

5.2 Where the claimant has sent the CNF to the wrong defendant, the claimant may, in this circumstance only, send the CNF to the correct defendant. The period in paragraph 6.11 or 6.13 starts from the date the CNF was sent to the correct defendant.

PERSONAL INJURY AND DEATH

Time periods

5.3 A reference to a fixed number of days is a reference to business days as defined in paragraph 1.1(3).

5.4 Where a party should respond within a fixed number of days, the period for response starts the first business day after the information was sent to that party.

5.5 All time periods, except those stated in—

(1) paragraph 6.11 (the insurer's response);
(2) paragraph 6.13 (MIB's response); and
(3) paragraph 7.37 (the further consideration period)

may be varied by agreement between the parties.

5.6 Where this Protocol requires the defendant to pay an amount within a fixed number of days the claimant must receive the cheque or the transfer of the amount from the defendant before the end of the period specified in the relevant provision.

Limitation period

5.7 Where compliance with this Protocol is not possible before the expiry of the limitation period the claimant may start proceedings and apply to the court for an order to stay (i.e. suspend) the proceedings while the parties take steps to follow this Protocol. Where proceedings are started in a case to which this paragraph applies the claimant should use the procedure set out under Part 8 in accordance with Practice Direction 8B ("the Stage 3 Procedure").

5.8 Where the parties are then unable to reach a settlement at the end of Stage 2 of this Protocol the claimant must, in order to proceed to Stage 3, apply to lift the stay and request directions in the existing proceedings.

Claimant's reasonable belief of the value of the claim

5.9 Where the claimant reasonably believes that the claim is valued at between £1,000 and the Protocol upper limit, but it subsequently becomes apparent that the value of the claim is less than £1,000, the claimant is entitled to the Stage 1 and (where relevant) the Stage 2 fixed costs.

Claimants without a legal representative

5.10 Where the claimant does not have a legal representative, on receipt of the CNF the defendant must explain—

(1) the period within which a response is required;
(2) that the claimant may obtain independent legal advice; and
(3) undertake a search of askCUEPI (website at: www.askCUE.co.uk) or an equivalent search system for defendants.

5.10A Where the claimant does not have a legal representative, paragraph 6.3A does not apply.

Discontinuing the Protocol process

5.11 Claims which no longer continue under this Protocol cannot subsequently re-enter the process.

SECTION III THE STAGES OF THE PROCESS

Stage 1: Completion of the Claim Notification Form

6.1 The claimant must complete and send—

(1) the CNF to the defendant's insurer; and
(2) the 'Defendant Only CNF' to the defendant by first class post, except where the defendant is a self-insurer in which case the CNF must be sent to the defendant as insurer and no 'Defendant Only CNF' is required.

6.2 The 'Defendant Only CNF' must be sent at the same time or as soon as practicable after the CNF is sent.

6.3 All boxes in the CNF that are marked as mandatory must be completed before it is sent. The claimant must make a reasonable attempt to complete those boxes that are not marked as mandatory.

6.3A

(1) Before the CNF is sent to the defendant pursuant to paragraph 6.1, the claimant's legal representative must undertake a search of askCUEPI (website at: www.askCUE.co.uk) and must enter in the additional information box in the CNF the unique reference number generated by that search.

(2) Where the claimant has sent the CNF without the unique reference number required by subparagraph (1), the defendant may require the claimant to resend the CNF with the reference number inserted. The period in paragraph 6.11 or 6.13 starts from the date the CNF was sent with the unique reference number.

(3) Where the claimant has sent the CNF without the unique reference number required by subparagraph (1) and the defendant does not require the claimant to resend the CNF pursuant to subparagraph (2), the defendant must respond in accordance with paragraph 6.11 or 6.13.

6.4 A claim for vehicle related damages will ordinarily be dealt with outside the provisions of this Protocol under industry agreements between relevant organisations and insurers. Where there is a claim for vehicle related damages the claimant must—

(1) state in the CNF that the claim is being dealt with by a third party; or

(2)

(a) explain in the CNF that the legal representative is dealing with the recovery of these additional amounts; and

(b) attach any relevant invoices and receipts to the CNF or explain when they are likely to be sent to the defendant.

6.5 Where the claimant is a child, this must be noted in the relevant section of the CNF.

6.6 The statement of truth in the CNF must be signed either by the claimant or by the claimant's legal representative where the claimant has authorised the legal representative to do so and the legal representative can produce written evidence of that authorisation. Where the claimant is a child the statement of truth may be signed by the parent or guardian. On the electronically completed CNF the person may enter their name in the signature box to satisfy this requirement.

Rehabilitation

6.7 The claimant must set out details of rehabilitation in the CNF. The parties should at all stages consider the Rehabilitation Code which may be found at: www.iua.co.uk/IUA_Member/Publicationsto complete the Claim Notification Form.

Failure to complete the Claim Notification Form

6.8

(1) Subject to paragraph (2) and paragraph 6.3A(2), where the defendant considers that inadequate mandatory information has been provided in the CNF, that shall be a valid reason for the defendant to decide that the claim should no longer continue under this Protocol.

(2) Where the claimant has sent the CNF to the defendant without the unique reference number required by paragraph 6.3A(1), but the defendant does not require the claimant to resend the CNF with the reference number inserted pursuant to paragraph 6.3A(2), the fact that the claimant has not provided this information shall not be a valid reason for the defendant to decide that the claim should no longer continue under this Protocol.

6.9 Rule 45.24(2) and (2A) sets out the sanctions available to the court where it considers that the claimant provided inadequate information in the CNF.

Response from insurer

6.10 The defendant must send to the claimant an electronic acknowledgment the next day after receipt of the CNF.

6.11 The defendant must complete the 'Insurer Response' section of the CNF ("the CNF response") and send it to the claimant within 15 days.

Application for a certificate of recoverable benefits

6.12 The defendant must, before the end of Stage 1, apply to the Compensation Recovery Unit (CRU) for a certificate of recoverable benefits.

Motor Insurers' Bureau

6.13 Where no insurer is identified and the claim falls to be dealt with by the MIB or its agents the CNF response must be completed and sent to the claimant within 30 days.

6.14 Where the MIB passes the claim to an insurer to act on its behalf, that insurer must notify the claimant of that fact. There is no extension to the time period in paragraph 6.13.

Contributory negligence, liability not admitted or failure to respond

6.15 The claim will no longer continue under this Protocol where the defendant, within the period in paragraph 6.11 or 6.13—

(1) makes an admission of liability but alleges contributory negligence (other than in relation to the claimant's admitted failure to wear a seat belt);
(2) does not complete and send the CNF response;
(3) does not admit liability; or
(4) notifies the claimant that the defendant considers that—
  (a) there is inadequate mandatory information in the CNF; or
  (b) if proceedings were issued, the small claims track would be the normal track for that claim.

6.16 Where the defendant does not admit liability under paragraph 6.15(3), the defendant must give brief reasons in the CNF response.

6.17 Where paragraph 6.15 applies the claim will proceed under the Pre-Action Protocol for Personal Injury Claims starting at paragraph 6.3 of that Protocol (which allows a maximum of three months for the defendant to investigate the claim) except that where paragraph 6.15(4)(a) applies the claim will proceed under paragraph 5.1 of that Protocol.

(For admissions made in the course of the process under this Protocol, see rule 14.1B.)

(Paragraph 2.10A of the Pre-Action Protocol on Personal Injury provides that the CNF can be used as the letter of claim except where the claim no longer continues under this Protocol because the CNF contained inadequate information.)

Stage 1 fixed costs

6.18 Except where the claimant is a child, the defendant must pay the Stage 1 fixed costs in rule 45.18 (and in a soft tissue injury claim, the cost of obtaining the fixed cost medical report and any cost for obtaining medical records in rule 45.19(2A) (collectively the "Stage 1 fixed recoverable costs") where—

(1) liability is admitted; or
(2) liability is admitted and contributory negligence is alleged only in relation to the claimant's admitted failure to wear a seat belt,

within 10 days after receiving the Stage 2 Settlement Pack, provided that invoices for the cost of obtaining the medical report and any medical records in a soft tissue injury claim have been included in the Stage 2 Settlement Pack.

6.19 Where the defendant fails to pay the Stage 1 fixed recoverable costs within the period specified in paragraph 6.18 the claimant may give written notice that the claim will no longer continue under this Protocol. Unless the claimant's notice is sent to the defendant within 10 days after the expiry of the period in paragraph 6.18 the claim will continue under this Protocol.

6.19A Where liability is admitted in a soft tissue injury claim, it is expected that in most cases the defendant's account will not be relevant to the procedure in Stage 2. In the limited cases where it is considered appropriate, the defendant may send their account to the claimant electronically at the same time as the CNF response. The defendant's insurer must have the defendant's written authority to provide this account and, in sending it, is certifying that it has that authority. For the purposes of this paragraph, the defendant's written authority may be provided electronically.

6.19B The procedure in paragraph 6.19A applies to the MIB, save that the MIB is certifying that the defendant user of the vehicle has provided such authority.

Stage 2: Medical reports – all claims

7.1 The claimant should obtain a medical report, if one has not already been obtained.

7.2 It is expected that most claimants will obtain a medical report from one expert, but additional medical reports may be obtained from other experts where the injuries require reports from more than one medical discipline.

7.3 The claimant must check the factual accuracy of any medical report before it is sent to the defendant. There will be no further opportunity for the claimant to challenge the factual accuracy of a medical report after it has been sent to the defendant.

7.4

(1) The medical expert should identify within the report—
 (a) the medical records that have been reviewed; and
 (b) the medical records considered relevant to the claim.
(2) The claimant must disclose with any medical report sent to the defendant any medical records which the expert considers relevant.

7.5 In most claims with a value of no more than £10,000, it is expected that the medical expert will not need to see any medical records.

7.6 Any relevant photograph(s) of the claimant's injuries upon which the claimant intends to rely should also be disclosed with the medical report.

7.7 Where the claimant was not wearing a seat belt the medical report must contain sufficient information to enable the defendant to calculate the appropriate reduction of damages in accordance with principles set out in existing case law.

All claims other than soft tissue injury claims – subsequent medical reports

7.8 A subsequent medical report from an expert who has already reported must be justified. A report may be justified where—

(1) the first medical report recommends that further time is required before a prognosis of the claimant's injuries can be determined; or
(2) the claimant is receiving continuing treatment; or
(3) the claimant has not recovered as expected in the original prognosis.

All claims other than soft tissue injury claims – subsequent medical reports

7.8A In addition to paragraphs 7.1 to 7.7, and subject to paragraph 7.8B, in a soft tissue injury claim—

(1) the first report must be a fixed cost medical report from an accredited medical expert selected for the claim via the MedCo Portal (website at: www.medco.org.uk); and
(2) where the defendant provides a different account under paragraph 6.19A, the claimant must provide this as part of the instructions to the medical

PERSONAL INJURY AND DEATH

expert for the sole purpose of asking the expert to comment on the impact, if any, on diagnosis and prognosis if—
(a) the claimant's account is found to be true; or
(b) the defendant's account is found to be true.

7.8B In a soft tissue injury claim—

(1) it is expected that only one medical report will be required;
(2) a further medical report, whether from the first expert instructed or from an expert in another discipline, will only be justified where—
(a) it is recommended in the first expert's report; and
(b) that report has first been disclosed to the defendant; and
(3) where the claimant obtains more than one medical report, the first report must be a fixed cost medical report from an accredited medical expert selected via the MedCo Portal and any further report from an expert in any of the following disciplines must also be a fixed cost medical report—
(a) Consultant Orthopaedic Surgeon;
(b) Consultant in Accident and Emergency Medicine;
(c) General Practitioner registered with the General Medical Council;
(d) Physiotherapist registered with the Health and Care Professions Council.

Non-medical expert reports

7.9

(1) In most cases, a report from a non-medical expert will not be required, but a report may be obtained where it is reasonably required to value the claim.
(2) Paragraph 7.3 applies to non-medical expert reports as it applies to expert medical reports.

Specialist legal advice

7.10 In most cases under this Protocol, it is expected that the claimant's legal representative will be able to value the claim. In some cases with a value of more than £10,000 (excluding vehicle related damages), an additional advice from a specialist solicitor or from counsel may be justified where it is reasonably required to value the claim.

Witness statements

7.11 In most cases, witness statements, whether from the claimant or otherwise, will not be, required. One or more statements may, however, be provided where reasonably required to value the claim.

Stay of process

7.12 Where the claimant needs to obtain a subsequent expert medical report or a non-medical report, the parties should agree to stay the process in this Protocol for a suitable period. The claimant may then request an interim payment in accordance with paragraphs 7.13 to 7.16.

Request for an interim payment

7.13 Where the claimant requests an interim payment of £1,000, the defendant should make an interim payment to the claimant in accordance with paragraph 7.18.

7.14 The claimant must send to the defendant the Interim Settlement Pack and initial medical report(s) (including any recommendation that a subsequent medical report is justified) in order to request the interim payment.

7.15 The claimant must also send evidence of pecuniary losses and disbursements. This will assist the defendant in considering whether to make an offer to settle the claim.

7.16 Where an interim payment of more than £1,000 is requested the claimant must specify in the Interim Settlement Pack the amount requested, the heads of damage which are the subject of the request and the reasons for the request.

7.17 Unless the parties agree otherwise—

(a) the interim payment of £1,000 is only in relation to general damages; and
(b) where more than £1,000 is requested by the claimant, the amount in excess of £1,000 is only in relation to pecuniary losses.

Interim payment of £1,000

7.18 Where paragraph 7.13 applies the defendant must pay £1,000 within 10 days of receiving the Interim Settlement Pack.

Interim payment of more than £1,000

7.19 Subject to paragraphs 7.24 and 7.25, where the claimant has requested an interim payment of more than £1,000 the defendant must pay—

(1) the full amount requested less any deductible amount which is payable to the CRU;
(2) the amount of £1,000; or
(3) some other amount of more than £1,000 but less than the amount requested by the claimant,

within 15 days of receiving the Interim Settlement Pack.

7.20 Where a payment is made under paragraphs 7.19(2) or (3) the defendant must briefly explain in the Interim Settlement Pack why the full amount requested by the claimant is not agreed.

7.21 Where the claim is valued at more than £10,000 the claimant may use the procedure at paragraphs 7.13 to 7.20 to request more than one interim payment.

7.22 Nothing in this Protocol is intended to affect the provisions contained in the Rehabilitation Code.

Vehicle related damages – interim payments

7.23 Claims for vehicle related damages will ordinarily be dealt with outside the provisions of this Protocol under industry agreements between relevant organisations and insurers. However, where the claimant has paid for the vehicle related damages, the sum may be included in a request for an interim payment under paragraph 7.16.

Application for a certificate of recoverable benefits

7.24 Paragraph 7.25 applies where the defendant agrees to make a payment in accordance with paragraph 7.19(1) or (3) but does not yet have a certificate of recoverable benefits or does not have one that will remain in force for at least 10 days from the date of receiving the Interim Settlement Pack.

7.25 The defendant should apply for a certificate of recoverable benefits as soon as possible, notify the claimant that it has done so and must make the interim payment under paragraph 7.19(1) or (3) no more than 30 days from the date of receiving the Interim Settlement Pack.

Request for an interim payment where the claimant is a child

7.26 The interim payment provisions in this Protocol do not apply where the claimant is a child. Where the claimant is a child and an interim payment is reasonably required proceedings must be started under Part 7 of the CPR and an application for an interim payment can be made within those proceedings.

(Rule 21.10 provides that no payment, which relates to a claim by a child, is valid without the approval of the court.)

7.27 Paragraph 7.26 does not prevent a defendant from making a payment direct to a treatment provider.

Interim payment – supplementary provisions

7.28 Where the defendant does not comply with paragraphs 7.18 or 7.19 the claimant may start proceedings under Part 7 of the CPR and apply to the court for an interim payment in those proceedings.

7.29 Where the defendant does comply with paragraph 7.19(2) or (3) but the claimant is not content with the amount paid, the claimant may still start proceedings. However, the court will order the defendant to pay no more than the Stage 2 fixed costs where the court awards an interim payment of no more than the amount offered by the defendant or the court makes no award.

7.30 Where paragraph 7.28 or 7.29 applies the claimant must give notice to the defendant that the claim will no longer continue under this Protocol. Unless the claimant's notice is sent to the defendant within 10 days after the expiry of the period in paragraphs 7.18, 7.19 or 7.25 as appropriate, the claim will continue under this Protocol.

Costs of expert medical and non-medical reports and specialist legal advice obtained

7.31

(1) Where the claimant obtains more than one expert report or an advice from a specialist solicitor or counsel—
   (a) the defendant at the end of Stage 2 may refuse to pay; or
   (b) the court at Stage 3 may refuse to allow,
   the costs of any report or advice not reasonably required.

(2) Therefore, where the claimant obtains more than one expert report or obtains an advice from a specialist solicitor or counsel—
   (a) the claimant should explain in the Stage 2 Settlement Pack why they obtained a further report or such advice; and
   (b) if relevant, the defendant should in the Stage 2 Settlement Pack identify the report or reports or advice for which they will not pay and explain why they will not pay for that report or reports or advice.

Submitting the Stage 2 Settlement Pack to the defendant

7.32 The Stage 2 Settlement Pack must comprise—

(1) the Stage 2 Settlement Pack Form;
(2) a medical report or reports;
(3) evidence of pecuniary losses; and
(4) evidence of disbursements (for example the cost of any medical report),
(4A) in a soft tissue injury claim, the invoice for the cost of obtaining the fixed cost medical report and any invoice for the cost of obtaining medical records;
(5) any non-medical expert report,
(6) any medical records/photographs served with medical reports; and
(7) any witness statements.

7.32A In a soft tissue injury claim, the Stage 2 Settlement Pack is of no effect unless the medical report is a fixed cost medical report. Where the claimant includes more than one medical report, the first report obtained must be a fixed cost medical report from an accredited medical expert selected via the MedCo Portal and any further report from an expert in any of the disciplines listed in paragraph 7.8B(3)(a) to (d) must also be a fixed cost medical report.

7.33 The claimant should send the Stage 2 Settlement Pack to the defendant within 15 days of the claimant approving —

(1) the final medical report and agreeing to rely on the prognosis in that report; or
(2) any non-medical expert report,

whichever is later.

7.34 Where the defendant alleges contributory negligence because of the claimant's failure to wear a seat belt, the Stage 2 Settlement Pack Form must also suggest a percentage reduction (which may be 0 per cent) in the amount of damages.

Consideration of claim

7.35 There is a 35 day period for consideration of the Stage 2 Settlement Pack by the defendant ("the total consideration period"). This comprises a period of up to 15 days for the defendant to consider the Stage 2 Settlement Pack ("the initial consideration period") and make an offer. The remainder of the total consideration period ("the negotiation period") is for any further negotiation between the parties.

7.36 The total consideration period can be extended by the parties agreeing to extend either the initial consideration period or the negotiation period or both.

7.37 Where a party makes an offer 5 days or less before the end of the total consideration period (including any extension to this period under paragraph 7.36), there will be a further period of 5 days after the end of the total consideration period for the relevant party to consider that offer. During this period ("the further consideration period") no further offers can be made by either party.

Defendant accepts offer or makes counter-offer

7.38 Within the initial consideration period (or any extension agreed under paragraph 7.36) the defendant must either accept the offer made by the claimant on the Stage 2 Settlement Pack Form or make a counter-offer using that form.

7.39 The claim will no longer continue under this Protocol where the defendant gives notice to the claimant within the initial consideration period (or any extension agreed under paragraph 7.36) that the defendant—

(a) considers that, if proceedings were started, the small claims track would be the normal track for that claim; or
(b) withdraws the admission of causation as defined in paragraph 1.1(1)(c).

7.40 Where the defendant does not respond within the initial consideration period (or any extension agreed under paragraph 7.36), the claim will no longer continue under this Protocol and the claimant may start proceedings under Part 7 of the CPR.

7.41 When making a counter-offer the defendant must propose an amount for each head of damage and may, in addition, make an offer that is higher than the total of the amounts proposed for all heads of damage. The defendant must also explain in the counter-offer why a particular head of damage has been reduced. The explanation will assist the claimant when negotiating a settlement and will allow both parties to focus on those areas of the claim that remain in dispute.

7.42 Where the defendant has obtained a certificate of recoverable benefits from the CRU the counter-offer must state the name and amount of any deductible amount.

7.43 On receipt of a counter-offer from the defendant the claimant has until the end of the total consideration period or the further consideration period to accept or decline the counter offer.

7.44 Any offer to settle made at any stage by either party will automatically include, and cannot exclude—

(1) the Stage 1 and Stage 2 fixed costs in rule 45.18;
(2) an agreement in principle to pay a sum equal to the Type C fixed costs of an additional advice on quantum of damages where such advice is justified under paragraph 7.10;

PERSONAL INJURY AND DEATH

(3) an agreement in principle to pay relevant disbursements allowed in accordance with rule 45.19;

(3A) in a soft tissue injury claim, the cost of obtaining a medical report in rule 45.19(2A)(a); or

(4) where applicable, any success fee in accordance with rule 45.31(1) (as it was in force immediately before 1 April 2013).

7.44A In a soft tissue injury claim, an offer to settle made by either party before a fixed cost medical report has been obtained and disclosed will have no adverse costs consequences until after the report has been disclosed.

7.45 Where there is a dispute about whether an additional advice on quantum of damages is justified or about the amount or validity of any disbursement, the parties may use the procedure set out in rule 45.29.

(Rule 45.29 provides that where the parties to a dispute have a written agreement on all issues but have failed to agree the amount of the costs, they may start proceedings under that rule so that the court can determine the amount of those costs.)

Withdrawal of offer after the consideration period

7.46 Where a party withdraws an offer made in the Stage 2 Settlement Pack Form after the total consideration period or further consideration period, the claim will no longer continue under this Protocol and the claimant may start proceedings under Part 7 of the CPR.

Settlement

7.47 Except where the claimant is a child or paragraphs 7.49 and 7.50 apply, the defendant must pay—

(1) the agreed damages less any—
   (a) deductible amount which is payable to the CRU; and
   (b) previous interim payment;

(2) any unpaid Stage 1 fixed costs in rule 45.18;

(3) the Stage 2 fixed costs in rule 45.18;

(4) where an additional advice on quantum of damages is justified under paragraph 7.10, a sum equal to the Type C fixed costs to cover the cost of that advice;

(5) the relevant disbursements allowed in accordance with rule 45.19, including any disbursements fixed under rule 45.19(2A); and

(6) where applicable, any success fee in accordance with rule 45.31(1) (as it was in force immediately before 1 April 2013),

within 10 days of the parties agreeing a settlement.

(Rule 21.10 provides that the approval of the court is required where, before proceedings are started, a claim is made by a child and a settlement is reached. The provisions in paragraph 6.1 of Practice Direction 8B set out what must be filed with the court when an application is made to approve a settlement.)

7.48 Except where paragraph 7.51 applies, where the parties agree a settlement for a greater sum than the defendant had offered during the total consideration period or further consideration period and after the Court Proceedings Pack has been sent to the defendant but before proceedings are issued under Stage 3—

(1) paragraph 7.47 applies; and

(2) the defendant must also pay the fixed late settlement costs in rule 45.23A.

Application for certificate of recoverable benefits

7.49 Paragraph 7.50 applies where, at the date of the acceptance of an offer in the Stage 2 Settlement Pack, the defendant does not have a certificate of recoverable benefits that will remain in force for at least 10 days.

7.50 The defendant should apply for a fresh certificate of recoverable benefits as soon as possible, notify the claimant that it has done so and must pay the amounts set out in paragraph 7.47 within 30 days of the end of the relevant period in paragraphs 7.35 to 7.37.

Vehicle related damages — additional damages

7.51 Paragraph 7.52 applies where at the end of the relevant period in paragraphs 7.35 to 7.37 the claim ("the original damages") has not settled and there remain vehicle related damages ("the additional damages") being dealt with by a third party separate from the claim. The original damages include all elements of the claim in the existing Stage 2 Settlement Pack.

7.52 Where paragraph 7.51 applies the claimant must, in relation to the additional damages—

(1) notify the defendant that this separate claim is being considered;
(2) obtain all relevant information from the third party; and
(3) make a separate offer by amending the Stage 2 Settlement Pack Form.

7.53 Within 15 days of the claimant sending the offer under paragraph 7.52(3), the defendant must either agree the offer made by the claimant or make a counter-offer.

7.54 The counter offer must explain why a particular head of damage has been reduced to assist the claimant when negotiating a settlement and to allow both parties to focus on those areas of the claim that remain in dispute.

Original damages and additional damages are agreed

7.55 Where the original damages and additional damages are agreed within the period in paragraph 7.53 the defendant must pay the claimant in accordance with paragraph 7.62.

7.56 Where the parties agree a settlement for a greater sum than the Defendant had offered during the period in paragraph 7.53 but after the Court Proceedings Pack has been sent to the Defendant and before proceedings are issued under Stage 3,

(1) paragraph 7.55 applies; and
(2) the defendant must also pay the fixed late settlement costs in rule 45.23A.

Original damages are not agreed, additional damages are agreed

7.57 Paragraph 7.58 applies where—

(1) the original damages are not agreed; but
(2) the additional damages are agreed.

7.58 Where paragraph 7.57 applies—

(1) the defendant must pay the agreed amount of the additional damages within 10 days of agreeing those damages, and
(2) the claimant must continue with the provisions in paragraphs 7.64 to 7.75 of this Protocol.

Original damages are agreed, additional damages are not agreed

7.59 Paragraph 7.60 applies where—

(1) the original damages are agreed; but
(2) the additional damages are not agreed.

7.60 Where paragraph 7.59 applies—

(1) the defendant must, in relation to the original damages, pay the claimant in accordance with paragraph 7.62 and

PERSONAL INJURY AND DEATH

(2) the claimant may start proceedings under Part 7 of the CPR in relation to the additional damages.

Original damages and additional damages are not agreed

7.61 Paragraphs 7.70 to 7.75 apply where the original and additional damages are not agreed.

Settlement after claim for additional damages

7.62 Except where the claimant is a child or paragraph 7.64 applies, the defendant must pay—

(1) the agreed damages less any—
  (a) deductible amount which is payable to the CRU; and
  (b) previous interim payment;
(2) any unpaid Stage 1 fixed costs in rule 45.18;
(3) the Stage 2 fixed costs in rule 45.18;
(4) where an additional advice on quantum of damages is justified under paragraph 7.10, a sum equal to the Type C fixed costs to cover the costs of that advice;
(5) the relevant disbursements allowed in accordance with rule 45.19, including any disbursements fixed under rule 45.19(2A); and
(6) where applicable, any success fee in accordance with rule 45.31 (as it was in force immediately before 1 April 2013) for Stage 1 and Stage 2 fixed costs,

within 10 days of agreeing to pay the damages.

(Rule 21.10 provides that the approval of the court is required where, before proceedings are started, a claim is made by a child and a settlement is reached. The provisions in paragraph 6.1 of Practice Direction 8B set out what must be filed with the court when an application is made to approve a settlement.)

Application for certificate of recoverable benefits

7.63 Where at the date on which damages are agreed the defendant does not have a certificate of recoverable benefits that remains in force for at least 10 days the defendant should apply for a fresh certificate as soon as possible, notify the claimant that it has done so and must pay the amounts set out in paragraph 7.62 within 30 days of the date on which damages are agreed.

Failure to reach agreement — general

7.64 Where the parties do not reach an agreement on—

(1) the original damages within the periods specified in paragraphs 7.35 to 7.37; or
(2) the original damages and, where relevant, the additional damages under paragraph 7.51,

the claimant must send to the defendant the Court Proceedings Pack (Part A and Part B) Form which must contain—

(a) in Part A, the final schedule of the claimant's losses and the defendant's responses comprising only the figures specified in subparagraphs (1) and (2) above, together with supporting comments and evidence from both parties on any disputed heads of damage; and
(b) in Part B, the final offer and counter offer from the Stage 2 Settlement Pack Form and, where relevant, the offer and any final counter offer made under paragraph 7.53.

7.65 The deductible amount should only be deducted from the personal injury damages.

7.66 Comments in the Court Proceedings Pack (Part A) Form must not raise anything that has not been raised in the Stage 2 Settlement Pack Form.

7.67 The defendant should then check that the Court Proceedings Pack (Part A and Part B) Form complies with paragraphs 7.64 to 7.66. If the defendant considers that the Court Proceedings Pack (Part A and Part B) Form does not comply it must be returned to the claimant within 5 days with an explanation as to why it does not comply.

7.68 Where the defendant intends to nominate a legal representative to accept service the name and address of the legal representative should be provided in the Court Proceedings Pack (Part A) Form.

7.69 Where the defendant fails to return the Court Proceedings Pack (Part A and Part B) Form within the period in paragraph 7.67, the claimant should assume that the defendant has no further comment to make.

Non-settlement payment by the defendant at the end of Stage 2

7.70 Except where the claimant is a child the defendant must pay to the claimant—

(1) the final offer of damages made by the defendant in the Court Proceedings Pack (Part A and Part B) Form less any—
   (a) deductible amount which is payable to the CRU; and
   (b) previous interim payment;

(2) any unpaid Stage 1 fixed costs in rule 45.18;

(3) the Stage 2 fixed costs in rule 45.18; and

(4) the disbursements in rule 45.19(2) that have been agreed, including any disbursements fixed under rule 45.19(2A).

7.71 Where the amount of a disbursement is not agreed the defendant must pay such amount for the disbursement as the defendant considers reasonable.

7.72 Subject to paragraphs 7.73 and 7.74 the defendant must pay the amounts in paragraph 7.70 and 7.71 within 15 days of receiving the Court Proceedings Pack (Part A and Part B) Form from the claimant.

7.73 Paragraph 7.74 applies where the defendant is required to make the payments in paragraph 7.70 but does not have a certificate of recoverable benefits that remains in force for at least 10 days.

7.74 The defendant should apply for a fresh certificate of recoverable benefits as soon as possible, notify the claimant that it has done so and must pay the amounts set out in paragraph 7.70 within 30 days of receiving the Court Proceedings Pack (Part A and Part B) Form from the claimant.

7.75 Where the defendant does not comply with paragraphs 7.72 or 7.74 the claimant may give written notice that the claim will no longer continue under this Protocol and start proceedings under Part 7 of the CPR.

General provisions

7.76 Where the claimant gives notice to the defendant that the claim is unsuitable for this Protocol (for example, because there are complex issues of fact or law) then the claim will no longer continue under this Protocol. However, where the court considers that the claimant acted unreasonably in giving such notice it will award no more than the fixed costs in rule 45.18.

Stage 3: Stage 3 Procedure

8.1 The Stage 3 Procedure is set out in Practice Direction 8B.

Forms

The standard forms used in the process set out in this Protocol are available from Her Majesty's Courts Service ('HMCS') website at http://www.hmcourts-service.gov.uk—

(1) Claim Notification Form ('Form RTA 1');
(2) Defendant Only Claim Notification Form ('Form RTA 2');
(3) Medical Report Form ('Form RTA 3');
(4) Interim Settlement Pack Form ('Form RTA 4');
(5) Stage 2 Settlement Pack Form ('Form RTA 5');
(6) Court Proceedings Pack (Part A) Form ('Form RTA 6'); and
(7) Court Proceedings Pack (Part B) Form ('Form RTA 7').

The information required in Form RTA 3 may be provided in a different format to that set out in that Form.

PRE-ACTION PROTOCOL FOR LOW VALUE PERSONAL INJURY (EMPLOYERS' LIABILITY AND PUBLIC LIABILITY) CLAIMS

SECTION I INTRODUCTION

1 Definitions

III PID [46]

1.1 In this Protocol—

(1) 'admission of liability' means the defendant admits that—
  (a) the breach of duty occurred;
  (b) the defendant thereby caused some loss to the claimant, the nature and extent of which is not admitted; and
  (c) the defendant has no accrued defence to the claim under the Limitation Act 1980;

(2) 'bank holiday' means a bank holiday under the Banking and Financial Dealings Act 1971;
(3) 'business day' means any day except Saturday, Sunday, a bank holiday, Good Friday or Christmas Day;
(4) 'certificate of recoverable benefits' has the same meaning as in rule 36.15(1)(e)(i) of the Civil Procedure Rules 1998.
(5) 'child' means a person under 18;
(6) 'claim' means a claim, prior to the start of proceedings, for payment of damages under the process set out in this Protocol;
(7) 'claimant' means a person starting a claim under this Protocol unless the context indicates that it means the claimant's legal representative;
(8) 'clinical negligence' has the same meaning as in section 58C of the Courts and Legal Services Act 1990;
(9) 'CNF' means a Claim Notification Form;
(10) 'deductible amount' has the same meaning as in rule 36.22(1)(d) of the Civil Procedure Rules 1998;
(11) 'defendant' includes, where the context indicates, the defendant's insurer or legal representative;
(12) 'disease claim' means a claim within sub-paragraph (14)(b);
(13) 'employee' has the meaning given to it by section 2(1) of the Employers' Liability (Compulsory Insurance) Act 1969;
(14) 'employers' liability claim' means a claim by an employee against their employer for damages arising from—
  (a) a bodily injury sustained by the employee in the course of employment; or
  (b) a disease that the claimant is alleged to have contracted as a consequence of the employer's breach of statutory or common law duties of care in the course of the employee's employment, other than a physical or psychological injury caused by an accident or other single event;

(15) 'legal representative' has the same meaning as in rule 2.3(1) of the Civil Procedure Rules 1998;

(16) 'medical expert' means a person who is—

(a) registered with the General Medical Council;

(b) registered with the General Dental Council; or

(c) a Psychologist or Physiotherapist registered with the Health Professions Council;

(17) 'pecuniary losses' means past and future expenses and losses; and

(18) 'public liability claim'—

(a) means a claim for damages for personal injuries arising out of a breach of a statutory or common law duty of care made against—

(i) a person other than the claimant's employer; or

(ii) the claimant's employer in respect of matters arising other than in the course the claimant's employment; but

(b) does not include a claim for damages arising from a disease that the claimant is alleged to have contracted as a consequence of breach of statutory or common law duties of care, other than a physical or psychological injury caused by an accident or other single event;

(19) 'Type C fixed costs' has the same meaning as in rule 45.18(2) of the Civil Procedure Rules 1998; and

(20) 'vulnerable adult' has the same meaning as in paragraph 3(5) of Schedule 1 to the Legal Aid, Sentencing and Punishment of Offenders Act 2012.

1.2 A reference to a rule or practice direction, unless otherwise defined, is a reference to a rule in the Civil Procedure Rules 1998 ('CPR') or a practice direction supplementing them.

1.3 Subject to paragraph 1.4 the standard forms used in the process set out in this Protocol are available from Her Majesty's Courts and Tribunals Service ('HMCTS') website at www.justice.gov.uk/forms/hmcts—

(1) Claim Notification Form ('Form EL1', 'Form ELD1' and 'Form PL1'– which are referred to in this Protocol as 'the CNF');

(2) Defendant Only Claim Notification Form ('Form EL2', 'Form ELD2' and 'Form PL2');

(3) Medical Report Form ('Form EPL3');

(4) Interim Settlement Pack Form ('Form EPL4');

(5) Stage 2 Settlement Pack Form ('Form EPL5');

(6) Court Proceedings Pack (Part A) Form ('Form EPL6'); and

(7) Court Proceedings Pack (Part B) Form ('Form EPL7').

1.4 The information required in Form EPL3 may be provided in a different format to that set out in that Form.

2 Preamble

2.1 This Protocol describes the behaviour the court expects of the parties prior to the start of proceedings where a claimant claims damages valued at no more than £25,000 in an employers' liability claim or in a public liability claim. The Civil Procedure Rules 1998 enable the court to impose costs sanctions where this Protocol is not followed.

3 Aims

3.1 The aim of this Protocol is to ensure that—

(1) the defendant pays damages and costs using the process set out in the Protocol without the need for the claimant to start proceedings;

(2) damages are paid within a reasonable time; and

(3) the claimant's legal representative receives the fixed costs at each appropriate stage.

4 Scope

4.1 This Protocol applies where—

(1) either—

PERSONAL INJURY AND DEATH

(a) the claim arises from an accident occurring on or after 31 July 2013; or

(b) in a disease claim, no letter of claim has been sent to the defendant before 31 July 2013;

(2) the claim includes damages in respect of personal injury;

(3) the claimant values the claim at not more than £25,000 on a full liability basis including pecuniary losses but excluding interest ('the upper limit'); and

(4) if proceedings were started the small claims track would not be the normal track for that claim.

(Rule 26.6 provides that the small claims track is not the normal track where the value of any claim for damages for personal injuries (defined as compensation for pain, suffering and loss of amenity) is more than £1,000.)

4.2 This Protocol ceases to apply to a claim where, at any stage, the claimant notifies the defendant that the claim has now been revalued at more than the upper limit.

4.3 This Protocol does not apply to a claim—

(1) where the claimant or defendant acts as personal representative of a deceased person;

(2) where the claimant or defendant is a protected party as defined in rule 21.1(2);

(3) in the case of a public liability claim, where the defendant is an individual ('individual' does not include a defendant who is sued in their business capacity or in their capacity as an office holder);

(4) where the claimant is bankrupt;

(5) where the defendant is insolvent and there is no identifiable insurer;

(6) in the case of a disease claim, where there is more than one employer defendant;

(7) for personal injury arising from an accident or alleged breach of duty occurring outside England and Wales;

(8) for damages in relation to harm, abuse or neglect of or by children or vulnerable adults;

(9) which includes a claim for clinical negligence;

(10) for mesothelioma;

(11) for damages arising out of a road traffic accident (as defined in paragraph 1.1(16) of the Pre-Action Protocol for Low Value Personal Injury Claims in Road Traffic Accidents).

4.4 The fixed costs in rule 45.18 apply in relation to a claimant only where a claimant has a legal representative.

SECTION II GENERAL PROVISIONS

Communication between the parties

5.1 Subject to paragraphs 6.1 and 6.2, where the Protocol requires information to be sent to a party it must be sent via www.claimsportal.org.uk (or any other Portal address that may be prescribed from time to time). The claimant will give an e-mail address for contact in the Claim Notification Form ('CNF'). All written communications not required by the Protocol must be sent by e-mail.

5.2 Where the claimant has sent the CNF to the wrong defendant, the claimant may, in this circumstance only, resend the relevant form to the correct defendant. The period in paragraph 6.12 starts from the date that the form was sent to the correct defendant.

Time periods

5.3 A reference to a fixed number of days is a reference to business days as defined in paragraph 1.1(3).

5.4 Where a party should respond within a fixed number of days, the period for response starts the first business day after the information was sent to that party.

5.5 All time periods, except those stated in—

(1) paragraph 6.11 (response);
(2) paragraph 7.34 (the further consideration period)

may be varied by agreement between the parties.

5.6 Where this Protocol requires the defendant to pay an amount within a fixed number of days the claimant must receive the cheque or the transfer of the amount from the defendant before the end of the period specified in the relevant provision.

Limitation period

5.7 Where compliance with this Protocol is not possible before the expiry of the limitation period the claimant may start proceedings and apply to the court for an order to stay (i.e. suspend) the proceedings while the parties take steps to follow this Protocol. Where proceedings are started in a case to which this paragraph applies the claimant should use the procedure set out under Part 8 in accordance with Practice Direction 8B ("the Stage 3 Procedure").

5.8 Where the parties are then unable to reach a settlement at the end of Stage 2 of this Protocol the claimant must, in order to proceed to Stage 3, apply to lift the stay and request directions in the existing proceedings.

Claimant's reasonable belief of the value of the claim

5.9 Where the claimant reasonably believes that the claim is valued at between £1,000 and £25,000 but it subsequently becomes apparent that the value of the claim is less than £1,000, the claimant is entitled to the Stage 1 and (where relevant) the Stage 2 fixed costs.

Claimants without a legal representative

5.10 Where the claimant does not have a legal representative, on receipt of the CNF the defendant must explain—

(1) the period within which a response is required; and
(2) that the claimant may obtain independent legal advice.

Discontinuing the Protocol process

5.11 Claims which no longer continue under this Protocol cannot subsequently re-enter the process.

SECTION III THE STAGES OF THE PROCESS

Stage 1: Completion of the Claim Notification Form

6.1

(1) The claimant must complete and send—
 (a) the CNF to the defendant's insurer, if known; and
 (b) the Defendant Only Claim Notification Form ("Defendant Only CNF") to the defendant,

 but the requirement to send the form to the defendant may be ignored in a disease claim where the CNF has been sent to the insurer and the defendant has been dissolved, is insolvent or has ceased to trade.

(2) If—

(a) the insurer's identity is not known; or
(b) the defendant is known not to hold insurance cover,

the CNF must be sent to the defendant's registered office or principal place of business and no Defendant Only CNF is required.

(3) Where the insurer's identity is not known, the claimant must make a reasonable attempt to identify the insurer and, in an employers' liability claim, the claimant must have carried out a database search through the Employers' Liability Tracing Office.

(4) In a disease claim, the CNF should be sent to the insurer identified as the insurer last on risk for the employer for the material period of employment.

6.2 If the CNF or Defendant Only CNF cannot be sent to the defendant via the prescribed Portal address, it must be sent via first class post; and this must be done, in a case where the CNF is sent to the insurer, at the same time or as soon as practicable after the CNF is sent.

6.3 All boxes in the CNF that are marked as mandatory must be completed before it is sent. The claimant must make a reasonable attempt to complete those boxes that are not marked as mandatory.

6.4 Where the claimant is a child, this must be noted in the relevant section of the CNF.

6.5 The statement of truth in the CNF must be signed either by the claimant or by the claimant's legal representative where the claimant has authorised the legal representative to do so and the legal representative can produce written evidence of that authorisation. Where the claimant is a child the statement of truth may be signed by the parent or guardian. On the electronically completed CNF the person may enter their name in the signature box to satisfy this requirement.

Rehabilitation

6.6 The claimant must set out details of rehabilitation in the CNF. The parties should at all stages consider the Rehabilitation Code which may be found at: www.iua.co.uk/IUA_Member/Publications.

Failure to complete the Claim Notification Form

6.7 Where the defendant considers that inadequate mandatory information has been provided in the CNF that shall be a valid reason for the defendant to decide that the claim should no longer continue under this Protocol.

6.8 Rule 45.24(2) sets out the sanctions available to the court where it considers that the claimant provided inadequate information in the CNF.

Response

6.9 The defendant must send to the claimant an electronic acknowledgment the next day after receipt of the CNF.

6.10 If the claimant has sent the CNF to the defendant in accordance with paragraph 6.1(2)—

(a) the defendant must send to the claimant an electronic acknowledgment the next day after receipt of the CNF and send the CNF to the insurer at the same time and advise the claimant that they have done so;
(b) the insurer must send to the claimant an electronic acknowledgment the next day after its receipt by the insurer; and
(c) the claimant must then submit the CNF to the insurer via the Portal as soon as possible and, in any event, within 30 days of the day upon which the claimant first sent it to the defendant.

6.11 The defendant must complete the 'Response' section of the CNF ("the CNF response") and send it to the claimant—

(a) in the case of an employers' liability claim, within 30 days of the step taken pursuant to paragraph 6.1; and

(b) in the case of a public liability claim, within 40 days of the step taken pursuant to paragraph 6.1.

Application for a certificate of recoverable benefits

6.12 The defendant must, before the end of Stage 1, apply to the Compensation Recovery Unit (CRU) for a certificate of recoverable benefits.

Contributory negligence, liability not admitted or failure to respond

6.13 The claim will no longer continue under this Protocol where the defendant, within the relevant period in paragraph 6.11—

(1) makes an admission of liability but alleges contributory negligence;

(2) does not complete and send the CNF response;

(3) does not admit liability; or

(4) notifies the claimant that the defendant considers that—

 (a) there is inadequate mandatory information in the CNF; or

 (b) if proceedings were issued, the small claims track would be the normal track for that claim.

6.14 Where the defendant does not admit liability the defendant must give brief reasons in the CNF response.

6.15 Where paragraph 6.13 applies the claim will proceed under the relevant Pre-Action Protocol and the CNF will serve as the letter of claim (except where the claim no longer continues under this Protocol because the CNF contained inadequate information). Time will be treated as running under the relevant Pre-Action Protocol from the date the form of acknowledgment is served under paragraph 6.9 or 6.10.

(For admissions made in the course of the process under this Protocol, see rule 14.1B.)

(Paragraph 2.10A of the Pre-Action Protocol on Personal Injury and paragraph 6.10A of the Pre-Action Protocol for Disease and Illness Claims provide that the CNF can be used as the letter of claim except where the claim no longer continues under this Protocol because the CNF contained inadequate information.)

Stage 1 fixed costs

6.16 Except where the claimant is a child, where liability is admitted the defendant must pay the Stage 1 fixed costs in rule 45.18 within 10 days after receiving the Stage 2 Settlement Pack.

6.17 Where the defendant fails to pay the Stage 1 fixed costs within the period specified in paragraph 6.16 the claimant may give written notice that the claim will no longer continue under this Protocol. Unless the claimant's notice is sent to the defendant within 10 days after the expiry of the period in paragraph 6.16 the claim will continue under this Protocol.

Stage 2: Medical reports

7.1 The claimant should obtain a medical report, if one has not already been obtained.

7.2 It is expected that most claimants will obtain a medical report from one expert but additional medical reports may be obtained from other experts where the injuries require reports from more than one medical discipline.

7.3 The claimant must check the factual accuracy of any medical report before it is sent to the defendant. There will be no further opportunity for the claimant to challenge the factual accuracy of a medical report after it has been sent to the defendant.

7.4

(1) The medical expert should identify within the report—
(a) the medical records that have been reviewed; and
(b) the medical records considered relevant to the claim.
(2) The claimant must disclose with any medical report sent to the defendant any medical records which the expert considers relevant.

7.5 Any relevant photograph(s) of the claimant's injuries upon which the claimant intends to rely should also be disclosed with the medical report.

Subsequent medical reports

7.6 A subsequent medical report from an expert who has already reported must be justified. A report may be justified where—

(1) the first medical report recommends that further time is required before a prognosis of the claimant's injuries can be determined; or
(2) the claimant is receiving continuing treatment; or
(3) the claimant has not recovered as expected in the original prognosis.

Non-medical reports

7.7

(1) In most cases, a report from a non-medical expert will not be required, but a report may be obtained where it is reasonably required to value the claim.
(2) Paragraph 7.2 applies to non-medical expert reports as it applies to expert medical reports.

Specialist legal advice

7.8 In most cases under this Protocol, it is expected that the claimant's legal representative will be able to value the claim. In some cases with a value of more than £10,000, an additional advice from a specialist solicitor or from counsel may be justified where it is reasonably required to value the claim.

Details of loss of earnings

7.9 In an employers' liability claim, the defendant must, within 20 days of the date of admission of liability, provide earnings details to verify the claimant's loss of earnings, if any.

Witness statements

7.10 In most cases, witness statements, whether from the claimant or otherwise, will not be, required. One or more statements may, however, be provided where reasonably required to value the claim.

Stay of process

7.11 Where the claimant needs to obtain a subsequent medical report or a report from a non-medical expert, the parties should agree to stay the process in this Protocol for a suitable period. The claimant may then request an interim payment in accordance with paragraphs 7.12 to 7.20.

Request for an interim payment

7.12 Where the claimant requests an interim payment of £1,000, the defendant should make an interim payment to the claimant in accordance with paragraph 7.17.

7.13 The claimant must send to the defendant the Interim Settlement Pack and initial medical report(s) (including any recommendation that a subsequent medical report is justified) in order to request the interim payment.

7.14 The claimant must also send evidence of pecuniary losses and disbursements. This will assist the defendant in considering whether to make an offer to settle the claim.

7.15 Where an interim payment of more than £1,000 is requested the claimant must specify in the Interim Settlement Pack the amount requested, the heads of damage which are the subject of the request and the reasons for the request.

7.16 Unless the parties agree otherwise—

(a) the interim payment of £1,000 is only in relation to general damages; and
(b) where more than £1,000 is requested by the claimant, the amount in excess of £1,000 is only in relation to pecuniary losses.

Interim payment of £1,000

7.17

(1) Where paragraph 7.12 applies the defendant must pay £1,000 within 10 days of receiving the Interim Settlement Pack.
(2) Sub-paragraph (1) does not apply in a claim in respect of a disease to which the Pneumoconiosis etc. (Workers' Compensation) Act 1979 applies unless there is a valid CRU certificate showing no deduction for recoverable lump sum payments.

Interim payment of more than £1,000

7.18 Subject to paragraphs 7.19 and 7.21, where the claimant has requested an interim payment of more than £1,000 the defendant must pay—

(1) the full amount requested less any deductible amount which is payable to the CRU;
(2) the amount of £1,000; or
(3) some other amount of more than £1,000 but less than the amount requested by the claimant,

within 15 days of receiving the Interim Settlement Pack.

7.19 Where a payment is made under paragraphs 7.18(2) or (3) the defendant must briefly explain in the Interim Settlement Pack why the full amount requested by the claimant is not agreed.

7.20 Where the claim is valued at more than £10,000 the claimant may use the procedure at paragraphs 7.12 to 7.19 to request more than one interim payment.

7.21 Nothing in this Protocol is intended to affect the provisions contained in the Rehabilitation Code.

Application for a certificate of recoverable benefits

7.22 Paragraph 7.23 applies where the defendant agrees to make a payment in accordance with paragraph 7.18(1) or (3) but does not yet have a certificate of recoverable benefits or does not have one that will remain in force for at least 10 days from the date of receiving the Interim Settlement Pack.

7.23 The defendant should apply for a certificate of recoverable benefits as soon as possible, notify the claimant that it has done so and must make the interim payment under paragraph 7.18(1) or (3) no more than 30 days from the date of receiving the Interim Settlement Pack.

Request for an interim payment where the claimant is a child

7.24 The interim payment provisions in this Protocol do not apply where the claimant is a child. Where the claimant is a child and an interim payment is reasonably required proceedings must be started under Part 7 of the CPR and an application for an interim payment can be made within those proceedings.

(Rule 21.10 provides that no payment, which relates to a claim by a child, is valid without the approval of the court.)

7.25 Paragraph 7.24 does not prevent a defendant from making a payment direct to a treatment provider.

Interim payment – supplementary provisions

7.26 Where the defendant does not comply with paragraphs 7.17 or 7.18 the claimant may start proceedings under Part 7 of the CPR and apply to the court for an interim payment in those proceedings.

7.27 Where the defendant does comply with paragraph 7.18(2) or (3) but the claimant is not content with the amount paid, the claimant may still start proceedings. However, the court will order the defendant to pay no more than the Stage 2 fixed costs where the court awards an interim payment of no more than the amount offered by the defendant or the court makes no award.

7.28 Where paragraph 7.26 or 7.27 applies the claimant must give notice to the defendant that the claim will no longer continue under this Protocol. Unless the claimant's notice is sent to the defendant within 10 days after the expiry of the period in paragraphs 7.17, 7.18 or 7.23 as appropriate, the claim will continue under this Protocol.

Costs of expert medical and non-medical reports and specialist legal advice obtained

7.29

(1) Where the claimant obtains more than one expert report or an advice from a specialist solicitor or counsel—
   - (a) the defendant at the end of Stage 2 may refuse to pay; or
   - (b) the court at Stage 3 may refuse to allow,

   the costs of any report or advice not reasonably required.

(2) Therefore, where the claimant obtains more than one expert report or obtains an advice from a specialist solicitor or counsel—
   - (a) the claimant should explain in the Stage 2 Settlement Pack why they obtained a further report or such advice; and
   - (b) if relevant, the defendant should in the Stage 2 Settlement Pack identify the report or reports or advice for which they will not pay and explain why they will not pay for that report or reports or advice.

Submitting the Stage 2 Settlement Pack to the defendant

7.30 The Stage 2 Settlement Pack must comprise—

(1) the Stage 2 Settlement Pack Form;
(2) a medical report or reports;
(3) evidence of pecuniary losses;
(4) evidence of disbursements (for example the cost of any medical report),
(5) any non-medical expert report,
(6) any medical records/photographs served with medical reports; and
(7) any witness statements.

7.31 The claimant should send the Stage 2 Settlement Pack to the defendant within 15 days of the claimant approving —

(1) the final medical report and agreeing to rely on the prognosis in that report; or
(2) any non-medical expert report,

whichever is later.

Consideration of claim

7.32 There is a 35 day period for consideration of the Stage 2 Settlement Pack by the defendant ("the total consideration period"). This comprises a period of up to 15 days for the defendant to consider the Stage 2 Settlement Pack ("the initial consideration period") and make an offer. The remainder of the total consideration period ("the negotiation period") is for any further negotiation between the parties.

7.33 The total consideration period can be extended by the parties agreeing to extend either the initial consideration period or the negotiation period or both.

7.34 Where a party makes an offer 5 days or less before the end of the total consideration period (including any extension to this period under paragraph 7.32), there will be a further period of 5 days after the end of the total consideration period for the relevant party to consider that offer. During this period ("the further consideration period") no further offers can be made by either party.

Defendant accepts offer or makes counter-offer

7.35 Within the initial consideration period (or any extension agreed under paragraph 7.33) the defendant must either accept the offer made by the claimant on the Stage 2 Settlement Pack Form or make a counter-offer using that form.

7.36 The claim will no longer continue under this Protocol where the defendant gives notice to the claimant within the initial consideration period (or any extension agreed under paragraph 7.33) that the defendant—

(a) considers that, if proceedings were started, the small claims track would be the normal track for that claim; or
(b) withdraws the admission of causation as defined in paragraph 1.1(1)(b).

7.37 Where the defendant does not respond within the initial consideration period (or any extension agreed under paragraph 7.33), the claim will no longer continue under this Protocol and the claimant may start proceedings under Part 7 of the CPR.

7.38 When making a counter-offer the defendant must propose an amount for each head of damage and may, in addition, make an offer that is higher than the total of the amounts proposed for all heads of damage. The defendant must also explain in the counter-offer why a particular head of damage has been reduced. The explanation will assist the claimant when negotiating a settlement and will allow both parties to focus on those areas of the claim that remain in dispute.

7.39 Where the defendant has obtained a certificate of recoverable benefits from the CRU the counter offer must state the name and amount of any deductible amount.

7.40 On receipt of a counter-offer from the defendant the claimant has until the end of the total consideration period or the further consideration period to accept or decline the counter offer.

7.41 Any offer to settle made at any stage by either party will automatically include, and cannot exclude—

(1) the Stage 1 and Stage 2 fixed costs in rule 45.18;
(2) an agreement in principle to pay a sum equal to the Type C fixed costs of an additional advice on quantum of damages where such advice is justified under paragraph 7.8;
(3) an agreement in principle to pay relevant disbursements allowed in accordance with rule 45.19; or
(4) where applicable, any success fee in accordance with rule 45.31(1) (as it was in force immediately before 1 April 2013).

7.42 Where there is a dispute about whether an additional advice on quantum of damages is justified or about the amount or validity of any disbursement, the parties may use the procedure set out in rule 46.14.

(Rule 46.14 provides that where the parties to a dispute have a written agreement on all issues but have failed to agree the amount of the costs, they may start proceedings under that rule so that the court can determine the amount of those costs.)

Withdrawal of offer after the consideration period

7.43 Where a party withdraws an offer made in the Stage 2 Settlement Pack Form after the total consideration period or further consideration period, the claim will no longer continue under this Protocol and the claimant may start proceedings under Part 7 of the CPR.

Settlement

7.44 Except where the claimant is a child or paragraphs 7.46 and 7.47 apply, the defendant must pay—

(1) the agreed damages less any—
  (a) deductible amount which is payable to the CRU; and
  (b) previous interim payment;

(2) any unpaid Stage 1 fixed costs in rule 45.18;

(3) the Stage 2 fixed costs in rule 45.18;

(4) where an additional advice on quantum of damages is justified under paragraph 7.8, a sum equal to the Type C fixed costs to cover the cost of that advice;

(5) the relevant disbursements allowed in accordance with rule 45.19; and

(6) where applicable, any success fee in accordance with rule 45.31(1) (as it was in force immediately before 1 April 2013),

within 10 days of the parties agreeing a settlement.

(Rule 21.10 provides that the approval of the court is required where, before proceedings are started, a claim is made by a child and a settlement is reached. The provisions in paragraph 6.1 of Practice Direction 8B set out what must be filed with the court when an application is made to approve a settlement.)

7.45 Where the parties agree a settlement for a greater sum than the defendant had offered during the total consideration period or further consideration period and after the Court Proceedings Pack has been sent to the defendant but before proceedings are issued under Stage 3—

(1) paragraph 7.44 applies; and

(2) the defendant must also pay the fixed late settlement costs in rule 45.23A.

Application for certificate of recoverable benefits

7.46 Paragraph 7.47 applies where, at the date of the acceptance of an offer in the Stage 2 Settlement Pack, the defendant does not have a certificate of recoverable benefits that will remain in force for at least 10 days.

7.47 The defendant should apply for a fresh certificate of recoverable benefits as soon as possible, notify the claimant that it has done so and must pay the amounts set out in paragraph 7.44 within 30 days of the end of the relevant period in paragraphs 7.32 to 7.34.

Failure to reach agreement — general

7.48 Where the parties do not reach an agreement on the damages to be paid within the periods specified in paragraphs 7.32 to 7.34, the claimant must send to the defendant the Court Proceedings Pack (Part A and Part B) Form which must contain—

(a) in Part A, the final schedule of the claimant's losses and the defendant's responses comprising only the figures specified during the periods in paragraphs 7.32 to 7.34, together with supporting comments and evidence from both parties on any disputed heads of damage; and

(b) in Part B, the final offer and counter offer from the Stage 2 Settlement Pack Form.

7.49 Comments in the Court Proceedings Pack (Part A) Form must not raise anything that has not been raised in the Stage 2 Settlement Pack Form.

7.50 The defendant should then check that the Court Proceedings Pack (Part A and Part B) Form complies with paragraphs 7.48 to 7.49. If the defendant considers that the Court Proceedings Pack (Part A and Part B) Form does not comply it must be returned to the claimant within 5 days with an explanation as to why it does not comply.

7.51 Where the defendant intends to nominate a legal representative to accept service the name and address of the legal representative should be provided in the Court Proceedings Pack (Part A) Form.

7.52 Where the defendant fails to return the Court Proceedings Pack (Part A and Part B) Form within the period in paragraph 7.50, the claimant should assume that the defendant has no further comment to make.

Non-settlement payment by the defendant at the end of Stage 2

7.53 Except where the claimant is a child the defendant must pay to the claimant—

(1) the final offer of damages made by the defendant in the Court Proceedings Pack (Part A and Part B) Form less any—
  (a) deductible amount which is payable to the CRU; and
  (b) previous interim payment(s);
(2) any unpaid Stage 1 fixed costs in rule 45.18;
(3) the Stage 2 fixed costs in rule 45.18; and
(4) the disbursements in rule 45.19(2) that have been agreed.

7.54 Where the amount of a disbursement is not agreed the defendant must pay such amount for the disbursement as the defendant considers reasonable.

7.55 Subject to paragraphs 7.56 and 7.57 the defendant must pay the amounts in paragraph 7.53 and 7.54 within 15 days of receiving the Court Proceedings Pack (Part A and Part B) Form from the claimant.

7.56 Paragraph 7.57 applies where the defendant is required to make the payments in paragraph 7.53 but does not have a certificate of recoverable benefits that remains in force for at least 10 days.

7.57 The defendant should apply for a fresh certificate of recoverable benefits as soon as possible, notify the claimant that it has done so and must pay the amounts set out in paragraph 7.53 within 30 days of receiving the Court Proceedings Pack (Part A and Part B) Form from the claimant.

7.58 Where the defendant does not comply with paragraphs 7.55 or 7.57 the claimant may give written notice that the claim will no longer continue under this Protocol and start proceedings under Part 7 of the CPR.

General provisions

7.59 Where the claimant gives notice to the defendant that the claim is unsuitable for this Protocol (for example, because there are complex issues of fact or law or where claimants contemplate applying for a Group Litigation Order) then the claim will no longer continue under this Protocol. However, where the court considers that the claimant acted unreasonably in giving such notice it will award no more than the fixed costs in rule 45.18.

Stage 3: Stage 3 Procedure

8.1 The Stage 3 Procedure is set out in Practice Direction 8B.

PERSONAL PROPERTY

TABLE OF CONTENTS

GENERAL NOTES ON PERSONAL PROPERTY

III PTY [1]–III PTY [18]

For the most part, rights in personal property derive from the general law of contract and the statutes concerning the sale, hire and hire-purchase of goods, as to which see the CONSUMER CONTRACTS title (at **III CON**). For the rest, the courts have jurisdiction in relation to the seizure and sale of goods in execution of judgments (see, for example, Tribunal, Courts and Enforcement Act 2007, s 62 at **II TCE [11]**), the attachment of debts (by third party debt order under **CPR 72**) or attachment of earnings (**CPR 89**). The PERSONAL PROPERTY title is concerned with other statutes which confer jurisdiction in relation to distress and disputes over personal property and choses in action.

The Law of Distress Amendment Act 1888 and the Distress for Rent Rules 1988, which were reproduced in the Civil Court Practice 2014 at paras **III PTY [2]** to **III PTY [18]** were repealed with effect from 6 April 2014 by the Tribunals, Courts and Enforcement Act 2007. The new regime for taking control of goods was brought into effect from the same date. Its main provisions are at **II TCE [11]–II TCE [18]** and in Schedule 12 at **II TCE [30]**.

For the substantive law see 35 *Halsbury's Laws* (4th edn, reissue) title PERSONAL PROPERTY, para 1201; 6 *Halsbury's Laws* (4th edn, reissue) title CHOSES IN ACTION, para 1; and 13 *Halsbury's Laws* (4th edn) title DISTRESS, para 201.

LAW OF PROPERTY ACT 1925

(c 20)

III PTY [19]

136. Legal assignments of things in action

(1) Any absolute assignment by writing under the hand of the assignor (not purporting to be by way of charge only) of any debt or other legal thing in action, of which express notice in writing has been given to the debtor, trustee or other person from whom the assignor would have been entitled to claim such debt or thing in action, is effectual in law (subject to equities having priority over the right of the assignee) to pass and transfer from the date of such notice—

(a) the legal right to such debt or thing in action;

(b) all legal and other remedies for the same; and

(c) the power to give a good discharge for the same without the concurrence of the assignor:

Provided that, if the debtor, trustee or other person liable in respect of such debt or thing in action has notice—

(a) that the assignment is disputed by the assignor or any person claiming under him; or

(b) of any other opposing or conflicting claims to such debt or thing in action;

PERSONAL PROPERTY

he may, if he thinks fit, either call upon the persons making claim thereto to interplead concerning the same, or pay the debt or other thing in action into court under the provisions of the Trustee Act 1925.

(2) This section does not affect the provisions of the Policies of Assurance Act 1867.

(3) The county court has jurisdiction (including power to receive payment of money or securities into court) under the proviso to subsection (1) of this section where the amount or value of the debt or thing in action does not exceed £30,000.

III PTY [19.1]

Jurisdiction The proviso to sub-s (1) enables the debtor who has notice of a questionable assignment to pay the money or other thing in action into court under the Trustee Act 1925 s 63. Although the High Court has unlimited jurisdiction the county court is limited to payments of debts of no more than £30,000. The procedure for paying into court under s 63 of the Trustee Act 1925 is regulated in the High Court by CPR Sch 1 RSC Ord 92 r 2 (see para **RSC 92R2**) and in the county court by CPR Sch 2 CCR Ord 49 r 20 (see para **CCR 49R20**), both rules being preserved by CPR 50(2) (see para **CPR 50**).

III PTY [19.2]

Absolute assignment by writing An assignment of part of a debt is not absolute: *Re Steel Wing Co Ltd* [1921] 1 Ch 349. But an assignment of specified debts may be absolute, although the debts have not yet accrued due: *Hughes v Pump House Hotel Co* [1902] 2 KB 190, CA.

III PTY [19.3]

Terms of assignment In *Global Financial Recoveries Ltd v Jones* [2000] 02 LS Gaz R 30, 144 Sol Jo LB 32, the assignee of the benefit of a mortgage deed sought to enforce the shortfall due under the agreement after the mortgagee had realised the security. It was held by the court on the construction of the assignment that whilst the assignment covered the benefit of the mortgage and the proceeds of the enforcement of the security, it did not include the benefit of the covenant in the mortgage by which the mortgagor was liable to make good any shortfall after realisation of the security.

III PTY [19.4]

Assignment of fruits of an action A legal assignment of a cause of action consists of the right to prosecute the action, to be named as the proper party and to give a good discharge to the judgment debtor. By contrast an assignment of the fruits of an action is an equitable assignment being an agreement to recover such fruits if and when they are recovered. Such an agreement does not give the assignee any right to prosecute or conduct the action and the assignee does not have to acquire any beneficial interest in the action itself: *ANC Ltd v Clark Golding and Page Ltd* (2000) Times, 31 May, CA.

On the other hand the law does not recognise, on the ground of public policy, an assignment of a bare right to litigate unsupported by sufficient interest to justify the assignee's pursuit of proceedings for his own benefit. The assignment of a cause of action in order to enable the assignee or a third party to make a profit out of the litigation would generally be void as savouring of champerty: *Simpson v Norfolk & Norwich University Hospital NHS Trust* [2011] EWCA Civ 1149, [2011] All ER (D) 102 (Oct).

III PTY [20]

188. Power to direct division of chattels

(1) Where any chattels belong to persons in undivided shares, the persons interested in a moiety or upwards may apply to the court for an order for division of the chattels or any of them, according to a valuation or otherwise, and the court may make such order and give any consequential directions as it thinks fit.

(2) The county court has jurisdiction under this section where the amount or value of the property or of the interest in the property which is to be dealt with in the court does not exceed £30,000.

III PTY [20.1]

Jurisdiction The jurisdiction of the High Court is unlimited, while that of the county court is limited to £30,000: High Court and county court Jurisdiction Order 1991, SI 1991/724, art 2(3) (see para **II HCJ [3]**).

III PTY [20.2]

Procedure The application should be made by a claim form. Arguably the Part 8 claim form (N208) is required to be used by Practice Direction 8B, section B, because proceedings under the old rules would have been by originating summons or originating application.

TORTS (INTERFERENCE WITH GOODS) ACT 1977

(c 32)

III PTY [21]

4. Interlocutory relief where goods are detained

(1) In this section "proceedings" means proceedings for wrongful interference.

(2) On the application of any person in accordance with rules of court, the High Court shall, in such circumstances as may be specified in the rules, have power to make an order providing for the delivery up of any goods which are or may become the subject matter of subsequent proceedings in the court, or as to which any question may arise in proceedings.

(3) Delivery shall be, as the order may provide, to the claimant or to a person appointed by the court for the purpose, and shall be on such terms and conditions as may be specified in the order.

(4) The power to make rules of court for the High Court in England and Wales or under section 7 of the Northern Ireland Act 1962 shall include power to make rules of court as to the manner in which an application for such an order can be made, and as to the circumstances in which such an order can be made; and any such rules may include such incidental, supplementary and consequential provisions as the authority making the rules may consider necessary or expedient.

(5) The preceding provisions of this section shall have effect in relation to county courts in Northern Ireland as they have effect in relation to the High Court in Northern Ireland, and as if in those provisions references to rules of court and to section 7 of the Northern Ireland Act 1962 included references to county court rules and to or Article 47 of the county courts (Northern Ireland) Order 1980.

(6) Subsections (1) to (4) have effect in relation to the county court in England and Wales as they have effect in relation to the High Court in England and Wales.

(6) Subsections (1) to (4) apply in relation to the family court in England and Wales as they apply in relation to the High Court in England and Wales, but as if references in those subsections to rules of court (including references to rules of court under any particular enactment) were references to Family Procedure Rules.

III PTY [21.1]

Interim orders for delivery Section 4 confers concurrent jurisdiction on the High Court and county court to make interim orders for the delivery up of property, pending a decision on the rights of the parties. The procedure is governed by CPR 25 (see para **CPR 25**). A precedent for such an application is provided at **BCCP C[20]**.

III PTY [21.2]

Clamping of vehicles The owner of a clamped vehicle may invoke s 4 to apply for its release. Clamping may be justified if the vehicle owner parks the vehicle on someone else's land knowing that this is a trespass and that the vehicle may be clamped: *Arthur v Anker* [1997] QB 564, [1996] 3 All ER 783, CA. If, however, the vehicle owner does not see the warning notice about clamping, the land owner cannot rely on consent to the risk of clamping and the clamping is, in such a case, an unlawful trespass to goods: *Vine v Waltham Forest London Borough Council* [2000] 4 All ER 169, [2000] 1 WLR 2383, CA. However, the clamping of vehicles on private land was made illegal by s 54 of the Protection of Freedoms Act 2012; parking charges may be imposed and collected instead, as provided in Sch 4 to the Act.

III PTY [21.3]

Statutory conversion by loss or conversion Section 2(2) provides that an action lies in conversion for loss or destruction of goods, but it has been held that the cause of action does not accrue until there has been a demand for their return and an unequivocal refusal and that the limitation period does not start until both requirements are fulfilled: *Schwartzchild v Harrods Ltd* [2008] EWHC 521 (QB), [2008] All ER (D) 299 (Mar).

III PTY [22]

13. Sale authorised by the court

(1) If a bailee of the goods to which section 12 applies satisfies the court that he is entitled to sell the goods under section 12, or that he would be so entitled if he had given any notice required in accordance with Schedule 1 to this Act, the court—

(a) may authorise the sale of the goods subject to such terms and conditions, if any, as may be specified in the order, and

(b) may authorise the bailee to deduct from the proceeds of sale any costs of sale and any amount due from the bailor to the bailee in respect of the goods, and

(c) may direct the payment into court of the net proceeds of sale, less any amount deducted under paragraph (b), to be held to the credit of the bailor.

(2) A decision of the court authorising a sale under this section shall, subject to any right of appeal, be conclusive, as against the bailor, of the bailee's entitlement to sell the goods, and gives a good title to the purchaser as against the bailor.

(3) In this section "the court", in relation to England and Wales, means the High Court or the county court and, in relation to Northern Ireland, means the High Court or a county court, save that a county court in Northern Ireland has jurisdiction in the proceedings only if the value of the goods does not exceed the county court limit mentioned in Article 10 (1) of the county courts (Northern Ireland) Order 1980.

III PTY [22.1]

Jurisdiction The High Court and county courts have unlimited jurisdiction under this section: High Court and County Courts Jurisdiction Order 1991, SI 1991/724, art 2(1) (see para **II HCJ [3]**).

III PTY [22.2]

Common law duty of bailee of uncollected goods In the absence of an express term requiring the bailee to return the goods a term may be implied that the bailor will collect them within a reasonable time, on the expiry of which the bailee's duty of care will cease: *Jerry Johan Developments SA v Avon Tyres Ltd* (1999) Times, 25 January, Evans-Lombe J.

III PTY [22.3]

Procedure A bailee seeking a court order under this section should use the Part 8 procedure and Form N208, in accordance with Practice Direction 8B, section B.

III PTY [22.4]

Charges by a bailor In the absence of express contractual provision, storage charges may not be claimed by a bailor when the bailor is also exercising a lien over the item that was being stored: *Morris v Beaconsfield Motors* [2001] All ER (D) 335 (July), CA.

REAL PROPERTY

TABLE OF CONTENTS

GENERAL NOTES ON REAL PROPERTY

III REA [1]

Scope of title This title deals with some of the most commonly encountered statutory provisions (other than those relating to landlord and tenant and housing matters) whereby the High Court and the county court are given jurisdiction in matters concerning real property. In addition, there are included for convenience ss 1 and 2 of the Law of Property (Miscellaneous Provisions) Act 1989 (which prescribe formal requirements for deeds and for contracts disposing of interests in land).

III REA [2]

High Court jurisdiction The jurisdiction of the High Court in matters concerning real property is generally unlimited. For the general jurisdiction of the High Court see the Senior Courts Act 1981 s 19 (para **II SCA [17]**). The principal exception within the scope of this title is that, outside Greater London, the county court has exclusive jurisdiction over actions in which a mortgagee claims possession of land including a dwelling house (other than actions for foreclosure or sale in which a claim for possession is also made): County Courts Act 1984 s 21 (see para **II CCA [11]**). Furthermore, applications under s 1 of the Access to Neighbouring Land Act 1992 (see para **III REA [43]**) must be commenced in the county court: High Court and County Courts Jurisdiction Order 1991 (SI 1991/724) art 6A (see para **II HCJ [6]**).

III REA [3]

County courts jurisdiction The jurisdiction of the county court is entirely statutory. The jurisdiction of the county court to hear and determine actions for the recovery of land and actions in which the title to any hereditament comes in question is unlimited: County Courts Act 1984 s 21 (1), (2) (see para **III CCA [11]**). The jurisdiction of the county court under specific statutes relating to real property is defined by the statutes in question. For mortgage possession proceedings, see further the note at para **III REA [23]**.

III REA [4]

Procedure Save where special provision is made by the rules, litigation concerning real property is governed by the general provisions of the CPR. For rules making special provision see in particular CPR Pt 55 (claims for the possession of land) (para **CPR 55**) and CPR PD 55 (para **CPR PD 55**). See also CPR 40 Pt II (sale of land etc) (para CPR 40.15) and CPR PD 40 (para **CPR PD 40**), CPR Pt 56 (miscellaneous provisions about land) (para **CPR 56**) and CPR PD 56, Sch 1 Ord 113 (writs of possession) and Sch 2 Ord 24 (warrants of possession) (para **CPR PD 56**).

III REA [4A]

Precedents For precedents for and further notes on proceedings relating to real property see **BCCP Division P**. For precedents for and further notes on proceedings under the Trusts of Land and Appointment of Trustees Act 1996 see **BCCP Q[751]–BCCP Q[850]**.

III REA [4B]

Substantive law For the substantive law see) *Halsbury's Laws of England* (5th edn).

SETTLED LAND ACT 1925

(c 18)

GENERAL NOTES ON SETTLED LAND ACT 1925

III REA [5]

The Settled Land Act 1925 consolidated the enactments relating to settled land in England and Wales. The meaning of "settlement" is defined by s 1 of the Act and the meaning of "settled land" by s 2. See *Dent v Dent* [1996] 1 All ER 659, [1996] 1 WLR 683. With limited exceptions, no settlement created after 1st January 1997 may be a settlement under this Act: see s 2 of the Trusts of Land and Appointment of Trustees Act 1996.

Numerous sections of the Act confer jurisdiction on the court with regard to particular aspects of the administration of settlements: These include ss 3 (vesting orders); 17 (orders discharging trustees); 24 (authority for trustees to exercise powers of tenant for life); 34 (appointment of trustees); 35 (execution of deeds appointing new trustees); 46 (variation of building or mining leases); 49 (rectification of payments attributable to timber or fixtures); 64 (authorisation of unauthorised transactions), as to which see *Hambro v Duke of Marlborough* [1994] Ch 158, [1994] 3 All ER 332, 65 (disposal of principal mansion house and park); 66 (cutting and sale of timber); 67 (sale and purchase of heirlooms); 75 (payment of capital money to trustees); 79 (directions as to application of purchase money); 84 (approval of mode of application of capital money); 87 (payment for improvements); 90 (directions respecting contracts); 92 (approval of legal proceedings); 93 (questions as to exercise of powers); 108 (exercise of powers); 114 (payment of costs).

III REA [6]

Jurisdiction By the combined effects of the Settled Land Act 1925 sub-ss 113(3) and (3A), the County Courts Jurisdiction Order 1981 (SI 1981/1123) and the County Courts Act 1984 s 145 (para **II CCA [139]**) and sub-s 147(1) (para **II CCA [141]**) county court has jurisdiction under the Settled Land Act 1925 as regards land not exceeding in capital value £30,000, as regards capital money and securities not exceeding in amount or value £30,000 and as regards personal chattels not exceeding in value £30,000. Section 24 of the County Courts Act 1984 (para **II CCA [13]**) enables the parties to confer additional jurisdiction by agreement on the county court in proceedings under the Settled Land Act 1925.

III REA [7]

Procedure Proceedings under the Settled Land Act 1925 should be commenced by a claim form under CPR Part 7 or Part 8 as appropriate.

LAW OF PROPERTY ACT 1925

(c 20)

GENERAL NOTES ON LAW OF PROPERTY ACT 1925

III REA [8]

The Law of Property Act 1925 consolidated the law relating to conveyancing and the law of property of England and Wales. Numerous sections of the Act confer jurisdiction on the court with regard to particular aspects of the law of property. Of these, the following are set out below: s 49 (applications to the court by vendor and purchaser) and ss 88–92 (provisions regarding mortgages). Further provisions of the Act which confer jurisdiction on the court include ss 3 (directions as to transfer or creation of legal estate); 38 (party structures); 50 (discharge of encumbrances by court on sales or exchanges); 66 (confirmation of past transactions); 84(2) (declaration as to enforceability of restrictive covenants), as to which see In *Re 6, 8, 10 and 12 Elm Avenue, New Milton, ex p New Forest District Council* [1984] 3 All ER 632, [1984] 1 WLR 1398; 136(1) (interpleader or payment into court on disputed assignment); 146 and 147 (relief from forfeiture), as to which see the title Landlord & Tenant and Housing in this volume; 181 (creation and vesting of legal estate on dissolution of corporations); 188 (power to direct division of chattels).

III REA [9]

49. Applications to the court by vendor and purchaser

(1) A vendor or purchaser of any interest in land, or their representatives respectively, may apply in a summary way to the court, in respect of any requisitions or objections, or any claim for compensation, or any other question arising out of or connected with the contract (not being a question affecting the existence or validity of the contract), and the court may make such order upon the application as to the court may appear just, and may order how and by whom all or any of the costs of and incident to the application are to be borne and paid.

(2) Where the court refuses to grant specific performance of a contract, or in any action for the return of a deposit, the court may, if it thinks fit, order the repayment of any deposit.

(3) This section applies to a contract for the sale or exchange of any interest in land.

(4) The county court has jurisdiction under this section where the land which is to be dealt with in the court does not exceed £30,000 in capital value.

III REA [9.1]

Exercise of discretion The ordinary contractual expectations of the parties to a contract for the sale of land are that the deposit is an earnest for the buyer's performance of the bargain and will be forfeited if the buyer defaults. The discretion conferred by s 49(2) of the Law of Property Act 1925 to order the return of the buyer's deposit will in general not be exercised solely on the ground that the seller has suffered no loss, or a loss less than the amount of the deposit, due to the buyer's default. There must be something special or exceptional to justify the return of the deposit: *Midill (97PL) Ltd v Park Lane Estates Ltd* [2008] EWCA Civ 1227, [2009] 2 All ER 1067, [2009] 1 WLR 2460.

III REA [9.2]

Precedents For precedents for proceedings between sellers and buyers of land see **BCCP P[1001]–BCCP P[1110]**.

III REA [10]

89. Realisation of leasehold mortgages

(1) Where a term of years absolute has been mortgaged by the creation of another term of years absolute limited thereout or by a charge by way of legal mortgage and the mortgagee sells under his statutory or express power of sale,—

(a) the conveyance by him shall operate to convey to the purchaser not only the mortgage term, if any, but also (unless expressly excepted with the leave of the court) the leasehold reversion affected by the mortgage, subject to any legal mortgage having priority to the mortgage in right of which the sale is made and to any money thereby secured, and thereupon

(b) the mortgage term, or the charge by way of legal mortgage and any subsequent mortgage term or charge, shall merge in such leasehold reversion or be extinguished unless excepted as aforesaid;

and such conveyance may, as respects the leasehold reversion, be made in the name of the estate owner in whom it is vested.

Where a licence to assign is required on a sale by a mortgagee, such licence shall not be unreasonably refused.

(2) Where any such mortgagee obtains an order for foreclosure absolute, the order shall, unless it otherwise provides, operate (without giving rise to a forfeiture for want of a licence to assign) to vest the leasehold reversion affected by the mortgage and any subsequent mortgage term in him, subject to any legal mortgage having priority to the mortgage in right of which the foreclosure is obtained and to any money thereby secured, and thereupon the mortgage term and any subsequent mortgage term or charge by way of legal mortgage bound by the order shall, subject to any express provision to the contrary contained in the order, merge in such leasehold reversion or be extinguished.

(3) Where any such mortgagee acquires a title under the Limitation Acts, he, or the persons deriving title under him, may by deed declare that the leasehold reversion affected by the mortgage and any mortgage term affected by the title so acquired shall vest in him, free from any right of redemption which is barred, and the same shall (without giving rise to a forfeiture for want of a licence to assign) vest accordingly, and thereupon the mortgage term, if any, and any other mortgage term or charge by way of legal mortgage affected by the title so acquired shall, subject to any express provision to the contrary contained in the deed, merge in such leasehold reversion or be extinguished.

(4) Where the mortgage includes fixtures or chattels personal, any statutory power of sale and any right to foreclose or take possession shall extend to the absolute or other interest therein affected by the charge.

(5) In the case of a sub-mortgage by subdemise of a term (less a nominal period) itself limited out of a leasehold reversion, the foregoing provisions of this section shall operate as if the derivative term created by the sub-mortgage had been limited out of the leasehold reversion, and so as (subject as aforesaid) to merge the principal mortgage term therein as well as the derivative term created by the sub-mortgage and to enable the sub-mortgagee to convey the leasehold reversion or acquire it by foreclosure, vesting, or otherwise as aforesaid.

(6) This section takes effect without prejudice to any incumbrance or trust affecting the leasehold reversion which has priority over the mortgage in right of which the sale, foreclosure, or title is made or acquired, and applies to a mortgage whether executed before or after the commencement of this Act, and to a mortgage term created by this Act, but does not apply where the mortgage term does not comprise the whole of the land included in the leasehold reversion unless the rent (if any) payable in respect of that reversion has been apportioned as respects the

land affected, or the rent is of no money value or no rent is reserved, and unless the lessee's covenants and conditions (if any) have been apportioned, either expressly or by implication, as respects the land affected.

In this subsection references to an apportionment include an equitable apportionment made without the consent of the lessor.

(7) The county court has jurisdiction under this section where the amount owing in respect of the mortgage or charge at the commencement of the proceedings does not exceed £30,000.

III REA [11]

90. Realisation of equitable charges by the court

(1) Where an order for sale is made by the court in reference to an equitable mortgage on land (not secured by a legal term of years absolute or by a charge by way of legal mortgage) the court may, in favour of a purchaser, make a vesting order conveying the land or may appoint a person to convey the land or create and vest in the mortgagee a legal term of years absolute to enable him to carry out the sale, as the case may require, in like manner as if the mortgage had been created by deed by way of legal mortgage pursuant to this Act, but without prejudice to any incumbrance having priority to the equitable mortgage unless the incumbrancer consents to the sale.

(2) This section applies to equitable mortgages made or arising before or after the commencement of this Act, but not to a mortgage which has been over-reached under the powers conferred by this Act or otherwise.

(3) The county court has jurisdiction under this section where the amount owing in respect of the mortgage or charge at the commencement of the proceedings does not exceed £30,000.

III REA [11.1]

For a practice form for an order for sale in an action by an equitable mortgagee see Form N300.

III REA [12]

91. Sale of mortgaged property in action for redemption or foreclosure

(1) Any person entitled to redeem mortgaged property may have a judgment or order for sale instead of for redemption in an action brought by him either for redemption alone, or for sale alone, or for sale or redemption in the alternative.

(2) In any action, whether for foreclosure, or for redemption, or for sale, or for the raising and payment in any manner of mortgage money, the court, on the request of the mortgagee, or of any person interested either in the mortgage money or in the right of redemption, and, notwithstanding that—

- (a) any other person dissents; or
- (b) the mortgagee or any person so interested does not appear in the action;

and without allowing any time for redemption or for payment of any mortgage money, may direct a sale of the mortgaged property, on such terms as it thinks fit, including the deposit in court of a reasonable sum fixed by the court to meet the expenses of sale and to secure performance of the terms.

(3) But, in an action brought by a person interested in the right of redemption and seeking a sale, the court may, in the application of any defendant, direct the plaintiff to give such security for costs as the court thinks fit, and may give the conduct of the sale to any defendant, and may give such directions as it thinks fit respecting the costs of the defendants or any of them.

(4) In any case within this section the court may, if it thinks fit, direct a sale without previously determining the priorities of incumbrancers.

(5) This section applies to actions brought either before or after the commencement of this Act.

(6) In this section "mortgaged property" includes the estate or interest which a mortgagee would have had power to convey if the statutory power of sale were applicable.

(7) For the purposes of this section the court may, in favour of a purchaser, make a vesting order conveying the mortgaged property, or appoint a person to do so, subject or not to any incumbrance, as the court may think fit; or, in the case of an equitable mortgage, may create and vest a mortgage term in the mortgagee to enable him to carry out the sale as if the mortgage had been made by deed by way of legal mortgage.

(8) The county court has jurisdiction under this section where the amount owing in respect of the mortgage or charge at the commencement of the proceedings does not exceed £30,000.

III REA [12.1]

Exercise of discretion For the approach of the court to the exercise of its discretion under s 91(2) where the mortgagor wishes a sale but the sale proceeds will not be sufficient to discharge the mortgage, see *Palk v Mortgage Services Funding plc* [1993] Ch 330, [1993] 2 All ER 481, CA. For the approach of the court to the exercise of its discretion under s 91(2) where the order sought would make a sale unimpeachable but a third party wished to impeach it, see *Arab Bank plc v Mercantile Holdings Ltd* [1994] Ch 71, [1994] 2 All ER 74.

III REA [13]–III REA [21]

92. Power to authorise land and minerals to be dealt with separately

(1) Where a mortgagee's power of sale in regard to land has become exercisable but does not extend to the purposes mentioned in this section, the court may, on his application, authorise him and the persons deriving title under him to dispose—

- (a) of the land, with an exception or reservation of all or any mines and minerals, and with or without rights and powers of or incidental to the working, getting or carrying away of minerals; or
- (b) of all or any mines and minerals, with or without the said rights or powers separately from the land;

and thenceforth the powers so conferred shall have effect as if the same were contained in the mortgage.

(2) The county court has jurisdiction under this section where the amount owing in respect of the mortgage or charge at the commencement of the proceedings does not exceed £30,000.

III REA [13.1]

Jurisdiction The jurisdiction of the county court under each of the sections printed above is as stated in those sections. See too the High Court and County Courts Jurisdiction Order 1991 (SI 1991/724) art 2 (para **II HCJ [3]**).

For the power of the parties to enlarge the jurisdiction of the county court under the Law of Property Act 1925 by agreement see the County Courts Act 1984 s 24 (para **II CCA [13]**).

III REA [13.2]

Procedure Proceedings under Law of Property Act 1925 should be commenced by a claim form under CPR Part 7 or 8 as appropriate.

REAL PROPERTY

ADMINISTRATION OF JUSTICE ACT 1970

(c 31)

PART IV
ACTIONS BY MORTGAGEES FOR POSSESSION

III REA [22]

36. Additional powers of court in action by mortgagee for possession of dwelling-house

(1) Where the mortgagee under a mortgage of land which consists of or includes a dwelling-house brings an action in which he claims possession of the mortgaged property, not being an action for foreclosure in which a claim for possession of the mortgaged property is also made, the court may exercise any of the powers conferred on it by sub-section (2) below if it appears to the court that in the event of its exercising the power the mortgagor is likely to be able within a reasonable period to pay any sums due under the mortgage or to remedy a default consisting of a breach of any other obligation arising under or by virtue of the mortgage.

(2) The court—

- (a) may adjourn the proceedings, or
- (b) on giving judgment, or making an order, for delivery of possession of the mortgaged property, or at any time before the execution of such judgment or order, may—
  - (i) stay or suspend execution of the judgment or order, or
  - (ii) postpone the date for delivery of possession,

for such period or periods as the court thinks reasonable.

(3) Any such adjournment, stay, suspension or postponement as is referred to in sub-section (2) above may be made subject to such conditions with regard to payment by the mortgagor of any sum secured by the mortgage or the remedying of any default as the court thinks fit.

(4) The court may from time to time vary or revoke any condition imposed by virtue of this section.

(5) This section shall have effect in relation to such an action as is referred to in sub-section (1) above begun before the date on which this section comes into force unless in that action judgment has been given, or an order made, for delivery of possession of the mortgaged property and that judgment or order was executed before that date.

(6) In the application of this section to Northern Ireland, "the court" means a judge of the High Court in Northern Ireland, and in sub-section (1) the words from "not being" to "made" shall be omitted.

III REA [22A]

38A

This Part of this Act shall not apply to a mortgage securing an agreement which is a regulated agreement within the meaning of the Consumer Credit Act 1974.

III REA [23]–III REA [25]

39. Interpretation of Part IV

(1) In this Part of this Act—

"dwelling-house" includes any building or part thereof which is used as a dwelling;

"mortgage" includes a charge and "mortgagor" and "mortgagee" shall be construed accordingly;

"mortgagor" and "mortgagee" includes any person deriving title under the original mortgagor or mortgagee.

(2) The fact that part of the premises comprised in a dwelling-house is used as a shop or office or for business, trade or professional purposes shall not prevent the dwelling-house from being a dwelling-house for the purposes of this Part of this Act.

III REA [23.1]

Introductory note Prima facie a legal mortgage gives the mortgagee a legal estate in the mortgaged property, by virtue of which he is entitled to go into possession whether or not the mortgagee is in default. "The mortgagee may go into possession before the ink is dry on the mortgage unless there is something in the mortgage, express or by implication, whereby he has contracted himself out of that right": per Harman J in *Four-Maids Ltd v Dudley Marshall (Properties) Ltd* [1957] Ch 317, [1957] 2 All ER 35.

The position of a legal chargee is identical. In what follows, references to mortgages include references to charges.

The mortgagee's right to take possession irrespective of default may be, and often is, modified by the terms of the mortgage. A common modification is to make it exercisable only in the event of default by the mortgagor. As to implied modification, see *Western Bank Ltd v Schindler* [1977] Ch 1, [1976] 2 All ER 393.

Where a mortgagee's right to possession has arisen, a court has no inherent power to refuse to grant possession to the mortgagee or to adjourn the proceedings, whether on terms of keeping up instalments or paying arrears, if the mortgagee cannot be persuaded to agree to that course. The only exceptions to this are: (a) adjournments which may be desirable in the ordinary course of procedure in circumstances such as temporary inability of a party to attend; and (b) the application may be adjourned for a short time to afford the mortgagor a chance of paying off the mortgage in full or otherwise satisfying the mortgagee: *Birmingham Citizen's Permanent Building Society v Caunt* [1962] Ch 883, [1962] 1 All ER 163.

Section 1 of the Mortgage Repossession (Protection of Tenants etc) Act 2010 (**III REA [89]**) gives the court power to postpone for a period not exceeding two months the operation of a possession order made in favour of a mortgagee of land which consists of or includes a dwelling-house on the application of a tenant of the mortgagor whose tenancy is not binding on the mortgagee.

III REA [23.2]

Part IV of the Administration of Justice Act 1970 Part IV of the Administration of Justice Act 1970, printed above (paras **III REA [22]–III REA [23]**), gives the court additional powers on claims for possession of property which "consists of or includes a dwelling house". Those powers are exercisable "where it appears to the court that in the event of its exercising the power the mortgagor is likely to be able within a reasonable period to pay any sums due under the mortgage or to remedy a default consisting of a breach of any other obligation arising under or by virtue of the mortgage". The powers of the court are to adjourn the proceedings, stay or suspend execution of an order for possession, or postpone the date for delivery of possession, for such period or periods as the court considers reasonable. Any such adjournment, stay, suspension or postponement may be made subject to such conditions with regard to payment by the mortgagor of any sum secured by the mortgage or the remedying of any default as the court thinks fit.

III REA [23.3]

Section 8 of the Administration of Justice Act 1973 Section 36 suffered from a defect, the nature and consequences of which have been described as follows: "By definition the cases in which [section 36] was likely to be invoked were cases where the whole principal sum had become due by default because most mortgages contain a provision making the whole principal sum due in the case of default. The reference in sub-s (1) of the section to a 'reasonable period to pay any sums due under the mortgage' had therefore the effect of confining the operation of the section to relatively few cases. If the mortgagor was already in difficulties with his instalments the chances of his being able to pay off the whole principal sum as well within a reasonable time must be considered fairly slim": per Oliver LJ in *Habib Bank Ltd v Tailor* [1982] 3 All ER 561 at 564, [1982] 1 WLR 1218 at 1222.

This limitation on the efficacy of s 36 led to the enactment of s 8 of the Administration of Justice Act 1973 (see para **III REA [30B]**). The intent of that section was "in the case of an instalment mortgage, to enable the court to defer possession if it was satisfied that there was a reasonable prospect of the mortgagee paying off, within a reasonable period, not the whole of the principal sum, but the outstanding instalments": per Oliver LJ in *Habib Bank Ltd v Tailor* [1982] 1 All ER 561 at 564, [1982] 1 WLR 1218 at 1223.

In practice, therefore, Pt IV of the Administration of Justice Act 1970 and s 8 of the Administration of Justice Act 1973 must be considered together, and they are dealt with together in the following notes.

III REA [23.3A]

Human rights There is no inconsistency between the common law, as mitigated by s 36 of the Administration of Justice Act 1970 and s 8 of the Administration of Justice Act 1973, and Article 8 of the European Convention on Human Rights (right to respect for private and family life, home and correspondence) or Article 1 of the First Protocol (entitlement to peaceful enjoyment of possessions): *Barclays Bank plc v Alcorn* [2002] EWCA Civ 817.

A sale by a mortgagee in exercise of the statutory power of sale conferred by the Law of Property Act 1925, s 101 overreaches the mortgagor's equity of redemption. A mortgagor who remains in possession after the exercise of such a power is a trespasser as against the purchaser from the mortgagee. Since the power of sale derives from the bargain made between the mortgagor and mortgagee, its exercise is not inconsistent with the right of the mortgagee to the peaceful enjoyment of his possessions guaranteed by the First Protocol to the European Convention of Human Rights. Accordingly s 101 of the Law of Property Act 1925 is not to be construed as requiring the authority of an order of the court for the exercise of the mortgagee's power of sale, and s 30 of the Administration of Justice Act 1970 is not to be construed as requiring a purchaser from a mortgagee to seek an order for possession, or as regulating the power of the court to make an order for possession in favour of such a purchaser: *Horsham Properties Group Ltd v Clark* [2008] EWHC 2327 (Ch), [2009] 1 All ER (Comm) 745, [2009] 1 WLR 1225. See further the Consultation Paper "Mortgages, Power of Sale and Residential Property" issued by the Ministry of Justice on 29 December 2009.

III REA [23.3B]

Equality and unlawful discrimination A lender who had made to a borrower a loan secured by a mortgage under which the principal sum was repayable by instalments and who had obtained an order for possession for non-payment of sums secured by the mortgage was not in breach of its obligations to the borrower under the Disability Discrimination Act 1995 or the Equality Act 2010 in failing to allow the borrower to convert the arrangement into an interest-only mortgage: *Green v Southern Pacific Mortgage Ltd* [2018] EWCA Civ 854, [2018] 2 P & CR 12.

III REA [23.4]

Scope of the sections The sections do not apply to a mortgage securing an agreement which is a regulated agreement within the meaning of the Consumer Credit Act 1974: s 38A (see para **III REA [22A]**). For the Consumer Credit Act 1974, see Part III Consumer Contracts (para **III CON [24]**).

The sections apply only where the mortgaged property "consists of or includes a dwelling house". The relevant date for determining whether property "consists of or includes a dwelling house" is the date on which the mortgagee brings an action claiming possession of the property. It is not a condition of the sections coming into play that the property should have consisted of or included a dwelling house when the mortgage was granted: *Royal Bank of Scotland v Miller* [2001] EWCA Civ 344, [2002] QB 255.

The sections apply whether or not the mortgagor is in default: *Western Bank Ltd v Schindler* [1977] Ch 1, [1976] 2 All ER 393.

The sections apply only where a mortgagee has brought an action for possession. They do not prevent a mortgagee who has not brought such proceedings from exercising his common law right to take possession: *Ropaigealach v Barclays Bank plc* [2000] 1 QB 263, [1999] 4 All ER 235.

For the purposes of the sections, the court, in ascertaining the provisions of a mortgage, must take into account not merely the stipulations therein as operating at law, but also their practical effect in equity: *Centrax Trustees Ltd v Ross* [1979] 2 All ER 952.

Two conditions must be present for s 8 to apply. "One is a provision that the mortgagor is entitled or is to be permitted to pay the principal by instalments or otherwise to defer payment thereof. The second is a provision for earlier payment in the event of any default by the mortgagor or of a demand by the mortgagee or otherwise. Both provisions must be terms of the contract between the parties. They must be made either by the mortgage or by an agreement between the mortgagor and the mortgagee": *Centrax Trustees Ltd v Ross* [1979] 2 All ER 952.

The words in s 8 "where . . . the mortgagor is entitled or is to be permitted . . . otherwise to defer payment of" the principal sum presuppose an existing liability to pay which is deferred. Accordingly a bank overdraft which is not repayable until demand but is repayable in full on demand does not satisfy either condition, and so is not within s 8 (although it may be within s 36): *Habib Bank Ltd v Tailor* [1982] 3 All ER 561, [1982] 1 WLR 1218.

Section 8 applies where (apart from default) the only obligation of the borrower to repay the principal sum arises at the end of a specified period of time. Accordingly an endowment mortgage can be within s 8: *Bank of Scotland v Grimes* [1985] 1 QB 1179, [1985] 2 All ER 254. See also *Royal Bank of Scotland v Miller* [2001] EWCA Civ 344, [2002] QB 255.

In s 8, an "agreement" means an agreement which is contractually or otherwise legally enforceable. Accordingly the giving by a lender to a borrower of an indulgence, unsupported by consideration, is not an "agreement" within the section: *Rees Investments Ltd v Groves* [2001] All ER (D) 292 (Jun), Neuberger J.

It appears that s 36 does not give the court jurisdiction to stay an order for possession in respect of part only of the mortgaged property: *Barclays Bank plc v Alcorn* [2002] All ER (D) 146 (Mar), Ch D. See also [2002] EWCA Civ 817 (dismissal of oral application for permission to appeal).

III REA [23.5]

Operation of the sections In the absence of unusual circumstances, the outstanding term of the mortgage is the starting point in determining how long it would be reasonable to keep a mortgagee out of possession so as to give the mortgagor time to pay any sums due under the mortgage: *Cheltenham and Gloucester Building Society v Norgan* [1996] 1 All ER 449, [1996] 1 WLR 343. For a checklist of factors relevant to ascertaining what is a "reasonable period" for the purposes of the sections, see *Cheltenham and Gloucester Building Society v Norgan* [1996] 1 All ER 449, [1996] 1 WLR 343 at 463, 357–8.

The starting point of the outstanding term of the mortgage is not available to a mortgagor who cannot discharge the arrears by periodic payment and whose only prospect of repaying the loan and accrued and accruing interest is from the proceeds of sale of the property. In such a case the only general guidance is that the reasonableness of the period is a matter for the court in the circumstances of the case: *Bristol & West Building Society v Ellis* (1996) 75 P & CR 158.

If the property is in negative equity and the mortgagor has no funds other than the proceeds of sale to make up the shortfall, the powers conferred by the sections should not be exercised for the sole purpose of giving the mortgagor rather than the mortgagee conduct of the sale: *Cheltenham and Gloucester Building Society v Krausz* [1997] 1 All ER 21, [1997] 1 WLR 1558.

III REA [23.6]

"Likely" The question whether the mortgagor is "likely" to be able to pay the sums specified in the sections is a question of fact to be decided on evidence: *Royal Trust Co of Canada v Markham* [1975] 3 All ER 433, [1975] 1 WLR 1416. However it is a matter for the court's discretion whether to act on the basis of informal material. "It must be open to [judges] to act without evidence, especially where . . . the mortgagor is present in court and available to be questioned, and no objection to the reception of informal material is made by the mortgagee": *Cheltenham & Gloucester Building Society v Grant* (1994) 26 HLR 703

III REA [23.6A]

Case management powers The case management powers of the court do not entitle the court to grant a stay of proceedings for reasons unconnected with case management. In exercise of its case management powers a court may stay a mortgagee's possession order for some procedural reason connected with the proceedings in which the order is made and, where there are related proceedings, case management considerations may dictate that one set of proceedings be stayed pending the determination of the other. However, in proceedings by a bank for possession against a borrower, a Lloyd's name, who could not satisfy s 36 of the Administration of Justice Act 1970 and s 8 of the Administration of Justice Act 1973, neither the court's inherent jurisdiction nor its case management powers enabled the court to grant a stay pending the outcome of other litigation concerning Lloyd's: *State Bank of New South Wales v Carey Harrison III* [2002] EWCA Civ 363, [2002] All ER (D) 113 (Mar).

III REA [23.7]

Counterclaim Subject to the provisions of the contract between the mortgagor and mortgagee, a counterclaim by the mortgagee (except possibly a claim for a liquidated sum by way of set-off against and in excess of the mortgage debt) does not defeat the mortgagee's legal right to possession. However the existence of such a cross-claim may be relevant to the exercise of discretion under the sections: *National Westminster Bank plc v Skelton* [1993] 1 All ER 242, [1993] 1 WLR 72n; *Ashley Guarantee plc v Zacaria* [1993] 1 All ER 254, [1993] 1 WLR 62

III REA [23.8]

Mortgagor bankrupt A mortgagor who has been declared bankrupt is entitled to be heard on an application for possession under the sections: *Nationwide Building Society v Purvis* [1998] BPIR 625.

III REA [23.9]

Jurisdiction The county court has unlimited jurisdiction in proceedings for possession by mortgagees. The High Court also has unlimited jurisdiction, except that it has no jurisdiction in an action in which a mortgagee claims possession of land which consists of or includes a dwelling house and no part of the land is situated in Greater London (other than actions for foreclosure or sale in which a claim for possession is also made): County Courts Act 1984 s 21 (see para **II CCA [11]**). Even if the High Court has jurisdiction, proceedings for possession should be commenced in the county court save in exceptional circumstances: CPR 55.3 (see para **CPR 55.3**).

III REA [23.10]

Procedure The procedure in claims for possession by mortgagees is governed by CPR Pt 55 and the associated Practice Direction.

III REA [23.11]

Precedents For precedents for claims in mortgage proceedings see **BCCP P[851]–BCCP P[908]**.

III REA [23.12]

Form of order If the court stays or suspends an order for possession the period for which it does so should be defined or ascertainable: *Royal Trust Co of Canada v Markham* [1975] 3 All ER 433, [1975] 1 WLR 1416. See also *Western Bank Ltd v Schindler* [1977] Ch 1, [1976] 2 All ER 393.

For a form of order see Form N31 (see the FORMS section of your CD-ROM and the Forms supplement). An order providing that possession is not to be given if the mortgagor pays arrears should specify the precise amount of the arrears, if necessary by a formula: *Rees Investments Ltd v Groves* [2001] All ER (D) 292 (Jun), Neuberger J.

A judgment for possession does not, without more, give rise to an issue estoppel with regard to any concurrent money claim: *UCB Bank Ltd v Chandler* (1999) 79 P & CR 270, CA.

Where an order for possession was made, not to be enforced for so long as the borrower paid the arrears by monthly instalments "in addition to the current instalments under the mortgage", the mortgagor was entitled to enforce the order for possession when the borrower fell into arrears with instalments payable under a consolidation of the outstanding arrears with the unpaid balance of the original loan. The instalments payable after the consolidation were "current instalments under the mortgage": *Bank of Scotland plc v Zinda* [2011] EWCA Civ 706, [2012] 1 WLR 728, [2011] 2 All ER (Comm) 839.

LAND CHARGES ACT 1972

(c 61)

GENERAL NOTES ON LAND CHARGES ACT 1972

III REA [26]

Jurisdiction of the High Court The High Court has a broad power, under s 1(6) of the Act to order the vacation of any registration in (a) the register of land charges, (b) the register of pending actions, (c) the register of writs and orders affecting land, (d) the register of deeds of arrangement affecting land and (e) the register of annuities. An application for such an order should be made by claim form in CPR Pt 7 or 8 (see para **CPR 7** and para **CPR 8**). In addition, the High Court has power, under s 5(10), to make an order vacating the registration of a pending land action, or a petition in bankruptcy, if satisfied that the action or petition is not prosecuted in good faith.

III REA [27]

Jurisdiction of the county court The jurisdiction of the county court is restated in the High Court and County Courts Jurisdiction Order 1991, SI 1991/724, art 2(6), as follows:

(6) A county court shall have jurisdiction under section 1(6) of the Land Charges Act 1972—

(a) in the case of a land charge of Class C (i), C (ii) or D (i), if the amount does not exceed £30,000;

(b) in the case of a land charge of Class C (iii), if it is for a specified capital sum of money not exceeding £30,000 or, where it is not for a specified capital sum, if the capital value of the land affected does not exceed £30,000;

(c) in the case of a land charge of Class A, Class B, Class C (iv), Class D (ii), Class D (iii) or Class E, if the capital value of the land affected does not exceed £30,000;

(d) in the case of a land charge of Class F, if the land affected by it is the subject of an order made by the court under s 1 of the Matrimonial Homes Act 1983 or an application for an order under that section relating to that land has been made to the court;

(e) in a case where an application under s 23 of the Deeds of Arrangement Act 1914 could be entertained by the court.

III REA [28]

Procedure Proceedings for the vacation of a land charge should be commenced by a Pt 8 Claim Form. See further **BCCP P[704]**.

III REA [29]

Precedents For precedents relating to land charges see **BCCP P[701]–BCCP P[754]**.

III REA [30]

Registration of access orders and applications An application for an access order under the Access to Neighbouring Land Act 1992 is to be regarded as a pending land action and is accordingly registrable as such (see sub-s 5(6) of that Act, para **III REA [47]**). An access order is registrable as a writ or order affecting land (Land Charges Act 1972 sub-s 6(1)(d)).

ADMINISTRATION OF JUSTICE ACT 1973

(c 15)

GENERAL NOTES ON ADMINISTRATION OF JUSTICE ACT 1973

III REA [30A]

Section 8 of this Act extends the powers of the court under s 36 of the Administration of Justice Act 1970 (see para **III REA [22]**). Section 8 is dealt with at paras **III REA [23.1]–III REA [23.12]**.

PART II
MISCELLANEOUS

III REA [30B]

8 Extension of powers of court in action by mortgagee of dwelling-house

(1) Where by a mortgage of land which consists of or includes a dwelling-house, or by any agreement between the mortgagee under such a mortgage and the mortgagor, the mortgagor is entitled or is to be permitted to pay the principal sum secured by instalments or otherwise to defer payment of it in whole or in part, but provision is also made for earlier payment in the event of any default by the mortgagor or of a demand by the mortgagee or otherwise, then for purposes of section 36 of the Administration of Justice Act 1970 (under which a court has power to delay giving a mortgagee possession of the mortgaged property so as to allow the mortgagor a reasonable time to pay any sums due under the mortgage) a court may treat as due under the mortgage on account of the principal sum secured and of interest on it only such amounts as the mortgagor would have expected to be required to pay if there had been no such provision for earlier payment.

(2) A court shall not exercise by virtue of subsection (1) above the powers conferred by section 36 of the Administration of Justice Act 1970 unless it appears to the court not only that the mortgagor is likely to be able within a reasonable period to pay any amounts regarded (in accordance with subsection (1) above) as due on account of the principal sum secured, together with the interest on those amounts, but also that he is likely to be able by the end of that period to pay any further amounts that he would have expected to be required to pay by then on account of that sum and of interest on it if there had been no such provision as is referred to in subsection (1) above for earlier payment.

(3) Where subsection (1) above would apply to an action in which a mortgagee only claimed possession of the mortgaged property, and the mortgagee brings an action for foreclosure (with or without also claiming possession of the property), then section 36 of the Administration of Justice Act 1970 together with subsections (1) and (2) above shall apply as they would apply if it were an action in which the mortgagee only claimed possession of the mortgaged property, except that—

(a) section 36(2)(b) shall apply only in relation to any claim for possession; and

(b) section 36(5) shall not apply.

(4) For purposes of this section the expressions "dwelling-house", "mortgage", "mortgagee" and "mortgagor" shall be construed in the same way as for the purposes of Part IV of the Administration of Justice Act 1970.

(5) . . .

(6) In the application of this section to Northern Ireland, subsection (3) shall be omitted.

LOCAL LAND CHARGES ACT 1975

(c 76)

GENERAL NOTES ON LOCAL LAND CHARGES ACT 1975

III REA [31]

Action for compensation Section 10 of the Act entitles the purchaser of land affected by a local charge to bring an action for compensation against the registering authority for any loss suffered as a result of the charge not being registered or not being shown as registered on an official search certificate. In the county court however the maximum recoverable is £5,000: High Court and County Courts Jurisdiction Order 1991, SI 1991/724, art 2(2)(a) (see para **II HCJ [3]**).

Since the entitlement to compensation is equivalent to a claim in tort the compensation should be assessed as at the date of the hearing, not the date of the breach of duty, where the claimant had acted reasonably in not selling before receiving adequate compensation: *Smith v South Gloucestershire District Council* [2002] EWCA Civ 1131, [2002] 38 EG 206, (2002) Times, 30 August.

The right to compensation under the Act is for compensation for loss suffered in consequence of a local land charge being enforceable despite not being registered. Accordingly, loss claimed by a claimant (namely the diminution in value of the claimant's property due to the development of adjoining land) was irrecoverable, even though the loss would not have occurred if a local land charge (namely the listing of the claimant's property as of architectural of historical interest) had been registered. Although the registration of the listing might have prevented the development, the loss claimed was not a consequence of the enforceability of the local land charge, but of the claimant's failure to exploit the benefit of it: *Pound v Ashford Borough Council* [2003] EWHC 1088 (Ch), [2004] 1 P & CR 2.

III REA [32]

Rules On 1 June 1998, the Local Land Charges (Amendment) Rules 1998, SI 1998/1190, made under s 14 of the Act, came into force. The 1992 rules, SI 1992/194, were revoked.

RENTCHARGES ACT 1977

(c 30)

GENERAL NOTES ON RENTCHARGES ACT 1977

III REA [33]

Provisions Under s 8 of this Act the owner of any land affected by a rentcharge may apply to the Secretary of State for a certificate certifying that the rentcharge has been redeemed. After the statutory procedure has been followed, the Secretary of State will serve on the applicant a notice ("instructions for redemption") specifying the sum required to redeem the rentcharge and naming the person, if any, to whom it should be paid (s 9(4)). On proof that within 28 days after service of the instructions the applicant has paid the amount specified to the person named or, if no person is named, has paid it into court, the Secretary of State must issue the applicant with a redemption certificate (s 9(5)). The Secretary of State may also authorise payment into court where the applicant is unable to effect payment in accordance with the instructions for redemption or it would be unreasonable to require him to do so (s 9(6)). The appropriate court is the county court if the sum concerned does not exceed £5,000 (s 10 as amended by the High Court and County Courts Jurisdiction Order 1991, SI 1991/724: see notes to County Courts Act 1984 s 15, at paras **II CCA [7.1]–II CCA [7.9]**).

III REA [34]

Procedure Where money is to be paid into the county court, it must be paid into the court for the district in which the land affected by the rentcharge or any part thereof is situated (CPR Sch 2 CCR Ord 49 r 16 at para **CCR 49r16**). The payment is made in accordance with rule 16(7) of the Court Funds Rules 1987 (title FUNDS IN COURT, see para **III FUN [22]**) on production of the Secretary of State's instructions or letter of authority and delivery of a form of lodgment (CFO Form 105) issued by the Secretary of State and completed by the applicant. The payment and relevant documents will be transmitted by the court to the Court Funds Office which will issue a full receipt to the person making the payment (except where the lodgment was made in cash) and certify to the Secretary of State that the lodgment has been made.

III REA [35]

Regulations The Rentcharges Regulations 1978, SI 1978/16 prescribe the forms of application for the redemption of rentcharges and the statement as to ownership required for that purpose.

III REA [36]

Payment out Where the owner of the rentcharge seeks payment out of redemption money paid into court under the Act, he or his solicitor should lodge a form of application and order in respect of a fund in court and provide written evidence of the identity of the rent owner. The district judge will consider the application ex parte and, if satisfied, will make an order for payment out forthwith. If he is not satisfied, he will indicate what further evidence he requires. The personal attendance of the applicant or his solicitor will be required only in the most exceptional circumstances. Once an order is obtained, payment out will be made in accordance with r 40 of the Court Funds Rules 1987 (title FUNDS IN COURT, see para **III FUN [45]**).

INSOLVENCY ACT 1986

(c 45)

CHAPTER V EFFECT OF BANKRUPTCY ON CERTAIN RIGHTS, TRANSACTIONS, ETC

RIGHTS UNDER TRUSTS OF LAND

III REA [36A]

335A. Rights under trusts of land

(1) Any application by a trustee of a bankrupt's estate under section 14 of the Trusts of Land and Appointment of Trustees Act 1996 (powers of court in relation to trusts of land) for an order under that section for the sale of land shall be made to the court having jurisdiction in relation to the bankruptcy.

(2) On such an application the court shall make such order as it thinks just and reasonable having regard to—

- (a) the interests of the bankrupt's creditors;
- (b) where the application is made in respect of land which includes a dwelling house which is or has been the home of the bankrupt or the bankrupt's spouse or civil partner or former spouse or former civil partner—
  - (i) the conduct of the spouse, civil partner, former spouse or former civil partner, so far as contributing to the bankruptcy,
  - (ii) the needs and financial resources of the spouse, civil partner, former spouse or former civil partner, and
  - (iii) the needs of any children; and
- (c) all the circumstances of the case other than the needs of the bankrupt.

(3) Where such an application is made after the end of the period of one year beginning with the first vesting under Chapter IV of this Part of the bankrupt's estate in a trustee, the court shall assume, unless the circumstances of the case are exceptional, that the interests of the bankrupt's creditors outweigh all other considerations.

(4) The powers conferred on the court by this section are exercisable on an application whether it is made before or after the commencement of this section.

III REA [36A.1]

Effect of section 335A This section was inserted in the Insolvency Act 1986 by the Trusts of Land and Appointment of Trustees Act 1996 ('TLATA'), s 25(1) Sch 3 para 23 and amended by the Civil Partnerships Act 2004, s 26(1) s 261, Sch 27, par 118. It governs an application by a trustee in bankruptcy for an order under TLATA, s 14 (see **III REA [50]**) for the sale of land held on a trust of land. Subsection (1) requires the application to be made to the court having jurisdiction in relation to the bankruptcy. Subsection (2) requires the court to make such order as it thinks just and reasonable on the application and specifies an apparently exhaustive list of matters to which the court is to have regard. Subsection (3) provides that where the application is made after the end of the period of one year beginning with the first vesting of the bankrupt's estate in a trustee the court shall assume, unless the circumstances of the case are exceptional, that the interests of the bankrupt's creditors outweigh all other considerations. Where the circumstances are exceptional the assumption specified in sub-s (3) does not apply, and the court has to make such order as it thinks just and reasonable applying the criteria in sub-s (2).

"creditors" The term "creditors" in sub-s 335A(2)(a) includes both secured and unsecured creditors, see further *Judd v Brown* [1998] 2 FLR 360.

"needs" The word "needs" in sub-s 335A(2) refers to needs of any kind, including not only financial but also medical needs and needs of any other description such as emotional, psychological and mental needs: *Everitt v Budhram (a Bankrupt)* [2009] EWHC 1219 (Ch), [2010] Ch 170, [2010] 2 WLR 637.

"the circumstances of the case other than the needs of the bankrupt" The circumstances of the case include the statutory scheme of the bankruptcy legislation, at the heart of which is the vesting of the bankrupt's property in his trustee, with the object that the trustee should then realise the property and distribute the net proceeds among the creditors on a pari passu basis: *Grant v Baker* [2016] EWHC 1782 (Ch), [2017] 2 FLR. 646 at [44].

"exceptional circumstances" The word "exceptional" in sub-s (3) is derived from the law prior to the enactment of s 335A, as to which see *Re Citro* [1991] Ch 142 at 147 per Nourse LJ (inability of spouse with young children to buy comparable home and difficulties over schooling not exceptional, they are "the melancholy consequences of debt and impoverishment with which every civilised society has been familiar") and see also at 161 per Bingham LJ ("the order sought by the trustees must be made unless there are, at least, compelling reasons, not found in the ordinary run of cases, for refusing it"). For examples of decisions on this requirement made under section 335A see *Judd v Brown* [1998] 2 FLR 360 (spouse suffering from cancer, circumstances held exceptional); *Re Raval* [1998] 2 FLR 718 (mental illness of spouse, circumstances held exceptional); *Claughton v Charalambous* [1999] 1 FLR 740 (ill health and immobility with associated special housing needs of spouse with reduced life expectancy, circumstances held exceptional); *Re Bremmer* [1999] 1 FLR 912 (need of spouse to care for bankrupt with short life expectancy, circumstances held exceptional); *Barca v Mears* [2004] EWHC 2170 (Ch), [2005] 2 FLR 1 (child with special educational needs, circumstances held not exceptional); *Nicholls v Lan* [2006] EWHC 1255 (Ch), (2006) Times, 4 August (mental illness of spouse, circumstances held exceptional).

For the possible impact of the Human Rights Act 1998 on s 335A see *Barca v Mears* [2004] EWHC 2170 (Ch), [2005] 2 FLR 1 at [33]–[42]; *Donohoe v Ingram* [2006] 2 FLR 1004 at [19]–[22]; *Nicholls v Lan* [2006] EWHC 1255 (Ch), (2006) Times, 4 August [41]–[44].

Where the beneficial co-owners of land are a divorced husband and wife and a property adjustment order made by consent in matrimonial proceedings between them postpones a sale of the property until the happening of specified events which have not yet occurred, the court nevertheless has jurisdiction under TLATA, s 14 to order a sale on the application of the trustee in bankruptcy of the husband in circumstances other than those specified in the consent order. The interest taken by the wife under the consent order is not absolute, but is subject to the right of the husband to apply to the court for an order for sale under TLATA, s 14. If that right becomes exercisable by the husband's trustee in bankruptcy, the trustee's application for an order for sale is regulated by s 335A of the Insolvency Act 1986. Although TLATA, sub-ss 6(6) and (7) impose restrictions on the exercise by trustees of land of their functions, an order for sale under TLATA, s 14 is equivalent to a direction to both co-owners to concur in a sale and may override those restrictions: *Avis v Turner* [2007] 4 All ER 1103, [2008] Ch 218, [2007] EWCA Civ 748.

As to the correct approach to the exercise of the court's discretion where the circumstances are exceptional, see *Grant v Baker* [2016] EWHC 1782 (Ch), [2017] 2 FLR 646 (adult daughter of co-owners with special needs, indefinite deferral of sale refused; deferral for 12 months granted); *Pickard v Constable* [2017] EWHC 2475 (Ch) (disabled co-owner, indefinite deferral of sale refused; deferral for 12 months granted, with permission to apply for further deferral).

III REA [36A.2]

Property transfer order The parties to a property transfer order made in ancillary relief proceedings give consideration for the purposes of the Insolvency Act 1986, s 339 (transactions at an undervalue): *Haines v Hill* [2007] EWHC Civ 1284, [2008] 2 All ER 901, [2007] 3 FCR 785.

Exclusion of home from bankrupt's estate Section 283A of the Insolvency Act 1986, which is set out at **III INS [79]** and came into force on 1 April 2004, provides that the bankrupt's home will cease to form part of his estate at the end of three years from the date of the bankruptcy unless within that period the trustee realises that interest or applies for an order for possession or sale. The purpose of this provision is to prevent trustees allowing interests in the family home to remain dormant until they have increased in value: see *Grant v Baker* [2016] EWHC 1782 (Ch), [2017] 2 FLR 646 at [22].

LAW OF PROPERTY (MISCELLANEOUS PROVISIONS) ACT 1989

(c 34)

GENERAL NOTES ON LAW OF PROPERTY (MISCELLANEOUS PROVISIONS) ACT 1989

III REA [37]

Section 1 of this Act reformed the law relating to the formal requirements for deeds and their execution, and s 2 reformed the law relating to the formal requirements for contracts for the sale or other disposition of interests in land. These sections are printed below.

III REA [37A]

1. Deeds and their execution

(1) Any rule of law which—

(a) restricts the substances on which a deed may be written;

(b) requires a seal for the valid execution of an instrument as a deed by an individual; or

(c) requires authority by one person to another to deliver an instrument as a deed on his behalf to be given by deed,

is abolished.

(2) An instrument shall not be a deed unless—

(a) it makes it clear on its face that it is intended to be a deed by the person making it or, as the case may be, by the parties to it (whether by describing itself as a deed or expressing itself to be executed or signed as a deed or otherwise); and

(b) it is validly executed as a deed—

(i) by that person or a person authorised to execute it in the name or on behalf of that person, or

(ii) by one or more of those parties or a person authorised to execute it in the name or on behalf of one or more of those parties.

(2A) For the purposes of subsection (2)(a) above, an instrument shall not be taken to make it clear on its face that it is intended to be a deed merely because it is executed under seal.

(3) An instrument is validly executed as a deed by an individual if, and only if—

(a) it is signed—

(i) by him in the presence of a witness who attests the signature; or

(ii) at his direction and in his presence and the presence of two witnesses who each attest the signature; and

(b) it is delivered as a deed < . . . >.

(4) In subsections (2) and (3) above "sign", in relation to an instrument, includes—

(a) an individual signing the name of the person or party on whose behalf he executes the instrument; and

(b) making one's mark on the instrument,

and "signature" is to be construed accordingly.

(4A) Subsection (3) above applies in the case of an instrument executed by an individual in the name or on behalf of another person whether or not that person is also an individual.

(5) Where a relevant lawyer, or an agent or employee of a relevant lawyer, in the course of or in connection with a transaction . . . , purports to deliver an instrument as a deed on behalf of a party to the instrument, it shall be conclusively presumed in favour of a purchaser that he is authorised so to deliver the instrument.

(6) In subsection (5) above—

"purchaser" has the same meaning as in the Law of Property Act 1925;

"relevant lawyer" means a person who, for the purposes of the Legal Services Act 2007, is an authorised person in relation to an activity which constitutes a reserved instrument activity (within the meaning of that Act);

< . . . >

(7) Where an instrument under seal that constitutes a deed is required for the purposes of an Act passed before this section comes into force, this section shall have effect as to signing, sealing or delivery of an instrument by an individual in place of any provision of that Act as to signing, sealing or delivery.

(8) . . .

(9) Nothing in subsection (1)(b), (2), (3), (7) or (8) above applies in relation to deeds required or authorised to be made under—

- (a) the seal of the county palatine of Lancaster;
- (b) the seal of the Duchy of Lancaster; or
- (c) the seal of the Duchy of Cornwall.

(10) The references in this section to the execution of a deed by an individual do not include execution by a corporation sole and the reference in subsection (7) above to signing, sealing or delivery by an individual does not include signing, sealing or delivery by such a corporation.

(11) Nothing in this section applies in relation to instruments delivered as deeds before this section comes into force.

III REA [37A.1]

Commencement This section came into force on 31 July 1990 and was amended with effect from 15 September 2005 by the Regulatory Reform (Execution of Deeds and Documents Order 2005, SI 2005/1906.

III REA [37A.2]

Estoppel A party to a deed may be estopped from relying on non-compliance with the requirement in s 1(3)(a) that an attesting witness sign in the presence of a signatory to a deed: *Shah v Shah* [2001] EWCA Civ 527, [2002] QB 35, [2001] 4 All ER 138.

III REA [37A.3]

Signing while the deed is still in draft A document is not validly executed as a deed if it consists of a page containing the signature and attestation taken from an earlier version of the document combined with revised pages taken from a later version of the document: *R (on the application of Mercury Tax Group Ltd) v Revenue and Customs Comrs* [2008] EWHC 2721 (Admin), [2009] STC 743.

III REA [38]

2. Contracts for sale etc of land to be made by signed writing

(1) A contract for the sale or other disposition of an interest in land can only be made in writing and only by incorporating all the terms which the parties have expressly agreed in one document or, where contracts are exchanged, in each.

(2) The terms may be incorporated in a document either by being set out in it or by reference to some other document.

(3) The document incorporating the terms or, where contracts are exchanged, one of the documents incorporating them (but not necessarily the same one) must be signed by or on behalf of each party to the contract.

(4) Where a contract for the sale or other disposition of an interest in land satisfies the conditions of this section by reason only of the rectification of one or more documents in pursuance of an order of a court, the contract shall come into being, or be deemed to have come into being, at such time as may be specified in the order.

(5) This section does not apply in relation to—

- (a) a contract to grant such a lease as is mentioned in section 54(2) of the Law Property Act 1925 (short leases);
- (b) a contract made in the course of a public auction; or

(c) a contract regulated under the Financial Services and Markets Act 2000, other than a regulated mortgage contract, a regulated home reversion plan or a regulated home purchase plan;

and nothing in this section affects the creation or operation of resulting, implied or constructive trusts.

(6) In this section—

"disposition" has the same meaning as in the Law of Property Act 1925;

"interest in land" means any estate, interest or charge in or over land . . .

"regulated mortgage contract", "regulated home reversion plan" and "regulated home purchase plan" must be read with—

(a) section 22 of the Financial Services and Markets Act 2000,

(b) any relevant order under that section, and

(c) Schedule 22 to that Act.

(7) Nothing in this section shall apply in relation to contracts made before this section comes into force.

(8) [. . .]

III REA [38.1]

Scope of section Section 2 was intended to simplify the law relating to the formal requirements for contracts for the sale or other disposition of interests in land. For a summary of the differences between this section and the former law, see *Firstpost Homes Ltd v Johnson* [1995] 1 WLR 1567, [1995] 4 All ER 000, CA.

Section 2 is concerned with contracts for the creation or sale of legal estates or interests in land, not with documents which actually create or transfer such estates or interests. So a contract to transfer a freehold or a lease in the future, a contract to grant a lease in the future, or a contract for a mortgage in the future, are all within the reach of the section, provided of course the ultimate subject matter is land. However, an actual transfer, conveyance or assignment, an actual lease, or an actual mortgage are not within the scope of s 2 at all: *Helden v Strathmore Ltd* [2011] EWCA Civ 542 at [27]. Thus, where, as part of a family arrangement, A agreed to pay a sum of money to B in consideration of B executing a declaration of land, the agreement between A and B was not required to comply with s 2: *Rollerteam Ltd v Riley* [2016] EWCA Civ 1291. The formal requirements for actual dispositions of interests in land are contained in the Law of Property Act 1925, ss 51 to 55.

Section 2 applies to a contract to grant an option, but not to the exercise of an option granted by a contract complying with the section: *Spiro v Glencrown Properties Ltd* [1991] Ch 537, [1991] 1 All ER 600, Ch D.

A consequence of s 2 is that it is not possible to create an equitable charge of an interest in land by an informal deposit of title deeds, such a charge may only be created in accordance with s 2: *United Bank of Kuwait plc v Sahib* [1997] Ch 107, [1996] 3 All ER 215, CA.

A contract which fails to comply with this section may be severable, with the result that the parts of it which do not purport to effect a sale or other disposition of an interest in land are enforceable: *Jelson Ltd v Derby County Council* [1999] 3 EGLR 91, QBD.

An agreement which is unenforceable for non-compliance with this section may give rise to an enforceable constructive trust: *Yaxley v Gotts* [2000] Ch 162, [2000] 1 All ER 711, CA; *David Kinane v Alimamy Mackie-Conteh* [2005] EWCA Civ 45, [2005] P & CR 09 (agreement to grant charge); *Dowding v Matchmove Ltd* [2016] EWCA Civ 1233, [2017] 1 WLR 749 (oral agreement for sale of land on which purchasers acted to their detriment). See also *Kilkarne Holdings Ltd v Targetfellow (Birmingham) Ltd* [2005] EWCA Civ 1355, [2005] All ER (D) 203 (Nov) (agreement to finance lease; claim for constructive trust failed).

Proprietary estoppel cannot be prayed in aid to render enforceable an agreement that is unenforceable for non-compliance with s 2(1): *Yeoman's Row Management Ltd v Cobbe* [2008] UKHL 55, [2008] 4 All ER 713, [2008] 1 WLR 1752 at [29].

Where an issue arises as to whether a written contract fails to comply with s 2 for failure to include a matter on which the parties agreed, it is unhelpful to ask whether that matter was the subject of a collateral contract. The correct approach is to ask: (a) upon what terms did the parties agree that the interest in land was to be sold; and (b) are all those terms incorporated in the document which the parties have signed: *Grossman v Hooper* [2001] EWCA Civ 615, [2001] 3 FCR 662.

Nothing in s 2 of the 1989 Act is designed to prevent parties to a composite transaction which includes a land contract from structuring their bargain so that the land contract is genuinely separated from the rest of the transaction in the sense that its performance is not made conditional upon the performance of some other expressly agreed part of the bargain.

By contrast, the parties to a composite transaction are not free to separate into a separate document expressly agreed terms, if upon the true construction of the whole of the agreement, performance of the land sale is conditional upon performance of such terms. Since the splitting into separate contracts of parts of a composite transaction is inherently likely to give rise to uncertainties as to whether performance of the one is conditional upon performance of the other, the parties are free to make plain by express terms whether or not that conditionality exists. An 'entire agreement' clause may serve the valuable purpose (in a composite transaction which includes, but does not entirely consist of, a land contract) of ensuring that the land contract will not accidentally be construed as conditional upon the other expressly agreed terms, so as to render the land contract void under s 2: *North Eastern Properties Ltd v Coleman* [2010] EWCA Civ 277, [2010] 3 All ER 528, [2010] 2 All ER (Comm) 494.

Where an agreement is void for non-compliance with s 2(1), the property in a deposit paid pursuant to the transaction by the purchaser to the vendor may nevertheless pass to the vendor. In such a case, if the payment is intended to be conditional upon completion of the transaction the vendor will obtain only a conditional title to the money and will be bound to return it if the transaction fails, but if the payment is intended to be unconditional the vendor is prima facie entitled to retain it. The passing of the property does not exclude the possibility of a claim for restitution on a recognised ground such as failure of consideration: *Sharma v Simposh Ltd* [2011] EWCA Civ 1383, [2013] Ch 23, [2012] 2 All ER (Comm) 288.

Where a contract for the sale of land is void for non-compliance with s 2(1), practical completion of the land elements of the purported contract does not cause its other terms to become enforceable: *Keay v Morris Homes (West Midlands) Ltd* [2012] EWCA Civ 900, [2012] 1 WLR 2855, [2012] 2 P & CR 363.

An agreement for the making of mutual wills disposing of land was a contract for the disposition of an interest in land within s 2, and was accordingly of no legal effect as a contract, as s 2 had not been complied with. However equity would intervene by the imposition of a constructive trust requiring the recipient of property which had been disposed of inconsistently with the agreement to give effect to it: *Healey v Brown* [2002] WTLR 849, (2002) 19 EG 147 (CS). The necessary equitable obligation to bind the conscience of the surviving testator and so call into existence the constructive trust of mutual wills can also arise from proprietary estoppel: *Legg v Burton* [2017] EWHC 2088 (Ch), [2017] 4 WLR 186.

An agreement between A and B whereby A agreed to sell his property at the best price reasonably obtainable and to discharge his indebtedness to B out of the proceeds of sale did not fall within s 2: *Newze v Nwoko* [2004] EWCA Civ 379, [2004] 17 LS Gaz R 30.

Section 2 does not apply to a boundary agreement whereby the parties agree on the demarcation of a boundary the position of which was unclear, even if one or both of the parties thereby consciously gives up areas of land which, in aggregate, are trivial: *Joyce v Rigolli* [2004] EWCA Civ 79, (2004) 148 Sol Jo LB 234; *Yeates v Line* [2012] EWHC 3085 (Ch), [2013] Ch 363, [2013] 2 All ER 84.

A compromise of litigation relating to land made conformably with CPR Part 36 will not fail to be enforceable for non-compliance with s 2: *Orrton v Collins* [2007] EWHC 803 (Ch), [2007] 3 All ER 863, [2007] 1 WLR 2953.

An agent may be orally authorised to sign a contract falling within s 2, notwithstanding that the Law of Property Act 1925, s 53(1)(a) provides that an agent must be authorised in writing to sign an instrument creating or disposing of an interest in land: *McLaughlin v Duffill* [2010] EWCA Civ 1627, [2009] 3 WLR 1139, [2009] 34 EG 80.

The Companies Act 2006, s 44 provides, by sub-s (2), that a document is validly executed by a company if it is signed on behalf of the company by two authorised signatories or by a director of the company in the presence of a witness who attests the signature, and, by sub-s (4), that a document signed in accordance with sub-s (2) and expressed, in whatever words, to be executed by the company has the same effect as if executed under the common seal of the company. A document may be validly executed in accordance with these provisions even if the relevant signatories are not expressed to be signing on behalf of the company, provided that it is clear on the construction of the document that they are signing in that capacity: *Redcard Ltd v Williams* [2011] EWCA Civ 466, [2011] 4 All ER 444.

The section applies to contracts for the disposal of land in the future; it does not apply to the disposal contract itself: *Rollerteam Ltd v Riley* (2017) Times, 2 February, CA.

III REA [38.2]

Precedents For precedents raising issues under s 2 of the Act see **BCCP P[1107]–BCCP P[1110]**.

ACCESS TO NEIGHBOURING LAND ACT 1992

(c 23)

GENERAL NOTES ON ACCESS TO NEIGHBOURING LAND ACT 1992

III REA [39]

This Act, which came into force on 31 January 1993, enables a person to obtain on application to the county court a right of access for the purpose of carrying out certain types of work, and on certain terms ('the access order'). The order will be made where the court is satisfied that the works are reasonably necessary for the preservation of any land ('the dominant land'), except where the making of the order would constitute an unreasonable interference with or disturbance of the rights of the owner or occupier of the land to which access is to be given ('the servient land'). Any access order is to be on terms as to the manner in which the works are to be carried out, and as to the payment of compensation for loss, damage or injury and disturbance. Only in the case of access for work to non-residential land is compensation referable to the financial advantage to the applicant to be paid to the owner of the servient land (s 2(4) and (5) see para **III REA [44]**). An access order is binding upon successors in title and is registrable under s 6(1) of the Land Charges Act 1972 and by a notice under Part 4 of the Land Registration Act 2002. It is not possible to contract out of the application of this Act (s 4(4) see para **III REA [46]**).

III REA [40]

Jurisdiction Section 7 of the Act allocates jurisdiction to both the High Court and to the county court but the High Court and County Courts Jurisdiction Order 1991, SI 1991/724, art 6A provides that all such applications under this Act are to be commenced in the county court (see para **II HCJ [5]**).

III REA [41]

Procedure Proceedings under the Act are governed by CPR PD 56 para 11 (see para **CPR PD 56**).

III REA [42]

Precedents For precedents for proceedings under the Act see **BCCP P[1]–BCCP P[56]**.

III REA [43]

1. Access orders

(1) A person

(a) who, for the purpose of carrying out works to any land (the "dominant land"), desires to enter upon any adjoining or adjacent land (the "servient land"), and

(b) who needs, but does not have, the consent of some other person to that entry,

may make an application to the court for an order under this section (an "access order") against that other person.

(2) On an application under this section, the court shall make an access order if, and only if, it is satisfied—

(a) that the works are reasonably necessary for the preservation of the whole or any part of the dominant land; and

(b) that they cannot be carried out, or would be substantially more difficult to carry out, without the entry upon the servient land;

but this subsection is subject to subsection (3) below.

(3) The court shall not make an access order in any case where it is satisfied that, were it to make such an order—

(a) the respondent or any other person would suffer interference with, or disturbance of, his use or enjoyment of the servient land or,

(b) the respondent, or any other person (whether of full age or capacity or not) in occupation of the whole or any part of the servient land, would suffer hardship,

to such a degree by reason of the entry (notwithstanding any requirement of this Act or term or condition that may be imposed under it) that it would be unreasonable to make the order.

(4) Where the court is satisfied on an application under this section that it is reasonably necessary to carry out any basic preservation works to the dominant land, those works shall be taken for the purposes of this Act to be reasonably necessary for the preservation of the land; and in this subsection "basic preservation works" means any of the following; that is to say—

(a) the maintenance, repair or renewal of any part of a building or other structure comprised in, or situate on, the dominant land;

(b) the clearance, repair or renewal of any drain, sewer, pipe or cable so comprised or situate;

(c) the treatment, cutting back, felling, removal or replacement of any hedge, tree, shrub or other growing thing which is so comprised and which is, or is in danger of becoming, damaged, diseased, dangerous, insecurely rooted or dead;

(d) the filling in, or clearance, of any ditch so comprised;

but this subsection is without prejudice to the generality of the works which may, apart from it, be regarded by the court as reasonably necessary for the preservation of any land.

(5) If the court considers it fair and reasonable in all the circumstances of the case, works may be regarded for the purposes of this Act as being reasonably necessary for the preservation of any land (or, for the purposes of subsection (4) above, as being basic preservation works which it is reasonably necessary to carry out to any land) notwithstanding that the works incidentally involve—

(a) and making of some alteration, adjustment or improvement to the land,

or

(b) the demolition of the whole or any part of a building or structure comprised in or situate upon the land.

(6) Where any works are reasonably necessary for the preservation of the whole or any part of the dominant land, the doing to the dominant land of anything which is requisite for, incidental to, or consequential on, the carrying out of those works shall be treated for the purpose of this Act as the carrying out of works

which are reasonably necessary for the preservation of that land; and references in this Act to works, or to the carrying out of such works, shall be construed accordingly.

(7) Without prejudice to the generality of the subsection (6) above, if it is reasonably necessary for a person to inspect the dominant land—

(a) for the purpose of ascertaining whether any works may be reasonably necessary for the preservation of the whole or any part of that land,

(b) for the purpose of making any map or plan, or ascertaining the course of any drain, sewer, pipe or cable, in preparation for, or otherwise in connection with, the carrying out of works which are so reasonably necessary, or

(c) otherwise in connection with the carrying out of any such works,

the making of such an inspection shall be taken for the purposes of this Act to be the carrying out to the dominant land of works which are reasonably necessary for the preservation of that land; and references in that Act to works, or to the carrying out of works, shall be construed accordingly.

III REA [43.1]

Access order This section sets out the basic criteria for the making of an order under the Act. The applicant must establish that (1) he wishes to carry out work to land (the dominant land), (2) that to do so he needs, but does not have, the consent of some other person, (3) that the works are reasonably necessary for the preservation of the whole, or part of the dominant land, and (4) cannot be carried out, or would be substantially more difficult without entry to adjoining or adjacent load (the servient land).

III REA [43.2]

Adjacent or adjoining land A distinction is drawn between "adjacent" and "adjoining". The latter in common usage means "physically contiguous", the former has been held to be a word including places "close or near to", one another. The degree of proximity is entirely a question of the circumstances in each case, see *Wellington Corpn v Lower Hutt Corpn* [1904] AC 773 at 775, 776, PC.

III REA [43.3]

Land Save for the reference in s 8(3) (see para **III REA [49]**) excluding a highway there is no general definition of "land" and accordingly that to be found in Schedule 1 to the Interpretation Act 1978 applies. It includes buildings and other structures, which in law form part of the land, including land covered with water, and any estate, interest, easement, or right over land. The Act does not extend to Crown lands as it is not stated expressly so to do. This definition includes a party wall: see *Dean v Walker* (1996) 73 P & CR 366, CA.

III REA [43.4]

Reasonably necessary for the preservation of the dominant land An access order will only be made in a case where the works are reasonably necessary for the purpose of preservation of the land (or incidental to such purpose). Development or alteration merely for the sake of improving the dominant land does not fall within this category, yet demolition, improvement, alteration or adjustment incidental to works of preservation will (s 1(6)). Basic preservation works are reasonably necessary for the preservation of the land. Demolition, followed by reconstruction after such demolition, may be treated as "basic preservation works", but only if falling within the wider ambit of "preservation works": see s 1(4).

III REA [43.5]

Cannot be carried out or substantially more difficult The applicant is obliged to show that it is not possible to do the works or that the works would be substantially more difficult. "Substantial" has been construed to mean "considerable" (*Granada Theatres v Freehold Investments (Leytonstone)* [1958] 2 All ER 551, [1958] 1 WLR 845), and "substantially" has been found to mean neither trivial or total: *R v Lloyd* [1967] 1 QB 175, CCA. See *Atkinson v Bettison* [1955] 3 All ER 340, [1955] 1 WLR 1127, CA and *Bewlay (Tobacconists) Ltd v British Bata Shoe Co Ltd* [1958] 3 All ER 652, [1959] 1 WLR 45, CA.

III REA [43.6]

Respondents to the application The respondents to the application are the owner and the occupier of the servient land: CPR Sch 2 CCR Ord 49 r 1(4) (see para **CCR 49r1**). Other parties may be joined if it is desired or necessary. The scheme of the Act is to confer immunity against suit in trespass, by treating entry pursuant to an access order as being with the consent of the requisite owner (see s 3 at para **III REA [45]**) or the appropriate interest. There may be more than one such person, and only persons party to the access order are bound by it.

III REA [43.7]

Applicant It is not necessary that the applicant for the order be the owner of an interest in the land.

III REA [43.8]

Inconvenience or hardship to servient occupier The ability to obtain an order is subject to the proviso in s 1(3) that an access order shall not be made where the occupier of the servient land would suffer inconvenience, or other hardship, to such a degree as to make it unreasonable to make the order. In considering whether this proviso applies, the court is not limited to considering the effects of the works during the period that they are being carried out but may also consider the effects of the work for the servient owner after the works have been completed: *BPT Ltd v Patterson*, Central London County Court, 29 July 2016.

III REA [43.9]

Subsection (7) This subsection confers upon the court a power to permit access for the purpose of examining whether any works are reasonably necessary, for the purpose of map making in relation to drains, sewers etc, and generally. This is in addition to the power to obtain an order for the inspection of property which may be the subject matter of a claim. See CPR 25.1 at para **CPR 25.1**.

III REA [44]

2. Terms and conditions of access orders

(1) An access order shall specify—

- (a) the works to the dominant land that may be carried out by entering upon the servient land in pursuance of the order;
- (b) the particular area of the servient land that may be entered upon by virtue of the order for the purpose of carrying out those works to the dominant land; and
- (c) the date upon which, or the period during which, the land may be so entered upon;

and in the following provisions of this Act any reference to the servient land is a reference to the area specified in the order in pursuance of paragraph (b) above.

(2) An access order may impose upon the applicant or the respondent such terms and conditions as appear to the court to be reasonably necessary for the purpose of avoiding or restricting—

- (a) any loss, damage or injury which might otherwise be caused to the respondent or any other person by reason of the entry authorised by the order; or
- (b) any inconvenience or loss of privacy that might otherwise be so caused to the respondent or any other person.

(3) Without prejudice to the generality of subsection (2) above, the terms and conditions which may be imposed under that subsection include provisions with respect to—

- (a) the manner in which the specified works are to be carried out;
- (b) the days on which, and the hours between which, the works involved may be executed;
- (c) the person who may undertake the carrying out of the specified works or enter upon the servient land under or by virtue of the order;
- (d) the taking of any such precautions by the applicant as may be specified in the order.

(4) An access order may also impose terms and conditions—

- (a) requiring the applicant to pay, or to secure that such person connected with him as may be specified in the order pays, compensation for—
  - (i) any loss, damage or injury, or

(ii) any substantial loss of privacy or other substantial inconvenience, which will, or might, be caused to the respondent or any other person by reason of the entry authorised by the order;

(b) requiring the applicant to secure that he, or such person connected with him as may be specified in the order, is insured against any such risks as may be so specified; or

(c) requiring such a record to be made of the condition of the servient land, or of such part of it as may be so specified, as the court may consider expedient with a view to facilitating the determination of any question that may arise concerning damage to that land.

(5) An access order may include provision requiring the applicant to pay the respondent such sum by way of consideration for the privilege of entering the servient land in pursuance of the order as appears to the court to be fair and reasonable having regard to all the circumstances of the case, including, in particular—

(a) the likely financial advantage of the order to the applicant and any persons connected with him; and

(b) the degree of inconvenience likely to be caused to the respondent or any other person by the entry;

but no payment shall be ordered under this subsection if and to the extent that the works which the applicant desires to carry out by means of the entry are works to residential land.

(6) For the purposes of subsection (5) (a) above, the likely financial advantage of an access order to the applicant and any persons connected with him shall in all cases be taken to be a sum of money equal to the greater of the following amounts, that is to say—

(a) the amount (if any) by which so much of any likely increase in the value of the land—

(i) which consists of or includes the dominant land, and

(ii) which is owned or occupied by the same person as the dominant land,

as may reasonably be regarded as attributable to the carrying out of the specified works exceeds the likely cost of carrying out those works with the benefit of the access order; and

(b) the difference (if it would have been possible to carry out the specified works without entering upon the servient land) between—

(i) the likely cost of carrying out those works without entering upon the servient land; and

(ii) the likely cost of carrying them out with the benefit of the access order.

(7) For the purposes of subsection (5) above, "residential land" means so much of any land as consists of—

(a) a dwelling or part of a dwelling;

(b) a garden, yard, private garage or outbuilding which is used and enjoyed wholly or mainly with a dwelling; or

(c) in the case of a building which includes one or more dwellings, any part of the building which is used and enjoyed wholly or mainly with those dwellings or any of them.

(8) The persons who are to be regarded for the purposes of this section as "connected with" the applicant are—

(a) the owner of any estate or interest in, or right over, the whole or any part of the dominant land;

(b) the occupier of the whole or any part of the dominant land; and

(c) any person whom the applicant may authorise under section 3 (7) below to exercise the power of entry conferred by the access order.

(9) The court may make provision—

(a) for the reimbursement by the applicant of any expenses reasonably incurred by the respondent in connection with the application which are not otherwise recoverable as costs;

(b) for the giving of security by the applicant for any sum that might become payable to the respondent or any other person by virtue of this section or section 3 below.

III REA [44.1]

Terms of access order The order must specify the works to the dominant land that are to be carried out as a result of entering the servient land, the particular area of servient land that may be entered, and the date upon which or the period during which the servient land may be entered.

III REA [44.2]

Terms and conditions The court may impose a range of terms and conditions according to the relevant circumstances, including those relating to the manner of execution of works so as to avoid inconvenience, loss or damage (sub-s (2)); payment of compensation (sub-s (4)); the obtaining by the applicant, or his contractor, of insurance cover (sub-s (4)); making a record of the condition of the servient land (sub-s (4)); the provision of security for such compensation (sub-ss (4) and (9); the payment of consideration for access (in the case of non-residential dominant land) (sub-s (5)).

III REA [44.3]

Compensation Compensation may cover three elements: (a) compensation for loss, damage or injury; (b) compensation for loss of privacy, 'or other substantial inconvenience'; and (c) where the dominant land is not residential land, consideration for the likely financial advantage derived from the privilege of entering the servient land, and the disadvantage to the occupier of that land (sub-s (5)). In order to establish the amount of compensation under sub-s (5) it will be necessary to satisfy the court that a financial advantage (as defined) is 'likely'. That has been construed to mean a 'reasonable prospect' (*Dunning v Board of Governors of the United Liverpool Hospitals* [1973] 2 All ER 454 at 460); 'it's on the cards', and 'it's more probable than not' (*R v Sheppard* [1981] AC 394, [1980] 3 All ER 899 at 904, HL per Lord Diplock).

III REA [44.4]

Subsection (7): garden A garden is 'a substantially homogenous area, substantially devoted to the growth of fruits, flowers and vegetables": see *Bomford v Osborne* [1942] AC 14 at 40, [1941] 2 All ER 426 at 442, HL per Lord Wright.

III REA [44.5]

Wholly or mainly The word "mainly" probably means "more than half" (*Fawcett Properties Ltd v Buckingham County Council* [1961] AC 636 at 669, [1960] 3 All ER 503 at 512, HL per Lord Morton of Henryton). See also *Re Hatschek's Patents, ex p Zerenner* [1909] 2 Ch 68; *Miller v Ottilie (Owners)* [1944] KB 188, [1944] 1 All ER 277, CA; *Franklin v Gramophone Co Ltd* [1948] 1 KB 542 at 555, [1948] 1 All ER 353 at 358, CA.

III REA [44.6]

Subsection (8): Occupier "Occupier" includes a person who has a licence entitling him to possession (*Stevens v London Borough of Bromley* [1972] Ch 400, [1972] 1 All ER 712, CA), and a statutory tenant (*Brown v Ministry of Housing and Local Government* [1953] 2 All ER 1385, [1953] 1 WLR 1370), but probably not a person whose entry on the premises was unlawful and forcible (*Woodcock v South Western Electricity Board* [1975] 2 All ER 545, [1975] 1 WLR 983).

III REA [44.7]

Security The Act does not specify when or how such a security is to be given.

III REA [45]

3. Effect of access order

(1) An access order requires the respondent, so far as he has power to do so, to permit the applicant or any of his associates to do anything which the applicant or associate is authorised or required to do under or by virtue of the order or this section.

(2) Except as otherwise provided by or under this Act, an access order authorises the applicant or any of his associates, without the consent of the respondent—

- (a) to enter upon the servient land for the purpose of carrying out the specified works;
- (b) to bring onto that land, leave there during the period permitted by the order and, before the end of that period, remove, such materials, plant and equipment as are reasonably necessary for the carrying out of those works; and
- (c) to bring on to that land any waste arising from the carrying out of those works, if it is reasonably necessary to do so in the course of removing it from the dominant land;

but nothing in this Act or in any access order shall authorise the applicant or any of his associates to leave anything in, on or over the servient land (other than in the discharge of their duty to make good that land) after their entry for the purpose of carrying out works to the dominant land ceases to be authorised under or by virtue of the order.

(3) An access order requires the applicant—

- (a) to secure that any waste arising from the carrying out of the specified works is removed from the servient land forthwith;
- (b) to secure that, before the entry ceases to be authorised under or by virtue of the order, the servient land is, so far as reasonably practicable, made good; and
- (c) to indemnify the respondent against any damage which may be caused to the servient land or any goods by the applicant or any of his associates which would not have been so caused had the order not been made;

but this subsection is subject to subsections (4) and (5) below.

(4) In making an access order, the court may vary or exclude, in whole or in part,—

- (a) any authorisation that would otherwise be conferred by subsection (2)(b) or (c) above; or
- (b) any requirement that would otherwise be imposed by subsection (3) above.

(5) Without prejudice to the generality of subsection (4) above, if the court is satisfied that it is reasonably necessary for any such waste as may arise from the carrying out of the specified works to be left on the servient land for some period before removal, the access order may, in place of subsection (3)(a) above, include provision—

- (a) authorising the waste to be left on that land for such period as may be permitted by the order; and
- (b) requiring the applicant to secure that waste is removed before the end of that period.

(6) Where the applicant or any of his associates is authorised or required under or by virtue of an access order or this section to enter, or do any other thing, upon the servient land, he shall not (as respects that access order) be taken to be a trespasser from the beginning on account of his, or any other person's, subsequent conduct.

(7) For the purposes of this section, the applicant's "associates" are such number of persons (whether or not servants or agents of his) whom he may reasonably authorise under this subsection to exercise the power of entry conferred by the access order as may be reasonably necessary for carrying out the specified works.

III REA [45.1]

General note The complex manner in which the provisions of this section interact emphasises the need for care in drafting both the original application and the reply. Subsection (2) sets out the limits of what the applicant may be authorised to do, and sub-s (3) defines the requirements that may be imposed upon him. In making the order, the court can (by sub-s (4)) vary or exclude all of those provisions except the right of entry conferred on the applicant by sub-s (2)(a). The proviso to sub-s (2) which prohibits the applicant from leaving anything in, on or over the servient land except for the purpose of making good the land is itself partly negated by sub-s (5), which gives the court power, in certain circumstances, to authorise the applicant to leave waste on the land for the period specified in the order.

III REA [46]

4. Persons bound by access order, unidentified persons and bar on contracting out

(1) In addition to the respondent, an access order shall, subject to the provisions of the Land Charges Act 1972 and the Land Registration Act 2002, be binding on—

(a) any of his successors in title to the servient land; and

(b) any person who has an estate or interest in, or right over, the whole or any part of the servient land which was created after the making of the order and who derives his title to that estate, interest or right under the respondent;

and references to the respondent shall be construed accordingly.

(2) If and to the extent that the court considers it just and equitable to allow him to do so, a person on whom an access order becomes binding by virtue of subsection (1)(a) or (b) above shall be entitled, as respects anything falling to be done after the order becomes binding on him, to enforce the order or any of its terms or conditions as if he were the respondent, and references to the respondent shall be construed accordingly.

(3) Rules of court may—

(a) provide a procedure which may be followed where the applicant does not know, and cannot reasonably ascertain, the name of any person whom he desires to make respondent to the application; and

(b) make provision enabling such an applicant to make such a person respondent by description instead of by name;

and in this subsection "applicant" includes a person who proposes to make an application for an access order.

(4) Any agreement, whenever made, shall be void if and to the extent that it would, apart from this subsection, prevent a person from applying for an access order or restrict his right to do so.

III REA [46.1]

General note If an access order is registered under the Land Charges Act 1972 (in the case of unregistered land) or under the Land Registration Act 2002 (in the case of registered land) it is binding on a successor in title to, and a person deriving title under, the person against whom it is made. For registration under the Land Charges Act 1972 see para **III REA [30]**. Under the Land Registration Act 2002, an access order must be registered by an agreed notice: see the Land Registration Rules 2003, SI 2003/1417, r 80. Subsection (2) above gives the court power to permit a successor in title to, and a person deriving title under, the person against whom the order is made to enforce the order or any of its terms and conditions as respects anything falling to be done after the order becomes binding on him.

III REA [46.2]

Contracting out It is not possible to prevent a person from applying for an access order or restrict his right to do so.

III REA [47]

5. Registration of access orders and of application for such orders

(1)–(3) < . . . >

(4) In any case where—

(a) an access order is discharged under section 6(1)(a) below, and

(b) the order has been protected by an entry registered under the Land Charges Act 1972 or by a notice under the Land Registration Act 2002,

the court may by order direct that the entry or notice shall be cancelled.

(5) The rights conferred on a person by or under an access order shall not be capable of falling within paragraph 2 of Schedule 1 or 3 to the Land Registration Act 2002 (overriding status of interest of person in actual occupation).

(6) An application for an access order shall be regarded as a pending land action for the purposes of the Land Charges Act 1972 and the Land Registration Act 2002.

III REA [47.1]

Registration of access orders and applications For registration under the Land Charges Act 1972 see para **III REA [30]**, and for registration under the Land Registration Act 1925 see para **III REA [46.1]**.

III REA [48]

6. Variation of orders and damages for breach

(1) Where an access order or an order under this subsection has been made, the court may, on the application of any party to the proceedings in which the order was made or of any other person on whom the order is binding—

(a) discharge or vary the order or any of its terms or conditions;

(b) suspend any of its terms of conditions; or

(c) revive any term or condition suspended under paragraph (b) above;

and in the application of subsections (1) and (2) of section 4 above in relation to an access order, any order under this subsection which relates to the access order shall be treated for the purposes of those subsections as included in the access order.

(2) If any person contravenes or fails to comply with any requirement, term or condition imposed upon him by or under this Act, the court may, without prejudice to any other remedy available, make an order for the payment of damages by him to any other person affected by the contravention or failure who makes an application for relief under this subsection.

III REA [48A]

7. Jurisdiction over, and allocation of, proceedings

(1) The High Court and the county court shall both have jurisdiction under this Act.

(2) In article 4 of the High Court and County Courts Jurisdiction Order 1991 (which provides that proceedings in which the county courts and the High Court both have jurisdiction may, subject to articles 5 and 6, be commenced either in a county court or in the High Court) for the words "and 6" there shall be substituted the words ", 6 and 6A"; and after article 6 of that Order there shall be inserted—

"6A Applications under section 1 of the Access to Neighbouring Land Act 1992 shall be commenced in a county court."

(3) The amendment by subsection (2) above of provisions contained in an order shall not be taken to have prejudiced any power to make further orders revoking or amending those provisions.

III REA [48A.1]

Jurisdiction Article 6A of the High Court and County Courts Jurisdiction Order 1981, SI 1991/1724, which was inserted by s 7 of the Act, requires that an application under the Act must be commenced in the county court. Article 6A is set out at **II HCJ [6]**. However, both the High Court and the county court have jurisdiction, and so an application commenced in the county court could, if the facts warranted it, be transferred to the High Court.

III REA [49]

8. Interpretation and application

(1) Any reference in this Act to an "entry" upon any servient land includes a reference to the doing on that land of anything necessary for carrying out the works to the dominant land which are reasonably necessary for its preservation; and "enter" shall be construed accordingly.

(2) This Act applies in relation to any obstruction of, or other interference with, a right over, or interest in, any land as it applies in relation to an entry upon that land; and "enter" and "entry" shall be construed accordingly.

(3) In this Act—

"access order" has the meaning given by section 1 (1) above;

"applicant" means a person making an application for an access order and, subject to section 4 above, "the respondent" means the respondent, or any of the respondents, to such an application;

"the court" means the High Court or the county court;

"the dominant land" and "the servient land" respectively have the meanings given by section 1 (1) above, but subject, in the case of servient land, to section 2 (1) above;

"land" does not include a highway;

"the specified works" means the works specified in the access order in pursuance of section 2 (1)(a) above.

TRUSTS OF LAND AND APPOINTMENT OF TRUSTEES ACT 1996

(c 47)

GENERAL NOTES ON TRUSTS OF LAND AND APPOINTMENT OF TRUSTEES ACT 1996

III REA [50]

The Trusts of Land and Appointment of Trustees Act 1996 ('TLATA'), which came into force on 1 January 1997, was intended to remedy defects in the previous law relating to land held on trust. These defects included the existence of three parallel systems whereby land might be held in trust, namely under the Settled Land Act 1925, under trusts for sale and bare trusts, and the imposition of a duty on trustees for sale of land to sell the land even when it had been purchased with a view to being occupied by the beneficiaries of the trust.

With limited exceptions (see sub-s 1(3) of the Act), all land held on trust is now held on a trust of land. The powers and duties, collectively called functions, of the trustees of a trust of land are defined by ss 6 to 9A of the Act. Provisions relating to obtaining the consents of beneficiaries and consultation with beneficiaries are contained in ss 10 and 11.

III REA [50.1]

Minors A minor cannot hold a legal estate: Law of Property Act 1925, s 1(6). The purported grant of a legal estate to a minor operates as a declaration of trust thereof for him: TLATA, Sch 1 para 1(1). Consequently, a local authority which purportedly granted a legal tenancy to a minor constituted itself a trustee of the tenancy for the minor. A notice to quit given by the local authority to the minor was ineffective to terminate the tenancy, as it was the duty of the local authority as trustee to preserve, and not destroy, the subject-matter of the trust: *Hammersmith and Fulham London Borough Council v Alexander-David* [2009] EWCA (Civ) 259, [2009] 3 All ER 1098, [2009] 2 FLR 329.

III REA [51]

Occupation by beneficiaries Section 12 of the Act (para **III REA [56]**) confers a statutory right of occupation of land on a beneficiary who is beneficially entitled to an interest in possession of land subject to a trust of land at any time when (a) the purposes of the trust include making the land available for his occupation (or for the occupation of a class of beneficiaries of which he is a member or of beneficiaries in general) or the land is held by the trustees so as to be so available. Section 13 (para **III REA [57]**) gives the trustees (subject in some respects to a requirement to obtain the consent of any person in occupation or the approval of the court) powers to regulate the exercise of those rights.

III REA [52]

Powers of the court Section 13 gives the court a specific power to approve the exercise in certain respects of the trustees' powers to regulate the exercise of a beneficiary's statutory right of occupation. Section 14 (para **III REA [58]**) gives the court a wide power to make orders relating to the exercise by the trustees of their functions, and declaring the nature or extent of a person's interest in property subject to the trust. Section 15 of the Act specifies matters to which the court is to have regard in exercising its powers under ss 13 and 14.

III REA [52A]

Sale of land Many applications for orders under s 14 arise out of disputes as to whether or not land should be sold. Prior to the coming into force of TLATA disputes as to whether land held on trust for sale should be sold were resolved by applying criteria developed under s 30 of the Law of Property Act 1925. The matters to which the court is now to have regard include those stated in TLATA, s 15. Under s 30 of the Law of Property Act 1925, where a sale was sought at the instance of the trustee in bankruptcy of a beneficial co-owner of a property, the principle was that the interests of the bankrupt's creditors would prevail even if the property was the home of the bankrupt's spouse and a sale within a short period would be ordered save in exceptional; circumstances: *Re Citro* [1991] Ch 142, [1990] 3 All ER 952. The same principle applied where a sale was sought at the instance of a mortgagee or chargee of the interest of one of the beneficial co-owners: *Lloyds Bank plc v Byrne* [1993] 1 FLR 369. TLATA treats these situations differently. An application by a trustee in bankruptcy under TLATA, s 14 for an order for the sale of land is governed by s 335A of the Insolvency Act 1996 (see **III REA [36A]**), and the criteria in s 15 of the Trusts of Land and Appointment of Trustees Act 1996 do not apply to it: see s 15(4). An application under s 14 for an order for sale by a mortgagee or chargee of the beneficial interest of a co-owner is, however, governed by the criteria in s 15, which require a more flexible approach: *Mortgage Corporation v Shaire* [2001] Ch 743, [2001] 4 All ER 364. On such an application "nevertheless a powerful consideration is and ought to be whether the creditor is receiving proper recompense for being kept out of his money, repayment of which is overdue": *Bank of Ireland Home Mortgages Ltd v Bell* [2001] 2 All ER (Comm) 920, [2001] 2 FLR 809 at [31]. See too *Edwards v Lloyds TSB* [2004] EWHC 1745 (Ch), [2005] 1 FCR 139 at [30].

III REA [53]

Jurisdiction The county court has unlimited jurisdiction under TLATA, ss 13 and 14: High Court and County Courts Jurisdiction Order 1991 (SI 1991/724) art 2 (para **II HCJ [3]**).

III REA [54]

Procedure An application under TLATA, ss 13 or 14 should be commenced by claim form, in accordance with CPR Part 7 or 8 as appropriate.

III REA [55]

Precedents For precedents, see **BCCP Q[751]–BCCP Q[850]**.

III REA [56]

12. The right to occupy

(1) A beneficiary who is beneficially entitled to an interest in possession in land subject to a trust of land is entitled by reason of his interest to occupy the land at any time if at that time—

(a) the purposes of the trust include making the land available for his occupation (or for the occupation of beneficiaries of a class of which he is a member or of beneficiaries in general), or

(b) the land is held by the trustees so as to be so available.

(2) Subsection (1) does not confer on a beneficiary a right to occupy land if it is either unavailable or unsuitable for occupation by him.

(3) This section is subject to section 13.

III REA [57]

13. Exclusion and restriction of right to occupy

(1) Where two or more beneficiaries are (or apart from this subsection would be) entitled under section 12 to occupy land, the trustees of land may exclude or restrict the entitlement of any one or more (but not all) of them.

(2) Trustees may not under subsection (1)—

(a) unreasonably exclude any beneficiary's entitlement to occupy land, or

(b) restrict any such entitlement to an unreasonable extent.

(3) The trustees of land may from time to time impose reasonable conditions on any beneficiary in relation to his occupation of land by reason of his entitlement under section 12.

(4) The matters to which trustees are to have regard in exercising the powers conferred by this section include—

(a) the intentions of the person or persons (if any) who created the trust,

(b) the purposes for which the land is held, and

(c) the circumstances and wishes of each of the beneficiaries who is (or apart from any previous exercise by the trustees of those powers would be) entitled to occupy the land under section 12.

(5) The conditions which may be imposed on a beneficiary under subsection (3) include, in particular, conditions requiring him—

(a) to pay any outgoings or expenses in respect of the land, or

(b) to assume any other obligation in relation to the land or to any activity which is or is proposed to be conducted there.

(6) Where the entitlement of any beneficiary to occupy land under section 12 has been excluded or restricted, the conditions which may be imposed on any other beneficiary under subsection (3) include, in particular, conditions requiring him to—

(a) make payments by way of compensation to the beneficiary whose entitlement has been excluded or restricted, or

(b) forgo any payment or other benefit to which he would otherwise be entitled under the trust so as to benefit that beneficiary.

(7) The powers conferred on trustees by this section may not be exercised—

(a) so as prevent any person who is in occupation of land (whether or not by reason of an entitlement under section 12) from continuing to occupy the land, or

(b) in a manner likely to result in any such person ceasing to occupy the land,

unless he consents or the court has given approval.

(8) The matters to which the court is to have regard in determining whether to give approval under subsection (7) include the matters mentioned in subsection (4)(a) to (c).

III REA [57.1]

Payment to beneficiaries not in occupation The question of what payment should be made by a beneficiary of a trust of land who is in occupation of the land to a beneficiary who is out of occupation should now be approached by applying the principles in TLATA, ss 12 to 15 rather than the court's equitable jurisdiction, although the outcome should in most cases be the same: *Stack v Dowden* [2007] UKHL 17, [2007] 2 AC 432, [2007] 2 All ER 929 at [93]–[94]; *Murphy v Gooch* [2007] EWCA Civ 603, [2007] 2 FLR 934.

However, where a co-owner who is not in occupation is bankrupt, recourse should be had to the court's equitable jurisdiction: *Re Barcham (a bankrupt)* [2008] EWHC 1505 (Ch), [2008] 1 All ER 145; *Davis v Jackson* [2017] EWHC 698 (Ch), [2017] 1 WLR 4005 at [41] to [48].

"but not all" The words "but not all" in sub-s 13(1) do not prevent the powers in s 13 being exercised so as to restrict each beneficiary to the occupation of part of the property: *Rodway v Landy* [2001] EWCA Civ 471, [2001] Ch 703.

III REA [57.1A]

Conditions A condition requiring a beneficiary to contribute to the cost of works necessary to adapt a property so that beneficiaries may occupy separate parts of it is within the scope of s 13(3): *Rodway v Landy* [2001] EWCA Civ 471, [2001] Ch 703.

III REA [57.1B]

Occupiers who are not beneficiaries Where a beneficiary has permitted someone else to occupy, that person does not have the protection of sub-s (7), since sub-s (1) is not engaged: *Omotajo v Omotajo* [2008] All ER (D) 156 (Oct), Underhill J.

III REA [57.2]

Applications to the court Subsections 15(1) and (2) specify matters to which the court is to have regard in determining applications relating to the exercise of the powers by this section.

III REA [58]

14. Applications for order

(1) Any person who is a trustee of land or has an interest in a property subject to a trust of land may make an application to the court for an order under this section.

(2) On an application for an order under this section the court may make any such order—

(a) relating to the exercise by the trustees of any of their functions (including an order relieving them of any obligation to obtain the consent of, or to consult, any person in connection with the exercise of any of their functions), or

(b) declaring the nature or extent of a person's interest in property subject to the trust,

as the court thinks fit.

(3) The court may not under this section make any order as to the appointment or removal of trustees.

(4) The powers conferred on the court by this section are exercisable on an application whether it is made before or after the commencement of this Act.

III REA [58.1]

Functions of the trustees Where a periodic tenancy is vested in two or more co-owners on trust for themselves, the giving of a notice to quit by one or more of them is not an exercise of a power or duty vested in them as trustees. Accordingly it is not a "function" of trustees of land, in respect of which a duty to consult beneficiaries arises under s 11 or the Act, nor *semble* in respect of which the court can made orders under s 14(2)(a) of the Act: *Notting Hill Housing Trust v Brackley* [2000] EWCA Civ 601, [2001] 35 EG 106.

The object and effect of ss 14 and 15 is to confer on the court a substantially wider discretion, exercised on the basis of wider considerations, than might be enjoyed by the trustees themselves, acting without either the consent of their beneficiaries or an order of the court. In exercising its powers in circumstances where, necessarily, the beneficiaries will be in dispute with each other about what should be done with the trust property, the court is not rigidly constrained by those rules of equity which may, pursuant to sub-s 6(6), constrain the trustees themselves. In general, the use and disposal of land held on a trust of land will be determined by the unanimous consent and direction of the beneficiaries. The court's powers are there to enable the property to be dealt with justly and effectively when that basis of consent breaks down: *Bagum v Hafiz* [2015] EWCA Civ 801, [2016] Ch 241, [2015] All ER (D) 249 (Jul).

The court has no power under s 14 to order that one beneficiary under a trust of land sell his interest to another, since the sale of a beneficiary's interest is not a function of the trustees. However, the court may in appropriate circumstances order trustees of land to sell the land, giving one beneficiary a right of first refusal. Such an order may have the same economic effect as a sale by one beneficiary of his interest to another: *Bagum v Hafiz* [2015] EWCA Civ 801, [2016] Ch 241, [2015] All ER (D) 249 (Jul).

Where two persons own leases of land and acquire the freehold, the court has power to order them to grant a longer lease to one of them, since under the trust of the freehold they have all the powers of an absolute owner of land, which include a power to grant leases: *Parkes v Wilkes* [2017] EWHC 1556 (Ch), [2017] 4 WLR 123.

III REA [58.2]

Declaring the nature and extent of a person's interest The same principles for determining the nature of a person's interest under a trust of land apply irrespective of the nature of the land and the purpose for which it was acquired.

Section 53(1)(b) of the Law of Property Act 1925 provides that 'a declaration of trust respecting any land or any interest therein must be manifested and proved by some writing declared by some person who is able to declare such trust or by his will'.

A written declaration of trust is (unless set aside on grounds such as fraud or mistake) conclusive as to the beneficial interests of the parties to it at the time it was made: *Goodman v Gallant* [1986] 1 All ER 311, [1986] Fam 106; *Pankhania v Chandegra (by her litigation friend, Ronald Andrew Eagle)* [2012] EWCA Civ 1438, [2013] 1 P & CR 16.

A declaration by two proprietors of registered land that the survivor may give a receipt for capital money is not, without more, a declaration that they hold the property as beneficial joint tenants, see *Stack v Dowden* [2007] UKHL 17, [2007] 2 AC 432, [2007] 2 All ER 929 at [49].

Section 53(1) of the Law of Property Act 1925 'does not affect the creation or operation of resulting implied or constructive trusts' (sub-s 53(2).

A resulting trust may arise where the purchase price of property is contributed in whole or part by a person other than the legal owner. There is a presumption that the property is held by the legal owner on trust for the persons who contributed to the purchase price in proportions corresponding to their contributions. The presumption does not arise in some relationships (such as parent and child) where a presumption of advancement (ie that the payment was a gift) may arise. Both presumptions may be displaced by evidence of the parties' actual intentions. The presumption of advancement as between husband and wife is abolished by the Equality Act 2010, s 199, from a date to be appointed.

A constructive trust may arise where it would be unconscionable for the legal owner of the property to deny the existence of another's beneficial interest in it

Where the interests of beneficial co-owners of land are concurrent, their interests may be either those of beneficial joint tenants or beneficial tenants in common. The interests of beneficial joint tenants pass between them by survivorship. If a beneficial joint tenancy is severed, the interests of the co-owners become those of tenants in common in equal shares, even if the co-owners contributed unequally to the purchase of the property: *Goodman v Gallant* [1986] 1 All ER 311, [1986] Fam 106.

The interests of beneficial tenants in common may be equal or unequal, and each beneficial tenant in common may dispose of his interest independently of the other.

III REA [58.2A]

Residential property The application of these principles to homes purchased for occupation by couples where there is no written declaration of trust has been considered in five decisions of the House of Lords: *Pettit v Pettit* [1970] AC 777, [1969] 2 All ER 966; *Gissing v Gissing* [1971] AC 886, [1970] 2 All ER 780; *Lloyds Bank plc v Rossett* [1991] 1 AC 107, [1990] 1 All ER 1111; *Stack v Dowden* [2007] UKHL 17v[2007] 2 AC 432, [2007] 2 All ER 929, and *Jones v Kernott* [2011] UKSC 53, [2012] 1 AC 776, [2012] 1 All ER 1265 which together support the following propositions:

The questions

Where a home is purchased for occupation by a couple but there is no written declaration of trust, the following questions arise (1) do both parties have a beneficial interest in it and (2) if so, what is the nature of their interests?

Ascertainment of intention

Both questions must be answered by reference to the common intentions of the parties at the time of acquisition of the property and (if it is alleged that their beneficial interests changed after acquisition) subsequently. Their intentions may be either expressed or inferred from their conduct viewed in the context of the surrounding circumstances. The courts may be willing to impute intentions to the parties to achieve an objectively fair result following a break-up: *Jones v Kernott* [2011] UKSC 53.

Question (1) - do both parties have a beneficial interest?

If the legal title was conveyed into the joint names of the couple, the starting point is that joint beneficial ownership was intended. The onus is on a party to show that the other was not intended to have a beneficial interest (see *Stack* at [54]–[70], *Jones* at [51]).

If the legal title was conveyed into the sole name of one of the couple, the starting point is that he or she was intended to be the sole beneficial owner. The onus is on the non-legal owner to show that he or she was intended to have a beneficial interest (see *Stack* at [56], Jones at [52]).

If the legal title was conveyed into the sole name of one of the couple, a distinction must be made between (1) cases where there was an express agreement, arrangement or understanding between the parties that the property was to be shared beneficially and (2) cases where there was no such express agreement arrangement or understanding. In a type (1) case it will only be necessary for the claimant to show that he acted to his detriment or altered his position in reliance on the agreement to give rise to a constructive trust or estoppel (see *Rossett* at 132G, 1119a).

In a type (2) case, it was said in *Rossett* (133A, 1119b) that it was doubtful whether anything less than a direct contribution to the purchase price of property would justify an inference that that the property was to be shared beneficially. However, dicta in *Stack* ([26], [63]) and *Abbott v Abbott* [2007] UKPC 53, [2007] All ER (D) 432 (Jul) suggest that this test should now be regarded as too strict.

Question (2) – What is the nature of the parties' beneficial interests?

The principles applicable where a family home is bought in the joint names of a cohabiting couple who are both responsible for any mortgage, but without any express declaration of their beneficial interests, were summarised in *Jones* at [51] as follows:

(1) The starting point is that equity follows the law and they are joint tenants both in law and in equity.

(2) That presumption can be displaced by showing (a) that the parties had a different common intention at the time when they acquired the home, or (b) that they later formed the common intention that their respective shares would change.

(3) Their common intention is to be deduced objectively from their conduct:

> 'the relevant intention of each party is the intention which was reasonably understood by the other party to be manifested by that party's words and conduct notwithstanding that he did not consciously formulate that intention in his own mind or even acted with some different intention which he did not communicate to the other party': Lord Diplock in *Gissing* at 906.

(4) In those cases where it is clear either (a) that the parties did not intend joint tenancy at the outset, or (b) had changed their original intention, but it is not possible to ascertain by direct evidence or by inference what their actual intention was as to the shares in which they would own the property, "the answer is that each is entitled to that share which the court considers fair having regard to the whole course of dealing between them in relation to the property": Chadwick LJ in *Oxley v Hiscock* [2004] EWCA

Civ 546, [2005] Fam 211 at [69], [2004] 3 All ER 703. "The whole course of dealing . . . in relation to the property" should be given a broad meaning, enabling a similar range of factors to be taken into account as may be relevant to ascertaining the parties' actual intentions.

(5) Each case will turn on its own facts. Financial contributions are relevant but there are many other factors which may enable the court to decide what shares were either intended (as in case (3)) or fair (as in case (4)).

Where a family home is put into the name of one party only, the starting point is different. The first issue is whether it was intended that the other party have any beneficial interest in the property at all. If he does, the second issue is what that interest is. There is no presumption of joint beneficial ownership. But their common intention has once again to be deduced objectively from their conduct. If the evidence shows a common intention to share beneficial ownership but does not show what shares were intended, the court will have to proceed as at para 51(4) and (5) above: see *Jones* at [52]; *Thompson v Hurst* [2012] EWCA Civ 1752.

Where the legal title is conveyed into the names of two people as joint tenants and the beneficial interests are expressly provided to be held by them in equal shares as tenants in common, the imposition of a constructive trust is not permissible because the beneficial interests have already been declared expressly: *Pankhania v Chandegra (by her litigation friend, Ronald Andrew Eagle)* [2012] EWCA Civ 1438, [2013] 1 P & CR 16.

III REA [58.2B]

Investment property The principle that a conveyance into joint names indicates a legal and beneficial joint tenancy unless the contrary is proved is not confined to the domestic context: *Marr v Collie* [2017] UKPC 17, [2017] 3 WLR 1507.

III REA [58.2BA]

Illegality Where a legal title to land has been acquired in pursuance of an illegal purpose, there is no general rule that the title cannot be enforced. Where a claimant claims an interest under a trust of land, there is no general rule that the claim will fail if the claimant has to rely on an illegal purpose to prove his claim. When deciding whether to give effect to an interest under a trust of land which is alleged to have arisen in pursuance of an illegal purpose, the court will consider (a) the underlying purpose of the prohibition which has been transgressed and whether that purpose would be enhanced by enforcing or denying the interest in question, (b) any relevant public policy on which the enforcement or denial would have an impact and (c) whether denial of enforcement would be a proportionate response to the illegality: *Patel v Mirza* [2016] UKSC 42, [2016] 3 WLR 399.

III REA [58.2C]

Proprietary estoppel Where the owner of property expressly or impliedly represents to another that the other has or will acquire an interest in that property, and the representee acts to his detriment in reasonable reliance on the representation, the owner may be estopped from denying that the representee has or will acquire such an interest: *Yeoman's Row Management Ltd v Cobbe* [2008] UKHL 55, [2008] 4 All ER 713, [2008] 1 WLR 1752; *Thorner v Major* [2009] UKHL18, [2009] 3 All ER 945, [2009] 1 WLR 776 esp. at [29].

Where the owner of land and another agree, subject to contract, that the land will be developed using the skills of the other, the other acts to his detriment in anticipation of the contract being made, and the landowner then unconscionably refuses to enter into the contract, the doctrine of proprietary estoppel cannot be used to obtain for the other the benefits he would have received had the contract been made. In such a case the expectation of benefits is dependent on the agreement being made: *Yeoman's Row Management Ltd v Cobbe* [2008] UKHL 55, [2008] 4 All ER 713, [2009] 1 All ER (Comm) 205.

The doctrines of proprietary estoppel and constructive trust overlap: see eg *Thorner* at [14], [20]; *Stack* at [37].

III REA [58.2D]

Practice Where an order relating to a trust of land is sought in the context of the breakdown of a marriage or civil partnership the provisions of the Matrimonial Causes Act 1973 of the Civil Partnership Act 2004 should be considered. Where the interests of a child are affected consideration should be given to the provisions of s 15 and Sch 1 of the Children Act 1989. Applications under TLATA, s 14 and s 15 and Sch 1 of the Children Act 1989 should ordinarily be dealt with together: *White v White (Joinder of Trusts of Land Act and Children's Act Applications)* [2003] EWCA Civ 924, [2004] 2 FLR 321.

On an application under TLATA between separated spouses, the court should embark upon the discretionary exercise by asking itself whether the issue raised by the application can reasonably be left to be resolved within an application for ancillary relief following divorce.

Furthermore if, at first sight, there appears to the court to be any measurable chance that, on an application for ancillary relief made within a time-frame tolerable in all the circumstances, the respondent to the application for an order for sale under TLATA will be able to preserve her or his occupation of the home by securing an outright transfer of ownership of it or a variation of the trust, it is hard to conceive that an order for sale would reflect a proper exercise of discretion: *Miller Smith v Miller Smith* [2009] EWCA Civ 1297, [2010] 1 FLR 1402, [2010] Fam Law 142.

III REA [58.3]

Equitable accounting The rights co-owners of land may have against each other in respect of such matters as expenditure on the outgoings relating to the land are adjusted by means of equitable accounting. This process is distinct from the ascertainment of the nature and amount of their respective beneficial interests in land. Where the land is to be sold, equitable accounting should not normally take place until after the sale. The date from which one co-owner should be accountable to the other depends on intentions of the parties as to how the relevant expenditure should be borne between them: *Wilcox v Tait* [2006] EWCA Civ 1867, [2007] 2 FLR 871, esp at [64]–[65].

Where one of two co-owners of land is in occupation and the other is not, the default position is that no occupation rent is payable by the co-owner who is in occupation; for the court to depart from that default position there has to be some conduct by the occupying party or some other feature of the case relating to the occupying party to make it just for the court to do so: *Davis v Jackson* [2017] EWHC 698 (Ch), [2017] 1 WLR 4005 at [41]–[48].

Where one of two co-owners has incurred expenditure which has improved the value of the land, the general principle is that that co-owner is entitled to a credit for one half of whichever is the less of his actual expenditure and the increase in value achieved thereby. Where one of two co-owners has discharged the payments due under a mortgage of the land, the general principle is that the co-owner is entitled to a credit for one half of the amount of the payments: *Davis v Jackson* [2017] EWHC 698 (Ch), [2017] 1 WLR 4005 at [32]–[36].

III REA [58.4]

Equity of exoneration If property is owned beneficially by A and B and is charged to secure the debts of B only, A may, by virtue of an equity of exoneration, be entitled to a charge over B's share of the property to the extent that B's debts are paid out of A's share: *Armstrong v Onyearu* [2017] EWCA Civ 268, [2018] Ch 137.

III REA [59]

15. Matters relevant in determining applications

(1) The matters to which the court is to have regard in determining an application for an order under section 14 include—

(a) the intentions of the person or persons (if any) who created the trust,

(b) the purposes for which the property subject to the trust is held,

(c) the welfare of any minor who occupies or might reasonably be expected to occupy any land subject to the trust as his home, and

(d) the interests of any secured creditor of any beneficiary.

(2) In the case of an application relating to the exercise in relation to any land of the powers conferred on the trustees by section 13, the matters to which the court is to have regard also include the circumstances and wishes of each of the beneficiaries who is (or apart from any previous exercise by the trustees of those powers would be) entitled to occupy the land under section 12.

(3) In the case of any other application, other than one relating to the exercise of the power mentioned in section 6(2), the matters to which the court is to have regard also include the circumstances and wishes of any beneficiaries of full age and entitled to an interest in possession in property subject to the trust or (in case of dispute) of the majority (according to the value of their combined interests).

(4) This section does not apply to an application if section 335A of the Insolvency Act 1986 (which is inserted by Schedule 3 and relates to applications by a trustee of a bankrupt) applies to it.

III REA [59.1]

"The intentions of the person or persons (if any) who created the trust" To fall within s 15(1)(a), an intention must have been held at the time of the creation of the trust, and, if the trust was created by more than one person, by such persons in common: *White v White (Joinder of Trusts of Land Act and Children's Act Applications)* [2003] EWCA Civ 924, [2004] 2 FLR 321.

III REA [59.1A]

"The purposes for which the property subject to the trust is held" To fall within s 15(1)(b), a purpose must have been either established at the time of the creation of the trust or agreed on subsequently by all the persons who created the trust: *White v White (Joinder of Trusts of Land Act and Children's Act Applications)* [2003] EWCA Civ 924, [2004] 2 FLR 321.

III REA [59.2]

"Any other application" In s 15(3), the words "any other application" mean any application not falling within s 15(2), not s 15(1) and (2): *Mortgage Corporation v Shaire* [2001] Ch 743, [2001] 4 All ER 364.

III REA [59.2A]

"The majority" Where the interests of beneficiaries of full age and entitled to interests in possession in property subject to a trust of land are of equal value, and the wishes and circumstances of such beneficiaries are opposed to each other, the court is entitled to have regard to the wishes and circumstances of all beneficiaries, and to give them such weight as it thinks fit, notwithstanding the reference to "the majority (according to the value of their combined interests)" in s 15(3): *White v White (Joinder of Trusts of Land Act and Children's Act Applications)* [2003] EWCA Civ 924, [2004] 2 FLR 321.

III REA [60]

22. Meaning of "beneficiary"

(1) In this Act "beneficiary", in relation to a trust, means any person who under the trust has an interest in property subject to the trust (including a person who has such an interest as a trustee or a personal representative).

(2) In this Act references to a beneficiary who is beneficially entitled do not include a beneficiary who has an interest in property subject to the trust only by reason of being a trustee or personal representative.

(3) For the purposes of this Act a person who is a beneficiary only by reason of being an annuitant is not to be regarded as entitled to an interest in possession in land subject to the trust.

PARTY WALL ETC ACT 1996

(c. 40)

GENERAL NOTE ON THE PARTY WALL ETC ACT 1996

III REA [60A]

This Act extends, with variations, the provisions of the London Building Acts to the whole of England and Wales. It provides procedures for authorising a property owner to carry out work to an existing party structure or otherwise on or near to the boundary with an adjoining property, but which at the same time protect the legitimate interests of the adjoining owner. The provisions are intended to constitute a means of dispute resolution which avoids recourse to the courts.

Broadly, the Act applies in three situations: where an owner of land wishes to build on the boundary line with an adjoining property and there is no existing party structure (s 1); where an owner wishes to carry out work to a party structure (ss 2 to 5); and where an owner wishes to carry out certain works of excavation near to a building or structure of an adjoining owner (s 6).

In outline, the procedure requires the service of a notice by a building owner wishing to do works to which the Act applies on adjoining owners affected by the works. Unless the adjoining owner gives his consent to the works, a scheme to define the works to be done, and the terms on which they should be carried out, can be fixed expeditiously, with both parties' interests being properly represented and protected. The scheme is fixed, either by agreement between the parties, by a single surveyor whom they appoint jointly or by each party having his own appointed surveyor to agree or negotiate the works between them, with a third surveyor also being appointed so that, if necessary, a final decision can be made, either by him as referee or by a majority decision of two of the three surveyors. By one of these means, the exact works, the appropriate terms and conditions for their execution and the appropriate responsibility for the costs of the work can be decided and recorded in a party wall award, to which reference can then be made for the parties respective rights and obligations: *Manu v Euroview Estates Ltd* [2008] 1 EGLR 165 at [9] (Judge Hazel Marshall QC, Central London County Court):

> 'The scheme provided by the Act is clever and intricate. It has to be because it has to provide a single, manageable code to cope, as far as possible, with all predictable routes that negotiations may take between parties that may have a range of different attitudes to works and to each other, so as to enable a final authoritative result to be produced in any instance with the kind of speedy timescale that building or repair projects demand': *Manu v Euroview Estates Ltd* [2008] 1 EGLR 165 at [11].

As to the availability of a claim for damages for breach of statutory duty arising from failure to operate the mandatory provisions of the Act, see *Crowley t/a Crowley Civil Engineers v Rushmoor Borough Council* [2009] EWHC 2237 (TCC) and *Bridgland v Earlsmead Estates Ltd* (Birmingham County Court, 1 July 2015).

CONSTRUCTION AND REPAIR OF WALLS ON LINE OF JUNCTION

III REA [60B]

1. New building on line of junction

(1) This section shall have effect where lands of different owners adjoin and—

(a) are not built on at the line of junction; or

(b) are built on at the line of junction only to the extent of a boundary wall (not being a party fence wall or the external wall of a building),

and either owner is about to build on any part of the line of junction.

(2) If a building owner desires to build a party wall or party fence wall on the line of junction he shall, at least one month before he intends the building work to start, serve on any adjoining owner a notice which indicates his desire to build and describes the intended wall.

(3) If, having been served with notice described in subsection (2), an adjoining owner serves on the building owner a notice indicating his consent to the building of a party wall or party fence wall—

- (a) the wall shall be built half on the land of each of the two owners or in such other position as may be agreed between the two owners; and
- (b) the expense of building the wall shall be from time to time defrayed by the two owners in such proportion as has regard to the use made or to be made of the wall by each of them and to the cost of labour and materials prevailing at the time when that use is made by each owner respectively.

(4) If, having been served with notice described in subsection (2), an adjoining owner does not consent under this subsection to the building of a party wall or party fence wall, the building owner may only build the wall—

- (a) at his own expense; and
- (b) as an external wall or a fence wall, as the case may be, placed wholly on his own land,

and consent under this subsection is consent by a notice served within the period of fourteen days beginning with the day on which the notice described in subsection (2) is served.

(5) If the building owner desires to build on the line of junction a wall placed wholly on his own land he shall, at least one month before he intends the building work to start, serve on any adjoining owner a notice which indicates his desire to build and describes the intended wall.

(6) Where the building owner builds a wall wholly on his own land in accordance with subsection (4) or (5) he shall have the right, at any time in the period which—

- (a) begins one month after the day on which the notice mentioned in the subsection concerned was served, and
- (b) ends twelve months after that day,

to place below the level of the land of the adjoining owner such projecting footings and foundations as are necessary for the construction of the wall.

(7) Where the building owner builds a wall wholly on his own land in accordance with subsection (4) or (5) he shall do so at his own expense and shall compensate any adjoining owner and any adjoining occupier for any damage to his property occasioned by—

- (a) the building of the wall;
- (b) the placing of any footings or foundations placed in accordance with subsection (6).

(8) Where any dispute arises under this section between the building owner and any adjoining owner or occupier it is to be determined in accordance with section 10.

III REA [60C]

2. Repair etc of party wall: rights of owner

(1) This section applies where lands of different owners adjoin and at the line of junction the said lands are built on or a boundary wall, being a party fence wall or the external wall of a building, has been erected.

(2) A building owner shall have the following rights—

(a) to underpin, thicken or raise a party structure, a party fence wall, or an external wall which belongs to the building owner and is built against a party structure or party fence wall;

(b) to make good, repair, or demolish and rebuild, a party structure or party fence wall in a case where such work is necessary on account of defect or want of repair of the structure or wall;

(c) to demolish a partition which separates buildings belonging to different owners but does not conform with statutory requirements and to build instead a party wall which does so conform;

(d) in the case of buildings connected by arches or structures over public ways or over passages belonging to other persons, to demolish the whole or part of such buildings, arches or structures which do not conform with statutory requirements and to rebuild them so that they do so conform;

(e) to demolish a party structure which is of insufficient strength or height for the purposes of any intended building of the building owner and to rebuild it of sufficient strength or height for the said purposes (including rebuilding to a lesser height or thickness where the rebuilt structure is of sufficient strength and height for the purposes of any adjoining owner);

(f) to cut into a party structure for any purpose (which may be or include the purpose of inserting a damp proof course);

(g) to cut away from a party wall, party fence wall, external wall or boundary wall any footing or any projecting chimney breast, jamb or flue, or other projection on or over the land of the building owner in order to erect, raise or underpin any such wall or for any other purpose;

(h) to cut away or demolish parts of any wall or building of an adjoining owner overhanging the land of the building owner or overhanging a party wall, to the extent that it is necessary to cut away or demolish the parts to enable a vertical wall to be erected or raised against the wall or building of the adjoining owner;

(j) to cut into the wall of an adjoining owner's building in order to insert a flashing or other weather-proofing of a wall erected against that wall;

(k) to execute any other necessary works incidental to the connection of a party structure with the premises adjoining it;

(l) to raise a party fence wall, or to raise such a wall for use as a party wall, and to demolish a party fence wall and rebuild it as a party fence wall or as a party wall;

(m) subject to the provisions of section 11(7), to reduce, or to demolish and rebuild, a party wall or party fence wall to—

  (i) a height of not less than two metres where the wall is not used by an adjoining owner to any greater extent than a boundary wall; or

  (ii) a height currently enclosed upon by the building of an adjoining owner;

(n) to expose a party wall or party structure hitherto enclosed subject to providing adequate weathering.

(3) Where work mentioned in paragraph (a) of subsection (2) is not necessary on account of defect or want of repair of the structure or wall concerned, the right falling within that paragraph is exercisable—

(a) subject to making good all damage occasioned by the work to the adjoining premises or to their internal furnishings and decorations; and

(b) where the work is to a party structure or external wall, subject to carrying any relevant flues and chimney stacks up to such a height and in such materials as may be agreed between the building owner and the adjoining owner concerned or, in the event of dispute, determined in accordance with section 10;

and relevant flues and chimney stacks are those which belong to an adjoining owner and either form part of or rest on or against the party structure or external wall.

(4) The right falling within subsection (2)(e) is exercisable subject to—

(a) making good all damage occasioned by the work to the adjoining premises or to their internal furnishings and decorations; and

(b) carrying any relevant flues and chimney stacks up to such a height and in such materials as may be agreed between the building owner and the adjoining owner concerned or, in the event of dispute, determined in accordance with section 10;

and relevant flues and chimney stacks are those which belong to an adjoining owner and either form part of or rest on or against the party structure.

(5) Any right falling within subsection (2)(f), (g) or (h) is exercisable subject to making good all damage occasioned by the work to the adjoining premises or to their internal furnishings and decorations.

(6) The right falling within subsection (2)(j) is exercisable subject to making good all damage occasioned by the work to the wall of the adjoining owner's building.

(7) The right falling within subsection (2)(m) is exercisable subject to—

(a) reconstructing any parapet or replacing an existing parapet with another one; or

(b) constructing a parapet where one is needed but did not exist before.

(8) For the purposes of this section a building or structure which was erected before the day on which this Act was passed shall be deemed to conform with statutory requirements if it conforms with the statutes regulating buildings or structures on the date on which it was erected.

III REA [60C.1]

Underpinning The term 'underpinning' in s 2(2)(a) contemplates whatever works are required in order to effect the underpinning, including excavation to get at the location of the underpinning. Excavation works proposed in order to effect underpinning may be covered by a notice under s 3, and no separate notice under s 6 is necessary in respect of them: *Manu v Euroview Estates Ltd* [2008] 1 EGLR 165 at [93]–[96].

III REA [60D]

3. Party structure notices

(1) Before exercising any right conferred on him by section 2 a building owner shall serve on any adjoining owner a notice (in this Act referred to as a "party structure notice") stating—

(a) the name and address of the building owner;

(b) the nature and particulars of the proposed work including, in cases where the building owner proposes to construct special foundations, plans, sections and details of construction of the special foundations together with reasonable particulars of the loads to be carried thereby; and

(c) the date on which the proposed work will begin.

(2) A party structure notice shall—

(a) be served at least two months before the date on which the proposed work will begin;

(b) cease to have effect if the work to which it relates—

(i) has not begun within the period of twelve months beginning with the day on which the notice is served; and

(ii) is not prosecuted with due diligence.

(3) Nothing in this section shall—

(a) prevent a building owner from exercising with the consent in writing of the adjoining owners and of the adjoining occupiers any right conferred on him by section 2; or

(b) require a building owner to serve any party structure notice before complying with any notice served under any statutory provisions relating to dangerous or neglected structures.

III REA [60E]

4. Counter notices

(1) An adjoining owner may, having been served with a party structure notice serve on the building owner a notice (in this Act referred to as a "counter notice") setting out—

(a) in respect of a party fence wall or party structure, a requirement that the building owner build in or on the wall or structure to which the notice relates such chimney copings, breasts, jambs or flues, or such piers or recesses or other like works, as may reasonably be required for the convenience of the adjoining owner;

(b) in respect of special foundations to which the adjoining owner consents under section 7(4) below, a requirement that the special foundations—

(i) be placed at a specified greater depth than that proposed by the building owner; or

(ii) be constructed of sufficient strength to bear the load to be carried by columns of any intended building of the adjoining owner,

or both.

(2) A counter notice shall—

(a) specify the works required by the notice to be executed and shall be accompanied by plans, sections and particulars of such works; and

(b) be served within the period of one month beginning with the day on which the party structure notice is served.

(3) A building owner on whom a counter notice has been served shall comply with the requirements of the counter notice unless the execution of the works required by the counter notice would—

(a) be injurious to him;

(b) cause unnecessary inconvenience to him; or

(c) cause unnecessary delay in the execution of the works pursuant to the party structure notice.

III REA [60F]

5. Disputes arising under sections 3 and 4

If an owner on whom a party structure notice or a counter notice has been served does not serve a notice indicating his consent to it within the period of fourteen days beginning with the day on which the party structure notice or counter notice was served, he shall be deemed to have dissented from the notice and a dispute shall be deemed to have arisen between the parties.

Adjacent excavation and construction

III REA [60G]

6. Adjacent excavation and construction

(1) This section applies where—

(a) a building owner proposes to excavate, or excavate for and erect a building or structure, within a distance of three metres measured horizontally from any part of a building or structure of an adjoining owner; and

(b) any part of the proposed excavation, building or structure will within those three metres extend to a lower level than the level of the bottom of the foundations of the building or structure of the adjoining owner.

(2) This section also applies where—

(a) a building owner proposes to excavate, or excavate for and erect a building or structure, within a distance of six metres measured horizontally from any part of a building or structure of an adjoining owner; and

(b) any part of the proposed excavation, building or structure will within those six metres meet a plane drawn downwards in the direction of the excavation, building or structure of the building owner at an angle of forty-five degrees to the horizontal from the line formed by the intersection of the plane of the level of the bottom of the foundations of the building or structure of the adjoining owner with the plane of the external face of the external wall of the building or structure of the adjoining owner.

(3) The building owner may, and if required by the adjoining owner shall, at his own expense underpin or otherwise strengthen or safeguard the foundations of the building or structure of the adjoining owner so far as may be necessary.

(4) Where the buildings or structures of different owners are within the respective distances mentioned in subsections (1) and (2) the owners of those buildings or structures shall be deemed to be adjoining owners for the purposes of this section.

(5) In any case where this section applies the building owner shall, at least one month before beginning to excavate, or excavate for and erect a building or structure, serve on the adjoining owner a notice indicating his proposals and stating whether he proposes to underpin or otherwise strengthen or safeguard the foundations of the building or structure of the adjoining owner.

(6) The notice referred to in subsection (5) shall be accompanied by plans and sections showing—

(a) the site and depth of any excavation the building owner proposes to make;

(b) if he proposes to erect a building or structure, its site.

(7) If an owner on whom a notice referred to in subsection (5) has been served does not serve a notice indicating his consent to it within the period of fourteen days beginning with the day on which the notice referred to in subsection (5) was served, he shall be deemed to have dissented from the notice and a dispute shall be deemed to have arisen between the parties.

(8) The notice referred to in subsection (5) shall cease to have effect if the work to which the notice relates—

(a) has not begun within the period of twelve months beginning with the day on which the notice was served; and

(b) is not prosecuted with due diligence.

(9) On completion of any work executed in pursuance of this section the building owner shall if so requested by the adjoining owner supply him with particulars including plans and sections of the work.

(10) Nothing in this section shall relieve the building owner from any liability to which he would otherwise be subject for injury to any adjoining owner or any adjoining occupier by reason of work executed by him.

III REA [60G.1]

Notice The purpose of s 6(6) is to give an adjoining owner notice of excavation works that might affect the stability of his building and to enable him to decide whether he foresees a risk in this regard that means he should invoke his rights under s 6(3). The notice is required to show 'the site and depth of any excavation' sufficiently to enable that assessment to be made. The notice must be clear and intelligible in the respects that will convey that information, on the assumption that the recipient either is or will have the advice of a person familiar with interpreting plans and drawings: it is not that they should be perfectly intelligible to the untutored layman: *Manu v Euroview Estates Ltd* [2008] 1 EGLR 165 at [105]–[106].

Rights etc

III REA [60H]

7. Compensation etc

(1) A building owner shall not exercise any right conferred on him by this Act in such a manner or at such time as to cause unnecessary inconvenience to any adjoining owner or to any adjoining occupier.

(2) The building owner shall compensate any adjoining owner and any adjoining occupier for any loss or damage which may result to any of them by reason of any work executed in pursuance of this Act.

(3) Where a building owner in exercising any right conferred on him by this Act lays open any part of the adjoining land or building he shall at his own expense make and maintain so long as may be necessary a proper hoarding, shoring or fans or temporary construction for the protection of the adjoining land or building and the security of any adjoining occupier.

(4) Nothing in this Act shall authorise the building owner to place special foundations on land of an adjoining owner without his previous consent in writing.

(5) Any works executed in pursuance of this Act shall—

(a) comply with the provisions of statutory requirements; and

(b) be executed in accordance with such plans, sections and particulars as may be agreed between the owners or in the event of dispute determined in accordance with section 10;

and no deviation shall be made from those plans, sections and particulars except such as may be agreed between the owners (or surveyors acting on their behalf) or in the event of dispute determined in accordance with section 10.

III REA [60H.1]

Compensation Section 7(1) imposes an obligation on the building owner as to the manner in which works are to be carried out. It does not impose an obligation on surveyors appointed under the Act not to authorise a design which is likely to cause unnecessary inconvenience to an adjoining owner: *Russell Gray v Elite Town Management* [2016] EWCA Civ 1318 at [35]–[39].

The principles which govern the award of compensation under s 7(2) are the general common law principles which govern the assessment of damages for torts to land: *Lea Valley (Developments) Ltd v Derbyshire* [2017] EWHC 1353, [2017] 4 WLR 120.

III REA [60I]

8. Rights of entry

(1) A building owner, his servants, agents and workmen may during usual working hours enter and remain on any land or premises for the purpose of executing any work in pursuance of this Act and may remove any furniture or fittings or take any other action necessary for that purpose.

(2) If the premises are closed, the building owner, his agents and workmen may, if accompanied by a constable or other police officer, break open any fences or doors in order to enter the premises.

(3) No land or premises may be entered by any person under subsection (1) unless the building owner serves on the owner and the occupier of the land or premises—

(a) in case of emergency, such notice of the intention to enter as may be reasonably practicable;

(b) in any other case, such notice of the intention to enter as complies with subsection (4).

(4) Notice complies with this subsection if it is served in a period of not less than fourteen days ending with the day of the proposed entry.

(5) A surveyor appointed or selected under section 10 may during usual working hours enter and remain on any land or premises for the purpose of carrying out the object for which he is appointed or selected.

(6) No land or premises may be entered by a surveyor under subsection (5) unless the building owner who is a party to the dispute concerned serves on the owner and the occupier of the land or premises—

(a) in case of emergency, such notice of the intention to enter as may be reasonably practicable;

(b) in any other case, such notice of the intention to enter as complies with subsection (4).

III REA [60J]

9. Easements

Nothing in this Act shall—

(a) authorise any interference with an easement of light or other easements in or relating to a party wall; or

(b) prejudicially affect any right of any person to preserve or restore any right or other thing in or connected with a party wall in case of the party wall being pulled down or rebuilt.

Resolution of disputes

III REA [60K]

10. Resolution of disputes

(1) Where a dispute arises or is deemed to have arisen between a building owner and an adjoining owner in respect of any matter connected with any work to which this Act relates either—

(a) both parties shall concur in the appointment of one surveyor (in this section referred to as an "agreed surveyor"); or

(b) each party shall appoint a surveyor and the two surveyors so appointed shall forthwith select a third surveyor (all of whom are in this section referred to as "the three surveyors").

(2) All appointments and selections made under this section shall be in writing and shall not be rescinded by either party.

(3) If an agreed surveyor—

(a) refuses to act;

(b) neglects to act for a period of ten days beginning with the day on which either party serves a request on him;

(c) dies before the dispute is settled; or

(d) becomes or deems himself incapable of acting,

the proceedings for settling such dispute shall begin *de novo*.

(4) If either party to the dispute—

(a) refuses to appoint a surveyor under subsection (1)(b), or

(b) neglects to appoint a surveyor under subsection (1)(b) for a period of ten days beginning with the day on which the other party serves a request on him,

the other party may make the appointment on his behalf.

(5) If, before the dispute is settled, a surveyor appointed under paragraph (b) of subsection (1) by a party to the dispute dies, or becomes or deems himself incapable of acting, the party who appointed him may appoint another surveyor in his place with the same power and authority.

(6) If a surveyor—

(a) appointed under paragraph (b) of subsection (1) by a party to the dispute; or

(b) appointed under subsection (4) or (5),

refuses to act effectively, the surveyor of the other party may proceed to act *ex parte* and anything so done by him shall be as effectual as if he had been an agreed surveyor.

(7) If a surveyor—

(a) appointed under paragraph (b) of subsection (1) by a party to the dispute; or

(b) appointed under subsection (4) or (5),

neglects to act effectively for a period of ten days beginning with the day on which either party or the surveyor of the other party serves a request on him, the surveyor of the other party may proceed to act *ex parte* in respect of the subject matter of the request and anything so done by him shall be as effectual as if he had been an agreed surveyor.

(8) If either surveyor appointed under subsection (1)(b) by a party to the dispute refuses to select a third surveyor under subsection (1) or (9), or neglects to do so for a period of ten days beginning with the day on which the other surveyor serves a request on him—

(a) the appointing officer; or

(b) in cases where the relevant appointing officer or his employer is a party to the dispute, the Secretary of State,

may on the application of either surveyor select a third surveyor who shall have the same power and authority as if he had been selected under subsection (1) or subsection (9).

(9) If a third surveyor selected under subsection (1)(b)—

(a) refuses to act;

(b) neglects to act for a period of ten days beginning with the day on which either party or the surveyor appointed by either party serves a request on him; or

(c) dies, or becomes or deems himself incapable of acting, before the dispute is settled,

the other two of the three surveyors shall forthwith select another surveyor in his place with the same power and authority.

(10) The agreed surveyor or as the case may be the three surveyors or any two of them shall settle by award any matter—

(a) which is connected with any work to which this Act relates, and

(b) which is in dispute between the building owner and the adjoining owner.

(11) Either of the parties or either of the surveyors appointed by the parties may call upon the third surveyor selected in pursuance of this section to determine the disputed matters and he shall make the necessary award.

(12) An award may determine—

(a) the right to execute any work;

(b) the time and manner of executing any work; and

(c) any other matter arising out of or incidental to the dispute including the costs of making the award;

but any period appointed by the award for executing any work shall not unless otherwise agreed between the building owner and the adjoining owner begin to run until after the expiration of the period prescribed by this Act for service of the notice in respect of which the dispute arises or is deemed to have arisen.

(13) The reasonable costs incurred in—

(a) making or obtaining an award under this section;

(b) reasonable inspections of work to which the award relates; and

(c) any other matter arising out of the dispute,

shall be paid by such of the parties as the surveyor or surveyors making the award determine.

(14) Where the surveyors appointed by the parties make an award the surveyors shall serve it forthwith on the parties.

(15) Where an award is made by the third surveyor—

(a) he shall, after payment of the costs of the award, serve it forthwith on the parties or their appointed surveyors; and

(b) if it is served on their appointed surveyors, they shall serve it forthwith on the parties.

(16) The award shall be conclusive and shall not except as provided by this section be questioned in any court.

(17) Either of the parties to the dispute may, within the period of fourteen days beginning with the day on which an award made under this section is served on him, appeal to the county court against the award and the county court may—

(a) rescind the award or modify it in such manner as the court thinks fit; and

(b) make such order as to costs as the court thinks fit.

III REA [60K.1]

"Dispute" In s 10, "dispute" meant a dispute arising under the provisions of the Act. Although there are circumstances in which appointed surveyors have power under s 10 to order payment by a building owner to an adjoining owner of legal costs reasonably and properly incurred (as in *Onigbanjo v Pearson* [2008] BLR 5007, Mayor's and City of London's Ct), such power is restricted to costs connected with the statutory dispute resolution mechanism. Court proceedings to enforce common law or equitable remedies fall outside the Act. Appointed surveyors do not have power to direct the payment by a building owner to an adjoining owner of costs incurred in connection with contemplated court proceedings for trespass and nuisance: *Reeves v Blake* [2009] EWCA Civ 611, [2010] 1 WLR 1, [2010] P & CR 81.

As to whether an award made under s 10(10) of the Act authorising works which were notifiable under s 6 of the Act may require the party carrying out the works to make good damage to an adjoining owner's property or make payment in lieu, see *Lea Valley (Developments) Ltd v Derbyshire* [2017] EWHC 1353, [2017] 4 WLR 120.

III REA [60K.2]

Appointment A surveyor may be appointed under s 10(1)(b) before the service of a party wall notice in respect of the proposals to which it relates, and the appointment will take effect under the Act when a dispute arises or is deemed to have arisen: *Manu v Euroview Estates Ltd* [2008] 1 EGLR 165 at [85]

III REA [60K.3]

"Refuses to act effectively" For the meaning of "refuses to act effectively" in s 10(6), see *Manu v Euroview Estates Ltd* [2008] 1 EGLR 165 at [119]–[125].

III REA [60K.3A]

"Neglects to act effectively" If a surveyor neglects to act effectively for more than 10 days after being served with a request to act, but acts effectively after the expiration of the 10 day period and before the requesting surveyor has proceeded to act ex parte, the requesting surveyor may not thereafter proceed to act ex parte: *Patel v Peters* [2014] EWCA Civ 335, [2015] 1 WLR 179.

III REA [60K.3B]

"Determine" The word 'determine' in s 10(12) and (13) is not limited to matters which are in dispute between a building owner and an adjoining owner. An award may determine matters which are not in dispute between them, such as the costs payable by a building owner to a surveyor appointed by him: *R (on the application of Farrs Lane Developments Ltd) v Justices of the Peace for Avon Somerset & Gloucestershire* [2016] EWHC 982 (Admin).

III REA [60K.3C]

"Costs" An award is not limited to directing payment of costs between a building owner and an adjoining owner: thus, if an award determines that the costs of a surveyor are to be paid by the party who appointed him, it may direct the appointing party to pay them, and the surveyor may enforce the payment of those costs as a civil debt under s 17: *R (on the application of Farrs Lane Developments Ltd) v Justices of the Peace for Avon Somerset & Gloucestershire* [2016] EWHC 982 (Admin).

III REA [60K.4]

Appeals An appeal to the county court under s 10(17) is governed by CPR Part 52: *Zissis v Lukomski* [2006] EWCA Civ 341, [2006] 1 WLR 2778, [2006] 15 EG 135 (CS). For the purposes of CPR Part 52 the surveyor or surveyors who made the award appealed from are the "lower court": see the extended definition of that term in CPR Part 52 rule 1. Permission to appeal is not required: see CPR Part 52 rule 3 and PD 52 para 4.

The appeal must be commenced with the period of 14 days specified in s 10(17). The period of 21 days referred to in CPR Part 52 rule 4(2), and the period of 28 days referred to in CPR PD 52 para 17.3 are subject to any enactment which sets out special provisions with regard to any category of appeal: CPR Part 52 rule (4); PD 52 para 17.1: *Zissis v Lukomski* (above) at [40]. It appears that the period of 14 days specified in s 10(17) may not be extended under CPR Part 52, rule 4(2) by the surveyor or surveyors from whose award the appeal is brought or under CPR Part 3(1) by the county court; see *Mucelli v Government of Albania* [2009] UKHL 2, [2009] 3 All ER 1035, [2009] 1 WLR 276 at [74], [78].

For when time under s 10(17) begins to run in respect of an award served by post, see **III REA [60P.1]**.

The appeal is a "statutory appeal", and the provisions of CPR Part 52 apply with the amendments set out in PD 52 paras 17.3–17.11: these inter alia require that the appellant's notice be served on the surveyor or surveyors from whom the appeal is brought: para 17(5).

CPR Part 52, rule 11 provides that every appeal is limited to a review of the decision of the lower court except where a practice direction makes provision for a different category of appeal. PD 52 para 9.1 provides that the hearing on an appeal will be a re-hearing, as opposed to a review, if the appeal is from a person who did not hold a hearing. Surveyors making an award under the Act will not normally hold a hearing, and accordingly the appeal will normally take the form of a re-hearing. For the nature of a re-hearing, as compared to a review, see *El Du Pont De Nemours & Co v ST Dupont* [2003] EWCA Civ 1368, [2006] 1 WLR 2793, esp. at [84]–[98], [2004] FSR 293, and see *Zissis v Lukomski* (above) at [41] and *Manu v Euroview Estates Ltd* [2008] 1 EGLR 165 at [74].

Under s 10(17), an appeal lies to the county court. An appeal can nevertheless be heard in the High Court by a judge of the High Court sitting as a judge of the country court under s 5(3) of the County Courts Act 1984, or by being transferred by the county court to the High Court under s 42(2) of the County Courts Act 1984: *Kaye v Lawrence* [2010] EWHC 2678 (TCC), [2010] NLJR 1532.

A further appeal from the county court to the Court of Appeal is a "second appeal", for which permission is required from the Court of Appeal: CPR Part 52, rule 13(1). The Court of Appeal will not give permission for a second appeal unless it considers that the appeal raises an important point of law or practice or there is some other compelling reason for the Court of Appeal to hear it: CPR Part 52, rule 13(2). The county court may give an indication of its opinion as to whether permission should be given: PD 52 para 4.3.

A party challenging an award which he claims to be invalid need not do so by an appeal under CPR Part 52: he may do so by seeking declaratory relief, or by resisting the award's enforcement or by bringing an action inconsistent with it: *Zissis v Lukomiski* (above) at [45].

Expenses

III REA [60L]

11. Expenses

(1) Except as provided under this section expenses of work under this Act shall be defrayed by the building owner.

(2) Any dispute as to responsibility for expenses shall be settled as provided in section 10.

(3) An expense mentioned in section 1(3)(b) shall be defrayed as there mentioned.

(4) Where work is carried out in exercise of the right mentioned in section 2(2)(a), and the work is necessary on account of defect or want of repair of the structure or wall concerned, the expenses shall be defrayed by the building owner and the adjoining owner in such proportion as has regard to—

- (a) the use which the owners respectively make or may make of the structure or wall concerned; and
- (b) responsibility for the defect or want of repair concerned, if more than one owner makes use of the structure or wall concerned.

(5) Where work is carried out in exercise of the right mentioned in section 2(2)(b) the expenses shall be defrayed by the building owner and the adjoining owner in such proportion as has regard to—

- (a) the use which the owners respectively make or may make of the structure or wall concerned; and
- (b) responsibility for the defect or want of repair concerned, if more than one owner makes use of the structure or wall concerned.

(6) Where the adjoining premises are laid open in exercise of the right mentioned in section 2(2)(e) a fair allowance in respect of disturbance and inconvenience shall be paid by the building owner to the adjoining owner or occupier.

(7) Where a building owner proposes to reduce the height of a party wall or party fence wall under section 2(2)(m) the adjoining owner may serve a counter notice under section 4 requiring the building owner to maintain the existing height of the wall, and in such case the adjoining owner shall pay to the building owner a due proportion of the cost of the wall so far as it exceeds—

- (a) two metres in height; or
- (b) the height currently enclosed upon by the building of the adjoining owner.

(8) Where the building owner is required to make good damage under this Act the adjoining owner has a right to require that the expenses of such making good be determined in accordance with section 10 and paid to him in lieu of the carrying out of work to make the damage good.

(9) Where—

- (a) works are carried out, and
- (b) some of the works are carried out at the request of the adjoining owner or in pursuance of a requirement made by him,

he shall defray the expenses of carrying out the works requested or required by him.

(10) Where—

- (a) consent in writing has been given to the construction of special foundations on land of an adjoining owner; and
- (b) the adjoining owner erects any building or structure and its cost is found to be increased by reason of the existence of the said foundations,

the owner of the building to which the said foundations belong shall, on receiving an account with any necessary invoices and other supporting documents within the period of two months beginning with the day of the completion of the work by the adjoining owner, repay to the adjoining owner so much of the cost as is due to the existence of the said foundations.

(11) Where use is subsequently made by the adjoining owner of work carried out solely at the expense of the building owner the adjoining owner shall pay a due proportion of the expenses incurred by the building owner in carrying out that work; and for this purpose he shall be taken to have incurred expenses calculated by reference to what the cost of the work would be if it were carried out at the time when that subsequent use is made.

III REA [60L.1]

"Responsibility" The concept of responsibility in s 11(4)(b) does not equate with legal liability. Rather, it is a simple and practical yardstick capable of being applied in a relatively summary way as a matter of common-sense impression. "Responsibility" in s 11(4) means responsibility according to use, but use in the slightly wider sense of "treatment" rather than the narrower sense of "turning to account for one's benefit. Looked at another way, responsibility is the mirror of causation and the test amounts to whether, as a matter of common-sense impression (and if so, to what extent) one party has been more the cause of the relevant defect, damage or disrepair than the other": *Manu v Euroview Estates Ltd* [2008] 1 EGLR 165 at [139].

Responsibility is to be decided only as between the parties to the proceedings and not with regard to other persons, such as predecessors in title: *Manu v Euroview Estates Ltd* [2008] 1 EGLR 165 at [140].

III REA [60L.2]

Expense of making good damage Section 11(8) confers jurisdiction for a surveyor or surveyors appointed under the Act to award a sum in lieu of making good damage occasioned by work, notwithstanding that the work in question is carried out following the service of a party structure notice under s 3 of the Act and that the adjoining owner serves a counternotice consenting thereto, with the consequence that no dispute is deemed to have arisen under s 5: *Onigbanjo v Pearson* [2008] BLR 507.

III REA [60M]

12. Security for expenses

(1) An adjoining owner may serve a notice requiring the building owner before he begins any work in the exercise of the rights conferred by this Act to give such security as may be agreed between the owners or in the event of dispute determined in accordance with section 10.

(2) Where—

(a) in the exercise of the rights conferred by this Act an adjoining owner requires the building owner to carry out any work the expenses of which are to be defrayed in whole or in part by the adjoining owner; or

(b) an adjoining owner serves a notice on the building owner under subsection (1),

the building owner may before beginning the work to which the requirement or notice relates serve a notice on the adjoining owner requiring him to give such security as may be agreed between the owners or in the event of dispute determined in accordance with section 10.

(3) If within the period of one month beginning with—

(a) the day on which a notice is served under subsection (2); or

(b) in the event of dispute, the date of the determination by the surveyor or surveyors,

the adjoining owner does not comply with the notice or the determination, the requirement or notice by him to which the building owner's notice under that subsection relates shall cease to have effect.

III REA [60M.1]

Security Security can be requested when works are being carried out only on the building owner's land, and not only when works are being carried out on the land of the adjoining owner: *Kaye v Lawrence* [2010] EWHC 2678, [2011] 1 WLR 1948 (TCC).

III REA [60N]

13. Account for work carried out

(1) Within the period of two months beginning with the day of the completion of any work executed by a building owner of which the expenses are to be wholly or partially defrayed by an adjoining owner in accordance with section 11 the building owner shall serve on the adjoining owner an account in writing showing—

- (a) particulars and expenses of the work; and
- (b) any deductions to which the adjoining owner or any other person is entitled in respect of old materials or otherwise;

and in preparing the account the work shall be estimated and valued at fair average rates and prices according to the nature of the work, the locality and the cost of labour and materials prevailing at the time when the work is executed.

(2) Within the period of one month beginning with the day of service of the said account the adjoining owner may serve on the building owner a notice stating any objection he may have thereto and thereupon a dispute shall be deemed to have arisen between the parties.

(3) If within that period of one month the adjoining owner does not serve notice under subsection (2) he shall be deemed to have no objection to the account.

III REA [60O]

14. Settlement of account

(1) All expenses to be defrayed by an adjoining owner in accordance with an account served under section 13 shall be paid by the adjoining owner.

(2) Until an adjoining owner pays to the building owner such expenses as aforesaid the property in any works executed under this Act to which the expenses relate shall be vested solely in the building owner.

Miscellaneous

III REA [60P]

15. Service of notices etc

(1) A notice or other document required or authorised to be served under this Act may be served on a person—

- (a) by delivering it to him in person;
- (b) by sending it by post to him at his usual or last-known residence or place of business in the United Kingdom; or
- (c) in the case of a body corporate, by delivering it to the secretary or clerk of the body corporate at its registered or principal office or sending it by post to the secretary or clerk of that body corporate at that office.

(1A) A notice or other document required or authorised to be served under this Act may also be served on a person ("the recipient") by means of an electronic communication, but only if—

- (a) the recipient has stated a willingness to receive the notice or document by means of an electronic communication,
- (b) the statement has not been withdrawn, and
- (c) the notice or document was transmitted to an electronic address specified by the recipient.

(1B) A statement under subsection (1A) may be withdrawn by giving a notice to the person to whom the statement was made.

(1C) For the purposes of subsection (1A)—

"electronic address" includes any number or address used for the purposes of receiving electronic communications;

"electronic communication" means an electronic communication within the meaning of the Electronic Communications Act 2000; and

"specified" means specified in a statement made for the purposes of subsection (1A).

(2) In the case of a notice or other document required or authorised to be served under this Act on a person as owner of premises, it may alternatively be served by—

- (a) addressing it "the owner" of the premises (naming them), and
- (b) delivering it to a person on the premises or, if no person to whom it can be delivered is found there, fixing it to a conspicuous part of the premises.

III REA [60P.1]

Service The Interpretation Act 1978, s 7 applies to the postal service provisions in s 15(1)(b), with the result that service of a notice or other document required or authorised to be served under this Act is deemed to be effected by properly addressing, pre-paying and posting a letter containing the document and, unless the contrary is proved, to have been effected at the time at which the letter would be delivered in the ordinary course of post: *Freetown Ltd v Assethold Ltd* [2012] EWCA Civ 1657, [2012] All ER (D) 134 (Dec).

Sub-sections 15(1A), (1B) and (1C) were inserted by the Party Wall etc Act 1996 (Electronic Communications) Order 2016, SI 2016/335 with effect from 6 April 2016.

The word "may" in s 15(1) is permissive as to the means by which a notice or other document may be validly served: *Knight v Goulandris* [2018] EWCA Civ 237, [2018] 1 WLR 3345.

III REA [60Q]

16. Offences

(1) If—

- (a) an occupier of land or premises refuses to permit a person to do anything which he is entitled to do with regard to the land or premises under section 8(1) or (5); and
- (b) the occupier knows or has reasonable cause to believe that the person is so entitled,

the occupier is guilty of an offence.

(2) If—

- (a) a person hinders or obstructs a person in attempting to do anything which he is entitled to do with regard to land or premises under section 8(1) or (5); and
- (b) the first-mentioned person knows or has reasonable cause to believe that the other person is so entitled,

the first-mentioned person is guilty of an offence.

(3) A person guilty of an offence under subsection (1) or (2) is liable on summary conviction to a fine of an amount not exceeding level 3 on the standard scale.

III REA [60R]

17. Recovery of sums

Any sum payable in pursuance of this Act (otherwise than by way of fine) shall be recoverable summarily as a civil debt.

III REA [60S]

18. Exception in case of Temples etc

(1) This Act shall not apply to land which is situated in inner London and in which there is an interest belonging to—

- (a) the Honourable Society of the Inner Temple,
- (b) the Honourable Society of the Middle Temple,
- (c) the Honourable Society of Lincoln's Inn, or
- (d) the Honourable Society of Gray's Inn.

(2) The reference in subsection (1) to inner London is to Greater London other than the outer London boroughs.

III REA [60T]

19. The Crown

(1) This Act shall apply to land in which there is—

- (a) an interest belonging to Her Majesty in right of the Crown,
- (b) an interest belonging to a government department, or
- (c) an interest held in trust for Her Majesty for the purposes of any such department.

(2) This Act shall apply to—

- (a) land which is vested in, but not occupied by, Her Majesty in right of the Duchy of Lancaster;
- (b) land which is vested in, but not occupied by, the possessor for the time being of the Duchy of Cornwall.

III REA [60U]

20. Interpretation

In this Act, unless the context otherwise requires, the following expressions have the meanings hereby respectively assigned to them—

"adjoining owner" and "adjoining occupier" respectively mean any owner and any occupier of land, buildings, storeys or rooms adjoining those of the building owner and for the purposes only of section 6 within the distances specified in that section;

"appointing officer" means the person appointed under this Act by the local authority to make such appointments as are required under section 10(8);

"building owner" means an owner of land who is desirous of exercising rights under this Act;

"foundation", in relation to a wall, means the solid ground or artificially formed support resting on solid ground on which the wall rests;

"owner" includes—

- (a) a person in receipt of, or entitled to receive, the whole or part of the rents or profits of land;
- (b) a person in possession of land, otherwise than as a mortgagee or as a tenant from year to year or for a lesser term or as a tenant at will;
- (c) a purchaser of an interest in land under a contract for purchase or under an agreement for a lease, otherwise than under an agreement for a tenancy from year to year or for a lesser term;

"party fence wall" means a wall (not being part of a building) which stands on lands of different owners and is used or constructed to be used for separating such adjoining lands, but does not include a wall constructed on the land of one owner the artificially formed support of which projects into the land of another owner;

"party structure" means a party wall and also a floor partition or other structure separating buildings or parts of buildings approached solely by separate staircases or separate entrances;

"party wall" means—

(a) a wall which forms part of a building and stands on lands of different owners to a greater extent than the projection of any artificially formed support on which the wall rests; and

(b) so much of a wall not being a wall referred to in paragraph (a) above as separates buildings belonging to different owners;

"special foundations" means foundations in which an assemblage of beams or rods is employed for the purpose of distributing any load; and

"surveyor" means any person not being a party to the matter appointed or selected under section 10 to determine disputes in accordance with the procedures set out in this Act.

III REA [60V]

21. Other statutory provisions

(1) The Secretary of State may by order amend or repeal any provision of a private or local Act passed before or in the same session as this Act, if it appears to him necessary or expedient to do so in consequence of this Act.

(2) An order under subsection (1) may—

(a) contain such savings or transitional provisions as the Secretary of State thinks fit;

(b) make different provision for different purposes.

(3) The power to make an order under subsection (1) shall be exercisable by statutory instrument subject to annulment in pursuance of a resolution of either House of Parliament.

General

III REA [60W]

22. Short title, commencement and extent

(1) This Act may be cited as the Party Wall etc Act 1996.

(2) This Act shall come into force in accordance with provision made by the Secretary of State by order made by statutory instrument.

(3) An order under subsection (2) may—

(a) contain such savings or transitional provisions as the Secretary of State thinks fit;

(b) make different provision for different purposes.

(4) This Act extends to England and Wales only.

LAND REGISTRATION ACT 2002

(c 9)

GENERAL NOTES ON LAND REGISTRATION ACT 2002

III REA [61]

Land Registration Act 2002 The Land Registration Act 1925 established a system of land registration. The Act of 1925 was amended by Land Registration Acts of 1936, 1986, 1988 and 1997, and by the Land Registration and Land Charges Act 1971. The Land Registration Act 2002 ("the Act"), which came into force on 13 October 2003, restated and partially reformed the previous law. The system will continue to be administered by H M Chief Land Registrar ("the registrar").

III REA [62]

The main reforms introduced by the Act were:

(a) to make provision for electronic conveyancing;

(b) to provide for there to be a separate register of cautions against first registration ("the cautions register") as well as to continue the register of title;

(c) to increase the kinds of disposition that are registrable, in particular by reducing the minimum length of leases that are registrable from 21 years to 7;

(d) to reduce the kinds of overriding interests (ie interests that bind a registered proprietor without being registered);

(e) to simplify, by reforming the provisions relating to notices and restrictions and abolishing inhibitions, the methods of protecting the interests of third parties over registered land;

(f) to make new provisions relating to the acquisition of title to registered land by persons in adverse possession (see **III LIM [49]–III LIM [52]**);

(g) to create the office of Adjudicator to HM Land Registry to determine certain kinds of disputes relating to land registration.

The policy underlying many of these changes was to improve the accuracy and completeness of the land register.

The provisions of the Act are extensively supplemented by rules, in particular the Land Registration Rules 2003 (SI 2003/1417), relevant extracts from which are given below.

The office of Adjudicator to HM Land Registry was abolished and his functions were transferred to the First-Tier Tribunal with effect from 1 July 2013 by the Transfer of Tribunal Functions Order 2013, SI 2013/1036.

III REA [63]

Powers of the courts and tribunals The principal circumstances in which the civil courts will be concerned with matters relating to land registration are:

III REA [64]

High Court and county court

(1) Making orders for the alteration of the cautions register and the register of title. See ss 20, 46 and Sch 4, printed below. Where a decision of the court on a matter of title gives rise to a need to alter the register, the court now has a duty to order the alteration. For the precise scope of the duty as regards the cautions register see the Land Registration Rules 2003, rule 48, printed below. For the precise scope of the duty as regards the register of title, see Sch 4 para 3(3) of the Act and the Land Registration Rules 2003 rule 126, printed below.

(2) Determining whether there is an entitlement to an indemnity payable under the Act, and the amount of an indemnity. See Sch 8, printed below.

(3) Awarding damages for breach of the duty imposed by the Act not to exercise certain rights conferred by the Act without reasonable cause. The rights concerned are to lodge a caution against first registration, to apply for the entry of a notice or restriction and to object to an application to the registrar. See s 77 of the Act.

(4) Hearing appeals from decisions of the First-tier Tribunal. See the notes on the First-tier Tribunal and on appeals below.

(5) Hearing appeals from decisions of the registrar relating to the production of documents (s 75 of the Act) and costs (s 76 of the Act).

III REA [65]

First-tier Tribunal The First-tier Tribunal now discharges functions originally conferred on the Adjudicator to HM Land Registry. Those functions include the following:

(1) To determine objections to applications to the registrar (see s 108 (1)(a) of the Act). When an application is made to the registrar, he must refer it to the Tribunal unless he is satisfied that it is groundless or is able to resolve it by agreement (see s 73(5)–(7)). The Tribunal may, instead of determining the reference itself, direct a party to commence proceedings to obtain the court's decision on the matter (see s 110(1) of the Act);

(2) To determine appeals against decisions of the registrar under Sch 4 para 5 of the Act (see s 108(1)(b) of the Act). Schedule 4 para 5 relates to access to facilities for electronic conveyancing.

(3) To determine applications for the rectification or setting aside of conveyancing documents (see s 108(2) of the Act).

The procedure of the Tribunal is regulated by Part 11 of the Act, the Land Registration (Referral to the Adjudicator to HM Land Registry) Rules 2003 (SI 2003/2114) and the Tribunal Procedure (First-tier Tribunal) (Property Chamber) Rules 2013 (SI 2013/1169).

A person aggrieved by a decision of the First-tier Tribunal may, with permission, appeal to the Upper Tribunal (see section 111 of the Act and section 11 of the Tribunals, Courts and Enforcement Act 2007). Where the appeal is from a decision of the First-tier Tribunal on an appeal under Sch 4 para 5 (relating to access to facilities for electronic conveyancing) the further appeal may only be on a point of law.

III REA [66]

Jurisdiction References in the Act to 'the court' are to the High Court or the county court: see s 232(3), below. Accordingly both the High Court and county court have jurisdiction to make orders in exercise of the powers conferred by the Act for the alteration of the cautions register and the land register.

Under the Land Registration Act 1925 it was held that the High Court also had an inherent jurisdiction to make orders for the rectification of the land register: *Clearbrook Property Holdings Ltd v Verrier* [1973] 3 All ER 614, [1974] 1 WLR 243; *Calgary and Edmonton Land Co Ltd v Dobinson* [1974] Ch 102 at 110, [1974] 1 All ER 484. The court has an inherent jurisdiction to order the vacation of unilateral notices registered under the 2002 Act. Where a unilateral notice has been registered to protect a claim to an interest in land and the registered proprietor seeks vacation of the notice in order to raise funds to defend the claim, the court's jurisdiction will be exercised by analogy with its jurisdiction to vary interim proprietary freezing orders to allow a defendant access to funds with which to defend the claim: *Nugent v Nugent* [2013] EWHC 4095 (Ch), [2015] Ch 121, [2014] 2 All ER 313.

In the High Court, a Master and a District Judge of the Chancery Division can make orders for alteration or rectification of the land register: PD 2B paras 7B.1, 7B.2.

Both the High Court and county court also have jurisdiction to make orders for the payment of an indemnity under the Act (Sch 8) and for damages for breach of the duty to act reasonably imposed by the Act (s 77). An order under either of these provisions will be for the payment of a sum recoverable by statute, where the county court has unlimited jurisdiction: County Courts Act 1984 s 16.

As noted above, appeals from the First-tier Tribunal lie to the Upper Tribunal.

III REA [67]

Transitional provisions Important transitional provisions are contained in Sch 12 of the Act and the Land Registration Act 2002 (Transitional Provisions) Order 2003 (SI 2003/1953).

III REA [68]

Substantive law For the substantive law relating to land registration, see Halsbury's Laws of England, 5th edn, and other practitioners' works. For practical guidance see the website of H M Land Registry at http://www.landregistry.gov.uk.

PART 2
FIRST REGISTRATION OF TITLE

CHAPTER 2 CAUTIONS AGAINST FIRST REGISTRATION

III REA [69]

15 Right to lodge

(1) . . . a person may lodge a caution against the registration of title to an unregistered legal estate if he claims to be—

(a) the owner of a qualifying estate, or

(b) entitled to an interest affecting a qualifying estate.

(2) For the purposes of subsection (1), a qualifying estate is a legal estate which—

(a) relates to land to which the caution relates, and

(b) is an interest of any of the following kinds—

(i) an estate in land,

(ii) a rentcharge,

(iii) a franchise, and

(iv) a profit a prendre in gross.

(3) . . .

(4) The right under subsection (1) is exercisable by application to the registrar.

III REA [70]

16 Effect

(1) Where an application for registration under this Part relates to a legal estate which is the subject of a caution against first registration, the registrar must give the cautioner notice of the application and of his right to object to it.

(2) The registrar may not determine an application to which subsection (1) applies before the end of such period as rules may provide, unless the cautioner has exercised his right to object to the application or given the registrar notice that he does not intend to do so.

(3) Except as provided by this section, a caution against first registration has no effect and, in particular, has no effect on the validity or priority of any interest of the cautioner in the legal estate to which the caution relates.

(4) For the purposes of subsection (1), notice given by a person acting on behalf of an applicant for registration under this Part is to be treated as given by the registrar if—

(a) the person is of a description provided by rules, and

(b) notice is given in such circumstances as rules may provide.

III REA [71]

19 Cautions register

(1) The registrar must keep a register of cautions against first registration.

(2) Rules may make provision about how the cautions register is to be kept and may, in particular, make provision about—

(a) the information to be included in the register,

(b) the form in which information included in the register is to be kept, and

(c) the arrangement of that information.

III REA [72]

20 Alteration of register by court

(1) The court may make an order for alteration of the cautions register for the purpose of—

(a) correcting a mistake, or

(b) bringing the register up to date.

(2) An order under subsection (1) has effect when served on the registrar to impose a duty on him to give effect to it.

(3) Rules may make provision about—

(a) the circumstances in which there is a duty to exercise the power under subsection (1),

(b) the form of an order under that subsection, and

(c) service of such an order.

III REA [73]

22 Supplementary

In this Chapter, "the cautioner", in relation to a caution against first registration, means the person who lodged the caution, or such other person as rules may provide.

III REA [73.1]

Cautions against first registration Section 19 of the Act requires the registrar to maintain a separate register of cautions against first registration of unregistered legal estates ("the cautions register"). Section 15 of the Act specifies who may lodge a caution against first registration, and s 16 sets out the effect of a caution against first registration. A caution does not give the cautioner priority for the right or interest claimed by him, but entitles him to be given notice of, and to object to, an application for first registration. The registrar must refer to the First-tier Tribunal an objection which he is unable to resolve by agreement, unless he is satisfied that it is groundless (see s 73(5)–(7) of the Act).

Sections 17 and 18 (not printed above) relate to the withdrawal and cancellation of cautions.

Section 20 of the Act gives the court power to make orders for alteration of the cautions register for the purpose of correcting a mistake or bringing the register up to date.

The Land Registration Rules 2003, Part 5 (relevant extracts from which are printed below) supplement the operation of these provisions. By virtue of rule 48, if in any proceedings the court decides that a cautioner does not own the interest claimed by the cautioner, or only owns part of it, or that such interest either wholly or in part does not exist or has come to an end, the court has a duty to make an order for the alteration of the cautions register. Rule 48 also makes provisions relating to the content and service of such orders.

RESTRICTIONS

III REA [74]

40 Nature

(1) A restriction is an entry in the register regulating the circumstances in which a disposition of a registered estate or charge may be the subject of an entry in the register.

(2) A restriction may, in particular—

(a) prohibit the making of an entry in respect of any disposition, or a disposition of a kind specified in the restriction;

(b) prohibit the making of an entry—

(i) indefinitely,

(ii) for a period specified in the restriction, or

(iii) until the occurrence of an event so specified.

(3) Without prejudice to the generality of subsection (2)(b)(iii), the events which may be specified include—

(a) the giving of notice,

(b) the obtaining of consent, and

(c) the making of an order by the court or registrar.

(4) The entry of a restriction is to be made in relation to the registered estate or charge to which it relates.

III REA [75]

41 Effect

(1) Where a restriction is entered in the register, no entry in respect of a disposition to which the restriction applies may be made in the register otherwise than in accordance with the terms of the restriction, subject to any order under subsection (2).

(2) The registrar may by order—

(a) disapply a restriction in relation to a disposition specified in the order or dispositions of a kind so specified, or

(b) provide that a restriction has effect, in relation to a disposition specified in the order or dispositions of a kind so specified, with modifications so specified.

(3) The power under subsection (2) is exercisable only on the application of a person who appears to the registrar to have a sufficient interest in the restriction.

III REA [76]

46 Power of court to order entry

(1) If it appears to the court that it is necessary or desirable to do so for the purpose of protecting a right or claim in relation to a registered estate or charge, it may make an order requiring the registrar to enter a restriction in the register.

(2) No order under this section may be made for the purpose of protecting the priority of an interest which is, or could be, the subject of a notice.

(3) The court may include in an order under this section a direction that an entry made in pursuance of the order is to have overriding priority.

(4) If an order under this section includes a direction under subsection (3), the registrar must make such entry in the register as rules may provide.

(5) The court may make the exercise of its power under subsection (3) subject to such terms and conditions as it thinks fit.

III REA [76.1]

Restrictions Restrictions under the Land Registration Act 2002 take the place of both inhibitions and restrictions under the former law. Section 40(1) provides that a restriction is an entry on the register regulating the circumstances in which a disposition of a registered estate or charge may be entered on the register. Examples of the form a restriction may take are given in ss 40(2) and (3). Section 41(1) provides that (subject to any order made by the registrar under sub-s (2)), no entry may be made by the registrar otherwise than in accordance with the terms of the disposition.

Section 46(1) gives the court power to order the entry of a restriction. For example, if the court has determined that a person is entitled to a beneficial interest in land under a trust, it might also order the entry of a restriction to ensure that there was no disposition of the registered estate without the prior consent of the beneficiary. Again, if the court has granted a "freezing" injunction, it might also order a restriction preventing the registration of any disposition of land affected by the injunction without the consent of the claimant or the court.

Section 46(3) gives the court the power to direct that a restriction ordered by it has overriding effect. If such a direction is made, the restriction overrides the priority protection given to an official search or the entry of a notice in respect of an estate contract: see further s 72 of the Act, especially s 72(4).

Section 46(5) enables the court to impose terms and conditions on the exercise of the power under section 46(3). For example, a term might be imposed requiring an applicant for the restriction to undertake to indemnify any person acting in good faith who has suffered loss as a result of the court's direction, or to require the applicant to give security, pay money into court, pay costs, or to withdraw some other entry in the register.

PART 6
REGISTRATION: GENERAL
ALTERATION OF REGISTER

III REA [77]

65 Alteration of register

Schedule 4 (which makes provision about alteration of the register) has effect.

III REA [77.1]

See the extracts from Schedule 4 below.

PART 10
LAND REGISTRY
FEES AND INDEMNITIES

III REA [78]

103 Indemnities

Schedule 8 (which makes provision for the payment of indemnities by the registrar) has effect.

III REA [78.1]

Schedule 8 is set out below.

PART 12
MISCELLANEOUS AND GENERAL
SUPPLEMENTARY

III REA [79]

131 "Proprietor in possession"

(1) For the purposes of this Act, land is in the possession of the proprietor of a registered estate in land if it is physically in his possession, or in that of a person who is entitled to be registered as the proprietor of the registered estate.

(2) In the case of the following relationships, land which is (or is treated as being) in the possession of the second-mentioned person is to be treated for the purposes of subsection (1) as in the possession of the first-mentioned person—

- (a) landlord and tenant;
- (b) mortgagor and mortgagee;
- (c) licensor and licensee;
- (d) trustee and beneficiary.

(3) In subsection (1), the reference to entitlement does not include entitlement under Schedule 6.

III REA [79.1]

Proprietor in possession The register may not be rectified so as to affect the title of a registered proprietor who is in possession, within the meaning of this section, unless the requirements of Schedule 4 para 3(2) are satisfied. See further the extracts from and notes to Schedule 4, below.

III REA [80]

132 General interpretation

(1) In this Act—

...

"assured tenancy" has the same meaning as in Part 1 of the Housing Act 1988;

"caution against first registration" means a caution lodged under section 15;

"cautions register" means the register kept under section 19(1);

"charge" means any mortgage, charge or lien for securing money or money's worth;

"demesne land" means land belonging to Her Majesty in right of the Crown which is not held for an estate in fee simple absolute in possession;

"dwelling-house" has the same meaning as in Part 1 of the Housing Act 1988;

"flexible tenancy" has the meaning given by section *107A* [115B] of the Housing Act 1985;

["introductory tenancy" has the same meaning as in Chapter 1 of Part 5 of the Housing Act 1996;]

"land" includes—

(a) buildings and other structures,

(b) land covered with water, and

(c) mines and minerals, whether or not held with the surface;

"land registration rules" means any rules under this Act, other than rules under section 93, Part 11, section 121 or paragraph 1, 2 or 3 of Schedule 5;

"legal estate" has the same meaning as in the Law of Property Act 1925 (c 20);

"legal mortgage" has the same meaning as in the Law of Property Act 1925;

"long tenancy" means a tenancy granted for a term certain of more than 21 years, whether or not it is (or may become) terminable before the end of that term by notice given by the tenant or by re-entry or forfeiture;

"mines and minerals" includes any strata or seam of minerals or substances in or under any land, and powers of working and getting any such minerals or substances;

"registrar" means the Chief Land Registrar;

"register" means the register of title, except in the context of cautions against first registration;

"registered" means entered in the register;

"registered charge" means a charge the title to which is entered in the register;

"registered estate" means a legal estate the title to which is entered in the register, other than a registered charge;

"registered land" means a registered estate or registered charge;

"registrable disposition" means a disposition which is required to be completed by registration under section 27;

"relevant social housing tenancy" means—

(a) a flexible tenancy, *or*

[(aa) a secure tenancy of a dwelling-house in England granted on or after the day on which paragraph 4 of Schedule 7 to the Housing and Planning Act 2016 comes fully into force,

(ab) an introductory tenancy of a dwelling-house in England granted on or after the day on which paragraph 4 of Schedule 7 to the Housing and Planning Act 2016 comes fully into force, or]

(b) an assured tenancy of a dwelling-house in England granted by a private registered provider of social housing, other than a long tenancy or a shared ownership lease;

"requirement of registration" means the requirement of registration under section 4;

["secure tenancy" has the meaning given by section 79 of the Housing Act 1985;]

"shared ownership lease" means a lease of a dwelling-house—

(a) granted on payment of a premium calculated by reference to a percentage of the value of the dwelling-house or of the cost of providing it, or

(b) under which the lessee (or the lessee's personal representatives) will or may be entitled to a sum calculated by reference, directly or indirectly, to the value of the dwelling-house;

"sub-charge" means a charge under section 23(2)(b);

"term of years absolute" has the same meaning as in the Law of Property Act 1925 (c 20);

"valuable consideration" does not include marriage consideration or a nominal consideration in money.

(2) In subsection (1), in the definition of "demesne land", the reference to land belonging to Her Majesty does not include land in relation to which a freehold estate in land has determined, but in relation to which there has been no act of entry or management by the Crown.

(3) In this Act—

(a) references to the court are to the High Court or the county court,

(b) references to an interest affecting an estate or charge are to an adverse right affecting the title to the estate or charge, and

(c) references to the right to object to an application to the registrar are to the right under section 73.

Amendment *Text in italic is deleted and text in square brackets is inserted by the Housing and Planning Act 2016, with effect from a date to be appointed.*

SCHEDULE 4
ALTERATION OF THE REGISTER

III REA [81]

Introductory

1 In this Schedule, references to rectification, in relation to alteration of the register, are to alteration which—

(a) involves the correction of a mistake, and

(b) prejudicially affects the title of a registered proprietor.

Alteration pursuant to a court order

2 (1) The court may make an order for alteration of the register for the purpose of—

(a) correcting a mistake,

(b) bringing the register up to date, or

(c) giving effect to any estate, right or interest excepted from the effect of registration.

(2) An order under this paragraph has effect when served on the registrar to impose a duty on him to give effect to it.

3 (1) This paragraph applies to the power under paragraph 2, so far as relating to rectification.

(2) If alteration affects the title of the proprietor of a registered estate in land, no order may be made under paragraph 2 without the proprietor's consent in relation to land in his possession unless—

(a) he has by fraud or lack of proper care caused or substantially contributed to the mistake, or

(b) it would for any other reason be unjust for the alteration not to be made.

(3) If in any proceedings the court has power to make an order under paragraph 2, it must do so, unless there are exceptional circumstances which justify its not doing so.

(4) In sub-paragraph (2), the reference to the title of the proprietor of a registered estate in land includes his title to any registered estate which subsists for the benefit of the estate in land.

4 Rules may—

(a) make provision about the circumstances in which there is a duty to exercise the power under paragraph 2, so far as not relating to rectification;

(b) make provision about the form of an order under paragraph 2;

(c) make provision about service of such an order.

Rectification and derivative interests

(8) The powers under this Schedule to alter the register, so far as relating to rectification, extend to changing for the future the priority of any interest affecting the registered estate or charge concerned.

Costs in non-rectification cases

9 (1) If the register is altered under this Schedule in a case not involving rectification, the registrar may pay such amount as he thinks fit in respect of any costs or expenses reasonably incurred by a person in connection with the alteration which have been incurred with the consent of the registrar.

(2) The registrar may make a payment under sub-paragraph (1) notwithstanding the absence of consent if—

(a) it appears to him—

(i) that the costs or expenses had to be incurred urgently, and

(ii) that it was not reasonably practicable to apply for his consent, or

(b) he has subsequently approved the incurring of the costs or expenses.

III REA [81.1]

Alteration of the land register Under the Land Registration Act 1925, the term 'rectification' applied to all alterations to the register. Under the Land Registration Act 2002, that term has a narrower meaning, namely an alteration of the register which (a) involves the correction of a mistake, and (b) prejudicially affects the title of a registered proprietor. An alteration to reflect an overriding interest will not, therefore, be "rectification": since the interest binds the registered proprietor irrespective of registration, he will not be prejudicially affected if it is entered on the register.

The court has power to order that the register be altered in the three cases set out in Schedule 4 paragraph 2.

The first of these is the correction of a mistake.

The term 'mistake' includes mistakes of a substantive, as well as of a procedural, character.

For alteration of the register to correct a mistake consisting of the registration of a transfer procured by forgery, see *Fitzwilliam v Richall Holdings Services Ltd* [2013] EWHC 86 (Ch), [2013] 1 P & CR 318, [2013] 2 EGLR 183.

If a person is registered as proprietor of land following an application made under Sch 6, para 1, the former registered proprietor may nevertheless obtain the alteration of the register to restore himself as the registered proprietor if he proves that the statutory preconditions to registration in Sch 6, para 1 were not met and that (if applicable) the conditions in Sch 4, paras 3(2) and (3) are satisfied. The jurisdiction to alter the register exists even if the former registered proprietor did not object to the applicant's application, so that the registration of the applicant was not made in consequence of any procedural mistake by the Land Registry: *Baxter v Mannion* [2011] EWCA Civ 120, [2011] 2 All ER 574, [2011] 1 WLR 594 (a decision on the corresponding provisions in Sch 4, paras 5 and 6).

An alteration to correct a mistake will be 'rectification' if it prejudicially affects the title of a registered proprietor. If the registered proprietor whose title would be prejudicially affected is 'in possession', the court may not make the alteration unless (a) the registered proprietor consents, (b) the registered proprietor has by fraud or lack of proper care caused or substantially contributed to the mistake, or (c) it would for any other reason be unjust for the alteration not to be made: see para 3(2) of Schedule 4. Thus the title of a registered proprietor who is in possession is given a degree of protection from being altered. For what is meant by land being "in possession" of a registered proprietor, see s 131 above.

A person who suffers loss by reason of rectification of the register may have right to an indemnity under the provisions of Schedule 8, printed below.

The second kind of case in which the court has power to order the alteration of the register is for the purpose of bringing it up to date. For example, if the court declares that a registered lease has been validly forfeited, it has power (and in the circumstances referred to below, the duty) to order that the register be altered by the removal of the entry of the lease.

The third kind of case in which the court has power to order the alteration of the register is for the purpose of giving effect to any estate, right or interest excepted from the effect of registration. For estates, rights or interests excepted from the effect of registration, see ss 9 to 12 of the Act.

If in any proceedings the court decides that there is a mistake in the register, that the register is not up to date, or there is an estate, right or interest excepted from the effect of registration that should be given effect to, the court must make an order for alteration of the register, unless there are exceptional circumstances that justify not doing so. See Schedule 4 para 3(3) (rectification cases) and the Land Registration Rules 2003, rule 126 (non-rectification cases).

The policy of the Land Registration Act 2002 is that the register should be a complete and accurate statement of the position at any given time. Consequently, where a disposition is voidable but has not been avoided, an entry in the register to reflect the disposition is not a "mistake" within the meaning of Schedule 4, nor will it become a mistake if the disposition is later rescinded, because the entry was correct at the time it was made. If the disposition is avoided by an order of the court, the court may, and in the circumstances covered by paragraph 3 must, make an order under paragraph 2(1)(b) for the purpose of bringing the register up to date: *NRAM Ltd v Evans* [2017] EWCA Civ 1013, [2018] 1 WLR 639.

Where (1) a person (T) was registered as proprietor of land pursuant to an order of the court in 2007, (2) T granted a legal charge of the land in favour of B, (C) T was registered as proprietor of the land and B was registered as proprietor of the charge and (C) some of the documents used to obtain the 2007 order were subsequently held to be forgeries, neither the registration of T as proprietor of the land nor the registration of the charge in favour of B were "mistakes" within the meaning of Schedule 4 to the Land Registration Act 2002, because at the time the registrations were made the 2007 order was a valid order of the court, even if it was liable to be set aside: *Antoine v Barclays Bank UK Plc* [2018] EWCA Civ 2846.

III REA [81.2]

Rectification and derivative interests Where the court orders rectification of the register by ordering the registration of a derivative interest that has been mistakenly removed from the register, the effect of para (8) is that the court's power extends to conferring on that interest the priority it would have had if the interest had not been mistakenly removed. So where:

(1) lease A is mistakenly removed from the register,
(2) lease B, of the same property, is registered and
(3) the proprietor of lease A is entitled to rectification of the register to correct the mistaken removal of lease A,

the court has power to order that the register be rectified by registering lease A with priority over interest B. Such rectification operates prospectively only, so it does not give lease A priority over lease B during the period between the registration of lease B and the making of the order for rectification: *Macleod v Gold Harp Properties Ltd* [2014] EWCA Civ 1084, [2015] 1 WLR 1249, [2014] 3 EGLR 133.

SCHEDULE 8
INDEMNITIES

III REA [82]

Entitlement

1 (1) A person is entitled to be indemnified by the registrar if he suffers loss by reason of—

(a) rectification of the register,

(b) a mistake whose correction would involve rectification of the register,

(c) a mistake in an official search,

(d) a mistake in an official copy,

(e) a mistake in a document kept by the registrar which is not an original and is referred to in the register,

(f) the loss or destruction of a document lodged at the registry for inspection or safe custody,

(g) a mistake in the cautions register, or

(h) failure by the registrar to perform his duty under section 50.

(2) For the purposes of sub-paragraph (1)(a)—

(a) any person who suffers loss by reason of the change of title under section 62 is to be regarded as having suffered loss by reason of rectification of the register, and

(b) the proprietor of a registered estate or charge claiming in good faith under a forged disposition is, where the register is rectified, to be regarded as having suffered loss by reason of such rectification as if the disposition had not been forged.

(3) No indemnity under sub-paragraph (1)(b) is payable until a decision has been made about whether to alter the register for the purpose of correcting the mistake; and the loss suffered by reason of the mistake is to be determined in the light of that decision.

Mines and minerals

2 No indemnity is payable under this Schedule on account of—

(a) any mines or minerals, or

(b) the existence of any right to work or get mines or minerals,

unless it is noted in the register that the title to the registered estate concerned includes the mines or minerals.

Costs

3 (1) In respect of loss consisting of costs or expenses incurred by the claimant in relation to the matter, an indemnity under this Schedule is payable only on account of costs or expenses reasonably incurred by the claimant with the consent of the registrar.

(2) The requirement of consent does not apply where—

(a) the costs or expenses must be incurred by the claimant urgently, and

(b) it is not reasonably practicable to apply for the registrar's consent.

(3) If the registrar approves the incurring of costs or expenses after they have been incurred, they shall be treated for the purposes of this paragraph as having been incurred with his consent.

4 (1) If no indemnity is payable to a claimant under this Schedule, the registrar may pay such amount as he thinks fit in respect of any costs or expenses reasonably incurred by the claimant in connection with the claim which have been incurred with the consent of the registrar.

(2) The registrar may make a payment under sub-paragraph (1) notwithstanding the absence of consent if—

(a) it appears to him—

(i) that the costs or expenses had to be incurred urgently, and

(ii) that it was not reasonably practicable to apply for his consent, or

(b) he has subsequently approved the incurring of the costs or expenses.

Claimant's fraud or lack of care

5 (1) No indemnity is payable under this Schedule on account of any loss suffered by a claimant—

(a) wholly or partly as a result of his own fraud, or

(b) wholly as a result of his own lack of proper care.

(2) Where any loss is suffered by a claimant partly as a result of his own lack of proper care, any indemnity payable to him is to be reduced to such extent as is fair having regard to his share in the responsibility for the loss.

(3) For the purposes of this paragraph any fraud or lack of care on the part of a person from whom the claimant derives title (otherwise than under a disposition for valuable consideration which is registered or protected by an entry in the register) is to be treated as if it were fraud or lack of care on the part of the claimant.

Valuation of estates etc

6 Where an indemnity is payable in respect of the loss of an estate, interest or charge, the value of the estate, interest or charge for the purposes of the indemnity is to be regarded as not exceeding—

(a) in the case of an indemnity under paragraph 1(1)(a), its value immediately before rectification of the register (but as if there were to be no rectification), and

(b) in the case of an indemnity under paragraph 1(1)(b), its value at the time when the mistake which caused the loss was made.

Determination of indemnity by court

7 (1) A person may apply to the court for the determination of any question as to—

(a) whether he is entitled to an indemnity under this Schedule, or

(b) the amount of such an indemnity.

(2) Paragraph 3(1) does not apply to the costs of an application to the court under this paragraph or of any legal proceedings arising out of such an application.

Time limits

8 For the purposes of the Limitation Act 1980 (c 58)—

(a) a liability to pay an indemnity under this Schedule is a simple contract debt, and

(b) the cause of action arises at the time when the claimant knows, or but for his own default might have known, of the existence of his claim.

Interest

9 Rules may make provision about the payment of interest on an indemnity under this Schedule, including—

(a) the circumstances in which interest is payable, and

(b) the periods for and rates at which it is payable.

Recovery of indemnity by registrar

10 (1) Where an indemnity under this Schedule is paid to a claimant in respect of any loss, the registrar is entitled (without prejudice to any other rights he may have)—

(a) to recover the amount paid from any person who caused or substantially contributed to the loss by his fraud, or

(b) for the purpose of recovering the amount paid, to enforce the rights of action referred to in sub-paragraph (2).

(2) Those rights of action are—

(a) any right of action (of whatever nature and however arising) which the claimant would have been entitled to enforce had the indemnity not been paid, and

(b) where the register has been rectified, any right of action (of whatever nature and however arising) which the person in whose favour the register has been rectified would have been entitled to enforce had it not been rectified.

(3) References in this paragraph to an indemnity include interest paid on an indemnity under rules under paragraph 9.

Interpretation

11 (1) For the purposes of this Schedule, references to a mistake in something include anything mistakenly omitted from it as well as anything mistakenly included in it.

(2) In this Schedule, references to rectification of the register are to alteration of the register which—

(a) involves the correction of a mistake, and

(b) prejudicially affects the title of a registered proprietor.

III REA [82.1]

Indemnities Paragraph 1 of Schedule 8 sets out eight circumstances by reason of which a person is entitled to be indemnified by the registrar in respect of loss.

The first (paragraph (a)) is rectification of the register. The meaning of this term is defined in paragraph 11 in the same way as in Schedule 4. It is narrower than the meaning of the term under the Land Registration Act 1925. Paragraph 1(2) expands the scope of paragraph 1(1)(a) to include loss suffered by reason of the upgrading of a title under s 62 of the Act. It also establishes that the proprietor of a registered estate or charge claiming in good faith under a forged disposition is, when the register is rectified, to be regarded as having suffered loss by reason of such rectification as if the disposition had not been forged. But for this provision, it would have been arguable that the proprietor suffered no loss, as the disposition, being forged, was ineffective to pass title.

Five further cases (paras (b), (c), (d), and (g)) relate to various kinds of mistake. The meaning of "mistake" is partially defined in para 11(1). It is not a necessary element of the concept of mistake that the Land Registry, or any other person, should have been at fault. Paragraph (b) (a mistake whose correction would involve rectification of the register) must be read with paragraph 1(3).

The remaining two cases relate to the loss or destruction of documents and to the registrar's duty under s 50 of the Act (whereby the registrar is required to give notice of the entry of an overriding statutory charge).

Paragraph 3 restricts a claimant's entitlement to an indemnity in respect of costs incurred without the registrar's consent. This paragraph is qualified in the case of the costs of court proceedings by para 7(1).

Paragraph 4 relates to the position of a claimant to whom an indemnity is payable but who has reasonably incurred costs (for example in reasonably investigating a matter which is then found not to give rise to a right of indemnity).

Paragraph 5 prevents an indemnity being payable in respect of a loss suffered by a claimant wholly or partly on account of his own fraud, or wholly on account of his lack of proper care. Where the loss is suffered partly on account of the claimant's lack of proper care, the indemnity payable may be reduced to such extent as is fair. Fraud or lack of care by persons from whom the claimant derived title otherwise than under a disposition for value which are registered or protected on the register is treated as if it were fraud or lack of care on the part of the claimant himself.

Paragraph 6 limits the maximum indemnity payable in respect of the loss of an estate, interest or charge.

Paragraph 7 gives the court jurisdiction to determine whether any person is entitled to an indemnity and its amount. For the meaning of "court" see s 132(2) and the note "jurisdiction" above.

Paragraphs 8, 9 and 10 relate to limitation issues, interest and rights by way of subrogation available to the registrar.

For consideration of the operation of the provisions for the payment of an indemnity in respect of an error in an official certificate of search under the Land Registration Act 1925, see *Prestige Properties Ltd v Scottish Provident Institution* [2002] EWHC 30 (Ch), [2003] Ch 1.

III REA [82.2]

Forged dispositions Under the general law, a forged disposition is of no legal effect. The effect of para 1(2)(b) of Schedule 8 is that, where the register is rectified by the cancellation of the interest of a person claiming in good faith under a forged disposition, that person is deemed to have suffered loss by reason of such rectification, notwithstanding that the disposition under which he claimed would, in the absence of registration, have had no legal effect. Accordingly if:

(1) A is the registered proprietor of land,
(2) a forged charge in favour of B is registered against the title to the land,
(3) B in good faith advances money on the security of the charge and
(4) the register is rectified by the cancellation of the charge,

B is entitled to an indemnity equal to the value the charge would have had if it had not been forged. Further, if A has an overriding interest which has priority over B's charge, the value of the indemnity to which B is entitled is not reduced on the ground of that overriding interest: *Swift 1st Ltd v Chief Land Registrar* [2015] EWCA Civ 330, [2015] Ch 602.

LAND REGISTRATION RULES 2003

(SI 2003/1417)

PART 5
CAUTIONS AGAINST FIRST REGISTRATION

III REA [83]

39 Definitions

In this Part -

"cautioner" has the same meaning as in section 22 of the Act (read with rule 52),

"cautioner's register" is the register so named in rule 41(2) the contents of which are described in rule 41(5),

"relevant interest" means the interest claimed by the cautioner in the unregistered legal estate to which the caution against first registration relates.

III REA [84]

48 Alteration of the cautions register by the court

(1) If in any proceedings the court decides that the cautioner does not own the relevant interest, or only owns part, or that such interest either wholly or in part did not exist or has come to an end, the court must make an order for alteration of the cautions register under section 20(1) of the Act.

(2) An order for alteration of the cautions register must state the caution title number of the individual caution register affected, describe the alteration that is to be made, and direct the registrar to make the alteration.

(3) For the purposes of section 20(2) of the Act an order for alteration of the cautions register may only be served on the registrar by making an application for him to give effect to the order.

III REA [85]

52 Definition of "the cautioner"

(1) The other person referred to in sections 22 and 73(2) of the Act shall be the person for the time being shown as cautioner in the cautioner's register, where that person is not the person who lodged the caution against first registration.

(2) Where the cautioner shown in the cautioner's register comprises more than one person, then each such person has a separate right to object to an application made under section 18 of the Act.

III REA [85.1]

Cautions against first registration Part V of the Land Registration Rules 2003 supplements Part 2 Chapter 2 of the Act, dealing with cautions against first registration. See the notes to that Part above.

PART 12
ALTERATIONS AND CORRECTIONS

III REA [86]

126 Alteration under a court order – not rectification

(1) Subject to paragraphs (2) and (3), if in any proceedings the court decides that –

- (a) there is a mistake in the register,
- (b) the register is not up to date, or
- (c) there is an estate, right or interest excepted from the effect of registration that should be given effect to,

it must make an order for alteration of the register under the power given by paragraph 2(1) of Schedule 4 to the Act.

(2) The court is not obliged to make an order if there are exceptional circumstances that justify not doing so.

(3) This rule does not apply to an alteration of the register that amounts to rectification.

III REA [87]

127 Court order for alteration of the register-form and service

(1) An order for alteration of the register must state the title number of the title affected and the alteration that is to be made, and must direct the registrar to make the alteration.

(2) Service on the registrar of an order for alteration of the register must be made by making an application for the registrar to give effect to the order, accompanied by the order.

III REA [87.1]

Alteration of the register Part 12 of the Land Registration Rules 2003 supplements Schedule 4, dealing with alteration of the register. See the notes to Schedule 4 above.

MORTGAGE REPOSSESSIONS (PROTECTION OF TENANTS ETC) ACT 2010

(c 19)

GENERAL NOTE ON MORTGAGE REPOSSESSIONS (PROTECTION OF TENANTS ETC) ACT 2010

III REA [88]

This Act serves two functions. First, it empowers the court, on the application of a tenant of residential property whose tenancy is not binding on a mortgagee, to postpone the date for delivery of possession to the mortgagee by up to two months. Second, it requires occupiers of residential property to be given notice of an application by a mortgage of an application for a warrant for possession. The Act, and the Dwelling Houses (Execution of Possession Orders by Mortgagees) Regulations 2010, SI 2010/1809, made under s 2, were brought into force on 1st October 2010.

III REA [89]

1 Power of court to postpone giving of possession

(1) This section applies if—

(a) the mortgagee under a mortgage of land which consists of or includes a dwelling-house brings an action (other than an action for foreclosure) in which the mortgagee claims possession of the mortgaged property, and

(b) there is an unauthorised tenancy of all or part of the property.

(2) When making an order for delivery of possession of the property, the court may, on the application of the tenant, postpone the date for delivery of possession for a period not exceeding two months.

(3) Subsection (4) applies where an order for delivery of possession of the property has been made but not executed.

(4) The court may, on the application of the tenant ("the applicant"), stay or suspend execution of the order for a period not exceeding two months if—

(a) the court did not exercise its powers under subsection (2) when making the order or, if it did, the applicant was not the tenant when it exercised those powers,

(b) the applicant has asked the mortgagee to give an undertaking in writing not to enforce the order for two months beginning with the date the undertaking is given, and

(c) the mortgagee has not given such an undertaking.

(5) When considering whether to exercise its powers under this section, the court must have regard to—

(a) the circumstances of the tenant, and

(b) if there is an outstanding breach by the tenant of a term of the unauthorised tenancy—
   (i) the nature of that breach, and
   (ii) whether the tenant might reasonably be expected to have avoided breaching that term or to have remedied the breach.

(6) The court may make any postponement, stay or suspension under this section conditional on the making of payments to the mortgagee in respect of the occupation of the property (or part of the property) during the period of the postponement, stay or suspension.

(7) The making of any payment pursuant to—
(a) a condition of an undertaking of a kind mentioned in subsection (4)(c), or
(b) a condition imposed by virtue of subsection (6),

is not to be regarded as creating (or as evidence of the creation of) any tenancy or other right to occupy the property.

(8) For the purposes of this section there is an "unauthorised tenancy" if—
(a) an agreement has been made which, as between the parties to it (or their successors in title), is or gives rise to—
   (i) an assured tenancy (within the meaning of the Housing Act 1988), or
   (ii) a protected or statutory tenancy (within the meaning of the Rent Act 1977), and
(b) the mortgagee's interest in the property is not subject to the tenancy.

(9) In this section "the tenant", in relation to an unauthorised tenancy, means the person who is, as between the parties to the agreement in question (or their successors in title), the tenant under the unauthorised tenancy (or, if there is more than one tenant, any of them).

III REA [89.1]

Section 1 of the Act: Background A tenancy granted by a mortgagor will be binding as between the mortgagor and the tenant, at least as a tenancy by estoppel, but it may not be binding on the mortgagee. It will usually be binding on the mortgagee if it was granted prior to the mortgage, or if it was granted after the mortgage in accordance with powers of letting conferred on the mortgagor by the mortgage. It will usually not be binding on the mortgagee if it was granted after the mortgage and otherwise than in accordance with any powers of letting conferred on the mortgagor by the mortgage.

If the tenancy is binding on the mortgagee, the mortgagee may not obtain possession from the tenant save in accordance with the terms of the tenancy. If the tenancy is not binding on the mortgagee, the mortgagee may obtain possession from the tenant notwithstanding the tenancy: *Dudley and District Building Society v Emerson* [1949] Ch 707, [1949] 2 All ER 252, CA. Section 1 of the Act is intended to ameliorate the position of tenants whose tenancy is not binding on the mortgagee by empowering the court to defer the obtaining of possession by up to two months.

III REA [89.2]

Summary of the section The section applies where a mortgagee of land which consists of or includes a dwelling house brings an action for possession and there is either an assured tenancy of the property within the meaning of the Housing Act 1980 or a protected or statutory tenancy of the property within the meaning of the Rent Act 1977 which is not binding on the mortgagee (sub-ss (1), (8) and (9)). When making an order for possession in favour of the mortgagee, the court may, on the application of the tenant, postpone the date for delivery of possession for a period not exceeding two months (sub-s (2)), and see CPR Part 55, rule 10(4A). Alternatively, if the court has not exercised that power, and an order for possession has been made in favour of the mortgagee but not executed, the court may, again on the application of the tenant, stay or suspend execution of the order for possession for a period not exceeding two months. It is a pre-condition of the exercise of the latter power that the tenant has asked the mortgagee to give a written undertaking not to enforce the order for two months and the mortgagee has not given the undertaking (sub-ss (3) and (4)). When considering whether to exercise either power, the court must have regard to the tenant's circumstances and any breach of the terms of the tenancy (subsection (5)), and it may make any postponement, stay or suspension conditional on the making of payments to the mortgagee in respect of the occupation of the property (sub-s (6)). However, the making of such payments is not to be regarded as creating or as evidence of the creation of any tenancy or other right to occupy the property (sub-s (7)).

The powers given by the section can only be exercised on the application of a tenant of the specified kinds whose tenancy is not binding on the mortgagee. Thus, the powers cannot be exercised on the application of the mortgagor (whose position is protected by Part IV of the Administration of Justice Act 1970 (**III REA [22]**) and Part II of the Administration of Justice Act 1973 (**III REA [30A]**), or on the application of a lodger or other licensee.

III REA [90]

2. Notice of execution of possession order

(1) This section applies where the mortgagee under a mortgage of land which consists of or includes a dwelling-house has obtained an order for possession of the mortgaged property.

(2) The order may be executed—

(a) only if the mortgagee gives notice at the property of any prescribed step taken for the purpose of executing the order, and

(b) only after the end of a prescribed period beginning with the day on which such notice is given.

(3) "Prescribed" means prescribed by regulations made by the Secretary of State.

(4) Regulations made by the Secretary of State may prescribe the form of notices and the way in which they must be given.

(5) The regulations may make supplementary, incidental, transitional or saving provision.

(6) Regulations under this section may be made only with the consent of the Lord Chancellor.

(7) Regulations under this section are to be made by statutory instrument.

(8) A statutory instrument containing regulations made under this section is subject to annulment in pursuance of a resolution of either House of Parliament.

III REA [90.1]

Section 2 of the Act: Background A mortgagee seeking possession of land which consists of or includes residential property must, independently of this Act, send notice of the proceedings to the property addressed to "the tenant or the occupier" (and to other persons): CPR Part 50, rule 10. This section introduces a further requirement intended to ensure that persons in occupation of mortgaged property become aware of possession proceedings by a mortgagee. It requires a mortgagee of property which consists of or includes a dwelling house who has obtained an order for possession to give notice to occupiers of an application for a warrant of possession. In contrast to section 1, the section applies irrespective of whether the property is occupied by a tenant whose tenant is not binding on the mortgagee.

III REA [90.2]

Regulations The Dwelling Houses (Execution of Possession Orders by Mortgagees) Regulations 2010, SI 2010/1809 have been made pursuant to this section. By virtue of para 2 of the regulations, the "prescribed step" referred to in s 2(2)(a) of the Act is the mortgagee making an application to the court for a warrant for possession of the property, and by virtue of para 3 the "prescribed period" referred to in s 2(2)(b) is 14 days. Paragraph 4 of the Regulations prescribes a form of notice under s 2(4) of the Act, and paragraph 5 provides that the notice under reg 4 it may be given either:

"(a) by sending the notice to the property by first class post or registered post in an envelope addressed—

(i) to the tenant by name, or

(ii) if the tenant's name is not known, to "The Tenant or Occupier";

(b) by leaving the notice at the property—

(i) in an envelope addressed as described in subparagraph (a), or

(ii) affixed to and displayed in a prominent place where its contents can be read by a person entering the property; or

(c) by personal service upon a person who appears to be in residence at the property."

Accordingly, the order for possession can only be executed 14 days after the mortgagee has given a notice in the prescribed form in one of the ways specified in reg 5. When applying for a warrant of possession, the claimant must certify that notice has been given in accordance with the regulations: CCR 26, r 17(2A); Form N325.

III REA [91]

3. Interpretation

(1) This section applies for the purposes of this Act.

(2) "Dwelling-house" includes any building, or part of a building, that is used as a dwelling.

(3) The fact that part of the premises comprised in a dwelling-house is used as a shop or office, or for other business, trade or professional purposes, does not prevent the dwelling-house from being a dwelling-house for the purposes of this Act.

(4) "Mortgage" includes a charge, and "mortgagee" is to be read accordingly.

(5) "Mortgagee" includes any person deriving title under the original mortgagee.

(6) "Order" includes a judgment, and references to the making of an order are to be read accordingly.

III REA [92]

4. Commencement, extent and short title

(1) This Act (except this section) comes into force on such day as the Secretary of State may by order made by statutory instrument appoint (and different days may be appointed for different purposes).

(2) An order under subsection (1) may make transitional or saving provision.

(3) This Act extends to England and Wales only.

(4) This Act may be cited as the Mortgage Repossessions (Protection of Tenants etc) Act 2010.

SOLICITORS AND OTHER LEGAL REPRESENTATIVES

TABLE OF CONTENTS

GENERAL NOTES ON LEGAL SERVICES PROVIDERS

III SOL [1]

The activities of individuals and bodies offering legal services are governed primarily by the Legal Services Act 2007 ('the 2007 Act') which establishes the regulatory framework governing reserved activities and the legal professions, the Legal Complaints Service (which runs the Legal Ombudsman scheme) and provides for the establishment of alternative business structures. The Solicitors Act 1974, as supplemented by the Administration of Justice Act 1985 sets out detailed provisions governing solicitors.

The 2007 Act sets out the regulatory objectives for legal services and the activities which are reserved to regulated providers. Under that Act, reserved legal services can only be carried out by Authorised Persons (ie those authorised to provide the services by an Approved Regulator. The Act establishes the Legal Services Board (LSB) which is charged with overseeing the work of the regulatory bodies for the different professions, together with the Legal Complaints Service.

The 2007 Act provides that the following activities can only be conducted by individuals who have been authorised by an Approved Regulator:

(a) the exercise of a right of audience in courts where those rights are restricted (the magistrates courts, county courts and above);
(b) the conduct of litigation;
(c) reserved instrument activities (conveyancing and other notarial activities);
(d) probate activities; and
(e) the administration of oaths.

These are distinguished from the concept of 'legal activities' which covers the bulk of unreserved legal work and is defined as advice on legal rights and advice in connection with a legal dispute. These activities can be undertaken by anyone. However, the Approved Regulators regulate the conduct of the individuals they regulate in respect of all legal activities, whether or not they are reserved.

The 2007 Act also provides that those regulated by the Law Society and the Bar Council may provide immigration services. Otherwise, those providing such advice and services must be registered with the Office of the Immigration Services Commissioner.

The Competition Act 2006 provided a structure for regulating claims managers. Individuals who offer claims management services who are not authorised persons much be registered with the Claims Management Regulator, currently an office within the Ministry of Justice. Claims managers do not have any rights to undertake reserved work. The Legal Aid, Sentencing and Punishment of Offenders Act 2012 (the 2012 Act) provides significant restrictions on the payment of referral fees by solicitors and others in paying referral fees in respect of financial claims.

III SOL [2]

The 2007 Act also provides for the existence of Alternative Business Structures (ABSs). ABSs are organisations in which at least one of the owners or managers is a lawyer and another is not. The concept enables legal services to be provided in a variety of contexts:

(a) by existing law firms who wish to take a non-lawyer on as a partner or director;
(b) by firms wishing to provide multi-disciplinary professional services involving two or more different professionals, one of whom is not a lawyer;
(c) by existing commercial organisations, such as banks or supermarkets, wishing to offer legal services as part of a larger portfolio of products; and

SOLICITORS

(d) by firms wishing to float on the stock market.

Bodies wishing to provide these services must be licensed by a Licensing Authority which is also an Approved Regulator for the activities that they wish to pursue. Approved Regulators may be designated as licensing authorities by the Lord Chancellor by Statutory Instrument on the recommendation of the LSB. At present the CLC, the Law Society, the Bar Council and the ICAEW have been designated as licensing authorities.

The Legal Complaints Service was established in 2010 and runs the Legal Ombudsman (LeO) scheme. It is appointed by the LSB. The Legal Ombudsman investigates complaints of poor service against legal services providers, including claims managers and can require providers to apologise, reduce or refund fees or pay compensation to the complainant up to £30,000. The other regulatory bodies are expressly prohibited from requiring payment of compensation as part of their disciplinary investigations.

Failure to comply with LeO's decisions may result in an immediate prison sentence; see ss 147–149 of the Legal Services Act 2007, and where the case does not require this the imposition of a penalty. In *Deputy Chief Legal Ombudsman v French* [2012] All ER (D) 85 (Jan), (2012) NLJR, 27 January, page 139, a solicitor was sentenced to 4 months imprisonment suspended for 12 months for failure to comply with a notice under s 147 of the Legal Services Act 2007, the Ombudsman having certified the failure to the court under s 149(2). In *Legal Ombudman v Young* [2011] EWHC 2923 (Admin), (2011) Gazette, 17 November, page 3 a fine of £5,000 was imposed by the High Court with an order for £15,500 costs. In this case there was virtually total failure to respond to the Legal Ombudsman. This case provides guidance as to the use of CPR Part 8 in matters proceeding under s 149 of the LSA 2007.

LEGAL SERVICES ACT 2007

(c 29)

GENERAL NOTE ON THE LEGAL SERVICES ACT 2007

III SOL [3]

Preliminary The Legal Services Act 2007 ('the 2007 Act') came into force on 1 January 2010 and provided a new framework for the provision of legal services. The entitlement to provide 'reserved legal services' (s 12 of the 2007 Act) is to be determined 'solely in accordance with the provisions' of the 2007 Act (s 13(2)) and whether a person is an 'authorised person' or an 'exempt person' (s 13).

The Legal Services Board was created by the 2007 Act and one of the functions is to regulate the 'approved regulators' which can grant to their members the right to carry out legal activities, including rights of audience. The Law Society is one of the approved regulators.

PART 1
THE REGULATORY OBJECTIVES

III SOL [4]

1. The regulatory objectives

(1) In this Act a reference to "the regulatory objectives" is a reference to the objectives of—

(a) protecting and promoting the public interest;
(b) supporting the constitutional principle of the rule of law;
(c) improving access to justice;
(d) protecting and promoting the interests of consumers;
(e) promoting competition in the provision of services within subsection (2);
(f) encouraging an independent, strong, diverse and effective legal profession;
(g) increasing public understanding of the citizen's legal rights and duties;
(h) promoting and maintaining adherence to the professional principles.

(2) The services within this subsection are services such as are provided by authorised persons (including services which do not involve the carrying on of activities which are reserved legal activities).

(3) The "professional principles" are—

(a) that authorised persons should act with independence and integrity,
(b) that authorised persons should maintain proper standards of work,
(c) that authorised persons should act in the best interests of their clients,
(d) that persons who exercise before any court a right of audience, or conduct litigation in relation to proceedings in any court, by virtue of being authorised persons should comply with their duty to the court to act with independence in the interests of justice, and
(e) that the affairs of clients should be kept confidential.

(4) In this section "authorised persons" means authorised persons in relation to activities which are reserved legal activities.

SOLICITORS

PART 3
RESERVED LEGAL ACTIVITIES

RESERVED LEGAL ACTIVITIES

III SOL [5]

12. Meaning of "reserved legal activity" and "legal activity"

(1) In this Act "reserved legal activity" means—

(a) the exercise of a right of audience;
(b) the conduct of litigation;
(c) reserved instrument activities;
(d) probate activities;
(e) notarial activities;
(f) the administration of oaths.

(2) Schedule 2 makes provision about what constitutes each of those activities.

(3) In this Act "legal activity" means—

(a) an activity which is a reserved legal activity within the meaning of this Act as originally enacted, and
(b) any other activity which consists of one or both of the following—

(i) the provision of legal advice or assistance in connection with the application of the law or with any form of resolution of legal disputes;

(ii) the provision of representation in connection with any matter concerning the application of the law or any form of resolution of legal disputes.

(4) But "legal activity" does not include any activity of a judicial or quasi-judicial nature (including acting as a mediator).

(5) For the purposes of subsection (3) "legal dispute" includes a dispute as to any matter of fact the resolution of which is relevant to determining the nature of any person's legal rights or liabilities.

(6) Section 24 makes provision for adding legal activities to the reserved legal activities.

III SOL [5.1]

Rights of Audience The rights of audience here are those in the magistrates courts, the county court and above. They do not include tribunals.

III SOL [5.2]

Right to Conduct Litigation The conduct of litigation is defined in para 4 of Schedule 3 to the 2007 Act as:

'(1)

(a) the issuing of proceedings before any court in England and Wales,

(b) the commencement, prosecution and defence of such proceedings, and

(c) the performance of any ancillary functions in relation to such proceedings (such as entering appearances to actions).'

In *Agassi v Robinson (Inspector of Taxes) (Bar Council intervening)* [2005] EWCA Civ 1507, [2006] 1 All ER 900, [2006] 1 WLR 2126, the court construed definition of ancillary functions narrowly. Essentially, it is limited to the formal steps required in the conduct of litigation.

CARRYING ON THE ACTIVITIES

III SOL [6]

13. Entitlement to carry on a reserved legal activity

(1) The question whether a person is entitled to carry on an activity which is a reserved legal activity is to be determined solely in accordance with the provisions of this Act.

(2) A person is entitled to carry on an activity ("the relevant activity") which is a reserved legal activity where—

(a) the person is an authorised person in relation to the relevant activity, or

(b) the person is an exempt person in relation to that activity.

(3) Subsection (2) is subject to section 23 (transitional protection for non-commercial bodies).

(4) Nothing in this section or section 23 affects section 84 of the Immigration and Asylum Act 1999 (c 33) (which prohibits the provision of immigration advice and immigration services except by certain persons).

INTERPRETATION

III SOL [7]

18. Authorised persons

(1) For the purposes of this Act "authorised person", in relation to an activity ("the relevant activity") which is a reserved legal activity, means—

(a) a person who is authorised to carry on the relevant activity by a relevant approved regulator in relation to the relevant activity (other than by virtue of a licence under Part 5), or

(b) a licensable body which, by virtue of such a licence, is authorised to carry on the relevant activity by a licensing authority in relation to the reserved legal activity.

(2) A licensable body may not be authorised to carry on the relevant activity as mentioned in subsection (1)(a).

(3) But where a body ("A") which is authorised as mentioned in subsection (1)(a) becomes a licensable body, the body is deemed by virtue of this subsection to continue to be so authorised from that time until the earliest of the following events—

(a) the end of the period of 90 days beginning with the day on which that time falls;

(b) the time from which the relevant approved regulator determines this subsection is to cease to apply to A;

(c) the time when A ceases to be a licensable body.

(4) Subsection (2) is subject to Part 2 of Schedule 5 (by virtue of which licensable bodies may be deemed to be authorised as mentioned in subsection (1)(a) in relation to certain activities during a transitional period).

(5) A person other than a licensable body may not be authorised to carry on the relevant activity as mentioned in subsection (1)(b).

(6) But where a body ("L") which is authorised as mentioned in subsection (1)(b) ceases to be a licensable body, the body is deemed by virtue of this subsection to continue to be so authorised from that time until the earliest of the following events—

(a) the end of the period of 90 days beginning with the day on which that time falls;

(b) the time from which the relevant licensing authority determines this subsection is to cease to apply to L;

(c) the time when L becomes a licensable body.

III SOL [7.1]

Authorised Persons – rights of audience Authorised persons are people authorised to conduct a reserved activity by an Approved Regulator. In respect of rights of audience these are:

(a) barristers;
(b) solicitors;
(c) legal executives; and
(d) patent agents and trade mark attorneys.

The rules governing barristers are set out in the BSB Handbook (3rd edition, which came into force on 1 April 2017; current latest edition is version 3.4 with effect from November 2018). Barristers have full rights of audience in all courts provided that they hold a practising certificate and:

(a) practise in a capacity approved by the BSB (ie in self-employed practice, as an employee, or within a body licensed by the BSB or by another approved regulator (BSB Handbook, rule S18);

(b) have completed the first six months of pupillage and are in their second six months of pupillage and carrying out the work with the approval of their pupil supervisor (BSB Handbook, rule S19);

SOLICITORS

(c) have completed both stages of pupillage and, if they have been in practice for less than three years, are working in the same office as a Qualified Person who is readily available to provide guidance. A qualified person is an individual who has been entitled to exercise full rights of audience and, amongst other things, has done so for the last five years (BSB Handbook, rule S20–S22).

Barristers who do not or cannot comply with these rules (for example, because they have not completed pupillage or are not working in an approved environment) are described as 'unregistered barristers'. They are not able to undertake any reserved activities but may offer other legal services on the same basis as any unqualified individual. They may appear in court at the discretion of the court (see the discussion on 'exempt persons' below). The Bar Handbook sets out rules which aim to ensure that clients of unregistered barristers are not misled as to their status. Unregistered barristers appearing in court are subject to the same duties as practising barristers in respect of assisting and not misleading the court. The BSB has issued guidance (https://www.barstandardsboard.org.uk/media/1666521/1__guidance_for_unregistered_barristers__barristers_without_practising_certificates__-_supplying_legal_services_and_holding_out.pdf) which sets out the general provisions applying to unregistered barristers.

The rules requiring barristers to provide legal services only when instructed by solicitors or others with rights to conduct litigation have been significantly liberalised in recent years. Barristers may provide legal services (including exercising rights of audience) where:

(a) the client has been licensed by the BSB as being suitable to instruct barristers (licensed access); or

(b) the barrister has been authorised by the BSB to provide services directly to the public (public access).

In both situations, the barrister must be satisfied that it is not in the interests of justice or of the client for a solicitor to be instructed.

Solicitors gain rights of audience in the county courts on qualification as individuals who are regulated by an Approved Regulator in respect of rights of audience. The SRA has imposed further requirements on those who wish to exercise rights of audience in the higher courts.

The SRA has made clear that all solicitors have rights of audience to appear in the Family Court (www.sra.org.uk/solicitors/code-of-conduct/guidance/guidance/rights-of-audience-in-the-single-family-court.page).

Legal Executives working in solicitors firms have the rights of exempt people (see below). Fellows and Graduate Members of CIlex can obtain an advocacy qualification which enables them to appear in the county court as if they were solicitors. The qualification is divided into a Civil Proceedings Certificate (which enables the individual to appear in the county court), a Criminal Proceedings Certificate and a Family Proceedings Certificate (which enables the individual to appear in proceedings in the Family Court).

Patent Agents and Trade Mark Attorneys have rights granted by the IPRB which enable them to appear in the Intellectual Property Enterprise Court and the county courts. These apply to all individuals who were on the register before 1 January 2013 and to others who have satisfied the IPRB that they have the appropriate skills.

III SOL [7.2]

Authorised Persons – rights to conduct litigation Solicitors have full rights to conduct litigation.

Practising barristers may obtain rights to conduct litigation by complying with the requirements of the Bar Handbook (essentially satisfying the BSB that they have the requisite skills and training).

Legal Executives do not have the right to conduct litigation.

Patent Attorneys and Trade Mark Attorneys may conduct litigation in the county court on the same basis that they can exercise rights of audience.

Section 181 of the 2007 Act provides that it is an offence for an unqualified person to pretend to be a barrister.

All advocates and litigators, whilst under a duty to do their best for their client, must never deceive or mislead the court. In civil proceedings they are under a duty to say on behalf of his client what the client should properly say for himself or herself if the client possessed the requisite skill and knowledge. See further Solicitors Code of Conduct 2011, chapter 5, Your client and the Court and the BSB Handbook at C1.

From 2 January 2008 all authorised advocates have had the right to wear wigs in court, albeit the wearing of wigs in civil cases has largely ceased.

III SOL [7.3]

For licensable bodies see the discussion on Alternative Business Structures. Essentially, the provisions enable bodies which are licensed (and, therefore, satisfy the requirements) to provide reserved legal services, assuming that the employee of that body who will be undertaking the work has the appropriate rights granted by an Authorised Regulator.

III SOL [8]

19. Exempt persons

In this Act, "exempt person", in relation to an activity ("the relevant activity") which is a reserved legal activity, means a person who, for the purposes of carrying on the relevant activity, is an exempt person by virtue of—

(a) Schedule 3 (exempt persons), or

(b) paragraph 13 or 18 of Schedule 5 (additional categories of exempt persons during transitional period).

III SOL [8.1]

Exempt Persons – rights of audience Exempt person in respect of rights of audience include those falling within the circumstances or provisions set out in **III SOL [8.2]** to **III SOL [8.7]** below.

III SOL [8.2]

Lay Representatives (Rights of Audience) Order 1999, SI 1999/1225 In exercise of his powers under ss 11 and 120 of the Courts and Legal Services Act 1990 the Lord Chancellor has revoked the Lay Representatives (Rights of Audience) Order 1992, SI 1992/1966 and authorises any person to exercise rights of audience in any proceedings dealt with as a small claim except:

(a) where the client does not attend the hearing;
(b) at any stage after judgment; or
(c) on appeal (SI 1999/1225).

The fact that the lay representative is also a witness or is being paid is irrelevant.

III SOL [8.3]

Right of audience granted by court: right removed by the court Where a person seeks rights of audience under s 19, Sch 3.1(3) of the LSA 2007 the court should, in conformity with the spirit of the Act, grant the application only in exceptional circumstances: D v S [1997] 2 FCR 217, [1997] 1 FLR 724, CA which was approved and applied in *Milne v Kennedy* (1999) Times, 11 February, [1999] CLY 87, CA. Generally where a right of audience is granted the litigant in person should still normally be present in court: but see *Clarkson v Gilbert* [2000] 3 FCR 10, [2000] 2 FLR 839, CA, a libel case where a husband was allowed to represent his wife in her absence. They had tried to obtain legal representation without success and the wife's health was very poor. The consent of the parties is immaterial to the court's consideration: *Re Pelling* [1997] 2 FCR 585, [1997] 2 FLR 458. Relevant considerations on an application to represent a litigant in person include: (a) any savings of time which may result; (b) the appropriateness of the individual as a representative, having regard to his or her legal training, objectivity of approach and ability; and (c) the objective of providing a fair hearing: *Izzo v Philip Ross & Co (a firm)* [2001] 35 LS Gaz R 37, (2001) Times, 9 August, Neuberger J. All these cases were decided before the implementation of the provisions of the LSA 2007 were brought into force but remain relevant.

Both the right of audience and the right to conduct litigation were considered by the Court of Appeal in *Paragon Finance plc v Noueiri (Practice Note)* [2001] EWCA Civ 1402, [2001] 1 WLR 2357. The Court referred to the decision of Peter Gibson J in *Mensah v Islington London Borough Council* (1 December 2000, unreported), when he stated that the court should be very slow to permit McKenzie friends to act as advocates. The Court of Appeal stated that the decision whether to grant a right of audience should be made by reference to ss 17 and 18 of the 1990 Act (now repealed). It did not find that the refusal of such an application would contravene the rights of any person under the European Convention on Human Rights, see art 6 (see para **III HUM [28]**) and art 8 of the Convention (see para **III HUM [30]**).

The right to conduct litigation is governed by s 19, Sch 3.2 of the LSA 2007 (*Agassi* case).

III SOL [8.4]

Assistance to party in person 'Any person, whether he be a professional man or not, may attend as the friend of either party; may take notes, may quietly make suggestions, and give advice; but no one can demand to take part in the proceedings as an advocate contrary to the regulations of the court as settled by the discretion of the justices. See Tenterden CJ in

Collier v Hicks (1831) 2 B & Ad 663; cited with approval in *McKenzie v McKenzie* [1971] P 33, [1970] 3 All ER 1034, CA. Furthermore, a litigant in person has, subject to the court's jurisdiction to maintain order and regulate proceedings before it, a right to advice of the kind described above: *R v Leicester City Justices, ex p Barrow* [1991] 2 QB 260, [1991] 3 All ER 935, CA; *R v Wolverhampton Stipendiary Magistrate, ex p Mould* (1992) Times, 16 November, and this applies to proceedings heard in chambers as well as to those heard in open court: *Re H* [1997] 3 FCR 619, [1997] 2 FLR 423, CA. The use of the expression 'McKenzie friend' is misleading and should be avoided: *R v Leicester City Justices, ex p Barrow* [1991] 2 QB 260, [1991] 3 All ER 935, CA.

In *R v Bow County Court, ex p Pelling* [1999] 4 All ER 751, [1999] 1 WLR 1807, CA, the Master of the Rolls fully considered the position and concluded that a litigant should be allowed a friend where the hearing was in public or in chambers, unless the proceedings were in private, but where the proceedings were in private their nature might make it undesirable in the interests of justice for a friend to assist. In all cases the court had a discretion but should give reasons if refusing.

In *Re G (a minor) (chambers proceedings: hearing assistance)* [1999] 1 WLR 1828, [1999] 2 FLR 59, CA the Court of Appeal did not interfere with a decision to exclude a McKenzie friend who was a solicitor and able to have himself put on the record.

In *Re G (A Child) (litigants in person)* [2003] EWCA Civ 1055, [2003] 2 FLR 963, (2003) Times, 30 July the President expressed concern at the difficulties that the Family Proceedings Rules and in particular r 4.23 presented to a litigant in person seeking legal advice and general assistance.

The danger where a person giving assistance is also a funder of the litigation is well illustrated by the decision in *Bournemouth & Boscombe Athletic Club v Lloyds TSB Bank plc* [2004] EWCA Civ 935, [2004] All ER (D) 323 (Jun) where the funder was held liable in costs where the claimant he was assisting failed in its claim.

The present position is set out fully in *Practice Guidance: McKenzie Friends (Civil and Family Courts)* dated 12 July 2010 (see Volume 1, para **CPR PG 39**) which includes the names and references of relevant cases and references to the Legal Services Act 2007, ss 12–19 and Sch 3. This Practice Guidance appears at [2010] 1 WLR 1881. It is apparent that rights of audience to individuals are to be granted in exceptional circumstances only, as to do otherwise would tend to subvert the will of Parliament.

See also *R (on the application of Koli) v Maidstone Crown Court* [2011] QBD (Admin), Ousley J, 10 May 2011, where it was held 'to grant an unqualified advocate rights of audience . . . where the claim was not of such complexity of fact or law as to require any assistance from an unqualified advocate . . . was inappropriate'. He could of course act as a McKenzie friend.

The decline in the availability of legal aid has led to an increase in the number of litigants in person. The Law Society recently espoused a concept of 'unbundling' whereby a solicitor could provide limited ad hoc assistance to a client without accepting a full retainer, provided that the limits of the solicitor's involvement were made clear in a retainer. As such, a lay client might instruct a solicitor for initial advice and, possibly, to appear as an advocate but the solicitor would not take responsibility for anything done outside the scope of the work instructed.

It is also open to litigants to instruct barristers to appear for them under the Public Access Scheme, where the barrister is satisfied that it is not in the interests of the client or the interests of justice for a solicitor to be instructed.

Concerns have also been raised about the growth of paid McKenzie Friends, that is, individuals who appear regularly as McKenzie Friends who charge clients to appear on their behalf. These concerns involve individuals who tend to use litigation as a means of forwarding their own causes or simply to cheat litigants. The senior judiciary issued a consultation paper on reforming the approach to McKenzie Friends in February 2016 but, so far, no further action has been taken.

III SOL [8.5]

Right of solicitor's employee to appear in chambers An employee who is engaged to assist in the conduct of litigation and is doing so under the instructions of a qualified litigator cannot be denied rights of audience in chambers; it is not a matter of discretion: *Re HS (minors (chambers proceedings: right of audience)* [1998] 3 FCR 245, [1998] 1 FLR 868, CA. It would seem from the decision in *Smith Graham (a firm) v Lord Chancellor's Department* [1999] NLJR 1443, where an enquiry agent was employed to do preparation work by a solicitor and was held to fall within the definition of fee earner, that it is not necessary for a clerk to be a full- or part-time employee to enjoy the rights of audience as long as he is acting under the instructions of a qualified litigator.

Some self-employed agents receive instructions not from a firm of solicitors but from an agency company. Their entitlement to appear is doubtful. Such an agent would be wise to comply with CPR PD 39A, para 5.1 and have available a written statement containing:

(a) his name and address;
(b) his qualifications to act as an advocate;
(c) the party for whom he acts.

It will be a matter of fact whether the requirement of instruction and supervision are satisfied.

III SOL [8.6]

County Courts Act 1984 Section 60(2) of the County Courts Act 1984 (see para **II CCA [39]**) gives an officer of a local authority, duly authorised, the right to address the district judge in housing possession claims and claims for rent, etc.

In *London Borough of Hackney v Spring* [2006] LTL 15 November where the borough had transferred the management (but not the ownership) of its housing stock to an arm's length management organisation (ALMO), that organisation was refused permission to represent the borough before the court without the express permission of the Secretary of State; see Courts and Legal Services Act 1990, ss 11 and 27 and Housing Act 1984, s 60(2). The Master of the Rolls subsequently issued a memorandum to district judges informing them that ALMO staff do not have the same rights as council officers under s 60(2) which grants rights only to employees; but now see s 60A of the County Courts Act 1984 inserted by s 191 of the LSA 2007 granting rights of audience to housing management bodies.

Section 61 (see para **II CCA [40]**) and the Rights of Audience Direction (see para **II CCA [40.1]**) made by the Lord Chancellor give a fellow of the Institute of Legal Executives a right to address the court on unopposed applications for adjournments and for judgments by consent.

III SOL [8.7]

Companies CPR 39.6 (see para **CPR 39.6**) provides that a company or other corporation may be represented at trial by an employee if:

(a) the employee has been authorised by the company or corporation to appear at the trial on its behalf; and
(b) the court gives permission.

The Practice Direction to Part 39 at para 5 describes the procedure to apply for such permission and the matters to be considered by the court when deciding such an application (see para **CPR PD 39**).

In a claim on the small claims track a body corporate may be represented by any of its officers or employees: para 3.2(4) of the Practice Direction to CPR 27 (see para **CPR PD 27**).

SOLICITORS

III SOL [9]

20. Approved regulators and relevant approved regulators

(1) In this Act, the following expressions have the meaning given by this section—

"approved regulator";

"relevant approved regulator".

(2) "Approved regulator" means—

(a) a body which is designated as an approved regulator by Part 1 of Schedule 4 or under Part 2 of that Schedule (or both) and whose regulatory arrangements are approved for the purposes of this Act, and
(b) if an order under section 62(1)(a) has effect, the Board.

(3) An approved regulator is a "relevant approved regulator" in relation to an activity which is a reserved legal activity if—

(a) the approved regulator is designated by Part 1, or under Part 2, of Schedule 4 in relation to that reserved legal activity, or
(b) where the approved regulator is the Board, it is designated in relation to that reserved legal activity by an order under section 62(1)(a).

(4) An approved regulator is a "relevant approved regulator" in relation to a person if the person is authorised by the approved regulator to carry on an activity which is a reserved legal activity.

(5) Schedule 4 makes provision with respect to approved regulators other than the Board.

In that Schedule—

(a) Part 1 designates certain bodies as approved regulators in relation to certain reserved legal activities,

(b) Part 2 makes provision for bodies to be designated by order as approved regulators in relation to one or more reserved legal activities, and

(c) Part 3 makes provision relating to the approval of changes to an approved regulator's regulatory arrangements.

(6) An approved regulator may authorise persons to carry on any activity which is a reserved legal activity in respect of which it is a relevant approved regulator.

III SOL [9.1]

The Approved Regulators The Approved Regulators are:

- the Law Society (in respect of all the reserved activities);
- the General Council of the Bar (the Bar Council) (in respect of all the reserved activities);
- the Council for Licensed Conveyancers (in respect of reserved instrument and probate transactions);
- the Chartered Institute of Legal Executives (CILEx) in respect of limited rights of audience;
- the Chartered Institute of Patent Agents (CIPA) in respect of rights of audience in intellectual property proceedings;
- the Institute of Trade Mark Attorneys (ITMA) in respect of rights of audience in intellectual property proceedings;
- the Association of Chartered Accountants in Scotland (in respect of probate matters);
- the Faculty Office of the Archbishop of Canterbury (in respect of reserved instrument transactions and administration of oaths).

The 2007 Act requires those regulatory bodies with combined regulatory and representative functions to ensure that their regulatory functions are, so far as practicable, independent of their regulatory functions. As a result, the Law Society established the Solicitors Regulation Authority (SRA) as its regulatory arm, the Bar Council established the Bar Standards Board (BSB), CILEx established CILEX Regulation and CIPA and ITMA jointly established the Intellectual Property Regulatory Board.

Those regulatory arms make the rules governing qualification, conduct and discipline of those they regulate. Changes to the rules must be approved by the LSB.

ALTERNATIVE BUSINESS STRUCTURES

III SOL [10]

The 2007 Act introduced the concept of Alternative Business Structures. Under Part 5 of the Act, the Lord Chancellor, on the recommendation of the LSB may designate Approved Regulators as licensing authorities which may license firms where one or more of the owners or managers are not Authorised Persons as being suitable to offer reserved legal services. The licensing authorities may only license bodies to offer reserved services which the authority can itself authorise individuals to undertake.

The 2007 Act sets out a number of requirements that licensing authorities must impose and consider before granting a licence. These include:

(a) ensuring that owners and managers are fit and proper people;
(b) indemnification and compensation arrangements;
(c) the appointment of a Head of Legal Practice (responsible for compliance with the regulatory obligations) and a Head of Finance and Administration (responsible for ensuring financial and administrative probity).

The following bodies have been designated as licensing authorities:

(a) the CLC;
(b) the Law Society (through the SRA);
(c) the ICAEW;
(d) the Bar Council (through the BSB).

Of these, only the SRA and the BSB are able to license bodies in respect of all the reserved legal activities. The BSB, however, has indicated that, initially, it will be looking to license bodies that concentrate primarily on advocacy or advisory work of the sort currently undertaken by barristers.

The SRA's arrangements for licensing bodies are considered below.

PART 8
MISCELLANEOUS PROVISIONS ABOUT LAWYERS ETC

DUTIES OF REGULATED PERSONS

III SOL [11]

176. Duties of regulated persons

(1) A person who is a regulated person in relation to an approved regulator has a duty to comply with the regulatory arrangements of the approved regulator as they apply to that person.

(2) A person is a regulated person in relation to an approved regulator if the person—

(a) is authorised by the approved regulator to carry on an activity which is a reserved legal activity, or

(b) is not so authorised, but is a manager or employee of a person who is so authorised.

(3) This section applies in relation to the Board in its capacity as a licensing authority and its licensing rules, as it applies in relation to an approved regulator and its regulatory arrangements.

III SOL [11.1]

Regulatory arrangements The regulatory arrangements include the qualification rules, Codes of Conduct and disciplinary requirements of the regulators. These are contained in, for example, the SRA Handbook and the BSB Handbook.

SOLICITORS

ADVOCATES AND LITIGATORS

III SOL [12]

188. Duties of advocates and litigators

(1) This section applies to a person who—

(a) exercises before any court a right of audience, or

(b) conducts litigation in relation to proceedings in any court,

by virtue of being an authorised person in relation to the activity in question.

(2) A person to whom this section applies has a duty to the court in question to act with independence in the interests of justice.

(3) That duty, and the duty to comply with relevant conduct rules imposed on the person by section 176(1), override any obligations which the person may have (otherwise than under the criminal law) if they are inconsistent with them.

(4) "Relevant conduct rules" are the conduct rules of the relevant authorising body which relate to the exercise of a right of audience or the conduct of litigation.

(5) The relevant authorising body is—

(a) the approved regulator by which the person is authorised to exercise the right of audience or conduct the litigation, or

(b) where the person is authorised to exercise the right of audience or conduct the litigation by the Board in its capacity as a licensing authority, the Board.

III SOL [13]

189. Employed advocates

(1) This section applies where an authorised person in relation to the exercise of a right of audience is employed as a Crown Prosecutor or in any other description of employment.

(2) Qualification regulations or conduct rules of the approved regulator by whom the person is authorised to carry on that activity which relate to the right of audience do not have effect in relation to the person if—

(a) they—

(i) limit the courts before which, or proceedings in which, that activity may be carried on by persons who are employed, or

(ii) limit the circumstances in which that activity may be carried on by persons who are employed by requiring such persons to be accompanied by some other person when carrying on that activity, and

(b) they do not impose the same limitation on persons who are authorised persons in relation to the activity in question but are not employed.

PRO BONO REPRESENTATION

III SOL [14]

194. Payments in respect of pro bono representation

(1) This section applies to proceedings in a civil court in which—

(a) a party to the proceedings ("P") is or was represented by a legal representative ("R"), and

(b) R's representation of P is or was provided free of charge, in whole or in part.

(2) This section applies to such proceedings even if P is or was also represented by a legal representative not acting free of charge.

(3) The court may order any person to make a payment to the prescribed charity in respect of R's representation of P (or, if only part of R's representation of P was provided free of charge, in respect of that part).

(4) In considering whether to make such an order and the terms of such an order, the court must have regard to—

(a) whether, had R's representation of P not been provided free of charge, it would have ordered the person to make a payment to P in respect of the costs payable to R by P in respect of that representation, and

(b) if it would, what the terms of the order would have been.

(5) The court may not make an order under subsection (3) against a person represented in the proceedings if the person's representation was at all times within subsection (6).

(6) Representation is within this subsection if it is—

(a) provided by a legal representative acting free of charge, or

(b) provided under arrangements made for the purposes of Part 1 of the Legal Aid, Sentencing and Punishment of Offenders Act 2012.

(7) Rules of court may make further provision as to the making of orders under subsection (3), and may in particular—

(a) provide that such orders may not be made in civil proceedings of a description specified in the rules;

(b) make provision about the procedure to be followed in relation to such orders;

(c) specify matters (in addition to those mentioned in subsection (4)) to which the court must have regard in deciding whether to make such an order, and the terms of any order.

(8) "The prescribed charity" means the charity prescribed by order made by the Lord Chancellor.

(9) An order under subsection (8) may only prescribe a charity which—

(a) is registered in accordance with section 30 of the Charities Act 2011, and

(b) provides financial support to persons who provide, or organise or facilitate the provision of, legal advice or assistance (by way of representation or otherwise) which is free of charge.

(10) In this section—

"legal representative", in relation to a party to proceedings, means a person exercising a right of audience or conducting litigation on the party's behalf;

"civil court" means—

(a) the Supreme Court when it is dealing with a relevant civil appeal,

(b) the civil division of the Court of Appeal,

(c) the High Court,

(ca) the family court, or

(d) the county court;

"free of charge" means otherwise than for or in expectation of fee, gain or reward.

"relevant civil appeal" means an appeal to the Supreme Court—

(a) from the High Court in England and Wales under Part 2 of the Administration of Justice Act 1969,

(b) from the Court of Appeal under section 40(2) of the Constitutional Reform Act 2005, or

(c) under section 13 of the Administration of Justice Act 1960 (appeal in cases of contempt of court) other than an appeal from an order or decision made in the exercise of jurisdiction to punish for criminal contempt of court.

(11) The court may not make an order under subsection (3) in respect of representation if (or to the extent that) it is provided before this section comes into force.

III SOL [14.1]

Costs Orders in pro bono work By virtue of the Legal Services Act 2007, s 194, from October 2008 the courts can make costs orders in all civil cases where the successful party was represented wholly or in part by a pro bono lawyer; for further information see the website for the Access to Justice Foundation at www.accesstojusticefoundation.org.uk (enquiries@atjf.org.uk). Generally the costs will be summarily assessed and will not exceed the amount that would have been awarded had the legal services not been provided pro bono.

The costs paid by the paying party will be paid to the nominated charity the Access to Justice Foundation which redistributes the funds to organisations providing pro bono legal services. Where pro bono costs have been ordered the lawyer concerned should notify the ATJF (e-mail: costs@ATJF.org.uk) and send a copy of the order to it at PO Box 64162, London, WC1A 9AN. The order for costs should begin 'The [party] shall pay costs for pro bono representation to the Access to Justice Foundation at [*specify address*]...'. For orders in respect of pro bono representation see **CPR 44.3C**.

'Civil court' has been extended to include the Supreme Court.

PART 9
GENERAL

OFFENCES

III SOL [15]

198. Local weights and measures authorities

(1) A local weights and measures authority may institute proceedings for an offence under section 14 if the activity which it is alleged that the accused was not entitled to carry on constitutes reserved instrument activities.

. . .

SOLICITORS

SCHEDULE 2
THE RESERVED LEGAL ACTIVITIES

Section 12

INTRODUCTION

III SOL [16]

1 This Schedule makes provision about the reserved legal activities.

2 In this Schedule "the appointed day" means the day appointed for the coming into force of section 13 (entitlement to carry on reserved legal activities).

RIGHTS OF AUDIENCE

3 (1) A "right of audience" means the right to appear before and address a court, including the right to call and examine witnesses.

(2) But a "right of audience" does not include a right to appear before or address a court, or to call or examine witnesses, in relation to any particular court or in relation to particular proceedings, if immediately before the appointed day no restriction was placed on the persons entitled to exercise that right.

CONDUCT OF LITIGATION

4 (1) The "conduct of litigation" means—

(a) the issuing of proceedings before any court in England and Wales,

(b) the commencement, prosecution and defence of such proceedings, and

(c) the performance of any ancillary functions in relation to such proceedings (such as entering appearances to actions).

(2) But the "conduct of litigation" does not include any activity within paragraphs (a) to (c) of sub-paragraph (1), in relation to any particular court or in relation to any particular proceedings, if immediately before the appointed day no restriction was placed on the persons entitled to carry on that activity.

. . .

SCHEDULE 3
EXEMPT PERSONS

Section 19

RIGHTS OF AUDIENCE

III SOL [17]

1 (1) This paragraph applies to determine whether a person is an exempt person for the purpose of exercising a right of audience before a court in relation to any proceedings (subject to paragraph 7).

(2) The person is exempt if the person—

(a) is not an authorised person in relation to that activity, but

(b) has a right of audience granted by that court in relation to those proceedings.

(3) The person is exempt if the person—

(a) is not an authorised person in relation to that activity, but

(b) has a right of audience before that court in relation to those proceedings granted by or under any enactment.

(4) The person is exempt if the person is the Attorney General or the Solicitor General and—

(a) the name of the person is on the roll kept by the Law Society under section 6 of the Solicitors Act 1974 (c 47), or

(b) the person has been called to the Bar by an Inn of Court.

(5) The person is exempt if the person is the Advocate General for Scotland and is admitted—

(a) as a solicitor in Scotland under section 6 of the Solicitors (Scotland) Act 1980 (c 46), or

(b) to practise as an advocate before the courts of Scotland.

(6) The person is exempt if the person—

(a) is a party to those proceedings, and

(b) would have a right of audience, in the person's capacity as such a party, if this Act had not been passed.

(7) The person is exempt if—

(a) the person is an individual whose work includes assisting in the conduct of litigation,

(b) the person is assisting in the conduct of litigation—

(i) under instructions given (either generally or in relation to the proceedings) by an individual to whom sub-paragraph (8) applies, and

(ii) under the supervision of that individual, and

(c) the proceedings are being heard in chambers in the High Court or a county court and are not reserved family proceedings.

(c) the proceedings are not reserved family proceedings and are being heard in chambers—

(i) in the High Court or county court, or

(ii) in the family court by a judge who is not, or by two or more judges at least one of whom is not, within section 31C(1)(y) of the Matrimonial and Family Proceedings Act 1984 (lay justices).

(8) This sub-paragraph applies to—

(a) any authorised person in relation to an activity which constitutes the conduct of litigation;

(b) any person who by virtue of section 193 is not required to be entitled to carry on such an activity.

(9) The person is an exempt person in relation to the exercise of a right of audience in proceedings on an appeal from the Comptroller-General of Patents, Designs and Trade Marks to the Patents Court under the Patents Act 1977 (c 37), if the person is a solicitor of the Court of Judicature of Northern Ireland.

(10) For the purposes of this paragraph—

"family proceedings" has the same meaning as in the Matrimonial and Family Proceedings Act 1984 (c 42) and also includes any proceedings in the family court and any other proceedings which are family proceedings for the purposes of the Children Act 1989 (c 41);

"reserved family proceedings" means such category of family proceedings as the Lord Chancellor may, after consulting the President of the Law Society and with the concurrence of the President of the Family Division, by order prescribe;

and any order made under section 27(9) of the Courts and Legal Services Act 1990 (c 41) before the day appointed for the coming into force of this paragraph is to have effect on and after that day as if it were an order made under this sub-paragraph.

CONDUCT OF LITIGATION

2 (1) This paragraph applies to determine whether a person is an exempt person for the purpose of carrying on any activity which constitutes the conduct of litigation in relation to any proceedings (subject to paragraph 7).

(2) The person is exempt if the person—
(a) is not an authorised person in relation to that activity, but
(b) has a right to conduct litigation granted by a court in relation to those proceedings.

(3) The person is exempt if the person—
(a) is not an authorised person in relation to that activity, but
(b) has a right to conduct litigation in relation to those proceedings granted by or under any enactment.

(4) The person is exempt if the person—
(a) is a party to those proceedings, and
(b) would have a right to conduct the litigation, in the person's capacity as such a party, if this Act had not been passed.

(5) The person is an exempt person in relation to any activity which is carried on in or in connection with proceedings on an appeal from the Comptroller-General of Patents, Designs and Trade Marks to the Patents Court under the Patents Act 1977 (c 37), if the person is a solicitor of the Court of Judicature of Northern Ireland.

. . .

GENERAL NOTES ON SOLICITORS

III SOL [18]–III SOL [19]

Preliminary The Solicitors Act 1974 is a consolidation Act containing most of the statutory provisions relating to solicitors. All references to sections of the Act that appear below are in respect of the Solicitors Act 1974 unless otherwise stated. The Legal Service Act 2007, by s 177 and Sch 16 Part 1, has made amendments to the 1974 Act. The text of the parts of the Act below includes the amendments that have been brought into force. The full text of the Solicitors Act 1974, with all amendments made to it is to be found in Halsbury's Statutes (4th edn) Vol II (4).

For precedents for claims against barristers and solicitors see **BCCP N[201]** et seq.

For further commentary on the Act, see 44(1) Halsbury's Laws (4th edn reissue) title SOLICITORS, 41 Halsbury's Statutes (4th edn 2004 reissue) 11(2)-11(4) Halsbury's Statutes title COURTS AND LEGAL SERVICES (4th edn 2008 reissue) and Cordery on Solicitors (9th edn, 1995).

Halsbury's Statutes 4th edn Vol 11(4) contains the text of the Solicitors Act 1974, the Courts and Legal Services Act 1990 and the Administration of Justice Act 1985 as if the amendments made by the Legal Services Act 2007 were all in force.

III SOL [20]

The status of solicitors Section 1 of the Solicitors Act 1974 provides that no person shall be qualified to act as a solicitor unless:

(a) he has been admitted to be a solicitor; and
(b) his name is on the Roll; and
(c) he has in force a practising certificate.

A 'solicitor' is a person admitted as a solicitor whose name appears on the roll of solicitors. Solicitors are officers of the Senior Courts of England and Wales and as such subject to their jurisdiction (s 50(2)).

The full title of a solicitor is now **'solicitor of the Senior Courts and England and Wales'**. This applies to all solicitors including those admitted before 1 October 2009.

In order to practise, solicitors must hold a current practising certificate (s 1) unless they are employed solicitors and s 1 applies. If not:

(a) they cannot recover any costs (s 25); and
(b) they are guilty of an offence and in contempt of court (s 20(2)).

However the absence of a current practising certificate does not prevent solicitors from recovering counsel's fees or any other disbursement incurred on behalf of a client (s 25(2)). Sections 20–21 provide penalties for an unqualified person who acts as or pretends to be a solicitor.

III SOL [22]

From 6 October 2011, a firm's letterhead has had to state it is 'Authorised and regulated by the Solicitors Regulation Authority'.

III SOL [23]

Unqualified persons not to act as a solicitor or pretend to be a solicitor Sections 20–21 of the Solicitors Act (which are not reproduced) prohibit in general terms (and subject to specific exceptions in the sections) any unqualified person:

(1) acting as a solicitor – penalty if guilty of the offence and convicted on indictment is imprisonment for more than two years or a fine or both (s 20);

(2) pretending to be a solicitor – penalty on summary conviction is a fine not exceeding the fourth level on the standard scale (s 21).

In each case the Act provides for criminal proceedings against the unqualified person and s 24 applies the penal provisions to bodies corporate.

III SOL [24]

Unqualified person acting as solicitor Section 25 restricts the recovery of costs in respect of anything done by any unqualified person acting as a solicitor. In *Piper Double Glazing Ltd v DC Contracts (1992) Ltd* [1994] 1 All ER 177, [1994] 1 WLR 777 it was said that this restriction applied only to the 'doing of acts which only a solicitor may perform and/or the doing of acts by a person pretending or holding himself out to be a solicitor', not merely acts which are commonly done by solicitors and involve no representation that the unqualified person is acting as a solicitor. See *Pilbrow v Pearless De Rougemont & Co (a firm)* [1999] 3 All ER 355, [1999] 2 FLR 139, CA at **III SOL [85.3]** followed in *Arian Allen v Fuglers (a firm)* No 5 of decisions reported by the Supreme Court Costs Office in 2003 [2003] 33 LS Gaz R 25.

III SOL [25]

Regulation of solicitors The Law Society by s 28 of the Solicitors Act 1974 is given power to make regulations as to:

(a) admission as a solicitor;
(b) the keeping of the roll;
(c) practising certificates;
(d) sole solicitor endorsements and applications for them; and
(e) the keeping of the register under 10A.

The **Solicitors Regulation Authority ('the SRA') principles** are mandatory principles which apply to all. As a solicitor, you must:

(1) uphold the rule of law and the proper administration of justice;
(2) act with integrity;
(3) not allow your independence to be compromised;
(4) act in the best interests of each client;
(5) provide a proper standard of service to your clients;
(6) behave in a way that maintains the trust the public places in you and in the provision of legal services;
(7) comply with your legal and regulatory obligations and deal with your regulators and ombudsmen in an open, timely and co-operative manner;
(8) run your business or carry out your role in the business effectively and in accordance with proper governance and sound financial and risk management principles;
(9) run your business or carry out your role in the business in a way that encourages equality of opportunity and respect for diversity; and
(10) protect client money and assets.

The Solicitors Regulation Authority Handbook containing the new Code of Conduct is now the basis of regulation replacing the Code of Conduct 2007 with new outcomes-focused regulation from October 2011. The SRA 'quick user guide' explaining the handbook and outlining the difference between the handbook and the 2007 Code is to be found at www.sra.org.uk.

III SOL [26]

The SRA regulates the conduct of solicitors and their employees, registered European lawyers, recognised bodies and their managers and employees, and licensed bodies and their managers and employees.

To enable this to be done, SRA Rules and Regulations were made with effect from 6 October 2011 for:

- Practice Framework;
- Authorisation for Legal Services Bodies and Licensable Bodies;
- Practising Regulations;
- Recognised Bodies Regulations;
- Keeping of the Rolls;
- Training Regulations, Parts 1 and 2;
- Admission;

SOLICITORS

- Qualified Lawyers transfer Scheme;
- Higher Rights of Audience; and
- Suitability Test.

The Solicitors Disciplinary Tribunal established under s 46 exercises jurisdiction over the professional conduct of solicitors, this is subject to an appeal to the High Court (s 49 (see para **III SOL [66]**)). The Tribunal consists of solicitor members who are practising solicitors of at least 10 years' standing, and lay members who are not solicitors or barristers. The Tribunal hears applications and complaints and can make such orders as it thinks fit. It can refer an application to it to the Office for Legal Complaints, which, with the Legal Ombudsman, has replaced the Legal Complaints Service (see para **III SOL [66.1]**) under s 28. It can do so even before deciding whether a prima facie case has been established: *R (on the application of Toth) v Solicitors Disciplinary Tribunal* [2001] EWHC Admin 240, [2001] 3 All ER 180. The Tribunal produces an annual report.

The Solicitors (Disciplinary Proceedings) Rules 2007, SI 2007/3588, regulate the procedure for making an application to the Solicitors Disciplinary Tribunal constituted under the Solicitors Act 1974. The Legal Service Act 2007, s 17(8) provides that an alteration of its rules by the Tribunal under s 45(9)(b) of the Solicitors Act 1974 does not have effect unless approved by the Legal Services Board.

In addition, the SRA has the power under s 44D of the Solicitors Act 1974 to impose rebukes and fines of up to £2,000 on individual solicitors or recognised bodies. Under s 95 of the 2007 Act, it may impose a fine of up to £250 million on licensed bodies and up to £50 million on employees or directors of such bodies.

The Solicitors Disciplinary Tribunal has powers to hear appeals against decisions of the SRA. It is proposed that these powers be extended to cover rebukes and decisions in respect of individuals and who are employees or owners of licensed bodies (ABSs) or in respect of decisions not to grant a license – for example, because, there has been a refusal to designate an individual as a Head of Legal Practice. The Tribunal consulted on rules to implement these proposals in June 2018 (www.solicitorstribunal.org.uk/sites/default/files-sd t/Content/documents/consultation%20paper%20final.pdf) and expects to reach a decision, w hich will need to be ratified by the LSB, in early 2019.

The Court of Appeal in *Napier v Pressdram Ltd* [2009] EWCA Civ 443, [2009] NLJR 859, (2009) Times, 2 June held that there is no confidentiality concerning the outcome of complaints to the Law Society arising from the process of such complaints. Where the SRA regards the complaint as sufficiently serious for it to be referred to the SDT the referral as well as its outcome are published so there has been no question of confidentiality.

However, in those cases where a solicitor is offered a Regulatory Settlement Agreement by the SRA acceptance of which would avoid reference to the SDT and consequent publicity, the absence of publicity has been a significant factor to be taken into account by a solicitor when deciding whether to accept this outcome. The decision in *Napier* has taken away that factor.

The SRA has published its policy statement on publication of regulatory and disciplinary decisions – for the latest updates see www.sra.org.uk. Where there has been a breach of reg ulatory or professional obligations the SRA can issue a written rebuke or impose a fine (based on the civil standard of proof) but more serious cases or where dishonesty is involved the case are likely to be referred to the SDT.

The SDT currently still uses the criminal standard of proof in looking at the facts of individual cases. This causes an inconsistency with the SRA's approach for its powers in respect of the sanctions available to it. The SDT's consultation paper referred to above, sought views on whether the standard of proof should be changed.

Solicitors needing advice on how to handle a service complaint can contact the Law Society's Lawyerline Support Service (Tel. 0870 606 2588). A booklet 'Handling Complaint Effectively' is available (Tel. 01577 883264). It can also be found by searching the Law Society's website.

III SOL [27]

Practice arrangements for solicitors Solicitors can practise in the following entities:

(a) a recognised body, which covers sole practitioners, partnerships, limited liability partnerships and other arrangements in which only solicitors, registered European lawyers, registered foreign lawyers or other individuals authorised to provide legal services are owners or managers;

(b) a licensed body, where non-lawyers are owners or managers (ie an Alternative Business Structure).

Under rules which were approved by the Legal Services Board on 5 November 2018, the Handbook will be amended to achieve two major amendments to practice arrangements:

(a) Solicitors will be permitted to provide unreserved legal services in an unregulated organisation. This will be subject to requirements to ensure that clients are properly informed about the level of insurance held and the fact that legal professional privilege may not apply.

(b) Solicitors who have been in practice for more than three years will be able to offer reserved legal services as free-lancers. They will be subject to the same rules in respect of insurance etc as other solicitors.

At the time of writing, the new rules were expect to come into effect by April 2019.

III SOL [28]

Recognised and licensed bodies The SRA Practice Framework Rules 2011 (which took effect on 6 October 2012), rule 13 sets out the 'eligibility criteria and fundamental requirements for recognised bodies and licensed bodies'. For practical purposes a recognised body is in the same position as a solicitor practising as an individual or solicitors practising in partnership (see para **III SOL [33]**).

See the SRA Recognised Bodies Regulations 2011 (not reproduced).

III SOL [29]

COLPs and COFAs The primary responsibility for compliance with the provisions of the Code (as defined by LSA 2007, s 21) rests with owners and managers. The SRA Authorisation Rules for Legal Services Bodies and Licensable Bodies 2011, rule 8.5 requires all authorised bodies to have at all times an authorised compliance officer for legal practice ('COLP') and an authorised officer for finance and administration ('COFA').

The COFA is required to monitor and report accounts irregularities in the light of the SRA Accounts Rules and may well be required to assess the financial viability of the practice.

The COLP has the responsibility of ensuring compliance with the principles and outcomes of the Code of Conduct and has recording and reporting responsibilities. He is obliged to ensure that the reporting and notification requirements are complied with (outcome 10.1) and report to the SRA promptly serious misconduct (outcome 10.3). He must maintain records on non-compliance; lesser breaches will be deemed to be duly disclosed as part of the renewal process but 'material' breaches fall to be reported as soon as is reasonably practical. The decision as into which class a non-compliance falls will at times be a difficult one and possibly a controversial one within the firm.

See SRA Authorisation Rules for Legal Services Bodies and Licensable Bodies 2011, 8.10 Guidance Notes, (vi).

See Solicitors Handbook 2012, Part 3, Chapter 6.

Note that both roles of COLP and COFA attract personal liability and potentially significant fines if the SRA decides that they are not being properly performed; see (2012) Sol Jo, 18 December, page 3.

III SOL [30]

Notes about partnership The partnership agreement between the members of a firm of solicitors is of great importance and justifies very careful drafting. By way of example, in *Hammonds (a firm) v Jones* [2009] EWCA Civ 1400, (2010) Times, 4 January, 154 Sol Jo (no 1 (29) the agreement provided that accounts were binding on partners. It was held on construction of the relevant clause that it covered those persons who were partners at any time of the year. Accordingly a partner who left the partnership part way through the year in question was nevertheless bound by the accounts for the year.

Careful consideration of proposed restrictive covenants in partnership agreements should be carried out. It may be too late when the solicitor is leaving the partnership to raise arguments against them. See article by Suzanne Foster and Clare Murray in (2011) Sol Jo, 6 December, page 13.

The dangers for solicitors entering into an arrangement, which they maintain is not 'a true partnership . . . but . . . an association of convenience', are considerable; see *Hodson v Hodson* [2009] EWHC 430 (Ch), [2009] All ER (D) 160 (Mar) and for detailed discussion the article 'Just good friends' by Stevens and Gee in (2010) NLJ, 12 February, page 210. The risk is of 'sham' partnerships between solicitors giving rise to disciplinary proceedings. See also an article in (2011) Sol Jo, 11 October, page 15 'Status symbol' by Anna Birtwhistle and Clare Murray where the problem of the status of salaried, fixed share and junior partners is addressed and the Employment Appeals Tribunal decisions in *Briars v Williamson & Soden Solicitors* (2011) UKEAT/0611/10/DM, [2011] All ER (D) 101 (Aug), EAT and *Tiffin v Lester Aldridge LLP* [2011] IRLR 105, EAT are considered.

The Court of Appeal, on an appeal from the Employment Tribunal decision in *Tiffin v Lester Aldridge LLP* (reported at [2012] EWCA Civ 35, [2012] 2 All ER 1113, [2012] 1 WLR 1887) upheld the tribunal's decision that the appellant as a fixed share partner was not an employee and accordingly was not able to claim for unfair dismissal or redundancy. The crucial question was the intent of the parties and whether they had intended to form a partnership. for consideration of the position see article by Mark Whitcombe entitled 'A matter of definition' in (2012) NLJ, 9 March, page 343.

By contrast, the Supreme Court in *Bates van Winkelhof v Clyde & Co LLP* [2014] UKSC 32, [2014] 3 All ER 225, [2014] 1 WLR 2047 held that 'ordinary' partners and the members of an LLP are workers for the purposes of s 230 of the Employment Rights Act 1996 and so have the limited protection given to 'whistle-blowers' by s 47B of the Employment Rights Act 1996 as amended by the Public Interest Disclosure Act 1998. This has the effect of, in addition, giving partners of an LLP rights under the Working Time Directive and similar provisions.

The Equality Act 2010 of particular concern to partnerships of solicitors and is dealt with at **III PAR [15B]**, **III PAR [15C]** and **III PAR [20C]** in the Partnership section. Note however *R (on the application of Age UK) v Secretary of State for Business, Innovation and Skills* [2009] EWHC 2336 (Admin), [2009] IRLR 1017, [2009] NLJR 1401 where it was held the 2006 Regulations were lawful under European Directive 2000/78/EC as being a legitimate social policy aim to protect the integrity of the labour market. For earlier authorities and articles on the 2006 Regulations see the Civil Court Practice 2011, Volume 2, Solicitors.

The mandatory retirement age of 65 ended on October 2011.

Between 6 April 2011 and 1 October 2011 only those who were notified before 6 April could be compulsorily retired on account of age and from 1 October 2011 employers can only operate a compulsory retirement age where they can objectively justify it as a 'proportionate means of achieving a legitimate aim'.

It should be noted that partners share discrimination rights with employees; see (2010) NLJ, 15 June, article 'Silent partner' by Michelle Chance.

The principal authority is *Seldon v Clarkson Wright and Jakes* [2010] EWCA Civ 899; the appellant, a former partner in the respondent firm of solicitors, claimed unlawful direct age discrimination. Sir Mark Waller stated that the actions of employers and firms must be consistent with the social or labour policy of the United Kingdom and if they were they would be lawful if they were a proportionate means of achieving their aims. The aims in *Seldon* were succession planning and retirement with dignity and they were regarded as legitimate. The decision was the subject of appeal to the Supreme Court which upheld the finding that age discrimination could be lawful if it was to achieve a legitimate aim, in an appropriate manner. The Supreme Court remitted the case to the tribunal on the question of proportionality.

III SOL [31]

SRA Authorisation and Practice Requirements The following rules and regulations were made by the SRA under provisions of the Solicitors Act 1974, the Administration of Justice Act 1985, the Courts and Legal Services Act 1990 and the Legal Services Act 2007 and with the approval of the Legal Services Board.

NB: As noted above, these rules are likely to be replaced by amended versions in the period between January and April 2019. Details of the rules can be found at www.legalservicesboard.org.uk/Projects/statutory_decision_making/pdf/2018/SRA_application_to_LSB_Aug18.pdf. The rules were approved by the LSB on 5 November 2018.

III SOL [32]

D0 Introduction These rules must be read in conjunction with the Principles. The Principles apply to all aspects of practice, including applications for authorisation or approval by firms and individuals and achievement of training requirements.

The desired outcomes that apply to authorisation and training are that:

- clients and the general public remain confident that legal services provided by our regulated community will be delivered to the required standard and in a principled manner;
- firms and individuals provide the SRA with sufficient information to enable the SRA to make appropriate judgements concerning whether to authorise, or continue to authorise, any firm or person;
- only those individuals and firms who/that meet the SRA's criteria for authorisation (including the requirements to be suitable and capable of providing legal services to the required standard) are authorised;
- firms are managed in such a way, and with appropriate systems and controls, so as to protect the public and safeguard the reputation of the legal profession;
- solicitors, regardless of the route by which they qualify, have been educated and trained to a standard that clients, the public, the profession and the judiciary properly expect;
- providers of training are authorised and monitored to an appropriate standard;
- solicitors have demonstrated their competence to exercise rights of audience in the higher courts; and

- solicitors have achieved the standard of competence required of advocates conducting criminal advocacy;
- solicitors demonstrate this competence through independent assessment;
- solicitors act so that clients, the judiciary and the wider public, have confidence that this been demonstrated.

III SOL [33]–III SOL [36]

D1 Practice Framework Rules 2011 Introduction and Part 1, rule 1.1 and guidance notes only reproduced below

Introduction

Part 1 of these rules sets out the types of business through which solicitors, RELs, RFLs and authorised bodies may practise. It restricts the types of business available in order to reflect statutory provisions and to ensure that clients and the public have the protections provided for by statute.

Part 2 permits authorised bodies, solicitors, RELs and RFLs to carry out certain types of work, including immigration work.

Part 3 governs the formation and practice requirements which must be satisfied by bodies to be eligible for authorisation by the SRA, and is based on the requirements of ss 9 and 9A of the AJA and s 72 of the LSA.

Part 4 sets out certain requirements relating to compliance with these rules and the SRA's regulatory arrangements.

Part 1, rule 1: Solicitors

1.1 Practice from an office in England and Wales

You may practise as a solicitor from an office in England and Wales in the following ways only:

(a) as a recognised sole practitioner or the employee of a recognised sole practitioner;

(b) as a solicitor exempted under Rule 10.2 from the obligation to be a recognised sole practitioner;

(c) as a manager, employee, member or interest holder of an authorised body provided that all work you do is:

  (i) of a sort the body is authorised by the SRA to carry out; or

  (ii) done for the body itself, or falls within Rule 4.1 to 4.11, and where this sub-paragraph applies, references in Rule 4 to 'employer' shall be construed as referring to that body, accordingly;

(d) as a manager, employee, member or interest holder of an authorised non-SRA firm, provided that all work you do is:

  (i) of a sort the firm is authorised by the firm's approved regulator to carry out; or

  (ii) done for the firm itself, or falls within Rule 4.1 to 4.11, and where this sub-paragraph applies, references in Rule 4 to 'employer' shall be construed as referring to that firm, accordingly;

(e) as the employee of another person, business or organisation, provided that you undertake work only for your employer, or as permitted by Rule 4 (In-house practice).

Guidance Notes

(i) See also Rules 10 (Sole practitioners), 13 (Eligibility criteria and fundamental requirements for recognised bodies), 14 (Eligibility criteria and fundamental requirements for licensed bodies), 15 (Formation, registered office and practising address), 16 (Composition of an authorised body) and 17 (Authorised bodies which are companies) below, Chapter 13 of the SRA Code of Conduct (Application and waivers provisions) and the SRA Practising Regulations.

(ii) See Rule 4.3 below and the definition of 'in-house practice' in the Glossary, in relation to in-house work that you carry out for clients which is outside of your firm's authorisation.

(iii) A recognised body which is a company may not have a corporate director (this also applies to a licensed body). However, when permitted, a corporate body owner and/or manager of a recognised body will need to be a legally qualified body (see the Glossary).

(iv) The rules do not prevent a solicitor establishing, for example, their own company for tax purposes (which is itself a recognised body) so that that company can be a corporate manager of another firm through which the solicitor practises.

III SOL [37]

D3 SRA Authorisation Rules for Legal Services Bodies and Licensable Bodies 2011 (not reproduced)

D4 SRA Practising Regulations 2011 (not reproduced)

D5 Recognised Bodies Regulations 2011 (not reproduced)

D5 Keeping of the Roll Regulations 2011 (not reproduced)

D6 Training Regulations 2011 (not reproduced)

D7 Admission Regulations 2011 (not reproduced)

D8 Qualified Lawyers Transfer Scheme Regulations 2011 (not reproduced)

D8A Qualified Lawyers Transfer Regulations 2011 (not reproduced)

D9 Higher Rights of Audience Regulations 2011 (not reproduced)

D9A Higher Courts Qualification Regulation 2011 (not reproduced)

III SOL [38]

D10 SRA Suitability Test 2011 Overview and the Principles only reproduced.

Overview

Outcomes-focused regulation concentrates on providing positive outcomes which when achieved will benefit and protect clients and the public. We must ensure that any individual admitted as a solicitor has, and maintains, the level of honesty, integrity and the professionalism expected by the public and other stakeholders and professionals, and does not pose a risk to the public or the profession.

The Suitability Test will apply the same high standards to all those seeking admission or restoration to the roll as a solicitor, as well as legally qualified and non-legally qualified applicants for roles in authorised bodies as authorised role holders.

The test is the same for non-solicitors as they will be working within the profession and must meet the same high standards that the general public expect of solicitors. This document is intended to make it clear to you what this standard is in terms of your character, suitability, fitness and propriety.

No applicant has the automatic right of admission, restoration or authorisation and it will always be for you to discharge the burden of satisfying suitability under this test. Any application that requires us to be satisfied as to character, suitability, fitness and propriety will be determined by reference to this test.

The Principles are set out at **III SOL [25]** above.

ADMINISTRATION OF JUSTICE ACT 1985

(c 61)

Incorporated practices

III SOL [39]

9. Recognition of legal services bodies and of sole solicitors' practices

(1) The Society may make rules—

(a) making provision as to the management and control of legal services bodies;

(b) prescribing the circumstances in which—

(i) legal services bodies may be recognised by the Society as being suitable bodies to undertake the provision of any solicitor services or other relevant legal services; and

(ii) sole solicitors' practices may be recognised by the Society as being suitable to undertake the provision of any such services;

(c) prescribing the requirements which (subject to any exceptions provided by the rules) must at all times be satisfied by bodies and sole solicitors' practices . . . so recognised if they are to remain so recognised; and

(d) regulating the conduct of the affairs of such bodies and sole solicitors' practices.

(1A) Where the Society makes rules under subsection (1), it must by rules under subsection (1)(c) prescribe the requirement that (subject to any exceptions provided by the rules) recognised bodies and recognised sole solicitors' practices must not provide services other than—

(a) solicitor services, or

(b) solicitor services and other relevant legal services.

(1B) "Relevant legal services" means—

(a) solicitor services, and

(b) where authorised persons other than solicitors or registered European lawyers are managers or employees of, or have an interest in, a recognised body, or are employees in a recognised sole solicitor's practice, services of the kind provided by individuals practising as such authorised persons (whether or not those services involve the carrying on of reserved legal activities within the meaning of the Legal Services Act 2007).

(1C) The Society may by rules under this section provide that services specified, or of a description specified, in the rules are not to be treated as solicitor services or other relevant legal services.

(2) Rules made by the Society may also make provision—

(a) for the manner and form in which applications for recognition under this section, or for the renewal of such recognition, are to be made, and requiring such applications to be accompanied by a fee of such amount as the Society may from time to time determine;

(aa) for the manner and form in which other applications under the rules are to be made, and requiring such applications to be accompanied by a fee of such amount as the Society may from time to time determine;

(ab) requiring recognised bodies, recognised sole solicitors' practices, or descriptions of such bodies or practices, to pay periodical fees of such amount as the Society may from time to time determine;

(b) for regulating the names that may be used by recognised bodies or recognised sole solicitors' practices;

(c) about the time when any recognition, or renewal of recognition, takes effect and the period for which it is (subject to the provisions made by or under this Part) to remain in force;

(d) for the suspension or revocation of any such recognition, on such grounds and in such circumstances as may be prescribed by the rules;

(e) about the effect on the recognition of a partnership or other unincorporated body ("the existing body") of any change in the membership of the existing body, including provision for the existing body's recognition to be transferred where the existing body ceases to exist and another body, or a sole solicitor's practice, succeeds to the whole or substantially the whole of its business;

(eza) about the effect on the recognition of a sole solicitor's practice where the sole solicitor ceases to practise as a sole principal and—

(i) another sole solicitor succeeds that sole solicitor as sole principal in the practice; or

(ii) a body or another sole solicitor succeeds to the whole or substantially the whole of the practice's business;

(ea) for the keeping by the Society of a register containing the names and places of business of all bodies and sole solicitors' practices which are for the time being recognised under this section, and such other information relating to them as may be specified in the rules;

(eb) for information (or information of a specified description) on such a register to be made available to the public, including provision about the manner in which, and times at which, information is to be made so available;

(f) for rules made under any provision of the 1974 Act to have effect in relation to recognised bodies or recognised sole solicitors' practices with such additions, omissions or other modifications as appear to the Society to be necessary or expedient;

(fa) about the education and training requirements to be met by managers and employees of recognised bodies or employees in recognised sole solicitors' practices;

(fb) for rules made under any provision of the 1974 Act to have effect in relation to managers and employees of recognised bodies or employees in recognised sole solicitors' practices with such additions, omissions or other modifications as appear to the Society to be necessary or expedient;

(fc) requiring recognised bodies to appoint a person or persons to monitor compliance, by the recognised body, its managers and its employees, with requirements imposed on them by or by virtue of this Act or any rules applicable to them by virtue of this section;

(fd) requiring the sole solicitor in a recognised sole solicitor's practice to appoint a person or persons to monitor compliance, by the sole solicitor and the employees in the practice, with requirements imposed on them by or by virtue of this Act, the 1974 Act or any rules applicable to them by virtue of this section or the 1974 Act;

(g) . . .

(h) for the manner of service on recognised bodies, or on sole solicitors in relation to recognised sole solicitors' practices, of documents authorised or required to be served on such bodies under or by virtue of this Part.

(2ZA) Rules under subsection (2)(fd) may provide that the person appointed under that paragraph may be the sole solicitor.

(2A) If rules under this section provide for the recognition of legal services bodies which have one or more managers who are not legally qualified, the rules must make provision—

(a) for the recognition of such bodies to be suspended or revoked, on such grounds and in such circumstances as may be prescribed by the rules;

(b) as to the criteria and procedure for the Society's approving, as suitable to be a manager of a recognised body, an individual who is not legally qualified (and for the Society's withdrawing such approval).

(2B) Rules under this section may make provision for appeals to the High Court against decisions made by the Society under the rules—

(a) to suspend or revoke the recognition of any body or sole solicitor's practice;

(b) not to approve, as suitable to be the manager of a recognised body, an individual who is not legally qualified (or to withdraw such approval).

(2C) The rules may provide for appeals against decisions within subsection (2B)(b) to be brought by the individual to whom the decision relates (as well as the body).

(2D) In relation to an appeal under rules made by virtue of subsection (2B), the High Court may make such order as it thinks fit as to payment of costs.

(2E) The decision of the High Court on such an appeal shall be final.

(2F) Where the Society decides to recognise a body or a sole solicitor's practice under this section it must grant that recognition subject to one or more conditions if—

(a) the case is of a kind prescribed for the purposes of this section by rules made by the Society, and

(b) the Society considers that it is in the public interest to do so.

(2G) While a body or a sole solicitor's practice is recognised under this section, the Society—

(a) must direct that the . . . recognition is to have effect subject to one or more conditions if—

(i) the case is of a prescribed kind, and

(ii) the Society considers that it is in the public interest to do so;

(b) may, in such circumstances as may be prescribed, direct that the . . . recognition is to have effect subject to such conditions as the Society may think fit.

"Prescribed" means prescribed by rules made by the Society.

(2H) The conditions which may be imposed under subsection (2F) or (2G) include—

(a) conditions requiring the body, or the sole solicitor, to take specified steps that will, in the opinion of the Society, be conducive to the carrying on by . . . of an efficient business;

(b) conditions which prohibit the body, or the sole solicitor, from taking any specified steps except with the approval of the Society;

(c) if rules under this section provide for the recognition of legal services bodies which have one or more managers who are not legally qualified, a condition that all the managers of the body must be legally qualified.

"Specified" means specified in the condition.

(2I) Rules made by the Society may make provision about when conditions imposed under this section take effect (including provision conferring power on the Society to direct that a condition is not to have effect until the conclusion of any appeal in relation to it).

(2J) Section 86A of the 1974 Act applies to rules under this section as it applies to rules under that Act.

(2K) Rules under this section may contain such incidental, supplemental, transitional or transitory provisions or savings as the Society considers necessary or expedient.

(3) Despite section 24(2) of the 1974 Act, section 20 of that Act (prohibition on unqualified person acting as solicitor) does not apply to a recognised body; and nothing in section 24(1) of that Act applies in relation to such a body.

(4) . . .

(5) A certificate signed by an officer of the Society and stating that any body or sole solicitor's practice . . . is or is not, or was or was not at any time, recognised under this section shall, unless the contrary is proved, be evidence of the facts stated in the certificate; and a certificate purporting to be so signed shall be taken to have been so signed unless the contrary is proved.

(6) Schedule 2 (which makes provision with respect to the application of provisions of the 1974 Act to recognised bodies, with respect to other matters relating to such bodies, and with respect to matters relating to recognised sole solicitors' practices) shall have effect.

(7) Subject to the provisions of that Schedule, the Lord Chancellor may by order made by statutory instrument subject to annulment in pursuance of a resolution of either House of Parliament provide for any enactment or instrument passed or made before or in the same session as the Legal Services Act 2007 was passed and having effect in relation to solicitors to have effect in relation to recognised bodies with such additions, omissions or other modifications as appear to the Lord Chancellor to be necessary or expedient.

(8) In this section—

"the 1974 Act" means the Solicitors Act 1974;

"authorised person" means an authorised person in relation to an activity which is a reserved legal activity (within the meaning of the Legal Services Act 2007);

references to employment in a recognised sole solicitor's practice are references to employment by a sole solicitor for the purposes of a practice recognised under this section;

"the Society" has the meaning given by section 87(1) of the 1974 Act; . . .

[. . .]

"legally qualified" and "legal services body" have the meaning given by section 9A;

"manager", in relation to a body, has the same meaning as in the Legal Services Act 2007 (see section 207 of that Act);

"recognised body" means a body . . . for the time being recognised under this section

"recognised sole solicitor's practice" means a sole solicitor's practice for the time being recognised under this section;

"registered European lawyer" means a person who is registered with the Law Society under regulation 17 of the European Communities (Lawyers' Practice) Regulations 2000;

"sole solicitor" has the meaning given by section 87(1) of the 1974 Act;

"solicitor services" means professional services such as are provided by individuals practising as solicitors or lawyers of other jurisdictions;

and a person has an interest in a body if the person has an interest in the body within the meaning of Part 5 of the Legal Services Act 2007 (see sections 72 and 109 of that Act).

III SOL [39.1]

Registered office SRA Authorised Bodies Regulations 2011, reg 15, extract:

'15.1 Where a body is granted initial recognition or its recognition is renewed, the SRA must issue a certificate of recogntion.

15.2 Each certificate of recognition must state, in respect of the recognised body:

(a) the name and number under which the body is recognised;

(b) its registered office if it is an LLP or company;

(c) its principal practising adress in England and Wales.'

III SOL [39.2]

Overseas practice A recognised body can practise overseas as well as in England and Wales but must then comply with local law and the requirements of:

(a) the Solicitors Code of Conduct 2011, in particular Chapter 13;
(b) the SRA Practice Framework Rules 2011, in particular rule 1.2 and rules 10, 13, 14, 15, 16 and 17;
(c) the SRA Recognised Bodies Regulations 2011; and
(d) the SRA Practising Regulations 2011.

III SOL [40]

9A. Legal services bodies

(1) For the purposes of section 9, a "legal services body" means a body (corporate or unincorporate) in respect of which—

(a) the management and control condition, and

(b) the relevant lawyer condition,

are satisfied.

(2) The management and control condition is satisfied if—

(a) at least 75% of the body's managers are legally qualified,

(b) the proportion of shares in the body held by persons who are legally qualified is at least 75%,

(c) the proportion of voting rights in the body which persons who are legally qualified are entitled to exercise, or control the exercise of, is at least 75%,

(d) all the persons with an interest in the body who are not legally qualified are managers of the body, and

(e) all the managers of the body who are not legally qualified are individuals approved by the Society as suitable to be managers of a recognised body.

(3) The Society may by rules under section 9 provide that, in relation to specified kinds of bodies, subsection (2) applies as if the references to 75% were to such greater percentage as may be specified (and different percentages may be specified for different kinds of bodies).

(4) The relevant lawyer condition is satisfied in relation to a body if at least one manager of the body is—

(a) a solicitor,

(b) a registered European lawyer, or

(c) a qualifying body.

(5) For that purpose a qualifying body is a body in respect of which—

(a) the management and control condition [is] satisfied . . . ,

(b) the relevant lawyer condition is satisfied by virtue of subsection (4)(a) or (b), and

(c) the services condition is satisfied.

(6) For the purposes of this section the following are legally qualified—

(a) an authorised person who is an individual;

(b) a registered foreign lawyer (within the meaning of section 89 of the Courts and Legal Services Act 1990 (c 41));

(c) a person entitled to pursue professional activities under a professional title to which the Directive applies in a state to which the Directive applies (other than the title of barrister or solicitor in England and Wales);

(d) an authorised person which is a body in respect of which—

(i) the services condition is satisfied, and

(ii) the management and control condition would be satisfied if the references in subsection (2) to persons who are legally qualified were to persons who are legally qualified by virtue of paragraphs (a) to (c);

(e) a body which provides professional services such as are provided by individuals who are authorised persons or lawyers of other jurisdictions, and in respect of which the management and control condition would be satisfied if the references in subsection (2) to persons who are legally qualified were to persons who are legally qualified by virtue of paragraphs (a) to (c).

(f) a legal partnership which—

(i) was in existence immediately before the commencement of this paragraph,

(ii) since that time has continued to be a partnership of the kind mentioned in rule 12.01(1)(b), 12.02(1)(b) or 12.04(1)(c)(i) of the pre-commencement conduct rules (framework of practice), and

(iii) has not, since that time, had a body corporate (other than a body within paragraph (g)) as a member;

(g) a body corporate which—

SOLICITORS

(i) was recognised under section 9 immediately before the commencement of this paragraph, and

(ii) has since that time continued to satisfy the requirements of rule 14.03(1) and 14.04(1) to (3) or the requirements of rule 14.05(1) to (3) of the pre-commencement conduct rules (restrictions on directors, owners etc of incorporated practices);

(h) a body which—

(i) is an authorised person and satisfies the services condition, or

(ii) provides professional services such as are provided by individuals who are authorised persons or lawyers of other jurisdictions,

and which satisfies the requirements of rules under subsection (6C).

(6A) For the purposes of subsection (6)(f), a partnership is to be treated as the same partnership despite a change in membership, if any person who was a member before the change remains a member.

(6B) For the purposes of subsection (6)(f) and (g), the references in the pre-commencement conduct rules to a recognised body are to be construed as references to a body which was recognised under section 9 immediately before the commencement of subsection (6)(f) and (g).

(6C) The Society must make rules for the purposes of paragraph (h) of subsection (6) prescribing the requirements relating to management and control which must be satisfied by or in relation to a body for it to fall within that paragraph.

(7) For the purposes of this section, the services condition is satisfied in relation to a body if the body provides only services which may be provided by a recognised body (having regard to rules under section 9(1A) and (1C)).

(8) For the purposes of this section—

"authorised person" has the same meaning as in section 9;

"the Directive" means Directive 98/5/EC of the European Parliament and the Council, to facilitate practice of the profession of lawyer on a permanent basis in a Member State other than that in which the qualification was obtained;

"legal partnership" means a partnership in which a solicitor, a registered European lawyer or a recognised body is permitted to practise by virtue of rules made under section 31 of the Solicitors Act 1974 (c 47), as those rules had effect immediately before the commencement of subsection (6)(f);

"manager", in relation to a body, has the meaning given by section 9;

"pre-commencement conduct rules" means rules under Part 2 of the Solicitors Act 1974 or section 9 of this Act, known as the Solicitors' Code of Conduct 2007, as those rules had effect immediately before the commencement of subsection (6)(f) and (g);

"recognised body" has the same meaning as in section 9 (subject to subsection (6B) above);

"registered European lawyer" has the same meaning as in section 9;

"shares" has the same meaning as for the purposes of Part 5 of the Legal Services Act 2007 (see sections 72 and 109 of that Act);

"the Society" has the meaning given by section 87(1) of the Solicitors Act 1974;

"specified" means specified in rules made by the Society;

and a person has an interest in a body if the person has an interest in the body for the purposes of section 9.

III SOL [41]

10. Penalty for pretending to be a body recognised under s 9

(1) A body shall not describe itself or hold itself out as a body for the time being recognised under section 9 unless it is so recognised.

(2) Any body which contravenes subsection (1) shall be guilty of an offence and liable on summary conviction to a fine not exceeding the fourth level on the standard scale.

(3) Where an offence under this section committed by a body corporate is proved to have been committed with the consent or connivance of or to be attributable to any neglect on the part of an officer of the body corporate, that officer (as well as the body corporate) is guilty of the offence and is liable to be proceeded against and punished accordingly.

(4) Where the affairs of a body corporate are managed by its members, subsection (3) applies in relation to the acts and defaults of a member in connection with the member's functions of management as it applies to an officer of the body corporate.

(5) Proceedings for an offence under this section alleged to have been committed by an unincorporated body are to be brought in the name of that body (and not in that of any of its members) and, for the purposes of any such proceedings, any rules of court relating to the service of documents have effect as if that body were a corporation.

(6) A fine imposed on an unincorporated body on its conviction of an offence under this section is to be paid out of the funds of that body.

(7) If an unincorporated body is charged with an offence under this section, section 33 of the Criminal Justice Act 1925 (c 86) and Schedule 3 to the Magistrates' Courts Act 1980 (c 43) (procedure on charge of an offence against a corporation) have effect in like manner as in the case of a corporation so charged.

(8) Where an offence under this section committed by an unincorporated body (other than a partnership) is proved to have been committed with the consent or connivance of, or to be attributable to any neglect on the part of, any officer of the body or any member of its governing body, that officer or member as well as the unincorporated body is guilty of the offence and liable to be proceeded against and punished accordingly.

(9) Where an offence under this section committed by a partnership is proved to have been committed with the consent or connivance of, or to be attributable to any neglect on the part of, a partner, that partner as well as the partnership is guilty of the offence and liable to be proceeded against and punished accordingly.

(10) In this section "officer", in relation to a body corporate, means—

(a) any director, secretary or other similar officer of the body corporate, or

(b) any person who was purporting to act in any such capacity.

III SOL [41.1]

Summary conviction Summary jurisdiction and procedure are mainly governed by the Magistrates' Court Act 1980.

GENERAL NOTES — CONTINUED

III SOL [42]

Solicitors retainer Discussion on retainers needs to be read with the requirements of the SRA Handbook and, in particular, with the first section, You and Your Client which sets out the principal expectations of the regulator in respect of treating client's fairly and transparently.

The relationship between a solicitor and his client is contractual and the provisions of the contract are expressed or implied in the solicitor's retainer. There is no strict requirement that there need be a formal written retainer for there to be an enforceable retainer as to

SOLICITORS

costs; the court in *Fladgate LLP v Harrison* [2012] EWHC 67 (QB), [2012] NLJR 262 rejected arguments to the contrary. The absence of a written retainer can however, 'cause costs chaos' as Simon Gibbs sets out in his article 'Put pen to paper' in (2012) NLJ, 5 June, page 805.

The point of a retainer (and/or a client care letter) is that both parties should have an authoritative statement of the basis on which the solicitor is acting and the court in *Manches* (above) continued:

'... once such a letter (drafted be it said by the solicitor) is signed there is a lot to be said for it being conclusive.'

It is important for solicitors to provide an accurate as possible costs estimate and subsequent written notice must be given if the estimate is exceeded; per Cranston J in *Minkin* at first instance. The client's instructions must be clearly recorded and any lack of clarity remedied in a subsequent supplemental document that is duly signed.

The court recognises that the business experience and acumen of the client can be a crucial factor in construing the retainer; see *Cheney v Newman* [2011] EWHC 2156 (QB), a case where the retainer was held not to extend to the commercial merits of the transaction, and articles by Victoria Brackett entitled 'Scope of the retainer' in (2012) Sol Jo, 10 June, page 29 and Philip Murrim and Tom Pangbourne entitled 'Word to the wise' in (2013) Sol Jo, 15 January, page 14.

An example of dispute over the extent of the retainer is provided by *Farnon v Devonshires Solicitors* [2011] EWHC 3167 (QB), [2011] All ER (D) 93 (Dec) where the client sought advice as to the notice provisions and the restrictive covenants in a partnership agreement and subsequently allegations of negligent advice as to sex discrimination, a compromise agreement and the ability of a company to recover overpaid tax. The issue in the case was the scope of the retainer. The Court held that the retainer was limited to the issues arising as to notice and the restrictive covenants; accordingly the claim was dismissed.

The further example is provided by *Mason v Mills & Reeve (a firm)* [2011] EWHC 410 (Ch), [2011] STC 1177, [2011] NLJR 365 where the careful drafting of the retainer excluded from the work to be provided by solicitors tax advice save as to management buy-out and the client's disposal of his shares. This did not cover advising as to the advisability of delaying the transaction because of an operation imminently to be taken by the client. Consideration of this case is provided by Mark Lucas in (2012) Sol Jo, 27 March, at page 29.

The retainer or client care letter should not only clearly set out what is covered but also what is excluded; a claim cannot be based on expressly excluded aspects. In an article entitled 'Knowing the limits' in (2012) Sol Jo, 16 October, page 12 Simon Butler and Tom Ramsbury consider the problem of drafting the retainer and provide a list of twelve practical steps distilled from the cases.

In recent years, particularly with the decline of legal aid, there has been interest in the concept of 'unbundling' whereby the solicitor agrees to undertake a particular part of a larger piece of legal work for a client (for example, initial advice in respect of a divorce) while the client undertakes the remainder. The Law Society in April 2016 published a practice note providing advice for solicitors wishing to offer services on this basis.

III SOL [43]

Terminating the retainer The Court of Appeal in *Richard Buxton (a firm) v Mills-Owens* [2010] EWCA Civ 122, [2010] 4 All ER 405, [2010] 1 WLR 1997 allowed the appeal by the appellant firm of solicitors against the decision that they were not entitled to recover their costs from the respondent when they terminated their retainer, which was held to be an 'entire contract', because the client insisted a case be put forward and argued although it was not properly arguable and 'doomed to disaster'.

The Court of Appeal found that even though there was an entire contract there was a right to terminate it for 'good reasons' and the instructions if followed would have resulted in a breach by the solicitors of their professional duty as officers of the court, of CPR 1.3 which requires the parties to help the court to deal with cases 'justly' and Rule 11.01(3) of the Solicitors Code of Conduct 2007 which was then in force. Accordingly the solicitors were entitled to terminate their retainer and to be paid their costs and to recover their disbursements to the date of termination.

The decision is welcome, in particular for signalling the end of the use of a code whereby the advocate could indicate he expected his submission to be rejected; for example 'I am instructed that . . . '. However the decision has not given any clear guidance on what amounts to 'good reason' either within the Code of Conduct 2011 or in the eyes of the court.

It is clear that termination is not a step to be taken lightly and that reasonable notice must be given; solicitors may, however, be wise to consider their standard retainer letter afresh for an appropriate amendment may assist them if they should be forced into a position where they must decide where they stand when faced with making a 'close' decision. For discussion see article 'To sack or not to sack?' by David Burrows in (2010) NLJ, 14 May, page 693.

At common law it was not 'good reason', giving a right to terminate a retainer, that the client had failed to pay part of the profit costs contained in a bill on account as the claim proceeded. If however, the solicitors' retainer contained provision for payments on an interim basis then non-payment of a reasonable sum on account after reasonable notice would entitle the solicitor to withdraw from the retainer: s 65(2) of the 1974 Act.

In *Minkin v Cawdery Kaye Fireman and Taylor* (reported at first instance at [2011] EWHC 177 (QB) and on appeal at [2012] LJR 681) at first instance it was held that the client had reasonable justification to delay payment of a bill for costs on account and the solicitors' refusal to continue to act for him amounted to a repudiatory breach of contract. The solicitors were ordered to pay back to the client all sums paid by him less monies used to pay counsel's fees. On appeal the Court of Appeal held that the client had no reasonable justification for not meeting the bill presented to him and the solicitors were entitled to and did suspend the operation of the retainer until receipt of the monies requested on account. The retainer remained in force until later terminated when the client informed the solicitors he had lost faith in them. That absolved the solicitors from further performance of the contract but did not absolve the client from payment of costs properly incurred to that point. The costs judge had been wrong not to order the payment of the costs as they were assessed and also wrong in ordering the solicitors to make repayment to the client.

Solicitors wishing to suspend doing work, upon failure to pay an instalment of costs, as opposed to terminating the retainer, may find guidance in Ward LJ's statement:

'Not being prepared to act until money is paid shows a willingness to act when there is money on account. This is the clear language of suspension...'

Their letter may well adopt this phraseology.

A further decision giving guidance on the termination of a retainer is *French v Carter Lemon Camerons LLP* [2012] EWCA Civ 1180, [2012] NLJR 1155, 156 Sol Jo (no 34) 27 and the appeal [2012] EWCA Civ 1180, [2012] All ER (D) 14 (Sep); the Court of Appeal held that the client had terminated the retainer and accordingly the solicitors were entitled to their outstanding fees and to a lien in respect of them.

It has been held that the client's supervening incapacity does not frustrate the underlying contract of retainer: *Blankley v Central Manchester and Manchester Children's University Hospitals NHS Trust* [2014] EWHC 168 (QB), [2014] 2 All ER 1104, [2014] 1 WLR 2683.

In *Budana v Leeds Teaching Hospitals NHS Trust* [2017] EWCA Civ 1980, 7 December 2017, the Court of Appeal held that the assignment of a case to another solicitor did not necessarily terminate a retainer where the client had consented to the transfer.

III SOL [44]

On-going retainers In *Shepherd Construction Ltd v Pinsent Masons LLP* [2012] EWHC 43 (TCC), 141 ConLR 232, [2012] BLR 213 the claim against the defendant solicitors depended on the former client being able to establish that the defendant solicitor were party to an on-going retainer making them responsible for reviewing all previous advice or services provided in the light of any changes that had occurred (typically new legislation) that required further action to be taken by the client.

Akenhead J found there was not an on-going retainer to, what must be regarded as, general relief to a legal profession faced with an argument which if successful could require all advice given or services provided to be kept under constant review.

A similar attempt was made to establish such a position existed with accountants in *Integral Memory plc v Haines Watts* [2012] EWHC 342 (Ch), [2012] SWTI 1385 and failed. The concept of a continuing duty extending beyond the limits of the retainer is, it seems, unlikely to find favour with the courts except where the contract evidenced by the retainer can properly be construed as creating a continuing contractual obligation. A look into the future position is provided by Claire Roake in her article 'Duty of Care ends in?' in the Gazette, 30 August 2012.

III SOL [45]

Information for clients and complaints Under the EU Services Directive, solicitors are required to make available details of their professional indemnity insurers and to identify the jurisdictions to which the insurance applies. This has now been supplemented by a requirement under the ADR Directive to provide details of approved ADR providers who could assist in respect of complaints which could not be resolved internally. The Law Society has issued a practice note to give detailed advice to solicitors on the provisions of both directives (www.lawsociety.org.uk/support-services/advice/practice-notes/information-on-letterheads-emails-and-websites/).

Every firm of solicitors must establish and maintain a procedure for resolving client complaints. A client must be informed of the procedure when instructions are given or confirmed so that he knows who to approach if he wants to complain.

From 6 December 2018, the SRA Transparency Rules 2018 require solicitors to publish information for clients about the prices of its services where it advertises that it offers services in respect of conveyancing, probate, immigration, employment, magistrates courts and debt-recovery work. The information should either cover the fixed costs of the work, or the basis of charging, including information about the seniority and qualifications of the individuals carrying out the work, the basis of any conditional fees charges and whether the price includes VAT.

Rules which have not yet come into force would require firms to publish information about the number of complaints they receive and any regulatory action taken against them.

III SOL [46]

Referral fees Section 56 of the Legal Aid, Sentencing and Punishment of Offenders Act 2012 (LASPO) requires the SRA to ensure that prohibited referral fees in personal injury cases are not paid. The provision came into effect on 1 April 2013. The SRA has indicated it intends to use an 'outcomes focused approach' to regulate the ban which will allow it 'to look at the substance of an arrangement... and focus on those arrangements that pose a real risk to the public'. Since the ban was introduced a number of firms have been investigated and prosecuted by the SRA. See Cordery on Legal Services Volume 1 for a discussion of the rules as they affect solicitors. In December 2018, for example, a solicitor was find £5000 by the SDT for approving 378 referral payments for Road Traffic Accident cases (www.lawgazette.co.uk/news/solicitor-fined-after-approving-378-referral-payments-for-rta-claims/5068727.article).

III SOL [47]

Funding the client's disbursements The issue of the liability of a solicitor, who has funded his client's disbursements, to an order for payment of the costs to the other party to the proceedings concerned has come before the courts on a number of occasions, including: *Germany v Flatman* [2011] EWHC 2945 (QB) (where the court favoured imposition of liability) and *Tinseltime v Roberts* [2012] EWHC 2628 (TCC) (where it did not).

The position is considered by Kevin Shannon in (2012) Sol Jo, 27 November, page 14 in an article entitled 'The uncertain cost'.

III SOL [48]

Solicitor-client agreements as to costs A solicitor may make an agreement with his client as to the amount of his costs. This may be a contentious business agreement under s 59 or a non-contentious business agreement under s 57 (see para **III SOL [74]**) (see s 87(1) (at para **III SOL [91]**) and the notes at para **III SOL [75]** as to the distinction).

Any clause in a contentious business agreement whereby a solicitor seeks to evade liability for negligence is void if the client is a natural person who, in entering into that agreement, is acting for purposes which are outside his trade, business or profession (s 60(5) (see para **III SOL [76]**)) but a solicitor may limit his contractual liability. Liability for fraud or reckless disregard of a professional obligation cannot be limited. See Law Society Gazette 103/05 2 Feb 2006 for an article on limiting liability by top law firms with little client resistance. Solicitors are not permitted to limit liability below the minimum level of professional indemnity insurance required by the SRA (see SRA Indemnity Insurance Rules 2011 and the SRA Indemnity Enactment Rules 2011 with the SRA Indemnity Rules 2011 annexed). In particular it is to be noted that the amount of the 'cap' in each individual agreement must be 'reasonable' to satisfy the requirements of the Unfair Contract Terms Act 1977.

In *Marplace (Number 512) Ltd v Chaffe Street* [2006] EWHC 1919 (Ch), [2006] All ER (D) 413 (Jul) the court considered the reasonableness of a liability cap in a solicitor's engagement letter in the light of s 11(1) of the 1977 Act. In that case they found it reasonable because:

(i) the clients were familiar with such clauses in professional contracts;
(ii) it had been the subject of discussion and had not been put forward as a non-negotiable term;
(iii) the engagement letter included machinery for the discussion of variations of the cap;
(iv) the cap was determined on reasonable commercial principles.

For detailed consideration see article 'Making sure the cap fits' by John Verry in Gazette (2007) 19 April, page 12 referred to above, and the provisions of the Solicitors Code of Conduct 2011.

A solicitor cannot sue on a contentious business agreement (s 61(1) (see para **III SOL [77]**)). Either party may apply to the court, which has complete jurisdiction to enforce or set aside the agreement (s 61(2) (see para **III SOL [77]**)). Similar powers may be exercised where the solicitor dies or becomes incapable of acting or the client changes his solicitor (s 63 (see para **III SOL [79]**)). If the client enters into the agreement as a representative on behalf of a person whose property may be chargeable, the agreement must be laid before a costs officer before payment (s 62(1) (see para **III SOL [78]**)).

A bill of costs in respect of contentious business which is not the subject of a s 59 agreement (see para **III SOL [75]**) may be for a gross sum instead of containing detailed items but the client has certain rights to require the solicitor to deliver a detailed bill and if he does so the gross sum bill is of no effect (s 64 (see para **III SOL [80]**)). No action may be brought on the bill until one month has expired since delivery although the court has power to allow earlier proceedings in special circumstances and to order the costs to be assessed (s 69 (see para **III SOL [85]**)). The court has power to order the costs to be assessed on the application of the solicitor, a party chargeable (s 70 (see para **III SOL [86]**)) or a third party who has paid or is liable to pay the bill (s 71 (see para **III SOL [87]**)). For procedure see CPR Part 67 in Volume 1. There are special provisions enabling a solicitor to obtain a charging order, over property "recovered or preserved", to secure his costs (s 73 (see para **III SOL [89]**)).

The provisions as to costs are contained in Part III of the Solicitors Act 1974 and proceedings under that part must be brought by a claim under CPR Part 8; note CPR 67.3 and the model claim form annexed to the Costs Practice Direction in Volume 1.

A solicitor will have to make a separate claim to recover unpaid costs even if they have been assessed by the court.

For precedents relating to the recovery of costs between solicitor and client see **BCCP E[3001]** et seq.

III SOL [49]

Jurisdiction in respect of solicitors' remuneration Jurisdiction under the Solicitors Act 1974 is primarily conferred on the High Court. However, the county court in which any part of the business was done has a limited jurisdiction (upper limit £5,000) under ss 69–71 (see paras **III SOL [85]–III SOL [87]** and CPR 67.3(a) in Volume 1 (para **CPR 67.3**)) relating to the assessment of bills rendered by a solicitor to his client in respect of proceedings in the county court. This jurisdiction derives from s 69(3) (see para **III SOL [85]**). The county court also has an unlimited jurisdiction under s 68 (see para **III SOL [84]**) to order a solicitor to deliver a bill relating wholly or partly to contentious business done by the solicitor in that county court. For procedure see CPR Part 67, at 67.2 in Volume 1.

III SOL [50]

Costs against solicitors Section 51 of the Senior Courts Act 1981 makes provision for disallowance of a solicitor's costs and for the making of an order that a legal representative pay costs in certain situations: see the Procedural Tables Supplement 2013 at **TAB 25**, General, paras 1.24.1-1.24.4 and **TAB 25**, Division C, 'Detailed assessment' at para 13.

See also **CPR 44.8** as to the duty of a legal representative to inform a client, who was not present, in writing of the costs order also CPR 46.8 as to the personal liability of legal representatives — wasted costs orders.

Wasted costs are further considered at **III SOL [55]** below and the topic is fully dealt with at **CPR 48.7** and **CPR 48.7[1]–CPR 48.7[9]** in Volume 1.

CPR 44.11 enables the court to exercise its powers where:

(a) in connection with a summary or detailed assessment, a party or that party's legal representative fails to comply with a rule, practice direction or court order; or

(b) it appears to the court that the conduct of a party or that party's legal representative, before or during the proceedings or in the assessment proceedings, was unreasonable or improper.

The court's powers include ordering a party's legal representative to pay costs he has caused any other party to incur.

III SOL [51]

Barristers' fees From 31 January 2013 the Bar Council's new contractual terms require payment of fees within 30 days of receipt of an invoice whether or not the solicitor has been put in funds. The 'Withdrawal of Credit List' is replaced by an advisory List of Defaulting Solicitors from whom barristers are not obliged to accept work. For further details and the ability for barristers to sue for their fees, see (2012) Gazette, 28 January, page 31.

III SOL [52]

Success fees Section 44 of the Legal Aid, Sentencing and Punishment of Offenders Act 2012 (LASPO) has amended ss 58 and 58A of the Courts and Legal Services Act 1990 preventing the recovery by a lawyer of a success fee paid from a losing party. This is subject to additional provisions that the lawyer may recover it from his successful client. The

SOLICITORS

lawyer's success fee is capped at a percentage of the damages. In personal injury cases the success fee is capped at 25% of the damages awarded for pain/suffering and loss of amenity and pecuniary loss other than future pecuniary loss and net of any sums recoverable by the CRU, inclusive of VAT. This 25% cap relates to proceedings at first instance and the cap in other personal injury claims (ie appeals) is set at 100%, inclusive of VAT. In all other proceedings the cap is 100%.

The amendments made by s 44 do not presently apply to diffuse mesothelioma proceedings.

Reference should be made to the Conditional Fee Agreements Order 2013.

III SOL [53]

After-the-event insurance After-the-event insurance premiums are no longer recoverable from a losing party but the Lord Chancellor may regulate for their payment in clinical negligence proceedings of a prescribed prescription subject to compliance with the conditions set out in s 58C(2) of LASPO and in the circumstances only set in the Recovery of Costs Insurance Premiums in Clinical Negligence Regulations 2013, SI 2013/92. These Regulations also contain provisions as to the amount of the premium that may be recoverable.

III SOL [54]

Damages-based agreements Damages-based Agreements (DBAs) enable a person providing advocacy, litigation or claims management services to recover an agreed percentage of a client's damages of the case is won but nothing if the case is lost. The agreements are enforceable by s 58AA of the Courts and Legal Services Act 1990.

The Damages-based Agreements Regulations 2013 came into force on 1 April 2013. The Regulations apply to all agreements entered into or signed after they come into force. Such agreements for personal injuries must not provide for a payment above an amount which, including VAT, is equal to 25% of the combined sums recovered for general damages for pain, suffering and loss of amenity and damages for pecuniary loss other than future pecuniary loss but net of sums recoverable by the CRU.

In any other claim or proceedings to which the Regulations apply the 'cap', including VAT, is equal to 50% of the sums ultimately recovered by the client.

The prescribed percentages only apply to claims or proceedings at first instance.

Regulation 4 of the Regulations sets out (in respect of claims or proceedings other than employment matters) the limits on the amount payable by the client ('the payment') and the deductions from it.

Regulations 5, 6, 7 and 8 of the Regulations apply only in employment matters.

The rules have been the subject of criticism and solicitors are advised to proceed with considerable caution if considering this approach.

III SOL [55]

Wasted costs A wasted costs order may be made by the court against any lawyer in the proceedings: s 51 of the Senior Courts Act 1981 as substituted by s 4 Courts and Legal Services Act 1990 and *Brown v Bennett* [2002] 2 All ER 273, [2002] 1 WLR 713, Neuberger J, but a party must be allowed to make submissions prior to a wasted costs order being made against him: *Re Wiseman Lee (Solicitors) (Wasted Costs) (No 5 of 2000)* (2001) Times, 5 April.

See the Supreme Court Costs Office Guide set out in Volume 1 (CPR 48 COG, paras 16.3-16.6) and in particular the guidelines laid down by the Court of Appeal in *Ridehalgh v Horsefield* [1994] Ch 205, CA. See also now ss 188–191 of the Legal Services Act 2007 and also paras CPR 44.11 and CPR 46.8 as supplemented by Practice Direction 46, para 5, in particular the three-stage test set out at para 5.5.

A wasted costs order can be made against solicitors only if they have breached their duty to the court; mere negligent handling of a client's case is not sufficient: *Redford & Co v Charles* (2003) Times, 26 November, CA, Neuberger J. In *R (on the application of Hide) v Staffordshire County Council* [2007] EWHC 2441, [2007] NLJR 1543 the court decided that despite finding the solicitor advocate had behaved unreasonably and negligently in the conduct of the litigation it would not make an order for wasted costs as the evidence was that such an order would result in the bankruptcy of the solicitor. This would be, the court stated, a disproportionate consequence of the conduct.

An application was made for a wasted costs order under s 145A of the Magistrates' Courts Act 1980 against a firm of solicitors which had failed to discover that its purported client was a non-existent company in *Chief Constable of British Transport Police v Soods Solicitors Ltd* [2012] EWHC 3780 (Admin), 156 Sol Jo (29) 31. The Court held that as no finding of fault had been made the order sought could not be made.

A wasted costs order was made against the claimant's solicitors in *Mbutu v De la Rue Browne* [2006] All ER (D) 170 (Mar) where the solicitors evaluated their client's expert evidence only one week before the trial date and having done so came off the record.

A wasted costs order cannot be made against a litigant's former solicitors where they had not issued the proceedings nor performed any ancillary functions amounting to the conduct of proceedings: *Byrne v South Sefton (Merseyside) Health Authority* [2001] EWCA Civ 1904, [2002] 1 WLR 775, [2002] 01 LS Gaz R 19.

Note the Court of Appeal decided in *Myatt v NCB (No 2)* [2007] EWCA Civ 307, [2007] 1 WLR 1559, [2007] 4 All ER 1094 that the court has jurisdiction under s 51 of the Supreme Court Act 1981 to make a costs order against a party's solicitor where the litigation has been pursued by the client in whole or substantial part for the benefit of the solicitor.

A wasted costs order under s 51(b) of the Supreme Court Act 1981 should only be made 'where, and to the extent that, the conduct so characterised has been established as directly causative of wasted costs': *Harrison v Harrison* [2009] EWHC 428 (QB), [2009] 1 FLR 1434, [2009] Fam Law 481.

In *Hallam-Peel & Co v Southwark London Borough Council* [2008] EWCA Civ 1120, [2009] 2 Costs LR 269 the solicitors successfully appealed against a wasted costs order having satisfied the court they had not acted unreasonably in raising a new point in possession proceedings and accordingly were not in breach of their duty to the court.

For a recent decision see *Fisher Meredith v JH and PH (financial remedy: appeal: wasted costs)* [2012] EWHC 408 (Fam), [2012] 2 FCR 241, [2012] 2 FLR 536 discussed by Geraldine Morris in 'The blame game' (2012) NLJ, 30 March.

SOLICITORS

III SOL [56]

Conflicts and confidentiality The Solicitors Code of Conduct 2011, Chapter 3 deals with 'Conflicts of interests' and Chapter 4 deals with 'Confidentiality and disclosure'.

If a solicitor puts himself in the position of having conflicting duties to two different clients his duty to both clients remained unmodified and he is liable in damages to the client whose duty he has failed to perform: *Hilton v Barker, Booth and Eastwood (a firm)* [2005] UKHL 8, [2005] 1 All ER 651, [2005] 1 WLR 567. For a case where Chinese Walls were held to be sufficient see *GUS Consulting GmbH v Leboeuf Lamb Greene & Macrae (a firm)* [2006] EWCA Civ 683, [2006] ArbLR 31.

In *Conway v Ratiu* [2005] EWCA Civ 1302, [2006] 1 All ER 571n, [2006] 1 EGLR 125 the court considered the solicitor's duty of confidentiality to the client and the question of conflict of interest. In the course of his judgment Auld LJ, with whom Laws and Sedley LJJ agreed, set out the position in great detail in paras [71]–[81].

Legal advice privilege is absolute and is the client's right so that only the client can waive it. Confidentiality is wider and is capable of being overridden. The client's right to instruct the solicitor of his or her choice overrides confidentiality where, for example, the confidential information is not material to the issue on which the solicitor is to be instructed.

III SOL [57]

Legal professional privilege The privilege is that of the client and only the client can waive it. For cases on waiver by the client see *Mortgage Express v Singh Savali* [2010] EWHC B23 (Ch) where there was found to be a waiver and *Quinn v The Law Society* [2010] EWCA Civ 805 where there was not found to be a waiver. See also the Procedural Tables Supplement, **TAB 15**, para 1.12 et seq.

The Supreme Court in *R (on the application of Prudential plc) v Special Comr of Income Tax* [2013] UKSC 1, [2013] 2 AC 185, [2013] 2 All ER 24 declined to extend legal professional privilege to accommodate accountants' given advice on tax law. The majority expressed the view that any change would require intervention by Parliament.

The question has recently been further considered by the Court of Appeal in the case of *Serious Fraud Office v Eurasian Natural Resources Corporation Ltd* [2018] EWCA Civ 2006. In that case, the court considered whether documents obtained for the purposes of an internal investigation were covered by privilege in the context of subsequent proceedings by the SFO. The court decided, on the facts of the case, that the documents collected did attract litigation privilege, because they were gathered in a context where a prosecution by the SFO was a possible outcome. It decided that they did not attract legal advice privilege in the light of the House of Lords decision in *Three Rivers District Council v Governor and Company of the Bank of England (No 5)* [2003] QB 1556 ('*Three Rivers (No 5)*'). It is notable, however, that the court raised criticisms of the *Three Rivers (No 5)* decision, noting that it was out of step with international practice.

III SOL [58]

Attending counsel at court in civil cases A solicitor does not need to attend counsel in small claims or fast track cases where the solicitor is satisfied it is reasonable. Where a legal representative attends court to assist the advocate at a fast track trial, CPR 45.39(2) (at para **CPR 46.3**) provides for payment of the sum of £345, in addition to the advocate's fee, if the court considers that it was 'necessary' to do so.

III SOL [59]

Power of advocate to make terms An advocate has power to make terms, one of which is that the party will not appeal: *Re West Devon Great Consols Mine* (1988) 38 Ch D 51, CA; *Matthews v Munster* (1887) 20 QBD 141, CA. See further as to counsel's power to compromise: *Lewis's v Lewis* (1890) 45 Ch D 281; *Huddersfield Banking Co Ltd v Henry Lister & Son Ltd* [1895] 2 Ch 273, CA; *Wilding v Sanderson* [1897] 2 Ch 534, CA; *Neale v Gordon Lennox* [1902] AC 465, HL; *Shepherd v Robinson* [1919] 1 KB 474, CA. See also *Waugh v HB Clifford & Sons Ltd* [1982] Ch 374, [1982] 1 All ER 1095, CA; and *Re Debtors (No 78 of 1980)* (1985) Times, 11 May. Counsel has authority to accept or refuse service of documents in the course of proceedings in the absence of his client and his instructing solicitor: *Penman v Parker* [1986] 2 All ER 862, [1986] 1 WLR 882.

An admission made by counsel in the course of interlocutory proceedings may be withdrawn unless the circumstances were such as to give rise to an estoppel: *H Clark (Doncaster) Ltd v Wilkinson* [1965] Ch 694, [1965] 1 All ER 934, CA.

The Court of Appeal in dismissing the appeal in *Worldwide Corpn Ltd v Marconi Communications Ltd* [1999] 28 LS Gaz R 25, CA, 14 July held the client was bound by counsel's assurance in court even if an action in negligence might lie against counsel to which he could plead immunity.

III SOL [60]

Advocate's immunity The advocate's immunity from claims in negligence was reconsidered by the House of Lords *in Arthur J S Hall & Co (a firm) v Simons* [2002] 1 AC 615, [2000] 3 All ER 673, HL. Their Lordships unanimously decided that in civil proceedings the immunity should be abolished and with three dissentients decided the immunity should be abolished in respect of criminal proceedings. Public interest, particularly that in preventing collateral attacks on decisions, was held to be adequately protected by other powers of the court, in particular the principles of abuse of process, issue estoppel and res judicata.

III SOL [61]

Recent decisions on the extent of the duty of care In *Pritchard, Joyce & Hinds (a firm) v Batcup* [2009] EWCA Civ 369, [2009] 20 LS Gaz R 19, [2009] 19 EG 110 (CS), Sedley LJ stated:

'The law does not however demand omniscience or infallibility in lawyers any more than it does in doctors or architects.'

'The law's standard of reasonable competence means not only that there will be errors which are not compensable but that legal advisers are not expected to divine every claim a client may theoretically have.'

These observations were intended to refer to solicitors and barristers.

The three cases that follow are of assistance in considering the extent of a solicitor's duty in the ordinary course of business. These are *Football League v Edge Ellison* [2006] EWHC 1462 (Ch), 150 Sol Jo LB 890 (no implied duty to advise as to seeking of guarantees); *Regent Leisuretime Ltd v Skerrett and Pearson* [2006] EWCA Civ 1184, [2006] All ER (D) 313 (Jul) (no general duty on a solicitor to consider all aspects of a client's needs); and *Marplace (Number 512) Ltd v Chaffe Street* [2006] EWHC 1919 (Ch), [2006] All ER (D) 413 (Jul) (no duty to offer unsought advice to a commercially astute client). In all these cases, however, the sophistication and experience of the clients was a key factor in the court's decision that solicitors had not been negligent and danger can be foreseen in a situation where the solicitors present themselves as, for example, 'dynamic corporate lawyers' or 'able to advise on all aspects of your business'.

In contrast in *Padden v Bevan Ashford* (2012) Gazette, 19 January, page 6, a case concerning the standard of care required of solicitors giving free advice to clients who walk in off the street, the Court of Appeal has reversed the trial judge's decision that no breach of duty had been established in the circumstances. A retrial was ordered.

It was held in *Tom Hoskins plc v EMW Law (a firm)* [2010] EWHC 479 (Ch), [2010] NLJR 584 that although a solicitor is not normally required to give general commercial advice to a client he could be negligent if he failed to adequately warn him of proceeding on the basis of the contract drafted. The defendant solicitors were held to be negligent in failing to do so. For a report of the judgment see (2010) NLJ, 23 April, page 584.

The Court of Appeal in *Levicom International Holdings BV v Linklaters (a firm)* [2010] EWCA Civ 494, [2010] All ER (D) 81 (May) decided, over-ruling the first instance judge who awarded nominal damages of £5 only, that where a solicitor advises a client it has a strong case and should issue proceedings rather than settle such advice was capable of being causative and the evidential burden was on the solicitor to prove that its advice was not. The allegation against the solicitor was that its advice was over-optimistic and resulted in a settlement at a far later stage on more onerous terms. The Court of Appeal remitted the claim for damages to be assessed and the solicitor seeks leave to appeal to the Supreme Court. For detailed discussion see article by Taylor and Maguire (2010) Sol Jo, 8 June.

The court in *Football League* (see above) stressed the importance of establishing the extent of the solicitor's retainer and this approach can also be clearly seen in the case of *Brunsdon v Pattinson and Brewer (a firm)* [2006] EWHC 1562 (CQB), [2006] All ER (D) 349 (Jun) and also in *Cabvision Ltd v Feetum* [2009] EWHC 3400 (Ch), [2009] All ER (D) 203 (Dec) where the solicitors recording of the extent of the retainer proved vital.

In *Lloyds TSB Bank plc v Markandum & Uddin (a firm)* [2010] EWHC 2517 (Ch) the necessity of scrupulous compliance with instructions, protocols and procedure was stressed most strongly. Solicitors acting for the purchaser and the lenders released the mortgage in breach of their instructions. For detailed discussion see (2010) NLJ, 5 November, page 1521, article by Rosenthal and Ollech.

In *Farnon v Devonshire Solicitors* [2011] EWHC 3167 (QB) the claimant failed because her allegations related to matters outside the scope of the retainer and in *Cherney v Neuman* [2011] EWHC 2156 (QB) the client again failed as her allegations were as to the commercial merits of the transactions where the solicitor's duty was only as to the conveyancing and corporate aspects of them.

It is not sufficient for the advice to be correct; it must also be clearly given: *Levicom International Holdings v Linklaters* [2009] EWHC 812 (Comm), [2009] NLJR 632, 153 Sol Jo (no 17) 28.

For consideration of the measure of damages for professional negligence see the principle in *Ruxley Electronic and Construction Ltd v Forsyth* [1994] 3 All ER 801, [1994] 1 WLR 650; revsd [1996] AC 344, [1995] 3 All ER 268 (award limited to loss of amenity) was agreed. Further on the quantification of damages for professional negligence see *Veitch v Avery* [2007] EWCA Civ 711, 115 ConLR 70, (2007) Times, 29 August, CA, where the damages were limited to nominal damages only and *Levicom International Holdings BV v Linklaters* [2009] EWHC 812 (Comm), [2009] NLJR 632, 153 Sol Jo (no 17) 28 where only £5 nominal damages was awarded. For discussion see article 'Liability matters' NLJ 18 September 2009, p 1288 by Simon Lowe.

The liability of negligent solicitors was fixed at 20% in the loss of chance case *Parkin v Lupton Fawcett (a firm)* [2008] EWCA Civ 408, (2008) Sol Jo, 6 May.

For the burden of proof in claims for negligence against solicitors see *Fulham Leisure Holdings Ltd v Nicholson Graham Jones (a firm)* [2008] EWCA Civ 84, [2008] 09 EG 201 (CS) where it was held that the judge had wrongly reversed the burden of proof. The burden of proving that the negligence of a solicitor caused a claimant to waste expenditure rests on the claimants: *Parker v SJ Berwin & Co* [2008] EWHC 3017 (QB), [2008] All ER (D) 176 (Dec). This decision can be distinguished from *Platform Funding Ltd v Bank of Scotland Plc* [2008] EWCA Civ 930, [2009] QB 426, [2009] 2 All ER 344 where the court found the defendant had warranted a particular result would be achieved. For further discussion see article 'Leaving it to chance' by Harrison and Wild in (2009) Sol Jo 26 May, page 11.

For claims, arising from mortgage advances, against the solicitor acting see *Nationwide Building Society v Dunlop Haywards Ltd* [2007] EWHC 1374 (Comm), [2007] All ER (D) 393 (Jul) and *Pulvers (a firm) v Chan* [2007] EWHC 2406 (Ch), [2007] All ER (D) 425 (Oct). Rule 6(3) of the Solicitors Practice Rules and the Council of Mortgage Lenders Handbook should be noted.

Solicitors must take care to ensure when they are acting for a company in litigation that they have the requisite authority to issue proceedings; see *Re Micosulis Ltd* [2008] EWHC 1129 (Ch), per Toulson J and the principle in *Yonge v Tonybee* [1910] 1 KB 215 that a solicitor can be liable on an implied contract that he had authority to act if when so acting he had represented he had such authority.

For the application of this principle in favour of lenders see *Penn v Bristol & West Building Society* [1997] 3 All ER 470, [1997] 1 WLR 1356, CA and *Bristol & West Building Society v Fancy & Jackson (a firm)* [1997] 4 All ER 582, [1997] NPC 109, discussed in an article entitled 'Safe as houses?' by Amanda Eillege in NLJ 14 August 2009, page 1160.

Following the recent decision in *Stuart v Goldberg* [2008] EWCA Civ 2, (2008) TImes, 23 January, 152 Sol Jo (no 4) 28 where the defendant solicitors unsuccessfully failed to stop the claimant from asserting two fresh causes of action against them which they said he could have brought in earlier proceedings that he successfully took against them, there has been considerable discussion about abuse of process in professional negligence claims. See, for example, 'Forms of Abuse' by Stacey and Nash in (2008) NLJ 18 April, page 533. See also *AIB Group v Mark Ridler & Co* [2013] EWCA Civ 45; noted in (2013) Sol Jo, 19 February, page 4.

For the assessment of damages against solicitors see *Murfin v Campbell* [2011] EWHC 1475 (Ch), [2011] All ER (D) 190 (Jun) – the task of the judge is to award as damages to each claimant that sum of money which would put him, as near as a money claim could do, in the position he would have been in had there been no negligence by the solicitor.

For consideration by the Court of Appeal of limitation periods in professional negligence claims, see *Nouri v Marvi* [2010] EWCA Civ 1107 where it was decided in a case concerning a fraudulent conveyance that the loss crystallised on execution of its deed and not on the date of subsequent registration.

The problem of there being an 'on-going' retainer, requiring advice given to be re-addressed and updated, without any fresh instruction from the client, is a particularly worrying one for solicitors. Whilst he did not rule out the possibility, Akenhead J in *Shepherd Construction Ltd v Pinsent Masons LLP* [2012] EWHC 43 (TCC), 141 ConLR 232, [2012] BLR 213 said it would be 'commercially and professionally worrying if professional people are to be held responsible for reviewing all previous advice or services provided'. See also **III SOL [42]** above.

He dismissed the claim but firms should ensure that the scope of retainers is clearly and precisely set out. Preferably the retainer should also specify any particular matters that are not covered.

For the liability of a firm of solicitors and of each of its partners, see ss 9 and 10 of the Partnership Act 1980 (at paras **III PAR [29]** and **III PAR [30]**), *Dubai Aluminium Co Ltd v Salaam* [2002] UKHL 48, [2003] 2 AC 366, [2003] 1 All ER 97 and *JJ Coughlan Ltd v Ruparelia* [2003] EWCA Civ 1057, [2003] 37 LS Gaz R 34, (2003) Times, 26 August. Reference should also be made to *Sweetman v Nathan* [2003] EWCA Civ 1115, (2003) Times, 1 September where the Court of Appeal held that a client jointly engaged with his solicitor in a fraud was not precluded from suing the solicitor and his partners for negligent conveyancing and *Chappell v Somers & Blake (a firm)* [2003] EWHC 1644 (Ch), [2004] Ch 19, [2003] 3 All ER 1076 where the executrix of an estate was held to be entitled to maintain an action for damages against solicitors who failed to administer the estate.

An action for negligence arising from clerical errors in the drafting of a will may be avoided by an application for rectification pursuant to s 20 of the Administration of Justice Act 1982. The application should be made within 6 months of the grant of probate; see generally *Bush v Jouliac* [2006] EWHC 363 (Ch), [2006] All ER (D) 108 (Jan) and as to the time limit *Hobart v Hobart* [2006] EWHC 1784 (Ch), [2006] All ER (D) 295 (May).

For cases where the principle of *ex turpi causa* has been put forward see *Stone & Rolls Ltd (in liq) v Moore Stephens (a firm)* [2009] UKHL 39, [2009] AC 1391, [2009] 4 All ER 431 and *Nayyar v Denton Sapte Wilde* [2009] EWHC 3218 (QB), [2010] PNLR 15 discussed in (2011) Gazette, 12 May, page 14 by Simon Howarth in an article entitled 'Rogues' Gallery'.

The House of Lords in *Cave v Robinson Jarvis and Rolf (a firm)* [2002] UKHL 18, [2002] 2 All ER 641, (2002) Times, 7 May held that "deliberate concealment" for the purposes of s 32(1)(b) and (2) of the Limitation Act 1980 did not include failure to disclose a breach of duty that was committed unknowingly. In so doing it overruled *Brocklesby v Armitage & Guest (a firm)* [2001] 1 All ER 172, [2002] 1 WLR 589n, CA. For a further decision on "deliberate concealment" see *Williams v Fanshaw Porter and Hazelhurst (a firm)* [2004] EWCA Civ 157, [2004] 2 All ER 616, (2004) Times, 27 February, CA where solicitors concealed from their client that they had agreed on her behalf to a consent order for the dismissal of her claim for medical negligence. The effect of deliberate concealment may well postpone the start of the limitation period.

As to the date from which the limitation period begins to run against a solicitor, see *Khan v RM Falvey & Co (a firm)* [2002] EWCA Civ 400, [2002] Lloyd's Rep PN 369, [2002] 19 LS Gaz R 30.

It was held in *Humblestone v Martin Tolhurst Partnership (a firm)* [2004] EWHC 151 (Ch), 6 ITELR 900, (2004) Times, 27 February that where solicitors were instructed to draft a will but did not supervise its execution they had a duty to check it was properly executed when it was returned to them for safe-keeping.

Lord Scott in *Riley v Pickersgill* [2004] UKPC 14, [2004] Lloyd's Rep IR 795, [2004] 14 EGCS 140 said that the scope of a solicitor's duty was variable; it would depend first and foremost on the instructions he was given but would also depend on the circumstances of the case and on the characteristics of the client that were apparent to the solicitor. On the same point see *John Mowlem Construction plc v Neil F Jones & Co (a firm)* [2004] EWCA Civ 768, [2004] BLR 387, (2004) Times, 27 August, CA.

The decision in *Credit Lyonnaise SA v Russell Jones & Walker (a firm)* [2002] EWHC 1310 (Ch), [2002] 33 EG 99, (2002) Times, 9 October illustrates the danger of a solicitor dealing with instructions that are concerned with an area of the law which is outside his particular expertise.

The decision in *Hamilton Jones v David & Snape (a firm)* [2003] EWHC 3147 (Ch), [2004] 1 All ER 657, [2004] 1 WLR 924 was that the claimant having lost custody of her children as a result of the defendant solicitors' negligence was entitled in contract to damages for the mental distress she suffered.

For liability for loss of chance to litigate, see *Dixon v Clement Jones Solicitors* [2004] EWCA Civ 1005, (2004) 148 Sol Jo LB 878, Times, 2 August, CA, *Batty v Danahar* [2005] EWHC 2763 (QB), [2006] All ER (D) 90 (Jan) and *Amin v Imran Khan & Partners* [2011] EWHC 2958 (QB), [2011] All ER (D) 34 (Dec).

See further in Volume 1 CPR 67 'Proceedings Relating to Solicitors' at **CPR 67 [7]**, last five paragraphs and note in particular *McFaddens v Graham Platford* [2009] EWHC 126 (TCC) as to reliance on counsel's advice. A further relevant case is *Locke v Camberwell Health Authority* [1991] 2 Med LR 249, which indicates that a solicitor must not blindly follow counsel's advice. For detailed consideration see 'Update: professional negligence' in (2010) Sol Jo, 2 March, page 25 by Victoria Brackett.

The claimant in *Langsam v Beachcroft LLP* [2011] EWHC 1451 (Ch) settled on leading counsel's advice but subsequently sued his solicitors although they had warned him of the possibility of achieving a better result. The claim failed although counsel's advice was described as 'conservative'. The appeal to the Court of Appeal [2012] EWCA Civ 1230 was dismissed and the Court stated where the principal advice was given by counsel (in this case leading counsel) the solicitors would only be in breach of duty if the advice had been obviously or glaringly wrong.

III SOL [62]

Professional indemnity insurance (PII) The Code of Conduct contains provisions requiring solicitors to take out and maintain qualifying insurance cover if they carry on practice during any insurance period. There are provisions dealing separately with employed solicitors provided the employer firm maintains qualifying insurance.

It is notable that the minimum terms required by the SRA are significantly different from those under normal indemnity insurance policies. For example, the insurance will be valid to cover innocent partners where one of their number is fraudulent and where there has been a material non-disclosure.

Where a solicitor cannot obtain insurance for the following year, the insurer under the firm's existing policy will offer a three months extended policy. For the first 30 days of the extended policy period such firms may continue to practise but for the remaining 60 days of the three month period the firms may only work on existing instructions and while it continues to try to obtain PII or conduct an orderly closure of the practice in preparation for failure to obtain PII.

For a detailed explanation of the operation of the scheme see articles by Richard Collins, and executive director of the SRA, entitled 'Pooling resources' in (2012) Gazette, 19 July, page 23 and by Neil Hodge in 'Sea Change' in (2012) Gazette Special on PII renewals, 19 July, page 11.

See also the SRA Indemnity Insurance Rules 2011 and the SRA Indemnity (Enactment) Rules 2011.

The complexity of the terms and conditions of professional indemnity generally can be seen from the decision in *Zurich Professional Ltd v Karim* [2006] EWHC 3355 (QB), [2006] All ER (D) 238 (Dec) where liability was excluded if it arose from dishonesty or fraud of or condoned by the insured. The firm in question comprised three partners, two of whom had no knowledge of the frauds although they were aware of and 'went along with' breaches of the rules and other improper dealings. Despite their lack of knowledge the two parties in question were held to have condoned the frauds committed by the third partner. The solicitors were not represented and the reasoning of the court was somewhat unconvincing. The reservations about the decision are discussed in an article in the LS Gazette (2007) 19 April, page 28, entitled 'Are you your mother's keeper?'.

III SOL [63]

Fiduciary duty of an employed solicitor A solicitor owes a fiduciary duty to the firm employing him which prevents him benefiting personally from his position: *Cobbetts LLP v Hodge* [2009] EWHC 786 (Ch), [2010] 1 BCLC 30, 153 Sol Jo (no 17) 29 where the benefit was the acquisition of shares in a client company.

See also Gazette (2009) 8 October, page 3 where there is reported the decision of the High Court in *Dass Solicitors v Southcott* where a three month injunction was granted against an associate solicitor, who was not subject to a restrictive covenant, preventing him from working for clients of the claimant for three months after he left the firm.

A solicitor should not administer an oath in proceedings in which he is acting for one of the parties. This is so whether the proceedings are contentious or non-contentious.

III SOL [64]

Client accounts In *Wood v Burdett* [2004] January, the Solicitors' Disciplinary Tribunal stated it was not a proper part of a solicitor's everyday practice to operate a banking facility for a third party whether or not he was a client. This view was reiterated in June 2006 following strongly expressed concern by Mr Justice Rivlin, see LSG 103/33 8 June 2006.

In *Patel v SRA* [2012] EWHC 3373 (Admin) the appellant solicitor's appeal against a fine of £7,500 for allowing a client to receive and distribute funds through his account, was dismissed. There was no underlying legal transaction in respect of the transactions and in effect the solicitor was supplying banking facilities contrary to rule 14.5 of the SRA Accounts Rules 2011 (previously rule 15.2 of the Solicitors Accounts Rules 1998).

SOLICITORS ACT 1974

(c 47)

III SOL [65]

35. Intervention in solicitor's practice

The powers conferred by Part II of Schedule 1 shall be exercisable in the circumstances specified in Part I of that Schedule.

III SOL [65.1]

The statute refers to 'the Society' but the powers are exercised by the SRA.

III SOL [65.2]

Intervention is the most severe action that is available to the SRA for it in effect puts an end to a solicitor's practice without compensation: see *Giles v Law Society* [1995] 38 LS Gaz R 25, 139 Sol Jo LB 218.

Intervention will involve the suspension of the solicitor's practising certificate unless there is a direction that the provision shall not apply: Solicitors Act 1974, s 15(1A) and (1B).

III SOL [65.3]

The resolution to intervene can be made by two adjudicators (one in an emergency). Intervention can take place without notice but will normally take place after an investigation has taken place and a report prepared.

III SOL [65.4]

Within 8 days of service of the intervention resolution and notice the solicitor can, on giving not less than 48 hours notice in writing to the SRA, apply to the High Court for an order directing the SRA to withdraw the notice; see paragraph 6(4) of the Solicitors Act 1974, Sch 1. If the SRA agrees that the intervention was not appropriate a consent order must be filed as there is no power for the SRA to reverse its decision.

If the application to challenge the notice is contested in the first instance an urgent application for directions should be made.

For guidance where intervention is threatened but the intervention resolution has not been made see article by Tony Guise in (2009) Sol Jo 16 February, page 18 entitled 'The co-operative approach'.

For avenues open for the intervened solicitor see article entitled 'Time for change' by Chris Gadd in (2012) NLJ 3 August, page 106.

See also **III SOL [94]** to **III SOL [94.6]**.

III SOL [66]

49. Appeals from Tribunal

(1) An appeal from the Tribunal shall lie to the High Court.

(2) Subject to subsection (3) and to section 43(5) of the Administration of Justice Act 1985, an appeal shall lie at the instance of the applicant or complainant or of the person with respect to whom the application or complaint was made.

(3) An appeal against an order under section 43(3A) shall lie only at the instance of the person with respect to whom the order was made[, and an appeal against an order under section 47 excluding any person or persons from criminal legal aid work (as defined in that section) shall lie only at the instance of any person so excluded.]

(4) The High Court shall have power to make such order on an appeal under this section as it may think fit.

(5) Subject to any rules of court, on an appeal against an order made by virtue of rules under section 46(10)(c) without hearing the applicant or complainant, the court—

(a) shall not be obliged to hear the appellant, and

(b) may remit the matter to the Tribunal instead of dismissing the appeal.

(6) Any decision of the High Court—

(a) on an application under section 43(3) or 47(1)(d), (e), (ea) or (f), or

(b) against an order under section 43(3A),

shall be final.

SOLICITORS

(7) . . .

Amendment *In sub-s (3) words in square brackets inserted by the Administration of Justice Act 1985 with effect from a date to be appointed.*

III SOL [66.1]

"The Tribunal" This is the Solicitors Disciplinary Tribunal (SDT) whose constitution is dealt with under s 46. Section 47 sets out its jurisdiction and powers. The SDT has acquired by the implementation of the Legal Services Act 2007 full operational independence having always had judicial independence from the Law Society. The SDT has power to strike off solicitors, suspend solicitors for a fixed or indefinite time, fine solicitors an unlimited amount, make reprimands and orders for payment of costs. It can, on application, restore solicitors to the roll. It has specific powers in respect of sole practitioners. The SDT itself may no longer impose sanctions for inadequate professional services: see **III SOL [2]**.

It is to be noted that pursuant to s 49A, inserted on 1 July 2009, the Society may with the approval of the Tribunal make rules which provide that certain appeals from the Tribunal in such circumstances as may be prescribed lie to the Tribunal and not the High Court.

The Solicitors (Disciplinary Proceedings) Rules 2007, SI 2007/3588, regulate the procedure for the making of applications to the SDT. In particular the rules make provision for:

(a) the constitution of the tribunal;
(b) applications to the tribunal;
(c) procedure and rules of evidence.

There are four practice directions and a policy note to the 2007 Rules.

Where there has been failure by the solicitor to comply with directions of a Law Society adjudication made pursuant to Sch 1A of the Solicitors Act 1974 (see **III SOL [93]** below, in particular para 5) the SDT may order that those directions should be treated for the purpose of enforcement as if they were contained in an order of the High Court: see Gazette 105/13, 3 April 2008, page 33 – Application Number 9652-2007.

The Court of Appeal in *Law Society v Bultitude* (2005) Times, 14 January held that the inevitable consequence of a solicitor committing breaches of professional accounts rules was the removal of his name from the roll of solicitors. The suggestion that a solicitor should not be struck off unless he had an intention to permanently deprive was rejected. There are, however, cases where there have been breaches of the accounts rules but no finding of dishonesty, where there has not been a decision to strike-off; see, for example, decisions of the SDT reported at LSG 103/31 21 Sept 2006 p 39. For discussion of three High Court decisions overruling the SDT see Law Society Gazette 103/21 25 May 2006 p 3.

These, however, are exceptional cases and should be compared with *Baxendale-Walker v Law Society* [2007] EWCA Civ 233, [2007] 3 All ER 330; *Law Society v Wilson* [2006] EWHC 1022 (Admin), [2006] All ER (D) 184 (May), where the Law Society successfully appealed against the penalty of suspension with the result that striking-off was substituted; and *Butt v Law Society* [2006] EWCA Civ 393, [2006] All ER (D) 79 (Feb) where although there had been no allegation of dishonesty the Court of Appeal found that striking-off was not an excessive penalty.

Following criticism by the High Court, in an appeal reported in the Gazette for 24 March 2011, the SDT has published 'A Guidance Note on Sanctions'; the document extends to 14 pages and brings together in a single document 'all existing SDT sanctioning principles...'.

For a case where a private prosecution was successfully brought before the SDT see (2013) Sol Jo, 26 February, page 4 under the heading 'City solicitor struck off for misleading the court'.

An interesting comparison of the functions of the SDT and the SRA was provided by the Court of Appeal in *Re a Solicitor (No 7 of 2007)* (2007) 151 Sol Jo LB 1263, CA. The SDT suspended the solicitor for three months but did not impose any conditions on his practising certificate. Subsequently the SRA granted him a conditional certificate. The solicitor's appeal against the imposition of conditions failed; the Court of Appeal stated that whilst the decision of the SDT had to be taken into account as a significant factor it was no more than that. The SRA is distinct from the SDT which has a punitive and disciplinary function. The Court of Appeal considered *Comacho v Law Society* [2004] EWHC 1042 (Admin) in coming to its decision.

For an examination of allegations of bias and disciplinary tribunals see *R (on the application of Kaur) v Institute of Legal Executives Appeal Tribunal* [2010] EWHC 3321 (Admin), (2010) Gazette Law Reports, 9 December, page 17 and on appeal (2011) Gazette LR, 24 November, page 20.

Another case, this relating to a doctor, *R (Bonhoeffor) v The General Medical Council* [2011] EWHC 1585 (Admin), [2011] All ER (D) 141 (Jun) concerned the case against the doctor relying on hearsay evidence preventing it being tested by cross-examination. It was held to render the proceedings unfair and the decision was quashed. This despite the relaxation of the rules against hearsay evidence by the Civil Evidence Act 1995.

The decision has also to be assessed having regard to the subsequent decision of the European Court of Human Rights in *Al-Khawaja and Tahery v United Kingdom (Application Nos 26766/05 and 22228/06)* where it was held that a conviction based solely or decisively on an absent witness would not automatically result in a breach of Article 6.1 of the European Convention on Human Rights provided appropriate safeguards were in place.

Without reference to Art 6, in cases where allegations of serious professional misconduct have to be determined the authorities establish that the criminal standard of proof is to be applied in professional disciplinary cases: see for example *Re A Solicitor* [1993] QB 69, [1992] 2 All ER 33 and Stewart Duffy's article 'An alternative prescription' in (2011) NLJ, 21 October, page 1442. This places the SDT in a different position to that of the SRA and, indeed, the bulk of other regulators. The BSB recently decided that the standard of proof for its Tribunals should become the civil standard. In response to that, the SDT announced that it will be consulting on a possible change to its own standard ((2017) Law Gazette, 2 August).

See further **CPR 67** and the notes to it in Volume 1.

Although the Disciplinary Proceedings Rules provide for sittings of the tribunal to be in private there is no power to direct that proceedings should be anonymised: *Solicitors Regulation Authority v Spector* [2016] EWHC 37 (Admin), 15 January 2016.

SOLICITORS

III SOL [66.1A]

The attitude of the High Court to decisions of the SDT The cases of *Salsbury v Law Society* [2008] EWCA Civ 1285, [2009] 2 All ER 487, [2009] 1 WLR 1286 and *Thobani v SRA* [2011] All ER (D) 12 (Dec) state: The High Court should only interfere with SDT penalties when they are clearly inappropriate. This is very similar to the approach to the courts in other professions – see most recently the Court of Appeal's approach in *Bawa-Garba v General Medical Council* [2018] EWCA Civ 1879. It is notable, however, that such cases tend to be decided on their individual facts and it is hard to see any consistent approach by the courts.

It is also well-established that the courts are unlikely to overturn decisions based on factual findings by the SDT. This was reiterated in *Solicitors Regulation Authority v Dav* [2018] EWCA 2726 (Admin) where the court noted that the CPR 52.21(3) says that the court must establish whether the decision was 'wrong' as to fact, law or an exercise of discretion. It stressed the approach endorsed by all the authorities that appellate courts should be slow to intervene in findings of fact by the fact-finding tribunal. In this case, it was noted that the SRA's appeal solely involved disagreements with the findings of fact by the SDT and no evidence was provided to reach the high bar of showing that those findings were wrong.

In *Gurpinar v Solicitors Regulation Authority* [2012] EWHC 192 (Admin), [2012] NLJR 293 '... it was established law that the tribunal was an expert body and its assessment of the appropriate penalty in any given case was entitled to considerable respect'. The court should not interfere with the tribunal's decision unless it had erred in law or the penalty it had imposed was clearly inappropriate.

In *Adeeko v Solicitors Regulation Authority* [2012] EWHC 841 (Admin), [2012] NLJR 363: '... except in a very strong case an appellate court should not interfere with the sentence imposed by the tribunal'.

In *Maistry v Solicitors Regulation Authority* [2012] EWHC 3041 (Admin): '... the tribunal had conducted a fair hearing and had made no error of law and its decision should be respected'. The Court applied Salisbury (see above) and the earlier case of *Bolton v Law Society* [1994] 2 All ER 486, [1994] 1 WLR 512.

The appeal by the solicitor in *Afolabi v SRA* [2012] EWHC 3502 (Admin), [2012] All ER (D) 5 (Dec) was refused although the third finding of misconduct was found not to have been established. The Court of Appeal drew attention to the decision in *Salsbury* and stated it was for the SDT to decide upon the appropriate sanction and it was fully entitled to find that striking off was appropriate on the findings found to be proved.

The degree of respect given to the SDT decisions is not to be taken that they are in effect unappealable. See, for example the following cases:

De Souza v Law Society (2009) 153 Sol Jo (no 30) 30, DC — failure to take account of the solicitor's means resulted in reduction of fine.

Donkin v Law Society [2007] EWHC 414 (Admin), [2007] NLJR 402, Div Ct and *Yerolemou v Law Society* [2008] EWHC 682 (Admin), [2008] All ER (D) 136 (Mar) — failure to take account of references and not applying the proper test in the former and failing to take account of mitigation and the circumstances in the latter resulted, in both cases, in removals from the Roll being set aside and replaced by less severe penalties.

The successful appeal in *Akodu v Solicitors Regulatory Authority* [2009] EWHC 3654 (Admin), [2009] All ER (D) 181 (Nov) clearly shows the High Court will overturn decisions made on insufficient evidence.

The successful appeal in *Davis v Solicitors Regulation Authority* [2011] EWHC 3645 (Admin), [2011] NLJR 29 against a refusal of the SRA to enrol the appellant as a solicitor is perhaps the strongest example of the necessity of the appeal machinery (motoring conviction not disclosed on the advice of her supervisor).

In *Solicitors Regulation Authority v James* [2018] EWHC 3058 (Admin), the Divisional Court overturned a decision of the SDT to suspend three solicitors who had been found to be dishonest and, instead, ordered that they be struck off the Roll.

III SOL [66.1B]

The effect of dishonesty In *Solicitors Regulation Authority v Sharma* [2010] EWHC 2022 (Admin), [2010] All ER (D) 143 (Nov) Coulson J stated:

> 'Save in exceptional circumstances, a finding of dishonesty will lead to a solicitor being struck off the Roll.'

This approach follows that taken by Sir Thomas Bingham MR in *Bolton v Law Society* [1993] EWCA Civ 32, [1994] 2 All ER 486, [1994] 1 WLR 512 who stressed the importance of honesty and integrity within the profession:

> 'Any solicitor who is shown to have discharged his professional duties with anything less than complete integrity, probity and trustworthiness must expect severe sanctions to be imposed upon him by the Solicitors Disciplinary Tribunal. Lapses from the required high standard may, of course, take different forms and be of varying degrees. The most serious involves proven dishonesty, whether or not leading to criminal proceedings and criminal penalties. In such cases the Tribunal has almost invariably, no matter how strong the mitigation advanced for the solicitor, ordered that he be struck off the Roll of Solicitors. Only infrequently, particularly in recent years, has it been willing to order the restoration to the Roll of a solicitor against whom serious dishonesty had been established, even after a passage of years, and even where the solicitor had made every effort to re-establish himself and redeem his reputation. If a solicitor is not shown to have acted dishonestly, but is shown to have fallen below the required standards of integrity, probity and trustworthiness, his lapse is less serious but it remains very serious indeed in a member of a profession whose reputation depends upon trust. A striking off order will not necessarily follow in such a case, but it may well. The decision whether to strike off or to suspend will often involve a fine and difficult exercise of judgment, to be made by the Tribunal as an informed and expert body on all the facts of the case. Only in a very unusual and venial case of this kind would the Tribunal be likely to regard as appropriate any order less severe than one of suspension.'

In *Ivey v Genting Casinos Ltd* [2017] UKSC 67, the Supreme Court decided that the previous two-stage test for deciding whether an individual is dishonest was not the law. Lord Hughes, stated that:

> 'When dishonesty is in question the fact-finding tribunal must first ascertain (subjectively) the actual state of the individual's knowledge or belief as to the facts. The reasonableness or otherwise of his belief is a matter of evidence (often in practice determinative) going to whether he held the belief, but it is not an additional requirement that his belief must be reasonable; the question is whether it is genuinely held. When once his actual state of mind as to knowledge or belief as to facts is established, the question whether his conduct was honest or dishonest is to be determined by the fact-finder by applying the (objective) standards of ordinary decent people. There is no requirement that the defendant must appreciate that what he has done is, by those standards, dishonest.'

This test is likely to be used by all courts and Tribunals seeking to establish whether an individual has acted dishonestly.

In *Salsbury v Law Society* [2008] EWHC 889 (Admin), [2008] All ER (D) 251 (Mar) after a minimal level of dishonesty was found by the trial court which imposed a conditional discharge, the High Court stated that there are only a small group of dishonesty cases where striking-off is not appropriate. They found this to be one of them and substituted a three year suspension for the striking-off order made by the SDT. The Law Society, however, appealed and the Court of Appeal restored the order for striking-off ([2008] EWCA Civ 1285, [2009] 1 WLR 1286). In the absence of an error of law this decision appears to have been consistently followed by the High Court, including the case of *Solicitors Regulation Authority v Dennison* [2012] EWCA Civ 421, [2012] NLJR 542 by the Court of Appeal and *Robinson v Solicitors Regulation Authority* [2012] EWHC 2690 (Admin), [2012] All ER (D) 108 (Oct) by the High Court.

A similar approach was taken by the Divisional Court in *Solicitors Regulation Authority v James* [2018] EWHC 3058 (Admin). In those cases, the solicitors concerned were under very substantial pressure from within dysfunctional firms to achieve particular targets and, under that pressure, succumbed to various types of dishonest conduct, including amending dates of service dishonestly. The SDT originally had accepted the mitigation and imposed orders of suspension. The Divisional Court, following the approach in *Bolton* and other cases substituted the sanction that they should be struck off the Roll.

The SDT has stated that dishonesty cannot be proved by inference but once it is proved the burden of establishing to the SDT that the circumstances are 'exceptional' is considerable and it is clear that any such success will be carefully considered by the SRA with a view to lodging an appeal if it is appropriate. For detailed discussion of the appropriate standard of proof see article entitled 'How high a hurdle' by Tim Kerr QC and Charles Banner in (2013) NLJ, 1 February, page 101.

In *Wingate v Solicitors Regulation Authority* [2018] EWCA Civ 366, the Court of Appeal considered the distinction between dishonesty and lack of integrity for the purposes of the SRA's Code of Conduct. Jackson LJ said that the concept of lack of integrity went beyond dishonesty and was a useful shorthand for the higher standards expected of professional people:

> 'The professions have a privileged and trusted role in society. In return they are required to live up to their own professional standards,' said Jackson. 'Integrity connotes adherence to the ethical standards of one's own profession. That involves more than mere honesty . . . a professional person is expected to be even more scrupulous about accuracy than a member of the general public in daily discourse.'

III SOL [66.1C]

Restoration to the Roll The SDT recently restated its stance in relation to applications to restore to the Roll; it did so giving reasons for refusing the application for restoration of Aurangzeb Iqbal on 3 September 2012, reported in the Gazette on 15 November 2012, page 22. It did so after referring to the relevant entry in *Cordery in Solicitors* at paragraph 459 and to *Bolton v Law Society* [1994] 2 All ER 486, [1994] 1 WLR 512.

It listed its key concerns as:

(i) whether the applicant was fit in the 'eyes of a member of the public' to be re-admitted;
(ii) whether the public would consider any profession to be proud to have the applicant as a member; and
(iii) whether the reputation of the profession would be damaged by the restoration.

The tribunal stated that an applicant for restoration would have to show that all members of the public would trust him without hesitate or further question.

III SOL [66.1D]

Conditions on a practising certificate If the SRA considered that the imposition of conditions was appropriate and those conditions were proportionate it was held to be wrong to remove them and replace them with undertakings. The court in *Bryant v Solicitors Regulation Authority* [2012] EWHC 1475 (Admin), 156 Sol Jo (no 23) 35 decided that the harsher climate in the insurance industry was not a sufficient reason for taking the step requested even though Eady J acknowledged that 'the imposition of conditions is now in practical terms recognised to be the kiss of death' and 'To all intents and purposes they render the prospect of further employment impossible'. For comment see (2012) NLJ, 15 June at page 589 and note that the applicant had made no personal gain from acting for the client in the transaction that led to the imposition of the conditions.

III SOL [66.2]

Procedure on Appeal to the High Court The procedure for most appeals from the Solicitors Disciplinary Tribunal is laid down in the Practice Direction supplementing CPR Part 52, para 27.1 (see para **CPR PD 52D.27**). The notice of appeal must be headed:

> 'Re a Solicitor *or* Re a Solicitor's clerk
>
> In the Matter of the Solicitors Act 1974.'

For the applicable test to be applied by the court on appeal from the Tribunal, guidance may be obtained from *Ghosh v General Medical Council* [2001] UKPC 29, [2001] 1 WLR 1915, *McMahon v Council of the Law Society of Scotland* 2002 SLT 363 and *Silver v General Medical Council* [2003] UKPC 33, (2003) Times, 9 May.

The decisions of the Court of Appeal in *Meadow v General Medical Council* [2006] EWCA Civ 1390) and *Fatnani v General Medical Council* [2007] EWCA Civ 46, [2007] 1 WLR 1460) provide a clear indication of the Court's attitude towards the issues decided by the original tribunal. For discussion see the article 'Healthy Competition' in (2007) Solicitors Journal for 7 September, at page 1110 and see **III SOL [66.1A]** above.

The Court of Appeal has power under CPR 52.10(2)(b) to refer any claim or issue back to the lower court for decision. The power is normally only used where the appeal court requires a particular issue to be decided and that it would be better decided by the lower court: *Hicks v Russell Jones and Walker* [2007] EWCA Civ 844, [2007] All ER (D) 60 (Nov).

III SOL [66.3]

Power of Court to substitute its own decision The Court's jurisdiction is not purely supervisory: it has power to substitute its own decision for that of the Tribunal: *Langford v Law Society* [2002] EWHC 2802 (Admin), [2003] NLJR 176, DC. but it has no free-standing power to restore a solicitor's practising certificate which had been automatically suspended by the Law Society's statutory notice of intervention in his practice without also directing the society to withdraw its intervention notice: *Sritharan v Law Society* [2005] EWCA Civ 476, [2005] 4 All ER 1105.

III SOL [66.4]

Where a solicitor is guilty of breaches of the Solicitors Accounts Rules, even though no dishonesty is alleged, he may be struck off the Roll of Solicitors: *Weston v Law Society* [1998] 31 LS Gaz R 35, CA. In *Law Society v Gilbert* (2001) Times, 12 January, Div Ct, the solicitor had admitted before the Tribunal conduct unbefitting a solicitor, including breaches of the accounts rules; he was not struck off because of strong mitigating circumstances. He was subsequently convicted of dishonesty on essentially the same facts. The Law Society brought a second set of disciplinary proceedings at which he was struck off. The Divisional Court held the second proceedings were not an abuse of process.

See also *Bultitude v Law Society* (2005) Times, 14 January, CA at **III SOL [66.1]** above.

III SOL [66.5]

Findings of fact made in disciplinary proceedings In *Conlon v Simms* [2006] EWCA Civ 1749, [2007] 3 All ER 802 the Court of Appeal considered the argument that it was an abuse of process for facts found by the SDT to be put in issue in a subsequent claim for damages against the solicitor. The court decided it was not an abuse to put in issue findings of fact made in previous proceedings between the party and a person who is not a party to the current litigation.

III SOL [67]

50. Jurisdiction of Senior Courts over solicitors

(1) Any person duly admitted as a solicitor shall be an officer of the Senior Courts; . . .

(2) Subject to the provisions of this Act, the High Court, the Crown Court and the Court of Appeal respectively, or any division or judge of those courts, may exercise the same jurisdiction in respect of solicitors as any one of the superior courts of law or equity from which the Senior Courts were constituted might have exercised immediately before the passing of the Supreme Court of Judicature Act 1873 in respect of any solicitor, attorney or proctor admitted to practise there.

(3) An appeal shall lie to the Court of Appeal from any order made against a solicitor by the High Court or the Crown Court in the exercise of its jurisdiction in respect of solicitors under subsection (2).

III SOL [67.1]

Solicitors undertakings Chapter 11, Relations with third parties, of the Code of Conduct 2011 includes the conduct of solicitors in relation to undertakings.

An undertaking is an unequivocal declaration of intention addressed to someone who reasonably places reliance on it and made by:

(1) a solicitor or member of a solicitor's staff in the course of practise; or
(2) a solicitor as "solicitor" but not in the course of practise.

The declaration does not need to include the word "undertake".

Both the High Court and the county court (county courts Act 1984 s 142 (see para **II CCA [136]**)) have power to enforce an undertaking given by a solicitor whether or not the undertaking was given to the court or included in any order of the court and even in the absence of misconduct (see *United Mining and Finance Corpn Ltd v Becher* [1910] 2 KB 296, [1908–10] All ER Rep 876, on appeal [1911] 1 KB 840, CA) or, indeed, given before a writ was issued (see *The Ring* [1931] P 58, 47 TLR 384). The undertaking must be given by the solicitor as such (*United Mining and Finance Corpn Ltd v Becher* [1910] 2 KB 296, [1908–10] All ER Rep 876, on appeal [1911] 1 KB 840, CA) and not merely as an individual (*Northfield v Orton* (1832) 1 Dowl 415; *Allaway v Duncan* (1867) 16 LT 264); personally (*Burrell v Jones* (1819) 3 B & Ald 47; *Hall v Ashurst* (1833) 1 Cr & M 714; *Re C* (1908) 53 Sol Jo 119), and not as an agent of his client (*Burnett v Proois, Re an Attorney* (1870) 22 LT 543; *Re Williams* (1850) 12 Beav 510). The undertaking is enforceable if the client dies (*Hellings v Jones* (1825) 3 Bing 70); instructs the solicitor not to perform it (*Re Kerly, Son and Verden* [1901] 1 Ch 467, CA); or changes his solicitor (*Williams v Williams and Partridge* (1910) 54 Sol Jo 506, CA). A solicitor may be held liable in damages at the suit of a third party if he breaches an undertaking, the object of which is to protect the third party (*Al-Kandari v JR Brown & Co* [1988] QB 665, [1988] 1 All ER 833, CA). An undertaking given by a solicitor employed by a firm within the normal course of his employment can be enforced against the firm (*United Bank of Kuwait v Hammand, City Trust Ltd v Levy* [1988] 3 All ER 418, [1988] 1 WLR 1051, CA). The court may relieve a solicitor from his undertaking (*United Mining and Finance Corpn Ltd v Becher* [1910] 2 KB 296, [1908–10] All ER Rep 876, on appeal [1911] 1 KB 840, CA). This power has been exercised, eg

(1) where it was given in ignorance of facts known to the other party (*Wade v Simeon* (1845) 13 M & W 647);
(2) where it was given by mistake (*Mullins v Howell* (1879) 11 Ch D 763); or
(3) where it has become impossible of performance (*Udall v Capri Lighting Ltd* [1988] QB 907, [1987] 3 All ER 262, CA) though the court can order compensation for the breach;

but not where the undertaking was given in the mistaken belief that the solicitor had authority to give it (*The Gertrud* [1927] WN 265). A solicitor who gives a personal undertaking which turns out to be impossible to perform will not be excused if he or she knew of the factors making it impossible but did not disclose them: *Citadel Management Inc v Equal Ltd* (1998) Times, 25 September, [1999] 1 FLR 21, CA. A bare assurance given by a borrower's solicitor to a lender that his undertaking guaranteeing a loan was given in the normal course of business was not of itself sufficient to confer on him authority he did not have so as to bind his partners: *Hirst v Etherington* [1999] 31 LS Gaz R 42, CA.

See *Global Marine Drillships Ltd v Landmark Solicitors LLP* [2011] EWHC 2685 (Ch) for a case concerning an alleged breach of an undertaking where an application for summary judgment against the solicitors was dismissed as the issues raised required examination at a full trial.

For a detailed consideration of 'the special circumstances' required to release a party from an undertaking see *Di Placito v Slater* [2003] EWCA Civ 1863, [2004] 1 WLR 1605, (2004) Times, 29 January, CA albeit that the undertaking was given by a party and not his solicitor. The Court of Appeal in *Mid-Suffolk District Council v Clarke* said it would never be an appropriate exercise of the jurisdiction of a first instance Judge to change an undertaking incorporated in a previous order without a change of circumstances. It should be left for an appeal.

A solicitor will be held personally liable to honour an undertaking given 'on behalf of' anyone unless such liability is clearly disclaimed: Solicitors' Code of Conduct 2007, rule 10.05 and guidance at para 35 on page 132 (the Code of Conduct 2007 has been replaced by the SRA Code of Conduct 2011 which in Chapter 11 'Relations with third parties' at Outcome O(11.2) states 'you will perform all undertakings given by you . . . ').

There is no general principle that disclosure at the earliest opportunity of a change in circumstances releases a solicitor from an undertaking: *Hole & Pugsley v Sumption* (2002) Times, 29 January, Ch D.

For the acceptance of undertakings on the completion of a conveyancing transaction see *Patel v Daybells* [2001] EWCA Civ 1229 and the article in [2002] 22 LS Gaz R 40.

Where there is a dispute as to whether or not an undertaking has been breached it is essential to establish its proper construction; see for example *Templeton Insurance Ltd v Penningtons Solicitors LLP* [2006] EWHC 685 (Ch), [2006] All ER (D) 191(Feb). In this case money was paid to the defendant on its undertaking to use it to finance specific property transactions but it used the funds for other purposes. On the proper construction of the undertaking it was held the claimant was entitled to the repayment of the money wrongly used.

Where a solicitor has to give an undertaking in a matter which is not entirely within his own control he would be well advised only to undertake 'to use his best endeavours to . . . '. For the steps that are required of a solicitor giving such an undertaking see *IBM United*

Kingdom Ltd v Rockware Glass Ltd [1980] FSR 335, CA and for the consideration of this case and the giving of undertakings generally see article by John Coulter entitled 'Undertakings: how to avoid the traps' in (2012) Sol Jo, 17 April, page 21.

For the danger of giving an undertaking without being fully aware of the consequences see *Clark v Lucas Solicitors LLP* [2009] EWHC 1953 (Ch), [2009] 46 EG 144, [2009] 32 EG 69 (CS) where summary judgment was granted against the solicitors who gave the undertaking although the sum required to comply with the undertaking to pay off the charges on completion was approximately double the value of the property conveyed.

The case of *Angel Solicitors (a firm) v Jenkins O'Dowd & Barth* [2009] EWHC 46 (Ch), [2009] 1 WLR 1220, [2009] 14 EG 88 is discussed in an article by Ryan Clement at Sol Jo, 24 February 2009, page 14.

See also *Thames Valley Housing Association v Elegant Homes* [2009] EWHC 2647 (Ch), [2010] 1 P&CR D39 where the solicitors were faced with a payment of £1.34 million for the removal of a charge in favour of lenders when the proceeds of sale had been released in their entirety without referring to the charge and the undertaking to remove it.

In *Udall v Capri Lighting Ltd* [1988] QB 907, [1987] 3 All ER 262, CA Balcombe LJ stated there are three ways to enforce an undertaking:

(a) by action at law;

(b) by application to the High Court to exercise its inherent jurisdiction over solicitors (normally to order the solicitor to do what he had undertaken to do);

(c) by application the Law Society.

See also the *Procedural Tables Supplement* , **TAB 36** and **CPR 81.4** and **CPR PD 81.2**.

III SOL [67.2]

Inherent power of the court The High Court's inherent power over solicitors entitles it to inquire into the propriety of instructing leading counsel despite the fact that there is a legal aid authority authorising the solicitor to take in leading counsel: see *Re Solicitors, Re Taxation of Costs* [1982] 2 All ER 683, [1982] 1 WLR 745, CA.

The High Court in *JSC BTA Bank v Solodchenko* (2011) Times, 27 September in the exercise of its inherent jurisdiction to give directions to solicitors as officers of the court (amongst other powers) gave directions that solicitors disclose contact details of their client. The primary purpose of the disclosure was to aid enforcement of a committal order. The court stressed that this power over solicitors should only be exercised in appropriate circumstances and so as to further the interests of justice.

III SOL [67.3]

Procedure Procedure for enforcing an undertaking is provided by CPR 81 and CPR PD 81 and where the application is for a breach of a solicitor's undertaking the applicant must obtain permission from the court before making the application. The application for permission may be made by application notice under CPR 23 and must be supported by an affidavit; it may be made without notice (CPR 81.11).

III SOL [68]

51. Procedure upon certain applications to High Court

(1) Where an application to strike the name of a solicitor off the roll or to require a solicitor to answer allegations contained in an affidavit is made to the High Court, then, subject to section 54, the following provisions of this section shall have effect in relation to that application.

(2) The court shall not entertain the application except on production of an affidavit proving that the applicant has served on the Society fourteen clear days' notice of his intention to make the application, together with copies of all affidavits intended to be used in support of the application.

(3) The Society may appear by counsel on the hearing of the application and any other proceedings arising out of or in reference to the application, and may apply to the court—

(a) to make absolute any order nisi which the court may have made on the application;

(b) to make an order that the name of the solicitor be struck off the roll; or

(c) to make such other order as the court may think fit.

(4) The court may order the costs of the Society of or relating to any of the matters mentioned in subsections (2) and (3) to be paid by the solicitor against whom, or by the person by whom, the application was made, or was intended to be made, or partly by one and partly by the other of them

III SOL [68.1]

Application to strike solicitor off roll These applications are rare and rely on the inherent jurisdiction of the High Court. The applicant must show it was reasonable to take this exceptional course rather than applying to the Solicitors Disciplinary Tribunal and if he fails to do so he may be ordered to pay the additional costs incurred: *Parsons v Davies* (1983) unreported, CA.

The applications are not within Sch 1 of the Solicitors Act 1974 and accordingly fall within Section B of Practice Direction 8B to CPR Pt 8 (see para **CPR PD 8B**) and are commenced by claim form.

An application to strike a solicitor off the Roll may only be made by counsel and not by the applicant in person despite the wording of the former RSC Ord 5 r 6: *Re Solicitor, ex p Peasgood* [1994] 1 All ER 298.

As to the power to treat an application requiring a solicitor to answer allegations as one to strike off, see s 55 below.

III SOL [69]

52. Power of Society to draw up order of court

Where an order, whether nisi or absolute, is made by the High Court or the Court of Appeal on a motion to strike the name of a solicitor off the roll, or to require a solicitor to answer allegations contained in an affidavit, and that order is not drawn up by the applicant within one week of its being made, the Society may cause the order to be drawn up, and all future proceedings on the order shall be taken as if the motion had been made by the Society.

III SOL [70]

53. Production of order of court to Society

Where an order is made by the High Court or the Court of Appeal that the name of a solicitor be struck off the roll, or that a solicitor be suspended from practice, the proper officer of the court shall forthwith send a copy of the order to the Society, and the Society shall enter a note of the order on the roll against the name of the solicitor and, where the order so directs, shall strike that name off the roll.

III SOL [71]

54. Restrictions on powers to strike names off roll

(1) No solicitor shall be liable to have his name struck off the roll on account of any failure to comply with the requirements with respect to persons seeking admission as solicitors of any training regulations or on account of any defect in his admission and enrolment, unless—

(a) the application to strike his name off the roll is made within twelve months of the date of his enrolment; or

(b) fraud is proved to have been committed in connection with the failure or defect.

(2) No solicitor shall be liable to have his name struck off the roll by reason only—

(a) that a solicitor who undertook a training responsibility for him under training regulations neglected or omitted to take out a practising certificate; or

(b) that the name of a solicitor who undertook such a responsibility for a period has been removed from or struck off the roll after the end of that period.

SOLICITORS

III SOL [71.1]

Within twelve months of the date of enrolment In calculating the period the date of enrolment is omitted: *Stewart v Chapman* [1951] 2 KB 792, [1951] 2 All ER 613.

III SOL [72]

55. Applications to require a solicitor to answer allegations

For the avoidance of doubt it is hereby declared that an application by any person to require a solicitor to answer allegations contained in an affidavit, whether that application is made to the Tribunal or to the High Court, may be treated as an application to strike the name of that solicitor off the roll on the grounds of the matters alleged.

III SOL [73]

56. Orders as to remuneration for non-contentious business

(1) For the purposes of this section there shall be a committee consisting of the following persons—

- (a) the Lord Chancellor;
- (b) the Lord Chief Justice;
- (c) the Master of the Rolls;
- (d) the President of the Society;
- (da) a member of the Legal Services Board nominated by that Board;
- (e) a solicitor, being the president of a local law society, nominated by the Lord Chancellor to serve on the committee during his tenure of office as president; and
- (f) for the purpose only of prescribing and regulating the remuneration of solicitors in respect of business done under the Land Registration Act 2002, the Chief Land Registrar appointed under that Act.

(2) The committee, or any three members of the committee (the Lord Chancellor being one), may make general orders prescribing the general principles to be applied when determining the remuneration of solicitors in respect of non-contentious business.

(3) The Lord Chancellor, before any order under this section is made, shall cause a draft of the order to be sent to the Society; and the committee shall consider any observations of the Society submitted to them in writing within one month of the sending of the draft, and may then make the order, either in the form of the draft or with such alterations or additions as they may think fit.

(4) The principles prescribed by an order under this section may provide that solicitors should be remunerated—

- (b) by a gross sum; or
- (c) by a fixed sum for each document prepared or perused, without regard to length; or
- (d) in any other mode; or
- (e) partly in one mode and partly in another.

(5) The general principles prescribed by an order under this section may provide that the amount of such remuneration is to be determined by having regard to all or any of the following, among other, considerations, that is to say—

- (a) the position of the party for whom the solicitor is concerned in the business, that is, whether he is vendor or purchaser, lessor or lessee, mortgagor or mortgagee, or the like;
- (b) the place where, and the circumstances in which, the business or any part of it is transacted;
- (c) the amount of the capital money or rent to which the business relates;

(d) the skill, labour and responsibility on the part of the solicitor, or any employee of his who is an authorised person, which the business involves;

(e) the number and importance of the documents prepared or perused, without regard to length.

(5A) In subsection (5) "authorised person" means a person who is an authorised person in relation to an activity which is a reserved legal activity, within the meaning of the Legal Services Act 2007 (see section 18 of that Act).

(6) An order under this section may authorise and regulate—

(a) the taking by a solicitor from his client of security for payment of any remuneration, to be ascertained by assessment or otherwise, which may become due to him under any such order; and

(b) the allowance of interest.

(7) So long as an order made under this section is in operation the assessment of bills of costs of solicitors in respect of non-contentious business shall, subject to the provisions of section 57, be subject to that order.

(8) Any order made under this section may be varied or revoked by a subsequent order so made.

(9) The power to make orders under this section shall be exercisable by statutory instrument which shall be subject to annulment in pursuance of a resolution of either House of Parliament; and the Statutory Instruments Act 1946 shall apply to a statutory instrument containing such an order in like manner as if the order had been made by a Minister of the Crown.

III SOL [73.1]

An order under this section... See Solicitors' (Non-Contentious Business) Remuneration Order 2009, SI 2009/1931 which prescribes the general principles to be applied when determining the remuneration of solicitors in respect of non-contentious business.

The Legal Services Act 2007 amended s 56 of the Solicitors Act 1974. The result of the amendment of s 56 and the Solicitors' (Non-Contentious Business) Remuneration Order 2009 (SI 2009/1931), which came into force on 11 August 2009, was to put an end to the remuneration certificate system. Any client wishing to challenge a solicitor's non-contentious bill will need to go to the Legal Ombudsman.

Bills or other notification sent to clients or other entitled persons should refer them to their right to challenge or complain about the solicitor's bill and the circumstances in which they may be liable to pay interest on an unpaid bill: SRA Code of Conduct 2011, Chapter 1, Client care, at O(1.14).

Article 4 of the 2009 Order deals with the solicitors' rights to take security from the client for the payment of costs and interest.

Article 5 of the 2009 Order empowers solicitors to charge interest and, subject to any agreement between the solicitor and client, interest will run from one month after the date of delivery of the bill and the rate of interest shall not exceed the rate for the time being payable on judgment debts.

III SOL [74]

57. Non-contentious business agreements

(1) Whether or not any order is in force under section 56, a solicitor and his client may, before or after or in the course of the transaction of any non-contentious business by the solicitor, make an agreement as to his remuneration in respect of that business.

(2) The agreement may provide for the remuneration of the solicitor by a gross sum or by reference to an hourly rate, or by a commission or percentage, or by a salary, or otherwise, and it may be made on the terms that the amount of the remuneration stipulated for shall or shall not include all or any disbursements made by the solicitor in respect of searches, plans, travelling, taxes, fees or other matters.

(3) The agreement shall be in writing and signed by the person to be bound by it or his agent in that behalf.

(4) Subject to subsections (5) and (7), the agreement may be sued and recovered on or set aside in the like manner and on the like grounds as an agreement not relating to the remuneration of a solicitor.

(5) If on any assessment of costs the agreement is relied on by the solicitor and objected to by the client as unfair or unreasonable, the costs officer may enquire into the facts and certify them to the court, and if from that certificate it appears just to the court that the agreement should be set aside, or the amount payable under it reduced, the court may so order and may give such consequential directions as it thinks fit.

(6) Subsection (7) applies where the agreement provides for the remuneration of the solicitor to be by reference to an hourly rate.

(7) If, on the assessment of any costs, the agreement is relied on by the solicitor and the client objects to the amount of the costs (but is not alleging that the agreement is unfair or unreasonable), the costs officer may enquire into—

(a) the number of hours worked by the solicitor; and

(b) whether the number of hours worked by him was excessive.

III SOL [74.1]

Agreement in writing As to the requirement of writing, see *Electrical Trades Union v Tarlo* [1964] Ch 720, [1964] 2 All ER 1, where it was held that an oral agreement as to non-contentious profit costs was invalid, and the notes to s 59 at para **III SOL [75.2]**.

The agreement must be in writing and be signed by the person to be bound or his agent and must contain all the terms agreed. Provided these requirements are satisfied it will be a binding contract.

III SOL [74.2]

Litigation before tribunals The definitions of contentious and non-contentious business in s 87(1) classify tribunal work as non-contentious.

III SOL [74.3]

Interest It seems an agreement under this section may validly provide for charging interest on unpaid fees: see *Walton v Egan* [1982] QB 1232, [1982] 3 All ER 849.

III SOL [74.4]

Assessment The effect of sub-ss (4) and (5) is that where the agreement is sued upon, the matter may be referred to the costs officer for inquiry and report but on the reference he acts as a delegate of the powers of the court and does not exercise his own originating powers of assessment: see *Walton v Egan* [1982] QB 1232, [1982] 3 All ER 849.

Where the agreement is relied upon by the solicitor, and the client does not claim it is unfair or unreasonable, if it provides for remuneration to be by reference to hourly rates, on any assessment, the taxing officer can enquire into the number of hours worked and whether that number of hours was excessive: sub-ss (6) and (7).

It remains appropriate for solicitors administering an estate and charging for time spent on the administration to charge a separate scale fee based on the value of the estate, provided it is fair and reasonable to do so having regard to all the circumstances: *Jemma Trust Co Ltd v Liptrott* [2003] EWCA Civ 1476, [2004] 1 All ER 510, Times, 29 October. As to the scale, see *Maltby v DJ Freeman & Co* [1978] 2 All ER 913, [1978] 1 WLR 431 but make an adjustment for inflation. Any agreement as to probate costs should deal specifically with any charge to be made by reference to the value of the estate.

For the costs of solicitors for work done in administering a deceased's estate see *Barrett v Rutt-Field* [2006] WTLR 1505, (2007) NLJ 225.

III SOL [74.5]

Re-opening agreement Where an agreement has been made by virtue of this section, the client is not entitled, under sub-s (5) to have an itemised bill delivered and referred to detailed assessment in order to see whether the agreement is unfair or unreasonable, unless he can establish special circumstances showing that there is something in the case which should be looked into, eg that he was induced to enter into the agreement by the solicitor's mis-statement as to the basis on which he was entitled to charge: *Rutter v Sheridan-Young* [1958] 2 All ER 13, [1958] 1 WLR 444, CA. If the court decides the agreement should be set aside or the amount payable reduced it can so order.

III SOL [75]

59. Contentious business agreements

(1) Subject to subsection (2), a solicitor may make an agreement in writing with his client as to his remuneration in respect of any contentious business done, or to be done, by him (in this Act referred to as a "contentious business agreement") providing that he shall be remunerated by a gross sum or by reference to an hourly rate, or by a salary, or otherwise, and whether at a higher or lower rate than that at which he would otherwise have been entitled to be remunerated.

(2) Nothing in this section or in sections 60 to 63 shall give validity to—

(a) any purchase by a solicitor of the interest, or any part of the interest, of his client in any action, suit or other contentious proceeding; or

(b) any agreement by which a solicitor retained or employed to prosecute any action, suit or other contentious proceeding, stipulates for payment only in the event of success in that action, suit or proceeding; or

(c) any disposition, contract, settlement, conveyance, delivery, dealing or transfer which under the law relating to bankruptcy is invalid against a trustee or creditor in any bankruptcy or composition

III SOL [75.1]

Contentious and non-contentious Contentious business is defined by s 87(1) of the Solicitors Act 1974 (see para **III SOL [91]**). Contentious business includes work done prior to the commencement of litigation (or arbitration) provided that litigation (or arbitration) is in fact commenced; see *Re Simpkin Marshall Ltd* [1959] Ch 229, [1958] 3 All ER 611 in which it was said, "All business is to now to be regarded as contentious which is done before proceedings are begun, provided that the business is done with a view to proceedings being begun, and that they are in fact begun, and also all business done in the course of the proceedings. All other business is non-contentious". It follows that work which would normally be regarded as "contentious", eg negotiations to settle a claim for personal injuries is non-contentious if no proceedings are in fact begun. On the other hand work which would normally be regarded as non-contentious, eg obtaining a grant of probate is contentious if carried out solely for the purpose of proceedings which are in fact begun. Proceedings before a tribunal except the Lands Tribunal, the Transport Tribunal (and, quaere, the Employment Appeals Tribunal) are not contentious: *A-G v BBC* [1981] AC 303 and *Peach Grey & Co (a firm) v Sommers* [1995] 2 All ER 513. Advising a liquidator in a compulsory winding-up whether an action should be brought to recover money paid by the company or whether a misfeasance summons would be issued is not business done "in or for the purpose of" the winding-up proceedings and therefore it is not contentious business quoad those proceedings (*Re Simpkin Marshall* [1959] Ch 229, [1958] 3 All ER 611).

There are recent dicta that the definition of 'contentious' work is expanding. See, for example, *Crosbie v Munroe* [2003] 8 of 2003 Supreme Court Cost Office Reports, CA, per Lord Brooke in the final paragraph of his judgment. This paragraph is set out in (2003) LS Gaz R, 4 September 2003 at 25 and 26.

See, however, *Gaynor v Central West London Buses Ltd* [2006] EWCA Civ 1120, [2007] 1 All ER 84 where work done by solicitors before a client decided whether to pursue a claim was held not to be the provision of litigation services; advising a client that he had a good prima facie case and writing a letter before action is not enough.

Stanley Burnton LJ provided clarity as to the classification of work as contentious or non-contentious in his judgment in *Bilkus v Stockler Brunton (a firm)* [2010] EWCA Civ 101, [2010] 3 All ER 64, [2010] 1 WLR 2526. He stated that it did not depend on the nature of the work done but on whether it was done 'in or for the purposes of proceedings begun before a court or an arbitrator'. Work done after the completion of the proceedings was done not for the purpose of those proceedings but in consequence of them.

Steps taken to enforce a judgment by one of the methods listed in CPR PD 70 were clearly themselves proceedings.

His Lordship also dealt with the necessity of solicitors continuing to act after judgment and wishing to change their charging rate. The solicitors must give the client an informed chance to agree or to change his solicitors.

In the instant case a valuation carried out under a court order and pursuant to directions of the court was contentious business.

Employment cases are deemed non-contentious; see article 'When the gloves are off' by Jon Robbins in (2010) NLJ, 12 March, page 365.

III SOL [75.2]

Agreement in writing For an agreement to be a contentious business agreement within s 59 it must be in writing and must contain all the terms of the bargain between the parties and the agreement to such terms: see *Re Raven, ex p Pitt* (1881) 45 LT 742; *Re Frape* [1893] 2 Ch 284. The "writing" may well consist of an exchange of letters (*Chamberlain v Boodle and King* [1982] 3 All ER 188, [1982] 1 WLR 1443, CA) or written acceptance by the client of a "client care letter" provided that the terms are clear. It need only be signed by the party to be charged: *Re Frape* [1893] 2 Ch 284.

Unlike the terms of s 57(3) (see para **III SOL [74]**) dealing with non-contentious business agreements, the section is purely permissive and the client may by relying on the common law be able to enforce a special agreement relating to contentious business even though it is not in writing (*Clare v Joseph* [1907] 2 KB 369, CA) and where an oral agreement relates both to contentious and non-contentious business the client may rely on it so far as the contentious business is concerned (*Electrical Trades Union v Tarlo* [1964] Ch 720, [1964] 2 All ER 1). It appears likely that a solicitor cannot escape from the provisions of ss 59 onwards by taking a cheque from the client and suing on it: *Ray v Newton* [1913] 1 KB 249, CA (decided under the previous legislation); *Martin Boston & Co v Levy* [1982] 3 All ER 193, [1982] 1 WLR 1434 (in which this was said to be a triable issue and a default judgment was set aside).

III SOL [75.3]

No win-no fee agreements Where a solicitor conducts litigation in the knowledge that there is no real likelihood of his costs being paid by or on behalf of his client, unless there is a valid conditional fee agreement he may be held personally liable for any costs awarded against his client: *Mainwaring v Goldtech Investments Ltd* (1991) Times, 19 February, CA; *British Waterways Board v Norman* (1993) 26 HLR 232, Times, 11 December. But see also *Count Tolstoy-Miloslavsky v Lord Aldington* [1996] 2 All ER 556, [1996] 1 WLR 736, CA as to the question of making a wasted costs order in such circumstances. See also *Burnstein v Times Newspapers Ltd* [2002] EWCA Civ 1739, [2002] All ER (D) 442 (Nov), (2002) Times, 6 December where it was held that there is no principle of law which precludes a solicitor from continuing to act for a client whenever he becomes aware that the client is no longer able to pay his costs.

By CPR 44.1(3) where advocacy or litigation services are provided to a client under a CFA costs are recoverable notwithstanding the client is only liable to pay the legal representative's fees and expenses only to the extent that sums are recovered in respect of the proceedings, whether by way of costs or otherwise.

Note the amendments of ss 58, 58A, 58AA and the insertion of 58C in the Courts and Legal Services Act 1990 by ss 44–46 of the Legal Aid, Sentencing and Punishment of Offenders Act 2012 (LASPO):

(i) s 44 of LASPO as to **conditional fee agreements; success fees (CFAs)**, supplemented by the Conditional Fee Agreements Order 2013;
(ii) s 45 of LASPO as to **damages-based agreements**, supplemented by the Damages-based Agreements Regulations 2013;
(iii) s 46 of LASPO as to the **recovery of insurance premiums by way of costs**.

The broad effect on claimants for damages for pain, suffering and loss of amenity can be encapsulated as:

(i) success fees to lawyers under CFAs cannot be recovered by successful litigants;
(ii) success fees to lawyers may be recovered from clients but subject to a percentage cap.

In *Budana v Leeds Teaching Hospitals NHS Trust* [2017] EWCA Civ 1980, the Court of Appeal considered whether a conditional fee agreement could be assigned between solicitors. Gloster LJ said that this was perfectly legitimate where the client had consented to the case being transferred and there had been no termination of the original retainer. This case involved a CFA which had been entered into before LASPO came into effect, but it appears that this case would also apply to post-LASPO cases.

III SOL [75.4]

Invalid against a trustee in bankruptcy See Insolvency Act 1986 ss 284 and 339–334.

Payments to a solicitor to defend bankruptcy proceedings have been upheld against a trustee in bankruptcy and payment for the costs of defending a criminal charge should also be upheld: *Re Charlwood, ex p Masters* [1894] 1 QB 643.

III SOL [75.5]

CPR Rule 48.8 It is of great importance that the distinction is made between a formal contentious business agreement and an agreement that is subject to CPR 48.8. See *Cook on Costs 2013* at para 2.38 for a detailed discussion of the differences.

III SOL [76]

60. Effect of contentious business agreement

(1) Subject to the provisions of this section and to sections 61 to 63, the costs of a solicitor in any case where a contentious business agreement has been made shall not be subject to assessment or (except in the case of an agreement which provides for the solicitor to be remunerated by reference to an hourly rate) to the provisions of section 69.

(2) Subject to subsection (3), a contentious business agreement shall not affect the amount of, or any rights or remedies for the recovery of, any costs payable by the client to, or to the client by, any person other than the solicitor, and that person may, unless he has otherwise agreed, require any such costs to be assessed according to the rules for their assessment for the time being in force.

(3) A client shall not be entitled to recover from any other person under an order for the payment of any costs to which a contentious business agreement relates more than the amount payable by him to his solicitor in respect of those costs under the agreement.

(4) A contentious business agreement shall be deemed to exclude any claim by the solicitor in respect of the business to which it relates other than—

(a) a claim for the agreed costs; or

(b) a claim for such costs as are expressly excepted from the agreement.

(5) A provision in a contentious business agreement that the solicitor shall not be liable for his negligence, or that of any employee of his, shall be void if the client is a natural person who, in entering that agreement, is acting for purposes which are outside his trade, business or profession.

(6) A provision in a contentious business agreement that the solicitor shall be relieved from any responsibility to which he would otherwise be subject as a solicitor shall be void.

III SOL [76.1]

"Shall not be subject to assessment" The effect of sub-s (1) is to exclude the operation of s 74(3) (see para **III SOL [90]**), where there is a written agreement under s 59 (see para **III SOL [75]**), unless the special provisions of ss 61–63 (see paras **III SOL [77]**–**III SOL [79]**) apply.

III SOL [76.2]

Indemnity principle Subsection (3) sets out the indemnity principle: that a client may not recover more from another party than is payable his own solicitor. The common law principle was set out in *Gundry v Sainsbury* [1910] 1 KB 645, CA. For the erosion of the indemnity principle see CPR 43.2[1A] (at para **CPR 43.2**) above. Where an agreement provides for the solicitor's remuneration to be on the basis of an hourly rate the section precludes recovery of uplifted hourly rates exceeding those agreed: *General of Berne Insurance Co v Jardine Reinsurance Management Ltd* [1998] 2 All ER 301, [1998] 1 WLR 1231, CA. The costs must be looked at on an item by item basis as opposed to applying an overall cap. See also *Practice Note* [1999] 1 All ER 126, [1998] 1 WLR 1674 as to the item by item basis where there is no contentious business agreement.

Statutory authority for the abrogation of the indemnity principle is contained in s 31 Access to Justice Act 1999 and contentious business may include a conditional fee agreement providing for payment to be conditional on success with or without a fee uplift.

Conditional fees are dealt with in Part III under FUNDING OF LEGAL SERVICES.

III SOL [76.3]

Uplift The addition to a bill of an item by way of uplift is excluded by s 60(4) in the case of costs claimed under a contentious business agreement: *Bilkus v Stockler Brunton (a firm)* [2010] EWCA Civ 101, [2010] 3 All ER 64, [2010] 1 WLR 2526.

SOLICITORS

III SOL [77]

61. Enforcement of contentious business agreement

(1) No action shall be brought on any contentious business agreement, but on the application of any person who—

(a) is a party to the agreement or the representative of such a party; or

(b) is or is alleged to be liable to pay, or is or claims to be entitled to be paid, the costs due or alleged to be due in respect of the business to which the agreement relates,

the court may enforce or set aside the agreement and determine every question as to its validity or effect.

(2) On any application under subsection (1), the court—

(a) if it is of the opinion that the agreement is in all respects fair and reasonable, may enforce it;

(b) if it is of the opinion that the agreement is in any respect unfair or unreasonable, may set it aside and order the costs covered by it to be assessed as if it had never been made;

(c) in any case, may make such order as to the costs of the application as it thinks fit.

(3) If the business covered by a contentious business agreement (not being an agreement to which section 62 applies) is business done, or to be done, in any action, a client who is a party to the agreement may make application to a costs officer of the court for the agreement to be examined.

(4) A costs officer before whom an agreement is laid under subsection (3) shall examine it and may either allow it, or, if he is of the opinion that the agreement is unfair or unreasonable, require the opinion of the court to be taken on it, and the court may allow the agreement or reduce the amount payable under it, or set it aside and order the costs covered by it to be assessed as if it had never been made.

(4A) Subsection (4B) applies where a contentious business agreement provides for the remuneration of the solicitor to be by reference to an hourly rate.

(4B) If on the assessment of any costs the agreement is relied on by the solicitor and the client objects to the amount of the costs (but is not alleging that the agreement is unfair or unreasonable), the costs officer may enquire into—

(a) the number of hours worked by the solicitor; and

(b) whether the number of hours worked by him was excessive.

(5) Where the amount agreed under any contentious business agreement is paid by or on behalf of the client or by any person entitled to do so, the person making the payment may at any time within twelve months from the date of payment, or within such further time as appears to the court to be reasonable, apply to the court, and, if it appears to the court that the special circumstances of the case require it to be re-opened, the court may, on such terms as may be just, re-open it and order the costs covered by the agreement to be assessed and the whole or any part of the amount received by the solicitor to be repaid by him.

(6) In this section and in sections 62 and 63 "the court" means—

(a) in relation to an agreement under which any business has been done in any court having jurisdiction to enforce and set aside agreements, any such court in which any of that business has been done;

(b) in relation to an agreement under which no business has been done in any such court, and under which more than £50 is payable, the High Court;

(c) in relation to an agreement under which no business has been done in any such court and under which not more than £50 is payable, any county court which would, but for the provisions of subsection (1) prohibiting the bringing of an action on the agreement, have had jurisdiction in any action on it;

and for the avoidance of doubt it is hereby declared that in paragraph (*a*) "court having jurisdiction to enforce and set aside agreements" includes the county court.

III SOL [77.1]

"Fair and reasonable" See *Re Stuart, ex p Cathcart* [1893] 2 QB 201, per Lord Esher.

See also *Higgins v Ministry of Defence* [2010] EWHC 654 (QB), 154 Sol Jo (no 14) 28 where on appeal it was held that the Master had been entitled to take into account the claimant's age and the urgency in his case when deciding it was reasonable for him to instruct Central London solicitors in respect of his personal injury claim. The list of factors set out by Kennedy LJ in *Truscott v Truscott, Wraith v Sheffield Forgemasters Ltd* [1998] 1 All ER 82, 1 WLR 132, CA in relation to this issue is useful but not of general application.

III SOL [77.2]

Re-opening of agreement The court can re-open an agreement under sub-s (5) even though it has been allowed by a costs officer under sub-s (4): *Re Simmons and Politzer* [1954] 2 QB 296, [1954] 2 All ER 811, CA.

III SOL [77.3]

"costs judge", "costs officer" CPR 44.1 (see para **CPR 44.1**) now defines taxing masters of the Senior Courts as costs judges; the costs judges are to remain district judges and authorised court officers.

III SOL [77.4]

"Court" Before a solicitor can rely on a contentious business agreement he must apply to the court for permission to enforce it and a client may apply to the court to set it aside.

Any application to a county court under CPR Part 8 may be determined by a district judge (see **CPR 2.4**) and may be dealt with in private if the general rule that hearings be in public is displaced by one of the factors listed in CPR 39.2(3)(a)–(g) (at para **CPR 39**).

III SOL [77.5]

Challenging the time taken If the client does not challenge the agreement or his challenge to it is rejected, where the agreement provides for remuneration by reference to a specified hourly rate the client cannot challenge the amount of the hourly rate, but he can still challenge the number of hours claimed to have been worked and whether the time taken was reasonable: sub-ss 4A and 4B.

III SOL [78]

62. Contentious business agreements by certain representatives

(1) Where the client who makes a contentious business agreement makes it as a representative of a person whose property will be chargeable with the whole or part of the amount payable under the agreement, the agreement shall be laid before a costs officer of the court before payment.

(2) A costs officer before whom an agreement is laid under subsection (1) shall examine it and may either allow it, or, if he is of the opinion that it is unfair or unreasonable, require the opinion of the court to be taken on it, and the court may allow the agreement or reduce the amount payable under it, or set it aside and order the costs covered by it to be assessed as if it had never been made.

(3) A client who makes a contentious business agreement as mentioned in subsection (1) and pays the whole or any part of the amount payable under the agreement without it being allowed by the officer or by the court shall be liable at any time to account to the person whose property is charged with the whole or any part of the amount so paid for the sum so charged, and the solicitor who accepts the payment may be ordered by the court to refund the amount received by him.

(4) A client makes a contentious business agreement as the representative of another person if he makes it—

(a) as his guardian,

(b) as a trustee for him under a deed or will,

(c) as a deputy for him appointed by the Court of Protection with powers in relation to his property and affairs, or

(d) as another person authorised under that Act to act on his behalf.

III SOL [78.1]

"Court" See para **III SOL [77.4]**.

III SOL [78.2]

"costs judge", "costs officer" See para **III SOL [77.3]**.

III SOL [79]

63. Effect on contentious business agreement of death, incapability or change of solicitor

(1) If, after some business has been done under a contentious business agreement but before the solicitor has wholly performed it—

(a) the solicitor dies, or becomes incapable of acting; or

(b) the client changes his solicitor (as, notwithstanding the agreement, he shall be entitled to do),

any party to, or the representative of any party to, the agreement may apply to the court, and the court shall have the same jurisdiction as to enforcing the agreement so far as it has been performed, or setting it aside, as the court would have had if the solicitor had not died or become incapable of acting, or the client had not changed his solicitor.

(2) The court, notwithstanding that it is of the opinion that the agreement is in all respects fair and reasonable, may order the amount due in respect of business under the agreement to be ascertained by assessment, and in that case—

(a) the costs officer, in ascertaining that amount, shall have regard so far as may be to the terms of the agreement; and

(b) payment of the amount found by him to be due may be enforced in the same manner as if the agreement had been completely performed.

(3) If in such a case as is mentioned in subsection (1)(b) an order is made for the assessment of the amount due to the solicitor in respect of the business done under the agreement, the court shall direct the costs officer to have regard to the circumstances under which the change of solicitor has taken place, and the costs officer, unless he is of the opinion that there has been no default, negligence, improper delay or other conduct on the part of the solicitor, or any of his employees, affording the client reasonable ground for changing his solicitor, shall not allow to the solicitor the full amount of the remuneration agreed to be paid to him.

III SOL [79.1]

"Court" See para **III SOL [77.4]**.

III SOL [79.2]

"costs judge", "costs officer" See para **III SOL [77.3]**.

III SOL [79.3]

"taxation" See para **III SOL [76.2]**.

III SOL [80]

64. Form of bill of costs for contentious business

(1) Where the remuneration of a solicitor in respect of contentious business done by him is not the subject of a contentious business agreement, then, subject to subsections (2) to (4), the solicitor's bill of costs may at the option of the solicitor be either a bill containing detailed items or a gross sum bill.

(2) The party chargeable with a gross sum bill may at any time—

(a) before he is served with a writ or other originating process for the recovery of costs included in the bill, and

(b) before the expiration of three months from the date on which the bill was delivered to him,

require the solicitor to deliver, in lieu of that bill, a bill containing detailed items; and on such a requirement being made the gross sum bill shall be of no effect.

(3) Where an action is commenced on a gross sum bill, the court shall, if so requested by the party chargeable with the bill before the expiration of one month from the service on that party of the writ or other originating process, order that the bill be assessed.

(4) If a gross sum bill is assessed, whether under this section or otherwise, nothing in this section shall prejudice any rules of court with respect to assessment, and the solicitor shall furnish the costs officer with such details of any of the costs covered by the bill as the costs officer may require.

III SOL [80.1]

Submission of detailed bill Before there can be recourse to sub-s (2) there must be something which can fairly be described as a request or requirement that the solicitor should deliver to the client a detailed bill to replace the gross sum bill already delivered; a request, after delivery of a gross sum bill, for "your bill to be prepared and lodged for taxation" is not enough. In any event, the solicitor cannot as against a client who relies on it waive the three months' limit imposed by the subsection and so cannot substitute for a gross sum bill a larger detailed bill delivered on a request made out of time: *Carlton v Theodore Goddard & Co* [1973] 2 All ER 877, [1973] 1 WLR 623. See also *Madurasinghe v Penguin Electronics (a firm)* [1993] 3 All ER 20, [1993] 1 WLR 989, CA as to the effect of a request for a detailed bill under this section where it was stressed that the detailed bill requested by the client replaced the gross sum bill which was then "of no effect". Contrast the situation where as part of the detailed assessment the costs officer directs preparation of a "detailed breakdown". In this situation the "detailed breakdown" is merely an aid to a detailed assessment of the original gross sum bill which remains in effect.

III SOL [81]

65. Security for costs and termination of retainer

(1) A solicitor may take security from his client for his costs, to be ascertained by assessment or otherwise, in respect of any contentious business to be done by him.

(2) If a solicitor who has been retained by a client to conduct contentious business requests the client to make a payment of a sum of money, being a reasonable sum on account of the costs incurred or to be incurred in the conduct of that business and the client refuses or fails within a reasonable time to make that payment, the refusal or failure shall be deemed to be a good cause whereby the solicitor may, upon giving reasonable notice to the client, withdraw from the retainer.

III SOL [81.1]

See paras **III SOL [43]** and **III SOL [44]** above

III SOL [82]

66. Assessments with regard to contentious business

Subject to the provisions of any rules of court, on every assessment of costs in respect of any contentious business, the costs officer may—

(a) allow interest at such rate and from such time as he thinks just on money disbursed by the solicitor for the client, and on money of the client in the hands of, and improperly retained by, the solicitor or an employee of the solicitor; and

(b) in determining the remuneration of the solicitor, have regard to the skill, labour and responsibility involved in the business done by him or by any employee of his who is an authorised person (within the meaning of section 56(5A)).

SOLICITORS

III SOL [82.1]

A solicitor suing for unpaid fee can claim statutory interest pursuant to s 35A of the Senior Courts Act 1981 or s 69(1) of the County Courts Act 1984; the court has a discretion as to whether to award such interest.

III SOL [83]

67. Inclusion of disbursements in bill of costs

A solicitor's bill of costs may include costs payable in discharge of a liability properly incurred by him on behalf of the party to be charged with the bill (including counsel's fees) notwithstanding that those costs have not been paid before the delivery of the bill to that party; but those costs—

(a) shall be described in the bill as not then paid; and

(b) if the bill is assessed, shall not be allowed by the costs officer unless they are paid before the assessment is completed.

III SOL [83.1]

Disbursement not shown as unpaid It is clear that the court has power to allow a solicitor to withdraw a bill in which it is not stated that disbursements are unpaid and substitute a fresh bill: *Polak v Marchioness of Winchester* [1956] 2 All ER 660, [1956] 1 WLR 818, CA. In the unreported case of *Tearle & Co v Sherring* (29 October 1993, unreported) 12 Litigation Letter (January 1994, p 78) the court allowed the solicitor to amend his bill to show that counsel's fees had been incurred but not paid.

III SOL [84]

68. Power of court to order solicitor to deliver bill etc

(1) The jurisdiction of the High Court to make orders for the delivery by a solicitor of a bill of costs, and for the delivery up of, or otherwise in relation to, any documents in his possession, custody or power, is hereby declared to extend to cases in which no business has been done by him in the High Court.

(2) The county court and the family court each have the same jurisdiction as the High Court to make orders making such provision as is mentioned in subsection (1) in cases where the bill of costs or the documents relate wholly or partly to contentious business done by the solicitor in the county court or (as the case may be) the family court.

(3) In this section and in sections 69 to 71 "solicitor" includes the executors, administrators and assignees of a solicitor.

III SOL [84.1]

Delivery of bill The Supreme Court has inherent jurisdiction to order the assessment of a solicitor's costs: see Halsbury's Laws (4th edn reissue), para 203. In *Re Solicitor, Re Taxation of Costs* [1953] Ch 480, [1953] 2 All ER 23, CA, the court exercised its discretion to order the delivery of an itemised bill although three years had elapsed since the solicitors originally rendered their account. In this case the Court of Appeal distinguished *Re a Solicitor, Re Taxation of Costs* [1947] Ch 274, [1947] 1 All ER 369, where an order was refused after six years. More recently see *Falmouth House Freehold Co Ltd v Morgan Walker LLP* [2010] EWHC 3092 (Ch), [2010] NLJR 1686, [2010] All ER (D) 256 (Nov).

III SOL [84.2]

County court Note that the county court can exercise the power of the High Court under this section irrespective of the size of the bill provided that the costs or documents relate wholly or partly to contentious business done in that county court.

III SOL [84.3]

Procedure For procedure see CPR Part 67, r 2 in Volume 1 (para **CPR 67**).

III SOL [84.4]

Disclosure of Documents The courts have recently been considering applications from clients for orders under the court's inherent jurisdiction that solicitors disclose documents on their files to clients for the purpose of enabling the client to investigate whether they have been over-charged.

In the cases of *Green v SGI Legal plc* (England and Wales High Court) Senior Courts Costs Office, 18 December 2017 and *Riaz v Ashwood Solicitors Ltd* [2018] EWHC Costs B5, [2018] Lexis Citation 25, Master Leonard rejected two such applications. In *Green*, he distinguished between documents that the client was entitled to and those which were the property of the solicitor even though to do with the client's case. His view was that the client was not entitled to see the latter documents and the court would not require the solicitor to disclose them.

In *Riaz*, the client was arguing that the solicitor had over-charged the client in a CFA following a Road Traffic Accident. The client claimed not to have received some information from the solicitor. Master Leonard took the view that (a) client had received all the documents to which he was entitled and that the solicitor was not required to replace them if the client had mislaid them, (b) there was limited evidence that the solicitor had over-charged, so the court should be careful in exercising its powers simply to enable the client to investigate and (c) the time limit for any challenge was likely to have passed. In those circumstances, the court would not exercise its jurisdiction to order the solicitor to provide the documents.

Both decisions were based on the facts of the individual cases, but the approach suggests a reluctance to require solicitors to provide information which they would not otherwise be required to provide in the absence of strong reasons to do so.

III SOL [85]

69. Action to recover solicitor's costs

(1) Subject to the provisions of this Act, no action shall be brought to recover any costs due to a solicitor before the expiration of one month from the date on which a bill of those costs is delivered in accordance with the requirements mentioned in subsection (2); but if there is probable cause for believing that the party chargeable with the costs—

(a) is about to quit England and Wales, to become bankrupt or to compound with his creditors, or

(b) is about to do any other act which would tend to prevent or delay the solicitor obtaining payment,

the High Court may, notwithstanding that one month has not expired from the delivery of the bill, order that the solicitor be at liberty to commence an action to recover his costs and may order that those costs be assessed.

(2) The requirements referred to in subsection (1) are that the bill must be—

(a) signed in accordance with subsection (2A), and

(b) delivered in accordance with subsection (2C).

(2A) A bill is signed in accordance with this subsection if it is—

(a) signed by the solicitor or on his behalf by an employee of the solicitor authorised by him to sign, or

(b) enclosed in, or accompanied by, a letter which is signed as mentioned in paragraph (a) and refers to the bill.

(2B) For the purposes of subsection (2A) the signature may be an electronic signature.

(2C) A bill is delivered in accordance with this subsection if—

(a) it is delivered to the party to be charged with the bill personally,

(b) it is delivered to that party by being sent to him by post to, or left for him at, his place of business, dwelling-house or last known place of abode, or

(c) it is delivered to that party—

(i) by means of an electronic communications network, or

(ii) by other means but in a form that nevertheless requires the use of apparatus by the recipient to render it intelligible,

and that party has indicated to the person making the delivery his willingness to accept delivery of a bill sent in the form and manner used.

(2D) An indication to any person for the purposes of subsection (2C)(c)—

SOLICITORS

(a) must state the address to be used and must be accompanied by such other information as that person requires for the making of the delivery;

(b) may be modified or withdrawn at any time by a notice given to that person.

(2E) Where a bill is proved to have been delivered in compliance with the requirements of subsections (2A) and (2C), it is not necessary in the first instance for the solicitor to prove the contents of the bill and it is to be presumed, until the contrary is shown, to be a bill bona fide complying with this Act.

(2F) A bill which is delivered as mentioned in subsection (2C)(c) is to be treated as having been delivered on the first working day after the day on which it was sent (unless the contrary is proved).

(3) Where a bill of costs relates wholly or partly to contentious business done in the county court and the amount of the bill does not exceed £5,000, the powers and duties of the High Court under this section and sections 70 and 71 in relation to that bill may be exercised and performed by the county court.

(4) . . .

(5) In this section references to an electronic signature are to be read in accordance with section 7(2) of the Electronic Communications Act 2000 (c 7).

(6) In this section—

"electronic communications network" has the same meaning as in the Communications Act 2003 (c 21);

"working day" means a day other than a Saturday, a Sunday, Christmas Day, Good Friday or a bank holiday in England and Wales under the Banking and Financial Dealings Act 1971 (c 80).

III SOL [85.1]

"Subject to the provisions of this Act" This section does not apply where a non-contentious business agreement has been made under s 57 (see para **III SOL [74]**): *Rutter v Sheridan-Young* [1958] 2 All ER 13, [1958] 1 WLR 444, CA. Where there is an agreement as to the remuneration of contentious business pursuant to s 59 of the Act: s 61 (1) see para **III SOL [77]**.

III SOL [85.2]

"no action" The decision in *Truex v Toll* [2009] EWHC 396 (Ch), [2009] 4 All ER 419, [2009] 1 WLR 2121 has clarified that a claim for solicitors fees not judicially assessed or determined is not a claim for a liquidated sum which could be the subject of a bankruptcy petition under s 167 of the Insolvency Act 1986 even if the time for challenge under the Solicitors Act 1974 had passed. Such a debt can only be converted into a liquidated sum by an admission, acknowledgment or agreement from which the debtor has bound himself not to resile.

III SOL [85.3]

"due to a solicitor" The restriction applies to costs due to the solicitor as such and not, eg as an election or parliamentary agent (*Re Oliver* (1866) 36 LJ Ch 261; *Re Baker Lee & Co* [1903] 1 KB 189, CA) or as a rent collector (*Re Shilson Coode & Co* [1904] 1 Ch 837).

Where a client requested advice from a solicitor but instead was advised by an employee who was not a solicitor and he was not aware of that, he was held not to be liable to pay the solicitor's bill. This was so even though he had been advised to the standard of a competent solicitor: *Pilbrow v Pearless de Rougemont & Co (A Firm)* [1999] 3 All ER 355, CA and *Adrian Allen v Fuglers (a firm)* No 5 of decisions reported by the Supreme Court Costs Office in 2003 [2003] 33 LS Gaz R 25. It would be otherwise if the client had merely requested legal advice. Such difficulties would have been avoided by a proper "client-care" letter. See also SRA Code of Conduct 2011, Chapter 1, Client care, at 1.B(1.3) which states 'ensuring that the client is told, in writing, the name and status of the person dealing with the matter and the name and status of the person responsible for its overall supervision.

A solicitor who has been represented by his own firm in the successful defence of proceedings brought against him personally was entitled, when an order for costs was made in his favour, to the profit costs of his firm in defending those proceedings: *Malkinson v Trim*

[2002] EWCA Civ 1273, [2003] 3All ER 356, [2003] 1 WLR 463. See **CPR 48.6** and note in particular CPR 48.6(6)(b) which provides a solicitor acting for himself is a litigant in person. For discussion see *Cook on Costs 2008*, paras 39.12 and 39.13.

A solicitor, who operated his practice under rule 27 of the Solicitors Indemnity Rules 2001 which permits solicitors to practice without indemnity insurance provided their business is limited to acting for personal friends or family or for registered charities without payment, is not regarded as a practising solicitor for the purposes of the Rules of the Supreme Court, which allow solicitors to charge as such for time spent in pursuing litigation on their own behalf: *Boyd & Hutchinson (a firm) v Joseph* [2003] 19 LS Gaz R 29, (2003) Times, 28 April.

In *Agassi v Robinson (Inspector of Taxes)* [2005] EWCA Civ 1507, [2005] NLJ 9 the taxpayer retained a tax expert to instruct counsel direct. The expert was a member of the Chartered Institute of Taxation and licensed so to do. The work he did which would normally have been done by a solicitor could not be charged against the other party.

In *Wilson v William Sturges & Co* [2006] EWHC 792 (QB), [2006] 16 EG 146 (CS) the court held there was no authority for the proposition that a solicitor who overcharged his client and then insisted on payment automatically terminated his retainer preventing him recovering sums found properly owing to him.

The fees of an external costs draftsman can be considered as profit costs of the instructing solicitor and therefore attract a success fee: *Crane v Canons Leisure Centre* [2007] EWCA Civ 1352, [2008] 2 All ER 931, article 'Life Draft' by Grania Langdon-Down, at pages 18–19. The problem of deciding the appropriate grade of fee earner remains to be decided on a case by case basis depending on all the circumstances.

Motto v Trafigura Ltd [2011] EWCA Civ 1150 is a group litigation case in which the Master of the Rolls, Lord Neuberger, followed the analysis in *Lowndes v Home Office Practice Note* [2002] 1 WLR 2450, para 3, by Lord Woolf, Lord Chief Justice, that where the costs as a whole appeared disproportionate the court would then want to be satisfied that the work in relation to each item had been necessary and, if necessary, that the costs of the item was reasonable.

It was further decided in *Motto* above that until a CFA is signed, 'the potential claimant . . . is not a client'. The effect of this is that the expenses of getting business should not normally be treated as attributable to, and payable by, the ultimate client. Such costs are general expenses that fall to be taken into acocunt when a solicitor calculates his hourly rates.

For the danger of the solicitor losing the right to costs by terminating the contract with his client, see **CPR 67 [7]** in Volume 1, *Richard Buxton Solicitors v Mills-Owen* [2010] EWCA Civ 122, where on appeal the solicitors were held to have good reason to terminate, and *Minkin v Cawdery Kaye Fireman and Taylor* [2012] EWCA Civ 546, [2012] 3 All ER 1117, [2012] NLJR 681 where the solicitors refused to continue with the consequence that they were ordered to repay all sums except for money used to pay counsel's fees. Good reason for termination was not established. This decision was reversed on appeal [2012] NLJR 681 by the Court of Appeal.

III SOL [85.3A]

Interim bills During the course of a retainer a solicitor may deliver interim bills of costs. If they are statute-compliant they may be assessed in accordance with s 70. To be compliant a bill must not only meet the formal requirements of section 69 but must also be self-contained and final as to its subject-matter. It may include profit costs and disbursements or one without the other. But a bill simply seeking a payment on account is not an interim statute bill and is outside the scope of ss 69 and 70: *Slade (t/a Richard Slade and Company) v Boodia* [2018] EWCA Civ 2667.

III SOL [85.4]

Application under subsection (1) Applications under sub-s (1) should be made ex parte to a judge in chambers (or in the county court to a district judge) by affidavit (see *Re Duckers* (1906) 50 Sol Jo 441).

III SOL [85.5]

The bill Earlier authorities suggest that the bill must be sufficient to enable the client to obtain advice and the court to tax. However in view of the ability of the client to require the solicitor to deliver a detailed bill in lieu of a gross sum bill (s 64(2) (see para **III SOL [80]**)) there must be some doubt as to whether these authorities still apply. The point is discussed in *Ralph Hume Garry (a firm) v Gwillim* [2002] EWCA Civ 1500, [2003] 1 All ER 1038, [2003] 1 WLR 510 and it is to be noted that Ward LJ stated that to avoid such "unseemly disputes" consideration should be given, in light of the need for transparency, to providing clients with printouts of computer records, kept by accounts departments, of how their fees are calculated. He said: "Surely in 2002 every second of time spent, certainly on contentious business, is recorded on the account department's computer with a description of the fee earner, the rate of charging and some description of the work done. A copy of the printout, adjusted as may be necessary to remove items recorded not chargeable to the client . . . is the least a client is entitled to expect."

See also *Long Eaton Plant Hire Ltd v Nelsons* (28 August 2002, unreported), Supreme Court Costs Office for the duty of solicitors where costs begin to "run away" from the costs estimate. A client who has been provided with a costs estimate is entitled to rely on it and that it will not be exceeded by more than a reasonable amount or 15%; *Wong v Vizards* (1997) 2 Costs LR 46. For the position where no estimate has been given but the client is aware of their solicitor's hourly rates, see *Gabutt and Gabutt v Edward* [2005] EWCA Civ 1206, [2006] 1 All ER 553. For helpful discussion of this very important decision see NLJ Vol 155 7201, 18 November 2005 pages 1742–1745, where articles by Tony Guise and David Chalk appear.

The SRA Code of Conduct 2011, Chapter 1, Client care at O(14) requires clients to be informed of their right to challenge or complain about their solicitor's bill and to be advised of the circumstances under which they may be liable to pay interest on an unpaid bill.

Further, Chapter 1, 1.1B(1.22)–1.B(1.24) sets out provisions for complaints handling and on request supplying the firm's complaints procedure.

The SRA will also issue guidance as to the circumstances in which solicitors will not need to include the wording with every bill, eg where monthly bills are being rendered to a 'sophisticated' corporate client.

III SOL [85.6]

Signature Where the solicitor carries on business alone in a firm name, the bill or covering letter may be signed by him in the firm's name (*Goodman v J Eban Ltd* [1954] 1 QB 550, [1954] 1 All ER 763, CA). The signature on the bill need not be in the full name of the firm provided that the full name appears on the bill and the abbreviation used is a convenient and obvious contraction of the full name (*Bartletts de Reya v Byrne* (1983)127 Sol Jo 69, 133 NLJ 1101, CA). As in any case on non-compliance with the formal requirements of the Act as to the contents and form of the bill the court has discretion to permit the bill to be withdrawn and a fresh bill delivered: *Zuliani v Veira* [1994] 1 WLR 1149, PC. It may be that the court could allow the solicitor to amend the bill in an appropriate case, see (in a different context): *Tearle & Co v Sherring* (29 October 1993, unreported) 12 Litigation Letter (January 1994) p 78. An unsigned bill may be taxed: *Ex p D'Aragon* (1887) 3 TLR 815. There is a line of cases which show that a client may be precluded by his actions from objecting to an unsigned bill (*Re Pender* (1846) 2 Ph 69; *Re Gedye* (1851) 14 Beav 56; *Young v Walker* (1847) 16 M & W 446).

The cases quoted in the last paragraph were all decided prior to the Civil Procedure Rules 1998.

Signature of bills delivered after 7 March 2008 by mechanical means is permitted by s 69(2B) of the Act and bills will be duly signed in accordance with s 69 if signed by the solicitor or on his behalf by an employee of his duly authorised by him to sign. Further it will be sufficient of the bill is enclosed in, or accompanied by, a letter which is so signed and refers to the bill: s 69(2A).

III SOL [85.7]

Delivery The bill must be delivered to the client or an agent authorised by him, delivery to his new solicitor, unless under the client's direction or the authority of the court is not sufficient: *Daubney v Phipps* (1849) 18 LJQB 337; *Spier v Bernard* (1863) 8 LT 396. Where the bill relates to contentious business and there is no contentious business agreement under s 59 (see para **III SOL [75]**), the solicitor may deliver a "gross sum" bill rather than an itemised bill (s 64 (see para **III SOL [80]**)). If the bill is defective the court has a discretion in special circumstances to permit its withdrawal and the delivery of a new bill in proper form (*Re Solicitor* [1951] 1 All ER 592; *Zuliani v Veira* [1994] 1 WLR 1149, PC) even after the bill has been taxed: *Chappell v Mehta* [1981] 1 All ER 349, CA.

In *Polak v Marchioness of Winchester* [1956] 2 All ER 660, [1956] 1 WLR 818, CA, the bill contained disbursements which had not been paid and did not state the fact, the court allowed the substitution of a fresh bill after the disbursements had been paid. In *Tearle & Co v Sherring* (29 October 1993, unreported, QBD) 12 Litigation Letter (January 1994) at p78 the court held that it had the power to permit the solicitor to amend the bill without withdrawing it and serving a new bill (and therefore without having to pay the costs thrown away).

A bill once delivered may be withdrawn and a fresh bill delivered with the consent of the client, such consent may be implied where the client applies for taxation of the later bill: *Revzi and Revzi v Brown Cooper (a firm)* [1997] 1 Costs LR 109. Mere errors of arithmetic may be corrected on taxation: *Re Grant, Bulcraig & Co* [1906] 1 Ch 124.

See s 69(2C)(c) as to delivery by electronic etc means, substituted on 7 March 2008.

III SOL [85.7A]

Incorporated practices In relation to the bills of a recognised body, s 69(2) above has effect so that signature must be "on behalf of the recognised body by any officer or employee of the body duly authorised by it to do so".

III SOL [85.8]

County court jurisdiction The county court has a severely limited jurisdiction to deal with taxations under the Solicitors Act. The powers of this section can be applied by a county court only where the amount of the bill does not exceed £5,000 and all or part of the work in respect of which the bill was delivered was carried out in the particular county court. The powers of the court may be exercised by a district judge (see **CPR 2.4**). See also the limited jurisdiction where there is a contentious business agreement under s 61(6) (see para **III SOL 77**).

III SOL [85.9]

Procedure under CPR For proceedings for an order under Part III of the Solicitors Act for the assessment of costs payable to a solicitor by his client see CPR 67.3 in Volume 1 (para **CPR 67.3**) and note that a model claim form is annexed to the Costs Practice Directions.

III SOL [85.10]

Directors' liability for the costs of a company An attempt to make a director liable for the cost of services provided to the limited company failed in *Manches LLP v Carl Freer* [2006] EWHC 991 (QB), [2006] All ER (D) 428 (Nov). The court held that if a director's signature to a legal document was to bind not only his company but the director personally, that intention should be documented by the parties beforehand. Verbal assurances as to payments were likely to be regarded as 'mere statements of comfort'. For discussion see Sol Jo 151 at p 24.

The advice and services in question in this case had been supplied to two companies and the director had not entered into a personal contract of guarantee to pay the costs if the companies failed to do so.

In the case of *Context Drouzhba v Wiseman* [2007] EWCA Civ 1201, [2007] NLJR 1695 the defendant being the active director responsible for the operation of a limited company signed an agreement for payment on behalf of the company knowing it had no funds to make the payment. It was found that the defendant was liable to the claimants in deceit and that the agreement signed constituted a statement in writing for the purposes of s 6 of the Statute of Frauds Amendment Act 1828. The defendant's appeal against the decision was dismissed but the Court of Appeal stressed that each case depended on its own facts ((2008) Times, 8 January, CA).

The decision is of considerable importance. The judgment delivered by Waller LJ is fully reported in [2007] NLJ 30 November at pages 1694-1695.

A detailed consideration of when a director can be said to have 'assumed responsibility' and rendered himself personally liable is provided by *Williams v Natural Life Health Foods Ltd* [1998] 2 All ER 577, [1998] 1 WLR 830, HL (not a case concerning solicitors). The same principles would apply to a member of an LLP. Such cases are described as 'exceptional' in (2012) Sol Jo, 17 April, page 11 by Lucas and Marsh under the heading 'Personal Liability'.

III SOL [85.11]

Lien The general rules as to liens is that they extend to money and other personal chattels that have come into a solicitors possession in the course of his employment in his capacity as a solicitor with the client's agreement.

At common law a solicitor has the right to exercise a lien for unpaid fees but the right may be lost by a failure to comply with rule 2.03(1)(e) of the Solicitors Code of Conduct 2007 which requires the client to be advised that there are circumstances where the right to exercise a lien for unpaid costs arises. The 2007 Code has been replaced by the 2011 Code but that would expect a similar practice to be followed by the solicitor. See further *R (on the application of Malik Law Chambers Solicitors) v Law Society* [2010] EWHC 981 (Admin), [2010] All ER (D) 29 (May) where Saunders J stated that there could be circumstances where it would be unreasonable for a solicitor to exercise his right to a lien and that there was no reason why the Legal Complaints Service should not regulate those circumstances having power to do so under the Solicitors Act 1974, Sch 1A, para 2(1)(d).

For a recent consideration of the limits to the circumstances in which a lien can exist see *Withers LLP v Langbar International Ltd* [2011] EWCA Civ 1419, [2011] All ER (D) 22 (Dec), (2011) NLJ LR, 16 December, page 1742 in which the Court of Appeal reversing the decision of the High Court held that no lien existed over money held in the solicitor's client account. The money was earmarked for a particular purpose and for it to be capable of being the subject of a lien was inconsistent with that purpose.

See also **III SOL [43]** above (penultimate paragraph) as to the survival of the solicitor's lien notwithstanding termination of his retainer by the client.

III SOL [86]

70. Assessment on application of party chargeable or solicitor

(1) Where before the expiration of one month from the delivery of a solicitor's bill an application is made by the party chargeable with the bill, the High Court shall, without requiring any sum to be paid into court, order that the bill be assessed and that no action be commenced on the bill until the assessment is completed.

(2) Where no such application is made before the expiration of the period mentioned in subsection (1), then, on an application being made by the solicitor or, subject to subsections (3) and (4), by the party chargeable with the bill, the court may on such terms, if any, as it thinks fit (not being terms as to the costs of the assessment), order—

(a) that the bill be assessed; and

(b) that no action be commenced on the bill, and that any action already commenced be stayed, until the assessment is completed.

(3) Where an application under subsection (2) is made by the party chargeable with the bill—

(a) after the expiration of 12 months from the delivery of the bill, or

(b) after a judgment has been obtained for the recovery of the costs covered by the bill, or

(c) after the bill has been paid, but before the expiration of 12 months from the payment of the bill,

no order shall be made except in special circumstances and, if an order is made, it may contain such terms as regards the costs of the assessment as the court may think fit.

(4) The power to order assessment conferred by subsection (2) shall not be exercisable on an application made by the party chargeable with the bill after the expiration of 12 months from the payment of the bill.

(5) An order for the assessment of a bill made on an application under this section by the party chargeable with the bill shall, if he so requests, be an order for the assessment of the profit costs covered by the bill.

(6) Subject to subsection (5), the court may under this section order the assessment of all the costs, or of the profit costs, or of the costs other than profit costs and, where part of the costs is not to be assessed, may allow an action to be commenced or to be continued for that part of the costs.

(7) Every order for the assessment of a bill shall require the costs officer to assess not only the bill but also the costs of the assessment and to certify what is due to or by the solicitor in respect of the bill and in respect of the costs of the assessment.

(8) If after due notice of any assessment either party to it fails to attend, the officer may proceed with the assessment ex parte.

(9) Unless—

(a) the order for assessment was made on the application of the solicitor and the party chargeable does not attend the assessment, or

(b) the order for assessment or an order under subsection (10) otherwise provides,

the costs of an assessment shall be paid according to the event of the assessment, that is to say, if the amount of the bill is reduced by one fifth, the solicitor shall pay the costs, but otherwise the party chargeable shall pay the costs.

(10) The costs officer may certify to the court any special circumstances relating to a bill or to the assessment of a bill, and the court may make such order as respects the costs of the assessment as it may think fit.

(11) . . .

(12) In this section "profit costs" means costs other than counsel's fees or costs paid or payable in the discharge of a liability incurred by the solicitor on behalf of the party chargeable, and the reference in subsection (9) to the fraction of the amount of the reduction in the bill shall be taken, where the assessment concerns only part of the costs covered by the bill, as a reference to that fraction of the amount of those costs which is being assessed.

III SOL [86.1]

"The High Court" The powers given by this section may also be exercised by a county court where the amount of the bill does not exceed £5,000 and all or part of the work which is the subject of the bill was carried out in that county court (s 69(3) (see para **III SOL [85]**)). The district judge of a county court may exercise the court's powers under this Act (see para **CPR 2.4**).

In all other cases the assessment must be in the Senior Courts Costs Office.

III SOL [86.2]

Procedure for obtaining an order An application under this section should be made by way of Part 8 claim form (N208) (Precedent J in the Schedule of Costs Precedents in the Practice Direction to CPR 47 (see para **CPR PD 47**) is a model form of claim form) unless it is made in pending proceedings in which case an application under CPR 23 could be made.

Formal defects in a claim form seeking detailed assessment of bills of costs delivered by a solicitor will not prevent it commencing the proceedings if it conveys the message that the client wanted the bills assessed: *Ilana Szekeres v Alan Smeath & Co* [2005] EWHC 1733 (Ch), [2005] 32 LS Gaz R 31.

For the procedure to be followed where the court has made an order under Part III of the Solicitors Act 1974 for the assessment of coasts payable to a solicitor by his client see **CPR 46.10**.

A pilot scheme for a new process for assessing bills of cost began in October 2016 with a view to a new scheme operating from October 2017. See CPR Practice Direction 51L.

III SOL [86.3]

Order See Precedent L in the Schedule of Costs Precedents in the Practice Direction to CPR 47 (see para **CPR PD 47**) for an order for detailed assessment on the application of a client. Precedent M is an order on the solicitor's application. Precedent K is an order for delivery of a bill. These precedents are reproduced in the Forms supplement. Precedent P is of a breakdown of costs. See also Appendix A-8 of the Supreme Court Costs Office Guide in Volume 1 at **CPR 48 COG**.

III SOL [86.4]

Twelve months In protracted proceedings the solicitor may deliver bills from time to time for work done to date. If he makes clear his intention that each should be regarded as a final bill for such work and not simply a request for payment on account each such bill may be treated as a separate bill for the purpose of sub-s (3): *Re Romer & Haslam* [1893] 2 QB 286, CA; *Davidsons (a firm) v Jones-Fenleigh* (1980) 124 Sol Jo 204, (1980) Times, 11 March, [1997] Costs LR 70, CA. If not and the bills form a series, the twelve months runs from the delivery of the last bill. The test is whether there were natural breaks in the work done by the solicitor so that each portion of it could and should be treated as distinct from the rest: *Chamberlain v Boodle and King* [1982] 3 All ER 188, [1982] 1 WLR 1443, CA. The High Court has no power under its inherent jurisdiction over solicitors to order assessment when the twelve months period has elapsed, even if there is alleged to have been overcharging so gross as to amount to fraud or professional misconduct: *Harrison v Tew* [1990] 2 AC 523, [1990] 1 All ER 321, HL.

Section 70(1) of the Act gives an absolute right, to the party chargeable with the bill, to the assessment of it where he makes application within one month of delivery of the bill; see *Holmes v LHC Solicitors* (2011) Sol Jo, page 17. If he makes his application after one but before the expiry of 12 months the court retains a discretion whether to allow a detailed assessment.

Only in 'special circumstances' will an order be made for assessment after the period of 12 months; s 70(3) of the Act. For 'special circumstances' see *Falmouth House Freehold Company Ltd v Morgan Walker LLP* [2010] All ER (D) 1256 (Nov).

A client who no longer has the right to claim assessment of a solicitor's bill of cost under this section because of the twelve months time limit has expired can still challenge the reasonableness of charges claimed: *Palomo SA v Turner & Co* [2000] 1 WLR 37, CA.

III SOL [86.5]

Payment Where a solicitor, without the knowledge or approbation of his client, pays his own bill out of moneys belonging to the client, that does not constitute payment within the meaning of s 70(3), (4): *Forsinard Estates Ltd v Dykes* [1971] 1 All ER 1018, [1971] 1 WLR 232. It may be otherwise if there has been a settled account in writing: *Re Webb* [1894] 1 Ch 73, CA or the client's express assent: *Re David* (1861) 30 Beav 278; *Hitchcock v Stretton* [1892] 2 Ch 343; *Re Baylis* [1896] 2 Ch 107, CA.

III SOL [86.6]

Special circumstances The court must exercise its discretion having regard to all the circumstances of the case (*Re Cheeseman* [1891] 2 Ch 289, CA). They are those which "appear . . . so special and exceptional as to justify taxation" (*Hirst and Capes v Fox* [1908] AC 416, HL). The circumstances may include payment with a reservation of the right to tax (*Sanders v Isaacs* [1971] 1 All ER 755, [1971] 1 WLR 240) although it would appear that though this would be a "highly important factor" it alone may not necessarily be a sufficient circumstance. Mere payment under protest would appear not to be such a circumstance: see *Re Cheeseman* [1891] 2 Ch 289, CA; *Re Warde Bowie & Co* (1910) 102 LT 881 CA. Generally it has been said that the applicant must show particular items of overcharge or that the bill is "redolent of overcharge": *Re Boycott* (1885) 29 Ch D 571, 55 LJCh 835; *Re a Solicitor* [1961] Ch 491, [1961] 2 All ER 321. It is not necessary to show misconduct or fraud: *Re Norman* (1886) 16 QBD 673; *Hirst and Capes v Fox* [1908] AC 416, HL. In *Riley v Dibb Lupton Alsop (a firm)* [1997] NLJR 1422 it was said that "special" circumstances implied something more than "exceptional" circumstances.

In *Falmouth House Freehold Company Ltd v Morgan Walker LLP* [2010] All ER (D) 256 (Nov), (2010) NLJ, 3 December, page 1686 the court stated that whether there were special circumstances justifying a detailed assessment for the purposes of s 70 was a value judgement depending on comparing the particular case with a run of the mill case.

III SOL [86.7]

One fifth taxed off The apparent strictness of this rule is to some extent mitigated by the fact that a taxing master or district judge may now exercise the powers of the court. The costs judge may make the order for detailed assessment – which could include a direction that sub-s (9) should not apply and he may in many cases in effect certify to himself any special circumstances under sub-s (10) and make such order as to costs as may appear appropriate.

In the case where no special order is made if the bill is not reduced by 20% or more the client will be responsible for the costs of the assessment. If there is a reduction of 20% or more the solicitor is responsible.

The scope of 'special circumstances' as a basis for departing from the 20% rule is considered by the Court of Appeal in a number of situations, reported under *Wilson Solicitors LLP v Bentine* [2015] EWCA Civ 1168, [2015] All ER (D) 39 (Dec).

III SOL [86.8]

Gross sum bill Where a gross sum bill is delivered to a client he has a right under s 64(2) (see para **III SOL [80]**) to require the solicitor to deliver a bill containing detailed items and the making of such a request renders the bill of no effect. If no such request is made the gross sum bill will be assessed but the solicitor must furnish the taxing officer with such details of any of the costs covered by the bill as the costs officer may require: sub-s (4).

III SOL [86.9]

Assessment of solicitor and client costs The following provision is made by the CPR:

- **CPR 67.3** as to a claim for an order under Part III of the Solicitors Act 1974
- **CPR 46** 'Costs — Special Cases', Section II

These rules are supplemented by **CPR PD 46**, para 6 (see para **CPR PD 46**) and the pilot scheme at **CPR PD 51L**.

The Schedule of Costs Precedents in the Schedule to **CPR PD 47** contains the following Solicitors Act 1974 precedents:

- **Precedent J** Part 8 claim form under Part III of the Solicitors Act 1974;
- **Precedent K** Order for delivery of bill;
- **Precedent L** Order for detailed assessment (client);
- **Precedent M** Order for detailed assessment (solicitors); and
- **Precedent P** Breakdown of costs.

III SOL [87]

71. Assessment on application of third parties etc

(1) Where a person other than the party chargeable with the bill for the purposes of section 70 has paid, or is or was liable to pay, a bill either to the solicitor or to the party chargeable with the bill, that person, or his executors, administrators or assignees may apply to the High Court for an order for the assessment of the bill as if he were the party chargeable with it, and the court may make the same order (if any) as it might have made if the application had been made by the party chargeable with the bill.

(2) Where the court has no power to make an order by virtue of subsection (1) except in special circumstances it may, in considering whether there are special circumstances sufficient to justify the making of an order, take into account circumstances which affect the applicant but do not affect the party chargeable with the bill.

(3) Where a trustee, executor or administrator has become liable to pay a bill of a solicitor, then, on the application of any person interested in any property out of which the trustee, executor or administrator has paid, or is entitled to pay, the bill, the court may order—

- (a) that the bill be assessed on such terms, if any, as it thinks fit; and
- (b) that such payments, in respect of the amount found to be due to or by the solicitor and in respect of the costs of the assessment, be made to or by the applicant, to or by the solicitor, or to or by the executor, administrator or trustee, as it thinks fit.

(4) In considering any application under subsection (3) the court shall have regard—

- (a) to the provisions of section 70 as to applications by the party chargeable for the assessment of a solicitor's bill so far as they are capable of being applied to an application made under that subsection;
- (b) to the extent and nature of the interest of the applicant.

(5) If an applicant under subsection (3) pays any money to the solicitor, he shall have the same right to be paid that money by the trustee, executor or administrator chargeable with the bill as the solicitor had.

(6) Except in special circumstances, no order shall be made on an application under this section for the assessment of a bill which has already been assessed.

(7) If the court on an application under this section orders a bill to be assessed, it may order the solicitor to deliver to the applicant a copy of the bill on payment of the costs of that copy.

SOLICITORS

III SOL [87.1]

"assessment" See para **III SOL [76.2]**.

III SOL [87.2]

"The High Court" The powers given by this section may also be exercised by a county court where the amount of the bill does not exceed £5,000 and all or part of the work which is the subject of the bill was carried out in that county court (s 69(3) (see para **III SOL [85]**)). The district judge of a county court may exercise the court's powers under this Act (see para **CPR 2.4**).

III SOL [87.3]

Application out of time Subsection (1) imports into itself sub-s (4) as well as sub-s (3) of s 70 (see para **III SOL [86]**): *Forsinard Estates Ltd v Dykes* [1971] 1 All ER 1018, [1971] 1 WLR 232. Similarly, sub-s (2) incorporates, as respects trustees, executors and administrators, the provisions as to special circumstances in s 70(3) (see para **III SOL [86]**): *Sanders v Isaacs* [1971] 1 All ER 755, [1971] 1 WLR 240. Where the client has paid the solicitor's bill, a third party is not entitled to have a detailed assessment unless he can show special circumstances: *Re Wellbourne* [1901] 1 Ch 312, CA.

III SOL [87.3A]

Procedure The non-party will apply by claim form under Part 8 unless the application is made in pending proceedings; see CPR 67 in Volume 1 (para **CPR 67**). If the proceedings are pending the court is likely to require the applicant to make himself a party for the purpose only of the assessment before it will allow him to make an application pursuant to CPR 23 on form N244. The Part 8 claim form can be drafted by amending Precedent J in the Schedule of Costs Precedents (see para **CPR PD 47**) and then the procedure will follow CPR 46.10, supplemented by CPR PD 46, para 6. It should be noted that Practice Direction 46, para 6 provides that "client" includes any person entitled to make application under Part III of the Solicitors Act 1974.

III SOL [87.3B]

Person other than party chargeable Where a person not chargeable with a bill decides to pay it, he is entitled to have the bill assessed in the same way as the party chargeable would have been if the latter was paying the bill himself. Similarly if the person is required to pay the costs of the party chargeable, for example, where the terms of a lease require a tenant to pay the landlord's solicitor's costs incurred when giving permission to assign the lease.

III SOL [87.4]

Inherent jurisdiction The inherent jurisdiction of the High Court over solicitors does not enable a party to have assessment of the bill of the solicitor of another: *Forsinard Estates Ltd v Dykes* [1971] 1 All ER 1018, [1971] 1 WLR 232. However, sub-s (1) does not presuppose a relationship of solicitor and client between the applicant and the solicitor whose fees are in question. It applies for example, where as part of a settlement one party agrees to pay a specific sum for the other party's costs, although in the exercise of its discretion on the facts the court may decline to order a detailed assessment: *Ingrams v Sykes* [1987] NLJ Rep 1135, CA.

III SOL [88]

72. Supplementary provisions as to assessments

(1) Every application for an order for the assessment of a solicitor's bill or for the delivery of a solicitor's bill and for the delivery up by a solicitor of any documents in his possession, custody or power shall be made in the matter of that solicitor.

(2) Where a costs officer is in the course of assessing a bill of costs, he may request the costs officer of any other court to assist him in assessing any part of the bill, and the costs officer so requested shall assess that part of the bill and shall return the bill with his opinion on it to the costs officer making the request.

(3) Where a request is made as mentioned in subsection (2), the costs officer who is requested to assess part of a bill shall have such powers, and may take such fees, in respect of that part of the bill, as he would have or be entitled to take if he were assessing that part of the bill in pursuance of an order of the court of which he is an officer; and the costs officer who made the request shall not take any fee in respect of that part of the bill.

(4) The certificate of the costs officer by whom any bill has been assessed shall, unless it is set aside or altered by the court, be final as to the amount of the costs covered by it, and the court may make such order in relation to the certificate as it thinks fit, including, in a case where the retainer is not disputed, an order that judgment be entered for the sum certified to be due with costs.

III SOL [89]

73. Charging orders

(1) Subject to subsection (2), any court in which a solicitor has been employed to prosecute or defend any suit, matter or proceedings may at any time—

- (a) declare the solicitor entitled to a charge on any property recovered or preserved through his instrumentality for his assessed costs in relation to that suit, matter or proceeding; and
- (b) make such orders for the assessment of those costs and for raising money to pay or for paying them out of the property recovered or preserved as the court thinks fit;

and all conveyances and acts done to defeat, or operating to defeat, that charge shall, except in the case of a conveyance to a bona fide purchaser for value without notice, be void as against the solicitor.

(2) No order shall be made under subsection (1) if the right to recover the costs is barred by any statute of limitations.

III SOL [89.1]

Procedure The jurisdiction under the Solicitors Act is in addition to that under the Charging Orders Act 1979 (as to which see CPR 73 at para **CPR 73**). A Charging Order under the 1979 Act requires a judgment whereas under the Solicitors Act requires only the conditions in sub-s (1) be met (*Harris v Yarm* [1960] Ch 256). The proceedings being under Part III of the Solicitors Act the procedural requirements for making the application are those set out in **CPR 67.3**. It must be made by Part 8 claim form or if in existing proceedings by Part 23 application. An application for an interim charge may be made without giving notice.

The application should, if reasonably possible, be made to the judge who tried the action. The application should be made in chambers. A county court has jurisdiction where the solicitor's remuneration is in respect of contentious business done in that court.

For a precedent see **BCCP E[3005]**.

III SOL [89.2]

Property recovered or preserved The question of what property has been "recovered or preserved" must be determined as a matter of fact by the court taking into account the nature of the litigation: *White v Hyde* [1933] P 105, *sub nom Re White* 49 TLR 325. A charging order has been made against costs recoverable by a client dormant company even though there is no order for taxation of the costs and there has been no detailed assessment: *Fairfold Properties Ltd v Exmouth Docks Co Ltd (No 2)* [1993] Ch 196, [1992] 4 All ER 289.

III SOL [89.3]

Joint property In a case where the client has a beneficial interest under a declaration of trust which the solicitor has prepared that interest may be charged. But the creditor may not enforce it by orders for sale or possession where the beneficial interest under the trust is discretionary and therefore a defeasible interest: *Skyparks Group plc v Marks* [2001] EWCA Civ 319, [2001] All ER (D) 102 (Mar).

III SOL [89.4]

Rights under s 73 exercisable despite taking security The rights under s 73 are not lost by taking security unless such steps are inconsistent with the rights under s 73 continuing: *Clifford Harris & Co v Solland International* [2005] EWHC 141 (Ch), [2005] 2 All ER 334.

III SOL [90]

74. Special provisions as to contentious business done in county courts

(1) The remuneration of a solicitor in respect of contentious business done by him in the county court shall be regulated in accordance with sections 59 to 73, and for that purpose those sections shall have effect subject to the following provisions of this section.

(2) The district judge of a county court shall be the costs officer of that court but any assessment of costs by him may be reviewed by a judge assigned to the county court district, or by a judge acting as a judge so assigned, on the application of any party to the assessment.

(3) The amount which may be allowed on the assessment of any costs or bill of costs in respect of any item relating to proceedings in the county court shall not, except in so far as rules of court may otherwise provide, exceed the amount which could have been allowed in respect of that item as between party and party in those proceedings, having regard to the nature of the proceedings and the amount of the claim and of any counterclaim.

III SOL [90.1]

Jurisdiction As to the limited jurisdiction see the notes to s 70 at para **III SOL [86.1]**.

SOLICITORS

III SOL [90.2]

"costs judge", "costs officer" See para **III SOL [77.2]**.

III SOL [90.3]

Assessment as between solicitor and own client CPR 46.9(2) (see para **CPR 46.9**) "otherwise provides" for the purpose of ss (3) where there is a written agreement expressly permitting payment to a solicitor of greater costs than the client could have recovered from the other party to the proceedings. The effect of the limitation is reduced by the fact that the subsection refers to "the amount which could have been allowed" and this takes into account the discretion of the costs officer under CPR 44.2 (see para **CPR 44.2**) and CPR 44.4 (see para **CPR 44.4**) where the business conducted is contentious.

See also *Lynch (Jane Sarah)v Paul Davidson Taylor (a firm)* [2004] EWHC 89 (QB), [2004] 1 WLR 1753 where the claimant succeeded in her claim but her costs were reduced on assessment from £7,600 to £3,000. She argued her solicitors could only recover £3,000 from her because of s 74(3). The court rejected the argument.

See CPR 44.3 for the basis of assessment.

III SOL [91]

87. Interpretation

(1) In this Act, except where the context otherwise requires—

. . .

"bank" means the Bank of England, a person (other than a building society) who has permission under Part 4A of the Financial Services and Markets Act 2000 to accept deposits or an EEA firm of the kind mentioned in paragraph 5(b) of Schedule 3 to that Act which has permission under paragraph 15 of that Schedule (as a result of qualifying for authorisation under paragraph 12 of that Schedule) to accept deposits;

"building society" means a building society within the meaning of the Building Societies Act 1986 . . . .

"the Charter" means the Royal Charter dated 26th February 1845, whereby the Society was incorporated, together with the Royal Charters supplemental to it dated respectively 26th November 1872, 4th June 1903, 2nd June 1909 and 10th March 1954;

"client" includes—

(a) in relation to contentious business, any person who as a principal or on behalf of another person retains or employs, or is about to retain or employ, a solicitor, and any person who is or may be liable to pay a solicitor's costs;

(b) in relation to non-contentious business, any person who, as a principal or on behalf of another, or as a trustee or executor, or in any other capacity, has power, express or implied, to retain or employ, and retains or employs or is about to retain or employ, a solicitor, and any person for the time being liable to pay to a solicitor for his services any costs;

"client account" means an account subject to rules under section 32(1)(a);

"contentious business" means business done, whether as solicitor or advocate, in or for the purposes of proceedings begun before a court or before an arbitrator . . . , not being business which falls within the definition of non-contentious or common form probate business contained in section 128 of the Senior Courts Act 1981;

"contentious business agreement" means an agreement made in pursuance of section 59;

. . .

"costs" includes fees, charges, disbursements, expenses and remuneration;

"the Council" means the Council of the Society elected in accordance with the provisions of the Charter and this Act;

. . .

"indemnity rules" means rules under section 37;

. . .

"local law society" means a society which is for the time being recognised by the Council as representative of solicitors in some particular part of England and Wales;

"non-contentious business" means any business done as a solicitor which is not contentious business as defined by this subsection;

"officer", in relation to a limited liability partnership, means a member of the limited liability partnership;

. . .

"practising certificate" has the meaning assigned to it by section 1;

. . .

"the roll" means the list of solicitors of the Senior Courts kept by the Society under section 6;

"Secretary" of the Society includes any deputy or person appointed temporarily to perform the duties of that office;

"the Society" means the Law Society, that is to say, the Society incorporated and regulated by the Charter;

"sole solicitor" means a solicitor who is the sole principal in a practice;

"sole solicitor endorsement" has the same meaning as in section 1B;

"solicitor" means solicitor of the Senior Courts;

"solicitor in Scotland" means a person enrolled or deemed to have been enrolled as a solicitor in pursuance of the Solicitors (Scotland) Act 1933;

. . .

"training regulations" means regulations under section 2;

"the Tribunal" means the Solicitors Disciplinary Tribunal;

"trust" includes an implied or constructive trust and a trust where the trustee has a beneficial interest in the trust property, and also includes the duties incident to the office of a personal representative, and "trustee" shall be construed accordingly;

"unqualified person" means a person who is not qualified under section 1 to act as a solicitor.

(1A) In this Act "authorised insurer" means—

(a) a person who has permission under *Part 4* [Part 4A] of the Financial Services and Markets Act 2000 to effect or carry out contracts of insurance of a relevant class;

(b) a person who carries on an insurance market activity, within the meaning of section 316(3) of that Act;

(c) an EEA firm of the kind mentioned in paragraph 5(d) of Schedule 3 to that Act, which has permission under paragraph 15 of that Schedule (as a result of qualifying for authorisation under paragraph 12 of that Schedule) to effect or carry out contracts of insurance of a relevant class; or

(d) a person who does not fall within paragraph (a), (b) or (c) and who may lawfully effect or carry out contracts of insurance of a relevant class in a member state other than the United Kingdom.

(1B) A contract of insurance is of a relevant class for the purposes of subsection (1A) if it insures against risks arising from—

(a) accident;

(b) credit;

(c) legal expenses;

(d) general liability to third parties;

(e) sickness;

(f) suretyship;

SOLICITORS

(g) miscellaneous financial loss.

(1C) The definition of "bank" in subsection (1) and subsections (1A) and (1B) must be read with—

(a) section 22 of the Financial Services and Markets Act 2000;

(b) any relevant order under that section; and

(c) Schedule 2 to that Act.

(2) In this Act—

(a) references to the removal of a solicitor's name from the roll are references to its removal at his own request or in pursuance of regulations under section 28(3A);

(b) references to striking a solicitor's name off the roll are references to striking it off as a disciplinary sanction; and

(c) references to removal or striking off include references to deleting an entry made by means of a computer by whatever means are appropriate.

(3) In this Act, except where otherwise indicated—

(a) a reference to a numbered Part, section or Schedule is a reference to the Part or section of, or the Schedule to, this Act so numbered;

(b) a reference in a section to a numbered subsection is a reference to the subsection of that section so numbered;

(c) a reference in a section, subsection or Schedule to a numbered paragraph is a reference to the paragraph of that section, subsection or Schedule so numbered; and

(d) a reference in a paragraph to a numbered sub-paragraph is a reference to the sub-paragraph of that paragraph so numbered.

(4) Except where the context otherwise requires, references in this Act to any enactment shall be construed as references to that enactment as amended or applied by or under any other enactment, including this Act.

Amendment *Text in italic is deleted and text in square brackets is inserted by the Financial Services Act 2012 with effect from a date to be appointed.*

III SOL [91.1]

Contentious business See para **III SOL [75.1]**.

III SOL [91.2]

"Client" See further *Three Rivers District Council v Governor and Company of the Bank of England (No 5)* (2003) Times, 19 April, CA for consideration of the relationship between solicitor and client and the limits of solicitor advice privilege. In the appeal of the Court of Appeal decision in *Three Rivers (No 6)* the House of Lords declined to clarify who constitutes a client: *Three Rivers District Council v Governor and Company of the Bank of England (No 6)* (2004) Times, 12 November, HL. See also (2004) Law Society Gazette, 18 November at p 1. More recently on the question of professional privilege see *National Westminster Bank plc v Radobank Nederland* [2006] EWHC 2332 (Comm), [2006] All ER (D) 11 (Oct).

III SOL [92]

88. Saving for solicitors to public departments and City of London

(1) Nothing in this Act shall prejudice or affect any rights or privileges of the solicitor to the Treasury, any other public department, the Church Commissioners or the Duchy of Cornwall, or require any such officer or any clerk or officer appointed to act for him to be admitted or enrolled or to hold a practising certificate in any case where it would not have been necessary for him to be admitted or enrolled or to hold such a certificate if this Act had not been passed.

(1A) The exemption from the requirement to hold a practising certificate conferred by subsection (1) above shall not apply to solicitors who are Crown Prosecutors.

(2) Sections 31 and 32 (1) shall not apply to, and nothing in this Act shall prejudice or affect any rights or privileges which immediately before the commencement of this Act attached to the office of, the Solicitor of the City of London.

Schedules

SCHEDULE 1
INTERVENTION IN SOLICITOR'S PRACTICE*

PART I
CIRCUMSTANCES IN WHICH THE SOCIETY MAY INTERVENE

III SOL [93]

1. (1) Subject to sub-paragraph (2), the powers conferred by Part II of this Schedule shall be exercisable where—
   (a) the Society has reason to suspect dishonesty on the part of—
      (i) a solicitor, or
      (ii) an employee of a solicitor, or
      (iii) the personal representatives of a deceased solicitor,

   in connection with that solicitor's practice or former practice or in connection with any trust of which that solicitor is or formerly was a trustee or that employee is or was a trustee in his capacity as such an employee;
   (aa) the Society has reason to suspect dishonesty on the part of a solicitor ("S") in connection with—
      (i) the business of any person of whom S is or was an employee, or of any body of which S is or was a manager, or
      (ii) any business which is or was carried on by S as a sole trader;
   (b) the Society considers that there has been undue delay on the part of the personal representatives of a deceased solicitor who immediately before his death was practising as a sole solicitor in connection with that solicitor's practice or in connection with any *controlled trust* [trust];
   (c) the Society is satisfied that a solicitor has failed to comply with rules made by virtue of section 31, 32 or 37(2)(c);
   (d) a solicitor has been adjudged bankrupt or has made a composition or arrangement with his creditors;
   (e) a solicitor has been committed to prison in any civil or criminal proceedings;
   (ee) the Society is satisfied that a sole solicitor is incapacitated by illness, injury or accident to such an extent as to be unable to attend to his practice;
   (f) a solicitor lacks capacity (within the meaning of the Mental Capacity Act 2005) to act as a solicitor and powers under sections 15 to 20 or section 48 of that Act are exercisable in relation to him; or
   (g) the name of a solicitor has been removed from or struck off the roll or a solicitor has been suspended from practice;
   (h) the Society is satisfied that a solicitor has abandoned his practice;
   (i) the Society is satisfied that a sole solicitor is incapacitated by age to such an extent as to be unable to attend to his practice;
   (j) any power conferred by this Schedule has been exercised in relation to a sole solicitor by virtue of sub-paragraph (1)(a) and he has acted as a sole solicitor within the period of eighteen months beginning with the date on which it was so exercised;

SOLICITORS

(k) the Society is satisfied that a person has acted as a solicitor at a time when he did not have a practising certificate which was in force;

(l) the Society is satisfied that a solicitor has failed to comply with any condition, subject to which his practising certificate was granted or otherwise has effect, to the effect that he may act as a solicitor only—

(i) in employment which is approved by the Society in connection with the imposition of that condition;

(ii) as a member of a partnership which is so approved;

(iii) as a manager of a body recognised by the Society under section 9 of the Administration of Justice Act 1985 and so approved; or

(iv) in any specified combination of those ways;]

(m) the Society is satisfied that it is necessary to exercise the powers conferred by Part 2 of this Schedule (or any of them) in relation to a solicitor to protect—

(i) the interests of clients (or former or potential clients) of the solicitor or his firm, or

(ii) the interests of the beneficiaries of any trust of which the solicitor is or was a trustee.

(1A) In sub-paragraph (1) "manager" has the same meaning as in the Legal Services Act 2007 (see section 207 of that Act).

(2) . . .

2 On the death of a sole solicitor paragraphs 6 to 8 shall apply to the client accounts of his practice.

3 The powers conferred by Part II of this Schedule shall also be exercisable, subject to paragraphs 5(4) and 10(9), where—

(a) the Society is satisfied that there has been undue delay—

(i) on the part of a solicitor in connection with any matter in which the solicitor or his firm is or was acting on behalf of a client or with any trust, or

(ii) on the part of an employee of a solicitor in connection with any trust of which the employee is or was a trustee in his capacity as such an employee; and

(b) the Society by notice in writing invites the solicitor to give an explanation within a period of not less than 8 days specified in the notice; and

(c) the solicitor fails within that period to give an explanation which the Society regards as satisfactory; and

(d) the Society gives notice of the failure to the solicitor and (at the same or any later time) notice that the powers conferred by Part II of this Schedule are accordingly exercisable.

4 (1) Where the powers conferred by Part II of this Schedule are exercisable in relation to a solicitor, they shall continue to be exercisable after his death or after his name has been removed from or struck off the roll.

(2) The references to the solicitor or his firm in paragraphs 5(1), 6(2) and (3), 6A, 8, 9(1), (5) and (6) and 10(2) and (7) include, in any case where the solicitor has died, references to his personal representatives.

PART II
POWERS EXERCISABLE ON INTERVENTION

MONEY

III SOL [94]

5 (1) The High Court, on the application of the Society, may order that no payment shall be made without the leave of the court by any person (whether or not named in the order) of any money held by him (in whatever manner and whether it was received before or after the making of the order) on behalf of the solicitor or his firm.

(2) No order under this paragraph shall take effect in relation to any person to whom it applies unless the Society has served a copy of the order on him (whether or not he is named in it) and, in the case of a bank [or other financial institution], has indicated at which of its branches the Society believes that the money to which the order relates is held.

(3) A person shall not be treated as having disobeyed an order under this paragraph by making a payment of money if he satisfies the court that he exercised due diligence to ascertain whether it was money to which the order related but nevertheless failed to ascertain that the order related to it.

(4) This paragraph does not apply where the powers conferred by this Part of this Schedule are exercisable by virtue of paragraph 3.

6 (1) Without prejudice to paragraph 5, if the Society passes a resolution to the effect that any sums of money to which this paragraph applies, and the right to recover or receive them, shall vest in the Society, all such sums shall vest accordingly (whether they were received by the person holding them before or after the Society's resolution) and shall be held by the Society on trust to exercise in relation to them the powers conferred by this Part of this Schedule and subject thereto and to rules under paragraph 6B upon trust for the persons beneficially entitled to them.

(2) This paragraph applies—

(a) where the powers conferred by this paragraph are exercisable by virtue of paragraph 1, to all sums of money held by or on behalf of the solicitor or his firm in connection with

(i) his practice or former practice,

(ii) any trust of which he is or formerly was a trustee, or

(iii) any trust of which a person who is or was an employee of the solicitor is or was a trustee in the person's capacity as such an employee;

(b) where they are exercisable by virtue of paragraph 2, to all sums of money in any client account; and

(c) where they are exercisable by virtue of paragraph 3, to all sums of money held by or on behalf of the solicitor or his firm in connection with the trust or other matter in connection with which the Society is satisfied there has been undue delay as mentioned in sub-paragraph (a) of that paragraph.

(3) The Society shall serve on the solicitor or his firm and on any other person having possession of sums of money to which this paragraph applies a certified copy of the Council's resolution and a notice prohibiting the payment out of any such sums of money.

(4) Within 8 days of the service of a notice under sub-paragraph (3), the person on whom it was served, on giving not less than 48 hours' notice in writing to the Society and (if the notice gives the name of the solicitor instructed by the Society) to that solicitor, may apply to the High Court for an order directing the Society to withdraw the notice.

SOLICITORS

(5) If the court makes such an order, it shall have power also to make such other order with respect to the matter as it may think fit.

(6) If any person on whom a notice has been served under sub-paragraph (3) pays out sums of money at a time when such payment is prohibited by the notice, he shall be guilty of an offence and liable on summary conviction to a fine not exceeding level 3 on the standard scale.

6A (1) Without prejudice to paragraph 5, if the Society passes a resolution to the effect that any rights to which this paragraph applies shall vest in the Society, those rights shall vest accordingly.

(2) This paragraph applies to any right to recover or receive debts due to the solicitor or his firm in connection with his practice or former practice.

(3) Any sums recovered by the Society by virtue of the exercise of rights vested under sub-paragraph (1) shall vest in the Society and shall be held by it on trust to exercise in relation to them the powers conferred by this Part of this Schedule and, subject to those powers and to rules under paragraph 6B, upon trust for the persons beneficially entitled to them.

(4) The Society shall serve on the solicitor or his firm, and any person who owes a debt to which the order applies, a certified copy of the Society's resolution.

6B (1) The Society may make rules governing its treatment of sums vested in it under paragraph 6 or 6A(3).

(2) The rules may in particular make provision in respect of cases where the Society, having taken such steps to do so as are reasonable in all the circumstances of the case, is unable to trace the person or persons beneficially entitled to any sum vested in the Society under paragraph 6 or 6A(3) (including provision which requires amounts to be paid into or out of compensation funds (within the meaning of section 36A)).

7 (1) If the Society takes possession of any sum of money to which paragraph 6 or 6A(3) applies, the Society shall pay it into a special account in the name of the Society or of a person nominated on behalf of the Society, or into a client account of a solicitor nominated on behalf of the Society, and any such person or solicitor shall hold that sum on trust to permit the Society to exercise in relation to it the powers conferred by this Part of this Schedule and subject thereto and to rules under paragraph 6B on trust for the persons beneficially entitled to it.

(2) A bank or other financial institution at which a special account is kept shall be under no obligation to ascertain whether it is being dealt with properly.

8 Without prejudice to paragraphs 5 to 7, if the High Court is satisfied, on an application by the Society, that there is reason to suspect that any person

(a) holds money on behalf of the solicitor or his firm, or

(b) has information which is relevant to identifying any money held by or on behalf of the solicitor or his firm,

the court may require that person to give the Society information as to any such money and the accounts in which it is held.

Documents

9 (1) The Society may give notice to the solicitor or his firm requiring the production or delivery to any person appointed by the Society at a time and place to be fixed by the Society—

(a) where the powers conferred by this Part of this Schedule are exercisable by virtue of paragraph 1, of all documents in the possession or under the control of the solicitor or his firm in connection with his practice or former practice or with any trust of which the solicitor is or was a trustee; and

(b) where they are exercisable by virtue of paragraph 3, of all documents in the possession or under the control of the solicitor or his firm in connection with the trust or other matters *to* of which the Society is satisfied (whether or not they relate also to other matters).

(2) The person appointed by the Society may take possession of any such documents on behalf of the Society.

(3) Except in a case where an application has been made to the High Court under sub-paragraph (4), if any person having possession or control of any such documents refuses, neglects or otherwise fails to comply with a requirement under sub-paragraph (1), he shall be guilty of an offence and liable on summary conviction to a fine not exceeding level 3 on the standard scale.

(4) The High Court, on the application of the Society, may order a person required to produce or deliver documents under sub-paragraph (1) to produce or deliver them to any person appointed by the Society at such time and place as may be specified in the order, and authorise him to take possession of them on behalf of the Society.

(5) If on an application by the Society the High Court is satisfied that there is reason to suspect that documents in relation to which the powers conferred by sub-paragraph (1) are exercisable have come into the possession or under the control of some person other than the solicitor or his firm, the court may order that person to produce or deliver the documents to any person appointed by the Society at such time and place as may be specified in the order and authorise him to take possession of them on behalf of the Society.

(5A) In the case of a document which consists of information which is stored in electronic form, a requirement imposed by a notice under sub-paragraph (1) or an order under sub-paragraph (4) or (5), is a requirement to produce or deliver the information in a form in which it is legible or from which it can readily be produced in a legible form.

(6) On making an order under this paragraph, or at any later time, the court, on the application of the Society, may authorise a person appointed by the Society to enter any premises (using such force as is reasonably necessary) to search for and take possession of—

(a) any documents to which the order relates;

(b) any property—

(i) in the possession of or under the control of the solicitor or his firm, or

(ii) in the case of an order under sub-paragraph (5), which was in the possession or under the control of such a person and has come into the possession or under the control of the person in respect of whom the order is made,

which the Society reasonably requires for the purpose of accessing information contained in such documents, and to use property obtained under paragraph (b) for that purpose.

(7) The Society, on taking possession of any documents or other property under this paragraph, shall serve upon the solicitor or personal representatives and upon any other person from whom they were received on the Society's behalf or from whose premises they were taken a notice that possession has been taken on the date specified in the notice.

(8) Subject to sub-paragraph (9) a person upon whom a notice under sub-paragraph (7) is served, on giving not less than 48 hours notice to the Society and (if the notice gives the name of the solicitor instructed by the Society) to that solicitor, may apply to the High Court for an order directing the Society to deliver the documents or other property to such person as the applicant may require.

(9) A notice under sub-paragraph (8) shall be given within 8 days of the service of the Society's notice under sub-paragraph (7).

(10) Without prejudice to the foregoing provisions of this Schedule, the Society may apply to the High Court for an order as to the disposal or destruction of any documents or other property in its possession by virtue of this paragraph or paragraph 10.

(11) On an application under sub-paragraph (8) or (10), the Court may make such order as it thinks fit.

(12) Except so far as its right to do so may be restricted by an order on an application under sub-paragraph (8) or (10), the Society may take copies of or extracts from any documents in its possession by virtue of this paragraph or paragraph 10 and require any person to whom it is proposed that such documents shall be delivered, as a condition precedent to delivery, to give a reasonable undertaking to supply copies or extracts to the Society.

Mail and other forms of communication

10 (1) The High Court, on the application of the Society, may from time to time make a communications redirection order.

(2) A communications redirection order is an order that specified communications to the solicitor or his firm are to be directed, in accordance with the order, to the Society or any person appointed by the Society.

(3) For the purposes of this paragraph—

- (a) "specified communications" means communications of such description as are specified in the order;
- (b) the descriptions of communications which may be so specified include—
  - (i) communications in the form of a postal packet;
  - (ii) electronic communications;
  - (iii) communications by telephone.

(4) A communications redirection order has effect for such time not exceeding 18 months as is specified in the order.

(5) Where a communications redirection order has effect, the Society or the person appointed by the Society may take possession or receipt of the communications redirected in accordance with the order.

(6) Where a communications redirection order is made, the Society must pay to—

- (a) in the case of an order relating to postal packets, the postal operator concerned, and
- (b) in any other case, the person specified in the order,

the like charges (if any) as would have been payable for the redirection of the communications to which the order relates if the addressee had permanently ceased to occupy or use the premises or other destination of the communications and had applied to the postal operator or the specified person (as the case may be) to redirect the communications to him as mentioned in the order.

(7) The High Court may, on the application of the Society, authorise the Society, or a person appointed by it, to take such steps as may be specified in the order in relation to any website purporting to be or have been maintained by or on behalf of the solicitor or his firm if the High Court is satisfied that the taking of those steps is necessary to protect the public interest or the interests of clients (or potential or former clients) of the solicitor or his firm.

(8) In this paragraph "postal operator" and "postal packet" have the meaning given by section 27 of the Postal Services Act 2011.

(9) This paragraph does not apply where the powers conferred by this Part of this Schedule are exercisable by virtue of paragraph 3.

Trusts

11 (1) If the solicitor or his personal representative is a trustee of a trust, the Society may apply to the High Court for an order for the appointment of a new trustee in substitution for him.

(2) The Trustee Act 1925 shall have effect in relation to an appointment of a new trustee under this paragraph as it has effect in relation to an appointment under section 41 of that Act.

General

12 The powers in relation to sums of money, documents and other property conferred by this Part of this Schedule shall be exercisable notwithstanding any lien on them or right to their possession.

13 Subject to any order for the payment of costs that may be made on an application to the court under this Schedule, any costs incurred by the Society for the purposes of this Schedule, including, without prejudice to the generality of this paragraph, the costs of any person exercising powers under this Part of this Schedule on behalf of the Society, shall be paid by the Solicitor or his personal representatives and shall be recoverable from him or them as a debt owing to the Society.

13A (1) The High Court, on the application of the Society, may order a former partner of the solicitor to pay a specified proportion of the costs mentioned in paragraph 13.

(2) The High Court may make an order under this paragraph only if it is satisfied that the conduct (or any part of the conduct) by reason of which the powers conferred by this Part were exercisable in relation to the solicitor was conduct carried on with the consent or connivance of, or was attributable to any neglect on the part of, the former partner.

(3) In this paragraph "specified" means specified in the order made by the High Court.

14 Where an offence under this Schedule committed by a body corporate is proved to have been committed with the consent or connivance of, or to be attributable to any neglect on the part of, any director, manager, secretary or other similar officer of the body corporate or any person who was purporting to act in any such capacity, he, as well as the body corporate, shall be guilty of that offence and shall be liable to be proceeded against and punished accordingly.

15 Any application to the High Court under this Schedule may be disposed of in chambers.

16 The Society may do all things which are reasonably necessary for the purpose of facilitating the exercise of its powers under this Schedule.

III SOL [94.1]

Procedure The procedure for applications under the Schedule is set out in CPR 67.4 (para **CPR 67.4**).

See also **III SOL [65]** *et seq* above.

III SOL [94.2]

Powers of intervention The powers of intervention held by the Law Society are exercised now by the SRA. It is not a pre-requisite to the exercise of the power under s 35 and Sch 1 that there should be on-going dishonesty – see *Penna v Law Society* (1999) Times, 29 June and *Bultitude v Law Society* (2005) Times, 14 January, CA – but if the intervention is based on dishonesty and there were not sufficient reasons to suspect it see *Sheikh v Law Society* [2005] EWHC 1409 (Ch), [2005] 4 All ER 717, [2005] NLJR 1095, Park J where the notice of intervention was withdrawn by the court. The decision was however reversed by the Court of

Appeal [2006] EWCA Civ 1577, [2007] 3 All ER 183, (2006) Times, 1 December having regard to the solicitor's past record which was held to be 'plainly relevant'. The Court was however critical of the very general reasons for intervention given to solicitors and Chadwick LJ called on the Society to consider the need for 'much more specificity'.

For the exercise of intervention powers in relation to a registered foreign lawyer and the practice of a multi-national partnership, see para 5 of Sch 14 to the Courts and Legal Services Act 1990.

For the exercise of intervention powers in relation to a "recognised body", see paras 32–35 of Sch 2 to the Administration of Justice Act 1985.

On intervention the SRA has powers and duties under statutory trust which are not the same as under a private trust: *Re Ahmed & Co (a firm)* [2006] EWHC 480 (Ch), [2006] NLJR 512. The statutory trusts have been held to apply to all moneys held by a solicitor in connection with his practice, although the practice was carried on within a limited partnership: *Williams v Law Society of England and Wales* (2015) Times, 16 September, Ch D.

As to the question of whether intervention in a solicitor's practice breaches the human right to peaceful enjoyment of his possessions see *Holder v Law Society* [2003] EWCA Civ 39, [2003] 3 All ER 62 where it was accepted that a fair balance needed to be struck (ie a proportionate response) in cases of intervention but the appeal of the Law Society, against a decision that the intervention had been contrary to the Human Rights Act 1998, was allowed. It is nevertheless open to a solicitor to claim his human rights have been breached on the facts of his particular case.

A solicitor cannot claim for a breach of a private duty of care against the Council of the Law Society arising from the conduct of an accountant appointed by it to inspect the solicitor's books: *Miller v Law Society* [2002] EWHC 1453 (Ch), [2002] 4 All ER 312.

In *Sheikh v Law Society* [2006] EWCA Civ 1577, [2007] 3 All ER 183, [2006] NLJR 1846, see above, the lengthy judgment of Chadwick LJ provides a detailed consideration of the nature of the court's jurisdiction in such intervention cases.

III SOL [94.3]

Rights and duties on intervention The SRA will appoint as its agent in the intervention a solicitor, who is a member of its investigation panel, to take responsibility for the client files. The agent does not take over or run the practice but a letter will be sent to each client informing him of the intervention and asking him to appoint a new solicitor to take over his files.

In *Dooley v Law Society* [2001] NLJR 1768, it was held that money was vested in the Law Society in accordance with para 6(1), if it was held by the solicitor at the date of the resolution or while the resolution was in force. The solicitor was not allowed either to deduct disbursements from such money or to deal with the debts before payment so as to undermine the protection of clients. On the other hand, the right of recovery still vested in the solicitor and the society might use its powers under para 16 to allow agreed disbursements to be deducted.

Whether or not there has been an intervention, if a solicitor misappropriates client's money and the SRA resolves to compensate the client, the time for recovering the compensation from the solicitor runs from the date of the resolution, not the earlier date of the misappropriation or the Law Society's knowledge of it: *Law Society v Sephton & Co (a Firm)* [2004] EWCA Civ 1627, (2005) Times, 11 January upheld in *Law Society v Sephton & Co* [2006] UKHL 22, [2006] 3 All ER 401.

See also SRA Intervention Powers (Statutory Trust) Rules 2011.

III SOL [94.3A]

Court's powers on an application under paragraph 6(4) When the SRA intervenes in a solicitor's practice it is entitled to recover the costs of so doing; para 13, Schedule 1 to the Solicitors act 1974. For a case where the solicitor challenged that entitlement see *Gauntlett v Law Society* [2006] EWHC 1954 (Ch), [2006] AlL ER (D) 420 (Jul).

On an application under paragraph 6(4) the court has power to make "such other order respecting the matter as it may think fit". But this does include the restoration of a practising certificate except on the withdrawal, or setting aside, of the intervention notice: *Sritharan v Law Society* [2005] EWCA Civ 476, (2005) Times, 11 May.

III SOL [94.4]

Right to an assessment of costs recoverable by the Law Society In LSG 103/48 (2006) 15 December, page 22 there is set out the Regulation Board's (now the Solicitors' Regulation Authority) confirmation that a solicitor or firm will normally be directed to pay costs if there is a finding of professional misconduct or failure to comply with any requirement of the Solicitors Act 1974. It also set out a revised list of fixed fees to be applied form 1 January 2007.

See also the judgment of Henderson J in *Shahrokh Mireskandari v Law Society* [2009] EWHC 2224 (Ch), 153 Sol Jo (no 34) 29 where the solicitor challenged the intervention but subsequently discontinued his challenge. His objection to an order for costs of the challenge against him was dismissed and he was ordered to pay costs on an indemnity basis.

The solicitor who has incurred a costs liability within para 13 may invoke s 71 and have the bill taxed: *Pine v Law Society* [2002] EWCA Civ 175, [2002] 2 All ER 658, [2002] NLJR 313.

The SRA (Costs of Investigations) Regulations 2011 has at Appendix 1 its Schedule of Charges which incorporates a sliding scale based on the time taken, eg 2 hours or more but under 8 hours £600.

III SOL [94.5]

Employment of staff after intervention An intervention does not terminate contracts of employment and the SRA's ancillary powers under para 16 do not enable it to dismiss or engage staff: *Rose v Dodd* [2005] EWCA Civ 957, [2006] 1 All ER 464, [2005] ICR 1776. If, however, the contract is rendered impossible or unlawful it may be frustrated.

III SOL [94.6]

Powers and duties on intervention Powers and duties on intervention are those of a statutory as opposed to a private trustee: see *Re Ahmed & Co (a firm)* [2006] EWHC 480 (Ch), 8 ITELR 779, [2006] NLJR 512.

NOTES ON BARRISTERS

III SOL [95]

Barristers do not have the same level of statutory regulation as solicitors. Beyond the provisions of the 2007 Act, the jurisdiction of the BSB applies through the undertakings given by the barrister on Call to the Bar.

Barristers gain their title by virtue of membership of an Inn of Court and complying with the requirements specified in the Bar Training Regulations. The qualification (which is treated as an academic degree) is bestowed by the barrister's Inn of Court and only an Inn can remove that qualification (disbarment) which is achieved either voluntarily or by an order of a Disciplinary Tribunal of the Four Inns of Court.

The Inns have undertaken to abide by the findings of Disciplinary Tribunals and work closely with the BSB on education and training of barristers. They are responsible for the administration of the disciplinary process, at which the BSB acts as prosecutor. The Inns have created the Bar Tribunal Adjudication Service (BTAS) which administers.

In contrast to solicitors, barristers are not officers of the court and the courts do not have any equivalent jurisdiction over them as compared to solicitors.

Historically, barristers have tended to act as expert advisers and advocates, instructed by solicitors on a referral basis. This has recognised the fact that barristers do not have the same level of administrative support as solicitors, have tended to act as sole practitioners and so are not able to provide the same level of client service as solicitors.

In recent years, that has changed. The BSB has recognised a number of professions and organisations as being suitable to instruct barristers without the intervention of the solicitors. It has also enabled barristers to take instructions directly from members of the public subject to them having taken an appropriate training course and being satisfied that it is not appropriate for a solicitor to be instructed.

In particular, it should be noted that barristers are not permitted to undertake the general management of a client's affairs or to hold client money. This enables the BSB to operate a relatively light-touch regulatory approach compared with that of the SRA.

The BSB's rules now allow barristers to practise through a corporate entity, including an ABS.

The Bar's Code of Conduct, in general, takes the same approach to ethical matters as the SRA's does for solicitors. It is worth noting the following differences:

- The Bar's 'cab-rank' rule positively requires barristers to accept work, subject to them being free, there being no conflicts of interest or other professional reason to refuse, the fee being appropriate (legal aid fees are not deemed to be so) and the work being undertaken under the Standard Terms of Work. In practice, there are a number of reasons why a barrister can refuse work under this work.
- Referral fees are completely prohibited, apart from fees payable to a clerk.

Where a barrister is instructed by a professional client or intermediary on behalf of a lay client, the contractual relationship is usually with the intermediary. Since the development of contractual relationships, it will be open to the courts to test the extent of barristers' retainers though, in practice, this is likely to arise only in respect of disputes over fees. The BSB Handbook in respect of barristers' duties to their clients (at C2) will be particularly relevant in that the Code specifies with some clarity the barrister's duties to the client when deciding whether to cease to act.

Where the relationship is directly with the lay client, the BSB Handbook specifies matters that need to be included in the agreement with the client. These are not very different in spirit from those that the SRA require in respect of relationships with clients but are particularly concerned to stress the limits of a barrister's ability to undertake work on behalf of the client.

Barristers are required to hold Professional Indemnity Insurance. Self-employed barristers are generally insured by the Bar Mutual Indemnity Fund.

TRUSTS AND ADMINISTRATION OF ESTATES

TABLE OF CONTENTS

GENERAL NOTES ON TRUSTS AND ADMINISTRATION OF ESTATES

III TRU [1]

Jurisdiction of the High Court The High Court has unlimited jurisdiction in matters concerning trusts and the administration of estates. For the jurisdiction of the High Court see the Senior Courts Act 1981 s 19 (para **II SCA [17]**). The High Court has an inherent jurisdiction to secure the proper administration of trusts: *Re MF Global UK Ltd (in special administration) (No 3)* [2013] EWHC 1655 (Ch), [2013] 1 WLR 3874, [2013] 2 BCLC 426.

III TRU [2]

Jurisdiction of the County Court The jurisdiction of the county court is wholly statutory. By the County Courts Act 1984 s 23 (para **II CCA [12]**) the county court has all the jurisdiction of the High Court to hear and determine proceedings for the administration of the estate of a deceased person where the estate does not exceed in amount in value the county court limit, and proceedings for the execution of any trust, or for a declaration that a trust subsists, or under the Variation of Trusts Act 1958, where the estate or fund subject, or alleged to be subject, to the trust does not exceed in amount or value the county court limit.

Various statutes in this field, notably the Trustee Act 1925 and the Administration of Estates Act 1925, confer jurisdiction on the county court up to a monetary limit. Section 24 of the County Courts Act 1984 (para **II CCA [13]**) enables the parties to proceedings to confer jurisdiction by agreement on the county court in excess of the monetary limits in certain of those statutes.

III TRU [3]

Scope of title This title deals with some of the most commonly encountered statutory provisions in addition to those referred to above whereby the High Court or the county court are given jurisdiction to grant relief in litigation concerning trusts and the administration of estates.

III TRU [3A]

Statutory Powers and duties of trustees The statutory provisions which regulate the appointment of trustees, otherwise than by court order, and their powers and duties, have not been reproduced in this title. It should be noted, however, that the general powers of trustees, particularly those of investment, have been substantially revised, with effect from 1 February 2000, by the Trustee Act 2000 and that a new statutory duty to exercise reasonable care and skill in the situations listed in Sch 1 has been imposed by ss 1 and 2 of that Act. For precedents for a claim for breach of this duty, see **BCCP Q[911]–BCCP Q[950]**.

III TRU [4]

Procedure In the High Court, proceedings for the execution of trusts and the administration of estates are assigned to the Chancery Division: see s 61 and Sch 1 to the Senior Courts Act 1981. Claims relating to the administration of estates and trusts are governed by CPR 64, rr 64.2–64.4 and the Practice Directions made thereunder. Further guidance on the conduct of proceedings within the scope of this title is given by the Chancery Guide (see para **CHG 1.1**).

The Chancery Division is part of the Business and Property Courts. Claims relating to trusts and the administration of estates should be issued in the Property, Trusts and Probate list: see Practice Direction 57AA – Business and Property Courts.

III TRU [5]

Precedents A range of precedents for proceedings in respect of trusts and the administration of estates is provided in **BCCP Division Q**.

III TRU [6]

Probate proceedings and the rectification of wills Contentious and non-contentious probate proceedings (other than proceedings for the rectification of wills) are not covered by this title. For the non-contentious probate jurisdiction of the High Court, see the Senior Courts Act 1981, s 25 (para **II SCA [23]**), Part V of that Act and the Non-Contentious Probate Rules 1987, SI 1987/2024. For the contentious probate jurisdiction of the county court, see the County Courts Act 1984, s 32 (para **II CCA [16]**). The practice in contentions probate proceedings is governed by CPR 57 (see para **CPR 57**). For notes on procedure in contentious probate proceedings and precedents, see **BCCP Q[2]–BCCP Q[250]**.

Claims for the rectification of wills are governed by the Administration of Justice Act 1982, s 20, see para **III TRU [43B]**.

III TRU [7]

The Judicial Trustees Act 1896 and the Public Trustee Act 1906 For notes on these Acts, see the 2000 edition of this work and previous editions of the *County Court Practice*. Remuneration of judicial trustees is regulated by a practice direction: *Practice Direction (Judicial Trustees: Remuneration)* [2003] 3 All ER 875, [2003] 1 WLR 1653.

III TRU [7A]

Substantive law For the substantive law, see *Halsbury's Laws of England* (5th edn).

TRUSTEE ACT 1925

(c 19)

GENERAL NOTES ON TRUSTEE ACT 1925

III TRU [8]

Introductory note The Trustee Act 1925 consolidates the principal enactments relating to trustees in England and Wales. Part IV of the Act confers on the court powers in relation to trustees and the administration of trusts, and the sections of that Part most commonly invoked are set out below. Proceedings under the Trustee Act 1925 are assigned to the Chancery Division: see CPR PD 8A, section B. For precedents for various forms of application under the Trustee Act 1925, see **BCCP Division Q [651]–[670], [910], [912]**.

PART IV
POWERS OF THE COURT

III TRU [9]

41. Power of court to appoint new trustees

(1) The court may, whenever it is expedient to appoint a new trustee or new trustees, and it is found inexpedient difficult or impracticable so to do without the assistance of the court, make an order appointing a new trustee or new trustees either in substitution for or in addition to any existing trustee or trustees, or although there is no existing trustee.

In particular and without prejudice to the generality of the foregoing provision, the court may make an order appointing a new trustee in substitution for a trustee who [. . .] lacks capacity to exercise his functions as trustee, or is a bankrupt, or is a corporation which is in liquidation or has been dissolved.

(2) ...

(3) An order under this section, and any consequential vesting order or conveyance, shall not operate further or otherwise as a discharge to any former or continuing trustee than an appointment of new trustees under any power for that purpose contained in any instrument would have operated.

(4) Nothing in this section gives power to appoint an executor or administrator.

III TRU [9.1]

Scope of section It will often be possible to appoint new trustees without the assistance of the court, either under an express power in the trust instrument or under the statutory power in s 36 of the Trustee Act 1925. This section confers on the court a power to appoint a new trustee or trustees whenever it is expedient to do so and it is found inexpedient, difficult or impracticable to do so without the assistance of the court (sub-s (1)). An order appointing new trustees will not, without more, vest the trust property in the trustees so appointed, and the order should therefore also make provision, under ss 44 to 46, for the trust property to vest in the newly constituted trustees. For the persons entitled to apply for orders under this section, see s 58 (para **III TRU [26]**).

III TRU [9.2]

Executors and administrators This section does not confer power to appoint an executor or administrator (sub-s (4)). For the court's power to appoint executors and administrators, see s 50 of the Administration of Justice Act 1985 (para **III TRU [45]**).

III TRU [9.3]

Jurisdiction For the jurisdiction of the county court under this section, see s 63A (para **III TRU [32]**).

III TRU [9.4]

Procedure A claim for relief under this section should normally be commenced by a Part 8 Claim Form, but if the matter is contentious a claim for relief under this section can be made in proceedings commenced by a Part 7 Claim Form.

III TRU [9.5]

Precedents For precedents for an application for the appointment of new trustees and vesting orders, see **BCCP Q[651]–BCCP Q[750]**.

III TRU [10]

42. Power to authorise remuneration

Where the court appoints a corporation, other than the Public Trustee, to be a trustee either solely or jointly with another person, the court may authorise the corporation to charge such remuneration for its services as trustee as the court may think fit.

III TRU [10.1]

Scope of section Trustees are entitled to be reimbursed for their proper expenses: Trustee Act 2000, s 31. However, there is no general entitlement for trustees to receive remuneration for their services. Such a right is often conferred by the trust instrument, and the Trustee Act 2000, Part V authorises trust corporations and professional trustees to receive remuneration for their services in the circumstances there stated. The court can also confer a power for trustees to receive remuneration under s 57 (see para **III TRU [25]**), and it has a limited inherent jurisdiction to do so.

This section additionally empowers the court, when appointing a corporation as trustee, to authorise the corporation to charge such remuneration for its services as the court may think fit. It should be noted that a corporation appointed by the court to act as a trustee will thereby become a trust corporation (see s 68(18) at para **III TRU [34]**) and so fall within the provisions of the Trustee Act 2000, Part V. The Public Trustee, who has a statutory power to charge, is excluded from the scope of the section.

III TRU [10.2]

Jurisdiction For the jurisdiction of the county court under this section, see s 63A (para **III TRU [32]**).

III TRU [11]

43. Powers of new trustee appointed by the Court

Every trustee appointed by a court of competent jurisdiction shall, as well before as after the trust property becomes by law, or by assurance, or otherwise, vested in him, have the same powers, authorities, and discretions, and may in all respects act as if he had been originally appointed a trustee by the instrument, if any, creating the trust.

VESTING ORDERS

III TRU [12]

44. Vesting orders of land

In any of the following cases, namely:

(i) Where the court appoints or has appointed a trustee, or where a trustee has been appointed out of court under any statutory or express power;

(ii) Where a trustee entitled to or possessed of any land or interest therein, whether by way of mortgage or otherwise, or entitled to a contingent right therein, either solely or jointly with any other person—

  (a) is under disability; or

  (b) is out of the jurisdiction of the High Court; or

  (c) cannot be found, or, being a corporation, has been dissolved;

(iii) Where it is uncertain who was the survivor of two or more trustees jointly entitled to or possessed of any interest in land;

(iv) Where it is uncertain whether the last trustee known to have been entitled to or possessed of any interest in land is living or dead;

(v) Where there is no personal representative of a deceased trustee who was entitled to or possessed of any interest in land, or where it is uncertain who is the personal representative of a deceased trustee who was entitled to or possessed of any interest in land;

(vi) Where a trustee jointly or solely entitled to or possessed of any interest in land, or entitled to a contingent right therein, has been required, by or on behalf of a person entitled to require a conveyance of the land or interest or a release of the right, to convey the land or interest or to release the right, and has wilfully refused or neglected to convey the land or interest or release the right for twenty-eight days after the date of the requirement;

(vii) Where land or any interest therein is vested in a trustee whether by way of mortgage or otherwise, and it appears to the court to be expedient;

the court may make an order (in this Act called a vesting order) vesting the land or interest therein in any such person in any such manner and for any such estate or interest as the court may direct, or releasing or disposing of the contingent right to such person as the court may direct:

Provided that—

(a) Where the order is consequential on the appointment of a trustee the land or interest therein shall be vested for such estate as the court may direct in the persons who on the appointment are the trustees; and

(b) Where the order relates to a trustee entitled or formerly entitled jointly with another person, and such trustee is under disability or out of the jurisdiction of the High Court or cannot be found, or being a corporation has been dissolved, the land interest or right shall be vested in such other person who remains entitled, either alone or with any other person the court may appoint.

III TRU [13]

Scope of section This section confers on the court a power to vest land in trustees in the wide range of circumstances therein stated. These include, but are not limited to, the appointment of new trustees by the court under s 41 (see para **III TRU [9]**). The effect of a vesting order is stated in s 49 (para **III TRU [17]**). The court may alternatively appoint a person to convey the land under s 50 (para **III TRU [18]**). For the corresponding power in relation to stock and things in action, see s 51 (para **III TRU [19]**). For the persons entitled to apply for orders under this section, see s 58 (para **III TRU [26]**).

III TRU [14]

Jurisdiction For the jurisdiction of the county court under this section, see s 63A (para **III TRU [32]**).

III TRU [15]

Procedure A claim for relief under this section should normally be commenced by a Part 8 Claim Form, but if the matter is contentious a claim for relief under this section can be made in proceedings commenced by a Part 7 Claim Form.

III TRU [16]

Precedents For precedents for an application for the appointment of new trustees and vesting orders, see **BCCP Q[651]–BCCP Q[750]**.

III TRU [17]

49. Effect of vesting order

A vesting order under any of the foregoing provisions shall in the case of a vesting order consequential on the appointment of a trustee, have the same effect—

(a) as if the persons who before the appointment were the trustees, if any, had duly executed all proper conveyances of the land for such estate or interest as the court directs; or

(b) if there is no such person, or no such person of full capacity, as if such person had existed and been of full capacity and had duly executed all proper conveyances of the land for such estate or interest as the court directs;

and shall in every other case have the same effect as if the trustee or other person or description or class of persons to whose rights or supposed rights the said provisions respectively relate had been an ascertained and existing person of full capacity, and had executed a conveyance or release to the effect intended by the order.

III TRU [17.1]

Any of the foregoing provisions These are ss 44 to 48. Section 44 is printed above (see para **III TRU [12]**). Sections 45 to 48 are not reproduced in this work. They concern orders as to contingent rights of unborn persons (s 45), vesting orders in place of conveyances by infant mortgagees (s 46), vesting orders consequential on orders for sale or mortgage of land (s 47) and vesting orders consequential on judgments for specific performance.

III TRU [18]

50. Power to appoint person to convey

In all cases where a vesting order can be made under any of the foregoing provisions, the court may, if it is more convenient, appoint a person to convey the land or any interest therein or release the contingent right, and a conveyance or release by that person in conformity with the order shall have the same effect as an order under the appropriate provision.

III TRU [18.1]

Any of the foregoing provisions See para **III TRU [17.1]**.

III TRU [19]

51. Vesting orders as to stock and things in action

(1) In any of the following cases, namely:—

- (i) Where the court appoints or has appointed a trustee, or where a trustee has been appointed out of court under any statutory or express power;
- (ii) Where a trustee entitled, whether by way of mortgage or otherwise, alone or jointly with another person to stock or to a thing in action—
  - (a) is under disability; or
  - (b) is out of the jurisdiction of the High Court; or
  - (c) cannot be found, or, being a corporation, has been dissolved; or
  - (d) neglects or refuses to transfer stock or receive the dividends or income thereof, or to sue for or recover a thing in action, according to the direction of the person absolutely entitled thereto for twenty- eight days next after a request in writing has been made to him by the person so entitled; or
  - (e) neglects or refuses to transfer stock or receive the dividends or income thereof, or to sue for or recover a thing in action for twenty-eight days next after an order of the court for that purpose has been served on him;
- (iii) Where it is uncertain whether a trustee entitled alone or jointly with another person to stock or to a thing in action is alive or dead;
- (iv) Where stock is standing in the name of a deceased person whose personal representative is under disability;
- (v) Where stock or a thing in action is vested in a trustee whether by way of mortgage or otherwise and it appears to the court to be expedient;

the court may make an order vesting the right to transfer or call for a transfer of stock, or to receive the dividends or income thereof, or to sue for or recover the thing in action, in any such person as the court may appoint:

Provided that—

(a) Where the order is consequential on the appointment of a trustee, the right shall be vested in the persons who, on the appointment, are the trustees; and

(b) Where the person whose right is dealt with by the order was entitled jointly with another person, the right shall be vested in that last-mentioned person either alone or jointly with any other person whom the court may appoint.

(2) In all cases where a vesting order can be made under this section, the court may, if it is more convenient, appoint some proper person to make or join in making the transfer:

Provided that the person appointed to make or join in making a transfer of stock shall be some proper officer of the bank, or the company or society whose stock is to be transferred.

(3) The person in whom the right to transfer or call for the transfer of any stock is vested by an order of the court under this Act, may transfer the stock to himself or any other person, according to the order, and the Bank of England and all other companies shall obey every order under this section according to its tenor.

(4) After notice in writing of an order under this section it shall not be lawful for the Bank of England or any other company to transfer any stock to which the order relates or to pay any dividends thereon except in accordance with the order.

(5) The court may make declarations and give directions concerning the manner in which the right to transfer any stock or thing in action vested under the provisions of this Act is to be exercised.

(6) The provisions of this Act as to vesting orders shall apply to shares in ships registered under the Merchant Shipping Act 1995 as if they were stock.

III TRU [19.1]

Scope of section This section confers on the court a power to vest stock and things in action in new trustees in the circumstances stated in sub-s (1). These include, but are not limited to, the appointment of new trustees by the court under s 41 (see para **III TRU [9]**). The effect of a vesting order is stated in s 49 (para **III TRU [17]**). For the equivalent power in relation to land, see s 44 (para **III TRU [12]**). For the persons entitled to apply for orders under this section, see s 58 (para **III TRU [26]**).

III TRU [19.2]

Jurisdiction For the jurisdiction of the county court under this section, see s 63A (para **III TRU [32]**).

III TRU [19.3]

Procedure A claim for relief under this section should normally be commenced by a Part 8 Claim Form, but if the matter is contentious a claim for relief under this section can be made in proceedings commenced by a Part 7 Claim Form.

III TRU [19.4]

Precedents For precedents for an application for the appointment of new trustees and vesting orders, see **BCCP Q[651]–BCCP Q[750]**.

III TRU [20]

52. Vesting orders of charity property

The powers conferred by this Act as to vesting orders may be exercised for vesting any interest in land, stock, or thing in action in any trustee of a charity or society over which the court would have jurisdiction upon action duly instituted, whether the appointment of the trustee was made by instrument under a power or by the court under its general or statutory jurisdiction.

TRUSTS

III TRU [20.1]

Scope of section The effect of this section is to confirm that the powers of the court to make vesting orders are exercisable in relation to charitable trusts. Alternatively, it may often be possible to resolve problems as to the vesting of property in charity trustees by an order of the Charity Commission under s 69 of the Charities Act 2011.

III TRU [21]–III TRU [22]

53. Vesting orders in relation to infants' beneficial interests

Where an infant is beneficially entitled to any property the court may, with a view to the application of the capital or income thereof for the maintenance, education, or benefit of the infant, make an order—

(a) appointing a person to convey such property; or

(b) in the case of stock, or a thing in action, vesting in any person the right to transfer or call for a transfer of such stock, or to receive the dividends or income thereof, or to sue for and recover such thing in action, upon such terms as the court may think fit.

III TRU [21]–III TRU [22.1]

Scope of section An infant does not, save in limited circumstances, have capacity to deal with property to which he is beneficially entitled. The court does not have a general inherent jurisdiction to deal with an infant's property merely because to do so is for his benefit: *Chapman v Chapman* [1954] AC 429. Where an infant becomes absolutely entitled to property under a will or intestacy, s 42 of the Administration of Estates Act 1925 empowers the personal representatives to appoint trustees of that property. Further, the court has a statutory jurisdiction to approve on behalf of an infant an arrangement varying trusts if the arrangement is for his benefit: see the Variation of Trusts Act 1958 (para **III TRU [37]**).

This section gives the court an additional power to vest property to which an infant is beneficially entitled in another, with a view to the application of the income or capital thereof for his maintenance, education or benefit. The requirement that there be a view to an application of income or capital for the stated purposes means that the court does not have jurisdiction under this section to approve transactions that do not involve such an application, even if they are beneficial to the infant for other reasons: *Re Heyworth's Contingent Reversionary Interest* [1956] Ch 364.

III TRU [21]–III TRU [22.2]

Jurisdiction For the jurisdiction of the county court under this section, see s 63A (para **III TRU [32]**).

III TRU [21]–III TRU [22.3]

Procedure A claim for relief under this section should normally be commenced by a Part 8 Claim Form.

III TRU [23]

55. Orders made upon certain allegations to be conclusive evidence

Where a vesting order is made as to any land under this Act or under sections 15 to 20 of the Mental Capacity Act 2005 or any corresponding provisions having effect in Northern Ireland, founded on an allegation of any of the following matters namely—

(a) that a trustee or mortgagee lacks capacity in relation to the matter in question; or

(b) that a trustee or mortgagee or the personal representative of or other person deriving title under a trustee or mortgagee is out of the jurisdiction of the High Court or cannot be found, or being a corporation has been dissolved; or

(c) that it is uncertain which of two or more trustees, or which of two or more persons interested in a mortgage, was the survivor; or

(d) that it is uncertain whether the last trustee or the personal representative of or other person deriving title under a trustee or mortgagee, or the last surviving person interested in a mortgage is living or dead: or

(e) that any trustee or mortgagee has died intestate without leaving a person beneficially interested under the intestacy or has died and it is not known who is his personal representative or the person interested;

the fact that the order has been so made shall be conclusive evidence of the matter so alleged in any court upon any question as to the validity of the order; but this section does not prevent the court from directing a reconveyance or surrender or the payment of costs occasioned by any such order if improperly obtained.

III TRU [24]

56. Application of vesting order to property out of England

The powers of the court to make vesting orders under this Act shall extend to all property in any part of His Majesty's dominions except Scotland.

JURISDICTION TO MAKE OTHER ORDERS

III TRU [25]

57. Power of court to authorise dealings with trust property

(1) Where in the management or administration of any property vested in trustees, any sale, lease, mortgage, surrender, release, or other disposition, or any purchase, investment, acquisition, expenditure, or other transaction, is in the opinion of the court expedient, but the same cannot be effected by reason of the absence of any power for that purpose vested in the trustees by the trust instrument, if any, or by law, the court may by order confer upon the trustees, either generally or in any particular instance, the necessary power for the purpose, on such terms, and subject to such provisions and conditions, if any, as the court may think fit and may direct in what manner any money authorised to be expended, and the costs of any transaction, are to be paid or borne as between capital and income.

(2) The court may, from time to time, rescind or vary any order made under this section, or may make any new or further order.

(3) An application to the court under this section may be made by the trustees, or by any of them, or by any person beneficially interested under the trust.

(4) This section does not apply to trustees of a settlement for the purposes of the Settled Land Act 1925.

III TRU [25.1]

Scope of section This section confers on the court a power to enlarge the powers of trustees either generally (for example by adding additional administrative powers) or specifically (for example by authorising the trustees to carry out a particular transaction which would otherwise be unauthorised). The powers available to trustees under the general law were enlarged by the Trusts of Land and Appointment of Trustees Act 1996 and the Trustee Act 2000; consequently the need for applications under this section has been correspondingly reduced.

The court must be satisfied that the transaction is expedient in the interests of the beneficiaries as a whole, not just in the interests of one of them: *Re Craven's Estate* [1937] Ch 431. Further, for the court to have jurisdiction under this section, there must be no power vested in the trustees to do what is sought: *Re Pratt's Will Trusts* [1943] Ch 326. The powers of the court under this section do not extend to varying beneficial interests: *Chapman v Chapman* [1954] AC 429. The conferring of powers of appropriation and partition, the effects of which on beneficial interests are only incidental, may be within this section: *Southgate v Sutton* [2011] EWCA Civ 637, [2012] 1 WLR 326, [2011] 2 P & CR D37.

For an example of the exercise of the power conferred by this section to authorise a sale of trust property when the settlor had excluded the trustees' statutory powers of sale see *Alexander v Alexander* [2011] EWHC 2721 (Ch), [2012] WTLR 187. For an example of the exercise of the power conferred by this section to enlarge the powers of the trustees of a group of trusts with complex assets see *Re Portman Estate* [2015] EWHC 536 (Ch), [2015] WTLR 871, [2015] All ER (D) 93 (Mar).

The powers of trustees may also be enlarged under the Variation of Trusts Act 1958 s 1 (see **III TRU [38]**). Where both jurisdictions are available, to proceed under this section will generally be simpler: *Anker-Petersen v Anker-Petersen* [2000] 1 WTLR 581.

III TRU [25.2]

Settled land This section does not apply to settled land act trustees. For the corresponding provision in relation to settled land, see the Settled Land Act 1925 s 64.

III TRU [25.3]

Jurisdiction For the jurisdiction of the county court under this section, see s 63A (para **III TRU [32]**).

III TRU [25.4]

Procedure A claim for relief under this section should normally be commenced by a Part 8 Claim Form.

III TRU [26]

58. Persons entitled to apply for orders

(1) An order under this Act for the appointment of a new trustee or concerning any interest in land, stock, or thing in action subject to a trust, may be made on the application of any person beneficially interested in the land, stock, or thing in action, whether under disability or not, or on the application of any person duly appointed trustee thereof.

(2) An order under this Act concerning any interest in land, stock, or thing in action subject to a mortgage may be made on the application of any person beneficially interested in the equity of redemption, whether under disability or not, or of any person interested in the money secured by the mortgage.

III TRU [27]

59. Power to give judgment in absence of a trustee

Where in any action the court is satisfied that diligent search has been made for any person who, in the character of trustee, is made a defendant in any action, to serve him with a process of the court, and that he cannot be found, the court may hear and determine the action and give judgment therein against that person in his character of a trustee as if he had been duly served, or had entered an appearance in the action, and had also appeared by his counsel and solicitor at the hearing, but without prejudice to any interest he may have in the matters in question in the action in any other character.

III TRU [27.1]

The court This section extends to the county court: see s 63(4) (para **III TRU [31]**).

III TRU [28]

60. Power to charge costs on trust estate

The court may order the costs and expenses of and incident to any application for an order appointing a new trustee, or for a vesting order, or of and incident to any such order, or any conveyance or transfer in pursuance thereof, to be raised and paid out of the property in respect whereof the same is made, or out of the income thereof, or to be borne and paid in such manner and by such persons as to the court may seem just.

III TRU [28.1]

The court For the jurisdiction of the county court under this section, see s 63A (para **III TRU [32]**).

III TRU [29]

61. Power to relieve trustee from personal liability

If it appears to the court that a trustee, whether appointed by the court or otherwise, is or may be personally liable for any breach of trust, whether the transaction alleged to be a breach of trust occurred before or after the commencement of this Act, but has acted honestly and reasonably, and ought fairly to be excused for the breach of trust and for omitting to obtain the directions of the court in the matter in which he committed such breach, then the court may relieve him either wholly or partly from personal liability for the same.

III TRU [29.1]

Scope of section This section confers on the court a power to relieve a trustee from personal liability for breach of trust. The requirements of the section must be satisfied cumulatively, not merely alternatively. The section extends to personal representatives: see s 68(17) (para **III TRU [34]**). Cases decided under this section inevitably turn on their own facts.

III TRU [29.2]

Jurisdiction For the jurisdiction of the county court under this section, see s 63A (para **III TRU [32]**).

III TRU [29.3]

Procedure A claim for relief under this section should normally be commenced by a Part 8 Claim Form. A trustee who is being sued for breach of trust and who wishes to claim relief under this section should plead the facts on which he relies in his defence.

III TRU [29.4]

Precedents For a precedent for a defence claiming relief under this section, see **BCCP Q[912]**.

III TRU [30]

62. Power to make beneficiary indemnify for breach of trust

(1) Where a trustee commits a breach of trust at the instigation or request or with the consent in writing of a beneficiary, the court may, if it thinks fit, . . . make such order as to the court seems just, for impounding all or any part of the interest of the beneficiary in the trust estate by way of indemnity to the trustee or persons claiming through him.

(2) [. . .]

III TRU [30.1]

Scope of section This section confers on the court a power to impound the beneficial interest of a beneficiary who has instigated, requested or consented in writing to a breach of trust, by way of indemnity to the trustee. For the operation of the section, see further *Re Somerset, Somerset v Earl Poulett* [1894] 1 Ch 231 and *Re Pauling's Settlement Trusts* [1963] Ch 576.

III TRU [30.2]

Jurisdiction For the jurisdiction of the county court under this section, see s 63A (see para **III TRU [32]**).

III TRU [30.3]

Procedure A claim under this section should be commenced by a Claim Form under Part 7 or Part 8, depending on the extent to which the matter is contentious.

III TRU [30.4]

Precedents For a precedent for a defence and counterclaim claiming relief under this section, see **BCCP Q[910]**.

TRUSTS

III TRU [31]

63. Payment into court by trustees

(1) Trustees, or the majority of trustees, having in their hands or under their control money or securities belonging to a trust, may pay the same into court; . . .

(2) The receipt or certificate of the proper officer shall be a sufficient discharge to trustees for the money or securities so paid into court.

(3) Where money or securities are vested in any persons as trustees, and the majority are desirous of paying the same into court, but the concurrence of the other or others cannot be obtained, the court may order the payment into court to be made by the majority without the concurrence of the other or others.

(4) Where any such money or securities are deposited with any banker, broker, or other depository, the court may order payment or delivery of the money or securities to the majority of the trustees for the purpose of payment into court.

(5) Every transfer payment and delivery made in pursuance of any such order shall be valid and take effect as if the same had been made on the authority or by the act of all the persons entitled to the money and securities so transferred, paid, or delivered.

III TRU [31.1]

Scope of section Trustees who are in doubt or difficulty as to the application of trust funds may pay the fund into court. The payment into court operates as a discharge of the trustees in relation to the funds paid in, but does not relieve them of liability for antecedent breaches of trust. A trustee should in general only pay trust funds into court if there is no other appropriate solution to the doubt or difficulty, and a trustee who does so without sufficient cause may be ordered to pay any additional costs resulting from taking this course. See further, s 68(2) (para **III TRU [34]**).

III TRU [31.2]

Procedure For the procedure, see CPR 37 and paras 9 and 10 of the Practice Direction to CPR 37.

III TRU [31.3]

Jurisdiction For the jurisdiction of the county court under this section, see s 63A (para **III TRU [32]**).

III TRU [32]

63A. Jurisdiction of County Court

(1) The county court has jurisdiction under the following provisions where the amount or value of the trust estate or fund to be dealt with in the court does not exceed the county court limit—

section 41;
section 42;
section 51;
section 57;
section 60;
section 61;
section 62.

(2) The county court has jurisdiction under the following provisions where the land or the interest or contingent right in land which is to be dealt with in the court forms part of a trust estate which does not exceed in amount or value the county court limit—

section 44;
section 45;
section 46;

(3) The county court has jurisdiction—

(a) under sections 47 and 48 of this Act, where the judgment is given or order is made by the court;

(b) under sections 50 and 56, where a vesting order can be made by the court;

(c) under section 53, where the amount or value of the property to be dealt with in the court does not exceed the county court limit; and

(d) under section 63 (including power to receive payment of money or securities into court) where the money or securities to be paid into court do not exceed in amount or value the county court limit.

(4) Any reference to the court in section 59 of this Act includes a reference to the county court.

(5) In this section, in its application to any enactment, "the county court limit" means the amount for the time being specified by an Order in Council under section 145 of the County Courts Act 1984 as the county court limit for the purposes of that enactment (or, where no such Order in Council has been made, the corresponding limit specified by Order in Council under section 192 of the County Courts Act 1959).

III TRU [32.1]

County court limit The county court limit for the purposes of this section is £30,000: County Courts Jurisdiction Order 1981, SI 1981/1123. The jurisdiction may be enlarged by agreement: County Courts Act 1984, s 24 (see para **II CCA [13]**).

PART V
GENERAL PROVISIONS

III TRU [33]

67. Jurisdiction of the "court"

(1) In this Act "the court" means the High Court . . . or the county court, where those courts respectively have jurisdiction.

(2) The procedure under this Act in . . . the county court shall be in accordance with the Acts and rules regulating the procedure of those courts.

III TRU [34]

68. Definitions

(1) In this Act, unless the context otherwise requires, the following expressions have the meanings hereby assigned to them respectively, that is to say:—

(1) "Authorised investments" mean investments authorised by the instrument, if any, creating the trust for the investment of money subject to the trust, or by law;

(2) "Contingent right" as applied to land includes a contingent or executory interest, a possibility coupled with an interest, whether the object of the gift or limitation of the interest, or possibility is or is not ascertained, also a right of entry, whether immediate or future, and whether vested or contingent;

(3) "Convey" and "conveyance" as applied to any person include the execution by that person of every necessary or suitable assurance (including an assent) for conveying, assigning, appointing, surrendering, or otherwise transferring or disposing of land whereof he is seised or possessed, or wherein he is entitled to a contingent right, either for his whole estate or for any less estate, together with the performance of all formalities required by law for the validity of the conveyance; "sale" includes an exchange;

(4) "Gazette" means the London Gazette;

TRUSTS

(5) "Instrument" includes Act of Parliament;

(6) "Land" includes land of any tenure, and mines and minerals, whether or not severed from the surface, buildings or parts of buildings, whether the division is horizontal, vertical or made in any other way, and other corporeal hereditaments; also a manor, an advowson, and a rent and other incorporeal hereditaments, and an easement, right, privilege, or benefit in, over, or derived from . . . ; and in this definition "mines and minerals" include any strata or seam of minerals or substances in or under any land, and powers of working and getting the same . . . ; and "hereditaments" mean real property which under an intestacy occurring before the commencement of this Act might have devolved on an heir;

(7) "Mortgage" and "mortgagee" include a charge or chargee by way of legal mortgage, and relate to every estate and interest regarded in equity as merely a security for money, and every person deriving title under the original mortgagee;

(8) . . .

(9) "Personal representative" means the executor, original or by representation, or administrator for the time being of a deceased person;

(10) "Possession" includes receipt of rents and profits or the right to receive the same, if any; "income" includes rents and profits; and "possessed" applies to receipt of income of and to any vested estate less than a life interest in possession or in expectancy in any land;

(11) "Property" includes real and personal property, and any estate share and interest in any property, real or personal, and any debt, and any thing in action, and any other right or interest, whether in possession or not;

(12) "Rights" include estates and interests;

(13) "Securities" include stocks, funds, and shares; . . . and "securities payable to bearer" include securities transferable by delivery or by delivery and endorsement;

(14) "Stock" includes fully paid up shares, and so far as relates to vesting orders made by the court under this Act, includes any fund, annuity, or security transferable in books kept by any company or society, or by instrument of transfer either alone or accompanied by other formalities, and any share or interest therein;

(15) "Tenant for life," "statutory owner," "settled land," "settlement," "trust instrument," "trustees of the settlement" . . . "term of years absolute" and "vesting instrument" have the same meanings as in the Settled Land Act 1925, and "entailed interest" has the same meaning as in the Law of Property Act 1925;

(16) "Transfer" in relation to stock or securities, includes the performance and execution of every deed, power of attorney, act, and thing on the part of the transferor to effect and complete the title in the transferee;

(17) "Trust" does not include the duties incident to an estate conveyed by way of mortgage, but with this exception the expressions "trust" and "trustee" extend to implied and constructive trusts, and to cases where the trustee has a beneficial interest in the trust property, and to the duties incident to the office of a personal representative, and "trustee" where the context admits, includes a personal representative, and "new trustee" includes an additional trustee;

(18) "Trust corporation" means the Public Trustee or a corporation either appointed by the court in any particular case to be a trustee, or entitled

by rules made under subsection (3) of section four of the Public Trustee Act 1906, to act as custodian trustee;

(19) "Trust for sale" in relation to land means an immediate . . . trust for sale, whether or not exercisable at the request or with the consent of any person . . . ;

(20) "United Kingdom" means Great Britain and Northern Ireland.

(2) Any reference in this Act to paying money or securities into court shall be construed as referring to paying the money or transferring or depositing the securities into or in the Senior Courts or into or in any other court that has jurisdiction, and any reference in this Act to payment of money or securities into court shall be construed—

(a) with reference to an order of the High Court, as referring to payment of the money or transfer or deposit of the securities into or in the Senior Courts; and

(b) with reference to an order of any other court, as referring to payment of the money or transfer or deposit of the securities into or in that court.

(3) Any reference in this Act to a person who lacks capacity in relation to a matter is to a person—

(a) who lacks capacity within the meaning of the Mental Capacity Act 2005 in relation to that matter, or

(b) in respect of whom the powers conferred by section 48 of that Act are exercisable and have been exercised in relation to that matter.

III TRU [35]

69. Application of Act

(1) This Act, except where otherwise expressly provided, applies to trusts including, so far as this Act applies thereto, executorships and administratorships constituted or created either before or after the commencement of this Act.

(2) The powers conferred by this Act on trustees are in addition to the powers conferred by the instrument, if any, creating the trust, but those powers, unless otherwise stated, apply if and so far only as a contrary intention is not expressed in the instrument, if any, creating the trust, and have effect subject to the terms of that instrument.

(3) [. . .]

ADMINISTRATION OF ESTATES ACT 1925

(c 23)

GENERAL NOTE ON ADMINISTRATION OF ESTATES ACT 1925

III TRU [36]

Jurisdiction The Administration of Estates Act 1925 consolidated the law relating to the administration of estates of deceased persons. Section 17 of the Act provides that if, while proceedings are pending in any court by or against an administrator to whom a temporary administration has been granted, that administration is revoked, the court may order that the proceedings be continued by or against the new personal representative in like manner as if the proceedings had originally been commenced by or against him, but subject to such variations and conditions, if any, as that court directs. The county court has jurisdiction under that section where the proceedings are pending in that court. This provision should be considered in conjunction with CPR Pt 5 (see para **CPR 5**). Section 23 gives the High Court power to appoint special or additional personal representatives of settled land. Section 38 provides that an assent or conveyance of property by a personal representative to a person other than a purchaser does not prejudice the right of any person to follow that property or property representing it, and gives the court power to make various orders to give effect to those rights. Section 41(1) gives the court power to consent on behalf of infants to appropriations in satisfaction of legacies. Section 43 gives the court power to give directions and make vesting orders in relation to real estate. The county court has jurisdiction under ss 38, 41 and 43 where the estate in respect of which the application is made does not exceed in amount or value the county court limit.

VARIATION OF TRUSTS ACT 1958

(c 53)

GENERAL NOTE ON VARIATION OF TRUSTS ACT 1958

III TRU [37]

The Variation of Trusts Act 1958 extended the jurisdiction of the court to vary trusts in the interests of beneficiaries and to sanction dealings with trust property.

III TRU [38]

1. Jurisdiction of courts to vary trusts

(1) Where property, whether real or personal, is held on trusts arising, whether before or after the passing of this Act, under any will, settlement or other disposition, the court may if it thinks fit by order approve on behalf of—

(a) any person having, directly or indirectly, an interest, whether vested or contingent, under the trusts who by reason of infancy or other incapacity is incapable of assenting, or

(b) any person (whether ascertained or not) who may become entitled, directly or indirectly, to an interest under the trusts as being at a future date or on the happening of a future event a person of any specified description or a member of any specified class of persons, so however that this paragraph shall not include any person who would be of that description, or a member of that class, as the case may be, if the said date had fallen or the said event had happened at the date of the application to the court, or

(c) any person unborn, or

(d) any person in respect of any discretionary interest of his under protective trusts where the interest of the principal beneficiary has not failed or determined,

any arrangement (by whomsoever proposed, and whether or not there is any other person beneficially interested who is capable of assenting thereto) varying or revoking all or any of the trusts, or enlarging the powers of the trustees of managing or administering any of the property subject to the trusts:

Provided that except by virtue of paragraph (d) of this subsection the court shall not approve an arrangement on behalf of any person unless the carrying out thereof would be for the benefit of that person.

(2) In the foregoing subsection "protective trusts" means the trusts specified in paragraphs (i) and (ii) of subsection (1) of section thirty-three of the Trustee Act 1925, or any like trusts, "the principal beneficiary" has the same meaning as in the said subsection (1) and "discretionary interest" means an interest arising under the trust specified in paragraph (ii) of the said subsection (1) or any like trust.

(3) [. . .] The jurisdiction conferred by subsection (1) of this section shall be exercisable by the High Court, except that the question whether the carrying out of any arrangement would be for the benefit of a person falling within paragraph (a) of the said subsection (1) lacks capacity (within the meaning of the Mental Capacity Act 2005) to give his assent is to be determined by the Court of Protection.

(4) [. . .]

(5) Nothing in the foregoing provisions of this section shall apply to trusts affecting property settled by Act of Parliament.

(6) Nothing in this section shall be taken to limit the powers of the Court of Protection.

III TRU [38.1]

Jurisdiction The county court has jurisdiction under the Variation of Trusts Act 1958 where the estate or fund subject, or alleged to be subject, to the trust does not exceed in amount or value the county court limit: County Courts Act 1984 sub-s 23(b)(d) (para **II CCA [12]**). The county court limit for this purpose is £30,000: County Courts Jurisdiction Order 1981 (SI 1981/1123). This limit on the jurisdiction of the county courts may not be extended by agreement: County Courts Act 1984 sub-s 24(3) (para **II CCA [13]**).

III TRU [38.1A]

Powers of the court The Act extends to the statutory trusts arising on intestacy under the Administration of Estates Act 1925: *S v T* [2006] WTLR 1461, and to property held by the personal representative of an estate in the course of administration: *Bernstein v Jacobson* [2008] EWHC 3454 (Ch), [2010] WTLR 559.

The principles to be applied in the exercise of the court's jurisdiction under this Act have been summarised as follows:

(a) The court's task under the Act is to be approached with "a fair, cautious and inquiring mind".

(b) The court's jurisdiction under the Act is to supply consent to an arrangement on behalf of a person unable to provide it himself. For the court to do so, the arrangement must confer on him a real benefit; it is not enough that it does him no real harm.

(c) "Benefit" is generally financial in nature: and when it is the court will be concerned in a practical and business-like consideration of the arrangement, including the total amounts of the advantages which the various parties obtain, and their bargaining strength. If the outcome of the arrangement cannot be predicted with certainty then the court is prepared to take on behalf of a minor a risk that an adult would be prepared to take.

(d) But "benefit" need not be financial: and when it is not (or where non-financial benefit falls to be weighed against financial disadvantage) business-like considerations do not provide a sure guide, though the recognition of risk will still have some part to play. In such cases the assessment of benefit and advantage must be approached with caution, lest the process simply becomes a reflection of the perceptions and preferences of the individual judge.

(e) One step towards objectifying the assessment of non-financial benefit would be to ask: would a prudent adult, motivated by intelligent self-interest, and after sustained consideration of the proposed trusts and powers and the circumstances in which they may fall to be implemented, be likely to accept the proposal?

See *Wright v Gater* [2011] EWHC 2881 (Ch), [2012] 1 WLR 802, [2012] STC 255.

For the weight to be placed on evidence of the settlor's intentions see *Goulding v James* [1997] 2 All ER 239. The court has jurisdiction to vary a bare trust: *D (a child) v O* [2004] EWHC 1036 (Ch), [2004] 3 All ER 780. For recent examples of the exercise of the court's power to approve an arrangement see *Re RGST Settlement Trust* [2007] EWHC 2666 (Ch), [2007] STC 1883 (insertion of prior life interest and power of advancement for benefit of reversioners for fiscal reasons, notwithstanding deferment of their interest); *Wyndham v Egremont* [2009] EWHC 2076 (Ch), [2009] WTLR 1473 (postponement of interest of unborn beneficiaries to defer charge to capital gains tax); *Wright v Gater* [2011] EWHC 2881 (Ch), [2012] 1 WLR 802 (postponement of vesting of interest of infant under statutory trusts on intestacy beyond age of majority).

III TRU [38.1B]

Court of Protection Where an application is made for the court to approve the variation of a trust pursuant to s 1 because one of the beneficiaries is an infant, the question as to whether the variation is for the benefit of that beneficiary is to be determined by the High Court, not the Court of Protection, even though the minor also suffers from mental incapacity within the meaning of s 2(1) of the Mental Capacity Act 2005. This is so even if (i) the beneficiary is nearly 18 and lacks capacity in relation to other matters within s 2(1) of the 2005 Act, or (ii) the beneficiary's circumstances have been considered in other respects by the Court of Protection and a deputy has been appointed in relation to that person: *T v P* [2018] EWHC 685 (Ch), [2018] Ch 565.

III TRU [38.2]

Practice See CPR 64.1–64.4 and the Practice Direction to CPR 64, para 4. Save in an exceptional case, it is not appropriate for approval of an arrangement under this Act to be sought on paper. The proponent of an arrangement and the persons on whose behalf approval is sought should be separately represented. The trustees of a trust of which variation is sought have a role of general oversight: see *Wright v Gater* [2011] EWHC 2881 (Ch), [2012] 1 WLR 802.

The general principle that hearings are in open court applies to applications under the Act. For a discussion of when the court will conduct the hearing in private, impose reporting restrictions, or anonymise the listing of an application or a judgment, and of the practice to be followed where it is intended to apply for the court to do one or more of these, see *V v T* [2014] EWHC 3432 (Ch), [2015] WTLR 173, [2014] All ER (D) 293 (Oct).

FORFEITURE ACT 1982

(c 34)

GENERAL NOTE ON FORFEITURE ACT 1982

III TRU [39]

The courts have evolved a rule of public policy which in certain circumstances precludes a person who has unlawfully killed another from acquiring a benefit in consequence of the killing. This Act gives the courts power to modify the application of that rule.

III TRU [40]

1. The "forfeiture rule"

(1) In this Act, the "forfeiture rule" means the rule of public policy which in certain circumstances precludes a person who has unlawfully killed another from acquiring a benefit in consequence of the killing.

(2) References in this Act to a person who has unlawfully killed another include a reference to a person who has unlawfully aided, abetted, counselled or procured the death of that other and references in this Act to unlawful killing shall be interpreted accordingly.

III TRU [41]

2. Power to modify the rule

(1) Where a court determines that the forfeiture rule has precluded a person (in this section referred to as "the offender") who has unlawfully killed another from acquiring any interest in property mentioned in subsection (4) below, the court may make an order under this section modifying the effect of that rule.

(2) The court shall not make an order under this section modifying the effect of the forfeiture rule in any case unless it is satisfied that, having regard to the conduct of the offender and of the deceased and to such other circumstances as appear to the court to be material, the justice of the case requires the effect of the rule to be so modified in that case.

(3) In any case where a person stands convicted of an offence of which unlawful killing is an element, the court shall not make an order under this section modifying the effect of the forfeiture rule in that case unless proceedings for the purpose are brought before the expiry of the period of three months beginning with his conviction.

(4) The interests in property referred to in subsection (1) above are—

- (a) any beneficial interest in property which (apart from the forfeiture rule) the offender would have acquired—
  - (i) under the deceased's will (including, as respects Scotland, any writing having testamentary effect) or the law relating to intestacy or by way of ius relicti, ius relictae or legitim;
  - (ii) on the nomination of the deceased in accordance with the provisions of any enactment;
  - (iii) as a donatio mortis causa made by the deceased; or
  - (iv) under a special destination (whether relating to heritable or moveable property); or
- (b) any beneficial interest in property which (apart from the forfeiture rule) the offender would have acquired in consequence of the death of the deceased, being property which, before the death, was held on trust for any person.

(5) An order under this section may modify the effect of the forfeiture rule in respect of any interest in property to which the determination referred to in subsection (1) above relates and may do so in either or both of the following ways, that is—

- (a) where there is more than one such interest, by excluding the application of the rule in respect of any (but not all) of those interests; and
- (b) in the case of any such interest in property, by excluding the application of the rule in respect of part of the property.

(6) On the making of an order under this section, the forfeiture rule shall have effect for all purposes (including purposes relating to anything done before the order is made) subject to the modifications made by the order.

(7) The court shall not make an order under this section modifying the effect of the forfeiture rule in respect of any interest in property which, in consequence of the rule, has been acquired before the coming into force of this section by a person other than the offender or a person claiming through him.

(8) In this section—

"property" includes any chose in action or incorporeal moveable property; and

"will" includes codicil.

III TRU [42]

3. Application for financial provision not affected by the rule

(1) The forfeiture rule shall not be taken to preclude any person from making any application under a provision mentioned in subsection (2) below or the making of any order on the application.

(2) The provisions referred to in subsection (1) above are—

(a) any provision of the Inheritance (Provision for Family and Dependants) Act 1975; and

(b) sections 31(6) and 36(1) of the Matrimonial Causes Act 1973 (variation by court in England and Wales of periodical payments orders and maintenance agreements in respect of marriages);

(c) paragraphs 60(2) and 73(2) of Schedule 5 to the Civil Partnership Act 2004 (variation by court in England and Wales of periodical payments orders and maintenance agreements in respect of civil partnerships); and

(d) section 13(4) of the Family Law (Scotland) Act 1985 (variation etc of periodical allowances in respect of marriages and civil partnerships).

III TRU [43]

5. Exclusion of murderers

Nothing in this Act or in any order made under section 2 or referred to in section 3(1) of this Act or in any decision made under section 4(1A) of this Act shall affect the application of the forfeiture rule in the case of a person who stands convicted of murder.

III TRU [43.1]

Section 1(1) of this Act defines the 'forfeiture rule' as 'the rule of public policy which in certain circumstances precludes a person who has unlawfully killed another from acquiring a benefit in consequence of the killing'. The rule applies to all cases of unlawful killing, the only possible exception being where the defendant is found to be criminally insane, leading to acquittal: *Re Land dec'd* [2006] EWHC 2069 (Ch), [2007] 1 All ER 324. Unlawful killing is defined for the purposes of the Act by s 1(2) and includes for example aiding and abetting suicide, contrary to s 2(1) of the Suicide Act 1961 (*Dunbar v Plant* [1998] Ch 412, [1997] 4 All ER 289, CA) and manslaughter by gross negligence (*Re Land dec'd* [2006] EWHC 2069 (Ch), [2007] 1 All ER 324).

In *Re DWS* [2001] Ch 568, [2001] 1 All ER 97 the Court of Appeal held that the where a child murdered his parent, who died intestate, not only the murderer but also a child of the murderer took no interest in the victim's estate. The effect of the decision was reversed by s 1 of the Estates of Deceased Persons (Forfeiture Rule and Law of Succession) Act 2011 (see below).

Section 2 of the Act gives the court power to modify the effect of the forfeiture rule, and s 3 provides that the rule shall not be taken to preclude any person from making an application under specified legislation or the making of an order on the application. The legislation specified includes the Inheritance (Provision for Family and Dependants) Act 1975 and certain provisions of the Matrimonial Causes Act 1973 and the Civil Partnership Act 2004. However s 5 provides that nothing in the Act or in any order made under s 2 or referred to in s 3(1) shall affect the operation of the forfeiture rule in the case of a person who stands convicted of murder.

For instances of the application of the Act see *Re K* [1986] Ch 180, [1985] 2 All ER 833, CA (manslaughter; relief granted); *Re S* [1996] 1 WLR 235, Ch D (manslaughter; relief granted in favour of trust set up for killer's son); *Dunbar v Plant* [1998] Ch 412, [1997] 4 All ER 289, CA (complicity in suicide; relief granted); *Re Murphy (dec'd), Dalton v Latham* [2003] EWCA Civ 796 (Ch), [2003] WTLR 687 (manslaughter by reason of diminished responsibility; relief refused); *Re Mack dec'd* [2009] EWHC 1524 (Ch) (manslaughter by reason of provocation, relief refused)); *Chadwick v Collinson* [2014] EWHC 3055 (Ch), [2015] WTLR 25, [2014] All ER (D) 172 (Sep) (manslaughter by reason of diminished responsibility, relief refused); *Henderson v Wilcox* [2015] EWHC 3469 (Ch), [2015] All ER (D) 42 (Dec), [2016] 4 WLR 475 (plea of guilty to manslaughter accepted on basis of absence of intention to kill, relief refused); *Macmillan Cancer Support v Hayes* [2017] EWHC 3110 (Ch) [2018] WTLR 243 (unlawful killing followed by suicide of perpetrator and beneficiary under will, relief granted to allow testamentary wishes of victim to take effect)).

For the interaction of the Act and the Inheritance (Provision for Family and Dependants) Act 1975 see *Re Royse* [1985] Ch 22, [1984] 3 All ER 339, CA; *Re Land dec'd* [2006] EWHC 2069 (Ch), [2007] 1 All ER 324.

The 'forfeiture rule' does not apply when a person settles property on a beneficiary during his lifetime and the beneficiary kills the settlor: *Henderson v Wilcox* [2015] EWHC 3469 (Ch), [2015] All ER (D) 42 (Dec), [2016] 4 WLR 475.

The Estates of Deceased Persons (Forfeiture Rule and Law of Succession) Act 2011 was enacted following a review of the law by the Law Commission in the light of the decision in *Re DWS* [2001] Ch 568, [2001] 1 All ER 97 (the Forfeiture Rule and the Law of Succession (2005, Law Com 295)). The Act:

(a) amends the Administration of Estates Act 1925 to provide that where a person would have been entitled to an interest in the residuary estate of an intestate had the person not been precluded by the forfeiture rule from acquiring it, the person is to be treated for the purposes of that Act as having died immediately before the intestate; and

(b) amends the Wills Act 1837 to provide that where a will contains a devise or bequest to a person who has been precluded by the forfeiture rule from acquiring it, the person is, unless a contrary intention appears by the will, to be treated for the purposes of that Act as having died immediately before the testator.

III TRU [43.2]

Jurisdiction The High Court has jurisdiction under the Act. Although the Act contains no definition of 'court', it would seem that the county court has jurisdiction under the Act in a matter within its equity jurisdiction under s 23 of the County Courts Act 1984.

III TRU [43.3]

Procedure Section 3(3) imposes a three-month time limit in the case of an application by a person who stands convicted of an offence of which unlawful killing is an element. The court has no jurisdiction to extend the time limit: *Re Land dec'd* [2006] EWHC 2069 (Ch), [2007] 1 All ER 324. Proceedings under the Act should be commenced by a claim form under CPR Part 7 or Part 8 as appropriate.

ADMINISTRATION OF JUSTICE ACT 1982

(c 53)

GENERAL NOTE ON ADMINISTRATION OF JUSTICE ACT 1982

III TRU [43A]

Part IV of the Administration of Justice Act 1982 contained provisions relating to the rectification and interpretation of wills. Section 20 (rectification of wills) is set out below.

III TRU [43B]

20. Rectification

(1) If a court is satisfied that a will is so expressed that it fails to carry out the testator's intentions, in consequence—

(a) of a clerical error; or

(b) of a failure to understand his instructions,

it may order that the will shall be rectified so as to carry out his intentions.

(2) An application for an order under this section shall not, except with the permission of the court, be made after the end of the period of six months from the date on which representation with respect to the estate of the deceased is first taken out.

TRUSTS

(3) The provisions of this section shall not render the personal representatives of a deceased person liable for having distributed any part of the estate of the deceased, after the end of the period of six months from the date on which representation with respect to the estate of the deceased is first taken out, on the ground that they ought to have taken into account the possibility that the court might permit the making of an application for an order under this section after the end of that period; but this subsection shall not prejudice any power to recover, by reason of the making of an order under this section, any part of the estate so distributed.

(4) The following are to be left out of account when considering for the purposes of this section when representation with respect to the estate of a deceased person was first taken out—

(a) a grant limited to settled land or to trust property,

(b) any other grant that does not permit any of the estate to be distributed,

(c) a grant limited to real estate or to personal estate, unless a grant limited to the remainder of the estate has previously been made or is made at the same time,

(d) a grant, or its equivalent, made outside the United Kingdom (but see subsection (5)).

(5) A grant sealed under section 2 of the Colonial Probates Act 1892 counts as a grant made in the United Kingdom for the purposes of subsection (4), but is to be taken as dated on the date of sealing.

III TRU [43B.1]

Rectification of wills A will, or part of a will, may be omitted from probate if the testator did not know or approve of it, see eg *Re Morris* [1971] P 62, [1970] 1 All ER 1057.

The approach to the construction of wills is the same as to the construction of other documents, and accordingly some mistakes in the drafting of wills can be corrected by way of construction: *Marley v Rawlings* [2014] UKSC 2, [2015] AC 157, [2014] 1 All ER 807. For illustrations see *Brooke v Purton* [2014] EWHC 547 (Ch), [2014] WTLR 745; *Reading v Reading* [2015] EWHC 946 (Ch), [2015] WTLR 1245, [2015] All ER (D) 64 (Feb). For the evidence which is admissible to interpret a will, see the Administration of Justice Act 1982, s 21.

The court has no inherent jurisdiction to rectify wills. Section 20 of this Act confers a statutory jurisdiction to rectify wills in the circumstances specified in sub-s (1).

Will The word 'will' in s 20 is not confined to a will which complies with the requirements of formal validity imposed by s 9 of the Wills Act 1837, as amended, but means any document which on its face was bona fide intended to be a will and which, once rectified, would be a valid will. In order to be a 'will' which is capable of being rectified pursuant to s 20, a document does not have to satisfy the formal requirements of s 9 of the Wills Act 1837 or of having the testator's knowledge and approval.

Accordingly, where 'mirror wills' were prepared for a husband and wife and, by mistake, each executed the will prepared for the other, the husband's will could be rectified by transposing into it the text contained in the document executed by the wife, notwithstanding that the husband had not known and approved the contents of the document he executed. Rectification was possible since there was certainty as to the husband's intention and as to how he would have expressed himself but for the mistake, and he had unambiguously intended the document he executed to have effect as his last will, and had signed it in the presence of two witnesses on the basis that it was his will: *Marley v Rawlings* [2014] UKSC 2, [2015] AC 157, [2014] 1 All ER 807.

Clerical error The term 'clerical error' in sub-s 20(1) (a) has a wide meaning, 'namely a mistake arising out of office work of a relatively routine nature, such as preparing, filing, sending, organising the execution of, a document (save, possibly, to the extent that the activity involves some special expertise': *Marley v Rawlings* [2014] UKSC 2, [2015] AC 157, at [75]. Accordingly, it has been applied to mistakenly causing a husband and wife each to execute a will prepared for the other: *Marley v Rawlings* (above). However, it has not been applied to the mistaken use by a solicitor of the word 'issue' to include step-children: *Reading v Reading* [2015] EWHC 946 (Ch), [2015] WTLR 1245.

For earlier decisions on the scope of the phrase 'clerical error' and the scope of the section generally, see *Wordingham v Royal Exchange Trust Co Ltd* [1992] Ch 412, [1992] 3 All ER 204; *Re Segelman* [1995] 3 All ER 676, [1996] Ch 171; *Re Bell, Bell v Georgiou*

[2002] WTLR 1105; *Goodman v Goodman* [2006] EWHC 1757 (Ch), [2006] WTLR 1807; *Price v Craig* [2006] EWHC 2561 (Ch), [2006] All ER (D) 249 (Oct); *Clarke v Brothwood* (21 November 2006, Ch D); *Pengelly v Pengelly* [2007] EWHC 3227 (Ch), [2007] Ch 375.

Where a claimant claims that a will fails to give effect to the testator's intention to benefit him by reason of negligence on the part of the draftsman of the will, the claimant may be expected to mitigate his damage by claiming rectification of the will under this section before bringing a claim for damages for negligence against the draftsman: *Walker v Geo H Medlicott & Son* [1999] 1 All ER 685, [1999] 1 WLR 727.

III TRU [43B.2]

Jurisdiction The High Court has unlimited jurisdiction under this section. No statute expressly gives the county court jurisdiction under this section, but it is submitted that the county court may give relief under this section in proceedings which are within its jurisdiction by virtue of s 23 of the County Courts Act 1984, eg as proceedings for the administration of the estate of a deceased person. Under that section, the county court has jurisdiction to hear and determine proceedings for the administration of the estate of a deceased person where the estate does not exceed in amount or value the county court limit, currently £30,000. That jurisdiction can be extended by agreement under s 25 of that Act.

III TRU [43B.3]

Extension of time The principles on which the court exercises its power to extend time for bringing claims under the Inheritance (Provision for Family and Dependants) Act 1975 (see para **III FMY [10]**) are applicable to the exercise of its power to extend time under sub-s (2): *Re Chittock* [2000] 1 WTLR 643, (2000) Times, 5 April. For cases where permission was granted to bring claims out of time see *Price v Craig* [2006] EWHC 2561 (Ch), [2006] All ER(D) 249 (Oct); *Pengelly v Pengelly* [2007] EWHC 3227 (Ch), [2007] Ch 375.

III TRU [43B.4]

Procedure An application under this section may be commenced by either a Pt 7 or Pt 8 claim form, as appropriate. In the High Court, proceedings should be commenced in the Property, Trusts and Probate list of the Business and Property Courts. Further procedural requirements are contained in CPR 57.12 (see para **CPR 57.12**) and CPR PD 57 paras 9 and 10 (see para **CPR PD 57**).

III TRU [43B.5]

Precedents For precedents for an application for rectification of a Will, see **BCCP Q[251]–BCCP Q[350]**.

TRUSTS

ADMINISTRATION OF JUSTICE ACT 1985

(c 61)

GENERAL NOTE ON ADMINISTRATION OF JUSTICE ACT 1985

III TRU [44]

Section 50 of the Administration of Justice Act 1985 confers on the High Court power to appoint substitutes for, or to remove, personal representatives.

III TRU [45]

50. Power of High Court to appoint substitute for, or to remove, personal representative

(1) Where an application relating to the estate of a deceased person is made to the High Court under this subsection by or on behalf of a personal representative of the deceased or a beneficiary of the estate, the court may in its discretion—

(a) appoint a person (in this section called a substituted personal representative) to act as personal representative of the deceased in place of the existing personal representative or representatives of the deceased or any of them; or
(b) if there are two or more existing personal representatives of the deceased, terminate the appointment of one or more, but not all, of those persons.

(2) Where the court appoints a person to act as a substituted personal representative of a deceased person, then—
(a) if that person is appointed to act with an executor or executors the appointment shall (except for the purpose of including him in any chain of representation) constitute him executor of the deceased as from the date of the appointment; and
(b) in any other case the appointment shall constitute that person administrator of the deceased's estate as from the date of the appointment.

(3) The court may authorise a person appointed as a substituted personal representative to charge remuneration for his services as such, on such terms (whether or not involving the submission of bills of charges for taxation by the court) as the court may think fit.

(4) Where an application relating to the estate of a deceased person is made to the court under subsection (1), the court may, if it thinks fit, proceed as if the application were, or included, an application for the appointment under the Judicial Trustees Act 1896 of a judicial trustee in relation to that estate.

(5) In this section "beneficiary", in relation to the estate of a deceased person, means a person who under the will of the deceased or under the law relating to intestacy is beneficially interested in the estate.

III TRU [45.1]

Jurisdiction The county court has no jurisdiction under this section.

III TRU [45.1A]

Scope of section: sub-section (1) For the principles on which the court acts on an application under s 50(1) see *Thomas and Agnes Carvel Foundation v Carvel* [2007] EWHC 1314 (Ch), [2008] Ch 395; *Kershaw v Micklethwaite* [2010] EWHC 506 (Ch), [2011] WTLR 413; *Heath v Heath* [2018] EWHC 779 (Ch).

The court has jurisdiction under this section to replace an executor named in a will before probate of the will has been granted: *Goodman v Goodman* [2013] EWHC 758 (Ch), [2014] Ch 186, [2013] 3 All ER 490.

III TRU [45.1B]

Scope of section: sub-section (4) One of the purposes of giving the court the power to proceed under the Judicial Trustees Act 1896 when the applicant has applied under the 1985 Act is to enable the court to cure purely procedural defects *Thomas and Agnes Carvel Foundation v Carvel* [2007] EWHC 1314 (Ch), [2008] Ch 395.

III TRU [45.2]

Procedure See CPR 57.13 and the Practice Direction to CPR Part 57, paras 12–14.

III TRU [45.3]

Precedents For precedents for an application for the appointment of a new personal representative, see **BCCP Q[351]–BCCP Q[400]**.

PRESUMPTION OF DEATH ACT 2013

(c 13)

GENERAL NOTES ON PRESUMPTION OF DEATH ACT 2013

III TRU [46]

Background and Summary The Presumption of Death Act 2013, which was brought fully into force on 1 October 2013, introduces a procedure enabling persons with a sufficient interest to do so to obtain a declaration from the High Court that a person who is thought to have died or has not been known to be alive for at least 7 years is presumed to be dead. The Act fills a gap in legislation, which previously only dealt with this topic in a fragmentary way.

The High Court has jurisdiction if either the missing person was domiciled or habitually resident in England and Wales or the application is made by a spouse or civil partner who is domiciled or habitually resident in England and Wales (s 1).

A declaration, when it can no longer be the subject of an appeal, is conclusive of the missing persons presumed death, and the date and time of the death, and is effective for all purposes and against all persons (s 3).

When making a declaration, the court has power to determine any question which relates to an interest in property and arises as a result of the declaration, and to determine the domicile of the missing person at the time of his or her presumed death. The court may also make such order as it considers reasonable in relation to any interest in property acquired as a result of the declaration (s 4).

A declaration of presumed death may be varied or revoked by a variation order, and the court making a variation order has power to determine any question which relates to an interest in property and arises as a result of the variation order, and to determine the domicile of the missing person at the time of his or her presumed death. The court may also make such order as it considers reasonable in relation to any interest in property acquired as a result of the declaration varied or revoked by the order (ss 5 to 8).

The Registrar General maintains a Register of Presumed Deaths (s 15).

III TRU [47]

Procedure The procedure on an application for a declaration of presumed death or variation order under the Act is governed by the new Section V which has been added to CPR Part 57 (CPR 57.17–CPR 57.23) and CPR PD 57B.

WALES

TABLE OF CONTENTS

GOVERNMENT OF WALES ACT 2006

(c 32)

GENERAL NOTE ON THE GOVERNMENT OF WALES ACT 2006

III WAL [1]

Changes made by the Government of Wales Act 2006 The Government of Wales Act 2006 has replaced the Government of Wales Act 1998 and repealed almost all of its provisions. The main structural changes are to establish the Welsh Assembly Government as an entity separate from, but accountable to, the National Assembly and to provide for provide for legislative competence to be conferred on the Assembly in respect of specified matters. Such legislation will be known as Welsh Measures. The only provisions reproduced below are those concerning the resolution of devolution issues (s 149 and Sch 9) and the power to vary retrospective decisions (s 153).

Devolution issues raised under the 1998 Act should in some circumstances be determined under the new Act: see art 3 of the Government of Wales Act 2006 (Transitional Provisions) Order 2007, SI 2007/1270.

In *National Assembly for Wales v Condron* (2006) Times, 13 December, the Court of Appeal stressed the importance of seeing that judicial review applications and appeals concerning decisions within the devolved powers of the Government of Wales should be listed for hearing in Wales, both at first instance and on appeal.

III WAL [2]

149. Resolution of devolution issues

For provision about the resolution of devolution issues see Schedule 9.

III WAL [3]

153. Power to vary retrospective decisions

(1) This section applies where any court or tribunal decides—

(a) that an Assembly Measure or Act of the Assembly, or any provision of an Assembly Measure or Act of the Assembly, is outside the Assembly's legislative competence,

WALES

(b) that any provision of subordinate legislation made, or purporting to be made, under an Assembly Measure or Act of the Assembly is outside the powers under which it was, or purported to be, made, or

(c) that any provision of subordinate legislation made, or purporting to be made, by the Welsh Ministers, the First Minister or the Counsel General is outside the powers under which it was, or purported to be, made.

(2) The court or tribunal may make an order—

(a) removing or limiting any retrospective effect of the decision, or

(b) suspending the effect of the decision for any period and on any conditions to allow the defect to be corrected.

(3) In determining whether to make an order under this section, the court or tribunal must (among other things) have regard to the extent to which persons who are not parties to the proceedings would otherwise be adversely affected by the decision.

(4) Where a court or tribunal is considering whether to make an order under this section, it must order notice (or intimation) of that fact to be given to the persons specified in subsection (5) (unless a party to the proceedings).

(5) The persons mentioned in subsection (4) are—

(a) in relation to proceedings in England and Wales, the Attorney General and the Counsel General,

(b) in relation to proceedings in Scotland, the [Attorney General] for Scotland, and

(c) in relation to proceedings in Northern Ireland, the Advocate General for Northern Ireland.

(6) A person to whom notice (or intimation) is given in pursuance of subsection (4) may take part as a party in the proceedings, so far as they relate to the making of the order.

(7) In deciding any question as to costs or expenses, the court or tribunal may—

(a) take account of any additional expense which it considers that any party to the proceedings has incurred as a result of the participation of any person in pursuance of subsection (6), and

(b) award the whole or part of the additional expense as costs or expenses to the party who incurred it (whether or not it makes an order under this section and whatever the terms of any such order it does make).

(8) Any power to make provision for regulating the procedure before any court or tribunal includes power to make provision for the purposes of this section including, in particular, provision for determining the manner in which and the time within which any notice (or intimation) is to be given.

(9) In subsection (1) "made" includes confirmed or approved.

SCHEDULE 9
DEVOLUTION ISSUES

PART 1 PRELIMINARY

III WAL [4]

1 (1) In this Schedule "devolution issue" means—

(a) a question whether an Assembly Measure or Act of the Assembly, or any provision of an Assembly Measure or Act of the Assembly, is within the Assembly's legislative competence,

(b) a question whether any function (being a function which any person has purported, or is proposing, to exercise) is exercisable by the Welsh Ministers, the First Minister or the Counsel General,

(c) a question whether the purported or proposed exercise of a function by the Welsh Ministers, the First Minister or the Counsel General is, or would be, within the powers of the Welsh Ministers, the First Minister or the Counsel General (including a question whether a purported or proposed exercise of a function is, or would be, outside those powers by virtue of section 80(8) or 81(1)),

(d) a question whether there has been any failure to comply with a duty imposed on the Welsh Ministers, the First Minister or the Counsel General (including any obligation imposed by virtue of section 80(1) or (7)), or

(e) a question of whether a failure to act by the Welsh Ministers, the First Minister or the Counsel General is incompatible with any of the Convention rights.

(2) In this Schedule—

(a) "the Judicial Committee" means the Judicial Committee of the Privy Council, and

(b) "civil proceedings" means proceedings other than criminal proceedings.

2 A devolution issue is not to be taken to arise in any proceedings merely because of any contention of a party to the proceedings which appears to the court or tribunal before which the proceedings take place to be frivolous or vexatious.

III WAL [4.1]

Compatibility with Convention rights An appeal may be made on a devolution issue as to whether a Ministerial failure to act is compatible with Convention rights, although any other right of appeal is excluded by statute: *BH v Lord Advocate* [2012] UKSC 24, [2012] 4 All ER 600, (2012) Times, 03 July, an appeal on a devolution issue under the Scotland Act 1998 regarding a decision of the High Court of Justiciary under Part 2 of the Extradition Act 2001.

PART 2
PROCEEDINGS IN ENGLAND AND WALES

Application of Part 2

III WAL [5]

3 This Part applies in relation to devolution issues in proceedings in England and Wales.

Institution of proceedings

4 (1) Proceedings for the determination of a devolution issue may be instituted by the Attorney General or the Counsel General.

(2) The Counsel General may defend any such proceedings instituted by the Attorney General.

(3) This paragraph does not limit any power to institute or defend proceedings exercisable apart from this paragraph by any person.

Notice of devolution issue

5 (1) A court or tribunal must order notice of any devolution issue which arises in any proceedings before it to be given to the Attorney General and the Counsel General (unless a party to the proceedings).

(2) A person to whom notice is given in pursuance of sub-paragraph (1) may take part as a party in the proceedings, so far as they relate to a devolution issue.

Reference of devolution issue to High Court or Court of Appeal

6 A magistrates' court may refer any devolution issue which arises in civil proceedings before it to the High Court.

7 (1) A court may refer any devolution issue which arises in civil proceedings before it to the Court of Appeal.

(2) Sub-paragraph (1) does not apply—

(a) to a magistrates' court, the Court of Appeal or the House of Lords, or

(b) to the High Court if the devolution issue arises in proceedings on a reference under paragraph 6.

8 A tribunal from which there is no appeal must refer any devolution issue which arises in proceedings before it to the Court of Appeal; and any other tribunal may make such a reference.

9 A court, other than the Court of Appeal or the House of Lords, may refer any devolution issue which arises in criminal proceedings before it to—

(a) the High Court if the proceedings are summary proceedings, or

(b) the Court of Appeal if the proceedings are proceedings on indictment.

References from Court of Appeal to Judicial Committee

10 The Court of Appeal may refer any devolution issue which arises in proceedings before it (otherwise than on a reference under paragraph 7, 8 or 9) to the Judicial Committee.

Appeals from superior courts to Judicial Committee

11 An appeal against a determination of a devolution issue by the High Court or the Court of Appeal on a reference under paragraph 6, 7, 8 or 9 lies to the Judicial Committee but only—

(a) with leave of the court from which the appeal lies, or

(b) failing such leave, with special leave of the Judicial Committee.

PART 5
GENERAL

Proceedings in the House of Lords

III WAL [6]

28A Any devolution issue which arises in judicial proceedings in the House of Lords is to be referred to the Judicial Committee unless the House considers it more appropriate, having regard to all the circumstances, that it should determine the issue.

Direct references to Judicial Committee

29 (1) The relevant officer may require any court or tribunal to refer to the Judicial Committee any devolution issue which has arisen in any proceedings before it to which that person is a party.

(2) In sub-paragraph (1) "the relevant officer" means—

(a) in relation to proceedings in England and Wales, the Attorney General or the Counsel General,

(b) in relation to proceedings in Scotland, the Advocate General for Scotland, and

(c) in relation to proceedings in Northern Ireland, the Attorney General for Northern Ireland.

30 (1) The Attorney General or the Counsel General may refer to the Judicial Committee any devolution issue which is not the subject of proceedings.
(2) Where a reference is made under sub-paragraph (1) by the Attorney General in relation to a devolution issue which relates to the proposed exercise of a function by the Welsh Ministers, the First Minister or the Counsel General—

(a) the Attorney General must notify the Counsel General of that fact, and

(b) the function must not be exercised by the Welsh Ministers, the First Minister or the Counsel General in the manner proposed during the period beginning with the receipt of the notification and ending with the reference being decided or otherwise disposed of.

COSTS

31 (1) A court or tribunal before which any proceedings take place may take account of any additional expense of the kind mentioned in sub-paragraph (3) in deciding any question as to costs or expenses.
(2) In deciding any such question the court or tribunal may award the whole or part of the additional expense as costs or expenses to the party who incurred it (whatever the decision on the devolution issue).
(3) The additional expense is any additional expense which the court or tribunal considers that any party to the proceedings has incurred as a result of the participation of any person in pursuance of paragraph 5, 14 or 24.

PROCEDURE OF COURTS AND TRIBUNALS

32 Any power to make provision for regulating the procedure before any court or tribunal includes power to make provision for the purposes of this Schedule including, in particular, provision—

(a) for prescribing the stage in the proceedings at which a devolution issue is to be raised or referred,

(b) for the staying or sisting of proceedings for the purpose of any proceedings under this Schedule, and

(c) for determining the manner in which and the time within which any notice or intimation is to be given.

REFERENCES TO BE FOR DECISION

33 Any function conferred by this Schedule to refer a devolution issue to a court is to be construed as a function of referring the issue to the court for decision.

PRACTICE DIRECTION—DEVOLUTION ISSUES

THIS PRACTICE DIRECTION IS DIVIDED INTO 4 PARTS.

WALES

PART I INTRODUCTION

Definitions

III WAL [7]

1 In this Practice Direction –

"the Assembly" means the National Assembly for Wales or Cynulliad Cenedlaethol Cymru

"the GWA" means the Government of Wales Act 1998

"the NIA" means the Northern Ireland Act 1998

"the SA" means the Scotland Act 1998

"the Acts" mean the GWA, the NIA and the SA

"the Judicial Committee" means the Judicial Committee of the Privy Council

"the CPR" means the Civil Procedure Rules 1998

"the FPR" means the Family Proceedings Rules 1991

"the FPC" means the Family Proceedings Courts (Children Act 1989) Rules 1991

"devolution issue" has the same meaning as in paragraph 1, schedule 8 to the GWA; paragraph 1, schedule 10 to the NIA; and paragraph 1, schedule 6 of the SA

"devolution issue notice" means a notice that a devolution issue has arisen in proceedings

Scope

2.1 This Practice Direction supplements the provisions dealing with devolution issues in the Acts. It deals specifically with the position if a devolution issue arises under the GWA. If a devolution issue arises under the NIA or the SA the procedure laid down in this Practice Direction should be adapted as required.

The devolution legislation

3.1 Schedule 8 to the GWA contains provisions dealing with devolution issues arising out of the GWA; schedule 10 to the NIA contains provisions dealing with devolution issues arising out of the NIA; and schedule 6 to the SA contains provisions dealing with devolution issues arising out of the SA.

3.2 Broadly a devolution issue will involve a question whether a devolved body has acted or proposes to act within its powers (which includes not acting incompatibly with Convention rights[1] and Community law[2]) or has failed to comply with a duty imposed on it. Reference should be made to the Acts where "devolution issue" is defined.

3.3

(1) If a devolution issue under the GWA arises in proceedings, the court must order notice of it to be given to the Attorney General and the Assembly if they are not already a party. They have a right to take part as a party in the proceedings so far as they relate to a devolution issue, if they are not already a party (paragraph 5, schedule 8 to the GWA.) If they do take part, they may require the court to refer the devolution issue to the Judicial Committee (paragraph 30, schedule 8 to the GWA)[3].

(2) There are similar provisions in the NIA and the SA although the persons to be notified are different (paragraphs 13, 14, and 33, schedule 10 to the NIA; paragraphs 16, 17 and 33, schedule 6 to the SA).

3.4 Under all the Acts the court may refer a devolution issue to another court as follows:

(1) A magistrates' court may refer a devolution issue arising in civil or summary proceedings to the High Court (paragraphs 6 and 9, schedule 8 to the GWA; paragraphs 15 and 18, schedule 10 to the NIA; and paragraphs 18 and 21, schedule 6 to the SA).

(2) The Crown Court may refer a devolution issue arising in summary proceedings to the High Court and a devolution issue arising in proceedings on indictment to the Court of Appeal (paragraph 9, schedule 8 to the GWA; paragraph 18, schedule 10 to the NIA; paragraph 21, schedule 6 to the SA).

(3) The County Court, the High Court (unless the devolution issue has been referred to the High Court)[4], and the Crown Court[5] may refer a devolution issue arising in civil proceedings to the Court of Appeal (paragraph 7, schedule 8 to the GWA; paragraph 16, schedule 10 to the NIA; paragraph 19, schedule 6 to the SA).

(4) A tribunal from which there is no appeal must, and any other tribunal may, refer a devolution issue to the Court of Appeal (paragraph 8, schedule 8 to the GWA; paragraph 17, schedule 10 to the NIA; paragraph 20, schedule 6 to the SA).

(5) The Court of Appeal may refer a devolution issue to the Judicial Committee, unless the devolution issue was referred to it by another court (paragraph 10, schedule 8 to the GWA; paragraph 19, schedule 10 to the NIA; paragraph 22, schedule 6 to the SA).

(6) An appeal against the determination of a devolution issue by the High Court or the Court of Appeal on a reference lies to the Judicial Committee with the leave of the court concerned, or, failing such leave, with special leave of the Judicial Committee (paragraph 11, schedule 8 to the GWA; paragraph 20, schedule 10 to the NIA; paragraph 23, schedule 6 to the SA).

3.5 A court may take into account additional expense which the court considers that a party has incurred as a result of the participation of the Attorney General or the Assembly in deciding any question as to costs (paragraph 35, schedule 8 to the GWA).

FOOTNOTES TO PART I (Part of Practice Direction)

---

1 The rights and fundamental freedoms set out in – (a) Articles 2 to 12 and 14 of the European Convention on Human Rights ("ECHR"), (b) Articles 1 to 3 of the First Protocol (agreed at Paris on 20th March 1952), and (c) Articles 1 and 2 of the Sixth Protocol (agreed at Strasbourg on 11th May 1994), as read with Articles 16 and 18 of the ECHR (Section 1 Human Rights Act 1998; s. 107(1) and (5) GWA; sections 6(2); 24(1) and 98(1) NIA; sections 29(2); 57(2) and 126 (1) SA).

2 All the rights, powers, liabilities, obligations and restrictions from time to time created or arising by or under the Community Treaties; and all the remedies and procedures from time to time provided for by or under the Community Treaties (sections 106(7) and 155(1), GWA; sections 6(2); 24(1) and 98(1), NIA; sections 29(2); 57(2) and 126(9) SA).

3 If the Attorney General or the Assembly had become a party to the original proceedings but did not exercise their right to require the devolution issue to be referred to the Judicial Committee and the court decided the case, they would have the same rights of appeal as parties. These would not allow them to appeal a decision made in proceedings on indictment, although the Attorney General has a power under section 36 of the Criminal Justice Act 1972 to refer a point of law to the Court of Appeal where the defendant has been acquitted in a trial on indictment.

Paragraph 31, schedule 8 to the GWA, allows the Attorney General and Assembly to refer to the Judicial Committee any devolution issue which is not the subject of proceedings. This power could possibly be used if a court reached a decision where they had not been parties and so had no rights of appeal but such a reference could not affect the decision of the court.

4 If an appeal by way of case stated in criminal proceedings goes to the Divisional Court there appears to be no power for the Divisional Court to refer a devolution issue to the Court of Appeal.

5 For example in appeals from a magistrates' court in a licensing matter.

PART II DIRECTIONS APPLICABLE TO ALL PROCEEDINGS

Scope

III WAL [8]

4 Paragraphs 5 to 13 apply to proceedings in England and Wales in the magistrates' courts, the County Court, the Crown Court, the High Court and the Court of Appeal (Civil and Criminal Division). Paragraph 10 also applies to the form and procedure for a reference to the Court of Appeal by a tribunal.

Raising the question as to whether a devolution issue arises

5.1 Where a party to any form of proceedings wishes to raise an issue which may be a devolution issue whether as a claim (or part of a claim) to enforce or establish a legal right or to seek a remedy or as a defence (or part of a defence), the provisions of this Practice Direction apply in addition to the rules of procedure applicable to the proceedings in which the issue arises.

5.2 A court may, of its own volition, require the question of whether a devolution issue arises to be considered, if the materials put before the court indicate such an issue may arise, even if the parties have not used the term "devolution issue".

Determination by a court of whether a devolution issue arises

6.1 The court may give such directions as it considers appropriate to obtain clarification or additional information to establish whether a devolution issue arises.

6.2 In determining whether a devolution issue arises the court, notwithstanding the contention of a party to the proceedings, may decide that a devolution issue shall not be taken to arise if the contention appears to the court to be frivolous or vexatious (paragraph 2 of schedule 8 to the GWA).

6.3 If the court determines that a devolution issue arises it must state what that devolution issue is clearly and concisely.

Notice of devolution issue to the Attorney General and the Assembly

7.1 If a court determines that a devolution issue arises in the proceedings, it must order a devolution issue notice substantially in the form numbered "DI 1" in Annex 1 to be given to the Attorney General and the Assembly unless they are already a party to the proceedings (paragraph 5(1), schedule 8 to the GWA).

7.2 A court receiving a reference does not have to serve a devolution issue notice unless it determines that a devolution issue that was not identified by the court making the reference has arisen. In that case the court receiving the reference must serve a devolution issue notice which must:

(1) state what devolution issue has been referred to it;
(2) state what further devolution issue has arisen; and
(3) identify the referring court.

7.3 If the devolution issue has arisen in criminal proceedings, the devolution issue notice must state:

(1) whether the proceedings have been adjourned;
(2) whether the defendant is remanded in custody; and
(3) if the defendant has been remanded in custody and his trial has not commenced, when the custody time limit expires[6].

7.4 If the devolution issue arises in an appeal, the devolution issue notice must:

(1) state that the devolution issue arises in an appeal;

(2) identify the court whose decision is being appealed; and
(3) state whether the devolution issue is raised for the first time on appeal; or, if it is not, state that the devolution issue was raised in the court whose decision is being appealed, what decision was reached by that court, and the date of the previous notice to the Attorney General and the Assembly.

7.5 The devolution issue notice will specify a date as the date by which the Attorney General or the Assembly must notify the court of any intention to take part as a party to the proceedings, so far as they relate to a devolution issue. Such date will be 14 days, or such longer period as the court may direct (see below), after the date of the notice.

7.6 The court may, in exceptional circumstances, specify a date longer than 14 days after the date of the notice as the date by which the Attorney General and the Assembly must notify the court of any intention to take part as a party to the proceedings. The court may do this before the notice is given, or before or after the expiry of the period given in the notice.

7.7

(1) On the date of the devolution issue notice—
(a) the notice for the Attorney General must be faxed to the Attorney General's Office by the court[7]; and
(b) the notice for the Assembly must be faxed by the court to the Counsel General for the Assembly.
(2) On the same day as a fax is sent a copy of the devolution issue notice must be sent by the court by first class post to the Attorney General and the Counsel General for the Assembly.

7.8 The court may, on such terms as it considers appropriate, order such additional documents to be served (eg in civil proceedings, the claim form) or additional information to be supplied with the devolution issue notice.

7.9

(1) When a court orders a devolution issue notice to be given the court may make such further orders as it thinks fit in relation to any adjournment, stay, continuance of the proceedings, or interim measures, during the period within which the Attorney General and the Assembly have to notify the court if they intend to take part as a party to the proceedings.
(2) Before ordering an adjournment in criminal proceedings, the court will consider all material circumstances, including whether it would involve delay that might extend beyond the custody time limits if the defendant is remanded in custody and his trial has not commenced.

7.10 If neither the Attorney General nor the Assembly notify the court within the specified time of any intention to take part as a party to the proceedings:

(1) the proceedings should immediately continue on expiry of the period within which they had to notify the court; and
(2) the court has no duty to inform them of the outcome of the proceedings apart from the duty to notify them if the court decides to refer the devolution issue to another court (see paragraph 10.3(5))[8].

Adding the Attorney General or the Assembly to the proceedings and their right to require referral of a devolution issue to the Judicial Committee

8.1 If the Attorney General or the Assembly intends to take part as a party to the proceedings so far as they relate to a devolution issue, the Attorney General or the Assembly must send to the court and the other parties (and to each other if only one of them has become a party) a notice substantially in the form numbered "DI 2" shown in Annex 1 within the time specified in the devolution issue notice.

8.2 On receipt of this form the court may give such consequential directions as it considers necessary.

WALES

8.3 If the Attorney General or the Assembly is a party to the proceedings, and either of them intends to require the court to refer the devolution issue to the Judicial Committee, the Attorney General or the Assembly must as soon as practicable send to the court and the other parties (and to each other if only one of them has become a party) a notice substantially in the form numbered "DI 3" shown in Annex 1.

Determination by the court of whether or not to make a reference of a devolution issue if the Attorney General or the Assembly do not require a reference

9.1 If the court is not required to refer the devolution issue to the Judicial Committee, the court will decide whether it should refer the devolution issue to the relevant court as specified in paragraph 3.4.

9.2 Before deciding whether to make a reference the court may hold a directions hearing or give written directions as to the making of submissions on the question of whether to make a reference.

9.3 The court may make a decision on the basis of written submissions if its procedures permit this and it wishes to do so, or the court may have a hearing before making a decision.

9.4 In exercising its discretion as to whether to make a reference, the court will have regard to all relevant circumstances and in particular to:

(1) the importance of the devolution issue to the public in general;
(2) the importance of the devolution issue to the original parties to the proceedings;
(3) whether a decision on the reference of the devolution issue will be decisive of the matters in dispute between the parties;
(4) whether all the relevant findings of fact have been made (a devolution issue will not, unless there are exceptional circumstances, be suitable for a reference if it has to be referred on the basis of assumed facts);
(5) the delay that a reference would entail particularly in cases involving children and criminal cases (including whether the reference is likely to involve delay that would extend beyond the expiry of the custody time limits if the defendant is remanded in custody and his trial has not commenced); and
(6) additional costs that a reference might involve[9].

9.5 The court should state its reasons for making or declining to make a reference.

9.6 If the court decides not to refer the case, it will give directions for the future conduct of the action, which will include directions as to the participation of the Attorney General and the Assembly if they are parties.

Form and procedure for references

10.1 If the court or tribunal is required by the Attorney General or the Assembly (in relation to any proceedings before the court to which he or it is a party) to refer the devolution issue to the Judicial Committee:

(1) the court or tribunal will make the reference as soon as practicable after receiving the notice from the Attorney General or the Assembly substantially in the form numbered "DI 3" shown in Annex 1, and follow the procedure for references in the Judicial Committee (Devolution Issues) Rules Order 1999; and
(2) the court or tribunal may order the parties, or any of them, to draft the reference.

10.2 If the Court of Appeal decides to refer the devolution issue to the Judicial Committee:

(1) it will follow the procedure in the Judicial Committee (Devolution Issues) Rules Order 1999; and

(2) the court may order the parties, or any of them, to draft the reference.

10.3 If any other court or tribunal decides, or if a tribunal is required, to refer the devolution issue to another court:

(1) the reference must be substantially in the form numbered "DI 4" shown in Annex 1 and must set out the following:
   (a) the question referred;
   (b) the addresses of the parties, except in the case of family proceedings, for which see paragraphs 15.2–4;
   (c) a concise statement of the background of the matter including –
      (i) the facts of the case, including any relevant findings of fact by the referring court or lower courts; and
      (ii) the main issues in the case and the contentions of the parties with regard to them;
   (d) the relevant law, including the relevant provisions of the GWA;
   (e) the reasons why an answer to the question is considered necessary for the purpose of disposing of the proceedings;

(2) all judgments already given in the proceedings will be annexed to the reference;

(3) the court may order the parties, or any of them, to draft the reference;

(4) the court or tribunal will transmit the reference to:
   (a) the Civil Appeals Office Registry if the reference is to the Court of Appeal from a county court, the High Court or the Crown Court in civil proceedings, or from a tribunal;
   (b) the Registrar of Criminal Appeals if the reference is to the Court of Appeal from the Crown Court in proceedings on indictment; and
   (c) the Administrative Court Office if the reference is to the High Court from a magistrates' court in civil or summary proceedings or from the Crown Court in summary proceedings[10].

   If the reference is transmitted to Cardiff an additional copy of the reference must be filed so that it can be retained by the Cardiff Office. The original reference will be forwarded to the Administrative Court Office in London.

(5) at the same time as the reference is transmitted to the court receiving the reference a copy of the reference will be sent by first class post to:
   (a) the parties;
   (b) the Attorney General if not already a party; and
   (c) the Assembly if it is not already a party;

(6) each person on whom a copy of the reference is served must within 21 days notify the court to which the reference is transmitted and the other persons on whom the reference is served whether they wish to be heard on the reference;

(7) the court receiving the reference (either the Court of Appeal or the High Court) will give directions for the conduct of the reference, including the lodging of cases or skeleton arguments; and transmit a copy of the determination on the reference to the referring court; and

(8) if there has been an appeal to the Judicial Committee against a decision of the High Court or the Court of Appeal on a reference, and a copy of the Judicial Committee's decision on that appeal has been sent to the High Court or Court of Appeal (as the case may be), that court will send a copy to the court which referred the devolution issue to it.

10.4 When a court receives notification of the decision on a reference, it will determine how to proceed with the remainder of the case.

Power of the court to deal with pending proceedings if a reference is made (whether by the Attorney General, the Assembly or the court).

11 If a reference is made the court will adjourn or stay the proceedings in which the devolution issue arose, unless it otherwise orders; and will make such further orders as it thinks fit in relation to any adjournment or stay.

The Welsh language

12.1 If any party wishes to put forward a contention in relation to a devolution issue that involves comparison of the Welsh and English texts of any Assembly subordinate legislation, that party must give notice to the court as soon as possible.

12.2 Upon receipt of the notification, the court will consider the appropriate means of determining the issue, including, if necessary, the appointment of a Welsh speaking judicial assessor to assist the court.

12.3 Parties to any proceedings in which the Welsh language may be used must also comply with the Practice Direction of 16th October 1998 (relating to proceedings in the Crown Court) and the Practice Direction of 26th April 1999 (relating to civil proceedings). These Practice Directions apply, as appropriate, to proceedings involving a devolution issue in which the Welsh language may be used.

Crown Proceedings Act 1947 (Section 19)

13. Where the court has determined that a devolution issue arises, the Attorney General will give any necessary consent to:

(1) the proceedings being transferred to The Law Courts, Cathays Park, Cardiff, CF 10 3PG, or to such other district registry as shall (exceptionally) be directed by the court; and

(2) to the trial taking place at Cardiff or at such other trial location as shall (exceptionally) be directed by the court.

FOOTNOTES TO PART II (Part of Practice Direction)

[6] Custody time limits are imposed by the Prosecution of Offences (Custody Time Limits) Regulations 1987 as amended.

[7] See Annex 2 for information about fax numbers and addresses.

[8] If there is an appeal, the appeal court will serve a devolution issue notice on the Attorney General and the Assembly (see paragraph 7.4).

[9] In criminal cases section 16 of the Prosecution of Offences Act 1985 does not enable a court receiving a reference to make a defendant's costs order. If the defendant is subsequently acquitted by the court who made the reference that court can make a defendant's costs order. However it would not cover the costs of the reference as "proceedings" is defined in section 21 as including proceedings in any court below but makes no mention of proceedings on a reference.

[10] See Annex 2 for the relevant addresses. It shows The Law Courts, Cathays Park, Cardiff, CF10 3PG and the Royal Courts of Justice, Strand, London WC2A 2LL as alternative addresses for transmitting documents to the Administrative Court Office. If the order is transmitted to Cardiff, the additional copy will be forwarded by the Cardiff Office to the Administrative Court Office in London.

PART III DIRECTIONS APPLICABLE TO SPECIFIC PROCEEDINGS

Judicial review proceedings

III WAL [9]

14.1 Practice Direction 54D contains provisions about where judicial review proceedings may be started in the Administrative Court.

Family proceedings in the Magistrates' Courts and the High Court

15.1 In any proceedings in which any question with respect to the upbringing of a child arises, the court shall have regard to the general principle that any delay in determining the question is likely to prejudice the welfare of the child[11].

15.2 If the FPR apply, the court will comply with rule 10.21[12].

15.3 If Part IV of the FPR applies, the court will comply with rule 4.23[13].

15.4 If the FPC apply, the court will comply with Rules 23 and 33A[14].

15.5 If the proceedings are listed in column (i) of Appendix 3 to the FPR or Schedule 2 to the FPC, a copy of any notice to be given to the parties must also be given to the persons set out in column (iv) of Appendix 3 or Schedule 2 as the case may be.

15.6 A party wishing to raise a devolution issue must, wherever possible, raise it (giving full particulars of the provisions relied on) in the application or answer or at the first directions hearing where appropriate.

15.7 If a party has not raised a devolution issue as above, the party must seek the permission of the court to raise it at a later stage.

15.8 Where a court has referred the devolution issue to another court and has received notification of the decision on the reference, the matter should so far as is practicable be placed before the same judge or magistrates who dealt with the case before the reference.

Civil proceedings in the County Court and the High Court

16.1 A party wishing to raise a devolution issue must specify in the claim form, or if he is a defendant, in the defence (or written evidence filed with the acknowledgement of service in a Part 8 claim) that the claim raises a devolution issue and the relevant provisions of the GWA.

16.2 The particulars of claim or defence if the devolution issue is raised by the defendant (or written evidence filed with the acknowledgement of service in a Part 8 claim) must contain the facts and circumstances and points of law on the basis of which it is alleged that a devolution issue arises in sufficient detail to enable the court to determine whether a devolution issue arises in the proceedings.

16.3 Whether or not the allocation rules apply, if a question is raised during the proceedings that might be a devolution issue, then a directions hearing must take place and the matter must be referred to a circuit judge (in county court actions) or a High Court judge (in High Court actions) for determination as to whether a devolution issue arises and for further directions.

16.4 If a party fails to specify in the appropriate document that a devolution issue arises but that party subsequently wishes to raise a devolution issue, that party must seek the permission of the court.

16.5 Where any party has specified that a devolution issue arises, no default judgment can be obtained.

Criminal proceedings in the Crown Court

17. If the defendant wishes to raise a devolution issue he should do so at the Plea and Directions Hearing.

Criminal and civil proceedings in the magistrates' courts

18.1

(1) Where a defendant, who has been charged or has had an information laid against him in respect of a criminal offence and has entered a plea of "Not Guilty", wishes to raise a devolution issue he should, wherever possible, give full particulars of the provisions relied on by notice in writing.

(2) Where a party to a complaint, or applicant for a licence wishes to raise a devolution issue he should, wherever possible, give full particulars of the provisions relied on by notice in writing.

(3) Such notice should be given to the prosecution (and other party if any) and the court as soon as practicable after the "Not Guilty" plea is entered or the complaint or application is made as the case may be.

18.2 Where proceedings are to be committed or transferred to the Crown Court by the magistrates, the question as to whether a devolution issue arises shall be a matter for the Crown Court.

FOOTNOTES TO PART III (Part of Practice Direction)

---

11 Section 1(2), Children Act 1989.

12 Rule 10.21 states: (1) Subject to rule 2.3 [of the FPR] nothing in these rules shall be construed as requiring any party to reveal the address of their private residence (or that of any child) save by order of the court. (2) Where a party declines to reveal an address in reliance upon paragraph (1) above, he shall give notice of that address to the court in Form C8 and that address shall not be revealed to any person save by order of the court.

13 Rule 4.23 states: (1) Notwithstanding any rule of court to the contrary, no document, other than a record of an order, held by the court and relating to proceedings to which [Part IV] applies shall be disclosed, other than to – (a) a party, (b) the legal representative of a party (c) the guardian ad litem, (d) the Legal Aid Board, or (e) a welfare officer, without the leave of the judge or the district judge. (2) Nothing in this rule shall prevent the notification by the court or the proper officer of a direction under section 37(1) to the authority concerned. (3) Nothing in this rule shall prevent the disclosure of a document prepared by a guardian ad litem for the purpose of – (a) enabling a person to perform functions required by regulations made under section 41(7); (b) assisting a guardian ad litem or a reporting officer (within the meaning of section 65(1)(b) of the Adoption Act 1976) who is appointed under any enactment to perform his functions.

14 Rule 23 states: (1) No document, other than a record of an order, held by the court and relating to relevant proceedings shall be disclosed, other than to – (a) a party, (b) the legal representative of a party, (c) the guardian ad litem, (d) the Legal Aid Board, or (e) a welfare officer, without leave of the justices' clerk or the court. (2) Nothing in this rule shall prevent the notification by the court or the justices' clerk of a direction under section 37(1) to the authority concerned. (3) Nothing in this rule shall prevent the disclosure of a document prepared by a guardian ad litem for the purpose of _ (a) enabling a person to perform functions required by regulations made under section 41(7); (b) assisting a guardian ad litem or a reporting officer (within the meaning of section 65(1)(b) of the Adoption Act 1976) who is appointed under any enactment to perform his functions.

Rule 33A states: (1) Nothing in these Rules shall be construed as requiring any party to reveal the address of their private residence (or that of any child) except by order of the court. (2) Where a party declines to reveal an address in reliance upon paragraph (1) he shall give notice of that address to the court in Form C8 and that address shall not be revealed to any person except by order of the court.

PART IV APPEALS

Appeals to the Court of Appeal (Civil and Criminal Division)

III WAL [10]

19.1 This paragraph applies if a devolution issue is raised in any appeal to either the Civil or the Criminal Division of the Court of Appeal.

19.2 The devolution issue may already have been raised in the court whose decision is being appealed. The devolution issue may, however, be raised for the first time on appeal.

19.3 Where an application for permission to appeal is made, or an appeal is brought where permission is not needed, the appellant must specify in the application notice (or the notice of appeal or notice of motion as the case may be):

(1) that the appeal raises a devolution issue and the relevant provisions of the GWA;

(2) the facts and circumstances and points of law on the basis of which it is alleged that a devolution issue arises in sufficient detail to enable the court to determine whether a devolution issue arises; and

(3) whether the devolution issue was considered in the court below, and, if so, provide details of the decision.

19.4 An appellant may not seek to raise a devolution issue without the permission of the court after he has filed an application notice; or a notice of appeal or notice of motion (if no application notice).

19.5 Where permission to appeal is sought and a party to the appeal wishes to raise a devolution issue which was not raised in the lower court, the court will determine if a devolution issue arises before deciding whether to grant leave to appeal.

Appeals to the Crown Court

20. A notice of appeal from a decision of the magistrates' courts to the Crown Court must specify whether the devolution issue was considered in the court below and if so, provide details of the decision. If it was not so considered, the notice should specify:

(1) that the appeal raises a devolution issue and the relevant provisions of the GWA; and

(2) the facts and circumstances and points of law on the basis of which it is alleged that a devolution issue arises in sufficient detail to enable the court to determine whether a devolution issue arises.

ANNEX 1

III WAL [11]

DI 1

Devolution Issues Notice of Devolution Issue to Attorney General and the National Assembly for Wales

[NAME OF CASE]

Take notice that the above mentioned case has raised a devolution issue as defined by Schedule 8 to the Government of Wales Act 1998. Details of the devolution issue are given in the attached schedule.

This notice meets the notification requirements under paragraph 5(1) of Schedule 8 to the Government of Wales Act 1998. You may take part as a party to these proceedings, so far as they relate to a devolution issue (paragraph 5(2) of Schedule 8). If you want to do this you must notify the court by completing the attached form, and returning it to the court at [*address*] by [*date*].

DATED

To: The Attorney General

The National Assembly for Wales

Other parties (where appropriate)

DI 2

Devolution Issues Notice of Intention of Attorney General or the National Assembly for Wales to become party to proceedings, so far as they relate to a devolution issue, under paragraph 5(2) Schedule 8 to the Government of Wales Act 1998

In the [name of court]

[case name]

Take notice that the [Attorney General] [the National Assembly for Wales] intends to take part as a party to proceedings so far as they relate to a devolution issue as permitted by paragraph 5(2) of Schedule 8 to the Government of Wales Act 1998 in relation to the devolution issue raised by [ ], of which notice was received by the [Attorney General] [Assembly] on [ ].

[The [ ] also gives notice that it [requires the matter to be referred to] [is still considering whether to require the matter to be referred to] the Judicial Committee of the Privy Council under paragraph 30 of Schedule 8 to the Government of Wales Act 1998.]

[DATE]

On behalf of the [Attorney General]

[National Assembly for Wales]

To: The clerk of the court at [ ]

The parties to the case

[Attorney General] [National Assembly for Wales]

DI 3

Devolution issues notice by Attorney General or National Assembly for Wales that they require devolution issue to be referred to the Judicial Committee of the Privy Council

In the [court]

[case name]

The [Attorney General] [National Assembly for Wales] gives notice that the devolution issue, which has been raised in the above case and to which [he] [it] is a party, must be referred to the Judicial Committee of the Privy Council under paragraph 30 of Schedule 8 to the Government of Wales Act 1998.

[DATE]

On behalf of the [Attorney General]

[National Assembly for Wales]

To: The clerk of the court at [ ]

The parties to the case

[Attorney General] [National Assembly for Wales]

DI 4

Devolution issues reference by the court or tribunal of devolution issue to [High Court] [Court Of Appeal] [Judicial Committee of the Privy Council]

In the [court]

[case name]

It is ordered that the devolution issue(s) set out in the schedule be referred to the [High Court] [Court of Appeal] [Judicial Committee of the Privy Council] for determination in accordance with paragraph [ ] of Schedule 8 to the Government of Wales Act 1998.

It is further ordered that the proceedings be stayed until the [High Court] [Court of Appeal] Judicial Committee of the Privy Council] determine the devolution issue[s] or until further order.

DATED

Judge/clerk to the magistrates court

Chairman of the Tribunal

[Address]

Skeleton reference to be attached to Form DI 4

In the [court]

[case name]

(a) [The question referred.]
(b) [The addresses of the parties]
(c) [A concise statement of the background to the matters including -
  (i) The facts of the case including any relevant findings of fact by the referring court or lower courts; and
  (ii) The main issues in the case and the contentions of the parties with regard to them;]
(d) [the relevant law including the relevant provisions of the Government of Wales Act 1998]
(e) [the reasons why an answer to the question is considered necessary for the purpose of disposing of the proceedings.]

[All judgments already given in the proceedings are annexed to this reference.]

ANNEX 2

Addresses

III WAL [12]

(1) Notices to the National Assembly for Wales (Cynulliad Cenedlaethol Cymru) must be sent to the Counsel General to the National Assembly for Wales, Crown Buildings, Cathays Park, Cardiff CF99 1NA. Fax number: (01222) 826798.

(2) Notices to the Attorney General must be sent to the Attorney General's Offices at 5–8 The Sanctuary, London SW1P 3JS. Fax number 020 7271 2432.

EXPLANATORY NOTE

(4) The addresses and fax numbers above are the best information available. However it is possible that these (particularly the fax numbers and address for Notices to the Assembly) may change. It would therefore be advisable to confirm the numbers before sending information.

Editorial note on the Practice Direction The Practice Direction was issued to assist where devolution issues were raised under the Government of Wales Act 1998 and it includes many references to the provisions of that Act although that Act has been repealed and replaced by the Government of Wales Act 2006. In accordance with s 17 of the Interpretation Act 1978 references to repealed provisions should be interpreted as references to the provisions of the new Act which replace them.

PRACTICE DIRECTION RELATING TO THE USE OF THE WELSH LANGUAGE IN CASES IN THE CIVIL COURTS IN WALES

III WAL [13]

THE PURPOSE OF THIS PRACTICE DIRECTION IS TO REFLECT THE PRINCIPLE OF THE WELSH LANGUAGE ACT 1993 THAT IN THE ADMINISTRATION OF JUSTICE IN WALES, THE ENGLISH AND WELSH LANGUAGES SHOULD BE TREATED ON THE BASIS OF EQUALITY.

1. GENERAL

1.1 This practice direction applies to civil proceedings in courts in Wales.

1.2 The existing practice of conducting a hearing entirely in the Welsh language on an ad hoc basis and without notice will continue to apply when all parties and witnesses directly involved at the time consent to the proceedings being so conducted.

1.3 In every case in which it is possible that the Welsh language may be used by any party or witness [or in any document which may be placed before the court], the parties or their legal representatives must inform the court of that fact so that appropriate arrangements can be made for the management and listing of the case.

1.4 If costs are incurred as a result of a party failing to comply with this direction, a costs Order may be made against him or his legal representative.

1.5 Where a case is tried with a jury, the law does not permit the selection of jurors in a manner which enables the court to discover whether a juror does or does not speak Welsh or to secure a jury whose members are bilingual to try a case in which the Welsh language may be used.

2. THE ALLOCATION QUESTIONNAIRE

2.1 In any proceedings in which a party is required to complete an allocation questionnaire, he must include details relating to the possible use of Welsh ie details of any person wishing to give oral evidence in Welsh and of any documents in Welsh (eg documents to be disclosed under Part 31 or witness statements) which that party expects to use.

2.2 A party must include the details mentioned in paragraph 2.1 in the allocation questionnaire even if he has already informed the court of the possible use of Welsh in accordance with the provisions of section 1 above.

3. CASE MANAGEMENT

3.1 At any interlocutory hearing, the court will take the opportunity to consider whether it should give case management directions. To assist the court, a party or his legal representative should draw the court's attention to the possibility of Welsh being used in the proceedings, even where he has already done so in compliance with other provisions of this direction.

3.2 In any case where a party is required to complete a pre-trial check list (listing questionnaire) and has already intimated the intention to use Welsh, he should confirm the intended use of Welsh in the pre-trial check list and provide any details which have not been set out in the allocation questionnaire.

4. LISTING BY THE COURT

4.1 The diary manager, in consultation with the Designated Civil Judge, will ensure that a case in which the Welsh language is to be used is listed:

(a) wherever practicable before a Welsh speaking judge; and
(b) where translation facilities are needed, at a court with simultaneous translation facilities.

5. INTERPRETERS

5.1 Whenever an interpreter is needed to translate evidence from English to Welsh or from Welsh to English, the Court Manager in whose court the case is to be heard will take steps to secure the attendance of an interpreter whose name is included in the list of approved court interpreters.

6. WITNESSES AND JURORS

6.1 When each witness is called, the court officer administering the oath or affirmation will inform the witness that he or she may be sworn or may affirm in Welsh or English as he or she wishes.

6.2 Where a case is tried with a jury, the court officer swearing in the jury will inform the jurors in open court that each juror may take the oath or may affirm in Welsh or English as he or she wishes.

7. ROLE OF THE LIAISON JUDGE

7.1 If any question or difficulty arises concerning the implementation of this practice direction, contact should in the first place be made with the Liaison Judge for the Welsh language.

SUPPLEMENTARY DIRECTION APPLICABLE TO CASES WHERE THE WELSH LANGUAGE IS TO BE USED AND WHICH ORIGINATE IN NORTH WALES

III WAL [14]

THE FOLLOWING DIRECTION APPLIES TO CASES TRANSFERRED OR COMMITTED FROM MAGISTRATES COURTS IN WALES WHERE AS A RESULT OF LISTING OR OTHER ARRANGEMENTS IT IS CONTEMPLATED THAT THE CASE MAY BE TRIED IN CHESTER OR AT ANOTHER LOCATION OUTSIDE WALES.

1. In accordance with the Practice Direction issued by the Lord Chief Justice in [1998] 1 WLR 1677, all cases involving evidence to be given in the Welsh Language should wherever practicable be heard in Wales. If for any reason any such case committed for trial or sentence or transferred from a Magistrates Court in Wales cannot be heard in Wales, then the case must be referred to one of the Presiding Judges. No hearing or trial in that case can take place in a court outside of Wales without the express consent of one of the Presiding Judges. The Presiding Judge must be provided with:

Detailed information about the case.

The scope of the intended use of the Welsh language.

Information about the views of the Prosecution and Defence about hearing/trial and the use of Welsh.

The name of the Judge who is to hear the case.

Consent to the hearing of a case outside of Wales will be on the basis that it is heard by the Judge specifically nominated for that case; no other Judge may hear the case without further reference being made to one of the Presiding Judges.

2. No Judge other than a Judge designated on the list provided by the Circuit Administrator as approved to try cases in the Welsh language may try any case involving the use of the Welsh language, unless the consent of one of the Presiding Judges or the liaison Judge for the Welsh language (Judge Roderick Evans QC) has been specifically obtained.

3. This supplementary Direction takes immediate effect and applies to any hearings or trials that take place after the date of this supplementary Direction.

MOBILE HOMES (WALES) ACT 2013

(anaw 6)

PART 1
INTRODUCTION

III WAL [15]

1. Overview of Act

(1) This Act makes provision about mobile home sites in Wales.

(2) In this Act—

(a) Part 2 makes provision for and in connection with the licensing of regulated sites etc,

(b) Part 3 makes provision for protection from eviction from protected sites,

(c) Part 4 makes provision about the terms of agreements for stationing mobile homes on protected sites,

(d) Part 5 makes provision under which local authorities may provide sites for mobile homes and may prohibit the stationing of mobile homes on commons, and

(e) Part 6 makes supplementary and general provision.

III WAL [15.1]

The law relating to mobile homes in Wales Much of the law relating to mobile homes in Wales concerns matters of licensing and administration. Performance in these areas may be subject to judicial review but decisions are not subject to rights of appeal except to residential property tribunals. In the circumstances the provisions of Part 2 (licensing of mobile home sites etc) and Part 5 (powers of local authorities) are not reproduced below. The definition in section 60 of 'mobile home' is the only provision included from Part 6 (Supplementary and General) and of the Schedules, only Schedule 2 (Terms of mobile home agreements) is reproduced. The Act has been fully in force since 1 October 2014 and consequential amendments of other legislation such as the Mobile Homes Act 1983 have already been incorporated in the text used in that title. The Parts where there is some involvement with the county court are reproduced below: Part 3 (Protection from Eviction) and Part 4 (Mobile Home Agreements).

WALES

III WAL [16]

2. Mobile home sites subject to Act

(1) In this Act "regulated site" means any land in Wales on which a mobile home is stationed for the purposes of human habitation (including any land in Wales used in conjunction with that land), other than—

(a) a site which Schedule 1 provides is not to be a regulated site, or
(b) a holiday site.

(2) In this Act "protected site" means land which is—
(a) a regulated site, or
(b) a site that would be a regulated site but for paragraph 11 of Schedule 1.

(3) In subsection (1) "holiday site" means a site in respect of which the relevant planning permission or the site licence for the site under the Caravan Sites and Control of Development Act 1960—
(a) is expressed to be granted for holiday use only, or
(b) requires that there are times of the year when no mobile home may be stationed on the site for human habitation.

(4) For the purpose of determining whether or not a site is a holiday site, any provision of the relevant planning permission or of the site licence which permits the stationing of a mobile home on the land for human habitation all year round is to be ignored if the mobile home is authorised to be occupied by—
(a) the person who is the owner of the site, or
(b) a person employed by that person but who does not occupy the mobile home under an agreement to which Part 4 applies.

(5) In this Act "local authority Gypsy and Traveller site" means land owned by a local authority for the stationing of mobile homes providing accommodation for Gypsies and Travellers.

III WAL [17]

3. Owners of sites

In this Act "owner", in relation to any land, means the person who, by virtue of an estate or interest in the land—
(a) is entitled to possession of the land, or
(b) would be entitled to possession of the land but for the rights of any other person under any licence or contract granted in respect of the land (including a licence or contract to station or occupy a mobile home there),

but see also sections 39(2), 42(7) and 55(2)(a).

PART 2
LICENSING OF MOBILE HOME SITES ETC

Editorial Note The text of Part 2, sections 4 to 39, has been omitted.

PART 3
PROTECTION FROM EVICTION

III WAL [18]

40.

This Part applies in relation to any licence or contract (whenever made) under which a person is entitled—
(a) to station a mobile home on a protected site and occupy it as the person's residence, or
(b) if the mobile home is stationed on the protected site by another, to occupy it as the person's residence.

III WAL [19]

41. Minimum length of notice

In any case where a residential contract is determinable by notice given by either party to the other, a notice is of no effect unless it is given not less than 4 weeks before the date on which it is to take effect.

III WAL [19.1]

Law applicable outside Wales The provisions on the minimum length of notice and the other provisions of Part 3 (protection from eviction and harassment and suspension of eviction orders) reflect the pre-existing law contained in the Caravan Sites 1968, which continues to apply to protected sites in England.

III WAL [20]

42. Protection of occupiers against eviction and harassment, false information etc

(1) A person to whom any of subsections (2) to (6) applies commits an offence.

(2) This subsection applies to a person if, during the subsistence of a residential contract, the person unlawfully deprives the occupier of the mobile home of occupation on the protected site of any mobile home which the occupier is entitled by the contract to station and occupy, or to occupy, as the occupier's residence on the protected site.

(3) This subsection applies to a person if, after the expiry or determination of a residential contract, the person enforces, otherwise than by proceedings in the court, any right to exclude the occupier of the mobile home from the protected site or from any such mobile home, or to remove or exclude any such mobile home from the protected site.

(4) This subsection applies to a person if (whether during the subsistence, or after the expiry or determination, of a residential contract) with intent to cause the occupier of the mobile home—

- (a) to abandon the occupation of the mobile home or remove it from the site, or
- (b) to refrain from exercising any right or pursuing any remedy in respect of that,

the person does acts likely to interfere with the peace or comfort of the occupier or persons residing with the occupier, or withdraws or withholds services or facilities reasonably required for the occupation of the mobile home as a residence on the site.

(5) This subsection applies to a person if the person is, or is the agent of, the owner of the protected site and (whether during the subsistence or after the expiration or determination of a residential contract)—

- (a) the person does acts likely to interfere with the peace or comfort of the occupier of the mobile home or persons residing with the occupier, or
- (b) withdraws or withholds services or facilities reasonably required for the occupation of the mobile home as a residence on the site,

and (in either case) the person knows, or has reasonable cause to believe, that that conduct is likely to cause the occupier to do any of the things mentioned in subsection (4)(a) or (b).

(6) This subsection applies to a person if the person is, or is the agent of, the owner of a protected site and, during the subsistence of a residential contract, the person—

- (a) knowingly or recklessly provides information or makes a representation which is false or misleading in a material respect to any person, and
- (b) knows, or has reasonable cause to believe, that doing so is likely to cause—

WALES

(i) the occupier to do any of the things mentioned in subsection (4)(a) or (b), or

(ii) a person who is considering whether to purchase or occupy the mobile home to which the residential contract relates to decide not to do so.

(7) In subsections (5) and (6) references to the owner of a protected site include references to a person with an estate or interest in the site which is superior to that of the owner.

(8) In this section references to the occupier of the mobile home include references to the person who was the occupier of the mobile home under a residential contract which has expired or been determined and, in the case of the death of the occupier (whether during the subsistence or after the expiry or determination of the contract), to any person then residing with the occupier.

(9) Nothing in this section applies to the exercise by the owner of a mobile home of a right to take possession of the mobile home, other than a right conferred by or arising on the expiry or determination of a residential contract, or to anything done pursuant to the order of any court.

III WAL [21]

43. Offences under section 42: supplementary

(1) In proceedings for an offence of contravening section 42(2) or (3) it is a defence to prove that the accused believed, and had reasonable cause to believe, that the occupier of the mobile home had ceased to reside on the site.

(2) In proceedings for an offence of contravening section 42(5) it is a defence to prove that the accused had reasonable grounds for doing the acts or withdrawing or withholding the services or facilities in question.

(3) A person guilty of an offence under section 42 is liable—

(a) on summary conviction, to a fine or to imprisonment for a term not exceeding 12 months, or to both, or

(b) on conviction on indictment, to a fine or to imprisonment for a term not exceeding 2 years, or to both.

III WAL [22]

44. Provision for suspension of eviction orders

(1) If in proceedings by the owner of a protected site the court makes an order for enforcing in relation to the site any such right as is mentioned in section 42(3), the court may (without prejudice to any power apart from this section to postpone the operation or suspend the execution of an order) suspend the enforcement of the order for such period not exceeding 12 months from the date of the order as the court thinks reasonable.

(2) Where the court by virtue of this section suspends the enforcement of an order, it may impose such terms and conditions, including conditions as to the payment of rent or other periodical payments or of arrears of such rent or payments, as the court thinks reasonable.

(3) The court may from time to time, on the application of either party, extend, reduce or terminate the period of suspension ordered, or vary any terms or conditions imposed, but may not extend the period of suspension for more than 12 months at a time.

(4) In considering whether or how to exercise its powers under this section, the court must have regard to all the circumstances which include (but are not limited to) the questions—

(a) whether the occupier of the mobile home has failed, whether before or after the expiry or determination of the relevant residential contract, to observe any terms or conditions of that contract, any conditions of the site licence, or any reasonable rules made by the owner of the protected site for the management and conduct of the site or the maintenance of mobile homes on it,

(b) whether the occupier of the mobile home has unreasonably refused an offer by the owner to renew the residential contract or make another residential contract for a reasonable period and on reasonable terms, and

(c) whether the occupier of the mobile home has failed to make reasonable efforts to obtain elsewhere other suitable accommodation for the mobile home or another suitable mobile home and accommodation for it.

(5) Where the court makes an order such as is mentioned in subsection (1) but suspends the enforcement of the order, the court may not make any order for costs unless it appears to the court, having regard to the conduct of the owner of the protected site or of the occupier of the mobile home, that the circumstances of the case are exceptional.

(6) The court may not suspend the enforcement of an order by virtue of this section if—

(a) no site licence is in force in respect of the site, and

(b) the site is not owned by a local authority;

and where a site licence in respect of the site is expressed to expire at the end of a specified period, the period for which enforcement may be suspended by virtue of this section does not extend beyond the expiry of the site licence.

III WAL [23]

45. Supplementary

(1) The power of the court under section 44 to suspend the enforcement of an order extends to any order made but not executed before the commencement of this Part.

(2) Nothing in this Part affects the operation of section 13 of the Compulsory Purchase Act 1965.

(3) The Protection from Eviction Act 1977 does not apply to any premises consisting of a mobile home stationed on a protected site.

III WAL [24]

46. Offences

Proceedings for an offence under this Part may be instituted by any local authority.

III WAL [25]

47. Interpretation

(1) In this Part—

"occupier" ("*meddiannydd*") in relation to a mobile home and a protected site, means the person entitled as mentioned in section 40 in relation to a mobile home and the protected site;

"residential contract" ("*contract preswyl*") means a licence or contract within that section.

(2) In this Part "the court" means the county court.

WALES

PART 4
MOBILE HOME AGREEMENTS

III WAL [26]

48. Agreements to which Part applies

(1) This Part applies to any agreement under which a person is entitled—

(a) to station a mobile home on a protected site, and

(b) to occupy the mobile home as the person's only or main residence.

(2) In this Part "occupier", in relation to a mobile home and a protected site, means the person entitled as mentioned in subsection (1) in relation to a mobile home and the protected site (but see also section 55(2)(b)).

III WAL [26.1]

Mobile homes agreements outside Wales The provisions of this Part are modelled on the pre-existing law applied by the Mobiles Homes Act 1983 to mobile homes in England and Wales and now only to those in England.

III WAL [27]

49. Particulars of agreements

(1) Before making an agreement to which this Part applies, the owner of the protected site must give to the proposed occupier under the agreement a written statement which—

(a) specifies the names and addresses of the parties,

(b) includes particulars of the land on which the proposed occupier is to be entitled to station the mobile home that are sufficient to identify that land,

(c) sets out the express terms to be contained in the agreement (including any site rules),

(d) sets out the terms to be implied by section 50(1), and

(e) complies with such other requirements as may be prescribed by regulations made by the Welsh Ministers.

(2) The written statement required by subsection (1) must be given—

(a) no later than 28 days before the date on which any agreement for the sale of the mobile home to the proposed occupier is made, or

(b) (if no such agreement is made before the making of the agreement to which this Part applies) no later than 28 days before the date on which the agreement to which this Part applies is made.

(3) But if the proposed occupier consents in writing to that statement being given by a date ("the chosen date") which is less than 28 days before the date mentioned in subsection (2)(a) or (b), the statement must be given to the proposed occupier not later than the chosen date.

(4) If any express term other than a site rule—

(a) is contained in an agreement to which this Part applies, but

(b) was not set out in a written statement given to the proposed occupier in accordance with subsections (1) to (3),

the term is unenforceable by the owner or any person within section 53(1); but this is subject to any order made by the appropriate judicial body under section 50(3).

(5) If the owner has failed to give the occupier a written statement in accordance with subsections (1) to (3) the occupier may, at any time after the making of the agreement, apply to the appropriate judicial body for an order requiring the owner—

(a) to give the occupier a written statement which complies with paragraphs (a) to (e) of subsection (1) (read with any modifications necessary to reflect the fact that the agreement has been made), and

(b) to do so not later than such date as is specified in the order.

(6) A statement required to be given to a person under this section may be either delivered to the person personally or sent to the person by post.

(7) Any reference in this section to the making of an agreement to which this Part applies includes a reference to any variation of an agreement by virtue of which the agreement becomes one to which this Part applies.

(8) Subsections (2), (3) and (5) do not apply in relation to a person occupying or proposing to occupy a transit pitch on a local authority Gypsy and Traveller site; and in such a case the reference in subsection (4) to subsections (1) to (3) is to be treated as a reference to subsection (1).

III WAL [28]

50. Terms of agreements

(1) The applicable terms set out in Part 1 of Schedule 2 are implied in any agreement to which this Part applies; and this subsection has effect despite any express term of the agreement.

(2) The appropriate judicial body may, on the application of either party made within the relevant period, order that terms concerning the matters mentioned in Part 2 of Schedule 2 are to be implied in the agreement.

(3) The appropriate judicial body may, on the application of either party made within the relevant period, make an order—

(a) varying or deleting any express term of the agreement other than a site rule,

(b) in the case of any express term to which section 49(4) applies other than a site rule, providing for the term to have full effect or to have such effect subject to any variation specified in the order.

(4) In subsections (2) and (3) "the relevant period" means the period beginning with the date on which the agreement is made and ending—

(a) 6 months after that date, or

(b) where a written statement relating to the agreement is given to the occupier after that date (whether or not in compliance with an order under section 49(5)), 6 months after the date on which the statement is given;

and subsection (7) of section 49 applies for the purposes of this subsection as it applies for the purposes of that section.

(5) On an application under this section, the appropriate judicial body must make such provision as it considers just and equitable in the circumstances.

(6) Subsections (2) to (4) do not apply in relation to a person occupying or proposing to occupy a transit pitch on a local authority Gypsy and Traveller site.

III WAL [28.1]

Schedule 2 See below at **III WAL [35]** for the text of Parts 1 and 2 of Schedule 2.

III WAL [29]

51. Power to amend implied terms

(1) The Welsh Ministers may by order make such amendments of Schedule 2, apart from paragraph 11, as they consider appropriate.

(2) Without prejudice to the generality of subsection (1), an order under this section may—

(a) make provision for or in connection with the determination by the court or a tribunal of such questions, or the making by the court or a tribunal of such orders, as are specified in the order, or

(b) make such amendments of any other provision of this Part as the Welsh Ministers consider appropriate in consequence of any amendment made in Schedule 2 by the order.

III WAL [30]

52. Site rules

(1) In the case of a protected site, other than a local authority Gypsy and Traveller site, for which there are site rules, each of the rules is to be an express term of each agreement to which this Part applies that relates to a pitch on the site (including an agreement made before commencement or one made before the making of the rules).

(2) The "site rules" for a protected site are rules made by the owner, in accordance with such procedure as may be prescribed by regulations made by the Welsh Ministers, which relate to—

(a) the management and conduct of the site, or

(b) such other matters as may be prescribed by regulations made by the Welsh Ministers.

(3) Any rules made by the owner before the coming into force of this section which relate to a matter mentioned in subsection (2) cease to have effect at the end of such period beginning with the day on which this section comes into force as may be prescribed by regulations made by the Welsh Ministers.

(4) Site rules come into force at the end of such period beginning with the first consultation day as may be prescribed by regulations made by the Welsh Ministers, if before the end of that period a copy of the rules is deposited with the local authority in whose area the protected site is situated.

(5) Where a site rule is varied, the rule as varied comes into force at the end of such period beginning with the first consultation day as may be prescribed by regulations made by the Welsh Ministers, if—

(a) the rule is varied in accordance with the procedure prescribed by regulations made by the Welsh Ministers, and

(b) a copy of the rule as varied is before the end of that period deposited with the local authority in whose area the protected site is situated.

(6) Where a site rule is deleted, the deletion comes into force at the end of such period beginning with the first consultation day as may be prescribed by regulations made by the Welsh Ministers, if—

(a) the rule is deleted in accordance with such procedure as may be prescribed by regulations made by the Welsh Ministers, and

(b) notice of the deletion is deposited before the end of that period deposited with the local authority in whose area the protected site is situated.

(7) The Welsh Ministers may by regulations provide that a site rule may not be made, varied or deleted unless a proposal to make, vary or delete the rule is notified to the occupiers of mobile homes on the site in question in accordance with the regulations.

(8) The Welsh Ministers may by regulations provide that site rules, or rules such as are mentioned in subsection (3), are of no effect in so far as they make provision in relation to matters prescribed by the regulations.

(9) The Welsh Ministers may by regulations make provision as to the resolution of disputes—

(a) relating to a proposal to make, vary or delete a site rule,

(b) as to whether the making, variation or deletion of a site rule was in accordance with the applicable procedure prescribed by the regulations,

(c) as to whether a deposit required to be made by virtue of subsection (4), (5) or (6) was made before the end of the relevant period.

(10) Provision under subsection (9) may confer functions on a tribunal.

(11) The Welsh Ministers may by regulations—

(a) require a local authority to establish and keep up to date a register of site rules in respect of protected sites in its area,

(b) require a local authority to publish the up-to-date register,

(c) provide that any deposit required to be made by virtue of subsection (4), (5) or (6) must be accompanied by a fee of such amount as the local authority may determine.

(12) In this section "first consultation day" means the day on which a proposal made under regulations under subsection (7) is notified to the occupiers of mobile homes on the site in accordance with the regulations.

III WAL [31]

53. Successors in title

(1) An agreement to which this Part applies is binding on, and has effect for the benefit of, any successor in title of the owner and any person claiming through or under the owner or any such successor.

(2) Where an agreement to which this Part applies is lawfully assigned to any person, the agreement has effect for the benefit of, and is binding on, that person.

(3) Where a person entitled to the benefit of and bound by an agreement to which this Part applies dies, the agreement has effect for the benefit of, and is binding on—

(a) any person residing in the mobile home as that person's only or main residence at that time, being—

(i) the widow, widower or surviving civil partner of the deceased or the surviving partner of an enduring family relationship of the deceased, or

(ii) in default of a person within sub-paragraph (i) residing in the mobile home as that person's only or main residence at that time, any member of the deceased's family, or

(b) in default of any such person residing in the mobile home as that person's only or main residence at that time, the person entitled to the mobile home by virtue of the deceased's will or under the law relating to intestacy, but subject to subsection (4).

(4) An agreement to which this [Part] applies does not have effect for the benefit of, and is not binding on, a person by virtue of subsection (3)(b) in so far as—

(a) it would, but for this subsection, enable or require that person to occupy the mobile home, or

(b) it includes terms implied by virtue of paragraph 6, 12, 13, 39 or 41 of Schedule 2.

III WAL [32]

54. Jurisdiction of a tribunal or the court

(1) A tribunal has jurisdiction—

(a) to determine any question arising under this Part or any agreement to which it applies, and

(b) to entertain any proceedings brought under this Part or any such agreement,

subject to subsections (2) to (6).

(2) Subsection (1) applies in relation to a question irrespective of anything contained in an arbitration agreement which has been entered into before that question arose.

(3) The court has jurisdiction—

(a) to determine any question arising by virtue of paragraph 5, 6, 7(1)(b), 38, 39 or 40(1)(b) of Schedule 2 under this Part or any agreement to which it applies, and

(b) to entertain any proceedings arising by virtue of any of those provisions brought under this Part or any such agreement,

subject to subsections (4) to (6).

(4) Subsection (5) applies if the owner and occupier have entered into an arbitration agreement before the question mentioned in subsection (3)(a) arises and the agreement applies to that question.

(5) A tribunal has jurisdiction to determine the question and entertain any proceedings arising instead of the court.

(6) Subsection (5) applies irrespective of anything contained in the arbitration agreement mentioned in subsection (4).

III WAL [32.1]

Jurisdiction of the court As in England the jurisdiction of the county court in Wales is confined to issues arising on claims for possession.

III WAL [33]

55. Interpretation

(1) In this Part—

"the appropriate judicial body" ("*corff barnwrol priodol*") means whichever of the court or a tribunal has jurisdiction under section 54;

"arbitration agreement" ("*cytundeb cymrodeddu*") means an agreement in writing to submit to arbitration any question arising under this Part or any agreement to which it applies;

"the court" ("*y llys*") means the county court for the district in which the protected site is situated or, where the parties have entered into an arbitration agreement that applies to the question to be determined, the arbitrator;

"occupier" ("*meddiannydd*") has the meaning given by section 48(2) (but see also subsection (2)(b));

"permanent pitch" ("*llain barhaol*") means a pitch which is not a transit pitch;

"pitch" ("*llain*") means the land, forming part of a protected site and including any garden area, on which an occupier is entitled to station a mobile home under the terms of an agreement;

"transit pitch" ("*llain dramwy*") means a pitch on which a person is entitled to station a mobile home under the terms of an agreement for a fixed period of up to 3 months;

"tribunal" ("*tribiwnlys*") means a residential property tribunal or, where the parties have entered into an arbitration agreement that applies to the question to be determined and that question arose before the agreement was made, the arbitrator;

"site rules" ("*rheolau safle*") has the meaning given by section 52(2).

(2) In relation to an agreement to which this Part applies—

(a) any reference in this Part to the owner includes a reference to any person who is bound by and entitled to the benefit of the agreement by virtue of subsection (1) of section 53, and

(b) subject to subsection (4) of that section, any reference in this Part to the occupier includes a reference to any person who is entitled to the benefit of and bound by the agreement by virtue of subsection (2) or (3) of that section.

(3) For the purposes of this Part the following are members of a person's family—

(a) the person's spouse or civil partner or any person who lives together with the person as a partner in an enduring family relationship,

(b) the person's parents, grandparents, children and grandchildren (including any person who is in that relationship by virtue of a marriage or civil partnership or an enduring family relationship) and any other person treated by the person as a child of the person's family, and

(c) the person's brothers, sisters, uncles, aunts, nephews and nieces (including any person who is in that relationship by virtue of a marriage or civil partnership or an enduring family relationship).

PART 5
POWERS OF LOCAL AUTHORITIES

Editorial Note The text of Part 5, sections 56 to 57 has been omitted.

PART 6
SUPPLEMENTARY AND GENERAL

III WAL [34]

60. Meaning of "mobile home"

(1) In this Act "mobile home" means any structure designed or adapted for human habitation which is capable of being moved from one place to another (whether by being towed, or by being transported on a motor vehicle or trailer) and any motor vehicle designed or adapted for human habitation, but does not include—

(a) any railway rolling stock which is for the time being on rails forming part of a railway system, or

(b) any tent.

(2) A structure designed or adapted for human habitation which—

(a) is composed of not more than 2 sections separately constructed and designed to be assembled on a site by means of bolts, clamps or other devices, and

(b) is, when assembled, physically capable of being moved by road from one place to another (whether by being towed, or by being transported on a motor vehicle or trailer),

is not to be regarded as not being (or as not having been) a mobile home for the purposes of this Act by reason only that it cannot lawfully be moved on a highway when assembled.

(3) For the purposes of this Act "mobile home" does not include a structure designed or adapted for human habitation which falls within subsection (2)(a) and (b) if its dimensions when assembled exceed any of the following limits, namely—

(a) length (exclusive of any drawbar): 20 metres,

(b) width: 6.8 metres, and

(c) overall height of living accommodation (measured internally from the floor at the lowest level to the ceiling at the highest level): 3.05 metres.

(4) The Welsh Ministers may by order substitute for any figure mentioned in subsection (3) such other figure as may be specified in the order.

SCHEDULE 2
TERMS OF MOBILE HOME AGREEMENTS

PART 1
TERMS IMPLIED BY ACT

CHAPTER 1 APPLICATION

III WAL [35]

1 (1) The implied terms set out in Chapter 2 apply to all agreements except an agreement which relates to a pitch on a local authority Gypsy and Traveller site.

(2) The implied terms set out in Chapter 3 apply to an agreement which relates to a transit pitch on a local authority Gypsy and Traveller site.

(3) The implied terms set out in Chapter 4 apply to an agreement which relates to a permanent pitch on a local authority Gypsy and Traveller site.

(4) In this Part—

"consumer prices index" ("*mynegai prisiau defyddwyr*") means the general index of consumer prices (for all items) published by the Statistics Board or, if that index is not published for a relevant month, any substituted index or index figures published by the Board;

"review date" ("*dyddiad yr adolygiad*"), in relation to an agreement, means the date specified in the written statement as the date on which the pitch fee will be reviewed in each year or, if no such date is specified, each anniversary of the date the agreement commenced;

"written statement" ("*datganiad ysgrifenedig*") means the written statement that the owner of the protected site is required to give to the occupier of the mobile home by section 49(1).

CHAPTER 2 AGREEMENTS RELATING TO PITCHES EXCEPT THOSE ON LOCAL AUTHORITY GYPSY AND TRAVELLER SITES

2 Subject to paragraph 3, the right to station the mobile home on land forming part of the protected site subsists until the agreement is determined under paragraph 4, 5, 6 or 7.

3 (1) If the owner's estate or interest is insufficient to enable the owner to grant the right for an indefinite period, the period for which the right subsists does not extend beyond the date when the owner's estate or interest determines.

(2) If planning permission for the use of the protected site as a site for mobile homes has been granted in terms such that it will expire at the end of a specified period, the period for which the right subsists does not extend beyond the date when the planning permission expires.

(3) If before the end of a period determined by this paragraph there is a change in circumstances which allows a longer period, account is to be taken of that change.

4 **Termination**

The occupier is entitled to terminate the agreement by notice in writing given to the owner not less than 4 weeks before the date on which it is to take effect.

5 The owner is entitled to terminate the agreement immediately if, on the application of the owner, the appropriate judicial body—

(a) is satisfied that the occupier has breached a term of the agreement and, after service of a notice to remedy the breach, has not complied with the notice within a reasonable time, and

(b) considers it reasonable for the agreement to be terminated.

6 The owner is entitled to terminate the agreement immediately if, on the application of the owner, the appropriate judicial body—

(a) is satisfied that the occupier is not occupying the mobile home as the occupier's only or main residence, and

(b) considers it reasonable for the agreement to be terminated.

7 (1) The owner is entitled to terminate the agreement immediately if—

(a) on the application of the owner, a tribunal has determined that, having regard to its condition, the mobile home is having a detrimental effect on the amenity of the site, and

(b) then, on the application of the owner, the appropriate judicial body, having regard to the tribunal's determination and to any other circumstances, considers it reasonable for the agreement to be terminated.

(2) Sub-paragraphs (3) and (4) apply if, on an application to the tribunal under sub-paragraph (1)(a)—

(a) the tribunal considers that, having regard to the present condition of the mobile home, it is having a detrimental effect on the amenity of the site, but

(b) it also considers that it would be reasonably practicable for particular repairs to be carried out on the mobile home that would result in the mobile home not having that detrimental effect, and

(c) the occupier indicates to the tribunal that the occupier intends to carry out those repairs.

(3) In such a case, the tribunal may make an interim order—

(a) specifying the repairs that must be carried out and the time within which they must be carried out, and

(b) adjourning the proceedings on the application for such period specified in the interim order as the tribunal considers reasonable to enable the repairs to be carried out.

(4) If the tribunal makes an interim order under sub-paragraph (3), it must not make a determination under sub-paragraph (1)(a) unless it is satisfied that the specified period has expired without the repairs having been carried out.

8 Recovery of overpayments by occupier

Where the agreement is terminated as mentioned in paragraph 4, 5, 6 or 7, the occupier is entitled to recover from the owner so much of any payment made by the occupier in pursuance of the agreement as is attributable to a period beginning after the termination.

9 Sale of mobile home

(1) Where the agreement is a new agreement, the occupier is entitled to sell the mobile home and to assign the agreement to the person to whom the mobile home is sold (the "new occupier") without the approval of the owner.

(2) In this paragraph and paragraphs 10, 12 and 13, "new agreement" means an agreement—

(a) which was made after the commencement of this paragraph, or

(b) which was made before, but which has been assigned after, that commencement.

(3) The new occupier must, as soon as reasonably practicable, notify the owner of the completion of the sale and assignment of the agreement.

(4) The new occupier is required to pay the owner a commission on the sale of the mobile home at a rate not exceeding such rate as may be prescribed by regulations made by the Welsh Ministers.

(5) Except to the extent mentioned in sub-paragraph (4), the owner may not require any payment to be made (whether to the owner or otherwise) in connection with the sale of the mobile home and the assignment of the agreement to the new occupier.

(6) The Welsh Ministers may by regulations prescribe procedural requirements to be complied with by the owner, the occupier or the new occupier in connection with—

(a) the sale of the mobile home and assignment of the agreement, or

(b) the payment of commission by virtue of sub-paragraph (4).

10 (1) Where the agreement is not a new agreement, the occupier is entitled to sell the mobile home and assign the agreement without the approval of the owner if—

(a) the occupier serves on the owner a notice (a "notice of proposed sale") that the occupier proposes to sell the mobile home, and assign the agreement, to the person named in the notice (the "proposed occupier"), and

(b) the first or second condition is satisfied.

(2) The first condition is that, within the period of 21 days beginning with the date on which the owner received the notice of proposed sale ("the 21-day period"), the occupier does not receive a notice from the owner that the owner has applied to a tribunal for an order preventing the occupier from selling the mobile home, and assigning the agreement, to the proposed occupier (a "refusal order").

(3) The second condition is that—

(a) within the 21-day period—

(i) the owner applies to a tribunal for a refusal order, and

(ii) the occupier receives a notice of the application from the owner, and

(b) the tribunal rejects the application.

(4) If the owner applies to a tribunal for a refusal order within the 21-day period but the occupier does not receive notice of the application from the owner within that period—

(a) the application is to be treated as not having been made, and

(b) the first condition is accordingly to be treated as satisfied.

(5) A notice of proposed sale must include such information as may be prescribed in regulations made by the Welsh Ministers.

(6) A notice of proposed sale or notice of an application for a refusal order—

(a) must be in writing, and

(b) may be served by post.

(7) An application for a refusal order may be made only on one or more of the grounds prescribed in regulations made by the Welsh Ministers; and a notice of an application for a refusal order must specify the ground or grounds on which the application is made.

(8) The person to whom the mobile home is sold ("the new occupier") is required to pay the owner a commission on the sale of the mobile home at a rate not exceeding such rate as may be prescribed by regulations made by the Welsh Ministers.

(9) Except to the extent mentioned in sub-paragraph (8), the owner may not require any payment to be made (whether to the owner or otherwise) in connection with the sale of the mobile home and the assignment of the agreement.

(10) The Welsh Ministers may by regulations prescribe procedural requirements to be complied with by the owner, the occupier, a proposed occupier or the new occupier in connection with—

(a) the sale of the mobile home and assignment of the agreement, and

(b) the payment of commission by virtue of sub-paragraph (8).

11 (1) This paragraph applies where the occupier proposes to sell the mobile home, and assign the agreement, pursuant to paragraph 9 or 10.

(2) The occupier must, not later than 28 days before the completion of the sale of the mobile home and assignment of the agreement, provide the proposed occupier with—

(a) such documents, or documents of such description, as may be prescribed in regulations made by the Welsh Ministers, and
(b) such other information as may be prescribed in the regulations, in the form prescribed in them.

(3) But if the proposed occupier consents in writing to the documents and other information concerned being provided by a date ("the chosen date") which is less than 28 days before the completion of the sale and assignment of the agreement, the occupier must provide the documents and other information to the proposed occupier not later than the chosen date.

(4) The documents and other information which may be prescribed in regulations under sub-paragraph (2) include (but are not limited to)—
(a) a copy of the agreement,
(b) a copy of the site rules (if any) for the protected site on which the mobile home is stationed,
(c) details of the pitch fee payable under the agreement,
(d) a forwarding address for the occupier,
(e) in a case within paragraph 9, information about the requirement imposed by virtue of sub-paragraph (3) of that paragraph,
(f) details of the commission which would be payable by the proposed occupier by virtue of paragraph 9(4) or 10(8),
(g) information about such requirements as are prescribed in regulations under paragraph 9(6) or 10(10).

(5) Documents or other information required to be provided under this paragraph may be delivered to the prospective purchaser personally or sent by post.

(6) A claim that a person has broken the duty under sub-paragraph (2) or (3) may be made the subject of civil proceedings in the same manner as any other claim in tort for breach of statutory duty.

12 Gift of mobile home

(1) Where the agreement is a new agreement, provided that the occupier has supplied the owner with the relevant evidence, the occupier is entitled to give the mobile home, and to assign the agreement, to a member of the occupier's family (the "new occupier") without the approval of the owner.

(2) The relevant evidence is—
(a) evidence, or evidence of a description, prescribed in regulations made by the Welsh Ministers that the person to whom the occupier proposes to give the mobile home, and to assign the agreement, is a member of the occupier's family, or
(b) any other satisfactory evidence that the person concerned is a member of the occupier's family.

(3) The new occupier must, as soon as reasonably practicable, notify the owner of the receipt of the mobile home and assignment of the agreement.

(4) The owner may not require any payment to be made (whether to the owner or otherwise) in connection with the gift of the mobile home, and the assignment of the agreement, as mentioned in sub-paragraph (1).

(5) The Welsh Ministers may by regulations prescribe procedural requirements to be complied with by the owner, the occupier or the new occupier in connection with the gift of the mobile home, and assignment of the agreement, as mentioned in sub-paragraph (1).

13 (1) Where the agreement is not a new agreement, the occupier is entitled to give the mobile home, and assign the agreement, to a member of the occupier's family (the "proposed occupier") without the approval of the owner if—
(a) the occupier serves on the owner a notice (a "notice of proposed gift") that the occupier proposes to give the mobile home to the proposed occupier, and
(b) the first or second condition is satisfied.

WALES

(2) The first condition is that, within the period of 21 days beginning with the date on which the owner received the notice of proposed gift ("the 21-day period"), the occupier does not receive a notice from the owner that the owner has applied to a tribunal for an order preventing the occupier from giving the mobile home, and assigning the agreement, to the proposed occupier (a "refusal order").

(3) The second condition is that—

(a) within the 21-day period—

(i) the owner applies to a tribunal for a refusal order, and

(ii) the occupier receives a notice of the application from the owner, and

(b) the tribunal rejects the application.

(4) If the owner applies to a tribunal for a refusal order within the 21-day period but the occupier does not receive notice of the application from the owner within that period—

(a) the application is to be treated as not having been made, and

(b) the first condition is accordingly to be treated as satisfied.

(5) A notice of proposed gift must include—

(a) the relevant evidence under paragraph 12(2), and

(b) such other information as may be prescribed in regulations made by the Welsh Ministers.

(6) A notice of proposed gift or notice of an application for a refusal order—

(a) must be in writing, and

(b) may be served by post.

(7) An application for a refusal order may be made only on one or more of the grounds prescribed in regulations made by the Welsh Ministers; and a notice of an application for a refusal order must specify the ground or grounds on which the application is made.

(8) The owner may not require any payment to be made (whether to the owner or otherwise) in connection with the gift of the mobile home, and the assignment of the agreement, as mentioned in sub-paragraph (1).

(9) The Welsh Ministers may by regulations prescribe procedural requirements to be complied with by the owner, the occupier, a proposed occupier or the person to whom the mobile home is given in connection with the gift of the mobile home, and assignment of the agreement, as mentioned in sub-paragraph (1).

14 Re-siting of mobile home

(1) The owner is entitled to require that the occupier's right to station the mobile home is exercisable for any period in relation to another pitch forming part of the protected site ("the other pitch") if—

(a) on the application of the owner, a tribunal is satisfied that the other pitch is broadly comparable to the occupier's original pitch and that it is reasonable for the mobile home to be stationed on the other pitch for that period, or

(b) the owner needs to carry out essential repair or emergency works that can only be carried out if the mobile home is moved to the other pitch for that period, and either—

(i) on an application by the owner a tribunal is satisfied of that need and that the other pitch is broadly comparable to the occupier's original pitch, or

(ii) the urgency of the need means that it is impracticable to make an application before the mobile home is re-sited.

(2) In a case where sub-paragraph (ii) of paragraph (b) of sub-paragraph (1) applies, the owner must immediately make an application to a tribunal and if the tribunal is not satisfied as mentioned in sub-paragraph (i) of that paragraph the owner must immediately secure that the mobile home is returned to the original pitch.

(3) If the owner requires the occupier to station the mobile home on the other pitch so that the owner can replace, or carry out repairs to, the base on which the mobile home is stationed, the owner must, if the occupier requires the owner to do so or a tribunal on the application of the occupier orders the owner to do so, secure that the mobile home is returned to the original pitch on the completion of the replacement or repairs.

(4) The owner must pay all the costs and expenses incurred by the occupier in connection with the mobile home being moved to and from the other pitch.

(5) In this paragraph and paragraph 16 "essential repair or emergency works" means—

- (a) repairs to the base on which the mobile home is stationed,
- (b) works or repairs needed to comply with any relevant legal requirements, or
- (c) works or repairs in connection with restoration following flood, landslide or other natural disaster.

15 Quiet enjoyment of the mobile home

The occupier is entitled to quiet enjoyment of the mobile home together with the pitch during the continuance of the agreement, subject to paragraphs 14 and 16.

16 Owner's right of entry to the pitch

(1) The owner may enter the pitch without prior notice between the hours of 9 am and 6 pm—

- (a) to deliver written communications, including post and notices, to the occupier, and
- (b) to read any meter for gas, electricity, water, sewerage or other services supplied by the owner.

(2) The owner may enter the pitch to carry out essential repair or emergency works on giving as much notice to the occupier (whether in writing or otherwise) as is reasonably practicable in the circumstances.

(3) Unless the occupier has agreed otherwise, the owner may enter the pitch for a reason other than one specified in sub-paragraph (1) or (2) only if the owner has given the occupier at least 14 clear days' written notice of the date, time and reason for the visit.

(4) The rights conferred by this paragraph do not extend to the mobile home.

17 The pitch fee

(1) The pitch fee can only be changed in accordance with this paragraph, either—

- (a) with the agreement of the occupier, or
- (b) if a tribunal, on the application of the owner or the occupier, considers it reasonable for the pitch fee to be changed and makes an order determining the amount of the new pitch fee.

(2) The pitch fee must be reviewed annually as at the review date.

(3) At least 28 clear days before the review date the owner must serve on the occupier a written notice setting out proposals in respect of the new pitch fee.

(4) A notice under sub-paragraph (3) which proposes an increase in the pitch fee is of no effect unless it is accompanied by a document which complies with paragraph 23.

(5) If the occupier agrees to the proposed new pitch fee, it is payable as from the review date.

(6) If the occupier does not agree to the proposed new pitch fee—

- (a) the owner or the occupier may apply to a tribunal for an order under sub-paragraph (1)(b) determining the amount of the new pitch fee,
- (b) the occupier must continue to pay the current pitch fee to the owner until such time as the new pitch fee is agreed by the occupier or an order determining the amount of the new pitch fee is made by the tribunal under sub-paragraph (1)(b), and

(c) the new pitch fee is payable as from the review date but the occupier is not to be regarded as being in arrears until the 28th day after the date on which the new pitch fee is agreed or, as the case may be, the 28th day after the date of the tribunal's order determining the amount of the new pitch fee.

(7) An application under sub-paragraph (6)(a) may be made at any time after the end of the period of 28 days beginning with the review date but no later than 3 months after the review date.

(8) Sub-paragraphs (9) to (12) apply if the owner—

(a) has not served the notice required by sub-paragraph (3) by the time by which it was required to be served, but

(b) at any time afterwards serves on the occupier a written notice setting out proposals in respect of a new pitch fee.

(9) A notice under sub-paragraph (8)(b) which proposes an increase in the pitch fee is of no effect unless it is accompanied by a document which complies with paragraph 23.

(10) If (at any time) the occupier agrees to the proposed pitch fee, it is payable as from the 28th day after the date on which the owner serves the notice under sub-paragraph (8)(b).

(11) If the occupier has not agreed to the proposed pitch fee—

(a) the owner or the occupier may apply to a tribunal for an order under sub-paragraph (1)(b) determining the amount of the new pitch fee,

(b) the occupier must continue to pay the current pitch fee to the owner until such time as the new pitch fee is agreed by the occupier or an order determining the amount of the new pitch fee is made by a tribunal under sub-paragraph (1)(b), and

(c) if the tribunal makes such an order, the new pitch fee is payable as from the 28th day after the date on which the owner serves the notice under sub-paragraph (8)(b).

(12) An application under sub-paragraph (11) may be made at any time after the end of the period of 56 days beginning with date on which the owner serves the notice under sub-paragraph (8)(b) but no later than 4 months after the date on which the owner serves that notice.

(13) A tribunal may permit an application under sub-paragraph (6)(a) or (11)(a) to be made to it outside the time limit specified in sub-paragraph (7) (in the case of an application under sub-paragraph (6)(a)) or in sub-paragraph (12) (in the case of an application under sub-paragraph (11)(a)) if it is satisfied that, in all the circumstances, there are good reasons for the failure to apply within the applicable time limit and for any delay since then in applying for permission to make the application out of time.

(14) The occupier is not to be treated as being in arrears—

(a) where sub-paragraph (10) applies, until the 28th day after the date on which the new pitch fee is agreed, or

(b) where sub-paragraph (11)(b) applies, until the 28th day after the date on which the new pitch fee is agreed or, as the case may be, the 28th day after the date of the tribunal's order determining the amount of the new pitch fee.

(15) Sub-paragraph (16) applies if a tribunal, on the application of the occupier, is satisfied that—

(a) a notice under sub-paragraph (3) or (8)(b) was of no effect as a result of sub-paragraph (4) or (9), but

(b) the occupier nonetheless paid the owner the pitch fee proposed in the notice.

(16) The tribunal may order the owner to pay the occupier, within the period of 21 days beginning with the date of the order, the difference between—

(a) the amount which the occupier was required to pay the owner for the period in question, and

(b) the amount which the occupier has paid the owner for that period.

18 (1) When determining the amount of the new pitch fee particular regard is to be had to—

(a) any sums expended by the owner since the last review date on improvements—

(i) which are for the benefit of the occupiers of mobile homes on the protected site,

(ii) which were the subject of consultation in accordance with paragraph 22(1)(e) and (f), and

(iii) to which a majority of the occupiers have not disagreed in writing or which, in the case of such disagreement, a tribunal, on the application of the owner, has ordered should be taken into account when determining the amount of the new pitch fee,

(b) any deterioration in the condition, and any decrease in the amenity, of the site or any adjoining land which is occupied or controlled by the owner since the date on which this sub-paragraph came into force (in so far as regard has not previously been had to that deterioration or decrease for the purposes of this sub-paragraph),

(c) any reduction in the services that the owner supplies to the site, pitch or mobile home, and any deterioration in the quality of those services, since the date on which this sub-paragraph came into force (in so far as regard has not previously been had to that reduction or deterioration for the purposes of this sub-paragraph), and

(d) any direct effect on the costs payable by the owner in relation to the maintenance or management of the site of an enactment which has come into force since the last review date.

(2) But no regard is to be had, when determining the amount of the new pitch fee, to any costs incurred by the owner since the last review date for the purpose of complying with provisions contained in this Part which were not contained in the Mobile Homes Act 1983 in its application in relation to Wales before the coming into force of this Part.

(3) When calculating what constitutes a majority of the occupiers for the purposes of sub-paragraph (1)(a)(iii) each mobile home is to be taken to have only 1 occupier and, in the event of there being more than 1 occupier of a mobile home, its occupier is to be taken to be whichever of them the occupiers agree or, in default of agreement, the one whose name appears first on the agreement.

(4) In a case where the pitch fee has not been previously reviewed, references in this paragraph to the last review date are to be read as references to the date when the agreement commenced.

19 (1) When determining the amount of the new pitch fee, any costs incurred by the owner in connection with expanding the protected site are not to be taken into account.

(2) When determining the amount of the new pitch fee, no regard may be had to—

(a) any costs incurred by the owner in relation to the conduct of proceedings under this Part or the agreement,

(b) any fee required to be paid by the owner by virtue of section 6 or 13, or

(c) any costs incurred by the owner in connection with—

(i) any action taken by a local authority under sections 15 to 25, or

(ii) the owner being convicted of an offence under section 18.

20 (1) Unless it would be unreasonable having regard to paragraph 18(1), there is a presumption that the pitch fee is to increase or decrease by a percentage which is no more than any percentage increase or decrease in the consumer prices index calculated by reference only to—

(a) the latest index, and

(b) the index published for the month which was 12 months before that to which the latest index relates.

(2) In sub-paragraph (1) "the latest index"—

(a) in a case where the owner serves a notice under paragraph 17(3), means the last index published before the day on which that notice is served, and

(b) in a case where the owner serves a notice under paragraph 17(8)(b) means the last index published before the day by which the owner was required to serve a notice under paragraph 17(3).

21 Occupier's obligations and owner's corresponding obligations

(1) The occupier must—

(a) pay the pitch fee to the owner,

(b) pay to the owner all sums due under the agreement in respect of gas, electricity, water, sewerage or other services supplied by the owner,

(c) keep the mobile home in a sound state of repair,

(d) maintain—

(i) the outside of the mobile home, and

(ii) the pitch, including all fences and outbuildings belonging to, or enjoyed with, it and the mobile home,

in a clean and tidy condition, and

(e) if requested by the owner, provide the owner with documentary evidence of any costs or expenses in respect of which the occupier seeks reimbursement.

(2) The owner must not do or cause to be done anything—

(a) which may adversely affect the ability of the occupier to perform the obligation under sub-paragraph (1)(c) or which may deter the occupier from making internal improvements to the mobile home or interfere with the occupier's ability to do so, or

(b) which may adversely affect the ability of the occupier to perform the obligations under sub-paragraph (1)(d) or which may deter the occupier from making external improvements to the mobile home or interfere with the occupier's ability to do so.

(3) Sub-paragraph (2) does not authorise the occupier to carry out works to the mobile home which are prohibited by the terms of the agreement or by or under any enactment.

(4) Where the terms of the agreement permit works to the mobile home to be carried out only with the permission of the owner, that permission must not be unreasonably withheld.

22 Owner's other obligations

(1) The owner must—

(a) if requested by the occupier, and on payment by the occupier of a charge of not more than £30, provide accurate written details of—

(i) the size of the pitch and the base on which the mobile home is stationed, and

(ii) the location of the pitch and the base within the protected site,

and the details must include measurements between identifiable fixed points on the protected site and the pitch and the base,

(b) if requested by the occupier, provide (free of charge) documentary evidence in support and explanation of—

(i) any new pitch fee,

(ii) any charges for gas, electricity, water, sewerage or other services payable by the occupier to the owner under the agreement, and

(iii) any other charges, costs or expenses payable by the occupier to the owner under the agreement,

(c) be responsible for repairing the base on which the mobile home is stationed and for maintaining any gas, electricity, water, sewerage or other services supplied by the owner to the pitch or to the mobile home,

(d) maintain in a clean and tidy condition those parts of the protected site, including access ways, site boundary fences and trees, which are not the responsibility of any occupier of a mobile home stationed on the protected site,

(e) consult the occupier about improvements to the protected site in general, and in particular about those which the owner wishes to be taken into account when determining the amount of any new pitch fee, and

(f) consult a qualifying residents' association (if there is one) or (otherwise) occupiers of mobile homes stationed on the protected site, about all matters which relate to the operation and management of, improvements to, or any proposed change of use of, the protected site and may affect the occupiers either directly or indirectly.

(2) For the purposes of sub-paragraph (1)(e), to "consult" the occupier means—

(a) to give the occupier at least 28 clear days' notice in writing of the proposed improvements which—

(i) describes the proposed improvements and how they will benefit the occupier in the long and short term,

(ii) details how the pitch fee may be affected when it is next reviewed, and

(iii) states when and where the occupier can make representations about the proposed improvements, and

(b) to take into account any representations made by the occupier about the proposed improvements, in accordance with paragraph (a)(iii), before undertaking them.

(3) For the purposes of sub-paragraph (1)(f), to "consult" a qualifying residents' association or occupiers means—

(a) to give the association or occupiers at least 28 clear days' notice in writing of the matters referred to in sub-paragraph (1)(f) which—

(i) describes the matters and how they may affect the occupiers either directly or indirectly in the long and short term, and

(ii) states when and where the association or occupiers can make representations about the matters, and

(b) to take into account any representations made by the association or occupiers, in accordance with paragraph (a)(ii), before proceeding with the matters.

23 The document referred to in paragraph 17(4) and (9) must—

(a) be in such form as the Welsh Ministers may by regulations prescribe,

(b) specify any percentage increase or decrease in the consumer prices index calculated in accordance with paragraph 20,

(c) explain the effect of paragraph 17,

(d) specify the matters to which the amount proposed for the new pitch fee is attributable,

(e) refer to the occupier's obligations in paragraph 21(1)(c) to (e) and the owner's obligations in paragraph 22(1)(c) and (d), and

(f) refer to the owner's obligations in paragraph 22(1)(e) and (f) (as glossed by paragraph 22(2) and (3)).

24 Owner's name and address

(1) The owner must by notice inform the occupier and any qualifying residents' association of the address in England or Wales at which notices (including notices of proceedings) may be served on the owner by the occupier or a qualifying residents' association.

WALES

(2) If the owner fails to comply with sub-paragraph (1), then (subject to sub-paragraph (5)) any amount otherwise due from the occupier to the owner in respect of the pitch fee is to be treated for all purposes as not being due from the occupier to the owner at any time before the owner complies with sub-paragraph (1).

(3) Where in accordance with the agreement the owner gives any written notice to the occupier or a qualifying residents' association, the notice must contain the following information—

(a) the name and address of the owner, and

(b) if that address is not in England or Wales, an address in England or Wales at which notices (including notices of proceedings) may be served on the owner.

(4) Subject to sub-paragraph (5), where—

(a) the occupier or a qualifying residents' association receives such a notice, but

(b) it does not contain the information required to be contained in it by virtue of sub-paragraph (3),

the notice is to be treated as not having been given until such time as the owner gives the information to the occupier or qualifying residents' association in respect of the notice.

(5) An amount or notice within sub-paragraph (2) or (4) is not to be treated as mentioned in relation to any time when, by virtue of an order of any court or tribunal, there is in force an appointment of a receiver or manager whose functions include receiving from the occupier the pitch fee, payments for services supplied or other charges.

(6) Nothing in sub-paragraphs (3) to (5) applies to any notice containing a demand to which paragraph 25(1) applies.

25 (1) Where the owner makes any demand for payment by the occupier of the pitch fee, or in respect of services supplied or other charges, the demand must contain—

(a) the name and address of the owner, and

(b) if that address is not in England or Wales, an address in England or Wales at which notices (including notices of proceedings) may be served on the owner.

(2) Subject to sub-paragraph (3), where—

(a) the occupier receives such a demand, but

(b) it does not contain the information required to be contained in it by virtue of sub-paragraph (1),

the amount demanded is to be treated for all purposes as not being due from the occupier to the owner at any time before the owner gives that information to the occupier in respect of the demand.

(3) The amount demanded is not to be treated as not being due in relation to any time when, by virtue of an order of any court or tribunal, there is in force an appointment of a receiver or manager whose functions include receiving from the occupier the pitch fee, payments for services supplied or other charges.

CHAPTER 3 AGREEMENTS RELATING TO TRANSIT PITCHES ON LOCAL AUTHORITY GYPSY AND TRAVELLER SITES

26 Duration of agreement

Subject to paragraph 27 the right to station the mobile home on the transit pitch subsists until—

(a) the fixed period set out in the agreement expires, or

(b) termination of the agreement under paragraph 28 or 29,

whichever is sooner.

27 (1) If the owner's estate or interest is insufficient to enable the owner to grant the right for the fixed period set out in the agreement, the period for which the right subsists does not extend beyond the date when the owner's estate or interest determines.

(2) If planning permission for the use of the protected site as a site for mobile homes has been granted in terms such that it will expire at the end of a specified period, the period for which the right subsists does not extend beyond the date when the planning permission expires.

(3) If planning permission for the use of the protected site as a site for mobile homes has been granted in terms such that it requires the owner to limit the duration of stay for mobile homes on the site, the period for which the right subsists does not extend beyond that duration.

28 Termination

The occupier is entitled to terminate the agreement before the expiry of the fixed period set out in the agreement by notice in writing given to the owner.

29 The owner is entitled to terminate the agreement before the expiry of the fixed period set out in the agreement—

(a) without being required to show any reason, by giving written notice not less than 4 weeks before the date on which that notice is to take effect, or

(b) immediately, where—

(i) the occupier has breached a term of the agreement and, after service of a notice to remedy the breach, has not complied with the notice within a reasonable time, and

(ii) the owner considers it reasonable for the agreement to be terminated.

30 Recovery of overpayments by occupier

Where the agreement is terminated as mentioned in paragraph 28 or 29, the occupier is entitled to recover from the owner so much of any payment made by the occupier in pursuance of the agreement as is attributable to a period beginning after the termination.

31 Quiet enjoyment of the mobile home

The occupier is entitled to quiet enjoyment of the mobile home together with the pitch during the continuance of the agreement, subject to paragraph 32.

32 Owner's right of entry to the pitch

(1) The owner may enter the pitch without prior notice between the hours of 9 am and 6 pm —

(a) to deliver written communications, including post and notices, to the occupier, and

(b) to read any meter for gas, electricity, water, sewerage or other services supplied by the owner.

(2) The owner may enter the pitch to carry out essential repair or emergency works on giving as much notice to the occupier (whether in writing or otherwise) as is reasonably practicable in the circumstances.

(3) In this paragraph "essential repair or emergency works" means—

(a) repairs to the base on which the mobile home is stationed,

(b) repairs to any outhouses and facilities provided by the owner on the pitch and to any gas, electricity, water, sewerage or other services or other amenities provided by the owner in such outhouses,

(c) works or repairs needed to comply with any relevant legal requirements, or

(d) works or repairs in connection with restoration following flood, landslide or other natural disaster.

(4) Unless the occupier has agreed otherwise, the owner may enter the pitch for a reason other than one specified in sub-paragraph (3) or (2) only if the owner has given the occupier at least 14 clear days' written notice of the date, time and reason for the visit.

(5) The rights conferred by this paragraph do not extend to the mobile home.

33 Owner's name and address

(1) The owner must by notice inform the occupier of the address in England or Wales at which notices (including notices of proceedings) may be served on the owner by the occupier.

(2) If the owner fails to comply with sub-paragraph (1), then any amount otherwise due from the occupier to the owner in respect of the pitch fee is to be treated for all purposes as not being due from the occupier to the owner at any time before the owner complies with sub-paragraph (1).

(3) Where in accordance with the agreement the owner gives any written notice to the occupier the notice must contain the name and address of the owner.

(4) Where—

(a) the occupier receives such a notice, but

(b) it does not contain the information required to be contained in it by virtue of sub-paragraph (3),

the notice is to be treated as not having been given until such time as the owner gives the information to the occupier in respect of the notice.

(5) Nothing in sub-paragraphs (3) and (4) applies to any notice containing a demand to which paragraph 34(1) applies.

34 (1) Where the owner makes any demand for payment by the occupier of the pitch fee, or in respect of services supplied or other charges, the demand must contain the name and address of the owner.

(2) Where—

(a) the occupier receives such a demand, but

(b) it does not contain the information required to be contained in it by virtue of sub-paragraph (1),

the amount demanded is to be treated for all purposes as not being due from the occupier to the owner at any time before the owner gives that information to the occupier in respect of the demand.

CHAPTER 4 AGREEMENTS RELATING TO PERMANENT PITCHES ON LOCAL AUTHORITY GYPSY AND TRAVELLER SITES

35 Duration of agreement

Subject to paragraph 36, the right to station the mobile home on land forming part of the protected site subsists until the agreement is determined under paragraph 37, 38, 39 or 40.

36 (1) If the owner's estate or interest is insufficient to enable the owner to grant the right for an indefinite period, the period for which the right subsists does not extend beyond the date when the owner's estate or interest determines.

(2) If planning permission for the use of the protected site as a site for mobile homes has been granted in terms such that it will expire at the end of a specified period, the period for which the right subsists does not extend beyond the date when the planning permission expires.

(3) If before the end of a period determined by this paragraph there is a change in circumstances which allows a longer period, account is to be taken of that change.

37 Termination

The occupier is entitled to terminate the agreement by notice in writing given to the owner not less than 4 weeks before the date on which it is to take effect.

38 The owner is entitled to terminate the agreement immediately if, on the application of the owner, the appropriate judicial body—

(a) is satisfied that the occupier has breached a term of the agreement and, after service of a notice to remedy the breach, has not complied with the notice within a reasonable time, and

(b) considers it reasonable for the agreement to be terminated.

39 The owner is entitled to terminate the agreement immediately if, on the application of the owner, the appropriate judicial body—

(a) is satisfied that the occupier is not occupying the mobile home as the occupier's only or main residence, and

(b) considers it reasonable for the agreement to be terminated.

40 (1) The owner is entitled to terminate the agreement immediately if—

(a) on the application of the owner, a tribunal has determined that, having regard to its condition, the mobile home is having a detrimental effect on the amenity of the site, and

(b) then, on the application of the owner, the appropriate judicial body, having regard to the tribunal's determination and to any other circumstances, considers it reasonable for the agreement to be terminated.

(2) Sub-paragraphs (3) and (4) apply if, on an application to the tribunal under sub-paragraph (1)(a)—

(a) the tribunal considers that, having regard to the present condition of the mobile home, it is having a detrimental effect on the amenity of the site, but

(b) it also considers that it would be reasonably practicable for particular repairs to be carried out on the mobile home that would result in the mobile home not having that detrimental effect, and

(c) the occupier indicates to the tribunal that the occupier intends to carry out those repairs.

(3) In such a case, the tribunal may make an interim order—

(a) specifying the repairs that must be carried out and the time within which they must be carried out, and

(b) adjourning the proceedings on the application for such period specified in the interim order as the tribunal considers reasonable to enable the repairs to be carried out.

(4) If the tribunal makes an interim order under sub-paragraph (3), it must not make a determination under sub-paragraph (1)(a) unless it is satisfied that the specified period has expired without the repairs having been carried out.

41 Assignment of agreement

(1) The occupier ("A") may assign the agreement—

(a) to a person who is a member of A's family, or

(b) to another person ("B") if the conditions in sub-paragraph (2) are met.

(2) The conditions are that—

(a) A must have the approval of the owner, and

(b) B must—

(i) be an occupier of a permanent pitch on a relevant site, and

(ii) have the approval of the owner to the assignment of B's agreement to A or to another occupier of a permanent pitch on a relevant site.

(3) A relevant site for the purposes of sub-paragraph (2) is a local authority Gypsy and Traveller site in the area of the local authority in which the site on which the pitch to which A's agreement relates is located.

WALES

(4) Neither the occupier nor the owner may require any payment to be made (whether to the occupier or owner or otherwise) in connection with the assignment of the agreement under this paragraph.

42 (1) The occupier may serve on the owner a request to approve for the purposes of paragraph 41, an assignment to a person named in the request ("the proposed occupier").

(2) Where the request relates to an assignment under paragraph 41(1)(a) the request must include satisfactory evidence that the proposed occupier is a member of the occupier's family.

(3) Where the owner receives a request under sub-paragraph (1), the owner must, within 28 days beginning with the date on which the request is received—

(a) approve the assignment, unless it is reasonable for the owner not to do so, and

(b) serve on the occupier notice of the owner's decision ("a decision notice").

(4) If a person ("P") receives a request under sub-paragraph (1) and P—

(a) while not being the owner, has an estate or interest in the land, and

(b) believes that another person is the owner,

and that other person has not received such a request, P owes a duty to the occupier (enforceable by a claim in tort for breach of statutory duty, as well as by action for breach of an implied term) to take such steps as are reasonable to secure that the other person receives the request within the period of 28 days beginning with the date on which P receives it.

(5) If the approval is withheld, the decision notice must specify the reasons for withholding it.

(6) Where a fee lawfully due from the occupier has not been paid or any term of the agreement has been broken or not performed, the approval required for the purpose of paragraph 41 may be given subject to a condition requiring the occupier to pay the outstanding fee, remedy the breach or perform the obligation.

(7) Except as provided by sub-paragraph (6), the approval required for the purpose of paragraph 41 cannot be given subject to a condition and a condition imposed otherwise than as so provided is to be disregarded.

(8) If the owner fails to serve the notice or withholds approval to the assignment the occupier may apply to the tribunal for an order declaring that the assignment is approved for the purposes of paragraph 41 and the tribunal may make such an order if it thinks fit.

(9) If the question arises as to whether the notice required by sub-paragraph (3)(b) was served within the required period of 28 days, it is for an owner to show that the notice was so served.

(10) If the owner did not approve the assignment and the question arises whether it was reasonable for the owner not to do so, it is for the owner to show that it was reasonable.

(11) A request or notice under this paragraph—

(a) must be in writing, and

(b) may be served by post.

(12) Subject to sub-paragraph (13), an application to the tribunal under sub-paragraph (8) by an occupier must be made—

(a) within the period of 3 months beginning with the day after the date on which the occupier receives the decision notice, or

(b) where the occupier receives no decision notice, within the period of 3 months beginning with the date which is 29 days after the date upon which the occupier served the request under sub-paragraph (1).

(13) A tribunal may permit an application under sub-paragraph (8) to be made to the tribunal after the applicable period specified in sub-paragraph (12) if it is satisfied that, in all the circumstances, there are good reasons for the failure to

apply before the end of that period and for any delay since then in applying for permission to make the application out of time.

43 Recovery of overpayments by occupier

Where the agreement is terminated as mentioned in paragraph 37, 38, 39 or 40, the occupier is entitled to recover from the owner so much of any payment made by the occupier in pursuance of the agreement as is attributable to a period beginning after the termination.

44 Re-siting of mobile home

(1) The owner is entitled to require that the occupier's right to station the mobile home is exercisable for any period in relation to another pitch forming part of the protected site or a pitch forming part of another protected site ("the other pitch") if—

(a) on the application of the owner, a tribunal is satisfied that the other pitch is broadly comparable to the occupier's original pitch and that it is reasonable for the mobile home to be stationed on the other pitch for that period, or

(b) the owner needs to carry out essential repair or emergency works that can only be carried out if the mobile home is moved to the other pitch for that period, and the other pitch is broadly comparable to the occupier's original pitch.

(2) A pitch forming part of another protected site is, for the purposes of sub-paragraph (1)(a), broadly comparable to the occupier's original pitch only if it provides access to health and education services required by the occupier which is, as far as reasonably practicable, broadly comparable to the access provided by the occupier's original pitch.

(3) If the owner requires the occupier to station the mobile home on the other pitch so that the owner can replace, or carry out repairs to, the base on which the mobile home is stationed, the owner must, if the occupier requires the owner to do so or a tribunal on the application of the occupier orders the owner to do so, secure that the mobile home is returned to the original pitch on the completion of the replacement or repairs.

(4) The owner must pay all the costs and expenses incurred by the occupier in connection with the mobile home being moved to and from the other pitch.

(5) In this paragraph and in paragraph 46 "essential repair or emergency works" means—

(a) repairs to the base on which the mobile home is stationed,

(b) repairs to any outhouses and facilities provided by the owner on the pitch and to any gas, electricity, water, sewerage or other services or other amenities provided by the owner in such outhouses,

(c) works or repairs needed to comply with any relevant legal requirements, or

(d) works or repairs in connection with restoration following flood, landslide or other natural disaster.

45 Quiet enjoyment of the mobile home

The occupier is entitled to quiet enjoyment of the mobile home together with the pitch during the continuance of the agreement, subject to paragraphs 44 and 46.

46 Owner's right of entry to the pitch

(1) The owner may enter the pitch without prior notice between the hours of 9 am and 6 pm —

(a) to deliver written communications, including post and notices, to the occupier, and

(b) to read any meter for gas, electricity, water, sewerage or other services supplied by the owner.

(2) The owner may enter the pitch to carry out essential repair or emergency works on giving as much notice to the occupier (whether in writing or otherwise) as is reasonably practicable in the circumstances.

(3) Unless the occupier has agreed otherwise, the owner may enter the pitch for a reason other than one specified in sub-paragraph (1) or (2) only if the owner has given the occupier at least 14 clear days' written notice of the date, time and reason for the owner's visit.

(4) The rights conferred by this paragraph do not extend to the mobile home.

47 The pitch fee

(1) The pitch fee can only be changed in accordance with this paragraph, either—

(a) with the agreement of the occupier, or

(b) if a tribunal, on the application of the owner or the occupier, considers it reasonable for the pitch fee to be changed and makes an order determining the amount of the new pitch fee.

(2) The pitch fee must be reviewed annually as at the review date.

(3) At least 28 clear days before the review date the owner must serve on the occupier a written notice setting out the owner's proposals in respect of the new pitch fee.

(4) If the occupier agrees to the proposed new pitch fee, it is payable as from the review date.

(5) If the occupier does not agree to the proposed new pitch fee—

(a) the owner may apply to a tribunal for an order under sub-paragraph (1)(b) determining the amount of the new pitch fee,

(b) the occupier must continue to pay the current pitch fee to the owner until such time as the new pitch fee is agreed by the occupier or an order determining the amount of the new pitch fee is made by a tribunal under sub-paragraph (1)(b), and

(c) the new pitch fee is payable as from the review date but the occupier is not to be regarded as being in arrears until the 28th day after the date on which the new pitch fee is agreed or, as the case may be, the 28th day after the date of the order of the tribunal determining the amount of the new pitch fee.

(6) An application under sub-paragraph (5)(a) may be made at any time after the end of the period of 28 days beginning with the review date but no later than 3 months after the review date.

(7) Sub-paragraphs (8) to (12) apply if the owner—

(a) has not served the notice required by sub-paragraph (3) by the time by which it was required to be served, but

(b) at any time afterwards serves on the occupier a written notice setting out the owner's proposals in respect of a new pitch fee.

(8) If (at any time) the occupier agrees to the proposed pitch fee, it is payable as from the 28th day after the date on which the owner serves the notice under sub-paragraph (7)(b).

(9) If the occupier has not agreed to the proposed pitch fee—

(a) the owner may apply to a tribunal for an order under sub-paragraph (1)(b) determining the amount of the new pitch fee,

(b) the occupier must continue to pay the current pitch fee to the owner until such time as the new pitch fee is agreed by the occupier or an order determining the amount of the new pitch fee is made by a tribunal under sub-paragraph (1)(b), and

(c) if a tribunal makes such an order, the new pitch fee is payable as from the 28th day after the date on which the owner serves the notice under sub-paragraph (7)(b).

(10) An application under sub-paragraph (9) may be made at any time after the end of the period of 56 days beginning with the date on which the owner serves the

notice under sub-paragraph (7)(b) but no later than 4 months after the date on which the owner serves that notice.

(11) A tribunal may permit an application under sub-paragraph (5)(a) or (9)(a) to be made to it outside the time limit specified in sub-paragraph (6) (in the case of an application under sub-paragraph (5)(a)) or in sub-paragraph (10) (in the case of an application under sub-paragraph (9)(a)) if it is satisfied that, in all the circumstances, there are good reasons for the failure to apply within the applicable time limit and for any delay since then in applying for permission to make the application out of time.

(12) The occupier is not to be treated as being in arrears—

(a) where sub-paragraph (8) applies, until the 28th day after the date on which the new pitch fee is agreed, or

(b) where sub-paragraph (9)(b) applies, until the 28th day after the date on which the new pitch fee is agreed or, as the case may be, the 28th day after the date of a tribunal order determining the amount of the new pitch fee.

48 (1) When determining the amount of the new pitch fee particular regard is to be had to—

(a) any sums expended by the owner since the last review date on improvements—

(i) which are for the benefit of the occupiers of mobile homes on the protected site,

(ii) which were the subject of consultation in accordance with paragraph 52(1)(f) and (g), and

(iii) to which a majority of the occupiers have not disagreed in writing or which, in the case of such disagreement, a tribunal, on the application of the owner, has ordered should be taken into account when determining the amount of the new pitch fee,

(b) any decrease in the amenity of the protected site since the last review date, and

(c) the effect of any enactment which has come into force since the last review date.

(2) When calculating what constitutes a majority of the occupiers for the purposes of sub-paragraph (1)(a)(iii) each mobile home is to be taken to have only 1 occupier and, in the event of there being more than 1 occupier of a mobile home, its occupier is to be taken to be whichever the occupiers agree or, in default of agreement, the occupier whose name first appears on the agreement.

(3) In a case where the pitch fee has not been previously reviewed, references in this paragraph to the last review date are to be read as references to the date when the agreement commenced.

49 When determining the amount of the new pitch fee no regard may be had to—

(a) any costs incurred by the owner in connection with expanding the protected site, or

(b) any costs incurred by the owner in relation to the conduct of proceedings under this Part or the agreement.

50 (1) Unless it would be unreasonable having regard to paragraph 48(1), there is a presumption that the pitch fee will increase or decrease by a percentage which is no more than any percentage increase or decrease in the consumer prices index calculated by reference only to—

(a) the latest index, and

(b) the index published for the month which was 12 months before that to which the latest index relates.

(2) In sub-paragraph (1) "the latest index" means—

WALES

(a) in the case where the owner serves a notice under paragraph 47(3), the latest index published before the day on which that notice is served, and

(b) in the case where the owner serves a notice under paragraph 47(7)(b), the latest index published before the day by which the owner was required to serve a notice under paragraph 47(3).

51 Occupier's obligations and owner's corresponding obligations

(1) The occupier must—

(a) pay the pitch fee to the owner,

(b) pay to the owner all sums due under the agreement in respect of gas, electricity, water, sewerage or other services supplied by the owner,

(c) keep the mobile home in a sound state of repair,

(d) maintain—

(i) the outside of the mobile home, and

(ii) the pitch, including all fences and outbuildings belonging to, or enjoyed with, it and the mobile home,

in a clean and tidy condition, and

(e) if requested by the owner, provide the owner with documentary evidence of any costs or expenses in respect of which the occupier seeks reimbursement.

(2) The owner must not do or cause to be done anything which may adversely affect the ability of the occupier to perform the occupier's obligations under sub-paragraph (1)(c) and (d).

52 Owner's other obligations

(1) The owner must—

(a) if requested by the occupier, and on payment by the occupier of a charge of not more than £30, provide accurate written details of—

(i) the size of the pitch and the base on which the mobile home is stationed, and

(ii) the location of the pitch and the base within the protected site,

and such details must include measurements between identifiable fixed points on the protected site and the pitch and the base,

(b) if requested by the occupier, provide (free of charge) documentary evidence in support and explanation of—

(i) any new pitch fee,

(ii) any charges for gas, electricity, water, sewerage or other services payable by the occupier to the owner under the agreement, and

(iii) any other charges, costs or expenses payable by the occupier to the owner under the agreement,

(c) be responsible for repairing the base on which the mobile home is stationed and for maintaining any gas, electricity, water, sewerage or other services supplied by the owner to the pitch or to the mobile home,

(d) be responsible for repairing other amenities provided by the owner on the pitch including any outhouses and facilities provided,

(e) maintain in a clean and tidy condition those parts of the protected site, including access ways, site boundary fences and trees, which are not the responsibility of any occupier of a mobile home stationed on the protected site,

(f) consult the occupier about improvements to the protected site in general, and in particular about those which the owner wishes to be taken into account when determining the amount of any new pitch fee, and

(g) consult a qualifying residents' association (if there is one) about all matters which relate to the operation and management of, or improvements to, the protected site and may affect the occupiers either directly or indirectly.

(2) For the purposes of sub-paragraph (1)(f), to "consult" the occupier means—

(a) to give the occupier at least 28 clear days' notice in writing of the proposed improvements which—

(i) describes the proposed improvements and how they will benefit the occupier in the long and short term,

(ii) details how the pitch fee may be affected when it is next reviewed, and

(iii) states when and where the occupier can make representations about the proposed improvements, and

(b) to take into account any representations made by the occupier about the proposed improvements, in accordance with paragraph (a)(iii), before undertaking them.

(3) For the purposes of sub-paragraph (1)(g), to "consult" a qualifying residents' association means—

(a) to give the association at least 28 clear days' notice in writing of the matters referred to in sub-paragraph (1)(g) which—

(i) describes the matters and how they may affect the occupiers either directly or indirectly in the long and short term, and

(ii) states when and where the association can make representations about the matters, and

(b) to take into account any representations made by the association, in accordance with paragraph (a)(ii), before proceeding with the matters.

53 Owner's name and address

(1) The owner must by notice inform the occupier and any qualifying residents' association of the address in England or Wales at which notices (including notices of proceedings) may be served on the owner by the occupier or a qualifying residents' association.

(2) If the owner fails to comply with sub-paragraph (1), then any amount otherwise due from the occupier to the owner in respect of the pitch fee is to be treated for all purposes as not being due from the occupier to the owner at any time before the owner does comply with that sub-paragraph.

(3) Where in accordance with the agreement the owner gives any written notice to the occupier or (as the case may be) a qualifying residents' association, the notice must contain the name and address of the owner.

(4) Where—

(a) the occupier or a qualifying residents' association receives such a notice, but

(b) it does not contain the information required to be contained in it by virtue of sub-paragraph (3),

the notice is to be treated as not having been given until such time as the owner gives the information to the occupier or (as the case may be) the association in respect of the notice.

(5) Nothing in sub-paragraphs (3) and (4) applies to any notice containing a demand to which paragraph 54(1) applies.

54 (1) Where the owner makes any demand for payment by the occupier of the pitch fee, or in respect of services supplied or other charges, the demand must contain the name and address of the owner.

(2) Where—

(a) the occupier receives such a demand, but

(b) it does not contain the information required to be contained in it by virtue of sub-paragraph (1), the amount demanded is to be treated for all purposes as not being due from the occupier to the owner at any time before the owner gives that information to the occupier in respect of the demand.

PART 2
MATTERS CONCERNING WHICH TERMS MAY BE IMPLIED BY THE APPROPRIATE JUDICIAL BODY

III WAL [36]

55 The sums payable by the occupier in pursuance of the agreement and the times at which they are to be paid.

56 The review at yearly intervals of the sums payable by the occupier in pursuance of the agreement.

57 The provision or improvement of services available on the protected site, and the use by the occupier of such services.

58 The preservation of the amenity of the protected site.

HOUSING (WALES) ACT 2014

2014 anaw 7

PART 1
REGULATION OF PRIVATE RENTED HOUSING

GENERAL NOTES ON THE HOUSING (WALES) ACT 2014

III WAL [37]

Part 1 of the Act introduces a compulsory registration and licensing scheme for private rented sector landlords and letting and management agents. The provisions came into force on 23 November 2016.

A landlord who lets a dwelling or offers to let a dwelling has to be registered: s 4. This is subject to limited exceptions: s 5. If the landlord carries out 'letting activities' or 'property management activities' then he has to be licensed to carry out those activities: ss 6 and 7. If the landlord delegates either or both activities to a lettings agent then he does not need to be licensed but the lettings agent must be licensed. Agents must be licensed for 'lettings work' (s 9) and for 'property management work' (s 11). Carrying out letting activities/work and property management activities/work without a licence are criminal offences enforceable in the Magistrates Court as is appointing an unlicensed agent: s 13. Under the current regulations Welsh Ministers have appointed Cardiff City Council as the sole licensing authority for Wales. Regulations made pursuant to s 19 prescribe how applications for licenses are to be made and the licensing authority has to apply a fit and proper person test when determining applications: s 20.

The licensing authority can grant a licence subject to condition, refuse to grant a licence, amend a licence or revoke a licence. All such decisions are subject to a right of appeal to a residential property tribunal: s 27.

Sections 30 and 32 provide for applications to be made to the residential property tribunal for rent stopping and rent repayment orders respectively. For such applications to succeed the applicant must show that an offence under s 7(5) or 13(3) has been committed. There is no need for an actual conviction. Applications for rent stopping orders can be made by the licensing authority or the local housing authority, the latter requires the consent of the former before making an application. A tenant as well as the licensing authority and local housing authority can apply for a rent repayment order.

Section 40 mandates Welsh Ministers to issue a code of practice and compliance with the code is one of the conditions on which licences are held.

The impact of contraventions of the registration and licensing regime on proceedings in the County Court are the subject of ss 43 and 44 (see paras **III WAL [40]** and **III WAL [41]** below).

The Act does not expressly deal with possession proceedings using the section 8 procedure in the event of the landlord and/or his agent not being appropriately licensed. Under sections 7 and 12 the collection of rent and serving notices to quit qualify as property management activities and property management work and such activities are unlawful unless the landlord and/or agent are licensed. It is at least arguable, therefore, that no possession proceedings or proceedings for the recovery for rent could be brought by a landlord/agent who are not licensed.

Part 2 of the Act reforms the law with regard to homelessness and places a stronger duty on local authorities to prevent homelessness. There is a right to review relevant local authority decisions pursuant to section 85. Section 88 provides for a right of appeal to the county court on a point of law (see para **III WAL [77]** below).

Introduction

III WAL [38]

1 Overview of this Part

(1) This Part regulates—

(a) the letting of dwellings under certain kinds of tenancy (which are defined as "domestic tenancies" in section 2), and

(b) the management of dwellings subject to such tenancies,

by means of a system of registration and licensing.

(2) It requires landlords to be—

(a) registered for each dwelling subject to, or marketed or offered for let under, a domestic tenancy in respect of which they are the landlord (section 4), subject to exceptions (section 5);

(b) licensed to carry out certain kinds of lettings activities for dwellings marketed or offered for let under domestic tenancies (section 6), subject to exceptions (section 8);

(c) licensed to carry out certain kinds of property management activities for dwellings subject to a domestic tenancy (section 7), subject to exceptions (section 8).

(3) It requires persons acting on behalf of a landlord to be licensed to carry out—

(a) lettings work in respect of a dwelling marketed or offered for let under a domestic tenancy (section 9);

(b) property management work in respect of a dwelling subject to a domestic tenancy (section 11).

(4) "Lettings work" and "property management work" are defined for the purposes of the Part in sections 10 and 12; the definitions exclude certain persons and activities from the licensing requirements imposed on persons acting on behalf of landlords.

(5) The system of registration and licensing is to be administered and enforced by a person designated by the Welsh Ministers as the licensing authority for the whole of Wales or by different persons designated as licensing authorities for different areas within Wales (section 3); provision is also made for local housing authorities to exercise certain enforcement powers.

(6) Sections 14 to 17 and Schedule 1 provide for a register to be established and maintained by the licensing authority and for registration generally.

(7) Sections 18 to 27 provide for licences generally; and

- (a) a licensing authority may only grant two kinds of licence (one for landlords and the other for persons acting on behalf of landlords) and licences have effect in respect of the area for which a licensing authority is responsible (section 18);
- (b) in order to be licensed a person must meet certain criteria, including being a fit and proper person (section 20) and requirements relating to training (see section 19).

(8) The requirements imposed by this Part are enforced by—

- (a) offences for contravention of registration and licensing requirements (see sections referred to in subsections (2) and (3) and sections 16(3), 23(3), 38(1) and (4) and 39(1) and (2));
- (b) fixed penalty notices (section 29);
- (c) rent stopping orders (sections 30 and 31);
- (d) rent repayment orders (sections 32 and 33).

(9) Sections 36 to 39 make provision about information required or given for the purposes of this Part.

(10) Section 40 provides for the Welsh Ministers to issue a code of practice and provision is made for guidance (section 41) and directions (section 42).

(11) Sections 43 to 48 make supplementary provision.

(12) Section 49 makes further provision about interpretation and indexes the defined terms used in this Part.

III WAL [38.1]

Commencement The Housing (Wales) Act 2014 is now fully in force. A series of eight commencement orders brought it into operation in stages, the first being Chapter 1, which introduced a requirement for private landlords to register and for private landlords and their agents to obtain licences. The last Part to be brought fully into force was Part 2 on Homelessness. The various dates for commencement, ending with 23 November 2016, are set out in the Housing (Wales) Act 2014 (Commencement No 8) Order 2016, SI 2016/1066.

WALES

III WAL [39]

2 Meaning of key terms

(1) In this Part—

"domestic tenancy" ("*tenantiaeth ddomestig*") means—

- (a) a tenancy which is an assured tenancy for the purposes of the Housing Act 1988 (which includes an assured shorthold tenancy), except where the tenancy—
  - (i) is a long lease for the purposes of Chapter 1 of Part 1 of the Leasehold Reform, Housing and Urban Development Act 1993 ("the 1993 Act"), or
  - (ii) in the case of a shared ownership lease (within the meaning given by section 7(7) of the 1993 Act), would be such a lease if

the tenant's share (within the meaning given by that section) were 100 per cent;

(b) a regulated tenancy for the purposes of the Rent Act 1977, or

(c) a tenancy under which a dwelling is let as a separate dwelling and which is of a description specified for the purposes of this Part in an order made by the Welsh Ministers;

"dwelling" ("*annedd*") means a building or part of a building occupied or intended to be occupied as a separate dwelling, together with any yard, garden, outhouses and appurtenances belonging to it or usually enjoyed with it, where the whole of the dwelling is in Wales;

"landlord" ("*landlord*") means—

(a) in relation to a dwelling subject to a domestic tenancy, the immediate landlord or, in relation to a statutory tenant, the person who, apart from the statutory tenancy, would be entitled to possession of the dwelling subject to the tenancy, and

(b) in relation to a dwelling that is not subject to a domestic tenancy, the person who would be the immediate landlord if the dwelling were let under a domestic tenancy;

"rental property" ("*eiddo ar rent*") means a dwelling subject to, or marketed or offered for let under, a domestic tenancy.

(2) In this section, "statutory tenant" and "statutory tenancy" mean a statutory tenant or statutory tenancy within the meaning of the Rent Act 1977.

Supplementary

III WAL [40]

43 Activity in contravention of this Part: effect on tenancy agreements

(1) No rule of law relating to the validity or enforceability of contracts in circumstances involving illegality is to affect the validity or enforceability of any provision of a domestic tenancy of a dwelling in respect of which a contravention of this Part has occurred.

(2) But periodical payments—

(a) payable in connection with such a tenancy may be stopped in accordance with section 30 (rent stopping orders), and

(b) paid in connection with such a tenancy may be recovered in accordance with sections 32 and 33 (rent repayment orders).

III WAL [40.1]

Rent stopping order A rent stopping order under s 30 may be made by a residential property tribunal on the application of the licensing authority or, with that authority's consent, by a local housing authority. Before making such an order the tribunal must be satisfied that an offence is being committed, contrary to s 7(5) or s 13(3) (unlicensed renting or appointment of an unlicensed agent), and that the authority has given the landlord and the tenant notice of its intention to apply for a stopping order. Section 31 provides for the circumstances in which a stopping order may be revoked.

III WAL [40.2]

Rent repayment order A rent repayment order under ss 31 and 32 may be made by a residential property tribunal on the application of the licensing authority or, with that authority's consent, by a local housing authority. The purpose of making such an order is for the recovery by the local housing authority of housing benefit or universal credit paid in respect of rent that was being collected in breach of s 7(5) or s 13(3) (unlicensed renting or appointment of an unlicensed agent). An authority may apply for leave to amend its application as to the amount of housing benefit or universal credit, in accordance with reg 2 of the Regulation of Private Rented Housing (Rent Repayment Orders) (Supplementary Provisions) (Wales) Regulations 2016, SI 2016/1022.

III WAL [40.3]

Periodical payments A failure to hold an appropriate property management licence on the part of a landlord or his agent would not, by virtue of any doctrine based on illegality, enable a tenant to justify withholding rent or counterclaiming for rent paid in civil court proceedings as rent stopping orders and rent repayment orders fall within the jurisdiction of the residential property tribunal.

The provisions ot section 44 of the Act, however, mean that contraventions of the licensing and registration regime are directly relevant to accelerated possession claims in respect of properties let on assured shorthold tenancies.

III WAL [41]

44 Restriction on terminating tenancies

(1) A section 21 notice may not be given in relation to a dwelling subject to a domestic tenancy which is an assured shorthold tenancy if—

(a) the landlord is not registered in respect of the dwelling, or

(b) the landlord is not licensed under this Part for the area in which the dwelling is located and the landlord has not appointed a person who is licensed under this Part to carry out all property management work in respect of the dwelling on the landlord's behalf.

(2) But subsection (1) does not apply for the period of 28 days beginning with the day on which the landlord's interest in the dwelling is assigned to the landlord.

(3) In this section, a "section 21 notice" means a notice under section 21(1)(b) or (4)(a) of the Housing Act 1988.

III WAL [41.1]

Section 21 notice An assured shorthold tenancy cannot be terminated by a landlord except by the service of a two month notice, as provided in s 21 of the Housing Act 1988. In the case of an unregistered or unlicensed landlord the service of such a notice is invalid and the tenancy continues.

III WAL [41.2]

There is an online facility operated by Rent Smart Wales to search whether the landlord and/or managing agent are registered and licensed. If they are not registered and licensed then the section 21 notice is invalid and the proceedings must be dismissed. Form 5NB Wales should be used in respect of possession proceedings relating to property located wholly in Wales and section 9 requires details to be given of the landlord and/or agent's registration and license numbers. The provisions relating to securing a deposit under sections 33 to 40 of the Deregulation Act 2015 and the requirement to serve a special form of notice entitled Form 6A which apply in England to any tenancy created after 1 October 2015 do not apply in Wales.

PART 2
HOMELESSNESS

CHAPTER 2 HELP FOR PEOPLE WHO ARE HOMELESS OR THREATENED WITH HOMELESSNESS

INTRODUCTION

III WAL [42]

53 Overview of this Chapter

(1) This Chapter confers duties on local housing authorities to help people who are homeless or threatened with homelessness and makes connected provision.

(2) Sections 55 to 59 define and otherwise explain the meaning of some key terms (further provision about interpretation and an index of terms defined in this Chapter is at section 99).

(3) Section 60 requires local housing authorities to secure the provision of a service providing people with information and advice connected with homelessness and assistance in accessing help under this Chapter.

(4) Section 61 introduces Schedule 2 which makes provision about eligibility for help under this Chapter.

(5) Section 62 places a duty on a local housing authority to assess the cases of people ("applicants") who apply to the authority for accommodation, or help in retaining or obtaining accommodation, where they appear to the authority to be homeless or threatened with homelessness.

(6) Section 63 provides for notice to be given to applicants about the outcome of the assessment.

(7) Section 64 gives examples of the kinds of ways in which the subsequent duties to secure or help to secure the availability of accommodation may be discharged and what may be done to discharge them; and section 65 explains what "help to secure" means.

(8) Sections 66 to 79 set out the main duties on local housing authorities to help applicants, the circumstances in which those duties come to an end and connected provision; the main duties are—

- (a) a duty to help to prevent applicants who are threatened with homelessness from becoming homeless (section 66);
- (b) a duty to secure interim accommodation for applicants in priority need (section 68) (section 70 provides for who is to have priority need for accommodation for the purposes of the Chapter);
- (c) a duty to help to secure that suitable accommodation is available for occupation by homeless applicants (section 73);
- (d) a duty to secure accommodation for applicants in priority need when the duty in section 73 comes to an end (section 75).

(9) Section 78 provides for the circumstances in which local housing authorities may have regard to whether an applicant became homeless intentionally when it is considering whether a duty to secure accommodation for applicants in priority need applies; section 77 provides for the meaning of intentionally homeless.

(10) Sections 80 to 82 provide for local housing authorities to end their duties to applicants by referring their cases to other authorities in Wales or England, where the applicants have a local connection with the areas of those other authorities; section 81 defines the meaning of "local connection" for the purposes of this Chapter.

(11) Sections 85 to 89 provide for reviews and appeals.

(12) Sections 90 to 99 make supplementary and general provision.

III WAL [42.1]

Housing the homeless Chapter 2 deals comprehensively with the housing of the homeless in Wales, including those threatened with homelessness. It is a free-standing exposition of the local housing authorities' powers and obligations with definitions provided for all the main building blocks and concepts. For the most part it replicates the provisions of Part VII of the Housing Act 1996, ss 175 to 217) for the assistance of those who are homeless or threatened with homelessness.

KEY TERMS

III WAL [43]

54 Application of key terms

Sections 55 to 59 apply for the purposes of this Part.

III WAL [44]

55 Meaning of homeless and threatened homelessness

(1) A person is homeless if there is no accommodation available for the person's occupation, in the United Kingdom or elsewhere, which the person—

(a) is entitled to occupy by virtue of an interest in it or by virtue of an order of a court,

(b) has an express or implied licence to occupy, or

(c) occupies as a residence by virtue of any enactment or rule of law giving the person the right to remain in occupation or restricting the right of another person to recover possession.

(2) A person is also homeless if the person has accommodation but—

(a) cannot secure entry to it, or

(b) it consists of a moveable structure, vehicle or vessel designed or adapted for human habitation and there is no place where the person is entitled or permitted both to place it and to reside in it.

(3) A person is not to be treated as having accommodation unless it is accommodation which it would be reasonable for the person to continue to occupy.

(4) A person is threatened with homelessness if it is likely that the person will become homeless within 56 days.

III WAL [45]

56 Meaning of accommodation available for occupation

(1) Accommodation may only be regarded as available for a person's occupation if it is available for occupation by that person together with—

(a) any other person who normally resides with that person as a member of his or her family, or

(b) any other person who might reasonably be expected to reside with that person.

(2) A reference in this Chapter to securing that accommodation is available for a person's occupation is to be interpreted accordingly.

III WAL [46]

57 Whether it is reasonable to continue to occupy accommodation

(1) It is not reasonable for a person to continue to occupy accommodation if it is probable that it will lead to the person, or a member of the person's household, being subjected to abuse.

(2) In this section "member of a person's household" means—

(a) a person who normally resides with him or her as member of his or her family, or

(b) any other person who might reasonably be expected to reside with that person.

(3) In determining whether it would be, or would have been, reasonable for a person to continue to occupy accommodation, a local housing authority—

(a) may have regard to the general circumstances prevailing in relation to housing in the area of the local housing authority to whom the person has applied for help in securing accommodation;

(b) must have regard to whether or not the accommodation is affordable for that person.

(4) The Welsh Ministers may by order specify—

(a) other circumstances in which it is to be regarded as reasonable or not reasonable for a person to continue to occupy accommodation, and

(b) other matters to be taken into account or disregarded in determining whether it would be, or would have been, reasonable for a person to continue to occupy accommodation.

III WAL [47]

58 Meaning of abuse and domestic abuse

(1) "Abuse" means physical violence, threatening or intimidating behaviour and any other form of abuse which, directly or indirectly, may give rise to the risk of harm; and abuse is "domestic abuse" where the victim is associated with the abuser.

(2) A person is associated with another person if—

(a) they are or have been married to each other;

(b) they are or have been civil partners of each other;

(c) they live or have lived together in an enduring family relationship (whether they are of different sexes or the same sex);

(d) they live or have lived in the same household;

(e) they are relatives;

(f) they have agreed to marry one another (whether or not that agreement has been terminated);

(g) they have entered into a civil partnership agreement between them (whether or not that agreement has been terminated);

(h) they have or have had an intimate personal relationship with each other which is or was of significant duration;

(i) in relation to a child, each of them is a parent of the child or has, or has had, parental responsibility for the child.

(3) If a child has been adopted or falls within subsection (4), two persons are also associated with each other for the purposes this Chapter if—

(a) one is a natural parent of the child or a parent of such a natural parent, and

(b) the other is—

(i) the child, or

(ii) a person who has become a parent of the child by virtue of an adoption order, who has applied for an adoption order or with whom the child has at any time been placed for adoption.

(4) A child falls within this section if—

(a) an adoption agency, within the meaning of section 2 of the Adoption and Children Act 2002, is authorised to place the child for adoption under section 19 of that Act (placing children with parental consent) or the child has become the subject of an order under section 21 of that Act (placement orders), or

(b) the child is freed for adoption by virtue of an order made—

(i) in England and Wales, under section 18 of the Adoption Act 1976,

(ii) in Northern Ireland, under Article 17(1) or 18(1) of the Adoption (Northern Ireland) Order 1987, or

(c) the child is the subject of a Scottish permanence order which includes granting authority to adopt.

(5) In this section—

"adoption order" ("*gorchymyn mabwysiadu*") means an adoption order within the meaning of section 72(1) of the Adoption Act 1976 or section 46(1) of the Adoption and Children Act 2002;

"civil partnership agreement" ("*cytundeb partneriaeth sifil*") has the meaning given by section 73 of the Civil Partnership Act 2004;

"parental responsibility" ("*cyfrifoldeb rhiant*") has the meaning given by section 3 of the Children Act 1989;

"relative" ("*perthynas*"), in relation to a person, means that person's parent, grandparent, child, grandchild, brother, half-brother, sister, half-sister, uncle, aunt, nephew, niece (including any person who is or has been in that relationship by virtue of a marriage or civil partnership or an enduring family relationship).

III WAL [48]

59 Suitability of accommodation

(1) In determining whether accommodation is suitable for a person, a local housing authority must have regard to the following enactments—

(a) Part 9 of the Housing Act 1985 (slum clearance);

(b) Part 10 of the Housing Act 1985 (overcrowding);

(c) Part 1 of the Housing Act 2004 (housing conditions);

(d) Part 2 of the Housing Act 2004 (licensing of houses in multiple occupation);

(e) Part 3 of the Housing Act 2004 (selective licensing of other residential accommodation);

(f) Part 4 of the Housing Act 2004 (additional control provisions in relation to residential accommodation);

(g) Part 1 of this Act (regulation of private rented housing).

(2) In determining whether accommodation is suitable for a person, a local housing authority must have regard to whether or not the accommodation is affordable for that person.

(3) The Welsh Ministers may by order specify—

(a) circumstances in which accommodation is or is not to be regarded as suitable for a person, and

(b) matters to be taken into account or disregarded in determining whether accommodation is suitable for a person.

III WAL [48.1]

Specified circumstances and matters By s 59(3)(a) of the Act the Welsh Ministers may specify circumstances in which accommodation is, or is not, to be regarded as suitable. By s 59(3)(b) the Ministers may also specify matters to be taken into account or, as the case may be, disregarded. The Homelessness (Suitability of Accommodation) (Wales) Order 2015 , SI 2015/1268 is divided into three parts. Part 1 specifies matters that must be taken into account. Part 2 specifies when B&B and shared accommodation are not suitable to be used as temporary accommodation. Part 3 specifies when private sector rented accommodation is not suitable for discharging the duties under s 75.

Information, Advice and Assistance in Accessing Help

III WAL [49]

60 Duty to provide information, advice and assistance in accessing help

(1) A local housing authority must secure the provision, without charge, of a service providing people in its area, or people who have a local connection with its area, with—

(a) information and advice relating to preventing homelessness, securing accommodation when homeless, accessing any other help available for people who are homeless or may become homeless, and

(b) assistance in accessing help under this Chapter or any other help for people who are homeless or may become homeless.

(2) In relation to subsection (1)(a), the service must include, in particular, the publication of information and advice on the following matters—

(a) the system provided for by this Chapter and how the system operates in the authority's area;

(b) whether any other help for people who are homeless or may become homeless (whether or not the person is threatened with homelessness within the meaning of this Chapter) is available in the authority's area;

(c) how to access the help that is available.

(3) In relation to subsection (1)(b), the service must include, in particular, assistance in accessing help to prevent a person becoming homeless which is available whether or not the person is threatened with homelessness within the meaning of this Chapter.

(4) The local housing authority must, in particular by working with other public authorities, voluntary organisations and other persons, ensure that the service is designed to meet the needs of groups at particular risk of homelessness, including in particular—

(a) people leaving prison or youth detention accommodation,

(b) young people leaving care,

(c) people leaving the regular armed forces of the Crown,

(d) people leaving hospital after medical treatment for mental disorder as an inpatient, and

(e) people receiving mental health services in the community.

(5) Two or more local housing authorities may jointly secure the provision of a service under this section for their areas; and where they do so—

(a) references in this section to a local housing authority are to be read as references to the authorities acting jointly, and

(b) references in this section to a local housing authority's area are to be read as references to the combined area.

(6) The service required by this section may be integrated with the service required by section 17 of the Social Services and Well-being (Wales) Act 2014.

Eligibility

III WAL [50]

61 Eligibility for help under this Chapter

Schedule 2 has effect for the purposes of determining whether an applicant is eligible for help under the following provisions of this Chapter.

III WAL [50.1]

Persons from abroad or subject to immigration control The Allocation of Housing and Homelessness (Eligibility) (Wales) Regulations 2014, SI 2014/2603, as amended by SI 2017/698, make provision for the eligibility for housing assistance of persons subject to immigration control and persons from abroad.

Applications for Help and Assessment

III WAL [51]

62 Duty to assess

(1) A local housing authority must carry out an assessment of a person's case if—

(a) the person has applied to a local housing authority for accommodation or help in retaining or obtaining accommodation,

(b) it appears to the authority that the person may be homeless or threatened with homelessness, and

(c) subsection (2) does not apply to the person.

(2) This subsection applies if the person has been assessed by a local housing authority under this section on a previous occasion and the authority is satisfied that—

(a) the person's circumstances have not changed materially since that assessment was carried out, and

(b) there is no new information that materially affects that assessment.

(3) In this Chapter, "applicant" means a person to whom the duty in subsection (1) applies.

(4) The authority must assess whether or not the applicant is eligible for help under this Chapter.

(5) If the applicant is eligible for help under this Chapter, the assessment must include an assessment of—

(a) the circumstances that have caused the applicant to be homeless or threatened with homelessness;

(b) the housing needs of the applicant and any person with whom the applicant lives or might reasonably be expected to live;

(c) the support needed for the applicant and any person with whom the applicant lives or might reasonably be expected to live to retain accommodation which is or may become available;

(d) whether or not the authority has any duty to the applicant under the following provisions of this Chapter.

(6) In carrying out an assessment, the local housing authority must—

(a) seek to identify the outcome the applicant wishes to achieve from the authority's help, and

(b) assess whether the exercise of any function under this Chapter could contribute to the achievement of that outcome.

(7) A local housing authority may carry out its assessment of the matters mentioned in subsections (5) and (6) before it has concluded that the applicant is eligible for help under this Chapter.

(8) A local housing authority must keep its assessment under review during the period in which the authority considers that it owes a duty to the applicant under the following provisions of this Chapter or that it may do so.

(9) A local housing authority must review its assessment in the following two cases—

Case 1 - where an applicant has been notified under section 63 that a duty is owed to the applicant under section 66 (duty to help to prevent an applicant from becoming homeless) and subsequently it appears to the authority that the duty under section 66 has or is likely to come to an end because the applicant is homeless;

Case 2 - where an applicant has been notified under section 63 that a duty is owed to the applicant under section 73 (duty to help to secure accommodation for homeless applicants) and subsequently it appears to the authority that the duty in section 73 has or is likely to come to an end in circumstances where a duty may be owed to the applicant under section 75 (duty to secure accommodation for applicants in priority need when the duty in section 73 ends).

(10) The duty in subsection (5)(d) does not require a local housing authority to assess whether or not a duty would be owed to the applicant under section 75 unless and until it reviews its assessment in accordance with subsection (9) in the circumstances described in case 2 of that subsection; but it may do so before then.

(11) Subsections (9) and (10) do not affect the generality of subsection (8).

III WAL [52]

63 Notice of the outcome of assessment

(1) The local housing authority must notify the applicant of the outcome of its assessment (or any review of its assessment) and, in so far as any issue is decided against the applicant's interests, inform the applicant of the reasons for its decision.

(2) If the authority decides that a duty is owed to the applicant under section 75, but would not have done so without having had regard to a restricted person, the notice under subsection (1) must also—

(a) inform the applicant that its decision was reached on that basis,
(b) include the name of the restricted person,
(c) explain why the person is a restricted person, and
(d) explain the effect of section 76(5).

(3) If the authority has notified or intends to notify another local housing authority under section 80 (referral of cases), it must at the same time notify the applicant of that decision and inform him or her of the reasons for it.

(4) A notice under subsection (1) or (3) must also—

(a) inform the applicant of his or her right to request a review of the decision and of the time within which such a request must be made (see section 85), and
(b) be given in writing and, if not received, is to be treated as having been given if it is made available at the authority's office for a reasonable period for collection by the applicant or on the applicant's behalf.

(5) In this Chapter, "a restricted person" means a person—

(a) who is not eligible for help under this Chapter,
(b) who is subject to immigration control within the meaning of the Asylum and Immigration Act 1996, and
(c) who either—
  (i) does not have leave to enter or remain in the United Kingdom, or
  (ii) has leave to enter or remain in the United Kingdom subject to a condition to maintain and accommodate himself or herself, and any dependants, without recourse to public funds.

Duties to Help Applicants

III WAL [53]

64 How to secure or help to secure the availability of accommodation

(1) The following are examples of the ways in which a local housing authority may secure or help to secure that suitable accommodation is available, or does not cease to be available, for occupation by an applicant—

(a) by arranging for a person other than the authority to provide something;
(b) by itself providing something;
(c) by providing something, or arranging for something to be provided, to a person other than the applicant.

(2) The following are examples of what may be provided or arranged to secure or help to secure that suitable accommodation is available, or does not cease to be available, for occupation by an applicant—

(a) mediation;
(b) payments by way of grant or loan;
(c) guarantees that payments will be made;
(d) support in managing debt, mortgage arrears or rent arrears;

(e) security measures for applicants at risk of abuse;
(f) advocacy or other representation;
(g) accommodation;
(h) information and advice;
(i) other services, goods or facilities.

(3) The Welsh Ministers must give guidance to local housing authorities in relation to how they may secure or help to secure that suitable accommodation is available, or does not cease to be available, for occupation by an applicant.

III WAL [54]

65 Meaning of help to secure

Where a local housing authority is required by this Chapter to help to secure (rather than "to secure") that suitable accommodation is available, or does not cease to be available, for occupation by an applicant, the authority—

(a) is required to take reasonable steps to help, having regard (among other things) to the need to make the best use of the authority's resources;
(b) is not required to secure an offer of accommodation under Part 6 of the Housing Act 1996 (allocation of housing);
(c) is not required to otherwise provide accommodation.

III WAL [55]

66 Duty to help to prevent an applicant from becoming homeless

(1) A local housing authority must help to secure that suitable accommodation does not cease to be available for occupation by an applicant if the authority is satisfied that the applicant is—

(a) threatened with homelessness, and
(b) eligible for help.

(2) Subsection (1) does not affect any right of the authority, whether by virtue of a contract, enactment or rule of law, to secure vacant possession of any accommodation.

III WAL [56]

67 Circumstances in which the duty in section 66 ends

(1) The duty to an applicant under section 66 comes to an end in any of the circumstances described in subsection (2), (3) or (4), if the applicant has been notified in accordance with section 84.

(2) The circumstances are that the local authority is satisfied that the applicant has become homeless.

(3) The circumstances are that the local housing authority is satisfied (whether as a result of the steps it has taken or not) that—

(a) the applicant is no longer threatened with homelessness, and
(b) suitable accommodation is likely to be available for occupation by the applicant for a period of at least 6 months.

(4) The circumstances are that—

(a) the applicant, having been notified in writing of the possible consequences of refusal or acceptance of the offer, refuses an offer of accommodation from any person which the authority is satisfied is suitable for the applicant, and
(b) the authority is satisfied that the accommodation offered is likely to be available for occupation by the applicant for a period of at least 6 months.

(5) The period of 6 months mentioned in subsections (3)(b) and (4)(b) begins on the day the notice under section 84 is sent or first made available for collection.

(6) See section 79 for further circumstances in which the duty in section 66 comes to an end.

III WAL [57]

68 Interim duty to secure accommodation for homeless applicants in priority need

(1) The local housing authority must secure that suitable accommodation is available for the occupation of an applicant to whom subsection (2) or (3) applies until the duty comes to an end in accordance with section 69.

(2) This subsection applies to an applicant who the authority has reason to believe may—

(a) be homeless,

(b) be eligible for help, and

(c) have a priority need for accommodation,

in circumstances where the authority is not yet satisfied that the applicant is homeless, eligible for help and in priority need for accommodation.

(3) This subsection applies to an applicant—

(a) who the authority has reason to believe or is satisfied has a priority need or whose case has been referred from a local housing authority in England under section 198(1) of the Housing Act 1996, and

(b) to whom the duty in section 73 (duty to help to end homelessness) applies.

(4) The duty under this section arises irrespective of any possibility of the referral of the applicant's case to another local housing authority (see sections 80 to 82).

III WAL [58]

69 Circumstances in which the duty in section 68 ends

(1) The duty to an applicant under section 68 comes to an end in any of the circumstances described in subsection (2), (3) (subject to subsection (4) and (5)), (7), (8) or (9) if the applicant has been notified in accordance with section 84.

(2) The circumstances are that the local housing authority has decided that no duty is owed to the applicant under section 73 and the applicant is notified of that decision.

(3) In the case of an applicant to whom section 68(3) applies, the circumstances are that the local housing authority has—

(a) decided that the duty owed to the applicant under section 73 has come to an end and that a duty is or is not owed to the applicant under section 75, and

(b) notified the applicant of that decision;

but this is subject to subsections (4) and (5).

(4) Subsection (5) applies where a local housing authority has decided that no duty is owed to the applicant under section 75 on the basis that the authority—

(a) is satisfied that the applicant became homeless intentionally in the circumstances which gave rise to the application, or

(b) has previously secured an offer of accommodation of the kind described in section 75(3)(f).

(5) The duty under section 68 does not come to an end in the circumstances described in subsection (3) until the authority is also satisfied that the accommodation it has secured under section 68 has been available to the applicant for a sufficient period, beginning on the day on which he or she is notified that section 75 does not apply, to allow the applicant a reasonable opportunity of securing accommodation for his or her occupation.

(6) The period mentioned in subsection (5) is not sufficient for the purposes of that subsection if it ends on a day during the period of 56 days beginning with the day on which the applicant was notified that the duty in section 73 applied.

(7) The circumstances are that the applicant, having been notified of the possible consequence of refusal, refuses an offer of accommodation secured under section 68 which the local housing authority is satisfied is suitable for the applicant.

(8) The circumstances are that the local housing authority is satisfied that the applicant has become homeless intentionally from suitable interim accommodation made available for the applicant's occupation under section 68.

(9) The circumstances are that the local housing authority is satisfied that the applicant voluntarily ceased to occupy as his or her only or principal home suitable interim accommodation made available for the applicant's occupation under section 68.

(10) The duty comes to an end in accordance with this section even if the applicant requests a review of any decision that has led to the duty coming to an end (see section 85).

(11) The authority may secure that suitable accommodation is available for the applicant's occupation pending a decision on a review.

(12) See section 79 for further circumstances in which the duty in section 68 comes to an end.

III WAL [59]

70 Priority need for accommodation

(1) The following persons have a priority need for accommodation for the purposes of this Chapter—

- (a) a pregnant woman or a person with whom she resides or might reasonably be expected to reside;
- (b) a person with whom a dependent child resides or might reasonably be expected to reside;
- (c) a person—
  - (i) who is vulnerable as a result of some special reason (for example: old age, physical or mental illness or physical or mental disability), or
  - (ii) with whom a person who falls within sub-paragraph (i) resides or might reasonably be expected to reside;
- (d) a person—
  - (i) who is homeless or threatened with homelessness as a result of an emergency such as flood, fire or other disaster, or
  - (ii) with whom a person who falls within sub-paragraph (i) resides or might reasonably be expected to reside;
- (e) a person—
  - (i) who is homeless as a result of being subject to domestic abuse, or
  - (ii) with whom a person who falls within sub-paragraph (i) resides (other than the abuser) or might reasonably be expected to reside;
- (f) a person—
  - (i) who is aged 16 or 17 when the person applies to a local housing authority for accommodation or help in obtaining or retaining accommodation, or
  - (ii) with whom a person who falls within sub-paragraph (i) resides or might reasonably be expected to reside;
- (g) a person—
  - (i) who has attained the age of 18, when the person applies to a local housing authority for accommodation or help in obtaining or

retaining accommodation, but not the age of 21, who is at particular risk of sexual or financial exploitation, or

(ii) with whom a person who falls within sub-paragraph (i) resides (other than an exploiter or potential exploiter) or might reasonably be expected to reside;

(h) a person—

(i) who has attained the age of 18, when the person applies to a local housing authority for accommodation or help in obtaining or retaining accommodation, but not the age of 21, who was looked after, accommodated or fostered at any time while under the age of 18, or

(ii) with whom a person who falls within sub-paragraph (i) resides or might reasonably be expected to reside;

(i) a person—

(i) who has served in the regular armed forces of the Crown who has been homeless since leaving those forces, or

(ii) with whom a person who falls within sub-paragraph (i) resides or might reasonably be expected to reside;

(j) a person who has a local connection with the area of the local housing authority and who is vulnerable as a result of one of the following reasons—

(i) having served a custodial sentence within the meaning of section 76 of the Powers of Criminal Courts (Sentencing) Act 2000,

(ii) having been remanded in or committed to custody by an order of a court, or

(iii) having been remanded to youth detention accommodation under section 91(4) of the Legal Aid, Sentencing and Punishment of Offenders Act 2012,

or a person with whom such a person resides or might reasonably be expected to reside.

(2) In this Chapter—

"looked after, accommodated or fostered" ("*yn derbyn gofal, yn cael ei letya neu'n cael ei faethu*") means—

(a) looked after by a local authority (within the meaning of section 74 of the Social Services and Well-Being (Wales) Act 2014 or section 22 of the Children Act 1989),

(b) accommodated by or on behalf of a voluntary organisation,

(c) accommodated in a private children's home,

(d) accommodated for a continuous period of at least three months—

(i) by any Local Health Board or Special Health Authority,

(ii) by or on behalf of a clinical commissioning group or the National Health Service Commissioning Board,

(iii) by or on behalf of a county or county borough council in Wales in the exercise of education functions,

(iv) by or on behalf of a local authority in England in the exercise of education functions,

(v) in any care home or independent hospital, or

(vi) in any accommodation provided by or on behalf of an NHS Trust or by or on behalf of an NHS Foundation Trust, or

(e) privately fostered (within the meaning of section 66 of the Children Act 1989).

(3) In subsection (2)—

"care home" ("*cartref gofal*")—

(a) has the same meaning as in the Care Standards Act 2000 in respect of a care home in England, and

(b) means a place in Wales at which a care home service within the meaning of Part 1 of the Regulation and Inspection of Social Care (Wales) Act 2016 (anaw 2) is provided;

"clinical commissioning group" ("*grwp comisiynu clinigol*") means a body established under section 14D of the National Health Service Act 2006;

"education functions" ("*swyddogaethau addysg*") has the meaning given by section 597(1) of the Education Act 1996;

"independent hospital" ("*ysbyty annibynnol*")—

(a) in relation to Wales, has the meaning given by section 2 of the Care Standards Act 2000, and

(b) in relation to England, means a hospital as defined by section 275 of the National Health Service Act 2006 that is not a health service hospital as defined by that section;

"local authority in England" ("*awdurdod lleol yn Lloegr*") means—

(a) a county council in England,

(b) a district council for an area in England for which there is no county council,

(c) a London borough council, or

(d) the Common Council of the City of London;

"Local Health Board" ("*Bwrdd Iechyd Lleol*") means a Local Health Board established under section 11 of the National Health Service (Wales) Act 2006.

III WAL [60]

71 Meaning of vulnerable in section 70

(1) A person is vulnerable as a result of a reason mentioned in paragraph (c) or (j) of section 70(1) if, having regard to all the circumstances of the person's case—

(a) the person would be less able to fend for himself or herself (as a result of that reason) if the person were to become street homeless than would an ordinary homeless person who becomes street homeless, and

(b) this would lead to the person suffering more harm than would be suffered by the ordinary homeless person;

this subsection applies regardless of whether or not the person whose case is being considered is, or is likely to become, street homeless.

(2) In subsection (1), "street homeless" ("digartref ac ar y stryd"), in relation to a person, means that the person has no accommodation available for the person's occupation in the United Kingdom or elsewhere, which the person—

(a) is entitled to occupy by virtue of an interest in it or by virtue of an order of a court,

(b) has an express or implied licence to occupy, or

(c) occupies as a residence by virtue of any enactment or rule of law giving the person the right to remain in occupation or restricting the right of another person to recover possession;

and sections 55 and 56 do not apply to this definition.

III WAL [61]

72 Power to amend or repeal provisions about priority need for accommodation

(1) The Welsh Ministers may by order—

(a) make provision for and in connection with removing any condition that a local housing authority must have reason to believe or be satisfied that an applicant is in priority need for accommodation before any power or duty to secure accommodation under this Chapter applies;

(b) amend or omit the descriptions of persons as having a priority need for accommodation for the purposes of this Chapter;

(c) specify further descriptions of persons as having a priority need for accommodation for the purposes of this Chapter.

(2) An order under subsection (1) may amend or repeal any provision of this Part.

(3) Before making an order under this section the Welsh Ministers must consult such associations representing councils of counties and county boroughs in Wales, and such other persons, as they consider appropriate.

III WAL [62]

73 Duty to help to secure accommodation for homeless applicants

(1) A local housing authority must help to secure that suitable accommodation is available for occupation by an applicant, if the authority is satisfied that the applicant is—

(a) homeless, and

(b) eligible for help.

(2) But the duty in subsection (1) does not apply if the authority refers the application to another local housing authority (see section 80).

III WAL [63]

74 Circumstances in which the duty in section 73 ends

(1) The duty to an applicant under section 73 comes to an end in any of the circumstances described in subsections (2), (3), (4), or (5), if the applicant has been notified in accordance with section 84.

(2) The circumstances are the end of a period of 56 days.

(3) The circumstances are that before the end of a period of 56 days the local housing authority is satisfied that reasonable steps have been taken to help to secure that suitable accommodation is available for occupation by the applicant.

(4) The circumstances are that the local housing authority is satisfied (whether as a result of the steps it has taken or not) that—

(a) the applicant has suitable accommodation available for occupation, and

(b) the accommodation is likely to be available for occupation by the applicant for a period of at least 6 months.

(5) The circumstances are that—

(a) the applicant, having been notified of the possible consequence of refusal or acceptance of the offer, refuses an offer of accommodation from any person which the authority is satisfied is suitable for the applicant, and

(b) the authority is satisfied that the accommodation offered is likely to be available for occupation by the applicant for a period of at least 6 months.

(6) The period of 56 days mentioned in subsections (2) and (3) begins on the day the applicant is notified under section 63 and for this purpose the applicant is to be treated as notified on the day the notice is sent or first made available for collection.

(7) The period of 6 months mentioned in subsection (4)(b) and (5)(b) begins on the day the notice under section 84 is sent or first made available for collection.

(8) See section 79 for further circumstances in which the duty in section 73 comes to an end.

III WAL [64]

75 Duty to secure accommodation for applicants in priority need when the duty in section 73 ends

(1) When the duty in section 73 (duty to help to secure accommodation for homeless applicants) comes to an end in respect of an applicant in the circumstances mentioned in subsection (2) o r (3) of section 74, the local housing authority must secure that suitable accommodation is available for occupation by the applicant if subsection (2) or (3) (of this section) applies.

(2) This subsection applies where the local housing authority—

(a) is satisfied that the applicant—

(i) does not have suitable accommodation available for occupation, or

(ii) has suitable accommodation, but it is not likely that the accommodation will be available for occupation by the applicant for a period of at least 6 months starting on the day the applicant is notified in accordance with section 84 that section 73 does not apply,

(b) is satisfied that the applicant is eligible for help,

(c) is satisfied that the applicant has a priority need for accommodation, and

(d) if the authority is having regard to whether or not the applicant is homeless intentionally (see section 77), is not satisfied that the applicant became homeless intentionally in the circumstances which gave rise to the application;

(3) This subsection applies where the local housing authority is having regard to whether or not the applicant is homeless intentionally and is satisfied that—

(a) the applicant became homeless intentionally in the circumstances which gave rise to the application,

(b) the applicant—

(i) does not have suitable accommodation available for occupation, or

(ii) has suitable accommodation, but it is not likely that the accommodation will be available for occupation by the applicant for a period of at least 6 months starting on the day on which the applicant is notified in accordance with section 84 that section 73 does not apply,

(c) the applicant is eligible for help,

(d) the applicant has a priority need for accommodation,

(e) the applicant is—

(i) a pregnant woman or a person with whom she resides or might reasonably be expected to reside,

(ii) a person with whom a dependent child resides or might reasonably be expected to reside,

(iii) a person who had not attained the age of 21 when the application for help was made or a person with whom such a person resides or might reasonably be expected to reside, or

(iv) a person who had attained the age of 21, but not the age of 25, when the application for help was made and who was looked after, accommodated or fostered at any time while under the age of 18, or a person with whom such a person resides or might reasonably be expected to reside, and

(f) the authority has not previously secured an offer of accommodation to the applicant under this section following a previous application for help under this Chapter, where that offer was made—

WALES

(i) at any time within the period of 5 years before the day on which the applicant was notified under section 63 that a duty was owed to him or her under this section, and

(ii) on the basis that the applicant fell within this subsection.

(4) For the purpose of subsections (2)(a)(ii) and (3)(b)(ii), the applicant is to be treated as notified on the day the notice is sent or first made available for collection.

III WAL [65]

76 Circumstances in which the duty in section 75 ends

(1) The duty to an applicant under section 75(1) comes to an end in any of the circumstances described in subsections (2), (3), (6) or (7), if the applicant has been notified in accordance with section 84.

(2) The circumstances are that the applicant accepts—

(a) an offer of suitable accommodation under Part 6 of the Housing Act 1996 (allocation of housing), or

(b) an offer of suitable accommodation under an assured tenancy (including an assured shorthold tenancy).

(3) The circumstances are that the applicant, having been given notice in writing of the possible consequence of refusal or acceptance of the offer, refuses—

(a) an offer of suitable interim accommodation under section 75,

(b) a private rented sector offer, or

(c) an offer of accommodation under Part 6 of the Housing Act 1996,

which the authority is satisfied is suitable for the applicant.

(4) For the purposes of this section an offer is a private rented sector offer if—

(a) it is an offer of an assured shorthold tenancy made by a private landlord to the applicant in relation to any accommodation which is available for the applicant's occupation,

(b) it is made, with the approval of the authority, in pursuance of arrangements made by the authority with the landlord with a view to bringing the authority's duty under section 75 to an end, and

(c) the tenancy being offered is a fixed term tenancy for a period of at least 6 months.

(5) In a restricted case, the local housing authority must, so far as reasonably practicable, bring its duty to an end by securing a private rented sector offer; for this purpose, a "restricted case" means a case where the local housing authority would not be satisfied as mentioned in section 75(1) without having regard to a restricted person (see section 63(5)).

(6) The circumstances are that the local housing authority is satisfied that the applicant has become homeless intentionally from suitable interim accommodation made available for the applicant's occupation—

(a) under section 68 and which continues to be made available under section 75, or

(b) under section 75.

(7) The circumstances are that the local housing authority is satisfied that the applicant has voluntarily ceased to occupy as his or her only or principal home, suitable interim accommodation made available for the applicant's occupation—

(a) under section 68 and which continues to be made available under section 75, or

(b) under section 75.

(8) See section 79 for further circumstances in which the duty in section 75(1) comes to an end.

(9) In this section "fixed term tenancy" has the meaning given by Part 1 of the Housing Act 1988.

III WAL [66]

77 Meaning of intentionally homeless

(1) A person is intentionally homeless for the purpose of this Chapter if subsection (2) or (4) apply.

(2) This subsection applies if the person deliberately does or fails to do anything in consequence of which the person ceases to occupy accommodation which is available for the person's occupation and which it would have been reasonable for the person to continue to occupy.

(3) For the purposes of subsection (2) an act or omission in good faith on the part of a person who was unaware of any relevant fact may not be treated as deliberate.

(4) This subsection applies if—

(a) the person enters into an arrangement under which the person is required to cease to occupy accommodation which it would have been reasonable for the person to continue to occupy, and

(b) the purpose of the arrangement is to enable the person to become entitled to help under this Chapter,

and there is no other good reason why the person is homeless.

III WAL [67]

78 Deciding to have regard to intentionality

(1) The Welsh Ministers must, by regulations, specify a category or categories of applicant for the purpose of this section.

(2) A local housing authority may not have regard to whether or not an applicant has become homeless intentionally for the purposes of sections 68 and 75 unless—

(a) the applicant falls within a category specified under subsection (1) in respect of which the authority has decided to have regard to whether or not applicants in that category have become homeless intentionally, and

(b) the authority has published a notice of its decision under paragraph (a) which specifies the category.

(3) Subsection (4) applies where a local housing authority has published a notice under subsection (2) unless the authority has—

(a) decided to stop having regard to whether or not applicants falling into the category specified in the notice have become homeless intentionally, and

(b) published a notice of its decision specifying the category.

(4) For the purposes of section 68 and 75, a local housing authority must have regard to whether or not an applicant has become homeless intentionally if the applicant falls within a category specified in the notice published by the authority under subsection (2).

III WAL [67.1]

Specified Categories of Intentionality Certain categories and specified by the Homelessness (Intentionality) (Specified Categories) (Wales) Regulations 2015, SI 2015/1265.

III WAL [68]

79 Further circumstances in which the duties to help applicants end

(1) The duties in sections 66, 68, 73 and 75 come to an end in the circumstances described in subsection (2), (3), (4) or (5), if the applicant is notified in accordance with section 84.

(2) The circumstances are that the local housing authority is no longer satisfied that the applicant is eligible for help.

(3) The circumstances are that the local housing authority is satisfied that a mistake of fact led to the applicant being notified under section 63 that the duty was owed to the applicant.

(4) The circumstances are that the local authority is satisfied that the applicant has withdrawn his or her application.

(5) The circumstances are that the local housing authority is satisfied that the applicant is unreasonably failing to co-operate with the authority in connection with the exercise of its functions under this Chapter as they apply to the applicant.

Referral to Another Local Housing Authority

III WAL [69]

80 Referral of case to another local housing authority

(1) Subsection (2) applies where—

- (a) a local housing authority considers that the conditions for referral to another local housing authority (whether in Wales or England) are met (see subsection (3)), and
- (b) the local housing authority would, if the case is not referred, be subject to the duty in section 73 in respect of an applicant who is in priority need of accommodation and unintentionally homeless (duty to help to secure accommodation for homeless applicants).

(2) The local housing authority may notify the other authority of its opinion that the conditions for referral are met in respect of the applicant.

(3) The conditions for referral of the case to another local housing authority (whether in Wales or England) are met if—

- (a) neither the applicant nor any person who might reasonably be expected to reside with the applicant has a local connection with the area of the authority to which the application was made,
- (b) the applicant or a person who might reasonably be expected to reside with the applicant has a local connection with the area of that other authority, and
- (c) neither the applicant nor any person who might reasonably be expected to reside with the applicant will run the risk of domestic abuse in that other area.

(4) But the conditions for referral mentioned in subsection (3) are not met if—

- (a) the applicant or any person who might reasonably be expected to reside with the applicant has suffered abuse (other than domestic abuse) in the area of the other authority, and
- (b) it is probable that the return to that area of the victim will lead to further abuse of a similar kind against him or her.

(5) The question of whether the conditions for referral of a case are satisfied is to be decided—

- (a) by agreement between the notifying authority and the notified authority, or
- (b) in default of agreement, in accordance with such arrangements—
  - (i) as the Welsh Ministers may direct by order, where both authorities are in Wales, or
  - (ii) as the Welsh Ministers and the Secretary of State may jointly direct by order, where the notifying authority is in Wales and the notified authority is in England.

(6) An order under subsection (5) may direct that the arrangements are to be—

- (a) those agreed by any relevant authorities or associations of relevant authorities, or

(b) in default of such agreement, such arrangements as appear to the Welsh Ministers or, in the case of an order under subsection (5)(b)(ii), to the Welsh Ministers and the Secretary of State to be suitable, after consultation with such associations representing relevant authorities, and such other persons, as they think appropriate.

(7) In subsection (6), "relevant authority" means a local housing authority or a social services authority; and it includes, in so far as that subsection applies to arrangements under subsection (5)(b)(ii), such authorities in Wales and England.

(8) The Welsh Ministers may by order specify other circumstances in which the conditions are or are not met for referral of the case to another local housing authority.

III WAL [70]

81 Local connection

(1) This section applies for the purposes of this Chapter.

(2) A person has a local connection with the area of a local housing authority in Wales or England if the person has a connection with it—

(a) because the person is, or in the past was, normally resident there, and that residence is or was of the person's own choice,

(b) because the person is employed there,

(c) because of family associations, or

(d) because of special circumstances.

(3) Residence in an area is not of a person's own choice if the person, or a person who might reasonably be expected to reside with that person, becomes resident there because the person is detained under the authority of an enactment.

(4) The Welsh Ministers may by order specify circumstances in which—

(a) a person is not to be treated as employed in an area, or

(b) residence in an area is not to be treated as of a person's own choice.

(5) A person has a local connection with the area of a local housing authority in Wales or England if the person was (at any time) provided with accommodation in that area under section 95 of the Immigration and Asylum Act 1999 (support for asylum seekers).

(6) But subsection (5) does not apply—

(a) to the provision of accommodation for a person in an area of a local housing authority if the person was subsequently provided with accommodation in the area of another local housing authority under section 95 of that Act, or

(b) to the provision of accommodation in an accommodation centre by virtue of section 22 of the Nationality, Immigration and Asylum Act 2002 (use of accommodation centres for section 95 support).

III WAL [71]

82 Duties to applicant whose case is considered for referral or referred

(1) Where a local housing authority notifies an applicant in accordance with section 84 that it intends to notify or has notified another local housing authority in Wales or England of its opinion that the conditions are met for the referral of the applicant's case to that other authority—

(a) it ceases to be subject to any duty under section 68 (interim duty to secure accommodation for homeless applicants in priority need), andd

(b) it is not subject to any duty under section 73 (duty to help to secure accommodation for homeless applicants);

but it must secure that suitable accommodation is available for occupation by the applicant until the applicant is notified of the decision whether the conditions for referral of the case are met.

(2) When it has been decided whether the conditions for referral are met, the notifying authority must notify the applicant in accordance with section 84.

(3) If it is decided that the conditions for referral are not met, the notifying authority is subject to the duty under section 73 (duty to help to secure accommodation for homeless applicants).

(4) If it is decided that those conditions are met and the notified authority is an authority in Wales, the notified authority is subject to the duty under section 73 (duty to help to secure accommodation for homeless applicants); for provision about cases where it is decided that those conditions are met and the notified authority is an authority in England, see section 201A of the Housing Act 1996 (cases referred from a local housing authority in Wales).

(5) The duty under subsection (1) ceases as provided in that subsection even if the applicant requests a review of the authority's decision (see section 85).

(6) The authority may secure that suitable accommodation is available for the applicant's occupation pending the decision on a review.

(7) If notice required to be given to an applicant under this section is not received by the applicant, it is to be treated as having been given if it is made available at the authority's office for a reasonable period for collection by the applicant or on the applicant's behalf.

III WAL [72]

83 Cases referred from a local housing authority in England

(1) This section applies where an application has been referred by a local housing authority in England to a local housing authority in Wales under section 198(1) of the Housing Act 1996 (referral of case to another local housing authority).

(2) If it is decided that the conditions in that section for referral of the case are met the notified authority is subject to the following duties in respect of the person whose case is referred—

- (a) section 68 (interim duty to secure accommodation for homeless applicants in priority need);
- (b) section 73 (duty to help to secure accommodation for homeless applicants);

for provision about cases where it is decided that the conditions for referral are not met, see section 200 of the Housing Act 1996 (duties to applicant whose case is considered for referral or referred).

(3) Accordingly, references in this Chapter to an applicant include a reference to a person to whom the duties mentioned in subsection (2) are owed by virtue of this section.

Notice

III WAL [73]

84 Notice that duties have ended

(1) Where a local housing authority concludes that its duty to an applicant under section 66, 68, 73 or 75 has come to an end (including where the authority has referred the applicant's case to another authority or decided that the conditions for referral are met), it must notify the applicant—

- (a) that it no longer regards itself as being subject to the relevant duty,
- (b) of the reasons why it considers that the duty has come to an end,
- (c) of the right to request a review, and
- (d) of the time within which such a request must be made.

(2) Where a notice under subsection (1) relates to the duty in section 73 coming to an end in the circumstances described in section 74(2) or (3), it must include notice of the steps taken by the local housing authority to help to secure that suitable accommodation would be available for occupation by the applicant.

(3) Notice under this section must be in writing.

(4) Where a notice is not received by an applicant, the applicant may be treated as having been notified under this section if the notice is made available at the authority's office for a reasonable period for collection by the applicant or on the applicant's behalf.

Right to Review and Appeal

III WAL [74]

85 Right to request review

(1) An applicant has the right to request a review of the following decisions—

- (a) a decision of a local housing authority as to the applicant's eligibility for help;
- (b) a decision of a local housing authority that a duty is not owed to the applicant under section 66, 68, 73, or 75 (duties to applicants who are homeless or threatened with homelessness);
- (c) a decision of a local housing authority that a duty owed to the applicant under section 66, 68, 73, or 75 has come to an end (including where the authority has referred the applicant's case to another authority or decided that the conditions for referral are met).

(2) Where the duty owed to an applicant under section 73 has come to an end in the circumstances described in section 74(2) or (3), an applicant has the right to request a review of whether or not reasonable steps were taken during the period in which the duty under section 73 was owed to help to secure that suitable accommodation would be available for his or her occupation.

(3) An applicant who is offered accommodation in, or in connection with, the discharge of any duty under this Chapter may request a review of the suitability of the accommodation offered to the applicant (whether or not he or she has accepted the offer).

(4) There is no right to request a review of the decision reached on an earlier review.

(5) A request for review must be made before the end of the period of 21 days (or such longer period as the authority may in writing allow) beginning with the day on which the applicant is notified of the authority's decision.

(6) On a request being made to them, the authority or authorities concerned must review their decision.

III WAL [75]

86 Procedure on review

(1) The Welsh Ministers may make provision by regulations as to the procedure to be followed in connection with a review under section 85.

(2) Regulations under subsection (1) may, for example,—

- (a) require the decision on review to be made by a person of appropriate seniority who was not involved in the original decision, and
- (b) provide for the circumstances in which the applicant is entitled to an oral hearing, and whether and by whom the applicant may be represented at such a hearing, and
- (c) provide for the period within which the review must be carried out and notice given of the decision.

(3) The authority, or as the case may be either of the authorities, concerned must notify the applicant of the decision on the review.

(4) The authority must also notify the applicant of the reasons for the decision, if the decision is—

- (a) to confirm the original decision on any issue against the interests of the applicant, or
- (b) to confirm that reasonable steps were taken.

(5) In any case they must inform the applicant of his or her right to appeal to the county court on a point of law, and of the period within which such an appeal must be made (see section 88).

(6) Notice of the decision is not be treated as given unless and until subsection (5), and where applicable subsection (4), is complied with.

(7) Notice required to be given to a person under this section must be given in writing and, if not received by that person, is to be treated as having been given if it is made available at the authority's office for a reasonable period for collection by the person or on his or her behalf.

III WAL [75.1]

Procedure on review The procedure to be followed on review is laid down in regulations made under this section: Homelessness (Review Procedure) (Wales) Regulations 2015, SI 2015/1266.

III WAL [76]

87 Effect of a decision on review or appeal that reasonable steps were not taken

(1) Subsection (2) applies where it is decided on review under section 85(2) or on an appeal of a decision under that section that reasonable steps were not taken.

(2) The duty in section 73 applies to the applicant again, with the modification that the 56 day period mentioned in subsection (2) of section 74 is to be interpreted as starting on the day the authority notifies the applicant of its decision on review under section 85(2) or, on an appeal, on such date as the court may order.

III WAL [77]

88 Right of appeal to county court on point of law

(1) An applicant who has requested a review under section 85 may appeal to the county court on any point of law arising from the decision or, as the case may be, the original decision or a question as to whether reasonable steps were taken if the applicant—

- (a) is dissatisfied with the decision on the review, or
- (b) is not notified of the decision on the review within the time prescribed under section 86.

(2) An appeal must be brought within 21 days of the applicant being notified of the decision or, as the case may be, of the date on which the applicant should have been notified of a decision on review.

(3) The court may give permission for an appeal to be brought after the end of the period allowed by subsection (2), but only if it is satisfied—

- (a) where permission is sought before the end of that period, that there is a good reason for the applicant to be unable to bring the appeal in time, or
- (b) where permission is sought after that time, that there is a good reason for the applicant's failure to bring the appeal in time and for any delay in applying for permission.

(4) On appeal the court may make such order confirming, quashing or varying the decision as it thinks fit.

(5) Where the authority was under a duty under section 68, 75 or 82 to secure that suitable accommodation is available for the applicant's occupation, it may secure that suitable accommodation is so available—

(a) during the period for appealing under this section against the authority's decision, and

(b) if an appeal is brought, until the appeal (and any further appeal) is finally determined.

III WAL [77.1]

Commencment The right of appeal under s 88 of the Act is a review of the reviewing officer's decision and is not a re-hearing. It is akin to the right of appeal under s 204 of the Housing Act 1996 and thus the observations made by the Court of Appeal in *Cramp v Hastings London Borough Council* [2005] EWCA Civ 1005 as to the need for judges to be astute as to the need to ensure that new evidence over and above the material contained in the housing file and the reviewing officer's decision should be strictly confined may well be relevant.

III WAL [77.2]

Appeals to the county court A right of appeal may be exercised within 21 days, on a point of law, in respect of any decision on review. The procedure for appeal is set out in CPR 52 and CPR PD 52D and Form N161 should be used. A right of appeal also lies in respect of a decision not to provide accommodation until the appeal is heard.

III WAL [78]

89 Appeals against refusal to accommodate pending appeal

(1) This section applies where an applicant has the right to appeal to the county court under section 88.

(2) An applicant may appeal to the county court against a decision of the authority—

(a) not to exercise their power under section 88(5) ("the section 88(5) power") in the applicant's case,

(b) to exercise that power for a limited period ending before the final determination by the county court of the applicant's appeal under section 88(1) ("the main appeal"), or

(c) to cease exercising that power before the final determination.

(3) An appeal under this section may not be brought after the final determination by the county court of the main appeal.

(4) On an appeal under this section the court—

(a) may order the authority to secure that suitable accommodation is available for the applicant's occupation until the determination of the appeal (or such earlier time as the court may specify), and

(b) must confirm or quash the decision appealed against.

(5) In considering whether to confirm or quash the decision the court must apply the principles applied by the High Court on an application for judicial review.

(6) If the court quashes the decision it may order the authority to exercise the section 88(5) power in the applicant's case for such period as may be specified in the order.

(7) An order under subsection (6)—

(a) may only be made if the court is satisfied that failure to exercise the section 88(5) power in accordance with the order would substantially prejudice the applicant's ability to pursue the main appeal;

(b) may not specify any period ending after the final determination by the county court of the main appeal.

Supplementary Provisions

III WAL [79]

90 Charges

A local housing authority may require a person in relation to whom it is discharging its functions under this Chapter—

(a) to pay reasonable charges determined by the authority in respect of accommodation which it secures for the person's occupation (either by making it available itself or otherwise), or

(b) to pay a reasonable amount determined by the authority in respect of sums payable by it for accommodation made available by another person.

III WAL [80]

91 Out-of-area placement

(1) A local housing authority must in discharging its functions under this Chapter secure or help to secure that suitable accommodation is available for the occupation of the applicant in its area, so far as is reasonably practicable.

(2) If the authority secures that accommodation is available for the occupation of the applicant outside its area in Wales or England, it must give notice to the local housing authority (whether in Wales or England) in whose area the accommodation is situated.

(3) The notice must state—

(a) the name of the applicant,

(b) the number and description of other persons who normally reside with the applicant as a member of his or her family or might reasonably be expected to reside with the applicant,

(c) the address of the accommodation,

(d) the date on which the accommodation was made available to the applicant, and

(e) which function under this Chapter the authority was discharging in securing that the accommodation is available for the applicant's occupation.

(4) The notice must be in writing, and must be given before the end of the period of 14 days beginning with the day on which the accommodation was made available to the applicant.

III WAL [81]

92 Interim accommodation: arrangements with private landlord

(1) This section applies where in carrying out any of its functions under section 68, 82 or 88(5) (interim accommodation) a local housing authority makes arrangements with a private landlord to provide accommodation.

(2) A tenancy granted to the applicant under the arrangements cannot be an assured tenancy before the end of the period of twelve months beginning with—

(a) the date on which the applicant was notified of the authority's decision under section 63(1) or 80(5), or

(b) if there is a review of that decision under section 85 or an appeal to the court under section 88, the date on which the applicant is notified of the decision on review or the appeal is finally determined,

unless, before or during that period, the tenant is notified by the landlord (or in the case of joint landlords, at least one of them) that the tenancy is to be regarded as an assured shorthold tenancy or an assured tenancy other than an assured shorthold tenancy.

III WAL [82]

93 Protection of property

(1) Where a local housing authority has become subject to a duty in respect of an applicant as described in subsection (2), it must take reasonable steps to prevent the loss of the personal property of the applicant or prevent or mitigate damage to it if the authority has reason to believe that—

(a) there is danger of loss of, or damage to, the property by reason of the applicant's inability to protect it or deal with it, and

(b) no other suitable arrangements have been or are being made.

(2) The duties in respect of an applicant are—

section 66 (duty to help to prevent an applicant from becoming homeless) in the case of an applicant in priority need;

section 68 (interim duty to secure accommodation for homeless applicants in priority need);

section 75 (duty to secure accommodation for applicants in priority need when the duty in section 73 ends);

section 82 (duties to applicant whose case is considered for referral or referred) in the case of an applicant in priority need.

(3) Where a local housing authority has become subject to the duty in subsection (1), it continues to be subject to that duty even if the duty in respect of the applicant as described in subsection (2) comes to an end.

(4) The duty of a local housing authority under subsection (1) is subject to any conditions it considers appropriate in the particular case, which may include conditions as to—

(a) the making and recovery by the authority of reasonable charges for the action taken, or

(b) the disposal by the authority, in such circumstances as may be specified, of property in relation to which it has taken action.

(5) A local housing authority may take any steps it considers reasonable for the purpose of protecting the personal property of an applicant who is eligible for help or prevent or mitigate damage to it if the authority has reason to believe that—

(a) there is danger of loss of, or damage to, the property by reason of the applicant's inability to protect it or deal with it, and

(b) no other suitable arrangements have been or are being made.

(6) References in this section to personal property of the applicant include personal property of any person who might reasonably be expected to reside with the applicant.

III WAL [82.1]

Protection of property Section 93 onwards set out the circumstances in which the local housing authority has to take reasonable steps to prevent loss of or damage to the personal property of the applicant. There is no equivalent provision in the Housing Act 1996 for the protection in England of the applicant's personal property.

III WAL [83]

94 Protection of property: supplementary provisions

(1) The authority may for the purposes of section 93—

(a) enter, at all reasonable times, any premises which are the usual place of residence of the applicant or which were the applicant's last usual place of residence, and

(b) deal with any personal property of the applicant in any way which is reasonably necessary, in particular by storing it or arranging for its storage.

(2) Where a local authority is proposing to exercise the power in subsection (1)(a), the officer it authorises to do so must, upon request, produce valid documentation setting out the authorisation to do so.

(3) A person who, without reasonable excuse, obstructs the exercise of the power under subsection (1)(a) commits an offence and is liable on summary conviction to a fine not exceeding level 4 on the standard scale.

(4) Where the applicant asks the authority to move his or her property to a particular location nominated by the applicant, the authority—

- (a) may, if it appears to it that the request is reasonable, discharge its responsibilities under section 93 by doing as the applicant asks, and
- (b) having done so, have no further duty or power to take action under that section in relation to that property.

(5) If such a request is made, the authority must before complying with it inform the applicant of the consequence of it doing so.

(6) If no such request is made (or, if made, is not acted upon) the authority cease to have any duty or power to take action under section 93 when, in its opinion, there is no longer any reason to believe that there is a danger of loss of or damage to a person's personal property by reason of his or her inability to protect it or deal with it.

(7) But property stored by virtue of the authority having taken such action may be kept in store and any conditions upon which it was taken into store continue to have effect, with any necessary modifications.

(8) Where the authority—

- (a) ceases to be subject to a duty to take action under section 93 in respect of an applicant's property, or
- (b) ceases to have power to take such action, having previously taken such action,

it must notify the applicant of that fact and of the reason for it.

(9) The notification must be given to the applicant—

- (a) by delivering it to the applicant, or
- (b) leaving it at, or sending it to, the applicant's last known address.

(10) References in this section to personal property of the applicant include personal property of any person who might reasonably be expected to reside with the applicant.

III WAL [84]

95 Co-operation

(1) A council of a county or county borough in Wales must make arrangements to promote co-operation between the officers of the authority who exercise its social services functions and those who exercise its functions as the local housing authority with a view to achieving the following objectives in its area—

- (a) the prevention of homelessness,
- (b) that suitable accommodation is or will be available for people who are or may become homeless,
- (c) that satisfactory support is available for people who are or may become homeless, and
- (d) the effective discharge of its functions under this Part.

(2) If a local housing authority requests the co-operation of a person mentioned in subsection (5) in the exercise of its functions under this Part, the person must comply with the request unless the person considers that doing so would—

- (a) be incompatible with the person's own duties, or
- (b) otherwise have an adverse effect on the exercise of the person's functions.

(3) If a local housing authority requests that a person mentioned in subsection (5) provides it with information it requires for the purpose of the exercise of any of its functions under this Part, the person must comply with the request unless the person considers that doing so would—

- (a) be incompatible with the person's own duties, or
- (b) otherwise have an adverse effect on the exercise of the person's functions.

(4) A person who decides not to comply with a request under subsection (2) or (3) must give the local housing authority who made the request written reasons for the decision.

(5) The persons (whether in Wales or England) are—

- (a) a local housing authority;
- (b) a social services authority;
- (c) a registered social landlord;
- (d) a new town corporation;
- (e) a private registered provider of social housing;
- (f) a housing action trust.

(6) The Welsh Ministers may amend subsection (5) by order to omit or add a person, or a description of a person.

(7) An order under subsection (6) may not add a Minister of the Crown.

(8) In this section—

"housing action trust" ("*ymddiriedolaeth gweithredu tai*") means a housing action trust established under Part 3 of the Housing Act 1988;

"new town corporation" ("*corfforaeth tref newydd*") has the meaning given in Part 1 of the Housing Act 1985;

"private registered provider of social housing" ("*darparwr tai cymdeithasol preifat cofrestredig*") has the meaning given by Part 2 of the Housing and Regeneration Act 2008;

"registered social landlord" ("*landlord cymdeithasol cofrestredig*") has the meaning given by Part 1 of the Housing Act 1996.

III WAL [85]

96 Co-operation in certain cases involving children

(1) This section applies where a local housing authority has reason to believe that an applicant with whom a person under the age of 18 normally resides, or might reasonably be expected to reside—

- (a) may be ineligible for help,
- (b) may be homeless and that a duty under section 68, 73 or 75 is not likely to apply to the applicant, or
- (c) may be threatened with homelessness and that a duty under section 66 is not likely to apply to the applicant.

(2) A local housing authority must make arrangements for ensuring that—

- (a) the applicant is invited to consent to the referral to the social services department of the essential facts of his or her case, and
- (b) if the applicant has given that consent, the social services department is made aware of those facts and of the subsequent decision of the authority in respect of his or her case.

(3) Nothing in subsection (2) affects any power apart from this section to disclose information relating to the applicant's case to the the social services department without the consent of the applicant.

(4) A council of a county or county borough must make arrangements for ensuring that, where it makes a decision as local housing authority that an applicant is ineligible for help, became homeless intentionally or became

threatened with homelessness intentionally, its housing department provides the social services department with such advice and assistance as the social services department may reasonably request.

(5) In this section, in relation to the council of a county or county borough—

"the housing department" ("*yr adran dai*") means those persons responsible for the exercise of its functions as local housing authority;

"the social services department" ("*yr adran gwasanaethau cymdeithasol*") means those persons responsible for the exercise of its social services functions under Part 3 of the Social Services and Well-Being (Wales) Act 2014.

General

III WAL [86]

97 False statements, withholding information and failure to disclose change of circumstances

(1) It is an offence for a person, with intent to induce a local housing authority to believe in connection with the exercise of its functions under this Chapter that the person or another person is entitled to accommodation or assistance in accordance with the provisions of this Chapter, or is entitled to accommodation or assistance of a particular description—

(a) knowingly or recklessly to make a statement which is false in a material particular, or

(b) knowingly to withhold information which the authority has reasonably required the person to give in connection with the exercise of those functions.

(2) If before an applicant receives notification of the local housing authority's decision on the application there is any change of facts material to the case, the applicant must notify the authority as soon as possible.

(3) The authority must explain to every applicant, in ordinary language, the duty imposed by subsection (2) and the effect of subsection (4).

(4) A person who fails to comply with subsection (2) after being given the explanation required by subsection (3) commits an offence.

(5) In proceedings against a person for an offence committed under subsection (4) it is a defence that the person had a reasonable excuse for failing to comply.

(6) A person guilty of an offence under this section is liable on summary conviction to a fine not exceeding level 4 on the standard scale.

III WAL [87]

98 Guidance

(1) In the exercise of its functions relating to homelessness, a council of a county or county borough must have regard to guidance given by the Welsh Ministers.

(2) Subsection (1) applies in relation to functions under this Part and any other enactment.

(3) The Welsh Ministers may—

(a) give guidance either generally or to specified descriptions of authorities;

(b) revise the guidance by giving further guidance under this Part;

(c) withdraw the guidance by giving further guidance under this Part or by notice.

(4) The Welsh Ministers must publish any guidance or notice under this Part.

III WAL [88]

99 Interpretation of this Chapter and index of defined terms

In this Chapter—

"abuse" ("*camdriniaeth*") has the meaning given by section 58;

"accommodation available for occupation" ("*llety sydd ar gael i'w feddiannu*") has the meaning given by section 56;

"applicant" ("*ceisydd*") has the meaning given by section 62(3) and section 83(3);

"associated" ("*cysylltiedig*"), in relation to a person, has the meaning given by section 58;

"assured tenancy" ("*tenantiaeth sicr*") and "assured shorthold tenancy" ("*tenantiaeth fyrddaliol sicr*") have the meaning given by Part 1 of the Housing Act 1988;

"domestic abuse" ("*camdriniaeth ddomestig*") has the meaning given by section 58;

"eligible for help" ("*yn gymwys i gael cymorth*") means not excluded from help under this Chapter by Schedule 2;

"enactment" ("*deddfiad*") means an enactment (whenever enacted or made) comprised in, or in an instrument made under—

(a) an Act of Parliament,

(b) a Measure or an Act of the National Assembly for Wales;

"help to secure" ("*cynorthwyo i sicrhau*"), in relation to securing that suitable accommodation is available, or does not cease to be available, for occupation, has the meaning given by section 65;

"help under this Chapter" ("*cynorth o dan y Bennod hon*") means the benefit of any function under sections 66, 68, 73, or 75;

"homeless" ("*digartref*") has the meaning given by section 55 and "homelessness" (digartrefedd) is to be interpreted accordingly;

"intentionally homeless" ("*digartref yn fwriadol*") has the meaning given by section 77;

"local connection" ("*cysylltiad lleol*") has the meaning given by section 81;

"local housing authority" ("*awdurdod tai lleol*") means—

(a) in relation to Wales, the council of a county or county borough, and

(b) in relation to England, a district council, a London borough council, the Common Council of the City of London or the Council of the Isles of Scilly,

but a reference to a "local housing authority" is to be interpreted as a reference to a local housing authority for an area in Wales only, unless this Chapter expressly provides otherwise;

"looked after, accommodated or fostered" ("*yn derbyn gofal, yn cael ei letya neu'n cael ei faethu*") has the meaning given by section 70(2);

"prescribed" ("*rhagnodedig*") means prescribed in regulations made by the Welsh Ministers;

"priority need for accommodation" ("*angen blaenoriaethol am lety*") has the meaning given by section 70;

"prison" ("*carchar*") has the same meaning as in the Prison Act 1952 (see section 53(1) of that Act);

"private landlord" ("*landlord preifat*") means a landlord who is not within section 80(1) of the Housing Act 1985 (the landlord condition for secure tenancies);

"reasonable to continue to occupy accommodation" ("*rhesymol parhau i feddiannu llety*") has the meaning given by section 57;

"regular armed forces of the Crown" ("*lluoedd arfog rheolaidd y Goron*") means the regular forces as defined by section 374 of the Armed Forces Act 2006;

"restricted person" ("*person cyfyngedig*") has the meaning given by section 63(5);

"social services authority" ("*awdurdod gwasanaethau cymdeithasol*") means—

(a) in relation to Wales, the council of a county or county borough council in the exercise of its social services functions, within the meaning of section 119 of the Social Services and Well-being (Wales) Act 2014, and

(b) in relation to England, a local authority for the purposes of the Local Authority Social Services Act 1970, as defined in section 1 of that Act,

but a reference to a "social services authority" is to be interpreted as a reference to a social services authority for an area in Wales only, unless this Chapter expressly provides otherwise;

"threatened with homelessness" ("*o dan fygythiad o ddigartrefedd*") has the meaning given by section 55(4);

"voluntary organisation" ("*corff gwirfoddol*") means a body (other than a public or local authority) whose activities are not carried on for profit.

"youth detention accommodation" ("*llety cadw ieuenctid*") means—

(a) a secure children's home;

(b) a secure training centre;

(c) a young offender institution;

(d) accommodation provided, equipped and maintained by the Welsh Ministers under section 82(5) of the Children Act 1989 for the purpose of restricting the liberty of children;

(e) accommodation, or accommodation of a description, for the time being specified by order under section 107(1)(e) of the Powers of Criminal Courts (Sentencing) Act 2000 (youth detention accommodation for the purposes of detention and training orders).

III WAL [89]

100 Consequential amendments

Part 1 of Schedule 3 makes consequential amendments relating to this Part.

PARTS 3 TO 9

No jurisdiction is conferred on the civil courts by Part 3 [Gypsies and Travellers], Part 4 [Standards for Social Housing], Part 5 [Housing Finance], Part 6 [Allowing Fully Mutual Housing Associations to Grant Tenancies, Part 7 [Council Tax for Certain Types of Dwelling], Part 8 [Amendment of the Leasehold Reform, Housing and Urban Development Act] and Part 9 [Miscellaneous And General]. They have therefore been omitted.

WELL-BEING OF FUTURE GENERATIONS (WALES) ACT 2015

2015 anaw 2

GENERAL NOTE ON THE WELL-BEING OF FUTURE GENERATIONS (WALES) ACT 2015

III WAL [89A]

This Act makes provision for requiring Welsh public bodies to do things in pursuit of the economic, social, environmental and cultural well-being of Wales in a way that accords with the sustainable development principle.

The sustainable development principle is defined in s 5 and involves ‘seeking to ensure that the needs of the present are met without compromising the ability of future generations to meet their own needs’.

Section 5(2) sets out certain ways of working which a public body must follow in order to act in accordance with the sustainable development principle.

Sustainable development is defined in s 2 as ‘the process of improving the economic, social and environmental and cultural well-being of Wales by taking action, in accordance with the sustainable development principle aimed at achieving the well-being goals’. The well-being goals are seven in number and are set out in s 4.

Under s 3 each public body must carry out sustainable development and must set and publish well-being objectives that are designed to maximise its contribution to achieving each of the well-being goals. Public bodies must take all reasonable steps (in the exercise of its functions) to meet its well-being objectives: s 3(2)(b).

Section 6 identifies the public bodies which are subject to the Act. This list may be amended by regulations passed by Welsh Ministers: s 52.

Section 17 establishes the post of Future Generations Commissioner for Wales and the powers and duties of the Commissioner are set out in Part 3 of the Act.

Section 29 establishes a public service board for each local authority area in Wales to consist of the local health authority, the Local Health Board, the local fire and rescue authority and the Natural Resources Body for Wales. The public service boards have a duty to improve the well-being of their area by contributing to the achievement of the well-being goals: s 36. To that end they must assess the social, economic, environmental and cultural well-being of their area: ss 37 and 38. The public service boards must prepare and publish a local well-being plan setting out their local objectives and outlining the steps they propose to take to meet them: s 39.

The Act plays a pervasive role in the exercise of the functions of public bodies in Wales and in the formulation of public policy. Regard to its provisions will often be required by when considering Welsh judicial review claims.

PART 1
INTRODUCTION

III WAL [90]

1 Overview

(1) This section is an overview of the main provisions of the Act.

(2) Part 2 of this Act—

(a) explains what is meant by "sustainable development" and requires public bodies to carry out sustainable development (sections 2 and 3);

(b) requires the bodies to set well-being objectives that are to contribute to the achievement of well-being goals and to take steps to meet those objectives (section 3)

(c) requires the bodies to do those things in accordance with the sustainable development principle (section 3);

(d) explains what the well-being goals are and what it means to do things in accordance with the sustainable development principle (sections 4 and 5);

(e) requires indicators that measure progress towards achieving the well-being goals (section 10), and reports on future trends in the well-being of Wales (section 11), to be published by the Welsh Ministers;

(f) requires the bodies to report annually on their progress towards meeting their well-being objectives (sections 12 and 13 and Schedule 1);

(g) requires the Auditor General for Wales to carry out examinations into the extent to which public bodies set objectives and take steps to meet them in accordance with the sustainable development principle (section 15).

(3) Part 3 of this Act—

(a) establishes the office of Future Generations Commissioner for Wales (section 17 and Schedule 2);

(b) provides for the Commissioner to promote the needs of future generations by monitoring and reporting on the extent to which the public bodies are setting and seeking to meet their well-being objectives in accordance with the sustainable development principle (section 18);

(c) provides for the Commissioner to carry out reviews of public bodies (section 20);

(d) establishes a panel of advisers to the Commissioner (sections 26 to 28).

(4) Part 4 of this Act—

(a) establishes a public services board for each local authority area in Wales and sets out who else a board may work with (Chapter 1);

(b) requires boards to improve the well-being of their area by contributing to the well-being goals, which they are to do by assessing well-being in their area, setting local objectives designed to maximise the board's contribution (within its area) to the achievement of the well-being goals and taking steps to meet those objectives (Chapter 2, section 36);

(c) requires boards to do those things in accordance with the sustainable development principle (Chapter 2, section 36);

(d) requires boards to publish local well-being plans setting out their local objectives and how they propose to take steps to meet them (Chapter 2, section 39);

(e) makes specific provision about how local well-being plans apply to community councils and how, in that way, a community council may contribute to the activity of the public services board in its area (Chapter 2, section 40);

(f) provides for boards to merge or otherwise collaborate (Chapter 3).

PART 2
IMPROVING WELL-BEING
SUSTAINABLE DEVELOPMENT AND WELL-BEING DUTY ON PUBLIC BODIES

III WAL [91]

2 Sustainable development

In this Act, "sustainable development" means the process of improving the economic, social, environmental and cultural well-being of Wales by taking action, in accordance with the sustainable development principle (see section 5), aimed at achieving the well-being goals (see section 4).

III WAL [92]

3 Well-being duty on public bodies

(1) Each public body must carry out sustainable development.

(2) The action a public body takes in carrying out sustainable development must include—

(a) setting and publishing objectives ("well-being objectives") that are designed to maximise its contribution to achieving each of the well-being goals, and

(b) taking all reasonable steps (in exercising its functions) to meet those objectives.

(3) A public body that exercises functions in relation to the whole of Wales may set objectives relating to Wales or any part of Wales.

(4) A public body that exercises functions in relation only to a part of Wales may set objectives relating to that part or any part of it.

III WAL [93]

4 The well-being goals

The well-being goals are listed and described in Table 1—

TABLE 1

Goal	Description of the goal
A prosperous Wales.	An innovative, productive and low carbon society which recognises the limits of the global environment and therefore uses resources efficiently and proportionately (including acting on climate change); and which develops a skilled and well-educated population in an economy which generates wealth and provides employment opportunities, allowing people to take advantage of the wealth generated through securing decent work.
A resilient Wales.	A nation which maintains and enhances a biodiverse natural environment with healthy functioning ecosystems that support social, economic and ecological resilience and the capacity to adapt to change (for example climate change).
A healthier Wales.	A society in which people's physical and mental well-being is maximised and in which choices and behaviours that benefit future health are understood.

A more equal Wales.	A society that enables people to fulfil their potential no matter what their background or circumstances (including their socio economic background and circumstances).
A Wales of cohesive communities.	Attractive, viable, safe and well-connected communities.
A Wales of vibrant culture and thriving Welsh language.	A society that promotes and protects culture, heritage and the Welsh language, and which encourages people to participate in the arts, and sports and recreation.
A globally responsible Wales.	A nation which, when doing anything to improve the economic, social, environmental and cultural well-being of Wales, takes account of whether doing such a thing may make a positive contribution to global well-being.

III WAL [94]

5 The sustainable development principle

(1) In this Act, any reference to a public body doing something "in accordance with the sustainable development principle" means that the body must act in a manner which seeks to ensure that the needs of the present are met without compromising the ability of future generations to meet their own needs.

(2) In order to act in that manner, a public body must take account of the following things—

- (a) the importance of balancing short term needs with the need to safeguard the ability to meet long term needs, especially where things done to meet short term needs may have detrimental long term effect;
- (b) the need to take an integrated approach, by considering how—
  - (i) the body's well-being objectives may impact upon each of the well-being goals;
  - (ii) the body's well-being objectives impact upon each other or upon other public bodies' objectives, in particular where steps taken by the body may contribute to meeting one objective but may be detrimental to meeting another;
- (c) the importance of involving other persons with an interest in achieving the well-being goals and of ensuring those persons reflect the diversity of the population of—
  - (i) Wales (where the body exercises functions in relation to the whole of Wales), or
  - (ii) the part of Wales in relation to which the body exercises functions;
- (d) how acting in collaboration with any other person (or how different parts of the body acting together) could assist the body to meet its well-being objectives, or assist another body to meet its objectives;
- (e) how deploying resources to prevent problems occurring or getting worse may contribute to meeting the body's well-being objectives, or another body's objectives.

III WAL [95]

6 Meaning of "public body"

(1) For the purposes of this Part and Part 3 of this Act, each of the following persons is a "public body"—

- (a) the Welsh Ministers;
- (b) a local authority;
- (c) a Local Health Board;
- (d) the following NHS Trusts—

(i) Public Health Wales;

(ii) Velindre;

(e) a National Park authority for a National Park in Wales;

(f) a Welsh fire and rescue authority;

(g) the Natural Resources Body for Wales;

(h) the Higher Education Funding Council for Wales;

(i) the Arts Council of Wales;

(j) the Sports Council for Wales;

(k) the National Library of Wales;

(l) the National Museum of Wales.

(2) Section 52 enables the Welsh Ministers to amend the meaning of a "public body".

(3) Chapter 1 of Part 4 provides for persons who are listed as public bodies in subsection (1) (as well as certain other persons who exercise functions of a public nature) to be either members, invited participants or other partners of the public services boards established under that Part.

Well-Being Objectives

III WAL [96]

7 Statements about well-being objectives

(1) When publishing the well-being objectives (including well-being objectives revised under section 8 or 9) a public body must also publish a statement—

(a) explaining why the body considers that meeting the objectives will contribute to the achievement of the well-being goals;

(b) explaining why the public body considers it has set well-being objectives in accordance with the sustainable development principle, including how the body proposes to involve other persons with an interest in achieving the well-being goals and ensure that those persons reflect the diversity of the population of—

(i) Wales (where the body exercises functions in relation to the whole of Wales), or

(ii) the part of Wales in relation to which the body exercises functions;

(c) setting out the steps the public body proposes to take to meet those objectives in accordance with the principle (including how it proposes to govern itself, how it will keep the steps under review and how it proposes to ensure that resources are allocated annually for the purpose of taking such steps);

(d) specifying the periods of time within which the body expects to meet the objectives;

(e) providing such other information as the body considers appropriate about taking the steps and meeting the objectives.

(2) The well-being objectives of a public body that is also a member of a public services board may be included in that board's local well-being plan (see Chapters 1 and 2 of Part 4).

III WAL [97]

8 Welsh Ministers' well-being objectives

(1) The Welsh Ministers' well-being objectives must be set and published—

(a) no later than 6 months after the date on which the first general election is held following the commencement of this section, and

(b) no later than 6 months after the date of each subsequent general election.

(2) The Welsh Ministers' well-being objectives must be set for the period—

(a) beginning with the day specified for that purpose in the statement published under section 7(1), and

(b) ending with the day of the next ordinary general election under section 3 of the Government of Wales Act 2006 (c 32).

(3) If the well-being goals are amended, the Welsh Ministers must review their well-being objectives.

(4) If, on a review under subsection (3), the Welsh Ministers determine that one or more of their well-being objectives are no longer appropriate, they must revise the objective or objectives concerned.

(5) The Welsh Ministers may at any other time review and revise their well-being objectives.

(6) Well-being objectives revised under subsection (4) or (5) must be set for the remainder of the period referred to in subsection (2).

(7) Where the Welsh Ministers revise their well-being objectives under subsection (4) or (5), they must publish them as soon as is reasonably practicable.

(8) In setting or revising their well-being objectives, the Welsh Ministers must take into account the Commissioner's report under section 23.

(9) In subsection (1), "general election" means—

(a) the poll held at an ordinary general election under section 3 of the Government of Wales Act 2006 (c 32), or

(b) the poll held at an extraordinary general election under section 5 of that Act.

III WAL [98]

9 Other public bodies' well-being objectives

(1) In this section references to a public body do not include the Welsh Ministers.

(2) A public body's well-being objectives must be set and published—

(a) no later than the beginning of the financial year following the commencement of this section, and

(b) at such subsequent times as the body considers appropriate.

(3) If the well-being goals are amended, a public body must review its well-being objectives.

(4) If, on a review under subsection (3), a public body determines that one or more of its well-being objectives are no longer appropriate, it must revise the objective or objectives concerned.

(5) A public body may at any other time review and revise its well-being objectives.

(6) Where a public body revises its well-being objectives under subsection (3) or (4), it must publish them as soon as is reasonably practicable.

(7) In setting or revising its well-being objectives, a public body must take into account the Commissioner's report under section 23.

Measuring Performance Towards Achieving the Goals

III WAL [99]

10 National indicators and annual well-being report

(1) The Welsh Ministers must—

(a) publish indicators ("national indicators") that must be applied for the purpose of measuring progress towards the achievement of the well-being goals, and

(b) lay a copy of the national indicators before the National Assembly.

(2) A national indicator—

(a) must be expressed as a value or characteristic that can be measured quantitatively or qualitatively against a particular outcome;

(b) may be measured over such period of time as the Welsh Ministers consider appropriate;

(c) may be measurable in relation to Wales or any part of Wales.

(3) The Welsh Ministers must set milestones in relation to the national indicators which the Welsh Ministers consider would assist in measuring whether progress is being made towards the achievement of the well-being goals.

(4) In setting a milestone the Welsh Ministers must specify—

(a) the criteria for determining whether the milestone has been achieved (by reference to the value or characteristic by which the indicator is measured), and

(b) the time by which the milestone is to be achieved.

(5) If the well-being goals are amended, the Welsh Ministers must review the national indicators and milestones.

(6) If, on a review under subsection (5), the Welsh Ministers determine that one or more of the national indicators or milestones are no longer appropriate, they must revise it or them.

(7) The Welsh Ministers may at any other time review and revise the national indicators and milestones.

(8) Where the Welsh Ministers revise the national indicators and milestones under subsection (6) or (7), they must as soon as reasonably practicable—

(a) publish the indicators and milestones as revised, and

(b) lay a copy of them before the National Assembly.

(9) Before publishing national indicators and milestones (including indicators and milestones revised under subsection (6) or (7)), the Welsh Ministers must consult—

(a) the Commissioner;

(b) the other public bodies;

(c) such other persons as they consider appropriate.

(10) The Welsh Ministers must, in respect of each financial year beginning after the date on which national indicators are published under subsection (1), publish a report (an "annual well-being report") on the progress made towards the achievement of the well-being goals by reference to the national indicators and milestones.

(11) An annual well-being report under subsection (10) must specify the periods of time to which the measurement of each indicator relates.

III WAL [100]

11 Future trends report

(1) The Welsh Ministers must, during the period of 12 months beginning with the date of a general election, publish a report (a "future trends report") that contains—

(a) predictions of likely future trends in the economic, social, environmental and cultural well-being of Wales, and

(b) any related analytical data and information that the Welsh Ministers consider appropriate.

(2) In preparing a future trends report the Welsh Ministers must—

(a) take account of any action taken by the United Nations in relation to the UN Sustainable Development Goals and assess the potential impact of that action on the economic, social, environmental and cultural well-being of Wales, and

(b) take account of the report containing an assessment of the risks for the United Kingdom of the current and predicted impact of climate change most recently sent to the Welsh Ministers under section 56(6) of the Climate Change Act 2008 (c 27).

(3) In subsection (2)(a), "UN Sustainable Development Goals" means [the goals set out in "Transforming our world: the 2030 Agenda for Sustainable Development", adopted by the General Assembly of the United Nations by resolution A/Res/70/1 of 25 September 2015].

(4) In subsection (1), the reference to the date of a general election is to the date on which an ordinary general election is held under section 3 of the Government of Wales Act 2006 (c 32) (or would be apart from section 5(5) of that Act).

III WAL [101]

12 Annual reports by the Welsh Ministers

(1) The Welsh Ministers must—

(a) publish, in respect of each financial year, a report of the progress they have made towards meeting their well-being objectives, and

(b) lay a copy of the report before the National Assembly.

(2) In preparing a report under this section, the Welsh Ministers must review their well-being objectives.

(3) If, on a review under subsection (2), the Welsh Ministers determine that one or more of their well-being objectives are no longer appropriate, they must revise the objective or objectives concerned and publish the revised objective or objectives as soon as practicable.

(4) Where the Welsh Ministers revise one or more of their objectives under subsection (3), the report must include an explanation of the revision and the reasons for making it.

(5) A report under this section must be published and laid before the National Assembly as soon as reasonably practicable following the end of the financial year to which the report relates.

III WAL [102]

13 Annual reports by other public bodies

(1) Schedule 1 makes provision requiring each public body other than the Welsh Ministers to publish annual reports of the progress it has made in meeting its well-being objectives.

(2) In preparing a report under Schedule 1, or under a provision amended by that Schedule, a public body must review its well-being objectives.

(3) If, on a review under subsection (2), a public body determines that one or more of its well-being objectives are no longer appropriate, it must revise the objective or objectives concerned and publish the revised objective or objectives as soon as practicable.

(4) Where a public body revises one or more of its objectives under subsection (3), the report must include an explanation of the revision and the reasons for making it.

Guidance

III WAL [103]

14 Guidance

(1) The Welsh Ministers must issue guidance to other public bodies about the exercise of functions under this Part.

(2) In exercising a function under this Part, a public body must take such guidance into account.

Role of the Auditor General for Wales

III WAL [104]

15 The sustainable development principle: Auditor General's examinations

(1) The Auditor General for Wales may carry out examinations of public bodies for the purposes of assessing the extent to which a body has acted in accordance with the sustainable development principle when—

(a) setting well-being objectives, and

(b) taking steps to meet those objectives.

(2) The Auditor General must carry out such an examination of each public body at least once during the period mentioned in subsection (6).

(3) Before the end of the period mentioned in subsection (6), the Auditor General must report on the results of the examinations carried out under subsection (1) during that period to the National Assembly.

(4) The Auditor General must lay any report prepared under subsection (3) before the National Assembly.

(5) In carrying out an examination under subsection (1), the Auditor General must—

(a) take into account any advice or assistance given to the public body, or any review of and recommendations made to the body, by the Future Generations Commissioner for Wales (see Part 3), and

(b) consult the Commissioner.

(6) The period referred to in subsections (2) and (3)—

(a) begins on the date falling one year before the date on which an ordinary general election is to be held under section 3 of the Government of Wales Act 2006, and

(b) ends on the date falling one day and one year before the date on which the next such election is to be held.

Promotion of Sustainable Development

III WAL [105]

16 Promotion of sustainable development

For section 79 of the Government of Wales Act 2006 (c 32) (sustainable development) substitute—

"79 Sustainable development

(1) The Welsh Ministers must, in the exercise of their functions, make appropriate arrangements to promote sustainable development.

(2) After each financial year the Welsh Ministers must publish a report containing a statement of the arrangements made in pursuance of subsection (1) that had effect during that financial year and must lay a copy of the report before the Assembly.

(3) The arrangements referred to in subsection (1) may be made by the Welsh Ministers exercising their functions under section (2) of the Well-being of Future Generations (Wales) Act 2015 (duty of Welsh public bodies to set objectives and take steps to meet them in accordance with the sustainable development principle).".

PART 3
THE FUTURE GENERATIONS COMMISSIONER FOR WALES

THE COMMISSIONER

III WAL [106]

17 Future Generations Commissioner for Wales

(1) There is to be a Future Generations Commissioner for Wales (referred to in this Act as the "Commissioner").

(2) The Commissioner is to be an individual appointed by the Welsh Ministers.

(3) Before making the appointment under subsection (2), the Welsh Ministers must consult with the National Assembly through its responsible committee.

(4) Schedule 2 makes further provision about the Commissioner.

III WAL [107]

18 Commissioner's general duty

The general duty of the Commissioner is—

(a) to promote the sustainable development principle, in particular to—

(i) act as a guardian of the ability of future generations to meet their needs, and

(ii) encourage public bodies to take greater account of the long-term impact of the things that they do, and

(b) for that purpose to monitor and assess the extent to which well-being objectives set by public bodies are being met.

RENTING HOMES (WALES) ACT 2016

WALES

PART 1
OVERVIEW OF ACT

GENERAL NOTES ON THE RENTING HOMES (WALES) ACT 2016

III WAL [108]

This lengthy Act re-writes the law of landlord and tenant for residential accommodation in Wales. It is based on the recommendations of the Law Commission's 2006 report on Renting Homes. The Act is not yet generally in force. The Renting Homes (Wales) Act 2016 (Commencement No 1) Order 2016, SI 2016/813 brought certain provisions into force on 5 August 2016 for the limited purposes of enabling regulations to be made and guidance to be issued. In the former category are ss 23, 29, 32(4), 45(3), 94, 112, 131, 203(5) and (6), 221, 236(3) and (4), paras 15(10) and 17 of Schedule 2, paras 10(2), 15(3) and (4) and 17 of Schedule 3, para 4(7) and (8) of Schedule 4, para 1(6) of Schedule 5, paragraph 5(7) and (8) of Schedule 7 and paras 15(2) and 33 of Schedule 12, In the latter category are ss 116(4) and 146(1).

When in force the Act will constitute a comprehensive reform of landlord and tenant law in Wales pertaining to dwellings. The aim of the Act is to bring greater clarity and fairness to the law.

Section 1 provides that there are two types of occupation contract – secure contracts and standard contracts. Standard contracts will either be periodic or fixed term standard contracts. Tenants and licensees will have occupation contracts. The occupier is described as the 'contract holder'. That term will largely replace tenant and licensee in the context of dwellings in Wales.

Section 2 describes two categories of landlord. Community landlords are local authorities and registered social landlords. Private landlords are those who are not community landlords. In general, community landlords will grant secure occupation contracts and private landlords will grant standard occupation contracts. Secure contracts are modelled on the current secure tenancy issued by local authorities and standard contracts are modelled on the current assured shorthold tenancy.

Each occupation contract will have to be in writing (s 31), and if the landlord fails to provide a written statement then he is liable to pay compensation to the contract-holder which in most circumstances will equate to the daily rent for the period of default up to a maximum of 2 months' rent: ss 35 and 87.

Each occupation contract comprises three elements:

- key matters pertaining to the dwelling, occupation date, rent and rental period: ss 26 and 27;
- fundamental terms which are the primary rights and responsibilities under the contract set out as fundamental provisions which can only be modified or excluded if in the opinion of the contract-holder their modification or exclusion improves his position: sections 18–22;
- supplementary terms which are further rights and responsibilities under the contract which will be set out in regulations to be made by Welsh Ministers: ss 23 and 24.

On 23 July 2018 Welsh Ministers issued a consultation on two documents: the Renting Homes (Supplementary Provisions) Wales Regulations and the Renting Homes (Supported Standard Contracts) (Supplementary Provisions) (Wales) Regulations. Each set of Regulations sets out supplementary provisions which will govern occupation contracts, unless the landlord and contract holder agree to modify or omit any of the terms pursuant to ss 21, 24 and 25.

Under s 29 of the Act Welsh Ministers must prescribe and publish model written contracts for different kinds of occupation contracts. These model contracts will include all fundamental and supplementary provisions applicable to that contract. Welsh Ministers have indicated that they will consult on the model contracts. Until these model contracts have been finalised and published it is unlikely that the main provisions of the Act will come into force. It is envisaged that the model contracts will form the basis of the written statement required under s 31. If the written statement excludes any fundamental or supplementary provision then that must be identified in the statement: s 32(3).

An occupation contract may also include a fourth element, additional terms, which are any express terms which do not fall within the previous three categories. To the extent, however, that the additional terms contradict any key matter, fundamental term or supplementary term then they are of no effect: s 28(2).

As well as simplifying housing law the Act makes a number of substantive changes.

Housing Associations will no longer be permitted to seek possession proceedings on the basis of 'Ground 8'. Though most social landlords do not pursue possession on 'Ground 8' as a matter of policy this change means that all community landlords will have the same legal rights as will all contract holders under secure contracts.

There will be six grounds of possession which will either be 'discretionary' or 'absolute'. Only three of the grounds apply to secure contracts. They are:

- breach of contract: s 157 (discretionary and applicable to secure and standard contracts);
- contract-holder's notice: ss 163, 165 and 170 (absolute and applicable to secure and standard contracts);
- landlord's notice under a periodic standard contract: s 178 (absolute and applicable to standard contracts only);
- landlord's notice under a fixed term standard contract: s 186 (absolute and applicable to standard contracts only);
- serious rent arrears under a standard contract: ss 181 and 187 (absolute and applicable to standard contracts only);
- estate management grounds: s 160 (discretionary and applicable to secure and standard contracts).

The absolute grounds under ss 178, 181, 186 and 187 which apply in respect of standard contracts are subject to section 217 which provides that if the court is satisfied that the possession proceedings are a retaliatory eviction in that the landlord is in breach of his repairing obligations or his obligation to keep the property in a state fit for human habitation and has sought to evict the contract holder to avoid those obligations the court may refuse to make a possession order. Accordingly, if the eviction is a retaliatory eviction then there are no absolute grounds and it is likely in most cases that landlords will struggle to persuade a court that a possession order is reasonable in such circumstances.

The Act provides that the landlord is obliged to ensure that the property is fit for human habitation on the occupation date of the contract and for the duration of the contract: s 91. Regulations must be passed under s 94 to prescribe in more detail what is meant by fitness for human habitation. Section 92 obliges the landlord to keep the structure and exterior of the dwelling in repair and to keep in repair and proper working order the service installations in the dwelling, thereby replicating s 11 of the Landlord and Tenant Act 1985.

Under the current law a joint tenancy can be brought to an end by the unilateral act of one of the tenants. The Act, by contrast, seeks to treat each joint contract-holder as an individual and one contract-holder cannot unilaterally bring the contract to an end for the other joint contract-holder: s 231. Likewise, the Act enables a joint contract-holder to be excluded from a contract on prohibited conduct grounds, or to be removed by the court, without affecting the other contract-holder: s 230. These provisions are intended to facilitate a more targeted approach to dealing with anti-social behaviour and domestic abuse.

Section 220 enables landlords to take possession of abandoned property without the need for a court order provided the procedural steps prescribed by the Act have been taken.

The Renting Homes Bill included a section allowing persons aged 16 and 17 to be contract-holders. That provision was not enacted, therefore the problems which were the subject matter of *Hammersmith and Fulham London Borough Council v Alexander-David* [2009] EWCA Civ 259 continue to apply in Wales as they do in England.

Introduction to Parts 1 and 2 and Key Concepts in this Act

III WAL [109]

1 Occupation contracts

(1) This Act (in Part 2) provides that—

(a) most individuals who rent their homes under a tenancy or licence, and their landlords, make a contract with each other known as an occupation contract (and in this Act such individuals are referred to as "contract-holders"; see section 7);

(b) there are two kinds of occupation contract, namely—

(i) secure contracts, and

(ii) standard contracts;

(c) there are two kinds of standard contract, namely—

(i) fixed term standard contracts, and

(ii) periodic standard contracts,

and the two kinds of standard contract differ in relation to their variation, transfer and termination.

(2) Each kind of occupation contract (and each kind of standard contract) gives different rights to, and imposes different obligations on, the contract-holder and landlord; a secure contract gives greater security of occupation to the contract-holder than a standard contract.

III WAL [110]

2 Kinds of landlord

(1) This Act (in Part 2) provides—

(a) for two kinds of landlord—

(i) community landlords (which are local authorities, registered social landlords and other kinds of authority), and

(ii) private landlords (which are any landlords who are not community landlords);

(b) that both kinds of landlord may make, or adopt, specific kinds of occupation contract (though this is subject to various exceptions).

(2) In general—

(a) occupation contracts made with or adopted by community landlords are secure contracts, and

(b) contracts made with or adopted by private landlords are standard contracts,

but this is subject to various exceptions.

III WAL [111]

3 Fundamental provisions and supplementary provisions of occupation contracts

(1) Part 2 of this Act establishes the concept of a "fundamental provision"; that is, a provision of this Act (generally a section) which is automatically included as a term of all occupation contracts, or of specified occupation contracts (and so forms part of the contract between a contract-holder and a landlord).

(2) Once a fundamental provision of this Act is included in an occupation contract, it is referred to as a "fundamental term" of the contract (see section 19).

(3) At the creation of the contract, the parties can agree that a fundamental provision will be included in the contract with changes (referred to in this Act as "modifications") or that it will not be included at all; however, the parties can only do either of these things if it will improve the contract-holder's position, and there are some fundamental provisions which must be included without changes.

(4) Once an occupation contract has been created the parties can vary its fundamental terms; but there are certain limits to this.

(5) Part 2 of this Act also establishes the concept of a "supplementary provision"; that is, a provision set out in regulations made by the Welsh Ministers which is automatically included as a term of all occupation contracts, or of specified occupation contracts.

(6) Once a supplementary provision is included in an occupation contract, it is referred to as a "supplementary term" of the contract (see section 23).

(7) At the creation of the contract, the parties can agree that a supplementary provision will be included in the contract with modifications or that it will not be included at all, and once an occupation contract has been created, the parties can vary its supplementary terms; but there are certain limits to this.

III WAL [112]

4 Identifying provisions of this Act which are fundamental provisions

(1) Each provision of this Act which is a fundamental provision—

(a) specifies that it is a fundamental provision, and

(b) specifies the occupation contracts it is applicable to.

(2) Schedule 1 contains three Parts, identifying the fundamental provisions in this Act as follows—

(a) Part 1 identifies the fundamental provisions that are applicable to secure contracts,

(b) Part 2 identifies the fundamental provisions that are applicable to periodic standard contracts, and

(c) Part 3 identifies the fundamental provisions that are applicable to fixed term standard contracts.

Overview of Rest of Act

III WAL [113]

5 Overview of Parts 3 to 9: operation and termination of occupation contracts

(1) Parts 3 to 9 concern occupation contracts.

(2) Part 3 applies to all occupation contracts; it deals with a range of matters about the rights and obligations of parties to occupation contracts.

(3) Parts 4 to 8 apply only to specific kinds of occupation contract—

- (a) Part 4 concerns landlords' obligations relating to the condition of dwellings; Chapter 2 (which sets out the obligations) applies to all occupation contracts except fixed term standard contracts for a term of seven years or more, and Chapters 1 and 3 are of general application,
- (b) Part 5 applies to secure contracts only (and section 118 applies only to secure contracts with a community landlord),
- (c) Part 6 applies to periodic standard contracts only,
- (d) Part 7 applies to fixed term standard contracts only, and
- (e) Part 8 applies to supported standard contracts only (a supported standard contract is an occupation contract which relates to accommodation provided in connection with support services).

(4) Part 9 concerns the termination of occupation contracts; in particular, it contains—

- (a) Chapters which apply to all occupation contracts, and
- (b) Chapters which apply only to specific kinds of occupation contract.

III WAL [114]

6 Overview of Parts 10 and 11: general provision

(1) Part 10 concerns miscellaneous matters which are either—

- (a) supplementary to Parts 2 to 9, or
- (b) about the application and operation of this Act.

(2) Part 11 contains—

- (a) provision about the interpretation of this Act, and
- (b) provision which applies generally for the purposes of this Act.

PART 2
OCCUPATION CONTRACTS AND LANDLORDS

CHAPTER 1 OCCUPATION CONTRACTS

III WAL [115]

7 Tenancies and licences that are occupation contracts

(1) A tenancy or licence is an occupation contract if—

- (a) it is within subsection (2) or (3), and
- (b) rent or other consideration is payable under it.

(2) A tenancy or licence is within this subsection if—

- (a) it is made between a landlord and an individual, and
- (b) it confers on the individual the right to occupy a dwelling as a home.

(3) A tenancy or licence is within this subsection if—

- (a) it is made between a landlord and two or more persons at least one of whom is an individual, and
- (b) it confers on the individual (or, if there is more than one individual, on one or more of them) the right to occupy a dwelling as a home.

(4) But there are exceptions to subsection (1) set out in Schedule 2, which provides—

(a) in Part 1, that certain tenancies and licences not within subsection (2) or (3) can be occupation contracts if notice is given,

(b) in Part 2, that certain tenancies and licences that are within subsection (2) or (3) are not occupation contracts unless notice is given,

(c) in Part 3, that certain tenancies and licences are never occupation contracts,

(d) in Parts 4 and 5, that certain tenancies and licences can be occupation contracts, but special rules apply in relation to them, and

(e) in Part 6, that the Welsh Ministers may amend that Schedule.

(5) Each person with whom a landlord makes an occupation contract is a contract-holder under the occupation contract.

(6) But an individual cannot be a contract-holder under an occupation contract if he or she has not reached the age of 18.

III WAL [116]

8 Secure contracts and standard contracts

(1) An occupation contract is either—

(a) a secure contract, or

(b) a standard contract.

(2) A secure contract is a periodic contract.

(3) A standard contract is either a fixed term contract or a periodic contract.

CHAPTER 2 NATURE OF CONTRACTS WHICH CAN BE MADE ETC BY COMMUNITY LANDLORDS AND PRIVATE LANDLORDS

Definitions

III WAL [117]

9 Community landlords

(1) In this Act "community landlord" means a landlord which is—

(a) an authority mentioned in subsection (2),

(b) a registered social landlord, other than a fully mutual housing association or a co-operative housing association, or

(c) a private registered provider of social housing (see section 80(3) of the Housing and Regeneration Act 2008 (c 17)).

(2) The authorities are—

(a) a local authority;

(b) a new town corporation;

(c) a housing action trust;

(d) an urban development corporation;

(e) a housing co-operative to which subsection (3) applies.

(3) This subsection applies to a housing co-operative (within the meaning of section 27B of the Housing Act 1985 (c 68)) to the extent that any dwelling subject to an occupation contract is comprised in a housing co-operative agreement within the meaning of that section.

(4) In this Act "registered social landlord" means a person registered in the register maintained under section 1 of the Housing Act 1996 (c 52).

(5) In this Act "fully mutual housing association" and "co-operative housing association" have the same meaning as in the Housing Associations Act 1985 (c 69) (see section 1(2) of that Act).

(6) The Welsh Ministers may by regulations amend this section for the purpose of—

- (a) providing that a person which is for the time being a community landlord is not a community landlord;
- (b) providing that a person which is not a community landlord is a community landlord;
- (c) changing a description of a person which is for the time being a community landlord.

III WAL [118]

10 Private landlords

In this Act "private landlord" means a landlord that is not a community landlord.

Contracts Made with or Adopted by Community Landlords

III WAL [119]

11 Contract made with community landlord

(1) An occupation contract made with a community landlord is a secure contract unless one of the following exceptions applies.

(2) The first exception applies if—

- (a) the occupation contract is within Schedule 3 (occupation contracts made with community landlords which may be standard contracts),
- (b) before or at the time the contract is made, the landlord gives the contract-holder a notice under section 13 (notice of standard contract), and
- (c) no other exception applies.

(3) The second exception applies if the contract is made as a result of an order under section 116 (prohibited conduct standard contract).

(4) The third exception applies if the contract arises under section 184(2) or is within section 184(6) (contracts at end of fixed term).

(5) The fourth exception applies if the contract is a tenancy or licence arising under section 238 (implied tenancies and licences).

(6) Section 16 makes further provision about contracts to which the first exception applies because the contract is within paragraph 3 of Schedule 3 (introductory standard contracts).

III WAL [120]

12 Contract adopted by community landlord

(1) If a community landlord becomes the landlord under an existing secure contract, the contract continues as a secure contract.

(2) If a community landlord becomes the landlord under an existing standard contract because of a transfer under section 62 or 66 (transfer of rights and obligations of landlord under a sub-occupation contract), the contract continues as a standard contract.

(3) If a community landlord becomes the landlord under an existing standard contract for any other reason, the existing contract—

- (a) ends when the community landlord becomes the landlord, and
- (b) is replaced with a secure contract that has an occupation date falling immediately after the existing contract ends,

unless one of the following exceptions applies.

(4) The first exception applies if—

- (a) the contract is within Schedule 3 (occupation contracts adopted by community landlords which may be standard contracts),

(b) before or at the time the community landlord becomes the landlord, the community landlord gives the contract-holder a notice under section 13, and

(c) no other exception applies.

(5) The second exception applies if the contract is made as a result of an order under section 116 (prohibited conduct standard contract).

(6) The third exception applies if the contract arises under section 184(2) or is within section 184(6) (contracts at end of fixed term).

(7) The fourth exception applies if the contract is a tenancy or licence arising under section 238 (implied tenancies and licences).

(8) The fifth exception applies if—

(a) the contract is a fixed term standard contract for which a premium was paid, and

(b) before the community landlord becomes the landlord, the contract-holder decides that the contract should remain a fixed term standard contract (section 15 makes further provision about such decisions).

(9) Section 16 makes further provision about contracts to which the first exception applies because the contract is within paragraph 3 of Schedule 3 (introductory standard contracts).

III WAL [121]

13 Notice of standard contract

(1) A notice under this section is a notice—

(a) specifying the paragraph of Schedule 3, and the description of occupation contract set out in that paragraph, on which the landlord relies, and

(b) stating that the contract is a standard contract.

(2) The notice must also inform the contract-holder of his or her right to apply for a review under section 14, and of the time by which the application must be made.

III WAL [122]

14 Review of notice

(1) This section applies where a community landlord gives a notice under section 13.

(2) The contract-holder may apply to the county court for a review of the landlord's decision to give the notice.

(3) The application must be made before the end of the period of 14 days starting with the day on which the landlord gives the contract-holder the notice.

(4) The county court may give permission for an application to be made after the end of the period allowed by subsection (3), but only if it is satisfied—

(a) where permission is sought before the end of that period, that there is a good reason for the contract-holder to be unable to make the application in time, or

(b) where permission is sought after that time, that there is a good reason for the contract-holder's failure to make the application in time and for any delay in applying for permission.

(5) The county court may confirm or quash the decision to give the notice.

(6) In considering whether to confirm or quash the decision, the county court must apply the principles applied by the High Court on an application for judicial review.

(7) If the county court quashes the decision, it may make any order the High Court could make when making a quashing order on an application for judicial review.

(8) If the county court quashes the decision and the landlord gives the contract-holder a further notice under section 13 before the end of the post-review period, the notice has effect (other than for the purposes of subsection (3)) as if given—

(a) in a case within section 11, at the time the contract was made, or

(b) in a case within section 12, at the time the community landlord became the landlord.

(9) The post-review period is the period of 14 days beginning with the day on which the county court quashes the decision.

III WAL [123]

15 Notice of right to decide to remain on a fixed term standard contract

(1) At least one month before a community landlord becomes the landlord under a fixed term standard contract for which a premium was paid, the community landlord must give the contract-holder a notice under this section.

(2) The notice must—

(a) inform the contract-holder of his or her right under section 12(8)(b) to decide that the contract should remain a fixed term standard contract, and of the time by which the decision must be made, and

(b) explain how section 12 will apply to the contract if the contract-holder does not make such a decision.

III WAL [124]

16 Introductory standard contracts

(1) An occupation contract which is a standard contract because the first exception in section 11 or 12 applies and because it is within paragraph 3 of Schedule 3 (new occupation contract made with community landlord)—

(a) is a periodic standard contract during the introductory period, and

(b) if it subsists immediately before the end of that period—

(i) ends at the end of that period, and

(ii) is replaced with a secure contract that has an occupation date falling immediately after that period ends.

(2) But subsection (1)(b) does not apply if an introductory period ends because of paragraph 1(6) of Schedule 4 (private landlord becomes landlord under the contract).

(3) Schedule 4 makes provision about introductory periods and about the terms of a secure contract which arises at the end of an introductory period.

(4) In this Act "introductory standard contract" means a contract—

(a) which is within subsection (1), and

(b) in relation to which the introductory period has not ended.

Contracts Made with or Adopted by Private Landlords

III WAL [125]

17 Contract made with or adopted by private landlord

(1) An occupation contract made with a private landlord is a standard contract unless, before or at the time the contract is made, the landlord gives the contract-holder a notice stating that the contract is a secure contract.

(2) If a private landlord becomes the landlord under an existing secure contract, the contract continues as a secure contract.

(3) If a private landlord becomes the landlord under an existing standard contract, the contract continues as a standard contract.

CHAPTER 3 FUNDAMENTAL PROVISIONS OF OCCUPATION CONTRACTS

III WAL [126]

18 Fundamental provisions

(1) Fundamental provisions are provisions of this Act (and provisions which are fundamental provisions by virtue of section 22(1)(a)) that are incorporated as terms of occupation contracts or particular kinds or descriptions of occupation contract (subject to sections 20(1) and (2) and 21).

(2) Each provision of this Act that is a fundamental provision identifies itself as such, and specifies the occupation contracts into which it is incorporated as a fundamental term.

(3) Nothing in this Act is to be read as enabling a landlord or contract-holder to do anything which would have the effect that a fundamental provision which is applicable to the occupation contract is not, or is not to be treated as, a fundamental provision which is applicable to the contract (but this does not prevent an agreement to modify or not to incorporate a fundamental provision, or a variation of a fundamental term, which is in accordance with this Act).

III WAL [127]

19 Fundamental terms and fundamental provisions: definitions

(1) This section applies for the purposes of interpreting this Act.

(2) "Fundamental provision" has the meaning given in section 18.

(3) A reference in this Act to a section or other provision which is a fundamental provision has effect, in relation to a contract in which the fundamental provision is incorporated (with or without modifications), as a reference to the fundamental term of the contract which incorporates the fundamental provision.

(4) "Fundamental term", in relation to an occupation contract, means a term of the contract which incorporates a fundamental provision (with or without modifications).

III WAL [128]

20 Incorporation and modification of fundamental provisions

(1) A fundamental provision is not incorporated as a term of an occupation contract if—

- (a) the landlord and the contract-holder agree that it should not be incorporated, and
- (b) in the contract-holder's opinion, the effect of its not being incorporated is that the position of the contract-holder is improved.

(2) A fundamental provision is incorporated as a term of an occupation contract with modifications if—

- (a) the landlord and the contract-holder agree that it should be incorporated with those modifications, and
- (b) in the contract-holder's opinion, the effect of its being incorporated with those modifications is that the position of the contract-holder is improved.

(3) Subsections (1) and (2) do not apply to the following fundamental provisions—

- (a) section 45 (requirement to use deposit scheme),
- (b) section 52 (joint contract-holder ceasing to be a party to the occupation contract),
- (c) section 55 (anti-social behaviour and other prohibited conduct),
- (d) sections 103(1)(b) and (2) and 108 (variation of secure contracts),

(e) sections 122(1)(b) and (2) and 127 (variation of periodic standard contracts),
(f) section 134(1)(b) and (2) and 135 (variation of fixed term standard contracts),
(g) section 148 (permissible termination),
(h) section 149 (possession claims),
(i) section 155 (death of sole contract-holder),
(j) section 158 (securing contract by use of false statement),
(k) section 175 (restriction on giving landlord's notice under a periodic standard contract during first four months of occupation),
(l) section 177 (breach of deposit requirements: periodic standard contracts),
(m) section 186(2) and (4) (restriction on ending fixed term standard contract during first six months of occupation),
(n) section 196 (restriction on use of landlord's break clause in a fixed term standard contract during first four months of occupation),
(o) section 198 (breach of deposit requirements: fixed term standard contracts with landlord's break clause), and
(p) paragraph 7 of Schedule 4 (variation of secure contract addressed in written statement of introductory standard contract).

(4) Subsections (1) and (2) are subject to section 34 (landlord's failure to provide written statement of contract) and section 36 (incomplete statement of contract).

III WAL [129]

21 Effect of non-incorporation and modification of fundamental provisions

(1) Subsections (2) and (3) apply where—
(a) a fundamental provision is not incorporated as a term of an occupation contract because of an agreement under section 20(1), or
(b) a fundamental provision is incorporated with modifications because of an agreement under section 20(2).

(2) If as a result it is necessary that another fundamental provision or a supplementary provision (see Chapter 4) is not incorporated, that other provision is not incorporated.

(3) If as a result it is necessary that another fundamental provision or a supplementary provision is incorporated with modifications, that provision is incorporated with the necessary modifications (in addition to any modifications made because of an agreement under section 20(2) or section 24(2)).

(4) But subsections (2) and (3) do not apply if their application would have the effect that a fundamental provision mentioned in section 20(3) would not be incorporated or would be incorporated with modifications; accordingly, the agreement mentioned in subsection (1)(a) or (b) has no effect.

III WAL [130]

22 Powers in relation to fundamental provisions

(1) The Welsh Ministers may by regulations provide that—
(a) a provision of any enactment is a fundamental provision applicable to an occupation contract;
(b) a provision of any enactment that is for the time being a fundamental provision applicable to an occupation contract ceases to be a fundamental provision applicable to an occupation contract.

(2) The Welsh Ministers may by regulations provide that—
(a) section 20(1) does not apply to a fundamental provision;
(b) section 20(2) does not apply to a fundamental provision.

(3) The power under section 256(2) to make consequential amendments includes, in its application to regulations under this section, the power to make consequential amendments to this Act.

CHAPTER 4 SUPPLEMENTARY PROVISIONS OF OCCUPATION CONTRACTS

III WAL [131]

23 Supplementary provisions

(1) The Welsh Ministers may by regulations provide that provisions set out in the regulations are incorporated as terms of occupation contracts (subject to sections 21, 24(1) and (2) and 25); for the purposes of this Act such provisions are "supplementary provisions".

(2) Before making regulations under subsection (1), the Welsh Ministers must consult such persons as appear to them to be appropriate.

(3) Sections 112 and 131 give the Welsh Ministers further powers to prescribe supplementary provisions relating to time limits for withdrawal of joint contract-holders from secure contracts and periodic standard contracts (and the Welsh Ministers must consult in accordance with subsection (2) before using those powers).

(4) The Welsh Ministers may, under subsection (1), prescribe a provision in an enactment as a supplementary provision applicable to an occupation contract.

(5) In this Act—

"supplementary provision" ("*darpariaeth atodol*") (except in relation to sections 255 and 256) has the meaning given in subsection (1) of this section;

"supplementary term" ("*teler atodol*"), in relation to an occupation contract, means a term of the contract which incorporates a supplementary provision (with or without modifications).

III WAL [132]

24 Incorporation and modification of supplementary provisions

(1) A supplementary provision is not incorporated as a term of an occupation contract if the landlord and the contract-holder agree that it should not be incorporated.

(2) A supplementary provision is incorporated as a term of an occupation contract with modifications if the landlord and the contract-holder agree that it should be incorporated with those modifications.

(3) An agreement under subsection (1) or (2) that would make a supplementary term of an occupation contract incompatible with a fundamental term of the contract is of no effect.

(4) Subsections (1) and (2) are subject to section 34 (landlord's failure to provide written statement of contract) and section 36 (incomplete written statement).

III WAL [133]

25 Effect of non-incorporation and modification of supplementary provisions

(1) Subsections (2) and (3) apply where—

(a) a supplementary provision is not incorporated as a term of an occupation contract because of an agreement under section 24(1), or

(b) a supplementary provision is incorporated as a term of the contract with modifications because of an agreement under section 24(2).

(2) If as a result it is necessary that another supplementary provision is not incorporated, the other provision is not incorporated.

(3) If as a result it is necessary that another supplementary provision is incorporated with modifications, the other provision is incorporated with the necessary modifications (in addition to any modifications made because of an agreement under section 24(2)).

CHAPTER 5 KEY MATTERS AND ADDITIONAL TERMS OF OCCUPATION CONTRACTS

III WAL [134]

26 Key matters of all occupation contracts

The following are key matters in relation to all occupation contracts—

(a) the dwelling,

(b) the occupation date,

(c) the amount of rent or other consideration, and

(d) the rental periods.

III WAL [135]

27 Further key matters of standard contracts

The following are key matters in relation to standard contracts (in addition to those set out in section 26)—

(a) whether the contract is periodic or made for a fixed term,

(b) if it is made for a fixed term, the term for which it is made, and

(c) if there are periods during which the contract-holder is not entitled to occupy the dwelling as a home, those periods (see sections 121 and 133).

III WAL [136]

28 Additional terms

(1) Additional terms of an occupation contract are any express terms of the contract other than—

(a) the terms addressing the key matters in relation to the contract,

(b) the fundamental terms of the contract, and

(c) the supplementary terms of the contract.

(2) An additional term of an occupation contract which is incompatible with any of the terms mentioned in paragraphs (a) to (c) of subsection (1) has no effect.

(3) In this Act "additional terms" has the meaning given by subsection (1).

CHAPTER 6 MODEL CONTRACTS

III WAL [137]

29 Model written statement of contract

(1) The Welsh Ministers must prescribe model written statements of contracts for such kinds or descriptions of occupation contract as they think fit.

(2) A model written statement of contract for an occupation contract of a particular kind or description is a written statement (see section 31) which incorporates without modification all the fundamental and supplementary provisions applicable to that contract.

PART 3
PROVISIONS APPLYING TO ALL OCCUPATION CONTRACTS

CHAPTER 1 OVERVIEW

III WAL [138]

30 Overview of this Part

This Part applies to all occupation contracts, and in particular—

(a) it requires landlords to give contract-holders a written statement setting out the terms of the occupation contract,

(b) it addresses deposits given to landlords by contract-holders, and provides that deposits must be held in an authorised deposit scheme,

(c) it makes provision about occupation contracts that have more than one contract-holder,

(d) it gives contract-holders a right to occupy their home without interference from the landlord,

(e) it prohibits anti-social behaviour and certain other kinds of conduct by contract-holders and other occupants and visitors,

(f) it prohibits dealing with an occupation contract, but this is subject to exceptions relating to sub-occupation contracts, transfers of the contract and succession to the contract,

(g) it addresses seeking and giving landlord's consent, and

(h) it addresses compensation which contract-holders may be entitled to under this Act.

CHAPTER 2 PROVISION OF INFORMATION

Written Statement of Contract

III WAL [139]

31 Written statement

(1) The landlord under an occupation contract must give the contract-holder a written statement of the contract before the end of the period of 14 days starting with the occupation date.

(2) If there is a change in the identity of the contract-holder under an occupation contract, the landlord must give the new contract-holder a written statement of the contract before the end of the period of 14 days starting with—

(a) the day on which the identity of the contract-holder changes, or

(b) if later, the day on which the landlord (or in the case of joint landlords, any one of them) becomes aware that the identity of the contract-holder has changed.

(3) The landlord may not charge a fee for providing a written statement under subsection (1) or (2).

(4) The contract-holder may request a further written statement of the contract at any time.

(5) The landlord may charge a reasonable fee for providing a further written statement.

(6) The landlord must give the contract-holder the further written statement before the end of the period of 14 days starting with—

(a) the day of the request, or

(b) if the landlord charges a fee, the day on which the contract-holder pays the fee.

(7) This section is a fundamental provision which is incorporated as a term of all occupation contracts.

III WAL [140]

32 Contents of written statement

(1) A written statement of an occupation contract must set out the names of the parties to the contract.

(2) It must also set out—

- (a) the terms of the contract addressing key matters in relation to the contract,
- (b) the fundamental terms of the contract,
- (c) the supplementary terms of the contract, and
- (d) any additional terms.

(3) It must identify—

- (a) any fundamental provision applicable to the contract which is not incorporated as a term of the contract because of section 20(1) or 21(2), and
- (b) any supplementary provision applicable to the contract which is not incorporated as a term of the contract because of section 21(2), 24(1) or 25(2).

(4) It must contain explanatory information about such matters as may be prescribed.

III WAL [141]

33 Editorial changes

(1) The written statement may set out the fundamental and supplementary terms of the occupation contract with editorial changes.

(2) Editorial changes are changes to the wording of a fundamental or supplementary term which do not change the substance of that term in any way; for example, substituting the names of the landlord or contract-holder for references to "the landlord", "the landlord under an occupation contract", "the contract-holder", "the contract-holder under a secure contract" etc

III WAL [142]

34 Failure to provide a written statement etc

(1) If the landlord under an occupation contract fails to comply with a requirement to provide a written statement under section 31, the contract-holder may apply to the court for a declaration as to the terms of the contract.

(2) On an application under subsection (1) each fundamental and supplementary provision applicable to the contract is to be treated as incorporated as a term of the contract without modification, unless the contract-holder claims that it was not incorporated or was incorporated with modifications.

(3) If the contract-holder makes a claim of a kind mentioned in subsection (2), the court must determine that claim.

(4) Subsection (3) does not apply if the landlord's failure to comply with section 31 is attributable to an act or omission of the contract-holder.

(5) The court may—

- (a) attach a statement of the occupation contract to its declaration, or
- (b) order the landlord to give the contract-holder a written statement of the contract.

III WAL [143]

35 Failure to provide statement: compensation

(1) If the landlord under an occupation contract fails to comply with a requirement to provide a written statement under section 31, the landlord is liable to pay the contract-holder compensation under section 87.

(2) The compensation is payable in respect of the relevant date and every day after the relevant date until—

(a) the day on which the landlord gives the contract-holder a written statement of the contract, or

(b) if earlier, the last day of the period of two months starting with the relevant date.

(3) Interest on the compensation is payable if the landlord fails to give the contract-holder a written statement of the contract on or before the day referred to in subsection (2)(b).

(4) The interest starts to run on the day referred to in subsection (2)(b), at the rate prevailing under section 6 of the Late Payment of Commercial Debts (Interest) Act 1998 (c 20) at the end of that day.

(5) This section does not apply if the landlord's failure to comply with section 31 is attributable to an act or omission of the contract-holder.

(6) The relevant date is the first day of the period before the end of which the landlord was required to give the written statement.

III WAL [144]

36 Incomplete statement

(1) If the landlord under an occupation contract provides a written statement of the contract that is incomplete, the contract-holder may apply to the court for a declaration as to the terms of the contract.

(2) A written statement is incomplete if it does not include everything required to be included by section 32.

(3) The contract-holder may not apply to the court under subsection (1) before the end of the period of 14 days starting—

(a) if the landlord was required to provide a written statement under section 31(1), with the occupation date;

(b) if the landlord was required to provide a written statement under section 31(2), with the day on which the landlord gave the new contract-holder the written statement;

(c) if the landlord was required to provide a further written statement under section 31(4) to (6), with the first day of the period mentioned in section 31(6).

(4) Subsection (5) applies if the written statement—

(a) does not set out a fundamental provision applicable to the contract and does not contain a statement that the provision is not incorporated because of section 20(1) or 21(2), or

(b) does not set out a supplementary provision applicable to the contract and does not contain a statement that the provision is not incorporated because of section 21(2), 24(1) or 25(2).

(5) That provision is to be treated as incorporated as a term of the contract without modification unless—

(a) section 21 or 25 applies in relation to it, or

(b) the contract-holder claims it was not incorporated or was incorporated with modifications.

(6) If the contract-holder makes a claim of a kind mentioned in subsection (5)(b) the court must determine that claim.

WALES

(7) Subsection (6) does not apply if the omission of the provision or statement is attributable to an act or omission of the contract-holder.

(8) The court may—

(a) attach a written statement of the occupation contract to its declaration, or

(b) order the landlord to give the contract-holder a written statement of the contract which is complete.

(9) If the court is satisfied that the written statement is incomplete because of the intentional default of the landlord, it may order the landlord to pay the contract-holder compensation under section 87.

(10) The compensation is payable in respect of the period, not exceeding two months, determined by the court; and the court may order the landlord to pay interest at such rate and calculated in such manner as it thinks fit.

III WAL [145]

37 Incorrect statement: contract-holder's application to court

(1) The contract-holder under an occupation contract may apply to the court for a declaration that a written statement of the contract—

(a) sets out a term of the contract incorrectly or sets out a term that is of no effect,

(b) incorrectly states that because of section 20(1) or 21(2), a fundamental provision applicable to the contract has not been incorporated as a term of the contract,

(c) incorrectly states that because of section 21(2), 24(1) or 25(2) a supplementary provision applicable to the contract has not been incorporated as a term of the contract, or

(d) sets out a term that is not a term of the contract.

(2) But a written statement is not incorrect merely because it does not set out a term varied in accordance with the contract or by or as a result of an enactment if—

(a) a written statement of the term varied was given in accordance with section 109, 128 or 136, or

(b) notice of the variation was given in accordance with section 104, 105(2) to (4) or 107(1)(b) and (2) to (6) (variation of secure contracts) or section 123, 124(2) to (4) or 126(1) to (4) (variation of periodic standard contracts),

unless the statement was given under section 31(2) or (4) after any such variation of a term took effect.

(3) The contract-holder may not apply to the court under subsection (1) before the end of the period of 14 days starting—

(a) if the landlord was required to provide a written statement under section 31(1), with the occupation date;

(b) if the landlord was required to provide a written statement under section 31(2), with the day on which the landlord gave the new contract-holder the written statement;

(c) if the landlord was required to provide a further written statement under section 31(4) to (6), with the first day of the period mentioned in section 31(6).

(4) If the court is satisfied that the ground in subsection (1)(a), (1)(b) or (1)(c) is made out, it may make a declaration setting out the correct term.

(5) If the court is satisfied that the ground in subsection (1)(d) is made out, it may make a declaration that the term is not a term of the contract.

(6) The court may—

(a) attach a written statement of the occupation contract to its declaration, or

(b) order the landlord to give the contract-holder a corrected written statement of the contract.

(7) If the court is satisfied that the written statement is incorrect as described in subsection (1) because of the intentional default of the landlord, it may order the landlord to pay the contract-holder compensation under section 87.

(8) The compensation is payable in respect of the period, not exceeding two months, determined by the court; and the court may order the landlord to pay interest at such rate and calculated in such manner as it thinks fit.

III WAL [146]

38 Incorrect statement: landlord's application to court for declaration that contract is a standard contract

(1) This section applies if the landlord under an occupation contract is a community landlord and has given the contract-holder—

(a) a notice under section 13 (notice of standard contract), but

(b) a written statement of the contract that is consistent with a secure contract.

(2) The landlord may apply to the court for a declaration that the contract is a standard contract.

(3) The court may not make the declaration if it is satisfied that, at the time the landlord gave the written statement to the contract-holder, it was the intention of the landlord that the contract should be a secure contract.

(4) If the court makes the declaration each fundamental and supplementary provision applicable to the contract is incorporated as a term of the contract without modification, unless the contract-holder claims it was not incorporated or was incorporated with modifications.

(5) If the contract-holder makes a claim of a kind mentioned in subsection (4), the court must determine that claim.

(6) The court may—

(a) attach a written statement of the occupation contract to its declaration, or

(b) order the landlord to give the contract-holder a corrected written statement of the contract.

Provision by Landlord of Information about Landlord

III WAL [147]

39 Provision by landlord of information about landlord

(1) The landlord under an occupation contract must, before the end of the period of 14 days starting with the occupation date of the contract, give the contract-holder notice of an address to which the contract-holder may send documents that are intended for the landlord.

(2) If there is a change in the identity of the landlord, the new landlord must, before the end of the period of 14 days starting with the day on which the new landlord becomes the landlord, give the contract-holder notice of the change in identity and of an address to which the contract-holder may send documents that are intended for the new landlord.

(3) If the address to which the contract-holder may send documents that are intended for the landlord changes, the landlord must, before the end of the period of 14 days starting with the day on which the address changes, give the contract-holder notice of the new address.

(4) This section is a fundamental provision which is incorporated as a term of all occupation contracts.

III WAL [148]

40 Compensation for breach of section 39

(1) If the landlord fails to comply with an obligation under section 39, the landlord is liable to pay the contract-holder compensation under section 87.

(2) The compensation is payable in respect of the relevant date and every day after the relevant date until—

- (a) the day on which the landlord gives the notice in question, or
- (b) if earlier, the last day of the period of two months starting with the relevant date.

(3) Interest on the compensation is payable if the landlord fails to give the contract-holder the notice on or before the day referred to in subsection (2)(b).

(4) The interest starts to run on the day referred to in subsection (2)(b), at the rate prevailing under section 6 of the Late Payment of Commercial Debts (Interest) Act 1998 (c 20) at the end of that day.

(5) The relevant date is the first day of the period before the end of which the landlord was required to give the notice.

(6) This section is a fundamental provision which is incorporated as a term of all occupation contracts.

Form of Notices, Statements and other Documents

III WAL [149]

41 Form of notices etc

(1) Any notice, statement or other document required or authorised to be given or made by an occupation contract must be in writing.

(2) Sections 236 and 237 make further provision about form of notices and other documents, and about how to deliver or otherwise give a document required or authorised to be given to a person by or because of this Act.

(3) This section is a fundamental provision which is incorporated as a term of all occupation contracts.

CHAPTER 3 WHEN CONTRACT BECOMES ENFORCEABLE

III WAL [150]

42 When terms of occupation contract become enforceable

(1) No term of an occupation contract is enforceable against the contract-holder before the earlier of—

- (a) the landlord giving the contract-holder a written statement of the contract under section 31(1), and
- (b) the occupation date.

(2) If there is a change in the identity of the contract-holder under an occupation contract, no term of the occupation contract is enforceable against the new contract-holder before the earlier of—

- (a) the landlord giving the new contract-holder a written statement of the contract under section 31(2), and
- (b) the day on which the new contract-holder becomes entitled to occupy the dwelling.

CHAPTER 4 DEPOSITS AND DEPOSIT SCHEMES

Security

III WAL [151]

43 Form of security

(1) The landlord under an occupation contract may not require security to be given in any form other than—

(a) money, or

(b) a guarantee.

(2) This section is a fundamental provision which is incorporated as a term of all occupation contracts.

III WAL [152]

44 Form of security: county court proceedings

(1) This section applies if—

(a) the landlord under an occupation contract requires security to be given in a form which is not permitted by section 43, and

(b) security is given in that form.

(2) The contract-holder (or any person who has given the security on his or her behalf) may apply to the county court for an order under subsection (3).

(3) An order under this subsection is an order requiring the person who appears to be holding the property constituting the security to return it.

Deposit Schemes

III WAL [153]

45 Requirement to use deposit scheme

(1) If the contract-holder under an occupation contract pays a deposit (or another person pays a deposit on his or her behalf), the deposit must be dealt with in accordance with an authorised deposit scheme.

(2) Before the end of the period of 30 days starting with the day on which the deposit is paid, the landlord must—

(a) comply with the initial requirements of an authorised deposit scheme, and

(b) give the contract-holder (and any person who has paid the deposit on his or her behalf) the required information.

(3) The required information is such information as may be prescribed relating to—

(a) the authorised deposit scheme which applies,

(b) the landlord's compliance with the initial requirements of the scheme, and

(c) the operation of this Chapter, including the contract-holder's rights (and the rights of any person who has paid the deposit on his or her behalf) in relation to the deposit.

(4) This section is a fundamental provision which is incorporated as a term of all occupation contracts; section 20 provides that this section—

(a) must be incorporated, and

(b) must not be incorporated with modifications.

III WAL [154]

46 Deposit schemes: further provision

(1) Schedule 5 contains further provision about deposit schemes.

(2) Sections 177 and 198 make provision relating to periodic standard contracts and fixed term standard contracts with a landlord's break clause, preventing a landlord from giving a notice requiring a contract-holder to give up possession if the landlord has not complied with certain requirements relating to the payment of security or to deposit schemes.

III WAL [155]

47 Deposit schemes: interpretation

(1) In this Act—

"authorised deposit scheme" ("*cynllun blaendal awdurdodedig*") means a deposit scheme in force in accordance with arrangements under paragraph 1 of Schedule 5 (and "deposit scheme" ("*cynllun blaendal*") has the meaning given in sub-paragraph (2) of that paragraph);

"deposit" ("*blaendal*") means money paid as security;

"initial requirements" ("*gofynion cychwynnol*"), in relation to an authorised deposit scheme, means the requirements of the scheme which must be complied with by the landlord when a deposit is paid;

"security" ("*sicrwydd*") means security for the performance of the contract-holder's obligations and the discharge of the contract-holder's liabilities.

(2) In this Act references to a deposit, in relation to a time after a deposit has been paid, are to a sum representing the deposit.

CHAPTER 5 JOINT CONTRACT-HOLDERS AND JOINT LANDLORDS

JOINT CONTRACT-HOLDERS

III WAL [156]

48 Joint contract-holders: joint liability etc

(1) If there are two or more joint contract-holders under an occupation contract, each joint contract-holder is fully liable to the landlord for the performance of every obligation owed to the landlord under the contract.

(2) References in this Act to the contract-holder, except where otherwise provided, are to the joint contract-holders.

(3) Subsection (2) applies even if the occupation contract is a tenancy and the leasehold estate is vested in one or more, but not all, of the joint contract-holders.

III WAL [157]

49 Adding a joint contract-holder

(1) The contract-holder under an occupation contract and another person may, with the consent of the landlord, make that person a joint contract-holder under the contract.

(2) If a person is made a joint contract-holder under this section he or she becomes entitled to all the rights and subject to all the obligations of a contract-holder under the contract from the day on which he or she becomes a joint contract-holder.

(3) This section is a fundamental provision which is incorporated as a term of all occupation contracts.

III WAL [158]

50 Adding a joint contract-holder: landlord's consent

Where a landlord refuses consent or consents subject to conditions to adding a joint contract-holder under section 49, what is reasonable for the purposes of section 84 (landlord's consent) is to be determined having regard to Schedule 6.

III WAL [159]

51 Adding a joint contract-holder: formalities

(1) The addition of a joint contract-holder under an occupation contract may be effected only by a document signed or executed by each of the parties to the transaction.

(2) If the contract requires the landlord's consent to the addition, the document must also be signed or executed by the landlord.

(3) But subsection (2) does not apply if the landlord is treated as having consented under section 84(6), (8) or (10).

Joint Contract-Holders: Survivorship

III WAL [160]

52 Joint contract-holder ceasing to be a party to the occupation contract

(1) If a joint contract-holder under an occupation contract dies, or ceases to be a party to the contract for some other reason, from the time he or she ceases to be a party the remaining joint contract-holders are—

- (a) fully entitled to all the rights under the contract, and
- (b) liable to perform fully every obligation owed to the landlord under the contract.

(2) The joint contract-holder is not entitled to any right or liable to any obligation in respect of the period after he or she ceases to be a party to the contract.

(3) Nothing in subsection (1) or (2) removes any right or waives any liability of the joint contract-holder accruing before he or she ceases to be a party to the contract.

(4) This section does not apply where a joint contract-holder ceases to be a party to the contract because his or her rights and obligations under the contract are transferred in accordance with the contract.

(5) This section is a fundamental provision which is incorporated as a term of all occupation contracts; section 20 provides that this section—

- (a) must be incorporated, and
- (b) must not be incorporated with modifications.

Joint Landlords

III WAL [161]

53 Joint landlords

(1) This section applies if two or more persons jointly constitute the landlord under an occupation contract.

(2) Each of them is fully liable to the contract-holder for the performance of every obligation owed to the contract-holder under the contract.

(3) References in this Act to the landlord are to the persons who jointly constitute the landlord.

CHAPTER 6 RIGHT TO OCCUPY WITHOUT INTERFERENCE

III WAL [162]

54 Right to occupy without interference from landlord

(1) The landlord under an occupation contract may not, by any act or omission, interfere with the contract-holder's right to occupy the dwelling.

(2) The landlord does not interfere with the contract-holder's right to occupy the dwelling by reasonably exercising the landlord's rights under the contract.

(3) The landlord does not interfere with the contract-holder's right to occupy the dwelling because of a failure to comply with repairing obligations (within the meaning of section 100(2)).

(4) The landlord is to be treated as having interfered with the contract-holder's right if a person who—

- (a) acts on behalf of the landlord, or
- (b) has an interest in the dwelling, or part of it, that is superior to the landlord's interest,

interferes with the contract-holder's right by any lawful act or omission.

(5) This section is a fundamental provision which is incorporated as a term of all occupation contracts.

CHAPTER 7 ANTI-SOCIAL BEHAVIOUR AND OTHER PROHIBITED CONDUCT

III WAL [163]

55 Anti-social behaviour and other prohibited conduct

(1) The contract-holder under an occupation contract must not engage or threaten to engage in conduct capable of causing nuisance or annoyance to a person with a right (of whatever description)—

- (a) to live in the dwelling subject to the occupation contract, or
- (b) to live in a dwelling or other accommodation in the locality of the dwelling subject to the occupation contract.

(2) The contract-holder must not engage or threaten to engage in conduct capable of causing nuisance or annoyance to a person engaged in lawful activity—

- (a) in the dwelling subject to the occupation contract, or
- (b) in the locality of that dwelling.

(3) The contract-holder must not engage or threaten to engage in conduct—

- (a) capable of causing nuisance or annoyance to—
  - (i) the landlord under the occupation contract, or
  - (ii) a person (whether or not employed by the landlord) acting in connection with the exercise of the landlord's housing management functions, and
- (b) that is directly or indirectly related to or affects the landlord's housing management functions.

(4) The contract-holder may not use or threaten to use the dwelling subject to the occupation contract, including any common parts and any other part of a building comprising the dwelling, for criminal purposes.

(5) The contract-holder must not, by any act or omission—

- (a) allow, incite or encourage any person who is living in or visiting the dwelling to act as mentioned in subsections (1) to (3), or
- (b) allow, incite or encourage any person to act as mentioned in subsection (4).

(6) This section is a fundamental provision which is incorporated as a term of all occupation contracts; section 20 provides that this section—

(a) must be incorporated, and

(b) must not be incorporated with modifications.

III WAL [164]

56 Power to amend section 55

The Welsh Ministers may by regulations amend section 55.

CHAPTER 8 DEALING

RIGHTS TO DEAL WITH OCCUPATION CONTRACT

III WAL [165]

57 Permissible forms of dealing

(1) The contract-holder under an occupation contract may not deal with the occupation contract, the dwelling or any part of the dwelling except—

(a) in a way permitted by the contract, or

(b) in accordance with a family property order (see section 251).

(2) A joint contract-holder may not deal with his or her rights and obligations under the occupation contract (or with the occupation contract, the dwelling or any part of the dwelling), except—

(a) in a way permitted by the contract, or

(b) in accordance with a family property order.

(3) If the contract-holder does anything in breach of subsection (1), or a joint contract-holder does anything in breach of subsection (2)—

(a) the transaction is not binding on the landlord, and

(b) the contract-holder or joint contract-holder is in breach of the contract (despite the transaction not being binding on the landlord).

(4) "Dealing" includes—

(a) creating a tenancy, or creating a licence which confers the right to occupy the dwelling;

(b) transferring;

(c) mortgaging or otherwise charging.

(5) This section is a fundamental provision which is incorporated as a term of all occupation contracts.

III WAL [166]

58 Dealing and landlord's consent

(1) Where a term of an occupation contract permits the contract-holder or a joint contract-holder to deal with anything mentioned in section 57(1) or (2) only with the landlord's consent, what is reasonable for the purposes of section 84 (landlord's consent) is to be determined having regard to Schedule 6.

(2) Section 19(1) of the Landlord and Tenant Act 1927 (c 36) (effect of covenants not to assign etc without consent) does not apply to a tenancy which is an occupation contract.

Sub-Occupation Contracts

III WAL [167]

59 Sub-occupation contracts: interpretation

(1) This section applies for the purposes of interpreting this Act.

(2) A "sub-occupation contract" is an occupation contract—

(a) made with a landlord who is the contract-holder under an occupation contract, and

(b) which relates to all or part of the dwelling to which that contract relates.

(3) "Sub-holder" means the contract-holder under the sub-occupation contract.

(4) "Head landlord" means the landlord under the head contract.

III WAL [168]

60 Sub-occupation contract never takes effect as transfer

(1) This section applies if the contract-holder under an occupation contract ("the head contract") enters into a sub-occupation contract, and the term of the sub-occupation contract ends at the same time as the term of the head contract.

(2) The sub-occupation contract takes effect as a sub-occupation contract (and not as a transfer to the sub-holder).

III WAL [169]

61 Failure to comply with conditions imposed by head landlord

(1) This section applies if an occupation contract ("the head contract") permits the contract-holder to enter into a sub-occupation contract with the consent of the head landlord.

(2) If the head landlord consents subject to conditions (see section 84), before entering into a sub-occupation contract with a person the contract-holder must notify that person of those conditions.

(3) If the contract-holder does not comply with the requirement in subsection (2) and a sub-occupation contract is entered into, the contract-holder is to be treated as having committed a repudiatory breach of the sub-occupation contract (see section 154).

(4) If the head landlord consents subject to conditions and a sub-occupation contract is entered into—

(a) section 32 is to be read in relation to that contract as if it provides (in addition to the other requirements under that section) that the written statement of the sub-occupation contract must set out the conditions imposed by the head landlord, and

(b) section 37 is to be read in relation to that contract as if it provides (in addition to the other provisions in that section)—

(i) in subsection (1), that the sub-holder can apply to the court for a declaration that the written statement sets out a condition incorrectly or sets out a condition which the head landlord did not impose,

(ii) that the head landlord is entitled to be a party to proceedings on the application, and

(iii) that the court, if satisfied that either of the grounds in sub-paragraph (i) is made out, may make a declaration setting out the correct condition or, as the case may be, may declare that the condition is not a condition imposed by the head landlord.

(5) A sub-occupation contract is not made otherwise than in accordance with the head contract only because—

(a) the head landlord consents subject to conditions, and
(b) the conditions are not complied with.

(6) In such a case the head landlord may choose to treat the sub-occupation contract as a periodic standard contract having the following characteristics—

(a) all the fundamental and supplementary provisions applicable to a periodic standard contract are incorporated without modification,
(b) any terms of the secure contract or fixed term standard contract which are incompatible with those fundamental or supplementary provisions have no effect, and
(c) otherwise, the terms of the periodic standard contract are the same as the terms of the secure contract or fixed term standard contract.

(7) If the head landlord chooses to treat it as a periodic standard contract under subsection (6), the head landlord must notify the contract-holder and the sub-holder of that choice.

(8) The head landlord may only give notice under subsection (7) after the sub-occupation contract is made and before the end of the period of two months starting with the day on which the head contract ends.

(9) If the head landlord gives notice in accordance with subsections (7) and (8), the contract is to be treated as a periodic standard contract with the characteristics mentioned in subsection (6) in any question arising between the sub-holder and any person other than the contract-holder.

III WAL [170]

62 End of head contract

(1) This section applies (subject to subsection (6)) if—

(a) the contract-holder under an occupation contract ("the head contract") enters into a sub-occupation contract in accordance with the head contract, and
(b) the head contract ends after the head contract's occupation date.

(2) If the sub-occupation contract subsists immediately before the head contract ends—

(a) the sub-occupation contract continues (as an occupation contract which is not a sub-occupation contract), and
(b) the contract-holder's rights and obligations as landlord under the sub-occupation contract are transferred to the head landlord.

(3) If the sub-holder asks the head landlord for a further written statement of the contract under section 31(4) (and subsection (5) of this section does not apply), the references to the contract-holder in sections 34(4) and 35(5) (failure to provide statement) include the person who was the contract-holder under the head contract.

(4) Subsection (5) applies where—

(a) a head landlord has given notice in accordance with section 61(7) and (8) in relation to a contract, and
(b) the contract continues because of subsection (2)(a) of this section.

(5) Where this subsection applies, for the purposes of section 31(1) (written statement of contract) the occupation date of the contract is to be treated—

(a) if the notice mentioned in section 61(7) is given to the sub-holder before the end of the head contract, as the day on which the head contract ends;
(b) if the notice is given to the sub-holder on or after the day on which the head contract ends, as the day on which the notice is given.

(6) This section does not apply if the head contract is a fixed term standard contract which ends at the end of the fixed term.

III WAL [171]

63 End of head contract: further provision

(1) Nothing in section 62 affects any right of the head landlord under section 61(6) (power to treat sub-occupation contract as periodic standard contract).

(2) Nothing in section 62 makes the head landlord liable to the sub-holder in respect of any breach of the sub-occupation contract committed by the contract-holder.

(3) Nothing in section 62 makes the sub-holder liable to the head landlord in respect of any breach by the sub-holder of the sub-occupation contract that occurred before the head contract ended.

(4) But the head landlord may be liable to the sub-holder, or the sub-holder to the head landlord, to the extent that any breach of the sub-occupation contract continues after the head contract ends.

(5) Subsections (3) and (4) do not affect any power conferred on the head landlord by the sub-occupation contract.

III WAL [172]

64 Possession claim against contract-holder where there is a sub-holder

(1) This section applies if—

(a) the contract-holder ("C") under an occupation contract ("the head contract") enters into a sub-occupation contract in accordance with the head contract, and

(b) after the sub-occupation contract is entered into, C's landlord gives C a possession notice, or other notice informing C that he or she must give up possession.

(2) At the same time as giving a notice mentioned in subsection (1)(b) to C, C's landlord must give the sub-holder a notice—

(a) stating that C's landlord intends to make a possession claim against C, and

(b) specifying the ground on which the claim will be made.

III WAL [173]

65 Extended possession order against sub-holder

(1) This section applies if—

(a) the contract-holder ("C") under an occupation contract ("the head contract") enters into a sub-occupation contract in accordance with the head contract, and

(b) after the sub-occupation contract is entered into, C's landlord makes a possession claim against C.

(2) In the proceedings on the claim against C, C's landlord may apply for an order for possession against the sub-holder ("S") (an "extended possession order"); but an application under this subsection may be made only if—

(a) the requirements set out in subsection (3) have been met, or

(b) the court considers it reasonable to dispense with those requirements.

(3) The requirements are as follows—

(a) C's landlord must have given S a copy of the notice mentioned in subsection (1)(b) of section 64 in accordance with subsection (2) of that section, and

(b) at the same time, C's landlord must have given S notice—

(i) of C's landlord's intention to apply for an extended possession order in the proceedings on the claim against C, and

(ii) of S's right to be a party to proceedings on the possession claim against C.

(4) Where C's landlord may apply for an extended possession order against S, S is entitled to be a party to proceedings on the possession claim against C (regardless of whether C's landlord makes an application for an extended possession order in the proceedings).

(5) The court may consider C's landlord's application for an extended possession order only if it has decided to make an order for possession against C.

(6) The court may make an extended possession order against S only if, had C made a possession claim against S, the court would have made an order for possession against S.

III WAL [174]

66 Exclusion of contract-holder after abandoning contracts

(1) This section applies if—

(a) a contract-holder ("C") under an occupation contract ("the head contract") enters into a sub-occupation contract in accordance with the head contract, and

(b) the sub-holder ("S") believes that C no longer considers himself or herself to be a party to the head contract and the sub-occupation contract.

(2) S may act to end the head contract in accordance with this section.

(3) S must give C a notice—

(a) stating that S believes that C no longer considers himself or herself to be a party to the head contract and the sub-occupation contract,

(b) requiring C to inform S in writing before the end of the warning period if he or she does consider himself or herself to be a party to one or both of those contracts, and

(c) informing C that after the warning period the head contract may be ended and his or her rights and obligations under the sub-occupation contract may be transferred to C's landlord.

(4) S must give a copy of the notice to C's landlord.

(5) During the warning period, S must make such inquiries as are necessary to satisfy himself or herself that C no longer considers himself or herself to be a party to the head contract and the sub-occupation contract.

(6) At the end of the warning period S may, if satisfied as described in subsection (5), apply to the court for an order—

(a) ending the head contract, and

(b) that C's rights and obligations as landlord under the sub-occupation contract are to be transferred to C's landlord in accordance with sections 62 and 63.

(7) The court may not hear S's application under subsection (6) if S has failed to comply with the requirement in subsection (4); but the court may dispense with that requirement if it considers it reasonable to do so.

(8) C's landlord is entitled to be a party to proceedings on an application made by S under subsection (6).

(9) If the court is satisfied that C does not consider himself or herself to be a party to the head contract and the sub-occupation contract, it may make the order applied for under subsection (6); and if it does so it must specify the date on which the head contract ends.

(10) But the court may not make an order under subsection (9) if—

(a) C's landlord is a party to the proceedings,

(b) C's landlord asserts that the court would have made an order for possession against S, had an application for such an order been made by C in a possession claim made by C against S, and

(c) the court is satisfied that it would have made an order for possession against S in those circumstances.

(11) The warning period is the period of four weeks starting with the day on which a notice under subsection (3) is given to C.

III WAL [175]

67 Excluded contract-holder's remedies

(1) This section applies if the court makes an order against C under section 66(9).

(2) Before the end of the period of six months starting with the day on which the order is made, C may apply to the court on a ground in subsection (3) for an order and declaration under subsection (4)(a).

(3) The grounds are—

(a) that S failed to give C a notice under section 66(3) or failed to make the inquiries required by section 66(5);

(b) that C considered himself or herself to be a party to the head contract or the sub-occupation contract or both of them and there is a good reason for his or her failure to respond (or to respond adequately) to the notice under section 66(3);

(c) that, when S applied to the court, he or she did not have reasonable grounds for being satisfied that C considered himself or herself not to be a party to the head contract and the sub-occupation contract.

(4) If the court finds that one or more of the grounds is made out, it may—

(a) by order rescind its order under section 66(9), and declare that the head contract continues to have effect in relation to the dwelling, and

(b) make such further order as it thinks fit.

III WAL [176]

68 Power to vary periods of time relating to exclusion after abandonment of contracts

The Welsh Ministers may by regulations—

(a) amend section 66(11) by substituting a different period for the period for the time being referred to;

(b) amend section 67(2) by substituting a different period for the period for the time being referred to.

Transfer

III WAL [177]

69 Form of transfer

(1) This section applies (subject to subsection (6)) to—

(a) a transfer of an occupation contract by the contract-holder;

(b) a transfer by a joint contract-holder of his or her rights and obligations under an occupation contract.

(2) The transfer must be signed or executed by each of the parties to the transfer.

(3) If the contract requires the landlord's consent to the transfer, the transfer must also be signed or executed by the landlord.

(4) But subsection (3) does not apply if the landlord is treated as having consented under section 84(6), (8) or (10).

(5) A transfer to which this section applies is of no effect if it does not comply with subsection (2) and, if it applies, subsection (3).

(6) This section does not apply to a transfer in accordance with a term included in the contract under section 139 or 142 (certain transfers of fixed term standard contracts).

III WAL [178]

70 Effect of authorised transfer

(1) If an occupation contract is transferred by the contract-holder to a person ("P") in accordance with the contract and section 69, on the transfer date—

- (a) P becomes entitled to all the rights and subject to all the obligations of the contract-holder under the contract, and
- (b) the contract-holder ceases to be entitled to any rights or subject to any obligations under the contract.

(2) If a joint contract-holder's rights and obligations under an occupation contract are transferred to a person ("P") in accordance with the contract and section 69, on the transfer date—

- (a) P becomes entitled to all the rights and subject to all the obligations of the joint contract-holder under the contract, and
- (b) the joint contract-holder ceases to be entitled to any rights or subject to any obligations under the contract.

(3) Subsection (2)(a) is subject to any term included in the contract because of section 141(3) or 142(3) (fixed term standard contracts: transfers of joint contract-holder's interest).

(4) Nothing in subsection (1)(b) or (2)(b) removes any right or waives any liability accruing before the transfer date.

(5) The transfer date is the day agreed by the contract-holder and P as the day on which the transfer takes effect.

III WAL [179]

71 Effect of unauthorised transfer

(1) This section applies to—

- (a) a transfer of an occupation contract by the contract-holder to a person ("P") which is not in accordance with the contract, and
- (b) a transfer by a joint contract-holder of his or her rights and obligations under an occupation contract to a person ("P") which is not in accordance with the contract.

(2) If the landlord accepts payments from P in respect of P's occupation of the dwelling, at a time when the landlord (or in the case of joint landlords, any one of them)—

- (a) knows that the transfer was not made in accordance with the contract, or
- (b) ought reasonably to know that the transfer was not made in accordance with the contract,

the transfer becomes binding on the landlord on the day immediately after the last day of the relevant period.

(3) Section 70 applies as if—

- (a) the transfer was made in accordance with the contract and section 69, and
- (b) the transfer date was the day immediately after the last day of the relevant period.

(4) The relevant period is the period of two months starting with the day on which payments are first accepted as described in subsection (2).

(5) Subsections (2) and (3) do not apply if before the end of the relevant period the landlord?—

(a) takes steps to end the occupation contract, or

(b) brings proceedings to evict P as a trespasser or otherwise shows an intention to treat P as a trespasser.

(6) References in this section to a transfer include a purported transfer which does not comply with section 69.

III WAL [180]

72 Deeds and covenants

(1) This section applies in relation to occupation contracts which are tenancies.

(2) Section 52 of the Law of Property Act 1925 (c 20) (land must be conveyed by deed) does not apply to a transfer of the contract.

(3) The Landlord and Tenant (Covenants) Act 1995 (c 30) does not apply to—

(a) a transfer by a contract-holder of any of the things mentioned in section 57(1), or by a joint contract-holder of any of the things mentioned in section 57(2), or

(b) a transfer which under section 28(6)(b) of that Act would be treated as an assignment of the premises.

Succession

III WAL [181]

73 Succession on death

(1) This section applies on the death of the sole contract-holder under an occupation contract (subject to section 139(2), which concerns fixed term standard contracts containing certain provision about transfer on the death of a sole contract-holder).

(2) If one person is qualified to succeed the contract-holder that person succeeds to the contract.

(3) If more than one person is qualified to succeed the contract-holder, the person identified in accordance with section 78 succeeds to the contract.

III WAL [182]

74 Persons qualified to succeed

(1) A person is qualified to succeed the contract-holder if that person—

(a) is a priority successor of the contract-holder or a reserve successor of the contract-holder, and

(b) is not excluded by subsection (3) or (4).

(2) But if the contract-holder was a reserve successor in relation to the occupation contract, no person is qualified to succeed him or her.

(3) A person is excluded if he or she has not reached the age of 18 at the time of the contract-holder's death.

(4) A person is excluded if at any time in the period of 12 months ending with the contract-holder's death he or she occupied the dwelling or part of it under a sub-occupation contract.

(5) A person is not excluded by subsection (4) if—

(a) he or she is a priority successor of the contract-holder, or he or she is a reserve successor of the contract-holder who meets the family member condition in section 76(2) because of section 250(1)(a) or (b) (spouses, civil partners etc), and

(b) the sub-occupation contract under which he or she occupied the dwelling or part of it ended before the contract-holder's death.

III WAL [183]

75 Priority successor

(1) A person is a priority successor of the contract-holder if—

(a) he or she—

(i) is the spouse or civil partner of the contract-holder, or

(ii) lives together with the contract-holder as if they were spouses or civil partners, and

(b) he or she occupied the dwelling as his or her only or principal home at the time of the contract-holder's death.

(2) But no person is a priority successor of the contract-holder if the contract-holder was a priority successor in relation to the occupation contract.

III WAL [184]

76 Reserve successor: family member

(1) A person is a reserve successor of the contract-holder if he or she is not a priority successor of the contract-holder and—

(a) he or she meets the family member condition,

(b) he or she occupied the dwelling as his or her only or principal home at the time of the contract-holder's death, and

(c) if he or she meets the family member condition because of section 250(1)(c) (family members other than spouses, civil partners etc), he or she also meets the basic residence condition.

(2) A person meets the family member condition if he or she is a member of the contract-holder's family.

(3) A person meets the basic residence condition if throughout the period of 12 months ending with the contract-holder's death—

(a) he or she occupied the dwelling, or

(b) he or she lived with the contract-holder.

(4) If the contract-holder was a priority successor in relation to the occupation contract, the references in subsections (2) and (3)(b) to the contract-holder include the person the contract-holder succeeded.

III WAL [185]

77 Reserve successor: carer

(1) A person is a reserve successor of the contract-holder if he or she is not a priority successor of the contract-holder and—

(a) he or she meets the carer condition,

(b) he or she occupied the dwelling as his or her only or principal home at the time of the contract-holder's death, and

(c) he or she meets the carer residence condition.

(2) A person meets the carer condition if at any time in the period of 12 months ending with the contract-holder's death he or she was a carer in relation to—

(a) the contract-holder, or

(b) a member of the contract-holder's family who, at the time the care was provided, lived with the contract-holder.

(3) If the contract-holder was a priority successor in relation to the occupation contract, the references in subsection (2) to the contract-holder include the person the contract-holder succeeded.

(4) A person meets the carer residence condition if—

(a) he or she meets the basic residence condition, as set out in section 76(3) and (4), and

(b) at the time of the contract-holder's death there was no other dwelling which the person was entitled to occupy as a home.

(5) "Carer" means a person who—

(a) provides or intends to provide a substantial amount of care for another person on a regular basis, and

(b) does not provide or will not provide that care because of a contract of employment or other contract with any person.

(6) A person does not provide care because of a contract merely because he or she is given board or lodging or because he or she may become qualified to succeed as a reserve successor.

III WAL [186]

78 More than one qualified successor

(1) This section applies where there is more than one person who is qualified to succeed the contract-holder.

(2) If one of the persons is a priority successor, the priority successor succeeds to the contract.

(3) If two or more of the persons are priority successors, the person who succeeds to the contract is (or the persons who succeed to the contract are)—

(a) the priority successor (or successors) selected by agreement between the priority successors, or

(b) if they fail to agree (or fail to notify the landlord of an agreement) within a reasonable time, whichever of them the landlord selects.

(4) If all the persons are reserve successors, the person who succeeds to the contract is (or the persons who succeed to the contract are)—

(a) the person (or persons) selected by agreement between the reserve successors, or

(b) if they fail to agree (or fail to notify the landlord of an agreement) within a reasonable time, whichever of them the landlord selects.

(5) Where the landlord makes a selection under subsection (3)(b), a priority successor who is not selected may appeal to the court against the landlord's selection.

(6) Where the landlord makes a selection under subsection (4)(b), a reserve successor who is not selected may appeal to the court against the landlord's selection.

(7) An appeal under subsection (5) or (6) must be brought before the end of the period of four weeks starting with the day on which the landlord notifies the person that he or she has not been selected.

(8) The court must determine the appeal on the merits (and not by way of review).

III WAL [187]

79 Effect of succession

(1) A person who succeeds to an occupation contract under section 73(2) or sections 73(3) and 78(2) becomes the contract-holder on the relevant date.

(2) A person who succeeds (or persons who succeed) to an occupation contract under sections 73(3) and 78(3) or (4) becomes a contract-holder (or become contract-holders) on the later of—

(a) the relevant date, and

(b) the day agreement is reached or the landlord makes a selection.

(3) A person who succeeds (or persons who succeed) to an occupation contract after an appeal under section 78(5) or (6) against the landlord's selection becomes a contract-holder (or become contract-holders) on the later of—

(a) the relevant date, and
(b) the day on which the appeal is finally determined.

(4) The relevant date is the day on which the contract would have ended under section 155 if no one had been qualified to succeed to the contract.

(5) During the period beginning with the relevant date and ending with a person (or persons) becoming the contract-holder under subsection (2) or (3), the relevant successors?—

(a) are not to be treated as trespassers in relation to the dwelling, and
(b) for the purposes of any liability under the contract are to be treated as if they were joint contract-holders under the contract.

(6) "The relevant successors" are the persons who—

(a) are qualified to succeed the contract-holder who died, and
(b) are living in the dwelling.

III WAL [188]

80 Substitute succession on early termination

(1) This section applies where—

(a) a person ("S") succeeds to an occupation contract under section 78(2) (priority successors),
(b) before the end of the period of six months starting with the death of the preceding contract-holder, S gives notice under a contract-holder's notice provision that he or she intends to end the contract or agrees with the landlord that the contract should end, and
(c) apart from this section, the contract would end in accordance with the contract-holder's notice provision or the agreement.

(2) The contract does not end if one or more persons are qualified to succeed the preceding contract-holder.

(3) If one person is qualified to succeed the preceding contract-holder, that person succeeds to the contract.

(4) If more than one person is qualified to succeed the preceding contract-holder, the person identified in accordance with section 78(4) succeeds to the contract.

(5) Whether there is a person qualified to succeed the preceding contract-holder is to be determined by applying section 74 in relation to the preceding contract-holder; but S is to be treated as not qualified to succeed the preceding contract-holder.

(6) In this section—

"the preceding contract-holder" ("*y deiliad contract blaenorol*") is the contract-holder as a result of whose death S succeeded to the contract, and

"contract-holder's notice provision" ("*darpariaeth hysbysiad deiliad y contract*") means section 163 or 168 (contract-holder's notice to end secure contract or periodic standard contract) or a contract-holder's break clause (under a fixed term standard contract).

III WAL [189]

81 Effect of substitute succession

(1) A person who succeeds to an occupation contract under section 80(3) becomes the contract-holder on the relevant date.

(2) A person who succeeds (or persons who succeed) to an occupation contract under sections 80(4) and 78(4) becomes a contract-holder (or become contract-holders) under the contract on the later of—

(a) the relevant date, and
(b) the day agreement is reached or the landlord makes a selection.

(3) A person who succeeds (or persons who succeed) to an occupation contract after an appeal under section 78(6) against the landlord's selection becomes a contract-holder (or become contract-holders) on the later of—

(a) the relevant date, and

(b) the day on which the appeal is finally determined.

(4) The relevant date is the day on which, but for section 80(2), the contract would have ended.

(5) During the period beginning with the relevant date and ending with a person (or persons) becoming the contract-holder under subsection (2) or (3), the relevant successors?—

(a) are not to be treated as trespassers in relation to the dwelling, and

(b) for the purposes of any liability under the contract are to be treated as if they were joint contract-holders under the contract.

(6) "The relevant successors" are the persons who—

(a) are qualified to succeed the contract-holder who died (and as a result of whose death the succession under section 78(2)) occurred), and

(b) are living in the dwelling.

III WAL [190]

82 Notice of rights under section 80

(1) This section applies where the landlord under an occupation contract—

(a) receives notice under a contract-holder's notice provision, or

(b) agrees with the contract-holder to end the contract,

in the circumstances mentioned in section 80(1)(a) and (b).

(2) The landlord must, before the end of the period of 14 days starting with the day on which the landlord receives S's notice or (as the case may be) the day on which the agreement is made, give a notice to—

(a) the occupiers of the dwelling (other than S), and

(b) any potential successors not occupying the dwelling whose address is known to the landlord (or in the case of joint landlords, any one of them).

(3) A potential successor is a person qualified to succeed the preceding contract-holder under section 80.

(4) The notice must—

(a) state that S has given notice that he or she intends to end the contract or that S and the landlord have agreed to end the contract, and

(b) explain the effect of section 80.

III WAL [191]

83 Succession: interpretation

(1) This section applies for the purposes of interpreting this Act.

(2) A contract-holder is a priority or reserve successor in relation to an occupation contract if he or she succeeded to the contract as a priority or reserve successor of the contract-holder in relation to that occupation contract who died.

(3) If a contract-holder is a priority or reserve successor in relation to a fixed term standard contract, he or she is also a priority or reserve successor in relation to—

(a) any periodic standard contract which arises under section 184(2) at the end of the fixed term, and

(b) unless the contract provides otherwise, any contract under section 184(6).

(4) If a contract-holder is a priority or reserve successor in relation to an occupation contract which is ended under section 220 (abandonment), he or she is also a priority or reserve successor in relation to any occupation contract under which he or she becomes the contract-holder as a result of an order under section 222(3)(b) (provision of suitable alternative accommodation on appeal).

(5) A contract-holder to whom an occupation contract is transferred by, or in accordance with, a family property order is a priority or reserve successor in relation to the contract if the person from whom the contract was transferred was such a successor.

(6) A contract-holder is a priority or reserve successor in relation to an occupation contract if his or her being treated as a priority or reserve successor was a condition of consent to a transaction relating to the contract.

(7) Subsection (8) applies if, before the end of the period of six months starting with the day on which a secure contract ("the first contract") ends—

- (a) the contract-holder under the first contract becomes a contract-holder under another secure contract ("the second contract"), and
- (b) either the dwelling or the landlord are the same under the second contract as under the first contract.

(8) If the contract-holder was a priority or reserve successor in relation to the first contract he or she is also such a successor in relation to the second contract, unless the second contract provides otherwise.

CHAPTER 9 LANDLORD'S CONSENT

III WAL [192]

84 Landlord's consent: reasonableness

(1) This section applies in relation to any term of an occupation contract which permits something to be done only with the landlord's consent.

(2) The landlord may not—

- (a) unreasonably refuse consent, or
- (b) consent subject to unreasonable conditions.

(3) A request for the landlord's consent must be made in writing, and references in this section to a request are to a written request.

(4) The landlord may ask for information to enable the landlord to deal with a request; but the landlord may not do so after the end of the period of 14 days starting with the day on which the request is made.

(5) If the landlord asks for information which it is not reasonable to ask for, the landlord is to be treated as not having asked for that information.

(6) If the landlord does not give or refuse consent in writing before the end of the relevant period, the landlord is to be treated as having consented without conditions.

(7) The relevant period is the period of one month starting with the later of—

- (a) the day on which the request for consent is made, or
- (b) if the landlord asks for information in accordance with subsection (4), the day on which the information is provided.

(8) If the landlord consents subject to conditions, the landlord must give the contract-holder written notice of the conditions at the same time that consent is given; and if the landlord does not do so, the landlord is to be treated as having consented without conditions.

(9) If the landlord refuses consent or consents subject to conditions, the person who made the request may ask for a written statement of the landlord's reasons.

(10) If the landlord does not give a written statement of reasons before the end of the period of one month starting with the day on which the statement is asked for, the landlord is to be treated as having consented without conditions.

III WAL [193]

85 Application to court relating to consent

(1) This section applies where under section 84 the landlord gives a written statement of reasons for refusing consent or consenting subject to conditions.

(2) The person who made the request for consent may apply to the court on the ground that?—

- (a) the landlord's refusal of consent is unreasonable, or
- (b) one or more of the conditions imposed is unreasonable.

(3) If the court is satisfied that the ground in subsection (2)(a) is made out it may declare that the landlord unreasonably refused consent, and may also—

- (a) declare that the landlord is to be treated as having consented without conditions, or
- (b) direct the landlord to reconsider the request for consent.

(4) If the court is satisfied that the ground in subsection (2)(b) is made out it may declare that one or more of the conditions imposed is unreasonable, and may also—

- (a) declare that the landlord is to be treated as having consented without conditions or subject to those conditions that were not declared unreasonable, or
- (b) direct the landlord to reconsider the request for consent.

(5) If the court makes a declaration under subsection (3) or (4) it may make any other order it thinks fit.

III WAL [194]

86 Landlord's consent: timing

(1) Where a term of an occupation contract permits something to be done with the landlord's consent, the landlord may give consent after the thing has been done.

(2) But this does not apply to—

- (a) section 49 (adding a joint contract-holder), or
- (b) any term of the occupation contract permitting the transfer of the contract, or of a joint contract-holder's rights and obligations under the contract.

CHAPTER 10 COMPENSATION

III WAL [195]

87 Compensation for failures relating to provision of written statements etc

(1) The following sections set out the circumstances in which a landlord may be liable to pay compensation under this section—

- (a) section 35 (failure to provide a written statement under section 31);
- (b) section 36 (providing an incomplete written statement);
- (c) section 37 (providing an incorrect written statement);
- (d) section 40 (failure to provide information under section 39);
- (e) section 110 (failure to provide written statement of variation of secure contract);
- (f) section 129 (failure to provide written statement of variation of periodic standard contract);

(g) section 137 (failure to provide written statement of variation of fixed term standard contract).

(2) Where the landlord under an occupation contract is liable to pay compensation to the contract-holder under this section, the amount of compensation payable in respect of a particular day is equivalent to the amount of rent payable under the contract in respect of that day.

(3) If the contract provides for rent to be paid in respect of periods other than a day, the amount of rent payable in respect of a single day is the appropriate proportion of the rent payable in respect of the period in which that day falls.

(4) If compensation is payable because of section 35, 110, 129 or 137 (failure to provide statement), the contract-holder may apply to the court for an order increasing the amount of the compensation on the ground that the landlord's failure to provide a written statement was intentional.

(5) If compensation is payable because of section 36 or 37 (incomplete or incorrect statement), the contract-holder may apply to the court for an order increasing the amount of the compensation.

(6) On an application under subsection (4) or (5) the court may increase the amount of the compensation payable in respect of a particular day by such percentage, not exceeding 100 per cent, as it thinks fit.

III WAL [196]

88 Right of set off

(1) If the landlord under an occupation contract is liable to pay the contract-holder compensation under section 87, the contract-holder may set off that liability against rent.

(2) This section is a fundamental provision which is incorporated as a term of all occupation contracts.

PART 4
CONDITION OF DWELLING
CHAPTER 1 INTRODUCTORY

III WAL [197]

89 Application of Part

(1) Chapter 2 applies to all secure contracts, all periodic standard contracts, and all fixed term standard contracts made for a term of less than seven years (see section 90).

(2) Chapter 3 applies to all occupation contracts.

III WAL [198]

90 Fixed term standard contracts: determining the length of term

(1) This section applies for the purpose of determining the term for which a fixed term standard contract is made.

(2) If a fixed term standard contract is a tenancy, it is to be treated as made for a term commencing with the grant of the tenancy.

(3) If a fixed term standard contract is a licence, it is to be treated as made for a term commencing with the occupation date of the contract.

(4) A fixed term standard contract is to be treated as made for a term of less than seven years if it is determinable at the option of the landlord before the end of the period of seven years starting with the commencement of the term.

(5) If a fixed term standard contract confers on the contract-holder an option for renewal for a term which, together with the original term, amounts to seven years or more, it is not to be treated as made for a term of less than seven years (unless subsection (4) applies).

CHAPTER 2 CONDITION OF DWELLING

LANDLORD'S OBLIGATIONS AS TO CONDITION OF DWELLING

III WAL [199]

91 Landlord's obligation: fitness for human habitation

(1) The landlord under a secure contract, a periodic standard contract or a fixed term standard contract made for a term of less than seven years must ensure that the dwelling is fit for human habitation—

- (a) on the occupation date of the contract, and
- (b) for the duration of the contract.

(2) The reference in subsection (1) to the dwelling includes, if the dwelling forms part only of a building, the structure and exterior of the building and the common parts.

(3) This section is a fundamental provision which is incorporated as a term of all secure contracts, all periodic standard contracts, and all fixed term standard contracts made for a term of less than seven years.

III WAL [200]

92 Landlord's obligation to keep dwelling in repair

(1) The landlord under a secure contract, a periodic standard contract or a fixed term standard contract made for a term of less than seven years must—

- (a) keep in repair the structure and exterior of the dwelling (including drains, gutters and external pipes), and
- (b) keep in repair and proper working order the service installations in the dwelling.

(2) If the dwelling forms part only of a building, the landlord must—

- (a) keep in repair the structure and exterior of any other part of the building (including drains, gutters and external pipes) in which the landlord has an estate or interest, and
- (b) keep in repair and proper working order a service installation which directly or indirectly serves the dwelling, and which either—
  - (i) forms part of any part of the building in which the landlord has an estate or interest, or
  - (ii) is owned by the landlord or is under the landlord's control.

(3) The standard of repair required by subsections (1) and (2) is that which is reasonable having regard to the age and character of the dwelling, and the period during which the dwelling is likely to be available for occupation as a home.

(4) In this Part, "service installation" means an installation for the supply of water, gas or electricity, for sanitation, for space heating or for heating water.

(5) This section is a fundamental provision which is incorporated as a term of all secure contracts, all periodic standard contracts, and all fixed term standard contracts made for a term of less than seven years.

III WAL [201]

93 Obligations under sections 91 and 92: supplementary

(1) The landlord must make good any damage caused by works and repairs carried out in order to comply with the landlord's obligations under section 91 or 92.

(2) The landlord may not impose any obligation on the contract-holder in the event of the contract-holder's enforcing or relying on the landlord's obligations under section 91 or 92.

(3) This section is a fundamental provision which is incorporated as a term of all secure contracts, all periodic standard contracts, and all fixed term standard contracts made for a term of less than seven years.

III WAL [202]

94 Determination of fitness for human habitation

(1) The Welsh Ministers must prescribe matters and circumstances to which regard must be had when determining, for the purposes of section 91(1), whether a dwelling is fit for human habitation.

(2) In exercising the power in subsection (1), the Welsh Ministers may prescribe matters and circumstances—

- (a) by reference to any regulations made by the Welsh Ministers under section 2 of the Housing Act 2004 (c 34) (meaning of "category 1 hazard" and "category 2 hazard");
- (b) which may arise because of a failure to comply with an obligation under section 92.

(3) The Welsh Ministers may by regulations—

- (a) impose requirements on landlords for the purpose of preventing any matters or circumstances which may cause a dwelling to be unfit for human habitation from arising;
- (b) prescribe that if requirements imposed under paragraph (a) are not complied with in respect of a dwelling, the dwelling is to be treated as if it were unfit for human habitation.

LIMITS ON LANDLORD'S OBLIGATIONS UNDER THIS CHAPTER

III WAL [203]

95 Limits on sections 91 and 92: general

(1) Section 91(1) does not impose any liability on a landlord in respect of a dwelling which the landlord cannot make fit for human habitation at reasonable expense.

(2) Sections 91(1) and 92(1) do not require the landlord—

- (a) to keep in repair anything which the contract-holder is entitled to remove from the dwelling, or
- (b) to rebuild or reinstate the dwelling or any part of it, in the case of destruction or damage by a relevant cause.

(3) If the dwelling forms part only of a building, sections 91(1) and 92(2) do not require the landlord to rebuild or reinstate any other part of the building in which the landlord has an estate or interest, in the case of destruction or damage by a relevant cause.

(4) Relevant causes are fire, storm, flood or other inevitable accident.

(5) Section 92(2) does not require the landlord to carry out works or repairs unless the disrepair or failure to keep in proper working order affects the contract-holder's enjoyment of—

- (a) the dwelling, or

(b) the common parts that the contract-holder is entitled to use under the occupation contract.

(6) This section is a fundamental provision which is incorporated as a term of all secure contracts, all periodic standard contracts, and all fixed term standard contracts made for a term of less than seven years.

III WAL [204]

96 Limits on sections 91 and 92: contract-holder's fault

(1) Section 91(1) does not impose any liability on the landlord if the dwelling is unfit for human habitation wholly or mainly because of an act or omission (including an act or omission amounting to lack of care) of the contract-holder or a permitted occupier of the dwelling.

(2) The landlord is not obliged by section 92(1) or (2) to carry out works or repairs if the disrepair, or the failure of a service installation to be in working order, is wholly or mainly attributable to lack of care by the contract-holder or a permitted occupier of the dwelling.

(3) "Lack of care" means a failure to take proper care—

(a) of the dwelling, or

(b) if the dwelling forms part only of a building, of the common parts that the contract-holder is entitled to use under the occupation contract.

(4) This section is a fundamental provision which is incorporated as a term of all secure contracts, all periodic standard contracts, and all fixed term standard contracts made for a term of less than seven years.

III WAL [205]

97 Limits on sections 91 and 92: notice

(1) The landlord's obligations under sections 91(1)(b) and 92(1) and (2) do not arise until the landlord (or in the case of joint landlords, any one of them) becomes aware that works or repairs are necessary.

(2) The landlord complies with the obligations under those provisions if the landlord carries out the necessary works or repairs within a reasonable time after the day on which the landlord becomes aware that they are necessary.

(3) Subsection (4) applies if—

(a) the landlord (the "old landlord") transfers the old landlord's interest in the dwelling to another person (the "new landlord"), and

(b) the old landlord (or where two or more persons jointly constitute the old landlord, any one of them) is aware before the date of the transfer that works or repairs are necessary in order to comply with section 91(1) or 92(1) or (2).

(4) The new landlord is to be treated as becoming aware of the need for those works or repairs on the date of the transfer, but not before.

(5) This section is a fundamental provision which is incorporated as a term of all secure contracts, all periodic standard contracts, and all fixed term standard contracts made for a term of less than seven years.

Access to Dwellings and Rights of Permitted Occupiers

III WAL [206]

98 Landlord's right to access dwelling

(1) The landlord may enter the dwelling at any reasonable time for the purpose of—

(a) inspecting its condition and state of repair, or

(b) carrying out works or repairs needed in order to comply with section 91 or 92.

(2) The landlord must give at least 24 hours' notice to the contract-holder before exercising that right.

(3) Subsection (4) applies where—

(a) the dwelling forms part only of a building, and

(b) in order to comply with section 91 or 92 the landlord needs to carry out works or repairs in another part of the building.

(4) The landlord is not liable for failing to comply with section 91 or 92 if the landlord does not have sufficient rights over that other part of the building to be able to carry out the works or repairs, and was unable to obtain such rights after making a reasonable effort to do so.

(5) This section is a fundamental provision which is incorporated as a term of all secure contracts, all periodic standard contracts, and all fixed term standard contracts made for a term of less than seven years.

III WAL [207]

99 Rights of permitted occupiers to enforce Chapter

(1) A permitted occupier who suffers personal injury, or loss of or damage to personal property, as a result of the landlord failing to comply with section 91 or 92 may enforce the section in question in his or her own right by bringing proceedings in respect of the injury, loss or damage.

(2) But a permitted occupier who is a lodger or sub-holder may do so only if the lodger is allowed to live in the dwelling, or the sub-occupation contract is made, in accordance with the occupation contract.

(3) This section is a fundamental provision which is incorporated as a term of all secure contracts, periodic standard contracts, and fixed term standard contracts made for a term of less than seven years.

CHAPTER 3 MISCELLANEOUS

III WAL [208]

100 Specific performance

(1) In any proceedings for breach of a repairing obligation under an occupation contract, the court may order specific performance of the obligation despite any equitable rule limiting the availability of that remedy.

(2) Repairing obligations are—

(a) obligations to repair (or keep or deliver up in repair), or to maintain, renew, construct or replace any property, and

(b) obligations to keep any dwelling fit for human habitation however expressed,

and include a landlord's obligations under sections 91 and 92.

III WAL [209]

101 Waste and tenant-like user

(1) The contract-holder under an occupation contract is not liable for waste in respect of the dwelling.

(2) The rule of law under which a tenant has an implied duty to use demised premises in a tenant-like manner does not apply to a contract-holder if the tenancy is an occupation contract.

PART 5
PROVISIONS APPLYING ONLY TO SECURE CONTRACTS

CHAPTER 1 OVERVIEW

III WAL [210]

102 Overview of Part

(1) Chapters 1 to 5 of this Part apply only to secure contracts, and address—

- (a) variation of secure contracts,
- (b) withdrawal of joint contract-holders,
- (c) dealing (that is, taking a lodger and transferring the contract), and
- (d) the imposition of prohibited conduct standard contracts (where the landlord is a community landlord or registered charity).

(2) Chapter 6 contains a fundamental provision about transfer of a secure contract to a person who is a contract-holder under another secure contract; this fundamental provision is applicable to secure contracts under which the landlord is a community landlord.

CHAPTER 2 VARIATION OF CONTRACTS

III WAL [211]

103 Variation

(1) A secure contract may not be varied except—

- (a) in accordance with sections 104 to 107, or
- (b) by or as a result of an enactment.

(2) A variation of a secure contract (other than by or as a result of any enactment) must be in accordance with section 108.

(3) This section is a fundamental provision which is incorporated as a term of all secure contracts; section 20 provides that subsections (1)(b) and (2) of this section—

- (a) must be incorporated, and
- (b) must not be incorporated with modifications.

III WAL [212]

104 Variation of rent

(1) The landlord may vary the rent payable under a secure contract by giving the contract-holder a notice setting out a new rent to take effect on the date specified in the notice.

(2) The period between the day on which the notice is given to the contract-holder and the specified date may not be less than two months.

(3) Subject to that—

- (a) the first notice may specify any date, and
- (b) subsequent notices must specify a date which is not less than one year after the last date on which a new rent took effect.

(4) This section is a fundamental provision which is incorporated as a term of all secure contracts under which rent is payable.

III WAL [213]

105 Variation of other consideration

(1) Where consideration other than rent is payable under a secure contract, the amount of consideration may be varied—

- (a) by agreement between the landlord and the contract-holder, or

(b) by the landlord in accordance with subsections (2) to (4).

(2) The landlord may give the contract-holder a notice setting out a new amount of consideration to take effect on the date specified in the notice.

(3) The period between the day on which the notice is given to the contract-holder and the specified date may not be less than two months.

(4) Subject to that—

(a) the first notice may specify any date, and

(b) subsequent notices must specify a date which is not less than one year after the last date on which a new amount of consideration took effect.

(5) This section is a fundamental provision which is incorporated as a term of all secure contracts under which consideration other than rent is payable.

III WAL [214]

106 Variation of fundamental terms

(1) A fundamental term of a secure contract may be varied by agreement between the landlord and the contract-holder (subject to section 108).

(2) This section is a fundamental provision which is incorporated as a term of all secure contracts.

III WAL [215]

107 Variation of supplementary and additional terms

(1) A supplementary or additional term of a secure contract may be varied (subject to section 108)—

(a) by agreement between the landlord and the contract-holder, or

(b) by the landlord giving a notice of variation to the contract-holder.

(2) Before giving a notice of variation the landlord must give the contract-holder a preliminary notice—

(a) informing the contract-holder that the landlord intends to give a notice of variation,

(b) specifying the proposed variation and informing the contract-holder of its nature and effect, and

(c) inviting the contract-holder to comment on the proposed variation within the time specified in the notice.

(3) The specified time must give the contract-holder a reasonable opportunity to comment.

(4) The notice of variation must specify the variation effected by it and the date on which the variation takes effect.

(5) The period between the day on which the notice of variation is given to the contract-holder and the date on which the variation takes effect may not be less than one month.

(6) When giving a notice of variation the landlord must also provide the contract-holder with such information as the landlord considers necessary to inform the contract-holder of the nature and effect of the variation.

(7) This section is a fundamental provision which is incorporated as a term of all secure contracts.

III WAL [216]

108 Limitation on variation

(1) A fundamental term of a secure contract incorporating any of the fundamental provisions to which subsection (2) applies may not be varied (except by or as a result of an enactment).

(2) This subsection applies to the following fundamental provisions—

(a) section 103(1)(b) and (2) and this section,

(b) section 45 (requirement to use deposit scheme),
(c) section 52 (joint contract-holder ceasing to be a party to the occupation contract),
(d) section 55 (anti-social behaviour and other prohibited conduct),
(e) section 148 (permissible termination),
(f) section 149 (possession claims),
(g) section 155 (death of sole contract-holder), and
(h) section 158 (securing contract by use of false statement).

(3) A variation of any other fundamental term (other than by or as a result of an enactment) is of no effect—

(a) unless as a result of the variation—
(i) the fundamental provision which the term incorporates would be incorporated without modification, or
(ii) the fundamental provision which the term incorporates would not be incorporated or would be incorporated with modification, but in the contract-holder's opinion the effect of this would be that the position of the contract-holder is improved;

(b) if the variation (regardless of whether it is within paragraph (a)) would render the fundamental term incompatible with a fundamental term which incorporates a fundamental provision to which subsection (2) applies.

(4) A variation of a term of a secure contract is of no effect if it would render any term of the contract incompatible with a fundamental term (unless that fundamental term is also varied in accordance with this section in a way that would avoid the incompatibility).

(5) Subsection (4) does not apply to a variation made by or as a result of an enactment.

(6) This section is a fundamental provision which is incorporated as a term of all secure contracts; section 20 provides that this section—
(a) must be incorporated, and
(b) must not be incorporated with modifications.

III WAL [217]

109 Written statement of variation

(1) If a secure contract is varied in accordance with the contract or by or as a result of an enactment the landlord must, before the end of the relevant period, give the contract-holder—
(a) a written statement of the term or terms varied, or
(b) a written statement of the occupation contract as varied,

unless the landlord has given notice of the variation in accordance with section 104, 105(2) to (4) or 107(1)(b) and (2) to (6).

(2) The relevant period is the period of 14 days starting with the day on which the contract is varied.

(3) The landlord may not charge a fee for providing a written statement under subsection (1).

(4) This section is a fundamental provision which is incorporated as a term of all secure contracts.

III WAL [218]

110 Failure to provide written statement etc

(1) If the landlord fails to comply with a requirement under section 109 the landlord is liable to pay the contract-holder compensation under section 87.

(2) The compensation is payable in respect of the relevant date and every day after the relevant date until—

(a) the day on which the landlord gives the contract-holder a written statement of the term or terms varied, or of the contract as varied, or

(b) if earlier, the last day of the period of two months starting with the relevant date.

(3) Interest on the compensation is payable if the landlord fails to give the contract-holder a written statement on or before the day referred to in subsection (2)(b).

(4) The interest starts to run on the day referred to in subsection (2)(b) at the rate prevailing under section 6 of the Late Payment of Commercial Debts (Interest) Act 1998 (c 20) at the end of that day.

(5) The relevant date is the day on which the contract was varied.

(6) Subsections (1) to (5) do not apply if the landlord's failure to comply with the requirement is attributable to an act or omission of the contract-holder.

(7) If under section 109 the landlord gives the contract-holder a written statement of the contract as varied, sections 36 and 37 (incomplete and incorrect statements) apply to the statement as if references in those sections to the relevant date were to the day on which the contract was varied.

CHAPTER 3 JOINT CONTRACT-HOLDERS: WITHDRAWAL

III WAL [219]

111 Withdrawal

(1) A joint contract-holder under a secure contract may withdraw from the contract by giving a notice (a "withdrawal notice") to the landlord.

(2) The withdrawal notice must specify the date on which the joint contract-holder intends to cease to be a party to the contract (the "withdrawal date").

(3) The joint contract-holder must give a written warning to the other joint contract-holders when he or she gives the withdrawal notice to the landlord; and a copy of the withdrawal notice must be attached to the warning.

(4) The landlord must give a written warning to the other joint contract-holders as soon as reasonably practicable after the landlord receives the withdrawal notice; and a copy of the withdrawal notice must be attached to the warning.

(5) The joint contract-holder ceases to be a party to the contract on the withdrawal date.

(6) A notice given to the landlord by one or more (but not all) of the joint contract-holders that purports to be a notice under section 163 (contract-holder's notice to end contract) is to be treated as a withdrawal notice, and the date specified in the notice is to be treated as the withdrawal date.

(7) Subsection (3) does not apply to a notice which is treated as a withdrawal notice because of subsection (6).

(8) This section is a fundamental provision which is incorporated as a term of all secure contracts.

III WAL [220]

112 Withdrawal: power to prescribe time limits

The Welsh Ministers must prescribe supplementary provisions specifying a minimum time period between the date on which a notice under section 111 is given to the landlord, and the date specified in the notice.

CHAPTER 4 DEALING

Lodgers

III WAL [221]

113 Lodgers

(1) The contract-holder under a secure contract may allow persons to live in the dwelling as lodgers.

(2) This section is a fundamental provision which is incorporated as a term of all secure contracts.

Transfers

III WAL [222]

114 Transfer to potential successor

(1) The contract-holder under a secure contract may transfer the contract as described in this section, but only if the landlord consents.

(2) The contract-holder may transfer the contract to—

- (a) a potential successor, or
- (b) if there are two or more potential successors, all of the potential successors who wish to be included in the transfer.

(3) If there is a sole contract-holder a potential successor is a person who, under section 74, would be qualified to succeed the contract-holder if the contract-holder died immediately before the transfer.

(4) If there are joint contract-holders a potential successor is a person who, under section 74, would be qualified to succeed a joint contract-holder if—

- (a) the joint contract-holder died immediately before the transfer, and
- (b) when the joint contract-holder died he or she was the sole contract-holder.

(5) This section is a fundamental provision which is incorporated as a term of all secure contracts.

III WAL [223]

115 Transfer to a potential successor: landlord's consent

Where a landlord refuses consent or consents subject to conditions to a transfer described in section 114, what is reasonable for the purposes of section 84 (landlord's consent) is to be determined having regard to Schedule 6.

CHAPTER 5 PROHIBITED CONDUCT STANDARD CONTRACTS

III WAL [224]

116 Order imposing periodic standard contract because of prohibited conduct

(1) If the landlord under a secure contract is a community landlord or a registered charity, the landlord may apply to the court for an order under this section on the ground that the contract-holder is in breach of section 55 (anti-social behaviour and other prohibited conduct).

(2) The effect of an order under this section is—

- (a) to end the secure contract from a date specified in the order, and
- (b) if the contract-holder remains in occupation after the specified date, to create a periodic standard contract whose occupation date is the date

specified in the order (and which is a periodic standard contract until the end of the probationary period).

(3) The court may make an order under this section only if it is satisfied that—

(a) the contract-holder is in breach of section 55,

(b) it would have made an order for possession on the ground in section 157 (breach of contract) in reliance only on that breach,

(c) the landlord will make available to the contract-holder a programme of social support the aim of which is the prevention of prohibited conduct, and

(d) it is reasonable to make the order.

(4) The Welsh Ministers may issue guidance as to the activities and services (including assistance, advice and counselling services) that may be included in a programme of social support for the purposes of subsection (3).

(5) Schedule 7 makes provision about probation periods, the procedure for obtaining an order under this section, and about the terms of a periodic standard contract created under this section.

(6) In this Act "prohibited conduct standard contract" means a contract which is a periodic standard contract created because of an order under this section, and in relation to which the probation period has not yet ended.

III WAL [225]

117 Conversion to secure contract

(1) A periodic standard contract which arose because of an order under section 116 and which subsists at the end of the probation period—

(a) ends at the end of the probation period, and

(b) is replaced with a secure contract that has an occupation date falling immediately after that period ends.

(2) But subsection (1) does not apply if the probation period ends because of paragraph 3(9) of Schedule 7.

(3) Schedule 7 makes provision about the terms of a secure contract which arises at the end of a probation period.

CHAPTER 6 PROVISIONS APPLYING ONLY TO SECURE CONTRACTS WITH COMMUNITY LANDLORDS

III WAL [226]

118 Transfer to another secure contract-holder

(1) The contract-holder under a secure contract under which the landlord is a community landlord may transfer the contract as described in this section, but only if the landlord consents.

(2) The contract-holder may transfer the contract to a person who—

(a) before the transfer is a contract-holder under a secure contract under which the landlord is a community landlord, and

(b) immediately before the transfer will cease to be the contract-holder under the contract mentioned in paragraph (a).

(3) This section is a fundamental provision which is incorporated as a term of all secure contracts under which the landlord is a community landlord.

WALES

III WAL [227]

119 Transfer to another secure contract-holder: landlord's consent
Where a landlord refuses consent or consents subject to conditions to a transfer described in section 118, what is reasonable for the purposes of section 84 (landlord's consent) is to be determined having regard to Schedule 6.

PART 6
PROVISIONS APPLYING ONLY TO PERIODIC STANDARD CONTRACTS

CHAPTER 1 OVERVIEW

III WAL [228]

120 Overview of Part
This Part applies only to periodic standard contracts, and addresses—
- (a) exclusion of the contract-holder from the dwelling for specified periods,
- (b) variation of periodic standard contracts, and
- (c) withdrawal of joint contract-holders.

CHAPTER 2 EXCLUSION FOR SPECIFIED PERIODS

III WAL [229]

121 Exclusion of contract-holder from dwelling for specified periods
(1) A periodic standard contract may provide that the contract-holder is not entitled to occupy the dwelling as a home for such periods as are specified in the contract.
(2) The contract may specify periods for the purpose of subsection (1) by reference to any matters reasonably ascertainable by the contract-holder (as well as by reference to specified dates).

CHAPTER 3 VARIATION OF CONTRACTS

III WAL [230]

122 Variation
(1) A periodic standard contract may not be varied except—
- (a) in accordance with sections 123 to 126, or
- (b) by or as a result of an enactment.

(2) A variation of a periodic standard contract (other than by or as a result of an enactment) must be in accordance with section 127.
(3) This section is a fundamental provision which is incorporated as a term of all periodic standard contracts; section 20 provides that subsections (1)(b) and (2) of this section—
- (a) must be incorporated, and
- (b) must not be incorporated with modifications.

III WAL [231]

123 Variation of rent
(1) The landlord may vary the rent payable under a periodic standard contract by giving the contract-holder a notice setting out a new rent to take effect on the date specified in the notice.

(2) The period between the day on which the notice is given to the contract-holder and the specified date may not be less than two months.

(3) Subject to that—

(a) the first notice may specify any date, and

(b) subsequent notices must specify a date which is not less than one year after the last date on which a new rent took effect.

(4) This section is a fundamental provision which is incorporated as a term of all periodic standard contracts under which rent is payable.

III WAL [232]

124 Variation of other consideration

(1) Where consideration other than rent is payable under a periodic standard contract, the amount of consideration may be varied—

(a) by agreement between the landlord and the contract-holder, or

(b) by the landlord in accordance with subsections (2) to (4).

(2) The landlord may give the contract-holder a notice setting out a new amount of consideration to take effect on the date specified in the notice.

(3) The period between the day on which the notice is given to the contract-holder and the specified date may not be less than two months.

(4) Subject to that—

(a) the first notice may specify any date, and

(b) subsequent notices must specify a date which is not less than one year after the last date on which a new amount of consideration took effect.

(5) This section is a fundamental provision which is incorporated as a term of all periodic standard contracts under which consideration other than rent is payable.

III WAL [233]

125 Variation of other terms

(1) The fundamental terms, supplementary terms and additional terms of a periodic standard contract may be varied (subject to section 127)—

(a) by agreement between the landlord and the contract-holder, or

(b) by the landlord in accordance with section 126.

(2) This section is a fundamental provision which is incorporated as a term of all periodic standard contracts; but subsection (1)(b) is not incorporated as a term of a periodic standard contract which does not incorporate section 173 (landlord's notice to end contract).

III WAL [234]

126 Variation by landlord of other terms: notice procedure

(1) The landlord may give the contract-holder notice that unless the contract-holder consents to a variation of the contract under section 125, the landlord will make a possession claim on the ground in section 178 (landlord's notice).

(2) But the landlord may not give notice under subsection (1) at any time when the landlord is prevented from giving the contract-holder notice under section 173 (landlord's notice to end contract) by section 175 (notice may not be given during first four months of occupation), section 176 (breach of information requirements) or section 177 (breach of security or deposit requirements).

(3) A notice under subsection (1) must—

(a) specify the nature of the variation and the date on which the variation is to take effect, and

(b) inform the contract-holder that the notice also has effect as a notice under section 173 (landlord's notice to end contract).

(4) The date specified as the date on which the variation is to take effect may not be less than two months after the day on which the notice is given to the contract-holder.

(5) If the contract-holder does not give written consent to the variation on or before the date on which it is to take effect, the landlord may make a possession claim on the ground in section 178 (landlord's notice).

(6) If the landlord satisfies the requirements of this section, the landlord is to be treated for the purposes of making the possession claim as having given notice to end the contract under section 173 (and section 179(1)(a) is to be read as if it referred to the date specified in the notice in accordance with subsection (3)(a) of this section).

(7) This section is a fundamental provision which is incorporated as a term of all periodic standard contracts, except periodic standard contracts which do not incorporate section 173 (landlord's notice to end contract).

III WAL [235]

127 Limitation on variation

(1) A fundamental term of a periodic standard contract incorporating any of the fundamental provisions to which subsection (2) applies may not be varied (except by or as a result of an enactment).

(2) This subsection applies to the following fundamental provisions—

- (a) section 122(1)(b) and (2) and this section,
- (b) section 45 (requirement to use deposit scheme) and section 177 (breach of deposit requirements),
- (c) section 52 (joint contract-holder ceasing to be a party to the occupation contract),
- (d) section 55 (anti-social behaviour and other prohibited conduct),
- (e) section 148 (permissible termination),
- (f) section 149 (possession claims),
- (g) section 155 (death of sole contract-holder),
- (h) section 158 (securing contract by use of false statement),
- (i) section 175 (restriction on giving landlord's notice under a periodic standard contract during first four months of occupation), and
- (j) paragraph 7 of Schedule 4 (variation of secure contract addressed in written statement of introductory standard contract).

(3) A variation of any other fundamental term (other than by or as a result of an enactment) is of no effect—

- (a) unless as a result of the variation—
  - (i) the fundamental provision which the term incorporates would be incorporated without modification, or
  - (ii) the fundamental provision which the term incorporates would not be incorporated or would be incorporated with modification, but in the contract-holder's opinion the effect of this would be that the position of the contract-holder is improved;
- (b) if the variation (regardless of whether it is within paragraph (a)) would render the fundamental term incompatible with a fundamental term which incorporates a fundamental provision to which subsection (2) applies.

(4) A variation of a term of a periodic standard contract is of no effect if it would render a term of the contract incompatible with a fundamental term (unless that fundamental term is also varied in accordance with this section in a way that would avoid the incompatibility).

(5) Subsection (4) does not apply to a variation made by or as a result of an enactment.

(6) This section is a fundamental provision which is incorporated as a term of all periodic standard contracts; section 20 provides that this section—

(a) must be incorporated, and

(b) must not be incorporated with modifications.

III WAL [236]

128 Written statement of variation

(1) If a periodic standard contract is varied in accordance with the contract or by or as a result of an enactment the landlord must, before the end of the relevant period, give the contract-holder—

(a) a written statement of the term or terms varied, or

(b) a written statement of the contract as varied,

unless the landlord has given notice of the variation in accordance with section 123, 124(2) to (4) or 126(1) to (4).

(2) The relevant period is the period of 14 days starting with the day on which the contract is varied.

(3) The landlord may not charge a fee for providing a written statement under subsection (1).

(4) This section is a fundamental provision which is incorporated as a term of all periodic standard contracts.

III WAL [237]

129 Failure to provide written statement etc

(1) If the landlord under a periodic standard contract fails to comply with a requirement under section 128 the landlord is liable to pay the contract-holder compensation under section 87.

(2) The compensation is payable in respect of the relevant date and every day after the relevant date until—

(a) the day on which the landlord gives the contract-holder a written statement of the term or terms varied, or of the contract as varied, or

(b) if earlier, the last day of the period of two months starting with the relevant date.

(3) Interest on the compensation is payable if the landlord fails to give the contract-holder a written statement on or before the day referred to in subsection (2)(b).

(4) The interest starts to run on the day referred to in subsection (2)(b) at the rate prevailing under section 6 of the Late Payment of Commercial Debts (Interest) Act 1998 (c 20) at the end of that day.

(5) The relevant date is the day on which the contract was varied.

(6) Subsections (1) to (5) do not apply if the landlord's failure to comply with the requirement is attributable to an act or omission of the contract-holder.

(7) If under section 128 the landlord gives the contract-holder a written statement of the contract as varied, sections 36 and 37 (incomplete and incorrect statements) apply to the statement as if references in those sections to the relevant date were to the day on which the contract was varied.

CHAPTER 4 JOINT CONTRACT-HOLDERS: WITHDRAWAL

III WAL [238]

130 Withdrawal

(1) A joint contract-holder under a periodic standard contract may withdraw from the contract by giving a notice (a "withdrawal notice") to the landlord.

(2) The withdrawal notice must specify the date on which the joint contract-holder intends to cease to be a party to the contract (the "withdrawal date").

(3) The joint contract-holder must give a written warning to the other joint contract-holders when he or she gives the withdrawal notice to the landlord; and a copy of the withdrawal notice must be attached to the warning.

(4) The landlord must give a written warning to the other joint contract-holders as soon as reasonably practicable after the landlord receives the withdrawal notice; and a copy of the withdrawal notice must be attached to the warning.

(5) The joint contract-holder ceases to be a party to the contract on the withdrawal date.

(6) A notice given to the landlord by one or more (but not all) of the joint contract-holders that purports to be a notice under section 168 (contract-holder's notice to end contract) is to be treated as a withdrawal notice, and the date specified in the notice is to be treated as the withdrawal date.

(7) Subsection (3) does not apply to a notice which is treated as a withdrawal notice because of subsection (6).

(8) This section is a fundamental provision which is incorporated as a term of all periodic standard contracts.

III WAL [239]

131 Withdrawal: power to prescribe time limits

The Welsh Ministers must prescribe supplementary provisions specifying a minimum time period between the date on which a notice under section 130 is given to the landlord, and the date specified in the notice.

PART 7
PROVISIONS APPLYING ONLY TO FIXED TERM STANDARD CONTRACTS

CHAPTER 1 OVERVIEW

III WAL [240]

132 Overview of Part

This Part applies only to fixed term standard contracts, and addresses—

(a) exclusion of the contract-holder from the dwelling for specified periods,

(b) variation of fixed term standard contracts,

(c) withdrawal of joint contract-holders from certain fixed term standard contracts, and

(d) dealing (that is, transfers).

CHAPTER 2 EXCLUSION FOR SPECIFIED PERIODS

III WAL [241]

133 Exclusion of contract-holder from dwelling for specified periods

(1) A fixed term standard contract may provide that the contract-holder is not entitled to occupy the dwelling as a home for such periods as are specified in the contract.

(2) The contract may specify periods for the purpose of subsection (1) by reference to any matters reasonably ascertainable by the contract-holder (as well as by reference to specified dates).

CHAPTER 3 VARIATION OF CONTRACTS

III WAL [242]

134 Variation

(1) A fixed term standard contract may not be varied except—

(a) by agreement between the landlord and the contract-holder, or

(b) by or as a result of an enactment.

(2) A variation of a fixed term standard contract (other than by or as a result of an enactment) must be in accordance with section 135.

(3) This section is a fundamental provision which is incorporated as a term of all fixed term standard contracts; section 20 provides that subsections (1)(b) and (2) of this section—

(a) must be incorporated, and

(b) must not be incorporated with modifications.

III WAL [243]

135 Limitation on variation

(1) A fundamental term of a fixed term standard contract which incorporates any of the fundamental provisions to which subsection (2) applies may not be varied (other than by or as a result of an enactment).

(2) This subsection applies to the following fundamental provisions—

(a) section 134(1)(b) and (2) and this section,

(b) section 45 (requirement to use deposit scheme),

(c) section 52 (joint contract-holder ceasing to be a party to the occupation contract),

(d) section 55 (anti-social behaviour and other prohibited conduct),

(e) section 148 (permissible termination),

(f) section 149 (possession claims),

(g) section 155 (death of sole contract-holder),

(h) section 158 (securing contract by use of false statement),

(i) section 186(2) and (4) (restriction on ending fixed term standard contract during first six months of occupation),

(j) section 196 (restriction on use of landlord's break clause in a fixed term standard contract during first four months of occupation), and

(k) section 198 (breach of deposit requirements: contracts with a landlord's break clause).

(3) A variation of any other fundamental term (other than by or as a result of an enactment) is of no effect—

(a) unless as a result of the variation—

(i) the fundamental provision which the term incorporates would be incorporated without modification, or

(ii) the fundamental provision which the term incorporates would not be incorporated or would be incorporated with modification, but in the contract-holder's opinion the effect of this would be that the position of the contract-holder is improved;

(b) if the variation (regardless of whether it is within paragraph (a)) would render the fundamental term incompatible with a fundamental term which incorporates a fundamental provision to which subsection (2) applies.

(4) A variation of a term of a fixed term standard contract is of no effect if it would render a term of the contract incompatible with a fundamental term (unless that fundamental term is also varied in accordance with this section in a way that would avoid the incompatibility).

WALES

(5) Subsection (4) does not apply to a variation made by or as a result of an enactment.

(6) This section is a fundamental provision which is incorporated as a term of all fixed term standard contracts, but subsection (2)(k) is not incorporated as a term of a contract which does not have a contract-holder's break clause; section 20 provides that this section—

- (a) must be incorporated, and
- (b) must not be incorporated with modifications.

III WAL [244

136 Written statement of variation

(1) If a fixed term standard contract is varied in accordance with the contract or by or as a result of an enactment the landlord must, before the end of the relevant period, give the contract-holder—

- (a) a written statement of the term or terms varied, or
- (b) a written statement of the contract as varied.

(2) The relevant period is the period of 14 days starting with the day on which the contract is varied.

(3) The landlord may not charge a fee for providing a written statement under subsection (1).

(4) This section is a fundamental provision which is incorporated as a term of all fixed term standard contracts.

III WAL [245]

137 Failure to provide written statement etc

(1) If the landlord under a fixed term standard contract fails to comply with a requirement under section 136 the landlord is liable to pay the contract-holder compensation under section 87.

(2) The compensation is payable in respect of the relevant date and every day after the relevant date until—

- (a) the day on which the landlord gives the contract-holder a written statement of the term or terms varied, or of the contract as varied, or
- (b) if earlier, the last day of the period of two months starting with the relevant date.

(3) Interest on the compensation is payable if the landlord fails to give the contract-holder a written statement on or before the day referred to in subsection (2)(b).

(4) The interest starts to run on the day referred to in subsection (2)(b), at the rate prevailing under section 6 of the Late Payment of Commercial Debts (Interest) Act 1998 (c 20) at the end of that day.

(5) The relevant date is the day on which the contract was varied.

(6) Subsections (1) to (5) do not apply if the landlord's failure to comply with the requirement is attributable to an act or omission of the contract-holder.

(7) If under section 136 the landlord gives the contract-holder a written statement of the contract as varied, sections 36 and 37 (incomplete and incorrect statements) apply to the statement as if references in those sections to the relevant date were to the day on which the contract was varied.

CHAPTER 4 JOINT CONTRACT-HOLDERS: WITHDRAWAL

III WAL [246]

138 Withdrawal of joint contract-holder using contract-holder's break clause

(1) If a fixed term standard contract contains a contract-holder's break clause, it may provide that if there are joint contract-holders, a notice given to the landlord by one or more (but not all) of them that purports to be a notice under the break clause is to be treated as a notice that the joint contract-holder intends (or the joint contract-holders intend) to withdraw from the contract ("a withdrawal notice").

(2) If it does so, it must also make provision equivalent to subsections (4) and (5) of sections 111 and 130.

CHAPTER 5 DEALING: TRANSFERS

Sole Contract-Holder

III WAL [247]

139 Transfer on death of sole contract-holder

(1) A fixed term standard contract may provide that on the death of a sole contract-holder, the contract may be transferred in the course of the administration of the contract-holder's estate.

(2) Section 73 (right to succeed) does not apply to a fixed term standard contract that contains such provision.

(3) Section 155 (termination of contract on death) is not incorporated as a term of a fixed term standard contract that contains such provision.

Joint Contract-Holders

III WAL [248]

140 Forced transfers

(1) A fixed term standard contract may provide that if there are joint contract-holders, one or more of them may require the other joint contract-holder or joint contract-holders to join in a transfer of the contract in accordance with the contract.

(2) If the contract contains such provision, the joint contract-holder or joint contract-holders wishing to transfer the occupation contract may apply to the court for an order that the other joint contract-holder or joint contract-holders join in the transfer.

(3) The court may make the order applied for if it thinks fit.

III WAL [249]

141 Joint contract-holder's interest

(1) This section applies if a fixed term standard contract provides that a joint contract-holder may transfer his or her rights and obligations under the contract.

(2) The contract must also provide that a transfer may not be made unless the transferor gives notice to the other joint contract-holders that a transfer will be made.

(3) The contract must also provide that the transferee is not entitled to occupy the dwelling without the consent of the other joint contract-holders.

III WAL [250]

142 Transfer on death of joint contract-holder

(1) This section applies if a fixed term standard contract provides that on the death of a joint contract-holder his or her rights and obligations under the contract may be transferred in the course of the administration of his or her estate.

(2) The contract must also provide that a transfer may not be made unless the joint contract-holder gives notice to the other joint contract-holders before his or her death that such a transfer will be made.

(3) The contract must also provide that the transferee is not entitled to occupy the dwelling without the consent of the other joint contract-holders.

PART 8
SUPPORTED STANDARD CONTRACTS

III WAL [251]

143 Supported standard contract and supported accommodation

(1) In this Act "supported standard contract" means a standard contract which relates to supported accommodation.

(2) For the purposes of this Act accommodation is "supported accommodation" if—

- (a) it is provided by a community landlord or a registered charity,
- (b) the landlord or charity (or a person acting on behalf of the landlord or charity) provides support services to a person entitled to occupy the accommodation, and
- (c) there is a connection between provision of the accommodation and provision of the support services.

(3) Accommodation in a care institution (within the meaning of paragraph 4 of Schedule 2) is not supported accommodation.

(4) "Support services" include—

- (a) support in controlling or overcoming addiction,
- (b) support in finding employment or alternative accommodation, and
- (c) supporting someone who finds it difficult to live independently because of age, illness, disability or any other reason.

(5) "Support" includes the provision of advice, training, guidance and counselling.

III WAL [252]

144 Mobility

(1) A supported standard contract may provide that the dwelling subject to the contract is the dwelling, within a building specified in the contract, as is from time to time specified by the landlord.

(2) If it does so, then references in this Act to the dwelling subject to the occupation contract are to be read as references to the dwelling for the time being specified by the landlord.

III WAL [253]

145 Temporary exclusion

(1) If the landlord under a supported standard contract reasonably believes that a contract-holder has done anything within subsection (2), the landlord may require the contract-holder—

- (a) to leave the dwelling, and
- (b) not to return to the dwelling for a specified period.

(2) The acts are—

(a) using violence against any person in the dwelling,

(b) doing something in the dwelling which creates a risk of significant harm to any person, and

(c) behaving in the dwelling in a way which seriously impedes the ability of another resident of supported accommodation provided by the landlord to benefit from the support provided in connection with that accommodation.

(3) The period specified under subsection (1)(b) may not be longer than 48 hours.

(4) The landlord must give a contract-holder required to leave the dwelling under this section a notice setting out the reasons why he or she is required to leave, and must do so?—

(a) when requiring him or her to leave, or

(b) as soon as reasonably practicable afterwards.

(5) The landlord may use the power conferred by this section, in relation to a particular contract-holder, no more than three times in any period of six months.

(6) In this section (except in subsection (2)(c) and this subsection) references to "the landlord" include references to any person designated by the landlord as entitled to exercise the power under this section in relation to the dwelling.

(7) In this section "dwelling" includes any common parts.

(8) This section is a fundamental provision which is incorporated as a term of all supported standard contracts.

III WAL [254]

146 Temporary exclusion: guidance

(1) The Welsh Ministers must issue guidance about the exercise by landlords of their functions under section 145.

(2) In the exercise of those functions, a landlord must have regard to guidance issued under subsection (1).

PART 9
TERMINATION ETC OF OCCUPATION CONTRACTS

CHAPTER 1 OVERVIEW AND INTRODUCTORY PROVISIONS

Overview

III WAL [255]

147 Overview of Part

The following table provides an overview of this Part—

TABLE 1

CHAPTER	OCCUPATION CONTRACTS TO WHICH IT APPLIES	CONTENT OF CHAPTER
1	All occupation contracts (except section 151, which applies only to introductory standard contracts and prohibited conduct standard contracts)	(a) ways in which occupation contracts may be ended, (b) circumstances in which landlords may make a claim to the court for recovery of possession of a dwelling, and (c) "possession notices", which are notices landlords must give to

WALES

		contract-holders before making a possession claim under section 157 (breach of contract), section 161 (in relation to estate management grounds), sections 165 or 170 (recovery of possession after contract-holder's notice), section 181 or 187 (serious rent arrears) or section 191 (recovery of possession after use of contract-holder's break clause).
2	All occupation contracts	Certain circumstances in which occupation contracts can end without a possession claim.
3	All occupation contracts	Landlords' possession claims on— (a) ground of contract-holder's breach of contract, and (b) estate management grounds.
4	Secure contracts	Contract-holder's right to end the contract.
5	Periodic standard contracts	(a) contract-holder's right to end the contract, and (b) rights of landlord to end the contract and make a possession claim.
6 and 7	Fixed term standard contracts	(a) what happens at the end of the term, (b) contract-holder's right to end the contract, and (c) rights of landlord to end the contract and make a possession claim.
8	Introductory standard contracts and prohibited conduct standard contracts	Review by landlord, when required by contract-holder, of landlord's decision to give a notice requiring possession on certain grounds.
9 and 10	All occupation contracts	(a) powers of court in relation to all possession claims, and (b) powers of court in relation to possession claims concerning discretionary grounds for possession.
11	Secure contracts	Powers and duties of court in relation to possession claims concerning a contract-holder's notice.
12	Standard contracts	Powers and duties of court in relation to possession claims concerning absolute grounds for possession.
13 to 15	All occupation contracts	(a) rights of landlord in relation to abandonment of dwelling by contract-holder, (b) termination and exclusion where there are joint contract-holders, and (c) forfeiture and notices to quit not available in relation to occupation contracts.

PERMISSIBLE TERMINATION, POSSESSION CLAIMS AND NOTICES REQUIRING POSSESSION

III WAL [256]

148 Permissible termination etc

(1) An occupation contract may be ended only in accordance with—

(a) the fundamental terms of the contract which incorporate fundamental provisions set out in this Part or other terms included in the contract in accordance with this Part, or

(b) an enactment.

(2) Nothing in this section affects—

(a) any right of the landlord or contract-holder to rescind the contract, or

(b) the operation of the law of frustration.

(3) This section is a fundamental provision which is incorporated as a term of all occupation contracts; section 20 provides that this section—

(a) must be incorporated, and

(b) must not be incorporated with modifications.

III WAL [257]

149 Possession claims

(1) The landlord under an occupation contract may make a claim to the court for recovery of possession of the dwelling from the contract-holder ("a possession claim") only in the circumstances set out in Chapters 3 to 5 and 7.

(2) This section is a fundamental provision which is incorporated as a term of all occupation contracts; section 20 provides that this section—

(a) must be incorporated, and

(b) must not be incorporated with modifications.

III WAL [258]

150 Possession notices

(1) This section applies in relation to a possession notice which a landlord is required to give to a contract-holder before making a possession claim.

(2) The notice must (in addition to specifying the ground on which the claim will be made)?—

(a) state the landlord's intention to make a possession claim,

(b) give particulars of the ground, and

(c) state the date after which the landlord is able to make a possession claim.

(3) This section is a fundamental provision which is incorporated as a term of all occupation contracts.

NOTICES REQUIRING POSSESSION: INTRODUCTORY STANDARD CONTRACTS AND PROHIBITED CONDUCT STANDARD CONTRACTS

III WAL [259]

151 Introductory standard contracts and prohibited conduct standard contracts: notices under sections 173 and 181

(1) Subsection (2) applies in relation to—

WALES

(a) a notice given under section 173 (landlord's notice) in connection with an introductory standard contract or a prohibited conduct standard contract;

(b) a possession notice given under section 181 (serious rent arrears) in connection with an introductory standard contract or a prohibited conduct standard contract.

(2) The notice must (in addition to complying with any other requirements under this Act) inform the contract-holder of the right to apply for a review under section 202 (review by landlord), and of the time by which the application must be made.

(3) This section is a fundamental provision which is incorporated as a term of all introductory standard contracts and prohibited conduct standard contracts.

CHAPTER 2 TERMINATION ETC WITHOUT A POSSESSION CLAIM

III WAL [260]

152 Early termination by contract-holder

(1) The contract-holder may end the occupation contract at any time before the earlier of—

(a) the landlord giving the contract-holder a written statement of the contract under section 31(1), or

(b) the occupation date.

(2) To end the contract under subsection (1), the contract-holder must give a notice to the landlord stating that he or she is ending the contract.

(3) On giving the notice to the landlord, the contract-holder—

(a) ceases to have any liability under the contract, and

(b) becomes entitled to the return of any deposit, rent or other consideration given to the landlord in accordance with the contract.

(4) This section is a fundamental provision which is incorporated as a term of all occupation contracts.

III WAL [261]

153 Termination by agreement

(1) If the landlord and the contract-holder under an occupation contract agree to end the contract, the contract ends—

(a) when the contract-holder gives up possession of the dwelling in accordance with the agreement, or

(b) if he or she does not give up possession and a substitute occupation contract is made, immediately before the occupation date of the substitute occupation contract.

(2) An occupation contract is a substitute occupation contract if—

(a) it is made in respect of the same (or substantially the same) dwelling as the original contract, and

(b) a contract-holder under it was also a contract-holder under the original contract.

(3) This section is a fundamental provision which is incorporated as a term of all occupation contracts.

III WAL [262]

154 Repudiatory breach by landlord

(1) If the landlord under an occupation contract commits a repudiatory breach of contract and the contract-holder gives up possession of the dwelling because of that breach, the contract ends when the contract-holder gives up possession of the dwelling.

(2) This section is a fundamental provision which is incorporated as a term of all occupation contracts.

III WAL [263]

155 Death of sole contract-holder

(1) If the sole contract-holder under an occupation contract dies, the contract ends—

- (a) one month after the death of the contract-holder, or
- (b) if earlier, when the landlord is given notice of the death by the authorised persons.

(2) The authorised persons are—

- (a) the contract-holder's personal representatives, or
- (b) the permitted occupiers of the dwelling aged 18 and over (if any) acting together.

(3) The contract does not end if under section 74 one or more persons are qualified to succeed the contract-holder.

(4) The contract does not end if, at the contract-holder's death, a family property order has effect which requires the contract-holder to transfer the contract to another person.

(5) If, after the contract-holder's death, the family property order ceases to have effect and there is no person qualified to succeed the contract-holder, the contract ends—

- (a) when the order ceases to have effect, or
- (b) if later, at the time the contract would end under subsection (1).

(6) This section is a fundamental provision which is incorporated as a term of all occupation contracts, except fixed term standard contracts that contain the provision mentioned in section 139(1) (transfer on death of sole contract holder); section 20 provides that this section—

- (a) must be incorporated, and
- (b) must not be incorporated with modifications.

III WAL [264]

156 Death of landlord where occupation contract is a licence

An occupation contract which is a licence ends on the death of the landlord.

CHAPTER 3 TERMINATION OF ALL OCCUPATION CONTRACTS (POSSESSION CLAIMS BY LANDLORDS)

BREACH OF CONTRACT

III WAL [265]

157 Breach of contract

(1) If the contract-holder under an occupation contract breaches the contract, the landlord may on that ground make a possession claim.

(2) Section 209 provides that the court may not make an order for possession on that ground unless it considers it reasonable to do so (and reasonableness is to be determined in accordance with Schedule 10).

(3) This section is a fundamental provision which is incorporated as a term of all occupation contracts.

III WAL [266]

158 False statement inducing landlord to make contract to be treated as breach of contract

(1) If the landlord under an occupation contract is induced to make the contract by means of a relevant false statement—

(a) the contract-holder is to be treated as being in breach of the occupation contract, and

(b) the landlord may accordingly make a possession claim on the ground in section 157 (breach of contract).

(2) A false statement is relevant if it is made knowingly or recklessly by—

(a) the contract-holder, or

(b) another person acting at the contract-holder's instigation.

(3) This section is a fundamental provision which is incorporated as a term of all occupation contracts; section 20 provides that this section—

(a) must be incorporated, and

(b) must not be incorporated with modifications.

III WAL [267]

159 Restrictions on section 157

(1) Before making a possession claim on the ground in section 157, the landlord must give the contract-holder a possession notice specifying that ground.

(2) The landlord may make a possession claim in reliance on a breach of section 55 (anti-social behaviour and other prohibited conduct) on or after the day on which the landlord gives the contract-holder a possession notice specifying a breach of that section.

(3) The landlord may not make a possession claim in reliance on a breach of any other term of the contract before the end of the period of one month starting with the day on which the landlord gives the contract-holder a possession notice specifying a breach of that term.

(4) In either case, the landlord may not make a possession claim after the end of the period of six months starting with the day on which the landlord gives the contract-holder the possession notice.

(5) This section is a fundamental provision which is incorporated as a term of all occupation contracts.

Estate Management Grounds

III WAL [268]

160 Estate management grounds

(1) The landlord under an occupation contract may make a possession claim on one or more of the estate management grounds.

(2) The estate management grounds are set out in Part 1 of Schedule 8 (paragraph 10 of that Schedule provides that Part 1 of that Schedule is a fundamental provision applicable to all occupation contracts).

(3) Section 210 provides that the court may not make an order for possession on an estate management ground unless—

(a) it considers it reasonable to do so (and reasonableness is to be determined in accordance with Schedule 10), and

(b) it is satisfied that suitable alternative accommodation (what is suitable is to be determined in accordance with Schedule 11) is available to the contract-holder (or will be available to the contract-holder when the order takes effect).

(4) If the court makes an order for possession on an estate management ground (and on no other ground), the landlord must pay to the contract-holder a sum equal to the reasonable expenses likely to be incurred by the contract-holder in moving from the dwelling.

(5) Subsection (4) does not apply if the court makes an order for possession on Ground A or B (the redevelopment grounds) of the estate management grounds (and on no other ground).

(6) This section is a fundamental provision which is incorporated as a term of all occupation contracts.

III WAL [269]

161 Restrictions on section 160

(1) Before making a possession claim on an estate management ground, the landlord must give the contract-holder a possession notice specifying that ground.

(2) The landlord may not make the claim—

(a) before the end of the period of one month starting with the day on which the landlord gives the contract-holder the possession notice, or

(b) after the end of the period of six months starting with that day.

(3) If a redevelopment scheme is approved under Part 2 of Schedule 8 subject to conditions, the landlord may give the contract-holder a possession notice specifying estate management Ground B before the conditions are met.

(4) The landlord may not give the contract-holder a possession notice specifying estate management Ground G (accommodation not required by successor)—

(a) before the end of the period of six months starting with the day on which the landlord (or in the case of joint landlords, any one of them) became aware of the previous contract-holder's death, or

(b) after the end of the period of twelve months starting with that day.

(5) The landlord may not give the contract-holder a possession notice specifying estate management Ground H (departing joint contract-holder) after the end of the period of six months starting with the day on which the joint contract-holder's rights and obligations under the contract ended.

(6) This section is a fundamental provision which is incorporated as a term of all occupation contracts.

III WAL [270]

162 Estate management grounds: redevelopment schemes

Part 2 of Schedule 8 (approval of redevelopment schemes) makes provision supplementing estate management Ground B.

CHAPTER 4 TERMINATION OF SECURE CONTRACTS (CONTRACT-HOLDER'S NOTICE)

III WAL [271]

163 Contract-holder's notice

(1) The contract-holder under a secure contract may end the contract by giving the landlord notice that he or she will give up possession of the dwelling on a date specified in the notice.

WALES

(2) This section is a fundamental provision which is incorporated as a term of all secure contracts.

III WAL [272]

164 Minimum notice period

(1) The date specified in a notice under section 163 may not be less than four weeks after the day on which the notice is given to the landlord.

(2) This section is a fundamental provision which is incorporated as a term of all secure contracts.

III WAL [273]

165 Recovery of possession

(1) If the contract-holder fails to give up possession of the dwelling on the date specified in a notice under section 163, the landlord may on that ground make a possession claim.

(2) Section 212 provides that if the court is satisfied that the ground is made out, it must make an order for possession of the dwelling (subject to any available defence based on the contract-holder's Convention rights).

(3) This section is a fundamental provision which is incorporated as a term of all secure contracts.

III WAL [274]

166 Restrictions on section 165

(1) Before making a possession claim on the ground in section 165 the landlord must give the contract-holder a possession notice specifying that ground.

(2) The landlord may make the possession claim on or after the day on which the landlord gives the contract-holder the possession notice.

(3) But the landlord may not make the possession claim after the end of the period of six months starting with that day.

(4) The landlord may not give the contract-holder a possession notice specifying the ground in section 165 after the end of the period of two months starting with the date specified in the notice under section 163 as the date on which the contract-holder would give up possession of the dwelling.

(5) This section is a fundamental provision which is incorporated as a term of all secure contracts.

III WAL [275]

167 Termination of contract on contract-holder's notice

(1) If the contract-holder gives up possession of the dwelling on or before the date specified in a notice under section 163, the contract ends on the date specified in the notice.

(2) If the contract-holder gives up possession of the dwelling after that date but in connection with the notice, the contract ends—

- (a) on the day on which the contract-holder gives up possession of the dwelling, or
- (b) if an order for possession is made, on the date determined in accordance with section 206.

(3) The notice ceases to have effect if, before the contract ends—

- (a) the contract-holder withdraws the notice by further notice to the landlord, and
- (b) the landlord does not object to the withdrawal in writing before the end of a reasonable period.

(4) This section is a fundamental provision which is incorporated as a term of all secure contracts.

CHAPTER 5 TERMINATION OF PERIODIC STANDARD CONTRACTS

TERMINATION BY CONTRACT-HOLDER: CONTRACT-HOLDER'S NOTICE

III WAL [276]

168 Contract-holder's notice

(1) The contract-holder under a periodic standard contract may end the contract by giving the landlord notice that he or she will give up possession of the dwelling on a date specified in the notice.

(2) This section is a fundamental provision which is incorporated as a term of all periodic standard contracts.

III WAL [277]

169 Minimum notice period

(1) The date specified in a notice under section 168 may not be less than four weeks after the day on which the notice is given to the landlord.

(2) This section is a fundamental provision which is incorporated as a term of all periodic standard contracts.

III WAL [278]

170 Recovery of possession

(1) If the contract-holder fails to give up possession of the dwelling on the date specified in a notice under section 168, the landlord may on that ground make a possession claim.

(2) Section 215 provides that if the court is satisfied that the ground is made out, it must make an order for possession of the dwelling (subject to any available defence based on the contract-holder's Convention rights).

(3) This section is a fundamental provision which is incorporated as a term of all periodic standard contracts.

III WAL [279]

171 Restrictions on section 170

(1) Before making a possession claim on the ground in section 170 the landlord must give the contract-holder a possession notice specifying that ground.

(2) The landlord may make the possession claim on or after the day on which the landlord gives the contract-holder the possession notice.

(3) But the landlord may not make the possession claim after the end of the period of six months starting with that day.

(4) The landlord may not give the contract-holder a possession notice specifying the ground in section 170 after the end of the period of two months starting with the date specified in the notice under section 168 as the date on which the contract-holder would give up possession of the dwelling.

(5) This section is a fundamental provision which is incorporated as a term of all periodic standard contracts.

III WAL [280]

172 Termination of contract on contract-holder's notice

(1) If the contract-holder gives up possession of the dwelling on or before the date specified in a notice under section 168 the contract ends on the date specified in the notice.

(2) If the contract-holder gives up possession of the dwelling after that date but in connection with the notice, the contract ends—

(a) on the day on which the contract-holder gives up possession of the dwelling, or

(b) if an order for possession is made, on the date determined in accordance with section 206.

(3) The notice ceases to have effect if, before the contract ends—

(a) the contract-holder withdraws the notice by giving further notice to the landlord, and

(b) the landlord does not object to the withdrawal in writing before the end of a reasonable period.

(4) This section is a fundamental provision which is incorporated as a term of all periodic standard contracts.

Termination by Landlord: Landlord's Notice

III WAL [281]

173 Landlord's notice

(1) The landlord under a periodic standard contract may end the contract by giving the contract-holder notice that he or she must give up possession of the dwelling on a date specified in the notice.

(2) This section is a fundamental provision which is incorporated as a term of all periodic standard contracts.

(3) If this section is not incorporated as a term of a periodic standard contract, the landlord may not vary the terms of the contract in accordance with sections 125(1)(b) and 126 (variation by landlord's notice).

III WAL [282]

174 Minimum notice period

(1) The date specified in a notice under section 173 may not be less than two months after the day on which the notice is given to the contract-holder.

(2) This section is a fundamental provision which is incorporated as a term of all periodic standard contracts.

III WAL [283]

175 Restrictions on section 173: notice may not be given in first four months of occupation

(1) The landlord may not give notice under section 173 before the end of the period of four months starting with the occupation date of the contract.

(2) If the contract is a substitute occupation contract, the landlord may not give notice under section 173 before the end of the period of four months starting with the occupation date of the original contract.

(3) For the purposes of subsection (2)—

(a) an occupation contract is a substitute occupation contract if—

(i) the occupation date of the contract falls immediately after the end of a preceding occupation contract,

(ii) immediately before the occupation date of the contract a contract-holder under the contract was a contract-holder under the preceding contract and a landlord under the contract was a landlord under the preceding contract, and

(iii) the contract relates to the same (or substantially the same) dwelling as the preceding contract, and

(b) "original contract" means—

(i) where the substitute occupation contract has an occupation date falling immediately after the end of a contract which is not a substitute occupation contract, the occupation contract which precedes the substitute occupation contract;

(ii) where there have been successive substitute occupation contracts, the occupation contract which preceded the first of the substitute occupation contracts.

(4) This section is a fundamental provision which is incorporated as a term of all periodic standard contracts, except periodic standard contracts which—

(a) do not incorporate section 173 as a term of the contract, or

(b) are within Schedule 9 (whether or not they incorporate section 173 as a term of the contract),

and section 20 provides that this section must be incorporated, and must not be incorporated with modifications.

III WAL [284]

176 Restrictions on section 173: breach of information requirements

(1) If the landlord does not comply with section 31(1) or (2) (duty to provide written statement of contract), the landlord may not give notice under section 173 before the end of the restricted period.

(2) The restricted period is six months starting with the day on which the landlord gives a written statement of the contract to the contract-holder.

(3) The landlord may not give the contract-holder notice under section 173 at any time when the landlord has not provided a notice required under section 39 (duty to provide information).

(4) This section is a fundamental provision which is incorporated as a term of all periodic standard contracts.

III WAL [285]

177 Restrictions on section 173: breach of security and deposit requirements

(1) The landlord may not give notice under section 173 at a time when security required by the landlord in a form not permitted by section 43 has not been returned to the person by whom it was given.

(2) The landlord may not give notice under section 173 at a time when any of subsections (3) to (5) apply unless—

(a) a deposit paid in connection with the contract has been returned to the contract-holder (or any person who paid the deposit on his or her behalf) either in full or with such deductions as may have been agreed, or

(b) an application to the county court has been made under paragraph 2 of Schedule 5 and has been determined by the county court, withdrawn, or settled by agreement between the parties.

(3) A deposit has been paid in connection with the contract but the initial requirements of an authorised deposit scheme have not been complied with.

(4) A deposit has been paid in connection with the contract but the landlord has not provided the information required by section 45(2)(b).

(5) A deposit paid in connection with the contract is not being held in accordance with an authorised deposit scheme.
(6) This section is a fundamental provision which is incorporated as a term of all periodic standard contracts which incorporate section 173 as a term of the contract; section 20 provides that this section—
- (a) must be incorporated, and
- (b) must not be incorporated with modifications.

III WAL [286]

178 Recovery of possession
(1) If the landlord gives the contract-holder a notice under section 173, the landlord may on that ground make a possession claim.
(2) Section 215 provides that if the court is satisfied that the ground is made out, it must make an order for possession of the dwelling, unless section 217 (retaliatory evictions: standard contracts) applies (and subject to any available defence based on the contract-holder's Convention rights).
(3) This section is a fundamental provision which is incorporated as a term of all periodic standard contracts.

III WAL [287]

179 Restriction on section 178
(1) The landlord may not make a possession claim on the ground in section 178—
- (a) before the date specified in the notice given by the landlord to the contract-holder under section 173, or
- (b) after the end of the period of two months starting with that date.

(2) This section is a fundamental provision which is incorporated as a term of all periodic standard contracts.

III WAL [288]

180 Termination of contract on landlord's notice
(1) If the contract-holder gives up possession of the dwelling on or before the date specified in a notice under section 173, the contract ends on the date specified in the notice.
(2) If the contract-holder gives up possession of the dwelling after that date but in connection with the notice, the contract ends—
- (a) on the day on which the contract-holder gives up possession of the dwelling, or
- (b) if an order for possession is made, on the date determined in accordance with section 206.

(3) The notice ceases to have effect if, before the contract ends—
- (a) the landlord withdraws the notice by further notice to the contract-holder, and
- (b) the contract-holder does not object to the withdrawal in writing before the end of a reasonable period.

(4) This section is a fundamental provision which is incorporated as a term of all periodic standard contracts.

TERMINATION BY LANDLORD: SERIOUS RENT ARREARS

III WAL [289]

181 Serious rent arrears

(1) If the contract-holder under a periodic standard contract is in serious rent arrears, the landlord may on that ground make a possession claim.

(2) The contract-holder is seriously in arrears with his or her rent—

- (a) where the rental period is a week, a fortnight or four weeks, if at least eight weeks' rent is unpaid;
- (b) where the rental period is a month, if at least two months' rent is unpaid;
- (c) where the rental period is a quarter, if at least one quarter's rent is more than three months in arrears;
- (d) where the rental period is a year, if at least 25% of the rent is more than three months in arrears.

(3) Section 216 provides that the court must (subject to any available defence based on the contract-holder's Convention rights) make an order for possession of the dwelling if it is satisfied that the contract-holder—

- (a) was seriously in arrears with his or her rent on the day on which the landlord gave the contract-holder the possession notice, and
- (b) is seriously in arrears with his or her rent on the day on which the court hears the possession claim.

(4) This section is a fundamental provision which is incorporated as a term of all periodic standard contracts.

III WAL [290]

182 Restrictions on section 181

(1) Before making a possession claim on the ground in section 181, the landlord must give the contract-holder a possession notice specifying that ground.

(2) The landlord under a periodic standard contract that is not an introductory standard contract or a prohibited conduct standard contract may not make the claim—

- (a) before the end of the period of 14 days starting with the day on which the landlord gives the contract-holder the possession notice, or
- (b) after the end of the period of six months starting with that day.

(3) The landlord under an introductory standard contract or a prohibited conduct standard contract may not make the claim—

- (a) before the end of the period of one month starting with the day on which the landlord gives the contract-holder the possession notice, or
- (b) after the end of the period of six months starting with that day.

(4) Subsection (1) is a fundamental provision which is incorporated as a term of all periodic standard contracts, and—

- (a) subsection (2) is a fundamental provision which is incorporated as a term of all periodic standard contracts that are not introductory standard contracts or prohibited conduct standard contracts;
- (b) subsection (3) is a fundamental provision which is incorporated as a term only of introductory standard contracts and prohibited conduct standard contracts.

Termination of Periodic Standard Contracts which Were Fixed Term Standard Contracts

III WAL [291]

183 Relevance of events under fixed term standard contract

(1) The landlord under a periodic standard contract which arises under section 184(2) (periodic standard contract arising at end of fixed term) may make a possession claim in reliance on—

(a) a possession notice, or

(b) a notice under section 186,

which the landlord gave to the contract-holder before the end of the fixed term contract.

(2) Sections 174 to 177, 179 and 180 apply to a notice under section 186(1), and a possession claim on the ground in section 186(5), as they apply to a notice under section 173 and a possession claim on the ground in section 178.

(3) In any possession notice the landlord gives to the contract-holder, the landlord may rely on events which occurred before the end of the fixed term standard contract.

(4) This section is a fundamental provision which is incorporated as a term of periodic standard contracts which arise under section 184(2).

CHAPTER 6 FIXED TERM STANDARD CONTRACTS: END OF THE FIXED TERM

III WAL [292]

184 End of fixed term

(1) A fixed term standard contract ends at the end of the term for which it is made.

(2) If the contract-holder remains in occupation of the dwelling after the end of the term, the landlord and the contract-holder are to be treated as having made a new periodic standard contract in relation to the dwelling.

(3) The new contract—

(a) has an occupation date falling immediately after the end of the fixed term, and

(b) has rental periods that are the same as those for which rent was last payable under the fixed term contract.

(4) The fundamental and supplementary provisions applicable to periodic standard contracts are incorporated as terms of the new contract without modification.

(5) Subject to subsections (3) and (4), the new contract has the same terms as the fixed term contract immediately before it ended.

(6) A new occupation contract does not arise as described in subsection (2) if the landlord and the contract-holder have made a new occupation contract in relation to the same (or substantially the same) dwelling which has an occupation date falling immediately after the fixed term contract ends.

(7) If, before or on the occupation date of a new occupation contract arising as described in subsection (2) or (6)—

(a) the contract-holder enters into an obligation to do an act which will cause the new contract to end, or

(b) the contract-holder gives any notice or other document that would, but for this subsection, cause the new contract to end, the obligation is unenforceable or (as the case may be) the notice or document is of no effect.

(8) The requirement in section 39(1) (landlord must give contract-holder a contact address at start of contract) does not apply in relation to a periodic standard contract arising under subsection (2).

III WAL [293]

185 Written statement may address periodic standard contract arising under section 184(2)

(1) A written statement of a fixed term standard contract may, as regards the periodic standard contract which may arise under section 184(2) ("the potential contract"), set out what the terms of that contract would be under section 184(3) to (5) by—

(a) identifying the terms of the fixed term standard contract that will not be terms of the potential contract, and setting out the terms that will apply only to the potential contract, or

(b) separately setting out all of the terms of the potential contract.

(2) Where a written statement of a fixed term standard contract addresses the potential contract in accordance with subsection (1)—

(a) the written statement is not incorrect (see section 37) merely because it addresses the potential contract;

(b) the landlord is to be treated as having complied with the requirement in section 31(1) (provision of written statement) in relation to the potential contract, and

(c) the terms of the potential contract may not be enforced against the contract-holder before the occupation date of that contract (and accordingly, section 42 does not apply).

CHAPTER 7 TERMINATION OF FIXED TERM STANDARD CONTRACTS

End of Fixed Term: Landlord's Notice

III WAL [294]

186 Landlord's notice in connection with end of term

(1) The landlord under a fixed term standard contract may, before or on the last day of the term for which the contract was made, give the contract-holder notice that he or she must give up possession of the dwelling on a date specified in the notice.

(2) The specified date may not be less than six months after—

(a) the occupation date of the contract, or

(b) if the contract is a substitute contract, the occupation date of the original contract.

(3) Subject to subsection (2), the specified date—

(a) may not be before the last day of the term for which the contract was made, and

(b) may not be less than two months after the day on which the notice is given to the contract-holder.

(4) For the purposes of subsection (2)—

(a) an occupation contract is a substitute occupation contract if—

(i) the occupation date of the contract falls immediately after the end of a preceding occupation contract,

WALES

(ii) immediately before the occupation date of the contract a contract-holder under the contract was a contract-holder under the preceding contract and a landlord under the contract was a landlord under the preceding contract, and

(iii) the contract relates to the same (or substantially the same) dwelling as the preceding contract, and

(b) "original contract" means—

(i) where the substitute occupation contract has an occupation date falling immediately after the end of a contract which is not a substitute occupation contract, the occupation contract which precedes the substitute occupation contract;

(ii) where there have been successive substitute occupation contracts, the occupation contract which preceded the first of the substitute occupation contracts.

(5) If the landlord gives the contract-holder a notice under subsection (1), the landlord may on that ground make a possession claim.

(6) Section 215 provides that if the court is satisfied that the ground is made out, it must make an order for possession of the dwelling (subject to any available defence based on the contract-holder's Convention rights).

(7) The landlord may not make a possession claim on that ground before the end of the fixed term standard contract.

(8) This section is a fundamental provision which is incorporated as a term of all fixed term standard contracts; subsections (2) and (4) are fundamental provisions which are incorporated as a term of all fixed term standard contracts, except fixed term standard contracts which—

(a) do not incorporate subsection (1) as a term of the contract, or

(b) are within Schedule 9 (whether or not they incorporate subsection (1) as a term of the contract),

and section 20 provides that those subsections must be incorporated, and must not be incorporated with modifications.

Termination by Landlord: Serious Rent Arrears

III WAL [295]

187 Serious rent arrears

(1) If the contract-holder under a fixed term standard contract is seriously in arrears with his or her rent, the landlord may on that ground make a possession claim.

(2) The contract-holder is seriously in arrears with his or her rent—

(a) where the rental period is a week, a fortnight or four weeks, if at least eight weeks' rent is unpaid;

(b) where the rental period is a month, if at least two months' rent is unpaid;

(c) where the rental period is a quarter, if at least one quarter's rent is more than three months in arrears;

(d) where the rental period is a year, if at least 25% of the rent is more than three months in arrears.

(3) Section 216 provides that the court must (subject to any available defence based on the contract-holder's Convention rights) make an order for possession of the dwelling if it is satisfied that the contract-holder—

(a) was seriously in arrears with his or her rent on the day on which the landlord gave the contract-holder the possession notice, and

(b) is seriously in arrears with his or her rent on the day on which the court hears the possession claim.

(4) This section is a fundamental provision which is incorporated as a term of all fixed term standard contracts.

III WAL [296]

188 Restrictions on section 187

(1) Before making a possession claim on the ground in section 187, the landlord must give the contract-holder a possession notice specifying that ground.

(2) The landlord may not make the claim—

(a) before the end of the period of 14 days starting with the day on which the landlord gives the contract-holder the possession notice, or

(b) after the end of the period of six months starting with that day.

(3) This section is a fundamental provision which is incorporated as a term of all fixed term standard contracts.

Contract-Holder's Break Clause

III WAL [297]

189 Contract-holder's break clause

(1) A fixed term standard contract may contain a term enabling the contract-holder to end the contract before the end of the fixed term by giving the landlord notice that he or she will give up possession of the dwelling on a date specified in the notice.

(2) References in this Act to a contract-holder's break clause, in relation to a fixed term standard contract, are to the term mentioned in subsection (1).

III WAL [298]

190 Minimum notice period

(1) The date specified in a notice under a contract-holder's break clause may not be less than four weeks after the day on which the notice is given to the landlord.

(2) This section is a fundamental provision which is incorporated as a term of all fixed term standard contracts with a contract-holder's break clause.

III WAL [299]

191 Recovery of possession

(1) If a contract-holder fails to give up possession of the dwelling on the date specified in a notice under a contract-holder's break clause, the landlord may on that ground make a possession claim.

(2) Section 215 provides that if the court is satisfied that the ground is made out, it must make an order for possession of the dwelling (subject to any available defence based on the contract-holder's Convention rights).

(3) This section is a fundamental provision which is incorporated as a term of all fixed term standard contracts with a contract-holder's break clause.

III WAL [300]

192 Restrictions on section 191

(1) Before making a possession claim on the ground in section 191 the landlord must give the contract-holder a possession notice specifying that ground.

(2) The landlord may make the possession claim on or after the day on which the landlord gives the contract-holder the possession notice.

(3) But the landlord may not make the possession claim after the end of the period of six months starting with that day.

(4) The landlord may not give the contract-holder a possession notice specifying the ground in section 191 after the end of the period of two months starting with the date specified in the notice under the contract-holder's break clause as the date on which the contract-holder would give up possession of the dwelling.

(5) This section is a fundamental provision which is incorporated as a term of all fixed term standard contracts with a contract-holder's break clause.

III WAL [301]

193 Termination of contract under contract-holder's break clause

(1) If the contract-holder gives up possession of the dwelling on or before the date specified in a notice under the contract-holder's break clause, the contract ends on the date specified in the notice.

(2) If the contract-holder gives up possession of the dwelling after that date but in connection with the notice, the contract ends—

- (a) on the day on which the contract-holder gives up possession of the dwelling, or
- (b) if an order for possession is made, on the date determined in accordance with section 206.

(3) The notice ceases to have effect if, before the contract ends—

- (a) the contract-holder withdraws the notice by further notice to the landlord, and
- (b) the landlord does not object to the withdrawal in writing before the end of a reasonable period.

(4) This section is a fundamental provision which is incorporated as a term of all fixed term standard contracts with a contract-holder's break clause.

Landlord's Break Clause

III WAL [302]

194 Landlord's break clause

(1) A fixed term standard contract may contain a term enabling the landlord to end the contract before the end of the fixed term by giving the contract-holder notice that he or she must give up possession of the dwelling on a date specified in the notice.

(2) References in this Act to a landlord's break clause, in relation to a fixed term standard contract, are to the term mentioned in subsection (1).

III WAL [303]

195 Minimum notice period

(1) The date specified in a notice under a landlord's break clause may not be less than two months after the day on which the notice is given to the contract-holder.

(2) This section is a fundamental provision which is incorporated as a term of all fixed term standard contracts with a landlord's break clause.

III WAL [304]

196 Restrictions on use of landlord's break clause: first four months of occupation

(1) The landlord may not give notice under a landlord's break clause before the end of the period of four months starting with the occupation date of the contract.

(2) If the contract is a substitute occupation contract, the landlord may not give notice under a landlord's break clause before the end of the period of four months starting with the occupation date of the original contract.

(3) For the purposes of subsection (2)—

(a) an occupation contract is a substitute occupation contract if—

(i) the occupation date of the contract falls immediately after the end of a preceding occupation contract,

(ii) immediately before the occupation date of the contract a contract-holder under the contract was a contract-holder under the preceding contract and a landlord under the contract was a landlord under the preceding contract, and

(iii) the contract relates to the same (or substantially the same) dwelling as the preceding contract, and

(b) "original contract" means—

(i) where the substitute occupation contract has an occupation date falling immediately after the end of a contract which is not a substitute occupation contract, the occupation contract which precedes the substitute occupation contract;

(ii) where there have been successive substitute occupation contracts, the occupation contract which preceded the first of the substitute occupation contracts.

(4) This section is a fundamental provision which is incorporated as a term of all fixed term standard contracts, except fixed term standard contracts which—

(a) do not have a landlord's break clause, or

(b) are within Schedule 9 (whether or not they have a landlord's break clause),

and section 20 provides that this section must be incorporated, and must not be incorporated with modifications.

III WAL [305]

197 Restrictions on use of landlord's break clause: breach of information requirements

(1) If the landlord does not comply with section 31(1) or (2) (duty to provide written statement of contract), the landlord may not give notice under a landlord's break clause before the end of the restricted period.

(2) The restricted period is six months starting with the day on which the landlord gives a written statement of the contract to the contract-holder.

(3) The landlord may not give notice under a landlord's break clause at any time when the landlord has not provided a notice required under section 39 (duty to provide information).

(4) This section is a fundamental provision which is incorporated as a term of all fixed term standard contracts with a landlord's break clause.

III WAL [306]

198 Restrictions on use of landlord's break clause: security and deposit requirements

(1) The landlord may not give notice under a landlord's break clause at a time when security required by the landlord in a form not permitted by section 43 has not been returned to the person by whom it was given.

(2) The landlord may not give notice under a landlord's break clause at a time when any of subsections (3) to (5) apply unless—

(a) a deposit paid in connection with the contract has been returned to the contract-holder (or any person who paid the deposit on his or her behalf) either in full or with such deductions as may have been agreed, or

(b) an application to the county court has been made under paragraph 2 of Schedule 5 and has been determined by the county court, withdrawn, or settled by agreement between the parties.

(3) A deposit has been paid in connection with the contract but the initial requirements of an authorised deposit scheme have not been complied with.

(4) A deposit has been paid in connection with the contract but the landlord has not provided the information required by section 45(2)(b).

(5) A deposit paid in connection with the contract is not being held in accordance with an authorised deposit scheme.

(6) This section is a fundamental provision which is incorporated as a term of all fixed term standard contracts with a landlord's break clause; section 20 provides that this section—

- (a) must be incorporated, and
- (b) must not be incorporated with modifications.

III WAL [307]

199 Recovery of possession

(1) If the landlord gives the contract-holder a notice under the landlord's break clause, the landlord may on that ground make a possession claim.

(2) Section 215 provides that if the court is satisfied that the ground is made out, it must make an order for possession of the dwelling, unless section 217 (retaliatory evictions) applies (and subject to any available defence based on the contract-holder's Convention rights).

(3) This section is a fundamental provision which is incorporated as a term of all fixed term standard contracts with a landlord's break clause.

III WAL [308]

200 Restriction on section 199

(1) The landlord may not make a possession claim on the ground in section 199—

- (a) before the date specified in the notice given by the landlord to the contract-holder under the landlord's break clause, or
- (b) after the end of the period of two months starting with that date.

(2) This section is a fundamental provision which is incorporated as a term of all fixed term standard contracts with a landlord's break clause.

III WAL [309]

201 Termination of contract under landlord's break clause

(1) If the contract-holder gives up possession of the dwelling on or before the date specified in a notice under the landlord's break clause, the contract ends on the date specified in the notice.

(2) If the contract-holder gives up possession of the dwelling after that date but in connection with the notice, the contract ends—

- (a) on the day on which the contract-holder gives up possession of the dwelling, or
- (b) if an order for possession is made, on the date determined in accordance with section 206.

(3) The notice ceases to have effect if, before the contract ends—

- (a) the landlord withdraws the notice by further notice to the contract-holder, and
- (b) the contract-holder does not object to the withdrawal in writing before the end of a reasonable period.

(4) This section is a fundamental provision which is incorporated as a term of all fixed term standard contracts with a landlord's break clause.

CHAPTER 8 REVIEW BY LANDLORD OF DECISION TO GIVE NOTICE REQUIRING POSSESSION

III WAL [310]

202 Review of decision to terminate introductory standard contract or prohibited conduct standard contract

(1) This section applies only in relation to introductory standard contracts and prohibited conduct standard contracts.

(2) If the landlord decides to give a contract-holder a notice under section 173 (landlord's notice) or a possession notice specifying the ground in section 181 (serious rent arrears), the contract-holder may request that the landlord carries out a review of that decision.

(3) A request for a review must be made to the landlord before the end of the period of 14 days (or such longer period as the landlord may allow in writing) starting with the day on which the landlord gives the contract-holder the notice.

III WAL [311]

203 Landlord's review of decision to give a notice

(1) If the contract-holder, in accordance with section 202, requests a review of the landlord's decision to give a notice, the landlord must carry out the review.

(2) Following a review, the landlord may—

(a) confirm the decision to give the notice, or

(b) reverse the decision.

(3) The landlord must notify the contract-holder of the outcome of the review before the date after which the landlord is able to make a possession claim.

(4) If the landlord confirms the decision, the notice must set out the reasons for the confirmation.

(5) The Welsh Ministers may prescribe the procedure to be followed in connection with a review under this section.

(6) Regulations under subsection (5) may, amongst other things—

(a) require the review to be carried out by a person of appropriate seniority who has not been involved in the decision, and

(b) set out circumstances in which a contract-holder is entitled to an oral hearing, and whether and by whom he or she may be represented at such a hearing.

CHAPTER 9 POSSESSION CLAIMS: POWERS OF COURT

III WAL [312]

204 Possession claims

(1) The court may not hear a possession claim made by the landlord under an occupation contract—

(a) if the landlord has failed to act in accordance with whichever of the following sections apply—

(i) section 126 (variation of periodic standard contract by landlord's notice);

(ii) section 159 (restrictions on making a possession claim following breach of contract);

(iii) section 161 (restrictions on making a possession claim on estate management grounds);

(iv) section 166 (restrictions on making a possession claim following contract-holder's notice: secure contracts);

WALES

(v) section 171 (restrictions on making a possession claim following contract-holder's notice: periodic standard contracts);

(vi) section 175 (restriction on giving landlord's notice under a periodic standard contract during first four months of occupation);

(vii) sections 176, 177 and 179 (restrictions relating to landlord's notice: periodic standard contracts);

(viii) section 182 (restrictions on making a possession claim following serious rent arrears: periodic standard contracts);

(ix) section 186 (restrictions relating to notice in connection with the end of fixed term);

(x) section 188 (restrictions on making a possession claim following serious rent arrears: fixed term standard contracts);

(xi) section 192 (restrictions on making a possession claim following use of contract-holder's break clause in a fixed term standard contract);

(xii) section 196 (restriction on use of landlord's break clause in a fixed term standard contract during first four months of occupation);

(xiii) sections 197, 198 and 200 (restrictions relating to landlord's break clause in a fixed term standard contract);

(xiv) section 203 (review of a decision to give a notice requiring possession: introductory standard contracts and prohibited conduct standard contracts), or

(b) if the landlord was required to give a possession notice and has failed to comply with section 150 or (in relation to an introductory standard contract or a prohibited conduct standard contract) section 151.

(2) Subsection (1) does not apply if the court considers it reasonable to dispense with the requirements mentioned in that subsection.

(3) Subsection (1) does not apply to an application for an order for possession against a sub-holder under section 65(2) (extended possession order).

III WAL [313]

205 Orders for possession

(1) The court may make an order requiring the contract-holder under an occupation contract to give up possession of the dwelling only on one or more of the grounds in—

(a) section 157 (breach of contract);

(b) section 160 (estate management);

(c) section 165 (contract-holder's notice: secure contracts);

(d) section 170 (contract-holder's notice: periodic standard contracts);

(e) section 178 (landlord's notice: periodic standard contracts);

(f) section 181 (serious rent arrears: periodic standard contracts);

(g) section 186 (landlord's notice in connection with end of fixed term);

(h) section 187 (serious rent arrears: fixed term standard contracts);

(i) section 191 (contract-holder's notice: fixed term standard contracts);

(j) section 199 (landlord's notice: fixed term standard contracts).

(2) Where the landlord is required to give the contract-holder a possession notice, the court may not make an order for possession on a ground that is not specified in the landlord's possession notice.

(3) But the court may allow the ground (or grounds) specified in the possession notice to be altered or added to at any time before the court makes an order for possession.

III WAL [314]

206 Effect of order for possession

(1) If the court makes an order requiring the contract-holder under an occupation contract to give up possession of the dwelling on a date specified in the order, the contract ends—

(a) if the contract-holder gives up possession of the dwelling on or before that date, on that date,

(b) if the contract-holder gives up possession of the dwelling after that date but before the order for possession is executed, on the day on which he or she gives up possession of the dwelling, or

(c) if the contract-holder does not give up possession of the dwelling before the order for possession is executed, when the order for possession is executed.

(2) Subsection (3) applies if—

(a) it is a condition of the order that the landlord must offer a new occupation contract in respect of the same dwelling to one or more joint contract-holders (but not all of them), and

(b) that joint contract-holder (or those joint contract-holders) continue to occupy the dwelling on and after the occupation date of the new contract.

(3) The occupation contract in relation to which the order for possession was made ends immediately before the occupation date of the new contract.

(4) This section is a fundamental provision which is incorporated as a term of all occupation contracts.

III WAL [315]

207 Participation in proceedings

(1) A person occupying a dwelling subject to an occupation contract who has home rights is entitled, so long as the person remains in occupation—

(a) to be a party to any proceedings on a possession claim relating to the dwelling, or in connection with an order for possession of the dwelling, or

(b) to seek an adjournment, postponement, stay or suspension under section 211, 214 or 219.

(2) "Home rights" has the meaning given by section 30(2) of the Family Law Act 1996 (c 27).

III WAL [316]

208 Misrepresentation or concealment of facts used to obtain order for possession

(1) This section applies if, after the landlord under an occupation contract obtains an order for possession against the contract-holder, the court is satisfied that the order was obtained by misrepresentation or concealment of material facts.

(2) The court may order the landlord to pay to the contract-holder such sum as appears sufficient compensation for damage or loss sustained by the contract-holder as a result of the order.

CHAPTER 10 POSSESSION CLAIMS: POWERS OF COURT IN RELATION TO DISCRETIONARY GROUNDS

III WAL [317]

209 Breach of contract ground

(1) This section applies if the landlord under an occupation contract makes a possession claim on the ground in section 157 (breach of contract).

(2) The court may not make an order for possession on that ground unless it considers it reasonable to do so.

(3) The court is not prevented from making an order for possession on that ground merely because the contract-holder ceased to be in breach of the contract before the landlord made the possession claim.

(4) Schedule 10 makes provision as regards the reasonableness of making an order for possession.

III WAL [318]

210 Estate management grounds

(1) This section applies if the landlord under an occupation contract makes a possession claim under section 160 on one or more of the estate management grounds.

(2) The court may not make an order for possession on that ground (or those grounds) unless—

(a) it considers it reasonable to do so, and

(b) it is satisfied that suitable alternative accommodation is available to the contract-holder (or will be available to the contract-holder when the order takes effect).

(3) Schedule 10 makes provision as regards the reasonableness of making an order for possession.

(4) Whether suitable alternative accommodation is, or will be, available to the contract-holder is to be determined in accordance with Schedule 11.

(5) If the landlord makes a possession claim on estate management Ground B and the redevelopment scheme is approved under Part 2 of Schedule 8 subject to conditions, the court may not make an order for possession unless it is satisfied that the conditions are or will be met.

(6) If the court makes an order for possession and the landlord is required to pay the contract-holder a sum under section 160(4), the sum payable—

(a) if not agreed between the landlord and contract-holder, is to be determined by the court, and

(b) is recoverable from the landlord as a civil debt.

III WAL [319]

211 Powers to adjourn proceedings and postpone giving up of possession

(1) If a landlord's possession claim relies on the ground in section 157 (breach of contract) or on one or more of the estate management grounds, the court may adjourn proceedings on the claim for such period or periods as it considers reasonable.

(2) If the court makes an order for possession under section 209 or 210, it may (on making the order or at any time before the order is executed) postpone the giving up of possession for such period or periods as it thinks fit.

(3) The giving up of possession may be postponed by the order for possession, or by suspending or staying execution of the order for possession.

(4) On an adjournment or postponement under this section, the court must impose conditions as regards—

(a) payment by the contract-holder of arrears of rent (if any), and

(b) continued payment of rent (if any),

unless it considers that to do so would cause exceptional hardship to the contract-holder or would otherwise be unreasonable.

(5) The court may impose any other conditions it thinks fit.

(6) If the contract-holder complies with the conditions, the court may discharge the order for possession.

(7) Schedule 10 makes provision as regards the reasonableness of an adjournment or postponement.

CHAPTER 11 POSSESSION CLAIMS: POWERS OF COURT IN RELATION TO ABSOLUTE GROUNDS

III WAL [320]

212 Contract-holder's notice ground

(1) This section applies if—

(a) the landlord under a secure contract makes a possession claim on the ground in section 165 (contract-holder's notice), and

(b) the court is satisfied that the ground is made out.

(2) The court must make an order for possession of the dwelling (subject to any available defence based on the contract-holder's Convention rights).

(3) This section is subject to section 213 (review by the county court).

III WAL [321]

213 Review of claim made on absolute ground

(1) This section applies if a landlord under a secure contract makes a possession claim in the county court on the ground in section 165 (contract-holder fails to give up possession following a contract-holder's notice), and—

(a) the landlord is a community landlord, or

(b) the landlord's decision to make a possession claim on that ground is subject to judicial review.

(2) The contract-holder may make an application in the possession proceedings for a review by the county court of the landlord's decision to make the claim.

(3) The county court may confirm or quash the decision.

(4) In considering whether to confirm or quash the decision, the county court must apply the principles applied by the High Court on an application for judicial review.

(5) If the county court quashes the decision it may—

(a) set aside the possession notice and dismiss the possession proceedings;

(b) make any order the High Court could make when making a quashing order on an application for judicial review.

(6) The contract-holder may not make an application under subsection (2) after an order for possession has been made in respect of the dwelling.

III WAL [322]

214 Powers to postpone giving up of possession

(1) This section applies if the court makes an order for possession of a dwelling under section 212.

(2) The court may not postpone the giving up of possession to a date later than 14 days after the making of the order, unless it appears to the court that exceptional hardship would be caused if the giving up of possession were not postponed to a later date.

(3) The giving up of possession may not in any event be postponed to a date later than six weeks after the making of the order.
(4) The giving up of possession may be postponed by the order for possession, or by suspending or staying execution of the order for possession.

CHAPTER 12 POSSESSION CLAIMS: POWERS OF COURT IN RELATION TO ABSOLUTE GROUNDS

Absolute Grounds for Possession Relating to Standard Contracts

III WAL [323]

215 Notice grounds

(1) Subsection (2) applies if—

(a) the landlord under a standard contract makes a possession claim on the ground in section 170 or 191 (contract-holder's notice) or section 186 (landlord's notice in connection with end of fixed term), and

(b) the court is satisfied that the ground is made out.

(2) The court must make an order for possession of the dwelling (subject to any available defence based on the contract-holder's Convention rights).

(3) Subsection (4) applies if—

(a) the landlord under a standard contract makes a possession claim on the ground in section 178 or 199 (landlord's notice), and

(b) the court is satisfied that the ground is made out.

(4) The court must make an order for possession of the dwelling unless section 217 (retaliatory evictions) applies (and subject to any available defence based on the contract-holder's Convention rights).

(5) This section is subject to section 218 (review by the county court).

III WAL [324]

216 Serious rent arrears grounds

(1) This section applies if the landlord under a standard contract makes a possession claim on the ground in section 181 or 187 (serious rent arrears).

(2) If the court is satisfied that the contract-holder—

(a) was seriously in arrears with his or her rent on the day on which the landlord gave the contract-holder a possession notice, and

(b) is seriously in arrears with his or her rent on the day on which the court hears the possession claim,

it must make an order for possession of the dwelling (subject to any available defence based on the contract-holder's Convention rights).

(3) Section 181(2) or (as the case may be) section 187(2) applies for determining whether a contract-holder is seriously in arrears with his or her rent.

(4) This section is subject to section 218 (review by the county court).

Retaliatory Eviction: Absolute Ground that Becomes a Discretionary Ground

III WAL [325]

217 Retaliatory possession claims to avoid obligations to repair etc

(1) This section applies if—

(a) a landlord under a standard contract makes a possession claim on the ground in section 178 or section 199 (landlord's notice), and

(b) the court considers that the claim is a retaliatory claim.

(2) The court may refuse to make an order for possession.

(3) A possession claim is a retaliatory claim if—

(a) the contract-holder has enforced or relied on the landlord's obligations under section 91 or 92, and

(b) the court is satisfied that the landlord has made the possession claim to avoid complying with those obligations.

(4) The Welsh Ministers may by regulations amend this section for the purpose of providing for further descriptions of retaliatory claim.

Review and Postponement

III WAL [326]

218 Review of claim made on absolute ground

(1) This section applies if a landlord under a standard contract makes a possession claim in the county court on a ground in a section to which subsection (2) applies, and—

(a) the landlord is a community landlord, or

(b) the landlord's decision to make a possession claim on that ground is subject to judicial review.

(2) This subsection applies to the following sections—

(a) section 170 (contract-holder's notice: periodic standard contracts),

(b) section 178 (landlord's notice: periodic standard contracts),

(c) section 181 (serious rent arrears: periodic standard contracts),

(d) section 186 (landlord's notice in connection with end of fixed term),

(e) section 187 (serious rent arrears: fixed term standard contracts),

(f) section 191 (contract-holder's notice: fixed term standard contracts), and

(g) section 199 (landlord's notice: fixed term standard contracts).

(3) The contract-holder may make an application in the possession proceedings for a review by the county court of the landlord's decision to make the claim.

(4) The contract-holder may make an application under this section regardless of whether he or she requested a review by the landlord under section 202 (introductory standard contracts and prohibited conduct standard contracts).

(5) The contract-holder may not make an application under this section on the ground that the possession claim was a retaliatory claim (within the meaning of section 217).

(6) The county court may confirm or quash the decision to make the claim.

(7) In considering whether to confirm or quash the decision, the county court must apply the principles applied by the High Court on an application for judicial review.

(8) If the county court quashes the decision it may—

(a) set aside the possession notice or (as the case may be) the landlord's notice and dismiss the possession proceedings;

(b) make any order the High Court could make when making a quashing order on an application for judicial review.

(9) The contract-holder may not make an application under subsection (3) after an order for possession has been made in respect of the dwelling.

III WAL [327]

219 Powers to postpone giving up of possession

(1) This section applies if the court makes an order for possession of a dwelling under section 215 or 216.

WALES

(2) The court may not postpone the giving up of possession to a date later than 14 days after the making of the order, unless it appears to the court that exceptional hardship would be caused if the giving up of possession were not postponed to a later date.

(3) The giving up of possession may not in any event be postponed to a date later than six weeks after the making of the order.

(4) The giving up of possession may be postponed by the order for possession, or by suspending or staying execution of the order for possession.

CHAPTER 13 ABANDONMENT

III WAL [328]

220 Possession of abandoned dwellings

(1) If the landlord under a relevant occupation contract believes that the contract-holder has abandoned the dwelling, the landlord may recover possession of the dwelling in accordance with this section.

(2) An occupation contract is relevant if it is a term of the contract (however expressed) that the contract-holder must occupy the dwelling as his or her only or principal home.

(3) The landlord must give the contract-holder notice—

- (a) stating that the landlord believes that the contract-holder has abandoned the dwelling,
- (b) requiring the contract-holder to inform the landlord in writing before the end of the warning period if the contract-holder has not abandoned the dwelling, and
- (c) informing the contract-holder of the landlord's intention to end the contract if at the end of the warning period the landlord is satisfied that the contract-holder has abandoned the dwelling.

(4) During the warning period the landlord must make such inquiries as are necessary to satisfy the landlord that the contract-holder has abandoned the dwelling.

(5) At the end of the warning period the landlord may, if satisfied as described in subsection (4), end the contract by giving the contract-holder a notice.

(6) The contract ends when the notice under subsection (5) is given to the contract-holder.

(7) If an occupation contract is ended under this section the landlord may recover possession of the dwelling without court proceedings.

(8) The warning period is the period of four weeks starting with the day on which a notice under subsection (3) is given to the contract-holder.

(9) The landlord must give a copy of a notice under subsection (3) and a copy of a notice under subsection (5) to any lodger or sub-holder of the contract-holder.

III WAL [329]

221 Disposal of property

(1) The Welsh Ministers may by regulations make provision in connection with safeguarding property (other than the landlord's property) that is in the dwelling when a contract ends under section 220, and delivering it to its owner.

(2) The regulations may, amongst other things—

- (a) provide that delivery of property is conditional on payment of expenses incurred by the landlord;
- (b) authorise the disposal of property after a prescribed period;
- (c) allow the landlord to apply any proceeds from selling property in satisfaction of expenses incurred by the landlord and amounts due

from the contract-holder under the contract.

III WAL [330]

222 Contract-holder's remedies

(1) A contract-holder may, before the end of the period of six months starting with the day on which he or she is given notice under section 220(5), apply to the court on a ground in subsection (2) for a declaration or order under subsection (3).

(2) The grounds are—

- (a) that the landlord failed to give notice under section 220(3) or failed to make the inquiries required by section 220(4);
- (b) that the contract-holder had not abandoned the dwelling and there is a good reason for his or her failure to respond (or to respond adequately) to the notice under section 220(3);
- (c) that when the landlord gave the notice to the contract-holder under section 220(5) the landlord did not have reasonable grounds for being satisfied that the contract-holder had abandoned the dwelling.

(3) If the court finds that one or more of the grounds is made out it may—

- (a) make a declaration that the notice under section 220(5) is of no effect and the occupation contract continues to have effect in relation to the dwelling,
- (b) order the landlord to provide suitable alternative accommodation to the contract-holder, or
- (c) make any other order it thinks fit.

(4) If the court does either of the things mentioned in paragraph (a) or (b) of subsection (3), it may make such further order as it thinks fit.

(5) The suitability of alternative accommodation is to be determined in accordance with Schedule 11.

III WAL [331]

223 Power to vary periods of time relating to abandonment

The Welsh Ministers may by regulations—

- (a) amend section 220(8) by substituting a different period of time for the period for the time being referred to;
- (b) amend section 222(1) by substituting a different period of time for the period for the time being referred to.

III WAL [332]

224 Rights of entry

(1) Subsection (2) applies if the landlord under a relevant occupation contract reasonably believes that the contract-holder has abandoned the dwelling.

(2) The landlord may enter the dwelling at any time in order to make it secure or to safeguard its contents and any fixtures or fittings, and may use reasonable force to do so.

(3) An occupation contract is relevant if it is a term of the contract (however expressed) that the contract-holder must occupy the dwelling as his or her only or principal home.

CHAPTER 14 JOINT CONTRACT-HOLDERS: EXCLUSION AND TERMINATION

Exclusion of Joint Contract-Holders

III WAL [333]

225 Non-occupation: exclusion by landlord

(1) If the landlord under an occupation contract believes that a joint contract-holder who is required to occupy the dwelling ("J")—

(a) does not occupy the dwelling, and

(b) does not intend to occupy it,

the landlord may end J's rights and obligations in accordance with this section.

(2) A joint contract-holder is required to occupy the dwelling if it is a term of the contract (however expressed) that he or she must occupy the dwelling as his or her only or principal home.

(3) The landlord must give J notice—

(a) stating that the landlord believes that J does not occupy, and does not intend to occupy, the dwelling,

(b) requiring J to inform the landlord in writing before the end of the warning period if J occupies or intends to occupy the dwelling, and

(c) informing J of the landlord's intention to end J's rights and obligations under the contract if at the end of the warning period the landlord is satisfied that J does not occupy, and does not intend to occupy, the dwelling.

(4) The warning period is the period of four weeks starting with the day on which a notice under subsection (3) is given to J.

(5) During the warning period the landlord must make such inquiries as are necessary to satisfy the landlord that J does not occupy the dwelling and does not intend to occupy it.

(6) At the end of the warning period the landlord may, if satisfied as described in subsection (5), end J's rights and obligations under the contract by giving him or her a notice.

(7) J ceases to be a party to the contract at the end of the period of eight weeks starting with the day on which he or she is given notice under subsection (6).

(8) The landlord must give a copy of a notice under subsection (3) and (if one was given to J) a copy of a notice under subsection (6) to each of the other joint contract-holders.

III WAL [334]

226 Remedies for exclusion under section 225

(1) J may, before the end of the period of eight weeks starting with the day on which he or she is given notice under section 225(6), apply to the court on a ground in subsection (2) for a declaration under subsection (3).

(2) The grounds are—

(a) that the landlord failed to give notice under section 225(3) or failed to make the inquiries required by section 225(5);

(b) that J occupied, or intended to occupy, the dwelling and there is a good reason for his or her failure to respond (or to respond adequately) to the notice under section 225(3);

(c) that when the landlord gave the notice to J under section 225(6) the landlord did not have reasonable grounds for being satisfied that J did not occupy, and did not intend to occupy, the dwelling.

(3) If the court finds that one or more of the grounds are made out it may—

(a) make a declaration that the notice under section 225(6) is of no effect and that J continues to be a party to the contract, and

(b) make such further order as it thinks fit.

III WAL [335]

227 Non-occupation: exclusion by joint contract-holder

(1) If a joint contract-holder ("C") believes that another joint contract-holder ("J") who is required under an occupation contract to occupy the dwelling—

(a) does not occupy the dwelling, and

(b) does not intend to occupy it,

J's rights and obligations under the contract may be ended in accordance with this section.

(2) A joint contract-holder is required to occupy the dwelling if it is a term of the contract (however expressed) that he or she must occupy the dwelling as his or her only or principal home.

(3) C must give J notice—

(a) stating that C believes that J does not occupy, and does not intend to occupy, the dwelling,

(b) requiring J to inform C in writing before the end of the warning period if J occupies or intends to occupy the dwelling, and

(c) informing J that if at the end of the warning period C is satisfied that J does not occupy, and does not intend to occupy, the dwelling, J's rights and obligations under the contract may be ended.

(4) C must give a copy of a notice under subsection (3)—

(a) to the landlord, and

(b) if there are joint contract-holders other than C and J, to each of those other joint contract-holders.

(5) During the warning period C must make such inquiries as are necessary to satisfy himself or herself that J does not occupy the dwelling and does not intend to occupy it.

(6) At the end of the warning period C may, if satisfied as described in subsection (5), apply to the court for an order ending J's rights and obligations under the occupation contract.

(7) If the court is satisfied that J does not occupy, and does not intend to occupy, the dwelling, it may make the order applied for under subsection (6).

(8) But it may not make the order if the fact that J does not occupy, and does not intend to occupy, the dwelling is attributable to C or another joint contract-holder failing to comply with section 55 (anti-social behaviour and other prohibited conduct).

(9) If the court makes the order, J ceases to be a party to the contract on the date specified in the order.

(10) The warning period is the period of four weeks starting with the day on which a notice under subsection (3) is given to J.

III WAL [336]

228 Remedies for exclusion under section 227

(1) Subsection (2) applies if the court makes an order under section 227(7) ending J's rights and obligations under the occupation contract.

(2) J may, before the end of the period of six months starting with the day on which the order is made, apply to the court on a ground in subsection (3) for an order and declaration under subsection (4)(a).

(3) The grounds are—

WALES

(a) that C failed to give notice under section 227(3) or failed to make the inquiries required by section 227(5);

(b) that J occupied or intended to occupy the dwelling and there is a good reason for his or her failure to respond (or to respond adequately) to the notice under section 227(3);

(c) that when C applied to the court he or she did not have reasonable grounds for being satisfied that J did not occupy, and did not intend to occupy, the dwelling.

(4) If the court finds that one or more of the grounds is made out it may—

(a) by order rescind its order under section 227, and declare that J continues to be a party to the occupation contract, and

(b) make such further order as it thinks fit.

III WAL [337]

229 Power to vary periods of time relating to exclusion of joint contract-holder

The Welsh Ministers may by regulations—

(a) amend section 225(4) by substituting a different period of time for the period for the time being referred to;

(b) amend section 226(1) by substituting a different period of time for the period for the time being referred to;

(c) amend section 227(10) by substituting a different period of time for the period for the time being referred to;

(d) amend section 228(2) by substituting a different period of time for the period for the time being referred to.

III WAL [338]

230 Prohibited conduct: exclusion by landlord

(1) If the landlord under an occupation contract believes that a joint contract-holder ("J") is in breach of section 55 (anti-social behaviour and other prohibited conduct), J's rights and obligations under the contract may be ended in accordance with this section.

(2) The landlord must give J a notice—

(a) stating that the landlord believes that J is in breach of section 55,

(b) specifying particulars of the breach, and

(c) stating that the landlord will apply to the court for an order ending J's rights and obligations under the contract.

(3) The landlord must give a notice to the other joint contract-holders stating that the landlord—

(a) believes that J is in breach of section 55, and

(b) will apply to the court for an order ending J's rights and obligations under the contract.

(4) The landlord may apply to the court for an order ending J's rights and obligations under the contract at any time before the end of the period of six months starting with the day on which the landlord gives J the notice under subsection (2).

(5) The court may make such an order if it would have made an order for possession against J, had the circumstances been those mentioned in subsection (6).

(6) The circumstances are that—

(a) J was the sole contract-holder under the contract, and

(b) the landlord had made a possession claim against J on the ground that J was in breach of section 55.

(7) If the court makes the order, J ceases to be a party to the contract on the date specified in the order.

Termination

III WAL [339]

231 Termination of occupation contract with joint contract-holders

(1) If there are joint contract-holders under an occupation contract, the contract cannot be ended by the act of one or more of the joint contract-holders acting without the other joint contract-holder or joint contract-holders.

(2) This section is a fundamental provision which is incorporated as a term of all occupation contracts.

CHAPTER 15 FORFEITURE AND NOTICES TO QUIT NOT AVAILABLE

III WAL [340]

232 Forfeiture and notices to quit

(1) A landlord under an occupation contract may not rely on—

- (a) any provision in the contract for re-entry or forfeiture, or
- (b) any enactment (other than this Act or an enactment made under it) or rule of law as to re-entry or forfeiture.

(2) A landlord under an occupation contract may not serve a notice to quit.

(3) Accordingly any provision in an occupation contract for re-entry or forfeiture, or relating to a landlord's notice to quit or the circumstances in which such a notice may be served, is of no effect.

PART 10
MISCELLANEOUS

CHAPTER 1 FURTHER PROVISIONS RELATING TO OCCUPATION CONTRACTS

Effect of Reaching 18

III WAL [341]

233 Effect of reaching 18

(1) This section applies to a tenancy or licence which is not an occupation contract because paragraph 7(2) of Schedule 2 (all those with whom tenancy or licence is made are under 18) applies to it.

(2) When the relevant person reaches the age of 18, the following questions are to be determined as if the tenancy or licence were made on the day the person reaches that age?—

- (a) whether the tenancy or licence is an occupation contract,
- (b) the identity of the contract-holders under the contract, and
- (c) whether it is a secure contract or a standard contract.

(3) The relevant person—

- (a) if the tenancy or licence is made with one person, is that person, and
- (b) if the tenancy or licence is made with more than one person, is the first of them to reach the age of 18.

Consultation Obligations of Community Landlords

III WAL [342]

234 Consultation arrangements

(1) A community landlord must make and maintain such arrangements as it considers appropriate—

(a) for informing contract-holders under occupation contracts with the landlord of relevant proposals on housing management matters, and

(b) for giving the contract-holders a reasonable opportunity to comment on the proposals.

(2) The duties in subsection (1)—

(a) apply only where a relevant proposal on a housing management matter is likely to substantially affect all the contract-holders under occupation contracts with the landlord, or a relevant group of such contract-holders, and

(b) apply only in relation to the contract-holders who are likely to be substantially affected.

(3) Before making any decision on a relevant proposal on a housing management matter, the landlord must consider any comments made by contract-holders in accordance with the arrangements.

(4) "Relevant proposal on a housing management matter" means a proposal that, in the opinion of the landlord, is about—

(a) a new programme of maintenance, improvement or demolition of dwellings subject to occupation contracts, or

(b) a change in the practice or policy of the landlord in relation to management, maintenance, improvement or demolition of such dwellings.

(5) But a proposal is not a relevant proposal on a housing management matter so far as it relates to—

(a) the rent payable or other consideration due to the landlord, or

(b) charges for services and facilities provided by the landlord.

(6) "Relevant group" means a group that—

(a) forms a distinct social group, or

(b) occupies dwellings which constitute a distinct class (whether by reference to the kind of dwelling, or the housing estate or other larger area in which they are situated).

(7) This section is subject to paragraph 12(7) in Part 2 of Schedule 8 (approval of redevelopment schemes).

III WAL [343]

235 Statement of consultation arrangements

(1) A landlord required to make arrangements under section 234 must prepare and publish a statement of the arrangements.

(2) If the landlord is a local housing authority, it must make a copy of the statement available at the landlord's principal office for inspection at all reasonable times, without charge, by members of the public.

(3) If the landlord is a registered social landlord or a private registered provider of social housing, it must send a copy of the statement to the Welsh Ministers and the local housing authority for the area in which the dwellings are situated.

(4) A local housing authority to which a copy is sent under subsection (3) must make it available at its principal office for inspection at all reasonable times, without charge, by members of the public.

(5) The landlord must give a copy of the statement—

(a) to any contract-holder under an occupation contract with the landlord who asks for one, free of charge, and

(b) to any other person who asks for one, on payment of a reasonable fee.

(6) The landlord must also—

(a) prepare a summary of the statement, and

(b) provide a copy of the summary without charge to any person who asks for one.

Notices, Statements and other Documents

III WAL [344]

236 Form of notices, statements and other documents

(1) This section applies to any notice or other document (including a copy of a document) required or authorised to be given or made by or because of this Act.

(2) The notice or document must be in writing.

(3) The Welsh Ministers may prescribe the form of the notice or document and, unless the regulations provide otherwise, a notice or document not in the prescribed form is of no effect.

(4) The notice or document may be in electronic form (subject to section 237(4)) provided it—

(a) has the certified electronic signature of each person by whom it is required to be signed or executed, and

(b) complies with such other conditions as may be prescribed.

(5) A notice or document within subsection (4) is to be treated as signed or executed by each person whose certified electronic signature it has.

(6) If a notice or document in electronic form is authenticated by a person as agent, it is to be regarded for the purposes of any enactment as authenticated by that person under the written authority of that person's principal.

(7) References to an electronic signature and to the certification of such a signature are to be read in accordance with section 7(2) and (3) of the Electronic Communications Act 2000 (c 7).

III WAL [345]

237 Giving notices, statements and other documents

(1) This section applies where this Act requires or authorises a person to—

(a) notify a person of something, or

(b) give a document to a person (including a notice or a copy of a document).

(2) The notification or document may be given to a person—

(a) by delivering it to the person,

(b) by leaving it at, or posting it to, one of the places mentioned in subsection (3), or

(c) if the conditions in subsection (4) are complied with, by sending it to the person in electronic form.

(3) The places are—

(a) the person's last known residence or place of business,

(b) any place specified by the person as a place where the person may be given notifications or documents, or

(c) if the notification or document is given to a person in that person's capacity as a contract-holder, the dwelling subject to the occupation contract.

(4) A notification or document may be given to a person by sending it in an electronic form if it complies with the conditions in, and any conditions under, section 236(4) and—

- (a) the person has indicated a willingness to receive the notification or document electronically,
- (b) the text is received by the person in legible form, and
- (c) the text is capable of being used for subsequent reference.

(5) The notification or document may be given to a body corporate by being given to the secretary or clerk of that body.

(6) A notification or document given to a person by leaving it at any of the places mentioned in subsection (3) is to be treated as having been given at the time at which it was left at that place.

CHAPTER 2 TRESPASSERS: IMPLIED TENANCIES AND LICENCES

III WAL [346]

238 Implied tenancies and licences

(1) This section applies if—

- (a) a dwelling which is not subject to an occupation contract is occupied as a home by a person ("T") who is a trespasser in relation to that dwelling, and
- (b) T makes payments in respect of his or her occupation of the dwelling to a person ("P") who would be entitled (whether alone or jointly) to bring proceedings to evict T as a trespasser.

(2) If P accepts such payments from T—

- (a) knowing that T is a trespasser in relation to the dwelling, or
- (b) at a time when P ought reasonably to know that T is a trespasser in relation to the dwelling,

P is to be treated as having made a periodic contract with T immediately after the end of the relevant period.

(3) The relevant period is the period of two months starting with the day on which P first accepts a payment from T as mentioned in subsection (2).

(4) Subsection (2) does not apply if before the end of the relevant period P brings proceedings to evict T as a trespasser or otherwise shows an intention to treat T as a trespasser.

(5) A contract under subsection (2) is either a tenancy or a licence.

(6) The tenancy or licence entitles T to occupy the dwelling as a home from the day immediately after the last day of the relevant period.

(7) The amount of rent and rental periods are to be determined having regard to the amount and frequency of the payment or payments made by T and any other relevant circumstances.

(8) A tenancy or licence under which T is entitled to occupy the dwelling as a home may not be implied except as provided in this section; but nothing in this section prevents P and T expressly making such a tenancy or licence before the end of the relevant period.

CHAPTER 3 TENANCIES AND LICENCES EXISTING BEFORE COMMENCEMENT OF THIS CHAPTER

III WAL [347]

239 Abolition of assured, secure and other tenancies

(1) On and after the appointed day, no tenancy or licence (whenever made) can be—

(a) a restricted contract;

(b) a protected shorthold tenancy;

(c) a secure tenancy;

(d) an assured tenancy (including an assured shorthold tenancy);

(e) an introductory tenancy;

(f) a demoted tenancy.

(2) If, immediately before the appointed day, the landlord under a protected or statutory tenancy might have recovered possession of the dwelling-house subject to the tenancy under Case 19 of Schedule 15 to the Rent Act 1977 (c 42) (former protected shorthold tenancies), the tenancy ceases to be a protected or statutory tenancy on the appointed day.

(3) Nothing in this section ends a tenancy or licence within subsection (1) or (2).

III WAL [348]

240 Conversion of tenancies and licences existing before commencement of Chapter

(1) For the purposes of determining the matters in subsection (2), a tenancy or licence which existed immediately before the appointed day is to be treated as if it were made on the appointed day.

(2) The matters are—

(a) whether the tenancy or licence is an occupation contract,

(b) the identity of the contract-holders under the contract, and

(c) whether the contract is a secure contract or a standard contract.

(3) Subsections (4) to (7) apply to a tenancy or licence which becomes an occupation contract on the appointed day.

(4) The fundamental provisions applicable to the contract are incorporated as terms of the contract.

(5) The existing terms of the contract continue to have effect, except to the extent that they—

(a) are incompatible with a fundamental provision incorporated as a term of the contract, or

(b) are terms of the contract because of an enactment repealed or revoked under this Act.

(6) The supplementary provisions applicable to the contract are incorporated as terms of the contract, except to the extent that they are incompatible with the existing terms of the contract.

(7) This section is subject to Schedule 12 (which makes further provision about existing tenancies and licences, modifies the application of this Act, and includes a fundamental provision incorporated into certain standard contracts).

WALES

III WAL [349]

241 Pre-existing contracts

(1) This section applies where, on or after the appointed day, a tenancy or licence is made in pursuance of a contract made before the day on which the order specifying the appointed day is made by the Welsh Ministers.

(2) Section 240 and Schedule 12 apply to the tenancy or licence as if—

(a) the day on which it is made is the appointed day, and
(b) immediately before that day it was a tenancy or licence of the kind it would have been on that day but for this Act.

(3) Paragraphs 2(3), 4(1) and (3), 11, 12, 13 and 23(3) and (7) of Schedule 12 do not apply in relation to the tenancy or licence.

III WAL [350]

242 Interpretation of Chapter

In this Chapter—

"the appointed day" ("*y diwrnod penodedig*") is the day appointed under section 257 as the day on which section 239 comes into force;

"assured shorthold tenancy" ("*tenantiaeth fyrddaliol sicr*") has the same meaning as in the Housing Act 1988 (c 50);

"assured tenancy" ("*tenantiaeth sicr*") has the same meaning as in the Housing Act 1988 (and includes an assured shorthold tenancy);

"demoted tenancy" ("*tenantiaeth isradd*") means a tenancy to which section 143A of the Housing Act 1996 (c 52) applies;

"introductory tenancy" ("*tenantiaeth ragarweiniol*") has the same meaning as in the Housing Act 1996;

"protected shorthold tenancy" ("*tenantiaeth fyrddaliol warchodedig*"), "protected tenancy" ("*tenantiaeth warchodedig*"), "restricted contract" ("*contract cyfyngedig*") and "statutory tenancy" ("*tenantiaeth statudol*") have the same meaning as in the Rent Act 1977 (c 42);

"secure tenancy" ("*tenantiaeth ddiogel*") has the same meaning as in the Housing Act 1985 (c 68), but it does not include a housing association tenancy within the meaning of section 86 of the Rent Act 1977.

PART 11
FINAL PROVISIONS

INTERPRETATION OF ACT

III WAL [351]

243 Local authority and other authorities

(1) This section applies for the purposes of interpreting this Act.

(2) The following are local authorities—

(a) a county council for an area in Wales,
(b) a county borough council, and
(c) a police and crime commissioner for a police area in Wales.

(3) "Local housing authority" (other than in paragraph 12 of Schedule 2) means a county council for an area in Wales or a county borough council.

(4) "Housing action trust" means a housing action trust established under Part 3 of the Housing Act 1988 (c 50) and includes any body established under section 88 of that Act.

(5) "New town corporation" has the same meaning as in the Housing Act 1985 (c 68) (see section 4 of that Act).

(6) "Urban development corporation" means an urban development corporation established under Part 16 of the Local Government, Planning and Land Act 1980 (c 65) and includes any body established under section 165B of that Act.

III WAL [352]

244 Landlord, lodger and permitted occupier

(1) This section applies for the purposes of interpreting this Act.

(2) The landlord, in relation to an occupation contract, is the person that is (or purports to be) entitled to confer on an individual a right to occupy the dwelling as a home.

(3) A person lives in a dwelling as a lodger if the tenancy or licence under which he or she occupies the dwelling falls within paragraph 6 of Schedule 2 (accommodation shared with landlord).

(4) But a person does not live in a dwelling as a lodger if he or she is given notice under paragraph 3 of Schedule 2 that his or her tenancy or licence is an occupation contract.

(5) A person is a permitted occupier of a dwelling subject to an occupation contract if—

(a) he or she lives in the dwelling as a lodger or sub-holder of the contract-holder, or

(b) he or she is not a lodger or sub-holder but is permitted by the contract-holder to live in the dwelling as a home.

III WAL [353]

245 Occupation date of an occupation contract

In this Act, the occupation date of an occupation contract is the day on which the contract-holder is entitled to begin occupying the dwelling.

III WAL [354]

246 Dwelling

(1) For the purposes of this Act "dwelling" means a dwelling which is wholly in Wales, and?—

(a) does not include any structure or vehicle which is capable of being moved from one place to another, but

(b) includes any land occupied together with the dwelling, unless the land is agricultural land exceeding 0.809 hectares.

(2) "Agricultural land" means—

(a) land used as arable, meadow or pasture ground only;

(b) land used for a plantation or a wood or for the growth of saleable underwood;

(c) land used for the purpose of poultry farming, market gardens, nursery grounds, orchards or allotments, including allotment gardens within the meaning of the Allotments Act 1922 (c 51),

but does not include land occupied together with a house as a park, gardens (other than as mentioned in paragraph (c)) or pleasure grounds, land used mainly or exclusively for purposes of sport or recreation or land used as a racecourse.

(3) Dwelling, in relation to an occupation contract, means the dwelling subject to the contract.

III WAL [355]

247 Meaning of "variation" of occupation contract

In this Act "variation", in relation to an occupation contract—

(a) includes the addition or removal of a term of the contract;

(b) does not include any change in the identity of the landlord or contract-holder under the contract.

III WAL [356]

248 The court

In this Act "the court" means the High Court or the county court.

III WAL [357]

249 Lease, tenancy and related expressions

(1) In this Act "lease" and "tenancy" have the same meaning.

(2) Both expressions include—

(a) a sub-lease or a sub-tenancy, and

(b) a lease or tenancy (or a sub-lease or sub-tenancy) in equity.

(3) The expressions "lessor" and "lessee" and "landlord" and "tenant", and references to letting, to the grant or making of a lease or to covenants or terms, are to be read accordingly.

(4) "Tenancy" and "licence" mean a tenancy or licence relating to a dwelling (see section 246).

III WAL [358]

250 Members of a family

(1) A person is a member of another's family for the purposes of this Act if—

(a) he or she is the spouse or civil partner of that person,

(b) he or she and that person live together as if they were spouses or civil partners, or

(c) he or she is that person's parent, grandparent, child, grandchild, brother, sister, uncle, aunt, nephew or niece.

(2) For the purposes of subsection (1)(c)—

(a) a relationship by marriage or civil partnership is to be treated as a relationship by blood,

(b) a relationship between persons who have only one parent in common is to be treated as a relationship between persons who have both parents in common, and

(c) except for the purposes of paragraph (b), the stepchild of a person is to be treated as his or her child.

III WAL [359]

251 Family property order

(1) For the purposes of this Act a family property order is an order under—

(a) section 24 of the Matrimonial Causes Act 1973 (c 18) (property adjustment orders in connection with matrimonial proceedings),

(b) section 17 or 22 of the Matrimonial and Family Proceedings Act 1984 (c 42) (property adjustment orders etc after overseas divorce),

(c) paragraph 1 of Schedule 1 to the Children Act 1989 (c 41) (orders for financial relief against parents),

(d) Schedule 7 to the Family Law Act 1996 (c 27) (transfer of tenancies on divorce or separation),

(e) Part 2 of Schedule 5 to the Civil Partnership Act 2004 (c 33) (property adjustment orders in connection with civil partnership), or

(f) paragraph 9 or 13 of Schedule 7 to that Act (property adjustment orders etc on overseas dissolution of civil partnership).

(2) An order under Schedule 1 to the Matrimonial Homes Act 1983 (c 19) (as it continues to have effect because of Schedule 9 to the Family Law Act 1996) is also a family property order.

III WAL [360]

252 Minor definitions

In this Act—

"common parts" ("*rhannau cyffredin*"), in relation to a dwelling subject to an occupation contract, means—

(a) any part of a building comprising that dwelling, and

(b) any other premises (including any other dwelling),

which the contract-holder is entitled under the terms of the contract to use in common with others;

"contract of employment" ("*contract cyflogaeth*") means a contract of service or apprenticeship, whether express or implied and (if it is express) whether oral or in writing;

"Convention rights" ("*hawliau Confensiwn*") has the same meaning as in the Human Rights Act 1998 (c 42);

"enactment" ("*deddfiad*") means an enactment (whenever enacted or made, unless the contrary intention appears) comprised in, or in an instrument made under—

(a) an Act of Parliament, or

(b) a Measure or an Act of the National Assembly for Wales (including this Act);

"fixed term contract" ("*contract cyfnod penodol*") means an occupation contract that is not a periodic contract;

"housing association" ("*cymdeithas dai*") has the same meaning as in the Housing Associations Act 1985 (c 69) (see section 1 of that Act);

"housing trust" ("*ymddiriedolaeth dai*") has the same meaning as in that Act (see section 2 of that Act);

"prescribed" ("*rhagnodedig*") means prescribed by regulations made by the Welsh Ministers;

"registered charity" ("*elusen gofrestredig*") means a charity registered under the Charities Act 2011 (c 25);

"rent" ("*rhent*") includes a sum payable under a licence;

"rental period" ("*cyfnod rhentu*") means a period in respect of which a payment of rent falls to be made.

III WAL [361]

253 Index of terms

The following table contains an index of terms used in this Act (other than in sections or paragraphs where the term used is defined or explained in that section or paragraph)—

TABLE 2

additional terms (of an occupation contract) ("*telerau ychwanegol (contract meddiannaeth)*")	section 28
anti-social behaviour ("*ymddygiad gwrthgymdeithasol*")	section 55
appointed day ("*diwrnod penodedig*")	section 242
assured shorthold tenancy ("*tenantiaeth fyrd-daliol sicr*")	section 242
assured tenancy ("*tenantiaeth sicr*")	section 242
authorised deposit scheme ("*cynllun blaendal awdurdodedig*")	section 47
common parts ("*rhannau cyffredin*")	section 252
community landlord ("*landlord cymunedol*")	section 9
contract-holder ("*deiliad contract*")	section 7 (see also section 48)

WALES

contract-holder's break clause ("*cymal terfynu deiliad contract*")	section 189
contract of employment ("*contract cyflogaeth*")	section 252
Convention rights ("*hawliau Confensiwn*")	section 252
co-operative housing association ("*cymdeithas dai gydweithredol*")	section 9
court ("*llys*")	section 248
demoted tenancy ("*tenantiaeth isradd*")	section 242
deposit ("*blaendal*")	section 47
dwelling ("*annedd*")	section 246
enactment ("*deddfiad*")	section 252
estate management grounds ("*seiliau rheoli ystad*")	section 160 and Schedule 8
family property order ("*gorchymyn eiddo teuluol*")	section 251
fixed term contract ("*contract cyfnod penodol*")	section 252
fully mutual housing association ("*cymdeithas dai gwbl gydfuddiannol*")	section 9
fundamental provision ("*darpariaeth sylfaenol*")	section 18 (see also section 19)
fundamental term ("*teler sylfaenol*")	section 19
head landlord ("*prif landlord*")	section 59
housing action trust ("*ymddiriedolaeth gweithredu tai*")	section 243
housing association ("*cymdeithas dai*")	section 252
housing trust ("*ymddiriedolaeth dai*")	section 252
initial requirements (in relation to an authorised deposit scheme) ("*gofynion cychwynnol (o ran cynllun blaendal awdurdodedig)*")	section 47
introduction date ("*dyddiad cyflwyno*")	paragraphs 1 and 2 of Schedule 4
introductory period ("*cyfnod rhagarweiniol*")	paragraph 1 of Schedule 4
introductory standard contract ("*contract safonol rhagarweiniol*")	section 16
introductory tenancy ("*tenantiaeth ragarweiniol*")	section 242
key matter (in relation to an occupation contract) ("*mater allweddol (o ran contract meddiannaeth)*")	sections 26 and 27
landlord ("*landlord*")	section 244 (see also section 53)
landlord's break clause ("*cymal terfynu'r landlord*")	section 194
lease ("*les*")	section 249
local authority ("*awdurdod lleol*")	section 243
local housing authority (other than in paragraph 12 of Schedule 2) ("*awdurdod tai lleol*")	section 243
lodger ("*lletywr*")	section 244
member of a family ("*aelod o deulu*")	section 250
new town corporation ("*corfforaeth tref newydd*")	section 243
occupation contract ("*contract meddiannaeth*")	section 7
occupation date ("*dyddiad meddiannu*")	section 245
permitted occupier ("*meddiannydd a ganiateir*")	section 244

possession claim ("*hawliad meddiant*")	section 149
possession notice ("*hysbysiad adennill meddiant*")	section 150
prescribed ("*rhagnodedig*")	section 252
priority successor (in relation to an occupation contract) ("*olynydd â blaenoriaeth (o ran contract meddiannaeth)*")	section 83
priority successor (of a contract-holder) ("*olynydd â blaenoriaeth (i ddeiliad contract)*")	section 75
private landlord ("*landlord preifat*")	section 10
private registered provider of social housing ("*darparwr tai cymdeithasol preifat cofrestredig*")	section 9
probation period ("*cyfnod prawf*")	paragraph 3 of Schedule 7
prohibited conduct ("*ymddygiad gwaharddedig*")	section 55
prohibited conduct standard contract ("*contract safonol ymddygiad gwaharddedig*")	section 116
protected shorthold tenancy ("*tenantiaeth fyrddaliol warchodedig*")	section 242
protected tenancy ("*tenantiaeth warchodedig*")	section 242
registered charity ("*elusen gofrestredig*")	section 252
registered social landlord ("*landlord cymdeithasol cofrestredig*")	section 9
rent ("*rhent*")	section 252
rental period ("*cyfnod rhentu*")	section 252
reserve successor (in relation to an occupation contract) ("*olynydd wrth gefn (o ran contract meddiannaeth)*")	section 83
reserve successor (of a contract-holder) ("*olynydd wrth gefn (i ddeiliad contract)*")	sections 76 and 77
restricted contract ("*contract cyfyngedig*")	section 242
secure contract ("*contract diogel*")	section 8
secure tenancy ("*tenantiaeth ddiogel*")	section 242
security ("*sicrwydd*")	section 47
service installation ("*gosodiad gwasanaeth*")	section 92
standard contract ("*contract safonol*")	section 8
statutory tenancy ("*tenantiaeth statudol*")	section 242
sub-holder ("*isddeiliad*")	section 59
sub-occupation contract ("*contract isfeddiannaeth*")	section 59
supplementary provision (other than in sections 255 and 256) ("*darpariaeth atodol*")	section 23
supplementary term ("*teler atodol*")	section 23
supported accommodation ("*llety â chymorth*")	section 143
supported standard contract ("*contract safonol â chymorth*")	section 143
tenancy ("*tenantiaeth*")	section 249
urban development corporation ("*corfforaeth datblygu trefol*")	section 243
variation ("*amrywiad*")	section 247

WALES

Crown Application

III WAL [362]

254 Crown application
This Act applies to the Crown.

Consequential and Transitional Provision etc

III WAL [363]

255 Power to make consequential and transitional provision etc
(1) If the Welsh Ministers consider it necessary or expedient for the purpose of giving full effect to any provision of this Act, or in consequence of any such provision, they may by regulations make—
- (a) any supplemental, incidental, or consequential provision, and
- (b) any transitory, transitional or saving provision.

(2) Regulations under subsection (1) may amend, repeal, revoke or modify any enactment (including a provision of this Act) enacted or made on or before the day on which this Act receives Royal Assent.

Regulations

III WAL [364]

256 Regulations
(1) Any power to make regulations under this Act—
- (a) is exercisable by statutory instrument,
- (b) may be exercised so as to make different provision for different cases or descriptions of case or different purposes or areas,
- (c) may be exercised so as to make different provision for different kinds or descriptions of occupation contract, unless the power applies only in relation to particular kinds or descriptions of occupation contract, and
- (d) includes power to make incidental, supplementary, consequential, transitory, transitional or saving provision.

(2) Regulations under this Act may make consequential amendments to, and modifications, repeals and revocations of, an enactment other than a provision of this Act.

(3) Regulations to which this subsection applies may not be made unless a draft of the statutory instrument containing the regulations (whether alone or with regulations to which this subsection does not apply) has been laid before, and approved by a resolution of, the National Assembly for Wales.

(4) Subsection (3) applies to regulations under—
- (a) section 9 (power to amend that section),
- (b) section 22 (powers in relation to fundamental provisions),
- (c) section 56 (power to amend section 55),
- (d) section 68 (power to amend sections 66 and 67),
- (e) section 217 (power to amend that section),
- (f) section 223 (power to amend sections 220 and 222),
- (g) section 229 (power to amend sections 225 to 228),
- (h) paragraph 17 of Schedule 2 (power to amend that Schedule),
- (i) paragraph 17 of Schedule 3 (power to amend that Schedule),
- (j) paragraph 3 of Schedule 4 (power to change time limit for giving notice of extension of introductory period),

(k) paragraph 5 of Schedule 5 (power to amend that Schedule),
(l) paragraph 4 of Schedule 7 (power to change time limit for giving notice of extension of probationary period),
(m) paragraph 13 of Schedule 9 (power to amend that Schedule), and
(n) paragraph 33 of Schedule 12 (power to amend that Schedule).

(5) Subsection (3) also applies to any other regulations under this Act which amend, modify or repeal any provision of an Act of Parliament or a Measure or Act of the National Assembly for Wales.

(6) A statutory instrument containing regulations made under a provision of this Act to which subsection (3) does not apply is subject to annulment in pursuance of a resolution of the National Assembly for Wales.

Coming into Force and Short Title

III WAL [365]

257 Coming into force

(1) This Part comes into force on the day after the day on which this Act receives Royal Assent.

(2) The remaining provisions of this Act come into force on a day appointed by the Welsh Ministers in an order made by statutory instrument.

(3) An order under this section may—
(a) include transitory, transitional or saving provision;
(b) make different provision for different cases or descriptions of case or different purposes or areas;
(c) make different provision for different kinds or descriptions of occupation contract;
(d) appoint different days for different purposes.

III WAL [366]

258 Short title

The short title of this Act is the Renting Homes (Wales) Act 2016.

SCHEDULE 1
OVERVIEW OF FUNDAMENTAL PROVISIONS INCORPORATED AS TERMS OF OCCUPATION CONTRACTS

PART 1
SECURE CONTRACTS

III WAL [367]

TABLE 3

FUNDAMENTAL PROVISION	NATURE OF PROVISION	NOTES
Section 31	Landlord ("L") must provide contract-holder ("C-H") with written statement of occupation contract	
Sections 39 and 40	L must provide C-H with L's name and address and other information	

WALES

Section 41	Notices and documents must be in writing	
Sections 43 and 45	Payment of deposits etc and requirement that L uses authorised deposit scheme	Section 45 must be incorporated without modification.
Section 49	C-H may, with L's consent, add joint C-H	
Section 52	Rights of joint C-H where another joint C-H dies or otherwise leaves contract	Must be incorporated without modification.
Section 54	L must not interfere with C-H's right to occupy the dwelling	
Section 55	Anti-social behaviour and other prohibited conduct	Must be incorporated without modification.
Section 57	C-H may only deal with the occupation contract in limited ways	
Section 88	C-H may set off compensation L is liable to pay under section 87 against C-H's rent	
Sections 91 to 93 and 95 to 99	L's obligations to keep the dwelling in good state of repair etc	
Sections 103 to 109	When and how contract may be varied	Sections 103(1)(b) and (2) and 108 must be incorporated without modification. Section 104 applies only to contracts under which rent is payable, and section 105 applies only to contracts under which consideration other than rent is payable.
Section 111	Withdrawal of joint C-H	
Section 113	C-H may have lodgers	
Section 114	C-H may transfer contract to potential successors	
Section 118	C-H's right to transfer to other secure C-Hs	Only applies where L is a community landlord.
Sections 148 to 150	General provision about termination of contract	Sections 148 and 149 must be incorporated without modification.
Sections 152 to 155	Termination without possession claim	Section 155 (death of C-H) must be incorporated without modification.
Sections 157 to 159	Termination by L on ground of breach of contract	Section 158 (false statement inducing L to make contract) must be incorporated without modification.

Sections 160 and 161 and Part 1 of Schedule 8	Termination by L on an estate management ground	
Sections 163 to 167	Termination by notice given by C-H	
Section 206	Effect of order for possession	
Section 231	Termination of contract which has joint C-Hs	

PART 2
PERIODIC STANDARD CONTRACTS

III WAL [368]
TABLE 4

FUNDAMENTAL PROVISION	NATURE OF PROVISION	NOTES
Section 31	Landlord ("L") must provide contract-holder ("C-H") with written statement of occupation contract	
Sections 39 and 40	L must provide C-H with L's name and address and other information	
Section 41	Notices and documents must be in writing	
Sections 43 and 45	Payment of deposits etc and requirement that L uses authorised deposit scheme	Section 45 must be incorporated without modification.
Section 49	C-H may, with L's consent, add joint C-H	
Section 52	Rights of joint C-H where another joint C-H dies or otherwise leaves contract	Must be incorporated without modification.
Section 54	L must not interfere with C-H's right to occupy the dwelling	
Section 55	Anti-social behaviour and other prohibited conduct	Must be incorporated without modification.
Section 57	C-H may only deal with the occupation contract in limited ways	
Section 88	C-H may set off compensation L is liable to pay under section 87 against C-H's rent	
Sections 91 to 93 and 95 to 99	L's obligations to keep dwelling in good state of repair etc	
Sections 122 to 128	When and how contract may be varied	Sections 122(1)(a) and (2) and 127 must be in-

WALES

		corporated without modification. Section 123 applies only to contracts under which rent is payable, and section 124 applies only to contracts under which consideration other than rent is payable. Sections 125(1)(b) and 126 are not incorporated into contracts that do not incorporate section 173 (L's notice).
Section 130	Withdrawal of joint C-H	
Section 145	L's right to temporarily exclude C-H from supported accommodation	Applies only to supported standard contracts (see section 143).
Sections 148 to 150	General provision about termination of contract	Sections 148 and 149 must be incorporated without modification.
Section 151	Further provision about notices requiring contract-holder to give up possession	Applies only to introductory standard contracts and prohibited conduct standard contracts.
Sections 152 to 155	Termination without possession claim	Section 155 (death of C-H) must be incorporated without modification.
Sections 157 to 159	Termination by L on ground of breach of contract	Section 158 (false statement inducing L to make contract) must be incorporated without modification.
Sections 160 and 161 and Part 1 of Schedule 8	Termination by L on an estate management ground	
Sections 168 to 172	Termination by notice given by C-H	
Sections 173 to 180	Termination by notice given by L	If section 173 is not incorporated, sections 125(1)(b), 126, 175 and 176 do not apply. Section 175 also does not apply to a contract that is within Schedule 9. If a contract incorporates section 173 and is not within Schedule 9, section 175 must be incorporated without modification. If a contract incorporates section 173, section 176 must be incorporated without modification.
Sections 181 and 182	Termination by L on serious rent arrears ground	In section 182, subsection (2) is not applicable to introductory standard contracts and prohibited conduct standard con-

		tracts, and subsection (3) is applicable only to such contracts.
Section 183	Possession claims where contract has arisen at end of a fixed term standard contract	Only applies to a contract that has arisen at end of a fixed term standard contract (see section 184(2)).
Section 206	Effect of order for possession	
Section 231	Termination of contract which has joint C-Hs	
Paragraph 7 of Schedule 4	Variation of secure contract addressed in written statement of introductory standard contract	Only applies to introductory standard contracts where the written statement addresses the secure contract that may arise at the end of the introductory period, in accordance with paragraph 6(2) of Schedule 4.

PART 3

FIXED TERM STANDARD CONTRACTS

III WAL [369]

TABLE 5

FUNDAMENTAL PROVISION	NATURE OF PROVISION	NOTES
Section 31	Landlord ("L") must provide contract-holder ("C-H") with written statement of occupation contract	
Sections 39 and 40	L must provide C-H with L's name and address and other information	
Section 41	Notices and documents must be in writing	
Sections 43 and 45	Payment of deposits etc and requirement that L uses authorised deposit scheme	Section 45 must be incorporated without modification.
Section 49	C-H may, with L's consent, add joint C-H	
Section 52	Rights of joint C-H where another joint C-H dies or otherwise leaves contract	Must be incorporated without modification.
Section 54	L must not interfere with C-H's right to occupy the dwelling	

WALES

Section 55	Anti-social behaviour and other prohibited conduct	Must be incorporated without modification.
Section 57	C-H may only deal with the occupation contract in limited ways	
Section 88	C-H may set off compensation L is liable to pay under section 87 against C-H's rent	
Sections 91 to 93 and 95 to 99	L's obligations to keep dwelling in good state of repair etc	Not applicable to fixed term standard contracts made for a term of seven years or more.
Sections 134 to 136	When and how contract may be varied	Sections 134(1)(b) and (2) and 135 must be incorporated without modification. Section 135(2)(k) applies only if contract has a contract-holder's break clause (see section 189).
Section 145	L's right to temporarily exclude C-H from supported accommodation	Only applies to supported standard contracts (see section 143).
Sections 148 to 150	General provision about termination of contract	Sections 148 and 149 must be incorporated without modification.
Sections 152 to 155	Termination without possession claim	Section 155 (death of C-H) must be incorporated without modification (but not into fixed term standard contracts that contain the provision mentioned in section 139(1)).
Sections 157 to 159	Termination by L on ground of breach of contract	Section 158 (false statement inducing L to make contract) must be incorporated without modification.
Sections 160 and 161 and Part 1 of Schedule 8	Termination by L on an estate management ground	
Section 186	Termination by notice given by L in connection with the end of the term of the contract	Subsections (2) and (4) of section 186 do not apply to a contract which does not incorporate subsection (1), or a contract that is within Schedule 9. If a contract incorporates subsection (1) and is not within Schedule 9, subsections (2) and (4) must be incorporated without modification.
Sections 187 and 188	Termination by L on serious rent arrears ground	

Sections 190 to 193	Termination by notice given by C-H under contract-holder's break clause	Only apply if contract has a contract-holder's break clause.
Sections 195 to 201	Termination by notice given by L under landlord's break clause	Only apply if contract has a landlord's break clause. Section 196 also does not apply to a contract within Schedule 9. If a contract has a landlord's break clause and is not within Schedule 9, section 196 must be incorporated without modification. If contract has a landlord's break clause, section 196 (breach of deposit rules) must be incorporated without modification.
Section 206	Effect of order for possession	
Section 231	Termination of contract which has joint C-Hs	

SCHEDULE 2
EXCEPTIONS TO SECTION 7

PART 1
TENANCIES AND LICENCES NOT WITHIN SECTION 7 THAT ARE OCCUPATION CONTRACTS IF NOTICE IS GIVEN

III WAL [370]

The rule

1 (1) A tenancy or licence which is not within section 7 may be an occupation contract if—

(a) it confers the right to occupy the dwelling as a home on an individual ("the beneficiary") other than the person with whom it is made, and

(b) the notice condition is met.

(2) A tenancy or licence which is not within section 7 because no rent or other consideration is payable under it (and to which sub-paragraph (1) does not apply) may be an occupation contract if the notice condition is met.

(3) The notice condition is met if, before or at the time when the tenancy or licence is made, the landlord gives a notice to the person with whom it is made stating that it is to be an occupation contract.

Contracts for another's benefit: further provision

2 (1) This paragraph applies where a notice under paragraph 1(3) is given in relation to a tenancy or licence within paragraph 1(1)(a).

(2) The notice may specify provisions of this Act and regulations made under it which are to have effect in relation to the occupation contract as if references to the contract-holder were references to the beneficiary.

(3) If it does so, the provisions specified in the notice have effect accordingly.

(4) Section 20(1)(b) and (2)(b) applies to fundamental provisions specified in the notice as if references to the contract-holder were references to the beneficiary.

WALES

PART 2
TENANCIES AND LICENCES WITHIN SECTION 7 THAT ARE NOT OCCUPATION CONTRACTS UNLESS NOTICE IS GIVEN

III WAL [371]

The rule

3 (1) A tenancy or licence within section 7, but to which sub-paragraph (2) applies, is not an occupation contract unless the notice condition is met.

(2) This sub-paragraph applies to a tenancy or licence—

(a) which confers the right to occupy a dwelling for the purposes of a holiday,

(b) which relates to the provision of accommodation in a care institution (see paragraph 4),

(c) which is a temporary expedient (see paragraph 5), or

(d) to which the shared accommodation exception applies (see paragraph 6).

(3) The notice condition is met if, before or at the time when the tenancy or licence is made, the landlord gives a notice to the person with whom it is made stating that it is to be an occupation contract.

Meaning of "care institution"

4 "Care institution" means—

(a) a health service hospital within the meaning of the National Health Service (Wales) Act 2006 (c 49) (see section 206(1) of that Act),

(b) *an independent hospital, a care home or a residential family centre within the meaning of the Care Standards Act 2000 (c 14) (see sections 2 to 4 of that Act), or* [an independent hospital within the meaning of the Care Standards Act 2000 (c 14) (see section 2 of that Act),]

(c) *a children's home in respect of which a person is registered under Part 2 of that Act.* [a place at which a care home service within the meaning of paragraph 1 of Schedule 1 to the Regulation and Inspection of Social Care (Wales) Act 2016 (anaw 2) is provided wholly or mainly to persons aged 18 or over,]

[(d) a place at which a residential family centre service within the meaning of paragraph 3 of Schedule 1 to the Regulation and Inspection of Social Care (Wales) Act 2016 is provided, or

(e) a place in respect of which a person is registered under Part 1 of the Regulation and Inspection of Social Care (Wales) Act 2016 to provide—

(i) a secure accommodation service within the meaning of paragraph 2 of Schedule 1 to that Act, or

(ii) a care home service within the meaning of paragraph 1 of Schedule 1 to that Act to persons wholly or mainly under the age of 18.]

Meaning of "temporary expedient"

5 (1) A tenancy or licence is a temporary expedient if it is made as a temporary expedient with a person who entered the dwelling to which it relates (or any other dwelling) as a trespasser.

(2) It is irrelevant whether or not, before the beginning of the tenancy or licence, another tenancy or licence to occupy the dwelling (or any other dwelling) had been made with the person.

(3) A tenancy or licence which arises under section 238 is not a temporary expedient.

Meaning of "shared accommodation

6 (1) The shared accommodation exception applies if—

(a) the terms of the tenancy or licence provide for the tenant or licensee to share any accommodation with the landlord, and

(b) immediately before the tenancy or licence is made the landlord occupies as the landlord's only or principal home a dwelling which includes all or part of the shared accommodation.

(2) But the exception applies under sub-paragraph (1) only while the person who is from time to time the landlord in relation to the tenancy or licence continues to occupy such a dwelling as that person's only or principal home.

(3) The shared accommodation exception also applies if—

(a) the terms of the tenancy or licence provide for the tenant or licensee to share any accommodation with another person ("the beneficiary"),

(b) immediately before the tenancy or licence is made the beneficiary occupies as his or her only or principal home a dwelling which includes all or part of the shared accommodation,

(c) that dwelling is subject to a trust, and

(d) under the trust the beneficiary—

(i) is entitled to an interest in the dwelling, and

(ii) by reason of that interest, is entitled to occupy the dwelling.

(4) But the exception applies under sub-paragraph (3) only while the beneficiary continues to occupy such a dwelling as the beneficiary's only or principal home.

(5) A tenant or licensee shares accommodation with the landlord or beneficiary if the tenant or licensee has the use of it in common with the landlord or beneficiary (whether or not in common with others).

(6) "Accommodation" does not include an area used for storage, or a staircase, passage, corridor or other means of access.

(7) If two or more persons are the landlord in relation to a tenancy or licence, references to the landlord are references to any one of them.

Amendment *Text in italic is deleted and text in square brackets is inserted by the Regulation and Inspection of Social Care (Wales) Act 2016 (Consequential Amendments) Regulations 2018 with effect from a date to be appointed.*

PART 3
TENANCIES AND LICENCES THAT ARE NEVER OCCUPATION CONTRACTS

III WAL [372]

The rule

7 (1) A tenancy or licence is not an occupation contract at any time when this paragraph applies to it.

(2) This paragraph applies to a tenancy or licence if all the persons with whom it is made are excluded from being contract-holders by section 7(6) (individuals who have not reached the age of 18).

(3) This paragraph also applies to—

(a) a tenancy to which Part 2 of the Landlord and Tenant Act 1954 (c 56) (business tenancies) applies;

(b) a protected occupancy or a statutory tenancy within the meaning of the Rent (Agriculture) Act 1976 (c 80);

(c) a protected tenancy or a statutory tenancy within the meaning of the Rent Act 1977 (c 42);

(d) a secure tenancy that is a housing association tenancy, within the meaning of section 86 of the Rent Act 1977;

(e) a tenancy of an agricultural holding within the meaning of the Agricultural Holdings Act 1986 (c 5);

WALES

(f) a farm business tenancy within the meaning of the Agricultural Tenancies Act 1995 (c 8);
(g) a long tenancy (see paragraph 8);
(h) a tenancy or licence which relates to armed forces accommodation (see paragraph 9);
(i) a tenancy or licence which relates to direct access accommodation (see paragraph 10).

Meaning of "long tenancy"

8 (1) "Long tenancy" means—
(a) a tenancy for a fixed term of more than 21 years (whether or not it is or may become terminable before the end of that term by notice given by the tenant or by re-entry or forfeiture),
(b) a tenancy for a term fixed by law because of a covenant or obligation for perpetual renewal, other than a tenancy by sub-demise from one which is not a long tenancy, or
(c) a tenancy made in pursuance of Part 5 of the Housing Act 1985 (c 68) (the right to buy), including a tenancy made in pursuance of that Part as that Part had effect because of section 17 of the Housing Act 1996 (c 52) (the right to acquire).

(2) But a tenancy terminable by notice after a death is not a long tenancy unless it is a shared ownership tenancy.

(3) A shared ownership tenancy is a tenancy which—
(a) was made with a housing association which was a registered social landlord or a private registered provider of social housing,
(b) was made for a premium calculated by reference to a percentage of the value of the dwelling or of the cost of providing it, and
(c) when made complied with the requirements of the shared ownership regulations then in force.

(4) A tenancy made before any shared ownership regulations were in force is to be treated as within sub-paragraph (3)(c) if, when the tenancy was made, it complied with the requirements of the first such regulations to come into force after it was made.

(5) "Shared ownership regulations" means regulations under—
(a) section 140(4)(b) of the Housing Act 1980 (c 51), or
(b) paragraph 5 of Schedule 4A to the Leasehold Reform Act 1967 (c 88) made for the purposes of paragraph 4(2)(b) of that Schedule.

Meaning of "armed forces accommodation"

9 Armed forces accommodation is accommodation which is provided to—
(a) a member of any of Her Majesty's forces,
(b) a member of the family of a member of any of Her Majesty's forces, or
(c) a civilian subject to service discipline (within the meaning of section 370 of the Armed Forces Act 2006 (c 52)),

for the purposes of any of Her Majesty's forces.

Meaning of "direct access accommodation"

10 (1) Direct access accommodation is accommodation which—
(a) is provided by a community landlord or a registered charity,
(b) (subject to availability) is provided on demand to any person who appears to satisfy criteria determined by the community landlord or charity, and
(c) is provided only for periods of 24 hours (or less) at a time.

(2) Accommodation may be direct access accommodation even if it is provided to the same person for several periods in succession.

PART 4

TENANCIES AND LICENCES TO WHICH SPECIAL RULES APPLY: HOMELESSNESS

11

III WAL [373]

A tenancy or licence within section 7, but made with an individual by a local housing authority because of the authority's functions under Part 2 of the Housing (Wales) Act 2014 (anaw 7) (homelessness), is not an occupation contract unless the authority is satisfied that it owes a duty to the individual under section 75(1) of that Act (duty to secure availability of suitable accommodation).

12 (1) This paragraph applies where a local housing authority, in pursuance of any of its homelessness housing functions, makes arrangements with a relevant landlord for the provision of accommodation.

(2) A tenancy or licence within section 7 but made with a relevant landlord in pursuance of the arrangements is not an occupation contract until immediately after the end of the notification period.

(3) Sub-paragraph (2) does not apply if, before the end of the notification period, the landlord gives the person with whom the tenancy or licence is made notice that it is an occupation contract.

(4) The notification period is the period of 12 months starting with—

(a) the day on which that person was notified of—

(i) the outcome of the authority's assessment under section 62 of the Housing (Wales) Act 2014 (anaw 7) or the authority's decision under section 80(5) of that Act, or (as the case may be)

(ii) the authority's decision under section 184(3) or 198(5) of the Housing Act 1996 (c 52), or

(b) if there is—

(i) a review of that decision under section 85 of the Housing (Wales) Act 2014 or an appeal to the county court under section 88 of that Act, or (as the case may be)

(ii) a review of that decision under section 202 of the Housing Act 1996 or an appeal to the court under section 204 of that Act,

the day on which that person is notified of the outcome of the assessment or the decision on review, or the day on which the appeal is finally determined.

(5) In this paragraph—

"homelessness housing functions" ("*swyddogaethau darparu tai i'r digartref*") means?—

(a) in relation to a local housing authority for an area in Wales, its functions under sections 68, 73, 75, 82 and 88(5) of the Housing (Wales) Act 2014, and

(b) in relation to a local housing authority for an area in England, its functions under sections 188, 190, 200 and 204(4) of the Housing Act 1996;

"local housing authority" ("*awdurdod tai lleol*") means—

(a) in relation to Wales, a county council for an area in Wales or a county borough council, and

(b) in relation to England, a district council, a London borough council, the Common Council of the City of London or the Council of the Isles of Scilly;

"relevant landlord" ("*landlord perthnasol*") means—

(a) a community landlord which is a registered social landlord or a private registered provider of social housing, or

(b) a private landlord.

WALES

PART 5
TENANCIES AND LICENCES TO WHICH SPECIAL RULES APPLY: SUPPORTED ACCOMMODATION

13

III WAL [374]

(1) A tenancy or licence within section 7, but which relates to supported accommodation (see section 143), is not an occupation contract if the landlord intends that the accommodation provided under the tenancy or licence is not to be subject to an occupation contract.

(2) But if the tenancy or licence continues after the end of the relevant period, it becomes an occupation contract immediately after the end of that period.

(3) The relevant period is (subject to paragraph 14)—

(a) the period of six months starting with the start date of the tenancy or licence, or

(b) if the relevant period has been extended under paragraph 15, the period starting with the start date of the tenancy or licence and ending with the date specified in the notice of extension.

(4) The occupation date of a tenancy or licence which becomes an occupation contract under sub-paragraph (2) is the day immediately after the last day of the relevant period.

(5) For the purposes of this Part, the start date of a tenancy or licence is the day on which the tenant or licensee is first entitled under the tenancy or licence to occupy the dwelling subject to the tenancy or licence.

Meaning of relevant period where there are previous contracts

14 (1) This paragraph applies in relation to a tenancy or licence mentioned in paragraph 13(1) ("the current tenancy or licence") if—

(a) the tenant or licensee was previously entitled to occupy supported accommodation under one or more relevant previous contracts, and

(b) the current tenancy or licence is the immediate successor of a relevant previous contract.

(2) A relevant previous contract is a tenancy or licence which relates to supported accommodation and to—

(a) the dwelling to which the current tenancy or licence relates ("the current dwelling");

(b) if the current dwelling forms part only of a building, another dwelling which is in?—

(i) that building, or

(ii) if that building is one of a number of buildings managed as a single entity, any of those buildings.

(3) If there is a sole tenant or licensee and one relevant previous contract, the relevant period is—

(a) the period of six months starting with the start date of the relevant previous contract, or

(b) if the relevant period has been extended under paragraph 15, the period set out in the notice of extension.

(4) If there is a sole tenant or licensee and two or more relevant previous contracts running in immediate succession, the relevant period is—

(a) the period of six months starting with the start date of the first of those contracts, or

(b) if the relevant period has been extended under paragraph 15, the period set out in the notice of extension.

(5) If there are joint tenants or licensees, the relevant period is—

(a) the period of six months starting with the date determined by—

(i) identifying, in relation to each joint tenant or licensee, the date on which the relevant period would start under sub-paragraph (3)(a) or (4)(a) if he or she were the sole tenant or licensee, and

(ii) taking the earliest of those dates, or

(b) if the relevant period has been extended under paragraph 15, the period set out in the notice of extension.

(6) A tenancy or licence ("contract 2") is the immediate successor of another tenancy or licence ("contract 1") if contract 1 ends immediately before the start date of contract 2.

Extending the relevant period

15 (1) The landlord may (on one or more occasions) extend the relevant period of a tenancy or licence mentioned in paragraph 13(1) by giving the tenant or licensee a notice of extension in accordance with this paragraph.

(2) The relevant period may not be extended by more than three months on any separate occasion.

(3) The notice of extension must be given at least four weeks before the date on which the relevant period would end under whichever of the following applies—

(a) paragraph 13(3)(a) or (b);

(b) paragraph 14(3)(a) or (b);

(c) paragraph 14(4)(a) or (b);

(d) paragraph 14(5)(a) or (b).

(4) Before giving a notice of extension, the landlord must consult the tenant or licensee.

(5) A landlord (other than a local housing authority) may not give a notice of extension without the consent of the local housing authority in whose area the accommodation is provided.

(6) The notice of extension must—

(a) state that the landlord has decided to extend the relevant period,

(b) set out the reasons for extending the relevant period,

(c) if the landlord is not a local housing authority, state that the local housing authority in whose area the accommodation is provided has consented to the extension, and

(d) specify the date on which the relevant period will come to an end.

(7) The notice of extension must also inform the tenant or licensee that he or she has a right to apply for a review in the county court under paragraph 16, and of the time by which the application must be made.

(8) In making the decision to extend the relevant period, the landlord may take into account?—

(a) the conduct of the tenant or licensee (or, if there is more than one tenant or licensee, the conduct of any of them), and

(b) the conduct of any person who appears to the landlord to live in the dwelling.

(9) A landlord may take a person's conduct into account under sub-paragraph (8)(b) whether or not the person lives continuously in the dwelling, and whatever the capacity in which the person lives in the dwelling.

(10) The Welsh Ministers may make provision by regulations for the purposes of sub-paragraph (5), including provision about the procedure to be followed in relation to obtaining the consent of a local housing authority.

County court review of decision to extend

16 (1) This section applies if a landlord gives a tenant or licensee a notice of extension under paragraph 15.

(2) The tenant or licensee may apply to the county court for a review—

(a) where the landlord is a local housing authority, of the decision to give a notice of extension, or

WALES

(b) where the landlord is not a local housing authority, of the local housing authority's decision to consent to the landlord giving the notice of extension.

(3) The application must be made before the end of the period of 14 days starting with the day on which the landlord gives the tenant or licensee a notice of extension.

(4) The county court may give permission for an application to be made after the end of the period allowed by sub-paragraph (3), but only if it is satisfied—

(a) where permission is sought before the end of that period, that there is a good reason for the tenant or licensee to be unable to make the application in time, or

(b) where permission is sought after that time, that there is a good reason for the tenant or licensee's failure to make the application in time and for any delay in applying for permission.

(5) The county court may—

(a) confirm or quash the decision, or

(b) vary the length of the extension (subject to paragraph 15(2)).

(6) In considering whether to confirm or quash the decision or vary the length of the extension, the county court must apply the principles applied by the High Court on an application for judicial review.

(7) If the county court varies the length of the extension, the notice of extension has effect accordingly.

(8) If the county court quashes the decision—

(a) the notice of extension is of no effect, and

(b) the county court may make any order the High Court could make when making a quashing order on an application for judicial review.

(9) If the county court quashes the decision and the landlord gives the tenant or licensee a further notice of extension under paragraph 15 before the end of the post-review period, the notice has effect as if given in accordance with paragraph 15(3) (other than for the purposes of sub-paragraph (3)).

(10) The post-review period is the period of 14 days beginning with the day on which the county court varies the length of the extension or quashes the decision.

PART 6
POWER TO AMEND SCHEDULE

17

III WAL [375]

The Welsh Ministers may by regulations amend this Schedule.

SCHEDULE 3

OCCUPATION CONTRACTS MADE WITH OR ADOPTED BY COMMUNITY LANDLORDS WHICH MAY BE STANDARD CONTRACTS

III WAL [376]

Occupation contracts by notice

1 An occupation contract which would not be an occupation contract but for a notice under paragraph 1 or 3 of Schedule 2.

Supported accommodation

2 An occupation contract which relates to supported accommodation.

Introductory occupation

3 (1) An occupation contract within this paragraph which does not relate to supported accommodation.

(2) An occupation contract is within this paragraph unless, immediately before the relevant date—

(a) a contract-holder under it was a contract-holder under a secure contract, and

(b) the landlord under the secure contract was a community landlord.

(3) The relevant date—

(a) in relation to a contract made with a community landlord, is the occupation date, and

(b) in relation to a contract under which a community landlord becomes the landlord, is the day on which it becomes the landlord.

Accommodation for asylum seekers

4 An occupation contract made in order to provide accommodation under Part 6 of the Immigration and Asylum Act 1999 (c 33) (support for asylum seekers).

Accommodation for displaced persons

5 An occupation contract made under the Displaced Persons (Temporary Protection) Regulations 2005 (SI 2005/1379).

Accommodation for homeless persons

6 An occupation contract made as described in paragraph 11 or 12 of Schedule 2 (accommodation for homeless persons).

Service occupancy: general

7 (1) An occupation contract where the contract-holder—

(a) is employed by a relevant employer, and

(b) is required by his or her contract of employment to occupy the dwelling.

(2) "Relevant employer" means—

(a) a local authority;

(b) a new town corporation;

(c) a housing action trust;

(d) an urban development corporation;

(e) a registered social landlord (other than a fully mutual housing association or a co-operative housing association);

(f) a private registered provider of social housing;

(g) a manager who exercises a local housing authority's management functions under a management agreement;

(h) the governing body of any of the following schools (see the School Standards and Framework Act 1998 (c 31))—

(i) a voluntary aided school,

(ii) a foundation school, or

(iii) a foundation special school.

(3) "Management agreement" means an agreement under section 27 of the Housing Act 1985 (c 68) and "manager" means a person with whom the agreement is made.

Service occupancy: police

8 An occupation contract where—

(a) the contract-holder is a member of a police force, and

(b) the dwelling is provided for the contract-holder free of rent under regulations made under section 50 of the Police Act 1996 (c 16) (general regulations as to government, administration and conditions of service).

Service occupancy: fire and rescue services

9 An occupation contract where—

(a) the contract-holder is an employee of a fire and rescue authority,

(b) the contract-holder's contract of employment requires him or her to live in close proximity to a particular fire station, and

(c) the dwelling is provided to him or her by the fire and rescue authority in consequence of that requirement.

Student accommodation

10 (1) An occupation contract where the right to occupy is conferred for the purpose of enabling the contract-holder to attend a designated course at an educational establishment.

(2) "Designated course" means a course of any kind prescribed for the purposes of this paragraph.

(3) "Educational establishment" means an institution or university which provides further education or higher education (or both); and "further education" and "higher education" have the same meaning as in the Education Act 1996 (c 56) (see sections 2 and 579 of that Act).

Temporary accommodation: land acquired for development

11 (1) An occupation contract where—

(a) the land the dwelling is on (including any land occupied together with the dwelling other than agricultural land exceeding 0.809 hectares) is, or is part of, land which has been acquired for development, and

(b) the dwelling is used by the landlord as temporary housing accommodation pending development of the land.

(2) "Development" has the meaning given by section 55 of the Town and Country Planning Act 1990 (c 8).

Temporary accommodation: persons taking up employment

12 An occupation contract where—

(a) immediately before the making of the contract the contract-holder was not living in the local housing authority area in which the dwelling is situated,

(b) before the making of the contract the contract-holder obtained employment or an offer of employment in that area or in an adjoining local housing authority area, and

(c) the right to occupy was conferred for the purpose of meeting the contract-holder's need for temporary accommodation in the local housing authority area in which the dwelling is situated or in an adjoining local housing authority area in order to work there, and enabling him or her to find permanent accommodation there.

Temporary accommodation: short-term arrangements

13 An occupation contract where—

(a) the dwelling has been let to the landlord with vacant possession for use as temporary housing accommodation,

(b) the terms on which it has been let include provision for the lessor to obtain vacant possession from the landlord at the end of a specified period or when required by the lessor,

(c) the lessor is not a community landlord, and

(d) the landlord has no interest in the dwelling other than under the lease in question or as mortgagor.

Temporary accommodation: accommodation during works

14 (1) An occupation contract where—

(a) the dwelling (the "temporary dwelling") has been made available for occupation by the contract-holder while works are carried out on the dwelling previously occupied by the contract-holder as a home,

(b) the landlord of the temporary dwelling is not the same as the landlord of the dwelling previously occupied by the contract-holder (the "old dwelling"), and

(c) the contract-holder was not a contract-holder under a secure contract of the old dwelling at the time when the contract-holder ceased to occupy it as a home.

(2) In this paragraph, references to the contract-holder include references to the contract-holder's predecessor.

(3) For the purposes of sub-paragraph (2), a person is a predecessor of a contract-holder under an occupation contract if that person was an earlier contract-holder under the same contract.

Accommodation which is not social accommodation

15 (1) An occupation contract where—

(a) the allocation rules did not apply to the making of the contract, or

(b) the dwelling is made available to the contract-holder because he or she is a key worker.

(2) The allocation rules are the landlord's rules for determining priority as between applicants in the allocation of housing accommodation, and include any rule or practice whereby the landlord provides accommodation to persons nominated by a local housing authority.

(3) Whether a contract-holder is a "key worker" is to be determined in accordance with regulations made by the Welsh Ministers.

(4) The regulations may include provision identifying key workers by reference to the nature of their employment, the identity of their employer, and the amount of their earnings.

Dwellings intended for transfer

16 An occupation contract where—

(a) the community landlord is a registered social landlord or a private registered provider of social housing,

(b) the landlord has acquired or built or otherwise developed the dwelling with the intention of transferring it to a fully mutual housing association or a co-operative housing association, and

(c) the occupation contract is made in anticipation of the transfer of the dwelling.

Power to amend Schedule

17 The Welsh Ministers may by regulations amend this Schedule.

SCHEDULE 4
INTRODUCTORY STANDARD CONTRACTS

III WAL [377]

Introductory period

1 (1) The introductory period, in relation to an occupation contract which is a periodic standard contract because the first exception in section 11 or 12 applies and because it is within paragraph 3 of Schedule 3, is—

(a) the period of 12 months starting with the introduction date of the contract, or

(b) if there is an extension under paragraph 3, the period of 18 months starting with the introduction date of the contract.

WALES

(2) Sub-paragraph (3) applies instead of sub-paragraph (1) if, at the end of what would be the introductory period under sub-paragraph (1)—

(a) a possession claim made by the landlord in respect of the dwelling has not been concluded, or

(b) the landlord has given the contract-holder a possession notice or a notice under section 173 (landlord's notice to end contract), and the period before the end of which the landlord may make a possession claim has not ended.

(3) Where this sub-paragraph applies, the introductory period is the period starting with the introduction date of the contract and ending—

(a) when a relevant event occurs, or

(b) if no relevant event occurs, immediately after the contract ends.

(4) In a case within sub-paragraph (2)(a) the relevant event is the conclusion of the possession claim in favour of the contract-holder.

(5) In a case within sub-paragraph (2)(b) each of the following is a relevant event—

(a) withdrawal of the notice;

(b) the period ending without a possession claim having been made;

(c) conclusion in favour of the contract-holder of a possession claim made in reliance on the notice.

(6) If a private landlord becomes the landlord under the contract before the time at which the introductory period would end apart from this sub-paragraph, the introductory period ends.

(7) The introduction date of an occupation contract is (subject to paragraph 2)—

(a) the occupation date of the contract, or

(b) if the contract became a periodic standard contract because the first exception in section 12 applied and because it was within paragraph 3 of Schedule 3 on a community landlord becoming the landlord under the contract, the day the community landlord became the landlord.

Meaning of introduction date where there are previous introductory standard contracts

2 (1) This paragraph applies in relation to an occupation contract which is a periodic standard contract because the first exception in section 11 or 12 applies and because it is within paragraph 3 of Schedule 3 if—

(a) a contract-holder under the contract ("the current contract") was previously a contract-holder under one or more introductory standard contracts ("previous contracts"), and

(b) the current contract is the immediate successor of a previous contract.

(2) If there is a sole contract-holder and one previous contract, the introduction date of the current contract is the introduction date of the previous contract.

(3) If there is a sole contract-holder and two or more previous contracts running in immediate succession, the introduction date of the current contract is the introduction date of the first of those contracts.

(4) If there are joint contract-holders, the introduction date of the contract is determined by?—

(a) identifying, in relation to each joint contract-holder, what the introduction date would be under sub-paragraphs (2) and (3) if he or she were the sole contract-holder, and

(b) taking the earliest of those dates.

(5) Sub-paragraph (6) applies if the introductory period of a previous contract with the same introduction date as the current contract was extended under paragraph 3.

(6) Where this sub-paragraph applies, the introductory period of the current contract is the period of 18 months starting with the introduction date of the current contract.

(7) An occupation contract ("contract 2") is the immediate successor of another contract ("contract 1") if contract 1 ends immediately before the occupation date of contract 2.

Extending the introductory period

3 (1) The landlord may extend the introductory period to the period of 18 months starting with the introduction date of the contract by giving the contract-holder a notice of extension.

(2) The notice of extension must be given to the contract-holder at least eight weeks before the day on which the introductory period would end under paragraph 1(1)(a).

(3) The notice of extension must state that the landlord has decided to extend the introductory period, and set out the reasons for that decision.

(4) The notice of extension must also inform the contract-holder that he or she has a right to request a review under paragraph 4 of the landlord's decision to extend the introductory period, and of the time by which the request must be made.

(5) In making the decision to extend the introductory period, the landlord may take into account—

(a) the conduct of the contract-holder (or, if there are joint contract-holders, the conduct of any of them), and

(b) the conduct of any person who appears to the landlord to live in the dwelling.

(6) A landlord may take a person's conduct into account under sub-paragraph (5)(b) whether or not the person lives continuously in the dwelling, and whatever the capacity in which the person lives in the dwelling.

(7) The Welsh Ministers may by regulations amend sub-paragraph (2) for the purpose of changing when a notice of extension must be given to a contract-holder; the power under section 256(2) to make consequential amendments includes, in its application to regulations under this sub-paragraph, the power to make consequential amendments to this Schedule.

Landlord's review of decision to extend introductory period

4 (1) If a landlord gives a notice of extension under paragraph 3, the contract-holder may request that the landlord carries out a review of the decision to give the notice.

(2) The request must be made to the landlord before the end of the period of 14 days (or such longer period as the landlord may allow in writing) starting with the day on which the landlord gives the contract-holder the notice of extension.

(3) If the contract-holder requests a review in accordance with sub-paragraph (2), the landlord must carry out the review.

(4) Following a review, the landlord may—

(a) confirm the decision to give the notice, or

(b) reverse the decision.

(5) The landlord must notify the contract-holder of the outcome of the review before the date on which the introductory period would end under paragraph 1(1)(a).

(6) If the landlord confirms the decision, the notice must—

(a) set out the reasons for the confirmation, and

(b) inform the contract-holder that he or she has a right to apply for a review in the county court under paragraph 5, and of the time by which the application must be made.

(7) The Welsh Ministers may prescribe the procedure to be followed in connection with a review under this paragraph.

(8) Regulations under sub-paragraph (7) may, amongst other things—

(a) require the review to be carried out by a person of appropriate seniority who has not been involved in the decision, and

(b) set out circumstances in which a contract-holder is entitled to an oral hearing, and whether and by whom he or she may be represented at such a hearing.

County court review of decision to extend

5 (1) This paragraph applies if a landlord, following a request for a review made in accordance with paragraph 4(2)—

(a) gives notice under paragraph 4(5) informing the contract-holder that the landlord has decided to confirm a decision to give a notice of extension under paragraph 3, or

(b) fails to give notice in accordance with paragraph 4(5).

(2) The contract-holder may apply to the county court for a review of the decision to give the notice of extension.

(3) The application must be made—

(a) before the end of the period of 14 days starting with the day on which the landlord gives the contract-holder notice under paragraph 4(5), or

(b) if no notice has been given in accordance with paragraph 4(5), before the end of the period of 14 days starting with the day after the date by which the landlord was required to give notice under that sub-paragraph.

(4) The county court may give permission for an application to be made after the end of the period allowed by sub-paragraph (3), but only if it is satisfied—

(a) where permission is sought before the end of that period, that there is a good reason for the contract-holder to be unable to make the application in time, or

(b) where permission is sought after that time, that there is a good reason for the contract-holder's failure to make the application in time and for any delay in applying for permission.

(5) The county court may confirm or quash the decision to give the notice of extension.

(6) In considering whether to confirm or quash the decision, the county court must apply the principles applied by the High Court on an application for judicial review.

(7) If the county court quashes the decision—

(a) the notice of extension is of no effect, and

(b) the county court may make any order the High Court could make when making a quashing order on an application for judicial review.

(8) If the county court quashes the decision and the landlord gives the contract-holder a further notice of extension under paragraph 3 before the end of the post-review period?—

(a) the notice has effect as if given in accordance with paragraph 3(2) (other than for the purposes of paragraph 4(2)), and

(b) paragraph 4(5) is to be read as if it requires the landlord to notify the contract-holder of the outcome of a review under that paragraph before the end of the period of 14 days starting with the day on which the contract-holder requested the review.

(9) The post-review period is the period of 14 days beginning with the day on which the county court quashes the decision.

Written statement may address secure contract arising at end of introductory standard contract

6 (1) Sub-paragraph (2) applies if, before the end of the introductory period, the landlord and the contract-holder have agreed (subject to the provisions of this Act as to the incorporation of fundamental and supplementary provisions) what the terms of the secure contract that may arise at the end of the introductory period are to be.

(2) A written statement of the introductory standard contract may set out the terms of the secure contract by—

(a) identifying the terms of the introductory standard contract that will not be terms of the secure contract, and setting out the terms that will apply only to the secure contract, or

(b) separately setting out all of the terms of the secure contract.

(3) Where a written statement of an introductory standard contract addresses the secure contract in accordance with sub-paragraph (2) (a "relevant written statement")—

(a) the relevant written statement is not incorrect (see section 37) merely because it addresses the secure contract,

(b) the landlord is to be treated as having complied with the requirement in section 31(1) (provision of written statement) in relation to the secure contract, and

(c) the terms of the secure contract may not be enforced against the contract-holder before the occupation date of that contract (and accordingly, section 42 does not apply).

(4) If the occupation date of a secure contract addressed in a relevant written statement changes because the landlord has extended the introductory period in accordance with paragraph 3, the relevant written statement is not incorrect merely because it does not set out the new occupation date.

7 (1) A secure contract addressed in a relevant written statement may be varied by agreement between the landlord and the contract-holder before the occupation date of the secure contract, subject to sub-paragraphs (2) to (5).

(2) Section 108(1) to (5) (limit on variation) applies in relation to such a variation.

(3) Sections 109(1) to (3) and 110 (written statement of variation) apply in relation to such a variation.

(4) Section 104(1) to (3) or (as the case may be) section 105(1)(b) and (2) to (4) applies in relation to a variation of the rent or other consideration which is to be payable under the secure contract.

(5) Sections 104(3)(a) and 105(4)(a), as applied by sub-paragraph (4), are to be read as if for "any date" there were substituted "the occupation date of the secure contract, or a later date".

(6) This paragraph is a fundamental provision which is incorporated as a term of all introductory standard contracts where the written statement of the contract is a relevant written statement; section 20 provides that this paragraph—

(a) must be incorporated, and

(b) must not be incorporated with modifications.

Terms of secure contract which was an introductory standard contract

8 (1) This paragraph applies where an introductory standard contract ends and is replaced with a secure contract because the introductory period has ended, and the landlord has not addressed the secure contract in the written statement of the introductory standard contract in accordance with paragraph 6(2).

(2) If the landlord and the contract-holder have agreed what the terms of the secure contract are to be in that event, the terms of the contract are the terms agreed.

(3) Sub-paragraph (2) is subject to the provisions of this Act as to the incorporation of fundamental and supplementary provisions.

(4) If the landlord and the contract-holder have not agreed what the terms of the secure contract are to be in that event—

(a) the fundamental and supplementary provisions applicable to secure contracts made with the landlord are incorporated as terms of the contract without modification,

(b) any terms of the contract which are incompatible with those fundamental or supplementary provisions cease to have effect, and

(c) otherwise, the terms of the secure contract are the same as the terms of the introductory standard contract.

Landlord's duty to give address at start of contract does not apply in relation to secure contract

9 The requirement in section 39(1) (landlord must give contract-holder a contact address at start of contract) does not apply in relation to a secure contract which replaces an introductory standard contract.

SCHEDULE 5
DEPOSIT SCHEMES: FURTHER PROVISION

III WAL [378]

Deposit schemes

1 (1) The Welsh Ministers must make arrangements for securing that one or more deposit schemes are available.

(2) "Deposit scheme" means a scheme for the purpose of—

- (a) safeguarding deposits paid in connection with occupation contracts, and
- (b) facilitating the resolution of disputes arising in connection with such deposits.

(3) "Arrangements" means arrangements with any person ("the scheme administrator") under which the scheme administrator undertakes to establish and maintain a deposit scheme of a description specified in the arrangements.

(4) The arrangements must require the scheme administrator to give the Welsh Ministers such information, and such facilities for obtaining information, as the Welsh Ministers may require.

(5) The Welsh Ministers may—

- (a) give financial assistance to the scheme administrator;
- (b) make other payments to the scheme administrator in pursuance of the arrangements;
- (c) guarantee the discharge of any financial obligation incurred by the scheme administrator in connection with the arrangements.

(6) The Welsh Ministers may make regulations conferring powers and imposing duties on scheme administrators.

Authorised deposit schemes: proceedings where the occupation contract has not ended

2 (1) Where a deposit has been paid in connection with an occupation contract that has not ended, the contract-holder (or any person who has paid the deposit on his or her behalf) may make an application to the county court on any of the following grounds.

(2) The first ground is that the landlord has not complied with section 45(2)(a) (initial requirements of an authorised deposit scheme).

(3) The second ground is that the landlord has not complied with section 45(2)(b) (provision of required information).

(4) The third ground is that the applicant—

- (a) has been notified by the landlord that a particular authorised deposit scheme applies to the deposit, but
- (b) has been unable to obtain confirmation from the scheme administrator that the deposit is being held in accordance with the scheme.

(5) The county court must act as follows if—

- (a) in the case of an application on the first or second ground, it is satisfied that the ground is made out, or
- (b) in the case of an application on the third ground, it is not satisfied that the deposit is being held in accordance with an authorised deposit scheme.

(6) The county court must either—

(a) order the person who appears to be holding the deposit to repay the deposit to the applicant before the end of the relevant period, or

(b) order the person who appears to be holding the deposit to pay the deposit, before the end of the relevant period, to the scheme administrator of a custodial deposit scheme (if such a scheme is in force in accordance with arrangements under paragraph 1) to be held in accordance with the scheme.

(7) The county court must also order the landlord to pay to the applicant, before the end of the relevant period, a sum of money not less than the amount of the deposit and not more than three times the amount of the deposit.

(8) The relevant period is the period of 14 days beginning with the date of the order.

(9) For the purposes of this paragraph, a custodial deposit scheme is a deposit scheme (within the meaning of paragraph 1(2)) under which deposits are paid to the scheme administrator by the landlord and held by the scheme administrator until, in accordance with the scheme, they fall to be paid to the landlord or contract-holder (or any person who paid the deposit on the contract-holder's behalf).

Authorised deposit schemes: proceedings where the occupation contract has ended

3 (1) Where a deposit has been paid in connection with an occupation contract that has ended, the person who was the contract-holder under the contract (or any person who paid the deposit on his or her behalf) may make an application to the county court on any of the following grounds.

(2) The first ground is that the landlord did not comply with section 45(2)(a) (initial requirements of an authorised deposit scheme).

(3) The second ground is that the landlord did not comply with section 45(2)(b) (provision of required information).

(4) The third ground is that the applicant—

(a) was notified by the landlord that a particular authorised deposit scheme applied to the deposit, but

(b) has been unable to obtain confirmation from the scheme administrator that the deposit is being held in accordance with the scheme.

(5) If the county court—

(a) in the case of an application on the first or second ground, is satisfied that the ground is made out, or

(b) in the case of an application on the third ground, is not satisfied that the deposit is being held in accordance with an authorised deposit scheme,

it may order the person who appears to be holding the deposit to repay all or part of the deposit to the applicant before the end of the relevant period.

(6) If sub-paragraph (5)(a) or (b) applies, the county court (whether or not it makes an order under that sub-paragraph) must order the landlord to pay to the applicant, before the end of the relevant period, a sum of money not less than the amount of the deposit and not more than three times the amount of the deposit.

(7) The relevant period is the period of 14 days beginning with the date of the order.

Existing deposit used in connection with a renewed or other kind of substitute occupation contract

4 (1) This paragraph applies where—

(a) a contract-holder paid a deposit in connection with an occupation contract ("the original contract"),

(b) the landlord, in respect of the deposit—

(i) dealt with it in accordance with an authorised deposit scheme,

(ii) complied with the initial requirements of the scheme, and

(iii) provided the information required by section 45(2)(b),

WALES

(c) the original contract is replaced with a substitute occupation contract, and

(d) the deposit that was paid in connection with the original contract continues to be held—

(i) in connection with the substitute occupation contract, and

(ii) in accordance with the same authorised deposit scheme as when the requirements mentioned in paragraph (b)(ii) and (iii) were last complied with in respect of it.

(2) This paragraph also applies where—

(a) a substitute occupation contract is replaced with a new substitute occupation contract, and

(b) the deposit that was paid in connection with the original contract continues to be held—

(i) in connection with the new substitute occupation contract, and

(ii) in accordance with the same authorised deposit scheme as when the requirements mentioned in sub-paragraph (1)(b)(ii) and (iii) were last complied with in respect of it.

(3) The landlord is to be treated as having complied with the requirements in section 45 in relation to the deposit held in connection with the substitute occupation contract.

(4) For the purposes of this paragraph, an occupation contract is replaced with a substitute occupation contract if—

(a) the occupation date of the substitute occupation contract falls immediately after the end of the preceding occupation contract,

(b) the landlord and contract-holder under the substitute occupation contract are the same as under the preceding contract, and

(c) the substitute occupation contract relates to the same (or substantially the same) dwelling as the preceding contract.

Power to amend Schedule

5 The Welsh Ministers may by regulations amend this Schedule.

SCHEDULE 6

REASONABLENESS OF WITHHOLDING CONSENT ETC

PART 1

INTRODUCTORY

1

III WAL [379]

(1) This Schedule applies for the purpose of determining whether—

(a) it is reasonable for a landlord to refuse consent to a transaction, or

(b) a condition subject to which a landlord gives consent is reasonable.

(2) Part 2 sets out circumstances which must be taken into account for that purpose, to the extent that they are relevant (and to the extent that there is no other requirement to take them into account for that purpose; for example, under the Human Rights Act 1998 (c 42)).

(3) Part 3 sets out circumstances (in addition to those in Part 2) which must be taken into account for that purpose in relation to specific kinds of transaction, to the extent that they are relevant (and to the extent that there is no other requirement to take them into account for that purpose).

(4) Parts 2 and 3 also set out certain circumstances in which it is always reasonable for a landlord to refuse consent or impose conditions (subject to

the Convention rights of the contract-holder and any other person affected by the landlord's decision).

PART 2
CIRCUMSTANCES WHICH MAY BE RELEVANT TO REASONABLENESS GENERALLY

III WAL [380]

Status of occupation contract

2 Whether any party to the contract has taken steps towards ending the contract or done any act which may cause the contract to end.

The dwelling

3 (1) The size and suitability of the dwelling affected by the transaction.

(2) Whether, as a result of the transaction, the dwelling will—

(a) constitute an overcrowded dwelling for the purposes of Part 10 of the Housing Act 1985 (c 68) (see section 324 of that Act),

(b) provide substantially more extensive accommodation than is reasonably required by the persons who will occupy the dwelling as a home, or

(c) provide accommodation that is not suitable to the needs of the persons who will occupy the dwelling as a home.

(3) Whether, if the transaction were to take place, an estate management ground would become available to the landlord (see Schedule 8).

(4) If the landlord has established requirements as to—

(a) the number of persons who are to occupy the dwelling affected by the transaction as a home, or

(b) the age or general characteristics of those persons,

whether the persons who will occupy the dwelling as a home will meet those requirements.

(5) But the landlord's requirements are to be taken into account under sub-paragraph (4) only to the extent that they are reasonable.

Circumstances of contract-holder and other occupiers

4 (1) The probable effect of the transaction on—

(a) the parties to the transaction, and

(b) any other person who occupies, or as a result of the transaction will occupy, the dwelling affected by the transaction as a home.

(2) The financial interests of the contract-holder; but this sub-paragraph does not apply (subject to the contract-holder's Convention rights) if the occupation contract is a secure contract and the landlord is a community landlord.

5 (1) The conduct of the contract-holder (including, in particular, whether he or she is or has been in breach of the occupation contract).

(2) Whether, if the landlord asked the contract-holder for information to enable the landlord to deal with the request for consent, the contract-holder provided that information.

6 If the contract-holder is in breach of the occupation contract when he or she requests the landlord's consent to the transaction, it is reasonable for the landlord to impose a condition that—

(a) the landlord's consent is to take effect only after the contract-holder ceases to be in breach, or

(b) despite anything in this Act or the occupation contract the person, or all the persons, who will be contract-holders after the transaction are to be liable in respect of the breach.

Circumstances of landlord

WALES

7 (1) The landlord's interests, including the landlord's financial interests.
(2) If the landlord is a community landlord, the probable effect of the transaction on its ability to fulfil its housing functions.
(3) Whether (and if so, when) a person would obtain a dwelling (or a dwelling similar to the dwelling affected by the transaction) from the landlord if the transaction did not take place.
(4) If the landlord is required to publish a summary of rules under section 106 of the Housing Act 1985 (c 68) (allocation of housing accommodation), those rules.
(5) If the landlord is a local housing authority, its allocation scheme (within the meaning of section 167 of the Housing Act 1996 (c 52)) and any information available under section 167(4A) of that Act to a person applying for an allocation of housing accommodation.
(6) If neither sub-paragraph (4) nor sub-paragraph (5) applies but the landlord has criteria for the allocation of accommodation, those criteria.

8 (1) The landlord's refusal of consent to a transaction is reasonable if—
(a) the landlord is a local housing authority, and
(b) as a result of the transaction a person who is ineligible (or is to be treated as ineligible) for an allocation of housing accommodation by the landlord will become a contract-holder.
(2) Sub-paragraph (1) does not apply to a transfer to a potential successor under section 114 or to a secure contract-holder under section 118.
(3) Whether a person is ineligible, or is to be treated as ineligible, for an allocation of housing accommodation by the landlord is to be determined in accordance with section 160A of the Housing Act 1996 (c 52) and regulations under that section.

PART 3
CIRCUMSTANCES WHICH MAY BE RELEVANT TO REASONABLENESS IN RELATION TO PARTICULAR TRANSACTIONS

III WAL [381]

Section 49: proposed joint contract-holder

9 (1) This paragraph applies where the contract-holder under the occupation contract seeks the landlord's consent to adding a joint contract-holder under section 49.
(2) Where this paragraph applies, the following circumstances (in addition to those in Part 2) must be taken into account (to the extent that they are relevant)—
(a) whether the proposed joint contract-holder is a suitable contract-holder;
(b) whether he or she is a member of the contract-holder's family (see section 250) and, if so, the nature of the relationship;
(c) whether the proposed joint contract-holder is likely to become a sole contract-holder in relation to the dwelling;
(d) whether he or she is likely, but for being made a joint contract-holder, to succeed to the contract under section 73.
(3) Circumstances relevant to sub-paragraph (2)(a) may include whether the proposed joint contract-holder—
(a) is likely to comply with the contract, and
(b) has complied with other occupation contracts (whether as contract-holder under those contracts or otherwise).
(4) Circumstances relevant to sub-paragraph (2)(c) may include—
(a) whether the landlord would have been able to refuse consent if the contract-holder requested the landlord's consent to a transfer of the contract to the proposed joint contract-holder, and

(b) any circumstances that would be relevant if the landlord were considering whether to make a new occupation contract in relation to the dwelling with that person.

(5) Circumstances relevant to sub-paragraph (2)(d) may include the probable effect of giving consent as regards—

(a) the persons who may in future be qualified to succeed to the occupation contract, and

(b) the period for which the occupation contract is likely to continue in force if one or more of those persons do succeed to it.

10 (1) This paragraph applies where the contract-holder under the occupation contract seeks the landlord's consent to adding a joint contract-holder under section 49.

(2) If the landlord considers that the probable effect of giving consent is to substantially lengthen the period during which the occupation contract is likely to continue in force, it is reasonable for the landlord to impose the condition mentioned in sub-paragraph (3).

(3) The condition is that the joint contract-holder is to be treated for the purposes of this Act as a priority successor or as a reserve successor in relation to the occupation contract.

Section 114: transfer to potential successor in relation to a secure contract

11 (1) This paragraph applies if a contract-holder under a secure contract seeks the landlord's consent to a transfer of the contract to a potential successor in accordance with section 114.

(2) Where this paragraph applies the following circumstances (in addition to those in Part 2) must be taken into account (to the extent that they are relevant)—

(a) the probable effect of giving consent as regards the persons who may in future be qualified to succeed to the occupation contract, and

(b) the period for which the occupation contract is likely to continue in force if one or more of those persons do succeed to it.

12 (1) This paragraph applies if a contract-holder under a secure contract seeks the landlord's consent to a transfer of the contract to a potential successor in accordance with section 114.

(2) If the landlord considers that the probable effect of giving consent is to lengthen substantially the period during which the occupation contract is likely to continue in force, it is reasonable for the landlord to impose the condition mentioned in sub-paragraph (3).

(3) The condition is that the potential successor is to be treated for the purposes of this Act as a priority successor or as a reserve successor in relation to the occupation contract.

Section 118: transfer to secure contract-holder in relation to a secure contract with a community landlord

13 (1) This paragraph applies if a contract-holder under a secure contract ("the transferor") seeks to transfer the contract in accordance with section 118 to a person ("the transferee") who is a contract-holder under another secure contract.

(2) Where this paragraph applies, the following circumstances (in addition to those in Part 2) must be taken into account (to the extent that they are relevant)—

(a) whether the transfer is to be part of a series of transactions and, if it is, all the circumstances relating to the other transactions intended to be part of the series (see also paragraph 14(2)), and

(b) whether the transferee is a priority or reserve successor in relation to the secure contract under which he or she is a contract-holder before the transfer (see also paragraph 14(3)).

14 (1) This paragraph applies if a contract-holder under a secure contract ("the transferor") seeks to transfer the contract in accordance with section 118 to a person ("the transferee") who is a contract-holder under another secure contract.
(2) If the transfer is to be part of a series of transactions it is reasonable to impose a condition that the transfer may take place only if the other transactions take place.
(3) If the transferee is a priority or reserve successor in relation to the secure contract under which he or she is a contract-holder before the transfer, it is reasonable to impose a condition requiring that the transferee is to be treated for the purposes of this Act as a successor of that kind in relation to the secure contract transferred to him or her by the transferor.

SCHEDULE 7
PROHIBITED CONDUCT STANDARD CONTRACTS

III WAL [382]

Procedure on application for an order under section 116

1 (1) The court may not hear a landlord's application for an order under section 116 unless—
(a) the landlord has given notice to the contract-holder of the landlord's intention to apply for such an order, or
(b) the court considers it reasonable to dispense with the requirement of notice.
(2) A notice under sub-paragraph (1) must give particulars of the conduct in respect of which the order is sought and state that proceedings may not be brought—
(a) before the day specified in the notice, or
(b) after the end of the period of six months starting with the day on which the notice is given to the contract-holder.
(3) The day specified for the purposes of sub-paragraph (2)(a) may be the day on which the notice is given to the contract-holder.
(4) The landlord may, in the same proceedings, apply to the court for an order under section 116 and make a possession claim.

Terms of prohibited conduct standard contract

2 (1) This section applies where a periodic standard contract is created by an order under section 116.
(2) If the landlord and the contract-holder agree the terms of the periodic standard contract, the terms of the contract are the terms agreed.
(3) Sub-paragraph (2) is subject to the provisions of this Act about the incorporation of fundamental and supplementary provisions.
(4) If the landlord and the contract-holder do not agree the terms of the periodic standard contract—
(a) the fundamental and supplementary provisions applicable to periodic standard contracts are incorporated as terms of the contract without modification,
(b) any terms of the contract which are incompatible with those fundamental or supplementary provisions cease to have effect, and
(c) otherwise, the terms of the periodic standard contract are the same as the terms of the secure contract.
(5) Whether or not the landlord and contract holder agree the terms of the periodic standard contract, it is a term of the contract that—
(a) any arrears of rent payable at the end of the secure contract become payable under the periodic standard contract, and

(b) any rent paid in advance or overpaid at the end of the secure contract is credited to the contract-holder's liability to pay rent under the periodic standard contract.

(6) The requirement in section 39(1) (landlord must give contract-holder a contact address at start of contract) does not apply.

(7) Section 151(3) (requirement to inform contract-holder of right to apply for landlord's review under section 202) provides that that section is a fundamental provision which is incorporated as a term of all prohibited conduct standard contracts.

(8) Prohibited conduct standard contracts are within Schedule 9; accordingly section 175 (restriction on giving landlord's notice during first four months of occupation) is not incorporated as a term of a prohibited conduct standard contract.

Probation period

3 (1) The probation period, in relation to an occupation contract which is a periodic standard contract because of an order under section 116, is—

(a) the period of 12 months starting with the occupation date of the contract (see section 116(2)(b)), or

(b) if there is an extension under paragraph 4, the period of 18 months starting with the occupation date of the contract.

(2) If the landlord gives the contract-holder notice that the probation period will end before the time at which it would end under sub-paragraph (1), the period ends on the date specified in the notice.

(3) If under paragraph 7 the court orders that the probation period will end before the time at which it would end under sub-paragraph (1), the period ends on the date specified in the order.

(4) If sub-paragraphs (2) and (3) both apply, the period ends on the earlier of the date specified in the notice and the date specified in the order.

(5) Sub-paragraph (6) applies instead of sub-paragraphs (1) to (4) if, at what would be the end of probation period under those sub-paragraphs—

(a) a possession claim made by the landlord in respect of the dwelling has not been concluded, or

(b) the landlord has given the contract-holder a possession notice or a notice under section 173 (landlord's notice to end contract), and the period before the end of which the landlord may make a possession claim has not ended.

(6) Where this sub-paragraph applies, the probation period is the period starting with the occupation date of the contract and ending—

(a) when a relevant event occurs, or

(b) if no relevant event occurs, immediately after the contract ends.

(7) In a case within sub-paragraph (5)(a) the relevant event is the conclusion of the possession claim in favour of the contract-holder.

(8) In a case within sub-paragraph (5)(b) each of the following is a relevant event—

(a) withdrawal of the notice;

(b) the period ending without a possession claim having been made;

(c) conclusion in favour of the contract-holder of a possession claim made in reliance on the notice.

(9) If a private landlord other than a registered charity becomes the landlord under the contract before the time at which the probation period would end apart from this sub-paragraph, the probation period ends.

Extending probation period

4 (1) The landlord may extend the probation period to the period of 18 months starting with the occupation date of the contract by giving the contract-holder a notice of extension.

(2) The notice of extension must be given to the contract-holder at least eight weeks before the date on which the probation period would end under paragraph 3(1)(a).

(3) The notice of extension must state that the landlord has decided to extend the probation period, and set out the reasons for the landlord's decision.

(4) The notice of extension must also inform the contract-holder that he or she has a right to request a review under paragraph 5 of the landlord's decision to extend the probation period, and of the time by which the request must be made.

(5) In making the decision to extend the probation period, the landlord may take into account—

(a) the conduct of the contract-holder (or, if there are joint contract-holders, the conduct of any of them), and

(b) the conduct of any person who appears to the landlord to live in the dwelling.

(6) A landlord may take into account a person's conduct under sub-paragraph (5)(b) whether or not the person lives continuously in the dwelling, and whatever the capacity in which the person lives in the dwelling.

(7) The Welsh Ministers may by regulations amend sub-paragraph (2) for the purpose of changing when a notice of extension must be given to a contract-holder; the power under section 256(2) to make consequential amendments includes, in its application to regulations under this sub-paragraph, the power to make consequential amendments to this Schedule.

Landlord's review of decision to extend probation period

5 (1) If a landlord gives a notice of extension under paragraph 4, the contract-holder may request that the landlord carries out a review of the decision to give the notice.

(2) The request must be made to the landlord before the end of the period of 14 days (or such longer period as the landlord may allow in writing) starting with the day on which the landlord gives the contract-holder the notice of extension.

(3) If the contract-holder requests a review in accordance with sub-paragraph (2), the landlord must carry out the review.

(4) Following a review, the landlord may—

(a) confirm the decision to give the notice, or

(b) reverse the decision.

(5) The landlord must notify the contract-holder of the outcome of the review before the date on which the probation period would end under paragraph 3(1)(a).

(6) If the landlord confirms the decision, the notice must—

(a) set out the reasons for the confirmation, and

(b) inform the contract-holder that he or she has a right to apply for a review in the county court under paragraph 6, and of the time by which the application must be made.

(7) The Welsh Ministers may prescribe the procedure to be followed in connection with a review under this paragraph.

(8) Regulations under sub-paragraph (7) may, amongst other things—

(a) require the review to be carried out by a person of appropriate seniority who has not been involved in the decision, and

(b) set out circumstances in which a contract-holder is entitled to an oral hearing, and whether and by whom he or she may be represented at such a hearing.

County court review of decision to extend probation period

6 (1) This paragraph applies if a landlord, following a request for a review made in accordance with paragraph 5(2)—

(a) gives notice under paragraph 5(5) informing the contract-holder that the landlord has decided to confirm a decision to give a notice of extension under paragraph 4, or

(b) fails to give a notice in accordance with paragraph 5(5).

(2) The contract-holder may apply to the county court for a review of the decision to give the notice of extension.

(3) The application must be made—

(a) before the end of the period of 14 days starting with the day on which the landlord gives the contract-holder notice under paragraph 5(5), or

(b) if no notice has been given in accordance with paragraph 5(5), before the end of the period of 14 days starting with the day after the date by which the landlord was required to give notice under that sub-paragraph.

(4) The county court may give permission for an application to be made after the end of the period allowed by sub-paragraph (3), but only if it is satisfied—

(a) where permission is sought before the end of that period, that there is a good reason for the contract-holder to be unable to make the application in time, or

(b) where permission is sought after that time, that there is a good reason for the contract-holder's failure to make the application in time and for any delay in applying for permission.

(5) The county court may confirm or quash the decision to give the notice of extension.

(6) In considering whether to confirm or quash the decision, the county court must apply the principles applied by the High Court on an application for judicial review.

(7) If the county court quashes the decision—

(a) the notice of extension is of no effect, and

(b) the county court may make any order the High Court could make when making a quashing order on an application for judicial review.

(8) If the county court quashes the decision and the landlord gives the contract-holder a further notice of extension under paragraph 4 before the end of the post-review period—

(a) the notice has effect as if given in accordance with paragraph 4(2) (other than for the purposes of paragraph 5(2)), and

(b) paragraph 5(5) is to be read as if it requires the landlord to notify the contract-holder of the outcome of a review under that paragraph before the end of the period of 14 days starting with the day on which the contract-holder requested the review.

(9) The post-review period is the period of 14 days beginning with the day on which the county court quashes the decision.

Application to court to end probation period

7 (1) The contract-holder under an occupation contract which is a periodic standard contract because of an order under section 116 may apply to the court for an order ending the probation period before the time at which it would end under paragraph 3(1).

(2) The application may be made at any time after the end of the period of six months starting with the occupation date of the contract (see section 116(2)(b)).

(3) The court may end the probation period only if it is satisfied that—

(a) it is no longer necessary for the contract-holder to occupy under a periodic standard contract, or

(b) the landlord has not made an appropriate programme of social support available to the contract-holder and it is unlikely that such support will be made available.

Terms of secure contract that was a prohibited conduct standard contract

8 (1) This paragraph applies where a prohibited conduct standard contract ends and is replaced with a secure contract because the probation period has ended.

(2) If the landlord and the contract-holder have agreed what the terms of the secure contract are to be in that event, the terms of the contract are the terms agreed.

(3) Sub-paragraph (2) is subject to the provisions of this Act as to the incorporation of fundamental and supplementary provisions.

(4) If the landlord and the contract-holder have not agreed what the terms of the secure contract are to be in that event—

(a) the fundamental and supplementary provisions applicable to secure contracts made with the landlord are incorporated as terms of the contract without modification,

(b) any terms of the contract which are incompatible with those fundamental or supplementary provisions cease to have effect, and

(c) otherwise, the terms of the secure contract are the same as the terms of the prohibited conduct standard contract.

(5) The requirement in section 39(1) (landlord must give contract-holder a contact address at start of contract) does not apply.

SCHEDULE 8
ESTATE MANAGEMENT GROUNDS

PART 1
THE GROUNDS

III WAL [383]

REDEVELOPMENT GROUNDS
Ground A (building works)

1 The landlord intends, within a reasonable time of obtaining possession of the dwelling—

(a) to demolish or reconstruct the building or part of the building comprising the dwelling, or

(b) to carry out work on that building or on land treated as part of the dwelling,

and cannot reasonably do so without obtaining possession of the dwelling.

Ground B (redevelopment schemes)

2 (1) This ground arises if the dwelling satisfies the first condition or the second condition.

(2) The first condition is that the dwelling is in an area which is the subject of a redevelopment scheme approved in accordance with Part 2 of this Schedule, and the landlord intends within a reasonable time of obtaining possession to dispose of the dwelling in accordance with the scheme.

(3) The second condition is that part of the dwelling is in such an area and the landlord intends within a reasonable time of obtaining possession to dispose of that part in accordance with the scheme, and for that purpose reasonably requires possession of the dwelling.

SPECIAL ACCOMMODATION GROUNDS
Ground C (charities)

3 (1) The landlord is a charity and the contract-holder's continued occupation of the dwelling would conflict with the objects of the charity.

(2) But this ground is not available to the landlord ("L") unless, at the time the contract was made and at all times after that, the person in the position of landlord (whether L or another person) has been a charity.

(3) In this paragraph "charity" has the same meaning as in the Charities Act 2011 (c 25) (see section 1 of that Act).

Ground D (dwelling suitable for disabled people)

4 The dwelling has features which are substantially different from those of ordinary dwellings and which are designed to make it suitable for occupation by a physically disabled person who requires accommodation of a kind provided by the dwelling and—

(a) there is no longer such a person living in the dwelling, and

(b) the landlord requires the dwelling for occupation by such a person (whether alone or with members of that person's family).

Ground E (housing associations and housing trusts: people difficult to house)

5 (1) The landlord is a housing association or housing trust which makes dwellings available only for occupation (whether alone or with others) by people who are difficult to house, and—

(a) either there is no longer such a person living in the dwelling or a local housing authority has offered the contract-holder a right to occupy another dwelling under a secure contract, and

(b) the landlord requires the dwelling for occupation by such a person (whether alone or with members of that person's family).

(2) A person is difficult to house if that person's circumstances (other than financial circumstances) make it especially difficult for him or her to satisfy his or her need for housing.

Ground F (groups of dwellings for people with special needs)

6 The dwelling constitutes part of a group of dwellings which it is the practice of the landlord to make available for occupation by persons with special needs and—

(a) a social service or special facility is provided in close proximity to the group of dwellings in order to assist persons with those special needs,

(b) there is no longer a person with those special needs living in the dwelling, and

(c) the landlord requires the dwelling for occupation by a person who has those special needs (whether alone or with members of his or her family).

UNDER-OCCUPATION GROUNDS

Ground G (reserve successors)

7 The contract-holder succeeded to the occupation contract under section 73 as a reserve successor (see sections 76 and 77), and the accommodation comprised in the dwelling is more extensive than is reasonably required by the contract-holder.

Ground H (joint contract-holders)

8 (1) This ground arises if the first condition and the second condition are met.

(2) The first condition is that a joint contract-holder's rights and obligations under the contract have been ended in accordance with—

(a) section 111, 130 or 138 (withdrawal), or

(b) section 225, 227 or 230 (exclusion).

(3) The second condition is that—

(a) the accommodation comprised in the dwelling is more extensive than is reasonably required by the remaining contract-holder (or contract-holders), or

(b) where the landlord is a community landlord, the remaining contract-holder does not (or the remaining contract-holders do not) meet the landlord's criteria for the allocation of housing accommodation.

OTHER ESTATE MANAGEMENT REASONS

Ground I (other estate management reasons)

9 (1) This ground arises where it is desirable for some other substantial estate management reason that the landlord should obtain possession of the dwelling.

(2) An estate management reason may, in particular, relate to—

(a) all or part of the dwelling, or

(b) any other premises of the landlord to which the dwelling is connected, whether by reason of proximity or the purposes for which they are used, or in any other manner.

FUNDAMENTAL PROVISION

Fundamental provision applicable to all occupation contracts

10 This Part of this Schedule is a fundamental provision which is incorporated as a term of all occupation contracts.

PART 2

APPROVAL OF REDEVELOPMENT SCHEMES FOR PURPOSES OF GROUND B

III WAL [384]

Approval of scheme and of variation of scheme

11 (1) The Welsh Ministers may, on the application of a landlord, approve for the purposes of estate management Ground B a scheme for the disposal and redevelopment of an area of land consisting of or including the whole or part of a dwelling subject to an occupation contract.

(2) For the purposes of this paragraph—

(a) "disposal" means a disposal of any interest in the land (including the grant of an option), and

(b) "redevelopment" means the demolition or reconstruction of buildings or the carrying out of other works to buildings or land,

and it is immaterial whether the disposal is to precede or follow the redevelopment.

(3) The Welsh Ministers may on the application of the landlord approve a variation of a scheme previously approved by them and may, amongst other things, approve a variation adding land to the area subject to the scheme.

Notice to contract-holders affected

12 (1) If a landlord proposes to apply to the Welsh Ministers for the approval of a scheme or variation of an approved scheme, the landlord must give a notice to the contract-holder under any affected occupation contract.

(2) An occupation contract is affected if the dwelling subject to it is affected by the proposal.

(3) The notice must state—

(a) the main features of the proposed scheme, or of the proposed variations of the approved scheme,

(b) that the landlord proposes to apply to the Welsh Ministers for approval of the scheme or variation, and

(c) that, because of section 160 and estate management Ground B, the effect of such approval will be to enable the landlord to make a possession claim in respect of the dwelling.

(4) The notice must also inform the contract-holder that—

(a) he or she may make representations to the landlord about the proposal, and

(b) the representations must be made before the end of the period of 28 days starting with the day on which the notice is given to him or her (or such longer period as the landlord may specify in the notice).

(5) The landlord may not apply to the Welsh Ministers until the landlord has considered any representations made before the end of that period.

(6) Sub-paragraph (7) applies in the case of a landlord under an occupation contract which would (but for this paragraph) be required under section 234 to

consult the contract-holder as regards a redevelopment scheme (or a variation of a redevelopment scheme).

(7) Where this sub-paragraph applies, this paragraph is to apply in relation to the landlord's consultation with the contract-holder instead of section 234.

Decision on approval or variation

13 (1) In considering whether to give its approval to a scheme or variation the Welsh Ministers must, among other things, take into account—

(a) the effect of the scheme on the extent and character of housing accommodation in the neighbourhood,

(b) the period of time proposed in the scheme as the period within which the proposed disposal and redevelopment will take place, and

(c) the extent to which the scheme includes provision for housing provided under the scheme to be sold to, or occupied under occupation contracts by, relevant persons.

(2) "Relevant persons" means existing contract-holders under an occupation contract with the landlord and, if the landlord is a community landlord, persons nominated by the landlord.

(3) The Welsh Ministers must also take into account—

(a) any representations made to them, and

(b) so far as they are brought to the Welsh Ministers' attention, any representations made to the landlord.

(4) The landlord must give to the Welsh Ministers such information as to the representations made to the landlord, and other relevant matters, as the Welsh Ministers may request.

Scheme affecting part of dwelling etc

14 The Welsh Ministers may not approve a scheme or variation so as to include in the area subject to the scheme—

(a) part only of any dwelling subject to an occupation contract, or

(b) any dwelling subject to an occupation contract that is not affected by the works involved in the redevelopment but is proposed to be disposed of along with other land which is so affected,

unless they are satisfied that the inclusion is justified in the circumstances.

Conditions in relation to approval

15 (1) The approval may be given subject to conditions and may be expressed to end after a specified period.

(2) The Welsh Ministers, on the application of the landlord or otherwise, may vary an approval so as to—

(a) add, remove or vary conditions to which the approval is subject, or

(b) extend or restrict the period after which the approval is to end.

Special provision for community landlords

16 For the purposes of this Part of this Schedule a community landlord is to be treated as being a landlord in relation to a dwelling if it has an interest of any description in that dwelling.

SCHEDULE 9

STANDARD CONTRACTS TO WHICH LIMITS IN SECTIONS 175, 186(2) AND 196 (LANDLORD'S NOTICE DURING FIRST SIX MONTHS OF OCCUPATION) DO NOT APPLY

III WAL [385]

Prohibited conduct standard contracts

WALES

1 A prohibited conduct standard contract.

Tenancies and licences which are occupation contracts because of notice given under Part 2 of Schedule 2

2 A standard contract which would not be an occupation contract but for a notice under paragraph 3 of Schedule 2 (holiday accommodation; care institutions; temporary expedients; shared accommodation).

Supported accommodation

3 A standard contract which relates to supported accommodation.

Accommodation for asylum seekers

4 A standard contract made in order to provide accommodation under Part 6 of the Immigration and Asylum Act 1999 (c 33) (support for asylum seekers).

Accommodation for displaced persons

5 A standard contract made under the Displaced Persons (Temporary Protection) Regulations 2005 (SI 2005/1379).

Accommodation for homeless persons

6 A standard contract made as described in paragraph 11 or 12 of Schedule 2 (accommodation for homeless persons).

Service occupancy

7 A standard contract where the contract-holder is required by his or her contract of employment to occupy the dwelling.

Service occupancy: police

8 A standard contract where—

(a) the contract-holder is a member of a police force, and

(b) the dwelling is provided for the contract-holder free of rent under regulations made under section 50 of the Police Act 1996 (c 16) (general regulations as to government, administration and conditions of service).

Service occupancy: fire and rescue services

9 A standard contract where—

(a) the contract-holder is an employee of a fire and rescue authority,

(b) the contract-holder's contract of employment requires him or her to live in close proximity to a particular fire station, and

(c) the dwelling is provided to him or her by the fire and rescue authority in consequence of that requirement.

Temporary accommodation: land acquired for development

10 (1) A standard contract where—

(a) the land the dwelling is on (including any land occupied together with the dwelling other than agricultural land exceeding 0.809 hectares) is, or is part of, land which has been acquired for development, and

(b) the dwelling is used by the landlord as temporary housing accommodation pending development of the land.

(2) "Development" has the meaning given by section 55 of the Town and Country Planning Act 1990 (c 8).

Temporary accommodation: short-term arrangements

11 A standard contract where—

(a) the dwelling has been let to the landlord with vacant possession for use as temporary housing accommodation,

(b) the terms on which it has been let include provision for the lessor to obtain vacant possession from the landlord at the end of a specified period or when required by the lessor,

(c) the lessor is not a community landlord, and

(d) the landlord has no interest in the dwelling other than under the lease in question or as mortgagor.

Temporary accommodation: accommodation during works

12 (1) A standard contract where—

(a) the dwelling (the "temporary dwelling") has been made available for occupation by the contract-holder while works are carried out on the dwelling previously occupied by the contract-holder as a home,

(b) the landlord of the temporary dwelling is not the same as the landlord of the dwelling previously occupied by the contract-holder (the "old dwelling"), and

(c) the contract-holder was not a contract-holder under a secure contract of the old dwelling at the time when the contract-holder ceased to occupy it as a home.

(2) In this paragraph, references to the contract-holder include references to the contract-holder's predecessor.

(3) For the purposes of sub-paragraph (2), a person is a predecessor of a contract-holder under a standard contract if that person was an earlier contract-holder under the same contract.

Power to amend Schedule

13 The Welsh Ministers may by regulations amend this Schedule.

SCHEDULE 10

ORDERS FOR POSSESSION ON DISCRETIONARY GROUNDS ETC: REASONABLENESS

III WAL [386]

Introductory

1 This Schedule applies for the purpose of determining whether it is reasonable—

(a) to make an order for possession under section 209 (breach of contract) or 210 (estate management grounds), or

(b) to make a decision under section 211 to adjourn proceedings on a possession claim or postpone the giving up of possession.

2 The court, in determining whether it is reasonable to make such an order or decision, or to make any other decision available to it, must (amongst other things) have regard to the circumstances set out in paragraphs 4 to 13 to the extent that the court considers them relevant (and to the extent that it is not otherwise required to have regard to those matters; for example, under the Human Rights Act 1998 (c 42)).

3 Paragraph 14 sets out a circumstance, concerning local authority assistance with homelessness, which the court should not have regard to (subject to any duty to have regard to that circumstance to which the court is subject).

Circumstances as regards the contract-holder

4 The probable effect of the order or decision on the contract-holder (and on any permitted occupiers of the dwelling).

5 If the case is one in which the court may decide to postpone the giving up of possession, the likelihood that the contract-holder will comply with any terms that may be imposed.

Circumstances as regards the landlord

WALES

6 The probable effect of not making the order, or of the decision, on the landlord's interests, including the landlord's financial interests.

7 If the landlord is a community landlord, the probable effect of not making the order, or of the decision, on the landlord's ability to fulfil its housing functions, including assisting other persons in need of accommodation.

Circumstances as regards other persons

8 (1) The probable effect of the order or decision on—

(a) contract-holders and permitted occupiers of other dwellings of the landlord,

(b) persons who have asked the landlord to provide them with housing accommodation, and

(c) persons living, visiting or otherwise engaging in a lawful activity in the locality (and persons who wish to live, visit or engage in lawful activities in the locality).

(2) If a possession claim is made on the ground in section 157 (breach of contract), the probable effect of the circumstances set out in paragraph 10 on the persons mentioned in sub-paragraph (1).

New occupation contract offered

9 Whether the landlord has offered or undertakes to offer a new occupation contract (whether for the same dwelling or other dwellings) to one or more of the persons occupying or living in the dwelling.

Circumstances in relation to a possession claim on ground of breach of contract

10 If a possession claim is made on the ground in section 157 (breach of contract)—

(a) the nature, frequency or duration of the breach or breaches,

(b) the degree to which the contract-holder (or a permitted occupier of the dwelling) is responsible for the breach,

(c) how likely it is that the breach will recur, and

(d) any action to end, or prevent a recurrence of, the breach that was taken by the landlord before making a possession claim.

Circumstances in relation to a possession claim concerning section 55

11 If the landlord makes a possession claim relying on a breach of section 55 (anti-social behaviour and other prohibited conduct), the general public interest in restraining the conduct prohibited by that section.

Circumstances relating to estate management Ground G

12 If the landlord makes a possession claim relying wholly or partly on estate management Ground G (accommodation not required by reserve successor)—

(a) the age of the contract-holder who succeeded to the contract under section 73,

(b) the period during which the contract-holder has occupied the dwelling as his or her only or principal home, and

(c) any financial or other support given by the contract-holder to the contract-holder who died (or, if the contract-holder who died was the successor of an earlier contract-holder, to that earlier contract-holder).

Circumstances relating to estate management Ground H

13 If the landlord makes a possession claim relying wholly or partly on estate management Ground H (departing joint contract-holder)—

(a) the age of the remaining contract-holder (or each of the remaining contract-holders), and

(b) the period during which the remaining contract-holder (or each of the remaining contract-holders) has occupied the dwellings as his or her only or principal home.

Assistance in relation to homelessness not relevant

14 The likelihood that a person will be assisted under Part 2 of the Housing (Wales) Act 2014 (anaw 7) or Part 7 of the Housing Act 1996 (c 52) (homelessness) is not a relevant circumstance (subject to any requirement to have regard to that circumstance to which the court is subject).

SCHEDULE 11
SUITABLE ALTERNATIVE ACCOMMODATION

III WAL [387]

Introductory

1 (1) This Schedule applies for the purposes of—

(a) an order for possession under section 210 (estate management grounds), or

(b) an order under section 222(3)(b) (appeal following possession for abandonment).

(2) In this Schedule the dwelling previously occupied by the contract-holder or of which possession is sought is referred to as "the existing dwelling", and the occupation contract to which that dwelling is or was subject is referred to as "the existing contract".

Estate management grounds: certificate of local housing authority

2 (1) This paragraph applies if—

(a) this Schedule applies because of section 210, and

(b) the landlord under the existing contract is not a local housing authority.

(2) A certificate of the local housing authority for the area in which the existing dwelling is situated, certifying that the authority will provide suitable alternative accommodation for the contract-holder by a date specified in the certificate, is conclusive evidence that suitable alternative accommodation will be available for him or her by that date.

Suitable accommodation

3 (1) This paragraph applies if—

(a) this Schedule applies because of section 210 and either—

(i) no certificate of the kind mentioned in paragraph 2(2) is produced to the court, or

(ii) the landlord in relation to the existing dwelling is a local housing authority, or

(b) this Schedule applies because of section 222.

(2) Accommodation is suitable if—

(a) it is to be occupied by the contract-holder under an occupation contract that gives him or her security of occupation reasonably equivalent to that given by the existing contract, and

(b) in the opinion of the court it is reasonably suitable to the needs of the contract-holder and his or her family (which must be determined in accordance with paragraph 4).

(3) If the existing contract relates to a separate dwelling, accommodation is not suitable unless it is a separate dwelling.

Needs of contract-holder and his or her family

4 (1) The court must determine whether accommodation is reasonably suitable in relation to the needs of the contract-holder and his or her family in accordance with this paragraph.

(2) The court must consider (among other things)—

WALES

(a) the needs of the contract-holder and his or her family as regards extent of accommodation,

(b) if the landlord is a private landlord, the needs of the contract-holder and his or her family as regards character of accommodation,

(c) the means of the contract-holder and his or her family,

(d) if the contract-holder or a member of his or her family works or is being educated, the distance of the accommodation from the place (or places) of work or education,

(e) if proximity to the home of any member of the contract-holder's family is essential to the well-being of the contract-holder or that member of his or her family, the proximity of the accommodation to that home,

(f) the terms of the existing contract and the terms of the occupation contract under which the accommodation is to be occupied, and

(g) if furniture was provided by the landlord under the existing contract, whether furniture is to be provided for use by the contract-holder and his or her family and, if so, the nature of that furniture.

(3) If the landlord is a community landlord, the court must also consider the nature of the accommodation which it is the practice of the landlord to allocate to persons with similar needs.

(4) If the landlord is a private landlord the court may consider, as an alternative to the matters in sub-paragraph (2)(a) to (c), whether the accommodation is similar as regards rent and extent to the accommodation provided in the neighbourhood by community landlords for comparable persons.

(5) "Comparable persons" are those whose needs, as regards extent, are in the opinion of the court similar to those of the contract-holder and the contract-holder's family.

(6) For the purposes of sub-paragraph (4) a certificate of a local housing authority stating—

(a) the extent of the accommodation provided by the authority to meet the needs of persons with families of such number as may be specified in the certificate, and

(b) the amount of rent charged by the authority for accommodation of that extent,

is to be conclusive evidence of the facts so stated.

(7) In considering the matters in sub-paragraph (2)(f) the court may not take into account any terms of the occupation contract that relate to lodgers and sub-holders.

Overcrowding

5 Accommodation is not suitable to the needs of the contract-holder and his or her family if, as a result of their occupation of the accommodation, the accommodation would constitute an overcrowded dwelling for the purposes of Part 10 of the Housing Act 1985 (c 68) (see section 324 of that Act).

Evidence of certificate of local housing authority

6 A document that purports to be a certificate of the local housing authority named in the certificate, issued for the purposes of this Schedule, and signed by the proper person on behalf of the authority—

(a) is to be received in evidence, and

(b) unless the contrary is shown, is to be treated as such a certificate without further proof.

SCHEDULE 12
CONVERSION OF TENANCIES AND LICENCES EXISTING BEFORE COMMENCEMENT OF CHAPTER 3 OF PART 10

III WAL [388]

Definitions

1 (1) In this Schedule—

"converted contract" ("*contract wedi ei drosi*") means a tenancy or licence which existed immediately before the appointed day and became an occupation contract on that day;

"converted secure contract" ("*contract diogel wedi ei drosi*") means a converted contract which became a secure contract on the appointed day;

"converted standard contract" ("*contract safonol wedi ei drosi*") means a converted contract which became a standard contract on the appointed day;

"information provision period" ("*cyfnod darparu gwybodaeth*") has the meaning given in paragraph 11(1);

"the initial notice period" ("*cyfnod hysbysu cychwynnol*") is the period of two months starting with the appointed day.

(2) See section 242 for definitions of other terms used in this Schedule.

Determination of whether existing tenancy or licence is occupation contract

2 (1) Schedule 2 applies to—

(a) a tenancy or licence which immediately before the appointed day was a secure tenancy, an assured tenancy, an introductory tenancy or a demoted tenancy, and

(b) a tenancy which existed immediately before the appointed day but is not within paragraph (a),

as if paragraphs 3(2)(b) and 4 (care institutions) were omitted.

(2) Schedule 2 applies to a tenancy which immediately before the appointed day was a secure tenancy, an assured tenancy, an introductory tenancy or a demoted tenancy as if paragraphs 3(2)(c) and 5 (temporary expedients) were omitted.

(3) The landlord may, in relation to a tenancy or licence which existed immediately before the appointed day, give notice under paragraph 1 or 3 of Schedule 2 at any time before the end of the initial notice period.

(4) If the landlord does so, the tenancy or licence is to be treated as having become an occupation contract on the appointed day.

Determination of whether converted contract is secure contract or standard contract

3 (1) Sections 11 to 17 (community landlords and private landlords) apply to a converted contract—

(a) under which the landlord is a private landlord, and

(b) which immediately before the appointed day was a secure tenancy under which the landlord was a private landlord,

as if the landlord were a community landlord.

(2) But in section 14 (review of notice of standard contract) subsection (1) applies as if after "section 13" there were inserted "and the landlord's decision to give the notice is subject to judicial review".

4 (1) The landlord under a converted contract may give notice under section 11(2)(b) (notice of standard contract) at any time before the end of the initial notice period.

(2) If the landlord does so, the contract is to be treated as having become a standard contract on the appointed day.

WALES

(3) The landlord under a converted contract may give notice under section 17(1) (notice of secure contract) at any time before the end of the initial notice period.

(4) If the landlord does so, the contract is to be treated as having become a secure contract on the appointed day.

5 A converted contract which immediately before the appointed day was an introductory tenancy has effect as an introductory standard contract (see paragraph 23).

6 A converted contract has effect as a prohibited conduct standard contract (see paragraph 24) if immediately before the appointed day—

(a) section 20B of the Housing Act 1988 (c 50) (demoted assured shorthold tenancies) applied to it, or

(b) section 143A of the Housing Act 1996 (c 52) (demoted tenancies) applied to it.

7 (1) A converted contract to which sub-paragraph (2) applies is an additional exception to section 11(1) (contracts made with community landlord are secure contracts).

(2) This sub-paragraph applies to a converted contract which immediately before the appointed day was a tenancy or licence for a fixed term, provided that—

(a) a premium was paid for the contract, and

(b) before the end of the period of one month starting with the appointed day, the contract-holder decides that the contract should become a fixed term standard contract.

(3) Before the appointed day, a community landlord which is the landlord under a tenancy or licence for a fixed term, and for which a premium was paid, must—

(a) inform the contract-holder of his or her right under sub-paragraph (2)(b) to decide that the contract should become a fixed term standard contract, and of the time by which that decision must be made, and

(b) explain how section 11 will apply to the contract if the contract-holder does not make such a decision.

8 (1) This paragraph applies where a community landlord becomes the landlord under a fixed term standard contract before the end of the period of one month starting with the appointed day.

(2) Section 12 (contracts adopted by community landlord) applies as if in subsection (8)(b), for "before the community landlord becomes the landlord" there were substituted "before the end of the period of one month starting with the appointed day (within the meaning of section 242)".

(3) The landlord must give the contract-holder the notice required by section 15(1) on or before the appointed day.

9 (1) The following are additional exceptions to sections 11(1) and 12(3) (contracts made or adopted by community landlord are secure contracts).

(2) A converted contract which before the appointed day—

(a) had been a secure tenancy, but

(b) had ceased to be such a tenancy because of section 89, 91 or 93 of the Housing Act 1985 (c 68) (succession, assignment and sub-letting).

(3) A converted contract which before the appointed day—

(a) had been an introductory tenancy, but

(b) had ceased to be such a tenancy because of section 133 of the Housing Act 1996 (c 52) (succession).

(4) A converted contract which before the appointed day—

(a) had been a demoted tenancy, but

(b) had ceased to be such a tenancy because of section 143I of the Housing Act 1996 (succession).

10 A converted secure contract which immediately before the appointed day was a secure tenancy becomes a standard contract if—

(a) the tenant died before the appointed day, and

(b) after that day an event occurs which, but for this Act, would under section 89 of the Housing Act 1985 (c 68) (succession) have caused the contract to cease to be a secure tenancy.

Written statement of converted contract and provision of information

11 (1) The landlord must give the contract-holder under a converted contract a written statement of the contract before the end of the period of six months starting with the appointed day ("the information provision period").

(2) Any references in this Act to the landlord's obligation under section 31(1) are to be read, in relation to converted contracts, as references to the landlord's obligation under sub-paragraph (1).

12 Sections 36 and 37 (applications to court) apply in relation to a written statement provided because of paragraph 11(1) as if for the words in section 36(3) and 37(2) there were substituted

"If the landlord was required to provide the written statement under paragraph 11(1) of Schedule 12, the contract-holder may not apply to the court under subsection (1) before—

(a) the end of the information provision period (within the meaning of Schedule 12), or

(b) if earlier, the period of 14 days starting with the day on which the landlord gave the contract-holder the written statement."

13 (1) Section 39(1) (information about landlord's address) applies in relation to a converted contract as if for "the period of 14 days starting with the occupation date of the contract" there were substituted "the information provision period (within the meaning of Schedule 12)".

(2) Section 40(2) (compensation) applies in relation to section 39(1), as modified by sub-paragraph (1), as if the relevant date were the first day of the period of 14 days ending with the last day of the information provision period (and accordingly section 40 is to be read as if subsection (5) were omitted).

Variation

14 (1) A converted contract may not be varied before the landlord has given the contract-holder a written statement of the contract.

(2) Sub-paragraph (1) does not apply to a variation under section 104 or 123 (variation of rent).

15 (1) Sections 104 and 123 (variation of rent) apply to a converted contract as if any variations in the rent payable under the contract before the appointed day were variations under whichever of those sections applies.

(2) The Welsh Ministers must by regulations make provision—

(a) enabling the contract-holder under a relevant converted contract, following receipt of a notice under section 104 or 123, to apply to a prescribed person or persons for a determination of the rent for the dwelling, and

(b) for the rent determined by the prescribed person or persons, in accordance with such assumptions as may be prescribed, to be the rent for the dwelling under the contract (unless the landlord and contract-holder otherwise agree).

(3) A converted contract is a relevant converted contract if immediately before the appointed day it was a tenancy to which section 13 of the Housing Act 1988 (c 50) (increases of rent under assured periodic tenancies) applied.

Waste and tenant-like user

WALES

16 Section 101 does not apply to a converted contract; accordingly—

(a) a contract-holder under a converted contract is subject to the same liability for waste in respect of the dwelling as he or she was subject to immediately before the appointed day, and

(b) the rule of law under which a tenant has an implied duty to use demised premises in a tenant-like manner applies to a contract-holder under a converted contract as it applied to him or her immediately before the appointed day.

Dealing

17 (1) This paragraph is a fundamental provision which is incorporated as a term of all converted standard contracts which immediately before the appointed day were secure tenancies.

(2) The contract-holder may allow persons to live in the dwelling as lodgers.

18 (1) This paragraph applies in relation to a converted contract—

(a) which is a secure contract or periodic standard contract, and

(b) under which there are joint contract-holders who were tenants in common in equity immediately before the appointed day.

(2) The provisions of fixed term standard contracts mentioned in subsection (1) of each of sections 140, 141 and 142 (transfers) are terms of the contract, and subsections (2) and (3) of each of those sections apply accordingly.

19 (1) This paragraph applies in relation to a converted contract which is a fixed term standard contract.

(2) The provisions of fixed term standard contracts mentioned in subsection (1) of each of sections 139, 140, 141 and 142 (transfers) are terms of the contract, and subsections (2) and (3) of each of those sections apply accordingly.

(3) Sub-paragraph (2) does not apply to the extent that any of those provisions is incompatible with an existing term of the contract.

Succession

20 (1) The contract-holder under a converted contract is to be treated as a priority successor in relation to the contract if—

(a) immediately before the appointed day the converted contract was of a description in column 1 of Table 6,

(b) before the appointed day it had vested in the contract-holder under the provision in column 2 of that Table, and

(c) the contract-holder qualified to succeed because of the provisions in column 3 of that Table.

TABLE 6

TYPE OF TENANCY	VESTING PROVISION	QUALIFYING PROVISIONS
Secure tenancy	Section 89 of the Housing Act 1985 (c 68)	Sections 87 and 113(1)(a) of that Act
Introductory tenancy	Section 133 of the Housing Act 1996 (c 52)	Sections 131 and 140(1)(a) of that Act
Demoted tenancy	Section 143H of the Housing Act 1996	Section 143P(1)(a) or (b) of that Act

(2) The contract-holder under a converted contract is also to be treated as a priority successor in relation to the contract if—

(a) immediately before the appointed day the contract was an assured tenancy,

(b) before the appointed day it had vested in the contract-holder under section 17 of the Housing Act 1988 (c 50) (succession to assured tenancy), and

(c) on the appointed day the landlord under the contract was a community landlord.

21 (1) The contract-holder under a converted contract is to be treated as a reserve successor in relation to the contract if—

(a) immediately before the appointed day the converted contract was of a description in column 1 of Table 7,

(b) before the appointed day it had vested in the contract-holder under the provision in column 2 of that Table, and

(c) the contract-holder qualified to succeed because of the provisions in column 3 of that Table.

TABLE 7

TYPE OF TENANCY	VESTING PROVISION	QUALIFYING PROVISIONS
Secure tenancy	Section 89 of the Housing Act 1985 (c 68)	Sections 87(b) and 113(1)(b) of that Act
Introductory tenancy	Section 133 of the Housing Act 1996 (c 52)	Sections 131(b) and 140(1)(b) of that Act
Demoted tenancy	Section 143H of the Housing Act 1996	Section 143P(1)(c) of that Act

(2) The contract-holder under a converted contract is to be treated as a reserve successor in relation to the contract if—

(a) immediately before the appointed day the contract was an assured tenancy, and

(b) before the appointed day the contract-holder had become entitled to the assured tenancy under paragraph 3 of Schedule 1 to the Rent Act 1977 (c 42) (succession).

(3) The contract-holder under a converted contract is to be treated as a reserve successor in relation to the contract if—

(a) immediately before the appointed day the contract was an assured tenancy,

(b) before the appointed day it had vested in the contract-holder under section 17 of the Housing Act 1988 (c 50) (succession to assured tenancy), and

(c) on the appointed day the landlord under the contract was a private landlord.

Requirement to occupy dwelling as main home under certain converted contracts

22 (1) Sub-paragraph (2) has effect in relation to a converted contract to which this paragraph applies as if it were a supplementary provision prescribed by the Welsh Ministers under section 23.

(2) The contract-holder (or if more than one, at least one of them) must occupy the dwelling subject to the contract as his or her only or principal home.

(3) This paragraph applies to a converted contract which immediately before the appointed day was—

(a) a protected or statutory tenancy,

(b) a secure tenancy,

(c) an assured tenancy,

(d) an introductory tenancy, or

WALES

(e) a demoted tenancy.

Introductory standard contracts

23 (1) This paragraph applies to a converted contract which has effect as an introductory standard contract because of paragraph 5.

(2) The introductory period of the contract ends if—

(a) the tenant died before the appointed day, and

(b) after that day an event occurs which, but for this Act, would under section 133 of the Housing Act 1996 (c 52) (succession) have caused the contract to cease to be an introductory tenancy,

and section 16(1)(b) of this Act (conversion to secure contract) does not apply where the introductory period ends because of this sub-paragraph.

(3) This Act applies as if the reference in paragraph 1(7) of Schedule 4 to the introduction date of the contract were to the day which was the beginning of the trial period under section 125(2)(a) or (b) of the Housing Act 1996.

(4) Paragraph 2 of Schedule 4 (introductory period where there are previous contracts) applies as if references to introductory standard contracts were to—

(a) assured shorthold tenancies under which the landlord was a registered social landlord or a private registered provider of social housing, or

(b) introductory tenancies.

(5) For the purposes of paragraph 2 of Schedule 4 the introduction date of an assured shorthold tenancy under which the landlord was a registered social landlord or a private registered provider of social housing is—

(a) the day on which the tenant was entitled to begin occupying the dwelling, or

(b) if the tenancy was not made with a registered social landlord or a private registered provider of social housing, the day a registered social landlord or a private registered provider of social housing became the landlord.

(6) For the purposes of paragraph 2 of Schedule 4 the introduction date of an introductory tenancy is the day which was the beginning of the trial period under section 125(2)(a) or (b) of the Housing Act 1996.

(7) Paragraph 2(5) and (6) of Schedule 4 does not apply, but any notice of extension given in relation to the converted contract under section 125A of the Housing Act 1996 has effect as if given under paragraph 3 of that Schedule.

Prohibited conduct standard contract

24 (1) This Act applies to a converted contract which has effect as a prohibited conduct standard contract because of paragraph 6 as if—

(a) the demotion order were an order under section 116 (order imposing periodic standard contract),

(b) references to the occupation date of the contract were to the day on which the demotion order took effect, and

(c) paragraphs 4 to 7 of Schedule 7 (changing the probation period) were omitted.

(2) The "demotion order" is—

(a) the order under section 82A of the Housing Act 1985 (c 68) or section 6A of the Housing Act 1988 (c 50) because of which section 20B of the Housing Act 1988 applied, or

(b) the order under section 82A of the Housing Act 1985 because of which section 143A of the Housing Act 1996 (c 52) applied.

Termination of contract by landlord

25 Sections 173 to 180 (termination by landlord's notice) are not applicable to a periodic standard contract which immediately before the appointed day was an assured tenancy but not an assured shorthold tenancy.

26 (1) Section 194 (landlord's break clause) does not apply to the following fixed term standard contracts (and accordingly sections 195 to 201 are not incorporated as terms of such contracts).

(2) A fixed term standard contract which immediately before the appointed day was a secure tenancy for a fixed term.

(3) A fixed term standard contract which—

(a) immediately before the appointed day was an assured tenancy for a fixed term, and

(b) is not an excluded contract.

(4) A contract is an excluded contract if, immediately before the appointed day, the landlord could have made a claim for possession relying on Ground 3 or 4 of Schedule 2 to the Housing Act 1988 (c 50).

27 Estate management Ground C (special accommodation: charities) applies to a converted contract as if the occupation contract was made on the appointed day.

Termination of contract that was assured tenancy by landlord: additional absolute grounds for possession

28 (1) This paragraph applies in relation to a converted contract which immediately before the appointed day was an assured tenancy.

(2) The landlord may claim possession of the dwelling subject to the contract relying on Ground 1, 2 or 5 of Schedule 2 to the Housing Act 1988 (c 50).

(3) But the landlord may not do so before the end of the period of two months starting with the day on which the landlord gives the contract-holder a possession notice (in accordance with section 150) specifying that Ground.

(4) Subject to section 204 (possession claims: powers of court) (which applies as if subsection (1)(a) included a reference to sub-paragraph (3)), if the court is satisfied that the Ground is made out it must make an order for possession (subject to any available defence based on the contract-holder's Convention rights).

29 (1) This paragraph also applies in relation to a converted contract which immediately before the appointed day was an assured tenancy.

(2) The landlord may claim possession of the dwelling subject to the contract relying on Ground 7 of Schedule 2 to the Housing Act 1988 (c 50) if—

(a) the tenant under the assured tenancy died before the appointed day, and

(b) before the appointed day the assured tenancy devolved, or after the appointed day the converted contract devolves, under the tenant's will or intestacy.

(3) But the landlord may not do so before the end of the period of two months starting with the day on which the landlord gives the contract-holder a possession notice specifying that Ground.

(4) Subject to section 204 (possession claims: powers of court) (which applies as if subsection (1)(a) included a reference to sub-paragraph (3)), if the court is satisfied that the Ground is made out it must make an order for possession (subject to any available defence based on the contract-holder's Convention rights).

Implied tenancies and licences

30 (1) This paragraph applies if, immediately before the appointed day, a dwelling is occupied as a home by a person who is a trespasser in relation to that dwelling.

(2) Section 238 (implied tenancies and licences)—

(a) applies to payments made by the person before the appointed day as to payments made by him or her after the appointed day, and

(b) applies as if the end of the relevant period were the end of the period mentioned in section 238(3) or, if later, the appointed day.

The occupation date

31 The occupation date, in relation to a converted contract, is the day on which the contract-holder became entitled to occupy the dwelling under the tenancy or licence which became an occupation contract on the appointed day.

Substitute occupation contracts

32 (1) If after a converted contract ends there are one or more substitute contracts, for the purposes of this Schedule (except paragraph 28), the substitute contract is (or the substitute contracts are) to be treated as if they were the same tenancy or licence as the converted contract.

(2) The following are substitute contracts.

(3) An occupation contract between—

(a) a contract-holder who immediately before the occupation date of the contract was a contract-holder under a converted contract or a substitute contract, and

(b) a landlord that immediately before that date was a landlord under the converted contract or substitute contract,

which relates to the same (or substantially the same) dwelling as the converted contract or substitute contract.

(4) But where a converted or substitute contract is a fixed term standard contract, an occupation contract which arises under section 184(2), or is within section 184(6) (further contracts at end of fixed term), is not a substitute contract.

(5) If a converted contract or a substitute contract ends under section 12(3)(a) (standard contract adopted by community landlord), the occupation contract which arises under section 12(3)(b).

(6) If a converted contract or a substitute contract is ended under section 220 (abandonment), and under section 222(3)(b) the court orders the landlord to provide suitable alternative accommodation, an occupation contract made in accordance with the order.

(7) If under section 210 (estate management grounds) the court makes an order for possession of a dwelling subject to a converted contract or a substitute contract, an occupation contract made to provide the contract-holder with suitable alternative accommodation.

Power to amend Schedule

33 The Welsh Ministers may by regulations amend this Schedule.

INDEX

This index covers material in **Volume 2 only**.
References are to paragraph number (eg III HUM[27.2B]) and to page number (in *italic*)
For statutory materials, please refer to the table at the front of this volume.

A

B

D

G

N

P

Q

R

S

U